Pronunciation

If more than one pronunciation is given for a word, they are all
the first form given is the most common. Not all possible Americ
are shown in this dictionary. For example, some speakers only u:
followed by /r/ (as in **horse** /hɔrs/) and use /ɑ/ in all other words
with /ɔ/ in this dictionary, so that they pronounce **caught** and **cot** ... .t/.

/ - / shows a second pronunciation when only part of the pronunciation changes. The part that remains the same is replaced by the hyphen, for example **pajamas** /pə'dʒɑməz, -æ-/.

/ ' / shows the strong stress in a word or group of words. It is in front of the part (or SYLLABLE) that you say most strongly. For example, **any** /'ɛni/ has a stress on the first syllable; **depend** /dɪ'pɛnd/ has a stress on the second syllable.

/ ˌ / shows a weaker (or SECONDARY) stress. Many longer words have a syllable that is pronounced with a secondary stress as well as a syllable with strong (or MAIN) stress. So in the word **pronunciation** /prəˌnʌnsi'eɪʃn/, the main stress is on the syllable /'eɪ/, and the secondary stress is on the syllable /ˌnʌn/.

/ ţ / American speakers use the sound /ţ/, which is like a quick /d/, in many words spelled with -t- or -tt-. It is used in words after a vowel or /r/ and before an unstressed vowel or syllabic /l/: **city** /'sɪţi/; **parting** /'parţɪŋ/; **little** /'lɪţl/.

Strong and Weak Forms

Some very common words, for example **an**, **for**, **of**, and **that**, have two or more pronunciations: a strong form and one or more weak forms. For example, **for** is pronounced /fər/ in the sentence *It's for you*. The strong form occurs when the word comes at the end of a sentence or when it is given special emphasis. For example, **for** is pronounced /fɔr/ in *Who's it for?* and *The present isn't from Anna, it's for her*.

Pronunciation of Derivatives and Compound Words

Many **derivatives** are formed by adding a common ending (or SUFFIX) to the end of a word. These are pronounced by simply saying the suffix after the word. For example, **safely** /'seɪfli/ is said by joining the suffix -ly to the word *safe* /seɪf/.

In **compounds** (= words made up of two or more words), the pronunciation of the individual words is not repeated. This dictionary shows how the compound is stressed using the marks / ' / and / ˌ /. For example, in **'hot dog**, the stress is on the first word. In **ˌcivil 'rights**, there is a secondary stress on the first syllable of *civil*, and the main stress is on *rights*.

Stress in Phrasal Verbs

One type of phrasal verb has a single strong stress on the first word. Examples are **'come to sth**, **'go for sth**, **'look at sth**. This stress pattern is kept in all situations.

Another type of phrasal verb is shown with two stresses. The pattern shown in the dictionary, with the main stress on the second word, is the one that is used when the verb is said on its own, or when the verb as a whole is the last important word in a phrase:

> *What time are you ˌcoming 'back?* > *He ˌmade it 'up.* > *ˌFill them 'out.*

But if a noun or other important word comes between the two parts of the phrasal verb, or after both of them, the strong stress usually goes on that word. The stress on the second word of the verb is then weakened or lost:

> *We ˌcame back 'early.* > *I ˌfilled out the 'form.* > *ˌFill this 'form out.*

Abbreviations used in the dictionary

abbr.	abbreviation	I	intransitive verb	sb	somebody/someone
adj.	adjective	*n.*	noun	*sing.*	singular
adv.	adverb	*pl.*	plural	sth	something
C	countable noun	*pp*	past participle	*symb.*	symbol
CanE	Canadian English	*prep.*	preposition	T	transitive verb
conj.	conjunction	*pron.*	pronoun	U	uncountable noun
det.	determiner	*pt*	past tense	*v.*	verb

→ To see how the abbreviations show how different types of verbs and nouns are used, look at pages **R6–9** and **R12–13**.

Symbols used in the dictionary

~	replaces the headword of an entry
•	shows a new part of speech in an entry
▶	derivative(s) section of an entry
·	in a headword (af·fect), shows where a word divides into syllables
↔	in phrasal verbs, shows that the object may come either before or after the particle
⊃	shows a cross reference to another related entry in the dictionary

ANT	shows an antonym
SYN	shows a synonym
IDM	idiom section of an entry
PHRV	phrasal verb section of an entry
🔑	shows a word from the *Oxford 3000*™ (see page **R18**)
AWL	shows a word from the *Academic Word List* (see page **R16**)

Labels used in the dictionary

The following labels are used with words that express a particular attitude or are appropriate in a particular situation.

approving expressions show that you feel approval or admiration, for example *feisty, petite*.

disapproving expressions show that you feel disapproval or dislike, for example *blinkered, newfangled*.

figurative language is used in a nonliteral or metaphorical way, as in *He didn't want to cast a shadow on* (= spoil) *their happiness*.

formal expressions are usually only used in serious or official language and would not be appropriate in normal, everyday conversation. Examples are *admonish, besmirch*.

humorous expressions are intended to be funny, for example *boy wonder, egghead*.

informal expressions are used between friends or in a relaxed or unofficial situation. They are not appropriate for formal situations. Examples are *bonkers, baloney*.

ironic language uses words to mean the opposite of the meaning that they seem to have, as in *You broke the switch. You're a great help* (= no help at all).

literary language is used mainly in literature and imaginative writing, for example *aflame, halcyon*.

offensive expressions are used by some people to address or refer to people in a way that is very insulting, especially in connection with their race, religion, sex, or disabilities. You should not use these words.

slang is very informal language, sometimes restricted to a particular group of people, for example people of the same age or those who have the same interests or do the same job. Examples are *dingbat, gnarly*.

technical language is used by people who specialize in particular subject areas, for example *accretion, adipose*.

The following labels show other restrictions on the use of words.

old-fashioned expressions are passing out of current use, for example *balderdash, five-and-dime*.

old use describes expressions that are no longer in current use, for example *ere, perchance*.

saying describes a well-known fixed or traditional phrase, such as a proverb, that is used to make a comment, give advice, etc., for example *actions speak louder than words*.

™ shows a trademark of a manufacturing company, for example *Band-Aid, Frisbee*.

Oxford

Advanced
AMERICAN
DICTIONARY

for learners
of English

OXFORD
UNIVERSITY PRESS

OXFORD
UNIVERSITY PRESS

Great Clarendon Street, Oxford OX2 6DP

Oxford University Press is a department of the University of Oxford.
It furthers the University's objective of excellence in research, scholarship,
and education by publishing worldwide in

Oxford New York

Auckland Cape Town Dar es Salaam Hong Kong Karachi
Kuala Lumpur Madrid Melbourne Mexico City
Nairobi New Delhi Shanghai Taipei Toronto

With offices in

Argentina Austria Brazil Chile Czech Republic France Greece
Guatemala Hungary Italy Japan Poland Portugal Singapore
South Korea Switzerland Thailand Turkey Ukraine Vietnam

OXFORD and OXFORD ENGLISH are registered trademarks of
Oxford University Press in the UK and in certain other countries

ISBN: 978 0 19 439966 1 Pack for paperback and CD-ROM
ISBN: 978 0 19 439962 3 Paperback in pack
ISBN: 978 0 19 439965 4 CD-ROM in pack

Printed in China

Contents

Acknowledgments

Publishing Manager
Alison Waters

Principal Editor
Diana Lea

Senior Editors
Jennifer Bradbery
Victoria Bull
Andrew Delahunty
Alison Macaulay
Sally Wehmeier
Judith Willis

Editors
Daniel Barron
Carol Braham
Jamie Greene
Kerri Hamberg
Lisa Isenman
Robin Longshaw
Susan Norton
Marina Padakis
Patrick Phillips
Suzanne Webb
Ben Weller

Phonetics Editor
Sharon Goldstein

Canadian English Adviser
Katherine Barber

Academic Word List
Averil Coxhead, Victoria University of Wellington, New Zealand

Oxford Writing Tutor and iWriter
Dr. Maggie Charles
Kerri Hamberg
Dilys Parkinson

Designers
A-Z design by Peter Burgess
Cover design by Maj-Britt Hagsted

Typesetting
Text capture and processing by Oxford University Press
Typesetting by Data Standards Limited

Oxford American Dictionaries Advisory Board
The publisher would like to thank the Board members for their invaluable advice and contribution to the development of the series.
Advisory Board members:
Jayme Adelson-Goldstein, ESL Curriculum Consultant, Lighthearted Learning, Northridge, CA
Cheryl Boyd Zimmerman, Ph.D., Associate Professor, TESOL Coordinator, California State University, Fullerton, CA
Keith S. Folse, Ph.D., Professor of TESOL, University of Central Florida, Orlando, FL
Alison Rice, Director, International English Language Institute Hunter College, City University of New York, NY

The publisher would like to acknowledge the following individuals for their invaluable feedback during the development of this series of dictionaries:

Gianna Acevedo Alamo, Volusia County Schools, FL; **Francesca Armendaries**, Golden West College, Orange County, CA; **Brian Arnold**, Virginia Commonwealth University, Richmond, VA; **Kenneth Aubens**, Westside Education and Career Center, Los Angeles, CA; **Beth Backes**, Tidewater Community College, VA; **Kitty Barrera**, University of Houston, Language and Culture Center, TX; **Susan Boland**, Tidewater Community College, VA; **Linda Bolet**, Houston Community College & South West College, TX; **Nancy Boyer**, Golden West College, Orange County, CA; **Sandra J Briggs**, San Mateo Union High School District, San Francisco, CA; **Adriana Casas**, School of Continuing Education, Orange County, CA; **Glyn Cassorla**, Hunter College, CUNY, NY; **Lucy Castillo**, Houston Community College & South West College, TX; **Cynthia Cen**, Newcomer High School, San Francisco, CA; **Gwen Charvis**, Lone Star College, North Harris, TX; **Roland Cirilo**, Lone Star College, Fairbanks, TX; **Tricia Collins**, Tidewater Community College, VA; **Mary Colonna**, Columbia University, NY; **Eugenia D Coutavas**, Hunter College, CUNY, NY; **Nancy Cuda**, Tidewater Community College, VA; **David Dahnke**, Lone Star College, North Harris, TX; **Karen Del Colle**, Bergen County Community College, NJ; **Stan Dicarlo**, Westside Education and Career Center, Los Angeles, CA; **Dorothy Doggett**, Houston Community College & South West College, TX; **Joyce Doyle**, Houston Community College and South West College, TX; **Tom Edminster**, Abraham Lincoln High School, San Francisco, CA; **Tatiana Erokina**, Golden West College & Santa Ana College, CA; **Gail Fernandez**, Bergen County Community College, NJ; **Katherine Fouche**, University of Texas, Austin, TX; **Ma. Alma Garza Cano**, Houston Community College & South West College, TX; **Jenny Georgerian**, Virginia Commonwealth University, Richmond, VA; **Caroline Gibbs**, City College of San Francisco, CA; **Linda Gilette**, City College of San Francisco, CA; **Betty Gilfillan**, Houston Community College & South West College, TX; **Terry Guthrie**, City College of San Francisco, CA; **Janet Harclerode**, Santa Monica College, Los Angeles, CA; **Deborah Hardin**, University of Houston, Language and Culture Center, TX; **Lisse Hildebrandt**, Virginia Commonwealth University, Richmond, VA; **Eva Hodjera**, Golden West College, Orange County, CA; **Kate Hoffman**, School District of Manatee County, FL; **Matt Holsten**, City College of San Francisco, CA; **Katie Hurter**, Lone Star College, North Harris, TX; **Bill Jiang**, Bergen County Community College, NJ; **Johnnie Johnson-Hafernik**, University of San Francisco, CA; **Harold Kahn**, Bergen County Community College, NJ; **Gursharan Kandola**, University of Houston, Language and Culture Center, TX; **John Keene**, California State University, Long Beach, CA; **Gail Kellersberger**, University of Houston, Downtown, TX; **Jane Kenefick**, Columbia University, NY; **Jeannie Keng-Suh**, Bergen County Community College, NJ; **Milena Kristov**, Bergen County Community College, NJ; **Kathy Lenz**, California State University, Long Beach, CA; **Deborah Levy**, City College of San Francisco, CA; **Lynn Levy**, City College of San Francisco, CA; **Victoria Loeb**, Houston Community College, TX; **Thi Thi Ma**, City College of San Francisco, CA; **Veronica Martir**, Hunter College, CUNY, NY; **Susan McAlister**, University of Houston, Language and Culture Center, TX; **Nadya Mcann**, San Francisco State University, American Language Institute, CA; **Jim McKinney**, City College of San Francisco, CA; **Shant Melkonian**, Hunter College, CUNY, NY; **Carmen Menendez**, Volusia County Schools, FL; **Florin Mihai**, University of Central Florida, FL; **Jay Mojica**, City College of San Francisco, CA; **Svetlana Montgomery**, St Lucie County Public Schools District Office, FL; **Susan Morgan**, Houston Community College & South West College, TX; **Susan Morse**, University of California, Irvine, CA; **Gretchen Mowens**, San Francisco State University, American Language Institute, CA; **Janet Muzal**, Lone Star College, North Harris, TX; **Dina Paglia**, Hunter College, CUNY, NY; **Irina Patten**, Lone Star College, Fairbanks, TX; **Arturo V. Ponce**, Whittier Union HS District, Los Angeles, CA; **Maria Ponce**, San Francisco Unified School District, CA; **Valentina Purtel**, School of Continuing Education, Orange County, CA; **Candace Revilla**, Golden West College, Orange County, CA; **Maureen Roller**, Bergen County Community College, NJ; **Barbara Russell**, Virginia Commonwealth University, VA; **Azize Ruttler**, Bergen County Community College, NJ; **Fayruz Sabha**, Golden West College, Santa Ana College & Long Beach CC, CA; **Peg Sarosy**, San Francisco State University, American Language Institute, CA; **Alice Savage**, Lone Star College, TX; **Shira Seaman**, Hunter College, CUNY, NY; **Kathy Sherak**, San Francisco State University, American Language Institute, CA; **Larry A. Sims**, University of California, Irvine, CA; **Lyna Soler Marin**, St Lucie County Public Schools District Office, FL; **Jennifer Swoyer**, Northside ISD Adult Education, Dallas, TX; **Mo-Shuet Tam**, City College of San Francisco, CA; **Dawn Venable**, Virginia Commonwealth University, VA; **Steve Vogel**, Hunter College, CUNY, NY; **Martha Young**, Virginia Commonwealth University, VA; **Jana Zanetto**, City College of San Francisco, CA.

Foreword

Cheryl Boyd Zimmerman

Long gone are the days when a dictionary was seen as a keeper of obscure words with opaque definitions, consulted primarily to check meanings and spelling. With the publication of the *Advanced Learner's Dictionary of Current English* in 1948, A.S. Hornby introduced a dictionary designed with the purpose of clearly explaining words and teaching language to learners of English. His dictionary, which featured simple definitions, pictures, and numerous sample sentences, stood in stark contrast to others. The learner dictionaries of today continue Hornby's legacy of teaching the language, while reflecting current changes in the field. There has been a shift toward *the teaching of language use* rather than language alone, and an effort to more effectively target specific audiences at specific levels. The *Oxford Advanced American Dictionary* brings Hornby's rich tradition of principled language analysis and practical information about words to an audience of high intermediate and advanced learners of American English.

One's actual knowledge of a word isn't revealed until an effort is made to use it. When a new word is encountered in reading, for example, knowledge of its subtle or multiple meanings may be summoned, along with its register and spelling. Attempts to use the word in writing further test this knowledge, along with what one knows of its derivative forms, grammatical behavior, and collocation patterns. Understanding a word in listening, or using it in speaking, requires knowledge of pronunciation. Complete word knowledge is acquired incrementally, requiring time, patience, and the accessibility of accurate information about how words are actually used.

The *OAAD* is an excellent source of such information. Its content is based on the American section of the Oxford English Corpus, which draws upon authentic sources including newspapers, magazines, broadcasts, novels, academic texts, specialist journals, and weblogs. The *OAAD* is accessible to learners in part because its design clearly highlights relevant information such as the *Oxford 3000* keywords (considered the most important words to learn in English and used as the defining vocabulary), and the words from the Academic Word List. In addition, challenging features of word use are made accessible in a variety of ways including authentic sample sentences, verb complementation "frames," brief "Help" notes, and longer note boxes featuring different categories of information. The note boxes list and illustrate useful collocations, explain tricky points of grammar, differentiate between close synonyms and confusable words, and help with vocabulary building and expressing ideas in writing.

This dictionary is far more than a problem-solver; it is a proactive teaching tool. It focuses in particular on the use of academic vocabulary and on related advanced language skills. For example, the Writing Tutor succinctly covers relevant topics such as the writing process, the answering of exam questions, and instruction in a range of genres from a letter of complaint to an argument essay to an American-style résumé. In addition, an interactive version of the Writing Tutor is provided on the accompanying CD-ROM, providing model texts, tips about useful language, and frameworks for learners to follow as they complete their own writing.

With the *OAAD*, the legacy of A.S. Hornby continues and expands its reach to learners of American English. This is a welcome volume with a rich history and promising future for new generations of English language learners.

Cheryl Boyd Zimmerman is Associate Professor of TESOL at California State University, Fullerton, where she specializes in second language vocabulary acquisition. She is the series editor of *Inside Reading: The Academic Word List in Context*, and *Word Knowledge: A Vocabulary Teacher's Handbook*, both published by Oxford University Press.

Guide to the Dictionary

Finding the Word

Information in the dictionary is given in **entries**, arranged in alphabetical order of **headwords**. **Compound words** are in separate entries, also arranged alphabetically.

headwords

book·bind·er /ˈbʊkˌbaɪndər/ noun a person whose job is fastening the pages of books together and putting covers on them ▶ **book·bind·ing** noun [U]

book·case /ˈbʊkkeɪs/ noun a piece of furniture with shelves for keeping books on

book club noun **1** (also ˈbook group) a group of people who meet together regularly to discuss a book they have all read **2** an organization that sells books cheaply to its members

entry

Some headwords can have more than one part of speech.

Circles show where the information on each part of speech begins.

break·through /ˈbreɪkθru/ noun, adj.
• **noun** an important development that may lead to an agreement or achievement: *to make/achieve a breakthrough* ◆ *a significant breakthrough in negotiations* ◆ *a major breakthrough in cancer research*
• **adj.** [only before noun] in which a performer or type of product is successful for the first time, when it is likely to be even more successful in the future: *It was a breakthrough album for the band.* ◆ *breakthrough technology/products*

headword and all possible parts of speech

There are some words in English that have the same spelling as each other but different pronunciations.

The small **homonym number** shows that this is the first of two headwords spelled *gill*.

gill¹ /gɪl/ noun [usually pl.] one of the openings on the side of a fish's head that it breathes through ⊃ picture at ANIMAL **IDM to the gills** (*informal*) completely full: *I was stuffed to the gills with chocolate cake.*

gill² /dʒɪl/ noun a unit for measuring liquids. There are four gills in a pint.

Different pronunciation is given at each headword.

There are also some words in English that have more than one possible spelling, and both spellings are acceptable. Information about these words is given at the most frequent spelling.

The variant spelling is given in parentheses.

a·moe·ba (also **a·me·ba**) /əˈmibə/ noun (*pl.* a·moe·bas or a-moe·bae /-bi/) a very small living creature that consists of only one cell

At the entry for the less frequent spelling, a cross reference directs you to the main entry.

a·me·ba, a·me·bic = AMOEBA, AMOEBIC

Irregular forms of verbs are treated in a similar way.

Some words that are **derivatives** of other words do not have their own entry in the dictionary because they can be easily understood from the meaning of the word from which they are derived (the **root** word). They are given in the same entry as the root word, in a specially marked section.

The triangle shows where the derivative section starts.

be·lat·ed /bɪˈleɪtəd/ adj. coming or happening late: *a belated birthday present* ▶ **be·lat·ed·ly** adv.

You can find **idioms** and **phrasal verbs** in separate sections, marked with special symbols.

phrasal verb section with symbol **PHRV** (see pages **R10–11**)

idiom section with symbol **IDM** (see page **R14**)

label giving information about usage (see page **ii**)

max **AWL** /mæks/ *abbr., verb*
- *abbr.* **1** (also **max.**) maximum: *max temperature 85°F* **2** (*informal*) at the most: *It'll cost $50 max.* **ANT** MIN.
  IDM **to the max** (*informal*) to the highest level or greatest amount possible: *She believes in living life to the max.*
- *verb*
  PHRV ˌmax (sth) ˈout (*informal*) to reach, or make something reach, the limit at which nothing more is possible: *The car maxed out at 150 mph.*

Finding the Meaning

Some words have very long entries. It is not usually necessary to read the whole entry from the beginning if you already know something about the general meaning that you are looking for.

Shortcuts show the context or general meaning.

Meanings that are closely related share the same shortcut.

spin /spɪn/ *verb, noun*
- *verb* (spin·ning, spun, spun /spʌn/)
  > **TURN AROUND QUICKLY 1** [I, T] to turn around and around quickly; to make something do this: (+ *adv./prep.*) *The plane was spinning out of control.* ◆ *a spinning ice skater* ◆ *My head is spinning* (= I feel as if my head is going around and I can't balance). ◆ **~ (around)** *The dancers spun around and around.* ◆ **~ sth (around)** *to spin a ball/coin/wheel* **2** [I, T] **~ (sb) around** | + *adv./prep.* to turn around quickly once; to make someone do this: *He spun around to face her.*
  > **MAKE THREAD 3** [I, T] to make thread from wool, cotton, silk, etc. by twisting it: *She sat by the window spinning.* ◆ **~ sth** *to spin and knit wool* ◆ **~ A into B** *spinning silk into thread* ◆ **~ B from A** *spinning thread from silk*

Understanding and Using the Word

Words printed in orange type and with a key symbol are part of the **Oxford 3000™** list of important words (see page **R18**).

con·cerned /kənˈsərnd/ *adj.*
1 worried and feeling concern about something: *Concerned parents held a meeting.* ◆ **~ about/for sth** *The president is deeply concerned about this issue.* ◆ **~ for sth** *He didn't seem in the least concerned for her safety.* ◆ **~ (that)…** *She was concerned that she might miss the turn and get lost.* ⊃ thesaurus box at WORRIED **2** **~ (about/with sth)** interested in something: *They were more concerned with how the others had dressed than with what the speaker was saying.*
ANT UNCONCERNED **IDM** see FAR

sig·nif·i·cant **AWL** /sɪgˈnɪfəkənt/ *adj.*
1 large or important enough to have an effect or to be noticed: *a highly significant discovery* ◆ *The results of the experiment are not **statistically significant**.* ◆ *There are no significant differences between the two groups of students.* ◆ *Your work has shown a significant improvement.* ◆ ***It is significant that** girls generally do better on examinations than boys.* ⊃ compare INSIGNIFICANT **2** having a particular meaning: *It is significant that he changed his will only days before his death.* **3** [usually before noun] having a special or secret meaning that is not understood by everyone **SYN** MEANINGFUL: *a significant look/smile*

Words from the Academic Word List are marked with **AWL** (see page **R16**).

pronunciation (see inside the front cover)

lieu·ten·ant /luˈtɛnənt/ *noun* (abbr. Lieut., Lt.) **1** an officer of middle rank in the army, navy, or AIR FORCE: *Lieutenant Paul Fisher* ⊃ see also SECOND LIEUTENANT **2** (in compounds) an officer just below the rank mentioned: *a lieutenant colonel* **3** (in the U.S.) a police officer or FIREFIGHTER of fairly high rank **4** a person who helps someone who is above them in rank or who performs their duties when that person is unable to

Stress marks show stress in compounds.

ˌbaby ˈgrand *noun* a small GRAND PIANO

shake /ʃeɪk/ verb, noun
- **verb** (shook /ʃʊk/, shak·en /ˈʃeɪkən/)
> OBJECT/BUILDING/PERSON **1** [I, T] to move or make someone or something move with short quick movements from side to side or up and down: *The whole house shakes when a train goes past.* ♦ *~ sth Shake the bottle well before use.* ♦ *He shook her violently by the shoulders.* ♦ *~ sb/sth + adj. She shook her hair loose.* **2** [T] *~ sth + adv./prep.* to move something in a particular direction by shaking: *She bent down to shake a pebble out of her shoe.*

irregular forms of verbs, with their pronunciations

examples of use in *italic* type

prepositions, adverbs, and structures that can be used with this word

a·nom·a·ly /əˈnɑməli/ noun (pl. a·nom·a·lies) *~ (in sth)* a thing, situation, etc. that is different from what is normal or expected: *the many anomalies in the tax system* ♦ *the apparent anomaly that those who produced the wealth, the workers, were the poorest*

Irregular plurals of nouns are also shown.

heart·y /ˈhɑrti/ adj. (heart·i·er, heart·i·est) **1** [usually before noun] showing friendly feelings for someone: *a hearty welcome* **2** (sometimes *disapproving*) loud, cheerful, and full of energy: *a hearty and boisterous fellow* ♦ *a hearty voice* **3** [only before noun] (of a meal or someone's APPETITE) large; making you feel full: *a hearty breakfast* ♦ *to have a hearty appetite* **4** [usually before noun] showing that you feel strongly about something: *He nodded his head in hearty agreement.* ♦ *Hearty congratulations to everyone involved.* ♦ *a hearty dislike of something* **IDM** see HALE ▶ **heart·i·ness** noun [U]

comparatives and superlatives of adjectives

information on the use of adjectives (see page **R13**)

age /eɪdʒ/ noun, verb
- **noun 1** [C, U] the number of years that a person has lived or a thing has existed: *He left school at the age of 18.* ♦ *She needs more friends her own age.* ♦ *children from 5–10 years of age* ♦ *This game is for children of all ages.* ♦ *When I was your age I was already married.* ♦ *He started playing the piano at an early age.* ♦ *Children over the age of 12 must pay the full fare.* ♦ *She was beginning to feel her age* (= feel that she was getting old). ♦ *He was tall for his age* (= taller than you would expect, considering his age). ♦ *There's a big age gap between them* (= a big difference in their ages). ♦ *ways of calculating the age of the earth* **2** [C, U] a particular period of a person's life: *middle age* ♦ *15 is an awkward age.* ♦ *He died of old age.* **3** [C] a particular period of history: *the nuclear age* ♦ *the age of the computer* ⊃ see also BRONZE AGE, IRON AGE, NEW AGE, STONE AGE **4** [U] the state of being old: *Wine improves with age.* ♦ *The jacket was showing signs of age.* ♦ *the wisdom that comes with age* **5 ages** [pl.] (*informal*) a very long time: *I waited for ages.* ♦ *It'll probably take ages to find a parking space.* ♦ *Carlos left ages ago.* ♦ *It's been ages since we've seen them.* **6** [C] (*geology*) a length of time which is a division of an EPOCH
- **verb** (ag·ing, aged, aged) **1** [I] to become older: *As he aged, his memory got worse.* ♦ *The population is aging* (= more people are living longer). **2** [T] to make someone or something look, feel, or seem older: *~ sb The shock has aged her.* ♦ *~ sth Exposure to the sun ages your skin.* **3** [I, T] to develop in flavor over a period of time; to allow something to do this **SYN** MATURE: *The cheese is left to age for at least a year.* ♦ *~ sth The wine is aged in oak casks.*

information on different types of nouns (see page **R12**)

common phrase in **bold type** in example (see page **R15**)

explanation of a particular phrase, in parentheses

fixed form of a noun

word used in a definition that is not in the **Oxford 3000™**

verb codes and frames (see pages **R6–9**)

Build Your Vocabulary

The dictionary also contains a lot of information that will help you increase your vocabulary and use the language productively.

sta·ble **AWL** /ˈsteɪbl/
adj., noun, verb
- **adj. 1** firmly fixed; not likely to move, change, or fail **SYN** STEADY: *stable prices* ♦ *a stable relationship* ♦ *This ladder doesn't seem very stable.* ♦ *The patient's condition is stable* (= it is not getting worse). **2** (of a person) calm and reasonable; not easily upset **SYN** BALANCED: *Mentally, she is not very stable.* **3** (*technical*) (of a substance) staying in the same chemical or ATOMIC state: *chemically stable* **ANT** UNSTABLE ▶ **sta·bly** /ˈsteɪbli/ adv.

WORD FAMILY
stable adj. (≠ unstable)
stability noun (≠ instability)
stabilize verb

Word Families show words related to the headword.

Special symbols show synonyms and antonyms.

Notes help you choose the right word and also help with difficult grammar points.
They are all listed on pages **xiii–xvii**.

words listed in order of
how frequent they are

> **THESAURUS**
>
> ## valuable
> **precious • priceless • irreplaceable**
>
> These words all describe something that is worth a lot of
> money or very important to someone.
>
> **valuable** worth a lot of money: *The thieves took three
> pieces of valuable jewelry.*
>
> **precious** rare and worth a lot of money; loved or valued
> very much: *a precious Chinese vase, valued at half a
> million dollars* ◆ *precious memories of our time together*
>
> **priceless** extremely valuable; loved or valued very
> much: *a priceless collection of antiques*
>
> **irreplaceable** too valuable or special to be replaced
>
> PATTERNS
> - valuable/precious/priceless/irreplaceable **posses-
>   sions**
> - valuable/precious/priceless **antiques/jewels**

Language Bank notes show you how to express similar ideas in a variety of ways.

> **LANGUAGE BANK**
>
> ## opinion
> **giving your personal opinion**
>
> - **In my opinion**, everyone should have some under-
>   standing of science.
> - Everyone should, **in my opinion**, have some under-
>   standing of science.
> - **It seems to me that** many people in this country have a
>   flawed understanding of science.
> - This is, **in my view**, the result of a failure of the scientific
>   community to get its message across.
> - Another reason why so many people have such a poor
>   understanding of science is, **I believe**, the lack of
>   adequate funding for science in schools.
> - Smith argues that science is separate from culture. **My
>   own view is that** science belongs with literature, art,
>   philosophy, and religion as an integral part of our
>   culture.
> - **In this writer's opinion**, the more the public knows
>   about science, the less they will fear and distrust it.
> - ⊃ Thesaurus at THINK
> - ⊃ Language Banks at ACCORDING TO, ARGUE, IMPER-
>   SONAL, NEVERTHELESS, PERHAPS

Cross references refer you to information in other parts of the dictionary.

Compare refers you to a
word with a contrasting
meaning.

> **bear** 🔑 /ber/ *verb, noun*
>
> • *noun* **1** a heavy wild animal with thick fur and sharp CLAWS
> (= pointed parts on the ends of its feet). There are many
> types of bears: *a black bear* ⊃ see also GRIZZLY BEAR, POLAR
> BEAR, TEDDY BEAR **2** (*finance*) a person who sells shares in a
> company, etc., hoping to buy them back later at a lower
> price ⊃ compare BULL **3** (*informal*) a thing that is very diffi-
> cult to deal with: *Their Victorian house is beautiful but it's a bear
> to clean.* ⊃ see also BEARISH

See also refers you to a
word with a similar or
related meaning.

Notes on Usage

In the dictionary you will find many notes on various aspects of usage in English. These notes are listed below according to the type of note.

Which Word?

These notes show the differences between words that are often confused. The word in **blue** shows you the entry where you can find the note.

above / over
actual / current / present
affect / effect
agenda / diary / schedule
almost / nearly / practically
alone / lone / lonely
also / as well / too
although / even though / though
altogether / all together
answer / reply
as / like
ashamed / embarrassed
awake / awaken / wake up / waken
back – the back / the rear / behind
baggage / luggage / bags
bath / bathe / swim / sunbathe
become / get / go / turn
begin / start
beside / besides
besides / except (for) / apart from
big / large / great
blind / blindly
borrow / lend
calm / calmness
can / may
care – take care of sb/sth / care for sb

cautious / careful
classic / classical
close/ shut
compliment / complement
condition / state
continuous / continual
country / state
court / court of law / courthouse
deep / deeply
disabled / handicapped
distrust / mistrust
double / dual
economic / economical
electric / electrical
especially / specially
fast / quick / rapid
first (of all) / firstly / at first
front – in front of / in the front of
further / farther / furthest / farthest
good / goodness
hard / hardly
hate / hatred
high / tall
historic / historical
infer / imply
interested / interesting / uninterested / disinterested / uninteresting

last / take
lastly / at last
light / lighting
long – (for) long / (for) a long time
loud / loudly / aloud
naked / bare
narrow / thin
near / close
next / nearest
noise / sound
old – older / elder
partly / partially
peace / peacefulness
persuade / convince
quick / quickly / fast
regrettably / regretfully
right / rightly
rise / raise
say / tell
sensible / sensitive
shade / shadow
slow / slowly
story / floor
surely / certainly
tight / tightly
used to / be used to
wide / broad
wrong / wrongly / wrongfully

Vocabulary Building

These notes help you to choose more interesting and varied words to use and so increase your vocabulary. The word in **blue** gives you the general area of meaning of the note and shows you where to find it.

approximately – ways of saying "approximately"
bad and very bad
a bar of chocolate
body – actions expressing emotions
break – words that mean "break"
cry – different ways of crying
do – household jobs: do or make?
face – expressions on your face
fat – saying that someone is fat
good and very good
hand – using your hands

laugh – different ways of laughing
learn – different ways of learning
nice and very nice
object – objects you can use
piece – pieces of things
rain and storms
smell – adjectives and nouns
teach and teachers
thin – saying that someone is thin
thing – other words for "thing"
walk – ways of walking

Grammar

These notes help explain points of grammar that often cause problems. The word in **blue** shows you the entry where you can find the note.

avenge / revenge
can / could / be able to / manage
dare
depend on sth
each / every
enjoy
half / whole / quarter
hardly / scarcely / barely / no sooner

if / whether
kind / type / sort
late / lately
likely
many / a lot of / lots of
modal verbs
much / a lot of / lots of
must / have (got) to / must not / don't have to

need
neither / either
none of
one / ones
percent – expressing percentages
proportion
school
shall / will

should / ought to / had better
should / would
sit
staff
used to
very / very much
well
whom
wish

More About

These notes give you more information about an aspect of life or language in the United States and show you the correct words to use. The word in **blue** shows you the topic of the note and the entry where you can find it.

American – talking about America
baseball – playing baseball
British – describing people from Britain
course – ways of saying "of course"
exam – words for exams and tests
football – playing football
gender – ways of talking about men and women
hello – greetings

lawyer – words for different kinds of lawyers
name – names and titles
Native American – describing the peoples of the U.S. and Canada
road – roads and streets
student – words for students at different levels
want – offers and invitations

Thesaurus

These notes show the differences between groups of words with similar meanings. The word in **blue** shows you the entry where you can find the note.

action /measure / step / act / move
admit / acknowledge / recognize / concede / confess
advertisement / publicity / ad / commercial / promotion / preview
afraid / scared / frightened / terrified / alarmed / paranoid
agree / accept / approve / go along with sb/sth / consent
angry / mad / furious / upset / indignant / irate
artificial / synthetic / fake / man-made / false / faux / imitation
ask / inquire / demand
basis / foundation / groundwork / base
beat / batter / pound / lash / hammer
beautiful / pretty / handsome / attractive / lovely / good-looking / gorgeous
bill / account / invoice / check
bitter / sour / pungent / sharp / acidic / tart
border / boundary / frontier / barrier
boring / dull / tedious
bottom / base / foundation / foot
bright / brilliant / vivid / vibrant
build / construct / assemble / put sth together / erect / put sth up / establish
building / property / premises / complex / structure

burn / char / scald / scorch / singe
call / cry out / exclaim / blurt (out)
campaign / battle / struggle / drive / war / fight
care / caution / prudence
certain / bound / sure / definite / guaranteed
cheap / competitive / budget / affordable / reasonable / inexpensive
cheat / lie / trick / fool / deceive / betray / con
check / examine / inspect / go over sth
choice / favorite / preference / selection / pick
choose / select / pick / decide / opt / go for sth
claim / allegation / assertion
clean / wash / rinse / cleanse / dry-clean
clear / obvious / apparent / evident / plain
clothes / clothing / garment / dress / wear / gear
coast / beach / shore / coastline / sand / seashore
cold / cool / freezing / chilly / lukewarm / tepid
collect / gather / accumulate / amass
color / shade / hue / tint / tinge
comment / note / remark / observe
complain / protest / object / grumble / whine
consist of sb/sth / comprise / make up sth / constitute / be composed of sb/sth
costs / spending / expenditure / expenses / overhead (costs) / outlay

country / landscape / countryside / terrain / land / scenery

crash / slam / collide / smash / wreck

crazy / insane / nuts / bananas / out of your mind / (not) in your right mind

cut / slash / cut sth back / scale sth back / streamline / downsize

damage / hurt / harm / impair

declare / state / indicate / announce

demand / expect / insist / ask / require

difficult / hard / challenging / demanding / taxing

dirty / dusty / filthy / muddy / soiled / grubby / stained

discussion / conversation / dialogue / talk / debate / consultation / chat / gossip

disease / illness / disorder / infection / condition / ailment / bug

disgusting / foul / revolting / repulsive / offensive / gross

economic / financial / commercial / monetary / fiscal

election / vote / referendum / ballot

entertainment / fun / recreation / relaxation / play / pleasure / amusement

environment / setting / surroundings / background

equipment / material / gear / kit / apparatus

essential / vital / crucial / critical / decisive / indispensable

examine / consider / look at sth / analyze / review / study / discuss

example / case / instance / specimen / illustration

excellent / outstanding / perfect / superb

excited / ecstatic / elated / euphoric / rapturous / exhilarated

exciting / dramatic / thrilling / exhilarating

expensive / costly / overpriced / pricey

explode / blow up / go off / burst / erupt / detonate

fabric / cloth / material / textile

factory / plant / mill / works / yard / workshop / shop / foundry

fear / terror / panic / alarm / fright

fight / clash / brawl / struggle / scuffle

floor / ground / land / earth

fun / pleasure / a good time / enjoyment / a great time

funny / amusing / entertaining / witty / humorous / comical / hilarious

glad / happy / pleased / delighted / proud / relieved / thrilled

great / cool / fantastic / fabulous / terrific / awesome

happy / satisfied / content / contented / joyful / blissful

hate / dislike / can't stand / despise / can't bear / loathe / detest

hide / conceal/ cover / disguise / mask / camouflage

hit / knock / bang / strike / bump / bash

hold / hold on / cling / clutch / grip / grasp / clasp / hang on

honest / direct / open / outspoken / straight / blunt / frank

hurt / ache / burn / sting / tingle / itch / throb

identify / know / recognize / name / make sb/sth out

illness / condition / health problems/issues / disability

imagine / think / see / envision

income / pay / salary / wage/wages / overtime / earnings

injure / wound / hurt / bruise / sprain / pull / strain

intelligent / smart / brilliant / bright / sharp

interest / hobby / pastime

interesting / fascinating / compelling / stimulating / gripping / absorbing

interview / interrogation / audience / consultation

job / position / post / vacancy / appointment

label / tag / sticker

land / lot / ground / space / plot

language / vocabulary / terms / wording / terminology

lid / top / cork / cap / plug

like / love / be fond of sth / be crazy about sth / adore

limit / restriction / control / constraint / restraint / limitation

look / watch / see / view / observe

look / glance / gaze / stare / glimpse / glare

luck / chance / coincidence / accident / fate / destiny

main / major / key / central / principal / chief / prime

make / do / create / develop / produce / generate / form

mark / stain / fingerprint / streak / speck / blot / smear / spot

mentally ill / insane / depressed / neurotic / psychotic / disturbed / unstable

mention / refer to sb/sth / speak of/about sb/sth / cite / quote

mistake / error / inaccuracy / slip / misprint

mix / stir / mingle / blend

money / cash / change / bills

nervous / neurotic / on edge / jittery

notice / note / detect / observe / witness

old / elderly / aged / long-lived / mature

option / choice / alternative / possibility

order / tell / instruct / direct / command

painful / sore / raw / inflamed / infected / excruciating / burning / itchy

patch / dot / mark / spot

payment / premium / contribution / subscription / repayment / deposit / installments

photograph / picture / photo / shot / snapshot / print

picture / painting / drawing / portrait / print / sketch

place / site / area / position / point / location / scene / spot / venue plain / simple / stark / bare / unequivocal

pleasure / delight / joy / privilege / treat / honor

poor / disadvantaged / needy / low-income /
impoverished / deprived / penniless / hard up

pressure / stress / tension / strain

price / cost / value / expense / worth

product / goods / commodity / merchandise /
produce

pull / drag / draw / haul / tow / tug

purpose / aim / intention / plan / point / idea

rate / charge / fee / rent / fine / fare / toll

reason / explanation / grounds / basis / excuse /
motive / justification / pretext

recommend / advise / advocate / urge

regard / call / find / consider / see / view

report / story / account / version

rest / break / respite / time out / breathing room

result / consequence / outcome / repercussion

return / come back / go back / get back / turn
back

rich / wealthy / prosperous / affluent / well off /
comfortable

right / correct

rude / sassy / insolent / disrespectful / impolite /
impertinent / discourteous

satisfaction / happiness / pride / contentment /
fulfillment

satisfying / rewarding / pleasing / gratifying /
fulfilling

save / budget / economize / tighten your belt

save / rescue / bail sb out / come through (for sb)

scare / frighten / alarm / terrify

see / spot / catch

serious / grave / earnest / solemn

shine / gleam / glow / sparkle / glisten / shimmer /
glitter / twinkle / glint

shock / appall / horrify / disgust / sicken / repulse

shout / yell / cry / scream / cheer / bellow / raise
your voice

sight / view / vision

sign / indication / symptom / symbol / indicator /
signal

sit / sit down / be seated / have/take a seat / perch

situation / circumstances / position / conditions /
things / the case / state of affairs

sleep / doze / nap / snooze

soil / dirt / mud / dust / clay / land / earth /
ground

speaker / communicator / gossip / talker

speech / lecture / address / talk / sermon

spoken / oral / vocal

stand / get up / stand up / rise / get to your feet /
be on your feet

stare / gaze / peer / glare

start / begin / start off / kick off / commence /
open

stress / emphasize

structure / framework / form / composition /
construction / fabric

successful / profitable / commercial / lucrative

sure / confident / convinced / certain / positive /
clear

surprise / startle / amaze / stun / astonish / take
sb aback / astound

take / lead / escort / drive / show / walk / guide /
usher / direct

talk / discuss / speak / communicate / debate /
consult

target / objective / goal / object / end

task / duties / mission / job / chore

tax / duty / customs duty/charge / tariff

terrible / awful / horrible / dreadful / foul /
horrendous

things / stuff / property / possessions / junk /
belongings / goods / valuables

think / believe / feel / be under the impression

throw / toss / hurl / fling / chuck / lob / pitch

trip / journey / tour / commute / expedition /
excursion / outing

true / right / correct

trust / depend on sb/sth / rely on sb/sth / count
on sb/sth / believe in sb

understand / see / get / follow / grasp /
comprehend

valuable / precious / priceless / irreplaceable

view / sight / scene / panorama

well / good / all right / OK / fine / healthy /
strong / in shape

wet / moist / damp / soaked / drenched /
saturated

witness / observer / onlooker / passerby /
bystander / eyewitness

word / term / phrase / expression / idiom

work / employment / career / profession /
occupation / trade

worried / concerned / nervous / anxious / uneasy

wrong / false / mistaken / incorrect / inaccurate /
misguided / untrue

Topic Collocations

These notes show useful words and phrases connected with particular topics, and a
selection of verbs to use with those words and phrases. The word in blue shows you
the entry where you can find the note.

age – The Ages of Life

art – Fine Arts

business – Business

child – Children

cooking – Cooking

crime – Crime

decorate – Decorating and
Home Improvement

diet – Diet and Exercise

driving – Driving

economy – The Economy

education – Education

e-mail – E-mail and the Internet
environment – The Environment
farming – Farming
fashion – Clothes and Fashion
finance – Finance
house – Houses and Apartments
injury – Injuries
international – International Relations
job – Jobs
justice – Criminal Justice
life – The Living World

literature – Literature
marriage – Marriage and Divorce
movie – The Movies
music – Music
phone – Phones
physical – Physical Appearance
politics – Politics
race – Race and Immigration
religion – Religion
restaurant – Restaurants
scientific – Scientific Research

shopping – Shopping
sick – Being Sick
television – Television
town – Town and Country
travel – Travel and Tourism
unemployment – Unemployment
vote – Voting in Elections
war – War and Peace
weather – The Weather

AWL Collocations

These notes help you to use words from the Academic Word List in typical combinations and phrases. The word in **blue** shows you the entry where you can find the note.

accurate / inaccurate / accuracy / accurately
achieve / achievement / achievable
acknowledge / acknowledged / acknowledgment
assume / assumption
available / availability
aware / unaware / awareness
clarify / clarification / clarity
conclude / conclusion / conclusive / inconclusive
contribute / contributing / contribution
create / creation / creative / creativity
distinct / distinction / distinctive
emphasis / emphasize
estimate / overestimate / underestimate / estimated
evaluate / reevaluate / evaluation
evident / evidence
globe / global / globally / globalization
identify / identifiable / identification / identity / identified / identifying

illustrate / illustration
indicate / indication / indicative / indicator
interpret / interpretation / misinterpret / misinterpretation
investigate / investigation
involve / involved / involvement
predict / prediction / predictable / unpredictable
relevant / irrelevant / relevance
rely / reliability / reliable / unreliable / reliance
significant / insignificant / significance / significantly
similar / dissimilar / similarity
summary / summarize
theory / theoretical / theoretically
valid / validate / validation / validity
vary / variable / variation / variability / varied

Language Bank

These notes show you how to express similar ideas in a variety of ways, particularly in writing. The word in **blue** shows you the entry where you can find the note.

about – saying what a text is about
according to – reporting someone's opinion
addition – adding another item
argue – verbs for reporting an opinion
because – explaining reasons
cause – X causes Y
conclusion – summing up an argument
consequently – describing the effect of something
contrast – highlighting differences
define – defining terms
e.g. – giving examples
emphasis – highlighting an important point
evidence – giving proof
except – making an exception
expect – discussing predictions
fall – describing a decrease
first – ordering your points

generally – ways of saying "in general"
however – ways of saying "but"
i.e. – explaining what you mean
illustrate – referring to a chart, graph, or table
impersonal – giving opinions using impersonal language
increase – describing an increase
nevertheless – conceding a point and making a counterargument
opinion – giving your personal opinion
perhaps – making an opinion sound less definite
process – describing a process
proportion – describing fractions and proportions
similarly – making comparisons
surprising – highlighting interesting data
therefore – ways of saying "for this reason..."
vital – saying that something is necessary

List of Illustrations

At or near these words in the dictionary, you will find pictures to help you to understand words and expand your vocabulary.

Many of these pictures have different parts labeled, for example the picture at **volcano** includes the items *lava*, *magma*, *vent*, and *geyser*.

At many other entries, you will find larger pictures including several related items, for example the picture near the entry for **plant** shows many different plants and flowers, and parts of a plant/flower.

Numbers

10,000-foot view /ˌtɛn ˌθaʊznd fʊt ˈvyu/ noun (business) a broad, general view or description of a problem **SYN** HELICOPTER VIEW: *Let me give you the 10,000-foot view.*

101 /ˌwʌn oʊ ˈwʌn/ noun a number used to indicate a college course that is at the most basic level: *Geometry 101*

1040 form /ˌtɛn ˈfɔrti ˌfɔrm/ noun an official document in which you give details of the amount of money that you have earned so that the government can calculate how much tax you have to pay

18 /eɪˈtin/ noun the age at which you are legally an adult in most states of the United States: *You'll be able to vote when you're 18.*

18-wheeler /ˌeɪtin ˈwilər/ noun a very large truck with nine wheels on each side

20/20 vision /ˌtwɛnti twɛnti ˈvɪʒn/ noun [U] the ability to see perfectly without using glasses or CONTACT LENSES

21 /ˌtwɛnti ˈwʌn/ noun the age at which you may legally buy alcohol in the United States: *No one under 21 is allowed in the club.*

212 /ˌtu wʌn ˈtu/ noun [sing.] the AREA CODE (= numbers that come before a phone number) for the city of New York. This number is used to mean New York: *We're here in the 212.* ◆ *"Law & Order" is filmed in the 212.*

24-hour clock /ˌtwɛnti fɔr aʊər ˈklɑk/ noun the system of using twenty-four numbers to talk about the hours of the day, instead of dividing it into two units of twelve hours

24/7 /ˌtwɛnti fɔr ˈsɛvən/ adv. (informal) twenty-four hours a day, seven days a week (used to mean "all the time"): *She's with me all the time — 24/7.*

3-D /ˌθri ˈdi/ noun [U] the quality of having, or appearing to have, length, width, and depth (= three DIMENSIONS): *These glasses allow you to see the movie in 3-D.* ◆ *a 3-D image*

3G /ˌθri ˈdʒi/ abbr. third generation (used to describe a level of performance for CELL PHONES that makes it possible to move data to and from the Internet): *3G technology*

360-degree feedback /ˌθri ˌsɪksti dɪˌgri ˈfidbæk/ (also 3ˌ60-deˌgree apˈpraisal) noun [U] (business) information provided by all the people that an employee deals with, used as a way of deciding how well the employee does their job: *360-degree feedback assessments*

4 x 4 /ˈfɔr baɪ ˌfɔr/ noun a vehicle with FOUR-WHEEL DRIVE (= a system in which power is applied to all four wheels, making it easier to control)

4-H /ˌfɔr ˈeɪtʃ/ noun a club for young people that is popular especially in farm areas. 4-H teaches life skills by allowing kids to learn by doing things like raising animals or working on building projects in their community: *I am showing my horse at the 4-H fair.*

401(k) /ˌfɔr oʊ wʌn ˈkeɪ/ noun an account in which an employee can save money for their retirement without paying tax until the money is taken out. Many private employers offer a 401(k); a 403(b) is offered for public service employees such as teachers: *Does your employer have a 401(k) plan?*

404 /ˌfɔr oʊ ˈfɔr/ adj. used to describe something or someone that is missing or not very intelligent: *My keys are 404.* ◆ *Don't ask Tom how to fix it — he's 404.* **ORIGIN** From the number that appears when something cannot be found on the Internet.

411 /ˌfɔr wʌn ˈwʌn/ noun **1** [U] the telephone number of the service that you use to find out a person's telephone number: *Call 411.* **2 the 411** [sing.] (informal) the true facts about a situation or the information you need: *He'll give us the 411 on what to expect.*

5 o'clock shadow /ˌfaɪv əklɑk ˈʃædoʊ/ noun [sing.] (informal) the dark color that appears on a man's chin and face when the hair has grown a little during the day

50-yard line /ˌfɪfti ˈyɑrd laɪn/ noun the line that marks the middle of a football field. If you sit near it, you have a good view of the game: *Try to get tickets near the 50-yard line.*

the $64,000 question /ðə ˌsɪksti fɔr ˌθaʊznd ˌdɑlər ˈkwestʃən/ noun (informal) the thing that people most want to know, or that is most important: *It's a great plan, but the $64,000 question is: Will it work?* **ORIGIN** From the name of a U.S. television show of the 1950s that gave prizes of money to people who answered questions correctly. The correct answer to the last question was worth $64,000. (The original term was **the $64 question**, from a radio show of the 1940s, in which the top prize was $64.)

800 number /ˌeɪt ˈhʌndrəd ˌnʌmbər/ noun a phone number that begins with 800. An 800 number is provided by businesses for customers to call them free of charge: *Does the electric company have an 800 number?*

86 /ˌeɪti ˈsɪks/ verb (86es, 86ing, 86ed) **~ sth/sb** (informal) to end or cancel something; to get rid of something or someone: *I would like a BLT, but please 86 the tomato.* ◆ *The men were 86ed from the bar for fighting.*

9 to 5 /ˌnaɪn tə ˈfaɪv/ adv., adj. the normal working hours in an office: *I work 9 to 5.* ◆ *a 9-to-5 job*

900 number /ˌnaɪn ˈhʌndrəd ˌnʌmbər/ noun a phone number that begins with 900. A 900 number is used by businesses that provide services for customers on the telephone, and a large fee is charged every minute: *Don't call that 900 number — it costs $4.99 a minute!*

911 /ˌnaɪn wʌn ˈwʌn/ noun the telephone number used to call the police, fire, or ambulance services in an emergency: *Call 911.*

9/11 /ˌnaɪn ɪˈlɛvn/ noun the abbreviation for the date September 11, 2001, when TERRORISTS flew planes into the World Trade Center in New York, the Pentagon in Washington, D.C., and a field in Pennsylvania, killing thousands of people

Aa

A /eɪ/ *noun, abbr.*
- **noun** (*pl.* As, A's /eɪz/) **1** also **a** (*pl.* a's) [C, U] the first letter of the English alphabet: *"Apple" begins with (an) A/"A."* **2** [C, U] (*music*) the 6th note in the SCALE of C MAJOR **3** [C, U] the highest grade that a student can get for a course, test, or piece of work: *She got an A in Biology.* ◆ *He had **straight A's** (= nothing but A's) all through high school.* **4** [U] used to represent the first of two or more possibilities: *Shall we go for plan A or plan B?* **5** [U] used to represent a person, for example in an imagined situation or to hide their identity: *Assume A knows B is guilty.* ⊃ see also A-FRAME
  IDM **from A to B** from one place to another: *For me a car is just a means of getting from A to B.* **from A to Z** including everything there is to know about something: *He knew his subject from A to Z.*
- **abbr.** (in writing) AMP(S)

a 🔑 /ə; *strong form* eɪ/ (also **an** /ən; *strong form* æn/ *indefinite article*
  HELP The form **a** is used before consonant sounds and the form **an** before vowel sounds. When saying abbreviations like "FM" or "UN," use **a** or **an** according to how the first letter is said. For example, **F** is a consonant, but begins with the sound /ɛ/ and so you say: *an FM radio.* U is a vowel but begins with /y/ and so you say: *a UN declaration.* **1** used before countable or singular nouns referring to people or things that have not already been mentioned: *a man/horse/unit* ◆ *an aunt/egg/hour/X-ray* ◆ *I can only carry two at a time.* ◆ *There's a visitor for you.* ◆ *She's a friend of my father's* (= one of my father's friends). **2** used before uncountable nouns when these have an adjective in front of them, or phrase following them: *a good knowledge of French* ◆ *a sadness that won't go away* **3** any; every: *A lion is a dangerous animal.* **4** used to show that someone or something is a member of a group or profession: *Their new car's a BMW.* ◆ *She's a Buddhist.* ◆ *He's a teacher.* ◆ *Is that a Monet* (= a painting by Monet)*?* **5** used in front of two nouns that are seen as a single unit: *a knife and fork* **6** used instead of *one* before some numbers: *A thousand people were there.* **7** used when talking about prices, quantities, and rates SYN PER: *They cost 50 cents a pound.* ◆ *I can type 50 words a minute.* ◆ *He was driving at 50 miles an hour.* **8** a person like someone: *He's a little Shaq.* **9** used before someone's name to show that the speaker does not know the person: *There's a Mrs. Green here to see you.* **10** used before the names of days of the week to talk about one particular day: *She died on a Tuesday.*

a- /eɪ/ *prefix* (in nouns, adjectives, and adverbs) not; without: *atheist* ◆ *atypical* ◆ *asexually*

A1 /ˌeɪ ˈwʌn/ *adj.* (*informal*) very good: *The car was in A1 condition.*

AA /ˌeɪ ˈeɪ/ *abbr.* ALCOHOLICS ANONYMOUS

AAA /ˌtrɪpl ˈeɪ; ˌeɪ eɪ ˈeɪ/ *abbr.* American Automobile Association (an organization that provides services for car owners) **HELP** When speaking, we usually say **triple A**.

A & R /ˌeɪ ən ˈɑr/ *abbr.* artists and repertoire (the department in a record company that is responsible for finding new singers and bands and getting them to sign a contract with the company)

aard·vark /ˈɑrdvɑrk/ *noun* an animal from southern Africa that has a long nose and tongue and that eats insects

aargh /ɑrg; ɑr/ *exclamation* used to express fear, anger, or some other strong emotion: *Aargh—get that cat off the table!*

a·back /əˈbæk/ *adv.*
  IDM **be taken aback (by sb/sth)** to be shocked or surprised by someone or something: *She was completely taken aback by his anger.* ⊃ see also TAKE SB ABACK ⊃ thesaurus box at SURPRISE

ab·a·cus /ˈæbəkəs/ *noun* a frame with small balls that slide along wires. It is used as a tool or toy for counting.

ab·a·lo·ne /ˌæbəˈlouni; ˌæbəˈlouni/ *noun* [C, U] a SHELLFISH that can be eaten and whose shell contains MOTHER-OF-PEARL

a·ban·don 🔑 **AWL** /əˈbændən/ *verb, noun*
- **verb 1** ~ sb to leave someone, especially someone you are responsible for, with no intention of returning: *The baby had been abandoned by its mother.* **2** to leave a thing or place, especially because it is impossible or dangerous to stay SYN LEAVE: ~ sth *Snow forced many drivers to abandon their vehicles.* ◆ *He gave the order to **abandon ship** (= to leave the ship because it was sinking).* ◆ ~ sth to sb/sth *They had to abandon their lands to the invading forces.* **3** to stop supporting or helping someone; to stop believing in something: ~ sb *The country abandoned its political leaders after the war.* ◆ ~ sth *By 1930 he had abandoned his Marxist principles.* **4** ~ sth to stop doing something, especially before it is finished; to stop having something: *They abandoned the game because of rain.* ◆ *She abandoned hope of any reconciliation.* **5** ~ yourself to sth (*literary*) to feel an emotion so strongly that you can feel nothing else: *He abandoned himself to despair.*
- **noun** [U] (*formal*) an uncontrolled way of behaving that shows that someone does not care what other people think: *He signed checks with careless abandon.*

a·ban·doned 🔑 **AWL** /əˈbændənd/ *adj.* **1** left and not wanted, not used, or no longer needed: *an abandoned car/house* ◆ *The child was found abandoned but unharmed.* **2** (of people or their behavior) wild; not following accepted standards

a·ban·don·ment **AWL** /əˈbændənmənt/ *noun* [U] (*formal*) **1** the act of leaving a person, thing, or place with no intention of returning **2** the act of giving up an idea or stopping an activity with no intention of returning to it: *the government's abandonment of its new economic policy*

a·base /əˈbeɪs/ *verb* ~ yourself (*formal*) to act in a way that shows that you accept someone's power over you
  ▶ **a·base·ment** *noun* [U]

a·bashed /əˈbæʃt/ *adj.* [not before noun] embarrassed and ashamed because of something that you have done
  ANT UNABASHED

a·bate /əˈbeɪt/ *verb* [I, T] (*formal*) to become less strong; to make something less strong: *The storm showed no signs of abating.* ◆ ~ sth *Steps are to be taken to abate pollution.*
  ▶ **a·bate·ment** *noun* [U]

ab·bess /ˈæbəs/ *noun* a woman who is the head of a CONVENT

ab·bey /ˈæbi/ *noun* a large church together with a group of buildings in which MONKS or NUNS live or lived in the past: *a sixteenth-century abbey*

ab·bot /ˈæbət/ *noun* a man who is the head of a MONASTERY or an ABBEY

ab·bre·vi·ate /əˈbrivieɪt/ *verb* [usually passive] ~ sth (to sth) to make a word, phrase, or name shorter by leaving out letters or using only the first letter of each word SYN SHORTEN: *The National Aeronautics and Space Administration is abbreviated to NASA.* ▶ **ab·bre·vi·at·ed** *adj.*: *Where appropriate, abbreviated forms are used.*

ab·bre·vi·a·tion /əˌbriviˈeɪʃn/ *noun* **1** [C] ~ (of/for sth) a short form of a word, etc.: *What's the abbreviation for "Saint"?* **2** [U] the process of abbreviating something

ABC /ˌeɪ bi ˈsi/ *noun, abbr.*
- **noun** [sing.] (also **ABCs, ABC's** [pl.]) **1** all the letters of the alphabet, especially as they are learned by children: *Do you know your ABCs?* **2** the basic facts about a subject: *the ABCs of gardening* **IDM** see EASY *adj.*
- **abbr.** American Broadcasting Company (a large national television company)

ABD /ˌeɪ bi ˈdi/ *abbr.* all but dissertation (having completed all the work for a higher degree except the DISSERTATION): *ABD students may apply.*

ab·di·cate /ˈæbdɪˌkeɪt/ *verb* **1** [I, T] to give up the position of being king or queen: *He abdicated in favor of his son.* ♦ **~ sth** *She was forced to abdicate the throne of Spain.* **2** [T] **~ responsibility/your responsibilities** to fail or refuse to perform a duty ▶ **ab·di·ca·tion** /ˌæbdɪˈkeɪʃn/ *noun* [U, C]

ab·do·men /ˈæbdəmən/ *noun* **1** the part of the body below the chest that contains the stomach, BOWELS, etc. **2** the end part of an insect's body that is attached to its THORAX

ab·dom·i·nal /æbˈdɑmənl; əb-/ *adj., noun*
● *adj.* [only before noun] (*anatomy*) relating to or connected with the abdomen: *abdominal pains*
● *noun* **ab·dom·i·nals** (also informal **abs**) [pl.] the muscles of the abdomen

ab·duct /əbˈdʌkt; æb-/ *verb* **~ sb** to take someone away illegally, especially using force **SYN** KIDNAP ▶ **ab·duc·tion** /əbˈdʌkʃn; æb-/ *noun* [U, C]

ab·duct·ee /ˌæbdʌkˈti/ *noun* a person who has been abducted

ab·duc·tor /əbˈdʌktər; æb-/ *noun* **1** a person who abducts someone **2** (also **abˈductor ˌmuscle**) (*anatomy*) a muscle that moves a body part away from the middle of the body or from another part ➔ **compare** ADDUCTOR

a·bed /əˈbɛd/ *adv.* (*old use*) in bed

ab·er·rant /əˈbɛrənt; ˈæbərənt/ *adj.* (*formal*) not usual or not socially acceptable: *aberrant behavior*

ab·er·ra·tion /ˌæbəˈreɪʃn/ *noun* [C, U] (*formal*) a fact, an action, or a way of behaving that is not usual, and that may be unacceptable

a·bet /əˈbɛt/ *verb* (-tt-) **~ sb** to help or encourage someone to do something wrong or illegal: *He was abetted in the deception by his wife.* **IDM** see AID v.

a·bey·ance /əˈbeɪəns/ *noun* [U]
IDM **in abeyance** (*formal*) not being used, or being stopped for a period of time

ab·hor /əbˈhɔr; æb-/ *verb* (-rr-) (not used in the progressive tenses) **~ sth** (*formal*) to hate something, for example a way of behaving or thinking, especially for moral reasons **SYN** DETEST, LOATHE

ab·hor·rence /əbˈhɔrəns; -ˈhɑr-/ *noun* [U, sing.] (*formal*) a feeling of strong hatred, especially for moral reasons

ab·hor·rent /əbˈhɔrənt; -ˈhɑr-/ *adj.* **~ (to sb)** (*formal*) causing hatred, especially for moral reasons **SYN** REPUGNANT: *Racism is abhorrent to a civilized society.*

a·bide /əˈbaɪd/ *verb* (**a·bid·ed**, **a·bid·ed**) **HELP** In sense 2 **ab·ode** is also used for the past tense and past participle. **1** [T] **can't/couldn't abide someone or something** to dislike someone or something so much that you hate having to be with or deal with them **SYN** BEAR, STAND: *I can't abide people with no sense of humor.* ♦ *He couldn't abide the thought of being cooped up in an office.* **2** [I] + **adv./prep.** (*old use* or *formal*) to stay or live in a place: *May joy and peace abide in us all.*
PHR V **aˈbide by sth** to accept and act according to a law, an agreement, etc.: *You'll have to abide by the rules of the club.* ♦ *We will abide by their decision.*

a·bid·ing /əˈbaɪdɪŋ/ *adj.* (*formal*) (of a feeling or belief) lasting for a long time and not changing

a·bil·i·ty 🔑 /əˈbɪləti/ *noun*
(*pl.* **a·bil·i·ties**) **1** [sing.] **~ to do sth** the fact that someone or something is able to do something: *The system has the ability to run more than one program at the same time.*
♦ *Everyone has the right to good medical care regardless of their ability to pay.* **ANT** INABILITY **2** [C, U] a level of skill or intelligence: *Almost everyone has some musical ability.* ♦ *He was a man of extraordinary abilities.* ♦ *students of mixed abilities* ♦ *A woman of her ability will easily find a job.* ♦ *I try to do my job to the best of my ability* (= as well as I can).

-ability, -ibility ➔ -ABLE

a·bi·ot·ic /ˌeɪbaɪˈɑtɪk/ *adj.* (*technical*) not involving biology or living things: *abiotic processes*

ab·ject /ˈæbdʒɛkt; æbˈdʒɛkt/ *adj.* [usually before noun] (*formal*) **1** terrible and without hope: *abject poverty/misery/failure* **2** without any pride or respect for yourself: *an abject apology* ▶ **ab·ject·ly** *adv.*

ab·jure /æbˈdʒʊr; əb-/ *verb* **~ sth** (*formal*) to promise publicly that you will give up or reject a belief or a way of behaving **SYN** RENOUNCE

ab·la·tion /əˈbleɪʃn/ *noun* [U] (*geology*) the loss of material from a large mass of ice, snow, or rock as a result of the action of the sun, wind, or rain

ab·la·tive /ˈæblətɪv/ *noun* (*grammar*) (in some languages) the form that a noun, a pronoun, or an adjective can take to show, for example, who or what something is done by or where something comes from ➔ **compare** ACCUSATIVE, DATIVE, GENITIVE, NOMINATIVE, VOCATIVE ▶ **ab·la·tive** *adj.*

a·blaze /əˈbleɪz/ *adj.* [not before noun] **1** burning quickly and strongly: *The whole building was soon ablaze.* ♦ *Cars and buses were set ablaze during the riot.* **2** full of bright light or colors: *There were lights still ablaze as they drove up to the house.* ♦ **~ with sth** *The trees were ablaze with fall colors.* **3 ~ (with sth)** full of strong emotion or excitement: *He turned to her, his eyes ablaze with anger.*

a·ble 🔑 /ˈeɪbl/ *adj.*

1 ~ to do sth (used as a modal verb) to have the skill, intelligence, opportunity, etc. needed to do something: *You must be able to speak French for this job.* ♦ *A viral infection left her barely able to walk.* ♦ *I didn't feel able to disagree with him.* ♦ *Will you be able to come?* **ANT** UNABLE ➔ note at CAN[1] **2** (**a·bler** /ˈeɪblər/, **a·blest** /ˈeɪbləst/) intelligent; good at something: *the ablest student in the class* ♦ *We aim to help the less able in society to lead an independent life.* ➔ see also ABLY

WORD FAMILY
able *adj.* (≠ unable)
ably *adv.*
ability *noun* (≠ inability)
disabled *adj.*
disability *noun*

-able, -ible /əbl/ *suffix* (in adjectives) **1** that can or must be: *calculable* ♦ *taxable* **2** having the quality of: *fashionable* ♦ *comfortable* ♦ *changeable* ▶ **-ability, -ibility** /əˈbɪləti/ (in nouns): *capability* ♦ *responsibility* **-ably, -ibly** /əbli/ (in adverbs): *noticeably* ♦ *incredibly*

able–bodied /ˌeɪbl ˈbɑdid/ *adj.* physically healthy, fit, and strong in contrast to someone who is weak or DISABLED

ab·lu·tions /əˈbluʃnz/ *noun* [pl.] (*formal* or *humorous*) the act of washing yourself

a·bly /ˈeɪbli/ *adv.* skillfully and well: *We were ably assisted by a team of volunteers.* ➔ see also ABLE

ABM /ˌeɪ bi ˈɛm/ *noun* (*CanE*) = ATM

ab·ne·ga·tion /ˌæbnɪˈgeɪʃn/ *noun* [U] (*formal*) the act of not allowing yourself to have something that you want; the act of rejecting something ▶ **ab·ne·gate** /ˈæbnɪˌgeɪt/ *verb* [T] **~ sth**

ab·nor·mal **AWL** /æbˈnɔrml/ *adj.* different from what is usual or expected, especially in a way that is worrying, harmful, or not wanted: *abnormal levels of sugar in the blood* ♦ *They thought his behavior was abnormal.* **ANT** NORMAL ▶ **ab·nor·mal·ly** **AWL** /-məli/ *adv.*: *abnormally high blood pressure*

ab·nor·mal·i·ty /ˌæbnɔrˈmæləti; -nər-/ *noun* (*pl.* **ab·nor·mal·i·ties**) [C, U] a feature or characteristic in a person's body or behavior that is not usual and may be harmful, worrying, or cause illness: *abnormalities of the heart* ♦ *congenital/fetal abnormality*

a·board /əˈbɔrd/ *adv., prep.* on or onto a ship, plane, bus, or train **SYN** ON BOARD: *We went aboard.* ♦ *He was already aboard the plane.* ♦ *The plane crashed, killing all 157 passengers aboard.* ♦ *All aboard!* (= the bus, boat, etc. is leaving soon) ♦ *Welcome aboard!* (= used to welcome passengers or a person joining a new organization, etc.)

a·bode /əˈboʊd/ *noun* [usually sing.] (*formal* or *humorous*) the place where someone lives: *You are most welcome to my humble abode.* ⊃ see also ABIDE

a·bol·ish /əˈbɑlɪʃ/ *verb* ~ **sth** to officially end a law, a system, or an institution: *This tax should be abolished.*

ab·o·li·tion /ˌæbəˈlɪʃn/ *noun* [U] **1** the ending of a law, a system, or an institution: *the abolition of capital punishment* **2** usually **Abolition** the official ending of the institution of SLAVERY in the U.S.

ab·o·li·tion·ist /ˌæbəˈlɪʃənɪst/ *noun* **1** a person who is in favor of the abolition of something **2** usually **Abolitionist** a person who supported or worked for the abolition of SLAVERY in the U.S.: *the Abolitionist John Brown*

ˈA-bomb *noun* = ATOMIC BOMB

a·bom·i·na·ble /əˈbɑmənəbl/ *adj.* extremely unpleasant and causing disgust **SYN** APPALLING, DISGUSTING: *The judge described the attack as an abominable crime.* ◆ *We were served the most abominable coffee.* ▶ **a·bom·i·na·bly** /-bli/ *adv.*: *She treated him abominably.*

Aˌbominable ˈSnowman *noun* = YETI

a·bom·i·nate /əˈbɑmə.neɪt/ *verb* (not used in the progressive tenses) ~ **sth/sb** (*formal*) to feel hatred or disgust for something or someone

a·bom·i·na·tion /əˌbɑmə'neɪʃn/ *noun* (*formal*) a thing that causes disgust and hatred, or is considered extremely offensive

ab·o·rig·i·nal /ˌæbəˈrɪdʒənl/ *adj., noun*
● *adj.* **1** usually **Ab·o·rig·i·nal** relating to the original people living in Australia: *the issue of Aboriginal land rights* **2** relating to the original people, animals, etc. of a place and to a period of time before Europeans arrived: *the aboriginal peoples of Canada* ◆ *aboriginal art/culture*
● *noun* usually **Ab·o·rig·i·nal** a member of a race of people who were the original people living in a country, especially Australia

ab·o·rig·i·ne /ˌæbəˈrɪdʒəni/ *noun* **1** a member of a race of people who were the original people living in a country **2** **Ab·o·rig·i·ne** a member of the race of people who were the original people of Australia

a·bort /əˈbɔrt/ *verb* **1** [I, T, often passive] to end or cause something to end before it has been completed, especially because it is likely to fail: (*computing*) *If the wrong password is given the program will abort.* ◆ ~ **sth** *We had no option but to abort the mission.* **2** [T] ~ **sth** to end a PREGNANCY early in order to prevent a baby from developing and being born alive: *to abort a pregnancy/fetus* **3** [I] (*technical*) to give birth to a child or young animal too early for it to survive: *The virus can cause pregnant animals to abort.* ⊃ compare MISCARRY

a·bor·tion /əˈbɔrʃn/ *noun* **1** [U] the deliberate ending of a PREGNANCY at an early stage: *to support/oppose abortion* ◆ *a woman's right to abortion* ◆ *abortion laws* ◆ *I've always been anti-abortion.* **2** [C] a medical operation to end a PREGNANCY so that the baby is not born alive: *She decided to have an abortion.* ⊃ compare MISCARRIAGE

a·bor·tion·ist /əˈbɔrʃənɪst/ *noun* a person who performs abortions, especially illegally

a·bor·tive /əˈbɔrtɪv/ *adj.* (*formal*) (of an action) not successful; failed **SYN** UNSUCCESSFUL: *an abortive military coup* ◆ *abortive attempts to divert the course of the river*

a·bound /əˈbaʊnd/ *verb* [I] to exist in great numbers or quantities: *Stories about his travels abound.*
PHR V **aˈbound with/in sth** to have something in great numbers or quantities: *The lakes abound with fish.* ⊃ see also ABUNDANCE, ABUNDANT

a·bout 🔑 /əˈbaʊt/ *adv., prep., adj.*
● *adv.* **1** a little more or less than; a little before or after **SYN** APPROXIMATELY: *It costs about $10.* ◆ *They waited (for) about an hour.* ◆ *He arrived (at) about ten.* **2** nearly; very close to: *I'm just about ready.* ◆ *This is about the best we can hope for.* **3** (*technical* or *formal*) facing the opposite direction: *He brought the ship about.*

IDM **that's about all | that's about it** used to say that you have finished telling someone about something and there is nothing to add: *"Anything else?" "No, that's about it for now."* ⊃ more at JUST, OUT

● *prep.* **1** on the subject of someone or something; in connection with someone or something: *a book about flowers* ◆ *Tell me all about it.* ◆ *What's she so angry about?* ◆ *There's something strange about him.* ◆ *I don't know what you're talking about.* ◆ *There's nothing you can do about it now.* **2** used to describe the purpose or an aspect of something: *Movies are all about making money these days.* ◆ *What was all that about?* (= what was the reason for what has just happened?) **3** busy with something; doing something: *Everywhere people were going about their daily business.* **4** in many directions or parts of a place; here and there **SYN** AROUND: *We wandered about the town for an hour or so.* ◆ *The papers were strewn about the room.* **5** next to a place or person; in the area mentioned **SYN** AROUND: *She's somewhere about the office.* **6** (*literary*) surrounding someone or something: *She wore a shawl about her shoulders.*
IDM **how/what about...?** **1** used when asking for information about someone or something: *How about Ruth? Have you heard from her?* ◆ *I'm having fish. What about you?* **2** used to make a suggestion: *How about we go for a walk?* ◆ *What about a break?*

● *adj.*
IDM **be about to do sth** to be close to doing something; to be going to do something very soon: *I was just about to ask you the same thing.* **not be about to do sth** to not be willing to do something; to not intend to do something: *I've never done any cooking and I'm not about to start now.*

┌───┐
LANGUAGE BANK

about

saying what a text is about

- The book **is about** homeless people in the cities.
- The report **deals with** the issue of homelessness in urban areas.
- The writer **discusses** the problems faced by homeless people.
- The article **presents an overview of** the issues surrounding homelessness.
- The novel **explores** the theme of friendship among homeless people.
- The first chapter **examines** the relationship between homelessness and drug addiction.
- The paper **considers** the question of why so many young people become homeless.
└───┘

aˌbout-ˈface *noun* [sing.] a complete change of opinion, plan, or behavior: *The government did an about-face on nuclear energy.*

a·bove 🔑 /əˈbʌv/ *prep., adv., adj.*
● *prep.* **1** at or to a higher place or position than something or someone: *The water came above our knees.* ◆ *We were flying above the clouds.* ◆ *the people in the apartment above mine* ◆ *A captain in the navy ranks above a captain in the army.* ◆ *They finished the year six places above their local rivals.* **2** more than something; greater in number, level, or age than someone or something: *Inflation is above 6%.* ◆ *Temperatures have been above average.* ◆ *We cannot accept children above the age of 10.* **3** of greater importance or of higher quality than someone or something: *I rate her above most other players of her age.* **4** too good or too honest to do something: *She's not above lying when it gets her out of trouble.* ◆ *He's above suspicion* (= he is completely trusted). **5** (of a sound) louder or clearer than another sound: *I couldn't hear her above the noise of the traffic.*
IDM **above all** most important of all; especially: *Above all, keep in touch.* ⊃ more at OVER ⊃ language bank at EMPHASIS
● *adv.* **1** at or to a higher place: *Put it on the shelf above.* ◆ *Seen from above the cars looked tiny.* ◆ *They were acting on*

instructions from above (= from someone in a higher position of authority). **2** greater in number, level, or age: *increases of 5% and above* ◆ *A score of 90 or above will get you an "A."* ◆ *children aged 12 and above* **3** earlier in something written or printed: *As was stated above...* ◆ *See above, page 97.*

● *adj.* [only before noun] mentioned or printed previously in a letter, book, etc.: *Please write to us at the above address.* ▶ **the a·bove** noun [C] (*pl.* **the a·bove**): *Please notify us if the above is not correct.* ◆ *All the above* (= the people mentioned) *have passed the exam.* **HELP** When **the above** refers to a plural noun, the verb is plural.

WHICH WORD?

above ◆ over

- **Above** and **over** can both be used to describe a position higher than something: *They built a new room above/over the garage.* When you are talking about movement from one side of something to the other, you can only use **over**: *They jumped over the stream.* **Over** can also mean "covering": *He put a blanket over the sleeping child.*
- **Above** and **over** can also mean "more than." **Above** is used in relation to a minimum level or a fixed point: *2,000 feet above sea level* ◆ *Temperatures will not rise above freezing tonight.* **Over** is used with numbers, ages, money, and time: *He's over 50.* ◆ *It costs over $100.* ◆ *We waited over 2 hours.*

a·bove·board /əˈbʌvbɔrd/ *adj., adv.* legal and honest; in a legal and honest way: *Don't worry; the deal was completely aboveboard.* **ORIGIN** If card players keep their hands above the table (the board), other players can see what they are doing.

a·bove-ˌmentioned *adj.* [only before noun] mentioned or named earlier in the same letter, book, etc.

a·bove-the-ˈfold *adj.* in a position where it is seen first, for example on the top half of the front page of a newspaper or in the part of a Web page that you see first when you open it: *above-the-fold images* ◆ *The company logo must be placed in an above-the-fold position.* ◆ compare BELOW-THE-FOLD **IDM** see FOLD

ab·ra·ca·dab·ra /ˌæbrəkəˈdæbrə/ *exclamation* a word that people say when they do a magic trick, in order to make it successful

a·brade /əˈbreɪd/ *verb* ~ sth (*technical*) to rub the surface of something, such as rock or skin, and damage it or make it rough

a·bra·sion /əˈbreɪʒn/ *noun* (*technical*) **1** [C] a damaged area of the skin where it has been rubbed against something hard and rough: *He suffered cuts and abrasions to the face.* **2** [U] damage to a surface caused by rubbing something very hard against it: *Diamonds have extreme resistance to abrasion.*

a·bra·sive /əˈbreɪsɪv/ *adj., noun*

● *adj.* **1** (of a person or their manner) rude and unkind; acting in a way that may hurt other people's feelings: *an abrasive style/tone/comment* **2** an abrasive substance is rough and can be used to clean a surface or to make it smooth: *abrasive kitchen cleaners* ▶ **a·bra·sive·ly** *adv.* **a·bra·sive·ness** *noun* [U]

● *noun* a substance used for cleaning surfaces or for making them smooth

a·breast /əˈbrɛst/ *adv.* next to someone or something and facing the same way: *biking two abreast* ◆ *~ of sb/sth A police car drew abreast of us and signaled us to stop.* **IDM keep/stay abreast of sth** to make sure that you know all the most recent facts about a subject: *It is almost impossible to keep abreast of all the latest developments in computing.*

a·bridge /əˈbrɪdʒ/ *verb* ~ sth to make a book, play, etc. shorter by leaving parts out ▶ **a·bridged** *adj.*: *an abridged edition/version* **ANT** UNABRIDGED **a·bridge·ment** (also **a·bridg·ment**) *noun* [U, C]

a·broad /əˈbrɔd/ *adv.*

1 in or to a foreign country: *to be/go/travel/live abroad* ◆ *She worked abroad for a year.* ◆ *He was famous, both at home and abroad* (= in his own country and in other countries). **2** (*formal*) being talked about or felt by many people: *There was news abroad that a change was coming.* **3** (*old use*) outside; outdoors

ab·ro·gate /ˈæbrəgeɪt/ *verb* ~ sth (*technical*) to officially end a law, an agreement, etc. **SYN** REPEAL ▶ **ab·ro·ga·tion** /ˌæbrəˈgeɪʃn/ *noun* [U]

ab·rupt /əˈbrʌpt/ *adj.* **1** sudden and unexpected, often in an unpleasant way: *an abrupt change/halt/departure* **2** speaking or acting in a way that seems unfriendly and rude; not taking time to say more than is necessary **SYN** BRUSQUE, CURT: *an abrupt manner* ◆ *She was very abrupt with me in our meeting.* ▶ **ab·rupt·ly** *adv.* **ab·rupt·ness** *noun* [U]

ABS /ˌeɪ bi ˈɛs/ *abbr.* antilock braking system ◆ see also ANTILOCK

abs /æbz/ *noun* [pl.] (*informal*) = ABDOMINAL

ab·scess /ˈæbsɛs/ *noun* a swollen and infected area on your skin or in your body, full of a thick yellow liquid (called PUS)

ab·scis·sa /æbˈsɪsə/ (*pl.* **ab·scis·sae** /-ˈsɪsi/ or **ab·scis·sas**) *noun* (*mathematics*) the COORDINATE that gives the distance along the horizontal AXIS ◆ compare ORDINATE

ab·scond /əbˈskɑnd; æb-/ *verb* [I] **1** ~ (from sth) to escape from a place that you are not allowed to leave without permission **2** ~ (with sth) to leave secretly and take with you something, especially money, that does not belong to you: *He absconded with the company funds.*

ab·sence /ˈæbsəns/ *noun*

1 [U, C] the fact of someone being away from a place where they are usually expected to be; the occasion or period of time when someone is away: *The decision was made in my absence* (= while I was not there). ◆ *We did not receive any news during his long absence.* ◆ *~ from... absence from work* ◆ *repeated absences from school* ◆ see also LEAVE **2** [U] the fact of someone or something not existing or not being available; a lack of something: *The case was dismissed in the absence of any definite proof.* ◆ *the absence of any women on the board of directors* **ANT** PRESENCE
IDM absence makes the heart grow fonder (*saying*) used to say that when you are away from someone that you love, you love them even more ◆ more at CONSPICUOUS

ab·sent /ˈæbsənt/ *adj., verb*

● *adj.* /ˈæbsənt/ **1** ~ (from sth) not in a place because of illness, etc.: *to be absent from school* **ANT** PRESENT **2** ~ (from sth) not present in something: *Love was totally absent from his childhood.* **ANT** PRESENT **3** showing that you are not really looking at or thinking about what is happening around you: *an absent expression* ◆ see also ABSENTLY

● *verb* /æbˈsɛnt/ ~ yourself (from sth) (*formal*) to not go to or be in a place where you are expected to be: *He had absented himself from the office for the day.*

ab·sen·tee /ˌæbsənˈti/ *noun* a person who is not at a place where they were expected to be

ˌabsentee ˈballot *noun* a vote in an election that you can send when you cannot be present

ab·sen·tee·ism /ˌæbsənˈtiɪzəm/ *noun* [U] the fact of being frequently away from work or school, especially without good reasons

ˌabsentee ˈlandlord *noun* a person who rents their property to someone, but does not live in it and rarely visits it

ab·sen·tia ◆ IN ABSENTIA

ab·sent·ly /ˈæbsəntli/ *adv.* in a way that shows you are not looking at or thinking about what is happening around you: *He nodded absently, his attention absorbed by the screen.*

ab·sent·mind·ed /ˌæbsəntˈmaɪndəd/ *adj.* tending to forget

t **tea**   ţ **butter**   d **did**   k **cat**   g **got**   tʃ **chin**   dʒ **June**   f **fall**

things, perhaps because you are not thinking about what is around you, but about something else **SYN FORGETFUL**
▶ **ab·sent·mind·ed·ly** adv. **ab·sent·mind·ed·ness** noun [U]

ab·sinthe /ˈæbsɪnθ/ noun [U] a very strong, green, alcoholic drink that tastes of ANISEED

ab·so·lute 🔑 /ˈæbsəˌlut; ˌæbsəˈlut/ adj., noun
• **adj.** **1** total and complete: *a class for absolute beginners* ♦ *absolute confidence/trust/silence/truth* ♦ *"You're wrong," she said with absolute certainty.* **2** [only before noun] used, especially in spoken English, to give emphasis to what you are saying: *There's absolute garbage on television tonight.* ♦ *He must earn an absolute fortune.* **3** definite and without any doubt or confusion: *There was no absolute proof.* ♦ *He taught us that the laws of physics were absolute.* ♦ *The divorce became absolute last week.* ⟳ see also DECREE ABSOLUTE **4** not limited or restricted: **absolute power/authority** ♦ *an absolute ruler/monarchy* (= one with no limit to their power) **5** existing or measured independently and not in relation to something else: *Although prices are falling* **in absolute terms**, *energy is still expensive.* ♦ *Beauty cannot be measured by any absolute standard.* ⟳ compare RELATIVE
• **noun** an idea or a principle that is believed to be true or valid in any circumstances: *Right and wrong are, for her, moral absolutes.*

ab·so·lute·ly 🔑 /ˈæbsəˌlutli; ˌæbsəˈlutli/ adv.
1 used to emphasize that something is completely true: *You're absolutely right.* ♦ *He made it absolutely clear.* **2** **absolutely no…, absolutely nothing** used to emphasize something negative: *She did absolutely no work.* ♦ *There's absolutely nothing more the doctors can do.* **3** used with adjectives or verbs that express strong feelings or extreme qualities to mean "extremely": *I was absolutely furious with him.* ♦ *She absolutely adores you.* ♦ *He's an absolutely fantastic cook.* **4** /ˌæbsəˈlutli/ used to emphasize that you agree with someone, or to give someone permission to do something: *"They could have told us, couldn't they?" "Absolutely!"* ♦ *"Can we leave a little early?" "Absolutely!"* **5** **absolutely not** used to emphasize that you strongly disagree with someone, or to refuse permission: *"Was it any good?" "No, absolutely not."*

ˌabsolute maˈjority noun more than half of the total number of votes or winning candidates

ˌabsolute ˈtemperature noun [U, C] temperature measured from absolute zero in KELVINS

ˌabsolute ˈzero noun [U] the lowest temperature that is thought to be possible, zero degrees on the KELVIN SCALE, equal to around -273°C or -459°F

ab·so·lu·tion /ˌæbsəˈluʃn/ noun [U] (especially in the Christian Church) a formal statement that a person is forgiven for what they have done wrong

ab·so·lut·ism /ˈæbsəˌlutɪzəm/ noun [U] **1** a political system in which a ruler or government has total power at all times **2** belief in a political, religious, or moral principle that is thought to be true in any circumstances
▶ **ab·so·lut·ist** /-ˌlutɪst/ noun, adj.

ab·solve /əbˈzɑlv/ verb **1** ~ sb **(from/of sth)** to state formally that someone is not guilty or responsible for something: *The court absolved him of all responsibility for the accident.* **2** ~ sb **(from/of sth)** to give ABSOLUTION to someone: *I absolve you from all your sins.*

ab·sorb 🔑 /əbˈsɔrb; əbˈzɔrb/ verb
❯ **LIQUID/GAS** **1** to take in a liquid, gas, or other substance from the surface or space around: ~ **sth** *Plants absorb oxygen.* ♦ ~ **sth into sth** *The lotion is easily absorbed into the skin.*
❯ **MAKE PART OF SOMETHING LARGER** **2** [often passive] to make something smaller become part of something larger: ~ **sth** *The country simply cannot absorb this influx of refugees.* ♦ ~ **sth into sth** *The surrounding small towns have been absorbed into the city.*
❯ **INFORMATION** **3** ~ **sth** to take something into the mind and

learn or understand it **SYN TAKE IN**: *It's a lot of information to absorb all at once.*
❯ **INTEREST SOMEONE** **4** ~ **sb** to interest someone very much so that they pay no attention to anything else **SYN ENGROSS**: *This work had absorbed him for several years.*
❯ **HEAT/LIGHT/ENERGY** **5** ~ **sth** to take in and keep heat, light, energy, etc. instead of reflecting it: *Black walls absorb a lot of heat during the day.*
❯ **SHOCK/IMPACT** **6** ~ **sth** to reduce the effect of a blow, hit, etc.: *This tennis racket absorbs shock on impact.* ⟳ see also SHOCK ABSORBER
❯ **MONEY/TIME/CHANGES** **7** ~ **sth** to use up a large supply of something, especially money or time: *The new proposals would absorb $80 billion of the federal budget.* **8** ~ **sth** to deal with changes, effects, costs, etc.: *The company is unable to absorb such huge losses.*

ab·sorb·a·ble /əbˈsɔrbəbl; -ˈzɔr-/ adj. able to be absorbed, especially into the body: *absorbable gases*

ab·sorb·ance /əbˈsɔrbəns; -ˈzɔr-/ noun [U] (physics) the ability of a substance to absorb light

ab·sorbed /əbˈsɔrbd; -ˈzɔrbd/ adj. [not usually before noun] ~ **in sth/sb** very interested in something or someone so that you are not paying attention to anything else: *She seemed totally absorbed in her book.*

ab·sorb·ent /əbˈsɔrbənt; -ˈzɔr-/ adj. able to take in something easily, especially liquid: *absorbent paper/materials/cotton* ▶ **ab·sorb·en·cy** /-bənsi/ noun [U]

ab·sorb·ing /əbˈsɔrbɪŋ; -ˈzɔr-/ adj. interesting and enjoyable, and holding your attention completely: *an absorbing book/game* ⟳ thesaurus box at INTERESTING

ab·sorp·tion /əbˈsɔrpʃn; -ˈzɔrp-/ noun [U] **1** the process of a liquid, gas, or other substance being taken in: *Vitamin D is necessary to aid the absorption of calcium from food.* **2** the process of a smaller group, country, etc. becoming part of a larger group or country: *the absorption of immigrants into the host country* **3** ~ **(in sth)** the fact of someone being very interested in something so that it takes all their attention: *His work suffered because of his total absorption in sports.*

ab·stain /əbˈsteɪn/ verb [I] **1** ~ **(from sth)** to choose not to use a vote, either in favor of or against something: *Ten people voted in favor, five against, and two abstained.* **2** ~ **(from sth)** to decide not to do or have something, especially something you like or enjoy, because it is bad for your health or considered morally wrong: *to abstain from alcohol/sex/drugs* ⟳ see also ABSTENTION, ABSTINENCE

ab·stain·er /əbˈsteɪnər/ noun **1** a person who chooses not to vote either in favor of or against something **2** a person who never drinks alcohol

ab·ste·mi·ous /əbˈstimiəs/ adj. (formal) not allowing yourself to have much food or alcohol, or to do things that are enjoyable

ab·sten·tion /əbˈstɛnʃn/ noun **1** [C, U] ~ **(from sth)** an act of choosing not to use a vote either in favor of or against something: *The voting was 15 in favor, 3 against, and 2 abstentions.* **2** [U] (formal) the act of not allowing yourself to have or do something enjoyable or something that is considered bad ⟳ see also ABSTAIN

ab·sti·nence /ˈæbstənəns/ noun [U] ~ **(from sth)** (formal) the practice of not allowing yourself something, especially food, alcoholic drinks, or sex, for moral, religious, or health reasons: *total abstinence from alcohol* ⟳ see also ABSTAIN

ab·sti·nent /ˈæbstənənt/ adj. not allowing yourself something, especially alcoholic drinks, for moral, religious, or health reasons

ab·stract **AWL** adj., noun, verb
• **adj.** /əbˈstrækt; æb-; ˈæbstrækt/ **1** based on general ideas and not on any particular real person, thing, or situation: *abstract knowledge/principles* ♦ *The research shows that preschool children are capable of thinking in abstract terms.* ⟳ compare CONCRETE **2** existing in thought or as an idea but not having a physical reality: *We may talk of beautiful things, but beauty itself is abstract.* **3** (of art) not representing

people or things in a realistic way, but expressing the artist's ideas about them ⊃ compare FIGURATIVE (2), REPRESENTATIONAL ▶ **ab·stract·ly** **AWL** adv.

● **noun** /'æbstrækt/ **1** an abstract work of art **2** a short piece of writing containing the main ideas in a document **SYN** SUMMARY

IDM **in the abstract** in a general way, without referring to a particular real person, thing, or situation

● **verb** **1** /əb'strækt; æb-/ ~ **sth (from sth)** to remove something from somewhere: *She abstracted the main points from the argument.* ◆ *a plan to abstract 8 million gallons of water from the river* **2** /'æbstrækt/ ~ **sth** (*technical*) to make a written summary of a book, etc.

ab·stract·ed /əb'stræktəd; æb-/ adj. (*formal*) thinking deeply about something and not paying attention to what is around you ▶ **ab·stract·ed·ly** adv.

ˌ**abstract ex'pressionism** noun [U] a style and movement in abstract art that developed in New York in the middle of the 20th century and tries to express the feelings of the artist rather than showing a physical object
▶ ˌ**abstract ex'pressionist** noun: *abstract expressionists like Jackson Pollock* ˌ**abstract ex'pressionist** adj. [usually before noun]: *abstract expressionist art*

ab·strac·tion **AWL** /əb'strækʃn; æb-/ noun **1** [C, U] (*formal*) a general idea not based on any particular real person, thing, or situation; the quality of being abstract **2** [U] (*formal*) the state of thinking deeply about something and not paying attention to what is around you **3** [U, C] (*technical*) the action of removing something from something else; the process of being removed from something else: *water abstraction from rivers*

ab·strac·tion·ism /əb'strækʃənɪzəm; æb-/ noun [U] **1** (*technical*) the principles and practices of ABSTRACT art **2** the expression of ideas in an abstract way ▶ **ab·strac·tion·ist** /-ʃənɪst/ noun, adj. [usually before noun]

ˌ**abstract 'noun** noun (*grammar*) a noun, for example *beauty* or *freedom*, that refers to an idea or a general quality, not to a physical object ⊃ compare COMMON NOUN, PROPER NOUN

ab·struse /əb'strus; æb-/ adj. (*formal*, often *disapproving*) difficult to understand: *an abstruse argument*

ab·surd /əb'sərd; əb'zərd/ adj. **1** completely ridiculous; not logical and sensible **SYN** RIDICULOUS: *That uniform makes the guards look absurd.* ◆ *Of course it's not true, what an absurd idea.* **2** **the absurd** noun [sing.] things that are or that seem to be absurd: *He has a good sense of the absurd.*
▶ **ab·surd·i·ty** /əb'sərdəti; -'zər-/ noun [U, C] (pl. **ab·surd·i·ties**): *It was only later that she could see the absurdity of the situation.* **ab·surd·ly** adv. **SYN** RIDICULOUSLY: *The paintings were sold for absurdly high prices.*

ab·surd·ism /əb'sərdɪzəm; -'zər-/ noun [U] the belief that humans exist in a world with no purpose or order ▶ **ab·surd·ist** /-dɪst/ noun **ab·surd·ist** adj. [usually before noun]: *absurdist literature*

a·bun·dance /ə'bʌndəns/ noun [sing., U] ~ **(of sth)** (*formal*) a large quantity that is more than enough
IDM **in abundance** in large quantities: *Fruit and vegetables grew in abundance on the island.*

a·bun·dant /ə'bʌndənt/ adj. (*formal*) existing in large quantities; more than enough **SYN** PLENTIFUL: *Fish are abundant in the lake.* ◆ *We have abundant evidence to prove his guilt.*

a·bun·dant·ly /ə'bʌndəntli/ adv. **1** ~ **clear** very clear: *She made her wishes abundantly clear.* **2** in large quantities: *Calcium is found most abundantly in dairy products.*

a·buse 🔑 noun, verb
● **noun** /ə'byus/ **1** [U, sing.] the use of something in a way that is wrong or harmful **SYN** MISUSE: *alcohol/drug abuse*
◆ *The system of paying cash bonuses is open to abuse* (= might be used in the wrong way). ◆ ~ **of sth** *He was arrested on charges of corruption and abuse of power.* ◆ *What she did was an abuse of her position as manager.* ⊃ see also SUBSTANCE ABUSE **2** [U, pl.] unfair, cruel, or violent treatment of

someone: *child abuse* ◆ *sexual abuse* ◆ *reported abuses by the secret police* ◆ *She suffered years of physical abuse.* **3** [U] rude and offensive remarks, usually made when someone is very angry **SYN** INSULT: *to scream/hurl/shout abuse* ◆ *a stream/torrent of abuse*

● **verb** /ə'byuz/ **1** ~ **sth** to make bad use of something, or to use so much of something that it harms your health: *to abuse alcohol/drugs* ◆ *He systematically abused his body with heroin and cocaine.* **2** ~ **sth** to use power or knowledge unfairly or wrongly: *She abused her position as principal by giving jobs to her friends.* ◆ *He felt they had abused his trust by talking about him to the press* (= tricked him, although he had trusted them). **3** ~ **sb/sth** to treat a person or an animal in a cruel or violent way, especially sexually: *All the children had been physically and emotionally abused.* ◆ *The boy had been sexually abused.* **4** ~ **sb** to make rude or offensive remarks to or about someone **SYN** INSULT: *The referee had been threatened and abused.* ▶ **a·bus·er** noun: *a drug abuser* ◆ *a child abuser*

a·bu·sive /ə'byusɪv/ adj. **1** (of speech or of a person) rude and offensive; criticizing rudely and unfairly: *abusive language/remarks* ◆ *He became abusive when he was drunk.* **2** (of behavior) involving violence: *an abusive relationship* ▶ **a·bu·sive·ly** adv.

a·but /ə'bʌt/ verb (-tt-) [I, T] ~ **(on) sth** (*formal*) (of land or a building) to be next to something or to have one side touching the side of something: *The hedges abut the road.*

a·but·ment /ə'bʌtmənt/ noun a structure built to support the ends of a bridge or an ARCH

a·buzz /ə'bʌz/ adj. [not before noun] ~ **(with sth)** | ~ **(about sb/sth)** filled with excitement or with the sound of people talking in an excited way: *The room was abuzz with gossip.*

a·bys·mal /ə'bɪzməl/ adj. extremely bad or of a very low standard **SYN** TERRIBLE ▶ **a·bys·mal·ly** adv.

a·byss /ə'bɪs/ noun [usually sing.] (*formal* or *literary*) a very deep wide space or hole that seems to have no bottom: *Ahead of them was a gaping abyss.* ◆ (*figurative*) *an abyss of ignorance/despair/loneliness* ◆ (*figurative*) *The country is stepping back from the edge of an abyss.*

AC /ˌeɪ 'si/ abbr. **1** AIR CONDITIONING **2** ALTERNATING CURRENT

a·ca·cia /ə'keɪʃə/ (also **a'cacia ˌtree**) noun a tree with yellow or white flowers. There are several types of acacia trees, some of which produce a sticky liquid used in making glue.

ac·a·de·mi·a **AWL** /ˌækə'dimiə/ (also *formal* or *humorous* **ac·a·deme** /'ækəˌdim; ˌækə'dim/) noun [U] the world of learning, teaching, research, etc. at colleges and universities; the people involved in it

ac·a·dem·ic 🔑 **AWL** /ˌækə'dɛmɪk/ adj., noun
● **adj.** **1** [usually before noun] connected with education, especially studying in colleges and universities: *The students return in October for the beginning of the new academic year.* ◆ *high/low academic standards* ◆ *an academic career* **2** [usually before noun] involving a lot of reading and studying rather than practical or technical skills: *academic subjects* **3** not connected to a real or practical situation and therefore not important: *It is a purely academic question.* ◆ *The whole thing's academic now—we can't win anyway.*
▶ **ac·a·dem·i·cally** **AWL** /-kli/ adv.: *You have to do well academically to get into medical school.*

● **noun** **1** [C] a person who teaches and/or does research at a college or university **2** **academics** [pl.] subjects that students study in school or college

ac·a·de·mi·cian /ˌækədə'mɪʃn; əˌkædə-/ noun a member of an academy

ˌ**academic 'year** noun the period of the year during which students go to school or college

a·cad·e·my **AWL** /ə'kædəmi/ noun (pl. **a·cad·e·mies**) **1** a school or college for special training: *the United States Naval Academy* ◆ *a police/military academy* **2** usually **Academy** a type of official organization that aims to encourage and

| h **h**at | m **m**an | n **n**o | ŋ si**ng** | l **l**eg | r **r**ed | y **y**es | w **w**et |

develop art, literature, science, etc.: *the National Academy of Sciences* **3** used in the name of some private high schools: *Deerfield Academy*

A·cad·e·my A'ward™ (also **Os·car™**) *noun* one of the awards given every year by the U.S. Academy of Motion Picture Arts and Sciences for achievement in the making of movies

A·ca·di·an /ə'keɪdiən/ *noun* **1** a French-speaking Canadian from New Brunswick, and parts of Québec near it, Nova Scotia, or Prince Edward Island **2** a person from Louisiana whose family originally came from the French COLONY of Acadia in what is now Nova Scotia, Canada

a cap·pel·la /ˌɑ kə'pɛlə/ *adj.* (*music*) for singing voices alone, without musical instruments ▶ **a cap·pel·la** *adv.*

ac·cede /ək'sid/ *verb* [I] (*formal*) **1** ~ **(to sth)** to agree to a request, proposal, etc.: *He acceded to demands for his resignation.* **2** ~ **(to sth)** to achieve a high position, especially to become king or queen: *The queen acceded to the throne.* ⊃ see also ACCESSION

ac·cel·er·ate /ək'sɛləˌreɪt/ *verb* **1** [I, T] to happen or to make something happen faster or earlier than expected: *Inflation continues to accelerate.* ♦ ~ **sth** *Exposure to the sun can accelerate the aging process.* **2** [I] (of a vehicle or person) to start to go faster: *The runners accelerated smoothly around the bend.* ♦ *The car accelerated to pass me.* **ANT** DECELERATE

ac·cel·er·a·tion /əkˌsɛlə'reɪʃn/ *noun* **1** [U, sing.] ~ **(in sth)** an increase in how fast something happens: *an acceleration in the rate of economic growth* **2** [U] the rate at which a vehicle increases speed: *a car with good acceleration* **3** [U] (*physics*) the rate at which the VELOCITY (= speed in a particular direction) of an object changes

ac·cel·er·a·tor /ək'sɛləˌreɪtər/ *noun* **1** the PEDAL in a car or other vehicle that you press with your foot to control the speed of the engine **SYN** GAS PEDAL ⊃ picture at CAR ⊃ collocations at DRIVING **2** (*physics*) a machine for making ELEMENTARY PARTICLES move at high speeds

ac'celerator ˌboard (also **ac'celerator ˌcard**) *noun* (*computing*) a CIRCUIT BOARD that can be put into a small computer to increase the speed at which it processes information

ac·cel·er·om·e·ter /əkˌsɛlə'rɑmətər/ *noun* (*physics*) an instrument for measuring ACCELERATION

ac·cent 🔑 *noun*, *verb*

● *noun* /'æksɛnt/ **1** [C, U] a way of pronouncing the words of a language that shows which country, area, or social class a person comes from: *a Southern/New York/Greek/British accent* ♦ *a heavy/thick accent* (= one that is very noticeable). ♦ *She spoke English with an accent.* ⊃ compare DIALECT **2** [sing.] a special importance that is given to something **SYN** EMPHASIS: *In all our products the accent is on quality.* **3** [C] the emphasis that you should give to part of a word when saying it **SYN** STRESS: *In "today" the accent is on the second syllable.* **4** [C] a mark on a letter to show that it should be pronounced in a particular way: *Canapé has an accent on the "e."*

● *verb* /'æksɛnt; æk'sɛnt/ ~ **sth** to emphasize a part of something

ac·cent·ed /'æksɛntəd; æk'sɛn-/ *adj.* **1** spoken with a foreign accent: *He spoke heavily accented English.* **2** (*technical*) spoken with particular emphasis: *accented vowels/syllables* **3** (*technical*) (of a letter of the alphabet) written or printed with a special mark on it to show it should be pronounced in a particular way: *accented characters*

ac·cen·tu·ate /ək'sɛntʃuˌeɪt/ *verb* ~ **sth** to emphasize something or make it more noticeable: *Her short hair accentuated her huge eyes.* ▶ **ac·cen·tu·a·tion** /əkˌsɛntʃu-'eɪʃn/ *noun* [U]

ac·cept 🔑 /ək'sɛpt/ *verb*

> OFFER/INVITATION **1** [I, T] to willingly take something that is offered; to say "yes" to an offer, invitation, etc.: *He asked me to marry him and I accepted.* ♦ ~ **sth** *Please accept our sincere*

apologies. ♦ *It was pouring rain so I accepted his offer of a ride.* ♦ *She decided not to accept the job.* ♦ ~ **sth from sb** *He was charged with accepting bribes from his suppliers.* ♦ ~ **sth for sth** *She said she'd accept $15 for it.* **ANT** REFUSE[1]

> RECEIVE AS SUITABLE **2** [T] to receive something as suitable or good enough: ~ **sth** *This machine only accepts coins.* ♦ *Will you accept a check?* ♦ ~ **sth for sth** *My article has been accepted for publication.*

> AGREE **3** [T] to agree to or approve of something: ~ **sth** *They accepted the court's decision.* ♦ *He accepted all the changes we proposed.* ♦ ~ **sth from sb** *She won't accept advice from anyone.* **ANT** REJECT ⊃ thesaurus box at AGREE

> RESPONSIBILITY **4** [T] ~ **sth** to admit that you are responsible or to blame for something: *He accepts full responsibility for what happened.* ♦ *You have to accept the consequences of your actions.*

> BELIEVE **5** [T] to believe that something is true: ~ **sth** *I don't accept his version of events.* ♦ ~ **sth as sth** *Can we accept his account as the true version?* ♦ ~ **that…** *I accept that this will not be popular.* ♦ *It is generally accepted that people are motivated by success.* ♦ **be accepted to be/have sth** *The Northeast is generally accepted to have some of the best colleges in the country.*

> DIFFICULT SITUATION **6** [T] to continue in a difficult situation without complaining, because you realize that you cannot change it: ~ **sth** *You just have to accept the fact that we're never going to be rich.* ♦ *Nothing will change as long as the workers continue to accept these terrible conditions.* ♦ ~ **sth as sth** *They accept the risks as part of the job.* ♦ ~ **that…** *He just refused to accept that his father was no longer there.*

> WELCOME **7** [T] to make someone feel welcome and part of a group: ~ **sb** *It may take years to be completely accepted by the local community.* ♦ ~ **sb into sth** *She had never been accepted into what was essentially a man's world.* ♦ ~ **sb as sth** *He never really accepted her as his own child.* **ANT** REJECT

> ALLOW SOMEONE TO JOIN **8** [T] to allow someone to join an organization, attend an institution, use a service, etc.: ~ **sb** *The college he applied to has accepted him.* ♦ ~ **sb into sth** *She was disappointed not to be accepted into the club.* ♦ ~ **sb as sth** *The landlord was willing to accept us as tenants.* ♦ ~ **sb to do sth** *She was accepted to study music.* **ANT** REJECT

ac·cept·a·ble 🔑 /ək'sɛptəbl/ *adj.*
1 agreed or approved of by most people in a society: *Children must learn socially acceptable behavior.* **2** that someone agrees is of a good enough standard or allowed: *To take this course, the lowest acceptable test score is 90.* ♦ *Air pollution in the city had reached four times the acceptable levels.* ♦ ~ **to sb** *We want a political solution that is acceptable to all parties.* **3** not very good, but good enough: *The food was acceptable, but no better than that.* **ANT** UNACCEPTABLE ▶ **ac·cept·a·bil·i·ty** /əkˌsɛptə'bɪləti/ *noun* [U] **ac·cept·a·bly** /ək'sɛptəbli/ *adv.*

ac·cept·ance /ək'sɛptəns/ *noun* **1** [U, C] the act of accepting a gift, an invitation, an offer, etc.: *Please confirm your acceptance of this offer in writing.* ♦ *He made a short acceptance speech.* **2** [U] the act of agreeing with something and approving of it: *The new laws have gained widespread acceptance.* **3** [U] the process of allowing someone to join something or be a member of a group: *Your acceptance into the insurance plan is guaranteed.* ♦ *Social acceptance is important for most young people.* **4** [U] willingness to accept an unpleasant or difficult situation: *acceptance of death/suffering*

ac·cess 🔑 **AWL** /'æksɛs/ *noun*, *verb*
● *noun* [U] **1** a way of entering or reaching a place: *The police gained access through a broken window.* ♦ ~ **to sth** *The only access to the farmhouse is across the fields.* ♦ *Disabled visitors are welcome; there is good wheelchair access to most facilities.* ⊃ compare EGRESS **2** ~ **(to sth)** the opportunity or right to use something or to see someone or something: *Students must have access to good resources.* ♦ *You need a password to get access to the computer system.* ♦ *access to confidential information* ♦ *Journalists were denied access to the president.*
● *verb* **1** ~ **sth** (*computing*) to open a computer file in order to

get or add information **2** ~ **sth** (*formal*) to reach, enter, or use something: *The loft can be accessed with a ladder.*

ac·ces·si·ble `AWL` /ək'sɛsəbl/ *adj.* **1** that can be reached, entered, used, seen, etc.: *The remote desert area is accessible only by helicopter.* ◆ *All the entrances are wheelchair accessible.* ◆ ~ **to sb** *These documents are not accessible to the public.* **2** easy to understand: *Her poetry is always very accessible.* ◆ ~ **to sb** *a program making science more accessible to young people* **3** (of a person) easy to talk to and get to know **ANT** INACCESSIBLE ▶ **ac·ces·si·bil·i·ty** `AWL` /ək,sɛsə'bıləti/ *noun* [U]

ac·ces·sion /ək'sɛʃn/ *noun* **1** [U] ~ **(to sth)** the act of becoming a ruler of a country: *the accession of the queen to the throne* ⊃ see also ACCEDE **2** [U] ~ **(to sth)** the act of becoming part of an international organization: *the accession of new member states to the EU in 2004* **3** [C] (*technical*) a thing that is added to a collection of objects, paintings, etc. in a library or museum

ac·ces·so·rize /ək'sɛsə,raız/ *verb* ~ **sth** to add fashionable items or extra decorations to something, especially to your clothes: *She accessorized her outfit with a scarf and some bracelets.*

ac·ces·so·ry /ək'sɛsəri/ *noun, adj.*
● *noun* (*pl.* **ac·ces·so·ries**) **1** [usually pl.] an extra piece of equipment that is useful but not essential, or that can be added to something else as a decoration: *bicycle accessories* ◆ *a line of furnishings and accessories for the home* **2** [usually pl.] a thing that you can wear or carry that matches your clothes, for example a belt or jewelry **3** (*law*) a person who helps someone to commit a crime or who knows about it, and protects the person from the police: *an accessory before/after the fact* (= before/after the crime was committed) ◆ ~ **to sth** *He was charged with being an accessory to murder.*
● *adj.* (*technical*) not the most important when compared with others: *the accessory muscles of respiration*

'access ,road *noun* a road used for driving into or out of a particular place

'access ,time *noun* [U, C] (*computing*) the time taken to obtain data stored in a computer

ac·ci·dent ✍ /'æksədənt; -,dɛnt/ *noun*
1 [C] an unpleasant event, especially in a vehicle, that happens unexpectedly and causes injury or damage: *a car/highway/traffic accident* ◆ *He was killed in an accident.* ◆ *One in seven accidents is caused by sleepy drivers.* ◆ *The accident happened at 3 p.m.* ◆ *to have an accident* ◆ *a serious/minor accident* ◆ *a fatal accident* (= in which someone is killed) ◆ *accidents in the home* ◆ *a climbing/riding accident* ◆ *Take out accident insurance before you go on your trip.* ◆ *I didn't mean to break it— it was an accident.* **2** [C, U] something that happens unexpectedly and is not planned in advance: *Their early arrival was just an accident.* ◆ *It is no accident that men fill most of the high-paying jobs in finance.* ◆ *an accident of birth/fate/history* (= describing facts and events that are due to chance or circumstances) ⊃ thesaurus box at LUCK
IDM accidents (will) happen people say **accidents (will) happen** to tell someone who has had an accident, for example breaking something, that it does not matter and they should not worry **by accident** in a way that is not planned or organized: *We met by accident at the airport.* ◆ *Helen got into acting purely by accident.* ◆ *She broke the vase by accident.* **ANT** DELIBERATELY ⊃ more at WAIT

ac·ci·den·tal ✍ /,æksə'dɛntl/ *adj.* happening by chance; not planned: *a verdict of accidental death* ◆ *I didn't think our meeting was accidental—he must have known I would be there.* ▶ **ac·ci·den·tal·ly** /-'dɛntli; -'dɛntl·i/ *adv.*: *As I turned around, I accidentally hit him in the face.* ◆ *The damage couldn't have been caused accidentally.*

'accident-,prone *adj.* more likely to have accidents than other people

ac·claim /ə'kleım/ *verb, noun*
● *verb* [usually passive] to praise or welcome someone or something publicly: ~ **sb/sth** *a highly/widely acclaimed*

performance ◆ ~ **sb/sth as sth** *The work was acclaimed as a masterpiece.*
● *noun* [U] praise and approval for someone or something, especially an artistic achievement: *international/popular/critical acclaim*

ac·cla·ma·tion /,æklə'meıʃn/ *noun* [U] **1** (*formal*) loud and enthusiastic approval or welcome **2** (*technical*) the act of electing someone using a spoken, not written, vote: *The decision was made by acclamation.*

ac·cli·mate /'æklə,meıt/ (also **ac·cli·ma·tize** /ə'klaımə,taız/) *verb* [I, T] to get used to a new place, situation, or climate: ~ **(to sth)** *Arrive two days early in order to acclimate.* ◆ ~ **yourself (to sth)** *She was fine once she had acclimated herself to the cold.* ▶ **ac·cli·ma·tion** /,æklə'meıʃn/ (also **ac·cli·ma·ti·za·tion** /ə,klaımətə'zeıʃn/) *noun* [U]

ac·co·lade /'ækə,leıd/ *noun* (*formal*) praise or an award for an achievement that people admire: *Meryl Streep has received many accolades for her performances.*

ac·com·mo·date `AWL` /ə'kɑmə,deıt/ *verb* **1** [T] ~ **sb** to provide someone with a room or place to sleep, live, or sit: *The hotel can accommodate up to 500 guests.* **2** [T] ~ **sb/sth** to provide enough space for someone or something: *The old town hall now accommodates a Folk Museum.* **3** [T] ~ **sth** (*formal*) to consider something, such as someone's opinion or a fact, and be influenced by it when you are deciding what to do or explaining something: *Our proposal tries to accommodate the special needs of the disabled.* **4** [T] ~ **sb** **(with sth)** (*formal*) to help someone by doing what they want **SYN** OBLIGE: *I have accommodated the press a great deal, giving numerous interviews.* **5** [I, T] ~ **(sth/yourself) to sth** (*formal*) to change your behavior so that you can deal with a new situation better: *I needed to accommodate myself to the new schedule.*

ac·com·mo·dat·ing `AWL` /ə'kɑmə,deıtıŋ/ *adj.* willing to help and do things for other people **SYN** OBLIGING

ac·com·mo·da·tion `AWL` /ə,kɑmə'deıʃn/ *noun* **1** **accommodations** [pl.] somewhere to live or stay, often also providing food or other services: *Hotel accommodations are included in the price of your vacation package.* ◆ *deluxe accommodations* **2** [C, U] (*formal*) an agreement or arrangement between people or groups with different opinions that is acceptable to everyone; the process of reaching this agreement: *They were forced to reach an accommodation with the rebels.* **3** [U] (*biology*) the way that the eyes automatically adjust so that you can see objects at varying distances

ac·com·pa·ni·ment `AWL` /ə'kʌmpənimənt/ *noun* **1** [C, U] ~ **(to sth)** music that is played to support singing or another instrument: *traditional songs with piano accompaniment* **2** [C] ~ **(to sth)** something that you eat, drink, or use together with something else: *The wine makes a good accompaniment to fish dishes.* **3** [C] ~ **(to sth)** (*formal*) something that happens at the same time as another thing: *High blood pressure is a common accompaniment to this disease.*
IDM to the accompaniment of sth 1 while a musical instrument is being played: *They performed to the accompaniment of guitars.* **2** while something else is happening: *She made her speech to the accompaniment of loud laughter.*

ac·com·pa·nist /ə'kʌmpənɪst/ *noun* a person who plays a musical instrument, especially a piano, while someone else plays or sings the main part of the music

ac·com·pa·ny ✍ `AWL` /ə'kʌmpəni/ *verb* (**ac·com·pa·nies**, **ac·com·pa·ny·ing**, **ac·com·pa·nied**, **ac·com·pa·nied**) **1** ~ **sb** (*formal*) to travel or go somewhere with someone: *His wife accompanied him on the trip.* **2** ~ **sth** to happen or appear with something else: *strong winds accompanied by heavy rain* ◆ *Each pack contains a book and accompanying CD.* **3** ~ **sb (at/on sth)** to play a musical instrument, especially a piano, while someone else sings or plays the main tune: *The singer was accompanied on the piano by her sister.*

ac·com·pli ⊃ FAIT ACCOMPLI

ʌ **cup**   ə **about**   eı **say**   aı **five**   ɔı **boy**   aʊ **now**   oʊ **go**   ər **bird**

ac·com·plice /əˈkʌmpləs/ *noun* a person who helps another to commit a crime or to do something wrong

ac·com·plish /əˈkʌmplɪʃ/ *verb* ~ **sth** to succeed in doing or completing something **SYN** ACHIEVE: *The first part of the plan has been safely accomplished.* ◆ *I don't feel I've accomplished very much today.* ◆ *That's it.* **Mission accomplished** (= we have done what we aimed to do).

ac·com·plished /əˈkʌmplɪʃt/ *adj.* very good at a particular thing; having a lot of skills: *an accomplished artist/actor/chef* ◆ *She was an elegant and highly accomplished woman.*

ac·com·plish·ment /əˈkʌmplɪʃmənt/ *noun* **1** [C] an impressive thing that is done or achieved after a lot of work **SYN** ACHIEVEMENT: *It was one of the president's greatest accomplishments.* **2** [U] (*formal*) the successful completing of something: *Money will be crucial to the accomplishment of our objectives.* **3** [C, U] a skill or special ability: *Drawing and singing were among her many accomplishments.* ◆ *a poet of rare accomplishment*

ac·cord /əˈkɔːd/ *noun, verb*
● *noun* a formal agreement between two organizations, countries, etc.: *The two sides signed a **peace accord** last July.* **IDM** in accord (with sth/sb) (*formal*) in agreement with: *This action would not be in accord with our policy.* of your own accord without being asked, forced, or helped: *He came back of his own accord.* ◆ *The symptoms will clear up of their own accord.*
● *verb* (*formal*) **1** [T] to give someone or something authority, status, or a particular type of treatment: ~ **sth to sb/sth** *Our society accords great importance to the family.* ◆ ~ **sb/sth sth** *Our society accords the family great importance.* **2** [I] ~ (with sth) to agree with or match something: *These results accord closely with our predictions.*

ac·cord·ance /əˈkɔːdns/ *noun*
IDM in accordance with sth (*formal*) according to a rule or the way that someone says that something should be done: *in accordance with legal requirements*

ac·cord·ing·ly /əˈkɔːdɪŋli/ *adv.* **1** in a way that is appropriate to what has been done or said in a particular situation: *We have to discover his plans and act accordingly.* **2** (used especially at the beginning of a sentence) for that reason **SYN** THEREFORE: *The cost of materials rose sharply last year. Accordingly, we were forced to increase our prices.*

according to /əˈkɔːdɪŋ tə/ *prep.*

1 as stated or reported by someone or something: *According to Mick, it's a great movie.* ◆ *You've been absent six times, according to our records.* ➔ language bank at ILLUSTRATE **2** following, agreeing with, or depending on something: *The work was done according to her instructions.* ◆ *Everything went according to plan.* ◆ *The salary will be set according to qualifications and experience.*

LANGUAGE BANK

according to
reporting someone's opinion
- Photography is, **according to** Vidal, the art form of untalented people.
- For Vidal, photography is the art form of untalented people.
- His **view is that** photography is not art but merely the mechanical reproduction of images.
- Smith **takes the view that** photography is both an art and a science.
- In Brown's **view**, photography should be treated as a legitimate art in its own right.
- James **is of the opinion that** a good painter can always be a good photographer if he or she so decides.
- Emerson **believed that** a photograph should reflect only what the human eye can see.

➔ Language Banks at ARGUE, OPINION

accordion   concertina

ac·cor·di·on /əˈkɔːdiən/ *noun* a musical instrument that you hold in both hands to produce sounds. You press the two ends together and pull them apart, and press buttons and/or keys to produce the different notes. ➔ see also PIANO ACCORDION

ac·cost /əˈkɒst; əˈkɑːst/ *verb* ~ **sb** (*formal*) to go up to someone and speak to them, especially in a way that is rude or threatening: *She was accosted in the street by a complete stranger.*

ac·count /əˈkaʊnt/ *noun, verb*
● *noun*
> AT BANK **1** (*abbr.* acct.) an arrangement that someone has with a bank, etc. to keep money there, take some out, etc.: *I don't have a bank account.* ◆ *to have an **account at/with** a bank* ◆ *to **open/close an account*** ◆ *What's your account number please?* ◆ *I deposited the check into my savings account.* ◆ *a **joint account** (= one that more than one person uses)* ➔ see also CHECKING ACCOUNT, SAVINGS ACCOUNT
> BUSINESS RECORDS **2** [usually pl.] a written record of all the money that a business pays out and receives: *to do the accounts* ◆ *accounts payable/accounts receivable* ➔ see also EXPENSE ACCOUNT, PROFIT AND LOSS ACCOUNT
> WITH STORE/COMPANY **3** (also ˈcharge acˌcount, *informal* charge) an arrangement with a store or business to pay bills for goods or services at a later time, for example in regular amounts every month: *Put it on my store account please.* ◆ *We have accounts with most of our suppliers.* ➔ thesaurus box at BILL
> REGULAR CUSTOMER **4** (*business*) a regular customer: *The agency has lost several of its most important accounts.*
> COMPUTING **5** an arrangement that someone has with a company that allows them to use the Internet, send, and receive messages by e-mail, etc.: *an **Internet/e-mail account***
> DESCRIPTION **6** a written or spoken description of something that has happened: *He gave the police a full account of the incident.* ➔ thesaurus box at REPORT **7** an explanation or a description of an idea, a theory, or a process: *the Biblical account of the creation of the world*
IDM by/from all accounts according to what other people say: *I've never been there, but it's a beautiful place, by all accounts.* by your own account according to what you say yourself: *By his own account, he had an unhappy childhood.* on account if you buy something or pay on account, you pay nothing or only a small amount immediately and the rest later on sb's account because of what you think someone wants: *Please don't change your plans on my account.* on account of sb/sth because of someone or something: *She retired early on account of ill health.* ➔ language bank at BECAUSE on no account | not on any account (used to emphasize something) not for any reason: *On no account should the house be left unlocked.* on your own account **1** for yourself: *In 2006 Smith set up in business on his own account.* **2** because you want to and you have decided, not someone else: *No one sent me, I am here on my own account.* on this/that account (*formal*) because of the particular thing that has been mentioned: *Weather conditions were poor, but he did not delay his departure on that account.* put/turn sth to good account (*formal*) to use something in a good or helpful way take account of sth | take sth into account to consider particular facts, circumstances, etc. when making a decision about something: *The company takes account of environmental issues wherever possible.* ◆ *Coursework is taken into account as well as exam results.* ◆ *The*

---

defendant asked for a number of other offenses to be taken into account. ➲ more at BLOW, CALL, SETTLE

● **verb** [usually passive] (*formal*) to have the opinion that someone or something is a particular thing: ~ *sb/sth* + **adj.** *In American law, a person is accounted innocent until they are proved guilty.* ◆ ~ *sb/sth* + **noun** *The event was accounted a success.*

IDM **there's no accounting for taste** (*saying*) used to say how difficult it is to understand why someone likes someone or something that you do not like at all: *She thinks he's wonderful—oh well, there's no accounting for taste.* ➲ more at PRESENT

PHR V **ac'count for sth** **1** to be the explanation or cause of something **SYN** EXPLAIN: *The bad weather may have accounted for the small crowd.* ◆ *Oh well, that accounts for it* (= I understand now why it happened). **2** to give an explanation of something **SYN** EXPLAIN: *How do you account for the show's success?* **3** to be a particular amount or part of something: *The Japanese market accounts for 35% of the company's revenue.* ➲ language bank at PROPORTION
ac'count for sb/sth **1** to know where someone or something is or what has happened to them, especially after an accident: *All passengers have now been accounted for.* **2** (*informal*) to defeat or destroy someone or something: *Our antiaircraft guns accounted for five enemy bombers.*
ac'count for sth (to sb) to give a record of how the money in your care has been spent: *We have to account for every penny we spend on business trips.*

ac·count·a·ble /əˈkaʊntəbl/ *adj.* [not usually before noun] responsible for your decisions or actions and expected to explain them when you are asked: ~ **to sb** *Politicians are ultimately accountable to the voters.* ◆ ~ **for sth** *Someone must be held accountable for the killings.* ▶ **ac·count·a·bil·i·ty** /əˌkaʊntəˈbɪləti/ *noun* [U]: *the accountability of a company's executives to the shareholders*

ac·count·an·cy /əˈkaʊntnsi/ *noun* [U] the work or profession of an accountant

ac·count·ant /əˈkaʊntnt/ *noun* (*abbr.* **acct.**) a person whose job is to keep or check financial accounts ➲ see also CPA

ac,count ex'ecutive *noun* a business person, especially one working in advertising, who is responsible for dealing with one of the company's regular customers

ac·count·ing /əˈkaʊntɪŋ/ *noun* [U] the process or work of keeping financial accounts: *a career in accounting* ◆ *accounting methods*

ac,counts 'payable *noun* [pl.] (*business*) money that is owed by a company

ac,counts re'ceivable *noun* [pl.] (*business*) money that is owed to a company

ac·cou·tre·ments (also **ac·cou·ter·ments**) /əˈkutrəmənts; əˈkuṭər-/ *noun* [pl.] (*formal or humorous*) pieces of equipment that you need for a particular activity

ac·cred·it /əˈkrɛdət/ *verb* **1** [usually passive] (*formal*) to believe that someone is responsible for doing or saying something: ~ **sth to sb** *The discovery of distillation is usually accredited to the Arabs of the 11th century.* ◆ ~ **sb with sth** *The Arabs are usually accredited with the discovery of distillation.* ➲ compare CREDIT *v.* **2** ~ **sth/sb** to officially approve something or someone as being of an accepted quality or standard: *Institutions that do not meet the standards will not be accredited for teacher training.* **3** [usually passive] ~ **sb to ...** (*technical*) to choose someone for an official position, especially as an AMBASSADOR: *He was accredited to Madrid.*

ac·cred·i·ta·tion /əˌkrɛdəˈteɪʃn/ *noun* [U] official approval given by an organization stating that someone or something has achieved a required standard: *a letter of accreditation* ◆ *an accreditation process*

ac·cred·it·ed /əˈkrɛdəṭəd/ *adj.* [usually before noun] **1** (of a person) officially recognized as something; with official permission to be something: *our accredited representative* ◆ *Only accredited journalists were allowed to enter.* **2** officially approved as being of a certain quality or standard: *a fully accredited school/college/course*

ac·cre·tion /əˈkriʃn/ *noun* (*technical or formal*) **1** [C] a layer of a substance that is slowly added to something **2** [U] the process of new layers being slowly added to something

ac·crue /əˈkru/ *verb* (*formal*) **1** [I] to increase over a period of time: *Interest will accrue if you keep your money in a savings account.* ◆ ~ **(to sb) (from sth)** *economic benefits accruing to the country from tourism* **2** [T] ~ **sth** to allow a sum of money or debts to grow over a period of time **SYN** ACCUMULATE: *The company had accrued debts of over $6 million.* ▶ **ac·cru·al** /əˈkruəl/ *noun* [U, C]: *the accrual of interest*

acct. *abbr.* (in writing) ACCOUNT

ac·cul·tur·ate /əˈkʌltʃəˌreɪt/ *verb* [I, T] ~ **(sb) (to sth)** (*formal*) to learn to live successfully in a different culture; to help someone to do this ▶ **ac·cul·tur·a·tion** /əˌkʌltʃəˈreɪʃn/ *noun* [U]

ac·cu·mu·late **AWL** /əˈkyumyəˌleɪt/ *verb* **1** [T] ~ **sth** to gradually get more and more of something over a period of time **SYN** AMASS: *I seem to have accumulated a lot of books.* ◆ *By investing wisely she accumulated a fortune.* ➲ note at COLLECT **2** [I] to gradually increase in number or quantity over a period of time **SYN** BUILD UP: *Debts began to accumulate.* ➲ thesaurus box at COLLECT ▶ **ac·cu·mu·la·tion** **AWL** /əˌkyumyəˈleɪʃn/ *noun* [U, C]: *the accumulation of wealth* ◆ *an accumulation of toxic chemicals*

ac·cu·mu·la·tive /əˈkyumyəˌleɪtɪv; -ləṭɪv/ *adj.* (*formal*) growing by increasing gradually: *the accumulative effects of pollution* ➲ compare CUMULATIVE

ac·cu·mu·la·tor /əˈkyumyəˌleɪṭər/ *noun* (*computing*) a section of a computer that is used for storing the results of what has been calculated

ac·cu·ra·cy **AWL** /ˈækyərəsi/ *noun* [U] the state of being exact or correct; the ability to do something skillfully without making mistakes: *They questioned the accuracy of the information in the file.* ◆ *She hits the ball with great accuracy.* **ANT** INACCURACY ➲ collocations at ACCURATE

ac·cu·rate 🔑 **AWL** /ˈækyərət/ *adj.*
1 correct and true in every detail: *an accurate description/account/calculation* ◆ *accurate information/data* ◆ *Accurate records must be kept.* **2** able to give completely correct information or to do something in an exact way: *a highly accurate electronic compass* ◆ *accurate to within 3mm* ◆ *My watch is not very accurate.* **3** an **accurate** throw, shot, weapon, etc. hits or reaches the thing that it was aimed at **ANT** INACCURATE ▶ **ac·cu·rate·ly** **AWL** *adv.*: *The article accurately reflects public opinion.* ◆ *You need to hit the ball accurately.*

AWL COLLOCATIONS

accurate
accurate *adj.*

- assessment | diagnosis | estimate, measurement | prediction | description | reflection, representation | information | record | result | method
Firms must acquire accurate information from clients about their needs.
- factually | historically | scientifically | statistically | technically
Although this book is historically accurate, it is not a history book.
- not entirely | not strictly
The figures he gave were not strictly accurate.
- prove
These predictions proved accurate.
- to
Results are accurate to within 0.2 seconds.

inaccurate *adj.*

- perception | estimate | representation | information | result | statement
Inaccurate estimates can lead to overproduction.

■ **grossly**
Errors in methodology can produce grossly inaccurate results.

■ **factually** | **historically** | **scientifically** | **technically**
He is technically inaccurate in several of his claims.

■ **prove**
These predictions may yet prove inaccurate.

accuracy *noun*

■ **absolute**, **pinpoint** | **unerring**
The needle has to be positioned with pinpoint accuracy.

■ **factual** | **historical** | **scientific** | **technical**
Get the manuscript checked for factual accuracy.

■ **confirm** | **ensure** | **check** | **test** | **verify**
Great care is taken to ensure the accuracy of research data.

accurately *adv.*

■ **assess** | **describe** | **diagnose** | **estimate**, **gauge**, **measure** | **predict** | **portray** | **reflect** | **reproduce**
Your title must accurately reflect the substance of your paper.

ac·curs·ed /əˈkɜrsəd; əˈkɜrst/ *adj.* (*old-fashioned*) having a CURSE (= a bad magic SPELL) on it

ac·cu·sa·tion /ˌækyəˈzeɪʃn/ *noun* [C, U] a statement saying that you think a person is guilty of doing something wrong, especially of committing a crime; the fact of accusing someone: *I don't want to **make an accusation** until I have some proof.* ◆ *There was a hint of accusation in her voice.* ◆ **~ of sth** *accusations of corruption/cruelty/racism* ◆ **~ against sb** *No one believed her wild accusations against her husband.* ◆ **~ that…** *He denied the accusation that he had ignored the problems.*

ac·cu·sa·tive /əˈkyuzətɪv/ *noun* (*grammar*) (in some languages) the form of a noun, a pronoun, or an adjective when it is the DIRECT OBJECT of a verb, or connected with the DIRECT OBJECT: *In the sentence, "I saw him today," the word "him" is **in the accusative**.* ⊃ compare ABLATIVE, DATIVE, GENITIVE, NOMINATIVE, VOCATIVE ▶ **ac·cu·sa·tive** *adj.*

ac·cu·sa·to·ry /əˈkyuzəˌtɔri/ *adj.* (*formal*) suggesting that you think someone has done something wrong

ac·cuse 🔑 /əˈkyuz/ *verb*

~ sb (of sth)
to say that someone has done something wrong or is guilty of something: *to accuse someone of murder/theft* ◆ *She accused him of lying.* ◆ *The government was accused of incompetence.* ◆ (*formal*) *They **stand accused** of crimes against humanity.* ▶ **ac·cus·er** *noun*

WORD FAMILY
accuse *verb*
accusation *noun*
accusing *adj.*
accusatory *adj.*
accused *noun*

the ac·cused /əˈkyuzd/ *noun* (*pl.* **the ac·cused**) a person who is on trial for committing a crime: *The accused was found innocent.* ◆ *All the accused have pleaded guilty.* ⊃ compare DEFENDANT

ac·cus·ing /əˈkyuzɪŋ/ *adj.* showing that you think someone has done something wrong: *an accusing look/finger/tone* ◆ *Her accusing eyes were fixed on him.* ▶ **ac·cus·ing·ly** *adv.*

ac·cus·tom /əˈkʌstəm/ *verb*
PHR V **ac'custom yourself/sb to sth** to make yourself/someone familiar with something or become used to it: *It took him a while to accustom himself to the idea.*

ac·cus·tomed /əˈkʌstəmd/ *adj.* **1 ~ to sth/to doing sth** familiar with something and accepting it as normal or usual **SYN** USED TO: **~ to sth** *to become/get accustomed to something* ◆ *My eyes slowly **grew accustomed** to the dark.* ◆ **~ to doing sth** *She was a person accustomed to having eight hours' sleep every night.* **2** [usually before noun] (*formal*) usual **SYN** HABITUAL: *He took his accustomed seat by the fire.* **ANT** UNACCUSTOMED

ace /eɪs/ *noun, verb*
● *noun* **1** a PLAYING CARD with a large single symbol on it,

which has either the highest or the lowest value in a particular card game: *the ace of spades/hearts/diamonds/clubs* ⊃ picture at PLAYING CARD **2** (*informal*) a person who is very good at doing something: *a soccer/flying ace* ◆ *an ace marksman* **3** (in TENNIS) a SERVE (= the first hit) that is so good that your opponent cannot reach the ball: *He served 20 aces in the match.*
IDM **an ace in the hole** (*informal*) a secret advantage, for example a piece of information or a skill, that you are ready to use if you need to **hold all the aces** to have all the advantages in a situation **play your ace** to use your best argument, etc. in order to get an advantage in a situation
● *adj.* (*informal*) very good: *an ace pilot/skier/sailor*
● *verb* **~ sth** (*informal*) to be successful in something: *He aced all his tests.*

a·cel·lu·lar /eɪˈsɛlyələr/ *adj.* (*biology*) not consisting of or divided into cells

a·cer·bic /əˈsɜrbɪk/ *adj.* (*formal*) (of a person or what they say) critical in a direct and rather cruel way: *The letter was written in her usual acerbic style.* ▶ **a·cer·bi·ty** /əˈsɜrbəti/ *noun* [U]

a·ce·ta·min·o·phen /əˌsitəˈmɪnəfən/ *noun* [U, C] a drug used to reduce pain and fever

ac·e·tate /ˈæsəˌteɪt/ *noun* **1** [U] a chemical made from acetic acid, used in making plastics, etc. **2** [U] a chemical used to make FIBERS that are used to make clothes, etc. **3** [C] a transparent plastic sheet that you can write or print something on and show on a screen using an OVERHEAD PROJECTOR

a·ce·tic ac·id /əˌsitɪk ˈæsɪd/ *noun* [U] the acid in VINEGAR that gives it its taste and smell

ac·e·tone /ˈæsəˌtoʊn/ *noun* [U] a clear liquid with a strong smell used for cleaning things, dissolving paint, and producing various chemicals

a·cet·y·lene /əˈsɛtlˌin; -ən/ (*also* **eth·yne**) *noun* [U] (*symb.* C_2H_2) a gas that burns with a very hot, bright flame, used for cutting or joining metal ⊃ compare OXYACETYLENE

ache /eɪk/ *verb, noun*
● *verb* **1** [I] to feel a continuous dull pain **SYN** HURT: *I'm aching all over.* ◆ **~ from sth** *Her eyes ached from lack of sleep.* ◆ (*figurative*) *It makes my heart ache* (= it makes me sad) *to see her suffer.* ⊃ thesaurus box at HURT **2** [I, T] (*formal*) to have a strong desire for someone or something, or to do something **SYN** LONG: **~ for sb/sth** *I was aching for home.* ◆ **~ to do sth** *He ached to see her.*
● *noun* (often in compounds) a continuous feeling of pain in a part of the body: *Mommy, I've got a tummy ache.* ◆ *Muscle aches and pains can be soothed by a relaxing massage.* ◆ (*figurative*) *an ache in my heart* (= a continuous sad feeling) ⊃ see also ACHY, BELLYACHE, HEARTACHE

a·chieve 🔑 **AWL** /əˈtʃiv/ *verb*
1 [T] **~ sth** to succeed in reaching a particular goal, status, or standard, especially by making an effort for a long time **SYN** ATTAIN: *He had finally achieved success.* ◆ *They could not achieve their target of less than 3% inflation.* **2** [T] **~ sth** to succeed in doing something or causing something to happen **SYN** ACCOMPLISH: *I haven't achieved very much today.* ◆ *All you've achieved is making my parents upset.* **3** [I] to be successful: *Their background gives them little chance of achieving in school.* ▶ **a·chiev·a·ble** **AWL** /əˈtʃivəbl/ *adj.*: *Profits of $20 million look achievable.* ◆ *achievable goals* **ANT** UNACHIEVABLE

AWL COLLOCATIONS

achieve

achieve *verb*
to succeed in reaching a particular goal, status, or standard, especially by making an effort for a long time
■ **aim**, **goal**, **objective** | **result**
Leaders are truly effective in achieving organizational objectives only when they are motivated by a concern for others.

strong steady beat, often played at parties where some people take harmful drugs

a·cid·ic /ə'sɪdɪk/ adj. **1** very sour: *Some fruit juices are very acidic.* ⊃ **thesaurus box** at BITTER **2** containing acid: *acidic soil*

a·cid·i·fy /ə'sɪdə,faɪ/ verb (a.cid·i·fies, a.cid·i·fy·ing, a·cid-i·fied, a.cid·i·fied) [I, T] **~ (sth)** *(technical)* to become or make something become an acid

a·cid·i·ty /ə'sɪdəti/ noun [U] the state of having a sour taste or of containing acid

acid 'jazz noun [U] a type of dance music that combines JAZZ, FUNK, SOUL, and HIP-HOP

ac·id·ly /'æsɪdli/ adv. in an unpleasant or critical way: *"Thanks for nothing," she said acidly.*

acid 'rain noun [U] rain that contains harmful chemicals from factory gases and that damages trees, crops, and buildings

'acid test (also **'litmus test**) noun [sing.] a way of deciding whether something is successful or true: *The acid test of a good driver is whether he or she remains calm in an emergency.*

ac·knowl·edge 🔑 **AWL** /ək'nɑlɪdʒ/ verb
> ADMIT **1** to accept that something is true: **~ sth** *She refuses to acknowledge the need for reform.* ◆ **~ that...** *The government acknowledged that the tax was unfair.* ◆ **~ sth to be, have, etc. sth** *It is generally acknowledged to be true.* ⊃ **thesaurus box** at ADMIT
> ACCEPT STATUS **2** to accept that someone or something has a particular authority or status **SYN** RECOGNIZE: **~ sb/sth** *The country acknowledged his claim to the presidency.* ◆ **~ sb/ sth as sth** *He is widely acknowledged as the best player in the world.* ◆ **~ sb/sth to be, have, etc. sth** *He is widely acknowledged to be the best player in the world.*
> REPLY TO LETTER **3 ~ sth** to tell someone that you have received something that they sent to you: *All applications will be acknowledged.* ◆ *Please acknowledge receipt of this letter.*
> SMILE/WAVE **4 ~ sb/sth** to show that you have noticed someone or something by smiling, waving, etc.: *I was standing right next to her, but she didn't even acknowledge me.*
> EXPRESS THANKS **5 ~ sth** to publicly express thanks for help you have been given: *I gratefully acknowledge financial support from several local businesses.*

▶ **ac·knowl·edged AWL** adj.: *a generally acknowledged fact*

AWL COLLOCATIONS

acknowledge
acknowledge verb
to accept or admit the existence or truth of something
- generally, universally, widely | openly, publicly | implicitly, tacitly | explicitly | readily
  Researchers have universally acknowledged the need for more studies in this area.
  Frederick Douglass openly acknowledged his Indian heritage.
- existence | importance | limitation | mistake
  The study's limitations must be acknowledged.
  North acknowledges the importance of technological change.
- that
  The authors acknowledge that some of the results are speculative.
- fail to | refuse to | be forced to
  Kamps's analysis fails to acknowledge a key distinction.

acknowledged adj.
- generally, universally, widely
  It is widely acknowledged that the Internet radically alters the commercial environment.
  Cézanne is the universally acknowledged father of Cubism.

- fail to | attempt to, try to, strive to | be able to | be difficult to | be necessary to
  Woodward concludes that economic policy broadly failed to achieve its goals of low unemployment and low inflation. An accurate estimate of their numbers is difficult to achieve.

achievement noun
a thing that someone has done successfully; the act or process of achieving something
- academic, educational, scholastic | technological
  No significant differences in academic achievement were found.
- impressive, notable, remarkable
  This agreement is a remarkable achievement from both a scientific and a social perspective.

achievable adj.
- easily, readily
  Web-based simulations can generate insights not readily achievable by other means.
- goal, objective
  Self-esteem arises from reaching out for difficult but achievable goals.

a·chieve·ment 🔑 **AWL** /ə'tʃivmənt/ noun
1 [C] a thing that someone has done successfully, especially using their own effort and skill: *the greatest scientific achievement of the decade* ◆ *It was a remarkable achievement for such a young player.* ◆ *They were proud of their children's achievements.* ⊃ **collocations** at ACHIEVE **2** [U] the act or process of achieving something: *the need to raise standards of achievement in education* ◆ *Even a small success gives you a sense of achievement* (= a feeling of pride).

a·chiev·er /ə'tʃivər/ noun **1** a person who achieves a high level of success, especially in their career **2** (after an adjective) a person who achieves the particular level of success that is stated: *a low achiever*

A·chil·les heel /ə,kɪliz 'hil/ noun [sing.] a weak point or fault in someone's character, which can be attacked by other people **ORIGIN** Named after the Greek hero **Achilles.** When he was a small child, his mother held him below the surface of the river Styx to protect him against any injury. She held him by his heel, which therefore was not touched by the water. Achilles died after being wounded by an arrow in the heel.

A,chilles 'tendon /ə,kɪliz 'tɛndən/ (also **A·chil·les**) noun the TENDON that connects the muscles at the back of the lower part of the leg to the heel

ach·ing·ly /'eɪkɪŋli/ adv. (of qualities or feelings) very great and affecting you deeply: *an achingly beautiful song*

achoo /a'tʃu; ə'tʃu/ exclamation the word for the sound people make when they SNEEZE

ach·y /'eɪki/ adj. (informal) suffering from a continuous slight pain: *I feel really achy.* ◆ *an achy back*

ac·id 🔑 /'æsɪd/ noun, adj.
- noun [U, C] (chemistry) a chemical, usually a liquid, that contains HYDROGEN and has a PH of less than seven. The HYDROGEN can be replaced by a metal to form a salt. Acids are usually sour and can often burn holes in or damage things they touch. ⊃ **compare** ALKALI ⊃ **see also** ACETIC ACID, AMINO ACID, ASCORBIC ACID, CITRIC ACID, HYDRO-CHLORIC ACID, LACTIC ACID, NITRIC ACID, NUCLEIC ACID, SULFURIC ACID
- adj. **1** (technical) that contains acid or has the essential characteristics of an acid; that has a pH of less than seven: *Rye can grow in acid soil.* ⊃ **compare** ALKALINE **2** that has a bitter, sharp taste **SYN** SOUR: *acid fruit* **3** (of a person's remarks) critical and unkind **SYN** CUTTING, SARCASTIC: *an acid wit*

'acid house noun [U] a type of electronic music with a

acknowledgment *noun*

the act of accepting that something exists or is true

• implicit, tacit | grudging, candid, frank

From the beginning, the characters' relationship is marked by a candid acknowledgment of Esther's strength.

ac·knowl·edg·ment [AWL] (also **ac·knowl·edge·ment**) /əkˈnɑlɪdʒmənt/ *noun* **1** [sing., U] an act of accepting that something exists or is true, or that something is there: *This report is an acknowledgment of the size of the problem.* • *She gave me a smile of acknowledgment* (= showed that she had seen and recognized me). ➔ **collocations at ACKNOWLEDGE**
2 [C, U] an act or a statement expressing thanks to someone; something that is given to someone as thanks: *I was sent a free copy in acknowledgment of my contribution.* • *The flowers were a small acknowledgment of your kindness.*
3 [C] a letter saying that something has been received: *I didn't receive an acknowledgment of my application.*
4 [C, usually pl.] a statement, especially at the beginning of a book, in which the writer expresses thanks to the people who helped

ACLU /ˌeɪ si ɛl ˈyu/ *abbr.* the abbreviation for "American Civil Liberties Union" (an organization that defends the CIVIL RIGHTS of U.S. citizens)

ac·me /ˈækmi/ *noun* [usually sing.] (*formal*) the highest stage of development or the most excellent example of something **SYN HEIGHT**

ac·ne /ˈækni/ *noun* [U] a skin condition, common among young people, that produces many PIMPLES (= swollen spots), especially on the face and neck: *to have bad acne*

ac·o·lyte /ˈækəˌlaɪt/ *noun* **1** (*formal*) a person who follows and helps a leader **2** (*technical*) a person who helps a priest in some church ceremonies

a·corn /ˈeɪkɔrn/ *noun* the small brown nut of the OAK tree, which grows in a base shaped like a cup **IDM** see **OAK**

a·cous·tic /əˈkustɪk/ *adj.* (also **a·cous·ti·cal** /əˈkustɪkl/)
1 related to sound or to the sense of hearing **2** [usually before noun] (of a musical instrument or performance) designed to make natural sound, not sound produced by electrical equipment: *an acoustic guitar* ▶ **a·cous·ti·cally** /-kli/ *adv.*

ac·ous·tics /əˈkustɪks/ *noun* **1** [pl.] also **acoustic** [sing.] the shape, design, etc. of a room or theater that make it good or bad for carrying sound: *The acoustics of the new concert hall are excellent.* **2** [U] the scientific study of sound

ac·quaint /əˈkweɪnt/ *verb* **~ sb/yourself with sth** (*formal*) to make someone/yourself familiar with or aware of something: *Please acquaint me with the facts of the case.* • *You will first need to acquaint yourself with the filing system.*

ac·quaint·ance /əˈkweɪntns/ *noun* **1** [C] a person that you know but who is not a close friend: *Claire has a wide circle of friends and acquaintances.* • *He's just a business acquaintance.* **2** [U, C] **~ (with sb)** (*formal*) slight friendship: *He hoped their acquaintance would develop further.* **3** [U, C] **~ with sth** (*formal*) knowledge of something: *I had little acquaintance with modern poetry.*
IDM **make sb's acquaintance | make the acquaintance of sb** (*formal*) to meet someone for the first time: *I am delighted to make your acquaintance, Mrs. Baker.* • *I made the acquaintance of several musicians around that time.* **of your acquaintance** (*formal*) that you know: *No one else of my acquaintance was as rich or successful.* **on/at first acquaintance** (*formal*) when you first meet someone: *Even on first acquaintance it was clear that he was not "the right type."*
➔ **more at NOD**

ac·quaintance ˌrape *noun* [U, C] the crime of raping (RAPE) someone, committed by a person the victim knows ➔ **compare DATE RAPE**

ac·quaint·ance·ship /əˈkweɪntnsˌʃɪp/ *noun* [U, C, usually sing.] (*formal*) a slight friendship with someone or knowledge of something: *It was unfair to judge her on such a brief acquaintanceship.*

ac·quaint·ed /əˈkweɪntəd/ *adj.* [not before noun] **1 ~ with sth** (*formal*) familiar with something, having read, seen, or experienced it: *The students are already acquainted with the work of Shakespeare.* • *Employees should be fully acquainted with emergency procedures.* **2** not close friends with someone, but having met a few times before: *We got acquainted at the conference* (= met and started to get to know each other). • **~ with sb** *I am well acquainted with her family.*

ac·qui·esce /ˌækwiˈɛs/ *verb* [I] **~ (in sth)** (*formal*) to accept something without arguing, even if you do not really agree with it: *Senior government figures must have acquiesced in the cover-up.*

ac·qui·es·cence /ˌækwiˈɛsns/ *noun* [U] (*formal*) the fact of being willing to do what someone wants and to accept their opinions, even if you are not sure that they are right: *There was general acquiescence to the UN sanctions.* ▶ **ac·qui·es·cent** /-ˈɛsnt/ *adj.*

ac·quire 🔑 [AWL] /əˈkwaɪər/ *verb* (*formal*)
1 ~ sth to obtain something by buying or being given it: *The company has just acquired new premises.* • *I've suddenly acquired a stepbrother.* **2 ~ sth** to gain something by your own efforts, ability, or behavior: *She has acquired a good knowledge of English.* • *He has acquired a reputation for dishonesty.* • *I have recently acquired a taste for* (= started to like) *olives.*
IDM **an acquired taste** a thing that you do not like much at first but gradually learn to like: *Abstract art is an acquired taste.*

ac·qui·si·tion [AWL] /ˌækwəˈzɪʃn/ *noun* **1** [U] the act of getting something, especially knowledge, a skill, etc.: *theories of child language acquisition* **2** [C] something that someone buys to add to what they already own, usually something valuable: *His latest acquisition is a racehorse.* **3** [C, U] (*business*) a company, piece of land, etc. bought by someone, especially another company; the act of buying it: *They have made acquisitions in several southern states.* • *the acquisition of shares by employees*

ac·quis·i·tive /əˈkwɪzətɪv/ *adj.* (*formal, disapproving*) wanting very much to buy or get new possessions ▶ **ac·quis·i·tive·ness** *noun* [U]

ac·quit /əˈkwɪt/ *verb* (-tt-) **1 ~ sb (of sth)** to decide and state officially in court that someone is not guilty of a crime: *The jury acquitted him of murder.* **ANT CONVICT** **2 ~ yourself well, badly, etc.** (*formal*) to perform or behave well, badly, etc.: *He acquitted himself extremely well in the exams.*

ac·quit·tal /əˈkwɪtl/ *noun* [C, U] an official decision in court that a person is not guilty of a crime: *The case resulted in an acquittal.* • *The jury voted for acquittal.* **ANT CONVICTION** ➔ **collocations at JUSTICE**

a·cre /ˈeɪkər/ *noun* a unit for measuring an area of land; 4,840 square yards (about 4,050 square meters): *3,000 acres of parkland* • *a three-acre area of woods* • (*informal*) *Each house has acres of space around it* (= a lot of space).

a·cre·age /ˈeɪkərɪdʒ/ *noun* [U, C] an area of land measured in acres

ac·rid /ˈækrɪd/ *adj.* having a strong, bitter smell or taste that is unpleasant **SYN PUNGENT**: *acrid smoke from burning tires*

ac·ri·mo·ni·ous /ˌækrəˈmoʊniəs/ *adj.* (*formal*) (of an argument, etc.) angry and full of strong, bitter feelings and words **SYN BITTER**: *His parents went through an acrimonious divorce.* ▶ **ac·ri·mo·ni·ous·ly** *adv.*

ac·ri·mo·ny /ˈækrəˌmoʊni/ *noun* [U] (*formal*) angry, bitter feelings or words: *The dispute was settled without acrimony.*

ac·ro·bat /ˈækrəˌbæt/ *noun* an entertainer who performs difficult acts such as balancing on high ropes, especially at a CIRCUS

ac·ro·bat·ic /ˌækrəˈbætɪk/ *adj.* involving or performing difficult acts or movements with the body: *acrobatic feats* • *an acrobatic dancer* ▶ **ac·ro·bat·i·cally** /-kli/ *adv.*

ac·ro·bat·ics /ˌækrəˈbætɪks/ *noun* [pl.] acrobatic acts and movements: *acrobatics on the high wire* • (*figurative*) *vocal* acrobatics (= performing skillfully with the voice when singing)

ac·ro·nym /'ækrənɪm/ *noun* a word formed from the first letters of the words that make up the name of something: For example, "AIDS" is an acronym for "acquired immune deficiency syndrome."

a·crop·o·lis /ə'krɑpələs/ *noun* (in an ancient Greek city) a castle, or an area that is designed to resist attack, especially one on top of a hill

a·cross 🔑 /ə'krɔs/ *adv., prep.*

- *adv.* **HELP** For the special uses of **across** in phrasal verbs, look at the entries for the verbs. For example, **come across** is in the phrasal verb section at **come**. **1** from one side to the other side: *It's too wide. We can't swim across.* ◆ *The yard measures about 50 feet across.* **2** in a particular direction toward or at someone or something: *When my name was called, he looked across at me.* **3** across from opposite: *There's a school just across from our house.* **4** (of an answer in a CROSSWORD) written from side to side: *I can't do 3 across.*

- *prep.* **1** from one side to the other side of something: *He walked across the field.* ◆ *I drew a line across the page.* ◆ *A grin spread across her face.* ◆ *Where's the nearest bridge across the river?* **2** on the other side of something: *There's a bank right across the street.* **3** on or over a part of the body: *He hit him across the face.* ◆ *It's too tight across the back.* **4** in every part of a place, group of people, etc. **SYN** THROUGHOUT: *Her family is scattered across the country.* ◆ *This view is common across all sections of the community.*

a·cros·tic /ə'krɔstɪk; ə'krɑs-/ *noun* a poem or other piece of writing in which particular letters in each line, usually the first letters, can be read downward to form a word or words

a·cryl·a·mide /ə'krɪlə,maɪd/ *noun* [U, C] a substance used in various industrial processes. Acrylamide is also found in food that has been cooked at high temperatures, and may be a cause of cancer.

a·cryl·ic /ə'krɪlɪk/ *adj., noun*

- *adj.* made of a substance produced by chemical processes from a type of acid: *acrylic paints/fibers* ◆ *an acrylic sweater*

- *noun* **1** [U] a type of FIBER produced by chemical processes, used to make clothes, etc. **2** [C, usually pl.] a type of paint used by artists

ACT /,eɪ si 'ti/ *abbr.* American College Test (an exam that some HIGH SCHOOL students take before they go to college)

act 🔑 /ækt/ *noun, verb*

- *noun*
> **SOMETHING THAT SOMEONE DOES 1** [C] a particular thing that someone does: *a criminal act* ◆ *~ of sth an act of kindness* ◆ *acts of terrorism* ◆ *~ of sb The murder was the act of a psychopath.* ⊃ thesaurus box at ACTION
> **LAW 2** [C] a law that has been passed by a government: *an act of Congress* ◆ *the Civil Rights Act*
> **PRETENDING 3** [sing.] a way of behaving that is not sincere but is intended to have a particular effect on others: *Don't take her seriously—it's all an act.* ◆ *You could tell she was just putting on an act.*
> **IN PLAY/ENTERTAINMENT 4** [C] one of the main divisions of a play, an OPERA, etc.: *a play in five acts* ◆ *The hero dies in Act 5, Scene 3.* **5** [C] one of several short pieces of entertainment in a show: *a circus/comedy/magic act* **6** [C] a performer or group of musicians: *They were one of rock's most impressive live acts.*
> **IDM** **act of God** (*law*) an event caused by natural forces beyond human control, such as a storm, a flood, or an EARTHQUAKE **be/get in on the act** (*informal*) to be/become involved in an activity that someone else has started, especially to get something for yourself **do, perform, stage, etc. a disappearing/vanishing act** (*informal*) to go away or be impossible to find when people need or want you **get your act together** (*informal*) to organize yourself and your activities in a more effective way in order to achieve something: *He needs to get his act together if he's going to pass.* **a hard/tough act to follow** a person who is

so good or successful at something that it will be difficult for anyone else coming after them to be as good or successful **in the act (of doing sth)** while you are doing something: *He was caught in the act of stealing a car.* ⊃ more at CLEAN *v.*, READ *v.*

- *verb*
> **DO SOMETHING 1** [I] to do something for a particular purpose or in order to deal with a situation: *It is vital that we act to stop the destruction of the rainforests.* ◆ *The girl's life was saved because the doctors acted so promptly.* ◆ *He claims he acted in self-defense.*
> **BEHAVE 2** [I] to behave in a particular way: + *adv. John's been acting very strangely lately.* ◆ *~ like sb/sth Stop acting like spoiled children!* ◆ *~ as if/though… She was acting as if she'd seen a ghost.* **HELP** In spoken English people often use **like** instead of **as if** or **as though** in this meaning: *She was acting like she'd seen a ghost.*
> **PRETEND 3** [I] to pretend by your behavior to be a particular type of person: + *adj. I decided to act dumb.*
> **PERFORM IN PLAY/MOVIE 4** [I, T] to perform a part in a play or movie: *Have you ever acted?* ◆ *Most of the cast act well.* ◆ *~ sth Who's acting (= taking the part of) Hamlet?* ◆ *The play was well acted.*
> **PERFORM FUNCTION 5** [I] to perform a particular role or function: *~ as sth Can you act as interpreter?* ◆ *~ like sth hormones in the brain that act like natural painkillers*
> **HAVE EFFECT 6** [I] *~ (on sth)* to have an effect on something: *Alcohol acts quickly on the brain.* **IDM** see AGE *n.*, FOOL *n.*, OWN *v.*
> **PHR V** **'act for/on behalf of sb** to be employed to deal with someone's affairs for them, for example by representing them in court **'act on/upon sth** to take action as a result of advice, information, etc.: *Acting on information from a member of the public, the police raided the club.* ◆ *Why didn't you act on her suggestion?* **,act sth↔'out 1** to perform a ceremony or show how something happened, as if performing a play: *The ritual of the party convention is acted out in the same way every year.* ◆ *The children started to act out the whole incident.* **2** to act a part in a real situation: *She acted out the role of the wronged lover.* **,act 'up** (*informal*) **1** to behave badly: *The kids started acting up.* **2** to not work as it should: *How long has your ankle been acting up?*

act·ing /'æktɪŋ/ *noun, adj.*

- *noun* [U] the activity or profession of performing in plays, movies, etc.

- *adj.* [only before noun] doing the work of another person for a short time **SYN** TEMPORARY: *the acting manager*

ac·tin·i·um /æk'tɪniəm/ *noun* [U] (*symb.* **Ac**) a chemical element. Actinium is a RADIOACTIVE metal.

ac·tion 🔑 /'ækʃn/ *noun*
> **WHAT SOMEONE DOES 1** [U] the process of doing something in order to make something happen or to deal with a situation: *The time has come for action if these beautiful animals are to survive.* ◆ *Firefighters took action immediately to stop the blaze from spreading.* ◆ *What is the best course of action under these circumstances?* ◆ *She began to explain her plan of action to the group.* ⊃ see also DIRECT ACTION, JOB ACTION **2** [C] a thing that someone does: *Her quick action saved the child's life.* ◆ *Each of us must take responsibility for our own actions.*
> **LEGAL PROCESS 3** [C, U] a legal process to stop a person or company from doing something, or to make them pay for a mistake, etc.: *An action is being brought against the magazine that published the article.* ◆ *He is considering taking legal action against the hospital.* ⊃ see also CLASS ACTION
> **IN WAR 4** [U] fighting in a battle or war: *missing in action* ◆ *soldiers killed in action*
> **IN STORY/PLAY 5** [U] the events in a story, play, etc.: *The action takes place in France.*
> **EXCITING EVENTS 6** [U] exciting events: *I like movies with plenty of action.* ◆ *New York is where the action is.*
> **EFFECT 7** [U] *~ of sth (on sth)* the effect that one substance or chemical has on another: *the action of sunlight on the skin*
> **OF PART OF THE BODY 8** [U, C] (*technical*) the way a part of the body moves or functions: *a study of the action of the liver*

> OF MACHINE **9** [sing.] the MECHANICAL parts of a piano, gun, clock, etc. or the way the parts move ⟳ see also PUMP-ACTION

IDM **actions speak louder than words** (*saying*) what a person actually does means more than what they say they will do **in action** if someone or something is **in action**, they are doing the activity or work that is typical for them: *Just press the button to see your favorite character in action.* ♦ *I have yet to see all the players in action.* **into action** if you put an idea or a plan **into action**, you start making it happen or work: *The new plan for traffic control is being put into action on an experimental basis.* **out of action** not able to work or be used because of injury or damage: *Jon will be out of action for weeks with a broken leg.* ♦ *The photocopier is out of action today.* ⟳ more at EVASIVE, PIECE *n.*, SPRING *v.*, SWING *v.*

THESAURUS

action

measure ♦ step ♦ act ♦ move

These are all words for a thing that someone does.

action a thing that someone does: *Her quick action saved the child's life.*

measure an official action that is done in order to achieve a particular aim: *The government introduced tougher security measures last summer.*

step one of a series of things that you do in order to achieve something: *This work is a first step towards our eventual goal.*

act a thing that someone does: *an act of kindness*

ACTION OR ACT?

These two words have the same meaning but are used in different patterns. An **act** is usually followed by *of* and/or used with an adjective. **Action** is not usually used with *of* but is often used with *his, her,* etc.: *a heroic act of bravery* ♦ a heroic action of bravery ♦ *her heroic actions/ acts during the war.* **Action** often combines with *take* but **act** does not: *We will take whatever action is necessary.* ♦ We will take whatever acts are necessary.

move (used especially in journalism) an action that you do or need to do to achieve something: *They are waiting for the results of the opinion polls before deciding their next move.*

PATTERNS

- to **take** action/measures/steps
- to **make** a move
- a **heroic/brave/daring** action/step/act/move

ac·tion·a·ble /ˈækʃənəbl/ *adj.* (*law*) giving someone a valid reason to bring a case to court

ac·tion·er /ˈækʃənər/ *noun* (*informal*) = ACTION MOVIE

action figure *noun* a DOLL representing a soldier or a character from a movie, TV show, etc.

action group *noun* (often as part of a name) a group that is formed to work for social or political change: *a local political action group*

action movie *noun* (also **ac·tion·er**) (*informal*) a movie that has a lot of exciting action and adventure

action-packed *adj.* full of exciting events and activity: *an action-packed weekend*

action point *noun* a suggestion for an action that must be taken, especially one that is made in a meeting

action research *noun* [U] studies done to improve the working methods of people who do a particular job or activity, especially in education

ac·ti·vate /ˈæktəˌveɪt/ *verb* ~ sth to make something such as a device or chemical process start working: *The burglar alarm is activated by movement.* ♦ *The gene is activated by a specific protein.* ▸ **ac·ti·va·tion** /ˌæktəˈveɪʃn/ *noun* [U]

ac·tive /ˈæktɪv/ *adj., noun*
● *adj.*
> BUSY **1** always busy doing things, especially physical activities: *Although he's almost 80, he is still very active.* **ANT** INACTIVE
> TAKING PART **2** involved in something; making a determined effort and not leaving something to happen by itself: *They were both politically active.* ♦ *active involvement/participation/support/resistance* ♦ *She takes an active part in school life.* ♦ *The parents were active in campaigning against cuts to the education budget.* ♦ *They took active steps to prevent the spread of the disease.*
> DOING AN ACTIVITY **3** doing something regularly; functioning: *sexually active teenagers* ♦ *animals that are active only at night* ♦ *The virus is still active in the blood.* ♦ *an active volcano* (= likely to ERUPT) **ANT** INACTIVE ⟳ compare DORMANT
> LIVELY **4** lively and full of ideas: *That child has a very active imagination.*
> CHEMICAL **5** having or causing a chemical effect: *What is the active ingredient in aspirin?* **ANT** INACTIVE
> GRAMMAR **6** connected with a verb whose subject is the person or thing that performs the action: *In "He was driving the car," the verb is active.* ⟳ compare PASSIVE
▸ **ac·tive·ly** *adv.*: *Your proposal is being actively considered.* ♦ *She was actively looking for a job.*
● *noun* (also **active voice**) [sing.] the form of a verb in which the subject is the person or thing that performs the action ⟳ compare PASSIVE

active list *noun* **1** a list of people that an organization may contact at any time to provide them with a service or information, or to ask them to do something: *Please e-mail us to be removed from our active list of blood donors.* **2** a list of officers or former officers connected to one of the armed forces who can be called for duty

active service (also **active duty**) *noun* [U] the work of a member of the armed forces, especially during a war: *troops on active service*

ac·tiv·ist /ˈæktəvɪst/ *noun* a person who works to achieve political or social change, especially as a member of an organization with particular aims: *animal rights activists* ▸ **ac·tiv·ism** /ˈæktəˌvɪzəm/ *noun* [U]

ac·tiv·i·ty /ækˈtɪvəti/ *noun* (*pl.* **ac·tiv·i·ties**) **1** [U] a situation in which something is happening or a lot of things are being done: *economic activity* ♦ *The streets were noisy and full of activity.* ♦ *Muscles contract and relax during physical activity.* ⟳ compare INACTIVE **2** [C, usually pl.] a thing that you do for interest or pleasure, or in order to achieve a particular aim: *leisure/outdoor/classroom activities* ♦ *The club provides a wide variety of activities including tennis, swimming, and squash.* ♦ *illegal/criminal activities*
IDM **a beehive/hive of activity** a place full of people who are busy

ac·tor /ˈæktər/ *noun* a person who performs on the stage, on television, or in movies, especially as a profession

actor-manager *noun* an actor who is in charge of a theater company and acts in the plays that it performs

ac·tress /ˈæktrəs/ *noun* a woman who performs on the stage, on television, or in movies, especially as a profession **HELP** Many women prefer to be called actors, although when the context is not clear, **an actor** is usually understood to refer to a man.

ac·tu·al /ˈæktʃuəl; ˈækʃuəl/ *adj.* [only before noun] **1** used to emphasize something that is real or exists in fact: *What were his actual words?* ♦ *The actual cost was higher than we expected.* ♦ *James looks younger than his wife but in actual fact* (= really) *he is five years older.* **2** used to emphasize the most important part of something: *The wedding preparations take weeks but the actual ceremony takes less than an hour.*

WHICH WORD?

actual + current + present

- **Actual** does not mean **current** or **present**. It means "real" or "exact," and is often used in contrast with something that is not seen as real or exact: *I need the actual figures, not an estimate.*
- **Present** means "existing or happening now": *How long have you been in your present job?*
- **Current** also means "existing or happening now," but can suggest that the situation is temporary: *The factory cannot continue its current level of production.*
- **Actually** does not mean "at the present time." Use **currently**, **at the present time**, or **at the moment** instead.

ac·tu·al·i·ty /ˌæktʃuˈæləti/ *noun* (*pl.* **ac·tu·al·i·ties**) (*formal*) **1** [U] the state of something existing in reality: *The building looked as impressive in actuality as it did in photographs.* **2** [C, usually pl.] things that exist **SYN** FACT, REALITY: *the grim actualities of prison life*

ac·tu·al·ize /ˈæktʃuəˌlaɪz/ *verb* ~ **sth** to make something real; to make something happen **SYN** REALIZE (2): *He finally actualized his dream.*

ac·tu·al·ly 🔑 /ˈæktʃuəli; ˈæktʃəli; ˈækʃəli/ *adv.* **1** used in speaking to emphasize a fact or a comment, or that something is really true: *What did she actually say?* ♦ *It's not actually raining now.* ♦ *That's the only reason I'm actually going.* ♦ *There are lots of people there who can actually help you.* ♦ *I didn't want to say anything without actually reading the letter first.* **2** used to show a contrast between what is true and what someone believes, and to show surprise about this contrast: *It was actually great fun after all.* ♦ *The food was not actually all that expensive.* ♦ *Our turnover actually increased last year.* **3** used to correct someone in a polite way: *We're not American, actually. We're Canadian.* ♦ *Actually, it would be much more sensible to do it later.* ♦ *They're not married, actually.* **4** used to get someone's attention, to introduce a new topic, or to say something that someone may not like, in a polite way: *Actually, I'll be a little late getting home.* ♦ *Actually, I'm busy at the moment—can I call you back?* ⊃ note at ACTUAL

ac·tu·ar·y /ˈæktʃuˌeri/ *noun* (*pl.* **ac·tu·ar·ies**) a person whose job involves calculating insurance risks and payments for insurance companies by studying how frequently accidents, fires, deaths, etc. happen ▶ **ac·tu·ar·i·al** /ˌæktʃuˈeriəl/ *adj.*

ac·tu·ate /ˈæktʃuˌeɪt/ *verb* (*formal*) **1** ~ **sth** to make a machine or device start to work **SYN** ACTIVATE **2** [usually passive] ~ **sb** to make someone behave in a particular way **SYN** MOTIVATE: *He was actuated entirely by malice.*

a·cu·i·ty /əˈkyuəti/ *noun* [U] (*formal*) the ability to think, see, or hear clearly

a·cu·men /əˈkyumən; ˈækyəmən/ *noun* [U] the ability to understand and decide things quickly and well: *business/commercial/financial acumen*

ac·u·pres·sure /ˈækyəˌprɛʃər/ (also **shi·at·su**) *noun* [U] a form of medical treatment, originally from Japan, in which pressure is applied to particular parts of the body using the fingers

ac·u·punc·ture /ˈækyəˌpʌŋktʃər/ *noun* [U] a Chinese method of treating pain and illness using special thin needles that are pushed into the skin in particular parts of the body

ac·u·punc·tur·ist /ˈækyəˌpʌŋktʃərɪst/ *noun* a person who is trained to perform acupuncture

a·cute /əˈkyut/ *adj.* **1** very serious or severe: *There is an acute shortage of water.* ♦ *acute pain* ♦ *the world's acute environmental problems* ♦ *acute competition for jobs* **2** an acute

illness is one that has quickly become severe and dangerous: *acute appendicitis* **ANT** CHRONIC **3** (of the senses) very sensitive and well developed **SYN** KEEN: *Dogs have an acute sense of smell.* **4** intelligent and quick to notice and understand things: *He is an acute observer of the social scene.* ♦ *Her judgment is acute.* **5** (*geometry*) (of an angle) less than 90° ▶ **a·cute·ness** *noun* [U]

a·cute ˈaccent *noun* the mark placed over a vowel to show how it should be pronounced, as over the *e* in *fiancé* ⊃ compare CIRCUMFLEX, GRAVE², TILDE, UMLAUT

a·cute ˈangle *noun* (*geometry*) an angle of less than 90° ⊃ picture at SHAPE ⊃ compare OBLIQUE ANGLE, OBTUSE ANGLE, REFLEX ANGLE, RIGHT ANGLE

a·cute·ly /əˈkyutli/ *adv.* **1** ~ **aware/conscious** noticing or feeling something very strongly: *I am acutely aware of the difficulties we face.* **2** (describing unpleasant feelings) very; very strongly: *acutely embarrassed*

-acy /əsi/ ⊃ -CY

a·cy·clic /eɪˈsaɪklɪk; -ˈsɪk-/ *adj.* **1** (*technical*) not occurring in cycles **2** (*chemistry*) (of a COMPOUND or MOLECULE) containing no rings of atoms

A.D. (also **AD**) /ˌeɪ ˈdi/ *abbr.* used in the Christian CALENDAR to show a particular number of years since the year when Christ was believed to have been born (from Latin "Anno Domini"): *in (the year) A.D. 55* ♦ *in 55 A.D.* ♦ *in the fifth century A.D.* ⊃ compare A.H., B.C., B.C.E., C.E.

ad 🔑 /æd/ *noun* (*informal*) = ADVERTISEMENT: *We put an ad in the local paper.* ♦ *an ad for a new chocolate bar* ⊃ see also BANNER AD ⊃ thesaurus box at ADVERTISEMENT

ad·age /ˈædɪdʒ/ *noun* a well-known phrase expressing a general truth about people or the world **SYN** SAYING

a·da·gio /əˈdadʒiˌoʊ; -dʒoʊ; -ˌʒioʊ/ *noun* (*pl.* **a·da·gi·os**) (*music*) a piece of music to be played slowly ▶ **a·da·gio** *adj.*, *adv.*

Ad·am /ˈædəm/ *noun* **IDM** see KNOW

ad·a·mant /ˈædəmənt/ *adj.* determined not to change your mind or to be persuaded about something: *Eva was adamant that she would not come.* ▶ **ad·a·mant·ly** *adv.*: *His family was adamantly opposed to the marriage.*

ad·a·man·tine /ˌædəˈmæntin; -taɪn; -tən/ *adj.* (*literary*) very strong and impossible to break

ˈAdam's ˌapple *noun* the lump at the front of the throat that sticks out, particularly in men, and moves up and down when you swallow

a·dapt 🔑 **AWL** /əˈdæpt/ *verb* **1** [T] to change something in order to make it suitable for a new use or situation **SYN** MODIFY: ~ **sth** *These styles can be adapted to suit individual tastes.* ♦ ~ **sth for sth** *Most of these tools have been specially adapted for use by disabled people.* **2** [I, T] to change your behavior in order to deal more successfully with a new situation **SYN** ADJUST: *It's amazing how soon you adapt.* ♦ *The organisms were forced to adapt in order to survive.* ♦ ~ **to sth** *We have had to adapt quickly to the new system.* ♦ *A large organization can be slow to adapt to change.* ♦ ~ **yourself to sth** *It took him a while to adapt himself to his new surroundings.* **3** [T] ~ **sth (for sth) (from sth)** to change a book or play so that it can be made into a play, movie, TV show, etc.: *Three of her novels have been adapted for television.*

a·dapt·a·ble **AWL** /əˈdæptəbl/ *adj.* (*approving*) able to change or be changed in order to deal successfully with new situations: *Older workers can be as adaptable and quick to learn as anyone else.* ♦ *Successful businesses are highly adaptable to economic change.* ▶ **a·dapt·a·bil·i·ty** **AWL** /əˌdæptəˈbɪləti/ *noun* [U]

ad·ap·ta·tion **AWL** /ˌædəpˈteɪʃn; ˌædæp-/ (also *less frequent* **a·dap·tion** /əˈdæpʃn/) *noun* **1** [C] a movie, play, or book that is based on a particular piece of work but that has been changed for a new situation: *a screen adaptation of*

| t **t**ea | t̮ bu**tt**er | d **d**id | k **c**at | g **g**ot | tʃ **ch**in | dʒ **J**une | f **f**all

Shakespeare's "Macbeth" **2** [U] the process of changing something, for example your behavior, to suit a new situation: *the adaptation of desert species to high temperatures*

a·dap·ter (also **a·dapt·or**) /əˈdæptər/ *noun* a device for connecting pieces of electrical equipment that were not designed to fit together

a·dapt·ive **AWL** /əˈdæptɪv/ *adj.* (*technical*) concerned with changing; able to change when necessary in order to deal with different situations

ADC /ˌeɪ di ˈsi/ *abbr.* AIDE-DE-CAMP

ADD /ˌeɪ di ˈdi/ *abbr.* attention deficit disorderATTENTION DEFICIT HYPERACTIVITY DISORDER

add /æd/ *verb*

1 [T] to put something together with something else so as to increase the size, number, amount, etc.: *~ sth Next add the flour.* ◆ *The juice contains no added sugar.* ◆ *The plan has the added* (= extra) *advantage of bringing employment to rural areas.* ◆ *~ sth to sth A new wing was added to the building.* ◆ *Shall I add your name to the list?* **2** [I, T] to put numbers or amounts together to get a total: *~ A to B Add 9 to the total.* ◆ *~ A and B together If you add all these amounts together, you get a huge figure.* **ANT** SUBTRACT **3** [T] to say something more; to make a further remark: *+ speech* "*And don't be late,*" *she added.* ◆ *~ sth (to sth) I have nothing to add to my earlier statement.* ◆ *~ that… He added that they would return a week later.* **4** [T] *~ sth (to sth)* to give a particular quality to an event, a situation, etc.: *This necklace will add a little class to your outfit.*

IDM **add insult to injury** to make a bad relationship with someone worse by offending them even more **added to this…**| **add to this…** used to introduce another fact that helps to emphasize a point you have already made: *Add to this the excellent service, and you can see why it's the most popular hotel on the island.*

PHRV ,**add sth↔'in** to include something with something else: *Remember to add in the cost of drinks.* ,**add sth↔'on (to sth)** to include or attach something extra: *A service charge of 15% was added on to the bill.* ⊃ related noun ADD-ON ,**add to sth** to increase something in size, number, amount, etc.: *The bad weather only added to our difficulties.* ◆ *The house has been added onto* (= new rooms, etc. have been built on to it) *from time to time.* ,**add 'up** (*informal*) **1** (especially in negative sentences) to seem reasonable; to make sense: *His story just doesn't add up.* **2** (not used in the progressive tenses) to increase by small amounts until there is a large total: *When you're feeding a family of six the bills soon add up.* ,**add 'up** | ,**add sth↔'up** to calculate the total of two or more numbers or amounts: *The waiter can't add up the check.* ◆ *Add up all the money I owe you.* ,**add 'up to sth 1** to make a total amount of something: *The numbers add up to exactly 100.* **2** to lead to a particular result; to show something **SYN** AMOUNT TO STH: *These clues don't really add up to very much* (= give us very little information).

ad·den·dum /əˈdɛndəm/ *noun* (*pl.* **ad·den·da** /-də/) (*formal*) a section of extra information that is added to something, especially to a book

ad·der /ˈædər/ *noun* a small poisonous snake

ad·dict /ˈædɪkt/ *noun* **1** a person who is unable to stop taking harmful drugs: *a heroin/drug/nicotine addict* **2** a person who is very interested in something and spends a lot of their free time on it: *a video game addict*

ad·dict·ed /əˈdɪktəd/ *adj.* [not before noun] *~ (to sth)* **1** unable to stop taking harmful drugs, or using or doing something as a habit: *to become addicted to drugs/gambling* **2** spending all your free time doing something because you are so interested in it: *He's addicted to computer games.*

ad·dic·tion /əˈdɪkʃn/ *noun* [U, C] the condition of being addicted to something: *cocaine addiction* ◆ *~ to sth He is now fighting his addiction to alcohol.*

ad·dic·tive /əˈdɪktɪv/ *adj.* **1** if a drug is **addictive**, it makes people unable to stop taking it: *Heroin is highly addictive.* **2** if an activity or type of behavior is **addictive**, people need to

do it as often as possible because they enjoy it: *You should try yoga - it's addictive.*

'add-in *noun* (*computing*) **1** a computer program that can be added to a larger program to allow it to do more things **2** = EXPANSION CARD ▶ **'add-in** *adj.* [only before noun]: *add-in software*

ad·di·tion /əˈdɪʃn/ *noun*

1 [U] the process of adding two or more numbers together to find their total: *children learning addition and subtraction* **ANT** SUBTRACTION **2** [C] *~ (to sth)* a thing that is added to something else: *the latest addition to our line of cars* ◆ *an addition to the family* (= another child) **3** [U] *~ (of sth)* the act of adding something to something else: *Pasta's basic ingredients are flour and water, sometimes with the addition of eggs or oil.* **4** [C] *~ (to sth)* a new part that is added to a building: *architects who specialize in home additions* **IDM** **in addition (to sb/sth)** used when you want to mention another person or thing after something else: *In addition to these arrangements, extra ambulances will be on duty until midnight.* ◆ *There is, in addition, one further point to make.*

LANGUAGE BANK

addition

adding another item

- Bilingual children do better on IQ tests than children who speak only one language. **In addition/What is more**, they seem to find it easier to learn third, or even fourth, languages.

- Learning another language **not only** improves children's job prospects in later life, **but also** boosts their self-esteem.

- Teaching children a second language improves their job prospects in later life. **Other** benefits **include** increased self-esteem and greater tolerance of other cultures.

- **Another/One further/One additional** reason for encouraging bilingual education is that it boosts children's self-esteem.

- Studies suggest that bilingual children find it easier to learn additional languages. There is, **moreover**, increasing evidence that bilingual children perform better across a range of school subjects, not just foreign languages.

- His claim that children find bilingual education confusing is based on very little evidence. **Moreover**, the evidence he does provide is seriously flawed.

- Research has shown that first-language development is not impeded by exposure to a second language. **Furthermore**, there is no evidence to support the claim that children find bilingual education confusing.

---

ad·di·tion·al /əˈdɪʃənl/ *adj.*

more than was first mentioned or is usual **SYN** EXTRA: *additional resources/funds/security* ◆ *The government provided an additional $25 million to expand the service.* ▶ **ad·di·tion·al·ly** *adv.* **SYN** IN ADDITION: *Additionally, the bus service will run on Sundays, every two hours.*

ad·di·tive /ˈædətɪv/ *noun* a substance that is added in small amounts to something, especially food, in order to improve it, give it color, make it last longer, etc.: *food additives* ◆ *additive-free orange juice* ◆ *chemical additives in gasoline* ⊃ collocations at DIET

ad·dle /ˈædl/ *verb* *~ sth* (often *humorous*) to make someone unable to think clearly; to confuse someone: *Being in love must have addled your brain.*

ad·dled /ˈædld/ *adj.* (often *humorous*) confused; unable to think clearly: *his addled brain*

'add-on *noun* a thing that is added to something else: *The company offers scuba diving as an add-on to the basic vacation package.* ◆ *add-on software* (= added to a computer)

---

ad·dress 🔑 *noun, verb*

- **noun** /əˈdrɛs; ˈædrɛs/ **1** [C] details of where someone lives or works and where letters, etc. can be sent: *What's your name and address?* ◆ *I'll give you my address and phone number.* ◆ *Is that your home address?* ◆ *Please note my change of address.* ◆ *Police found him at an address* (= a house or apartment) *in Philadelphia.* ➔ see also FORWARDING ADDRESS, RETURN ADDRESS **2** [C] (*computing*) a series of words and symbols that tells you where you can find something using a computer, for example on the Internet: *What's your e-mail address?* ◆ *The project has a new Web address.* **3** [C] a formal speech that is made in front of an audience: *tonight's televised presidential address* ➔ collocations at VOTE ➔ thesaurus box at SPEECH **4** [U] **form/mode of ~** the correct title, etc. to use when you talk to someone

- **verb** /əˈdrɛs/ **1** [usually passive] to write on an envelope, etc. the name and address of the person, company, etc. that you are sending it to by mail: *~ sth The letter was correctly addressed, but delivered to the wrong house.* ◆ *~ sth to sb/sth Address your application to the Personnel Manager.* ➔ compare READDRESS ➔ see also SASE **2** to make a formal speech to a group of people: *to address a meeting* **3** (*formal*) to say something directly to someone: *~ sb I was surprised when he addressed me in English.* ◆ *~ sth to sb Any questions should be addressed to your teacher.* **4** *~ sb* **(as sth)** to use a particular name or title for someone when you speak or write to them: *The judge should be addressed as "Your Honor."* ◆ *Many women prefer to be addressed as "Ms." rather than "Miss" or "Mrs."* **5** (*formal*) to think about a problem or a situation and decide how you are going to deal with it: *~ sth Your essay does not address the real issues.* ◆ *~ yourself to sth We must address ourselves to the problem of traffic congestion.*

ad·dress·a·ble /əˈdrɛsəbl/ *adj.* **1** (of a problem or situation) that can be addressed: *Let's start with the more easily addressable issues.* **2** (*computing*) (of a part of a computer system) that is identified using its own address

ad'dress ˌbar *noun* a line near the top of a page on an Internet BROWSER where you can type in the address of a Web site or where the Web site address is displayed

ad'dress ˌbook *noun* **1** a book in which you keep addresses, phone numbers, etc. **2** a computer file where you store e-mail and Internet addresses

ad·dress·ee /ˌædrɛˈsi; əˌdrɛˈsi/ *noun* a person that a letter, etc. is addressed to

ad·duce /əˈdus/ *verb* [often passive] *~ sth* (*formal*) to provide evidence, reasons, facts, etc. in order to explain something or to show that something is true **SYN** CITE: *Several factors have been adduced to explain the fall in the birth rate.*

ad·duc·tor /əˈdʌktər/ (also **ad'ductor ˌmuscle**) *noun* (*anatomy*) a muscle that moves a body part toward the middle of the body or toward another part ➔ compare ABDUCTOR

ad·e·noids /ˈædnˌɔɪdz/ *noun* [pl.] pieces of soft TISSUE at the back of the nose and throat, which are part of the body's IMMUNE SYSTEM and can swell up and cause breathing difficulties, especially in children ▶ **ad·e·noi·dal** /ˌædnˈɔɪdl/ *adj.*

a·dept /əˈdɛpt/ *adj.* *~ (at/in sth)* | *~ (at/in doing sth)* good at doing something that is quite difficult **SYN** SKILLFUL ▶ **a·dept** /ˈædɛpt; əˈdɛpt/ *noun* **a·dept·ly** /əˈdɛptli/ *adv.*

ad·e·quate 🔑 **AWL** /ˈædəkwət/ *adj.* enough in quantity, or good enough in quality, for a particular purpose or need: *an adequate supply of hot water* ◆ *The room was small but adequate.* ◆ *There is a lack of adequate access for disabled students.* ◆ *He didn't give an adequate answer to the question.* ◆ *~ for sth The space available is not adequate for our needs.* ◆ *~ to do sth training that is adequate to meet the future needs of the industry* **ANT** INADEQUATE ▶ **ad·e·qua·cy** **AWL** /ˈædəkwəsi/ *noun* [U]: *The adequacy of the security arrangements has been questioned.* **ANT** INADEQUACY **ad·e·quate·ly** **AWL** *adv.*: *Are you adequately insured?* **ANT** INADEQUATELY

ADHD /ˌeɪ di ˈeɪtʃ di/ *abbr.* ATTENTION DEFICIT HYPERACTIVITY DISORDER

ad·here /ədˈhɪr/ *verb* [I] *~ (to sth)* (*formal*) to stick firmly to something: *Once in the bloodstream, the bacteria adhere to the surface of the red cells.* **PHR V** **ad'here to sth** (*formal*) to behave according to a particular law, rule, set of instructions, etc.; to follow a particular set of beliefs or a fixed way of doing something: *For ten months he adhered to a strict no-fat low-salt diet.* ◆ *She adheres to teaching methods she learned over 30 years ago.*

ad·her·ence /ədˈhɪrəns/ *noun* [U] the fact of behaving according to a particular rule, etc., or of following a particular set of beliefs, or a fixed way of doing something: *strict adherence to the rules*

ad·her·ent /ədˈhɪrənt/ *noun* (*formal*) a person who supports a political party or set of ideas **SYN** SUPPORTER

ad·he·sion /ədˈhiʒn/ *noun* [U] (*technical*) the ability to stick or become attached to something

ad·he·sive /ədˈhisɪv; -zɪv/ *noun, adj.*
- **noun** [C, U] a substance that you use to make things stick together
- **adj.** that can stick to something **SYN** STICKY: *adhesive tape* ➔ see also SELF-ADHESIVE

ad hoc /ˌæd ˈhɑk; ˌæd ˈhoʊk/ *adj.* (from *Latin*) arranged or happening when necessary and not planned in advance: *an ad hoc meeting to deal with the problem* ◆ *The meetings will be held on an ad hoc basis.* ▶ **ad hoc** *adv.*

ad ho·mi·nem /ˌæd ˈhɑmənəm/ *adj., adv.* (from *Latin, formal*) directed against a person's character rather than their argument: *an ad hominem attack*

a·dieu /əˈdu; əˈdyu/ *exclamation* (*old use* or *literary*) goodbye: *I bid you adieu.*

ad in·fi·ni·tum /ˌæd ˌɪnfəˈnaɪtəm/ *adv.* (from *Latin*) without ever coming to an end; again and again: *You cannot stay here ad infinitum without paying rent.* ◆ *The problem would be repeated ad infinitum.*

ad·i·pose /ˈædəˌpoʊs/ *adj.* (*technical*) (of body TISSUE) used for storing fat

ad·ja·cent **AWL** /əˈdʒeɪsnt/ *adj.* (of an area, a building, a room, etc.) next to or near something: *The planes landed on adjacent runways.* ◆ *~ to sth Our farmland was adjacent to the river.*

ad·jacent ˈangle *noun* (*geometry*) one of the two angles formed on the same side of a straight line when another line meets it

ad·jec·tive /ˈædʒɪktɪv/ *noun* (*grammar*) a word that describes a person or thing, for example *big, red,* and *bright* in *a big house, red wine,* and *a bright idea* ▶ **ad·jec·ti·val** /ˌædʒɪkˈtaɪvl/ *adj.*: *an adjectival phrase* **ad·jec·ti·val·ly** /-ˈtaɪvəli/ *adv.*: *In "bread knife," the word "bread" is used adjectivally.*

ad·join /əˈdʒɔɪn/ *verb* [T, I] *~ (sth)* (*formal*) to be next to or joined to something: *A barn adjoins the farmhouse.* ▶ **ad·join·ing** *adj.* [usually before noun]: *They stayed in adjoining rooms.* ◆ *We'll have more space if we knock down the adjoining wall* (= the wall between two rooms).

ad·journ /əˈdʒɜrn/ *verb* [I, T, often passive] to stop a meeting or an official process, especially a trial, for a period of time: *The court adjourned for lunch.* ◆ *~ sth The trial has been adjourned until next week.* ▶ **ad·journ·ment** *noun* [C, U]: *The judge granted us a short adjournment.* **PHR V** **ad'journ to...** (*formal* or *humorous*) to go to another place, especially in order to relax

ad·judge /əˈdʒʌdʒ/ *verb* [usually passive] (*formal*) to make a decision about someone or something based on the facts that are available: *~ sth + adj. The company was adjudged bankrupt.* ◆ *~ sth + noun The tour was adjudged a success.* ◆ *sth is adjudged to be, have, etc. sth The reforms were generally adjudged to have failed.*

ad·ju·di·cate /əˈdʒudɪˌkeɪt/ *verb* **1** [I, T] to make an official decision about who is right in a disagreement between two groups or organizations: *~ (on/upon/in sth) A special*

h **hat**   m **man**   n **no**   ŋ **sing**   l **leg**   r **red**   y **yes**   w **wet**

subcommittee adjudicates on planning applications. ◆ ~ (sth) **(between A and B)** *Their purpose is to adjudicate disputes between employers and employees.* **2** [I] to be a judge in a competition: *Who is adjudicating at this year's contest?* ▶ **a·ju·di·ca·tion** /əˌdʒuːdɪˈkeɪʃn/ *noun* [U, C]: *The case was referred to a higher court for adjudication.* **ad·ju·di·ca·tor** /əˈdʒuːdɪˌkeɪtər/ *noun*: *You may refer your complaint to an independent adjudicator.*

ad·junct /ˈædʒʌŋkt/ *noun* **1** (*grammar*) an adverb or a phrase that adds meaning to the verb in a sentence or part of a sentence: *In "She went home yesterday" and "He ran away in a panic," "yesterday" and "in a panic" are adjuncts.* **2** (*formal*) a thing that is added or attached to something larger or more important: *The memory expansion cards are useful adjuncts to the computer.*

ad·jure /əˈdʒʊr/ *verb* ~ **sb to do sth** (*formal*) to ask or to order someone to do something: *He adjured them to tell the truth.*

ad·just /əˈdʒʌst/ *verb* **AWL**
1 [T] to change something slightly to make it more suitable for a new set of conditions or to make it work better: ~ **sth** *Watch out for sharp turns and adjust your speed accordingly.* ◆ *This button is for adjusting the volume.* ◆ ~ **sth to sth** *Adjust your language to the age of your audience.* **2** [I, T] to get used to a new situation by changing the way you behave and/or think **SYN** ADAPT: *They'll be fine—they just need time to adjust.* ◆ ~ **to sth** *After a while, his eyes adjusted to the dark.* ◆ ~ **to doing sth** *It took her a while to adjust to living alone.* ◆ ~ **yourself to sth** *I had to adjust myself to the idea that he wasn't coming back.* ◆ *My eyes were still trying to adjust themselves to the strong sunlight.* **3** [T] ~ **sth** to move something slightly so that it looks neater or feels more comfortable: *He smoothed his hair and adjusted his tie.*
➔ see also WELL-ADJUSTED

ad·just·a·ble /əˈdʒʌstəbl/ *adj.* that can be moved to different positions or changed in shape or size: *adjustable seat belts* ◆ *The height of the bicycle seat is adjustable.*

ad·just·ment **AWL** /əˈdʒʌstmənt/ *noun* [C, U] **1** a small change made to something in order to correct or improve it: *I've made a few adjustments to the design.* ◆ *Some adjustment of the lens may be necessary.* **2** a change in the way a person behaves or thinks: *She went through a period of emotional adjustment after her marriage broke up.*

ad·ju·tant /ˈædʒətənt/ *noun* an army officer who does office work and helps other officers

Adjutant General *noun* (*pl.* **Adjutants General**) the officer of very high rank in the army who is in charge of organization

ad lib /ˌæd ˈlɪb/ *verb* (**-bb-**) [I, T] to say something in a speech or a performance that you have not prepared or practiced **SYN** IMPROVISE: *She abandoned her script and began ad libbing.* ◆ ~ **sth** *I lost my notes and had to ad lib the whole speech.* ▶ **ad lib** *noun*: *The speech was full of ad libs.* **ad lib** *adj.*: *an ad lib speech* **ad lib** *adv.*: *She delivered her lines ad lib.*

ad·man /ˈædmæn/ *noun* (*pl.* **ad·men** /-mɛn/) (*informal*) a person who works in advertising

ad·min /ˈædmɪn/ *noun* [U] (*informal*) = ADMINISTRATION: *a few admin problems* ◆ *She works in admin.*

ad·min·is·ter /ədˈmɪnəstər/ *verb* **1** [often passive] ~ **sth** to manage and organize the affairs of a company, an organization, a country, etc. **SYN** MANAGE: *to administer a charity/fund/school* ◆ *The pension funds are administered by commercial banks.* **2** ~ **sth** to make sure that something is done fairly and in the correct way: *to administer justice/the law* ◆ *The questionnaire was administered by trained interviewers.* **3** ~ **sth (to sb)** (*formal*) to give or to provide something, especially in a formal way: *The teacher has the authority to administer punishment.* **4** [often passive] (*formal*) to give drugs, medicine, etc. to someone: ~ **sth** *Police believe his wife could not have administered the poison.* ◆ ~ **sth to sb** *The dose was administered to the child intravenously.* **5** ~ **a kick, a punch, etc. (to sb/sth)** (*formal*) to kick or to hit

someone or something: *He administered a severe blow to his opponent's head.*

ad·min·is·tra·tion /ədˌmɪnəˈstreɪʃn/ **AWL** *noun*
1 often **(the) Administration** [C, sing.] the government of a country under a particular leader: *the Obama administration* ◆ *The Administration will fight hard for the tax plan.* ◆ *Successive administrations have failed to solve the country's economic problems.* **2** often **the administration** [C, sing.] the people who plan, organize, and run a business, an institution, etc.: *the hospital/university administration* **3** (also *informal* **ad·min**) [U] the activities that are done in order to plan, organize, and run a business, school, or other institution: *Administration costs are passed on to the customer.* ◆ *the day-to-day administration of a company* **4** [U] the process or act of organizing the way that something is done: *the administration of justice* **5** [U] (*formal*) the act of giving a drug to someone: *the administration of antibiotics*

ad·min·is·tra·tive **AWL** /ədˈmɪnəˌstreɪtɪv; -strə-/ *adj.* connected with organizing the work of a business or an institution: *an administrative job/assistant/error* ▶ **ad·min·is·tra·tive·ly** **AWL** *adv.*

ad·min·is·tra·tor **AWL** /ədˈmɪnəˌstreɪtər/ *noun* a person whose job is to manage and organize the public or business affairs of a company or an institution: *a hospital administrator*

ad·mi·ra·ble /ˈædmərəbl/ *adj.* having qualities that you admire and respect **SYN** COMMENDABLE: *Her dedication to her work was admirable.* ◆ *He made his points with admirable clarity.* ▶ **ad·mi·ra·bly** /-bli/ *adv.*: *Joe coped admirably with a difficult situation.*

ad·mi·ral /ˈædmərəl/ *noun* an officer of very high rank in the navy: *The admiral visited the ships under his command.* ◆ *Admiral Rickover* ➔ see also REAR ADMIRAL

ad·mi·ra·tion /ˌædməˈreɪʃn/ *noun* [U] a feeling of respect and liking for someone or something: *to watch/gaze in admiration* ◆ ~ **for sb/sth** *I have great admiration for her as a writer.*

ad·mire /ədˈmaɪər/ *verb*
1 to respect someone for what they are or for what they have done: ~ **sb/sth** *I really admire your enthusiasm.* ◆ *You have to admire the way he handled the situation.* ◆ ~ **sb/sth for sth** *The school is widely admired for its excellent teaching.* ◆ ~ **sb for doing sth** *I don't agree with her, but I admire her for sticking to her principles.* **2** ~ **sth** to look at something and think that it is attractive and/or impressive: *He stood back to admire his handiwork.* ▶ **ad·mir·ing** *adj.*: *She was used to receiving admiring glances from men.* **ad·mir·ing·ly** *adv.*

ad·mir·er /ədˈmaɪrər/ *noun* **1** ~ **of sb/sth** a person who admires someone or something, especially a well-known person or thing: *He is a great admirer of Picasso's early paintings.* **2** a man who is attracted to a woman and admires her: *She never married but had many admirers.*

ad·mis·si·ble /ədˈmɪsəbl/ *adj.* that can be allowed or accepted, especially in court **ANT** INADMISSIBLE ▶ **ad·mis·si·bil·i·ty** /ədˌmɪsəˈbɪləti/ *noun* [U]

ad·mis·sion /ədˈmɪʃn/ *noun* **1** [U, C] the act of accepting someone into an institution, organization, etc.; the right to enter a place or to join an institution or organization: *Hospital admission is not necessary in most cases.* ◆ *Hospital admissions for asthma attacks have doubled.* ◆ *the college admissions policy/office* ◆ *They tried to get into the club but were refused admission.* ◆ *She failed to gain admission to the school of her choice.* ◆ ~ **to sth** *high school seniors applying for admission to college* ◆ *There is no admission to the park after 4 p.m.* **2** [C] a statement in which someone admits that something is true, especially something wrong or bad that they have done: *He is a thief by his own admission* (= he has admitted it). ◆ ~ **of sth** *an admission of guilt/failure/defeat* ◆ ~ **that ...** *The minister's resignation was an admission that he had lied.* **3** [U] the amount of money that you pay to go into a building or to an event: *admission charges/prices* ♦ *$5 admission* ♦ *What's the admission?*

admit

acknowledge ♦ recognize ♦ concede ♦ confess

These words all mean to agree, often unwillingly, that something is true.

admit to agree, often unwillingly, that something is true: *It was a stupid thing to do, I admit.*

acknowledge (*somewhat formal*) to accept that something exists, is true, or has happened: *She refuses to acknowledge the need for reform.*

recognize to admit or be aware that something exists or is true: *They recognized the need to take the problem seriously.*

concede (*somewhat formal*) to admit, often unwillingly, that something is true or logical: *He was forced to concede that there might be difficulties.*

ADMIT OR CONCEDE?

When someone **admits** something, they are usually agreeing that something that is generally considered bad or wrong is true or has happened, especially when it relates to their own actions. When someone **concedes** something, they are usually accepting, unwillingly, that a particular fact or statement is true or logical.

confess (*somewhat formal*) to admit something that you feel ashamed or embarrassed about: *She was reluctant to confess her ignorance.*

PATTERNS

- to admit/acknowledge/recognize/concede/confess that…
- to admit/confess **to sth**
- to admit/concede/confess sth **to sb**
- to admit/acknowledge/recognize **the truth**
- to admit/confess your **mistakes/ignorance**

ad·mit /əd'mɪt/ *verb* (**-tt-**)
> **ACCEPT TRUTH** **1** [I, T] ~ **(to sb) (that…)** to agree, often unwillingly, that something is true **SYN** CONFESS: *It was a stupid thing to do, I admit.* ♦ **+ speech** *"I'm very nervous," she admitted reluctantly.* ♦ ~ **to sth** *Don't be afraid to admit to your mistakes.* ♦ ~ **to doing sth** *She admits to being strict with her children.* ♦ ~ **sth** *He admitted all his mistakes.* ♦ *She stubbornly refuses to admit the truth.* ♦ *Why don't you just admit defeat* (= recognize that you cannot do something) *and let someone else try?* ♦ *Admit it! You were terrified!* ♦ ~ **(that)…** *They freely admit (that) they still have a lot to learn.* ♦ *You must admit that it all sounds very strange.* ♦ ~ **to sb that…** *I couldn't admit to my parents that I was failing the course.* ♦ **it is admitted that…** *It was generally admitted that the government had acted too quickly.* ♦ **be admitted to be, have, etc. sth** *The appointment is now generally admitted to have been a mistake.*
> **ACCEPT BLAME** **2** [I, T] to say that you have done something wrong or illegal **SYN** CONFESS: ~ **to sth** *He refused to admit to the other charges.* ♦ ~ **to doing sth** *She admitted to having stolen the car.* ♦ ~ **sth** *She admitted theft.* ♦ *He refused to admit his guilt.* ♦ ~ **doing sth** *She admitted having driven the car without insurance.*
> **ALLOW TO ENTER/JOIN** **3** [T] to allow someone or something to enter a place: ~ **sb/sth** *Each ticket admits one adult.* ♦ ~ **sb/sth to/into sth** *You will not be admitted to the theater after the performance has started.* ♦ *The narrow windows admit little light into the room.* **4** [T] to allow someone to become a member of a club, a school, or an organization: ~ **sb** *The society admits all U.S. citizens over 21.* ♦ ~ **sb to/into sth** *Women were only admitted into the club last year.*
> **TO A HOSPITAL** **5** [T, often passive] ~ **sb to/into a hospital, an institution, etc.** to take someone to a hospital or other

institution where they can receive special care: *Two crash victims were admitted to the local hospital.*
  PHR V **ad'mit of sth** (*formal*) to show that something is possible or likely as a solution, an explanation, etc.: *The situation was too urgent to admit of any delay.*

ad·mit·tance /əd'mɪtns/ *noun* [U] (*formal*) the right to enter or the act of entering a building, an institution, etc.: *Hundreds of people were unable to **gain admittance** to the hall.*

ad·mit·ted·ly /əd'mɪtədli/ *adv.* used, especially at the beginning of a sentence, when you are accepting that something is true: *Admittedly, it is pretty expensive, but you don't need to use much.*

ad·mix·ture /æd'mɪkstʃər/ *noun* (*formal*) **1** a mixture: *an admixture of aggression and creativity* **2** something, especially a small amount of something, that is mixed with something else: *a French-speaking region with an admixture of German speakers*

ad·mon·ish /əd'mɑnɪʃ/ *verb* (*formal*) **1** ~ **sb (for sth/for doing sth)** | **+ speech** to tell someone firmly that you do not approve of something that they have done **SYN** REPROVE: *She was admonished for chewing gum in class.* **2** ~ **sb (to do sth)** to strongly advise someone to do something: *A warning voice admonished him not to let this happen.*

ad·mo·ni·tion /ˌædmə'nɪʃn/ (*also less frequent* **ad·mon·ish·ment** /əd'mɑnɪʃmənt/) *noun* [C, U] (*formal*) a warning to someone about their behavior ▶ **ad·mon·i·to·ry** /əd'mɑnəˌtɔri/ *adj.*

ad nau·se·am /æd 'nɔziəm/ *adv.* (*from Latin*) if a person says or does something **ad nauseam**, they say or do it again and again so that it becomes boring or annoying: *Sports commentators repeat the same phrases ad nauseam.*

a·do /ə'du/ *noun*
  IDM **without further ado** (*old-fashioned*) without delaying; immediately

a·do·be /ə'doʊbi/ *noun* [U] mud that is dried in the sun, mixed with STRAW, and used as a building material

ad·o·les·cence /ˌædl'ɛsns/ *noun* [U] the time in a person's life when he or she develops from a child into an adult **SYN** PUBERTY ◯ collocations at AGE

ad·o·les·cent /ˌædl'ɛsnt/ *noun* a young person who is developing from a child into an adult: *adolescents between the ages of 13 and 18 and the problems they face*
  ▶ **ad·o·les·cent** *adj.*: *adolescent boys/girls/experiences*

A·don·is /ə'dɑnəs; ə'doʊnəs/ *noun* an extremely attractive young man **ORIGIN** From the name of the beautiful young man in ancient Greek myths, who was loved by both Aphrodite and Persephone. He was killed by a wild boar but Zeus ordered that he should spend the winter months in the underworld with Persephone and the summer months with Aphrodite.

a·dopt /ə'dɑpt/ *verb*
> **CHILD** **1** [I, T] to take someone else's child into your family and become its legal parent(s): *a campaign to encourage childless couples to adopt* ♦ ~ **sb** *to adopt a child* ◯ collocations at CHILD ◯ compare FOSTER
> **METHOD** **2** [T] ~ **sth** to start to use a particular method or to show a particular attitude toward someone or something: *All three teams adopted different approaches to the problem.*
> **SUGGESTION** **3** [T] ~ **sth** to formally accept a suggestion or policy by voting: *to adopt a resolution* ♦ *The council is expected to adopt the new policy at its next meeting.*
> **NEW NAME/COUNTRY** **4** [T] ~ **sth** to choose a new name, a country, a custom, etc. and begin to use it as your own: *to adopt a name/title/language* ♦ *Early settlers adopted many of the farming methods of the Native Americans.*
> **WAY OF BEHAVING** **5** [T] ~ **sth** (*formal*) to use a particular manner, way of speaking, expression, etc.: *He adopted an air of indifference.*

a·dopt·ed /ə'dɑptəd/ *adj.* **1** an **adopted** child has legally become part of a family that is not the one in which they were born: *Danny is their adopted son.* **2** an **adopted** country is one in which someone chooses to live although it is not the one they were born in

a·dopt·ee /əˌdɑpˈti/ *noun* someone who has been adopted: *adoptees and their families*

a·dopt·er /əˈdɑptər/ *noun* **1** a person who adopts a child **2** a person who starts using a new technology: *early/late adopters of DVD players*

a·dop·tion /əˈdɑpʃn/ *noun* **1** [C, U] the act of adopting a child: *She put/gave the baby up pure adoption.* ➔ collocations at CHILD **2** [U] the decision to start using something such as an idea, a plan, or a name: *the adoption of new technology*

a·dop·tive /əˈdɑptɪv/ *adj.* [usually before noun] an **adoptive** parent or family is one that has legally adopted a child

a·dor·a·ble /əˈdɔrəbl/ *adj.* very attractive and easy to feel love for: *What an adorable baby!* ▶ **a·dor·a·bly** /-bli/ *adv.*

ad·o·ra·tion /ˌædəˈreɪʃn/ *noun* [U] a feeling of great love or worship: *He gazed at her with pure adoration.* ◆ *The painting is called "Adoration of the Infant Christ."*

a·dore /əˈdɔr/ *verb* (not used in the progressive tenses) **1** ~ **sb** to love someone very much: *It's obvious that she adores him.* **2** (*informal*) to like something very much: ~ **sth** *I simply adore his music!* ◆ ~ **doing sth** *She adores working with children.* ➔ thesaurus box at LIKE

a·dor·ing /əˈdɔrɪŋ/ *adj.* [usually before noun] showing much love and admiration ▶ **a·dor·ing·ly** *adv.*

a·dorn /əˈdɔrn/ *verb* [often passive] (*formal*) to make something or someone look more attractive by decorating it or them with something: ~ **sth/sb** *Gold rings adorned his fingers.* ◆ (*ironic*) *Graffiti adorned the walls.* ◆ ~ **sth/sb/ yourself with sth** *The walls were adorned with paintings.* ◆ *The children adorned themselves with flowers.* ▶ **a·dorn·ment** *noun* [U, C]: *A plain necklace was her only adornment.*

ad·re·nal gland /əˈdrinl ˌglænd/ *noun* either of the two small organs above the KIDNEYS that produce adrenaline and other HORMONES

a·dren·al·ine /əˈdrɛnlˌən/ (also **a·dren·al·in**) *noun* [U] a substance produced in the body when you are excited, afraid, or angry. It makes the heart beat faster and increases your energy and ability to move quickly: *The excitement at the start of a race can really get the adrenaline flowing.*

a·drift /əˈdrɪft/ *adj.* [not before noun] **1** if a boat or a person in a boat is **adrift**, the boat is not tied to anything and is floating without being controlled by anyone: *The survivors were adrift in a lifeboat for six days.* **2** (of a person) feeling alone and without a direction or an aim in life: *young people adrift in the big city*
IDM **cast/set sb adrift** (usually passive) to leave someone to be carried away on a boat that is not being controlled by anyone: (*figurative*) *Without language, human beings are cast adrift.*

a·droit /əˈdrɔɪt/ *adj.* (*formal*) skillful and smart, especially in dealing with people: *an adroit negotiator* ▶ **a·droit·ly** *adv.* **a·droit·ness** *noun* [U]

ADSL /ˌeɪ di ɛs ˈɛl/ *abbr.* asymmetric digital subscriber line (a system for connecting a computer to the Internet using a telephone line)

ad·sorb /ædˈsɔrb; -ˈzɔrb/ *verb* ~ **sth** (*technical*) if something **adsorbs** a liquid, gas, or other substance, it holds it on its surface: *The dye is adsorbed onto the fiber.*

a·u·ki /əˈduki/ *noun* = ADZUKI

ad·u·la·tion /ˌædʒəˈleɪʃn/ *noun* [U] (*formal*) admiration and praise, especially when this is greater than is necessary ▶ **ad·u·la·to·ry** /ˈædʒələˌtɔri/ *adj.*

a·dult 🔑 **AWL** /əˈdʌlt; ˈædʌlt/ *noun, adj.*
● *noun* **1** a fully grown person who is legally responsible for their actions **SYN** GROWN-UP²: *Children must be accompanied by an adult.* ◆ *Why can't you act like civilized adults?* **2** a fully grown animal: *The fish return to the river as adults in order to breed.*

● *adj.* **1** fully grown or developed: *preparing young people for adult life* ◆ *the adult population* ◆ *adult monkeys* **2** behaving in an intelligent and responsible way; typical of what is expected of an adult **SYN** GROWN-UP¹: *When my parents split up, it was all very adult and open.* **3** [only before noun] intended for adults only, because it is about sex or contains violence: *an adult movie* ➔ see also ADULTHOOD

a·dult edu·ca·tion *noun* [U] = CONTINUING EDUCATION

a·dul·ter·ate /əˈdʌltəˌreɪt/ *verb* [often passive] ~ **sth (with sth)** to make something, such as food or drink, less pure by adding another substance to it **SYN** CONTAMINATE ➔ see also UNADULTERATED ▶ **a·dul·ter·a·tion** /əˌdʌltəˈreɪʃn/ *noun* [U]

a·dul·ter·er /əˈdʌltərər/ *noun* (*formal*) a person who commits adultery

a·dul·ter·ess /əˈdʌltərəs; -trəs/ *noun* (*formal*) a woman who commits adultery

a·dul·ter·y /əˈdʌltəri/ *noun* [U] sex between a married person and someone who is not their husband or wife: *He was accused of committing adultery.* ▶ **a·dul·ter·ous** /əˈdʌltərəs/ *adj.*: *an adulterous relationship*

a·dult·hood **AWL** /əˈdʌlthʊd/ *noun* [U] the state of being an adult: *a child reaching adulthood*

ad·um·brate /ˈædəmˌbreɪt; əˈdʌmbreɪt/ *verb* ~ **sth** (*formal*) to give a general idea or description of something without details **SYN** OUTLINE

ad·vance 🔑 /ədˈvæns/ *noun, verb, adj.*

● *noun*
▷ FORWARD MOVEMENT **1** [C] the forward movement of a group of people, especially armed forces: *We feared that an advance on the capital would soon follow.* ➔ collocations at WAR
▷ DEVELOPMENT **2** [C, U] ~ **(in sth)** progress or a development in a particular activity or area of understanding: *recent advances in medical science* ◆ *We live in an age of rapid technological advance.*
▷ MONEY **3** [C, usually sing.] money paid for work before it has been done or money paid earlier than expected: *They offered an advance of $5,000 after the signing of the contract.* ◆ *She asked for an advance on her salary.*
▷ SEXUAL **4** advances [pl.] attempts to start a sexual relationship with someone: *He had made advances to several women.*
▷ PRICE INCREASE **5** [C] ~ **(on sth)** (*business*) an increase in the price or value of something: *Share prices showed significant advances.*
IDM **in advance (of sth) 1** before the time that is expected; before something happens: *a week/month/year in advance* ◆ *It's cheaper if you book the tickets in advance.* ◆ *People were evacuated from the coastal regions in advance of the hurricane.* **2** more developed than someone or something else: *Galileo's ideas were well in advance of the age in which he lived.*

● *verb*
▷ MOVE FORWARD **1** [I] to move forward toward someone or something, often in order to attack or threaten them or it: *The troops were finally given the order to advance.* ◆ *They had advanced 20 miles by nightfall.* ◆ *the advancing Allied troops* ◆ ~ **on/toward sb/sth** *The mob advanced on us, shouting angrily.* ➔ compare RETREAT
▷ DEVELOP **2** [I, T] if knowledge, technology, etc. **advances**, it develops and improves: *Our knowledge of the disease has advanced considerably over recent years.* ◆ ~ **sth** *This research has done much to advance our understanding of language learning.*
▷ HELP TO SUCCEED **3** [T] to help something to succeed **SYN** FURTHER: *Studying for another degree is one way of advancing your career.* ◆ *They worked together to advance the cause of democracy.*
▷ MONEY **4** [T] to give someone money before the time it would usually be paid: ~ **sth to sb** *We are willing to advance the money to you.* ◆ ~ **sb sth** *We will advance you the money.*

> SUGGEST **5** [T] ~ sth (formal) to suggest an idea, a theory, or a plan for other people to discuss **SYN** PUT FORWARD: *The article advances a new theory to explain changes in the climate.*

> MAKE EARLIER **6** [T] ~ sth (formal) to change the time or date of an event so that it takes place earlier **SYN** BRING FORWARD: *The date of the trial has been advanced by one week.* **ANT** POSTPONE

> MOVE FORWARD **7** [I, T] (formal) to move forward to a later part of something; to move something forward to a later part: *Users advance through the program by answering a series of questions.* ◆ ~ sth *This button advances the CD to the beginning of the next track.*

> INCREASE **8** [I] (business) (of prices, costs, etc.) to increase in price or amount: *Oil shares advanced amid economic recovery hopes.*

● *adj.* [only before noun] **1** done or given before something is going to happen: *Please give us **advance warning** of any changes.* ◆ *We need **advance notice** of the numbers involved.* ◆ *No **advance booking** is necessary on most departures.*
2 ~ **party/team** a group of people who go somewhere first, before the main group

ad·vanced ✎ /əd'vænst/ adj.
1 having the most modern and recently developed ideas, methods, etc.: *advanced technology* ◆ *advanced industrial societies* **2** (of a course of study) at a high or difficult level: *There were only three of us on the advanced course.* ◆ *an advanced student of English* **3** at a late stage of development: *the advanced stages of the disease*
IDM **of advanced years| sb's advanced age** used in polite expressions to describe someone as "very old": *He was a man of advanced years.* ◆ (humorous) *Even at my advanced age, I still know how to enjoy myself!*

ad,vanced 'placement noun [U] (abbr. **AP**) an advanced course for high school students by which students can gain college CREDITS before they actually go to college

ad,vance 'guard noun a group of soldiers who go somewhere to make preparations before other soldiers arrive

ad·vance·ment /əd'vænsmənt/ noun (formal) **1** [U, C] the process of helping something to make progress or succeed; the progress that is made: *the **advancement of** knowledge/education/science* **2** [U] progress in a job, social class, etc.: *There are good opportunities for advancement if you have the right skills.*

ad·vanc·ing /əd'vænsɪŋ/ adj. ~ **years/age** used as a polite way of referring to the fact of time passing and of someone growing older: *She is still very active, in spite of her advancing years.*

ad·van·tage ✎ /əd'væntɪdʒ/ noun, verb
● *noun* [C, U] **1** a thing that helps you to be better or more successful than other people: *a big/great/definite advantage* ◆ *an unfair advantage* (= something that benefits you, but not your opponents) ◆ *You will **be at an advantage** (= have an advantage) in the interview if you have thought about the questions in advance.* ◆ ~ **over sb** *Being tall gave him an advantage over the other players.* **ANT** DISADVANTAGE **2** a quality of something that makes it better or more useful: *A small car **has the** added **advantage of** being cheaper to run.* ◆ *One advantage of/One of the advantages of living in the country is the fresh air.* ◆ *Each of these systems has its advantages and disadvantages.* **ANT** DISADVANTAGE **3** (abbr. **ad**) (in TENNIS) the first point scored after a score of 40–40: *Advantage Federer.*
IDM **be/work to your advantage** to give you an advantage; to change a situation in a way that gives you an advantage: *It would be to your advantage to attend this meeting.* ◆ *Eventually, the new regulations will work to our advantage.* **take advantage of sth/sb 1** to make use of something well; to make use of an opportunity: *She took advantage of the children's absence to clean their rooms.* ◆ *We took full advantage of the hotel facilities.* **2** to make use of someone or something in a way that is unfair or dishonest **SYN** EXPLOIT: *He took advantage of my generosity* (= for

example, by taking more than I had intended to give). **to (good/best) advantage** in a way that shows the best of something: *The photo showed him to advantage.* **use/turn/ put sth to your advantage** to use or change a bad situation so that it helps you

● *verb* ~ **sb** (formal) to put someone in a better position than other people or than they were in before

ad·van·taged /əd'væntɪdʒd/ adj. being in a good social or financial situation: *We aim to improve opportunities for the less advantaged in society.* **ANT** DISADVANTAGED

ad·van·ta·geous /ˌædvən'teɪdʒəs; -væn-/ adj. ~ **(to sb)** good or useful in a particular situation **SYN** BENEFICIAL: *A free trade agreement would be advantageous to both countries.* **ANT** DISADVANTAGEOUS ▶ **ad·van·ta·geous·ly** adv.

ad·vent /'ædvent/ noun **1** [sing.] **the ~ of sth/sb** the coming of an important event, person, invention, etc.: *the advent of new technology* **2 Advent** [U] (in the Christian religion) the period of approximately four weeks before Christmas

'Advent ,calendar noun a piece of stiff paper with a picture and 24 small doors with numbers on them. Children open a door each day during advent and find a picture or a piece of candy behind each one.

ad·ven·ti·tious /ˌædvən'tɪʃəs; -ven-/ adj. (formal) happening by accident; not planned

ad·ven·ture ✎ /əd'vɛntʃər/ noun
1 [C] an unusual, exciting, or dangerous experience, journey, or series of events: *her adventures traveling in Africa* ◆ *When you're a kid, life is one big adventure.* ◆ *adventure stories* **2** [U] excitement and the willingness to take risks, try new ideas, etc.: *a sense/spirit of adventure*

ad'venture ,game noun a type of computer game in which you play a part in an adventure

ad·ven·tur·er /əd'vɛntʃərər/ noun **1** a person who enjoys exciting new experiences, especially going to unusual places **2** (often disapproving, old-fashioned) a person who is willing to take risks or act in a dishonest way in order to gain money or power

ad·ven·ture·some /əd'vɛntʃərsəm/ adj. = ADVENTUROUS

ad·ven·tur·ess /əd'vɛntʃərəs/ noun (old-fashioned) **1** a woman who enjoys exciting new experiences, especially going to unusual places **2** (often disapproving) a woman who is willing to take risks or act in a dishonest way in order to gain money or power

ad·ven·tur·ism /əd'vɛntʃəˌrɪzəm/ noun [U] (disapproving) a willingness to take risks in business or politics in order to gain something for yourself

ad·ven·tur·ous /əd'vɛntʃərəs/ adj. **1** (also **ad·ven·ture-some**) (of a person) willing to take risks and try new ideas; enjoying being in new, exciting situations: *For the more adventurous tourists, there are trips into the mountains with a local guide.* ◆ *Many teachers would like to be more adventurous and creative.* **2** including new and interesting things, methods, and ideas: *The menu contained traditional favorites as well as more adventurous dishes.* **3** full of new, exciting, or dangerous experiences: *an adventurous trip/lifestyle* **ANT** UNADVENTUROUS ▶ **ad·ven·tur·ous·ly** adv.

ad·verb /'ædvərb/ noun (grammar) a word that adds more information about place, time, manner, cause, or degree to a verb, an adjective, a phrase, or another adverb: *In "speak kindly," "incredibly deep," "just in time," and "too quickly," "kindly," "incredibly," "just," and "too" are all adverbs.* ↪ see also SENTENCE ADVERB ▶ **ad·ver·bi·al** /əd'vərbiəl/ adj.: *"Very quickly indeed" is an adverbial phrase.*

ad,verbial 'particle noun (grammar) an adverb used especially after a verb to show position, direction of movement, etc.: *In "come back," "break down," and "fall off," "back," "down," and "off" are all adverbial particles.*

ad·ver·sar·i·al /ˌædvər'sɛriəl/ adj. (formal or technical) (especially of political or legal systems) involving people who are in opposition and who make attacks on each other: *the*

t **t**ea   t̮ bu**tt**er   d **d**id   k **c**at   g **g**ot   tʃ **ch**in   dʒ **J**une   f **f**all

adversarial nature of the two-party system ◆ an adversarial system of justice

ad·ver·sar·y /'ædvər,sɛri/ noun (pl. **ad·ver·sar·ies**) (formal) a person that someone is opposed to and competing with in an argument or a battle **SYN** OPPONENT

ad·verse /əd'vɜrs; æd-; 'ædvɜrs/ adj. [usually before noun] negative and unpleasant; not likely to produce a good result: *adverse change/circumstances/weather conditions* ◆ *Lack of money will have an **adverse effect** on our research program.* ◆ *They have attracted strong adverse criticism.* ◆ *This drug is known to have adverse side effects.* ▶ **ad·verse·ly** adv.: *Her health was **adversely affected** by the climate.*

ad·ver·si·ty /əd'vɜrsəti; æd-/ noun [U, C] (pl. **ad·ver·si·ties**) (formal) a difficult or unpleasant situation: *courage **in the face of adversity*** ◆ *He overcame many personal adversities.*

ad·ver·tise 🔧 /'ædvər,taɪz/ verb
1 [I, T] to tell the public about a product or a service in order to encourage people to buy or to use it: *If you want to attract more customers, try advertising in the local paper.* ◆ *~ sth (as sth) The cruise was advertised as "the journey of a lifetime."* **2** [I, T] to let people know that something is going to happen or that a job is available by giving details about it in a newspaper, on a notice in a public place, on the Internet, etc.: *~ (for sb/sth) We are currently advertising for a new sales manager.* ◆ *~ sth We advertised the concert very widely.* **3** [T] *~ sth* to show or tell something about yourself to other people **SYN** PUBLICIZE: *I wouldn't advertise the fact that you don't have a work permit.*

THESAURUS

advertisement

publicity ◆ ad ◆ commercial ◆ promotion ◆ preview

These are all words for a notice, picture, or short movie telling people about a product, job, or service.

advertisement a notice, picture, or short movie telling people about a product, job, or service; an example of something that shows its good qualities; the act of advertising something and making it public

publicity [U] the business of attracting the attention of the public to someone or something, such as a company, book, movie, movie star, or product; the things that are done to attract attention: *She works in publicity.* ◆ *Her new movie has received a lot of publicity.*

ad (informal) a notice, picture, or short movie telling people about a product, job, or service: *We put an ad in the local paper.* ◆ *an ad for a new candy bar*

commercial an advertisement played during a television, radio, or online show

promotion a set of advertisements for a particular product or service; activities done in order to increase the sales of a product or service: *a special promotion of local products* ◆ *The store is running a promotion on its gourmet coffees.*

preview a series of short scenes from a movie or television program, shown in advance to advertise it

PATTERNS
- (a/an) advertisement/publicity/ad/commercial/promotion/preview **for** sth
- a TV/**television**/**radio**/**cinema** advertisement/ad/commercial/promotion
- to **run**/**show** a(n) advertisement/ad/commercial/preview

---

ad·ver·tise·ment 🔧 /,ædvər'taɪzmənt; əd'vɜrtəs-/ noun
1 (also informal **ad**) [C] *~ (for sth)* a notice, picture, or short movie telling people about a product, job, or service: *Put an advertisement in the local paper to sell your car.* ⊃ see also CLASSIFIED ADVERTISEMENTS **2** [C] *~ for sth* an example of something that shows its good qualities: *Dirty streets and homelessness are no advertisement for a prosperous society.* **3** [U] the act of advertising something and making it public

ad·ver·tis·er /'ædvər,taɪzər/ noun a person or company that advertises

ad·ver·tis·ing 🔧 /'ædvər,taɪzɪŋ/ noun [U] the activity and industry of advertising things to people on television, in newspapers, on the Internet, etc.: *A good **advertising campaign** will increase our sales.* ◆ *Cigarette advertising has been banned.* ◆ ***radio/TV advertising*** ◆ *Val works for an **advertising agency** (= a company that designs advertisements).* ◆ *a career in advertising*

ad·ver·to·ri·al /,ædvər'tɔriəl/ noun an advertisement that is designed to look like an article in the newspaper or magazine in which it appears

ad·vice 🔧 /əd'vaɪs/ noun [U] *~ (on sth)*
an opinion or a suggestion about what someone should do in a particular situation: *advice on road safety* ◆ *They **give advice** to people with HIV and AIDS.* ◆ *Ask your teacher 's advice / Ask your teacher **for advice** on how to prepare for the exam.* ◆ *We were advised to **seek legal advice.*** ◆ *Let me give you **a piece of advice.*** ◆ ***A word of advice.** Don't wear that dress.* ◆ ***Take my advice.** Don't do it.* ◆ *I chose it **on his advice.***

ad'vice ˌcolumn noun part of a newspaper or magazine in which someone gives advice to readers who have sent letters about their personal problems

ad'vice ˌcolumnist noun a person who writes in a newspaper or magazine giving advice in reply to people's letters about their personal problems

ad·vis·a·ble /əd'vaɪzəbl/ adj. [not usually before noun] sensible and a good idea in order to achieve something: *Booking tickets early is advisable.* ◆ *~ to do sth It is advisable to book early.* **ANT** INADVISABLE ▶ **ad·vis·a·bil·i·ty** /əd,vaɪzə'bɪləti/ noun [U]

ad·vise 🔧 /əd'vaɪz/ verb
1 [I, T] to tell someone what you think they should do in a particular situation: *~ (sb) against sth/against doing sth I would **strongly advise** against going out on your own.* ◆ *~ sb Her mother was away and couldn't advise her.* ◆ *~ sth I'd advise extreme caution.* ◆ ***+ speech** "Get there early," she advised (them).* ◆ *~ sb to do sth Police are advising people to stay at home.* ◆ *She advised me not to tell him.* ◆ *~ that... The airline advises that you carry your passport at all times.* ◆ **it is advised that...** *It is strongly advised that you take out insurance.* ◆ *~ doing sth I'd advise buying your tickets well in advance if you want to travel in August.* ⊃ see also ILL-ADVISED, WELL-ADVISED ⊃ thesaurus box at RECOMMEND **2** [I, T] to give someone help and information on a subject that you know a lot about: *~ (sb) on/about sth/about doing sth We employ an expert to advise on new technology.* ◆ *She advises the government on environmental issues.* ◆ *~ (sb) what, which, whether, etc.... The pharmacist will advise which medicines are safe to take.* ◆ *Your lawyer can advise you whether to take any action.* **3** [T] (formal) to officially tell someone something **SYN** INFORM: *~ sb of sth Please advise us of any change of address.* ◆ *~ sb when, where, how, etc.... I will contact you later to advise you when to come.* ◆ *~ sb that... I regret to advise you that the course is now full.*

ad·vis·ed·ly /əd'vaɪzədli/ adv. (formal) if you say that you are using a word **advisedly**, you mean that you have thought carefully before choosing it

ad·vise·ment /əd'vaɪzmənt/ noun [U] (formal) advice: *a word of advisement*
IDM **take sth under advisement** to think carefully about something before making a decision about it: *The judge has taken the matter under advisement.*

ad·vis·er (also **ad·vis·or**) /əd'vaɪzər/ noun **1** a person who gives advice, especially someone who knows a lot about a particular subject: *a financial adviser* ◆ *~ (to sb) (on sth) a special adviser to the president on education* **2** (in school, college, or university) a teacher who helps a student plan a course of study

ad·vi·so·ry /əd'vaɪzəri/ adj., noun
- **adj.** having the role of giving professional advice: *an advisory committee/board/panel* ♦ *He acted in an advisory capacity only.*
- **noun** (pl. **ad·vi·so·ries**) an official warning that something bad is going to happen: *a tornado advisory*

ad·vo·ca·cy **AWL** /'ædvəkəsi/ noun [U] **1** ~ (of sth) (formal) the giving of public support to an idea, a course of action, or a belief **2** (technical) the work of lawyers who speak about cases in court

'advocacy ,group noun a group of people who work together to achieve something, especially by putting pressure on the government, etc., usually on behalf of people who are unable to speak for themselves: *an advocacy group for the rights of the mentally ill* ➔ compare INTEREST GROUP, PRESSURE GROUP

ad·vo·cate **AWL** verb, noun
- **verb** /'ædvə,keɪt/ (formal) to support something publicly: ~ **sth** *The group does not advocate the use of violence.* ♦ ~ **(sb) doing sth** *Many experts advocate rewarding your child for good behavior.* ♦ ~ **that...** *The report advocated that all buildings be equipped with smoke detectors.* ➔ thesaurus box at RECOMMEND
- **noun** /'ædvəkət/ **1** a person who supports or speaks in favor of someone or of a public plan or action: ~ **(for sth/sb)** *an advocate for hospital workers* ♦ ~ **(of sth/sb)** *a staunch advocate of free speech* ➔ see also DEVIL'S ADVOCATE **2** a person who defends someone in court ➔ note at LAWYER

adze (also **adz**) /ædz/ noun a heavy tool with a curved blade at RIGHT ANGLES to the handle, used for cutting or shaping large pieces of wood

ad·zu·ki /əd'zuki/ (also **ad'zuki ,bean, ad·u·ki**) noun a type of small, round, dark red BEAN that you can eat

ae·gis /'idʒəs/ noun
  IDM **under the aegis of sb/sth** (formal) with the protection or support of a particular organization or person

ae·o·li·an = EOLIAN

aer·ate /'ɛreɪt/ verb **1** ~ **sth** to make it possible for air to become mixed with soil, water, etc.: *Earthworms do the important job of aerating the soil.* **2** ~ **sth** to add a gas, especially CARBON DIOXIDE, to a liquid under pressure: *aerated water* ▶ **aer·a·tion** /ɛr'eɪʃn/ noun [U]

aer·i·al /'ɛriəl/ noun, adj.
- **adj.** **1** from a plane: *aerial attacks/bombardment/photography* ♦ *an aerial view of Palm Island* **2** in the air; existing above the ground: *The banyan tree has aerial roots.*
- **noun** = ANTENNA

aer·ie (also **eyr·ie**) /'ɛri; 'ɪri/ noun **1** a nest that is built high up among rocks by a BIRD OF PREY (= a bird that kills other creatures for food) such as an EAGLE **2** a room or building in a high place that is often difficult to reach and from which someone can see what is happening below

aero- /'ɛroʊ; 'ɛrə/ combining form (in nouns, adjectives, and adverbs) connected with air or aircraft: *aerodynamic* ♦ *aerospace*

aer·o·bat·ics /,ɛrə'bætɪks/ noun [pl.] exciting and skillful movements performed in an aircraft, such as flying upside down, especially in front of an audience ▶ **aer·o·bat·ic** adj.: *an aerobatic display*

aer·o·bic /ɛ'roʊbɪk; ə-/ adj. **1** (biology) needing OXYGEN: *aerobic bacteria* **2** (of physical exercise) especially designed to improve the function of the heart and lungs
  ANT ANAEROBIC

aer·o·bics /ɛ'roʊbɪks; ə-/ noun [U] physical exercises intended to make the heart and lungs stronger, often done in classes, with music: *to do aerobics*

aer·o·dy·nam·ics /,ɛroʊdaɪ'næmɪks/ noun **1** [pl.] the qualities of an object that affect the way it moves through the air: *Research has focused on improving the car's aerodynamics.*

2 [U] the science that deals with how objects move through air ▶ **aer·o·dy·nam·ic** adj.: *the car's aerodynamic shape* (= making it able to move faster) **aer·o·dy·nam·i·cal·ly** /-kli/ adv.

aer·o·gramme (also **aer·o·gram**) /'ɛrə,græm/ (also **'air ,letter**) noun a sheet of light paper that can be folded and sent by air as a letter

aer·o·naut /'ɛrə,nɔt; -,nɑt/ noun (in the past) a traveler in a HOT-AIR BALLOON or AIRSHIP

aer·o·nau·tics /,ɛrə'nɔtɪks; -'nɑtɪks/ noun [U] the science or practice of building and flying aircraft ▶ **aer·o·nau·ti·cal** /-'nɔtɪkl; -'nɑtɪkl/ adj.: *an aeronautical engineer*

aer·o·sol /'ɛrə,sɔl; -,sɑl/ noun a metal container in which a liquid such as paint or HAIRSPRAY is kept under pressure and released as a spray: *ozone-friendly aerosols* ♦ *an aerosol can/spray* ➔ picture at PACKAGING

aer·o·space /'ɛroʊ,speɪs/ noun [U] the industry of building aircraft, and vehicles and equipment to be sent into space: *jobs in aerospace and defense* ♦ *the aerospace industry*

aer·o·stat /'ɛrə,stæt/ noun (technical) an aircraft filled with hot air, such as an AIRSHIP or HOT-AIR BALLOON

aes·thete (also **es·thete**) /'ɛsθit/ noun (formal, sometimes disapproving) a person who has a love and understanding of art and beautiful things

aes·thet·ic (also **es·thet·ic**) /ɛs'θɛtɪk; ɪs-/ adj., noun
- **adj.** **1** concerned with beauty and art, and the understanding of beautiful things: *an aesthetic appreciation of the landscape* ♦ *The benefits of conservation are both financial and aesthetic.* **2** made in an artistic way and beautiful to look at: *Their furniture was more aesthetic than functional.* ▶ **aes·thet·i·cally** (also **es·thet·i·cally**) /-kli/ adv.: *aesthetically pleasing color combinations*
- **noun 1** [C] the **aesthetic** qualities and ideas of something: *The students debated the aesthetic of the poems.* **2** aesthetics [U] the branch of philosophy that studies the principles of beauty, especially in art ▶ **aes·thet·i·cism** (also **es·thet·i·cism**) /ɛs'θɛtə,sɪzəm; ɪs-/ noun [U]

a·far /ə'fɑr/ adv.
  IDM **from afar** (literary) from a long distance away: *He loved her from afar* (= did not tell her he loved her).

AFC /,eɪ ɛf 'si/ abbr. **1** the AFC the American Football Conference (one of the two groups of teams in the NFL) ➔ see also NFC **2** automatic frequency control (a system that allows radios and televisions to continue to receive the same signal)

af·fa·ble /'æfəbl/ adj. pleasant, friendly, and easy to talk to **SYN** GENIAL ▶ **af·fa·bil·i·ty** /,æfə'bɪləti/ noun [U] **af·fa·bly** /'æfəbli/ adv.

af·fair 🔑 /ə'fɛr/ noun
> **PUBLIC/POLITICAL ACTIVITIES 1** affairs [pl.] events that are of public interest or political importance: *world/international/business affairs* ♦ *an expert on foreign affairs* (= political events in other countries) ♦ *affairs of state*
> **EVENT 2** [C, usually sing.] an event that people are talking about or describing in a particular way: *The newspapers exaggerated the whole affair wildly.* ♦ *The debate was a pretty disappointing affair.* ♦ *She wanted the celebration to be a simple family affair.*
> **RELATIONSHIP 3** [C] a sexual relationship between two people, usually when one or both of them is married to someone else: *She is having an affair with her boss.* ➔ see also LOVE AFFAIR
> **PRIVATE BUSINESS 4** affairs [pl.] matters connected with a person's private business and financial situation: *I took care of my father's financial affairs.* ♦ *She wanted to put her affairs in order before she died.* **5** [sing.] a thing that someone is responsible for (and that other people should not be concerned with) **SYN** BUSINESS: *How I spend my money is my affair.*
> **OBJECT 6** [C] (old-fashioned) (with an adjective) an object that is unusual or difficult to describe: *Her hat was an amazing affair with feathers and a huge brim.* **IDM** see STATE n.

| h hat | m man | n no | ŋ sing | l leg | r red | y yes | w wet |

af·fect 🔑 **AWL** /əˈfekt/ *verb*

1 [often passive] **~ sb/sth** to produce a change in someone or something: *How will these changes affect us?* ◆ *Your opinion will not affect my decision.* ◆ *The south of the country was worst affected by the drought.* **2** [often passive] **~ sb/sth** (of a disease) to attack someone or a part of the body; to make someone become sick: *The condition affects one in five women.* ◆ *Rub the ointment into the affected areas.* **3 ~ sb** [often passive] to make someone have strong feelings of sadness, anger, etc.: *They were deeply affected by the news of her death.* **4 ~ (to do) sth** (*formal*) to pretend to be feeling or thinking something: *She affected a calmness she did not feel.* **5 ~ sth** (*formal*, *disapproving*) to use or wear something that is intended to impress other people **SYN** PUT ON: *I wish he wouldn't affect that ridiculous accent.*

> ### WHICH WORD?
>
> **affect ▪ effect**
>
> - **affect** *verb* = "to have an influence on someone or something": *Does television affect children's behavior?* It is not a noun.
> - **effect** *noun* = "result, influence": *Does television have an effect on children's behavior?*
> - **effect** *verb* is formal and means "to achieve or produce": *The negotiators hope to effect a reconciliation.* ◆ *Governments have the tools to use to effect change.*

af·fec·ta·tion /ˌæfekˈteɪʃn/ *noun* [C, U] behavior or an action that is not natural or sincere and that is often intended to impress other people: *His little affectations irritated her.* ◆ *Kayla has no affectations at all.* ◆ *He raised his eyebrows with an affectation of surprise* (= pretending to be surprised).

af·fect·ed **AWL** /əˈfektəd/ *adj.* (of a person or their behavior) not natural or sincere: *an affected laugh/smile* **ANT** UNAFFECTED ▸ **af·fect·ed·ly** *adv.*

af·fect·ing **AWL** /əˈfektɪŋ/ *adj.* (*formal*) producing strong feelings of sadness and sympathy

af·fec·tion 🔑 /əˈfekʃn/ *noun*

1 [U, sing.] the feeling of liking or loving someone or something very much and caring about them: *Children need lots of love and affection.* ◆ *He didn't* **show** *his wife any* **affection**. ◆ **~ for sb/sth** *Superman's affection for Lois Lane* ◆ *I have a great affection for New York.* ⊃ collocations at MARRIAGE **2 affections** [pl.] (*formal*) a person's feelings of love: *Ava had two men trying to win her affections.*

af·fec·tion·ate /əˈfekʃənət/ *adj.* showing caring feelings and love for someone **SYN** LOVING: *He is very affectionate toward his children.* ◆ *an affectionate kiss* ▸ **af·fec·tion·ate·ly** *adv.*: *William was affectionately known as Billy.*

af·fec·tive **AWL** /əˈfektɪv; ˈæfektɪv/ *adj.* (*technical*) connected with emotions and attitudes: *affective disorders* ▸ **af·fec·tive·ly** **AWL** *adv.*

af·fi·da·vit /ˌæfəˈdeɪvət/ *noun* (*law*) a written statement that you swear is true, and that can be used as evidence in court

af·fil·i·ate *verb, noun*
● *verb* /əˈfiliˌeɪt/ **1** [T, usually passive] **~ sb/sth (with/to sb/ sth)** to link a group, a company, or an organization very closely with another larger one: *The hospital is affiliated with the local university.* ◆ *The group is not affiliated to any political party.* **2** [T, I] **~ (yourself) (with sb/sth)** to join, to be connected with, or to work for an organization: *The majority of people questioned affiliated themselves with a religious group.*
● *noun* /əˈfiliət/ a company, an organization, etc. that is connected with or controlled by another larger one

af·fil·i·at·ed /əˈfiliˌeɪtəd/ *adj.* [only before noun] closely connected to or controlled by a group or an organization: *All affiliated members can vote.* ◆ *a government-affiliated institute* **ANT** UNAFFILIATED

af·fil·i·a·tion /əˌfiliˈeɪʃn/ *noun* [U, C] (*formal*) **1** a person's connection with a political party, religion, etc.: *He was arrested because of his political affiliation.* **2** one group or organization's official connection with another

af·fin·i·ty /əˈfɪnəti/ *noun* (*pl.* **af·fin·i·ties**) (*formal*) **1** [sing.] **~ (for/with sb/sth)** | **~ (between A and B)** a strong feeling that you understand someone or something and like them or it **SYN** RAPPORT: *Sam was born in the country and had a deep affinity with nature.* **2** [U, C] **~ (with sb/sth)** | **~ (between A and B)** a close relationship between two people or things that have similar qualities, structures, or features: *There is a close affinity between Spanish and Portuguese.*

af·finity ˌcard *noun* a CREDIT CARD printed with the name of an organization, for example a charity, which receives a small amount of money each time the card is used

af·finity ˌgroup *noun* a group of people who share the same interest or purpose

af·firm /əˈfərm/ *verb* (*formal*) to state firmly or publicly that something is true or that you support something strongly **SYN** CONFIRM: **~ sth** *Both sides affirmed their commitment to the cease-fire.* ◆ **~ that…** *I can affirm that no one will lose their job.* ▸ **af·firm·a·tion** /ˌæfərˈmeɪʃn/ *noun* [U, C]: *She nodded in affirmation.*

af·firm·a·tive /əˈfərmətɪv/ *adj., noun*
● *adj.* (*formal*) an **affirmative** word or reply means "yes" or expresses agreement **ANT** NEGATIVE ▸ **af·firm·a·tive·ly** *adv.*: *90% voted affirmatively.*
● *noun* (*formal*) a word or statement that means "yes"; an agreement or a CONFIRMATION: *She answered* **in the affirmative** (= said "yes"). **ANT** NEGATIVE

af·firmative ˈaction *noun* [U] the practice or policy of making sure that a particular number of jobs, etc. are given to people from groups that are often treated unfairly because of their race, sex, etc. ⊃ compare REVERSE DISCRIMINATION

af·fix *verb, noun*
● *verb* /əˈfɪks/ [often passive] **~ sth (to sth)** (*formal*) to stick or attach something to something else: *The label should be firmly affixed to the package.*
● *noun* /ˈæfɪks/ (*grammar*) a letter or group of letters added to the beginning or end of a word to change its meaning. The PREFIX *un-* in *unhappy* and the SUFFIX *-less* in *careless* are both affixes.

af·flict /əˈflɪkt/ *verb* [often passive] (*formal*) to affect someone or something in an unpleasant or harmful way: **~ sb/sth** *Aid will be sent to the afflicted areas.* ◆ **be afflicted with/by sth** *About 40% of the country's population is afflicted with the disease.*

af·flic·tion /əˈflɪkʃn/ *noun* [U, C] (*formal*) pain and suffering or something that causes it

af·flu·ent /ˈæfluənt/ *adj.* having a lot of money and a good standard of living **SYN** PROSPEROUS, WEALTHY: *affluent Western countries* ◆ *a very affluent neighborhood* ⊃ thesaurus box at RICH ▸ **af·flu·ence** /ˈæfluəns/ *noun* [U] **SYN** PROSPERITY

af·ford 🔑 /əˈfɔrd/ *verb*

1 [no passive] (usually used with *can, could*, or *be able to*, especially in negative sentences or questions) to have enough money or time to be able to buy or to do something: **~ sth** *Can we afford a new car?* ◆ *None of them could afford $50 for a ticket.* ◆ *She felt she couldn't afford any more time off work.* ◆ **~ to do sth** *We can't afford to go on vacation this summer.* ◆ *She never took a taxi, even though she could afford to.* ◆ **~ sth to do sth** *He couldn't afford the money to go on the trip.* **2** [no passive] (usually used with *can* or *could*, especially in negative sentences and questions) if you say that you **can't afford** to do something, you mean that you should not do it because it will cause problems for you if you do: **~ to do sth** *We cannot afford to ignore this warning.* ◆ *They could* **ill afford** *to lose any more staff.* ◆ **~ sth** *We cannot afford any more delays.* **3** (*formal*) to provide someone with something: **~ sth** *The tree affords some shelter from the sun.* ◆ **~ sb sth** *The program affords young people the chance to gain work*

experience. ▶ **af·ford·a·bil·i·ty** /əˌfɔrdəˈbɪləti/ noun [U]
af·ford·a·ble /əˈfɔrdəbl/ adj.: affordable prices/housing
ANT UNAFFORDABLE ⊃ thesaurus box at CHEAP
af·ford·a·bly /əˈfɔrdəbli/: affordably priced apartments

af·for·est·a·tion /əˌfɔrəˈsteɪʃn; -ˌfar-/ noun [U] (technical) the
process of planting areas of land with trees in order to form
a forest ⊃ compare DEFORESTATION ▶ **af·for·est** /əˈfɔrəst;
-ˈfar-/ verb [usually passive] **~ sth**

af·fray /əˈfreɪ/ noun [C, usually sing., U] (law) a fight or violent
behavior in a public place

af·fri·cate /ˈæfrɪkət/ noun (phonetics) a speech sound that is
made up of a PLOSIVE followed immediately by a FRICA-
TIVE, for example /tʃ/ and /dʒ/ in chair and job

af·front /əˈfrʌnt/ noun, verb
• **noun** [usually sing.] **~ (to sb/sth)** a remark or an action that
insults or offends someone or something
• **verb** [usually passive] **~ sb/sth** (formal) to insult or offend
someone: He hoped they would not feel affronted if they were
not invited. ✦ an affronted expression

Af·ghan hound /ˈæfgæn ˌhaʊnd/ noun a tall dog with long
soft hair and a pointed nose

a·fi·cio·na·do /əˌfɪʃəˈnadoʊ; əˌfɪsjə-/ noun (pl. a·fi·cio·na-
dos) a person who likes a particular sport, activity, or
subject very much and knows a lot about it

a·field /əˈfild/ adv.
IDM **far/farther/further afield** far away from home; to or
in places that are not near: You can rent a car if you want to
explore further afield. ✦ Journalists came from as far afield as
China.

a·flame /əˈfleɪm/ adj. [not before noun] (literary) **1** burning;
on fire **SYN** ABLAZE: The whole building was soon aflame.
2 full of bright colors and lights **SYN** ABLAZE: The woods
were aflame with fall colors. **3** showing excitement or embarrassment: eyes/cheeks aflame

AFL–CIO /ˌeɪ ɛf ˌel ˌsi aɪ ˈoʊ/ abbr. American Federation of
Labor and Congress of Industrial Organizations (an organization of LABOR UNIONS)

a·float /əˈfloʊt/ adj. [not before noun] **1** floating on water:
Somehow we kept the boat afloat. **2** (of a business, etc.)
having enough money to pay debts; able to survive: They
will have to borrow $10 million next year, just to stay afloat.

a·foot /əˈfʊt/ adj. [not before noun] being planned; happening: There are plans afoot to increase taxation. ✦ Changes
were afoot.

a·fore·men·tioned /əˈfɔrˌmenʃənd/ (also **a·fore·said**
/əˈfɔrsed/, **said**) adj. [only before noun] (formal or law)
mentioned before, in an earlier sentence: The aforementioned person was seen acting suspiciously.

a·fore·thought /əˈfɔrθɔt/ adj. **IDM** see MALICE

a for·ti·o·ri /ˌeɪ ˌfɔrtiˈɔraɪ; ˌa ˌfɔrtiˈɔri; -ˈfɔrʃi-/ adv. (from Latin,
formal or law) for or with an even stronger reason

a·foul /əˈfaʊl/ adv.
IDM **fall/run afoul of sth** to do something that is not
allowed by a law or rule or something that people in
authority disapprove of: to run afoul of the law

a·fraid 🔑 /əˈfreɪd/ adj. [not before noun]
1 feeling fear; frightened because you think that you might
be hurt or suffer: Don't be afraid. ✦ **~ of sb/sth** It's all over.
There's nothing to be afraid of now. ✦ Are you afraid of spiders?
✦ **~ of doing sth** I started to feel afraid of going out alone at
night. ✦ **~ to do sth** She was afraid to open the door. **2** worried
about what might happen: **~ of doing sth** She was afraid of
upsetting her parents. ✦ **~ to do sth** Don't be afraid to ask if you
don't understand. ✦ **~ (that...)** We were afraid (that) we were
going to capsize the boat. **3** **~ for sb/sth** worried or frightened that something unpleasant, dangerous, etc. will
happen to a particular person or thing: I'm not afraid for me,
but for the baby. ✦ They had already fired three people and he
was afraid for his job.
IDM **I'm afraid** used as a polite way of telling someone
something that is unpleasant or disappointing, or that you

are sorry about: I can't help you, I'm afraid. ✦ I'm afraid we
can't come. ✦ I'm afraid that it's not finished yet. ✦ He's no better,
I'm afraid to say. ✦ "Is there any left?" "I'm afraid not." ✦ "Will it
hurt?" "I'm afraid so."

THESAURUS

afraid

scared ✦ frightened ✦ terrified ✦ alarmed ✦ paranoid

These words all describe feeling or showing fear.

afraid [not before noun] feeling fear; worried that
something bad might happen: There's nothing to be
afraid of. ✦ Aren't you afraid (that) you'll fall?

scared feeling fear; worried that something bad might
happen: The thieves got scared and ran away. ✦ She was
scared that the glass would break.

frightened feeling fear; worried that something bad
might happen: a frightened child

AFRAID, SCARED, OR FRIGHTENED?

Scared is more informal, more common in speech, and
often describes small fears. **Afraid** cannot come before a
noun. It can only take the preposition of, not about. If you
are **afraid/scared/frightened of** something, or **afraid/
scared/frightened to** do something, you think you are
in danger of being hurt or suffering in some way. If you
are **scared/frightened about** something, it is less a fear
for your personal safety and more a worry that something unpleasant might happen.

terrified very frightened: I was terrified (that) she might
follow me. ✦ She looked at him with wide, terrified eyes. ✦ I
was terrified of flying.

alarmed afraid that something dangerous or unpleasant might happen: She was alarmed at the prospect of
traveling alone.

paranoid (somewhat informal) afraid or suspicious in a
way that is not reasonable: You're just being paranoid.

PATTERNS
■ afraid/scared/frightened/terrified **of** spiders, etc.
■ scared/frightened/paranoid **about** ...
■ afraid/scared/frightened/terrified **that** ...
■ afraid/scared/frightened **to** open the door, etc.
■ Don't be afraid/scared/frightened/alarmed.

A-frame (also ˌA-frame ˈhouse) noun a house with very
steep sides that meet at the top in the shape of the letter A

A-frame ˈtent noun a tent which forms an upside-down V
shape ⊃ compare DOME TENT, WALL TENT

a·fresh /əˈfreʃ/ adv. (formal) again, especially from the
beginning or with new ideas: It was a chance to start afresh.

Af·ri·can /ˈæfrɪkən/ adj., noun
• **adj.** of or connected with Africa
• **noun** a person from Africa, especially a black person

African Aˈmerican noun a person from America who is a
member of a race of people who have dark skin, originally
from Africa ▶ ˌAfrican Aˈmerican adj.

African Caˈnadian noun a person from Canada who is a
member of a race of people with dark skin, originally from
Africa ▶ ˌAfrican Caˈnadian adj.

African ˈrenaissance noun [sing.] a period of time when
Africa will experience great development in its economy
and culture. Some people believe that this started at the
end of the 20th century.

Af·ri·kaans /ˌæfrɪˈkɑns; -ˈkɑnz/ noun [U] a language that has
developed from Dutch, spoken in South Africa

Af·ri·ka·ner /ˌæfrɪˈkɑnər/ noun a person from South Africa,
usually of Dutch origin, whose first language is Afrikaans

Af·ro /ˈæfroʊ/ noun (pl. **Af·ros**) a HAIRSTYLE sometimes worn
by black people and popular in the 1970s, in which the hair
forms a round mass of tight curls

ʌ cup   ə about   eɪ say   aɪ five   ɔɪ boy   aʊ now   oʊ go   ər bird

Afro- /ˈæfrou/ *combining form* (in nouns and adjectives) African: *Afro-Asian*

Af·ro·beat /ˈæfrouˌbit/ *noun* [U] a type of music that combines traditional Nigerian rhythms and singing styles with JAZZ and FUNK

Afro-Carib'bean *noun* a person who comes, or whose family comes, from the Caribbean, and who is a member of a race of people with dark skin who originally came from Africa ▶ **Afro-Carib'bean** *adj.*

Af·ro·cen·tric /ˌæfrouˈsɛntrɪk/ *adj.* focusing on African or black culture, history, etc.: *Afrocentric clothing and jewelry* ▶ **Af·ro·cen·trism** /ˌæfrouˈsɛntrɪzəm/ *noun* [U]

aft /æft/ *adv.* (*technical*) in, near, or toward the back of a ship or an aircraft ▶ **aft** *adj.* ⊃ compare FORE

af·ter 🔑 /ˈæftər/ *prep., conj., adv., adj.*

● *prep.* **1** later than something; following something in time: *We'll leave after lunch.* ◆ *They arrived shortly after 5.* ◆ *Not long after that* he resigned. ◆ *Let's meet the day after tomorrow/ the week after next.* ◆ *After winning the prize, she became famous overnight.* ◆ *After an hour I went home* (= when an hour had passed). ◆ *It's ten after seven in the morning* (= 7:10 a.m.) **2 ... after...** used to show that something happens many times or continuously: *day after day of hot weather* ◆ *I've told you time after time not to do that.* ⊃ **see also** ONE AFTER ANOTHER at ONE **3** behind someone when they have left; following someone: *Shut the door after you.* ◆ *I'm always having to clean up after the kids* (= clean the place after they have left it dirty or messy). ◆ *He ran after her with the book.* ◆ *She was left staring after him.* **4** next to and following someone or something in order or importance: *Your name comes after mine on the list.* ◆ *He's the tallest, after Richard.* ◆ *After you* (= Please go first). ◆ *I'll jump into the pool after she does.* **5** in contrast to something: *It was pleasantly cool in the house after the sticky heat outside.* **6** as a result of or because of something that has happened: *I'll never forgive him after what he said.* **7** despite something; although something has happened: *I can't believe she'd do that, not after all I've done for her.* **8** trying to find or catch someone or something: *The police are after him.* ◆ *He's after a job at our place.* **9** about someone or something: *She asked after you* (= how you were). **10** in the style of someone or something; following the example of someone or something: *a painting after Goya* ◆ *We named the baby "Lillian" after her grandmother.* **11 after-** (in adjectives) happening or done later than the time or event mentioned: *after-hours drinking* (= after closing time) ◆ *an after-school club* ◆ *after-dinner mints* **IDM** **after all 1** despite what has been said or expected: *So you made it after all!* **2** used when you are explaining something, or giving a reason: *He should have paid. He suggested it, after all.*

● *conj.* at a time later than something; when something has finished: *I'll call you after I've spoken to them.* ◆ *Several years after they split up, they met again by chance in Paris.*

● *adv.* later in time; afterward: *That was in 1996. Soon after, I heard that he'd died.* ◆ *I could come next week, or the week after.* ◆ *And they all lived happily ever after.*

● *adj.* [only before noun] (*old use*) following; later: *in after years*

af·ter·birth /ˈæftərˌbərθ/ *noun* usually **the afterbirth** [sing.] the material that comes out of a woman or female animal's body after a baby has been born, and that was necessary to feed and protect the baby **SYN** PLACENTA

af·ter·burn·er /ˈæftərˌbərnər/ *noun* (*technical*) a device for increasing the power of a JET ENGINE

af·ter·care /ˈæftərˌkɛr/ *noun* [U] **1** care or treatment given to a person who has just left the hospital, prison, etc.: *aftercare services* **2** care of children after school until their parents finish work ⊃ compare DAY CARE

af·ter·ef·fect /ˈæftərɪˌfɛkt/ *noun* [usually pl.] the **aftereffects** of a drug, an illness, or an unpleasant event are the feelings that you experience later as a result of it

af·ter·glow /ˈæftərˌglou/ *noun* [usually sing.] (*literary*) **1** the light that is left in the sky after the sun has set **2** a pleasant feeling after a good experience

after-'hours *adj.* [only before noun] happening or open after the normal or legal closing time for a business: *an after-hours tour of the new facilities* ◆ *an after-hours bar*

af·ter·im·age /ˈæftərˌɪmɪdʒ/ *noun* (*technical*) an image that your eye still sees after the thing that you were looking at is no longer there

af·ter·life /ˈæftərˌlaɪf/ *noun* [sing.] a life that some people believe exists after death

af·ter·mar·ket /ˈæftərˌmarkət/ *noun* [sing.] **1** the demand for equipment and services that are related to a purchase: *the aftermarket for computer accessories* ◆ *the automotive aftermarket* **2** (*finance*) the financial markets such as STOCK EXCHANGES where shares in companies are bought and sold, after their original issue: *I sold the stock in the aftermarket at $19.25.* ◆ *declining aftermarket prices*

af·ter·math /ˈæftərˌmæθ/ *noun* [usually sing.] the situation that exists as a result of an important (and usually unpleasant) event, especially a war, an accident, etc.: *A lot of rebuilding took place in the aftermath of the war.* ◆ *the assassination of the president and its immediate aftermath*

af·ter·noon 🔑 /ˌæftərˈnun/ *noun* [U, C] the part of the day from 12 p.m. until about 6 p.m.: *this/ yesterday/tomorrow afternoon* ◆ *In the afternoon they went shopping.* ◆ *She takes an art class two afternoons a week.* ◆ *Are you ready for this afternoon's meeting?* ◆ *The baby always has an afternoon nap.* ◆ *Come over on Sunday afternoon.* ◆ *Where were you on the afternoon of May 21?* ⊃ **see also** GOOD AFTERNOON

af·ter·noons /ˌæftərˈnunz/ *adv.* during the afternoon every day: *She usually works afternoons.*

after-'school *adj.* [only before noun] starting at the end of the school day and usually finishing before dinner: *sports and other after-school activities*

af·ter·shave /ˈæftərˌʃeɪv/ *noun* [U, C] a liquid with a pleasant smell that men sometimes put on their faces after they shave

af·ter·shock /ˈæftərˌʃak/ *noun* a small EARTHQUAKE that happens after a bigger one

af·ter·taste /ˈæftərˌteɪst/ *noun* [sing.] a taste (usually an unpleasant one) that stays in your mouth after you have eaten or drunk something

af·ter·thought /ˈæftərˌθɔt/ *noun* [usually sing.] a thing that is thought of, said, or added later, and is often not carefully planned: *They only invited Jack and Sarah as an afterthought.*

af·ter·ward 🔑 /ˈæftərwərd/ (also **af·ter·wards**) /ˈæftərwərdz/ *adv.*
at a later time; after an event that has already been mentioned: *She was sorry afterward for what she said.* ◆ *Let's go out now and eat afterward.* ◆ *Shortly afterward he saw her again.*

af·ter·word /ˈæftərˌwərd/ *noun* a section at the end of a book that says something about the main text, and may be written by a different author ⊃ compare FOREWORD

a·gain 🔑 /əˈgɛn/ *adv.*
1 one more time; on another occasion: *Could you say it again, please?* ◆ *When will I see you again?* ◆ *This must never happen again.* ◆ *Once again* (= as had happened several times before), *the train was late.* ◆ *I've told you again and again* (= many times) *not to do that.* ◆ *I'll have to write it all over again* (= again from the beginning). **2** showing that someone or something is in the same place or state that they were in originally: *He was glad to be home again.* ◆ *She spends two hours a day getting to work and back again.* ◆ *You'll feel well again soon.* **3** used to show that a comment or fact is connected with what you have just said: *And again, we must think of the cost.* **4 then/there ~** used to introduce a fact or an opinion that contrasts with what you have just said: *We might buy it, but then again, we might not.* **5** used when you ask someone to tell you something or repeat something

that you think they have told you already: *What was the name again?* **IDM** see NOW, TIME n.

a·gainst 🔑 /əˈgenst/ prep.

HELP For the special uses of **against** in phrasal verbs, look at the entries for the verbs. For example, **count against sb** is in the phrasal verb section at **count**. **1** opposing or disagreeing with someone or something: *the fight against terrorism* ◆ *We're playing against the league champions next week.* ◆ *We were rowing against the current.* ◆ *That's against the law.* ◆ *She was forced to marry against her will.* ◆ *Are you for or against the death penalty?* ◆ *She is against seeing* (= does not want to see) *him.* ◆ *I'd advise you against doing that.* **2** not to the advantage or favor of someone or something: *The evidence is against him.* ◆ *Her age is against her.* ⊃ compare FOR **3** close to, touching, or hitting someone or something: *Put the piano there, against the wall.* ◆ *The rain beat against the windows.* **4** in order to prevent something from happening or to reduce the damage caused by something: *a vaccination against the measles* ◆ *They took precautions against fire.* ◆ *Are we insured against theft?* **5** with something in the background, as a contrast: *His red clothes stood out clearly against the snow.* ◆ *(figurative) The love story unfolds against a background of civil war.* **6** used when you are comparing two things: *You must weigh the benefits against the cost.* ◆ *Check your receipts against the statement.* ◆ *What's the exchange rate against the euro?* **IDM** see AS, STACKED

a·ga·pe /əˈgeɪp/ *adj.* [not before noun] (*formal*) if a person's mouth is **agape**, it is wide open, especially because they are surprised or shocked

a·gar /ˈɑgər/ (also **agar-ˈagar**) *noun* [U] a substance like jelly, used by scientists for growing CULTURES

ag·ate /ˈægət/ *noun* [U, C] a hard stone with bands or areas of color, used in jewelry

a·ga·ve /əˈgɑvi/ *noun* a plant that grows in hot dry areas of N. and S. America, with sharp points on the leaves and tall groups of flowers

age 🔑 /eɪdʒ/ *noun, verb*

● *noun* **1** [C, U] the number of years that a person has lived or a thing has existed: *He left school at the age of 18.* ◆ *She needs more friends her own age.* ◆ *children from 5–10 years of age* ◆ *This game is for children of all ages.* ◆ *When I was your age, I was already married.* ◆ *He started playing the piano at an early age.* ◆ *Children over the age of 12 must pay the full fare.* ◆ *She was beginning to feel her age* (= feel that she was getting old). ◆ *He was tall for his age* (= taller than you would expect, considering his age). ◆ *There's a big age gap between them* (= a big difference in their ages). ◆ *ways of calculating the age of the earth* **2** [C, U] a particular period of a person's life: *middle age* ◆ *15 is an awkward age.* ◆ *He died of old age.* **3** [C] a particular period of history: *the nuclear age* ◆ *the age of the computer* ⊃ see also BRONZE AGE, IRON AGE, NEW AGE, STONE AGE **4** [U] the state of being old: *The jacket was showing signs of age.* ◆ *the wisdom that comes with age* **5** **ages** [pl.] (*informal*) a very long time: *I waited for ages.* ◆ *It'll probably take ages to find a parking space.* ◆ *Carlos left ages ago.* ◆ *It's been ages since we saw them.* **6** [C] (*geology*) a length of time which is a division of an EPOCH **IDM** **be/act your age** to behave in a way that is suitable for someone of your age and not as though you were much younger **come of age 1** when a person **comes of age**, they reach the age when they have an adult's legal rights and responsibilities ⊃ see also COMING OF AGE **2** if something **comes of age**, it reaches the stage of development at which people accept and value it **look your age** to seem as old as you really are and not younger or older **under age** not legally old enough to do a particular thing: *It is illegal to sell cigarettes to children who are under age.* ⊃ see also UNDERAGE ⊃ more at ADVANCED, CERTAIN, DAY, FEEL, GRAND, RIPE

● *verb* (ag·ing, aged, aged) **1** [I] to become older: *As he aged, his memory got worse.* ◆ *The population is aging* (= more people are living longer). **2** [T] to make someone or something look, feel, or seem older: *~ sb The shock has aged her.* ◆ *~ sth Exposure to the sun ages your skin.* **3** [I, T] to develop in flavor

over a period of time; to allow something to do this **SYN** MATURE: *The cheese is left to age for at least a year.* ◆ *~ sth The wine is aged in oak casks.*

TOPIC COLLOCATIONS

The Ages of Life

childhood/youth
- be born (and raised) in New York; into a wealthy/middle-class family
- have a happy/an unhappy/a tough childhood
- grow up in a musical family/in an orphanage/on a farm
- be/grow up an only child (= with no brothers or sisters)
- reach/hit/enter/go through adolescence/puberty
- be in your teens/early twenties/mid-twenties/late twenties
- undergo/experience physical/psychological changes
- give in to/succumb to/resist peer pressure
- assert your independence/individuality

adulthood
- leave home
- graduate from school/college
- go to work (at the age of 21)
- get/find a job/partner
- be/get engaged/married
- have a wife/husband/mortgage/steady job
- settle down and have kids/start a family
- begin/start/launch/build a career (in politics/science/the music industry)
- prove (to be)/represent/mark/reach a (major) turning point in your life/career
- reach/be well into/settle into middle age
- have/suffer/go through a midlife crisis
- take/consider early retirement
- approach/announce/enjoy your retirement

old age
- see/spend time with your grandchildren
- take up/pursue/develop a hobby
- get/receive/draw/collect/live on a pension
- approach/save for/die of old age
- live to a ripe old age
- reach the grand old age of 102/23 (*often humorous*)
- be/become/be getting/be going senile (*often humorous*)
- die (peacefully)/pass away in your sleep/after a brief illness

---

-age /ɪdʒ/ *suffix* (in nouns) **1** the action or result of: *breakage* **2** a state or condition of: *bondage* **3** a set or group of: *baggage* **4** an amount of: *mileage* **5** the cost of: *postage* **6** a place where: *anchorage*

aged 🔑 *adj.*
1 /eɪdʒd/ [not before noun] of the age of: *They have two children aged six and nine.* ◆ *volunteers aged between 25 and 40* **2** /ˈeɪdʒəd/ (*formal*) very old: *my aged aunt* ⊃ thesaurus box at OLD **3** **the aged** /ˈeɪdʒəd/ *noun* [pl.] very old people: *services for the sick and the aged*

ˈage group (also *less frequent* ˈage ˌbracket) *noun* people of a similar age or within a particular range of ages: *men in the older age group* ◆ *education for the 14–18 age group* ◆ *Which age bracket are you? (Please check the box.)*

age·ism (also **ag·ism**) /ˈeɪdʒɪzəm/ *noun* [U] unfair treatment of people because they are considered too old ▶ **age·ist** (also **ag·ist**) /ˈeɪdʒɪst/ *adj.* **age·ist** (also **ag·ist**) *noun*

age·less /ˈeɪdʒləs/ *adj.* (*literary*) **1** never looking old or never seeming to grow old **SYN** TIMELESS: *Her beauty appeared ageless.* **2** existing for ever; impossible to give an age to **SYN** TIMELESS: *the ageless mystery of the universe*

t tea   ṱ butter   d did   k cat   g got   tʃ chin   dʒ June   f fall

¹age ˌlimit *noun* the oldest or youngest age at which you are allowed to do something: *to raise/lower the age limit*

a·gen·cy 🔑 /ˈeɪdʒənsi/ *noun*
(*pl.* **a·gen·cies**) **1** a business or an organization that provides a particular service, especially on behalf of other businesses or organizations: *an advertising/employment agency* ◆ *You can book at your local travel agency.* ◆ *international aid agencies caring for refugees* ⟳ see also NEWS AGENCY **2** a government department that provides a particular service: *the Central Intelligence Agency (CIA)* **IDM** **through the agency of** (*formal*) as a result of the action of someone or something

a·gen·da 🔑 /əˈdʒɛndə/ *noun*
a list of items to be discussed at a meeting: *The next item on the agenda is the publicity budget.* ◆ *For the government, education is now at the top of the agenda* (= most important). ◆ *In our company, quality is high on the agenda.* ◆ *Newspapers have been accused of trying to set the agenda for the government* (= decide what is important). ⟳ see also HIDDEN AGENDA

WHICH WORD?

agenda ◆ diary ◆ schedule

- A book with a space for each day where you write down things that you have to do in the future is called a **planner** or a **datebook** (not an *agenda*). You may also have a **calendar** on your desk or hanging up in your room, where you write down your appointments. A **diary** or a **journal** is also the record that some people keep of what has happened during the day: *The Diary of Anne Frank.*
- Your **schedule** is a plan that lists all the work that you have to do and when you must do each thing, or it is a list showing the fixed times at which events will happen: *a schedule of events for the conference*

---

a·gent 🔑 /ˈeɪdʒənt/ *noun*
1 a person whose job is to act for, or manage the affairs of, other people in business, politics, etc.: *an insurance agent* ◆ *Our agent in London deals with all U.K. sales.* ⟳ see also TRAVEL AGENT **2** a person whose job is to arrange work for an actor, musician, sports player, etc. or to find someone who will publish a writer's work: *a theatrical/literary agent* ⟳ see also PRESS AGENT **3** = SECRET AGENT: *an enemy agent* ⟳ see also DOUBLE AGENT, SPECIAL AGENT **4** (*formal*) a person or thing that has an important effect on a situation: *The charity has been an agent for social change.* **5** (*technical*) a chemical or a substance that produces an effect or a change or is used for a particular purpose: *cleaning/oxidizing agents* **6** (*grammar*) the person or thing that does an action (expressed as the subject of an active verb, or in a "by" phrase with a passive verb) ⟳ compare PATIENT ⟳ see also FREE AGENT

Agent ˈOrange *noun* [U] a chemical that destroys plants, used as a weapon by the U.S. during the war in Vietnam

a·gent pro·vo·ca·teur /ˌɑʒɑ̃ prouˌvɑkəˈtər/ *noun* (*pl.* a·gents pro·vo·ca·teurs* /ˌɑʒɑ̃ prouˌvɑkəˈtər/) (also pro·vo·ca·teur) (from *French*) a person who is employed by a government to encourage people in political groups to do something illegal so that they can be arrested

¹age of conˈsent *noun* [sing.] the age at which someone is legally old enough to agree to have a sexual relationship

¹age-old *adj.* [usually before noun] having existed for a very long time: *an age-old custom/problem*

ag·glom·er·ate *verb, noun, adj.* (*formal*)
- *verb* /əˈɡlɑməˌreɪt/ [I, T] to form into a mass or group; to collect things and form them into a mass or group: *These small particles agglomerate together to form larger clusters.* ◆ *~ sth They agglomerated many small pieces of research into a single large study.*
- *noun* /əˈɡlɑmərət/ a mass or collection of things: *a multimedia agglomerate* (= group of companies)

- *adj.* /əˈɡlɑmərət/ formed into a mass or group

ag·glom·er·a·tion /əˌɡlɑməˈreɪʃn/ *noun* [C, U] (*formal*) a group of things put together in no particular order or arrangement

ag·glu·ti·na·tive /əˈɡlutnˌeɪtɪv; -ətɪv/ *adj.* (*linguistics*) = SYNTHETIC *adj.* (2)

ag·gran·dize·ment /əˈɡrændəzmənt; -daɪz-/ *noun* [U] (*formal, disapproving*) an increase in the power or importance of a person or country: *Her sole aim is personal aggrandizement.*

ag·gra·vate /ˈæɡrəˌveɪt/ *verb* **1** ~ sth to make an illness or a bad or unpleasant situation worse **SYN** WORSEN: *Pollution can aggravate asthma.* ◆ *Military intervention will only aggravate the conflict even further.* **2** ~ sb (*informal*) to annoy someone, especially deliberately **SYN** IRRITATE ▶ **ag·gra·vat·ing** *adj.* **ag·gra·va·tion** /ˌæɡrəˈveɪʃn/ *noun* [U, C]: *The drug may cause an aggravation of the condition.* ◆ *I don't need all this aggravation at work.*

ag·gra·vat·ed /ˈæɡrəˌveɪtəd/ *adj.* **1** [not usually before noun] (*informal*) slightly angry; annoyed: *I get so aggravated when he does that!* **2** (*law*) [only before noun] an **aggravated** crime involves further unnecessary violence or unpleasant behavior

ag·gre·gate **AWL** *noun, adj., verb*
- *noun* /ˈæɡrɪɡət/ **1** [C] a total number or amount made up of smaller amounts that are collected together **2** [U, C] (*technical*) sand or broken stone that is used to make concrete or for building roads, etc.
  IDM **in (the) aggregate** (*formal*) added together as a total or single amount

- *adj.* /ˈæɡrɪɡət/ [only before noun] (*economics*) made up of several amounts that are added together to form a total number: *aggregate demand/investment/turnover*

- *verb* /ˈæɡrɪˌɡeɪt/ [usually passive] ~ sth (with sth) (*formal* or *technical*) to put together different items, amounts, etc. into a single group or total: *The scores were aggregated with the first round totals to decide the winner.* ▶ **ag·gre·ga·tion** **AWL** /ˌæɡrɪˈɡeɪʃn/ *noun* [U, C]: *the aggregation of data*

ag·gre·ga·tor /ˈæɡrɪˌɡeɪtər/ *noun* (*computing*) an Internet company that collects information about other companies' products and services and puts it on a single Web site: *a news aggregator*

ag·gres·sion /əˈɡrɛʃn/ *noun* [U] **1** feelings of anger and hatred that may result in threatening or violent behavior: *The research shows that computer games may cause aggression.* **2** a violent attack or threats by one person against another person or by one country against another country: *unprovoked military aggression*

ag·gres·sive 🔑 /əˈɡrɛsɪv/ *adj.*
1 angry, and behaving in a threatening way; ready to attack: *He gets aggressive when he's drunk.* ◆ *a dangerous, aggressive dog* **2** acting with force and determination in order to succeed: *an aggressive advertising campaign* ◆ *A good salesperson has to be aggressive in today's competitive market.* ▶ **ag·gres·sive·ly** *adv.*: *"What do you want?" he demanded aggressively.* ◆ *aggressively marketed products* **ag·gres·sive·ness** *noun* [U]

ag·gres·sor /əˈɡrɛsər/ *noun* a person, country, etc. that attacks first

ag·grieved /əˈɡrivd/ *adj.* **1** ~ (at/by sth) feeling that you have been treated unfairly **2** (*law*) suffering unfair or illegal treatment and making a complaint: *the aggrieved party* (= person) *in the case*

a·ghast /əˈɡæst/ *adj.* [not before noun] filled with horror and surprise when you see or hear something **SYN** HORRIFIED: *Erica looked at him aghast.* ◆ *~ at sth He stood aghast at the sight of so much blood.*

ag·ile /ˈædʒl; ˈædʒaɪl/ *adj.* **1** able to move quickly and easily **SYN** NIMBLE **2** able to think quickly and in an intelligent way: *an agile mind/brain* ▶ **a·gil·i·ty** /əˈdʒɪləti/ *noun* [U]: *He had the agility of a man half his age.*

ag·ing /ˈeɪdʒɪŋ/ noun, adj.
- **noun** [U] the process of growing old: *signs of aging*
- **adj.** [usually before noun] becoming older and usually less useful, safe, healthy, etc.: *aging equipment* ♦ *an aging rock star*

ag·ism, agist = AGEISM, AGEISM

ag·i·tate /ˈædʒəˌteɪt/ verb **1** [I, T] to argue strongly for something you want, especially for changes in a law, in social conditions, etc. **SYN** CAMPAIGN: ~ **(for/against sth)** *political groups agitating for social change* ♦ **to do sth** *Her family is agitating to have her released from custody.* **2** [T] ~ **sb** to make someone feel angry, anxious, or nervous **3** [T] ~ **sth** (technical) to make something, especially a liquid, move around by stirring or shaking it

ag·i·tat·ed /ˈædʒəˌteɪtəd/ adj. showing in your behavior that you are anxious and nervous: *Calm down! Don't get so agitated.*

ag·i·ta·tion /ˌædʒəˈteɪʃn/ noun **1** [U] worry and anxiety that you show by behaving in a nervous way: *Daria arrived in a state of great agitation.* **2** [U, C] ~ **(for/against sth)** public protest in order to achieve political change: *widespread agitation for social reform* **3** [U] (technical) the act of stirring or shaking a liquid

ag·i·ta·tor /ˈædʒəˌteɪtər/ noun **1** (disapproving) a person who tries to persuade people to take part in political protest **2** the part in the center of a WASHING MACHINE that helps to move the clothes and water around

ag·it·prop /ˈædʒətˌprɑp/ noun [U] the use of art, movies, music, etc. to spread LEFT-WING political ideas

a·glow /əˈɡloʊ/ adj. [not before noun] (literary) shining with warmth and color, or happiness

ag·no·sia /æɡˈnoʊʒə/ noun [U] (medical) the lack of the ability to recognize things and people

ag·nos·tic /æɡˈnɑstɪk; əɡ-/ noun a person who believes that it is not possible to know whether God exists or not ⊃ compare ATHEIST ► **ag·nos·tic** adj. **ag·nos·ti·cism** /æɡˈnɑstəˌsɪzəm; əɡ-/ noun [U]

a·go 🔑 /əˈɡoʊ/ adv.
used in expressions of time with the simple past tense to show how far in the past something happened: *two weeks/months/years ago* ♦ *The letter came a few days ago.* ♦ *She was here just a minute ago.* ♦ *a short/long time ago* ♦ *How long ago did you buy it?* ♦ *It was on TV not (so) long ago.* ♦ *He stopped working some time ago* (= quite a long time ago). ♦ *They're getting married? It's not that long ago* (= it's only a short time ago) *that they met!*

a·gog /əˈɡɑɡ/ adj. [not before noun] excited and very interested to find out something

ag·o·nize /ˈæɡəˌnaɪz/ verb [I] ~ **(over/about sth)** to spend a long time thinking and worrying about a difficult situation or problem: *I spent days agonizing over whether to take the job or not.*

ag·o·nized /ˈæɡəˌnaɪzd/ adj. suffering or expressing severe pain or anxiety: *agonized cries*

ag·o·niz·ing /ˈæɡəˌnaɪzɪŋ/ adj. causing great pain, anxiety, or difficulty: *his father's agonizing death* ♦ *It was the most agonizing decision of her life.*

ag·o·niz·ing·ly /ˈæɡəˌnaɪzɪŋli/ adv. used meaning "extremely" to emphasize something negative: *an agonizingly slow process*

ag·o·ny /ˈæɡəni/ noun (pl. **ag·o·nies**) [U, C] extreme physical or mental pain: *Jack collapsed in agony on the floor.* ♦ *It was agony not knowing where the children were.* ♦ *She waited in an agony of suspense.* ♦ *The worst agonies of the war were now beginning.* ♦ *Tell me now! Don't prolong the agony* (= make it last longer).

a·go·ra /ˈæɡərə; əˈɡɔrə/ noun (pl. **a·go·rae** /ˈæɡəri; əˈɡɔri/ or **a·go·ras**) in ancient Greece, an open space used for markets and public meetings

ag·o·ra·pho·bi·a /ˌæɡərəˈfoʊbiə; əˌɡɔrə-/ noun [U] (technical) a fear of being in public places where there are many other people ⊃ compare CLAUSTROPHOBIA

ag·o·ra·pho·bic /ˌæɡərəˈfoʊbɪk; əˌɡɔrə-/ noun a person who suffers from agoraphobia ► **ag·o·ra·pho·bic** adj.

a·grar·i·an /əˈɡreriən/ adj. [usually before noun] (technical) connected with farming and the use of land for farming

---

THESAURUS

agree

accept • approve • go along with sb/sth • consent

These words all mean to say that you will do what someone wants or that you will allow something to happen.

agree to say that you will do what someone wants or that you will allow something to happen: *He agreed to let me go early.*

accept to be satisfied with something that has been done, decided, or suggested: *They accepted the court's decision.*

approve to officially agree to a plan, suggestion, or request: *The committee unanimously approved the plan.*

go along with sb/sth to agree to something that someone else has decided; to agree with someone else's ideas: *He just goes along with everything she suggests.*

consent (formal) to agree to something or give your permission for something: *She finally consented to be interviewed.*

PATTERNS
- to agree/consent **to** sth
- to agree/consent **to do** sth
- to agree to/accept/approve/go along with/consent to a **plan/proposal**
- to agree to/accept/approve a **request**

---

a·gree 🔑 /əˈɡri/ verb
▷ **SHARE OPINION 1** [I, T] to have the same opinion as someone; to say that you have the same opinion: *When he said that, I had to agree.* ♦ + **speech** *"That's true," she agreed.* ♦ ~ **(with sb) (about/on sth)** *He agreed with them about the need for change.* ♦ ~ **with sth** *I agree with her analysis of the situation.* ♦ ~ **(that)...** *We agreed (that) the proposal was a good one.* ♦ *"It's terrible." "I couldn't agree more* (= I completely agree)*!"* **ANT** DISAGREE **2** [T] if people **are agreed** or something **is agreed**, everyone has the same opinion about something: **be agreed (on/about sth)** *Are we all agreed on this?* ♦ **be agreed (that...)** *It was agreed (that) we should hold another meeting.*
▷ **SAY YES 3** [I, T] to say "yes"; to say that you will do what someone wants or that you will allow something to happen: *I asked for a pay raise and she agreed.* ♦ ~ **to sth** *Do you think he'll agree to their proposal?* ♦ ~ **(that)...** *She agreed (that) I could go early.* ♦ ~ **to do sth** *She agreed to let me go early.*
▷ **DECIDE 4** [I, T] to decide with someone else to do something or to have something: ~ **on sth** *Can we agree on a date?* ♦ ~ **sth** *They met at the agreed time.* ♦ *Can we agree a price?* ♦ *They left at ten, as agreed.* ♦ ~ **to do sth** *We agreed to meet on Thursday.* ♦ ~ **what, where, etc....** *We couldn't agree what to do.*
▷ **ACCEPT 5** [I] ~ **on/upon sth** to officially accept a plan, request, etc. **SYN** APPROVE: *Next year's budget has been agreed upon.*
▷ **BE THE SAME 6** [I] to be the same as something **SYN** TALLY: *The figures do not agree.* ♦ ~ **with sth** *Your account of the accident does not agree with hers.* **ANT** DISAGREE
▷ **GRAMMAR 7** [I] ~ **(with sth)** to match a word or phrase in NUMBER, GENDER, or PERSON: *In "Tom likes jazz," the singular verb "likes" agrees with the subject "Tom."*
IDM **agree to differ/disagree** if two people **agree to differ/disagree**, they accept that they have different opinions, but they decide not to discuss it any longer

---

h hat   m man   n no   ŋ sing   l leg   r red   y yes   w wet

PHR V not a'gree with sb (of food) to make you feel sick: *I love strawberries, but they don't agree with me.*

a·gree·a·ble /əˈɡriəbl/ *adj.* (*formal*) **1** pleasant and easy to like: *We spent an agreeable day together.* ♦ *He seemed extremely agreeable.* **ANT** DISAGREEABLE **2** [not before noun] **~ (to sth)** willing to do something or allow something: *Do you think they will be agreeable to our proposal?* **3 ~ (to sb)** able to be accepted by someone: *The deal must be agreeable to both sides.*

a·gree·a·bly /əˈɡriəbli/ *adv.* (*formal*) in a pleasant, nice way: *an agreeably warm day* ♦ *They were agreeably surprised by the quality of the food.*

a·gree·ment 🔑 /əˈɡriəmənt/ *noun*
1 [C] an arrangement, a promise, or a contract made with someone: *an international peace agreement* ♦ *The agreement* (= the document recording the agreement) *was signed during a meeting at the U.N.* ♦ **~ with sb** *They have a free trade agreement with Australia.* ♦ **~ between A and B** *An agreement was finally reached between management and employees.* ♦ **~ to do sth** *They had made a verbal agreement to sell.* ♦ *They had an agreement never to talk about work at home.* ♦ **~ that…** *They had an agreement that he would be paid $30 for mowing the lawn.* ⊃ see also GENTLEMAN'S AGREEMENT, PRENUPTIAL AGREEMENT **2** [U] the state of sharing the same opinion or feeling: *The two sides failed to reach agreement.* ♦ **in ~** *Are we in agreement about the price?* **ANT** DISAGREEMENT **3** [U] the fact of someone approving of something and allowing it to happen: *There could be no action without the agreement of all three governments.* **4** [U] **~ (with sth)** (*grammar*) (of words in a phrase) the state of having the same NUMBER, GENDER, or PERSON **SYN** CONCORD: *In the sentence "They live in the country," the plural form of the verb "live" is in agreement with the plural subject "they."*

agri- /ˈæɡrə/ ⊃ AGRO-

ag·ri·busi·ness /ˈæɡrəˌbɪznəs/ *noun* [U, C] (*technical*) an industry concerned with the production and sale of farm products, especially involving large companies

ag·ri·cul·tur·al·ist /ˌæɡrəˈkʌltʃərəlɪst/ *noun* an expert in agriculture who gives advice to farmers or companies

ag·ri·cul·ture /ˈæɡrəˌkʌltʃər/ *noun* [U] the science or practice of farming: *The number of people employed in agriculture has fallen in the last decade.* ⊃ collocations at TOWN ▶ **ag·ri·cul·tur·al** /ˌæɡrəˈkʌltʃərəl/ *adj.: agricultural policy/land/production/development*

ag·ri·tour·ism /ˈæɡrɪˌtʊrɪzəm/ *noun* [U] tourist activities that are based on a farm or RANCH

agro- /ˈæɡrou/ (also **agri-**) *combining form* (in nouns, adjectives, and adverbs) connected with farming: *agro-industry* ♦ *agriculture*

ag·ro·chem·i·cal /ˌæɡrouˈkɛmɪkl/ *noun* any chemical used in farming, especially for killing insects or for making plants grow better

ˈagro-ˌindustry *noun* [U] industry connected with farming ▶ **ˌagro-inˈdustrial** *adj.*

a·gron·o·my /əˈɡrɑnəmi/ *noun* [U] the scientific study of the relationship between crops and the environment ▶ **a·gron·o·mist** /-mɪst/ *noun*

a·ground /əˈɡraʊnd/ *adv.* if a ship **runs/goes aground**, it touches the ground in shallow water and cannot move ▶ **a·ground** *adj.* [not before noun]

a·gue /ˈeɪɡyu/ *noun* [U] (*old-fashioned*) a disease such as MALARIA that causes fever and SHIVERING (= shaking of the body)

A.H. (also **AH**) /ˌeɪ ˈeɪtʃ/ *abbr.* used in the Muslim CALENDAR to show a particular number of years since the year when Muhammad left Mecca in A.D.622 (from Latin "Anno Hegirae"): *a Koran dated 556 A.H.* ⊃ compare A.D., B.C., B.C.E., C.E.

ah /ɑ/ *exclamation* used to express surprise, pleasure, admiration, or sympathy, or when you disagree with

someone: *Ah, there you are.* ♦ *Ah, this coffee is good.* ♦ *Ah well, better luck next time.* ♦ *Ah, but that may not be true.*

a·ha /ɑˈhɑ/ *exclamation* used when you are expressing pleasure that you have understood something or found something out: *Aha! So that's where I left it!*

a·head 🔑 /əˈhɛd/ *adv.*
HELP For the special uses of **ahead** in phrasal verbs, look at the entries for the verbs. For example, **press ahead (with sth)** is in the phrasal verb section at **press**. **1** further forward in space or time; in front: *I'll run ahead and warn them.* ♦ *The road ahead was blocked.* ♦ *We've got a lot of hard work ahead.* ♦ *This will create problems in the months ahead.* ♦ *He was looking straight ahead* (= straight forward, in front of him). **2** earlier **SYN** IN ADVANCE: *The party was planned weeks ahead.* **3** winning; further advanced: *Our team was ahead by six points.* ♦ *You need to work hard to stay ahead.*

a·head of *prep.* **1** further forward in space or time than someone or something; in front of someone or something: *Two boys were ahead of us.* ♦ *Ahead of us were ten days of intensive training.* **2** earlier than someone or something: *I finished several days ahead of the deadline.* **3** further advanced than someone or something; in front of someone, for example in a race or competition: *She was always well ahead of the rest of the class.* ♦ *His ideas were way ahead of their time* (= very new and so not widely understood or accepted).

a·hem /əˈhɛm; əˈhm/ *exclamation* used in writing to show the sound of a short cough made by someone who is trying to get attention, or to say something that is difficult or embarrassing: *Ahem, can I make a suggestion?*

a·his·tor·i·cal /ˌeɪhɪˈstɔrɪkl; -ˈstɑr-/ *adj.* (*formal*) not showing any knowledge of history or of what has happened before

-aholic /əˈhɔlɪk; əˈhɑlɪk/ *suffix* (in nouns) liking something very much and unable to stop doing or using it: *a shopaholic* ♦ *a chocaholic*

a·hoy /əˈhɔɪ/ *exclamation* used by people in boats to attract attention: *Ahoy there!* ♦ *Ship ahoy!* (= there is a ship in sight)

AI /ˌeɪ ˈaɪ/ *abbr.* **1** ARTIFICIAL INSEMINATION: *The baby was conceived via artificial insemination.* **2** ARTIFICIAL INTELLIGENCE

aid 🔑 **AWL** /eɪd/ *noun, verb*
● *noun* **1** [U] money, food, etc. that is sent to help countries in difficult situations: *economic/humanitarian/emergency aid* ♦ *An extra $10 million in foreign aid has been promised.* ♦ *aid agencies* (= organizations that provide help) ♦ *medical aid programs* ⊃ collocations at INTERNATIONAL ⊃ see also FINANCIAL AID, LEGAL AID **2** [U] help that you need to perform a particular task: *He was breathing only with the aid of a ventilator.* ♦ *This job would be impossible without the aid of a computer.* **3** [U] (*formal*) help that is given to a person: *One of the staff saw he was in difficulty and came to his aid* (= helped him). ⊃ see also FIRST AID **4** [C] an object, a machine, etc. that you use to help you do something: *a hearing aid* ♦ *Photos make useful teaching aids.*
● *verb* [I, T] **~ (sb/sth) (in sth/in doing sth)** | **~ sb (with sth)** (*formal*) to help someone or something to do something, especially by making it easier **SYN** ASSIST: **~ in sth/in doing sth** *The new test should aid in the early detection of the disease.* ♦ **~ sb (to do sth)** *This feature is designed to aid inexperienced users.* ♦ **~ sth** *Aided by heat and strong winds, the fire quickly spread.* ♦ *They were accused of aiding his escape.* ♦ **~ sb/sth in sth/in doing sth** *They were accused of aiding him in his escape.*
IDM **aid and abet** (*law*) to help someone to do something illegal or wrong: *She stands accused of aiding and abetting the crime.*

aide /eɪd/ *noun* a person who helps another person, especially a politician, in their job: *White House aides*

aide-de-camp /ˌeɪd dɪ ˈkæmp/ *noun* (*pl.* **aides-de-camp** /ˌeɪd dɪ ˈkæmp; ˌeɪdz-/) (*abbr.* **ADC**) an officer in the army or navy who helps a more senior officer

aide-me·moire /ˌeɪd mɛmˈwɑːr/ noun (from French) (pl. aides-me·moire, aides-me·moires /ˌeɪd mɛmˈwɑːr/) a thing, especially a book or document, that helps you to remember something

AIDS /eɪdz/ noun [U] the abbreviation for "Acquired Immune Deficiency Syndrome" (a very serious illness that attacks the body's ability to resist infection): *AIDS research/education/victims* ◆ *He developed full-blown AIDS five years after contracting HIV.*

ai·ki·do /aɪˈkiːdoʊ/ noun [U] (from Japanese) a Japanese system of fighting in which you hold and throw your opponent

ail /eɪl/ verb **1 ~ sth** (formal) to cause problems for someone or something: *They discussed the problems ailing the steel industry.* **2 ~ sb** (old use) to make someone sick: *What is ailing you?*

ai·ler·on /ˈeɪləˌrɑn/ noun (technical) a part of the wing of a plane that moves up and down to control the plane's balance ⇨ picture at PLANE

ail·ing /ˈeɪlɪŋ/ adj. (formal) **1** sick and not improving: *She took care of her ailing father.* **2** (of a business, government, etc.) having problems and getting weaker: *measures to help the ailing economy*

ail·ment /ˈeɪlmənt/ noun an illness that is not very serious: *childhood/common/minor ailments* ⇨ thesaurus box at DISEASE

aim 🔧 /eɪm/ verb, noun
• **verb 1** [I, T] to try or plan to achieve something: *He has always aimed high* (= tried to achieve a lot). ◆ **~ for sth** *We should aim for a bigger share of the market.* ◆ **~ at sth** *The government is aiming at a 50% reduction in unemployment.* ◆ **~ to do sth** *They are aiming to reduce unemployment by 50%.* ◆ *We aim to be there around six.* ◆ **~ at doing sth** *They're aiming at training everyone by the end of the year.* **2** [T] **be aimed at sth/at doing sth** to have something as an aim: *These measures are aimed at preventing violent crime.* **3** [I, T] to point or direct a weapon, a shot, a kick, etc. at someone or something: **~ at sb/sth** *I was aiming at the tree but hit the car by mistake.* ◆ **~ for sb/sth** *Aim for the middle of the target.* ◆ **~ sth (at sb/sth)** *The gun was aimed at her head.* **4** [T, usually passive] **~ sth at sb** to say or do something that is intended to influence or affect a particular person or group: *The book is aimed at very young children.* ◆ *My criticism wasn't aimed at you.*
• **noun 1** [C] the purpose of doing something; what someone is trying to achieve: *the aims of the lesson* ◆ *She went to Atlanta with the aim of finding a job.* ◆ *Our main aim is to increase sales in the Northwest.* ◆ *Bob's one aim in life is to earn a lot of money.* ◆ *Teamwork is required in order to achieve these aims.* ◆ *She set out the company's aims and objectives in her speech.* ⇨ thesaurus box at PURPOSE **2** [U] the action or skill of pointing a weapon at someone or something: *Her aim was good and she hit the bullseye with her first shot.* ◆ *The gunman took aim* (= pointed his weapon) *and fired.*
IDM take aim at sb/sth to direct your criticism at someone or something

aim·less /ˈeɪmləs/ adj. having no direction or plan: *My life seemed aimless.* ▶ **aim·less·ly** adv.: *He drifted aimlessly from one job to another.* **aim·less·ness** noun [U]

ain't /eɪnt/ short form (non-standard or humorous) **1** am not/is not/are not: *Things ain't what they used to be.* **2** has not/have not: *I ain't got no money.* ◆ *You ain't seen nothing yet!*
IDM if it ain't broke, don't fix it (informal) used to say that if something works well enough, it should not be changed

ai·o·li /aɪˈoʊli; eɪ-/ noun [U] (from French) a thick cold sauce made of MAYONNAISE and GARLIC

air 🔧 /ɛr/ noun, verb
• **noun**
> **GAS 1** [U] the mixture of gases that surrounds the earth and that we breathe: *air pollution* ◆ *Let's go out for some fresh air.* ◆ *I need to put some air in my tires.* ◆ *currents of warm air* ⇨ note at OUTSIDE

> **SPACE 2** usually **the air** [U] the space above the ground or that is around things: *I kicked the ball high in/into the air.* ◆ *Spicy smells wafted through the air.* ◆ *Music filled the night air.* ⇨ see also OPEN AIR
> **FOR PLANES 3** [U] the space above the earth where planes fly: *It only takes three hours by air* (= in a plane). ◆ *air travel/traffic* ◆ *The temple was clearly visible from the air.* ◆ *A surprise air attack* (= from aircraft) *was launched at night.*
> **IMPRESSION 4** [sing.] the particular feeling or impression that is given by someone or something; the way someone does something: *The room had an air of luxury.* ◆ *She looked at him with a defiant air.*
> **AIR CONDITIONING 5** often **the air** [U] = AIR CONDITIONING: *Tell them to turn up the air.*
> **TUNE 6** [C] (old-fashioned) (often used in the title of a piece of music) a tune: *Bach's Air on a G string*
> **BEHAVIOR 7 airs** [pl.] (disapproving) a way of behaving that shows that someone thinks that they are more important, etc. than they really are: *I hate the way she puts on airs.*
IDM come up for air to stop doing something for a while: *After studying all morning, it was time to come up for air.* **float/walk on air** to feel very happy **in the air** felt by a number of people to exist or to be happening: *There's romance in the air.* **on/off (the) air** broadcasting or not broadcasting on television or radio: *We will be back on air tomorrow morning at 7.* ◆ *The program was taken off the air over the summer.* **up in the air** not yet decided: *Our travel plans are still up in the air.* ⇨ more at BREATH, CASTLE, CLEAR v., NOSE n., PLUCK, THIN
• **verb**
> **CLOTHES 1** [T, I] **~ (sth)** to put clothing, etc. in a place that is warm or has plenty of air so that it dries completely and smells fresh; to be left to dry somewhere: *Leave the towels out to air.*
> **OPINIONS 2** [T] **~ sth** to express your opinions publicly **SYN** VOICE: *The weekly meeting enables employees to air their grievances.*
> **RADIO/TV PROGRAM 3** [T, I] **~ (sth)** to broadcast a program on the radio or on television; to be broadcast: *The show will be aired next Tuesday night.* ◆ *The program aired last week.*
IDM air your dirty laundry/linen in public (disapproving) to discuss your personal affairs in public, especially something embarrassing
PHR V air (sth) 'out to allow fresh air into a room or a building; to be filled with fresh air: *The rooms had all been cleaned and aired out.*

air·bag (also 'air bag) /ˈɛrbæg/ noun a safety device in a car that fills with air if there is an accident, to protect the people in the car

'**air ball** noun (informal) (in basketball) a shot that misses the BACKBOARD and BASKET

air·base /ˈɛrbeɪs/ noun a place where military aircraft fly from and are kept, and where some staff live

'**air bed** noun = AIR MATTRESS

air·borne /ˈɛrbɔrn/ adj. **1** [not before noun] (of a plane or passengers) in the air: *Do not leave your seat until the plane is airborne.* **2** [only before noun] carried through the air: *airborne seeds/viruses* ⇨ compare WATERBORNE **3** [only before noun] (of soldiers) trained to jump out of aircraft onto enemy land in order to fight: *an airborne division*

'**air brake** noun a BRAKE in a vehicle that is worked by air pressure

air·brush /ˈɛrbrʌʃ/ noun, verb
• **noun** an artist's tool for spraying paint onto a surface, which works by air pressure
• **verb** to paint something with an airbrush; to change a detail in a photograph with an airbrush: **~ sth** *an airbrushed photograph of a model* ◆ **~ sb/sth out** *Someone had been airbrushed out of the picture.*

air·bus™ /ˈɛrbʌs/ noun a large plane that carries passengers over short and medium distances

'**air con·ditioner** noun a machine that cools and dries air

'**air con·ditioning** noun [U] (abbr. AC, a/c) a system that

cools and dries the air in a building or car
▶ ˈair-conˌditioned adj.: air-conditioned offices

ˈair-cooled adj. made cool by a current of air

ˈair ˌcorridor noun an area in the sky that aircraft must stay inside when they fly over a country

ˈair ˌcover noun [U] protection that aircraft give to soldiers and military vehicles on the land or ocean

air·craft 🔧 /ˈɛrkræft/ noun (pl. air·craft)
any vehicle that can fly and carry goods or passengers: fighter/transport/military aircraft ⊃ see also LIGHT AIRCRAFT

ˈaircraft ˌcarrier noun a large ship that carries aircraft that use it as a base to land on and take off from

ˈair·crew /ˈɛrkru/ noun the pilot and other people who fly a plane, especially in the air force

air·drome /ˈɛrdroʊm/ noun (old-fashioned) a small airport

air·drop /ˈɛrdrɑp/ noun the act of dropping supplies, soldiers, etc. from an aircraft by PARACHUTE: The UN has begun making airdrops of food to refugees. ▶ air·drop verb (-pp-) ~ sth

Aire·dale /ˈɛrdeɪl/ noun a large TERRIER (= type of dog) with rough black and brown hair

air·fare /ˈɛrfɛr/ noun the money that you pay to travel by plane: Take advantage of off-season airfares.

air·field /ˈɛrfild/ noun an area of flat ground where military or private planes can take off and land

air·flow /ˈɛrfloʊ/ noun [U] the flow of air around a moving aircraft or vehicle

air·foil /ˈɛrfɔɪl/ noun the basic curved structure of an aircraft's wing that helps to lift it into the air

ˈair force noun the part of a country's armed forces that fights using aircraft: the U.S. Air Force ♦ air force officers ⊃ collocations at WAR

ˌAir Force ˈOne noun the name given to a special aircraft in the U.S. AIR FORCE when the U.S. president is using it

air·freight /ˈɛrfreɪt/ noun [U] goods that are transported by aircraft; the system of transporting goods by aircraft ▶ air·freight verb ~ sth

ˈair ˌfreshener noun [C, U] a substance or device for making a place smell more pleasant

ˈair guiˌtar noun [C, U] used to describe the actions of a person playing an imaginary electric GUITAR, especially while listening to ROCK music

ˈair gun (also ˈair ˌrifle) noun a gun that uses air pressure to fire small metal balls (called PELLETS) SYN BB GUN

air·head /ˈɛrhɛd/ noun (informal, disapproving) a silly or stupid person: She's a total airhead!

air·i·ly /ˈɛrəli/ adv. (formal) in a way that shows that you are not worried or that you are not treating something as serious

air·ing /ˈɛrɪŋ/ noun [sing.] 1 the expression or discussion of opinions in front of a group of people: an opportunity to give your views an airing 2 the act of allowing warm air to make clothes, beds, etc. fresh and dry

ˈair kiss noun a way of saying hello or goodbye to someone by kissing them near the side of their face but not actually touching them ▶ ˈair-kiss verb [T, I] ~ (sb/sth)

ˈair lane noun a route regularly used by aircraft

air·less /ˈɛrləs/ adj. not having any fresh or moving air or wind, and therefore unpleasant: a stuffy, airless room ♦ The night was hot and airless.

ˈair ˌletter noun = AEROGRAMME

air·lift /ˈɛrlɪft/ noun, verb
• noun an operation to take people, soldiers, food, etc. to or from an area by aircraft, especially in an emergency or when roads are closed or dangerous
• verb ~ sb/sth to take someone or something to or from an area by aircraft, especially in an emergency or when roads

are closed or dangerous: Two casualties were airlifted to safety. ⊃ compare SEALIFT

air·line /ˈɛrlaɪn/ noun a company that provides regular flights to take passengers and goods to different places: international airlines ♦ an airline pilot ⊃ collocations at TRAVEL

air·lin·er /ˈɛrˌlaɪnər/ noun a large plane that carries passengers

air·lock /ˈɛrlɑk/ noun 1 a small room with a tightly closed door at each end, which you go through to reach another area at a different air pressure, for example on a SPACECRAFT or SUBMARINE 2 a bubble of air that blocks the flow of liquid in a PUMP or pipe

air·mail /ˈɛrmeɪl/ noun [U] the system of sending letters, etc. by air: Send it airmail/by airmail.

air·man /ˈɛrmən/, air·wom·an /ˈɛrˌwʊmən/ noun (pl. air·men /-mən/, air·wom·en /-ˌwɪmən/) a member of one of the lowest ranks in the U.S. AIR FORCE: Airman Rodriguez

ˈair ˌmarshal (also ˈsky ˌmarshal) noun an armed guard, especially a government official, who travels on a plane with the passengers in order to protect the plane from TERRORISTS

ˈair ˌmattress (also ˈair bed) noun a large plastic or rubber bag that can be filled with air and used as a bed: You can sleep on the air mattress. ♦ She was lying on an air mattress in the swimming pool. ⊃ picture at BED

ˈAir Miles™ noun [pl.] points that you collect by buying plane tickets and other products, which you can then use to pay for air travel

ˈair ˌpistol noun a small gun that uses air pressure to fire small metal balls (called PELLETS)

air·plane /ˈɛrpleɪn/ (also plane) noun a flying vehicle with wings and one or more engines: They went to Florida by airplane. ♦ an airplane crash/flight ♦ a commercial/jet/military airplane

ˈair·play /ˈɛrpleɪ/ noun [U] time that is spent broadcasting a particular record, performer, or type of music on the radio: The band is starting to get a lot of airplay.

ˈair ˌpocket noun 1 a closed area that becomes filled with air 2 an area of low air pressure that makes a plane suddenly drop while flying

air·port 🔧 /ˈɛrpɔrt/ noun
a place where planes land and take off and that has buildings for passengers to wait in: Chicago's O'Hare Airport ♦ waiting in the airport lounge

ˈair ˌpower noun [U] military forces involving aircraft

ˈair pump noun a piece of equipment for sending air into or out of something

ˈair ˌquality noun [U] the degree to which the air is clean and free from pollution

ˈair quotes noun [pl.] imaginary quotation marks made in the air with your fingers when you are speaking, to show that you are using a word or phrase in an unusual way

ˈair raid noun an attack by a number of aircraft dropping many bombs on a place: Much of the city was destroyed in an air raid. ♦ an air raid shelter/warning

ˈair ˌrifle noun = AIR GUN

ˌair-sea ˈrescue noun [C, U] the process of rescuing people from the sea using aircraft

air·ship /ˈɛrʃɪp/ noun a large aircraft without wings, filled with a gas that is lighter than air, and driven by engines ⊃ compare BLIMP (1)

ˈair show noun a show at which people can watch aircraft flying

air·sick /ˈɛrsɪk/ adj. [not usually before noun] feeling sick when you are traveling on an aircraft ▶ air·sick·ness noun [U]

air·space /ˈɛrspeɪs/ noun [U] the part of the sky where planes fly, usually the part above a particular country that is legally controlled by that country: *The jet entered American airspace without permission.*

air·speed /'ɛrspid/ *noun* the speed of an aircraft relative to the air through which it is moving ⊃ compare GROUND SPEED

air·stream /'ɛrstrim/ *noun* a movement of air, especially a strong one

'**air strike** *noun* an attack made by aircraft

air·strip /'ɛrstrɪp/ (also 'landing ˌstrip) *noun* a narrow piece of cleared land that an aircraft can land on

'**air supˌport** *noun* [U] help that aircraft give to soldiers and military vehicles on the land or ocean

'**air ˌterminal** *noun* a building at an airport that provides services for passengers traveling by plane

air·tight /'ɛrtaɪt/ *adj.* not allowing air to get in or out: *Store the cake in an airtight container.* ◆ (*figurative*) *an airtight alibi* (= one that cannot be proved to be false)

air·time /'ɛrtaɪm/ *noun* [U] **1** the amount of time that is given to a particular subject on radio or television **2** the amount of time that is paid for when you are using a cell phone

ˌ**air-to-'air** *adj.* [usually before noun] from one aircraft to another while they are both flying: *an air-to-air missile*

ˌ**air-to-'ground** *adj.* [usually before noun] directed or operating from an aircraft to the surface of the land: *air-to-ground weapons*

ˌ**air-to-'surface** *adj.* [usually before noun] moving or passing from a flying aircraft to the surface of the ocean or land: *air-to-surface missiles*

ˌ**air traffic conˈtrol** *noun* [U] **1** the activity of giving instructions by radio to pilots of aircraft so that they know when and where to take off or land **2** the group of people or the organization that provides an air traffic control service: *The pilot was given clearance to land by air traffic control.*

ˌ**air traffic conˈtroller** *noun* a person whose job is to give instructions by radio to pilots of aircraft so that they know when and where to take off or land

air·waves /'ɛrweɪvz/ *noun* [pl.] radio waves that are used in broadcasting radio and television: *More and more TV and radio stations are crowding the airwaves.* ◆ *A well-known voice came over the airwaves.*

air·way /'ɛrweɪ/ *noun* **1** (*medical*) the passage from the nose and throat to the lungs, through which you breathe **2** (often used in names of AIRLINES) a route regularly used by planes: *British Airways*

air·wom·an ⊃ AIRMAN

air·wor·thy /'ɛrˌwɚði/ *adj.* (of aircraft) safe to fly ▸ **air·wor·thi·ness** /-ˌwɚðinəs/ *noun* [U]

air·y /'ɛri/ *adj.* (**air·i·er**, **air·i·est**) **1** with plenty of fresh air because there is a lot of space: *The office was light and airy.* **2** (*formal*) acting or done in a way that shows that you are not worried or that you are not treating something as serious: *He dismissed her with an airy wave.* ⊃ see also AIRILY **3** (*formal*, *disapproving*) not serious or practical: *airy promises/speculation*

aisle /aɪl/ *noun* a passage between rows of seats in a church, theater, train, etc., or between rows of shelves in a supermarket: *an aisle seat* (= in a plane) ◆ *Coffee and tea are in the next aisle.*

IDM **go/walk down the aisle** (*informal*) to get married ⊃ more at ROLL

a·jar /ə'dʒɑr/ *adj.* [not before noun] (of a door) slightly open: *I'll leave the door ajar.*

AK *abbr.* (in writing) Alaska

aka /ˌeɪ keɪ 'eɪ/ *abbr.* also known as: *Antonio Fratelli, aka "Big Tony"*

a·kee (also **ac·kee**) /'æki; æ'ki/ *noun* **1** [C] a type of tree that produces bright red fruit, originally from W. Africa **2** [U]

the fruit from this tree, which is poisonous to eat unless it is completely RIPE

a·kim·bo /ə'kɪmboʊ/ *adv.*
IDM (**with**) **arms akimbo** with your hands on your hips and your elbows pointing away from your body

a·kin /ə'kɪn/ *adj.* ~ **to sth** (*formal*) similar to: *What he felt was more akin to pity than love.*

AL *abbr.* (in writing) Alabama

-al /əl/ *suffix* **1** (in adjectives) connected with: *magical* ◆ *verbal* ⊃ see also -ALLY **2** (in nouns) a process or state of: *survival*

à la /'ɑ lɑ; 'ɑ lə; 'æ lə/ *prep.* (from *French*) in the same style as someone or something else: *a new singer à la Elvis*

al·a·bas·ter /'ælə,bæstɚ/ *noun* [U] a type of white stone that is often used to make statues and decorative objects: *an alabaster tomb* ◆ (*literary*) *her pale, alabaster* (= white and smooth) *skin*

à la carte /ˌɑ lɑ 'kɑrt; ˌæ lə-/ *adj.*, *adv.* (from *French*) if food in a restaurant is **à la carte**, or if you eat **à la carte**, you choose from a list of dishes that have separate prices, rather than having a complete meal at a fixed price

a·lack /ə'læk/ *exclamation* (*old use* or *humorous*) used to show you are sad or sorry: *Alas and alack, we had missed our bus.*

a·lac·ri·ty /ə'lækrəti/ *noun* [U] (*formal*) great willingness or enthusiasm: *They accepted the offer with alacrity.*

A·lad·din /ə'lædn/ *noun* a character from a traditional story, who had a magic lamp. When he rubbed the lamp, a GENIE appeared and did whatever Aladdin wanted.

à la mode /ˌɑ lə 'moʊd; æ lə-/ *adj.*, *adv.* (from *French*) **1** [after noun] served with ice cream: *apple pie à la mode* **2** [not before noun] (*old-fashioned*) fashionable; in the latest fashion

a·larm 🔊 /ə'lɑrm/ *noun*, *verb*

● *noun* **1** [U] fear and anxiety that someone feels when something dangerous or unpleasant might happen: *"What have you done?" Ellie cried in alarm.* ◆ *I felt a growing sense of alarm when he did not return that night.* ◆ *The doctor said there was no cause for alarm.* ⊃ thesaurus box at FEAR **2** [C, usually sing.] a loud noise or a signal that warns people of danger or of a problem: *She decided to sound the alarm* (= warn people that the situation was dangerous). ◆ *I hammered on all the doors to raise the alarm.* ⊃ see also FALSE ALARM **3** [C] a device that warns people of a particular danger: *a burglar/fire/smoke alarm* ◆ *The cat set off the alarm* (= made it start ringing). ◆ *A car alarm went off in the middle of the night* (= started ringing). **4** = ALARM CLOCK: *The alarm went off at 7 o'clock.*

IDM **alarm bells ring/start ringing | (sth) sets off alarm bells** if you say that **alarm bells are ringing** or that something **sets off alarm bells**, you mean that people are starting to feel worried and suspicious

● *verb* **1** ~ **sb (to do sth)** to make someone worried or afraid **SYN** WORRY: *The captain knew there was an engine fault but didn't want to alarm the passengers.* ⊃ thesaurus box at SCARE **2** ~ **sth** to put a device on something, such as a door, that warns people when someone is trying to enter illegally

aˈlarm call *noun* a cry of warning made by a bird or animal

aˈlarm clock (also **a·larm**) *noun* a clock that you can set to ring a bell, etc. at a particular time and wake you up: *I set the alarm clock for 7 a.m.* ⊃ picture at CLOCK

a·larmed 🔊 /ə'lɑrmd/ *adj.* [not before noun]
1 ~ **(at/by sth)** anxious or afraid that something dangerous or unpleasant might happen: *She was alarmed at the prospect of traveling alone.* ⊃ thesaurus box at AFRAID **2** protected by an alarm: *This door is alarmed.*

a·larm·ing 🔊 /ə'lɑrmɪŋ/ *adj.*
causing worry and fear: *an alarming increase in crime* ◆ *The rainforests are disappearing at an alarming rate.* ▸ **a·larm·ing·ly** *adv.*: *Prices have risen alarmingly.*

a·larm·ist /əˈlɑrmɪst/ adj. (disapproving) causing unnecessary fear and anxiety: A spokesperson for the food industry said the documentary was alarmist. ▶ **a·larm·ist** noun

a·las /əˈlæs/ exclamation (old use or literary) used to show you are sad or sorry: For many people, alas, hunger is part of everyday life.

al·ba·tross /ˈælbəˌtrɔs; -ˌtrɑs/ noun **1** a very large white bird with long wings that lives in the Pacific and Southern Oceans **2** [usually sing.] (formal) a thing that causes problems or prevents you from doing something

al·be·it ⟨AWL⟩ /ɔlˈbiət; æl-/ conj. (formal) although: He finally agreed, albeit reluctantly, to help us.

al·bi·nism /ˈælbəˌnɪzəm/ noun [U] (technical) the condition of being an albino

al·bi·no /ælˈbaɪnoʊ/ noun (pl. **al·bi·nos**) a person or an animal that is born with no color (= PIGMENT) in the hair or skin, which are white, or in the eyes, which are pink ▶ **al·bi·no** adj. [only before noun]

al·bum /ˈælbəm/ noun **1** a book in which you keep photographs, stamps, etc.: a photo album ◆ an online album (= a Web site where you can store and view photographs) ⊃ picture at HOBBY **2** a collection of pieces of music released as a single item, usually on a CD, etc. or on the Internet: the band's latest album ◆ an online album (= an album that you can listen to on the Internet) ⊃ collocations at MUSIC ⊃ compare SINGLE

al·bu·men /ælˈbyumən/ noun [U] (technical) the clear inside part of an egg that is white when cooked SYN WHITE ⊃ compare YOLK

Al·ca·traz /ˈælkəˌtræz/ noun a small U.S. island near San Francisco where there is a former prison: The clinic felt like Alcatraz. There was no escape.

al·che·mist /ˈælkəmɪst/ noun a person who studied alchemy

al·che·my /ˈælkəmi/ noun [U] **1** a form of chemistry studied in the Middle Ages that involved trying to discover how to change ordinary metals into gold **2** (literary) a mysterious power or magic that can change things

al·co·hol 🔑 /ˈælkəˌhɔl; -ˌhɑl/ noun [U]
1 drinks such as beer, wine, etc. that can make people drunk: He never drinks alcohol. ◆ alcohol abuse ⊃ collocations at DIET **2** the clear liquid that is found in drinks such as beer, wine, etc. and is used in medicines, cleaning products, etc.: Wine contains about 10% alcohol. ◆ a high blood alcohol level ◆ He pleaded guilty to driving under the influence of alcohol. ◆ Do you have any beers without alcohol? ⊃ see also ABSOLUTE ALCOHOL, RUBBING ALCOHOL

al·co·hol·ic 🔑 /ˌælkəˈhɔlɪk; -ˈhɑlɪk/ adj., noun
● adj. **1** connected with or containing alcohol: alcoholic drinks ANT NONALCOHOLIC ⊃ see also SOFT DRINK **2** caused by drinking alcohol: The guests left in an alcoholic haze.
● noun (also informal **lush**) a person who regularly drinks too much alcohol and cannot easily stop drinking, so that it has become an illness

Alco·holics A·nonymous noun [U] (abbr. **AA**) an international organization, begun in Chicago in 1935, for people who are trying to stop drinking alcohol. They have meetings to help each other.

al·co·hol·ism /ˈælkəhɔˌlɪzəm; -hɑ-/ noun [U] the medical condition caused by drinking too much alcohol regularly

al·cove /ˈælkoʊv/ noun an area in a room that is formed by part of a wall being built farther back than the rest of the wall: The bookcase fits neatly into the alcove.

al den·te /ɑl ˈdɛntər; æl-/ adj. (from Italian) (of cooked food, especially PASTA) firm, but not hard, when bitten ▶ **al den·te** adv.

al·der /ˈɔldər/ noun a tree like a BIRCH that grows in northern countries, usually in wet ground

al·der·man /ˈɔldərmən/ noun (pl. **al·der·men** /-mən/) (feminine **al·der·wom·an** /ˈɔldərˌwʊmən/, pl. **al·der·wom·en** /-ˌwɪmən/) (in the U.S., Canada, and Australia) an elected member of a town or city council: Alderman Tim Evans

ale /eɪl/ noun **1** [U, C] a type of beer, usually sold in bottles or cans. There are several kinds of ale: brown/pale ale **2** [C] a glass, bottle, or can of ale **3** [U] (old-fashioned) beer generally ⊃ see also GINGER ALE

al·ec, al·eck ⊃ SMART ALECK

a·lert /əˈlərt/ adj., verb, noun
● adj. **1** able to think quickly; quick to notice things: Suddenly he found himself awake and fully alert. ◆ Two alert scientists spotted the mistake. **2** ~ to sth aware of something, especially a problem or danger: We must be alert to the possibility of danger. ▶ **a·lert·ly** adj. **a·lert·ness** noun [U]
● verb [often passive] **1** ~ sb (to do sth) | ~ sb (that)... to warn someone about a dangerous or urgent situation: Neighbors quickly alerted the police. ◆ Alerted by a noise downstairs, he sat up and turned on the light. **2** ~ sb to sth to make someone aware of something: They had been alerted to the possibility of further price rises.
● noun **1** [sing., U] a situation in which people are watching for danger and are ready to deal with it: Police are warning the public to **be on the alert for** suspicious packages. ◆ More than 5,000 troops have been placed **on (full) alert**. **2** [C] a warning of danger or of a problem ⊃ see also RED ALERT

Al·eut /ˈæliˌut; ˈæliˌut; əˈlut/ noun (pl. **Al·eut** or **Al·euts**) a member of a Native American people from the Aleutian Islands and parts of Alaska

Al·ex·an·der tech·nique /ˌælɪgˈzændər tɛkˈnik/ noun [sing., U] a method of improving someone's health by teaching them how to stand, sit, and move correctly

al·ex·an·drine /ˌælɪgˈzændrɪn; -drən/ adj. (technical) (of lines of poetry) containing six IAMBIC FEET ▶ **al·ex·an·drine** noun

al·fal·fa /ælˈfælfə/ noun [U] a plant with small divided leaves and purple flowers, grown as food for farm animals, and as a salad vegetable

al·fres·co /ælˈfrɛskoʊ/ adj. outdoors: an alfresco dinner party ▶ **al·fres·co** adv.: dining alfresco

al·gae /ˈældʒi/ noun [U, pl.] (sing. **al·ga** /ˈælgə/) (technical) very simple plants with no real leaves, STEMS, or roots that grow in or near water, including SEAWEED ▶ **al·gal** /ˈælgəl/ adj. [only before noun]: **algal blooms/growth**

al·ge·bra /ˈældʒəbrə/ noun [U] a type of mathematics in which letters and symbols are used to represent quantities ▶ **al·ge·bra·ic** /ˌældʒəˈbreɪɪk/ adj.: an algebraic equation/expression

al·go·rithm /ˈælgəˌrɪðəm/ noun (computing) a set of rules that must be followed when solving a particular problem

-alia /ˈeɪlyə/ suffix (in plural nouns) items connected with the particular area of activity or interest mentioned: kitchenalia

a·li·as /ˈeɪliəs; ˈeɪlyəs/ adv., noun
● adv. used when a person, especially a criminal or an actor, is known by two names: Norma Jean Baker, alias Marilyn Monroe ◆ Benjamin Siegel, alias Bugsy ◆ Miley Cyrus uses the alias "Hannah Montana" on her popular TV show. ⊃ see also AKA
● noun **1** a false or different name, especially one that is used by a criminal: He checked into the hotel under an alias. **2** (computing) a name that can be used instead of the usual name for a file, Internet address, etc.

A·li Ba·ba /ˌɑli ˈbɑbə; ˌæli-/ noun a character in an old Arabian story who discovers that saying the magic words "Open Sesame!" will open the door of the CAVE where thieves have hidden gold and jewelry

al·i·bi /ˈæləˌbaɪ/ noun **1** evidence that proves that a person was in another place at the time of a crime and so could not have committed it: The suspects all had alibis for the day of the robbery. **2** an excuse for something that you have done wrong

Al·ice in Won·der·land /ˌæləs ɪn ˈwʌndərˌlænd/ noun [U]

used to describe a situation that is very strange, in which things happen that do not make any sense and are the opposite of what you would expect: *The country's economic system is pure Alice in Wonderland.* ▶ **Al·ice-in-Won·der·land** *adj.* [only before noun]: *I felt I was in an Alice-in-Wonderland world.* **ORIGIN** From the title of a children's story by Lewis Carroll.

a·li·en /ˈeɪliən; ˈeɪlyən/ *adj., noun*
• *adj.* **1** ~ **(to sb/sth)** strange and frightening; different from what you are used to **SYN** HOSTILE: *an alien environment* ◆ *In a world that had suddenly become alien and dangerous, he was her only security.* **2** (often *disapproving*) from another country or society; foreign: *an alien culture* **3** (*disapproving*) not usual or acceptable: ~ **to sb/sth** *The idea is alien to our religion.* ◆ *Cruelty was alien to him.* **4** connected with creatures from another world: *alien beings from outer space*
• *noun* **1** (also **non-ˈcitizen**) (*law* or *technical*) a person who is not a citizen of the country in which they live or work: *an illegal alien* ⊃ **compare** RESIDENT ALIEN **2** a creature from another world: *aliens from outer space*

al·ien·ate /ˈeɪliəˌneɪt; ˈeɪlyə-/ *verb* **1** ~ **sb** to make someone less friendly or sympathetic toward you: *His comments have alienated a lot of young voters.* **2** ~ **sb (from sth/sb)** to make someone feel that they do not belong in a particular group: *Very talented children may feel alienated from the others in their class.* ▶ **al·ien·a·tion** /ˌeɪliəˈneɪʃn; ˌeɪlyə-/ *noun* [U]: *The new policy resulted in the alienation of many voters.* ◆ *Many immigrants suffer from a sense of alienation.*

a·light /əˈlaɪt/ *adj., verb*
• *adj.* [not before noun] **1** on fire: *A cigarette set the dry grass alight.* ◆ *The tablecloth caught alight when the candle fell over.* **2** (*formal*) (of faces or eyes) showing a feeling of happiness or excitement **IDM** SEE WORLD
• *verb* (*formal* or *literary*) **1** [I] ~ **(in/on/upon sth)** (of a bird or an insect) to land in or on something after flying to it **SYN** LAND **2** [I] ~ **(from sth)** to get out of a bus, a train, or other vehicle: *Do not alight from a moving bus.*
PHR V **aˈlight on/upon sth** to think of, find, or notice something, especially by chance: *Eventually, we alighted on the idea of seeking sponsorship.* ◆ *Her eyes suddenly alighted on the bundle of documents.*

a·lign /əˈlaɪn/ *verb* **1** [I, T] ~ **(sth) (with sth)** to arrange something in the correct position, or to be in the correct position, in relation to something else, especially in a straight line: *Make sure the shelf is aligned with the top of the cupboard.* ◆ *The top and bottom line of each column on the page should align.* **2** [T] ~ **sth (with/to sth)** to change something slightly so that it is in the correct relationship to something else: *Domestic prices have been aligned with those in global markets.*
PHR V **aˈlign yourself with sb/sth** to publicly support an organization, a set of opinions, or a person that you agree with

a·lign·ment /əˈlaɪnmənt/ *noun* [U, C] **1** arrangement in a straight line: *A bone in my spine was out of alignment.* **2** political support given to one country or group by another: *Japan's alignment with the West*

a·like /əˈlaɪk/ *adj., adv.*
• *adj.* [not before noun] very similar: *My sister and I do not look alike.* ⊃ **compare** UNLIKE
• *adv.* **1** in a very similar way: *They always manage to think alike.* **2** used after you have referred to two people or groups, to mean "both" or "equally": *Good management benefits employers and employees alike.* **IDM** SEE GREAT *adj.*, SHARE *v.*

al·i·men·ta·ry ca·nal /ˌæləˌmentri kəˈnæl; -ˌmentəri-/ *noun* the passage in the body that carries food from the mouth to the ANUS

al·i·mo·ny /ˈæləˌmouni/ *noun* [U] the money that a court orders someone to pay regularly to their former wife or husband when the marriage is ended ⊃ **compare** PALIMONY

ˈA-line *adj.* (of a skirt or dress) wider at the bottom than at the top

al·i·quot /ˈæliˌkwɑt; -kwət/ *noun* **1** (*technical*) a small amount of something that is taken from a larger amount, especially when it is taken in order to do chemical tests on it **2** (*mathematics*) a quantity that can be exactly divided into another

ˈA-list *adj.* [usually before noun] used to describe the group of people who are considered to be the most famous, successful, or important: *He only invited A-list celebrities to his parties.* ⊃ **compare** B-LIST

a·live 🔑 /əˈlaɪv/ *adj.* [not before noun]
1 living; not dead: *We don't know whether he's alive or dead.* ◆ *Is your mother still alive?* ◆ *Doctors kept the baby alive for six weeks.* ◆ *I was glad to hear you're alive and well.* ◆ *She had to steal food just to stay alive.* ◆ *He was buried alive in the earthquake.* **2** ~ **(with sth)** full of emotion, excitement, activity, etc.: *Ed was alive with happiness.* **3** continuing to exist: *to keep a tradition alive* **4** ~ **with sth** full of living or moving things: *The pool was alive with goldfish.* **5** ~ **to sth** aware of something; knowing something exists and is important: *to be alive to the dangers/facts/possibilities*
IDM **alive and kicking** very active or healthy **bring sth alive** to make something interesting: *The pictures bring the book alive.* **come alive 1** (of a subject or an event) to become interesting and exciting: *The game came alive in the second quarter.* **2** (of a place) to become busy and full of activity **SYN**: *The city starts to come alive after dark.* **3** (of a person) to show interest in something and become excited about it: *She came alive as she talked about her job.* ⊃ **more at** EAT

al·ka·li /ˈælkəˌlaɪ/ *noun* [C, U] (*chemistry*) a chemical substance that reacts with acids to form a salt and gives a SOLUTION with a pH of more than seven when it is dissolved in water ⊃ **compare** ACID

al·ka·line /ˈælkələn; -ˌlaɪn/ *adj.* **1** (*chemistry*) having the nature of an alkali **2** (*technical*) containing alkali: *alkaline soil* ⊃ **compare** ACID

al·ka·lin·i·ty /ˌælkəˈlɪnəti/ *noun* [U] the state of being or containing an ALKALI

al·ka·loid /ˈælkəˌlɔɪd/ *noun* (*biology* or *medical*) a poisonous substance found in some plants. There are many different alkaloids and some are used as the basis for drugs.

al·kane /ˈælkeɪn/ *noun* (*chemistry*) any of a series of COMPOUNDS that contain CARBON and HYDROGEN: *Methane and propane are alkanes.*

Alka-Seltzer™ /ˈælkə ˌseltsər/ *noun* [C, U] a medicine that you mix with water to make a drink that helps with INDIGESTION

al·kene /ˈælkin/ *noun* (*chemistry*) any of a series of gases that contain HYDROGEN and CARBON and that have a double BOND (= force of attraction) between two of the CARBON atoms

all 🔑 /ɔl/ *det., pron., adv.*
• *det.* **1** (used with plural nouns. The noun may have *the, this, that, my, her, his,* etc. in front of it, or a number.) the whole number of: *All horses are animals, but not all animals are horses.* ◆ *Cars were coming from all directions* (= every direction). ◆ *All the people you invited are coming.* ◆ *All my plants have died.* ◆ *All five men are hard workers.* **2** (used with uncountable nouns. The noun may have *the, this, that, my, her, his,* etc. in front of it.) the whole amount of: *All wood tends to shrink.* ◆ *You had all the fun and I did all the hard work.* ◆ *All this mail must be answered.* ◆ *He has lost all his money.* **3** used with singular nouns showing something has been happening for a whole period of time: *He's worked hard all year.* ◆ *She was unemployed for all that time.* **4** the greatest possible: *In all honesty* (= being as honest as I can), *I can't agree.* **5** consisting or appearing to consist of one thing only: *The magazine was all advertisements.* ◆ *She was all smiles* (= smiling a lot). **6** any whatever: *He denied all knowledge of the crime.*

h **hat**   m **man**   n **no**   ŋ **sing**   l **leg**   r **red**   y **yes**   w **wet**

IDM **and all that (jazz, stuff, etc.)** (*informal*) and other similar things: *I'm bored by history—dates and battles and all that stuff.* **not all that good, well, etc.** not particularly good, well, etc.: *He doesn't sing all that well.* **not as bad(ly), etc. as all that** not as much as has been suggested: *They're not as rich as all that.* **of all people, things, etc.** (*informal*) used to express surprise because someone or something seems the least likely person, example, etc.: *I didn't think you, of all people, would become a vegetarian.* **of all the…** (*informal*) used to express anger: *I locked myself out. Of all the stupid things to do!* ➜ more at SIDE *n.*

● **pron. 1** the whole number or amount: *All of the food has gone.* ◆ *They ate all of it.* ◆ *They ate it all.* ◆ *I invited some of my colleagues but not all.* ◆ *Not all of them were invited.* ◆ *All of them enjoyed the party.* ◆ *They all enjoyed it.* ◆ *His last movie was best of all.* **2** (followed by a relative clause, often without *that*) the only thing; everything: *All I want is peace and quiet.* ◆ *It was all that I had.* ➜ note at ALTOGETHER ➜ see also YOU-ALL **IDM** **all in all** when everything is considered: *All in all it had been a great success.* **all in one** having two or more uses, functions, etc.: *It's a corkscrew and bottle opener all in one.* **all or nothing** used to say that if something is not complete or completely successful, it is not worth anything: *You have to have a passion for your work — for me, it's all or nothing.* **and all** also; included; in addition: *She jumped into the river, clothes and all* (= with her clothes on). **(not) at all** in any way; to any degree: *I didn't enjoy it at all.* **in all** as a total **SYN** ALTOGETHER: *There were twelve of us in all for dinner.* ◆ *That's $25.40 in all.* **not at all** used as a polite reply to an expression of thanks: *"Thanks very much for your help." "Not at all, it was a pleasure."* **your all** everything you have: *They gave their all* (= fought and died) *in the war.* ➜ more at ABOVE *prep.*, AFTER *prep.*, END *n.*, FOR *prep.*

● **adv. 1** completely: *She was dressed all in white.* ◆ *He lives all alone.* ◆ *The coffee spilled all over my skirt.* **2** (*informal*) very: *She was all excited.* ◆ *Now don't get all upset about it.* **3 ~ too…** used to show that something is more than you would like: *I'm all too aware of the problems.* ◆ *The end of the trip came all too soon.* **4** (in sports and games) to each side: *The score was four all.* **IDM** **all along** all the time; from the beginning: *I realized it was in my pocket all along.* **all around** in every way; in all respects: *a good performance all around* **all the better, harder, etc.** so much better, harder, etc.: *We'll have to work all the harder with two people out sick.* **all but 1** almost: *The party was all but over when we arrived.* ◆ *It was all but impossible to read his writing.* **2** everything or everyone except something or someone: *All but one of the plates were damaged.* **all of sth** (often *ironic*) used to emphasize an amount, a size, etc. usually when it is very small: *It must be all of 100 feet to the car!* **all over 1** everywhere: *We looked all over for the ring.* **2** what you would expect of the person mentioned: *That sounds like my sister all over.* **all there** (*informal*) having a healthy mind; thinking clearly: *He behaves very oddly at times—I don't think he's all there.* **be all about sb/sth** used to say what the most important aspect of something is: *It's all about money these days.* **be all for sth/for doing sth** to believe strongly that something should be done: *They're all for saving money where they can.* **be all over sb/sth** (*informal*) to show a lot of affection for or enthusiasm about someone or something: *He was all over her at the party.* **be all that** (*informal*) to be very attractive or impressive: *He thinks he's all that.* **be all up (with sb)** (old-fashioned, *informal*) to be the end for someone: *It looks as though it's all up with us now* (= we are ruined, have no further chances, etc.). ➜ more at SUDDEN

all- /ɔl/ *combining form* (in adjectives and adverbs) **1** completely: *an all-American team* ◆ *an all-inclusive price* **2** in the highest degree: *all-important* ◆ *all-powerful*

Al·lah /ˈɑlə; ˈælə; ɑˈlɑ/ *noun* the name of God among Muslims

all-A·mer·i·can *adj.* **1** having good qualities that people think are typically American: *a clean-cut, all-American boy*
2 (of a sports player) chosen as one of the best players in the U.S.

all-a·round *adj.* [only before noun] **1** including many different subjects, skills, etc.: *an all-around expert* **2** (of a person) with a wide range of skills or abilities: *She's a great all-around player.*

al·lay /əˈleɪ/ *verb* **~ sth** (*formal*) to make something, especially a feeling, less strong: *to allay fears/concern/suspicion*

the all-clear *noun* [sing.] **1** a signal (often a sound) that shows that a place or situation is not dangerous anymore **2** if a doctor gives someone **the all-clear**, they tell the person that they do not have any health problems **3** permission to do something: *The ship was given the all-clear to sail.*

all comers *noun* [pl.] anyone who wants to take part in an activity or a competition

all-con·sum·ing *adj.* (of an interest) taking up all of your time or energy: *an all-consuming love of jazz*

all-day *adj.* [only before noun] continuing for the whole day: *an all-day meeting*

al·le·ga·tion /ˌæləˈɡeɪʃn/ *noun* a public statement that is made without giving proof, accusing someone of doing something that is wrong or illegal **SYN** ACCUSATION: *to investigate/deny/withdraw an allegation* ◆ **~ of sth** *Several newspapers made allegations of corruption in the city's police department.* ◆ **~ (of sth) against sb** *allegations of dishonesty against him* ◆ **~ about sb/sth** *The committee has made serious allegations about interference in its work.* ◆ **~ that…** *an allegation that he had been dishonest* ➜ thesaurus box at CLAIM

al·lege /əˈledʒ/ *verb* [often passive] (*formal*) to state something as a fact but without giving proof: **~ (that)…** *The prosecution alleges (that) she was driving carelessly.* ◆ **it is alleged (that)…** *It is alleged that he mistreated the prisoners.* ◆ **be alleged to be, have, etc. sth** *He is alleged to have mistreated the prisoners.* ◆ **~ sth** *This procedure should be followed in cases where dishonesty has been alleged.*
▸ **al·leged** /əˈledʒd/ *adj.* [only before noun] (*formal*): *the alleged attacker/victim/killer* (= that someone says is one) ◆ *the alleged attack/offense/incident* (= that someone says has happened) **al·leg·ed·ly** /əˈledʒədli/ *adv.*: *crimes allegedly committed during the war*

al·le·giance /əˈlidʒəns/ *noun* [U, C] a person's continued support for a political party, religion, ruler, etc.: *to switch/transfer/change allegiance* ◆ *an oath/a vow/a statement of allegiance* ◆ *People of various party allegiances joined the campaign.* ◆ **~ to sb/sth** *to pledge/swear allegiance to someone or something* ➜ see also PLEDGE OF ALLEGIANCE

al·le·go·ry /ˈæləˌɡɔri/ *noun* [C, U] (*pl.* **al·le·go·ries**) a story, play, picture, etc. in which each character or event is a symbol representing an idea or a quality, such as truth, evil, death, etc.; the use of such symbols: *a political allegory* ◆ *the poet's use of allegory* ➜ see also FABLE ▸ **al·le·gor·i·cal** /ˌæləˈɡɔrɪkl/ *adj.*: *an allegorical figure/novel* **al·le·gor·i·cal·ly** /-kli/ *adv.*

al·le·gro /əˈleɪɡroʊ/ *noun* (*pl.* **al·le·gros**) (*music*) a piece of music to be played in a fast and lively manner ▸ **al·le·gro** *adj., adv.*

al·lele /əˈlil/ *noun* (*biology*) one of two or more possible forms of a gene that are found at the same place on a CHROMOSOME

al·le·lu·ia /ˌæləˈluyə/ *noun, exclamation* = HALLELUJAH

all-em·brac·ing *adj.* (*formal*) including everything

all-en·com·passing *adj.* (*formal*) including everything

Al·len screw™ /ˈælən ˌskru/ *noun* a screw with a hole that has six sides

Al·len wrench™ *noun* a small tool used for turning an Allen screw™

al·ler·gen /ˈælərdʒən/ *noun* a substance that causes an allergy

al·ler·gic /əˈlərdʒɪk/ *adj.* **1 ~ (to sth)** having an allergy to something: *I like cats but unfortunately I'm allergic to them.* **2** caused by an allergy: *an allergic reaction* **3** [not before noun] **~ to sth** (*informal*, *humorous*) having a strong dislike of something or someone: *You could see he was allergic to homework.*

al·ler·gist /ˈælərdʒɪst/ *noun* a doctor who treats people with allergies

al·ler·gy /ˈælərdʒi/ *noun* (*pl.* **al·ler·gies**) **~ (to sth)** a medical condition that causes you to react badly or feel sick when you eat or touch a particular substance: *I have an allergy to peanuts.*

al·le·vi·ate /əˈliːvieɪt/ *verb* **~ sth** to make something less severe SYN EASE: *to alleviate suffering* ◆ *A number of measures were taken to alleviate the problem.* ▶ **al·le·vi·a·tion** /əˌliːvi-ˈeɪʃn/ *noun* [U]

al·ley /ˈæli/ *noun* **1** (also **al·ley·way** /ˈæliweɪ/) a narrow passage behind or between buildings: *a narrow/dark alley* ⊃ see also BLIND ALLEY, BOWLING ALLEY **2** (*informal*) the pair of parallel lines on a TENNIS or BADMINTON COURT that mark the extra area that is used when four people are playing
  IDM **(right) up your alley** very suitable for you because it is something that you know a lot about or are very interested in ⊃ see also ALLY

alley cat *noun* a cat that lives on the streets

all-fired *adv.*, *adj.* (*informal*)
  ● *adv.* extremely: *If she's so all-fired smart, why does she have to study so much?*
  ● *adj.* [only before noun] extreme: *She had the all-fired nerve to insult me!*

all get-out *noun* (*informal*) used to emphasize how extreme a quality or action is: *He's as crazy as all get-out!* ◆ *We rushed like all get-out.*

al·li·ance /əˈlaɪəns/ *noun* **1** an agreement between countries, political parties, etc. to work together in order to achieve something that they all want: *to form/make an alliance* ◆ **~ with sb/sth** *The unions are now in alliance with the Democrats.* ◆ **~ between A and B** *an alliance between education and business to develop the use of technology in schools* **2** a group of people, political parties, etc. who work together in order to achieve something that they all want

al·lied 🔑 *adj.*
  1 /ˈælaɪd/ often **Allied** [only before noun] connected with countries that unite to fight a war together, especially the countries that fought together against Germany in World Wars I and II: *Italy joined the war on the Allied side in 1915.* ◆ *allied forces/troops* **2** /əˈlaɪd; ˈælaɪd/ (*formal*) (of two or more things) similar or existing together; connected with something: *medicine, nursing, physiotherapy, and other allied professions* ◆ **~ to/with sth** *This job requires social skills allied with technical knowledge.* ⊃ see also ALLY

al·li·ga·tor /ˈæləɡeɪtər/ *noun* a large REPTILE similar to a CROCODILE, with a long tail, hard skin, and very big JAWS, that lives in rivers and lakes in N. and S. America and China ⊃ picture at ANIMAL

all-im·port·ant *adj.* extremely important

all-in·clus·ive *adj.* including everything or everyone: *Our trips are all-inclusive—there are no hidden costs.*

all-in-one *adj.* [only before noun] able to do the work of two or more things that are usually separate: *an all-in-one shampoo and conditioner* ▶ **all-in-one** *noun*: *We sell printers and scanners, and all-in-ones that combine the two.*

al·lit·er·a·tion /əˌlɪtəˈreɪʃn/ *noun* [U] (*technical*) the use of the same letter or sound at the beginning of words that are close together, as in *sing a song of sixpence* ▶ **al·lit·er·a·tive** /əˈlɪtərətɪv; -ˌreɪtɪv/ *adj.*

al·li·um /ˈæliəm/ *noun* (*technical*) any plant that belongs to the same group as onions and GARLIC

all-night *adj.* [only before noun] **1** (of a place) open through the night: *an all-night café* **2** (of an activity) continuing through the night: *an all-night party*

all-nighter *noun* (*informal*) a time when you stay awake all night studying

al·lo·cate AWL /ˈæləkeɪt/ *verb* to give something officially to someone or something for a particular purpose: **~ sth (for sth)** *A large sum has been allocated for buying new books for the library.* ◆ **~ sth (to sb/sth)** *They intend to allocate more places for older students this year.* ◆ *More resources are being allocated to the project.* ◆ **~ sb/sth sth** *The project is being allocated more resources.*

al·lo·ca·tion AWL /ˌæləˈkeɪʃn/ *noun* **1** [C] an amount of money, space, etc. that is given to someone for a particular purpose **2** [U] the act of giving something to someone for a particular purpose: *the allocation of food to those who need it most*

al·lo·morph /ˈæləmɔːrf/ *noun* (*linguistics*) one possible form of a particular MORPHEME. The forms /s/, /z/, and /əz/ in *cats*, *dogs*, and *horses* are allomorphs of the plural ending *s*.

al·lo·phone /ˈæləfoʊn/ *noun* (*phonetics*) **1** a sound that is slightly different from another sound, although both sounds belong to the same PHONEME and the difference does not affect meaning. For example, the /l/ at the beginning of *little* is different from the /l/ at the end. **2** (*CanE*) a person who comes to live in Canada, especially Québec, from another country, whose first language is neither French nor English ▶ **al·lo·phone** *adj.*: *Within French-speaking Québec, anglophone, and Aboriginal minorities also exist.*

all-or-nothing *adj.* used to describe two extreme situations that are the only possible ones: *an all-or-nothing decision* (= one that could either be very good or very bad)

al·lo·saur·us /ˌæləˈsɔːrəs/ *noun* a type of large DINOSAUR

al·lot /əˈlɑt/ *verb* (-tt-) to give time, money, tasks, etc. to someone or something as a share of what is available: **~ sth** *I completed the test within the time allotted.* ◆ **~ sth to sb/sth** *How much money has been allotted to us?* ◆ **~ sb/sth sth** *How much money have we been allotted?*

al·lot·ment /əˈlɑtmənt/ *noun* [C, U] (*formal*) an amount of something that someone is given or allowed to have; the process of giving something to someone: *Water allotments to farmers were cut back in the drought.* ◆ *the allotment of shares to company employees*

al·lo·trope /ˈæləˌtroʊp/ *noun* (*chemistry*) one of the different forms in which a chemical element exists. For example, diamond and GRAPHITE are allotropes of CARBON.

all-out *adj.* [only before noun] using or involving every possible effort and done in a very determined way: *all-out war* ◆ *an all-out attack on the opposition* ▶ **all out** *adv.*: *We're going all out to win.*

all-over *adj.* [only before noun] covering the whole of something: *an all-over tan*

al·low /əˈlaʊ/ *verb*
  ➤ LET SOMEONE OR SOMETHING DO SOMETHING **1** to let someone or something do something; to let something happen or be done: **~ sb to do sth** *His parents won't allow him to stay out late.* ◆ *He is not allowed to stay out late.* ◆ *They shouldn't be allowed to get away with it.* ◆ **~ sth to do sth** *He allowed his mind to wander.* ◆ **~ yourself to do sth** *She won't allow herself to be dictated to.* ◆ **~ sth** *Smoking is not allowed in the hall.* **2** **~ sb/yourself sth** to let someone have something: *You're allowed an hour to complete the test.* ◆ *I'm not allowed visitors.* **3** [usually passive] to let someone or something go into, through, out of, etc. a place: **~ sth** *No dogs allowed* (= you cannot bring them in). ◆ **~ sb/sth + adv./prep.** *The prisoners are allowed out of their cells for two hours a day.* ◆ *The crowd parted to allow her through.*
  ➤ MAKE POSSIBLE **4** **~ sth** to make something possible: *A ramp allows easy access for wheelchairs.* ⊃ language bank at PROCESS¹
  ➤ TIME/MONEY/FOOD, ETC. **5** **~ sth (for sb/sth)** to make sure that you have enough of something for a particular purpose: *You need to allow three yards of fabric for the dress.*
  ➤ ACCEPT/ADMIT **6** (*formal*) to accept or admit something; to agree that something is true or correct: **~ sth** *The judge*

Λ **cup**   ə **about**   eɪ **say**   aɪ **five**   ɔɪ **boy**   aʊ **now**   oʊ **go**   ər **bird**

allowed my claim. ♦ *"Objection!" "I'll allow it."* ♦ **~ that...** *He refuses to allow that such a situation could arise.* ♦ **~ sb sth** *She was very helpful when my mother was sick—I'll allow you that.* ⊃ compare DISALLOW

IDM **allow me** used to offer help politely ⊃ more at REIN *n.*
PHR V **al'low for sb/sth** to consider or include someone or something when calculating something: *It will take about an hour to get there, allowing for traffic delays.* ♦ *All these factors must be allowed for.* **al'low of sth** (*formal*) to make something possible: *The facts allow of only one explanation.*

al·low·a·ble /əˈlaʊəbl/ *adj.* that is allowed, especially by law or by a set of rules

al·low·ance /əˈlaʊəns/ *noun* **1** an amount of money that is given to someone regularly or for a particular purpose: *an allowance of $20 a day* ♦ *a clothing/living/travel allowance* ♦ *Do you get an allowance for clothing?* **2** the amount of something that is allowed in a particular situation: *a baggage allowance of 50 pounds* **3** a small amount of money that parents give their children, usually every week or every month

IDM **make allowance(s) for sth** to consider something, for example when you are making a decision or planning something: *The budget made allowances for inflation.* ♦ *The plan makes no allowance for people working at different rates.* **make allowances (for sb)** to allow someone to behave in a way that you would not usually accept, because of a problem or because there is a special reason

al·loy *noun, verb*
• *noun* /ˈælɔɪ/ [C, U] a metal that is formed by mixing two types of metal together, or by mixing metal with another substance: *Brass is an alloy of copper and zinc.*
• *verb* /əˈlɔɪ; ˈælɔɪ/ **~ sth (with sth)** (*technical*) to mix one metal with another, especially one of lower value

all-'party *adj.* [usually before noun] involving all political parties: *all-party support*

all-points 'bulletin *noun* (*abbr.* APB) a radio message sent to every officer of a police force, giving details of people who are suspected of a crime, of stolen vehicles, etc.

all-'powerful *adj.* having complete power: *the all-powerful secret police*

all-'purpose *adj.* [only before noun] having many different uses; able to be used in many situations

all-purpose 'flour *noun* [U] flour that does not contain BAKING POWDER ⊃ compare SELF-RISING FLOUR

all 'right (also *non-standard* or *informal* **al·right**) *adj., adv., exclamation*
• *adj., adv.* **1** acceptable; in an acceptable manner **SYN** OK: *Is the coffee all right?* ♦ *Are you getting along all right in your new job?* **2** safe and well **SYN** OK: *I hope the children are all right.* ♦ *Do you feel all right?* ⊃ thesaurus box at WELL **3** only just good enough **SYN** OK: *Your work is all right but I'm sure you could do better.* **4** that can be allowed **SYN** OK: *Are you sure it's all right for me to leave early?* **5** used to emphasize that there is no doubt about something: *"Are you sure it's her?" "Oh, it's her all right."*

IDM **it'll be all right on the night** (*saying*) used to say that a performance, an event, etc. will be successful even if the preparations for it have not gone well

• *exclamation* **1** used to check that someone agrees or understands **SYN** OK: *We've got to get up early, all right?* **2** used to say that you agree **SYN** OK: *"Can you do it?" "Oh, all right."* **3** used when accepting thanks for help or a favor, or when someone says they are sorry **SYN** OK: *"I'm really sorry." "That's all right, don't worry."* **4** used to get someone's attention **SYN** OK: *All right class, turn to page 20.*

All 'Saints' Day *noun* a Christian festival in honor of the SAINTS, held on November 1

All 'Souls' Day *noun* a Christian festival in honor of the dead, held on November 2

all·spice /ˈɔlspaɪs/ *noun* [U] the dried BERRY of a tree from the West Indies, used in cooking as a spice

all-star *adj.* [only before noun] including many famous actors, players, etc.: *an all-star cast*

all-star 'game *noun* a game played between the best players in their sport: *the East-West All-Star Game*

all-terrain 'board *noun* = MOUNTAINBOARD

all-terrain 'vehicle *noun* = ATV

all-'time *adj.* [only before noun] (used when you are comparing things or saying how good or bad something is) of any time: *one of the all-time great players* ♦ *my all-time favorite song* ♦ *Unemployment reached an all-time record of 14.5 million.* ♦ *Profits are at an all-time high/low.*

al·lude /əˈlud/ *verb*
PHR V **al'lude to sb/sth** (*formal*) to mention something in an indirect way ⊃ see also ALLUSION

al·lure /əˈlʊr/ *noun* [U] (*formal*) the quality of being attractive and exciting: *sexual allure* ♦ *the allure of the big city*

al·lur·ing /əˈlʊrɪŋ/ *adj.* attractive and exciting in a mysterious way: *an alluring smile* ▶ **al·lur·ing·ly** *adv.*

al·lu·sion /əˈluʒn/ *noun* [C, U] **~ (to sb/sth)** something that is said or written that refers to or mentions another person or subject in an indirect way (= ALLUDES to it): *His statement was seen as an allusion to the recent political unrest.* ♦ *Her poetry is full of obscure literary allusion.*

al·lu·sive /əˈlusɪv/ *adj.* (*formal*) containing allusions: *an allusive style of writing*

al·lu·vi·al /əˈluviəl/ *adj.* [usually before noun] (*technical*) made of sand and earth that is left by rivers or floods

al·lu·vi·um /əˈluviəm/ *noun* [U] (*geology*) sand and earth that is left by rivers or floods

all-,weather *adj.* [usually before noun] suitable for all types of weather: *all-weather tires*

all-wheel 'drive *noun* [U] a system in which power is always applied to all four wheels of a vehicle

al·ly *noun, verb*
• *noun* /ˈælaɪ/ (*pl.* **al·lies**) **1** [C] a country that has agreed to help and support another country, especially in case of a war **2** [C] a person who helps and supports someone who is in a difficult situation, especially a politician: *a close ally and friend of the prime minister* **3** **the Allies** [pl.] the group of countries including the U.S. and Britain that fought together in World Wars I and II

WORD FAMILY
ally *verb, noun*
allied *adj.*
alliance *noun*

• *verb* /əˈlaɪ; ˈælaɪ/ (**al·lies, al·ly·ing, al·lied, al·lied**) [T, I] **~ (yourself) with sb/sth** to give your support to another group or country: *The president allied himself with the unions.*

-ally /əli; li/ *suffix* (makes adverbs from adjectives that end in *-al*): *magically* ♦ *sensationally*

al·ma ma·ter /ˌælmə ˈmɑtər; ˌɑl-/ also **Al·ma Ma·ter** *noun* [sing.] the school, college, or university that someone went to

al·ma·nac (also *less frequent* **al·ma·nack**) /ˈɔlmə næk; ˈæl-/ *noun* **1** a book that is published every year giving information for that year about a particular subject or activity **2** a book that gives information about the sun, moon, times of the TIDES (= the rise and fall of the sea level), etc. for each day of the year

al·might·y /ɔlˈmaɪti/ *adj.* **1** (in prayers) having complete power: *Almighty God, have mercy on us.* **2** [only before noun] (*informal*) very great or severe: *an almighty bang/crash/roar* **3** **the Almighty** *noun* [sing.] God

al·mond /ˈɑmənd; ˈæ-; ˈɑl-/ *noun* the flat, pale, sweet nut of the **almond tree**, used in cooking and to make almond oil: *ground almonds* ♦ *blanched almonds* (= with their skins removed) ♦ *almond paste* ♦ *almond eyes* (= eyes shaped like almonds) ⊃ picture at NUT

al·most /ˈɔlmoʊst; ɔlˈmoʊst/ *adv.*
not quite **SYN** NEARLY: *I like almost all of them.* ♦ *It's a mistake they almost always make.* ♦ *The story is almost certainly false.*

♦ *It's almost time to go.* ♦ *Dinner's almost ready.* ♦ *He slipped and almost fell.* ♦ *Their house is almost opposite ours.* ♦ *They'll eat almost anything.* ♦ *Almost no one* (= hardly anyone) *believed him.*

WHICH WORD?

almost ◆ nearly ◆ practically

These three words have similar meanings and are used frequently with the following words:

almost ~	**nearly ~**	**practically ~**
certainly	(numbers)	all
all	all	every
every	always	no
entirely	every	nothing
impossible	finished	impossible
empty	died	anything

- They are used in positive sentences: *She almost/nearly/practically missed her train.* They can be used before words like *all*, *every*, and *everybody*: *Nearly all the students have bikes.* ♦ *I've got practically every CD they've made.* **Practically** is used more in spoken than in written English. **Nearly** is the most common with numbers: *There were nearly 200 people at the meeting.* They can also be used in negative sentences but it is more common to make a positive sentence with **barely**: *We barely made it in time.* (or: *We almost/nearly didn't make it in time.*)
- **Almost** and **practically** can be used before words like *any*, *anybody*, *anything*, etc.: *I'll eat almost anything.* You can also use them before *no*, *nobody*, *never*, etc. but it is much more common to use **hardly** with *any*, *anybody*, *ever*, etc.: *She's hardly ever in.* (or: *She's almost never in.*)
- **Almost** can be used when you are saying that one thing is similar to another: *The boat looked almost like a toy.*

➲ note at HARDLY

alms /ɑmz/ *noun* [pl.] (*old-fashioned*) money, clothes, and food that are given to poor people

al·oe /ˈæloʊ/ *noun* a tropical plant with thick leaves with sharp points that contain a lot of water. The juice of some types of aloes is used in medicine and COSMETICS.

al·oe ver·a /ˌæloʊ ˈvɪrə; -ˈvɛrə/ *noun* **1** [U] a substance that comes from a type of aloe, used in products such as skin creams **2** [C] the aloe that this substance comes from

a·loft /əˈlɔft/ *adv.* (*formal*) high in the air

a·lo·ha /əˈloʊhɑ/ *exclamation* a Hawaiian word meaning "love," used to say hello or goodbye

aˈloha ˌshirt *noun* = HAWAIIAN SHIRT

a·lone 🔑 /əˈloʊn/ *adj.* [not before noun], *adv.* **1** without any other people: *I don't like going out alone at night.* ♦ *He lives alone.* ♦ *Finally the two of us were* ***alone together.*** ♦ *She was sitting* ***all alone*** *in the hall.* ♦ *Tom is* ***not alone in*** *finding Rick hard to work with.* **2** without the help of other people or things: *It's hard bringing up children alone.* ♦ *The assassin said he had acted alone.* **3** lonely and unhappy or without any friends: *Carol felt all alone in the world.* ♦ *I've been so alone since you went away.* **4** used after a noun or pronoun to show that the person or thing mentioned is the only one: *You can't blame anyone else; you alone made the decision.* **5** used after a noun or pronoun to emphasize one particular thing: *The shoes alone cost $200.*
IDM go it alone to do something without help from anyone: *Andrew decided to go it alone and start his own business.* **leave/let sb alone** to stop annoying someone or trying to get their attention: *She's asked to be left alone but the press photographers follow her everywhere.* **leave/let sth alone** to stop touching, changing, or moving something: *I've told you before—leave my things alone!* **let alone** used after a statement to emphasize that because the first thing is not true or possible, the next thing cannot be true or possible either: *There isn't enough room for us, let alone any guests.* **stand alone 1** to be independent or not connected with other people, organizations, or ideas: *These islands are too small to stand alone as independent states.* **2** to be not near other objects or buildings: *The arch once stood alone at the entrance to the castle.*

WHICH WORD?

alone ◆ lone ◆ lonely

- **Alone**, and **on your own/by yourself** (which are less formal and are the normal phrases used in spoken English) describe a person or thing that is separate from others. They do not mean that the person is unhappy: *I like being alone in the house.* ♦ *I'm going to London by myself next week.* ♦ *I want to finish this on my own* (= without anyone's help).
- **Lone/solitary/single** mean that there is only one person or thing there; **lone** and **solitary** may sometimes suggest that the speaker thinks the person involved is lonely: *a lone jogger in the park* ♦ *long, solitary walks*
- **Lonely/lonesome** mean that you are alone and sad: *a lonely child* ♦ *Sam was very lonely when he first moved to New York.* ♦ *The dog let out a lonesome howl.* It can also describe places or activities that make you feel lonely: *a lonely house* ♦ *the lonesome prairie*

a·long 🔑 /əˈlɔŋ/ *prep., adv.*
● ***prep.*** **1** from one end to or toward the other end of something: *They walked slowly along the road.* ♦ *I looked along the shelves for the book I needed.* **2** in a line that follows the side of something long: *Houses had been built along both sides of the river.* **3** at a particular point on or beside something long: *You'll find his office along this hallway on the right.*
● ***adv.*** **HELP** For the special uses of **along** in phrasal verbs, look at the entries for the verbs. For example, **get along with sb** is in the phrasal verb section at **get**. **1** forward: *I was just walking along singing to myself.* ♦ *He pointed out various landmarks as we drove along.* **2** with someone: *We're going for a swim. Why don't you come along?* ♦ *I'll be along* (= I'll join you) *in a few minutes.* **3** toward a better state or position: *The book's coming along nicely.*
IDM along with sb/sth in addition to someone or something; in the same way as someone or something: *She lost her job when the factory closed, along with hundreds of others.*

a·long·side 🔑 /əˌlɔŋˈsaɪd/ *prep.*
1 next to or at the side of something or someone: *A police car pulled up alongside us.* **2** together with or at the same time as something or someone: *Traditional beliefs still flourish alongside a modern urban lifestyle.* ▶ **a·long·side** *adv.*: *Nick caught up with me and rode alongside.*

a·loof /əˈluf/ *adj.* [not usually before noun] not friendly or interested in other people **SYN** DISTANT, REMOTE
▶ **a·loof·ness** *noun* [U]
IDM keep/hold (yourself) aloof | remain/stand aloof to not become involved in something; to show no interest in people: *The Emperor kept himself aloof from the people.*

al·o·pe·ci·a /ˌæləˈpiʃə/ *noun* [U] (*medical*) loss of hair from the head and body, often caused by illness

a·loud 🔑 /əˈlaʊd/ *adv.*
1 in a voice that other people can hear: *The teacher listened to the children* ***reading aloud.*** ♦ *He read the letter aloud to us.* ♦ *"What am I going to do?" she wondered aloud.* ➲ note at LOUD **2** in a loud voice: *She cried aloud in protest.* **IDM** see THINK

al·pac·a /ælˈpækə/ *noun* **1** [C] a S. American animal that is related to the LLAMA and has long hair **2** [U] a type of soft wool or cloth made from the hair of the alpaca, used especially for making expensive clothes: *an alpaca coat*

al·pha /ˈælfə/ *noun* the first letter of the Greek alphabet (Α, α)

al·pha·bet 🔊 /ˈælfəˌbɛt/ *noun*
a set of letters or symbols in a fixed order used for writing a language **ORIGIN** From *alpha* and *beta*, the first two letters of the Greek alphabet.

al·pha·bet·ic /ˌælfəˈbɛtɪk/ (also **al·pha·bet·ic·al**) *adj.* (of a written or printed character) being one of the letters of the alphabet, rather than a number or other symbol

al·pha·bet·i·cal 🔊 /ˌælfəˈbɛtɪkl/ *adj.*
1 according to the correct order of the letters of the alphabet: *The names on the list are* **in alphabetical order.** **2** = ALPHABETIC ▶ **al·pha·bet·i·cal·ly** /-kli/ *adv.*: *arranged/ listed/stored alphabetically*

al·pha·bet·ize /ˈælfəbəˌtaɪz/ *verb* ~ sth to arrange a list of words in alphabetical order

ˈalphabet ˌsoup *noun* [U] **1** (*informal*) language that is extremely difficult to understand, especially because it contains many symbols or abbreviations **2** soup that contains PASTA in the shape of letters

ˌalpha ˈmale *noun* [usually sing.] the man or male animal in a particular group who has the most power

al·pha·nu·mer·ic /ˌælfənuˈmɛrɪk/ (also **al·pha·nu·mer·ic·al** /ˌælfənuˈmɛrɪkl/) *adj.* containing both letters and numbers: *an alphanumeric code*

ˈalpha ˌparticle *noun* (*technical*) the NUCLEUS of a HELIUM atom; a PARTICLE with a positive electrical charge passing through it, which is produced in a nuclear reaction

ˈalpha ˌtest *noun* (*technical*) a test done by a company on a new product that they are developing ⊃ compare BETA TEST ▶ **ˈalpha-ˌtest** *verb* ~ sth

al·pine /ˈælpaɪn/ *adj., noun*
● *adj.* existing in or connected with high mountains, especially the Alps in Central Europe
● *noun* any plant that grows best on mountains

al·pin·ist /ˈælpənɪst/ *noun* a person who climbs high mountains as a sport, especially in the Alps ▶ **al·pin·ism** /ˈælpəˌnɪzəm/ *noun* [U]

al·read·y 🔊 /ɔlˈrɛdi/ *adv.*
1 before now or before a particular time in the past: *"Lunch?" "No thanks, I've already eaten."* ◆ *We got there early but Mike had already left.* **HELP** In informal spoken English, you can use the simple past tense with **already**: *I already ate.* This is not usually considered correct in written English. **2** used to express surprise that something has happened so soon or so early: *Is it 10 o'clock already?* ◆ *You're not leaving already, are you?* **3** used to emphasize that a situation or problem exists: *I'm already late.* ◆ *There are far too many people already. We can't take any more.* **IDM** see ENOUGH *pron.*

al·right /ɔlˈraɪt/ *adv.* (*informal*) = ALL RIGHT **HELP** This form should not be used in formal writing.

al·so 🔊 /ˈɔlsoʊ/ *adv.*
(not used with negative verbs) in addition; too: *She's fluent in French and German. She also speaks a little Italian.* ◆ *rubella,* **also known as** *German measles* ◆ *I didn't like it that much. Also, it was much too expensive.* ◆ *Jake's father had also been a doctor* (= both Jake and his father were doctors). ◆ *She was* **not only** *intelligent* **but also** *very musical.* ⊃ language bank at ACCORDING TO

WHICH WORD?

also ◆ as well ◆ too
- Also usually comes before the main verb or after *be*: *I went to New York last year, and I also spent some time in Washington.* **Too** is much more common in spoken and informal English. It is usually used at the end of a sentence: *"I'm going home now." "I'll come too."* As well often sounds formal or old-fashioned: *"Will your husband be attending as well?"*

- When you want to add a second negative point in a negative sentence, use **not...either**: *She hasn't called and she hasn't written either.* If you are adding a negative point to a positive one, you can use **not... too/as well**: *You can have a burger, but you can't have a hot dog too.*

ˈalso-ˌran *noun* a person who is not successful, especially in a competition or an election

al·tar /ˈɔltər/ *noun* a holy table in a church or TEMPLE: *the high altar* (= the most important one in a particular church) **IDM at/on the altar of sth** (*formal*) because of something that you think is worth suffering for: *He was willing to sacrifice his happiness on the altar of fame.*

ˈaltar ˌboy *noun* a boy who helps the priest in church services, especially in the Roman Catholic Church

al·tar·piece /ˈɔltərˌpis/ *noun* a painting or other work of art, located near the ALTAR in a church

al·ter 🔊 **AWL** /ˈɔltər/ *verb*
1 [I, T] to become different; to make someone or something different: *Prices did not alter significantly during 2010.* ◆ *He had altered his looks so much I barely recognized him.* ◆ ~ **sb/ sth** *It doesn't alter the way I feel.* ◆ *Nothing can* **alter the fact that** *we are to blame.* ◆ *The landscape has been radically altered, severely damaging wildlife.* **2** [T] ~ sth to make changes to a piece of clothing so that it will fit you better ▶ **al·ter·able** **AWL** /ˈɔltərəbl/ *adj.* (*formal*)

al·ter·a·tion **AWL** /ˌɔltəˈreɪʃn/ *noun* **1** [C] a change to something that makes it different: *major/minor alterations* ◆ *They are* **making** *some* **alterations to** *the house.* ◆ *an alteration in the baby's heartbeat* **2** [U] the act of making a change to something: *The dress will not need much alteration.*

al·ter·ca·tion /ˌɔltərˈkeɪʃn/ *noun* [C, U] (*formal*) a noisy argument or disagreement

al·ter e·go /ˌɔltər ˈigoʊ/ *noun* (*pl.* **al·ter e·gos**) (from *Latin*) **1** a person whose personality is different from your own but who shows or acts as another side of your personality: *Superman's alter ego was Clark Kent.* **2** a close friend who is very like yourself

al·ter·nate **AWL** *adj., verb, noun*
● *adj.* /ˈɔltərnət/ [usually before noun] **1** (of two things) happening or following one after the other regularly: *alternate layers of fruit and yogurt* **2** if something happens on **alternate** days, nights, etc. it happens on one day, etc. but not on the next: *John has to work on alternate Sundays.* **3** = ALTERNATIVE ▶ **al·ter·nate·ly** *adv.*: *He felt alternately hot and cold.*
● *verb* /ˈɔltərˌneɪt/ **1** [T] to make things or people follow one after the other in a repeated pattern: ~ **A and B** *Alternate cubes of meat and slices of red pepper on the kebabs.* ◆ ~ **A with B** *Alternate cubes of meat with slices of red pepper on the kebabs.* **2** [I] (of things or people) to follow one after the other in a repeated pattern: *alternating dark and pale stripes* ◆ ~ **with sth** *Dark stripes alternate with pale ones.* **3** [I] ~ **between A and B** to keep changing from one thing to another and back again: *Her mood alternated between happiness and despair.* ▶ **al·ter·na·tion** /ˌɔltərˈneɪʃn/ *noun* [U, C]: *the alternation of day and night*
● *noun* /ˈɔltərnət/ a person who does a job for someone who is away

ˌalternate ˈangles *noun* [pl.] (*geometry*) equal angles formed on opposite sides of a line that crosses two parallel lines, in the position of the inner angles of a Z ⊃ picture at SHAPE ⊃ compare CORRESPONDING ANGLES

ˌalternating ˈcurrent *noun* [U, C] (*abbr.* AC) an electric current that changes its direction at regular intervals many times a second ⊃ compare DIRECT CURRENT

al·ter·na·tive 🔊 **AWL** /ɔlˈtərnətɪv/ *noun, adj.*
● *noun* a thing that you can choose to do or have out of two or more possibilities: *You can be paid in cash weekly or by check monthly; those are the two alternatives.* ◆ *We had* **no alternative**

---

but to fire Gibson. ◆ *There is a vegetarian alternative on the menu every day.* ➔ thesaurus box at OPTION
- *adj.* [only before noun] **1** (also **al·ter·nate**) that can be used instead of something else: *an alternative method of doing something* ◆ *Do you have an alternative solution?* **2** different from the usual or traditional way in which something is done: *alternative comedy/music/lifestyles/values* ◆ *alternative energy* (= electricity or power that is produced using the energy from the sun, wind, water, etc.)

al·ternative 'fuel *noun* [C, U] fuel that can be used instead of FOSSIL FUELS such as coal and oil, and instead of nuclear fuel

al·ter·na·tive·ly 🔑 **AWL** /ɔlˈtɜrnətɪvli/ *adv.*
used to introduce a suggestion that is a second choice or possibility: *The agency will make travel arrangements for you. Alternatively, you can arrange your own transportation.*

al·ternative 'medicine *noun* [C, U] any type of treatment that does not use the usual scientific methods of Western medicine, for example one using plants instead of artificial drugs

al·ter·na·tor /ˈɔltərˌneɪtər/ *noun* a device, used especially in a car, that produces an ALTERNATING CURRENT

al·though 🔑 /ɔlˈðoʊ/ *conj.*
1 used for introducing a statement that makes the main statement in a sentence seem surprising **SYN** THOUGH: *Although the sun was shining, it wasn't very warm.* ◆ *Although small, the kitchen is well designed.* ➔ language bank at HOWEVER **2** used to mean "but" or "however" when you are commenting on a statement: *I felt he was wrong, although I didn't say so at the time.*

WHICH WORD?
although ◆ even though ◆ though
- You can use these words to show contrast between two clauses or two sentences. You can use **although**, **even though**, and **though** at the beginning of a sentence or clause that has a verb. Notice where the commas go: *Although/Even though/Though everyone played well, we lost the game.* ◆ *We lost the game, although/even though/though everyone played well.*
- You cannot use **even** on its own instead of **although**, **even though**, or **though** at the beginning of a sentence or clause: ~~Even everyone played well, we lost the game.~~

al·tim·e·ter /ælˈtɪmətər/ *noun* an instrument for showing height above sea level, used especially in an aircraft

al·ti·tude /ˈæltəˌtud/ *noun* **1** [C, usually sing.] the height above sea level: *We are flying at an altitude of 18,000 feet.* ◆ *The plane made a dive to a lower altitude.* **2** [C, usually pl., U] a place that is high above sea level: *Snow leopards live at high altitudes.* ◆ *The athletes trained at altitude in Mexico City.*

'altitude ˌsickness *noun* [U] illness caused by a lack of OXYGEN, because of being very high above sea level, for example on a mountain

Alt key /ˈɔlt ki/ *noun* also **ALT key** a key on a computer keyboard that you press while pressing other keys, in order to change their function

al·to /ˈæltoʊ/ *noun, adj.*
- *noun* (pl. **al·tos**) **1** (also **con·tral·to**) [C] a singing voice with a lower range than that of a SOPRANO; a person with an alto voice **2** [sing.] a musical part that is written for an alto voice ➔ compare BARITONE, BASS¹, COUNTER-TENOR, TENOR
- *adj.* [only before noun] (of a musical instrument) with the second highest range of notes in its group: *an alto saxophone* ➔ compare SOPRANO, TENOR

al·to·geth·er 🔑 /ˌɔltəˈɡeðər; ˈɔltəˌɡeðər/ *adv., noun*
- *adv.* **1** (used to emphasize something) completely; in every way: *The train went slower and slower until it stopped*

altogether. ◆ *I am not altogether happy about the decision.* ◆ *It was an altogether different situation.* **2** used to give a total number or amount: *You owe me $68 altogether.* **3** used to introduce a summary when you have mentioned a number of different things: *The food was good and we loved the music. Altogether, it was a great evening.*
- *noun*
IDM **in the altogether** (*old-fashioned, informal*) without any clothes on

WHICH WORD?
altogether ◆ all together
- **Altogether** and **all together** do not mean the same thing. **Altogether** means "in total" or "completely": *We have invited fifty people altogether.* ◆ *I am not altogether convinced by this argument.* ◆ *Have you lost your mind altogether?*
- **All together** means "all in one place" or "all at once": *Can you put your books all together in this box?* ◆ *Let's sing "Happy Birthday." All together now!*

al·tru·ism /ˈæltruˌɪzəm/ *noun* [U] (*formal*) the fact of caring about the needs and happiness of other people more than your own ▸ **al·tru·is·tic** /ˌæltruˈɪstɪk/ *adj.*: *altruistic behavior*

a·lum¹ /ˈæləm/ *noun* [U] a substance formed from ALUMINUM and another metal, used, for example, to prepare leather and to change the color of things

a·lum² /əˈlʌm/ *noun* (*informal*) a former student of a school, college, or university; an alumnus or alumna

a·lu·mi·na /əˈlumənə/ *noun* [U] (*technical*) a white substance found in many types of rock, especially CLAY

a·lu·mi·num /əˈlumənəm/ *noun* [U] (*symb.* **Al**) a chemical element. Aluminum is a light gray metal used for making pans, etc.: *aluminum pots/windows* ◆ *aluminum foil* (= for example, for wrapping food)

a·lum·na /əˈlʌmnə/ *noun* (*pl.* **a·lum·nae** /-ni/) (*formal*) a former female student of a school, college, or university

a·lum·ni /əˈlʌmnaɪ/ *noun* [pl.] the former male and female students of a school, college, or university: *Harvard Alumni Association*

a·lum·nus /əˈlʌmnəs/ *noun* (*pl.* **a·lum·ni** /-naɪ/) (*formal*) a former male student of a school, college, or university

al·ve·o·lar /ælˈviələr/ *noun* (*phonetics*) a speech sound made with the tongue touching the part of the mouth behind the upper front teeth, for example /t/ and /d/ in *tie* and *die* ▸ **al·ve·o·lar** *adj.*

al·ve·o·lus /ˌælˈviələs/ *noun* (*pl.* **al·ve·o·li** /-ˌlaɪ; -ˌli/) (*anatomy*) one of the many small spaces in each lung where gases can pass into or out of the blood

al·ways 🔑 /ˈɔlweɪz; -wɪz/ *adv.*
1 at all times; on every occasion: *There's always somebody at home in the evening.* ◆ *Always lock your car.* ◆ *She always arrives at 7:30.* ◆ *The children always seem to be hungry.* ◆ *We're not always this busy.* **2** for a long time; since you can remember: *This is the way we've always done it.* ◆ *This painting is very good —Ellie always was very good at art* (= so it is not very surprising). ◆ *Did you always want to be an actor?* **3** for all future time: *I'll always love you.* **4** if you say a person is **always doing** something, or something is **always happening**, you mean that they do it, or it happens, very often, and that this is annoying: *She's always criticizing me.* ◆ *That phone is always ringing.* **5** **can/could always...**, **there's always...** used to suggest a possible course of action: *If it doesn't fit, you can always take it back.* ◆ *If he can't help, there's always John.*
IDM **as always** as usually happens or is expected **SYN** AS USUAL: *As always, Polly was late for school.* ➔ more at ONCE

Alz·hei·mer's dis·ease /ˈɑltshaɪmərz dɪˌziz; ˈælts-; ˈɔlts-/ (also **Alz·hei·mer's**) *noun* [U] a serious disease, especially affecting older people, that prevents the brain from functioning normally and causes loss of memory, loss of ability to speak clearly, etc. **SYN** SENILE DEMENTIA

AM /ˌeɪ ˈem/ *abbr.* amplitude modulation (one of the main methods of broadcasting sound by radio)

am /əm; *strong form* æm/ ➔ BE

a.m. 🔑 (also **A.M.**) /ˌeɪ ˈem/ *abbr.*
between midnight and NOON (from Latin "ante meridiem"): *It starts at 10 a.m.* ➔ compare P.M.

a·mal·gam /əˈmælgəm/ *noun* **1** [C, usually sing.] ~ **(of sth)** (*formal*) a mixture or combination of things: *The film script is an amalgam of all three books.* **2** [U] (*technical*) a mixture of MERCURY and another metal, used especially to fill holes in teeth

a·mal·ga·mate /əˈmælgəˌmeɪt/ *verb* ~ **(sth) (with/into sth)** **1** [I, T] if two organizations **amalgamate** or are **amalgamated**, they join together to form one large organization **SYN** MERGE: *A number of colleges have amalgamated to form the new university.* ◆ ~ **with/into sth** *The company has now amalgamated with another local firm.* ◆ ~ **sth** *They decided to amalgamate the two schools.* ◆ ~ **sth with/into sth** *The two companies were amalgamated into one.* **2** [T] ~ **sth (into/with sth)** to put two or more things together so that they form one **SYN** MERGE: *This information will be amalgamated with information obtained earlier.* ▶ **a·mal·ga·ma·tion** /əˌmælgəˈmeɪʃn/ *noun* [U, C]: *the amalgamation of small farms into larger units*

a·man·u·en·sis /əˌmænjuˈensəs/ *noun* (*pl.* **a·man·u·en·ses** /-siz/) (*formal*) **1** a person who writes down your words when you cannot write, for example if you are injured and have an exam **2** an assistant, especially one who writes or types for someone

a·ma·ryl·lis /ˌæməˈrɪləs/ *noun* [C, U] a tall white, pink, or red flower shaped like a TRUMPET

a·mass /əˈmæs/ *verb* ~ **sth** to collect something, especially in large quantities **SYN** ACCUMULATE: *He amassed a fortune from silver mining.* ➔ thesaurus box at COLLECT

am·a·teur /ˈæmətʃər; -ˌtər; -ˌtʃur/ *noun, adj.*
● *noun* **1** a person who takes part in a sport or other activity for enjoyment, not as a job: *The tournament is open to both amateurs and professionals.* **2** (usually *disapproving*) a person who is not skilled: *This work was done by a bunch of amateurs!* **ANT** PROFESSIONAL ▶ **am·a·teur·ism** /ˈæmətʃərˌɪzəm; -tər-; -tʃur-/ *noun* [U]: *New rules on amateurism allow payment for promotional work.*
● *adj.* **1** [usually before noun] doing something for enjoyment or interest, not as a job: *an amateur photographer* **2** [usually before noun] done for enjoyment, not as a job: *amateur athletics* **3** (usually *disapproving*) = AMATEURISH **ANT** PROFESSIONAL

am·a·teur·ish /ˌæməˈtʃurɪʃ; -ˈtərɪʃ; -ˈtʃurɪʃ/ (also **am·a·teur**) *adj.* (usually *disapproving*) not done or made well or with skill: *Detectives described the burglary as "crude and amateurish."* **ANT** PROFESSIONAL

am·a·to·ry /ˈæməˌtɔri/ *adj.* [only before noun] (*formal* or *humorous*) relating to or connected with sexual desire or activity: *his amatory exploits*

a·maze 🔑 /əˈmeɪz/ *verb*
to surprise someone very much: ~ **sb** *Just the size of the place amazed her.* ◆ ~ **sb what, how, etc....** *It never ceases to amaze me what some people will do for money.* ◆ *What amazes me is how long she succeeded in hiding it from us.* ◆ **it amazes sb that.../to see, find, learn, etc.** *It amazed her that he could be so calm at such a time.* ➔ thesaurus box at SURPRISE

a·mazed 🔑 /əˈmeɪzd/ *adj.*
very surprised: *an amazed silence* ◆ ~ **at sb/sth** *I was amazed at her knowledge of French literature.* ◆ ~ **by sb/sth** *We were amazed by his generosity.* ◆ ~ **(that)...** *I was banging so loudly I'm amazed (that) they didn't hear me.* ◆ ~ **how...** *She was amazed how little he had changed.* ◆ ~ **to see, find, learn, etc.** *We were amazed to find that no one was hurt.*

a·maze·ment /əˈmeɪzmənt/ *noun* [U] a feeling of great surprise: *To my amazement, he remembered me.* ◆ *She looked at him in amazement.*

a·maz·ing 🔑 /əˈmeɪzɪŋ/ *adj.*
very surprising, especially in a way that makes you feel pleasure or admiration **SYN** ASTOUNDING, INCREDIBLE: *an amazing achievement/discovery/success/performance* ◆ *That's amazing, isn't it?* ◆ *It's amazing how quickly people adapt.* ▶ **a·maz·ing·ly** *adv.*: *Amazingly, no one noticed.* ◆ *Our dinner was amazingly cheap.*

Am·a·zon /ˈæməˌzɑn/ *noun* **1** (in ancient Greek stories) a woman from a group of female WARRIORS (= soldiers) **2** **am·a·zon** (*literary*) a tall strong woman

am·bas·sa·dor /æmˈbæsədər; əm-/ *noun* an official who lives in a foreign country as the senior representative there of his or her own country: *the American Ambassador to Italy/in Rome* ◆ *a former ambassador to the UN* ◆ (*figurative*) *The best ambassadors for the sport are the players.* ➔ see also GOODWILL AMBASSADOR ▶ **am·bas·sa·do·ri·al** /æmˌbæsəˈdɔriəl; əm-/ *adj.*

am·ber /ˈæmbər/ *noun* [U] **1** a hard, clear, yellowish-brown substance, used in making decorative objects or jewelry: *amber beads* **2** a yellowish-brown color: *amber eyes* ▶ **am·ber** *adj.*

am·ber·gris /ˈæmbərˌgrɪs; -ˌgris/ *noun* [U] a substance that is used in making some PERFUMES. It is produced naturally by a type of WHALE.

ambi- /ˈæmbi/ *prefix* (in nouns, adjectives, and adverbs) referring to both of two: *ambidextrous* ◆ *ambivalent*

am·bi·dex·trous /ˌæmbiˈdekstrəs/ *adj.* able to use the left hand or the right hand equally well

am·bi·ence (also **am·bi·ance**) /ˈæmbiəns; ˈɑmbiˌɑns/ *noun* [sing.] the character and atmosphere of a place: *the relaxed ambience of the city*

am·bi·ent /ˈæmbiənt/ *adj.* **1** [only before noun] (*technical*) relating to the surrounding area; on all sides: *ambient temperature/light/conditions* **2** (especially of music) creating a relaxed atmosphere: *a compilation of ambient electronic music* ◆ *soft ambient lighting*

am·bi·gu·i·ty **AWL** /ˌæmbiˈgyuəti/ *noun* (*pl.* **am·bi·gu·i·ties**) **1** [U] the state of having more than one possible meaning: *Write clear definitions in order to avoid ambiguity.* **2** [C] a word or statement that can be understood in more than one way: *There were several inconsistencies and ambiguities in her speech.* **3** [C, U] the state of being difficult to understand or explain because of involving many different aspects: *You must understand the ambiguity of my position.*

am·big·u·ous **AWL** /æmˈbɪgyuəs/ *adj.* **1** that can be understood in more than one way; having different meanings: *an ambiguous word/term/statement* ◆ *Her account was deliberately ambiguous.* **2** not clearly stated or defined: *His role has always been ambiguous.* **ANT** UNAMBIGUOUS ▶ **am·big·u·ous·ly** *adv.*: *an ambiguously worded agreement*

am·bit /ˈæmbɪt/ *noun* [sing.] (*formal*) the range of the authority or influence of something: *This case falls clearly within the ambit of the 2001 act.*

am·bi·tion 🔑 /æmˈbɪʃn/ *noun*
1 [C] something that you want to do or achieve very much: *It had been her lifelong ambition.* ◆ *political/presidential/nuclear ambitions* ◆ ~ **of being/doing sth** *She never achieved her ambition of becoming a famous writer.* ◆ ~ **to be/do sth** *His burning ambition was to study medicine.* **2** [U] the desire or determination to be successful, rich, powerful, etc.: *motivated by personal ambition* ◆ *She was intelligent but suffered from a lack of ambition.*

am·bi·tious /æmˈbɪʃəs/ *adj.* **1** determined to be successful, rich, powerful, etc.: *a fiercely ambitious young manager* ◆ *They were very ambitious for their children* (= they wanted them to be successful). **2** needing a lot of effort, money, or time to succeed: *the government's ambitious plans for social reform* **ANT** UNAMBITIOUS ▶ **am·bi·tious·ly** *adv.*

am·biv·a·lent /æmˈbɪvələnt/ *adj.* ~ **(about/toward sb/sth)** having or showing both good and bad feelings about someone or something: *She seems to feel ambivalent about her new job.* ◆ *He has an ambivalent attitude toward her.* ▶ **am·biv·a·lence** /-ləns/ *noun* [U, sing.]: ~ **(about/toward sb/sth)** *Many people feel some ambivalence toward television and its effect on our lives.* **am·biv·a·lent·ly** *adv.*

am·ble /ˈæmbl/ *verb* [I] + **adv./prep.** to walk at a slow relaxed speed **SYN** STROLL: *We ambled down to the beach.*

am·bro·sia /æmˈbroʊʒə/ *noun* [U] **1** (*literary*) something that is very pleasant to eat **2** (in ancient Greek and Roman stories) the food of the gods

am·bu·lance 🎧 /ˈæmbyələns/ *noun* a vehicle with special equipment, used for taking sick or injured people to a hospital: *an ambulance service* ◆ *ambulance crew* ◆ *Call an ambulance!*

ˈambulance ˌchaser *noun* (*informal, disapproving*) a lawyer who earns money by encouraging people who have been in an accident to make claims in court

am·bu·lant /ˈæmbyələnt/ (also **am·bu·la·to·ry**) *adj.* (*medical*) (of a patient) able to walk; not having to stay in bed

am·bu·la·to·ry /ˈæmbyələˌtɔri/ *adj.* **1** (*formal*) that is not fixed in one place and can move around easily **SYN** MOBILE: *an ambulatory care service* **2** (*medical*) = AMBULANT

am·bush /ˈæmbʊʃ/ *noun, verb*
• *noun* [C, U] the act of hiding and waiting for someone and then making a surprise attack on them: *Two soldiers were killed in a terrorist ambush.* ◆ *They were lying in ambush, waiting for the aid convoy.*
• *verb* ~ **sb/sth** to make a surprise attack on someone or something from a hidden position: *The guerrillas ambushed them near the bridge.* ◆ (*figurative*) *She was ambushed by reporters.*

a·me·ba, a·me·bic = AMOEBA, AMOEBIC

a·me·lio·rate /əˈmilyəˌreɪt/ *verb* ~ **sth** (*formal*) to make something better: *Steps have been taken to ameliorate the situation.* ▶ **a·me·lio·ra·tion** /əˌmilyəˈreɪʃn/ *noun* [U]

a·men /ˌeɪˈmɛn; ˌɑˈmɛn/ *exclamation, noun* also **Amen** a word used at the end of prayers and HYMNS, meaning "may it be so": *We ask this through our Lord, Amen.* ◆ (*figurative*) *Amen to that* (= I certainly agree with that).

a·me·na·ble /əˈminəbl; əˈmɛ-/ *adj.* **1** (of people) easy to control; willing to be influenced by someone or something: *They had three very amenable children.* ◆ ~ **to sth** *He seemed amenable to my idea.* **2** ~ **to sth** (*formal*) that you can treat in a particular way: *"Hamlet" is the least amenable of all Shakespeare's plays to being summarized.*

a·mend **AWL** /əˈmɛnd/ *verb* ~ **sth** to change a law, document, statement, etc. slightly in order to correct a mistake or to improve it: *He asked to see the amended version.*

a·mend·ment **AWL** /əˈmɛndmənt/ *noun* **1** [C, U] a small change or improvement that is made to a law or a document; the process of changing a law or a document: *to introduce/propose/table an amendment* (= to suggest it) ◆ *Legislation is delaying the proposed amendments to the new bill.* ◆ ~ **to sth** *She made several minor amendments to her essay.* **2 Amendment** [C] a statement of a change to the United States CONSTITUTION: *The 19th Amendment gave women the right to vote.*

a·mends **AWL** /əˈmɛndz/ *noun* [pl.]
IDM **make amends (to sb) (for sth/for doing sth)** to do something for someone in order to show that you are sorry for something wrong or unfair that you have done **SYN** MAKE UP FOR STH

a·men·i·ty /əˈmɛnəti; əˈmi-/ *noun* [usually pl.] (*pl.* **a·men·i·ties**) a feature that makes a place pleasant, comfortable, or easy to live in: *The campsite is close to all the local amenities.*

◆ *Many of the houses lacked even basic amenities* (= for example, bathrooms, showers, hot water).

a·men·or·rhe·a /eɪˌmɛnəˈriə/ *noun* [U] (*medical*) a condition in which an adult woman does not MENSTRUATE (= there is no flow of blood from her WOMB every month)

Am·er·a·sian /ˌæməˈreɪʒn/ *noun* a person with one Asian parent and one American parent ▶ **Am·er·a·sian** *adj.*

A·mer·i·can /əˈmɛrɪkən/ *noun, adj.*
• *noun* a person from America, especially the U.S. ➋ see also AFRICAN AMERICAN, NATIVE AMERICAN.
• *adj.* of or connected with N. or S. America, especially the U.S.: *I'm American.* ◆ *American culture/tourists* **IDM** **as American as apple pie** used to say that something is typical of America

A·mer·i·ca·na /əˌmɛrɪˈkɑnə; -ˈkænə/ *noun* [pl.] things connected with the U.S. that are thought to be typical of it

Aˈmerican ˌcheese *noun* [U] a kind of orange cheese that is usually sold in thin slices wrapped in plastic

the Aˌmerican ˈdream *noun* [sing.] the values and social standards that people traditionally try to achieve in the U.S., such as democracy, equal rights, and wealth

Aˌmerican ˈEnglish *noun* [U] the English language as spoken in the U.S.

Aˌmerican ˈIndian *noun* (sometimes *offensive*) = NATIVE AMERICAN

A·mer·i·can·ism /əˈmɛrɪkəˌnɪzəm/ *noun* **1** [C] a word, phrase, or spelling that is typical of American English, used in another variety of English **2** [U] the essential quality of being American

A·mer·i·can·ize /əˈmɛrɪkəˌnaɪz/ *verb* ~ **sb/sth** to make someone or something American in character ▶ **A·mer·i·can·i·za·tion, -isation** /əˌmɛrɪkənəˈzeɪʃn/ *noun* [U]

the Aˈmerican ˌLeague *noun* (in the U.S.) one of the two organizations for professional baseball ➋ see also NATIONAL LEAGUE

Aˈmerican ˌplan *noun* [U] (in hotels) a system of paying a single daily price that includes the room and all meals ➋ compare EUROPEAN PLAN

the Aˌmerican Revoˈlution (also **the Revoˌlutionary ˈWar**) *noun* [sing.] the war (1775-83) in which 13 colonies (COLONY) in North America won independence from British rule and established the United States of America

am·er·i·ci·um /ˌæməˈrɪʃiəm/ *noun* [U] (*symb.* **Am**) a chemical element. Americium is a RADIOACTIVE metal.

ʌ **cup**   ə **about**   eɪ **say**   aɪ **five**   ɔɪ **boy**   aʊ **now**   oʊ **go**   ər **bird**

A·mer·i·Corps /ə'mɛrɪˌkɔr/ *noun* [U] an organization whose members help in their communities, for example by building and repairing homes, cleaning parks, and preventing crime. Members can receive money to pay for their education.

Am·er·in·di·an /ˌæmə'rɪndiən/ *noun* (*old-fashioned*) = NATIVE AMERICAN

am·e·thyst /'æməθɪst/ *noun* [C, U] a purple SEMI-PRECIOUS STONE, used in making jewelry: *an amethyst ring*

a·mi·a·ble /'eɪmiəbl/ *adj.* pleasant; friendly and easy to like **SYN** AGREEABLE: *an amiable tone of voice* ◆ *Her parents seemed very amiable.* ▶ **a·mi·a·bil·i·ty** /ˌeɪmiə'bɪləti/ *noun* [U] **a·mi·a·bly** /'eɪmiəbli/ *adv.*: *"That's fine," he replied amiably.*

am·i·ca·ble /'æmɪkəbl/ *adj.* done or achieved in a polite or friendly way and without arguing: *an amicable relationship* ◆ *An amicable settlement was reached.* ▶ **am·i·ca·bly** /-bli/ *adv.*

a·mid /ə'mɪd/ (*also* **mid**, **a·midst** /ə'mɪdst/) *prep.* (*formal*) **1** in the middle of or during something, especially something that causes excitement or fear: *He finished his speech amid tremendous applause.* ◆ *The firm collapsed amid allegations of fraud.* **2** surrounded by something: *The hotel was in a beautiful setting amid lemon groves.*

a·mid·ships /ə'mɪdʃɪps/ *adv.* (*technical*) in or near the middle part of a ship

a·mi·go /ə'miɡoʊ/ *noun* (*pl.* **a·mi·gos**) (from *Spanish, informal*) a friend

a·mi·no ac·id /əˌminoʊ 'æsɪd/ *noun* (*chemistry*) any of the substances that combine to form the basic structure of PROTEINS

a·mir = EMIR

the A·mish /'ɑmɪʃ/ *noun* [pl.] the members of a strict Christian religious group. The Amish live a simple farming life and reject most forms of modern technology. ▶ **A·mish** *adj.*

a·miss /ə'mɪs/ *adj.* [not before noun] wrong; not as it should be: *She sensed something was amiss and called the police.*

am·i·ty /'æməti/ *noun* [U] (*formal*) a friendly relationship between people or countries

am·me·ter /'æˌmitər/ *noun* an instrument for measuring the strength of an electric current

am·mo /'æmoʊ/ *noun* [U] (*informal*) = AMMUNITION

am·mo·nia /ə'moʊnyə/ *noun* [U] (*symb.* **NH₃**) a gas with a strong smell; a clear liquid containing ammonia, used as a cleaning substance

am·mo·nite /'æməˌnaɪt/ *noun* [C] a FOSSIL of a simple sea creature that no longer exists, and that was related to SNAILS

ammonite

am·mo·ni·um /ə'moʊniəm/ *noun* [U] (*chemistry*) a salt made from AMMONIA containing NITROGEN and HYDROGEN together with another element

am·mu·ni·tion /ˌæmyə'nɪʃn/ *noun* [U] **1** a supply of bullets, etc. to be fired from guns **2** information that can be used against another person in an argument: *The letter gave her all the ammunition she needed.*

am·ne·sia /æm'niʒə/ *noun* [U] a medical condition in which someone partly or completely loses their memory ▶ **am·ne·si·ac** /æm'niʒiˌæk; -zi-/ *noun*: *This new discovery helps amnesiacs keep their memory.*

am·nes·ty /'æmnəsti/ *noun* (*pl.* **am·nes·ties**) **1** [C, usually sing., U] an official statement that allows people who have been put in prison for crimes against the state to go free: *The president granted a general amnesty for all political prisoners.* **2** [C, usually sing.] a period of time during which people can admit to a crime or give up weapons without being punished: *2,000 knives have been handed in during the month-long amnesty.*

Amnesty Inter'national *noun* [U] an international human rights organization that works to help people who have been put in prison for their beliefs or race and not because they have committed a crime. It also works to prevent TORTURE and punishment by death.

am·ni·o·cen·te·sis /ˌæmnioʊsen'tisəs/ *noun* [U, sing.] a medical test that involves taking some liquid from a pregnant woman's UTERUS in order to find out if the baby has particular illnesses or health problems

am·ni·ot·ic flu·id /ˌæmniɑtɪk 'fluəd/ *noun* [U] the liquid that surrounds a baby inside the mother's UTERUS

a·moe·ba (*also* **a·me·ba**) /ə'mibə/ *noun* (*pl.* **a·moe·bas** or **a·moe·bae** /-bi/) a very small living creature that consists of only one cell

a·moe·bic (*also* **a·me·bic**) /ə'mibɪk/ *adj.* related to or similar to an amoeba

a,moebic 'dysentery (*also* **a,mebic 'dysentery**) *noun* [U] an infection of the INTESTINE caused by a type of amoeba

a·mok /ə'mʌk; ə'mɑk/ *adv.*
IDM **run amok** to suddenly become very angry or excited and start behaving violently, especially in a public place

a·mong /ə'mʌŋ/ (*also* **a·mongst** /ə'mʌŋst/) *prep.* **1** surrounded by someone or something; in the middle of someone or something: *a house among the trees* ◆ *They strolled among the crowds.* ◆ *I found the letter amongst his papers.* ◆ *It's OK, you're among friends now.* **2** being included or happening in groups of things or people: *An American woman was among the survivors.* ◆ *He was among the last to leave.* ◆ *This attitude is common among teenagers.* ◆ *"What was wrong with the job?" "Well, the pay wasn't good, among other things."* ◆ *Discuss it* **among yourselves** *first* (= with each other). **3** used when you are dividing or choosing something, and three or more people or things are involved: *They divided the money up among the children.*

a·mor·al /eɪ'mɔrəl; eɪ'mɑr-/ *adj.* not following any moral rules and not caring about right and wrong ➲ compare IMMORAL, MORAL ▶ **a·mo·ral·i·ty** /ˌeɪmɔ'ræləti/ *noun* [U]

am·o·rous /'æmərəs/ *adj.* showing sexual desire and love toward someone: *Mary rejected Tony's amorous advances.* ▶ **am·o·rous·ly** *adv.*

a·mor·phous /ə'mɔrfəs/ *adj.* [usually before noun] (*formal*) having no definite shape, form, or structure **SYN** SHAPELESS: *an amorphous mass of cells with no identity at all*

am·or·tize /'æmərˌtaɪz/ *verb* ~ sth (*business*) to pay back a debt by making small regular payments over a period of time ▶ **am·or·ti·za·tion** /ˌæmərtə'zeɪʃn/ *noun* [U, C]

a·mount /ə'maʊnt/ *noun, verb*
● *noun* [C, U] **1** a sum of money: *The insurance company will refund any amount due to you.* ◆ *You will receive a bill for the full amount.* **2** ~ (of sth) (used especially with uncountable nouns) a quantity of something: *an amount of time/money/ information* ◆ *We've had an enormous amount of help from people.* ◆ *The server is designed to store huge amounts of data.*
IDM **any amount of sth** a large quantity of something: *There's been any amount of research into the subject.* **no amount of sth** used for saying that something will have no effect: *No amount of encouragement would make him jump into the pool.*
● *verb*
PHR V **a'mount to sth** **1** to add up to something; to make something as a total: *His earnings are said to amount to $300,000 a year.* ◆ *They gave me the money in the beginning but it* **did not amount to much** (= they did not give me much help). **2** to be equal to or the same as something: *Her answer amounted to a complete refusal.* ◆ *Their actions amount to a breach of contract.* ◆ *It'll either cost a lot or take a lot of time—it* **amounts to the same thing.**

ɪr **near**   ɛr **hair**   ɑr **car**   ɔr **north**   ʊr **tour**   ɑ̃ denouem**ent**   p **pen**   b **bad**   45

a·mour /əˈmʊr; ɑ-/ noun (old-fashioned, from French) a love affair, especially a secret one

a·mour pro·pre /ˌɑˌmʊr ˈproʊprə; əˌmʊr-/ noun [U] (from French) a feeling of pride in your own character and abilities

amp /æmp/ noun **1** (also **am·pere** /ˈæmpɪr/) (abbr. A) the unit for measuring electric current: *a 13 amp fuse/plug* **2** (informal) = AMPLIFIER

amp·ed /æmpt/ (also ˌamped ˈup) adj. (informal) excited, especially because of an event: *an amped audience of hard-core fans* ◆ *I get pretty amped up before I compete.*

am·per·age /ˈæmpərɪdʒ/ noun [U] the strength of an electric current, measured in AMPS

am·per·sand /ˈæmpərˌsænd/ noun the symbol (&) used to mean "and": *She works for Standard & Poor.*

am·phet·a·mine /æmˈfɛtəˌmin; -mən/ noun [C, U] a drug that makes you feel excited and full of energy. Amphetamines are sometimes taken illegally.

am·phib·i·an /æmˈfɪbiən/ noun any animal that can live both on land and in water. Amphibians have cold blood and skin without SCALES. FROGS, TOADS, and NEWTS are all amphibians. ⊃ collocations at LIFE ⊃ compare REPTILE

am·phib·i·ous /æmˈfɪbiəs/ adj. **1** able to live both on land and in water **2** (of military operations) involving soldiers landing at a place from the ocean **3** suitable for use on land or water: *amphibious vehicles*

am·phi·the·a·ter (CanE usually **am·phi·the·a·tre**) /ˈæmfəˌθiətər/ noun **1** a round building without a roof and with rows of seats that rise in steps around an open space. Amphitheaters were used especially in ancient Greece and Rome for public entertainments. ⊃ picture at BUILDING **2** a room, hall, or theater with rows of seats that rise in steps **3** (technical) an open space that is surrounded by high sloping land

am·pho·ra /ˈæmfərə; æmˈfɔrə/ noun (pl. **am·pho·rae** /ˈæmfəri; æmˈfɔri/ or **am·pho·ras**) a tall ancient Greek or Roman container with two handles and a narrow neck

am·pi·cil·lin /ˌæmpəˈsɪlən/ noun [U] a form of PENICILLIN that is used to treat certain infections

am·ple /ˈæmpl/ adj. **1** enough or more than enough **SYN** PLENTY OF: *ample opportunity/evidence/space/proof* ◆ *There was ample time to get to the airport.* ◆ *Ample free parking is available.* **2** (of a person's figure) large, often in an attractive way: *an ample bosom* ▶ **am·ply** /ˈæmpli/ adv.: *His efforts were amply rewarded.*

am·pli·fi·er /ˈæmpləˌfaɪər/ (also informal **amp**) noun an electrical device or piece of equipment that makes sounds or radio signals louder: *a 25 watt amplifier* ⊃ picture at INSTRUMENT

am·pli·fy /ˈæmpləˌfaɪ/ verb (am·pli·fies, am·pli·fy·ing, am·pli·fied, am·pli·fied) **1** [T] ~ sth to increase something in strength, especially sound: *to amplify a guitar/an electric current/a signal* **2** [I, T] (formal) to add details to a story, statement, etc.: *She refused to amplify further.* ◆ ~ sth *You may need to amplify this point.* ▶ **am·pli·fi·ca·tion** /ˌæmpləfəˈkeɪʃn/ noun [U]: *electronic amplification* ◆ *That comment needs some amplification.*

am·pli·tude /ˈæmpləˌtud/ noun [U, C] (physics) the greatest distance that a wave, especially a sound or radio wave, VIBRATES (= moves up and down)

am·ply adv. ⊃ AMPLE

am·poule (also **am·pule**) /ˈæmpyul/ -pul/ noun a small container, usually made of glass, containing a drug that will be used for an INJECTION

am·pu·tate /ˈæmpyəˌteɪt/ verb [T, I] ~ (sth) to cut off someone's arm, leg, finger, or toe in a medical operation: *He had to have both legs amputated.* ◆ *They may have to amputate.* ◆ collocations at INJURY ▶ **am·pu·ta·tion** /ˌæmpyəˈteɪʃn/ noun [U, C]

am·pu·tee /ˌæmpyəˈti/ noun a person who has had an arm or a leg amputated

am·u·let /ˈæmyələt/ noun a piece of jewelry that some people wear because they think it protects them from bad luck, illness, etc.

a·muse 🔑 /əˈmyuz/ verb
1 to make someone laugh or smile: ~ sb *My funny drawings amused the kids.* ◆ *This will amuse you.* ◆ **it amuses sb to do sth** *It amused him to think that they were probably talking about him at that very moment.* **2** to make time pass pleasantly for someone/yourself **SYN** ENTERTAIN: ~ sb *She suggested several ideas to help Laura amuse the twins.* ◆ ~ **yourself** *I'm sure I'll be able to amuse myself for a few hours.*

a·mused 🔑 /əˈmyuzd/ adj.
thinking that someone or something is funny, so that you smile or laugh: *There was an amused look on the president's face.* ◆ *Janet was **not** amused* (= she was annoyed or angry). ◆ ~ **at/by sth** *We were all amused at his stories.* ◆ ~ **to see, find, learn, etc.** *He was amused to see how seriously she took the game.*
IDM **keep sb amused** to give someone interesting things to do, or to entertain them so that they do not become bored: *Playing with water can keep children amused for hours.*

a·muse·ment /əˈmyuzmənt/ noun **1** [U] the feeling that you have when something is funny or amusing, or it entertains you: *She could not hide her amusement at the way he was dancing.* ◆ **To my amusement**, *he couldn't get the door open.* ◆ *Her eyes twinkled **with amusement**.* **2** [C, usually pl.] a game, an activity, etc. that provides entertainment and pleasure: *traditional boardwalk amusements including bumper cars, an arcade, and rides* **3** [U] the fact of being entertained by something: *What do you do for amusement around here?* ⊃ thesaurus box at ENTERTAINMENT

a·muse·ment park noun a large park that has a lot of things that you can ride and play on, and many different activities to enjoy ⊃ compare THEME PARK

a·mus·ing 🔑 /əˈmyuzɪŋ/ adj.
funny and enjoyable: *an amusing story/game/incident* ◆ *I didn't find the joke at all amusing.* ⊃ thesaurus box at FUNNY ▶ **a·mus·ing·ly** adv.

a·myg·da·la /əˈmɪgdələ/ noun (pl. **a·myg·da·lae** /-li/) (anatomy) either of two areas in the brain that are linked to memory, the emotions, and the sense of smell

am·yl·ase /ˈæməˌleɪs; -ˌleɪz/ noun [U] (chemistry) an ENZYME (= a substance that helps a chemical change to take place) that allows the body to change some substances into simple sugars

an 🔑 indefinite article ⊃ A

-an, -ana ⊃ -IAN, -IANA

an·a·bol·ic ste·roid /ˌænəbɑlɪk ˈstɛrɔɪd; -ˈstɪr-/ noun an artificial HORMONE (= a chemical substance) that increases the size of the muscles. It is sometimes taken illegally by people who play sports. ⊃ see also STEROID

a·nach·ro·nism /əˈnækrəˌnɪzəm/ noun **1** a person, a custom, or an idea that seems old-fashioned and does not belong to the present: *The monarchy is seen by many people as an anachronism in the modern world.* **2** something that is placed, for example in a book or play, in the wrong period of history ▶ **a·nach·ro·nis·tic** /əˌnækrəˈnɪstɪk/ adj.

an·a·con·da /ˌænəˈkɑndə/ noun a large S. American snake of the BOA family, that crushes other animals to death before eating them

an·aer·o·bic /ˌænəˈroʊbɪk; -ɛˈroʊ-/ adj. **1** (biology) not needing OXYGEN: *anaerobic bacteria* **2** (of physical exercise) not especially designed to improve the function of the heart and lungs **ANT** AEROBIC

an·a·gram /ˈænəˌgræm/ noun a word or phrase that is made by arranging the letters of another word or phrase in a different order: *An anagram of "Elvis" is "lives."*

a·nal /ˈeɪnl/ adj. **1** connected with the ANUS: *the anal region* **2** (also ˌanal-reˈtentive) (disapproving) caring too much about small details and about how things are organized ▶ **a·nal·ly** /ˈeɪmli/ *adv.*

an·al·ge·si·a /ˌænlˈdʒiːzə; -ziə/ *noun* [U] (*medical*) the loss of the ability to feel pain while still conscious

an·al·ge·sic /ˌænlˈdʒiːzɪk/ *noun* (*medical*) a substance that reduces pain **SYN** PAINKILLER: *Aspirin is a mild analgesic.* ▶ **an·al·ge·sic** *adj.*: *analgesic drugs/effects*

an·a·log (*especially CanE* **an·a·logue**) /ˈænlɔːɡ; -ɑːɡ/ *adj., noun*

● *adj.* (*technical*) **1** (of an electronic process) using a continuously changing range of physical quantities to measure or store data: *an analog circuit/computer/signal* **2** (of a clock or watch) showing the time using hands on a DIAL and not with a display of numbers ⊃ compare DIGITAL

● *noun* (*formal or technical*) a thing that is similar to another thing: *Scientists are attempting to compare features of extinct animals with living analogs.*

a·nal·o·gous **AWL** /əˈnæləɡəs/ *adj.* (*formal*) ~ **(to/with sth)** similar in some way to another thing or situation and therefore able to be compared with it: *Sleep has often been thought of as being in some way analogous to death.*

a·nal·o·gy **AWL** /əˈnælədʒi/ *noun* (*pl.* **a·nal·o·gies**) **1** [C] a comparison of one thing with another thing that has similar features; a feature that is similar: ~ **(between A and B)** *The teacher drew an analogy between the human heart and a pump.* ◆ ~ **(with sth)** *There are no analogies with any previous legal cases.* **2** [U] the process of comparing one thing with another thing that has similar features in order to explain it: *learning by analogy*

an·al·pha·bet·ic /ˌænælfəˈbetɪk/ *adj.* **1** (*technical*) completely unable to read or write **2** (*linguistics*) representing sounds with signs made of several parts rather than by single letters or symbols

anal-re'tentive *adj.* (*disapproving*) = ANAL

an·a·lyse (*CanE*) = ANALYZE

a·nal·y·sis 🔑 **AWL** /əˈnæləsəs/ *noun* (*pl.* **a·nal·y·ses** /-siːz/)
1 [U, C] the detailed study or examination of something in order to understand more about it; the result of the study: *statistical analysis* ◆ *The book is an analysis of poverty and its causes.* **2** [U, C] a careful examination of a substance in order to find out what it consists of: *The blood samples are sent to the laboratory **for analysis.*** ◆ *You can ask for a chemical analysis of your tap water.* **3** [U] = PSYCHOANALYSIS: *In analysis, the individual resolves difficult emotional conflicts.*
IDM **in the final/last analysis** used to say what is most important after everything has been discussed or considered: *In the final analysis, it's a matter of personal choice.*

an·a·lyst **AWL** /ˈænlɪst/ *noun* **1** a person whose job involves examining facts or materials in order to give an opinion on them: *a political/food analyst* ◆ *City analysts forecast huge profits this year.* ⊃ see also SYSTEMS ANALYST **2** = PSYCHOANALYST

an·a·lyt·ic **AWL** /ˌænlˈɪtɪk/ *adj.* **1** (also **i·so·lat·ing**) (*linguistics*) (of languages) using word order rather than word endings to show the functions of words in a sentence ⊃ compare SYNTHETIC **2** = ANALYTICAL

an·a·lyt·i·cal **AWL** /ˌænlˈɪtɪkl/ (also **an·a·lyt·ic**) *adj.* **1** using a logical method of thinking about something in order to understand it, especially by looking at all the parts separately: *She has a clear analytical mind.* ◆ *an analytic approach to the problem* **2** using scientific analysis in order to find out about something: *analytical methods of research* ▶ **an·a·lyt·i·cally** **AWL** /-kli/ *adv.*

an·a·lyze 🔑 **AWL** (*CanE also* **an·a·lyse**) /ˈænlaɪz/ *verb* **1** to examine the nature or structure of something, especially by separating it into its parts, in order to understand or explain it: ~ **sth** *The job involves gathering and analyzing data.* ◆ *He tried to analyze his feelings.* ◆ ~ **what, how, etc.…** *We need to analyze what went wrong.* ⊃ thesaurus box at EXAMINE **2** ~ **sb** = PSYCHOANALYZE

an·a·pest /ˈænəˌpest/ *noun* (*technical*) a unit of sound in poetry consisting of two weak or short syllables followed by one strong or long syllable ▶ **an·a·pes·tic** /ˌænəˈpestɪk/ *adj.*

a·naph·o·ra /əˈnæfərə/ *noun* [U] the use of a word that refers to or replaces another word used earlier in a sentence, for example the use of "does" in the sentence "I disagree and so does John." ▶ **an·a·phor·ic** /ˌænəˈfɔːrɪk/ *adj.*

an·a·phy·lax·is /ˌænəfəˈlæksəs/ *noun* [U, C] (*pl.* **an·a·phy·lax·es** /-ˈlæksiz/) (*medical*) an extreme ALLERGIC reaction to something that you eat or touch ▶ **an·a·phy·lac·tic** /ˌænəfəˈlæktɪk/ *adj.*: *anaphylactic shock*

an·ar·chism /ˈænərˌkɪzəm/ *noun* [U] the political belief that laws and governments are not necessary

an·ar·chist /ˈænərkɪst/ *noun* a person who believes that laws and governments are not necessary ▶ **an·ar·chis·tic** /ˌænərˈkɪstɪk/ *adj.*

an·ar·chy /ˈænərki/ *noun* [U] a situation in a country, an organization, etc. in which there is no government, order, or control: *The overthrow of the military regime was followed by a period of anarchy.* ◆ *There was complete anarchy in the classroom when their usual teacher was away.* ▶ **an·ar·chic** /əˈnɑːrkɪk/ (also *less frequent* **an·ar·chi·cal** /-kɪkl/) *adj.*

a·nath·e·ma /əˈnæθəmə/ *noun* [U, C, usually sing.] (*formal*) a thing or an idea that you hate because it is the opposite of what you believe: *Racial prejudice is (an) anathema to me.*

a·nat·o·mist /əˈnætəmɪst/ *noun* a scientist who studies anatomy

a·nat·o·my /əˈnætəmi/ *noun* (*pl.* **a·nat·o·mies**) **1** [U] the scientific study of the structure of human or animal bodies **2** [C, U] the structure of an animal or a plant: *the anatomy of the horse* ◆ *human anatomy* **3** [C] (*humorous*) a person's body: *Various parts of his anatomy were clearly visible.* **4** [C] (*formal*) an examination of what something is like or why it happens: *an anatomy of the current recession* ▶ **an·a·tom·i·cal** /ˌænəˈtɑːmɪkl/ *adj.*: *anatomical diagrams* **an·a·tom·i·cally** /-kli/ *adv.*

-ance, -ence /əns/ *suffix* (in nouns) the action or state of: *assistance* ◆ *confidence*

an·ces·tor /ˈænsestər/ *noun* **1** a person in your family who lived a long time ago **SYN** FOREBEAR: *His ancestors had come to America from Ireland.* **2** an animal that lived in the past, that a modern animal has developed from: *a reptile that was the common ancestor of lizards and turtles* **3** an early form of a machine that later became more developed **SYN** FORERUNNER: *The ancestor of the modern bicycle was called a penny-farthing.* ⊃ compare DESCENDANT ▶ **an·ces·tral** /ænˈsestrəl/ *adj.*: *her ancestral home* (= that had belonged to her ANCESTORS)

an·ces·try /ˈænsestri/ *noun* [C, usually sing., U] (*pl.* **an·ces·tries**) the family or the race of people that you come from: *to have Italian ancestry* ◆ *He was able to trace his ancestry back over 1,000 years.*

an·chor /ˈæŋkər/ *noun, verb*
● *noun* **1** a heavy metal object that is attached to a rope or chain and dropped over the side of a ship or boat to keep it in one place: *to drop anchor* ◆ *The ship lay at anchor two miles off the rocky coast.* ◆ *We weighed anchor* (= pulled it out of the water). **2** a person or thing that gives someone a feeling of safety: *the anchor of the family* **3** = ANCHORMAN, ANCHORWOMAN

anchor

● *verb* **1** [I, T] ~ **(sth)** to let an anchor down from a boat or ship in order to prevent it from moving away: *We anchored off the coast of Newport.* **2** [T] ~ **sth** to fix something firmly in position so that it cannot move: *Make sure the table is securely*

---

v **voice**   θ **thin**   ð **then**   s **so**   z **zoo**   ʃ **she**   ʒ **vision**   x **Chanukah** anchored. **3** [T, usually passive] ~ **sb/sth (in/to sth)** to firmly base something on something else: *Her novels are anchored in everyday experience.* **4** [I, T] ~ **(sth)** to be the person who introduces reports or reads the news on television or radio: *She anchored the evening news for seven years.*

an·chor·age /ˈæŋkərɪdʒ/ *noun* [C, U] **1** a place where ships or boats can anchor **2** a place where something can be fastened to something else: *anchorage points for a baby's car seat*

an·chor·man /ˈæŋkərˌmæn/, **an·chor·wom·an** /ˈæŋkərˌwʊmən/ *noun* (*pl.* **an·chor·men** /-ˌmɛn/, **an·chor·wom·en** /-ˌwɪmən/) (also **an·chor**) a man or woman who presents a radio or television program, and introduces reports by other people

an·cho·vy /ˈæntʃoʊvi; ænˈtʃoʊvi/ *noun* [C, U] (*pl.* **an·cho·vies**) a small fish with a strong salty flavor: *a pizza topped with cheese and anchovies*

an·cient 🔑 /ˈeɪnʃənt/ *adj.*

1 belonging to a period of history that is thousands of years in the past: *ancient civilization* ♦ *ancient Greece* **ANT** MODERN **2** very old; having existed for a very long time: *an ancient oak tree* ♦ (*humorous*) *He's ancient—he must be at least fifty!* **3 the ancients** *noun* [pl.] the people who lived in ancient times, especially the Egyptians, Greeks, and Romans ▶ **an·cient·ly** *adv.: The area where the market was anciently held* (= in ancient times).

ˌancient ˈhistory *noun* [U] **1** the history of societies that existed thousands of years ago, especially in Rome, Greece, and Egypt **2** (*informal*) if something is **ancient history**, it happened or existed a long time ago and is no longer important: *Don't worry, our disagreements are ancient history.*

an·cil·lar·y /ˈænsəˌlɛri/ *adj.* ~ **(to sth) 1** providing necessary support to the main work or activities of an organization **SYN** AUXILIARY: *ancillary staff/services/equipment* ♦ *ancillary workers in the hospital, such as cooks and cleaning staff* **2** in addition to something else but not as important: *ancillary rights*

-ancy, -ency /ənsi/ *suffix* (in nouns) the state or quality of: *expectancy* ♦ *complacency*

and 🔑 /ən; ənd; n; *especially after* /t/ *and* /d/, *strong form* /ænd/ *conj.*

(used to connect words or parts of sentences) **1** also; in addition to: *bread and butter* ♦ *a table, two chairs, and a desk* ♦ *Sue and I left early.* ♦ *Do it slowly and carefully.* ♦ *Can he read and write?* ♦ *I cooked lunch. And I made a cake.* **HELP** Some people think it is incorrect to begin a sentence with **and**. It is used in this way for emphasis, especially in spoken English. **HELP** When **and** is used in common phrases connecting two things or people that are closely linked, the determiner is not usually repeated before the second: *a knife and fork* ♦ *my father and mother*, but: *a knife and a spoon* ♦ *my father and my uncle* **2** added to **SYN** PLUS[1]: *5 and 5 makes 10.* ♦ *What's 47 and 16?* **HELP** When numbers (but not dates) are spoken, **and** is used between the hundreds and the figures that follow: *2,264—two thousand, two hundred, and sixty-four,* but: *1964—nineteen sixty-four.* **3** then; following this: *She came in and took her coat off.* **4 go, come, try, stay, etc.** ~ used before a verb instead of *to*, to show purpose: *Go and get me a pen, please.* ♦ *I'll come and see you soon.* ♦ *We stopped and bought some bread.* **HELP** In this structure **try** can only be used in the infinitive or to tell someone what to do. **5** used to introduce a comment or a question: *"We talked for hours." "And what did you decide?"* **6** as a result: *Miss another class and you'll fail.* **7** used between repeated words to show that something is repeated or continuing: *He tried and tried, but without success.* ♦ *The pain got worse and worse.* **8** used between repeated words or phrases to show that there are important differences between things or people of the same kind: *I like city life but there are cities and there are cities.* ➔ see also AND/OR **9** used when you want someone to add more

details to what they have said: *"I've decided to quit my job." "And?" "I want to become a writer."*

an·dan·te /ɑnˈdɑnteɪ/ *noun* (*music*) a piece of music to be played fairly slowly ▶ **an·dan·te** *adv., adj.*

and/or /ˌænd ˈɔr/ *conj.* (*informal*) used when you say that two situations exist together, or as an alternative to each other: *There is no help for those with lots of luggage and/or small children.*

an·dro·gen /ˈændrədʒən/ *noun* (*biology*) a male sex HORMONE, for example TESTOSTERONE

an·drog·y·nous /ænˈdrɑdʒənəs/ *adj.* having both male and female characteristics; looking neither strongly male nor strongly female

an·droid /ˈændrɔɪd/ *noun* (also **droid**) a ROBOT that looks like a real person

an·ec·do·tal /ˌænɪkˈdoʊtl/ *adj.* based on anecdotes and possibly not true or accurate: *anecdotal evidence* ▶ **an·ec·do·tal·ly** -ˈdoʊtl-i/ *adv.: This reaction has been reported anecdotally by a number of patients.*

an·ec·dote /ˈænɪkˌdoʊt/ *noun* [C, U] **1** a short, interesting, or amusing story about a real person or event: *amusing anecdotes about his brief career as an actor* **2** a personal account of an event: *This research is based on anecdote not fact.*

a·ne·mi·a /əˈnimiə/ *noun* [U] a medical condition in which someone has too few red cells in their blood, making them look pale and feel weak

a·ne·mic /əˈnimɪk/ *adj.* **1** suffering from anemia: *She looks anemic.* **2** weak and not having much effect **SYN** FEEBLE: *an anemic performance*

an·e·mom·e·ter /ˌænəˈmɑmətər/ (also **ˈwind gauge**) *noun* an instrument for measuring the speed of the wind or of a current of gas

a·nem·o·ne /əˈnɛməni/ *noun* a small plant with white, red, blue, or purple flowers that are shaped like cups and have dark centers ➔ see also SEA ANEMONE

an·es·the·sia /ˌænəsˈθiʒə/ *noun* [U] **1** the use of an anesthetic during medical operations **2** (*technical*) the state of being unable to feel anything, especially pain

an·es·the·si·ol·o·gist /ˌænəsˌθiziˈɑlədʒɪst/ *noun* a doctor who studies the use of anesthetics

an·es·thet·ic /ˌænəsˈθɛtɪk/ *noun, adj.*

● *noun* [C, U] a drug that makes a person or an animal unable to feel anything, especially pain, either in the whole body or in a part of the body: *How long will I be under the anesthetic?* ♦ *They gave him a general anesthetic* (= one that makes you become unconscious). ♦ *(a) local anesthetic* (= one that affects only a part of the body)

● *adj.* [only before noun] containing a substance that makes a person or an animal unable to feel pain in all or part of the body: *an anesthetic drug/spray*

an·es·the·tist /əˈnɛsθətɪst/ *noun* a person who is trained to give anesthetics to patients

an·es·the·tize /əˈnɛsθəˌtaɪz/ *verb* ~ **sb** to make a person unable to feel pain, etc., especially by giving them an anesthetic before a medical operation

an·eu·rysm /ˈænyəˌrɪzəm/ *noun* (*medical*) an area of extreme swelling on the wall of an ARTERY

a·new /əˈnu/ *adv.* (*formal*) if someone does something **anew**, they do it again from the beginning or do it in a different way: *They started life anew in Canada.*

an·gel /ˈeɪndʒl/ *noun* **1** a spirit who is believed to be a servant of God, and is sent by God to deliver a message or perform a task. Angels are often shown dressed in white, with wings. ➔ see also GUARDIAN ANGEL **2** a person who is very good and kind; a child who behaves well: *John is no angel, believe me* (= he does not behave well). **3** (*informal*) used when you are talking to someone and you are grateful to them: *Thanks Dad, you're an angel.* ♦ *Be an angel and make me a cup of coffee.*

h **hat**   m **man**   n **no**   ŋ **sing**   l **leg**   r **red**   y **yes**   w **wet**

An·ge·le·no (also **An·ge·li·no**) /ˌændʒəˈlinoʊ/ *noun* (pl. An·ge·le·nos) (*informal*) a person who lives in Los Angeles

an·gel·fish /ˈeɪndʒlˌfɪʃ/ *noun* (pl. an·gel·fish or an·gel·fish·es) a type of brightly colored FRESHWATER or SALT WATER fish with a thin deep body and long FINS

ˈangel food ˌcake *noun* [U, C] a light cake made with the white part of eggs and no fat, often baked in a ring shape

an·gel·ic /ænˈdʒɛlɪk/ *adj.* good, kind, or beautiful; like an angel: *an angelic smile* ▶ **an·gel·i·cally** *adv.* /-kli/

an·gel·i·ca /ænˈdʒɛlɪkə/ *noun* [U] pieces of a plant with a sweet smell, used in cooking

an·ge·lus /ˈændʒələs/ *noun* also **the Angelus** [sing.] (in the Roman Catholic Church) prayers said in the morning, at NOON, and in the evening; a bell rung when it is time for these prayers

an·ger 🔎 /ˈæŋɡər/ *noun, verb*

- *noun* [U] the strong feeling that you have when something has happened that you think is bad and unfair: *Jan slammed her fist on the desk in anger.* ◆ *the growing anger and frustration of young unemployed people* ◆ **~ at sb/sth** *He was filled with anger at the way he had been treated.*

- *verb* **~ sb** [often passive] to make someone angry: *The question clearly angered him.*

an·gi·na /ænˈdʒaɪnə/ (also *technical* **an·gi·na pec·to·ris** /ænˌdʒaɪnə ˈpɛktərəs/) *noun* [U] (*medical*) severe pain in the chest caused by a low supply of blood to the heart during exercise because the arteries (ARTERY) are partly blocked

an·gi·o·plas·ty /ˈændʒiəˌplæsti/ *noun* [C, U] (pl. an·gi·o·plas·ties) (*medical*) a medical operation to repair or open a blocked BLOOD VESSEL, especially either of the two arteries (ARTERY) that supply blood to the heart

an·gle 🔎 /ˈæŋɡl/ *noun, verb*

- *noun* **1** the space between two lines or surfaces that join, measured in degrees: *a 45° angle* ⊃ see also ACUTE ANGLE, ADJACENT ANGLE, CORRESPONDING ANGLES, OBTUSE ANGLE, RIGHT ANGLE, WIDE-ANGLE LENS **2** the direction that something is leaning or pointing in when it is not in a vertical or horizontal line: *The tower of Pisa leans at an angle.* ◆ *The plane was coming in at a steep angle.* ◆ *His hair was sticking out from all angles.* **3** a position from which you look at something: *The photo was taken from an unusual angle.* **4** a particular way of presenting or thinking about a situation, problem, etc.: *We need a new angle for our next advertising campaign.* ◆ *You can look at the issue from many different angles.* ◆ *The article concentrates on the human angle* (= the part that concerns people's emotions) *of the story.*

- *verb* **1** [T] **~ sth** to move or place something so that it is not straight or not directly facing someone or something: *He angled his chair so that he could sit and watch her without distracting her.* **2** [T] **~ sth** to present information, a report, etc. based on a particular way of thinking or for a particular audience: *The program is angled toward younger viewers.* **3** usually **go angling** [I] to catch fish with a line and a hook **PHR V ˈangle for sth** to try to get a particular reaction or response from someone, without directly asking for what you want: *She was angling for a promotion.*

ˈangle ˌbracket *noun* [usually pl.] one of a pair of marks, < >, used around words or figures to separate them from the surrounding text

an·gler /ˈæŋɡlər/ *noun* a person who catches fish (= goes angling) as a hobby ⊃ compare FISHERMAN

An·gli·can /ˈæŋɡlɪkən/ *noun* a member of the Church of England or of a Church connected with it in another country ⊃ see also EPISCOPALIAN ▶ **An·gli·can** *adj.*: *the Anglican Church*

An·gli·cism /ˈæŋɡləˌsɪzəm/ *noun* a word or phrase from the English language that is used in another language: *Many French people try to avoid Anglicisms such as "weekend" and "shopping."*

an·gli·cize /ˈæŋɡləˌsaɪz/ *verb* **~ sb/sth** to make someone or something English in character: *Gutmann anglicized his name to Goodman.*

an·gling /ˈæŋɡlɪŋ/ *noun* [U] the art or sport of catching fish with a line and hook, usually in rivers and lakes rather than in the ocean

An·glo /ˈæŋɡloʊ/ *noun* (pl. An·glos) a white person of European origin

Anglo- /ˈæŋɡloʊ/ *combining form* (in nouns and adjectives) English or British: *Anglo-American* ◆ *Anglophile*

ˌAnglo-ˈCatholic *noun* a member of the part of the Church of England that is most similar to the Roman Catholic Church in its beliefs and practices

an·glo·ma·ni·a /ˌæŋɡloʊˈmeɪniə/ *noun* [U] an extremely strong admiration for England or English customs

ˌAnglo-ˈNorman *noun* [U] a form of Norman French spoken in England in the MIDDLE AGES

An·glo·phile /ˈæŋɡləˌfaɪl/ *noun* a person who is not British but who likes Britain or British things very much

An·glo·pho·bi·a /ˌæŋɡləˈfoʊbiə/ *noun* [U] hatred or fear of England or Britain ▶ **An·glo·phobe** /ˈæŋɡləˌfoʊb/ *noun*: *Her father was an Anglophobe.* **An·glo·pho·bic** /ˌæŋɡləˈfoʊbɪk/ *adj.*

an·glo·phone /ˈæŋɡləˌfoʊn/ *noun* a person who speaks English, especially in countries where English is not the only language that is spoken ▶ **an·glo·phone** *adj.*: *anglophone communities*

ˌAnglo-ˈSaxon *noun* **1** [C] a person whose ANCESTORS were English **2** [C] an English person of the period before the Norman Conquest **3** [U] Old English ▶ **ˌAnglo-ˈSaxon** *adj.*: *Anglo-Saxon kings*

the An·glo·sphere /ˈæŋɡləˌsfɪr/ *noun* [sing.] the group of countries where English is the main language

an·go·ra /ænˈɡɔrə/ *noun* **1** [C] a breed of cat, GOAT, or RABBIT that has long smooth hair **2** [U] a type of soft wool or cloth made from the hair of the angora GOAT or RABBIT: *an angora sweater*

an·gos·tu·ra /ˌæŋɡəˈstʊrə/ *noun* [U] a bitter liquid, flavored with the BARK of a tropical tree, that is used to give flavor to alcoholic drinks

an·gry 🔎 /ˈæŋɡri/ *adj.* (an·gri·er, an·gri·est)

HELP You can also use **more angry** and **most angry**.

1 having strong feelings about something that you dislike very much or about an unfair situation: *Her behavior really made me angry.* ◆ *Thousands of angry demonstrators filled the square.* ◆ *The comments provoked an angry response from union leaders.* ◆ **~ with/at sb** *Please don't be angry with me. It wasn't my fault.* ◆ **~ with/at sb about/for sth** *I was very angry with myself for making such a stupid mistake.* ◆ **~ at/about/over sth** *He felt angry at the injustice of the situation.* ◆ *The passengers grew angry about the delay.* **2** (of a wound) red and infected **3** (*literary*) (of the sea or the sky) dark and STORMY ▶ **an·gri·ly** /-ɡrəli/ *adv.*: *Some senators reacted angrily to the president's remarks.* ◆ *He swore angrily.*

THESAURUS

angry

mad ◆ furious ◆ upset ◆ indignant ◆ irate

These words all describe people feeling and/or showing anger.

angry feeling or showing anger: *Please don't be angry with me.* ◆ *Thousands of angry demonstrators filled the square.*

mad [not before noun] (*informal*) very angry: *He got mad and walked out.* ◆ *She's mad at me for being late.*

furious extremely angry: *He was furious at having been taken out of the game.* ◆ *He was furious with her for ruining the party.*

upset somewhat angry or annoyed: *I was quite upset with him for being late.*

ˌangry young ˈman *noun* a young man who is not happy with society and does not accept its rules

angst /aŋst; æŋst/ *noun* [U] (from *German*) a feeling of anxiety and worry about a situation, or about your life: *songs full of teenage angst*

ˈangst-ˌridden *adj.* having feelings of angst: *a generation of angst-ridden adolescents*

ang·strom /ˈæŋstrəm/ *noun* (*chemistry*, *physics*) a very small unit of length, equal to 1 x 10^{-10} meters, used for measuring WAVELENGTHS and the distance between atoms

angst·y /ˈaŋsti; ˈæŋ-/ *adj.* having or showing feelings of angst: *Stefan plays the role of a rebellious, angsty outsider who joins a terrorist cell.* ◆ *angsty poetry/lyrics*

an·guish /ˈæŋgwɪʃ/ *noun* [U] (*formal*) severe pain, mental suffering, or unhappiness: *He groaned in anguish.* ◆ *Tears of anguish filled her eyes.* ▶ **an·guished** *adj.*: *anguished cries* ◆ *an anguished letter from her prison cell*

an·gu·lar /ˈæŋgyələr/ *adj.* **1** (of a person) thin and without much flesh so that the bones are noticeable: *an angular face* ◆ *a tall angular woman* **2** having angles or sharp corners: *a design of large angular shapes*

An·gus /ˈæŋgəs/ *noun* = BLACK ANGUS

an·i·mal 🔑 /ˈænəml/ *noun, adj.*
- *noun* **1** a creature that is not a bird, a fish, a REPTILE, an insect, or a human: *the animals and birds of South America* ◆ *a small furry animal* ◆ *Fish oils are less saturated than animal fats.* ◆ *domestic animals such as dogs and cats* **2** any living thing that is not a plant or a human: *the animal kingdom* ◆ *This product has not been tested on animals.* ⊃ **picture on page 52** **3** any living creature, including humans: *Humans are the only animals to have developed speech.* ⊃ **collocations at LIFE** ⊃ **compare** VEGETABLE **4** a person who behaves in a cruel or unpleasant way, or who is very dirty: *The person who did this is an animal, a brute.* **5** a particular type of person, thing, organization, etc.: *She's not a political animal.* ◆ *The government which followed the election was a very different animal.* ⊃ **see also** HIGHER ANIMALS, PARTY ANIMAL
- *adj.* [only before noun] relating to the physical needs and basic feelings of people: *animal desires/passion/instincts* ◆ *animal magnetism* (= a quality in someone that other people find attractive, usually in a sexual way)

ˌanimal conˈtrol ˌofficer *noun* (*formal*) a person whose job is to catch animals that are walking freely in the streets and do not seem to have a home ⊃ **compare** DOGCATCHER

ˌanimal ˈhusbandry *noun* [U] (*technical*) farming that involves keeping animals to produce food

ˌanimal ˈrights *noun* [pl.] the rights of animals to be treated well, for example by not being hunted or used for medical research: *His research work was attacked by animal rights activists.*

an·i·mate *verb, adj.*
- *verb* /ˈænəˌmeɪt/ **1** ~ sth to make something more lively or full of energy: *A smile suddenly animated her face.* **2** [usually passive] ~ sth to make models, toys, etc. seem to move in a movie by rapidly showing slightly different pictures of them in a series, one after another
- *adj.* /ˈænəmət/ (*formal*) living; having life: *animate beings* **ANT** INANIMATE

an·i·mat·ed /ˈænəˌmeɪtəd/ *adj.* **1** full of interest and energy **SYN** LIVELY: *an animated discussion/conversation* ◆ *Her face suddenly became animated.* **2** (of pictures, drawings, etc. in a movie) made to look as if they are moving: *animated cartoons/graphics/models* ▶ **an·i·mat·ed·ly** *adv.*: *People were talking animatedly.*

an·i·ma·tion /ˌænəˈmeɪʃn/ *noun* **1** [U] energy and enthusiasm in the way you look, behave, or speak: *His face was drained of all color and animation.* ⊃ **see also** SUSPENDED ANIMATION **2** [U] the process of making movies, videos, and computer games in which drawings or models of people and animals seem to move: *computer/cartoon animation* **3** [C] a movie in which drawings of people and animals seem to move: *The electronic dictionary included some animations.*

an·i·ma·tor /ˈænəˌmeɪtər/ *noun* a person who makes animated movies

an·i·ma·tron·ics /ˌænəməˈtrɑnɪks/ *noun* [U] the process of making and operating ROBOTS that look like real people or animals, used in movies and other types of entertainment ▶ **an·i·ma·tron·ic** *adj.*

an·i·me /ˈænəˌmeɪ/ *noun* [U] Japanese movie and television ANIMATION, often with a SCIENCE FICTION subject

an·i·mism /ˈænəˌmɪzəm/ *noun* [U] **1** the belief that plants, objects, and natural things such as the weather have a living soul **2** belief in a power that organizes and controls the universe ▶ **an·i·mist** /-mɪst/ *noun* **an·i·mis·tic** /ˌænəˈmɪstɪk/ *adj.*

an·i·mos·i·ty /ˌænəˈmɑsəti/ *noun* [U, C] (*pl.* **an·i·mos·i·ties**) a strong feeling of opposition, anger, or hatred **SYN** HOSTILITY: **~ (toward(s) sb/sth)** *He felt no animosity toward his critics.* ◆ **~ (between A and B)** *personal animosities between members of the two groups*

an·i·mus /ˈænəməs/ *noun* [U, sing.] **~ (against sb/sth)** (*formal*) a strong feeling of opposition, anger, or hatred

an·i·on /ˈænˌaɪən/ *noun* (*chemistry*, *physics*) an ION with a negative electrical CHARGE ⊃ **compare** CATION

an·ise /ˈænəs/ *noun* [U] a plant with seeds that smell sweet

an·i·seed /ˈænəsid/ *noun* [U] the dried seeds of the anise plant, used to give flavor to alcoholic drinks and candy

A·ni·shi·na·be /aˌnɪʃəˈnɑbeɪ/ *noun* (*pl.* **A·ni·shi·na·be**) (also **Chip·pe·wa, O·jib·wa**) a member of a Native American people, many of whom live in the U.S. states of Michigan, Wisconsin, and Minnesota, and in Québec, Ontario, Manitoba, and Saskatchewan in Canada

ankh /aŋk/ *noun* an object or design like a cross but with a LOOP instead of the top arm, sometimes worn as jewelry. The ankh was used in ancient Egypt as the symbol of life.

ankh

an·kle 🔑 /ˈæŋkl/ *noun* the joint connecting the foot to the leg: *to sprain/break your ankle* ◆ *My ankles have swollen.* ◆ *We found ourselves ankle-deep in water.* ◆ *ankle boots* (= that cover the ankle) ⊃ **picture at BODY**

an·klet /ˈæŋklət/ *noun* **1** a piece of jewelry worn around the ankle **2** a type of very short sock

an·ky·lo·saur /ˈæŋkəlouˌsɔr/ *noun* a type of plant-eating DINOSAUR covered with hard plates made of bone for protection

an·nals /ˈænlz/ *noun* [pl.] **1** an official record of events or activities year by year; historical records: *His deeds went down in the annals of American history.* **2** used in the title of academic JOURNALS: *Annals of Family Medicine, vol. viii*

an·neal /əˈnil/ *verb* ~ sth (*technical*) to heat metal or glass

ʌ cup   ə about   eɪ say   aɪ five   ɔɪ boy   aʊ now   oʊ go   ər bird

and allow it to cool slowly, in order to make it stronger or softer

an·nex *verb, noun*
- *verb* /əˈnɛks; ˈænɪks/ ~ **sth** to take control of a country, region, etc., especially by force **SYN** OCCUPY: *Germany annexed Austria in 1938.* ▶ **an·nex·a·tion** /ˌænɪkˈseɪʃn; ˌænɛk-/ *noun* [U, C]
- *noun* /ˈænɛks; ˈænɪks/ **1** a building that is added to, or is near, a larger one and that provides extra living or work space: *Our rooms were in the annex.* **2** (*formal*) an extra section of a document

an·ni·hi·late /əˈnaɪəˌleɪt/ *verb* **1** ~ **sb/sth/yourself** to destroy someone or something completely: *The human race has enough weapons to annihilate itself.* **2** ~ **sb/sth** to defeat someone or something completely: *She annihilated her opponent, who failed to win a single game.* ▶ **an·ni·hi·la·tion** /əˌnaɪəˈleɪʃn/ *noun* [U]: *the annihilation of the whole human race*

an·ni·ver·sa·ry 🔑 /ˌænɪˈvərsəri/ *noun* (*pl.* **an·ni·ver·sa·ries**)
a date that is an exact number of years after the date of an important or special event: *on the anniversary of his wife's death* ◆ *to celebrate your wedding anniversary* ◆ *the school's 25th anniversary celebrations* ➔ collocations at MARRIAGE

an·no·tate /ˈænəˌteɪt/ *verb* ~ **sth** to add notes to a book or text, giving explanations or comments ▶ **an·no·tat·ed** *adj.*: *an annotated edition* **an·no·ta·tion** /ˌænəˈteɪʃn/ *noun* [C, U]: *It will be published with annotations and an index.*

an·nounce 🔑 /əˈnaʊns/ *verb*
1 to tell people something officially, especially about a decision, plans, etc.: ~ **sth** *They haven't formally announced their engagement yet.* ◆ (*figurative*) *The sound of the doorbell announced Jack's arrival.* ◆ ~ **sth to sb** *The government yesterday announced to the media plans to create a million new jobs.* **HELP** You cannot "announce someone something": ~~*They announced us their decision.*~~ ◆ ~ **that…** *We are pleased to announce that all five candidates were successful.* ◆ **it is announced that…** *It was announced that new speed restrictions would be introduced.* ➔ note at DECLARE **2** to give information about something in a public place, especially through a LOUDSPEAKER: ~ **sth** *Has our flight been announced yet?* ◆ **+ speech** *"Flight 897 to Seattle is now boarding," the loudspeaker announced.* ◆ ~ **that…** *They announced that the flight would be delayed.* **3** to say something in a loud and/or serious way: **+ speech** *"I quit smoking," she announced.* ◆ ~ **that…** *She announced that she had quit smoking.* ➔ thesaurus box at DECLARE **4** ~ **yourself/sb** to tell someone your name or someone else's name when you or they arrive at a place: *Would you announce the guests as they arrive?* (= call out their names, for example at a formal party) **5** ~ **sth** to introduce, or give information about, a program on radio or television

an·nounce·ment 🔑 /əˈnaʊnsmənt/ *noun*
1 [C] a spoken or written statement that informs people about something: *to make an announcement* ◆ *Today's announcement of a peace agreement came after weeks of discussion.* ◆ *Announcements of births, marriages, and deaths appear in some newspapers.* **2** [U] the act of publicly informing people about something: *Announcement of the verdict was accompanied by shouts and cheers.*

an·nounc·er /əˈnaʊnsər/ *noun* **1** a person who introduces, or gives information about, programs on radio or television ➔ see also HOST **2** a person who gives information about something in a train station, an airport, etc., especially through a LOUDSPEAKER

an·noy 🔑 /əˈnɔɪ/ *verb*
1 to make someone slightly angry **SYN** IRRITATE: ~ **sb** *His constant joking was beginning to annoy her.* ◆ *It really annoys me when people forget to say thank you.* ◆ ~ **sb to do sth** *It annoys me to have to pay the check every time.* **2** ~ **sb** to make someone uncomfortable or unable to relax **SYN** BOTHER: *He swatted a fly that was annoying him.*

an·noy·ance /əˈnɔɪəns/ *noun* **1** [U] the feeling of being slightly angry **SYN** IRRITATION: *He could not conceal his annoyance at being interrupted.* ◆ *Much to our annoyance, they decided not to come after all.* ◆ *She stamped her foot in annoyance.* **2** [C] something that makes you slightly angry

an·noyed 🔑 /əˈnɔɪd/ *adj.* [not usually before noun]
slightly angry **SYN** IRRITATED: ~ **(with sb) (at/about sth)** *He was beginning to get very annoyed with me about my carelessness.* ◆ *I was annoyed with myself for giving in so easily.* ◆ *I bet she was annoyed at having to write it out again.* ◆ ~ **that…** *I was annoyed that they hadn't shown up.* ◆ ~ **to find, see, etc.** *He was annoyed to find himself blushing.*

an·noy·ing 🔑 /əˈnɔɪɪŋ/ *adj.*
making someone feel slightly angry **SYN** IRRITATING: *This interruption is very annoying.* ◆ *Her most annoying habit was eating with her mouth open.* ▶ **an·noy·ing·ly** *adv.*

an·nu·al 🔑 **AWL** /ˈænyuəl/ *adj., noun*
- *adj.* [usually before noun] **1** happening or done once every year: *an annual meeting/event/report* **2** relating to a period of one year: *an annual income/subscription/budget* ◆ *an average annual growth rate of 8%* ◆ *annual rainfall* ➔ compare BIANNUAL
- *noun* **1** any plant that grows and dies within one year or season ➔ compare BIENNIAL, PERENNIAL **2** a book that is published once a year, with the same title each time, but different contents: *the museum's design annual*

an·nu·al·ized /ˈænyuəˌlaɪzd/ *adj.* (*technical*) calculated for a period of a year but based on the amounts for a shorter period

an·nu·al·ly 🔑 **AWL** /ˈænyuəli/ *adv.*
once a year: *The exhibition is held annually.*

an·nu·ity /əˈnuəti/ *noun* (*pl.* **an·nu·i·ties**) **1** a fixed amount of money paid to someone each year, usually for the rest of their life **2** a type of insurance or investment that pays a fixed amount of money to someone each year

an·nul /əˈnʌl/ *verb* (-ll-) ~ **sth** to state officially that something is no longer legally valid: *Their marriage was annulled after just two months.* ▶ **an·nul·ment** *noun* [C, U]

an·nu·lar /ˈænyələr/ *adj.* (*technical*) shaped like a ring

the An·nun·ci·a·tion /əˌnʌnsiˈeɪʃn/ *noun* [sing.] (in the Christian religion) the occasion when Mary was told that she was to be the mother of Christ, celebrated on March 25

an·ode /ˈænoʊd/ *noun* (*technical*) the ELECTRODE in an electrical device where oxidation (OXIDIZE) occurs; the positive electrode in an electrolytic (ELECTROLYTE) cell and the negative electrode in a battery ➔ compare CATHODE

an·o·dize /ˈænəˌdaɪz/ *verb* ~ **sth** to cover a metal, especially ALUMINUM, with a layer of OXIDE in order to protect it

an·o·dyne /ˈænəˌdaɪn/ *adj.* (*formal*) unlikely to cause disagreement or offend anyone; not expressing strong opinions **SYN** BLAND

a·noint /əˈnɔɪnt/ *verb* ~ **sb/sth (with sth)** to put oil or water on someone's head as part of a religious ceremony: *The priest anointed her with oil.*

a·nom·a·lous /əˈnɑmələs/ *adj.* (*formal*) different from what is normal or expected ▶ **a·nom·a·lous·ly** *adv.*

a·nom·a·ly /əˈnɑməli/ *noun* (*pl.* **a·nom·a·lies**) ~ **(in sth)** a thing, situation, etc. that is different from what is normal or expected: *the many anomalies in the tax system* ◆ *the apparent anomaly that those who produced the wealth, the workers, were the poorest*

an·o·mie (also **an·o·my**) /ˈænəmi/ *noun* [U] (*formal*) a lack of social or moral standards

a·non /əˈnɑn/ *adv.* (*old-fashioned* or *literary*) soon: *See you anon.*

anon. *abbr.* (in writing) ANONYMOUS

an·o·nym·i·ty /ˌænəˈnɪməti/ *noun* [U] **1** the state of remaining unknown to most other people: *Names of people in*

The Animal Kingdom

birds

webbed foot · talons

beak (*also* bill) · wing · tail · toe · claw

crest

crest · feather · egg · nest

poultry and game

pheasant · duck

turkey · chicken

birds of prey

bald eagle · vulture · barn owl

seabirds

gull · albatross · puffin

mammals

ear · muzzle · whisker · dog

bat · coat

tail · mane · paw · claw · lion

antlers · deer · horn · goat · tusk · trunk · elephant

hooves

primates

chimpanzee · monkey · prehensile tail

marsupials

koala (*also* koala bear) · eucalyptus tree · joey · pouch · kangaroo

cetacean

blowhole · sperm whale

t tea   ţ butter   d did   k cat   g got   tʃ chin   dʒ June   f fall

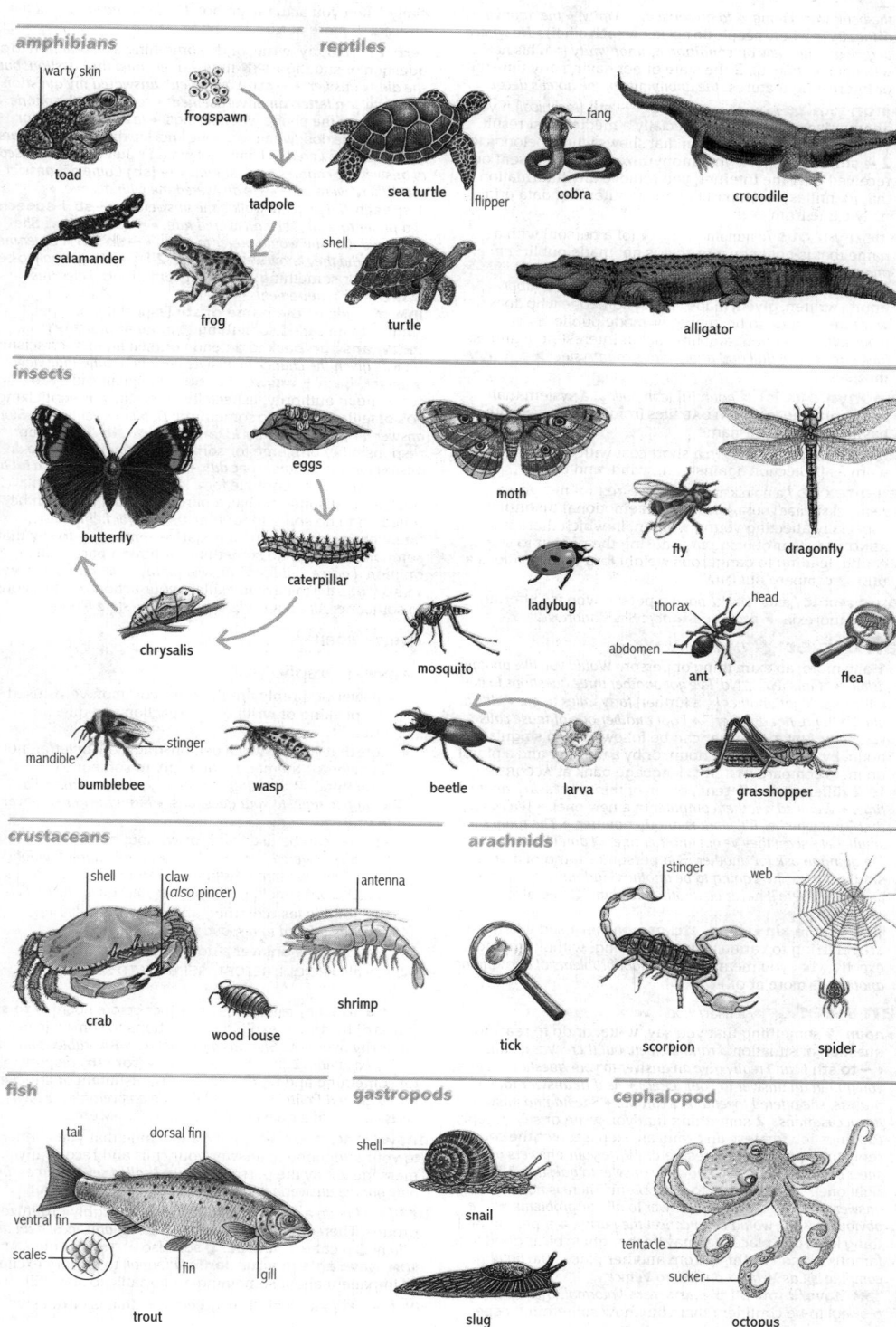

amphibians

warty skin

toad

frogspawn

tadpole

salamander

frog

reptiles

sea turtle

flipper

fang

cobra

crocodile

shell

turtle

alligator

insects

eggs

butterfly

caterpillar

chrysalis

mosquito

moth

ladybug

thorax

abdomen

head

ant

fly

dragonfly

flea

mandible

stinger

bumblebee

wasp

beetle

larva

grasshopper

crustaceans

shell

claw
(*also* pincer)

antenna

shrimp

crab

wood louse

arachnids

stinger

web

tick

scorpion

spider

fish

tail

dorsal fin

ventral fin

scales

fin

gill

trout

gastropods

shell

snail

slug

cephalopod

tentacle

sucker

octopus

the book were changed to preserve anonymity. ◆ the anonymity of the city (= where people do not know each other) ◆ He agreed to give an interview **on condition of anonymity** (= if his name was not mentioned). **2** the state of not having any unusual or interesting features: *the anonymity of the hotel's decor*

a·non·y·mize /əˈnɑnəˌmaɪz/ verb **1 ~ sth** (technical) if you **anonymize** a test result, especially a medical test result, you remove any information that shows who it belongs to **2 ~ sth** (computing) if you **anonymize** data that is sent or received over the Internet, you remove any information that identifies which particular computer that data originally came from

a·non·y·mous /əˈnɑnəməs/ adj. **1** (of a person) with a name that is not known or that is not made public: *an anonymous donor* ◆ *The money was donated by a local businessman who wishes to **remain anonymous**.* **2** (abbr. anon.) written, given, made, etc. by someone who does not want their name to be known or made public: *an anonymous letter* **3** without any unusual or interesting features: *long stretches of dull and anonymous countryside* ▶ **a·non·y·mous·ly** adv.

a,nonymous FTˈP noun [U] (computing) a system that allows anyone to DOWNLOAD files from the Internet without having to give their name

an·o·rak /ˈænəˌræk/ noun a short coat with a HOOD that is worn as protection against rain, wind, and cold

an·o·rex·i·a /ˌænəˈrɛksiə/ (also **an·o·rex·i·a ner·vo·sa** /ˌænəˌrɛksiə nərˈvousə/) noun [U] an emotional DISORDER, especially affecting young women, in which there is an ABNORMAL fear of being fat, causing the person to stop eating, leading to dangerous weight loss ➲ collocations at DIET ➲ compare BULIMIA

an·o·rex·ic /ˌænəˈrɛksɪk/ noun a person who is suffering from anorexia ▶ **an·o·rex·ic** adj.: *She's anorexic.*

an·oth·er 🔑 /əˈnʌðər/ det., pron.

1 one more; an extra thing or person: *Would you like another drink?* ◆ *"Finished?" "No, I've got another three questions to do."* ◆ *We've still got another* (= a further) *forty miles to go.* ◆ *"It's a bill." "Oh no, not another!"* ◆ *I got another one of those calls yesterday.* **HELP** Another can be followed by a singular noun, by of and a plural noun, or by a number and a plural noun. ➲ compare OTHER ➲ language bank at ACCORDING TO **2** different; a different person or thing: *Let's do it another time.* ◆ *We need another computer* (= a new one). ◆ *We can try that—but whether it'll work is another matter.* ◆ *The room's too small. Let's see if they've got another one.* ◆ *I don't like this room. I'm going to ask for another.* **3** a person or thing of a very similar type: *She's going to be another Madonna* (= as famous as her). ◆ *There'll never be another like him.* ➲ see also ONE ANOTHER

IDM **of one kind, type, etc. or another** used when you are referring to various types of a thing, without saying exactly what you mean: *We've all got problems of one kind or another.* ➲ more at ONE

an·swer 🔑 /ˈænsər/ noun, verb

● **noun 1** something that you say, write, or do to react to a question or situation: *I rang the bell, but there was no answer.* ◆ **~ to sth** *I can't really give an answer to your question.* ◆ *Have you gotten an answer to your letter?* ◆ *As if in answer to our prayers, she offered to lend us $10,000.* ◆ *She had no answer to the accusations.* **2** something that you write or say in reply to a question in a test, an exam, an exercise, etc.; the correct reply to a question in a test, etc.: *Write your answers on the sheet provided.* ◆ *Do you know the answer to question 12* (= the right one)? **3** a solution to a problem: *There is no easy answer.* ◆ *This could be the answer to all our problems.* ◆ *The obvious answer would be to cancel the party.* **4** a person or thing from one place that may be thought to be as good as a famous person or thing from another place: *The hotel complex is Las Vegas's answer to Venice.* **IDM** **have/know all the answers** (informal, often disapproving) to be confident that you know something, espe-

cially when you actually do not: *He thinks he knows all the answers.* ➲ more at NO

● **verb 1** [I, T] to say, write, or do something as a reaction to a question or situation **SYN** REPLY: *I repeated the question, but she didn't answer.* ◆ **~ sth** *You haven't answered my question.* ◆ *to answer a letter/an advertisement* ◆ *to answer the phone* (= to pick up the phone when it rings) ◆ *to answer the door* (= to open the door when someone knocks/rings) ◆ *My prayers have been answered* (= I have got what I wanted). ◆ *He refused to answer the charges against him.* ◆ **~ (sb)** *Come on, answer me! Where were you?* ◆ *He answered me with a smile.* ◆ **+ speech** *"I'd prefer to walk," she answered.* ◆ **~ sb + speech** *"I'd prefer to walk," she answered him.* ◆ **~ (sb) that...** *She answered that she would prefer to walk.* ◆ **~ sb sth** *Answer me this: How did they know we were here?* **2** [T] **~ sth** (formal) to be suitable for something; to match something: *Does this answer your requirements?*

IDM **answer to the name of sth** (especially of a pet animal) to be called something ➲ more at DESCRIPTION **PHR V** **answer ˈback** to defend yourself against criticism: *He was given the chance to answer back in a radio interview.* **,answer ˈback | ,answer sb ˈback** to speak rudely to someone in authority, especially when they are criticizing you or telling you to do something: *Don't answer back!* ◆ *Stop answering your mother back!* **ˈanswer for sth 1** to accept responsibility or blame for something: *You will have to answer for your behavior one day.* ◆ *This government has a lot to answer for* (= is responsible for a lot of bad things). **2** to promise that someone has a particular quality or can be relied on to do something: *I can answer for her honesty.* **ˈanswer for sb** (usually in negative sentences) to say that someone else will do something or have a particular opinion: *I agree, but I can't answer for my colleagues.* **ˈanswer to sb (for sth)** to have to explain your actions or decisions to someone: *All sales clerks answer to the store manager.*

WHICH WORD?

answer ◆ reply

■ **Answer** and **reply** are the most common verbs used for speaking or writing as a reaction to a question, letter, etc.

■ Note that you **answer** a person, question, or letter, not "answer to" them, but you **reply to** someone or something: *I'm writing to answer your questions.* ◆ *I'm writing to reply to your questions.* ◆ ~~I'm writing to answer to your questions.~~

■ **Answer** can be used with or without an object: *I haven't answered her e-mail yet.* ◆ *I knocked on the door but no one answered.* **Reply** is often used with the actual words spoken: *"I won't let you down," he replied.*

■ **Respond** is less common and more formal: *The directors refused to respond to questions.*

■ You can only **answer** a door or a phone.

➲ see also REJOIN, RETORT, GET BACK TO SB

---

an·swer·a·ble /ˈænsərəbl/ adj. **1** [not before noun] **~ to sb (for sth)** having to explain your actions to someone in authority over you: *She was a free agent, answerable to no one for her behavior.* **2** [not before noun] **~ (for sth)** responsible for something and ready to accept punishment or criticism for it: *Elected Politicians must be made answerable for their decisions.* **3** (of a question) that can be answered

ˈanswering ma,chine noun a machine that you connect to your telephone to answer your calls and record any message left by the person calling: *I called several times, but only got the answering machine.* ➲ compare VOICE MAIL

ant /ænt/ noun a small insect that lives in highly organized groups. There are many types of ants: *an ants' nest* ◆ *an ant colony* ➲ picture at ANIMAL ➲ see also ANTHILL, FIRE ANT **IDM** **have ants in your pants** (informal) to be very excited or impatient about something and unable to stay still

-ant, -ent /ənt/ suffix **1** (in adjectives) that is or does

---

h **hat**   m **man**   n **no**   ŋ **sing**   l **leg**   r **red**   y **yes**   w **wet**

something: *significant* ◆ *different* **2** (in nouns) a person or thing that: *inhabitant* ◆ *deterrent*

ant·ac·id /ænt'æsɪd/ *noun* a medicine that prevents or corrects ACIDITY, especially in the stomach

an·tag·o·nism /æn'tægə͵nɪzəm/ *noun* [U, pl.] **~ (to/toward(s) sb/sth)** | **~ (between A and B)** feelings of hatred and opposition **SYN** HOSTILITY: *The antagonism he felt toward his old enemy was still very strong.* ◆ *the racial antagonisms in society*

an·tag·o·nist /æn'tægənɪst/ *noun* (*formal*) a person who strongly opposes someone or something **SYN** OPPONENT

an·tag·o·nis·tic /æn͵tægə'nɪstɪk/ *adj.* **~ (to/toward(s) sb/sth)** (*formal*) showing or feeling opposition **SYN** HOSTILE ▶ **an·tag·o·nis·ti·cally** /-kli/ *adv.*

an·tag·o·nize /æn'tægə͵naɪz/ *verb* **~ sb** to do something to make someone angry with you: *Not wishing to antagonize her further, he said no more.*

the Ant·arc·tic /ænt'ɑrktɪk; -'ɑrtɪk/ *noun* [sing.] the regions of the world around the South Pole ▶ **Ant·arc·tic** *adj.* [only before noun]: *Antarctic explorers* ⊃ compare ARCTIC

the Ant͵arctic 'Circle *noun* [sing.] the line of LATITUDE 66° 33′ South ⊃ picture at EARTH ⊃ compare ARCTIC CIRCLE

an·te /'ænti/ *noun, verb*
● *noun*
IDM **raise/up the ante** to increase the level of something, especially demands or sums of money
● *verb*
PHRV **ante 'up (sth)** to pay a sum of money, especially in a card game in which you pay in advance: *About 100 poker players anted up $300.* ◆ *The owners have to ante up if they want to attract the best people.*

ante- /'ænti; 'ænti/ *prefix* (in nouns, adjectives, and verbs) before; in front of: *ante-room* ◆ *antedate* ⊃ compare POST-, PRE-

ant·eat·er /'ænt͵itər/ *noun* an animal with a long nose and tongue that eats ANTS

an·te·bel·lum /͵ænti'bɛləm/ *adj.* [only before noun] connected with the years before a war, especially the American Civil War: *the laws of the antebellum South*

an·te·ced·ent /͵æntə'sidnt/ *noun, adj.*
● *noun* **1** [C] (*formal*) a thing or an event that exists or comes before another, and may have influenced it **2 antecedents** [pl.] (*formal*) the people in someone's family who lived a long time ago **SYN** ANCESTORS (1) **3** [C] (*grammar*) a word or phrase to which the following word, especially a pronoun, refers: *In "He grabbed the ball and threw it in the air," "ball" is the antecedent of "it."*
● *adj.* (*formal*) previous: *antecedent events*

an·te·cham·ber /'ænti͵tʃeɪmbər/ *noun* (*formal*) = ANTEROOM

an·te·date /'ænti͵deɪt/ *verb* **~ sth** = PREDATE

an·te·di·lu·vi·an /͵æntidə'luviən/ *adj.* (*formal or humorous*) very old-fashioned

an·te·lope /'ænti͵loʊp/
noun (*pl.* **an·te·lope** or
an·te·lopes) an African or
Asian animal like a DEER,
that runs very fast. There
are many types of ante-
lopes.

antelope

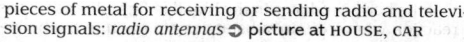

an·ten·na /æn'tɛnə/ *noun*
1 (*pl.* **an·ten·nae** /-ni/)
either of the two long thin
parts on the heads of some
insects and some animals
that live in shells, used to
feel and touch things with **SYN** FEELER ⊃ picture at
ANIMAL: (*figurative*) *The senator was praised for his acute political antennae* (= ability to understand complicated political situations). **2** (*pl.* **an·ten·nas** or **an·ten·nae**) (also
aer·i·al) a piece of equipment made of wire or long straight

pieces of metal for receiving or sending radio and television signals: *radio antennas* ⊃ picture at HOUSE, CAR

an·te·ri·or /æn'tɪriər/ *adj.* [only before noun] (*technical*) (of a part of the body) at or near the front **ANT** POSTERIOR

an·te·room /'ænti͵rum; -͵rʊm/ (also *formal* **an·te·cham·ber**) *noun* a room where people can wait before entering a larger room, especially in an important public building

an·them /'ænθəm/ *noun* **1** a song that has a special importance for a country, an organization, or a particular group of people and is sung on special occasions: *The Olympic anthem was played at the opening and closing ceremonies.* ⊃ see also NATIONAL ANTHEM **2** a short religious song for a CHOIR (= a group of singers), often with an organ

an·the·mic /æn'θiɪmɪk; -'θɛ-/ *adj.* (*formal*) (of a piece of music) that makes you feel happy and enthusiastic

an·ther /'ænθər/ *noun* (*biology*) the part of a flower at the top of a STAMEN that produces POLLEN ⊃ picture at PLANT

ant·hill /'ænthɪl/ *noun* a pile of earth formed by ANTS over their nests

an·thol·o·gize /æn'θɑlə͵dʒaɪz/ *verb* **~ sb/sth** to include a writer or piece of writing in an anthology

an·thol·o·gy /æn'θɑlədʒi/ *noun* (*pl.* **an·thol·o·gies**) a col-
lection of poems, stories, etc. that have been written by different people and published together in a book

an·thra·cite /'ænθrə͵saɪt/ *noun* [U] a very hard type of coal that burns slowly without producing a lot of smoke or flames

an·thrax /'ænθræks/ *noun* [U] a serious disease that affects sheep and cows and sometimes people, and can cause death

anthropo- /'ænθrəpoʊ; -pə/ *combining form* (in nouns, adjectives, and adverbs) connected with humans: *anthropology* ◆ *anthropocentric*

an·thro·po·cen·tric /͵ænθrəpə'sɛntrɪk/ *adj.* believing that humans are more important than anything else ▶ **an·thro·po·cen·trism** /͵ænθrəpə'sɛntrɪzəm/ *noun* [U]

an·thro·poid /'ænθrə͵pɔɪd/ *adj., noun* (*technical*)
● *adj.* (of an APE) looking like a human
● *noun* any type of APE that is similar to a human

an·thro·pol·o·gist /͵ænθrə'pɑlədʒɪst/ *noun* a person who studies anthropology

an·thro·pol·o·gy /͵ænθrə'pɑlədʒi/ *noun* [U] the study of the human race, especially of its origins, development, customs, and beliefs ▶ **an·thro·po·log·i·cal** /͵ænθrəpə-
'lɑdʒɪkl/ *adj.*

an·thro·po·mor·phic /͵ænθrəpə'mɔrfɪk/ *adj.* (of beliefs or ideas) treating gods, animals, or objects as if they had human qualities ▶ **an·thro·po·mor·phism** /͵ænθrəpə-
'mɔrfɪzəm/ *noun* [U]

an·ti /'æntaɪ; 'ænti/ *prep.* (*informal*) if someone is **anti** someone or something, they do not like or agree with that person or thing ⊃ compare PRO

anti- 🔑 /'ænti; 'æntaɪ; 'ænti/ *prefix*
(in nouns and adjectives) **1** opposed to; against: *antitank weapons* ◆ *antisocial* ⊃ compare PRO- **2** the opposite of: *antihero* ◆ *anticlimax* **3** preventing: *antifreeze*

an·ti·air·craft /'æntiˈɛrkræft; 'æntaɪ/ *adj.* [only before noun] designed to destroy enemy aircraft: *antiaircraft fire/guns/
missiles*

an·ti·bac·te·ri·al /͵æntibæk'tɪriəl; ͵æntaɪ-/ *adj.* that kills bacteria: *antibacterial treatments*

an·ti·bi·ot·ic /͵æntibaɪ'ɑtɪk; ͵æntaɪ-/ *noun* [usually pl.] a substance, for example PENICILLIN, that can destroy or prevent the growth of bacteria, and cure infections: *The doctor put her on antibiotics* (= told her to take them). ▶ **an·ti·bi·ot·ic** *adj.*: *an antibiotic drug* ◆ *effective antibiotic treatment*

an·ti·bod·y /'ænti͵bɑdi/ *noun* (*pl.* **an·ti·bod·ies**) a substance that the body produces in the blood to fight disease, or as a reaction when certain substances are put into the body

an·ti·choice /ˌænti'tʃɔɪs; ˈæntaɪ-/ *adj.* (*disapproving*) against giving women the right to have an ABORTION ⊃ compare PRO-CHOICE, PRO-LIFE

An·ti·christ /ˈænti̩kraɪst; ˈæntaɪ-/ usually **the Antichrist** *noun* [sing.] (in Christianity) the DEVIL; Christ's greatest enemy

an·tic·i·pate 🔑 ▪AWL▪ /æn'tɪsə̩peɪt/ *verb*
1 to expect something: ~ **sth** *We don't anticipate any major problems.* ◆ *Our anticipated arrival time is 8:30.* ◆ *The eagerly anticipated movie will be released next month.* ◆ ~ **doing sth** *They anticipate moving to bigger premises by the end of the year.* ◆ ~ **sth doing sth** *I don't anticipate it being a problem.* ◆ ~ **that...** *We anticipate that sales will rise next year.* ◆ **it is anticipated that...** *It is anticipated that inflation will stabilize at 3%.* ⊃ compare UNANTICIPATED **2** to see what might happen in the future and take action to prepare for it: ~ **sth** *We need someone who can anticipate and respond to changes in the fashion industry.* ◆ ~ **what, how, that, etc....** *Try to anticipate what the interviewers will ask.* **3** ~ **(doing) sth** | ~ **(sth doing) sth** to think with pleasure and excitement about something that is going to happen: *We eagerly anticipated the day we would finish school.* **4** ~ **sb (doing sth)** (*formal*) to do something before it can be done by someone else SYN FORESTALL: *When Scott reached the South Pole, he found that Amundsen had anticipated him.* ▶ **an·tic·i·pa·to·ry** /æn'tɪsəpə̩tɔri/ *adj.* (*formal*): *a fast anticipatory movement by the goaltender*

an·tic·i·pa·tion ▪AWL▪ /æn̩tɪsə'peɪʃn/ *noun* [U] **1** the fact of seeing that something might happen in the future and perhaps doing something about it now: *He bought extra food in anticipation of more people coming than he'd invited.* **2** a feeling of excitement about something (usually something good) that is going to happen: *happy/eager/excited anticipation* ◆ *The courtroom was filled with anticipation.*

an·ti·cler·i·cal /ˌænti'klerɪkl; ˌæntaɪ-/ *adj.* opposed to priests and their influence in political life: *anticlerical movements in the seventeenth century* ▶ **an·ti·cler·i·cal·ism** /-'klerɪkl̩ɪzəm/ *noun* [U]

an·ti·cli·max /ˌænti'klaɪmæks; ˌæntaɪ-/ *noun* [C, U] a situation that is disappointing because it happens at the end of something that was much more exciting, or because it is not as exciting as you expected: *Traveling in Europe was something of an anticlimax after the years he'd spent in Africa.* ◆ *a sense/feeling of anticlimax* ⊃ compare CLIMAX ▶ **an·ti·cli·mac·tic** /-klaɪ'mæktɪk/ *adj.*

an·ti·cline /ˈænti̩klaɪn/ *noun* (*geology*) an area of ground where layers of rock in the earth's surface have been folded into a curve that is higher in the middle than at the ends ⊃ compare SYNCLINE

an·ti·co·ag·u·lant /ˌæntikoʊ'ægyələnt; ˌæntaɪ-/ *noun* (*medical*) a substance that stops the blood from becoming thick and forming CLOTS

an·ti·con·vul·sant /ˌæntikən'vʌlsənt; ˌæntaɪ-/ *noun* a drug used to prevent FITS or similar illnesses ▶ **an·ti·con·vul·sant** *adj.*

an·tics /ˈæntɪks/ *noun* [pl.] **1** behavior that is silly and funny in a way that people usually like: *The kids were laughing and cheering to the antics of the clown and his dog.* **2** behavior that is ridiculous or dangerous

an·ti·cy·clone /ˌænti'saɪkloʊn; ˌæntaɪ-/ *noun* an area of high air pressure that produces calm weather conditions with clear skies ⊃ compare DEPRESSION

an·ti·de·pres·sant /ˌæntidɪ'presnt; ˌæntaɪ-/ *noun* a drug used to treat DEPRESSION ▶ **an·ti·de·pres·sant** *adj.* [only before noun]: *antidepressant drugs*

an·ti·dote /ˈænti̩doʊt/ *noun* **1** ~ **(to sth)** a substance that controls the effects of a poison or disease: *There is no known antidote to the poison.* **2** ~ **(to sth)** anything that takes away the effects of something unpleasant: *A Caribbean cruise was the perfect antidote to a long cold winter.*

an·ti·freeze /ˈænti̩friz/ *noun* [U] a chemical that is added to the water in the RADIATORS of cars and other vehicles to stop it from freezing

an·ti·gen /ˈæntɪdʒən/ *noun* (*medical*) a substance that enters the body and starts a process that can cause disease. The body then usually produces antibodies (ANTIBODY) to fight the antigens.

an·ti·glob·al·i·za·tion /ˌæntigloʊbələ'zeɪʃn; ˌæntaɪ-/ *noun* [U] opposition to the increase in the power of large international companies and institutions because of the bad effects on the economies of individual countries, especially poorer ones: *antiglobalization protests at the G8 summit* ◆ *the antiglobalization movement*

an·ti·grav·i·ty /ˌænti'grævəti; ˌæntaɪ-/ *noun* [U] (*physics*) an imaginary force that works against GRAVITY

an·ti·he·ro /ˈænti̩hɪroʊ; ˈæntaɪ-/ *noun* the main character in a story, but one who does not have the qualities of a typical hero, and is either more like an ordinary person or is morally bad

an·ti·his·ta·mine /ˌænti'hɪstəmin; -mən/ *noun* [C, U] a drug used to treat allergies (ALLERGY): *antihistamine cream/injections/shots*

ˌanti-in'flammatory *adj.* (of a drug) used to reduce INFLAMMATION ▶ **ˌanti-in'flammatory** *noun* (*pl.* ˌanti-in'flammatories)

an·ti·lock /ˈænti̩lɑk; ˈæntaɪ-/ *adj.* [only before noun] **antilock BRAKES** stop the wheels of a vehicle locking if you have to stop suddenly, and so make the vehicle easier to control: *an antilock braking system or ABS*

an·ti·mat·ter /ˈænti̩mætər; ˈæntaɪ-/ *noun* [U] (*physics*) matter that is made up of antiparticles

an·ti·mo·ny /ˈæntə̩moʊni/ *noun* [U] (*symb.* **Sb**) a chemical element. Antimony is a silver-white metal that breaks easily, used especially in making ALLOYS.

an·ti·ox·i·dant /ˌænti'ɑksədənt; ˌæntaɪ-/ *noun* **1** (*biology*) a substance such as VITAMIN C or E that removes dangerous MOLECULES, etc., such as FREE RADICALS, from the body **2** (*chemistry*) a substance that helps prevent OXIDATION, especially one used to help prevent stored food products from going bad

an·ti·par·ti·cle /ˈænti̩pɑrtɪkl; ˈæntaɪ-/ *noun* (*physics*) a very small part of an atom that has the same mass as a normal PARTICLE but the opposite electrical CHARGE

an·ti·pas·to /ˌænti'pɑstoʊ; ˌɑn-/ *noun* (*pl.* **an·ti·pas·ti** /-ti/) (in Italian cooking) a small amount of food that you eat before the main part of a meal SYN APPETIZER

an·tip·a·thy /æn'tɪpəθi/ *noun* [U, C, usually sing.] (*pl.* **an·tip·a·thies**) ~ **(between A and B)** | ~ **(to/toward(s) sb/sth)** (*formal*) a strong feeling of dislike SYN HOSTILITY: *personal/mutual antipathy* ◆ *a growing antipathy toward the idea* ▶ **an·ti·pa·thet·ic** /ˌæntɪpə'θetɪk; æn̩tɪpə-/ *adj.*: ~ **(to sb/sth)** *antipathetic to change*

an·ti·per·son·nel /ˌæntipərsə'nel; ˌæntaɪ-/ *adj.* [only before noun] (of weapons) designed to kill or injure people, not to destroy buildings or vehicles, etc.

an·ti·per·spi·rant /ˌænti'pərspərənt/ *noun* [U, C] a substance that people use, especially under their arms, to prevent or reduce sweat ⊃ see also DEODORANT

the An·tip·o·des /æn'tɪpədiz/ *noun* [pl.] Australia and New Zealand ▶ **An·tip·o·de·an** /æn̩tɪpə'diən/ *adj.*

an·ti·pro·ton /ˈænti̩proʊtɑn; ˈæntaɪ-/ *noun* (*physics*) a PARTICLE that has the same mass as a PROTON, but a negative electrical CHARGE

an·ti·quar·i·an /ˌænti'kweriən/ *adj.*, *noun*
• *adj.* [usually before noun] connected with the study, collection, or sale of valuable old objects, especially books
• *noun* (also *less frequent* **an·ti·quar·y** /ˈænti̩kweri/) a person who studies, collects, or sells old and valuable objects

an·ti·quark /ˈænti̩kwɔrk; ˈæntaɪ-; -ˌkwɑrk/ *noun* (*physics*) the ANTIPARTICLE of a QUARK

ʌ **cup**   ə **about**   eɪ **say**   aɪ **five**   ɔɪ **boy**   aʊ **now**   oʊ **go**   ər **bird**

an·ti·quat·ed /ˈæntɪˌkweɪtəd/ *adj.* (usually *disapproving*) (of things or ideas) old-fashioned and no longer suitable for modern conditions **SYN** OUTDATED

an·tique /ænˈtik/ *adj.*, *noun*
- *adj.* [usually before noun] (of furniture, jewelry, etc.) old and often valuable: *an antique mahogany desk*
- *noun* an object such as a piece of furniture that is old and often valuable: *Priceless antiques were destroyed in the fire.* ◆ *an antique shop* ◆ *an antique dealer*

an·tiq·ui·ty /ænˈtɪkwəti/ *noun* (*pl.* **an·tiq·ui·ties**) **1** [U] the ancient past, especially the times of the Greeks and Romans: *The statue was brought to Rome in antiquity.* **2** [U] the state of being very old or ancient: *A number of the monuments are of considerable antiquity.* **3** [C, usually pl.] an object from ancient times: *Egyptian/Roman antiquities*

an·ti·re·tro·vi·ral /ˌæntiˌretroʊˈvaɪrəl; ˌæntaɪ-/ *adj.* designed to stop viruses such as HIV from damaging the body: *antiretroviral drugs*

an·ti·roll bar /ˌæntiˈroʊl bɑr; ˌæntaɪ-/ *noun* a metal bar that is part of a car's SUSPENSION and that stops the car from leaning too much when it goes around corners

an·ti·Sem·i·tism /ˌæntiˈsɛməˌtɪzəm; ˌæntaɪ-/ *noun* [U] hatred of Jews; unfair treatment of Jews ▶ **an·ti·Sem·ite** /-ˈsɛmaɪt/ *noun*: *He was a notorious anti-Semite.* **an·ti·Se·mit·ic** /-səˈmɪtɪk/ *adj.*: *anti-Semitic propaganda*

an·ti·sep·tic /ˌæntəˈsɛptɪk/ *noun*, *adj.*
- *noun* [C, U] a substance that helps to prevent infection in wounds by killing bacteria **SYN** DISINFECTANT
- *adj.* **1** able to prevent infection: *antiseptic cream/lotion/wipes* **2** very clean and free from bacteria **SYN** STERILE: *Cover the burn with an antiseptic dressing.*

an·ti·so·cial /ˌæntiˈsoʊʃl; ˌæntaɪ-/ *adj.* **1** harmful or annoying to other people, or to society in general: *antisocial behavior* **2** not wanting to spend time with other people: *They'll think you're being antisocial if you don't go.* ⊃ compare SOCIABLE

an·ti·tank /ˌæntiˈtæŋk; ˌæntaɪ-/ *adj.* [only before noun] (of weapons) for use against enemy tanks: *antitank missiles/mines*

an·tith·e·sis /ænˈtɪθəsəs/ *noun* [C, U] (*pl.* **an·tith·e·ses** /-siz/) (*formal*) **1** the opposite of something: *Love is the antithesis of selfishness.* ◆ *Students finishing their education at 16 is the very antithesis of what society needs.* **2** a contrast between two things: *There is an antithesis between the needs of the state and the needs of the people.* ▶ **an·ti·thet·i·cal** /ˌæntəˈθɛtɪkl/ *adj.* **~ (to sth)**

an·ti·trust /ˌæntiˈtrʌst; ˌæntaɪ-/ *adj.* [only before noun] (of laws) preventing companies or groups of companies from controlling prices unfairly

an·ti·vi·ral /ˌæntiˈvaɪrəl; ˌæntaɪ-/ *adj.* (of a drug) used to treat infectious diseases caused by a virus

an·ti·vi·rus /ˈæntiˌvaɪrəs; ˌæntaɪ-/ *adj.* [only before noun] (*computing*) designed to find and destroy computer viruses: *antivirus software*

ant·ler /ˈæntlər/ *noun* [usually pl.] one of the two horns that grow on the head of male DEER ⊃ picture at ANIMAL

an·to·nym /ˈæntənɪm/ *noun* (*technical*) a word that means the opposite of another word **SYN** OPPOSITE: *"Old" has two possible antonyms: "young" and "new."* ⊃ compare SYNONYM

ant·sy /ˈæntsi/ *adj.* (*informal*) impatient; not able to keep still

a·nus /ˈeɪnəs/ *noun* (*anatomy*) the opening in a person's bottom through which solid waste leaves the body ⊃ picture at BODY ⊃ see also ANAL

an·vil /ˈænvl/ *noun* an iron block on which a BLACKSMITH puts hot pieces of metal before shaping them with a HAMMER

anx·i·e·ty /æŋˈzaɪəti/ *noun* (*pl.* **anx·i·e·ties**) **1** [U] **~ (about/over sth)** the state of feeling nervous or worried that something bad is going to happen: *acute/intense/deep anxiety* ◆ *Some hospital patients*

experience high levels of anxiety. ⊃ see also SEPARATION ANXIETY **2** [C] a worry or fear about something: *If you're worried about your health, share your anxieties with your doctor.* **3** [U] a strong feeling of wanting to do something or of wanting something to happen: **~ to do sth** *the candidate's anxiety to win the vote* ◆ **~ for sth** *the people's anxiety for the war to end*

anx·ious /ˈæŋkʃəs/ *adj.* **1** feeling worried or nervous: **~ (about sth)** *He seemed anxious about the meeting.* ◆ **~ (for sb)** *Parents are naturally anxious for their children.* ⊃ thesaurus box at WORRIED **2** causing anxiety; showing anxiety: *There were a few anxious moments in the game.* ◆ *an anxious look/face/expression* **3** wanting something very much: **~ to do sth** *She was anxious to finish school and get a job.* ◆ *He was anxious not to be misunderstood.* ◆ **~ for sth** *There are plenty of graduates anxious for work.* ◆ **~ for sb to do sth** *I'm anxious for her to do as little as possible.* ◆ **~ that...** *She was anxious that he might meet her father.* ▶ **anx·ious·ly** *adv.*: *to ask/look/wait anxiously* ◆ *Residents are anxiously awaiting a decision.*

an·y /ˈɛni/ *det.*, *pron.*, *adv.*
- *det.* **1** used with uncountable or plural nouns in negative sentences and questions, after *if* or *whether*, and after some verbs such as *prevent*, *ban*, *forbid*, etc. to refer to an amount or a number of something, however large or small: *I didn't eat any meat.* ◆ *Are there any stamps?* ◆ *I've got hardly any money.* ◆ *You can't go out without any shoes.* ◆ *He forbids any talking in class.* ◆ *She asked if we had any questions.* **HELP** In positive sentences, **some** is usually used instead of **any**: *I've got some paper if you want it.* It is also used in questions that expect a positive answer: *Would you like some milk in your tea?* **2** used with singular countable nouns to refer to one of a number of things or people, when it does not matter which one: *Take any book you like.* ◆ *Any color will do.* ◆ *Any teacher will tell you that students learn at different rates.* ⊃ see also CASE *n.*, EVENT, RATE *n.* **3** not just **~** used to show that someone or something is special: *It's not just any day—it's my birthday!*
- *pron.* **1** used in negative sentences and in questions and after *if* or *whether* to refer to an amount or a number, however large or small: *We need some more paint; there isn't any left.* ◆ *I need some stamps. Do you have any in your purse?* ◆ *Please let me know how many are coming, if any.* ◆ *She spent hardly any of the money.* ◆ *He returned home without any of the others.* **HELP** In positive sentences, **some** is usually used instead of **any**. It is also used in questions that expect a positive reply: *I've got plenty of paper—would you like some?* **2** one or more of a number of people or things, especially when it does not matter which: *I'll take any you don't want.* ◆ *"Which color do you want?" "Any of them would be OK."* **IDM sb isn't having any (of it)** (*informal*) someone is not interested or does not agree: *I suggested sharing the cost, but he wasn't having any of it.*
- *adv.* **1** used to emphasize an adjective or adverb in negative sentences or questions, meaning "at all": *He wasn't any good at French.* ◆ *I can't run any faster.* ◆ *Is your father feeling any better?* ◆ *I don't want any more.* ◆ *If you don't tell them, no one will be any the wiser.* **2** (*informal*) used at the end of a negative sentence to mean "at all": *That won't hurt you any.*

an·y·bod·y /ˈɛniˌbɑdi; -ˌbʌdi; -bədi/ *pron.* = ANYONE: *Is there anybody who can help me?* ◆ *Anybody can use the pool—you don't need to be a member.* ◆ *She wasn't anybody before she got that job.*

an·y·how /ˈɛniˌhaʊ/ *adv.* = ANYWAY

an·y·more /ˈɛniˈmɔr/ (also **any 'more**) *adv.* often used at the end of negative sentences and at the end of questions, to mean "any longer": *She doesn't live here anymore.* ◆ *Why doesn't he speak to me anymore?* ◆ *Now she won't have to go out to work anymore.* **HELP** Do not use "no more" with this meaning: ~~She doesn't live here no more.~~

an·y·one /'ɛnɪ,wʌn; -wən/ (also **an·y·bod·y**) pron.
1 used instead of *someone* in negative sentences and in questions after *if/whether*, and after verbs such as *prevent, forbid, avoid: Is anyone there?* ◆ *Does anyone want to come?* ◆ *Did anyone see you?* ◆ *Hardly anyone came.* ◆ *I forbid anyone to touch that clock.* **HELP** The difference between **anyone** and **someone** is the same as the difference between *any* and *some.* Look at the notes there. **2** any person at all; it does not matter who: *Anybody can see that it's wrong.* ◆ *The exercises are so simple that almost anyone can do them.* **3** (in negative sentences) an important person: *She wasn't anyone before she got that job.*

an·y·place /'ɛnɪ,pleɪs/ adv. = ANYWHERE

an·y·thing /'ɛnɪ,θɪŋ/ pron.
1 used instead of *something* in negative sentences and in questions; after *if/whether*; and after verbs such as *prevent, ban, avoid: Would you like anything else?* ◆ *There's never anything worth watching on TV.* ◆ *If you remember anything at all, please let us know.* ◆ *We hope to prevent anything unpleasant from happening.* **HELP** The difference between **anything** and **something** is the same as the difference between *any* and *some.* Look at the notes there. **2** any thing at all, when it does not matter which: *I'm so hungry, I'll eat anything.* **3** any thing of importance: *Is there anything* (= any truth) *to these rumors?*
IDM **anything but** definitely not: *The hotel was anything but cheap.* ◆ *It wasn't cheap. Anything but.* **anything like sb/sth** (*informal*) (used in questions and negative statements) similar to someone or something: *He isn't anything like my first boss.* **as happy, quick, etc. as anything** (*informal*) very happy, quick, etc.: *I felt as pleased as anything.* **not anything like** used to emphasize that something is not as good, not enough, etc.: *The book wasn't anything like as good as her first one.* **not for anything** (*informal*) definitely not: *I wouldn't give it up for anything.* **or anything** (*informal*) or another thing of a similar type: *If you want to call a meeting or anything, just let me know.*

an·y·time /'ɛnɪ,taɪm/ adv. at a time that is not fixed: *Call me anytime.*
IDM **anytime soon** used in negative sentences and questions to refer to the near future: *Will she be back anytime soon?*

an·y·way /'ɛnɪ,weɪ/ (also **an·y·how**) (also *informal* **an·y·ways**) adv.
1 used when adding something to support an idea or argument **SYN** BESIDES: *It's too expensive, and anyway the color doesn't look good on you.* ◆ *It's too late now, anyway.*
2 despite something; even so: *The water was cold but I took a shower anyway.* ◆ *I'm afraid we can't come, but thanks for the invitation anyway.* **3** used when changing the subject of a conversation, ending the conversation, or returning to a subject: *Anyway, let's forget about that for the moment.* ◆ *Anyway, I'd better go now—I'll see you tomorrow.* **4** used to correct or slightly change what you have said: *She works in a bank. She did when I last saw her, anyway.*

an·y·where /'ɛnɪ,wɛr/ (also **an·y·place**) adv.
1 used in negative sentences and in questions instead of *somewhere: I can't see it anywhere.* ◆ *Did you go anywhere interesting?* ◆ *Many of these animals are not found anywhere else.* ◆ *He's never been anywhere outside the U.S.* **HELP** The difference between **anywhere** and **somewhere** is the same as the difference between *any* and *some.* Look at the notes there. **2** in, at, or to any place, when it does not matter where: *Put the box down anywhere.* ◆ *An accident can happen anywhere.* ▶ **an·y·where** pron.: *I don't have anywhere to stay.* ◆ *Do you know anywhere I can buy a secondhand computer?*

A-OK /,eɪ oʊ 'keɪ/ adj., adv. (*informal*) in good condition; in an acceptable manner: *Everything's A-OK now.* ◆ *We hit it off A-OK.*

a·or·ta /eɪ'ɔrtə/ noun (*anatomy*) the main ARTERY that carries blood from the heart to the rest of the body once it has passed through the LUNGS

AP /,eɪ 'pi/ abbr. **1** ASSOCIATED PRESS **2** ADVANCED PLACE-MENT

a·pace /ə'peɪs/ adv. (*formal*) at a fast speed; quickly: *to continue/grow/proceed/develop apace*

A·pach·e /ə'pætʃi/ noun (pl. **A·pach·e** or **A·pach·es**) a member of a Native American people, many of whom live in the southwestern U.S.

a·part /ə'part/ adv.
1 separated by a distance, of space or time: *The two houses stood 500 feet apart.* ◆ *Their birthdays are only three days apart.* ◆ (*figurative*) *The two sides in the talks are still a long way apart* (= are far from reaching an agreement). **2** not together; separate or separately: *We're living apart now.* ◆ *Over the years, Emily and I had drifted apart.* ◆ *She keeps herself apart from other people.* ◆ *I can't* **tell** *the twins* **apart** (= see the difference between them). **3** into pieces: *The whole thing just came apart in my hands.* ◆ *We had to take the engine apart.* ◆ *When his wife died, his world fell apart.* **IDM** see POLE, RIP v., WORLD

a·part from (also **a·side from**) prep.
1 except for: *I've finished apart from the last question.* ⊃ language bank at EXCEPT **2** in addition to; as well as: *Apart from their house in Connecticut, they also have a cottage in Nantucket.* ◆ *It was a difficult time. Apart from everything else, we had financial problems.* ⊃ note at BESIDES

a·part·heid /ə'parteɪt; -taɪt/ noun [U] the former political system in South Africa in which only white people had full political rights and other people, especially black people, were forced to live away from white people, go to separate schools, etc.

a·part·ment /ə'partmənt/ noun (abbr. **apt.**) a set of rooms for living in, usually on one floor of a building ⊃ compare CONDOMINIUM

a·partment building noun a large building with apartments on each floor ⊃ picture at HOUSE

a·partment house noun a small apartment building

ap·a·thet·ic /,æpə'θɛtɪk/ adj. showing no interest or enthusiasm: *The illness made her apathetic and unwilling to meet people.* ▶ **ap·a·thet·i·cally** /-kli/ adv.

ap·a·thy /'æpəθi/ noun [U] the feeling of not being interested in or enthusiastic about anything: *There is widespread apathy among the electorate.*

ap·a·to·sau·rus /ə,pætə'sɔrəs/ (also **bron·to·sau·rus**) noun a very large DINOSAUR with a long neck and tail

APB /,eɪ pi 'bi/ abbr. ALL-POINTS BULLETIN

ape /eɪp/ noun, verb
● *noun* a large animal like a MONKEY, with no tail. There are different types of apes: *the great apes* (= for example, ORANGUTANS or CHIMPANZEES)
IDM **go ape** (*slang*) to become extremely angry or excited
● *verb* ~ sb/sth to copy the way someone else behaves or talks, in order to make fun of them **SYN** MIMIC: *We used to ape the teacher's Southern accent.*

ape·man /'eɪpmæn/ noun (pl. **ape·men** /-mɛn/) a large animal that no longer exists that was half way between an APE and a human

a·pe·ri·tif /ə,pɛrə'tif; ,apɛr-/ noun a drink, usually one containing alcohol, that people sometimes have just before a meal

ap·er·ture /'æpərtʃər/ noun **1** (*formal*) a small opening in something **2** (*technical*) an opening that allows light to reach a LENS, especially in cameras: *For flash photography, set the aperture at f.5.6.*

a·pex /'eɪpɛks/ noun (pl. **a·pex·es**) [usually sing.] the top or highest part of something: *the apex of the roof/triangle* ◆ (*figurative*) *At 37, she'd reached the apex of her career.*

a·pha·sia /ə'feɪʒə/ noun [U] (*medical*) the loss of the ability to understand or produce speech, because of brain damage

| t tea | t̮ butter | d did | k cat | g got | tʃ chin | dʒ June | f fall

a·phid /'eɪfɪd/ *noun* a very small insect that is harmful to plants. There are several types of aphids.

aph·o·rism /'æfə,rɪzəm/ *noun* (*formal*) a short phrase that says something true or wise ▶ **aph·o·ris·tic** /,æfə'rɪstɪk/ *adj.*

aph·ro·dis·i·ac /,æfrə'dɪziæk; -dɪ-/ *noun* a food or drug that is said to give people a strong desire to have sex ▶ **aph·ro·dis·i·ac** *adj.*: *the aphrodisiac qualities of ginseng*

a·pi·ar·y /'eɪpi,ɛri/ *noun* (*pl.* **a·pi·ar·ies**) a place where BEES are kept

a·piece /ə'pis/ *adv.* (used after a noun or number) having, costing, or measuring a particular amount each: *Jeter and Matsui scored a run apiece.* ◆ *The largest stones weigh over five tons apiece.*

a·plen·ty /ə'plɛnti/ *adv.*, *adj.* [after noun] (*formal*) in large amounts, especially more than is needed

a·plomb /ə'plɑm; ə'plʌm/ *noun* [U] if someone does something **with aplomb**, they do it in a confident and successful way, often in a difficult situation: *with* ***considerable/great/ remarkable aplomb*** ◆ *He delivered the speech with his* ***usual aplomb***.

ap·ne·a /'æpniə/ *noun* [U] (*medical*) a condition in which someone stops breathing temporarily while they are sleeping

a·poc·a·lypse /ə'pɑkəlɪps/ *noun* **1** [sing., U] the destruction of the world: *Civilization is on the brink of apocalypse.* **2 the Apocalypse** [sing.] the end of the world, as described in the Bible **3** [sing.] a situation causing very serious damage and destruction: *an environmental apocalypse*

a·poc·a·lyp·tic /ə,pɑkə'lɪptɪk/ *adj.* **1** describing very serious damage and destruction in past or future events: *an apocalyptic view of history* ◆ *apocalyptic warnings of the end of society* **2** like the end of the world: *an apocalyptic scene*

a·poc·ry·pha /ə'pɑkrəfə/ *noun* [pl.] **1 the Apocrypha** [sing.] Christian religious texts that are related to the Bible but not officially considered to be part of it **2** writings that are not considered to be genuine

a·poc·ry·phal /ə'pɑkrəfl/ *adj.* (of a story) well known, but probably not true: *Most of the stories about him are apocryphal.*

ap·o·gee /'æpədʒi/ *noun* [sing.] **1** (*formal*) the highest point of something, where it is greatest or most successful **2** (*astronomy*) the point in the ORBIT of the moon, a planet, or other object in space when it is furthest from the planet, for example the earth, around which it turns ⊃ compare PERIGEE

a·po·lit·i·cal /,eɪpə'lɪtɪkl/ *adj.* **1** (of a person) not interested in politics; not thinking politics are important **2** not connected with a political party

Ap·ol·lo·ni·an /,æpə'louniən/ *adj.* **1** connected with the ancient Greek god Apollo **2** (*formal*) connected with the controlled and reasonable aspects of human nature ⊃ compare DIONYSIAC

a·pol·o·get·ic /ə,pɑlə'dʒɛtɪk/ *adj.* feeling or showing that you are sorry for doing something wrong or for causing a problem: *"Sorry," she said, with an apologetic smile.* ◆ **~ about/for sth** *They were very apologetic about the trouble they caused.* ▶ **a·pol·o·get·i·cally** /-kli/ *adv.*: *"I'm sorry I'm late," he murmured apologetically.*

ap·o·lo·gi·a /,æpə'loudʒə; -dʒiə/ *noun* (*formal*) a formal written defense of your own or someone else's actions or opinions: *His book was seen as an apologia for the war.*

a·pol·o·gist /ə'pɑlədʒɪst/ *noun* **~ (for sb/sth)** a person who tries to explain and defend something, especially a political system or religious ideas

a·pol·o·gize ✐ /ə'pɑlə,dʒaɪz/ *verb* [I] **~ (to sb) (for sth)**
to say that you are sorry for doing something wrong or causing a problem: *Why should I apologize?* ◆ *Go and apologize to her.* ◆ *We apologize for the late departure of this flight.*

a·pol·o·gy /ə'pɑlədʒi/ *noun* (*pl.* **a·pol·o·gies**) **1** [C, U] **~ (to sb) (for sth)** a word or statement saying sorry for something that has been done wrong or that causes a problem: *to offer/make/demand/accept an apology* ◆ *You owe him an* ***apology*** *for what you said.* ◆ *We would like to offer our apologies for the delay to your flight today.* ◆ *We received a letter of apology.* **2** [C, usually pl.] information that you cannot go to a meeting or must leave early: (*formal*) *She* ***made her apologies*** *and left early.*

IDM make no apology/apologies for sth if you say that you **make no apology/apologies** for something, you mean that you do not feel that you have said or done something wrong

ap·o·plec·tic /,æpə'plɛktɪk/ *adj.* **1** very angry: *He was apoplectic with rage at the decision.* **2** (*old-fashioned*) connected with apoplexy: *an* ***apoplectic attack/fit***

ap·o·plex·y /'æpə,plɛksi/ *noun* [U] (*old-fashioned*) the sudden loss of the ability to feel or move caused by an injury in the brain **SYN A STROKE**

a·po·ri·a /ə'pɔriə/ *noun* (*technical*) a situation in which two or more parts of a theory or argument do not agree, meaning that the theory or argument cannot be true

a·pos·tate /ə'pɑsteɪt; -tət/ *noun* (*formal*) a person who has rejected their religious or political beliefs ▶ **a·pos·ta·sy** /ə'pɑstəsi/ *noun* [U]

a pos·te·ri·o·ri /,eɪ pɑ,stiri'ɔraɪ; ,ɑ pou,stiri'ɔri/ *adj.*, *adv.* (from *Latin*, *formal*) analyzing something by starting from known facts and then thinking about the possible causes of the facts, for example saying, "Look, the streets are wet, so it must have been raining." ⊃ compare A PRIORI

a·pos·tle /ə'pɑsl/ *noun* **1 Apostle** any one of the twelve men that Christ chose to tell people about him and his teachings **2 ~ (of sth)** (*formal*) a person who strongly believes in a policy or an idea and tries to make other people believe in it: *an apostle of free enterprise*

ap·os·tol·ic /,æpə'stɑlɪk/ *adj.* (*technical*) **1** connected with the Apostles or their teaching **2** connected with the Pope or popes, who are considered to have had authority passed down to them from Christ's Apostles

a·pos·tro·phe /ə'pɑstrəfi/ *noun* **1** the mark (') used to show that one or more letters or numbers have been left out, as in *she's* for *she is* and *'63* for *1963* **2** the mark (') used before or after the letter "s" to show that something belongs to someone, as in *Sam's watch* and *the horses' tails* **3** the mark (') used before the letter "s" to show the plural of a letter or number, as in *How many 3's are there in 9?* and *There are two m's in "comma."*

a·pos·tro·phize /ə'pɑstrə,faɪz/ *verb* **1** (*formal* or *literary*) **~ sb** to address what you are saying, or a poem, a speech in a play, etc. to a particular person **2 ~ sth** to add apostrophes to a piece of writing

a·poth·e·car·y /ə'pɑθə,kɛri/ *noun* (*pl.* **a·poth·e·car·ies**) a person who made and sold medicines in the past

a·poth·e·o·sis /ə,pɑθi'ousəs/ *noun* (*pl.* **a·poth·e·o·ses** /-siz/) (*formal*) **1** the highest or most perfect development or example of something **2** the best time in someone's life or career **3** a formal statement that a person has become a god: *the apotheosis of a Roman Emperor*

app /æp/ *noun* a computer program designed to do a particular job, especially one that you can use on a SMARTPHONE or other small computing device: *Business travelers can download apps to their PDAs.* ⊃ see also KILLER APP

ap·pall /ə'pɔl/ *verb* to shock someone very much **SYN HORRIFY** ⊃ thesaurus box at SHOCK: **~ sb** *The brutality of the crime appalled the public.* ◆ *The idea of sharing a room appalled her.* ◆ **it appalls sb that.../to do sth** *It appalled me that they could simply ignore the problem.*

ap·palled /ə'pɔld/ *adj.* feeling or showing horror or disgust at something unpleasant or wrong **SYN HORRIFIED**: *an* ***appalled expression/silence*** ◆ *We watched appalled as the boy* ran in front of the car. ◆ **~ at sth** *They were appalled at the waste of recyclable material.*

ap·pall·ing /əˈpɔːlɪŋ/ *adj.* **1** shocking; extremely bad: *The prisoners were living in appalling conditions.* **2** (*informal*) very bad: *The bus service is appalling now.* ▶ **ap·pall·ing·ly** *adv.*: **appallingly bad/difficult** ◆ *The essay was appallingly written.*

ap·pa·rat /ˌapəˈrɑːt; ˈæpəˌræt/ *noun* [usually sing.] the system of officials, offices, etc. that a government, especially a Communist government, uses to run a country

ap·pa·rat·chik /ˌɑːpəˈrɑːtʃɪk/ *noun* (from *Russian*, *disapproving* or *humorous*) an official in a large political organization: *party apparatchiks*

ap·pa·rat·us /ˌæpəˈrætəs; -ˈreɪtəs/ *noun* (*pl.* **ap·pa·rat·us·es**) (*formal*) **1** [U] the tools or other pieces of equipment that are needed for a particular activity or task: *a piece of laboratory apparatus* ◆ *Firefighters needed breathing apparatus to enter the burning house.* ⟳ thesaurus box at EQUIPMENT **2** [C, usually sing.] the structure of a system or an organization, particularly that of a political party or a government: *the power of the state apparatus* **3** [C, usually sing.] (*technical*) a system of organs in the body: *the sensory apparatus*

ap·par·el /əˈpærəl/ *noun* [U] **1** clothing, when it is being sold in stores: *The store sells women's and children's apparel.* **2** (*old-fashioned* or *formal*) clothes, particularly those worn on a formal occasion: *dressed in fine apparel for the wedding*

ap·par·ent **AWL** /əˈpɛrənt; əˈpær-/ *adj.* **1** [not usually before noun] easy to see or understand **SYN** OBVIOUS: *Their devotion was apparent.* ◆ *Then, for no apparent reason, the train suddenly stopped.* ◆ **~ (from sth) (that…)** *It was apparent from her face that she was really upset.* ◆ **~ (to sb) (that…)** *It soon became apparent to everyone that he couldn't sing.* ⟳ thesaurus box at CLEAR ⟳ language bank at ILLUSTRATE **2** [usually before noun] that seems to be real or true but may not be **SYN** SEEMING: *My parents were concerned at my apparent lack of enthusiasm for school.* ⟳ see also APPEAR

ap·par·ent·ly 🔊 **AWL** /əˈpɛrəntli; əˈpær-/ *adv.* according to what you have heard or read; according to the way something appears: *Apparently they are getting divorced.* ◆ *He paused, apparently lost in thought.* ◆ *I thought she had retired, but apparently (= in fact) she hasn't.*

ap·pa·ri·tion /ˌæpəˈrɪʃn/ *noun* a GHOST or an image of a person who is dead

ap·peal 🔊 /əˈpiːl/ *noun*, *verb*

● *noun* **1** [C, U] a formal request to a court or to someone in authority for a judgment or a decision to be changed: *to file an appeal* ◆ *an appeals court/judge* ◆ **~ against sth** *an appeal against the 3-game ban* ⟳ collocations at JUSTICE ⟳ see also COURT OF APPEALS **2** [U] a quality that makes someone or something attractive or interesting: *mass/wide/popular appeal* ◆ *The Beatles have never really lost their appeal.* ◆ *The prospect of living in a city holds little appeal for me.* ⟳ see also SEX APPEAL **3** [C, U] an urgent and deeply felt request for money, help, or information, especially one made by a charity or by the police: *a look of silent appeal* ◆ **~ (to sb) (for sth)** *an appeal for donations by the March of Dimes* ◆ *The boy's mother made an emotional appeal on TV for his return.* ◆ **~ to sb to do sth** *The police made an appeal to the public to remain calm.* **4** [C] **~ to sth** an indirect suggestion that any good, fair, or reasonable person would act in a particular way: *I relied on an appeal to his deeper feelings.*

● *verb* **1** [I] **~ (to sb/sth) (against sth)** to make a formal request to a court or to someone in authority for a judgment or a decision to be changed: *He said he would appeal after being found guilty on four counts of murder.* ◆ *The company is appealing against the ruling.* ◆ **~ (sth) (to sb/sth)** *The company has ten days to appeal the decision to the tribunal.* **2** [I] to attract or interest someone: *The prospect of a long wait in the rain did not appeal.* ◆ **~ to sb** *The design has to appeal to all ages and social groups.* **3** [I] to make a serious and urgent request: *I am appealing for donations on behalf of the famine victims* (= asking for money). ◆ **~ (to sb) (for sth)** *Nationalist leaders appealed for calm.* ◆ *Police have appealed for witnesses*

to come forward. ◆ **~ to sb to do sth** *Organizers appealed to the crowd not to panic.* **4** [I] **~ (to sth)** to try to persuade someone to do something by suggesting that it is a fair, reasonable, or honest thing to do: *They needed to appeal to his sense of justice.*

ap·peal·ing /əˈpiːlɪŋ/ *adj.* **1** attractive or interesting: *Spending the holidays with my in-laws wasn't a prospect that I found particularly appealing.* **ANT** UNAPPEALING **2** showing that you want people to help you or to show you sympathy: *"Would you really help?" he said with an appealing look.* ▶ **ap·peal·ing·ly** *adv.*: *an appealingly witty story* ◆ *The dog looked up at her appealingly.*

apˈpeals court *noun* = COURT OF APPEALS

ap·pear 🔊 /əˈpɪr/ *verb*
▶ **LOOK/SEEM 1** linking verb (not used in the progressive tenses) to give the impression of being or doing something **SYN** SEEM: + adj. *She didn't appear at all surprised at the news.* ◆ *It appears unlikely that interest rates will fall further.* ◆ **~ to be sth** *I don't think he's sick. He appears to be normal.* ◆ *She appeared to be in her late thirties.* ◆ **~ to do sth** *They appeared not to know what was happening.* ◆ *There appears to have been a mistake.* ◆ **it appears (that)…** *It appears that there has been a mistake.* ◆ *It would appear that this was a major problem.* ⟳ language bank at PERHAPS
▶ **BE SEEN 2** [I] to start to be seen: *Three days later a rash appeared.* ◆ **+ adv./prep.** *A bus appeared around the corner.* ◆ *Smoke appeared on the horizon.*
▶ **BEGIN TO EXIST 3** [I] **+ adv./prep.** to begin to exist or be known or used for the first time: *When did mammals appear on the earth?* ◆ *This problem first appeared in the inner cities.*
▶ **OF BOOK/PROGRAM 4** [I] **+ adv./prep.** to be published or broadcast: *His new book will be appearing in the spring.* ◆ *It was too late to prevent the story from appearing in the national newspapers.*
▶ **IN MOVIE/PLAY 5** [I] **+ adv./prep.** to take part in a movie, play, television program, etc.: *He has appeared in over 60 movies.* ◆ *She regularly appears on TV.* ◆ *Next month he will be appearing as George Bush in a new play on Broadway.*
▶ **ARRIVE 6** [I] **+ adv./prep.** to arrive at a place: *By ten o'clock, Lee still hadn't appeared.*
▶ **BE WRITTEN/MENTIONED 7** [I] **+ adv./prep.** to be written or mentioned somewhere: *Your name will appear at the front of the book.*
▶ **IN COURT 8** [I] **+ adv./prep.** to be present in court in order to give evidence or answer a charge: *A man who is charged with the murder will appear in court today.* ◆ *She appeared on six charges of theft.* ◆ *They will appear before the judge tomorrow.* ◆ *He has been asked to appear as a witness for the defense.* **9** [I] **~ for/on behalf of sb** to act as someone's lawyer in court: *Alan Dershowitz is the lawyer appearing for the defendant.* ⟳ see also APPARENT ⟳ compare DISAPPEAR

ap·pear·ance 🔊 /əˈpɪrəns/ *noun*
▶ **WAY SOMETHING LOOKS/SEEMS 1** [C, U] the way that someone or something looks on the outside; what someone or something seems to be: *the physical/outward/external appearance of something* ◆ *She had never been greatly concerned about her appearance.* ◆ *The dog was similar in appearance to a spaniel.* ◆ *He gave every appearance of* (= seemed very much to be) *enjoying himself.* ◆ *Judging by appearances can be misleading.* ◆ **By all appearances** (= as far as people could tell), *he was dead.* ◆ *When she lost all her money, she was determined to keep up appearances* (= hide the true situation and pretend that everything was going well).
▶ **SOMEONE OR SOMETHING ARRIVING 2** [C, usually sing.] the fact of someone or something arriving, especially when it is not expected: *The sudden appearance of a security guard caused them to drop the money and run.* ◆ *I don't want to go to the party, but I suppose I should make an appearance* (= go there for a short time). **3** [C, usually sing.] the moment at which something begins to exist or starts to be seen or used: *the early appearance of daffodils in spring* ◆ *the appearance of organic vegetables in the supermarkets*
▶ **IN PUBLIC 4** [C] an act of appearing in public, especially as a performer, politician, etc., or in court: *President Obama*

makes frequent public appearances. ◆ *Fans were disappointed that the actress didn't make a personal appearance at the premiere.* ◆ *the defendant's appearance in court*

> **BEING PUBLISHED/BROADCAST 5** [C, usually sing.] an act of being published or broadcast: *the appearance of claims about the minister's private life in the press*

ap·pease /əˈpiz/ *verb* (*formal*, usually *disapproving*) **1** ~ sb to make someone calmer or less angry by giving them what they want: *The move was widely seen as an attempt to appease critics of the regime.* **2** ~ sb/sth to give a country what it wants in order to avoid war ▸ **ap·pease·ment** *noun* [U]: *a policy of appeasement*

ap·pel·lant /əˈpɛlənt/ *noun* (*law*) a person who appeals against a decision made in court

ap·pel·late court /əˈpɛlət ˌkɔrt/ *noun* (*technical*) a court in which people can appeal against decisions made in other courts of law ⊃ **see also COURT OF APPEALS**

ap·pel·la·tion /ˌæpəˈleɪʃn/ *noun* (*formal*) a name or title

ap·pel·la·tive /əˈpɛlətɪv/ *adj., noun*
● *adj.* (*formal*) relating to the giving of a name
● *noun* (*technical*) a common noun that is used to address a person or thing, for example "mother" or "doctor"

ap·pend **AWL** /əˈpɛnd/ *verb* ~ sth (to sth) (*formal*) to add something to the end of a piece of writing: *Footnotes have been appended to the document.*

ap·pend·age /əˈpɛndɪdʒ/ *noun* (*formal*) a smaller or less important part of something larger

ap·pen·dec·to·my /ˌæpənˈdɛktəmi/ *noun* (*pl.* **ap·pen·dec·to·mies**) [C, U] (*medical*) the removal of the APPENDIX by SURGERY

ap·pen·di·ci·tis /əˌpɛndəˈsaɪtəs/ *noun* [U] a painful swelling of the appendix that can be very serious

ap·pen·dix **AWL** /əˈpɛndɪks/ *noun* (*pl.* **ap·pen·di·ces** /-dəsiz/) **1** a small bag of TISSUE that is attached to the large INTESTINE. In humans, the appendix has no clear function: *He had to have his appendix out* (= removed). ⊃ **picture at BODY** **2** a section giving extra information at the end of a book or document: *Full details are given in Appendix 3.*

ap·per·tain /ˌæpərˈteɪn/ *verb*
PHR V **apper'tain to sb/sth** (*formal*) to belong or refer to someone or something: *rights appertaining to the property* ◆ *These figures appertain to last year's sales.*

ap·pe·tite /ˈæpəˌtaɪt/ *noun* **1** [U, C, usually sing.] physical desire for food: *He suffered from headaches and loss of appetite.* ◆ *The walk gave me a good appetite.* ◆ *Don't spoil your appetite by eating between meals.* **2** [C] a strong desire for something: *sexual appetites* ◆ *The preview was intended to whet your appetite* (= make you want more). ◆ ~ for sth *The public has an insatiable appetite for scandal.*

ap·pe·tiz·er /ˈæpəˌtaɪzər/ *noun* a small amount of food or a drink that you have before a meal or before the main course of a meal

ap·pe·tiz·ing /ˈæpəˌtaɪzɪŋ/ *adj.* (of food, etc.) that smells or looks attractive; making you feel hungry or thirsty **ANT** UNAPPETIZING

ap·plaud /əˈplɔd/ *verb* **1** [I, T] to show your approval of someone or something by CLAPPING (= hitting your hands together): *He started to applaud and the others joined in.* ◆ ~ sb *They rose to applaud the speaker.* ◆ *She was applauded as she came on stage.* **2** [T] (*formal*) to express praise for someone or something because you approve of them or it: ~ sth *We applaud her decision.* ◆ *His efforts to improve the situation are to be applauded.* ◆ ~ sb (for sth) *I applaud her for having the courage to say no.*

ap·plause /əˈplɔz/ *noun* [U] the noise made by a group of people CLAPPING (= hitting their hands together) and sometimes shouting to show their approval or enjoyment: *Give her a big round of applause!* ◆ *The audience broke into thunderous applause.*

ap·ple /ˈæpl/ *noun*
a round fruit with shiny red or green skin and firm white flesh: *an apple pie* ◆ *a yard with three apple trees* ⊃ **picture at FRUIT** ⊃ see also **ADAM'S APPLE, BIG APPLE, CANDY APPLE, CRAB APPLE**
IDM **the apple doesn't fall/never falls far from the tree** (*saying*) a child usually behaves in a similar way to his or her parent(s) **the apple of sb's eye** a person or thing that is loved more than any other **apples and oranges** used to describe a situation in which two people or things are completely different from each other: *They really are apples and oranges.* ◆ *They are both great but you can't compare apples and oranges.* **bad apple** one bad person who has a bad effect on others in a group: *You shouldn't punish the whole class because of one bad apple.* ⊃ **more at AMERICAN**

apple cart *noun* **IDM** see UPSET v.

apple-cheeked *adj.* having round pink cheeks and looking healthy: *cute little apple-cheeked babies*

apple cider *noun* [U, C] = CIDER (1)

apple pie *noun* **1** [C, U] apples baked in a dish with PIE CRUST on the bottom, sides, and top: *a slice of apple pie* **2** [U] used to represent an idea of perfect home life and comfort: *Who could argue against motherhood and apple pie?* **IDM** see AMERICAN

ap·ple·sauce /ˈæplˌsɔs/ *noun* [U] a thick sauce made by cooking apples and sugar in a small amount of water

ap·plet /ˈæplət/ *noun* (*computing*) a program that is run from within another program, for example from within an Internet BROWSER

ap·pli·ance /əˈplaɪəns/ *noun* a machine that is designed to do a particular thing in the home, such as preparing food, heating, or cleaning: *electrical/household appliances* ◆ *They sell a wide range of home appliances —washing machines, dishwashers, and so on.*

ap·pli·ca·ble /ˈæplɪkəbl; əˈplɪkəbl/ *adj.* [not usually before noun] that can be said to be true in the case of someone or something **SYN** RELEVANT: *Give details about children where applicable* (= if you have any). ◆ ~ to sb/sth *Much of the form was not applicable* (= did not apply) *to me.* ⊃ see also **N/A** (1) ▸ **ap·pli·ca·bil·i·ty** /ˌæplɪkəˈbɪləti; əˌplɪkə-/ *noun* [U]: *The new approach had wide applicability to all kinds of different problems.*

ap·pli·cant /ˈæplɪkənt/ *noun* ~ (for sth) a person who makes a formal request for something (= applies for it), especially for a job, ADMISSION to (= permission to enter) a college or university, etc.: *There were over 500 applicants for the job.*

ap·pli·ca·tion /ˌæpləˈkeɪʃn/ *noun*
> **FOR JOB/SCHOOL 1** [C, U] a formal (often written) request for something, such as a job, permission to do something, or ADMISSION to (= permission to enter) a college or university: *a visa/passport application* ◆ *an application form* (= a piece of paper on which to apply for something) ◆ ~ for sth/to do sth *an application for membership/a loan/a license* ◆ ~ to sb (for sth/to do sth) *His application to the court for bail has been refused.*
> **PRACTICAL USE 2** [U, C] ~ (of sth) (to sth) the practical use of something, especially a theory, discovery, etc.: *the application of new technology to teaching* ◆ *The invention would have a wide range of applications in industry.*
> **OF PAINT/CREAM 3** [C, U] an act of putting or spreading something, such as paint or medical creams, onto something else: *lotion for external application only* (= to be put on the skin, not swallowed) ◆ *It took three applications of paint to cover the graffiti.*
> **OF RULE/LAW 4** [U] the act of making a rule, etc. operate or become effective: *strict application of the law*
> **COMPUTING 5** [C] (*abbr.* **app**) a program designed to do a particular job; a piece of software: *a database application*
> **HARD WORK 6** [U] (*formal*) determination to work hard at something; great effort: *Success as a writer demands great application.*

ap·pli·ca·tor /'æplɪˌkeɪtər/ noun a small tool that is used to put a substance onto a surface, or to put something into an object: *Use the applicator to apply ointment to the affected area.* ⊃ **picture at** MAKEUP

ap·plied /ə'plaɪd/ adj. [usually before noun] (especially of a subject of study) used in a practical way; not THEORETICAL: *applied mathematics* (= as used by engineers, etc.) ⊃ **compare** PURE

ap·plied lin'guistics noun [U] the scientific study of language as it relates to practical problems, in areas such as teaching and dealing with speech problems

ap·pli·qué /ˌæplə'keɪ/ noun [U] a type of NEEDLEWORK in which small pieces of cloth are sewn or stuck in a pattern onto a larger piece ▶ **ap·pli·quéd** adj.

ap·ply 🔑 /ə'plaɪ/ verb
(ap·plies, ap·ply·ing, ap·plied, ap·plied)
> FOR JOB/SCHOOL **1** [I, T] to make a formal request, usually in writing, for something such as a job, ADMISSION to (= permission to enter) a college or university, etc.: *You should apply in person/in writing.* ◆ ~ **for sth** *to apply for a job/passport/grant* ◆ ~ **to sb/sth (for sth)** *to apply to a company/college* ◆ ~ **to do sth** *He has applied to join the army.*
> USE **2** [T] to use something or make something work in a particular situation: ~ **sth** *to apply economic sanctions/political pressure* ◆ ~ **sth to sth** *The new technology was applied to farming.*
> PAINT/CREAM **3** [T] ~ **sth (to sth)** to put or spread something such as paint, cream, etc. onto a surface: *Apply the lotion sparingly to your face and neck.*
> BE RELEVANT **4** [I, T] (not used in the progressive tenses) to concern or relate to someone or something: *Special conditions apply if you are under 18.* ◆ ~ **to sb/sth** *What I am saying applies only to some of you.* ◆ ~ **sth to sth** *The word "unexciting" could never be applied to her novels.*
> WORK HARD **5** [T] to work at something or study something very hard: ~ **yourself** *You would pass your exams if you applied yourself.* ◆ ~ **yourself/sth to sth/to doing sth** *We applied our minds to finding a solution to our problem.*
> PRESS HARD **6** [T] to press on something hard with your hand, foot, etc. to make something work or have an effect on something: ~ **sth** *to apply the brakes (of a vehicle)* ◆ ~ **sth to sth** *Pressure applied to the wound will stop the bleeding.*

ap·point 🔑 /ə'pɔɪnt/ verb
1 to choose someone for a job or position of responsibility: ~ **sb** *They have appointed a new principal at my son's school.* ◆ ~ **sb to sth** *She has recently been appointed to the committee.* ◆ ~ **sb + noun** | ~ **sb as sth** *They appointed him (as) captain of the math team.* ◆ ~ **sb to do sth** *A lawyer was appointed to represent the child.* **2** [usually passive] ~ **sth** (formal) to arrange or decide on a time or place for doing something: *A date for the meeting is still to be appointed.* ◆ *Everyone was assembled at the **appointed time**.*

ap·point·ee /əˌpɔɪn'ti/ noun a person who has been chosen for a job or position of responsibility: *the new appointee to the post*

ap·point·ment 🔑 /ə'pɔɪntmənt/ noun
1 [C] a formal arrangement to meet or visit someone at a particular time, especially for a reason connected with their work: *I've got a dentist appointment at 3 o'clock.* ◆ *to **make/ keep an appointment*** ◆ *Viewing is by appointment only* (= only at a time that has been arranged in advance). ◆ ~ **with sb** *an appointment with my lawyer* ◆ ~ **for sth** *an appointment for a blood test* ◆ ~ **for sb to do sth** *She made an appointment for her son to see the doctor.* **2** [C, U] ~ **(as/to sth)** the act of choosing a person for a job or position of responsibility; the fact of being chosen for a job, etc.: *Following her recent appointment to the post...* ◆ *his appointment as principal* **3** [C] a job or position of responsibility: *a faculty/judicial appointment* ⊃ **thesaurus box at** JOB

ap'pointment ˌbook (also **ap'pointment ˌcalendar**, **date·book**) noun a book with spaces for each day of the

year in which you can write down things you have to do in the future **SYN** CALENDAR

ap·por·tion /ə'pɔrʃn/ verb (formal) to divide something among people; to give a share of something to someone: ~ **sth** *The program gives the facts but does not **apportion** blame.* ◆ ~ **sth among/between/to sb** *They apportioned the land among members of the family.* ▶ **ap·por·tion·ment** noun [U, sing.] (formal): *The contract defines the apportionment of risks between employer and contractor.* ◆ *an apportionment of land* ◆ *The apportionment of seats in the House of Representatives is based on the population of each state.*

ap·po·site /'æpəzət/ adj. ~ **(to sth)** (formal) very appropriate for a particular situation or in relation to something

ap·po·si·tion /ˌæpə'zɪʃn/ noun [U] (grammar) the use of a noun phrase immediately after another noun phrase that refers to the same person or thing: *In the phrase "Paris, the capital of France," "the capital of France" is in apposition to "Paris."*

ap·prais·al /ə'preɪzl/ noun [C, U] a judgment of the value, performance, or nature of someone or something: *He had read many detailed critical appraisals of her work.* ◆ *She was honest in her appraisal of her team's chances.* ◆ *We took Grandma's ring to a jeweler for an appraisal.*

ap·praise /ə'preɪz/ verb ~ **sb/sth** (formal) to form an opinion about how valuable, successful, or effective someone or something is: *The house and property were appraised at $750,000.* ◆ *an **appraising glance/look*** ◆ *She stepped back to appraise her workmanship.*

ap·prais·er /ə'preɪzər/ noun a person whose job is to examine a building and say how much it is worth

ap·pre·cia·ble [AWL] /ə'priʃəbl/ adj. large enough to be noticed or thought important **SYN** CONSIDERABLE: *The new regulations will not make an appreciable difference to most people.* ◆ *an **appreciable effect/increase/amount*** ▶ **ap·pre·cia·bly** [AWL] /-bli/ adv.: *The risk of infection is appreciably higher among children.*

ap·pre·ci·ate 🔑 [AWL] /ə'priʃiˌeɪt/ verb
1 [T] (not used in the progressive tenses) ~ **sb/sth** to recognize the good qualities of someone or something: *You can't really appreciate foreign literature in translation.* ◆ *His talents are not **fully appreciated** in that company.* ◆ *Her family doesn't appreciate her.* **2** [T] (not usually used in the progressive tenses) to be grateful for something that someone has done; to welcome something: ~ **sth** *I'd appreciate some help.* ◆ *Your support is greatly appreciated.* ◆ *Thanks for coming. I appreciate it.* ◆ *I would appreciate it if you paid in cash.* ◆ ~ **doing sth** *I don't appreciate being treated like a second-class citizen.* ◆ ~ **sb doing sth** *We would appreciate you letting us know of any problems.* **3** [T] (not used in the progressive tenses) to understand that something is true **SYN** REALIZE: ~ **sth** *What I failed to understand was the distance between the two cities.* ◆ ~ **how, what, etc....** *I don't think you appreciate how expensive it will be.* ◆ ~ **that...** *We didn't **fully appreciate** that he was seriously ill.* **4** [I] to increase in value over a period of time: *Their investments have appreciated over the years.* **ANT** DEPRECIATE

ap·pre·ci·a·tion [AWL] /əˌpriʃi'eɪʃn/ noun **1** [U] ~ **(of/for sth)** the feeling of being grateful for something: *Please accept this gift in appreciation of all you've done for us.* **2** [U, sing.] ~ **of sth** a full or sympathetic understanding of something, such as a situation or a problem, and of what it involves: *I had no appreciation of the problems they faced.* **3** [U] pleasure that you have when you recognize and enjoy the good qualities of someone or something: *She shows little appreciation of good music.* ◆ *The crowd murmured in appreciation.* **4** [U, sing.] ~ **(in sth)** increase in value over a period of time **ANT** DEPRECIATION **5** [C] ~ **(of sth)** (formal) a piece of writing or a speech in which the strengths and weaknesses of someone or something, especially an artist or a work of art, are discussed and judged

ap·pre·cia·tive /ə'priʃətɪv/ adj. **1** ~ **(of sth)** feeling or showing that you are grateful for something: *The company was very appreciative of my efforts.* **2** showing pleasure or enjoyment: *an appreciative audience/smile* ◆ *appreciative laughter/comments* ▶ ap·pre·cia·tive·ly *adv.*

ap·pre·hend /ˌæprɪˈhɛnd/ *verb* (*formal*) **1** ~ **sb** (of the police) to catch someone and arrest them **2** ~ **sth** (*old-fashioned*) to understand or recognize something

ap·pre·hen·sion /ˌæprɪˈhɛnʃn/ *noun* **1** [U, C] worry or fear that something unpleasant may happen **SYN** ANXIETY: *There is growing apprehension that fighting will begin again.* ◆ *He watched the election results **with some apprehension**.* **2** [U] (*formal*) the act of capturing or arresting someone, usually by the police

ap·pre·hen·sive /ˌæprɪˈhɛnsɪv/ *adj.* worried or frightened that something unpleasant may happen: *an apprehensive face/glance/look* ◆ ~ **about/of sth** *I was a little apprehensive about the effects of what I had said.* ◆ *You have no reason to be apprehensive of the future.* ◆ ~ **that...** *She was deeply apprehensive that something might go wrong.* ▶ ap·pre·hen·sive·ly *adv.*

ap·pren·tice /əˈprɛntəs/ *noun, verb*
● *noun* a young person who works for an employer for a fixed period of time in order to learn the particular skills needed in their job: *an apprentice electrician/chef*
● *verb* [usually passive] ~ **sb** (**to sb**) (**as sth**) (*old-fashioned*) to make someone an apprentice

ap·pren·tice·ship /əˈprɛntəʃˌʃɪp; -təˌʃɪp/ *noun* [C, U] a period of time working as an apprentice; a job as an apprentice: *She was in the second year of her apprenticeship as a carpenter.* ◆ *He had **served his apprenticeship** as a plumber.*

ap·prise /əˈpraɪz/ *verb* ~ **sb of sth** (*formal*) to tell or inform someone of something

ap·proach 🗝 **AWL** /əˈproʊtʃ/ *verb, noun*
● *verb*
▷ **MOVE NEAR 1** [I, T] to come near to someone or something in distance or time: *We heard the sound of an approaching car/ a car approaching.* ◆ *Winter is approaching.* ◆ ~ **sb/sth** *As you approach the town, you'll see the college on the left.*
▷ **OFFER/ASK 2** [T] to speak to someone about something, especially to ask them for something or to offer to do something: ~ **sb** *We have been approached by a number of companies that are interested in our product.* ◆ *I'd like to ask his opinion but I find him difficult to approach* (= not easy to talk to in a friendly way). ◆ ~ **sb for sth/about (doing) sth** *She approached the bank for a loan.*
▷ **AMOUNT/QUALITY 3** [T] ~ **sth** to come close to something in amount, level, or quality: *profits approaching 30 million dollars* ◆ *Few writers approach his richness of language.*
▷ **PROBLEM/TASK 4** [T] ~ **sth** to start dealing with a problem, task, etc. in a particular way: *What's the best way of approaching this problem?*
● *noun*
▷ **TO PROBLEM/TASK 1** [C] a way of dealing with someone or something; a way of doing or thinking about something such as a problem or a task: *She took the wrong approach in her dealings with them.* ◆ ~ **to sth** *The school has decided to adopt a different approach to discipline.*
▷ **MOVEMENT NEARER 2** [sing.] movement nearer to someone or something in distance or time: *She hadn't heard his approach and jumped as the door opened.* ◆ *the approach of spring*
▷ **OFFER/REQUEST 3** [C] the act of speaking to someone about something, especially when making an offer or a request: *The club has **made an approach** to a local company for sponsorship.* ◆ *She resented his persistent approaches.*
▷ **PATH/ROAD 4** [C] a path, road, etc. that leads to a place: *All the approaches to the palace were guarded by troops.* ◆ *a new approach road to the port*
▷ **OF AIRCRAFT 5** [C] the part of an aircraft's flight immediately before landing: *to begin the final approach to the runway*
▷ **SOMETHING SIMILAR 6** [sing.] a thing that is like something else that is mentioned: *That's the **nearest approach** to an apology you'll get from him.* **IDM** see CARROT

ap·proach·a·ble **AWL** /əˈproʊtʃəbl/ *adj.* **1** friendly and easy to talk to; easy to understand: *Despite being a big star,*

she's very approachable. ◆ *an approachable piece of music* **ANT** UNAPPROACHABLE **2** [not before noun] that can be reached by a particular route or from a particular direction: *The summit was approachable only from the south.*

ap·pro·ba·tion /ˌæprəˈbeɪʃn/ *noun* [U] (*formal*) approval or agreement

ap·pro·pri·a·cy **AWL** /əˈproʊpriəsi/ *noun* [U] **1** (*formal*) the extent to which something is suitable or acceptable **2** (*linguistics*) the extent to which a word or phrase sounds correct and natural in relation to the situation it is used in

ap·pro·pri·ate 🗝 **AWL** *adj., verb*
● *adj.* /əˈproʊpriət/ suitable, acceptable, or correct for the particular circumstances: *an appropriate response/measure/ method* ◆ *Now that the problem has been identified, appropriate action can be taken.* ◆ *Is now an appropriate time to make a speech?* ◆ *Please charge my Mastercard/Visa/American Express card (delete as appropriate).* ◆ ~ **for sth** *Jeans are not appropriate for a formal party.* ◆ *This movie is appropriate for children over 13.* ◆ ~ **to sth** *The book was written in a style appropriate to the era.* **ANT** INAPPROPRIATE ▶ ap·pro·pri·ate·ly **AWL** *adv.*: *The government has been accused of not responding appropriately to the needs of the homeless.* ◆ *The chain of volcanoes is known, **appropriately enough**, as the "Ring of Fire."* ap·pro·pri·ate·ness **AWL** *noun* [U]
● *verb* /əˈproʊpriˌeɪt/ (*formal*) **1** ~ **sth** to take something, someone's ideas, etc. for your own use, especially illegally or without permission: *He was accused of appropriating club funds.* ◆ *Some of the opposition party's policies have been appropriated by the government.* **2** ~ **sth** (**for sth**) to take or give something, especially money, for a particular purpose: *Five million dollars have been appropriated for research into the disease.* ⊃ compare MISAPPROPRIATE

ap·pro·pri·a·tion /əˌproʊpriˈeɪʃn/ *noun* **1** [U, sing.] (*formal* or *law*) the act of taking something that belongs to someone else, especially without permission: *dishonest appropriation of property* ⊃ compare MISAPPROPRIATE **2** [U, sing.] (*formal*) the act of keeping or saving money for a particular purpose: *a meeting to discuss the appropriation of funds* **3** [C] (*formal*) a sum of money to be used for a particular purpose, especially by a government or company: *an appropriation of $20,000 for debt payment*

ap·prov·al 🗝 /əˈpruvl/ *noun*
1 [U] the feeling that someone or something is good or acceptable; a positive opinion of someone or something: *She desperately wanted to win her father's approval.* ◆ *Do the plans **meet with your approval**?* ◆ *Several people nodded **in approval**.* **ANT** DISAPPROVAL **2** [U, C] agreement to, or permission for something, especially a plan or request: *The plan will be submitted to the committee for official approval.* ◆ *congressional/government approval* ◆ *Senior management has given its **seal of approval** (= formal approval) to the plans.* ◆ *I can't agree to anything without my partner's approval.* ◆ *planning approvals* ◆ *The proposal is **subject to approval** by the shareholders* (= they need to agree to it). ◆ ~ **(for sth) (from sb)** *They required/received approval for the proposal from the shareholders.* **3** [U] if you buy goods, or if goods are sold, **on approval**, you can use them for a time without paying, until you decide if you want to buy them or not

ap·prove 🗝 /əˈpruv/ *verb*
1 [I] to think that someone or something is good, acceptable, or suitable: *I told my mother I wanted to drop out of school, but she didn't approve.* ◆ ~ **of sb/sth** *Do you approve of my idea?* ◆ ~ **of sb doing sth** *She doesn't approve of me dropping out of school this year.* ◆ (*formal*) ~ **of sb's doing sth** *She doesn't approve of my dropping out of school this year.* **ANT** DISAPPROVE **2** [T] ~ **sth** to officially agree to a plan, request, etc.: *The committee unanimously approved the plan.* ⊃ thesaurus box at AGREE **3** [T, often passive] ~ **sth** to say that something is good enough to be used, or is correct: *The course is approved by the Board of Education.*

ap·prov·ing 🗝 /əˈpruvɪŋ/ *adj.*
showing that you believe that someone or something is

good or acceptable: *He gave me an approving nod.* **ANT** DISAPPROVING ▸ **ap·prov·ing·ly** *adv.*: *She looked at him approvingly and smiled.*

ap·prox. *abbr.* APPROXIMATE, APPROXIMATELY

ap·prox·i·mant /əˈprɑksəmənt/ *noun* **1** (*phonetics*) a speech sound made by bringing the parts of the mouth that produce speech close together but not actually touching, for example /r/ and /w/ in *right* and *wet* in many accents of English **2** (*mathematics*) a solution that is close to but not exactly the solution of a problem

ap·prox·i·mate 🔑 **AWL** *adj., verb*
- *adj.* /əˈprɑksəmət/ (*abbr.* **approx.**) almost correct or accurate, but not completely so: *an approximate number/total/cost* ♦ *The cost given is only approximate.* ♦ *Use these figures as an approximate guide in your calculations.* **ANT** EXACT
- *verb* /əˈprɑksəˌmeɪt/ (*formal*) **1** [T, I] to be similar or close to something in nature, quality, amount, etc., but not exactly the same: *~ sth The animals were reared in conditions that approximated the wild as closely as possible.* ♦ *The total cost will approximate $15 billion.* **2** [T] *~ sth* to calculate or estimate something fairly accurately: *a formula for approximating the weight of a horse*

ap·prox·i·mate·ly 🔑 **AWL** /əˈprɑksəmətli/ *adv.* used to show that something is almost, but not completely, accurate or correct: *The trip takes approximately seven hours.*

VOCABULARY BUILDING

ways of saying "approximately"
- The flight takes **approximately** three hours.
- The tickets cost **about** $20 each.
- You can expect to earn **around** $40,000 a year.
- The repairs will cost $200, **give or take** a few dollars.
- How much will it cost, **more or less**?
- We are expecting thirty **or so** people to come.
- She must be 25 **or thereabouts**.
- Profits have fallen by **roughly** 15%.
- The price is **somewhere around** $800.
- She earns **somewhere in the region of** $25,000.

All these words and phrases are used in both speaking and writing; **about** is the most common and **approximately** the most formal.

ap·prox·i·ma·tion **AWL** /əˌprɑksəˈmeɪʃn/ *noun* **1** an estimate of a number or an amount that is almost correct, but not exact: *That's just an approximation, you understand.* **2** *~ (of/to sth)* a thing that is similar to something else, but is not exactly the same: *Our results should be a good approximation of the true state of affairs.*

ap·pur·te·nance /əˈpɜrtnəns/ *noun* [usually pl.] (*formal* or *humorous*) a thing that forms a part of something larger or more important

APR /ˌeɪ pi ˈɑr/ *noun* [sing.] the abbreviation for "annual percentage rate" (the amount of interest a bank charges on money that it lends, calculated for a period of a year): *an APR of 26.4%*

a·près-ski /ˌɑpreɪ ˈski; ˌæ-/ *noun* [U] (from *French*) social activities and entertainment that take place in hotels and restaurants after a day's SKIING

ap·ri·cot /ˈæprɪˌkɑt; ˈeɪ-/ *noun* **1** [C] a small round fruit with yellow or orange skin, soft flesh, and a large seed (called a PIT) inside: *dried apricots* ◻ **picture at** FRUIT **2** [U] a yellowish-orange color ▸ **ap·ri·cot** *adj.*: *The room was painted apricot and white.*

A·pril 🔑 /ˈeɪprəl/ *noun* [U, C] (*abbr.* **Apr.**) the fourth month of the year, between March and May: *She was born in April.* ♦ *The meeting is on April fifth.* ♦ *We went to Japan last April.* ♦ *I arrived at the end of April.* ♦ *last April's election* ♦ *April showers* ♦ *an April wedding*

April Fool *noun* a person who has a trick played on them on April Fool's Day

April Fool's Day *noun* April 1, a day on which people traditionally play tricks on each other

a pri·o·ri /ˌeɪ praɪˈɔraɪ; ˌɑ priˈɔri/ *adj., adv.* (from *Latin, formal*) using facts or principles that are known to be true in order to decide what the likely effects or results of something will be, for example saying, "They haven't eaten anything all day so they must be hungry." ◻ **compare** A POSTERIORI

a·pron /ˈeɪprən/ *noun* **1** a piece of clothing worn over the front of the body, from the chest or the waist down, and tied around the waist. Aprons are worn over other clothes to keep them clean, for example when cooking. **2** (*technical*) an area with a hard surface at an airport, where aircraft are turned around, loaded, etc. **3** (also **apron stage**) (*technical*) (in a theater) the part of the stage that is in front of the curtain
IDM (tied to) sb's apron strings (too much under) the influence and control of someone: *Foreign governments needing aid often cling to America's apron strings.*

ap·ro·pos /ˌæprəˈpou/ (also **apro·pos of**) *prep.* concerning or related to someone or something: *Apropos (of) what you were just saying…* ♦ *Apropos of nothing…* (= with no connection to what was previously said or done)

apse /æps/ *noun* a small area, often in the shape of a SEMICIRCLE, usually at the east end of a church

apt /æpt/ *adj.* **1** suitable or appropriate in the circumstances: *a particularly apt description/name/comment* **2** likely or having a natural tendency to do something: *~ to be… apt to be forgetful/careless* ♦ *~ to do sth Babies are apt to put objects into their mouths.* **3** *~ student/pupil* a person who has a natural ability to learn and understand ▸ **apt·ly** *adv.*: *the aptly named Grand Hotel* **apt·ness** *noun* [U]

apt. *abbr.* (in writing) apartment

ap·ti·tude /ˈæptəˌtud/ *noun* [U, C] natural ability or skill at doing something **SYN** TALENT: *an aptitude test* (= one designed to show whether someone has the natural ability for a particular job or course of education) ♦ *~ for sth She showed a natural aptitude for the work.* ♦ *~ in sth an aptitude in math and science* ♦ *~ for doing sth His aptitude for dealing with children got him the job.* ♦ *~in doing sth Applicants are tested on their aptitude in solving problems.*

aq·ua /ˈækwə; ˈɑ-/ *noun* [U] **1** water (used especially on the labels on packages of food, drinks, medicines, etc. in order to show how much water they contain) **2** a blue-green color

aq·ua·cul·ture /ˈækwəˌkʌltʃər; ˈɑ-/ *noun* [U] the growing of plants in water for food

aq·ua·lung /ˈækwəˌlʌŋ; ˈɑ-/ *noun* a piece of breathing equipment that DIVERS wear on their backs when swimming underwater

aq·ua·ma·rine /ˌækwəməˈrin; ˌɑ-/ *noun* **1** [C, U] a pale greenish-blue SEMI-PRECIOUS STONE **2** [U] a pale greenish-blue color ▸ **aq·ua·ma·rine** *adj.*: *an aquamarine sea*

aq·ua·plane /ˈækwəˌpleɪn; ˈɑ-/ *verb, noun*
- *verb* [I] to stand on a board that is pulled along on water behind a SPEEDBOAT in the sport of aquaplaning
- *noun* a board that someone stands on in the sport of aquaplaning

aq·ua·plan·ing /ˈækwəˌpleɪnɪŋ; ˈɑ-/ *noun* [U] the sport of being pulled along on a board behind a SPEEDBOAT on water

a·quar·i·um /əˈkwɛriəm/ *noun* (*pl.* **a·quar·i·ums** or **a·quar·i·a** /-iə/) **1** a large glass container in which fish and other water creatures, and plants are kept **2** a building where people can go to see fish and other water creatures

A·quar·i·us /əˈkwɛriəs/ (also the **Water Bearer**, the **Water Carrier**) *noun* **1** [U] the 11th sign of the ZODIAC **2** [sing.] a person born under the influence of this sign, that is between January 21 and February 19 ▸ **A·quar·i·an** /əˈkwɛriən/ *noun, adj.*

t **t**ea   ṱ **b**u**tt**er   d **d**id   k **c**at   g **g**ot   tʃ **ch**in   dʒ **J**une   f **f**all

a·quat·ic /əˈkwætɪk; əˈkwɑtɪk/ adj. [usually before noun] **1** growing or living in, on, or near water: *aquatic plants/ life/ecosystems* **2** connected with water: *aquatic sports*

aq·ua·tint /ˈækwəˌtɪnt; ˈɑ-/ noun [U, C] (technical) a method of producing a picture using acid on a metal plate; a picture produced using this method

aq·ue·duct /ˈækwəˌdʌkt/ noun a structure for carrying water, usually one built like a bridge across a valley or low ground

a·que·ous /ˈeɪkwiəs; ˈæ-/ adj. (technical) containing water; like water

aqueous ˈhumor (CanE usually **aqueous ˈhumour**) noun [U] (anatomy) the clear liquid inside the front part of the eye ➔ compare VITREOUS HUMOR

aq·ui·fer /ˈækwəfər; ˈɑ-/ noun (geology) a layer of rock or soil that can absorb and hold water

aq·ui·line /ˈækwəˌlaɪn; -lən/ adj. (formal) a person with an **aquiline nose** or **aquiline features** has a nose that is thin and curved, similar to that of an EAGLE

AR abbr. (in writing) Arkansas

-ar /ɑr/ suffix **1** (in nouns) a person who: *beggar* ➔ compare -EE, -ER, -OR **2** (in adjectives) connected with or similar to: *circular*

Ar·ab /ˈærəb/ noun, adj.
- **noun** a person from the Middle East or N. Africa, whose ANCESTORS lived in the Arabian Peninsula
- **adj.** of or connected with Arabia or Arabs: *Arab countries*

ar·a·besque /ˌærəˈbesk/ noun **1** [C] (in BALLET) a position in which the dancer balances on one leg with the other leg lifted and stretched out behind, parallel to the ground **2** [C, U] (in art) a type of design where lines wind around each other

A·ra·bi·an /əˈreɪbiən/ adj., noun
- **adj.** of or connected with Arabia **HELP** Arabian is used to describe places: *the Arabian peninsula*. The people are **Arabs** and the adjective to describe them is **Arab**: *Arab children*. The language is **Arabic**: *Arabic script*
- **noun** a type of horse originally from Arabia

A·ra·bic /ˈærəbɪk/ noun, adj.
- **noun** [U] the language of the Arabs
- **adj.** of or connected with the literature and language of Arab people: *Arabic poetry*

Arabic ˈnumeral noun any of the symbols 0, 1, 2, 3, 4, etc. used for writing numbers in many countries ➔ compare ROMAN NUMERAL

ar·a·ble /ˈærəbl/ adj. (of land or soil) used or able to be used for growing crops: *arable land/fields*

a·rach·nid /əˈræknɪd/ noun (technical) any small creature of the class that includes spiders, SCORPIONS, MITES, and TICKS ➔ compare INSECT

a·rach·no·pho·bi·a /əˌræknəˈfoubiə/ noun [U] an extreme fear of spiders

A·rap·a·ho /əˈræpəˌhou/ noun (pl. **A·rap·a·ho** or **A·rap·a·hos**) a member of a Native American people, most of whom live on the Great Plains, especially in Wyoming

ar·bi·ter /ˈɑrbətər/ noun ~ **(of sth)** a person with the power or influence to make judgments and decide what will be done or accepted: *The law is the final arbiter of what is considered obscene.* ◆ *an arbiter of taste/style/fashion*

ar·bi·trage /ˈɑrbəˌtrɑʒ/ noun [U] (business) the practice of buying something (for example, shares or foreign money) in one place and selling it in another place where the price is higher ▶ **ar·bi·tra·geur** /ˌɑrbətrɑˈʒɜr/ (also **ar·bit·ra·ger** /ˈɑrbəˌtrɑʒər/) noun

ar·bi·trar·y **AWL** /ˈɑrbəˌtreri/ adj. **1** (of an action, a decision, a rule, etc.) not seeming to be based on a reason, system, or plan and sometimes seeming unfair: *The choice of players for the team seemed completely arbitrary.* ◆ *He makes unpredictable, arbitrary decisions.* **2** (formal) using power without restriction and without considering other people:

the arbitrary powers of officials ▶ **ar·bi·trar·i·ly** **AWL** /ˌɑrbəˈtrerəli/ adv.: *The leaders of the groups were chosen arbitrarily.* **ar·bi·trar·i·ness** **AWL** /ˈɑrbəˌtrerinəs/ noun [U]

ar·bi·trate /ˈɑrbəˌtreɪt/ verb [I, T] to officially settle an argument or a disagreement between two people or groups: ~ **(in/on) (sth)** *to arbitrate in a dispute* ◆ ~ **between A and B** *A committee was created to arbitrate between management and the unions.*

ar·bi·tra·tion /ˌɑrbəˈtreɪʃn/ noun [U] the official process of settling an argument or a disagreement by someone who is not involved: *Both sides in the dispute have agreed to go to arbitration.*

ar·bi·tra·tor /ˈɑrbəˌtreɪtər/ noun a person who is chosen to settle a disagreement

ar·bor (CanE usually **ar·bour**) /ˈɑrbər/ noun a shelter in a yard for people to sit under, made by growing climbing plants over a frame

ˈArbor ˌDay noun a day when people in the U.S., Canada, and some other countries plant trees

ar·bo·re·al /ɑrˈbɔriəl/ adj. (technical) relating to trees; living in trees

ar·bo·re·tum /ˌɑrbəˈritəm/ noun (pl. **ar·bo·re·tums** or **ar·bo·re·ta** /-ˈritə/) a garden where many different types of trees are grown, for people to look at or for scientific study

ar·bor·i·cul·ture /ˈɑrbərəˌkʌltʃər; ɑrˈbɔrə-/ noun [U] (technical) the study or practice of growing trees and SHRUBS ▶ **ar·bor·i·cul·tur·al** /ˌɑrbərəˈkʌltʃərəl; ɑrˌbɔrə-/ adj.: *an ar-boricultural specialist* **ar·bor·i·cul·tur·ist** /-ˈkʌltʃərɪst/ noun

ar·bor·ist /ˈɑrbərɪst/ noun (formal or technical) = TREE SURGEON

ar·bour (CanE) = ARBOR

arc /ɑrk/ noun, verb
- **noun 1** (geometry) part of a circle or a curved line ➔ picture at SHAPE **2** a curved shape: *the arc of a rainbow* ◆ *The beach swept around in an arc.* **3** (technical) an electric current passing across a space between two TERMINALS ➔ see also ARC LIGHT
- **verb** (arc·ing /ˈɑrkɪŋ/, arced, arced /ɑrkt/) (technical) **1** [I] to move in the shape of an arc **2** [I] to form an electric arc

ar·cade /ɑrˈkeɪd/ noun **1** a place where you can play games on machines that are operated by coins: *arcade games* **2** a covered passage with ARCHES along the side of a row of buildings (usually a row of stores) **3** a covered passage between streets, with stores on either side

Ar·ca·di·a /ɑrˈkeɪdiə/ noun [sing.] a part of southern Greece used in poetry and stories to represent an idea of perfect country life

Ar·ca·di·an /ɑrˈkeɪdiən/ adj. of or connected with Arcadia or an idea of perfect country life

ar·ca·na /ɑrˈkeɪnə/ noun **1** [pl.] things that are secret or mysterious **2** [sing.] either of the two groups of cards in a TAROT DECK, the **major arcana** and the **minor arcana**

ar·cane /ɑrˈkeɪn/ adj. (formal) secret and mysterious, and therefore difficult to understand

arch /ɑrtʃ/ noun, verb, adj.
- **noun 1** a curved structure that supports the weight of something above it, such as a bridge or the upper part of a building **2** a structure with a curved top that is supported by straight sides, sometimes forming an entrance or built as a MONUMENT: *Go through the arch and follow the path.* ◆ *The Gateway Arch is a famous St. Louis landmark.* ➔ picture at ARCHITECTURE **3** the raised part of the foot formed by a curved section of bones **4** anything that forms a curved shape at the top: *the delicate arch of her eyebrows*
- **verb 1** [T, I] ~ **(sth)** if you arch part of your body, or if it arches, it moves and forms a curved shape: *The cat arched its back and hissed.* **2** [I] to be in a curved line or shape across or over something: *Tall trees arched over the path.*
- **adj.** [usually before noun] (often disapproving) seeming amused because you know more about a situation than

other people: *an arch tone of voice* ▸ **arch·ly** *adv*.: *"Guess what?" she said archly.*

arch- /ɑrtʃ/ *combining form* (in nouns) main; most important or most extreme: *archbishop* ◆ *archenemy*

ar·chae·ol·o·gist (also **ar·che·ol·o·gist**) /ˌɑrkiˈɑlədʒɪst/ *noun* a person who studies archaeology

ar·chae·ol·o·gy (also **ar·che·ol·o·gy**) /ˌɑrkiˈɑlədʒi/ *noun* [U] the study of cultures of the past, and of periods of history, by examining the remains of buildings and objects found in the ground ⊃ see also INDUSTRIAL ARCHAEOLOGY ▸ **ar·chae·o·log·i·cal** (also **ar·che·o·log·i·cal**) /ˌɑrkiə ˈlɑdʒɪkl/ *adj*.: *archaeological excavations/evidence*

ar·chae·op·ter·yx /ˌɑrkiˈɑptərɪks/ *noun* the oldest known bird, which existed about 150 million years ago

ar·cha·ic /ɑrˈkeɪɪk/ *adj*. **1** old and not used anymore: *"Thou art" is an archaic form of "you are."* **2** very old-fashioned **SYN** OUTDATED: *The system is archaic and unfair and needs changing.* **3** from a much earlier or ancient period of history: *archaic art*

ar·cha·ism /ˈɑrkiˌɪzəm; -keɪ-/ *noun* (*technical*) a very old word or phrase that is not used anymore

arch·an·gel /ˈɑrkˌeɪndʒl/ *noun* an ANGEL of the highest rank: *the Archangel Gabriel*

arch·bish·op /ˌɑrtʃˈbɪʃəp/ *noun* a BISHOP of the highest rank, responsible for all the churches in a large area: *Archbishop Desmond Tutu*

arch·bish·op·ric /ˌɑrtʃˈbɪʃəprɪk/ *noun* **1** the position of an archbishop **2** the district for which an archbishop is responsible

arch·dea·con /ˌɑrtʃˈdikən/ *noun* a priest just below the rank of BISHOP, especially in the Anglican Church

arch·di·o·cese /ˌɑrtʃˈdaɪəsəs; -siz; -sis/ *noun* a district under the care of an ARCHBISHOP

arch·duch·ess /ˌɑrtʃˈdʌtʃəs/ *noun* (in the past) the wife of an archduke or a daughter of the EMPEROR of Austria

arch·duke /ˌɑrtʃˈduk/ *noun* (in the past) a son of the EMPEROR of Austria: *Archduke Franz Ferdinand* ⊃ compare GRAND DUKE

arched /ɑrtʃt/ *adj*. in the shape of an ARCH: *a chair with an arched back*

arch·en·e·my *noun* /ˌɑrtʃˈɛnəmi/ (*pl*. **arch·en·e·mies**) a person's main enemy

ar·che·ol·o·gist, ar·che·ol·o·gy = ARCHAEOLOGIST, ARCHAEOLOGY

arch·er /ˈɑrtʃər/ *noun* a person who shoots with a BOW² and arrows ⊃ picture at SPORT

arch·er·y /ˈɑrtʃəri/ *noun* [U] the art or sport of shooting arrows with a BOW² ⊃ picture at SPORT

ar·che·typ·al /ˌɑrkəˈtaɪpl/ *adj*. having all the important qualities that make someone or something a typical example of a particular kind of person or thing: *We're going on the archetypal beach vacation with the kids.*

ar·che·type /ˈɑrkəˌtaɪp/ *noun* the most typical or perfect example of a particular kind of person or thing: *She is the archetype of an American movie star.*

ar·chi·pel·a·go /ˌɑrkəˈpɛləɡoʊ/ *noun* (*pl*. **ar·chi·pel·a·gos** or **ar·chi·pel·a·goes**) a group of islands and the ocean surrounding them

ar·chi·tect /ˈɑrkəˌtɛkt/ *noun* **1** a person whose job is designing buildings, etc. **2** a person who is responsible for planning or creating an idea, an event, or a situation: *He was one of the principal architects of the revolution.* ◆ *Jones was the architect of the team's first goal.*

ar·chi·tec·ton·ic /ˌɑrkətɛkˈtɑnɪk/ *adj*. (*technical*) of or connected with architecture or architects

ar·chi·tec·tur·al /ˌɑrkəˈtɛktʃərəl/ *adj*. connected with architecture: *architectural features* ▸ **ar·chi·tec·tur·al·ly** *adv*.: *The house is of little interest architecturally.*

ar·chi·tec·ture /ˈɑrkəˌtɛktʃər/ *noun* **1** [U] the art and study

of designing buildings: *to study architecture* **2** [U] the design or style of a building or buildings: *the architecture of the eighteenth century* ◆ *modern architecture* ⊃ picture on page 67 **3** [C, U] (*computing*) the design and structure of a computer system

ar·chi·trave /ˈɑrkəˌtreɪv/ *noun* (*technical*) the frame around a door or window

ar·chive /ˈɑrkaɪv/ *noun, verb*
● *noun* (also **ar·chives**) [pl.] a collection of historical documents or records of a government, a family, a place, or an organization; the place where these records are stored: *the National Archives in Washington, D.C.* ◆ *archive film* ◆ *sepia photographs from the family archives*
● *verb* **1** ~ sth to put or store a document or other material in an archive **2** ~ sth (*computing*) to move information that is not often needed to a tape or disk to store it

ar·chi·vist /ˈɑrkəvɪst; -kaɪ-/ *noun* a person whose job is to develop and manage an archive

arch·ri·val /ˌɑrtʃˈraɪvl/ *noun* the main opponent of a person, team, or organization

arch·way /ˈɑrtʃweɪ/ *noun* a passage or an entrance with an ARCH over it: *We went through a stone archway into the courtyard.*

arc light (also **arc lamp**) *noun* a lamp that gives very bright light that is produced by an electric ARC

Arc·tic /ˈɑrktɪk; ˈɑrtɪk/ *adj., noun*
● *adj*. **1** [only before noun] related to or happening in the regions around the North Pole: *Arctic explorers* ⊃ compare ANTARCTIC **2** arctic extremely cold: *The news reported arctic conditions in the city.*
● *noun* [sing.] **the Arctic** the regions of the world around the North Pole

the ˌArctic ˈCircle *noun* [sing.] the line of LATITUDE 66° 33′ North ⊃ picture at EARTH ⊃ compare ANTARCTIC CIRCLE

ar·dent /ˈɑrdnt/ *adj*. [usually before noun] very enthusiastic and showing strong feelings about something or someone **SYN** PASSIONATE: *an ardent supporter of civil rights* ▸ **ar·dent·ly** *adv*.

ar·dor (CanE usually **ar·dour**) /ˈɑrdər/ *noun* [U] (*formal*) very strong feelings of enthusiasm or love **SYN** PASSION

ar·du·ous /ˈɑrdʒuəs/ *adj*. involving a lot of effort and energy, especially over a period of time: *an arduous journey across the Andes* ◆ *The work was arduous.* ▸ **ar·du·ous·ly** *adv*.

are /ər; strong form ɑr/ ⊃ BE

ar·e·a 🔑 AWL /ˈɛriə/ *noun*
▷ **PART OF PLACE 1** [C] part of a place, town, etc., or a region of a country or the world: *mountainous/desert areas* ◆ *rural/ urban/inner-city areas* ◆ *There is heavy traffic in the downtown area tonight.* ◆ *She knows the local area very well.* ◆ *John is the Cleveland area manager.* ◆ *Wreckage from the plane was scattered over a wide area.* ◆ *The farm and surrounding area were flooded.* ⊃ see also CATCHMENT AREA, CONSERVATION AREA, DEVELOPMENT AREA **2** [C] a part of a room, building, or particular space that is used for a special purpose: *the hotel reception area* ◆ *a play/parking/dining area* ⊃ see also PENALTY AREA, REST AREA, SERVICE AREA ⊃ thesaurus box at PLACE
▷ **PARTICULAR PLACE 3** [C] a particular place on an object: *Move the cursor to a blank area of the computer screen.* ◆ *The tumor had not spread to other areas of the body.*
▷ **SUBJECT/ACTIVITY 4** [C] ~ (of sth) a particular subject or activity, or an aspect of it: *the areas of training and development* ◆ *Finance is Mark's area.* ◆ *The big growth area of recent years has been in health clubs.* ⊃ see also GRAY AREA
▷ **MEASUREMENT 5** [C, U] the amount of space covered by a flat surface or piece of land, described as a measurement: *the area of a triangle* ◆ *The room is 120 square feet in area.*

ˈarea ˌcode *noun* the numbers for a particular area or city, that you use when you are making a telephone call from outside the local area: *What is your three-digit area code?*

a·re·na /əˈrinə/ *noun* **1** a place with a flat open area in the

architecture

cupola

dome

dome

rotunda

vaulted ceiling

keystone

arch

gargoyle

obelisk

relief

portico

geodesic dome

colonnade

capital

plinth column

cloister

middle and seats around it where people can watch sports and entertainment: *a concert at Pittsburgh's Mellon Arena* **2** (*formal*) an area of activity that concerns the public, especially one where there is a lot of opposition between different groups or countries: *the political/international arena*

aren't /ɑːnt; ˈɑːrənt/ *short form* **1** are not **2** (in questions) am not: *I'm invited, aren't I?*

a·re·o·la /əˈriːələ; ˌɛriˈoʊlə/ *noun* (*pl.* **a·re·o·lae** /-liː/) the round area of skin around the **NIPPLE** (= on a breast)

ar·gon /ˈɑːɡɒn/ *noun* [U] (*symb.* **Ar**) a chemical element. Argon is a gas that does not react with anything and is used in electric lights.

ar·got /ˈɑːɡoʊ; -ɡət/ *noun* [sing., U] (from *French*) words and phrases that are used by a particular group of people and not easily understood by others **SYN** JARGON

ar·gu·a·ble /ˈɑːɡjuəbl/ *adj.* (*formal*) **1** that you can give good reasons for: *It is arguable that giving too much detail may actually be confusing.* **2** not certain; that you do not accept without question **SYN** DEBATABLE: *It is arguable whether the case should have ever gone to trial* (= perhaps it should not have).

ar·gu·a·bly /ˈɑːɡjuəbli/ *adv.* used, often before a compar-

ative or superlative adjective, when you are stating an opinion that you believe you could give reasons to support: *He is arguably the best actor of his generation.*

ar·gue 🔑 /ˈɑːɡjuː/ *verb*
1 [I] to speak angrily to someone because you disagree with them: *My brothers are always arguing.* ◆ **~ (with sb) (about/over sth)** *We're always arguing with each other about money.* ◆ **~ with sb** *I don't want to argue with you—just do it!* **2** [I, T] to give reasons why you think that something is right/wrong, true/not true, etc., especially to persuade people that you are right: *They argued for the right to strike.* ◆ **~ sth** *She argued the case for bringing back the death penalty.* ◆ *He was too tired to* **argue the point** (= discuss the matter). ◆ *a well-argued article* ◆ **~ that...** *He argued that they needed more time to finish the project.* ◆ *It could be argued that laws are made by and for men.* ⊃ language bank on page 68 and at NEVERTHELESS, PERHAPS **3** [T] **~ sth** (*formal*) to show clearly that something exists or is true: *These latest developments argue a change in government policy.*

PHRV **'argue with sth** (usually used in negative sentences) (*informal*) to disagree with a statement: *He's a really successful man—you can't argue with that.*

argue

verbs for reporting an opinion

- Some critics **argue** that Picasso remained a great master all his life.
- Others **maintain** that his post-war work showed a significant deterioration in quality.
- Picasso himself **claimed** that good art is created, but great art is stolen.
- As Smith **has noted**, Picasso borrowed imagery from African art.
- As the author **points out**, Picasso borrowed imagery from African art.
- The writer **challenges the notion that** Picasso's sculpture was secondary to his painting.
- **It has been suggested that/**Sanchez **suggests that** Picasso's painting was influenced by jazz music.

➲ Language Banks at ABOUT, ACCORDING TO

ar·gu·ment ♪ /ˈɑrgyəmənt/ *noun*

1 [C, U] a conversation or discussion in which two or more people disagree, often angrily: *to win/lose an argument* ◆ *After some heated argument, they finally made a decision.* ◆ **~ (with sb) (about/over sth)** *We had an argument with the waiter about the check.* ◆ **~ with sb** *She got into an argument with the teacher.* **2** [C] a reason or set of reasons that someone uses to show that something is true or correct: *Her main argument was a moral one.* ◆ **~ for/against sth** *There are strong arguments for and against euthanasia.* ◆ **~ that...** *His argument was that public spending must be reduced.* **3** [U] **~ (about sth)** the act of disagreeing in a conversation or discussion using a reason or set of reasons: *Let's assume for the sake of argument* (= in order to discuss the problem) *that we can't start till March.*

ar·gu·men·ta·tion /ˌɑrgyəmənˈteɪʃn/ *noun* [U] logical arguments used to support a theory, an action, or an idea

ar·gu·men·ta·tive /ˌɑrgyəˈmɛntətɪv/ *adj.* a person who is **argumentative** likes arguing or often starts arguing

ar·gyle /ˈɑrgaɪl/ *noun* [U] a pattern of diamond shapes on a plain background, especially on a sweater or on socks

a·ri·a /ˈɑriə/ *noun* a song for one voice, especially in an OPERA or ORATORIO

–arian /ˈɛriən/ *suffix* (in nouns and adjectives) believing in; practicing: *humanitarian* ◆ *disciplinarian*

ar·id /ˈærɪd/ *adj.* **1** (of land or a climate) having little or no rain; very dry: *arid and semi-arid deserts* **2** (*formal*) with nothing new or interesting in it: *an arid discussion* ▶ **a·rid·i·ty** /əˈrɪdəti/ *noun* [U]

Ar·ies /ˈɛriz/ *noun* **1** [U] the first sign of the ZODIAC, the RAM **2** [sing.] a person born under the influence of this sign, that is between March 21 and April 20

a·right /əˈraɪt/ *adv.* (*old-fashioned*) correctly **IDM** **set sth aright** to put something back into good condition or proper order: *The system is not fair, and we want to set it aright.*

a·rise ♪ /əˈraɪz/ *verb* (**a·rose** /əˈroʊz/, **a·ris·en** /əˈrɪzn/)

1 [I] (somewhat *formal*) (especially of a problem or a difficult situation) to happen; to start to exist **SYN** OCCUR: *A new crisis has arisen.* ◆ *We keep them informed of any changes as they arise.* ◆ *Children should be disciplined when the need arises/should the need arise* (= when it is necessary). ◆ *A storm arose during the night.* **2** [I] **~ (out of/from sth)** (somewhat *formal*) to happen as a result of a particular situation: *injuries arising out of a road accident* ◆ *Emotional or mental problems can arise from a physical cause.* ◆ *Are there any questions arising from the minutes of the last meeting?* **3** [I] (*formal*) to begin to exist or develop: *Several new industries arose in the town.* **4** [I] (*old use or literary*) to get out of bed; to stand up: *He arose at dawn.* **5** [I] **~ (against sb/sth)** (*old use*) to come together to protest

about something or to fight for something: *The peasants arose against their masters.* **6** [I] (*literary*) (of a mountain, a tall building, etc.) to become visible gradually as you move toward it

ar·is·toc·ra·cy /ˌærəˈstɑkrəsi/ *noun* (*pl.* **ar·is·toc·ra·cies**) (in some countries) people born in the highest social class, who have special titles **SYN** NOBILITY: *members of the aristocracy*

a·ris·to·crat /əˈrɪstəˌkræt/ *noun* a member of the aristocracy ➲ compare COMMONER

a·ris·to·crat·ic /əˌrɪstəˈkrætɪk/ *adj.* belonging to or typical of the ARISTOCRACY **SYN** NOBLE: *an aristocratic name/ family/lifestyle*

Ar·is·to·te·lian /ˌærəstəˈtilyən; əˌrɪstə-/ *adj.* connected with Aristotle or his philosophy

a·rith·me·tic /əˈrɪθmətɪk/ *noun* [U] **1** the type of mathematics that deals with the adding, multiplying, etc. of numbers: *He's not very good at arithmetic.* **2** math problems involving the adding, multiplying, etc. of numbers: *a quick bit of mental arithmetic* ◆ *I think there's something wrong with your arithmetic.*

ar·ith·met·i·cal /ˌærɪθˈmɛtɪkl/ (also **ar·ith·met·ic** /ˌærɪθˈmɛtɪk/) *adj.* relating to arithmetic: *an arithmetical calculation* ▶ **ar·ith·met·i·cal·ly** /-kli/ *adv.*

ˌarithmetic ˈmean *noun* (*mathematics*) = MEAN *n.* (2)

ˌarithmetic proˈgression (also **ˌarithmetic ˈseries**) *noun* a series of numbers that decrease or increase by the same amount each time, for example 2, 4, 6, 8 ➲ compare GEOMETRIC PROGRESSION

the ark /ɑrk/ (also **Noah's ˈark**) *noun* [sing.] (in the Bible) a large boat that Noah built to save his family and two of every type of animal from the flood

arm ♪ /ɑrm/ *noun, verb*

▸ *noun* ➲ see also ARMS

▸ PART OF BODY **1** either of the two long parts that stick out from the top of the body and connect the shoulders to the hands: *He escaped with only a broken arm.* ◆ *She threw her arms around his neck.* ◆ *The officer grabbed him by the arm* (= grabbed his arm). ◆ *She touched him gently on the arm.* ◆ *He held the dirty rag at arm's length* (= as far away from his body as possible). ◆ *They walked along arm in arm* (= with the arm of one person linked with the arm of the other). ◆ *She cradled the child in her arms.* ◆ *They fell asleep in each other's arms* (= holding each other). ◆ *He was carrying a number of files under his arm* (= between his arm and his body). ◆ *He walked in with a tall blond lady on his arm* (= next to him and holding his arm). ➲ picture at BODY ➲ collocations at PHYSICAL

▸ OF CLOTHING **2** the part of a piece of clothing that covers the arm **SYN** SLEEVE

▸ OF CHAIR **3** the part of a chair, etc. on which you rest your arms ➲ picture at BRIDGE

▸ OF MACHINERY **4** a long narrow part of an object or a piece of machinery, especially one that moves, for example a CRANE

▸ OF WATER/LAND **5** a long narrow piece of water or land that is joined to a larger area: *A bridge spans the arm of the river.*

▸ OF ORGANIZATION **6** [usually sing.] **~ (of sth)** a section of a large organization that deals with one particular activity **SYN** WING: *the research arm of the company* **IDM** **cost/pay an arm and a leg** (*informal*) to cost/pay a lot of money **keep sb at arm's length** to avoid having a close relationship with someone: *He keeps all his clients at arm's length.* ➲ more at AKIMBO, BABE, BEAR *v.*, FOLD *v.*, LONG *adj.*, OPEN *adj.*, RIGHT *adj.*, SHOT *n.*, TWIST *v.*

▸ *verb* **1** [I, T] to provide weapons for yourself/someone in order to fight a battle or a war: **~ yourself/sb (with sth)** *The men armed themselves with sticks and stones.* ◆ *The country was arming itself against the enemy.* ◆ (*figurative*) *She had armed herself for the meeting with all the latest statistics.* ➲ see also ARMED **2** [T] **~ sth** to make a bomb, etc. ready to explode ➲ compare DISARM

ar·ma·da /ɑrˈmɑdə/ noun a large group of armed ships sailing together: *The Spanish Armada was sent to attack England in 1588.* ◆ (*figurative*) *a vast armada of football fans*

ar·ma·dil·lo /ˌɑrməˈdɪloʊ/ noun (*pl.* **ar·ma·dil·los**) a small animal that lives in the southern U.S. and Central and South America and eats insects. Its body is covered in a shell of hard plates for protection.

armadillo

Ar·ma·ged·don /ˌɑrməˈgɛdn/ noun [sing., U] **1** (in the Bible) a battle between good and evil at the end of the world **2** a terrible war that could destroy the world

Ar·mag·nac /ˈɑrmənˌyæk/ noun [U] a type of French BRANDY

ar·ma·ment /ˈɑrməmənt/ noun **1** [C, usually pl.] weapons, especially large guns, bombs, tanks, etc.: *the armaments industry* **2** [U] the process of increasing the amount of weapons an army or a country has, especially to prepare for war ➔ compare DISARMAMENT

ar·ma·ture /ˈɑrmətʃər/ noun (*technical*) a frame that is covered to make a figure: *The figures are made from clay over a wire armature.*

arm·band /ˈɑrmbænd/ noun a cloth band worn around the arm as a sign of something, for example that someone has an official position: *The stewards all wore armbands.* ◆ *Many people at the funeral service were wearing black armbands.*

'arm ˌcandy noun [U] (*informal*) a beautiful woman that a man takes with him when he goes to a public event in order to impress other people

arm·chair /ˈɑrmtʃer/ noun, adj.
● *noun* a comfortable chair with sides on which you can rest your arms: *to sit in an armchair* ➔ picture at CHAIR
● *adj.* [only before noun] knowing about a subject through books and television, rather than by doing it for yourself: *an armchair critic/traveler*

armed 🔊 /ɑrmd/ adj.
1 involving the use of weapons: *an armed robbery* ◆ *an international armed conflict* (= a war) **ANT** UNARMED
2 carrying a weapon, especially a gun: *The man is armed and dangerous.* ◆ *armed guards* ◆ *Police were heavily armed.* ◆ *~ with a gun, etc.* *He was armed with a rifle.* **ANT** UNARMED
3 *~* (**with sth**) knowing something or carrying something that you need in order to help you to perform a task: *He was armed with all the facts.*
IDM armed to the teeth having many weapons

the ˌarmed 'forces (also the ˌarmed 'services) noun [pl.] a country's army, navy, and AIR FORCE

arm·ful /ˈɑrmfʊl/ noun a quantity that you can carry in one or both arms

arm·hole /ˈɑrmhoʊl/ noun the place in a coat, shirt, dress, etc. that your arm goes through

ar·mi·stice /ˈɑrməstəs/ noun [sing.] a formal agreement during a war to stop fighting and discuss making peace **SYN** CEASE-FIRE

arm·lock /ˈɑrmlɑk/ noun (in WRESTLING) a way of holding an opponent's arm so that they cannot move: *He had him in an armlock.*

ar·moire /ɑrmˈwɑr; ˈɑrmwɑr/ noun (from *French*) a cupboard with drawers or shelves underneath, especially one that has a lot of decoration

ar·mor (*CanE* usually **ar·mour**) /ˈɑrmər/ noun [U] **1** special metal clothing that soldiers wore in the past to protect their bodies while fighting: *a suit of armor* ◆ (*figurative*) *Monkeys do not have any kind of protective armor and use their brains to solve problems.* **2** metal covers that protect ships and military vehicles such as tanks **3** (*technical*) military vehicles used in war: *an attack by infantry and armor*
IDM see CHINK *n.*, **KNIGHT** *n.*

ar·mored (*CanE* usually **ar·moured**) /ˈɑrmərd/ adj. **1** (especially of a military vehicle) protected by metal covers: *The cruiser was heavily armored.* ◆ *an armored car* **2** using armored vehicles: *an armored division*

ˌarmored per'sonˌnel ˌcarrier (*CanE* usually ˌarmoured per'sonˌnel ˌcarrier) noun a military vehicle used to transport soldiers

ar·mor·er (*CanE* usually **ar·mour·er**) /ˈɑrmərər/ noun a person who makes or repairs weapons and armor

ar·mo·ri·al /ɑrˈmɔriəl/ adj. connected with HERALDRY

ˈarmor-ˌplated (*CanE* usually ˈarmour-ˌplated) adj. (of vehicles) covered with sheets of metal to provide protection against bullets, etc.

ar·mor·y (*CanE* usually **ar·mour·y**) /ˈɑrməri/ noun (*pl.* ar·mor·ies, *CanE* usually ar·mour·ies) **1** a place where weapons and armor are kept **SYN** ARSENAL **2** a building that is the HEADQUARTERS for training people who are not professional soldiers, for example the National Guard **3** (*formal*) the things that someone has available to help them achieve something: *Doctors have an armory of drugs available.* **4** all the weapons and military equipment that a country has: *China's nuclear armory*

ar·mour (*CanE*) = ARMOR

arm·pit /ˈɑrmpɪt/ (also *informal* pit) noun the part of the body under the arm where it joins the shoulder ➔ picture at BODY ➔ see also UNDERARM
IDM the armpit of sth (*informal*) the most unpleasant or ugly place in a country or region: *The city has been called the armpit of the South.*

arm·rest /ˈɑrmrɛst/ noun the part of some types of seats, especially in planes or cars, that supports your arm

arms 🔊 /ɑrmz/ noun [pl.]
1 (*formal*) weapons, especially as used by the army, navy, etc.: *arms and ammunition* ◆ *Police officers in New York usually carry arms.* ➔ see also FIREARM, SMALL ARMS **2** = COAT OF ARMS
IDM be under arms to have weapons and be ready to fight in a war **lay down your arms** to stop fighting **take up arms (against sb)** to prepare to fight **(be) up in arms (about/over sth)** (*informal*) (of a group of people) to be very angry about something and ready to protest strongly about it ➔ more at BEAR *v.*, PRESENT *v.*

ˈarms conˌtrol noun [U] international agreements to destroy weapons or limit the number of weapons that countries have

ˈarms race noun [sing.] a situation in which countries compete to get the most and best weapons

ˈarm-ˌtwisting noun [U] (*informal*) the use of a lot of pressure or even physical force to persuade someone to do something

ˈarm-ˌwrestling noun a competition to find out which of two people is the stronger, in which they try to force each other's arm down onto a table

ar·my 🔊 /ˈɑrmi/ noun (*pl.* ar·mies)
1 [C] a large organized group of soldiers who are trained to fight on land: *The two opposing armies faced each other across the battlefield.* **2 the army** [sing.] the part of a country's armed forces that fights on land: *Her husband is in the army.* ◆ *After leaving school, Mike went into the army.* ◆ *an army officer* ➔ collocations at WAR **3** [C] a large number of people or things, especially when they are organized in some way or involved in a particular activity: *an army of advisers/volunteers* ◆ *An army of ants marched across the path.*

ˌarmy 'surplus noun [U] clothing and equipment that the army does not need anymore and that is sold to the public

ar·ni·ca /ˈɑrnɪkə/ noun [U] a natural medicine made from a plant, used to treat BRUISES (= marks that appear on the skin after someone has fallen, been hit, etc.)

a·ro·ma /əˈroʊmə/ noun a pleasant, noticeable smell: *the aroma of fresh coffee*

a·ro·ma·ther·a·py /əˌroʊməˈθerəpi/ *noun* [U] the use of natural oils that smell pleasant for controlling pain or for rubbing into the body during MASSAGE ▶ **a·ro·ma·ther·a·pist** /-ˈθerəpɪst/ *noun*

ar·o·mat·ic /ˌærəˈmætɪk/ *adj.* having a pleasant, noticeable smell **SYN** FRAGRANT: *aromatic oils/herbs*

a·rose pt of ARISE

a·round 🔑 /əˈraʊnd/ *adv., prep.*

• *adv.* **HELP** For the special uses of **around** in phrasal verbs, look at the entries for the verbs. For example, **come around to something** is in the phrasal verb section at **come**.
1 approximately: *He arrived around five o'clock.* ◆ *The cost would be somewhere around $1,500.* **2** on every side; surrounding someone or something: *I could hear laughter all around.* ◆ *a yard with a fence all around* **3** moving in a circle: *How do you make the wheels go around?* **4** measured in a circle: *an old tree that was at least ten feet around* **5** in or to many places: *We were all running around trying to get ready in time.* ◆ *This is our new office—Kay will show you around.* ◆ *There were papers lying around all over the floor.* **6** used to describe activities that have no real purpose: *There were several young people sitting around looking bored.* **7** present in a place; available: *There was more money around in those days.* ◆ *I knocked but there was no one around.* ◆ *Digital television has been around for some time now.* **8** active and well known in a sport, profession, etc.: *a new tennis champion who could be around for a long time* ◆ *Madonna has been around since the 1980s.* **9** in a circle or curve to face another way or the opposite way: *She turned the car around and drove off.* ◆ *They looked around when he called.* ➔ **see also** ABOUT *adv.* (1), ROUND *adv.*
IDM have been around to have gained knowledge and experience of the world

• *prep.* **1** surrounding someone or something; on each side of something: *The house is built around a central courtyard.* ◆ *He put his arms around her.* **2** on, to, or from the other side of someone or something: *Our house is just around the corner.* ◆ *The bus came around the bend.* ◆ *There must be a way around the problem.* **3** in a circle: *They walked around the lake.* **4** to fit in with particular people, ideas, etc.: *I can't arrange everything around your schedule!* **5** in or to many places in an area: *They walked around the town looking for a place to eat.* ➔ **see also** ROUND *prep.*

a·round-the-ˈclock *adj.* = ROUND-THE-CLOCK

a·rouse /əˈraʊz/ *verb* **1** ~ sth to make someone have a particular feeling or attitude: *to arouse someone's interest/curiosity/anger* ◆ *Her strange behavior aroused our suspicions.* **2** ~ sb to make someone feel sexually excited **SYN** EXCITE **3** ~ sb to make you feel more active and want to start doing something: *The whole community was aroused by the crime.* **4** ~ sb (from sth) (*formal*) to wake someone from sleep ➔ **see also** ROUSE ▶ **a·rou·sal** /əˈraʊzl/ *noun* [U]: *emotional/sexual arousal*

ar·peg·gi·o /ɑrˈpedʒiˌoʊ/ *noun* (*pl.* **ar·peg·gi·os**) (*music*) the notes of a CHORD played quickly, one after the other

arr. *abbr.* **1** (*music*) (in writing) arranged by: *Handel, arr. Mozart* **2** (in writing) arrives; arrival: *arr. Boston 6:03 p.m.* ◆ **compare** DEP.

ar·raign /əˈreɪn/ *verb* [usually passive] ~ sb (for sth) (*law*) to bring someone to court in order to formally accuse them of a crime: *He was arraigned for murder.* ◆ *He was arraigned on a charge of murder.* ▶ **ar·raign·ment** *noun* [C, U]

ar·range 🔑 /əˈreɪndʒ/ *verb*
1 [T, I] to plan or organize something in advance: ~ sth *The party was arranged quickly.* ◆ *We met at six, as arranged.* ◆ ~ how, where, etc.... *We've still got to arrange how to get to the airport.* ◆ ~ to do sth *Have you arranged to meet him?* ◆ *I arranged to borrow their car for the weekend.* ◆ ~ for sth (to do sth) *She arranged for a loan from the bank.* ◆ *We arranged for a car to pick us up from the airport.* ◆ ~ for sb to do sth *I arranged for the neighbors to feed the cat while we are away.* **2** [T] ~ sth to put something in a particular order; to make

something neat or attractive: *The books are arranged alphabetically by author.* ◆ *I need to arrange my financial affairs and make a will.* ◆ *She arranged the flowers in a vase.* **3** [T] ~ sth (for sth) to write or change a piece of music so that it is suitable for a particular instrument or voice: *He arranged traditional folk songs for the piano.*

ar·ranged ˈmarriage *noun* a marriage in which the parents choose the husband or wife for their child

ar·range·ment 🔑 /əˈreɪndʒmənt/ *noun*
1 [C, usually pl.] a plan or preparation that you make so that something can happen: *travel arrangements* ◆ ~ for sth *I'll make arrangements for you to be met at the airport.* **2** [C, usually pl.] the way things are done or organized: *She's happy with her unusual living arrangements.* ◆ *There are special arrangements for people working overseas.* **3** [C, U] an agreement that you make with someone that you can both accept: *We can come to an arrangement over the price.* ◆ ~ between A and B *an arrangement between the school and the parents* ◆ ~ with sb (to do sth) *You can cash checks here by prior arrangement with the bank.* ◆ ~ that... *They had an arrangement that the children would spend two weeks with each parent.* **4** [C, U] a group of things that are organized or placed in a particular order or position; the act of placing things in a particular order: *plans of the possible seating arrangements* ◆ *the art of flower arrangement* **5** [C, U] a piece of music that has been changed, for example for another instrument to play

ar·rang·er /əˈreɪndʒər/ *noun* **1** a person who arranges music that has been written by someone different **2** a person who arranges something: *the arranger of a loan/mortgage*

ar·rant /ˈærənt/ *adj.* [only before noun] (*old-fashioned*) used to emphasize how bad something or someone is: *arrant nonsense*

ar·ray /əˈreɪ/ *noun, verb*
• *noun* **1** [usually sing.] a group or collection of things or people, often one that is large or impressive: *a vast array of bottles of different shapes and sizes* ◆ *a dazzling array of talent* **2** (*computing*) a way of organizing and storing related data in a computer memory **3** (*technical*) a set of numbers, signs, or values arranged in rows and columns
• *verb* [usually passive] (*formal*) **1** ~ sth to arrange a group of things in a pleasing way or so that they are in order: *Jars of all shapes and sizes were arrayed on the shelves.* **2** ~ sb to arrange soldiers in a position from which they are ready to attack

ar·rayed /əˈreɪd/ *adj.* [not before noun] ~ (in sth) (*literary*) dressed in a particular way, especially in beautiful clothes: *She was arrayed in a black velvet gown.*

ar·rears /əˈrɪrz/ *noun* [pl.] money that someone owes that they have not paid at the right time: *rent/mortgage/tax arrears*
IDM be in arrears | get/fall into arrears to be late in paying money that you owe: *We're two months in arrears with the rent.* **in arrears** if money or a person is paid **in arrears** for work, the money is paid after the work has been done

ar·rest 🔑 /əˈrest/ *verb, noun*
• *verb* **1** [T, often passive] if the police **arrest** someone, the person is taken to a POLICE STATION and kept there because the police believe they may be guilty of a crime: ~ sb *A man has been arrested in connection with the robbery.* ◆ ~ sb for sth *She was arrested for drug-related offenses.* ◆ ~ sb for doing sth *You could get arrested for doing that.* ➔ **collocations** at JUSTICE **2** [T] ~ sth (*formal*) to stop a process or a development: *They failed to arrest the company's decline.* **3** [T] ~ sth (*formal*) to make someone notice something and pay attention to it: *An unusual noise arrested his attention.*
• *noun* [C, U] **1** the act of arresting someone: *The police made several arrests.* ◆ *She was under arrest on suspicion of murder.* ◆ *Opposition leaders were put under house arrest* (= not allowed to leave their houses). ➔ **see also** CITIZEN'S ARREST **2** an act

| t tea | ţ butter | d did | k cat | g got | tʃ chin | dʒ June | f fall

of something stopping or being interrupted: *He died after suffering a **cardiac arrest*** (= when his heart suddenly stopped).

ar·rest·a·ble of·fense /ə,rɛstəbl əˈfɛns/ *noun* (*law*) an offense for which someone can be arrested without a WARRANT from a judge

ar·rest·ing /əˈrɛstɪŋ/ *adj.* (*formal*) attracting a lot of attention; very attractive

ar·ri·val 🔑 /əˈraɪvl/ *noun*
1 [U, C] an act of coming or being brought to a place: *Guests receive a bottle of champagne **on/upon arrival** at the hotel.* ◆ *We apologize for the late arrival of the train.* ◆ *the arrival of the mail in the morning* ◆ *daily arrivals of refugees* ◆ *There are 120 **arrivals and departures** every day.* **ANT** DEPARTURE **2** [C] a person or thing that comes to a place: *The first arrivals at the concert got the best seats.* ◆ ***early/late/new arrivals*** ◆ *We're expecting **a new arrival*** (= a baby) *in the family soon.* **3** [U] the time when a new technology or idea is introduced: *the arrival of high-definition TV* **IDM** see DEAD *adj.*

ar·rive 🔑 /əˈraɪv/ *verb*
1 [I] (*abbr.* **arr.**) to get to a place, especially at the end of a journey: *I'll wait until they arrive.* ◆ *I was pleased to hear you arrived home safely.* ◆ *to **arrive early/late** for a meeting* ◆ *The police arrived to arrest him.* ◆ **~ at/in/on…** *She'll arrive in New York at noon.* ◆ *The train arrived at the station 20 minutes late.* ◆ *By the time I **arrived at the scene**, it was all over.* ◆ *We didn't arrive back at the hotel until very late.* **2** [I] (of things) to be brought to someone: *A letter arrived for you this morning.* ◆ *Send your application to arrive by October 31.* ◆ *We waited an hour for our lunch to arrive.* ◆ *The new product will arrive on supermarket shelves* (= be available) *early next year.* **3** [I] (of an event or a moment) to happen or to come, especially when you have been waiting for it: *The wedding day finally arrived.* ◆ *The baby arrived* (= was born) *early.*
IDM **sb has arrived** (*informal*) someone has become successful: *He knew he had arrived when he was shortlisted for the Pulitzer prize.*
PHR V **ar'rive at sth** to decide on or find something, especially after discussion and thought **SYN** REACH: *to arrive at an agreement/a decision/a conclusion* ◆ *to arrive at the truth*

ar·ri·viste /,æriˈvist/ *noun* (from *French*, *disapproving*) a person who is determined to be accepted as a member of a social group, etc. to which they do not really belong

ar·ro·gance /ˈærəgəns/ *noun* [U] the behavior of a person when they feel that they are more important than other people, and are rude to them or do not consider them

ar·ro·gant /ˈærəgənt/ *adj.* behaving in a proud, unpleasant way, showing little thought for other people
▶ **ar·ro·gant·ly** *adv.*

ar·ro·gate /ˈærəˌgeɪt/ *verb*
PHR V **'arrogate to yourself sth** (*formal*) to claim or take something that you have no right to: *I do not arrogate to myself the right to decide.*

ar·row 🔑 /ˈæroʊ/ *noun*
1 a thin stick with a sharp point at one end, which is shot from a BOW²: *a bow and arrow* ◆ *to fire/shoot an arrow* ◆ *The road continues as straight as an arrow.* ⊃ *picture at* BOW², SPORT **2** a mark or sign like an arrow (→), used to show direction or position: *Follow the arrows.* ◆ *Use the arrow keys to move the cursor.*

ar·row·head /ˈæroʊˌhɛd/ *noun* the sharp pointed end of an arrow

ar·row·root /ˈæroʊˌrut; -ˌrʊt/ *noun* [U] a plant whose roots can be cooked and eaten or made into a type of flour, used especially to make sauces thick; the flour itself

ar·roy·o /əˈrɔɪoʊ/ *noun* (*pl.* **ar·roy·os**) (from *Spanish*) a narrow channel with steep sides cut by a river in a desert region

ar·se·nal /ˈɑrsnl/ *noun* **1** a collection of weapons such as guns and EXPLOSIVES: *the United States' nuclear arsenal* **2** a

building where military weapons and EXPLOSIVES are made or stored

ar·se·nic /ˈɑrsənɪk; ˈɑrsnɪk/ *noun* [U] (*symb.* **As**) a chemical element. Arsenic is an extremely poisonous white powder.

ar·son /ˈɑrsn/ *noun* [U] the crime of deliberately setting fire to something, especially a building: *to carry out an **arson attack*** ⊃ collocations at CRIME

ar·son·ist /ˈɑrsənɪst/ *noun* a person who commits the crime of arson

art 🔑 /ɑrt/ *noun, verb*
● *noun* **1** [U] the use of the imagination to express ideas or feelings, particularly in painting, drawing, or SCULPTURE: *modern/contemporary/American art* ◆ *an art critic/historian/lover* ◆ *Can we call television art?* ◆ *stolen **works of art*** ◆ *Her performance displayed great art.* ⊃ see also CLIP ART, FINE ART **2** [U] examples of objects such as paintings, drawings, or SCULPTURE: *an art gallery/exhibition* ◆ *a collection of art and antiques* **3** [U] the skill of creating objects such as paintings and drawings, especially when you study it: *She's good at art and design.* ◆ *an art teacher/student/college/class* **4 the arts** [pl.] art, music, theater, literature, etc. when you think of them as a group: *private funding for the arts* ⊃ see also PERFORMING ARTS **5** [C] a type of VISUAL or performing art: *Dance is a very theatrical art.* **6** [C, usually pl.] the subjects you can study at school or college that are not scientific, such as languages, history, or literature: *an arts degree* ⊃ compare SCIENCE ⊃ see also LIBERAL ARTS **7** [C, U] an ability or a skill that you can develop with training and practice: *a therapist trained in the art of healing* ◆ *Letter-writing is a lost art.* ◆ *Appearing confident at interviews is quite an art* (= somewhat difficult). **IDM** see FINE *adj.*
● *verb* **thou art** (*old use*) used to mean "you are," when talking to one person

- **develop/adopt/paint in** a stylized manner/an abstract style

showing and selling art
- **commission** an altarpiece/a bronze bust of sb/a portrait/a religious work/an artist to paint sth
- **frame** a painting/a portrait/a piece/an artwork
- **hang** art/a picture/a painting/a piece/an artwork
- **display/exhibit** modern art/sb's work/a collection/ original artwork/ drawings/sculptures/a piece
- **be displayed/hung** in a gallery/museum
- **install/place** a sculpture in/at/on sth
- **erect/unveil/dedicate** a bronze/marble statue
- **hold/host/mount/open/curate/see** an exhibition/ exhibit
- **be/go on** exhibit
- **feature/promote/showcase** contemporary works/a conceptual artist
- **collect** African art/modern American paintings/ Japanese prints
- **restore/preserve** great works of art/a fresco

art dec·o also **Art Deco** /,ɑrt 'dɛkoʊ; -'deɪkoʊ/ noun [U] a popular style of decorative art in the 1920s and 1930s that has GEOMETRIC shapes with clear outlines and bright strong colors

'art di,rector noun **1** the person responsible for the pictures, photos, etc. in a magazine **2** the person responsible for the SET and PROPS when a movie is being made

ar·te·ri·ole /ɑr'tɪri,oʊl/ noun (anatomy) a thin branch of an ARTERY that leads off into capillaries (CAPILLARY)

ar·te·ri·o·scle·ro·sis /ɑr,tɪriouskləˈroʊsəs/ noun [U] (medical) a condition in which the walls of the arteries become thick and hard, making it difficult for blood to flow

ar·ter·y /'ɑrtəri/ noun (pl. **ar·ter·ies**) **1** any of the tubes that carry blood from the heart to other parts of the body: blocked arteries ⊃ compare VEIN ⊃ see also CORONARY ARTERY **2** a large and important road, river, railroad line, etc. ▶ **ar·te·ri·al** /ɑr'tɪriəl/ adj. [only before noun]: arterial blood/disease ◆ an arterial road

ar·te·sian well /ɑr,tiʒn 'wɛl/ noun a hole made in the ground through which water rises to the surface by natural pressure

'art form noun **1** [C] a particular type of artistic activity: The short story is a difficult art form to master. **2** [sing.] an activity that someone does very well and gives them the opportunity to show imagination: She has elevated the dinner party into an art form.

art·ful /'ɑrtfl/ adj. [usually before noun] **1** (disapproving) skillful at getting what you want, sometimes by not telling the truth SYN CRAFTY **2** (of things or actions) designed or done in a skillful way ▶ **art·ful·ly** /-fəli/ adv.

'art ,gallery (also **gallery**) noun a building where paintings and other works of art are shown to the public

,art 'history noun [U] the study of the history of painting, SCULPTURE, etc.

'art-house adj. art-house movies are usually made by small companies and are not usually seen by a wide audience

ar·thrit·ic /ɑr'θrɪtɪk/ adj. suffering from or caused by arthritis: arthritic hands/pain

ar·thri·tis /ɑr'θraɪtəs/ noun [U] a disease that causes pain and swelling in one or more joints of the body ⊃ see also OSTEOARTHRITIS, RHEUMATOID ARTHRITIS

ar·thro·pod /'ɑrθrə,pɑd/ noun (biology) an INVERTEBRATE animal such as an insect, spider, or CRAB, that has its SKELETON on the outside of its body and has joints on its legs

ar·ti·choke /'ɑrtə,tʃoʊk/ (also ,globe 'artichoke) noun [C, U] a round vegetable with a lot of thick green leaves. The bottom part of the leaves and the inside of the artichoke (= the heart) can be eaten when cooked. ⊃ picture at FRUIT ⊃ compare JERUSALEM ARTICHOKE

ar·ti·cle /'ɑrtɪkl/ noun

1 ~ (on/about sth) a piece of writing about a particular subject in a newspaper or magazine: Have you seen that article about young fashion designers? **2** (law) a separate item in an agreement or a contract: Article 3 of the U.S. Constitution describes the American court system. **3** (formal) a particular item or separate thing, especially one of a set SYN ITEM: articles of clothing ◆ You may bring one personal article on board, such as a handbag. ◆ The articles found in the car helped the police to identify the body. **4** (grammar) the words a and an (the indefinite article) or the (the definite article)

,article of 'faith noun (pl. ,articles of 'faith) something you believe very strongly, as if it were a religious belief

ar·tic·u·late verb, adj.

● **verb** /ɑr'tɪkyə,leɪt/ **1** [T] ~ **sth (to sb)** (formal) to express or explain your thoughts or feelings clearly in words: She struggled to articulate her thoughts. **2** [I, T] to speak, pronounce, or play something in a clear way: He was too drunk to articulate properly. ◆ ~ **sth** Every note was carefully articulated. **3** [I] ~ **(with sth)** (formal) to be related to something so that together the two parts form a whole: These courses are designed to articulate with advanced degrees. **4** [I, T] (technical) to be joined to something else by a joint, so that movement is possible; to join something in this way: ~ **(with sth)** bones that articulate with others ◆ ~ **sth** All these bones are articulated with each other.

● **adj.** /ɑr'tɪkyələt/ **1** (of a person) good at expressing ideas or feelings clearly in words **2** (of speech) clearly expressed or pronounced: All we could hear were loud sobs, but no articulate words. ANT INARTICULATE ▶ **ar·tic·u·late·ly** adv.

ar·tic·u·lat·ed /ɑr'tɪkyə,leɪtəd/ adj. with two or more sections joined together in a way that makes it easier to bend or to turn corners: an articulated truck ◆ a robot with articulated limbs ⊃ see also TRACTOR-TRAILER

ar·tic·u·la·tion /ɑr,tɪkyə'leɪʃn/ noun **1** [U] (formal) the expression of an idea or a feeling in words: the articulation of his theory **2** [U] (formal) the act of making sounds in speech or music: The singer worked hard on the clear articulation of every note. **3** [U, C, usually sing.] (technical) a joint or connection that allows movement

ar·ti·fact /'ɑrtə,fækt/ noun (technical) an object that is made by a person, especially something of historical or cultural interest

ar·ti·fice /'ɑrtəfɪs/ noun [U, C] (formal) the use of intelligent or dishonest tricks to cheat someone SYN CUNNING

ar·ti·fi·cial /,ɑrtə'fɪʃl/ adj.

1 made or produced to copy something natural; not real: an artificial limb/flower/sweetener/fertilizer ◆ artificial lighting/light **2** created by people; not happening naturally: A job interview is a very artificial situation. ◆ the artificial barriers of race, class, and gender **3** not what it appears to be SYN FAKE: artificial emotion ▶ **ar·ti·fi·ci·al·i·ty** /,ɑrtə,fɪʃi-'æləti/ noun [U] **ar·ti·fi·cial·ly** /,ɑrtə'fɪʃəli/ adv.: artificially created lakes ◆ artificially low prices

false (*somewhat formal*) not natural; not genuine, but made to look real to cheat people: *false teeth/eyelashes* ◆ *a suitcase with a false bottom*

faux not natural, but made to look or seem real: *chairs covered in faux leopard skin*

imitation [only before noun] made to look like something else; not real: *She would never wear imitation pearls.*

PATTERNS

- artificial/synthetic/man-made **fabrics/fibers/materials/products**
- artificial/synthetic/fake/faux/imitation **fur/leather/diamonds/pearls**

ˌartiˌficial insemiˈnation *noun* [U] (*abbr.* AI) the process of making a woman or female animal pregnant by an artificial method of putting male SPERM inside her, and not by sexual activity: *artificial insemination by a donor, abbreviated to "AID"*

ˌartiˌficial inˈtelligence *noun* [U] (*abbr.* AI) (*computing*) an area of study concerned with making computers copy intelligent human behavior

ˌartiˌficial ˈlanguage *noun* a language invented for international communication or for use with computers

ˌartiˌficial respiˈration *noun* [U] the process of helping a person who has stopped breathing begin to breathe again, usually by blowing into their mouth or nose ⊃ compare MOUTH-TO-MOUTH RESUSCITATION

ar·til·ler·y /ɑrˈtɪləri/ *noun* **1** [U] large heavy guns, which are often moved on wheels: *The town is under heavy artillery fire.* **2** the artillery [sing.] the section of an army trained to use these guns

ar·ti·san /ˈɑrtəzn; -sn/ *noun* (*formal*) a person who does skilled work, making things with their hands **SYN** CRAFTSMAN ▶ ar·ti·san·al /ˈɑrtɪzənl/ *adj.*: *artisanal bread*

art·ist 🔑 /ˈɑrtɪst/ *noun*

1 a person who creates works of art, especially paintings or drawings: *an exhibition of work by contemporary young artists* ◆ *a graphic artist* ◆ *a makeup artist* ◆ *Police have issued an artist's impression of her attacker.* ◆ (*figurative*) *Whoever made this cake is a real artist.* ⊃ collocations at ART **2** = ARTISTE: *a recording/solo artist*

ar·tiste /ɑrˈtist/ (*also* artist) *noun* a professional entertainer such as a singer, a dancer, or an actor

ar·tis·tic 🔑 /ɑrˈtɪstɪk/ *adj.*

1 connected with art or artists: *the artistic works of the period* ◆ *a work of great artistic merit* ◆ *the artistic director of the theater* **2** showing a natural skill in, or enjoyment of, art, especially being able to paint or draw well: *artistic abilities/achievements/skills/talent* ◆ *She comes from a very artistic family.* **3** done with skill and imagination; attractive or beautiful: *an artistic arrangement of dried flowers* **IDM** see LICENSE *n.* ▶ ar·tis·ti·cally /-kli/ *adv.*

arˌtistic diˈrector *noun* the person in charge of deciding which plays, OPERAS, etc. a theater company will perform, and the general artistic policy of the company

art·ist·ry /ˈɑrtəstri/ *noun* [U] the skill of an artist: *He played the piece with effortless artistry.*

art·less /ˈɑrtləs/ *adj.* (*formal*) **1** simple, natural, and honest: *the artless sincerity of a young child* **2** made without skill or art

art nou·veau (*also* Art Nouveau) /ˌɑrt nuˈvou; ˌɑr-/ *noun* [U] a style of decorative art and ARCHITECTURE popular in Europe and the U.S. at the end of the 19th century and beginning of the 20th century, that uses complicated designs and curved patterns based on natural shapes like leaves and flowers

ˌarts and ˈcrafts *noun* [pl.] objects such as jewelry and POTTERY that are made using both artistic and practical skills; the activity of making such objects

art·sy /ˈɑrtsi/ (*also* arty) *adj.* (*informal*, usually *disapproving*) seeming or wanting to be very artistic or interested in the arts: *She hangs out with the artsy types she met at drama school.*

art·sy-fart·sy /ˌɑrtsi ˈfɑrtsi/ *adj.* (*informal*, *disapproving*) connected with, or having an interest in, the arts: *I assume he's out with his artsy-fartsy friends.*

ˌart ˈtherapy *noun* [U] a type of PSYCHOTHERAPY in which you are encouraged to express yourself using art materials

art·work /ˈɑrtwərk/ *noun* **1** [U] photographs and pictures prepared for books, magazines, etc. **2** [C] a work of art, especially one in a museum

art·y /ˈɑrti/ *adj.* = ARTSY

a·ru·gu·la /əˈrugələ/ *noun* [U] a plant with long green leaves that have a strong flavor and are eaten raw in salads

-ary /ˈɛri; əri/ *suffix* (in adjectives and nouns) connected with: *planetary* ◆ *budgetary*

Ar·yan /ˈɛriən; ˈɑr-/ *noun* **1** a member of the group of people that went to S. Asia in around 1500 B.C. **2** a person who spoke any of the languages of the Indo-European group **3** (especially according to the ideas of the German Nazi party) a member of a Caucasian, not Jewish, race of people, especially one with fair hair and blue eyes ▶ Ar·y·an *adj.*

as 🔑 /əz; *strong form* æz/ *prep., adv., conj.*

● *prep.* **1** used to describe someone or something appearing to be someone or something else: *They were all dressed as clowns.* ◆ *The bomb was disguised as a package.* **2** used to describe the fact that someone or something has a particular job or function: *She works as a courier.* ◆ *Treat me as a friend.* ◆ *I respect him as a doctor.* ◆ *You can use that glass as a vase.* ◆ *The news came as a shock.* ◆ *She had been there often as a child* (= when she was a child).

● *adv.* **1** as… as… used when you are comparing two people or things, or two situations: *You're as tall as your father.* ◆ *He was as white as a sheet.* ◆ *She doesn't play as well as her sister.* ◆ *I haven't known him as long as you* (= as you have known him). ◆ *He doesn't earn as much as me.* ◆ *He doesn't earn as much as I do.* ◆ *It's not as hard as I thought.* ◆ *Run as fast as you can.* ◆ *We'd like it as soon as possible.* **2** used to say that something happens in the same way: *As always, he said little.* ◆ *The "h" in honest is silent, as in "hour."*

● *conj.* **1** while something else is happening: *He sat watching her as she got ready.* ◆ *As she grew older, she gained in confidence.* ⊃ language bank at PROCESS¹ **2** in the way in which: *They did as I had asked.* ◆ *Leave the papers as they are.* ◆ *She lost it, just as I said she would.* **3** used to state the reason for something: *As you were out, I left a message.* ◆ *She may need some help as she's new.* **4** used to make a comment or to add information about what you have just said: *As you know, Julia is leaving soon.* ◆ *She's very tall, as is her mother.* **5** used to say that in spite of something being true, what follows is also true **SYN** THOUGH: *Happy as they were, there was something missing.* ◆ *Try as he might* (= however hard he tried), *he couldn't open the door.*

IDM as aˈgainst sth in contrast with something: *They got 27% of the vote, as against 32% at the last election.* as and ˈwhen used to say that something may happen at some time in the future, but only when something else has happened: *We'll decide on the team as and when we qualify.* ◆ *I'll tell you more as and when* (= as soon as I can). as for sb/sth used to start talking about someone or something **SYN** REGARDING: *As for Jo, she's doing fine.* ◆ *As for food for the party, that's all being taken care of.* as of… used to show the time or date from which something starts: *Our fax number is changing as of May 12.* as ˈif/as ˈthough in a way that suggests something: *He behaved as if nothing had happened.* ◆ *It sounds as though you had a good time.* ◆ *It's my birthday. As if you didn't know!* ◆ *"Don't say anything." " As if I would! "* (= surely you do not expect me to) as it ˈis considering the present situation; as things are: *We were hoping to finish it by* next week—*as it is, it may be the week after.* ◆ *I can't help—I've got too much to do as it is* (= already). **as it were** used when a speaker is giving his or her own impression of a situation, or expressing something in a particular way: *Teachers must put the brakes on, as it were, when they notice students looking puzzled.* **as to sth| as regards sth** used when you are referring to something: *As to tax, that will be deducted from your salary.* **as you do** used as a comment on something that you have just said: *He smiled and I smiled back. As you do.* ⊃ more at WELL *adv.*, YET *adv.*

ASAP /ˌeɪ ɛs eɪ ˈpi; ˈeɪsæp/ *abbr.* as soon as possible

as·bes·tos /æsˈbɛstəs/ *noun* [U] a soft gray mineral that does not burn, used especially in the past in building as a protection against fire or to prevent heat loss

as·bes·to·sis /ˌæsbɛˈstoʊsəs/ *noun* [U] a disease of the lungs caused by breathing in asbestos dust

as·cend /əˈsɛnd/ *verb* [I, T] (*formal*) to rise; to go up; to climb up: *The path started to ascend more steeply.* ◆ *The air became colder as we ascended.* ◆ *The results, ranked in ascending order* (= from the lowest to the highest) *are as follows:* ◆ **~ from sth** *Mist ascended from the valley.* ◆ **~ to sth** (*figurative*) *He ascended to the peak of sports achievement.* ◆ **~ sth** *Her heart was thumping as she ascended the stairs.* ◆ (*figurative*) *to ascend the throne* (= become king or queen) **ANT** DESCEND

as·cend·an·cy (also **as·cend·en·cy**) /əˈsɛndənsi/ *noun* [U] **~ (over sb/sth)** (*formal*) the position of having power or influence over someone or something: *moral/political/intellectual ascendancy* ◆ *The opposition party was in the ascendancy* (= gaining control).

as·cend·ant (also **as·cend·ent**) /əˈsɛndənt/ *noun* **IDM in the ascendant** (*formal*) being or becoming more powerful or popular

as·cen·sion /əˈsɛnʃn/ *noun* [sing.] **1 the Ascension** (in the Christian religion) the journey of Jesus from the earth into heaven **2** the act of moving up or of reaching a high position: *her ascension to the throne*

As'cension ˌDay *noun* (in the Christian religion) the 40th day after Easter when Christians remember when Jesus left the earth and went into heaven

as·cent /əˈsɛnt/ *noun* **1** [C, usually sing.] the act of climbing or moving up; an upward journey: *the first ascent of Mount Everest* ◆ *The cart began its gradual ascent up the hill.* ◆ *The rocket steepened its ascent.* **ANT** DESCENT **2** [C, usually sing.] an upward path or slope: *At the other side of the valley was a steep ascent to the top of the hill.* **ANT** DESCENT **3** [U] (*formal*) the process of moving forward to a better position or of making progress: *man's ascent to civilization*

as·cer·tain /ˌæsərˈteɪn/ *verb* (*formal*) to find out the true or correct information about something: **~ sth** *It can be difficult to ascertain the facts.* ◆ **~ that...** *I ascertained that the driver was not badly hurt.* ◆ **it is ascertained that...** *It should be ascertained that the plans comply with the law.* ◆ **~ what, whether, etc....** *The police are trying to ascertain what really*

happened. ◆ *Could you ascertain whether she will be coming to the meeting?* ◆ **it is ascertained what, whether, etc....** *It must be ascertained if the land is still owned by the government.* ▶ **as·cer·tain·a·ble** /ˌæsərˈteɪnəbl/ *adj.* **as·cer·tain·ment** *noun* [U]

as·cet·ic /əˈsɛtɪk/ *adj.* [usually before noun] not allowing yourself physical pleasures, especially for religious reasons; related to a simple and strict way of living: *The monks lived a very ascetic life.* ▶ **as·cet·ic** *noun: monks, hermits, and ascetics* **as·cet·i·cism** /əˈsɛtəˌsɪzəm/ *noun* [U]

ASCII /ˈæski/ *noun* [U] (*computing*) the abbreviation for "American Standard Code for Information Interchange" (a standard code used so that data can be moved between computers that use different programs)

a·scor·bic ac·id /əˌskɔrbɪk ˈæsɪd/ *noun* [U] = VITAMIN C

as·cot /ˈæskɑt/ *noun* = CRAVAT

as·cribe /əˈskraɪb/ *verb* (*formal*)
PHR V a'scribe sth to sb to consider or state that a book, etc. was written by a particular person **SYN** ATTRIBUTE: *This play is usually ascribed to Shakespeare.* **a'scribe sth to sb/sth** (*formal*) **1** to consider that something is caused by a particular thing or person: *He ascribed his failure to bad luck.* **2** to consider that someone or something has, or should have, a particular quality: *We ascribe great importance to these policies.* **SYN** ATTRIBUTE ▶ **a·scrib·a·ble** /əˈskraɪbəbl/ *adj.*: **~ to sb/sth** *Their success is ascribable to the quality of their goods.* **as·crip·tion** /əˈskrɪpʃn/ *noun* [C, U]: **~ (to sb/sth)** *the ascription of meaning to objects and events*

ASEAN /ˈɑsiˌɑn; ˈæ-/ *abbr.* Association of Southeast Asian Nations

a·sep·tic /eɪˈsɛptɪk; ə-/ *adj.* (*medical*) free from harmful bacteria **ANT** SEPTIC

a·sex·u·al /eɪˈsɛkʃuəl/ *adj.* **1** (*technical*) not involving sex; not having sexual organs: *asexual reproduction* **2** not having sexual qualities; not interested in sex: *the tendency to see old people as asexual* ▶ **a·sex·u·al·ly** /eɪˈsɛkʃuəli; -ʃəli/ *adv.*: *to reproduce asexually*

ash /æʃ/ *noun* **1** [U] the gray or black powder that is left after something, especially TOBACCO, wood, or coal, has burned: *cigarette ash* ◆ *black volcanic ash* **2 ashes** [pl.] what is left after something has been destroyed by burning: *The town was reduced to ashes in the fighting.* ◆ *the glowing ashes of the campfire* ◆ (*figurative*) *The party had risen, like a phoenix, from the ashes of electoral disaster.* **3 ashes** [pl.] the powder that is left after a dead person's body has been CREMATED (= burned): *She wanted her ashes to be scattered at sea.* **4** [C, U] (also **'ash tree**) a forest tree with gray BARK ⊃ see also MOUNTAIN ASH ⊃ picture at TREE **5** [U] the hard pale wood of the ash tree **6** [C] (*technical*) the letter æ, used in Old English, and as a PHONETIC symbol to represent the vowel sound in *cat* **IDM** SEE SACKCLOTH

a·shamed 🔑 /əˈʃeɪmd/ *adj.* [not before noun]
1 feeling shame or embarrassment about someone or something, or because of something you have done: **~ of sth** *She was deeply ashamed of her behavior at the party.* ◆ *Mental illness is nothing to be ashamed of.* ◆ **~ of sb** *His daughter looked like such a mess that he was ashamed of her.*

♦ **~ of yourself** *You should be ashamed of yourself for telling such lies.* ♦ **~ that…** *I feel almost ashamed that I've been so lucky.* ♦ **~ to be sth** *The Super Bowl riots made me ashamed to be a football fan.* **2** **~ to do sth** unwilling to do something because of shame or embarrassment: *I'm ashamed to say that I lied to her.* ♦ *I cried at the end and I'm not ashamed to admit it.*

ash ˈblond (also ˌash ˈblonde) *adj., noun*
• *adj.* **1** (of hair) very pale blond in color **2** (of a person) having ash-blond hair
• *noun* a woman with hair that is ash blond in color

ash·en /ˈæʃn/ *adj.* (usually of someone's face) very pale; without color because of illness or fear: *They listened ashen-faced to the news.* ♦ *His face was ashen and wet with sweat.*

Ash·ke·naz·i /ˌɑʃkəˈnɑzi; ˌæʃ-/ *noun* (pl. **Ash·ke·naz·im** /-zɪm/) a Jew whose ANCESTORS came from central or eastern Europe ⊃ compare SEPHARDI ▶ **Ash·ke·naz·i** (also **Ash·ke·naz·ic**) /-ˈnɑzɪk/ *adj.*

a·shore /əˈʃɔr/ *adv.* toward, onto, or on land, having come from an area of water such as the ocean or a river: *to come/go ashore* ♦ *driftwood washed ashore on the beach* ♦ *The cruise included several days ashore.*

ash·ram /ˈɑʃrəm/ *noun* a place where Hindus who wish to live away from society live together as a group; a place where other Hindus go for a short time to say prayers before returning to society

ash·tray /ˈæʃtreɪ/ *noun* a container into which people who smoke put ASH, cigarette ends, etc.

Ash ˈWednesday *noun* [U, C] the first day of Lent ⊃ see also SHROVE TUESDAY

A·sia Mi·nor /ˌeɪʒə ˈmaɪnər/ *noun* [U] the western PENIN-SULA of Asia, which now forms most of Turkey

A·sian /ˈeɪʒn/ *noun, adj.*
• *noun* a person from Asia, or whose family originally came from Asia: *Chinese, Japanese, Koreans, and other Asians*
• *adj.* of or connected with Asia: *Asian music*

ˌAsian Aˈmerican *noun* a person from America whose family comes from Asia, especially E. Asia ▶ **ˌAsian Aˈmerican** *adj.*

A·si·at·ic /ˌeɪʒiˈætɪk; ˌeɪzi-/ *adj.* (technical) of or connected with Asia: *the Asiatic tropics*

ˈA-side *noun* the side of a VINYL pop record that was considered more likely to be successful ⊃ compare B-SIDE

a·side 🔊 /əˈsaɪd/ *adv., noun*
• *adv.* **1** to one side; out of the way: *She pulled the curtain aside.* ♦ *Stand aside and let these people pass.* ♦ *He took me aside* (= away from a group of people) *to give me some advice.* ♦ (figurative) *Putting aside* (= not considering at this stage) *the cost of the program, let us examine its benefits.* ♦ *All our protests were brushed aside* (= ignored). **2** to be used later: *We set aside some money for repairs.* **3** used after nouns to say that except for one thing, something is true: *Money worries aside, things are going well.*
• *noun* **1** (in the theater) something that a character in a play says to the audience, but that the other characters on stage are not intended to hear **2** a remark, often made in a low voice, that is not intended to be heard by everyone present **3** a remark that is not directly connected with the main subject that is being discussed: *I mention it only as an aside…*

aˈside from 🔊 *prep.*
= APART FROM: *Aside from a few scratches, I'm OK.* ⊃ language bank at EXCEPT

as·i·nine /ˈæsəˌnaɪn/ *adj.* (formal) stupid or silly **SYN** RIDICULOUS

ask 🔊 /æsk/ *verb*
❯ QUESTION **1** [I, T] **~ (sb) (about sb/sth)** to say or write something in the form of a question, in order to get information: *How old are you—if you don't mind me/my asking?* ♦ **~ about sb/sth** *He asked about her family.* ♦ **~ sth** *Can I ask a question?* ♦ *Did you ask the price?* ♦ **+ speech** *"Where are you going?" she asked.* ♦ **~ sb + speech** *"Are you sure?" he asked her.* ♦ **~ sb sth** *She asked the students their names.* ♦ *I often get asked that!* ♦ **~ sb (about sth)** *The interviewer asked me about my future plans.* ♦ **~ where, what, etc.…** *He asked where I lived.* ♦ **~ sb where, what, etc.…** *I had to ask the teacher what to do next.* ♦ *I was asked if/whether I could drive.* **HELP** You cannot say "ask to sb": ~~I asked to my friend what had happened.~~
❯ REQUEST **2** [T] to tell someone that you would like them to do something or that you would like something to happen: **~ sb to do sth** *All the students were asked to complete a questionnaire.* ♦ *Eric asked me to marry him.* ♦ **~ whether, what, etc.…** *I asked whether they could change my ticket.* ♦ **~ sb whether, what, etc.…** *She asked me if I would give her English lessons.* ♦ **~ that…** (formal) *She asked that she be kept informed of developments.* **3** [I, T] to say that you would like someone to give you something: **~ for sth** *to ask for a job/a drink/an explanation* ♦ *I am writing to ask for some information about courses.* ♦ **~ sth** *Why don't you ask his advice?* ♦ **~ sb for sth** *Why don't you ask him for his advice?* ♦ **~ sth of sb** *Can I ask a favor of you?* ♦ **~ sb sth** *Can I ask you a favor?*
❯ PERMISSION **4** [T] to request permission to do something: **~ to do sth** *Did you ask to use the car?* ♦ *I asked to see the manager.* ♦ **~ if, whether, etc.…** *I'll ask if it's all right to park here.* ♦ **~ sb if, whether, etc.…** *She asked her boss whether she could have the day off.*
❯ INVITE **5** [T] to invite someone: **~ sb (+ adv./prep.)** *They've asked me to dinner.* ♦ *I didn't ask them in* (= to come into the house). ♦ *We must ask the neighbors over* (= to our house). ♦ **~ sb to do sth** *She's asked him to come to the party.*
❯ MONEY **6** [T] **~ sth (for sth)** to request a particular amount of money for something that you are selling: *He's asking $4,000 for the car.*
❯ EXPECT/DEMAND **7** [T] to expect or demand something: **~ sth** *I know I'm asking a great deal.* ♦ **~ sth of sb** *You're asking too much of him.* ♦ **~ sth to do sth** *I know it's asking a lot to expect them to win again.* ⊃ thesaurus box at DEMAND
IDM **be asking a lot (of sb/sth)** (informal) to be expecting someone or something to achieve or deal with a difficult thing: *Beating the world champions is certainly asking a lot of the team.* **be asking for trouble | be asking for it** (informal) to behave in a way that is very likely to result in trouble **don't ask** (informal) if you say **don't ask** to someone, you mean that you do not want to reply to their question, because it would be awkward, embarrassing, etc. **don't ask me** (informal) if you say **don't ask me**, you mean that you do not know the answer to a question and are annoyed you have been asked **for the asking** if you can have something **for the asking**, it is very easy for you to get it if you ask for it: *The job is yours for the asking.* **I ask you** (informal) if you say **I ask you**, you are expressing disapproval, shock, or anger about something or someone **if you ask me** (informal) in my personal opinion: *Their marriage was a mistake, if you ask me.* **ask for it** (informal) to deserve something bad that happens to you or that someone does to you
PHR V **ˌask aˈround** to speak to a number of different people in order to try and get some information: *I don't know of any vacancies in the company but I'll ask around.* **ˈask for sb/sth** to say that you want to speak to someone or be directed to a place: *When you arrive, ask for Jane.* **ˌask sb ˈout** to invite someone to go out with you, especially as a way of starting a romantic relationship: *He's too shy to ask her out.*

THESAURUS

ask

inquire ♦ demand

These words all mean to say or write something in the form of a question, in order to point information.

ask to say or write something in the form of a question, in order to get information: *"Where are you going?" she asked.* ♦ *She asked the students their names.* ♦ *Can I ask a question?*

---

inquire (*somewhat formal*) to ask someone for information: *I am writing to inquire about the research position.* ◆ *May I inquire who's calling, please?* (= on the telephone)

demand to ask a question very firmly: *The client demanded an explanation.* ◆ *"I demand to know who wrote this," he said.*

PATTERNS
- to ask/inquire **about/after** sb/sth
- to ask/demand sth **of** sb
- to ask/inquire/demand to know **what/who/how**, etc.
- to ask/inquire **politely**
- to ask/inquire/demand **angrily**

a·skance /əˈskæns/ *adv.*
  IDM **look askance (at sb/sth) | look (at sb/sth) askance** to look at or react to someone or something with suspicion or doubt, or in a critical way

a·skew /əˈskyu/ *adv., adj.* [not before noun] not in a straight or level position **SYN** CROOKED: *His glasses had been knocked askew by the blow.* ◆ *Her hat was slightly askew.*

'asking ˌprice *noun* the price that someone wants to sell something for ⊃ compare SELLING PRICE

a·slant /əˈslænt/ *adv.* not exactly vertical or horizontal; at an angle: *The picture hung aslant.*

a·sleep 🔑 /əˈslip/ *adj.* [not before noun]
  sleeping: *The baby was sound asleep* (= sleeping deeply) *upstairs.* ◆ *I waited until they were all fast asleep* (= sleeping deeply). ◆ *He was so exhausted that he fell asleep at his desk.* ◆ *She was still half asleep* (= not fully awake) *when she arrived at work.* ◆ *The police found him asleep in a garage.* **ANT** AWAKE

asp /æsp/ *noun* a small poisonous snake found especially in N. Africa

as·par·a·gus /əˈspærəgəs/ *noun* [U] a plant whose young green or white STEMS are cooked and eaten as a vegetable ⊃ picture at FRUIT

as·par·tame /ˈæspərˌteɪm/ *noun* [U] a sweet substance used instead of sugar in drinks and food products, especially ones for people who are trying to lose weight

as·pect 🔑 **AWL** /ˈæspɛkt/ *noun*
  1 [C] a particular part or feature of a situation, an idea, a problem, etc.; a way in which it may be considered: *The book aims to cover all aspects of city life.* ◆ *the most important aspect of the debate* ◆ *She felt she had looked at the problem from every aspect.* ◆ *This was one aspect of her character he hadn't seen before.* **2** [U, sing.] (*formal*) the appearance of a place, a situation, or a person: *Events began to take on a more sinister aspect.* **3** [C, usually sing.] (*formal*) the direction in which a building, window, piece of land, etc. faces; the side of a building that faces a particular direction **SYN** ORIENTATION **4** [U, C] (*grammar*) the form of a verb that shows, for example, whether the action happens once or repeatedly, is completed or still continuing ⊃ see also PERFECT, PROGRESSIVE

as·pen /ˈæspən/ *noun* a type of POPLAR tree, with leaves that move even when there is very little wind

As·per·ger's syn·drome /ˈæspərgərz ˌsɪndroʊm/ *noun* [U] a mild type of AUTISM (= a mental condition in which a person finds it difficult to communicate or form relationships with others)

as·per·gil·lo·sis /ˌæspərdʒɪˈloʊsəs/ *noun* [U] a serious condition in which parts of the body, usually the lungs, become infected by FUNGUS

as·per·i·ty /əˈspɛrəti/ *noun* [U] (*formal*) the fact of being rough or severe, especially in the way you speak to or treat someone **SYN** HARSHNESS

as·per·sions /əˈspərʒnz/ *noun* [pl.] (*formal*) critical or unpleasant remarks or judgments: *I wouldn't want to cast aspersions on your honesty.*

as·phalt /ˈæsfɔlt/ *noun* [U] a thick, black, sticky substance used especially for making the surface of roads

as·phyx·i·a /əˈsfɪksiə/ *noun* [U] the state of being unable to breathe, causing death or loss of CONSCIOUSNESS

as·phyx·i·ate /əˈsfɪksiˌeɪt/ *verb* ~ sb to make someone become unconscious or die by preventing them from breathing **SYN** SUFFOCATE ▶ **as·phyx·i·a·tion** /əˌsfɪksiˈeɪʃn/ *noun* [U]

as·pic /ˈæspɪk/ *noun* [U] a clear substance that food can be put into when it is being served cold: *chicken breast in aspic* ⊃ see also JELLY (3)

as·pi·dis·tra /ˌæspəˈdɪstrə/ *noun* a plant with broad, green, pointed leaves, often grown indoors

as·pir·ant /ˈæspərənt; əˈspaɪrənt/ *noun* ~ (to/for sth) (*formal*) a person with a strong desire to achieve a position of importance or to win a competition: *aspirants to the title of world champion* ▶ **as·pir·ant** *adj.* [only before noun] = ASPIRING

as·pi·rate *noun, verb*
- *noun* /ˈæspərət/ (*phonetics*) the sound /h/, as in *house*: *The word "hour" is pronounced without an initial aspirate.*
- *verb* /ˈæspəˌreɪt/ **1** ~ sth (*medical*) to remove liquid from a person's body with a machine **2** ~ sth (*phonetics*) to pronounce something with an /h/ sound or with a breath

as·pi·ra·tion /ˌæspəˈreɪʃn/ *noun* **1** [C, usually pl.] a strong desire to have or do something: *I didn't realize you had political aspirations.* ◆ ~ to do sth *He has never had any aspiration to earn a lot of money.* ◆ ~ for sth *What changes are needed to meet women's aspirations for employment?* **2** [U] (*phonetics*) the action of pronouncing a word with an /h/ sound, as in *house*

as·pi·ra·tion·al /ˌæspəˈreɪʃənl/ *adj.* wanting very much to achieve success in your career or to improve your social status and standard of living

as·pire /əˈspaɪər/ *verb* [I, T] to have a strong desire to achieve or to become something: ~ to sth *She aspired to a scientific career.* ◆ ~ to be/do sth *He aspired to be their next leader.*

as·pi·rin /ˈæsprən/ *noun* (*pl.* as·pi·rin or as·pi·rins) [U, C] a drug used to reduce pain, fever, and INFLAMMATION: *Do you have any aspirin?* ◆ *Take two aspirin(s) for a headache.*

as·pir·ing /əˈspaɪrɪŋ/ (*also less frequent* as·pir·ant) *adj.* [only before noun] **1** wanting to start the career or activity that is mentioned: *Aspiring musicians need hours of practice every day.* **2** wanting to be successful in life

ass /æs/ *noun* **1** (*slang*) an impolite word for the part of the body that you sit on; your bottom: *Get off your ass* (= stop sitting around doing nothing). **2** (*informal*) a stupid person **SYN** FOOL, JACKASS: *Don't be such an ass!* ◆ *I made an ass of myself at the meeting—standing up and then forgetting the question.* **3** (*old use*) a DONKEY **IDM** see KICK v.

as·sail /əˈseɪl/ *verb* (*formal*) **1** ~ sb/sth to attack someone or something violently, either physically or with words: *He was assailed with fierce blows to the head.* ◆ *The proposal was assailed by the opposition party.* ◆ (*figurative*) *A vile smell assailed my nostrils.* **2** (*usually passive*) ~ sb to disturb or upset someone severely: *to be assailed by worries/doubts/fears*

as·sail·ant /əˈseɪlənt/ *noun* (*formal*) a person who attacks someone, especially physically **SYN** ATTACKER

as·sas·sin /əˈsæsn/ *noun* a person who murders someone important or famous, for money or for political reasons

as·sas·si·nate /əˈsæsəˌneɪt/ *verb* [often passive] ~ sb to murder an important or famous person, especially for political reasons: *The prime minister was assassinated by extremists.* ◆ *a plot to assassinate the president* ▶ **as·sas·si·na·tion** /əˌsæsəˈneɪʃn/ *noun* [U, C]: *The president survived a number of assassination attempts.* ◆ *the assassination of John F. Kennedy*

as·sault /əˈsɔlt/ *noun, verb*
- *noun* **1** [U, C] the crime of attacking someone physically: *Both men were charged with assault.* ◆ *sexual assaults* ◆ ~ on/

| t tea | ṭ butter | d did | k cat | g got | tʃ chin | dʒ June | f fall |

upon sb *A significant number of physical assaults on women go unreported.* ⊃ collocations at CRIME **2** [C] **~ (on/upon/against sb/sth)** (by an army, etc.) the act of attacking a building, an area, etc. in order to take control of it **SYN** ATTACK: *An assault on the capital was launched in the early hours of the morning.* **3** [C] **~ (on/upon sth)** the act of trying to achieve something that is difficult or dangerous: *The government has mounted a new assault on unemployment* (= in order to reduce it). ◆ *Three people died during an assault on the mountain* (= while trying to climb it). **4** [C] an act of criticizing someone or something severely **SYN** ATTACK: *The suggested closures came under assault from all parties.* ◆ **~ on/upon/against sb/sth** *The paper's assault on the president was totally unjustified.*

● *verb* **1 ~ sb** to attack someone violently, especially when this is a crime: *He has been charged with assaulting a police officer.* ◆ *Four women have been sexually assaulted in the area recently.* **2 ~ sth** (*formal*) to affect your senses in a way that is very unpleasant or uncomfortable: *Loud rock music assaulted our ears.*

as·sault and battery *noun* [U] (*law*) the crime of threatening to harm someone and then attacking them physically

as·say /ˈæseɪ; æˈseɪ/ *noun* [C, U] (*technical*) the testing of metals and chemicals for quality, often to see how pure they are ▶ **as·say** /æˈseɪ/ *verb* **~ sth**

as·sem·blage /əˈsemblɪdʒ/ *noun* (*formal, technical*) a collection of things; a group of people: *Tropical rainforests have the most varied assemblage of plants in the world.*

as·sem·ble **AWL** /əˈsembl/ *verb* **1** [I, T] to come together as a group; to bring people or things together as a group: *All the students were asked to assemble in the main hall.* ◆ *She then addressed the assembled company* (= all the people there). ◆ **~ sth** *to assemble evidence/data* ◆ *The manager has assembled a world-class team.* **2** [T] **~ sth** to fit together all the separate parts of something, for example a piece of furniture: *The shelves are easy to assemble.* **ANT** DISASSEMBLE ⊃ thesaurus box at BUILD

as·sem·bler /əˈsemblər/ *noun* **1** a person who assembles a machine or its parts **2** (*computing*) a program for changing instructions into MACHINE CODE **3** (*computing*) = ASSEMBLY LANGUAGE

As·sem·blies of God *noun* [pl.] the largest Pentecostal Church in the U.S. (= one that emphasizes the gifts of the Holy Spirit, such as the power to heal people who are sick)

as·sem·bly **AWL** /əˈsembli/ *noun* (*pl.* **as·sem·blies**) **1** also **Assembly** [C] a group of people who have been elected to meet together regularly and make decisions or laws for a particular region or country: *State/legislative/federal/local assemblies* ◆ *Power has been handed over to provincial and regional assemblies.* ◆ *The national assembly has voted to adopt the budget.* ◆ *the California Assembly* ◆ *the UN General Assembly* **2** [U, C] the meeting together of a group of people for a particular purpose; a group of people who meet together for a particular purpose: *They were fighting for freedom of speech and freedom of assembly.* ◆ *He was to address a public assembly on the issue.* ◆ *an assembly point* (= a place where people have been asked to meet) **3** [C, U] a meeting of the teachers and students in a school to give information, discuss school events, or watch a performance together **4** [U] the process of putting together the parts of something such as a vehicle or piece of furniture: *Putting the bookcase together should be a simple assembly job.* ◆ *a car assembly plant* ◆ *Some assembly required.* (= instruction on the box of a toy, etc.)

as·sem·bly language *noun* [C, U] (also **as·sem·bler**) (*computing*) the language in which a program is written before it is changed into MACHINE CODE

as·sem·bly line *noun* = PRODUCTION LINE: *workers on the assembly line*

as·sem·bly·man /əˈsemblimən/, **as·sem·bly·wo·man** /əˈsembliˌwʊmən/ *noun* (*pl.* **as·sem·bly·men** /-mən/,

as·sem·bly·wom·en /-ˌwɪmən/) a person who is an elected representative in a state assembly

as·sent /əˈsent/ *noun, verb*
● *noun* [U] **~ (to sth)** (*formal*) official agreement to or approval of something: *The director has given her assent to the proposals.* ◆ *He nodded (his) assent.* ◆ *There were murmurs of both assent and dissent from the crowd.*
● *verb* [I] **~ (to sth)** | **(+ speech)** (*formal*) to agree to a request, an idea, or a suggestion: *Nobody would assent to the terms they proposed.*

as·sert /əˈsərt/ *verb* **1** to state clearly and firmly that something is true: **~ that…** *She continued to assert that she was innocent.* ◆ **~ sth** *She continued to assert her innocence.* ◆ **+ speech** *"That is wrong," he asserted.* ◆ **it is asserted that…** *It is commonly asserted that older people prefer to receive care from family members.* **2 ~ yourself** to behave in a confident and determined way so that other people pay attention to your opinions **3 ~ sth** to make other people recognize your right or authority to do something, by behaving firmly and confidently: *to assert your independence/rights* ◆ *I was determined to assert my authority from the beginning.* **4 ~ itself** to start to have an effect: *Good sense asserted itself.*

as·ser·tion /əˈsərʃn/ *noun* **1** [C] a statement saying that you strongly believe something to be true **SYN** CLAIM: *He was correct in his assertion that the senator had been lying.* ◆ *Do you have any evidence to support your assertions?* ⊃ thesaurus box at CLAIM **2** [U, C] the act of stating, using, or claiming something strongly: *the assertion of his authority* ◆ *The demonstration was an assertion of the right to peaceful protest.*

as·ser·tive /əˈsərtɪv/ *adj.* expressing opinions or desires strongly and with confidence, so that people take notice: *You should try and be more assertive.* ◆ *assertive behavior* **ANT** SUBMISSIVE ▶ **as·ser·tive·ly** *adv.* **as·ser·tive·ness** *noun* [U]: *an assertiveness training course*

as·sess **AWL** /əˈses/ *verb* **1** to make a judgment about the nature or quality of someone or something: **~ sb/sth** *It's difficult to assess the effects of these changes.* ◆ *to assess a patient's needs* ◆ **~ sb/sth as sth** *The young men were assessed as either safe or unsafe drivers.* ◆ *I'd assess your chances as low.* ◆ **~ whether, how, etc.…** *The committee assesses whether a building is worth preserving.* ◆ *We are trying to assess how well the system works.* **2** to calculate the amount or value of something **SYN** ESTIMATE: **~ sth** *They have assessed the amount of compensation to be paid.* ◆ **~ sth at sth** *Damage to the building was assessed at $40,000.* ▶ **as·sess·able** /əˈsesəbl/ **AWL** *adj.*

as·sess·ment **AWL** /əˈsesmənt/ *noun* **1** [C] an opinion or a judgment about someone or something that has been thought about very carefully **SYN** : *a detailed assessment of the risks involved* ◆ *his assessment of the situation* **2** [U] the act of judging or forming an opinion about someone or something: *written exams and other forms of assessment* ◆ *Objective assessment of the severity of the problem was difficult.* **3** [C] an amount that has been calculated and that must be paid: *a tax assessment*

as·sessment center (*CanE usually* **assessment centre**) *noun* (*business*) a place where people applying for a job are given a number of tests and interviews to find out what their strengths and weaknesses are: *After the first interview, you may be asked back to an assessment center.*

as·ses·sor /əˈsesər/ *noun* **1** an expert in a particular subject who is asked by a court or other official group to give advice **2** a person who calculates the value or cost of something or the amount of money to be paid: *an insurance/a tax assessor* **3** a person who judges how well someone has done in an exam, a competition, etc.: *Professors acted as external assessors of the exam results.*

as·set /ˈæset/ *noun* **1** a person or thing that is valuable or useful to someone or something: *In his job, patience is an invaluable asset.* ◆ **~ to sb/sth** *She'll be an asset to the team.* **2** [usually pl.] a thing of value, especially property, that a person or company owns, and that can be used or sold to pay debts: *the net asset value of the company* ◆ *Her assets*

---

v **v**oice   θ **th**in   ð **th**en   s **s**o   z **z**oo   ʃ **sh**e   ʒ vi**s**ion   x **Ch**anukah   77

include shares in the company and a house in Florida. ◆ **asset sales/management** ◆ **financial/capital assets** ⊃ compare LIABILITY

'asset-ˌstripping noun [U] (usually disapproving, business) the practice of buying a company that is in financial difficulties at a low price and then selling everything that it owns in order to make a profit

as·sid·u·ous /əˈsɪdʒuəs/ adj. (formal) working very hard and taking great care that everything is done as well as it can be **SYN** DILIGENT ▶ **as·si·du·i·ty** /ˌæsəˈduəti; -ˈdʒu-/ noun [U] **as·sid·u·ous·ly** adv.

as·sign **AWL** /əˈsaɪn/ verb **1** to give someone something that they can use, or some work or responsibility: **~ sth (to sb)** The two large classrooms have been assigned to us. ◆ The teacher assigned a different task to each of the children. ◆ **~ sb sth** We have been assigned the two large classrooms. ◆ The teacher assigned each of the children a different task. **2** to provide a person for a particular task or position: **~ sb (to sth/as sth)** They've assigned their best man to the job. ◆ **~ sb to do sth** U.S. forces have been assigned to help with peacekeeping. **3** [usually passive] **~ sb to sb/sth** to send a person to work under the authority of someone or in a particular group: I was assigned to B platoon. **4** to say that something has a particular value or function, or happens at a particular time or place: **~ sth to sth** Assign a different color to each different type of information. ◆ **~ sth sth** The painting cannot be assigned an exact date. **5** **~ sth to sb** (law) to say that your property or rights now belong to someone else: The agreement assigns copyright to the publisher.

as·sig·na·tion /ˌæsɪgˈneɪʃn/ noun (formal or humorous) a meeting, especially a secret one, often with a lover

as·sign·ment **AWL** /əˈsaɪnmənt/ noun **1** [C, U] a task or piece of work that someone is given to do, usually as part of their job or studies: You will need to complete three written assignments per semester. ◆ She is in Greece on an assignment for one of the Sunday newspapers. ◆ one of our reporters **on assignment** in China ◆ I had given myself a tough assignment. **2** [U] the act of giving something to someone; the act of giving someone a particular task: his assignment to other duties in the same company

as·sim·i·late /əˈsɪməˌleɪt/ verb **1** [T] **~ sth** to fully understand an idea or some information so that you are able to use it yourself: The committee will need time to assimilate this report. **2** [I, T] to become, or allow someone to become, a part of a country or community rather than remaining in a separate group: **~ (into/to sth)** New arrivals find it hard to assimilate. ◆ **~ sb (into/to sth)** Immigrants have been successfully assimilated into the community. **3** [T, often passive] **~ sth into/to sth** to make an idea, a person's attitude, etc. fit into something or be acceptable: These changes were gradually assimilated into everyday life.

as·sim·i·la·tion /əˌsɪməˈleɪʃn/ noun **1** [U] the act of assimilating someone or something, or being assimilated: the rapid assimilation of new ideas ◆ his assimilation into the community **2** [U, C] (phonetics) the act of making two sounds in speech that are next to each other more similar to each other in certain ways, for example the pronunciation of the /t/ in football as a /p/; an example of this process

as·sist 🔑 **AWL** /əˈsɪst/ verb, noun
- *verb* **1** [I, T] to help someone to do something: Anyone willing to assist can contact this number. ◆ **~ in/with sth** Would someone be willing to assist with child care today? ◆ **~ sb** We'll do all we can to assist you. ◆ The play was directed by Mike Johnson, assisted by Sharon Gale. ◆ **~ sb in doing sth** We will assist you in finding somewhere to live. ◆ **~ sb in/with sth** I will be assisting Mrs. Jones with her class today. ◆ **~ sb to do sth** We want to assist students to take more responsibility for their work. **2** [T] **~ sth** to help something to happen more easily: activities that will assist the decision-making process
- *noun* an action in HOCKEY, baseball, etc. in which a player helps another player on the same team to score a goal or point

as·sis·tance 🔑 **AWL** /əˈsɪstəns/ noun [U] (formal) help or support: technical/economic/military assistance ◆ **financial assistance** for people on low incomes ◆ Can I be of any assistance? ◆ Despite his cries, no one came to his assistance. ◆ He can walk only **with the assistance of** crutches. ◆ **~ with sth** She offered me practical assistance with my research. ◆ **~ in doing sth/to do sth** The company provides advice and assistance in finding work.

as·sis·tant 🔑 **AWL** /əˈsɪstənt/ noun, adj.
- *noun* **1** a person who helps or supports someone, usually in their job: My assistant will now demonstrate the machine in action. ◆ a research assistant ⊃ see also PDA, PERSONAL ASSISTANT, TEACHING ASSISTANT **2** = SALES CLERK: a sales assistant in a department store
- *adj.* [only before noun] (abbr. **Asst.**) (often in titles) having a rank below a senior person and helping them in their work: the assistant manager ◆ assistant chief of staff ◆ Assistant District Attorney Serena Southerlyn

as·sistant pro·fessor noun a teacher at a college or university who has a rank just below the rank of an ASSOCIATE PROFESSOR

as·sistant refer·ee (also refer·ee's as·sistant) noun (in SOCCER) the official name for a LINESMAN (= an official who helps the REFEREE, for example in deciding whether or where a ball has passed outside the field of play)

as·sis·tant·ship /əˈsɪstəntˌʃɪp/ noun a paid position for a graduate student that involves some teaching or research

as·sisted 'living noun [U] housing for people who need help, for example with tasks like washing and dressing themselves: assisted living apartments

as·sisted 'suicide noun [U] the act, which is illegal in many places, of a person killing himself/herself with the help of someone such as a doctor, especially because he/she is suffering from a disease that has no cure

Assoc. abbr. (in writing) ASSOCIATION or ASSOCIATE

as·so·ci·ate 🔑 verb, adj., noun
- *verb* /əˈsoʊʃiˌeɪt; -siˌeɪt/ **1** [T] **~ sb/sth (with sb/sth)** to make a connection between people or things in your mind: I always associate the smell of baking with my childhood. ◆ He is closely associated with horror movies by the public. **2** [I] **~ with sb** to spend time with someone, especially a person or people that someone else does not approve of **SYN** MIX: I don't like you associating with those people. **3** [T] **~ yourself with sth** (formal) to show that you support or agree with something: May I associate myself with the president's remarks? (= I agree with them) **ANT** DISSOCIATE
- *adj.* /əˈsoʊʃiət; -siət/ [only before noun] **1** (often in titles) of a lower rank, having fewer rights in a particular profession or organization: associate membership in the club ◆ an associate member/director/editor **2** joined to or connected with a profession or an organization: an associate company in Japan
- *noun* /əˈsoʊʃiət; -siət/ **1** a person that you work with, do business with, or spend a lot of time with: business associates **2** also **Associate** (abbr. Assoc.) an associate member **3** Associate (abbr. Assoc.) a person who has an Associate's degree (= one that is given after completing two years of study at a junior college)

as·so·ci·ated /əˈsoʊʃiˌeɪtəd; -siˌeɪ-/ adj. **1** if one thing is associated with another, the two things are connected because they happen together or one thing causes the other: the risks associated with taking drugs **SYN** CONNECTED: Salaries and associated costs have risen substantially. **2** if a person is associated with an organization, etc., they support it: He no longer wished to be associated with the party's policy on education. **3** Associated used in the name of a business company that is made up of a number of smaller companies: Associated Newspapers

As·sociated 'Press noun (abbr. AP) a U.S. news service. Its offices throughout the world send news to its members, which include newspapers and television, and radio stations.

as·sociate pro'fessor *noun* a teacher at a college or university who has a rank just below the rank of a professor

As'sociate's de·gree *noun* a degree from a two-year college, such as a COMMUNITY COLLEGE

as·so·ci·a·tion 🔑 /əˌsoʊsiˈeɪʃn; -ʃiˈeɪ-/ *noun*

1 [C] (*abbr.* Assoc.) an official group of people who have joined together for a particular purpose **SYN** ORGANIZATION: *Do you belong to any professional or trade associations?* ♦ *the Harvard alumni association* ♦ *a residents' association* **2** [C, U] **~ (with sb/sth)** a connection or relationship between people or organizations: *his alleged association with terrorist groups* ♦ *They have maintained a close association with a college in the U.K.* ♦ *The book was published* **in association with** (= together with) *the ASPCA.* ♦ *She became famous through her association with the group of poets.* **3** [C, usually pl.] an idea or a memory that is suggested by someone or something; a mental connection between ideas: *The beach has pleasant associations with childhood vacations for me.* ♦ *The cat soon made the association between human beings and food.* ➔ **see also** FREE ASSOCIATION **4** [C] a connection between things where one is caused by the other: *a proven association between passive smoking and cancer*

as·so·ci·a·tive /əˈsoʊʃətɪv; -ʃiˌeɪtɪv; -siˌeɪtɪv/ *adj.* **1** relating to the association of ideas or things **2** (*mathematics*) giving the same result, no matter what order the parts of a calculation are done in, for example (a × b) × c = a × (b × c)

as·so·nance /ˈæsənəns/ *noun* [U] (*technical*) the effect created when two syllables in words that are close together have the same vowel sound, but different consonants, for example *barn* and *farm*

as·sort·ed /əˈsɔrtəd/ *adj.* of various different sorts: *The meat is served with salad or assorted vegetables.* ♦ *The sweater comes in assorted colors.*

as·sort·ment /əˈsɔrtmənt/ *noun* [usually sing.] a collection of different things or of different types of the same thing **SYN** MIXTURE: *a wide assortment of gifts to choose from* ♦ *He was dressed in an odd assortment of clothes.*

Asst. *abbr.* (in writing) ASSISTANT: *Asst. Manager*

as·suage /əˈsweɪdʒ/ *verb* **~ sth** (*formal*) to make an unpleasant feeling less severe

as·sume 🔑 **AWL** /əˈsum/ *verb*

1 to think or accept that something is true but without having proof of it: **~ (that)…** *It is reasonable to assume (that) the economy will continue to improve.* ♦ **Let us assume** *for a moment that the plan succeeds.* ♦ *She would, he assumed, be home at the usual time.* ♦ **it is assumed (that)…** *It is generally assumed that stress is caused by too much work.* ♦ **~ sth** *Don't always* **assume the worst** (= that something bad has happened). ♦ *In this example we have assumed a unit price of $10.* ♦ **~ sb/sth to be/have sth** *I had assumed him to be foreign.* **2 ~ sth** (*formal*) to take or begin to have power or responsibility **SYN** TAKE: *The court assumed responsibility for the girl's welfare.* ♦ *Rebel forces have assumed control of the capital.* **3 ~ sth** (*formal*) to take financial responsibility for something; to agree to pay for something: *Corporations are assuming more and more debt as they are forced to invest and innovate.* ♦ *Students must assume their own healthcare costs and buy their own equipment.* **4 ~ sth** (*formal*) to begin to have a particular quality or appearance **SYN** TAKE ON: *This matter has assumed considerable importance.* ♦ *In the story, the god assumes the form of an eagle.* **5 ~ sth** (*formal*) to pretend to have a particular feeling or quality **SYN** PUT ON: *He assumed an air of concern.*

as·sumed **AWL** /əˈsumd/ *adj.* [only before noun] that you suppose to be true or to exist: *the assumed differences between the two states*

AWL COLLOCATIONS

assume

assume *verb*

■ **commonly, generally | erroneously, incorrectly, mistakenly | safely | implicitly, tacitly**
Contrary to what is generally assumed by theoretical models, our results demonstrate that…
We can safely assume that emissions from developing countries will keep rising as economic activity grows.
This approach implicitly assumes that medication use is constant during the assessment period.

■ **be reasonable to, be safe to | be unreasonable to**
It is reasonable to assume that those with a continuous work history should have a higher commitment to the labor market.
On the basis of available evidence, it would not be unreasonable to assume that Chinese writing began in the seventeenth century B.C.

assumption *noun*

■ **implicit, underlying | valid**
This implicit assumption is rarely tested.
There seem to be some underlying assumptions, but there does not seem to be any evidence.

■ **reexamine, test | satisfy, validate | challenge, question | contradict, violate**
The first experiment was designed to test the assumptions of these hypotheses.
Our findings challenge an important assumption shared by all of the theories we have examined.

as·sumed 'name *noun* a name that someone uses that is not their real name **SYN** PSEUDONYM: *He was living* **under an assumed name.**

as·sum·ing **AWL** /əˈsumɪŋ/ *conj.* **~ (that)** used to suppose that something is true so that you can talk about what the results might be: *Assuming (that) he's still alive, how old would he be now?* ♦ *I hope to go to college next year, assuming that I pass my exams.* ➔ collocations at ASSUME

as·sump·tion **AWL** /əˈsʌmpʃn/ *noun* **1** [C] a belief or feeling that something is true or that something will happen, although there is no proof: *an* **underlying/implicit assumption** ♦ *We need to* **challenge** some of the basic **assumptions** of Western philosophy. ♦ *We are working* **on the assumption that** *everyone invited will show up.* ♦ *It was impossible to* **make assumptions about** *people's reactions.* ♦ *His actions were based on a* **false assumption.** ➔ collocations at ASSUME **2** [C, U] **~ of sth** (*formal*) the act of taking or beginning to have power or responsibility: *their* **assumption** *of power/control*

as·sur·ance **AWL** /əˈʃʊrəns/ *noun* **1** [C] a statement that something will certainly be true or will certainly happen, particularly when there has been doubt about it **SYN** GUARANTEE, PROMISE: *They called for assurances that the government is committed to its education policy.* ♦ *Unemployment seems to be rising, despite repeated* **assurances to the contrary.** **2** (also **self-as'surance**) [U] belief in your own abilities or strengths **SYN** CONFIDENCE: *There was an air of easy assurance and calm about him.* ➔ see also QUALITY ASSURANCE

as·sure 🔑 **AWL** /əˈʃʊr/ *verb*

1 to tell someone that something is definitely true or is definitely going to happen, especially when they have doubts about it: **~ sb (that)…** *You think I did it deliberately, but I assure you (that) I did not.* ♦ *We were assured that everything possible was being done.* ♦ *She's perfectly safe,* **I can assure you.** ♦ **~ sb (of sth)** *We assured him of our support.* ♦ **~ sb + speech** *"He'll come back," Susan assured her.* **2** to make something certain to happen **SYN** GUARANTEE: **~ sth** *Victory would assure a place in the finals.* ♦ **~ sb sth** *Victory would assure them a place in the finals.* **3** to make yourself certain about something: ~ **yourself of sth** *He assured himself of her safety.* ◆ ~ **yourself that...** *She assured herself that the letter was still in the drawer.* **IDM** see REST v.

as·sured **AWL** /əˈʃʊrd/ *adj.* **1** (also ˌself-asˈsured) confident in yourself and your abilities: *He spoke in a calm, assured voice.* **2** certain to happen **SYN** GUARANTEE: *Success seemed assured.* **3** ~ **of sth** (of a person) certain to get something: *You are assured of a warm welcome at this hotel.*

as·sur·ed·ly **AWL** /əˈʃʊrədli/ *adv.* (*formal*) certainly; definitely

as·ta·tine /ˈæstəˌtin/ *noun* [U] (*symb.* **At**) a chemical element. Astatine is a RADIOACTIVE element that is found in small amounts in nature, and is produced artificially for use in medicine.

as·ter /ˈæstər/ *noun* a garden plant that has pink, purple, blue, or white flowers with many long narrow PETALS

as·ter·isk /ˈæstərɪsk/ *noun* the symbol (*) placed next to a particular word or phrase to make people notice it or to show that more information is given in another place: *I've placed an asterisk next to the tasks I want you to do first.* ▶ **as·ter·isk** *verb*: ~ **sth** *I've asterisked the tasks I want you to do first.*

a·stern /əˈstərn/ *adv.* (*technical*) **1** in, at, or toward the back part of a ship or boat **2** if a ship or boat is moving **astern**, it is moving backward

as·ter·oid /ˈæstəˌrɔɪd/ *noun* any one of the many small planets that go around the sun

asth·ma /ˈæzmə/ *noun* [U] a medical condition of the chest that makes breathing difficult: *a severe asthma attack*

asth·mat·ic /æzˈmætɪk/ *noun* a person who suffers from asthma ▶ **asth·mat·ic** *adj.*: *asthmatic patients* ◆ *asthmatic wheezing*

a·stig·ma·tism /əˈstɪɡməˌtɪzəm/ *noun* [U] a fault in the shape of a person's eye that prevents them from seeing clearly

as·ton·ish /əˈstɑnɪʃ/ *verb* to surprise someone very much **SYN** AMAZE ⊃ thesaurus box at SURPRISE: ~ **sth** *The news astonished everyone.* ◆ *She astonished us by saying she was leaving.* ◆ **it astonishes sb (that)...** *It astonishes me (that) he could be so thoughtless.*

as·ton·ished /əˈstɑnɪʃt/ *adj.* very surprised **SYN** AMAZED: *The helicopter landed before our astonished eyes.* ◆ ~ **at/by sth** *My parents looked astonished at my news.* ◆ ~ **(that)...** *She seemed astonished (that) I had never been to New York.* ◆ ~ **to find/hear/learn/see...** *He was astonished to learn he'd won the competition.*

as·ton·ish·ing /əˈstɑnɪʃɪŋ/ *adj.* very surprising; difficult to believe **SYN** AMAZING: *She ran 100 meters in an astonishing 10.6 seconds.* ◆ *I find it absolutely astonishing that you didn't like it.* ▶ **as·ton·ish·ing·ly** *adv.*: *Jack took the news astonishingly well.* ◆ *Astonishingly, a crowd of several thousand turned out to hear him.*

as·ton·ish·ment /əˈstɑnɪʃmənt/ *noun* [U] a feeling of very great surprise **SYN** AMAZEMENT: *To my utter astonishment, she remembered my name.* ◆ *He stared in astonishment at the stranger.*

as·tound /əˈstaʊnd/ *verb* ~ **sb** to surprise or shock someone very much **SYN** ASTONISH: *His arrogance astounded her.* ◆ *She was astounded by his arrogance.* ⊃ thesaurus box at SURPRISE

as·tound·ed /əˈstaʊndəd/ *adj.* very surprised or shocked by something, because it seems very unlikely **SYN** ASTONISHED: *an astounded expression* ◆ *How can you say that? I'm absolutely astounded.* ◆ ~ **at/by sth** *She looked astounded at the news.* ◆ ~ **(that)...** *The doctors were astounded (that) he survived.* ◆ ~ **to find, hear, learn, see...** *I was astounded to see her appear from the house.*

as·tound·ing /əˈstaʊndɪŋ/ *adj.* so surprising that it is difficult to believe **SYN** ASTONISHING: *There was an astounding 20% increase in sales.* ▶ **as·tound·ing·ly** *adv.*

as·tra·khan /ˈæstrəkən; -ˌkæn/ *noun* [U] a type of black curly fur of a particular type of young sheep, used especially for making coats and hats; a type of cloth that is made to look like this

as·tral /ˈæstrəl/ *adj.* [only before noun] **1** (*technical*) connected with the stars: *astral navigation* **2** connected with the spiritual rather than the physical world of existence: *the astral plane*

a·stray /əˈstreɪ/ *adv.*
IDM **go astray 1** to become lost; to be stolen: *Several letters went astray or were not delivered.* ◆ *We locked up our valuables so they would not go astray.* **2** to go in the wrong direction or to have the wrong result: *Fortunately the gunman's shots went astray.* ◆ *Jack's parents thought the other boys might **lead him astray** (= make him do things that are wrong).*

a·stride /əˈstraɪd/ *prep.*, *adv.*
● *prep.* with one leg on each side of something: *to sit astride a horse/bike/chair* ◆ (*figurative*) *a town astride the river*
● *adv.* **1** with legs or feet wide apart **2** with one leg on each side

as·trin·gent /əˈstrɪndʒənt/ *adj.*, *noun*
● *adj.* **1** (*technical*) (of a liquid or cream) able to make the skin feel less OILY or to stop the loss of blood from a cut **2** (*formal*) critical in a severe or intelligent way: *astringent writers/comments* **3** (*formal*) (of a taste or smell) slightly bitter but fresh: *the astringent taste of lemon juice* ▶ **as·trin·gen·cy** /-dʒənsi/ *noun*
● *noun* a liquid or cream used in COSMETICS or medicine to make the skin less OILY or to stop the loss of blood from a cut

astro- /ˈæstroʊ; ˈæstrə/ *combining form* (in nouns, adjectives, and adverbs) connected with the stars or outer space: *astronaut* ◆ *astrophysics*

as·tro·labe /ˈæstrəˌleɪb/ *noun* (*astronomy*) a device used in the past for measuring the distances of stars, planets, etc. and for calculating the position of a ship

as·trol·o·ger /əˈstrɑlədʒər/ *noun* a person who uses astrology to tell people about their character, about what might happen to them in the future, etc.

as·trol·o·gy /əˈstrɑlədʒi/ *noun* [U] the study of the positions of the stars and the movements of the planets in the belief that they influence human affairs ▶ **as·tro·log·i·cal** /ˌæstrəˈlɑdʒɪkl/ *adj.*: *astrological influences*

as·tro·naut /ˈæstrəˌnɔt; -ˌnɑt/ *noun* a person whose job involves traveling and working in a SPACECRAFT

as·tron·o·mer /əˈstrɑnəmər/ *noun* a scientist who studies astronomy

as·tro·nom·i·cal /ˌæstrəˈnɑmɪkl/ *adj.* **1** connected with astronomy: *astronomical observations* **2** (also **as·tro·nom·ic**) (*informal*) (of an amount, a price, etc.) very large: *the astronomical costs of land for building* ◆ *The figures are astronomical.* ▶ **as·tro·nom·i·cally** /-kli/ *adv.*: *Interest rates are astronomically high.*

astroˌnomical ˈunit *noun* (*abbr.* **AU**) (*astronomy*) a unit of measurement equal to 149.6 million kilometers, which is the distance from the center of the earth to the sun

as·tron·o·my /əˈstrɑnəmi/ *noun* [U] the scientific study of the sun, moon, stars, planets, etc.

as·tro·phys·ics /ˌæstroʊˈfɪzɪks/ *noun* [U] the scientific study of the physical and chemical structure of the stars, planets, etc. ▶ **as·tro·phys·i·cist** /-ˈfɪzəsɪst/ *noun*

As·tro·Turf™ /ˈæstroʊˌtərf/ *noun* [U] an artificial surface that looks like grass, for playing sports on

ˈA ˌstudent *noun* a student who gets or is likely to get the highest grades on his/her work or exams

as·tute /əˈstut/ *adj.* very intelligent and quick at seeing what to do in a particular situation, especially how to get an advantage **SYN** SHREWD: *an astute businessman/politician/observer* ◆ *It was an astute move to sell the shares then.* ▶ **as·tute·ly** *adv.* **as·tute·ness** *noun* [U]

ʌ c**up**   ə **about**   eɪ **say**   aɪ **five**   ɔɪ **boy**   aʊ **now**   oʊ **go**   ər **bird**

a·sun·der /əˈsʌndər/ adv. (old-fashioned or literary) into pieces; apart: families cast/torn asunder by the revolution

a·sy·lum /əˈsaɪləm/ noun **1** (also formal po,litical aˈsylum) [U] protection that a government gives to people who have left their own country, usually because they were in danger for political reasons: to seek/apply for/be granted asylum ◆ There was a nationwide debate on whether the asylum laws should be changed. **2** [C] (old use) a hospital where people who were mentally ill could be cared for, often for a long time

aˈsylum ,seeker noun a person who has been forced to leave their own country because they are in danger and who arrives in another country asking to be allowed to stay there

a·sym·met·ric /ˌeɪsɪˈmɛtrɪk/ (also a·sym·met·ri·cal /ˌeɪsɪ-ˈmɛtrɪkl/) adj. **1** having two sides or parts that are not the same in size or shape: Most people's faces are asymmetric. **ANT** SYMMETRICAL **2** (technical) not equal, for example in the way each side or part behaves: Linguists are studying the asymmetric use of Creole by parents and children (= parents use one language and children reply in another). ▶ a·sym-met·ri·cally /-kli/ adv. a·sym·me·try /eɪˈsɪmətri/ noun [C, U]

a·symp·to·mat·ic /ˌeɪsɪmptəˈmætɪk/ adj. (medical) (of a person or illness) having no SYMPTOMS

a·syn·chro·nous /eɪˈsɪŋkrənəs/ adj. (formal) (of two or more objects or events) not existing or happening at the same time ▶ a·syn·chro·nous·ly adv.

at /ət; strong form æt/ prep.
1 used to say where something or someone is or where something happens: at the corner of the street ◆ We transferred at Grand Central. ◆ They arrived late at the airport. ◆ At the traffic circle, take a right. ◆ I'll be at home all morning. ◆ She's at Tom's (= Tom's house). ◆ I met her at the hospital. ◆ How many people were there at the concert? **2** used to say where someone works or studies: He's been at the bank longer than anyone else. ◆ She's at Yale (= Yale University). **3** used to say when something happens: We left at 2 o'clock. ◆ at the end of the week ◆ We woke at dawn. ◆ I don't know where she is at the moment (= now). ◆ At night you can see the stars. ◆ What are you doing at 8? **4** used to state the age at which someone does something: She got married at 25. ◆ He left home at the age of 18. **5** in the direction of or toward someone or something: What are you looking at? ◆ He pointed a gun at her. ◆ Somebody threw stones at the protesters. **6** used after a verb to show that someone tries to do something, or partly does something, but does not succeed or complete it: He clutched wildly at the rope as he fell. ◆ She nibbled at a sandwich (= ate only small bits of it). **7** used to state the distance away from something: I held it at arm's length. **8** used to show the situation someone or something is in, what someone is doing, or what is happening: The country is now at war. ◆ I felt like I was at a disadvantage. ◆ I think Mr. Harris is at lunch. **9** used to show a rate, speed, etc.: He was driving at 70 mph. ◆ The noise came at two-minute intervals (= once every two minutes). ◆ Prices start at $1,000. **10 ~ sb's/sth's best/worst, etc.** used to say that someone or something is as good, bad, etc. as they can be: This was Murray at his best. ◆ The garden's at its most beautiful in June. **11** used with adjectives to show how well someone does something: I'm good at French. ◆ She's hopeless at managing people. **12** used with adjectives to show the cause of something: They were impatient at the delay. ◆ She was delighted at the result. **13** (formal) in response to something: They attended the dinner at the chairman's invitation. **14** used when giving a telephone number: You can reach me at 637-2335, extension 354. **15** (computing) the symbol (@) used in e-mail addresses
IDM **at that** used when you are giving an extra piece of information: He managed to buy a car after all—and a nice one at that. **be at it again** (informal) to be doing something, especially something bad: Look at all that graffiti—those kids have been at it again. **where it's at** (informal) a place or an activity that is very popular or fashionable: Judging by the crowds waiting to get in, this seems to be where it's at.

at·a·vis·tic /ˌætəˈvɪstɪk/ adj. (formal) related to the attitudes and behavior of the first humans: an atavistic urge/instinct/fear

a·tax·i·a /əˈtæksiə/ (also a·tax·y /əˈtæksi/) noun [U] (medical) the loss of full control of the body's movements ▶ a·tax·ic /-sɪk/ adj.

ate pt of EAT

-ate /ət; eɪt/ suffix **1** (in adjectives) full of or having the quality of: passionate ◆ Italianate **2** /eɪt/ (in verbs) to give the thing or quality mentioned to: hyphenate ◆ activate **3** (in nouns) the status or function of: a doctorate **4** (in nouns) a group with the status or function of: the electorate **5** (chemistry) (in nouns) a salt formed by the action of a particular acid: sulfate

A-team noun [usually sing.] **1** the best sports team in a school, club, etc. **2** a group of the best workers, soldiers, etc.

at·el·ier /ˌætlˈyeɪ/ noun a room or building in which an artist works **SYN** STUDIO

a·tem·po·ral /eɪˈtɛmpərəl/ adj. (formal) existing or considered without relation to time

a·the·ism /ˈeɪθiˌɪzəm/ noun [U] the belief that God does not exist **ANT** THEISM ▶ a·the·is·tic /ˌeɪθiˈɪstɪk/ adj.

a·the·ist /ˈeɪθiɪst/ noun a person who believes that God does not exist ⟳ compare AGNOSTIC

ath·lete /ˈæθlit/ noun **1** a person who competes in sports: Olympic athletes **2** a person who is good at sports and physical exercise: She is a natural athlete.

ˈathlete's ˌfoot noun [U] an infectious skin disease that affects the feet, especially between the toes

ath·let·ic /æθˈlɛtɪk/ adj. physically strong, fit, and active: an athletic figure/build ◆ a tall, slim, athletic girl ▶ ath·let·i·cally /æθˈlɛtɪkli/ adv. ath·let·i·cism /æθˈlɛtəˌsɪzəm/ noun [U]: She moved with great athleticism around the court.

ath·let·ics /æθˈlɛtɪks/ noun [U] any sports that people compete in: students involved in all forms of college athletics

athˈletic ˌshoe noun a shoe that you wear for sports

athˈletic supˌporter noun = JOCKSTRAP

at-ˈhome adj. [only before noun] **1** done or taking place at home: an at-home job **2** (of a parent) staying at home rather than going out to work: at-home dads ⟳ see also STAY-AT-HOME

-athon /əθɑn/ suffix (in nouns) an event in which a particular activity is done for a very long time, especially one organized to raise money for charity: a danceathon

a·thwart /əˈθwɔrt/ prep. (formal) **1** across; from one side to the other: They put a table athwart the doorway. **2** not agreeing with; opposite to: His statement ran athwart what was previously said.

-ation /ˈeɪʃn/ ⟳ -ION

-ative /ətɪv; eɪtɪv/ suffix (in adjectives) doing or tending to do something: illustrative ◆ talkative ▶ -atively suffix (in adverbs): creatively

At·kins Di·et™ /ˈætkɪnz ˌdaɪət/ noun a diet in which you eat foods that contain a high level of PROTEIN (meat, eggs, cheese, etc.) and avoid foods that contain a high level of CARBOHYDRATES (bread, rice, fruit, etc.)

At·lan·tic Can·a·da /ətˌlæntɪk ˈkænədə/ noun [U] (also the At,lantic ˈProvinces [pl.]) the Canadian PROVINCES (= government divisions) of New Brunswick, Nova Scotia, Prince Edward Island, and Newfoundland and Labrador ⟳ compare MARITIMES

Atˈlantic ˌtime noun [U] the standard time system that is used in the eastern part of Canada, and also in Puerto Rico and the Virgin Islands ⟳ compare CENTRAL TIME, EASTERN TIME, MOUNTAIN TIME, PACIFIC TIME

At·lan·tis /ətˈlæntəs/ noun [U] (in stories) an island full of beauty and wealth, which was said to have been covered

---

by the ocean and lost. There are many stories about people's attempts to find it.

at·las /'ætləs/ *noun* a book of maps: *a world atlas ◆ a road atlas of the U.S.*

ATM /ˌeɪ ti 'ɛm/ (*CanE* ABM) *noun* automated teller machine; a machine in or outside a bank, etc., from which you can get money from your bank account using a special plastic card **SYN** CASH MACHINE

AT'M card *noun* a plastic card used to get money from an ATM ⊃ compare CHECK CARD, DEBIT CARD, CREDIT CARD

at·mos·phere /'ætməsˌfɪr/ *noun*
1 the atmosphere [sing.] the mixture of gases that surrounds the earth: *the upper atmosphere ◆ pollution of the atmosphere* **2** [C] a mixture of gases that surrounds another planet or a star: *Saturn's atmosphere* **3** [C] the air in a room or in a small space; the air around a place: *a smoky/stuffy atmosphere ◆ These plants love warm, humid atmospheres.* **4** [C, U] the feeling or mood that you have in a particular place or situation; a feeling between two people or in a group of people: *a party atmosphere ◆ The hotel offers a friendly atmosphere and personal service. ◆ Use music and lighting to create a romantic atmosphere. ◆ There was an atmosphere of mutual trust between them. ◆ The children grew up in an atmosphere of love and happiness. ◆ The old house is full of atmosphere* (= it's very interesting). **IDM** see HEAVY *adj.*

at·mos·pher·ic /ˌætməs'fɪrɪk; -'fɛr-/ *adj.* **1** [only before noun] related to the earth's atmosphere: *atmospheric pollution/conditions/pressure* **2** creating an exciting or emotional mood: *atmospheric music*

at·mos·pher·ics /ˌætməs'fɪrɪks; -'fɛr-/ *noun* [pl.] **1** qualities in something that create a particular atmosphere **2** noises that sometimes interrupt a radio broadcast

at·oll /'ætɔl; 'ætɑl/ *noun* an island made of CORAL and shaped like a ring with a lake of sea water (called a LAGOON) in the middle

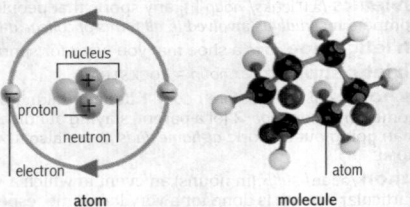

atom **molecule**

at·om /'ætəm/ *noun*
the smallest part of a chemical element that can take part in a chemical reaction: *the splitting of the atom ◆ Two atoms of hydrogen combine with one atom of oxygen to form a molecule of water.*

a·tom·ic /ə'tɑmɪk/ *adj.* [usually before noun] **1** connected with atoms or an atom: *atomic structure* **2** connected with weapons that use atomic energy: *the atomic bomb*

a·tomic 'bomb (also ˌatom 'bomb, 'A-bomb) *noun* a bomb that explodes using atomic energy

a·tomic 'clock *noun* an extremely accurate clock that uses the movement of atoms or MOLECULES to measure time

a·tomic 'energy (also ˌatomic 'power) *noun* [U] a powerful form of energy produced when atoms are split **SYN** NUCLEAR ENERGY

at·o·mic·i·ty /ˌætə'mɪsəti/ *noun* (*chemistry*) the number of atoms in one MOLECULE of a substance

a·tomic 'mass *noun* (*chemistry*) = RELATIVE ATOMIC MASS

a·tomic 'number *noun* (*chemistry*) the number of PROTONS in the NUCLEUS (= center) of an atom, which is characteristic of a chemical element. Elements are placed in the PERIODIC TABLE according to their atomic numbers.

a·tomic 'theory *noun* (*chemistry, physics*) the theory that all elements are made up of small PARTICLES called atoms, which are made up of a central NUCLEUS surrounded by moving ELECTRONS

a·tomic 'weight *noun* (*chemistry*) = RELATIVE ATOMIC MASS

at·om·ism /'ætəˌmɪzəm/ *noun* [U] (*technical*) the idea of analyzing something by separating it into its different parts ⊃ compare HOLISM ▶ **at·om·is·tic** /ˌætə'mɪstɪk/ *adj.*

at·om·ize /'ætəˌmaɪz/ *verb* ~ **sth** to reduce something to atoms or very small pieces

at·om·iz·er /'ætəˌmaɪzər/ *noun* a container that forces a liquid such as water or paint out as a very fine spray

a·ton·al /eɪ'toʊnl/ *adj.* (of a piece of music) not written in any particular KEY **ANT** TONAL ▶ **a·to·nal·i·ty** /ˌeɪtoʊ'næləti/ *noun* [U]

a·tone /ə'toʊn/ *verb* [I] ~ **(for sth)** (*formal*) to act in a way that shows you are sorry for doing something wrong in the past **SYN** MAKE AMENDS: *to atone for a crime* ▶ **a·tone·ment** *noun* [U]: *to make atonement for his sins ◆ Yom Kippur, the Jewish day of atonement*

a·top /ə'tɑp/ *prep.* on top of; at the top of: *a flag high atop a pole ◆ a scoop of ice cream atop a slice of apple pie*

a·top·ic /eɪ'tɑpɪk/ *adj.* (*medical*) relating to a form of ALLERGY where there is a reaction in a part of the body that does not have direct contact with the thing causing the ALLERGY

-ator /eɪtər/ *suffix* (in nouns) a person or thing that does something: *creator ◆ percolator*

A to Z /ˌeɪ tə 'zi/ *noun* [sing.] a book containing all the information you need about a subject or place: *an A to Z of needlework*

ˌat-'risk *adj.* [only before noun] (of a person or group) in danger of being attacked or hurt, especially in their own home: *Social services keep lists of at-risk children.*

a·tri·um /'eɪtriəm/ *noun* (*pl.* a·tri·a /'eɪtriə/ or a·tri·ums) **1** a large high space, usually with a glass roof, in the center of a modern building **2** an open space in the center of an ancient Roman VILLA **3** (*anatomy*) either of the two upper spaces in the heart that are used in the first stage of sending the blood around the body **SYN** AURICLE

a·tro·cious /ə'troʊʃəs/ *adj.* **1** very bad or unpleasant **SYN** TERRIBLE: *She speaks French with an atrocious accent. ◆ Isn't the weather atrocious?* **2** very cruel and shocking: *atrocious acts of brutality* ▶ **a·tro·cious·ly** *adv.*

a·troc·i·ty /ə'trɑsəti/ *noun* [U] (*pl.* a·troc·i·ties) [C, usually pl.] a cruel and violent act, especially in a war

at·ro·phy /'ætrəfi/ *noun, verb*
• *noun* [U] (*medical*) the condition of losing flesh, muscle, strength, etc. in a part of the body because it does not have enough blood: (*figurative, formal*) *TV viewing may lead to atrophy of children's imaginations.*
• *verb* (at·ro·phies, at·ro·phy·ing, at·ro·phied, at·ro·phied) [I] if a part of the body atrophies, it becomes weak because it is not used or because it does not have enough blood: (*figurative*) *Memory can atrophy through lack of use.* ▶ **at·ro·phied** *adj.*: *atrophied muscles ◆ atrophied religious values*

at·ta·boy /'ætəˌbɔɪ/ *exclamation* (*informal*) used when you want to encourage someone or show your admiration of them, especially a boy or man ⊃ see also ATTAGIRL

at·tach /ə'tætʃ/ **AWL** *verb*
1 to fasten or join one thing to another: ~ **sth** *I attach a copy of my notes for your information. ◆ I attach a copy of the spreadsheet* (= send it with an e-mail). ◆ ~ **sth to sth** *Attach the coupon to the front of your letter. ◆* (*figurative*) *They have attached a number of conditions to the agreement* (= said that the conditions must be part of the agreement). ⊃ compare DETACH **2** ~ **importance, significance, value, weight, etc. (to something)** to believe that something is important or worth thinking about: *I attach great importance to this research.* **3** ~ **yourself to sb** to join someone for a time, sometimes when you are not welcome or have not been

t tea   ţ butter   d did   k cat   g got   tʃ chin   dʒ June   f fall

invited: *He attached himself to me at the party and I couldn't get rid of him.* **4** (*formal*) to be connected with someone or something; to connect something to something: **~ sth to sb/sth** *This does not attach any blame to you.* ♦ *No blame is attached to you.* ♦ *No one is suggesting that any health risks are attached to this product.*

at·ta·ché /ˌætæˈʃeɪ; ˌætəˈʃeɪ/ *noun* a person who works at an EMBASSY, usually with a special responsibility for a particular area of activity: *a cultural attaché*

atta'ché case *noun* a small, hard, flat case used for carrying business documents ⊃ compare BRIEFCASE

at·tached 🔑 AWL /əˈtætʃt/ *adj.*
1 ~ (to sb/sth) full of affection for someone or something: *I've never seen two people so attached to each other.* ♦ *We've grown very attached to this house.* ⊃ compare UNATTACHED **2** [not before noun] **~ to sth** working for or forming part of an organization: *The research unit is attached to the university.* **3 ~ (to sth)** joined to something: *Please complete the attached application form.*

at·tach·ment AWL /əˈtætʃmənt/ *noun* **1** [C] a tool that you can fix onto a machine, to make it do another job: *an electric drill with a range of different attachments* **2** [U, C] the act of joining one thing to another; a thing that joins two things together: *All cars built since 1981 have points for the attachment of safety restraints.* ♦ *They discussed the attachment of new conditions to the peace plans.* ♦ *They had to check the strength of the seat attachments to the floor of the plane.* **3** [C, U] a strong feeling of affection for someone or something: *a child's strong attachment to its parents* **4** [C, U] belief in and support for an idea or a set of values: *the popular attachment to democratic government* **5** [C] (*computing*) a document that you send to someone using e-mail ⊃ collocations at E-MAIL

at·tack 🔑 /əˈtæk/ *noun, verb*
● *noun*
▷ VIOLENCE **1** [C, U] **~ (on sb)** an act of using violence to try to hurt or kill someone: *a series of racist attacks*
▷ IN WAR **2** [C, U] **~ (on sb/sth)** an act of trying to kill or injure the enemy in war, using weapons such as guns and bombs: *to launch/make/mount an attack* ♦ *The patrol came under attack from all sides.* ⊃ collocations at WAR ⊃ see also COUNTERATTACK
▷ CRITICISM **3** [C, U] **~ (on sb/sth)** strong criticism of someone or something in speech or in writing: *a scathing attack on the government's policies* ♦ *The school has come under attack for failing to encourage bright students.*
▷ ACTION TO STOP SOMETHING **4** [C] **~ (on sth)** an action that you take to try to stop or change something that you feel is bad: *to launch an all-out attack on poverty/unemployment*
▷ OF ILLNESS **5** [C] a sudden, short period of illness, usually severe, especially an illness that you have often: *to suffer an asthma attack* ♦ *an acute attack of food poisoning* ♦ *a panic attack* ♦ (*figurative*) *an attack of the giggles* ⊃ see also HEART ATTACK
▷ OF EMOTION **6** [C] a sudden period of feeling an emotion such as fear: *an attack of nerves*
▷ DAMAGE **7** [U, C] the action of something such as an insect, or a disease, that causes damage to something or someone: *The roof timbers were affected by rot and insect attack.*
● *verb*
▷ USE VIOLENCE **1** [I, T, often passive] to use violence to try to hurt or kill someone: *Most dogs will not attack unless provoked.* ♦ **~ sb** *A woman was attacked and robbed.* ♦ **~ sb with sth** *The man attacked him with a knife.*
▷ IN WAR **2** [I, T] to use weapons, such as guns and bombs, against an enemy in a war, etc.: *The guerrillas attack at night.* ♦ **~ sb/sth** *At dawn the army attacked the town.*
▷ CRITICIZE **3** [T] to criticize someone or something severely: **~ sb/sth** *a newspaper article attacking the governor* ♦ **~ sb/sth for sth/for doing sth** *She has been attacked for ignoring her own party members.*
▷ DAMAGE **4** [T] **~ sth** to have a harmful effect on something: *a disease that attacks the brain* ♦ *The vines were attacked by mildew.*

▷ DO SOMETHING WITH ENERGY **5** [T] **~ sth** to deal with something with a lot of energy and determination: *Let's attack one problem at a time.*
▷ IN SPORTS **6** [I] to go forward in a game in order to try to score goals or points: *The Penguins attacked more in the second half and deserved a goal.* ⊃ compare DEFEND

at'tack dog *noun* **1** a dog that has been trained to attack people or other animals **2** (*disapproving*) a person who often makes strong personal attacks on other people in public: *His image has changed from statesman to attack dog.*

at·tack·er /əˈtækər/ *noun* a person who attacks someone: *She didn't really see her attacker.*

at·ta·girl /ˈætəˌgərl/ *exclamation* (*informal*) used when you want to encourage a girl or woman, or show your admiration of them ⊃ see also ATTABOY

at·tain AWL /əˈteɪn/ *verb* **1 ~ sth** to succeed in getting something, usually after a lot of effort: *Most of our students attained five B's or higher on their exams.* **2 ~ sth** (*formal*) to reach a particular age, level, or condition: *The cheetah can attain speeds of up to 60 mph.*

at·tain·a·ble AWL /əˈteɪnəbl/ *adj.* that you can achieve: *attainable goals/objectives/targets* ♦ *This standard is easily attainable by most students.* ANT UNATTAINABLE

at·tain·ment AWL /əˈteɪnmənt/ *noun* (*formal*) **1** [U] success in achieving something: *The attainment of his ambitions was still a dream.* **2** [C] something that you achieved: *a young woman of impressive educational attainments*

at·tar /ˈætər; ˈɑːtɑr/ (also **otto**) *noun* an ESSENTIAL OIL usually made from ROSE PETALS

at·tempt 🔑 /əˈtɛmpt/ *noun, verb*
● *noun* **1** [C, U] an act of trying to do something, especially something difficult, often with no success: *I passed my driving test on the first attempt.* ♦ **~ to do sth** *Two factories were closed in an attempt to cut costs.* ♦ *They made no attempt to escape.* ♦ **~ at sth/at doing sth** *The couple made an unsuccessful attempt at a compromise.* **2** [C] **~ (on sb/on sb's life)** an act of trying to kill someone: *Someone has made an attempt on the president's life.* **3** [C] **~ (on sth)** an effort to do better than something, such as a very good performance in sports: *his attempt on the world land speed record*
● *verb* to make an effort or try to do something, especially something difficult: **~ to do sth** *I will attempt to answer all your questions.* ♦ *Do not attempt to repair this yourself.* ♦ **~ sth** *The prisoners attempted an escape, but failed.*

at·tempt·ed 🔑 /əˈtɛmptəd/ *adj.* [only before noun] (of a crime, etc.) that someone has tried to do but without success: *attempted murder/robbery*

at·tend 🔑 /əˈtɛnd/ *verb*
1 [I, T] to be present at an event: *We'd like as many people as possible to attend.* ♦ **~ sth** *The meeting was attended by 90% of shareholders.* ♦ *to attend a wedding/funeral* **2** [T] **~ sth** to go regularly to a place: *Our children attend the same school.* ♦ *How many people attend church every Sunday?* **3** [I] **~ (to sb/sth)** (*formal*) to pay attention to what someone is saying or to what you are doing: *She hadn't been attending during the lesson.* **4** [T] **~ sth** (*formal*) to happen at the same time as something: *She dislikes the loss of privacy that attends TV celebrity.* **5** [T] **~ sb** (*formal*) to be with someone and help them: *The president was attended by several members of his staff.*
PHR V **at'tend to sb/sth** to deal with someone or something; to take care of someone or something: *I have some urgent business to attend to.* ♦ *A nurse attended to his needs constantly.*

at·tend·ance /əˈtɛndəns/ *noun* **1** [U, C] the act of being present at a place, for example at school: *Attendance at these lectures is not compulsory.* ♦ *Teachers must keep a record of students' attendance.* **2** [C, U] the number of people present at an organized event: *high/low/falling/poor attendances* ♦ *There was an attendance of 42 at the meeting.*
IDM **be in attendance** (*formal*) to be present at a special

event: *Several heads of state were in attendance at the funeral.* **be in attendance (on sb)** (*formal*) to be with or near someone in order to help them if necessary: *He always has at least two bodyguards in attendance.* **take attendance** to check who is present and who is not present at a place and to mark this information on a list of names

at·tend·ant /əˈtɛndənt/ *noun, adj.*

● **noun** **1** a person whose job is to serve or help people in a public place: *a cloakroom/parking/museum attendant* ➔ see also FLIGHT ATTENDANT **2** a person who takes care of and lives or travels with an important person, or a sick or elderly person

● **adj.** [usually before noun] (*formal*) closely connected with something that has just been mentioned: *attendant problems/risks/circumstances* ◆ **~ on sth** *We had all the usual problems attendant on starting a new business.*

at·tend·ee /əˌtɛnˈdi; ˌætɛn-/ *noun* a person who attends a meeting, etc.

at·ten·tion 🔑 /əˈtɛnʃn/ *noun, exclamation*

● **noun**

▷ LISTENING/LOOKING CAREFULLY **1** [U] the act of listening to, looking at, or thinking about something or someone carefully: *the report's attention to detail* ◆ *He turned his attention back to the road again.* ◆ *Small children have a very short attention span.* ◆ *Please pay attention* (= listen carefully) *to what I am saying.* ◆ *Don't pay any attention to what they say* (= don't think that it is important). ◆ *She tried to attract the waiter's attention.* ◆ *I tried not to draw attention to* (= make people notice) *the weak points in my argument.* ◆ *An article in the newspaper caught my attention.* ◆ *I couldn't give the program my undivided attention.* ◆ (*formal*) *It has come to my attention* (= I have been informed) *that...* ◆ (*formal*) *He brought/called (their) attention to the fact that many files were missing.* ◆ (*formal*) *Can I have your attention please?* ➔ language bank at EMPHASIS

▷ INTEREST **2** [U] interest that people show in someone or something: *Movies with big stars always attract great attention.* ◆ *As the youngest child, she was always the center of attention.* **3** [C, usually pl.] things that someone does to try to please you or to show their interest in you: *She tried to escape the unwanted attentions of her former boyfriend.*

▷ TREATMENT **4** [U] special care, action, or treatment: *She was in need of medical attention.* ◆ *The roof needs attention* (= needs to be repaired). ◆ *for the attention of...* (= written on the envelope of an official letter to say who should deal with it)

▷ SOLDIERS **5** [U] the position soldiers take when they stand very straight with their feet together and their arms at their sides: *to stand at attention* ➔ compare (STAND) AT EASE at EASE *n.*

● **exclamation** **1** used for asking people to listen to something that is being announced: *Attention, please! Passengers for flight KL412 should report to gate 21 immediately.* **2** used for ordering soldiers to stand to attention

at·ten·tion ·deficit hyperac·tivity dis·order (also at·ten·tion ˈdeficit dis·order) *noun* [U] (*abbr.* ADHD, ADD) a medical condition, especially in children, that makes it difficult for them to pay attention to what they are doing, to stay still for long, and to learn things

at·ten·tive /əˈtɛntɪv/ *adj.* **1** listening or watching carefully and with interest: *an attentive audience* **2** helpful; making sure that people have what they need: *The hotel staff are friendly and attentive.* ◆ **~ to sb/sth** *Ministers should be more attentive to the needs of families.* ▶ **at·ten·tive·ly** *adv.* **at·ten·tive·ness** *noun* [U] **ANT** INATTENTIVE

at·ten·u·ate /əˈtɛnyuˌeɪt/ *verb* **~ sth** (*formal*) to make something weaker or less effective: *The drug attenuates the effects of the virus.* ▶ **at·ten·u·a·tion** /əˌtɛnyuˈeɪʃn/ *noun* [U]

at·ten·u·at·ed /əˈtɛnyuˌeɪtəd/ *adj.* (*formal*) **1** made weaker or less effective: *an attenuated form of the virus* **2** (of a person) very thin

at·ten·u·a·tor /əˈtɛnyuˌeɪtər/ *noun* (*technical*) a device consisting of a number of RESISTORS that reduce the strength of a radio sound or signal

at·test /əˈtɛst/ *verb* (*formal*) **1** [I, T] **~ (to sth)** | **~ (that...)** | **~ (sth)** to show or prove that something is true SYN BEAR WITNESS TO: *Contemporary accounts attest to his courage and determination.* **2** [T] **~ (sth)** | **~ (that...)** to state that you believe that something is true or genuine, for example in court: *to attest a will* ◆ *The signature was attested by two witnesses.*

at·tic /ˈætɪk/ *noun* a room or space just below the roof of a house, often used for storing things: *furniture stored in the attic* ◆ *an attic bedroom* ➔ compare GARRET

at·tire /əˈtaɪər/ *noun* [U] (*formal*) clothes: *dressed in formal evening attire*

at·tired /əˈtaɪərd/ *adj.* [not before noun] (*formal* or *literary*) dressed in a particular way

at·ti·tude 🔑 **AWL** /ˈætəˌtud/ *noun*

1 [C] **~ (to/toward sb/sth)** the way that you think and feel about someone or something; the way that you behave toward someone or something that shows how you think and feel: *changes in public attitudes to marriage* ◆ *the government's attitude toward single parents* ◆ *to have a good/ bad/positive/negative attitude toward someone or something* ◆ *If you want to pass your exams, you'd better change your attitude!* ◆ *You've got a pretty selfish attitude about this, don't you?* ◆ *A lot of drivers have a serious attitude problem* (= they do not behave in a way that is acceptable to other people). **2** [U] confident, sometimes aggressive, behavior that shows you do not care about other people's opinions and that you want to do things in an individual way: *a band with attitude* ◆ *You'd better get rid of that attitude and shape up, young man.* **3** [C] (*formal*) a position of the body: *Her hands were folded in an attitude of prayer.* **IDM** see COP *v.*

at·ti·tu·di·nal /ˌætəˈtudnəl/ *adj.* (*formal*) related to the attitudes that people have

attn. *abbr.* (*business*) (in writing) for the attention of: *Sales Dept., attn. C. Biggs*

at·tor·ney 🔑 /əˈtərni/ *noun*

1 a lawyer, especially one who can act for someone in court ➔ see also DISTRICT ATTORNEY ➔ note at LAWYER **2** a person who is given the power to act on behalf of another in business or legal matters: *She was made her father's attorney when he became ill.* ➔ see also POWER OF ATTORNEY

at·torney ˈgeneral *noun* (*pl.* attorneys general or attorney generals) **1** the chief lawyer for the U.S. or for a particular state, appointed by the government **2** At·torney ˈGeneral (*CanE*) the chief lawyer for Canada or for a particular area, who also gives legal advice to the government

at·tract 🔑 /əˈtrækt/ *verb*

1 [usually passive] if you are **attracted** by something, it interests you and makes you want it; if you are **attracted** by someone, you like or admire them: **~ sb** *I had always been attracted by the idea of working abroad.* ◆ **~ sb to sb/sth** *What first attracted me to her was her sense of humor.* **2** **~ sb/sth (to sth)** to make someone or something come somewhere or take part in something: *The warm damp air attracts a lot of mosquitoes.* ◆ *The exhibition has attracted thousands of visitors.* **3** **~ sth** to make people have a particular reaction: *This proposal has attracted a lot of interest.* ◆ *His comments are bound to attract criticism.* ◆ *She tried to attract the attention of the waiter.* **4** (*physics*) if a MAGNET or GRAVITY attracts something, it makes it move toward it **ANT** REPEL **IDM** see OPPOSITE *n.*

at·tract·ant /əˈtræktənt/ *noun* (*technical*) a substance that attracts something, especially an animal: *This type of trap uses no bait or other attractant.*

at·trac·tion 🔑 /əˈtrækʃn/ *noun*

1 [U, sing.] a feeling of liking someone, especially sexually: *She felt an immediate attraction for him.* ◆ *Sexual attraction is a large part of falling in love.* **2** [C] an interesting or enjoyable place to go or thing to do: *The Grand Canyon is a major tourist*

h hat   m man   n no   ŋ sing   l leg   r red   y yes   w wet

attraction. ◆ *The **main attraction** at Yellowstone Park is Old Faithful.* **3** [C, U] a feature, quality, or person that makes something seem interesting and enjoyable, and worth having or doing: *I can't see the attraction of sitting on a beach all day.* ◆ *City life holds little attraction for me.* ◆ *She is the star attraction of the show.* **4** [U] (*physics*) a force that pulls things toward each other: *gravitational/magnetic attraction* ⊃ compare REPULSION

at·trac·tive 🔑 /ə'træktɪv/ *adj.*
1 (of a person) pleasant to look at, especially in a sexual way: *an attractive woman* ◆ *I like John but I don't **find him** **attractive** physically.* ⊃ thesaurus box at BEAUTIFUL **2** (of a thing or a place) pleasant: *a big house with an attractive garden* ◆ *That's one of the less attractive aspects of her personality.* **3** having features or qualities that make something seem interesting and worth having **SYN** APPEALING: *an attractive offer/proposition* **ANT** UNATTRACTIVE ▶ **at·trac·tive·ly** *adv.*: *The room is arranged very attractively.* ◆ *attractively priced hotel rooms* **at·trac·tive·ness** *noun* [U]: *the attractiveness of traveling abroad*

at·trib·ut·a·ble **AWL** /ə'trɪbyətəbl/ *adj.* [not before noun] **~ to sb/sth** probably caused by the thing mentioned: *Their illnesses are attributable to a poor diet.*

at·trib·ute **AWL** *verb, noun*
● *verb* /ə'trɪbyut/ **1 ~ sth to sth** to say or believe that something is the result of a particular thing: *She attributes her success to hard work and a little luck.* **2** to say or believe that someone is responsible for doing something, especially for saying, writing, or painting something: **~ sth** *The committee refused to **attribute blame** without further information.* ◆ **~ sth to sb** *This play is usually attributed to Shakespeare.* ▶ **at·tri·bu·tion** **AWL** /ˌætrə'byuʃn/ *noun* [U]: *The attribution of this painting to Rembrandt has never been questioned.*
● *noun* /'ætrəˌbyut/ a quality or feature of someone or something: *Patience is one of the most important attributes in a teacher.*

at·trib·u·tive /ə'trɪbyətɪv/ *adj.* (*grammar*) (of adjectives or nouns) used before a noun to describe it: *In "the blue sky" and "a family business," "blue" and "family" are attributive.* ⊃ compare PREDICATIVE ▶ **at·trib·u·tive·ly** *adv.*: *Some adjectives can only be used attributively.*

at·tri·tion /ə'trɪʃn/ *noun* [U] (*formal*) **1** a process of making someone or something, especially your enemy, weaker by repeatedly attacking them or creating problems for them: *It was a **war of attrition**.* **2** the process of reducing the number of people who are employed by an organization by, for example, not replacing people who leave their jobs

at·tuned /ə'tund/ *adj.* [not before noun] **~ (to sb/sth)** familiar with someone or something so that you can understand or recognize them or it, and act in an appropriate way: *She wasn't yet attuned to her baby's needs.*

ATV /ˌeɪ ti 'vi/ *noun* the abbreviation for "all-terrain vehicle" (a small open vehicle with one seat and four wheels with very thick tires, designed especially for use on rough ground without roads)

a·typ·i·cal /ˌeɪ'tɪpɪkl/ *adj.* not typical or usual: *atypical behavior* **ANT** TYPICAL

AU /ˌeɪ 'yu/ *abbr.* ASTRONOMICAL UNIT

au·ber·gine /'oubərʒin/ *noun* [U] a dark purple color ▶ **au·ber·gine** *adj.*

au·burn /'ɔbərn/ *adj.* (of hair) reddish-brown in color ▶ **au·burn** *noun* [U]: *the rich auburn of her hair*

auc·tion /'ɔkʃn/ *noun, verb*
● *noun* [C, U] a public event at which things are sold to the person who offers the most money for them: *an auction of paintings* ◆ *The house is **up for auction** (= will be sold at an auction).* ◆ *A classic Rolls-Royce **fetched** (= was sold for) $45,000 **at auction**.* ◆ *an Internet auction site*

● *verb* [usually passive] **~ sth** to sell something at an auction: *The costumes from the movie are to be auctioned for charity.* **PHR V** ˌauction sth↔'off to sell something at an auction, especially something that is not needed or wanted anymore: *The Army is auctioning off a lot of surplus equipment.*

auc·tion·eer /ˌɔkʃə'nɪr/ *noun* a person whose job is to direct an auction and sell the goods

'auction ˌhouse *noun* a company that sells things in auctions

'auction ˌroom *noun* a building in which AUCTIONS are held

au·da·cious /ɔ'deɪʃəs/ *adj.* (*formal*) willing to take risks or to do something shocking **SYN** DARING: *an audacious decision* ▶ **au·da·cious·ly** *adv.*

au·dac·i·ty /ɔ'dæsəti/ *noun* [U] brave but rude or shocking behavior **SYN** NERVE: *He had the **audacity** to say I was too fat.*

au·di·ble /'ɔdəbl/ *adj.* that can be heard clearly: *Her voice was **barely audible** above the noise.* **ANT** INAUDIBLE ▶ **au·di·bil·i·ty** /ˌɔdə'bɪləti/ *noun* [U] **au·di·bly** /'ɔdəbli/ *adv.*

au·di·ence 🔑 /'ɔdiəns/ *noun*
1 the group of people who have gathered to watch or listen to something (a play, concert, someone speaking, etc.): *The audience was clapping for 10 minutes.* ◆ *an audience of 10,000* ◆ *The debate was televised in front of a **live audience**.* **2** a number of people or a particular group of people who watch, read, or listen to the same thing: *An audience of millions watched the wedding on TV.* ◆ *TV/theater/movie audiences* ◆ *His book reached an even wider audience when it was made into a movie.* ◆ *The **target audience** for this advertisement was mainly teenagers.* **3** a formal meeting with an important person: *an audience with the Pope* ⊃ thesaurus box at INTERVIEW

au·di·o /'ɔdiˌou/ *adj.* [only before noun] connected with sound that is recorded: *audio and video cassettes* ▶ **audio** *noun* [U]

audio- /'ɔdiou/ *combining form* (in nouns, adjectives, and adverbs) connected with hearing or sound: *an audiobook (= a reading of a book on CD, MP3 PLAYER, etc.)* ◆ *audiovisual*

au·di·ol·o·gy /ˌɔdi'ɑlədʒi/ *noun* [U] the science and medicine that deals with the sense of hearing ▶ **au·di·ol·o·gist** /-dʒɪst/ *noun*

au·di·om·e·try /ˌɔdi'ɑmətri/ *noun* [U] (*technical*) the measurement of how good a person's sense of hearing is

au·di·o·tape /'ɔdiouˌteɪp/ *noun* [U] MAGNETIC tape on which sound can be recorded

au·di·o·vis·u·al /ˌɔdiou'vɪʒuəl/ *adj.* (*abbr.* AV) using both sound and pictures: *audiovisual aids for the classroom*

au·dit /'ɔdət/ *noun, verb*
● *noun* [C, U] **1** an official examination of business and financial records to see that they are true and correct: *an annual audit* ◆ *a tax audit* **2** an official examination of the quality or standard of something ⊃ see also GREEN AUDIT
● *verb* **1 ~ sth** to officially examine the financial accounts of a company **2 ~ sth** to attend a course at college but without taking any exams or receiving credit

au·di·tion /ɔ'dɪʃn/ *noun, verb*
● *noun* a short performance given by an actor, a singer, etc., so that someone can decide whether they are suitable to act in a play, sing in a concert, etc.
● *verb* **1** [I] **~ (for sth)** to take part in an audition: *She was auditioning for the role of Lady Macbeth.* **2** [T] **~ sb (for sth)** to watch, listen to, and judge someone at an audition: *We auditioned over 200 children for the part.*

au·di·tor /'ɔdətər/ *noun* **1** a person who officially examines the business and financial records of a company **2** a person who attends a college course, but without having to take exams and without receiving credit

au·di·to·ri·um /ˌɔdə'tɔriəm/ *noun* (*pl.* **au·di·to·ri·ums** or **au·di·to·ri·a** /-'tɔriə/) **1** a large building or room in which public meetings, concerts, etc. are held **2** the part of a theater, concert hall, etc. in which the audience sits

au·di·to·ry /ˈɔdəˌtɔri/ *adj.* (*technical*) connected with hearing: *auditory stimuli*

'audit ˌtrail *noun* the detailed record of information on paper or on a computer that can be examined to prove what happened, for example what pieces of business were done and what decisions were made

au fait /oʊ ˈfeɪ/ *adj.* [not before noun] **~ (with sth)** (from French) completely familiar with something: *I'm new here so I'm not completely au fait with the system.*

au·ger /ˈɔgər/ *noun* a tool for making holes in wood, which looks like a large CORKSCREW

aught /ɔt/ *pron.* (*old use*) anything

aug·ment /ɔgˈmɛnt/ *verb* **~ sth** (*formal*) to increase the amount, value, size, etc. of something ▶ **aug·men·ta·tion** /ˌɔgmɛnˈteɪʃn/ *noun* [U, C]

aug·ment·a·tive /ɔgˈmɛntətɪv/ *adj.* (*linguistics*) (of an AFFIX or a word using an affix) increasing a quality expressed in the original word, especially by meaning "a large one of its kind"

au·gur /ˈɔgər/ *verb* [I] **~ well/badly** (*formal*) to be a sign that something will be successful or not successful in the future **SYN** BODE: *Conflicts among the various groups do not augur well for the future of the peace talks.*

au·gu·ry /ˈɔgyəri/ *noun* (*pl.* **au·gu·ries**) (*literary*) a sign of what will happen in the future **SYN** OMEN

Au·gust 🔑 /ˈɔgəst/ *noun* [U, C] (*abbr.* Aug.) the 8th month of the year, between July and September **HELP** To see how **August** is used, look at the examples at **April**.

au·gust /ɔˈgʌst/ *adj.* [usually before noun] (*formal*) impressive; making you feel respect

Au·gus·tan /ɔˈgʌstən/ *adj.* **1** connected with or happening during the time of the Roman EMPEROR Augustus **2** connected with English literature of the 17th and 18th centuries that was written in a style that was considered CLASSICAL

au jus /oʊ ˈʒu; oʊ ˈʒus/ *adj.* (from French) served with a thin sauce, especially one made from meat juices: *roast beef au jus*

auk /ɔk/ *noun* a northern bird with short narrow wings that lives near the ocean

auld lang syne /ˌɔld læŋ ˈzaɪn; ˌoʊld-/ *noun* an old Scottish song expressing feelings of friendship, traditionally sung at midnight on New Year's Eve

au na·tu·rel /ˌoʊ ˌnætʃəˈrɛl/ *adj., adv.* [not before noun] (from French) in a natural way: *The fish is served au naturel, uncooked and with nothing added.*

aunt 🔑 /ænt; ɑnt/ *noun* **1** the sister of your father or mother; the wife of your uncle: *Aunt Alice* ◆ *My aunt lives in Canada.* **2** (*informal*) used by children, with a first name, to address a woman who is a friend of their parents

aunt·ie (also **aunt·y**) /ˈænti; ˈɑnti/ *noun* (*informal*) aunt: *Auntie Mary*

au pair /ˌoʊ ˈpɛr/ *noun* a young person, usually a woman, who lives with a family in a foreign country. An au pair helps in the house and takes care of children, and receives a small salary.

au·ra /ˈɔrə/ *noun* **~ (of sth)** a feeling or particular quality that is very noticeable and seems to surround a person or place: *She always has an aura of confidence.*

au·ral /ˈɔrəl/ *adj.* (*technical*) connected with hearing and listening: *aural and visual images* ◆ *aural comprehension tests* ▶ **au·ral·ly** *adv.*

au·re·ate /ˈɔriət/ *adj.* (*formal*) **1** decorated in a complicated way: *an aureate style of writing* **2** made of gold or of the color of gold **SYN** GOLDEN

au·re·ole /ˈɔriˌoʊl/ *noun* (*literary*) a circle of light

au re·voir /ˌoʊ rəˈvwɑr; ˌɔ-/ *exclamation* (from French) goodbye (until we meet again)

au·ri·cle /ˈɔrɪkl/ *noun* (*anatomy*) **1** either of the two upper spaces in the heart used to send blood around the body **SYN** ATRIUM ⟳ compare VENTRICLE **2** the outer part of the ear

au·ro·ra aus·tral·is /əˌrɔrə ɔˈstreɪləs/ *noun* [sing.] = THE SOUTHERN LIGHTS

au·ro·ra bor·e·al·is /əˌrɔrə bɔriˈæləs/ *noun* [sing.] = THE NORTHERN LIGHTS

aus·pic·es /ˈɔspəsəz; -siz/ *noun* [pl.] **IDM** **under the auspices of sb/sth** with the help, support, or protection of someone or something: *The community center was set up under the auspices of a government initiative.*

aus·pi·cious /ɔˈspɪʃəs/ *adj.* (*formal*) showing signs that something is likely to be successful in the future **SYN** PROMISING: *an auspicious start to the new school year* **ANT** INAUSPICIOUS /ˈɔsɪ; ˈɔzɪ/

Aus·sie /ˈɔsi; ˈɔzi/ *noun* (*informal*) a person from Australia ▶ **Aus·sie** *adj.*

aus·tere /ɔˈstɪr/ *adj.* **1** simple and plain; without any decorations: *her austere bedroom with its simple narrow bed* **2** (of a person) strict and serious in appearance and behavior: *My father was a distant, austere man.* **3** allowing nothing that gives pleasure; not comfortable: *the monks' austere way of life* ▶ **aus·tere·ly** *adv.*

aus·ter·i·ty /ɔˈstɛrəti/ *noun* (*pl.* **aus·ter·i·ties**) **1** [U] a situation when people do not have much money to spend because there are bad economic conditions: *War was followed by many years of austerity.* **2** [U] the quality of being austere: *the austerity of the monks' life* **3** [C, usually pl.] something that is part of an austere way of life: *the austerities of the South in wartime*

aus·tral /ˈɔstrəl/ *adj.* (*formal*) relating to the south

Aus·tral·a·sia /ˌɔstrəˈleɪʒə/ *noun* the region including Australia, New Zealand, and the islands of the S.W. Pacific ▶ **Aus·tral·a·sian** *adj., noun*

Aus·tral·ian /ɔˈstreɪlyən/ *adj., noun*
● *adj.* of or connected with Australia
● *noun* a person from Australia

Aus·tra·lo·pith·e·cus /ɔˌstreɪloʊˈpɪθɪkəs; ˌɔstrəloʊ-/ *noun* [U, C] a creature similar to humans and APES that existed over one million years ago in Africa

Austro- /ˈɔstroʊ-/ *combining form* (in nouns and adjectives) Austrian: *the Austro-Hungarian border*

aut- /ɔt/ *combining form* = AUTO-

au·tar·chy (also **au·tar·ky**) /ˈɔˌtɑrki/ *noun* (*pl.* **au·tar·chies**) **1** [U, C] = AUTOCRACY **2** [U] (*economics*) economic independence ▶ **au·tar·chic** (also **au·tar·kic**) /ɔˈtɑrkɪk/ *adj.*

au·teur /oʊˈtər/ *noun* a movie director who plays such an important part in making their movies that they are considered to be the author **ORIGIN** From the French word *auteur*, meaning author.

au·then·tic /ɔˈθɛntɪk/ *adj.* **1** known to be real and genuine, and not a copy: *I don't know if the painting is authentic.* **ANT** INAUTHENTIC **2** true and accurate: *an authentic account of life in the desert* **ANT** INAUTHENTIC: *the authentic voice of inner-city youth* **3** made to be exactly the same as the original: *an authentic model of the ancient town* ▶ **au·then·ti·cally** /-kli/ *adv.*: *authentically flavored Mexican dishes*

au·then·ti·cate /ɔˈθɛntɪˌkeɪt/ *verb* to prove that something is genuine, real, or true: **~ sth** *The letter has been authenticated by handwriting experts.* ◆ **~ sth as sth** *Experts have authenticated the writing as that of Byron himself.* ▶ **au·then·ti·ca·tion** /ɔˌθɛntɪˈkeɪʃn/ *noun* [U]

au·then·tic·i·ty /ˌɔθɛnˈtɪsəti/ *noun* [U] the quality of being genuine or true

au·thor 🔑 **AWL** /ˈɔθər/ *noun, verb*

● *noun* **1** a person who writes books or the person who wrote a particular book: *Who is your favorite author?* ◆ *He is the author of three books on art.* ◆ *best-selling author Stephen King* ◆ *Who's the author?* ⊃ collocations at LITERATURE **2** the person who creates or starts something, especially a plan or an idea: *As the author of the proposal I cannot agree with you.*

● *verb* ~ **sth** (*formal*) to be the author of a book, report, etc.

au·thor·ess /ˈɔθərəs/ *noun* (*old-fashioned*) a woman author

au·tho·ri·al /ɔˈθɔriəl/ *adj.* [usually before noun] (*technical*) coming from or connected with the author of something

au·thor·ing /ˈɔθərɪŋ/ *noun* [U] (*computing*) creating computer programs without using programming language, for use in MULTIMEDIA products

au·thor·i·tar·i·an /əˌθɔrəˈtɛriən; əˌθɑr-/ *adj.* believing that people should obey authority and rules, even when these are unfair, and even if it means that they lose their personal freedom: *an authoritarian regime/government/state* ▶ **au·thor·i·tar·i·an** *noun: Father was a strict authoritarian.* **au·thor·i·tar·i·an·ism** /-ˌtɛriəˌnɪzəm/ *noun* [U]

au·thor·i·ta·tive **AWL** /əˈθɔrəˌteɪtɪv; əˈθɑr-/ *adj.* **1** that you can trust and respect as true and correct: *the most authoritative book on the subject* **2** showing that you expect people to obey and respect you: *an authoritative tone of voice* ▶ **au·thor·i·ta·tive·ly** *adv.*

au·thor·i·ty 🔑 **AWL** /əˈθɔrəti; əˈθɑr-/ *noun* (*pl.* **au·thor·i·ties**)

▷ **POWER 1** [U] the power to give orders to people: *in a position of authority* ◆ *She now has authority over the people who used to be her bosses.* ◆ *Nothing will be done because no one in authority* (= who has a position of power) *takes the matter seriously.* ◆ *There are very few male authority figures* (= people who have power over others) *in his movies.* **2** [U] ~ **(to do sth)** the power or right to do something: *Only the manager has the authority to sign checks.*
▷ **PERMISSION 3** [U] official permission to do something: *It was done without the principal's authority.* ◆ *We acted under the authority of the UN.*
▷ **ORGANIZATION 4** [C, usually pl.] the people or an organization who have the power to make decisions or who have a particular area of responsibility in a country or region: *The health authorities are investigating the problem.* ◆ *I have to report this to the authorities.*
▷ **KNOWLEDGE 5** [U] the power to influence people because they respect your knowledge or official position: *He spoke with authority on the topic.*
▷ **EXPERT 6** [C] ~ **(on sth)** a person with special knowledge **SYN** SPECIALIST: *She's an authority on criminal law.*
IDM have sth on good authority to be able to believe something because you trust the person who gave you the information

au·thor·i·za·tion /ˌɔθərəˈzeɪʃn/ *noun* **1** [U, C] official permission or power to do something; the act of giving permission: *You may not enter the security area without authorization.* ◆ *Who gave the authorization to release the data?* **2** [C] a document that gives someone official permission to do something: *Can I see your authorization?*

au·thor·ize /ˈɔθəˌraɪz/ *verb* [often passive] to give official permission for something, or for someone to do something: ~ **sth** *I can authorize payments up to $5,000.* ◆ *an authorized biography* ◆ ~ **sb to do sth** *I have authorized him to act for me while I am away.* ◆ *The soldiers were authorized to shoot at will.* ⊃ see also UNAUTHORIZED

au·thor·ship **AWL** /ˈɔθərˌʃɪp/ *noun* [U] **1** the identity of the person who wrote something, especially a book: *The authorship of the poem is unknown.* **2** the activity or fact of writing a book

au·tism /ˈɔˌtɪzəm/ *noun* [U] a mental condition in which a person finds it very difficult to communicate or form relationships with others ▶ **au·tis·tic** /ɔˈtɪstɪk/ *adj.*: *autistic behavior/children*

au·to /ˈɔtoʊ/ *noun* (*pl.* **au·tos**) a car: *the auto industry*

auto- /ˈɔtoʊ; ˈɔtə/ (also **aut-**) *combining form* (in nouns, adjectives, and adverbs) **1** of or by yourself: *autobiography* **2** by itself without a person to operate it: *automatic*

au·to·bi·og·ra·phy /ˌɔtəbaɪˈɑgrəfi/ *noun* [C, U] (*pl.* **au·to·bi·og·ra·phies**) the story of a person's life, written by that person; this type of writing ⊃ compare BIOGRAPHY ▶ **au·to·bi·o·graph·i·cal** /ˌɔtəˌbaɪəˈgræfɪkl/ *adj.*: *an autobiographical novel* (= one that contains many of the writer's own experiences)

au·to·clave /ˈɔtəˌkleɪv/ *noun* a strong closed container, used for processes that involve high temperatures or pressure

au·toc·ra·cy /ɔˈtɑkrəsi/ *noun* (*pl.* **au·toc·ra·cies**) (also **autarchy**) **1** [U] a system of government of a country in which one person has complete power **2** [C] a country that is ruled by one person who has complete power

au·to·crat /ˈɔtəˌkræt/ *noun* **1** a ruler who has complete power **SYN** DESPOT **2** a person who expects to be obeyed by other people and does not care about their opinions or feelings ▶ **au·to·crat·ic** /ˌɔtəˈkrætɪk/ *adj.*: *an autocratic manager* **au·to·crat·i·cal·ly** /ˌɔtəˈkrætɪkli/ *adv.*

au·to·cross /ˈɔtoʊˌkrɔs/ *noun* [U] a form of motor racing in which cars are driven over rough ground ⊃ compare RALLYCROSS

au·to·di·dact /ˌɔtoʊˈdaɪdækt/ *noun* (*formal*) a person who has taught himself or herself something rather than having lessons ▶ **au·to·di·dac·tic** /ˌɔtoʊdaɪˈdæktɪk/ *adj.*

au·to·ex·po·sure /ˌɔtoʊɪkˈspoʊʒər/ *noun* **1** [C] part of a camera that automatically adjusts the amount of light that reaches the film **2** [U] the ability of a camera to do this

au·to·fo·cus /ˈɔtoʊˌfoʊkəs/ *noun* **1** [C] part of a camera that automatically adjusts itself, so that the picture will be clear **2** [U] the ability of a camera to do this

au·to·gen·ic /ˌɔtəˈdʒɛnɪk/ *adj.* (*formal*) created by or from the thing itself

autogenic ˈtraining *noun* [U] a way of relaxing and dealing with stress using positive thoughts and mental exercises

au·to·graph /ˈɔtəˌgræf/ *noun, verb*

● *noun* a famous person's signature, especially when someone asks them to write it: *Could I have your autograph?*

● *verb* ~ **sth** (of a famous person) to sign your name on something for someone to keep: *The whole team has autographed a football, which will be used as a prize.*

au·to·im·mune /ˌɔtoʊɪˈmyun/ *adj.* [only before noun] (*medical*) an **autoimmune** disease or medical condition is one that is caused by substances that usually prevent illness

au·to·mak·er /ˈɔtoʊˌmeɪkər/ *noun* a company that makes cars

au·to·mat /ˈɔtəˌmæt/ *noun* (in the past) a restaurant in which food and drinks were bought from machines

au·to·mate **AWL** /ˈɔtəˌmeɪt/ *verb* [usually passive] ~ **sth** to use machines and computers instead of people to do a job or task: *The entire manufacturing process has been automated.* ◆ *The factory is now fully automated.*

automated ˈteller maˌchine *noun* = ATM

au·to·mat·ic 🔑 **AWL** /ˌɔtəˈmætɪk/ *adj., noun*

● *adj.* **1** (of a machine, device, etc.) having controls that work without needing a person to operate them: *automatic doors* ◆ *a fully automatic driverless train* ◆ *automatic transmission* (= in a car, etc.) ◆ *an automatic rifle* (= one that continues to fire as long as the TRIGGER is pressed) **2** done or happening without thinking **SYN** INSTINCTIVE: *Breathing is an automatic function of the body.* ◆ *My reaction was automatic.* **3** always happening as a result of a particular action or situation: *A fine for this offense is automatic.*

▶ au·to·mat·i·cally **AWL** /-kli/ adv.: The heating switches off automatically. ◆ I turned left automatically without thinking. ◆ You will automatically get free dental treatment if you are under 18.

● **noun 1** a gun that can fire bullets continuously as long as the TRIGGER is pressed **2** a car with a system of gears that operates without direct action from the driver ⊃ compare STICK SHIFT

ˌautomatic ˈpilot noun = AUTOPILOT

ˌautomatic transˈmission noun [U, C] a system in a vehicle that changes the gears for the driver automatically

ˌautomatic ˈwriting noun [U] writing that is believed to have been done in an unconscious state or under a SUPERNATURAL influence

au·to·ma·tion **AWL** /ˌɔːtəˈmeɪʃn/ noun [U] the use of machines to do work that was previously done by people: Automation meant the loss of many factory jobs.

au·tom·a·tism /ɔːˈtɑːməˌtɪzəm/ noun [U] (art) a method of painting that avoids conscious thought and allows a free flow of ideas

au·tom·a·ton /ɔːˈtɑːməˌtɑːn; -tən/ noun (pl. au·tom·a·tons or au·tom·a·ta /-mətə/) **1** a person who behaves like a machine, without thinking or feeling anything **SYN** ROBOT **2** a machine that moves without human control; a small ROBOT

au·to·mo·bile /ˌɔːtəməˈbiːl; ˈɔːtəməˌbiːl/ noun a car: the automobile industry ◆ an automobile accident

au·to·mo·tive /ˌɔːtəˈmoʊtɪv/ adj. (formal) connected with vehicles that are driven by engines: the automotive industry

au·to·nom·ic nerv·ous sys·tem /ˌɔːtənɑːmɪk ˈnɜːrvəs ˌsɪstəm/ noun the part of your NERVOUS SYSTEM that controls processes that are unconscious, for example the process of your heart beating

au·ton·o·mous /ɔːˈtɑːnəməs/ adj. **1** (of a country, a region, or an organization) able to govern itself or control its own affairs **SYN** INDEPENDENT: an autonomous republic/state/ province **2** (of a person) able to do things and make decisions without help from anyone else ▶ au·ton·o·mous·ly adv.

au·ton·o·my /ɔːˈtɑːnəmi/ noun [U] **1** the freedom for a country, a region, or an organization to govern itself independently **SYN** INDEPENDENCE: a campaign in the county for greater autonomy from the state **2** the ability to act and make decisions without being controlled by anyone else: giving individuals greater autonomy in their own lives

au·to·pi·lot /ˈɔːtoʊˌpaɪlət/ (also ˌautomatic ˈpilot) noun a device in an aircraft or a ship that keeps it on a fixed course without the need for a person to control it
IDM (be) on autopilot to do something without thinking because you have done the same thing many times before: I got up and got dressed on autopilot.

au·top·sy /ˈɔːˌtɑːpsi/ noun (pl. au·top·sies) an official examination of a dead body by a doctor in order to discover the cause of death **SYN** POSTMORTEM: an autopsy report ◆ to perform an autopsy

ˈauto ˌracing noun [U] the sport of racing fast cars on a special track

au·to·save /ˈɔːtoʊˌseɪv/ noun [sing.] (computing) the fact that changes to a document are saved automatically as you work ▶ au·to·save verb ~ sth

au·to·sug·ges·tion /ˌɔːtoʊsəgˈdʒestʃən; -səˈdʒes-/ noun [U] (psychology) a process that makes you believe something or act in a particular way according to ideas that come from within yourself without you realizing it

au·tumn /ˈɔːtəm/ noun **1** [U, C] the season of the year between summer and winter, when leaves change color and the weather becomes colder **SYN** FALL: in early/late autumn ◆ autumn colors/leaves/air ◆ an autumn walk in the countryside **2** [sing.] the time in someone's life that follows the period when they were strongest or most successful: He

was in the autumn of his brilliant career. ◆ the autumn of life (= when you are old)

au·tum·nal /ɔːˈtʌmnəl/ adj. [usually before noun] like or connected with autumn: autumnal colors

aux·il·ia·ry /ɔːgˈzɪlyəri; ɔːgˈzɪləri/ adj., noun
● **adj. 1** (of workers) giving help or support to the main group of workers **SYN** ANCILLARY: auxiliary nurses/workers/services **2** (technical) (of a piece of equipment) used if there is a problem with the main piece of equipment
● **noun** (pl. aux·il·ia·ries) **1** (also auxˈiliary ˌverb) (grammar) a verb such as be, do, and have used with main verbs to show tense, etc. and to form questions, and negatives **2** an individual worker or a group of workers who gives help or support to the main group of workers: nursing auxiliaries

aux·in /ˈɔːksn/ noun [U] a HORMONE found in plants

AV /ˌeɪ ˈviː/ abbr. AUDIOVISUAL

a·vail /əˈveɪl/ noun, verb
● **noun**
IDM of little/no avail (formal) of little or no use: Your ability to argue is of little avail if the facts are wrong. **to little/no avail** (formal) with little or no success: The doctors tried everything to keep him alive, but to no avail.
● **verb** ~ sb (sth) | ~ sth (formal or old-fashioned) to be helpful or useful to someone
PHR V aˈvail yourself of sth (formal) to make use of something, especially an opportunity or offer: Guests are encouraged to avail themselves of the full range of hotel facilities.

a·vail·a·ble 🔑 **AWL** /əˈveɪləbl/ adj.
1 (of things) that you can get, buy, or find: available resources/facilities ◆ readily/freely/publicly/generally available ◆ Tickets are available free of charge from the school. ◆ When will the information be made available? ◆ Further information is available on request. ◆ This was the only room available. ◆ We'll send you a copy as soon as it becomes available. ◆ Every available doctor was called to the scene. **2** (of a person) free to see or talk to people: Will she be available this afternoon? ◆ The director was not available for comment. ▶ a·vail·a·bil·i·ty **AWL** /əˌveɪləˈbɪləti/ noun [U]: the availability of cheap flights

AWL COLLOCATIONS

available
available adj.
▪ become
Figure 4 shows the income of the university from the 1870s, when reliable data became available.
▪ make sth
Schools recognize the importance of making physics and mathematics available to all students.
▪ currently, immediately, presently | easily, freely, readily | publicly, widely | commercially
By the 1960s, computers were widely available in industry and at universities.
Quartz sand is often used in water treatment because it is inexpensive and readily available.
▪ data, information | option
Of the 234 nations for which data is available from the World Bank, the U.S. claimed a third of the income earned worldwide in 2001.
Because Georgian Americans are small in number, less information is available about them than other ethnic groups.

availability noun
▪ widespread | limited | ready
Economic development was impressive, with the widespread availability of health and education facilities.
The limited availability of clean water creates unsanitary conditions that can cause disease.

av·a·lanche /ˈævəˌlæntʃ/ (also snow·slide) noun a mass of

　t tea 　　ţ butter 　　d did 　　k cat 　　g got 　　tʃ chin 　　dʒ June 　　f fall

snow, ice, and rock that falls down the side of a mountain: *alpine villages destroyed in an avalanche* ◆ (*figurative*) *We received an avalanche of letters in reply to our advertisement.*

Av·a·lon /ˈævəˌlɑn/ *noun* [U] (in ancient stories) the place where King Arthur is said to have gone after his death

a·vant- /ˈɑvɑnt; ˈæ-/ *combining form* (used especially with types of popular music) in a style that is modern and very different from what has been done before: *experimental music like avant-rock* ◆ *avant-jazz* ◆ *avant-pop*

the a·vant-garde /ˌɑvɑnt ˈgɑrd; ˌæ-/ *noun* [sing.] (from French) **1** new and very modern ideas in art, music, or literature that are sometimes surprising or shocking **2** a group of artists, etc. who introduce new and very modern ideas ▸ **a·vant-garde** *adj.*

av·a·rice /ˈævərəs/ *noun* [U] (*formal*) extreme desire for wealth **SYN** GREED ▸ **av·a·ri·cious** /ˌævəˈrɪʃəs/ *adj.*

av·a·tar /ˈævəˌtɑr/ *noun* **1** a picture of a person or an animal that represents a person, on a computer screen, especially in a computer game or CHAT ROOM **2** (in Hinduism and Buddhism) a god appearing in a physical form

Ave. (also **Av.**) *abbr.* (used in written addresses) AVENUE: *Fifth Ave.*

a·venge /əˈvɛndʒ/ *verb* (*formal*) to punish or hurt someone in return for something bad or wrong that they have done to you, your family, or your friends: *~ sth He promised to avenge his father's murder.* ◆ *~ yourself on sb She was determined to avenge herself on the man who had betrayed her.* ▸ **a·veng·er** *noun*

GRAMMAR

avenge • revenge

Avenge is a verb; revenge is (usually) a noun.
■ People **avenge** something, or **avenge** themselves **on** someone: *She vowed to avenge her brother's death.* ◆ *He later avenged himself on his wife's killers.* You **take revenge on** a person.
■ In literary or old-fashioned English, **revenge** can also be a verb. People **revenge** themselves **on** someone or **are revenged on** them (with the same meaning): *He was later revenged on his wife's killers.* You cannot **revenge** something: ~~*She vowed to revenge her brother's death.*~~

av·e·nue /ˈævəˌnu/ *noun* **1** (*abbr.* Ave., Av.) a street in a town or city: *a hotel on Fifth Avenue* **2** a choice or way of making progress toward something: *Several avenues are open to us.* ◆ *We will explore every avenue until we find an answer.* **3** a wide straight road with trees on both sides, especially one leading to a big house

a·ver /əˈvər/ *verb* (-rr-) ~ *that...* | ~ *sth* | + *speech* (*formal*) to state firmly and strongly that something is true **SYN** ASSERT, DECLARE: *She averred that she had never seen the man before.*

av·er·age 🔑 /ˈævrɪdʒ/ *adj., noun, verb*
● *adj.* **1** [only before noun] calculated by adding several amounts together, finding a total, and dividing the total by the number of amounts: *an average rate/cost/price* ◆ *Average annual earnings are around $50,000.* ◆ *at an average speed of 100 miles per hour* **2** typical or normal: *40 hours is a fairly average working week for most people.* ◆ *children of above/below average intelligence* ◆ *$30 for dinner is about average.* **3** ordinary; not special: *I was just an average student.* ▸ **av·er·age·ly** *adv.*: *He was attractive and averagely intelligent.*
● *noun* [C, U] **1** the result of adding several amounts together, finding a total, and dividing the total by the number of amounts: *The average of 4, 5, and 9 is 6.* ◆ *Parents spend an average of $220 a year on toys.* ◆ *If I get an A on this essay, that will bring my average* (= average grade) *up to a B+.* ⊃ see also GRADE POINT AVERAGE **2** a level that is usual: *Temperatures are above/below average for the time of year.*

◆ *400 people a year die of this disease on average.* ◆ *Class sizes in the school are below the national average.* **IDM** see LAW
● *verb* **1** [T] ~ *sth* [no passive] to be equal to a particular amount as an average: *Economic growth is expected to average 2% next year.* ◆ *Drivers in Los Angeles can expect to average about 12 miles per hour* (= to have that as their average speed). **2** [T, I] ~ *(sth)* to calculate the average of something: *Earnings are averaged over the whole period.* **PHR V** ˌaverage ˈout (at sth) to result in an average amount over a period of time or when several things are considered: *The cost should average out at about $6 per person.* ◆ *Sometimes I pay, sometimes he pays—it seems to average out* (= result in us paying the same amount). ˌaverage sth↔ˈout (at sth) to calculate the average of something

a·verse /əˈvərs/ *adj.* [not before noun] **1** not ~ to sth / to doing sth liking something or wanting to do something; not opposed to doing something: *I mentioned it to Kate and she wasn't averse to the idea.* **2** ~ to sth / to doing sth (*formal*) not liking something or wanting to do something; opposed to doing something: *He was averse to any change.*

a·ver·sion /əˈvərʒn/ *noun* [C, U] a strong feeling of not liking someone or something: *a strong aversion* ◆ ~ to sb/sth *He had an aversion to getting up early.*

aˈversion ˌtherapy *noun* [U] a way of helping someone to lose a bad habit, by making the habit seem to be associated with an effect that is not pleasant

a·vert /əˈvərt/ *verb* **1** ~ *sth* to prevent something bad or dangerous from happening: *A disaster was narrowly averted.* ◆ *He did his best to avert suspicion.* **2** ~ *your eyes, gaze, face* (**from something**) to turn your eyes, etc. away from something that you do not want to see: *She averted her eyes from the terrible scene in front of her.*

a·vi·an /ˈeɪviən/ *adj.* [usually before noun] (*technical*) of or connected with birds

ˌavian ˈflu *noun* [U] (*formal*) = BIRD FLU

a·vi·ar·y /ˈeɪviˌɛri/ *noun* (*pl.* **a·vi·a·ries**) a large CAGE or building for keeping birds in, for example in a ZOO

a·vi·a·tion /ˌeɪviˈeɪʃn/ *noun* [U] the designing, building, and flying of aircraft: *civil/military aviation* ◆ *the aviation business/industry*

a·vi·a·tor /ˈeɪviˌeɪtər/ *noun* (*old-fashioned*) a person who flies an aircraft

av·id /ˈævɪd/ *adj.* **1** [usually before noun] very enthusiastic about something (often a hobby) **SYN** KEEN: *an avid reader/ collector* ◆ *She has taken an avid interest in the project* (= she is extremely interested in it). **2** ~ for sth wanting to get something very much: *He was avid for more information.* ▸ **a·vid·i·ty** /əˈvɪdəti/ *noun* [U] **av·id·ly** *adv.*: *She reads avidly.*

a·vi·on·ics /ˌeɪviˈɑnɪks/ *noun* **1** [U] the science of ELEC-TRONICS when used in designing and making aircraft **2** [pl.] the electronic devices in an aircraft or a SPACECRAFT ▸ **a·vi·on·ic** *adj.*

av·o·ca·do /ˌɑvəˈkɑdou; ˌæ-/ *noun* (*pl.* **av·o·ca·dos**) a tropical fruit with hard, dark green skin, soft, light green flesh, and a large seed inside. Avocados are not sweet. ⊃ picture at FRUIT

av·o·ca·tion /ˌævouˈkeɪʃn/ *noun* (*formal*) a hobby or other activity that you do for interest and enjoyment

av·o·cet /ˈævəˌsɛt/ *noun* a bird that lives on or near water, with long legs, and black and white feathers

a·void 🔑 /əˈvɔɪd/ *verb*
1 to prevent something bad from happening: ~ *sth The accident could have been avoided.* ◆ *They narrowly avoided defeat.* ◆ *The name was changed to avoid confusion with another company.* ◆ ~ *doing sth They built a wall to avoid soil being washed away.* **2** to keep away from someone or something; to try not to do something: ~ *sb/sth He's been avoiding me all week.* ◆ *She kept avoiding my eyes* (= avoided looking at me). ◆ *I left early to avoid the rush hour.* ◆ ~ *doing sth I've been avoiding getting down to work all day.* ◆ *You should avoid*

mentioning his divorce. **3** ~ **sth** to prevent yourself from hitting something: *I had to swerve to avoid a cat.* **IDM** avoid sb/sth like the plague (*informal*) to try very hard not to meet someone, do something, etc. ◐ more at TRAP *n.*

a·void·a·ble /əˈvɔɪdəbl/ *adj.* that can be prevented: *Many deaths from heart disease are actually avoidable.* **ANT** UNAVOIDABLE

a·void·ance /əˈvɔɪdns/ *noun* [U] ~ **(of sth)** not doing something; preventing something from existing or happening: *A person's health improves with the avoidance of stress.* ◐ see also TAX AVOIDANCE

av·oir·du·pois /ˌævərdəˈpɔɪz; ˈpwɑ/ *noun* [U] the system of weights based on the pound

a·vow /əˈvaʊ/ *verb* ~ **that…** | ~ **sth** | + **speech** (*formal*) to say firmly and often publicly what your opinion is, what you think is true, etc.: *An aide avowed that the president had known nothing of the deals.* ▶ **a·vow·al** /əˈvaʊəl/ *noun* (*formal*): *an avowal of love*

a·vowed /əˈvaʊd/ *adj.* [only before noun] (*formal*) that has been admitted or stated in public: *an avowed atheist* ◆ *an avowed aim/intention/objective/purpose* ▶ **a·vow·ed·ly** /əˈvaʊədli/ *adv.*

a·vun·cu·lar /əˈvʌŋkyələr/ *adj.* (*formal*) behaving in a kind and friendly way toward young people, similar to the way an uncle treats his nieces or nephews

aw /ɔ/ *exclamation* used to express affection, sympathy, disappointment, etc.: *Aw, what a cute baby!* ◆ *Aw, come on, Andy!*

a·wait /əˈweɪt/ *verb* (*formal*) **1** ~ **sth** to wait for someone or something: *He is in custody awaiting trial.* ◆ *Her latest novel is eagerly awaited.* **2** ~ **sb** to be going to happen to someone: *A warm welcome awaits all our guests.*

a·wake 🔑 /əˈweɪk/ *adj., verb*
• *adj.* [not before noun] not asleep (especially immediately before or after sleeping): *to be half/fully awake* ◆ *to be wide awake* (= fully awake) ◆ *I was still awake when he came to bed.* ◆ *The noise was keeping everyone awake.* ◆ *I was finding it hard to stay awake.* ◆ *He lies awake at night worrying about his job.* ◆ *She was awake* (= not unconscious) *during the operation on her leg.*
• *verb* (**a·woke** /əˈwoʊk/, **a·wo·ken** /əˈwoʊkən/) (*formal*) **1** [I, T] to wake up; to make someone wake up: ~ **(sb) (from/to sth)** *I awoke from a deep sleep.* ◆ ~ **to do sth** *He awoke to find her gone.* ◆ ~ **sb** *Her voice awoke the sleeping child.* **2** [I, T] ~ **(sth)** if an emotion awakes or something awakes an emotion, you start to feel that emotion: *His speech is bound to awake old fears and hostilities.* **PHR V** a'wake to sth to become aware of something and its possible effects or results: *It took her some time to awake to the dangers of her situation.* ◐ compare WAKE

WHICH WORD?

awake ◆ awaken ◆ wake up ◆ waken
▪ **Wake (up)** is the most common of these verbs. It can mean someone has finished sleeping: *What time do you usually wake up?* or that somebody or something has disturbed your sleep: *The children woke me up.* ◆ *I was woken (up) by the telephone.*
▪ The verb **awake** is usually used only in writing and in the past tense **awoke**: *She awoke to a day of brilliant sunshine.* **Waken** and **awaken** are much more formal. **Awaken** is used especially in literature: *The Prince awakened Sleeping Beauty with a kiss.*
▪ **Awake** is also an adjective: *I was awake half the night worrying.* ◆ *Is the baby awake yet?* **Waking** is not used in this way.
▪ Look also at ASLEEP and the verb SLEEP.

a·wak·en /əˈweɪkən/ *verb* (*formal*) **1** [I, T, often passive] to wake up; to make someone wake up: ~ **(sb) (from/to sth)**

She awakened to the sound of birds singing. ◆ ~ **to do sth** *We awakened to find the others gone.* ◆ ~ **sb** *He was awakened at dawn by the sound of crying.* ◐ note at AWAKE **2** [I, T] ~ **(sth)** if an emotion **awakens** or something **awakens** an emotion, you start to feel that emotion: *The dream awakened terrible memories.*
PHR V a'waken (sb) to sth to become aware or to make someone aware of something and its possible effects or results: *I gradually awakened to the realization that our marriage was over.* ◐ compare WAKEN

a·wak·en·ing /əˈweɪkənɪŋ/ *noun* **1** [C, usually sing.] an occasion when you realize something or become aware of something: *If they had expected a warm welcome, they were in for a rude awakening* (= they would soon realize that it would not be warm). **2** [C, U] the act of beginning to understand or feel something; the act of something starting or waking: *sexual awakening* ◆ *the awakening of interest in the environment*

a·ward 🔑 /əˈwɔrd/ *noun, verb*
• *noun* **1** [C] (often in names of particular awards) a prize such as money, etc. for something that someone has done: *He was nominated for the best actor award.* ◆ *an award presentation/ceremony* ◆ *the Tony Awards* ◆ ~ **for sth** *to win/receive/get an award for something* ◐ see also ACADEMY AWARD™ **2** [C, U] the amount of money that a court decides should be given to someone who has won a case; the decision to give this money: *an award of $600,000 for pain and suffering* **3** [U] the official decision to give something (such as a DIPLOMA) to someone: *the award of an honorary doctorate*
• *verb* [T] to make an official decision to give something to someone as a payment, prize, etc.: ~ **sth (to sb)** *The judges awarded equal points to both finalists.* ◆ ~ **(sb) sth** *The judges awarded both finalists equal points.* ◆ *He was awarded damages of $50,000.*

a·ward·ee /əˌwɔrˈdi/ *noun* a person who is awarded something, such as a prize

a'ward–ˌwinning *adj.* having won a prize: *the award-winning TV drama*

a·ware 🔑 **AWL** /əˈwɛr/ *adj.*
1 [not before noun] knowing or realizing something: *As you're aware, this is not a new problem.* ◆ *As far as I'm aware, no one has done anything about it.* ◆ *acutely/painfully* (= very) *aware* ◆ ~ **of sth** *I don't think people are really aware of just how much it costs.* ◆ *He was well aware of the problem.* ◆ *Everybody should be made aware of the risks involved.* ◆ ~ **that…** *Were you aware that something was wrong?* **2** [not before noun] noticing that something is present, or that something is happening: ~ **of sb/sth** *She slipped away without him being aware of it.* ◆ *They suddenly became aware of people looking at them.* ◆ ~ **that…** *I was aware that she was trembling.* **3** (used with an adverb) interested in and knowing about something, and thinking it is important: *Young people are very environmentally aware.* **ANT** UNAWARE

AWL COLLOCATIONS

aware
aware *adj.*
conscious; informed
▪ acutely, keenly | fully, perfectly | consciously
By the late nineteenth century, physicists were keenly aware that light, like sound, propagates in waves.
▪ become
Members become aware of their group identity only by achieving a shared understanding with other group members.
▪ make sb
In conclusion, this policy makes students aware of a growing controversy in the scientific community.

h **hat**   m **man**   n **no**   ŋ **sing**   l **leg**   r **red**   y **yes**   w **wet**

aware adj.

■ **increasingly**
We are now increasingly aware of the impact of lifestyle on health status.

■ **environmentally, politically, socially**
Recent scholarship has demonstrated that Wheatley was a socially aware poet, writing for an audience she knew and understood.

unware adj.

■ **completely, totally | apparently, evidently, seemingly**
Apparently unaware of Newcomb's work, Benford ended up proposing the same logarithm law.

awareness noun

■ **enhance, heighten, increase, raise | promote, foster**
The program fosters international awareness among students.

a·ware·ness AWL /əˈwɛrnəs/ noun [U, sing.] **~ (of sth) | ~ (that…)** knowing something; knowing that something exists and is important; being interested in something: an awareness of the importance of eating a healthy diet ◆ There was an almost complete **lack of awareness** of the issues involved. ◆ It is important that students **develop an awareness** of how the Internet can be used. ◆ to **raise/heighten/increase** public awareness of something ◆ **a greater/a growing/an increasing awareness** of something ◆ environmental awareness (= knowing that taking care of the environment is important) ◆ Energy Awareness Week ⊃ collocations at AWARE

a·wash /əˈwɑʃ; əˈwɔʃ/ adj. [not before noun] **1 ~ (with water)** covered with water **2 ~ with sth** having something in large quantities: The city is awash with drugs.

a·way ♪ /əˈweɪ/ adv.
HELP For the special uses of **away** in phrasal verbs, look at the entries for the verbs. For example, **get away with sth** is in the phrasal verb section at **get**. **1** to or at a distance from someone or something in space or time: The beach is a mile away. ◆ Christmas is still months away. ◆ **~ from sb/sth** The subway station is a few minutes' walk away from here. **2** to a different place or in a different direction: Go away! ◆ Put your toys away. ◆ The bright light made her look away. **3** not present **SYN** ABSENT: They were away (= on vacation) last week. ◆ Sorry, he's away. ◆ **~ from sb/sth** She was away from work for a week. **4** used after verbs to say that something is done continuously or with a lot of energy: She was still writing away furiously when the bell rang. ◆ They were soon chatting away like old friends. **5** until disappearing completely: The water boiled away. ◆ The music faded away. ◆ They danced the night away (= all night). **6** (sports) at the opponent's field or STADIUM: The Steelers are playing away this Saturday. ◆ an away game ⊃ compare HOME
IDM away with… (literary) used to say that you would like to be rid of someone or something: Away with all these rules and regulations! ⊃ more at COBWEB, DANCE v., FAR adv., RIGHT adv., STRAIGHT adv.

awe /ɔ/ noun, verb
● **noun** [U] feelings of respect and slight fear; feelings of being very impressed by something or someone: awe and respect ◆ awe and wonder ◆ He speaks of her **with awe**. ◆ "It's magnificent," she whispered in awe.
IDM be/stand in awe of sb/sth to admire someone or something and be slightly frightened of them/it: While Diana was in awe of her grandfather, she adored her grandmother.

● **verb ~ sb** [usually passive] (formal) to fill someone with awe: She seemed awed by the presence of so many famous people. ▶ **awed** /ɔd/ adj.: We watched in awed silence.

ˈawe-in·spiring adj. impressive; making you feel respect and admiration: The building was awe-inspiring in size and design.

awe·some /ˈɔsəm/ adj. **1** very impressive or very difficult, and perhaps somewhat frightening: an awesome sight ◆ awesome beauty/power ◆ They had an awesome task ahead. **2** (informal) very good, enjoyable, etc.: I just bought this awesome new CD! ◆ Wow! That's totally awesome! ⊃ thesaurus box at GREAT ▶ **awe·some·ly** adv.: awesomely beautiful

awe·struck /ˈɔstrʌk/ adj. (literary) feeling very impressed by something: People were awestruck by the pictures the satellite sent back to earth.

aw·ful ♪ /ˈɔfl/ adj., adv.
● **adj. 1** (informal) very bad or unpleasant: That's an awful color. ◆ "They didn't even offer to pay." "Oh, that's awful." ◆ It's awful, isn't it? ◆ The weather last summer was awful. ◆ I feel awful about forgetting her birthday. ◆ **to look/feel awful** (= to look/feel sick) ◆ There's an awful smell in here. ◆ The awful thing is, it was my fault. ⊃ thesaurus box at TERRIBLE **2** (informal) used to emphasize something, especially that there is a large amount or too much of something: It's going to cost **an awful lot of** money. ◆ There's not an awful lot of room. ◆ I feel an awful lot better than I did yesterday. **3** very shocking **SYN** TERRIBLE: the awful horrors of war ▶ **aw·ful·ness** noun [U]: the sheer awfulness of the situation
● **adv.** (informal, non-standard) very; extremely: Clint is awful smart.

aw·fully /ˈɔfli/ adv. very; extremely **SYN** TERRIBLY: I'm awfully sorry about that problem the other day.

a·while /əˈwaɪl/ adv. for a short time

awk·ward ♪ /ˈɔkwərd/ adj.
1 making you feel embarrassed: There was an awkward silence. **2** difficult to deal with **SYN** DIFFICULT: Don't ask awkward questions. ◆ You've put me in an awkward position. ◆ an awkward pause in our conversation ◆ Please don't be awkward about letting him come. **3** not convenient **SYN** INCONVENIENT: Have I come at an awkward time? **4** difficult or dangerous because of its shape or design: This box is very awkward for one person to carry. **5** not moving in an easy way; not comfortable: He tried to dance, but he was too clumsy and awkward. ◆ I must have slept in an awkward position—I'm aching all over. ▶ **awk·ward·ly** adv.: "I'm sorry," he said awkwardly. ◆ She fell awkwardly and broke her ankle. ◆ an awkwardly shaped room **awk·ward·ness** noun [U]: She laughed to cover up her feelings of awkwardness.

awl /ɔl/ noun a small pointed tool used for making holes, especially in leather

awn·ing /ˈɔnɪŋ/ noun a sheet of strong cloth that stretches out from above a door or window to keep off the sun or rain

a·woke pt of AWAKE

a·wo·ken pp of AWAKE

AWOL /ˈeɪwɔl/ abbr. absent without leave (used especially in the armed forces when someone has left their group without permission): He's gone AWOL from his base. ◆ The guitarist went AWOL in the middle of the recording.

a·wry /əˈraɪ/ adv., adj. **1** if something **goes awry**, it does not happen in the way that was planned: All my plans for the party had gone awry. **2** [only before noun] not in the right position **SYN** UNTIDY: She rushed out, her hair awry.

ax /æks/ noun, verb
● **noun** (also **axe**) **1** a tool with a wooden handle and a heavy metal blade, used for chopping wood, cutting down trees, etc. ⊃ picture at TOOL ⊃ see also BATTLEAX, ICE AX, PICKAX **2 the ax** [sing.] (informal) if someone gets **the ax**, they lose their job; if an institution or a project gets **the ax**, it is closed or stopped, usually because of a lack of money: Up to 300 workers are **facing the ax** at a struggling finance company. ◆ Patients are delighted their local hospital has been saved from the ax.
IDM have an ax to grind to have private reasons for being involved in something or for arguing for a particular cause: She had no ax to grind and was only acting out of concern for their safety.
● **verb** (also **axe**) [often passive] **1 ~ sth** to get rid of a service,

system, etc. or to reduce the money spent on it by a large amount: *Other less profitable services will be axed later this year.* **2 ~ sb** to remove someone from their job: *Jones has been axed from the team.* **3 ~ sb** to kill someone with an ax

ax·el /'æksl/ *noun* a movement in SKATING in which you jump from the front outside edge of one foot, turn in the air, and land on the outside edge of your other foot

ax·i·al /'æksiəl/ *adj.* of or related to an AXIS: *an axial road*

ax·i·om /'æksiəm/ *noun* (*formal*) a rule or principle that most people believe to be true

ax·i·o·mat·ic /ˌæksiə'mætɪk/ *adj.* [not usually before noun] (*formal*) true in such an obvious way that you do not need to prove it **SYN** SELF-EVIDENT: *It is axiomatic that life is not always easy.* ▶ **ax·i·o·mat·i·cally** /-kli/ *adv.*

axis

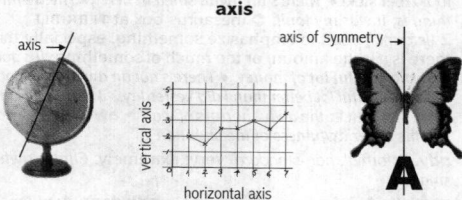

axis →

axis of symmetry →

vertical axis

horizontal axis

ax·is /'æksəs/ *noun* (*pl.* **ax·es** /'æksiz/) **1** an imaginary line through the center of an object, around which the object turns: *Mars takes longer to revolve on its axis than the earth does.* ➋ picture at EARTH **2** (*technical*) a fixed line against which the positions of points are measured, especially points on a GRAPH: *the vertical/horizontal axis* **3** (*geometry*) a line that divides a shape into two equal parts: *an axis of symmetry* ◆ *The axis of a circle is its diameter.* **4** [usually sing.]

(*formal*) an agreement or ALLIANCE between two or more countries: *the Axis Powers of World War II*

ax·le /'æksl/ *noun* a long straight piece of metal that connects a pair of wheels on a vehicle: *the front/rear axle*

ax·man (also **axe·man**) /'æksmən/ (*pl.* **ax·men** /-mən/) *noun* (*informal*) a man who attacks other people with an ax

ax·on /'æksɑn/ *noun* (*biology*) the long thin part of a nerve cell along which signals are sent to other cells ➋ compare DENDRITE

a·ya·tol·lah /ˌaɪə'toʊlə/ *noun* a religious leader of Shiite Muslims in Iran

aye /aɪ/ *exclamation, noun*
● **exclamation** (*old use* or *dialect*) **1** yes: *"Did you see what happened?" "Oh aye, I was there."* **2** always; still
● **ayes** *noun* [pl.] the total number of people voting "yes" in a formal debate, for example in a parliament: *The ayes have it* (= more people have voted for something than against it). ➋ compare NAY, YEA

A·yur·ve·dic med·i·cine /ˌaɪərveɪdɪk 'mɛdəsn/ *noun* [U] a type of traditional Hindu medicine that treats illnesses using a combination of foods, HERBS, and breathing exercises

AZ *abbr.* (in writing) Arizona

a·zal·ea /ə'zeɪlyə/ *noun* a plant or bush with large flowers that may be pink, purple, white, or yellow

az·i·muth /'æzəməθ/ *noun* (*astronomy*) an angle related to a distance around the earth's HORIZON, used to find out the position of a star, planet, etc.

AZT™ /ˌeɪ zi 'ti/ *noun* [U] a drug that is used to treat AIDS

az·ure /'æʒər/ *adj.* bright blue in color like the sky ▶ **az·ure** *noun* [U]

Bb

B /bi/ noun (pl. **Bs, B's** /biz/) **1** also **b** (pl. **b's**) [C, U] the second letter of the English alphabet: *"Butter" begins with (a) B/"B."* **2** [C, U] (*music*) the 7th note in the SCALE of C MAJOR **3** [C, U] the second highest grade that a student can get for a class, test, or piece of work: *She got a B in History.* **4** [U] used to represent the second of two or more possibilities: *Shall we go for plan A or plan B?* **5** [U] used to represent a person, for example in an imagined situation, or to hide their identity: *Let's pretend A meets B in the park.* **IDM** see A

b. *abbr.* (in writing) born: *Abraham Lincoln, b. 1809*

B2B /ˌbi tə ˈbi/ *abbr.* BUSINESS-TO-BUSINESS

B.A. (also **BA**) /ˌbi ˈeɪ/ *noun* a college degree in an ARTS subject (the abbreviation for "Bachelor of Arts"): *to have a B.A. in Psychology*

baa /bɑ; bæ/ *noun* the sound made by sheep or LAMBS ▶ **baa** *verb* (**baa·ing, baaed**) [I]

B&B (also **b. & b.**) /ˌbi ən ˈbi/ *abbr.* (*informal*) BED AND BREAKFAST

bab·ble /ˈbæbl/ *noun, verb*
● *noun* [sing.] **1** the sound of many people speaking at the same time: *a babble of voices* **2** talking that is confused or silly, and is difficult to understand: *I can't listen to his constant babble.* **3** the sounds a baby makes before beginning to say actual words ⊃ **see also** PSYCHOBABBLE
● *verb* **1** [I, T] ~ **(away/on) (sth)** to talk quickly in a way that is difficult to understand: *They were all babbling away in a foreign language.* ◆ *I realized I was babbling like an idiot.* **2** [I] to make the sound of water flowing over rocks, like a stream: *a babbling brook*

babe /beɪb/ *noun* **1** (*slang*) a word used to address a young woman, or your wife, husband, or lover, usually expressing affection but sometimes considered offensive if used by a man to a woman he does not know: *What are you doing tonight, babe?* **2** (*informal*) an attractive young woman **3** (*old use*) a baby
IDM **a babe in arms** (*old-fashioned*) a very small baby that cannot yet walk **a babe in the woods** (*informal*) someone who lacks knowledge or experience of life: *He's still a babe in the woods compared to the other guys here.* ⊃ **more at** MOUTH *n.*

ba·bel /ˈbeɪbl; ˈbæbl/ *noun* [sing.] (*formal*) the sound of many voices talking at one time, especially when more than one language is being spoken **ORIGIN** From the Bible story in which God punished the people who were trying to build a tower to reach heaven (the **tower of Babel**) by making them unable to understand each other's languages.

babe magnet *noun* (*slang*) a man or a man's possession that is considered to be attractive to women: *Bob's such a babe magnet.* ◆ *A sports car like that is a total babe magnet.*

ba·boon /bæˈbun/ *noun* a large African or Asian MONKEY with a long face like a dog's

ba·bush·ka *noun* (from *Russian*) **1** /bəˈbʊʃkə/ a traditional Russian woman's HEADSCARF, tied under the chin **2** /bəˈbʊʃkə; ˈbabʊʃkə/ a Russian old woman or grandmother

ba·by 🔑 /ˈbeɪbi/ *noun, adj., verb*
● *noun* (pl. **bab·ies**) **1** a very young child or animal: *The baby's crying!* ◆ *a newborn baby* ◆ *My sister's expecting a baby.* ◆ *She had a baby last year.* ◆ *a baby boy/girl* ◆ *baby food/clothes* ◆ *a baby monkey/blackbird* ⊃ collocations at CHILD **2** (*informal*) the youngest member of a family or group: *He's the baby of the family.* **3** (*disapproving*) a person who behaves like a young child and is easily upset: *Stop crying! Don't be such a baby.* **4** (*slang*) a word used to address someone, especially your wife, husband, or lover, in a way that expresses affection but that can be offensive if used by a man to a woman he does not know
IDM **be your/sb's baby** (*informal*) to be a plan or project that someone is responsible for and cares about because they have created it **throw the baby out with the bathwater** (*informal*) to lose something that you want at the same time as you are trying to get rid of something that you do not want ⊃ **more at** CANDY, SLEEP *v.*
● *adj.* [only before noun] baby vegetables are a very small version of particular vegetables, or are picked when they are very small: *baby carrots*
● *verb* (**bab·ies, ba·by·ing, bab·ied, bab·ied**) ~ **sb** to treat someone with too much care, as if they were a baby

baby 'blue *adj.* very pale blue in color ▶ **baby 'blue** *noun* [U]

baby 'blues *noun* [pl.] (*informal*) a depressed feeling that some women get after the birth of a baby **SYN** POSTPARTUM DEPRESSION

baby boom *noun* a period when many more babies are born than usual. In the U.S., this usually means the time between the end of World War II and about 1964.

baby boomer (also **boom·er**) *noun* a person born during a baby boom, especially after World War II

baby carriage (also **baby buggy**, *old-fashioned*) *noun* a small vehicle on four wheels for a baby to go out in, pushed by a person on foot ⊃ picture at STROLLER ⊃ compare STROLLER

baby-doll *adj.* used to describe a style of women's dress or NIGHTDRESS that is short with a high waist and is similar to the type of dress traditionally worn by DOLLS

baby-faced *adj.* with a face that looks young and innocent

baby fat *noun* [U] fat on a child's body that disappears as the child grows older

baby grand *noun* a small GRAND PIANO

ba·by·hood /ˈbeɪbiˌhʊd/ *noun* [U] the period of your life when you are a baby

ba·by·ish /ˈbeɪbiɪʃ/ *adj.* (usually *disapproving*) typical of or suitable for a baby

baby shower *noun* a party given for a woman who is going to have a baby, at which her friends give her presents for the baby

ba·by·sit /ˈbeɪbiˌsɪt/ *verb* (**ba·by·sit·ting, ba·by·sat, ba·by·sat**) (also **sit**) [I, T] to take care of babies or children for a short time while their parents are out: ~ **(for sb)** *She regularly babysits for us.* ◆ ~ **sb** *He's babysitting the neighbor's kids.* ▶ **ba·by·sit·ting** *noun* [U]

ba·by·sit·ter /ˈbeɪbiˌsɪtər/ (also **sit·ter**) *noun* a person who takes care of babies or children while their parents are away from home and is usually paid to do this: *I can't find a babysitter for tonight.*

baby talk *noun* [U] the words or sounds a baby says when it is learning to talk; the special language adults sometimes use when talking to babies

baby tooth *noun* any of the first set of teeth in young children that drop out and are replaced by others

bac·ca·lau·re·ate /ˌbækəˈlɔriət/ *noun* (*formal*) a B.A. degree

bac·ca·rat /ˈbɑkəˌrɑ; bæ-; ˌbɑkəˈrɑ; bæ-/ *noun* [U] a card game in which players hold two or three cards each and bet on whose cards will have the highest number left over when their value is divided by ten

bac·cha·na·li·an /ˌbækəˈneɪliən; ˌbɑ-/ *adj.* (*formal*) (of a party, etc.) wild and involving large amounts of alcohol **ORIGIN** From the name of the Greek god **Bacchus** (also called Dionysus), the god of wine and wild enjoyment.

bach·e·lor /ˈbætʃlər; ˈbætʃələr/ *noun* **1** a man who has never been married: *an eligible bachelor* (= one that many people want to marry, especially because he is rich) ◆ *a confirmed bachelor* (= a person who does not intend to marry; often used in newspapers to refer to a HOMOSEXUAL man)

⊃ compare SPINSTER **2** usually **Bachelor** a person who has a Bachelor's degree (= a first college degree): *a Bachelor of Arts/Engineering/Science* ⊃ see also B.A., B.ED., B.SC **3** (also **'bachelor a'partment**) (*CanE*) a small apartment suitable for a person living alone

bach·e·lor·ette /ˌbætʃləˈrɛt; ˌbætʃələ-/ *noun* a young woman who is not married

bachelor'ette ˌparty *noun* a party that a woman has with her female friends just before she gets married

'bachelor ˌgirl *noun* an independent young woman who is not married

bach·e·lor·hood /ˈbætʃlərˌhʊd; ˈbætʃələr-/ *noun* [U] the time in a man's life before he is married

'bachelor ˌparty (also **'stag ˌparty**) *noun* a party that a man has with his male friends just before he gets married, often the night before

ba·cil·lus /bəˈsɪləs/ *noun* (*pl.* **ba·cil·li** /-laɪ/) a type of bacteria. There are several types of bacilli, some of which cause disease.

back 🔑 /bæk/ *noun, adj., adv., verb*

● *noun*

▸ **PART OF BODY 1** the part of the human body that is on the opposite side to the chest, between the neck, and the tops of the legs; the part of an animal's body that CORRESPONDS to this: *Do you sleep on your back or your stomach?* ◆ *He stood with his back to the door.* ◆ *They had their hands tied behind their backs.* ◆ *back pain* ◆ *a back massage* ◆ *A small boy rode on the elephant's back.* ⊃ picture at BODY ⊃ collocations at PHYSICAL ⊃ see also BAREBACK, HORSEBACK **2** the row of bones in the middle of the back **SYN** BACKBONE, SPINE: *She broke her back in a riding accident.* ◆ *He threw his back out* (= DISLOCATED something in his back) *lifting the crates.*

▸ **PART FURTHEST FROM FRONT 3** [usually sing.] **~ (of sth)** the part or area of something that is furthest from the front: *We could only get seats in the back* (= of the room). ◆ *I found some old photos at the back of the drawer.* ◆ *He was shot in the back of the knee.* ◆ *The house has three bedrooms in the front and two in the back.* ◆ *There's room for three people in back.* ◆ *If you'd like to come out back* (= to the area behind the house), *I'll show you the garden.* ⊃ see also HARDBACK, PAPERBACK

▸ **OF PIECE OF PAPER 4** [usually sing.] **~ (of sth)** the part of a piece of paper, etc. that is on the opposite side to the one that has information or the most important information on it: *Write your name on the back of the check.*

▸ **OF BOOK 5** [usually sing.] **~ (of sth)** the last few pages of a book, etc.: *The television guide is at the back of the paper.*

▸ **OF CHAIR 6** the part of a chair, etc. against which you lean your back

▸ **-BACKED 7** (in adjectives) used to describe furniture that has the type of back mentioned: *a high-backed sofa*

▸ **IN SPORTS 8** a player whose main role is to defend their team's goal ⊃ compare FORWARD ⊃ see also FULLBACK, HALFBACK, QUARTERBACK

IDM **back to back 1** if two people stand **back to back**, they stand with their backs facing or touching each other **2** if two or more things happen **back to back**, they happen one after the other ⊃ see also BACK-TO-BACK **behind sb's back** without someone's knowledge or permission: *Have you been talking about me behind my back?* ◆ *They went ahead and sold it behind my back.* ⊃ compare TO SB'S FACE at FACE n. **be on sb's back** (*informal*) to keep asking or telling someone to do something that they do not want to do, in a way that they find annoying **get off sb's back** (*informal*) to stop annoying someone, for example by criticizing them, or asking them to do something: *Just get off my back, will you!* **have (got) sb's back** (*informal*) to protect and support someone: *Don't worry, I've got your back.* **have your back to/against the wall** (*informal*) to be in a difficult situation in which you are forced to do something but are unable to make the choices that you would like **in/at the back of your mind** if a thought, etc. is **in the back of your mind**, you are aware of it but it is not what you are mainly thinking about **off the back of a truck** (*informal, humorous*) goods that **fell off the**

back of a truck were probably stolen. People say or accept that they came "off the back of a truck" to avoid saying or asking where they really came from. **on the back of sth** as a result of an achievement or a success: *The profits growth came on the back of a 26 percent rise in sales.* **(flat) on your back** (*informal*) in bed because you are sick: *She's been flat on her back for over a week now.* ◆ (*figurative*) *The bonds market was flat on its back* (= business was very bad). **put your back into sth** to use a lot of effort and energy on a particular task **turn your back** to turn so that you are facing in the opposite direction **turn your back on sb/sth 1** to move so that you are standing or sitting with your back facing someone or something: *When on stage, try not to turn your back on the audience.* **2** to reject someone or something that you have previously been connected with: *She turned her back on them when they needed her.* ⊃ more at COVER v., EYE n., KNOW v., PAT n., PAT v., PUSH v., SCRATCH v., SHIRT, SKIN n., STAB n., STAB v., STRAW, WATER n., SKIN n.

WHICH WORD?

the back ◆ the rear ◆ behind

■ **The back** and **the rear** have a similar meaning, but **the rear** is used more in formal or official language: *What's that in the back of the fridge?* ◆ *The exits are located at the rear of the aircraft.* It is usual to talk about the **back door** of a house, but the **rear exit** of an aircraft or a public building. If something is **behind** something else, it is near to the back of it but not part of it. Compare: *Our room was at the back of the hotel* and *There's a pretty little pond just behind our hotel.*

● *adj.* [only before noun]

▸ **AWAY FROM FRONT 1** located behind or at the back of something: *We were sitting in the back row.* ◆ *back teeth* ◆ *a back room* (= one at the back of a building) ◆ *the back page of a newspaper* ⊃ compare FRONT

▸ **FROM PAST 2** of or from a past time: *a back issue of the magazine*

▸ **OWED 3** owed for a time in the past: *back pay/taxes/rent*

▸ **PHONETICS 4** (of a vowel) produced with the back of the tongue in a higher position than the front, for example /ɑ/ in English ⊃ compare CENTRAL, FRONT

IDM **on the back burner** (*informal*) (of an idea, a plan, etc.) left for the present time; to be done or considered later ⊃ see also BACK-BURNER ⊃ compare ON THE FRONT BURNER at FRONT *adj.*

● *adv.* **HELP** For the special uses of **back** in phrasal verbs, look at the entries for the verbs. For example, **pay sb back** is in the phrasal verb section at **pay.**

▸ **AWAY FROM FRONT 1** away from the front or center; behind you: *I stepped back to let them pass.* ◆ *Sit back and relax.* ◆ *He combed his hair back.* ◆ *He turned and looked back.* ◆ *She fell back toward the end of the race.* **ANT** FORWARD

▸ **AT A DISTANCE 2** at a distance away from something: *The barriers kept the crowd back.* ◆ *Stand back and give me some room.*

▸ **UNDER CONTROL 3** under control; prevented from being expressed or coming out: *He could no longer hold back his tears.*

▸ **AS BEFORE 4** to or into the place, condition, situation, or activity where something was before: *Put the book back on the shelf.* ◆ *Please give me my ball back.* ◆ *He'll be back on Monday.* ◆ *It takes me an hour to walk there and back.* ◆ *Could you go back to the beginning of the story?* ◆ *She woke up briefly and then went back to sleep.* ◆ *We were right back where we started,* only this time without any money.

▸ **IN PAST 5** in or into the past; ago: *The village has a history going back to the Middle Ages.* ◆ *She left back in November.* ◆ *That was a few years back.*

▸ **AT A PREVIOUS PLACE 6** at a place previously left or mentioned: *We should have turned left five miles back.* ◆ *Back at home, her parents were worried.* ◆ *I can't wait to get back home.*

t **t**ea   t̬ bu**tt**er   d **d**id   k **c**at   g **g**ot   tʃ **ch**in   dʒ **J**une   f **f**all

> **IN RETURN** **7** in return or reply: *If he kicks me, I'll kick him back.* ◆ *Could you call back later, please?*
IDM **back and forth** from one place to another and back again repeatedly: *ferries sailing back and forth between the islands* **in back of sth** (*informal*) behind something: *the houses in back of the church* ➪ more at DAY, EARTH
● *verb*
> **MOVE BACKWARD** **1** [I, T] to move or make something move backward: **+ adv./prep.** *He backed against the wall, terrified.* ◆ **~ sth + adv./prep.** *If you can't drive in forward, try backing it in.* ➪ compare REVERSE
> **SUPPORT** **2** [T] **~ sb/sth** to give help or support to someone or something: *Her parents backed her in her choice of career.* ◆ *Doctors have backed plans to raise the tax on cigarettes.* ◆ *The program of economic reform is backed* (= given financial support) *by foreign aid.* ◆ *a United Nations-backed peace plan*
> **BET MONEY** **3** [T] **~ sth** to bet money on a horse in a race, a team in a competition, etc.: *I backed the winner and won fifty dollars.*
> **MUSIC** **4** [T] **~ sth** to play or sing music that supports the main singer or instrument ➪ see also BACKING
> **COVER BACK** **5** [T] **~ sth (with sth)** [usually passive] to cover the back of something in order to support or protect it
> **BE BEHIND** **6** [T, usually passive] **~ sth** to be located behind something: *The house is backed by fields.*
PHR V ˌback aˈway (from sb/sth) to move away backward from someone or something that is frightening or unpleasant; to avoid doing something that is unpleasant ˌback ˈdown (on/from sth) (also ˌback ˈoff) to take back a demand, an opinion, etc. that other people are strongly opposed to; to admit defeat: *She refused to back down on a point of principle.* ˌback ˈoff **1** to move backward in order to get away from someone or something frightening or unpleasant: *As the riot police approached the crowd backed off.* **2** to stop threatening, criticizing, or annoying someone: *Back off! There's no need to yell at me.* ◆ *The press have agreed to back off and leave the couple alone.* ˌback ˈoff (from sth) to choose not to take action, in order to avoid a difficult situation: *The government backed off from a confrontation.* ˌback ˈonto sth (of a building) to have something directly behind it: *Our house backs onto the river.* ˌback ˈout (of sth) to decide that you are no longer going to take part in something that has been agreed: *He lost confidence and backed out of the deal at the last minute.* ˌback ˈup | ˌback sth↔ˈup **1** to move backward, especially in a vehicle: *You can back up another two feet or so.* ◆ *I backed the car up to the door.* **2** to stop something from moving or flowing freely, usually by blocking it; to be unable to move or flow freely: *Traffic was backed up for about two miles because of the accident.* ◆ *Do your drains ever back up?* ➪ related noun BACKUP (3) ˌback sb/sth↔ˈup **1** to support someone or something; to say that what someone says, etc. is true: *I'll back you up if they don't believe you.* ◆ *The writer doesn't back up his opinions with examples.* **2** to provide support for someone or something: *two doctors backed up by a team of nurses* ◆ *The rebels backed up their demands with threats.* ➪ related noun BACKUP (1) ˌback sth↔ˈup (*computing*) to prepare a second copy of a file, program, etc. that can be used if the main one fails or needs extra support ➪ related noun BACKUP (2)

back·ache /ˈbækeɪk/ *noun* [C, U] a continuous pain in the back: *to have a backache*

ˌback-ˈalley *adj.* [only before noun] happening or done secretly, often illegally: *a back-alley abortion*

back·beat /ˈbækbiːt/ *noun* (*music*) a strong emphasis on one or two of the beats that are not normally emphasized, used especially in JAZZ and rock music

back·bit·ing /ˈbækˌbaɪtɪŋ/ *noun* [U] unpleasant and unkind talk about someone who is not present

back·board /ˈbækbɔrd/ *noun* the board behind the BASKET in the game of basketball

back·bone /ˈbækboʊn/ *noun* **1** [C] the row of small bones that are connected together down the middle of the back **SYN** SPINE **2** [sing.] the most important part of a system, an organization, etc. that gives it support and strength: *Agriculture forms the backbone of the rural economy.* **3** [U] the strength of character that you need to do something difficult: *He doesn't have the backbone to face the truth.*

ˈback-ˌbreaking *adj.* (of physical work) very hard and tiring

ˌback-ˈburner *verb* **~ sth** (*informal*) to leave an idea or a plan for a time, to be done or considered later ➪ compare ON THE BACK BURNER at BACK *adj.*

ˈback ˌcatalog (also ˈback ˌcatalogue) *noun* all the recorded music previously produced by a musician: *The Beatles' entire back catalog has been put online.*

back·chan·nel /ˈbækˌtʃænl/ *noun* **1** a secret or unusual way of passing information to other people **2** (*linguistics*) a sound or sign that someone makes to show that they are listening to the person who is talking to them

back·coun·try /ˈbækˌkʌntri/ *noun* [U] an area away from roads and towns, especially in the mountains

back·court /ˈbækkɔrt/ *noun* **1** (in TENNIS, basketball, etc.) the area at either end of the COURT **2** (in basketball) the players who form the defense

back·date /ˈbækdeɪt/ *verb* **~ sth** to write a date on a check or other document that is earlier than the actual date ➪ compare POSTDATE

ˌback ˈdoor *noun* the door at the back or side of a building **IDM** **by/through the back door** in an unfair or indirect way: *His friends helped him get a job in the company through the back door.*

ˌback-ˈdoor *adj.* [only before noun] using indirect or secret means in order to achieve something

back·draft /ˈbækdræft/ *noun* **1** a current of air that flows backward down a CHIMNEY, pipe, etc. **2** an explosion caused by more OXYGEN being supplied to a fire, for example by a door being opened

back·drop /ˈbækdrɑp/ *noun* **1** a painted piece of cloth that is hung behind the stage in a theater as part of the SCENERY **2** everything that can be seen around an event that is taking place, but which is not part of that event: *The mountains provided a dramatic backdrop for our picnic.* **3** the general conditions in which an event takes place, that sometimes help to explain that event: *It was **against this backdrop** of racial tension that the civil war began.*

ˌback ˈend *noun* the part of something that is behind the part that you can see

ˈback-end *adj.* [only before noun] **1** relating to the end of a period or process **2** (*computing*) (of a device or program) not used directly by a user, but used by a program or computer ➪ compare FRONT-END

back·er /ˈbækər/ *noun* a person or company that gives support to someone or something, especially financial support

back·field /ˈbækfild/ *noun* [sing., U] **1** (in football) the area of play behind the LINE OF SCRIMMAGE **2** the players who play in or around this area

back·fill /ˈbækfɪl/ *verb* **~ sth** to fill a hole with the material that has been dug out of it

back·fire /ˈbækˌfaɪər/ *verb* **1** [I] **~ (on sb)** to have the opposite effect to the one intended, with bad or dangerous results: *Unfortunately the plan backfired.* **2** [I] (of an engine or a vehicle) to make a sudden noise like an explosion ➪ compare MISFIRE

back·flip /ˈbækflɪp/ *noun* if someone does a **backflip**, they turn their body over backward in the air and land on their feet again

ˈback-forˌmation *noun* [U, C] (*linguistics*) a word formed by removing or changing the end of a word that already exists. For example, *commentate* is a back-formation from *commentator*.

back·gam·mon /ˈbækˌgæmən/ *noun* [U] a game for two people played on a board marked with long thin triangles.

Players throw DICE and move pieces around the board.
⮕ picture at TOY

back·ground ♪ /'bækgraʊnd/ noun

> FAMILY/EDUCATION, ETC. **1** [C] the details of a person's family, education, experience, etc.: *a person's family/social/cultural/educational/class background* ◆ *The job would suit someone with a business background.*

> PAST **2** [C, usually sing., U] the circumstances or past events which help explain why something is how it is; information about these: *the historical background to the war* ◆ *background information/knowledge* ◆ *The elections are taking place against a background of violence.* ◆ *Can you give me more background on the company?*

> OF PICTURE/PHOTO **3** [C, usually sing.] the part of a picture, photograph, or view behind the main objects, people, etc.: *a photograph with trees in the background* ⮕ compare FORE-GROUND ⮕ thesaurus box at ENVIRONMENT

> LESS IMPORTANT POSITION **4** [sing.] a position in which people are not paying attention to someone or something or not as much attention as they are paying to someone or something else: *He prefers to remain in the background and let his assistant talk to the press.* ◆ *A piano tinkled gently in the background.* ◆ *background music* ◆ *There was a lot of background noise* (= that you could hear, but were not listening to). ⮕ compare FOREGROUND

> COLOR UNDER SOMETHING **5** [C, usually sing.] a color or design on which something is painted, drawn, etc.: *The name of the company is written in red on a white background.*
IDM in the background (*computing*) (of a computer program) not being used at the present time and appearing on the screen behind programs that are being used ⮕ compare IN THE FOREGROUND ⮕ more at MERGE

back·hand /'bækhænd/ noun [usually sing.] (in TENNIS, etc.) a stroke played with the back of the hand turned in the direction toward which the ball is hit: *He has a good backhand* (= he can make good backhand strokes). ◆ *a backhand volley/drive* ⮕ compare FOREHAND

back·hand·ed /'bæk‚hændəd/ adj. having a meaning that is not directly or clearly expressed, or that is not intended **IDM** see COMPLIMENT n.

back·hoe /'bækhoʊ/ noun a large vehicle with machinery for digging, used in building roads, etc. ⮕ picture at CONSTRUCTION

back·ing /'bækɪŋ/ noun **1** [U] help **SYN** SUPPORT: *financial backing* ◆ *The police gave the proposals their full backing.* **2** [U, C] material attached to the back of something in order to protect it or make it stronger **3** [U, C, usually sing.] (especially in pop music) music that accompanies the main singer or tune: *a backing group/singer/track*

‚back 'issue noun a copy of a newspaper or magazine from a date in the past

back·lash /'bæklæʃ/ noun [sing.] ~ (against sth) | ~ (from sb) a strong negative reaction by a large number of people, for example to something that has recently changed in society: *The government is facing an angry backlash from voters over the new tax.*

back·less /'bækləs/ adj. (of a dress) not covering most of the back

back·light /'bæklaɪt/ noun, verb
● noun [U] light from behind something in a photograph or painting
● verb (back·lit, back·lit /-lɪt/ or back·light·ed, back·light-ed) ~ sth to shine light on something from behind ▶ **back·lit** /-lɪt/ adj.: *a backlit photograph*

back·list /'bæklɪst/ noun the list of books that have been published by a company in the past and are still available

back·log /'bæklɔg; -lag/ noun a quantity of work that should have been done already, but has not yet been done

back·lot /'bæklat/ noun an outdoor area in a movie studio, where pieces of SCENERY are made and some scenes are filmed

back·most /'bækmoʊst/ adj. [usually before noun] furthest back: *the backmost teeth*

‚back 'office noun (*business*) the part of a business company that does not deal directly with the public

'back ‚order noun [C, U] an order for a product that is not yet available: *Those items are a back order and we're not sure when they will be in.* ◆ *Those items are on back order.* ▶ 'back ‚order verb: ~ sth *Your books have been back ordered and should be here within a week.*

back·pack /'bækpæk/ noun, verb
● noun a bag, sometimes supported on a light metal frame, carried on the back and used especially by people who are traveling or HIKING ⮕ picture at BAG
● verb [I] usually **go backpacking** to travel on vacation carrying your equipment and clothes in a backpack: *They went backpacking in the Adirondacks last year.* ▶ **back-pack·er** noun

back·ped·al /'bæk‚pedl/ verb (-l-, CanE usually -ll-) **1** [I] ~ (on sth) to change an earlier statement or opinion; to not do something that you promised to do: *The protests have forced the government to backpedal on the new tax.* **2** [I] to PEDAL backward on a bicycle; to walk or run backward

back·plane /'bækpleɪn/ noun (*computing*) a CIRCUIT BOARD that other devices can be connected to

back·rest /'bækrɛst/ noun part of a seat that supports someone's back

‚back 'room noun a room at the back of a building, away from the entrance, often where secret activities take place: *back-room deals between political parties*

back·scratch·ing /'bæk‚skrætʃɪŋ/ noun [U] (*informal, often disapproving*) the fact of giving someone help in return for help that they have given you, often in connection with something that might be illegal

‚back 'seat noun a seat at the back of a vehicle
IDM take a back seat to allow someone else to play a more active and important role in a particular situation than you do

back·seat driv·er /‚bæksit 'draɪvər/ noun **1** a passenger in a vehicle who keeps giving advice to the driver about how he or she should drive **2** a person who wants to be in control of something that is not really their responsibility

back·shift /'bækʃɪft/ noun [U] (*linguistics*) the changing of a tense when reporting what someone said, for example when reporting the words "What are you doing?" as "He asked me what I was doing."

back·side /'bæksaɪd/ noun (*informal*) the part of the body that you sit on **SYN** BEHIND, BOTTOM: *Get up off your backside and do some work!*

back·slap·ping /'bæk‚slæpɪŋ/ noun [U] loud and enthusi-astic behavior when people are praising each other for something good they have done ▶ **back·slap·ping** adj. [only before noun]: *backslapping tributes*

back·slash /'bækslæʃ/ noun a mark (\), used in computer commands ⮕ compare FORWARD SLASH

back·slid·ing /'bæk‚slaɪdɪŋ/ noun [U] the situation when someone fails to do something that they agreed to do and returns to their former bad behavior

back·space /'bækspeɪs/ noun, verb
● noun the key on the keyboard of a computer or TYPE-WRITER which allows you to move backward. On a computer keyboard this key also removes the last letter that you typed.
● verb [I] to use the backspace key on a computer keyboard or on a TYPEWRITER

back·spin /'bækspɪn/ noun [U] a backward spinning movement of a ball that has been hit, which makes it go less far than it normally would

back·stab·bing /'bæk‚stæbɪŋ/ noun [U] the action of criticizing someone when they are not there, while pretending to be their friend at other times

---

96

h hat   m man   n no   ŋ sing   l leg   r red   y yes   w wet

back·stage /ˌbækˈsteɪdʒ/ adv. **1** in the part of a theater where the actors and artists get ready and wait to perform: *After the show, we were allowed to go backstage to meet the cast.* **2** away from the attention of the public; in secret: *I'd like to know what really goes on backstage in government.* ▶ **backstage** adj.

back·stairs noun, adj.
● **noun** /ˈbækˈstɛrz/ [pl.] stairs at the back or side of a building, sometimes used by servants
● **adj.** /ˈbækstɛrz/ secret or dishonest: *backstairs deals between politicians*

back·stitch /ˈbækstɪtʃ/ noun [U, C] a method of sewing in which each STITCH begins at the middle of the previous one

back·stop /ˈbækstɑp/ noun (sports) **1** a fence or screen used to keep balls from going outside the playing area **2** (informal) (in baseball) a CATCHER

back·sto·ry /ˈbækˌstɔri/ noun (pl. **back·sto·ries**) [C, U] **1** the things that are supposed to have happened to the characters in a movie, novel, etc., before the movie, etc. starts: *The film spends too long establishing the characters' backstories.* **2** (especially in journalism) the background to a news story: *First, some backstory:…*

back·street noun, adj.
● **noun** /ˈbækstrit/ a small quiet street, usually in a poor part of a town or city, away from main roads
● **adj.** /ˈbækstrit/ [only before noun] acting or happening secretly, often illegally or illegally: *backstreet dealers*

back·stroke /ˈbækstroʊk/ noun [U, sing.] a style of swimming in which you lie on your back: *Can you do the backstroke?* ◆ *He won the 100-meter backstroke (= the race).* ⊃ picture at SPORT

back·swing /ˈbækswɪŋ/ noun (sports) the backward movement of your arm or arms before you hit the ball

back talk noun [U] a way of answering that shows no respect for someone in authority

back-to-ˈback adj. [usually before noun] following one after another in a series: *The conference consisted of back-to-back meetings over a period of three days.* ⊃ see also BACK n.

back·track /ˈbæktræk/ verb **1** [I] to go back along the same route that you have just come along **2** [I] to change an earlier statement, opinion, or promise because of pressure from someone or something

back·up /ˈbækʌp/ noun **1** [U, C] extra help or support that you can get if necessary: *The police had backup from the army.* ◆ *We can use him as a backup if one of the other players drops out.* ◆ *a backup power supply* **2** (computing) [C] a copy of a file, etc. that can be used if the original is lost or damaged: *Always make a backup of your work.* ◆ *a backup copy* ⊃ see also BACK UP **3** [C] a situation in which something is not moving or flowing freely, usually because something is blocking it: *a traffic backup* ◆ *a toilet backup* ⊃ collocations at DRIVING **4** [U] (especially in pop music) music that accompanies the main singer or tune: *They sang backup for Elvis Presley.* ◆ *backup vocals*

backup ˌlight noun a light at the back of a vehicle that comes on when the vehicle moves backward

back·ward 🔊 /ˈbækwərd/ adj., adv.
● **adj.** **1** [only before noun] directed or moving toward the back: *She strode past him without a backward glance.* **2** moving in a direction that means that no progress is being made **SYN** RETROGRADE: *She felt that going back to live in her hometown would be a backward step.* **3** having made less progress than normal; developing slowly: *a backward part of the country, with no paved roads and no electricity* ◆ *a backward child* **ANT** FORWARD
● **adv.** (also **backwards**) **1** toward a place or position that is behind: *I lost my balance and fell backward.* ◆ *He took a step backward.* **ANT** FORWARD **2** in the opposite direction to the usual one: *"Ambulance" is written backward so you can read it in the mirror.* ◆ *In the movie they take a journey backward through time.* **3** toward a worse state: *I felt that going to live*

with my parents would be a step backward. **ANT** FORWARD **4** if you put on a piece of clothing **backward**, you make a mistake and put the back where the front should be **IDM** **backward and forward** from one place or position to another and back again many times: *She rocked backward and forward on her chair.* **bend/lean over backward (to do sth)** to make a great effort, especially in order to be helpful or fair: *I've bent over backward to help him.* ⊃ more at KNOW v.

backward comˈpatible (also **backwards comˈpatible**) adj. (computing) able to be used with systems, machines, or programs that are older

backward-ˌlooking adj. (disapproving) opposed to progress or change

back·ward·ness /ˈbækwərdnəs/ noun [U] the state of having made less progress than normal

back·wash /ˈbækwɑʃ; -wɔʃ/ noun [sing.] **1** the unpleasant result of an event **2** waves caused by a boat moving through water; the movement of water back into the ocean after a wave has hit the beach

back·wa·ter /ˈbækˌwɑtər; -ˌwɑtər/ noun **1** a part of a river away from the main part, where the water only moves slowly **2** (often disapproving) a place that is away from the places where most things happen, and is therefore not affected by events, progress, new ideas, etc.: *a sleepy/ quiet/rural backwater*

back·woods /ˌbækˈwʊdz/ noun [pl.] a place that is away from any big towns and from the influence of modern life

back·woods·man /ˌbækˈwʊdzmən/ noun (pl. **back·woods·men** /-mən/) a person who lives in a region far from towns where not many people live, especially one who does not have much education or good manners

back·yard /ˌbækˈyɑrd/ noun the whole area behind and belonging to a house, including an area of grass and the garden: *a backyard barbecue* ⊃ see also YARD **IDM** **in your (own) backyard** in or near the place where you live or work: *The residents didn't want a new factory in their backyard.* ◆ *The party leader is facing opposition in his own backyard (= from his own members).* ⊃ see also NIMBY

ba·con /ˈbeɪkən/ noun [U] meat from the back or sides of a pig that has been CURED (= preserved using salt or smoke), usually served in thin slices: *a slice of bacon* ◆ *bacon and eggs* ◆ *smoked/unsmoked bacon* ⊃ compare HAM, PORK **IDM** see HOME adv., SAVE v.

bac·te·ri·a 🔊 /bækˈtɪriə/ noun [pl.] (sing. **bac·te·ri·um** /-iəm/) the simplest and smallest forms of life. Bacteria exist in large numbers in air, water, and soil, and also in living and dead creatures and plants, and are often a cause of disease ⊃ collocations at LIFE ▶ **bac·te·ri·al** /bækˈtɪriəl/ adj.: *bacterial infections/growth*

bac·te·ri·ol·o·gy /bækˌtɪriˈɑlədʒi/ noun [U] the scientific study of bacteria ▶ **bac·te·ri·o·log·i·cal** /bækˌtɪriəˈlɑdʒɪkl/ adj. **bac·te·ri·ol·o·gist** /bækˌtɪriˈɑlədʒɪst/ noun

bad 🔊 /bæd/ adj., noun, adv.
● **adj.** (**worse** /wərs/, **worst** /wərst/)
⟩ **UNPLEASANT 1** unpleasant; full of problems: *bad news/ weather/dreams/habits* ◆ *I'm having a really bad day.* ◆ *It was the worst experience of her life.* ◆ *Smoking gives you bad breath.* ◆ *Things are bad enough without our own guns shelling us.*
⟩ **POOR QUALITY 2** of poor quality; below an acceptable standard: *bad conditions/driving* ◆ *a bad copy/diet* ◆ *I thought it was a very bad article.* ◆ *This isn't as bad as I thought.* ◆ *That's not a bad idea.*
⟩ **NOT GOOD AT SOMETHING 3 ~ at sth/at doing sth** (of a person) not able to do something well or in an acceptable way **SYN** POOR: *a bad teacher* ◆ *You're a bad liar!* ◆ *He's a bad loser (= he complains when he loses a game).* ◆ *She is so bad at keeping secrets.*
⟩ **SERIOUS 4** serious; severe: *You're heading for a bad attack of sunburn.* ◆ *The engagement was a bad mistake.* ◆ *My headache is getting worse.*
⟩ **NOT APPROPRIATE 5** [only before noun] not appropriate in a

particular situation: *I know that this is a bad time to ask for help.* ◆ *He now realized that it had been a bad decision.*
>WICKED **6** morally unacceptable: *The hero gets to shoot all the bad guys.* ◆ *He said I must have done something bad to deserve it.*
>CHILDREN **7** [usually before noun] (especially of children) not behaving well **SYN** NAUGHTY: *Have you been a bad boy?*
>HARMFUL **8** [not before noun] ~ **for sb/sth** harmful; causing or likely to cause damage: *Those shoes are bad for her feet.* ◆ *Weather like this is bad for business.*
>PAINFUL **9** [usually before noun] (of parts of the body) not healthy; painful: *I've got a bad back.*
>FOOD **10** not safe to eat because it has decayed: *Put the meat in the fridge so it doesn't go bad.*
>TEMPER/MOOD **11** ~ **temper/mood** the state of feeling annoyed or angry: *It put me in a bad mood for the rest of the day.*
>GUILTY/SORRY **12** feel ~ to feel guilty or sorry about something: *She felt bad about leaving him.* ◆ *Why should I want to make you feel bad?*
>ILL/SICK **13** feel/look ~ to feel or look sick: *I'm afraid I'm feeling pretty bad.*
>EXCELLENT **14** (bad·der, bad·dest) (*slang*) good; excellent **IDM** Most idioms containing **bad** are at the entries for the nouns and verbs in the idioms. For example, **be bad news (for someone or something)** is at **news**. **can't be bad** (*informal*) used to try to persuade someone to agree that something is good: *You'll save fifty dollars, which can't be bad, can it?* **have got it bad** (*informal, humorous*) to be very much in love: *You're not seeing him again tonight, are you? That's five times this week—you've got it bad!* **not bad** (*informal*) quite good; better than you expected: *"How are you?" "Not too bad."* ◆ *That wasn't bad for a first attempt.* **too bad** (*informal*) a shame; unfortunately: *Too bad every day can't be as good as this.*
● **noun** the bad [U] bad people, things, or events: *You will always have the bad as well as the good in the world.* **IDM** **go to the bad** (*old-fashioned*) to begin behaving in an immoral way: *I hate to see you going to the bad.* **my bad** (*informal*) used when you are admitting that something is your fault or that you have made a mistake: *I'm sorry—my bad.* **take the bad with the good** to accept the bad aspects of something as well as the good ones
● **adv.** (*informal, non-standard*) badly: *She wanted it real bad.* ◆ *Are you hurt bad?*

VOCABULARY BUILDING

bad and very bad

Instead of saying that something is **bad** or **very bad**, try to use more precise and interesting adjectives to describe things:
■ an **unpleasant**/a **foul**/a **disgusting** smell
■ **appalling**/**dreadful**/**severe** weather
■ an **unpleasant**/a **frightening**/a **traumatic** experience
■ **poor**/**weak** eyesight
■ a **terrible**/**serious**/**horrific** accident
■ a **wicked**/an **evil**/an **immoral** person
■ an **awkward**/an **embarrassing**/a **difficult** situation
■ We were working in **difficult**/**appalling** conditions.
To refer to your health, you can say: *I feel sick/terrible* ◆ *I don't feel (very) good.*
In conversation, words like **terrible**, **horrible**, and **awful** can be used in most situations to mean "very bad."

bad ˈbreath *noun* [U] breath that smells unpleasant: *Have I got bad breath?* **SYN** HALITOSIS
bad ˈdebt *noun* [C, U] a debt that is unlikely to be paid
bad·dy /ˈbædi/ *noun* (*pl.* bad·dies) (*informal*) a bad or evil character in a movie, book, play, etc.: *As usual, the cops get the baddies in the end.*
bade *pt of* BID²

badge /bædʒ/ *noun* **1** a small piece of metal or plastic, with a design or words on it, that a person wears to show that they belong to an organization, support something, have achieved something, have a particular rank, etc.: *a Girl Scout badge* ◆ *All employees have to wear name badges.* ⊃ compare BUTTON **2** a small piece of metal that you carry or wear to prove who you are, used, for example, by police officers: *He pulled out a badge and said he was a cop.* **3** ~ **of honor/courage** (*formal*) something that you are proud of or that shows how brave you are: *He wore his working-class background like a badge of honor.*
badg·er /ˈbædʒər/ *noun, verb*
● **noun** an animal with gray fur and wide black and white lines on its head. Badgers are NOCTURNAL (= active mostly at night) and live in holes in the ground.
● **verb** to put pressure on someone by repeatedly asking them questions or asking them to do something **SYN** PESTER: ~ **sb (into doing sth)** *I finally badgered him into coming with us.* ◆ ~ **sb about sth** *Reporters constantly badger her about her private life.* ◆ ~ **sb to do sth** *His daughter was always badgering him to let her join the club.*
ˌbad ˈhair day *noun* (*informal*) a day on which everything seems to go wrong
bad·i·nage /ˌbædnˈɑʒ/ *noun* [U] (from *French, literary*) friendly joking between people **SYN** BANTER
bad·lands /ˈbædlændz/ *noun* [pl.] **1** large areas of land where very few plants will grow, which cannot be used for farming **2** the Badlands a large area of land in the western U.S. where plants will not grow
ˌbad ˈlanguage *noun* [U] words that many people find offensive **SYN** SWEAR WORD
bad·ly /ˈbædli/ *adv.*
(worse, worst) **1** not skillfully or not carefully: *to play/sing badly* ◆ *badly designed/organized* **ANT** WELL **2** not successfully: *Things have been going badly.* ◆ *I did badly* (= was not successful) *on my exams.* **ANT** WELL **3** not in an acceptable way: *to behave/sleep badly* ◆ *badly paid/treated* ◆ *The kids took the dog's death very badly* (= they were very unhappy). **ANT** WELL **4** in a way that makes people get a bad opinion about something: *The economic crisis reflects badly on the government's policies.* ◆ *She's only trying to help, so don't think badly of her.* **ANT** WELL **5** used to emphasize how much you want, need, etc. someone or something: *The building is badly in need of repair.* ◆ *They wanted to win so badly.* ◆ *I miss her badly.* **6** used to emphasize how serious a situation or an event is: *badly damaged/injured/hurt* ◆ *The country has been badly affected by recession.*
ˌbadly ˈoff *adj.* (worse ˈoff, worst ˈoff) **1** not having much money **SYN** POOR: *We aren't too badly off but we can't afford a house like that.* **ANT** WELL OFF **2** not in a good situation: *I've got quite a big room so I'm not too badly off.* **ANT** WELL OFF
bad·min·ton /ˈbæd.mɪtn; -ˌmɪntn/ *noun* [U] a game like TENNIS played by two or four people, usually indoors. Players hit a small light object (= a SHUTTLECOCK) across a high net using a RACKET. ⊃ picture at SPORT
bad-mouth /ˈbædmaʊθ; -maʊð/ *verb* ~ **sb** (*informal*) to say unpleasant things about someone: *No one wants to employ someone who bad-mouths their former employer.*
bad·ness /ˈbædnəs/ *noun* [U] the fact of being morally bad: *There was not a hint of badness in him.*
ˌbad-ˈtempered *adj.* often angry; in an angry mood: *She gets very bad-tempered when she's tired.*
baf·fle /ˈbæfl/ *verb, noun*
● **verb** to confuse someone completely; to be too difficult or strange for someone to understand or explain: ~ **sb** *His behavior baffles me.* ◆ **be baffled (as to) why, how, where, etc....** *I'm baffled as to why she hasn't called.* ◆ *I'm baffled why she hasn't called.* ▶ **baf·fle·ment** *noun* [U]: *His reaction was one of bafflement.* **baff·ling** *adj.*

bags

suitcase

duffel bag

backpack

tote bag

briefcase

purse

strap

clutch bag

grocery bag

fanny pack

change purse

wallets (*also* bill folds)

garbage bag (*also* trash bag)

● **noun** (*technical*) a screen used to control or prevent the flow of sound, light, or liquid

bag /bæg/ noun, verb

● **noun**

> **CONTAINER 1** [C] (often in compounds) a container made of paper or plastic, which opens at the top, used especially in stores: *a **plastic/paper bag** ◆ a **shopping/lunch bag** ◆ a black plastic **trash/garbage bag*** ⊃ picture at PACKAGING **2** [C] a strong container made from cloth, plastic, leather, etc., usually with one or two handles, used to carry things in when shopping or traveling: *a tote/makeup bag ◆ an overnight bag ◆ He's upstairs unpacking his bags. ◆ She opened her bag* (= her HANDBAG) *and took out her comb.* ⊃ see also AIRBAG, BEANBAG, GARMENT BAG, GOODY BAG, PUNCHING BAG, SANDBAG, TEA BAG ⊃ note at BAGGAGE

> **AMOUNT 3** [C] ~ **(of sth)** the amount contained in a bag: *She ate a bag of chips.* ⊃ see also MIXED BAG, RAGBAG

> **UNDER EYES 4** bags [pl.] dark circles or loose folds of skin under the eyes, as a result of getting old or lack of sleep

> **UNPLEASANT WOMAN 5** [C] (*informal*) an insulting word for an unpleasant or bad-tempered older woman ⊃ see also SCUMBAG, WINDBAG

> **BIRDS/ANIMALS 6** [C, usually sing.] all the birds, animals, etc. shot or caught on one occasion

HELP There are many other compounds ending in **bag**. You will find them at their place in the alphabet.

IDM **a bag of bones** (*informal*) a very thin person or animal **a bag of tricks** (*informal*) a set of methods or equipment that someone can use **be in the bag** (*informal*) if something is in the bag, it is almost certain to be won or achieved **leave sb holding the bag** (*informal*) to suddenly make someone responsible for something important, such as finishing a difficult job, that is really your responsibility **(not) sb's bag** (*informal*) (not) something that you are interested in or good at: *Poetry isn't really my bag.* ⊃ more at CAT, NERVE *n.*, PACK *v.*

● **verb** (-gg-)

> **PUT INTO BAGS 1** ~ **sth (up)** to put something into bags: *The fruit is washed, sorted, and bagged at the farm.*

> **CATCH ANIMAL 2** ~ **sth** (*informal*) to catch or kill an animal

> **CLAIM SOMETHING 3** ~ **sth** (*informal*) to claim something as yours before someone else claims it; to take something

before someone else can get it: *Sally had managed to bag the two best seats.* ◆ *Quick, bag that table over there!*

> **DECIDE NOT TO DO SOMETHING 4** ~ **sth** (*informal*) to decide not to do something because you think it will not be successful or because you think it will be better to do it later: *They decided to bag the trip because they were short of cash.*

bag·a·telle /ˌbæɡəˈtɛl/ noun **1** [U] a game played on a board with small balls that you try to hit into holes **2** [C, usually sing.] (*literary*) a small and unimportant thing or amount: *It cost a mere bagatelle.*

ba·gel /ˈbeɪɡl/ noun a hard bread roll shaped like a ring

bag·gage /ˈbæɡɪdʒ/ noun [U]
1 bags, cases, etc. that contain someone's clothes and things when they are traveling: *excess baggage* (= weighing more than the limit allowed on a plane) ◆ *baggage handlers* (= people employed to load and unload baggage at airports) ◆ *We loaded our baggage into the car.* ⊃ collocations at TRAVEL **2** the beliefs and attitudes that someone has as a result of their past experiences: *She was carrying a lot of emotional baggage.*

WHICH WORD?

baggage ◆ luggage ◆ bags

- **Baggage** is the term used for the packed suitcases that travelers carry with them: *I try not to check any baggage if I can.* ◆ *baggage handlers* ◆ *the baggage claim area in the airport*
- **Luggage** is more formal than **baggage** and is often used to describe the empty bags themselves: *I need to buy some new luggage for my vacation next month.*
- Both **baggage** and **luggage** are noncount nouns: *Do you have a lot of baggage?* ◆ *The couple had matching luggage.*
- **Bags** are individual pieces of baggage: *You're allowed one checked bag and one carry-on.* ◆ *How many bags do you have?*

baggage ˌcar noun a car on a train for carrying passengers' baggage

baggage ˌcarousel (also **car·ou·sel**) noun a moving belt from which you collect your bags at an airport

baggage claim *noun* [U] the place at an airport where you get your baggage, etc. again after you have flown

Bag·gie™ /'bægi/ *noun* a small bag made of clear plastic that is used for storing SANDWICHES, etc.

bag·gy /'bægi/ *adj.* (bag·gi·er, bag·gi·est) (of clothes) fitting loosely: *a baggy T-shirt* **ANT** TIGHT

bag lady *noun* a woman who has no home and who walks around carrying her possessions with her

bag lunch *noun* a meal of SANDWICHES, fruit, etc. that you take to school, work, etc. in a bag ⭗ **compare** BOX LUNCH

bag·pipes /'bægpaɪps/ (also pipes) *noun* [pl.] (also bag·pipe [sing.]) a musical instrument played especially in Scotland. The player blows air into a bag held under the arm and then slowly forces the air out through pipes to produce a noise. ▶ **bag·pipe** *adj.*: *bagpipe music*

ba·guette /bæ'gɛt/ *noun* **1** a LOAF of white bread in the shape of a long thick stick that is crisp on the outside and soft inside **2** a small baguette or part of one that is filled with food and eaten as a SANDWICH: *a cheese baguette*

bah /bɑ; bæ/ *exclamation* used to show a sound that people make to express disapproval

Ba·ha·'i (also Ba·ha·i) /bə'haɪ/ *noun* [U] a religion that teaches that people and religions are the same, and that there should be peace

bail /beɪl/ *noun, verb*
• *noun* [U] money that someone agrees to pay if a person accused of a crime does not appear at their trial. When bail has been arranged, the accused person is allowed to go free until the trial: *Can anyone post bail for you?* ♦ *She was released on $2,000 bail.* ♦ *Bail was set at $1 million.* ♦ *He committed another offense while he was out on bail* (= after bail had been agreed). ♦ *The judge granted/refused bail.* ⭗ **collocations at** JUSTICE
  IDM jump/skip bail to not appear at your trial after you have paid bail
• *verb* **1** [T] to release someone on bail: *His son called home to get bailed out of jail.* **2** [I] (*informal*) to leave a place, especially quickly: *Sorry, I really have to bail.*
  PHR V **bail 'out (of sth) 1** to jump out of a plane that is going to crash **2** to escape from a situation that you do not want to be involved in anymore: *I'd understand if you wanted to bail out of this relationship.* **bail 'out | bail (sth)↔'out** to empty water from something by lifting it out with your hand or a container: *He had to stop rowing to bail water out of the boat.* ♦ *The boat will sink unless we bail out.* **bail sb↔'out** to pay someone's bail for them **bail sb↔'out (of sth)** to rescue someone from a difficult situation: *The government had to bail the company out of financial difficulty.* ♦ *Ryan's late goal bailed out his team.* ⭗ **thesaurus box at** SAVE

bai·ley /'beɪli/ *noun* the open area of a castle, inside the outer wall

bail·iff /'beɪləf/ *noun* an official who keeps order in court, takes people to their seats, watches prisoners, etc.

bail·i·wick /'beɪliˌwɪk; 'beɪlə-/ *noun* (*formal*) someone's particular area of responsibility or interest: *He never writes up our reports—that's my bailiwick.*

bail·out /'beɪlaʊt/ *noun* an act of giving money to a company, a foreign country, etc. that has very serious financial problems

bait /beɪt/ *noun, verb*
• *noun* [U, C] **1** food put on a hook to catch fish, or in nets, traps, etc. to catch animals or birds: *The fish took the bait.* **2** a person or thing that is used to catch someone or to attract them, for example to make them do what you want
• *verb* **1** ~ sth (with sth) to place food on a hook, in a trap, etc. in order to attract or catch an animal: *He baited the trap with a piece of meat.* **2** ~ sb to deliberately try to make someone angry by making cruel or insulting remarks **3** -baiting (in compound nouns) the activity of attacking a wild animal with dogs: *bear-baiting*

bait-and-'switch *noun* [C, usually sing.] a selling method where advertisements for cheap products are used to attract customers, who are then persuaded to buy something more expensive

baize /beɪz/ *noun* [U] a type of thick cloth made of wool that is usually green, used especially for covering card tables and POOL tables

bake 🔊 /beɪk/ *verb*
1 [T, I] to cook food in an oven without extra fat or liquid; to be cooked in this way: ~ (sth) *baked apples* ♦ *the delicious smell of baking bread* ♦ ~ sth for sb *I'm baking a birthday cake for Alex.* ♦ ~ sb sth *I'm baking Alex a cake.* ⭗ **picture at** COOKING ⭗ **collocations at** COOKING **2** [I, T] to become or to make something become hard by heating: *The bricks are left in the kiln to bake.* ♦ ~ sth (+ adj.) *The sun had baked the ground hard.* **3** [I] (*informal*) to be or become very hot: *We sat baking in the sun.* ⭗ **see also** HALF-BAKED

baked A·las·ka /ˌbeɪkt ə'læskə/ *noun* [C, U] a DESSERT made of cake and ice cream covered in MERINGUE and cooked quickly in a very hot oven

baked 'beans (also Bos·ton baked beans) *noun* [pl.] small white BEANS cooked in a sweet brown sauce and usually sold in cans

baked po'tato *noun* a potato cooked in its skin in an oven: *a baked potato with sour cream*

Ba·ke·lite™ /'beɪkəˌlaɪt; 'beɪklaɪt/ *noun* [U] a type of hard plastic used in the past for electrical equipment, etc.

bak·er /'beɪkər/ *noun* a person whose job is baking and selling bread and cakes

baker's 'dozen *noun* [sing.] (*old-fashioned*) a group of thirteen (= one more than a dozen, which is twelve) **ORIGIN** This phrase comes from bakers' old custom of adding one extra loaf to an order of a dozen.

bak·er·y /'beɪkəri/ *noun* (*pl.* bak·er·ies) a place where bread and cakes are made and/or sold

bake sale *noun* an event at which cakes, etc. are baked and sold to make money, usually for a school or charity

bake·ware /'beɪkwɛr/ *noun* [U] tins and other containers used for baking

bak·ing /'beɪkɪŋ/ *noun, adj.*
• *noun* [U] the process of cooking using dry heat in an oven: *a baking dish/pan*
• *adj.* extremely hot **SYN** BOILING

baking powder *noun* [U] a mixture of powders that are used to make cakes rise and become light as they are baked

baking sheet *noun* = COOKIE SHEET

baking soda *noun* [U] = SODIUM BICARBONATE

Bak·ke de·cis·ion /'bæki dɪˌsɪʒn/ *noun* an important decision made by the U.S. Supreme Court in 1978. A white man called Allan Bakke claimed that he had been illegally refused a place to study at medical school because black students with worse grades were accepted. The Court decided that he should have been accepted, but that it is not wrong to consider a person's race when deciding whether to accept them. ⭗ **see also** AFFIRMATIVE ACTION

ba·kla·va /'bɑkləˌvɑ; ˌbɑklə'vɑ/ *noun* [C, U] a sweet dish from the Middle East, made from very thin PASTRY, nuts, and HONEY

bal·a·cla·va /ˌbæləˈklɑvə/ *noun* a type of hat made of wool that covers most of the head, neck, and face

bal·a·lai·ka /ˌbæləˈlaɪkə/ *noun* a musical instrument like a GUITAR with a body shaped like a triangle and two, three, or four strings, popular especially in Russia ⭗ **picture at** INSTRUMENT

bal·ance 🔊 /'bæləns/ *noun, verb*
• *noun*
➢ **EQUAL AMOUNTS 1** [U, sing.] a situation in which different things exist in equal, correct, or good amounts ⭗ **see also** IMBALANCE: *This newspaper maintains a good balance in its presentation of different opinions.* ♦ *Tourists often disturb the*

delicate balance of nature on the island. ◆ **~ between A and B** *Try to keep a balance between work and relaxation.* ⟳ see also BALANCE OF POWER

▸ OF BODY **2** [U] the ability to keep steady with an equal amount of weight on each side of the body: *Athletes need a good sense of balance.* ◆ *I struggled to* **keep my balance** *on my new skates.* ◆ *She rode around the corner,* **lost her balance**, *and fell off her bike.*

▸ MONEY **3** [C, usually sing.] the amount that is left after taking numbers or money away from a total: *to check your* **account balance** (= to find out how much money there is in your account) **4** [C, usually sing.] an amount of money still owed after some payment has been made: *The balance of $500 must be paid within 90 days.*

▸ INSTRUMENT FOR WEIGHING **5** [C] an instrument for weighing things, with a bar that is supported in the middle and has dishes hanging from each end

IDM **(be/hang) in the balance** if the future of something or someone, or the result of something, is/hangs **in the balance**, it is uncertain: *The long-term future of the space program hangs in the balance.* **(catch/throw sb) off balance 1** to make someone or something unsteady and in danger of falling: *I was thrown off balance by the sudden gust of wind.* **2** to make someone surprised or confused: *The senator was clearly caught off balance by the unexpected question.* **on balance** after considering all the information: *On balance, the company has had a successful year.* ⟳ more at REDRESS, STRIKE, SWING, TIP

• *verb*

▸ KEEP STEADY **1** [I, T] to put your body or something else into a position where it is steady and does not fall: **~ (on sth)** *How long can you balance on one leg?* ◆ **~ sth (on sth)** *The television was precariously balanced on top of a pile of books.* ◆ *She balanced the cup on her knee.*

▸ BE/KEEP EQUAL **2** [I, T] to be equal in value, amount, etc. to something else that has the opposite effect **SYN** OFFSET: **~ out** *The good and bad effects of any decision will usually balance out.* ◆ **~ sth (out)** *This year's profits will balance our previous losses.* ◆ *His lack of experience was balanced by a willingness to learn.* **3** [T] **~ A with/and B** to give equal importance to two contrasting things or parts of something: *She tries to balance home life and career.*

▸ COMPARE **4** [T] **~ A against B** to compare the relative importance of two contrasting things: *The cost of obtaining legal advice needs to be balanced against its benefits.*

▸ MONEY **5** [T] **~ sth** (*finance*) to show that in an account the total money spent is equal to the total money received; to calculate the difference between the two totals

balance ˌbeam *noun* a wooden bar that is used in the sport of GYMNASTICS for people to move and balance on

bal·anced /ˈbælənst/ *adj.* [usually before noun] (*approving*) keeping or showing a balance so that different things or different parts of something exist in equal or correct amounts: *The program presented a balanced view of the two sides of the conflict.* ◆ *a balanced diet* (= one with the quantity and variety of food needed for good health)

balance of ˈpayments *noun* [sing.] the difference between the amount a country pays for imports and the amount it receives for exports in a particular period of time

balance of ˈpower *noun* [sing.] **1** a situation in which political or military strength is divided between two countries or groups of countries: *a commitment to maintaining the balance of power in Europe* ⟳ collocations at INTERNATIONAL **2** the power held by a small group that can give its support to either of two larger and equally strong groups: *With 18% of the votes, the Independents could* **hold the balance of power** *in the House.*

balance of ˈtrade (also **ˈtrade ˌbalance**) *noun* [sing.] the difference in value between imports and exports: *a balance-of-trade deficit* (= when a country spends more on imports than it earns from exports)

balance ˌsheet *noun* (*finance*) a written statement showing the amount of money and property that a company has and listing what has been received and paid out

balancing ˌact *noun* a process in which one tries to please two or more people or groups who want different things: *The UN must perform a delicate balancing act between the different sides in the conflict.*

bal·co·ny /ˈbælkəni/ *noun* (*pl.* **bal·co·nies**) **1** a platform that is built on the upstairs outside wall of a building, with a wall or rail around it. You can get out onto a balcony from an upstairs room. ⟳ picture at HOUSE **2** an area of seats upstairs in a theater ⟳ compare CIRCLE ⟳ see also FIRST BALCONY

bald /bɔld/ *adj.* **1** having little or no hair on the head: *He started* **going bald** *in his twenties.* **2** without any of the usual hair, marks, etc. covering the skin or surface of something: *Our dog has a bald patch on its leg.* ◆ *a bald tire* (= a tire whose surface has become smooth) **3** without any extra explanation or detail to help you understand or accept what is being said: *The bald truth is that we don't need you any longer.* ◆ *The letter was a bald statement of our legal position.* ⟳ see also BALDLY ⟳ picture at HAIR ▶ **bald·ness** *noun* [U]

bald ˈeagle *noun* a N. American BIRD OF PREY (= a bird that kills other creatures for food) with a white head and white tail feathers. It is used as a symbol of the U.S. ⟳ picture at ANIMAL

bal·der·dash /ˈbɔldərˌdæʃ/ *noun* [U] (*old-fashioned*) nonsense

bald-faced *adj.* (*disapproving*) making no attempt to hide your dishonest behavior **SYN** BAREFACED, BLATANT: *bald-faced lies*

bald·ing /ˈbɔldɪŋ/ *adj.* starting to lose the hair on your head: *a short balding man with glasses*

bald·ly /ˈbɔldli/ *adv.* in a few words with nothing extra or unnecessary: *"You're lying," he said baldly.*

bald·y (also **bald·ie**) /ˈbɔldi/ *noun* (*pl.* **bald·ies**) (*informal*) a person who has no hair or almost no hair on their head

bale /beɪl/ *noun, verb*
• *noun* a large amount of a light material pressed tightly together and tied up: *bales of hay/straw/cotton/wool*
• *verb* **~ sth** to make something into bales: *The waste paper is baled, then used for recycling.*

bale·ful /ˈbeɪlfl/ *adj.* (*literary*) threatening to do something evil or to hurt someone: *a baleful look/influence* ▶ **bale·ful·ly** /-fəli/ *adv.*

bal·er /ˈbeɪlər/ *noun* a machine for making paper, cotton, HAY, etc. into BALES

balk /bɔk/ *verb* **1** [I] **~ (at sth)** to be unwilling to do something or become involved in something because it is difficult, dangerous, etc.: *Many parents may balk at the idea of paying $100 for a pair of shoes.* **2** [I] **~ (at sth)** (of a horse) to stop suddenly and refuse to jump a fence, etc. **3** [T] **~ sb (of sth)** [usually passive] (*formal*) to prevent someone from getting something or doing something: *She looked like a lion balked of its prey.*

Bal·kan·ize /ˈbɔlkəˌnaɪz/ *verb* **~ sth** to divide a region into smaller regions that are unfriendly or aggressive toward each other ▶ **Bal·kan·i·za·tion** /ˌbɔlkənəˈzeɪʃn/ *noun* [U]

the Bal·kans /ˈbɔlkənz/ *noun* [pl.] a region of S.E. Europe, including the countries to the south of the rivers Sava and Danube ▶ **Bal·kan** *adj.*: *the Balkan Peninsula*

balk·y /ˈbɔki/ *adj.* (of a person or machine) refusing or failing to do what you want them to do

ball /bɔl/ *noun, verb*
• *noun* **1** a round object used for throwing, hitting, or kicking in games and sports: *a golf/tennis/soccer ball* ◆ *Bounce the ball and try to hit it over the net.* ⟳ picture at SPORT **2** a round object or an object that has been formed into a round shape: *The sun was a huge ball of fire low on the horizon.* ◆ *a ball of string* ◆ *Some animals roll themselves into a ball for protection.* **3** a kick, hit, or throw of the ball in some sports: *He hit a foul ball.* **4** (in baseball) a throw by the PITCHER that is outside the STRIKE ZONE (= the area between the BATTER's upper arms and knees) **5 ~ of the**

foot/hand the part underneath the big toe or the thumb **6** a large formal party with dancing

IDM a ball and chain a problem that prevents you from doing what you would like to do **the ball is in your/sb's court** it is your/someone's responsibility to take action next: *They've offered me the job, so the ball's in my court now.* **a ball of fire** (*informal*) a person who is full of energy and enthusiasm **get/set/start/keep the ball rolling** to make something start happening; to make sure that something continues to happen **have a ball** (*informal*) to enjoy yourself a lot **have something/a lot on the ball** (*informal*) to be capable of doing a job very well; to be intelligent **(be) on the ball** to be aware of and understand what is happening and able to react quickly: *The new publicity manager is really on the ball.* **pick up/take the ball and run with it** to develop an idea or plan that already exists: *It's up to the private sector to take the ball and run with it.* **play ball (with sb)** **1** to play with a ball: *Chris was in the park playing ball with the kids.* **2** (*informal*) to be willing to work with other people in a helpful way, especially so that someone can get what they want **the whole ball of wax** (*informal*) the whole thing; everything: *I panicked, I cried—the whole ball of wax.* ⊃ more at CARRY, DROP *v.*, EYE *n.*

- **verb** [I, T] to form something or be formed into the shape of a ball: **~ (into sth)** *Her hands balled into fists.* ◆ **~ sth (into sth)** *My hands were balled into fists.*

bal·lad /'bæləd/ *noun* **1** a song or poem that tells a story: *a medieval ballad about a knight and a lady* **2** a slow song about love: *Her latest single is a ballad.* ⊃ collocations at MUSIC

bal·lad·eer /ˌbælə'dɪr/ *noun* a person who sings or writes ballads

ball-and-'socket ˌjoint
noun (*anatomy*) a joint such as the hip joint, in which a ball-shaped part moves inside a curved hollow part

ball-and-socket joint

bal·last /'bæləst/ *noun* [U] **1** heavy material placed in a ship or HOT-AIR BALLOON to make it heavier and keep it steady **2** a layer of stones that makes a strong base on which a road, railroad, etc. can be built

ball ˈbearing *noun* a ring of small metal balls used in a machine to enable the parts to turn smoothly; one of these small metal balls

ball bearing

ball boy *noun* a boy who picks up the balls for the players in a TENNIS match ⊃ see also BALL GIRL

ball cock *noun* a device with a floating ball that controls the amount of water going into a con-tainer, for example the water tank of a toilet

bal·le·ri·na /ˌbælə'rinə/ *noun* a female dancer in BALLET ⊃ see also PRIMA BALLERINA

bal·let /bæ'leɪ/ *noun* **1** [U] a style of dancing that tells a dramatic story with music but no talking or singing: *She wants to be a ballet dancer.* ◆ *ballet shoes* **2** [C] a story or work of art performed by a group of ballet dancers: *"Swan Lake" is one of the great classical ballets.* **3** [C] a group of dancers who work and perform ballet together: *members of the New York City Ballet*

bal·let·ic /bæ'lɛtɪk/ *adj.* (*formal, approving*) smooth and elegant, like a movement or a dancer in ballet: *The first symphony had a balletic slow movement.*

ˈball game *noun* **1** any game played with a ball **2** a game of baseball: *Are you going to the ball game?*

IDM a (whole) different/new ball game (*informal*) a completely different kind of situation

ˈball girl *noun* a girl who picks up the balls for the players in a TENNIS match ⊃ see also BALL BOY

ball·hawk /'bɔlhɔk/ *noun* (*informal*) a player who is good at getting or catching balls, especially in football, baseball, or basketball

bal·lis·tic /bə'lɪstɪk/ *adj.* connected with ballistics
IDM go ballistic (*informal*) to become very angry: *He went ballistic when I told him.*

bal,listic 'missile *noun* a MISSILE that is fired into the air at a particular speed and angle in order to fall in the right place

bal·lis·tics /bə'lɪstɪks/ *noun* [U] the scientific study of things that are shot or fired through the air, such as bullets and MISSILES

bal·loon /bə'lun/ *noun, verb*
- **noun 1** a small bag made of very thin rubber that becomes larger and rounder when you fill it with air or gas. Balloons are brightly colored and used as decorations or toys: *to blow up/pop a balloon* ⊃ compare TRIAL BALLOON **2** = HOT-AIR BALLOON **IDM** see LEAD²
- **verb 1** [I] **~ (out/up)** to suddenly swell out or get bigger: *Her skirt ballooned out in the wind.* **2** [I] usually **go balloon-ing** to travel in a HOT-AIR BALLOON as a sport

bal·loon·ist /bə'lunɪst/ *noun* a person who travels in a balloon as a sport

bal'loon ˌwhisk *noun* a WHISK that you hold in your hand, made of thin pieces of curved wire

bal·lot /'bælət/ *noun, verb*
- **noun 1** [U, C] the system of voting in writing and usually in secret; an occasion on which a vote is held: *The chairperson is chosen by secret ballot.* ◆ *next year's primary ballot* ⊃ thesaurus box at ELECTION ⊃ collocations at VOTE ⊃ see also ABSENTEE BALLOT **2** [C] the piece of paper on which someone marks who they are voting for: *What percentage of eligible voters cast their ballots?* **3** the ballot [sing.] the total number of votes in an election: *She won 58.8% of the ballot.*
- **verb 1** [T] **~ sb (on sth)** to ask someone to vote in writing and secretly about something **SYN** POLL: *The union balloted its members on the proposed changes.* **2** [I] to vote secretly about something: *The workers balloted for a strike.*

ˈballot ˌbox *noun* **1** [C] a box in which people put their ballot after voting **2** the ballot box [sing.] the system of voting in an election: *The people make their wishes known through the ballot box.*

ball·park /'bɔlpɑrk/ *noun* **1** [C] a place where baseball is played **2** [sing.] an area or a range within which an amount is likely to be correct or something can be measured: *The offers for the contract were all in the same ballpark.* ◆ *If you said five million, you'd be in the ballpark.* ◆ *Give me a ballpark figure* (= a number that is approximately right).

ball·play·er /'bɔlˌpleɪər/ *noun* (*informal*) a person who plays baseball, especially a professional

ball·point /'bɔlpɔɪnt/ (also ˌballpoint 'pen) *noun* a pen with a very small metal ball at its point that rolls ink onto the paper ⊃ picture at STATIONERY

ball·room /'bɔlrum; -rʊm/ *noun* a very large room used for dancing on formal occasions ⊃ compare DANCE HALL

ˌballroom 'dancing *noun* [U] a type of dancing done with a partner and using particular fixed steps and movements to particular types of music such as the WALTZ

bal·ly·hoo /'bæli,hu; ˌbæli'hu/ *noun* [U] (*informal, disapproving*) unnecessary noise and excitement

balm /bɑm/ *noun* [U, C, usually sing.] **1** (also bal·sam) oil with a pleasant smell that is obtained from some types of trees and plants, used in the past to help heal wounds, for example **2** a liquid, cream, etc. that has a pleasant smell and is used to make wounds less painful or skin softer: *lip balm* **3** (*literary*) something that makes you feel calm or relaxed

balm·y /ˈbɑmi/ *adj.* (*approving*) (of the air, weather, etc.) warm and pleasant **SYN** MILD: *a balmy summer evening*

ba·lo·ney /bəˈlouni/ *noun* [U] **1** (*informal*) nonsense; lies: *Don't give me that baloney!* **2** = BOLOGNA

bal·sa /ˈbɔlsə/ (also ˈbalsa ˌwood) *noun* [U] the light wood of the tropical American **balsa tree**, used especially for making models

bal·sam /ˈbɔlsəm/ *noun* **1** [U, C] = BALM **2** [C] any plant or tree from which BALM is obtained

bal·sam·ic vin·e·gar /ˌbɔlˌsæmɪk ˈvɪnɪgər/ *noun* [U] a dark sweet Italian VINEGAR, stored in BARRELS (= round wooden containers) to give it flavor

Bal·tic /ˈbɔltɪk/ *adj.* relating to the Baltic Sea in northern Europe and the countries surrounding it: *the Baltic republics of Estonia, Latvia, and Lithuania*

bal·us·ter /ˈbæləstər/ *noun* any of the short posts that form a balustrade

bal·us·trade /ˈbæləˌstreɪd/ *noun* a row of posts, joined together at the top, built along the edge of a BALCONY, bridge, etc. to prevent people from falling off, or as a decoration

bam /bæm/ *exclamation* (*informal*) **1** used to represent the sound of a sudden loud hit or a gun being fired: *She pointed the gun at him and—bam!* **2** used to show that something happens very suddenly: *I saw him yesterday and—bam!—I realized I was still in love with him.*

bam·boo /ˌbæmˈbu/ *noun* [C, U] (*pl.* **bam·boos**) a tall tropical plant that is a member of the grass family and has hard hollow STEMS that are used for making furniture, poles, etc.: *a bamboo grove* ♦ *a bamboo chair* ♦ *bamboo shoots* (= young bamboo plants that can be eaten) ➔ picture at PLANT

bam·boo·zle /bæmˈbuzl/ *verb* ~ **sb** (*informal*) to confuse someone, especially by tricking them

ban ⚘ /bæn/ *verb, noun*
- *verb* (-nn-) **1** ~ **sth** to decide or say officially that something is not allowed **SYN** PROHIBIT: *Chemical weapons are banned internationally.* **2** [usually passive] to order someone not to do something, go somewhere, etc., especially officially: ~ **sb from sth** *He was banned from the meeting.* ♦ ~ **sb from doing sth** *She's been banned from leaving Texas while the allegations are investigated.*
- *noun* ~ (**on sth**) an official rule that says that something is not allowed: *There is to be a total ban on smoking in the office.* ♦ *to impose/lift a ban*

ba·nal /bəˈnæl; bəˈnɑl; ˈbeɪnl/ *adj.* (*disapproving*) very ordinary and containing nothing that is interesting or important

ba·nal·i·ty /bəˈnæləti/ *noun* (*pl.* **ba·nal·i·ties**) [U, C] (*disapproving*) the quality of being banal; things, remarks, etc. that are banal: *the banality of modern city life* ♦ *They exchanged banalities for a couple of minutes.*

ba·nan·a /bəˈnænə/ *noun* a long curved fruit with a thick yellow skin and soft flesh, that grows on trees in hot countries: *a bunch of bananas* ➔ picture at FRUIT ➔ see also SECOND BANANA, TOP BANANA

baˈnana ˌbelt *noun* (*informal*) a region where the weather is warm

baˌnana reˈpublic *noun* (*disapproving, offensive*) a poor country with a weak government, that depends on foreign money

ba·nan·as /bəˈnænəz/ *adj.* (*slang*) angry, crazy, or silly: *He lost his job and just went bananas.* ➔ thesaurus box at CRAZY

baˌnana ˈsplit *noun* a cold DESSERT (= a sweet dish) made from a BANANA that is cut in half along its length and filled with ice cream, nuts, etc.

band ⚘ /bænd/ *noun, verb*
- *noun*
> GROUP OF MUSICIANS **1** a small group of musicians who play popular music together, often with a singer or singers: *a rock/jazz band* ♦ *She's a singer with a band.* ➔ see also BOY BAND, GIRL BAND **2** a group of musicians who play BRASS and PERCUSSION instruments: *a military band* ➔ see also BRASS BAND, MARCHING BAND, ONE-MAN BAND
> GROUP OF PEOPLE **3** a group of people who do something together or who have the same ideas: *a band of outlaws* ♦ *He persuaded a small band of volunteers to help.*
> STRIP OF MATERIAL/COLOR **4** a thin flat strip or circle of any material that is put around things, for example to hold them together or to make them stronger: *She always ties her hair back in a band.* ♦ *All babies in the hospital have name bands on their wrists.* ♦ *She wore a simple band of gold on her finger.* ➔ see also ARMBAND, HAIRBAND, HATBAND, RUBBER BAND, SWEATBAND, WAISTBAND **5** a strip of color or material on something that is different from what is around it: *a white plate with a blue band around the edge*
> OF RADIO WAVES **6** (also ˈwave·band) a range of radio waves: *channels in the UHF band*
- *verb*
> WITH COLOR/MATERIAL [usually passive] **be banded** (+ adj.) to put a band of a different color or material around something: *Many insects are banded with black and yellow.* **PHR V** ˌband toˈgether to form a group in order to achieve something: *Local people banded together to fight the drug dealers.*

band·age ⚘ /ˈbændɪdʒ/ *noun, verb*
- *noun* a strip of cloth used for covering or tying around a part of the body that has been hurt in order to protect or support it
- *verb* ~ **sth** (**up**) to wrap a bandage around a part of the body in order to protect it because it is injured ➔ collocations at INJURY

ˈBand–Aid™ *noun* **1** a small bandage that can be stuck to the skin to protect a small wound or cut **2** (*disapproving*) a temporary solution to a problem that does not really solve it at all

ban·dan·na /bænˈdænə/ *noun* a piece of brightly colored cloth worn around the neck or head

ban·deau /bænˈdou/ *noun* **1** a narrow band worn around the head to hold the hair in place **2** a piece of women's clothing that is tied around the body to cover the breasts: *a bandeau bikini top*

ban·di·coot /ˈbændɪˌkut/ *noun* **1** a small Australasian animal with a long nose and long tail, that eats mainly insects **2** (also ˌbandicoot ˈrat) an Asian RAT

ban·dit /ˈbændət/ *noun* a member of an armed group of thieves who attack travelers

ban·di·to /bænˈditou; bænˈdidou/ (also **ban·di·do**) *noun* (*pl.* **ban·di·tos**) (from *Spanish*) a Mexican BANDIT

ban·dit·ry /ˈbændətri/ *noun* [U] (*formal*) acts of stealing and violence by bandits

band·lead·er /ˈbændˌlidər/ *noun* a player who is in charge of a band, especially a JAZZ band

band·mas·ter /ˈbændˌmæstər/ *noun* a person who CONDUCTS a military or BRASS band

ban·do·lier (also **ban·do·leer**) /ˌbændəˈlɪr/ *noun* a belt made for carrying bullets and worn over the shoulder

bands·man /ˈbændzmən/ *noun* (*pl.* **bands·men** /-mən/) a musician who plays in a military or BRASS band

band·stand /ˈbændstænd/ *noun* a covered platform outdoors, where musicians, especially a BRASS or military band, can stand and play

band·wag·on /ˈbændˌwægən/ *noun* [usually sing.] an activity that more and more people are becoming involved in: *The World Cup bandwagon is starting to roll.* **IDM** climb/jump on the bandwagon (*informal, disapproving*) to join others in doing something that is becoming fashionable because you hope to become popular or successful yourself: *politicians eager to jump on the environmental bandwagon* **ORIGIN** In the U.S., political PARADES often included a band on a wagon. Political leaders would join them in the hope of winning popular support.

band·width /ˈbændwɪdθ; -wɪtθ/ *noun* [C, U] (*computing*) **1** a band of frequencies (FREQUENCY) used for sending electronic signals **2** a measurement of the amount of information that a particular computer network or Internet connection can send in a particular time. It is often measured in BITS per second.

ban·dy /ˈbændi/ *adj., verb*
● *adj.* (of the legs) curving, with the knees wide apart: *a bandy-legged teenager*
● *verb* (ban·dies, ban·dy·ing, ban·died, ban·died)
IDM **bandy words (with sb)** (*old-fashioned*) to argue with someone or speak rudely to them
PHR V ˌbandy sth↔aˈbout/aˈround [usually passive] if a name, a word, a story, etc. is **bandied about/around**, it is mentioned frequently by many people: *His name was being bandied about as a future mayor.*

bane /beɪn/ *noun* [sing.] **the ~ of sb/sth** something that causes trouble and makes people unhappy: *The neighbors' kids are the **bane of my existence**.*

bane·ful /ˈbeɪnfl/ *adj.* (*literary*) evil or causing evil

bang /bæŋ/ *verb, noun, adv., exclamation*
● *verb* **1** [I, T] to hit something in a way that makes a loud noise: **~ on sth** *She banged on the door angrily.* ◆ **~ sth (with sth)** *The baby was banging the table with his spoon.* ⊃ thesaurus box at HIT **2** [I, T] to close something or to be closed with a loud noise **SYN** SLAM: *A window was banging somewhere* (= opening and closing noisily). ◆ **+ adj.** *The door banged shut behind her.* ◆ **~ sth** *Don't bang the door when you go out!* **3** [T] **~ sth + adv./prep.** to put something somewhere suddenly and violently **SYN** SLAM: *He banged the money down on the counter.* ◆ *She banged saucepans around irritably.* **4** [T] **~ sth (+ adv./prep.)** to hit something, especially a part of the body, against something by accident **SYN** BUMP: *She tripped and banged her knee on the desk.* **IDM** see DRUM *n.*, HEAD *n.*
PHR V ˌbang /aˈround to move around noisily: *We could hear the kids banging around upstairs.* ˌbang ˈinto sth to crash into or hit something by mistake: *I banged into a chair and hurt my leg.* ˌbang sth↔ˈup (*informal*) to damage or injure something
● *noun* **1** a sudden loud noise: *The door swung shut with a bang.* ◆ *Suddenly there was a loud bang and a puff of smoke.* ⊃ see also BIG BANG **2** a sudden painful blow on a part of the body: *a bang on the head* **3 bangs** [pl.] the front part of someone's hair that is cut so that it hangs over their FOREHEAD ⊃ picture at HAIR **4** (*informal, computing*) the symbol (!)
IDM **bang for your buck** (*informal*) if you get more, better, etc. **bang for your buck**, you get better value for the money you spend or the effort you put in to something **with a bang** (*informal*) **1** very successfully: *The party went off with a bang.* **2** in a way that everyone notices; with a powerful effect: *The team won their last four games, ending the season with a bang.* ⊃ more at EARTH
● *adv.*
IDM **go bang** (*informal*) to burst or explode with a loud noise; to make a sudden loud noise: *A balloon suddenly went bang.* ⊃ see also SLAP *adv.*
● *exclamation* used to show the sound of something loud, like a gun: *"Bang, bang, you're dead!" shouted the little boy.*

ˌbanged ˈup *adj.* (*informal*) injured or damaged: *Two days after the accident she still looked pretty banged up.*

Bangla /ˈbɑŋglə; ˈbæŋglə/ *noun* [U] **1** the Bengali language **2** Bangladesh

ban·gle /ˈbæŋgl/ *noun* a piece of jewelry in the form of a large ring of gold, silver, etc. worn loosely around the wrist ⊃ picture at JEWELRY

ˈbang-up *adj.* (*informal*) very good

ban·ish /ˈbænɪʃ/ *verb* **1** [usually passive] **~ sb (from…) (to…)** to order someone to leave a place, especially a country, as a punishment **SYN** EXILE: *He was banished to Australia, where he died five years later.* ◆ *The children were banished from the dining room.* **2 ~ sb/sth (from sth)** to make someone or something go away; to get rid of someone or something: *The sight of food banished all other thoughts from my mind.*

ban·ish·ment /ˈbænɪʃmənt/ *noun* [U] the punishment of being sent away from a place, especially from a country

ban·is·ter (also **ban·nis·ter**) /ˈbænəstər/ *noun* the posts and rail that you can hold for support when going up or down stairs: *to hold on to the banister*

ban·jo /ˈbændʒoʊ/ *noun* (*pl.* **ban·jos**) a musical instrument like a GUITAR, with a long neck, a round body, and four or more strings ⊃ picture at INSTRUMENT

bank 🔑 /bæŋk/ *noun, verb*
● *noun*
▷ FOR MONEY **1** an organization that provides various financial services, for example keeping or lending money: *My salary is paid directly into my bank.* ◆ *I need to go to the bank* (= the local office of a bank). ◆ *a bank loan* ◆ see also COMMERCIAL BANK, INVESTMENT BANK, SAVINGS BANK
▷ IN GAMBLING **2** a supply of money or things that are used as money in some games, especially those in which gambling is involved
▷ SOMETHING COLLECTED/STORED **3** an amount of something that is collected; a place where something is stored ready for use: *a bank of knowledge* ◆ *a blood/sperm bank* ⊃ see also DATA BANK
▷ OF RIVER/CANAL **4** the side of a river, CANAL, etc. and the land near it: *He jumped in and swam to the opposite bank.* ◆ *It's on the north bank of Lake Michigan.* ◆ *a house on the banks of the Mississippi River* (= on land near the river)
▷ SLOPE **5** a raised area of ground that slopes at the sides, often at the edge of something or dividing something: *There were low banks of earth between the rice fields.* ◆ *The girls ran down the steep grassy bank.* **6** an artificial slope built at the side of a road, so that cars can drive fast around bends
▷ OF CLOUD/SNOW, ETC. **7** a mass of cloud, snow, etc., especially one formed by the wind: *The sun disappeared behind a bank of clouds.*
▷ OF MACHINES, ETC. **8** a row or series of similar objects, especially machines: *a bank of lights/switches/computers*
IDM **not break the bank** (*informal, humorous*) if you say something **won't break the bank**, you mean that it won't cost a lot of money, or more than you can afford ⊃ more at LAUGH *v.*
● *verb*
▷ MONEY **1** [T] **~ sth** to put money into a bank account: *She is believed to have banked* (= been paid) *$10 million in two years.* **2** [I] **~ (with/at…)** to have an account with a particular bank: *The family has banked with First National for generations.*
▷ OF PLANE **3** [I] to travel with one side higher than the other when turning: *The plane banked steeply to the left.*
▷ FORM PILES **4** [T] **~ sth (up)** to form something into piles: *They banked the earth (up) into a mound.*
▷ A FIRE **5** [T] **~ sth (up)** to pile coal, etc. on a fire so that the fire burns slowly for a long time: *The fire was banked up to last throughout the night.*
PHR V ˈbank on sb/sth to rely on someone or something: *I'm banking on your help.* ◆ *"I'm sure he'll help." "Don't bank on it* (= it is not likely to happen).*"* ◆ **~ sb to do sth** *I'm banking on you to help me.* ◆ **~ doing sth** *I was banking on getting something to eat on the train.* ˌbank ˈup to form into piles, especially because of the wind: *The snow had banked up against the wall.*

bank·a·ble /ˈbæŋkəbl/ *adj.* (*informal*) likely to make money for someone: *The movie's success has made her one of the world's most bankable stars.*

ˈbank acˌcount *noun* an arrangement that you have with a bank that allows you to keep your money there, to pay in or take out money, etc.: *to open/close a bank account*

ˈbank ˌbalance *noun* the amount of money that someone has in their bank account at a particular time

ʌ **cup**   ə **about**   eɪ **say**   aɪ **five**   ɔɪ **boy**   aʊ **now**   oʊ **go**   ər **bird**

'bank card *noun* a plastic card provided by your bank that may be used as a CREDIT CARD or DEBIT CARD or to get money from your account out of a machine

'bank draft *noun* a check paid by a bank to another bank or to a particular person or organization

bank·er /'bæŋkər/ *noun* **1** a person who owns a bank or has an important job at a bank: *an investment banker* **2** a person who is in charge of the money in particular games

bank·ing /'bæŋkɪŋ/ *noun* [U] the business activity of banks: *She's thinking about a career in banking.*

bank ma,chine *noun* (*CanE*) = CASH MACHINE

bank·note /'bæŋknoʊt/ *noun* a piece of paper money **SYN** BILL *n.* (2): *forged* (= illegally copied) *banknotes*

'bank rate *noun* the rate of interest charged by a bank for lending money, which is fixed by a central bank in a country

bank·roll /'bæŋkroʊl/ *verb, noun*
• *verb* ~ sb/sth (*informal*) to support someone or something by giving money **SYN** FINANCE: *They claimed his campaign had been bankrolled with dirty money.*
• *noun* a supply of money: *He is the candidate with the biggest campaign bankroll.*

bank·rupt /'bæŋkrʌpt/ *adj., noun, verb*
• *adj.* **1** without enough money to pay what you owe **SYN** INSOLVENT: *They went bankrupt in 2009.* ◆ *The company was declared bankrupt by the court.* **2** ~ (of sth) (*formal, disapproving*) completely lacking in anything that has value: *a government bankrupt of new ideas* ◆ *a society that is morally bankrupt*
• *noun* (*law*) a person who has been judged by a court to be unable to pay his or her debts
• *verb* ~ sb to make someone bankrupt: *The company was almost bankrupted by legal costs.*

bank·rupt·cy /'bæŋkrəptsi; -rəpsi/ *noun* [U, C] (*pl.* bank·rupt·cies) the state of being bankrupt: *The company filed for bankruptcy* (= asked to be officially declared bankrupt) *in 2009.* ◆ *moral/political bankruptcy* ◆ *There could be further bankruptcies among small farmers.* ➔ collocations at BUSINESS

'bank ,statement (also state·ment) *noun* a printed record of all the money paid into and out of a customer's bank account within a particular period

ban·ner /'bænər/ *noun* a long piece of cloth with a message on it that is carried between two poles or hung in a public place to show support for something: *Protesters carried a banner reading "Save our Wildlife."*

banner ,ad *noun* an advertisement across the top or bottom or down the side of a page on the Internet

banner 'headline *noun* a line of words printed in large letters across the front page of a newspaper

banner 'year *noun* a year in which something is especially successful

ban·nis·ter = BANISTER

ban·quet /'bæŋkwət/ *noun* **1** a formal meal for a large number of people, usually for a special occasion, at which speeches are often made: *a state banquet in honor of the visiting president* **2** a large impressive meal

ban·quette /bæŋ'kɛt/ *noun* a long soft seat along a wall in a restaurant, etc.

ban·shee /'bænʃi/ *noun* (in Irish stories) a female spirit who gives a long sad cry as a warning to people that someone in their family is going to die soon

ban·tam /'bæntəm/ *noun* a type of small chicken

ban·tam·weight /'bæntəm,weɪt/ *noun* a BOXER weighing between 112 and 118 pounds (51-53.5 kg), or a WRESTLER who weighs between 114 and 125 pounds (52-57 kg): *a bantamweight champion* ➔ compare FEATHERWEIGHT, FLY-WEIGHT

ban·ter /'bæntər/ *noun, verb*
• *noun* [U] friendly remarks and jokes: *He enjoyed exchanging banter with the customers.*
• *verb* [I] ~ (with sb) to joke with someone: *He bantered with reporters and posed for photographers.*

ban·ter·ing /'bæntərɪŋ/ *adj.* (of a way of talking) amusing and friendly: *There was a friendly, bantering tone in his voice.*

ban·yan /'bænyən/ (also 'banyan ,tree) *noun* a S. Asian tree with structures that grow down from the branches to the ground and then grow into new roots and TRUNKS

ba·o·bab /'beɪoʊ,bæb; 'baʊbæb/ *noun* a short thick tree, found especially in Africa and Australia, that lives for many years

bap·tism /'bæptɪzəm/ *noun* a Christian ceremony in which a few drops of water are poured on someone or they are covered with water, to welcome them into the Christian Church and often to name them ➔ compare CHRISTENING **IDM** a baptism of fire a difficult introduction to a new job or activity

bap·tis·mal /bæp'tɪzməl/ *adj.* [only before noun] connected with baptism: *a baptismal service/ceremony*

Bap·tist /'bæptɪst/ *noun* a member of a Christian Protestant Church that believes that baptism should take place when a person is old enough to understand what it means, and not as a baby ► **Bap·tist** *adj.* [usually before noun]: *a Baptist church*

bap·tize /'bæptaɪz; bæp'taɪz/ *verb* [usually passive] ~ sb (+ noun) to give someone BAPTISM: *She was baptized Mary.* ◆ *I was baptized a Catholic.* ➔ see also CHRISTEN

bar /bɑr/ *noun, verb, prep.*
• *noun*
> **FOR DRINKS/FOOD 1** [C] a place where you can buy and drink alcoholic and other drinks: *We met at a bar called the Flamingo.* ◆ *the island's only bar* ◆ *a cocktail bar* ➔ see also BARROOM, MINIBAR **2** [C] a long wide wooden surface where drinks, etc. are served: *She was sitting at the bar.* ◆ *It was so crowded I couldn't get to the bar.* **3** [C] (especially in compounds) a place in which a particular kind of food or drink is the main thing that is served: *a sandwich bar* ◆ *a salad bar* ◆ *a coffee bar* ➔ see also OXYGEN BAR, RAW BAR, SNACK BAR, WINE BAR
> **OF CHOCOLATE/SOAP 4** [C] a piece of something with straight sides: *a bar of chocolate/soap* ◆ *candy bars*
> **OF METAL/WOOD 5** [C] a long straight piece of metal or wood. Bars are often used to stop someone from getting through a space: *He smashed the window with an iron bar.* ◆ *All the ground-floor windows had bars on them.* ◆ *a five-bar gate* (= one made with five horizontal bars of wood) ➔ see also ROLL BAR, SPACE BAR, TOW BAR
> **OF COLOR/LIGHT 6** [C] a band of color or light: *Bars of sunlight slanted down from the tall narrow windows.*
> **THAT PREVENTS SOMETHING 7** [C, usually sing.] ~ (to sth) a

bars

drinks bar

salad bar

five-bar gate

bars on a window

bar of chocolate

bar of soap

bar code

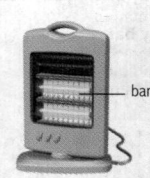

bars on an electric fire

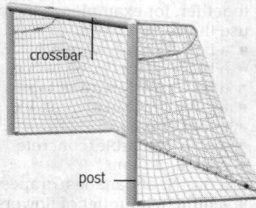

crossbar of a goal

thing that stops someone from doing something: *At that time being a woman was a bar to promotion in most professions.* ⊃ see also COLOR BAR
> IN MUSIC **8** (also **meas·ure**) [C] one of the short sections of equal length that a piece of music is divided into, and the notes that are in it: *four beats to the bar* ◆ *the opening bars of a piece of music*
> LAW **9** the bar [sing.] the profession of any kind of lawyer: *to be admitted to the bar* (= allowed to work as a lawyer) ◆ *You need to pass the bar if you really want to practice law.* ◆ *He is a member of the Georgia State Bar.* ⊃ note at LAWYER
> MEASUREMENT **10** [C] a unit for measuring the pressure of the atmosphere, equal to a hundred thousand NEWTONS per square meter ⊃ see also MILLIBAR
> IN SPORTS **11** the bar [sing.] the CROSSBAR of a goal: *His shot hit the bar.*
  IDM **behind bars** (*informal*) in prison: *The murderer is now safely behind bars.* **set the bar** to set a standard of quality or performance: *The show really sets the bar for artistic invention.* ⊃ more at LOWER¹, RAISE v.
● *verb* (-rr-)
> CLOSE WITH BARS **1** [usually passive] ~ sth to close something with a bar or bars: *All the doors and windows were barred.*
> BLOCK **2** ~ sth to block a road, path, etc. so that no one can

pass: *Two police officers were barring her exit.* ◆ *We found our way barred by rocks.*
> PREVENT **3** ~ sb (from sth/from doing sth) to ban or prevent someone from doing something: *Asylum seekers are barred from entering the country.* IDM see HOLD n.
● *prep.* except for someone or something: *The students all attended, bar two who were sick.* ◆ *It's the best result we've ever had, bar none* (= none was better).

barb /bɑrb/ *noun* **1** the point of an arrow or a hook that is curved backward to make it difficult to pull out **2** a remark that is meant to hurt someone's feelings ⊃ see also BARBED

bar·bar·i·an /bɑrˈbɛriən/ *noun* **1** a person who behaves very badly and has no respect for art, education, etc. **2** a person long ago in the past who belonged to a European people which was considered wild and UNCIVILIZED: *barbarian invasions of the fifth century*

bar·bar·ic /bɑrˈbærɪk; -ˈbɛrɪk/ *adj.* **1** cruel and violent, and not as expected from people who are educated and respect each other: *a barbaric act/custom/ritual* ◆ *The way these animals are killed is barbaric.* **2** connected with barbarians ▸ **bar·bar·i·cally** /-kli/ *adv.*

bar·ba·rism /ˈbɑrbəˌrɪzəm/ *noun* [U] **1** a state of not having any education, respect for art, etc. **2** cruel or violent behavior: *the barbarism of war*

bar·bar·i·ty /bɑrˈbærəti; -ˈbɛr-/ *noun* (*pl.* **bar·bar·i·ties**) [U, C] behavior that deliberately causes extreme pain or suffering to others

bar·ba·rous /ˈbɑrbərəs/ *adj.* (*formal*) **1** extremely cruel and shocking: *the barbarous treatment of these prisoners of war* **2** showing a lack of education and good manners ▸ **bar·ba·rous·ly** *adv.*

bar·be·cue /ˈbɑrbɪˌkyu/ *noun, verb*
● *noun* (*abbr.* BBQ) **1** a metal frame for cooking food on over an open fire outdoors: *I put another steak on the barbecue.* ◆ *barbecue ribs* (= cooked in this way) ⊃ picture at COOKING **2** an outdoor meal or party when food is cooked in this way: *Let's have a barbecue!* ⊃ compare COOKOUT
● *verb* [T, I] ~ (sth) to cook food on a barbecue ⊃ compare BROIL

barbecue ˌsauce *noun* [C, U] a spicy sauce served with food that has been cooked on a barbecue

barbed /bɑrbd/ *adj.* **1** (of an ARROW or a hook) having a point that is curved backward (called a BARB) **2** (of a remark or comment) meant to hurt someone's feelings

barbed ˈwire *noun* [U] strong wire with short sharp points on it, used especially for fences: *a barbed-wire fence*

barbed wire

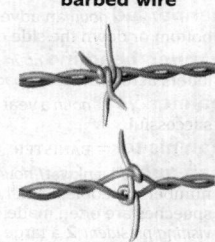

bar·bell /ˈbɑrbɛl/ *noun* a long metal bar with weights at each end, used in the sport of WEIGHTLIFTING and for exercise ⊃ picture at EXERCISE

bar·ber /ˈbɑrbər/ *noun* a person whose job is to cut men's hair and sometimes to shave them ⊃ compare HAIRDRESSER

bar·ber·shop /ˈbɑrbərˌʃɑp/ *noun* **1** [C] a place where men go to have their hair cut **2** [U] a type of light music for four parts sung by men, without instruments: *a barbershop quartet*

Bar·bie doll™ /ˈbɑrbi ˌdɑl/ (also **Bar·bie**) *noun* **1** a DOLL that looks like an attractive young woman **2** (*informal*) a woman who is sexually attractive, especially one who is thought to be stupid or boring

bar·bi·tu·rate /bɑrˈbɪtʃərət/ *noun* a powerful drug that makes you feel calm and relaxed, or puts you to sleep. There are several types of barbiturates.

t tea   t̬ butter   d did   k cat   g got   tʃ chin   dʒ June   f fall

bar chart noun = BAR GRAPH

bar code noun a pattern of thick and thin lines that is printed on things you buy. It contains information that a computer can read. ⊃ picture at BAR

bard /bɑːd/ noun (literary) a person who writes poems

bare /beə(r)/ adj., verb
- **adj.** (bar·er, bar·est) **1** not covered by any clothes: She likes to walk around in **bare feet**. ⊃ see also BAREFOOT **2** (of trees or countryside) not covered with leaves; without plants or trees: the bare branches of winter trees ◆ a bare mountainside **3** (of surfaces) not covered with or protected by anything: bare wooden floorboards ◆ Bare wires were sticking out of the cable. ◆ The walls were bare except for a clock. **4** (of a room, cupboard, etc.) empty: The fridge was completely bare. ◆ bare shelves **5** [only before noun] just enough; the most basic or simple: The family was short of even the **bare necessities** of life. ◆ We only had the **bare essentials** in the way of equipment. ◆ He did the **bare minimum** of work but still passed the exam. ◆ She gave me only the bare facts of the case. ◆ It was the barest hint of a smile. ⊃ note at NAKED ⊃ thesaurus box at PLAIN ◆ **bare·ness** noun [U] **IDM** **the bare bones (of sth)** the basic facts: the bare bones of the story **with your bare hands** without weapons or tools: He was capable of killing a man with his bare hands. **lay sth bare** (formal) to show something that was covered or to make something known that was secret: Every aspect of their private lives has been laid bare.
- **verb** ~ sth to remove the covering from something, especially from part of the body: She was paid several thousand dollars to bare all (= take all her clothes off) for the magazine. **IDM** **bare your soul (to sb)** to tell someone your deepest and most private feelings **bare your teeth** to show your teeth in an aggressive and threatening way: The dog bared its teeth and growled.

bare·back /'beəbæk/ adj., adv. on a horse without a SADDLE: a bareback rider ◆ riding bareback

bare·faced /'beəfeɪst/ adj. [only before noun] (disapproving) showing that you do not care about offending someone or about behaving badly **SYN** BALD-FACED, BLATANT: a bare-faced lie

bare·foot /'beəfʊt/ (also less frequent **bare·foot·ed**) adj., adv. not wearing anything on your feet: going barefoot on the beach

bare·hand·ed /ˌbeə'hændəd/ adj., adv. not wearing gloves or carrying anything in your hands: a barehanded catch ◆ He caught the ball barehanded.

bare·head·ed /ˌbeə'hedəd/ adj., adv. not wearing anything to cover your head

bare-'knuckle (also **bare-'knuckled**) adj. **1** [only before noun] (of a BOXER OR BOXING match) without gloves **2** (informal) showing no doubt about doing something that may be morally wrong: a believer in bare-knuckle capitalism

bare·ly /'beəli/ adv.
1 in a way that is just possible but only with difficulty: The music was barely audible. ◆ She was barely able to stand. ◆ We barely had time to catch the train. **2** in a way that almost does not happen or exist: She barely acknowledged his presence. ◆ There was barely any smell. **3** just; certainly not more than (a particular amount, age, time, etc.): Barely 50% of the population voted. ◆ He was barely 20 years old and already running his own company. ◆ They arrived barely a minute later. **4** only a very short time before: I had barely started speaking when he interrupted me. ⊃ note at HARDLY

barf /bɑːf/ verb [I] (informal) to VOMIT ► barf noun [U]

bar·fly /'bɑːflaɪ/ noun (pl. bar·flies) (informal) a person who spends a lot of time drinking in bars

bar·gain /'bɑːɡən/ noun, verb
- **noun 1** a thing bought for less than the usual price: I picked up a few good bargains at the sale. ◆ The car was a bargain at that price. ◆ bargain prices ⊃ collocations at SHOPPING

2 ~ (with sb) an agreement between two or more people or groups, to do something for each other: He and his partner had **made a bargain** to tell each other everything. ◆ I've done what I promised and I expect you to **keep your side of the bargain** (= do what you agreed in return). ◆ Finally the two sides **struck a bargain** (= reached an agreement). **IDM** **in the bargain** (used to emphasize an extra piece of information) also; as well: Volunteers learn a lot and enjoy themselves in the bargain. ⊃ more at HARD adj., STRIKE v.
- **verb** [I] to discuss prices, conditions, etc. with someone in order to reach an agreement that is acceptable **SYN** NEGOTIATE: He said he wasn't prepared to bargain. ◆ ~ (with sb) (about/over/for sth) In the market, dealers were bargaining with growers over the price of coffee. **PHRV** **bargain sth↔a'way** to give something away and not get something of equal value in return: They felt that their leaders had bargained away their freedom. **'bargain for/ on sth** (usually in negative sentences) to expect something to happen and be prepared for it: We hadn't bargained for this sudden change in the weather. ◆ When he agreed to answer a few questions, he got more than he bargained for (= he got more questions, or more difficult ones, than he had expected). ◆ ~ doing sth I didn't bargain on finding them here as well. ◆ ~ sb/sth doing sth I hadn't bargained on them being here.

bargain 'basement noun a part of a large store, usually in the floor below street level, where goods are sold at reduced prices: bargain-basement prices

'bargain ˌhunter noun a person who is looking for goods that are good value for money, usually because they are being sold at prices that are lower than usual ► **'bargain ˌhunting** noun [U]

bar·gain·ing /'bɑːɡənɪŋ/ noun [U] discussion of prices, conditions, etc. with the aim of reaching an agreement that is acceptable **SYN** NEGOTIATION: After much **hard bargaining** we reached an agreement. ◆ Exporters are in a strong **bargaining position** at the moment. ⊃ see also COLLECTIVE BARGAINING, PLEA BARGAINING

'bargaining ˌchip noun a fact or a thing that a person or a group of people can use to get an advantage for themselves when they are trying to reach an agreement with another group

'bargaining ˌpower noun [U] the amount of control a person or group has when trying to reach an agreement with another group in a business or political situation

barge /bɑːdʒ/ noun, verb
- **noun** a large boat with a flat bottom, used for carrying goods and people on CANALS and rivers
- **verb** [I, T] + adv./prep. to move in an awkward way, pushing people out of the way or crashing into them **SYN** PUSH: He barged past me to get to the bar. ◆ They **barged their way** through the crowds. **PHRV** **barge 'in (on sb/sth)** to enter a place or join a group of people rudely interrupting what someone else is doing or saying: I hope you don't mind me barging in like this. ◆ He barged in on us while we were having a meeting.

bar graph (also **bar chart**) noun a diagram which uses lines or narrow RECTANGLES (= bars) of different heights (but equal widths) to show different amounts, so that they can be compared ⊃ picture at GRAPH ⊃ compare HISTOGRAM

'bar-hop verb [I] (-pp-) (informal) to drink in a series of bars in a single day or evening

ba·ri·sta /bə'riːstə/ noun a person who works in a COFFEE BAR

bar·i·tone /'bærətəʊn/ noun **1** a man's singing voice with a range between TENOR and BASS[1]; a man with a baritone voice **2** a musical instrument that is second lowest in PITCH in its family ► **baritone** adj. ⊃ compare ALTO, BASS[1], TENOR

bar·i·um /'beəriəm; 'bær-/ noun [U] (symb. Ba) a chemical element. Barium is a soft silver-white metal.

bark /bɑrk/ *noun, verb*

- *noun* [U, C] **1** the outer covering of a tree ⭢ picture at TREE **2** the short loud sound made by dogs and some other animals **3** a short loud sound made by a gun or a voice: *a bark of laughter*

  IDM **sb's bark is worse than their bite** (*informal*) used to say that someone is not really as angry or as aggressive as they sound

- *verb* **1** [I] ~ **(at sb/sth)** when a dog **barks**, it makes a short loud sound: *The dog suddenly started barking at us.* **2** [T] to give orders, ask questions, etc. in a loud, unfriendly way: ~ **out sth** *She barked out an order.* ◆ ~ **sth (at sb)** *He barked questions at her.* ◆ **+ speech** *"Who are you?" he barked.*

  IDM **be barking up the wrong tree** (*informal*) to have the wrong idea about how to get or achieve something: *You're barking up the wrong tree if you think we'd lend you money again.*

bark·er /ˈbɑrkər/ *noun* a person who stands outside a place where there is entertainment and shouts to people to go in: *He acted like a carnival barker, whipping the crowd into a frenzy.*

bar·ley /ˈbɑrli/ *noun* [U] a plant grown for its grain that is used for making food, beer, and WHISKEY; the grains of this plant ⭢ picture at CEREAL

bar mitz·vah /ˌbɑr ˈmɪtsvə/ *noun* **1** a ceremony and celebration for a Jewish boy who has reached the age of 13, at which he accepts the religious responsibilities of an adult **2** the boy who is celebrating this occasion ⭢ compare BAT MITZVAH

barn /bɑrn/ *noun* **1** a large farm building for storing grain or keeping animals in: *a hay barn* ◆ *They live in a converted barn* (= a barn that has been turned into a house). ⭢ picture at BUILDING **2** a large, plain, ugly building: *They live in a big barn of a house.* **3** a building in which buses, trucks, etc. are kept when not being used

  IDM **close, etc. the barn door after the horse has escaped** to try to prevent or avoid loss or damage when it is already too late to do so

bar·na·cle /ˈbɑrnəkl/ *noun* a small SHELLFISH that attaches itself to objects underwater, for example to rocks and the bottoms of ships

barn dance *noun* an informal social event at which people dance traditional dances, such as SQUARE DANCE s

barn owl *noun* a BIRD OF PREY (= a bird that kills other creatures for food) of the OWL family, that often makes its nest in BARNS and other buildings ⭢ picture at ANIMAL

barn·storm /ˈbɑrnstɔrm/ *verb* [I, T] ~ **(sth)** to travel quickly through an area making political speeches, or getting a lot of attention for your organization, ideas, etc.: *He barnstormed across the southern states in an attempt to woo the voters.* ◆ *The Governor will barnstorm her way through Florida today.* ▶ **barn·storm·ing** *noun* [U], *adj.*

barn·yard /ˈbɑrnyard/ *noun, adj.*

- *noun* an area on a farm that is surrounded by farm buildings

- *adj.* (*informal*) used to describe a way of talking about the body, sex, etc. that some people find rude or offensive: *Some members of the audience didn't appreciate the comedian's barnyard sense of humor.*

ba·rom·e·ter /bəˈrɑmətər/ *noun* **1** an instrument for measuring air pressure to show when the weather will change: *The barometer is falling* (= showing that it will probably rain). **2** something that shows the changes that are happening in an economic, social or political situation: *Infant mortality is a reliable barometer of socioeconomic conditions.* ▶ **bar·o·met·ric** /ˌbærəˈmɛtrɪk/ *adj.*: *barometric pressure*

bar·on /ˈbærən/ *noun* **1** a NOBLEMAN of the lowest rank **2** a person who owns or controls a large part of a particular industry: *a press baron* ◆ *drug barons*

bar·on·ess /ˈbærənəs; ˌbærəˈnɛs/ *noun* **1** a woman who has the same rank as a baron **2** the wife of a baron

bar·on·et /ˈbærənət; ˌbærəˈnɛt/ *noun* (in Britain) a man who has the lowest rank of honor, which can be passed to his son when he dies ⭢ compare KNIGHT

ba·ro·ni·al /bəˈrouniəl/ *adj.* [usually before noun] connected with or typical of a BARON: *a baronial hall*

ba·roque /bəˈrouk/ *adj.* [usually before noun] used to describe European ARCHITECTURE, art, and music of the 17th and early 18th centuries that has a grand and highly decorated style: *baroque churches/music* ◆ *the baroque period* ▶ **ba·roque** *noun* [sing.]: *paintings representative of the baroque*

barque /bɑrk/ *noun* a sailing ship with three or more MASTS (= posts that support the sails)

bar·racks /ˈbærəks/ *noun* (*pl.* **bar·racks**) [C, U] a large building or group of buildings for soldiers to live in: *an army barracks* ◆ *The troops were ordered back to barracks.*

bar·ra·cu·da /ˌbærəˈkudə/ *noun* a large aggressive fish with sharp teeth that lives in warm seas

bar·rage /bəˈrɑʒ/ *noun* **1** [C, usually sing.] the continuous firing of a large number of guns in a particular direction, especially to protect soldiers while they are attacking or moving toward the enemy **2** [sing.] ~ **(of sth)** a large number of something, such as questions or comments, that are directed at someone very quickly, one after the other, often in an aggressive way: *a barrage of questions/criticisms/complaints*

bar·rel /ˈbærəl/ *noun, verb*

- *noun* **1** a large round container, usually made of wood or metal, with flat ends and, usually, curved sides: *a beer/wine barrel* ⭢ see also RAIN BARREL **2** the contents of or the amount contained in a barrel. An oil barrel contains 42 gallons (158.9 l): *They got through a barrel* (= 31 gallons or 117.3 l) *of beer.* ◆ *Oil prices fell to $9 a barrel.* **3** the part of a gun like a tube through which the bullets are fired

  IDM **a barrel of laughs** (often *ironic*) very amusing; a lot of fun: *Life hasn't exactly been a barrel of laughs lately.* **(get/have sb) over a barrel** (*informal*) (to put/have someone) in a situation in which they must accept or do what you want: *They've got us over a barrel. Either we agree to their terms or we lose the money.* ⭢ more at LOCK *n.*, SCRAPE *v.*, SHOOT *v.*

- *verb* [I] **+ adv./prep.** (*informal*) to move very fast in a particular direction, especially in a way that you cannot control: *He came barreling down the hill and smashed into the fence.*

barrel-chested *adj.* (of a man) having a large rounded chest

barrel organ *noun* a musical instrument that is played by turning a handle, usually played in the streets for money ⭢ see also ORGAN GRINDER

bar·ren /ˈbærən/ *adj.* **1** (of land or soil) not good enough for plants to grow on it: *a barren desert* ◆ *a barren landscape* (= one that is empty, with few plants) **2** (of plants or trees) not producing fruit or seeds **SYN** INFERTILE **3** (*old-fashioned* or *formal*) (of women or female animals) not able to produce children or young animals **SYN** INFERTILE **4** [usually before noun] not producing anything useful or successful: *young heads filled with barren facts* ▶ **bar·ren·ness** /ˈbærənnəs/ *noun* [U]

bar·rette /bəˈrɛt/ *noun* a small decorative piece of metal or plastic used by girls and women for holding their hair in place

bar·ri·cade /ˈbærəˌkeɪd/ *noun, verb*

- *noun* a line of objects placed across a road, etc. to stop people from getting past: *The police stormed the barricades the demonstrators put up.*

- *verb* ~ **sth** to defend or block something by building a barricade: *They barricaded all the doors and windows.*

  PHR V **barri·cade yourself 'in/in'side (sth)** to build a barricade in front of you in order to prevent anyone from coming in: *He had barricaded himself in his room.*

bar·ri·er /ˈbæriər/ noun
1 an object like a fence that prevents people from moving forward from one place to another: *The crowd had to stand behind barriers.* ◆ *Show your ticket at the barrier.* **2** a problem, rule, or situation that prevents someone from doing something, or that makes something impossible: *the removal of trade barriers* ◆ *~* **to sth** *Lack of confidence is a psychological barrier to success.* ➔ collocations at INTERNATIONAL **3** something that exists between one thing or person and another and keeps them separate: *The Yangtze river is a natural barrier to the northeast.* ◆ *the* **language barrier** (= when people cannot communicate because they do not speak the same language) ◆ *~* **between A and B** *There was no real barrier between reality and fantasy in his mind.* ◆ *~* **against sth** *Ozone is the earth's barrier against ultraviolet radiation.* ➔ thesaurus box at BORDER **4** a particular amount, level, or number which it is difficult to get past: *the first player whose earnings passed the $10 million barrier*

barrier method noun a method of avoiding becoming pregnant by stopping the SPERM from reaching the egg, for example by using a CONDOM

barrier reef noun a line of rock and CORAL in the sea, often not far from land

bar·ring /ˈbɑrɪŋ/ prep. except for; unless there is/are: *Barring accidents, we should arrive on time.*

bar·ri·o /ˈbɑriou; ˈbær-/ noun (pl. **bar·ri·os**) (from *Spanish*) a district of a city where a lot of Spanish-speaking people live

bar·ris·ter /ˈbærəstər/ noun a lawyer in Britain who has the right to argue cases in the higher courts of law ➔ note at LAWYER

bar·room /ˈbɑrrum; -rʊm/ noun a room in which alcoholic drinks are served at a bar: *a topic much discussed in barrooms across the country* ◆ *a barroom brawl*

bar·row /ˈbærou/ noun **1** = WHEELBARROW **2** a large pile of earth built over a place where people were buried in ancient times

bar·stool /ˈbɑrstul/ noun a tall seat for customers at a bar to sit on

bar·tend·er /ˈbɑrˌtɛndər/ noun someone who works in a bar, serving drinks

bar·ter /ˈbɑrtər/ verb [I, T] to exchange goods, property, services, etc. for other goods, etc. without using money: *~* **(with sb) (for sth)** *The prisoners tried to barter with the guards for items like writing paper and books.* ◆ *~* **sth (for sth)** *The local people bartered wheat for tools.* ▶ **barter** noun [U]: *The islanders use a system of barter instead of money.*

ba·sal /ˈbeɪsl; -zl/ adj. (technical) forming or belonging to a bottom layer or base: *basal cells of the skin*

ba·salt /bəˈsɔlt/ noun [U] a type of dark rock that comes from VOLCANOES

base /beɪs/ noun, verb, adj.
● *noun*
▷ **LOWEST PART 1** [C, usually sing.] the lowest part of something, especially the part or surface on which it rests or stands: *the base of a column/glass* ◆ *a pain at the base of the spine* ◆ *The lamp has a heavy base.* ➔ thesaurus box at BOTTOM
▷ **ORIGINAL IDEA/SITUATION 2** [C] an idea, a fact, a situation, etc. from which something is developed **SYN** BASIS: *She used her family's history as a base for her novel.* ◆ *His arguments have a sound economic base.* ➔ thesaurus box at BASIS
▷ **OF SUPPORT/INCOME/POWER 3** [C, usually sing.] the people, activity, etc. from which someone or something gets most of their support, income, power, etc.: *These policies have a broad base of support.* ◆ *an economy with a solid manufacturing base* ➔ see also CUSTOMER BASE, POWER BASE **4** *~* **pay/salary/wage** the pay that you get before anything extra is added: *All we got was base pay—we didn't reach profitability levels to earn a bonus.*
▷ **FIRST/MAIN SUBSTANCE 5** [C, usually sing.] the first or main part of a substance to which other things are added: *a drink*

with *a rum base* ◆ *Put some moisturizer on as a base before applying your makeup.*
▷ **MAIN PLACE 6** [C] the main place where you live or stay or where a business operates from: *I spend a lot of time in Los Angeles, but Paris is still my base.* ◆ *The town is an ideal base for touring the area.* ◆ *The company has its base in New York, and branch offices all over the world.*
▷ **OF ARMY, NAVY, ETC. 7** [C,U] a place where an army, a navy, etc. operates from: *a military/naval base* ◆ *an air base* ◆ *After the attack, they returned to base.*
▷ **CHEMISTRY 8** [C] a chemical substance, for example an ALKALI, that can combine with an acid to form a salt
▷ **MATHEMATICS 9** [C, usually sing.] a number on which a system of counting and expressing numbers is built up, for example 10 in the DECIMAL system and 2 in the BINARY system
▷ **IN BASEBALL 10** [C] one of the four positions that a player must reach in order to score points ➔ see also DATABASE
IDM off base (informal) completely wrong about something: *If that's what you think, you're way off base.* ➔ more at COVER v., FIRST BASE, TOUCH v.

● *verb* [usually passive] *~* **sb/sth/yourself in...** to use a particular city, town, etc. as the main place for a business, vacation, etc.: *They decided to base the new company in Houston.* ◆ *We're going to base ourselves in Tokyo and make trips from there.*
PHR V base sth on/upon sth to use an idea, a fact, a situation, etc. as the point from which something can be developed: *What are you basing this theory on?* ➔ see also BASED

● *adj.* (**bas·er**, **bas·est**) (formal) not having moral principles or rules: *He acted from base motives.* ▶ **base·ly** adv.

base·ball /ˈbeɪsbɔl/ noun
1 [U] a game played especially in the U.S. by two teams of nine players, using a BAT and ball. Each player tries to hit the ball and then run around four BASES before the other team can return the ball: *a baseball bat/team/stadium* ➔ picture on page 110 **2** [C] the ball used in this game

MORE ABOUT

baseball

- There are nine players on a baseball team. One team is **at bat** and the other team **fields**. The **pitcher** stands on the pitcher's **mound** and **pitches** (= throws) the ball to a **batter** from the other team, who stands next to **home plate**. The **catcher** stands behind home plate and catches and returns balls that were not batted to the pitcher.
- The batter tries to score **runs** (= points) by hitting the ball and running around the four **bases**, which are at each corner of a 90-foot square called the **diamond**. The batter can stop at any of the bases and then run on to the next base when the next batter hits the ball. If a batter hits the ball so far forward that it goes out of the field, this is a **home run**, and the batter is allowed to touch all four bases and automatically gains a point for himself or herself as well as any batter who was standing on a base.
- If the batter tries to hit the ball but misses it, this is called a **strike**. After three strikes, the batter is **out** and the next batter comes to bat. The expressions **three strikes and you're out** and **the three strikes rule** comes from baseball, and is used to describe a law that says that people who commit three crimes will automatically go to prison.
- If the batter hits the ball behind or anywhere outside first or third base, this is a **foul ball** and counts as a strike, unless the batter is already on two strikes. If the ball is pitched outside a certain area (= the **strike zone**) above home plate and the batter does not try to hit it, this is called a **ball**. If the batter gets four balls, they automatically get to go to first base.

i **see**	ɪ **sit**	ɛ **ten**	æ **cat**	ɑ **hot**	ɔ **saw**	ʊ **put**	u **too**

baseball

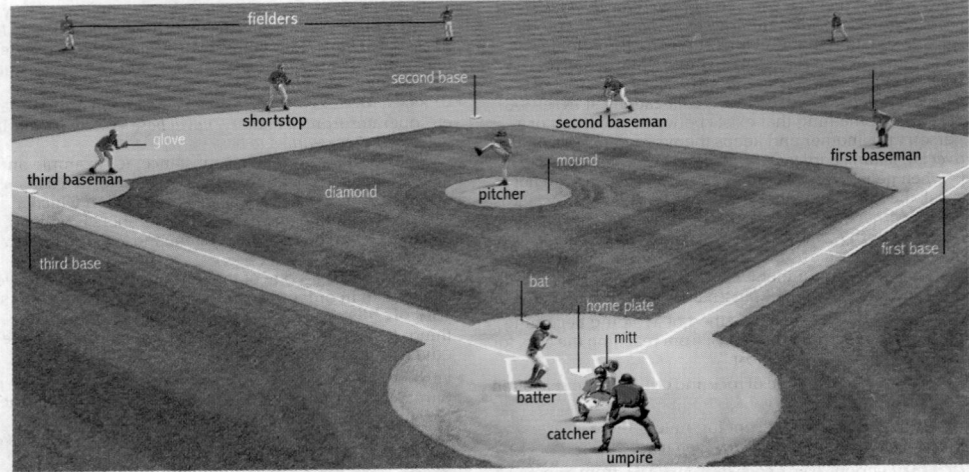

fielders
second base
shortstop
second baseman
glove
first baseman
third baseman
mound
diamond
pitcher
third base
first base
bat
home plate
mitt
batter
catcher
umpire

- A batter can also be out if one of the **fielders** catches the ball after the batter has hit it and it has not touched the ground; if a fielder picks up or catches the ball and steps on one of the bases as the batter is running toward it; or if a fielder **tags** (= touches) a batter with the ball as the batter is running between bases.
- When the team in the field has had three **outs** (= gotten three batters out), the teams switch places and the team in the field is now up (= has a turn at bat). One turn of batting for each team is called an **inning**. One game usually consists of nine innings, at the end of which the team with the most runs is the winner.

'baseball ,cap noun a cap with a long BILL (= a curved part sticking out in front), originally worn by baseball players ⊃ picture at HAT

base·board /'beɪsbɔrd/ noun a narrow piece of wood that is attached along the bottom of the walls in a house

'base camp noun a camp where people start their journey when climbing high mountains

based /beɪst/ adj. [not before noun] **1** ~ (on sth) if one thing is **based** on another, it uses it or is developed from it: *The movie is based on a real-life incident.* ◆ *The report is based on figures from six different European cities.* **2** (also in compounds) if a person or business is **based** in a particular place, that is where they live or work, or where the work of the business is done: *We're based in Chicago.* ◆ *a Chicago-based company* **3** -**based** (in compounds) containing something as an important part or feature: *lead-based paints* ◆ *a class-based society* ⊃ see also BROAD-BASED

'base form noun (grammar) the basic form of a word to which endings can usually be added, for example *wall* is the base form of *walls* and *walled*. The base form is the form in which words in the dictionary are usually shown.

'base ,jumping noun also **'BASE jumping** [U] the sport of jumping with a PARACHUTE from a high place such as a building or a bridge ▶ **'base jumper** noun

base·less /'beɪsləs/ adj. (formal) not supported by good reasons or facts **SYN** UNFOUNDED: *The rumors were completely baseless.*

base·line /'beɪslaɪn/ noun [usually sing.] **1** (sports) a line marking each end of the COURT in TENNIS or the edge of the area where a player can run in baseball **2** (technical) a line or measurement that is used as a starting point when

comparing facts: *The figures for 2009 were used as a baseline for the study.*

base·man /'beɪsmən/ noun (pl. **base·men** /-mən/) (in baseball) a player who defends first, second, or third base: *one of the best third basemen in the league*

base·ment /'beɪsmənt/ noun a room or rooms in a building, partly or completely below the level of the ground: *Kitchen goods are sold in the basement.* ◆ *a basement apartment* ⊃ picture at HOUSE ⊃ compare CELLAR (1)

,base 'metal noun a metal, for example iron or LEAD, that is not a PRECIOUS METAL such as gold

ba·ses 1 pl. of BASIS **2** pl. of BASE

bash /bæʃ/ verb, noun
● verb (informal) **1** [T, I] to hit someone or something very hard: ~ **sb/sth** *He bashed her over the head with a hammer.* ◆ ~ **into sb/sth** *I braked too late and bashed into the car in front of me.* ⊃ thesaurus box at HIT **2** [T] ~ **sb/sth** to criticize someone or something strongly: *Bashing politicians is normal practice in the press.* ◆ *a liberal-bashing administration* ⊃ see also BASHING
PHR V **,bash sth↔'down/'in** to destroy something by hitting it very hard and often: *The police bashed the door down.* ◆ *I'll bash your head in if you do that again.*
● noun (informal) **1** a large party or celebration: *a birthday bash* **2** a hard hit: *He gave Mike a bash in the nose.*

bash·ful /'bæʃfl/ adj. shy and easily embarrassed ▶ **bash·ful·ly** /-fəli/ adv.: *She smiled bashfully.* **bash·ful·ness** noun [U]

bash·ing /'bæʃɪŋ/ noun [U, C] (often in compounds) **1** (used especially in newspapers) very strong criticism of a person or group: *union-bashing* **2** a physical attack, or a series of attacks, on a person or group of people: *gay-bashing* (= attacking HOMOSEXUALS)

BASIC /'beɪsɪk/ noun [U] a simple language, using familiar English words, for writing computer programs

ba·sic 🔑 /'beɪsɪk/ adj.
1 forming the part of something that is most necessary and from which other things develop: *basic information/facts/ ideas* ◆ *the basic principles of law* ◆ ~ **to sth** *Drums are basic to African music.* **2** of the simplest kind or at the simplest level: *The campsite provided only basic facilities.* ◆ *My knowledge of French is pretty basic.* **3** [only before noun] necessary and important to all people: *basic human rights* ◆ *the cost of basic foods*

ʌ cup   ə about   eɪ say   aɪ five   ɔɪ boy   aʊ now   oʊ go   ər bird

ba·si·cally 🔑 /'beɪsɪkli/ adv.
1 in the most important ways, without considering things that are less important **SYN** ESSENTIALLY: *Yes, that's basically correct.* ◆ *The two approaches are basically very similar.* ◆ *There have been some problems but basically it's a good system.* **2** used when you are giving your opinion or stating what is important about a situation: *Basically, there's not a lot we can do about it.* ◆ *He basically just sits there and does nothing all day.* ◆ *And that's it, basically.*

¡**Basic 'English** noun [U] a set of 850 carefully chosen words of English, used for international communication

ba·sics /'beɪsɪks/ noun [pl.] **1 ~ (of sth)** the most important and necessary facts, skills, ideas, etc. from which other things develop: *the basics of computer programming* **2** the simplest and most important things that people need in a particular situation: *Some schools lack money for basics like books and pencils.*
IDM **go/get back to basics** to think about the simple or most important ideas within a subject or an activity instead of new ideas or complicated details

bas·il /'berzl; 'bæzl/ noun [U] a plant with shiny green leaves that smell sweet and are used in cooking as an HERB ➔ picture at HERB

ba·sil·i·ca /bə'sɪlɪkə/ noun a large church or hall with a curved end and two rows of columns inside

bas·i·lisk /'bæsəlɪsk; 'bæzə-/ noun (in ancient stories) a creature like a snake, that can kill people by looking at them or breathing on them

ba·sin /'beɪsn/ noun **1** a large round bowl for holding liquids; the amount of liquid, etc. in a basin **2** an area of land around a large river with streams running down into it: *the Amazon Basin* **3** (technical) a place where the earth's surface is lower than in other areas of the world: *the Pacific Basin* **4** = SINK ➔ see also WASHBASIN **5** a sheltered area of water providing a safe HARBOR for boats: *a yacht basin*

ba·sis 🔑 /'beɪsəs/ noun
(pl. **ba·ses** /'beɪsiz/) **1** [sing.] the reason why people make a particular choice: *She was chosen for the job on the basis of her qualifications.* ◆ *Some movies have been banned on the basis that they are too violent.* ➔ thesaurus box at REASON **2** [sing.] the way things are organized or arranged: *on a regular/permanent/part-time/temporary basis* ◆ *on a daily/day-to-day/weekly basis* **3** [C, usually sing., U] the important facts, ideas, or events that support something and that it can develop from: *The basis of a good marriage is trust.* ◆ *This article will form the basis for our discussion.* ◆ *The theory seems to have no basis in fact.*

base [usually sing.] an idea, a fact, or a situation from which something is developed: *This work provided us with a strong base upon which to build the company.*

PATTERNS
▪ a/the basis/foundation/groundwork/base **for** sth
▪ a **secure/solid/sound/strong/weak** basis/foundation/base
▪ to **form** the basis/foundation/base of sth
▪ to **lay** the foundation/groundwork for sth
▪ to **be without** basis/foundation

bask /bæsk/ verb [I] **~ (in sth)** to enjoy sitting or lying in the heat or light of something, especially the sun: *We sat basking in the warm sunshine.*
PHR V '**bask in sth** to enjoy the good feelings that you have when other people praise or admire you, or when they give you a lot of attention: *He had always basked in his parents' attention.* ◆ *I never minded basking in my wife's reflected glory* (= enjoying the praise, attention, etc. she got).

baskets

shopping basket   picnic basket

laundry basket   hamper

hanging basket   wastebasket

bas·ket /'bæskət/ noun **1** a container for holding or carrying things. Baskets are made of thin strips of material that bends and twists easily, for example plastic, wire, or WICKER: *a shopping basket* ◆ *a picnic basket* ◆ *a laundry basket* (= in which dirty clothes are put before being washed) ◆ *a wicker/wire basket* ◆ *a cat basket* (= in which a cat sleeps) ➔ see also WASTEBASKET **2** the net and the metal ring it hangs from, high up at each end of a basketball COURT; a point that is scored by throwing the ball through this net: *to make/shoot a basket* ➔ picture at SPORT **3** (economics) a number of different goods or CURRENCY: *the value of the dollar against a basket of currencies* **IDM** see EGG n.

bas·ket·ball 🔑 /'bæskət,bɔl/ noun
1 [U] a game played by two teams of five players, using a large ball which players try to throw into a high net hanging from a ring: *a basketball game/coach/team* ➔ picture at SPORT **2** [C] the ball used in this game
'**basket ,case** noun (informal) **1** a person who is slightly

crazy and who has problems dealing with situations **2** a country or an organization whose economic situation is very bad

bas·ket·ry /ˈbæskətri/ *noun* [U] **1** material twisted together in the style of a basket **2** the craft of making baskets, etc.

bas·ma·ti /basˈmɑti/ (also **bas mati ˈrice**) *noun* [U] a type of rice with long grains and a delicate flavor

ˌbas ˈmitzvah /ˌbas ˈmɪtsvə/ *noun* = BAT MITZVAH

Basque /bæsk/ *noun, adj.*
• *noun* **1** [C] a person who was born in the Basque country of France and Spain **2** [U] the language of the people living in the Basque country
• *adj.* connected with these people or their language

basque /bæsk/ *noun* a piece of women's underwear that covers the body from just under the arms to the tops of the legs

bas·re·lief /ˌbɑ rɪˈlif/ *noun* [U, C] a form of SCULPTURE in which the shapes are cut so that they are slightly raised from the background; a SCULPTURE made in this way

bass¹ /beɪs/ *noun, adj.* ➭ see also BASS²
• *noun* **1** [U] the lowest tone or part in music, for instruments or voices: *He always plays his stereo with the bass turned up.* ◆ *He sings bass.* ◆ *a pounding bass line* ➭ see also DRUM AND BASS ➭ compare TREBLE **2** [C] a man's singing voice with a low range; a man with a bass voice ➭ compare ALTO, BARITONE, TENOR **3** [sing.] a musical part that is written for a bass voice **4** (also ˌbass guiˈtar) [C] an electric GUITAR that plays very low notes: *a bass player* ◆ *bass and drums* ◆ *Les Claypool on* (= playing) *bass* **5** [C] = DOUBLE BASS
• *adj.* [only before noun] low in tone: *a bass voice* ◆ *the bass clef* (= the symbol in music showing that the notes following it are low) ➭ compare TREBLE

bass² /bæs/ *noun* [C, U] (*pl.* bass) a sea or FRESHWATER fish that is used for food ➭ see also BASS¹

ˌbass ˈdrum *noun* a large drum that makes a very low sound, used in ORCHESTRAS ➭ picture at INSTRUMENT

bas·set hound /ˈbæsət ˌhaʊnd/ *noun* a dog with short legs, a long body, and long ears

bas·si·net /ˌbæsəˈnet/ *noun* a small bed for a baby, that looks like a BASKET

bass·ist /ˈbeɪsɪst/ *noun* a person who plays the BASS GUITAR or the DOUBLE BASS

bas·soon /bəˈsun/ *noun* a musical instrument of the WOODWIND family. It is shaped like a large wooden tube with a double REED that you blow into, and produces notes with a low sound. ➭ picture at INSTRUMENT

bas·soon·ist /bəˈsunɪst/ *noun* a person who plays the bassoon

bas·tard /ˈbæstərd/ *noun* (*old-fashioned, disapproving, usually offensive*) a person whose parents were not married to each other when he or she was born

bas·tard·ize /ˈbæstərˌdaɪz/ *verb* ~ sth (*formal*) to copy something, but change parts of it so that it is not as good as the original

baste /beɪst/ *verb* **1** ~ sth to pour liquid fat or juices over meat, etc. while it is cooking **2** ~ sth to sew pieces of cloth together temporarily with long loose STITCHES

bas·tion /ˈbæstʃən/ *noun* **1** (*formal*) a group of people or a system that protects a way of life or a belief when it seems that it may disappear: *a bastion of male privilege* ◆ *a bastion of freedom* **2** a place that military forces are defending

bat /bæt/ *noun, verb*
• *noun* **1** a piece of wood with a handle, made in various shapes and sizes, and used for hitting the ball in games such as baseball: *a baseball bat* ➭ picture at BASEBALL ➭ compare RACKET **2** an animal like a mouse with wings, that flies and feeds at night (= it is NOCTURNAL). There are many types of bats. ➭ picture at ANIMAL ➭ see also FRUIT BAT, VAMPIRE BAT
IDM **at bat** (in baseball) **1** trying to hit the ball with a bat: *It's his first time at bat in the major leagues.* **2** often **at-bat** an

occasion when a player is trying to hit the ball with a bat: *Who had the most at-bats last season?* **have bats in the/your belfry** (*informal, old-fashioned*) to be strange or crazy **like a bat out of hell** (*informal*) very fast ➭ more at BLIND *adj.*, RIGHT *adv.*
• *verb* (-tt-) [I, T] ~ (sth) to hit a ball with a bat, especially in a game of baseball: *He bats very well.* ◆ *Who's batting first for the Orioles?*
IDM **bat your eyes/eyelashes** to open and close your eyes quickly, in a way that is supposed to be attractive **bat a thousand** (*informal*) to be very successful **go to bat for sb** (*informal*) to give someone help and support **not bat an eye** (*informal*) to show no surprise or embarrassment when something unusual happens: *She didn't bat an eye when I told her my news.*
PHRV **bat sth↔aˈround** (*informal*) to discuss whether an idea or a plan is good or not, before deciding what to do: *It's just an idea we've been batting around.*

bat·boy /ˈbætbɔɪ/ *noun* a boy who is employed by a baseball team to take care of their BATS and other equipment

batch /bætʃ/ *noun, verb*
• *noun* **1** a number of people or things that are dealt with as a group: *Each summer a new batch of students tries to find work.* ◆ *We deliver the goods in batches.* **2** an amount of food, medicine, etc. produced at one time: *a batch of cookies* **3** (*computing*) a set of jobs that are processed together on a computer: *to process a batch job* ◆ *a batch file/program*
• *verb* [T, I] ~ (sth) to put things into groups in order to deal with them: *The service will be improved by batching and sorting queries.*

ˌbatch ˈprocessing *noun* [U] (*computing*) a way of running a group of programs at the same time, usually automatically

bat·ed /ˈbeɪtəd/ *adj.*
IDM **with bated breath** (*formal*) feeling very anxious or excited: *We waited with bated breath for the winner to be announced.*

bat·girl /ˈbætgərl/ *noun* a girl who is employed by a baseball team to take care of their BATS and other equipment

bath /bæθ/ *noun* [C]
(*pl.* **baths** /bæðz; bæθs/) **1** an act of washing your whole body by sitting or lying in water: *I think I'll take a bath and go to bed.* ➭ see also BUBBLE BATH **2** the water in a BATHTUB, ready to use: *a long soak in a hot bath* ◆ *Please run a bath for me* (= fill the BATHTUB with water). ➭ see also BIRDBATH **3** = BATHROOM: *a master suite with a private bath* ◆ *a house with four bedrooms and two full baths* **4** **baths** [usually pl.] a public place where people went in the past to wash or have a bath: *Roman villas and baths* ➭ see also TURKISH BATH **5** (*technical*) a container with a liquid, such as water or a DYE in it, in which something is washed or placed for a period of time. Baths are used in industrial, chemical, and medical processes. ➭ see also BLOODBATH
IDM **take a bath** to lose money on a business agreement

WHICH WORD?

bath ◆ bathe ◆ swim ◆ sunbathe

- When you wash yourself, you can say that you **bathe**, but it is much more common to say **take a bath**.
- You can also **bathe** another person, for example a baby: *Have you bathed the baby yet?*
- You can **bathe** a part of your body, especially to clean a wound: *Bathe the wound and apply a clean dressing.*
- When you go swimming, you say that you **swim**, **go for a swim**, or **go swimming**: *Let's go for a quick swim in the pool.* ◆ *She goes swimming every morning before breakfast.* What you wear for this activity is usually called a **swimsuit** or a **bathing suit**.
- When you lie in the sun in order to turn brown, you **sunbathe**.

bathe /beɪð/ *verb* **1** [I] to take a bath: *I bathe every day.* ➔ note at BATH **2** [T] ~ *sb* to give someone a bath: *Have you bathed the baby yet?* **3** [T] ~ *sth* to wash something with water, especially a part of your body: *Bathe the wound and apply a clean dressing.* **4** [T] ~ *sth* (in *sth*) (*literary*) to fill or cover something with light: *The moon bathed the country-side in silver light.* **5** [I] (*old-fashioned*) to go swimming in the sea, a river, etc. for enjoyment ➔ see also SUNBATHE

bathed /beɪðd/ *adj.* **1** ~ in *sth* (*literary*) covered with light: *The castle was bathed in moonlight.* **2** ~ in *sth* wet because covered with sweat or tears: *I was so nervous that I was bathed in sweat.*

bath·er /ˈbeɪðər/ *noun* (*old-fashioned*) a person who is swimming in the sea, a river, etc.

bath·house /ˈbæθhaʊs/ *noun* **1** a public building in which there are baths, steam rooms, etc. **2** a building in which you change your clothes for swimming

ˈbathing ˌcap *noun* a soft rubber or plastic cap that fits closely over your head to keep your hair dry while you are swimming

ˈbathing ˌsuit *noun* = SWIMSUIT

ˈbath mat *noun* **1** a piece of material that you put beside the BATHTUB to stand on when you get out **2** a piece of rubber that you put on the bottom of the BATHTUB so that you do not slip

ba·thos /ˈbeɪθɑs/ *noun* [U] (*literary*) (in writing or speech) a sudden change, that is not always intended, from a serious subject or feeling to something that is silly or not important

bath·robe /ˈbæθroʊb/ (also **robe**) a long loose piece of clothing, usually with a belt, worn before and after taking a bath, or indoors over night clothes ➔ picture at CLOTHES

bath·room ♪ /ˈbæθrum; -rʊm/ *noun*
a room in which there is a toilet, a SINK, and sometimes a BATHTUB or shower: *I have to go to the bathroom* (= use the toilet). ◆ *Where's the bathroom?* (= for example in a restaurant) ◆ *Go and wash your hands in the bathroom.* ➔ compare RESTROOM

bath·tub /ˈbæθtʌb/ *noun* (also *informal* **tub**) a large, long container that you put water in and then get into to wash your whole body

bath·wat·er /ˈbæθˌwɔtər; -ˌwɑtər/ *noun* [U] water in a BATHTUB **IDM** see BABY *n.*

ba·tik /bəˈtik/ *noun* [U, C] a method of printing patterns on cloth using WAX (= a solid substance made from fat or oil) on the parts that will not have any color; a piece of cloth printed in this way

bat mitz·vah /ˌbɑt ˈmɪtsvə/ (also **bas mitz·vah**) *noun* **1** a ceremony and celebration that is held for a Jewish girl at the age of 13 at which she accepts the religious responsibilities of an adult **2** the girl who is celebrating this occasion ➔ compare BAR MITZVAH

ba·ton /bəˈtɑn/ *noun* **1** a thin light stick used by the person (called a CONDUCTOR) who is in control of an ORCHESTRA, etc. **2** a short light stick that one member of a team in a RELAY¹ race passes to the next person to run: *to pass/hand over the baton* ◆ (*figurative*) *The president passed the baton* (= passed responsibility) *to his successor.* **3** a long stick that is held and thrown in the air by a person marching in front of a band, or by a MAJORETTE **4** a NIGHTSTICK

bat·tal·ion /bəˈtælyən/ *noun* **1** a large group of soldiers that is made up of several companies **2** (*formal*) a large group of people, especially an organized group with a particular purpose: *a battalion of supporters*

bat·ten /ˈbætn/ *noun, verb*
● *noun* (*technical*) a long strip of wood that is used to keep other building materials in place on a wall or roof
● *verb*
IDM **batten down the hatches 1** to prepare yourself for a period of difficulty or trouble **2** (on a ship) to firmly shut all the entrances to the lower part, especially because a storm is expected

PHR V **ˌbatten sth↔ˈdown** to fix something firmly in position with wooden boards: *He was busy battening down all the shutters and doors.*

bat·ter /ˈbætər/ *verb, noun*
● *verb* [I, T, often passive] to hit someone or something hard many times, especially in a way that causes serious damage: ~ *at/on sth She battered at the door with her fists.* ◆ ~ *sb He had been badly battered around the head and face.* ◆ *She had been battered* (= physically abused) *by her husband for several years.* ◆ ~ *sth Severe winds have been battering the north coast.* ➔ thesaurus box at BEAT
PHR V **ˌbatter sth↔ˈdown** to hit something hard many times until it breaks or comes down
● *noun* **1** [U, C] a mixture of eggs, milk, and flour used in cooking to make PANCAKES, cakes, etc., or to cover food such as fish or chicken before you fry it **2** [C] (in baseball) the player who is hitting the ball ➔ note at BASEBALL ➔ picture at BASEBALL

bat·tered /ˈbætərd/ *adj.* **1** [usually before noun] attacked violently and injured; attacked and badly damaged by weapons or by bad weather: *battered women/children* ◆ *The child had suffered what has become known as "battered baby syndrome."* ◆ *Rockets and shells continued to hit the battered port.* **2** old, used a lot, and not in very good condition: *a battered old car*

bat·ter·ing /ˈbætərɪŋ/ *noun* [U, sing.] a violent attack that injures or damages someone or something: *wife battering* ◆ (*figurative*) *The film took a battering from critics.*

ˈbattering ˌram *noun* a long, heavy piece of wood used in war in the past for breaking down doors and walls

bat·ter·y ♪ /ˈbætəri/ *noun* (*pl.* **bat·ter·ies**)
1 [C] a device that is placed inside a car engine, clock, radio, etc. and that produces the electricity that makes it work: *to change the batteries* ◆ *a rechargeable battery* ◆ *battery-powered/-operated* ◆ *a car battery* ◆ *The battery is dead* (= it is no longer producing electricity). ➔ picture at FLASHLIGHT **2** [C] ~ (of *sth*) a large number of things or people of the same type: *He faced a battery of questions.* ◆ *a battery of reporters* **3** [C] (*technical*) a number of large guns that are used together **4** [U] (*law*) the crime of attacking someone physically ➔ see also ASSAULT AND BATTERY **IDM** see RECHARGE

ˈbatting ˌaverage *noun* **1** (in baseball) a number that shows how often a BATTER hits the ball successfully **2** the level of success or achievement that someone has in an activity: *He's a very good accountant, but as a dancer his batting average is pretty low.*

bat·tle ♪ /ˈbætl/ *noun, verb*
● *noun* **1** [C, U] a fight between armies, ships, or planes, especially during a war; a violent fight between groups of people: *the battle of Gettysburg* ◆ *to be killed in battle* ◆ *a gun battle* ➔ see also PITCHED BATTLE **2** [C] ~ (with *sb*) (for *sth*) a competition, an argument, or a struggle between people or groups of people trying to win power or control: *a legal battle for compensation* ◆ *a battle with an insurance company* ◆ *a battle of wits* (= when each side uses their ability to think quickly to try to win) ◆ *a battle of wills* (= when each side is very determined to win) ➔ thesaurus box at CAMPAIGN **3** [C, usually sing.] a determined effort that someone makes to solve a difficult problem or succeed in a difficult situation: ~ (**against** *sth*) *her long battle against cancer* ◆ *to fight an uphill battle against prejudice* ◆ ~ (**for** *sth*) *a battle for survival* ◆ ~ (**with** *sth*) *his battle with alcoholism* **IDM** **the battle lines are drawn** used to say that people or groups have shown which side they intend to support in an argument or contest that is going to begin **do battle (with sb) (over sth)** to fight or argue with someone **half the battle** the most important or difficult part of achieving something ➔ more at FIGHT *v.*, JOIN *v.*
● *verb* [I, T] to try very hard to achieve something difficult or to deal with something unpleasant or dangerous: *Both teams battled hard.* ◆ *I had to battle hard just to stay afloat.* ◆

~ **with/against sb/sth (for sth)** *She's still battling with a knee injury.* ♦ ~ **for sth** *The two leaders are battling for control of the government.* ♦ *The two teams will **battle it out** in the Superbowl next week.* ♦ ~ **sth** *He battled cancer for four years.*

bat·tle·ax (also **bat·tle·axe**) /ˈbætl̩æks/ *noun* **1** (*informal, disapproving*) an aggressive and unpleasant older woman **2** a heavy AX with a long handle, used in the past as a weapon

bat·tle·cruis·er /ˈbætl̩kruzər/ *noun* a large fast ship used in war in the past, faster and lighter than a BATTLESHIP

battle cry *noun* **1** a shout that soldiers used to give in battle to encourage their own army or to frighten the enemy **2** a word or phrase used by a group of people who work together for a particular purpose, especially a political one

battle fa·tigue *noun* [U] = COMBAT FATIGUE

battle fa·tigues *noun* [pl.] = COMBAT FATIGUES

bat·tle·field /ˈbætl̩fild/ (also **bat·tle·ground** /ˈbætl̩graʊnd/) *noun* **1** a place where a battle is being fought or has been fought **2** a subject that people feel strongly about and argue about

battle-hardened *adj.* (of soldiers) having experience of war and therefore effective at fighting battles

bat·tle·ments /ˈbætl̩mənts/ *noun* [pl.] a low wall around the top of a castle with spaces in it that people inside could shoot through ➔ picture at BUILDING

battle-scarred *adj.* a person or place that is **battle-scarred** has been in a war or fight and shows the signs of injury or damage

bat·tle·ship /ˈbætl̩ʃɪp/ *noun* a very large ship used in war, with big guns and heavy ARMOR (= metal plates that cover the ship to protect it)

bat·ty /ˈbæti/ *adj.* (*informal*) (of people or ideas) slightly crazy, in a harmless way

bau·ble /ˈbɔbl̩/ *noun* a piece of jewelry that is cheap and has little artistic value

baud /bɔd/ *noun* (*computing*) a unit for measuring the speed at which electronic signals and information are sent from one computer to another

Bau·haus /ˈbaʊhaʊs/ *noun* [U] (from *German*) a style and movement in German ARCHITECTURE and design in the early 20th century that was influenced by the methods and materials used in industry, and placed emphasis on how things would be used

baux·ite /ˈbɔksaɪt/ *noun* [U] a soft mineral from which ALUMINUM is obtained

bawd·y /ˈbɔdi/ *adj.* (**bawd·i·er, bawd·i·est**) (*old-fashioned*) (of songs, plays, etc.) loud, and dealing with sex in an amusing way

bawl /bɔl/ *verb* **1** [I, T] to cry loudly, especially in an unpleasant and annoying way: *A child was bawling in the next room.* ♦ *He was **bawling his eyes out** (= crying very loudly).* **2** [I, T] to shout loudly, especially in an unpleasant or angry way: ~ **(at sb)** *She bawled at him in front of everyone.* ♦ ~ **(out) sth (at sb)** *He sat in his office bawling orders at his secretary.* ♦ **+ speech (+ out)** *"Get in here now!" she bawled out.*

PHRV **bawl sb↔'out** (*informal*) to speak angrily to someone because they have done something wrong: *The teacher bawled him out for being late.*

bay /beɪ/ *noun, verb, adj.*
• *noun* **1** [C] a part of the sea, or of a large lake, partly surrounded by a wide curve of the land: *the Bay of Bengal* ♦ *Hudson Bay* ♦ *a magnificent view across the bay* **2** [C] a marked section of ground either inside or outside a building, for example for a vehicle to park in, for storing things, etc.: *a parking/loading bay* ♦ *Put the equipment in the cargo bay.* ➔ see also SICKBAY **3** [C] a curved area of a room or building that sticks out from the rest of the building ➔ see also BAY WINDOW **4** [C] a horse of a dark brown

color: *He was riding a big bay.* **5** (also **sweet bay**) [C] = BAY TREE **6** [U] an HERB used to give flavor to food, made of the leaves of the bay tree ➔ picture at HERB
IDM **hold/keep sb/sth at bay** to prevent an enemy from coming close or a problem from having a bad effect **SYN** WARD OFF: *I'm trying to keep my creditors at bay.* ♦ *Charlotte bit her lip to hold the tears at bay.*
• *verb* **1** [I] (of a dog or WOLF) to make a long deep sound, especially while hunting **SYN** HOWL: *a pack of baying hounds* **2** [I] ~ **(for sth)** (usually used in the progressive tenses) to demand something in a loud and angry way: *The referee's decision left the crowd **baying for blood** (= threatening violence toward him).*
• *adj.* (of a horse) dark brown in color: *a bay mare*

bay leaf *noun* the dried leaf of the BAY TREE that is used in cooking as an HERB

bay·o·net /ˈbeɪənət; ˈbeɪənɛt/ *noun, verb*
• *noun* a long, sharp knife that is fastened onto the end of a RIFLE and used as a weapon in battle
• *verb* ~ **sb** to push a bayonet into someone in order to kill them

bay·ou /ˈbaɪu; ˈbaɪoʊ/ *noun* a branch of a river in the southern U.S. that moves very slowly and has many plants growing in it

bay tree (also **bay**) *noun* a small tree with dark green leaves with a sweet smell that are used in cooking ➔ see also BAY LEAF

bay window *noun* a large window, usually with glass on three sides, that sticks out from the outside wall of a house ➔ picture at HOUSE

ba·zaar /bəˈzɑr/ *noun* **1** (in some Eastern countries) a street or an area of a town where there are many small shops **2** a sale of goods, often items made by hand, to raise money for a charity or for people who need help

ba·zoo·ka /bəˈzukə/ *noun* a long gun, shaped like a tube, which is held on the shoulder, and used to fire ROCKETS at military vehicles

BBC /ˌbi bi ˈsi/ *abbr.* British Broadcasting Corporation (a national organization in the U.K. that broadcasts television and radio programs)

BB gun /ˈbibi ˌɡʌn/ *noun* a gun that uses air pressure to shoot small metal balls called BBs **SYN** AIR GUN

BBQ *abbr.* BARBECUE

BBS /ˌbi bi ˈɛs/ *noun* [C, U] (*computing*) bulletin board system (a system which allows a group of people to leave messages which the others in the group can read and reply to)

B.C. (also **BC**) /ˌbi ˈsi/ *abbr.* before Christ (used in the Christian CALENDAR to show a particular number of years before the year when Christ is believed to have been born): *in (the year) 2,000 B.C.* ♦ *the third century B.C.* ➔ compare A.D., A.H., B.C.E., C.E.

B.C.E. (also **BCE**) /ˌbi si ˈi/ *abbr.* before the Common Era (before the birth of Christ, when the Christian CALENDAR starts counting years. B.C.E. can be used to give dates in the same way as B.C.): *in (the year) 2,000 B.C.E.* ♦ *the third century B.C.E.* ➔ compare A.D., B.C., C.E.

BD /ˌbi ˈdi/ (also **BD-'ROM**) *abbr.* the abbreviation for "Blu-ray Disc" or "Blu-ray Disc read-only memory" (a type of CD on which large amounts of data can be stored, used especially to play high quality video)

be /bi/ *verb, auxiliary verb* ➔ IRREGULAR VERBS on page R5
• *verb* **1** *linking verb* there is/are + *noun* to exist; to be present: *Is there a God?* ♦ *Once upon a time there was a princess...* ♦ *I tried calling her but there was no answer.* ♦ *There's a bank down the road.* **2** [I] **+ adv./prep.** to be located; to be in a place: *The town is three miles away.* ♦ *If you're looking for your file, it's on the table.* ♦ *Mary's upstairs.* **3** [I] **+ adv./prep.** to happen at a time or

h hat   m man   n no   ŋ sing   l leg   r red   y yes   w wet

in a place: *The party is on Friday evening.* ◆ *The meetings are always in the main conference room.* **4** [I] + **adv./prep.** to remain in a place: *She has been in her room for hours.* ◆ *They're here till Christmas.* **5** [I] + **adv./prep.** to attend an event; to be present in a place: *I'll be at the party.* ◆ *He'll be here soon* (= will arrive soon). **6** [I] (only used in the perfect tenses) + **adv./prep.** to visit or call: *I've never been to Spain.* ◆ *He had been to Asia many times.* **7** [I] ~ **from...** used to say where someone was born or where their home is: *She's from Oregon.* **8** *linking verb* used when you are naming people or things, describing them, or giving more information about them: + **noun** *Today is Monday.* ◆ *"Who is that?" "It's my brother."* ◆ *Susan is a doctor.* ◆ *He wants to be* (= become) *a pilot when he grows up.* ◆ + **adj.** *It's beautiful!* ◆ *Life is unfair.* ◆ *He is ten years old.* ◆ *"How are you?" "I'm very well, thanks."* ◆ *Be quick!* ◆ ~ **(that)... The fact is (that) we don't have enough money.** ◆ ~ **doing sth** *The problem is getting it all done in the time available.* ◆ ~ **to do sth** *The problem is to get it all done in the time available.* **9** *linking verb* **it is/was** used when you are describing a situation or saying what you think about it: + **adj.** *It was really hot in the sauna.* ◆ *It's strange how she never comes to see us any more.* ◆ *He thinks it's clever to make fun of people.* ◆ + **noun** *It would be a shame if you lost it.* ◆ *It's going to be a great match.* **10** *linking verb* **it is/was** used to talk about time: + **noun** *It's two thirty.* ◆ + **adj.** *It was late at night when we finally arrived.* **11** *linking verb* + **noun** used to say what something is made of: *Is your jacket real leather?* **12** *linking verb* [I] used to say who something belongs to or who it is intended for: ~ **mine, yours, etc.** *The money's not yours—it's John's.* ◆ ~ **for me, you, etc.** *This package is for you.* **13** *linking verb* + **noun** to cost: *"How much is that dress?" "Eighty dollars."* **14** *linking verb* + **noun** to be equal to: *Three and three is six.* ◆ *How much is a thousand dollars in euros?* ◆ *Let x be the sum of a and b.* ◆ *Las Vegas is not Nevada* (= do not think that all of Nevada is like Las Vegas). **15** *linking verb* ~ **everything, nothing, etc. (to someone)** used to say how important something is to someone: *Money isn't everything* (= it is not the only important thing). ◆ *A thousand dollars is nothing to someone as rich as he is.* **IDM** Most idioms containing **be** are at the entries for the nouns and adjectives in the idioms. For example, **be the death of someone** is at **death**. **the be-all and end-all (of sth)** (*informal*) the most important part; all that matters: *Her career is the be-all and end-all of her existence.* **if it wasn't/ weren't for...** used to say that someone or something stopped someone or something from happening: *If it weren't for you, I wouldn't be alive today.* **leave/let sb/sth be** to leave someone or something alone without disturbing them or it: *Leave her be—she obviously doesn't want to talk about it.* ◆ *Let the poor dog be* (= don't annoy it). **-to-be** (in compounds) future: *his bride-to-be* ◆ *mothers-to-be* (= pregnant women)

● *auxiliary verb* **1** used with a past participle to form the passive: *He was killed in the war.* ◆ *Where were they made?* ◆ *The house was still being built.* ◆ *You will be told what to do.* **2** used with a present participle to form progressive tenses: *I am studying Chinese.* ◆ *I'll be seeing him soon.* ◆ *What have you been doing this week?* ◆ *I'm always being criticized.* **3** used to make QUESTION TAGS (= short questions added to the end of statements): *You're not hungry, are you?* ◆ *Ben's coming, isn't he?* ◆ *The old theater was torn down, wasn't it?* **4** used to avoid repeating the full form of a verb in the passive or a progressive tense: *Karen wasn't beaten in any of her games, but all the others were.* ◆ *"Are you coming with us?" "No, I'm not."* **5** ~ **to do sth** used to say what must or should be done: *I am to call them once I reach the airport.* ◆ *You are to report this to the police.* ◆ *What is to be done about this problem?* **6** ~ **to do sth** used to say what is arranged to happen: *They are to be married in June.* **7** ~ **to do sth** used to say what happened later: *He was to regret that decision for the rest of his life* (= he did regret it). **8** ~ **not, never, etc. to be done/to be** used to say what could not or did not happen: *Anna was nowhere to be found* (= we could not find her anywhere). ◆ *His wife was never to be seen again* (= although he did not know it would be so at the time, he did not see her again). ◆ *She wanted to write a successful novel, but it was not to be* (= it turned out never to happen). **9** **if sb/we were to do sth...** | **were sb/it to do sth...** (*formal*) used to express a condition: *If we were to offer you more money, would you stay?* ◆ *Were we to offer you more money, would you stay?*

be- /bɪ-/ *prefix* **1** (in verbs) to make or treat someone or something as: *Don't belittle his achievements* (= say they are not important). ◆ *An older girl befriended me.* **2** (in adjectives ending in *-ed*) wearing or covered with: *heavily bejeweled fingers* ◆ *bespattered with mud* **3** (in verbs and adjectives ending in *-ed*) to cause something to be: *The ship was becalmed.* ◆ *The rebels besieged the fort.* **4** used to turn INTRANSITIVE verbs (= without an object) into TRANSITIVE verbs (= with an object): *She is always bemoaning her lot in life.*

beach 🔊 /bitʃ/ *noun, verb*
● *noun* an area of sand or small stones beside the ocean or a lake: *tourists sunbathing on the beach* ◆ *a sandy/pebble beach* ◆ *a beach bar* ➾ thesaurus box at COAST
● *verb* [T, I] ~ **(sth)** to come or bring something out of the water and onto the beach: *He beached the boat and lifted the boy onto the shore.* ◆ *a beached whale* (= one that has become stuck on land and cannot get back into the water)

'**beach ball** *noun* a large, light, colored plastic ball that people play games with on the beach

'**beach buggy** *noun* = DUNE BUGGY

beach·comb·er /'bitʃˌkoumər/ *noun* a person who walks along beaches collecting interesting or valuable things, either for pleasure or to sell

beach·front /'bitʃfrʌnt/ *noun* [sing.] often **the beachfront** the part of a town facing the beach: *beachfront hotels/ apartments*

beach·head /'bitʃhɛd/ *noun* a strong position on a beach from which an army that has just landed prepares to go forward and attack ➾ see also BRIDGEHEAD

'**beach volleyball** *noun* [U] a form of VOLLEYBALL played on sand by teams of two players

beach·wear /'bitʃwɛr/ *noun* [U] (used especially in stores) clothes for wearing on the beach

bea·con /'bikən/ *noun* **1** a light that is placed somewhere to guide vehicles and warn them of danger: *a navigation beacon* **2** ~ **of/for sth** a person, principle, etc. that guides others or is a good model for them to follow: *He was a beacon of hope* for the younger generation. ◆ *America is a beacon for freedom.* **3** a radio station whose signal helps ships and aircraft to find their position **4** (in the past) a fire lit on top of a hill as a signal

Beacon 'Hill *noun* an old, fashionable area of Boston, where many rich families and politicians live

bead /bid/ *noun* **1** [C] a small piece of glass, wood, etc. with a hole through it, that can be put on a string with others of the same type and worn as jewelry, etc.: *a necklace of wooden beads* ◆ *A bead curtain separated the two rooms.* ➾ see also WORRY BEADS **2** [C] a small drop of liquid: *There were beads of sweat on his forehead.* **3 beads** [pl.] a ROSARY **IDM draw/get a bead on sb/sth** to aim carefully at someone or something before shooting a gun

bead·ed /'bidəd/ *adj.* **1** decorated with beads: *a beaded dress* **2** ~ **with sth** with small drops of a liquid on it: *His face was beaded with sweat.*

bead·ing /'bidɪŋ/ *noun* [U] **1** (also **bead·work** /'bidwərk/) BEADS that are sewn together and used as a decoration on clothes **2** a strip of wood, stone, or plastic with a pattern on it, used for decorating walls, doors, and furniture

bead·y /'bidi/ *adj.* (of eyes) small, round, and bright; watching everything closely or with suspicion

beady-eyed *adj.* (*informal*) watching carefully and noticing every small detail

bea·gle /'bigl/ *noun* a small dog with short legs, used in hunting

beak 🔊 /bik/ *noun*
1 the hard pointed or curved outer part of a bird's mouth **SYN** BILL: *The gull held the fish in its beak.* ➲ picture at ANIMAL **2** (*humorous*) a person's nose, especially when it is large and/or pointed

beaked /bikt/ *adj.* (usually in compounds) having a beak, or the type of beak mentioned: *flat-beaked*

beak·er /'bikər/ *noun* a glass cup with straight sides and a lip, used in chemistry, for example for measuring liquids ➲ picture at LABORATORY

beam /bim/ *noun*, *verb*
● *noun* **1** a line of light, electric waves, or PARTICLES: *narrow beams of light/sunlight* ◆ *the beam of a flashlight* ◆ *a laser/electron beam* ◆ *a car with its high beams on* **2** a long piece of wood, metal, etc. used to support weight, especially as part of the roof in a building: *The cottage had exposed oak beams.* **3** = BALANCE BEAM **4** a wide and happy smile: *a beam of satisfaction*
● *verb* **1** [I, T, no passive] to have a big, happy smile on your face: *~ (at sb) He beamed at the journalists.* ◆ *~ (with sth) She was positively beaming with pleasure.* ◆ *~ sth (at sb) The teacher beamed her approval at her students.* ◆ *"I'd love to come," she beamed* (= said with a large smile). **2** [T] *+ adv./prep.* to send radio or television signals over long distances using electronic equipment: *Live pictures of the ceremony were beamed around the world.* **3** [I] *+ adv./prep.* to produce a stream of light and/or heat: *The morning sun beamed down on us.* ◆ *Light beamed through a hole in the curtain.* **IDM** see EAR
PHR V ,beam sb 'up/'down (in SCIENCE FICTION stories) to transport someone to or from a SPACESHIP using special electronic equipment **ORIGIN** From the television series *Star Trek.*

beamed /bimd/ *adj.* having beams of wood: *a high-beamed ceiling*

bean /bin/ *noun*, *verb*
● *noun* **1** a seed, or POD containing seeds, of a climbing plant, eaten as a vegetable. There are several types of beans, and the plants that they grow on are also called beans: *lima beans* ◆ *green beans* ◆ *I'll have a burrito with beans and rice.* ➲ see also BAKED BEANS **2** (usually in compounds) a seed from a coffee plant, or some other plants: *coffee/cocoa/vanilla beans* ➲ see also JELLY BEAN **IDM** full of beans/life having a lot of energy ➲ more at HILL, KNOW v., SPILL v.
● *verb ~ sb* (*informal*) to hit someone on the head: *I got beaned by a rock someone threw.*

bean·bag /'binbæg/ *noun* **1** a very large bag made of cloth and filled with small pieces of plastic, used for sitting on **2** a small bag made of cloth filled with beans or small pieces of plastic and used as a ball

'bean ,counter *noun* (*informal, disapproving*) a person who works with money, for example as an ACCOUNTANT, and who wants to keep strict control of how much money a company spends

'bean curd *noun* [U] = TOFU

bean·ie /'bini/ *noun* a small round hat that fits close to the head ➲ picture at HAT

bean·pole /'binpoʊl/ *noun* (*informal, usually disapproving*) a tall thin person

'bean sprouts *noun* [pl.] BEAN seeds that are just beginning to grow, often eaten raw ➲ picture at FRUIT

bean·stalk /'binstɔk/ *noun* the tall STEM of a BEAN plant which usually grows quickly

bear 🔊 /bɛr/ *verb*, *noun*
● *verb* (bore /bɔr/, borne /bɔrn/)
> ACCEPT/DEAL WITH **1** [T] (used with can/could in negative sentences and questions) to be able to accept and deal with something unpleasant **SYN** STAND: *~ sth The pain was almost more than he could bear.* ◆ *She couldn't bear the thought of losing him.* ◆ *~ doing sth I can't bear having cats in the*

house. ◆ *He can't bear being laughed at.* ◆ *~ to do sth He can't bear to be laughed at.* ◆ *~ sb doing sth I can't bear you doing that.* ➲ thesaurus box at HATE
> BE RESPONSIBLE FOR SOMETHING **2** [T] *~ sth* (*formal*) to take responsibility for something: *She bore the responsibility for most of the changes.* ◆ *Do parents have to bear the whole cost of tuition fees?* ◆ *Tuition fees are usually borne by the parents.* ◆ *You shouldn't have to bear the blame for other people's mistakes.*
> NOT BE SUITABLE **3** [T] **not ~** to not be suitable for something: *~ sth Her later work does not bear comparison with her earlier novels* (= because it is not nearly as good). ◆ *The plan won't bear close inspection* (= it will be found to be unacceptable when carefully examined). ◆ *~ doing sth The joke doesn't bear repeating* (= because it is not funny or may offend people). ◆ *His sufferings don't bear thinking about* (= because they are so terrible).
> NEGATIVE FEELING **4** [T] to have a feeling, especially a negative feeling: *~ sth (against/toward sb) He bears no resentment toward them.* ◆ *~ sb sth She bore him no ill will.*
> SUPPORT WEIGHT **5** [T] *~ sth* to support the weight of someone or something: *The ice is too thin to bear your weight.* ◆ *The weight of the bridge is borne by steel beams.*
> SHOW **6** [T] *~ sth* (*formal*) to show something; to carry something so that it can be seen: *The document bore her signature.* ◆ *He was badly wounded in the war and still bears the scars.* ◆ *She bears little resemblance to* (= is not much like) *her mother.* ◆ *The title of the essay bore little relation to* (= was not much connected with) *the contents.*
> NAME **7** [T] *~ sth* (*formal*) to have a particular name: *a family that bore an ancient and honored name*
> CARRY **8** [T] *~ sb/sth* (*old-fashioned* or *formal*) to carry someone or something, especially while moving: *three kings bearing gifts*
> YOURSELF **9** [T] *~ yourself well, etc.* (*formal*) to move, behave, or act in a particular way: *He bears himself* (= stands, walks, etc.) *proudly, like a soldier.* ◆ *She bore herself with dignity throughout the funeral.*
> CHILD **10** [T] (*formal*) to give birth to a child: *~ sth She was not able to bear children.* ◆ *~ sb sth She had borne him six sons.*
> OF TREES/PLANTS **11** [T] *~ sth* (*formal*) to produce flowers or fruit
> TURN **12** [I] *~ (to the) left, north, etc.* to go or turn in the direction mentioned: *When you get to the fork in the road, bear right.*
IDM bear arms (*old use*) to be a soldier; to fight bear fruit to have a successful result bear hard, heavily, severely, etc. on sb (*formal*) to be a cause of difficulty or suffering to someone: *Taxes bear heavily on us all.* bring sth to bear (on sb/sth) (*formal*) to use energy, pressure, influence, etc. to try to achieve something or make someone do something: *We must bring all our energies to bear upon the task.* ◆ *Pressure was brought to bear on us to finish the work on time.* ➲ more at BRUNT, CROSS n., GRIN v., MIND n., WITNESS n.
PHR V ,bear 'down on sb/sth **1** to press on someone or something: *Bear down on it with all your strength so it doesn't move.* **2** to move quickly toward someone or something in a determined or threatening way 'bear on sth (*formal*) to relate to something **SYN** AFFECT: *These are matters that bear on the welfare of the community.* ,bear sb/sth 'out to show that someone is right or that something is true: *The other witnesses will bear me out.* ◆ *The other witnesses will bear out what I say.* ,bear 'up (against/under sth) to remain as cheerful as possible during a difficult time: *He's bearing up well under the strain of losing his job.* 'bear with sb/sth to be patient with someone or something: *She's under a lot of strain. Just bear with her.* ◆ *If you will bear with me* (= be patient and listen to me) *a little longer, I'll answer your question.*
● *noun* **1** a heavy wild animal with thick fur and sharp CLAWS (= pointed parts on the ends of its feet). There are many types of bears: *a black bear* ➲ see also GRIZZLY BEAR, POLAR BEAR, TEDDY BEAR **2** (*finance*) a person who sells shares in a company, etc., hoping to buy them back later at a lower price ➲ compare BULL **3** (*informal*) a thing that is very difficult to deal with: *Their Victorian house is beautiful but it's a bear to clean.* ➲ see also BEARISH

bear·a·ble /ˈbeərəbl/ *adj.* a person or thing that is **bearable** can be accepted or dealt with: *She was the only thing that made life bearable.* **ANT** UNBEARABLE

beard 🔊 /bɪrd/
noun [U, C] hair that grows on the chin and cheeks of a man's face; similar hair that grows on some animals: *He has decided to grow a beard and a mustache.* ◆ *a week's growth of beard* ◆ *a goat's beard* ⊃ picture at HAIR ⊃ collocations at PHYSICAL ⊃ compare MUSTACHE ▶ **beard·ed** *adj.*: *a bearded face/man*

bear·er /ˈbeərər/ *noun* **1** (*formal*) a person who has something with them or is the official owner of something, such as a document: *A pass will allow the bearer to enter the building.* **2** a person whose job it is to carry something, especially at a ceremony: *flag bearers* ⊃ see also PALL-BEARER, RING BEARER, STANDARD-BEARER, STRETCHER-BEARER **3** a person who brings a message, a letter, etc.: *I'm sorry to be the bearer of bad news.* **4** a person who has knowledge of something, such as an idea or a tradition, and makes sure that it is not forgotten, by teaching others about it

bear hug *noun* an act of showing affection for someone by holding them very tightly and strongly in your arms

bear·ing /ˈbeərɪŋ/ *noun* **1** [U] ~ **on sth** the way in which something is related to something or influences it: *Recent events had no bearing on our decision.* ◆ *Regular exercise has a direct bearing on fitness and health.* **2** [sing.] the way in which you stand, walk, or behave: *Her whole bearing was alert.* **3** [C] (*technical*) a direction measured from a fixed point using a COMPASS **4** [C] (*technical*) a part of a machine that supports a moving part, especially one that is turning ⊃ see also BALL BEARING
IDM **get/find your bearings** to make yourself familiar with your surroundings in order to find out where you are or to feel comfortable in a place **lose your bearings** to become lost or confused

bear·ish /ˈbeərɪʃ/ *adj.* (*finance*) showing or expecting a fall in the prices of shares: *a bearish market* ◆ *Japanese banks remain bearish.* ⊃ compare BULLISH

bear 'market *noun* (*finance*) a period during which people are selling shares, etc. rather than buying, because they expect the prices to fall ⊃ compare BULL MARKET

bear·skin /ˈbeərskɪn/ *noun* the skin and fur of a BEAR: *a bearskin rug*

beast /bist/ *noun* **1** (*old-fashioned* or *formal*) an animal, especially one that is large or dangerous, or one that is unusual: *wild/savage/ferocious beasts* ◆ *mythical beasts* such as unicorns and dragons **2** a person who is cruel and whose behavior is uncontrolled **SYN** ANIMAL **3** (*informal*, often *humorous*) an unpleasant person or thing: *The math exam was a real beast.* **4** (*informal*) a thing of a particular kind **SYN** ANIMAL: *His new guitar is a very expensive beast.*

beast·ly /ˈbistli/ *adj.* (*old-fashioned*, *informal*) unpleasant **SYN** HORRIBLE, NASTY ▶ **beast·li·ness** *noun* [U]

beast of 'burden *noun* an animal used for heavy work such as carrying or pulling things

beat 🔊 /bit/ *verb, noun, adj.*
● *verb* (beat, beat·en /ˈbitn/)
▷ IN GAME **1** [T] ~ **sb (at sth)** to defeat someone in a game or competition: *He beat me at chess.* ◆ *Their recent wins have proved they're still the ones to beat* (= the most difficult team to beat).
▷ CONTROL **2** [T] ~ **sth** to get control of something **SYN** DEFEAT: *The government's main aim is to beat inflation.*
▷ BE TOO DIFFICULT **3** [T] to be too difficult for someone **SYN** DEFEAT: ~ **sb** *a problem that beats even the experts* ◆ ~ **sb** **why, how, etc....** *It beats me* (= I don't know) *why he did it.* ◆ *What beats me is how it was done so quickly* (= I don't understand how).
▷ BE BETTER **4** [T] ~ **sth** to do or be better than something: *Nothing beats home cooking.* ◆ *You can't beat Italian shoes.*

◆ *They want to **beat** the speed **record** (= go faster than anyone before).*
▷ AVOID **5** [T] ~ **sth** to avoid something: *If we go early, we should beat the traffic.* ◆ *We were up and off early to **beat** the **heat**.*
▷ HIT **6** [I, T] to hit someone or something many times, usually very hard: + adv./prep. *Somebody was beating at the door.* ◆ *Hailstones beat against the window.* ◆ ~ **sth** *Someone was beating a drum.* ◆ ~ **sth** + adv./prep. *She was beating dust out of the carpet* (= removing dust from the carpet by beating it). ◆ ~ **sb** *At that time children were regularly beaten for minor offenses* (= a punishment). ◆ ~ **sb** + adv./prep. *An elderly man was found **beaten to death**.* ◆ ~ **sb** + adj. *They beat him unconscious* (= hit him until he became unconscious).
▷ OF HEART/DRUMS/WINGS **7** [I, T] to make, or cause something to make, a regular sound or movement: *She's alive— her heart is still beating.* ◆ *We heard the **drums beating**.* ◆ *The bird was **beating its wings** (= moving them up and down) frantically.*
▷ MIX **8** [T] to mix something with short, quick movements with a fork, etc.: ~ **sth (up)** *Beat the eggs up to a frothy consistency.* ◆ ~ **A and B together** *Beat the flour and milk together.*
▷ SHAPE METAL **9** [T] to change the shape of something, especially metal, by hitting it with a hammer, etc.: ~ **sth (out) (into sth)** *beaten silver* ◆ *The gold is beaten out into thin strips.* ◆ ~ **sth** + adj. *The metal had been beaten flat.*
▷ MAKE PATH **10** [T] ~ **sth (through, across, along, etc. sth)** to make a path, etc. by walking somewhere, or by pressing branches down and walking over them: *a well-beaten track* (= one that has been worn hard by much use) ◆ *The hunters beat a path through the undergrowth.*
IDM **beat around the bush** to talk about something for a long time without coming to the main point: *Stop beating about the bush and tell me what you want.* **beat sb at their own game** to defeat or do better than someone in an activity which they have chosen or in which they think they are strong **beat your brains out** (*informal*) to think very hard about something for a long time **beat your breast** to show that you feel sorry about something that you have done, especially in public and in an exaggerated way **beat the clock** to finish a task, race, etc. before a particular time **beat it** (*slang*) (usually used in orders) to go away immediately: *This is private land, so beat it!* **beat a path to sb's door** if a lot of people **beat a path to someone's door**, they are all interested in something that person has to sell, or can do or tell them: *Top theatrical agents are beating a path to the teenager's door.* **beat the rap** (*slang*) to escape without being punished **beat a (hasty) retreat** to go away or back quickly, especially to avoid something unpleasant **beat time (to sth)** to mark or follow the rhythm of music, by waving a stick, tapping your foot, etc.: *She beat time with her fingers.* **beat sb to the punch** (*informal*) to get or do something before someone else can **can you beat that/it!** (*informal*) used to express surprise or anger **if you can't beat them, join them** (*saying*) if you cannot defeat someone or be as successful as they are, then it is more sensible to join them in what they are doing and perhaps get some advantage for yourself by doing so **off the beaten track** far away from other people, houses, etc.: *They live miles off the beaten track.* **a rod/stick to beat sb with** a fact, an argument, etc. that is used in order to blame or punish someone **take some beating** to be difficult to beat: *That score is going to take some beating.* ◆ *For sheer luxury, this hotel takes some beating.* ⊃ more at BLACK *adj.*, DAYLIGHTS, DEAD, DRUM *n.*, HELL
PHRV **beat sth↔'down** to hit a door, etc. many times until it breaks open **beat 'down (on sb/sth)** if the sun **beats down**, it shines with great heat **beat sb/sth 'down (to sth)** to persuade someone to reduce the price at which they are selling something: *He wanted $8,000 for the car but I beat him down to $6,000.* ◆ *I beat down the price to $6,000.* **beat sb/sth↔'off** to force someone or something back or away by fighting: *The attacker was beaten off.* ◆ *She beat off a challenge to her leadership.* **'beat on sb** = BEAT UP ON SB **beat sth↔'out 1** to produce a rhythm by hitting some-

thing many times **2** to put a fire out by beating: *We beat the flames out.* **3** to remove something by hitting it with a HAMMER, etc.: *They can beat out the dent in the car's fender.* ˌbeat sth ˈout of sb to hit someone until they tell you what you want to know ˈbeat sb out of sth (*informal*) to cheat someone by taking something from them: *Her brother beat her out of $200.* ˈbeat sb to sth | ˌbeat sb ˈto it to get somewhere or do something before someone else: *She beat me to the top of the hill.* ♦ *I was about to take the last cookie, but he beat me to it.* ˌbeat sb↔ˈup to hit or kick someone hard, many times: *He was badly beaten up by a gang of thugs.* ˌbeat ˈup on sb (also ˈbeat on sb) to blame someone too much for something: *Don't beat up on Paul—he tried his best.* ˌbeat yourself ˈup (about/over sth) (also ˌbeat ˈup on yourself (about/over sth)) (*informal*) to blame yourself too much for something: *Look, there's no need to beat yourself up over this.*

● **noun**

> OF DRUMS/HEART/WINGS **1** [C] a single blow to something, such as a drum, or a movement of something, such as your heart; the sound that this makes: *several loud beats on the drum* ♦ *His heart skipped a beat when he saw her.* **2** [sing.] a series of regular blows to something, such as a drum; the sound that this makes: *the steady beat of the drums* ↻ see also HEARTBEAT

> RHYTHM **3** [C] the main rhythm, or a unit of rhythm, in a piece of music, a poem, etc.: *This type of music has a strong beat to it.* ♦ *The piece has four beats to the bar.*

> OF POLICE OFFICER **4** [C] the area which a police officer walks around regularly and which he or she is responsible for: *More police officers out on the beat may help to cut crime.* **IDM** see HEART, MARCH, MISS v., WALK v.

● **adj.** [not before noun] (*informal*) very tired: *You look beat.*

THESAURUS

beat

batter ◆ pound ◆ lash ◆ hammer

These words all mean to hit someone or something many times, especially hard.

beat to hit someone or something many times, especially very hard: *Someone was beating at the door.* ♦ *A young man was found beaten to death last night.* ♦ *At that time, children were often beaten for quite minor offenses* (= as a punishment).

batter to hit someone or something hard many times, especially in a way that causes serious damage: *He was badly battered about the head and face.* ♦ *Severe winds are battering the coast.*

pound to hit someone or something hard many times, especially in a way that makes a lot of noise: *Heavy rain pounded on the roof.* ♦ *She pounded on the table with her fist.*

lash to hit someone or something with great force: *The rain lashed at the window.* **NOTE** The subject of **lash** is often *rain, wind, hail, sea,* or *waves*.

hammer to hit someone or something hard many times, in a way that is noisy or violent: *He hammered at the lock, but it would not open.* ♦ (*figurative*) *She hammered him with difficult questions.*

POUND OR HAMMER?

There is not much difference in meaning between these two, but to **pound** is sometimes a steadier action. To **hammer** can be more violent and it is often used figuratively.

PATTERNS

■ to beat/batter/pound/lash/hammer sb/sth **with** sth
■ to beat/batter/pound/lash/hammer **against** sth
■ to beat/batter/pound/hammer **on** sth
■ to beat/batter/hammer sth **down**
■ the **rain/wind/sea** beats/batters/pounds/lashes (at) sth

beat·box /ˈbitˌbɑks/ *noun, verb*
● **noun 1** [C] (*informal*) an electronic machine that produces drum sounds **2** [C] (*informal*) a large radio, etc. that can be carried around and is used for playing loud music **3** (also **beat·box·er**) [C] a person who uses the voice to make sounds in HIP-HOP **4** [U] music that is created using sounds made with the human voice
● **verb** [I] to make the sound of a drum with the voice

beat·box·ing /ˈbitˌbɑksɪŋ/ *noun* [U] the use of the human voice to create the beat in HIP-HOP: *an amazing beatboxing performance*

ˌbeaten-ˈup *adj.* = BEAT-UP

beat·er /ˈbitər/ *noun* **1** (often in compounds) a tool used for beating things: *an egg beater* ♦ *a carpet beater* **2** a person who hits someone, especially a person who does this often: *a wife beater* **3** (*informal*) an old car that is in bad condition ↻ see also WORLD-BEATER

the ˈbeat generˌation *noun* [sing.] a group of young people in the 1950s and early 1960s who rejected the way most people lived in society, wanted to express themselves freely, and liked modern JAZZ

be·a·tif·ic /ˌbiəˈtɪfɪk/ *adj.* (*formal*) showing great joy and peace: *a beatific smile/expression*

be·at·i·fy /biˈætəˌfaɪ/ *verb* (be·at·i·fies, be·at·i·fy·ing, be·at·i·fied, be·at·i·fied) ~ **sb** (of the Pope) to give a dead person a special honor by stating officially that he/she is very holy ↻ compare BLESS, CANONIZE ▶ **be·at·i·fi·ca·tion** /biˌætəfəkˈeɪʃn/ *noun* [C, U]

beat·ing /ˈbitɪŋ/ *noun* **1** [C] an act of hitting someone hard and repeatedly, as a punishment or in a fight: *to give someone a beating* **2** [C] (*informal*) a very heavy defeat: *The team has taken a few beatings this season.* **3** [U] a series of regular blows to something such as a drum, or movements of something, such as your heart; the sound that this makes: *He could hear the beating of his own heart.* ♦ *the beating of drums/wings*

be·at·i·tude /biˈætəˌtud/ *noun* the Beatitudes [pl.] (in the Bible) the eight statements made by Christ about people who are BLESSED

beat·nik /ˈbitnɪk/ *noun* a young person in the 1950s and early 1960s who rejected the way of life of ordinary society and showed this by behaving and dressing in a different way from most people

ˌbeat-ˈup (also ˌbeaten-ˈup) *adj.* [usually before noun] (*informal*) old and damaged: *a beat-up old truck*

beau /boʊ/ *noun* (*pl.* beaux or beaus /boʊz/) (*old-fashioned*) a woman's male lover or friend

beau·coup /ˈboʊku; boʊˈku/ *det.* (*informal*) many or a lot: *You can spend beaucoup bucks* (= a lot of money) *on software.*

the Beau·fort scale /ˈboʊfərt ˌskeɪl/ *noun* [sing.] a range of numbers used for measuring how strongly the wind is blowing. The lowest number 0 means that there is no wind and the highest number 12 means that there is a HURRI-CANE (= a violent storm with very strong winds): *The storm measured 10 on the Beaufort scale.* **ORIGIN** From Sir Francis Beaufort, the English admiral who invented it.

Beau·jo·lais /ˌboʊʒəˈleɪ; ˈboʊʒəˌleɪ/ *noun* (*pl.* Beau·jo·lais) [C, U] a light wine, usually red, from the Beaujolais district of France

beaut /byut/ *noun* (*informal*) an excellent or beautiful person or thing

beau·te·ous /ˈbyutiəs/ *adj.* (*literary*) beautiful

beau·ti·cian /byuˈtɪʃn/ *noun* a person, usually a woman, whose job is to give beauty treatments to the face and body

beau·ti·ful 🔑 /ˈbyutəfl/ *adj.*
1 having beauty; pleasing to the senses or to the mind: *a beautiful woman/face/baby/voice/poem/evening* ♦ *beautiful countryside/weather/music* **2** very good or skillful: *What beautiful timing!*

beautiful

pretty ◆ handsome ◆ attractive ◆ lovely ◆ good-looking ◆ gorgeous

These words all describe people who are pleasant to look at.

beautiful (especially of a woman or girl) very pleasant to look at: *She looked stunningly beautiful that night.*

pretty (especially of a girl or woman) pleasant to look at: *She's got a very pretty face.* **NOTE** Pretty is used most often to talk about girls. When it is used to talk about a woman, it usually suggests that she is attractive, but not beautiful.

handsome (of a man) pleasant to look at; (of a woman) pleasant to look at, with strong features rather than small, delicate ones: *He was described as "tall, dark and handsome."* ◆ *Joan Crawford was a handsome woman.*

attractive (of a person) pleasant to look at, especially in a sexual way: *She's a very attractive woman.*

lovely (of a woman) beautiful; very attractive; (of a man or woman) with a pleasant personality: *She looked particularly lovely that night.* ◆ *They really are a lovely couple.* **NOTE** When you describe someone as **lovely**, you are usually showing that you also have a feeling of affection for them.

good-looking (of a person) pleasant to look at, often in a sexual way: *She arrived with a very good-looking man.*

gorgeous (informal) (of a person) extremely attractive, especially in a sexual way: *You look gorgeous!*

ATTRACTIVE OR GOOD-LOOKING?

If you describe someone as **attractive** or **lovely**, you often also mean that they have a pleasant personality as well as being pleasant to look at; **good-looking** describes only someone's physical appearance.

PATTERNS

- a(n) beautiful/pretty/handsome/attractive/lovely/good-looking/gorgeous **girl/woman/lady**
- a(n) beautiful/handsome/attractive/good-looking/gorgeous **boy/man**
- a(n) beautiful/pretty/handsome/attractive/lovely/good-looking **face**
- a(n) beautiful/attractive/lovely **smile**

beau·ti·fully 🔊 /ˈbyuṭəfli/ adv.
1 in a beautiful way: *She sings beautifully.* ◆ *a beautifully decorated house* **2** very well; in a pleasing way: *It's all working out beautifully.*

beau·ti·fy /ˈbyuṭəˌfaɪ/ verb (beau·ti·fies, beau·ti·fy·ing, beau·ti·fied, beau·ti·fied) ~ sb/sth to make someone or something beautiful or more beautiful

beau·ty 🔊 /ˈbyuṭi/ noun
(pl. beau·ties) **1** [U] the quality of being pleasing to the senses or to the mind: *the beauty of the sunset/of poetry/of his singing* ◆ *a woman of great beauty* ◆ *The woods were designated an area of outstanding natural beauty.* ◆ *beauty products/treatments* (= intended to make a person more beautiful) **2** [C] a person or thing that is beautiful: *She had been a beauty in her day.* **3** [C] an excellent example of its type: *That last goal was a beauty!* **4** [C] a pleasing feature **SYN** ADVANTAGE: *One of the beauties of living here is that it's so peaceful.* ◆ *The project will require very little work to start up; that's the beauty of it.* **IDM beauty is in the eye of the beholder** (saying) people all have different ideas about what is beautiful **beauty is only skin-deep** (saying) how a person looks is less important than their character

Beauty and the Beast noun **1** a traditional story about a young girl who saves a large ugly creature from a magic SPELL by her love. He becomes a HANDSOME prince and they get married. **2** (informal, humorous) two people of whom one is much more attractive than the other

beauty contest noun **1** a competition to choose the most beautiful from a group of women ⇒ compare PAGEANT **2** a contest between competing companies or political candidates that depends heavily on presentation

beauty mark noun = BEAUTY SPOT

beauty queen noun a woman who is judged to be the most beautiful in a BEAUTY CONTEST

beauty salon (also **beauty parlor**, **beauty shop**) noun a place where you can pay for treatment to your face, hair, nails, etc., which is intended to make you more beautiful

beauty school noun a place that trains people to cut hair, take care of nails, etc. as a job

beauty sleep noun [U] (humorous) enough sleep at night to make sure that you look and feel healthy and beautiful

beauty spot noun **1** a place in the countryside which is famous because it is beautiful **2** (also **beauty mark**) a small dark spot on a woman's face, which used to be thought to make her more beautiful

beaux pl. of BEAU

bea·ver /ˈbivər/ noun, verb
● **noun 1** [C] an animal with a wide flat tail and strong teeth. Beavers live in water and on land, and can build DAMS (= barriers across rivers), made of pieces of wood and mud. It is an official symbol of Canada. ⇒ **picture at RODENT** ⇒ see also EAGER BEAVER **2** [U] the fur of the beaver, used in making hats and clothes
● **verb**
PHR V beaver away (at sth) (informal) to work very hard at something: *He's been beavering away at the accounts all morning.*

be·bop /ˈbibɑp/ (also bop) noun [U] a type of JAZZ with complicated rhythms

be·calmed /bɪˈkɑmd/ adj. (of a ship with a sail) unable to move because there is no wind

be·came pt of BECOME

be·cause 🔊 /bɪˈkʌz; -ˈkɔz/ conj.
for the reason that: *I did it because he told me to.* ◆ *Just because I don't complain, people think I'm satisfied.* ▶ **because of** prep.: *They are here because of us.* ◆ *He walked slowly because of his bad leg.* ◆ *Because of the children's presence, I said nothing about it.*

because of

explaining reasons

- The number of people with diabetes is growing, partly **because of** an increase in levels of obesity.
- The number of overweight children has increased dramatically in recent years, largely **as a result of** changes in diet and lifestyle.
- The increase in childhood obesity is largely **due to/the result of** changes in lifestyle and diet over the last twenty years.
- Many obese children are bullied at school **on account of** their weight.
- Part of the problem with treating childhood obesity **stems from** the fact that parents do not always recognize that their children are obese.
- Childhood obesity may be **caused by** genetic factors as well as environmental ones.
⇒ Language Banks at CAUSE, CONSEQUENTLY, THEREFORE

bé·cha·mel /ˌbeɪʃəˈmɛl; ˈbeɪʃəˌmɛl/ (also **bécha·mel sauce**) noun [U] a thick sauce made with milk, flour, and butter **SYN** WHITE SAUCE

beck /bɛk/ *noun*
  IDM **at sb's beck and call** always ready to obey someone's orders: *Don't expect to have me at your beck and call.*

beck·on /ˈbɛkən/ *verb* **1** [I, T] to give someone a signal using your finger or hand, especially to tell them to move nearer or to follow you **SYN** SIGNAL: *~ to sb (to do sth) He beckoned to the waiter to bring the check.* ◆ *~ sb (+ adv./prep.) He beckoned her over with a wave.* ◆ *The boss beckoned him into her office.* ◆ *~ sb to do sth She beckoned him to come and join them.* **2** [I, T] to appear very attractive to someone: *The clear blue sea beckoned.* ◆ *~ sb The thought of a month without work was beckoning her.* **3** [I] to be something that is likely to happen or will possibly happen to someone in the future: *For many kids leaving college the prospect of unemployment beckons.*

be·come 🔑 /bɪˈkʌm/ *verb* (be·came /bɪˈkeɪm/, be·come)
1 *linking verb* to start to be something: *+ adj. It was becoming more and more difficult to live on his salary.* ◆ *It soon became apparent that no one was going to come.* ◆ *She was becoming confused.* ◆ *+ noun Obama became president in 2009.* ◆ *The bill will become law next year.* **2** [T, no passive] (not used in the progressive tenses) *~ sb (formal)* to be suitable for someone: *Such behavior did not become her.* **3** [T, no passive] (not used in the progressive tenses) *~ sb (formal)* to look attractive on someone **SYN** SUIT: *Short hair really becomes you.*
  IDM **what became, has become, will become of sb/sth?** used to ask what has happened or what will happen to someone or something: *What became of that student who used to live with you?* ◆ *I dread to think what will become of them if they lose their home.*

WHICH WORD?

become ◆ get ◆ go ◆ turn

These verbs are used frequently with the following adjectives:

become ~	get ~	go ~	turn ~
involved	used to	wrong	blue
clear	better	right	sour
accustomed	worse	bad	bad
extinct	dark	crazy	cold
famous	angry	bald	red
ill	sick	blind	

- **Become** is more formal than **get**. Both describe changes in people's emotional or physical state, or natural or social changes.
- **Go** is usually used for negative changes.
- **Turn** is used for changes of color and changes in the weather.

---

be·com·ing /bɪˈkʌmɪŋ/ *adj.* (*formal*) **1** (of clothes, etc.) making the person wearing them look more attractive **SYN** FLATTERING **2** suitable or appropriate for someone or their situation **SYN** FITTING: *It was not very becoming behavior for a teacher.* **ANT** UNBECOMING

bec·que·rel /ˌbɛkəˈrɛl; ˈbɛkəˌrɛl/ *noun* (*abbr.* Bq) (*physics*) a unit for measuring

B.Ed. /ˌbi ˈɛd; ˌbi ɛ ˈdi/ *noun* a college degree in education (the abbreviation for "Bachelor of Education"): *Sarah is working toward a B.Ed.*

bed 🔑 /bɛd/ *noun, verb*
● *noun*
> FURNITURE **1** [C, U] a piece of furniture for sleeping on: *a single/double bed* ◆ *She lay on the bed (= on top of the covers).* ◆ *He lay in bed (= under the covers).* ◆ *I'm tired—I'm going to bed.* ◆ *It's time for bed (= time to go to sleep).* ◆ *I'll just put the kids to bed.* ◆ *He likes to have a cup of cocoa before bed (= before going to bed).* ◆ *to get into/out of bed* ◆ *to make the bed (= arrange the covers in a tidy way)* ◆ *Could you give me a bed for the night (= somewhere to sleep)?* ◆ *There's a shortage of*

hospital beds (= not enough room for patients to be admitted). ◆ *He has been confined to bed with flu for the past couple of days.* ⇒ picture on page 121 ⇒ see also SOFA BED, TWIN BED, WATERBED
> OF RIVER/LAKE/SEA **2** [C] the bottom of a river, the ocean, etc.: *the ocean bed* ◆ *oyster beds (= an area in the ocean where there are many OYSTERS)*
> FOR FLOWERS/VEGETABLES **3** [C] an area of ground in a yard or park for growing flowers, vegetables, etc.: *flower beds* ⇒ see also SEEDBED
> BOTTOM LAYER **4** [C] *~ of sth* a layer of something that other things lie or rest on: *grilled chicken, served on a bed of rice* ◆ *The blocks should be laid on a bed of concrete.*
> GEOLOGY **5** [C] a layer of CLAY, rock, etc. in the ground ⇒ see also BEDROCK
  IDM **(not) a bed of roses** (not) an easy or a pleasant situation: *Their life together hasn't exactly been a bed of roses.* **get up on the wrong side of the bed** to be in a bad mood for the whole day for no particular reason **go to bed with sb** (*informal*) to have sex with someone **in bed** used to refer to sexual activity: *What's he like in bed?* ◆ *I caught them in bed together (= having sex).* **you've made your bed and you must lie in it** (*saying*) you must accept the results of your actions **take to your bed** to go to bed and stay there because you are sick ⇒ more at DIE v., WET v.
● *verb* (-dd-) **1** *~ sth (in sth)* to fix something firmly in something: *The bricks were bedded in sand to improve drainage.* ◆ *Make sure that you bed the roots firmly in the soil.* **2** *~ sb* (*old-fashioned*) to have sex with someone
  PHRV **bed 'down** to sleep in a place where you do not usually sleep: *You have my room and I'll bed down in the living room.*

bed and 'breakfast *noun* (*abbr.* B & 'B, ˌb. & 'b.*) a private house or small hotel that provides a room to sleep in and a meal the next morning: *There are several good bed and breakfasts in the area.* ◆ *That B&B costs $150 a night.*

be·daz·zle /bɪˈdæzl/ *verb* [usually passive] *~ sb* to impress someone very much with intelligence, beauty, etc.: *He was so bedazzled by her looks that he couldn't speak.* ▶ **be·daz·zle·ment** *noun* [U]

bed·bug /ˈbɛdbʌɡ/ *noun* a small flat insect that lives especially in beds, where it bites people and sucks their blood

bed·cham·ber /ˈbɛdˌtʃeɪmbər/ *noun* (*old use*) a bedroom: *the royal bedchamber*

bed·clothes /ˈbɛdkloʊz; -kloʊðz/ *noun* [pl.] the sheets and other covers that you put on a bed

bed·cov·er /ˈbɛdˌkʌvər/ *noun* = BEDSPREAD

bed·ding /ˈbɛdɪŋ/ *noun* [U] **1** the sheets and covers that you put on a bed, often also the MATTRESS and the PILLOWS **2** STRAW, etc. for animals to sleep on

'bedding ˌplant *noun* a plant that is planted out in a garden bed, usually just before it gets flowers. It usually grows and dies within one year.

bed·dy-bye /ˈbɛdi ˌbaɪ/ *noun* [U] a child's word for bed, used when talking about the time someone goes to bed: *Time for beddy-bye.*

be·deck /bɪˈdɛk/ *verb* [usually passive] *~ sth/sb (with/in sth)* (*literary*) to decorate something or someone with flowers, flags, PRECIOUS STONES, etc.

be·dev·il /bɪˈdɛvl/ *verb* *~ sb/sth* (*formal*) to cause a lot of problems for someone or something over a long period of time **SYN** BESET: *The expedition was bedeviled by bad weather.*

bed·fel·low /ˈbɛdˌfɛloʊ/ *noun* a person or thing that is connected with or related to another, often in a way that you would not expect: *strange/unlikely bedfellows*

bed·lam /ˈbɛdləm/ *noun* [U] a scene full of noise and confusion **SYN** CHAOS: *It was bedlam at our house on the morning of the wedding.*

'bed ˌlinen *noun* [U] sheets and PILLOWCASES for a bed

Bed·ou·in /ˈbɛduən/ *noun* (*pl.* Bed·ou·in) a member of an Arab people that traditionally lives in tents in the desert

---

  h **h**at   m **m**an   n **n**o   ŋ si**ng**   l **l**eg   r **r**ed   y **y**es   w **w**et

beds

four-poster bed

double bed
(*also* **full-size bed**)

twin bed
(*also* **single bed**)

bunk beds

canopy · bedpost · patchwork quilt · mattress · quilt · pillow · headboard · sheet · blanket · bedspread

sofa bed

futon

pump

air mattress

hammock

cradle

crib

travel crib

sleeping bag

cot

---

bed·pan /'bɛdpæn/ *noun* a container used as a toilet by a person who is too sick to get out of bed

bed·post /'bɛdpoʊst/ *noun* one of the four vertical supports at the corners of a bed (especially an old type of bed with a wooden or metal frame) ⊃ **picture at BED**

be·drag·gled /bɪ'dræɡld/ *adj.* made wet, dirty, or messy by rain, mud, etc.: *bedraggled hair/clothes*

bed·rid·den /'bɛd,rɪdn/ *adj.* having to stay in bed all the time because you are sick, injured, or old

bed·rock /'bɛdrɑk/ *noun* **1** [sing.] a strong base for something, especially the facts or the principles on which it is based: *Poor urban areas traditionally **formed the bedrock of the** candidate's support.* ◆ *Honesty is the bedrock of any healthy relationship.* **2** [U] the solid rock in the ground below the loose soil and sand

bed·roll /'bɛdroʊl/ *noun* a thick piece of material or a SLEEPING BAG that you can roll up for carrying and use for sleeping on or in, for example when you are camping

bed·room /'bɛdrum; -rʊm/ *noun, adj.*

● *noun* **1** a room for sleeping in: *the spare bedroom* ◆ *a hotel with 20 bedrooms* ◆ *This is the **master bedroom** (= the main bedroom of the house).* **2 -bedroom** having the number of bedrooms mentioned: *a three-bedroom house*

● *adj.* [only before noun] used as a way of referring to sexual activity: *the bedroom scenes in the movie*

bedroom com·munity (*also* **bedroom suburb**) *noun* a town that people live in and from where they travel to work in a bigger town or city

bed·side /'bɛdsaɪd/ *noun* [usually sing.] the area beside a bed: *His mother has been **at his bedside** throughout his illness.* ◆ *a bedside lamp*

bedside manner *noun* [sing.] the way in which a doctor or other person talks to someone who is sick

bed·sore /'bɛdsɔr/ *noun* a painful and sometimes infected place on a person's skin, caused by lying in bed for a long time

bed·spread /'bɛdsprɛd/ (*also* **bed·cov·er, spread**) *noun* an attractive cover put on top of all the sheets and covers on a bed ⊃ **picture at BED**

bed·stead /'bɛdstɛd/ *noun* the wooden or metal frame of an old-fashioned type of bed

bed·time /'bɛdtaɪm/ *noun* [U] the time when someone usually goes to bed: *It's way past your bedtime.* ◆ *Will you read me a bedtime story?*

bed-wetting *noun* [U] the problem of urinating (URINATE) in bed, usually by children while they are asleep ▶ **bed-wetter** *noun*

bee /bi/ *noun* **1** a black and yellow flying insect that can sting. Bees live in large groups and make HONEY (= a sweet sticky substance that is good to eat): *a swarm of bees* ◆ *a bee sting* ◆ *Bees were buzzing in the clover.* ⊃ **picture at ANIMAL** ⊃ **see also BEEHIVE, BEESWAX, BUMBLEBEE, QUEEN BEE 2** a meeting in a group where people combine work, competition, and pleasure: *a sewing bee* ⊃ **see also SPELLING BEE**
IDM the bee's knees (*informal, old-fashioned*) an excellent person or thing: *She thinks she's the bee's knees* (= she has a very high opinion of herself). **have a bee in your bonnet (about sth)** (*informal*) to think or talk about something all the time, and to think that it is very important ⊃ **more at BIRD, BUSY** *adj.*

beech /bitʃ/ *noun* **1** [C, U] (*also* **beech tree**) a tall forest tree with smooth gray BARK, shiny leaves, and small nuts: *forests planted with beech* ◆ *The great beeches towered up toward the sky.* ⊃ **see also COPPER BEECH** ⊃ **picture at TREE 2** (*also* **beech·wood**) [U] the wood of the beech tree

beef /bif/ *noun, verb*

● *noun* **1** [U] meat that comes from a cow: *roast/ground beef* ◆ *beef and dairy cattle* ⊃ **see also CHIPPED BEEF, CORNED BEEF 2** [C] (*informal*) a complaint: *What's his latest beef?*

● *verb* [I] **~ (about sb/sth)** (*informal*) to complain a lot about someone or something
PHR V beef sth↔up (*informal*) to make something bigger, better, more interesting, etc.

---

beef·cake /'bifkeɪk/ noun [U] (slang) attractive men with big muscles, especially those that appear in magazines

beef·steak /'bifsteɪk/ noun [C, U] = STEAK

beefsteak to'mato noun a type of large tomato

beef·y /'bifi/ adj. (beef·i·er, beef·i·est) (informal) (of a person or their body) big or fat: beefy men/arms/thighs

bee·hive /'bihaɪv/ noun **1** = HIVE **2** a HAIRSTYLE for women, with the hair piled high on top of the head **IDM** see ACTIVITY

bee·keep·er /'bi,kipər/ noun a person who owns and takes care of BEES ▶ **bee·keep·ing** noun [U]

bee·line /'bilaɪn/ noun
IDM **make a beeline for sth/sb** (informal) to go straight toward something or someone as quickly as you can

Be·el·ze·bub /bɪ'ɛlzə,bʌb/ noun a name for the DEVIL

been /bɪn/ ⊃ BE ⊃ see also GO

beep /bip/ noun, verb
• noun a short high sound such as that made by a car horn or by electronic equipment
• verb **1** [I] (of an electronic machine) to make a short high sound: The microwave beeps to let you know when it's done. **2** [I, T] when a car horn, etc. **beeps** or when you **beep** it, it makes a short noise: The car behind started beeping at us. ◆ ~ **sth** He beeped his horn at the cyclist. **3** [T] ~ **sb** to call someone on their beeper

beep·er /'bipər/ noun a small electronic device that you carry around with you and that lets you know when someone is trying to contact you, by making a sound

beer /bɪr/ noun
1 [U, C] an alcoholic drink made from MALT and flavored with HOPS. There are many types of beer: a bottle/glass/six-pack of beer ◆ beers brewed in Vermont ◆ a beer glass ◆ Are you a beer drinker? **2** [C] a glass, bottle, or can of beer: Shall we have a beer? ⊃ picture at CUP ⊃ see also GINGER BEER, ROOT BEER

'beer ,belly (also **'beer gut**) noun (informal) a man's very fat stomach, caused by drinking a lot of beer over a long period

'beer ,garden noun an outdoor area at a bar with tables and chairs

'beer mat noun a small piece of thick paper that you put under a glass, usually in a bar, etc. in order to protect the surface below

beer·y /'bɪri/ adj. smelling of beer; influenced by the drinking of beer

bees·wax /'bizwæks/ noun [U] a yellow sticky substance that is produced by BEES and is used especially for making CANDLES and polish for wood

beet /bit/ noun [C, U] **1** a plant with a round, dark red root that is cooked and eaten as a vegetable ⊃ picture at FRUIT **2** a plant with a root that is used as a vegetable, especially for feeding animals or making sugar ⊃ see also SUGAR BEET

bee·tle /'bitl/ noun, verb
• noun an insect, often large and black, with a hard case on its back covering its wings. There are several types of beetles. ⊃ picture at ANIMAL ⊃ see also DEATHWATCH BEETLE
• verb [I] + adv./prep. (informal) to move somewhere quickly SYN SCURRY: I last saw him beetling off down the road.

be·fall /bɪ'fɔl/ verb (be·fell /bɪ'fɛl/, be·fal·len /bɪ'fɔlən/) ~ **sb** (used only in the third person) (literary) (of something unpleasant) to happen to someone: They were unaware of the fate that was to befall them.

be·fit /bɪ'fɪt/ verb (-tt-) (used only in the third person and in participles) **sth befits sb** (formal) to be suitable and good enough for someone or something: It was a lavish reception as befitted a visitor of her status. ◆ He lived in the style befitting a gentleman.

be·fog /bɪ'fɔg; -'fɑg/ verb ~ **sb** to make someone confused: Her brain was befogged by lack of sleep.

be·fore /bɪ'fɔr/ prep., conj., adv.
• prep. **1** earlier than someone or something: before lunch ◆ the day before yesterday ◆ The year before last he won a gold medal, and the year before that he won a silver. ◆ She's lived there since before the war. ◆ He arrived before me. ◆ She became a lawyer as her father had before her. ◆ Leave your keys at the reception desk before departure. ◆ Something should have been done before now. ◆ We'll know **before long** (= soon). ◆ Turn left just before (= before you reach) the bank. **2** (somewhat formal) used to say that someone or something is in a position in front of someone or something: They knelt before the altar. ◆ Before you is a list of the points we have to discuss. ⊃ compare BEHIND **3** used to say that someone or something is ahead of someone or something in an order or arrangement: Your name is before mine on the list. ◆ He puts his work before everything (= regards it as more important than anything else). **4** used to say that something is facing someone in the future: The task before us is a daunting one. ◆ The whole summer lay before me. **5** in the presence of someone who is listening, watching, etc.: He was brought before the judge. ◆ She said it before witnesses. ◆ They had the advantage of playing before their home crowd. **6** (formal) used to say how someone reacts when they have to face someone or something: They retreated before the enemy.
• conj. **1** earlier than the time when: Do it before you forget. ◆ Did she leave a message before she went? **2** until: It may be many years before the situation improves. ◆ It was some time before I realized the truth. **3** used to warn or threaten someone that something bad could happen: Put that away before it gets broken. **4** (formal) rather than: I'd die before I apologized!
• adv. at an earlier time; in the past; already: You should have told me so before. ◆ It was fine the week before (= the previous week). ◆ That had happened long before (= a long time earlier). ◆ I think we've met before.

be·fore·hand /bɪ'fɔrhænd/ adv. earlier; before something else happens or is done: two weeks/three days/a few hours beforehand ◆ I wish we'd known about it beforehand.

be·friend /bɪ'frɛnd/ verb [usually passive] ~ **sb** to become a friend of someone, especially someone who needs your help: Shortly after my arrival at the school, I was befriended by an older girl.

be·fud·dled /bɪ'fʌdld/ adj. confused and unable to think normally: He was befuddled by alcohol.

beg /bɛg/ verb (-gg-) **1** [I, T] to ask someone for something, especially in an anxious way because you want or need it very much: ~ **(for sth)** He wants to see them beg for mercy. ◆ ~ **sb (for sth)** They begged him for help. ◆ ~ **sth (of/from sb)** She begged forgiveness from him. ◆ ~ **(sb) + speech** "Give me one more chance," he begged (her). ◆ ~ **sb to do sth** She begged him not to go. ◆ ~ **to do sth** He begged to be told the truth. ◆ ~ **that…** (formal) She begged that she be allowed to go. ◆ She begged that she should be allowed to go. ◆ ~ **of sb** (formal) Don't leave me here, I beg of you! **2** [I, T] to ask someone for money, food, etc., especially in the street: Chicago is full of homeless people begging in the streets. ◆ ~ **sth (from sb)** The children were begging for food. ◆ ~ **sth (from sb)** We managed to beg a meal from the café. **3** [I] if a dog **begs**, it sits on its back legs with its front legs in the air, waiting to be given something
IDM **beg leave to do sth** (formal) to ask someone for permission to do something **be going begging** (informal) if something is going begging, it is available because no one else wants it **beg the question 1** to make someone want to ask a question that has not yet been answered: All of which begs the question as to who will fund the project. **2** to talk about something as if it were definitely true, even though it might not be: These assumptions beg the question that children learn languages more easily than adults. **I beg to differ** used to say politely that you do not agree with something that has just been said **I beg your pardon 1** (formal) used to tell

someone that you are sorry for something you have said or done: *I beg your pardon, I thought that was my coat.* **2** used to ask someone to repeat what they have just said because you did not hear: *"It's on Bleecker Street." "I beg your pardon." "Bleecker Street."* **3** used to tell someone that you are offended by what they have just said or by the way that they have said it: *"Just go away." "I beg your pardon!"*

PHR V **beg 'off** to say that you are unable to do something that you have agreed to do: *He's always begging off at the last minute.*

be·gan pt of BEGIN

be·get /bɪˈɡɛt/ *verb* (**be·get·ting, be·got, be·got** /bɪˈɡɑt/
HELP In sense 1 **begat** /bɪˈɡæt/ is used for the past tense, and **begotten** /bɪˈɡɑtn/ is used for the past participle.)
1 ~ sth (*formal* or *old-fashioned*) to make something happen: *Violence begets violence.* **2** (old use, for example in the Bible) ~ sb to become the father of a child: *Isaac begat Jacob.*
▶ **be·get·ter** *noun*

beg·gar /ˈbɛɡər/ *noun, verb*
● *noun* a person who lives by asking people for money or food
IDM **beggars can't be choosers** (*saying*) people say **beggars can't be choosers** when there is no choice and someone must be satisfied with what is available ➔ more at WISH *n.*
● *verb* ~ sb/sth/yourself to make someone or something very poor: *Why should I beggar myself for you?*
IDM **beggar belief/description** to be too extreme, shocking, etc. to believe/describe: *It beggars belief how things could have gotten this bad.*

beg·gar·ly /ˈbɛɡərli/ *adj.* (*literary*) very small in amount

'begging ˌbowl *noun* a bowl held out by someone asking for food or money: (*figurative*) *He is handing around the begging bowl on behalf of the candidate's campaign fund.*

be·gin 🔑 /bɪˈɡɪn/ *verb*
(**be·gin·ning, be·gan** /bɪˈɡæn/, **be·gun** /bɪˈɡʌn/) **1** [I, T] to start doing something; to do the first part of something: *Shall I begin?* ◆ ~ at/with sth *Let's begin at page 9.* ◆ ~ by doing sth *She began by thanking us all for coming.* ◆ ~ sth *We began work on the project in May.* ◆ *I began* (= started reading) *this novel last month and I still haven't finished it.* ◆ ~ sth at/with sth *He always begins his lessons with a warm-up exercise.* ◆ ~ sth as sth *He began his political career as a student* (= when he was a student). ◆ ~ to do sth *I began to feel dizzy.* ◆ *Finally the guests began to arrive.* ◆ *She began to cry.* ◆ *It was beginning to snow.* ◆ *I was beginning to think you'd never come.* ◆ ~ doing sth *Everyone began talking at once.* ◆ *When will you begin recruiting?* ➔ thesaurus box at START ➔ language bank at FIRST **2** [I] to start to happen or exist, especially from a particular time: *When does the concert begin?* ◆ *Work on the new bridge is due to begin in September.* ◆ *The evening began well.* **3** [I] ~ as sth to be something first, before becoming something else: *He began as an actor, before starting to direct films.* ◆ *What began as a minor scuffle turned into a full-scale riot.* **4** [I] to have something as the first part or the point where something starts: *Where does Europe end and Asia begin?* ◆ ~ with sth *Use "an" before words beginning with a vowel.* ◆ *"I'm thinking of a country in Asia." "What does it begin with* (= what is the first letter)?" ◆ *Each chapter begins with a quotation.* ◆ ~ at… *The path begins at the edge of the village.* **5** [T] + speech to start speaking: *"Ladies and gentlemen," he began, "welcome to the Town Hall."* **6** [I, T] to start or make something start for the first time: *The school began in 1920, with only ten students.* ◆ ~ sth *He began a new magazine on postwar architecture.* **7** [T] not ~ to do something to make no attempt to do something or have no chance of doing something: *I can't begin to thank you enough.* ◆ *He couldn't even begin to understand my problem.*
IDM **to begin with 1** at first: *I found it tiring to begin with, but I soon got used to it.* ◆ *We'll go slowly to begin with.* **2** used to introduce the first point you want to make: *"What was it you didn't like?" "Well, to begin with, our room was far too small."* ➔ more at CHARITY

be·gin·ner /bɪˈɡɪnər/ *noun* a person who is starting to learn something and cannot do it very well yet: *She's in the beginners' class.*

be,ginner's 'luck *noun* [U] good luck or unexpected success when you start to do something new

be·gin·ning 🔑 /bɪˈɡɪnɪŋ/ *noun*
1 [C, usually sing.] ~ (of sth) the time when something starts; the first part of an event, a story, etc.: *We're going to Japan at the beginning of July.* ◆ *She's been working there since the beginning of last summer.* ◆ *We missed the beginning of the movie.* ◆ *Let's start again from the beginning.* ◆ *The birth of their first child marked the beginning of a new era in their married life.* ◆ *I've read the whole book from beginning to end and still can't understand it.* **HELP** **At the beginning (of)** is used for the time and place when something begins. **In the beginning** = at first and suggests a contrast with a later situation. **2 beginnings** [pl.] the first or early ideas, signs, or stages of something: *Did democracy have its beginnings in ancient Greece?* ◆ *He built up his multimillion-dollar music business from small beginnings.*
IDM **the beginning of the end** the first sign of something ending

be·gone /bɪˈɡɔn; -ˈɡɑn/ *exclamation* (old use) a way of telling someone to go away immediately

be·go·nia /bɪˈɡoʊnyə/ *noun* a plant with large shiny flowers that may be pink, red, yellow, or white, grown indoors or in a garden

be·got pt of BEGET

be·got·ten pp of BEGET

be·grudge /bɪˈɡrʌdʒ/ *verb* (often used in negative sentences) **1** to feel unhappy that someone has something because you do not think that they deserve it: ~ sb sth *You surely don't begrudge him his happiness.* ◆ ~ sb doing sth *I don't begrudge her being so successful.* **2** to feel unhappy about having to do, pay, or give something: ~ sth *I begrudge every second I spent trying to help him.* ◆ ~ doing sth *They begrudge paying so much money for a second-rate service.*

be·grudg·ing·ly /bɪˈɡrʌdʒɪŋli/ *adv.* = GRUDGING

be·guile /bɪˈɡaɪl/ *verb* (formal) **1** ~ sb (into doing sth) to trick someone into doing something, especially by being nice to them: *She beguiled them into believing her version of events.* **2** ~ sb to attract or interest someone: *He was beguiled by her beauty.*

be·guil·ing /bɪˈɡaɪlɪŋ/ *adj.* (formal) attractive and interesting but sometimes mysterious or trying to trick you: *beguiling advertisements* ◆ *Her beauty was beguiling.* ▶ **be·guil·ing·ly** *adv.*

be·gun pp of BEGIN

be·half 🔑 **AWL** /bɪˈhæf/ noun

IDM **in behalf of sb | in sb's behalf** in order to help someone: *We collected money in behalf of the homeless.* **on behalf of sb | on sb's behalf** **1** as the representative of someone or instead of them: *On behalf of the department, I would like to thank you all.* ◆ *Mr. Knight cannot be here, so his wife will accept the prize on his behalf.* **2** because of someone; for someone: *Don't worry on my behalf.* **3** in order to help someone: *They campaigned on behalf of asylum seekers.*

be·have 🔑 /bɪˈheɪv/ verb

1 [I] + adv./prep. to do things in a particular way **SYN** ACT: *The doctor behaved very unprofessionally.* ◆ *They behaved very badly toward their guests.* ◆ *He behaved like a true gentleman.* ◆ *She behaved with great dignity.* ◆ *He behaved as if/though nothing had happened.* ◆ *They behave differently when you're not around.* **HELP** In spoken English, people often use **like** instead of **as if** or **as though**: *He behaved like nothing had happened.* **2** [I, T] to do things in a way that people think is correct or polite: *Will you kids just behave!* ◆ *She doesn't know how to behave in public.* ◆ **~ yourself** *I want you to behave yourselves while I'm away.* **ANT** MISBEHAVE **3** **-behaved** (in adjectives) behaving in the way mentioned: *well-/badly-behaved children* **4** [I] + adv./prep. (*technical*) to naturally react, move, etc. in a particular way: *a study of how metals behave under pressure* **IDM** see OWN v.

be·hav·ior 🔑 /bɪˈheɪvyər/ noun

1 [U] the way that someone behaves, especially toward other people: *good/bad behavior* ◆ *social/sexual/criminal behavior* ◆ *His behavior toward her was becoming more and more aggressive.* **2** [U, C] the way a person, an animal, a plant, a chemical, etc. behaves or functions in a particular situation: *the behavior of dolphins/chromosomes* ◆ *studying human and animal behavior* ◆ (*technical*) *studying learned behaviors* ▶ **be·hav·ior·al** /bɪˈheɪvyərəl/ adj.: *children with behavioral difficulties* ◆ *behavioral science* (= the study of human behavior) **be·hav·ior·al·ly** adv.

IDM **be on your best behavior** to behave in the most polite way you can

be·hav·ior·ism /bɪˈheɪvyəˌrɪzəm/ noun [U] (*psychology*) the theory that all human behavior is learned by adapting to outside conditions and that learning is not influenced by thoughts and feelings ▶ **be·hav·ior·ist** /-yərɪst/ noun

be·head /bɪˈhɛd/ verb [usually passive] **~ sb** to cut off someone's head, especially as a punishment **SYN** DECAPITATE

be·held pt, pp of BEHOLD

be·he·moth /bɪˈhiməθ/ noun (*formal*) a very big and powerful company or organization

be·hest /bɪˈhɛst/ noun [sing.]

IDM **at sb's behest** (*old use* or *formal*) because someone has ordered or requested it

be·hind 🔑 /bɪˈhaɪnd/ prep., adv., noun

● **prep.** **1** at or toward the back of someone or something, and often hidden by it or them: *Who's the girl standing behind Jan?* ◆ *Stay close behind me.* ◆ *a small street behind the station* ◆ *She glanced behind her.* ◆ *Don't forget to lock the door behind you* (= when you leave). ◆ *The sun disappeared behind the clouds.* ⊃ compare IN FRONT OF ⊃ note at BACK **2** making less progress than someone or something: *He's behind the rest of the class in reading.* ◆ *We're behind schedule* (= late). **3** giving support to, or approval of, someone or something: *She knew that, whatever she decided, her family was right behind her.* **4** responsible for starting or developing something: *What's behind that happy smile* (= what is causing it)? ◆ *He was the man behind the plan to build a new hospital.* **5** used to say that something is in someone's past: *The accident is behind you now, so try to forget it.* ◆ *She has ten years of useful experience behind her.*

● **adv.** **1** at or toward the back of someone or something; farther back: *She rode off down the road with the dog running behind.* ◆ *The others are a long way behind.* ◆ *He was shot from behind as he ran away.* ◆ *I had fallen so far behind that trying to*

catch up seemed pointless. **2** in the place where someone or something is or was: *I was told to stay behind after school* (= remain in school). ◆ *This bag was left behind after the class.* **3** late in paying money or completing work: **~ (with sth)** *She has fallen behind with the payments.* ◆ **~ (in sth)** *He was really behind in his work.*

● **noun** (*informal*) a person's BUTTOCKS. People often say "behind" to avoid saying "buttocks." **SYN** BACKSIDE: *The dog bit him on his behind.*

be·hind·hand /bɪˈhaɪndhænd/ adj. [not before noun] **~ (with/in sth)** late in doing something or in paying money that is owed: *They were behindhand in settling their debts.*

be·hold /bɪˈhoʊld/ verb (**be·held** /bɪˈhɛld/, **be·held**) **~ sb/ sth** (*old use* or *literary*) to look at or see someone or something: *Her face was a joy to behold.* ◆ *They beheld a bright star shining in the sky.* **IDM** see LO

be·hold·en /bɪˈhoʊldən/ adj. **~ to sb (for sth)** (*formal*) owing something to someone because of something that they have done for you: *She didn't like to be beholden to anyone.*

be·hold·er /bɪˈhoʊldər/ noun **IDM** see BEAUTY

be·hoove /bɪˈhuv/ verb

IDM **it behooves sb to do sth** (*formal*) it is right or necessary for someone to do something: *It behooves us to study these findings carefully.*

beige /beɪʒ/ adj. light yellowish-brown in color ▶ **beige** noun [U]

be·ing /ˈbiɪŋ/ noun **1** [U] existence: *The state of Texas came into being in 1845.* ◆ *A new era was brought into being by the war.* ⊃ see also WELL-BEING **2** [C] a living creature: *human beings* ◆ *a strange being from another planet* **3** [U] (*formal*) your mind and all of your feelings: *I hated him with my whole being.* ⊃ see also BE

be·jew·eled /bɪˈdʒuəld/ adj. (*literary*) decorated with PRECIOUS STONES; wearing jewelry

bel /bɛl/ noun (*technical*) a measurement of sound equal to 10 DECIBELS

be·la·bor /bɪˈleɪbər/ verb

IDM **belabor the point** (*formal*) to repeat an idea, argument, etc. many times to emphasize it, especially when it has already been mentioned or understood

be·lat·ed /bɪˈleɪtəd/ adj. coming or happening late: *a belated birthday present* ▶ **be·lat·ed·ly** adv.

be·lay /bɪˈleɪ/ verb [I, T] **~ (sth/sb)** (*technical*) (in climbing) to attach a rope to a rock, etc.; to make a person safe while climbing by attaching a rope to the person and to a rock

bel can·to /ˌbɛl ˈkɑntoʊ/ noun [U] (*music*) a style of OPERA or opera singing in the 19th century in which producing a beautiful tone was considered very important

belch /bɛltʃ/ verb **1** [I] to let air come up noisily from your stomach and out through your mouth: *He wiped his hand across his mouth, then belched loudly.* **SYN** BURP **2** [I, T] **~ (out/forth) (sth)** to send out large amounts of smoke, flames, etc.; to come out of something in large amounts **SYN** SPEW OUT ▶ **belch** noun: *He sat back and let out a loud belch.*

be·lea·guered /bɪˈligərd/ adj. **1** (*formal*) experiencing a lot of criticism and difficulties: *The beleaguered manager was forced to resign.* **2** surrounded by an enemy: *supplies for the beleaguered city*

bel·fry /ˈbɛlfri/ noun (pl. **bel·fries**) a tower in which bells hang, especially as part of a church **IDM** see BAT n.

Bel·gian en·dive /ˌbɛldʒən ˈɛndaɪv; -anˈdiv/ noun [C, U] = ENDIVE

be·lie /bɪˈlaɪ/ verb (**be·lies**, **be·ly·ing**, **be·lied**, **be·lied**) (*formal*) **1 ~ sth** to give a false impression of someone or something: *Her energy and youthful good looks belie her 65 years.* **2 ~ sth** to show that something cannot be true or correct: *Government claims that there is no poverty are belied by the number of homeless people on the streets.*

   t tea   t̬ butter   d did   k cat   g got   tʃ chin   dʒ June   f fall

be·lief 🔊 /bɪˈliːf/ *noun*

1 [U] ~ **(in sth/sb)** a strong feeling that something or someone exists or is true; confidence that something or someone is good or right: *I admire his passionate belief in what he is doing.* ◆ *belief in God/democracy* **2** [sing., U] ~ **(that…)** an opinion about something; something that you think is true: *She acted in the belief that she was doing good.* ◆ *Contrary to popular belief* (= in spite of what people may think), *he was not responsible for the tragedy.* ◆ *There is a general belief that things will soon get better.* **3** [C, usually pl.] something that you believe, especially as part of your religion: *religious/political beliefs* ⊃ compare DISBELIEF, UNBELIEF

IDM **beyond belief** (in a way that is) too great, difficult, etc. to be believed: *Dissatisfaction with the government has grown beyond belief.* ◆ *icy air that was cold beyond belief* ⊃ more at BEGGAR *v.*, BEST *n.*

be·liev·a·ble /bɪˈliːvəbl/ *adj.* that can be believed **SYN** PLAUSIBLE: *Her explanation certainly sounded believable.* ◆ *a play with believable characters* **ANT** UNBELIEVABLE

be·lieve 🔊 /bɪˈliːv/ *verb*
(not used in the progressive tenses)
▷ **FEEL CERTAIN 1** [T] to feel certain that something is true or that someone is telling you the truth: ~ **sb** *I don't believe you!* ◆ *The man claimed to be a social worker and the old woman believed him.* ◆ *Believe me, she's not right for you.* ◆ ~ **sth** *I believed his lies for years.* ◆ *I find that hard to believe.* ◆ *Don't believe a word of it* (= don't believe any part of what someone is saying). ◆ ~ **(that)…** *People used to believe (that) the earth was flat.* ◆ *He refused to believe (that) his son was taking drugs.* ◆ *I do believe you're right* (= I think something is true, even though it is surprising).
▷ **THINK POSSIBLE 2** [I, T] to think that something is true or possible, although you are not completely certain: *"Where does she come from?" "Spain, I believe."* ◆ *"Does he still work there?" "I believe so/not."* ◆ ~ **(that)…** *Police believe (that) the man may be armed.* ◆ **it is believed (that)…** *It is believed that the couple has left the country.* ◆ ~ **sb/sth to be, have, etc. sth** *The vases are believed to be worth over $20,000 each.* ◆ ~ **sb/sth + adj.** *Three sailors are missing, believed drowned.* ⊃ thesaurus box at THINK
▷ **HAVE OPINION 3** [T] ~ **(that)…** to have the opinion that something is right or true: *The candidate believes (that) education is the most important issue facing the government.* ⊃ language bank at ACCORDING TO, OPINION
▷ **BE SURPRISED/ANNOYED 4** [T] **don't/can't** ~ used to say that you are surprised or annoyed at something: ~ **(that)…** *She couldn't believe (that) it was all happening again.* ◆ ~ **how, what, etc.…** *I can't believe how much better I feel.*
▷ **RELIGION 5** [I] to have a religious faith: *The god appears only to those who believe.*

IDM **believe it or not** (*informal*) used to introduce information that is true but that may surprise people: *Believe it or not, he asked me to marry him!* **believe (you) me** (*informal*) used to emphasize that you strongly believe what you are saying: *You haven't heard the last of this, believe you me!* **don't you believe it!** (*informal*) used to tell someone that something is definitely not true **I don't believe it!** (*informal*) used to say that you are surprised or annoyed about something: *I don't believe it! What are you doing here?* **if you believe that, you'll believe anything** (*informal*) used to say that you think someone is stupid if they believe that something is true **make believe (that…)** to pretend that something is true ⊃ related noun MAKE-BELIEVE **not believe your ears/eyes** (*informal*) to be very surprised at something you hear/see: *I couldn't believe my eyes when she walked in.* **seeing is believing** (*saying*) used to say that someone will have to believe that something is true when they see it, although they do not think it is true now **would you believe (it)?** (*informal*) used to show that you are surprised and annoyed about something: *And, would you believe, he didn't even apologize!* **you/you'd better believe it!** (*informal*) used to tell someone that something is definitely true ⊃ more at GIVE *v.*

PHR V **be·lieve in sb/sth** to feel certain that someone or

something exists: *Do you believe in God?* **be·lieve in sb** to feel that you can trust someone and/or that they will be successful: *They need a leader they can believe in.* ⊃ thesaurus box at TRUST **be·lieve in sth** to think that something is good, right, or acceptable: [+ **-ing**] *I don't believe in hitting children.* **be·lieve sth of sb** to think that someone is capable of something: *Are you sure he was lying? I can't believe that of him.*

be·liev·er /bɪˈliːvər/ *noun* a person who believes in the existence or truth of something, especially someone who believes in a god or religious faith **ANT** NONBELIEVER, UNBELIEVER

IDM **be a (great/firm) believer in sth** to believe strongly that something is good, important, or valuable

be·lit·tle /bɪˈlɪtl/ *verb* ~ **sb/sth** to make someone or the things that someone does seem unimportant: *She felt her husband constantly belittled her achievements.*

bell 🔊 /bel/ *noun*

1 a hollow metal object, often shaped like a cup, that makes a ringing sound when hit by a small piece of metal inside it; the sound that it makes: *A peal of church bells rang out in the distance.* ◆ *a bicycle bell* ◆ *His voice came down the line as clear as a bell.* ◆ *the bell of a trumpet* (= the bell-shaped part at the end of it) ◆ *a bell-shaped flower* **2** an electrical device which makes a ringing sound when a button on it is pushed; the sound that it makes, used as a signal or a warning: *Ring the bell to see if they're in.* ◆ *The bell's ringing!* ◆ *The bell rang at the end of the class.* ◆ *An alarm bell went off.* ◆ (*figurative*) *Warning bells started ringing in her head as she sensed that something was wrong.*

IDM **have/get your bell rung** (*slang*) to be hit very hard on the head: *Gonzales had his bell rung in the third round of the fight.* **with bells on** (*informal*) eager and full of enthusiasm about something: *Just tell me where the party is and I'll be there with bells on.* ⊃ more at ALARM *n.*, RING² , SOUND *adj.*

bel·la·don·na /ˌbeləˈdɑːnə/ *noun* [U] **1** = DEADLY NIGHTSHADE **2** a poisonous drug made from DEADLY NIGHTSHADE

bell-bottoms *noun* [pl.] pants with legs that become very wide below the knee

bell·boy /ˈbelbɔɪ/ (also **bell·hop**) *noun* a person whose job is to carry people's cases to their rooms in a hotel

bell curve *noun* (*mathematics*) a line on a GRAPH that rises to a high round curve in the middle, showing NORMAL DISTRIBUTION

belle /bel/ *noun* (*old-fashioned*) a beautiful woman; the most beautiful woman in a particular place: *a dainty Southern belle from Georgia*

belles-let·tres /ˌbel ˈletrə/ *noun* [pl., U] (from *French, old-fashioned*) studies or writings on the subject of literature or art, contrasted with those on technical or scientific subjects

bell·hop /ˈbelhɑːp/ *noun* = BELLBOY

bel·li·cose /ˈbeləkoʊs/ *adj.* (*formal*) having or showing a desire to argue or fight **SYN** AGGRESSIVE, WARLIKE ▶ **bel·li·cos·i·ty** /ˌbeləˈkɑːsəti/ *noun* [U]

-bellied /ˈbelid/ ⊃ BELLY

bel·lig·er·ent /bəˈlɪdʒərənt/ *adj., noun*
● *adj.* **1** unfriendly and aggressive **SYN** HOSTILE: *a belligerent attitude* **2** [only before noun] (*formal*) (of a country) fighting a war: *the belligerent countries/states/nations* ▶ **bel·lig·er·ence** /-rəns/ *noun* [U] **bel·lig·er·ent·ly** *adv.*
● *noun* (*formal*) a country or group that is fighting a war

bell jar *noun* a tall, round, glass cover, used by scientists

bel·low /ˈbeloʊ/ *verb* **1** [I, T] to shout in a loud, deep voice, especially because you are angry **SYN** YELL: ~ **(at sb)** *They bellowed at her to stop.* ◆ ~ **sth (at sb)** *The coach bellowed instructions from the sidelines.* ◆ + **speech** *"Get over here!" he bellowed.* ⊃ thesaurus box at SHOUT **2** [I] when a large animal such as a BULL **bellows**, it makes a loud deep sound ▶ **bel·low** *noun*: *to let out a bellow of rage/pain*

bel·lows /ˈbɛloʊz/ *noun* (*pl.* bel·lows) a piece of equipment for blowing air into or through something. Bellows are used for making a fire burn better or for producing sound in some types of musical instruments: *a pair of bellows* (= a small bellows with two handles to be pushed together)

bellows

bell 'pepper (also ˌsweet 'pepper) *noun* a hollow fruit, usually red, green, or yellow, eaten as a vegetable, either raw or cooked ⊃ picture at FRUIT

'bell pull *noun* a rope or handle that you pull to make a bell ring, for example to make someone in another room hear you

'bell-ˌringer (also ring·er) *noun* a person who rings church bells as a hobby ▶ **'bell-ˌringing** *noun* [U] ⊃ see also CAMPANOLOGY

ˌbells and 'whistles *noun* [pl.] (*computing*) attractive extra features

bell·weth·er /ˈbɛlˌwɛðər/ *noun* [usually sing.] something that is used as a sign of what will happen in the future: *College campuses are often the bellwether of change.*

bel·ly /ˈbɛli/ *noun, verb*
• *noun* (*pl.* bel·lies) **1** the part of the body below the chest **SYN** GUT, STOMACH: *They crawled along on their bellies.* ⊃ see also BEER BELLY, **2** (*literary*) the round or curved part of an object: *the belly of a ship* **3** -bellied (in adjectives) having the type of belly mentioned: *flat-bellied* ♦ *fat-bellied*
IDM **go belly up** (*informal*) to fail completely: *Last year the business went belly up after one of the partners resigned.*
• *verb* (bel·lies, bel·ly·ing, bel·lied, bel·lied) [I] ~ **(out)** (especially of sails) to fill with air and become rounder

bel·ly·ache /ˈbɛliˌeɪk/ *noun, verb*
• *noun* [C, U] (*informal*) a pain in the stomach: *I have a bellyache.*
• *verb* [I] (*informal*) to complain a lot about something in an annoying or unreasonable way

'belly ˌbutton *noun* (*informal*) = NAVEL

'belly ˌdance *noun* a dance, originally from the Middle East, in which a woman moves her belly and hips around ▶ **'belly ˌdancer** *noun*

bel·ly·flop /ˈbɛliˌflɑp/ *noun* (*informal*) a bad DIVE into water, in which the front of the body hits the water flat

bel·ly·ful /ˈbɛliˌfʊl/ *noun*
IDM **have had a bellyful of sb/sth** (*informal*) to have had more than enough of someone or something, so that you cannot deal with any more: *I've had a bellyful of your whining.*

'belly ˌlaugh *noun* (*informal*) a deep, loud laugh

be·long /bɪˈlɔŋ/ *verb*
(not used in the progressive tenses) **1** [I] + adv./prep. to be in the right or suitable place: *Where do these plates belong* (= where are they kept)? ♦ *Are you sure these documents belong together?* **2** [I] to feel comfortable and happy in a particular situation or with a particular group of people: *I don't feel as if I belong here.* ▶ **be·long·ing** *noun* [U]: *to feel a sense of belonging*
PHR V **be'long to sb 1** to be owned by someone: *Who does this watch belong to?* ♦ *The islands belong to Spain.* **2** an event, a competition, etc. that **belongs** to someone is one in which they are the most successful or popular: *American actors did well at the award ceremony, but the evening belonged to the British.* **be'long to sth 1** to be a member of a club, an organization, etc.: *Have you ever belonged to a political party?* **2** to be part of a particular group, type, or system: *Lions and tigers belong to the cat family.*

be·long·ings /bɪˈlɔŋɪŋz/ *noun* [pl.] the things that you own that can be moved, for example not land or buildings **SYN** POSSESSION: *insurance for property and personal belongings* ♦ *She packed her few belongings in a bag and left.* ⊃ thesaurus box at THING

be·lov·ed *adj., noun*
• *adj.* (*formal*) **1** /bɪˈlʌvd/ ~ **by/of sb** loved very much by someone; very popular with someone: *the deep purple flowers so beloved by artists* **2** /bɪˈlʌvd/ [only before noun] loved very much: *in memory of our dearly beloved son, John*
• *noun* /bɪˈlʌvəd/ (*old use* or *literary*) a person who is loved very much by someone: *It was a gift from her beloved.*

be·low /bɪˈloʊ/ *prep., adv.*
• *prep.* **1** at or to a lower level or position than someone or something: *He dived below the surface of the water.* ♦ *Please do not write below this line.* ♦ *Skirts should be worn below* (= long enough to cover) *the knee.* **2** of a lower amount or standard than someone or something: *The temperature remained below freezing all day.* ♦ *Her work was well below average for the class.* **3** of a lower rank or of less importance than someone or something: *A police sergeant is below a lieutenant.*
• *adv.* **1** at or to a lower level, position, or place: *They live on the floor below.* ♦ *I could still see the airport buildings far below.* ♦ *See below* (= at the bottom of the page) *for references.* ♦ *The passengers who felt seasick stayed below* (= on a lower DECK). **2** (of a temperature) lower than zero: *The thermometer had dropped to a record 40 below* (= −40 degrees). **3** at a lower rank: *This ruling applies to the ranks of Captain and below.*

be·low-the-'fold *adj.* not in a position where it is seen first, for example on the bottom part of a newspaper page or web page: *below-the-fold links* ♦ *That story would have been better in a less prominent, below-the-fold-position.* ⊃ compare ABOVE-THE-FOLD **IDM** see FOLD *n.*

belt /bɛlt/ *noun, verb*
• *noun* **1** a long narrow piece of leather, cloth, etc. that you wear around the waist: *to buckle/fasten/tighten a belt* ♦ *a belt buckle* ⊃ picture at CLOTHES ⊃ see also BLACK BELT, SEAT BELT **2** a continuous band of material that moves around and is used to carry things along, or to drive machinery ⊃ see also CONVEYOR BELT, FAN BELT **3** an area with particular characteristics or where a particular group of people live: *the country's corn/sun belt* ♦ *a belt of rain moving across the country* ⊃ see also BIBLE BELT, GREEN BELT **4** (*informal*) an act of hitting something or someone hard: *She gave the ball a huge belt.*
IDM **below the belt** (of a remark) unfair or cruel: *That really hit him below the belt!* **have sth under your belt** (*informal*) to have already achieved or obtained something: *She already has a couple of good wins under her belt.* ⊃ more at TIGHTEN
• *verb* **1** ~ **sb/sth** (*informal*) to hit someone or something hard: *He belted the ball right out of the park.* ♦ *I'll belt you if you do that again.* **2** [T] ~ **sth (+ adv.)** (*informal*) to drink very fast: *He belted down three shots of whiskey.* **3** [T] ~ **sth** to fasten a belt around something: *The dress was belted at the waist.*
PHR V **ˌbelt sth↔'out** (*informal*) to sing a song or play music loudly

belt·ed /ˈbɛltəd/ *adj.* with a belt around it: *a belted jacket*

belt-ˌtightening *noun* [U] changes that are made in order to spend less money: *We've all had to do some belt-tightening this year.* ▶ **'belt-ˌtightening** *adj.* [only before noun]: *belt-tightening measures* ⊃ see also TIGHTEN

belt·way /ˈbɛltweɪ/ *noun* **1** a highway that goes around a city ⊃ note at ROAD **2** usually **the Beltway** [sing.] the political world and social life of Washington, D.C.: *She had a difficult time adjusting to life inside the Beltway.*

be·lu·ga /bəˈluɡə/ *noun* (*pl.* be·lu·ga or be·lu·gas) **1** [C] a type of small WHALE **2** [C] a type of large fish that lives in rivers and lakes in eastern Europe **3** (also beˌluga 'caviar) [U] a type of CAVIAR (= fish eggs), from a beluga

be·moan /bɪˈmoʊn/ *verb* ~ **sth** (*formal*) to complain or say that you are not happy about something: *They sat bemoaning the fact that no one would give them a chance.*

be·mused /bɪˈmyuzd/ *adj.* showing that you are confused and unable to think clearly **SYN** : *a bemused expression/smile* ▶ **be·muse** *verb* ~ **sb** **be·mus·ed·ly** /bɪˈmyuzədli/ *adv.*

bench /bɛntʃ/ *noun, verb*

- *noun* **1** [C] a long seat for two or more people, usually made of wood: *a park bench* ⮕ picture at CHAIR **2 the bench** [sing.] (*law*) a judge in court or the seat where he/she sits; the position of being a judge or MAGISTRATE: *His lawyer turned to address the bench.* ◆ *She has recently been appointed to the bench.* **3 the bench** [sing.] (*sports*) the seats where players sit when they are not playing in the game; the players on that bench: *the substitutes' bench* ◆ *The team has a deep bench* (= good players who are waiting to play). **4** [C] = WORKBENCH: *a carpenter's bench*
- *verb* ~ **sb** to withdraw a player from a game, or to not allow them to play: *The quarterback was benched for the first time in his career.*

bench·mark /ˈbɛntʃmɑrk/ *noun, verb*

- *noun* something which can be measured and used as a standard that other things can be compared with: *Tests at the age of seven provide a benchmark against which the child's progress at school can be measured.*
- *verb* ~ **sth (against sth)** to judge the quality of something in relation to that of other similar things: *Projects are assessed and benchmarked against the targets.*

bench press *noun* an exercise in which you lie on a raised surface with your feet on the floor and raise a weight with both arms

bench·warm·er /ˈbɛntʃˌwɔrmər/ *noun* (*informal*) a sports player who is not chosen to play in a particular game, but is available if their team needs them **SYN** SUBSTITUTE

bend 🔑 /bɛnd/ *verb, noun*

- *verb* (**bent, bent** /bɛnt/) **1** [I, T] (especially of someone's body or head) to lean, or make something lean, in a particular direction: *He bent and kissed her.* ◆ + *adv./prep. fields of poppies bending in the wind* ◆ *His dark head bent over her.* ◆ *She bent forward to pick up the newspaper.* ◆ *Slowly bend from the waist and bring your head down to your knees.* ◆ ~ **sth (+ adv./prep.)** *He bent his head and kissed her.* ◆ *She was bent over her desk writing a letter.* **2** [T, I] ~ **(sth)** if you **bend** your arm, leg, etc. or if it **bends**, you move it so that it is no longer straight: *Bend your knees, keeping your back straight.* ◆ *Lie flat and let your knees bend.* **3** [T] ~ **sth** to force something that was straight into an angle or a curve: *Mark the pipe where you want to bend it.* ◆ *The knives were bent out of shape.* ◆ *He bent the wire into the shape of a square.* **4** [I, T] to change direction to form a curve or an angle; to make something change direction in this way: *The road bent sharply to the right.* ◆ ~ **sth** *Glass and water both bend light.*
  IDM **bend sb's ear (about sth)** (*informal*) to talk to someone a lot about something, especially about a problem that you have **bend your mind/efforts to sth** (*formal*) to think very hard about or put a lot of effort into one particular thing **bend the truth** to say something that is not completely true **on bended knee(s)** if you ask for something **on bended knee(s)**, you ask for it in a very anxious and/or HUMBLE way ⮕ more at BACKWARD *adv.*, RULE *n.*
  PHRV **ˈbend sb to sth** (*formal*) to force or persuade someone to do what you want or to accept your opinions: *He manipulates people and tries to bend them to his will* (= make them do what he wants).
- *noun* **1** [C] a curve or turn, especially in a road or river: *a sharp bend in the road* **2 the bends** [pl.] severe pain and difficulty in breathing experienced by a DIVER who comes back to the surface of the water too quickly
  IDM **around the bend** (*informal*) crazy: *She has gone completely around the bend.* ◆ *The children are driving me around the bend today* (= annoying me very much).

bend·er /ˈbɛndər/ *noun* (*slang*) a period of drinking a lot of alcohol or taking a lot of drugs: *to go on a bender*

bend·y /ˈbɛndi/ *adj.* (*informal*) that can be bent easily **SYN** FLEXIBLE

be·neath 🔑 /bɪˈniθ/ *prep.* (*formal*)
1 in or to a lower position than someone or something;

under someone or something: *They found the body buried beneath a pile of leaves.* ◆ *The boat sank beneath the waves.* **2** not good enough for someone: *He considers such jobs beneath him.* ◆ *They thought she had married beneath her* (= married a man of lower social status). ▶ **be·neath** *adv.*: *Her careful makeup hid the signs of age beneath.*

Ben·e·dic·tine /ˌbɛnəˈdɪktin; -tən/ *noun* a member of a Christian group of MONKS or NUNS following the rules of St. Benedict ▶ **Ben·e·dic·tine** *adj.*: *a Benedictine monastery*

ben·e·dic·tion /ˌbɛnəˈdɪkʃn/ *noun* [C, U] (*formal*) a Christian prayer of BLESSING

ben·e·fac·tion /ˌbɛnəˈfækʃn/ *noun* (*formal*) a gift, usually of money, that is given to a person or an organization in order to do good

ben·e·fac·tor /ˈbɛnəˌfæktər/ *noun* (*formal*) a person who gives money or other help to a person or an organization such as a school or charity

ben·e·fice /ˈbɛnəfəs/ *noun* the paid position of a Christian priest in charge of a PARISH

be·nef·i·cent /bɪˈnɛfəsnt/ *adj.* (*formal*) giving help; showing kindness **SYN** GENEROUS ▶ **be·nef·i·cence** /-fəsns/ *noun* [U]

ben·e·fi·cial **AWL** /ˌbɛnəˈfɪʃl/ *adj.* ~ **(to sth/sb)** improving a situation; having a helpful or useful effect **SYN** ADVANTAGEOUS, FAVORABLE: *A good diet is beneficial to your health.* **ANT** DETRIMENTAL

ben·e·fi·ci·ar·y **AWL** /ˌbɛnəˈfɪʃiˌɛri; -ˈfɪʃəri/ *noun* (*pl.* **ben·e·fi·ci·ar·ies**) **1** ~ **(of sth)** a person who gains as a result of something: *Who will be the main beneficiary of the income tax cuts?* **2** ~ **(of sth)** a person who receives money or property when someone dies

ben·e·fit 🔑 **AWL** /ˈbɛnəfɪt/ *noun, verb*

- *noun* **1** [U, C] an advantage that something gives you; a helpful and useful effect that something has: *I've had the benefit of a good education.* ◆ *The new regulations will be for the benefit of everyone concerned.* ◆ *It will be to your benefit to arrive early.* ◆ *He couldn't see the benefit of arguing any longer.* ◆ *the benefits of modern medicine* ◆ *It was good to see her finally reaping the benefits* (= enjoying the results) *of all her hard work.* ⮕ see also COST-BENEFIT **2** [C, usually pl.] an advantage that you get from a company in addition to the money that you earn; money from an insurance company: *Your benefits package includes medical and dental insurance.* ◆ *The insurance plan will provide a substantial cash benefit to your family in case of your death.* ⮕ see also FRINGE BENEFIT **3** [C] an event such as a performance, a dinner, etc., organized in order to raise money for a particular person or charity: *a benefit game/concert*
  IDM **for sb's benefit** especially in order to help or be useful to someone: *I have typed out some lecture notes for the benefit of those people who were absent last week.* ◆ *Don't go to any trouble for my benefit!* **give sb the benefit of the doubt** to accept that someone has told the truth or has not done something wrong because you cannot prove that they have not
- *verb* (**-t-** or **-tt-**) **1** [T] ~ **sb** to be useful to someone or improve their life in some way: *We should spend the money on something that will benefit everyone.* **2** [I] ~ **(from/by sth)** to be in a better position because of something: *Who exactly stands to benefit from these changes?*

Ben·e·lux /ˈbɛnlˌʌks/ *noun* [U] a name for Belgium, the Netherlands, and Luxembourg, when they are thought of as a group

be·nev·o·lent /bəˈnɛvələnt/ *adj.* **1** (*formal*) (especially of people in authority) kind, helpful, and generous: *a benevolent smile/attitude* ◆ *belief in the existence of a benevolent god* **ANT** MALEVOLENT **2** used in the names of some organizations that give help and money to people in need: *the Police Benevolent Association* ▶ **be·nev·o·lence** /-ləns/ *noun* [U] **be·nev·o·lent·ly** *adv.*

Ben·ga·li /bɛŋˈgɔli; -ˈgɑli/ *noun* **1** [C] a person from Bangladesh or West Bengal in eastern India **2** [U] the language of people from Bangladesh or West Bengal in eastern India ▶ **Ben·ga·li** *adj.*

be·night·ed /bɪˈnaɪtəd/ *adj.* (*old-fashioned*) **1** (of people) without understanding **2** (of places) without the benefits of modern life

be·nign /bɪˈnaɪn/ *adj.* **1** (*formal*) (of people) kind and gentle; not hurting anyone **2** (*medical*) (of TUMORS growing in the body) not dangerous or likely to cause death
ANT MALIGNANT ▶ **be·nign·ly** *adv.*: *He smiled benignly.*

bent 🔑 /bɛnt/ *adj., noun* ⊃ see also BEND
• *adj.* **1** not straight: *a piece of bent wire* ♦ *Do this exercise with your knees bent* (= not with your legs straight). ⊃ **picture at** CURVED **2** (of a person) not able to stand up straight, usually as a result of being old or sick: *a small, bent, old woman* ♦ *He was **bent double** with laughter.*
IDM **bent on sth/on doing sth** determined to do something (usually something bad): *She seems bent on making life difficult for me.* ⊃ **see also** HELL-BENT **get (all) bent out of shape (about/over sth)** (*informal*) to become angry, anxious, or upset: *Don't get bent out of shape about it. It was just a mistake!*
• *noun* [usually sing.] ~ **(for sth)** a natural skill or interest in something: *She has a bent for mathematics.*

bent·wood /ˈbɛntwʊd/ *noun* [U] wood that is artificially shaped for making furniture: *bentwood chairs*

ben·zene /ˈbɛnzin; bɛnˈzin/ *noun* [U] a clear liquid obtained from PETROLEUM and COAL TAR, used in making plastics and many chemical products

be·queath /bɪˈkwið; -ˈkwiθ/ *verb* (*formal*) **1** to say in a WILL that you want someone to have your property, money, etc. after you die **SYN** LEAVE: ~ **sth (to sb)** *He bequeathed his entire estate to his daughter.* ♦ ~ **sb sth** *He bequeathed his daughter his entire estate.* **2** ~ **sth (to sb)** | ~ **sb sth** to leave the results of your work, knowledge, etc. for other people to use or deal with, especially after you have died

be·quest /bɪˈkwɛst/ *noun* (*formal*) money or property that you ask to be given to a particular person when you die: *He left a bequest to each of his grandchildren.*

be·rate /bɪˈreɪt/ *verb* ~ **sb/yourself** (*formal*) to criticize or speak angrily to someone because you do not approve of something they have done

be·reave /bɪˈriv/ *verb* **be bereaved** if someone is **bereaved**, a relative or close friend has just died: *The ceremony was an ordeal for those who had been recently bereaved.*

be·reaved /bɪˈrivd/ *adj.* (*formal*) **1** having lost a relative or close friend who has recently died: *recently bereaved families* **2** **the bereaved** *noun* (pl. **the bereaved**) a person who is bereaved: *an organization offering counseling for the bereaved*

be·reave·ment /bɪˈrivmənt/ *noun* **1** [U] the state of having lost a relative or close friend because they have died: *the pain of an emotional crisis such as divorce or bereavement* **2** [C] the death of a relative or close friend: *A family bereavement meant that he could not attend the conference.*

be·reft /bɪˈrɛft/ *adj.* [not before noun] (*formal*) **1** ~ **of sth** completely lacking something; having lost something: *bereft of ideas/hope* **2** (of a person) sad and lonely because you have lost something: *He was completely bereft when his wife died.*

be·ret /bəˈreɪ/ *noun* a round flat cap made out of soft cloth and with a tight band around the head ⊃ **picture at** HAT

ber·ga·mot /ˈbərgəˌmɑt/ *noun* [U] **1** (also **ˈbergamot oil**) oil from the skin of a small orange **2** a type of HERB

ber·i·ber·i /ˌbɛriˈbɛri/ *noun* [U] a disease that affects the nerves and heart, caused by a lack of VITAMIN B

ber·ke·li·um /ˈbərkliəm; bərˈkiliəm/ *noun* [U] (*symb.* **Bk**) a chemical element. Berkelium is a RADIOACTIVE metal that is produced artificially from AMERICIUM and HELIUM.

berm /bərm/ *noun* (*technical*) **1** an area of ground at the side of a road; a raised area of ground at the side of a river or CANAL **2** a narrow raised area of sand formed on a beach by the waves coming in from the ocean

Ber·mu·da shorts /bərˌmyudə ˈʃɔrts/ (also **Ber·mu·das** /bərˈmyudəz/) *noun* [pl.] SHORTS (= short pants) that come down to just above the knee: *a pair of Bermudas*

the Ber·muda ˈTriangle *noun* [sing.] an area in the Atlantic Ocean between Bermuda, Florida, and Puerto Rico where a large number of ships and aircraft are believed to have disappeared in a mysterious way: *This area of town is known as the Bermuda Triangle—drinkers seem to disappear into the bars and clubs and be lost to the world.*

ber·ry /ˈbɛri/ *noun* (pl. **ber·ries**) (often in compounds) a small fruit that grows on a bush. There are several types of berries, some of which can be eaten: *Birds feed on nuts and berries in the winter.* ♦ *blackberries/raspberries*

ber·serk /bərˈzərk; -ˈsərk/ *adj.* [not usually before noun] **1** very angry, often in a violent or uncontrolled way: *He went berserk when he found out where I was.* **2** very excited: *The kids were going berserk with excitement.*

berth /bərθ/ *noun, verb*
• *noun* **1** a place to sleep on a ship or train, or in a CAMPER **SYN** BUNK **2** a place where a ship or boat can stop and stay, usually in a HARBOR **IDM** see WIDE *adj.*
• *verb* [T, I] ~ **(sth)** to put a ship in a berth or keep it there; to sail into a berth: *The USS* Constitution *is berthed in Boston.*

ber·yl /ˈbɛrəl/ *noun* [U] a transparent pale green, blue, or yellow SEMI-PRECIOUS STONE, used in making jewelry

be·ryl·li·um /bəˈriliəm/ *noun* [U] (*symb.* **Be**) a chemical element. Beryllium is a hard gray metal found mainly in the mineral BERYL.

be·seech /bɪˈsitʃ/ *verb* (**be·sought, be·sought** /bɪˈsɔt/) or (**be·seeched, be·seeched**) ~ **sb (to do sth)** (*formal*) to ask someone for something in an anxious way because you want or need it very much **SYN** BEG, IMPLORE: *Let him go, I beseech you!*

be·seech·ing /bɪˈsitʃɪŋ/ *adj.* [only before noun] (*formal*) (of a look, tone of voice, etc.) showing that you want something very much ▶ **be·seech·ing·ly** *adv.*

be·set /bɪˈsɛt/ *verb* (**be·set·ting, be·set, be·set**) [usually passive] ~ **sb/sth** (*formal*) to affect someone or something in an unpleasant or harmful way: *The team was beset by injury all season.* ♦ *It's one of the most difficult problems besetting our modern way of life.*

be·side 🔑 /bɪˈsaɪd/ *prep.*
1 next to or at the side of someone or something: *He sat beside her all night.* ♦ *a mill beside a stream* **2** compared with someone or something: *My painting looks childish beside yours.*
IDM **beside yourself (with sth)** unable to control yourself because of the strength of emotion you are feeling: *He was beside himself with rage when I told him what I had done.* ⊃ **more at** POINT *n.*

WHICH WORD?

beside ♦ besides
- The preposition **beside** usually means "next to something/someone" or "at the side of something/someone": *Sit here beside me.* **Besides** means "in addition to something": *What other sports do you play besides hockey?* Do not use **beside** with this meaning.
- The adverb **besides** is not usually used on its own to mean "in addition." It is mainly used to give another reason or argument for something: *I don't think I'll come on Saturday. I have a lot of work to do. Besides, I don't really like parties.* ♦ ~~She likes football. Besides, she likes tennis and basketball.~~

be·sides /bɪˈsaɪdz/ *prep., adv.*
• *prep.* in addition to someone or something; except for someone or something: *We have lots of things in common*

besides music. ◆ Besides working as a doctor, he also writes novels in his spare time. ◆ I've got no family besides my parents. ⊃ note at BESIDE
• **adv. 1** used for making an extra comment that adds to what you have just said: I don't really want to go. Besides, it's too late now. ⊃ note at BESIDE **2** in addition; also: discounts on televisions, stereos, and much more besides

besides ◆ except (for) ◆ apart from

■ The preposition **besides** means "in addition to": What other sports do you like besides football? You use **except (for)** when you mention the only thing that is not included in a statement: I like all sports except (for) football. You can use **apart from** with both these meanings: What other sports do you like apart from football? ◆ I like all sports apart from football.

be·siege /bɪˈsidʒ/ verb **1** ~ sth to surround a building, city, etc. with soldiers until the people inside are forced to let you in SYN LAY SIEGE TO: Paris was besieged for four months and forced to surrender. ◆ (figurative) Fans besieged the box office to get tickets for the concert. **2** [usually passive] ~ sb/sth (especially of something unpleasant or annoying) to surround someone or something in large numbers: The actress was besieged by reporters at the airport. **3** ~ sb (with sth) to send so many letters, ask so many questions, etc. that it is difficult for someone to deal with them all: The radio station was besieged with calls from angry listeners.

be·smirch /bɪˈsmərtʃ/ verb ~ sb/sth (formal) to damage the opinion that people have of someone or something SYN SULLY

be·som /ˈbizəm/ noun a brush for sweeping floors, made from sticks tied onto a long handle

be·sot·ted /bɪˈsatəd/ adj. ~ (by/with sb/sth) loving someone or something so much that you do not behave in a sensible way: He is completely besotted with his new girlfriend.

be·sought pt, pp of BESEECH

be·speak /bɪˈspik/ verb (be·spoke /bɪˈspoʊk/, be·spo·ken /bɪˈspoʊkən/) ~ sth (literary) to show or suggest something: His style of dressing bespoke great self-confidence.

be·spec·ta·cled /bɪˈspɛktəkld/ adj. (formal) wearing glasses

be·spoke /bɪˈspoʊk/ adj. [usually before noun] (formal) **1** (also ˌcustom-ˈmade) (of a product) made specially, according to the needs of an individual customer: a bespoke suit ◆ bespoke software SYN TAILOR-MADE **2** making products specially, according to the needs of an individual customer: a bespoke tailor

best ♪ /bɛst/ adj., adv., noun, verb
• **adj.** (superlative of good) **1** of the most excellent type or quality: That's the best movie I've ever seen! ◆ She was one of the best tennis players of her generation. ◆ Is that your best suit? ◆ They've been best friends (= closest friends) since they were children. ◆ the company's best-ever results ◆ We want the kids to have the best possible education. **2** most enjoyable; happiest: Those were the best years of my life. **3** most suitable or appropriate: What's the best way to cook steak? ◆ The best thing to do would be to apologize. ◆ He's the best man for the job. ◆ It's best if you go now. ◆ I'm not in the best position to advise you. IDM Idioms containing **best** adj. are at the entries for the nouns and verbs in the idioms. For example, **on your best behavior** is at **behavior**.
• **adv.** (superlative of well, often used in adjectives) **1** most; to the greatest extent: Which one do you like best? ◆ Well-drained soil suits the plant best. ◆ her best-known poem **2** in the most excellent way; to the highest standard: He works best in the mornings. ◆ Hollywood's best-dressed woman ◆ The beaches are beautiful, but best of all, there are very few tourists. **3** in the most suitable or appropriate way: Painting is best done in daylight. ◆ Do what you think best (= what you think is the most suitable thing to do).

IDM **as best (as) you can** not perfectly but as well as you are able: We'll manage as best we can. **had best (do sth)** used to tell someone what you think they should do: You'd best clear up that mess before Mom gets home.
• **noun** [sing.] usually the best **1** the most excellent thing or person: We all want the best for our children. ◆ They only buy the best. ◆ They're all good players, but she's the best of all. ◆ We're the best of friends (= very close friends). **2** the highest standard that someone or something can reach: She always brings out the best in people (= gives people a chance to show their good qualities). ◆ The town looks its best (= is most attractive) in the spring. ◆ Don't worry about the exam—just do your best (= do as well as you can). ◆ Yesterday I wasn't at my best (= performing or working as well as I can). ◆ I will do the job to the best of my ability (= as well as I can). ◆ I'm not feeling my best (= not feeling very well) today. ◆ Exercise helps me to feel my best (= feel healthy) ◆ My mom's not in the best of health (= not healthy). **3** something that is as close as possible to what you need or want: Fifty dollars is the best I can offer you. ◆ The best we can hope for in the game is a tie. **4** the highest standard that a particular person has reached, especially in a sport: She won the race with a personal best of 2 minutes 22 seconds.
IDM **all the best** (informal) used when you are saying goodbye to someone or ending a letter, to give someone your good wishes **at best** used for saying what is the best opinion you can have of someone or something, or the best thing that can happen, when the situation is bad: Their response to the proposal was, at best, cool. ◆ We can't arrive before Friday at best. **be (all) for the best** used to say that although something appears bad or unpleasant now, it will be good in the end: I don't want you to leave, but perhaps it's for the best. **the best of three, five, etc.** (especially in games and sports) up to three, five, etc. games played to decide who wins, the winner being the person who wins most of them **the best that money can buy** the very best: We make sure our clients get the best that money can buy. **do, mean, etc. sth for the best** to do or say something in order to achieve a good result or to help someone: I just don't know what to do for the best. ◆ I'm sorry if my advice offended you—I meant it for the best. **get the best of sb/sth** to defeat someone or something, or gain an advantage: I thought you had the best of that discussion. ◆ I'm sorry I opened your mail—my curiosity got the best of me (= I didn't intend to open it, but I was so interested that I did). **make the best of sth/it | make the best of things** to accept a bad or difficult situation, and do as well as you can **to the best of your knowledge/belief** as far as you know: He never made a will, to the best of my knowledge. **with the best (of them)** as well as anyone: He'll be out there, dancing with the best of them. ⊃ more at BUNCH n., HOPE v., LUCK n., SUNDAY
• **verb** [usually passive] ~ sb (formal) to defeat or be more successful than someone

bes·tial /ˈbɛstʃəl; ˈbis-/ adj. (formal) cruel and disgusting; of or like a BEAST: bestial acts/cruelty/noises

bes·ti·al·i·ty /ˌbɛstʃiˈæləti; ˌbis-/ noun [U] **1** (technical) sexual activity between a human and an animal **2** (formal) cruel or disgusting behavior

bes·ti·ar·y /ˈbɛstʃiˌɛri; ˈbis-/ noun (pl. bes·ti·ar·ies) a collection of descriptions of, or stories about, various types of animals, especially one written in the Middle Ages

be·stir /bɪˈstər/ verb (-rr-) ~ yourself (formal or humorous) to start doing things again after a period during which you have been doing nothing SYN ROUSE

ˌbest ˈman noun [sing.] a male friend or relative of the BRIDEGROOM at a wedding, who helps him during the wedding ceremony ⊃ compare BRIDESMAID

be·stow /bɪˈstoʊ/ verb ~ sth (on/upon sb) (formal) to give something to someone, especially to show how much they are respected: an honorary degree bestowed upon her by the college

ˌbest ˈpractice noun [U, C] a way of doing something that is seen as a very good example of how it should be done and can be copied by other companies or organizations

be·stride /bɪˈstraɪd/ *verb* (*pt* **be·strode** /-ˈstroʊd/) **~ sth** (*literary*) to sit with one leg on either side of something: *He bestrode his horse.*

best ˈseller (also **best·sel·ler**) /ˌbestˈsɛlər/ *noun* a product, usually a book, which is bought by large numbers of people: *Her previous book was a best seller.* ♦ *the best-seller list* ▸ **best-ˈselling** *adj.*: *a best-selling novel/author*

be·suit·ed /bɪˈsuːtəd/ *adj.* (*formal*) wearing a suit: *besuited businessmen*

bet 🔑 /bet/ *verb, noun*

● *verb* (**bet·ting, bet, bet·ted**) **1** [I, T] to risk money on a race or an event by trying to predict the result: *You have to be over 18 to bet.* ♦ **~ on/against sth** *I wouldn't bet on them winning the next election.* ♦ **~ sth (on sth)** *He bet $2,000 on the final score of the game.* ♦ **~ (sb) (sth) (that...)** *She bet me $20 that I wouldn't do it.* ⊃ see also BETTING, GAMBLE **2** [T] (*informal*) used to say that you are almost certain that something is true or that something will happen: **~ (that)...** *I bet (that) we're too late.* ♦ *You can bet (that) the minute I sit down, the phone will ring.* ♦ **~ sb (that)...** *I'll bet you (that) he knows all about it.*
IDM **I/I'll bet!** (*informal*) **1** used to show that you can understand what someone is feeling, describing, etc.: *"I almost died when he told me." "I bet!"* **2** used to tell someone that you do not believe what they have just said: *"I'm going to tell her what I think of her." "Yeah, I bet!"* **I wouldn't bet on it| don't bet on it** (*informal*) used to say that you do not think that something is very likely: *"She'll get used to the idea." "I wouldn't bet on it."* **want to bet?** (also **wanna bet?**) (*informal*) used to disagree with what someone has stated or claimed: *"The Giants are going to win the Super Bowl." " Want to bet?"* **you bet!** (*informal*) used instead of "yes" to emphasize that someone has guessed something correctly or made a good suggestion: *"Are you nervous?" "You bet!"* **you can bet your life/your bottom dollar (on sth/(that)...)** (*informal*) used to say that you are certain that something will happen: *You can bet your bottom dollar that he'll be late.*

● *noun* **1** an arrangement to risk money, etc. on the result of a particular event; the money that you risk in this way: *to win/lose a bet* ♦ **~ on sth** *We've got a bet on who's going to arrive first.* ♦ *He had a bet on the horses.* ♦ *They all put a bet on the race.* ♦ *I hear you're taking bets on whether she'll marry him.* ♦ *I did it for a bet* (= because someone had agreed to pay me money if I did). **2** (*informal*) an opinion about what is likely to happen or to have happened: *My bet is that they got held up in traffic.*
IDM **all bets are off** used to say that if a particular event happens, then your current forecast, agreement, etc. will no longer apply: *We expect shares to rise unless the economy slows down again, in which case all bets are off.* **the/your best bet** (*informal*) used to tell someone what is the best action for them to take to get the result they want: *If you want to get around D.C. fast, the Metro is your best bet.* **a good/safe bet** something that is likely to happen, to succeed, or to be suitable: *Money is a safe bet as a present for a teenager.* ⊃ more at HEDGE *v.*

be·ta /ˈbeɪtə/ *noun* the second letter of the Greek alphabet (B, β)

beta ˌblocker *noun* a drug used to control heart rhythm, treat severe chest pain, and reduce high blood pressure

beta ˈcarotene *noun* [U] a substance found in carrots and other plants, which is needed by humans

beta deˌcay *noun* [sing.] (*physics*) the breaking up of an atom in which an ELECTRON is given off

be·take /bɪˈteɪk/ *verb* (**be·took** /bɪˈtʊk/, **be·tak·en** /bɪˈteɪkən/) **~ yourself + adv./prep.** (*literary*) to go somewhere: *He betook himself to his room.*

beta ˌparticle (also **beta ray**) *noun* (*physics*) a fast-moving ELECTRON that is produced when some RADIOACTIVE substances decay

beta ˌtest *noun* a test on a new product, done by someone who does not work for the company that is developing the product ⊃ compare ALPHA TEST ▸ **beta-ˌtest** *verb* **~ sth**

beta ˌversion *noun* [usually sing.] the version of a new product, especially computer software, that is almost ready for the public to buy or use, but is given to a few customers to test first

bet·cha /ˈbetʃə/ (*informal, non-standard*) a way of saying or writing "bet you" in informal speech
IDM **you betcha** (*informal*) used to say "yes" when you are very enthusiastic about something: *"Are you going to the game this weekend?" "You betcha!"*

be·tel /ˈbiːtl/ *noun* [U] the leaves of a climbing plant, also called betel, chewed by people in Asia

betel ˌnut *noun* the slightly bitter nut of a tropical Asian PALM, that is cut into small pieces, wrapped in betel leaves, and chewed

bête noire /ˌbet ˈnwɑr; ˌbeɪt-/ *noun* (*pl.* **bêtes noires** /ˌbet ˈnwɑrz; ˌbeɪt-/) (from *French*) a person or thing that particularly annoys you and that you do not like

be·tide /bɪˈtaɪd/ *verb* **IDM** see WOE

be·to·ken /bɪˈtoʊkən/ *verb* **~ sth** (*literary*) to be a sign of something: *a clear blue sky betokening a fine day*

be·tray /bɪˈtreɪ/ *verb* **1** to give information about someone or something to an enemy: **~ sb/sth** *He was offered money to betray his colleagues.* ♦ **~ sb/sth to sb** *For years they had been betraying state secrets to Russia.* **2 ~ sb/sth** to hurt someone who trusts you, especially by not being loyal or faithful to them: *She felt betrayed when she found out the truth about him.* ♦ *She betrayed his trust over and over again.* ♦ *I have never known her to betray a confidence* (= tell other people something that should be kept secret). ⊃ thesaurus box at CHEAT **3 ~ sth** to ignore your principles or beliefs in order to achieve something or gain an advantage for yourself: *He has been accused of betraying his former socialist ideals.* **4** to tell someone or make them aware of a piece of information, a feeling, etc., usually without meaning to **SYN** GIVE AWAY: **~ sth** *His voice betrayed the worry he was trying to hide.* ♦ **~ yourself** *She was terrified of saying something that would make her betray herself* (= show her feelings or who she was).

be·tray·al /bɪˈtreɪəl/ *noun* [U, C] the act of betraying someone or something or the fact of being betrayed: *a sense/a feeling/an act of betrayal* ♦ *I saw her actions as a betrayal of my trust.* ♦ *the many disappointments and betrayals in his life*

be·troth·al /bɪˈtroʊðl/ *noun* **~ (to sb)** (*formal* or *old-fashioned*) an agreement to marry someone **SYN** ENGAGEMENT

be·trothed /bɪˈtroʊðd/ *adj.* (*formal* or *old-fashioned*) **1 ~ (to sb)** having promised to marry someone **SYN** ENGAGED **2 someone's betrothed** *noun* [sing.] the person that someone has promised to marry

bet·ter 🔑 /ˈbetər/ *adj., adv., noun, verb*

● *adj.* (comparative of *good*) **1** of a higher standard or less poor quality; not as bad as something else: *We're hoping for better weather tomorrow.* ♦ *Her work is getting better and better.* ♦ *He is in a much better mood than usual.* ♦ *The meal couldn't have been better.* ♦ *There's nothing better than a long soak in a hot bath.* ♦ *If you can only exercise once a week, that's better than nothing* (= better than doing no exercise at all). **2** more able or skilled: *She's far better at science than her brother.* **3** more suitable or appropriate: *Can you think of a better word than "nice"?* ♦ *It would be better for him to talk to his parents about his problems.* ♦ *You'd be better to go by bus.* **4** less sick or unhappy: *She's a lot better today.* ♦ *His leg was getting better.* ♦ *You'll feel better after a good night's sleep.* **5** fully recovered after an illness; in good health again: *Don't go back to work until you are better.* ⊃ see also WELL *adj.*
IDM Most idioms containing **better** are at the entries for the nouns and verbs in the idioms. For example, **better luck next time** is at luck. **little/no better than** almost or just the same as; almost or just as bad as: *The dinner was no*

better than fast food. **that's (much) better 1** used to give support to someone who has been upset and is trying to become calmer: *Dry your eyes now. That's better.* **2** used to praise someone who has made an effort to improve: *That's much better—you played all the right notes this time.* **the bigger, smaller, faster, slower, etc. the better** used to say that something should be as big, small, etc. as possible: *As far as the hard disk is concerned, the bigger the better.*

● *adv.* (comparative of *well*) **1** in a more excellent or pleasant way; not as badly: *She sings much better than I do.* ♦ *Sound travels better in water than in air.* ♦ *People are better educated now.* **2** more; to a greater degree: *You'll like her when you know her better.* ♦ *A cup of tea? There's nothing I'd like better!* ♦ *Healthy people are better able to cope with stress.* **3** used to suggest that something would be a suitable or appropriate thing to do: *The money could be better spent on more urgent cases.* ♦ *Some things are better left unsaid.* ♦ *You'd do better to tell her everything before she finds out from someone else.*
IDM Most idioms containing **better** are at the entries for the nouns, adjectives and verbs in the idioms, for example **better the devil you know** is at **devil**. **be better off** to have more money: *Families will be better off under the new law.* ♦ *Her promotion means she's $100 a week better off.* **ANT** BE WORSE OFF **be better off (doing sth)** used to say that someone is/would be happier or more satisfied if they were in a particular position or did a particular thing: *She's better off without him.* ♦ *The weather was so bad we'd have been better off staying at home.* **had better/best (do sth)** used to tell someone what you think they should do: *You'd better go to the doctor about your cough.* ♦ *We'd better leave now or we'll miss the bus.* ♦ *You'd better not do that again.* ♦ *"I'll give you back the money tomorrow." "You'd better!"* (= as a threat)
➔ note at SHOULD

● *noun* **1** [sing., U] something that is better: *the better of the two books* ♦ *I expected better of him* (= I thought he would have behaved better). **2 your betters** [pl.] (*old-fashioned*) people who are more intelligent or more important than you **3** [C] = BETTOR
IDM **for better or (for) worse** used to say that something cannot be changed, whether the result is good or bad **get the better of sb/sth** to defeat someone or something or gain an advantage: *No one can get the better of her in an argument.* ♦ *She always gets the better of an argument.* ♦ *His curiosity got the better of him* (= he didn't intend to ask questions, but he wanted to know so badly that he did). **so much better/worse** used to say that something is even better/worse: *We don't actually need it on Tuesday, but if it arrives by then, so much the better.* ➔ more at CHANGE *n.*, THINK *v.*

● *verb* **1** [often passive] **~ sth** to be better or do something better than someone or something else: *The work he produced early in his career has never really been bettered.* **2 ~ yourself** to improve your social position through education, a better job, etc.: *Thousands of unemployed mothers are getting job training in an attempt to better themselves.*

better ˈhalf *noun* (*informal, humorous*) the person that you are married to, or your boyfriend or girlfriend

bet·ter·ment /ˈbɛtərmənt/ *noun* [U] (*formal*) the process of becoming or making something or someone better
SYN IMPROVEMENT

bet·ting /ˈbɛtɪŋ/ *noun* [U]
the act of risking money, etc. on the unknown result of an event: *illegal betting*

bet·tor (also **bet·ter**) /ˈbɛtər/ *noun* a person who bets on a race or other sports event, especially someone who does this regularly

be·tween 🔑 /bɪˈtwin/ *prep., adv.*

● *prep.* **1** in or into the space separating two or more points, objects, people, etc.: *Q comes between P and R in the English alphabet.* ♦ *I sat down between Melinda and Sasha.* ♦ *Switzerland lies between France, Germany, Austria, and Italy.* ♦ *The paper had fallen down between the desk and the wall.*

♦ (*figurative*) *My job is somewhere between a secretary and a personal assistant.* **2** in the period of time that separates two days, years, events, etc.: *It's cheaper between 6 p.m. and 8 a.m.* ♦ *Don't eat between meals.* ♦ *Children must attend school between the ages of 5 and 16.* ♦ *Many changes took place between the two world wars.* **3** at some point along a scale from one amount, weight, distance, etc. to another: *It weighed between nine and ten pounds.* ♦ *The temperature remained between 75°F and 80°F all week.* **4** (of a line) separating one place from another: *the border between Oregon and Washington* **5** from one place to another: *We fly between Chicago and Dallas twice daily.* **6** used to show a connection or relationship: *a difference/distinction/contrast between two things* ♦ *a link between unemployment and crime* ♦ *There's a lot of bad feelings between them.* ♦ *I had to choose between the two jobs.* **7** shared by two or more people or things: *We ate a pizza between us.* ♦ *This is just between you and me / between ourselves* (= it is a secret). **8** by putting together the efforts or actions of two or more people or groups: *We should be able to manage it between us.* **9 ~ doing sth** used to show that several activities are involved: *Between working full-time and taking care of the kids, he didn't have much time for hobbies.*

● *adv.* usually **in between** in the space or period of time separating two or more points, objects, etc. or two dates, events, etc.: *The house was near a park but there was a road in between.* ♦ *I see her most weekends but not very often in between.*
IDM see BETWIXT

be·twixt /bɪˈtwɪkst/ *adv., prep.* (*literary* or *old use*) between
IDM **betwixt and between** (*old-fashioned*) in a middle position; neither one thing nor the other

bev·el /ˈbɛvl/ *noun* **1** a sloping edge or surface, for example at the side of a picture frame or sheet of glass **2** a tool for making sloping edges on wood or stone

bev·eled /ˈbɛvld/ *adj.* [usually before noun] having a sloping edge or surface

beveled

bev·er·age /ˈbɛvərɪdʒ; ˈbɛvrɪdʒ/ *noun* (*formal*) any type of drink except water: *laws governing the sale of alcoholic beverages*

bev·y /ˈbɛvi/ *noun* [sing.] (*informal*) a large group of people or things of the same kind: *a bevy of beauties* (= beautiful young women)

be·wail /bɪˈweɪl/ *verb* **~ sth** (*formal* or *humorous*) to express great sadness about something

be·ware /bɪˈwɛr/ *verb* [I, T] (used only in infinitives and in orders) if you tell someone to **beware**, you are warning them that someone or something is dangerous and that they should be careful: **~ of sb/sth** *Drivers have been warned to beware of icy roads.* ♦ **~ (of) doing sth** *Beware of saying anything that might reveal where you live.* ♦ **~ sb/sth** *It's a great place for swimming, but beware dangerous currents.*

be·wigged /bɪˈwɪgd/ *adj.* (*formal*) (of a person) wearing a WIG

be·wil·der /bɪˈwɪldər/ *verb* [usually passive] **~ sb** to confuse someone: *She was totally bewildered by his sudden change of mood.* ▶ **be·wil·dered** *adj.*: *He turned around, with a bewildered look on his face.*

be·wil·der·ing /bɪˈwɪldərɪŋ/ *adj.* making you feel confused because there are too many things to choose from or because something is difficult to understand
SYN CONFUSING: *a bewildering array/assortment* ♦ *There is a bewildering variety of software available.* ▶ **be·wil·der·ing·ly** *adv.*: *All the houses looked bewilderingly similar.*

be·wil·der·ment /bɪˈwɪldərmənt/ *noun* [U] a feeling of being completely confused **SYN** CONFUSION: *to look/stare in bewilderment*

be·witch /bɪ'wɪtʃ/ *verb* **1** [often passive] ~ **sb** to attract or impress someone so much that they cannot think in a sensible way: *He was completely bewitched by her beauty.* **2** ~ **sb** to put a magic SPELL on someone **SYN** ENCHANT

be·witch·ing /bɪ'wɪtʃɪŋ/ *adj.* so beautiful or interesting that you cannot think about anything else: *a bewitching girl/ smile* ◆ *a bewitching performance*

be·yond 🔑 /bɪ'yɑnd/ *prep., adv.*

- **prep. 1** on or to the further side of something: *The road continues beyond the village up into the hills.* **2** later than a particular time: *It won't go on beyond midnight.* ◆ *I know what I'll be doing for the next three weeks but I haven't thought beyond that.* **3** more than something: *Our success was far beyond what we thought possible.* ◆ *She has nothing beyond social security.* **4** used to say that something is not possible: *The bicycle was beyond repair* (= is too badly damaged to repair). ◆ *The situation is beyond our control.* **5** too far or too advanced for someone or something: *The handle was just beyond my reach.* ◆ *The exercise was beyond the abilities of most of the class.*
  IDM **be beyond sb** (*informal*) to be impossible for someone to imagine, understand, or do: *It's beyond me why she wants to marry Jeff.*
- **adv.** on the other side; further on: *Rainier and the mountains beyond were covered in snow.* ◆ *The immediate future is clear, but it's hard to tell what lies beyond.* ◆ *the year 2012 and beyond*

bez·el /'bɛzl/ *noun* (*technical*) a ring with a long narrow cut around the inside, used to hold something in place, such as the cover of a watch or cell phone

bhan·gra /'bʌŋgrə; 'bɑŋ-/ *noun* [U] a type of dance music that combines traditional Punjabi music from India and Pakistan with Western pop music

bi /baɪ/ *adj.* (*informal*) = BISEXUAL

bi- /baɪ/ *combining form* (in nouns and adjectives) two; twice; double: *bilingual* ◆ *bicentenary* **HELP** Bi- with a period of time can mean either "happening twice" in that period of time, or "happening once in every two" periods.

bi·an·nu·al /baɪ'ænyuəl/ *adj.* [only before noun] happening twice a year ⊃ compare ANNUAL ⊃ see also BIENNIAL

bi·as **AWL** /'baɪəs/ *noun, verb*

- **noun 1** [U, C, usually sing.] a strong feeling in favor of or against one group of people, or one side in an argument, often not based on fair judgment: *accusations of political bias in news programs* (= that reports are unfair and show favor to one political party) ◆ *Employers must consider all candidates impartially and without bias.* ◆ *Some institutions still have a strong bias against women.* **2** [C, usually sing.] an interest in one thing more than others; a special ability: *The course has a strong practical bias.* **3** [U, sing.] the **bias** of a piece of cloth is an edge cut DIAGONALLY across the threads: *The skirt is cut on the bias.*
- **verb 1** ~ **sb/sth (toward(s)/against/in favor of sb/sth)** to unfairly influence someone's opinions or decisions **SYN** PREJUDICE: *The newspapers have biased people against her.* **2** ~ **sth** to have an effect on the results of research or an experiment so that they do not show the real situation: *The experiment contained an error which could bias the results.*

bias-·cut *adj.* (of cloth or of an item of clothing) cut across the natural direction of the lines in the cloth

bi·ased **AWL** /'baɪəst/ *adj.* **1** ~ **(toward(s)/against/in favor of sb/sth)** having a tendency to show favor toward or against one group of people or one opinion for personal reasons; making unfair judgments: *biased information/ sources/press reports* ◆ *a biased jury/witness* **ANT** UNBIASED **2** ~ **toward sth/sb** having a particular interest in one thing more than others: *a school biased toward music and art*

bi·ath·lon /baɪ'æθlɑn; -lən/ *noun* a sporting event that combines CROSS-COUNTRY SKIING and RIFLE shooting ⊃ compare DECATHLON, HEPTATHLON, PENTATHLON, TETRATHLON, TRIATHLON

bib /bɪb/ *noun* **1** a piece of cloth or plastic that you put under babies' chins to protect their clothes while they are eating

2 the part of an APRON or a pair of OVERALLS that is above the waist **3** a piece of cloth or plastic with a number or special colors on it that people wear on their chests and backs when they are taking part in a sport, so that people know who they are

bi·ble /'baɪbl/ *noun* **1 the Bible** [sing.] the holy book of the Christian religion, consisting of the Old Testament and the New Testament **2 the Bible** [sing.] the holy book of the Jewish religion, consisting of the Torah (or Law), the PROPHET, and the Writings **3** [C] a copy of the holy book of the Christian or Jewish religion **4** [C] a book containing important information on a subject, that you refer to very often: *the stamp-collector's bible*

the Bible Belt *noun* [sing.] an area of the southern and midwestern U.S. where people have strong and strict Christian beliefs

Bible-·thumping *noun* [U] (*informal, disapproving*) the act of teaching or talking about the Bible in public in a very enthusiastic or aggressive way ▶ **Bible-·thumper** *noun*

bib·li·cal also **Bib·li·cal** /'bɪblɪkl/ *adj.* **1** connected with the Bible; in the Bible: *biblical scholarship/times/scenes* ◆ *biblical stories/passages* **2** very great; on a large scale: *a thunderstorm of biblical proportions*

biblio- /'bɪbliou; -liə/ *combining form* (in nouns, adjectives and adverbs) connected with books: *bibliophile*

bib·li·og·ra·phy /ˌbɪbli'ɑgrəfi/ *noun* (*pl.* **bib·li·og·ra·phies**) **1** [C] a list of books or articles about a particular subject or by a particular author; the list of books, etc. that have been used by someone writing an article, etc. **2** [U] the study of the history of books and their production ▶ **bib·li·og·ra·pher** /-fər/ *noun* **bib·li·o·graph·i·cal** /ˌbɪbliə'græfɪkl/ (also **bib·li·o·graph·ic**) *adj.*

bib·li·o·phile /'bɪbliə faɪl/ *noun* (*formal*) a person who loves or collects books

bib overalls *noun* [pl.] = OVERALLS (3)

bib·u·lous /'bɪbyələs/ *adj.* (*old-fashioned* or *humorous*) liking to drink too much alcohol

bi·cam·er·al /baɪ'kæmərəl/ *adj.* (*technical*) (of a LEGISLATURE) having two main parts, such as the Senate and the House of Representatives in the U.S. Congress

bi·carb /ˌbaɪ'kɑrb; 'baɪkɑrb/ *noun* [U] (*informal*) = SODIUM BICARBONATE

bi·car·bo·nate /ˌbaɪ'kɑrbənət/ *noun* [U] (*chemistry*) a salt made from CARBONIC ACID containing CARBON, HYDROGEN, and OXYGEN, together with another element

bi·carbonate of soda *noun* [U] = SODIUM BICARBONATE

bi·cen·ten·ni·al /ˌbaɪsɛn'tɛniəl/ (also **bi·cen·ten·ar·y** /ˌbaɪsɛn'tɛnəri/) *noun* the year, or the day, when you celebrate an important event that happened exactly 200 years earlier ▶ **bi·cen·ten·ni·al** *adj.* [only before noun]: *bicentennial celebrations*

bi·ceps /'baɪsɛps/ *noun* (*pl.* **bi·ceps**) the main muscle at the front of the top part of the arm ⊃ compare TRICEPS

bick·er /'bɪkər/ *verb* [I] ~ **(about/over sth)** to argue about things that are not important **SYN** SQUABBLE: *The children are always bickering about something or another.* ▶ **bick·er·ing** *noun* [U]

bi·coast·al /ˌbaɪ'koʊstl/ *adj.* involving people and places on both the east and west coasts of the U.S.

bi·cy·cle 🔑 /'baɪsɪkl/ *noun, verb*

- **noun** (also *informal* **bike**) a road vehicle with two wheels that you ride by pushing the PEDALS with your feet: *He got on his bicycle and rode off.* ◆ *We went for a bicycle ride on Sunday.* ⊃ picture on page 133
- **verb** [I] **(+ adv./prep.)** (*old-fashioned*) to go somewhere on a bicycle ⊃ compare BIKE, CYCLE

bicycle clip *noun* one of the two bands that people wear around their ankles when they are riding a bicycle to stop their pants getting caught in the chain

bicycle lane *noun* = BIKE LANE

Bikes

handlebars

brake lever
brake cable
front brake
fork
hub
spoke
rim
tire

saddle
water bottle
crossbar
rear brake
frame

chain wheel
crank
pedal
reflector
chain
stand
gears
valve

bicycle

child's bike training wheels

tricycle

unicycle

helmet

D-lock

light

pump

mountain bike

quad bike

dirt bike

drop handlebars

tandem

gas tank
engine
muffler

motorcycle

mirror
kickstand

scooter

bi·cy·clist /ˈbaɪsɪklɪst/ *noun* (*formal*) a person who rides a bicycle ⊃ compare CYCLIST

bid¹ 🎵 /bɪd/ *verb, noun* ⊃ see also BID²

● *verb* (bid·ding, bid, bid) **1** [I, T] to offer to pay a particular price for something, especially at an AUCTION: ~ (sth) (for sth) *I bid $2,000 for the painting.* ◆ ~ (against sb) *We wanted to buy the chairs but another couple was bidding against us.* **2** [I] ~ (for sth) | ~ (on sth) | ~ (to do sth) to offer to do work or provide a service for a particular price, in competition with other companies, etc. SYN TENDER: *A French firm will be bidding for the contract.* **3** [T] ~ to do sth (used especially in newspapers) to try to do, get, or achieve something SYN ATTEMPT: *The team is bidding to make the playoffs.* **4** [T, I] ~ (sth) (in some card games) to say how many points you expect to win: *She bid four hearts.*

● *noun* **1** ~ (for sth) an offer by a person or a business company to pay a particular amount of money for something: *Granada mounted a hostile takeover bid for Forte.* ◆ *At the auction* (= a public sale where things are sold to the person who offers most), *the highest bid for the picture was $200.* ◆ *Any more bids?* **2** ~ (for sth) | ~ (on sth) an offer to do work or provide a service for a particular price, in competition with other companies, etc. SYN TENDER: *The company submitted a bid for the contract to clean the hospital.* **3** (used especially in newspapers) an effort to do something or to obtain something: ~ for sth *a bid for power* ◆ ~ to do sth *a desperate bid to escape from his attackers* **4** (in some card games) a statement of the number of points a player thinks he or she will win

bid² /bɪd/ *verb* ⊃ see also BID¹ (bid·ding, bade /bæd; beɪd/, bid·den /ˈbɪdn/ or (bid·ding, bid, bid)) **1** ~ (someone) good morning, farewell, etc. (*formal*) to say "good morning", etc. to someone: *I bade farewell to all the friends I had made in Paris.* ◆ *I bade all my friends farewell.* **2** ~ sb (do sth) (*old use* or *literary*) to tell someone to do something: *He bade me come closer.*

bid·da·ble /ˈbɪdəbl/ *adj.* (*formal*) (of people) willing to obey and to do what they are told to

bid·der /ˈbɪdər/ *noun* **1** a person or group that offers to pay an amount of money to buy something: *It went to the highest bidder* (= the person who offered the most money). **2** a person or group that offers to do something or to provide something for a particular amount of money, in competition with others: *There were six bidders for the catering contract.*

bid·ding /ˈbɪdɪŋ/ *noun* [U] **1** the act of offering prices, especially at an AUCTION: *There was fast bidding between private collectors and dealers.* ◆ *Several companies remained in the bidding.* **2** the act of offering to do something or to provide something for a particular price: *competitive bidding for the contract* **3** (in some card games) the process of stating the number of points that players think they will win **4** (*old-fashioned* or *formal*) what someone asks or orders you to do: *to do someone's bidding* (= to obey someone)

bid·dy /ˈbɪdi/ *noun* (*pl.* bid·dies) (*informal*, *disapproving*) an old woman, especially an annoying one

bide /baɪd/ *verb* [I] (*old use*) = ABIDE
IDM **bide your time** to wait for the right time to do something

bi·det /bɪˈdeɪ/ *noun* a low bowl in the bathroom, usually with taps, that you fill with water and sit on to wash your bottom

bi·di·rec·tion·al /ˌbaɪdəˈrekʃənl; -daɪ-/ *adj.* (*technical*) functioning in two directions

bi·en·ni·al /baɪˈeniəl/ *adj., noun*
● *adj.* [usually before noun] happening once every two years: *a biennial convention* ▶ **bi·en·ni·al·ly** *adv.* ⊃ see also ANNUAL, BIANNUAL
● *noun* any plant that lives for two years, producing flowers in the second year ⊃ compare ANNUAL, PERENNIAL

bier /bɪr/ *noun* a frame on which the dead body or the COFFIN is placed or carried at a funeral

biff /bɪf/ *verb* ~ sb (*old-fashioned*, *informal*) to hit someone hard with your FIST: *He biffed me on the nose.* ▶ **biff** *noun*

bi·fo·cals /ˈbaɪˌfouklz/ *noun* [pl.] a pair of glasses with each LENS made in two parts. The upper part is for looking at things at a distance, and the lower part is for looking at things that are close to you. ⊃ compare VARIFOCALS ▶ **bi·fo·cal** *adj.*

bi·fur·cate /ˈbaɪfərˌkeɪt/ *verb* [I] (*formal*) (of roads, rivers, etc.) to divide into two separate parts ▶ **bi·fur·ca·tion** /ˌbaɪfərˈkeɪʃn/ *noun* [C, U]

WHICH WORD?

big ◆ large ◆ great

These adjectives are frequently used with the following nouns:

big ~	large ~	great ~
man	numbers	success
house	part	majority
car	area	interest
boy	room	importance
dog	company	difficulty
smile	family	problem
problem	population	pleasure
surprise	volume	beauty
question	fries	artist
difference	soda	surprise

■ **Large** is more formal than **big** and should be used in writing unless it is in an informal style. It is not usually used to describe people, except to avoid saying "fat."
■ **Great** often suggests quality and not just size. Note also the phrases: *a large amount of* ◆ *a large number of* ◆ *a large quantity of* ◆ *a great deal of* ◆ *in great detail* ◆ *a person of great age.*

---

big 🎵 /bɪg/ *adj., adv.* ⊃ see also BIGS *n.*
● *adj.* (big·ger, big·gest)
▷ LARGE **1** large in size, degree, amount, etc.: *a big man/house/increase* ◆ *This shirt isn't big enough.* ◆ *It's the world's biggest computer company.* ◆ (*informal*) *He had this great big grin on his face.* ◆ *They were earning big money.* ◆ *The news came as a big blow.*
▷ OLDER **2** (*informal*) older: *You're a big girl now.* ◆ *my big brother*
▷ IMPORTANT **3** [only before noun] important; serious: *a big decision* ◆ *Tonight is the biggest match of his career.* ◆ *You are making a big mistake.* ◆ *She took the stage for her big moment.* ◆ (*informal*) *Do you really think we can take on the big boys* (= compete with the most powerful people)?
▷ AMBITIOUS **4** (*informal*) (of a plan) needing a lot of effort, money, or time to succeed: *They're full of big ideas.*
▷ POPULAR **5** (*informal*) popular with the public; successful: *Orange is the big color this year.* ◆ ~ in… *The band's very big in Japan.*
▷ ENTHUSIASTIC **6** (*informal*) enthusiastic about someone or something: *I'm a big fan of hers.*
▷ DOING SOMETHING A LOT **7** doing something often or to a large degree: *a big eater/drinker/spender*
▷ GENEROUS **8** ~ of sb (usually *ironic*) kind or generous: *He gave me an extra five dollars for two hours of work. I thought, "That's big of you."*

▶ **big·ness** *noun* [U]
IDM **be/get too big for your boots/britches** to be/become too proud of yourself; to behave as if you are more important than you really are **a big cheese** (*informal*, *humorous*) an important and powerful person, especially in an organization **the big enchilada** (*informal*, *humorous*) the most important person or thing **a big fish (in a small pond)** an important person (in a small community) **a big shot/name** an important person **the big picture** (*informal*) the situation as a whole: *Right now, we need to forget the details and take a look at the big picture.* **the big stick** (*informal*) the use or threat of force or power: *The authorities used quiet persuasion instead of the big stick.* **the big three, four, etc.**

ʌ cup   ə about   eɪ say   aɪ five   ɔɪ boy   aʊ now   oʊ go   ər bird

the three, four, etc. most important countries, people, companies, etc.: *She works for one of the Big Six.* **give sb/get a big hand** to show your approval of someone by CLAPPING; to be APPLAUDED in this way: *Ladies and gentlemen, let's give a big hand to our special guests tonight…* ➔ more at EYE *n.*, FISH *n.*, MR., THING, WAY *n.*

• *adv.* in an impressive way: *We need to think big.* **IDM go over big (with sb)** (*informal*) to make a good impression on someone; to be successful: *This story went over big with my kids.* **make it big** to be very successful: *He's hoping to make it big on TV.* ➔ more at HIT *v.*

big·a·mist /ˈbɪɡəmɪst/ *noun* a person who commits the crime of bigamy

big·a·my /ˈbɪɡəmi/ *noun* [U] the crime of marrying someone when you are still legally married to someone else ➔ compare MONOGAMY, POLYGAMY ▶ **big·a·mous** /ˈbɪɡəməs/ *adj.*: *a bigamous relationship*

the Big Apple *noun* [sing.] (*informal*) New York City

the Big Bad Wolf *noun* [sing.] (*informal*) a dangerous and frightening enemy **ORIGIN** From the wolf in several children's stories and the song *Who's Afraid of the Big Bad Wolf?*

big band *noun* a large group of musicians playing JAZZ or dance music: *the big-band sound*

big bang *noun* [sing.] usually **Big Bang** the single large explosion that some scientists suggest created the universe

Big Board *noun* **the Big Board** [sing.] (*informal*) the New York Stock Exchange: *There was a lot of activity on the Big Board today.*

big box (also **big-box store**) *noun* (*informal*) a very large store, built on one level and located outside a town, which sells goods at low prices: *When a big-box store opens, smaller retailers often go out of business.* ◆ *Efforts were made to limit big-box expansion.*

Big Brother *noun* [sing.] a leader, a person in authority, or a government that tries to control people's behavior and thoughts, but pretends to act for their benefit **ORIGIN** From George Orwell's novel *Nineteen Eighty-Four*, in which the leader of the government, **Big Brother**, had total control over the people. The slogan "Big Brother is watching you" reminded people that he knew everything they did.

big bucks *noun* [pl.] (*informal*) a large amount of money

big business *noun* [U] **1** large companies that have a lot of power, considered as a group: *links between politics and big business* **2** something that has become important because people are willing to spend a lot of money on it: *Health and fitness have become big business.*

big cat *noun* any large wild animal of the cat family. LIONS, TIGERS, and LEOPARDS are all big cats.

Big Chief *noun* (*informal*) the person in charge of a business or other organization

big deal *noun* [sing.] (*informal*) **1** something that is very special or important: *Her first party dress was a big deal for the little girl.* **2** (*ironic*) used to say that something is not important: *So he earns more than me. Big deal!* ◆ *We lost the first game of the season, but it's no big deal.* ◆ *Yes, we're a little late, but what's the big deal?* **IDM make a big deal out of sth | make sth into a big deal** to try to make something seem more important than it really is: *She always makes a big deal out of her kids' piano recitals.* ◆ *Why do you have to make this little incident into such a big deal?*

Big Dipper *noun* [sing.] a group of seven bright stars that can only be seen from the northern half of the world

Big·foot /ˈbɪɡfʊt/ *noun* (*pl.* **Big·feet** /-fiːt/) (also **Sas·quatch**) a large creature covered with hair like an APE, which some people believe lives in western N. America

big game *noun* [U] large wild animals that people hunt for sport, for example ELEPHANTS and LIONS

big·gie /ˈbɪɡi/ *noun* (*informal*) an important thing, person, or event

IDM no biggie (*informal*) used to say that you are not concerned or angry about something: *"I haven't finished the report yet." "No biggie—we don't need it until tomorrow."*

big government *noun* [U] (*disapproving*) a type of government that has a lot of control over people's lives and the economy

big gun *noun* (*informal*) a person who has a lot of power or influence

big hair *noun* [U] hair in a style that makes a large shape around the head

big-headed *adj.* (*informal*, *disapproving*) having a very high opinion of how important and smart you are; too proud ▶ **big-head** *noun*

big-hearted *adj.* very kind; generous

big hitter *noun* (*informal*) a person who is successful and has a lot of influence: *They've appointed one of the industry's big hitters to the board.*

the big house *noun* [sing.] (*slang*) prison: *He got twenty years in the big house.*

bight /baɪt/ *noun* a long curve in a coast: *the Southern California Bight*

big league *noun* [C] **1** a group of teams in a professional sport, especially baseball, that play at the highest level **2 the big league** (*informal*) a very successful and important group: *Over the past year, the company has joined the big leagues.*

big-league *adj.* **1** connected with sports teams that are in a big league **2** very important and successful

Big Man on Campus *noun* (*abbr.* BMOC) (*informal*) a successful, popular, male student at a college or university

big mouth (also **big-mouth**) *noun* (*informal*) a person who talks a lot, especially about himself or herself, and who cannot keep secrets **IDM have a big mouth** **HELP** In this idiom the main stress is on **mouth**. **1** to be bad at keeping secrets **2** to talk too much, especially about your own abilities and achievements **me and my big mouth** **HELP** In this idiom the main stress is on **mouth**. (*informal*) used when you realize that you have said something that you should not have said ▶ **big-mouthed** /ˈbɪɡ maʊðd/ *adj.*

Big Muddy *noun* (*informal*) the Mississippi River

big·ot /ˈbɪɡət/ *noun* (*disapproving*) a person who has very strong, unreasonable beliefs or opinions about race, religion, or politics, and who will not listen to or accept the opinions of anyone who disagrees: *a religious/racial bigot*

big·ot·ed /ˈbɪɡətəd/ *adj.* (*disapproving*) showing strong, unreasonable beliefs or opinions, and a refusal to change them

big·ot·ry /ˈbɪɡətri/ *noun* [U] (*disapproving*) the state of feeling, or the act of expressing, strong, unreasonable beliefs or opinions

bigs /bɪɡz/ *noun* [pl.] (*informal*) **1 the bigs** the major league in a professional sport **2** large companies with a lot of money and influence: *software bigs* ◆ *the Internet travel bigs*

the big screen *noun* [sing.] the movies (when contrasted with television): *The movie hits the big screen in July.* ◆ *her first big-screen success*

big tent *noun* a group or philosophy that accepts and includes individuals and organizations that have a wide variety of opinions or styles: *The movement soon became a big tent under which many campaign groups gathered.*

big-ticket *adj.* [only before noun] costing a lot of money: *big-ticket items*

big time *noun*, *adv.* (*informal*)
• *noun* **the big time** [sing.] great success in a profession, especially the entertainment business: *a bit-part actor who finally made/hit the big time* ➔ compare SMALL-TIME
• *adv.* on a large scale; to a great extent: *This time they messed up big time!*

,big 'toe *noun* the largest toe on a person's foot ⊃ **picture at** BODY

'big top *usually* **the big top** *noun* [usually sing.] the large tent in which a CIRCUS gives performances

,big 'wheel (*informal*) an important person in a company or an organization

big·wig /'bɪgwɪg/ *noun* (*informal*) an important person: *She had to entertain some boring local bigwigs.*

bike /baɪk/ *noun, verb*
● *noun* (*informal*) **1** a bicycle: *She got on her bike and rode off.* ◆ *I usually go to work by bike.* ⊃ **see also** MOUNTAIN BIKE **2** a motorcycle ⊃ **see also** DIRT BIKE ⊃ **picture at** BICYCLE
● *verb* [I] (+ adv./prep.) to go somewhere on a bicycle or motorcycle: *My dad bikes to work every day.*
▶ **bik·ing** *noun* [U]: *The activities on offer include sailing and mountain biking.* ⊃ **compare** BICYCLE, CYCLE

'bike lane (also 'bicycle ,lane) *noun* a part of a road that only bicycles are allowed to use

bik·er /'baɪkər/ *noun* **1** a person who rides a motorcycle, usually as a member of a large group **2** a person who rides a bicycle, especially a MOUNTAIN BIKE

bi·ki·ni /bɪ'kini/ *noun* a piece of clothing in two pieces that women wear for swimming and lying in the sun

bi'kini ,line *noun* the area of skin around the bottom half of a BIKINI and the hair that grows there, which some women remove

bi·la·bi·al /ˌbaɪ'leɪbiəl/ *noun* (*phonetics*) a speech sound made by using both lips, such as /b/, /p/, and /m/ in *buy, pie,* and *my* ▶ **bi·la·bi·al** *adj.*

bi·lat·er·al /ˌbaɪ'lætərəl/ *adj.* **1** involving two groups of people or two countries: *bilateral relations/agreements/trade/talks* **2** (*medical*) involving both of two parts or sides of the body or brain ▶ **bi·lat·er·al·ly** *adv.* ⊃ **compare** MULTILATERAL, TRILATERAL, UNILATERAL

bil·ber·ry /'bɪl,beri/ *noun* (*pl.* bil·ber·ries) (also whor·tle·ber·ry) a small dark blue BERRY that grows on bushes on hills and in woods and can be eaten. The bush is also called a bilberry. ⊃ **compare** BLUEBERRY

bile /baɪl/ *noun* [U] **1** the greenish-brown liquid with a bitter, unpleasant taste that is produced by the LIVER to help the body to deal with the fats we eat, and that can come into your mouth when you VOMIT with an empty stomach **2** (*formal*) anger or hatred: *The critic's review of the play was just a paragraph of bile.*

'bile duct *noun* the tube that carries bile from the LIVER and the GALL BLADDER to the DUODENUM ⊃ **picture at** BODY

bilge /bɪldʒ/ *noun* **1** [C] also **bilges** [pl.] the almost flat part of the bottom of a boat or a ship, inside or outside **2** (also 'bilge water) [U] dirty water that collects in a ship's bilge

bil·har·zi·a /bɪl'hɑrziə; -'hɑrtsiə/ *noun* [U] a serious disease, common in parts of Africa and S. America, caused by small WORMS that get into the blood

bil·i·ar·y /'bɪli,eri/ *adj.* (*medical*) relating to BILE or to the BILE DUCT

bi·lin·gual /ˌbaɪ'lɪŋgwəl/ *adj.* **1** able to speak two languages equally well: *She is bilingual in English and Punjabi.* **2** using two languages; written in two languages: *bilingual education/communities* ◆ *a bilingual dictionary* ▶ **bi·lin·gual** *noun: Spanish/English bilinguals* ⊃ **compare** MONOLINGUAL, MULTILINGUAL

bil·ious /'bɪlyəs/ *adj.* **1** feeling as if you might VOMIT soon **2** (of colors, usually green or yellow) creating an unpleasant effect: *a bilious green dress* **3** (*formal*) in a bad mood; full of anger

bil·i·ru·bin /ˌbɪli'rubən/ *noun* [U] (*medical*) an orange substance produced in the LIVER

bilk /bɪlk/ *verb* (*informal*) ~ **sb (out of sth)** | ~ **sth (from sb)** to cheat someone, especially by taking money from them: *a con man who bilked investors out of millions of dollars*

bill 🔑 /bɪl/ *noun, verb*
● *noun*
> FOR PAYMENT **1** a piece of paper that shows how much you owe someone for goods or services: *the telephone/electricity/gas bill* ◆ *We ran up a huge hotel bill.* ◆ *She always pays her bills on time.* ◆ *The bills are piling up* (= there are more and more that have still not been paid). ◆ *The bill for the meal came to $35.* ◆ *Let's ask for the bill.* ⊃ **collocations at** RESTAURANT ⊃ **compare** CHECK *n.*
> MONEY **2** a piece of paper money **SYN** BANKNOTE: *a ten-dollar bill* ⊃ **picture at** MONEY ⊃ **thesaurus box at** MONEY
> IN GOVERNMENT **3** a written suggestion for a new law that is presented to a country's government so that its members can discuss it: *to pass/approve/veto a bill* ◆ *a civil rights bill*
> AT THEATER, ETC. **4** a program of entertainment at a theater, etc.: *a horror double bill* (= two horror movies shown one after the other) ◆ *Topping the bill* (= the most important performer) *is Paul Simon.*
> ADVERTISEMENT **5** a notice in a public place to advertise an event **SYN** POSTER ⊃ **see also** HANDBILL
> OF BIRDS **6** the hard pointed or curved outer part of a bird's mouth ⊃ **picture at** ANIMAL **SYN** BEAK **7** -billed (in adjectives) having the type of bill mentioned: *long-billed waders*
> ON HAT **8** (also vi·sor) the stiff front part of a cap that sticks out above your eyes ⊃ **picture at** HAT
IDM fill/fit the bill to be what is needed in a particular situation or for a particular purpose: *On paper, several of the applicants fit the bill.* ⊃ **more at** CLEAN *adj.*, FOOT *v.*
● *verb*
> ASK FOR PAYMENT **1** ~ **sb (for sth)** to send someone a bill for something: *Please bill me for the books.*
> ADVERTISE **2** [usually passive] ~ **sb/sth as sth** to advertise or describe someone or something in a particular way: *He was billed as the new Brad Pitt.* **3** [usually passive] ~ **sb/sth to do sth** to advertise that someone or something will do something: *She was billed to be performing for three nights at Radio City.*
IDM bill and coo (*old-fashioned, informal*) if two people who are in love **bill and coo**, they kiss and speak in a loving way to each other

t tea   ṭ butter   d did   k cat   g got   tʃ chin   dʒ June   f fall

bill·a·ble *adj.* (of work done by professional people) that a client or customer can be charged for: *All the firm's attorneys are expected to put in a certain number of billable hours each month.*

bill·board /'bɪlbɔrd/ *noun* a large board on the outside of a building or at the side of the road, used for putting advertisements on: *giant billboards along the highway*

bil·let /'bɪlət/ *noun, verb*
● *noun* a place, often in a private house, where soldiers live temporarily
● *verb* [T, usually passive] **+ adv./prep.** to send soldiers to live somewhere temporarily, especially in private houses during a war

bil·let-doux /ˌbɪli 'du; ˌbɪleɪ-/ *noun* (*pl.* **bil·lets-doux** /ˌbɪli 'duz; ˌbɪleɪ-; -'du/) (from *French*, *humorous* or *literary*) a love letter

bill·fold /'bɪlfoʊld/ *noun* = WALLET

bill·hook /'bɪlhʊk/ *noun* a tool with a long handle and a curved blade, used for cutting the small branches off trees

bil·liards /'bɪlyərdz/ *noun* [U] a game for two people played with CUES (= long sticks) and three balls on a long table covered with green cloth. Players try to hit the balls against each other and into pockets at the edge of the table: *a game of billiards* ⊃ compare POOL ► **bil·liard** *adj.* [only before noun]: *a billiard cue*

bill·ing /'bɪlɪŋ/ *noun* **1** [U] the position, especially an important one, that someone is advertised or described as having in a show, etc.: *to have top/star billing* **2** [U] the act of preparing and sending bills to customers **3** [C, usually pl.] the total amount of business that a company does in a particular period of time: *billings around $7 million*

bil·lion /'bɪlyən/ *number* (*usually plural verb*) **1** (*abbr.* **bn**) 1,000,000,000; one thousand million: *Worldwide sales reached 2.5 billion.* ◆ *half a billion dollars* ◆ *They have spent billions on the problem* (= billions of dollars, etc.). **HELP** You say **a, one, two, several,** etc. **billion** without a final "s" on "billion." **Billions (of…)** can be used if there is no number or quantity before it. Always use a plural verb with **billion** or **billions,** except when a number or an amount of money is mentioned: *Two billion (people) worldwide are expected to watch the game.* ◆ *Two billion (dollars) was withdrawn from the account.* ◆ *A billion is 10 to the power of 9.* There are more examples of how to use numbers at the entry for **hundred**. **2 a billion** or **billions (of…)** (*informal*) a very large amount: *Our immune systems are killing billions of germs right now.*

bil·lion·aire /ˌbɪlyə'nɛr; 'bɪlyəˌnɛr/ *noun* an extremely rich person, who has at least a thousand million dollars, etc. in money or property

bill of ex·change *noun* (*pl.* **bills of ex·change**) (*business*) a written order to pay a sum of money to a particular person on a particular date

bill of 'fare *noun* (*pl.* **bills of 'fare**) (*old-fashioned*) a list of the food that can be ordered in a restaurant **SYN** MENU

bill of lad·ing /ˌbɪl əv 'leɪdɪŋ/ *noun* (*pl.* **bills of lad·ing**) (*business*) a list giving details of the goods that a ship, etc. is carrying

bill of 'rights (also **Bill of 'Rights**) *noun* [sing.] a written statement of the basic rights of the citizens of a country; in particular, the first ten AMENDMENTS to the U.S. Constitution

bill of 'sale *noun* (*pl.* **bills of 'sale**) (*business*) an official document showing that something has been bought

bil·low /'bɪloʊ/ *verb, noun*
● *verb* **1** [I] (of a sail, skirt, etc.) to fill with air and swell out: *The curtains billowed in the breeze.* **2** [I] if smoke, cloud, etc. **billows,** it rises and moves in a large mass: *A huge cloud of smoke billowed out of the chimney.*
● *noun* [usually pl.] a moving mass or cloud of smoke, steam, etc. like a wave

bil·ly club /'bɪli ˌklʌb/ *noun* a short wooden stick used as a weapon by police officers

billy ˌgoat *noun* a male GOAT ⊃ compare NANNY GOAT

bim·bo /'bɪmboʊ/ *noun* (*pl.* **bim·bos**) (*informal, disapproving*) a young woman, who is sexually attractive but not very intelligent: *He's going out with an empty-headed bimbo half his age.*

bi·month·ly /ˌbaɪ'mʌnθli/ *adj., adv.* produced or happening every two months or twice each month

bin /bɪn/ *noun* **1** a large container, usually with a lid, for storing things in: *a bread bin* **2** a container that you put waste in: *a recycling bin*

bi·na·ry /'baɪnɛri; -nəri/ *adj.* **1** (*computing, mathematics*) using only 0 and 1 as a system of numbers: *the binary system* ◆ *binary arithmetic* **2** (*technical*) based on only two numbers; consisting of two parts: *binary code/numbers* ⊃ compare UNARY ► **bi·na·ry** *noun* [U]: *The computer performs calculations in binary and converts the results to decimal.*

bind /baɪnd/ *verb, noun*
● *verb* (bound, bound /baʊnd/)
▷ **TIE WITH ROPE/CLOTH 1** [T] to tie someone or something with rope, string, etc. so that they cannot move or are held together firmly: **~ sb/sth to sth** *She was bound to a chair.* ◆ **~ sb/sth together** *They bound his hands together.* ◆ **~ sb/sth** *He was left **bound and gagged** (= tied up and with a piece of cloth tied over his mouth).* **2** [T] **~ sth (up)** to tie a long thin piece of cloth around something: *She bound up his wounds.* ◆ *newspapers bound up with twine*
▷ **MAKE SOMEONE DO SOMETHING 3** [T, usually passive] to force someone to do something by making them promise to do it or by making it their duty to do it: **~ sb (to sth)** *He had been bound to secrecy* (= made to promise not to tell people about something). ◆ **~ sb to do sth** *The agreement binds her to repay the debt within six months.* ⊃ see also BINDING, BOUND
▷ **UNITE 4** [T] to unite people, organizations, etc. so that they live or work together more happily or effectively: **~ A and B (together)** *Organizations such as schools and clubs bind a community together.* ◆ **~ A to B** *She thought that having his child would bind him to her forever.*
▷ **STICK TOGETHER 5** [I, T] to stick together or to make things stick together in a solid mass: **~ (together)** *Add an egg yolk to make the mixture bind.* ◆ **~ sth (together)** *Add an egg yolk to bind the mixture together.*
▷ **BOOK 6** [T, usually passive] **~ sth (in sth)** to fasten the pages of a book together and put them inside a cover: *two volumes bound in leather*
▷ **SEW EDGE 7** [T, often passive] **~ sth (with sth)** to sew the edge of something to decorate it or to make it stronger: *The blankets were bound with satin.* **IDM** see HAND *n.*
PHRV **bind sb 'over** [usually passive] (*law*) to give someone BAIL while they are waiting to go to trial: *He was bound over for trial.*
● *noun* [sing.] (*informal*) an annoying situation that is often difficult to avoid ⊃ see also DOUBLE BIND
IDM **in a bind** in a difficult situation that you do not know how to get out of: *When the babysitter quit, it really put us in a bind.*

bind·er /'baɪndər/ *noun* **1** [C] a hard cover for holding sheets of paper, magazines, etc. together **2** [C] a *ring binder* **2** a person or machine that puts covers on books **3** [C, U] a substance that makes things stick or mix together in a solid form **4** [C] a machine that fastens WHEAT into bunches after it has been cut **5** [C] a temporary insurance policy that is legal and provides protection until a permanent contract is issued **6** [C] a payment made by the buyer of a house or other property to the seller, which shows that their agreement is official

bin·di /'bɪndi/ *noun* a decorative mark worn in the middle of the FOREHEAD, usually by Hindu women

bind·ing /'baɪndɪŋ/ *adj., noun*
● *adj.* **~ (on/upon sb)** that must be obeyed because it is accepted in law: *a binding promise/agreement/contract* **ANT** NONBINDING

● **noun 1** [C, U] the cover that holds the pages of a book together **2** [C, U] cloth that is fastened to the edge of something to protect or decorate it **3** [C] a device on a SKI that holds the heel and toe of your boot in place and releases the boot automatically if you fall ⸠ picture at SPORT

binding theory noun ⸠ GOVERNMENT AND BINDING THEORY

bind·weed /'baɪndwiːd/ noun [U] a wild plant that twists itself around other plants

binge /bɪndʒ/ noun, verb
● **noun** (informal) a short period of time when someone does too much of a particular activity, especially eating or drinking alcohol: to go on a binge ◆ One of the symptoms is binge eating.
● **verb** (binge·ing or bing·ing, binged, binged) [I] ~ (on sth) to eat or drink too much, especially without being able to control yourself: When she's depressed she binges on chocolate.

bin·go /'bɪŋɡoʊ/ noun, exclamation
● **noun** [U] a game in which each player has a card with numbers on it. Numbers are called out in no particular order and the first player whose numbers are all called out, or who has a line of numbers called out, wins a prize: to play bingo ◆ a bingo hall
● **exclamation** used to express pleasure and/or surprise because you have found something that you were looking for, or done something that you were trying to do: The computer program searches, and bingo! We get a match.

bin·oc·u·lar /bɪ'nɑkyələr/ adj. (technical) using two eyes to see: binocular vision

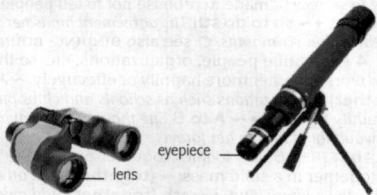

eyepiece
lens
binoculars   telescope

bin·oc·u·lars /bɪ'nɑkyələrz/ noun [pl.] an instrument, like two small TELESCOPES fixed together, that makes objects that are far away seem nearer when you look through it: a pair of binoculars ◆ We looked at the birds through binoculars.

bi·no·mi·al /baɪ'noʊmiəl/ noun **1** (mathematics) an expression that has two groups of numbers or letters, joined by the sign + or − **2** (linguistics) a pair of nouns joined by a word like "and," where the order of the nouns is always the same, for example "knife and fork" ▶ **bi·no·mi·al** adj. ⸠ compare POLYNOMIAL

bio- /'baɪoʊ/ combining form (in nouns, adjectives, and adverbs) connected with living things or human life: biodegradable ◆ biography

bi·o·chem·ist /ˌbaɪoʊ'kɛmɪst/ noun a scientist who studies biochemistry

bi·o·chem·is·try /ˌbaɪoʊ'kɛməstri/ noun **1** [U] the scientific study of the chemistry of living things **2** [U, C] the chemical structure and behavior of a living thing ▶ **bi·o·chem·i·cal** /-'kɛmɪkl/ adj.

bi·o·da·ta /'baɪoʊˌdeɪtə; -ˌdætə/ noun [U, pl.] information about a person and about what they have done in their life

bi·o·de·grad·a·ble /ˌbaɪoʊdɪ'greɪdəbl/ adj. a substance or chemical that is biodegradable can be changed to a harmless natural state by the action of bacteria, and will therefore not damage the environment ANT NONBIODEGRADABLE ⸠ collocations at ENVIRONMENT

bi·o·de·grade /ˌbaɪoʊdɪ'greɪd/ verb [I] (of a substance or chemical) to change back to a harmless natural state by the action of bacteria

bi·o·die·sel /'baɪoʊˌdizl; -ˌdɪsl/ noun [U] a type of fuel made from plant or animal material, and used in DIESEL engines

bi·o·di·ver·si·ty /ˌbaɪoʊdə'vərsəti; -daɪ'vər-/ (also less frequent ˌbioˌlogical di'versity) noun [U] the existence of a large number of different kinds of animals and plants that make a balanced environment ⸠ collocations at ENVIRONMENT

bi·o·en·gi·neer·ing /ˌbaɪoʊˌɛndʒə'nɪrɪŋ/ noun [U] the use of engineering methods to solve medical problems, for example the use of artificial arms and legs

bi·o·eth·ics /ˌbaɪoʊ'ɛθɪks/ noun [U] (technical) the moral principles that influence research in medicine and biology

bi·o·feed·back /ˌbaɪoʊ'fidbæk/ noun [U] (technical) the use of electronic equipment to record and display activity in the body that is not usually under your conscious control, for example your heart rate, so that you can learn to control that activity

bi·o·fu·el /'baɪoʊˌfyuəl; -ˌfyul/ noun [C, U] fuel made from plant or animal sources and used in engines: biofuels made from sugar cane and sugar beet

bi·o·gas /'baɪoʊˌɡæs/ noun [U] gas, especially METHANE, that is produced by dead plants and that can be burned to produce heat

bi·og·ra·pher /baɪ'ɑɡrəfər/ noun a person who writes the story of another person's life

bi·og·ra·phy /baɪ'ɑɡrəfi/ noun [C, U] (pl. bi·og·ra·phies) the story of a person's life written by someone else; this type of writing: Boswell's biography of Johnson ⸠ compare AUTOBIOGRAPHY ▶ **bi·o·graph·i·cal** /ˌbaɪə'ɡræfɪkl/ adj.

bi·o·haz·ard /'baɪoʊˌhæzərd/ noun a risk to human health or to the environment, from a BIOLOGICAL source

bi·o·log·i·cal /ˌbaɪə'lɑdʒɪkl/ adj. **1** connected with the science of biology: the biological sciences **2** connected with the processes that take place within living things: the biological effects of radiation ◆ the biological control of pests (= using living ORGANISMS to destroy them, not chemicals) ◆ a child's biological parents (= natural parents, not the people who adopted him/her) **3** (of laundry soap, etc.) using ENZYMES (= chemical substances that are found in plants and animals) to get clothes, etc. clean: biological and non-biological detergents ▶ **bi·o·log·i·cally** /-kli/ adv.

ˌbioˌlogical 'clock noun (technical) a natural system in living things that controls regular physical activities such as sleeping: (figurative) At 38, Kate's biological clock was ticking (= she was beginning to think that she would soon be too old to have children).

ˌbioˌlogical di'versity noun = BIODIVERSITY

ˌbioˌlogical 'warfare (also ˌgerm 'warfare) noun [U] the use of harmful bacteria as weapons of war

ˌbioˌlogical 'weapon noun a weapon of war that uses harmful bacteria ⸠ compare CHEMICAL WEAPON

bi·ol·o·gist /baɪ'ɑlədʒɪst/ noun a scientist who studies biology

bi·ol·o·gy /baɪ'ɑlədʒi/ noun [U]
1 the scientific study of the life and structure of plants and animals: a degree in biology ⸠ compare BOTANY, ZOOLOGY **2** the way in which the body and cells of a living thing behave: How far is human nature determined by biology? ◆ the biology of marine animals

bi·o·lu·mi·nes·cence /ˌbaɪoʊˌlumə'nɛsns/ noun [U] (biology) the natural production of light by living creatures such as GLOWWORMS

bi·o·mass /'baɪoʊˌmæs/ noun [U, sing.] (technical) **1** the total quantity or MASS (= weight) of plants and animals in a particular area or volume **2** natural materials from living or recently dead plants, trees, and animals, used as fuel and in industrial production, especially in the generation of electricity: biomass crops ⸠ compare FOSSIL FUEL

bi·ome /ˈbaɪoʊm/ *noun* (*biology*) the characteristic plants and animals that exist in a particular type of environment, for example in a forest or desert

bi·o·me·chan·ics /ˌbaɪoʊməˈkænɪks/ *noun* [U] the scientific study of the physical movement and structure of living creatures

bi·o·med·i·cal /ˌbaɪoʊˈmɛdɪkl/ *adj.* [usually before noun] relating to how biology affects medicine

bi·o·met·ric /ˌbaɪoʊˈmɛtrɪk/ *adj.* [usually before noun] using measurements of human features, such as fingers or eyes, in order to identify people

bi·on·ic /baɪˈɑnɪk/ *adj.* having parts of the body that are electronic, and therefore able to do things that are not possible for normal humans

bi·o·phys·ics /ˌbaɪoʊˈfɪzɪks/ *noun* [U] the science which uses the laws and methods of physics to study biology

bi·o·pic /ˈbaɪoʊˌpɪk/ *noun* a movie about the life of a particular person

bi·op·sy /ˈbaɪɑpsi/ *noun* (*pl.* bi·op·sies) the removal and examination of TISSUE from the body of someone who is sick, in order to find out more about their disease

bi·o·rhythm /ˈbaɪoʊˌrɪðəm/ *noun* [usually pl.] the changing pattern of how physical processes happen in the body, that some people believe affects human behavior

bi·o·sci·ence /ˈbaɪoʊˌsaɪəns; ˌbaɪoʊˈsaɪəns/ *noun* [C, U] any of the LIFE SCIENCES (= sciences concerned with studying humans, animals, or plants)

bi·o·se·cur·i·ty /ˌbaɪoʊsəˈkyʊrəti/ *noun* [U] the activities involved in preventing the spread of animal and plant diseases from one area to another

bi·o·sphere /ˈbaɪəˌsfɪr/ *noun* [sing.] (*technical*) the part of the earth's surface and atmosphere in which plants and animals can live

bi·o·tech·nol·o·gy /ˌbaɪoʊtɛkˈnɑlədʒi/ (also *informal* bi·o·tech /ˈbaɪoʊˌtɛk/) *noun* [U] (*technical*) the use of living cells and bacteria in industrial and scientific processes ▶ bi·o·tech·no·log·i·cal /ˌbaɪoʊˌtɛknəˈlɑdʒɪkl/: *biotechnological research*

bi·ot·ic /baɪˈɑtɪk/ *adj.* (*biology*) of or related to living things

bi·o·type /ˈbaɪoʊˌtaɪp/ *noun* (*biology*) a group of living things with exactly the same combination of GENES

bi·par·ti·san /baɪˈpɑrtəzn; -ˈpɑrtəsn/ *adj.* involving two political parties: *a bipartisan policy*

bi·par·tite /baɪˈpɑrtaɪt/ *adj.* (*technical*) involving or made up of two separate parts

bi·ped /ˈbaɪpɛd/ *noun* (*technical*) any creature with two feet ⊃ compare QUADRUPED

bi·ped·al /ˌbaɪˈpɛdl/ *adj.* (*technical*) (of animals) using only two legs for walking

bi·plane /ˈbaɪpleɪn/ *noun* an early type of plane with two sets of wings, one above the other ⊃ picture at PLANE ⊃ compare MONOPLANE

bi·po·lar /ˌbaɪˈpoʊlər/ (also ˌmanic-deˈpressive) *adj.* (*psychology*) suffering from or connected with bipolar disorder ▶ bi·po·lar (also ˌmanic-deˈpressive) *noun*

biˌpolar disˈorder (also biˌpolar afˌfective disˈorder) *noun* [U, C] (also ˌmanic-deˈpression [U]) (*psychology*) a mental illness causing someone to change suddenly from being extremely depressed to being extremely happy

bi·ra·cial /ˌbaɪˈreɪʃl/ *adj.* concerning or containing members of two different races

birch /bɜrtʃ/ *noun* 1 [C, U] (also ˈbirch tree [C]) a tree with smooth BARK and thin branches, that grows in northern regions ⊃ see also SILVER BIRCH ⊃ picture at TREE 2 (also ˈbirch·wood /ˈbɜrtʃwʊd/) [U] the hard pale wood of the birch tree 3 the birch [sing.] the practice of hitting someone with a bunch of birch sticks, used as a punishment, especially in the past

bird 🔑 /bɜrd/ *noun, verb*
● *noun* 1 a creature that is covered with feathers and has two wings, and two legs. Most birds can fly: *a bird's nest with two eggs in it* ◆ *a species of bird* ◆ *The area has a wealth of bird life.* ⊃ collocations at LIFE ⊃ see also GAME BIRD, SEABIRD, SONGBIRD, WATERBIRD 2 (*informal*) a person of a particular type, especially someone who is strange or unusual in some way: *a wise old bird* ◆ *She is that rare bird: a politician with a social conscience.*
IDM **be for the birds** (*informal*) to not be important or practical **a bird in the hand is worth two in the bush** (*saying*) it is better to keep something that you already have than to risk losing it by trying to get much more **the birds and the bees** (*humorous*) the basic facts about sex, especially as told to children **a bird's-eye view (of sth)** a view of something from a high position looking down **birds of a feather (flock together)** (*saying*) people of the same sort (are found together) **give/flip sb the bird** (*informal*) to make a rude sign at someone with your middle finger ⊃ more at EARLY *adj.*, KILL *v.*, LITTLE *adj.*
● *verb* [I] (*informal*) to go BIRDWATCHING

bird·bath /ˈbɜrdbæθ/ *noun* a bowl filled with water for birds to wash in and drink from, usually in a yard

bird·brain /ˈbɜrdbreɪn/ *noun* a stupid person

bird·cage /ˈbɜrdkeɪdʒ/ *noun* a CAGE in which birds are kept, usually one in a house

ˈbird dog *noun* 1 a dog used in hunting to bring back birds that have been shot 2 (*informal*) a person whose job involves searching for good players for a sports team

bird·er /ˈbɜrdər/ *noun* (*informal*) = BIRDWATCHER ⊃ compare ORNITHOLOGIST

ˈbird ˌfeed·er *noun* a container or platform in a yard or garden in/on which people put food for birds

ˈbird flu (also *formal* ˈavian ˈflu) *noun* [U] a serious illness that affects birds, especially chickens, that can be spread from birds to humans and that can cause death: *Ten new cases of bird flu were reported yesterday.*

bird·house /ˈbɜrdhaʊs/ *noun* a small box, often made to look like a house, for birds to build their nest in

bird·ie /ˈbɜrdi/ *noun* 1 (*informal*) a child's word for a little bird 2 (in GOLF) a score of one stroke less than PAR (= the standard score for a hole) ⊃ compare BOGEY, EAGLE 3 = SHUTTLECOCK IDM see LITTLE *adj.*

bird·ing /ˈbɜrdɪŋ/ *noun* (*informal*) = BIRDWATCHING

ˌbird of ˈparadise *noun* (*pl.* ˌbirds of ˈparadise) a bird with very bright feathers, found mainly in New Guinea

ˌbird of ˈpassage *noun* (*pl.* ˌbirds of ˈpassage) 1 a bird that travels regularly from one part of the world to another at different seasons of the year 2 a person who passes through a place without staying there long

ˌbird of ˈprey *noun* (*pl.* ˌbirds of ˈprey) a bird that hunts and kills other creatures for food. EAGLES, HAWKS, and OWLS are all birds of prey.

bird·seed /ˈbɜrdsid/ *noun* [U] special seeds for feeding birds that are in CAGES

bird·song /ˈbɜrdsɔŋ/ *noun* [U] the musical sounds made by birds

ˈbird strike *noun* an occasion when a bird hits an aircraft

bird·watch·er /ˈbɜrdˌwɑtʃər/ (also *informal* bird·er) *noun* a person who watches birds in their natural environment and identifies different breeds, as a hobby ⊃ compare ORNITHOLOGIST ▶ bird·watch·ing (also *informal* bird·ing) *noun* [U]

bi·ret·ta /bəˈrɛtə/ *noun* a square cap worn by Roman Catholic priests

bi·ri·a·ni = BIRYANI

birth 🔑 /bɜrθ/ *noun*
1 [U, C] the time when a baby is born; the process of being born: *The baby weighed 8 pounds at birth.* ◆ *John was present at the birth of both his children.* ◆ *It was a difficult birth.* ◆ *a*

hospital/home birth ♦ *Mark has been blind **from birth**.* ♦ *Please state your **date and place of birth**.* ➔ collocations at CHILD **2** [sing.] the beginning of a new situation, idea, place, etc.: *the birth of a new society in South Africa* **3** [U] a person's origin or the social position of their family: *Anne was French **by birth** but lived most of her life in Italy.* ♦ *a woman of noble birth* **IDM** **give birth (to sb/sth)** to produce a baby or young animal: *She died shortly after giving birth.* ♦ *Mary gave birth to a healthy baby girl.* ♦ *(figurative) It was the study of history that gave birth to the social sciences.*

ˈbirth cerˌtificate *noun* an official document that shows when and where a person was born

ˈbirth conˌtrol *noun* [U] the practice of controlling the number of children a person has, using various methods of CONTRACEPTION: *a reliable method of birth control*

birth·day 🔑 /ˈbɜrθdeɪ/ *noun*
the day in each year that is the same date as the one on which you were born: *Happy Birthday!* ♦ *Oliver's 13th birthday* ♦ *a birthday card/party/present*
IDM **in your birthday suit** (*humorous*) not wearing any clothes

birth·ing /ˈbɜrθɪŋ/ *noun* [U] the action or process of giving birth: *a birthing pool*

birth·mark /ˈbɜrθmɑrk/ *noun* a red or brown mark on a person's skin that has been there since they were born

ˈbirth ˌmother *noun* the woman who gave birth to a child who has been adopted

ˈbirth ˌpartner *noun* a person whom a woman chooses to be with her when she is giving birth to a baby

birth·place /ˈbɜrθpleɪs/ *noun* **1** the house or area where a person was born, especially a famous person **2** the place where something first happened: *Hawaii was the birthplace of surfing.*

ˈbirth rate *noun* the number of live births every year for every 1,000 people in the population of a place: *a low/high birth rate*

birth·right /ˈbɜrθraɪt/ *noun* a thing that someone has a right to because of the family or country they were born in, or because it is a basic right of all humans: *The property is the birthright of the eldest child.* ♦ *Education is every child's birthright.*

birth·stone /ˈbɜrθstoʊn/ *noun* a SEMI-PRECIOUS STONE that is associated with the month of someone's birth or their sign of the ZODIAC

birth·weight /ˈbɜrθweɪt/ *noun* [U, C] the recorded weight of a baby when it is born

bi·ry·a·ni (also **bi·ri·a·ni**) /ˌbɪriˈɑni/ *noun* [U, C] a S. Asian dish made from rice with meat, fish, or vegetables: *chicken biryani*

bis /bɪs/ *adv.* (*music*) (used as an instruction) again

bis·cot·ti /bɪˈskɑti/ *noun* [pl.] small crisp cookies that often contain nuts, made originally in Italy

bis·cuit /ˈbɪskət/ *noun* **1** [C] a type of soft bread, in a small, round shape, often eaten with GRAVY **2** [U] a pale yellowish-brown color **3** [C] (*British*) a CRACKER or cookie ➔ see also DOG BISCUIT

bi·sect /ˈbaɪsɛkt; baɪˈsɛkt/ *verb* ~ **sth** (*technical*) to divide something into two equal parts

bi·sex·u·al /ˌbaɪˈsɛkʃuəl/ *adj., noun*
• *adj.* **1** (also *informal* **bi**) sexually attracted to both men and women **2** (*biology*) having both male and female sexual organs ▶ **bi·sex·u·al·i·ty** /ˌbaɪsɛkʃuˈæləti/ *noun* [U]
• *noun* a person who is bisexual ➔ compare HETEROSEXUAL, HOMOSEXUAL

bish·op /ˈbɪʃəp/ *noun* **1** a senior priest in charge of the churches and priests in a city or district: *the Bishop of Newark* ♦ *Presiding Bishop Jefferts Schori* ➔ see also ARCHBISHOP **2** a piece used in the game of CHESS, that is shaped like a bishop's hat and can move any number of squares in a DIAGONAL line ➔ picture at TOY

bish·op·ric /ˈbɪʃəprɪk/ *noun* **1** the position of a bishop **2** the district for which a bishop is responsible **SYN** DIOCESE

bis·muth /ˈbɪzməθ/ *noun* [U] (*symb.* **Bi**) a chemical element. Bismuth is a reddish-white metal that breaks easily and is used in medicine.

bi·son /ˈbaɪsn; -zn/ *noun* (*pl.* **bi·son**) a large wild animal of the cow family that is covered with hair. The N. American bison is also called a BUFFALO: *a herd of bison*

bisque /bɪsk/ *noun* [U, C] a thick soup, especially one made from SHELLFISH: *lobster bisque*

bis·tro /ˈbistroʊ; ˈbɪs-/ *noun* (*pl.* **bis·tros**) a small informal restaurant

bit 🔑 /bɪt/ *noun*
> **SMALL AMOUNT 1** **a bit** [sing.] (used as an adverb) rather, slightly **SYN** A LITTLE: *These pants are a little bit tight.* ♦ *"Do you want to lie down?" "Yes, I am a bit tired."* ♦ *It costs a little bit more than I wanted to spend.* ♦ *I can lend you fifty dollars—that should help a bit.* **2** **a bit** [sing.] a short time or distance: *Wait a bit!* ♦ *Can you move up a bit?* ♦ *Greg thought for a bit before answering.* **3** [C] ~ **of sth** a small amount or piece of something: *some useful bits of information* ♦ *With **a bit of** luck, we'll be there by 12.* ♦ *I have a little bit of shopping to do.* ♦ *I just want a little bit of cake.* ♦ *bits of grass/paper*
> **LARGE AMOUNT 4** [sing.] **a ~ (of sth)** (*informal*) a large amount: *The new system will **take a bit of** getting used to* (= it will take a long time to get used to).
> **COMPUTING 5** [C] the smallest unit of information used by a computer
> **FOR HORSE 6** [C] a metal bar that is put in a horse's mouth so that the rider can control it ➔ picture at HORSE
> **TOOL 7** [C] a tool or part of a tool for DRILLING (= making) holes ➔ see also DRILL
> **MONEY 8** (*informal*) an amount of money equal to 12½ cents ➔ see also BITE *v.*
IDM **the (whole)… bit** (*informal, disapproving*) behavior or ideas that are typical of a particular group, type of person, or activity: *She found the whole motherhood bit difficult.* **bit by bit** a piece at a time; gradually: *He assembled the model aircraft bit by bit.* ♦ *Bit by bit memories of the night came back to me.* **a bit much** (*informal*) not fair or not reasonable: *Isn't it a bit much, calling me at three in the morning?* **a bit of a…** (*informal*) used when talking about unpleasant or negative things or ideas, to make what you are saying sound less strong : *We may have a bit of a problem on our hands.* **bits and pieces** (*informal*) small objects or items of various kinds: *She stuffed all the bits and pieces into a bag and left.* **do your bit** (*informal*) to do your share of a task: *We can finish this job on time if everyone does their bit.* **every bit as good, bad, etc. (as sb/sth)** just as good, bad, etc.; equally good, bad, etc.: *Rome is every bit as beautiful as Paris.* **get the bit between your teeth** (*informal*) to become very enthusiastic about something that you have started to do so that you are unlikely to stop until you have finished **not a bit| not one (little) bit** not at all; not in any way: *"Are you cold?" "Not a bit."* ♦ *I don't like that idea one bit.* **quite a bit** a fairly large amount or degree: *"How much does he earn?" "Quite a bit, I'm told."* ♦ *He's lost quite a bit of weight on this diet.* ♦ *The trip was quite a bit longer than we expected.* **to bits 1** into small pieces: *The car was blown to bits in the explosion.* ♦ *He smashed it to bits with a hammer.* **2** (*informal*) very much: *I love my kids to bits.* ➔ more at CHAMP *v.*

bitch /bɪtʃ/ *noun, verb*
• *noun* **1** [C] a female dog: *a greyhound bitch* **2** [C] (*slang, disapproving*) an offensive way of referring to a woman, especially an unpleasant one: *She can be a real bitch sometimes.* **3** [sing.] (*slang*) a thing that causes problems or difficulties: *Life's a bitch.*
• *verb* [I] ~ **(about sb/sth)** (*informal*) to make unkind and critical remarks about someone or something, especially when they are not there

bitch·in' (also **bitch·ing**) /ˈbɪtʃɪn/ *adj.* (*slang*) very good

bitch·y /ˈbɪtʃi/ *adj.* (**bitch·i·er, bitch·i·est**) (*informal, offensive*)

ʌ **cup**　　ə **about**　　eɪ **say**　　aɪ **five**　　ɔɪ **boy**　　aʊ **now**　　oʊ **go**　　ɜr **bird**

saying unpleasant and unkind things about other people: *bitchy remarks* ▶ **bitch·i·ness** *noun* [U]

bite 🔑 /baɪt/ *verb, noun*

● *verb* (**bit** /bɪt/, **bit·ten** /ˈbɪtn/)

> USE TEETH **1** [I, T] to use your teeth to cut into or through something: *Does your dog bite?* ◆ *Come here! I won't bite!* (= you don't need to be afraid) ◆ **~ into/through sth** *She bit into a ripe, juicy pear.* ◆ **~ sb/sth** *She was bitten by the family dog.* ◆ *Stop biting your nails!* ◆ **~ off sth/sth off** *He bit off a large chunk of bread./He bit a large chunk of bread off.*

> OF INSECT/SNAKE **2** [I, T] to wound someone by making a small hole or mark in their skin: *Most European spiders don't bite.* ◆ **~ sb** *We were badly bitten by mosquitoes.*

> OF FISH **3** [I] if a fish **bites**, it takes food from the hook of a FISHING LINE and may get caught

> ACCEPT/BELIEVE STH **4** [I] (*informal*) to accept, believe, etc. something, especially when someone tries hard to persuade you to accept or believe it: *They tried to sell us a fake Picasso, but we didn't bite.*

> HAVE EFFECT **5** [I] to have an unpleasant effect: *The recession is beginning to bite.*

> BE VERY BAD **6** **sth bites** [I] (*slang, offensive*) used to say that something is very bad: *Let's leave…this movie really bites!* ◆ *You lost your job? That bites!*

IDM **be bitten by sth** to develop a strong interest in, or enthusiasm for, something: *He's been bitten by the travel bug.* **bite the bullet** (*informal*) to start to deal with an unpleasant or difficult situation which cannot be avoided **ORIGIN** From the custom of giving soldiers a bullet to bite on during a medical operation without anesthetic. **bite the dust** (*informal*) **1** to fail, or to be defeated or destroyed: *Thousands of small businesses bite the dust every year.* **2** (*humorous*) to die **bite the hand that feeds you** to harm someone who has helped you or supported you **bite your lip** to stop yourself from saying something or from showing an emotion **bite off more than you can chew** to try to do too much, or something that is too difficult **bite your tongue** to stop yourself from saying something that might upset someone or cause an argument, although you want to speak: *I didn't believe her explanation, but I bit my tongue.* **I/he/she could have bitten my/his/her tongue out/off** used when someone says something stupid or embarrassing and immediately wishes they had not said it ⊃ more at HEAD, ONCE

PHR V **bite 'back (at sb/sth)** to react angrily, especially when someone has criticized or harmed you **bite sth↔'back** to stop yourself from saying something or from showing your feelings: *She bit back her anger.* **bite 'into sth** to cut into the surface of something: *The horses' hooves bit deep into the soft earth.*

● *noun*

> USING TEETH **1** [C] an act of biting: *The dog gave me a playful bite.* ◆ *He has to wear a brace to correct his bite* (= the way the upper and lower teeth fit together).

> FOOD **2** [C] a small piece of food that you can bite from a larger piece: *She took a couple of bites of the sandwich.* ◆ *He didn't eat a bite of his dinner* (= he ate nothing). **3 a ~ (to eat)** [sing.] (*informal*) a small amount of food; a small meal: *a bite to eat before the movie.* ◆ *Let's go grab a bite.*

> OF INSECT/ANIMAL **4** [C] a wound made by an animal or insect: *Dog bites can get infected.* ◆ *a mosquito/snake bite*

> STRONG TASTE **5** [U] a pleasant strong taste: *Cheese will add extra bite to any pasta dish.*

> COLD **6** [sing.] a sharp, cold feeling: *There's a bite in the air tonight.*

> POWERFUL EFFECT **7** [U] a quality that makes something effective or powerful: *The performance had no bite to it.*

> OF FISH **8** [C] the act of a fish biting food on a hook ⊃ see also FROSTBITE, SOUND BITE

IDM **take a bite out of sth** (*informal*) to reduce something by a large amount: *Insurance costs can take a bite out of your retirement funds.* ⊃ more at BARK n.

bite-sized (also **bite-size**) *adj.* [usually before noun] **1** small enough to put into the mouth and eat: *Cut the meat into bite-sized pieces.* **2** (*informal*) very small or short: *The exams are taken in bite-size chunks over two years.*

bit·ing /ˈbaɪtɪŋ/ *adj.* **1** (of a wind) very cold and unpleasant **2** (of remarks) cruel and critical: *biting sarcasm/wit* ▶ **bit·ing·ly** *adv.*

bit·map /ˈbɪtmæp/ *noun* (*computing*) a way in which an image is stored with a fixed number of BITS (= units of information) for each unit of the image ▶ **bit·map** *verb* (**-pp-**) **~ sth**

bi·ton·al /baɪˈtoʊnl/ *adj.* (*music*) having parts in two different KEYS sounding together ▶ **bi·ton·al·i·ty** /ˌbaɪtoʊˈnæləti/ *noun* [U]

'bit part *noun* a small part in a movie

'bit ˌplayer *noun* **1** an actor with a small part in a movie **2** a person or an organization that is involved in a situation but does not have an important role and has little influence

bit·stream /ˈbɪtstrim/ *noun* (*computing*) a flow of data in BINARY form

bit·ten pp of BITE

---

bit·ter 🔑 /ˈbɪtər/ *adj., noun*

● *adj.* **HELP** **more bitter** and **most bitter** are the usual comparative and superlative forms, but **bitterest** can also be used. **1** (of arguments, disagreements, etc.) very serious and unpleasant, with a lot of anger and hatred involved: *a long and bitter dispute* ◆ *a bitter divorce* **2** (of people) feeling angry and unhappy because you feel that you have been treated unfairly: *She is very bitter about losing her job.* **3** [usually before noun] making you feel very unhappy; caused by great unhappiness: *to weep/shed bitter tears* ◆ *Losing the game was a bitter disappointment for the team.* ◆ *I've learned from bitter experience not to trust what he says.* **4** (of food, etc.) having a strong, unpleasant taste; not sweet: *Black coffee leaves a bitter taste in the mouth.*

⊃ compare SWEET **5** (of weather conditions) extremely cold and unpleasant: *bitter cold* ♦ *a bitter wind* ♦ *It's really bitter out today.* ▶ **bit·ter·ness** *noun* [U]: *The pay cut caused bitterness among the staff.* ♦ *The flowers of the hop plant add bitterness to the beer.*

IDM **a bitter pill (for sb) (to swallow)** a fact or an event that is unpleasant and difficult to accept **to/until the bitter end** continuing until you have done everything you can, or until something is completely finished, despite difficulties and problems: *They were prepared to fight to the bitter end for their rights.*

● *noun* **1** [U, C] a type of beer with a dark color and a strong, bitter taste **2** **bitters** [U] a strong, bitter, alcoholic liquid that is made from plants and added to other alcoholic drinks to give flavor: *gin with a dash of bitters*

bit·ter·ly 🔊 /'bɪtərli/ *adv.*
1 in a way that shows feelings of sadness or anger: *She wept bitterly.* ♦ *They complained bitterly.* ♦ *The development was bitterly opposed by the local community.* **2** (describing unpleasant or sad feelings) extremely: *bitterly disappointed/ashamed* **3** ~ **cold** very cold

bit·tern /'bɪtərn/ *noun* a bird of the HERON family, that lives on wet ground and has a loud call

bit·ter·sweet /ˌbɪtər'swit/ *adj.* **1** bringing pleasure mixed with sadness: *bittersweet memories* **2** (of tastes or smells) bitter and sweet at the same time

bit·ty /'bɪti/ *adj.* (*informal*) (bit·ti·er, bit·ti·est) very small ⊃ see also ITTY-BITTY

bi·tu·men /bɪ'tumən; baɪ-; 'bɪtʊmən/ *noun* [U] a black sticky substance obtained from oil, used for covering roads or roofs

bi·tu·mi·nous /bɪ'tumənəs; baɪ-/ *adj.* containing bitumen

bi·valve /'baɪvælv/ *noun* (*technical*) any SHELLFISH with a shell in two parts, for example a MUSSEL ⊃ compare MOLLUSK

biv·ou·ac /'bɪvu,æk/ *noun*, *verb*
● *noun* a temporary camp or shelter, without using a tent, that is made and used especially by people climbing mountains or by soldiers
● *verb* (-ck-) [I] to spend the night in a bivouac

the biz /bɪz/ *noun* [sing.] (*informal*) a particular type of business, especially one connected with entertainment: *people in the music biz*

bi·zarre /bɪ'zɑr/ *adj.* very strange or unusual **SYN** WEIRD: *a bizarre situation/incident/story* ♦ *bizarre behavior* ▶ **bi·zarre·ly** *adv.*: *bizarrely dressed*

blab /blæb/ *verb* (-bb-) [I, T] ~ **(to sb) (about sth)** | ~ **(sth) (to sb)** (*informal*) to tell someone information that should be kept secret: *Someone must have blabbed to the police.*

blab·ber /'blæbər/ *verb* [I] ~ **(on) (about sth)** (*informal*) to talk in a way that other people think is silly and annoying: *What was she blabbering on about this time?*

blab·ber·mouth /'blæbər,maʊθ/ *noun* (*informal*, *disapproving*) a person who tells secrets because they talk too much

black 🔊 /blæk/ *adj.*, *noun*, *verb*
● *adj.* (black·er, black·est)
❭ COLOR **1** having the very darkest color, like night or coal: *a shiny black car* ♦ *black storm clouds*
❭ WITH NO LIGHT **2** without light; completely dark: *a black night*
❭ PEOPLE **3** belonging to a race of people who have dark skin; connected with black people: *a black writer* ♦ *black culture* **HELP** The term **African American** is generally preferred to **black** for Americans whose families originally came from Africa.
❭ TEA/COFFEE **4** without milk: *Two black coffees, please.* ⊃ compare WHITE
❭ DIRTY **5** very dirty; covered with dirt: *chimneys black with smoke* ♦ *Go and wash your hands; they're completely black!*

❭ ANGRY **6** full of anger or hatred: *She's been in a really black mood all day.* ♦ *Rory shot her a black look.*
❭ DEPRESSING **7** without hope; very depressing: *The future looks pretty black.* ♦ *It's been another black day with the announcement of further job losses.*
❭ EVIL **8** (*literary*) evil or immoral: *black deeds/lies*
❭ HUMOR **9** dealing with unpleasant or terrible things, such as murder, in a humorous way: *"Good place to bury the bodies," she joked with black humor.* ♦ *The play is a black comedy.* ⊃ see also BLACKLY
▶ **black·ness** *noun* [U, sing.]: *She peered out into the blackness of the night.*

IDM **(beat sb) black and blue** (to hit someone until they are) covered with BRUISES (= blue, brown, or purple marks on the body) **not as black as he/she/it is painted** not as bad as people say he/she/it is: *Is he really as black as he's painted?* ⊃ more at POT *n.*

● *noun*
❭ COLOR **1** [U] the very darkest color, like night or coal: *the black of the night sky* ♦ *Everyone at the funeral was dressed in black.*
❭ PEOPLE **2** [C, usually pl.] a member of a race of people who have dark skin **HELP** In this meaning **black** is more common in the plural. It can sound offensive in the singular. Instead, you can use the adjective ("a black man/woman"), but **African American** is the most generally accepted term for an American whose family originally came from Africa.

IDM **be in the black** to have money, for example in your bank account ⊃ compare BE IN THE RED at RED **black and white** having no colors except black, white, and shades of gray (in photographs, on television, etc.): *a film made in black and white* ♦ *black-and-white photos* **in black and white** in writing or in print: *I never thought they'd put it in black and white on the front page.* **(in) black and white** in a way that makes people or things seem completely bad or good, or completely right or wrong: *It's a complex issue, but he only sees it in black and white.* ♦ *This is not a black-and-white decision* (= where the difference between two choices is completely clear).

● *verb* ~ **sth** to make something black **SYN** BLACKEN **PHRV** ˌblack 'out to become unconscious for a short time **SYN** FAINT: *The driver blacked out at the wheel and crashed into a tree.* ⊃ related *noun* BLACKOUT ˌblack sth↔'out **1** to make a place dark by turning off lights, covering windows, etc.: *A power failure blacked-out the city last night.* ♦ *a house with blacked out windows* ⊃ related *noun* BLACKOUT **2** to prevent something such as a piece of writing or a television broadcast from being read or seen: *Some lines of the document have been blacked out for security reasons.*

Black Angus (also An·gus) *noun* a breed of black beef CATTLE with no horns

the ˌblack 'arts *noun* [pl.] = BLACK MAGIC

black·ball /'blækbɔl/ *verb* ~ **sb** to prevent someone from joining a club or a group by voting against them

ˈblack belt *noun* **1** a belt that you can earn in a sport such as JUDO or KARATE, which shows that you have reached a very high standard **2** a person who has gained a black belt

Black·Ber·ry™ /'blæk,bɛri/ *noun* (*pl.* Black·Ber·ries) a very small computer that you can hold in your hand and that you can use for storing information, sending and receiving e-mails and TEXT MESSAGES, making and receiving phone calls, and looking at the Internet: *Check your e-mails via your BlackBerry.* ♦ *a BlackBerry handset*

black·ber·ry /'blæk,bɛri/ (*pl.* black·ber·ries) *noun* a small, soft, black fruit that grows on a bush with THORNS. The bush is called a blackberry or a BRAMBLE: *blackberry and apple pie* ⊃ picture at FRUIT

black·ber·ry·ing /'blæk,bɛriɪŋ/ *noun* [U] the act of picking blackberries: *Would you like to go blackberrying?*

black·bird /'blækbərd/ *noun* **1** a mainly black, N. American bird, related to the STARLING **2** a European bird, smaller than the N. American blackbird

black·board /'blækbɔrd/ (also **chalk·board**) noun a large board with a smooth black or dark green surface that teachers write on with a piece of CHALK: *to write on the blackboard* ➔ compare WHITEBOARD

black 'box noun **1** [C] (also **'flight re,corder**) a small machine in a plane that records all the details of each flight and is useful for finding out the cause of an accident **2** [usually sing.] (*technical*) a complicated piece of equipment, usually electronic, that you know produces particular results, but that you do not completely understand

black 'cherry noun **1** [C] a type of N. American CHERRY tree **2** [C] a sour fruit of the black cherry tree **3** [U] the hard wood of the black cherry tree

black 'currant // noun a small black BERRY that grows in bunches on a garden bush and can be eaten: *black-currant jam* ◆ *a black-currant bush*

the ,Black 'Death noun [sing.] the name used for the very serious infectious disease (called BUBONIC PLAGUE) that killed millions of people in Europe and Asia in the 14th century

black 'diamond noun **1** [C] (*informal*) a lump of coal **2** [U, C] a dark form of diamond **3** [C] a slope that is difficult to SKI down: *a black diamond run*

black em'powerment (also ,black eco,nomic em-'powerment) noun [U] a policy that aims to give black people the chance to earn more money, own more property, etc., and have a greater role in the economy than they did before

black·en /'blækən/ verb **1** [T, I] ~ (sth) to make something black; to become black: *Their faces were blackened with soot.* ◆ *Smoke had blackened the walls.* **2** [T] ~ someone's name/reputation/character to say unpleasant things that give people a bad opinion of someone: *He accused the newspaper of trying to blacken his name.*

black·ened /'blækənd/ adj. (of food, especially of fish) covered with a mixture of hot spices and cooked quickly over high heat so that the outside becomes very dark: *blackened red snapper*

Black 'English noun [U] any of various forms of English spoken by black people, especially a form spoken in U.S. cities ➔ see also EBONICS

black 'eye noun an area of dark skin (called a BRUISE) that can form around someone's eye when it has been hit

black-eyed 'pea noun = COWPEA

black-eyed Su·san /,blæk aɪd 'suzn/ noun a North American plant that has yellow flowers with a dark center

black·face /'blækfeɪs/ noun [U] a dark substance used by actors to make their skin look dark, especially in musical shows in the past. The practice of appearing **in blackface** is now considered offensive.

black 'flag noun **1** a flag with a SKULL AND CROSSBONES on it **2** a black flag used in motor racing to stop a driver who has done something wrong

black 'fly noun (pl. 'black flies) **1** a small, black or dark green insect that damages plants **2** a small black fly that sucks blood from humans and animals

Black·foot /'blækfʊt/ noun (pl. Black·feet /-fit/ or Black-foot) a member of a Native American people, many of whom live in the state of Montana and in Alberta in Canada

Black Forest 'cake noun [U, C] a type of chocolate cake with layers of cherries (CHERRY) and cream

black 'gold noun [U] (*informal*) oil

black·guard /'blægərd; -gard/ noun (*old-fashioned*) a man who is dishonest and has no sense of what is right and what is wrong

black·head /'blækhɛd/ noun a small spot on the skin, often on the face, with a black top

black 'hole noun an area in space that nothing, not even light, can escape from, because GRAVITY (= the force that pulls objects in space toward each other) is so strong there:

(*figurative*) *The company viewed the venture as a financial black hole* (= it would use a lot of the company's money with no real result).

black 'ice noun [U] ice in a thin layer on the surface of a road

black·jack /'blækdʒæk/ noun **1** [U] a card game in which players try to collect cards with a total value of 21 and no more **2** [C] a type of CLUB used as a weapon, especially a metal pipe covered with leather

black light noun [U] ULTRAVIOLET or INFRARED RAYS, which cannot be seen

black·list /'blæklɪst/ noun, verb
● noun a list of the names of people, companies, products, or countries that an organization or a government considers unacceptable and that must be avoided
● verb ~ sb/sth to put the name of a person, a company, a product, or a country on a blacklist: *She was blacklisted by all the major Hollywood studios because of her political views.*

black 'lung noun [U] a lung disease caused by breathing in coal dust over a long period of time

black·ly /'blækli/ adv. ~ comic/funny/humorous/satirical dealing with unpleasant or terrible things, such as murder, in a humorous way: *The movie takes a blackly humorous look at climate change.*

black 'magic noun [U] (also the ,black 'arts [pl.]) a type of magic which is believed to use the power of the DEVIL in order to do evil

black·mail /'blækmeɪl/ noun, verb
● noun [U] **1** the crime of demanding money from a person by threatening to tell someone else a secret about them **2** the act of putting pressure on a person or a group to do something they do not want to do, for example by making threats or by making them feel guilty: *emotional/moral blackmail*
● verb to force someone to give you money or do something for you by threatening them, for example by saying you will tell people a secret about them: ~ sb *She blackmailed him for years by threatening to tell the newspapers about their affair.* ◆ ~ sb into doing sth *The president said he wouldn't be blackmailed into agreeing to the terrorists' demands.*

black·mail·er /'blæk,meɪlər/ noun a person who commits blackmail

black 'mark noun a note, either in writing on an official record, or in someone's mind, of something you have done or said that makes people think badly of you: *She got a black mark on her record for opposing company policy.* ◆ *The public scandal was a black mark against him.*

black 'market noun [usually sing.] an illegal form of trade in which foreign money, or goods that are difficult to obtain, are bought and sold: *to buy or sell goods on the black market* ◆ *a flourishing black market in foreign currency*

black market'eer noun a person who sells goods on the black market

black 'mass noun a ceremony in which people worship the DEVIL

Black 'Muslim noun a member of a group of black people, especially in the U.S., who follow the religion of Islam and want a separate black society

black·out /'blækaʊt/ noun **1** a period when there is no light as a result of an electrical power failure **2** a temporary loss of CONSCIOUSNESS, sight, or memory: *She had a blackout and couldn't remember anything about the accident.* **3** a situation when the government or the police will not allow any news or information on a particular subject to be given to the public **4** a period of time during a war when all lights must be put out or covered at night, so that they cannot be seen by an enemy attacking by air **5** [usually pl.] a covering for windows that stops light from being seen from outside, or light from outside from coming into a room

black 'pepper noun [U] a black powder made from dried berries (BERRY) (called PEPPERCORNS) used to give a spicy flavor to food: *salt and freshly ground black pepper*

Black 'Power *noun* [U] a movement supporting rights and political power for black people

black 'sheep *noun* [usually sing.] a person who is different from the rest of their family or another group, and who is considered bad or embarrassing: *the black sheep of the family*

black·shirt also **Black·shirt** /'blækʃərt/ *noun* a member of a FASCIST organization, especially in the 1920s and 30s

black·smith /'blæksmɪθ/ (also **smith**) *noun* a person whose job is to make and repair things made of iron, especially HORSESHOES ⊃ compare FARRIER

black·thorn /'blækθɔrn/ *noun* [U] a bush with THORNS and black branches, white flowers, and sour purple fruit called SLOES

black 'tie *noun* a black BOW TIE worn with a TUXEDO ▶ **black 'tie** *adj.*: *The party is black tie* (= formal clothes should be worn). ♦ *a black-tie dinner*

black·top /'blæktɑp/ *noun* [U] ASPHALT, or another black material used for making road surfaces SYN TARMAC™

black 'widow *noun* a poisonous American spider. The female black widow often eats the male.

blad·der /'blædər/ *noun* **1** an organ that is shaped like a bag in which URINE (= liquid waste) collects before it is passed out of the body ⊃ picture at BODY ⊃ see also GALL BLADDER **2** a bag made of rubber, leather, etc. that can be filled with air or liquid, such as the one inside a football

blades

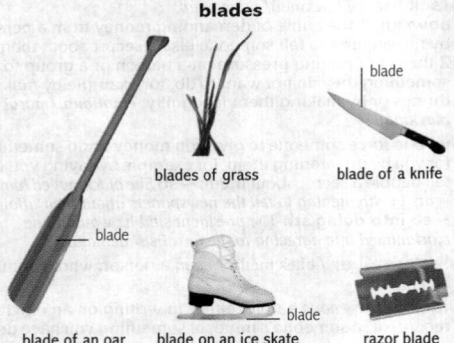

blades of grass   blade of a knife

blade of an oar   blade on an ice skate   razor blade

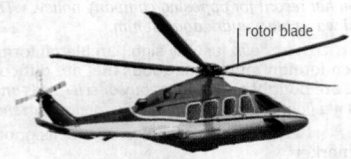

rotor blades

blade /bleɪd/ *noun* **1** the flat part of a knife, tool, or machine, which has a sharp edge or edges for cutting ⊃ picture at TOOL ⊃ see also RAZOR BLADE, SWITCHBLADE **2** one of the flat parts that turn around in an engine or on a HELICOPTER: *the blades of a propeller* ♦ *rotor blades on a helicopter* **3** the flat wide part of an OAR (= one of the long poles that are used to ROW a boat) that goes in the water ⊃ picture at BOAT **4** a single flat leaf of grass **5** the flat metal part on the bottom of an ICE SKATE ⊃ see also SHOULDER BLADE

blad·ing /'bleɪdɪŋ/ *noun* [U] the sport of moving on Rollerblades (ROLLERBLADE™)

blah /blɑ/ *noun*, *adj.*
● *noun* [U] (*informal*) people say **blah, blah, blah**, when they do not want to give the exact words that someone has said or written because they think they are not important or are

boring: *They said, "Come in, sit down, blah, blah, blah, sign here."*
● *adj.* (*informal*) **1** not interesting: *The movie was pretty blah.* **2** not feeling well; feeling slightly unhappy

blame /bleɪm/ *verb*, *noun*
● *verb* to think or say that someone or something is responsible for something bad: **~ sb/sth (for sth)** *She doesn't blame anyone for her father's death.* ♦ *A dropped cigarette is being blamed for the fire.* ♦ **~ sth on sb/sth** *Police are blaming the accident on dangerous driving.*
IDM **be to blame (for sth)** to be responsible for something bad: *If anyone's to blame, it's me.* ♦ *Which driver was to blame for the accident?* **don't blame me** (*informal*) used to advise someone not to do something, when you think they will do it despite your advice: *Call her if you like, but don't blame me if she's angry.* **I don't blame you/her, etc. (for doing sth)** (*informal*) used to say that you think that what someone did was reasonable and the right thing to do: *"I just slammed the phone down when he said that." "I don't blame you!"* **only have yourself to blame** used to say that you think something is someone's own fault: *If you lose your job, you'll only have yourself to blame.*
● *noun* [U] **~ (for sth)** responsibility for doing something badly or wrongly; saying that someone is responsible for something: *to lay/place/put the blame for something on someone* ♦ *The government will have to take the blame for the riots.* ♦ *Why do I always get the blame for everything that goes wrong?* ⊃ compare CREDIT

blame·less /'bleɪmləs/ *adj.* doing no wrong; free from responsibility for doing something bad SYN INNOCENT: *to lead a blameless life* ♦ *None of us is entirely blameless in this matter.* ▶ **blame·less·ly** *adv.*

blame·wor·thy /'bleɪmˌwɜrði/ *adj.* (*formal*) deserving disapproval and criticism; responsible for doing something wrong

blanch /blæntʃ/ *verb* **1** [I] **~ (at sth)** (*formal*) to become pale because you are shocked or frightened **2** [T] **~ sth** to prepare food, especially vegetables, by putting it into boiling water for a short time

bland /blænd/ *adj.* (**bland·er, bland·est**) **1** with little color, excitement, or interest; without anything to attract attention SYN NONDESCRIPT: *bland background music* **2** not having a strong or interesting taste: *a rather bland diet of soup, fish, and bread* **3** showing no strong emotions or excitement; not saying anything very interesting: *a bland smile* ♦ *After the meeting, a bland statement was issued.* ▶ **bland·ly** *adv.* **bland·ness** *noun* [U]

bland·ish·ments /'blændɪʃmənts/ *noun* [pl.] (*formal*) pleasant things that you say to someone or do for them to try to persuade them to do something

blank /blæŋk/ *adj.*, *noun*, *verb*
● *adj.* **1** empty, with nothing written, printed, or recorded on it: *Sign your name in the blank space below.* ♦ *a blank CD* ♦ *Write on one side of the paper and leave the other side blank.* ♦ *She turned to a blank page in her notebook.* **2** (of a wall or screen) empty; with no pictures, marks, or decoration: *blank, whitewashed walls* ♦ *Suddenly the screen went blank.* **3** showing no feeling, understanding, or interest: *She stared at me with a blank expression on her face.* ♦ *Steve looked blank and said he had no idea what I was talking about.* ♦ *Suddenly my mind went blank* (= I could not remember anything). **4** [only before noun] (of negative things) complete and total: *a blank refusal/denial* ⊃ see also POINT-BLANK ▶ **blank·ly** *adv.*: *She stared blankly into space, not knowing what to say next.* **blank·ness** *noun* [U]
● *noun* **1** [C] an empty space on a printed form or document for you to write answers, information, etc. in: *Please fill in the blanks.* ♦ *If you can't answer the question, leave a blank.* **2** [sing.] a state of not being able to remember anything: *My mind was a blank and I couldn't remember her name.* **3** [C] (also **blank 'cartridge**) a CARTRIDGE in a gun that contains

an EXPLOSIVE but no bullet: *The troops fired blanks in the air.* **IDM** see DRAW v.

- **verb 1** [T] **~ sb** (*informal*) (in sports) to defeat your opponent without allowing them to score: *Baltimore blanked Toronto in a 7-0 victory.* **2** [I] **~ (out)** to be suddenly unable to remember or think of something: *I knew the answer, but I totally blanked during the test.*
PHRV ˌblank ˈout to suddenly become empty: *The screen blanked out.* ˌblank sthˈout **1** to cover something completely so that it cannot be seen: *All the names in the letter had been blanked out.* **2** to deliberately forget something unpleasant: *She had tried to blank out the whole experience.*

ˌblank ˈcheck (*CanE usually* ˌblank ˈcheque) *noun* **1** a check that is signed but which does not have the amount of money to be paid written on it **2** permission or authority to do something that is necessary in a particular situation: *The president was given a blank check by Congress to continue the war.*

blan·ket /ˈblæŋkət/ *noun, adj., verb*
- **noun 1** a large cover, often made of wool, used especially on beds to keep people warm ➔ picture at BED ➔ see also ELECTRIC BLANKET **2** [usually sing.] **~ of sth** a thick layer or covering of something: *a blanket of fog/snow/clouds* ◆ (*figurative*) *The trial was conducted under a blanket of secrecy.* ➔ see also WET BLANKET
- **adj.** [only before noun] including or affecting all possible cases, situations, or people: *a blanket ban on tobacco advertising* ◆ *a blanket refusal*
- **verb** [often passive] **~ sth** (*formal*) to cover something completely with a thick layer: *The frozen ground was blanketed with snow.*

blank·e·ty-blank /ˌblæŋkəti ˈblæŋk/ *adj.* [only before noun] (*informal*) used in place of a rude word that the speaker does not want to say: *It's not my blankety-blank fault!*

ˌblank ˈverse *noun* [U] (*technical*) poetry that has a regular rhythm, usually with ten syllables and five stresses in each line, but which does not RHYME ➔ compare FREE VERSE

blare /blɛr/ *verb, noun*
- **verb** [I, T] to make a loud unpleasant noise: *police cars with lights flashing and sirens blaring* ◆ **~ out** *Music blared out from the open window.* ◆ **~ sth (out)** *The radio was blaring (out) rock music.*
- **noun** [sing.] a loud unpleasant noise: *the blare of car horns*

blar·ney /ˈblɑrni/ *noun* [U] (*informal*) talk that is friendly and amusing but probably not true, and which may be used to persuade or trick you **ORIGIN** From **Blarney**, a castle in Ireland where there is a stone which is said to have magic powers: anyone who kisses the "Blarney stone" is given the gift of speaking persuasively ("the gift of the gab").

bla·sé /blɑˈzeɪ/ *adj.* **~ (about sth)** not impressed, excited, or worried about something, because you have seen or experienced it many times before

blas·pheme /ˈblæsfim; blæsˈfim/ *verb* [I, T] **~ (sb/sth)** to speak about God or the holy things of a particular religion in an offensive way; to swear using the names of God or holy things ▸ **blas·phem·er** *noun*

blas·phe·my /ˈblæsfəmi/ *noun* (*pl.* blas·phe·mies) [U, C] behavior or language that insults or shows a lack of respect for God or religion ▸ **blas·phe·mous** /ˈblæsfəməs/ *adj.*: *Many people found the film blasphemous.* **blas·phe·mous·ly** *adv.*

blast /blæst/ *noun, verb, exclamation*
- **noun**
> EXPLOSION **1** [C] an explosion or a powerful movement of air caused by an explosion: *a bomb blast* ◆ *27 schoolchildren were injured in the blast.*
> OF AIR **2** [C] a sudden strong movement of air: *A blast of hot air hit us as we stepped off the plane.* ◆ *the wind's icy blasts*
> LOUD NOISE **3** [C] a sudden loud noise, especially one made by a musical instrument that you blow, or by a whistle or a car horn: *three short blasts on the ship's siren*

> FUN **4** [sing.] (*informal*) a very enjoyable experience that is a lot of fun: *The party was a blast.* ◆ *We had a blast at the party.*
> E-MAIL **5** [C] (*informal*) advertising or information that is sent to a large number of people at the same time by e-mail **IDM** **a blast from the past** (*informal*) a person or thing from your past that you see, hear, meet, etc. again in the present **(at) full blast** with the greatest possible volume or power: *She had the car stereo on at full blast.*
- **verb**
> EXPLODE **1** [T, I] **~ (sth) (+ adv./prep.)** | **~ sth (+ adj.)** to violently destroy or break something into pieces, using EXPLOSIVES: *They blasted a huge crater in the runway.* ◆ *They had to blast a tunnel through the mountain.* ◆ *All the windows were blasted inward with the force of the explosion.* ◆ *The fighter plane was blasted out of the sky.* ◆ *Danger! Blasting in Progress!*
> MAKE LOUD NOISE **2** [I, T] to make a loud unpleasant noise, especially music: **~ (out)** *Music suddenly blasted out from the speakers.* ◆ **~ sth (out)** *The radio blasted out rock music at full volume.*
> CRITICIZE **3** [T] **~ sb/sth (for sth/for doing sth)** (*informal*) to criticize someone or something severely: *The movie was blasted by all the critics.*
> HIT/KICK **4** [T] **~ sb/sth (+ adv./prep.)** (*informal*) to hit or kick someone or something with a lot of force: *He blasted the ball past the goalie.* ◆ *He blasted the policeman right between the eyes.*
> AIR/WATER **5** [T] **~ sb/sth (+ adv./prep.)** to direct air, water, etc. at someone or something with a lot of force: *Police blasted the demonstrators with water cannons.*
> DESTROY WITH DISEASE, ETC. **6** [T, usually passive] **~ sth** to destroy something such as a plant with disease, cold, heat, etc.: *Their whole crop had been blasted by a late frost.*
PHRV ˌblast aˈway if a gun or someone using a gun blasts away, the gun fires continuously and loudly ˌblast ˈoff (of SPACECRAFT) to leave the ground **SYN** LIFT OFF, TAKE OFF ➔ related noun BLASTOFF
- **exclamation** (*informal*) people sometimes say **Blast!** when they are annoyed about something: *Oh blast! The car won't start.*

blast·ed /ˈblæstəd/ *adj.* [only before noun] (*informal*) used when you are very annoyed about something: *Make your own blasted coffee!*

ˈblast ˌfurnace *noun* a large structure like an oven in which iron ORE (= rock containing iron) is melted in order to take out the metal

blast·off /ˈblæstɔf; -ɑf/ *noun* [U] the moment when a SPACECRAFT leaves the ground **SYN** LIFT-OFF

bla·tant /ˈbleɪtnt/ *adj.* (*disapproving*) (of actions that are considered bad) done in an obvious and open way without caring if people are shocked **SYN** FLAGRANT: *a blatant attempt to buy votes* ◆ *It was a blatant lie.* ▸ **bla·tant·ly** *adv.*: *a blatantly unfair decision* ◆ *He just blatantly lied about it.*

blath·er /ˈblæðər/ (*also* blith·er) *verb* [I] **~ (on) (about sth)** (*informal*) to talk continuously about things that are silly or unimportant ▸ **blath·er** (*also* blith·er) *noun* [U]

blax·ploi·ta·tion /ˌblæksplɔɪˈteɪʃn/ *noun* [U] the use of black people in movies, especially in a way that shows them in fixed ways that are different from real life

blaze /bleɪz/ *verb, noun*
- **verb 1** [I] to burn brightly and strongly: *A huge fire was blazing in the fireplace.* ◆ *Within minutes the whole building was blazing.* ◆ *He rushed back into the blazing house.* **2** [I] to shine brightly: *The sun blazed down from a clear blue sky.* ◆ *The garden blazed with color.* **3** [I] **~ (with sth)** (*formal*) if someone's eyes blaze, they look extremely angry: *Her eyes were blazing with fury.* **4** (*also* blaz·on) [T, usually passive] **~ sth (across/all over sth)** to make news or information widely known by telling people about it in a way that they are sure to notice: *The story was blazed all over the daily papers.* **5** [I] **~ (away)** if a gun or someone using a gun blazes, the gun fires continuously: *In the distance machine guns were blazing.*
IDM **blaze a trail** to be the first to do or to discover

something that others follow: *The department is blazing a trail in the field of laser surgery.* ⊃ compare TRAILBLAZER ⊃ more at GUN

PHRV ˌblaze ˈup 1 to suddenly start burning very strongly 2 to suddenly become very angry

• **noun 1** [C] (*used especially in newspapers*) a very large fire, especially a dangerous one: *Five people died in the blaze.* **2** [sing.] strong bright flames in a fire: *Dry wood makes a good blaze.* **3** [sing.] **a ~ of sth** a very bright show of lights or color; an impressive or noticeable show of something: *The gardens are a blaze of color.* ◆ *a blaze of lights in the city center* ◆ *the bright blaze of the sun* ◆ *a blaze of glory* ◆ *They got married in a blaze of publicity.* **4** [sing.] **(a) ~ of sth** a sudden show of very strong feeling: *a blaze of anger/passion/hate* **5** [C, usually sing.] a white mark on an animal's face

IDM **what/where/who the blazes…?** (*old-fashioned, informal*) used to emphasize that you are annoyed and surprised, to avoid using the word "hell": *What the blazes have you done?* **like blazes** (*old-fashioned, informal*) very hard; very fast

blaz·er /ˈbleɪzər/ noun a jacket, often dark blue, that does not form part of a suit

blaz·ing /ˈbleɪzɪŋ/ adj. [only before noun] **1** (also ˌblazing ˈhot) extremely hot: *blazing heat* ◆ *a blazing hot day* **2** extremely angry or full of strong emotion: *a blazing fury*

bla·zon /ˈbleɪzn/ verb **1** [usually passive] **~ sth (on/across/over sth)** = EMBLAZON: *He had the word "Cool" blazoned across his chest.* **2** = BLAZE v. (4)

bleach /blitʃ/ verb, noun

• **verb** [I, T] to become white or pale by a chemical process or by the effect of light from the sun; to make something white or pale in this way: *bones of animals bleaching in the sun* ◆ **~ sth** *His hair was bleached by the sun.* ◆ *bleached cotton/paper* ◆ **~ sth + adj.** *She bleached her hair blond.*

• **noun** [U, C] a chemical that is used to make something become white or pale, and as a DISINFECTANT (= to prevent infection from spreading)

bleach·ers /ˈblitʃərz/ noun [pl.] rows of seats at a sports field, usually without a roof over them ▶ **bleach·er** adj. [only before noun]: *bleacher seats*

bleak /blik/ adj. (bleak·er, bleak·est) **1** (of a situation) not encouraging or giving any reason to have hope: *a bleak outlook/prospect* ◆ *The future looks bleak for the fishing industry.* ◆ *The medical prognosis was bleak.* **2** (of the weather) cold and unpleasant: *a bleak winter's day* **3** (of a place) exposed, empty, or with no pleasant features: *a bleak landscape/hillside/expanse* ◆ *bleak concrete housing* ▶ **bleak·ly** adv.: *"There seems no hope," she said bleakly.* ◆ *bleakly lit hallways* **bleak·ness** noun [U]

blear·i·ly /ˈblɪrəli/ adv. with bleary eyes; in a tired way: *"I was asleep," she explained blearily.*

blear·y /ˈblɪri/ adj. (of eyes) not able to see clearly, especially because you are tired: *She had bleary, red eyes from lack of sleep.*

ˈbleary-ˌeyed adj. with bleary eyes and seeming tired: *He appeared at breakfast bleary-eyed and with a hangover.*

bleat /blit/ verb **1** [I] to make the sound that sheep and GOATS make **2** [I, T] **~ (on) (about sth)** | **~ that…** | + **speech** to speak in a weak or complaining voice: *"But I only just got here," he bleated feebly.* ▶ **bleat** noun: *The lamb gave a faint bleat.* **bleat·ing** noun [U, C]: *the distant bleating of sheep*

bleed /blid/ verb (bled, bled /blɛd/) **1** [I] to lose blood, especially from a wound or an injury: *My finger is bleeding.* ◆ *She slowly bled to death.* ◆ *He was bleeding copiously from a gash on his head.* **2** [T] **~ sb** (in the past) to take blood from someone as a way of treating disease **3** [T] **~ sb (for sth)** (*informal*) to force someone to pay a lot of money over a period of time: *My ex-wife is bleeding me for every penny I have.* **4** [T] **~ sth** to remove air or liquid from something so that it works correctly **5** [I] **~ (into sth)** to spread from one area of something to another area: *Keep the paint fairly dry so that the colors don't bleed into each other.*

IDM **bleed sb dry** (*disapproving*) to take away all someone's money: *The big corporations are bleeding some of these small countries dry.* ⊃ more at HEART

bleed·ing /ˈblidɪŋ/ noun [U] the process of losing blood from the body: *Press firmly on the wound to stop the bleeding.*

ˌbleeding ˈedge noun [sing.] **the ~ (of sth)** (*computing*) technology that is so advanced that there may be problems when you use it: *They were working at the bleeding edge of chip design.* ⊃ compare CUTTING EDGE

ˌbleeding ˈheart noun (*disapproving*) a person who is too kind and sympathetic toward people that other people think do not deserve kindness: *a bleeding-heart liberal*

bleep /blip/ noun, verb

• **noun** [C, U] **1** a short, high sound made by a piece of electronic equipment **2** a short, high, electronic sound used in television as a substitute for a SWEAR WORD that is not allowed to be broadcast: *We watched the movie on TV and every other word was a bleep.* **3** (*informal*) used when someone is speaking to replace a SWEAR WORD: *What the bleep are we going to do?" he asked.*

• **verb 1** [I] to make a short, high, electronic sound **SYN** BEEP: *The microwave will bleep when your meal is ready.* **2** [T] **~ sth (out)** to broadcast a short, high, electronic sound in place of a SWEAR WORD on a television or radio show, so that people will not be offended

blem·ish /ˈblɛmɪʃ/ noun, verb

• **noun** a mark on the skin or on an object that spoils it and makes it look less beautiful, or perfect: *makeup to cover blemishes* ◆ (*figurative*) *His reputation is without a blemish.*

• **verb** [usually passive] **~ sth** (*formal*) to spoil something that is beautiful or perfect in all other ways

blench /blɛntʃ/ verb [I] (*formal*) to react to something in a way that shows you are frightened

blend /blɛnd/ verb, noun

• **verb 1** [T] to mix two or more substances together: **~ A with B** *Blend the flour with the milk to make a smooth paste.* ◆ **~ A and B (together)** *Blend together the eggs, sugar, and flour.* ⊃ thesaurus box at MIX **2** [I] to form a mixture with something: **~ with sth** *Oil does not blend with water.* ◆ **~ (together)** *Oil and water do not blend.* **3** [I, T] to combine with something in an attractive or effective way; to combine something in this way: **~ (sth) (together)** *The old and new buildings blend together perfectly.* ◆ **~ sth (and/with sth)** *Their music blends traditional and modern styles.* **4** [T, usually passive] **~ sth** to produce something by mixing different types together: *blended whiskey/tea* **IDM** see WOODWORK

PHRV ˌblend ˈin (with sth/sb) if something blends in, it is similar to its surroundings or matches its surroundings: *Choose curtains that blend in with your decor.* ◆ *The thieves soon blended in with the crowd and got away.* ˌblend sth↔ˈin (in cooking) to add another substance and mix it in with the others: *Beat the butter and sugar; then blend in the egg.* ˌblend ˈinto sth to look so similar to the background that it is difficult for you to see it separately: *He blended into the crowd.*

• **noun 1** a mixture of different types of the same thing: *a blend of tea* **2** [usually sing.] a pleasant or useful combination of different things: *a blend of youth and experience*

ˌblended ˈfamily noun a family that consists of two people and their children from their own relationship and from previous ones

ˌblended ˈlearning noun [U] a way of studying a subject that combines being taught in class with the use of different technologies, including learning over the Internet: *Blended learning is a cost-effective way of delivering training.*

blend·er /ˈblɛndər/ noun an electric machine for mixing soft food or liquid ⊃ picture at KITCHEN

bless /blɛs/ verb

• (blessed, blessed /blɛst/) **1** **~ sb/sth** to ask God to protect someone or something: *They brought the children to Jesus and he blessed them.* ◆ *God bless you!* **2** **~ sth** to make something holy by saying a prayer over it: *The priest blessed the bread and wine.* **3** ~ **sb/sth** (*formal*) to call God holy; to praise God: *We bless your holy name, O Lord.* **4** ~ **sb/sth** (*old-fashioned, informal*) used to express surprise: *Bless my soul! Here comes Bill!*

IDM **be blessed with sth/sb** to have something good such as ability, great happiness, etc.: *She's blessed with excellent health.* ♦ *We're blessed with five beautiful grand-children.* **bless you** said to someone after they have SNEEZED **bless you, her, him, etc.** (*informal*) used to show that you are pleased with someone, especially because of something they have done: *Sarah, bless her, had made a cup of tea.* ♦ *Bless her heart, she came over straight away.* ⊃ more at GOD

bless·ed /'blesəd/ *adj.* **1** Blessed holy: *the Blessed Virgin Mary* **2** (in religious language) lucky: *Blessed are the poor.* **3** [only before noun] enjoyable in a way that gives you a sense of peace or a feeling of freedom from anxiety or pain: *a moment of blessed calm* **4** [only before noun] (*old-fashioned, informal*) used to express mild anger: *I can't see a blessed thing without my glasses.* ▶ **bless·ed·ly** *adv.*: *The kitchen was warm and blessedly familiar.* **bless·ed·ness** *noun* [U]

bless·ing /'blesɪŋ/ *noun* **1** [usually sing.] God's help and protection, or a prayer asking for this: *to pray for God's blessing* ♦ *The bishop said the blessing.* ⊃ collocations at RELIGION **2** [usually sing.] approval of or permission for something: *The government gave its blessing to the new plans.* ♦ *He went with his parents' blessing.* **3** something that is good or helpful: *Lack of traffic is one of the blessings of country life.* ♦ *It's a blessing that nobody was in the house at the time.*
IDM **a blessing in disguise** something that seems to be a problem at first, but that has good results in the end **a mixed blessing/a blessing and a curse** something that has advantages and disadvantages: *Wealth can be a mixed blessing.* ♦ *A home studio can be a blessing and a curse for a workaholic.* ⊃ more at COUNT *v.*

blew pt of BLOW

blight /blaɪt/ *verb, noun*
● *verb* ~ **sth** to spoil or damage something, especially by causing a lot of problems: *His career has been blighted by injuries.* ♦ *an area blighted by unemployment*
● *noun* **1** [U, C] any disease that kills plants, especially crops: *potato blight* **2** [sing., U] ~ **(on sb/sth)** something that has a bad effect on a situation, a person's life, or the environment: *His death cast a blight on the whole of that year.* ♦ *urban blight* (= areas in a city that are ugly or not cared for well)

blimp /blɪmp/ *noun* **1** a small AIRSHIP (= an aircraft without wings) ⊃ picture at PLANE **2** a very fat person

blin *noun* sing of BLINI

blinds

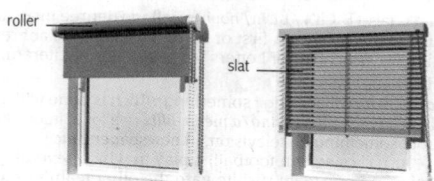

roller blind (*also* shade)   Venetian blind

blind 🔊 /blaɪnd/ *adj., verb, noun, adv.*
● *adj.* (blind·er, blind·est) **1** not able to see: *Doctors think he will go blind.* ♦ *blind and partially sighted people* ♦ *One of her parents is blind.* **2** **the blind** *noun* [pl.] people who are blind: *recorded books for the blind* ♦ *guide dogs for the blind* **3** ~ **(to sth)** not noticing or realizing something: *She is blind to her husband's faults.* ♦ *I must have been blind not to realize the danger we were in.* **4** [usually before noun] (of strong feelings) seeming to be unreasonable, and accepted without question; seeming to be out of control: *blind faith/*

obedience ♦ *It was a moment of blind panic.* **5** [usually before noun] (of a situation or an event) that cannot be controlled by reason: *blind chance* ♦ *the blind force of nature* **6** that a driver in a car cannot see, or cannot see around: *a blind driveway* ♦ *a blind spot/corner* ▶ **blind·ness** *noun* [U]: *total/temporary/partial blindness* ⊃ see also BLINDLY
IDM **(as) blind as a bat** (*humorous*) not able to see well **the blind leading the blind** a situation in which people with almost no experience or knowledge give advice to others who also have no experience or knowledge **turn a blind eye (to sth)** to pretend not to notice something bad that is happening, so you do not have to do anything about it ⊃ more at LOVE *n.*

● *verb* **1** ~ **sb** to permanently destroy someone's ability to see: *She was blinded in the explosion.* **2** ~ **sb/sth** to make it difficult for someone to see for a short time: *When she went outside she was temporarily blinded by the sun.* **3** ~ **sb (to sth)** to make someone no longer able to think clearly or behave in a sensible way: *His sense of loyalty blinded him to the truth.*
IDM **blind sb with science** to confuse someone by using technical or complicated language that they do not understand
● *noun* **1** (also shade, 'window ,shade) [C] a covering for a window, especially one made of a roll of cloth that is fixed at the top of the window and can be pulled up and down ⊃ see also VENETIAN BLIND **2** [sing.] something people say or do to hide the truth about something in order to trick other people
● *adv.* (in connection with flying) without being able to see; using instruments only
IDM **blind drunk** extremely drunk ⊃ more at ROB

blind 'alley *noun* a way of doing something that seems useful at first, but does not produce useful results, like following a path that suddenly stops

blind 'date *noun* a meeting between two people who have not met each other before. The meeting is sometimes organized by their friends because they want them to develop a romantic relationship.

blind·ers /'blaɪndərz/ *noun* [pl.] **1** (also blink·ers) pieces of leather that are placed at the side of a horse's eyes to stop it from looking sideways **2** something that prevents you from understanding the truth about something: *We need to have a fresh look at the plan, without blinders* (= we need to consider every aspect of it).

blind·fold /'blaɪndfoʊld/ *noun, verb*
● *noun* something that is put over someone's eyes so that they cannot see
● *verb* ~ **sb** to cover someone's eyes with a piece of cloth or other covering so that they cannot see: *The hostages were tied up and blindfolded.*

blind·fold·ed /'blaɪndfoʊldəd/ *adj., adv.* with the eyes covered: *The reporter was taken blindfolded to a secret location.* ♦ *I knew the way home blindfolded* (= because it was so familiar). ♦ *I could do that blindfolded* (= very easily, with no problems).

blind·ing /'blaɪndɪŋ/ *adj.* [usually before noun] very bright; so strong that you cannot see: *a blinding flash of light* ♦ (*figurative*) *a blinding* (= very bad) *headache*

blind·ing·ly /'blaɪndɪŋli/ *adv.* very; extremely: *The reason is*

---

blindingly obvious. ♦ The latest computers can work at a blindingly fast speed.

blind·ly /ˈblaɪndli/ adv. **1** without being able to see what you are doing: She groped blindly for the light switch in the dark room. **2** without thinking about what you are doing: He wanted to decide for himself instead of blindly following his parents' advice. ⊃ note at BLIND

,**blind man's 'bluff** (also ,blind man's 'buff) noun [U] a children's game in which a player whose eyes are covered with a piece of cloth tries to catch and identify the other players

'**blind side** noun a direction in which someone cannot see very much, especially approaching danger

blind·side /ˈblaɪndsaɪd/ verb **1** ~ sb to attack someone from the direction where they cannot see you coming **2** [usually passive] ~ sb to give someone an unpleasant surprise: Just when it seemed life was going well, she was blindsided by a devastating illness.

'**blind spot** noun **1** an area that someone cannot see, especially an area of the road when they are driving a car **2** if someone has a **blind spot** about something, they ignore it or they are unwilling or unable to understand it **3** the part of the RETINA in the eye that is not sensitive to light **4** an area where a radio signal cannot be received

,**blind 'test** noun a way of deciding which product out of a number of competing products is the best or most popular, or how a new product compares with others. People are asked to try the different products and to say which ones they prefer, but they are not told the names of the products.

,**blind 'trust** noun a type of TRUST that takes care of someone's investments, without the person knowing how their money is being invested. It is used by politicians, for example, so that their private business does not influence their political decisions.

bling /blɪŋ/ (also 'bling-bling) noun (informal) expensive, shiny jewelry and bright, fashionable clothes worn in order to attract attention to yourself ▶ bling (also 'bling-bling) adj.: women with big hair and bling jewelry ♦ bling culture/lifestyles

blin·i /ˈblini; ˈblɪni/ (also blin·is) noun [pl.] (sing. blin /blɪn/) small Russian PANCAKES (= thin flat round cakes), served with SOUR CREAM

blink /blɪŋk/ verb, noun
● **verb 1** [I, T] ~ (sth) when you blink, or blink your eyes, or your eyes blink, you shut and open your eyes quickly: He blinked in the bright sunlight. ♦ I'll be back before you can blink (= very quickly). ⊃ compare WINK **2** [I] to shine with an unsteady light; to flash on and off: Suddenly a warning light blinked.
  IDM not (even) blink (an eye) to show no surprise at something that someone else says or does: When I told Dad I had wrecked the car, he didn't even blink an eye. ♦ When I told her the news, she didn't even blink .
  PHR V blink sth↔a'way/'back to try to control tears or clear your eyes by blinking: She bravely blinked back her tears.
● **noun** [usually sing.] the act of shutting and opening your eyes very quickly
  IDM in the blink of an eye very quickly; in a short time on the blink (informal) (of a machine) no longer working correctly

blink·er /ˈblɪŋkər/ noun **1** [C] (informal) = TURN SIGNAL **2** blink·ers [pl.] = BLINDERS

blink·ered /ˈblɪŋkərd/ adj. (disapproving) not aware of every aspect of a situation; not willing to accept different ideas about something **SYN** NARROW-MINDED: a blinkered policy/attitude/approach

blintz /blɪnts/ noun a thin cake is been filled with cheese or fruit, rolled, and then fried or baked

blip /blɪp/ noun **1** a bright light flashing on the screen of a piece of equipment, sometimes with a short, high sound **2** a change in a process or situation, usually when it gets worse for a short time before it gets better; a temporary problem: a temporary blip

bliss /blɪs/ noun, verb
● **noun** [U] extreme happiness: married/wedded/domestic bliss ♦ My idea of bliss is a month in the Bahamas. ♦ Swimming on a hot day is sheer bliss. **IDM** see IGNORANCE
● **verb**
  PHR V bliss 'out (also be ,blissed 'out) to reach a state of perfect happiness, when you are not aware of anything else

bliss·ful /ˈblɪsfl/ adj. extremely happy; showing happiness: We spent three blissful weeks away from work. ♦ a blissful smile ♦ We preferred to remain in blissful ignorance of (= not to know) what was going on. ⊃ thesaurus box at HAPPY ▶ bliss·ful·ly /-fəli/ adv.: blissfully happy ♦ blissfully ignorant/unaware

'**B-list** adj. [usually before noun] used to describe the group of people who are considered to be fairly famous, successful, or important, but not as much as the A-LIST people: a TV talk show full of B-list celebrities

blis·ter /ˈblɪstər/ noun, verb
● **noun 1** a swelling on the surface of the skin that is filled with liquid and is caused, for example, by rubbing or burning ⊃ see also FEVER BLISTER **2** a similar swelling, filled with air or liquid, on metal, painted wood, or another surface
● **verb 1** [I, T] to form blisters; to make something form blisters: His skin was beginning to blister. ♦ ~ sth Her face had been blistered by the sun. **2** [I, T] ~ (sth) when a surface blisters or something blisters it, it swells and cracks **3** [T] ~ sb to criticize someone strongly ▶ blis·tered adj.: cracked and blistered skin ♦ blistered paintwork

blis·ter·ing /ˈblɪstərɪŋ/ adj. [usually before noun] **1** (describing actions in sports) done very fast or with great energy: The runners set off at a blistering pace. **2** extremely hot in a way that is uncomfortable **SYN** BAKING: a blistering July day ♦ blistering heat **3** very critical: a blistering attack ▶ blis·ter·ing·ly adv.

'**blister ,pack** noun a pack in which small goods, such as pills, are sold, with each individual item in its own separate plastic or FOIL section on a piece of card ⊃ picture at PACKAGING

blithe /blaɪð; blaɪθ/ adj. [usually before noun] **1** (disapproving) showing you do not care or are not anxious about what you are doing: He drove with blithe disregard for the rules of the road. **2** (literary) happy; not anxious: a blithe and carefree girl ▶ blithe·ly adv.: He was blithely unaware of the trouble he'd caused. ♦ "It'll be easy," she said blithely.

blith·er /ˈblɪðər/ verb, noun = BLATHER

blith·er·ing /ˈblɪðərɪŋ/ adj. [only before noun] (old-fashioned, informal) complete: He was a blithering idiot.

B.Litt. (also B.Lit.) /ˌbi ˈlɪt/ noun a college degree in an ARTS subject that may be a first or second degree (the abbreviation for "Bachelor of Letters" or "Bachelor of Literature")

blitz /blɪts/ noun, verb
● **noun 1** [C, usually sing.] something which is done with a lot of energy: an advertising/a media blitz (= a lot of information about something on television, in newspapers, etc.) **2** [C, usually sing.] (in football) a play in which several players on one team rush toward the other team's QUARTERBACK **3** [C, usually sing.] a sudden attack: Five stores were damaged in a firebomb blitz. **4** the Blitz [sing.] the German air attacks on the United Kingdom in 1940–41
● **verb** ~ sth to attack or damage a city by dropping a large number of bombs on it in a short time

blitzed /blɪtst/ adj. (slang) very drunk: They went out and got blitzed that night.

blitz·krieg /ˈblɪtskriɡ/ noun (from German) a sudden military attack intended to win a quick victory

bliz·zard /ˈblɪzərd/ noun **1** a SNOWSTORM with very strong winds: blizzard conditions ♦ a raging/howling blizzard ⊃ collocations at WEATHER **2** (figurative) a large quantity of things that may seem to be attacking you: *a blizzard of e-mails*

bloat /bloʊt/ *verb* [T, I] **~ sth** to swell or make something swell, especially in an unpleasant way: *Her features had been bloated by years of drinking.*

bloat·ed /ˈbloʊtəd/ *adj.* **1** full of liquid or gas and therefore bigger than normal, in a way that is unpleasant: *a bloated body floating in the canal* ♦ (*figurative*) *a bloated organization* (= with too many people in it) **2** full of food and feeling uncomfortable: *I felt bloated after the huge meal they served.*

blob /blɑb/ *noun* a small amount or drop of something, especially a liquid; a small area of color: *a blob of ink* ♦ *a pink blob*

bloc /blɑk/ *noun* a group of countries that work closely together because they have similar political interests ⊃ collocations at INTERNATIONAL

block 🔑 /blɑk/ *noun, verb*

● *noun*

>SOLID MATERIAL **1** [C] a large piece of a solid material that has flat, square sides: *a block of ice/concrete/stone* ♦ *a butcher's block* (= for cutting food on) ⊃ see also BUILDING BLOCK, CINDER BLOCK

>STREETS **2** [C] a group of buildings with streets on all sides: *She took the dog for a walk around the block.* **3** [C] the length of one side of a piece of land or group of buildings, from the place where one street crosses it to the next: *His apartment is three blocks away from the police station.*

>AMOUNT **4** [C] a quantity of something or an amount of time that is considered as a single unit: *a block of shares* ♦ *a block of text in a document* ♦ *The three-hour class is divided into four blocks of 45 minutes each.*

>THAT STOPS PROGRESS **5** [C, usually sing.] something that makes movement or progress difficult or impossible **SYN** OBSTACLE: *Lack of training acts as a block to progress in a career.* ⊃ see also ROADBLOCK, STUMBLING BLOCK, WRITER'S BLOCK

>IN SPORTS **6** [C] a movement that stops another player from going forward **7 the blocks** [pl.] = STARTING BLOCKS

>BUILDING **8** [C] a building, especially part of a group of buildings, that is used for a particular purpose: *a cell block*

>FOR PUNISHMENT **9 the block** [sing.] (in the past) the piece of wood on which a person's head was cut off as a punishment

IDM **go on the block** to be sold, especially at an AUCTION (= a sale in which items are sold to the person who offers the most money) **have been around the block (a few times)** (*informal*) to have a lot of experience **put/lay your head/neck on the block** to risk losing your job, damaging your reputation, etc. by doing or saying something ⊃ more at CHIP *n.*, KNOCK *v.*, NEW

● *verb* **1 ~ sth** to stop something from moving or flowing through it or across it: *After today's heavy snow, many roads are still blocked.* ♦ *a blocked sink* **2 ~ the/someone's way, exit, view, etc.** to stop someone from going somewhere or seeing something by standing in front of them or in their way: *One of the guards moved to block her path.* ♦ *An ugly new building blocked the view from the window.* **3 ~ sth** to prevent something from happening, developing, or making progress: *The proposed merger has been blocked by the government.* **4 ~ sth** to stop a ball, blow, etc. from reaching somewhere by moving in front of it: *His shot was blocked by the goalie.*

PHRV **block sb/sth↔'in** to prevent a car from being able to be driven away by parking too close to it **block sth↔'in** to draw or paint something roughly, without showing any detail: *I have blocked in the shapes of the larger buildings.* **block sth↔'off** to close a road or an opening by placing a barrier at one end or in front of it **block sth↔'out 1** to stop light or noise from coming in: *Black clouds blocked out the sun.* **2** to stop yourself from thinking about or remembering something unpleasant: *Over the years she had tried to block out that part of her life.* **block sth↔'up** to completely

fill a hole or an opening and so prevent anything from passing through it: *One door had been blocked up.* ♦ *My nose is blocked up.*

block·ade /blɑˈkeɪd/ *noun, verb*

● *noun* **1** the action of surrounding or closing a place, especially a port, in order to stop people or goods from coming in or out: *a naval blockade* ♦ *to impose/lift a blockade* ♦ *an economic blockade* (= stopping goods from entering or leaving a country) **2** a barrier that stops people or vehicles from entering or leaving a place: *The police set up blockades on highways leading out of the city.*

● *verb* **~ sth** to surround a place, especially a port, in order to stop people or goods from coming in or out

block·age /ˈblɑkɪdʒ/ *noun* **1** a thing that blocks flow or movement, for example of a liquid in a narrow place **SYN** OBSTRUCTION: *a blockage in an artery/a pipe/a drain* **2** the state of being blocked: *to cause/clear the blockage*

block and 'tackle *noun* [sing.] a piece of equipment for lifting heavy objects, which works by a system of ropes and PULLEYS (= small wheels around which the ropes are stretched)

block and tackle

pulley

block·bust·er /ˈblɑk-ˌbʌstər/ *noun* (*informal*) something very successful, especially a very successful book or movie: *a Hollywood blockbuster* ▶ **block·bust·ing** *adj.*: *a blockbusting performance*

block 'capitals *noun* [pl.] = BLOCK LETTERS

block·head /ˈblɑkhɛd/ *noun* (*informal*) a very stupid person

block·house /ˈblɑkhaʊs/ *noun* **1** a strong concrete shelter used by soldiers, for example during a battle **2** a house made of LOGS (= thick pieces of wood)

block 'letters (also **block 'capitals**) *noun* [pl.] separate capital letters: *Please fill out the form in block letters.*

block ˌparty *noun* a party for the all the residents of a block or neighborhood, usually held on a city street that has been closed to traffic

block 'vote *noun* a voting system in which each person who votes represents a number of people

blog /blɑg; blɔg/ *noun, verb*

● *noun* (also **web·log**) a Web site where a person writes regularly about recent events or a particular topic, sometimes with new information added every few minutes as events happen, and with the opportunity for readers to send in their own comments and opinions: *Post your comments on our live blog right now.* ⊃ collocations at E-MAIL

● *verb* (-gg-) [I] to keep a blog ▶ **blog·ger** *noun* **blog·ging** *noun* [U]

blog·o·sphere /ˈblɑgəˌsfɪr; ˈblɔ-/ *noun* usually **the blogo-sphere** [sing.] (*informal*) all the personal Web sites that exist on the Internet, viewed as a network of people communicating with each other: *It's one of the top stories in the blogosphere.* ♦ *the growing influence of the political blogosphere*

blog·roll /ˈblɑgroʊl; ˈblɔg-/ *noun* (*computing*) a list on a Web site of other linked Web sites that the site owner thinks are useful or interesting

blond 🔑 /blɑnd/ *adj., noun*

● *adj.* **1** (of hair) pale gold in color **2** (of a person) having blond hair: *a small, blond boy*

● *noun* a person with hair that is pale gold in color

blonde /blɑnd/ *adj., noun*

● *adj.* **1** (of a woman's hair) pale gold in color **2** (of a woman) having blond hair

• **noun** (sometimes *offensive*) a woman with hair that is pale gold in color: *Is she a natural blonde* (= Is her hair naturally blonde)? **HELP** The spelling **blond** is usually preferred for both men and women, for both the adjective and the noun. In particular, referring to a woman as *a blonde* may be considered offensive.

blood 🔑 /blʌd/ *noun*
1 [U] the red liquid that flows through the bodies of humans and animals: *He lost a lot of blood in the accident.* ◆ *Blood was pouring out of a cut on her head.* ◆ *to give blood* (= to have blood taken from you so that it can be used in the medical treatment of other people) ◆ *to draw blood* (= to wound a person so that they lose blood) ◆ *a blood cell/sample* **2** –**blooded** (in adjectives) having the type of blood mentioned: *cold-blooded reptiles* ➔ see also BLUE-BLOODED, HOT-BLOODED, RED-BLOODED **3** [U] (*formal*) family origins: *She is of noble blood.*
IDM **bad blood (between A and B)** (*old-fashioned*) feelings of hatred or strong dislike **be after/out for sb's blood** (*informal*, often *humorous*) to be angry with someone and want to hurt or punish them **be/run in your blood** to be a natural part of your character and of the character of other members of your family **blood is thicker than water** (*saying*) family relationships are stronger than any others **blood, sweat, and tears** very hard work; a lot of effort **have sb's blood on your hands** to be responsible for someone's death: *a dictator with the blood of thousands on his hands* **like getting blood out of/from a stone** almost impossible to obtain: *Getting an apology from him was like getting blood from a stone.* **make sb's blood boil** to make someone extremely angry **make sb's blood run cold** to make someone very frightened or fill them with horror **new/fresh blood** new members or employees, especially young ones, with new ideas or ways of doing things ➔ more at COLD *adj.*, FLESH *n.*, FREEZE *v.*, SPILL *v.*, SPIT *v.*, STIR *v.*, SWEAT *v.*

blood bank *noun* a place where blood is kept for use in hospitals, etc.

blood·bath /'blʌdbæθ/ *noun* [sing.] a situation in which many people are killed violently **SYN** MASSACRE

blood ,brother *noun* a man who has promised to treat another man as his brother, sometimes in a ceremony in which their blood is mixed together

blood clot (also **clot**) *noun* a lump that is formed when blood dries or becomes thicker: *a blood clot on the brain*

blood count *noun* the number of red and white cells in someone's blood; a medical test to count these

blood-,curdling *adj.* (of a sound or a story) filling you with horror; extremely frightening: *a blood-curdling scream/story*

blood ,donor *noun* a person who gives some of his or her blood to be used in the medical treatment of other people

blood drive *noun* an organized event where people can give some of their blood for use in hospitals, etc.: *The Red Cross blood drive was very successful.*

blood feud *noun* a long conflict between families, involving murders that are intended as punishment for past murders

blood·hound /'blʌdhaʊnd/ *noun* a large dog with a very good sense of smell, used to follow or look for people

blood·ied /'blʌdid/ *adj.* covered in blood: *his bruised and bloodied nose*

blood·i·ly *adv.* ➔ BLOODY

blood·less /'blʌdləs/ *adj.* **1** without any killing: *a bloodless coup/revolution* **2** (of a person or a part of the body) very pale: *bloodless lips* **3** lacking human emotion **SYN** COLD, UNEMOTIONAL

blood·let·ting /'blʌd,lɛtɪŋ/ *noun* [U] **1** (*formal*) the killing or wounding of people **SYN** BLOODSHED **2** a medical treatment used in the past in which some of a patient's blood

was removed **3** (*informal*) the act of forcing a lot of people to leave a company or organization: *He lost his job in the corporate bloodletting last year.*

blood·line /'blʌdlaɪn/ *noun* (*technical*) the set of ANCESTORS of a person or an animal

blood·lust /'blʌdlʌst/ *noun* [U] a strong desire to kill or be violent

blood ,money *noun* [U] (*disapproving*) **1** money paid to a person who is hired to murder someone **2** money paid to the family of a murdered person

blood ,orange *noun* a type of orange with red flesh

blood ,poisoning *noun* an illness where the blood becomes infected with harmful bacteria

blood ,pressure *noun* [U] the pressure of blood as it travels around the body: *to have high/low blood pressure* ◆ *to take* (= measure) *someone's blood pressure* ➔ collocations at DIET

blood-'red *adj.* bright red in color, like fresh blood

blood re'lation (also **blood 'relative**) *noun* a person related to someone by birth rather than by marriage

blood ,sausage *noun* [U, C] a type of large dark SAUSAGE made from pig's blood, fat, and grain

blood·shed /'blʌdʃɛd/ *noun* [U] the killing or wounding of people, usually during fighting or a war: *The two sides called a truce to avoid further bloodshed.*

blood·shot /'blʌdʃɑt/ *adj.* (of eyes) with the part that is usually white full of red lines because of lack of sleep, etc.

blood sport *noun* [usually pl.] a sport in which animals or birds are killed

blood·stain /'blʌdsteɪn/ *noun* a mark or spot of blood on something ▶ **blood·stained** *adj.*: *a bloodstained shirt*

blood·stock /'blʌdstɑk/ *noun* [U] horses of pure breed, bred especially for racing

blood·stream /'blʌdstrim/ *noun* [sing.] the blood flowing through the body: *They injected the drug directly into her bloodstream.*

blood·suck·er /'blʌd,sʌkər/ *noun* **1** an animal or insect that sucks blood from people or animals **2** (*informal*, *disapproving*) a person who takes advantage of other people in order to gain financial benefit ▶ **blood·suck·ing** *adj.* [only before noun]: *bloodsucking insects* ◆ (*disapproving*) *bloodsucking lawyers*

blood ,sugar *noun* [U] the amount of GLUCOSE in your blood

blood test *noun* an examination of a small amount of your blood by doctors in order to make judgments about your medical condition

blood·thirst·y /'blʌd,θərsti/ *adj.* **1** wanting to kill or wound; enjoying seeing or hearing about killing, and violence **2** (of a book, movie, etc.) describing or showing killing and violence

blood trans,fusion (also **trans·fu·sion**) *noun* [C, U] the process of putting new blood into the body of a person or an animal: *He was given a blood transfusion.*

blood type *noun* any of the different types that human blood is separated into for medical purposes: *What blood type are you?* ◆ *What blood type do you have?* ◆ *blood type O*

blood ,vessel *noun* any of the tubes through which blood flows through the body ➔ see also ARTERY, CAPILLARY, VEIN

blood·y /'blʌdi/ *adj.* (**blood·i·er**, **blood·i·est**) **1** involving a lot of violence and killing: *a bloody battle* ◆ *The terrorists have halted their bloody campaign of violence.* **2** covered with blood; BLEEDING: *to give someone a bloody nose* (= in a fight) ▶ **blood·i·ly** /'blʌdl·i/ *adv.* **IDM** see SCREAM *v.*

Blood·y Mar·y /,blʌdi 'mɛri/ *noun* (*pl.* **Blood·y Mar·ys**) an alcoholic drink made by mixing VODKA with tomato juice

bloody-'minded *adj.* (*informal*) behaving in a way that makes things difficult for other people; refusing to be helpful ▸ **bloody-'mindedness** noun [U]

bloom /blum/ noun, verb
• noun (formal or technical) **1** [C] a flower (usually one on a plant that people admire for its flowers): *the exotic blooms of the orchid* **2** [sing., U] a healthy, fresh appearance: *the bloom in her cheeks*
IDM **in (full) bloom** (of trees, plants, gardens, etc.) with the flowers fully open
• verb **1** [I] to produce flowers **SYN** FLOWER: *Most roses will begin to bloom in late May.* **2** [I] to become healthy and happy, or develop fully **SYN** BLOSSOM: *Their love had bloomed during their college years.*

bloo·mers /'blumərz/ noun [pl.] **1** (informal) an old-fashioned piece of women's underwear like long loose UN-DERPANTS **2** short, loose pants that fit tightly at the knee, worn by women for sports, riding bicycles, etc.: *a pair of bloomers*

bloop /blup/ verb [I] (informal) to make a mistake

bloop·er /'blupər/ noun an embarrassing mistake that you make in public

blos·som /'blasəm/ noun, verb
• noun [C, U] a flower or a mass of flowers, especially on a fruit tree or bush: *cherry/orange/apple blossom* ♦ *The trees are in blossom.* ⊃ picture at TREE
• verb **1** [I] (of a tree or bush) to produce blossom **2** [I] to become more healthy, confident, or successful: *She has visibly blossomed over the last few months.* ♦ ~ **into sth** *Their friendship blossomed into love.*

blot /blat/ verb, noun
• verb (-tt-) **1** ~ **sth (up)** to remove liquid from a surface by pressing soft paper or cloth on it **2** ~ **sth** to make a spot or spots of ink fall on paper
PHR V **blot sth↔'out 1** to cover or hide something completely: *Clouds blotted out the sun.* **2** to deliberately try to forget an unpleasant memory or thought: *He tried to blot out the image of Helen's sad face.*
• noun **1** a spot or dirty mark on something, made by ink, etc. ⊃ thesaurus box at MARK **2** ~ **(on sth)** something that spoils the opinion that other people have of you, or your happiness: *Her involvement in the fraud has left a serious blot on her reputation.*
IDM **a blot on the landscape** an object, especially an ugly building, that spoils the beauty of a place

blotch /blatʃ/ noun a mark, usually not regular in shape, on skin, plants, material, etc.: *His face was covered with dark red blotches.*

blotch·y /'blatʃi/ (also blotched /blatʃt/) adj. covered in blotches: *her blotchy, swollen face*

blot·ter /'blatər/ noun **1** a large piece of blotting paper in a cover with a stiff back that is kept on a desk **2** a book used for daily records, especially for police activities: *a police blotter*

blotting paper noun [U] soft, thick paper used for drying ink after you have written something on a piece of paper

blot·to /'blatou/ adj. [not before noun] (old-fashioned, informal) very drunk

blouse /blaus/ noun a piece of clothing like a shirt, worn by women

blous·on /'blausan/ noun a short, loose jacket that is gathered together at the waist

blo·vi·ate /'blouvi,eɪt/ [I] (informal, disapproving) to talk or write in a way that shows that you think you know a lot and have something important to say, when in fact you do not know much and have nothing important to say

blow 🔊 /blou/ verb, noun
• verb (blew /blu/, blown /bloun/)
▸ FROM MOUTH **1** [I, T] to send out air from the mouth: + adv./prep. *You're not blowing hard enough!* ♦ *The policeman asked*

me to blow into the Breathalyzer. ♦ ~ **sth + adv./prep.** *He inhaled from his cigarette and blew out a stream of smoke.*
▸ OF WIND **2** [I] (+ adv./prep.) when the wind or a current of air blows, it is moving; when it blows, the wind is blowing: *A cold wind blew from the east.* ♦ *It was blowing hard.* ♦ *Gales of wind were blowing through the valley.*
▸ MOVE WITH WIND/BREATH **3** [I, T] to be moved by the wind, someone's breath, etc.; to move something in this way: + adv./prep. *My hat blew off.* ♦ + adj. *The door blew open.* ♦ ~ **sth + adv./prep.** *I was almost blown over by the wind.* ♦ *She blew the dust off the book.* ♦ *The ship was blown onto the rocks.* ♦ ~ **sth + adj.** *The wind blew the door shut.*
▸ WHISTLE/INSTRUMENT **4** [T, I] ~ **(sth)** if you blow a whistle, musical instrument, etc. or if a whistle, etc. blows, you produce a sound by blowing into the whistle, etc.: *The referee blew his whistle.* ♦ *the sound of trumpets blowing*
▸ YOUR NOSE **5** [T] ~ **your nose** to clear your nose by blowing strongly through it into a TISSUE or HANDKERCHIEF
▸ A KISS **6** [T] ~ **(someone) a kiss** to kiss your hand and then pretend to blow the kiss toward someone
▸ SHAPE SOMETHING **7** [T] ~ **sth** to make or shape something by blowing: *to blow smoke rings* ♦ *to blow bubbles* (= for example, by blowing onto a thin layer of water mixed with soap) ♦ *to blow glass* (= to send a current of air into melted glass to shape it)
▸ ELECTRICITY **8** [I, T] ~ **(sth)** if a FUSE (= a thin wire) blows, or you blow a fuse, the electricity stops flowing suddenly because the fuse has melted because the current was too strong
▸ TIRE **9** [I, T] ~ **(sth)** to break open or apart, especially because of pressure from inside; to make a tire break open or apart in this way: *The car spun out of control when a tire blew.* ♦ *The truck blew a tire and lurched off the road.*
▸ WITH EXPLOSIVES **10** [T] ~ **sth** to break something open with EXPLOSIVES: *The safe had been blown by the thieves.*
▸ SECRET **11** [T] ~ **sth** (informal) to make known something that was secret: *One mistake could blow your cover* (= make your real name, job, intentions, etc. known).
▸ MONEY **12** [T] ~ **sth (on sth)** (informal) to spend or waste a lot of money on something: *He inherited over a million dollars and blew it all on alcohol and gambling.*
▸ OPPORTUNITY **13** [T] ~ **sth** (informal) to waste an opportunity: *She blew her chances by arriving late for the interview.* ♦ *You had your chance and you blew it.*
▸ LEAVE SUDDENLY **14** [T, I] ~ **(sth)** (slang) to leave a place suddenly: *Let's blow this joint.*
IDM **blow your/sb's brains out** (informal) to kill yourself/someone by shooting yourself/them in the head **blow chunks** (slang) to VOMIT **blow a fuse** (informal) to get very angry **blow hot and cold (about sth)** (informal) to change your opinion about something often **blow sb/sth out of the water** (informal) **1** to destroy someone or something completely **2** to show that someone or something is not good by being very much better than it/them: *A DVD music system plays disks that look like CDs, but blows them out of the water.* **blow your mind** (informal) to produce a very strong pleasant or shocking feeling: *Wait till you hear this. It'll blow your mind.* ⊃ see also MIND-BLOWING **blow your top/stack** (informal) to get very angry **blow up in sb's face**, etc. **blows up in your face**, it goes wrong in a way that causes you damage, embarrassment, etc. **blow the whistle on sb/sth** (informal) to tell someone in authority about something wrong or illegal that someone is doing ⊃ see also WHISTLE-BLOWER **IDM** see COBWEB, HORN, ILL adj., LID, PUFF v., SOCK n., STEAM, WAY n.
PHR V **blow sth↔a'part 1** to completely destroy something in an explosion **2** to show that an idea is completely false: *What we discovered blew apart all our preconceptions about this fascinating species.* **blow sb↔a'way** (informal) **1** to kill someone by shooting them **2** to impress someone a lot or to make them very happy **3** to defeat someone easily **blow 'in | blow 'into sth** (informal) to arrive or enter a place suddenly: *Look who just blew in!* ♦ *Have you heard who has blown into town?* **blow sb↔'off** (informal) to deliberately not meet someone when you said you would; to end a romantic relationship with someone **blow sth↔'off**

(*informal*) to deliberately not do something that you said you would: *He looks for any excuse he can to blow off work.* ,blow 'out **1** if a flame, etc. **blows out**, it is put out by the wind, etc.: *Somebody opened the door and the candle blew out.* **2** if an oil or gas WELL **blows out**, it sends out gas suddenly and with force ➔ related noun BLOWOUT ,blow itself 'out when a storm **blows itself out**, it finally loses its force ,blow sb↔'out (*informal*) to defeat someone easily ,blow sth↔'out to put out a flame, etc. by blowing ,blow 'over to go away without having a serious effect: *The storm blew over in the night.* ♦ *The scandal will soon blow over.* ,blow 'up **1** to explode; to be destroyed by an explosion: *The bomb blew up.* ♦ *A police officer was killed when his car blew up.* ➔ thesaurus box at EXPLODE **2** to start suddenly and with force: *A storm was blowing up.* ♦ *A crisis has blown up over the president's latest speech.* ,blow sth↔'up **1** to destroy something by an explosion: *The police station was blown up by terrorists.* ➔ thesaurus box at EXPLODE **2** to fill something with air or gas so that it becomes firm: *to blow up a balloon* **3** to make a photograph bigger **SYN** ENLARGE ➔ related noun BLOWUP **4** to make something seem more important, better, worse, etc. than it really is: *The whole affair was blown up out of all proportion.* ,blow 'up (at sb) (*informal*) to get angry with someone **SYN** LOSE YOUR TEMPER: *I'm sorry I blew up at you.* ➔ related noun BLOWUP

● **noun 1** a hard hit with the hand, a weapon, etc.: *She received a severe blow on the head.* ♦ *He was knocked out by a single blow to the head.* ♦ *The two men were exchanging blows.* ♦ *He landed a blow on Hill's nose.* **2** ~ (to sb/sth) a sudden event which has damaging effects on someone or something, causing sadness or disappointment: *Losing his job came as a terrible blow to him.* ♦ *It was a shattering blow to her pride.* ➔ see also BODY BLOW **3** the action of blowing: *Give your nose a good blow* (= clear it completely).
IDM a blow-by-blow account, description, etc. (of sth) (*informal*) a description of an event that gives you all the details in the order in which they happen come to blows (over sth) to start fighting because of something soften/ cushion the blow to make something that is unpleasant seem less unpleasant and easier to accept ➔ more at DEAL *v.*, STRIKE *v.*

blow·back /'bloʊbæk/ *noun* [U, C] **1** a process in which gases expand or travel in a direction that is opposite to the usual one: *blowback gas* ♦ *Blowback may be caused by a defective mechanism.* **2** the results of a political action or situation that are not what was intended or wanted: *The policy has led to blowback.* ♦ *The war created a ferocious blowback.*

'blow-dry *verb* ~ sth to dry hair with a HAIR DRYER and shape it into a particular style ▶ 'blow-dry *noun*: *a cut and blow-dry*

blow·er /'bloʊər/ *noun* a device that produces a current of air: *a hot-air blower* ➔ see also WHISTLE-BLOWER

blow·fly /'bloʊflaɪ/ *noun* (*pl.* blow·flies) a large fly that lays its eggs on meat and other food

blow·hard /'bloʊhɑrd/ *noun* (*informal, disapproving*) a person who talks too proudly about something they own or something they have done

blow·hole /'bloʊhoʊl/ *noun* **1** a hole in the top of a WHALE's head through which it breathes **2** a hole in a large area of ice, through which SEALS, etc. breathe

blown *pp* of BLOW

blow·out /'bloʊaʊt/ *noun* **1** an occasion when a tire suddenly bursts on a vehicle while it is moving **SYN** PUNCTURE: *to have a blowout* **2** [usually sing.] (*informal*) a large meal at which people eat too much: *a four-course blowout* **3** (*informal*) a large party or social occasion: *We're going to have a huge blowout for Valentine's Day.* **4** (*informal*) an easy victory: *The game was a blowout, 8–1.* **5** a sudden escape of oil or gas from an OIL WELL

blow·pipe /'bloʊpaɪp/ *noun* **1** a weapon consisting of a long tube through which an arrow is blown **2** a long tube for blowing glass into a particular shape

blows·y (also **blowz·y**) /'blaʊzi/ *adj.* (*informal, disapproving*) a woman who is **blowsy** is big and fat, and looks messy

blow·torch /'bloʊtɔrtʃ/ (also **torch**) *noun* a tool for directing a very hot flame onto part of a surface, for example to remove paint

blow·up (also 'blow-up) /'bloʊʌp/ *noun* **1** an ENLARGEMENT of a photograph, picture, or design: *Can you do a blowup of his face?* **2** an occasion when someone suddenly becomes angry

BLT /ˌbi ɛl 'ti/ *noun* the abbreviation for "bacon, lettuce, and tomato" (used to refer to a SANDWICH filled with this): *I'll have a BLT with extra mayonnaise.*

blub·ber /'blʌbər/ *noun, verb*
● **noun** [U] the fat of WHALES and other sea animals
● **verb** [I, T] (*informal, disapproving*) to cry noisily: *There he sat, blubbering like a baby.*

bludg·eon /'blʌdʒən/ *verb* **1** ~ sb to hit someone several times with a heavy object **2** ~ sb (into sth/into doing sth) to force someone to do something, especially by arguing with them: *They tried to bludgeon me into joining their protest.*

blue 🔊 /blu/ *adj., noun*
● **adj.** (blu·er, blu·est) **1** having the color of a clear sky or the ocean on a clear day: *piercing blue eyes* ♦ *a blue shirt* **2** (of a person or part of the body) looking slightly blue in color because the person is cold or cannot breathe easily: *Her hands were blue with cold.* **3** (*informal*) sad **SYN** DEPRESSED: *He'd been feeling blue all week.* **4** movies, jokes, or stories that are **blue** are about sex: *a blue movie* **5** (*politics*) (of an area in the U.S.) having more people who vote for the Democratic candidate than the Republican one: *blue states/ counties* **ANT** RED ➔ see also TRUE-BLUE ▶ blue·ness *noun* [U, sing.]: *the blueness of the water*
IDM do sth till you are blue in the face (*informal*) to try to do something as hard and as long as you possibly can but without success: *You can argue till you're blue in the face, but you won't change my mind.* ➔ more at BLACK *adj.*, DEVIL, ONCE *adv.*

● **noun** [C, U] the color of a clear sky or the ocean on a clear day: *bright/dark/light/pale blue* ♦ *The room was decorated in vibrant blues and yellows.* ♦ *She was dressed in blue.* ➔ see also BLUES
IDM out of the blue unexpectedly; without warning: *The decision came out of the blue.* ➔ more at BOLT *n.*, BOY *n.*

'blue ,baby *noun* a baby whose skin is slightly blue at birth because there is something wrong with its heart

blue·bell /'blubɛl/ *noun* a garden or wild flower with a short STEM and small, blue or white flowers shaped like bells ➔ picture at PLANT

blue·ber·ry /'blu,bɛri/ *noun* (*pl.* blue·ber·ries) a dark blue BERRY that grows on bushes and can be eaten ➔ picture at FRUIT ➔ compare BILBERRY

blue·bird /'blubərd/ *noun* a small N. American bird with blue feathers on its back or head

,blue-'blooded *adj.* from a royal or socially important family ▶ 'blue blood *noun* [U]

'blue book *noun* **1** a book with a blue cover used by students for writing the answers to examination questions **2** a book that lists the prices that people should expect to pay for used cars

blue·bot·tle /'blu,bɑtl/ *noun* a large fly with a blue body

,blue 'box *noun* (*CanE*) a blue, plastic box in which you put garbage that can be RECYCLED (= processed so that it can be used again) such as paper, cans, and bottles

'blue cheese *noun* [U, C] cheese with lines of blue MOLD in it

'blue-chip *adj.* [only before noun] (*finance*) a **blue-chip** investment is thought to be safe and likely to make a profit: *blue-chip companies*

,blue-'collar *adj.* [only before noun] connected with people who do physical work in industry: *blue-collar workers/ voters/votes* ➔ compare PINK-COLLAR, WHITE-COLLAR

blue·fish /'blufɪʃ/ noun (pl. **blue·fish**) a fish that lives in the ocean and is caught for food and for sport

blue 'funk noun (old-fashioned, informal) = FUNK

blue·grass /'blugræs/ noun [U] a type of traditional American country music played on GUITARS and BANJOS

blue 'helmet noun a member of a United Nations force that is trying to prevent war or violence in a place

blue·jay /'bludʒeɪ/ noun a large N. American bird with blue feathers on its back and a row of feathers (called a CREST) standing up on its head

blue jeans noun [pl.] pants made of blue DENIM

blue law noun [usually pl.] a law that bans business and certain other activities, such as sports, on Sundays

blue ,pages noun [pl.] the blue pages in a TELEPHONE DIRECTORY that give a list of government departments and their telephone numbers

blue·print /'bluprɪnt/ noun **1** a PHOTOGRAPHIC print of a plan for a building or a machine, with white lines on a blue background **2** ~ **(for sth)** a plan which shows what can be achieved and how it can be achieved: *a blueprint for the socialization of health care* **3** (technical) the pattern in every living cell, which decides how the plant, animal, or person will develop and what it will look like: *DNA carries the genetic blueprint that tells any organism how to build itself.*

blue 'ribbon noun an honor (sometimes in the form of a blue RIBBON) given to the winner of the first prize in a competition

'blue-,ribbon adj. [only before noun] **1** (of a committee, panel, etc.) carefully or specially selected: *a blue-ribbon commission on healthcare reform* **2** of the highest quality: *blue-ribbon service*

blues /bluz/ noun **1** often **the blues** [U] a type of slow, sad music with strong rhythms, developed by African American musicians in the southern U.S.: *a blues band/singer* **2** [C] (pl. **blues**) a blues song **3 the blues** [pl.] feelings of sadness: *the Monday morning blues* ⊃ see also BABY BLUES

,blue-'sky adj. [only before noun] involving new and interesting ideas which are not yet possible or practical: *The government has been doing some blue-sky thinking on how to improve school standards.*

blue·stock·ing /'blu,stakɪŋ/ noun (old-fashioned, sometimes disapproving) a well-educated woman who is more interested in ideas and studying than in traditionally FEMININE things

blues·y /'bluzi/ adj. having the slow, strong rhythms and sad mood of blues music: *a bluesy sound/voice*

Blue·tooth™ /'blutuθ/ noun [U] a radio technology that makes it possible for cell phones, computers, and other electronic devices to be linked over short distances, without needing to be connected by wires: *Bluetooth-enabled devices*

,blue 'whale noun a type of WHALE that is the largest known living animal

bluff /blʌf/ verb, noun, adj.
• **verb** [I, T] ~ **(sth)** to try to make someone believe that you will do something that you do not really intend to do, or that you know something that you do not really know: *I don't think he'll shoot—I think he's just bluffing.*
PHR V bluff sb into doing sth to make someone do something by tricking them, especially by pretending you have more experience, knowledge, etc. than you really have **,bluff your way 'in/'out/'through | ,bluff your way 'into/'out of/'through sth** to succeed in dealing with a difficult situation by making other people believe something which is not true: *She successfully bluffed her way through the interview.*
• **noun 1** [U, C] an attempt to trick someone by making them believe that you will do something when you really have no intention of doing it, or that you know something when you do not, in fact, know it: *It was just a game of bluff.* ◆ *He said he*

would resign if he didn't get more money, but it was only a bluff. ⊃ see also DOUBLE BLUFF **2** [C] a steep CLIFF or slope, especially by the ocean or a river ⊃ see also BLIND MAN'S BLUFF **IDM** See CALL v.
• **adj.** (of people or their manner) very direct and cheerful, with good intentions, although not always very polite: *Beneath his bluff exterior he was a sensitive man.*

blu·ish /'bluɪʃ/ adj. fairly blue in color: *a bluish-green carpet*

blun·der /'blʌndər/ noun, verb
• **noun** a stupid or careless mistake: *to make a terrible blunder* ◆ *a series of political blunders*
• **verb** [I] to make a stupid or careless mistake: *The government had blundered in its handling of the affair.*
PHR V ,blunder a'bout, a'round, etc. to move around in an awkward way, knocking into things, as if you cannot see where you are going **,blunder 'into sth 1** to knock into something because you are awkward or are not able to see **2** to find yourself in a difficult or unpleasant situation by accident **,blunder 'on** to continue doing something in a careless or stupid way

blun·der·buss /'blʌndər,bʌs/ noun an old type of gun with a wide end

blunt /blʌnt/ adj., verb
• **adj.** (blunt·er, blunt·est) **1** without a sharp edge or point: *a blunt knife* ◆ *This pencil is blunt!* ◆ *The police said he had been hit with a blunt instrument.* **ANT** SHARP **2** (of a person or remark) very direct; saying exactly what you think without trying to be polite: *She has a reputation for being blunt.* ◆ *To be blunt, your work is terrible.* ⊃ thesaurus box at HONEST
▶ **blunt·ness** noun [U]
• **verb 1** ~ **sth** to make something weaker or less effective: *Age hadn't blunted his passion for adventure.* **2** ~ **sth** to make a point or an edge less sharp

blunt·ly /'blʌntli/ adv. in a very direct way, without trying to be polite or kind: *To put it bluntly, I want a divorce.* ◆ *"Is she dead?" he asked bluntly.*

blur /blər/ noun, verb
• **noun** [usually sing.] **1** a shape that you cannot see clearly, often because it is moving too fast: *His arm was a rapid blur of movement as he swung.* ◆ *Everything is a blur when I take my glasses off.* **2** something that you cannot remember clearly: *The events of that day were just a blur.*
• **verb** (-rr-) **1** [I, T] if the shape or outline of something **blurs**, or if something **blurs** it, it becomes less clear and sharp: *The writing blurred and danced before his eyes.* ◆ ~ **sth** *The mist blurred the edges of the buildings.* **2** [T, I] ~ **(sth)** if something **blurs** your eyes or VISION, or your eyes or vision **blur**, you cannot see things clearly: *Tears blurred her eyes.* **3** [I, T] to become or make something become difficult to distinguish clearly: *The differences between art and life seem to have blurred.* ◆ ~ **sth** *She tends to blur the distinction between her friends and her colleagues.*

Blu-ray™ /'blu reɪ/ noun [U] technology that uses a blue LASER (= a very strong line of light) to record and play large amounts of high quality data on a type of CD: *These high-definition movies are all out on Blu-ray.*

'Blu-ray ,Disc™ noun (abbr. BD, BD-ROM) a type of CD on which large amounts of data can be stored, used especially to play high quality video

blurb /blərb/ noun a short description of a book, a new product, etc., written by the people who have produced it, that is intended to attract your attention and make you want to buy it

blurred /blərd/ adj. **1** not clear; without a clear outline or shape: *She suffered from dizziness and blurred vision.* ◆ *a blurred image/picture* **2** difficult to remember clearly: *blurred memories* **3** difficult to distinguish, so that differences are not clear: *blurred distinctions/boundaries*

blur·ry /'bləri/ adj. (informal) without a clear outline; not clear: *blurry, distorted photographs* ◆ (figurative) *a blurry policy*

blurt /blərt/ verb ~ **sth (out)** | ~ **that...** | + **speech** to say something suddenly and without thinking carefully enough: *She blurted it out before I could stop her.* ⊃ **thesaurus** box at CALL

blush /blʌʃ/ *verb, noun*
- **verb 1** [I] to become red in the face because you are embarrassed or ashamed **SYN** GO RED: *~ (with sth) (at sth) to blush with embarrassment/shame* ◆ *She blushed furiously at the memory of the conversation.* ◆ + **adj./noun** *He blushed crimson at the thought.* **2** [T] *~* **to do sth** to be ashamed or embarrassed about something: *I blush to admit it, but I really like her music.*
- **noun 1** the red color that spreads over your face when you are embarrassed or ashamed: *She felt a warm blush rise to her cheeks.* ◆ *He turned away to hide his blushes.* **2** = BLUSHER ⊃ **picture at** MAKEUP

blush·er /ˈblʌʃər/ (also **blush**) *noun* [U, C] a colored cream or powder that some people put on their cheeks to give them more color ⊃ **picture at** MAKEUP

blush wine *noun* [C, U] slightly pink wine that is usually made from red GRAPES with the skins removed ⊃ **compare** RED WINE, ROSE, WHITE WINE

blus·ter /ˈblʌstər/ *verb* **1** [T, I] *~* **(sth)** | + **speech** to talk in an aggressive or threatening way, but with little effect: *"I don't know what you're talking about," he blustered.* ◆ *a blustering bully* **2** [I] (of the wind) to blow violently ▶ **blus·ter** *noun* [U]: *I wasn't frightened by what he said—it was all bluster.*

blus·ter·y /ˈblʌstəri/ *adj.* (of weather) with strong winds: *blustery winds/conditions* ◆ *The day was cold and blustery.*

Blvd. *abbr.* (used in written addresses) BOULEVARD

BMI /ˌbi ɛm ˈaɪ/ *abbr.* BODY MASS INDEX

BMOC /ˌbi ɛm oʊ ˈsi/ *abbr.* BIG MAN ON CAMPUS

B-ˌmovie *noun* a movie that is made cheaply and is not very good: *a B-movie actress*

B.Mus. /ˌbi ˈmʌz/ *noun* a college degree in music that is usually a first degree (the abbreviation for "Bachelor of Music")

BMX /ˌbi ɛm ˈɛks/ *noun* **1** [C] a strong bicycle that can be used for riding on rough ground **2** (also **BMX·ing**) [U] the sport of racing BMX bicycles on rough ground

bn *abbr.* (in writing) BILLION

BO /ˌbi ˈoʊ/ *noun* [U] the abbreviation for "body odor" (an unpleasant smell from a person's body, especially of sweat): *She's got BO.*

bo·a /ˈboʊə/ *noun* **1** = BOA CONSTRICTOR **2** = FEATHER BOA

bo·a con·stric·tor /ˈboʊə kənˌstrɪktər/ (also **bo·a**) *noun* a large S. American snake that kills animals for food by winding its long body around them and crushing them

boar /bɔr/ *noun* (*pl.* **boar** or **boars**) **1** (also **wild ˈboar**) a wild pig **2** a male pig that has not been CASTRATED ⊃ **compare** HOG, SOW²

board 🔑 /bɔrd/ *noun, verb*
- **noun**
- ⟩ PIECE OF WOOD, ETC. **1** [C, U] a long, thin piece of strong, hard material, especially wood, used, for example, for making floors, building walls and roofs, and making boats: *He had ripped up the carpet, leaving only the bare boards.* ⊃ **see also** FLOORBOARD, HARDBOARD, PARTICLEBOARD **2** [C] (especially in compounds) a piece of wood, or other strong material, that is used for a special purpose: *a blackboard* ◆ *I'll write it up on the board.* ◆ *a bulletin board* ◆ *The exam results went up on the board.* ◆ *a diving board* ◆ *She jumped off the top board.* ◆ *a chessboard* ◆ *He removed the piece from the board.* ⊃ **see also** MESSAGE BOARD, PEGBOARD
- ⟩ IN WATER SPORTS **3** [C] = BODYBOARD, SAILBOARD, SURFBOARD
- ⟩ GROUP OF PEOPLE **4** [C] a group of people who have power to make decisions and control a company or other organization: *She has a seat on the board of directors.* ◆ *The board is unhappy about falling sales.* ◆ *members of the board* ◆ *discussions at the board level* ◆ *the youth advisory board* (= for

example, of a political campaign) ◆ *the board of education* (= a group of elected officials who are in charge of all the public schools in a particular area) ⊃ **see also** SCHOOL BOARD
- ⟩ ORGANIZATION **5** [C] used in the name of some organizations: *the Federal Reserve Board*
- ⟩ MEALS **6** [U] the meals that are provided when you pay to stay in a place; what you pay for the meals: *Her tuition includes room and board.*
- ⟩ EXAMS **7 boards** [pl.] (*old-fashioned*) exams that you take when you apply to go to college or medical school
- ⟩ IN THEATER **8 the boards** [pl.] (*old-fashioned, informal*) the stage in a theater: *His play is on the boards on Broadway.* ◆ *She's treading the boards* (= working as an actress).
- ⟩ HOCKEY **9 the boards** [pl.] the low wooden wall surrounding the area where a game of HOCKEY is played: *The puck went wide, hitting the boards.* **HELP** There are many other compounds ending in **board**. You will find them at their place in the alphabet.

IDM **across the board** involving everyone or everything in a company, an industry, etc.: *The industry needs more investment across the board.* ◆ *an across-the-board salary increase* **go by the board** (of plans or principles) to be rejected or ignored; to be no longer possible: *All her efforts to be polite went by the board and she started to shout at him.* **on board 1** on or in a ship, an aircraft, or a train **SYN** ABOARD: *Have the passengers gone on board yet?* **2** giving your support to an idea or a project: *We must get more sponsors on board.* ◆ *You need to bring the whole staff on board.* **take sth on board** to accept and understand an idea or a suggestion: *I told her what I thought, but she didn't take my advice on board.* ⊃ **more at** SWEEP v.

- **verb**
- ⟩ GET ON PLANE/SHIP, ETC. **1** [I, T] to get on a ship, train, plane, bus, etc.: *Passengers are waiting to board.* ◆ *~* **sth** *The ship was boarded by customs officials.* **2** [I] **be boarding** when a plane or ship **is boarding**, it is ready for passengers to get on: *Flight UA193 for Paris is now boarding at Gate 37.*
- ⟩ LIVE SOMEWHERE **3** [I] *~* **at.../with sb** to live and take meals in someone's home, in return for payment: *She always had one or two students boarding with her.* **4** [I] to live at a school during the school year

PHR V **board sth↔ˈup** to cover a window, door, etc. with wooden boards

board·er /ˈbɔrdər/ *noun* **1** a child who lives at school and goes home for the holidays: *boarders and day students* **2** a person who pays money to live in a room in someone else's house

ˈboard game *noun* any game played on a board, often using DICE and small pieces that are moved around

board·ing /ˈbɔrdɪŋ/ *noun* [U] **1** long pieces of wood that are put together to make a wall, etc. **2** the arrangement by which school students live at their school, going home during the holidays: *boarding fees* **3** the act of getting on a train, plane, ship, etc.: *Boarding will begin at 12 o'clock.*

board·ing·house (also **ˈboarding-house**) /ˈbɔrdɪŋhaʊs/ *noun* a private house where people can pay to sleep and have meals

ˈboarding ˌkennel *noun* = KENNEL (1)

ˈboarding ˌpass *noun* a card that you show before you get on a plane or boat

ˈboarding ˌschool *noun* a school where children can live during the school year ⊃ **compare** DAY SCHOOL

board·room /ˈbɔrdrum; -rʊm/ *noun* a room in which the meetings of the board of a company (= the group of people who control it) are held: *a boardroom battle*

board·sail·ing /ˈbɔrdˌseɪlɪŋ/ *noun* [U] = WINDSURFING

board·walk /ˈbɔrdwɔk/ *noun* a path made of wooden boards, especially on a beach or near water

boast /boʊst/ *verb, noun*
- **verb 1** [I, T] to talk with too much pride about something that you have or can do: *I don't want to boast, but I can actually speak six languages.* ◆ *~* **about sth** *She is always boasting about how wonderful her children are.* ◆ *~* **of sth** *He openly*

t tea	ʈ butter	d did	k cat	g got	tʃ chin	dʒ June	f fall

Boats and Ships

tugboat (*also* tug)

container ship

paddle wheel

paddle wheeler (*also* paddleboat)

twin hulls

catamaran

skirt

hovercraft

hydrofoil

the bridge

ferry

bow   stern

liner

submarine

speedboat

yacht

life jacket (*also* life vest)

blade

paddle

kayak

canoe

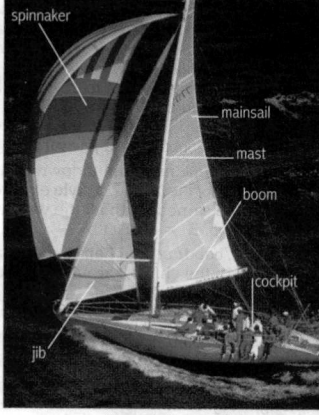
spinnaker

mainsail

mast

boom

cockpit

jib

sailboat (*also* yacht)

raft

oar

rowboat

boasted of getting a promotion at work. ♦ **~ that…** *Sam boasted that she could beat anyone at poker.* ♦ **+ speech** *"I won!" she boasted.* **2** [T] (not used in the progressive tenses) **~ sth** to have something that is impressive and that you can be proud of: *The hotel also boasts two swimming pools and a golf course.*

● **noun ~ (that…)** (often *disapproving*) something that a person talks about in a very proud way, often to seem more important or smart: *Despite his boasts that his children were brilliant, neither of them went to college.* ♦ *It was her **proud boast** that she had never missed a day of work because of illness.*

boast·ful /ˈboʊstfl/ adj. (*disapproving*) talking about yourself in a very proud way: *I tried to emphasize my good points without sounding boastful.*

boat 🎣 /boʊt/ noun
1 a vehicle (smaller than a ship) that travels on water, moved by OARS, sails, or a motor: *an inflatable boat* ♦ *a fishing boat* ♦ *You can take a **boat trip** along the coast.* ➔ see also CANAL BOAT, HOUSEBOAT, LIFEBOAT, MOTORBOAT, POWERBOAT, ROWBOAT, SAILBOAT, SPEEDBOAT, STEAM-BOAT **2** any ship: *"How are you going to Nantucket?" "We're going by boat* (= by FERRY).*"* ➔ picture on page 155 ➔ see also GRAVY BOAT, SAUCEBOAT
IDM **be in the same boat** to be in the same difficult situation ➔ more at FLOAT v., MISS v., ROCK v.

boat·er /ˈboʊtər/ noun a hard STRAW hat with a flat top ➔ picture at HAT

boat·hook /ˈboʊthʊk/ noun a long pole with a hook at one end, used for pulling or pushing boats

boat·house /ˈboʊthaʊs/ noun a building beside a river or lake for keeping a boat in

boat·ing /ˈboʊtɪŋ/ noun [U] the activity of using a small boat for pleasure: *to go boating* ♦ *Local activities include walking, boating, and golf.*

boat·load /ˈboʊtloʊd/ noun **1** as many goods or passengers as a ship or boat can carry: *a boatload of bananas* ➔ compare SHIPLOAD **2** (*informal*) a large number of people; a large amount of something: *They made boatloads of food for the Super Bowl party.*

boat·man /ˈboʊtmən/ noun (pl. **boat·men** /-mən/) a man who earns money from small boats, either by carrying passengers or goods on them, or by renting them out

boat people noun [pl.] people who escape from their own country in small boats to try to find safety in another country

boat·swain /ˈboʊsn/ noun = BOSUN

boat·yard /ˈboʊtyɑrd/ noun a place where boats are built, repaired, or kept

bob /bɑb/ verb, noun
● **verb** (-bb-) **1** [I, T] to move or make something move quickly up and down, especially in water: **~ up and down** *Tiny boats bobbed up and down in the harbor.* ♦ **~ sth (up and down)** *She bobbed her head nervously.* **2** [T] **~ sth** to cut someone's hair so that it is the same length all the way around ➔ picture at HAIR
PHRV **bob 'up** to come to the surface suddenly: *The dark head of a seal bobbed up a few yards away.*
● **noun 1** a quick movement down and up of your head and body: *a bob of the head* **2** a style of a woman's hair in which it is cut the same length all the way around: *She wears her hair in a bob.* **3** = BOBSLED

bobbed /bɑbd/ adj. (of hair) cut so that it hangs loosely to the level of the chin all around the back and sides

bob·ber /ˈbɑbər/ noun a floating object used in fishing to hold the hook at the right depth

bob·bin /ˈbɑbən/ noun a small device on which you wind thread, used, for example, in a sewing machine

bob·ble /ˈbɑbl/ verb (*informal*) **1** [I] **+ adv./prep.** to move along the ground with small BOUNCES: *The ball somehow*

bobbled into the net. **2** [T] **~ sth** to drop a ball or to fail to stop it: *She tried to catch the ball but bobbled it.*

bobby pin /ˈbɑbi ˌpɪn/ noun a small, thin piece of metal or plastic folded in the middle, used by women for holding their hair in place ➔ compare HAIRPIN

bobby socks noun [pl.] short white socks worn with a dress or skirt, especially by girls and young women in the U.S. in the 1940s and 50s

bob·cat /ˈbɑbkæt/ noun a N. American wild cat

bob·sled /ˈbɑbslɛd/ (also **bob**) noun a racing SLED (= a vehicle for two or more people that slides over snow) ➔ picture at SPORT

bob·tail /ˈbɑbteɪl/ noun **1** a dog, cat, or horse with a tail that has been cut short **2** a tail that has been cut short

bod /bɑd/ noun (*informal*) a person's body: *He's got a great bod.*

bo·da·cious /boʊˈdeɪʃəs/ adj. (*informal*) **1** excellent; extremely good **2** willing to take risks or to do something shocking **SYN** AUDACIOUS

bode /boʊd/ verb
IDM **bode well/ill (for sb/sth)** (*formal*) to be a good/bad sign for someone or something **SYN** AUGUR: *These figures do not bode well for the company's future.*

bo·de·ga /boʊˈdeɪɡə/ noun (from *Spanish*) a small grocery store in a neighborhood where most of the people speak Spanish

bo·dhi·satt·va (also **Bo·dhi·satt·va**) /ˌboʊdɪˈsʌtvə; -ˈsɑt-/ noun (in Mahayana Buddhism) a person who is able to reach NIRVANA (= a state of peace and happiness) but who delays doing this because of the suffering of other humans

bod·ice /ˈbɑdəs/ noun the top part of a woman's dress, above the waist

bodice-ripper noun (*informal*) a romantic novel or movie with a lot of sex in it, which is set in the past

bod·i·ly /ˈbɑdlæwi/ adj., adv.
● **adj.** [only before noun] connected with the human body: *bodily functions/changes/needs* ♦ *bodily fluids* ♦ *bodily harm* (= physical injury)
● **adv. 1** by moving the whole of someone's body; by force: *The force of the blast hurled us bodily to the ground.* ♦ *He lifted her bodily into the air.* **2** in one piece; completely: *The monument was moved bodily to a new site.*

bod·kin /ˈbɑdkɪn/ noun a thick needle with no point

body 🎣 /ˈbɑdi/ noun (pl. **bod·ies**)
> **OF PERSON/ANIMAL 1** [C] the whole physical structure of a human or an animal: *a human/female/male/naked body* ♦ *parts of the body* ♦ *His whole body was trembling.* ♦ *body fat/weight/temperature/size/heat* **2** [C] the main part of a body not including the head, arms, and legs: *She had injuries to her head and body.* ♦ *He has a large body, but thin legs.* ➔ picture on page 157 **3** [C] the body of a dead person or animal: *a dead body* ♦ *The family of the missing girl has been called in by the police to identify the body.*
> **MAIN PART 4** [sing.] **the ~ of sth** the main part of something, especially of a building, a vehicle, or a book, an article, etc.: *the body of a plane* (= the central part where the seats are) ♦ *the main body of the text*
> **GROUP OF PEOPLE 5** [U] a group of people who work or act together, often for an official purpose, or who are connected in some other way: *a regulatory/an advisory/a review body* ♦ *The governing body of the school is concerned about discipline.* ♦ *recognized professional bodies such as the Bar Association* ♦ *An independent body has been set up to investigate the affair.* ♦ *A large body of people will be affected by the tax cuts.* ♦ *The protesters marched in **a body*** (= all together) *to the White House.* ➔ see also STUDENT BODY
> **LARGE AMOUNT 6** [C] **~ of sth** a large amount or collection of something: *a vast body of evidence/information/research* ♦ *large bodies of water* (= lakes or oceans) ♦ *There is a powerful body of opinion against the ruling.*

The Body

the body

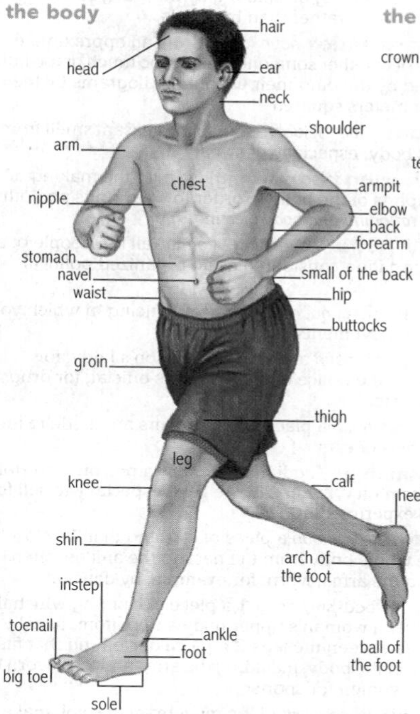

- hair
- head
- ear
- neck
- shoulder
- arm
- chest
- armpit
- elbow
- back
- forearm
- nipple
- stomach
- navel
- waist
- small of the back
- hip
- buttocks
- groin
- thigh
- leg
- knee
- calf
- heel
- shin
- arch of the foot
- instep
- toenail
- ankle
- foot
- big toe
- ball of the foot
- sole

the face

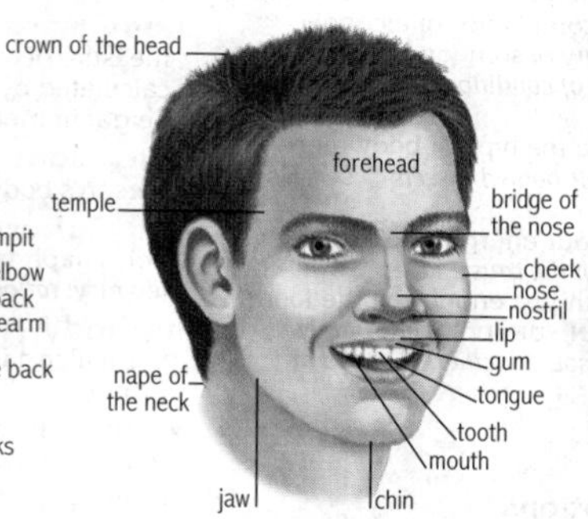

- crown of the head
- forehead
- temple
- bridge of the nose
- cheek
- nose
- nostril
- lip
- gum
- tongue
- tooth
- mouth
- nape of the neck
- jaw
- chin

the hand

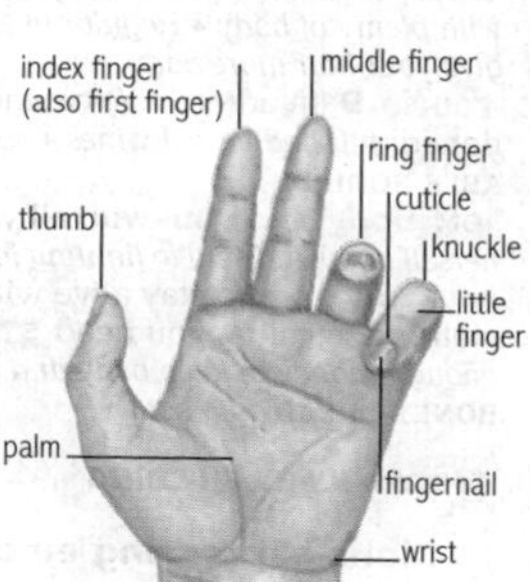

- index finger (also first finger)
- middle finger
- ring finger
- cuticle
- thumb
- knuckle
- little finger
- palm
- fingernail
- wrist

the eye

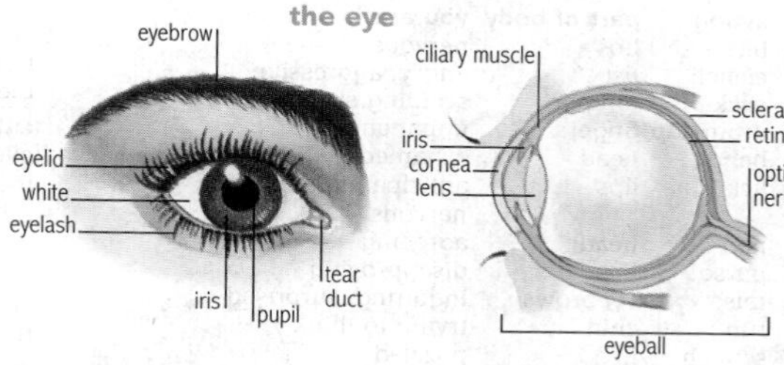

- eyebrow
- ciliary muscle
- eyelid
- white
- eyelash
- iris
- pupil
- tear duct
- iris
- cornea
- lens
- sclera
- retina
- optic nerve
- eyeball

the skeleton

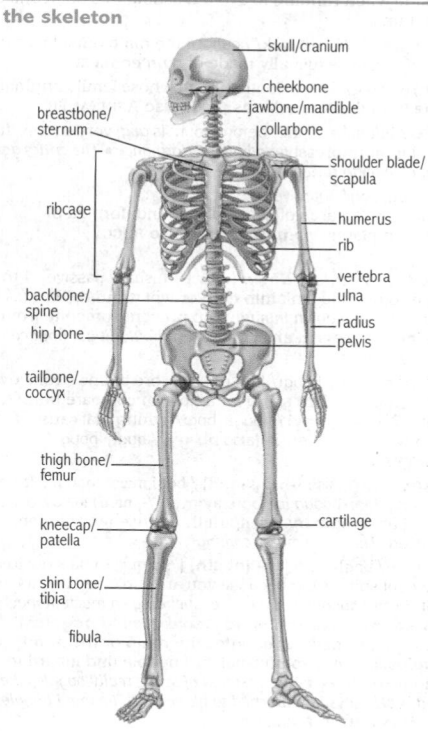

- skull/cranium
- cheekbone
- jawbone/mandible
- collarbone
- breastbone/sternum
- shoulder blade/scapula
- ribcage
- humerus
- rib
- vertebra
- backbone/spine
- ulna
- hip bone
- radius
- pelvis
- tailbone/coccyx
- thigh bone/femur
- cartilage
- kneecap/patella
- shin bone/tibia
- fibula

the internal organs

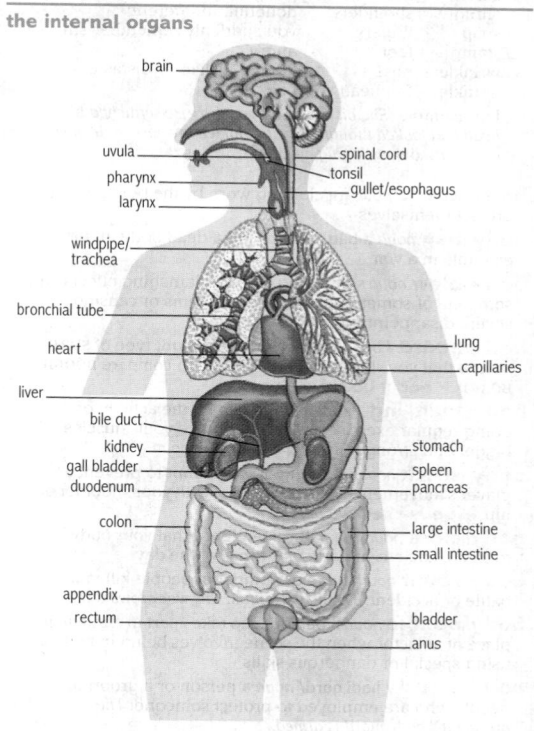

- brain
- uvula
- spinal cord
- pharynx
- tonsil
- larynx
- gullet/esophagus
- windpipe/trachea
- bronchial tube
- heart
- lung
- capillaries
- liver
- bile duct
- kidney
- gall bladder
- duodenum
- stomach
- spleen
- pancreas
- colon
- large intestine
- small intestine
- appendix
- rectum
- bladder
- anus

> **OBJECT 7** [C] (*formal*) an object: *heavenly bodies* (= stars, planets, etc.) ♦ *an operation to remove a foreign body* (= something that would not usually be there) *from a wound*

> **OF DRINKS/HAIR 8** [U] the full strong flavor of alcoholic drinks or the thick healthy quality of someone's hair: *a wine with plenty of body* ♦ *Regular use of conditioner is supposed to give your hair more body.*

> **-BODIED 9** (in adjectives) having the type of body mentioned: *full-bodied red wines* ♦ *soft-bodied insects* ⮞ see also ABLE-BODIED

IDM **body and soul** with all your energy: *She committed herself body and soul to fighting for the cause.* **keep body and soul together** to stay alive with just enough of the food, clothing, etc. that you need **SYN** SURVIVE: *They barely have enough money to keep body and soul together.* ⮞ more at BONE *n.*, DEAD *adj.*, SELL *v.*

VOCABULARY BUILDING

actions expressing emotions

Often, parts of the body are closely linked to particular verbs. The combination of the verb and part of the body expresses an emotion or attitude.

action	part of body	you are...
bite	lips	nervous
clench	fist	angry, aggressive
click	tongue	scolding sb
drum/tap	fingers	impatient
hang	head	ashamed
lick	lips	anticipating sth good, nervous
nod	head	agreeing
purse	lips	disapproving
raise	eyebrows	inquiring, surprised
rub	chin	trying to think
scratch	head	puzzled
shake	head	disagreeing
shrug	shoulders	doubtful, indifferent
snap	fingers	you suddenly remember sth
stamp	foot	angry
wrinkle	nose	feeling dislike or distaste
wrinkle	forehead	puzzled

For example: *She bit her lip nervously.* ♦ *He scratched his head and looked thoughtful.* ♦ *I wrinkled my nose in disgust.* ♦ *She raised questioning eyebrows.*

'**body** ,**armor** *noun* [U] clothing worn by the police, etc. to protect themselves

'**body** ,**bag** *noun* a bag for carrying a dead body in, for example in a war

'**body** ,**blow** *noun* something that has damaging effects on someone or something, creating problems or causing severe disappointment

bod·y·board /'badi,bɔrd/ *noun* a short light type of SURF-BOARD that you ride lying on your front ⮞ compare BOOGIE BOARD ▸ **bod·y·board·ing** *noun* [U]

bod·y·build·ing /'badi,bɪldɪŋ/ *noun* [U] the activity of doing regular exercises in order to make your muscles bigger and stronger ▸ **bod·y·build·er** *noun*

'**body** ,**check** *noun* (in HOCKEY) an attempt to prevent a player's movement by blocking them with your shoulder or hip ▸ '**body-check** *verb*

'**body** ,**clock** *noun* the natural tendency that your body has to sleep, eat, etc. at particular times of the day

'**body** ,**count** *noun* the total number of people killed in a battle or accident: *The body count in this war grows weekly.*

'**body** ,**double** *noun* a person who takes part in a movie in place of an actor when the scene involves being naked, or using special or dangerous skills

bod·y·guard /'badi,gɑrd/ *noun* a person or a group of people who are employed to protect someone: *The president's bodyguard is armed.*

'**body** ,**language** *noun* [U] the process of communicating what you are feeling or thinking by the way you place and move your body rather than by words

,**body mass** '**index** *noun* (*abbr.* BMI) an approximate measure of whether someone weighs too much or too little, calculated by dividing their weight in kilograms by their height in meters squared

'**body** ,**odor** *noun* [U] (*abbr.* BO) an unpleasant smell from a person's body, especially of sweat

'**body** ,**piercing** (also pierc·ing) *noun* [U] the making of holes in parts of the body in order to wear rings and other jewelry: *tattooing and body piercing*

the ,**body** '**politic** *noun* [sing.] (*formal*) all the people of a particular nation considered as an organized political group

'**body-**,**popping** *noun* [U] a way of dancing in which you make stiff movements like a ROBOT

'**body** ,**search** *noun* a search of a person's body, for example by the police or by a customs official, for drugs, weapons, etc.

'**body** ,**shop** *noun* a place where repairs are made to the main bodies of cars

bod·y·snatch·er /'badi,snætʃər/ *noun* a person who stole bodies from GRAVEYARDS in the past, especially to sell for medical experiments

'**body** ,**stocking** *noun* a piece of clothing that fits closely over the whole body from the neck to the ankles, often including the arms, worn, for example, by dancers

bod·y·suit /'badi,sut/ *noun* **1** a piece of clothing which fits tightly over a woman's upper body and bottom, usually fastening between the legs **2** a piece of clothing that fits closely over the body, including the arms and legs, worn by men and women for sports

'**body** ,**swerve** *noun* a sudden movement that you make to the side when running to avoid crashing into someone or something

bod·y·work /'badi,wərk/ *noun* [U] the main outside structure of a vehicle, usually made of painted metal

Boer /bɔr; bʊr/ *noun* a South African whose family originally came from the Netherlands ⮞ see also AFRIKANER

bof·fo /'bafoʊ/ *adj.* [only before noun] (*slang*) very successful, popular, or impressive: *a boffo performance* ♦ *The critics gave the movie boffo reviews.*

bog /bag; bɔg/ *noun, verb*
● *noun* [C, U] (an area of) wet, soft ground, formed of decaying plants: *a peat bog* ⮞ see also BOGGY
● *verb* (-gg-)
PHR V ,**bog sth/sb** '**down (in sth)** [usually passive] **1** to make something sink into mud or wet ground: *The tank became bogged down in mud.* **2** to prevent someone from making progress in an activity: *We shouldn't **get bogged down** in details.*

bo·gey *noun* **1** /'boʊgi/ (in GOLF) a score of one stroke over PAR (= the standard score for a hole) ⮞ compare BIRDIE, EAGLE **2** (also **bo·gy**) /'boʊgi; 'bʊgi/ a thing that causes fear, often without reason **3** (also **bo·gy**) /'bʊgi; 'boʊgi/ = BOGEYMAN

bo·gey·man (also **bo·gy·man**) /'bʊgi,mæn; 'boʊgi-/ (also **boo·gey·man**) *noun* (*pl.* **bo·gey·men** /-,mɛn/) (also **bo·gey**, **bo·gy**) an imaginary evil spirit that is used to frighten children: *The bogeyman's coming!*

bog·gle /'bagl/ *verb* [I] **~ (at sth)** (*informal*) to be slow to do or accept something because you are surprised or shocked by it: *Even I boggle at the idea of spending so much money.*
IDM **sth boggles the mind** (also **the mind boggles**) (*informal*) if something **boggles the mind** or **the mind boggles** at it, it is so unusual that people find it hard to imagine or accept: *The vastness of space really boggles the mind.* ♦ *"He says he's married to his cats!" "The mind boggles!"* ⮞ compare MIND-BOGGLING

ʌ **cup**   ə **about**   eɪ **say**   aɪ **five**   ɔɪ **boy**   aʊ **now**   oʊ **go**   ər **bird**

bog·gy /'bɑgi; 'bɔgi/ adj. (bog·gi·er, bog·gi·est) (of land) soft and wet, like a BOG: boggy ground

bo·gus /'bougəs/ adj. pretending to be real or genuine
  SYN FALSE: a bogus doctor/contract ◆ bogus claims of injury by workers

bo·gy, bo·gy·man = BOGEY, BOGEYMAN

bo·he·mi·an /bou'himiən/ noun a person, often someone who is involved with the arts, who lives in a very informal way without following accepted rules of behavior ▶ bo·he·mi·an adj.: a bohemian existence/lifestyle

bohr·i·um /'bɔriəm/ noun [U] (symb. **Bh**) a RADIOACTIVE chemical element. Bohrium is produced when atoms COLLIDE (= crash into each other).

boil /bɔɪl/ verb, noun
● verb 1 [I, T] when a liquid boils or when you boil it, it is heated to the point where it forms bubbles and turns to steam or VAPOR: The water was bubbling and boiling away. ◆ ~ sth Boil plenty of salted water, then add the spaghetti. ⊃ picture at COOKING 2 [I, T] when a KETTLE, pan, etc. boils or when you boil a KETTLE, etc., it is heated until the water inside it boils: The kettle is boiling. ◆ ~ sth Boil a large pot of water. ◆ + adj. She left the burner on by mistake and the pot boiled dry (= the water boiled until there was none left). 3 [I, T] to cook or wash something in boiling water; to be cooked or washed in boiling water: She put some potatoes on to boil. ◆ ~ sth boiled carrots/cabbage ◆ to boil an egg for someone ◆ ~ sb sth to boil someone an egg ⊃ collocations at COOKING 4 [I] ~ (with sth) if you boil with anger, etc. or anger, etc. boils inside you, you are very angry: He was boiling with rage. **IDM** see BLOOD, WATCH v.
  PHR V ,boil 'down | ,boil sth↔'down to be reduced or to reduce something by boiling. ,boil sth 'down (to sth) to make something, especially information, shorter by leaving out the parts that are not important: The original speech I had written got boiled down to about ten minutes. ,boil 'down to sth (not used in the progressive tenses) (of a situation, problem, etc.) to have something as a main or basic part: In the end, what it all boils down to is money, or the lack of it. ,boil 'over 1 (of liquid) to boil and flow over the side of a pan, etc. 2 (informal) to become very angry 3 (of a situation, an emotion, etc.) to change into something more dangerous or violent **SYN** EXPLODE: Racial tension finally boiled over in the inner city riots. ,boil 'up if a situation or an emotion boils up, it becomes dangerous, worrying, etc.: I could feel anger boiling up inside me. ,boil sth↔'up to heat a liquid or some food until it boils
● noun 1 [sing.] a period of boiling; the point at which liquid boils: Bring the soup to a boil. 2 [C] a painful, infected swelling under the skin which is full of a thick yellow liquid (called PUS)

boil·er /'bɔɪlər/ noun a container in which water is heated to provide hot water and heating in a building, or to produce steam in an engine ⊃ compare FURNACE (1) ⊃ see also DOUBLE BOILER

boil·er·mak·er /'bɔɪlər,meɪkər/ noun 1 a person or company that makes boilers 2 a person who makes and repairs metal objects for industry 3 a drink of WHISKEY followed immediately by a glass of beer

boil·er·plate /'bɔɪlər,pleɪt/ noun [C, U] a standard form of words that can be used as a model for writing parts of a business document, legal agreement, etc.

'**boiler ,room** noun 1 a room in a building or ship containing the boiler 2 a room or office used by people using telephones to sell something, especially shares, in an aggressive or a dishonest way

boil·ing /'bɔɪlɪŋ/ (also ,boiling 'hot) adj. very hot
  SYN BAKING: You must be boiling in that sweater! ◆ a boiling hot day **ANT** FREEZING

'**boiling ,point** noun 1 the temperature at which a liquid starts to boil 2 the point at which a person becomes very angry, or a situation is likely to become violent: Racial tension has reached boiling point.

bois·ter·ous /'bɔɪstərəs/ adj. (of people, animals, or behavior) noisy and full of life and energy: It was a challenge, keeping ten boisterous seven-year-olds amused. ▶ bois·ter·ous·ly adv.

bok choy /,bak 'tʃɔɪ/ noun [U] a type of CHINESE CABBAGE with long, dark green leaves and thick white STEMS

bold /bould/ adj., noun
● adj. (bold·er, bold·est) 1 (of people or behavior) brave and confident; not afraid to say what you feel or to take risks: It was a bold move on their part to open a business in France. ◆ The wine made him bold enough to approach her. 2 (of shape, color, lines, etc.) that can be easily seen; having a strong clear appearance: the bold outline of a mountain against the sky ◆ She paints with bold strokes of the brush. 3 (technical) (of printed words or letters) in a thick, dark TYPE: Highlight the important words in bold type. ◆ bold lettering ▶ bold·ly adv. bold·ness noun [U]
  IDM be/make so bold (as to do sth) (formal) used especially when politely asking a question or making a suggestion which you hope will not offend anyone (although it may criticize them slightly): If I may be so bold as to suggest that he made a mistake in his calculations… (as) bold as brass (informal) without showing any respect, shame, or fear
● noun [U] (technical) = BOLDFACE

bold·face /'bouldfeɪs/ (also **bold**) noun [U] (technical) thick, dark TYPE used for printing words or letters: Headwords are printed in boldface.

bole /boul/ noun the main STEM of a tree **SYN** TRUNK

bo·le·ro /bə'lɛrou/ noun (pl. bo·le·ros) 1 a traditional Spanish dance; a piece of music for this dance 2 a women's short jacket that is not fastened at the front

bo·lete /bou'lit/ (also bo·le·tus /bou'liṭəs/) noun [C, U] a MUSHROOM with small round holes under the top part. Some types of boletes can be eaten.

boll /boul/ noun the part of the cotton plant that contains the seeds

bol·lard /'balərd/ noun a short thick post on a ship, or on land close to water, to which a ship's rope may be tied

,boll 'weevil noun an insect that damages cotton plants

Bol·ly·wood /'bali,wʊd/ noun [U] (informal) used to refer to the Hindi movie industry, which mainly takes place in the Indian city of Mumbai (formerly called Bombay)

bo·lo·gna (also ba·lo·ney) /bə'louni/ noun [U] a type of SAUSAGE that is put in SANDWICHES, made of a mixture of meats

bo·lo tie /'boulou ,taɪ/ noun a string worn around the neck and fastened with a decorative CLASP or bar

Bol·she·vik /'boulʃəvɪk/ noun a member of the group in Russia that took control after the 1917 Revolution ▶ Bol·she·vik adj. Bol·she·vism /'boulʃə,vɪzəm/ noun [U]

bol·ster /'boulstər/ verb, noun
● verb to improve something or make it stronger: ~ sth to bolster someone's confidence/courage/morale ◆ ~ sth up Falling interest rates may help to bolster up the economy.
● noun a long thick PILLOW that is placed across the top of a bed under the other pillows

bolt /boult/ noun, verb, adv.
● noun 1 a long, narrow piece of metal that you slide across the inside of a door or window in order to lock it 2 a piece of metal like a screw without a point that is used with a circle of metal (= a NUT) to fasten things together: nuts and bolts ⊃ picture at TOOL 3 ~ of lightning a sudden flash of LIGHTNING in the sky, appearing as a line 4 a short heavy arrow shot from a CROSSBOW 5 a long piece of cloth wound in a roll
  IDM a bolt from the blue an event or a piece of news that is sudden and unexpected; a complete surprise: Her dismissal came as a bolt from the blue. make a bolt for sth | make a bolt for it to run away very fast, in order to escape ⊃ more at NUT

• *verb* **1** [T, I] **~ (sth)** to fasten something such as a door or window by sliding a bolt across; to be able to be fastened in this way: *Don't forget to bolt the door.* ◆ *The gate bolts on the inside.* **2** [T] to fasten things together with a bolt: **~ A to B** *The vise is bolted to the workbench.* ◆ **~ A and B together** *The various parts of the car are then bolted together.* **3** [I] if an animal, especially a horse, **bolts**, it suddenly runs away because it is frightened **4** [I] **(+ adv./prep.)** (of a person) to run away, especially in order to escape: *When he saw the police arrive, he bolted down an alley.* **5** [T] **~ sth (down)** to eat something very quickly: *Don't bolt down your food!* **6** [T, I] **~ (sth)** to stop supporting a particular group or political party: *Many Democrats bolted the party to vote Republican.* **7** [I] (of a plant, especially a vegetable) to grow too quickly and start producing seeds, and so become less good to eat

• *adv.*
   IDM **sit/stand bolt upright** to sit or stand with your back straight

'bolt-‚action *adj.* (of a gun) having a back part that is opened by turning a BOLT and sliding it back

'bolt-on *adj.* [only before noun] able to be easily added to a machine, etc. to make it able to do something new

bo·lus /'boʊləs/ *noun* **1** (*medical*) a single amount of a drug that is given at one time **SYN** DOSE **2** (*technical*) a small, round mass of substance, especially chewed food that is swallowed

bomb 🔑 /bɑm/ *noun, verb*

• *noun* **1** [C] a weapon designed to explode at a particular time or when it is dropped or thrown: *a bomb attack/blast/explosion* ◆ *a bomb goes off/explodes* ◆ *extensive bomb damage* ◆ *Hundreds of bombs were dropped on the city.* ⊃ see also DIRTY BOMB **2 the bomb** [sing.] nuclear weapons (ATOMIC or HYDROGEN bombs): *countries that have the bomb* **3 a bomb** [sing.] (*informal*) a complete failure: *The musical was a complete bomb on Broadway.* **4** [C] (in football) a long forward throw of the ball **5** [C] a container in which a liquid such as paint or insect poison is kept under pressure and released as a spray or as FOAM: *a bug bomb* (= used for killing insects) ⊃ see also CHERRY BOMB
   IDM **be the bomb** (*informal*) to be very good; to be the best: *Check out the new Web site. It's the bomb!*

• *verb* **1** [T] **~ sth** to attack a place by leaving a bomb there or by dropping bombs from a plane: *Terrorists bombed several army barracks.* ◆ *The city was heavily bombed in the war.* **2** [T, I] **~ (sth)** (*informal*) to fail a test or an exam very badly: *The exam was impossible! I definitely bombed it.* **3** [I] (*informal*) (of a play, show, etc.) to fail very badly: *His latest movie bombed and lost millions of dollars.*
   PHR V **be ‚bombed 'out (of sth)** **1** if you are **bombed out**, your home is destroyed by bombs **2** if a building is **bombed out**, it has been destroyed by bombs

bom·bard /bɑm'bɑrd/ *verb* **1 ~ sb/sth (with sth)** to attack a place by firing large guns at it or dropping bombs on it continuously **2 ~ sb/sth (with sth)** to attack someone with a lot of questions, criticisms, etc. or by giving them too much information: *We have been bombarded with letters of complaint.* ▶ **bom·bard·ment** *noun* [U, C]: *The city came under heavy bombardment.*

bom·bar·dier /‚bɑmbər'dɪr/ *noun* the person on a military plane in the AIR FORCE who is responsible for aiming and dropping bombs

bom·bast /'bɑmbæst/ *noun* [U] (*formal*) words that sound important but have little meaning, used to impress people ▶ **bom·bas·tic** /bɑm'bæstɪk/ *adj.*: *a bombastic speaker* **SYN** HIGH-FLOWN

'bomb bay *noun* a part of an aircraft in which bombs are held and from which they can be dropped

'bomb dis‚posal *noun* [U] the job of removing or exploding bombs in order to make an area safe: *a bomb disposal expert/squad/team*

bombed /bɑmd/ *adj.* [not before noun] (*informal*) extremely drunk

bomb·er /'bɑmər/ *noun* **1** a plane that carries and drops bombs **2** a person who puts a bomb somewhere illegally

'bomber ‚jacket *noun* a short jacket that fits tightly around the waist and fastens with a ZIPPER

bomb·ing /'bɑmɪŋ/ *noun* [C, U] an occasion when a bomb is dropped or left somewhere; the act of doing this: *recent bombings in major cities* ◆ *enemy bombing*

bomb-proof /'bɑmpruf/ *adj.* strong enough to give protection against an attack by a bomb

'bomb scare (also **'bomb threat**) *noun* an occasion when someone says that they have put a bomb somewhere and everyone has to leave the area

bomb·shell /'bɑmʃɛl/ *noun* [usually sing.] (*informal*) **1** an event or a piece of news which is unexpected and usually unpleasant: *The news of his death came as a bombshell.* ◆ *She dropped a bombshell at the meeting and announced that she was leaving.* **2 a blond(e) bombshell** a very attractive woman with blond hair

'bomb site *noun* an area where all the buildings have been destroyed by bombs

bo·na fide /'boʊnə ‚faɪd; 'bɑnə-/ *adj.* [usually before noun] (from *Latin*) genuine, real, or legal; not false: *a bona fide reason* ◆ *Is it a bona fide, reputable organization?*

bo·na fi·des /‚boʊnə 'faɪdiz/ *noun* [pl.] (from *Latin*) evidence that someone is who they say that they are; evidence that someone or something is honest

bo·nan·za /bə'nænzə/ *noun* [sing.] **1** a situation in which people can make a lot of money or be very successful: *a cash bonanza for investors* ◆ *a bonanza year for the computer industry* **2** a situation where there is a large amount of something pleasant: *the usual bonanza of barbecues in the summer*

bon·bon /'bɑnbɑn/ *noun* a piece of candy, especially one with a soft center

bond 🔑 AWL /bɑnd/ *noun, verb*

• *noun*
> STRONG CONNECTION **1** [C] **~ (between A and B)** something that forms a connection between two people or groups, such as a feeling of friendship or shared ideas and experiences: *A bond of friendship had been formed between them.* ◆ *The agreement strengthened the bonds between the two countries.* ◆ *the special bond between mother and child*
> MONEY **2** [C] an agreement by a government or a company to pay you interest on the money you have lent; a document containing this agreement ⊃ see also JUNK BOND, SAVINGS BOND **3** [U] (*law*) a sum of money that is paid as BAIL: *He was released on $5,000 bond.*
> ROPES/CHAINS **4 bonds** [pl.] (*formal*) the ropes or chains keeping someone prisoner; anything that stops you from being free to do what you want: *to release someone from their bonds* ◆ *the bonds of oppression/injustice*
> LEGAL AGREEMENT **5** [C] (*formal*) a legal written agreement or promise: *We entered into a solemn bond.*
> ATTACHMENT **6** [C] the way in which two things are joined together: *a firm bond between the two surfaces*
> CHEMISTRY **7** [C] the way in which atoms are held together in a chemical COMPOUND **IDM** see WORD *n.*

• *verb*
> JOIN FIRMLY **1** [T, I] to join two things firmly together; to join firmly to something else: **~ sth** *This new glue bonds a variety of surfaces in seconds.* ◆ **~ (A) to B** *It cannot be used to bond wood to metal.* ◆ **~ (A and B) together** *The atoms bond together to form a molecule.*
> DEVELOP RELATIONSHIP **2** [I, T] **~ (with sb)** to develop or create a relationship of trust with someone: *Mothers who are depressed sometimes fail to bond with their children.*

bond·age /'bɑndɪdʒ/ *noun* **1** (*old-fashioned* or *formal*) the state of being a SLAVE or prisoner **SYN** SLAVERY: (*figurative*) *women's liberation from the bondage of domestic life* **2** the

| t tea | ţ butter | d did | k cat | g got | tʃ chin | dʒ June | f fall |

practice of being tied with ropes, chains, etc. in order to gain sexual pleasure

bonded 'labor *noun* [U] forced work for an employer for a fixed time without being paid, often as a way of paying a debt: *Many of the immigrants are used as bonded labor.*
▶ **bonded 'laborer** *noun*

bonded 'warehouse *noun* a government building where imported goods are stored until tax has been paid on them

bond·ing AWL /'bɑndɪŋ/ *noun* [U] **1** the process of forming a special relationship with someone or with a group of people: *mother-child bonding* ◆ *male bonding* **2** (*chemistry*) the process of atoms joining together: *hydrogen bonding*

'bond ˌpaper *noun* [U] writing paper of very high quality

bone 🎵 /boʊn/ *noun, verb*
• *noun* **1** [C] any of the hard parts that form the SKELETON of the body of a human or an animal: *He survived the accident with no broken bones.* ◆ *This fish has a lot of bones in it.* **2** [U] the hard substance that bones are made of: *knives with bone handles* **3** -**boned** (in adjectives) having bones of the type mentioned: *He was a physically imposing man, tall and big-boned.* ⊃ see also RAWBONED
  IDM **a bone of contention** a subject that causes disagreement and arguments between people **close to the bone** (*informal*) (of a remark, joke, story, etc.) so honest or clearly expressed that it is likely to cause offense to some people **cut, pare, etc. sth to the bone** to reduce something, such as costs, as much as you possibly can **have a bone to pick with sb** (*informal*) to be angry with someone about something and want to discuss it with them **make no bones about (doing) sth** to be honest and open about something; to not hesitate to do something: *She made no bones about telling him exactly what she thought of him.* **not have a … bone in your body** to have none of the quality mentioned: *She was honest and hard-working, and didn't have an unkind bone in her body.* **throw sb a bone** to give someone a small part of what they want as a way of showing that you want to help them, without offering them the main thing they want **to the bone** affecting you very strongly: *His threats chilled her to the bone.* ⊃ more at BAG *n.*, BARE *adj.*, FEEL *v.*, FINGER *n.*, FLESH *n.*, SKIN *n.*
• *verb* ~ **sth** to take the bones out of fish or meat
  PHR V ˌbone 'up on sth (*informal*) to try to learn about something or to remind yourself of what you already know about it: *She had boned up on the city's history before her visit.*

ˌbone 'china *noun* [U] thin delicate CHINA made of CLAY mixed with crushed bone; cups, plates, etc. made of this

ˌbone 'dry (also **ˌbone-'dry**) *adj.* [not usually before noun] completely dry

bone·head /'boʊnhɛd/ *noun* (*informal*) a stupid person

bone·less /'boʊnləs/ *adj.* (of meat or fish) without any bones: *boneless chicken breasts*

ˈbone ˌmarrow (also **mar·row**) *noun* [U] a soft substance that fills the hollow parts of bones: *a bone-marrow transplant*

bone·meal /'boʊnmil/ *noun* [U] a substance made from crushed animal bones that is used to make soil richer

bon·er /'boʊnər/ *noun* (*informal*) an embarrassing mistake

bon·fire /'bɑnˌfaɪər/ *noun* a large outdoor fire for burning waste or as part of a celebration

bong /bɑŋ; bɔŋ/ *noun* **1** the sound made by a large bell: *the bongs of the Liberty Bell* **2** a long pipe for smoking CANNABIS and other drugs, which passes the smoke through a container of water

bon·go /'bɑŋgoʊ; 'bɔŋ-/ *noun* (*pl.* **bon·gos**) (also **ˈbongo ˌdrum**) a small drum, usually one of a pair, that you play with your fingers

bon·ho·mie /ˌbɑnəˈmi; ˌboʊ-/ *noun* [U] (from *French, formal*) a feeling of cheerful friendship

bonk /bɑŋk/ *noun, verb*
• *noun* the act of hitting someone on the head or of hitting

your head on something
• *verb* ~ **sth** to hit someone lightly on the head or to hit yourself by mistake: *I bonked my head on the doorway.*

bon·kers /'bɑŋkərz/ *adj.* [not before noun] (*informal*) completely crazy and silly: *I'll go bonkers if I have to wait any longer.*

bon mot /ˌbɑn ˈmoʊ; ˌbɑn-/ *noun* (*pl.* **bons mots** /ˌbɑn ˈmoʊz; ˌbɑn-/) (from *French, formal*) a funny and intelligent remark

bon·net /'bɑnət/ *noun* a hat tied with strings under the chin, worn by babies and, especially in the past, by women
  IDM see BEE

bon·sai /'boʊnsaɪ; 'bɑn-; boʊnˈsaɪ; bɑn-/ *noun* (*pl.* **bon·sai**)
1 [C] a small tree that is grown in a pot and prevented from reaching its normal size **2** [U] the Japanese art of growing bonsai

bo·nus /'boʊnəs/ *noun* **1** an extra amount of money that is added to a payment, especially to someone's pay as a reward: *a $100 Christmas bonus* ◆ *performance bonuses* **2** anything pleasant that is extra and more or better than you were expecting: *Being able to walk to work is an added bonus of the new job.*

bon vi·vant /ˌbɑn viˈvɑnt; ˌboʊn-/ *noun* (from *French*) a person who enjoys going out with friends and eating good food, drinking good wine, etc.

bon vo·yage /ˌboʊn vɔɪˈɑʒ; ˌbɑn-/ *exclamation* (from *French*) said to someone who is leaving on a journey, to wish them a good journey

bon·y /'boʊni/ *adj.* (**bon·i·er, bon·i·est**) **1** (of a person or part of the body) very thin so that the bones can be seen under the skin **2** (of fish) full of small bones **3** consisting of or like bone

boo /bu/ *exclamation, noun, verb*
• *exclamation, noun* **1** a sound that people make to show that they do not like an actor, speaker, etc.: *"Boo!" they shouted. "Get off the stage!"* ◆ *The speech was greeted with loud boos from the audience.* **2** people shout **Boo!** when they want to surprise or frighten someone IDM see SAY *v.*
• *verb* [I, T] to show that you do not like a person, performance, idea, etc. by shouting **Boo**: *The audience booed as she started her speech.* ◆ ~ **sb** *He was booed off the stage.*

boob /bub/ *noun* **1** (*slang*) a woman's breast **2** (*informal*) a stupid or silly person

boo-boo *noun* **1** (*informal*) a stupid mistake: *I think I made a boo-boo.* **2** a child's word for a small cut or injury

ˈboob tube *noun* (also **tube**) (*informal, disapproving*) the television

boo·by /'bubi/ *noun* (*pl.* **boo·bies**) **1** (*informal*) a stupid person: *Don't be such a booby!* **2** [usually pl.] (*informal*) a word for a woman's breast, used especially by children **3** a large tropical bird with brightly colored feet that lives near the ocean

ˈbooby ˌprize *noun* a prize that is given as a joke to the person who is last in a competition

ˈbooby ˌtrap *noun* **1** a hidden bomb that explodes when the object that it is connected to is touched **2** a hidden device that is meant as a joke to surprise someone, for example an object placed above a door so that it will fall on the first person who opens the door

ˈbooby-ˌtrap *verb* (**-pp-**) ~ **sth** to place a booby trap in or on something

boog·er /'bʊgər/ *noun* (*informal*) a piece of dried MUCUS from inside your nose

boo·gey·man /'bʊgiˌmæn/ *noun* = BOGEYMAN

boog·ie /'bʊgi/ *noun, verb*
• *noun* (also **boog·ie-woog·ie** /ˌbʊgi ˈwʊgi/) [U] a type of blues music played on the piano, with a fast strong rhythm
• *verb* [I] (*informal*) **1** to dance to fast pop music **2** to move or leave a place quickly: *Boogie on down the road.* ◆ *We'd better boogie on out of here before it gets too late.*

boogie board *noun* a small board used for riding on waves in a lying position

boo·hoo /ˌbuˈhu/ *exclamation* used in written English to show the sound of someone crying

book ⚘ /bʊk/ *noun, verb*

● *noun*
> PRINTED WORK **1** [C] a set of printed pages that are fastened inside a cover so that you can turn them and read them: *a pile of books* ◆ *hardcover/paperback books* **2** [C] a written work published in printed or electronic form: *a book by Stephen King* ◆ *a book about/on wildlife* ◆ *reference/children's/library books* ⊃ collocations at LITERATURE
> FOR WRITING IN **3** [C] a set of sheets of paper that are fastened together inside a cover and used for writing in: *an exercise book* ◆ *a notebook* ⊃ see also ADDRESS BOOK
> OF STAMPS/TICKETS/MATCHES, ETC. **4** [C] a set of things that are fastened together like a book: *a book of stamps/tickets* ◆ *a checkbook*
> ACCOUNTS **5 books** [pl.] the written records of the financial affairs of a business **SYN** ACCOUNTS: *to do the books* (= to check the accounts)
> SECTION OF BIBLE, ETC. **6** [C] a section of a large written work: *the books of the Bible*
> **IDM** **be in sb's good/bad books** (*informal*) used to say that someone is pleased/annoyed with you: *I'm in her good books at the moment because I cleaned up the kitchen.* **bring sb to book (for sth)** (*formal*) to punish someone for doing something wrong and make them explain their behavior **by the book** following rules and instructions in a very strict way: *She always does everything by the book.* **in my book** (*informal*) used when you are giving your opinion: *That's cheating in my book.* **(be) on sb's books** (to be) on an organization's list, for example of people who are available for a particular type of work: *We have very few nurses on our books at the moment.* ◆ *Most of the houses on our books are north of the city.* **on the books** contained in a book of laws or records: *Many discriminatory laws are still on the books.* ◆ *He's got the longest pitching career on the books.* **take a page/leaf from/out of sb's book** to copy someone's behavior and do things in the same way that they do, because they are successful **SYN** EMULATE **throw the book at sb** (*informal*) to punish someone who has committed an offense as severely as possible ⊃ more at CLOSE¹ *v.*, CLOSED, COOK *v.*, HISTORY, JUDGE *v.*, OPEN *adj.*, READ *v.*, TRICK *n.*

● *verb* **1** [I, T] to arrange to have or use something on a particular date in the future; to buy a ticket in advance: *Book early to avoid disappointment.* ◆ *~ sth She booked a flight to Chicago.* ◆ *The performance is fully booked* (= there are no more tickets available). ◆ *I'm sorry—we're booked solid.* **HELP** Book is not used if you do not have to pay in advance; instead use **make a reservation**. ⊃ compare RESERVE **2** [T] to arrange for someone to have a seat on a plane, etc.: *~ sb + adv./prep. I booked you on the 10 o'clock flight.* ◆ *~ sb sth (+ adv./prep.) I booked you a room at the Plaza Hotel.* **3** [T] *~ sb/sth (for sth)* to arrange for a singer, etc. to perform on a particular date: *We booked a band for the wedding reception.* **4** [T] *~ sb (for sth)* (*informal*) to write down someone's name and address because they have committed a crime or an offense: *He was booked for possession of cocaine.*
IDM **be booked up 1** if a restaurant, etc. is **booked up**, it is full and there are no places available: *That new restaurant is booked up for weeks.* **2** if a person is **booked up**, they are very busy and not available to do anything else **PHR V** **book sb 'in/'into sth** to arrange for someone to have a room at a hotel, etc.

book·a·ble /ˈbʊkəbl/ *adj.* if a crime is a **bookable** offense, the person responsible can be arrested

book·bind·er /ˈbʊkˌbaɪndər/ *noun* a person whose job is fastening pages of books together and putting covers on them ▶ **book·bind·ing** *noun* [U]

book·case /ˈbʊkkeɪs/ *noun* a piece of furniture with shelves for keeping books on

book club *noun* **1** (also **book group**) a group of people who meet together regularly to discuss a book they have all read **2** an organization that sells books cheaply to its members

book·cros·sing /ˈbʊkˌkrɔsɪŋ/ *noun* [U] the practice of leaving a book in a public place so that another person can find it, read it, and then leave it where someone else will find it

book·end /ˈbʊkɛnd/ *noun* [usually pl.] one of a pair of objects used to keep a row of books standing up

book group *noun* = BOOK CLUB (1)

book·ie /ˈbʊki/ *noun* (*informal*) = BOOKMAKER

book·ing /ˈbʊkɪŋ/ *noun* **1** [C, U] an arrangement that you make in advance to buy a ticket to travel somewhere, reserve a room, etc.: *Can I make a booking for Friday?* ◆ *Online booking is recommended.* ◆ *No advance booking is necessary.* ⊃ compare RESERVATION **2** [C] an arrangement for someone to perform at a theater, in a concert, etc.

book·ish /ˈbʊkɪʃ/ *adj.* (sometimes *disapproving*) interested in reading and studying, rather than in more active or practical things

book·keep·er /ˈbʊkˌkipər/ *noun* a person whose job is to keep an accurate record of the accounts of a business ▶ **book·keep·ing** *noun* [U]

book learning *noun* [U] knowledge from books or study rather than from experience

book·let /ˈbʊklət/ *noun* a small, thin book with a paper cover that contains information about a particular subject

book·mak·er /ˈbʊkˌmeɪkər/ (also *informal* **book·ie**) *noun* a person whose job is to take bets on the result of horse races, etc. and pay out money to people who win ▶ **book·mak·ing** *noun* [U]

book·mark /ˈbʊkmɑrk/ *noun* **1** a strip of paper, etc. that you put between the pages of a book when you finish reading so that you can easily find the place again **2** (*computing*) a record of the address of a file, a page on the Internet, etc. that enables you to find it quickly **SYN** FAVORITE ▶ **book·mark** *verb*: *~ sth Do you want to bookmark this site?*

book·mo·bile /ˈbʊkmoʊˌbil/ *noun* a truck that contains a library and travels from place to place so that people in different places can borrow books

book·plate /ˈbʊkpleɪt/ *noun* a decorative piece of paper that is stuck in a book to show the name of the person who owns it

book·sell·er /ˈbʊkˌsɛlər/ *noun* a person whose job is selling books

book·shelf /ˈbʊkʃɛlf/ *noun* (*pl.* **book·shelves** /-ˌʃɛlvz/) a shelf that you keep books on

book·smart *adj.* (becoming *old-fashioned*, often *disapproving*) having a lot of academic knowledge learned from books and studying, but not necessarily knowing much about people and living in the real world: *He's book-smart but he's got no common sense.* ⊃ compare STREET-SMART

book·stall /ˈbʊkstɔl/ *noun* a small store that is open at the front, where you can buy books

book·store /ˈbʊkstɔr/ (also **book·shop** /ˈbʊkʃɑp/) *noun* a store that sells books

book·worm /ˈbʊkwɜrm/ *noun* a person who likes reading very much

Bool·e·an /ˈbuliən/ *adj.* (*mathematics, computing*) connected with a system, used especially in COMPUTING and ELECTRONICS, that uses only the numbers 1 (to show something is true) and 0 (to show something is false)

Boolean operator *noun* (*computing*) a symbol or word such as "or" or "and," used in computer programs and searches to show what is or is not included

boom /bum/ *noun, verb*
● *noun*
> IN BUSINESS/ECONOMY **1** a sudden increase in trade and

economic activity; a period of wealth and success: *Living standards improved rapidly during the postwar boom.* ♦ **~ in sth** *a boom in car sales* ♦ *a* **boom year** *(for trade, exports, etc.)* ♦ *a* **property/housing boom** ♦ *a chaotic period of* **boom and bust** ➲ collocations at ECONOMY ➲ compare SLUMP ➲ see also BABY BOOM

> POPULAR PERIOD **2** [usually sing.] a period when something such as a sport or a type of music suddenly becomes very popular and successful: *The only way to satisfy the golf boom was to build more courses.*
> ON BOAT **3** a long pole that the bottom of a sail is attached to and that you move to change the position of the sail ➲ picture at BOAT
> SOUND **4** [usually sing.] a loud, deep sound: *the distant boom of the guns* ➲ see also SONIC BOOM
> IN RIVER/HARBOR **5** a floating barrier that is placed across a river or the entrance to a HARBOR to prevent ships or other objects from coming in or going out
> FOR MICROPHONE **6** a long pole that carries a MICROPHONE or other equipment

● *verb*
> MAKE LOUD SOUND **1** [I] to make a loud, deep sound: *Outside, thunder boomed and crashed.* **2** [T, I] to say something in a loud, deep voice: + **speech** *"Get out of my sight!" he boomed.* ♦ **~ (out)** *A voice boomed out from the darkness.* ♦ *He had a* **booming** *voice.*
> OF BUSINESS/ECONOMY **3** [I] to have a period of rapid growth; to become bigger, more successful, etc.: *By the 1980s, the computer industry was booming.* ♦ *Business is booming!*

ˈboom box *noun* (*informal*) a large radio and CD player that can be carried around, especially to play loud music in public

boom·er /ˈbuːmər/ *noun* **1** = BABY BOOMER **2** a large male KANGAROO

boo·mer·ang /ˈbuːməˌræŋ/ *noun, verb*

boomerang

● *noun* a curved, flat piece of wood that you throw and that can fly in a circle and come back to you. Boomerangs were first used by Australian Aborigines as weapons when they were hunting.

● *verb* [I] if a plan **boomerangs** on someone, it hurts them instead of the person it was intended to hurt **SYN** BACKFIRE

ˈboomerang ˌkid *noun* (*informal*) an adult child who returns home to live with their parents after being away for some time

ˈboom town (also **boom·town** /ˈbuːmtaʊn/) *noun* a town that has become rich and successful because trade and industry has developed there

boon /buːn/ *noun* [usually sing.] **~ (to/for sb)** something that is very helpful and makes life easier for you: *The new software will prove a boon to Internet users.*

ˌboon comˈpanion *noun* (*literary*) a very good friend

boon·docks /ˈbuːndɑks/ (also **boon·ies** /ˈbuːniz/) *noun* [pl.] usually **the boondocks** (*informal, disapproving*) an area far away from cities or towns

boon·dog·gle /ˈbuːnˌdɑgl; -ˌdɔgl/ *noun* (*informal*) a piece of work that is unnecessary and that wastes time and/or money

boor /bʊr/ *noun* (*old-fashioned*) a rude, unpleasant person

boor·ish /ˈbʊrɪʃ/ *adj.* (of people and their behavior) very unpleasant and rude

boost /buːst/ *verb, noun*
● *verb* **1 ~ sth** to make something increase, or become better or more successful: *to boost exports/profits* ♦ *The movie helped boost her screen career.* ♦ *to boost someone's confidence/morale* ♦ *Getting that job really boosted his ego* (= made him feel more confident). **2 ~ sth** (*informal, becoming old-fashioned*) to steal something
● *noun* [usually sing.] **1** something that helps or encourages

someone or something: *a great/tremendous/welcome boost* ♦ *The tax cuts will give a much-needed boost to the economy.* ♦ *Winning the competition was a wonderful boost to the team's morale.* **2** an increase in something: *a boost in car sales* **3** an increase in power in an engine or a piece of electrical equipment **4** an act of pushing someone up from behind: *He gave her a boost over the fence.*

boost·er /ˈbuːstər/ *noun* **1** a thing that helps, encourages, or improves someone or something: *a morale/confidence booster* **2** an extra small amount of a drug that is given to increase the effect of one given earlier, for example to protect you from a disease for longer: *a tetanus booster* **3** a person who gives their support to someone or something, especially in politics: *a meeting of Republican boosters* **4** (also ˈbooster rocket) a ROCKET that gives a SPACECRAFT extra power when it leaves the earth, or that makes a MISSILE go further **5** a device that gives extra power to a piece of electrical equipment

ˈbooster ˌseat *noun* a seat that you put on a car seat, or on a chair at a table, so that a small child can sit higher

boot 🔧 /buːt/ *noun, verb*

● *noun* **1** a strong shoe that covers the foot and ankle, and often the lower parts of the leg: *hiking boots* ♦ *a pair of black leather boots* ➲ picture at SHOE ➲ see also COWBOY BOOT, DESERT BOOT, RUBBER BOOT **2** [usually sing.] (*informal*) a quick, hard kick: *He gave the ball a tremendous boot.* **3** = DENVER BOOT

IDM **be given the boot**| **get the boot** (*informal*) to be told that you must leave your job or that a relationship you are having with someone is over **to boot** (*old-fashioned or humorous*) used to add a comment to something that you have said: *He was a vegetarian, and a fussy one to boot.* ➲ more at BIG *adj.*, LICK *v.*

● *verb* **1** [T] **~ sth + adv./prep.** to kick someone or something hard with your foot: *He booted the ball clear across the field.* **2** [I, T] **~ (sth) (up)** (*computing*) to prepare a computer for use by loading its OPERATING SYSTEM; to be prepared in this way **3** [T] **be/get booted** (*informal*) if you or your car is **booted**, a piece of equipment is fixed to the car's wheel so that you cannot drive it away, usually because the car is illegally parked ➲ see also DENVER BOOT
PHRV **ˌboot sb↔ˈout (of sth)** (*informal*) to force someone to leave a place or job **SYN** THROW OUT

ˈboot camp *noun* **1** a training camp for new members of the armed forces, where they have to work hard **2** a type of prison for young criminals, where there is strict discipline

ˈboot-cut *adj.* [usually before noun] **boot-cut** pants are slightly wider at the bottom of the legs where the material goes over the feet or shoes

booth /buːθ/ *noun* **1** a small, closed place where you can do something privately, for example make a telephone call, or vote: *a phone booth* ♦ *a polling/voting booth* ➲ see also PHOTO BOOTH, TOLLBOOTH **2** a small tent or temporary structure at a market, an exhibition, or a fair, where you can buy things, get information, or watch something **3** a place to sit in a restaurant that consists of two long seats with a table between them

ˌBoot ˈHill *noun* [U] (*informal, humorous*) (in the Wild West) a place where people are buried

boot·ie (also **boot·ee**) *noun* **1** /ˈbuːti/ a baby's sock, worn instead of shoes: *a pair of booties* **2** /ˈbuːti; buˈti/ a woman's short boot

boot·lace /ˈbuːtleɪs/ *noun* [usually pl.] a long, thin piece of leather or string used to fasten boots or shoes

boot·leg /ˈbuːtlɛg/ *adj., verb*
● *adj.* [only before noun] made and sold illegally: *a bootleg CD* (= for example, one recorded illegally at a concert) ➲ see also PIRATE ▶ **boot·leg** *noun*: *a bootleg of the concert*
● *verb* (-gg-) **~ sth** to make or sell goods, especially alcohol, illegally ▶ **boot·leg·ging** *noun* [U]

boot·lick·er /ˈbuːtˌlɪkər/ *noun* (*informal, disapproving*) a person who is too friendly to someone in authority and is always ready to do what they want ▶ **boot·lick·ing** *noun* [U]

boot·strap /ˈbutstræp/ *noun*
IDM **pull yourself up by your (own) bootstraps** (*informal*) to improve your situation yourself, without help from other people

boo·ty /ˈbuti/ (*pl.* **boo·ties**) *noun* **1** [U] valuable things that are stolen, especially by soldiers in a time of war **SYN** LOOT **2** [U] (*informal*) valuable things that someone wins, buys, or obtains: *When we got home from shopping, we laid all our booty out on the floor.* **3** [C] (*informal*) the part of the body that you sit on **SYN** BUTTOCKS: *to shake your booty* (= to dance with great energy)

boo·ty·li·cious /ˌbutiˈlɪʃəs/ *adj.* (*informal*) sexually attractive

booze /buz/ *noun, verb*
• *noun* [U] (*informal*) alcoholic drinks
• *verb* [I] (*informal*) (usually used in the progressive tenses) to drink alcohol, especially in large quantities: *He's out boozing with his buddies.*

ˈbooze cruise *noun* (*informal, humorous*) a social occasion when people travel on a ship or boat and enjoy themselves by drinking alcohol, eating, and dancing

booz·er /ˈbuzər/ *noun* (*informal*) a person who drinks a lot of alcohol

booz·y /ˈbuzi/ *adj.* (*informal*) liking to drink a lot of alcohol; involving a lot of alcoholic drink: *one of my boozy friends* ◆ *a boozy lunch*

bop /bɑp/ *noun, verb*
• *noun* **1** [C] (*informal*) a gentle hit: *Mike gave Jimmy a bop on the head.* **2** [U] = BEBOP
• *verb* (-pp-) **1** [T] **~ sb** to hit someone lightly **2** [I] (*informal*) to dance to pop music

bor·age /ˈbɔrɪdʒ; ˈbɑr-/ *noun* [U] a Mediterranean plant with blue flowers that are shaped like stars, and leaves covered with small hairs. Borage leaves are eaten raw as a salad vegetable.

bo·rax /ˈbɔræks/ *noun* [U] a white mineral, usually in powder form, used in making glass and for cleaning things

bor·del·lo /bɔrˈdɛloʊ/ *noun* (*pl.* **bor·del·los**) = BROTHEL

bor·der 🔑 /ˈbɔrdər/ *noun, verb*
• *noun* [C] **1** the line that divides two countries or areas; the land near this line: *a national park on the border between Kenya and Tanzania* ◆ *Denmark's border with Germany* ◆ *in Vermont, near the Canadian border* ◆ *Nevada's northern border* ◆ *to cross the border* ◆ *to flee across/over the border* ◆ *border guards/controls* ◆ *a border dispute/incident* ◆ *a border town/state* ➲ collocations at INTERNATIONAL **2** a strip around the edge of something such as a picture or a piece of cloth: *a pillowcase with a lace border* ➲ picture at EDGE **3** (in a garden) a strip of soil that is planted with flowers, along the edge of the grass **4** the separation or distance between one thing or person and another: *It is difficult to define the border between love and friendship.*
• *verb* **1 ~ sth** (of a country or an area) to share a border with another country or area: *the states bordering the Gulf of Mexico* **2 ~ sth** to form a line along or around the edge of something: *Meadows bordered the path to the woods.* ◆ *The large garden is bordered by a stream.*
PHR V **ˈborder on sth 1** to come very close to being something, especially a strong or unpleasant emotion or quality: *She felt an anxiety bordering on hysteria.* **2** to be next to something: *areas bordering on the Pacific*

THESAURUS

border

boundary ◆ **frontier** ◆ **barrier**

These are all words for a line that marks the edge of something and separates it from other areas or things.
border the line that separates two countries or areas;

---

the land near this line: *a national park on the border between Montana and Wyoming*

boundary a line that marks the edges of an area of land and separates it from other areas: *The fence marked the boundary between my property and hers.*

BORDER OR BOUNDARY?

The point where you cross from one country to another is usually called the **border**. The line on a map that shows the border of a country can be called the **boundary**, but "boundary" is not used when you cross from one country to another: *After the war, the national boundaries were redrawn.* ◆ ~~Thousands of immigrants cross the boundary every day.~~ **Boundary** can also be a physical line between two places, for example between property belonging to two different people, marked by a fence or wall: *the boundary fence/wall between the properties*

frontier the border between two countries or areas; a line that marks the beginning of an unexplored or dangerous area: *the frontier between Guatemala and Mexico* ◆ *The Ingalls family crossed the frontier in a covered wagon.*

barrier something that exists between two places and prevents easy movement between them: *The mountains form a natural barrier between the ocean and the desert.*

PATTERNS
■ **across/along/on/over** a/the border/boundary/frontier/barrier
■ **at** the boundary/frontier/barrier
■ the border/boundary/frontier **with** a place
■ the **northern/southern/eastern/western** border/boundary/frontier
■ a **national/common/disputed** border/boundary/frontier

ˈBorder ˌcollie *noun* a medium-sized black and white dog, often used as a SHEEPDOG

bord·er·land /ˈbɔrdərˌlænd/ *noun* **1** [C] an area of land close to a border between two countries **2** [sing.] an area between two qualities, ideas, or subjects that has features of both but is not clearly one or the other: *the murky borderland between history and myth*

bord·er·line /ˈbɔrdərˌlaɪn/ *adj., noun*
• *adj.* not clearly belonging to a particular condition or group; not clearly acceptable: *In borderline cases, teachers will make the final decision, based on the student's previous work.* ◆ *a borderline pass/fail on an exam*
• *noun* the division between two qualities or conditions: *This biography sometimes crosses the borderline between fact and fiction.*

bore 🔑 /bɔr/ *verb, noun* ➲ see also BEAR *v.*
• *verb* **1** [T] to make someone feel bored, especially by talking too much: **~ sb** *I'm not boring you, am I?* ◆ **~ sb with sth** *Has he been boring you with his stories about his trip?* **2** [I, T] to make a long deep hole with a tool or by digging: **~ into/through sth** *The drill is strong enough to bore through solid rock.* ◆ **~ sth (in/through sth)** *to bore a hole in something* **3** [I] **~ into sb/sth** (of eyes) to stare in a way that makes someone feel uncomfortable: *His blue eyes seemed to bore into her.*
• *noun* **1** [C] a person who is very boring, usually because they talk too much **2** [sing.] a situation or thing that is boring or that annoys you: *It's such a bore having to stay late tonight.* **3** [C] the hollow inside of a tube, such as a pipe or a gun; the width of the hole **SYN** GAUGE: *a tube with a wide/narrow bore* ◆ *a twelve-bore shotgun* **4** [C] a strong, high wave that rushes along a river from the sea at particular times of the year **5** [C] (also **ˈbore-hole**) a deep hole made in the ground, especially to find water or oil

ʌ **cup**   ə **about**   eɪ **say**   aɪ **five**   ɔɪ **boy**   aʊ **now**   oʊ **go**   ər **bird**

bo·re·al /ˈbɔːriəl/ adj. relating to the climate zone south of the Arctic: northern boreal forests

bored /bɔːd/ adj.
feeling tired and impatient because you have lost interest in someone or something or because you have nothing to do: There was a bored expression on her face. ◆ ~ **with sb/sth** | ~ **with doing sth** The children quickly **got bored** with staying indoors.
IDM bored stiff | bored to death/tears | bored out of your mind extremely bored

bore·dom /ˈbɔːdəm/ noun [U] the state of feeling bored; the quality of being very boring: I started to eat too much out of sheer boredom. ◆ Television helps to relieve the boredom of long winter evenings.

bore·hole /ˈbɔːhəʊl/ noun = BORE n. (5)

bor·ing /ˈbɔːrɪŋ/ adj.
not interesting; making you feel tired and impatient: a boring man ◆ a boring job/book/evening ▶ **bor·ing·ly** adv.: boringly normal

---

THESAURUS

boring

dull • tedious

These words all describe a subject, activity, person, or place that is not interesting or exciting.

boring not interesting; making you feel tired and impatient: He's such a boring man! ◆ She found her job very boring.

dull not interesting or exciting: Life in a small town can be extremely dull.

tedious lasting or taking too long and not interesting, so that you feel bored and impatient: The journey soon became tedious.

PATTERNS
- to be boring/dull/tedious **for** sb
- boring/dull/tedious **subjects/books**
- boring/dull/tedious **jobs/work/games**
- a boring/dull **place/man/woman/person**

---

born /bɔːn/ verb, adj.
● **verb be born** (used only in the passive, without by) **1** (abbr. **b.**) to come out of your mother's body at the beginning of your life: I was born in 1976. ◆ She was born with a weak heart. ◆ ~ **into sth** She was born into a very musical family. ◆ ~ **to sb** He was born to German parents. ◆ + **adj.** Her brother was **born blind** (= was blind when he was born). ◆ + **noun** John Wayne was born Marion Michael Morrison (= that was his name at birth). ⊃ collocations at AGE **2** (of an idea, an organization, a feeling, etc.) to start to exist: the city where the protest movement was born ◆ ~ **(out) of sth** She acted with a courage born (out) of desperation. **3** –**born** (in compounds) born in the order, way, place, etc. mentioned: firstborn ◆ nobly-born ◆ French-born ⊃ see also NEWBORN, STILLBORN
IDM be born to be/do sth to have something as your DESTINY (= what is certain to happen to you) from birth: He was born to be a great composer. **born and bred** born and having grown up in a particular place with a particular background and education: He was born and bred in Boston. ◆ I'm a Chicagoan, born and bred. **born with a silver spoon in your mouth** (saying) having rich parents **not be born yesterday** (informal) used to say that you are not stupid enough to believe what someone is telling you: Oh yeah? I wasn't born yesterday, you know. **there's one born every minute** (saying) used to say that someone is very stupid ⊃ more at MANNER, WAY n.
● **adj.** [only before noun] having a natural ability or skill for a particular activity or job: a born athlete/writer/leader ◆ a born loser (= a person who always loses or is unsuccessful)
IDM in all my born days (old-fashioned, informal) used when you are very surprised at something you have never heard or seen before: I've never heard such nonsense in all my born days.

born-a·gain adj. [usually before noun] having found a new, strong belief in a particular religion (especially EVANGELICAL Christianity) or idea, and wanting other people to have the same belief: a born-again Christian ◆ a born-again vegetarian

borne /bɔːn/ **1** pp of BEAR **2** –**borne** (in adjectives) carried by: waterborne diseases

bo·ron /ˈbɔːrɒn/ noun [U] (symb. **B**) a chemical element. Boron is a solid substance used in making steel ALLOYS and parts for nuclear REACTORS.

bor·ough /ˈbʌrə/ noun a town or part of a city that has its own local government: The Bronx is one of the five boroughs of New York. ◆ the borough president

bor·row /ˈbɒrəʊ; ˈbɔːr-/ verb
1 [T] to take and use something that belongs to someone else, and return it to them at a later time: ~ **sth** Can I borrow your umbrella? ◆ ~ **sth from sb/sth** Members can borrow up to ten books from the library at any one time. ⊃ compare LEND
2 [T, I] to take money from a person or bank and agree to pay it back to them at a later time: ~ **sth (from sb/sth)** She borrowed $2,000 from her parents. ◆ ~ **(from sb/sth)** I don't like to borrow from friends. ⊃ compare LEND, LOAN v. (1)
3 [I, T] to take words, ideas, etc. from another language, person, etc. and use them, as your own: ~ **(from sb/sth)** The author borrows heavily from Henry James. ◆ ~ **sth (from sb/sth)** Some musical terms are borrowed from Italian.
IDM be (living) on borrowed time **1** to still be alive after the time when you were expected to die **2** to be doing something that other people are likely to stop you from doing soon

---

WHICH WORD?

borrow • lend

- These two words are often confused. You **borrow** something from someone else, while they **lend** it to you: Can I borrow your pen? ◆ Can I borrow a pen from you? ◆ Here, I'll lend you my pen.

---

bor·row·er /ˈbɒrəʊə(r); ˈbɔːr-/ noun a person or an organization that borrows money, especially from a bank ⊃ compare LENDER

bor·row·ing /ˈbɒrəʊɪŋ; ˈbɔːr-/ noun **1** [C, U] the money that a company, an organization, or a person borrows; the act of borrowing money: an attempt to reduce bank borrowing ◆ High interest rates help to keep borrowing down. ◆ collocations at ECONOMY **2** [C] a word, a phrase, or an idea that someone has taken from another person's work or from another language and used in their own

borscht /bɔːʃt/ noun [U] a Russian or Polish soup made from BEETS (= a dark red root vegetable)

bor·zoi /ˈbɔːzɔɪ/ noun a large Russian dog with soft white hair

bos·om /ˈbʊzəm/ noun **1** [C] a woman's chest or breasts: her ample bosom ◆ She pressed him to her bosom. **2** [C] the part of a piece of clothing that covers a woman's bosom: a rose pinned to her bosom **3** the ~ of sth [sing.] a situation in which you are with people who love and protect you: to live in the bosom of your family

bosom buddy (also bosom friend) noun a very close friend

bos·om·y /ˈbʊzəmi/ adj. (old-fashioned, informal) (of a woman) having large breasts

boss /bɒs/ noun, verb, adj.
● **noun 1** a person who is in charge of other people at work and tells them what to do: I'll ask my boss if I can have the day off. ◆ I like being my own boss (= working for myself and making my own decisions). ◆ Who's the boss (= who's in control) in this house? **2** (informal) a person who is in charge

---

of a large organization: *the new boss at IBM* ◆ *Hospital bosses protested at the decision.* **IDM** see SHOW v.

- **verb** ~ **sb (around)** to tell someone what to do in an aggressive and/or annoying way: *I'm sick of you bossing me around!*
- **adj.** (*slang*) very good

bos·sa no·va /ˌbasə ˈnoʊvə/ *noun* [U, C] a style of Brazilian music popular in the 1960s

boss·y /ˈbɔsi/ *adj.* (*disapproving*) (**boss·i·er**, **boss·i·est**) always telling people what to do ▶ **boss·i·ly** /-səli/ *adv.* **boss·i·ness** /-sinəs/ *noun* [U]

Bos·ton baked beans /ˌbɔstən beɪkt ˈbinz/ *noun* [pl.] = BAKED BEANS

bo·sun (also **bo'sun**, **boat·swain**) /ˈboʊsn/ *noun* an officer on a ship whose job is to take care of the equipment and the people who work on the ship

bot /bat/ *noun* (*computing*) a computer program that performs a particular task again and again many times

bo·tan·i·cal /bəˈtænɪkl/ *adj.* connected with the science of botany

bo,tanical ˈgarden (also **bo,tanic ˈgarden**) *noun* [usually pl.] a park where plants, trees, and flowers are grown for scientific study

bot·a·nist /ˈbatn·ɪst/ *noun* a scientist who studies botany

bot·a·ny /ˈbatn·i/ *noun* [U] the scientific study of plants and their structure ⊃ compare BIOLOGY, ZOOLOGY

botch /batʃ/ *verb*, *noun*
- **verb** ~ **sth (up)** (*informal*) to spoil something by doing it badly: *He completely botched up the interview.* ◆ *She has the ability to take on any task without botching it.*
- **noun** (also **ˈbotch-up**) (*informal*) a piece of work or a job that has been done badly

both 🔑 /boʊθ/ *det.*, *pron.*
1 used with plural nouns to mean "the two" or "the one as well as the other": *Both women were French.* ◆ *Both the women were French.* ◆ *Both of the women were French.* ◆ *I talked to the women. Both of them were French/They were both French.* ◆ *I liked them both.* ◆ *We were both tired.* ◆ *Both of us were tired.* ◆ *We have both seen the movie.* ◆ *I have two sisters. Both of them live in Seattle/They both live in Seattle.* ◆ *Both (my) sisters live in Seattle.* **2 both... and...** not only... but also...: *Both his mother and his father will be there.* ◆ *For this job, you will need a good knowledge of both Italian and Spanish.* ⊃ language bank at SIMILARLY

both·er 🔑 /ˈbaðər/ *verb*, *noun*
- **verb 1** [I, T] (often used in negative sentences and questions) to spend time and/or energy doing something: *"Should I wait?" "No, don't bother."* ◆ *I don't know why I bother! Nobody ever listens!* ◆ ~ **with/about sth** *It's not worth bothering with* (= using) *an umbrella—the car's just outside.* ◆ *I don't know why you bother with that crowd* (= why you spend time with them). ◆ ~ **to do sth** *He didn't even bother to let me know he was coming.* ◆ ~ **doing sth** *Why bother asking if you're not really interested?* **2** [T] to annoy, worry, or upset someone; to cause someone trouble or pain: ~ **sb** *The thing that bothers me is...* ◆ *That sprained ankle is still bothering her* (= hurting). ◆ *"I'm sorry he was so rude to you." "It doesn't bother me."* ◆ ~ **sb with sth** *I don't want to bother him with my problems at the moment.* ◆ ~ **sb about sth** *You don't sound too bothered about it.* ◆ ~ **sb that...** *Does it bother you that she earns more than you?* ◆ **it bothers sb to do sth** *It bothers me to think of her alone in that big house.* **3** [T] to interrupt someone; to talk to someone when they do not want to talk to you: ~ **sb** *Stop bothering me when I'm working.* ◆ *Let me know if he bothers you again.* ◆ *Sorry to bother you, but there's a call for you on line two.*
IDM can't be bothered (to do sth) used to say that you do not want to spend time and/or energy doing something: *I should really do some work this weekend, but I can't be bothered.* ◆ *All this happened because you couldn't be bothered to give me the message.* ⊃ more at HOT

- **noun 1** [U] trouble or difficulty: *Don't go to the bother of cleaning up on my account* (= don't make the effort to do it). ◆ *"Thanks for your help!" "It's no bother."* ◆ *Call them and save yourself the bother of going out.* ◆ *Repairing those old shoes is more bother than it's worth.* **2 a bother** [sing.] an annoying situation, thing, or person **SYN** NUISANCE: *I hope I haven't been a bother.*

both·er·some /ˈbaðərsəm/ *adj.* (*old-fashioned*) causing trouble or difficulty **SYN** ANNOYING

bot·net /ˈbatnɛt/ *noun* (*computing*) a group of computers that are controlled by MALWARE (= software such as a virus that the users do not know about or want)

Bo·tox™ /ˈboʊtaks/ *noun* [U] a substance that makes muscles relax. It is sometimes INJECTED into the skin around someone's eyes to remove lines and make the skin look younger. ▶ **Bo·tox** *verb* [usually passive]: ~ **sb/sth** *Do you think she's been Botoxed?*

bot·tle 🔑 /ˈbatl/ *noun*, *verb*
- **noun 1** [C] a glass or plastic container, usually round, with straight sides and a narrow neck, used especially for storing liquids: *a wine/beer/soda bottle* ◆ *Put the top back on the bottle.* ⊃ picture at PACKAGING **2** [C] (also **bot·tle·ful** /ˈbatlfʊl/) the amount contained in a bottle: *He drank a whole bottle of wine.* **3 the bottle** [sing.] (*informal*) alcoholic drink: *After his wife died, he really hit the bottle* (= started drinking heavily). **4** [C, usually sing.] a bottle used to give milk to a baby; the milk from such a bottle (used instead of mother's milk): *It's time for her bottle.*
- **verb** ~ **sth** to put a liquid into a bottle: *The wines are bottled after three years.* ▶ **bot·tled** *adj.*: *bottled beer/water* ◆ *bottled gas* (= sold in metal containers for use in heating and cooking) **PHR V bottle sth⟷up** to not allow other people to see that you are unhappy, angry, etc., especially when this happens over a long period of time: *Try not to bottle up your emotions.*

ˌbottle ˈblonde (also **ˌbottle ˈblond**) *adj.* (*disapproving*) (of hair) artificially colored blond ▶ **ˌbottle ˈblonde** *noun*

ˈbottle-feed *verb* [T, I] ~ **(sb)** to feed a baby with artificial milk from a bottle ⊃ compare BREASTFEED

ˌbottle-ˈgreen *adj.* dark green in color: *a bottle-green coat* ▶ **ˌbottle ˈgreen** *noun* [U]

bot·tle·neck /ˈbatlnɛk/ *noun* **1** a narrow or busy section of road where the traffic often gets slower and stops **2** anything that delays development or progress, particularly in business or industry

ˈbottle ˌopener *noun* a small tool for opening bottles with metal tops, for example beer bottles ⊃ picture at KITCHEN

bot·tom 🔑 /ˈbatəm/ *noun*, *adj.*, *verb*
- **noun**
⊳LOWEST PART **1** [C, usually sing.] ~ **(of sth)** the lowest part of something: *Footnotes are given at the bottom of each page.* ◆ *I waited for them at the bottom of the hill.* ◆ *The book I want is right at the bottom* (= of the pile). **ANT** TOP **2** [C, usually sing.] ~ **(of sth)** the part of something that faces downward and is not usually seen: *The manufacturer's name is on the bottom of the plate.*
⊳OF CONTAINER **3** [C, usually sing.] ~ **(of sth)** the lowest surface on the inside of a container: *I found some coins at the bottom of my bag.*
⊳OF RIVER/POOL **4** [sing.] the ground below the water in a lake, river, swimming pool, etc.: *He dived in and hit his head on the bottom.*
⊳LOWEST POSITION **5** [sing.] ~ **(of sth)** the lowest position in a class, on a list, etc.; a person, team, etc. that is in this position: *a battle between the teams at the bottom of the league* ◆ *You have to be prepared to start at the bottom and work your way up.* ◆ *I was always at the bottom of the class in math.* **ANT** TOP
⊳PART OF BODY **6** [C] the part of the body that you sit on **SYN** BACKSIDE, BEHIND
⊳CLOTHING **7** [C, usually pl.] the lower part of a set of clothes

t **tea**   ţ **butter**   d **did**   k **cat**   g **got**   tʃ **chin**   dʒ **June**   f **fall**

that consists of two pieces: *pajama/bikini bottoms* ✦ *tops and bottoms* ➔ compare TOP
> OF SHIP **8** [C] the lower part of a ship that is below the surface of the water **SYN** HULL
> **-BOTTOMED 9** (in adjectives) having the type of bottom mentioned: *a flat-bottomed boat*
IDM **at bottom** used to say what someone or something is really like: *Their offer to help was, at bottom, self-centered.* **be at the bottom of sth** to be the original cause of something, especially something unpleasant **the bottom drops/falls out (of sth)** people stop buying or using the products of a particular industry: *The bottom has fallen out of the travel market.* **bottoms up!** (*informal*) used to express good wishes when drinking alcohol, or to tell someone to finish their drink **get to the bottom of sth** to find out the real cause of something, especially something unpleasant ➔ more at HEAP *n.*, HEART, PILE *n.*, SCRAPE *v.*, TOP *n.*, TOUCH *v.*
● *adj.* [only before noun] in the lowest, last, or furthest place or position: *the bottom line (on a page)* ✦ *your bottom lip* ✦ *the bottom step (of a flight of stairs)* ✦ *on the bottom shelf* ✦ *Put your clothes in the bottom drawer.* ✦ *in the bottom right-hand corner of the page* ✦ *the bottom end of the price range* ✦ *We came in at the bottom* (= got the worst result) *with 12 points.* **IDM** see BET *v.* ➔ see also ROCK BOTTOM
● *verb*
PHR V ˌbottom ˈout (of prices, a bad situation, etc.) to stop getting worse: *The recession is finally beginning to show signs of bottoming out.*

THESAURUS

bottom

base ✦ foundation ✦ foot

These are all words for the lowest part of sth.

bottom [usually sing.] the lowest part of sth: *Footnotes are given at the bottom of each page.* ✦ *I waited for them at the bottom of the hill.*

base [usually sing.] the lowest part of sth, especially the part or surface on which it rests or stands: *The lamp has a heavy base.*

foundation [usually pl.] a layer of bricks, concrete, etc. that forms the solid underground base of a building: *to lay the foundations of the new school*

foot [sing.] the lowest part of sth: *She waited for him at the foot of the stairs.*

BOTTOM OR FOOT?

Foot is used to talk about a limited number of things: it is used most often with *tree, hill/mountain, steps/stairs,* and *page.* **Bottom** can be used to talk about a much wider range of things, including those mentioned above for **foot**.

PATTERNS
- at/near/toward the bottom/base/foot of sth
- on the bottom/base of sth
- (a) firm/solid/strong base/foundation(s)

ˈbottom ˌfeeder *noun* **1** (*informal*) a person who earns money by taking advantage of bad things that happen to other people, or by using things that other people throw away **2** a fish that feeds at the bottom of a river, lake, or the ocean

bot·tom·less /ˈbɑtəmləs/ *adj.* (*formal*) very deep; seeming to have no bottom or limit
IDM **a bottomless pit (of sth)** a thing or situation which seems to have no limits or seems never to end: *There isn't a bottomless pit of money for public spending.* ✦ *the bottomless pit of his sorrow*

ˌbottom ˈline *noun* [sing.] **1 the bottom line** the most important thing that you have to consider or accept; the essential point in a discussion, etc.: *The bottom line is that we have to make a decision today.* **2** (*business*) the amount of

money that is a profit or a loss after everything has been calculated: *The bottom line for 2010 was a pretax profit of $85 million.* **3** the lowest price that someone will accept: *Two thousand—and that's my bottom line!*

ˌbottom-ˈup *adj.* (of a plan, project, etc.) starting with details and then later moving on to more general principles: *a bottom-up approach to tackling the problem* ➔ compare TOP-DOWN

bot·u·lin /ˈbɑtʃələn/ *noun* [U] the poisonous substance in the bacteria that cause BOTULISM

bot·u·lism /ˈbɑtʃəˌlɪzəm/ *noun* [U] a serious illness caused by bacteria in badly preserved food

bou·doir /ˈbudwɑr; buˈdwɑr/ *noun* (*old-fashioned*) a woman's small private room or bedroom

bouf·fant /buˈfɑnt/ *adj.* (of a person's hair) in a style that raises it up and back from the head in a high, round shape

bou·gain·vil·le·a (also bou·gain·vil·lae·a) /ˌbugənˈvɪlyə/ *noun* a tropical climbing plant with red, purple, white, or pink flowers

bough /baʊ/ *noun* (*literary*) a large branch of a tree

bought *pt, pp of* BUY

bouil·la·baisse /ˌbuyəˈbeɪs; ˈbuyəˌbeɪs/ *noun* [U] (*from French*) a spicy fish soup from the south of France

bouil·lon /ˈbulyɑn/ *noun* [U, C] a liquid made by boiling meat or vegetables in water, used for making clear soups or sauces: *beef bouillon*

ˈbouillon ˌcube *noun* a solid CUBE made from the dried juices of meat or vegetables, sold in packs, and used for making soups, sauces, etc.

boul·der /ˈboʊldər/ *noun* a very large rock which has been shaped by water or the weather

boul·der·ing /ˈboʊldərɪŋ/ *noun* [U] the sport or activity of climbing on large rocks

boul·e·vard /ˈbʊləˌvɑrd/ *noun* **1** a wide city street, often with trees on either side **2** (*abbr.* Blvd.) a wide main road (often used in the name of streets): *Sunset Boulevard*

bounce /baʊns/ *verb, noun*
● *verb*
> MOVE OFF SURFACE **1** [I, T] if something **bounces** or you **bounce** it, it moves quickly away from a surface it has just hit or you make it do this: *The ball bounced twice before he could reach it.* ✦ **~ off sth** *Short sound waves bounce off even small objects.* ✦ *The light bounced off the river and dazzled her.* ✦ **~ sth (against/on/off sth)** *She bounced the ball against the wall.*
> MOVE UP AND DOWN **2** [I] **~ (up and down) (on sth)** (of a person) to jump up and down on something: *She bounced up and down excitedly on the bed.* **3** [T] **~ sb (up and down) (on sth)** to move a child up and down while he or she is sitting on your knee in order to entertain him or her **4** [I, T] **~ (sth) (up and down)** to move up and down; to move something up and down: *Her hair bounced as she walked.* **5** [I] **+ adv./prep.** to move up and down in a particular direction: *The bus bounced down the hill.*
> MOVE WITH ENERGY **6** [I] **+ adv./prep.** (of a person) to move somewhere in a lively and cheerful way: *He bounced across the room to greet them.*
> CHECK **7** [I, T] **~ (sth)** (*informal*) if a check **bounces**, or a bank **bounces** it, the bank refuses to accept it because there is not enough money in the account
> IDEAS **8** [T] **~ ideas (off someone)/(around)** to tell someone your ideas in order to find out what they think about them: *He bounced ideas off colleagues every chance he got.*
> COMPUTING **9** [I, T] **~ (sth) (back)** if an e-mail **bounces** or the system **bounces** it, it returns to the person who sent it because the system cannot deliver it
> MAKE SOMEONE LEAVE **10** [T] **~ sb (from sth)** (*informal*) to force someone to leave a job, team, place, etc.: *He was bounced from the team after testing positive for steroids.*
IDM **be bouncing off the walls** (*informal*) to be so full of energy or so excited that you cannot keep still

---

PHR V ˌbounce ˈback to become healthy, successful, or confident again after being sick or having difficulties **SYN** RECOVER: *He's had a lot of problems, but he always seems to bounce back pretty quickly.* ˌbounce ˈback (from sth) (*business*) (of prices, shares, etc.) to return to their previous high level or value after a period of difficulty: *The airline's shares have bounced back after two days of heavy losses.*

● *noun*
> MOVEMENT **1** [C] the action of bouncing: *one bounce of the ball* ◆ *a bounce* (= increase) *in popularity* **2** [U] the ability to bounce or to make something bounce: *There's not much bounce left in these balls.* ◆ *Players complained about the uneven bounce of the tennis court.*
> ENERGY **3** [U, C] the energy that a person has: *All her old bounce was back.* ◆ *There was a bounce in his step.*
> OF HAIR **4** [U] the quality in a person's hair that shows that it is in good condition and means that it does not lie flat: *thin, fine hair, lacking in bounce*

bounc·er /ˈbaʊnsər/ *noun* **1** a person employed to stand at the entrance to a club, bar, etc. to stop people who are not wanted from going in, and to throw out people who are causing trouble inside **2** (in baseball) a ball that bounces before it is caught **3** a plastic castle or other shape which is filled with air and which children can jump and play on

bounc·ing /ˈbaʊnsɪŋ/ *adj.* ~ (**with sth**) healthy and full of energy: *a bouncing baby boy*

bounc·y /ˈbaʊnsi/ *adj.* (**bounc·i·er**, **bounc·i·est**) **1** that bounces well or that has the ability to make something bounce: *a very bouncy ball* ◆ *his bouncy blond curls* **2** lively and full of energy

bound 🔑 /baʊnd/ *adj., verb, noun* ⊃ see also BIND
● *adj.* [not before noun] **1** ~ **to do/be sth** certain or likely to happen, or to do or be something: *There are bound to be changes when the new system is introduced.* ◆ *It's bound to be sunny again tomorrow.* ◆ *You've done so much work—you're bound to pass the exam.* ◆ *It was bound to happen sooner or later* (= we should have expected it). ◆ *You're bound to be nervous at the first time* (= it's easy to understand). ⊃ thesaurus box at CERTAIN **2** forced to do something by law, duty, or a particular situation: ~ **by sth** *We are not bound by the decision.* ◆ *You are bound by the contract to pay before the end of the month.* ◆ ~ (**by sth**) **to do sth** (*formal*) *I am bound to say I disagree with you on this point.* ⊃ see also DUTY-BOUND **3** (in compounds) prevented from going somewhere or from working normally by the conditions mentioned: *Strike-bound travelers face long delays.* ◆ *fogbound airports* **4** (also in compounds) traveling, or ready to travel, in a particular direction or to a particular place: *homeward bound* (= going home) ◆ *Paris-bound* ◆ *northbound/southbound/eastbound/westbound* ◆ ~ **for...** *a plane bound for Atlanta*
IDM be bound up in sth to be very busy with something; very interested or involved in something: *He's too bound up in his work to have much time for his children.* bound and determined very determined to do something be bound together by/in sth to be closely connected: *communities bound together by customs and traditions* bound up with sth closely connected with something: *From that moment, my life became inextricably bound up with hers.* ⊃ more at HONOR *n.*

● *verb* **1** [I] + adv./prep. to run with long steps, especially in an enthusiastic way: *The dogs bounded ahead.* **2** [T, usually passive] ~ **sth** (*formal*) to form the edge or limit of an area: *The field was bounded on the left by woods.*

● *noun* (*formal*) a high or long jump ⊃ see also BOUNDS
IDM SEE LEAP *n.*

bound·ary /ˈbaʊndri/ *noun* (*pl.* **bound·aries**) **1** a real or imaginary line that marks the limits or edges of a place or piece of land: *national boundaries* ◆ *county boundaries* ◆ *boundary changes/disputes* ◆ *The fence marks the boundary between my property and hers.* ⊃ thesaurus box at BORDER **2** an imaginary line that marks the limits of something and separates it from other things: *the boundary between*

acceptable and unacceptable behavior **3** [usually pl.] the farthest limit of something; the limit of what is possible or acceptable: *Scientists continue to push back the boundaries of human knowledge.* ◆ *how to set boundaries with your teenager* ◆ *to violate the boundaries of a professional relationship*

bound·en /ˈbaʊndən/ *adj.*
IDM a/your bounden duty (*old-fashioned*, *formal*) something that you feel you must do; a responsibility which cannot be ignored

bound·er /ˈbaʊndər/ *noun* (*old-fashioned*, *informal*) a man who behaves badly and cannot be trusted

bound·less /ˈbaʊndləs/ *adj.* without limits; seeming to have no end **SYN** INFINITE: *Kids seem to have boundless energy.*

bounds /baʊndz/ *noun* [pl.] the accepted or furthest limits of something: *beyond/outside/within the bounds of decency* ◆ *Public spending should be kept within reasonable bounds.* ◆ *It was not beyond the bounds of possibility that they would meet again one day.* ◆ *His enthusiasm knew no bounds* (= was very great).
IDM out of bounds **1** (in some sports) outside the area of play which is allowed: *His shot went out of bounds.* **2** not reasonable or acceptable: *His demands were out of bounds.* out of bounds (to/for sb) if a place is out of bounds, people are not allowed to go there ⊃ see also OFF-LIMITS

boun·te·ous /ˈbaʊntiəs/ *adj.* (*formal* or *literary*) giving very generously

boun·ti·ful /ˈbaʊntɪfl/ *adj.* (*formal* or *literary*) **1** in large quantities; large: *a bountiful supply of food* **2** giving generously **SYN** GENEROUS: *belief in a bountiful god*

boun·ty /ˈbaʊnti/ *noun* (*pl.* **boun·ties**) **1** [U, C] (*literary*) generous actions; something provided in large quantities **2** [C] money given as a reward: *a bounty hunter* (= someone who catches criminals or kills people for a reward)

bou·quet /buˈkeɪ; boʊ-/ *noun* **1** [C] a bunch of flowers arranged in an attractive way so that it can be carried in a ceremony or presented as a gift: *A little girl presented the actress with a large bouquet of flowers.* **2** [C, U] the pleasant smell of a type of food or drink, especially of wine

bou·quet gar·ni /ˌbukeɪ gɑrˈni; ˌboʊ-/ *noun* (*pl.* **bou·quets gar·nis** /ˌbukeɪ gɑrˈni; ˌboʊ-/) (from *French*) a bunch of different HERBS in a small bag, used in cooking to give extra flavor to food

bour·bon /ˈbɜrbən/ *noun* **1** [U, C] a type of WHISKEY made with CORN and RYE **2** [C] a glass of bourbon

bour·geois /ˌbʊrˈʒwɑ; ˈbʊrʒwɑ/ *adj.* **1** belonging to the middle class: *a traditional bourgeois family* ⊃ see also PETIT BOURGEOIS **2** (*disapproving*) interested mainly in possessions and social status, and supporting traditional values: *bourgeois attitudes/tastes* ◆ *They've become very bourgeois since they got married.* **3** (*politics*) supporting the interests of CAPITALISM: *bourgeois ideology* ▶ **bour·geois** *noun* (*pl.* **bour·geois**)

bour·geoi·sie /ˌbʊrʒwɑˈzi/ *noun* the bourgeoisie [sing.] **1** the middle classes in society: *the rise of the bourgeoisie in the nineteenth century* **2** (*politics*) the CAPITALIST class: *the proletariat and the bourgeoisie*

bourse /bʊrs/ *noun* (from *French*) a STOCK EXCHANGE, especially the one in Paris

bout /baʊt/ *noun* **1** a short period of great activity; a short period during which there is a lot of a particular thing, usually something unpleasant: *a drinking bout* ◆ ~ **of sth/of doing sth** *the latest bout of inflation* **2** an attack or period of illness: ~ (**of sth**) *a severe bout of flu/coughing* ◆ *He suffered occasional bouts of depression.* ◆ ~ **with sth** *a bout with the flu* **3** a BOXING or WRESTLING match

bou·tique /buˈtik/ *noun, adj.*
● *noun* a small store that sells fashionable clothes or expensive gifts

h hat	**m** man	**n** no	**ŋ** sing	**l** leg	**r** red	**y** yes	**w** wet

bows

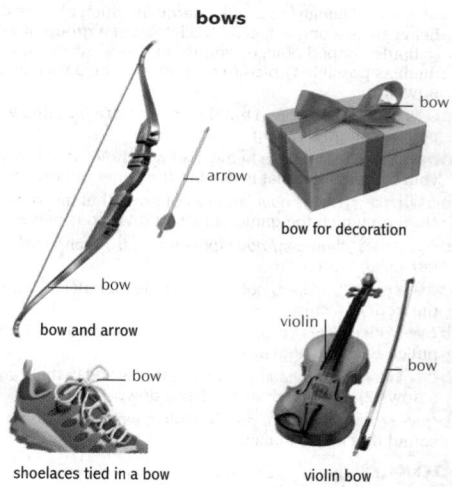

bow for decoration

arrow

bow

bow and arrow

violin

bow

bow

shoelaces tied in a bow

violin bow

• *adj.* [only before noun] (of a business) small and offering products or services of a high quality to a small number of customers: *a boutique hotel that offers an escape from the outside world* ◆ *a boutique investment bank*

bou·ton·nière /ˌbutnˈɪr/ *noun* a flower that is worn in the BUTTONHOLE of a coat or jacket

bou·zou·ki /buˈzuki/ *noun* a Greek musical instrument with strings that are played with the fingers

bo·vine /ˈboʊvaɪn/ *adj.* [usually before noun] **1** (*technical*) connected with cows: *bovine diseases* **2** (*disapproving*) (of a person) stupid and slow

bow

bow

bow of a ship

take a bow

bow¹ /baʊ/ *verb, noun* ➲ see also BOW²

• *verb* **1** [I] to move your head or the top half of your body forward and downward as a sign of respect or to say hello, or goodbye: ~ **(to/before sb/sth)** *He bowed low to the assembled crowd.* ◆ ~ **down (to/before sb/sth)** *The people all bowed down before the altar.* **2** [T] ~ **your head** to move your head forward and downward: *She bowed her head in shame.* ◆ *They stood in silence with their heads bowed.* **3** [I, T] to bend or make something bend: (**+ adv./prep.**) *The pines bowed in the wind.* ◆ ~ **sth (+ adv./prep.)** *Their backs were bowed under the weight of their packs.*
IDM **bow and scrape** (*disapproving*) to be too polite to an important person in order to gain their approval **PHR V** **bow 'down to sb/sth** (*disapproving*) to allow someone to tell you what to do **bow 'out (of sth)** to stop taking part in an activity, especially one in which you have been successful in the past: *She finally decided it was time to bow out of international tennis.* **'bow to sth** to agree unwillingly to do something because other people want you to: *They finally bowed to pressure from the public.* ◆ *She bowed to the inevitable* (= accepted a situation in which she had no choice) *and resigned.*

• *noun* **1** the act of bending your head or the upper part of your body forward in order to say hello or show respect **2** (also **bows** [pl.]) the front part of a boat or ship ➲ picture at BOAT ➲ compare STERN **IDM** **take a/your bow** (of a performer) to bow to the audience as they are APPLAUDING you ➲ more at SHOT *n.*

bow² /boʊ/ *noun, verb* ➲ see also BOW¹

• *noun* **1** a weapon used for shooting arrows, consisting of a long, curved piece of wood with a tight string joining its ends: *He was armed with a bow and arrow.* **2** a knot with two LOOPS and two loose ends that is used for decoration on clothes, in hair, etc. or for tying shoes: *to tie your shoelaces in a bow* ◆ *Her hair was tied back in a neat bow.* ➲ picture at KNOT **3** a long, thin piece of wood with HORSEHAIR stretched along it, used for playing musical instruments such as the VIOLIN ➲ picture at INSTRUMENT

• *verb* [I, T] ~ **(sth)** to use a bow to play a musical instrument that has strings

bowd·ler·ize /ˈboʊdləˌraɪz; ˈbaʊd-/ *verb* ~ **sth** (usually *disapproving*) to remove the parts of a book, play, etc. that you think are likely to shock or offend people **SYN** EXPURGATE **ORIGIN** Named after Dr. Thomas Bowdler, who in 1818 produced a version of Shakespeare from which he had taken out all the material which he considered not suitable for family use.

bow·el /ˈbaʊəl/ *noun* **1** [C, usually pl.] the tube along which food passes after it has been through the stomach, especially the end where waste is collected before it is passed out of the body: (*medical*) *to empty/move your bowels* (= to pass solid waste out of the body) ◆ *bowel cancer/cancer of the bowel* **2 the bowels of sth** [pl.] (*literary*) the part that is

deepest inside something: *A rumble came from the bowels of the earth* (= deep underground).

'bowel ˌmovement (also **move·ment**) *noun* (*medical*) an act of emptying waste material from the bowels; the waste material that is emptied

bow·er /ˈbaʊər/ *noun* (*literary*) a pleasant place in the shade under trees or climbing plants in the forest or a yard

bow·fin /ˈboʊfɪn/ *noun* (*pl.* **bow·fin** or **bow·fins**) an American fish with a large head, that can survive for a long time out of water

bow·ie knife /ˈboʊi ˌnaɪf; ˈbui-/ *noun* a large, heavy knife with a long blade, used in hunting

bowl /boʊl/ *noun, verb*

• *noun*
➢ CONTAINER **1** [C] (especially in compounds) a deep, round dish with a wide, open top, used especially for holding food or liquid: *a salad/fruit/sugar bowl* ◆ *a mixing bowl*
➢ AMOUNT **2** [C] (also **bowl·ful** /ˈboʊlfʊl/) the amount contained in a bowl: *a bowl of soup*
➢ SHAPE **3** [C] the part of some objects that is shaped like a bowl: *the bowl of a spoon* ◆ *a toilet bowl*
➢ THEATER **4** [C] (in names) a large round theater or STADIUM without a roof, used for concerts, etc. outdoors: *the Hollywood Bowl*
➢ FOOTBALL GAME **5** [C] (in names) a game of football played after the main season between the best teams: *the Super Bowl*
➢ BALL **6** [C] a heavy wooden ball that is used in the game of LAWN BOWLING
➢ GAME **7 bowls** [U] = LAWN BOWLING

• *verb*
➢ ROLL BALL **1** [I, T] ~ **(sth)** to roll a ball in the games of BOWLING and LAWN BOWLING
➢ MOVE QUICKLY **2** [I] + **adv./prep.** to move quickly in a particular direction, especially in a vehicle: *Soon we were bowling along the country roads.*
PHR V **ˌbowl sb 'over 1** to run into someone and knock them down **2** to surprise or impress someone a lot

bow legs /ˈboʊ lɛgz/ *noun* [pl.] legs that curve out at the knees ▶ **bow-leg·ged** /ˈboʊ ˌlɛgəd/ *adj.*

bowl·er /ˈboʊlər/ *noun* **1** a person who plays the game of BOWLING **2** (also **ˌbowler 'hat**) = DERBY

bow·line /ˈboʊlɪn; -laɪn/ *noun* **1** a rope that attaches one side of a sail to the BOW¹ of a boat **2** a type of knot, used for making a LOOP at the end of a rope

---

| i see | ɪ sit | ɛ ten | æ cat | ɑ hot | ɔ saw | ʊ put | u too | 169 |

bowl·ing /ˈboʊlɪŋ/ noun [U] a game in which players roll heavy balls along a special track toward a group of PINS (= bottle-shaped objects) and try to knock over as many of them as possible ⊃ picture at HOBBY ⊃ compare LAWN BOWLING

bowling ,alley noun a building or part of a building where people can go bowling

bowling ,ball noun a heavy ball with holes that you put your fingers into, that is used in the game of BOWLING

bowling ,green noun an area of grass that has been cut short on which the game of LAWN BOWLING is played

bow·man /ˈboʊmən/ noun (pl. bow·men /-mən/) (old-fashioned) = ARCHER

bow·sprit /ˈbaʊsprɪt/ noun a thick pole that sticks forward at the front of a ship

bow·string /ˈboʊstrɪŋ/ noun the string on a BOW²(1) that is pulled back to shoot arrows

bow tie /ˈboʊ taɪ/ noun a man's tie that is tied in the shape of a BOW²(2) and that does not hang down

bow-wow /ˈbaʊ waʊ/ noun a child's word for a dog or the sound that a dog makes

box 🔑 /baks/ noun, verb

• noun
>CONTAINER **1** [C] (especially in compounds) a container made of wood, CARDBOARD, metal, etc. with a flat, stiff base and sides, and often a lid, used especially for holding solid things: She kept all the letters in a box. ♦ a lunch box ♦ cardboard boxes ♦ a toolbox ♦ a jewelry box ⊃ picture at PACKAGING **2** [C] a box and its contents: a box of chocolates/matches ♦ a box set of DVDs **3** [C] electronic equipment or controls inside a box: a cable box
>IN THEATER/COURT **4** [C] a small area in a theater, court or STADIUM separated off from where other people sit: a box at the opera ♦ the witness/jury box ♦ box seats at Yankee Stadium ⊃ see also PRESS BOX
>SHAPE **5** [C] a small square or RECTANGLE drawn on a page for people to write information in: Put a check mark in the appropriate box. ♦ to check a box **6** [C] an area on a printed page surrounded by straight lines: A box in the upper right-hand corner of the page explained some of the terms used in the article.
>TELEVISION **7 the box** [sing.] (informal) the television: What's on the box tonight?
>IN SPORTS **8** [C] an area on a sports field that is marked by lines and used for a particular purpose: the penalty box ♦ the batter's box
>FOR MAIL **9** [C] = BOX NUMBER
>ON ROAD **10** [C] a place where two roads cross or join, marked with a pattern of yellow lines to show that vehicles must not stop: There is a $100 fine for blocking the box.
>SHELTER **11** [C] a small shelter used for a particular purpose: a sentry box
>TREE/WOOD **12** [C, U] a small EVERGREEN tree or bush with thick, dark leaves, used especially for garden HEDGES **13** (also **box·wood**) [U] the hard wood of this bush **IDM** see THINK v.

• verb
>FIGHT **1** [I, T] ~ (sb) to fight someone in the sport of BOXING
>PUT IN CONTAINER **2** [T] ~ sth (up) to put something in a box **IDM box sb's ears** (old-fashioned) to hit someone with your hand on the side of their head as a punishment **PHRV box sb/sth 'in 1** to prevent someone or something from being able to move by surrounding them with people, vehicles, etc.: Someone parked behind us and boxed us in. **2** [usually passive] (of a situation) to prevent someone from doing what they want by creating unnecessary problems: She felt boxed in by all their petty rules. ♦ Don't box yourself in when you are asked what salary you want.

box·car /ˈbakskar/ noun a closed car on a train, with a sliding door, used for carrying goods

boxed /bakst/ adj. put and/or sold in a box: a boxed set of original recordings

box·er /ˈbaksər/ noun **1** a person who boxes, especially as a job: a professional/amateur/heavyweight boxer **2** a large dog with smooth hair, a short, flat nose, and a tail that has usually been cut very short

boxer ,shorts (also box·ers, shorts) noun [pl.] men's UNDERPANTS similar to the SHORTS worn by boxers: a pair of boxer shorts

box·ful /ˈbaksfʊl/ noun a full box (of something)

box·ing /ˈbaksɪŋ/ noun [U] a sport in which two people fight each other with their hands, while wearing very large, thick gloves (called **boxing gloves**): a boxing champion/ match ♦ heavyweight boxing ⊃ picture at SPORT

Boxing ,Day noun [U, C] the first day after Christmas Day that is not a Sunday. Boxing Day is an official holiday in Canada and some other countries.

box kite noun a KITE in the shape of a long box that is open at both ends

box 'lunch noun a meal of SANDWICHES, fruit, etc. that you take to school, work, etc. in a box ⊃ compare BAG LUNCH

box ,number (also box) noun a number used as an address, especially one given in newspaper advertisements to which replies can be sent ⊃ compare PO BOX

box ,office noun **1** [C] the place at a theater, movie theater, etc. where the tickets are sold **2** [sing.] used to refer to the commercial success of a movie, play, or actor: Anything she's in will do well at the box office. ♦ The movie has been a huge box-office success/hit (= many people have been to see it).

box score noun the results of a baseball game or other sporting event shown in the form of rows and columns which include details of each player's performance

box 'seat noun a seat in a box in a theater or sports STADIUM: We were treated to box seats at the opera.

box spring noun [usually pl.] each of a set of metal springs inside a box that is covered with cloth and used under a MATTRESS as part of a bed

box·wood /ˈbakswʊd/ noun [U] = BOX n. (12)

box·y /ˈbaksi/ adj. having a square shape: a boxy car

boy 🔑 /bɔɪ/ noun, exclamation

• noun **1** [C] a male child or a young male person: a little/ small/young boy ♦ I used to play here as a boy. ♦ The older boys at school used to tease him. ♦ Now that she's a teenager, she's starting to be interested in boys. ⊃ see also OLD BOY, TOY BOY **2** [C] a young son: They have two boys and a girl. ♦ Her eldest boy is at college. **3** [C] (in compounds; offensive when used of an older man) a boy or young man who does a particular job: a delivery boy ⊃ see also BEST BOY **4** [C] a way of talking about someone who comes from a particular place, etc.: He's a **college boy**. ♦ a city/country boy **5 the boys** [pl.] (informal) a group of male friends who often go out together: a night out with the boys **6 our boys** [pl.] a way of talking with affection about your country's soldiers **IDM the boys in blue** (informal) the police **boys will be boys** (saying) you should not be surprised when boys or men behave in a noisy or rough way as this is part of typical male behavior ⊃ more at SEPARATE v., WORK n.

• exclamation (informal) used to express feelings of surprise, pleasure, pain, etc.: Boy, it sure is hot! ♦ Oh boy! That's great!

boy band noun a group of attractive young men who sing pop music and dance, and who are especially popular with girls

boy·cott /ˈbɔɪkat/ verb, noun
• verb ~ sth to refuse to buy, use, or take part in something as a way of protesting: We are asking people to boycott goods from companies that use child labor.
• noun an act of boycotting someone or something: ~ (of sth) a trade boycott of foreign goods ♦ ~ (on sth) a boycott on the use of tropical wood

---

boy·friend 🔑 /'bɔɪfrɛnd/ *noun*
a man or boy that someone has a romantic or sexual relationship with

boy·hood /'bɔɪhʊd/ *noun* [U] the time in a man's life when he is a boy: *boyhood days/memories/friends*

boy·ish /'bɔɪɪʃ/ *adj.* (*approving*) looking or behaving like a boy, in a way that is attractive: *boyish charm/enthusiasm* ◆ *her slim, boyish figure* ▶ **boy·ish·ly** *adv.*

Boy Scout *noun* [C] **1** a member of an organization (called **Boy Scouts of America**) that trains boys in practical skills and does a lot of activities with them, for example camping ⊃ compare GIRL SCOUT **2** often **boy scout** (*informal*) an honest, friendly man who always follows the rules and tends to believe everything that he is told

Boy Scouts of A'merica *noun* [sing.] an organization for boys between the ages of 11 and 17 that encourages outdoor activities, service to others, and the development of good character

boy·sen·ber·ry /'bɔɪznˌbɛri/ *noun* (*pl.* **boy·sen·ber·ries**) a large red fruit like a BLACKBERRY. The bush it grows on is also called a boysenberry.

boy shorts *noun* [pl.] a piece of women's underwear that covers the body from the hips to the top of the legs

boy toy *noun* (*informal*) **1** (*humorous*) a woman's male lover who is much younger than she is **2** (*disapproving*) a young woman who is happy to be considered only for her sexual attraction and not for her character or intelligence

boy 'wonder *noun* (*informal, humorous*) a boy or young man who is extremely good at something

bo·zo /'boʊzoʊ/ *noun* (*pl.* **bo·zos**) (*informal*) a stupid person

B.Ph. /ˌbi pi 'eɪtʃ/ (also **B.Phil.**) *noun* a college degree in philosophy that is usually a second degree (the abbreviation for "Bachelor of Philosophy")

bpi /ˌbi pi 'aɪ/ *abbr.* (*computing*) bits per inch (a measure of the amount of data that can fit onto a tape or disk)

bps /ˌbi pi 'ɛs/ *abbr.* (*computing*) bits per second (a measure of the speed at which data is sent or received)

Bq *abbr.* = BECQUEREL

Br. *abbr.* (in writing) British

bra /brɑ/ *noun* **1** (also *formal* **bras·siere**) a piece of women's underwear worn to cover and support the breasts **2** (also **'car bra**) a tightly fitting cover that is put over the front end of a car to protect it, sometimes made of a material that absorbs the waves from police RADAR equipment, so that it is more difficult to tell if a driver is going too fast

brace /breɪs/ *noun, verb*
● *noun* **1** [C] a device that holds things firmly together or holds, and supports them in position: *a neck brace* (= worn to support the neck after an injury) **2** [C] **braces** [pl.] a metal device worn, often by children, inside the mouth to help their teeth grow straight **3** [C, usually pl.] a metal support for weak or injured legs **4** [C] either of the two marks, { }, used to show that the words, etc. between them are connected ⊃ compare BRACKET **5** [C] (*pl.* **brace**) a pair of birds or animals that have been killed in hunting
● *verb* **1** ~ sb/yourself (for sth) | ~ sb/yourself (to do sth) to prepare someone/yourself for something difficult or unpleasant that is going to happen: *UN troops are braced for more violence.* ◆ *They are bracing themselves for a long legal battle.* **2** ~ sth/yourself (against sth) to press your body or part of your body firmly against something in order to stop yourself from falling: *They braced themselves against the wind.* **3** ~ sth to contract the muscles in your body or part of your body before doing something that is physically difficult: *He stood with his legs and shoulders braced, ready to lift the weights.* **4** ~ sth (*technical*) to make something stronger or more solid by supporting it with something: *The roof was braced by lengths of timber.*

brace·let /'breɪslət/ *noun* a piece of jewelry worn around the wrist or arm ⊃ picture at JEWELRY

brac·er /'breɪsər/ *noun* a drink, usually alcoholic, that is intended to give strength to the person who drinks it

bra·chi·o·pod /'breɪkiəˌpɑd; 'bræ-/ *noun* (*biology*) a SHELL-FISH that has two joined shells and uses small TENTACLES (= long, thin parts) to find food

bra·chi·o·sau·rus /ˌbreɪkiə'sɔrəs/ *noun* a very large DINOSAUR whose front legs were much longer than its back legs

brac·ing /'breɪsɪŋ/ *adj.* (especially of weather) making you feel full of energy because it is cold: *bracing sea air*

brack·en /'brækən/ *noun* [U] a wild plant with large leaves that grows thickly on hills and in woods, and turns brown in the fall

brack·et /'brækət/ *noun, verb*
● *noun* **1** price, age, income, etc. ~ prices, etc. within a particular range: *people in the lower income bracket* ◆ *Most of the houses are out of our price bracket.* ◆ *the 30–34 age bracket* (= people aged between 30 and 34) **2** (also **square 'bracket**) [usually pl.] either of a pair of marks, [ ], placed at the beginning and end of extra information in a text, especially comments made by an editor: *Publication dates are given in brackets after each title.* ⊃ see also ANGLE BRACKET ⊃ compare BRACE, PARENTHESIS **3** a piece of wood, metal, or plastic fixed to the wall to support a shelf, lamp, etc.
● *verb* **1** ~ sth to put words, information, etc. between brackets **2** ~ A and B (together) | ~ A (together) with B [often passive] to consider people or things to be similar or connected in some way: *It is unfair to bracket together those who cannot work with those who will not.*

brack·ish /'brækɪʃ/ *adj.* (of water) salty in an unpleasant way: *brackish lakes/lagoons/marshes*

brad /bræd/ *noun* a small, thin nail with a small head and a flat tip

brad·awl /'brædɔl/ *noun* a small, pointed tool used for making holes ⊃ picture at TOOL

brag /bræg/ *verb, noun*
● *verb* [I, T] (-gg-) ~ (to sb) (about/of sth) | ~ that... | + speech (*disapproving*) to talk too proudly about something you own or something you have done SYN BOAST: *He bragged to his friends about his new car.*
● *noun* [U] a card game which is a simple form of POKER

brag·ga·do·ci·o /ˌbrægə'doʊʃiou; -tʃiou; -siou/ *noun* [U] (*literary*) behavior that seems too proud or confident

brag·gart /'brægərt/ *noun* (*old-fashioned*) a person who brags

Brah·man (also **Brah·min**) /'brɑmən/ *noun* a Hindu who belongs to the CASTE (= division of society) that is considered the highest, originally that of priests

Brah·min /'brɑmən/ *noun* **1** = BRAHMAN **2** a person who is rich and has a lot of influence in society, especially someone from New England whose family belongs to the highest social class: *a Boston Brahmin*

braid /breɪd/ *noun, verb*
● *noun* **1** [C] a long piece of something, especially hair, that is divided into three parts and twisted together: *She wears her hair in braids.* ⊃ picture at HAIR **2** [U] thin, colored rope that is used to decorate furniture and military uniforms: *The general's uniform was trimmed with gold braid.*
● *verb* ~ sth to twist three or more long pieces of hair, rope, etc. together to make one long piece: *She braided her hair.*

Braille /breɪl/ *noun* also **braille** [U] a system of printing for blind people in which the letters of the alphabet and the numbers are printed as raised dots that can be read by touching them

brain 🔑 /breɪn/ *noun, verb*
● *noun*
▷ IN HEAD **1** [C] the organ inside the head that controls movement, thought, memory, and feeling: *damage to the*

brain ♦ brain cells ♦ She died of a brain tumor. ♦ a device to measure brain activity during sleep ➲ **picture at** BODY
> FOOD **2 brains** [pl.] the brain of an animal, eaten as food: sheep's brains
> INTELLIGENCE **3** [U, C, usually pl.] the ability to learn quickly and think about things in a logical, and intelligent way: It doesn't take a lot of brains to figure out that both stories can't be true. ♦ Teachers spotted that he had a good brain at an early age. ♦ You need brains as well as brawn (= intelligence as well as strength) to do this job. ➲ **see also** NO-BRAINER
> INTELLIGENT PERSON **4** [C] (informal) an intelligent person: one of the best scientific brains in the country **5 the brains** [sing.] the most intelligent person in a particular group; the person who is responsible for thinking of and organizing something: He's always been the brains of the family. ♦ The band's drummer is **the brains behind** their latest venture.
IDM have sth on the brain (informal) to think about something all the time, especially in a way that is annoying: He has football on the brain. ➲ **more at** BEAT v., BLOW v., PICK v., RACK v.
● **verb** ~ sb/sth/yourself (informal) to hit a person or an animal very hard on the head

brain·child /ˈbreɪntʃaɪld/ noun [sing.] an idea or invention of one person or a small group of people
brain ˌdamage noun [U] permanent damage to the brain caused by illness or an accident ► **brain-ˌdamaged** adj.
brain-dead adj. **1** suffering from serious damage to the brain and needing machines to stay alive **2** (humorous) very stupid and boring; not intelligent
brain death noun [U] very serious damage to the brain that cannot be cured. A person who is suffering from brain death needs machines to keep them alive, even though their heart is still beating.
brain drain noun [sing.] (informal) the movement of highly skilled and qualified people to a country where they can work in better conditions and earn more money
brain·i·ac /ˈbreɪniæk/ noun (informal) a very intelligent person **ORIGIN** From the name of a character in the Superman stories.
brain·less /ˈbreɪnləs/ adj. stupid; not able to think or talk in an intelligent way
brain·pow·er /ˈbreɪnˌpaʊər/ noun [U] the ability to think; intelligence
brain·stem /ˈbreɪnstɛm/ (also **brain stem**) noun (anatomy) the central part of the brain, which continues downward to form the SPINAL CORD
brain·storm /ˈbreɪnstɔrm/ noun, verb
● **noun** [sing.] a sudden good idea **SYN** BRAINWAVE
● **verb** [T, I] ~ (sth) to try to come up with as many ideas as possible about a problem or project, often together with other people: Brainstorm as many ideas as possible. ► **brain·storm·ing** noun [U]: a brainstorming session
brain ˌsurgery noun [U]
IDM it's not brain surgery (informal) used to emphasize that something is easy to do or understand **SYN** ROCKET SCIENCE: Look, we're not doing brain surgery here.
brain-ˌteaser noun a problem that is difficult but fun to solve
brain·wash /ˈbreɪnwɑʃ; -wɔʃ/ verb to force someone to accept your ideas or beliefs, for example by repeating the same thing many times or by preventing the person from thinking clearly: ~ sb The group is accused of brainwashing its young members. ♦ ~ sb into doing sth Women have been brainwashed into thinking that they need to work in order to fulfill themselves. ► **brain·wash·ing** noun [U]: the victims of brainwashing and torture
brain·wave /ˈbreɪnweɪv/ noun **1** an electrical signal in the brain **2** = BRAINSTORM: I just had a brainwave!
brain·y /ˈbreɪni/ adj. (informal) (brain·i·er, brain·i·est) very intelligent
braise /breɪz/ verb ~ sth to cook meat or vegetables very

slowly with a little liquid in a closed container: braised lamb shank
brake /breɪk/ noun, verb
● **noun 1** a device for slowing or stopping a vehicle: to put/slam on the brakes ♦ the brake pedal ➲ **picture at** CAR ➲ **collocations at** DRIVING ➲ **see also** AIR BRAKE, DISC BRAKE, FOOTBRAKE, HANDBRAKE **2** ~ (on sth) a thing that stops something or makes it difficult: High interest rates are a brake on the economy. **IDM see** JAM v.
● **verb** [I, T] to go slower or make a vehicle go slower using the brake: The car braked and swerved. ♦ The truck **braked to a halt**. ♦ You don't need to brake at every bend. ♦ She had to brake hard to avoid running into the car in front of her. ♦ ~ sth He braked the car and pulled over to the side of the road.
brake ˌfluid noun [U] liquid used in BRAKES to make the different parts move smoothly
brake light noun a red light on the back of a vehicle that comes on when the brakes are used
brake pad noun a thin block that presses onto the disk in a DISC BRAKE in a vehicle, in order to stop the vehicle
bram·ble /ˈbræmbl/ noun a wild bush with THORNS and berries (BERRY), especially a BLACKBERRY bush
bran /bræn/ noun [U] the outer covering of grain which is left when the grain is made into flour
branch 🔑 /bræntʃ/ noun, verb
● **noun**
> OF TREE **1** a part of a tree that grows out from the main STEM and on which leaves, flowers, and fruit grow ➲ **picture at** TREE
> OF COMPANY **2** a local office or store belonging to a large company or organization: The bank has branches all over the country. ♦ Our New York branch is dealing with the problem.
> OF GOVERNMENT **3** a part of a government or other large organization that deals with one particular aspect of its work **SYN** DEPARTMENT: the antiterrorist branch
> OF KNOWLEDGE **4** a division of an area of knowledge or a group of languages: the branch of computer science known as "artificial intelligence"
> OF RIVER/ROAD **5** a smaller or less important part of a river, road, railroad, etc. that leads away from the main part: a branch of the Mississippi ♦ a branch line (= a small line off a main railroad, often in country areas)
> OF FAMILY **6** a group of members of a family who all have the same ANCESTORS: My uncle's branch of the family emigrated to Canada.
● **verb** [I] to divide into two or more parts, especially smaller or less important parts: The accident happened where the road branches.
PHR V branch ˈoff 1 (of a road or river) to be joined to another road or river but lead in a different direction: Just after the lake, the path branches off to the right. **2** (of a person) to leave a road or path and travel in a different direction **branch ˈout (into sth)** to start to do an activity that you have not done before, especially in your work or business **SYN** DIVERSIFY: The company branched out into selling insurance. ♦ I decided to branch out on my own.
brand 🔑 /brænd/ noun, verb
● **noun 1** a type of product made by a particular company: Which brand of toothpaste do you use? ♦ You pay less for the store brand. ♦ brand loyalty (= the tendency of customers to continue buying the same brand) ♦ Champagne houses owe their success to brand image. ♦ the leading brand of detergent ➲ **see also** STORE-BRAND **2** a particular type or kind of something: an unorthodox brand of humor **3** a mark made with a piece of hot metal, especially on farm animals to show who owns them
● **verb** [often passive] **1** to describe someone as being something bad or unpleasant, especially unfairly: ~ sb as sth They were branded as liars and cheats. ♦ ~ sb + noun/adj. The newspapers branded her a hypocrite. **2** ~ sth (with sth) to mark an animal with a BRAND to show who owns it
brand·ed /ˈbrændəd/ adj. [only before noun] (of a product)

t tea ʈ butter d did k cat g got tʃ chin dʒ June f fall

made by a well-known company and having that company's name on it: *branded drugs/goods/products*

brand·ing /ˈbrændɪŋ/ *noun* [U] the activity of giving a particular name and image to goods and services so that people will be attracted to them and want to buy them ⊃ see also CO-BRANDING

ˈbranding ˌiron *noun* a metal tool that is heated and used to BRAND farm animals

bran·dish /ˈbrændɪʃ/ *verb* ~ sth to hold or wave something, especially a weapon, in an aggressive or excited way

ˈbrand name *noun* the name given to a product by the company that produces it

ˌbrand ˈnew /ˌbræn ˈnu/ *adj.* completely new: *a brand new computer* ◆ *She bought her car brand new.*

bran·dy /ˈbrændi/ *noun* (*pl.* **bran·dies**) **1** [U, C] a strong, alcoholic drink made from wine **2** [C] a glass of brandy

brash /bræʃ/ *adj.* (*disapproving*) **1** confident in an aggressive way: *Beneath his brash exterior, he's still a little boy inside.* **2** (of things and places) too bright or too noisy in a way that is not attractive ▶ **brash·ly** *adv.* **brash·ness** *noun* [U]

brass /bræs/ *noun*

> METAL **1** [U] a bright yellow metal made by mixing COPPER and ZINC; objects made of brass: *solid **brass** fittings/door handles* ◆ *a **brass** plaque* (= a sign outside a building giving the name and profession of the person who works there) ◆ *to clean/polish the brass*

> MUSICAL INSTRUMENTS **2** [U] the musical instruments made of metal, such as TRUMPETS or FRENCH HORNS, that form a band or section of an ORCHESTRA; the people who play them: *music for piano, strings, and brass* ⊃ compare PERCUSSION, STRING, WIND INSTRUMENT, WOODWIND

> IMPORTANT PEOPLE **3** [sing.] (also *informal* ˌtop ˈbrass) the people who are in the most important positions in a company, an organization, etc.

> IN CHURCH **4** [C] a flat piece of brass with words or a picture on it, attached to the floor or wall of a church in memory of someone who has died ⊃ see also BRASSY

IDM **the ˈbrass ring** (*informal*) the opportunity to be successful; success that you have worked hard to get: *The girls' track team has **grabbed the brass ring** seven times.* **ORIGIN** From the custom of giving a free ride to any child who grabbed one of the rings hanging around the side of a merry-go-round at a fairground. **(get down to) brass tacks** (*informal*) (to start to consider) the basic facts or practical details of something ⊃ more at BOLD

ˌbrass ˈband *noun* a group of musicians who play brass instruments

bras·se·rie /ˌbræsəˈri/ *noun* a type of restaurant, often one in a French style that is not very expensive

bras·si·ca /ˈbræsɪkə/ *noun* a plant of a type that includes BROCCOLI, CABBAGE, BROCCOLI and MUSTARD

bras·sière /brəˈzɪr/ *noun* (*formal*) = BRA

ˌbrass ˈknuckles *noun* [pl.] (also **knuck·le·dust·er**) a metal cover that is put on the fingers and used as a weapon

ˈbrass ˌrubbing *noun* [U, C] the art of rubbing a soft pencil or CHALK on a piece of paper placed over a BRASS in a church; the pattern you get by doing this

brass·y /ˈbræsi/ *adj.* **1** (sometimes *disapproving*) (of music) loud and unpleasant **2** (*informal*, *disapproving*) (of a woman) dressing in a way that makes her sexual attraction obvious, but without style: *the brassy blonde behind the bar* **3** like BRASS in color; too yellow and bright **4** (*informal*) saying what you think, without caring about other people

brat /bræt/ *noun* (*informal*, *disapproving*) a person, especially a child, who behaves badly: *a spoiled brat* ▶ **brat·ty** *adj.*: *a bratty kid*

bra·va·do /brəˈvɑdoʊ/ *noun* [U] a confident way of behaving that is intended to impress people, sometimes as a way of hiding a lack of confidence: *an act of sheer bravado*

brave 🔑 /breɪv/ *adj., verb, noun*

● *adj.* (**brav·er**, **brav·est**) **1** (of a person) willing to do things that are difficult, dangerous, or painful; not afraid **SYN** COURAGEOUS: *brave men and women* ◆ *Be brave!* ◆ *I wasn't brave enough to tell her what I thought of her.* **2** (of an action) requiring or showing courage: *a brave decision* ◆ *She died after a brave fight against cancer.* ◆ *He felt homesick, but made a brave attempt to appear cheerful.* **3** ~ **new** (sometimes *ironic*) new in an impressive way: *a vision of a brave new America* ▶ **brave·ly** *adv.* **brav·er·y** /ˈbreɪvəri/ *noun* [U] **SYN** COURAGE: *an award for outstanding bravery* ◆ *acts of skill and bravery*

IDM **(a) brave new world** a situation or society that changes in a way that is meant to improve people's lives but is often a source of extra problems: *the brave new world of technology* **put on a brave face**| **put a brave face on sth** to pretend that you feel confident and happy when you do not

● *verb* ~ **sb/sth** to have to deal with something difficult or unpleasant in order to achieve something: *He did not feel up to braving the journalists at the airport.* ◆ *Over a thousand people **braved the elements** (= went outside in spite of the bad weather) to attend the march.*

● *noun* **1 the brave** [pl.] people who are brave: *America, the land of the free and the home of the brave* **2** [C] (*old-fashioned*) a Native American WARRIOR

bra·vo /ˈbrɑvoʊ; ˌbrɑˈvoʊ/ *exclamation* (becoming *old-fashioned*) people say **Bravo!** at the end of something they have enjoyed, such as a play at the theater

bra·vu·ra /brəˈvyʊrə; -ˈvʊrə/ *noun* [U] (*formal*) great skill and enthusiasm in doing something artistic: *a bravura performance*

brawl /brɔl/ *noun, verb*

● *noun* a noisy and violent fight involving a group of people, usually in a public place: *a drunken brawl* ⊃ thesaurus box at FIGHT

● *verb* [I] to take part in a noisy and violent fight, usually in a public place: *They were arrested for brawling in the street.* ▶ **brawl·er** *noun*

brawn /brɔn/ *noun* [U] physical strength: *In this job you need brains as well as brawn.*

brawn·y /ˈbrɔni/ *adj.* (*informal*) having strong muscles **SYN** BURLY: *He was a huge, brawny brute of a man.*

bray /breɪ/ *verb* **1** [I] when a DONKEY **brays**, it makes a loud sound **2** [I] (of a person) to talk or laugh in a loud unpleasant voice: *He brayed with laughter.* ◆ *a braying voice* ▶ **bray** *noun*

bra·zen /ˈbreɪzn/ *adj., verb*

● *adj.* **1** (*disapproving*) open and without shame, usually about something that people find shocking **SYN** SHAMELESS: *She had become brazen about the whole affair.* ◆ *his brazen admission that he was cheating* **2** (*literary*) made of, or having the color of, BRASS ▶ **bra·zen·ly** *adv.*: *She brazenly admitted letting him back into the house.* **bra·zen·ness** *noun* [U]

● *verb*

PHRV **ˌbrazen it ˈout** to behave as if you are not ashamed or embarrassed about something even though you should be: *Now that everyone knew the truth, the only thing to do was to brazen it out.*

bra·zier /ˈbreɪʒər/ *noun* a large metal container that holds a fire and is used to keep people warm when they are outside

Bra·zil·ian /brəˈzɪlyən/ *adj., noun*

● *adj.* from or connected with Brazil

● *noun* a person from Brazil

Bra·zil nut /brəˈzɪl nʌt/ *noun* the curved nut of a large S. American tree. It has a hard shell with three sides. ⊃ picture at NUT

breach /britʃ/ *noun, verb*

● *noun* **1** [C, U] ~ **of sth** a failure to do something that must be done by law: *a breach of contract/copyright/warranty*

◆ *They are* **in breach of** *Article 119.* **2** [C, U] **~ of sth** an action that breaks an agreement to behave in a particular way: *a* **breach of confidence/trust** ◆ *a breach of security* (= when something that is normally protected is no longer secure) **3** [C] a break in a relationship between people or countries: *a breach in Franco-German relations* **4** [C] an opening that is created during a military attack or by strong winds or seas: *They escaped through a breach in the wire fence.* **IDM** see **STEP** v.

● **verb 1 ~ sth** to not keep to an agreement or not keep a promise **SYN** BREACH: *The government is accused of breaching the terms of the treaty.* **2 ~ sth** to make a hole in a wall, fence, etc. so that someone or something can go through it: *The dam had been breached.*

bread /brɛd/ *noun*

1 [U, C] a type of food made from flour, water, and usually YEAST mixed together and baked: *a loaf/slice/piece of bread* ◆ *white/wheat/rye bread* ◆ *The bakery is known for its specialty breads* (= types of bread). ◆ see also FRENCH BREAD, GINGERBREAD **2** [U] *(old-fashioned, slang)* money **IDM** take the bread out of sb's mouth to take away someone's job so that they are no longer able to earn enough money to live ◆ more at DAILY *adj.*, KNOW *v.*, SLICE

bread and ˈbutter *noun* [U] **1** *(informal)* a person or company's main source of income **2** slices of bread that have been spread with butter: *a piece of bread and butter*

ˌbread-and-ˈbutter *adj.* [only before noun] basic; very important: *Employment and taxation are the bread-and-butter issues of politics.*

bread·bas·ket /ˈbrɛdˌbæskət/ *noun* [sing.] the part of a country or region that produces large amounts of food, especially grain, for the rest of the country or region

bread·board /ˈbrɛdbɔrd/ *noun* a flat board used for cutting bread on

bread·box /ˈbrɛdbɑks/ *noun* a wooden, metal, or plastic container for keeping bread in so that it stays fresh

bread·crumbs /ˈbrɛdkrʌmz/ *noun* [pl.] very small pieces of bread that can be used in cooking

bread·ed /ˈbrɛdəd/ *adj.* covered in breadcrumbs

bread·fruit /ˈbrɛdfrut/ *noun* [C, U] *(pl.* **bread·fruit**) a large tropical fruit with a thick skin, that tastes and feels like bread when it is cooked. It grows on a tree which is called a **breadfruit tree**.

bread·line /ˈbrɛdlaɪn/ *noun* (in the past) a line of people waiting to receive free food

bread·stick /ˈbrɛdstɪk/ *noun* **1** a long, thin, crisp piece of bread **2** a piece of fresh bread, baked in the shape of a small stick

breadth /brɛdθ; brɛtθ/ *noun* [U, C] **1** the distance or measurement from one side to the other; how broad or wide something is **SYN** WIDTH: *She estimated the breadth of the lake to be 500 feet.* ◆ compare LENGTH **2** a wide range (of knowledge, interests, etc.): *He was surprised at her* **breadth of knowledge** *about music.* ◆ *The curriculum needs breadth and balance.* ◆ *a new political leader whose breadth of vision* (= willingness to accept new ideas) *can persuade others to change* **IDM** see LENGTH

bread·win·ner /ˈbrɛdˌwɪnər/ *noun* a person who supports their family with the money they earn

break /breɪk/ *verb, noun*

● **verb** (broke /broʊk/, bro·ken /ˈbroʊkən/)
▷ IN PIECES **1** [I, T] to be damaged and separated into two or more parts as a result of force; to damage something in this way: *All the windows broke with the force of the blast.* ◆ **~ in/ into sth** *She dropped the plate and it broke into pieces.* ◆ **~ sth** *to break a cup/window* ◆ *She fell off a ladder and broke her arm.* ◆ **~ sth in/into sth** *He broke the pencil in two.* ◆ collocations at INJURY
▷ STOP WORKING **2** [I, T] to stop working as a result of being damaged; to damage something and stop it from working:

My watch broke last week. ◆ **~ sth** *I think I broke the washing machine.*
▷ SKIN **3** [T] **~ sth** to cut the surface of the skin and make it BLEED: *The dog bit me, but didn't break the skin.*
▷ LAW/PROMISE **4** [T] **~ sth** to do something that is against the law; to not keep a promise, etc.: *to break the law/rules/ conditions* ◆ *to break an agreement/a contract/a promise/your word* ◆ *to break an appointment* (= not to come to it) ◆ *He was breaking the speed limit* (= traveling faster than the law allows).
▷ A RECORD **5** [T] **~ a record** to do something better, faster, etc. than anyone has ever done it before: *She had broken the world 100 meters record.* ◆ *The movie broke all box-office records.*
▷ STOP FOR SHORT TIME **6** [I] to stop doing something for a while, especially when it is time to eat or have a drink: **~ (for sth)** *Let's break for lunch.*
▷ END SOMETHING **7** [T] **~ sth** to interrupt something so that it ends suddenly: *She* **broke the silence** *by coughing.* ◆ *A tree* **broke his fall** (= stopped him as he was falling). ◆ *The phone rang and broke my train of thought.* **8** [T] **~ sth** to make something end by using force or strong action: *an attempt to break the year-long siege* ◆ *Management has not succeeded in breaking the strike.* **9** [T] **~ sth** to end a connection with something or a relationship with someone: *He broke all ties with his parents.* **10** [T] **~ sb of sth** to cause someone to stop doing something that they have done for a long time, especially something that is harmful to them: *His friends tried to help break him of his drug habit, but eventually he had to go into rehab.*
▷ DESTROY, BE DESTROYED **11** [T, I] **~ (sb/sth)** to destroy something or make someone or something weaker; to become weak or be destroyed: *to break someone's morale/ resistance/resolve/spirit* ◆ *The government was determined to break the power of the trade unions.* ◆ *The scandal broke him* (= ruined his reputation and destroyed his confidence). ◆ *She broke under questioning* (= was no longer able to bear it) *and confessed to everything.*
▷ MAKE SOMEONE FEEL BAD **12** [T] **~ sb** to make someone feel so sad, lonely, etc. that they cannot live a normal life: *The death of his wife broke him completely.*
▷ ESCAPE **13** [I] **~ free (from someone or something)** (of a person or an object) to get away from or out of a position in which they are stuck or trapped: *He finally managed to break free from his attacker.*
▷ OF DAY/DAWN/STORM **14** [I] when the day or DAWN or a storm **breaks**, it begins: *Dawn was breaking when they finally left.* ◆ see also DAYBREAK
▷ OF WAVES **15** [I] when waves **break**, they fall and are dissolved into FOAM, usually near land: *the sound of waves breaking on the beach* ◆ *The ocean was breaking over the wrecked ship.*
▷ OF WEATHER **16** [I] to change suddenly, usually after a period when it has been fine
▷ SHOW OPENING **17** [I] to show an opening: *The clouds broke and the sun came out.*
▷ OF NEWS **18** [I] if a piece of news **breaks**, it becomes known: *There was a public outcry when the scandal broke.* ◆ **breaking news** (= news that is arriving about events that have just happened) **19** [T] **~ it/the news to someone** to be the first to tell someone some bad news: *Who's going to break it to her?* ◆ *I'm sorry to be the one to break the news to you.*
▷ OF VOICE **20** [I] if someone's voice **breaks**, it changes its tone because of emotion: *Her voice broke as she told us the dreadful news.* **21** [I] when a boy's voice **breaks**, it becomes permanently deeper at about the age of 13 or 14
▷ SOMETHING SECRET **22** [T] **~ a code/cipher** to find the meaning of something secret: *It took experts weeks to break the code and read the message.*
▷ MONEY **23** [T] **~ sth** to change a BANKNOTE for coins: *Can you break a twenty-dollar bill?*
IDM Idioms containing **break** are at the entries for the nouns and adjectives in the idioms. For example, **break sb's heart** is at **heart**.
PHR V break aˈway (from sb/sth) **1** to escape suddenly from someone who is holding you or keeping you prisoner: *The prisoner broke away from his guards.* **2** to leave a political

party, state, etc., especially to form a new one: *The people of the province wanted to break away and form a new state.* ⊃ related noun BREAKAWAY **3** to move away from a crowd or group, especially in a race: *She broke away from the pack and opened up a two-second lead.*

,break 'down 1 (of a machine or vehicle) to stop working because of a fault: *The telephone system has broken down.* ♦ *We* (= the car) *broke down on the freeway.* ⊃ related noun BREAKDOWN **2** to fail: *Negotiations between the two sides have broken down.* ⊃ related noun BREAKDOWN **3** to become very bad: *Her health broke down under the pressure of work.* ⊃ see also NERVOUS BREAKDOWN **4** to lose control of your feelings and start crying: *He broke down and wept when he heard the news.* **5** to divide into parts to be analyzed: *Expenditure on the project breaks down as follows: salaries $10m, plant $4m, raw materials $5m.* ⊃ related noun BREAKDOWN ⊃ language bank at ILLUSTRATE **,break sth↔'down 1** to make something fall down, open, etc. by hitting it hard: *Firefighters had to break the door down to reach the people trapped inside.* **2** to destroy something or make it disappear, especially a particular feeling or attitude that someone has: *to break down resistance/opposition* ♦ *to break down someone's reserve/shyness* ♦ *Attempts must be made to break down the barriers of fear and hostility which divide the two communities.* **3** to divide something into parts in order to analyze it or make it easier to do: *Break your expenditures down into bills, food, and other.* ♦ *Each lesson is broken down into several units.* ⊃ related noun BREAKDOWN **4** to make a substance separate into parts or change into a different form in a chemical process: *Sugar and starch are broken down in the stomach.* ⊃ related noun BREAKDOWN
'break for sth to suddenly run toward something when you are trying to escape: *She had to hold him back as he tried to break for the door.*
,break 'in to enter a building by force: *Burglars had broken in while we were away.* ⊃ related noun BREAK-IN **,break sb/sth 'in 1** to train someone or something in something new that they must do: *to break in new recruits* ♦ *The young horse was not yet broken in* (= trained to carry a rider). **2** to wear something, especially new shoes, until they become comfortable **,break 'in (on sth)** to interrupt or disturb something: *She longed to break in on their conversation, but didn't want to appear rude.* ♦ [+ **speech**] *"I didn't do it!" she broke in.*
,break 'into sth 1 to enter a building by force; to open a car, etc. by force: *Our car was broken into last week.* ⊃ related noun BREAK-IN **2** to begin laughing, singing, etc. suddenly: *As the president's car pulled up, the crowd broke into loud applause.* **3** to suddenly start running; to start running faster than before: *He broke into a run when he saw the police.* ♦ *Her horse broke into a trot.* **4** to open and use something that has been kept for an emergency: *They had to break into the emergency food supplies.* **5** to be successful when you get involved in something: *The company is having difficulty breaking into new markets.*
,break 'off 1 to become separated from something as a result of force: *The back section of the plane had broken off.* **2** to stop speaking or stop doing something for a time: *He broke off in the middle of a sentence.* **,break sth↔'off 1** to separate something, using force: *She broke off a piece of chocolate and gave it to me.* **2** to end something suddenly: *Britain threatened to break off diplomatic relations.* ♦ *They've broken off their engagement.*
,break 'out (of war, fighting, or other unpleasant events) to start suddenly: *They had escaped to America shortly before war broke out in 1939.* ♦ *Fighting had broken out between rival groups of fans.* ♦ *Fire broke out during the night.* ⊃ related noun OUTBREAK **,break 'out (of sth)** to escape from a place or situation: *Several prisoners broke out of the jail.* ♦ *She needed to break out of her daily routine and do something exciting.* ⊃ related noun BREAKOUT **,break 'out in sth** to suddenly become covered in something: *Her face broke out in a rash.* ♦ *He broke out in a cold sweat* (= for example, from fear).
,break 'through to make new and important discoveries: *Scientists think they are beginning to break through in the fight against cancer.* ⊃ related noun BREAKTHROUGH **,break**

'through | ,break 'through sth 1 to make a way through something using force: *Demonstrators broke through the police lines.* **2** (of the sun or moon) to appear from behind clouds: *The sun finally broke through in the afternoon.* **,break 'through sth** to succeed in dealing with an attitude that someone has and the difficulties it creates SYN OVERCOME: *He had finally managed to break through her reserve.*
,break 'up 1 to separate into smaller pieces: *The ship broke up on the rocks.* **2** to come to an end: *Their marriage has broken up.* ⊃ related noun BREAKUP **3** to go away in different directions: *The meeting broke up at eleven o'clock.* **4** to laugh very hard **5** when a person who is talking on a cell phone **breaks up**, you can no longer hear them clearly because the signal has been interrupted **,break sb↔'up** to make someone laugh very hard: *Woody Allen just breaks me up.* **,break sth↔'up 1** to make something separate into smaller pieces; to divide something into smaller parts: *The ship was broken up for scrap metal.* ♦ *Sentences can be broken up into clauses.* **2** to end a relationship, a company, etc.: *They decided to break up the partnership.* ⊃ related noun BREAKUP **3** to make people leave something or stop doing something, especially by using force: *Police were called in to break up the fight.* **,break 'up (with sb)** to end a relationship with someone: *She just broke up with her boyfriend.* ⊃ related noun BREAKUP
'break with sth to end a connection with something: *to break with tradition/old habits/the past*

● *noun*

> SHORT STOP/PAUSE **1** [C] a short period of time when you stop what you are doing and rest, eat, etc.: *a coffee/lunch break* ♦ *Let's take a break.* ♦ *a break for lunch* ♦ *She worked all day without a break.* ⊃ thesaurus box at REST **2** [C] a pause or period of time when something stops before starting again: *a break in my daily routine* ♦ *Her comment caused an awkward break in their conversation.* **3** [C] a pause for advertisements in the middle of a television or radio program: *More news after the break.*

> VACATION **4** [C] a short vacation: *We had a weekend break in New York.* ♦ *a well-earned break*

> OPENING/SPACE **5** [C] ~ **(in sth)** a space or an opening between two or more things: *We could see the moon through a break in the clouds.*

> OPPORTUNITY **6** [C] (*informal*) an opportunity to do something, usually to get something that you want or to achieve success: *I got my lucky break when I won a "Young Journalist of the Year" competition.* ♦ *We've had a few bad breaks* (= pieces of bad luck) *along the way.*

> CHANGE IN SITUATION **7** [sing.] the moment when a situation, or a relationship that has existed for a time changes, ends or is interrupted: ~ **(with sb/sth)** *He needed to make a complete break with the past.* ♦ *a break with tradition/convention* (= a change from what is accepted, in something such as art, behavior, etc.) ♦ ~ **(in sth)** *a break in the weather* (= a change from one type of weather to a different one) ♦ *a break in diplomatic relations*

> OF BONE **8** [C] a place where something, especially a bone in your body, has broken: *The X-ray showed there was no break in his leg.*

> **IN TENNIS 9** (also **break of 'serve**) [C] a win in a game in which your opponent is SERVING: *It was her second break in the set.* ⊃ see also BREAK POINT (2)

> **IN BILLIARDS 10** [C] a series of successful shots by one player; the number of points scored in a series of successful shots: *He put together a magnificent break.*

> **IDM** **break of day/dawn** (*literary*) the moment in the early hours of the morning when it begins to get light **give me a break!** (*informal*) used when someone wants someone else to stop doing or saying something that is annoying, or to stop saying something that is not true **give sb a break** to give someone a chance; to not judge someone too severely: *Give the guy a break—it's only his second day on the job.* **make a break for sth/for it** to run toward something in order to try and escape: *He suddenly leapt up and made a break for the door.* ♦ *They decided to make a break for it* (= to try and escape) *that night.* ⊃ more at CLEAN *adj.*

break·a·ble /'breɪkəbl/ *adj.* likely to break; easily broken

break·age /'breɪkɪdʒ/ *noun* **1** [U, C] the act of breaking something: *Wrap it up carefully to protect against breakage.* **2** [C, usually pl.] an object that has been broken: *The last time we moved house, there were very few breakages.*

break·a·way /'breɪkəˌweɪ/ *adj., noun*
- *adj.* [only before noun] (of a political group, an organization, or a part of a country) having separated from a larger group or country: *a breakaway faction/group/party* ♦ *a breakaway republic*
- *noun* [sing.] **1** an occasion when members of a political party or an organization leave it in order to form a new party, etc. **2** a change from an accepted style: *a breakaway from his earlier singing style*

break·beat /'breɪkbit/ *noun* **1** [C] a series of drum beats that are repeated to form the rhythm of a piece of dance music **2** [U] dance music, for example HIP-HOP, that uses breakbeats

breakbone ˌfever /'breɪkboun ˌfivər/ *noun* [U] = DENGUE

break·danc·ing /'breɪkˌdænsɪŋ/ *noun* [U] a style of dancing with ACROBATIC movements, often performed in the street ▶ **break·dance** *verb* [I] **break·danc·er** *noun*

break·down /'breɪkdaʊn/ *noun* **1** [C] an occasion when a vehicle or machine stops working: *a breakdown on the highway* ♦ *a breakdown recovery service* **2** [C, U] a failure of a relationship, discussion, or system: *the breakdown of a marriage* ♦ *marriage breakdown* ♦ *a breakdown in communications* ♦ *The breakdown of the negotiations was not unexpected.* ♦ *the breakdown of law and order* **3** [C, usually sing.] detailed information that you get by studying a set of figures: *First, let's look at a breakdown of the costs.* **4** [U] (*technical*) the breaking of a substance into the parts of which it is made: *the breakdown of proteins in the digestive system* **5** [C] = NERVOUS BREAKDOWN: *She's still recovering from her breakdown.*

break·er /'breɪkər/ *noun* a large wave covered with white bubbles that is moving toward land ⊃ see also CIRCUIT-BREAKER, DEAL-BREAKER, HOUSEBREAKING, ICEBREAKER, LAWBREAKER, RECORD-BREAKER, STRIKE-BREAKER,

break-'even *noun* [U] (*business*) a time when a company or piece of business earns just enough money to pay for its costs: *The company expects to reach break-even next year.* ⊃ see also EVEN *adj.*

break·fast 🔊 /'brɛkfəst/ *noun, verb*
- *noun* [C, U] the first meal of the day: *a big/hearty/light breakfast* ♦ *a pancake breakfast* ♦ *Do you want bacon and eggs for breakfast?* ♦ *They were having breakfast when I arrived.* ♦ *She doesn't eat much breakfast.* ⊃ see also BED AND BREAKFAST, CONTINENTAL BREAKFAST, POWER BREAKFAST
- *verb* [I] **~ (on sth)** (*formal*) to eat breakfast

break-in *noun* an entry into a building using force, usually to steal something

breaking and 'entering *noun* [U] the crime of entering a building illegally and using force

breaking ˌpoint (also **'break point**) *noun* [U] the time when problems become so great that a person, an organization, or a system can no longer deal with them: *to be at, reach the breaking point* ♦ *to be stretched to the breaking point*

break·neck /'breɪknɛk/ *adj.* [only before noun] very fast and dangerous: *to drive at breakneck speed*

break·out /'breɪkaʊt/ *noun, adj.*
- *noun* an escape from prison, usually by a group of prisoners: *a mass breakout from a high-security prison*
- *adj.* [only before noun] **1** (*informal*) suddenly and extremely popular and successful; establishing someone's reputation: *a breakout hit/movie* **2** taking place separately from the main meeting, with a smaller number of people: *a breakout session before the convention* ♦ *a breakout group on ethical issues*

'break point *noun* **1** the point where something, especially a computer program, is interrupted **2** **break 'point** (especially in TENNIS) a point that the person who is SERVING must win in order not to lose a game **3** = BREAKING POINT

break·through /'breɪkθru/ *noun, adj.*
- *noun* an important development that may lead to an agreement or achievement: *to make/achieve a breakthrough* ♦ *a significant breakthrough in negotiations* ♦ *a major breakthrough in cancer research*
- *adj.* [only before noun] in which a performer or type of product is successful for the first time, when it is likely to be even more successful in the future: *It was a breakthrough album for the band.* ♦ *breakthrough technology/products*

break·up /'breɪkʌp/ *noun* **1** the ending of a relationship or an association: *the breakup of their marriage* ♦ *family breakups* **2** the division of a large organization or country into smaller parts

break·wa·ter /'breɪkˌwɔtər; -ˌwɑtər/ *noun* a wall built out into the ocean to protect the SHORE or HARBOR from the force of the waves

bream /brim; brɪm/ *noun* (*pl.* **bream**) a FRESHWATER or ocean fish that is used for food

breast 🔊 /brɛst/ *noun, verb*
- *noun*
> **PART OF BODY 1** [C] either of the two round, soft parts at the front of a woman's body that produce milk when she has had a baby: *She put the baby to her breast.* ♦ *breast milk* **2** [C] the similar, smaller part on a man's body, which does not produce milk **3** [C] (*literary*) the top part of the front of your body, below your neck **SYN** CHEST: *She cradled the child against her breast.*
> **MEAT 4** [C, U] meat from the front part of the body of a bird or an animal: *chicken/turkey breasts* ♦ *breast of lamb*
> **OF BIRD 5** [C] the front part of a bird's body: *breast feathers* ♦ *The robin has a red breast.*
> **CLOTHING 6** [C] the part of a piece of clothing that covers your chest: *A row of medals was pinned to the breast of his coat.*
> **-BREASTED 7** (in adjectives) having the type of chest or breasts mentioned: *a small-breasted/full-breasted woman* ♦ *the yellow-breasted male of the species* ⊃ see also DOUBLE-BREASTED, SINGLE-BREASTED
> **HEART 8** [C] (*literary*) the part of the body where the feelings and emotions are thought to be: *a troubled breast* ⊃ see also CHIMNEY BREAST **IDM** see BEAT
- *verb* (*formal*) **1** **~ sth** to reach the top of a hill, etc.: *As they breasted the ridge, they saw the valley and lake before them.* **2** **~ sth** to push through something, touching it with your chest: *He strode into the ocean, breasting the waves.*

breast·bone /'brɛstboun/ *noun* the long, flat bone in the chest that the seven top pairs of RIBS are connected to **SYN** STERNUM ⊃ picture at BODY

breast·feed /'brɛstfid/ *verb* (**breast·fed, breast·fed** /-fɛd/) [I, T] **~ (sb)** when a woman **breastfeeds**, she feeds her baby with milk from her breasts. ⊃ compare BOTTLE-FEED, NURSE

breast·plate /'brɛstpleɪt/ *noun* a piece of ARMOR worn by

ʌ **cup**   ə **about**   eɪ **say**   aɪ **five**   ɔɪ **boy**   aʊ **now**   oʊ **go**   ər **bird**

soldiers in the past to protect the upper front part of the body

breast 'pocket *noun* a pocket on a shirt, or on the outside or inside of the part of a jacket that covers the chest ⊃ picture at CLOTHES

'breast pump *noun* a device for getting milk from a woman's breasts, so that her baby can be fed later from a bottle

breast·stroke /'brɛststroʊk; 'brɛstroʊk/ *noun* [U, sing.] a style of swimming that you do on your front, moving your arms and legs away from your body and then back toward it in a circle ⊃ picture at SPORT

breath /brɛθ/ *noun*
1 [U] the air that you take into your lungs and send out again: *His breath smelled of garlic.* ◆ *bad breath* (= that smells bad) ◆ *She was very **short of breath** (= had difficulty breathing).* **2** [C] an amount of air that enters the lungs at one time: *to take a deep breath* ◆ *He recited the whole poem in one breath.* ◆ *We had to stop for a breath before we got to the top.* **3** [sing.] **~ of sth** (*formal*) a small amount of something; slight evidence of something: *a breath of suspicion/scandal* **4** [sing.] **a ~ of air/wind** (*literary*) a slight movement of air
IDM **a breath of (fresh) air** clean air breathed in after being indoors or in a dirty atmosphere: *We'll get a breath of fresh air at lunchtime.* **a breath of fresh air** a person, thing, or place that is new and different and therefore interesting and exciting **the breath of life to/for sb** (*literary*) an essential part of a person's existence **catch your breath** to breathe normally again after running or doing some tiring exercise **hold your breath 1** to stop breathing for a short time: *Hold your breath and count to ten.* **2** to be anxious while you are waiting for something that you are worried about: *He held his breath while the results were read out.* **3** (*informal*) people say **don't hold your breath!** to emphasize that sth will take a long time or may not happen: *She said she'd do it this week, but don't hold your breath!* **in the same breath** immediately after saying something that suggests the opposite intention or meaning: *He praised my work and in the same breath told me I would have to leave.* **his/her last/dying breath** the last moment of a person's life **out of breath** having difficulty breathing after exercise: *We were out of breath after only five minutes.* **say sth, speak, etc. under your breath** to say something quietly so that people cannot hear: *"Liar!" he murmured under his breath.* **take sb's breath away** to be very surprising or beautiful: *My first view of the island from the air took my breath away.* ⊃ more at BATED, CATCH *v.*, DRAW *v.*, SAVE *v.*, WASTE *v.*

breath·a·ble /'briðəbl/ *adj.* (*technical*) **1** (of material used in making clothes) allowing air to pass through: *Breathable, waterproof clothing is essential for most outdoor sports.* **2** (of air) fit or pleasant to breathe

breath·a·lyze /'brɛθəˌlaɪz/ *verb* [usually passive] **~ sb** to check how much alcohol a driver has drunk by making him or her breathe into a breathalyzer: *Both drivers were breathalyzed at the scene of the accident.*

Breath·a·lyz·er™ /'brɛθəˌlaɪzər/ *noun* a device used by the police to measure the amount of alcohol in a driver's breath

breathe /brið/ *verb*
> AIR/BREATH **1** [I, T] to take air into your lungs and send out again through your nose or mouth: *He breathed deeply before speaking again.* ◆ *The air was so cold we could hardly breathe.* ◆ *She was beginning to breathe more easily.* ◆ **~ sth** *Most people don't realize that they are breathing polluted air.* **2** [T] **~ sth (+ adv./prep.)** to send air, smoke, or a particular smell out of your mouth: *He came close, breathing alcohol fumes all over me.*
> SAY QUIETLY **3** [T] **~ sth | + speech** (*literary*) to say something quietly: *"I'm over here," she breathed.*
> OF WINE **4** [I] if you allow wine to **breathe**, you open the bottle and let air get in before you drink it
> OF CLOTH/SKIN **5** [I] if cloth, leather, skin, etc. can **breathe**, air can move around or through it: *Cotton clothing allows your skin to breathe.*

> FEELING/QUALITY **6** [T] **~ sth** (*formal*) to be full of a particular feeling or quality: *Her performance breathed wit and charm.*
IDM **breathe (easy/easily/freely) again** to feel calm again after something unpleasant or frightening has ended **breathe down sb's neck** (*informal*) to watch closely what someone is doing in a way that makes them feel anxious and/or annoyed **breathe (new) life into sth** to improve something by introducing new ideas and making people more interested in it **breathe your last** (*literary*) to die ⊃ more at EASY *adv.*, LIVE¹
PHR V **breathe 'in** to take air into your lungs through your nose or mouth SYN INHALE **breathe sth⟷'in** to take air, smoke, etc. into your lungs through your nose or mouth: *His illness is a result of breathing in paint fumes over many years.* **breathe 'out** to send air out of your lungs through your nose or mouth SYN EXHALE **breathe sth⟷'out** to send air, smoke, etc. out of your lungs through your nose or mouth: *Humans take in oxygen and breathe out carbon dioxide.*

breath·er /'briðər/ *noun* (*informal*) a short pause for rest or to relax: *to take/have a breather* ◆ *Tell me when you need a breather.* ◆ *a five-minute breather*

breath·ing /'briðɪŋ/ *noun* [U]
the action of breathing air into the lungs and sending it out again: *Her breathing became steady and she fell asleep.* ◆ *Deep breathing exercises will help you relax.* ◆ *Heavy* (= loud) *breathing was all I could hear.*

'breathing room *noun* [U] **1** (also **'breathing ˌspace** [U, sing.]) a short rest in the middle of a busy period ⊃ thesaurus box at REST **2** (also **'breathing ˌspace** [U]) enough space to breathe comfortably

breath·less /'brɛθləs/ *adj.* **1** having difficulty in breathing; making it difficult for someone to breathe: *He arrived breathless at the top of the stairs.* ◆ *They maintained a breathless* (= very fast) *pace for half an hour.* **2** (*formal*) experiencing, or making someone experience, a strong emotional reaction: *the breathless excitement of seeing each other again* ◆ **~ with sth** *breathless with terror* **3** (*formal*) with no air or wind: *the breathless heat of a summer afternoon* ▶ **breath·less·ly** *adv.* **breath·less·ness** *noun* [U]

breath·tak·ing /'brɛθˌteɪkɪŋ/ *adj.* very exciting or impressive (usually in a pleasant way); very surprising: *a breathtaking view of the mountains* ◆ *The scene was one of breathtaking beauty.* ◆ *He spoke with breathtaking arrogance.* ▶ **breath·tak·ing·ly** *adv.*: *a breathtakingly expensive diamond*

'breath test *noun* a test used by the police to show the amount of alcohol in a driver's breath

breath·y /'brɛθi/ *adj.* speaking or singing with a noticeable sound of breathing

bred *pt, pp* of BREED

breech /britʃ/ *noun* the part of a gun at the back where the bullets are loaded

'breech birth (also **ˌbreech de'livery**) *noun* a birth in which the baby's bottom or feet come out of the mother first

breech·es (also **britch·es**) /'brɪtʃɪz/ *noun* [pl.] short pants fastened just below the knee: *a pair of breeches* ◆ *riding breeches*

breed /brid/ *verb, noun*
● *verb* (**bred, bred** /brɛd/) **1** [I] (of animals) to have sex and produce young: *Many animals breed only at certain times of the year.* ⊃ see also INTERBREED **2** [T] **~ sth (for/as sth)** to keep animals or plants in order to produce young ones in a controlled way: *The rabbits are bred for their long coats.* ⊃ collocations at FARMING ⊃ see also CROSS-BREED, PURE-BRED, THOROUGHBRED **3** [T] **~ sth** to be the cause of something: *Nothing breeds success like success.* **4** [T, usually passive] **~ sth into sb** to educate someone in a particular way as they are growing up: *Fear of failure was bred into him at an early age.* ⊃ see also WELL BRED IDM see BORN, FAMILIARITY
● *noun* **1** a particular type of animal that has been developed

by people in a controlled way, especially a type of dog, cat, or farm animal: *Labradors and other large breeds of dog* ◆ *a breed of cattle/sheep, etc.* **2** [usually sing.] a type of person: *He represents a new breed of politician.* ◆ *Players as skillful as this are a rare breed.*

breed·er /'briːdər/ *noun* a person who breeds animals: *a dog/horse/cattle, etc.* **breeder**

breed·ing /'briːdɪŋ/ *noun* [U] **1** the keeping of animals in order to breed from them: *the breeding of horses* **2** the producing of young animals, plants, etc.: *the breeding season* **3** the family or social background that is thought to result in good manners: *a sign of good breeding*

'**breeding ground** *noun* **1** [usually pl.] a place where wild animals go to produce their young **2** ~ **(for sth)** [usually sing.] a place where something, especially something bad, is able to develop: *This area of the city has become a breeding ground for violent crime.*

breeze /briːz/ *noun, verb*
● *noun* **1** [C] a light wind: *a sea breeze* ◆ *The flowers were gently swaying in the breeze.* ◆ *A light breeze was blowing.* ➔ **collocations at** WEATHER **2** [sing.] (*informal*) a thing that is easy to do: *It was a breeze.* **IDM** see SHOOT *v.*
● *verb* [I] + **adv./prep.** to move in a cheerful and confident way in a particular direction: *She just breezed in and asked me to help.*
 PHR V breeze '**through sth** to do something successfully and easily: *He breezed through the tests.*

breeze·way /'briːzweɪ/ *noun* an outside passage with a roof and open sides between two separate parts of a building

breez·y /'briːzi/ *adj.* (**breez·i·er**, **breez·i·est**) **1** with the wind blowing somewhat strongly: *It was a bright, breezy day.* ◆ *the breezy east coast* **2** having or showing a cheerful and relaxed manner: *You're very bright and breezy today!* ▶ **breez·i·ly** /-zəli/ *adv.*: *"Hi folks," he said breezily.* **breez·i·ness** /-zinəs/ *noun* [U]

breth·ren /'brɛðrən/ *noun* [pl.] (*old-fashioned*) **1** used to talk to people in church or to talk about the members of a male religious group: *Let us pray, brethren.* **2** people who are part of the same society as yourself: *We should do all we can to help our less fortunate brethren.*

breve /briːv; brɛv/ *noun* (*music*) a note that lasts as long as eight QUARTER NOTES, which is rarely used in modern music

brev·i·ty **AWL** /'brɛvəti/ *noun* [U] (*formal*) **1** the quality of using few words when speaking or writing **SYN** : *The report is a masterpiece of brevity.* **2** the fact of lasting a short time: *the brevity of human life* ➔ **see also** BRIEF

brew /bruː/ *verb, noun*
● *verb* **1** [T, I] ~ **(sth)** to make beer: *The beer is brewed in Wisconsin.* **2** [T] ~ **sth** to make a hot drink of tea or coffee: *freshly brewed coffee* **3** [I] (of tea or coffee) to be mixed with hot water and become ready to drink: *Always let tea brew for a few minutes.* **4** [I] (usually used in the progressive tenses) if something unpleasant **is brewing**, it seems likely to happen soon
● *noun* **1** [C, U] a type of beer, especially one made in a particular place: *I thought I'd try the local brew.* ◆ *home brew* (= beer made at home) **2** [C, usually sing.] a mixture of different ideas, events, etc.: *The movie is a potent brew of adventure, romance, and comedy.* ◆ *His music is a heady brew* (= a powerful mixture) *of heavy metal and punk.*

brew·er /'bruːər/ *noun* a person or company that makes beer

brew·er·y /'bruːəri/ *noun* (*pl.* **brew·er·ies**) a factory where beer is made; a company that makes beer

brew·house /'bruːhaʊs/ *noun* a factory where beer is made **SYN** BREWERY

brew·ski /'bruːski/ *noun* (*slang*) a bottle, can, or glass of beer

bri·ar (also **bri·er**) /'braɪər/ *noun* **1** a wild bush with THORNS, especially a wild ROSE bush **2** a bush with a hard root that is used for making TOBACCO pipes; a tobacco pipe made from this root

bribe /braɪb/ *noun, verb*
● *noun* a sum of money or something valuable that you give or offer to someone to persuade them to help you, especially by doing something dishonest: *It was alleged that he had* **taken bribes** *while in office.* ◆ *She had been offered a $50,000 bribe to drop the charges.* ➔ **collocations at** CRIME
● *verb* to give someone money or something valuable in order to persuade them to help you, especially by doing something dishonest: ~ **sb (with sth)** *They bribed the guards with cigarettes.* ◆ ~ **sb into doing sth** *She was bribed into handing over secret information.* ◆ ~ **sb to do sth** *She bribed him to sign the certificate.* ◆ ~ **your way…** *He managed to bribe his way onto the ship.*

brib·er·y /'braɪbəri/ *noun* [U] the giving or taking of bribes: *She was arrested on bribery charges.* ◆ *allegations of bribery and corruption*

bric-a-brac /'brɪk ə ˌbræk/ *noun* [U] ORNAMENTS and other small decorative objects of little value: *a flea market selling cheap bric-a-brac*

brick /brɪk/ *noun, verb*
● *noun* **1** [C, U] a block of baked CLAY used for building walls, houses, and other buildings; bricks used as a building material: *a pile of bricks* ◆ *The school is built of brick.* ◆ *a brick wall* ➔ **see also** REDBRICK **2** [C] a plastic or wooden block, used as a toy for young children to build things with **IDM** **be up against a brick wall** to be unable to make any progress because there is a difficulty that stops you **bricks and mortar** buildings, when you are thinking of them in connection with how much they cost to build or how much they are worth: *They put their money into bricks and mortar.* ◆ (*business*) *a new Internet company without a lot of bricks-and-mortar businesses* (= businesses with buildings that customers go to) ◆ **brick-and-mortar businesses you can't make bricks without straw** used to say that you cannot work without the necessary material, money, information, etc. ➔ **more at** HEAD *n.*, TON
● *verb*
 PHR V brick sth↔**'in/'up** to fill an opening in a wall with bricks: *The windows had been bricked up.*

brick·bat /'brɪkbæt/ *noun* [usually pl.] an insulting remark made in public

brick·lay·er /'brɪkˌleɪər/ *noun* a person whose job is to build walls, etc. with bricks ▶ **brick·lay·ing** *noun* [U]

brick·work /'brɪkwərk/ *noun* [U] the bricks in a wall, building, etc.: *Plaster had fallen away in places, exposing the brickwork.*

brid·al /'braɪdl/ *adj.* [only before noun] connected with a bride or a wedding: *a bridal gown* ◆ *the* **bridal party** (= the bride and the bridegroom and the people helping them at their wedding, sometimes used to refer only to the bride and those helping her) ◆ *a* **bridal suite** (= a set of rooms in a hotel for a couple who have just gotten married) ◆ *a* **bridal shower** (= a party for a woman who will get married soon)

bride /braɪd/ *noun* a woman on her wedding day, or just before or just after it: *a toast to the* **bride and groom** ◆ *He introduced his new bride.*

bride·groom /'braɪdɡrum/ (also **groom**) *noun* a man on his wedding day, or just before or just after it

brides·maid /'braɪdzmeɪd/ *noun* a young woman or girl who helps a BRIDE before and during the marriage ceremony ➔ **compare** BEST MAN, RING BEARER

bridge /brɪdʒ/ *noun, verb*
● *noun*
❯ OVER ROAD/RIVER **1** [C] a structure that is built over a road, railroad, river, etc. so that people or vehicles can cross from one side to the other: *We crossed the bridge over the Ohio river.* ➔ **see also** LAND BRIDGE, SUSPENSION BRIDGE, SWING BRIDGE
❯ CONNECTION **2** [C] a thing that provides a connection or contact between two different things: *Cultural exchanges are a way of* **building bridges** *between countries.*

t **t**ea   ʈ **b**u**tt**er   d **d**id   k **c**at   ɡ **g**ot   tʃ **ch**in   dʒ **J**une   f **f**all

bridges

bridge

bridge over a river

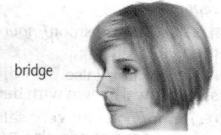

bridge of the nose

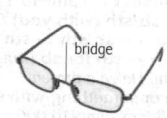

bridge

bridge of a pair of glasses

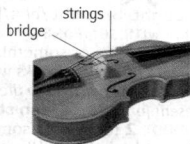

strings

bridge

bridge of a violin

> OF SHIP **3** [C, usually sing.] usually **the bridge** the part of a ship where the captain and other officers stand when they are controlling and steering the ship ⊃ **picture at BOAT**
> CARD GAME **4** [U] a card game for two pairs of players who have to predict how many tricks they will win. They score points if they succeed in winning that number of cards and lose points if they fail. ⊃ see also CONTRACT BRIDGE
> OF NOSE **5 the ~ of someone's nose** [sing.] the hard part at the top of the nose, between the eyes
> OF GLASSES **6** [C] the part of a pair of glasses that rests on your nose
> OF GUITAR/VIOLIN **7** [C] a small piece of wood on a GUITAR, VIOLIN, etc. over which the strings are stretched ⊃ picture at INSTRUMENT
> FALSE TEETH **8** [C] a false tooth or false teeth, held permanently in place by being fastened to natural teeth on either side **IDM** see BURN v., CROSS v., WATER n.
● **verb**
> BUILD/FORM BRIDGE **~ sth** to build or form a bridge over something: *The valley was originally bridged by the Romans.* ◆ *A plank of wood bridged the stream.* **IDM** **bridge the gap/gulf/divide (between A and B)** to reduce or get rid of the differences that exist between two things or groups of people

bridge-building *noun* [U] activities intended to make relations between two groups, countries, etc. friendlier

bridge-head /'brɪdʒhed/ *noun* **1** a strong position that an army has captured in enemy land, from which it can go forward or attack the enemy **2** [usually sing.] a good position from which to make progress

bridge loan *noun* an amount of money that a bank lends you for a short time, especially so that you can buy a new house while you are waiting to sell your old one

bridge-work /'brɪdʒwɜrk/ *noun* [U] **1** artificial teeth and the parts that keep them in place in the mouth **2** the work of making these teeth or putting them in place

bri-dle /'braɪdl/ *noun, verb*
● **noun** a set of leather bands, attached to REINS, which is put around a horse's head and used for controlling it ⊃ picture at HORSE
● **verb 1** [T] **~ sth** to put a bridle on a horse **2** [I] **~ (at sth)** (*literary*) to show that you are annoyed and/or offended at something, especially by moving your head up and backward in a proud way: *She bridled at the suggestion that she was lying.*

bridle path *noun* a rough path that is suitable for people riding horses or walking, but not for cars

Brie /briː/ *noun* [U, C] a type of soft French cheese

brief ✎ **AWL** /briːf/ *adj., noun, verb*
● **adj.** (**brief·er**, **brief·est**) **1** lasting only a short time; short:

a brief visit/meeting/conversation ◆ a brief pause/silence ◆ Mozart's life was brief. **2** using few words: *a brief description/summary/account* ◆ *Please be brief* (= say what you want to say quickly). **3** (of clothes) short and not covering much of the body: *a brief skirt* ⊃ see also BREVITY, BRIEFLY **IDM** **in brief** in a few words, without details: *In brief, the meeting was a disaster.* ◆ *Now the rest of the news in brief.*
● **noun** ⊃ see also BRIEFS **1** (*law*) a written summary of the facts that support one side of a legal case, that will be presented to a court **2** = BRIEFING (2): *Officials are pushing for this target to be included in the next presidential brief.* **IDM** **hold no brief for sb/sth** (*formal*) to not support or be in favor of someone or something: *I hold no brief for either side in this war.*
● **verb** to give someone information about something so that they are prepared to deal with it: **~ sb** *I expect to be kept fully briefed at all times.* ◆ **~ sb on/about sth** *The officer briefed her on what to expect.* ⊃ compare DEBRIEF

brief·case /'briːfkeɪs/ *noun* a flat case used for carrying papers and documents ⊃ picture at BAG ⊃ compare ATTACHE CASE

brief·ing **AWL** /'briːfɪŋ/ *noun* **1** [C] a meeting in which people are given instructions or information: *a press briefing* **2** (also **brief**) [C, U] the detailed instructions or information that are given at such a meeting: *Captain Kirk gave his men a full briefing.* ◆ *a briefing session/paper*

brief·ly ✎ **AWL** /'briːfli/ *adv.*
1 for a short time: *He had spoken to Emma only briefly.* **2** in few words: *Briefly, the argument is as follows…* ◆ *Let me tell you briefly what happened.*

briefs /briːfs/ *noun* [pl.] men's UNDERPANTS or women's PANTIES: *a pair of briefs*

bri·er = BRIAR

brig /brɪg/ *noun* **1** a ship with two MASTS (= posts that support the sails) and square sails **2** a prison, especially one on a WARSHIP

bri·gade /brɪ'geɪd/ *noun* **1** a large group of soldiers that forms a unit of an army **2** [usually sing.] (often *disapproving*) used, always with a word or phrase in front of it, to describe a group of people who share the same opinions or are similar in some other way: *the antiwar brigade*

brig·a·dier gen·er·al /ˌbrɪgədɪr 'dʒenərəl; -'dʒenrəl/ *noun* an officer of high rank in the army, AIR FORCE, or MARINES

brig·and /'brɪgənd/ *noun* (*old-fashioned*) a member of a group of criminals that steals from people, especially one that attacks travelers **SYN** BANDIT

bright ✎ /braɪt/ *adj., adv., noun*
● **adj.** (**bright·er**, **bright·est**) **1** full of light; shining strongly: *bright light/sunshine* ◆ *a bright room* ◆ *Her eyes were bright with tears.* ◆ *a bright morning* (= with the sun shining) **2** (of a color) strong and easy to see: *I like bright colors.* ◆ *a bright yellow dress* ◆ *Jack's face turned bright red.* **3** cheerful and lively: *His eyes were bright and excited.* ◆ *She gave me a bright smile.* ◆ *Why are you so bright and cheerful today?* ◆ *His face was bright with excitement.* **4** intelligent; quick to learn: *the brightest student in the class* ◆ *Do you have any bright ideas* (= intelligent ideas)? ⊃ thesaurus box at INTELLIGENT **5** giving reason to believe that good things will happen; likely to be successful: *This young musician has a bright future.* ◆ *Prospects for the coming year look bright.* ◆ *a bright start to the week* ◆ **bright·ly** *adv.*: *a brightly lit room* ◆ *"Hi!" she called brightly.* **bright·ness** *noun* [U] **IDM** **bright and early** very early in the morning: *You're up bright and early today!* **the bright lights** the excitement of city life: *Although he grew up in the country, he's always had a taste for the bright lights.* **a/the bright spot** a good or pleasant part of something that is unpleasant or bad in all other ways: *The win last week was the only bright spot in their last ten games.* **look on the bright side** to be cheerful or positive about a bad situation, for example by thinking only of the advantages and not the disadvantages

- **adv.** (**bright·er**, **bright·est**) (*literary*) (usually with the verbs *burn* and *shine*) brightly: *The stars were shining bright.*
- **noun** **brights** [pl.] the HEADLIGHTS on a vehicle set to a position in which they are shining as brightly as possible and not directed downward **SYN** HIGH BEAMS

THESAURUS

bright

brilliant ◆ vivid ◆ vibrant

These words all describe things that are shining or full of light or colors that are strong and easy to see.

bright full of light; shining strongly; (of colors) strong and easy to see: *a bright yellow dress*

brilliant very bright: *The sky was a brilliant blue.*

vivid (*approving*) (of colors) bright and strong: *His eyes were a vivid green.*

vibrant (*approving*) (of colors) bright and strong: *The room was decorated in vibrant blues and greens.*

VIVID OR VIBRANT?

These two words are very similar, but **vivid** emphasizes how bright a color is, while **vibrant** suggests a more lively and exciting color or combination of colors.

PATTERNS

- bright/brilliant/vivid/vibrant **colors**
- bright/brilliant **light/sunlight/sunshine/eyes**

bright·en /ˈbraɪtn/ *verb* **1** [I, T] to become or make something lighter or brighter in color: *In the distance, the sky was beginning to brighten.* ◆ **~ sth** *a shampoo to brighten and condition your hair* **2** [I, T] to become, feel, or look happier; to make someone look happier: *Her eyes brightened.* ◆ **~ up** *He brightened up at their words of encouragement.* ◆ **~ sth (up)** *A smile brightened her face.* **3** [T, I] **~ (sth) (up)** to become or make something become more pleasant or enjoyable; to bring hope: *A personal letter will usually brighten up a person's day.* ◆ [T] **~ sth (up)** to make something look more brightly colored and attractive: *Fresh flowers will brighten up any room in the house.* **5** [I] **~ (up)** (of the weather) to improve and become brighter: *According to the forecast, it should brighten up later.*

bright-eyed (also **bright-eyed and bushy-tailed**) *adj.* (of a person) full of interest and enthusiasm

bright young thing *noun* an enthusiastic and intelligent young person who wants to be successful in their career **ORIGIN** From the name used in the 1920s for rich young people whose behavior was considered shocking.

bril·liant /ˈbrɪlyənt/ *adj.* **1** extremely intelligent or impressive: *What a brilliant idea!* ◆ *a brilliant performance/invention* **2** very successful: *a brilliant career* ◆ *The play was a brilliant success.* **3** (of a person) very intelligent or skillful: *a brilliant young scientist* ◆ *She has one of the most brilliant minds in the country.* ⭥ thesaurus box at INTELLIGENT **4** (of light or colors) very bright: *brilliant sunshine* ◆ *brilliant blue eyes* ⭥ thesaurus box at BRIGHT ▶ **bril·liance** /ˈbrɪlyəns/ *noun* [U] **bril·liant·ly** *adv.*: *The plan worked brilliantly.* ◆ *It was brilliantly sunny.*

brim /brɪm/ *noun, verb*
- **noun** **1** the top edge of a cup, bowl, glass, etc.: *two wine glasses, filled to the brim* **2** the flat edge around the bottom of a hat that sticks out ⭥ picture at HAT **3 -brimmed** (in adjectives) having the type of brim mentioned: *a wide-brimmed hat*
- **verb** (**-mm-**) [I] to be full of something; to fill something: *Tears brimmed in her eyes.* ◆ **~ with sth** *Her eyes brimmed with tears.* ◆ *The team was brimming with confidence before the game.*
PHR V **brim over (with sth)** (of a cup, container, etc.) to be so full of a liquid that it flows over the edge **SYN** OVERFLOW: (*figurative*) *Her heart was brimming over with happiness.*

brim·ful /ˌbrɪmˈfʊl; ˈbrɪmfʊl/ *adj.* **~ of sth** completely full of something: *She's certainly brimful of energy.* ◆ *a pitcher brimful of cream*

brim·stone /ˈbrɪmstoʊn/ *noun* (*old use*) the chemical element SULFUR

brin·dle /ˈbrɪndl/ (also **brin·dled** /ˈbrɪndld/) *adj.* (of dogs, cats, and cows) brown with bands or marks of another color

brine /braɪn/ *noun* [U] very salty water, used especially for preserving food ⭥ see also BRINY

bring /brɪŋ/ *verb* (**brought**, **brought** /brɔt/)

> **COME WITH SOMEONE OR SOMETHING 1** to come to a place with someone or something: **~ sb/sth (with you)** *Don't forget to bring your books with you.* ◆ **~ sb/sth to sth** *She brought her boyfriend to the party.* ◆ **~ sth for sb** *Bring a present for Helen.* ◆ **~ sb sth** *Bring Helen a present.*
> **PROVIDE 2** to provide someone or something with something: **~ sb/sth sth** *His writing brings him $10,000 a year.* ◆ **~ sth to sb/sth** *The team's new manager brings ten years of experience to the job.*
> **CAUSE 3 ~ sth** to cause something: *The revolution brought many changes.* ◆ *The news brought tears to his eyes* (= made him cry). ◆ *Retirement usually brings with it a huge drop in income.* **4 ~ sb/sth + adv./prep.** to cause someone or something to be in a particular condition or place: *to bring a meeting to an end* ◆ *Bring the water to a boil.* ◆ *The article brought her into conflict with the authorities.* ◆ *Hello, Sam! What brings you here?*
> **MAKE SOMEONE OR SOMETHING MOVE 5** to make someone or something move in a particular direction or way: **~ sb/sth + adv./prep.** *The judge brought his hammer down on the table.* ◆ **~ sb/sth running** *Her cries brought the neighbors running* (= made them run to her).
> **ACCUSATION 6 ~ sth (against sb)** to officially accuse someone of a crime: *to bring a charge/a legal action/an accusation against someone*
> **FORCE YOURSELF 7 ~ yourself to do sth** to force yourself to do something: *She could not bring herself to tell him the news.* **IDM** Idioms containing **bring** are at the entries for the nouns and adjectives in the idioms. For example, **bring someone or something to heel** is at **heel**. **PHR V** **bring sth↔about** to make something happen **SYN** CAUSE: *What brought about the change in his attitude?* ⭥ language bank at CAUSE **PHR V** **bring sb around** (also **bring sb to**) to make someone who is unconscious become conscious again **bring sb around (to…)** to bring someone to someone's house: *Bring the family around sometime; we'd love to meet them.* **bring sth around to sth** to direct a conversation to a particular subject **bring sb/sth↔back** to return someone or something: *Please bring back all library books by the end of the week.* ◆ *He brought me back* (= gave me a ride home) *in his car.* **bring sth↔back 1** to make someone remember something or think about it again: *The photographs brought back many pleasant memories.* **2** to make something that existed before be introduced again **SYN** REINTRODUCE: *Most people are against bringing back smoking on airplanes.* **bring sb sth↔back | bring sth↔back (for sb)** to return with something for someone: *What did you bring the kids back from Hawaii?* ◆ *I brought a T-shirt back for Mark.* **bring sb/sth before sb** (*formal*) to present someone or something for discussion or judgment: *The matter will be brought before the committee.* ◆ *He was brought before the court and found guilty.* **bring sb↔down 1** to make someone lose power or be defeated: *The scandal may bring down the government.* **2** (in sports) to make someone fall down: *He was brought down in the penalty area.* **bring sth↔down 1** to reduce something: *We aim to bring down prices on all our computers.* **2** to land an aircraft: *The pilot managed to bring the plane down in a field.* **3** to make an aircraft fall out of the sky: *Twelve enemy fighters had been brought down.* **4** to make an animal or a

bird fall down or fall out of the sky by killing or wounding it: *He brought down the bear with a single shot.*
,bring sb/sth↔'forth (*old use* or *formal*) to give birth to someone; to produce something: *She brought forth a son.* ♦ *trees bringing forth fruit*
,bring sth↔'forward 1 to move something to an earlier date or time: *The meeting has been brought forward from May 10 to May 3.* 2 to suggest something for discussion: *Please bring the matter forward at the next meeting.* 3 to move a total sum from the bottom of one page or column of numbers to the top of the next: *A credit balance of $50 was brought forward from his September account.*
,bring sb↔'in 1 to ask someone to do a particular job or to be involved in something: *Local residents were angry at not being brought in on (= asked for their opinion about) the new housing proposal.* ♦ [+ to inf] *Experts were brought in to advise the government.* 2 (of the police) to bring someone to a police station in order to ask them questions or arrest them: *Two men were brought in for questioning.* ,bring sb/sth↔'in 1 to introduce a new law: *They want to bring in a bill to limit arms exports.* 2 to attract someone or something to a place or business: *We need to bring in a lot more new business.* 3 to give a decision in court: *The jury brought in a verdict of guilty.* ,bring 'in sth to make or earn a particular amount of money: *His freelance work brings in about $20,000 a year.* ♦ *How much does she bring in now?*
,bring sth↔'off to succeed in doing something difficult **SYN** PULL OFF: *It was a difficult task but we brought it off.* ♦ *The goalie brought off an amazing save.*
,bring sb↔'on to help someone develop or improve while they are learning to do sth ,bring sth↔'on 1 to make something develop, usually something unpleasant **SYN** CAUSE: *He was suffering from stress brought on by overwork.* 2 to make crops, fruit, etc. grow well 'bring sth on yourself/sb to be responsible for something unpleasant that happens to you/someone: *I have no sympathy—you brought it all on yourself.*
,bring sb 'out of himself, herself, etc. to help someone to feel more confident: *She's a shy girl who needs friends to bring her out of herself.* ,bring sth↔'out 1 to make something appear: *A crisis brings out the best in her.* 2 to make something easy to see or understand: *That dress really brings out the color of your eyes.* 3 to produce something; to publish something: *The band has just brought out their second album.*
,bring sb 'through (sth) to help someone deal with something that is difficult or dangerous: *A team of dedicated doctors and nurses helped bring the child through a very serious illness.*
,bring sb 'to (also ,bring sb a'round) to make someone who is unconscious become conscious again
,bring A and B to'gether to help two people or groups to end a disagreement: *The loss of their son brought the two of them together.*
,bring sb↔'up 1 [often passive] to care for a child, teaching him or her how to behave, etc. **SYN** RAISE: *She brought up five children.* ♦ *He was brought up by his aunt.* ♦ *a well/badly brought up child* ♦ ~ to do sth *They were brought up to* (= taught as children to) *respect authority.* ♦ + noun *I was brought up a Catholic.* ⊃ related noun UPBRINGING 2 (*law*) to make someone appear for trial: *He was brought up on a charge of drunk driving.* ,bring sth↔'up 1 to mention a subject or start to talk about it **SYN** RAISE: *Bring it up at the meeting.* 2 to make something appear on a computer screen: *Click with the right mouse button to bring up a new menu.* 3 to VOMIT: *to bring up your lunch* ,bring sb 'up against sth to force someone to know about something and have to deal with it: *Working in the slums brought her up against the realities of poverty.*

brink /brɪŋk/ *noun* [sing.] **1** the ~ (of sth) if you are on the **brink** of something, you are almost in a very new, dangerous, or exciting situation: *on the brink of collapse/war/death/disaster* ♦ *Scientists are on the brink of making a major new discovery.* ♦ *He's pulled the company back from the brink* (= he has saved it from disaster). ♦ *He was finally pushed over the brink* (= he became crazy) *when he lost his daughter.* **2** (*literary*) the extreme edge of land, for example at the top

of a CLIFF or by a river: *the brink of the precipice* **IDM** see TEETER

brink·man·ship /'brɪŋkmən,ʃɪp/ (also **brinks·man·ship** /'brɪŋks-/) *noun* [U] the activity, especially in politics, of getting into a situation that could be very dangerous in order to frighten people and make them do what you want

brin·y /'braɪni/ *adj.* (of water) containing a lot of salt **SYN** SALTY ⊃ see also BRINE

bri·o /'briou/ *noun* [U] (*formal*) enthusiasm and individual style

bri·oche /bri'ouʃ/ *noun* [C, U] a type of sweet bread made from flour, eggs, and butter, usually in the shape of a small roll

bri·quette /brɪ'kɛt/ *noun* a small hard block made from coal dust and used as fuel

brisk /brɪsk/ *adj.* (*comparative* **brisk·er**, no *superlative*) **1** quick; busy: *a brisk walk* ♦ *to set off at a brisk pace* ♦ *Ice-cream vendors were doing a brisk business* (= selling a lot of ice cream). **2** (of a person, their voice, or manner) practical and confident; showing a desire to get things done quickly: *His tone became brisk and businesslike.* **3** (of wind and the weather) cold but pleasantly fresh: *a brisk wind/breeze* ▶ **brisk·ly** *adv.* **brisk·ness** *noun* [U]

bris·ket /'brɪskət/ *noun* [U] meat that comes from the chest of an animal, especially a cow

bris·tle /'brɪsl/ *noun, verb*
● *noun* **1** a short stiff hair: *the bristles on his chin* **2** one of the short stiff hairs or wires in a brush ⊃ picture at COMB
● *verb* **1** [I] ~ (with sth) (at sth) to suddenly become very annoyed or offended at what someone says or does: *His lies made her bristle with rage.* **2** [I] (of an animal's fur) to stand up on the back and neck because the animal is frightened or angry
PHR V 'bristle with sth to contain a large number of something: *The whole subject bristles with problems.*

bris·tly /'brɪsli/ *adj.* like or full of bristles; rough: *a bristly chin/mustache*

Brit /brɪt/ *noun* (*informal*) a person from Britain

Brit·ain /'brɪtn/ *noun* [sing.] the island containing England, Scotland, and Wales ⊃ see also GREAT BRITAIN, UNITED KINGDOM

Bri·tan·ni·a /brɪ'tænyə/ *noun* [sing.] a figure of a woman used as a symbol of Britain. She is usually shown sitting down wearing a HELMET and holding a SHIELD and a TRIDENT (= a long weapon with three points).

Bri·tan·nic /brɪ'tænɪk/ *adj.* (*old-fashioned, formal*) (used mainly in names or titles) relating to Britain or the British Empire: *her Britannic Majesty* (= the Queen)

britch·es *noun* = BREECHES **IDM** see BIG *adj.*

Brit·ish /'brɪtɪʃ/ *adj.* **1** (*abbr.* Br.) connected with the United Kingdom of Great Britain and Northern Ireland or the people who live there: *the British Government* ♦ *He was born in France but his parents are British.* ♦ *British-based/British-born/British-made* **2** the British *noun* [pl.] the people of the United Kingdom ▶ **Brit·ish·ness** *noun* [U]

MORE ABOUT

the British

■ There is no singular noun which is commonly used to refer to a person from Britain. Instead, the adjective **British** is used: *She's British.* ♦ *The British have a very odd sense of humor.* The adjective **English** refers only to people from England, not people from the rest of the United Kingdom. They may be **Scottish, Welsh**, or **Northern Irish**.

■ The noun **Briton** is used mainly in newspapers: *The survivors of the avalanche included 12 Britons.* It also describes the early inhabitants of Britain: *the ancient Britons.* **Brit** is informal and can sound negative. **Britisher** is now very old-fashioned.

British 'English *noun* [U] the English language as spoken in Britain and certain other countries

Brit·ish·er /'brɪtɪʃər/ *noun* (*old-fashioned*, *informal*) a person from Britain

Brit·on /'brɪtn/ *noun* (*formal*) a person from Britain: *the ancient Britons* ◆ *the first Briton to climb Everest without oxygen* ➔ note at BRITISH

Brit·pop /'brɪtpɑp/ *noun* [U] a type of pop music played by British groups in the 1990s, influenced by a variety of British musical traditions

brit·tle /'brɪtl/ *adj.*, *noun*
● **1** hard but easily broken: *brittle bones/nails* **2** a brittle mood or state of mind is one that appears to be happy or strong but is actually nervous and easily damaged: *a brittle personality* **3** (of a sound) hard and sharp in an unpleasant way: *a brittle laugh* ▶ **brit·tle·ness** *noun* [U]
● *noun* [U] a type of candy made with cooked sugar and nuts: *peanut brittle*

brittle 'bone dis·ease *noun* [U] (*medical*) **1** a rare disease in which someone's bones break extremely easily **2** = OSTEOPOROSIS

Brit·ton·ic /brɪ'tɑnɪk/ *adj.* = BRYTHONIC

bro /broʊ/ *noun* (*pl.* **bros**) (*informal*) **1** a brother **2** a friendly way of addressing a male person: *Thanks, bro !*

broach /broʊtʃ/ *verb* **~ sth (to/with sb)** to begin talking about a subject that is difficult to discuss, especially because it is embarrassing or because people disagree about it: *She was dreading having to broach the subject of money with her father.*

broad 🔑 /brɔd/ *adj.*, *noun*
● *adj.* (**broad·er**, **broad·est**)
➢ WIDE **1** wide: *a broad street/ avenue/river* ◆ *broad shoulders* ◆ *He is tall, broad, and muscular.* ◆ *a broad smile/grin* (= one in which your mouth is stretched very wide because you are very pleased or amused) **ANT** NARROW **2** used after a measurement of distance to show how wide something is: *two yards broad and one yard high*
➢ WIDE RANGE **3** including a great variety of people or things: *a broad range of products* ◆ *a broad spectrum of interests* ◆ *There is broad support for the government's policies.* ◆ *She took a broad view of the duties of being a teacher* (= she believed her duties included a wide range of things). **ANT** NARROW
➢ GENERAL **4** [only before noun] general; not detailed: *the broad outline of a proposal* ◆ *The negotiators were in broad agreement on the main issues.* ◆ *She's a feminist, in the broadest sense of the word.* ◆ *In broad terms, the paper argues that each country should develop its own policy.*
➢ LAND/WATER **5** covering a wide area: *a broad expanse of water*
➢ ACCENT **6** if someone has a **broad accent**, you can hear very easily which area they come from **SYN** STRONG
➢ HINT **7** if someone gives a **broad hint**, they make it very clear what they are thinking or what they want
➢ HUMOR **8** dealing with sex in an amusing way: *The movie mixes broad humor with romance.* ➔ note at WIDE
IDM **(in) broad 'daylight** (in) the clear light of day, when it is easy to see: *The robbery occurred in broad daylight, on a crowded street.* ➔ more at PAINT *v.*
● *noun* (*old-fashioned*, *slang*) an offensive way of referring to a woman

WORD FAMILY
broad *adj.*
broadly *adv.*
broaden *verb*
breadth *noun*

broad·band /'brɔdbænd/ *noun* [U] **1** (*technical*) signals that use a wide range of frequencies (FREQUENCY) ➔ compare NARROWBAND **2** a way of connecting a computer to the Internet, which allows you to receive information, including pictures, etc., very quickly: *We have broadband at home now.* ➔ collocations at E-MAIL

broad-based (also **broadly-'based**) *adj.* based on a wide variety of people, things, or ideas; not limited

broad bean *noun* = FAVA BEAN

broad-brush *adj.* [only before noun] dealing with a subject or problem in a general way rather than considering details: *a broad-brush approach*

broad·cast 🔑 /'brɔdkæst/ *verb*, *noun*
● *verb* (**broad·cast**, **broad·cast** or **broad·cast·ed**, **broad·cast·ed**) **1** [T, I] **~ (sth)** to send out programs on television or radio: *The concert will be broadcast live* (= at the same time as it takes place) *tomorrow evening.* ◆ *They began broadcasting in 1922.* ➔ collocations at TELEVISION **2** [T] **~ sth** to tell a lot of people about something: *I don't like to broadcast the fact that my father owns the company.*
● *noun* a radio or television program: *a political debate broadcast* (= for example, before an election) ◆ *We watched a live broadcast of the speech* (= one shown at the same time as the speech was made).

broad·cast·er /'brɔdˌkæstər/ *noun* **1** a person whose job is reporting or talking on television or radio programs **2** a company that sends out television or radio programs

broad·cast·ing /'brɔdˌkæstɪŋ/ *noun* [U] the business of making and sending out radio and television programs: *to work in broadcasting* ◆ *a documentary on the local public broadcasting station*

broad·en /'brɔdn/ *verb* **1** [I] to become wider **SYN** WIDEN: *Her smile broadened.* **2** [T, I] to affect or make something affect more people or things **SYN** WIDEN: **~ (sth)** *a promise to broaden access to higher education* ◆ *The candidate needs to broaden his appeal to voters.* ◆ **~ sth out** *Let's broaden out the political discussion.* **3** [T] **~ sth** to increase your experience, knowledge, etc.: *Few would disagree that travel broadens the mind* (= helps you to understand other people's customs, etc.). ◆ *Spending a year working in the city helped to broaden his horizons.*

the 'broad jump *noun* [sing.] = LONG JUMP

broad·leaved /'brɔdlivd/ (also *less frequent* **broad·leaf** /-lif/) *adj.* (*technical*) (of plants) having broad, flat leaves

broad·ly 🔑 /'brɔdli/ *adv.*
1 generally, without considering details: *Broadly speaking, I agree with you.* ◆ *broadly similar/comparable/equivalent/ consistent* **2** if you smile **broadly**, you smile with your mouth stretched very wide because you are very pleased or amused

broad-'minded *adj.* willing to listen to other people's opinions and accept behavior that is different from your own **SYN** OPEN-MINDED, TOLERANT **ANT** NARROW-MINDED ▶ **broad-'mindedness** *noun* [U]

broad·ness /'brɔdnəs/ *noun* [U] the quality of being broad

broad-scale (also **broad·scale**) /'brɔdskeɪl/ *adj.* on a large scale: *The broad-scale cutting down of trees is damaging the environment.*

broad·sheet /'brɔdʃit/ *noun* **1** a newspaper printed on a large size of paper, generally considered more serious than smaller newspapers ➔ compare TABLOID **2** a large piece of paper printed on one side only with information or an advertisement

broad·side /'brɔdsaɪd/ *noun*, *adv.*, *verb*
● *noun* an aggressive attack in words, whether written or spoken: *The president fired a broadside at his critics.*
● *adv.* with one side facing something **SYN** SIDEWAYS: *The car skidded and crashed broadside into another car.*
● *verb* **~ sth** to crash into the side of something: *The driver ran a stop light and broadsided the truck.*

broad-'spectrum *adj.* [only before noun] (*technical*) (of a drug or chemical) effective against a large variety of bacteria, insects, etc.

broad·sword /'brɔdsɔrd/ *noun* a large SWORD with a broad, flat blade

Broad·way /'brɔdweɪ/ *noun* [U] a street in New York City where there are many theaters, sometimes used to refer to the theater industry in general: *a Broadway musical* ◆ *The*

play opened **on Broadway** in 2010. ➔ see also OFF-BROADWAY

bro·cade /broʊˈkeɪd/ noun [U, C] a type of thick, heavy cloth with a raised pattern, made especially from gold or silver silk thread

bro·cad·ed /broʊˈkeɪdəd/ adj. [usually before noun] made of or decorated with brocade

Bro·ca's ar·e·a /ˈbroʊkəz ˌɛriə/ noun (anatomy) an area in the front part of the brain connected with speech

broc·co·li /ˈbrɑkəli; ˈbrɑkli/ noun [U] a vegetable with a thick green STEM and several dark green or purple flower heads ➔ picture at FRUIT

broccoli rabe /ˈbrɑkəli ˌrɑb; ˈbrɑkli-/ noun [U] a green vegetable with small bunches of flowers and bitter leaves

bro·chette /broʊˈʃɛt/ noun (from French) **1** [C, U] a dish consisting of pieces of food cooked on a thin stick over a fire **2** [C] one of the sticks used for cooking food in this way

bro·chure /broʊˈʃʊr/ noun a small magazine or book containing pictures and information about something or advertising something: a travel brochure

bro·de·rie an·glaise /ˌbroʊdəri ɑŋˈglɛz; -ˈglɛz/ noun [U] (from French) decoration with sewing on fine white cloth; the cloth decorated in this way

brogue /broʊg/ noun **1** [usually sing.] the accent that someone has when they are speaking, especially the accent of Irish or Scottish speakers of English **2** [usually pl.] a strong shoe which usually has a pattern in the leather: a pair of brogues

broil /brɔɪl/ verb **1** [T] ~ sth to cook meat or fish under direct heat or over heat on metal bars: broiled chicken ➔ compare BARBECUE **2** [I, T] ~ (sb) to become or make someone become very hot: They lay broiling in the sun.

broil·er /ˈbrɔɪlər/ noun **1** (also **broiler ˌchicken**) a young chicken suitable for broiling or ROASTING **2** the part inside the oven of a stove that directs heat downward to cook food that is placed underneath it

broke /broʊk/ adj. [not before noun] (informal) having no money: I'm always broke by the end of the month. ♦ During the recession thousands of small businesses **went broke** (= had to stop doing business). ♦ **flat broke** (= completely broke) ➔ see also BREAK
> **IDM** **go for broke** (informal) to risk everything in one determined effort to do something ➔ more at AIN'T

broken   chip   chipped   chip   crack   cracked

bro·ken ✍ /ˈbroʊkən/ adj. ➔ see also BREAK v.
> **DAMAGED** **1** that has been damaged or injured; no longer whole or working correctly: a broken window/plate ♦ a broken leg/arm ♦ pieces of broken glass ♦ How did this dish get broken? ♦ The TV's broken. ➔ see also BROKEN HEART
> **PROMISE/AGREEMENT** **2** [usually before noun] not kept
> **NOT CONTINUOUS** **3** [usually before noun] not continuous; disturbed or interrupted: a night of broken sleep ♦ a single broken white line across the road
> **PERSON** **4** [only before noun] made weak and tired by illness or difficulties: He was a broken man after the failure of his business.
> **LANGUAGE** **5** [only before noun] (of a language that is not your own) spoken slowly and with a lot of mistakes; not FLUENT: to speak in broken English
> **RELATIONSHIP** **6** [usually before noun] ended or destroyed: a broken marriage/engagement ➔ see also BROKEN HOME
> **GROUND** **7** having a rough surface: an area of broken, rocky ground

broken-ˈdown adj. [usually before noun] in a very bad

condition; not working correctly; very tired and sick: a broken-down old car/horse

broken ˈheart noun a feeling of great sadness, especially when someone you love has died or left you: No one ever died of a broken heart. ▶ **broken-ˈhearted** adj.: He was broken-hearted when his wife died. ➔ compare HEARTBROKEN

broken ˈhome noun a family in which the parents are divorced or separated: She comes from a broken home.

bro·ken·ly /ˈbroʊkənli/ adv. (formal) (of someone's manner of speaking) in phrases that are very short or not complete, with a lot of pauses; not FLUENTLY

bro·ker /ˈbroʊkər/ noun, verb
• **noun 1** a person who buys and sells things for other people: an insurance broker **2** = STOCKBROKER ➔ see also HONEST BROKER, PAWNBROKER, POWER BROKER
• **verb** ~ sth to arrange the details of an agreement, especially between different countries: a peace plan brokered by the UN

bro·ker·age /ˈbroʊkərɪdʒ/ noun [U] **1** the business of being a broker: a brokerage firm/house **2** an amount of money charged by a broker for work that they do

broker-ˈdealer noun (finance) a person who works on the Stock Exchange buying shares from and selling shares to BROKERS and the public

bro·mide /ˈbroʊmaɪd/ noun **1** [C, U] a chemical which contains bromine, used, especially in the past, to make people feel calm **2** [C] an idea or remark that is intended to make someone feel calmer or more comfortable, but that is not original and has no effect: Feel-good bromides can create the illusion of problem solving.

bro·mine /ˈbroʊmin/ noun [U] (symb. **Br**) a chemical element. Bromine is a dark red, poisonous liquid and has a very strong, unpleasant smell. It is mainly found in the form of salts in ocean water.

bronc /brɑŋk/ noun (informal) = BRONCO

bron·chi·al /ˈbrɑŋkiəl/ adj. [usually before noun] (medical) of or affecting the two main branches of the WINDPIPE (called **bronchial tubes**) leading to the lungs: bronchial pneumonia

bron·chi·tis /brɑŋˈkaɪtəs/ noun [U] an illness that affects the bronchial tubes leading to the lungs: He was suffering from chronic bronchitis. ▶ **bron·chit·ic** /brɑŋˈkɪtɪk/ adj.: a bronchitic cough

bron·chus /ˈbrɑŋkəs/ noun (pl. **bron·chi** /-kaɪ; -ki/) (anatomy) any one of the system of tubes which make up the main branches of the WINDPIPE through which air passes in and out of the lungs

bron·co /ˈbrɑŋkoʊ/ noun (pl. **bron·cos**) (also informal **bronc**) a wild horse of the western U.S.: a bucking bronco in the rodeo

bron·to·sau·rus /ˌbrɑntəˈsɔrəs/ noun = APATOSAURUS

Bronx cheer /ˌbrɑŋks ˈtʃɪr/ noun (informal) = RASPBERRY

bronze /brɑnz/ noun, adj.
• **noun 1** [U] a dark reddish-brown metal made by mixing COPPER and tin: a bronze statue ♦ a figure cast in bronze **2** [U] a dark reddish-brown color, like bronze **3** [C] a work of art made of bronze, for example a statue **4** [C, U] = BRONZE MEDAL
• **adj.** dark reddish-brown in color: bronze skin

the ˈBronze Age noun [sing.] the period in history between the Stone Age and the Iron Age when people used tools and weapons made of bronze

bronzed /brɑnzd/ adj. having skin that has been turned brown in an attractive way by the sun **SYN** TANNED

bronze ˈmedal (also **bronze**) noun [C, U] a MEDAL given as third prize in a competition or race: an Olympic bronze medal winner ♦ She won (a) bronze at the Olympics. ➔ compare GOLD MEDAL, SILVER MEDAL ▶ **bronze ˈmedalist** noun: She's an Olympic bronze medalist.

brooch /broʊtʃ; brutʃ/ noun a piece of jewelry with a pin on the back of it, that can be fastened to your clothes **SYN** PIN

brood /bruːd/ *verb, noun*

● **verb 1** [I] ~ **(over/on/about sth)** to think a lot about something that makes you annoyed, anxious, or upset: *You're not still brooding over what he said, are you?* **2** [I, T] ~ **(sth)** if a bird broods, or broods its eggs, it sits on the eggs in order to HATCH them (= make the young come out of them)

● **noun 1** all the young birds or creatures that a mother produces at one time **SYN** CLUTCH **2** (*humorous*) a large family of children

brood·ing /'bruːdɪŋ/ *adj.* (*literary*) sad and mysterious, or threatening: *dark, brooding eyes* ◆ *a brooding silence* ◆ *Alaska's brooding tundra*

'**brood mare** *noun* a female horse kept for breeding

brood·y /'bruːdi/ *adj.* **1** quiet and thinking about something because you are unhappy or disappointed **2** (of a female bird) wanting to lay eggs and sit on them: *a broody hen* ▶ **brood·i·ness** *noun* [U]

brook /brʊk/ *noun, verb*
● *noun* a small river
● *verb* **not brook something/brook no…** (*formal*) to not allow something: *The tone in his voice brooked no argument.*

broom /bruːm; brʊm/ *noun* **1** [C] a brush on the end of a long handle, used for sweeping floors ⸃ picture at CLEANING **2** [U] a wild bush with small yellow flowers

'**broom closet** *noun* **1** a large built-in closet used for keeping cleaning equipment, etc. in **2** (often *humorous*) a very small room: *I couldn't afford more than a broom closet to set up my office in.*

broom·stick /'bruːmstɪk; 'brʊm-/ *noun* a broom with a long handle and small thin sticks at the end, or the handle of a broom. In stories WITCHES (= women with evil magic powers) ride through the air on broomsticks.

Bros (also **Bros.**) *abbr.* (used in the name of a company) Brothers: *Warner Bros*

broth /brɔːθ; brɑːθ/ *noun* [U, C] soup made by boiling meat or fish and vegetables in water: *chicken broth* **IDM** see COOK *n.*

broth·el /'brɔːθl; 'brɑː-; -ðl/ (also **bor·del·lo**) *noun* a house where people pay to have sex with PROSTITUTES

broth·er 🔑 /'brʌðər/ *noun, exclamation*
● *noun*
▷ IN FAMILY **1** a boy or man who has the same mother and father as another person: *We're brothers.* ◆ *He's my brother.* ◆ *an older/younger brother* ◆ *a twin brother* ◆ *Does she have any brothers and sisters?* ◆ *Edward was the youngest of the Kennedy brothers.* ◆ *He was like a brother to me* (= very close). ⸃ see also HALF-BROTHER, STEPBROTHER
▷ IN RELIGIOUS GROUP **2** also **Brother** (*pl.* **breth·ren** or **broth·ers**) a male member of a religious group, especially a MONK: *Brother Luke* ◆ *The Brethren meet regularly for prayer.*
▷ AT COLLEGE **3** a member of a FRATERNITY (= a club for a group of male students at a college)
▷ FORM OF ADDRESS **4** (*informal*) used by black people as a form of address for a black man
▷ OTHER MEN **5** (*pl.* **broth·ers** or *old-fashioned* **breth·ren**) used for talking to or talking about other male members of an organization or other men who have the same ideas, purpose, etc. as yourself: *We must work together, brothers!* ◆ *He was greatly respected by his brother officers.* ◆ *We must support our weaker brethren.*

● **exclamation** (*old-fashioned*) used to express the fact that you are annoyed or surprised: *Oh brother!*

broth·er·hood /'brʌðərhʊd/ *noun* **1** [U] friendship and understanding between people: *to live in peace and brotherhood* **2** [C] an organization formed for a particular purpose, especially a religious society or political organization **3** [U] the relationship of brothers: *the ties of brotherhood*

'**brother-in-law** (*pl.* '**brothers-in-law**) *noun* the brother of your husband or wife; your sister's husband; the

husband of your husband or wife's sister ⸃ compare SISTER-IN-LAW

broth·er·ly /'brʌðərli/ *adj.* [usually before noun] showing feelings of affection and kindness that you would expect a brother to show: *brotherly love/advice* ◆ *He gave her a brotherly kiss on the cheek.*

brought pt, pp of BRING **IDM** see LOW *adj.*

brou·ha·ha /'bruːhɑːhɑː/ *noun* [U, sing.] (*old-fashioned, informal*) noisy excitement or complaints about something

brow /braʊ/ *noun* **1** (*literary*) the part of the face above the eyes and below the hair **SYN** FOREHEAD: *The nurse mopped his fevered brow.* ◆ *Her brow furrowed in concentration.* **2** [usually pl.] = EYEBROW: *One dark brow rose in surprise.* **3** [usually sing.] the top part of a hill: *The path disappeared over the brow of the hill.* ⸃ see also HIGHBROW, LOWBROW, MIDDLEBROW **IDM** see KNIT *v.*

brow·beat /'braʊbiːt/ *verb* (**brow·beat**, **brow·beat·en** /-ˌbiːtn/) ~ **sb (into doing sth)** to frighten or threaten someone in order to make them do something **SYN** INTIMIDATE: *They were browbeaten into accepting the offer.*

brown 🔑 /braʊn/ *adj., noun, verb*
● *adj.* (**brown·er, brown·est**) **1** having the color of earth or coffee: *brown eyes* ◆ *brown bread* ◆ *dark brown shoe polish* ◆ *a package wrapped in brown paper* **2** having skin that is naturally brown or has been made brown by the sun: *I don't get brown very easily.* ◆ *After a summer at the beach, the children were brown as berries.*

● *noun* [U, C] the color of earth or coffee: *leaves of various shades of brown* ◆ *Brown doesn't* (= brown clothes do not) *really suit you.*

● *verb* [I, T] to become brown; to make something brown: *Heat the butter until it browns.* ◆ *The grass was browning in patches.* ◆ ~ **sth** *Brown the onions before adding the meat.*

'**brown bag** *verb* (**-gg-**) ~ **it** (*informal*) to bring your lunch with you to work or school, usually in a brown paper bag: *My kids have been brown bagging it this week.* ▶ '**brown-bag** *adj.* [only before noun]: *brown-bag lunches*

ˌ**brown 'dwarf** *noun* (*astronomy*) an object in space that is between a large planet and a small star in size, and that produces heat

brown·field /'braʊnfild/ *adj.* [only before noun] used to describe an area of land in a city that was used by industry or for offices in the past and that may now be cleared for new building development: *a brownfield site*

Brown·i·an mo·tion /ˌbraʊniən 'moʊʃn/ *noun* [U] (*physics*) the movement without any regular pattern made by very small pieces of matter in a liquid or gas

brown·ie /'braʊni/ *noun* **1** [C] a thick, soft, flat cake made with chocolate and sometimes nuts and served in small squares: *a fudge brownie* **2 the Brownies** [pl.] a branch of the GIRL SCOUTS for girls between the ages of seven and ten or eleven: *to join the Brownies* **3** [C] **Brownie** a member of the Brownies ⸃ compare CUB SCOUT, GIRL SCOUT, SCOUT

'**brownie point** *noun* [usually pl.] (*informal*) if someone does something to earn **brownie points**, they do it to make someone in authority have a good opinion of them **ORIGIN** The Brownies is a club for young girls who are not yet old enough to be Girl Scouts. They are awarded points for good behavior and achievements.

brown·ish /'braʊnɪʃ/ *adj.* fairly brown in color: *You can't see in this light, but my new coat is a sort of brownish color.*

'**brown-nose** *verb* [I, T] (*informal, disapproving*) ~ **(sb)** to treat someone in authority with special respect in order to make them approve of you or treat you better

brown·out *noun* a period of time when the amount of electrical power that is supplied to an area is reduced

ˌ**brown 'rat** (also ˌ**common 'rat, 'Nor·way rat**) *noun* a common type of RAT

ˌ**brown 'recluse** (also ˌ**brown 'recluse ˌspider**) *noun* a poisonous, brown, N. American spider that has a dark brown mark on its head

,brown 'rice *noun* [U] rice that is light brown because it has not had all of its outside part removed

'brown sauce *noun* [U] a sauce made with fat and flour, cooked until it becomes brown

brown·stone /'braʊnstoʊn/ *noun* a house built of, or with a front made of, a type of reddish-brown stone, which is also called brownstone: *New York brownstones*

,brown 'sugar *noun* [U] sugar that has a brown color and has only been partly REFINED

Brown v. ,Board of Edu'cation *noun* a law case in 1954 which led to a decision of the U.S. Supreme Court that made separate education for black and white children illegal

browse /braʊz/ *verb* **1** [I, T] to look at a lot of things in a store rather than looking for one particular thing: *You are welcome to come in and browse.* ◆ **~ sth** *She browsed the shelves for something interesting to read.* **2** [I, T] **~ (through) sth** to look through the pages of a book, newspaper, etc. without reading everything: *I found the article while I was browsing through some old magazines.* **3** [I, T] **~ (sth)** (*computing*) to look for information on a computer, especially on the Internet **4** [I] **~ (on sth)** (of cows, GOATS, etc.) to eat leaves, etc. that are growing high up ► **browse** *noun* [sing.]: *The gift shop is well worth a browse.*

brows·er /'braʊzər/ *noun* **1** (*computing*) a program that lets you look at or read documents on the Internet: *a Web browser* ᕳ **collocations** at E-MAIL **2** a person who looks through books, magazines, etc. or at things for sale, but may not seriously intend to buy anything

brrr /bərr/ *exclamation* a sound that people make to show that they are very cold: *Brrr, it's freezing here.*

bru·cel·lo·sis /ˌbrusəˈloʊsəs/ *noun* [U] a disease caused by bacteria that affects cows and that can cause fever in humans

bruise /bruz/ *verb, noun*
● *verb* **1** [I, T] to develop a bruise, or make a bruise or bruises appear on the skin of someone or something: *Strawberries bruise easily.* ◆ **~ sth** *She had slipped and badly bruised her knee.* ◆ **collocations** at INJURY ᕳ **thesaurus box** at INJURE **2** [T, usually passive] **~ sb** to affect someone badly and make them feel unhappy, and less confident: *They had been badly bruised by the defeat.* ► **bruised** *adj.*: *He suffered badly bruised ribs in the crash.* ◆ *a bruised ego*
● *noun* **1** a blue, brown, or purple mark that appears on the skin after someone has fallen, been hit, etc.: *to be covered in bruises* ◆ *cuts and bruises* ᕳ **thesaurus box** at INJURE **2** a mark on a fruit or vegetable where it is damaged

bruis·er /'bruzər/ *noun* (*informal*) a large, strong, aggressive man

bruis·ing /'bruzɪŋ/ *adj., noun*
● *adj.* difficult and unpleasant, making you feel tired or weak: *a bruising meeting/experience*
● *noun* [U] bruises on part of a person's body, a piece of fruit, etc.: *She suffered severe bruising, but no bones were broken.* ◆ *internal bruising*

bruit /brut/ *verb* **~ sth (about)** (*formal*) to spread a piece of news widely: *This rumor has been bruited about for years.*

brunch /brʌntʃ/ *noun* [C, U] a meal that you eat in the late morning as a combination of breakfast and lunch

bru·nette /bru'nɛt/ *noun* a woman with dark brown hair

brunt /brʌnt/ *noun*
IDM **bear, take, etc. the brunt of sth** to receive the main force of something unpleasant: *Schools will bear the brunt of cuts in government spending.*

bru·schet·ta /bru'skɛtə; -'ʃɛtə/ *noun* [U] (from *Italian*) an Italian dish consisting of pieces of warm bread covered with oil and chopped raw tomatoes: *a first course of bruschetta*

brush /brʌʃ/ *noun, verb*
● *noun* **1** [C] an object made of short stiff hairs (called BRISTLES) or wires set in a block of wood or plastic, usually attached to a handle. Brushes are used for many different jobs, such as cleaning, painting, and arranging your hair: *a paintbrush* ◆ *a hairbrush* ◆ *a toothbrush* ◆ *brush strokes* (= the marks left by a brush when painting) ◆ *a dustpan and brush* ◆ *Apply the paint with a fine brush.* ᕳ **picture** at MAKEUP **2** [sing.] an act of brushing: *to give your teeth a good brush* **3** [U] land covered by small trees or bushes: *a brush fire* **4** [sing.] a light touch made in passing something or someone: *the brush of his lips on her cheek* **5** [C] **~ with sb/ sth** a short unfriendly meeting with someone; an occasion when you nearly experience something unpleasant: *She had a nasty brush with her boss this morning.* ◆ *In his job he's had frequent brushes with death.* ◆ *a brush with the law* **6** [C] the tail of a FOX **IDM** see PAINT v., TAR v.
● *verb* **1** [T] to clean, polish, or make something smooth with a brush: **~ sth** *to brush your hair/teeth/shoes* ◆ **~ sth + adj.** *A tiled floor is easy to brush clean.* **2** [T] to put something, for example oil, milk, or egg, on something using a brush: **~ A with B** *Brush the pastry with beaten egg.* ◆ **~ B over A** *Brush beaten egg over the pastry.* **3** [T] **~ sth + adv./prep.** to remove something from a surface with a brush or with your hand: *He brushed the dirt off his jacket.* ◆ *She brushed the fly away.* **4** [I, T] to touch someone or something lightly while moving close to them/it: **~ against/by/past sb/sth** *She brushed past him.* ◆ *His hand accidentally brushed against hers.* ◆ **~ sth** *The leaves brushed her cheek.* ◆ **~ sth with sth** *He brushed her lips with his.*
PHR V **,brush sb/sth↔'aside** to ignore someone or something; to treat someone or something as unimportant **SYN** DISMISS: *He brushed aside my fears.* **,brush sth↔'down** to clean something by brushing it: *to brush a coat/horse down* **,brush 'off** to be removed by brushing: *Mud brushes off easily when it is dry.* **,brush sb↔'off** to rudely ignore someone or refuse to listen to them: *She brushed him off impatiently.* ᕳ **related noun** BRUSH-OFF **,brush sb/yourself 'off** to make someone/yourself clean, especially after you have fallen, by brushing your clothes, etc. with your hands **,brush sth↔'up** | **,brush 'up on sth** to quickly improve a skill, especially when you have not used it for a time: *I need to brush up on my Spanish before I go to Seville.*

'brush-off *noun* [sing.] (*informal*) rude or unfriendly behavior that shows that a person is not interested in someone: *Paul asked Tara out to dinner, but she* **gave him the brush-off.**

brush·wood /'brʌʃwʊd/ *noun* [U] small broken or dead branches of trees, often used to make fires

brush·work /'brʌʃwərk/ *noun* [U] the particular way in which an artist uses a brush to paint ᕳ **collocations** at ART

brusque /brʌsk/ *adj.* using very few words and sounding rude **SYN** ABRUPT, CURT: *The doctor spoke in a brusque tone.* ► **brusque·ly** *adv.*: *"What's your name?" he asked brusquely.* **brusque·ness** *noun* [U]

Brus·sels sprout /'brʌslz ˌspraʊt/ (also **Brus·sel sprout**) *noun* a small round green vegetable like a very small CABBAGE

bru·tal /'brutl/ *adj.* **1** violent and cruel: *a brutal attack/ murder/rape/killing* **2** direct and clear about something unpleasant; not thinking of people's feelings: *With brutal honesty, she told him she did not love him.* ► **bru·tal·i·ty** /bru'tæləti/ *noun* [U, C] (*pl.* **bru·tal·i·ties**): *police brutality* ◆ *the brutalities of war* **bru·tal·ly** /'brutl·i/ *adv.*: *He was brutally assaulted.* ◆ *Let me be brutally frank about this.*

bru·tal·ism /'brutlˌɪzəm/ *noun* [U] (*architecture*) (sometimes *disapproving*) a style of architecture used especially in the 1950s and 60s that uses large concrete blocks, steel, etc., and is sometimes considered ugly and unpleasant ► **bru·tal·ist** /-ɪst/ *adj., noun*

bru·tal·ize /'brutlˌaɪz/ *verb* **1** **~ sb** to treat someone in a cruel or violent way **2** [usually passive] **~ sb** to make someone unable to feel normal human emotions such as sympathy: *soldiers brutalized by war*

brute /brut/ *noun, adj.*
- *noun* **1** (sometimes *humorous*) a man who treats people in an unkind, cruel way: *His father was a drunken brute.* ◆ *You've forgotten my birthday again, you brute!* **2** a large strong animal **3** a thing which is awkward and unpleasant
- *adj.* [only before noun] **1** involving physical strength only and not thought or intelligence: *brute force/strength* **2** basic and unpleasant: *the brute facts of inequality*

brut·ish /'brutɪʃ/ *adj.* unkind and violent and not showing thought, or intelligence ▶ **brut·ish·ness** *noun* [U]

Bryl·creem™ /'brɪlkrim/ *noun* [U] a type of cream that men can put on their hair to make it smooth and shiny

B.S. (also **BS**) /ˌbi 'ɛs/ (also **B.Sc.**, **BSc**) *noun* a college degree in science (the abbreviation for "Bachelor of Science"): *to have/do a B.S. in Zoology*

B.Sc (also **BSc**) /ˌbi ɛs 'si/ *noun* = B.S.

BSE /ˌbi ɛs 'i/ (also *informal* ˌmad 'cow disˌease) *noun* [U] the abbreviation for "bovine spongiform encephalopathy" (a brain disease of cows that causes death)

'B-side *noun* the side of a VINYL pop record that was considered less likely to be successful ⊃ compare A-SIDE

Btu (also **BTU**) *abbr.* British thermal unit (the quantity of heat needed to raise one pound of water one degree FAHREN-HEIT)

BTW (also **btw**) *abbr.* (*informal*) used in writing to mean "by the way"

bub /bʌb/ *noun* (*slang*) an aggressive or rude way of addressing a boy or man: *Hey bub, what are you doing here?*

bub·ble 🔑 /'bʌbl/ *noun, verb*
- *noun* **1** a ball of air or gas in a liquid, or a ball of air inside a solid substance such as glass: *champagne bubbles* ◆ *a bubble of oxygen* ◆ *blowing bubbles into water through a straw* ⊃ picture at FROTH ⊃ see also SPEECH BUBBLE **2** a round ball of liquid, containing air, produced by soap and water: *The children like to have bubbles in their bath.* **3** a small amount of a feeling that someone wants to express: *a bubble of laughter/hope/enthusiasm* **4** a good or lucky situation that is unlikely to last long: *At the time, the telecoms bubble was at its height.*
  IDM the bubble bursts there is a sudden end to a good or lucky situation: *When the bubble finally burst, hundreds of people lost their jobs.* ⊃ more at BURST *v.*
- *verb* **1** [I] to form bubbles: *The water in the pan was beginning to bubble.* ◆ *Add the white wine and let it bubble up.* **2** [I] (+ *adv./prep.*) to make a bubbling sound, especially when moving in the direction mentioned: *I could hear the soup bubbling away.* ◆ *A stream came bubbling between the stones.* **3** [I] ~ (over) with sth to be full of a particular feeling: *She was bubbling over with excitement.* **4** [I] + *adv./prep.* (of a feeling) to be felt strongly by a person; to be present in a situation: *Laughter bubbled up inside him.* ◆ *the anger that bubbled beneath the surface*
  IDM bubble under the radar (*informal*) to be likely to be very successful or popular soon: *Here are two records that are bubbling under the radar.*

'bubble ˌbath *noun* **1** [U] a liquid soap that smells pleasant and makes a lot of bubbles when it is added to BATH-WATER **2** [C] a bath with bubble bath in the water

bub·ble·gum /'bʌblˌgʌm/ *noun, adj.*
- *noun* [U] a type of GUM that can be blown into bubbles
- *adj.* [only before noun] simple in style, not serious, and liked mainly by young people: *This CD is pure bubblegum pop.*

bub·ble·jet print·er /'bʌbldʒɛt ˌprɪntər/ *noun* a type of printer that uses bubbles of air to blow small dots of ink in order to form letters, numbers, etc. on paper

'bubble ˌwrap (also **'bubble ˌpack**) *noun* [U] a sheet of plastic that has lots of small raised parts filled with air, used for protecting things that are being carried or sent by mail

bub·bly /'bʌbli/ *adj.* (**bub·bli·er**, **bub·bli·est**) *noun*
- *adj.* **1** full of bubbles **2** (of a person) always cheerful, friendly, and enthusiastic
- *noun* [U] (*informal*) = CHAMPAGNE

bu·bon·ic plague /byuˌbɑnɪk 'pleɪg; bu-/ (also **the plague**) *noun* [U] a disease spread by RATS that causes fever, swellings on the body, and usually death

buc·ca·neer /ˌbʌkə'nɪr/ *noun* **1** (in the past) a sailor who attacked ships at sea and stole from them **SYN** PIRATE **2** (especially in business) a person who achieves success in a skillful but not always honest way

buc·ca·neer·ing /ˌbʌkə'nɪrɪŋ/ *adj.* enjoying taking risks, especially in business: *Apple's buccaneering founder, Steve Jobs*

buck /bʌk/ *noun, verb*
- *noun* **1** [C] (*informal*) a dollar: *They cost ten bucks.* ◆ *We're talking big bucks* (= a lot of money) *here.* **2** [C] a male DEER, HARE, or RABBIT (also called a **buck rabbit**) ⊃ compare DOE, HART, STAG **3** the buck [sing.] used in some expressions to refer to the responsibility or blame for something: *It was my decision. The buck stops here* (= no one else can be blamed). ◆ *I was tempted to pass the buck* (= make someone else responsible). **ORIGIN** From **buck**, an object that in a poker game is placed in front of the player whose turn it is to deal.
  IDM make a fast/quick buck (*informal*, often *disapproving*) to earn money quickly and easily ⊃ more at BANG *n.*, MILLION
- *verb* **1** [I] (of a horse) to jump with the two back feet or all four feet off the ground **2** [I] to move up and down suddenly or in a way that is not controlled: *The boat bucked and heaved beneath them.* **3** [T] ~ sth (*informal*) to resist or oppose something: *One or two companies have managed to buck the trend of the recession.* ◆ *He admired her willingness to buck the system* (= oppose authority or rules).
  PHR V buck 'up (*informal*) (often in orders) to become more cheerful **SYN** CHEER UP: *Buck up, kid! It's not the end of the game.* ˌbuck sb 'up (*informal*) to make someone more cheerful **SYN** CHEER UP: *The good news bucked us all up.*

buck·et /'bʌkət/ *noun* **1** (also **pail**) [C] an open container with a handle, used for carrying or holding liquids, sand, etc.: *a plastic bucket* ◆ *Get the mop and bucket—I just spilled water all over the floor.* ⊃ picture at CLEANING **2** [C] a large container that is part of a CRANE or DIGGER, and is used for lifting things **3** (also **buck·et·ful** /-fʊl/, **pail**, **pail·ful**) [C] the amount contained in a bucket: *two buckets/bucketfuls of water* ◆ *They used to drink coffee by the bucket/bucketful* (= in large quantities). **4** buckets [pl.] (*informal*) a large amount: *To succeed in show business, you need buckets of confidence.* ◆ *We wept buckets.* ◆ *He was sweating buckets by the end of the race.* ◆ *The rain was coming down in buckets* (= it was raining very heavily). **IDM** see DROP *n.*, KICK *v.*

ˌbucket 'seat *noun* a seat with a curved back for one person, especially in a car

buck·eye /'bʌkaɪ/ *noun* **1** a N. American tree that has bright red or white flowers and produces nuts **2** an orange and brown BUTTERFLY with large spots on its wings that look like eyes **3** Buckeye (*informal*) a person from the state of Ohio

Buck·ing·ham Pal·ace /ˌbʌkɪŋəm 'pæləs; ˌbʌkɪŋhæm-/ *noun* **1** the official home of the British royal family in London **2** the British royal family or the people who advise them: *Buckingham Palace refused to comment.*

buck·le /'bʌkl/ *verb, noun*
- *verb* **1** [T, I] to fasten something or be fastened with a buckle: ~ (sth) *She buckled her belt.* ◆ ~ (sth on/up) *He buckled on his sword.* ◆ *These shoes buckle at the side.* ⊃ picture at CLOTHES **2** [I, T] to become crushed or bent under a weight or force; to crush or bend something in this way: *The steel frames began to buckle under the strain.* ◆ (*figurative*) *A weaker man would have buckled under the pressure.* ◆ ~ sth *The crash buckled the front of my car.* **3** [I] when your knees or legs **buckle** or when you **buckle** at the knees, your knees become weak and you start to fall

h **hat**   m **man**   n **no**   ŋ **sing**   l **leg**   r **red**   y **yes**   w **wet**

PHR V **buckle 'down (to sth)** (*informal*) to start to do something seriously: *I'd better buckle down and finish those reports.* ,buckle 'up (*informal*) to fasten your SEAT BELT (= a belt worn by a passenger in a vehicle)

- **noun** a piece of metal or plastic used for joining the ends of a belt or for fastening a part of a bag, shoe, etc.

,buck 'naked *adj.* (*informal*) (of a person) not wearing any clothes at all

buck·ram /'bʌkrəm/ *noun* [U] a type of stiff cloth made especially from cotton or LINEN, used in the past for covering books and for making clothes stiffer

buck·shot /'bʌkʃɑt/ *noun* [U] balls of LEAD ² that are fired from a SHOTGUN

buck·skin /'bʌkskɪn/ *noun* [U] soft leather made from the skin of DEER or GOATS, used for making gloves, bags, etc.

,buck 'teeth *noun* [pl.] top teeth that stick forward ▶ 'buck-toothed *adj.*

buck·wheat /'bʌkwit/ *noun* [U] small dark grain that is grown as food for animals and for making flour

bu·col·ic /byu'kɑlɪk/ *adj.* (*literary*) connected with the countryside or country life

bud /bʌd/ *noun, verb*
- **noun** **1** a small lump that grows on a plant and from which a flower, leaf, or STEM develops: *the first buds appearing in spring* ♦ *The tree is in bud already.* ⊃ collocations at LIFE ⊃ picture at TREE **2** a flower or leaf that is not fully open **3** (*informal*) = BUDDY: *Listen, bud, enough of the wisecracks, OK?* ⊃ see also ROSEBUD, TASTE BUD **IDM** see NIP *v.*
- **verb** [I] to produce buds

Bud·dha /'budə; 'bʊ-/ *noun* **1** (also **the Buddha**) the person on whose teachings the Buddhist religion is based **2** [C] a statue or picture of the Buddha **3** [C] a person who has achieved ENLIGHTENMENT (= spiritual knowledge) in Buddhism

Bud·dhism /'budɪzəm; 'bʊ-/ *noun* [U] an Asian religion based on the teaching of Siddhartha Gautama (or Buddha) ▶ **Bud·dhist** /'budɪst; 'bʊ-/ *noun*: *a devout Buddhist* **Buddhist** *adj.* [usually before noun]: *a Buddhist monk/temple*

bud·ding /'bʌdɪŋ/ *adj.* [only before noun] beginning to develop or become successful: *a budding artist/writer* ♦ *our budding romance*

bud·dle·ia /'bʌdliə/ (also **'butterfly ,bush**) *noun* [C, U] a bush with purple or white flowers that grow in groups

bud·dy /'bʌdi/ *noun, verb*
- **noun** (*pl.* **bud·dies**) **1** (also **bud**) (*informal*) a friend: *an old college buddy of mine* **2** (also **bud**) (*informal*) used to speak to a man you do not know: *"Where to, buddy?" the driver asked.* **3** a partner who does an activity with you so that you can help each other: *The school uses a buddy system to pair newcomers with older students.*
- **verb** (**bud·dies, bud·dy·ing, bud·died, bud·died**) **PHR V** ,buddy 'up (to/with sb) **1** (*informal*) to become friendly with someone: *You might want to buddy up with your neighbor to make the trip more enjoyable.* **2** to become friendly with someone in order to get an advantage for yourself

,buddy-'buddy *adj.* (*informal*, often *disapproving*) ~ (with sb) very friendly: *He's very buddy-buddy with the boss, so of course he got promoted.*

'buddy ,movie *noun* (*informal*) a movie in which there is a close friendship between two people

budge /bʌdʒ/ *verb* (usually used in negative sentences) **1** [I, T] to move slightly; to make something or someone move slightly: *She pushed at the door, but it wouldn't budge.* ♦ *The dog refused to budge.* ♦ ~ sth *I heaved with all my might, but still couldn't budge it.* **2** [I, T] to change your opinion about something; to make someone change their opinion: *He won't budge an inch on the issue.* ♦ ~ sb *He wouldn't be budged on the issue.*

budg·er·i·gar /'bʌdʒəri,gɑr/ *noun* (also *informal* **budg·ie**) a small bird of the PARROT family, often kept in a CAGE as a pet

budg·et 🔑 /'bʌdʒət/ *noun, verb, adj.*
- **noun** **1** [C, U] the money that is available to a person or an organization and a plan of how it will be spent over a period of time: *a monthly/an annual/a family budget* ♦ *the education/defense budget* (= the amount of money that can be spent on this) ♦ *an advertising budget of $2 million* ♦ *a big-budget movie* ♦ *We decorated the house on a tight budget* (= without much money to spend). ♦ *The work was finished on time and within budget* (= did not cost more money than was planned). ♦ *They went over budget* (= spent too much money). ♦ *budget cuts* ⊃ collocations at BUSINESS **2** an official statement by the government of a country's income from taxes, etc. and how it will be spent: *tax cuts in this year's budget* ♦ *a budget deficit* (= when the government spends more money than it earns) ⊃ collocations at ECONOMY
- **verb** [I, T] to be careful about the amount of money you spend; to plan to spend an amount of money for a particular purpose: *If we budget carefully, we'll be able to afford the trip.* ♦ ~ for sth *I budgeted for two new members of staff.* ♦ ~ sth (for sth) *Ten million dollars has been budgeted for the project.* ♦ ~ sth (at sth) *The project has been budgeted at ten million dollars.* ⊃ thesaurus box at SAVE ▶ **bud·get·ing** *noun* [U]
- **adj.** [only before noun] (used in advertising, etc.) low in price: *a budget flight/hotel* ⊃ thesaurus box at CHEAP

budg·et·ar·y /'bʌdʒə,tɛri/ *adj.* connected with a budget: *budgetary control/policies/reform*

budg·ie /'bʌdʒi/ *noun* (*informal*) = BUDGERIGAR

buff /bʌf/ *noun, adj., verb*
- **noun** **1** [C] (used in compounds) a person who is very interested in a particular subject or activity and knows a lot about it: *an opera buff* **2** [U] a pale yellow-brown color **SYN** BEIGE **3** [U] soft, strong, yellowish-brown leather **IDM** in the buff (*informal*) wearing no clothes **SYN** NAKED
- **adj.** **1** pale yellow-brown in color: *a buff envelope* **SYN** BEIGE **2** (*slang*) physically fit and attractive with big muscles
- **verb** ~ sth (up) to polish something with a soft cloth **PHR V** ,buff 'up | ,buff yourself 'up (*slang*) to make yourself more attractive, especially by exercising in order to make your muscles bigger: *He buffed up to take the role of the commando captain.* ,buff sb/sth 'up (*informal*) to work on someone or something to make them/it seem more attractive or impressive: *The team will have to buff up their tarnished image.*

buf·fa·lo /'bʌfə,loʊ/ *noun* (*pl.* buffalo, buf·fa·loes or buf·fa·los) **1** a large wild animal of the cow family that is covered with hair. It is also called a BISON. **2** a large animal of the cow family. There are two types of buffalo, the African and the Asian, which has wide, curved horns. ⊃ see also WATER BUFFALO

buffalo

'buffalo ,wings *noun* [pl.] chicken wings cooked in a spicy sauce

buff·er /'bʌfər/ *noun, verb*
- **noun** **1** a thing or person that reduces a shock or protects someone or something against difficulties: ~ (against sth) *Support from family and friends acts as a buffer against stress.* ♦ ~ (between sth and sth) *She often had to act as a buffer between father and son.* ♦ *a buffer state* (= a small country between two powerful states that helps keep peace between them) ♦ *a buffer zone* (= an area of land between two opposing armies or countries) **2** (*computing*) an area in a computer's memory where data can be stored for a short time

verb 1 ~ sth to reduce the harmful effects of something: *to buffer the effects of stress on health* **2** ~ sb (against sth) to protect someone from something: *They tried to buffer themselves against problems and uncertainties.* **3** ~ sth (computing) (of a computer) to hold data for a short time before using it

buf·fet¹ /ˈbəˈfeɪ; bʊ-/ ⊃ see also BUFFET² *noun* **1** a meal at which people serve themselves from a table and then stand or sit somewhere else to eat: *a lunch/dinner buffet* ◆ *Dinner will be buffet style, not a sit-down meal.* **2** a long table in a restaurant, etc. that a buffet is served fom **3** = SIDEBOARD

buf·fet² /ˈbʌfət/ ⊃ see also BUFFET¹ *verb* [often passive] ~ sb/sth to knock or push someone or something roughly from side to side: *to be buffeted by the wind* ◆ (figurative, formal) *The nation had been buffeted by a wave of strikes.* ▶ **buf·fet·ing** *noun* [U, C, usually sing.]

buf·foon /bəˈfuːn/ *noun* (old-fashioned) a person who does silly but amusing things ▶ **buf·foon·er·y** /bəˈfuːnəri/ *noun* [U]

bug /bʌɡ/ *noun, verb*
• *noun* **1** [C] any small insect **2** [C] (informal) an infectious illness that is usually fairly mild: *a flu bug* ◆ *There's a stomach bug going around* (= people are catching it from each other). ◆ *I picked up a bug in the office.* ⊃ thesaurus box at DISEASE **3** usually **the… bug** [sing.] (informal) an enthusiastic interest in something such as a sport or a hobby: *the travel bug* ◆ *She was never interested in the gym before, but she was bitten by the fitness bug.* **4** [C] (informal) a small hidden device for listening to other people's conversations **5** [C] a fault in a machine, especially in a computer system or program
• *verb* (-gg-) **1** ~ sth to put a special device (= a bug) somewhere in order to listen secretly to other people's conversations: *They bugged her hotel room.* ◆ *They were bugging his phone conversations.* ◆ *a bugging device* **2** ~ sb (informal) to annoy or irritate someone: *Stop bugging me!* ◆ *It's something that's been bugging me a lot recently.*
PHR V bug ˈoff! (informal) a rude way of telling someone to go away **bug ˈout** (informal) **1** (especially of someone's eyes) to be wide open and stick out: *Their eyes were bugging out of their heads when they saw it.* **2** to leave a place or situation, especially because it is becoming dangerous: *We should bug out now before it's too late.* **3** to become too frightened to do something: *Susan started to bug out when she heard a noise in the bushes.*

bug·a·boo /ˈbʌɡəˌbuː/ *noun* (informal) a thing that people are afraid of

bug·bear /ˈbʌɡber/ *noun* a thing that annoys people and that they worry about: *Inflation is the government's main bugbear.*

ˈbug-eyed *adj.* (informal) having eyes that stick out

bug·gy /ˈbʌɡi/ *noun* (pl. bug·gies) **1** a light CARRIAGE for one or two people, pulled by one horse **2** a small car, often without a roof or doors, used for a particular purpose ⊃ see also DUNE BUGGY **3** a type of light folding chair on wheels in which a baby or small child is pushed along ⊃ compare STROLLER

bu·gle /ˈbjuːɡl/ *noun* a musical instrument like a small TRUMPET, used in the army for giving signals

bu·gler /ˈbjuːɡlər/ *noun* a person who plays the bugle

build 🔑 /bɪld/ *verb, noun*
• *verb* (built, built /bɪlt/) **1** [T, I] to make something, especially a building, by putting parts together: ~ (sth) *They have permission to build 200 new houses.* ◆ *Robins build nests almost anywhere.* ◆ *They're going to build on the site of the old power station.* ◆ ~ sth of/in/from sth *a house built of stone* ◆ ~ sth for sb *They had a house built for them.* ◆ ~ sb sth *David built us a shed in the backyard.* **2** [T] ~ sth to create or develop something: *She built a new career for herself.* ◆ *We want to build a better life.* ◆ *This information will help us build a picture of his attacker.* **3** [I] (of a feeling) to become gradually stronger: *The tension and excitement built gradually all day.*
IDM see CASTLE, ROME

PHR V build sth aˈround sth [usually passive] to create something, using something else as a basis: *The story is built around a group of high school dropouts.* **build sth↔ˈin | build sth ˈinto sth** [often passive] **1** to make something a permanent part of a larger structure: *We're having new wardrobes built in.* ◆ *The pipes were built into the concrete.* **2** to make something a permanent part of a system, plan, etc.: *A certain amount of flexibility is built into the system.* ⊃ see also BUILT-IN **build on sth** to use something as a basis for further progress: *This study builds on earlier work.* **build sth on sth** [usually passive] to base something on something: *an argument built on sound logic* **build sth↔ˈon | build sth ˈonto sth** to add something (for example, an extra room) to an existing structure by building: *They built an extension on the back of the house.* ◆ *The new wing was built onto the hospital last year.* **build ˈup (to sth)** to gradually become greater, more powerful, or larger in number or quantity: *The pressure had built up, and he was out of work for weeks from stress.* ◆ *The music builds up to a rousing climax.* ◆ *She had been away for several weeks and dust had built up on all the furniture.* ⊃ related noun BUILDUP **build ˈup to sth | build yourself ˈup to sth** to prepare for a particular moment or event: *Build yourself up to peak performance on the day of the race.* ⊃ related noun BUILDUP **build sb/sth ˈup** [usually passive] to give a very positive and enthusiastic description of someone or something, often exaggerating your claims: *The play was built up to be a masterpiece, but I found it very disappointing.* ⊃ related noun BUILDUP **build sb/yourself↔ˈup** to make someone/yourself healthier or stronger: *You need more protein to build you up.* **build sth↔ˈup 1** to create or develop something: *She's built up a very successful business.* ◆ *These finds help us build up a picture of life in the Middle Ages.* ◆ *I am anxious not to build up false hopes* (= to encourage people to hope for too much). **2** to make something higher or stronger than it was before

THESAURUS

build

construct ◆ **assemble** ◆ **put sth together** ◆ **erect** ◆ **put sth up** ◆ **establish**

These words all mean to make or create something, especially by putting different parts together.

build to make something, especially a building, by putting parts together: *a house built of stone* ◆ *They're going to build a museum on the site of the old power plant.*

construct [often passive] (somewhat formal) to build something such as a road, building, or machine

assemble (somewhat formal) to fit together all the separate parts of something, such as a piece of furniture or a machine: *The cupboard is easy to assemble.*

put sth together to make or prepare something by fitting or collecting parts together: *to put together a model plane*

erect (formal) to build something; to put something in position and make it stand upright: *Police had to erect barriers to keep crowds back.*

put sth up to build something or place something somewhere: *I put up a fence so that my dog would have somewhere to exercise.*

establish to create an organization or place that is meant to last for a long time: *President Roosevelt established the first national park at Yellowstone.*

PATTERNS
- to build/construct/erect/put up a **house/wall**
- to build/construct/erect/put up some **shelves**
- to build/construct/erect/put up a **barrier/fence/shelter**
- to build/assemble a(n) **engine/machine**
- to build/construct a **road/railway/railroad/tunnel**
- to erect/put up a **tent/statue/monument/memorial**

ʌ **cup**   ə **about**   eɪ **say**   aɪ **five**   ɔɪ **boy**   aʊ **now**   oʊ **go**   ər **bird**

buildings

palace

battlements turret
castle | moat

portico
mansion

amphitheater

pyramid

fort

greenhouse

lighthouse

oil rig (also oil platform)

skyscraper

warehouse

log cabin

pagoda

hut

barn

● **noun** [U, C, usually sing.] the shape and size of the human body: *a man with a stocky build*

build·er /ˈbɪldər/ *noun* **1** a person or company whose job is to build or repair houses or other buildings **2** (usually in compounds) a person or thing that builds, creates or develops something: *a shipbuilder* ♦ *a confidence builder* ➸ see also BODYBUILDING

build·ing 🔎 /ˈbɪldɪŋ/ *noun*
1 [C] a structure such as a house, school, or factory that has a roof and walls: *tall/old/historic buildings* ➸ collocations at DECORATE **2** [U] the process and work of building: *the building of the school* ♦ *There's building work going on next door.* ♦ *the building trade* ♦ *building materials/costs/regulations*

premises [pl.] (*formal*) the building or buildings and surrounding land that a business or person owns or uses: *The police searched the premises.*

complex a group of buildings of a similar type together in one place: *an apartment complex*

structure a thing that is made of several parts, especially a building: *The pier is a wooden structure.*

PATTERNS

(a/an) **commercial/industrial/residential** building/property/premises/complex
- an **apartment** building/complex
- a/the **school** building/premises
- to **build** a property/complex/structure
- to **put up** a building/property/structure
- to **demolish/knock down** a building/property/complex/structure

'building ,block *noun* **1** [C] a piece of wood or plastic used as a toy for children to build things with ⊃ **picture at** TOY **2 building blocks** [pl.] parts that are joined together in order to make a large thing exist: *Single words are the building blocks of language.*

'building ,site = CONSTRUCTION SITE

build·up /'bɪldʌp/ *noun* **1** [sing., U] an increase in the amount of something over a period of time: *a steady buildup of traffic in the evenings* **2** [C, usually sing.] ~ (**to sth**) the time before an important event, when people are preparing for it: *the buildup to the president's visit* **3** [C, usually sing.] a very positive and enthusiastic description of something that is going to happen, that is intended to make people excited about it: *The media has given the show a huge buildup.*

built /bɪlt/ *verb, combining form, adj.*
- *verb* pt, pp of BUILD
- *combining form* (after adverbs and in compound adjectives) made in the particular way that is mentioned: *a newly built station* ◆ *Japanese-built cars* ⊃ **see also** WELL BUILT
- *adj.* made, constructed, or provided by people: *transforming the built environment* (= the housing, roads, manufactured goods, etc. that make up a community)

,built-'in *adj.* [only before noun] **1** included as part of something and not separate from it: *built-in cupboards* **2** a **built-in** quality exists as an essential part of something or someone: *His height gives him a built-in advantage over his opponent.*

,built-'up *adj.* [usually before noun] (of an area of land) covered in buildings, roads, etc.: *to reduce the speed limit in built-up areas*

bulb /bʌlb/ *noun* **1** (also **'light bulb**) the glass part that fits into an electric lamp, etc. to give light when it is switched on: *a 60-watt bulb* ◆ *a room lit by a bare bulb* (= with no decorative cover) ⊃ **picture at** LIGHT **2** the round underground part of some plants, shaped like an onion, that grows into a new plant every year: *a garlic bulb* ⊃ **picture at** PLANT **3** an object shaped like a bulb, for example the end of a THERMOMETER

bul·bous /'bʌlbəs/ *adj.* shaped like a bulb; round and fat in an ugly way: *a bulbous red nose*

bul·gar (also **bul·gur**) /'bʌlgər; 'bʊl-/ (also **'bulgur ,wheat**) *noun* [U] a type of food consisting of grains of WHEAT that are boiled then dried

bulge /bʌldʒ/ *verb, noun*
- *verb* **1** [I] ~ (**with sth**) (usually used in the progressive tenses) to be completely full (of something): *Her pockets were bulging with presents.* ◆ *a bulging briefcase* **2** [I] to stick out from something in a round shape: *His eyes bulged.* **IDM** see SEAM
- *noun* **1** a lump that sticks out from something in a round shape: *the bulge of a gun in his pocket* **2** (*informal*) fat on the body that sticks out in a round shape: *That skirt is too tight. It shows all your bulges.* **3** a sudden temporary increase in the

amount of something: *After the war there was a bulge in the birth rate.*

bulg·ing /'bʌldʒɪŋ/ *adj.* that sticks out from something in a round shape: *bulging eyes*

bu·lim·i·a /bʊ'limiə/ (also **bu·lim·i·a ner·vo·sa** /bʊ,limiə nər'voʊsə/) *noun* [U] an emotional DISORDER in which a person repeatedly eats too much and then forces him- or herself to VOMIT ⊃ **collocations at** DIET ⊃ **compare** ANOREXIA ▶ **bu·lim·ic** /bʊ'limɪk/ *adj., noun*

bulk ᴬᵂᴸ /bʌlk/ *noun, verb*
- *noun* **1** [sing.] **the ~ (of sth)** the main part of something; most of something: *The bulk of the population lives in cities.* **2** [U] the (large) size or quantity of something: *Despite its bulk and weight, the car is extremely fast.* ◆ *a bulk order* (= one for a large number of similar items) ◆ *bulk buying* (= buying in large amounts, often at a reduced price) ◆ *It's cheaper to buy in bulk.* **3** [sing.] the weight or shape of someone or something large: *She heaved her bulk out of the chair.*
- *verb*
  PHR V ,bulk sth↔'out/'up to make something bigger, thicker, or heavier ,bulk (yourself) 'up to gain weight and build your muscles by eating and exercising more, often when training for sports events: *The coach told us to bulk up before the season started.*

bulk·head /'bʌlkhɛd/ *noun* (*technical*) a wall that divides a ship or an aircraft into separate parts

bulk·y ᴬᵂᴸ /'bʌlki/ *adj.* (**bulk·i·er, bulk·i·est**) **1** (of a thing) large and difficult to move or carry: *Bulky items will be collected separately.* **2** (of a person) tall and heavy: *The guard's bulky figure appeared at the door.*

bull /bʊl/ *noun* **1** [C] the male of any animal in the cow family: *a bull neck* (= a short thick neck like a bull) ⊃ **compare** BULLOCK, COW, OX, STEER **2** [C] the male of the ELEPHANT, WHALE, and some other large animals ⊃ **compare** COW **3** [C] (*finance*) a person who buys shares in a company, hoping to sell them soon afterward at a higher price ⊃ **compare** BEAR **4** [C] an official order or statement from the POPE (= the head of the Roman Catholic Church): *a papal bull* **5** [U] (*slang*) nonsense: *That's a load of bull!* **6** [C] = BULL'S-EYE ⊃ **see also** COCK AND BULL STORY
IDM a **bull in a china shop** a person who is careless, or who moves or acts in a rough or awkward way, in a place or situation where skill and care are needed **take the bull by the horns** to face a difficult or dangerous situation directly and with courage ⊃ **more at** SHOOT v., WAVE v.

bull·dog /'bʊldɔg/ *noun* a short strong dog with a large head, a short, flat nose and a short, thick neck

bull·doze /'bʊldoʊz/ *verb* **1** [T] ~ **sth** to destroy buildings, trees, etc. with a bulldozer: *The trees are being bulldozed to make way for a new superstore.* **2** [I, T] to force your way somewhere; to force something somewhere: + adv./prep. *Eli Manning bulldozed through to score.* ◆ ~ **sth** + adv./prep. *They bulldozed the tax through Congress.* ◆ *He bulldozed his way to victory.* **3** [T] ~ **sb** (**into doing sth**) to force someone to do something: *They bulldozed him into selling.*

bull·doz·er /'bʊl,doʊzər/ *noun* a powerful vehicle with a broad steel blade in front, used for moving earth or knocking down buildings ⊃ **picture at** CONSTRUCTION

bul·let 🔑 /'bʊlət/ *noun*
a small metal object that is fired from a gun: *bullet wounds* ◆ *There were bullet holes in the door.* ◆ *He was killed by a bullet in the head.* ⊃ **see also** MAGIC BULLET, PLASTIC BULLET, RUBBER BULLET, SILVER BULLET **IDM** see BITE v.

bul·le·tin /'bʊlətn; -tən/ *noun* **1** a short news report on the radio or television **2** an official statement about something important: *a bulletin on the president's health* **3** a printed report that gives news about an organization or a group

'bulletin ,board *noun* **1** (also **board**) a board for putting notices on **2** (*computing*) a place in a computer system where any user can write or read messages

'bullet ,point *noun* an item in a list in a document, that is printed with a square, diamond, or circle in front of it in order to show that it is important. The square, etc. is also called a bullet point.

bul·let·proof /ˈbʊlətˌpruf/ adj. that can stop bullets from passing through it: *a bulletproof vest*

ˈbullet ˌtrain noun (*informal*) a train that carries passengers at high speeds, especially a very fast train in Japan

bull·fight /ˈbʊlfaɪt/ noun a traditional public entertainment, popular especially in Spain, in which BULLS are fought and usually killed ▶ **bull·fight·er** noun **bull·fight·ing** noun [U] ➔ see also MATADOR

bull·frog /ˈbʊlfrɔg; -frag/ noun a large American FROG with a loud CROAK

bull·head·ed /ˈbʊlˌhɛdəd/ adj. unwilling to change your opinion about something, in a way that other people think is annoying and unreasonable SYN OBSTINATE, STUBBORN ▶ **bull·head·ed·ness** noun [U]

bull·horn /ˈbʊlhɔrn/ noun an electronic device, shaped like a horn, with a MICROPHONE at one end, that you speak into in order to make your voice louder so that it can be heard at a distance ➔ compare MEGAPHONE

bul·lion /ˈbʊlyən/ noun [U] gold or silver in large amounts or in the form of bars: *gold bullion*

bull·ish /ˈbʊlɪʃ/ adj. **1** feeling confident and positive about the future: *in a bullish mood* **2** (*finance*) causing, or connected with, an increase in the price of shares: *a bullish market* ➔ compare BEARISH

ˌbull ˈmarket noun (*finance*) a period during which share prices are rising and people are buying shares ➔ compare BEAR MARKET

ˌbull ˈmastiff noun a large strong dog with short smooth hair

bul·lock /ˈbʊlək/ noun a young BULL (= a male cow) that has been CASTRATED (= had part of its sex organs removed) ➔ compare OX, STEER

bull·pen /ˈbʊlpɛn/ noun **1** the part of a baseball field where pitchers practice PITCHING (= throwing) **2** extra PITCHERS (= players who throw the ball) in a baseball team who are used, if necessary, to replace the usual pitchers: *The team's bullpen is solid this year.* **3** a type of large office which is OPEN-PLAN (= it does not have walls dividing the office area) **4** a room where prisoners wait before they go into the court for their trial

bull·ring /ˈbʊlrɪŋ/ noun the large round area, like an outdoor theater, where BULLFIGHTS take place

bull·rush = BULRUSH

ˈbull ˌsession noun (*informal*) an occasion when people meet and talk in an informal way

ˈbull's-eye (also **bull's·eye**) /ˈbʊlzaɪ/ noun [usually sing.] the center of the target that you shoot or throw at in shooting, ARCHERY, or DARTS; a shot or throw that hits this: *He scored a bull's-eye.* ➔ picture at DART

ˌbull ˈterrier noun a strong dog with short hair, a thick neck, and a long nose ➔ see also PIT BULL

bull·whip /ˈbʊlwɪp/ noun a long leather WHIP

bul·ly /ˈbʊli/ noun, verb, exclamation
- **noun** (pl. **bul·lies**) a person who uses their strength or power to frighten or hurt weaker people: *the school bully*
- **verb** (bul·lies, bul·ly·ing, bul·lied, bul·lied) to frighten or hurt a weaker person; to use your strength or power to make someone do something: ~ **sb** *My son is being bullied at school.* ◆ ~ **sb into sth/into doing sth** *I won't be bullied into signing anything.* ➔ collocations at EDUCATION ▶ **bul·ly·ing** noun [U]: *Bullying is a problem in many schools.* ◆ *He refused to give in to bullying and threats.* ◆ *bullying behavior/tactics*
- **exclamation**
  IDM **bully for you, etc.** (*informal*) used to show that you do not think that what someone has said or done is very impressive: *He got a job in New York? Well, bully for him!*

ˈbully ˌpulpit noun [sing.] a position of authority that gives someone the opportunity to speak in public about an issue

bul·rush (also **bull·rush**) /ˈbʊlrʌʃ/ noun a tall plant with long, narrow leaves, and a long brown head of flowers, that grows in or near water ➔ picture at PLANT

bul·wark /ˈbʊlwərk/ noun **1** ~ **(against sth)** (*formal*) a person or thing that protects or defends something: *a bulwark against extremism* **2** a wall built as a defense **3** [usually pl.] the part of a ship's side that is above the level of the DECK

bum /bʌm/ noun, verb, adj.
- **noun** [C] (*informal*) **1** a person who has no home or job, and who asks other people for money or food **2** a lazy person who does nothing for other people or for society: *He's nothing but a no-good bum!* **3** (in compounds) a person who spends a lot of time doing a certain activity instead of on serious work: *a ski bum* ◆ *a beach bum* **4** (*CanE, informal*) the part of the body that you sit on
  IDM **give sb/get the bum's rush** (*informal*) to force someone/be forced to leave a place quickly: *He soon got the bum's rush from the club.*
- **verb** (-mm-) **1** ~ **sth (off sb)** (*informal*) to get something from someone by asking: *Can I bum a cigarette off you?* **2** ~ **sb (out)** (*informal*) to make someone feel upset or disappointed
  PHRV **bum aˈround** (*informal*) to travel around or spend your time with no particular plans: *He bummed around Europe for a year until he ran out of money.*
- **adj.** [only before noun] (*informal*) **1** of bad quality; wrong or useless: *Her campaign has really gotten a bum rap* (= has been described in an unfair way) ◆ *a bum deal* (= a situation where you do not get what you deserve or have paid for) **2** injured or not functioning correctly: *My bum knee keeps me from playing tennis.*

bum·ble /ˈbʌmbl/ verb [I] + **adv./prep.** to act or move in an awkward or confused way: *I could hear him bumbling around in the kitchen.*

bum·ble·bee /ˈbʌmblˌbi/ noun a large BEE covered with small hairs that makes a loud noise as it flies ➔ picture at ANIMAL

bum·bling /ˈbʌmblɪŋ/ adj. [only before noun] behaving in an awkward confused way, often making careless mistakes

bum·mer /ˈbʌmər/ noun **a bummer** [sing.] (*informal*) a disappointing or unpleasant situation: *It's a real bummer that she can't come.*

bump /bʌmp/ verb, noun
- **verb 1** [I] to hit someone or something by accident: ~ **into sb/sth** *I bumped into a chair in the dark.* ◆ ~ **against sb/sth** *The car bumped against the curb.* ➔ thesaurus box at HIT **2** [T] ~ **sth (against/on sth)** to hit something, especially a part of your body, against or on something: *Be careful not to bump your head on the beam when you stand up.* **3** [I, T] to move across a rough surface: + **adv./prep.** *The jeep bumped along the dirt track.* ◆ ~ **sth** + **adv./prep.** *The car slowly bumped its way down the drive.* **4** [T] ~ **sb** + **adv./prep.** to move someone from one group or position to another; to remove someone from a group: *The airline apologized and bumped us up to first class.* ◆ *If you are bumped off an airline because of overbooking, you are entitled to compensation.* ◆ *The coach told him he had been bumped from the starting lineup.*
  PHRV **bump ˈinto sb** (*informal*) to meet someone by chance **ˌbump sb↔ˈoff** (*informal*) to murder someone **ˌbump sth↔ˈup** to increase or raise something **ˌbump ˈup against sth** to experience a problem or factor that you did not expect: *We kept bumping up against inflexible regulations.*
- **noun 1** the action or sound of something hitting a hard surface: *He fell to the ground with a bump.* ◆ *We could hear loud bumps from upstairs where the children were playing.* **2** a swelling on the body, often caused by a blow SYN LUMP: *She was covered in bumps and bruises.* ◆ *How did you get that bump on your forehead?* **3** a part of a flat surface that is not even, but raised above the rest of it: *a bump in the road* ➔ see also BUMPY, SPEED BUMP IDM see EARTH, THING

bump·er /ˈbʌmpər/ *noun, adj.*

• *noun* a bar attached to the front and back of a car, etc. to reduce the effect if it hits anything: *The cars were bumper to bumper on the road to the coast* (= so close that their bumpers were almost touching). ➲ picture at CAR

• *adj.* [only before noun] (*approving*) unusually large; producing an unusually large amount: *a bumper issue* (= of a magazine, etc.) ♦ *a bumper crop/harvest/season/year*

ˈbumper ˌcar *noun* one of the small electric cars that you drive in a special area at an AMUSEMENT PARK, and try to hit other cars with

ˈbumper ˌsticker *noun* a sign with a message on it that people stick on the bumper of their car: *Their bumper sticker says, "Make Love, Not War."*

bump·kin /ˈbʌmpkɪn/ *noun* = COUNTRY BUMPKIN

bump·tious /ˈbʌmpʃəs/ *adj.* (*disapproving*) showing that you think that you are very important; often giving your opinions in a loud, confident, and annoying way

bump·y /ˈbʌmpi/ *adj.* (bump·i·er, bump·i·est) **1** (of a surface) not even; with a lot of bumps: *a bumpy road/track* ♦ *bumpy ground* **2** (of a journey) uncomfortable, with a lot of sudden, unpleasant movements caused by the road surface, weather conditions, etc.: *a bumpy ride/flight* **IDM** **have/give sb a bumpy ride** to have a difficult time; to make a situation difficult for someone

bun /bʌn/ *noun* **1** [C] a small, round, flat type of bread: *a hamburger bun* ➲ compare ROLL **2** [C] a small, round, sweet cake: *a cinnamon bun* ♦ *a sticky bun* ➲ see also HOT CROSS BUN **3** [C] long hair that has been twisted into a round shape and is worn on top, or at the back of the head: *She wore her hair in a bun.* ➲ picture at HAIR **4** buns [pl.] (*informal*) the two sides of a person's bottom **IDM** **have a bun in the oven** (*informal, humorous*) to be pregnant

bunch 🔖 /bʌntʃ/ *noun, verb*

• *noun* **1** [C] ~ of sth a number of things of the same type that are growing or fastened together: *a bunch of bananas/grapes, etc.* ♦ *She picked me a bunch of flowers.* **2** [sing.] **a ~ (of sth)** (*informal*) a large amount of something; a large number of things or people: *I have a whole bunch of stuff to do this morning.* **3** [sing.] (*informal*) a group of people: *The people that I work with are a great bunch.* **IDM** **the best/pick of the bunch** the best out of a group of people or things

• *verb* [I, T] to become tight or to form tight folds; to make something do this: *His muscles bunched under his shirt.* ♦ ~ **(sth) up** *Her skirt had bunched up around her waist.* ♦ ~ **sth** *His forehead was bunched in a frown.* **PHR V** **bunch ˈup/toˈgether** | **bunch sb/sth ˈup/toˈgether** to move closer and form into a group; to make people or things do this: *The sheep bunched together as soon as they saw the dog.*

bun·dle /ˈbʌndl/ *noun, verb*

• *noun* **1** [C] a number of things tied or wrapped together; something that is wrapped up: *a bundle of rags/newspapers/firewood, etc.* ♦ *She held her little bundle* (= her baby) *tightly in her arms.* **2** [C] a number of things that belong, or are sold together: *a bundle of ideas* ♦ *a bundle of graphics packages for your PC* **3** [sing.] **a ~ of laughs, fun, etc.** (*informal*) a person or thing that makes you laugh: *He wasn't exactly a bundle of laughs* (= a happy person to be with) *last night.* ➲ see also BUNDLE OF JOY **4 a bundle** [sing.] (*informal*) a large amount of money: *That car must have cost a bundle.* **IDM** see NERVE *n.*

• *verb* **1** [T] ~ **sb + adv./prep.** to push or send someone somewhere quickly and not carefully: *They bundled her into the back of a car.* ♦ *He was bundled off to boarding school.* **2** [I] **+ adv./prep.** to move somewhere quickly in a group: *We bundled out onto the street.* **3** [T] ~ **sth (with sth)** to supply extra equipment, especially software when selling a new computer, at no extra cost: *A nine applications are bundled with the system.*

PHR V **ˌbundle sth↔ˈup** | **ˌbundle sth↔toˈgether** to make or tie something into a bundle: *He bundled up the dirty clothes and stuffed them into the bag.* ♦ *The newspapers were all bundled together, ready to be thrown out.* **ˌbundle sb ˈup (in sth)** to put warm clothes or coverings on someone: *I bundled her up in a blanket and gave her a hot drink.*

ˌbundle of ˈjoy *noun* (*informal, humorous, sometimes ironic*) a baby son or daughter: *Here are the latest pictures of our little bundle of joy.*

bung /bʌŋ/ *noun* a round piece of wood, rubber, etc. used for closing the hole in a container such as a BARREL or JAR

bun·ga·low /ˈbʌŋɡəloʊ/ *noun* a small house, usually built all on one level, without stairs ➲ picture at HOUSE ➲ compare RANCH HOUSE

bun·gee /ˈbʌndʒi/ (also **ˈbungee ˌcord**) *noun* **1** a long rope which can stretch, that people tie to their feet when they do bungee jumping ➲ picture at SPORT **2** a thick ELASTIC rope with a hook at each end that can be used to hold packages together, keep things in position, etc.

ˈbungee ˌjumping *noun* [U] a sport in which a person jumps from a high place, such as a bridge or a CLIFF, with a bungee tied to their feet: *to go bungee jumping* ➲ picture at SPORT ▶ **ˈbungee jump** *noun*: *to do a bungee jump*

bun·gle /ˈbʌŋɡl/ *verb, noun*

• *verb* [T, I] ~ **(sth)** to do something badly or without skill; to fail at something **SYN** BOTCH: *They bungled the job.* ♦ *a bungled robbery/raid/attempt* ▶ **bun·gler** /ˈbʌŋɡlər/ *noun* **bun·gling** *adj.*: *bungling incompetence*

• *noun* [usually sing.] something that is done badly and that causes problems: *Their paychecks were late because of a computer bungle.*

bun·ion /ˈbʌnyən/ *noun* a painful swelling on the foot, usually on the big toe

bunk /bʌŋk/ *noun, verb*

• *noun* **1** [C] (also **ˈbunk bed**) one of two beds that are attached together, one above the other, especially for children ➲ picture at BED **2** [C] a narrow bed that is attached to a wall, especially on a ship or train **3** [U] (*old-fashioned, informal*) nonsense **SYN** BUNKUM

• *verb* [I] to sleep somewhere for the night: *We can bunk with friends for the night.* ♦ *They bunked together at summer camp.*

bun·ker /ˈbʌŋkər/ *noun, verb*

• *noun* **1** a strongly built shelter for soldiers or guns, usually underground: *a concrete/underground/secret bunker* **2** a container for storing coal, especially on a ship or outside a house: *a coal bunker* **3** (also **ˈsand trap, trap**) a small area filled with sand on a GOLF COURSE ➲ picture at SPORT

• *verb* **be bunkered** (in GOLF) to have hit your ball into a bunker (and therefore to be in a difficult position)

ˈbunker ˌbuster *noun* (*informal*) a bomb that goes through concrete or rock and explodes underground. It is used to destroy bunkers.

bunk·house /ˈbʌŋkhaʊs/ *noun* a building for workers to sleep in

bun·kum /ˈbʌŋkəm/ *noun* [U] (*old-fashioned, informal*) nonsense **SYN** BUNK

bun·ny /ˈbʌni/ *noun* (*pl.* bun·nies) (also **ˈbunny ˌrabbit**) a child's word for a RABBIT

ˈbunny-ˌhop *noun* a small jump forward in a CROUCHING position ▶ **ˈbunny-hop** *verb* (-pp-) [I]

ˈbunny ˌslope *noun* a slope that is not very steep and is used by people who are learning to SKI

Bun·sen burn·er /ˈbʌnsn ˌbərnər/ *noun* an instrument used in scientific work that produces a hot gas flame ➲ picture at LABORATORY

bunt /bʌnt/ *verb* [T, I] ~ **(sth)** (in baseball) to deliberately hit the ball only a short distance ▶ **bunt** *noun*

bunt·ing /ˈbʌntɪŋ/ *noun* **1** [U] colored flags or paper used for decorating streets and buildings in celebrations **2** [C] a small bird related to the FINCH and SPARROW families.

There are several types of buntings: *a corn/reed/snow bunting*

bu·oy /'bui; bɔɪ/ *noun, verb*
- *noun* an object that floats on the ocean or a river to mark the places where it is dangerous and where it is safe for boats to go ➲ see also LIFEBUOY
- *verb* [usually passive] **1 ~ sb (up)** to make someone feel cheerful or confident: *Buoyed by their win yesterday, the team feels confident of further success.* **2 ~ sb/sth (up)** to keep someone or something floating on water **3 ~ sth (up)** to keep prices at a high or acceptable level

buoy·ant /'bɔɪənt/ *adj.* **1** (of prices, business activity, etc.) tending to increase or stay at a high level, usually showing financial success: *a buoyant economy/market* ◆ *buoyant sales/prices* ◆ *a buoyant demand for homes* **2** cheerful and feeling sure that things will be successful: *They were all in buoyant mood.* **3** floating, able to float, or able to keep things floating: *The boat bobbed like a cork on the waves: light and buoyant.* ◆ *Salt water is more buoyant than fresh water.*
▶ **buoy·an·cy** /'bɔɪənsi/ *noun* [U]: *the buoyancy of the stock market* ◆ *a mood of buoyancy* ◆ *a buoyancy aid* (= something to help you float)

bur = BURR

bur·ble /'bərbl/ *verb* **1** [I] to make the gentle sound of a stream flowing over stones **2** [I, T] **~ (on) (about sth)** | **+ speech** (*disapproving*) to speak in a confused or silly way that is difficult to hear or understand: *What's he burbling on about?*

burbs /bərbz/ *noun* **the burbs** [pl.] (*informal*) = SUBURBS

bur·den /'bərdn/ *noun, verb*
- *noun* **1** the **~ (of sth)** | a **~ (on/to sb)** a duty, responsibility, etc. that causes worry, difficulty, or hard work: *to bear/carry/ease/share the burden* ◆ *The main burden of caring for old people falls on the family.* ◆ *the heavy tax burden on working people* ◆ *I don't want to become a burden to my children when I'm old.* **2** (*formal*) a heavy load that is difficult to carry ➲ see also BEAST OF BURDEN
- *verb* **1 ~ sb/yourself (with sth)** to give someone a duty, responsibility, etc. that causes worry, difficulty, or hard work: *They have burdened themselves with a high mortgage.* ◆ *I don't want to burden you with my worries.* ◆ *to be burdened by high taxes* **ANT** UNBURDEN **2 be burdened with sth** to be carrying something heavy: *She got off the bus, burdened with two heavy suitcases.*

the ˌburden of ˈproof *noun* [sing.] (*law*) the task or responsibility of proving that something is true

bur·den·some /'bərdnsəm/ *adj.* (*formal*) causing worry, difficulty, or hard work **SYN** ONEROUS

bur·dock /'bərdɑk/ *noun* [U] a plant with flowers that become PRICKLY and stick to passing animals

bu·reau /'byʊroʊ/ *noun* **1** a government department or part of a government department: *the Federal Bureau of Investigation* **2** an office or organization that provides information on a particular subject: *a news bureau* ◆ *a visitor's bureau* (= an office that provides information for tourists) ➲ see also CREDIT BUREAU **3** = CHEST OF DRAWERS

bu·reauc·ra·cy /byʊ'rɑkrəsi/ *noun* (*pl.* bu·reauc·ra·cies) **1** [U] (often *disapproving*) the system of official rules and ways of doing things that a government or an organization has, especially when these seem to be too complicated: *unnecessary/excessive bureaucracy* **2** [U, C] a system of government in which there are a large number of state officials who are not elected; a country with such a system: *the power of the state bureaucracy* ◆ *living in a modern bureaucracy* **3** [C] a government or a department within a government that is divided into many smaller departments and run by officials who are appointed rather than elected

bu·reau·crat /'byʊrəˌkræt/ *noun* (often *disapproving*) an official working in an organization or a government department, especially one who follows the rules of the department too strictly

bu·reau·crat·ic /ˌbyʊrə'kræt̬ɪk/ *adj.* (often *disapproving*) connected with a bureaucracy or bureaucrats and involving complicated official rules which may seem unnecessary: *bureaucratic power/control/procedures/organizations* ◆ *The report revealed a great deal of bureaucratic inefficiency.*
▶ **bu·reau·crat·i·cally** /-kli/ *adv.*

bu·rette (also **bu·ret**) /byʊ'rɛt/ *noun* a glass tube with measurements on it and a FAUCET at one end, used, for example, in chemical experiments for measuring out amounts of a liquid ➲ picture at LABORATORY

burg /bərg/ *noun* (*informal*) a town or city

bur·geon /'bərdʒən/ *verb* [I] (*formal*) to begin to grow or develop rapidly ▶ **bur·geon·ing** *adj.*: *a burgeoning population* ◆ *burgeoning demand*

burg·er /'bərgər/ *noun* **1** = HAMBURGER **2** -burger (in compounds) finely chopped fish, vegetables, nuts, etc. made into flat round shapes like HAMBURGERS: *a spicy beanburger* ➲ see also CHEESEBURGER, VEGGIE BURGER

burgh /'bərou/ *noun* (*old-fashioned*) a town or part of a city that has its own local government

burgh·er /'bərgər/ *noun* (*old use* or *humorous*) a citizen of a particular town

bur·glar /'bərglər/ *noun* a person who enters a building illegally in order to steal

ˈburglar aˌlarm *noun* an electronic device, often fixed to a wall, that rings a loud bell if someone tries to enter a building by force

bur·glar·ize /'bərgləˌraɪz/ (also **bur·gle**) *verb* **~ sb/sth** to enter a building illegally, usually using force, and steal from it: *We were burglarized while we were away* (= our house was burglarized). ◆ *The house next door was burglarized.*

bur·gla·ry /'bərgləri/ *noun* [U, C] (*pl.* bur·gla·ries) the crime of entering a building illegally and stealing things from it: *The teen was charged with three counts of burglary.* ◆ *a rise in the number of burglaries committed in the area* ➲ compare ROBBERY, THEFT

bur·gle /'bərgl/ *verb* = BURGLARIZE

bur·goo /bər'gu/ *noun* (*pl.* bur·goos) **1** [U] a type of thick soup, especially one eaten outdoors **2** [C] an event at which burgoo is eaten outdoors

bur·gun·dy /'bərgəndi/ *noun* (*pl.* bur·gun·dies) **1** [U] a dark red color **2** Burgundy [U, C] a red or white wine from the Burgundy area of eastern France ▶ **bur·gun·dy** *adj.*: *a burgundy leather briefcase*

bur·i·al /'bɛriəl/ *noun* [U, C] the act or ceremony of burying a dead body: *a burial place/mound/site* ◆ *Her body was sent home for burial.* ◆ *His family insisted he should be given a proper burial.*

ˈburial ˌground *noun* a place where dead bodies are buried, especially an ancient place

bur·ka (also **bur·qa**) /'bərkə; 'bur-/ *noun* a long, loose piece of clothing that covers the whole body, including the head and face, worn in public by Muslim women in some countries

bur·lap /'bərlæp/ *noun* [U] a type of strong, rough, brown cloth, used especially for making SACKS

bur·lesque /bər'lɛsk/ *noun* **1** [C] a performance or piece of writing that tries to make something look ridiculous by representing it in a humorous way **SYN** PARODY: *a burlesque of literary life* **2** [U] a type of entertainment involving humorous acts, singing, dancing, etc., and often including STRIPTEASE ▶ **bur·lesque** *adj.* [usually before noun]

bur·ly /'bərli/ *adj.* (bur·li·er, bur·li·est) (of a man or a man's body) big, strong, and heavy **SYN** BRAWNY

burn 🖉 /bərn/ *verb, noun*
- *verb* (burned, burned /bərnd/ or burnt, burnt /bərnt/)
  > FIRE **1** [I] to produce flames and heat: *A welcoming fire was burning in the fireplace.* ◆ *Fires were burning all over the city.* **2** [I] (used especially in the progressive tenses) to be on fire: *By nightfall the whole city was burning.* ◆ *Two children were rescued from the burning car.* ◆ *The smell of burning rubber filled*

the air. **3** [T, I] to destroy, damage, injure, or kill someone or something by fire; to be destroyed, etc. by fire: **~ (sb/sth)** *to burn trash/dead leaves* ◆ *All his belongings were burned in the fire.* ◆ *The cigarette burned a hole in the carpet.* ◆ *The house was burned to the ground* (= completely destroyed). ◆ *The house burned to the ground.* ◆ *Ten people burned to death in the hotel fire.* ◆ **~ sb/sth + adj.** *His greatest fear is of being burned alive.*
▷ **FUEL 4** [T, I] **~ (sth)** if you **burn** a fuel, or a fuel **burns**, it produces heat, light, or energy: *a furnace that burns gas/oil* ◆ *(figurative) Some people burn calories* (= use food to produce energy) *faster than others.* ◆ *Which fuel burns most efficiently?*
▷ **FOOD 5** [I, T] if food **burns**, or if you **burn** it, it is spoiled because it gets too hot: *I can smell something burning in the kitchen.* ◆ **~ sth** *Sorry—I burned the toast.*
▷ **SUN/HEAT/ACID 6** [I, T] to be damaged or injured by the sun, heat, acid, etc.; to damage or injure someone or something in this way: *My skin burns easily* (= in the sun). ◆ **~ sth** *I got badly burned by the sun yesterday.* ◆ **~ sth** *The soup is hot. Don't burn your mouth.* ◆ **~ yourself** *I burned myself on the stove.*
▷ **OF PART OF BODY 7** [I] if part of your body **burns** or is **burning**, it feels very hot and painful: *Your forehead is burning. Do you have a fever?* ◆ *Her cheeks burned with embarrassment.* ⊃ thesaurus box at HURT
▷ **OF A LIGHT 8** [I] to produce light: *Lights were burning upstairs, but no one answered the door.*
▷ **FEEL EMOTION/DESIRE 9** [I, T] *(literary)* to feel a very strong emotion or desire: **~ with sth** *to be burning with rage/ambition/love* ◆ **~ to do sth** *He was burning to go climbing again.*
▷ **GO FAST 10** [I] **+ adv./prep.** *(informal)* to move very fast in a particular direction: *His car burned past us on the highway.*
▷ **MAKE ANGRY 11** [T] **~ sb** *(informal)* to make someone very angry: *So you did it just to burn me?*
▷ **CHEAT 12** [T, usually passive] *(informal)* to cheat or take advantage of someone: **be/get burned** *A lot of investors were burned by his scams.* ◆ *She's been jilted before and is afraid of getting burned again.*
▷ **CD, ETC. 13** [T, I] **~ (sth) (to sth)** to put information onto a CD, etc.
IDM **burn your bridges** to do something that makes it impossible to return to the previous situation later: *Think carefully before you resign—you don't want to burn your bridges.* **burn the candle at both ends** to become very tired by trying to do too many things and going to bed late, and getting up early **burn your fingers | get your fingers burned** to suffer as a result of doing something without realizing the possible bad results, especially in business: *He really got his fingers burned dabbling in the stock market.* **burn a hole in your pocket** if money **burns a hole in your pocket**, you want to spend it as soon as you have it **burn the midnight oil** to study or work until late at night **burn rubber** *(informal)* to drive very fast **burn sth to a crisp** to cook something for too long or with too much heat, so that it becomes badly burned ⊃ more at CRASH *v.*, EAR, MONEY
PHR V ,burn a'way to disappear as a result of burning; to make something do this: *Half the candle had burned away.* ◆ *The clothing on his back got burned away in the fire.* ,burn 'down if a fire **burns down**, it becomes weaker and has smaller flames ,burn 'down | ,burn sth↔'down to be destroyed, or to destroy something, by fire: *The house burned down in 1895.* ,burn sth↔'off **1** to remove something by burning: *Burn off the old paint before repainting the door.* **2** to use energy by doing exercise: *This workout helps you to burn off fat and tone muscles.* ,burn 'out | ,burn itself 'out (of a fire) to stop burning because there is nothing more to burn: *The fire had burned (itself) out before the fire engines arrived.* ,burn 'out | ,burn sth↔'out to stop working or to make something stop working because it gets too hot or is used too much: *The clutch finally burned out.* ,burn 'out | ,burn yourself/sb 'out to become extremely tired or sick by working too hard over a period of time: *If he doesn't stop working so hard, he'll burn himself out.* ◆ *By the age of 25 she was completely burned out and retired from the sport.* ⊃ related noun BURNOUT ,burn sth 'out [usually passive] to destroy something completely by fire so that only the outer frame remains: *The hotel was completely burned out.* ◆ *the*

burnt-out wreck of a car ,burn 'up **1** to be destroyed by heat: *The spacecraft burned up as it entered the earth's atmosphere.* **2** (usually used in the progressive tenses) *(informal)* to have a high temperature: *You're burning up—have you gone to the doctor yet?* **3** (of a fire) to burn more strongly and with larger flames ,burn sb 'up *(informal)* to make someone very angry: *The way he treats me really burns me up.* ,burn sth↔'up **1** to get rid of or destroy something by burning: *The fire burned up 1,500 acres of farmland.* **2** to use CALORIES or energy by doing exercise: *Which burns up more calories—swimming or cycling?*

● **noun**
▷ **INJURY 1** [C] an injury or a mark caused by fire, heat, or acid: *minor/severe/third-degree burns* ◆ *cigarette burns on the furniture* ◆ *burn marks* ◆ *a burn unit in a hospital* **2** [C, U] a mark that is red and painful, caused by something rubbing against the skin: *a smooth shave without razor burn*
▷ **IN MUSCLES 3** **the burn** [sing.] the feeling that you get in your muscles when you have done a lot of exercise
▷ **RIVER 4** [C] a small river **SYN** STREAM **IDM** see SLOW *adj.*

THESAURUS

burn

char ◆ scald ◆ scorch ◆ singe

These words all mean to damage, injure, destroy, or kill something or someone with heat or fire.

burn to damage, injure, destroy, or kill something or someone with fire, heat, or acid; to be damaged, etc. by fire, heat, or acid: *She burned all his letters.* ◆ *The house burned down* in 1995.

char [usually passive] to make something black by burning it; to become black by burning: *The pasta was topped with charred peppers.*

scald to burn part of your body with very hot liquid or steam

scorch to burn and slightly damage a surface by making it too hot: *I scorched my dress when I was ironing it.*

singe to burn the surface or edges of something slightly, usually by mistake; to be burned in this way: *He singed his hair as he tried to light his cigarette.*

SCORCH OR SINGE?

Things are **scorched** by either heat or fire. Things can be **singed** only by fire or a flame.

PATTERNS
- to burn/scald **yourself/your hand**
- to burn/scorch/singe your **hair/clothes**
- burned out/charred/scorched **remains/ruins/buildings**

burned = BURNT
,burned-'out (also ,burnt-'out) *adj.* **1** destroyed or badly damaged by fire: *a burned-out car* **2** feeling as if you have done something for too long and need to have a rest: *I'm feeling burned-out at work—I need a vacation.*
burn·er /'bərnər/ *noun* **1** the part of a stove, etc. that produces a flame **2** a large, solid, metal piece of equipment for burning wood or coal, used for heating a room: *a wood burner* ⊃ see also BUNSEN BURNER, CD BURNER, DVD BURNER **IDM** see BACK, FRONT
burn·ing /'bərnɪŋ/ *adj., adv.*
● *adj.* [only before noun] **1** (of feelings, etc.) very strong; extreme: *a burning desire to win* ◆ *He's always had a burning ambition to start his own business.* **2** a **~ issue/question** a very important and urgent problem **3** (of pain, etc.) very strong and giving a feeling of burning ⊃ thesaurus box at PAINFUL **4** very hot; looking and feeling very hot: *the burning sun* ◆ *her burning face* **5 ~ eyes** *(literary)* eyes that seem to be staring at you very hard
● *adv.* **burning hot** very hot

bur·nish /ˈbɜrnɪʃ/ verb ~ sth (formal) to polish metal until it is smooth and shiny ▶ **bur·nished** adj. [usually before noun]: *burnished gold/copper*

bur·noose (also **bur·nous**) /bərˈnus/ noun a long loose item of outer clothing with a HOOD (= covering for the head), worn by Arabs

burn·out /ˈbɜrnaʊt/ noun [C, U] **1** the state of being extremely tired or sick, either physically or mentally, because you have worked too hard **2** the point at which a ROCKET has used all of its fuel and has no more power

burnt /bɜrnt/ (also **burned**) verb, adj.
• verb pt, pp of BURN
• adj. damaged or injured by burning: *burnt toast*

burnt 'ocher noun [U] **1** a deep yellow-brown color **2** a yellow-brown PIGMENT, used in art

burnt 'offering noun **1** something (usually an animal) that is burned in a religious ceremony as a gift offered to a god **2** (humorous) food that has been badly burned by accident

burnt si'enna noun [U] **1** a deep red-brown color **2** a deep red-brown PIGMENT, used in art

burnt 'umber noun [U] **1** a dark brown color **2** a dark brown PIGMENT, used in art

burp /bɜrp/ verb (informal) **1** [I] to let out air from the stomach through the mouth, making a noise SYN BELCH **2** [T] ~ sb to make a baby bring up air from the stomach, especially by rubbing or PATTING its back ▶ **burp** noun

bur·qa = BURKA

burr /bɜr/ noun **1** (also **bur**) [C] the seed container of some plants that is covered in very small hooks that stick to clothes or fur **2** [usually sing.] the soft regular noise made by parts of a machine moving quickly SYN WHIRR **3** [C] a rough spot left on metal by the action of a tool or machine **4** [usually sing.] a strong pronunciation of the "r" sound, typical of some accents in English; an accent with this type of pronunciation: *She speaks with a Scottish burr.*

bur·ri·to /bəˈritoʊ/ noun (pl. **bur·ri·tos**) (from Spanish) a Mexican dish consisting of a TORTILLA filled with meat or BEANS

bur·ro /ˈbɜroʊ; ˈbʊroʊ/ noun (pl. **bur·ros**) (from Spanish) a small DONKEY

bur·row /ˈbɜroʊ/ verb, noun
• verb **1** [I, T] to make a hole or a tunnel in the ground by digging SYN DIG: (+ adv./prep.) *Earthworms burrow deep into the soil.* ◆ ~ sth + adv./prep. *The rodent burrowed its way into the sand.* **2** [I, T] to press yourself close to someone or under something: + adv./prep. *He burrowed down beneath the blankets.* ◆ ~ sth + adv./prep. *She burrowed her face into his chest.* **3** [I] + adv./prep. to search for something under or among things: *She burrowed in the drawer for a pair of socks.* ◆ *He was afraid that they would burrow into his past.*
• noun a hole or tunnel in the ground made by animals such as RABBITS for them to live in

bur·sa /ˈbɜrsə/ noun (pl. **bur·sae** /-si/ or **bur·sas**) (anatomy) a part inside the body like a bag or sleeve, which is filled with liquid, especially around a joint so that it can work smoothly

bur·sar /ˈbɜrsər/ noun a person whose job is to manage the financial affairs of a school or college

bur·si·tis /bərˈsaɪtəs/ noun [U] (medical) a condition in which a bursa becomes swollen and sore

burst /bɜrst/ verb, noun
• verb (**burst**, **burst**) **1** [I, T] to break open or apart, especially because of pressure from inside; to make something break in this way: *That balloon will burst if you blow it up any more.* ◆ *The dam burst under the weight of water.* ◆ *My grocery bag burst and spilled food all over the floor.* ◆ (figurative) *He felt he would burst with anger and shame.* ◆ *a pipe that had burst* ◆ ~ sth *Don't burst that balloon!* ◆ *The river burst its banks and flooded nearby towns.* ⊃ thesaurus box at EXPLODE **2** [I]

+ adv./prep. to go or move somewhere suddenly with great force; to come from somewhere suddenly: *He burst into the room without knocking.* ◆ *The sun burst through the clouds.* ◆ *The words burst from her in an angry rush.* **3** [I] be **bursting (with sth)** to be very full of something; to be very full and almost breaking open: *The roads are bursting with cars.* ◆ *to be bursting with ideas/enthusiasm/pride* ◆ *The hall was filled to bursting point.* ◆ *The hall was full to bursting.*

IDM **be bursting to do sth** to want to do something so much that you can hardly stop yourself: *She was bursting to tell him the good news.* **burst sb's bubble** to bring an end to someone's hopes, happiness, etc. **burst open| burst (sth) open** to open suddenly or violently; to make something open in this way: *The door burst open.* ◆ *Firefighters burst the door open and rescued them.* ⊃ more at BUBBLE n., SEAM

PHR V **burst 'in | burst into a 'room, 'building, etc.** to enter a room or building suddenly and noisily **burst 'in on sb/sth** to interrupt someone or something by entering a place suddenly and noisily: *He burst in on the meeting.* **burst into sth** to start producing something suddenly and with great force: *The aircraft crashed and burst into flames* (= suddenly began to burn). ◆ *She burst into tears* (= suddenly began to cry). **burst on/onto sth** to appear somewhere suddenly in a way that is very noticeable: *A major new talent has burst onto the literary scene.* **burst 'out 1** to speak suddenly, loudly, and with strong feeling: [+ **speech**] *"For heavens' sake!" he burst out.* ⊃ related noun OUTBURST **2** to begin doing something suddenly: [+ **-ing**] *Karen burst out laughing.*

• noun **1** a short period of a particular activity or strong emotion that often starts suddenly: *a sudden burst of activity/energy/anger/enthusiasm* ◆ *Her breath was coming in short bursts.* ◆ *I tend to work in bursts.* ◆ *spontaneous bursts of applause* **2** an occasion when something bursts; the hole left where something has burst: *a burst in a water pipe* **3** a short series of shots from a gun: *frequent bursts of machine-gun fire*

burst·y /ˈbɜrsti/ adj. (**burst·i·er**, **burst·i·est**) **1** (technical) used to describe data that is sent in small, sudden groups of signals: *a bursty connection* ◆ *bursty Internet traffic* **2** (informal) occurring at intervals, for short periods of time

bur·y /ˈbɛri/ verb
(**bur·ies**, **bur·y·ing**, **bur·ied**, **bur·ied**)
▷ DEAD PERSON **1** ~ sb/sth to place a dead body in a grave: *He was buried in Woodlawn Cemetery.* ◆ (figurative) *Their ambitions were finally dead and buried.* **2** ~ sb (old-fashioned) to lose someone by death: *She's 85 and has buried three husbands.*
▷ HIDE IN GROUND **3** ~ sth to hide something in the ground: *buried treasure* ◆ *The dog had buried its bone in the garden.*
▷ COVER **4** [often passive] to cover someone or something with soil, rocks, leaves, etc.: ~ sb/sth *The house was buried under ten feet of snow.* ◆ ~ sb/sth + adj. *The miners were buried alive when the tunnel collapsed.* **5** ~ sth to cover something so that it cannot be seen: *Your letter got buried under a pile of papers.* ◆ *He buried his face in his hands and wept.*
▷ HIDE FEELING **6** ~ sth to ignore or hide a feeling, a mistake, etc.: *She had learned to bury her feelings.*
▷ PUT DEEPLY INTO SOMETHING **7** ~ sth (in sth) to put something deeply into something else: *He walked slowly, his hands buried in his pockets.* ◆ *She always has her head buried in a book.*
IDM **bury the hatchet/your differences** to stop being unfriendly and become friends again ⊃ more at HEAD n.
PHR V **bury yourself in sth 1** to give all your attention to something: *Since she left, he's buried himself in his work.* **2** to go to or be in a place where you will not meet many people: *She buried herself in the country to write a book.*

bus /bʌs/ noun, verb
• noun (pl. **bus·es**, **bus·ses**) **1** a large road vehicle that carries passengers, especially one that travels along a fixed route and stops regularly to let people get on and off: *Shall we walk or go by bus?* ◆ *A regular bus service connects the train station with the town center.* ◆ *a bus company/driver* ◆ *a school*

buses

school bus   tour bus

van

bus ⊃ see also BUS LANE, BUS SHELTER, BUS STATION, BUS STOP, MINIBUS **2** (*computing*) a set of wires that carries information from one part of a computer system to another **IDM** **throw sb under the bus** (*informal*) to blame someone unfairly or hurt them emotionally: *She really threw him under the bus by suggesting that he had stolen the information.*
● *verb* (-s- or -ss-) **1** ~ **sb (from/to…)** to transport someone by bus: *We were bused from the airport to our hotel.* **2** ~ **sb** to transport young people by bus to another area so that students of different races can be educated together **3** ~ **sth** to take the dirty plates, etc. off the tables in a restaurant, as a job

bus·boy /ˈbʌsbɔɪ/ *noun* a person who works in a restaurant and whose job is to clear the dirty dishes, etc.

bush /bʊʃ/ *noun*
1 [C] a plant that grows thickly with several hard STEMS coming up from the root: *a rose bush* ◆ *holly bushes* ⊃ compare TREE **2** [C] a thing that looks like a bush, especially an area of thick hair or fur **3** often the bush [U] an area of wild land that has not been cleared, especially in Africa and Australia **IDM** see BEAT *v.*, BIRD *n.*

ˈbush baby *noun* a small African animal with large eyes, that lives in trees

bushed /bʊʃt/ *adj.* [not before noun] (*informal*) very tired **SYN** EXHAUSTED

bush·el /ˈbʊʃl/ *noun* **1** [C] a unit for measuring grain and fruit (equal in volume to 8 gallons) **2** bushels [pl.] ~ (of sth) (*informal*) a large amount of something **IDM** see HIDE *v.*

ˈbush fire *noun* a fire in a large area of rough open ground, especially one that spreads quickly

bu·shi·do /buˈʃiːdoʊ; ˈbʊʃiˌdoʊ/ *noun* [U] (from *Japanese*) the system of honor and morals of the Japanese SAMURAI

ˈbush-league *adj.* (*informal*) of very low quality

Bush·man /ˈbʊʃmən/ *noun* (*pl.* Bush·men /-mən/) **1** a member of one of the races of people from southern Africa who live and hunt in the African BUSH **2** bushman a person who lives, works or travels in the Australian BUSH

ˈbush·meat /ˈbʊʃmiːt/ *noun* [U] the meat of wild animals used as food, for example African animals

ˌbush ˈtelegraph *noun* [U, sing.] (*informal, humorous*) the process by which information and news are passed quickly from person to person

bush·whack /ˈbʊʃwæk/ *verb* **1** [I] to live or travel in wild country **2** [I] + adv./prep. to cut your way through bushes, plants, etc. in wild country: *We had to bushwhack through undergrowth.* **3** [T] ~ sb to attack someone very suddenly from a hidden position **SYN** AMBUSH **4** [I] to fight as a GUERRILLA ▶ **bush·whack·ing** *noun* [U]

bush·whack·er /ˈbʊʃwækər/ *noun* **1** a person who lives or travels in an area of wild country **2** a person who fights in a GUERRILLA war

bush·y /ˈbʊʃi/ *adj.* (bush·i·er, bush·i·est) **1** (of hair or fur)

growing thickly: *a bushy beard/tail* ◆ *bushy eyebrows* **2** (of plants) growing thickly, with a lot of leaves

ˈbushy-ˌtailed *adj.* ⊃ BRIGHT-EYED
bus·i·ly ⊃ BUSY

TOPIC COLLOCATIONS

Business

running a business
- buy/acquire/own/sell a company/firm/franchise
- set up/establish/start/start up/launch a business/company
- run/operate a business/company/franchise
- head/run a firm/department/team
- make/secure/win/lose/block a deal

- expand/grow/build the business
- boost/increase investment/spending/sales/turnover/earnings/exports/trade
- increase/expand production/output/sales
- boost/maximize production/productivity/efficiency/income/revenue/profit/profitability
- achieve/maintain/sustain growth/profitability
- cut/reduce/bring down/lower/slash costs/prices
- announce/impose/make cuts/cutbacks

sales and marketing
- break into/enter/capture/dominate a market
- capture/gain/grab/take/win/boost/lose market share
- identify/find/build/create a market for sth
- start/launch an advertising/a marketing campaign
- develop/launch/promote a product/Web site
- estimate/assess/create/generate demand for your product
- attract/get/retain/keep/help customers/clients
- drive/generate/boost/increase demand/sales
- beat/keep ahead of/out-think/outperform/(*informal*) stymie the competition
- meet/reach/exceed/miss sales targets

finance
- draw up/set/present/propose/agree on/approve a budget
- keep to/balance/cut/reduce/slash the budget
- be/come in below/under/over/within budget
- generate income/revenue/profit(s)/funds/business
- fund/finance a campaign/a venture/an expansion/spending/a deficit
- provide/raise/allocate capital/funds
- attract/encourage investment/investors
- recover/recoup costs/losses/an investment/an outlay
- get/obtain/offer sb/grant sb credit/a loan
- apply for/raise/secure/arrange/provide financing

failure
- lose business/trade/customers/sales/revenue
- accumulate/accrue/incur/run up debts
- suffer/sustain enormous/heavy/serious losses
- face cuts/a deficit/bankruptcy/a shortfall
- declare/file for/enter/avoid/escape bankruptcy
- liquidate a company/a business/assets
- survive/weather a recession/downturn
- propose/seek/block/oppose a merger
- launch/make/accept/contest/defeat a takeover bid

busi·ness /ˈbɪznəs/ *noun*
▷ TRADE **1** [U] the activity of making, buying, selling, or supplying goods or services for money **SYN** COMMERCE, TRADE: *business contacts/affairs/interests* ◆ *a business investment* ◆ *It's been a pleasure to do business with you.* ◆ *She has started a business as a hairdresser.* ◆ *When he left school, he went into business with his brother.* ◆ *She works in the computer business.* ⊃ see also AGRIBUSINESS, BIG BUSINESS, SHOW BUSINESS

t **t**ea   ţ bu**tt**er   d **d**id   k **c**at   g **g**ot   tʃ **ch**in   dʒ **J**une   f **f**all

> **WORK** **2** [U] work that is part of your job: *Is the trip to Rome business or pleasure?* ◆ *a business lunch* ◆ *He's away on business.* **3** [U] the amount of work done by a company, etc.; the rate or quality of this work: *Business was bad.* ◆ *Business was booming.* ◆ *Her job was to drum up* (= increase) *business.* ◆ *How's business?*
> **COMPANY** **4** [C] a commercial organization such as a company, store, or factory: *to have/start/run a business* ◆ *business premises* ◆ *She works in the family business.* ◆ *They have a small catering business.*
> **RESPONSIBILITY** **5** [U] something that concerns a particular person or organization: *It is the business of the police to protect the community.* ◆ *I will make it my business to find out who is responsible.* ◆ *My private life is none of your business* (= does not concern you). ◆ *It's no business of yours who I invite to the party.*
> **IMPORTANT MATTERS** **6** [U] important matters that need to be dealt with or discussed: *the main business of the meeting* ◆ *He has some unfinished business to deal with.*
> **EVENT** **7** [sing.] (usually with an adjective) a matter, an event, or a situation: *That plane crash was a terrible business.* ◆ *I found the whole business very depressing.* ◆ *The business of the missing tickets hasn't been sorted out.*
> **BEING A CUSTOMER** **8** [U] the fact of a person or people buying goods or services at a store or business: *We're grateful for your business.*

IDM any other business the things that are discussed at the end of an official meeting that do not appear on the agenda: *I think we've finished item four. Now is there any other business?* be in business (*informal*) to have everything that you need in order to be able to start something immediately: *All we need is a car and we'll be in business.* business as usual a way of saying that things will continue as normal despite a difficult situation business is business a way of saying that financial and commercial matters are the important things to consider and you should not be influenced by friendship, etc. get down to business to start dealing with the matter that needs to be dealt with, or doing the work that needs to be done go about your business to do the things that you normally do: *streets filled with people going about their daily business* have no business doing sth | have no business to do sth to have no right to do something: *You have no business being here.* not be in the business of doing sth not intending to do something (which it would be surprising for you to do): *I'm not in the business of getting other people to do my work for me.* out of business having stopped operating as a business because there is no more money or work available: *The new regulations will put many small businesses out of business.* ◆ *Some travel companies will probably go out of business this summer.* ⊃ more at LAND OFFICE, MEAN *v.*, MIND *v.*

ˈbusiness adminiˌstration *noun* [U] the study of how to manage a business: *a master's degree in business administration (= an MBA)*

ˈbusiness ˌcard (also card) *noun* a small card printed with someone's name and details of their job and company ⊃ compare CALLING CARD

ˈbusiness ˌclass *noun* [U] the part of a plane where passengers have a high level of comfort and service, designed for people traveling on business, and less expensive than first class ▶ ˈbusiness class *adv.*: *I always fly business class.*

the ˈbusiness ˌend *noun* [sing.] ~ (of sth) (*informal*) the end of a tool or weapon that performs its main function

ˈbusiness ˌhours *noun* [pl.] the hours in a day that a store or company is open

ˈbusi·ness·like /ˈbɪznəsˌlaɪk/ *adj.* (of a person) working in an efficient and organized way and not wasting time, or thinking about personal things: *She adopted a brisk, businesslike tone.*

busi·ness·man 🔊 /ˈbɪznəsˌmæn; -mən/,
busi·ness·wom·an /ˈbɪznəsˌwʊmən/ *noun*
(*pl.* **busi·ness·men** /-ˌmɛn; -mən/, **busi·ness·wom·en** /-ˌwɪmən/) **1** a person who works in business, especially at

a high level **2** a person who is skillful in business and financial matters: *I could have gotten a better price for the car, but I'm not much of a businessman.*

ˈbusiness ˌpark *noun* an area of land that is specially designed for offices and small factories

ˈbusiness ˌperson *noun* (*pl.* business ˌpeople) a person who works in business, especially at a high level

ˈbusiness ˌschool *noun* a part of a college or university that teaches business, often to GRADUATES (= people who already have a first degree)

ˈbusiness ˌstudies *noun* [U] the study of subjects connected with money and managing a business: *a degree in business studies*

ˌbusiness-to-ˈbusiness *adj.* [usually before noun] (*abbr.* B2B) done between one business and another rather than between a business and its ordinary customers

bus·ing (also bus·sing) /ˈbʌsɪŋ/ *noun* [U] a system of transporting young people by bus to another area so that students of different races can be educated together

busk /bʌsk/ *verb* [I] to perform music in a public place and ask for money from people passing by ▶ busk·er *noun* busk·ing *noun* [U]

ˈbus lane *noun* a part of a road that only buses are allowed to use

bus·load /ˈbʌsloʊd/ *noun* a large group of people on a bus

bus·man's hol·i·day /ˌbʌsmənz ˈhɑlədeɪ/ *noun* [sing.] a vacation that is spent doing the same thing that you do at work

ˈbus pass *noun* **1** a ticket that allows you to travel on any bus within a particular area for a fixed period of time **2** a ticket that allows people from particular groups (for example, students or old people) to travel free or at a reduced cost

ˈbus ˌshelter *noun* a structure with a roof where people can stand while they are waiting for a bus

bus·sing = BUSING

ˈbus ˌstation *noun* the place in a town or city where buses (especially to or from other towns) leave and arrive

ˈbus stop *noun* a place at the side of a road that is marked with a sign, where buses stop

bust /bʌst/ *verb, noun, adj.*
● *verb* (*informal*) **1** ~ sth to break something: *I busted my camera.* ◆ *The lights are busted.* ◆ *Come out, or I'll bust the door down!* **2** ~ sb/sth (for sth) (of the police) to suddenly enter a place and search it, or arrest someone: *He was busted for drugs.* **3** ~ sb to make someone lower in military rank as a punishment **SYN** DEMOTE **4** -busting (in compound adjectives) used to show that something is being prevented or stopped: *a crime-busting superhero*
IDM bust sb's chops (*informal*) **1** to hit someone hard in the JAW: *If you call me that again, I'll bust your chops.* **2** to criticize or annoy someone in a way that is not serious: *My dad sometimes busts my chops about not working hard enough.* bust a gut (also bust your gut) (*informal*) **1** to laugh very hard: *The movie was so funny I busted my gut laughing.* **2** to put a lot of effort into something: *We busted a gut trying to fix the car, but it just wouldn't move.* ◆ *I busted a gut to get you out of this mess!* ... or bust (*informal*) used to say that you will try very hard to get somewhere or achieve something: *For him it's the Olympics or bust.*
PHR V bust 'out (*informal*) **1** to escape from a place such as a prison: *He busted out of reform school at 16.* **2** to begin doing something suddenly: ~ doing sth *We busted out laughing at his silly joke.* ˌbust 'up (*informal* of a couple, friends, partners, etc.) to have an argument and separate **SYN** BREAK UP: *They busted up after five years of marriage.* ⊃ related noun BUST-UP ˌbust sth↔'up (*informal*) to make something end by disturbing or ruining it **SYN** BREAK STH UP: *It was his drinking that busted up his marriage.*
● *noun* **1** (*informal*) an unexpected visit made by the police in order to arrest people for doing something illegal: *a drug*

bust 2 (used especially when talking about clothes or measurements) a woman's breasts or the measurement around the breasts and back **3** a stone or metal model of a person's head, shoulders, and chest **4** a thing that is not good: *As a show it was a bust.*

● **adj.** [not usually before noun] (*informal*) (of a person or business) failed because of a lack of money **SYN** BANKRUPT: *We lost our money when the travel company went bust.*

bus·tard /ˈbʌstərd/ *noun* a large European bird that can run fast

bust·ed /ˈbʌstəd/ *adj.* [not before noun] (*informal*) caught in the act of doing something wrong and likely to be punished: *You are so busted!*

bust·er /ˈbʌstər/ *noun* **1** (*informal*) used to speak to a man you do not like: *Get lost, buster!* **2** (usually in compounds; often used in newspapers) a person or thing that stops or gets rid of something: *crime-busters*

bus·tier /ˌbusˈtyeɪ/ *noun* a woman's tight top which does not cover the arms or shoulders

bus·tle /ˈbʌsl/ *verb, noun*
● **verb** [I, T] to move around in a busy way or to hurry someone in a particular direction: + **adv./prep.** *She bustled around in the kitchen.* ◆ **~ sb + adv./prep.** *The nurse bustled us out of the room.*
● **noun 1** [U] busy and noisy activity: *the hustle and bustle of city life* **2** [C] a frame that was worn under a skirt by women in the past in order to hold the skirt out at the back

bust·ling /ˈbʌslɪŋ/ *adj.* full of people moving about in a busy way: *a bustling city* ◆ **~ with sth** *The market was bustling with life.*

bust-up *noun* (*informal*) the end of a relationship **SYN** BREAKUP: *the final bust-up of their marriage*

bust·y /ˈbʌsti/ *adj.* (*informal*) (of a woman) having large breasts

bus·y 🔑 /ˈbɪzi/ *adj., verb*
● **adj.** (bus·i·er, bus·i·est)
❯ DOING SOMETHING **1** having a lot to do; perhaps not free to do something else because you are working on something: *Are you busy tonight?* ◆ *I'm afraid the doctor is busy at the moment. Can he call you back?* ◆ *I'll be too busy to come to the meeting.* ◆ *The principal is a very busy woman.* ◆ *She was always too busy to listen.* ◆ *a very busy life* ◆ **~ with sth/sb** *Kate's busy with her homework.* **2 ~ (doing sth)** spending a lot of time on something: *James is busy practicing for the school concert.* ◆ *Let's get busy with the cleaning up.*
❯ PLACE **3** full of people, activity, vehicles, etc.: *a busy main road* ◆ *Grand Central is one of New York's busiest stations.*
❯ PERIOD OF TIME **4** full of work and activity: *Have you had a busy day?* ◆ *This is one of the busiest times of the year for the department.*
❯ TELEPHONE **5** being used: *The line is busy—I'll try again later.* ◆ *the busy signal* ⊃ collocations at PHONE
❯ PATTERN/DESIGN **6** too full of small details
   ▶ **bus·i·ly** /ˈbɪzəli/ *adv.*: *He was busily engaged in fixing his bike.*
IDM as busy as a bee very busy keep yourself busy to find enough things to do: *Since she retired she's kept herself very busy.*
● **verb** (bus·ies, bus·y·ing, bus·ied, bus·ied) to fill your time doing an activity or a task: **~ yourself (with sth)** *She busied herself with the preparations for the party.* ◆ **~ yourself (in/ with) doing sth** *While we talked, Bill busied himself making lunch.*

bus·y·bod·y /ˈbɪzi ˌbɑdi/ *noun* (pl. bus·y·bod·ies) (*disapproving*) a person who is too interested in what other people are doing: *He's an interfering old busybody!*

bus·y·work /ˈbɪzi ˌwɜrk/ *noun* [U] work that is given to someone to keep them busy, without really being useful

but 🔑 /bət; *strong form* bʌt/ *conj., prep., adv., noun*
● **conj. 1** used to introduce a word or phrase that contrasts with what was said before: *I got it wrong. It wasn't the red one, but the blue one.* ◆ *His mother won't be there, but his father might be.* ◆ *It isn't that he lied, but he does tend to exaggerate.* **2** however; despite this: *I invited everyone, but only two people came.* ◆ *By the end of the day, we were tired but happy.* ⊃ language bank at NEVERTHELESS **3** used when you are saying sorry about something: *I'm sorry, but I can't stay any longer.* **4** used to introduce a statement that shows that you are surprised or annoyed, or that you disagree: *But that's not possible!* ◆ *"Here's the money I owe you." "But that's not right —it was only $10."* **5** except: *I had no choice but to sign the contract.* **6** used before repeating a word in order to emphasize it: *Nothing, but nothing would make him change his mind.* **7** (*literary*) used to emphasize that something is always true: *She never passed her old home but she thought of the happy years she had spent there* (= she always thought of them).
IDM but for **1** if it were not for: *He would have played but for a knee injury.* **2** except for: *The square was empty but for a couple of cabs.* but then (again) **1** however; on the other hand: *He might agree. But then again, he might have a completely different opinion.* **2** used before a statement that explains or gives a reason for what has just been said: *She speaks very good Italian. But then, she did live in Rome for a year* (= so it's not surprising). you cannot/could not but… (*formal*) used to show that everything else is impossible except the thing that you are saying: *What could he do but forgive her?* (= that was the only thing possible)
● **prep.** except; apart from: *We've had nothing but trouble with this car.* ◆ *The problem is anything but easy.* ◆ *Who but Rosa could think of something like that?* ◆ *Everyone was there but him.*
● **adv.** only: *He was but a shadow of his former self after the accident.* ◆ *There were a lot of famous people there: Tom Hanks and Julia Roberts, to name but two.*
● **noun** /bʌt/ [usually pl.] a reason that someone gives for not doing something or not agreeing: *"There are no buts about it,"* he said firmly. *"You are going."* ◆ *With so many ifs and buts, we'll just have to wait and see.*

bu·tane /ˈbyutein/ *noun* [U] a gas produced from PETROLEUM, used in liquid form as a fuel for cooking, etc.

butch /bʊtʃ/ *adj.* (*informal*) **1** (of a woman) behaving or dressing like a man **2** (of a man) big, and often behaving in an aggressive way

butch·er /ˈbʊtʃər/ *noun, verb*
● **noun 1** a person whose job is cutting up and selling meat in a store, or killing animals for this purpose **2** a person who kills people in a cruel and violent way
● **verb 1 ~ sb** to kill people in a very cruel and violent way **2 ~ sth** to kill animals and cut them up for use as meat **3 ~ sth** to spoil something by doing it very badly: *The script was good, but those guys butchered it.*

butcher ˌblock *noun* [U] a material used for surfaces in kitchens, especially those that you work on: *a slab of butcher block*

butcher's ˌblock *noun* a thick block of wood on which a butcher cuts meat, also used in kitchens as a surface for cutting food on

butch·er·y /ˈbʊtʃəri/ *noun* [U] **1** cruel, violent, and unnecessary killing **2** the work of preparing meat to be sold

but·ler /ˈbʌtlər/ *noun* the main male servant in a large house

butt 🔑 /bʌt/ *noun, verb*
● **noun 1** (*informal*) the part of the body that you sit on **SYN** BUTTOCK: *Get off your butt and do some work!* ◆ *Get your butt over here!* (= Come here!) **2** the thick end of a weapon or tool: *a rifle butt* **3** the part of a cigarette or CIGAR that is left after it has been smoked **4** the act of hitting someone with your head: *a butt from his head* ⊃ see also HEADBUTT
IDM be the butt of sth to be the person or thing that other people often joke about or criticize **SYN** TARGET: *She was the butt of some very unkind jokes.* ⊃ more at KICK v., PAIN n.

h hat   m man   n no   ŋ sing   l leg   r red   y yes   w wet

• **verb 1 ~ sb/sth** to hit or push someone or something hard with your head **2 ~ sb/sth** if an animal **butts** someone or something, it hits them or it hard with its horns and head
PHR V ˌ**butt 'in (on sb/sth) 1** to interrupt a conversation rudely: *How can I explain if you keep butting in?* ♦ **+ speech** *"Is that normal?" Josie butted in.* **2** (*informal*) to become involved in a situation that does not concern you **SYN** INTERFERE (IN): *I didn't ask you to butt in on my private business.* ˌ**butt 'out** (*informal*) used to tell someone rudely to go away or to stop INTERFERING in something that does not concern them: *Butt out, Neil! This is none of your business.*

butte /byut/ *noun* a hill that is flat on top and is separate from other high ground

but·ter 🔑 /ˈbʌt̬ər/ *noun, verb*
• **noun** [U] a soft yellow food made from cream, used in cooking, and for spreading on bread: *Fry the onions in butter.* ➲ see also BREAD AND BUTTER, COCOA BUTTER, PEANUT BUTTER, SHEA BUTTER
IDM butter wouldn't melt (in sb's mouth) (*informal*) used to say that someone seems to be innocent, kind, etc. when they are not really ➲ more at KNIFE *n.*
• **verb ~ sth** to spread butter on something: *She buttered four thick slices of bread.* **IDM** see KNOW *v.*
PHR V ˌ**butter sb↔'up** (*informal*) to say nice things to someone so that they will help you or give you something

ˈ**butter** ˌ**bean** *noun* a large, pale yellow BEAN. Butter beans are often sold dried.

but·ter·cream /ˈbʌt̬ərˌkrim/ *noun* [U] a soft mixture of butter and sugar, used inside and on top of cakes

but·ter·cup /ˈbʌt̬ərˌkʌp/ *noun* a wild plant with small, shiny, yellow flowers that are shaped like cups ➲ picture at PLANT

but·ter·fat /ˈbʌt̬ərˌfæt/ *noun* [U] the natural fat contained in milk and milk products

but·ter·fin·gers /ˈbʌt̬ərˌfɪŋgərz/ *noun* [sing.] (*informal*) a person who often drops things

but·ter·fly /ˈbʌt̬ərˌflaɪ/ *noun* (*pl.* **but·ter·flies**) **1** [C] a flying insect with a long thin body and four large, usually brightly colored, wings: *butterflies and moths* ♦ *She's like a butterfly. She flits in and out of people's lives.* ➲ picture at ANIMAL **2** [U] a swimming stroke in which you swim on your front and lift both arms forward at the same time while your legs move up and down together: *She came in third in the 200 meter butterfly* (= a swimming race). ➲ picture at SPORT **3** also ˈ**social butterfly** [C] a person who is not serious and spends a lot of time going to parties, and talking to people
IDM have butterflies (in your stomach) (*informal*) to have a nervous feeling in your stomach before doing something

ˈ**butterfly** ˌ**bush** *noun* [C, U] = BUDDLEIA

ˈ**butter** ˌ**knife** *noun* a knife that has a flat blade with a round end, used for spreading butter on bread

but·ter·milk /ˈbʌt̬ərˌmɪlk/ *noun* [U] the liquid that remains after butter has been separated from milk, used in cooking or as a drink

but·ter·nut /ˈbʌt̬ərˌnʌt/ *noun* a N. American tree grown as a decoration and for its wood

ˌ**butternut 'squash** *noun* [C, U] a long fruit that grows on the ground and is eaten as a vegetable. It has a hard yellow skin and orange flesh, and is fatter at one end than the other ➲ picture at FRUIT

but·ter·scotch /ˈbʌt̬ərˌskɑtʃ/ *noun* [U] **1** a type of hard, pale brown candy made by boiling butter and brown sugar together **2** a sauce flavored with butterscotch, used for pouring on ice cream, etc.

ˌ**butter 'tart** *noun* (*CanE*) a small PIE with a soft and sticky filling made with brown sugar and usually RAISINS (= dried grapes)

but·ter·y /ˈbʌt̬əri/ *adj.* like, containing, or covered with butter

but·tock /ˈbʌt̬ək/ *noun* [usually pl.] either of the two round soft parts at the top of a person's legs ➲ picture at BODY

but·ton 🔑 /ˈbʌtn/ *noun, verb*
• **noun 1** a small round piece of metal, plastic, etc. that is sewn onto a piece of clothing and used for fastening two parts together: *to button/unbutton your buttons* ♦ *to sew on a button* ♦ *shirt buttons* ➲ picture at CLOTHES **2** a small part of a machine that you press to make it work: *the play/stop/rewind button* ♦ *Adam pressed a button and waited for the elevator.* ♦ *Choose "printer" from the menu and click with the right mouse button.* ♦ *The windows slide down **at the touch of a button**.* ➲ picture at HANDLE ➲ see also PUSH-BUTTON **3** a small area on a computer screen that you click on to make it do something: *Click on the back button to go back to the previous screen.* **4** a round, flat, metal pin, especially one with a message printed on it ➲ see also BELLY BUTTON
IDM on the button (*informal*) **1** at exactly the right time or at the exact time mentioned: *We arrived at 4 o'clock on the button.* **2** exactly right: *You're on the button there!* ➲ more at PUSH *v.*
• **verb 1** [T] **~ sth (up)** to fasten something with buttons: *She hurriedly buttoned (up) her blouse.* **2** [I] **~ (up)** to be fastened with buttons: *The dress buttons (up) at the back.*
IDM button it! (*informal*) used to tell someone rudely to be quiet

ˈ**button-**ˌ**down** *adj.* a **button-down** COLLAR, shirt, etc. has the ends of the collar fastened to the shirt with buttons

ˌ**buttoned-'up** *adj.* (*informal*) not expressing your emotions openly

but·ton·hole /ˈbʌtnˌhoʊl/ *noun, verb*
• **noun** a hole on a piece of clothing for a button to be put through ➲ picture at CLOTHES
• **verb ~ sb** (*informal*) to make someone stop and listen to you, especially when they do not want to

ˈ**button** ˌ**lift** *noun* a machine with poles that pulls people up the mountain on their SKIS

ˈ**button** ˌ**mushroom** *noun* a small young MUSHROOM used in cooking

but·tress /ˈbʌtrəs/ *noun, verb*
• **noun** a stone or brick structure that supports a wall
• **verb ~ sb/sth** (*formal*) to support or give strength to someone or something: *The sharp increase in crime seems to buttress the argument for more police officers on the street.*

bux·om /ˈbʌksəm/ *adj.* (of a woman) large in an attractive way, and with large breasts

buy 🔑 /baɪ/ *verb, noun*
• **verb** (**bought, bought** /bɔt/)
› **WITH MONEY 1** [T, I] to obtain something by paying money for it: **~ (sth)** *Where did you buy that dress?* ♦ *If you're thinking of getting a new car, now is a good time to buy.* ♦ **~ sth from sb** *I bought it from a friend for $10.* ♦ **~ sb sth** *He bought me a new coat.* ♦ **~ sth for sb** *He bought a new coat for me.* ♦ **~ sth + adj.** *I bought my car secondhand.* **ANT** SELL **2** [T] **~ sth** (of money) to be enough to pay for something: *He gave his children the best education that money can buy.* ♦ *Five dollars doesn't buy much nowadays.* **3** [T] **~ sb** to persuade someone to do something dishonest in return for money **SYN** BRIBE: *He can't be bought* (= he's too honest to accept money in this way).
› **OBTAIN 4** [T, usually passive] **~ sth** to obtain something by losing something else of great value: *Her fame was bought at the expense of her marriage.*
› **BELIEVE 5** [T] **~ sth** (*informal*) to believe that something is true, especially something that is not very likely: *You could say you were sick, but I don't think they'd **buy it*** (= accept the explanation).
IDM (have) bought it (*informal*) to be killed, especially in an accident or a war **buy the farm** (*informal*) to die **buy time** to do something in order to delay an event, a decision, etc. ➲ more at BEST *n.*, PIG
PHR V ˌ**buy 'into sth 1** to buy shares in a company, especially in order to gain some control over it **2** (*informal*) to believe something, especially an idea that many other

people believe in: *She had never bought into the idea that to be attractive you have to be thin.* ⊃ related noun BUY-IN ,buy sb↔'off to pay someone money, especially dishonestly, to prevent them from doing something you do not want them to do ,buy sb↔'out **1** to pay someone for their share in a business, usually in order to get total control of it for yourself ⊃ related noun BUYOUT **2** to pay money so that someone can leave an organization, especially the army, before the end of an agreed period ,buy sth↔'up to buy all or as much as possible of something: *Developers are buying up all the land on the island.*

● *noun*
> SOMETHING BOUGHT **1** a good, better, etc. ~ a thing that is worth the money that you pay for it: *That jacket was a really good buy.* ◆ *The best buys this week are carrots and cabbages.* **2** something that is bought or that is for sale; the act of buying something: *Computer games are a popular buy this Christmas.*

buy·er 🔑 /'baɪər/ *noun*
1 a person who buys something, especially something expensive: *Have you found a buyer for your house?* ⊃ compare PURCHASER **ANT** SELLER, VENDOR **2** a person whose job is to choose goods that will be sold in a large store **IDM** a buyer's market a situation in which there is a lot of a particular item for sale, so that prices are low and people buying have a choice

,buyer's re'morse *noun* [U] the feeling of disappointment someone has after they have bought something when they think they have made a mistake

'buy-in *noun* [U] (*business*) the fact of accepting a policy or change because you agree with it: *If you want to make major changes, you need buy-in from everyone in the organization.* ◆ *You need to win people's buy-in.* ⊃ see also BUY v.

buy·out /'baɪaʊt/ *noun* a situation in which a person or group gains control of a company by buying all or most of its shares: *a management buyout*

buzz /bʌz/ *verb, noun*
● *verb* **1** [I] (of a BEE) to make a continuous low sound: *Bees buzzed lazily among the flowers.* **2** [I] to make a sound like a BEE buzzing: *The doorbell buzzed loudly.* ◆ *My ears were buzzing* (= were filled with a continuous sound). **3** [I] to be full of excitement, activity, etc.: *New York buzzes from dawn to dusk.* ◆ *My head was still buzzing after the day's events.* ◆ ~ with sth *The place was buzzing with journalists.* **4** [I, T] ~ (sth) (for sb/sth) to call someone to come by pressing a BUZZER: *The doctor buzzed for the next patient to come in.* **5** [T] ~ sb + adv./prep. to let someone in or out of a place by pressing a buzzer to open a door or gate: *The doorman will buzz you in.* ◆ *I buzzed myself through the gate.* **6** [T] ~ sb/sth (*informal*) to fly very close to someone or something, especially as a warning or threat
PHR V ,buzz a'round to move around quickly, especially because you are very busy: *I've been buzzing around town all day planning my trip.* ,buzz 'off (*informal*) used to tell someone rudely to go away: *Just buzz off and let me get back to my work.*
● *noun* **1** [C, usually sing.] (also buzz·ing [U, sing.]) a continuous sound like the one that a BEE, a BUZZER, or other electronic device makes: *the buzz of bees hunting nectar* ◆ *The buzz of the intercom interrupted our conversation.* ◆ *hums and buzzes from the amplifier* **2** [sing.] the sound of people talking, especially in an excited way: *The buzz of conversation suddenly stopped when she came into the room.* **3** [sing.] (*informal*) a strong feeling of pleasure, excitement, or achievement: *a buzz of excitement/expectation* ◆ *She gets a buzz out of her work.* ◆ *Flying gives me a real buzz.* ◆ *You can sense the creative buzz in the city.* **4 the buzz** [sing.] (*informal*) news that people tell each other that may or may not be true **SYN** RUMOR
IDM give sb a buzz (*informal*) to telephone someone: *I'll give you a buzz on Monday, OK?*

buz·zard /'bʌzərd/ *noun* **1** a large American bird like a VULTURE that eats the flesh of animals that are already dead **2** a large European BIRD OF PREY (= a bird that kills other creatures for food) of the HAWK family

'buzz cut *noun* a style of cutting the hair in which all the hair is cut very short, close to the skin of the head

buzz·er /'bʌzər/ *noun* an electrical device that produces a BUZZING sound as a signal
IDM at the buzzer at the end of a game or period of play: *He missed a three-point attempt at the buzzer.*

'buzz group *noun* one of the small groups of people that a large group can be divided into in order to discuss and give their opinions about a particular subject. The information obtained is used by people doing MARKET RESEARCH.

'buzz saw *noun* = CIRCULAR SAW

buzz·word /'bʌzwərd/ *noun* a word or phrase, especially one connected with a particular subject, that has become fashionable and popular, and is used a lot in newspapers, etc.

b/w *abbr.* (in writing) black and white

by 🔑 /baɪ/ *prep., adv.*
● *prep.* **1** near someone or something; at the side of someone or something; beside someone or something: *a house by the river* ◆ *The telephone is by the window.* ◆ *Come and sit by me.* **2** used, usually after a passive verb, to show who or what does, creates, or causes something: *He was knocked down by a bus.* ◆ *a play by Ibsen* ◆ *Who's that book by?* ◆ *I was frightened by the noise.* **3** used for showing how or in what way something is done: *The house is heated by gas.* ◆ *May I pay by check?* ◆ *I will contact you by mail.* ◆ *to travel by boat/ bus/car/plane* ◆ *to travel by air/land/sea* ◆ *Switch it on by pressing this button.* **4** used before particular nouns without the, to say that something happens as a result of something: *They met by chance.* ◆ *I did it by mistake.* ◆ *The coroner's verdict was "death by strangulation."* **5** not later than the time mentioned; before: *Can you finish the work by five o'clock?* ◆ *I'll have it done by tomorrow.* ◆ *By this time next week we'll be in New York.* ◆ *He should have arrived by now/by this time.* ◆ *By the time (that)* this letter reaches you, I will have left the country. **6** past someone or something: *He walked by me without speaking.* **7** during something; in a particular situation: *to travel by day/night* ◆ *We had to work by candlelight.* **8** used to show the degree or amount of something: *The bullet missed him by two inches.* ◆ *House prices went up by 10%.* ◆ *It would be better by far* (= much better) *to…* **9** from what something shows or says; according to something: *By my watch it is two o'clock.* ◆ *I could tell by the look on her face that something terrible had happened.* ◆ *By law, you are a child until you are 18.* **10** used to show the part of someone or something that someone touches, holds, etc.: *I took him by the hand.* ◆ *She seized her by the arm.* ◆ *Pick it up by the handle!* **11** used with *the* to show the period or quantity used for buying, selling, or measuring something: *We rented the car by the day.* ◆ *They're paid by the hour.* ◆ *We only sell it by the yard.* **12** used to state the rate at which something improves: *They're improving day by day.* ◆ *We'll do it bit by bit.* ◆ *It was getting worse by the minute* (= very fast). ◆ *The children came in two by two* (= in groups of two). **13** used for giving more information about where someone comes from, what someone does, etc.: *He's German by birth.* ◆ *They're both doctors by profession.* **14** used when swearing to mean "in the name of": *I swear by Almighty God…* **15** used to show the measurements of something: *The room measures fifteen feet by twenty feet.* **16** used when multiplying or dividing: *6 multiplied by 2 equals 12.* ◆ *6 divided by 2 equals 3.*
IDM by the by/bye = BY THE WAY at WAY
● *adv.* **1** past: *Just drive by. Don't stop.* ◆ *He hurried by without speaking.* ◆ *Excuse me, I can't get by.* ◆ *Time goes by so quickly.* **2** in order to visit someone for a short time: *I'll come by this evening and pick up the books.*
IDM by and by (*old-fashioned*) before long; soon: *By and by she met an old man with a beard.*

by- (also bye-) /baɪ/ *prefix* (in nouns and verbs) **1** less important: *a byproduct* **2** near: *a bystander*

ʌ cup   ə about   eɪ say   aɪ five   ɔɪ boy   aʊ now   oʊ go   ər bird

by·catch /'baɪkætʃ/ *noun* [U] fish that are caught by ships by accident when other types of fish are being caught: *Thousands of small fish are thrown back into the sea as bycatch.*

bye /baɪ/ *exclamation, noun*
- *exclamation* (also **bye-bye, 'bye-bye**) (*informal*) goodbye: *Bye! See you next week.* ◆ *She waved bye-bye and got into the car.* ◆ *Bye for now, Dad!*
- *noun* (*sports*) a situation in which a player or team does not have an opponent in one part of the competition and continues to the next part as if they had won **IDM** see BY *prep.*

by·gone /'baɪgɔn; -gɑn/ *adj.* [only before noun] happening or existing a long time ago: *a bygone age/era*

by·gones /'baɪgɔnz; -gɑnz/ *noun* [pl.]
   IDM **let bygones be bygones** to decide to forget about disagreements that happened in the past

by·law (also **'by-law**) /'baɪlɔ/ *noun* **1** a law or rule of a club or company **2** a law that is made by a local authority and that applies only to that area

by·line /'baɪlaɪn/ *noun* a line at the beginning or end of a piece of writing in a newspaper or magazine that gives the writer's name

by·name /'baɪneɪm/ *noun* a name given to someone who has the same first name as someone else, so that it is clear who is being referred to

BYOB *abbr.* (*informal*) bring your own bottle/booze/beer (written or said as part of an invitation, meaning that you should bring your own alcoholic drink to a party)

by·pass /'baɪpæs/ *noun, verb*
- *noun* **1** a medical operation on the heart in which blood is directed along a different route so that it does not flow through a part that is damaged or blocked; the new route that the blood takes: *heart bypass surgery* ◆ *a triple bypass operation* ⊃ see also GASTRIC BYPASS **2** a road that passes around a town or city rather than through the center ⊃ note at ROAD
- *verb* **1** ~ **sth** to go around or avoid a place: *A new road now bypasses the town.* **2** ~ **sth** to ignore a rule, an official system, or someone in authority, especially in order to get something done quickly

by·product *noun* **1** a substance that is produced during the process of making or destroying something else: *When burned, plastic produces dangerous byproducts.* **2** a thing that happens, often unexpectedly, as the result of something else: *One of the byproducts of unemployment is an increase in crime.*

by·road /'baɪroʊd/ *noun* a minor road

by·stand·er /'baɪˌstændər/ *noun* a person who sees something that is happening but is not involved **SYN** ONLOOKER: *innocent bystanders at the scene of the accident* ⊃ thesaurus box at WITNESS

byte /baɪt/ *noun* a unit of information stored in a computer, equal to 8 BITS. A computer's memory is measured in bytes.

by·way /'baɪweɪ/ *noun* **1** [C] a small road that is not used very much **2** **byways** [pl.] the less important areas of a subject

by·word /'baɪwərd/ *noun* [usually sing.] **1 a** ~ **for sth** a person or thing that is a well-known lexample of a particular quality: *The name Chanel became a byword for elegance.* **2** a word or phrase that is well known or often used

Byz·an·tine /'bɪznˌtin/ *adj.* [usually before noun] **1** connected with Byzantium or the Eastern Roman Empire **2** used to describe ARCHITECTURE of the 5th to the 15th centuries in the Byzantine Empire, especially churches with high central DOMES and MOSAICS **3** also **byzantine** (*formal*) (of an idea, a system, etc.) complicated, secret, and difficult to change: *an organization of byzantine complexity*

Cc

C /si/ *noun, abbr., symbol*

● **noun** [C, U] (*pl.* Cs, C's /siz/) **1** also **c** (*pl.* **c's**) the third letter of the English alphabet: *"Cat" begins with (a) C/"C."* **2** (*music*) the first note in the SCALE of C MAJOR ⊃ see also MIDDLE C **3** the third highest grade that a student can get for a course, test, or piece of work: *She got a C in Physics.*

● **abbr. 1** CELSIUS: *Water freezes at 0° C.* **2** (also ©, C.) COPYRIGHT: *© Oxford University Press 2011* **3** C. CAPE: *C. Horn* (= for example, on a map) ⊃ see also C&W

● **symbol 1** also **c** the number 100 in ROMAN NUMERAL **2** the symbol for the chemical element CARBON

c. 🔊 *abbr.*

1 (in writing) CENT(S) **2** (in writing) century: *in the 19th c.* ⊃ see also CENT. **3** (also **c, ca.**) (especially before dates) about; approximately (from Latin *circa*): *c. 1890* **4** (in cooking) cup: *add 2 c. flour*

CA *abbr.* (in writing) California

cab /kæb/ *noun* **1** a taxi: *Let's take a cab home.* ♦ *a cab driver* **2** the place where the driver sits in a bus, train, or truck

ca·bal /kə'bæl; -'bæl/ *noun* (*formal*, usually *disapproving*) a small group of people who are involved in secret plans to get political power

Ca·ba·la = KABBALAH

cab·a·lis·tic /ˌkæbə'lɪstɪk/ *adj.* relating to secret or MYSTICAL beliefs

ca·ba·na /kə'bænə/ *noun* (from *Spanish*) a small, simple building or shelter at a beach or swimming pool

cab·a·ret /ˌkæbə'reɪ/ *noun* **1** [C, U] entertainment with singing and dancing that is performed in restaurants or clubs in the evenings: *a cabaret act/singer/band* **2** [C] a restaurant or club where cabaret entertainment is performed

cab·bage /'kæbɪdʒ/ *noun* [U, C] a round vegetable with large green, purple-red, or white leaves that can be eaten raw or cooked: *Do you like cabbage?* ♦ *two cabbages* ♦ *white/red cabbage* ⊃ picture at FRUIT ⊃ see also CHINESE CABBAGE, BOK CHOY

cab·bie (also **cab·by**) /'kæbi/ *noun* (*pl.* **cab·bies**) (*informal*) a person who drives a taxi

cab driver (also **cab·driv·er**) /'kæbdraɪvər/ *noun* a person who drives a taxi as his or her job

cab·in /'kæbən/ *noun* **1** a small house or shelter, usually made of wood: *a log cabin* **2** a small room on a ship in which you live or sleep **3** one of the areas for passengers to sit in a plane ⊃ picture at PLANE **4** (*CanE*) a summer cottage

cabin boy *noun* a boy or young man who works as a servant on a ship

cabin crew *noun* the people whose job is to take care of passengers on a plane

cabin cruiser *noun* = CRUISER

cab·i·net 🔊 /'kæbənət/ *noun*

1 a piece of furniture with doors, drawers, and/or shelves, that is used for storing or showing things: *kitchen cabinets* ♦ *a medicine cabinet* ♦ *The china was displayed in a glass cabinet.* ⊃ see also FILING CABINET **2** usually **the Cabinet** a group of chosen members of a government, that is responsible for advising and deciding on government policy: *a cabinet meeting* ♦ *Hillary Clinton was appointed to the Cabinet as Secretary of State.*

cab·i·net·mak·er /'kæbənətˌmeɪkər/ *noun* a person who makes fine wooden furniture, especially as a job

cab·i·net·ry /'kæbənətri/ *noun* [U] cabinets, especially ones fitted in a kitchen

ca·ble 🔊 /'keɪbl/ *noun, verb*

● **noun 1** [U] = CABLE TELEVISION: *We can receive up to 500 cable channels.* **2** [C, U] a set of wires, covered in plastic or rubber, that carries electricity, telephone signals, etc.: *overhead/underground cables* ♦ *a 10,000 volt cable* ♦ *fiber-optic cable* ⊃ picture at CORD **3** [U, C] thick, strong, metal rope used on ships, for supporting bridges, etc. **4** [C] (*old-fashioned*) a message sent by electrical signals and printed out

● **verb** [T, I] ~ (**sb**) (*old-fashioned*) to send someone a CABLE

cable car *noun* **1** a vehicle that runs on tracks and is pulled by a moving cable **2** (also **tram**) a vehicle that hangs from and is pulled by a moving cable and that carries passengers up and down a mountain

cable modem *noun* a device that connects a computer to the Internet, using the kind of cable used for cable television

cable television (also **ca·ble, cable T'V**) *noun* [U] a system of broadcasting television programs along wires rather than by radio waves

cab·ling /'keɪblɪŋ/ *noun* [U] all the cables that are required for particular equipment or a particular system

ca·boo·dle /kə'budl/ *noun*

IDM **the whole (kit and) caboodle** (*informal*) everything: *I had new clothes, a new hairstyle—the whole kit and caboodle.*

ca·boose /kə'bus/ *noun* the part at the back of a train where the person who is in charge of the train rides

ca·ca·o /kə'kaʊ/ *noun* [U, C] a tropical tree with seeds that are used to make chocolate and COCOA; the seeds from this tree

cache /kæʃ/ *noun, verb*

● **noun 1** a hidden store of things such as weapons: *an arms cache* **2** (*computing*) a part of a computer's memory that stores copies of data that is often needed while a program is running. This data can be accessed very quickly.

● **verb 1** ~ **sth** to store things in a secret place, especially weapons **2** ~ **sth** (*computing*) to store data in a cache: *This page is cached.*

ca·chet /kæ'ʃeɪ/ *noun* [U, sing.] if something has **cachet**, it has a special quality that people admire and approve of SYN PRESTIGE

cack·le /'kækl/ *verb, noun*

● **verb 1** [I] (of a chicken) to make a loud, unpleasant noise **2** [I, T] (+ **speech**) to laugh in a loud, unpleasant way: *She cackled with evil laughter.*

● **noun 1** the loud noise that a chicken makes **2** a loud, unpleasant laugh

ca·coph·o·ny /kə'kɑfəni/ *noun* [U, sing.] (*formal*) a mixture of loud unpleasant sounds ► **ca·coph·o·nous** /-nəs/ *adj.*

cac·tus /'kæktəs/ *noun* (*pl.* **cac·tus·es** or **cac·ti** /-taɪ/) a plant that grows in hot dry regions, especially one with thick STEMS covered in SPINES but without leaves. There are many different types of cactuses. ⊃ picture at PLANT

CAD /kæd; ˌsi eɪ 'di/ *noun* [U] the use of computers to design machines, buildings, vehicles, etc. (the abbreviation for "computer-aided design")

cad /kæd/ *noun* (*old-fashioned*) a man who behaves in a dishonest or unfair way

ca·dav·er /kə'dævər/ *noun* (*technical*) a dead human body SYN CORPSE

ca·dav·er·ous /kə'dævərəs/ *adj.* (*literary*) (of a person) extremely pale, thin, and looking sick

CAD/CAM /'kædkæm/ *noun* [U] the use of computers in the design and manufacture of products (the abbreviation for "computer-aided design/computer-aided manufacture")

cad·die (also **cad·dy**) /'kædi/ *noun, verb*

● **noun** (*pl.* **cad·dies**) (in GOLF) a person who helps a player by carrying his or her CLUB and equipment during a game

| t tea | ṭ butter | d did | k cat | g got | tʃ chin | dʒ June | f fall |

● **verb** (cad·dies, cad·dy·ing, cad·died, cad·died) [I] to act as a caddie in the game of GOLF

cad·dis·fly /ˈkædəsˌflaɪ/ (also ˈcaddis fly) noun a small insect. The young forms, called **caddis worms**, are often used for catching fish.

cad·dy /ˈkædi/ noun (pl. cad·dies) **1** a small bag or box for storing or carrying small objects: a sewing/makeup caddy **2** = CADDIE

ca·dence /ˈkeɪdns/ noun **1** (formal) the rise and fall of the voice in speaking: He delivered his words in slow, measured cadences. **2** the end of a musical phrase

ca·den·za /kəˈdɛnzə/ noun (music) a short passage, usually near the end of a piece of CLASSICAL music, that is played or sung by the SOLOIST alone, and is intended to show the performer's skill

ca·det /kəˈdɛt/ noun a young person who is training to become an officer in the police or armed forces

Ca·dil·lac™ /ˈkædlˌæk/ noun **1** a large and expensive American car **2 the ~ of sth** something that is thought of as an example of the highest quality of a type of thing: This is the Cadillac of watches.

cad·mi·um /ˈkædmiəm/ noun [U] (symb. Cd) a chemical element. Cadmium is a soft, poisonous, blue-white metal that is used in batteries and nuclear REACTORS.

ca·dre /ˈkɑdreɪ; ˈkæ-; -dri/ noun (formal) **1** a small group of people who are specially chosen and trained for a particular purpose **2** a member of this kind of group

Cae·sar·e·an (CanE) = CESAREAN

Cae·sar sal·ad /ˌsizər ˈsæləd/ noun [U, C] a salad of LETTUCE and CROUTONS served with a mixture of oil, lemon juice, egg, etc.

cae·su·ra /siˈʒʊrə/ noun (technical) a pause near the middle of a line of poetry ➔ compare ENJAMBEMENT

ca·fé /kæˈfeɪ/ noun a place where you can buy drinks and simple meals ➔ compare RESTAURANT

caf·e·te·ri·a /ˌkæfəˈtɪriə/ noun a restaurant where you choose and pay for your meal at a counter and carry it to a table. Cafeterias are often found in factories, colleges, hospitals, etc.

caf·fein·at·ed /ˈkæfəˌneɪtəd/ adj. (of coffee or tea) containing caffeine ➔ compare DECAFFEINATED

caf·feine /kæˈfin/ noun [U] a drug found in coffee and tea that makes you feel more active ➔ collocations at DIET ➔ see also DECAFFEINATED

caffe ˈlatte /ˌkæfeɪ ˈlɑteɪ; ˌkɑfeɪ-/ noun = LATTE

caf·tan noun = KAFTAN

cage /keɪdʒ/ noun, verb
● **noun** a structure made of metal bars or wire in which animals or birds are kept: a birdcage ➔ see also RIB CAGE
IDM see RATTLE v.
● **verb** [usually passive] **~ sth (up)** to put or keep an animal in a cage: The dogs are caged (up) at night. ▶ **caged** adj.: He paced the room like a caged animal.

cag·ey /ˈkeɪdʒi/ adj. (cag·i·er, cag·i·est) **~ (about sth)** (informal) not wanting to give someone information **SYN** EVASIVE, SECRETIVE: Tony is very cagey about his family. ▶ **cag·i·ly** /-dʒəli/ adv.

ca·hoots /kəˈhuts/ noun
IDM be in cahoots (with sb) (informal) to be planning or doing something dishonest with someone else **SYN** BE IN COLLUSION

cai·man (also **cay·man**) /ˈkeɪmən/ noun (pl. cai·mans) a N. and S. American REPTILE similar to an ALLIGATOR

cairn /kɛrn/ noun a pile of stones that mark a special place such as the top of a mountain or a place where someone is buried

cais·son /ˈkeɪsən; -sn/ noun a large concrete structure that does not allow water to get in, in which construction work can be done under water

ca·jole /kəˈdʒoʊl/ verb [T, I] to make someone do something by talking to them and being very nice to them **SYN** COAX: **~ sb (into sth/into doing sth)** He cajoled me into agreeing to do the work. ◆ **~ sth out of sb** I managed to cajole his address out of them. ◆ **(+ speech)** "Please say yes," she cajoled.

Ca·jun /ˈkeɪdʒən/ noun, adj.
● **noun 1** [C] a person of French origin from Louisiana who speaks an old form of French, also called Cajun **2** [U] a type of music originally played by Cajuns, that is a mixture of BLUES and FOLK MUSIC
● **adj.** connected with the Cajuns, their language, music, or spicy cooking: Cajun chicken/cuisine

cake /keɪk/ noun, verb
● **noun 1** [C, U] a sweet food made from a mixture of flour, eggs, butter, sugar, etc. that is baked in an oven. Cakes are made in various shapes and sizes and are often decorated, for example with ICING: a piece/slice of cake ◆ to make/bake a cake ◆ a chocolate cake ◆ a birthday cake ◆ a cake pan ➔ see also ANGEL FOOD CAKE, FRUIT CAKE, SPONGE CAKE, WEDDING CAKE **2** [C] a food mixture that is cooked in a round flat shape: potato cakes ➔ see also FISH CAKE
IDM have your cake and eat it too to have the advantages of something without its disadvantages; to have both things that are available **the icing/frosting on the cake** something extra and not essential that is added to an already good situation or experience and that makes it even better **take the cake** (informal) to be the most surprising, annoying, etc. thing that has happened or that someone has done ➔ more at HOT, PIECE n.
● **verb 1** [T, usually passive] **~ sth (in/with sth)** to cover something with a thick layer of something soft that becomes hard when it dries: Her shoes were caked with mud. **2** [I] if a substance cakes, it becomes hard when it dries ▶ **caked** adj.: caked blood

cake·walk /ˈkeɪkwɔk/ noun [sing.] (informal) something that is extremely easy to do

cal·a·bash /ˈkæləˌbæʃ/ noun **1** a container made from the hard covering of a fruit or vegetable; the fruit or vegetable from which a calabash is made ➔ see also GOURD **2** (also ˈcalabash tree) a tropical tree that produces a large round fruit with very hard skin, also called calabash

cal·a·mine /ˈkæləˌmaɪn/ (also ˈcalamine ˌlotion) noun [U] a pink liquid that is used to treat burned, sore, or ITCHY skin

ca·lam·i·tous /kəˈlæmətəs/ adj. (formal) causing great damage to people's lives, property, etc. **SYN** DISASTROUS

ca·lam·i·ty /kəˈlæməti/ noun [C, U] (pl. ca·lam·i·ties) an event that causes great damage to people's lives, property, etc. **SYN** DISASTER

cal·ci·fy /ˈkælsəˌfaɪ/ verb (cal·ci·fies, cal·ci·fy·ing, cal·ci·fied, cal·ci·fied) [I, T] **~ (sth)** (technical) to become hard or make something hard by adding CALCIUM salts ▶ **cal·ci·fi·ca·tion** /ˌkælsəfəˈkeɪʃn/ noun [U]

cal·cite /ˈkælsaɪt/ noun [U] (chemistry) a white or clear mineral consisting of CALCIUM CARBONATE. It forms a major part of rocks such as LIMESTONE, MARBLE, and CHALK.

cal·ci·um /ˈkælsiəm/ noun [U] (symb. Ca) a chemical element. Calcium is a soft silver-white metal that is found in bones, teeth, and CHALK.

calcium ˈcarbonate noun [U] (symb. $CaCO_3$) (chemistry) a white solid substance that exists naturally as CHALK, LIMESTONE, and MARBLE

cal·cu·la·ble /ˈkælkyələbl/ adj. that can be calculated: a calculable risk ➔ compare INCALCULABLE

cal·cu·late /ˈkælkyəˌleɪt/ verb
1 to use numbers to find out a total number, amount, distance, etc. **SYN** WORK OUT: ~ sth Use the formula to calculate the volume of the container. ◆ Benefits are calculated on the basis of average weekly earnings. ◆ **~ how much, what, etc.** You'll need to calculate how much time the assignment will take. **2** to guess something or form an opinion by using all

the information available **SYN** ESTIMATE: ~ *that...* *Conservationists calculate that hundreds of species could be lost in this area.* ◆ ~ **how much, what, etc.** *It is impossible to calculate what influence he had on her life.*

cal·cu·lat·ed /ˈkælkyəˌleɪtəd/ *adj.* [usually before noun] carefully planned to get what you want: *a calculated insult* ◆ *He took a calculated risk* (= a risk that you decide is worth taking even though you know it might have bad results). **IDM** **be calculated to do sth** to be intended to do something; to be likely to do something: *Her latest play is calculated to shock.* ◆ *This kind of entertainment is not calculated to be appealing to children.*

cal·cu·lat·ing /ˈkælkyəˌleɪtɪŋ/ *adj.* (*disapproving*) good at planning things so that you have an advantage, without caring about other people: *a cold and calculating killer* ◆ *I never realized you could be so calculating.*

cal·cu·la·tion 🔊 /ˌkælkyəˈleɪʃn/ *noun* **1** [C, U] the act or process of using numbers to find out an amount: *Cathy did a rough calculation.* ◆ *By my calculations, we made a profit of $20,000 last year.* ◆ *Our guess was confirmed by calculation.* ➔ **collocations at** SCIENTIFIC **2** [C, U] the process of using your judgment to decide what the results would be of doing something **3** [U] (*disapproving*) careful planning for yourself without caring about other people: *an act of cold calculation*

cal·cu·la·tor /ˈkælkyəˌleɪtər/ *noun* a small electronic device for calculating with numbers: *a pocket calculator* ➔ **picture at** STATIONERY

cal·cu·lus /ˈkælkyələs/ *noun* [U] the type of mathematics that deals with rates of change, for example in the slope of a curve or the speed of a falling object

cal·de·ra /kɔlˈdɛrə; kæl-; -ˈdɪrə/ *noun* (*technical*) a very large hole in the top of a VOLCANO, usually caused by an eruption (ERUPT)

cal·dron = CAULDRON

Cal·e·do·ni·an /ˌkæləˈdoʊniən/ *adj.* connected with Scotland

cal·en·dar /ˈkæləndər/ *noun* **1** a page or series of pages showing the days, weeks, and months of a particular year, especially one that you hang on a wall: *a 2014 calendar* ➔ **see also** ADVENT CALENDAR **2** a record of what you have to do each day; the book or piece of software in which you write this down: *an appointment calendar* ➔ **compare** APPOINTMENT BOOK, SCHEDULE **3** [usually sing.] a list of important events or dates of a particular type during the year: *This is one of the biggest weeks in the baseball calendar.* **4** a system by which time is divided into fixed periods, showing the beginning and end of a year: *the Islamic calendar*

ˌ**calendar** ˈ**month** *noun* (*technical*) **1** one of the twelve months of the year ➔ **compare** LUNAR MONTH **2** a period of time from a particular date in one month to the same date in the next one

ˌ**calendar** ˈ**year** *noun* (*technical*) the period of time from January 1 to December 31 in the same year

calf /kæf/ *noun* (*pl.* **calves** /kævz/) **1** [C] the back part of the leg between the ankle and the knee: *I tore a calf muscle.* ◆ *She wore a calf-length skirt.* ➔ **picture at** BODY **2** [C] a young cow **3** [C] a young animal of some other type, such as a young ELEPHANT or WHALE **4** [U] = CALFSKIN **IDM** **in/with calf** (of a cow) pregnant

calf·skin /ˈkæfskɪn/ (also **calf**) *noun* [U] soft thin leather made from the skin of calves, used especially for making shoes and clothing

cal·i·ber (also **cal·i·bre**) /ˈkæləbər/ *noun* **1** [U] the quality of something, especially a person's ability **SYN** STANDARD: *He was impressed by the high caliber of applicants for the job.* ◆ *The company needs more people of your caliber.* **2** [C] the width of the inside of a tube or gun; the width of a bullet

cal·i·brate /ˈkæləˌbreɪt/ *verb* (*technical*) **1** ~ **sth** to mark units of measurement on an instrument such as a THER-

MOMETER so that it can be used for measuring something accurately **2** ~ **sth** to check the measurement on an instrument against a standard instrument, and adjust the first instrument to keep it accurate

cal·i·bra·tion /ˌkæləˈbreɪʃn/ *noun* (*technical*) **1** [U] the act of calibrating: *a calibration error* **2** [C] the units of measurement marked on a THERMOMETER or other instrument

cal·i·co /ˈkælɪˌkoʊ/ *noun* [U] a type of light cotton cloth that has a pattern printed on it

ˌ**calico** ˈ**cat** *noun* a cat with black, brown, orange, and white fur **SYN** TORTOISESHELL

cal·i·for·ni·um /ˌkæləˈfɔrniəm/ *noun* [U] (*symb.* **Cf**) a chemical element. Californium is a RADIOACTIVE metal produced artificially with CURIUM or AMERICIUM

cal·i·pers (also **cal·li·pers**) /ˈkæləpərz/ *noun* [pl.] an instrument with two long thin parts joined at one end, used for measuring the DIAMETER of tubes and round objects (= the distance across them): *a pair of calipers*

ca·liph /ˈkeɪləf/ *noun* a title used by Muslim rulers, especially in the past

cal·iph·ate /ˈkæləˌfeɪt; ˈkeɪ-/ *noun* **1** the position of a caliph **2** an area of land that is ruled over by a caliph

call 🔊 /kɔl/ *verb, noun*

● **verb**

> TELEPHONE **1** [I, T] to telephone someone: *I'll call again later.* ◆ ~ **sb/sth** *I called the office to tell them I'd be late.* ◆ *My brother called me from Spain last night.*

> DESCRIBE SB/STH **2** [T] to describe someone or something in a particular way; to consider someone or something to be something: ~ **sb/sth** + **noun** *I wouldn't call German an easy language.* ◆ *Are you calling me a liar?* ◆ *He was in the family room, or the den, or whatever you want to call it.* ◆ *You owe me ten dollars and forty-three cents. Let's just call it ten dollars.* ◆ ~ **sb/sth** + **adj.** *Would you call it blue or green?* ➔ **thesaurus box at** REGARD

> GIVE NAME **3** [T] to give someone or something a particular name; to use a particular name or title when you are talking to someone: ~ **sb/sth** + **noun** *They called their daughter Hannah.* ◆ *His name is Hiroshi but everyone calls him Hiro.* ◆ *What do they call that new fabric?* ◆ ~ **sb** *We call each other by our first names here.* ➔ **see also** CALLED

> ASK/ORDER BY TELEPHONE **4** [T] to ask someone or something to come quickly to a particular place by telephoning: ~ **sb/sth** *to call the fire department/the police/a doctor/an ambulance* ◆ *The doctor has been called to an urgent case.* ◆ *I'll call a taxi for you.* ◆ ~ **sb sth** *I'll call you a taxi.*

> ASK/ORDER SOMEONE TO COME **5** [T, I] ~ (**sb**) to ask someone to come by shouting or speaking loudly: *Will you call the kids in for lunch?* ◆ *Did you call?* **6** [T, usually passive] ~ **adv./prep.** (*formal*) to order someone to come to a place: *Several candidates were called for a second interview.* ◆ *The ambassador was called back to Washington by the president.* ◆ *He felt called to the priesthood* (= had a strong feeling that he must become a priest). **7** [T] to order someone to come into a court to give evidence: ~ **sb** *Call the next witness!* ◆ ~ **sb as sth** *Seventeen people were called as witnesses.* ◆ ~ **sb to do sth** *He was called to testify at the trial.*

> MEETING/STRIKE, ETC. **8** [T] ~ **sth** to order something to happen; to announce that something will happen: *to call a meeting/an election/a strike*

> SHOUT **9** [I, T] to shout or say something loudly to attract someone's attention: *I thought I heard someone calling.* ◆ ~ (**out**) **to sb** (**for sth**) *She called out to her father for help.* ◆ ~ (**sth**) **out** *He called out a warning from the kitchen.* ◆ ~ **sth** *Did someone call my name?* ◆ + **speech** *"See you later!" she called.*

> DESCRIBE YOURSELF **10** [T] ~ **yourself** + **noun** to claim that you are a particular type of person, especially when other people question whether this is true: *You call yourself a friend? So why won't you help me, then?* ◆ *She has no right to call herself a feminist.*

> OF BIRD/ANIMAL **11** [I] to make the cry that is typical for it

---

h **hat**   m **man**   n **no**   ŋ **sing**   l **leg**   r **red**   y **yes**   w **wet**

> **IN SPORTS 12** [T] to make an official decision about a play or shot: ~ *sth The umpire called a foul ball.* ◆ ~ **sb/sth + adj.** *The serve was called out.*

> **PREDICT 13** [T] ~ **sth** to predict the result of a future event, especially an election or a vote: *The presidential race is still **too close to call** (= the candidates are doing equally well and it is impossible to guess who will win).* ◆ *Wow! You called it! How did you know that would happen?*

> **CANCEL 14** [T] ~ **sth** to stop or cancel a game: *The game was called because of rain.*

> **VISIT 15** [I] (*old-fashioned*) to make a short visit to a person or place: ~ **on sb** *Miss Crane called on Mrs. Alcott this afternoon.* ◆ ~ **to do sth** *He was out when I called to see him.*

> **COIN 16** [T, I] ~ **(sth)** to say which side of a coin you think will face upward after it is thrown: *to call heads/tails*

> **IN CARDS 17** [T, I] ~ **(sb/sth)** (in a game of POKER) to bet the same amount of money as the previous player, and so force the player to show his or her cards

IDM **call sb's bluff** to tell someone to do what they are threatening to do, because you believe that they will not be cruel or brave enough to do it **call sth into play** (*formal*) to make use of something: *Chess is a game that calls into play all your powers of concentration.* **call sth into question** to doubt something or make others doubt something **SYN** QUESTION: *His honesty has never been called into question.* **call it a day** (*informal*) to decide or agree to stop doing something: *After forty years in politics I think it's time for me to call it a day* (= to retire). **call it quits** (*informal*) **1** to agree to end a contest, disagreement, etc. because both sides seem equal **2** to decide to stop doing something **call sb names** to use insulting words about someone **call the shots/tune** (*informal*) to be the person who controls a situation **call a spade a spade** to say exactly what you think without trying to hide your opinion **call sb to account (for/over sth)** to make someone explain a mistake, etc. because they are responsible for it **call sb/sth to order** to ask people in a meeting to be quiet so that the meeting can start or continue ⭢ more at CARPET *n.*, MIND *n.*, PAY *v.*, POT *n.*, WHAT

PHR V **'call at...** (of a ship or boat) to stop at a place for a short time: *The ship calls at New York and Cancun.* **,call sb a'way** to ask someone to stop what they are doing and to go somewhere else: *She was called away from the meeting to take an urgent phone call.* **,call 'back | ,call sb 'back** to telephone someone again or to telephone someone who telephoned you earlier: *She said she'd call back.* ◆ *I'm waiting for someone to call me back with a price.* **'call for sb** (*old-fashioned*) to pick up someone in order to go somewhere: *I'll call for you at 7 o'clock.* **'call for sth 1** to need something: *The situation calls for prompt action.* ◆ *"I've been promoted." "This calls for a celebration!"* ⭢ see also UNCALLED FOR **2** to publicly ask for something to happen: *They called for the immediate release of the hostages.* ◆ *The opposition party has called for him to resign.* **,call sth↔'forth** (*formal*) to produce a particular reaction: *His speech called forth an angry response.* **,call 'in 1** to telephone a place, especially the place where you work: *Several people have **called in sick** today.* **2** to make a phone call to a radio or television program: *They invite listeners to call in with questions for the celebrity guests.* **,call sb↔'in** to ask for the services of someone: *to call in the bomb squad/the police* **,call sth↔'in** to order or ask for the return of something: *The bank called in all of its loans.* **,call sb/sth↔'off** to order a dog or a person to stop attacking, searching, etc. **,call sth↔'off** to cancel something; to decide that something will not happen: *to call off a trip/strike* ◆ *They have called off their engagement* (= decided not to get married). ◆ *The game was called off because of bad weather.* **'call on/upon sb** (*formal*) **1** to formally invite or ask someone to speak, etc.: *I now call upon the chairman to address the meeting.* **2** to ask or demand that someone do something: *I feel called upon to* (= feel that I should) *warn you that...* **,call sb 'out** to ask someone to come, especially to an emergency: *The governor had to call out troops to quell the disturbances.* **,call sb↔'up 1** to make a telephone call to someone **2** to move a baseball player from a MINOR LEAGUE team to a MAJOR LEAGUE team ⭢ **related noun**

CALL-UP **,call sth↔'up 1** to bring something back to your mind **SYN** RECALL: *The smell of the ocean called up memories of her childhood.* **2** to use something that is stored or kept available: *I called his address up on the computer.* ◆ *She called up her last reserves of strength.*

● **noun**

> **ON TELEPHONE 1** [C] (also **'phone call**) the act of speaking to someone on the telephone: *to get/have/receive a call from someone* ◆ *to give sb/to make a call* ◆ *Were there any calls for me while I was out?* ◆ *I'll take* (= answer) *the call upstairs.* ◆ *I left a message but he didn't **return my call.*** ◆ *a local call* ◆ *a long-distance call* ⭢ note at PHONE ⭢ see also WAKE-UP CALL

> **LOUD SOUND 2** [C] a loud sound made by a bird or an animal, or by a person to attract attention: *the distinctive call of the bluejay* ◆ *a call for help*

> **REQUEST/DEMAND 3** [C] ~ **(for sth)** a request, an order, or a demand for someone to do something or to go somewhere: *calls for the senator to resign* ◆ *calls for national unity* ◆ *This is the last call for passengers traveling on U.S. Airways flight 199 to Chicago.* ◆ (*formal*) *a **call to arms** (= a strong request to fight in the army, etc.)* ⭢ see also CURTAIN CALL **4** [U] **no ~ for sth | no ~ (for sb) to do sth** no demand for something; no reason for someone's behavior: *There isn't a lot of call for videotapes nowadays.* ◆ *There was no call for him to be so rude.*

> **OF A PLACE 5** [sing.] ~ **(of sth)** (*literary*) a strong feeling of attraction that a particular place has for you: *the call of the sea/your homeland*

> **TO A PARTICULAR JOB 6** [sing.] ~ **(to do sth)** a strong feeling that you want to do something, especially a particular job ⭢ see also CALLING

> **DECISION 7** [C] (*informal*) a decision: *It's your call!* ◆ *a good/bad call* ◆ *That's a tough call.*

> **IN SPORTS 8** [C] a decision made by the UMPIRE or REFEREE: *There was a disputed call in the second set.*

> **VISIT 9** [C] (*old-fashioned*) a short visit to someone: *to pay a call on an old friend* ⭢ see also HOUSE CALL

IDM **the call of nature** (*humorous*) the need to go to the bathroom **(be) on call** (of a doctor, police officer, etc.) available for work if necessary, especially in an emergency: *I'll be on call the night of the party.* ⭢ see also ON-CALL ⭢ more at BECK, CLOSE² *adj.*

THESAURUS

call

cry out ● exclaim ● blurt (out)

These words all mean to shout or say something loudly or suddenly.

call to shout or say something loudly to attract someone's attention: *I thought I heard someone calling.*

cry out (sth) to shout something loudly, especially when you need help or are in trouble: *She cried out for help.* ◆ *I cried out his name.*

exclaim to say something suddenly and loudly, especially because of a strong emotion: *"It isn't fair!" he exclaimed angrily.*

blurt (out) to say something suddenly and without thinking carefully enough: *He blurted out the answer.*

PATTERNS

- to call/cry out/exclaim/blurt out (sth) **to** sb
- to call/cry out **for** sb/sth
- to cry out/exclaim/blurt out **in/with** sth
- to call/cry out/exclaim/blurt out **suddenly**
- to call/cry out/exclaim/burst out **loudly**

---

call·back /'kɔlbæk/ *noun* **1** [C] an occasion when you are asked to return somewhere, for example for a second interview when you are trying to get a job **2** [U, C] (*computing*) a process by which the user of a computer or telephone system proves their identity by contacting a computer, which then contacts them **3** [C] a telephone call that you make to someone who has just called you

---

call box *noun* a small box beside a road, with a telephone in it, to call for help after an accident, etc.

call ˌcenter (*CanE usually* **ˈcall ˌcentre**) *noun* an office in which a large number of people work using telephones, for example arranging insurance for people, or taking customers' orders, and answering questions

called /kɔld/ *adj.* [not before noun] having a particular name: *What's their son called?* ♦ *I don't know anyone called Scott.* ♦ *I forgot what the company he works for is called.* ♦ *What's it called again? Yeah, that's right. A modem.* ⊃ see also SO-CALLED

call·er /ˈkɔlər/ *noun* **1** a person who is making a telephone call: *The caller hung up.* ♦ *an anonymous caller* **2** (*old-fashioned*) a person who goes to a house or a building **3** a person who shouts out the steps for people performing a SQUARE DANCE

ˌcaller I'D *noun* [U] a system that uses a device on your telephone to identify and display the telephone number of the person who is calling you

ˈcall girl *noun* a PROSTITUTE who makes her arrangements by telephone

cal·lig·ra·phy /kəˈlɪgrəfi/ *noun* [U] beautiful HANDWRITING that you do with a special pen or brush; the art of producing this ▶ **cal·lig·ra·pher** /-fər/ *noun*

call-in *noun* a radio or television program in which people can telephone and make comments or ask questions about a particular subject

call·ing /ˈkɔlɪŋ/ *noun* **1** a strong desire or feeling of duty to do a particular job, especially one in which you help other people **SYN** VOCATION: *He realized that his calling was to preach the gospel.* **2** (*formal*) a profession or career

ˈcalling ˌcard *noun* **1** (also **ˈphone card**) a card with a number on it that you use in order to pay to make a call from any phone. The cost of the call is charged to your account and you pay it later. **2** (also **card**) (especially in the past) a small card with your name on it that you leave with someone after, or instead of, a formal visit

cal·li·pers *noun* = CALIPERS

ˈcall ˌletters *noun* [pl.] the letters that are used to identify a radio or television station: *the call letters WNBC*

cal·lous /ˈkæləs/ *adj., noun*
● *adj.* not caring about other people's feelings or suffering **SYN** CRUEL, UNFEELING: *a callous killer/attitude/act* ♦ *a callous disregard for the feelings of others* ▶ **cal·lous·ly** *adv.* **cal·lous·ness** *noun* [U]
● *noun* = CALLUS

cal·loused (also **cal·lused**) /ˈkæləst/ *adj.* (of the skin) made rough and hard, usually by hard work: *calloused hands*

cal·low /ˈkæloʊ/ *adj.* (*formal, disapproving*) young and without experience **SYN** INEXPERIENCED: *a callow youth*

ˈcall sign *noun* the letters and numbers used in radio communication to identify the person who is sending a message

ˈcall-up *noun* the opportunity for a baseball player from a MINOR LEAGUE team to play for a MAJOR LEAGUE team: *a call-up from the RiverDogs to the Yankees*

cal·lus (also **cal·lous**) /ˈkæləs/ *noun* an area of thick hard skin on a hand or foot, usually caused by rubbing

cal·lused = CALLOUSED

ˌcall ˈwaiting *noun* [U] a telephone service that lets you take another call when you are already using the telephone, without ending the first call

calm 🔑 /kɑm/ *adj., verb, noun*
● *adj.* (**calm·er, calm·est**) **1** not excited, nervous, or upset: *It is important to keep calm in an emergency.* ♦ *Try to remain calm.* ♦ *Her voice was surprisingly calm.* ♦ *The city is calm again* (= free from trouble and fighting) *after yesterday's riots.* **2** (of the ocean) without large waves **3** (of the weather) without wind: *a calm, cloudless day* ▶ **calm·ly** *adv.*: *"I'll call the doctor,"* *he said calmly.* **calm·ness** *noun* [U]

● *verb* ~ **sb/sth** to make someone or something become quiet and more relaxed, especially after strong emotion or excitement: *I took a few seconds to calm my nerves.* ♦ *His presence had a calming influence.*
PHR V ˌcalm ˈdown | ˌcalm sb/sth↔ˈdown to become or make someone become calm: *Look, calm down! We'll find her.* ♦ *We waited inside until things calmed down.* ♦ *He took a few deep breaths to calm himself down.*
● *noun* [C, U] **1** a quiet and peaceful time or situation: *the calm of the early morning* ♦ *The police appealed for calm.* **2** a quiet and relaxed manner: *Her previous calm gave way to terror.*
IDM **the calm before the storm** a calm time immediately before an expected period of violent activity or argument

WHICH WORD?

calm ♦ **calmness**
■ The noun **calm** is usually used to talk about a peaceful time or situation: *There was a short period of uneasy calm after the riot.* It can also be used to describe a person's manner: *She spoke with an icy calm.* **Calmness** is usually used to talk about a person: *We admired her calmness under pressure.*

cal·o·rie /ˈkæləri/ *noun* **1** a unit for measuring how much energy food will produce: *No dessert for me, thanks—I'm counting my calories.* ♦ *a low-calorie drink/diet* ⊃ collocations at DIET **2** (*technical*) a unit for measuring a quantity of heat; the amount of heat needed to raise the temperature of a gram of water by one degree Celsius ▶ **ca·lor·ic** /kəˈlɔrɪk/ *adj.*: *a caloric value of 7 calories per gram* ♦ *In order to lose weight, you should reduce your caloric intake.*

cal·o·rif·ic /ˌkælæˈrɪfɪk/ *adj.* [usually before noun] **1** (of food and drink) containing a lot of calories and likely to make you fat: *calorific chocolate cake* **2** (*technical*) relating to the amount of energy contained in food or fuel: *the calorific value of food* (= the quantity of heat or energy produced by a particular amount of food)

cal·o·rim·e·ter /ˌkæləˈrɪmətər/ *noun* (*technical*) a device which measures the amount of heat in a chemical reaction

calque /kælk/ (also **ˈloan transˌlation**) *noun* (*linguistics*) a word or expression in a language that is a translation of a word or expression in another language: *"Traffic calming" is a calque of the German "Verkehrsberuhigung."*

cal·um·ny /ˈkæləmni/ *noun* (*pl.* **cal·um·nies**) (*formal*) **1** [C] a false statement about a person that is made to damage their reputation **2** [U] the act of making such a statement **SYN** SLANDER

Cal·va·dos /ˈkælvəˌdoʊs; ˌkælvəˈdoʊs/ *noun* [U] a French drink made by DISTILLING apple juice

calve /kæv/ *verb* [I] (of a cow) to give birth to a CALF

calves pl. of CALF

Cal·vin·ist /ˈkælvɪnɪst/ (also **Cal·vin·is·tic** /ˌkælvəˈnɪstɪk/) *adj.* **1** connected with a Church that follows the teachings of the French Protestant, John Calvin **2** having very strict moral attitudes ▶ **Cal·vin·ism** /ˈkælvəˌnɪzəm/ *noun* [U] **Cal·vin·ist** *noun*

ca·lyp·so /kəˈlɪpsoʊ/ *noun* (*pl.* **cal·yp·sos**) [C, U] a Caribbean song about a subject of current interest; this type of music

ca·lyx /ˈkeɪlɪks/ *noun* (*pl.* **ca·lyx·es** or **ca·ly·ces** /ˈkeɪləsiz; ˈkæ-/) (*technical*) the ring of small green leaves (called **sepals**) that protect a flower before it opens

CAM /kæm/ *noun* [U] the use of computers to manufacture products (the abbreviation for "computer-aided manufacturing")

cam /kæm/ *noun* a part on a wheel that sticks out and changes the CIRCULAR movement of the wheel into up-and-down or backwards-and-forwards movement

ca·ma·ra·de·rie /ˌkɑməˈrɑdɛri; ˌkæ-/ *noun* [U] a feeling of friendship and trust among people who work or spend a lot of time together

cam·ber /'kæmbər/ *noun* a slight downward curve from the middle of a road to each side

cam·bric /'keɪmbrɪk/ *noun* [U] a type of thin white cloth made from cotton or LINEN

cam·cord·er /'kæm,kɔrdər/ *noun* a video camera that records pictures and sound and that can be carried around

came pt of COME

cam·el /'kæml/ *noun* **1** [C] an animal with a long neck and one or two HUMPS on its back, used in desert countries for riding on, or for carrying goods ⟳ compare DROMEDARY **2** [U] = CAMEL HAIR: *a camel coat* **IDM** see STRAW

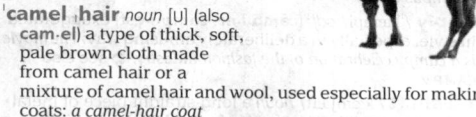
camel

camel ,hair *noun* [U] (also **cam·el**) a type of thick, soft, pale brown cloth made from camel hair or a mixture of camel hair and wool, used especially for making coats: *a camel-hair coat*

ca·mel·lia /kə'mɪlyə/ *noun* a bush with shiny leaves and white, red, or pink flowers that look like ROSES and are also called camellias

Cam·em·bert /'kæməm,ber/ *noun* [U, C] a type of soft French cheese with a strong flavor

cam·e·o /'kæmiou/ *noun* (*pl.* **cam·e·os**) **1** a small part in a movie or play for a famous actor: *a cameo role/appearance* **2** a piece of jewelry that consists of a raised design, often of a head, on a background of a different color: *a cameo ring* **3** a short piece of writing that gives a good description of someone or something

cam·er·a /'kæmrə; 'kæmərə/ *noun* a piece of equipment for taking photographs, moving pictures, or television pictures: *Just point the camera and press the button.* ◆ *Cameras started clicking as soon as she stepped out of the car.* ◆ *a TV/digital camera* ◆ *a camera crew* **IDM** **in camera** (*law*) in a judge's private room, without the press or the public being present: *The trial was held in camera.* **on camera** being filmed or shown on television: *Are you prepared to tell your story on camera?*

cam·er·a·man /'kæmrə,mæn; -mən/, **cam·er·a·wom·an** /'kæmrə,wumən/ *noun* (*pl.* **cam·er·a·men** /-,mɛn; -mən/, **cam·er·a·wom·en** /-,wɪmən/) a person whose job is operating a camera for making movies or television programs

cam·er·a ob·scu·ra /,kæmrə əb'skyurə/ *noun* an early form of camera consisting of a dark box with a tiny hole or LENS in the front and a small screen inside, on which the image appears

camera ,operator *noun* (also **cam·er·a·per·son** /'kæmrə,pərsn/ *pl.* **cam·er·a·peo·ple** /-,pipl/) a person whose job is operating a camera for making movies or television programs

cam·er·a·work /'kæmrə,wərk/ *noun* [U] the style in which someone takes photographs or uses a movie camera

cam·i·sole /'kæmə,soul/ *noun* a short piece of women's underwear that is worn on the top half of the body and is held up with narrow strips of material over the shoulders

cam·o·mile = CHAMOMILE

cam·ou·flage /'kæmə,flɑʒ/ *noun, verb*
• *noun* **1** [U] a way of hiding soldiers and military equipment, using paint, leaves, or nets, so that they look like part of their surroundings: *a camouflage jacket* (= covered with green and brown marks and worn by soldiers) ◆ *troops dressed in camouflage* **2** [U, sing.] the way in which an animal's color or shape matches its surroundings and makes it difficult to see **3** [U, sing.] behavior that is deliberately meant to hide the truth: *Her angry words were camouflage for the way she felt.*

• *verb* ~ sth (with sth) to hide someone or something by making them or it look like the things around, or like something else: *The soldiers camouflaged themselves with leaves.* ◆ *Her size was camouflaged by the long loose dress she wore.* ⟳ thesaurus box at HIDE

camp /kæmp/ *noun, verb*
• *noun*
> IN TENTS **1** [C, U] a place where people live temporarily in tents or temporary buildings: *Let's return to camp.* ◆ *to pitch/ make/set up camp* (= put up tents) ◆ *to break camp* (= to take down tents)
> VACATION **2** [C, U] a place where young people go on vacation and take part in various activities, or a particular activity: *a tennis camp* ◆ *He spent two weeks at camp this summer.* ◆ *summer camp* ⟳ see also DAY CAMP, FAT CAMP
> PRISON, ETC. **3** [C] (used in compounds) a place where people are kept in temporary buildings or tents, especially by a government and often for long periods: *a refugee camp* ◆ *a camp guard* ⟳ see also CONCENTRATION CAMP, PRISON CAMP
> ARMY **4** [C, U] a place where soldiers live while they are training or fighting: *an army camp*
> GROUP OF PEOPLE **5** [C] a group of people who have the same ideas about something and oppose people with other ideas: *the socialist camp* ◆ *We were in opposing camps.* **6** [C] one of the sides in a competition and the people connected with it: *There was an air of confidence in the Red Sox camp.* **IDM** see FOOT n.
• *verb*
> LIVE IN TENT **1** [I] to put up a tent and live in it for a short time: *I camped overnight in a field.* **2** [I] **go camping** to stay in a tent, especially while you are on vacation: *They go camping in Wyoming every year.*
> STAY FOR SHORT TIME **3** [I] ~ (out) to live in someone's house for a short time, especially when you do not have a bed there: *I'm camping out at a friend's apartment at the moment.*
PHR V **,camp 'out** to live outside for a short time: *Dozens of reporters camped out on her doorstep.* **,camp it 'up** (*informal*) to behave in a very exaggerated manner, especially to attract attention to yourself or to make people laugh ⟳ see also CAMPY

cam·paign /kæm'peɪn/ *noun, verb*
• *noun* **1** ~ (against/for sth) a series of planned activities that are intended to achieve a particular social, commercial, or political aim: *to conduct a campaign* ◆ *a campaign against ageism in the workplace* ◆ *the campaign for congressional reform* ◆ *an antismoking campaign* ◆ *Today police launched* (= began) *a campaign to reduce traffic accidents.* ◆ *an advertising campaign* ◆ *an election campaign* ◆ *the president's campaign team/manager* ⟳ collocations at VOTE **2** a series of attacks and battles that are intended to achieve a particular military aim during a war
• *verb* [I, T] to take part in or lead a campaign, for example to achieve political change or in order to win an election: *The party campaigned vigorously in the Midwest.* ◆ ~ for/against sb/sth *We have campaigned against whaling for the last 15 years.* ◆ ~ to do sth *They are campaigning to save the area from building development.* ▶ **cam·paign·ing** *noun* [U]

THESAURUS

campaign

battle ◆ struggle ◆ drive ◆ war ◆ fight

These are all words for an effort made to achieve or prevent something.

campaign a series of planned activities that are intended to achieve a particular social, commercial, or political aim: *the campaign for health care reform* ◆ *an advertising campaign*

battle a competition or argument between people or groups of people trying to win power or control: *She* *finally won her legal battle.* ♦ *the endless battle between man and nature*

struggle a competition or argument between people or groups of people trying to win power or control: *the struggle for independence* ♦ *the struggle between good and evil*

BATTLE OR STRUGGLE?

These words are very similar and in many cases you can use either word. However, **battle** often refers to a shorter, more direct fight. A **struggle** may be a longer fight against powerful forces instead of individuals or one particular problem: *the battle for the Republican nomination* ♦ *her long struggle for recognition*

drive an organized effort by a group of people to achieve something: *the drive for success* ♦ *a drive to reduce energy consumption* ♦ *a major fund drive*

CAMPAIGN OR DRIVE?

A **campaign** is usually an attempt to get other people to do something, that takes place over a period of time; a **drive** may be a shorter or more local effort. A **campaign** may be larger, more formal, and more organized than a **drive**.

war [sing.] an effort over a long period of time to get rid of or stop something bad: *the war against poverty*

fight [sing.] the work of trying to stop or prevent something bad or achieve something good; an act of competing, especially in a sport: *Workers won their fight for better benefits and higher pay.*

WAR OR FIGHT?

- A **war** is about stopping things, like drugs and crime, that everyone agrees are bad. A **fight** can be about achieving justice for yourself.

PATTERNS

- a campaign/battle/struggle/drive/war/fight **against** sth
- a campaign/battle/struggle/drive/fight **for** sth
- a **one-man/one-woman/personal** campaign/battle/struggle/war
- a **bitter** campaign/battle/struggle/drive/war/fight
- to **launch/embark on** a campaign/battle/drive
- to **lead/continue** the campaign/battle/struggle/drive/fight
- to **win/lose** a battle/struggle/war/fight

cam·paign·er /kæmˈpeɪnər/ *noun* a person who leads or takes part in a campaign, especially one for political or social change: *a leading human rights campaigner* ♦ *a campaigner on environmental issues* ♦ *a campaigner for women priests* ♦ *an old/veteran/seasoned campaigner* (= a person with a lot of experience of a particular activity) ♦ *Obama campaigners* (= people working for Obama in a campaign)

cam·pa·ni·le /ˌkæmpəˈniːli/ *noun* a tower that contains a bell, especially one that is not part of another building

cam·pa·nol·o·gy /ˌkæmpəˈnɑlədʒi/ *noun* [U] (*formal*) the study of bells and the art of ringing bells ▶ **cam·pa·nol·o·gist** /-dʒɪst/ *noun* ➔ see also BELL-RINGER

camp·er /ˈkæmpər/ *noun* **1** a person who spends a vacation living in a tent or at a camp **2** a child or young person at a summer camp **3** a large vehicle designed for people to live and sleep in when they are on vacation ➔ compare MOTOR HOME, RV **4** (also **trail·er**) a road vehicle without an engine that is pulled by a car, designed for people to live and sleep in, especially when they are on vacation **IDM** see HAPPY

camp·fire /ˈkæmpˌfaɪər/ *noun* an outdoor fire made by people who are sleeping outside or living in a tent

camp follower *noun* **1** a person who spends time with a particular group but is not really part of the group and does not have much to contribute to it **2** (in the past) a person

who was not a soldier but followed an army from place to place to sell goods or services

camp·ground /ˈkæmpgraʊnd/ *noun* a place where people on vacation can put up their tents, park their camper, etc., often with toilets, water, etc. ➔ see also CAMPSITE

cam·phor /ˈkæmfər/ *noun* [U] a white substance with a strong smell, used in medicine, for making plastics, and to keep insects away from clothes

camp·ing /ˈkæmpɪŋ/ *noun* [U] living in a tent, etc. on vacation: *Do you go camping?* ♦ *a camping trip*

camp·site /ˈkæmpsaɪt/ *noun* a place in a campground where you can put up one tent or park one CAMPER, etc.

cam·pus /ˈkæmpəs/ *noun* [C, U] the buildings of a university, college, hospital, or large business, and the land around them: *She lives on campus* (= within the main university area). ♦ *campus life*

camp·y /ˈkæmpi/ *adj.* (**camp·i·er**, **camp·i·est**) exaggerated in style, especially in a deliberately amusing way: *The movie is a campy celebration of the fashion industry.* ➔ see also CAMP v.

cam·shaft /ˈkæmʃæft/ *noun* a long straight piece of metal with a CAM on it joining parts of machinery, especially in a vehicle

can¹ /kən; strong form kæn/ *modal verb*

➔ see also CAN² (*negative* **can·not** /ˈkænɑt; kəˈnɑt; kæˈnɑt/, *short form* **can't** /kænt/, *pt* **could** /kəd; strong form kʊd/, *negative* **could not**, *short form* **could·n't** /ˈkʊdnt/) **1** used to say that it is possible for someone or something to do something, or for something to happen: *I can run fast.* ♦ *Can you call back tomorrow?* ♦ *He couldn't answer the question.* ♦ *The stadium can be emptied in four minutes.* ♦ *I can't promise anything, but I'll do what I can.* ♦ *Please let us know if you cannot attend the meeting.* **2** used to say that someone knows how to do something: *She can speak Spanish.* ♦ *Can he cook?* ♦ *She could read before she started kindergarten.* **3** used with the verbs "feel", "hear", "see", "smell", "taste": *She could feel the cool air on her face.* ♦ *I can hear music.* **4** used to show that someone is allowed to do something: *You can take the car if you want.* ♦ *We can't wear jeans at work.* **5** (*informal*) used to ask permission to do something: *Can I read your newspaper?* ♦ *Can I take you home?* **6** (*informal*) used to ask someone to help you: *Can you help me with this box?* ♦ *Can you feed the cat, please?* **7** used in the negative for saying that you are sure something is not true: *That can't be Mary—she's in New York.* ♦ *He can't have slept through all that noise.* **8** used to express doubt or surprise: *What can they be doing?* ♦ *Can he be serious?* ♦ *Where could she have put it?* **9** used to say what someone or something is often like: *He can be very tactless sometimes.* ♦ *It can be really cold here in the winter.* **10** used to make suggestions: *We can eat in a restaurant if you like.* ♦ *I can take the car if necessary.* **11** (*informal*) used to say that someone must do something, usually when you are angry: *You can be quiet or get out!* ➔ note at MODAL

IDM **as happy, simple, sweet, etc. as can be** as happy, etc. as possible: *Shopping online is as simple as can be.* **no can do** (*informal*) used to say that you are not able or willing to do something: *Sorry, no can do. I just don't have the time.*

WHICH WORD?

can • may

- **Can** and **cannot** (or **can't**) are the most common words used for asking for, giving, or refusing permission: *Can I borrow your calculator?* ♦ *You can come with us if you want to.* ♦ *You can't park your car there.*
- **May** (negative **may not**) is used as a polite and fairly formal way to ask for or give permission: *May I borrow your newspaper?* ♦ *You may come if you wish.* It is often used in official signs and rules: *Visitors may use the swimming pool between 7 a.m. and 7 p.m.* ♦ *Students may not use the college car park.* The form **mayn't** is hardly ever used in modern English.

can • could • be able to • manage

- **Can** is used to say that somebody knows how to do something: *Can you play the piano?* It is also used with verbs of seeing, noticing, etc: *I can hear someone calling*, and with passive infinitives: *The DVD can be found online.*
- **Can** or **be able to** are used to say that something is possible or that somebody has the opportunity to do something: *Can you/Are you able to come on Saturday?*
- You use **be able to** to form the future and perfect tenses and the infinitive: *You'll be able to get a taxi outside the station.* ◆ *I haven't been able to get much work done today.* ◆ *She'd love to be able to play the piano.*
- **Could** is used to talk about what someone was generally able to do in the past: *Our daughter could walk when she was nine months old.*
- You use **was/were able to** or **manage** (but not **could**) when you are saying that something was possible on a particular occasion in the past: *I was able to/managed to find some useful books in the library.* ◆ ~~I could find some useful books in the library.~~ **Manage** is more formal and less frequent than **be able to**. In negative sentences, **could not** can also be used: *We weren't able to/didn't manage to/couldn't get there in time.* **Could** is also used with this meaning with verbs of seeing, noticing, understanding, etc.: *I could see there was something wrong.*
- **Could have** is used when you are saying that it was possible for somebody to do something in the past but they did not try: *I could have won the game but decided to let him win instead.*

can² 🔊 /kæn/ *noun, verb* ⊃ see also CAN¹
- **noun** **1** [C] a metal container in which food or drinks are sold: *a can of beans* ◆ *a beer/paint can* ⊃ picture at PACKAGING **2** [C] the amount contained in a can: *We drank a can of soda each.* **3** [C] a metal or plastic container for holding or carrying liquids: *an oil can* ◆ *a watering can* **4** [C] a metal container in which liquids are kept under pressure and let out in a fine spray when you press a button on the lid: *a can of hairspray* **5 the can** [sing.] (*slang*) prison **6 the can** [sing.] (*slang*) the toilet
IDM a can of worms (*informal*) if you open up **a can of worms**, you start doing something that will cause a lot of problems and be very difficult **be in the can** (*informal*) (especially of filmed or recorded material) to be completed and ready for use
- **verb** (-nn-) **1** ~ sth to preserve food by putting it in a metal or glass container **2** ~ sb (*informal*) to dismiss someone from their job **SYN** FIRE

Canada ˈDay *noun* (in Canada) a national holiday held on July 1 to celebrate the original joining together of PROVINCES to form Canada in 1867

ˌCanada ˈgoose (also **ˌCanadian ˈgoose**) *noun* a common N. American GOOSE with a black head and neck

ˌCanada ˈPension ˌPlan *noun* [sing.] (*abbr.* CPP) (*CanE*) a system for saving money to live on in old age, which both workers and their employers pay into, and which is managed by the government

ˌCanada ˈRevenue ˌAgency *noun* (*CanE*) = CRA

Ca·na·di·an /kəˈneɪdiən/ *adj., noun*
- **adj.** from or connected with Canada
- **noun** a person from Canada

Caˌnadian ˈbacon *noun* [U] meat from the back of a pig that has been CURED (= preserved using salt or smoke) and has little fat on it, usually served in thin slices ⊃ compare BACON

the ˌCanadian ˈCharter of ˌRights and ˈFreedoms (also **the Charˌter**) *noun* [sing.] (*CanE*) an official document that is part of Canada's CONSTITUTION (= its set of basic

laws), and which guarantees basic political, legal, and language rights, as well as the rights of Aboriginals

Caˌnadian Seˌcurity Inˈtelligence ˌService *noun* (*CanE*) = CSIS

ca·nal /kəˈnæl/ *noun* **1** a long straight passage dug in the ground and filled with water for boats and ships to travel along; a smaller passage used for carrying water to fields, crops, etc.: *the Panama/Suez Canal* ◆ *an irrigation canal* **2** a tube inside the body through which liquid, food, or air can pass ⊃ see also ALIMENTARY CANAL

caˈnal ˌboat *noun* a long narrow boat used on canals

can·al·ize /ˈkænlˌaɪz/ *verb* **1** ~ sth (*technical*) to make a river wider, deeper or straighter; to make a river into a canal **2** ~ sth (*formal*) to control an emotion, activity, etc. so that it is aimed at a particular purpose **SYN** CHANNEL
▶ **ca·nal·i·za·tion** /ˌkænl.əˈzeɪʃn/ *noun* [U]

can·a·pé /ˈkænəˌpeɪ; -pi/ *noun* [usually pl.] a small piece of bread or a CRACKER with cheese, meat, fish, etc. on it, usually served with drinks at a party

ca·nard /kəˈnɑrd/ *noun* (*formal*) a false report or piece of news

ca·nar·y /kəˈnɛri/ *noun* (pl. **ca·nar·ies**) a small yellow bird with a beautiful song, often kept in a CAGE as a pet **IDM** see CAT

ca·nas·ta /kəˈnæstə/ *noun* [U] a card game played with two packs of cards, in which players try to collect sets of cards

can·can /ˈkænkæn/ *noun* often **the cancan** [sing.] a fast dance in which a line of women kick their legs high in the air

can·cel 🔊 /ˈkænsl/ *verb* (-l-, *CanE usually* -ll-)
1 [T] ~ sth to decide that something that has been arranged will not now take place: *All flights have been canceled because of bad weather.* ◆ *Don't forget to cancel the newspaper* (= arrange for it not to be delivered) *before going away.* ⊃ compare POSTPONE **2** [T, I] ~ (sth) to say that you no longer want to continue with an agreement, especially one that has been legally arranged: *to cancel a policy/subscription* ◆ *Is it too late to cancel my order?* ◆ *The U.S. has agreed to cancel debts* (= say that they no longer need to be paid) *totaling $10 million.* ◆ *No charge will be made if you cancel within 10 days.* **3** [T] ~ sth to mark a ticket or stamp so that it cannot be used again
PHR V cancel ˈout | ˌcancel sth↔ˈout if two or more things **cancel out** or one **cancels out** the other, they are equally important but have an opposite effect on a situation so that the situation does not change: *Recent losses have canceled out any profits made at the start of the year.* ◆ *The advantages and disadvantages would appear to cancel each other out.*

can·cel·la·tion /ˌkænsəˈleɪʃn/ *noun* **1** [U, C] a decision to stop something that has already been arranged from happening; a statement that something will not happen: *We need at least 24 hours' notice of cancellation.* ◆ *a cancellation fee* ◆ *Heavy seas can cause cancellation of ferry services.* ◆ *Cancellations must be made in writing.* **2** [C] something that has been canceled: *Are there any cancellations for this evening's performance?* (= tickets that have been returned) **3** [U] the fact of making something no longer valid: *the cancellation of the contract*

Can·cer /ˈkænsər/ *noun* **1** [U] the fourth sign of the ZODIAC, the CRAB **2** [sing.] a person born under the influence of this sign, that is between June 22 and July 22, approximately
▶ **Can·cer·i·an** /kænˈsɪriən; -ˈsɛr-/ *noun, adj.*

can·cer 🔊 /ˈkænsər/ *noun*
1 [U, C] a serious disease in which GROWTHS of cells, also called cancers, form in the body and kill normal body cells. The disease often causes death: *lung/breast cancer* ◆ *cancer of the colon/stomach* ◆ *Most skin cancers are completely curable.* ◆ *The cancer has spread to his stomach.* ◆ *cancer patients* ◆ *cancer research* **2** [C] (*literary*) an evil or dangerous thing that spreads quickly: *Violence is a cancer in our society.*

| v **v**oice | θ **th**in | ð **th**en | s **s**o | z **z**oo | ʃ **sh**e | ʒ vi**s**ion | x **Ch**anukah | 209 |

► **can·cer·ous** /ˈkænsərəs/ *adj.*: *to become cancerous* ◆ *cancerous cells/growths/tumors*

can·de·la /kænˈdɛlə; -ˈdiːlə/ *noun* (*abbr.* **cd**) (*physics*) a unit for measuring the amount of light that shines in a particular direction

can·de·la·bra /ˌkændəˈlɑːbrə; -ˈlæbrə/ (also *less frequent* **can·de·la·brum** /-ˈlɑːbrəm; -ˈlæbrəm/) *noun* (*pl.* **can·de·la·bra, can·de·la·bras**) an object with several branches for holding CANDLES or lights

can·did /ˈkændɪd/ *adj.* **1** saying what you think openly and honestly; not hiding your thoughts: *a candid statement/interview* ⊃ see also CANDOR **2** a candid photograph is one that is taken without the person in it knowing that they are being photographed ► **can·did·ly** *adv.*

can·di·da /ˈkændədə/ *noun* [U] (*medical*) the FUNGUS that can cause a YEAST INFECTION

can·di·da·cy /ˈkændədəsi/ *noun* (*pl.* **can·di·da·cies**) [C, U] the fact of being a candidate in an election: *to announce/declare/withdraw your candidacy for the post*

can·di·date 🔑 /ˈkændədeɪt; -dət/ *noun*
1 ~ (for sth) a person who is trying to be elected or is applying for a job: *one of the leading candidates for the presidency* ◆ *a presidential candidate* ◆ *He was a candidate in the school board elections.* ◆ *There were a large number of candidates for the job.* ⊃ collocations at VOTE **2** ~ (for sth) a person or group that is considered suitable for something or that is likely to get something or to be something: *a PhD. candidate* (= someone doing a PhD. degree) ◆ *Our manager is a prime candidate for promotion this year.* ◆ *Your father is an obvious candidate for a heart attack.*

can·died /ˈkændid/ *adj.* [only before noun] (of fruit or other food) preserved by boiling in sugar; cooked in sugar: *candied fruit*

can·dle /ˈkændl/ *noun* a round stick of WAX with a piece of string (called a WICK) through the middle that is lit to give light as it burns ⊃ see also VOTIVE CANDLE
IDM **not hold a candle to sb/sth** to not be as good as someone or something else: *His singing doesn't hold a candle to Bocelli's.* ⊃ more at BURN *v.*

can·dle·light /ˈkændlˌlaɪt/ *noun* [U] the light that a candle produces: *to read by candlelight*

can·dle·lit /ˈkændlˌlɪt/ *adj.* [only before noun] lit by candles: *a romantic candlelit dinner*

can·dle·stick /ˈkændlˌstɪk/ *noun* an object for holding a candle

can·dle·wick /ˈkændlˌwɪk/ *noun* [U] a type of soft cotton cloth with a raised pattern of threads, used especially for making BEDSPREADS

can-'do *adj.* [only before noun] (*informal*) willing to try new things and expecting that they will be successful: *a can-do attitude/spirit*

can·dor (*CanE usually* **can·dour**) /ˈkændər/ *noun* [U] the quality of saying what you think openly and honestly **SYN** FRANKNESS: *"I don't trust him," he said, in a rare moment of candor.* ⊃ see also CANDID

C & W *abbr.* COUNTRY AND WESTERN

can·dy 🔑 /ˈkændi/ *noun* (*pl.* **can·dies**) [U, C]
sweet food made of sugar and/or chocolate, eaten between meals; a piece of this **SYN** SWEET: *a box of candy* ◆ *a candy store* ◆ *a candy bar* ◆ *Who wants the last piece of candy?* ⊃ see also ARM CANDY, EYE CANDY, PENNY CANDY
IDM **be like taking candy from a baby** (*informal*) used to emphasize how easy it is to do something

candy apple *noun* an apple covered with a thin layer of hard red candy or CARAMEL and fastened on a stick

candy cane *noun* a stick of hard, striped candy, with a curved end

can·dy·man /ˈkændiˌmæn/ *noun* (*pl.* **can·dy·men** /-mɛn/) (*slang*) a person who sells illegal drugs

candy-striped *adj.* (becoming *old-fashioned*) (of cloth or clothes) with a pattern of white and pink stripes

candy strip·er /ˈkændi ˌstraɪpər/ *noun* a young person, usually a girl, who works in a hospital as a nurse's assistant without being paid

cane /keɪn/ *noun, verb*
● *noun* **1** [C] a long thin stick, used to help someone to walk ⊃ see also WALKING STICK **2** [C] the hard hollow STEMS of some plants, for example BAMBOO or sugar **3** [U] these STEMS used as a material for making furniture, etc.: *a cane chair* **4** [C] a long thin stick, used in the past in some schools for beating children as a punishment: *to get the cane* (= be punished with a cane)
● *verb* ~ sb to hit someone with a cane as a punishment ► **can·ing** /ˈkeɪnɪŋ/ *noun* [U, C]: *the abolition of caning in schools*

cane rat *noun* a type of large RODENT found in wild areas of Africa, which can be used for food ⊃ see also GRASSCUTTER

cane sugar *noun* [U] sugar obtained from the juice of SUGAR CANE

ca·nine /ˈkeɪnaɪn/ *adj., noun*
● *adj.* connected with dogs
● *noun* **1** (also 'canine tooth) one of the four pointed teeth in the front of a human's or animal's mouth ⊃ compare INCISOR, MOLAR **2** (*formal*) a dog

can·is·ter /ˈkænəstər/ *noun* **1** a container with a lid for holding flour, sugar, etc. **2** a strong metal container holding gas or a chemical substance, especially one that bursts when it is fired from a gun or thrown: *tear-gas canisters* **3** a round metal container used for storing film: *a film canister*

can·ker /ˈkæŋkər/ *noun* **1** = CANKER SORE **2** [U] a disease that destroys the wood of plants and trees **3** [C] (*literary*) an evil or dangerous influence that spreads and affects people's behavior **4** [U] a disease that causes sore areas in the ears of animals, especially dogs and cats

canker sore *noun* a small sore area in the mouth

can·na·bis /ˈkænəbəs/ *noun* [U] a drug made from the dried leaves and flowers, or RESIN of the HEMP plant, which is smoked or eaten and which gives the user a feeling of being relaxed. Use of the drug is illegal in many countries. **SYN** MARIJUANA

canned /kænd/ *adj.* **1** (of food) preserved in a can: *canned tuna/soup* **2** ~ laughter/music the sound of people laughing or music that has been previously recorded, and used in television and radio programs **3** not original or interesting: *The plot of the movie is bland, canned and predictable.*

can·nel·lo·ni /ˌkænlˈoʊni/ *noun* [U] (from *Italian*) large tubes of PASTA filled with meat or cheese

can·ner·y /ˈkænəri/ *noun* (*pl.* **can·ner·ies**) a factory where food is put into cans

can·ni·bal /ˈkænəbl/ *noun* **1** a person who eats human flesh: *a tribe of cannibals* **2** an animal that eats the flesh of other animals of the same kind ► **can·ni·bal·ism** /ˈkænəbəˌlɪzəm/ *noun* [U]: *to practice cannibalism* **can·ni·bal·is·tic** /ˌkænəbəˈlɪstɪk/ *adj.*

can·ni·bal·ize /ˈkænəbəˌlaɪz/ *verb* **1** ~ sth to take the parts of a machine, vehicle, etc. and use them to repair or build another **2** ~ sth (*business*) (of a company) to reduce the sales of one of its products by introducing a similar new product **3** ~ sth to take creative ideas from another source, often without showing much respect for that source: *With this latest remake coming to theaters, the studio is again cannibalizing its past.* ► **can·ni·bal·i·za·tion** /ˌkænəbələˈzeɪʃn/ *noun* [U]

can·non /ˈkænən/ *noun* (*pl.* **can·non** or **can·nons**) **1** an old type of large heavy gun, usually on wheels, that fires solid metal or stone balls ⊃ see also LOOSE CANNON, WATER CANNON **2** an automatic gun that is fired from an aircraft

can·non·ade /ˌkænəˈneɪd/ *noun* a continuous firing of large guns

can·non·ball /ˈkænənˌbɔl/ *noun* a large metal or stone ball that is fired from a cannon

'cannon ˌfodder *noun* [U] soldiers who are thought of not as people whose lives are important, but as material to be used up in war

can·not = CAN NOT: *I cannot believe the price of the tickets!*

can·nu·la /ˈkænyələ/ *noun* (*pl.* can·nu·lae /-li/ or can·nu·las) (*medical*) a thin tube that is put into a VEIN or other part of the body, for example to give someone medicine

can·ny /ˈkæni/ *adj.* intelligent, careful, and showing good judgment, especially in business or politics: *a canny politician* ◆ *a canny move* ▶ **can·ni·ly** /ˈkænl-i/ *adv.*

ca·noe /kəˈnu/ *noun, verb*
● *noun* a light narrow boat which you move along in the water with a PADDLE ⊃ **picture at** BOAT ⊃ **see also** KAYAK
● *verb* (ca·noe·ing, ca·noed, ca·noed) [I] often **go canoeing** to travel in a canoe

ca·noe·ing /kəˈnuɪŋ/ *noun* [U] the sport of traveling in or racing a canoe: *to go canoeing*

ca·noe·ist /kəˈnuɪst/ *noun* a person traveling in a canoe

can·o·la /kəˈnoʊlə/ (also **ca'nola ˌoil**) *noun* [U] a type of cooking oil made from a variety of RAPESEED that was developed in Canada and is grown widely in N. America. The plant is also referred to as **canola**.

can·on /ˈkænən/ *noun* **1** (*formal*) a generally accepted rule, standard, or principle by which something is judged **2** a list of the books or other works that are generally accepted as the genuine work of a particular writer or as being important: *the Shakespeare canon* ◆ *"The House of Mirth" is a central book in the canon of American literature.* **3** a piece of music in which singers or instruments take turns repeating the MELODY (= tune) **4** a Christian priest with special duties in a CATHEDRAL

ca·non·i·cal /kəˈnɑnɪkl/ (also **ca·non·ic**) *adj.* **1** included in a list of holy books that are accepted as genuine; connected with works of literature that are highly respected **2** according to the law of the Christian Church **3** (*technical*) in the simplest accepted form in mathematics

ca,nonical 'form *noun* (*linguistics*) the most basic form of a GRAMMATICAL structure or expression, for example the infinitive in the case of a verb

can·on·ize /ˈkænəˌnaɪz/ *verb* [usually passive] **~ sb** (of the POPE) to state officially that someone is now a SAINT ⊃ **compare** BEATIFY ▶ **can·on·i·za·tion** /ˌkænənəˈzeɪʃn/ *noun* [C, U]

'canon ˌlaw *noun* [U] the law of the Christian church

ca·noo·dle /kəˈnudl/ *verb* [I] (*old-fashioned, informal*) (of two people) to kiss and touch each other in a sexual way

'can ˌopener *noun* a kitchen UTENSIL (= a tool) for opening cans of food ⊃ **picture at** KITCHEN

can·o·py /ˈkænəpi/ *noun* (*pl.* can·o·pies) **1** a cover that is placed or hangs above a bed, seat, etc. as a shelter or decoration ⊃ **picture at** BED **2** a layer of something that spreads over an area like a roof, especially branches of trees in a forest **3** a roof that is supported on posts and is sometimes also attached at one side to a building: *a new steel entrance canopy for the building* **4** a cover for the COCKPIT of an aircraft

canst /kænst/ *verb* **thou canst** (*old use*) used to mean "you can," when talking to one person

cant /kænt/ *noun, verb*
● *noun* [U] statements, especially about moral or religious issues, that are not sincere and that you cannot trust **SYN** HYPOCRISY
● *verb* [I, T] **~ (sth)** (*formal*) to be or put something in a sloping position

can't *short form* cannot

can·ta·loupe /ˈkæntlˌoʊp/ *noun* a MELON (= a type of fruit) with a green skin and orange flesh

can·tan·ker·ous /kænˈtæŋkərəs/ *adj.* bad-tempered and always complaining: *a cantankerous old man*

can·ta·ta /kənˈtɑtə/ *noun* a short musical work, often on a religious subject, sung by SOLO singers, often with a CHOIR and ORCHESTRA ⊃ **compare** MOTET, ORATORIO

can·teen /kænˈtin/ *noun* **1** a small container used by soldiers, travelers, etc. for carrying water or other liquid **2** a place in a military base where soldiers can go for drinks and entertainment **3** a store in a school, camp, etc. where people can buy food, drink, and other supplies

can·ter /ˈkæntər/ *noun, verb*
● *noun* [usually sing.] a movement of a horse at a speed that is fairly fast but not very fast; a ride on a horse moving at this speed: *She set off at a canter.*
● *verb* [I, T] **~ (sth)** (of a horse or rider) to move or make a horse move at a canter: *We cantered along the beach.* ⊃ **compare** GALLOP, TROT

can·ti·cle /ˈkæntɪkl/ *noun* a religious song with words taken from the Bible

can·ti·le·ver /ˈkæntəˌlivər/ *noun* a long piece of metal or wood that sticks out from a wall to support the end of a bridge or other structure: *a cantilever bridge*

can·ti·na /kænˈtinə/ *noun* (from *Spanish*) a Mexican-style bar, especially in the southwestern U.S.

can·to /ˈkæntoʊ/ *noun* (*pl.* can·tos) one of the sections of a long poem

can·ton /ˈkæntən; ˈkæntn/ *noun* one of the official regions which some countries, such as Switzerland, are divided into

Can·ton·ese /ˌkæntəˈniz; -ˈnis/ *noun, adj.*
● *noun* **1** (also **Yue**) [U] a form of Chinese spoken mainly in southern China, including Hong Kong **2** [C] (*pl.* Can·ton·ese) a person whose first language is Cantonese
● *adj.* of or relating to people who speak Cantonese, or their language or culture: *Cantonese cooking*

can·ton·ment /kænˈtɑnmənt; -ˈtoʊn-/ *noun* a military camp

can·tor /ˈkæntər/ *noun* the person who leads the singing in a SYNAGOGUE or in a church CHOIR

Ca·nuck /kəˈnʌk/ *noun* (*informal*) a person from Canada

can·vas /ˈkænvəs/ *noun* **1** [U] a strong, heavy, rough material used for making tents, sails, etc. and by artists for painting on ⊃ **collocations at** ART **2** [C] a piece of canvas used for painting on; a painting done on a piece of canvas, using oil paints: *a sale of the artist's early canvases* ⊃ **picture at** HOBBY **3** a situation seen as a whole: *The movie depicts the grim canvas of war.* ◆ **broad/wide, etc. ~** *The novel presents a broad social canvas.*
IDM **under canvas** in a tent

can·vass /ˈkænvəs/ *verb* **1** [I, T] to ask someone to support a particular person, political party, etc., especially by going around an area and talking to people: **~ (for sth)** *He spent the whole month canvassing for votes.* ◆ **~ sb (for sth)** *Party workers are busy canvassing local residents for their support.* **2** [T] to ask people about something in order to find out what they think about it: **~ sth** *He has been canvassing the neighborhood about property taxes.* ◆ **~ sb** *People are being canvassed on their opinions on the proposed new road.* **3** [T] **~ support** to try to get support from a group of people **SYN** DRUM UP **4** [T] **~ sth** to discuss an idea thoroughly: *The proposal is currently being canvassed.* ▶ **can·vass** *noun: to carry out a canvass* **can·vass·er** *noun*

can·yon /ˈkænyən/ *noun* a deep valley with steep sides of rock **SYN** GORGE

can·yon·ing /ˈkænyənɪŋ/ *noun* [U] a sport in which you jump into a mountain stream in a canyon and allow yourself to be carried down at high speed

cap /kæp/ noun, verb

● **noun**

> HAT **1** a type of soft flat hat with a BILL (= a hard curved part sticking out in front): *a baseball cap* ⊃ picture at HAT **2** (usually in compounds) a soft hat that fits closely and is worn for a particular purpose: *a shower cap* ⊃ see also MOB CAP, STOCKING CAP **3** a soft hat with a square flat top worn by some college or university teachers, and students at special ceremonies: *The photo showed her wearing a graduation cap and gown.* ⊃ compare MORTARBOARD

> ON PEN/BOTTLE **4** a cover or top for a pen, bottle, etc.: *a lens cap* ⊃ picture at PACKAGING ⊃ see also GAS CAP, HUBCAP ⊃ thesaurus box at LID

> ON TOOTH **5** an artificial covering on a tooth that makes it look more attractive

> LIMIT ON MONEY **6** an upper limit on an amount of money that can be spent or borrowed by a particular institution or in a particular situation: *The government has placed a cap on military spending.*

> IN TOY GUNS **7** a small paper container with EXPLOSIVE powder inside it, used especially in toy guns ⊃ see also CAPS, ICE CAP, THINKING CAP **IDM** see FEATHER *n.*

● **verb** (-pp-)

> COVER TOP **1** [usually passive] ~ sth (with sth) to cover the top or end of something with something: *mountains capped with snow* ♦ *snow-capped mountains*

> LIMIT MONEY **2** [often passive] ~ sth to limit the amount of money that can be charged for something or spent on something: *The company has capped travel expenses.*

> TOOTH **3** [usually passive] ~ sth to put an artificial covering on a tooth to make it look more attractive: *He's had his front teeth capped.* **SYN** CROWN

IDM to cap/top it all (off) (*informal*) used to introduce the final piece of information that is worse than the other bad things that you have just mentioned

ca·pa·bil·i·ty **AWL** /ˌkeɪpəˈbɪləti/ noun (pl. ca·pa·bil·i·ties) [C, U] **1** ~ (to do sth/of doing sth) the ability or qualities necessary to do something: *Animals in the zoo have lost the capability to catch/of catching food for themselves.* ♦ *beyond/within the capabilities of current technology* ♦ *Age affects the range of a person's capabilities.* **2** the power or weapons that a country has for war or for military action: *The U.S.'s nuclear/military capability*

ca·pa·ble **AWL** /ˈkeɪpəbl/ adj. **1** having the ability or qualities necessary for doing something: ~ of sth *You are capable of better work than this.* ♦ ~ of doing sth *He's fully capable of lying to get out of trouble.* ♦ *I'm perfectly capable of doing it myself, thank you.* **2** having the ability to do things well **SYN** SKILLED, COMPETENT: *She's a very capable teacher.* ♦ *I'll leave the planning in your capable hands.* **ANT** INCAPABLE ▶ ca·pa·bly /-bli/ adv.

ca·pa·cious /kəˈpeɪʃəs/ adj. (*formal*) having a lot of space to put things in **SYN** ROOMY: *capacious pockets*

ca·pac·i·tance /kəˈpæsətəns/ noun [U] (*physics*) **1** the ability of a system to store an electrical charge **2** a comparison between change in electrical charge and change in electrical POTENTIAL

ca·pac·i·tor /kəˈpæsətər/ noun (*physics*) a device used to store an electrical charge

ca·pac·i·ty **AWL** /kəˈpæsəti/ noun (pl. ca·pac·i·ties)

> OF CONTAINER **1** [U, C, usually sing.] the number of things or people that a container or space can hold: *The theater has a seating capacity of 2,000.* ♦ *a fuel tank with a capacity of 50 gallons* ♦ *The hall was filled to capacity* (= was completely full). ♦ *They played to a capacity crowd* (= one that filled all the space or seats).

> ABILITY **2** [C, usually sing., U] the ability to understand or to do something: *intellectual capacity* ♦ ~ for sth *She has an enormous capacity for hard work.* ♦ ~ for doing sth *Limited resources are restricting our capacity for developing new products.* ♦ ~ to do sth *your capacity to enjoy life* ⊃ see also DIMINISHED CAPACITY

> ROLE **3** [C, usually sing.] the official position or function that someone has **SYN** ROLE: *acting in her capacity as manager* ♦ *We are simply involved in an advisory capacity on the project.*

> OF FACTORY/MACHINE **4** [sing., U] the quantity that a factory, machine, etc. can produce: *The factory is working at full capacity.*

> OF ENGINE **5** [C, U] the size or power of a piece of equipment, especially the engine of a vehicle: *an engine with a capacity of 1,600 cc*

ca·par·i·soned /kəˈpærəsnd/ adj. in the past a caparisoned horse or other animal was one covered with a decorated cloth

cape /keɪp/ noun **1** a loose outer piece of clothing that has no sleeves, fastens at the neck, and hangs from the shoulders, like a CLOAK but shorter: *a bullfighter's cape* **2** (often in place names) a piece of high land that sticks out into the ocean: *Cape Cod*

caped /keɪpt/ adj. wearing a cape

ca·per /ˈkeɪpər/ noun, verb

● **noun** **1** [usually pl.] the small, green, flower BUD of a Mediterranean bush, preserved in VINEGAR, and used to flavor dishes and sauces **2** (*informal*) an activity, especially one that is illegal or dangerous: *A call to the police should put an end to their little caper.* **3** an amusing movie that contains a lot of action: *a classic spy caper* **4** a short jumping or dancing movement: *He cut a little celebratory caper* (= jumped or danced a few steps) *in the middle of the road.*

● **verb** [I] (+ adv./prep.) (*formal*) to run or jump around in a happy and excited way

cap·il·lar·y /ˈkæpəˌleri/ noun (pl. cap·il·lar·ies) (*anatomy*) any of the smallest tubes in the body that carry blood ⊃ picture at BODY

capillary ˈaction noun [U] (*technical*) the force that makes a liquid move up a narrow tube

cap·i·tal /ˈkæpətl/ noun, adj.

● **noun**

> CITY **1** (also ˌcapital ˈcity) [C] the city where the central government of a country or state operates from: *Baton Rouge is the capital of Louisiana.* ♦ (*figurative*) *Paris, the fashion capital of the world*

> MONEY **2** [sing.] a large amount of money that is invested or is used to start a business: *to set up a business with a capital investment of $100,000* **3** [U] wealth or property that is owned by a business or a person: *capital assets* ♦ *capital expenditure* (= money that an organization spends on buildings, equipment, etc.) **4** [U] (*technical*) people who use their money to start businesses, considered as a group: *capital and labor*

> LETTER **5** (also ˌcapital ˈletter) [C] a letter of the form and size that is used at the beginning of a sentence or a name (= A, B, C rather than a, b, c): *Acronyms are usually written in capitals.* ♦ *Please write in capitals/in capital letters.*

> ARCHITECTURE **6** the top part of a column ⊃ picture at ARCHITECTURE

IDM make capital (out) of sth to use a situation for your own advantage: *The opposition parties are making political capital out of the government's problems.*

● **adj.**

> PUNISHMENT **1** [only before noun] involving punishment by death: *a capital offense*

> LETTER **2** [only before noun] (of letters of the alphabet) having the form and size used at the beginning of a sentence or a name: *English is written with a capital "E."* ⊃ compare LOWERCASE

> EXCELLENT **3** (*old-fashioned*) excellent

IDM with a capital A, B, etc. used to emphasize that a word has a stronger meaning than usual in a particular situation: *He was romantic with a capital R.*

capital ˈgain noun [usually pl.] (*economics*) a profit from the sale of property or of an investment: *to pay capital gains tax* ♦ *They realized a capital gain from the sale of their investments.*

capital ˈgoods noun [pl.] (*business*) goods such as factory

machines that are used for producing other goods
⊃ compare CONSUMER GOODS

ˌcapital-inˈtensive *adj.* (of a business, an industry, etc.) needing large amounts of money in order to operate well ⊃ compare LABOR-INTENSIVE

cap·i·tal·ism /ˈkæpətlˌɪzəm/ *noun* [U] an economic system in which a country's businesses and industry are controlled and run for profit by private owners rather than by the government ⊃ compare SOCIALISM

cap·i·tal·ist /ˈkæpətl·ɪst/ *noun, adj.*
• *noun* **1** a person who supports capitalism **2** a person who owns or controls a lot of wealth and uses it to produce more wealth
• *adj.* (also *less frequent* cap·i·tal·is·tic /ˌkæpətl·ˈɪstɪk/) based on the principles of capitalism: *a capitalist society/system/economy*

cap·i·tal·ize /ˈkæpətlˌaɪz/ *verb* **1** ~ sth to write or print a letter of the alphabet as a capital; to begin a word with a capital letter **2** ~ sth (*business*) to sell possessions in order to change them into money **3** [usually passive] ~ sth (*business*) to provide a company etc. with the money it needs to function ▶ cap·i·tal·i·za·tion /ˌkæpətl·ə·ˈzeɪʃn/ *noun* [U, sing.]
PHR V ˈcapitalize on/upon sth to gain a further advantage for yourself from a situation **SYN** TAKE ADVANTAGE OF STH: *The team failed to capitalize on their early lead.*

ˌcapital ˈletter *noun* = CAPITAL

ˌcapital ˈloss *noun* (*economics*) a financial loss from the sale of an investment for less than it cost to buy

ˈcapital ˌmarket *noun* (*economics*) the part of a financial system that is concerned with raising money by dealing in STOCKS and BONDS

ˌcapital ˈpunishment *noun* [U] punishment by death **SYN** DEATH PENALTY

ˌcapital ˈsum *noun* a single payment of money that is made to someone, for example by an insurance company

cap·i·ta·tion /ˌkæpəˈteɪʃn/ *noun* [C, U] (*technical*) a tax or payment of an equal amount for each person; the system of payments of this kind: *a capitation fee for each student*

cap·i·tol /ˈkæpətl/ *noun* **1** usually the Capitol [sing.] the building in Washington, D.C., where the U.S. Congress meets to work on new laws **2** [usually sing.] a building in each U.S. state where politicians meet to work on new laws: *the California state capitol*

ˌCapitol ˈHill (also *informal* the Hill) *noun* [sing.] used to refer to the U.S. Capitol and the activities that take place there

ca·pit·u·late /kəˈpɪtʃəˌleɪt/ *verb* **1** [I] ~ (to sb/sth) to agree to do something that you have been refusing to do for a long time **SYN** GIVE IN, YIELD: *They were finally forced to capitulate to the terrorists' demands.* **2** [I] ~ (to sb/sth) to stop resisting an enemy and accept that you are defeated **SYN** SURRENDER: *The town capitulated after a three-week siege.* ▶ ca·pit·u·la·tion /kəˌpɪtʃəˈleɪʃn/ *noun* [C, U]

cap·let (also Cap·let™) /ˈkæplət/ *noun* a long narrow pill, with rounded ends, that you swallow

ca·po·ei·ra /ˌkapuˈeɪrə/ *noun* [U] a Brazilian system of movements which is similar to dance and MARTIAL ARTS

ca·pon /ˈkeɪpən/ *noun* a male chicken that has been CASTRATED and made fat for eating

cap·pel·la ⊃ A CAPPELLA

cap·puc·ci·no /ˌkæpəˈtʃinoʊ; ˌka-/ *noun* (*pl.* cap·puc·ci·nos)
1 [U] a type of coffee made with hot FROTHY milk
2 [C] a cup of cappuccino

ca·price /kəˈpris/ *noun* (*formal*) **1** [C] a sudden change in attitude or behavior for no obvious reason **SYN** WHIM **2** [U] the tendency to change your mind suddenly or behave unexpectedly

ca·pri·cious /kəˈprɪʃəs; -ˈpri-/ *adj.* (*formal*) **1** showing sudden changes in attitude or behavior
SYN UNPREDICTABLE **2** changing suddenly and quickly

SYN CHANGEABLE: *a capricious climate* ▶ ca·pri·cious·ly *adv.* ca·pri·cious·ness *noun* [U]

Cap·ri·corn /ˈkæprɪˌkɔrn/ *noun* **1** [U] the 10th sign of the ZODIAC, the Goat **2** [C] a person born under the influence of this sign, that is between December 21 and January 20, approximately

ca·pris /kəˈpriz/ (also capri pants /kəˈpri ˌpænts/) *noun* [pl.] a type of pants for women ending between the knee and the foot

caps /kæps/ *noun* [pl.] (*technical*) capital letters: *a title printed in bold caps*

cap·si·cum /ˈkæpsɪkəm/ *noun* (*technical*) a type of plant that has hollow fruit. Some types of these are eaten as vegetables, either raw or cooked, for example BELL PEPPERS or CHILIS.

cap·size /ˈkæpsaɪz; kæpˈsaɪz/ *verb* [I, T] ~ (sth) if a boat capsizes or something capsizes it, it turns over in the water

cap·stan /ˈkæpstən; -stæn/ *noun* a thick CYLINDER that winds up a rope, used for lifting heavy objects such as an ANCHOR on a ship

cap·stone /ˈkæpstoʊn/ *noun* **1** the best and final thing that someone achieves, thought of as making their career or life complete **2** a stone placed at the top of a building or wall

cap·sule /ˈkæpsl/ *noun, adj.*
• *noun* **1** a small container that has a measured amount of a medicine inside and dissolves when you swallow it **2** a small plastic container with a substance or liquid inside **3** the part of a SPACECRAFT in which people travel and that often separates from the main ROCKET **4** (*technical*) a shell or container for seeds or eggs in some plants and animals ⊃ see also TIME CAPSULE
• *adj.* (of a description or piece of writing) made shorter than the original version, but keeping the most important features: *a capsule review of a movie*

Capt. *abbr.* captain

cap·tain 🔊 /ˈkæptən/ *noun, verb*
• *noun* **1** the person in charge of a ship or commercial aircraft: *Captain Cook* ◆ *The captain gave the order to abandon ship.* **2** an officer of fairly high rank in the navy, the army, and the U.S. AIR FORCE: *Captain Lance Price* **3** the leader of a group of people, especially a sports team: *She was captain of the hockey team at school.* **4** an officer of high rank in a U.S. police or fire department
• *verb* ~ sth to be a captain of a sports team or a ship

cap·tain·cy /ˈkæptənsi/ *noun* (*pl.* cap·tain·cies) [C, usually sing., U] the position of captain of a team; the period during which someone is captain

ˌcaptain of ˈindustry *noun* (*pl.* ˌcaptains of ˈindustry) used in newspapers, etc. to describe a person who manages a large business company

cap·tion /ˈkæpʃn/ *noun, verb*
• *noun* words that are printed underneath a picture, CARTOON, etc. that explain or describe it ⊃ see also CLOSED-CAPTIONED
• *verb* [usually passive] ~ sth to write a caption for a picture, photograph, etc.

cap·ti·vate /ˈkæptəˌveɪt/ *verb* [often passive] ~ sb to keep someone's attention by being interesting, attractive, etc. **SYN** ENCHANT: *The children were captivated by her stories.*

cap·ti·vat·ing /ˈkæptəˌveɪtɪŋ/ *adj.* taking all your attention; very attractive and interesting **SYN** ENCHANTING: *He found her captivating.*

cap·tive /ˈkæptɪv/ *adj., noun*
• *adj.* **1** kept as a prisoner or in a small space; unable to escape: *captive animals* ◆ *They were taken captive by masked gunmen.* ◆ *captive breeding* (= the catching and breeding of wild animals) **2** [only before noun] not free to leave a particular place or to choose what you want do to: *A salesman loves to have a captive audience* (= listening because they have no choice).

• **noun** a person who is kept as a prisoner, especially in a war

cap·tiv·i·ty /kæpˈtɪvəti/ *noun* [U] the state of being kept as a prisoner or in a place you cannot escape from: *He was held in captivity for three years.* ◆ *The bird had escaped from captivity.*

cap·tor /ˈkæptər/ *noun* (*formal*) a person who captures a person or an animal and keeps them as a prisoner

cap·ture ✏ /ˈkæptʃər/ *verb, noun*

• **verb**

> CATCH **1** to catch a person or an animal and keep them as a prisoner or in a place they cannot escape from: *~ sb Allied troops captured over 300 enemy soldiers.* ◆ *~ sth The animals are captured in nets and sold to local zoos.*

> TAKE CONTROL **2** *~ sth* to take control of a place, building, etc. using force: *The city was captured in 1941.* **3** *~ sth* to succeed in getting control of something that other people are also trying to control: *The company has captured 90% of the market.*

> MAKE SOMEONE INTERESTED **4** *~ sb's attention/imagination/interest* to make someone interested in something: *They use puppets to capture the imagination of younger audiences.*

> FEELING/ATMOSPHERE **5** *~ sth* to succeed in accurately expressing a feeling, an atmosphere, etc. in a picture, piece of writing, movie, etc. **SYN** CATCH: *The article captured the mood of the nation.*

> FILM/RECORD/PAINT **6** [often passive] *~ sb or sth on film/tape/canvas, etc.* to film/record/paint, etc. someone or something: *The attack was captured on film by security cameras.*

> SOMEONE'S HEART **7** *~ sb's heart* to make someone love you

> COMPUTING **8** *~ sth* to put something into a computer in a form it can use

• **noun** [U] the act of capturing someone or something or of being captured: *the capture of enemy territory* ◆ *He evaded capture for three days.* ◆ *data capture*

cap·y·ba·ra /ˌkæpəˈberə; -ˈbɑrə/ *noun* (*pl.* **cap·y·ba·ra** or **cap·y·ba·ras**) an animal like a very large RABBIT with thick legs and small ears, which lives near water in S. and Central America

car ✏ /kɑr/ *noun*

1 (also *formal* **au·to·mo·bile**) a road vehicle with an engine and four wheels that can carry a small number of passengers: *Paula got into the car and drove off.* ◆ *"How did you come?" "By car."* ◆ *a car driver/manufacturer/dealer* ◆ *a car accident/crash* ◆ *Where can I park the car?* ⊃ picture on page 215 ⊃ collocations at DRIVING ⊃ see also COMPANY CAR, MOTOR CAR **2** (also **rail·car**) a separate section of a train: *Several cars went off the rails.* **3** (in compounds) a car on a train of a particular type: *a sleeping/dining car*

ca·rafe /kəˈræf/ *noun* a glass container with a wide neck in which wine or water is served at meals; the amount contained in a carafe

car·a·mel /ˈkærəml; ˈkærəˌmɛl; ˈkɑrml/ *noun* **1** [U, C] a type of hard sticky candy made from butter, sugar, and milk; a small piece of this **2** [U] burned sugar used for adding color and flavor to food ⊃ see also FLAN **3** [U] a light brown color

car·a·mel·ize /ˈkærəməˌlaɪz; ˈkɑrmə-/ *verb* **1** [I] (of sugar) to turn into caramel **2** [T] *~ sth* to cook something slowly for a long time so that it gets very sweet, thick, and brown

car·a·pace /ˈkærəˌpeɪs/ *noun* (*technical*) the hard shell on the back of some animals such as CRABS, that protects them

car·at /ˈkærət/ *noun* (*abbr.* **ct.**) a unit for measuring the weight of diamonds and other PRECIOUS STONES, equal to 200 milligrams

car·a·van /ˈkærəˌvæn/ *noun* a group of people with vehicles or animals who are traveling together, especially across the desert

car·a·van·sa·ry /ˌkærəˈvænsəri/ (*pl.* **car·a·van·sa·ries**) (also **car·a·van·se·rai** /-səˌraɪ/) *noun* **1** in the past, a place where travelers could stay in desert areas of Asia and N. Africa **2** (*formal*) a group of people traveling together

car·a·way /ˈkærəˌweɪ/ *noun* [U] the dried seeds of the caraway plant, used to give flavor to food: *caraway seeds*

carb /kɑrb/ *noun* = CARBOHYDRATE

car·bine /ˈkɑrbin; -baɪn/ *noun* a short, light RIFLE

car·bo·hy·drate /ˌkɑrboʊˈhaɪdreɪt; -bə-/ *noun* **1** (also *informal* **carb**) [C, U] a substance such as sugar or STARCH that consists of CARBON, HYDROGEN, and OXYGEN. Carbohydrates in food provide the body with energy and heat. **2 carbohydrates** (also *informal* **carbs**) [pl.] foods such as bread, potatoes, and rice that contain a lot of carbohydrates ⊃ see LOW-CARB

car·bol·ic /kɑrˈbɑlɪk/ (also **car·bolic ˈacid**) *noun* [U] a chemical that kills bacteria, used as an ANTISEPTIC, and as a DISINFECTANT (= to prevent infection from spreading): *carbolic soap*

ˈcar bomb *noun* a bomb hidden inside or under a car

car·bon /ˈkɑrbən/ *noun* **1** [U] (*symb.* **C**) a chemical element. Carbon is found in all living things, existing in a pure state in two main forms (diamond and GRAPHITE): *carbon fiber* **2** [U] used when referring to the gas CARBON DIOXIDE in terms of the effect it has on the earth's climate in causing GLOBAL WARMING: *carbon emissions/levels/taxes* ◆ *How do we move to a low-carbon economy?* **3** [C] = CARBON COPY **4** [C] a piece of CARBON PAPER

car·bo·nate /ˈkɑrbənət; -ˌneɪt/ *noun* (*chemistry*) a salt that contains CARBON and OXYGEN together with another chemical

car·bo·nat·ed /ˈkɑrbəˌneɪtəd/ *adj.* (of a drink) containing small bubbles of CARBON DIOXIDE

ˌcarbon ˈcopy *noun* **1** (also **car·bon**) a copy of a document, letter, etc. made with CARBON PAPER ⊃ see also CC **2** a person or thing that is very similar to someone or something else: *She is a carbon copy of her sister.*

ˈcarbon ˌcredit *noun* **1** a key element in the system of national and international EMISSIONS TRADING. A country or organization has the right to produce a particular amount of CARBON DIOXIDE and other gases that cause GLOBAL WARMING, which is expressed in terms of **carbon credits**, which may be traded between countries or organizations: *The sale of carbon credits can finance renewable energy projects.* **2** a CARBON OFFSET, which a person or company may choose to buy as a way of reducing the level of CARBON DIOXIDE for which they are responsible: *Wind energy companies sell carbon credits to consumers.*

ˈcarbon ˌcycle *noun* [C, U] the processes by which carbon is changed from one form to another within the environment, for example in plants and when wood or oil is burned

ˈcarbon ˌdating (also *formal* **radio·carbon ˌdating**) *noun* [U] a method of calculating the age of very old objects by measuring the amounts of different forms of carbon in them

ˌcarbon diˈoxide *noun* [U] (*symb.* CO_2) a gas breathed out by people and animals from the lungs or produced by burning CARBON

ˌcarbon ˈfootprint *noun* a measure of the amount of carbon dioxide that is produced by the daily activities of a person or company: *carpooling and other ways to reduce your carbon footprint* ⊃ collocations at ENVIRONMENT

car·bon·ic ac·id /kɑrˌbɑnɪk ˈæsɪd/ *noun* [U] (*chemistry*) a very weak acid that is formed when carbon dioxide is dissolved in water

car·bon·if·er·ous /ˌkɑrbəˈnɪfərəs/ *adj.* (*geology*) **1** producing or containing coal **2 Carboniferous** of the period in the earth's history when layers of coal were formed underground

car·bon·ize /ˈkɑrbəˌnaɪz/ *verb* **1** [I, T] *~ (sth)* to become CARBON, or to make something become carbon **2** [T] *~ sth* to cover something with CARBON ▶ **car·bon·i·za·tion** /ˌkɑrbənəˈzeɪʃn/ *noun* [U]

| t tea | ṭ butter | d did | k cat | g got | tʃ chin | dʒ June | f fall |

Cars

1. rearview mirror
2. side-view mirror
3. visor
4. windshield wiper
5. door handle
6. vent
7. glove compartment
   (*also* glove box)
8. GPS
9. dashboard
10. odometer
11. speedometer
12. fuel gauge
13. steering wheel
14. ignition
15. horn
16. gearshift
17. gas pedal
   (*also* accelerator)
18. brake
19. emergency brake
   (*also* parking brake)
20. headrest
21. driver's seat
22. passenger seat
23. seat belt

antenna
rear window
side window
fender
headlight
bumper
hubcap

hatchback

windshield
hood
tire

convertible

trunk
taillight

sedan

SUV

windshield
wheel

sports car

station wagon

exhaust pipe
(*also* tailpipe)
turn signal

minivan

Jeep™

taxi (*also* cab, taxicab)

RV

carbon monoxide /ˌkɑrbən məˈnɑksaɪd/ *noun* [U] (*symb.* **CO**) a poisonous gas formed when CARBON burns partly but not completely. It is produced when gas is burned in car engines.

ˌcarbon-ˈneutral *adj.* in which the amount of CARBON DIOXIDE produced has been reduced to nothing or is balanced by actions that protect the environment **SYN** ZERO-CARBON: *All of these fuels are renewable and carbon neutral.*

ˌcarbon ˈoffset *noun* [C, U] a way for a company or person to reduce the level of CARBON DIOXIDE for which they are responsible by paying money to a company that works to reduce the total amount produced in the world, for example by planting trees: *carbon offset initiatives for air travelers* ⊃ compare CARBON CREDIT

ˈcarbon ˌpaper *noun* thin paper with a dark substance on one side, that is used between two sheets of paper for making copies of written or typed documents

ˈcarbon ˌtrading (also eˈmissions ˌtrading) *noun* [U] a system that gives countries and organizations the right to produce a particular amount of CARBON DIOXIDE and other gases that cause GLOBAL WARMING, and allows them to sell this right

car·bo·run·dum /ˌkɑrbəˈrʌndəm/ *noun* [U] (*chemistry*) a very hard, black, solid substance, used as an ABRASIVE

car·boy /ˈkɑrbɔɪ/ *noun* a large round bottle, usually protected by an outer frame of wood, and used for storing and transporting dangerous liquids

ˈcar bra *noun* = BRA (2)

car·bun·cle /ˈkɑrˌbʌŋkl/ *noun* **1** a large painful swelling under the skin **2** a bright red JEWEL, usually cut into a round shape

car·bu·re·tor /ˈkɑrbəˌreɪtər/ *noun* the part of an engine, for example in a car, where gas and air are mixed together

car·cass /ˈkɑrkəs/ *noun* the dead body of an animal, especially of a large one or of one that is ready for cutting up as meat

car·cin·o·gen /kɑrˈsɪnədʒən; ˈkɑrsənəˌdʒɛn/ *noun* a substance that can cause cancer

car·cin·o·gen·ic /ˌkɑrsənəˈdʒɛnɪk/ *adj.* likely to cause cancer

car·ci·no·ma /ˌkɑrsəˈnoʊmə/ *noun* (*medical*) a cancer that affects the top layer of the skin or the LINING of the organs inside the stomach

card ✎ /kɑrd/ *noun, verb*

● *noun*
> **WITH INFORMATION 1** [C] a small piece of stiff paper or plastic with information on it, especially information about someone's identity: *a membership card* ◆ *an appointment card* ⊃ see also GREEN CARD, ID CARD, INDEX CARD, LOYALTY CARD, RED CARD, REPORT CARD, YELLOW CARD **2** [C] = BUSINESS CARD: *Here's my card if you need to contact me again.* **3** [C] = CALLING CARD
> **FOR MONEY 4** [C] a small piece of plastic, especially one given by a bank or store, used for buying things or obtaining money: *I put dinner on* (= paid for it using) *my card.* ◆ *a phone card* ⊃ see also ATM CARD, CHARGE CARD, CHIP CARD, CREDIT CARD, DEBIT CARD, SMART CARD, SWIPE CARD
> **WITH A MESSAGE 5** [C] a piece of stiff paper that is folded in the middle and has a picture on the front of it, used for sending someone a message with your good wishes, an invitation, etc.: *a birthday/get-well/good luck card* ⊃ see also CHRISTMAS CARD, GREETING CARD **6** [C] = POSTCARD: *Did you get my card from Italy?*
> **IN GAMES AND HOBBIES 7** [C] = PLAYING CARD: *Pick a card.* ◆ *a deck of cards* ⊃ see also TRUMP CARD, WILD CARD **8 cards** [pl.] a game or games in which PLAYING CARDS are used: *Who wants to play cards?* ◆ *I've never been very good at cards.* ◆ *She won $20 playing cards.* **9** [C] = TRADING CARD: *a collection of baseball cards*

> **COMPUTING 10** [C] a small device containing an electronic CIRCUIT that is part of a computer or added to it, enabling it to perform particular functions: *a graphics/network/sound card* ⊃ see also EXPANSION CARD
> **PERSON 11** [C] (*old-fashioned*, *informal*) an unusual or amusing person
> **HORSE RACES 12** [C] a list of all the races at a RACETRACK: *a race card*
> **FOR WOOL/COTTON 13** [C] (*technical*) a machine or tool used for cleaning and COMBING wool or cotton before it is spun
IDM **sb's best/strongest/winning card** something that gives someone an advantage over other people in a particular situation **have a/another card up your sleeve** to have an idea, a plan, etc. that will give you an advantage in a particular situation and that you keep secret until it is needed **hold all the cards** (*informal*) to be able to control a particular situation because you have an advantage over other people **hold/keep/play your cards close to your chest** to keep your ideas, plans, etc. secret **lay/put your cards on the table** to tell someone honestly what your plans, ideas, etc. are **in the cards** (*informal*) likely to happen: *The merger has been in the cards for some time now.* **play the … card** to mention a particular subject, idea, or quality in order to gain an advantage: *He accused his opponent of playing the immigration card during the campaign.* ⊃ see also RACE CARD **play your cards right** to deal successfully with a particular situation so that you achieve some advantage or something that you want ⊃ more at SHOW *v.*, STACKED

● *verb* **1** ~ **sb** (*informal*) to ask a person to show their ID card as a means of checking how old they are, for example if they want to buy alcohol **2** ~ **sth** (*technical*) to clean wool using a wire instrument

car·da·mom /ˈkɑrdəməm/ *noun* [U] the dried seeds of a S.E. Asian plant, used in cooking as a spice ⊃ picture at HERB

card·board /ˈkɑrdbɔrd/ *noun, adj.*
● *noun* [U] stiff material like very thick paper, often used for making boxes: *a cardboard box* ◆ *a piece of cardboard*
● *adj.* [only before noun] not seeming real or genuine: *a novel with superficial, cardboard characters*

ˈcard-ˌcarrying *adj.* [only before noun] known to be an official and usually active member of a political organization: *a card-carrying member of the Republican party*

ˈcard ˌcatalog *noun* a box of cards with information on them, arranged in alphabetical order

ˈcard game *noun* a game in which playing cards are used

card·hold·er /ˈkɑrdˌhoʊldər/ *noun* a person who has a credit card from a bank, etc.

car·di·ac /ˈkɑrdiˌæk/ *adj.* [only before noun] (*medical*) connected with the heart or heart disease: *cardiac disease/failure/surgery* ◆ *to suffer cardiac arrest* (= an occasion when a person's heart stops temporarily or permanently)

car·di·gan /ˈkɑrdɪgən/ (also ˌcardigan ˈsweater) *noun* a sweater, usually with no COLLAR and fastened with buttons at the front ⊃ picture at CLOTHES

car·di·nal /ˈkɑrdnəl; ˈkɑrdn-l/ *noun, adj.*
● *noun* **1** a priest of the highest rank in the Roman Catholic Church. Cardinals elect and advise the POPE: *Cardinal O'Connor* **2** a N. American bird. The male cardinal is bright red. **3** (also ˌcardinal ˈnumber) a number, such as 1, 2, and 3, used to show quantity rather than order ⊃ compare ORDINAL
● *adj.* [only before noun] (*formal*) most important; having other things based on it: *Freedom of expression is a cardinal principle of U.S. law.*

ˌcardinal ˈpoints *noun* [pl.] (*technical*) the four main points (North, South, East, and West) of the COMPASS

ˌcardinal ˈsin *noun* **1** (sometimes *humorous*) an action that is a serious mistake or that other people disapprove of: *He committed the cardinal sin of criticizing his teammates.* **2** a serious SIN in the Christian Church

h **hat**	m **man**	n **no**	ŋ **sing**	l **leg**	r **red**	y **yes**	w **wet**

car·di·o /ˈkɑrdioʊ/ noun [U] (informal) exercises to make your heart work harder, that you do to keep yourself healthy: *Cardio is the answer if you want to lose weight.* ♦ *cardio exercise/workouts* ⊃ see also CARDIOVASCULAR

cardio- /ˈkɑrdioʊ; ˈkɑrdiə/ combining form (in nouns, adjectives, and adverbs) connected with the heart: *cardiogram*

car·di·ol·o·gist /ˌkɑrdiˈɑlədʒɪst/ noun a doctor who studies and treats heart diseases ▶ **car·di·ol·o·gy** /-dʒi/ noun [U]

car·di·o·vas·cu·lar /ˌkɑrdioʊˈvæskyələr/ adj. (medical) connected with the heart and the BLOOD VESSELS (= the tubes that carry blood around the body)

'card key noun = KEY CARD

'card sharp (also **'card shark**) noun a person who cheats in games of cards in order to make money

'card swipe noun an electronic device through which you pass a credit card, etc. in order to record the information on it, open a door, etc.

'card ˌtable noun a small table for playing card games on, especially one that you can fold

---

care 🔑 /kɛr/ noun, verb

- **noun 1** [U] the process of caring for someone or something and providing what they need for their health or protection: *medical/patient care* ♦ *How much do men share child care?* ♦ *the provision of care for the elderly* ♦ *skin/hair care products* ⊃ see also DAY CARE, EASY-CARE, HEALTHCARE, INTENSIVE CARE, MANAGED CARE **2** [U] attention or thought that you give to something that you are doing so that you will do it well and avoid mistakes or damage: *She chose her words with care.* ♦ *Great care is needed when choosing a used car.* ♦ *Fragile—handle with care* (= written on a container holding something that is easily broken or damaged) **3** [C, usually pl., U] (formal) a feeling of worry or anxiety; something that causes problems or anxiety: *I felt free from the cares of the day as soon as I left the building.* ♦ *Sam looked as if he didn't have a care in the world.* **IDM** **care of sb** (also **in care of sb**) (abbr. c/o) used when writing to someone at another person's address: *Write to him care of his lawyer.* **in the care of sb/in sb's care** being cared for by someone: *The child was left in the care of friends.* **take care** (informal) used when saying goodbye: *Bye! Take care!* **take care (that.../to do sth)** to be careful: *Take care*

WORD FAMILY
care noun, verb
careful adj. (≠ careless)
carefully adv. (≠ carelessly)
caring adj. (≠ uncaring)

(that) you don't drink too much! ♦ *Care should be taken to close the lid securely.* **take care of sb/sth/yourself 1** to care for someone or something/yourself; to be careful about something: *Who's taking care of the children while you're away?* ♦ *She takes great care of her clothes.* ♦ *He's old enough to take care of himself.* **2** to be responsible for or to deal with a situation or task: *Don't worry about the travel arrangements. They're all being taken care of.* ♦ *Celia takes care of the marketing side of things.* **under the care of sb** receiving medical care from someone: *He's under the care of Dr. Parks.*

- **verb** (not used in the progressive tenses) **1** [I, T] to feel that something is important and worth worrying about: *I don't care* (= I will not be upset) *if I never see him again!* ♦ *He threatened to fire me, as if I care!* ♦ **~ about sth** *She cares deeply about environmental issues.* ♦ **~ what/whether, etc.** *I don't care what he thinks.* ♦ **~ that...** *She doesn't seem to care that he's been married four times before.* **2** [I] **~ (about sb)** to like or love someone and worry about what happens to them: *He genuinely cares about his employees.* **3** [T] **~ to do sth** to make the effort to do something: *I've done this job more times than I care to remember.* **IDM** **couldn't care less** (informal) used to say, often rudely, that you do not think that someone or something is important or worth worrying about: *Honestly, I couldn't care less what they do.* **for all you, I, they, etc. care** (informal) used to say that a person is not worried about or interested in what happens to someone or something: *I could be dead for all he cares! who cares?* | **What do I, you, etc. care?** (informal) used to say, often rudely, that you do not think that something is important or interesting: *Who cares what she thinks? Would you care for sth?* | **Would you care to do sth?** (formal) used to ask someone politely if they would like to do something, or would like to do something, or if they would be willing to do something: *Would you care for another drink?* ♦ *If you'd care to follow me, I'll show you where his office is.* ⊃ note at WANT ⊃ more at HOOT *n.* **PHR V** **'care for sb 1** to look after someone who is sick, very old, very young, etc. **SYN** TAKE CARE OF: *She moved back home to care for her elderly parents.* ⊃ see also UNCARED FOR **2** to love or like someone very much: *He cared for her more than she realized.* **not 'care for sb/sth** (formal) to not like someone or something: *He didn't much care for her friends.*

ca·reen /kəˈrin/ (also formal **ca·reer**) verb [I] + adv./prep. (of a person or vehicle) to move forward very quickly, especially in a way that is dangerous or uncontrolled **SYN** HURTLE

ca·reer 🔑 /kəˈrɪr/ noun, verb

- **noun 1** the series of jobs that a person has in a particular area of work, usually involving more responsibility as time passes: *a career in politics* ♦ *a teaching career* ♦ *What made you decide on a career as a vet?* ♦ *She has been concentrating on her career.* ♦ *a career change* ♦ *That will be a good career move* (= something that will help your career). ♦ *a career soldier/diplomat, etc.* (= a professional one) ♦ *a career counselor* (= a person whose job is to give people advice and information about jobs) ⊃ collocations at JOB ⊃ thesaurus box at WORK **2** the period of time that you spend in your life working or doing a particular thing: *She started her career as*

---

an English teacher. ◆ *He is playing the best tennis of his career.* ◆ *My school career was not very impressive.*

IDM make a career of doing sth to do something so many times that you get a reputation for doing it: *She seems to be making a career of being late for work.*

● *verb* [I] (*formal*) = CAREEN

ca'reer ˌbreak *noun* a period of time when you do not do your usual job, for example because you have children to care for

ca·reer·ist /kəˈrɪrɪst/ *noun* (*often disapproving*) a person whose career is more important to them than anything else ▶ ca·reer·ism /kəˈrɪrˌɪzəm/ *noun* [U]

ca'reer ˌwoman *noun* a woman whose career is more important to her than getting married and having children

care·free /ˈkɛrfri/ *adj.* having no worries or responsibilities: *He looked happy and carefree.* ◆ *a carefree attitude/life*

care·ful 🔊 /ˈkɛrfl/ *adj.*

1 [not before noun] giving attention or thought to what you are doing so that you avoid hurting yourself, damaging something, or doing something wrong: *Be careful!* ◆ **~ to do sth** *He was careful to keep out of sight.* ◆ **~ not to do sth** *Be careful not to wake the baby.* ◆ **~ when/what/how, etc.** *You need to be careful when handling chemicals.* ◆ **~ of/about/ with sth** *Be careful of the traffic.* ◆ *Please be careful with my glasses* (= Don't break them). ◆ **~ (that)...** *Be careful you don't bump your head.* ⊃ note at CAUTIOUS **2** giving a lot of attention to details: *a careful piece of work* ◆ *a careful examination of the facts* ◆ *After careful consideration, we have decided to offer you the job.* **ANT** CARELESS ▶ care·ful·ly /ˈkɛrfəli/ *adv.*: *Please listen carefully.* ◆ *She put the glass down carefully.* ◆ *Drive carefully.* **ANT** CARELESS ▶ care·ful·ness *noun* [U]

IDM you can't be too careful used to warn someone that they should take care to avoid danger or problems: *Don't stay out in the sun for too long—you can't be too careful.* careful with money not spending money on unimportant things

care·giv·er /ˈkɛrˌgɪvər/ *noun* a person who takes care of a sick or old person at home

'care ˌlabel *noun* a label attached to the inside of a piece of clothing, giving instructions about how it should be washed, and ironed

care·less 🔊 /ˈkɛrləs/ *adj.*

1 not giving enough attention and thought to what you are doing, so that you make mistakes: *It was careless of me to leave the door open.* ◆ *Don't be so careless about/with spelling.* ◆ *a careless worker/driver* **ANT** CAREFUL **2** resulting from a lack of attention and thought: *a careless mistake/error* **3** not showing interest or effort **SYN** CASUAL: *She gave a careless shrug.* ◆ *a careless laugh/smile* ▶ care·less·ly *adv.*: *Someone had carelessly left a window open.* ◆ *She threw her coat carelessly onto the chair.* ◆ *"Whatever," he said carelessly.* care·less·ness *noun* [U]: *a moment of carelessness*

ca·ress /kəˈrɛs/ *verb, noun*

● *verb* **~ sb/sth** to touch someone or something gently, especially in a sexual way or in a way that shows affection: *His fingers caressed the back of her neck.*

● *noun* a gentle touch or kiss to show you love someone

car·et /ˈkærət/ *noun* a mark (^) placed below a line of printed or written text to show that words or letters should be added at that place in the text

care·tak·er /ˈkɛrˌteɪkər/ *noun, adj.*

● *noun* **1** a person who takes care of a house or land while the owner is away ⊃ see also JANITOR **2** a person such as a teacher, parent, nurse, etc., who takes care of other people

● *adj.* [only before noun] in charge for a short time, until a new leader or government is chosen: *a caretaker manager/ government*

care·worn /ˈkɛrwɔrn/ *adj.* looking tired because you have a lot of worries

car·go /ˈkɑrgoʊ/ *noun* (*pl.* car·goes, car·gos) [C, U] the goods carried in a ship or plane: *The tanker began to spill its cargo of oil.* ◆ *a cargo ship*

'cargo ˌpants (also car·goes) *noun* [pl.] loose pants that have pockets in various places, for example on the side of the leg above the knee ⊃ picture at CLOTHES

Car·ib·be·an /ˌkærəˈbiən; kəˈrɪbiən/ *noun, adj.*

● *noun* the Caribbean the region consisting of the Caribbean Sea and its islands, including the West Indies, and the coasts that surround it

● *adj.* connected with the Caribbean

car·i·bou /ˈkærəˌbu/ *noun* (*pl.* car·i·bou) a N. American REINDEER

car·i·ca·ture /ˈkærəkətʃər; -ˌtʃʊr/ *noun, verb*

● *noun* **1** [C] a funny drawing or picture of someone that exaggerates some of their features **2** [C] a description or presentation of a person or thing that makes them seem ridiculous by exaggerating some of their characteristics: *a caricature of middle-American suburbia* **3** [U] the art of drawing or writing caricatures ▶ car·i·ca·tur·ist /-ˌtʃʊrɪst/ *noun*

● *verb* [often passive] **~ sb/sth (as sth)** to produce a caricature of someone; to describe or present someone as a type of person you would laugh at or not respect: *She was unfairly caricatured as a dumb blonde.*

car·ies /ˈkɛriz/ *noun* [U] (*medical*) decay in teeth or bones: *dental caries*

car·il·lon /ˈkærəˌlɑn/ *noun* **1** a set of bells on which tunes can be played, sometimes using a keyboard **2** a tune played on bells

car·ing /ˈkɛrɪŋ/ *adj.* [usually before noun] kind, helpful, and showing that you care about other people: *He's a very caring person.* ◆ *Children need a caring environment.* ◆ *a caring profession* (= a job that involves taking care of or helping other people)

car·jack·ing /ˈkɑrˌdʒækɪŋ/ *noun* [U, C] the crime of forcing the driver of a car to take you somewhere or give you their car, using threats and violence ⊃ compare HIJACK ▶ car·jack *verb* **~ sb/sth** car·jack·er *noun*

car·load /ˈkɑrloʊd/ *noun* the number of people or things that a car is carrying or is able to carry

car·mine /ˈkɑrmaɪn; -mən/ *adj.* (*formal*) dark red in color ▶ car·mine *noun* [U]

car·nage /ˈkɑrnɪdʒ/ *noun* [U] the violent killing of a large number of people **SYN** SLAUGHTER: *a scene of carnage*

car·nal /ˈkɑrnl/ *adj.* [usually before noun] (*formal* or *law*) connected with the body or with sex: *carnal desires/ appetites* ▶ car·nal·ly /-nəli/ *adv.*

ˌcarnal ˈknowledge *noun* [U] (*old-fashioned* or *law*) = SEXUAL INTERCOURSE

car·na·tion /kɑrˈneɪʃn/ *noun* a white, pink, or red flower, often worn as a decoration on formal occasions: *He was wearing a carnation in his buttonhole.* ⊃ picture at PLANT

car·nel·ian /kɑrˈnilyən/ (also cor·nel·ian) *noun* [C, U] a red, brown, or white stone, used in jewelry

car·ni·val /ˈkɑrnəvl/ *noun* **1** [C] a type of entertainment in a field or park at which people can ride on large machines and play games to win prizes **SYN** FAIR *n.* **2** [C, U] a public festival, usually one that happens at a regular time each year, that involves music and dancing in the streets, for which people wear brightly colored clothes: *There is a local carnival every year.* ◆ *the carnival in Rio* ◆ *a carnival atmosphere* **3** [sing.] **~ of sth** (*formal*) an exciting or brightly colored mixture of things: *this summer's carnival of sports*

car·ni·vore /ˈkɑrnəˌvɔr/ *noun* any animal that eats meat ⊃ compare HERBIVORE, INSECTIVORE, OMNIVORE ▶ car·niv·o·rous /kɑrˈnɪvərəs/ *adj.*: *a carnivorous diet* ⊃ compare OMNIVOROUS

car·ny /ˈkɑrni/ *noun* (*pl.* car·nies) (*informal*) **1** a carnival: *The whole trade show had a carny atmosphere.* **2** a person who

ʌ cup   ə about   eɪ say   aɪ five   ɔɪ boy   aʊ now   oʊ go   ər bird

works in a carnival: *He came from a family of carnies and knew no other life.*

car·ob /ˈkærəb/ *noun* the dark brown fruit of a southern European tree that can be made into a powder that tastes like chocolate

car·ol /ˈkærəl/ *noun, verb*
- *noun* (also **Christmas ˌcarol**) a Christian religious song sung at Christmas
- *verb* [I, T] (-l-, *CanE usually* -ll-) **~ (sth)** | **+ speech** to sing something in a cheerful way

car·om /ˈkærəm/ *verb* [I] to hit a surface and come off it fast at a different angle

car·o·tene /ˈkærəˌtin/ *noun* [U] a red or orange substance found in carrots and other plants ⊃ see also BETA CAROTENE

car·ot·id ar·ter·y /kəˌrɑtəd ˈɑrtəri/ *noun* (*anatomy*) either of the two large arteries (ARTERY) in the neck that carry blood to the head

ca·rouse /kəˈrauz/ *verb* [I] (*literary*) to spend time drinking alcohol, laughing, and enjoying yourself in a noisy way with other people

car·ou·sel /ˌkærəˈsɛl/ *noun* **1** = MERRY-GO-ROUND **2** = BAGGAGE CAROUSEL

carp /kɑrp/ *noun, verb*
- *noun* (*pl.* carp) [C, U] a large FRESHWATER fish that is used for food
- *verb* [I] **~ (at sb) (about sth)** to keep complaining about someone or something in an annoying way

car·pal /ˈkɑrpl/ *noun* (*anatomy*) any of the eight small bones that form the wrist

ˌcarpal ˈtunnel ˌsyndrome *noun* [U] (*medical*) a painful condition of the hand and fingers caused by pressure on a nerve because of repeated movements over a long period

car·pe di·em /ˌkɑrpeɪ ˈdiɛm/ *exclamation* (from *Latin*) an expression used when you want to say that someone should not wait, but should take an opportunity as soon as it appears

car·pel /ˈkɑrpl/ *noun* (*biology*) the part of a plant in which seeds are produced ⊃ picture at PLANT

car·pen·ter /ˈkɑrpəntər/ *noun* a person whose job is making and repairing wooden objects and structures

car·pen·try /ˈkɑrpəntri/ *noun* [U] **1** the work of a carpenter **2** things made by a carpenter

car·pet 🔑 /ˈkɑrpət/ *noun, verb*
- *noun* **1** [U] a thick WOVEN material made of wool, etc. for covering floors or stairs: *a roll of carpet* **2** [C] a piece of carpet used as a floor covering, especially when shaped to fit a room: *to lay a carpet* ◆ *a bedroom carpet* ◆ *We have wall-to-wall carpets in our house.* ⊃ see also CARPETING, RED CARPET, RUG **3** [C] **~ (of sth)** (*literary*) a thick layer of something on the ground: *a carpet of snow*
  IDM (be/get called) on the carpet (*informal*) called to see someone in authority because you have done something wrong: *I got called on the carpet for being late.*
- *verb* [usually passive] **1** **~ sth** to cover the floor of a room with a carpet: *The hall was carpeted in blue.* **2** **~ sth (with/in sth)** (*literary*) to cover something with a thick layer of something: *The forest floor was carpeted with wild flowers.*

ˈcarpet ˌbag *noun* a bag used in the past for carrying your things when traveling

car·pet·bag·ger /ˈkɑrpətˌbægər/ *noun* **1** a person from the northern states of the U.S. who went to the South after the Civil War in order to make money or get political power **2** (*disapproving*) a politician who tries to be elected in an area where he or she is not known and is therefore not welcome

ˈcarpet-ˌbomb *verb* **1** **~ sth** to drop a large number of bombs onto every part of an area **2** **~ sb** (*business*) to send an advertisement to a very large number of people, especially by e-mail ▶ **ˈcarpet-ˌbombing** *noun* [U]

car·pet·ing /ˈkɑrpətɪŋ/ *noun* [U] carpets in general or the material used for carpets: *new offices with wall-to-wall carpeting* ◆ *We need new carpeting* (= a new carpet) *in the living room.*

ˈcarpet ˌsweeper *noun* a simple machine for cleaning carpets, with a long handle, and brushes that go around

ˈcar phone *noun* a radio telephone for use in a car

ˈcar pool *noun* a group of car owners who take turns to drive everyone in the group to work, or everyone's children to school, so that only one car is used at a time

car·pool /ˈkɑrpul/ *verb* [I] if a group of people **carpool**, they travel to work together in one car and divide the cost between them

car·port /ˈkɑrpɔrt/ *noun* a shelter for a car, usually built beside a house, and consisting of a roof supported by posts

car·rel /ˈkærəl/ *noun* a small area with a desk, separated from other desks by a dividing wall or screen, where one person can work in a library

car·riage /ˈkærɪdʒ/ *noun* **1** [C] a road vehicle, usually with four wheels, that is pulled by one or more horses, and was used in the past to carry people: *a horse-drawn carriage* **2** [C] a moving part of a machine that supports or moves another part, for example on a TYPEWRITER **3** [sing.] (*old-fashioned*) the way in which someone holds and moves their head and body SYN BEARING ⊃ see also BABY CARRIAGE, UNDERCARRIAGE

ˈcarriage ˌclock *noun* a small clock inside a case with a handle on top

ˈcarriage ˌhouse *noun* a building for storing a carriage in the past; such a building that has been converted into a place for people to live in

car·ri·er /ˈkæriər/ *noun* **1** a company that carries goods or passengers from one place to another, especially by air **2** a person or thing that carries something: *Aquarius, the Water Carrier* ◆ *a baby carrier* (= for carrying a baby on your back or in front of you) **3** a company that provides a telephone or Internet service: *a telecommunications carrier* **4** a person or animal that passes a disease to other people or animals but does not suffer from it **5** a military vehicle or ship that carries soldiers or equipment from one place to another: *an armored personnel carrier* ⊃ see also AIRCRAFT CARRIER **6** a metal frame that is attached to a bicycle and used for carrying bags

ˈcarrier ˌpigeon *noun* a PIGEON (= a type of bird) that has been trained to carry messages

car·ri·on /ˈkæriən/ *noun* [U] the decaying flesh of dead animals: *crows feeding on carrion*

car·rot 🔑 /ˈkærət/ *noun*
1 [C, U] a long, pointed, orange root vegetable: *grated carrots* ◆ *a pound of carrots* ⊃ picture at FRUIT **2** [C] a reward promised to someone in order to persuade them to do something SYN INCENTIVE: *They are holding out a carrot of $120 million in economic aid.*
IDM the carrot and (the) stick (approach) if you use the **carrot and stick approach**, you persuade someone to try harder by offering them a reward if they do, or a punishment if they do not

car·rot·y /ˈkærəti/ *adj.* (sometimes *disapproving*) (of hair) orange in color

car·ry 🔑 /ˈkæri/ *verb*
(car·ries, car·ry·ing, car·ried, car·ried)
▸ TAKE WITH YOU **1** [T] **~ sb/sth** to support the weight of someone or something and take them or it from place to place; to take someone or something from one place to another: *He was carrying a suitcase.* ◆ *She carried her baby in her arms.* ◆ *The injured were carried away on stretchers.* ◆ *a train carrying commuters to work* **2** [T] **~ sth** to have something with you and take it wherever you go: *Police in many countries carry guns.* ◆ *I never carry much money on me.*
▸ OF PIPES/WIRES **3** [T] **~ sth** to contain and direct the flow of

water, electricity, etc.: *a pipeline carrying oil* ◆ *The veins carry blood to the heart.*
> DISEASE **4** [T] ~ **sth** if a person, an insect, etc. **carries** a disease, they are infected with it and might spread it to others although they might not become sick themselves: *Ticks can carry a nasty disease which affects humans.*
> REMEMBER **5** [T] ~ **sth in your head/mind** to be able to remember something
> SUPPORT WEIGHT **6** [T] ~ **sth** to support the weight of something: *A road bridge has to carry a lot of traffic.*
> RESPONSIBILITY **7** [T] ~ **sth** to accept responsibility for something; to suffer the results of something: *He is carrying the department* (= it is only working because of his efforts). ◆ *Their group was targeted to* **carry the burden** *of job losses.*
> HAVE AS QUALITY/FEATURE **8** [T] ~ **sth** to have something as a quality or feature: *Her speech carried the ring of authority.* ◆ *My views don't* **carry much weight** *with* (= have much influence on) *the boss.* ◆ *Each bike carries a ten-year guarantee.* **9** [T] ~ **sth** to have something as a result: *Violent crimes carry heavy penalties.* ◆ *As a combat sport, karate* **carries with it** *the risk of injury.*
> OF THROW/KICK **10** [I] + **noun** + **adv./prep.** if something that is thrown, kicked, etc. **carries** a particular distance, it travels that distance before stopping: *The fullback's kick carried 50 yards into the crowd.*
> OF SOUND **11** [I] (+ **adv./prep.**) if a sound **carries**, it can be heard a long distance away
> TAKE TO PLACE/POSITION **12** [T] ~ **sth/sb to/into sth** to take something or someone to a particular point or in a particular direction: *The war was carried into enemy territory.* ◆ *Her abilities carried her to the top of her profession.*
> APPROVAL/SUPPORT **13** [T, usually passive] ~ **sth** to approve of something by more people voting for it than against it: *The resolution was carried by 340 votes to 210.* **14** [T] ~ **sb/sth** to win the support or sympathy of someone; to persuade people to accept your argument: *His moving speech was enough to carry the audience.*
> HAVE LABEL **15** [T] ~ **sth** to have a particular label or piece of information attached: *Cigarettes carry a health warning.*
> NEWS STORY **16** [T] ~ **sth** if a newspaper or broadcast **carries** a particular story, it publishes or broadcasts it
> ITEM IN STORE **17** [T] ~ **sth** if a store **carries** a particular item, it has it for sale: *We carry a range of educational software.*
> INSURANCE **18** [T] ~ **sth** to provide or take responsibility for the cost of something: *The company* **carries** *health* **insurance** *for all its employees.*
> BABY **19** [T] **be carrying someone** to be pregnant with someone: *She was carrying twins.*
> YOURSELF **20** [T] ~ **yourself** + **adv./prep.** to hold or move your head or body in a particular way: *to carry yourself well*
> ADDING NUMBERS **21** [T] ~ **sth** to add a number to the next column on the left when adding up numbers, for example when the numbers add up to more than ten
> IDM **be/get carried away** to get very excited or lose control of your feelings: *I got carried away and started shouting at the TV.* **carry the ball** (*informal*) to take responsibility for getting something done: *My coworker was sick, so I had to carry the ball.* **carry a torch for sb** to be in love with someone, especially someone who does not love you in return **carry the torch** to support something over a long period of time, even if others do not: *Coach Thomas still carries the torch for his team, in spite of a dismal season so far.* **carry a tune** to be able to sing all the right notes in a piece of music: *They asked him to join the chorus, but he insisted that he couldn't carry a tune.* ⊃ more at DAY, FAR *adv.*, FAST *adv.*, FETCH
> PHR V **carry sth↔'forward** (also **carry sth↔'over**) to move a total amount from one column or page to the next **,carry sth↔'off 1** to win something: *He carried off most of the prizes.* **2** to succeed in doing something that most people would find difficult: *She's had her hair cut really short, but she can carry it off.* **,carry 'on** (*informal*) to argue or complain noisily: *He was shouting and carrying on.* **,carry 'on (with sth)** | **,carry sth↔'on** to continue doing something: *Carry on with your work while I'm away.* ◆ *After he left I just tried*

to carry on as normal (= do the things I usually do). ◆ *Carry on with the good work!* ◆ ~ **doing sth** *He carried on peeling the potatoes.* **,carry 'on (with sb)** (*old-fashioned*) to have a sexual relationship with someone when you should not: *His wife found out he'd been carrying on with another woman.* **,carry sth↔'out 1** to do something that you have said you will do or have been asked to do: *to carry out a promise/a threat/a plan/an order* **2** to do and complete a task: *to carry out an investigation/a survey* ◆ *Extensive tests have been carried out on the patient.* **,carry 'over** to continue to exist in a different situation: *Attitudes learned at home carry over onto the playground.* **,carry sth↔'over 1** to keep something from one situation and use it or deal with it in a different situation **2** to delay something until a later time: *The game had to be carried over until Sunday.* **3** = **,carry sth 'through** | **,carry sb 'through sth** to help someone to survive a difficult period: *His determination carried him through the ordeal.* **,carry sth 'through** to complete something successfully: *It's a difficult job, but she's the person to carry it through.* **,carry 'through (on/with sth)** to do what you have said you will do: *He has proved he can carry through on his promises.*

car·ry·all /'kæri,ɔl/ *noun* a large bag with handles, usually made of soft material

'carry-,on *noun* a small bag or case that you carry onto a plane with you: *Only one carry-on is allowed.* ◆ *carry-on luggage*

'carry-,out *noun* = TAKEOUT: [U] *Let's get some carry-out.* ◆ *carry-out Chinese food*

'carry-,over *noun* **1** [usually sing.] something that remains or results from a situation in the past: *His neatness is a carry-over from his army days.* **2** an amount of money that has not been used and so can be used later: *The $20 million included a $7 million carry-over from last year's budget.*

'car seat *noun* **1** a special safety seat for a child, that can be fitted into a car ⊃ **picture at** CHAIR **2** a seat in a car

car·sick /'karsɪk/ *adj.* [not usually before noun] feeling sick because you are traveling in a car: *Do you get carsick?* ▶ **car·sick·ness** *noun* [U]

cart /kart/ *noun, verb*
• *noun* **1** a vehicle with two or four wheels that is pulled by a horse and used for carrying loads: *a horse and cart* **2** a BASKET or table with wheels that can be pushed or pulled along and is used for carrying things: *a shopping/baggage cart* ◆ *a dessert cart* **3** (also **hand·cart**) a light vehicle with wheels that you pull or push by hand ⊃ **see also** GOLF CART
  IDM **put the cart before the horse** to put or do things in the wrong order
• *verb* **1** ~ **sth** (+ **adv./prep.**) to carry something in a cart or other vehicle: *The trash is then carted away for recycling.* **2** ~ **sth** + **adv./prep.** (*informal*) to carry something that is large, heavy, or awkward in your hands: *We had to cart our luggage up six flights of stairs.* **3** ~ **sb** + **adv./prep.** (*informal*) to take someone somewhere, especially with difficulty: *The demonstrators were carted off to the local police station.*

carte blanche /,kart 'blanʃ/ *noun* [U] (from *French*) ~ **(to do sth)** the complete freedom or authority to do whatever you like

car·tel /kar'tɛl/ *noun* a group of separate companies that agree to increase profits by fixing prices and not competing with each other

Car·te·sian /kar'tiʒən/ *adj.* connected with the French PHILOSOPHER Descartes and his ideas about philosophy and mathematics

car·ti·lage /'kartl·ɪdʒ/ *noun* [U, C] the strong white TISSUE that is important in support and especially in joints to prevent the bones rubbing against each other ⊃ **picture at** BODY

car·ti·lag·i·nous /,kartl'ædʒənəs/ *adj.* (*anatomy*) made of cartilage

cart·load /'kartloʊd/ *noun* **1** the amount of something that

fills a CART 2 [usually pl.] (*informal*) a large amount of something

car·tog·ra·pher /kɑrˈtɑgrəfər/ *noun* a person who draws or makes maps

car·tog·ra·phy /kɑrˈtɑgrəfi/ *noun* [U] the art or process of drawing or making maps ▶ **car·to·graph·ic** /ˌkɑrtəˈgræfɪk/ *adj.*

car·ton /ˈkɑrtn/ *noun* **1** a heavy paper or plastic box or pot for holding goods, especially food or liquid; the contents of a carton: *a milk carton/an egg carton* ♦ *a carton of milk/yogurt* ◯ picture at PACKAGING **2** a large container in which goods are packed in smaller containers: *a carton of cigarettes*

car·toon /kɑrˈtun/ *noun* **1** an amusing drawing in a newspaper or magazine, especially one about politics or events in the news **2** = COMIC STRIP **3** a movie made by photographing a series of gradually changing drawings or models, so that they look as if they are moving: *Saturday morning cartoons* ♦ *a cartoon character* **4** (*technical*) a drawing made by an artist as a preparation for a painting

car·toon·ish /kɑrˈtunɪʃ/ *adj.* very silly or exaggerated, often in a way that is not appropriate: *Her cartoonish makeup made her look ridiculous.*

car·toon·ist /kɑrˈtunɪst/ *noun* a person who draws cartoons

car·touche /kɑrˈtuʃ/ *noun* an OBLONG or OVAL shape which contains a set of ancient Egyptian HIEROGLYPHS, often representing the name and title of a king or queen

car·tridge /ˈkɑrtrɪdʒ/ *noun* **1** (also **shell**) a tube or case containing EXPLOSIVES and a bullet, or SHOT, for shooting from a gun **2** a case containing something that is used in a machine, for example an electronic game, ink for a printer, etc. Cartridges are put into the machine and can be removed and replaced when they are finished or empty. **3** a thin tube containing ink that you put inside a pen

cart·wheel /ˈkɑrtwil/ *noun* **1** a fast physical movement in which you turn in a circle sideways by putting your hands on the ground and bringing your legs, one at a time, over your head: *to do/turn cartwheels* **2** the wheel of a CART ▶ **cart·wheel** *verb* [I]

carve /kɑrv/ *verb* **1** [T, I] to make objects, patterns, etc. by cutting away material from wood or stone: ~ *sth a carved doorway* ♦ ~ *sth from/out of sth The statue was carved out of a single piece of stone.* ♦ ~ *sth into/in sth The wood had been carved into the shape of a flower.* ♦ ~ *in sth She carves in both stone and wood.* ◯ collocations at ART **2** [T] ~ *sth (on sth)* to write something on a surface by cutting into it: *They carved their initials on the desk.* **3** to cut a large piece of cooked meat into smaller pieces for eating: [T, I] ~ *(sth)* | ~ *(sb) sth Who's going to carve the turkey?* **4** [T, no passive] to work hard in order to have a successful career, reputation, etc.: ~ *sth* **(out)** *He succeeded in carving out a career in media.* ♦ ~ *sth* **(out) for yourself** *She has carved out a place for herself in the fashion world.* **IDM** see STONE *n.*
PHR V **carve sth↔up** (*disapproving*) to divide a company, an area of land, etc. into smaller parts in order to share it between people

carv·ing /ˈkɑrvɪŋ/ *noun* **1** [C, U] an object or a pattern made by cutting away material from wood or stone **2** [U] the art of making objects in this way

ˈcarving ˌknife *noun* a large sharp knife for cutting cooked meat ◯ picture at KITCHEN

ˈcar wash *noun* a place with special equipment, where you can pay to have your car washed

car·y·at·id /ˌkæriˈætəd; ˈkæriəˌtɪd/ *noun* (*architecture*) a statue of a female figure used as a supporting PILLAR in a building

Cas·a·no·va /ˌkæsəˈnoʊvə; ˌkæzə-/ *noun* a man who has romantic or sexual relationships with a lot of women
ORIGIN From Giovanni Jacopo Casanova, an Italian man in the 18th century who was famous for having sex with many women.

cas·bah (also **kas·bah**) /ˈkæzbɑ; ˈkɑz-/ *noun* a castle on high ground in a N. African city or the area around it

cas·cade /kæˈskeɪd/ *noun, verb*
● *noun* **1** a small WATERFALL, especially one of several falling down a steep slope with rocks **2** a large amount of water falling or pouring down: *a cascade of rainwater* **3** (*formal*) a large amount of something hanging down: *Her hair tumbled in a cascade down her back.* **4** (*formal*) a large number of things falling or coming quickly at the same time: *He crashed to the ground in a cascade of oil cans.*
● *verb* **1** [I] + **adv./prep.** to flow downward in large amounts: *Water cascaded down the mountainside.* **2** [I] + **adv./prep.** (*formal*) to fall or hang in large amounts: *Blond hair cascaded over her shoulders.*

case /keɪs/ *noun, verb*
● *noun*
▷ SITUATION **1** [C] a particular situation or a situation of a particular type: *In some cases, people have had to wait several weeks for an appointment.* ♦ *The company only dismisses its employees in cases of gross misconduct.* ♦ *It's a* **classic case** (= a very typical case) *of bad planning.* ◯ see also WORST-CASE ◯ thesaurus box at EXAMPLE, SITUATION **2** **the case** [sing.] ~ **(that…)** the true situation: *If that is the case* (= if the situation described is true), *we need more staff.* ♦ *It is simply not the case that prison conditions are improving.* **3** [C, usually sing.] a situation that relates to a particular person or thing: *In your case, we are prepared to be lenient.* ♦ *I cannot make an exception in your case* (= for you and not for others). ♦ *Every application will be decided* **on a case-by-case basis** (= each one will be considered separately). ◯ thesaurus box at EXAMPLE
▷ POLICE INVESTIGATION **4** [C] a matter that is being officially investigated, especially by the police: *a murder case* ♦ *a case of theft* ◯ collocations at CRIME
▷ IN COURT **5** [C] a question to be decided in court: *The case will be heard next week.* ♦ *a court case* ♦ *to win/lose a case* ◯ see also TEST CASE
▷ ARGUMENTS **6** [C, usually sing.] ~ **(for/against sth)** a set of facts or arguments that support one side in a trial, a discussion, etc.: *the case for the defense/prosecution* ♦ *Our lawyer didn't think we had a case* (= had enough good arguments to win in a court of law). ♦ *the case for/against private education* ♦ *The report* **makes a strong case** (= gives good arguments) *for spending more money on hospitals.* ♦ *You will each be given the chance to* **state** *your case.*
▷ CONTAINER **7** [C] (often in compounds) a container or covering used to protect or store things; a container with its contents or the amount that it contains: *a pencil case* ♦ *a jewelry case* ♦ *a packing case* (= a large wooden box for packing things in) ♦ *The museum was full of fossils in glass cases.* ♦ *a case* (= 12 bottles) *of champagne* ◯ picture at CLOCK ◯ see also VANITY CASE
▷ OF DISEASE **8** [C] the fact of someone having a disease or an injury; a person suffering from a disease or an injury: *a severe case of typhoid* ♦ *The most serious cases were treated at the scene of the accident.*
▷ PERSON **9** [C] a person who needs, or is thought to need, special treatment or attention: *He's a hopeless case.*
▷ GRAMMAR **10** [C, U] the form of a noun, an adjective, or a pronoun in some languages, that shows its relationship to another word: *the nominative/accusative/genitive case* ♦ *Latin nouns have case, number, and gender.*
IDM **as the case may be** used to say that one of two or more possibilities is true, but which one is true depends on the circumstances: *There may be an announcement about this tomorrow—or not, as the case may be.* **be on sb's case** (*informal*) to criticize someone all the time: *She's always on my case about cleaning my room.* **be on the case** to be dealing with a particular matter, especially a criminal investigation: *We have two agents on the case.* **get off my case** (*informal*) used to tell someone to stop criticizing you **a case in point** a clear example of the problem, situation, etc. that is being discussed ◯ language bank at E.G. **in any case** whatever happens or may have happened: *There's no point in complaining now—we're leaving tomorrow in any case.* **(just) in case (…)** because of the possibility of something happening: *You'd better take the keys in case I'm out.* ♦ *You probably won't need to call—but take my number, just in case.*

◆ *In case* (= if it is true that) *you're wondering why Joe is here—let me explain...* **in case of sth** (often on official notices) if something happens: *In case of fire, ring the alarm bell.* **in that case** if that happens or has happened; if that is the situation: *"I've made up my mind." "In that case, there's no point discussing it."* ➔ more at REST v.

● *verb*

IDM **case the joint** (*informal*) to look carefully around a building so that you can plan how to steal things from it at a later time

case·book /'keɪsbʊk/ *noun* a written record kept by doctors, lawyers, etc. of cases they have dealt with

cased /keɪst/ *adj.* **~ in sth** completely covered with a particular material: *The towers are made of steel cased in granite.* ➔ see also CASING

ˌcase 'history *noun* a record of a person's background, past illnesses, etc. that a doctor or SOCIAL WORKER studies

case law *noun* [U] (*law*) law based on decisions made by judges in earlier cases ➔ compare COMMON LAW, STATUTE LAW ➔ see also TEST CASE

case·load /'keɪsloʊd/ *noun* all the people that a doctor, SOCIAL WORKER, etc. is responsible for at one time: *a heavy caseload*

case·ment /'keɪsmənt/ (also 'casement ˌwindow) *noun* a window that opens on HINGES like a door

ˌcase-'sensitive *adj.* (*computing*) a program that is **case-sensitive** recognizes the difference between capital letters and small letters

ˌcase 'study *noun* a detailed account of the development of a person, a group of people, or a situation over a period of time

case·work /'keɪswɜrk/ *noun* [U] social work (= work done to help people in the community with special needs) involving the study of a particular person's family and background

case·work·er /'keɪsˌwɜrkər/ *noun* a SOCIAL WORKER who helps a particular person or family in the community with special needs

cash 🔊 /kæʃ/ *noun, verb*

● *noun* **1** [U] money in the form of coins or bills: *How much cash do you have on you?* ◆ *Payments can be made by check or in cash.* ◆ *Customers are offered a 10% discount if they* **pay cash.** ◆ *The thieves stole $500* **in cash.** ➔ see also COLD CASH, PETTY CASH ➔ thesaurus box at MONEY **2** [U] money in any form: *The museum needs to find ways of raising cash.* ◆ *I'm short of cash right now.* ◆ *I'm constantly* **strapped for cash** (= without enough money). **3** [C] (*CanE, informal*) = CASH REGISTER

IDM **cash up front** with immediate payment of cash: *to pay for something cash up front* **cash on delivery** (*abbr.* COD) a system of paying for goods when they are delivered

● *verb* **~ a check** to exchange a check for the amount of money that it is worth

IDM **cash in your chips 1** to give someone your CHIPS (= small flat pieces of plastic used in gambling) for money **2** (*informal*) to die

PHR V ˌcash 'in (on sth) (*disapproving*) to gain an advantage for yourself from a situation, especially in a way that other people think is wrong or immoral: *The film studio is being accused of cashing in on the singer's death.* ˌcash sth↔'in to exchange something, such as an insurance policy, for money ˌcash 'out to add up the amount of money that has been received in a store, club, etc., especially at the end of the day

ˌcash and 'carry *noun* [C, U], a large WHOLESALE store that sells goods in large quantities at low prices to customers from other businesses who pay in cash and take the goods away themselves; the system of buying and selling goods in this way

'cash back (also 'cash-back) *noun* **1** [U] if you ask for **cash back** when you are paying for goods in a store with a DEBIT CARD (= a plastic card that takes money directly from your

bank account), you get a sum of money in cash, that is added to your bill **2** [U, C] a sum of money that is offered to people who buy particular products or services: *There's $200 cash back on this computer if you buy before January 31.*

'cash bar *noun* a bar at a wedding, party, etc., at which the guests have to pay for their own drinks rather than getting them free

'cash box *noun* a box with a lock for keeping money in, usually made of metal

'cash cow *noun* (*business*) the part of a business that always makes a profit and that provides money for the rest of the business

'cash crop *noun* a crop grown for selling, rather than for use by the person who grows it ➔ compare SUBSISTENCE

cash·ew /'kæʃu; kæ'ʃu/ (also 'cashew ˌnut) *noun* the small curved nut of the tropical American **cashew tree**, used in cooking, and often eaten salted ➔ picture at NUT

'cash flow *noun* [C, U] the movement of money into and out of a business as goods are bought and sold: *a healthy cash flow* (= having enough money to make payments when necessary) ◆ *cash-flow problems*

cash·ier /kæ'ʃɪr/ *noun, verb*

● *noun* a person whose job is to receive and pay out money in a bank, store, hotel, etc.

● *verb* [usually passive] **~ sb** to make someone leave the army, navy, etc. because they have done something wrong

cash'ier's check (*CanE* **cash'ier's cheque**) *noun* a check that is guaranteed because it uses the bank's own funds and is signed by a bank official

cash·less /'kæʃləs/ *adj.* done or working without using cash: *We are moving toward a cashless society.*

'cash ma,chine (*CanE* 'bank ma,chine) *noun* a machine in or outside a bank, etc., from which you can get money from your bank account using a special plastic card **SYN** ATM

cash·mere /'kæʒmɪr; 'kæʃ-/ *noun* [U] fine soft wool made from the long hair of a type of GOAT, used especially for making expensive clothes

'cash ˌregister (also reg·is·ter, *CanE, informal* cash) *noun* a machine used in stores, restaurants, etc. that has a drawer for keeping money in, and that shows and records the amount of money received for each thing that is sold

'cash-starved *adj.* [only before noun] without enough money, usually because another organization, such as the government, has failed to provide it: *cash-starved public services*

'cash-strapped *adj.* [only before noun] without enough money: *cash-strapped governments/shoppers*

'cash ˌtransfer (also 'money ˌtransfer) *noun* [C, U] the act of moving money from one bank or place to another; the money moved in this way: *He made a cash transfer of $1,000 to his relatives in Haiti.*

cas·ing /'keɪsɪŋ/ *noun* [C, U] a covering that protects something

ca·si·no /kə'sinoʊ/ *noun* (*pl.* ca·si·nos) a public building or room where people play gambling games for money

cask /kæsk/ *noun* a small wooden BARREL used for storing liquids, especially alcoholic drinks; the amount contained in a cask: *a wine cask/a cask of wine*

cas·ket /'kæskət/ *noun* **1** = COFFIN **2** a small decorated box for holding jewelry or other valuable things, especially in the past

cas·sa·va /kə'savə/ (also man·i·oc) *noun* [U] **1** a tropical plant with many branches and long roots that you can eat **2** the roots of this plant, which can be boiled, fried, ROASTED or made into flour

cas·se·role /'kæsəˌroʊl/ *noun* **1** [C, U] a hot dish made with meat, vegetables, etc. that are cooked slowly in liquid in an oven: *a chicken casserole* ◆ *Is there any casserole left?* **2** [C] (also 'casserole dish) a container with a lid used for cooking meat, etc. in liquid in an oven

cas·sette /kəˈsɛt/ noun **1** a small, flat, plastic case containing tape for playing or recording music or sound: *a cassette recorder/player/deck* ♦ *available on cassette* ♦ *a video cassette* (= for recording sound and pictures) **2** a plastic case containing film that can be put into a camera

cas·sock /ˈkæsək/ noun a long piece of clothing, usually black or red, worn by some Christian priests and other people with special duties in a church

cas·so·war·y /ˈkæsəˌwɛri/ noun (pl. **cas·so·war·ies**) a very large bird related to the EMU, that does not fly. It is found mainly in New Guinea.

cast 🔊 /kæst/ verb, noun

● **verb** (cast, cast)

› **VOTE 1** [T] ~ **a/your vote/ballot (for sb or sth)** to vote for someone or something

› **LIGHT/A SHADOW 2** [T] ~ **sth (over sth)** to make light, a shadow, etc. appear in a particular place: *The setting sun cast an orange glow over the mountains.* ♦ *(figurative) The sad news cast a shadow over the proceedings* (= made people feel unhappy).

› **DOUBT 3** [T] ~ **doubt/aspersions (on/upon sth)** to say, do or suggest something that makes people doubt something or think that someone is less honest, good, etc.: *This latest evidence casts serious doubt on his version of events.*

› **FISHING LINE 4** [I, T] ~ **(sth)** to throw one end of a FISHING LINE into a river, etc.

› **ACTORS 5** [T] to choose actors to play the different parts in a movie, play, etc.; to choose an actor to play a particular role: ~ **sth** *The play is being cast in both the U.S. and Britain.* ♦ ~ **sb (as sb)** *He cast her as an ambitious lawyer in his latest movie.*

› **A LOOK/GLANCE/SMILE 6** [T] ~ **(sb) sth** to look, smile, etc. in a particular direction: *She cast a welcoming smile in his direction.*

› **DESCRIBE 7** [T] to describe or present someone/yourself in a particular way: ~ **sb/yourself (as sth)** *He cast himself as the innocent victim of a hate campaign.* ♦ ~ **sb/yourself (in sth)** *The press were quick to cast her in the role of "the other woman."*

› **SHAPE METAL 8** [T] ~ **sth (in sth)** to shape hot liquid metal, etc. by pouring it into a hollow container (called a MOLD): *a statue cast in bronze*

› **THROW 9** [T] ~ **sb/sth** (literary) to throw someone or something somewhere, especially using force: *The priceless treasures had been cast into the Nile.* ♦ *They cast anchor at nightfall.*

› **SKIN 10** [T] ~ **sth** when a snake **casts** its skin, the skin comes off as part of a natural process **SYN** SHED

› **SHOE 11** [T] ~ **sth** if a horse **casts** a shoe, the shoe comes off by accident

IDM **cast your mind back (to sth)** to make yourself think about something that happened in the past: *I want you to cast your minds back to the first time you met.* **cast your net wide** to consider a lot of different people, activities, possibilities, etc. when you are looking for something **cast a spell (on sb/sth)** to use words that are thought to be magic and have the power to change, or influence someone or something ⊃ more at ADRIFT, DIE *n.*, EYE *n.*, LIGHT *n.*, LOT *n.*

PHR V **cast aˈbout/aˈround for sth** to try hard to think of or find something, especially when this is difficult: *She cast around desperately for a safe topic of conversation.* **cast sb/ sth↔aˈside** (formal) to get rid of someone or something because you no longer want or need them **SYN** DISCARD be **cast aˈway** to be left somewhere after a SHIPWRECK ⊃ related noun CASTAWAY be **cast ˈdown (by sth)** (literary) to be sad or unhappy about something ⊃ see also DOWNCAST **cast ˈoff** | **cast sth↔ˈoff 1** to undo the ropes that are holding a boat in a fixed position, in order to sail away **2** (in knitting) to remove STITCHES from the needles in a way that forms an edge that will not come undone **cast sth↔ˈoff** (formal) to get rid of something because you no longer want or need it: *The town is still trying to cast off its dull image.* **cast ˈon** | **cast sth↔ˈon** (in knitting) to put the first row of STITCHES on a needle **cast sb/sth↔ˈout** (literary) to

get rid of someone or something, especially by using force: *He claimed to have the power to cast out demons.* ⊃ related noun OUTCAST

● **noun**

› **ACTORS 1** [C] all the people who act in a play or movie: *The whole cast performed brilliantly.* ♦ *members of the cast* ♦ *an all-star cast* (= including many well-known actors) ♦ *the supporting cast* (= not the main actors, but the others) ♦ *a cast list*

› **ON ARM/LEG 2** (also ˌplaster ˈcast) [C] a hard cover that is put on an arm, a leg, etc. to protect a broken bone: *Her leg is in a cast.*

› **IN SHAPING METAL 3** [C] an object that is made by pouring hot liquid metal, etc. into a MOLD (= a specially shaped container) **4** [C] a shaped container used to make an object **SYN** MOLD

› **THROW 5** [C] an act of throwing something, especially a fishing line

› **APPEARANCE 6** [sing.] (formal) the way that a person or thing is or appears: *He has an unusual cast of mind.* ♦ *I disliked the arrogant cast to her mouth.*

cas·ta·nets /ˌkæstəˈnɛts/ noun [pl.] a musical instrument that consists of two small round pieces of wood that you hold in the hand and hit together with the fingers to make a noise. Castanets are used especially by Spanish dancers. ⊃ picture at INSTRUMENT

cast·a·way /ˈkæstəˌweɪ/ noun a person whose ship has sunk (= who has been SHIPWRECKED) and who has had to swim to a lonely place, usually an island

caste /kæst/ noun **1** [C, U] any of the four main divisions of Hindu society, originally those made according to functions in society; the system of dividing Hindu society in this way: *the caste system* ♦ *high-caste Brahmins* **2** [C] a social class, especially one whose members do not allow others to join it: *the ruling caste*

cas·tel·lat·ed /ˈkæstəˌleɪtəd/ adj. (architecture) built in the style of a castle with BATTLEMENTS

cas·tel·la·tions /ˌkæstəˈleɪʃnz/ noun [pl.] the top edge of a castle wall, that has regular spaces along it

cast·er /ˈkæstər/ noun one of the small wheels attached to the bottom of a piece of furniture so that it can be moved easily

cas·ti·gate /ˈkæstəˌɡeɪt/ verb ~ **sb/sth/yourself (for sth)** (formal) to criticize someone or something severely: *He castigated himself for being so stupid.* ▶ **cas·ti·ga·tion** /ˌkæstəˈɡeɪʃn/ noun [U]

cast·ing /ˈkæstɪŋ/ noun **1** [U] the process of choosing actors for a play or movie **2** [C] an object made by pouring hot liquid metal, etc. into a MOLD (= a specially shaped container)

ˈcasting ˌcouch noun used to refer to a process in which actors are chosen for a movie, etc. if they have sex with the person in charge of choosing the actors

ˌcasting ˈvote noun [usually sing.] the vote given by the person in charge of an official meeting to decide an issue when votes on each side are equal

ˌcast ˈiron noun [U] a hard type of iron that does not bend easily and is shaped by pouring the hot liquid metal into a MOLD (= a specially shaped container)

ˌcast-ˈiron adj. **1** made of cast iron: *a cast-iron bridge* **2** very strong or certain; that cannot be broken or fail: *a cast-iron guarantee/promise* ♦ *a cast-iron excuse/alibi* ⊃ compare IRONCLAD

cas·tle /ˈkæsl/ noun **1** a large strong building with thick high walls and towers, built in the past by kings or queens, or other important people, to defend themselves against attack ⊃ picture at BUILDING ⊃ see also SANDCASTLE **2** (also rook) (in CHESS) any of the four pieces placed in the corner squares of the board at the start of the game, usually made to look like a castle ⊃ picture at TOY

IDM **(build) castles in the air** (to have) plans or dreams that are not likely to happen or come true ⊃ more at MAN *n.*

cast-off /ˈkæstɔf/ noun [usually pl.] (usually disapproving) a piece of clothing that the original owner no longer wants to wear ➔ compare HAND-ME-DOWN ▶ cast-off adj.: a castoff overcoat

castor oil noun [U] a thick yellow oil obtained from a tropical plant and used in the past as a type of medicine, usually as a LAXATIVE

cas-trate /ˈkæstreɪt/ verb ~ sb/sth to remove the TESTICLES of a male animal or person ▶ cas-tra-tion /kæˈstreɪʃn/ noun [U, C]

ca-su-al /ˈkæʒuəl; -ʒəl/ adj., noun
● **adj.**
> NOT FORMAL **1** not formal: casual clothes (= comfortable clothes that you choose to wear in your free time) ◆ family parties and other casual occasions
> WITHOUT CARE/ATTENTION **2** [usually before noun] not showing much care or thought; seeming not to be worried; not wanting to show that something is important to you: a casual manner ◆ It was just a casual remark—I wasn't really serious. ◆ He tried to sound casual, but I knew he was worried. ◆ They have a casual attitude toward safety (= they don't care enough). **3** [usually before noun] without paying attention to detail: a casual glance ◆ It's obvious even to the casual observer.
> RELATIONSHIP **4** [usually before noun] without deep affection: a casual acquaintance ◆ a casual friendship ◆ to have casual sex (= to have sex without having a steady relationship with that partner)
> BY CHANCE **5** [only before noun] happening by chance; doing something by chance: a casual encounter/meeting ◆ a casual passerby ◆ The exhibition is interesting to both the enthusiast and the casual visitor. ◆ The disease is not spread by casual contact.
> WORK **6** [usually before noun] not permanent; not done regularly; not doing something regularly: casual workers/labor ◆ Students sometimes do casual work in the tourist business. ◆ They are employed on a casual basis (= they do not have a permanent job with the company).
▶ cas-u-al-ly adv.: "What did he say about me?" she asked as casually as she could. ◆ They chatted casually on the phone. ◆ dressed casually in jeans and a T-shirt **cas-u-al-ness** noun [U]: He was sure that the casualness of the gesture was deliberate.
● **noun** a casual worker (= one who does not work permanently for a company)

cas-u-al-i-za-tion /ˌkæʒuələˈzeɪʃn/ noun [U] the practice of employing temporary staff for short periods instead of permanent staff, in order to save costs

cas-u-al-ty /ˈkæʒəlti; -ʒuəl-/ noun (pl. cas-u-al-ties) **1** a person who is killed or injured in war or in an accident: highway casualties ◆ Both sides had suffered heavy casualties (= many people had been killed). ➔ collocations at WAR **2** a person who suffers or a thing that is destroyed when something else takes place SYN VICTIM: She became a casualty of the reduction in part-time work (= she lost her job). ◆ Small businesses have been a casualty of the recession.

cas-u-ist-ry /ˈkæʒuəstri/ noun [U] (formal, disapproving) a way of solving moral or legal problems by using intelligent arguments that may be false

ca-sus bel-li /ˌkɑsəs ˈbɛli; ˌkeɪsəs ˈbɛlaɪ/ noun (pl. ca-sus bel-li) (formal) an act or situation that is used to justify a war

cat /kæt/ noun
1 a small animal with soft fur that people often keep as a pet. Cats catch and kill birds and mice: cat food ➔ see also KITTEN, TOMCAT **2** a wild animal of the cat family: the big cats (= LIONS, TIGERS, etc.) ➔ see also FAT CAT, WILDCAT
IDM be the cat's meow/pajamas (informal) to be the best thing, person, idea, etc.: He really thinks he's the cat's meow (= he has a high opinion of himself). let the cat out of the bag to tell a secret carelessly or by mistake: I wanted it to be a surprise, but my sister let the cat out of the bag. like a cat on a hot tin roof very nervous: She was like a cat on a hot tin roof before her driving test. like the cat that got/ate/swallowed the canary very pleased with yourself SYN SMUG (has the)

cat got your tongue? (informal) said to someone, especially a child, who stays silent when expected to speak, for example after being asked a question: What's the matter? Cat got your tongue? look like sth the cat brought/dragged in (informal) (of a person) to look dirty and messy play (a game of) cat and mouse with sb | play a cat-and-mouse game with sb to play a cruel game with someone in your power by changing your behavior very often, so that they become nervous and do not know what to expect when the cat's away the mice will play (saying) people enjoy themselves more and behave with greater freedom when the person in charge of them is not there ➔ more at CURIOSITY, FIGHT v., RAIN v., ROOM n., WAY n.

ca-tab-o-lism /kəˈtæbəˌlɪzəm/ noun [U] (biology) the process by which chemical structures are broken down and energy is released

cat-a-clysm /ˈkætəˌklɪzəm/ noun (formal) a sudden disaster or a violent event that causes change, for example a flood or a war ▶ cat-a-clys-mic /ˌkætəˈklɪzmɪk/ adj. [usually before noun]

cat-a-combs /ˈkætəˌkoumz/ noun [pl.] a series of underground tunnels used for burying dead people, especially in ancient times

cat-a-falque /ˈkætlˌfɔk; -ˌfælk/ noun a decorated platform on which the dead body of a famous person is placed before a funeral

Cat-a-lan /ˈkætlˌæn; -ən/ noun, adj.
● **noun 1** [U] a language spoken in Catalonia, Andorra, the Balearic Islands, and parts of southern France **2** [C] a person who was born in or who lives in Catalonia
● **adj.** connected with Catalonia, its people, its language, or its culture

cat-a-lep-sy /ˈkætlˌɛpsi/ noun [U] (medical) a condition in which someone's body becomes stiff and they temporarily become unconscious ▶ cat-a-lep-tic /ˌkætlˈɛptɪk/ adj.

cat-a-log (especially CanE **cat-a-logue**) /ˈkætlˌɔg; -ˌɑg/ noun, verb
● **noun 1** a complete list of items, for example of things that people can look at or buy: a mail-order catalog (= a book showing goods for sale to be sent to people's homes) ◆ to consult the library catalog ◆ An illustrated catalog accompanies the exhibition. ◆ an online catalog **2** a long series of things that happen (usually bad things): a catalog of disasters/errors/misfortunes
● **verb 1** ~ sth to arrange a list of things in order in a catalog; to record something in a catalog **2** ~ sth to give a list of things connected with a particular person, event, etc.: Interviews with the refugees catalog a history of discrimination and violence.

cat-a-lyst /ˈkætlˌɪst/ noun **1** (chemistry) a substance that makes a chemical reaction happen faster without being changed itself **2** ~ (for sth) a person or thing that causes a change: I see my role as being a catalyst for change.

catalytic converter /ˌkætəlɪtɪk kənˈvərtər/ noun a device used in the EXHAUST system of vehicles to reduce the damage caused to the environment

cat-a-lyze (CanE also **cat-a-lyse**) /ˈkætlˌaɪz/ verb ~ sth (chemistry) to make a chemical reaction happen faster

cat-a-ma-ran /ˌkætəməˈræn; ˈkætəməˌræn/ noun a fast sailing boat with two HULLS ➔ picture at BOAT ➔ compare TRIMARAN

cat-a-mite /ˈkætəˌmaɪt/ noun (old use) a boy kept as a SLAVE for a man to have sex with

cat-a-pult /ˈkætəˌpʌlt; -ˌpʊlt/ noun, verb
● **noun 1** a weapon used in the past to throw heavy stones **2** a machine used for sending planes up into the air from a ship
● **verb** [T, I] to throw someone or something or be thrown suddenly and violently through the air: ~ (sb/sth) + adv./prep. She was catapulted out of the car as it hit the wall. ◆ (figurative) The movie catapulted him to international stardom.

cat·a·ract /ˈkætəˌrækt/ *noun* **1** a medical condition that affects the LENS of the eye and causes a gradual loss of sight **2** (*literary*) a large, steep WATERFALL

ca·tarrh /kəˈtɑr/ *noun* [U] (*formal* or *medical*) thick liquid (called PHLEGM) that you have in your nose and throat because, for example, you have a cold

ca·tas·tro·phe /kəˈtæstrəfi/ *noun* **1** a sudden event that causes many people to suffer SYN DISASTER: *Early warnings of rising water levels prevented another major catastrophe.* **2** an event that causes one person or a group of people personal suffering, or that makes difficulties: *The attempt to expand the business was a catastrophe for the company.* ◆ *We've had a few catastrophes with the food for the party.* ▶ **cat·a·stroph·ic** /ˌkætəˈstrɑfɪk/ *adj.* SYN DISASTROUS: *catastrophic effects/ losses/results* **cat·a·stroph·i·cally** /-kli/ *adv.*

cat·a·to·ni·a /ˌkætəˈtoʊniə/ *noun* [U] (*medical*) a condition resulting from a mental illness, especially SCHIZOPHRENIA, in which a person does not move for long periods

cat·a·ton·ic /ˌkætəˈtɑnɪk/ *adj.* (*medical*) not able to move or show any reaction to things because of illness, shock, etc.

cat·bird /ˈkætbərd/ *noun* a North American bird with dark gray or black feathers, a long tail, and a call that sounds like a cat
   IDM **be in the catbird seat** to have an advantage over other people or be in control of a situation

ˈcat ˌburglar *noun* a thief who climbs up the outside of a building in order to enter it and steal something

cat·call /ˈkætkɔl/ *noun* [usually pl.] a noise or shout expressing anger at or disapproval of someone who is speaking or performing in public

catch 🔑 /kætʃ/ *verb, noun*

● *verb* (**caught, caught** /kɔt/)
▸ HOLD **1** [T] ~ sth to stop and hold a moving object, especially in your hands: *She managed to catch the keys as they fell.* ◆ *"Would you throw me a towel?" "OK. Catch!"* ◆ *The dog caught the stick in its mouth.* **2** [T] ~ sth to hold a liquid when it falls: *The roof was leaking and I had to use a bucket to catch the drips.* **3** [T] ~ sb/sth (+ adv./prep.) to take hold of someone or something: *He caught her arm as she tried to push past him.*
▸ CAPTURE **4** [T] ~ sb/sth to capture a person or an animal that tries or would try to escape: *The murderer was never caught.* ◆ *Our cat is useless at catching mice.* ◆ *How many fish did you catch?*
▸ SOMEONE DOING SOMETHING **5** [T] to find or discover someone doing something, especially something wrong: ~ sb doing sth *I caught her smoking in the bathroom.* ◆ *You wouldn't catch me working* (= I would never work) *on a Sunday!* ◆ ~ yourself doing sth *She caught herself wondering whether she had made a mistake.* ◆ ~ sb + adv./prep. *He was caught with bomb-making equipment in his home.* ◆ *thieves caught in the act* ◆ *You've caught me at a bad time* (= at a time when I am busy).
▸ BE IN TIME **6** [T] ~ sb/sth to be in time to do something, talk to someone, etc.: *I caught him just as he was leaving the building.* ◆ *I was hoping to catch you at home* (= to telephone you at home when you were there). ◆ *The disease can be treated provided it's caught* (= discovered) *early enough.* ◆ (*informal*) *Bye! I'll catch you later* (= speak to you again later).
▸ BUS/TRAIN/PLANE **7** [T] ~ sth to be in time for a bus, train, plane, etc. and get on it: *We caught the 12:15 from Grand Central.* ◆ *I have to go—I have a train to catch.*
▸ HAPPEN UNEXPECTEDLY **8** [T] ~ sb to happen unexpectedly and put someone in a difficult situation: *His arrival caught me by surprise.* ◆ *She got caught in a thunderstorm.*
▸ SEE/HEAR **9** [T] ~ sth (*informal*) to see or hear something; to attend something: *Let's eat now and maybe we could catch a movie later.* ➋ thesaurus box at SEE **10** [T] ~ sth to hear or understand something: *Excuse me, I didn't catch what you said.*
▸ ILLNESS **11** [T] to get an illness: ~ sth *to catch the measles* ◆ ~ sth from sb *I think I must have caught this cold from you.*
▸ BECOME STUCK **12** [I, T] to become stuck in or on something;

to make something become stuck: ~ (in/on sth) *Her dress caught on a nail.* ◆ ~ sth (in/on sth) *He caught his thumb in the door.*
▸ HIT **13** [T] to hit someone or something: ~ sb/sth + adv./ prep. *The stone caught him on the side of the head.*
▸ NOTICE **14** [T] ~ sth to notice something only for a moment: *She caught sight of a car in the distance.* ◆ *He caught a glimpse of himself in the mirror.* ◆ *I caught a look of surprise on her face.* ◆ *He caught a whiff of her perfume.*
▸ INTEREST **15** [T] ~ sb's interest, imagination, attention, etc. if something **catches** your interest, etc., you notice it and feel interested in it
▸ SHOW ACCURATELY **16** [T] ~ sth to show or describe something accurately SYN CAPTURE: *The artist has caught her smile perfectly.*
▸ LIGHT **17** [T] ~ sth if something **catches** the light or the light **catches** it, the light shines on it and makes it shine too: *The knife gleamed as it caught the light.*
▸ BURN **18** [T, I] ~ (fire) to begin to burn: *The wooden rafters caught fire.* ◆ *These logs are wet—they won't catch.*
   IDM **catch your breath 1** to stop breathing for a moment because of fear, shock, etc. **2** to breathe normally again after running or doing some tiring exercise **catch your death (of cold)** (*old-fashioned, informal*) to catch a very bad cold **catch sb's eye** to attract someone's attention: *Can you catch the waiter's eye?* **catch hell** (also **catch it, get it**) (*informal*) to be punished or spoken to angrily about something: *If your dad finds out you'll really catch hell!* **catch sb napping** to get an advantage over someone by doing something when they are not expecting it and not ready for it **catch sb on the hop** (*informal*) to surprise someone by doing something when they are not expecting it and not ready for it **catch sb red-handed** to catch someone in the act of doing something wrong or committing a crime **catch sb with their pants down** (*informal*) to arrive or do something when someone is not expecting it and not ready, especially when they are in an embarrassing situation ➋ more at BALANCE *n.*, FANCY *n.*, ROCK *n.*, SHORT *adv.*

   PHR V ˈcatch at sth = CLUTCH AT STH ˌcatch ˈon to become popular or fashionable: *He invented a new game, but it never really caught on.* ˌcatch ˈon (to sth) (*informal*) to understand something: *He is very quick to catch on to things.* ˌcatch sb ˈout **1** to surprise someone and put them in a difficult position: *Many investors were caught out by the fall in share prices.* **2** to show that someone does not know much or is doing something wrong: *They tried to catch her out with a difficult question.* ˌcatch ˈup (on sth) **1** to spend extra time doing something because you have not done it earlier: *I have a lot of work to catch up on.* **2** to find out about things that have happened: *We spent the evening catching up on each other's news.* be/get ˌcaught ˈup in sth to become involved in something, especially when you do not want to be: *Innocent passersby got caught up in the riots.* ˌcatch ˈup (with sb) **1** to reach someone who is ahead by going faster: *Go on ahead. I'll catch up with you.* **2** to reach the same level or standard as someone who was better or more advanced: *After missing the fall semester, he had to work hard to catch up.* ˌcatch ˈup with sb **1** to finally start to cause problems for someone after they have managed to avoid this for some time: *She was terrified that one day her old problems would catch up with her.* **2** if the police or authorities **catch up with** someone, they find and punish them after some time: *The law caught up with him years later when he had moved to Spain.*

● *noun*
▸ OF BALL **1** [C] an act of catching something, for example a ball: *to make a great catch*
▸ AMOUNT CAUGHT **2** [C] the total amount of things that are caught: *a huge catch of fish*
▸ FASTENING **3** [C] a device used for fastening something: *a catch on the door* ◆ *safety catches for the windows*
▸ DIFFICULTY **4** [C, usually sing.] a hidden difficulty or disadvantage: *All that money for two hours of work—what's the catch?*
▸ CHILD'S GAME **5** [U] a child's game in which two people throw a ball to each other

▸ **PERSON 6** [sing.] (*old-fashioned*) a person that other people see as a good person to marry, employ, etc.
IDM **(a) catch-22 | a catch-22 situation** (*informal*) a difficult situation from which there is no escape because you need to do one thing before doing a second, but you need to do the second thing before you can do the first: *I can't get a job because I don't have anywhere to live, but I can't afford a place to live until I get a job—it's a catch-22 situation.*

'catch-all *noun* **1** a group or description that includes different things and that does not state clearly what is included or not **2** a thing for holding many small objects ▸ **'catch-all** *adj.* [only before noun]: *a catch-all phrase/term*

catch-er /ˈkætʃər/ *noun* **1** (in baseball) the player who stands behind the BATTER and catches the ball if he or she does not hit it ⊃ picture at BASEBALL **2** (usually in compounds) a person or thing that catches something: *a dog catcher*

catch-ing /ˈkætʃɪŋ/ *adj.* [not before noun] **1** (of a disease) easily caught by one person from another **SYN** INFECTIOUS **2** (of an emotion or a mood) passing quickly from one person to another **SYN** INFECTIOUS: *Try to be as enthusiastic as possible (enthusiasm is catching)!*

catch-line /ˈkætʃlaɪn/ *noun* (*technical*) a short line of text which can be easily noticed, for example at the top of a page

catch-ment ar-e-a /ˈkætʃmənt ˌeriə/ (also **catch-ment**) *noun* **1** the area from which a school takes its students **2** (*technical*) the area from which rain flows into a particular river or lake

catch-pen-ny /ˈkætʃˌpeni/ *adj.* (*old-fashioned*) (of a product or service) produced or provided just to make money, without being of good quality

catch-phrase /ˈkætʃfreɪz/ *noun* a popular phrase that is connected with the politician or entertainer who used it and made it famous

'catch-up *noun* [U] the act of trying to reach the same level or standard as someone who is ahead of you: *It was a month of catch-up for them.*
IDM **play catch-up** to try to equal someone that you are competing against in a sport or game, in business or politics: *After our bad start to the season we were always playing catch-up.*

catch-y /ˈkætʃi/ *adj.* (**catch-i-er**, **catch-i-est**) (*informal*) (of music or the words of an advertisement) pleasing and easily remembered: *a catchy tune/slogan*

'cat door *noun* a hole cut in the bottom of the door to a house, covered by a piece of plastic that swings, so a pet cat can go in and out

cat-e-chism /ˈkætəˌkɪzəm/ *noun* [usually sing.] a set of questions and answers that are used for teaching people about the beliefs of the Christian religion

cat-e-gor-i-cal /ˌkætəˈɡɔrɪkl/ *adj.* [usually before noun] (*formal*) expressed clearly and in a way that shows that you are very sure about what you are saying: *to make a categorical statement* ♦ *to give a categorical assurance* ▸ **cat-e-gor-i-cally** /-kli/ *adv.*: *He categorically rejected our offer.*

cat-e-go-rize **AWL** /ˈkætəɡəˌraɪz/ *verb* to put people or things into groups according to what type they are **SYN** CLASSIFY: *~ sb/sth Participants were categorized according to age.* ♦ *~ sb/sth as sth His latest work cannot be categorized as either a novel or an autobiography.* ▸ **cat-e-go-ri-za-tion** **AWL** /ˌkætəɡərəˈzeɪʃn/ *noun* [C, U]

cat-e-go-ry 🔑 **AWL** /ˈkætəˌɡɔri/ *noun* (*pl.* **cat-e-go-ries**) a group of people or things with particular features in common **SYN** CLASS: *Students over 25 fall into a different category.* ♦ *The results can be divided into three main categories.*

ca-ter /ˈkeɪtər/ *verb* [I, T] to provide food and drinks for a social event: *~ for sb/sth Most of our work now involves catering for weddings.* ♦ *~ sth Who will be catering the party?*

PHR V **'cater for sb/sth** to provide the things that a particular person or situation needs or wants: *The class caters for all ability ranges.* **'cater to sb/sth** to provide the things that a particular type or person wants, especially things that you do not approve of: *They only publish novels which cater to the mass market.*

ca-ter-er /ˈkeɪtərər/ *noun* a person or company whose job is to provide food and drinks at a business meeting or for a special occasion such as a wedding

ca-ter-ing /ˈkeɪtərɪŋ/ *noun* [U] the work of providing food and drinks for meetings or social events: *Who did the catering for your son's bar mitzvah?*

cat-er-pil-lar /ˈkætəˌpɪlər; ˈkætər-/ *noun* a small creature like a WORM with legs, that develops into a BUTTERFLY or MOTH (= flying insects with large, sometimes brightly colored, wings). Caterpillars eat the leaves of plants. ⊃ picture at ANIMAL

cat-er-waul /ˈkætərˌwɔl/ *verb* [I] to make the loud unpleasant noise that is typical of a cat

cat-fight /ˈkætfaɪt/ *noun* (*informal*) a fight between women

cat-fish /ˈkætfɪʃ/ *noun* (*pl.* **cat-fish**) a large fish with long stiff hairs, like a cat's WHISKERS, around its mouth. There are several types of catfish, most of which are FRESHWATER fish.

cat-gut /ˈkætɡʌt/ *noun* [U] thin strong string made from animals' INTESTINES and used in making musical instruments

ca-thar-sis /kəˈθɑrsəs/ *noun* [U, C] (*pl.* **ca-thar-ses** /-siz/) (*technical*) the process of releasing strong feelings, for example through plays or other artistic activities, as a way of providing relief from anger, suffering, etc. ▸ **ca-thar-tic** /kəˈθɑrtɪk/ *adj.*: *It was a cathartic experience.*

ca-the-dral /kəˈθidrəl/ *noun* the main church of a district, under the care of a BISHOP (= a priest of high rank): *St. Paul's Cathedral*

cath-e-ter /ˈkæθətər/ *noun* a thin tube that is put into the body in order to remove liquid such as URINE

cath-ode /ˈkæθoʊd/ *noun* (*technical*) the ELECTRODE in an electrical device where REDUCTION occurs; the negative electrode in an electrolytic (ELECTROLYTE) cell and the positive electrode in a battery ⊃ compare ANODE

'cathode ray ˌtube *noun* a VACUUM tube inside a television or computer screen, etc. from which a stream of ELECTRONS produces images on the screen

Cath-o-lic /ˈkæθlɪk/ *noun* = ROMAN CATHOLIC: *They're Catholics.* ▸ **Ca-thol-i-cism** /kəˈθɑləˌsɪzəm/ *noun* [U] = ROMAN CATHOLIC

cath-o-lic /ˈkæθlɪk/ *adj.* **1 Catholic** = ROMAN CATHOLIC: *Are they Catholic or Protestant?* ♦ *a Catholic church* **2** (*formal*) including many or most things: *to have catholic tastes* (= like many different things)

cat-i-on /ˈkætˌaɪən/ *noun* (*chemistry, physics*) an ION with a positive electrical CHARGE ⊃ compare ANION

cat-kin /ˈkætkɪn/ *noun* a long, thin, hanging bunch, or short, standing group of soft flowers on the branches of trees such as the WILLOW

cat-nap /ˈkætnæp/ *noun* a short sleep ▸ **cat-nap** *verb* (-pp-) [I]

cat-nip /ˈkætnɪp/ (also **cat-mint** /ˈkætmɪnt/) *noun* [U] a plant that has white flowers with purple spots, leaves covered with small hairs, and a smell that is attractive to cats

cat-o'-nine-tails /ˌkæt ə ˈnaɪn teɪlz/ *noun* [sing.] a WHIP made of nine strings with knots in them, that was used to punish prisoners in the past

'CAT scan /ˈkæt skæn/ (also **CT scan**) *noun* a medical examination that uses a computer to produce an image of the inside of someone's body from X-RAY or ULTRASOUND pictures ⊃ compare MRI

'cat's ˈcradle *noun* **1** [U] a game in which you wrap string around the fingers of both hands to make different

t **tea**   ţ **butter**   d **did**   k **cat**   g **got**   tʃ **chin**   dʒ **June**   f **fall**

patterns **2** [C] a pattern made with string in a game of cat's cradle

cat·suit /ˈkætsut/ *noun* a piece of women's clothing that fits closely and covers the body and legs

cat·sup = KETCHUP

cat·tail /ˈkætteɪl/ *noun* a tall plant that grows in wet areas and has long flat leaves, and a long, dark brown head of many tiny flowers

cat·te·ry /ˈkætəri/ *noun* (*pl.* **cat·te·ries**) a place where people can pay to leave their cats to be cared for while they are away

cat·tle 🔑 /ˈkætl/ *noun* [pl.]
cows and BULLS that are kept as farm animals for their milk or meat: *a herd of cattle* ♦ *twenty head of cattle* (= twenty cows) ♦ *dairy/beef cattle* ⊃ collocations at FARMING

'cattle call *noun* (*informal*) an event at which many people try to get parts in a play, movie, or other production by giving a short performance **SYN** AUDITION

'cattle ˌguard *noun* metal bars that are placed over a hole that has been made in the road. Cars can pass over the metal bars but animals such as sheep and cows cannot.

cat·tle·man /ˈkætlmən/ *noun* (*pl.* **cat·tle·men** /-mən/) a person who owns or takes care of cattle

cat·ty /ˈkæti/ *adj.* (**cat·ti·er, cat·ti·est**) (*informal*) (of a woman) saying unkind things about other people **SYN** SPITEFUL: *a catty comment* ► **cat·ti·ness** *noun* [U]

catty-ˌcorner(ed) *adj., adv.* (*informal*) = KITTY-CORNER(ED)

CATV /ˌsi eɪ ti ˈvi/ *abbr.* community antenna television (= cable television)

cat·walk /ˈkætwɔk/ *noun* **1** (also **run·way**) the long stage that models walk on during a fashion show ⊃ collocations at FASHION **2** a narrow platform for people to walk on, for example along the outside of a building or a bridge

Cau·ca·sian /kɔˈkeɪʒn/ *noun* a member of any of the races of people who have pale skin ► **Cau·ca·sian** *adj.*

cau·cus /ˈkɔkəs/ *noun, verb*
● *noun* **1** a meeting of the members or leaders of a political party to choose candidates or to decide policy; the members or leaders of a political party as a group **2** a group of people with similar interests, often within a larger organization or political party: *the Congressional Black Caucus*
● *verb* [I, T] **~ (sb)** to meet in a caucus or other group to discuss something

caught *pt, pp* of CATCH

caul·dron (also **cal·dron**) /ˈkɔldrən/ *noun* a large deep pot for boiling liquids or cooking food over a fire: *a witch's cauldron*

cau·li·flow·er /ˈkɔliˌflaʊər; ˈkɑ-/ *noun* [U, C] a vegetable with green leaves around a large hard white head of flowers: *Do you like cauliflower?* ♦ *steamed cauliflower* ⊃ picture at FRUIT

'cauliflower ˈear *noun* an ear that is permanently swollen because it has been hit many times

caulk /kɔk/ *verb, noun*
● *verb* **~ sth** to fill the holes or cracks in something, especially a ship, with a substance that keeps out water
● *noun* (also **caulk·ing**) [U] a substance that keeps out water and is used in building work and repairs to fill holes and cracks

caus·al /ˈkɔzl/ *adj.* **1** (*formal*) connected with the relationship between two things, where one causes the other to happen: *the causal relationship between poverty and disease* **2 ~ conjunction/connective** (*grammar*) a word such as *because* that introduces a statement about the cause of something ► **caus·al·ly** /ˈkɔzəli/: *Are the two factors causally connected?*

cau·sal·i·ty /kɔˈzæləti/ (also **cau·sa·tion**) *noun* [U] (*formal*) the relationship between something that happens and the reason for it happening; the principle that nothing can happen without a cause

cau·sa·tion /kɔˈzeɪʃn/ *noun* [U] (*formal*) **1** the process of one event causing or producing another event **2** = CAUSALITY

caus·a·tive /ˈkɔzətɪv/ *adj.* **1** (*formal*) acting as the cause of something: *Smoking is a causative factor in several major diseases.* **2** (*grammar*) a **causative verb** expresses a cause, for example *sharpen* which means "to cause to become sharp" ⊃ compare ERGATIVE, INCHOATIVE

'cause /kəz; kʌz; kɔz/ *conj.* (*informal*) because: *I can't see her at all, 'cause it's too dark.*

cause 🔑 /kɔz/ *noun, verb*
● *noun* **1** [C] the person or thing that makes something happen: *Unemployment is a major cause of poverty.* ♦ *There was discussion about the fire and its likely cause.* ♦ *Drinking and driving is one of the most common causes of traffic accidents.* ♦ *There is no simple cause-and-effect relationship between these two events.* **2** [U] **~ (for sth)** a reason for having particular feelings or behaving in a particular way: *There is no cause for concern.* ♦ *The food was excellent—I had no cause for complaint.* ♦ *with/without good cause* (= with/without a good reason) **3** [C] an organization or idea that people support or fight for: *Animal welfare advocates raised $70,000 for their cause last year.* ♦ *a good cause* (= an organization that does good work, such as a charity) ♦ *campaigning for the Republican cause* ⊃ see also LOST CAUSE **4** [C] (*law*) a case that goes to court
IDM **be for/in a good cause** worth doing, because it is helping other people ⊃ more at COMMON *adj.*
● *verb* to make something happen, especially something bad or unpleasant: **~ sth** *Do they know what caused the fire?* ♦ *Are you causing trouble again?* ♦ *deaths caused by dangerous driving* ♦ **~ sth for sb** *The bad weather is causing problems for many farmers.* ♦ **~ sb sth** *The project is still causing him a lot of problems.* ♦ **~ sth to do sth** *The poor harvest caused prices to rise sharply.*

LANGUAGE BANK

cause

X causes Y

- Childhood obesity can **cause/lead to** long-term health problems.
- Changes in lifestyle and diet over the last twenty years have **caused/led to/resulted in** a sharp increase in childhood obesity.
- Several factors, including changes in diet and lifestyle, **have contributed to** the increase in childhood obesity.
- Research suggests that fast food and soft drinks directly **contribute to** childhood obesity.
- Genetics, lifestyle, and diet **are** all important **factors** in cases of childhood obesity.
- Even small changes in lifestyle and diet can **bring about** significant weight loss.

⊃ Language Banks at BECAUSE OF, CONSEQUENTLY, THEREFORE

---

cause célèbre /ˌkɔz səˈlɛb; -səˈlɛbrə/ *noun* (from *French*) (*pl.* **causes célèbres** /ˌkɔz səˈlɛb; -səˈlɛbrə/) an issue that attracts a lot of attention and is supported by a lot of people

cause·way /ˈkɔzweɪ/ *noun* a raised road or path across water or wet ground

caus·tic /ˈkɔstɪk/ *adj.* **1** critical in a bitter or SARCASTIC way **SYN** SCATHING: *caustic comments/wit* **2** (of a chemical substance) able to destroy or dissolve other substances **SYN** CORROSIVE ► **caus·ti·cally** /-kli/ *adv.*

ˌcaustic ˈsoda *noun* [U] a chemical used in making paper and soap

cau·ter·ize /ˈkɔtəˌraɪz/ *verb* **~ sth** (*medical*) to burn a wound, using a chemical or heat, in order to stop the loss of blood or to prevent infection

cau·tion /'kɔʃn/ *noun, verb*
- **noun 1** [U] care that you take in order to avoid danger or mistakes; not taking any risks: *extreme/great caution* ◆ *Statistics should be treated with caution.* ◆ *Use caution* (= Be careful) *when you drive on icy roads.* ⊃ thesaurus box at CARE **2** [U, sing.] (*formal*) a warning or a piece of advice about a possible danger or risk: *a word/note of caution* ◆ *He offered a caution: "We can't say 100 percent this will succeed."*
  IDM throw caution to the wind(s) to stop caring about how dangerous something might be; to start taking risks
- **verb** [I, T] to warn someone about the possible dangers or problems of something: ~ **against sth** *I would caution against getting too involved.* ◆ ~ **sb against/about sth** *Sam cautioned him against making a hasty decision.* ◆ ~ **(sb) that...** *The government cautioned that pay increases could lead to job losses.* ◆ ~ **sb to do sth** *Employees were cautioned to be careful about what they said to people outside the company.* ◆ ~ **(sb) + speech** *"I'd be careful if I were you," she cautioned (him).*

cau·tion·ar·y /'kɔʃə,nɛri/ *adj.* giving advice or a warning: *a cautionary tale about the problems of buying a computer* ◆ *In her conclusion, the author sounds a cautionary note.*

cau·tious /'kɔʃəs/ *adj.* being careful about what you say or do, especially to avoid danger or mistakes; not taking any risks: *The government has been cautious in its response to the report.* ◆ *They've taken a very cautious approach.* ◆ *They expressed cautious optimism about a solution to the crisis.* ◆ ~ **about sb/sth** | ~ **about doing sth** *He was very cautious about committing himself to anything.* **ANT** RECKLESS
  ▶ **cau·tious·ly** *adv.*: *She looked cautiously around and then walked away from the house.* ◆ *I'm cautiously optimistic.*
  cau·tious·ness *noun* [U]

WHICH WORD?

cautious • careful
- A **cautious** person is nervous that something may be dangerous or unwise, so they do it only very slowly or after a lot of thought. (antonym = **reckless**)
- A **careful** person is not nervous but does take extra care to make sure that everything is correct or nothing goes wrong. (antonym = **careless**)

Notice also:
- *Be careful/Use caution when you drive on icy roads.*
- *Caution/Warning — thin ice.*

ca·va /'kɑvə/ *noun* [U, C] a type of SPARKLING white wine (= with bubbles) from Spain

cav·al·cade /,kævl'keɪd; 'kævl,keɪd/ *noun* a line of people on horses or in vehicles forming part of a ceremony

cav·a·lier /,kævə'lɪr/ *adj.* [usually before noun] not caring enough about something important or about the feelings of other people: *The government takes a cavalier attitude to the problems of prison overcrowding.* ▶ **cav·a·lier·ly** *adv.*

cav·al·ry /'kævlri/ *noun* usually **the cavalry** [sing.] (in the past) the part of the army that fought on horses; the part of the modern army that uses ARMORED vehicles

cave /keɪv/ *noun, verb*
- **noun** a large hole in the side of a hill or under the ground: *the mouth* (= the entrance) *of the cave* ◆ *a cave-dweller* (= a person who lives in a cave)
- **verb**
  PHR V ,cave 'in (on sb/sth) (of a roof, wall, etc.) to fall down and toward the center: *The ceiling suddenly caved in on top of them.* ⊃ related noun CAVE-IN ,cave 'in (to sth) to finally do what someone wants after you have been strongly opposing them: *The President is unlikely to cave in to demands for a public investigation.* ⊃ see also CAVING

ca·ve·at /'kævi,ɑt; 'kævi,æt; 'kɑvi,ɑt/ *noun* (*formal*, from *Latin*) a warning that particular things need to be considered before something can be done

ca·ve·at emp·tor /,kæviɑt 'ɛmptɔr; ,kæviæt-; ,kɑviɑt-/ *noun* (from *Latin*) the principle that a person who buys something is responsible for finding any faults in the thing they buy

'cave-in *noun* the fact of something suddenly collapsing

cave·man /'keɪvmæn/ *noun* (*pl.* **cave·men** /-mɛn/) **1** a person who lived in a CAVE thousands of years ago **2** (*informal*) a man who behaves in an aggressive way

'cave ,painting *noun* a PREHISTORIC painting on the walls of a CAVE, often showing animals and hunting scenes

cav·er /'keɪvər/ (also spe·lunk·er) *noun* a person who goes into CAVES under the ground as a sport or hobby ⊃ compare SPELEOLOGIST

cav·ern /'kævərn/ *noun* a CAVE, especially a large one

cav·ern·ous /'kævərnəs/ *adj.* (*formal*) (of a room or space) very large and often empty and/or dark; like a CAVE

cav·i·ar /'kævi,ɑr/ *noun* [U] the eggs of some types of fish, especially the STURGEON, that are preserved using salt and eaten as a very special and expensive type of food

cav·il /'kævl/ *verb* [I] ~ **(at sth)** (*formal*) to make unnecessary complaints about something **SYN** QUIBBLE

cav·ing /'keɪvɪŋ/ (also spe·lunk·ing) *noun* [U] the sport or activity of going into CAVES under the ground: *He had always wanted to go caving.* ⊃ picture at HOBBY

cav·i·ty /'kævəti/ *noun* (*pl.* **cav·i·ties**) **1** a hole in a tooth **2** a hole or empty space inside something solid: *the abdominal cavity*

'cavity ,wall *noun* a wall consisting of two walls with a space between them, designed to prevent heat from escaping: *cavity wall insulation*

cav·ort /kə'vɔrt/ *verb* [I] + **adv./prep.** to jump or move around in a noisy, excited, and often sexual way: *The photos showed her cavorting on the beach with her new boyfriend.*

caw /kɔ/ *noun* the unpleasant sound that is made by birds such as CROWS and ROOKS ▶ **caw** *verb* [I]

cay·enne /kaɪ'ɛn; keɪ-/ (also ,cayenne 'pepper) *noun* [U] a type of red pepper used in cooking to give a hot flavor to food

cay·man /'keɪmən/ = CAIMAN

CB /,si 'bi/ *noun* [U] the abbreviation for "Citizens' Band" (a range of waves on a radio on which people can talk to each other over short distances, especially when driving): *A truck driver used his CB radio to call for help.*

CBO /,si bi 'ou/ *abbr.* Congressional Budget Office (a government agency that provides economc data to the U.S. Congress and helps to estimate the federal budget)

CBS /,si bi 'ɛs/ *abbr.* Columbia Broadcasting System (a recording and broadcasting company that produces records, television programs, etc.)

CBT /,si bi 'ti/ *abbr.* computer-based testing (a method of giving a standard test using a computer or other electronic device, that records and sometimes scores the responses)

cc /,si 'si/ *abbr., verb*
- **abbr. 1** carbon copy (to) (used on business letters and e-mails to show that a copy is being sent to another person): *to Luke Peters, cc: Janet Gold* **2** cubic centimeter(s): *an 850cc engine*
- **verb** (cc's, cc'ing, cc'ed, cc'ed /,si 'sid/) ~ **sth (to sb)** | ~ **sb sth** (*informal*) to send someone a copy of a letter or e-mail message that you are sending to someone else: *Her message was sent to the company president and cc'ed to us.*

CCRA /,si si ɑr 'eɪ/ *abbr.* Canada Customs and Revenue Agency (the department of the Canadian government that deals with personal income tax, and with taxes on goods that are bought and sold)

CCTV /,si si ti 'vi/ *abbr.* CLOSED-CIRCUIT TELEVISION

CD /,si 'di/ *noun*
1 (also disk) the abbreviation for "compact disc" (a small disk on which sound or information is recorded. CDs are played on a special machine called a **CD player**): *His albums*

| h **hat** | m **man** | n **no** | ŋ **sing** | l **leg** | r **red** | y **yes** | w **wet** |

are available **on CD** and online. ➲ collocations at MUSIC **2** the abbreviation for "certificate of deposit" (a certificate issued by a bank guaranteeing a particular amount of interest to a person leaving money in the bank for a particular length of time)

ˈCD ˌburner (also **ˌCD ˌwriter**) *noun* a piece of equipment used for copying sound or information from a computer onto a CD

CD-I /ˌsi di ˈaɪ/ *noun* **1** [U] the abbreviation for "compact disk interactive" (a MULTIMEDIA system that uses CDs that can react to instructions given by the user) **2** [C] the type of CD that this type of system uses

CD-R /ˌsi di ˈɑr/ *noun* [C, U] the abbreviation for "compact disk recordable" (a CD on which information, sound, and pictures can be recorded once only)

Cdr. (also **CDR**) *abbr.* (in writing) COMMANDER: *Cdr. (John) Stone*

CD-ROM /ˌsi di ˈrɑm/ *noun* [C, U] the abbreviation for "compact disk read-only memory" (a CD on which large amounts of information, sound, and pictures can be stored, for use on a computer): *The software package contains 5 CD-ROMs.* ◆ *The encyclopedia is available on CD-ROM.* ◆ *a CD-ROM drive* (= in a computer) ➲ picture at COMPUTER ➲ compare ROM

CD-RW /ˌsi di ɑr ˈdʌblyu; -ˈdʌbəyu/ *noun* [C, U] the abbreviation for "compact disk rewritable" (a CD on which information, sound, and pictures can be recorded and removed more than once)

CDT /ˌsi di ˈti/ *abbr.* CENTRAL DAYLIGHT TIME

C.E. (also **CE**) /ˌsi ˈi/ *abbr.* Common Era (the period since the birth of Christ when the Christian CALENDAR starts counting years). C.E. can be used to give dates in the same way as A.D. ➲ compare A.D., B.C., B.C.E.

cease AWL /sis/ *verb* [I, T] (*formal*)
to stop happening or existing; to stop something from happening or existing: *Welfare payments cease as soon as an individual starts a job.* ◆ ~ **to do sth** *You never cease to amaze me!* ◆ ~ **sth** *They voted to cease contributions immediately.* ◆ *He ordered his men to cease fire* (= stop shooting). ◆ ~ **doing sth** *The company ceased trading in June.* ➲ see also CESSATION
IDM **cease and desist** (*law*) used in official orders to tell someone to stop doing something ➲ more at WONDER *n.*

cease-fire /ˈsisˌfaɪər/ *noun* a time when enemies agree to stop fighting, usually while a way is found to end the fighting permanently SYN TRUCE: *a call for an immediate cease-fire.* ◆ *Observers have reported serious violations of the cease-fire.* ➲ collocations at WAR

cease-less AWL /ˈsisləs/ *adj.* (*formal*) not stopping; seeming to have no end SYN CONSTANT, INTERMINABLE ▶ **cease-less-ly** *adv.*

ce-cum /ˈsikəm/ *noun* (*pl.* **ce-ca** /ˈsikə/) a small bag which is part of the INTESTINE, between the small and the large intestine

ce-dar /ˈsidər/ *noun* **1** [C] a tall EVERGREEN tree with wide spreading branches **2** (also **cedar-wood** /ˈsidərˌwʊd/) [U] the hard red wood of the cedar tree, that has a sweet smell

cede /sid/ *verb* ~ **sth (to sb)** (*formal*) to give someone control of something or give them power, a right, etc., especially unwillingly: *Cuba was ceded by Spain to the U.S. in 1898.* ➲ see also CESSION

ce-dil-la /sɪˈdɪlə/ *noun* the mark placed under the letter *c* in French, Portuguese, etc. to show that it is pronounced like an *s* rather than a *k*, as in *français*; a similar mark under *s* in Turkish and some other languages

ceil-ing /ˈsilɪŋ/ *noun*
1 the top inside surface of a room: *She lay on her back staring up at the ceiling.* ◆ *a large room with a high ceiling* **2** the highest limit or amount of something: *price ceilings* ◆ *They raised the ceiling on the federal debt.* ➲ compare FLOOR

3 (*technical*) the greatest height at which a particular aircraft is able to fly ➲ see also GLASS CEILING **IDM** see HIT *v.*

ce-leb /səˈlɛb/ *noun* (*informal*) = CELEBRITY

cel-e-brant /ˈsɛləbrənt/ *noun* **1** a priest who leads a church service, especially the COMMUNION service; a person who attends a service **2** a person who is celebrating something, for example at a party

cel-e-brate /ˈsɛləˌbreɪt/ *verb*
1 [I, T] to show that a day or an event is important by doing something special on it: *Jake passed his exams. We're going out to celebrate.* ◆ ~ **sth** *We celebrated our 25th wedding anniversary in Florence.* ◆ *How do people celebrate New Year's in your country?* **2** [T] ~ **sb/sth** (*formal*) to praise someone or something: *a movie celebrating the life and work of Martin Luther King, Jr.* **3** [T] ~ **sth** to perform a religious ceremony, especially the Christian COMMUNION service

cel-e-bra-ted /ˈsɛləˌbreɪtəd/ *adj.* famous for having good qualities: *a celebrated painter*

cel-e-bra-tion /ˌsɛləˈbreɪʃn/ *noun*
1 [C] a special event that people organize in order to celebrate something: *birthday/wedding celebrations* **2** [U, C] the act of celebrating something: *Her triumph was a cause for celebration.* ◆ *a party in celebration of their fiftieth wedding anniversary* ◆ *The memorial service was a celebration of his life* (= praised what he had done in his life).

cel-e-bra-to-ry /ˈsɛləbrəˌtɔri/ *adj.* celebrating something or marking a special occasion: *a celebratory drink/dinner*

ce-leb-ri-ty /səˈlɛbrəti/ *noun* (*pl.* **ce-leb-ri-ties**) **1** (also *informal* **ce-leb**) [C] a famous person: *TV celebrities* **2** [U] the state of being famous SYN FAME: *Does he find his new celebrity intruding on his private life?*

ce-ler-i-ac /səˈlɛriˌæk; -ˈlɪr-/ *noun* [U] a large white root vegetable that is a type of CELERY and that is eaten raw or cooked

cel-er-y /ˈsɛləri/ *noun* [U] a vegetable with long, crisp, light green STEMS that are often eaten raw: *a stalk of celery* ➲ picture at FRUIT

ce-les-ta /səˈlɛstə/ (also **ce-leste** /səˈlɛst/) *noun* a small musical instrument with a keyboard, that produces a sound like bells

ce-les-tial /səˈlɛstʃəl/ *adj.* [usually before noun] (*formal* or *literary*) of the sky or of heaven: *celestial bodies* (= the sun, moon, stars, etc.) ◆ *celestial light/music* ➲ compare TERRESTRIAL

ce-li-ac dis-ease /ˈsiliæk dɪˌziz/ *noun* [U] a disease in which someone cannot DIGEST food (= break it down in their body) because their body is very sensitive to GLUTEN (= a substance that is found in flour, especially WHEAT flour)

cel-i-bate /ˈsɛləbət/ *adj., noun*
● *adj.* **1** not married and not having sex, especially for religious reasons: *celibate priests* **2** not having sex: *I've been celibate for the past six months.* ▶ **cel-i-ba-cy** /ˈsɛləbəsi/ [U]: *a vow of celibacy*
● *noun* (*formal*) a person who has chosen not to marry; a person who never has sex

cell /sɛl/ *noun*
1 the smallest unit of living matter that can exist on its own. All plants and animals are made up of cells: *blood cells* ◆ *the nucleus of a cell* ➲ see also STEM CELL **2** a room for one or more prisoners in a prison or police station ➲ see also PADDED CELL **3** a small room without much furniture in which a MONK or NUN lives **4** (*informal*) = CELL PHONE **5** a device for producing an electric current, for example by the action of chemicals or light: *a photoelectric cell* **6** a small group of people who work as part of a larger political organization, especially secretly: *a terrorist cell* **7** each of the small sections that together form a larger structure, for example a HONEYCOMB **8** one of the small squares in a SPREADSHEET computer program in which you enter a single piece of data

cel·lar /ˈsɛlər/ noun **1** an underground room often used for storing things: *a root cellar* ⊃ compare BASEMENT **2** = WINE CELLAR ⊃ see also SALT CELLAR

cel·list /ˈtʃɛlɪst/ noun a person who plays the CELLO

cell·mate /ˈsɛlmeɪt/ noun a prisoner with whom another prisoner shares a cell

cel·lo /ˈtʃɛloʊ/ (*pl.* cel·los) (also *formal* vi·o·lon·cel·lo) noun a musical instrument with strings, shaped like a large VIOLIN. The player sits down and holds the cello between his or her knees. ⊃ picture at INSTRUMENT

cel·lo·phane /ˈsɛləˌfeɪn/ noun [U] a thin, transparent, plastic material used for wrapping things

'cell phone 🔑 (also ˌcellular ˈphone, *informal* cell) noun
a telephone that does not have wires and works by radio, that you can carry with you and use anywhere: *cell phone users* ◆ *I talked to her on my cell phone.* ◆ *The use of cellular phones is not permitted on most aircraft.* ◆ *I'll be out all day, but you can reach me on my cell.* ⊃ collocations at PHONE

cel·lu·lar /ˈsɛlyələr/ adj. **1** connected with or consisting of the cells of plants or animals: *cellular structure/processes* **2** connected with a telephone system that works by radio instead of wires: *a cellular network* ◆ *cellular radio*

cel·lu·lite /ˈsɛlyəˌlaɪt; -ˌlit/ noun [U] a type of fat that some people get below their skin, which stops the surface of the skin looking smooth

cel·lu·loid /ˈsɛlyəˌlɔɪd/ noun [U] **1** a thin, transparent, plastic material made in sheets, used in the past for movie film **2** (*old-fashioned*) used as a way of referring to movies

cel·lu·lose /ˈsɛlyəˌloʊs/ noun [U] **1** a natural substance that forms the cell walls of all plants and trees and is used in making plastics, paper, etc. **2** any COMPOUND of cellulose used in making paint, LACQUER, etc.

Cel·si·us /ˈsɛlsiəs/ (also cen·ti·grade) adj. (*abbr.* C) of or using a scale of temperature in which water freezes at 0° and boils at 100°: *the Celsius Scale* ◆ *Bees can raise their body temperature to above 37 degrees Celsius (98.6 degrees Fahrenheit).* ▶ **Cel·si·us** noun [U]: *temperatures in Celsius and Fahrenheit*

Celt /kɛlt; sɛlt/ noun **1** a member of a race of people from western Europe who settled in ancient Britain before the Romans came **2** a person whose ANCESTORS were Celts, especially one from Ireland, Wales, Scotland, Cornwall, or Brittany

Celt·ic /ˈkɛltɪk; ˈsɛltɪk/ adj. connected with the Celts or their language: *Celtic history*

ce·ment /səˈmɛnt/ noun, verb
● noun [U] **1** a gray powder made by burning CLAY and LIME that sets hard when it is mixed with water. Cement is used in building to stick bricks together and to make very hard surfaces. **2** the hard substance that is formed when cement becomes dry and hard: *a floor of cement* ◆ *a cement floor* ⊃ see also CONCRETE, MORTAR **3** a soft substance that becomes hard when dry and is used for sticking things together or filling in holes: *dental cement* (= for filling holes in teeth) **4** (*formal*) something that unites people in a common interest: *values which are the cement of society*
● verb **1** [often passive] **~ A and B (together)** to join two things together using cement, glue, etc. **2 ~ sth** to make a relationship, an agreement, etc. stronger SYN STRENGTHEN: *The President's visit was intended to cement the alliance between the two countries.*

ce·men·ta·tion /ˌsimɛnˈteɪʃn/ noun [U] **1** (*chemistry*) the process of changing a metal by heating it together with a powder **2** (*geology*) the process of grains of sand, etc. sticking together to form SEDIMENTARY rocks

ce'ment ˌmixer (also ˈconcrete ˌmixer) noun a machine with a drum that holds sand, water, and cement and turns to mix them together ⊃ picture at TRUCK

cem·e·ter·y /ˈsɛməˌteri/ noun (*pl.* cem·e·ter·ies) an area of land used for burying dead people, especially one that is not beside a church ⊃ compare CHURCHYARD, GRAVEYARD

ce·no·taph /ˈsɛnəˌtæf/ noun a MONUMENT built in memory of soldiers killed in war who are buried somewhere else

cen·ser /ˈsɛnsər/ noun a container for holding and burning INCENSE (= a substance that produces a pleasant smell), used especially during religious ceremonies

cen·sor /ˈsɛnsər/ noun, verb
● noun a person whose job is to examine books, movies, etc. and remove parts which are considered to be offensive, immoral, or a political threat
● verb **~ sth** to remove the parts of a book, movie, etc. that are considered to be offensive, immoral, or a political threat: *The news reports had been heavily censored.*

cen·so·ri·ous /sɛnˈsɔriəs/ adj. (*formal*) tending to criticize people or things a lot SYN CRITICAL

cen·sor·ship /ˈsɛnsərˌʃɪp/ noun [U] the act or policy of CENSORING books, etc.: *press censorship* ◆ *The decree imposed strict censorship of the media.*

cen·sure /ˈsɛnʃər/ noun, verb
● noun [U] (*formal*) strong criticism: *a vote of censure on the government's foreign policy*
● verb **~ sb (for sth)** (*formal*) to criticize someone severely, and often publicly, because of something they have done SYN REBUKE: *He was censured for leaking information to the press.*

cen·sus /ˈsɛnsəs/ noun (*pl.* cen·sus·es) the process of officially counting something, especially a country's population, and recording various facts; the results of this process: *to take a census* ◆ *According to the 2008 census, there are 15.5 million Asian Americans living in the United States.*

cent 🔑 /sɛnt/ noun (*abbr.* c, ct.)
1 a coin and unit of money worth 1% of $1 SYN PENNY **2** a coin and unit of money worth 1% of the main unit of money in some other countries ⊃ see also PERCENT, RED CENT
IDM **put in your two cents/your two cents' worth** (*informal*) to give your opinion about something, even if other people do not want to hear it

cent. *abbr.* century: *in the 20th cent.*

cen·taur /ˈsɛntɔr/ noun (in ancient Greek stories) a creature with a man's head, arms, and upper body on a horse's body and legs

cen·te·nar·i·an /ˌsɛntəˈnɛriən/ noun a person who is 100 years old or more

cen·ten·ar·y /sɛnˈtɛnəri; ˈsɛntəˌneri/ noun (*pl.* cen·ten·ar·ies) noun = CENTENNIAL: *The club will celebrate its centenary next year.* ⊃ see also BICENTENARY, TERCENTENARY

cen·ten·ni·al /sɛnˈtɛniəl/ (also cen·ten·ar·y) noun the 100th anniversary of an event: *The year 1889 was the centennial of the inauguration of George Washington.* ◆ *the centennial year* ⊃ see also BICENTENNIAL

cen·ter 🔑 (*CanE usually* centre) /ˈsɛntər/ noun, verb
● noun
▷ MIDDLE **1** [C] the middle point or part of something: *the center of a circle* ◆ *a long table in the center of the room* ◆ *chocolates with soft centers*
▷ BUILDING **2** [C] a building or place used for a particular purpose or activity: *a shopping/sports/community center* ◆ *a recreation/rec center* ◆ *the center for International Studies*
▷ TOWN/CITY **3** [C] a place or an area where a lot of people live; a place where a lot of business or cultural activity takes place: *major urban/industrial centers* ◆ *a center of population* ◆ *Small towns in Guatemala serve as economic and cultural centers for the surrounding villages.* **4** [C] = DOWNTOWN: *in the town/city center* ◆ *the center of town* ◆ *a town-center parking lot*
▷ OF EXCELLENCE **5** [C] **~ of excellence** a place where a particular kind of work is done extremely well
▷ OF ATTENTION **6** [C, usually sing.] the point toward which people direct their attention: *Children like to be the center of*

ʌ cup ə about eɪ say aɪ five ɔɪ boy aʊ now oʊ go ər bird

attention. ♦ *The vice president is **at the center of** a political scandal over leaked documents.* ⊃ see also CENTER STAGE

>**-CENTERED 7** (in adjectives) having the thing mentioned as the most important feature or center of attention: *a child-centered approach to teaching* ⊃ see also CENTERED, SELF-CENTERED

>**IN POLITICS 8** usually **the center** [sing.] a MODERATE (= middle) political position or party, between the extremes of LEFT-WING and RIGHT-WING parties

>**IN SPORTS 9** [C] (in some team sports) a player or position in the middle of the field, court, etc. **IDM** see FRONT

● **verb 1** ~ **sth** to move something so that it is in the center of something else: *Carefully center the photograph on the page and glue it in place.* **2** [usually passive] ~ **sth + adv./prep.** to make somewhere the place where an activity or event takes place: *Most of the fighting was centered north of the capital.*

PHR V '**center around/on/upon sb/sth** | '**center sth around/on/upon sb/sth** to be or make someone or something become the person or thing around which most activity, etc. takes place: *State occasions always centered around the king.* ♦ *Discussions were centered on developments in Eastern Europe.* ⊃ picture at SHAPE

ˌcenter 'back (*CanE usually* ˌcentre 'back) (also ˌcenter 'half, *CanE usually* ˌcentre 'half) *noun* (in SOCCER and some other sports) a player or position in the middle of the back line of players

cen·ter·board (*CanE usually* **cen·tre·board**) /ˈsɛntərˌbɔrd/ *noun* a board that can be passed through a hole in the bottom of a SAILBOAT to keep it steady when sailing

cen·tered /ˈsɛntərd/ *adj.* calm, sensible, and emotionally in control: *My family helps to keep me centered.* ⊃ see also CENTER (7)

'center field (*CanE usually* 'centre field) *noun* (in baseball) the central part of the outer area of a baseball field, where one player (called the **center fielder**) stands to catch balls that are hit in that area

cen·ter·fold (*CanE usually* **cen·tre·fold**) /ˈsɛntərˌfoʊld/ *noun* **1** a large picture, often of a young woman with few or no clothes on, folded to form the middle pages of a magazine **2** a person whose picture is the centerfold of a magazine

ˌcenter 'forward (*CanE usually* ˌcentre 'forward) *noun* (in SOCCER and some other sports) a player or position in the middle of the front line of players ⊃ compare CENTER n. (9)

ˌcenter 'half (*CanE usually* ˌcentre 'half) *noun* = CENTER BACK

ˌcenter-'left (*CanE usually* ˌcentre-'left) (also ˌleft-of-'center, *CanE usually* ˌleft-of-'centre) *adj.* (*politics*) supporting both CAPITALISM and gradual social change: *a center-left coalition government* ▶ ˌcenter-'left *noun* [U]: *Most of the center-left will give their support.*

ˌcenter of 'gravity (*CanE usually* ˌcentre of 'gravity) *noun* (*pl.* centers of gravity) the point in an object at which its weight is considered to act

ˌcenter of 'mass (*CanE usually* ˌcentre of 'mass) *noun* [sing.] (*physics*) a point that represents the middle position of the matter in a body or system

cen·ter·piece (*CanE usually* **cen·tre·piece**) /ˈsɛntərˌpis/ *noun* **1** [sing.] the most important item: *This treaty is the centerpiece of the government's foreign policy.* **2** a decoration for the center of a table

ˌcenter-'right (*CanE usually* ˌcentre-'right) (also ˌright-of-'center, *CanE usually* ˌright-of-'centre) *adj.* (*politics*) supporting CAPITALISM and accepting some social change: *Europe's center-right parties* ▶ ˌcenter-'right *noun* [U]: *a politician of the center-right*

'center ˌspread (*CanE usually* 'centre ˌspread) *noun* the two facing middle pages of a newspaper or magazine

ˌcenter 'stage (*CanE usually* ˌcentre 'stage) *noun* [U] **1** the middle part of the stage in a theater: *At center stage stand two folding tables.* **2** an important position where someone or something can easily get people's attention: *Education is taking center stage in the government's plans.* ♦ *This region continues to occupy center stage in world affairs.* ▶ ˌcenter 'stage *adv.*: *She stood center stage to receive the applause.* ♦ *The President said, "We are putting full employment center stage."*

centi- /ˈsɛntə-/ *combining form* (in nouns) **1** hundred: *centipede* **2** (often used in units of measurement) one one-hundredth: *centimeter*

cen·ti·grade /ˈsɛntəˌgreɪd/ *adj.* = CELSIUS: *a temperature of 40 degrees centigrade* ▶ **cen·ti·grade** *noun* [U]: *temperatures in centigrade and Fahrenheit*

cen·ti·gram /ˈsɛntəˌɡræm/ *noun* a unit for measuring weight. There are 100 centigrams in a gram.

cen·ti·li·ter (*CanE usually* **cen·ti·li·tre**) /ˈsɛntəˌlitər/ *noun* (*abbr.* cl) a unit for measuring liquids. There are 100 centiliters in a liter.

cen·ti·me·ter 🔑 (*CanE usually* **cen·ti·me·tre**) /ˈsɛntəˌmitər; ˈsɑn-/ *noun* (*abbr.* cm) a unit for measuring length. There are 100 centimeters in a meter.

cen·ti·pede /ˈsɛntəˌpid/ *noun* a small creature like an insect, with a long thin body, and many legs

cen·tral 🔑 /ˈsɛntrəl/ *adj.*

1 most important: *The central issue is that of widespread racism.* ♦ *She has been a central figure in the campaign.* ♦ *Prevention also plays a central role in traditional medicine.* ♦ *Reducing inflation is central to* (= is an important part of) *the government's economic policy.* ⊃ thesaurus box at MAIN **2** having power or control over other parts: *the central command* (= of an army) ♦ *The organization has a central office in Omaha.* **3** in the center of an area or object: *central California* ♦ *Central America/Europe/Asia* ♦ *the central area of the brain* **4** easily reached from many areas: *The apartment is in a central location—just five minutes from Main Street.* **5** (*phonetics*) (of a vowel) produced with the center of the tongue in a higher position than the front or the back ⊃ compare BACK, FRONT ▶ **cen·tral·i·ty** /sɛnˈtræləti/ *noun* [U] (*formal*): *the centrality of the family as a social institution* **cen·tral·ly** /ˈsɛntrəli/ *adv.*: *The hotel is centrally located near all major attractions.* ♦ *a centrally planned economy* ♦ *Is the house centrally heated* (= does it have central heating)?

ˌCentral A'merica *noun* [U] the part of N. America that consists of Guatemala, Belize, Honduras, El Salvador, Nicaragua, Costa Rica, and Panama ▶ ˌCentral A'merican *adj., noun*

ˌcentral 'bank *noun* a national bank that does business with the government and other banks, and issues the country's coins and paper money

ˌcentral 'government *noun* [U, C] the government of a whole country, rather than LOCAL GOVERNMENT, which is concerned with smaller areas

ˌcentral 'heating *noun* [U] a system for heating a building from one source that then sends the hot water or hot air around the building through pipes ⊃ collocations at DECORATE

the ˌCentral In'telligence ˌAgency *noun* [sing.] = CIA

cen·tral·ism /ˈsɛntrəˌlɪzəm/ *noun* [U] a way of organizing something, such as government or education, that involves one central group of people controlling the whole system ▶ **cen·tral·ist** *adj.*: *centralist control of schools*

cen·tral·ize /ˈsɛntrəˌlaɪz/ *verb* ~ **sth** to give the control of a country or an organization to a group of people in one particular place: *a highly centralized system of government* ▶ **cen·tral·i·za·tion** /ˌsɛntrələˈzeɪʃn/ *noun* [U]: *the centralization of political power*

ˌcentral 'locking *noun* [U] a system for locking a car in which all the doors can be locked or opened at the same time

ˌcentral 'nervous ˌsystem *noun* (*anatomy*) the part of the system of nerves in the body that consists of the brain and the SPINAL CORD ⊃ see also NERVOUS SYSTEM

,central 'processing ,unit *noun* (*computing*) (*abbr.* CPU) the part of a computer that controls all the other parts of the system

,Central 'Standard ,Time *noun* [U] (*abbr.* CST) the time used in winter in the central U.S. and Canada, which is six hours earlier than GMT

'Central ,time *noun* [U] the standard time system that is used in the central part of the U.S. and Canada ⊃ compare ATLANTIC TIME, EASTERN TIME, MOUNTAIN TIME, PACIFIC TIME

cen·tre (*CanE*) = CENTER

-centric /ˈsɛntrɪk/ *suffix* **1** having a particular center: *geo-centric* **2** (often *disapproving*) based on a particular way of thinking: *egocentric* ◆ *ethnocentric*

cen·trif·u·gal /sɛnˈtrɪfyəgl; -ˈtrɪfə-/ *adj.* (*technical*) moving or tending to move away from a center

cen,trifugal 'force *noun* (*physics*) a force that appears to cause an object traveling around a center to fly away from the center and off its CIRCULAR path

cen·tri·fuge /ˈsɛntrəˌfyudʒ/ *noun* a machine with a part that spins around to separate substances, for example liquids from solids, by forcing the heavier substance to the outer edge

cen·trip·e·tal /sɛnˈtrɪpətl/ *adj.* (*technical*) moving or tending to move toward a center

cen·trist /ˈsɛntrɪst/ *noun* a person with political views that are not extreme **SYN** MODERATE ▸ **cen·trist** *adj.*

cen·tu·ri·on /sɛnˈtʊriən/ *noun* (in ancient Rome) an army officer who commanded 100 soldiers

cen·tu·ry 🔑 /ˈsɛntʃəri/ *noun* (*pl.* **cen·tu·ries**) **1** a period of 100 years **2** (*abbr.* c, cent.) any of the periods of 100 years before or after the birth of Christ: *the 20th century* (= A. D.1901–2000 or 1900–1999) ◆ *eighteenth-century writers* **IDM** see TURN *n.*

CEO /ˌsi i ˈoʊ/ *abbr.* chief executive officer (the person with the highest rank in a business company)

cep /sɛp/ *noun* a type of MUSHROOM, which many people consider to be one of the best to eat

ce·phal·ic /səˈfælɪk/ *adj.* (*anatomy*) in or related to the head

ceph·a·lo·pod /ˈsɛfələˌpɑd/ *noun* (*biology*) a type of MOLLUSK with a combined head and body, and large eyes. Cephalopods have arms and/or TENTACLES (= long thin parts like arms), which may have SUCKERS (= round parts that suck) on them. OCTOPUS and SQUIDS are cephalopods.

ce·ram·ic /səˈræmɪk/ *noun* **1** [C, usually pl.] a pot or other object made of CLAY that has been made permanently hard by heat: *an exhibition of ceramics by Picasso* **2** **ce·ram·ics** [U] the art of making and decorating ceramics ▸ **ce·ram·ic** *adj.*: *ceramic tiles*

ce·re·al /ˈsɪriəl/ *noun* **1** [C] one of various kinds of grasses that produce grains that can be eaten or are used to make flour or bread. WHEAT, BARLEY, and RYE are all cereals: *cereal crops* **2** [U] the grain produced by cereal crops **3** [C, U] food made from the grain of cereals, often eaten for breakfast with milk: *breakfast cereal* ◆ *a bowl of cereal*

cer·e·bel·lum /ˌsɛrəˈbɛləm/ *noun* (*pl.* **cer·e·bel·lums** or **cer·e·bel·la** /-ˈbɛlə/) (*anatomy*) the part of the brain at the back of the head that controls the activity of the muscles

ce·re·bral /səˈribrəl; ˈsɛrə-/ *adj.* **1** relating to the brain: *a cerebral hemorrhage* **2** relating to the mind rather than the feelings **SYN** INTELLECTUAL: *His poetry is very cerebral.*

cerebral palsy /ˌsɛrəbrəl ˈpɔlzi/ *noun* [U] a medical condition usually caused by brain damage before or at birth that causes the loss of control of movement in the arms and legs

ce·re·brum /səˈribrəm/ *noun* (*pl.* **ce·re·bra** /-brə/) (*anatomy*) the front part of the brain, responsible for thoughts, emotions, and personality

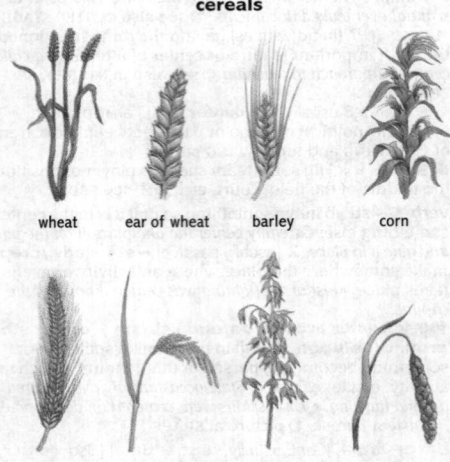

cereals

wheat   ear of wheat   barley   corn

rye   rice   oats   millet

cer·e·mo·ni·al /ˌsɛrəˈmoʊniəl/ *adj., noun*
● *adj.* relating to or used in a ceremony: *ceremonial occasions* ◆ *a ceremonial sword* ▸ **cer·e·mo·ni·al·ly** *adv.*
● *noun* [U, C] the system of rules and traditions that states how things should be done at a ceremony or formal occasion: *The visit was conducted with all due ceremonial.*

cer·e·mo·ni·ous /ˌsɛrəˈmoʊniəs/ *adj.* (*formal*) behaving or performed in an extremely formal way **ANT** UNCEREMONIOUS ▸ **cer·e·mo·ni·ous·ly** *adv.*

cer·e·mo·ny 🔑 /ˈsɛrəˌmoʊni/ *noun* (*pl.* **cer·e·mo·nies**) **1** [C] a public or religious occasion that includes a series of formal or traditional actions: *an award/opening ceremony* ◆ *a wedding/marriage ceremony* ⊃ collocations at MARRIAGE **2** [U] formal behavior; traditional actions and words used on particular formal occasions
IDM **stand on ceremony** to behave formally: *Please don't stand on ceremony* (= Please be natural and relaxed) *with me.* **without ceremony** in a very rough or informal way: *The network dropped her from the show last year without ceremony.* ⊃ see also MASTER OF CEREMONIES

ce·rise /səˈris; -ˈriz/ *adj.* pinkish-red in color ▸ **ce·rise** *noun* [U]

ce·ri·um /ˈsɪriəm/ *noun* [U] (*symb.* Ce) a chemical element. Cerium is a silver-white metal used in the production of glass and CERAMICS.

cert. *abbr.* **1** CERTIFICATE **2** CERTIFY

cer·tain 🔑 /ˈsɔrtn/ *adj., pron.*
● *adj.* **1** that you can rely on to happen or to be true: *The climbers face certain death if the rescue today is unsuccessful.* ◆ *~ (that)… It is certain that they will agree/They are certain to agree.* ◆ *~ to do sth She looks certain to win an Oscar.* ◆ *~ of sth/of doing sth If you want to be certain of getting a ticket, reserve now.* ⊃ thesaurus box at SURE **2** firmly believing something; having no doubts: *~ (that)… She wasn't certain (that) he had seen her.* ◆ *~ of/about sth Are you absolutely certain about this?* ◆ *~ who/where, etc.… I'm not certain who was there.* **3** used to mention a particular thing, person, or group without giving any more details about it or them: *For certain personal reasons, I will not be able to attend.* ◆ *Certain people might disagree with this.* ◆ *They refused to release their hostages unless certain conditions were met.* **4** (*formal*) used with a person's name to show that the speaker does not know the person: *It was a certain Dr. Davis who performed the operation.* **5** slight; noticeable, but difficult to describe: *That's true, to a certain extent.* ◆ *I felt there was a certain coldness in her manner.*

IDM **for certain** without doubt: *I can't say for certain when we'll arrive.* **make certain (that…)** to find out whether something is definitely true: *I think there's a bus at 8 but you'd better call to make certain.* **make certain of sth/of doing sth** to do something in order to be sure that something else will happen: *You'll have to leave soon to make certain of getting there on time.* **of a certain age** if you talk about a person being **of a certain age**, you mean that they are no longer young but not yet old: *The show appeals to an audience of a certain age.*

• *pron.* **certain of…** (*formal*) used for talking about some members of a group of people or things without giving their names: *Certain of those present were unwilling to discuss the matter further.*

cer·tain·ly 🔊 /'sɜrtnli/ *adv.*
1 without doubt **SYN** DEFINITELY: *Without treatment, she will almost certainly die.* ♦ *Certainly, the early years are crucial to a child's development.* ♦ *I'm certainly never going there again.* ➔ **note at** SURELY ➔ **language bank at** NEVERTHELESS
2 (used in answer to questions) of course: *"May I see your passport, Mr. Scott?" "Certainly."* ♦ *"Do you think all this money will change your life?" "Certainly not."*

cer·tain·ty /'sɜrtnti/ *noun* (*pl.* **cer·tain·ties**) **1** [C] a thing that is certain: *political/moral certainties* ♦ *Her return to the team now seems a certainty.* **2** [U] the state of being certain: *There is no certainty that the president's removal would end the civil war.* ♦ *I can't say* **with** *any* **certainty** *where I'll be next week.*

cer·ti·fi·a·ble /ˌsɜrtə'faɪəbl/ *adj.* **1** a person who is **certifiable** can or should be officially stated to be INSANE: (*informal*) *He's certifiable* (= he's crazy). **2** good enough to be officially accepted or recommended **3** clearly true or genuine: *There is little hope for certifiable progress in the stalemate.* ▶ **cer·ti·fi·a·bly** /-əbli/ *adv.*: *certifiably insane*

cer·tif·i·cate 🔊 *noun* /sər'tɪfəkət/ (*abbr.* **cert.**)
1 an official document that may be used to prove that the facts it states are true: *a birth/marriage/death certificate*
2 an official document proving that you have completed a course of study or passed an exam; a qualification obtained after a course of study or an exam: *an elementary teaching certificate*

cer·ti·fi·ca·ted /sər'tɪfəˌkeɪtəd/ *adj.* (*formal*) having the certificate that shows that the necessary training for a particular job has been done

cer·ti·fi·ca·tion /ˌsɜrtəfə'keɪʃn/ *noun* **1** [U] (*technical*) the act of CERTIFYING something: *the medical certification of the cause of death* **2** [C] a document that says a person is a professional and is allowed to do something such as teach or practice law: *She received her teaching certification last month.*

ˌcertified 'check (CanE usually ˌcertified 'cheque) *noun* a check that a bank guarantees

ˌcertified fiˌnancial 'planner *noun* a person whose job is to give financial advice, and who has completed a training course and passed an exam in order to do this

ˌcertified 'mail *noun* [U] a method of sending a letter or package in which the person sending it gets an official note to say it has been mailed and the person receiving it must sign a form when it is delivered: *I'd like to send this (by) certified mail.* ➔ **compare** REGISTERED MAIL

ˌcertified ˌpublic ac'countant *noun* a fully trained and qualified ACCOUNTANT

cer·ti·fy /'sɜrtəˌfaɪ/ *verb* (**cer·ti·fies**, **cer·ti·fy·ing**, **cer·ti·fied**, **cer·ti·fied**) **1** to state officially, especially in writing, that something is true: **~ (that)…** *He handed her a piece of paper certifying (that) she was in good health.* ♦ *This* (= this document) *is to certify that…* ♦ **~ sb/sth + adj.** *She had her farm certified organic.* ♦ **~ sb/sth (as) sth** *The accounts were certified (as) correct by the finance department.* ♦ **~ to be/do sth** *The plants must be certified to be virus free.* **2** [usually passive] **~ sb (as sth)** to give someone an official document proving that they are qualified to work in a particular profession: *He was certified as a geriatric nurse last year.* **3** [usually passive] **~ sb (+ adj.)** (*law*) to officially state that someone is mentally ill, so that they can be given medical treatment: *Patients must be certified before they can be admitted to the hospital.* ▶ **cer·ti·fied** *adj.*

cer·ti·tude /'sɜrtəˌtud/ *noun* [U, C] (*formal*) a feeling of being certain; a thing about which you are certain: *"You will like Rome," he said, with absolute certitude.* ♦ *the collapse of moral certitudes*

ce·ru·le·an /sə'ruliən/ *adj.* (*literary*) deep blue in color

ce·ru·men /sə'rumən/ *noun* [U] (*technical*) a substance like WAX which is produced in the ear **SYN** EARWAX

cer·vi·cal /'sɜrvɪkl/ *adj.* [only before noun] (*anatomy*)
1 connected with the cervix: *cervical cancer* **2** connected with the neck: *the cervical spine*

cer·vix /'sɜrvɪks/ *noun* (*pl.* **cer·vices** /-vəsiz/ or **cer·vixes**) (*anatomy*) the narrow passage at the opening of a woman's UTERUS

ce·sar·e·an /sɪ'zɛriən/ (*also* ceˌsarean 'section, 'C-section) (CanE Cae·sar·e·an, Caeˌsarean 'section) (*also informal* **sec·tion**) *noun* [C, U] a medical operation in which an opening is cut in a woman's body in order to take out a baby: *an emergency cesarean* ♦ *The baby was born by cesarean section.* ♦ *She had to have a C-section.*

ce·si·um /'siziəm/ *noun* [U] (*symb.* **Cs**) a chemical element. Cesium is a soft silver-white metal that reacts strongly in water, used in PHOTOELECTRIC CELL s.

ces·sa·tion /sɛ'seɪʃn/ *noun* [U, C] (*formal*) the stopping of something; a pause in something: *Mexico called for an immediate cessation of hostilities.*

ces·sion /'sɛʃn/ *noun* [U, C] (*formal*) the act of giving up land or rights, especially to another country after a war **SYN** SURRENDER ➔ **see also** CEDE

cess·pool /'sɛspul/ (*also* **cess·pit** /'sɛspɪt/) *noun* **1** a covered hole or container in the ground for collecting waste from a building, especially from the toilets **2** a place where dishonest or immoral people gather: *a cesspool of corruption*

ce·ta·cean /sɪ'teɪʃn/ *adj.*, *noun* (*biology*)
• *adj.* (*also* ce·ta·ceous /sɪ'teɪʃəs/) connected with the group of creatures that includes WHALES and DOLPHINS
• *noun* a WHALE, DOLPHIN, or other sea creature that belongs to the same group

ce·vi·che (also **se·vi·che**) /sɛ'vitʃer; sə-/ noun [U] a dish, originally from South America, made of raw fish that has been left for several hours in a mixture of LIME or lemon juice, oil, and spices

cf. abbr. (in writing) compare

CFC /ˌsi ɛf 'si/ noun [C, U] the abbreviation for "chlorofluoro-ocarbon" (a type of gas used especially in AEROSOLS (= types of containers that release liquid in the form of a spray). CFCs are harmful to the layer of the gas OZONE in the earth's atmosphere.

CFL /ˌsi ɛf 'ɛl/ abbr. Canadian Football League (the organization of professional football teams in Canada)

CFO /ˌsi ɛf 'ou/ abbr. Chief Financial Officer (the person who has the most authority over the finances of a large company)

CGI /ˌsi dʒi 'aɪ/ abbr. computer-generated imagery: The movie combines CGI animation with live-action location shots.

ch. abbr. (in writing) chapter

Cha·blis /ʃæ'bli; ʃə-/ noun [U, C] a type of dry, white, French wine

cha-cha /'tʃɑ tʃɑ/ (also ˌcha-cha-'cha) noun a S. American dance with small fast steps: to dance/do the cha-cha

cha-ching /tʃə 'tʃɪŋ/ exclamation (informal) = KA-CHING

chad /tʃæd/ noun the small piece that is removed when a hole is made in a piece of paper, especially a test paper or BALLOT paper

chad·or /'tʃɑdɔr; tʃɑ'dɔr/ noun a large piece of cloth that covers a woman's head and upper body so that only the face can be seen, worn by some Muslim women

chafe /tʃeɪf/ verb **1** [I, T] if skin **chafes**, or if something **chafes** it, it becomes sore because the thing is rubbing against it: Her wrists chafed where the rope had been. ♦ ~ sth The collar was much too tight and chafed her neck. **2** [I] ~ (at/under sth) (formal) to feel annoyed and impatient about something, especially because it limits what you can do: Young people often go through a phase of chafing under parental control. **3** [T] ~ sth (literary) to rub a part of the body in order to make it warm or restore feeling to it: Kate pulled the blankets over the girl and chafed her hands.

chaff /tʃæf/ noun [U] **1** the outer covering of the seeds of grain such as WHEAT, which is separated from the grain before it is eaten **2** STRAW (= dried STEMS of WHEAT) and HAY (= dried grass) cut up as food for cows **IDM** see WHEAT

chaf·ing dish /'tʃeɪfɪŋ ˌdɪʃ/ noun a metal pan used for keeping food warm at the table

cha·grin /ʃə'grɪn/ noun [U] (formal) a feeling of being disappointed or annoyed ▶ **cha·grined** adj.

chain 🔊 /tʃeɪn/ noun, verb

● **noun**
>METAL RINGS **1** [C, U] a series of connected metal rings, used for pulling or fastening things; a length of chain used for a particular purpose: a short length of chain ♦ She wore a heavy gold chain around her neck. ♦ a bicycle chain ♦ The prisoners were kept **in chains** (= with chains around their arms and legs, to prevent them from escaping). ⊃ see also KEY CHAIN ⊃ picture at BICYCLE, JEWELRY, ROPE
>CONNECTED THINGS **2** [C] a series of connected things or people: to set in motion a **chain of events** ♦ a **chain of command** (= a system in an organization by which instructions are passed from one person to another) ♦ mountain/island chains ♦ Volunteers formed a **human chain** to rescue precious items from the burning house. ⊃ see also FOOD CHAIN
>OF STORES/HOTELS **3** [C] a group of stores or hotels owned by the same company: a chain of supermarkets/a supermarket chain
>RESTRICTION **4** [C, usually pl.] (formal or literary) a thing that restricts someone's freedom or ability to do something: the chains of fear/misery **IDM** see BALL n., LINK n., WEAK

● **verb** [often passive] to fasten something with a chain; to fasten someone or something to another person or thing with a chain, so that they do not escape or get stolen: ~ sb/

sth The doors were always locked and chained. ♦ ~ sb/sth up The dog was chained up for the night. ♦ ~ sb/sth to sb/sth She chained her bicycle to the gate. ♦ (figurative) I've been chained to my desk all week (= because there was so much work).

chain gang noun a group of prisoners chained together and forced to work

chain ˌletter noun a letter sent to several people asking them to make copies of the letter and send them on to more people

ˌchain-link 'fence noun a fence made of wire in a diamond pattern

chain mail (also **mail**) noun [U] ARMOR (= covering to protect the body when fighting) made of small metal rings linked together

ˌchain re'action noun **1** (chemistry, physics) a chemical or nuclear change that forms products which themselves cause more changes and new products **2** a series of events, each of which causes the next: It set off a chain reaction in the international money markets.

chain·saw /'tʃeɪnsɔ/ noun a tool made of a chain with sharp teeth set in it, that is driven by a motor and used for cutting wood

chain-smoke verb [I, T] ~ (sth) to smoke cigarettes continuously, lighting the next one from the one you have just smoked ▶ **ˈchain-ˌsmoker** noun

chain store noun a store that is one of a series of similar stores owned by the same company

chair 🔊 /tʃɛr/ noun, verb

● **noun 1** [C] a piece of furniture for one person to sit on, with a back, a seat, and four legs: a table and chairs ♦ Sit on your chair! ♦ an old man asleep in a chair (= an ARMCHAIR) ⊃ picture on page 235 ⊃ see also ARMCHAIR, DECK CHAIR, EASY CHAIR, HIGH CHAIR, MUSICAL CHAIRS, ROCKING CHAIR, WHEELCHAIR **2** [C] = CHAIRMAN, CHAIRPERSON **3** [C] the person in charge of a department in a university: He is the chair of philosophy at Stanford. **4** the chair [sing.] (informal) = THE ELECTRIC CHAIR

● **verb** ~ sth to act as the chairman or chairwoman of a meeting, discussion, etc.: Who's chairing the meeting?

chair·lift /'tʃɛrlɪft/ noun a series of chairs hanging from a moving cable, for carrying people up and down a mountain

chair·man 🔊 /'tʃɛrmən/ noun (pl. chair·men /-mən/) **1** (also **chair**) the person in charge of a meeting, who tells people when they can speak, etc. **2** the person in charge of a committee, a company, etc.: the chairman of the board of directors ♦ The chairman of the company presented the annual report. ⊃ note at GENDER

chair·man·ship /'tʃɛrmənˌʃɪp/ noun **1** [C] the position of a chairman or chairwoman: the chairmanship of the committee **2** [U] the state of being a chairman or chairwoman: under her skillful chairmanship

chair·per·son /'tʃɛrˌpərsn/ noun (pl. chair·per·sons) (also **chair**) a chairman or chairwoman

chair·wom·an 🔊 /'tʃɛrˌwumən/ noun (pl. chair·women /-ˌwɪmən/) a woman in charge of a meeting, a committee, or an organization ⊃ note at GENDER

chaise /ʃeɪz/ noun **1** = CHAISE LONGUE **2** a CARRIAGE pulled by a horse or horses, used in the past

chaise longue /ˌʃeɪz 'lɔŋ; ʃeɪz 'laundʒ; ˌtʃeɪs-/ noun (pl. chaises longues /ˌʃeɪz 'lɔŋ/) (also **chaise**) (from French) **1** a long low seat with a back and one arm, on which the person sitting can stretch out their legs ⊃ picture at CHAIR **2** (also **chaise 'lounge, ˌloung·er, 'lounge chair**) a long chair with a back that can be vertical for sitting on or flat for lying on outdoors

chak·ra /'tʃʌkrə; 'tʃɑ-/ noun (in YOGA) each of the main centers of spiritual power in the human body

cha·let /ʃæ'leɪ/ noun a wooden house with a roof that slopes steeply down over the sides, usually built in mountain areas, especially in Switzerland

chal·ice /ˈtʃæləs/ *noun* a large cup for holding wine, especially one from which wine is drunk in the Christian COMMUNION service

chalk /tʃɔk/ *noun, verb*
- *noun* **1** [U] a type of soft white stone: *chalk cliffs* **2** [U, C] a substance similar to chalk made into white or colored sticks for writing or drawing: *a piece/stick of chalk* ◆ *drawing diagrams with chalk on the blackboard* ◆ *a box of colored chalks*
- *verb* ~ **sth (up) (on sth)** to write or draw something with chalk: *She chalked (up) the day's menu on the board.* **PHRV** ,chalk ˈup sth (*informal*) to achieve or record a success, points in a game, etc.: *The team chalked up their tenth win this season.* ,chalk sth ˈup to sth (*informal*) to consider that something is caused by something: *We can chalk up that win to a lot of luck.* **IDM** see EXPERIENCE *n.*

chalk·board /ˈtʃɔkbɔrd/ *noun* = BLACKBOARD

ˈchalk talk *noun* a talk or lecture, especially one given by a sports coach to a team, in which the speaker draws diagrams on a BLACKBOARD to explain particular points

chalk·y /ˈtʃɔki/ *adj.* containing chalk or like chalk

chal·lah /ˈhɑlə; ˈxɑlə/ *noun* [U] a type of white bread that is made with egg and often made in a twisted shape, traditionally eaten by Jews on the SABBATH and on holidays

chal·lenge **AWL** /ˈtʃæləndʒ/ *noun, verb*
- *noun* **1** a new or difficult task that tests someone's ability and skill: *an exciting/interesting challenge* ◆ *The role will be the biggest challenge of his acting career.* ◆ *to face a challenge* (= to have to deal with one) ◆ *Destruction of the environment is one of the most **serious challenges** we face.* ◆ *Schools must **meet the challenge** of new technology* (= deal with it successfully). ◆ *We rose to the challenge and figured out a way to do it.* **2** an invitation or a suggestion to someone that they should enter a competition, fight, etc.: *to accept/take up a challenge* ◆ *to mount a challenge* **3** ~ **(to sth)** a statement or an action that shows that someone refuses to accept something and questions whether it is right, legal, etc.: *It was a direct challenge to the president's authority.* ◆ *Their legal challenge was unsuccessful.* **4** a demand that someone stop and provide proof of their identity: *The sentry's challenge forced them to stop and show their identification.* **5** (*law*) an occasion at the beginning of a court case when a lawyer formally questions whether a possible member of a jury is qualified or suitable for that position

chairs

chair

armchair

rocking chair

stool

cushion

sofa (*also* couch, settee)

recliner

chaise longue

deck chair

director's chair

lounger

bench

car seat

high chair

swivel chair

wheelchair

• **verb 1** ~ **sth** to question whether a statement or an action is right, legal, etc.; to refuse to accept something **SYN** DISPUTE: *The story was completely untrue and was successfully challenged in court.* ◆ *She does not like anyone challenging her authority.* ◆ *This discovery challenges traditional beliefs.* ⊃ language bank at ARGUE **2** to invite someone to enter a competition, fight, etc.; to suggest strongly that someone should do something (especially when you think that they might be unwilling to do it): ~ **sb (to sth)** *Mike challenged me to a game of chess.* ◆ ~ **sb to do sth** *The Senate minority leader challenged the Vice President to call a roll-call vote.* **3** ~ **sb** to test someone's ability and skills, especially in an interesting way: *The job doesn't really challenge her.* **4** ~ **sb** to order someone to stop and say who they are or what they are doing: *We were challenged by police at the border.* **5** ~ **sb** (*law*) to formally object to someone serving on a jury because they may not be qualified or suitable for that position

chal·lenged **AWL** /'tʃæləndʒd/ *adj.* (used with an adverb) a polite way of referring to someone who has a disability of some sort: *a competition for physically challenged athletes* ◆ (*humorous*) *I'm financially challenged at the moment* (= I have no money).

chal·leng·er **AWL** /'tʃæləndʒər/ *noun* a person who competes with someone else in sport or in politics for an important position that the other person already holds: *the official challenger for the world championship title*

chal·leng·ing **AWL** /'tʃæləndʒɪŋ/ *adj.* **1** difficult in an interesting way that tests your ability: *challenging work/ questions/problems* ◆ *a challenging and rewarding career as a teacher* ⊃ thesaurus box at DIFFICULT **2** done in a way that invites people to disagree or argue with you, or shows that you disagree with them: *She gave him a challenging look. "Are you really sure?" she demanded.*

cham·ber 🔑 /'tʃeɪmbər/ *noun*
1 [C] (in compounds) a room used for the particular purpose that is mentioned: *a burial chamber* ◆ *Divers transfer from the water to a decompression chamber.* ⊃ see also GAS CHAMBER **2** [C] a space under the ground that is almost completely closed on all sides: *They found themselves in a vast underground chamber.* **3** [C] a space in the body, in a plant, or in a machine, that is separated from the rest: *the chambers of the heart* ◆ *the rocket's combustion chamber* ◆ *the chamber of a gun* (= the part that holds the bullets) **4** **chambers** [pl.] an office used by a judge **5** [C] a room in a public building that is used for formal meetings: *the Senate/ House chamber* ⊃ see also CHAMBER OF COMMERCE **6** [C] one of the parts of a parliament: *the Chamber of Deputies in the Italian parliament* ◆ *Under Senate rules, the chamber must vote on the bill by this Friday.* **7** [C] (*old use*) a bedroom or private room

cham·ber·lain /'tʃeɪmbərlən/ *noun* an official who managed the home and servants of a king, queen, or important family in past centuries

cham·ber·maid /'tʃeɪmbər,meɪd/ *noun* a woman whose job is to clean bedrooms, usually in a hotel

chamber music *noun* [U] CLASSICAL music written for a small group of instruments

Chamber of Commerce *noun* a group of local business people who work together to help business and trade in a particular town or city

chamber of horrors *noun* [sing.] a part of a museum displaying objects used to kill people in a cruel and painful way or scenes showing how they died

chamber orchestra *noun* a small group of musicians who play CLASSICAL music together

chamber pot *noun* a round container that people in the past had in the bedroom and used to URINATE in at night

cha·me·le·on /kə'milyən/ *noun* **1** a small LIZARD (= a type of REPTILE) that can change color according to its surroundings **2** (often *disapproving*) a person who changes their behavior or opinions according to the situation: *a social/political chameleon*

cham·fer /'tʃæmfər/ *noun* (*technical*) a cut made along an edge or on a corner so that it slopes rather than being at 90°

cham·ois /'ʃæmi/ *noun* (*pl.* **cham·ois**) **1** [U] a type of soft, thick, cotton cloth, used especially for making shirts **2** [C] an animal like a small DEER, that lives in the mountains of Europe and Asia **3** [U, C] a type of soft leather, made from the skin of GOATS, sheep, etc.; a piece of this, used especially for cleaning windows

cham·o·mile (also **cam·o·mile**) /'kæmə,mil; -,maɪl/ *noun* [U] a plant with a sweet smell and small white and yellow flowers. Its dried leaves and flowers are used to make tea, medicine, etc.: *chamomile tea*

champ /tʃæmp/ *verb, noun*
• *verb* [T, I] ~ **(sth)** (especially of horses) to bite or eat (something) noisily
  IDM **champing at the bit** (*informal*) impatient to do or start doing something
• *noun* an informal way of referring to a champion, often used in newspapers: *Baseball champs celebrate victory!*

cham·pagne /ʃæm'peɪn/ *noun* [U, C] a French SPARKLING white wine (= one with bubbles) that is drunk on special occasions: *a glass of champagne*

cham·pi·on /'tʃæmpiən/ *noun, verb*
• *noun* **1** a person, team, etc. that has won a competition, especially in a sport: *the world basketball champions* ◆ *a champion jockey/boxer/swimmer, etc.* ◆ *the reigning champion* (= the person who is champion now) **2** ~ **(of sth)** a person who fights for, or speaks in support of, a group of people or a belief: *She was a champion of the poor all her life.*
• *verb* ~ **sth** to fight for or speak in support of a group of people or a belief: *He has always championed the cause of gay rights.*

cham·pi·on·ship /'tʃæmpiən,ʃɪp/ *noun* **1** (also **championships** [pl.]) a competition to find the best player or team in a particular sport: *the National Basketball Association Championship* ◆ *He won a silver medal at the World Championships.* **2** the position of being a champion: *They've held the championship for the past two years.*

chance 🔑 /tʃæns/ *noun, verb, adj.*
• *noun* **1** [C, U] a possibility of something happening, especially something that you want: ~ **of doing sth** *Is there any chance of getting tickets for tonight?* ◆ *She has only a slim chance of passing the exam.* ◆ ~ **that…** *There's a slight chance that he'll be back in time.* ◆ *There is no chance that he will change his mind.* ◆ ~ **of sth happening** *What chance is there of anybody being found alive?* ◆ ~ **of sth** *Nowadays a premature baby has a very good chance of survival.* ◆ *The operation has a fifty-fifty chance of success.* ◆ *an outside chance* (= a very small one) ◆ *The chances are a million to one against being struck by lightning.* **2** [C] a suitable time or situation when you have the opportunity to do something: *It was the chance she had been waiting for.* ◆ *Jeff deceived me once already—I won't give him a second chance.* ◆ *This is your big chance* (= opportunity for success). ◆ *I just had to accept the offer. It was the chance of a lifetime* (= an opportunity that you only get once). ◆ ~ **of sth** *We won't get another chance of a vacation this year.* ◆ ~ **to do sth** *Please give me a chance to explain.* ◆ *Tonight is your last chance to catch the play at your local theater.* ◆ *She jumped at the chance* (= eagerly took the chance) *to play the role.* ◆ ~ **for sb to do sth** *There will be a chance for parents to look around the school.* **3** [C] an unpleasant or dangerous possibility: *When installing electrical equipment don't take any chances. A mistake could kill.* **4** [U] the way that some things happen without any cause that you can see or understand: *I met her by chance* (= without planning to) *at the airport.* ◆ *Chess is not a game of chance.* ◆ *It was pure chance that we were both there.* ◆ *We'll plan everything very carefully and leave nothing to chance.* ⊃ thesaurus box at LUCK
  IDM **as chance would have it** happening in a way that was lucky, although it was not planned: *As chance would have it, John was going to San Francisco too, so I went with him.*

by any chance used especially in questions, to ask whether something is true, possible, etc.: *Are you in love with him, by any chance?* **chances are (that)...** (*informal*) it is likely that...: *Chances are you won't have to pay.* **give sb/sth half a chance** to give someone or something some opportunity to do something: *That dog will give you a nasty bite, given half a chance.* **no chance** (*informal*) there is no possibility: *"Do you think he'll do it?" "No chance."* **on the off chance (that)** because of the possibility of something happening, although it is unlikely: *I didn't think you'd be at home but I just stopped by on the off chance.* **stand a chance (of doing sth)** to have the possibility of succeeding or achieving something: *The driver didn't stand a chance of stopping in time.* **take a chance (on sth)** to decide to do something, knowing that it might be the wrong choice: *We took a chance on the weather and planned to have the party outside.* **take your chances** to take a risk or to use the opportunities that you have and hope that things will happen in the way that you want: *He took his chances and jumped into the water.* ⊃ more at EVEN *adj.*, FAT *adj.*, FIGHT *v.*, SNOWBALL *n.*, SPORTING

• **verb 1** (*informal*) to risk something, although you know the result may not be successful: **~ sth** *"Take an umbrella." "No, I'll chance it* (= take the risk that it may rain).*"* ◆ **~ doing sth** *I stayed hidden; I couldn't chance coming out.* **2** (*formal*) to happen or to do something by chance: **it chanced (that)...** *It chanced (that) they were staying at the same hotel.* ◆ **~ to do sth** *They chanced to be staying at the same hotel.* ◆ *If I do chance to find out where she is, I'll inform you immediately.*
PHR V ˈchance on/upon sb/sth (*formal*) to find or meet someone or something unexpectedly or by chance: *One day he chanced upon Emma's diary and began reading it.*

• **adj.** [only before noun] not planned **SYN** UNPLANNED: *a chance meeting/encounter*

chan·cel /ˈtʃænsl/ *noun* the part of a church near the ALTAR, where the priests and the CHOIR (= singers) sit during services

chan·cel·ler·y /ˈtʃænsləri; -sləri/ *noun* (*pl.* **chan·cel·ler·ies**) **1** [C, usually sing.] the place where a chancellor has his or her office **2** [sing.] the staff in the department of a chancellor

chan·cel·lor /ˈtʃænslər; -sələr/ *noun* (often used in a title) **1** the head of government in Germany or Austria: *Chancellor Adenauer* **2** the head of some American universities

chan·cer·y /ˈtʃænsəri/ *noun* [sing.] **1** (also ˈchancery court) a court that decides legal cases based on the principle of EQUITY **2** an office where public records are kept **3** the offices where the official representative of a country works, in another country

chanc·y /ˈtʃænsi/ *adj.* (*informal*) involving risks and UNCERTAINTY **SYN** RISKY

chan·de·lier /ˌʃændəˈlɪr/ *noun* a large round frame with branches that hold lights or CANDLES. Chandeliers are decorated with many small pieces of glass and hang from the ceiling.

chan·dler /ˈtʃændlər/ (also ˈship's ˌchandler) *noun* a person or store that sells equipment for ships

change 🔊 /tʃeɪndʒ/ *verb, noun*

• **verb**
> **BECOME/MAKE DIFFERENT 1** [I] to become different: *Rick hasn't changed. He looks exactly the same as he did at school.* ◆ *changing attitudes toward education* ◆ *Her life changed completely since she won the lottery.* **2** [T] **~ sb/sth** to make someone or something different: *Fame hasn't really changed him.* ◆ *Computers have changed the way people work.* **3** [I, T] to pass or make someone or something pass from one state or form into another: *Wait for the traffic lights to change.* ◆ **~ (from A) to/into B** *The lights changed from red to green.* ◆ *Caterpillars change into butterflies.* ◆ **~ sb/sth (from A) to/into B** *With a wave of her magic wand, she changed the frog into a handsome prince.* **4** [T] **~ sth** to stop having one state, position, or direction and start having another: *Leaves*

change color in the fall. ◆ *The wind has changed direction.* ◆ *Our ship changed course.*
> **REPLACE 5** [T] to replace one thing, person, service, etc. with something new or different: **~ sb/sth** *I want to change my doctor.* ◆ *That back tire needs to be changed.* ◆ **~ sb/sth (for sb/sth)** *We change our car every two years.* ◆ *We changed the car for a bigger one.* ◆ **~ sth (to sth)** *Marie changed her name when she got married.* ◆ *She changed her name to his.*
> **EXCHANGE 6** [T] (used with a plural object) to exchange positions, places, etc. with someone else, so that you have what they have, and they have what you have: **~ sth** *At half-time the teams change sides.* ◆ *Can we change seats?* ◆ **~ sth with sb** *Can I change seats with you?*
> **CLOTHES 7** [I, T] to put on different or clean clothes: *I went into the bedroom to change.* ◆ **~ into sth** *She changed into her swimsuit.* ◆ **~ out of sth** *You need to change out of those wet things.* ◆ **~ sth** *I didn't have time to change clothes before the party.* ◆ *I didn't have time to get changed before the party* (= to put different clothes on).
> **BABY 8** [T] **~ sb/sth** to put clean clothes or a clean DIAPER on a baby: *She can't even change a diaper.* ◆ *The baby needs to be changed.* ◆ *There are baby changing facilities in all our stores.*
> **BED 9** [T] **~ sth** to put clean sheets, etc. on a bed: *to change the sheets*
> **MONEY 10** [T] to exchange money into the money of another country: **~ sth** *Where can I change my money?* ◆ **~ sth into sth** *to change dollars into yen* **11** [T] to exchange money for the same amount in different coins or notes: **~ sth** *Can you change a $20 note?* ◆ **~ sth for/into sth** *to change a dollar bill for four quarters*
> **BUS/TRAIN/PLANE 12** [I, T] to go from one bus, train, etc. to another in order to continue a journey: *Where do I have to change?* ◆ *Change at New Haven (for Hartford).* ◆ **~ sth** *I stopped in Moscow only to change planes.* ⊃ see also UN-CHANGING
IDM **change hands** to pass to a different owner: *The house has changed hands several times.* **change your/sb's mind** to change a decision or an opinion: *Nothing will make me change my mind.* **change your tune** (*informal*) to express a different opinion or behave in a different way when your situation changes: *Wait until it happens to him—then he'll change his tune.* **change your ways** to start to live or behave in a different way from before ⊃ more at GEAR *n.*, HORSE *n.*, LEOPARD, PLACE *n.*
PHR V ˌchange sth↔aˈround to move things or people into different positions: *You've changed all the furniture around.* ˌchange ˈback (into sb/sth) to return to a previous situation, form, etc. ˌchange ˈback (into sth) to take off your clothes and put on what you were wearing earlier: *She changed back into her work clothes.* ˌchange sth ˈback (into sth) to exchange an amount of money into the CURRENCY that it was in before: *You can change back unused euros into dollars at the bank.* ˌchange ˈover (from sth) (to sth) to change from one system or position to another: *The farm has changed over to organic methods.* ⊃ related noun CHANGEOVER

• **noun**
> **DIFFERENCE 1** [C, U] **~ (in/to sth)** the act or result of something becoming different: *a change in the weather* ◆ *important changes to the tax system* ◆ *There was no change in the patient's condition overnight.* ◆ *She is someone who hates change.* ◆ *social/political/economic change*
> **SOMETHING NEW AND INTERESTING 2 a change** [sing.] **~ (from sth)** the fact of a situation, a place, or an experience being different from what is usual and therefore likely to be interesting, enjoyable, etc.: *Finishing early was a welcome change.* ◆ *Let's stay in tonight for a change.* ◆ *Can you just listen for a change?*
> **REPLACING SOMETHING 3** [C] **~ (of sth)** | **~ (from sth to sth)** the process of replacing something with something new or different; a thing that is used to replace something: *a change of address* ◆ *a change of government* ◆ *a change from agriculture to industry* ◆ *There will be a crew change when we land in Dallas.* ◆ *Let's get away for the weekend. A change of scenery* (= time in a different place) *will do you good.*
> **OF CLOTHES 4 ~ of clothes, etc.** [C] an extra set of clothes,

etc.: *She packed a change of clothes for the weekend.* ✦ *I keep a change of shoes in the car.*

> MONEY **5** [U] the money that you get back when you have paid more money for something than the amount it costs: *Don't forget your change!* ✦ *That's 40 cents change.* ✦ *Keep the change!* ✦ *The ticket machine gives change.* ⊃ see also CHUMP CHANGE **6** [U] coins rather than paper money: *Do you have any change for the phone?* ✦ *a dollar in change* (= coins that together are worth one dollar) ✦ *I didn't have any small change* (= coins of low value) *to leave as a tip.* ✦ *He puts his loose change on his dresser.* ✦ *Could you give me change for a ten dollar bill* (= coins or bills that are worth this amount)? ⊃ thesaurus box at MONEY

> OF BUS/TRAIN/PLANE **7** [C] an occasion when you go from one bus, train, or plane to another during a trip: *The trip involved three changes.*

> IN WOMAN'S LIFE **8** the change [sing.] (*informal*) = MENO-PAUSE

IDM **a change for the better/worse** a person, thing, situation, etc. that is better/worse than the previous or present one **a change of heart** if you have **a change of heart**, your attitude toward something changes, usually making you feel more friendly, helpful, etc. **a change of mind** an act of changing what you think about a situation, etc. ⊃ more at WIND¹ *n.*

change·a·ble /'tʃeɪndʒəbl/ *adj.* likely to change; often changing **SYN** UNPREDICTABLE: *The weather is very changeable at this time of year.* ⊃ compare UNCHANGEABLE ▶ **change·a·bil·i·ty** /ˌtʃeɪndʒə'bɪləti/ *noun* [U]

changed /tʃeɪndʒd/ *adj.* [only before noun] (of people or situations) very different from what they were before: *She's a changed woman since she got that job.* ✦ *This will not be possible in the changed economic climate.* **ANT** UNCHANGED

change·less /'tʃeɪndʒləs/ *adj.* (*formal*) never changing

change·ling /'tʃeɪndʒlɪŋ/ *noun* (*literary*) a child who is believed to have been secretly left in exchange for another, especially (in stories) by fairies (FAIRY)

the change of life *noun* [sing.] (*informal*) = MENOPAUSE

change·o·ver /'tʃeɪndʒˌoʊvər/ *noun* a change from one system or method of working to another **SYN** SWITCH: *the changeover from a manual to a computerized system* ✦ *a changeover period*

change purse (also **purse**) *noun* a small bag made of leather, plastic, etc. for carrying coins ⊃ picture at BAG ⊃ compare WALLET

chang·er /'tʃeɪndʒər/ *noun* (often in compounds) a person or thing that changes something, usually in order, to improve it: *The whole experience was a life changer for me.* **1** a piece of equipment that holds several disks, etc. and is able to switch between them: *The car comes with white leather seats and a 6-CD changer.*

changing room *noun* a room for changing clothes in, especially before playing sports, or in a store before deciding to buy the clothes ⊃ compare FITTING ROOM, LOCKER ROOM

changing table *noun* a table that you put a baby on in order to change its DIAPER

chan·nel 🔊 **AWL** /'tʃænl/ *noun, verb*

● *noun*

> ON TELEVISION/RADIO **1** [C] a television station: *a movie/sports channel* ✦ *to change/switch channels* ⊃ collocations at TELEVISION **2** [C] a band of radio waves used for broadcasting television or radio programs: *digital/satellite channels*

> FOR COMMUNICATING **3** [C] also **channels** [pl.] a method or system that people use to get information, to communicate, or to send something somewhere: *Complaints must be made through the proper channels.* ✦ *The newsletter is a useful channel of communication between teacher and students.* ✦ *The company has worldwide distribution channels.*

> FOR IDEAS/FEELINGS **4** [C] a way of expressing ideas and

feelings: *The campaign provided a channel for protest against the war.* ✦ *Music is a great channel for releasing your emotions.*

> WATER **5** [C] a passage that water can flow along, especially in the ground, on the bottom of a river, etc.: *drainage channels in the rice fields* **6** [C] a deep passage of water in a river or near the coast that can be used as route for ships **7** [C] a passage of water that connects two areas of water: *the English Channel*

● *verb*

> IDEAS/FEELINGS **1** ~ sth (into sth) to direct money, feelings, ideas, etc. toward a particular thing or purpose: *He channels his aggression into sports.*

> MONEY/HELP **2** ~ sth (through sth) to send money, help, etc. using a particular route: *Money for the project will be channeled through the local government.*

> WATER/LIGHT **3** ~ sth to carry or send water, light, etc. through a passage: *A sensor channels the light signal along an optical fiber.*

> SPIRIT **4** ~ sb to allow the spirit of a dead person to communicate through you: *The medium claimed to be able to channel the woman's dead husband.*

channel-surf (also **channel-hop**) *verb* [I] to repeatedly switch from one television channel to another

chant /tʃænt/ *noun, verb*

● *noun* **1** [C] words or phrases that a group of people shout or sing again and again: *The crowd broke into chants of "Out! Out!"* ✦ *soccer chants* **2** [C, U] a religious song or prayer, or a way of singing, using only a few notes that are repeated many times: *a Buddhist chant* ⊃ see also GREGORIAN CHANT

● *verb* **1** [I, T] to sing or shout the same words or phrases many times: *A group of protesters, chanting and carrying placards, waited outside.* ✦ *~ sth The crowd chanted their hero's name.* ✦ *"Resign! Resign!" they chanted.* **2** [I, T] ~ (sth) to sing or say a religious song or prayer using only a few notes that are repeated many times ▶ **chant·ing** *noun* [U]: *The chanting rose in volume.*

chan·te·relle /ˌʃæntə'rɛl/ *noun* a yellowish MUSHROOM that grows in woods and has a hollow part in the center

chan·teuse /ʃan'tuz; ʃæn-/ *noun* (from *French*) a female singer of popular songs, especially in a NIGHTCLUB

chant·ey (also **chant·y, shant·y**) /'ʃænti; 'tʃæn-/ *noun* (*pl.* **chant·ies**) (also **sea chantey**) a song that sailors traditionally used to sing while pulling ropes, etc.

chan·try /'tʃæntri/ *noun* (*pl.* **chan·tries**) (also **chantry chapel**) a small church or part of a church paid for by someone, so that priests could say prayers for them there after their death

Cha·nu·kah /'xɑnəkə/ = HANUKKAH

cha·os /'keɪɑs/ *noun* [U] a state of complete confusion and lack of order: *economic/political/domestic chaos* ✦ *Heavy snow has caused total chaos on the highways.* ✦ *The house was in chaos after the party.*

chaos theory *noun* [U] (*mathematics*) the study of a group of connected things that are very sensitive so that small changes in conditions affect them very much

cha·ot·ic /keɪ'ɑtɪk/ *adj.* in a state of complete confusion and lack of order: *The traffic in the city is chaotic at rush hour.* ▶ **cha·ot·i·cally** /-kli/ *adv.*

chap. *abbr.* (in writing) chapter

chap·ar·ral /ˌʃæpə'ræl/ *noun* [U] an area of dry land that is covered with small bushes, especially in southern California

chap·el /'tʃæpl/ *noun* **1** [C] a small building or room used for Christian worship in a school, prison, hospital, etc.: *a college chapel* **2** [C] a separate part of a church or CATHE-DRAL, with its own ALTAR, used for some services and private prayer **3** [C] a small building or room used for funeral services, especially at a CEMETERY or CREMATORIUM

chap·er·one (also **chap·er·on**) /'ʃæpəˌroʊn/ *noun, verb*

● *noun* **1** a person, such as a parent or a teacher, who goes with a group of young people on a trip or to a dance to encourage good behavior **2** (in the past) an older woman who, on social occasions, took care of a young woman who was not married **3** a person who takes care of children in public, especially when they are working, for example as actors

● *verb* **~ sb/sth** to act as a chaperone for someone, especially a woman, or for an event: *We need volunteers to chaperone the dance.*

chap·lain /'tʃæplən/ *noun* a priest or other Christian minister who is responsible for the religious needs of people in a prison, hospital, etc. or in the armed forces ⊃ compare PADRE, PRIEST

chap·lain·cy /'tʃæplənsi/ *noun* (*pl.* **chap·lain·cies**) the position or work of a chaplain; the place where a chaplain works

chap·let /'tʃæplət/ *noun* a circle of leaves, flowers, or JEWELS worn on the head

chapped /tʃæpt/ *adj.* (of the skin or lips) rough, dry, and sore, especially because of wind or cold weather

chaps /tʃæps; ʃæps/ *noun* [pl.] leather coverings worn as protection over pants by COWBOYS, etc. when riding a horse: *a pair of chaps*

chap·ter 🔑 **AWL** /'tʃæptər/ *noun*
1 (*abbr.* **ch., chap.**) a separate section of a book, usually with a number or title: *I've just finished Chapter 3.* ◆ *in the previous/next/last chapter* ◆ *Have you read the chapter on the legal system?* **2** a period of time in a person's life or in history: *a difficult chapter in our country's history* **3** a local branch of a society, club, etc.: *the local chapter of the Rotary club* **4** all the priests of a CATHEDRAL or members of a religious community: *a meeting of the dean and chapter*
IDM **chapter and verse** the exact details of something, especially the exact place where particular information may be found: *I can't give chapter and verse, but that's the rough outline of our legal position.*

Chapter 11 /,tʃæptər ɪ'levn/ *noun* [U] (*law*) a section of the law dealing with BANKRUPTCY (= being unable to pay debts), that allows companies to stop paying their debts in the normal way while they try to find a solution to their financial problems: *The company has filed for Chapter 11 bankruptcy protection.*

Chapter 7 /,tʃæptər 'sevn/ *noun* [U] (*law*) a section of the law dealing with BANKRUPTCY (= being unable to pay debts), that allows a court to take property belonging to a company or person, which is then sold to pay their debts

chapter house *noun* a building where all the priests of a CATHEDRAL or members of a religious community meet

char /tʃɑr/ *verb* (**-rr-**) [I, T] **~ (sth)** to become black by burning; to make something black by burning it ⊃ see also CHARRED ⊃ thesaurus box at BURN

char·ac·ter 🔑 /'kærəktər/ *noun*
➤ QUALITIES/FEATURES **1** [C, usually sing.] all the qualities and features that make a person, groups of people, and places different from others: *to have a strong/weak character* ◆ *character traits/defects* ◆ *The book gives a fascinating insight into Mrs. Obama's character.* ◆ *Generosity is part of the American character.* ◆ *The character of the neighborhood hasn't changed at all.* **2** [C, usually sing., U] the way that something is, or a particular quality or feature that a thing, an event, or a place has **SYN** NATURE: *the delicate character of the light in the evening* ◆ *buildings that are very simple in character* **3** [U] (*approving*) strong personal qualities such as the ability to deal with difficult or dangerous situations: *Everyone admires her strength of character and determination.* ◆ *He showed great character returning to the sport after his accident.* ◆ *Adventure camps are considered character-building* (= meant to improve someone's strong qualities). **4** [U] (usually *approving*) the interesting or unusual quality that a place or a person has: *The modern hotels here have no real character.* ◆ *a face with a lot of character*
➤ STRANGE/INTERESTING PERSON **5** [C] (*informal*) (used with an adjective) a person, particularly an unpleasant or strange one: *There were some really strange characters hanging around*

the bar. **6** [C] (*informal*) an interesting or unusual person: *She's a real character!*
➤ REPUTATION **7** [C, U] (*formal*) the opinion that people have of you, particularly of whether you can be trusted or relied on: *She was a victim of character assassination* (= an unfair attack on the good opinion people had of her). ◆ *an attack on his character* ◆ *My teacher agreed to be a character witness for me in court.* ◆ *a character reference* (= a letter that a person who knows you well writes to an employer to tell them about your good qualities)
➤ IN BOOK/PLAY/MOVIE **8** [C] a person or an animal in a book, play, or movie: *a major/minor character in the book* ◆ *cartoon characters* ⊃ collocations at LITERATURE
➤ SYMBOL/LETTER **9** [C] a letter, sign, mark, or symbol used in writing, printing, or on computers: *Chinese characters* ◆ *a line 30 characters long*
IDM **in character** | **out of character** typical/not typical of a person's character: *Her behavior last night was completely out of character.* **in character (with sth)** in the same style as something **SYN** KEEPING: *The new wing of the museum was not really in character with the rest of the building.*

character actor *noun* an actor who always takes the parts of interesting or unusual people

char·ac·ter·ful /'kærəktərfl/ *adj.* very interesting and unusual

char·ac·ter·is·tic 🔑 /,kærəktə'rɪstɪk/ *adj., noun*
● *adj.* **~ (of sth/sb)** very typical of something or of someone's character: *She spoke with characteristic enthusiasm.* **ANT** UNCHARACTERISTIC ▶ **char·ac·ter·is·ti·cally** /-kli/ *adv.*: *Characteristically, Helen paid for everyone.*
● *noun* **~ (of sth/sb)** a typical feature or quality that something or someone has: *The need to communicate is a key characteristic of human society.* ◆ *The two groups of children have quite different characteristics.* ◆ *Personal characteristics such as age and sex are taken into account.* ◆ *genetic characteristics*

char·ac·ter·i·za·tion /,kærəktərə'zeɪʃn/ *noun* [U, C] **1** the way that a writer makes characters in a book or play seem real **2** (*formal*) the way in which someone or something is described or defined **SYN** PORTRAYAL: *the characterization of physics as the study of simplicity*

char·ac·ter·ize /'kærəktə,raɪz/ *verb* (*formal*) **1 ~ sb/sth** to be typical of a person, place, or thing: *the rolling hills that characterize this part of Virginia* **2 ~ sb/sth** [often passive] to give something its typical or most noticeable qualities or features: *The city is characterized by tall modern buildings of steel and glass.* **3 ~ sb/sth (as sth)** to describe or show the qualities of someone or something in a particular way: *activities that are characterized as "male" or "female" work*

char·ac·ter·less /'kærəktərləs/ *adj.* having no interesting qualities

character recognition *noun* [U] the ability of a computer to read numbers or letters that are printed or written by hand

cha·rade /ʃə'reɪd/ *noun* **1** [C] a situation in which people pretend that something is true when it clearly is not **SYN** PRETENSE: *Their whole marriage had been a charade—they had never loved each other.* **2 charades** [U] a game in which one player acts out a word or title and the other players try to guess what it is: *Let's play charades.*

char·broil /'tʃɑrbrɔɪl/ *verb* **~ sth** to cook meat or other food over CHARCOAL

char·coal /'tʃɑrkoʊl/ *noun* [U] **1** a black substance made by burning wood slowly in an oven with little air. Charcoal is used as a fuel or for drawing: *charcoal grilled steaks* ◆ *a charcoal drawing* **2** (also **charcoal gray**) a very dark gray color

chard /tʃɑrd/ (also **Swiss chard**) *noun* [U] a vegetable with thick white STEMS and large leaves

Char·don·nay /,ʃɑrdn'eɪ/ *noun* [U, C] a type of white wine, or the type of GRAPE from which it is made

charge /tʃɑrdʒ/ *noun, verb*

● *noun*

▷ MONEY **1** [C, U] ~ **(for sth)** the amount of money that someone asks for goods and services: *We have to add a small charge for refreshments.* ♦ *admission charges* ♦ *Delivery is free of charge.* ◯ thesaurus box at RATE **2** [C, U] (*informal*) = ACCOUNT: *Would you like to put that on your charge?* ♦ *"Are you paying cash?" "No, it'll be a charge."*

▷ RESPONSIBILITY **3** [U] a position of having control over someone or something; responsibility for someone or something: *She has charge of the day-to-day running of the business.* ♦ *They left the au pair in charge of the children for a week.* ♦ *He took charge of the farm after his father's death.* ♦ *I'm leaving the school in your charge.* **4** [C] (*formal* or *humorous*) a person that you have responsibility for and care for

▷ OF CRIME/SOMETHING WRONG **5** [C, U] an official claim made by the police that someone has committed a crime: *criminal charges* ♦ *a murder/an assault charge* ♦ *He will be sent back to Colorado to face a charge of* (= to be on trial for) *armed robbery.* ♦ *They decided to drop the charges against the newspaper and settle out of court.* ♦ *After being questioned by the police, she was released without charge.* ◯ collocations at JUSTICE **6** [C] a statement accusing someone of doing something wrong or bad **SYN** ALLEGATION: *She rejected the charge that the story was untrue.* ♦ *Be careful you don't leave yourself open to charges of political bias.*

▷ ELECTRICITY **7** [C, U] the amount of electricity that is put into a battery or carried by a substance: *a positive/negative charge*

▷ RUSH/ATTACK **8** [C] a sudden rush or violent attack, for example by soldiers, wild animals, or players in some sports: *He led the charge down the field.*

▷ EXPLOSIVE **9** [C] the amount of EXPLOSIVE needed to fire a gun or make an explosion ◯ see also DEPTH CHARGE

▷ STRONG FEELING **10** [sing.] the power to cause strong feelings: *the emotional charge of the piano piece*

▷ TASK **11** [sing.] (*formal*) a task or duty: *His charge was to obtain specific information.*

IDM bring/press charges against sb (*law*) to accuse someone formally of a crime so that there can be a trial in court get a charge out of sth to get a strong feeling of excitement or pleasure from something

● *verb*

▷ MONEY **1** [T, I] to ask an amount of money for goods or a service: ~ **sth for sth** *What did they charge for the repairs?* ♦ *The restaurant charged $20 for dinner.* ♦ ~ **sb for sth** *We won't charge you for delivery.* ♦ ~ **sth at sth** *Calls are charged at 36 cents per minute.* ♦ ~ **sb sth (for sth)** *He only charged me half price.* ♦ ~ **for sth** *Do you think museums should charge for admission?* ♦ ~ **(sb) to do sth** *The bank doesn't charge to stop a payment.* **2** [T] to record the cost of something as an amount that someone has to pay: ~ **sth to sth** *They charge the calls to their credit-card account.* ♦ ~ **sth** *Don't worry. I'll charge it* (= pay by credit card).

▷ WITH CRIME/SOMETHING WRONG **3** [T] to accuse someone formally of a crime so that there can be a trial in court: ~ **sb** *Several people were arrested but nobody was charged.* ♦ ~ **sb with sth/with doing sth** *He was charged with murder.* **4** [T] ~ **sb (with sth/with doing sth)** (*formal*) to accuse someone publicly of doing something wrong or bad: *Opposition senators charged the Secretary with neglecting his duty.*

▷ RUSH/ATTACK **5** [I, T] to rush forward and attack someone or something: *The bull put its head down and charged.* ♦ ~ **(at) sb/sth** *We charged at the enemy.* **6** [I] + adv./prep. to rush in a particular direction: *The children charged down the stairs.* ♦ *He came charging into my room and demanded to know what was going on.*

▷ WITH RESPONSIBILITY/TASK **7** [T] [usually passive] (*formal*) to give someone a responsibility or task.: ~ **sb with sth** *The committee has been charged with the development of sports in the region.* ♦ ~ **sb with doing sth** *The governing body is charged with managing the school within its budget.*

▷ WITH ELECTRICITY **8** [T] to pass electricity through something so that it is stored there: ~ **sth** *Before use, the battery*

must be charged. ♦ *I need to charge my phone.* ♦ ~ **sth up** *The shaver can be charged up and used when traveling.*

▷ WITH STRONG FEELING **9** [T] [usually passive] ~ **sth (with sth)** (*literary*) to fill someone with an emotion: *The room was charged with hatred.* ♦ *a highly charged atmosphere*

▷ GUN **10** [T] ~ **sth** (*old use*) to load a gun

charge·a·ble /ˈtʃɑrdʒəbl/ *adj.* **1** ~ **(to sb/sth)** (of a sum of money) that must be paid by someone: *Any expenses you may incur will be chargeable to the company.* **2** (of a criminal act) serious enough to be formally treated as a crime: *Assault and battery is a chargeable offense.*

ˈcharge ac·count *noun* = ACCOUNT

ˈcharge ˌcard *noun* a small plastic card provided by a store that you use to buy goods there, paying for them later ◯ see also CREDIT CARD

charged /tʃɑrdʒd/ *adj.* ~ **(with sth)** full of or causing strong feelings or opinions: *a highly charged atmosphere* ♦ *a politically charged issue* ♦ *The dialogue is charged with menace.*

char·gé d'af·faires /ˌʃɑrˌʒeɪ dəˈfɛr/ *noun* (*pl.* **char·gés d'af·faires** /ˌʃɑrˌʒeɪ dəˈfɛr; ʃɑrˌʒeɪz-/) (from *French*) **1** an official who takes the place of an AMBASSADOR in a foreign country when he or she is away **2** an official below the rank of AMBASSADOR who acts as the senior representative of his or her country in a foreign country where there is no AMBASSADOR

charg·er /ˈtʃɑrdʒər/ *noun* **1** a piece of equipment for loading a battery with electricity **2** a large plate used in a place SETTING as a decoration **3** (*old use*) a horse that a soldier rode in battle in the past

ˈcharge sheet *noun* a record kept in a police station of the names of people that the police have stated to be guilty of a crime (= that they have charged)

char·grill /ˈtʃɑrgrɪl/ *verb* ~ **sth** [usually passive] to cook meat, fish, or vegetables over a very high heat so that the outside is slightly burned

char·i·ot /ˈtʃæriət/ *noun* an open vehicle with two wheels, pulled by horses, used in ancient times in battle and for racing

char·i·ot·eer /ˌtʃæriəˈtɪr/ *noun* the driver of a chariot

cha·ris·ma /kəˈrɪzmə/ *noun* [U] the powerful personal quality that some people have to attract and impress other people: *The President has great personal charisma.* ♦ *a lack of charisma*

char·is·mat·ic /ˌkærəzˈmætɪk/ *adj., noun*

● *adj.* **1** having charisma: *a charismatic leader* **ANT** UNCHARISMATIC **2** (of a Christian religious group) believing in special gifts from God; worshiping in a very enthusiastic way ▶ **char·is·mat·i·cally** /-kli/ *adv.*

● *noun* often **Charismatic** a charismatic Christian

char·i·ta·ble /ˈtʃærətəbl/ *adj.* **1** connected with a charity or charities: *a charitable institution/foundation/trust* ♦ *a charitable donation/gift* **2** helping people who are poor or in need: *His later years were devoted largely to charitable work.* **3** kind in your attitude to other people, especially when you are judging them: *Let's be charitable and assume she just made a mistake.* **ANT** UNCHARITABLE ▶ **char·i·ta·bly** /-bli/ *adv.*: *Try to think about him a little more charitably.*

char·i·ty /ˈtʃærəti/ *noun* (*pl.* **char·i·ties**) **1** [C] an organization for helping people in need: *Many charities send money to help the victims of the famine.* ♦ *The concert will raise money for local charities.* **2** [U] the aim of giving money, food, help, etc. to people who are in need: *Many of the runners in the Boston Marathon are raising money for charity.* ♦ *Do you give much to charity?* ♦ *a charity concert* (= organized to get money for charity) ♦ *to live on/off charity* (= to live on money which other people give you because you are poor) **3** [U] (*formal*) kindness and sympathy toward other people, especially when you are judging them: *Her article showed no charity toward her former friends.*

IDM charity begins at home (*saying*) you should help and

| h hat | m man | n no | ŋ sing | l leg | r red | y yes | w wet |

care for your own family, etc. before you start helping other people

char·la·tan /ˈʃɑrlətən/ *noun* a person who claims to have knowledge or skills that they do not really have

charles·ton /ˈtʃɑrlstən/ *noun* usually **the charleston** [sing.] a fast dance that was popular in the 1920s

char·ley horse /ˈtʃɑrli ˌhɔrs/ *noun* [usually sing.] (*informal*) = CRAMP: *Ow! I just got a charley horse in my leg.*

charm /tʃɑrm/ *noun, verb*

• *noun* **1** [U] the power of pleasing or attracting people: *a man of great charm* ◆ *The hotel is full of charm and character.* **2** [C] a feature or quality that is pleasing or attractive: *her physical charms* (= her beauty) **3** [C] a small object worn on a chain or BRACELET, that is believed to bring good luck: *a lucky charm* ◆ *a charm bracelet* ⊃ picture at JEWELRY **4** [C] an act or words believed to have magic power SYN SPELL
IDM **work like a charm** to be immediately and completely successful ⊃ more at THIRD

• *verb* **1** [T, I] ~ **(sb)** to please or attract someone in order to make them like you or do what you want: *He was charmed by her beauty and wit.* ◆ *Her words had lost their power to charm.* **2** [T] ~ **sb/sth** to control or protect someone or something using magic, or as if using magic: *He has led a charmed life* (= he has been lucky even in dangerous or difficult situations).
PHR V **charm sth 'out of sb** to obtain something such as information, money, etc. from someone by using charm

charmed 'circle *noun* [sing.] a group of people who have special influence

charm·er /ˈtʃɑrmər/ *noun* a person who acts in a way that makes them attractive to other people, sometimes using this to influence others ⊃ see also SNAKE CHARMER

charm·ing /ˈtʃɑrmɪŋ/ *adj.* **1** very pleasant or attractive: *The cottage is tiny, but it's charming.* ◆ *She's a charming person.* **2** (*ironic, informal*) used to show that you have a low opinion of someone's behavior: *They left me to clean it all up myself. Charming, wasn't it?* ▸ **charm·ing·ly** *adv.*

charm·less /ˈtʃɑrmləs/ *adj.* (*formal*) not at all pleasant or interesting: *a charmless industrial town*

charm of'fensive *noun* a situation in which a person, for example a politician, is especially friendly and pleasant in order to get other people to like them and to support their opinions

charm school *noun* a school where young people are taught to behave in a polite way

char·nel house /ˈtʃɑrnl ˌhaʊs/ *noun* a place used in the past for keeping dead human bodies or bones

charred /tʃɑrd/ *adj.* [usually before noun] burned and black: *the charred remains of a burned-out car*

chart 🔊 **AWL** /tʃɑrt/ *noun, verb*

• *noun* **1** [C] a page or sheet of information in the form of diagrams, lists of figures, etc.: *a weather chart* ◆ *a sales chart* (= showing the level of a company's sales) ⊃ picture at GRAPH ⊃ see also BAR CHART, FLOW CHART, PIE CHART **2** **the charts** [pl.] a list, produced each week, of the music CDs that have sold the most copies: *The album went straight on to the charts at number 1.* ◆ *to top the charts* (= to be the record that has sold more copies than all the others) **3** [C] a detailed map of the ocean or stars: *a naval chart*
IDM **off the charts** (*informal*) extremely high in level: *World demand for the product is off the charts.*

• *verb* **1** ~ **sth** to record or follow the progress or development of someone or something: *The exhibition charts the history of the palace.* **2** ~ **sth** to plan a course of action: *She had carefully charted her route to the top of her profession.* **3** ~ **sth** to make a map of an area SYN MAP: *Cook charted the coast of New Zealand in 1768.*

char·ter /ˈtʃɑrtər/ *noun, verb*

• *noun* **1** [C] a written statement of the principles and aims of an organization SYN CONSTITUTION: *the United Nations Charter* ◆ *the Employees Credit Union charter* **2** [C] an official document stating that a ruler or government allows a new

organization, town, or university to be established and gives it particular rights: *The Rhode Island colony received its royal charter in 1663.* **3** [U] the renting of a plane, boat, etc.: *a yacht available for charter* **4** (*CanE*) also **the Charter** = CANADIAN CHARTER OF RIGHTS AND FREEDOMS

• *verb* **1** ~ **sth** to rent a plane, boat, etc. for your own use: *a chartered plane* **2** ~ **sth** to state officially that a new organization, town, or university has been established and has special rights

char·tered /ˈtʃɑrtərd/ *adj.* [only before noun] (of an aircraft, a ship, or a boat) rented for a particular purpose: *a chartered plane*

charter 'flight *noun* a flight in an aircraft in which all the seats are paid for by a travel company and then sold to their customers, usually at a lower cost than that of a SCHEDULED FLIGHT

charter 'member (also ˌfounding 'member) *noun* one of the first members of a society, an organization, etc., especially one who helped start it

charter 'school *noun* a school that has been established by teachers, parents, or community groups, but receives public funds, and places special emphasis on a particular subject or teaching method: *Both of her children attend a performing arts charter school.* ◆ *a Chinese immersion charter school*

char·treuse /ʃɑrˈtruz; -ˈtrus/ *noun* [U] **1** a pale yellow or pale green color **2** a green or yellow LIQUEUR (= a strong, sweet, alcoholic drink)

chart-ˌtopping *adj.* [only before noun] (of a CD, singer, etc.) having reached the highest position in the music CHARTS: *his latest chart-topping hit* ▸ **chart-ˌtopper** *noun*

char·y /ˈtʃɛri/ *adj.* ~ **of sth/of doing sth** not willing to risk doing something; fearing possible problems if you do something SYN WARY

chase 🔊 /tʃeɪs/ *verb, noun*

• *verb*
❯ **RUN/DRIVE AFTER 1** [T, I] to run, drive, etc. after someone or something in order to catch them: ~ **sb/sth** *My dog likes chasing rabbits.* ◆ *The kids chased each other around the kitchen table.* ◆ ~ **after sb/sth** *He chased after the burglar but couldn't catch him.*
❯ **MONEY/WORK/SUCCESS 2** [T] ~ **sth** to try to obtain or achieve something, for example money, work, or success: *Too many people are chasing too few jobs nowadays.* ◆ *The team is chasing its first win in five games.*
❯ **MAN/WOMAN 3** [I, T] (*informal*) to try to persuade someone to have a sexual relationship with you: ~ **after sb** *Kevin's been chasing after Jan for months.* ◆ ~ **sb** *Girls are always chasing him.*
❯ **REMIND SOMEONE 4** [T] ~ **sb** (*informal*) to persuade someone to do something that they should have done already: *I need to chase him about organizing the meeting.*
❯ **RUSH 5** [I] + adv./prep. (*informal*) to rush or hurry somewhere: *I've been chasing around town all morning looking for a present for Sharon.*
❯ **METAL 6** [T] ~ **sth** (*technical*) to cut patterns or designs on metal: *chased silver*
IDM **chase your (own) tail** (*informal*) to be very busy but in fact achieve very little
PHR V **chase sb/sth↔a'way, 'off, 'out, etc.** to force someone or something to run away ˌchase sth↔'down to find something that is needed; to deal with something that has been forgotten: *My job was to chase down late replies.* ˌchase sb↔'up to contact someone in order to remind them to do something that they should have done already: *We need to chase up all members who have not yet paid.*

• *noun*
❯ **RUNNING/DRIVING AFTER 1** [C] (often used with *the*) an act of running or driving after someone or something in order to catch them: *The thieves were caught by police after a short chase.* ◆ *a high-speed car chase* ◆ *We lost him in the narrow streets and had to give up the chase* (= stop chasing him). ◆ *to take up the chase* (= start chasing someone)

> **FOR SUCCESS/MONEY/WORK 2** [sing.] a process of trying hard to get something: *Three teams are involved in the chase for the championship.*

> **IN SPORTS 3 the chase** [sing.] hunting animals as a sport **⊃** see also PAPER CHASE, WILD GOOSE CHASE

IDM **cut to the chase** (*informal*) to stop wasting time and start talking about the most important thing: *Right, let's cut to the chase. How much is it going to cost?* **give chase** (*literary*) to begin to run after someone or something in order to catch them: *We gave chase along the sidewalk.*

chas·er /'tʃeɪsər/ noun a drink that you have after another of a different kind, for example a stronger alcoholic drink after a weak one: *a beer with a whiskey chaser*

Cha·s·idism /'hɑsɪˌdɪzəm; 'xɑ-/ noun [U] = HASIDISM

chasm /'kæzəm/ noun **1** [C] (*literary*) a deep crack or opening in the ground **2** [sing.] **~ (between A and B)** (*formal*) a very big difference between two people or groups, for example because they have different attitudes **SYN** GULF

chas·sis /'tʃæsi; 'ʃæsi/ noun (*pl.* **chas·sis** /-siz/) the frame that a vehicle is built on

chaste /tʃeɪst/ adj. **1** (*old-fashioned*) not having sex with anyone; only having sex with the person that you are married to: *to remain chaste* **2** (*formal*) not expressing sexual feelings: *a chaste kiss on the cheek* **3** (*formal*) simple and plain in style; not decorated: *the cool, chaste interior of the hall* ▶ **chaste·ly** adv.: *He kissed her chastely on the cheek.*

chas·ten /'tʃeɪsn/ verb [often passive] **~ sb** (*formal*) to make someone feel sorry for something they have done: *He felt suitably chastened and apologized.* ◆ *She gave them a chastening lecture.* ◆ *It was a chastening experience.*

chas·tise /tʃæ'staɪz; 'tʃæstaɪz/ verb **1 ~ sb (for sth/for doing sth)** (*formal*) to criticize someone for doing something wrong: *He chastised the team for their lack of commitment.* **2 ~ sb** (*old-fashioned*) to punish someone physically **SYN** BEAT ▶ **chas·tise·ment** noun [U]

chas·ti·ty /'tʃæstəti/ noun [U] the state of not having sex with anyone or only having sex with the person that you are married to; being CHASTE: *vows of chastity* (= those taken by some priests)

chastity belt noun a device worn by some women in the past to prevent them from being able to have sex

chat 🔑 /tʃæt/ verb, noun

● **verb** (-tt-) **1** [I] to talk in a friendly, informal way to someone: **~ (to/with sb)** *My kids spend hours chatting on the phone to their friends.* ◆ **~ away (to/with sb)** *Within minutes of being introduced they were chatting away like old friends.* ◆ **~ about sth/sb** *What were you chatting about?* **2** [I] **~ (away) (to/with sb)** | **~ (about sth/sb)** to exchange messages with other people on the Internet, especially in a CHAT ROOM: *He's been on the computer all morning, chatting with his friends.*

● **noun 1** [C] a friendly, informal conversation: *I just stopped by for a chat.* ◆ *I had a long chat with her.* **⊃** thesaurus box at DISCUSSION **2** [U] talking, especially informal conversation: *That's enough chat from me—on with the music!* **3** [U, C] communication between people on the Internet: *chat software* ◆ *Internet chat services* ◆ *Fans are invited to an online chat.*

châ·teau /ʃæ'toʊ/ noun (*pl.* **châ·teaux** or **châ·teaus** /-'toʊz/) (from *French*) a castle or large country house in France

chat·line /'tʃætlaɪn/ noun **1** a telephone service that allows a number of people who call in separately to have a conversation, especially for fun **2** a telephone service that people can call to talk to someone about sex in order to feel sexually excited

chat room noun an area on the Internet where people can communicate with each other, usually about one particular topic **⊃** collocations at E-MAIL

chat·tel /'tʃætl/ noun [C, U] (*law* or *old-fashioned*) something that belongs to you

chat·ter /'tʃætər/ verb, noun

● **verb 1** [I] **~ (away/on) (to sb) (about sth)** to talk quickly and continuously, especially about things that are not important: *They chattered away happily for a while.* ◆ *The children chattered to each other excitedly about the next day's events.* **2** [I] (of teeth) to knock together continuously because you are cold or frightened **3** [I] (of birds or MONKEYS) to make a series of short high sounds

● **noun** [U] **1** continuous rapid talk about things that are not important: *Jane's constant chatter was beginning to annoy him.* ◆ *idle chatter* **2** a series of quick, short, high sounds that some animals make: *the chatter of monkeys* **3** a series of short sounds made by things knocking together: *the chatter of teeth*

chat·ter·box /'tʃætərbɑks/ noun (*informal*) a person who talks a lot, especially a child

chat·ty /'tʃæti/ adj. (**chat·tier**, **chat·tiest**) (*informal*) **1** talking a lot in a friendly way: *You're very chatty today, Alice.* **2** having a friendly informal style: *a chatty letter*

chauf·feur /'ʃoʊfər; ʃoʊ'fər/ noun, verb

● **noun** a person whose job is to drive a car, especially for someone rich or important

● **verb ~ sb** to drive someone in a car, usually as your job: *He was chauffeured to all his meetings.* ◆ *a chauffeured limousine*

chau·vin·ism /'ʃoʊvəˌnɪzəm/ noun [U] (*disapproving*) **1** = MALE CHAUVINISM **2** an aggressive and unreasonable belief that your own country is better than all others

chau·vin·ist /'ʃoʊvənɪst/ noun **1** = MALE CHAUVINIST **2** a person who has an aggressive and unreasonable belief that their own country is better than all others ▶ **chau·vin·is·tic** /ˌʃoʊvə'nɪstɪk/ (also *less frequent* **chau·vin·ist**) adj. **chau·vin·is·ti·cally** /-kli/ adv.

chaw /tʃɔ/ noun something that you chew, especially a large piece of TOBACCO

THESAURUS

cheap

competitive ◆ budget ◆ affordable ◆ reasonable ◆ inexpensive

These words all describe a product or service that costs little money or less money than you expected.

cheap costing little money or less money than you expected; charging low prices. **NOTE** Cheap can also be used in a disapproving way to suggest that something is poor quality as well as low in price: *a bottle of cheap perfume.*

competitive (of prices, goods, or services) as cheap as, or cheaper than, those offered by other companies; able to offer goods or services at competitive prices.

budget [only before noun] (used especially in advertising) cheap because it offers only a basic level of service: *a budget hotel*

affordable cheap enough for most people to afford

reasonable (of prices) not too expensive

inexpensive (*somewhat formal*) cheap **NOTE** Inexpensive is often used to mean that something is good value for its price. It is sometimes used instead of **cheap**, because it **cheap** can suggest that something is poor quality.

PATTERNS
- cheap/competitive/budget/affordable/reasonable **prices/fares/rates**
- cheap/competitive/budget/affordable/inexpensive **products/services**

---

cheap 🔑 /tʃip/ adj., adv.

● **adj.** (**cheap·er**, **cheap·est**)

> **LOW PRICE 1** costing little money or less money than you expected **SYN** INEXPENSIVE: *cheap fares* ◆ *Personal compu-*

ters are cheap and getting cheaper. ◆ Riding a bike is a cheap way to get around. ◆ The printer isn't exactly cheap at $400. ◆ immigrant workers, used as a source of **cheap labor** (= workers who are paid very little, especially unfairly) ⊃ see also DIRT CHEAP **ANT** EXPENSIVE **2** charging low prices: a cheap restaurant/hotel **ANT** EXPENSIVE
> POOR QUALITY **3** (disapproving) low in price and quality: cheap perfume/jewelry/shoes
> NOT GENEROUS **4** (informal, disapproving) not liking to spend money: Don't be so cheap!
> UNKIND **5** unpleasant or unkind and somewhat obvious: I was tired of his cheap jokes at my expense.
> LOW STATUS **6** (disapproving) having a low status and therefore not deserving respect: He's just a cheap crook. ◆ His treatment of her made her **feel cheap** (= ashamed, because she had lost her respect for herself).
▶ cheap·ness noun [U]
IDM cheap at the price (also cheap at 'twice the price) so good or useful that the cost does not seem too much on the cheap spending less money than you usually need to spend to do something: a guide to decorating your house on the cheap ⊃ more at LIFE
• **adv.** (comparative cheap·er, , no superlative) (informal) for a low price: I got this dress cheap in a sale.
IDM be going cheap to be offered for sale at a lower price than usual sth does not come cheap something is expensive: Violins like this don't come cheap.

cheap·en /ˈtʃipən/ verb **1** ~ sb/yourself to make someone lose respect for himself or herself **SYN** DEGRADE: She never cheapened herself by lowering her standards. **2** ~ sth to make something lower in price: to cheapen the cost of raw materials **3** ~ sth to make something appear to have less value: The movie was accused of cheapening human life.

cheap·ly /ˈtʃipli/ adv.
without spending or costing much money: I'm sure I could buy this more cheaply somewhere else. ◆ a cheaply made movie
cheap·o /ˈtʃipoʊ/ adj. [only before noun] (informal, disapproving) cheap and often of poor quality
cheap·skate /ˈtʃipskeɪt/ noun (informal, disapproving) a person who does not like to spend money

---

THESAURUS

cheat
lie ◆ trick ◆ fool ◆ deceive ◆ betray ◆ con

These words all mean to make someone believe something that is not true, especially in order to get what you want.

cheat to make someone believe something that is not true, in order to get money or something else from them: She cheated on her taxes. ◆ I was cheated out of my fair share. **NOTE** Cheat also means to act in a dishonest way in order to gain an advantage, especially in a game, competition, or exam: Copying someone else's answers is one kind of cheating.

lie to say or write something that you know is not true: He lied about his age. ◆ Don't lie to me.

trick to make someone believe something that is not true, especially in a skillful way, in order to get what you want: She tricked him into handing over all his savings.

fool to make someone believe something that is not true, especially in order to laugh at them or to get what you want: Just don't be fooled by these statistics.

deceive to make someone believe something that is not true, especially someone who trusts you, in order to get what you want: I don't know how he deceived me so well.

betray to hurt someone who trusts you, especially by deceiving them or not being loyal to them: She felt betrayed when she found out the truth about him.

con (informal) to deceive someone, especially in order to

---

get money from them or get them to do something for you: My grandfather was conned out of $10,000 by criminals.

WHICH WORD?

Many of these words involve making someone believe something that is not true, but some of them are more disapproving than others. **Deceive** is probably the worst because people typically deceive friends, relations, and others who know and trust them. People may **feel cheated/betrayed** by someone in authority whom they trusted to look after their interests. If someone **cheats/tricks/fools/cons** you, they may get something from you and make you feel stupid. However, someone might **fool** you just as a joke; and to **trick** someone is sometimes seen as a skillful thing to do, if the person being tricked is seen as a bad person who deserves it.

PATTERNS
▪ to cheat/trick/fool/con sb **out of** sth
▪ to fool/trick/con sb **into doing** sth
▪ to **feel** cheated/tricked/fooled/deceived/betrayed/conned
▪ to fool/deceive **yourself**
▪ to cheat/trick/con **your way** into sth

cheat /tʃit/ verb, noun
• **verb 1** [T] ~ sb/sth to trick someone or make them believe something that is not true: Many people feel cheated by the government's refusal to hold a referendum. ◆ He cheated his way into the job. **2** [I] ~ (at/on sth) to act in a dishonest way in order to gain an advantage, especially in a game, a competition, an exam, etc.: He cheats at cards. ◆ She always finds ways to cheat on her taxes. ◆ You're not allowed to look at the answers—that's cheating. **3** [I] ~ (on sb) (of someone who is married or who has a regular sexual partner) to have a secret sexual relationship with someone else
IDM cheat death (often used in newspapers) to survive in a situation where you could have died
PHR V 'cheat sb ('out) of sth to prevent someone from having something, especially in a way that is not honest or fair: They cheated him out of his share of the profits.
• **noun 1** (also cheat·er) [C] a person who cheats, especially in a game: You little cheat! **2** [sing.] something that seems unfair or dishonest, for example a way of doing something with less effort than it usually needs: It's really a cheat, but you can use a ready-made pie crust if you want. **3** [C] (computing) a program you can use to move immediately to the next stage of a computer game without needing to play the game: There's a cheat you can use to get to the next level.

'cheat sheet noun (informal) a set of notes to help you remember important information, especially one taken secretly into an exam room

check /tʃɛk/ verb, noun, exclamation
• **verb**
> EXAMINE **1** [T] ~ sth (for sth) to examine something to see if it is correct, safe, or acceptable: Check the container for cracks or leaks. ◆ She gave me the minutes of the meeting to read and check. ◆ Check the oil and water before leaving. ◆ Check your work before handing it in.
> MAKE SURE **2** [I, T] to find out if something is correct or true, or if something is how you think it is: "Is Mary in the office?" "Just a moment. I'll go and check." ◆ ~ (that)... Go and check (that) I've locked the windows. ◆ ~ (with sb) (what/whether, etc....) You'd better check with Jane what time she's expecting us tonight. ⊃ see also CROSS-CHECK, DOUBLE-CHECK
> COATS/BAGS/CASES **3** [T] ~ sth to leave coats, bags, etc. in an official place (called a CHECKROOM) while you are visiting a club, restaurant, etc.: Do you want to check your coats? **4** [T] ~ sth to leave bags or cases with an official so that they can be put on a plane

---

> **MAKE MARK 5** [T] ~ sth to put a mark (✓) next to an item on a list, an answer, etc.: *Check the box next to the right answer.*
> **CONTROL 6** [T] ~ sth to control something; to stop something from increasing or getting worse: *The government is determined to check the growth of public spending.* ◆ [T] to stop yourself from saying or doing something, or from showing a particular emotion: *~ sth to check your anger/laughter/ tears* ◆ **~ yourself** *She wanted to tell him the whole truth but she checked herself—it wasn't the right moment.*
> **IN HOCKEY 8** [T] ~ sb to push or hit someone hard with your body or a stick in order to stop them: *He checked his opponent and stole the puck.*

PHR V ,check 'in (at...) to go to a desk in a hotel, an airport, etc. and tell an official there that you have arrived: *Please check in at least an hour before departure.* ◆ *We've checked in at the hotel.* ◆ related noun **CHECK-IN** ,check sth↔'in to leave bags or cases with an official to be put on a plane: *We checked in our luggage and went through security.* **7** [T] ◆ related noun **CHECK-IN** 'check into... to arrive at a hotel or private hospital to begin your stay there: *He checked into a top Los Angeles clinic yesterday for an operation on his knee.* ,check sb/ sth↔'off to put a mark (✓) beside a name or an item on a list to show that something has been dealt with: *Check the names off as the guests arrive.* 'check on sb/sth to make sure that there is nothing wrong with someone or something: *I'll just go and check on the kids.* ,check 'out **1** to be found to be true or acceptable after being examined: *The local police found her story didn't check out.* **2** to take the things you want to buy at a supermarket to a counter and pay for them: *As soon as I get a couple more items, I'll be ready to check out.* ◆ related noun **CHECKOUT** (1) ,check 'out (of...) to pay your bill and leave a hotel, etc.: *Guests should check out of their rooms by noon.* ◆ related noun **CHECKOUT** (2) ,check sb↔'out to enter the price of goods being bought in a supermarket into a **CASH REGISTER**, so the total can be calculated and the customer can pay: *We'll be able to check more customers out if we open another register.* ◆ related noun **CHECKOUT** (1) ,check sb/sth↔'out **1** to find out if something is correct, or if someone is acceptable: *The police are checking out his alibi.* ◆ *We'll have to check him out before we employ him.* **2** (*informal*) to look at or examine a person or thing that seems interesting or attractive: *Check out the prices at our new store!* ◆ *Hey, check out that car!* ,check sth↔'out to borrow something from an official place, for example a book from a library: *The book has been checked out in your name.* ,check 'over/'through↔sth to examine something carefully to make sure that it is correct or acceptable: *Check over your work for mistakes.* ,check 'up on sb to make sure that someone is doing what they should be doing: *My parents are always checking up on me.* ,check 'up on sth to find out if something is true or correct: *I need to check up on a few things before I can decide.*

check

examine ◆ inspect ◆ go over sth

These words all mean to look closely to make sure that everything is correct, in good condition, or acceptable.

check to look at something closely to make sure that everything is correct, in good condition, safe, or satisfactory: *Check your work before handing it in.*

examine to look at someone or something closely to see if there is anything wrong or to find the cause of a problem: *The goods were examined for damage.*

inspect to look at someone or something closely to make sure that everything is satisfactory; to officially visit a school, factory, etc. in order to check that rules are being followed and that standards are acceptable: *Make sure you inspect the goods before signing for them.* ◆ *The state health board inspects all restaurants at least once a year.*

CHECK, EXAMINE, OR INSPECT?
All these words can be used when you are looking for possible problems, but only **check** is used for mistakes: *~~Examine/Inspect your work before handing it in.~~* Only **examine** is used when looking for the cause of a problem: *~~The doctor checked/inspected her but could find nothing wrong.~~* **Examine** is used more often when talking about the activities of a professional person: *The surveyor examined the walls for signs of termites.* **Inspect** is used more often about an official: *Public health officials were called in to inspect the nursing home.*

go over sth to check something carefully for mistakes, damage, or anything dangerous: *My boss goes over each report in detail.*

PATTERNS
- to check/examine/inspect/go over sth **for** sth
- to check/examine/inspect/go over sth **to see if/ whether...**
- to check/examine/inspect/go over sth **carefully/ thoroughly**

● *noun*
> **EXAMINATION 1** [C] ~ (for/on sth) an act of making sure that something is safe, correct, or in good condition by examining it: *Could you give the tires a check?* ◆ *a health check* ◆ *The drugs were found in their car during a routine check by police.* ◆ *a check for spelling mistakes* ◆ *I'll just have a quick check to see if the letter's arrived yet.* ◆ *It is vital to keep a check on your speed* (= look at it regularly in order to control it). ◆ see also **REALITY CHECK**
> **INVESTIGATION 2** [C] ~ (on sb/sth) an investigation to find out more information about something: *The police ran a check on the license plate number of the car.* ◆ *Was any check made on Mr. Morris when he applied for the position?*
> **MONEY 3** (*CanE usually* cheque) [C] a printed form that you can write on and sign as a way of paying for something instead of using money: *a check for $50* ◆ *to write a check* ◆ *to make a check out to someone* ◆ *to pay by check* ◆ *to cash a check* (= to get or give money for a check) ◆ see also **BLANK CHECK, CASHIER'S CHECK, PERSONAL CHECK , TRAVELER'S CHECK**
> **4** [C] a piece of paper that shows how much you have to pay for the food and drinks that you have had in a restaurant: *Can I have the check, please?* ◆ compare **BILL** *n.* ◆ thesaurus box at **BILL**
> **CONTROL 5** [C] ~ (on/to sth) (*formal*) something that delays the progress of something else or stops it from getting worse: *A cold spring will provide a natural check on the number of insects.* **6** checks [pl.] (*formal*) rules that are designed to control the amount of power, especially political power, that one person or group has ◆ see also **CHECKS AND BALANCES**
> **MARK 7** (also 'check mark) [C] a mark (✓) put beside a written answer or an item on a list, usually to show that it has been checked, or done, or is correct ◆ compare **CROSS, X**
> **PATTERN 8** [C, U] a pattern of squares, usually of two colors: *Do you prefer checks or stripes?* ◆ see also **CHECKED**
> **FOR COATS/BAGS 9** [C] coat ~ a place in a club, restaurant, etc. where you can leave your coat or bag **10** [C] a ticket that you get when you leave your coat, bag, etc. in, for example, a restaurant or theater
> **IN HOCKEY 11** [C] an act of pushing or hitting someone hard with your body or a stick in order to stop them
> **IN GAME 12** [U] (in CHESS) a position in which a player's king (= the most important piece) can be directly attacked by the other player's pieces: *There, you're in check.* ◆ see also **CHECKMATE**

IDM hold/keep sth in check to keep something under control so that it does not spread or get worse ◆ more at **RAIN CHECK**

• *exclamation* used to show that you agree with someone or that something on a list has been dealt with: *"Do you have your tickets?" "Check." "Passport?" "Check."*

check·book (*CanE* **cheque·book**) /'tʃɛkbʊk/ *noun* a book of printed checks

ˌ**checkbook** ˈ**journalism** *noun* [U] (*disapproving*) the practice of journalists paying people large amounts of money to give them personal or private information for a newspaper story

check·box /'tʃɛkbɑks/ *noun* a small square on a computer screen that you click on with the mouse to choose whether a particular function is switched on or off

ˈ**check card** *noun* = DEBIT CARD

checked /tʃɛkt/ *adj.* having a pattern of squares, usually of two colors: *checked material* ♦ *a checked shirt* ⊃ see also CHECK

check·er /'tʃɛkər/ *noun* ⊃ see also CHECKERS **1** a person who works at the CHECKOUT in a supermarket **2** (in compounds) a computer program that you use to check something, for example the spelling and grammar of something you have written: *a spelling/grammar/virus checker* **3** a person who checks things: *a quality control checker* ♦ *a fact checker*

check·er·board /'tʃɛkər,bɔrd/ *noun* a board with black and white squares, used for playing CHECKERS

check·ered /'tʃɛkərd/ *adj.* **1** ~ *past/history/career* a person's past, etc. that contains both successful and not successful periods **2** having a pattern of squares of different colors

the ˌ**checkered** ˈ**flag** *noun* a flag with black and white squares that is waved when a driver has finished a motor race

check·ers /'tʃɛkərz/ *noun* [U] a game for two players using 24 round pieces on a board marked with black and white squares ⊃ picture at TOY

ˈ**check-in** *noun* **1** [C, U] the place where you go first when you arrive at an airport, hotel, or hospital, to show your ticket, get your room key, etc. **2** [U] the act or process of arriving and registering at an airport, hotel, or hospital: *Do you know your check-in time?* ♦ *the check-in counter/desk*

ˈ**checking ac·count** (*CanE* ˈ**chequing ac·count**) *noun* a type of bank account that you can take money out of at any time, and that provides you with a CHECKBOOK and an ATM CARD ⊃ compare SAVINGS ACCOUNT

check·list /'tʃɛklɪst/ *noun* a list of the things that you must remember to do, to take with you, or to find out

check·mate /'tʃɛkmeɪt/ (also **mate**) *noun* [U] **1** (in CHESS) a position in which one player cannot prevent his or her king (= the most important piece) being captured and therefore loses the game ⊃ see also CHECK ⊃ compare STALEMATE **2** a situation in which someone has been completely defeated ▸ **check·mate** *verb:* ~ *sb/sth His king had been checkmated.* ♦ *She hoped the plan would checkmate her opponents.*

check·out /'tʃɛkaʊt/ *noun* **1** [C] the place where you pay for the things that you are buying in a supermarket: *long lines at the checkouts* **2** [U] the time when you leave a hotel at the end of your stay: *At checkout, your bill will be printed for you.*

check·point /'tʃɛkpɔɪnt/ *noun* a place, especially on a border between two countries, where people have to stop so their vehicles and documents can be checked

check·room /'tʃɛkrum, -rʊm/ *noun* (also ˈ**cloak·room**, ˈ**coat check**, ˈ**coat·room**) a room in a public building where people can leave coats, bags, etc. for a time

ˌ**checks and** ˈ**balances** *noun* [pl.] **1** the principle of government by which the President, Congress, and the Supreme Court each have some control over the others ⊃ compare SEPARATION OF POWERS **2** influences in an organization or political system that help to keep it fair and stop a small group from keeping all the power

check·sum /'tʃɛksʌm/ *noun* (*computing*) the total of the numbers in a piece of digital data, used to check that the data is correct

ˈ**check-up** *noun* an examination of something, especially a medical one to make sure that you are healthy: *to go for/to have a check-up* ♦ *a medical/dental/routine/thorough check-up*

ched·dar /'tʃɛdər/ (also ˌ**cheddar** ˈ**cheese**) *noun* [U] a type of hard yellow or orange cheese

cheek /tʃik/ *noun* **1** [C] either side of the face below the eyes: *chubby/rosy/pink cheeks* ♦ *He kissed her on both cheeks.* ♦ *Couples were dancing cheek to cheek.* ⊃ picture at BODY ⊃ collocations at PHYSICAL **2** -**cheeked** (in adjectives) having the type of cheeks mentioned: *chubby-cheeked/rosy-cheeked/hollow-cheeked* **3** [C] (*informal*) either of the BUTTOCKS
IDM **cheek by jowl (with sb/sth)** very close to someone or something **turn the other cheek** to make a deliberate decision to remain calm and not to act in an aggressive way when someone has hurt you or made you angry ⊃ more at TONGUE

cheek·bone /'tʃikboʊn/ *noun* the bone below the eye ⊃ picture at BODY

cheek·y /'tʃiki/ *adj.* (**cheek·i·er, cheek·i·est**) (*informal*) rude in an amusing or an annoying way: *a cheeky grin* ▸ **cheek·i·ly** /-kəli/ *adv.* **cheek·i·ness** *noun* [U]

cheep /tʃip/ *verb* [I] (of young birds) to make short, high sounds ▸ **cheep** *noun*

cheer /tʃɪr/ *noun, verb*
• *noun* **1** [C] a shout of joy, support, or praise: *A great cheer went up from the crowd.* ♦ *cheers of encouragement* ♦ *Three cheers for the winners!* (= used when you are asking a group of people to cheer three times, in order to CONGRATULATE someone, etc.) **ANT** BOO **2** [C] a special song or poem used by CHEERLEADERS **3** [U] (*formal* or *literary*) an atmosphere of happiness
• *verb* **1** [I, T] to shout loudly, to show support or praise for someone, or to give them encouragement: *We all cheered as the team came on to the field.* ♦ *Cheering crowds greeted their arrival.* ♦ ~ **sb** *The crowd cheered the President as he drove slowly by.* ⊃ thesaurus box at SHOUT **ANT** BOO **2** [T] ~ **sb** [usually passive] to give hope, or encouragement to someone: *She was cheered by the news from home.* ▸ **cheer·ing** *noun* [U]: *He came on stage amid clapping and cheering.* **cheer·ing** *adj.*: *The results of the test were very cheering.*
PHRV ˌ**cheer sb↔ˈon** to give shouts of encouragement to someone in a race, competition, etc. ˌ**cheer ˈup** | ˌ**cheer sb/sth↔ˈup** to become more cheerful; to make someone or something more cheerful: *Oh, come on—cheer up!* ♦ *Give Mary a call; she needs some cheering up.* ♦ *Bright curtains can cheer up a dull room.*

cheer·ful /'tʃɪrfl/ *adj.*
1 happy, and showing it by the way that you behave: *You're not your usual cheerful self today.* ♦ *a cheerful, hardworking employee* ♦ *a cheerful smile/voice* **2** giving you a feeling of happiness: *a bright, cheerful restaurant* ♦ *walls painted in cheerful* (= light and bright) *colors* ♦ *a chatty, cheerful letter* ▸ **cheer·ful·ly** /-fəli/ *adv.* **cheer·ful·ness** *noun* [U]

cheer·lead·er /'tʃɪr,lidər/ *noun* **1** one of the members of a group of young people (usually women) wearing special uniforms, who encourage the crowd to CHEER for their team at a sports event **2** a person who supports a particular politician, idea, or way of doing something ▸ **cheer·lead·ing** *noun* [U]: *She was into cheerleading in high school.* ♦ *the President's continued cheerleading for the "strong dollar"*

cheer·less /'tʃɪrləs/ *adj.* (*formal*) (of a place, etc.) without warmth or color so it makes you feel depressed **SYN** GLOOMY: *a dark and cheerless room*

cheers /tʃɪrz/ *exclamation* a word that people say to each other as they lift up their glasses to drink

cheer·y /ˈtʃɪri/ adj. (cheer·ier, cheer·iest) (informal) (of a person or their behavior) happy and cheerful: *a cheery remark/smile/wave* ◆ *He left with a cheery "See you again soon."* ▶ **cheer·i·ly** /ˈtʃɪrəli/ adv.

cheese 🔑 /tʃiz/ noun
1 [U, C] a type of food made from milk, that can be either soft or hard and is usually white or yellow in color; a particular type of this food: *Cheddar cheese* ◆ *a grilled cheese sandwich* ◆ *a chunk/piece/slice of cheese* ◆ *a selection of French cheeses* ◆ *a cheese knife* (= a knife with a special curved blade with two points on the end, used for cutting and picking up pieces of cheese) ⊃ see also AMERICAN CHEESE, BLUE CHEESE, COTTAGE CHEESE, CREAM CHEESE, GOAT CHEESE, MACARONI AND CHEESE, STRING CHEESE **2** **cheese!** what you ask someone to say before you take their photograph **IDM** see BIG adj.

cheese·board /ˈtʃizbɔrd/ noun **1** a board that is used to cut cheese on **2** a variety of cheeses that are served at the end of a meal

cheese·burg·er /ˈtʃizˌbərgər/ noun a HAMBURGER with a slice of cheese on top of the meat

cheese·cake /ˈtʃizkeɪk/ noun [C, U] a cold DESSERT (= a sweet dish) made from a soft mixture of CREAM CHEESE, sugar, eggs, etc. on a base of PASTRY, cake, or crushed cookies, sometimes with fruit on top: *a strawberry cheese-cake* ◆ *Is there any cheesecake left?*

cheese·cloth /ˈtʃizklɔθ/ noun [U] a type of loose cotton cloth used in cooking and making cheese

cheese straw noun a stick of PASTRY with cheese in it, eaten as a SNACK

chees·y /ˈtʃizi/ adj. (chees·ier, chees·iest) **1** (informal) not very good or original, in a way that is embarrassing but amusing: *a cheesy horror movie* **2** (informal) too emotional or romantic, in a way that is embarrassing: *a cheesy love song* **3** (of a smile) done in an exaggerated and probably not sincere way: *She had a **cheesy grin** on her face.* **4** smelling or tasting of cheese

chee·tah /ˈtʃitə/ noun a wild animal of the cat family, with black spots, that runs very fast

chef /ʃɛf/ noun a professional cook, especially the most senior cook in a restaurant, hotel, etc. ⊃ see also PASTRY CHEF

chef-d'oeuvre /ʃeɪ ˈdərv; -ˈduvrə/ noun (pl. chefs-d'oeuvre /ʃeɪ ˈdərv; -ˈduvrə/) (from French, formal) a very good piece of work, especially the best work by a particular artist, writer, etc. **SYN** MASTERPIECE

chef's ˌsalad (also ˈchef ˌsalad) noun a large salad consisting of LETTUCE, tomato, and other vegetables with slices of cheese and meat, such as chicken or HAM, on top

chem·i·cal 🔑 **AWL** /ˈkɛmɪkl/ adj., noun
● **adj. 1** connected with chemistry: *a chemical element* ◆ *the chemical industry* **2** produced by or using processes that involve changes to atoms or MOLECULES: *chemical reactions/processes* ▶ **chem·i·cally** **AWL** /-kli/ adv.: *The raw sewage is chemically treated.*
● **noun** a substance obtained by or used in a chemical process

ˌchemical engiˈneering noun [U] the study of the design and use of machines in industrial chemical processes ▶ **ˌchemical engiˈneer** noun

ˌchemical ˈwarfare noun [U] the use of poisonous gases and chemicals as weapons in a war

ˌchemical ˈweapon noun a weapon that uses poisonous gases and chemicals to kill and injure people ⊃ compare BIOLOGICAL WEAPON

che·mise /ʃəˈmiz/ noun a loose dress or piece of women's underwear

chem·ist 🔑 /ˈkɛmɪst/ noun
a scientist who studies chemistry: *a research chemist*

chem·is·try 🔑 /ˈkɛməstri/ noun [U]
1 the scientific study of the structure of substances, how they react when they are combined or in contact with one another, and how they behave under different conditions: *a degree in chemistry* ◆ *the university's chemistry department* ◆ *inorganic/organic chemistry* ⊃ see also BIOCHEMISTRY **2** (technical) the chemical structure and behavior of a particular substance: *the chemistry of copper* ◆ *The patient's blood chemistry was monitored regularly.* **3** the relationship between two people, usually a strong sexual attraction: *sexual chemistry* ◆ *The chemistry just wasn't right.*

ˈchemistry ˌset noun a box of equipment that children can use to perform simple chemistry experiments

che·mo /ˈkimoʊ/ noun [U] (informal) = CHEMOTHERAPY

che·mo·re·cep·tor /ˌkimoʊrɪˈsɛptər/ noun (biology) a cell or sense organ that is sensitive to chemical stimuli (STIMULUS), making a response possible

che·mo·ther·a·py /ˌkimoʊˈθɛrəpi/ (also informal che·mo) noun [U] the treatment of disease, especially cancer, with the use of chemical substances ⊃ compare RADIATION, RADIOTHERAPY

che·nille /ʃəˈnil/ noun [U] a type of thick, soft thread; cloth made from this: *a chenille sweater*

cheong·sam /ˈtʃɔŋsam/ noun a straight, tightly fitting, silk dress with a high neck and short sleeves, and an opening at the bottom on each side, worn by women from China and Indonesia

cheque (CanE) = CHECK n. (3)

cheque·book (CanE) = CHECKBOOK

ˈchequing acˌcount noun (CanE) = CHECKING ACCOUNT

cher·ish /ˈtʃɛrɪʃ/ verb (formal) **1** ~ sb/sth to love someone or something very much and want to protect them or it: *Children need to be cherished.* ◆ *her most cherished possession* **2** ~ sth to keep an idea, a hope, or a pleasant feeling in your mind for a long time: ***Cherish the memory*** *of those days in Paris.*

Cher·o·kee /ˈtʃɛrəki/ noun (pl. Cher·o·kee or Cher·o·kees) a member of a Native American people, many of whom now live in Oklahoma and North Carolina

che·root /ʃəˈrut/ noun a type of CIGAR with two open ends

cher·ry /ˈtʃɛri/ noun, adj.
● **noun** (pl. cher·ries) **1** [C] a small, soft, round fruit with shiny red or black skin and a large seed inside ⊃ picture at FRUIT **2** (also ˈcherry tree) [C] a tree on which cherries grow, or a similar tree, grown for its flowers: *cherry blossoms* ◆ *a winter-flowering cherry* **3** (also cher·ry·wood /ˈtʃɛriˌwʊd/) [U] the wood of the cherry tree **4** (also ˌcherry ˈred) [U] a bright red color
● **adj.** (also ˌcherry ˈred) bright red in color: *cherry lips*

ˈcherry ˌbomb noun a small, round, red FIRECRACKER that explodes with a very loud noise

ˈcherry-ˌpick verb [T, I] ~ (sb/sth) to choose the best people or things from a group and leave those that are not so good

ˈcherry ˌpicker noun **1** a type of tall CRANE that lifts people up so that they can work in very high places **2** a person who picks cherries

ˈcherry toˌmato noun a type of very small tomato

cher·ub /ˈtʃɛrəb/ noun **1** (pl. cher·ubs or cher·u·bim /ˈtʃɛrəbɪm/) (in art) a type of ANGEL, shown as a small, fat, usually male, child with wings ⊃ compare SERAPH **2** (pl. cher·ubs) (informal) a pretty child; a child who behaves well ▶ **che·ru·bic** /tʃəˈrubɪk/ adj. (formal): *a cherubic face* (= looking round and innocent, like a small child's)

cher·vil /ˈtʃɜrvl/ noun [U] a plant with leaves that are used in cooking as an HERB

chess /tʃɛs/ noun [U] a game for two people played on a board marked with black and white squares on which each playing piece (representing a king, queen, castle, etc.) is

h hat　　m man　　n no　　ŋ sing　　l leg　　r red　　y yes　　w wet

moved according to special rules. The aim is to put the other player's king in a position from which it cannot escape (= to CHECKMATE it). ◇ picture at TOY

chess·board /'tʃesbɔːrd/ *noun* a board with 64 black and white squares that chess is played on ◇ picture at TOY

chess·man /'tʃesmæn; -mən/ *noun* (*pl.* **chess·men** /-mɛn; -mən/) any of the 32 pieces used in the game of chess

chest 🔑 /tʃɛst/ *noun*
1 the top part of the front of the body, between the neck and the stomach: *The bullet hit him in the chest.* ◆ *She gasped for breath, her chest heaving.* ◆ *a chest infection* ◆ *chest pains* ◆ *a hairy chest* ◇ picture at BODY ◇ collocations at PHYSICAL **2 -chested** (in adjectives) having the type of chest mentioned: *flat-chested* ◆ *broad-chested* **3** a strong box, often made of wood, used for storing things in and/or moving them from one place to another: *a medicine chest* ◆ *a treasure chest* ◇ see also HOPE CHEST, ICE CHEST, WAR CHEST **IDM** **get sth off your chest** to talk about something that has been worrying you for a long time so that you feel less anxious ◇ more at CARD *n.*

chest·nut /'tʃɛsnʌt/ *noun, adj.*
● *noun* **1** (also **chestnut tree**) [C] a large tree with spreading branches, that produces smooth brown nuts inside cases that are covered with SPIKES. There are several types of chestnut trees. ◇ see also HORSE CHESTNUT **2** [C] a smooth brown nut of a chestnut tree, some types of which can be eaten: *roasted chestnuts* ◇ picture at NUT ◇ see also WATER CHESTNUT **3** [U] a deep reddish-brown color **4** [C] a horse of a reddish-brown color **5 old chestnut** [C] (*informal*) an old joke or story that has been told so many times that it is no longer amusing or interesting
● *adj.* reddish-brown in color

chest of drawers *noun* (*pl.* **chests of drawers**) (also **bu·reau, dres·ser**) a piece of furniture with drawers for keeping clothes in

chev·ron /'ʃɛvrən/ *noun* **1** a line or pattern in the shape of a V **2** a piece of cloth in the shape of a V that soldiers and police officers wear on their uniforms to show their rank

chew 🔑 /tʃuː/ *verb, noun*
● *verb* **1** [I, T] to bite food into small pieces in your mouth with your teeth to make it easier to swallow: **~ (at/on/through sth)** *After the operation you may find it difficult to chew and swallow.* ◆ **~ sth (up)** *teeth designed for chewing meat* ◆ *He is always chewing gum.* **2** [I, T] to bite something continuously, for example because you are nervous or to taste it: **~ on sth** *Rosa chewed on her lip and stared at the floor.* ◆ *The dog was chewing on a bone.* ◆ **~ sth** *to chew your nails* **IDM** **chew the fat** (*informal*) to have a long friendly talk with someone about something ◇ more at BITE *v.* **PHR V** **chew sb 'out** (*informal*) to tell someone angrily that you do not approve of their actions: *He got chewed out by the boss for lying.* **chew sth⟷'over** to think about or discuss something slowly and carefully
● *noun* **1** an act of chewing something **2** a type of candy or cookie that you chew **3** a piece of TOBACCO that you chew

chewing gum *noun* [U] = GUM

chew·y /'tʃuːi/ *adj.* (**chew·i·er, chew·i·est**) (of food) needing to be chewed a lot before it can be swallowed

Chey·enne /ʃaɪˈæn; -ˈɛn/ *noun* (*pl.* **Chey·enne** or **Chey·ennes**) a member of a Native American people, many of whom now live in Oklahoma and Montana

chez /ʃeɪ/ *prep.* (from *French*) at the home of: *I spent a pleasant evening chez the Stewarts.*

chi /kaɪ/ *noun* the 22nd letter of the Greek alphabet (Χ, χ)

Chi·an·ti /kiˈɑːnti/ *noun* [U, C] a dry red wine from the region of Tuscany in Italy

chi·a·ro·scu·ro /kiˌɑːrəˈskʊroʊ; -ˈskjʊroʊ/ *noun* [U] (*art*) the way light and shade are shown; the contrast between light and shade

chi·as·mus /kaɪˈæzməs; ki-/ *noun* (*pl.* **chi·as·mi** /kaɪˈæzmaɪ; kiˈæzmi/) [U, C] (*technical*) a technique used in writing or in speeches, in which words, ideas, etc. are repeated in reverse order

chic /ʃiːk/ *adj.* very fashionable and elegant **SYN** STYLISH: *She always looks so chic.* ◆ *a chic new restaurant* ► **chic** *noun* [U]: *a perfectly dressed woman with an air of chic that was unmistakably French*

chi·ca /'tʃiːkə/ *noun* (from *Spanish, informal*) a girl or young woman

Chi·ca·na /tʃɪˈkɑːnə/ *noun* (from *Spanish*) a woman or girl living in the U.S. whose family come from Mexico ◇ compare CHICANO, LATINO

chi·can·er·y /ʃɪˈkeɪnəri/ *noun* [U] (*formal*) the use of complicated plans and clever talk in order to trick people

Chi·ca·no /tʃɪˈkɑːnoʊ/ *noun* (*pl.* **Chi·ca·nos**) (from *Spanish*) a person living in the U.S. whose family came from Mexico ◇ compare CHICANA, LATINO

chi·chi /'ʃiːʃi/ *adj.* used to describe a style of decoration that contains too many details and lacks taste

chick /tʃɪk/ *noun* **1** a baby bird, especially a baby chicken **2** (*old-fashioned*, sometimes *offensive*) a way of referring to a young woman

chick·a·dee /'tʃɪkədi/ *noun* a small N. American bird of the TIT family. There are many types of chickadees.

chick·en 🔑 /'tʃɪkən/ *noun, verb, adj.*
● *noun* **1** [C] a large bird that is often kept for its eggs or meat: *They keep chickens in the back yard.* ◆ *free-range chickens* ◇ picture at ANIMAL ◇ compare ROOSTER, HEN **2** [U] meat from a chicken: *fried/roast chicken* ◆ *chicken stock/soup* ◆ *chicken breasts/livers/thighs* ◆ *chicken and dumplings* ◇ see also SPRING CHICKEN **IDM** **a chicken-and-egg situation, problem, etc.** a situation in which it is difficult to tell which one of two things was the cause of the other **play chicken** to play a game in which people do something dangerous for as long as they can to show how brave they are. The person who stops first has lost the game. ◇ more at COUNT *v.*, HOME *adv.*
● *verb* **PHR V** **chicken 'out (of sth/of doing sth)** (*informal*) to decide not to do something because you are afraid
● *adj.* [not before noun] (*informal*) not brave; afraid to do something **SYN** COWARDly

chicken feed *noun* [U] (*informal*) an amount of money that is not large enough to be important

chicken-fried steak *noun* [C, U] a thin piece of beef that is covered in BREADCRUMBS and fried until it is crisp

chicken pox (also **chick·en·pox**) /'tʃɪkən.pɑks/ *noun* [U] a disease, especially of children, that causes a slight fever and many spots on the skin: *to catch/get/have the chicken pox*

chicken run *noun* an area surrounded by a fence in which chickens are kept

chicken wire *noun* [U] thin wire made into sheets like nets with a pattern of shapes with six sides

chick flick *noun* (*informal*) a movie that is intended especially for women

chick lit *noun* [U] (*informal*) novels that are intended especially for women, often with a young, single woman as the main character

chick·pea /'tʃɪkpi/ *noun* (also **gar·ban·zo, gar'banzo bean**) a hard round seed, like a light brown PEA, that is cooked and eaten as a vegetable

chick·weed /'tʃɪkwid/ *noun* [U] a small plant with white flowers that often grows as a WEED over a wide area

chi·co /'tʃiːkoʊ/ *noun* (*pl.* **chi·cos**) (from *Spanish, informal*) a boy or young man

chic·o·ry /'tʃɪkəri/ *noun* [U] **1** [C, U] a small pale green plant with bitter leaves that are eaten raw or cooked as a vegetable. The root can be dried and used with or instead of coffee. **2** = ENDIVE

chide /tʃaɪd/ *verb* (*formal*) to criticize or blame someone because they have done something wrong **SYN** REBUKE: ~ **sb/yourself (for sth/for doing sth)** *She chided herself for being so impatient with the children.* ◆ ~ **(sb) + speech** *"Isn't that a little selfish?" he chided.*

chief 🔑 /tʃiːf/ *adj., noun*
- *adj.* [only before noun] **1** most important: *the chief cause/ problem/reason* ◆ *one of the President's chief rivals* ➔ thesaurus box at MAIN **2** often **Chief** highest in rank: *the Chief Education Officer* ◆ *the chief financial officer of the company* **3** -**in**-'**chief** (in nouns) of the highest rank: *commander-in-chief* ➔ see also CHIEFLY
- *noun* **1** a person with a high rank or the highest rank in a company or an organization: *army/industry/police chiefs* ➔ see also CHIEF OF STAFF **2** (often as a title) a leader or ruler of a people or community: *Chief Buthelezi* ◆ *Chief Crazy Horse*

the ˌChief ˈDiplomat *noun* the president of the United States, as the person who directs and manages how the country deals with foreign governments

ˌ**chief exˈecutive** *noun* **1** = CHIEF EXECUTIVE OFFICER **2** Chief Executive the President of the United States

ˌ**chief exˌecutive ˈofficer** *noun* (*abbr.* CEO) (also ˌchief exˈecutive) the person in a company who has the most power and authority

ˌ**chief ˈjustice** (also ˌChief ˈJustice) *noun* the most important judge in a court, especially the U.S. Supreme Court or a state supreme court

chief·ly /ˈtʃiːfli/ *adv.* not completely, but as a most important part **SYN** PRIMARILY, MAINLY: *We are chiefly concerned with improving educational standards.* ◆ *He's traveled widely, chiefly in Africa and Asia.*

ˌ**chief of ˈstaff** *noun* (*pl.* ˌchiefs of ˈstaff) an officer of very high rank, responsible for advising the person who commands each of the armed forces ➔ see also JOINT CHIEFS OF STAFF

ˌ**chief of ˈstate** *noun* (*pl.* ˌchiefs of ˈstate) the person who holds the formal title of head of a country, as distinguished from the head of a government: *Queen Elizabeth is the chief of state of the United Kingdom.*

ˌ**Chief ˈRabbi** *noun* the main religious leader of the Jewish community in a particular country or city

chief·tain /ˈtʃiːftən/ *noun* the leader of a people or a CLAN in Scotland

chif·fon /ʃɪˈfɑn/ *noun* [U] a type of fine, transparent cloth made from silk or NYLON, used especially for making clothes

chig·ger /ˈtʃɪgər/ (also jig·ger) *noun* a small FLEA (= a type of very small insect) that lays eggs under a person's or animal's skin, causing painful areas on the skin

chi·gnon /ˈʃinyɑn/ *noun* (from *French*) a style for women's hair in which the hair is pulled back and twisted into a smooth knot at the back ➔ picture at HAIR

chi·hua·hua /tʃɪˈwɑwə/ *noun* a very small dog with smooth hair

chil·blain /ˈtʃɪlbleɪn/ *noun* [usually pl.] a painful red swelling on the hands or feet that is caused by cold or bad CIRCULATION of the blood

child 🔑 /tʃaɪld/ *noun* (*pl.* chil·dren /ˈtʃɪldrən/) **1** a young human who is not yet an adult: *a three-year-old child* ◆ *men, women, and children* ◆ *an unborn child* ◆ *not suitable for young children* ◆ *I lived in Miami as a child.* ◆ *a child star* ➔ see also BRAINCHILD, LATCHKEY CHILD, POSTER CHILD, SCHOOLCHILD **2** a son or daughter of any age: *They have three grown-up children.* ◆ *a support group for adult children of alcoholics* ◆ *They can't have children.* ➔ see also GODCHILD, GRANDCHILD, LOVE CHILD, ONLY CHILD, STEPCHILD ➔ compare KID **3** a person who is strongly influenced by

the ideas and attitudes of a particular time or person: *a child of the 90s* **4** (*disapproving*) an adult who behaves like a child and is not MATURE or responsible
IDM **be with child** (*old-fashioned*) to be pregnant **be child's play** (*informal*) to be very easy to do, so not even a child would find it difficult

---

TOPIC COLLOCATIONS

Children

having a baby/child
- **want (to have)** a baby/a child/children/kids
- **start** a family
- **conceive/be expecting/be going to have** a baby/ child
- **miss** your period
- **become/get/ be/find out that you are** pregnant
- **have** a baby/a child/kids/a son/a daughter/twins/a family
- **have** a normal/a difficult/an unwanted pregnancy; an easy/a difficult birth/labor
- **be in/go into/induce** labor
- **have/suffer/cause** a miscarriage
- **give birth to** a child/a baby/a daughter/a son/twins

parenting
- **bring up/raise** a child/a family
- **care for/watch** a baby/child/kid
- **change** a diaper/a baby
- **nurse/feed/breastfeed/bottle-feed** a baby
- **be entitled to/go on** maternity/paternity leave
- **go back/return to work** after maternity leave
- **need/find/get** a babysitter/high-quality, affordable childcare/a nanny
- **balance/combine work and** childcare/child-rearing/family (life)
- **educate/teach/home-school** a child/a kid/children
- **punish/discipline/spoil** a child/a kid/children
- **adopt/foster** a baby/a child/a kid/children
- **offer a baby for/put a baby up for** adoption
- **be placed with/be raised by** foster parents

ˈ**child aˌbuse** *noun* [U] the crime of harming a child in a physical, sexual, or emotional way: *victims of child abuse*

child·bear·ing /ˈtʃaɪldˌbɛrɪŋ/ *noun* [U] the process of giving birth to children: *women of childbearing age*

child·birth /ˈtʃaɪldbərθ/ *noun* [U] the process of giving birth to a baby: *pregnancy and childbirth* ◆ *His wife died in childbirth.*

child·care /ˈtʃaɪldkɛr/ *noun* [U] the care of children, especially while parents are at work: *childcare facilities for working parents* ➔ collocations at CHILD

child·hood 🔑 /ˈtʃaɪldhʊd/ *noun* [U, C]
the period of someone's life when they are a child: *childhood, adolescence, and adulthood* ◆ *in early childhood* ◆ *childhood memories/experiences* ◆ *She had a happy childhood.* ◆ *childhood cancer* ➔ collocations at AGE
IDM **a/sb's second childhood** a time in the life of an adult person when they behave like a child again

child·ish /ˈtʃaɪldɪʃ/ *adj.* **1** (*disapproving*) (of an adult) behaving in a stupid or silly way **SYN** IMMATURE: *Don't be so childish!* **ANT** MATURE ➔ compare CHILDLIKE **2** connected with or typical of a child: *childish handwriting* ▶ **child·ish·ly** *adv.*: *to behave childishly* **child·ish·ness** *noun* [U]

child·less /ˈtʃaɪldləs/ *adj.* having no children: *a childless couple/marriage*

child·like /ˈtʃaɪldlaɪk/ *adj.* (usually *approving*) having the qualities that children usually have, especially INNOCENCE: *childlike enthusiasm/simplicity/delight* ➔ compare CHILDISH

child·proof /ˈtʃaɪldpruf/ *adj.* designed so that young children cannot open, use, or damage it: *childproof bottles of medicine*

ʌ **cup**   ə **about**   eɪ **say**   aɪ **five**   ɔɪ **boy**   aʊ **now**   oʊ **go**   ər **bird**

'**child re**｜**straint** *noun* a belt, or small seat with a belt, that is used in a car to control and protect a child

'**child seat** *noun* = CAR SEAT

'**child sup**｜**port** *noun* [U] money that a court orders a parent to pay regularly to help support their children, when the children are no longer living with that parent

chil·i /'tʃɪli/ *noun* (*pl.* **chil·ies**) **1** (also **chili** ｜**pepper**) [C, U] the small green or red fruit of a type of pepper plant that is used in cooking to give a hot taste to food, often dried or made into powder, also called chili or **chili powder 2** (also **chil·i con car·ne** /ˌtʃɪli kɑn 'kɑrni/) [U] a hot, spicy dish made with BEANS, chilies, and often meat, originally from Mexico

'**chili** ｜**dog** *noun* a HOT DOG with chili (2) on top of it

chill /tʃɪl/ *noun, verb, adj.*

• *noun* **1** [sing.] a feeling of being cold: *There's a chill in the air this morning.* ♦ *A small fire was burning to **take the chill off** the room.* **2** [C] an illness caused by being cold and wet, causing fever and the SHIVERS (= shaking of the body) **3** [sing.] a feeling of fear: *a chill of fear/apprehension* ♦ *His words sent a chill down her spine.* **IDM** see THRILL *n.*

• *verb* **1** [T, usually passive] **~ sb** to make someone very cold: *They were chilled by the icy wind.* ♦ *Let's go home, I'm **chilled to the bone** (= very cold).* **2** [I, T] when food or a drink **chills** or when someone **chills** it, it is made very cold but it does not freeze: *Let the pudding chill for an hour until set.* ♦ **~ sth** *This wine is best served chilled.* ♦ *chilled foods* (= for example in a supermarket) **3** [I] (*informal*) = CHILL OUT: *We went home and chilled in front of the TV.* ♦ *Just chill, Mom, everything's going to be OK.* **4** [T] **~ sb/sth** (*literary*) to frighten someone: *His words chilled her.* ♦ *What he saw chilled his blood/chilled him to the bone.*

PHR V ｜**chill** '**out** (*informal*) to relax and stop feeling angry or nervous about something: *They sometimes meet up to chill out and watch a movie.* ♦ *Sit down and chill out!*

• *adj.* (*formal*) (especially of weather and the wind) cold, in an unpleasant way: *the chill gray dawn* ♦ *a chill wind*

chill·ax /tʃɪ'læks/ *verb* [I] (*slang*) to relax and stop feeling angry or nervous about something: *Chillax, dude—I'm on your team.*

｜**chilled-**'**out** (also **chilled**) *adj.* (*informal*) very relaxed: *a chilled-out atmosphere* ♦ *He felt totally chilled.*

chill·er /'tʃɪlər/ *noun* a book or movie that is intended to frighten people

chill·ing /'tʃɪlɪŋ/ *adj.* frightening, usually because it is connected with something violent or cruel: *a chilling story* ♦ *The movie evokes chilling reminders of the war.*

chill·out /'tʃɪlaʊt/ *noun* [U] a style of electronic music that is not fast or lively, and is intended to make you relaxed and calm

chill·y /'tʃɪli/ *adj.* (**chill·i·er**, **chill·i·est**) **1** (especially of the weather or a place, but also of people) too cold to be comfortable: *It's chilly today.* ♦ *I was feeling chilly.* ⊃ thesaurus box at COLD **2** not friendly: *The visitors got a chilly reception.* ▶ **chill·i·ness** *noun* [U]

chime /tʃaɪm/ *verb, noun*

• *verb* [I, I] (of a bell or a clock) to ring; to show the time by making a ringing sound: *I heard the clock chime.* ♦ *Eight o'clock had already chimed.* ♦ **~ sth** *The clock chimed midnight.* **PHR V** ｜**chime** '**in** (**with sth**) to join or interrupt a conversation: *He kept chiming in with his own opinions.* ♦ **+ speech** *"And me!" she chimed in.*

• *noun* a ringing sound, especially one that is made by a bell: *door chimes* ⊃ see also WIND CHIMES

chi·me·ra (also **chi·mae·ra**) /kaɪ'mɪrə; kə-/ *noun* **1** (in ancient Greek stories) a creature with a LION's head, a GOAT's body, and a snake's tail, that can breathe out fire **2** (*formal*) an impossible idea or hope

chim·ney /'tʃɪmni/ *noun* **1** a structure through which smoke or steam is carried up away from a fire, etc. and through the roof of a building; the part of this that is above the roof: *He threw the paper onto the fire and it flew up the*

chimney. ♦ *the factory chimneys of an industrial landscape* ⊃ picture at HOUSE **2** (*technical*) a narrow opening in an area of rock that a person can climb up

'**chimney** ｜**stack** (also **smoke·stack**) *noun* a very tall chimney, especially one in a factory

'**chimney** ｜**sweep** (also **sweep**) *noun* a person whose job is to clean the inside of chimneys

chim·pan·zee /ˌtʃɪmpæn'zi/ (also *informal* **chimp**) *noun* a small, intelligent, African APE (= an animal like a large MONKEY without a tail) ⊃ picture at ANIMAL

chin /tʃɪn/ *noun*
the part of the face below the mouth and above the neck ⊃ picture at BODY ⊃ collocations at PHYSICAL ⊃ see also DOUBLE CHIN
IDM (**keep your**) **chin up** (*informal*) used to tell someone to try to stay cheerful even though they are in a difficult or unpleasant situation: *Keep your chin up! Only two exams left.* **take sth on the chin** (*informal*) **1** to accept a difficult or unpleasant situation without complaining, trying to make excuses, etc. **2** to be damaged or badly affected by something ⊃ more at CHUCK *v.*

chi·na /'tʃaɪnə/ *noun* [U] **1** white CLAY that is baked and used for making delicate cups, plates, etc.: *a china vase* ⊃ see also BONE CHINA **2** cups, plates, etc. that are made of china: *She got out the best china.* **IDM** see BULL, TEA

｜**china** '**clay** *noun* [U] = KAOLIN

Chi·na·town /'tʃaɪnəˌtaʊn/ *noun* [U, C] the area of a city where many Chinese people live and there are Chinese stores and restaurants

chin·chil·la /tʃɪn'tʃɪlə/ *noun* **1** [C] an animal like a RABBIT with soft silver-grey fur. Chinchillas are often kept on farms for their fur. **2** [U] the skin and fur of the chinchilla, used for making expensive coats, etc.

Chi·nese /ˌtʃaɪ'niz; -'nis/ *adj., noun*
• *adj.* from or connected with China
• *noun* (*pl.* **Chi·nese**) **1** [C] a person from China, or whose family was originally from China **2** [U] the language of China

｜**Chinese** '**cabbage** *noun* [U] a type of vegetable with long leaves and thick white stems, that is eaten cooked or in salads ⊃ compare BOK CHOY

｜**Chinese** '**checkers** *noun* [U] a game for two to six players who try to move the playing pieces from one corner to the opposite corner of the board, which is shaped like a star ⊃ picture at TOY

｜**Chinese** '**lantern** *noun* **1** a lamp that is inside a paper case, with a handle to carry it **2** a plant with white flowers and round orange fruits inside a material like paper

Chinglish /'tʃɪŋglɪʃ/ *noun* [U] (*informal*) language that is a mixture of ENGLISH and CHINESE, especially a type of English that includes many Chinese words and/or follows Chinese grammar rules

chink /tʃɪŋk/ *noun, verb*
• *noun* **1** a narrow opening in something, especially one that lets light through: *a chink in the curtains* **2 ~ of light** a small area of light shining through a narrow opening **3** [usually sing.] the light ringing sound that is made when glass objects or coins touch: *the chink of glasses* **IDM** a **chink in sb's armor** a weak point in someone's argument, character, etc., that can be used in an attack
• *verb* [I, T] when glasses, coins, or other glass or metal objects touch or when you **chink** them, they make a light ringing sound **SYN** CLINK: *the sound of bottles chinking* ♦ **~ sth** *We chinked glasses and drank to each other's health.*

chin·less /'tʃɪnləs/ *adj.* (of a man) having a very small chin (often thought of as a sign of a weak character)

chi·noi·se·rie /ʃin'wɑzəri/ *noun* [U] (*art*) the use of Chinese images, designs, and techniques in Western art, furniture, and ARCHITECTURE

Chi·nook /ʃəˈnʊk; tʃə-/ *noun* (*pl.* **Chi·nook** or **Chi·nooks**) a member of a group of Native Americans who originally lived in the area around the lower Columbia River in Washington and Oregon

chi·nook /ʃəˈnʊk; tʃə-/ *noun* **1** (also **chi·nook ˈwind**) a warm dry wind that blows down the east side of the Rocky Mountains at the end of winter **2** (also **chi·nook ˈsalmon**) a large N. Pacific SALMON which is eaten as food

chi·nos /ˈtʃiːnoʊz/ *noun* [pl.] informal pants made from strong cotton: *a pair of chinos*

chintz /tʃɪnts/ *noun* [U, C] a type of shiny cotton cloth with a printed design, especially of flowers, used for making curtains, covering furniture, etc.

chintz·y /ˈtʃɪntsi/ *adj.* **1** (*informal*) cheap and not attractive **2** (*informal*) not willing to spend money SYN CHEAP, STINGY **3** covered in or decorated with chintz

ˈchin-up *noun* = PULL-UP

chip ✏ /tʃɪp/ *noun*, *verb*
● *noun* **1** a thin piece of potato or TORTILLA that is fried until hard then dried and eaten cold. Chips are sold in bags and have many different flavors. **2** = MICROCHIP: *chip technology* ⊃ see also V-CHIP **3** the place from which a small piece of wood, glass, etc. has broken from an object: *This mug has a chip in it.* **4** a small piece of wood, glass, etc. that has broken off an object: *chips of wood* ♦ *chocolate chip cookies* (= cookies containing small pieces of chocolate) **5** a small flat piece of plastic used to represent a particular amount of money in some types of gambling: (*figurative*) *The release of prisoners was used as a bargaining chip.* **6** (also **ˈchip shot**) (especially in GOLF and SOCCER) an act of hitting or kicking a ball high in the air so that it lands within a short distance ⊃ see also BLUE-CHIP
IDM **a chip off the old block** (*informal*) a person who is very similar to their mother or father in the way that they look or behave **have a chip on your shoulder (about sth)** (*informal*) to be sensitive about something that happened in the past and become easily offended if it is mentioned because you think that you were treated unfairly **let the chips fall (where they may)** to accept the results of your plans or actions without worrying or complaining: *You may think I'm making a big mistake, but I'm going ahead with my plan, so let the chips fall where they may.* **when the chips are down** (*informal*) used to refer to a difficult situation in which you are forced to decide what is important to you: *I'm not sure what I'll do when the chips are down.* ⊃ more at CASH *v.*
● *verb* (-pp-) **1** [T, I] ~ (sth) to damage something by breaking a small piece off it; to become damaged in this way: *a badly chipped saucer* ♦ *She chipped one of her front teeth.* ♦ *These plates chip easily.* ⊃ picture at BROKEN **2** [T] ~ sth + adv./prep. to cut or break small pieces off something with a tool: *Chip away the damaged area.* ♦ *The fossils had been chipped out of the rock.* **3** [T, I] ~ (sth) (especially in GOLF and SOCCER) to hit or kick the ball so that it goes high in the air and then lands within a short distance **4** [T] ~ sth to put a MICROCHIP under the skin of a dog or other animal so that it can be identified if it is lost or stolen
PHR V **ˌchip aˈway at sth** to keep breaking small pieces off something: *He was chipping away at the stone.* ♦ (*figurative*) *They chipped away at the power of the government* (= gradually made it weaker). **ˌchip ˈin (with sth)** (*informal*) **1** to join in or interrupt a conversation; to add something to a conversation or discussion: *Pete and Anne chipped in with suggestions.* ♦ + speech *"That's different," she chipped in.* **2** (also **ˈchip ˈin sth**) to give some money so that a group of people can buy sth together SYN CONTRIBUTE: *If everyone chips in, we'll be able to buy her a really nice present.* ♦ *We each chipped in (with) $5.* **ˌchip ˈoff** | **ˌchip sth↔ˈoff** to damage something by breaking a small piece off it; to be damaged in this way: *He chipped off a piece of his tooth.* ♦ *The paint had chipped off.*

chip·munk /ˈtʃɪpmʌŋk/ *noun* a small N. American animal of the SQUIRREL family, with light and dark marks on its back ⊃ picture at RODENT

chipped ˈbeef *noun* [U] thin pieces of dried, smoked beef, usually served in a cream sauce

chip·per /ˈtʃɪpər/ *adj.*, *noun*
● *adj.* (*informal*) cheerful and lively
● *noun* a machine that cuts wood into very small pieces

Chip·pe·wa /ˈtʃɪpəˌwɑ; -ˌwɔ/ *noun* (*pl.* **Chip·pe·wa** or **Chip·pe·was**) = ANISHINABE

ˈchip shot *noun* = CHIP

chi·ro·man·cy /ˈkaɪrəˌmænsi/ *noun* [U] the practice of telling what will happen in the future by looking at the lines on someone's PALM SYN PALMISTRY ▶ **chi·ro·man·cer** /-sər/ *noun*

chi·ro·prac·tic /ˌkaɪrəˈpræktɪk; ˈkaɪrəˌpræktɪk/ *noun* [U] the medical profession that involves treating some diseases and physical problems by pressing and moving the bones in a person's SPINE or joints; the work of a chiropractor

chi·ro·prac·tor /ˈkaɪrəˌpræktər/ *noun* a person whose job involves treating some diseases and physical problems by pressing and moving the bones in a person's SPINE or joints ⊃ compare OSTEOPATH

chirp /tʃɜrp/ (also **chir·rup**) *verb* **1** [I] (of small birds and some insects) to make short high sounds **2** [I, T] to speak in a lively and cheerful way ▶ **chirp** (also **chir·rup**) *noun*

chirp·y /ˈtʃɜrpi/ *adj.* (*informal*) lively and cheerful; in a good mood ▶ **chirp·i·ly** /-pəli/ *adv.* **chirp·i·ness** *noun* [U]

chir·rup /ˈtʃɪrəp; ˈtʃɜrəp/ *verb*, *noun* = CHIRP

chis·el /ˈtʃɪzl/ *noun*, *verb*
● *noun* a tool with a sharp, flat edge at the end, used for shaping wood, stone, or metal ⊃ picture at HOBBY, TOOL
● *verb* [T, I] ~ (sth) (+ adv./prep.) to cut or shape wood or stone with a chisel: *A name was chiseled into the stone.* ♦ *She was chiseling some marble.* ▶ **chis·el·er** /ˈtʃɪzlər/ *noun*

chis·eled /ˈtʃɪzld/ *adj.* (of a person's face) having clear, strong features

chi-square test /ˈkaɪ skwer ˌtɛst/ *noun* (*statistics*) a calculation that is used to test how well a set of data fits the results that were expected according to a theory

chit /tʃɪt/ *noun* **1** a short written note, signed by someone, showing an amount of money that is owed, or giving someone permission to do something **2** (*old-fashioned*, *disapproving*) a young woman or girl, especially one who is thought to have no respect for older people

ˈchit-chat *noun* [U] (*informal*) conversation about things that are not important SYN CHAT

chit·ter·lings (also **chit·lins**) /ˈtʃɪtlənz/ *noun* [pl.] pig's INTESTINES, eaten as food

chiv·al·rous /ˈʃɪvlrəs/ *adj.* (of men) polite, kind, and behaving with honor, especially toward women SYN GALLANT ▶ **chiv·al·rous·ly** *adv.*

chiv·al·ry /ˈʃɪvlri/ *noun* [U] **1** polite and kind behavior that shows a sense of honor, especially by men toward women **2** (in the Middle Ages) the religious and moral system of behavior that the perfect KNIGHT was expected to follow

chives /tʃaɪvz/ *noun* [pl.] the long, thin leaves of a plant with purple flowers. Chives taste like onions and are used to give flavor to food. ⊃ picture at HERB ▶ **chive** *adj.* [only before noun]: *a chive and garlic dressing*

chiv·vy /ˈtʃɪvi/ *verb* (**chiv·vies**, **chiv·vy·ing**, **chiv·vied**, **chiv·vied**) ~ sb (into sth/along) | ~ sb to do sth to try and make someone hurry or do something quickly, especially when they do not want to do it: *He chivvied them into the car.*

chla·myd·i·a /kləˈmɪdiə/ *noun* [U] (*medical*) a disease caused by bacteria, that is caught by having sex with an infected person

chlo·ride /ˈklɔraɪd/ *noun* [U, C] (*chemistry*) a COMPOUND of CHLORINE and another chemical element ⊃ see also SODIUM CHLORIDE

t tea   ṭ butter   d did   k cat   g got   tʃ chin   dʒ June   f fall

chlo·ri·nate /ˈklɔrəˌneɪt/ *verb* ~ **sth** to put chlorine in something, especially water ▶ **chlo·ri·na·tion** /ˌklɔrə-ˈneɪʃn/ *noun* [U]: *a chlorination plant*

chlo·rine /ˈklɔrin; klɔˈrin/ *noun* [U] (*symb.* **Cl**) a chemical element. Chlorine is a poisonous greenish gas with a strong smell. It is often used in swimming pools to keep the water clean.

chlo·ro·fluor·o·car·bon /ˌklɔroʊˈflɔrəˌkarbən; -ˈflʊrə-/ *noun* (*chemistry*) a CFC; a COMPOUND containing CARBON, FLUORINE, and CHLORINE, that is harmful to the OZONE LAYER

chlo·ro·form /ˈklɔrəˌfɔrm/ *noun* [U] (*symb.* **CHCl₃**) a clear liquid used in the past in medicine, etc. to make people unconscious, for example before an operation

chlo·ro·phyll /ˈklɔrəfɪl/ *noun* [U] the green substance in plants that absorbs light from the sun to help them grow ⊃ see also PHOTOSYNTHESIS

chlo·ro·plast /ˈklɔrəˌplæst/ *noun* (*biology*) the structure in plant cells that contains CHLOROPHYLL and in which PHO-TOSYNTHESIS takes place

choc·a·hol·ic = CHOCOHOLIC

chock·a·block /ˈtʃɑkəˌblɑk/ (also **chock-a-block**) *adj.* [not before noun] ~ **(with sth/sb)** (*informal*) very full of things or people pressed close together: *The shelves were chockablock with ornaments.* ◆ *It was chockablock in town today* (= full of people).

chock–full /ˌtʃɑkˈfʊl; ˌtʃʌk-/ *adj.* [not before noun] ~ **(of sth/sb)** (*informal*) completely full

choc·o·hol·ic (also **choc·a·hol·ic**) /ˌtʃɑkəˈhɑlɪk; -ˈhɔlɪk/ *noun* (*informal*) a person who likes chocolate very much and eats a lot of it

choc·o·late 🔑 /ˈtʃɑklət; ˈtʃɔk-/ *noun*

1 [U] a hard, brown, sweet food made from COCOA BEANS, used in cooking to add flavor to cakes, etc. or eaten as a candy: *a piece of chocolate* ◆ *a chocolate cake/bar* ◆ *a chocolate factory* ⊃ see also DARK CHOCOLATE, MILK CHOCOLATE **2** [C] a type of candy that is made of or covered with chocolate: *a box of chocolates* **3** [U] a dark brown color

---

THESAURUS

choice

favorite ◆ preference ◆ selection ◆ pick

These are all words for a person or thing that is chosen, or that is liked more than others.

choice a person or thing that is chosen: *She's the best choice for the job.*

favorite a person or thing that you like more than the others of the same type: *Which one's your favorite?*

preference a thing that is liked better or best: *Would you like Italian or Chinese? I don't have a preference.*

FAVORITE OR PREFERENCE?

Your **favorites** are the things you like best, and that you have, do, listen to, etc. often; your **preferences** are the things that you would rather have or do if you have a choice.

selection a number of people or things that have been chosen from a larger group: *A selection of readers' comments are published below.*

pick (*somewhat informal*) a person or thing that is chosen: *Who's your pick for best actress this year?*

PATTERNS

- sb's choice/favorite/pick **for** sth
- sb's choice/selection/pick **as** sth
- an **obvious** choice/favorite/preference/selection
- a(n) **excellent/good/popular/fine** choice/selection

choice 🔑 /tʃɔɪs/ *noun, adj.*

● *noun* **1** [C] ~ **(between A and B)** an act of choosing between two or more possibilities; something that you can choose: *women forced to make a choice between family and career* ◆ *We are faced with a difficult choice.* ◆ *We aim to help students make more informed career choices.* ◆ *There is a wide range of choices open to you.* ⊃ thesaurus box at OPTION **2** [U, sing.] the right to choose or the possibility of choosing: *If I had the choice, I would stop working tomorrow.* ◆ *He had no choice but to leave* (= this was the only thing he could do). ◆ *She's going to do it. She doesn't have much choice.* ◆ *This government is committed to extending parental choice in education.* ⊃ see also HOBSON'S CHOICE, MULTIPLE-CHOICE **3** [C] a person or thing that is chosen: *She's the obvious choice for the job.* ◆ *Hawaii remains a popular choice for winter vacation travel.* ◆ *This color wasn't my first choice.* ◆ *She wouldn't be my choice as manager.* **4** [sing., U] the number or range of different things from which to choose: *The menu has a good choice of desserts.* ◆ *There wasn't much choice of color.* ⊃ see also HOBSON'S CHOICE, MULTIPLE-CHOICE **IDM** by **choice** because you have chosen: *I wouldn't go there by choice.* **of choice (for sb/sth)** (used after a noun) that is chosen by a particular group of people or for a particular purpose: *It's the software of choice for business use.* **of your choice** that you choose yourself: *First prize will be dinner for two at the restaurant of your choice.*

● *adj.* (**choic·er**, **choic·est**) [only before noun] **1** (especially of food) of very good quality **2** (of meat) of good, but not the highest, quality **3** ~ **words/phrases** carefully chosen words or phrases: *She summed up the situation in a few choice phrases.* ◆ (*humorous*) *He used some pretty choice* (= rude or offensive) *language.*

choir /ˈkwaɪər/ *noun* **1** a group of people who sing together, for example in church services or public performances: *She sings in the school choir.* ⊃ collocations at MUSIC **2** the part of a church where the choir sits during services

choir·boy /ˈkwaɪərˌbɔɪ/, **choir·girl** /ˈkwaɪərˌgərl/ *noun* a boy or girl who sings in the choir of a church ⊃ see also CHORISTER

choir·mas·ter /ˈkwaɪərˌmæstər/ *noun* a person who trains a CHOIR to sing

choke /tʃoʊk/ *verb, noun*

● *verb* **1** [I, T] to be unable to breathe because the passage to your lungs is blocked or you cannot get enough air; to make someone unable to breathe: *She almost choked to death on the thick fumes.* ◆ ~ **on sth** *He was choking on a piece of toast.* ◆ ~ **sb** *Very small toys can choke a baby.* **2** [T] ~ **sb** to make someone stop breathing by squeezing their throat **SYN** STRANGLE: *He may have been choked or poisoned.* **3** [I, T] to be unable to speak normally especially because of strong emotion; to make someone feel too emotional to speak normally: ~ **(with sth)** *His voice was choking with rage.* ◆ ~ **sth** *Despair choked her words.* ◆ *"I can't bear it," he said in a choked voice.* ⊃ see also CHOKED **4** [T] to block or fill a passage, space, etc. so that movement is difficult: ~ **sth (with sth)** *The pond was choked with rotten leaves.* ◆ ~ **sth up (with sth)** *The roads are choked up with traffic.* **5** [I] (*informal*) to fail at something, for example because you are nervous: *It looked like an easy goal, but he choked and missed the shot.* **IDM** **enough (sth) to choke a horse** (*informal*) **1** extremely: *a tournament big enough to choke a horse* **2** a large quantity of sth: *His movies have enough prestige to choke a horse.*

PHR V ˌchoke sth↔ˈback to try hard to prevent your feelings from showing: *to choke back tears/anger/sobs* ˌchoke sth↔ˈdown to swallow something with difficulty ˌchoke sth↔ˈoff **1** to prevent or limit something: *High prices have choked off demand.* **2** to interrupt something; to stop something: *Her screams were suddenly choked off.* ˌchoke ˈout | choke out sth to say something with great difficulty because you feel a strong emotion: *He choked out a reply.* ◆ + speech *"I hate you!" she choked out.* ˌchoke ˈup | be/get choked up to find it difficult to speak, because of the strong emotion that you are feeling: *She got choked up when she began to talk about her mother.*

• **noun 1** a device that controls the amount of air flowing into the engine of a vehicle **2** an act or the sound of choking

choke·cher·ry /ˈtʃoʊkˌtʃɛri/ *noun* (*pl.* **choke·cher·ries**) a North American CHERRY tree with very sour fruit that is usually eaten cooked

ˈ**choke ˌcollar** (also ˈ**choke chain**) *noun* a chain formed into a circle by passing one end through a ring on the other end, placed around a dog's neck and used for control by putting pressure on the throat when the dog pulls

choked /tʃoʊkt/ *adj.* [not before noun] **~ up (about sth)** | **~ (about sth)** (*informal*) upset or angry about something, so that you find it difficult to speak

chok·er /ˈtʃoʊkər/ *noun* a piece of jewelry or narrow band of cloth worn closely around the neck

cho·la /ˈtʃoʊlə/ *noun* (*pl.* **cho·las**) (from *Spanish*) a woman from Latin America who has both Spanish and Native American ANCESTORS ⊃ compare CHOLO

chol·er·a /ˈkɑlərə/ *noun* [U] a disease caught from infected water that causes severe DIARRHEA and VOMITING, and often causes death

chol·er·ic /ˈkɑlərɪk; kəˈlɛrɪk/ *adj.* (*formal*) easily made angry **SYN** BAD-TEMPERED

cho·les·ter·ol /kəˈlɛstəˌrɔl/ *noun* [U] a substance found in blood, fat, and most TISSUES of the body. Too much cholesterol can cause heart disease. ⊃ collocations at DIET

cho·lo /ˈtʃoʊloʊ/ *noun* (*pl.* **cho·los**) a person from Latin America who has both Spanish and Native American ANCESTORS ⊃ compare CHOLA

chomp /tʃɑmp/ *verb* [I, T] to eat or bite food noisily **SYN** MUNCH: **~ (away) (on/through sth)** *She was chomping away on a bagel.* ♦ **~ sth** *He chomped his way through two hot dogs.*

choo-choo /ˈtʃutʃu/ *noun* (*pl.* **choo-choos**) a child's word for a train

choose 🔑 /tʃuz/ *verb* (**chose** /tʃoʊz/, **cho·sen** /ˈtʃoʊzn/)

1 [I, T] to decide which thing or person you want out of the ones that are available: *You choose—I can't decide.* ♦ *There are plenty of restaurants to choose from.* ♦ **~ between A and/or B** *She had to choose between quitting her job or hiring a nanny.* ♦ **~ sth** *Sarah chose her words carefully.* ♦ *This site has been chosen for the new school.* ♦ **~ A from B** *We have to choose a new manager from a shortlist of five candidates.* ♦ **~ sb/sth as/for sth** *He chose banking as a career.* ♦ *We chose Paul Stubbs as/for chairperson.* ♦ **~ whether, what, etc....** *You'll have to choose whether to buy it or not.* ♦ **~ to do sth** *We chose to go by train.* ♦ **~ sb to be/do sth** *We chose Paul Stubbs to be chairperson.* **2** [I, T] to prefer or decide to do something: *Employees can retire at 60 if they choose.* ♦ **~ to do sth** *Many people choose not to marry.* ⊃ see also CHOICE

IDM **there is nothing/not much/little to choose between A and B** there is very little difference between two or more things or people ⊃ more at PICK *v.*

THESAURUS

choose

select ♦ pick ♦ decide ♦ opt ♦ go for sth

These words all mean to decide which thing or person you want out of the ones that are available.

choose to decide which thing or person you want out of the ones that are available: *I can't decide—you choose.*

select [often passive] (*formal*) to choose a person or thing, usually carefully, from a group of people or things: *He was selected for the team.* ♦ *a randomly selected sample of 23 schools*

pick (*somewhat informal*) to choose a person or thing from a group of people or things: *Pick a number between one and ten.*

CHOOSE, SELECT, OR PICK?

Choose is the most general of these words and the only one that can be used without an object. When you **select** something, you choose it carefully, unless you actually say that it is *selected randomly/at random.* **Pick** is a more informal word and often a less careful action, used especially when the choice being made is not very important.

decide to choose between two or more possibilities: *We're still trying to* **decide on** *a movie.*

opt to choose to take or not to take a particular course of action: *After graduating, she* **opted for** *a career in music.* ♦ *After a lot of thought, I* **opted against** *buying a motorcycle.*

go for sth (*somewhat informal*) to choose something: *I think I'll go for the fruit salad.*

PATTERNS

- to choose/pick/decide **between** A and/or B
- to choose/select/pick A **from** B
- to opt/go **for** sb/sth
- to choose/decide/opt **to do sth**
- to choose/select/pick sb/sth **carefully/at random**
- **randomly** chosen/selected/picked

choos·er /ˈtʃuzər/ *noun* **IDM** see BEGGAR *n.*

choos·y /ˈtʃuzi/ *adj.* (**choos·i·er**, **choos·i·est**) (*informal*) careful in choosing; difficult to please **SYN** FUSSY, PICKY: *I'm very choosy about my clothes.*

chop 🔑 /tʃɑp/ *verb, noun*

• *verb* (-pp-) **1** to cut something into pieces with a sharp tool such as a knife: **~ sth** *He was chopping logs for firewood.* ♦ *Add the finely chopped onions.* ♦ **~ sth (up) (into sth)** *Chop the carrots up into small pieces.* ♦ (*figurative*) *The country was chopped up into small administrative areas.* ⊃ picture at COOKING ⊃ collocations at COOKING **2** [usually passive] **~ sth (from sth) (to sth)** (*informal*) to reduce something by a large amount; to stop something **SYN** CUT: *The share price was chopped from 50 cents to 20 cents.* **3** **~ sb/sth** to hit someone or something with a short downward stroke or blow

PHR V ˈ**chop (away) at sth** to aim blows at something with a heavy sharp tool such as an AX ˌ**chop sth↔ˈdown** to make something, such as a tree, fall by cutting it at the base with a sharp tool ˌ**chop sth↔ˈoff (sth)** to remove something by cutting it with a sharp tool: *He chopped a branch off the tree.* ♦ (*informal*) *Anne Boleyn had her head chopped off.*

• *noun* **1** [C] a thick slice of meat with a bone attached to it, especially from a pig or sheep: *a pork/lamb chop* **2** [C] an act of cutting something with a quick downward movement using an AX or a knife **3** [C] an act of hitting someone or something with the side of your hand in a quick downward movement: *a karate chop* **4** **chops** [pl.] (*informal*) the part of a person's or an animal's face around the mouth: *The dog sat licking its chops.* **IDM** see BUST *v.*

ˌ**chop-ˈchop** *exclamation* (*informal*) hurry up!: *Chop-chop! We haven't got all day!* **ORIGIN** From pidgin English based on a Chinese word for "quick."

chop·per /ˈtʃɑpər/ *noun* **1** [C] (*informal*) = HELICOPTER **2** [C] a large heavy knife or small AX **3** [C] a type of motorcycle with a long piece of metal connecting the front wheel to the HANDLEBARS **4** **choppers** [pl.] (*informal*) teeth

ˈ**chopping ˌblock** *noun* a thick wooden board used for cutting meat or vegetables on ⊃ picture at KITCHEN **SYN** CUTTING BOARD

chop·py /ˈtʃɑpi/ *adj.* (**chop·pi·er**, **chop·pi·est**) **1** (of the ocean, etc.) with a lot of small waves; not calm: *choppy waters* **2** (*disapproving*) (of a style of writing) containing a lot of short sentences and changing topics too often

chop·stick /ˈtʃɑpstɪk/ *noun* [usually pl.] either of a pair of thin sticks that are used for eating with, especially in some Asian countries

h **h**at	m **m**an	n **n**o	ŋ si**ng**	l **l**eg	r **r**ed	y **y**es	w **w**et

chop su·ey /ˌtʃɑp ˈsui/ *noun* [U] a Chinese-style dish of small pieces of meat fried with vegetables and served with rice

cho·ral /ˈkɔrəl/ *adj.* connected with, written for, or sung by a CHOIR (= a group of singers): *choral music*

cho·rale /kəˈræl; -ˈrɑl/ *noun* **1** a piece of church music sung by a group of singers **2** a group of singers; a CHOIR

chord /kɔrd/ *noun* **1** (*music*) two or more notes played together **2** (*mathematics*) a straight line that joins two points on a curve ➔ picture at SHAPE
IDM **strike/touch a chord (with sb)** to say or do something that makes people feel sympathy or enthusiasm: *The speaker had obviously struck a chord with his audience.*

chore /tʃɔr/ *noun* **1** a task that you do regularly: *doing the household/domestic chores* ➔ thesaurus box at TASK **2** an unpleasant or boring task: *Shopping is a real chore for me.*

cho·re·a /kəˈriə/ *noun* [U] (*medical*) a condition in which parts of the body make quick, sudden movements that cannot be controlled

cho·re·o·graph /ˈkɔriəˌgræf/ *verb* ~ sth to design and arrange the steps and movements for dancers in a BALLET or a show: (*figurative*) *There was some carefully choreographed flag-waving as the president drove by.*

cho·re·og·ra·phy /ˌkɔriˈɑgrəfi/ *noun* [U] the art of designing and arranging the steps and movements in dances, especially in BALLET; the steps and movements in a particular ballet or show ▶ **cho·re·og·ra·pher** /ˌkɔri ˈɑgrəfər/ *noun* **cho·re·o·graph·ic** /ˌkɔriəˈgræfɪk/ *adj.*

cho·ric /ˈkɔrɪk/ *adj.* (*technical*) relating to a CHORUS that is spoken in a play, etc.

chor·is·ter /ˈkɔrəstər; ˈkɑr-/ *noun* a person, especially a boy, who sings in the CHOIR of a church

cho·ri·zo /tʃəˈrisou; -zou/ *noun* (*pl.* **cho·ri·zos**) [U, C] (from *Spanish*) a spicy Spanish or Latin American SAUSAGE

chor·tle /ˈtʃɔrtl/ *verb* [I, T] to laugh loudly with pleasure or because you are amused: *Bill chortled with delight.* ▶ **chor·tle** *noun*

cho·rus /ˈkɔrəs/ *noun, verb*
● *noun* **1** [C] part of a song that is sung after each VERSE **SYN** REFRAIN: *Everyone joined in the chorus.* **2** [C] a piece of music, usually part of a larger work, that is written for a CHOIR (= a group of singers): *the Hallelujah Chorus* **3** [C] (often in names) a large group of singers **SYN** CHOIR: *the Tanglewood Festival Chorus* **4** [C] a group of performers who sing and dance in a musical show: *the chorus line* (= a line of singers and dancers performing together) **5 a ~ of sth** [sing.] the sound of a lot of people expressing approval or disapproval at the same time: *a chorus of praise/complaint* ◆ *a chorus of voices calling for her resignation* ➔ see also DAWN CHORUS **6** [sing.] (in ancient Greek drama) a group of performers who comment together on the events of the play **7** [sing.] (especially in 16th century drama) an actor who speaks the opening and closing words of the play
IDM **in chorus** all together **SYN** IN UNISON: *"Thank you,"* they said in chorus.
● *verb* ~ sth to sing or say something all together: *"Hello, Paul,"* they chorused.

chorus girl *noun* a girl or young woman who is a member of the chorus in a musical show, etc.

chorus line *noun* a group of performers who sing and dance together in a musical show, especially when they stand in a straight line to do this

chose /tʃouz/ *pt of* CHOOSE

cho·sen /ˈtʃouzn/ *verb, adj.*
● *verb pp of* CHOOSE
● *adj.* [only before noun] having been selected as the best or most appropriate: *Music is his chosen vocation.* ◆ *Admission to the club was limited to the chosen few* (= only a few people were selected).

chow /tʃaʊ/ *noun, verb*
● *noun* **1** [U] (*slang*) food **2** (also **chow chow**) [C] a dog with long thick hair, a curled tail, and a blue-black tongue, originally from China
● *verb*
PHR V **chow ˈdown** | **chow sth↔ˈdown** (*informal*) to eat, especially in an eager or noisy way: *He chowed down on lobster.* ◆ *Lions chow down their kills.*

chow·der /ˈtʃaʊdər/ *noun* [U] a thick soup made with fish and vegetables: *clam chowder*

chow·der·head /ˈtʃaʊdərˌhɛd/ *noun* (*informal*) a stupid person

chow mein /ˌtʃaʊ ˈmeɪn/ *noun* [U] a Chinese-style dish of fried NOODLES served with small pieces of meat and vegetables: *chicken chow mein*

Christ /kraɪst/ (also **Je·sus, Jesus ˈChrist**) *noun* the man that Christians believe is the son of God and on whose teachings the Christian religion is based

chris·ten /ˈkrɪsn/ *verb* **1** to give a name to a baby at his or her baptism to welcome him or her into the Christian Church: ~ sb + noun *The child was christened Mary.* ◆ ~ sb *Did you have your children christened?* **2** ~ sb/sth (+ noun) to give a name to someone or something: *This area has been christened "America's last wilderness."* ◆ *They christened the boat "Oceania."* **3** ~ sth (*informal*) to use something for the first time

Chris·ten·dom /ˈkrɪsndəm/ *noun* [U] (*old-fashioned*) all the Christian people and countries of the world

chris·ten·ing /ˈkrɪsənɪŋ/ *noun* a Christian ceremony in which a baby is officially named and welcomed into the Christian Church ➔ compare BAPTISM

Chris·tian /ˈkrɪstʃən; ˈkrɪstʃən/ *adj., noun*
● *adj.* **1** based on or believing the teachings of Jesus Christ: *the Christian Church/faith/religion* ◆ *She had a Christian upbringing.* ◆ *a Christian country* **2** connected with Christians: *the Christian sector of the city* **3** also **christian** showing the qualities that are thought of as typical of a Christian; good and kind
● *noun* a person who believes in the teachings of Jesus Christ or has been BAPTIZED in a Christian church: *What percentage of the population are practicing Christians?*

the Christian ˈera *noun* [sing.] the period of time that begins with the birth of Christ

Chris·ti·an·i·ty /ˌkrɪstʃiˈænəti; ˌkrɪstʃi-/ *noun* [U] the religion that is based on the teachings of Jesus Christ and the belief that he was the son of God

ˈChristian ˌname *noun* (in Western countries) a name given to someone when they are born or when they are CHRISTENED; a personal name, not a family name: *His Christian name is Charles.* ➔ see also FIRST NAME

ˌChristian ˈScience *noun* [U] the beliefs of a religious group called **the Church of Christ Scientist**, which include the belief that the physical world is not real and that you can cure illness only by prayer ▶ **ˌChristian ˈScientist** *noun*

Christ·mas /ˈkrɪsməs/ *noun* [U, C] **1** (also **ˌChristmas ˈDay**) December 25th, the day when Christians celebrate the birth of Christ: *Christmas dinner/presents* **2** (also **Christmas·time**) the period that includes Christmas Day and the days close to it: *the Christmas vacation* ◆ *Are you spending Christmas with your family?* ◆ *Merry Christmas and Happy New Year!* ➔ see also WHITE CHRISTMAS

ˈChristmas ˌcard *noun* a card with a picture on it that you send to friends and relatives at Christmas with your good wishes

ˈChristmas ˌcarol *noun* = CAROL

ˌChristmas ˈEve *noun* [U, C] the day before Christmas Day, December 24th; the evening of this day

'Christmas ,stocking (also stock·ing) *noun* a long sock that children leave out when they go to bed on Christmas Eve so that it can be filled with presents

Christ·mas·sy /'krɪsməsi/ *adj.* (*informal*) typical of Christmas: *We put up the decorations and the tree, and it finally started to feel Christmassy.*

Christ·mas·time /'krɪsməs,taɪm/ *noun* [U, C] = CHRISTMAS

'Christmas ,tree *noun* an EVERGREEN tree, or an artificial tree that looks similar, that people cover with decorations and lights, and have in their homes or outside at Christmas

chro·ma /'krəʊmə/ *noun* [U] (*technical*) the degree to which a color is pure or strong, or the fact that it is pure or strong

chro·mat·ic /krəʊ'mætɪk; krə-/ *adj.* (*music*) of the chromatic scale, a series of musical notes that rise and fall in HALF TONES ➲ compare DIATONIC

chro·ma·tog·ra·phy /,krəʊmə'tɑɡrəfi/ *noun* [U] (*chemistry*) the separation of a mixture by passing it through a material through which some parts of the mixture travel further than others ▶ chro·mat·o·graph·ic /,krəʊ,mætə'ɡræfɪk/ *adj.*

chrome /krəʊm/ *noun* [U] a hard shiny metal used especially as a covering that protects another metal; chromium or an ALLOY of chromium and other metals

,chrome 'steel (also ,chromium 'steel) *noun* [U] a hard steel containing CHROMIUM that is used for making tools

chro·mi·um /'krəʊmiəm/ *noun* [U] (*symb.* Cr) a chemical element. Chromium is a hard gray metal that shines brightly when polished and is often used to cover other metals in order to prevent them from RUSTING: *chromium-plated steel*

,chromium 'steel *noun* [U] = CHROME STEEL

chro·mo·some /'krəʊmə,səʊm/ *noun* (*biology*) one of the very small structures like threads in the nuclei (NUCLEUS) (= central parts) of animal and plant cells, that carry the GENE ➲ see also SEX CHROMOSOME, X CHROMOSOME, Y CHROMOSOME ▶ chro·mo·so·mal /,krəʊmə'səʊməl/ *adj.*: *chromosomal abnormalities*

chron·ic /'krɑnɪk/ *adj.* 1 (especially of a disease) lasting for a long time; difficult to cure or get rid of: *chronic bronchitis/arthritis/asthma* ◆ *the country's chronic unemployment problem* ◆ *a chronic shortage of housing in rural areas* ANT ACUTE 2 having had a disease for a long time: *a chronic alcoholic/depressive* ▶ chron·i·cally /-kli/ *adv.*: *a hospital for the chronically ill*

,chronic fa'tigue ,syndrome *noun* [U] an illness that makes people feel extremely weak and tired and that can last a long time

chron·i·cle /'krɑnɪkl/ *noun, verb*
• *noun* a written record of events in the order in which they happened: *the Anglo-Saxon Chronicle* ◆ *Her latest novel is a chronicle of life in a small town in North Carolina.*
• *verb* ~ sth (*formal*) to record events in the order in which they happened: *Her achievements are chronicled in a new biography out this week.* ▶ chron·i·cler /'krɑnɪklər/ *noun*

chrono- /'krɑnəʊ/ *combining form* (in nouns, adjectives, and adverbs) concerned with time: *chronological*

chron·o·graph /'krɑnə,ɡræf/ *noun* 1 a device for recording time extremely accurately 2 a STOPWATCH

chron·o·log·i·cal /,krɑnl'ɑdʒɪkl/ *adj.* 1 (of a number of events) arranged in the order in which they happened: *The facts should be presented in chronological order.* 2 ~ age (*formal*) the number of years a person has lived as opposed to their level of physical, mental, or emotional development ➲ compare MENTAL AGE ▶ chron·o·log·i·cally /-kli/ *adv.*

chro·nol·o·gy /krə'nɑlədʒi/ *noun* (*pl.* chro·nol·o·gies) [U, C] the order in which a series of events happened; a list of these events in order: *Historians seem to have confused the chronology of these events.* ◆ *a chronology of Mozart's life*

chro·nom·e·ter /krə'nɑmətər/ *noun* a very accurate clock, especially one used at sea

chrys·a·lis /'krɪsələs/ (also chrys·a·lid /'krɪsəlɪd/) *noun* the form of an insect, especially a BUTTERFLY or MOTH, while it is changing into an adult inside a hard case, also called a chrysalis ➲ picture at ANIMAL ➲ compare PUPA

chry·san·the·mum /krɪ'sænθəməm/ *noun* a large, brightly colored, garden flower that is shaped like a ball and made up of many long, narrow PETALS ➲ picture at PLANT

chub /tʃʌb/ *noun* (*pl.* chub) a FRESHWATER fish with a thick body

chub·by /'tʃʌbi/ *adj.* (chub·bi·er, chub·bi·est) slightly fat in a way that people usually find attractive: *chubby cheeks/fingers/hands* ▶ chub·bi·ness *noun* [U]

chuck /tʃʌk/ *verb, noun*
• *verb* 1 (*informal*) to throw something carelessly or without much thought: ~ sth (+ adv./prep.) *He chucked the paper in a drawer.* ◆ ~ sb sth *Would you chuck me the newspaper?* ➲ thesaurus box at THROW 2 ~ sth (*informal*) to throw something away: *That's no good—just chuck it.* 3 (*informal*) to give up or stop doing something: ~ sth *You haven't chucked your job yet?*
IDM chuck sb under the chin (*old-fashioned*) to touch someone gently under the chin in a friendly way PHRV ,chuck sth↔a'way | ,chuck sth↔'out (*informal*) to throw something away: *Those old clothes can be chucked out.* ,chuck sb 'off (sth) | ,chuck sb 'out (of sth) (*informal*) to force someone to leave a place or a job: *They got chucked off the bus.* ◆ *You can't just chuck him out.*
• *noun* 1 [C] a part of a tool such as a DRILL that can be adjusted to hold something tightly 2 (also ,chuck 'steak) [U] meat from the shoulder of a cow

chuck·le /'tʃʌkl/ *verb* [I] ~ (at/about sth) to laugh quietly: *She chuckled at the memory.* ▶ chuck·le *noun*: *She gave a chuckle of delight.*

'chuck ,wagon *noun* (*old-fashioned*) a vehicle with cooking facilities for providing food on a RANCH or for people who are camping or working outdoors

chug /tʃʌɡ/ *verb, noun*
• *verb* (-gg-) 1 [I] (+ adv./prep.) to move making the sound of an engine running slowly: *The boat chugged down the river.* 2 [T] ~ sth (*slang*) to drink all of something quickly without stopping
• *noun* the sound made by a chugging engine

chum /tʃʌm/ *noun* 1 [C] (*old-fashioned, informal*) a friend: *an old school chum* 2 [U] small pieces of fish that are thrown into the water from a boat in order to attract other fish that will be caught

chum·my /'tʃʌmi/ *adj.* (*old-fashioned, informal*) very friendly ▶ chum·mi·ly /'tʃʌməli/ *adv.* chum·mi·ness *noun* [U]

chump /tʃʌmp/ *noun* (*informal*) a stupid person: *Don't be such a chump!*

'chump change *noun* [U] (*informal*) a small or unimportant amount of money: *For all my hard work, all I got was chump change.*

chunk /tʃʌŋk/ *noun* 1 a thick, solid piece that has been cut or broken off something: *a chunk of cheese/concrete* 2 (*informal*) a fairly large amount of something: *I've already written a fair chunk of the article.* 3 (*linguistics*) a phrase or group of words that can be learned as a unit by someone who is learning a language. Examples of chunks are "Can I have the bill, please?" and "Pleased to meet you." IDM see BLOW v.

chunk·ing /'tʃʌŋkɪŋ/ *noun* [U] (*linguistics*) the use of chunks in language

chunk·y /'tʃʌŋki/ *adj.* (chunk·i·er, chunk·i·est) 1 thick and heavy: *a chunky gold bracelet* ◆ *a chunky sweater* 2 having a short, strong body: *a squat, chunky man* 3 (of food) containing thick pieces: *chunky peanut butter*

church /tʃɜrtʃ/ *noun*
1 [C] a building where Christians go to worship: *a church tower* ◆ *The procession moved into the church.* ◆ *church services* 2 [U] a service or services in a church: *How often do*

you **go to church**? ♦ They're **at church** (= attending a church service). ♦ They're **in church**. ♦ *Church is at 9 o'clock.* ⊃ collocations at RELIGION ♦ note at SCHOOL **3 Church** [C] a particular group of Christians: *the Episcopal Church* ♦ *the Catholic Church* ♦ *the Reformed Churches* ⊃ see also DENOMINATION **4 (the) Church** [sing.] the ministers of the Christian religion; the institution of the Christian religion: *The Church has a duty to condemn violence.* ♦ *the conflict between Church and State* ♦ *to go into the Church* (= to become a Christian minister)

church·go·er /'tʃɜrtʃˌgoʊər/ *noun* a person who goes to church services regularly ▶ **church·go·ing** *noun* [U]

church·man /'tʃɜrtʃmən/, **church·wom·an** /'tʃɜrtʃˌwʊmən/ *noun* (pl. **church·men** /-mən/, **church·wom·en** /-ˌwɪmən/) = CLERGYMAN, CLERGYWOMAN

the ˌChurch of ˈEngland *noun* [sing.] the official Church in England

ˈchurch school *noun* a private school that is run by a church or other religious group

church·y /'tʃɜrtʃi/ *adj.* (**church·i·er**, **church·i·est**) (*disapproving*) (of a person) religious in a way that involves going to church, PRAYING, etc. a lot, but often not accepting other people's views

church·yard /'tʃɜrtʃyard/ *noun* an area of land around a church, often used for burying people in ⊃ compare CEMETERY, GRAVEYARD

churl /tʃɜrl/ *noun* (*old-fashioned*) a rude, unpleasant person

churl·ish /'tʃɜrlɪʃ/ *adj.* (*formal*) rude or unfriendly: *It would be churlish to refuse such a generous offer.* ▶ **churl·ish·ly** *adv.* **churl·ish·ness** *noun* [U]

churn /tʃɜrn/ *verb*, *noun*
• *verb* **1** [I, T] if water, mud, etc. **churns**, or if something **churns it (up)**, it moves or is moved around violently: **~ (up)** *The water churned beneath the huge ship.* ♦ **~ (up)** *Huge crowds had churned the field into a sea of mud.* **2** [I, T] **~ (sth)** if your stomach **churns** or if something **churns** your stomach, you feel a strong, unpleasant feeling of worry, disgust, or fear: *My stomach churned as the names were read out.* **3** [I, T] **~ (sb) (up)** to feel or to make someone feel upset or emotionally confused: *Conflicting emotions churned inside him.* **4** [T] **~ sth** to turn and stir milk in a special container in order to make butter
PHRV ˌchurn sth↔ˈout (*informal*, often *disapproving*) to produce something quickly and in large amounts
• *noun* a machine in which milk or cream is shaken to make butter

ˈchurn rate *noun* (*business*) the number of people who stop using a product and change to another, or who leave the company they work for and go to another

chute /ʃut/ *noun* **1** a tube or passage down which people or things can slide: *a laundry/garbage chute* (= from the upper floors of a high building) **2** (*informal*) = PARACHUTE

ˌChutes and ˈLadders™ *noun* [U] a children's game played on a special board with pictures of chutes and ladders on it. Players move their pieces up the ladders to go forward and down the chutes to go back.

chut·ney /'tʃʌtni/ *noun* [U] a cold thick sauce made from fruit, sugar, spices, and VINEGAR, eaten with cold meat, cheese, etc.

chutz·pah /'hʊtspə; 'xʊt-/ *noun* [U] (often *approving*) behavior, or a person's attitude, that is rude or shocking but so confident that people may feel forced to admire it **SYN** NERVE

Ci *abbr.* CURIE(S)

CIA /ˌsi aɪ 'eɪ/ *abbr.* Central Intelligence Agency (a department of the U.S. government that collects information about other countries, often secretly)

cia·bat·ta /tʃəˈbɑtə/ *noun* [U, C] (from *Italian*) a type of Italian bread made in a long, flat shape; a SANDWICH made with this type of bread

ciao /tʃaʊ/ *exclamation* (*informal*, from *Italian*) goodbye

ci·ca·da /səˈkeɪdə/ *noun* a large insect with transparent wings, common in hot countries. The male makes a continuous high sound by making two MEMBRANES (= pieces of thin skin) on its body VIBRATE (= move very fast).

-cide /saɪd/ *combining form* (in nouns) **1** the act of killing: *suicide* ♦ *genocide* **2** a person or thing that kills: *insecticide* ▶ **-cidal** /'saɪdl/ (in adjectives): *homicidal*

ci·der /'saɪdər/ *noun* **1** (also ˌapple ˈcider) [U, C] a drink made from the juice of apples: *a cider press* (= for squeezing the juice from apples) **2** [U, C] = HARD CIDER

ci·gar /sɪˈgɑr/ *noun* a roll of dried TOBACCO leaves that people smoke, like a cigarette but bigger and without paper around it: *cigar smoke* **IDM** see CLOSE² *adj.*

cig·a·rette 🔊 /ˌsɪgəˈrɛt; 'sɪgəˌrɛt/ *noun* a thin tube of paper filled with TOBACCO, for smoking: *a pack of cigarettes* ♦ *to light a cigarette*

ciga'rette butt *noun* the part of a cigarette that is left when someone has finished smoking it

ciga'rette ˌholder *noun* a narrow tube for holding a cigarette in while you are smoking

ciga'rette ˌlighter *noun* = LIGHTER

ciga'rette ˌpaper *noun* a thin piece of paper in which people roll TOBACCO to make their own cigarettes

cig·a·ril·lo /ˌsɪgəˈrɪloʊ/ *noun* (pl. **cig·a·ril·los**) a small CIGAR

ci·lan·tro /sɪˈlɑntroʊ; -ˈlæn-/ *noun* [U] the leaves of the CORIANDER plant, used in cooking as an HERB ⊃ picture at HERB

cil·i·a·ry mus·cle /'sɪlieri ˌmʌsl/ *noun* (*anatomy*) a muscle in the eye that controls how much the LENS curves ⊃ picture at BODY

C-in-C /ˌsi ɪn 'si/ *abbr.* COMMANDER-IN-CHIEF

cinch /sɪntʃ/ *noun*, *verb*
• *noun* [sing.] (*informal*) **1** something that is very easy: *The first question is a cinch.* **2** a thing that is certain to happen; a person who is certain to do something: *He's a cinch to win the race.*
• *verb* **1** **~ sth** to fasten something tightly around your waist; to be fastened around someone's waist **2** **~ sth** to fasten a GIRTH around a horse **3** **~ sth** (*informal*) to make something certain

cin·der /'sɪndər/ *noun* [usually pl.] a small piece of ASH or partly burned coal, wood, etc. that is no longer burning but may still be hot: *a cinder track* (= a track for runners made with finely crushed cinders)

ˈcinder ˌblock *noun* a light building block, made of sand, coal ASHES, and CEMENT

Cin·der·el·la /ˌsɪndəˈrɛlə/ *noun* [usually sing.] a person or thing that has been ignored and deserves to receive more attention: *For years radio has been the Cinderella of the media world.* **ORIGIN** From the European fairy tale about a beautiful girl, **Cinderella**, who was treated in a cruel way by her two ugly sisters. She had to do all the work and received no reward or thanks until she met and married Prince Charming.

cin·e·aste (also **cin·e·ast**) /'sɪniˌæst/ *noun* (from *French*) a person who knows a lot about movies and is very enthusiastic about them

cin·e·ma /'sɪnəmə/ *noun* **1** [U, sing.] movies as an art or an industry: *one of the great successes of American cinema* **2** = THEATER (2): *the local cinema*

Cin·e·ma·Scope™ /'sɪnəməˌskoʊp/ *noun* a method of showing movies that makes the picture on the screen very wide

cin·e·mat·ic /ˌsɪnəˈmætɪk/ *adj.* (*technical*) connected with movies and how they are made: *cinematic effects/techniques*

cin·e·ma·tog·ra·phy /ˌsɪnəməˈtɑgrəfi/ *noun* [U] (*technical*) the art or process of making movies ▶ **cin·e·ma·tog·ra·pher** /-fər/ *noun* **cin·e·mat·o·graph·ic** /ˌsɪnəˌmætəˈgræfɪk/ *adj.*

ɪr **near**   ɛr **hair**   ɑr **car**   ɔr **north**   ʊr **tour**   ɑ̃ **denouement**   p **pen**   b **bad**

cin·e·phile /ˈsɪnəˌfaɪl/ *noun* a person who is very interested in movies

cin·na·bar /ˈsɪnəˌbɑr/ *noun* [U] **1** a bright red mineral that is sometimes used to give color to things **2** the bright red color of cinnabar

cin·na·mon /ˈsɪnəmən/ *noun* [U] the inner BARK of a S.E. Asian tree, used in cooking as a spice, especially to give flavor to sweet foods ➷ picture at HERB

ci·pher (also **cy·pher**) /ˈsaɪfər/ *noun* **1** [U, C] a secret way of writing, especially one in which a set of letters or symbols is used to represent others **SYN** CODE: *a message in cipher* ➷ see also DECIPHER **2** [C] (*formal, disapproving*) a person or thing of no importance

cir·ca /ˈsɜrkə/ *prep.* (from *Latin*) (*abbr.* c) (used with dates) about: *born circa 150 B.C.*

cir·ca·di·an /sərˈkeɪdiən/ *adj.* [only before noun] (*technical*) connected with the changes in the bodies of people or animals over each period of 24 hours

cir·cle 🖉 /ˈsɜrkl/ *noun, verb*

● *noun* **1** a completely round flat shape: *Cut out two circles of paper.* ➷ picture at SHAPE ➷ see also SEMICIRCLE **2** the line that forms the edge of a circle: *Draw a circle.* ◆ *She walked the horse around in a circle.* ➷ see also ANTARCTIC CIRCLE, ARCTIC CIRCLE, TURNING CIRCLE **3** a thing or a group of people or things shaped like a circle: *a circle of trees/chairs* ◆ *The children stood in a circle.* **4** an upper floor of a theater or movie theater where the seats are arranged in curved rows: *We had seats in the circle.* ➷ see also DRESS CIRCLE ➷ compare BALCONY (2) **5** a group of people who are connected because they have the same interests, jobs, etc.: *the family circle* ◆ *She's well known in theatrical circles.* ◆ *a large circle of friends* ➷ see also CHARMED CIRCLE, INNER CIRCLE, VICIOUS CIRCLE
IDM **come full circle** to return to the situation in which you started, after a series of events or experiences **go around in circles** to work hard at something or discuss something without making any progress **run around in circles** (*informal*) to be busy doing something without achieving anything important or making progress

● *verb* **1** [I, T] to move in a circle, especially in the air: *~ (around) (above/over sb/sth) Seagulls circled around above his head.* ◆ *~ sth The plane circled the airport to burn up excess fuel.* **2** [T] *~ sth* to draw a circle around something: *Spelling mistakes are circled in red ink.*
IDM **circle the wagons** to join together with people who have the same ideas and beliefs as you, and avoid contact with those who do not, who may threaten, or attack you: *When your way of life is threatened you have to circle the wagons and defend yourself.* **ORIGIN** From the practice of arranging a WAGON TRAIN in a circle, to defend against attack.

cir·clet /ˈsɜrklət/ *noun* a round band made of PRECIOUS METAL, flowers, etc., worn around the head for decoration

cir·cuit /ˈsɜrkət/ *noun* **1** a line, route, or trip around a place: *The race ended with eight laps of a downtown circuit.* ◆ *The earth takes a year to make a circuit of* (= go around) *the sun.* **2** the complete path of wires and equipment along which an electric current flows: *an electrical circuit* ◆ *a circuit diagram* (= one showing all the connections in the different parts of the circuit) ➷ see also INTEGRATED CIRCUIT, PRINTED CIRCUIT, SHORT CIRCUIT **3** (in sports) a series of games or matches in which the same players regularly take part: *the women's tennis circuit* **4** a track for cars or motorcycles to race around **5** a series of places or events of a particular kind at which the same people appear or take part: *the lecture/cabaret circuit* ➷ see also CLOSED-CIRCUIT TELEVISION **6** a regular trip made by a judge to hear court cases in each of the courts of law in a particular area: *a circuit court/judge*

circuit ˌboard *noun* a board that holds electrical circuits inside a piece of electrical equipment

circuit–ˌbreaker *noun* a device that can automatically stop an electric current if it becomes dangerous

circuit ˌcourt *noun* a court of law that meets in various places within the district it is responsible for

cir·cu·i·tous /sərˈkyuətəs/ *adj.* (*formal*) (of a route or journey) long and not direct **SYN** ROUNDABOUT ▶ **cir·cu·i·tous·ly** *adv.*

cir·cuit·ry /ˈsɜrkətri/ *noun* [U] a system of electrical CIRCUITS or the equipment that forms this

circuit ˌtraining *noun* [U] a type of training in sports in which different exercises are each done for a short time

cir·cu·lar /ˈsɜrkyələr/ *adj., noun*

● *adj.* **1** shaped like a circle; round: *a circular building* **2** moving around in a circle: *a circular tour of the city* **3** (of an argument or a theory) using an idea or a statement to prove something that is then used to prove the idea or statement at the beginning ▶ **cir·cu·lar·i·ty** /ˌsɜrkyəˈlærəti/ *noun* [U]: *There is a dangerous circularity about this argument.*

● *noun* a printed letter, notice, or advertisement that is sent to a large number of people at the same time

ˌcircular ˈsaw (also **ˈbuzz saw**) *noun* a SAW in the form of a metal disk that turns quickly, driven by a motor, and is used for cutting wood, etc.

cir·cu·late /ˈsɜrkyəˌleɪt/ *verb* **1** [I, T] when a liquid, gas, or air **circulates** or **is circulated**, it moves continuously around a place or system: *The condition prevents the blood from circulating freely.* ◆ *~ sth Cooled air is circulated throughout the building.* **2** [I, T] *~ (sth)* if a story, an idea, information, etc. **circulates** or if you **circulate** it, it spreads or it is passed from one person to another: *Rumors began to circulate about his financial problems.* **3** [T] *~ sth (to sb)* to send goods or information to all the people in a group: *The document will be circulated to all members.* **4** [I] to move around a group, especially at a party, talking to different people

cir·cu·la·tion /ˌsɜrkyəˈleɪʃn/ *noun* **1** [U] the movement of blood around the body: *Regular exercise will improve blood circulation.* ◆ *to have good/bad circulation* **2** [U] the passing or spreading of something from one person or place to another: *the circulation of money/information/ideas* ◆ *A number of forged tickets are in circulation.* ◆ *The coins were taken out of circulation.* ◆ *Copies of the magazine were withdrawn from circulation.* **3** [U] the fact that someone takes part in social activities at a particular time: *Anne has been sick but now she's back in circulation.* ◆ *I was out of circulation for months after the baby was born.* **4** [C, usually sing.] the usual number of copies of a newspaper or magazine that are sold each day, week, etc.: *a daily circulation of more than one million* **5** [U, C] the movement of something (for example air, water, gas, etc.) around an area or inside a system or machine

cir·cu·la·to·ry /ˈsɜrkyələˌtɔri/ *adj.* relating to the circulation of the blood

cir·cum·cise /ˈsɜrkəmˌsaɪz/ *verb* **1** *~ sb* to remove the FORESKIN of a boy or man for religious or medical reasons **2** *~ sb* to cut off part of the sex organs of a girl or woman

cir·cum·ci·sion /ˌsɜrkəmˈsɪʒn; ˈsɜrkəmˌsɪʒn/ *noun* [U, C] the act of circumcising someone; the religious ceremony when someone, especially a baby, is circumcised

cir·cum·fer·ence /sərˈkʌmfrəns/ *noun* [C, U] a line that goes around a circle or any other curved shape; the length of this line: *the circumference of the earth* ◆ *The earth is almost 25,000 miles in circumference.* ➷ picture at SHAPE ➷ compare PERIMETER

cir·cum·flex /ˈsɜrkəmˌflɛks/ (also ˌcircumflex ˈaccent) *noun* the mark placed over a vowel in some languages to show how it should be pronounced, as over the *o* in *rôle* ➷ compare ACUTE ACCENT, GRAVE¹, TILDE, UMLAUT

cir·cum·lo·cu·tion /ˌsɜrkəmlouˈkyuʃn/ *noun* [U, C] (*formal*) using more words than are necessary, instead of speaking or writing in a clear, direct way ▶ **cir·cum·loc·u·to·ry** /ˌsɜrkəmˈlɑkyəˌtɔri/ *adj.*

cir·cum·nav·i·gate /ˌsərkəmˈnævəˌgeɪt/ *verb* ~ **sth** (*formal*) to sail all the way around something, especially all the way around the world ▶ **cir·cum·nav·i·ga·tion** /ˌsərkəmˌnævə-ˈgeɪʃn/ *noun* [U]

cir·cum·scribe /ˈsərkəmˌskraɪb/ *verb* **1** [often passive] ~ **sth** (*formal*) to limit someone's or something's freedom, rights, power, etc. **SYN** RESTRICT: *The power of the monarchy was circumscribed by the new law.* **2** ~ **sth** (*technical*) to draw a circle around another shape ▶ **cir·cum·scrip·tion** /ˌsərkəmˈskrɪpʃn/ *noun* [U]

cir·cum·spect /ˈsərkəmˌspɛkt/ *adj.* (*formal*) thinking very carefully about something before doing it, because there may be risks involved **SYN** CAUTIOUS ▶ **cir·cum·spec·tion** /ˌsərkəmˈspɛkʃn/ *noun* [U] **cir·cum·spect·ly** /ˈsərkəmˌspɛktli/ *adv.*

cir·cum·stance 🔑 **AWL** /ˈsərkəmˌstæns/ *noun* **1** [C, usually pl.] the conditions and facts that are connected with and affect a situation, an event, or an action: *The company reserves the right to cancel this agreement in certain circumstances.* ♦ *changing social and political circumstances* ♦ *I know I can trust her in any circumstance.* ♦ *Police said there were no suspicious circumstances surrounding the boy's death.* ♦ *The ship sank in mysterious circumstances.* ♦ *She never discovered the true circumstances of her birth.* ⊃ thesaurus box at SITU-ATION **2** circumstances [pl.] the conditions of a person's life, especially the money they have: *Grants are awarded according to your financial circumstances.* ♦ *family/domestic/personal circumstances* **3** [U] (*formal*) situations and events that affect and influence your life and that are not in your control: *a victim of circumstance* (= a person who has suffered because of a situation that they cannot control) ♦ *He had to leave the country through force of circumstance* (= events made it necessary).

IDM in/under the circumstances used before or after a statement to show that you have thought about the conditions that affect a situation before making a decision or a statement: *Under the circumstances, it seemed better not to tell him about the accident.* ♦ *She did the job very well in the circumstances.* in/under no circumstances used to emphasize that something should never happen or be allowed: *Under no circumstances should you lend Paul any money.* ♦ *Don't open the door, in any circumstances.* reduced circumstances the state of being poorer than you were before. People say "living in reduced circumstances" to avoid saying "poor." ⊃ more at POMP

cir·cum·stan·tial /ˌsərkəmˈstænʃl/ *adj.* **1** (*law*) containing information and details that strongly suggest that something is true but do not prove it: *circumstantial evidence* ♦ *The case against him was largely circumstantial.* **2** (*formal*) connected with particular circumstances: *Their problems were circumstantial rather than personal.*

cir·cum·vent /ˌsərkəmˈvɛnt; ˈsərkəmˌvɛnt/ *verb* (*formal*) **1** ~ **sth** to find a way of avoiding a difficulty or a rule: *They found a way of circumventing the law.* **2** ~ **sth** to go or travel around something that is blocking your way ▶ **cir·cum·ven·tion** /ˌsərkəmˈvɛnʃn/ *noun* [U]

cir·cus /ˈsərkəs/ *noun* **1** [C] a group of entertainers, sometimes with trained animals, who perform skillful or amusing acts in a show that travels around to different places **2** the circus [sing.] a show performed by circus entertainers, usually in a large tent called a BIG TOP: *We took the children to the circus.* **3** [sing.] (*informal, disapproving*) a group of people or an event that attracts a lot of attention: *A media circus surrounded the celebrity couple wherever they went.* ♦ *the American electoral circus* **4** [C] (in ancient Rome) a place like a big, round, outdoor theater for public games, races, etc.

cirque /sərk/ *noun* (also **cor·rie, cwm**) (*geology*) a round hollow area in the side of a mountain

cir·rho·sis /səˈroʊsəs/ *noun* [U] a serious disease of the LIVER, caused especially by drinking too much alcohol

cir·rus /ˈsɪrəs/ *noun* [U] (*technical*) a type of light cloud that forms high in the sky

CIS /ˌsi aɪ ˈɛs/ *abbr.* Commonwealth of Independent States (a group of independent countries that were part of the Soviet Union until 1991)

cis·tern /ˈsɪstərn/ *noun* a container in which water is stored in a building, especially one in the roof or connected to a toilet

cit·a·del /ˈsɪtədəl; -ˌdɛl/ *noun* (in the past) a castle on high ground in or near a city, where people could go when the city was being attacked: (*figurative*) *citadels of private economic power*

ci·ta·tion **AWL** /saɪˈteɪʃn/ *noun* **1** [C] words or lines taken from a book or a speech **SYN** QUOTATION **2** [C] = SUMMONS: *The judge issued a contempt citation against the woman for violating a previous court order.* **3** [C] an official statement about something special that someone has done, especially about acts of courage in a war: *a citation for bravery* **4** [U] (*formal*) an act of citing or being cited: *Space does not permit the citation of the examples.*

cite **AWL** /saɪt/ *verb* (*formal*) **1** ~ **sth (as sth)** to mention something as a reason or an example, or in order to support what you are saying: *She cited her heavy workload as the reason for her breakdown.* ⊃ thesaurus box at MENTION **2** ~ **sth** to speak or write the exact words from a book, an author, etc. **SYN** QUOTE **3** ~ **sb (for sth)** (*law*) to order someone to appear in court; to name someone officially in a legal case: *She was cited in the divorce proceedings.* **4** ~ **sb (for sth)** to mention someone officially or publicly because they deserve special praise: *He was cited for bravery.*

cit·i·fied /ˈsɪtɪˌfaɪd/ *adj.* (usually *disapproving*) characteristic of a city: *his citified surroundings*

cit·i·zen 🔑 /ˈsɪtəzn/ *noun* **1** a person who has the legal right to belong to a particular country: *She's Italian by birth but is now a United States citizen.* ♦ *U.S. citizens living in Mexico and the Caribbean* **2** a person who lives in a particular place: *the citizens of Denver* ♦ *When you're old, people treat you like a second-class citizen.* ⊃ see also SENIOR CITIZEN ⊃ compare SUBJECT

citizen ˈjournalism *noun* [U] reports and pictures of events recorded by ordinary people and shown on the Internet: *citizen journalism Web sites* ▶ **citizen ˈjournalist** *noun*

cit·i·zen·ry /ˈsɪtəzənri/ *noun* [sing.] all the citizens of a particular town, country, etc.

citizen's arˈrest *noun* an arrest made by a member of the public, not by the police

ˈCitizens' ˌBand *noun* [U] = CB

cit·i·zen·ship /ˈsɪtəzənˌʃɪp/ *noun* [U] **1** the legal right to belong to a particular country: *American citizenship* ♦ *You can apply for citizenship after five years' residency.* **2** the state of being a citizen and accepting the responsibilities of it: *an education that prepares young people for citizenship*

cit·ric /ˈsɪtrɪk/ *adj.* relating to fruit such as lemons, oranges, and LIMES: *a citric flavor*

citric ˈacid *noun* [U] a weak acid found in the juice of lemons and other sour fruits

cit·ron /ˈsɪtrən/ *noun* [C, U] a yellow fruit like a large lemon

cit·ron·el·la /ˌsɪtrəˈnɛlə/ (also **citroˈnella ˌoil**) *noun* [U] a natural oil that smells like lemons and is used to keep away insects and in PERFUME, and soap

cit·rus /ˈsɪtrəs/ *noun* [U] fruit belonging to the group of fruit that includes oranges, lemons, LIMES, and GRAPEFRUIT: *citrus fruit/trees/growers* ♦ *fabric in bright citrus shades* (= orange, yellow, or green)

cit·y 🔑 /ˈsɪti/ *noun* (pl. **cit·ies**) **1** [C] a large and important town: *one of the world's most beautiful cities* ♦ *a major city* ♦ *the country's capital city* ♦ *Mexico City* ⊃ collocations at TOWN ⊃ see also INNER CITY, SISTER CITY **2** [C] a town that has been given special rights by the state government: *an unincorporated area within the City of Monterey* **3** [sing.] all the people who live in a city: *The city* turned out to welcome the victorious team home. **4** [C] the government or employees of a city: *The city is working on implementing more recycling.* ♦ *city workers* **5** [U] (*informal*) used after other nouns to say that a place is full of a particular thing: *It's not exactly fun city here, is it?*

ˌcity ˈcouncil *noun* a group of elected officials who make the laws of a city and help to govern it

ˈcity ˌdesk *noun* the department of a newspaper that deals with local news

ˌcity ˈeditor *noun* a journalist who is responsible for local news in a newspaper or magazine

ˌcity ˈfather *noun* [usually pl.] a person with experience of governing a city

ˌcity ˈhall *noun* often **City Hall** [C, U] the local government of a city and the offices it uses

ˌcity ˈplanner (also **plan·ner**, ˌtown ˈplanner) *noun* a person whose job is to plan the growth and development of a town

ˌcity ˈplanning (also **plan·ning**, ˌtown ˈplanning) *noun* [U] the control of the development of towns and their buildings, roads, etc. so that they can be pleasant and convenient places for people to live in; the subject that studies this

cit·y·scape /ˈsɪtiˌskeɪp/ *noun* the appearance of a city or urban area, especially in a picture; a picture of a city

ˌcity ˈslicker *noun* (*informal*, often *disapproving*) a person who behaves in a way that is typical of people who live in big cities

ˈcity ˌstate *noun* (especially in the past) an independent state consisting of a city and the area around it (for example, Athens in ancient times)

cit·y·wide /ˌsɪtiˈwaɪd/ *adj.* involving or happening in all parts of a city or town: *a citywide parking ban* ♦ *citywide festivities* ▶ **cit·y·wide** *adv.*: *The mayor called for 15 percent budget cuts citywide.*

civ·et /ˈsɪvət/ *noun* **1** [C] a wild animal like a cat, that lives in central Africa and Asia **2** [U] a substance with a strong smell, obtained from a civet, and used in making PERFUME

civ·ic /ˈsɪvɪk/ *adj.* [usually before noun] **1** officially connected with a town or city: *civic buildings/leaders* **2** connected with the people who live in a town or city: *a sense of civic pride* (= pride that people feel for their town or city) ♦ *civic duties/responsibilities*

ˈcivic ˌcenter (*CanE* usually ˈcivic ˌcentre) *noun* a large building where public entertainments and meetings are held: *Atlanta Civic Center*

ˌcivic ˈholiday (*CanE*) *noun* a holiday that is taken on the first Monday in August in all of Canada apart from Québec, Alberta, and Prince Edward Island

civ·ics /ˈsɪvɪks/ *noun* [U] the school subject that studies the way government works and deals with the rights and duties that you have as a citizen and a member of a particular society

civ·il 🔑 AWL /ˈsɪvl/ *adj.*
1 [only before noun] connected with the people who live in a country: *civil unrest* (= that is caused by groups of people within a country) ⊃ see also CIVIL WAR **2** [only before noun] connected with the state rather than with religion or with the armed forces: *a civil marriage ceremony* **3** [only before noun] involving personal legal matters and not criminal law: *a civil court* ⊃ compare CRIMINAL ⊃ see also CIVIL LAW **4** polite in a formal way but possibly not friendly ANT UNCIVIL ▶ **civ·il·ly** /ˈsɪvəli/ *adv.*: *She greeted him civilly but with no sign of affection.*

ˌcivil deˈfense *noun* [U] the organization and training of ordinary people to protect themselves from attack during a war or from natural disasters such as HURRICANES

ˌcivil disoˈbedience *noun* [U] refusal by a large group of people to obey particular laws or pay taxes, usually as a form of peaceful political protest

ˌcivil engiˈneering *noun* [U] the design, building, and repair of roads, bridges, CANALS, etc.; the study of this as a subject ▶ **ˌcivil engiˈneer** *noun*

ci·vil·ian /səˈvɪlyən/ *noun* a person who is not a member of the armed forces or the police ⊃ collocations at WAR ▶ **ci·vil·ian** *adj.* [usually before noun]: *He left the army and returned to civilian life.* ⊃ compare MILITARY

ci·vil·i·ty /səˈvɪləti/ *noun* (*formal*) **1** [U] polite behavior: *Staff members are trained to treat customers with civility at all times.* **2** civilities [pl.] remarks that are said only in order to be polite

civ·i·li·za·tion /ˌsɪvələˈzeɪʃn/ *noun* **1** [U] a state of human society that is very developed and organized: *the technology of modern civilization* ♦ *The settlers saw themselves as bringing progress and civilization to the wilderness.* **2** [U, C] a society, its culture, and its way of life during a particular period of time or in a particular part of the world: *the civilizations of ancient Greece and Rome* ♦ *diseases that are common in Western civilization* **3** [U] all the people in the world and the societies they live in, considered as a whole: *Environmental damage threatens the whole of civilization.* **4** [U] (often *humorous*) a place that offers you the comfortable way of life of a modern society: *It's good to be back in civilization after two weeks in a tent!*

civ·i·lize /ˈsɪvəˌlaɪz/ *verb* ~ **sb/sth** to educate and improve a person or a society; to make someone's behavior or manners better: *The girls in a class tend to have a civilizing influence on the boys.*

civ·i·lized /ˈsɪvəˌlaɪzd/ *adj.* **1** well organized socially with a very developed culture and way of life: *the civilized world* ♦ *rising crime in our so-called civilized societies* ♦ *civilized peoples* **2** having laws and customs that are fair and morally acceptable: *No civilized country should allow such terrible injustices.* **3** having or showing polite and reasonable behavior: *We couldn't even have a civilized conversation any more.* **4** typical of a comfortable and pleasant way of life: *Breakfast on the terrace—how civilized!* ANT UNCIVILIZED

ˌcivil ˈlaw *noun* [U, C] a system of law that deals with the rights of private citizens rather than with crime; a law belonging to this system ⊃ compare CRIMINAL LAW

ˌcivil ˈliberty *noun* [C, usually pl., U] the right of people to be free to say or do what they want while respecting others and staying within the law

ˌcivil ˈmarriage *noun* a marriage with no religious ceremony

ˌcivil ˈpartnership *noun* a relationship between two people of the same sex, recognized as having the same legal status as a marriage between a man and a woman

ˌcivil ˈrights *noun* [pl.] the rights that every person in a society has, for example to be treated equally, to be able to vote, work, etc. whatever their sex, race, or religion: *the civil rights leader Martin Luther King*

the ˌcivil ˈrights ˌmovement *noun* [sing.] the campaign in the 1950s and 1960s to change the laws so that African Americans have the same rights as others

ˌcivil ˈservant *noun* a person who works in the civil service

the ˌcivil ˈservice *noun* [sing.] the government departments in a country, except the armed forces, and the people who work for them

ˌcivil ˈwar *noun* **1** [C, U] a war between groups of people in the same country: *the Spanish Civil War* ♦ *30 years of bitter civil war* ⊃ collocations at WAR **2 the Civil War** the war fought in the U.S. between the northern and the southern states in the years 1861 to 1865

civ·vies /ˈsɪviz/ *noun* [pl.] (*slang*) (used by people in the armed forces) ordinary clothes, not military uniform

CJD /ˌsi dʒeɪ ˈdi/ *abbr.* CREUTZFELDT-JAKOB DISEASE ⊃ see also NEW VARIANT CJD

cl *abbr.* (*pl.* **cl** or **cls**) CENTILITER: *75cl*

clack /klæk/ *verb* [I, T] ~ **(sth)** if two hard objects **clack**, they make a short loud sound when they hit each other: *Her heels clacked on the marble floor.* ▶ **clack** *noun* [sing.]: *the clack of high heels on the floor* ♦ *the click-clack of her knitting needles*

| h hat | m man | n no | ŋ sing | l leg | r red | y yes | w wet |

clad /klæd/ adj. (usually *formal*) **1** ~ **(in sth)** (often used after an adverb or in compounds) wearing a particular type of clothing **SYN** DRESSED: *She was clad in blue velvet.* ◆ *warmly/scantily clad* ◆ *leather-clad motorcyclists* **2** -**clad** (in compounds) covered in a particular thing: *snow-clad hills*

clad·ding /'klædɪŋ/ noun [U] a covering of a hard material, used as protection

claim 🔑 /kleɪm/ *verb, noun*

● **verb**

> **SAY SOMETHING IS TRUE 1** [T] to say that something is true although it has not been proved and other people may not believe it: ~ **(that)**... *He claims (that) he was not given a fair hearing.* ◆ ~ **(sb/sth) to be/do sth** *I don't claim to be an expert.* ◆ ~ **sth** *Scientists are claiming a major breakthrough in the fight against cancer.* ◆ **it is claimed that...** *It was claimed that some doctors were working 80 hours a week.* ⊃ language bank at ARGUE

> **DEMAND LEGAL RIGHT 2** [T] ~ **sth** to demand or ask for something because you believe it is your legal right to own or to have it: *A lot of lost property is never claimed.* ◆ *He claimed political asylum.*

> **MONEY 3** [T, I] to ask for money from the government or a company because you have a right to it: ~ **sth** *He's not entitled to claim unemployment.* ◆ ~ **sth from sth** *She claimed damages from the company for the injury she had suffered.* ◆ *You could have claimed the cost of the hotel room from your insurance.* ◆ ~ **(on sth) (for sth)** *You can claim on your insurance for that coat you left on the train.*

> **ATTENTION/THOUGHT 4** [T] ~ **sth** to get or take someone's attention: *A most unwelcome event claimed his attention.*

> **GAIN/WIN 5** [T] ~ **sth** to gain, win, or achieve something: *She has finally claimed a place on the team.*

> **CAUSE DEATH 6** [T] ~ **sth** (of a disaster, an accident, etc.) to cause someone's death: *The car crash claimed three lives.*

PHR V ,claim sth↔'back to ask or demand to have something returned because you have a right to it: *You can claim back the tax on your purchases.*

● **noun**

> **SAYING SOMETHING IS TRUE 1** [C] ~ **(that...)** a statement that something is true although it has not been proved and other people may not agree with or believe it: *The singer has denied the magazine's claim that she is leaving the band.*

> **LEGAL RIGHT 2** [C, U] ~ **(on/to sth)** a right that someone believes they have to something, especially property, land, etc.: *They had no claim on the land.* ◆ *She has more claim to the book's success than anybody* (= she deserves to be praised for it).

> **FOR MONEY 3** [C] ~ **(for sth)** a request for a sum of money that you believe you have a right to, especially from a company, the government', etc.: *You can make a claim on your insurance policy.* ◆ *to put in a claim for an allowance* ◆ *a claim for $2,000* ◆ *Make sure your claims for expenses are submitted by the end of the month.* ◆ *Complete a claim form* (= an official document which you must use in order to request money from an organization).

IDM claim to fame (often *humorous*) one thing that makes a person or place important or interesting: *His main claim to fame is that he went to school with the President.* have a claim on sb to have the right to demand time, attention, etc. from someone lay claim to sth to state that you have a right to own something make no claim used when you are saying that you cannot do something: *I make no claim to understand modern art.* ⊃ more at STAKE v.

THESAURUS

claim

allegation ◆ assertion

■ These are all words for a statement that something is true, although it has not been proven.

claim a statement that something is true, although it has not been proven

---

allegation (*somewhat formal*) a public statement that has not been proven, that accuses someone of doing something that is wrong or illegal

assertion (*somewhat formal*) a statement of something that you strongly believe to be true, although it has not been proven

CLAIM OR ASSERTION?

When the point in doubt is a matter of opinion, not fact, use **assertion**: ~~She made sweeping claims about the role of women in society.~~ When you are talking about a matter of fact, you can use either word; an **assertion** may be slightly stronger than a **claim** and it is a more formal word.

PATTERNS

■ a(n) claim/allegation/assertion **that**...
■ a(n) claim/allegation/assertion **about/of** sth
■ **false/unfounded/conflicting** claims/allegations/assertions
■ to **make/deny** a(n) claim/allegation/assertion
■ to **withdraw** a(n) claim/allegation

claim·ant /'kleɪmənt/ noun **1** a person who claims something because they believe they have a right to it **2** a person who is receiving money from the state because they are unemployed, etc.

'**claims ad·jus·ter** noun = INSURANCE ADJUSTER

clair·voy·ance /klɛr'vɔɪəns/ noun [U] the power that some people are believed to have to be able to see future events or to communicate with people who are dead or far away ▶ **clair·voy·ant** noun: *to consult a clairvoyant* **clair·voy·ant** *adj.*

clam /klæm/

● **noun** a SHELLFISH that can be eaten. It has a shell in two parts that can open and close: *clam chowder/sauce* ⊃ picture at SHELLFISH **IDM** see HAPPY

● **verb** (-mm-)
PHR V ,clam 'up (on sb) (*informal*) to refuse to speak, especially when someone asks you about something

clam·bake /'klæmbeɪk/ noun an outdoor party, especially for eating clams and other SEAFOOD

clam·ber /'klæmbər/ verb [I] + **adv./prep.** to climb or move with difficulty or a lot of effort, using your hands and feet **SYN** SCRAMBLE: *The children clambered up the steep bank.*

clam·my /'klæmi/ adj. (clam·mi·er, clam·mi·est) damp in an unpleasant way: *His skin felt cold and clammy.* ◆ *clammy hands*

clam·or (CanE also **clam·our**) /'klæmər/ verb, noun
● **verb 1** [I, T] to demand something loudly: ~ **(for sth)** *People began to clamor for his resignation.* ◆ ~ **to do sth** *Everyone was clamoring to know how much they would get.* ◆ + **speech** *"Play with us!" the children clamored.* **2** [I] (of many people) to shout loudly, especially in a confused way
● **noun** [sing., U] (*formal*) **1** a loud noise, especially one that is made by a lot of people or animals: *the clamor of the market* **2** ~ **(for sth)** a demand for something made by a lot of people: *The clamor for her resignation grew louder.* ▶ **clam·or·ous** /'klæmərəs/ adj.

clamp /klæmp/ verb, noun
● **verb 1** [T] to hold something tightly, or fasten two things together, with a clamp: ~ **A to B** *Clamp one end of the plank to the edge of the table.* ◆ ~ **A and B (together)** *Clamp the two halves together until the glue dries.* **2** [T, I] to hold or fasten something very tightly so that it does not move; to be held tightly: ~ **sth** + **adv./prep.** *He had a cigar clamped between his teeth.* ◆ *She clamped a pair of headphones over her ears.* ◆ + **adv./prep.** *Her lips clamped tightly together.* ◆ ~ **(sth)** + **adj.** *He clamped his mouth shut.*

PHR V ,clamp 'down (on sb/sth) to take strict action in order to prevent something, especially crime: *a campaign by police to clamp down on street crime* ⊃ related noun CLAMPDOWN 'clamp sth on sb to force someone to accept something such as a restriction or law: *The army clamped a curfew on the city.*

● **noun** a tool for holding things tightly together, usually by means of a screw ⊃ picture at LABORATORY

clamp·down /'klæmpdaʊn/ noun [usually sing.] sudden action that is taken in order to stop an illegal activity: *a clampdown on drinking and driving*

clam·shell /'klæmʃel/ adj. [only before noun] having a lid or other part that opens and shuts like the shell of a CLAM: *a clamshell phone* ► **clam·shell** noun

clan /klæn/ noun **1** a group of families who are related to each other, especially in Scotland: *the Macleod clan* ◆ *clan warfare* **2** (informal, sometimes humorous) a very large family, or a group of people who are connected because of a particular thing: *one of a growing clan of stars who have left Hollywood*

clan·des·tine /klæn'destən/ adj. (formal) done secretly or kept secret: *a clandestine meeting/relationship*

clang /klæŋ/ verb [I, T] to make a loud ringing sound like that of metal being hit; to cause something to make this sound **SYN** CLANK: *Bells were clanging in the tower.* ◆ **+ adj.** *The gates clanged shut.* ◆ **~ sth + adv./prep.** *The trolleys clanged their way along the streets.* ◆ *He clanged a spoon against a glass.* ► **clang** (also **clang·ing**) noun [usually sing.]

clang·or (CanE usually **clang·our**) /'klæŋər/ noun (formal) a continuous loud crashing or ringing sound ► **clang·or·ous** /'klæŋərəs/ adj.

clank /klæŋk/ verb [I, T] to make a loud sound like pieces of metal hitting each other; to cause something to make this sound: *clanking chains* ◆ **+ adj.** *I heard a door clank shut.* ◆ **~ sth** *The guard clanked his heavy ring of keys.* ► **clank** (also **clanking**) noun [usually sing.]

clan·nish /'klænɪʃ/ adj. (often disapproving) (of members of a group) not showing interest in people who are not in the group

clans·man /'klænzmən/ noun (pl. clans·men /-mən/) a member of a CLAN

clap /klæp/ verb, noun

● **verb** (-pp-) **1** [I] to hit your open hands together several times to show that you approve of or have enjoyed something: *The audience clapped and cheered.* ◆ *Everyone clapped for us when we went up to get our prize.* **2** [I, T] to hit your open hands together: *Everyone clapped in time to the music.* ◆ **~ your hands** *She clapped her hands in delight.* ◆ *He clapped his hands for silence.* **3** [T] **~ sb on the back/shoulder** to lightly hit someone with your open hand, usually in a friendly way **4** [T] **~ sth + adv./prep.** to put something or someone somewhere quickly and suddenly: *"Oh dear!" she cried, clapping a hand over her mouth.* ◆ *to clap someone in irons/jail/prison* ► **clap·ping** noun [U]: *I could hear the sound of clapping from the other room.*

● **noun 1** [C] an act of clapping the hands; the sound this makes: *There were plenty of claps and cheers for the young singer.* **2** [C] a sudden loud noise: *a clap of thunder* **3** also **the clap** [U] (informal) a disease of the sexual organs, caught by having sex with an infected person **SYN** GONORRHOEA

clap·board /'klæbərd/ noun [C, U] one of a series of long, narrow, horizontal pieces of wood, each with one edge thicker than the other. They are fastened to the outside walls of a house with the bottom of one over the top of the one below, to cover the wall and protect it from rain and wind: *a clapboard house*

clap·per /'klæpər/ noun the piece of metal inside a bell that hits the sides and makes the bell ring

clap·per·board /'klæpər,bɔrd/ noun a device that is used when making movies. It consists of two connected boards that are hit together at the start of a scene, and its purpose is to help to match the pictures with the sound.

clap·trap /'klæptræp/ noun [U] (informal) stupid talk that has no value

claque /klæk/ noun a group of people who are paid to clap for or BOO a performer or public speaker

clar·et /'klærət/ noun **1** [U, C] a dry red wine, especially from the Bordeaux area of France. There are several types of claret. **2** [U] a dark red color

clar·i·fy **AWL** /'klærə,faɪ/ verb (clar·i·fies, clar·i·fy·ing, clar·i·fied, clar·i·fied) **1** (formal) to make something clearer or easier to understand: **~ sth** *to clarify a situation/problem/issue* ◆ *I hope this clarifies my position.* ◆ **~ what/how, etc.…** *She asked him to clarify what he meant.* ⊃ language bank at DEFINE **2 ~ sth** to make something, especially butter, pure by heating it: *clarified butter* ► **clar·i·fi·ca·tion** **AWL** /,klærəfə'keɪʃn/ noun [U, C]: *I am seeking clarification of the regulations.*

AWL COLLOCATIONS

clarify

clarify verb

to make something clearer or easier to understand
■ **definitively, fully | greatly | further**
The following sections of this paper will further clarify the methodology.
■ **aim to, attempt to, seek to | serve to | help to**
Additional research in several areas may help to clarify some remaining questions.
■ **ambiguity | misconception | distinction | relationship | role | issue, matter | position, situation | meaning**
Garcia clarified the relationship that exists between language and culture.

clarification noun
■ **further**
Further clarification of these relationships is required.
■ **need, require | seek**
This analysis is confusing and needs further clarification.

clarity noun
■ **lack | obscure | enhance, improve | bring, lend, offer, provide | achieve, gain**
Kangle's translation is considered the most authentic, but lacks clarity in some instances.
■ **lack of ~**
One reason for the lack of clarity is that measurement varies greatly across studies.

---

clar·i·net /,klærə'nɛt/ noun a musical instrument of the WOODWIND group. It is shaped like a pipe and has a REED and a MOUTHPIECE at the top that you blow into. ⊃ picture at INSTRUMENT

clar·i·net·ist /,klærə'nɛtɪst/ noun a person who plays the clarinet

clar·i·on call /'klæriən ,kɔl/ noun [sing.] (formal) a clear message or request for people to do something

clar·i·ty **AWL** /'klærəti/ noun [U] **1** the quality of being expressed clearly: *a lack of clarity in the law* ⊃ collocations at CLARIFY **2** the ability to think about or understand something clearly: *clarity of thought/purpose/vision* **3** if a picture, substance, or sound has **clarity**, you can see or hear it very clearly, or see through it easily: *the clarity of sound on a CD*

clash /klæʃ/ noun, verb

● **noun**
> **FIGHT 1 ~ (with sb) | ~ (between A and B)** a short fight between two groups of people: *Clashes broke out between police and demonstrators.* ⊃ thesaurus box at FIGHT
> **ARGUMENT 2 ~ (with sb) (over sth) | ~ (between A and B) (over sth)** an argument between two people or groups of

ʌ **cup**   ə **about**   eɪ **say**   aɪ **five**   ɔɪ **boy**   aʊ **now**   oʊ **go**   ər **bird**

people who have different beliefs and ideas **SYN** CONFLICT: *a clash between the two leaders over education policy*
> DIFFERENCE **3** the difference that exists between two things that are opposed to each other **SYN** CONFLICT: *a clash of opinions/cultures* ♦ *a personality clash with the boss*
> OF COLORS **4** the situation when two colors, designs, etc. look ugly when they are put together
> LOUD NOISE **5** a loud noise made by two metal objects being hit together: *a clash of cymbals/swords*
> IN SPORTS **6** (used in newspapers, about sports) an occasion when two teams or players compete against each other: *the Steelers' clash with the Cardinals in the Super Bowl*
> OF TWO EVENTS **7** a situation in which two events happen at the same time so that you cannot go to or see them both: *a clash in the schedule*

● *verb*
> FIGHT/COMPETE **1** [I] ~ (with sb) to come together and fight or compete in a contest: *The two sets of fans clashed outside the stadium.* ♦ *The two teams clash in tomorrow's final.*
> ARGUE **2** [I] ~ (with sb) (over/on sth) to argue or disagree seriously with someone about something, and to show this in public: *The leaders and members clashed on the issue.* ♦ *The leaders clashed with party members on the issue.*
> BE DIFFERENT **3** [I] ~ (with sth) (of beliefs, ideas, or personalities) to be very different and opposed to each other: *His left-wing views clashed with his father's politics.* ♦ *His views and his father's clashed.* ♦ *They have clashing personalities.*
> OF COLORS **4** [I] ~ (with sth) (of colors, patterns, or styles) to look ugly when put together: *The wallpaper clashes with the carpet.* ♦ *The wallpaper and the carpet clash.*
> MAKE LOUD NOISE **5** [I, T] to hit together and make a loud ringing noise; to make two metal objects do this: ~ (together) *The long blades clashed together.* ♦ ~ sth (together) *She clashed the cymbals.*
> OF TWO EVENTS **6** [I] ~ (with sth) (of events) to happen at the same time so that you cannot go to or see them both: *Unfortunately your party clashes with a wedding I'm going to.* ♦ *There are two good movies on TV tonight, but they clash.*

clasp /klɑːsp/ *verb, noun*
● *verb* **1** ~ sth to hold something tightly in your hand: *He leaned forward, his **hands clasped** tightly together.* ♦ *They clasped hands* (= held each other's hands). ♦ *I stood there, clasping the door handle.* ⊃ thesaurus box at HOLD **2** ~ sb/ sth to hold someone or something tightly with your arms around them: *She clasped the children in her arms.* ♦ *He clasped her to him.* **3** ~ sth (+ adv./prep.) to fasten something with a clasp: *She clasped the bracelet around her wrist.* ⊃ picture at JEWELRY
● *noun* **1** [C] a device that fastens something, such as a bag or the ends of a belt or a piece of jewelry: *the clasp of a necklace/handbag* **2** [sing.] a tight hold with your hand or in your arms: *He took her hand in his firm, warm clasp.*

class /klæs/ *noun, verb, adj.*
● *noun*
> IN EDUCATION **1** [C] a group of students who are taught together: *We're in the same class at school.* ♦ *She is the youngest in her class.* ♦ *The whole class was told to stay behind after school.* **2** [C, U] an occasion when a group of students meets to be taught **SYN** LESSON: *I was late for a class.* ♦ *See me after class.* ♦ *She works hard in class* (= during the class). ♦ *I have a history class at 9 o'clock.* ⊃ collocations at EDUCATION **3** [C] (also classes [pl.]) a series of classes on a particular subject **SYN** COURSE: *I've been taking classes in pottery.* ♦ *Are you still doing your French night class?* **4** [C] a group of students who finish their studies at a school or college in a particular year: *the class of 2008* ♦ *He graduated at the top of the class.*
> IN SOCIETY **5** [C] one of the groups of people in a society that are thought of as being at the same social or economic level: *the working/middle/upper class* ♦ *The party tries to appeal to all classes of society.* ♦ *the professional classes* **6** [U] the way that people are divided into different social and economic groups: *differences of class, race, or gender* ♦ *the*

class system ♦ *a society in which class is more important than ability*
> GROUP OF PEOPLE/ANIMALS **7** [C] a group of people, animals, or things that have similar characteristics or qualities: *It has good food for a restaurant of this class.* ♦ *different classes of drugs* ♦ *Dickens was in a different class from* (= was much better than) *most of his contemporaries.* ♦ *As a jazz singer, she's in a class of her own* (= better than most others). ⊃ see also FIRST-CLASS, HIGH-CLASS, LOW-CLASS, SECOND-CLASS
> SKILL/STYLE **8** [U] an elegant quality or a high level of skill that is impressive: *She wouldn't make a scene in public. She has class.* ♦ *Some fresh flowers would add a touch of class to this room.*
> IN TRAIN/PLANE **9** [C] (especially in compounds) each of several different levels of comfort that are available to travellers in a plane, etc.: *He always travels business class.* ♦ *The first-class compartment is situated at the front of the train.* ⊃ see also ECONOMY CLASS SYNDROME, SECOND-CLASS, THIRD-CLASS, TOURIST CLASS
> BIOLOGY **10** [C] a group into which animals, plants, etc. that have similar characteristics are divided, below a PHYLUM ⊃ compare FAMILY, GENUS, SPECIES
● *verb* [often passive] ~ sb/sth (as sth)
> PUT INTO GROUP to think or decide that someone or something is a particular type of person or thing **SYN** CLASSIFY: *Immigrant workers were classed as aliens.*
● *adj.* [only before noun] (*informal*)
> WITH SKILL/STYLE very good: *a class player/performer* ♦ *She's a real class act.*

ˌclass ˈaction *noun* a type of LAWSUIT that is started by a group of people who have the same problem
ˈclass-ˌconscious *adj.* very aware of belonging to a particular social class and of the differences between social classes ▶ ˌclass-ˈconsciousness *noun* [U]

clas·sic ✎ **AWL** /ˈklæsɪk/ *adj., noun*
● *adj.* [usually before noun] **1** accepted or deserving to be accepted as one of the best or most important of its kind: *a classic novel/study/goal* **2** (also clas·sic·al) with all the features you would expect to find; very typical: *a classic example of poor communication* ♦ *She displayed the classic symptoms of depression.* ♦ *I made the classic mistake of clapping in a pause in the music!* **3** elegant, but simple and traditional in style or design; not affected by changes in fashion: *a classic gray suit* ♦ *classic design* ♦ *classic cars* (= cars which are no longer made, but which are still popular) **4** (*informal*) people say **That's classic!** when they find something very amusing, when they think someone has been very stupid, or when something annoying, but not surprising, happens: *She's not going to help? Oh, that's classic!*
● *noun* **1** [C] a book, movie, or song that is well known and considered to be of very high quality, setting standards for other books, etc.: *American classics such as "Little House on the Prairie"* ♦ *The novel may become a modern classic.* **2** [C] a thing that is an excellent example of its kind: *That match was a classic.* **3** Classics [U] the study of ancient Greek and Roman culture, especially their languages and literature: *a degree in Classics*

WHICH WORD?

classic ♦ classical
These adjectives are frequently used with the following nouns:

classic ~	classical ~
example	music
case	ballet
novel	architecture
work	scholar
car	period

■ **Classic** describes something that is accepted as being of very high quality and one of the best of its kind: *a* *classic movie/work*. It is also used to describe a typical example of something: *a classic example/mistake*, or something elegant but simple and traditional: *classic design*

■ **Classical** describes a form of traditional Western music and other things that are traditional in style: *a classical composer* ◆ *a classical theory*. It is also used to talk about things that are connected with the culture of Ancient Greece and Rome: *a classical scholar* ◆ *classical mythology*

clas·si·cal AWL /ˈklæsɪkl/ *adj.* [usually before noun] **1** widely accepted and used for a long time; traditional in style or idea: *the classical economics of Smith and Ricardo* ◆ *the classical theory of unemployment* ◆ *classical and modern ballet* **2** connected with or influenced by the culture of ancient Greece and Rome: *classical studies* ◆ *a classical scholar* (= an expert in Latin and Greek) **3** (of music) written in a Western musical tradition, usually using an established form (for example a SYMPHONY), and not played on electronic instruments. Classical music is generally considered to be serious and to have lasting value: *He plays classical music, as well as rock and jazz.* ◆ *a classical composer/violinist* ➜ collocations at MUSIC **4** = CLASSIC: *These are classical examples of food allergy.* **5** (of a language) ancient in its form and no longer used in a spoken form: *classical Arabic* **6** simple and attractive: *the classical elegance of the design* ▶ **clas·si·cal·ly** /-kli/ *adv.*: *Her face is classically beautiful.* ◆ *a classically trained singer* ➜ note at CLASSIC

clas·si·cism /ˈklæsəˌsɪzəm/ *noun* [U] **1** a style of art and literature that is simple and elegant, and is based on the styles of ancient Greece and Rome. Classicism was popular in Europe in the 18th century. **2** a style or form that has simple, natural qualities, and pleasing combinations of parts

clas·si·cist /ˈklæsəsɪst/ *noun* **1** a person who studies ancient Greek or Latin **2** a person who follows classicism in art or literature

clas·si·fi·a·ble /ˈklæsəˌfaɪəbl; ˌklæsəˈfaɪəbl/ *adj.* that you can or should CLASSIFY: *The information was not easily classifiable.* ◆ *top-secret or classifiable information*

clas·si·fi·ca·tion /ˌklæsəfəˈkeɪʃn/ *noun* **1** [U] the act or process of putting people or things into a group or class (= of CLASSIFYING them): *a style of music that defies classification* (= is like no other) **2** [C] a group, class, division, etc. into which someone or something is put **3** [U] (*biology*) the act of putting animals, plants, etc. into groups, classes, or divisions according to their characteristics **4** [C] (*technical*) a system of arranging books, tapes, magazines, etc. in a library into groups according to their subject

clas·si·fied /ˈklæsəˌfaɪd/ *adj.* [usually before noun] **1** (of information) officially secret and available only to particular people: *classified information/documents/material* ANT UNCLASSIFIED **2** with information arranged in groups according to subjects: *a classified catalog* **3 classifieds** *noun* [pl.] = CLASSIFIED ADVERTISEMENTS

classified adver·tisements (also ˌclassified ˈads, ˈclas·si·fieds, ˈwant ads) *noun* [pl.] the section in a newspaper with small advertisements arranged in groups according to their subject, that are placed by people or small companies who want to buy or sell something, find or offer a job, etc.

clas·si·fi·er /ˈklæsəˌfaɪər/ *noun* (*grammar*) an AFFIX or word that shows that a word belongs to a group of words with similar meanings. For example the prefix "un" is a classifier that shows the word is negative.

clas·si·fy /ˈklæsəˌfaɪ/ *verb* (**clas·si·fies, clas·si·fy·ing, clas·si·fied, clas·si·fied**) **1 ~ sth** to arrange things in groups according to features that they have in common: *The books in the library are classified according to subject.* ◆ *Patients are classified into three categories.* **2 ~ sb/sth as sth** to decide which type or group someone or something belongs to: *Only eleven of these accidents were classified as major.* **3 ~ sth**

to make documents or information officially secret or available only to people with special authority: *Government officials classified 6.3 million documents in 2008.*

class·less /ˈklæsləs/ *adj.* **1** (*approving*) with no divisions into social classes: *The United States is claimed to be a classless society.* **2** not clearly belonging to a particular social class: *a classless accent* ▶ **class·less·ness** *noun* [U]

class·mate /ˈklæsmeɪt/ *noun* a person who is or was in the same class as you at school or college

class·room 🔑 /ˈklæsrum; -rʊm/ *noun* a room where a class of children or students is taught: *classroom activities* ◆ *the use of computers in the classroom*

ˌclass ˈstruggle (also ˌclass ˈwar) *noun* [U, sing.] (*politics*) opposition between the different social classes in society, especially that described in Marxist theory

class·work /ˈklæswɜrk/ *noun* [U] work that students do at school rather than at home: *When you have finished your classwork, you may read a book.* ➜ compare HOMEWORK (1)

class·y /ˈklæsi/ *adj.* (**class·i·er, class·i·est**) (*informal*) of high quality; expensive and/or fashionable: *a classy player* ◆ *a classy hotel/restaurant*

clat·ter /ˈklætər/ *verb* **1** [I] if hard objects clatter, they knock together and make a loud noise: *He dropped the knife and it clattered on the stone floor.* ◆ *Her cup clattered in the saucer.* **2** [I] + adv./prep. to move making a loud noise like hard objects knocking together: *The cart clattered over the cobblestones.* ◆ *She heard him clattering around downstairs.* ▶ **clat·ter** (also **clat·ter·ing**) *noun* [sing.]: *the clatter of horses' hoofs*

clause AWL /klɔz/ *noun* **1** (*grammar*) a group of words that includes a subject and a verb, and forms a sentence or part of a sentence: *In the sentence "They often go to Italy because they love the food," "They often go to Italy" is the main clause and "because they love the food" is a subordinate clause.* **2** an item in a legal document that says that a particular thing must or must not be done ➜ see also GRANDFATHER CLAUSE

claus·tro·pho·bi·a /ˌklɔstrəˈfoʊbiə/ *noun* [U] an extreme fear of being in a small confined place; the unpleasant feeling that a person gets in a situation that restricts them: *to suffer from claustrophobia* ◆ *She felt she had to escape from the claustrophobia of family life.* ➜ compare AGORAPHOBIA

claus·tro·pho·bic /ˌklɔstrəˈfoʊbɪk/ *adj.* giving you claustrophobia; suffering from claustrophobia: *the claustrophobic atmosphere of the room* ◆ *to feel claustrophobic*

clave /ˈklɑveɪ; kleɪv/ *noun* **1** one of a pair of wooden sticks that are hit together to make a sound **2** a rhythm that forms the basis of Latin music

clav·i·chord /ˈklævəˌkɔrd/ *noun* an early type of musical instrument, like a piano with a very soft tone

clav·i·cle /ˈklævɪkl/ *noun* (*anatomy*) the COLLARBONE ➜ picture at BODY

claw /klɔ/ *noun, verb*
● *noun* **1** one of the sharp, curved nails on the end of an animal's or a bird's foot **2** a long, sharp, curved part of the body of some types of SHELLFISH, used for catching and holding things: *the claws of a crab* ➜ picture at ANIMAL **3** part of a tool or machine, like a claw, used for holding, pulling, or lifting things: *a claw hammer* (= used for pulling out nails)
IDM **get your claws into sb 1** (*disapproving*) if a woman gets her claws into a man, she tries hard to make him marry her or have a relationship with her **2** to criticize someone severely: *Wait until the media gets its claws into her.*
● *verb* [I, T] to scratch or tear someone or something with claws or with your nails: *~ at sb/sth The cat was clawing at the leg of the chair.* ◆ *~ sb/sth She had clawed Stephen across the face.* ◆ (*figurative*) *His hands clawed the air.*
IDM **claw your way back, into sth, out of sth, to sth, etc.** to gradually achieve something or move somewhere by using a lot of determination and effort: *She clawed her*

way to the top of her profession. ♦ Slowly, he clawed his way out from under the collapsed building.
PHR V ˌclaw sth↔'back to get something back that you have lost, usually by using a lot of effort

'claw ˌhammer noun a hammer with one split, curved side that is used for pulling out nails

clay /kleɪ/ noun [U] a type of heavy, sticky earth that becomes hard when it is baked and is used to make things such as pots and bricks つ thesaurus box at SOIL **IDM** see FOOT n.

'clay court noun a TENNIS COURT that has a surface made of clay

clay·ey /kleɪi/ adj. containing clay; like clay: clayey soil

ˌclay 'pigeon noun a disk of baked clay that is thrown into the air for people to shoot at in the sport of SKEET SHOOTING

clean 🖊 /klin/ adj., verb, adv., noun

• **adj.** (clean·er, clean·est)

> NOT DIRTY **1** not dirty: Are your hands clean? ♦ to wipe something clean ♦ The hotel was spotlessly (= extremely) clean. ♦ Keep your room neat and clean. ♦ I can't find a clean shirt (= one I haven't worn since it was washed). **2** having a clean appearance and clean surroundings: Cats are very clean animals.

> NOT HARMFUL **3** free from harmful or unpleasant substances: clean drinking water ♦ clean air ♦ cleaner cars (= not producing so many harmful substances)

> PAPER **4** [usually before noun] with nothing written on it: a clean sheet of paper

> SMOOTH/SIMPLE **5** having a smooth edge, surface, or shape; simple and regular: A sharp knife makes a clean cut. ♦ a modern design with clean lines

> NOT ILLEGAL **6** not showing or having any record of doing something that is against the law: a clean driver's license ♦ a clean police record **7** (informal) not owning or carrying anything illegal such as drugs or weapons: The police searched her, but she was clean.

> FAIR **8** played or done in a fair way and within the rules: It was a tough but clean game.

> NOT OFFENSIVE **9** not offensive or referring to sex; not doing anything that is considered immoral or bad: The movie was good, clean fun for the whole family. ♦ Keep the jokes clean, please! ♦ The sport has a very clean image.

> ACCURATE **10** done in a skillful and accurate way: The plane made a clean takeoff.

> TASTE/SMELL **11** tasting, smelling, or looking pleasant and fresh: The wine has a clean taste and a lovely golden color.
つ compare UNCLEAN
IDM as clean as a whistle (informal) very clean a clean bill of health a report that says someone is healthy or that something is in good condition a clean break **1** a complete separation from a person, an organization, a way of life, etc.: She wanted to make a clean break with the past. **2** a break in a bone in one place a clean slate a record of your work or behavior that does not show any mistakes or bad things that you have done: No government operates with a completely clean slate. make a clean sweep (of sth) **1** to win all the prizes or parts of a game or competition; to win an election completely: China made a clean sweep of the medals in the gymnastics events. ♦ The opinion poll suggests a clean sweep for the Democrats. **2** to remove all the people or things from an organization that are thought to be unnecessary or need changing **IDM** see MR., NOSE n., WIPE v.

• **verb 1** [T, I] ~ (sth) to make something free from dirt or dust by washing or rubbing it: to clean the windows/bathroom/floor ♦ to clean a wound ♦ The villa is cleaned twice a week. ♦ I spent all day cooking and cleaning. つ see also DRY-CLEAN, SPRING-CLEANING **2** [I] to become clean: This oven cleans easily (= is easy to clean). **3** [T] ~ sth = DRY-CLEAN: This coat is filthy. I'll have it cleaned. **4** [T] ~ sth to remove the inside parts of a fish, chicken, etc. before you cook it
IDM clean house **1** to remove people or things that are not necessary or wanted: The new manager said he wanted to clean house. **2** to make your house clean clean up your act

(informal) to start behaving in a moral or responsible way: He cleaned up his act and got a job.
PHR V 'clean sth off/from sth | ˌclean sth↔'off to remove something from something by brushing, rubbing, etc.: I cleaned the mud off my shoes. ˌclean sth↔'out to clean the inside of something thoroughly: I need to clean the fish tank out. ˌclean sb 'out (informal) to use all of someone's money: Paying for all those drinks has cleaned me out. ˌclean sb/sth 'out (informal) to steal everything from a person or place: The burglars totally cleaned her out. ˌclean (yourself) 'up (informal) to make yourself neat and clean, usually by washing: I need to change and clean up. ♦ Go and clean yourself up. ♦ You'd better get cleaned up. つ related noun CLEAN-UP ˌclean 'up | ˌclean sth↔'up **1** to remove dirt, etc. from somewhere: He always expected other people to clean up after him (= when he had made the place dirty or messy). ♦ Who's going to clean up this mess? ♦ to clean up beaches after an oil spill つ related noun CLEAN-UP **2** (informal) to win or make a lot of money: This movie should clean up at the box office. ˌclean sth↔'up to remove crime and immoral behavior from a place or an activity: The new mayor is determined to clean up the city. ♦ Soccer needs to clean up its image. つ related noun CLEAN-UP

• **adv.** (informal) used to emphasize that an action takes place completely: The thief got clean away. ♦ I clean forgot about calling him.
IDM come clean (with sb) (about sth) to admit and explain something that you have kept as a secret: Isn't it time the government came clean about their plans for education?

• **noun** [sing.] the act or process of cleaning something: The house needed a good clean.

clean

wash ♦ rinse ♦ cleanse ♦ dry-clean

These words all mean to remove dirt from something, especially by using water and/or soap.

clean to remove dirt or dust from something, especially by using water or chemicals: The house is cleaned twice a week.

wash to remove dirt from something using water and usually soap: He quickly washed his hands and face. ♦ These jeans need to be washed.

rinse to remove dirt, etc. from something using clean water only, not soap; to remove the soap from something with clean water after washing it: Rinse the cooked pasta with boiling water. ♦ Make sure you rinse out all the soap.

cleanse to clean something or make it pure, especially your skin or a wound

dry-clean to clean clothes using chemicals instead of water

PATTERNS
- to clean/wash/rinse/cleanse sth in/with sth
- to clean/wash/rinse/cleanse sth from sth
- to clean/wash/cleanse a wound
- to clean/wash the car/floor
- to wash/rinse your hair
- to have sth cleaned/washed/dry-cleaned

ˌclean and 'jerk noun an exercise in WEIGHTLIFTING in which a bar with weights is lifted to the shoulder, and then raised above the head

ˌclean-'cut adj. (especially of a young man) looking neat and clean and therefore socially acceptable: Simon's clean-cut good looks

clean·er /'klinər/ noun **1** a person whose job is to clean other people's houses or offices, etc.: an office cleaner **2** a machine or substance that is used for cleaning: a vacuum cleaner ♦ a bottle of kitchen cleaner **3** cleaners (pl. cleaners)

cleaning and renovating

broom · mop · squeegee mop · bucket (*also* pail) · dustpan and brush · duster · vacuum cleaner

squeegee · sponge · feather duster

iron · dishwashing liquid · dish towel · ironing board · paintbrushes · step · rung · stepladder

scrub brush · cloths · rubber gloves · ladder · roller

(also **dry cleaners**) a store where clothes, curtains, etc. are cleaned, especially with chemicals: *Can you pick up my suit from the cleaners?*

IDM **take sb to the cleaners** (*informal*) **1** to steal all of someone's money, etc., or to get it using a trick **2** to defeat someone completely: *Our team got taken to the cleaners.*

clean·ing /ˈkliːnɪŋ/ *noun* [U] the work of making the inside of a house, etc. clean: *They pay someone to **do the cleaning**.*

ˈcleaning lady (also **ˈcleaning woman**) *noun* a woman whose job is to clean the rooms and furniture in an office, a house, etc.

clean-ˈlimbed *adj.* (of a person) thin and with a good shape: *a clean-limbed model*

clean·li·ness /ˈklɛnlinəs/ *noun* [U] the state of being clean or the habit of keeping things clean: *Some people are obsessive about cleanliness.*

clean-ˈliving *adj.* (of a person) living a healthy life, by not drinking alcohol, not having sex with a lot of different people, etc.

clean·ly /ˈkliːnli/ *adv.* **1** easily and smoothly in one movement: *The boat moved cleanly through the water.* **2** in a clean way: *fuel that burns cleanly*

cleanse /klɛnz/ *verb* [T, I] ~ **(sth)** to clean something or make it pure, especially your skin or a wound: *a cleansing*

cream ⊃ thesaurus box at CLEAN **2** [T] ~ **sb (of/from sth)** (*literary*) to take away someone's guilty feelings or SIN ⊃ see also ETHNIC CLEANSING

cleans·er /ˈklɛnzər/ *noun* [C, U] **1** a liquid or cream for cleaning your face, especially for removing makeup **2** a substance that contains chemicals and is used for cleaning things

clean-ˈshaven *adj.* a man who is **clean-shaven** does not have a beard or MUSTACHE (= hair that has been allowed to grow on the face) ⊃ picture at HAIR

ˈclean-up *noun* [usually sing.] the process of removing dirt, or things that are considered bad or immoral from a place: *the clean-up of the river* ◆ *a clean-up campaign*

clear /klɪr/ *adj., verb, adv.*
● *adj.* (**clear·er**, **clear·est**)
> **WITHOUT CONFUSION/DOUBT**
1 easy to understand and not causing any confusion: *She gave me clear and precise directions.*
◆ *Are these instructions clear enough?* ◆ *You'll do as you're told, is that clear?* ◆ *This behavior must stop—do I **make myself clear** (= express myself clearly so there is no doubt about what I mean)?* ◆ *I hope I **made it clear** to him that he was no longer welcome here.* ⊃ thesaurus box on page 266 **2** obvious and

WORD FAMILY
clear *adj.* (≠ unclear)
clearly *adv.*
clarity *noun*
clarify *verb*

leaving no doubt at all: *This is a clear case of fraud.* ◆ *She won the election by a clear majority.* ◆ *His height gives him a clear advantage.* ◆ **~ (to sb) (that)…** *It was quite clear to me that she was lying.* ◆ **~ what, how, whether, etc.…** *It is not clear what they want us to do.* ⊃ language bank at EVIDENCE, IMPERSONAL **3** having or feeling no doubt or confusion: **~ about/on sth** *Are you clear about the arrangements for tomorrow?* ◆ *My memory is not clear on that point.* ◆ **~ what, how, whether, etc.…** *I'm still not clear what the job involves.* ◆ *We need a clear understanding of the problems involved.* ⊃ thesaurus box at SURE

> MIND **4** thinking in a sensible and logical way, especially in a difficult situation: *a clear thinker* ◆ *You'll need to keep a clear head for your interview.*

> EASY TO SEE/HEAR **5** easy to see or hear: *The photo wasn't very clear.* ◆ *The voice on the phone was clear and strong.* ◆ *She was in Australia but I could hear her voice as clear as a bell.*

> TRANSPARENT **6** that you can see through: *The water was so clear we could see the bottom of the lake.* ◆ *clear glass* ◆ *a clear, colorless liquid*

> SKY/WEATHER **7** without cloud or MIST: *a clear blue sky* ◆ *On a clear day you can see the Farallon Islands.*

> SKIN **8** without spots or marks: *clear skin* ◆ *a clear complexion*

> EYES **9** bright and lively

> NOT BLOCKED **10** **~ (of sth)** free from things that are blocking the way or covering the surface of something: *The road was clear and I ran over.* ◆ *All exits must be kept clear of baggage.* ◆ *You won't get a clear view of the stage from here.* ◆ *I always leave a clear desk at the end of the day.*

> CONSCIENCE **11** if you have a **clear** CONSCIENCE or your CONSCIENCE is **clear**, you do not feel guilty

> FREE FROM SOMETHING BAD **12** **~ of sth** free from something that is unpleasant: *They were still not clear of all suspicion.* ◆ *We are finally clear of debt.*

> NOT TOUCHING/NEAR **13** [not before noun] **~ (of sb/sth)** not touching something; a distance away from something: *The plane climbed until it was clear of the clouds.* ◆ *Make sure you park your car clear of the entrance.*

> PERIOD OF TIME **14** without any events or activities planned: *I need three clear weeks to work on this project.*

> SUM OF MONEY **15** [only before noun] remaining when taxes, costs, etc. have been taken away **SYN** NET: *They had made a clear profit of $2,000.*

> PHONETICS **16** (of a speech sound) produced with the central part of the tongue close to the top of the mouth. In many accents of English, clear /l/ is used before a vowel, as in *leave*. **ANT** DARK

IDM **(as) clear as day** easy to see or understand **(as) clear as mud** (*informal, humorous*) not clear at all; not easy to understand: *Oh well, that's all as clear as mud, then.* **in the clear** (*informal*) no longer in danger or thought to be guilty of something: *It seems that the original suspect is in the clear.* ⊃ more at FIELD *n.*, HEAD *n.*, LOUD *adv.*, SAILING

● *verb*
> REMOVE SOMETHING OR SOMEONE **1** [T] to remove something that is not wanted or needed from a place: **~ sth** *I had cleared my desk before I left.* ◆ *It was several hours before the road was cleared after the accident.* ◆ *It's your turn to clear the table* (= to take away the dirty plates, etc. after a meal). ◆ *She cleared a space on the sofa for him to sit down.* ◆ **~ A (of B)** *I cleared my desk of papers.* ◆ *The streets had been cleared of snow.* ◆ **~ B (from/off A)** *Clear all those papers off the desk.* ◆ *The remains of the snow had been cleared from the streets.* ⊃ see also CLEAR AWAY **2** [T] **~ sth** to make people leave a place: *After the bomb warning, police cleared the streets.*

> NOT BE BLOCKED **3** [I] to move freely again; to no longer be blocked: *The traffic took a long time to clear after the accident.* ◆ *The boy's lungs cleared and he began to breathe more easily.*

> OF SKY/WEATHER **4** [I] when the sky or the weather **clears**, it becomes brighter and free of cloud or rain: *The sky cleared after the storm.* ◆ *The rain is clearing slowly.*

> OF SMOKE, ETC. **5** [I] **~ (away)** when smoke, FOG, etc. **clears**, it disappears so that it is easier to see things: *The mist will clear by mid-morning.*

> OF LIQUID **6** [I] when a liquid **clears**, it becomes transparent and you can see through it: *The muddy water slowly cleared.*

> YOUR HEAD/MIND **7** [I, T] if your head or mind **clears**, or you **clear** it, you become free of thoughts that worry or confuse you or the effects of alcohol, a blow, etc. and you are able to think clearly: *As her mind cleared, she remembered what had happened.* ◆ **~ sth** *I went for a walk to clear my head.*

> OF FACE/EXPRESSION **8** [I] if your face or expression **clears**, you stop looking angry or worried

> PROVE SOMEONE INNOCENT **9** [T] **~ sb (of sth)** to prove that someone is innocent: *She was cleared of all charges against her.* ◆ *Throughout his years in prison, he fought to clear his name.*

> GIVE OFFICIAL PERMISSION **10** [T] to give or get official approval for something to be done: **~ sth** *His appointment had been cleared by the board.* ◆ **~ sth with sb/sth** *I'll have to clear it with the manager.* **11** [T] **~ sth** to give official permission for a person, a ship, a plane, or goods to leave or enter a place: *The plane had been cleared for takeoff.* ◆ *to clear goods through customs* **12** [T] **~ sb** to decide officially, after finding out information about someone, that they can be given special work or allowed to see secret papers: *She hasn't been cleared by security.*

> MONEY **13** [I, T] **~ (sth)** if a check that you deposit to your bank account **clears**, or a bank **clears** it, the money is available for you to use: *Checks usually take three working days to clear.* **14** [T] **~ sth** to gain or earn a sum of money as profit: *She cleared $1,000 on the deal.* **15** [T] **~ sth** if you **clear** a debt or a loan, you pay all the money back

> GET OVER/PAST **16** [T] **~ sth** to jump over or get past something without touching it: *The horse cleared the fence easily.* ◆ *The car only just cleared* (= avoided hitting) *the gatepost.*

> IN SPORTS **17** [T, I] **~ (sth)** (in SOCCER and some other sports) if you **clear** a ball, or a ball **clears**, it is kicked or hit away from the area near your own goal

IDM **clear the air** to improve a difficult or TENSE situation by talking about worries, doubts, etc. **clear the decks** (*informal*) to prepare for an activity, event, etc. by removing anything that is not essential to it **clear your throat** to cough so that you can speak clearly **clear the way (for sth/for sth to happen)** to remove things that are stopping the progress or movement of something: *The ruling could clear the way for extradition proceedings.* ⊃ more at COAST *n.*, COBWEB

PHR V **,clear a'way** | **,clear sth↔a'way** to remove something because it is not wanted or needed, or in order to leave a clear space: *He cleared away and made coffee.* ◆ *It's time your toys were cleared away.* **,clear 'out (of…)** (*informal*) to leave a place quickly: *He cleared out with all the money and left her with the kids.* **,clear 'out | ,clear sth↔'out** to make something empty and clean by removing things or throwing things away: *to clear out a drawer/room* ◆ *We cleared out all our old clothes.* ◆ *I found the letters when I was clearing out after my father died.* ⊃ related noun CLEAR-OUT **,clear 'up 1** (of the weather) to become fine or bright: *I hope it clears up this afternoon.* **2** (of an illness, infection, etc.) to disappear: *Has your rash cleared up yet?* **,clear 'up | ,clear sth↔'up** to make something clean and neat: *It's time to clear up.* ◆ *Clear up your own mess!* **,clear sth↔'up** to solve or explain something: *to clear up a mystery/difficulty/misunderstanding*

● *adv.*
> NOT NEAR/TOUCHING **1** **~ (of sth)** away from something; not near or touching something: *Stand clear of the train doors.* ◆ *He injured his arm as he jumped clear of the car.* ◆ *By lap two, Walker was two meters clear of the rest of the runners.*

> ALL THE WAY **2** all the way to something that is far away: *She could see clear down the highway into the town.*

IDM **keep/stay/steer clear (of sb/sth)** to avoid a person or thing because it may cause problems ⊃ more at WAY *n.*

clear·ance /ˈklɪrəns/ *noun* **1** [C, U] the removal of things that are not wanted: *forest clearances* ◆ *a clearance sale* (= in a store, when goods are sold cheaply to get rid of them quickly) **2** [U, C] the amount of space or distance that is needed between two objects so that they do not touch each other: *There is not much clearance for vehicles passing under this*

clear

obvious ◆ **apparent** ◆ **evident** ◆ **plain**

These words all describe something that is easy to see or understand and leaves no doubts or confusion.

clear easy to see or understand and leaving no doubts: *Her instructions were very clear.*

obvious easy to see or understand: *I don't understand how you missed such an obvious error.*

apparent [not usually before noun] (*somewhat formal*) easy to see or understand: *It soon became apparent that everything had gone wrong.*

evident (*somewhat formal*) easy to see or understand: *The orchestra played with evident enjoyment.*

plain easy to see or understand: *He made it very plain that he wanted us to leave.*

WHICH WORD?

These words all have almost exactly the same meaning. There are slight differences in register and patterns of use. If you *make sth clear/plain*, you do so deliberately because you want people to understand something; if you *make sth obvious*, you usually do it without meaning to: ~~I hope I make myself obvious.~~ ◆ ~~Try not to make it so clear/plain.~~ In the expressions *clear majority*, *for obvious reasons*, *for no apparent reason*, and *plain to see*, none of the other words can be used instead. You can have *a clear/an obvious/a plain case of sth* but not: ~~an evident case of sth~~.

PATTERNS

- clear/obvious/apparent/evident/plain **to sb/sth**
- clear/obvious/apparent/evident/plain **that/what/who/how/where/why...**
- to **seem/become/make sth** clear/obvious/apparent/evident/plain
- **perfectly/quite/very** clear/obvious/apparent/evident/plain

---

bridge. ◆ *a clearance of four feet* **3** [U, C] official permission that is given to someone before they can work somewhere, have particular information, or do something they want to do: *I'm waiting for clearance from headquarters.* ◆ *All employees at the submarine base require **security clearance**.* **4** [U] official permission for a person or vehicle to enter or leave an airport or a country: *The pilot was waiting for clearance for takeoff.* **5** [U, C] the process of a check being paid by a bank **6** [C] a **clearance** in SOCCER and some other sports is when a player kicks or hits the ball away from the goal of his or her own team

ˌclear-ˈcut *adj.* definite and easy to see or identify: *There is no clear-cut answer to this question.*

ˌclear-ˈheaded *adj.* able to think in a clear and sensible way, especially in a difficult situation

clear·ing /ˈklɪrɪŋ/ *noun* an open space in a forest where there are no trees **SYN** GLADE

ˈclearing house *noun* **1** a central office that banks use in order to pay each other money and exchange checks, etc. **2** an organization that collects and exchanges information on behalf of people or other organizations

clear·ly 🔑 /ˈklɪrli/ *adv.*
1 in a way that is easy to see or hear: *Please speak clearly after the tone.* **2** in a way that makes sense and is easy to understand: *She explained everything very clearly.* **3** used to emphasize that what you are saying is obvious and true **SYN** OBVIOUSLY: *Clearly, this will cost a lot more than we realized.*

clear·ness /ˈklɪrnəs/ *noun* [U] (much less frequent than *clarity*) the state of being clear

---

ˌclear-ˈsighted *adj.* understanding or thinking clearly; able to make good decisions and judgments

cleat /klit/ *noun* **1** [C] a piece of rubber on the bottom of a shoe, etc. to stop it from slipping **2** **cleats** [pl.] shoes with cleats, often worn for playing sports ⟳ picture at FOOTBALL ⟳ compare SPIKE **3** [C] a small wooden or metal bar fastened to something, on which ropes may be fastened by winding

cleav·age /ˈklivɪdʒ/ *noun* **1** [C, U] the space between a woman's breasts that can be seen above a shirt or dress that does not completely cover them **2** [C] (*formal*) a difference or division between people or groups

cleave /kliv/ *verb* (**cleaved**, **cleaved HELP** Less commonly, **cleft** /klɛft/ and **clove** /kloʊv/ are used for the past tense, and **cleft** and **cloven** /ˈkloʊvn/ for the past participle.) **1** [T] **~ sth** (*old-fashioned* or *literary*) to split or cut something in two using something sharp and heavy: *She cleaved his skull (in two) with an ax.* ◆ (*figurative*) *His skin was cleft with deep lines.* **2** [I, T] (*old-fashioned* or *literary*) to move quickly through something: *~ through sth a ship cleaving through the water* ◆ *~ sth The huge boat cleaved the darkness.* **3** [I] **~ to sth/sb** (*literary*) to stick close to something or someone: *Her tongue clove to the roof of her mouth.* **4** (**cleaved**, **cleaved**) [I] **~ to sth** (*formal*) to continue to believe in or be loyal to something: *to cleave to a belief/idea*

cleav·er /ˈklivər/ *noun* a heavy knife with a broad blade, used for cutting large pieces of meat ⟳ picture at KITCHEN

clef /klɛf/ *noun* (*music*) a symbol at the beginning of a line of printed music (called a STAVE or STAFF) that shows the PITCH of the notes on it: *the treble/bass clef*

cleft /klɛft/ *noun* a natural opening or crack, for example in the ground or in rock, or in a person's chin: *a cleft in the rocks* ⟳ see also CLEAVE

ˌcleft ˈlip *noun* a condition in which someone is born with their upper lip split

ˌcleft ˈpalate *noun* a condition in which someone is born with the roof of their mouth split, making them unable to speak clearly

ˌcleft ˈsentence *noun* (*grammar*) a sentence that begins with "it" or "that" and has a following clause, for example, "it is you that I love," or "that is my mother you're insulting"

clem·a·tis /ˈklɛmətəs; kləˈmætəs/ *noun* [C, U] a climbing plant with large white, purple, or pink flowers

clem·en·cy /ˈklɛmənsi/ *noun* [U] (*formal*) kindness shown to someone when they are being punished; willingness not to punish someone so severely **SYN** MERCY: *a plea for clemency*

clem·ent /ˈklɛmənt/ *adj.* (*formal*) **1** (especially of weather) mild and pleasant **ANT** INCLEMENT **2** showing kindness and MERCY to someone who is being punished

clem·en·tine /ˈklɛmənˌtaɪn; -ˌtin/ *noun* a fruit like a small orange

clench /klɛntʃ/ *verb* **1** [T, I] **~ (sth)** when you **clench** your hands, teeth, etc., or when they **clench**, you press or squeeze them together tightly, usually showing that you are angry, determined, or upset: *He clenched his fists in anger.* ◆ *Through clenched teeth she told him to leave.* ◆ *His fists clenched slowly until his knuckles were white.* **2** [T] **~ sth (in/between sth)** to hold something tightly and firmly: *Her pen was clenched between her teeth.*

clere·sto·ry /ˈklɪrˌstɔri/ *noun* (*pl.* **clere·sto·ries**) (*architecture*) the upper part of a wall in a large church, with a row of windows in it, above the level of the lower roofs

cler·gy /ˈklərdʒi/ *noun* often **the clergy** [pl.] the priests or ministers of a religion, especially of the Christian Church: *All the local clergy were asked to attend the ceremony.* ◆ *The new proposals affect both clergy and laity.* ⟳ collocations at RELIGION ⟳ compare LAITY

cler·gy·man /ˈklərdʒimən/ (also **church·man**) *noun* (*pl.* **cler·gy·men** /-mən/) a male priest or minister in the Christian Church ⟳ compare PRIEST

ʌ **cup**   ə **about**   eɪ **say**   aɪ **five**   ɔɪ **boy**   aʊ **now**   oʊ **go**   ər **bird**

cler·gy·wom·an /'klɜːdʒiˌwʊmən/ noun (pl. **cler·gy·wom-en** /-ˌwɪmən/) a female priest or minister in the Christian Church

cler·ic /'klerɪk/ noun **1** (old-fashioned or formal) a member of the clergy **2** a religious leader in any religion: *Muslim clerics*

cler·i·cal /'klerɪkl/ adj. **1** connected with office work: *clerical workers/staff/assistants* ◆ *a clerical error* (= one made in copying or calculating something) **2** connected with the CLERGY (= priests): *a clerical collar* (= one that fastens at the back, worn by some priests)

clerk /klɑːk/ noun, verb
● *noun* **1** a person whose job is to keep the records or accounts in an office, store, etc.: *an office clerk* ⊃ see also FILING CLERK **2** a person whose job is to serve customers in a store: *The clerk at the counter gave me too little change.* **3** an official in charge of the records of a town, court, etc.: *the Town Clerk* ◆ *the Clerk of the Court* ⊃ see also COUNTY CLERK **4** (also **'desk clerk**) a person whose job is dealing with people arriving at or leaving a hotel **SYN** RECEPTIONIST
● *verb* [I] to work as a clerk: *a clerking job*

clev·er /'klevər/ adj. (**clev·er·er, clev·er·est**) **HELP** You can also use **more clever** and **most clever**. **1** showing intelligence or skill, for example in the design of an object, in an idea, or someone's actions: *a clever little gadget* ◆ *What a clever idea!* ◆ *That* (= what you just did) *wasn't very clever, was it?* (= it wasn't sensible) **2** quick at learning and understanding things **SYN** INTELLIGENT: *She's a clever girl!* ◆ *How clever of you to work it out!* **3** ~ **(at sth)** skillful: *She's clever at getting what she wants.* ◆ *He's clever with his hands.* ▶ **clev·er·ly** adv. **clev·er·ness** noun [U]

cli·ché (also **cli·che**) /kli'ʃeɪ/ noun (disapproving) **1** [C] a phrase or an idea that has been used so often that it no longer has much meaning and is not interesting: *the old cliché that "a trouble shared is a trouble halved"* **2** [U] the use of clichés in writing or speaking ▶ **cli·chéd** adj.: *a clichéd view of upper-class life*

click /klɪk/ verb, noun
● *verb* **1** [I, T] to make or cause something to make a short, sharp sound: **(+ adv./prep.)** *The cameras clicked away.* ◆ *The bolt clicked into place.* ◆ **+ adj.** *The door clicked shut.* ◆ ~ **sth** *He clicked his fingers at the waiter.* ◆ *Polly clicked her tongue in annoyance.* **2** [T, I] to choose a particular function or item on a computer screen, etc., by pressing one of the buttons on a mouse: ~ **sth** *Click the OK button to start.* ◆ ~ **(on sth)** *I clicked on the link to the next page of the Web site.* ◆ *To run a program, just double-click on the icon.* ⊃ see also DOUBLE-CLICK **3** [I] (informal) to suddenly become clear or understood: *Suddenly it clicked —we'd been talking about different people.* ◆ *It all clicked into place.* **4** [I] (informal) to become friends with someone at once; to become popular with someone: *We met at a party and clicked immediately.* ◆ ~ **with sb** *He's never really clicked with his students.* **5** [I] (informal) to work well together: *The team doesn't seem to have clicked yet.* **PHR V** ˌclick 'through (to sth) to visit a Web site by clicking on an electronic link or advertisement on another Web page
● *noun* **1** a short sharp sound: *The door closed with a click.* **2** the act of pressing the button on a computer mouse **3** (phonetics) a speech sound made by pressing the tongue against the top of the mouth or the part of the mouth behind the upper front teeth, then releasing it quickly, causing air to be sucked in. Clicks are found especially in southern African languages: *click languages* **4** = KLICK

click·a·ble /'klɪkəbl/ adj. (computing) if text or an image is clickable, you can click on it with the mouse in order to make something happen

click·er /'klɪkər/ noun (informal) a device that allows you to operate a television, etc. from a distance **SYN** REMOTE CONTROL

click·stream /'klɪkstriːm/ noun a record of all the Web sites a person visits when spending time on the Internet

cli·ent /'klaɪənt/ noun
1 a person who uses the services or advice of a professional person or organization: *a lawyer with many famous clients* ◆ *to act on behalf of a client* ◆ *Social workers must always consider the best interests of their clients.* **2** (computing) a computer that is linked to a SERVER

cli·en·tele /ˌklaɪən'tel/ noun [sing.] all the customers or clients of a store, restaurant, organization, etc.: *an international clientele*

ˌclient-'server adj. [only before noun] (computing) (of a computer system) in which a central SERVER provides data to a number of computers connected together in a network ⊃ see also PEER-TO-PEER

'client ˌstate noun a country that depends on a larger and more powerful country for support and protection

cliff /klɪf/ noun a high area of rock with a very steep side, often at the edge of the ocean: *the cliff edge/top* ◆ *the redstone cliffs of Colorado* ◆ *a castle perched high on the cliffs above the river*

cliff·hang·er /'klɪfˌhæŋər/ noun a situation in a story, movie, competition, etc. that is very exciting because you cannot guess what will happen next, or you do not find out immediately what happens next: *The first part of the serial ended with a real cliffhanger.* ▶ **cliff·hang·ing** adj.

cliff·top /'klɪftɑp/ noun the area of land at the top of a cliff

cli·mac·tic /klaɪ'mæktɪk/ adj. (formal) (of an event or a point in time) very exciting; most important

cli·mate /'klaɪmət/ noun
1 [C, U] the regular pattern of weather conditions of a particular place: *a mild/temperate/warm/wet climate* ◆ *the harsh climate of the Arctic regions* **2** [C] an area with particular weather conditions: *They wanted to move to a warmer climate.* **3** [C] a general attitude or feeling; an atmosphere or a situation that exists in a particular place: *the present political climate* ◆ *the current climate of opinion* (= what people generally are thinking about a particular issue) ◆ *a climate of suspicion/violence* ◆ *We need to create a climate in which business can prosper.*

'climate ˌchange noun [U] changes in the earth's weather, including changes in temperature, wind patterns, and RAINFALL, especially the increase in the temperature of the earth's atmosphere that is caused by the increase of particular gases, especially CARBON DIOXIDE: *the threat of global climate change* ⊃ compare GLOBAL WARMING

cli·mat·ic /klaɪ'mætɪk/ adj. [only before noun] connected with the weather of a particular area: *climatic changes/conditions* ▶ **cli·mat·i·cally** /-kli/ adv.

cli·ma·tol·o·gy /ˌklaɪmə'tɑlədʒi/ noun [U] the scientific study of climate ▶ **cli·ma·to·log·i·cal** /ˌklaɪmətl'ɑdʒɪkl/ adj. **cli·ma·tol·o·gist** /ˌklaɪmə'tɑlədʒɪst/ noun

cli·max /'klaɪmæks/ noun, verb
● *noun* **1** the most exciting or important event or point in time: *to come to/reach a climax* ◆ *the climax of his political career* **2** the most exciting part of a play, piece of music, etc. that usually happens near the end **3** the highest point of sexual pleasure **SYN** ORGASM ⊃ compare ANTICLIMAX
● *verb* **1** [I, T] to come to or form the best, most exciting, or most important point in something: ~ **with/in sth** *The festival will climax on Sunday with a gala concert.* ◆ ~ **sth** *The sensational verdict climaxed a six-month trial.* **2** [I] to have an ORGASM

climb /klaɪm/ verb, noun
● *verb*
▷ GO UP **1** [T, I] ~ **(up) (sth)** to go up something toward the top: *to climb a mountain/hill/tree/wall* ◆ *She climbed up the stairs.* ◆ *The car slowly climbed the hill.* ◆ *As they climbed higher, the air became cooler.*

> **GO THROUGH/DOWN/OVER** **2** [I] + *adv./prep.* to move somewhere, especially with difficulty or effort: *I climbed through the window.* ◆ *Sue climbed into bed.* ◆ *Can you climb down?* ◆ *The boys climbed over the wall.*

> **MOUNTAIN, ROCK, ETC.** **3** go climbing [I] to go up mountains or climb rocks as a hobby or sport: *He goes climbing almost every weekend.*

> **AIRCRAFT/SUN, ETC.** **4** [I] to go higher in the sky: *The plane climbed to 33,000 feet.*

> **SLOPE UP** **5** [I] to slope upward: *From here the path climbs steeply to the summit.*

> **OF PLANTS** **6** [I] to grow up a wall or frame: *a climbing rose*

> **INCREASE** **7** [I] (of temperature, a country's money, etc.) to increase in value or amount: *The dollar has been climbing all week.* ◆ *The paper's circulation continues to climb.*

> **IMPROVE POSITION/STATUS** **8** [I] ~ **(to sth)** to move to a higher position or social rank by your own effort: *In a few years, he had climbed to the top of his profession.* ◆ *The team has now climbed to fourth in the league.* **IDM** see **BANDWAGON**

● *noun*

> **MOUNTAIN/STEPS** **1** an act of climbing up a mountain, rock, or large number of steps; a period of time spent climbing: *an exhausting climb* ◆ *It's an hour's climb to the summit.* **2** a mountain or rock that people climb up for sport: *Titan's Wall is the mountain's hardest rock climb.*

> **INCREASE** **3** [usually sing.] an increase in value or amount: *the dollar's climb against the euro*

> **TO A HIGHER POSITION OR STATUS** **4** [usually sing.] progress to a higher status, standard, or position: *a rapid climb to stardom* ◆ *the long slow climb out of the recession*

climb·er /'klaɪmər/ *noun* **1** a person who climbs (especially mountains) or an animal that climbs: *climbers and hikers* ◆ *Monkeys are efficient climbers.* **2** a climbing plant ⊃ see also **SOCIAL CLIMBER**

climb·ing /'klaɪmɪŋ/ *noun* [U] the sport or activity of climbing rocks or mountains: *to go climbing* ◆ *a climbing accident*

'**climbing ,wall** *noun* a wall with parts to hold onto, usually inside a building, for people to practice climbing on

clime /klaɪm/ *noun* [usually pl.] (*literary* or *humorous*) a country with a particular kind of climate: *I'm heading for sunnier climes next month.*

clinch /klɪntʃ/ *verb, noun*
● *verb* **1** ~ **sth** to succeed in achieving or winning something: *to clinch an argument/a deal/a victory* **2** ~ **sth** to provide the answer to something; to settle something that was not certain: *"I'll pay your airfare." "Okay, that clinches it—I'll come with you."* ◆ *a clinching argument*
● *noun* **1** (*informal*) a position in which two lovers hold each other tightly **SYN EMBRACE** **2** a position in a fight in which two opponents hold each other tightly

clinch·er /'klɪntʃər/ *noun* [usually sing.] (*informal*) a fact, a remark, or an event that settles an argument, a decision, or a competition

cline /klaɪn/ *noun* a series of similar items in which each is almost the same as the ones next to it, but the last is very different from the first **SYN CONTINUUM**

cling /klɪŋ/ *verb* (clung, clung /klʌŋ/) **1** [I] to hold on tightly to someone or something: ~ **to sb/sth** *survivors clinging to a raft* ◆ ~ **on to sb/sth** *She clung on to her baby.* ◆ ~ **on** *Cling on tight!* ◆ ~ **together** *They clung together, shivering with cold.* ⊃ thesaurus box at **HOLD** **2** [I] to stick to something: *a dress that clings* (= fits closely and shows the shape of your body) ◆ ~ **to sth** *The wet shirt clung to his chest.* ◆ *The smell of smoke still clung to her clothes.* **3** [I] ~ **(to sb)** (usually *disapproving*) to stay close to someone, especially because you need them emotionally: *After her mother's death, Sara clung to her aunt more than ever.*
PHRV '**cling to sth** | ,**cling 'on to sth** to be unwilling to get rid of something, or stop doing something: *Throughout the trial, she had clung to the belief that he was innocent.* ◆ *He had one last hope to cling on to.* ◆ *She managed to cling on to life for another couple of years.*

cling·y /'klɪŋi/ (also **cling·ing** /'klɪŋɪŋ/) *adj.* **1** (of clothes or material) sticking to the body and showing its shape **2** (usually *disapproving*) needing another person too much: *a clinging child*

clin·ic /'klɪnɪk/ *noun* **1** a building or part of a hospital where people can go for medical treatment or advice: *the local family planning clinic* **2** a building shared by a group of doctors who work together **3** a period of time during which doctors give special medical treatment or advice: *The prenatal clinic is on Wednesdays.* **4** a private hospital or one that treats health problems of a particular kind: *He is being treated at a New York clinic.* ◆ *a rehabilitation clinic for alcoholics* **5** an occasion in a hospital when medical students learn by watching a specialist examine and treat patients **6** an occasion at which a professional person, especially an **ATHLETE** or coach, gives advice and training: *a serving clinic for young tennis players*

clin·i·cal /'klɪnɪkl/ *adj.* **1** [only before noun] relating to the examination and treatment of patients and their illnesses: *clinical research* (= done on patients, not just considering theory) ◆ *clinical training* (= the part of a doctor's training done in a hospital) ◆ *clinical trials of a drug* **2** (*disapproving*) cold and calm and without feeling or sympathy: *He watched her suffering with clinical detachment.* **3** (*disapproving*) (of a room, building, etc.) very plain; without decoration ▶ **clin·i·cal·ly** /-kli/ *adv.*: *clinically dead* (= judged to be dead from the condition of the body) ◆ *clinically depressed*

cli·ni·cian /klɪ'nɪʃn/ *noun* a doctor, **PSYCHOLOGIST**, etc. who has direct contact with patients

clink /klɪŋk/ *verb, noun*
● *verb* [I, T] to make or cause something to make a sharp ringing sound, like that of glasses being hit against each other **SYN CHINK**: *clinking coins* ◆ ~ **sth** *They clinked glasses and drank to each other's health.*
● *noun* [sing.] **1** (also **clink·ing**) a sharp ringing sound like the sound made by glasses being hit against each other **2** (*old-fashioned, slang*) prison

clink·er /'klɪŋkər/ *noun* **1** [sing.] a wrong musical note: *The singer hit a clinker.* **2** [C] (*informal*) something that is of very poor quality or a failure: *The band has recorded some great albums, but this one is a real clinker.* **3** [U, C] the hard rough substance left after coal has burned at a high temperature; a piece of this substance

clip /klɪp/ *noun, verb*
● *noun* **1** [C] (often in compounds) a small metal or plastic object used for holding things together or in place: *a hair clip* ◆ *toe clips on a bicycle* ⊃ see also **BICYCLE CLIP, PAPER CLIP** **2** [C] a short part of a movie that is shown separately: *Here is a clip from her latest movie.* **3** [C] a set of bullets in a metal container that is placed in or attached to a gun for firing **4** [sing.] the act of cutting something to make it shorter: *He gave the hedge a clip.*
IDM at a fast, good, steady, etc. clip quickly **$5, $100, etc. a clip** used to talk about how much each one of an item costs: *The tickets are going for $5 a clip.*
● *verb* (-pp-) **1** [T, I] to fasten something to something else with a clip; to be fastened with a clip: ~ **sth** + *adv./prep.* *He clipped the microphone (on) to his collar.* ◆ *Clip the pages together.* ◆ + *adv./prep.* *Do those earrings clip on?* **2** [T] to cut something with scissors or **SHEARS**, in order to make it shorter or neater; to remove something from somewhere by cutting it off: ~ **sth** *to clip a hedge* ◆ ~ **sth from sth/off (sth)** *He clipped off a length of wire.* **3** [T] to hit the edge or side of something: ~ **sth** *The car clipped the curb as it turned.* ◆ ~ **sth** + *adv./prep.* *She clipped the ball into the net.* **4** [T] ~ **sth (out of/from sth)** to cut something out of something else using scissors: *to clip a coupon (out of the paper)*
IDM clip sb's wings to restrict a person's freedom or power
PHRV ,**clip sth 'off sth** (*informal*) to reduce the time that it takes to do something by a particular length of time: *She clipped two seconds off her previous best time.*

| t tea | ţ butter | d did | k cat | g got | tʃ chin | dʒ June | f fall |

'clip art *noun* [U] (*computing*) pictures and symbols that are stored in computer programs or on Web sites for computer users to copy and add to their own documents

clip·board /'klɪpbɔrd/ *noun* **1** a small board with a clip at the top for holding papers, used by someone who wants to write while standing or moving around ⊃ picture at STATIONERY **2** (*computing*) a place where information from a computer file is stored for a time until it is added to another file

clip-clop /'klɪp klɑp/ *noun* a sound like the sound of a horse's HOOF on a hard surface

'clip joint *noun* (*informal, old-fashioned, disapproving*) a NIGHTCLUB that charges prices that are too high

'clip-on *adj.* [only before noun] fastened to something with a CLIP: *clip-on earrings*

clipped /klɪpt/ *adj.* (of a person's way of speaking) clear and fast but not very friendly: *his clipped military tones*

clip·per /'klɪpər/ *noun* **1 clippers** [pl.] a tool for cutting small pieces off things: *a pair of clippers* ⊃ see also NAIL CLIPPERS **2** a fast sailing ship, used in the past

clip·ping /'klɪpɪŋ/ *noun* **1** [usually pl.] a piece cut off something: *hedge/nail clippings* **2** (also **'press ˌclipping**) an article or a story that you cut from a newspaper or magazine and keep

clique /klik; klɪk/ *noun* (often *disapproving*) a small group of people who spend their time together and do not allow others to join them

cli·quey /'kliki; 'klɪki/ (also **cli·quish** /'klikɪʃ; 'klɪ-/) *adj.* (*disapproving*) tending to form a clique; controlled by cliques: *He found the school very cliquey and elitist.*

clit·o·ris /'klɪtərəs/ *noun* the small sensitive organ just above the opening of a woman's VAGINA, which becomes larger when she is sexually excited ▶ **clit·o·ral** /'klɪtərəl/ *adj.* [only before noun]

cloak /kloʊk/ *noun, verb*
● *noun* **1** [C] a type of coat that has no sleeves, fastens at the neck, and hangs loosely from the shoulders, worn especially in the past **2** [sing.] (*literary*) a thing that hides or covers someone or something: *They left under the cloak of darkness.*
● *verb* ~ **sth (in sth)** [often passive] (*literary*) to cover or hide something: *The hills were cloaked in thick mist.* ◆ *The meeting was cloaked in mystery.* ▶ **cloaked** /kloʊkt/ *adj.*: *a tall cloaked figure* (= a person wearing a cloak)

ˌcloak-and-'dagger *adj.* [only before noun] **cloak-and-dagger** activities are secret and mysterious, sometimes in a way that people think is unnecessary or ridiculous

cloak·room /'kloʊkrum; -rʊm/ *noun* = CHECKROOM

clob·ber /'klɑbər/ *verb* (*informal*) **1** ~ **sb** to hit someone very hard **2** [often passive] ~ **sb/sth** to affect someone badly or to punish them, especially by making them lose money: *The paper got clobbered with libel damages of half a million dollars.* **3** [usually passive] ~ **sb/sth** to defeat someone completely: *We got clobbered in the game on Saturday.*

cloche /kloʊʃ/ *noun* **1** (also **ˌcloche 'hat**) a woman's hat, shaped like a bell, and fitting close to the head, worn especially in the 1920s **2** a glass or plastic cover placed over young plants to protect them from cold weather

clock /klɑk/ *noun, verb*
● *noun* **1** [C] an instrument for measuring and showing time, in a room or on the wall of a building (not worn or carried like a watch): *It was ten after six by the kitchen clock.* ◆ *The clock struck twelve/midnight.* ◆ *The clock is fast/slow.* ◆ *The clock has stopped.* ◆ *the clock face* (= the front part of a clock with the numbers on it) ◆ *The hands of the clock crept slowly around.* ◆ *Ellen heard the loud ticking of the clock in the hall.* ⊃ see also ALARM CLOCK, BIOLOGICAL CLOCK, BODY CLOCK, CARRIAGE CLOCK, CUCKOO CLOCK, GRANDFATHER CLOCK, O'CLOCK, TIME CLOCK **2 the clock** [sing.] (*informal*) = MILOMETER: *a used car with 20,000 miles on the clock*

clocks and watches

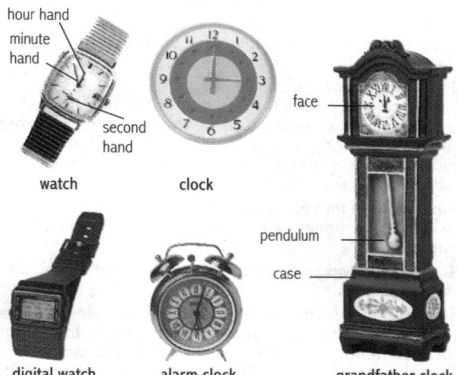

hour hand
minute hand
second hand
watch
clock
face
pendulum
case
digital watch
alarm clock
grandfather clock

IDM against the clock if you do something **against the clock**, you do it fast in order to finish before a particular time **around the clock** all day and all night without stopping **put/turn/set the clock back 1** to return to a situation that existed in the past; to remember a past age: *I wish we could turn the clock back two years and give the marriage another chance.* **2** (*disapproving*) to return to old-fashioned methods or ideas: *The new censorship law will turn the clock back 50 years.* **run down/run out/kill the clock** if a sports team tries to **run down/out the clock** or **kill the clock** at the end of a game, it stops trying to score and just tries to keep hold of the ball to stop the other team from scoring **set/move the clocks ahead/back** to change the time shown by clocks, usually by one hour, when the time changes officially, for example at the beginning and end of summer **the clocks go forward/back** the time changes officially, for example at the beginning and end of summer ⊃ more at BEAT, RACE, STOP v., WATCH v.
● *verb* **1** ~ **sth** to reach a particular time or speed: *He clocked 10.09 seconds in the 100 meters final.* **2** to measure the speed at which someone or something is traveling: ~ **sb doing sth** *The police clocked him doing over 100 miles an hour.* ◆ ~ **sb/ sth (at sth)** *Wind gusts at 80 m.p.h. were clocked at Rapid City.* **3** ~ **sb** (*informal*) to hit someone, especially on the head: *Someone clocked him for no good reason.*
PHR V ˌclock 'in (also **ˌpunch 'in**) to record the time at which you arrive at work, especially by putting a card into a machine **ˌclock 'out** (also **ˌpunch 'out**) to record the time at which you leave work, especially by putting a card into a machine **ˌclock 'up sth** to reach a particular amount or number: *On the trip we clocked up over 1,800 miles.* ◆ *He has clocked up more than 25 years on the committee.*

ˌclock 'radio *noun* a clock combined with a radio that can be set to come on at a particular time in order to wake someone up

'clock speed *noun* [U] (*computing*) the speed at which a computer operates: *This machine has a clock speed of 1.6GHz.*

'clock ˌtower *noun* a tall tower, usually part of another building, with a clock at the top

'clock-ˌwatcher *noun* (*disapproving*) a worker who is always checking the time to make sure that they do not work longer than they need to

clock·wise /'klɑkwaɪz/ *adv., adj.* moving around in the same direction as the hands of a clock: *Turn the key clockwise.* ◆ *a clockwise direction* ANT COUNTERCLOCKWISE

clock·work /'klɑkwərk/ *noun* [U] machinery with wheels and SPRINGS like that inside a clock: *clockwork toys* (= toys that you wind up with a key) ◆ *He is home by six every day like clockwork.*
IDM (go/run) like clockwork to happen according to plan; to happen without difficulties or problems

clod /klɑd/ noun **1** [usually pl.] a lump of earth or CLAY **2** (informal) a stupid person

clod·hop·per /ˈklɑdˌhɑpər/ noun (informal) **1** [usually pl.] a large heavy shoe **2** (disapproving) an awkward or CLUMSY person

clog /klɑg; klɔg/ verb, noun
● verb (-gg-) [T, often passive, I] to block something or to become blocked: ~ sth (up) (with sth) The narrow streets were clogged with traffic. ◆ The sink is clogged. ◆ Tears clogged her throat. ◆ ~ (up) (with sth) Within a few years, the pipes began to clog up.
● noun a shoe that is completely made of wood or one that has a thick wooden SOLE and a leather top ⊃ picture at SHOE

'clog dance noun a dance that is performed by people wearing clogs

clois·ter /ˈklɔɪstər/ noun **1** [C, usually pl.] a covered passage with ARCHES around a square garden, usually forming part of a CATHEDRAL, CONVENT, or MONASTERY ⊃ picture at ARCHITECTURE **2** [sing.] life in a CONVENT or MONASTERY

clois·tered /ˈklɔɪstərd/ adj. (formal) protected from the problems and dangers of normal life: a cloistered life ◆ the cloistered world of the university

clone /kloʊn/ noun, verb
● noun **1** (biology) a plant or an animal that is produced naturally or artificially from the cells of another plant or animal and is therefore exactly the same as it **2** (sometimes disapproving) a person or thing that seems to be an exact copy of another **3** (computing) a computer designed to work in exactly the same way as another, usually one made by a different company and more expensive
● verb **1** ~ sth to produce an exact copy of an animal or a plant from its cells: A team from the U.K. was the first to successfully clone an animal. ◆ Dolly, the cloned sheep **2** ~ sth to illegally make an electronic copy of stored information from a person's credit card or cell phone so that you can make payments or phone calls but the owner of the card or phone receives the bill

clonk /klɑŋk/ noun (informal) a short loud sound of heavy things hitting each other ▶ **clonk** verb [I, T] ~ (sth)

close¹ 🔊 /kloʊz/ verb, noun ⊃ see also CLOSE²
● verb
▷ WINDOW/DOOR, ETC. **1** [T, I] ~ (sth) to put something into a position so that it covers an opening; to get into this position SYN SHUT: Would anyone mind if I closed the window? ◆ She closed the gate behind her. ◆ It's dark now—let's close the curtains. ◆ I closed my eyes against the bright light. ◆ The doors open and close automatically. ANT OPEN
▷ BOOK/UMBRELLA, ETC. **2** [T] ~ sth (up) to move the parts of

something together so that it is no longer open SYN SHUT: to close a book/an umbrella ANT OPEN
▷ STORE/BUSINESS, ETC. **3** [T, often passive, I] to make the work of a store, etc. stop for a period of time; to not be open for people to use: ~ sth (for sth) The museum has been closed for renovation. ◆ ~ sth (to sb/sth) The gallery will be closed to the public on December 16. ◆ ~ (for sth) What time does the bank close? ◆ We close for lunch between one and two. ANT OPEN
4 [T, I] ~ (sth) (also close 'down, close sth↔'down) if a company, store, etc. closes, or if you close it, it stops operating as a business: The club was closed by the police. ◆ The hospital closed at the end of last year. ◆ The play closed after just three nights. ANT OPEN
▷ ROAD/BORDER **5** [T] to prevent entrance to or exit from a place: ~ sth The army took control of the government and closed the border. ◆ The street was closed for repairs. ◆ ~ sth to sb/sth The road was closed to traffic for two days.
▷ END **6** [T, I] to end or make something end: The meeting will close at 10:00 p.m. ◆ The offer closes at the end of the week. ◆ ~ sth to close a meeting/debate ◆ to close a case/an investigation ◆ to close an account (= to stop keeping money in a bank account) ◆ The subject is now closed (= we will not discuss it again). ANT OPEN
▷ BUSINESS DEAL **7** [T] ~ sth to complete and formally agree on a piece of business: They closed a deal yesterday with a new supplier. ◆ He was able to close the sale in just a few minutes.
▷ FINANCE **8** [I] ~ (at sth) to be worth a particular amount at the end of the day's business: Shares in the company closed at 75 cents. ◆ closing prices
▷ COMPUTING **9** [T] ~ sth to make a document or program disappear from the screen, so that it is stored in a secure way until it is needed again
▷ DISTANCE/DIFFERENCE **10** [T, I] ~ (sth) to make the distance or difference between two people or things smaller; to become smaller or narrower: These measures are aimed at closing the gap between rich and poor. ◆ The gap between the two top teams is closing all the time. ⊃ note at NEAR
▷ HOLD FIRMLY **11** [T, I] ~ (sth) about/around/over sb/sth to hold something or someone firmly: She closed her hand over his. ◆ Her hand closed over his.
IDM **close the book/books on sth** to stop doing something because you no longer believe you will be successful or will find a solution: The police have closed the book on the case (= they have stopped trying to solve it). **close its doors** (of a business, etc.) to stop trading: The factory closed its doors for the last time in 2009. **close your mind to sth** to refuse to think about something as a possibility **close ranks 1** if a group of people close ranks, they work closely together to defend themselves, especially when they are being criticized: It's not unusual for the police to close ranks when one of their officers is being investigated. **2** if soldiers close ranks, they move closer together in order to defend themselves ⊃ more at DOOR, EAR, EYE
PHR V **close 'down | close sth↔'down** = CLOSE¹(4): All the steel mills around here were closed down in the 1980s. ⊃ related noun CLOSEDOWN ANT OPEN UP **close 'in 1** when the days close in, they become gradually shorter during the fall **2** if the weather closes in, it gets worse **3** when the night closes in, it gets darker: They huddled around the fire as the night closed in. **close 'in (on sb/sth)** to move nearer to someone or something, especially in order to attack them: The lions closed in on their prey. **close sth↔'off** to separate something from other parts so that people cannot use it: The entrance to the train station was closed off following the explosion. **close 'out sth 1** to sell goods very cheaply in order to get rid of them quickly ⊃ related noun CLOSEOUT **2** to finish or settle something: A rock concert closed out the festivities. **close 'over sb/sth** to surround and cover someone or something: The water closed over his head. **close 'up** when a wound closes up, it heals **2** to hide your thoughts or emotions: She closed up when I asked her about her family. **close 'up | close sth↔'up 1** to shut and lock something such as a store or a building, especially for a short period of time: Why don't we close up and go out for lunch? ◆ Can the last one out close up the office? ANT OPEN UP **2** to come closer together; to bring people or

things closer together: *Traffic was heavy and cars were closing up behind each other.* **3** to become narrower and less open: *Every time he tried to speak, his throat closed up with fear.* **ANT** OPEN UP

● **noun** [sing.] (*formal*) the end of a period of time or an activity: *at the close of the 17th century* ◆ *His life was **drawing to a close**.* ◆ *Can we **bring** this meeting **to a close**?*

close² /klous/ *adj., adv., noun* ⊃ see also CLOSE¹
● *adj.* (clos·er, clos·est)
› NEAR **1** [not usually before noun] *~* (to sb/sth) | *~* (together) near in space or time: *Our new house is close to the school.* ◆ *I had no idea the beach was so close.* ◆ *The two buildings are close together.* ◆ *This is the closest we can get to the beach by car.* ◆ *We all have to work **in close proximity** (= near each other).* ◆ *The President was shot **at close range** (= from a short distance away).* ◆ *The children are close in age.* ◆ *Their birthdays are very **close together**.* ⊃ note at NEAR
› ALMOST/LIKELY **2** [not before noun] *~* to sth | *~* to doing sth almost in a particular state; likely to do something soon: *He was close to tears.* ◆ *The new library is close to completion.* ◆ *She knew she was close to death.* ◆ *We are close to signing the agreement.*
› RELATIONSHIP **3** *~* (to sb) knowing someone very well and liking them very much: *Jo is a very **close friend**.* ◆ *She is very close to her father.* ◆ *She and her father are very close.* ◆ *We're a very **close family**.* **4** near in family relationship: *close relatives, such as your mother and father, and brothers and sisters* **ANT** DISTANT **5** very involved in the work or activities of someone else, usually seeing and talking to them regularly: *He is one of the governor's closest advisers.* ◆ *The college has **close links** with many other institutions.* ◆ *She has kept in **close contact** with the victims' families.* ◆ *We keep in **close touch** with the police.*
› CAREFUL **6** [only before noun] careful and thorough: *Take a **close look** at this photograph.* ◆ *On closer examination, the painting proved to be a fake.* ◆ *Pay **close attention** to what I am telling you.*
› SIMILAR **7** *~* (to sth) very similar to something else or to an amount: *There's a **close resemblance** (= they look very similar).* ◆ *His feeling for her was close to hatred.* ◆ *The total was close to 20% of the workforce.* ◆ *We tried to match the colors, but this is the closest we could get.*
› COMPETITION/ELECTION, ETC. **8** won by only a small amount or distance: *a close contest/match/election* ◆ *It was a very **close finish**.* ◆ *I think it's going to be close.* ◆ *Our team came in a **close second** (= nearly won).* ◆ *The game was closer than the score suggests.* ◆ *The result is going to be **too close to call** (= either side may win).*
› ALMOST BAD RESULT **9** used to describe something, usually a dangerous or unpleasant situation, that nearly happens: *Phew! That was close—that car nearly hit us.* ◆ *We caught the bus in the end but it was close (= we nearly missed it).*
› WITHOUT SPACE **10** with little or no space in between: *over 1,000 pages of close print* ◆ *The soldiers advanced in close formation.*
› CUT SHORT **11** cut very short, near to the skin: *a close haircut/shave*
› GUARDED **12** [only before noun] carefully guarded: *The donor's identity is a **close secret**.* ◆ *She was kept under **close arrest**.*
› WEATHER/ROOM **13** warm in an uncomfortable way because there does not seem to be enough fresh air **SYN** STUFFY
› PHONETICS **14** (also *high*) (of a vowel) produced with the mouth in a relatively closed position ⊃ compare OPEN
► **close·ly** *adv.*: *I sat and watched everyone very closely* (= carefully). ◆ *He walked into the room, closely followed by the rest of the family.* ◆ *a closely contested election* ◆ *She closely resembled her mother at the same age.* ◆ *The two events are closely connected.* **close·ness** *noun* [U]
IDM **at/from close quarters** very near: *fighting at close quarters* **close, but no cigar** (*informal*) used to tell someone that their attempt or guess was almost but not quite successful **a close call/shave** (*informal*) a situation in which

you only just manage to avoid an accident, etc. **close to home** if a remark or topic of discussion is **close to home**, it is accurate or connected with you in a way that makes you uncomfortable or embarrassed: *Her remarks about me were embarrassingly close to home.* **keep a close eye/watch on sb/sth** to watch someone or something carefully: *Over the next few months we will keep a close eye on sales.* ⊃ more at HEART

● *adv.* (clos·er, closest) near; not far away: *They sat close together.* ◆ *Don't come too close!* ◆ *She held Tom close and pressed her cheek to his.* ◆ *I couldn't get close enough to see.* ◆ *A second police car followed close behind.*
IDM **close at hand** near; in a place where someone or something can be reached easily: *I keep snacks for the kids close at hand.* **close by (sb/sth)** at a short distance (from someone or something): *Our friends live close by.* ◆ *The route passes close by the town.* **close to** almost; nearly: *She is close to sixty.* ◆ *It is close to midnight.* ◆ *a profit close to $200 million* **close up** in a position very near to something: *The picture looks very different when you see it close up.* **close up to sb/sth** very near in space to someone or something: *She snuggled close up to him.* **come close (to sth/to doing sth)** to almost reach or do something: *He'd come close to death.* ◆ *We didn't win, but we came close.* ⊃ more at CARD *n.*, MARK *n.*, SAIL

● *noun* the grounds and buildings that surround and belong to a CATHEDRAL

close-cropped /ˌklous ˈkrɑpt/ *adj.* (of hair, grass, etc.) cut very short

closed /klouzd/ *adj.*
1 [not before noun] shut: *Keep the door closed.* **2** [not before noun] not open for business or public access: *The museum is closed on Mondays.* ◆ *This road is closed to traffic.* **3** not willing to accept outside influences or new ideas: *a closed society* ◆ *He has a **closed mind**.* **4** [usually before noun] limited to a particular group of people; not open to everyone: *a closed membership* **ANT** OPEN ⊃ note at CLOSE¹
IDM **behind closed doors** without the public being allowed to attend or know what is happening; in private **a closed book (to sb)** a subject or person that you know nothing about

closed-ˈcaptioned *adj.* (of a TV program) having CAPTIONS that can only be read if you have a special machine (= a DECODER)

closed-ˌcircuit ˈtelevision *noun* [U] (*abbr.* CCTV) a television system that works within a limited area, for example a public building, to protect it from crime

close·down /ˈklouzdaun/ *noun* [U, sing.] the stopping of work, especially permanently, in an office, a factory, etc.

closed ˈseason *noun* [sing.] the time of year when it is illegal to kill particular kinds of animals, birds, and fish because they are breeding **ANT** OPEN SEASON

closed ˈshop *noun* a factory, business, etc. in which employees must all be members of a particular LABOR UNION

closed ˈsyllable *noun* (*phonetics*) a syllable that ends with a consonant, for example *sit*

close-fit·ting /ˌklous ˈfɪtɪŋ/ *adj.* (of clothes) fitting tightly, showing the shape of the body

close har·mo·ny /ˌklous ˈhɑrməni/ *noun* [U] (*music*) a style of singing in HARMONY in which the different notes are close together

close-knit /ˌklous ˈnɪt/ (also *less frequent* ˌclosely-ˈknit) *adj.* (of a group of people) having strong relationships with each other and taking a close, friendly interest in each other's activities and problems: *the close-knit community of a small village*

close-mouthed /ˈklouz mauθt; ˈklous mauðd/ *adj.* [not usually before noun] not willing to say much about something because you want to keep a secret

close·out /ˈkloʊzaʊt/ noun an occasion when goods are sold cheaply in order to get rid of them quickly

close-range /ˌkloʊs ˈreɪndʒ/ adj. [only before noun] at or from a short distance: *The close-range shot was blocked by the goalie.*

close-set /ˌkloʊs ˈsɛt/ adj. very close together: *close-set eyes*

clos·et 🔑 /ˈklɑzət/ noun, adj., verb
- **noun** a small room or a space in a wall with a door that reaches the floor, used for storing things: *a walk-in closet* ➔ see also WATER CLOSET
  IDM **come out of the closet** to admit something openly that you kept secret before, especially because of shame or embarrassment: *Homosexuals in public life are now coming out of the closet.* ➔ more at SKELETON
- **adj.** [only before noun] used to describe people who want to keep some fact about themselves secret: *closet gays* ♦ *I suspect he's a closet fascist.*
- **verb** ~ sb/yourself + adv./prep. to put someone in a room away from other people, especially so that they can talk privately with someone, or so that they can be alone: *He was closeted with the President for much of the day.* ♦ *She had closeted herself away in her room.*

close-up /ˈkloʊs ʌp/ noun [C, U] a photograph, or picture in a movie, taken very close to someone or something so that it shows a lot of detail: *a close-up of a human eye* ♦ *It was strange to see her own face in close-up on the screen.* ♦ *close-up pictures of the planet*

clos·ing /ˈkloʊzɪŋ/ adj., noun
- **adj.** [only before noun] coming at the end of a speech, a period of time, or an activity: *his closing remarks* ♦ *the closing stages of the game* **ANT** OPENING
- **noun 1** [U] the act of shutting something such as a factory, hospital, school, etc. permanently: *the closing of the local school* **2** [C] the way that a letter, speech, etc. ends **ANT** OPENING

closing date noun the last date by which something must be done, such as applying for a job or entering a competition

closing time noun [C, U] the time when a store, bar, etc. ends business for the day and people have to leave

clo·sure /ˈkloʊʒər/ noun **1** [C, U] the situation when a factory, school, hospital, etc. shuts permanently: *factory closures* ♦ *The hospital has been threatened with closure.* **2** [C, U] the temporary closing of a road or bridge **3** [U] the feeling that a difficult or an unpleasant experience has come to an end or been dealt with in an acceptable way: *The conviction of their son's murderer helped to give them a sense of closure.*

clot /klɑt/ noun, verb
- **noun** = BLOOD CLOT: *They removed a clot from his brain.*
- **verb** (-tt-) [I, T] ~ (sth) when blood or cream **clots** or when something **clots** it, it forms thick lumps or clots: *a drug that stops blood from clotting during operations* ♦ *the blood clotting agent, Factor 8*

cloth 🔑 /klɔθ/ noun (pl. cloths /klɔðz; klɔθs/)
1 [U] material made by weaving (WEAVE) or KNITTING cotton, wool, silk, etc.: *woolen/cotton cloth* ♦ *bandages made from strips of cloth* ♦ *the cloth industry* ♦ *a cloth bag* ➔ thesaurus box at FABRIC **2** [C] (often in compounds) a piece of cloth, often used for a special purpose, especially cleaning things or covering a table: *Wipe the surface with a damp cloth.* ➔ picture at CLEANING ➔ see also DISHCLOTH, DROP CLOTH, TABLECLOTH **3** the cloth [sing.] (literary) used to refer to Christian priests as a group: *a man of the cloth*

clothe /kloʊð/ verb **1** ~ sb/yourself (in sth) (formal) to dress someone/yourself: *They clothe their children in the latest fashions.* ♦ (figurative) *Climbing plants clothed the courtyard walls.* **2** ~ sb to provide clothes for someone to wear: *the costs of feeding and clothing a family*

clothed /kloʊðd/ adj. [not usually before noun] ~ (in sth) dressed in a particular way: *a man clothed in black* ♦ *She jumped fully clothed into the water.* ♦ (figurative) *The valley was clothed in trees and shrubs.*

clothes 🔑 /kloʊz; kloʊðz/ noun [pl.]
the things that you wear, such as pants, dresses, and jackets: *I bought some new clothes for the trip.* ♦ *to put on/take off your clothes* ♦ *Bring a change of clothes with you.* ♦ *She has no clothes sense* (= she does not know what clothes look attractive). ➔ picture on page 273 ➔ collocations at FASHION ➔ see also STREET CLOTHES **IDM** SEE EMPEROR

THESAURUS

clothes

clothing ♦ garment ♦ dress ♦ wear ♦ gear

These are all words for the things that you wear, such as shirts, jackets, dresses, and pants.

clothes [pl.] the things that you wear, such as shirts, jackets, dresses, and pants: *Please pick your clothes up off the floor.*

clothing [U] (somewhat formal) clothes, especially a particular type of clothes: *warm clothing*

CLOTHES OR CLOTHING?

Clothing is more formal than **clothes** and is used especially to mean "a particular type of clothes." There is no singular form of **clothes** or **clothing**: *a piece/an item/an article of clothing* is used to talk about one thing that you wear, such as a dress or shirt.

garment (formal) a piece of clothing: *He was wearing a strange shapeless garment.* **NOTE** Garment should only be used in formal or literary contexts; in everyday contexts use *a piece of clothing.*

dress [U] clothes, especially when worn in a particular style or for a particular occasion: *Casual dress is allowed on Fridays.*

wear [U] (usually in compounds) clothes for a particular purpose or occasion, especially when it is being sold in stores: *the children's wear department*

gear [U] clothes for a particular purpose: *the most advanced cold-weather gear* (= warm boots, coats, gloves, etc.)

PATTERNS

- **casual** clothes/clothing/dress/wear
- **evening/formal** clothes/dress/wear
- **designer/sports** clothes/clothing/garments/wear/gear
- **children's/men's/ladies'** clothes/clothing/garments/wear
- to **have on/be in/wear** …clothes/garments/gear

clothes hanger noun = HANGER

clothes horse noun (disapproving) a person, especially a woman, who is too interested in fashionable clothes

clothes·line /ˈkloʊzlaɪn/ (also line) noun a piece of thin rope or wire, attached to posts, that you hang clothes on to dry outside after you have washed them

clothes·pin /ˈkloʊzpɪn/ noun a piece of wood or plastic used for attaching wet clothes to a clothesline

cloth·ier /ˈkloʊðiər/ noun (formal) a person or company that makes or sells clothes or cloth

cloth·ing 🔑 /ˈkloʊðɪŋ/ noun [U]
clothes, especially a particular type of clothes: *protective clothing* ♦ *the high cost of food and clothing* ♦ *an item/article of clothing* ➔ thesaurus box at CLOTHES **IDM** SEE WOLF

clotting factor noun [C, U] (biology) any of the substances in the blood that help it to CLOT (= become thick and form lumps)

272   ʌ cup   ə about   eɪ say   aɪ five   ɔɪ boy   aʊ now   oʊ go   ər bird

Clothes

suit
- lapel
- jacket
- crease
- pants

- tie
- suspenders
- rolled-up sleeve

- button-down collar
- breast pocket
- shirt
- sleeve
- belt
- cuff
- fly
- jeans
- cargo pants
- pocket

- hoodie

pajamas   **nightgown**

overcoat

raincoat

- short-sleeved blouse
- collar

skirt

- shoulder strap

dress

bathrobe

fleece vest

- crew neck

crew neck sweater

- turtleneck

turtleneck sweater

vest

T-shirt

shorts

leather jacket

denim jacket

- hood
- lining

windbreaker

cardigan

- hanger

polo shirt

scarves

silk scarf

scarf

bow ties

stripes

polka dots

plaid

closures

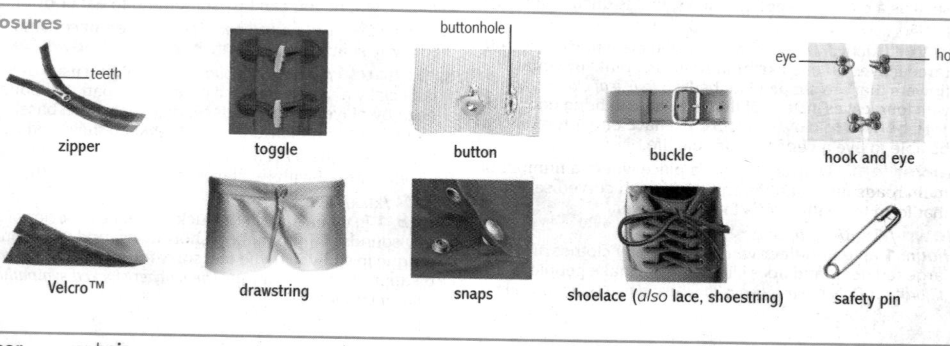

- teeth

zipper

toggle

- buttonhole

button

buckle

- eye
- hook

hook and eye

Velcro™

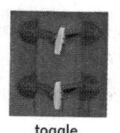
drawstring

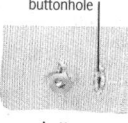
snaps

shoelace (*also* lace, shoestring)

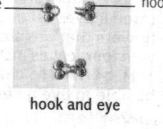
safety pin

cloud 🔑 /klaʊd/ *noun, verb*

● *noun* **1** [C, U] a gray or white mass made of very small drops of water, that floats in the sky: *The sun went behind a cloud.* ◆ *The plane was flying in cloud most of the way.* ⊃ collocations at WEATHER ⊃ see also STORM CLOUD, THUNDERCLOUD **2** [C] a large mass of something in the air, for example dust or smoke, or a number of insects flying all together **3** [C] something that makes you feel sad or anxious: *Her father's illness cast a cloud over her wedding day.* ◆ *The only dark cloud on the horizon was that they might have to move.* ◆ *He still has a cloud of suspicion hanging over him.* **IDM** **every cloud has a silver lining** (*saying*) every sad or difficult situation has a positive side **on cloud nine** (*informal*) extremely happy **under a cloud** if someone is **under a cloud**, other people think that they have done something wrong and are suspicious of them ⊃ more at HEAD

● *verb* **1** [T] ~ sth if something **clouds** your judgment, memory, etc., it makes it difficult for you to understand or remember something clearly: *Doubts were beginning to cloud my mind.* ◆ *His judgment was clouded by jealousy.* **2** [I, T] (*formal*) (of someone's face) to show sadness, fear, anger, etc.; to make someone look sad, afraid, angry, etc.: ~ (over) *Her face clouded over with anger.* ◆ ~ sth *Suspicion clouded his face.* **3** [T] ~ the issue to make something you are discussing or considering less clear, especially by introducing subjects that are not connected with it **4** [I] ~ (over) (of the sky) to fill with clouds: *It was beginning to cloud over.* **5** [T] ~ sth to make something less pleasant or enjoyable: *His last years were clouded by financial worries.* **6** [I, T] if glass, water, etc. **clouds**, or if something **clouds** it, it becomes less transparent: ~ (with sth) *Her eyes clouded with tears.* ◆ ~ sth *Steam had clouded the mirror.*

cloud·burst /ˈklaʊdbərst/ *noun* a sudden very heavy fall of rain

ˌcloud comˈputing *noun* [U] a computer system in which data and software are stored mainly on a central computer, to which users have access over the Internet

ˈcloud ˌforest *noun* [C, U] a forest in tropical or SUBTROP-ICAL parts of the world that usually has thick cloud at the level of the tops of the trees ⊃ compare RAINFOREST

cloud·less /ˈklaʊdləs/ *adj.* clear; with no clouds: *a cloudless sky*

cloud·y /ˈklaʊdi/ *adj.* (cloudier, cloudiest) **1** (of the sky or the weather) covered with clouds; with a lot of clouds **ANT** CLEAR: *a gray, cloudy day* **2** (of liquids) not clear or transparent ▶ cloud·i·ness *noun* [U]

clout /klaʊt/ *noun, verb*

● *noun* [U] power and influence: *political/financial clout* ◆ *I knew his opinion carried a lot of clout with them.*

clove /kloʊv/ *noun* **1** [C, U] the dried flower of a tropical tree, used in cooking as a spice, especially to give flavor to sweet foods. Cloves look like small nails. ⊃ picture at HERB **2** [C] a garlic ~ | a ~ of garlic one of the small separate sections of a BULB (= the round underground part) of GARLIC ⊃ picture at FRUIT ⊃ see also CLEAVE

cloven hoof /ˌkloʊvən ˈhʊf; -ˈhuf/ *noun* the foot of an animal such as a cow, a sheep, or a GOAT, that is divided into two parts

clo·ver /ˈkloʊvər/ *noun* [U] a small wild plant that usually has three leaves on each STEM and purple, pink, or white flowers that are shaped like balls: *a four-leaf clover* (= one with four leaves instead of three, thought to bring good luck) **IDM** be/live in clover (*informal*) to have enough money to be able to live a very comfortable life

clo·ver·leaf /ˈkloʊvərˌlif/ *noun* a place where a number of main roads meet at different levels, with curved sections that form the pattern of a four-leaf clover

clown /klaʊn/ *noun, verb*

● *noun* **1** an entertainer who wears funny clothes and a large red nose, and does silly things to make people laugh: (*figurative*) *Robert was always the class clown* (= he did silly

things to make the other students laugh). **2** (*disapproving*) a person that you disapprove of because they act in a stupid way: *What do those clowns in the government think they are doing?*

● *verb* [I] ~ (around) (often *disapproving*) to behave in a silly way, especially in order to make other people laugh

clown·ish /ˈklaʊnɪʃ/ *adj.* like a clown; silly

cloy /klɔɪ/ [I] (of something pleasant or sweet) to start to become slightly disgusting or annoying, because there is too much of it: *After a while, the rich sauce begins to cloy.*

cloy·ing /ˈklɔɪɪŋ/ *adj.* (*formal*) **1** (of food, a smell, etc.) so sweet that it is unpleasant **2** using emotion in a very obvious way, so that the result is unpleasant: *the cloying sentimentality of her novels* ▶ cloy·ing·ly *adv.*

cloze test /ˈkloʊz test/ *noun* a type of test in which you have to put suitable words in spaces in a text where words have been left out

club 🔑 /klʌb/ *noun, verb*

● *noun*
> FOR ACTIVITY/SPORTS **1** [C] (especially in compounds) a group of people who meet together regularly, for a particular activity, sports, etc.: *a golf/tennis, etc. club* ◆ *a chess/movie, etc. club* ◆ to join/belong to a club ◆ *The club has voted to admit new members.* ⊃ see also FAN CLUB, GLEE CLUB, YOUTH CLUB **2** [C] the building or rooms that a particular club uses: *We had lunch at the golf club.* ◆ *the club bar* ⊃ see also COUNTRY CLUB, HEALTH CLUB **3** [C] a professional sports organization that includes the players, managers, owners, and members: *The New York Yankees are a famous ball club.*
> MUSIC/DANCING **4** [C] a place where people, especially young people, go and listen to music, dance, etc.: *a jazz club* ◆ *the club scene in New Haven* ⊃ see also CLUBBING, NIGHT-CLUB, STRIP CLUB
> SOCIAL **5** [C] an organization and a place where people can meet together socially or stay: *He's a member of The University Club.*
> SELLING BOOKS/CDS **6** [C] an organization that sells books, CDs, etc. cheaply to its members: *a music club* ⊃ see also BOOK CLUB
> WEAPON **7** [C] a heavy stick with one end thicker than the other, that is used as a weapon ⊃ see also BILLY CLUB
> IN GOLF **8** [C] = GOLF CLUB
> IN CARD GAMES **9** clubs [pl.] one of the four sets of cards (called SUITS) in a DECK of cards. The clubs have a black design shaped like three black leaves on a short STEM: *the five/queen/ace of clubs* ⊃ picture at PLAYING CARD **10** [C] one card from the SUIT called clubs: *I played a club.* **IDM** see JOIN v.

● *verb* (-bb-) **1** [T] ~ sb/sth to hit a person or an animal with a heavy stick or similar object: *The victim was clubbed to death with a baseball bat.* **2** [I] go clubbing (*informal*) to spend time dancing and drinking in NIGHTCLUBS

club·bing /ˈklʌbɪŋ/ *noun* [U] the activity of going to NIGHT-CLUBS regularly: *They go clubbing almost every weekend.* ▶ club·ber *noun*: *The venue was packed with 3,000 clubbers.*

ˈclub car *noun* a car on a train with comfortable chairs and tables, where you can buy something to eat or drink

ˈclub foot *noun* [C, U] a foot that has been DEFORMED (= badly shaped) since birth ▶ club-ˌfooted *adj.*

club·house /ˈklʌbhaʊs/ *noun* **1** the building used by a club, especially a sports club **2** a building or part of a building used by players on a sports team, especially a baseball team, to put on their uniforms and keep their clothes

ˌclub ˈsandwich *noun* a SANDWICH consisting of three slices of bread with two layers of food between them

cluck /klʌk/ *verb, noun*

● *verb* **1** [I] when a chicken **clucks**, it makes a series of short low sounds **2** [I] to make a short low sound with your tongue to show that you feel sorry for someone or that you disapprove of something: *The teacher clucked sympatheti-cally at the child's story.*

t **t**ea   ţ **b**u**tt**er   d **d**id   k **c**at   g **g**ot   tʃ **ch**in   dʒ **J**une   f **f**all

- **noun** the low, short sounds that a chicken makes: (*figurative*) *a cluck of impatience/annoyance*

clue /klu/ *noun, verb*

- **noun** **1** ~ **(to sth)** an object, a piece of evidence, or some information that helps the police solve a crime: *The police think the videotape may hold some vital clues to the identity of the killer.* **2** ~ **(to sth)** a fact or a piece of evidence that helps you discover the answer to a problem: *Diet may hold the clue to the causes of migraine.* **3** some words or a piece of information that helps you find the answers to a CROSS-WORD, a game, or a question: *"You'll never guess who I saw today!" "Give me a clue."*
  IDM **not have a clue** (*informal*) **1** to know nothing about something or about how to do something: *I don't have a clue where she lives.* **2** (*disapproving*) to be very stupid: *Don't ask him to do it—he doesn't have a clue!*
- **verb**
  PHR V **,clue sb 'in (on sth)** (*informal*) to give someone the most recent information about something: *He's just clued me in on the latest developments.*

,clued-'in *adj.* ~ **(on sth)** (*informal*) knowing a lot about something; having a lot of information about something

clue·less /ˈkluləs/ *adj.* (*informal, disapproving*) very stupid; not able to understand or to do something: *He's completely clueless about computers.*

clump /klʌmp/ *noun, verb*

- **noun** **1** a small group of things or people very close together, especially trees or plants; a bunch of something such as grass or hair: *a clump of trees/bushes* **2** the sound made by someone putting their feet down very heavily
- **verb** **1** [I] + *adv./prep.* to put your feet down noisily and heavily as you walk: *The children clumped down the stairs.* **2** [I, T] ~ **(together)** | ~ **A and B (together)** to come together or be brought together to form a tight group: *Galaxies tend to clump together in clusters.*

clump·y /ˈklʌmpi/ *adj.* (of shoes and boots) big, thick, and heavy

clum·sy /ˈklʌmzi/ *adj.* (**clumsier, clumsiest**) **1** (of people and animals) moving or doing things in a very awkward way: *I spilled your coffee. Sorry—that was clumsy of me.* ◆ *His clumsy fingers couldn't untie the knot.* **2** (of actions and statements) done without skill or in a way that offends people: *She made a clumsy attempt to apologize.* **3** (of objects) difficult to move or use easily; not well designed **4** (of processes) awkward; too complicated to understand or use easily: *The complaints procedure is clumsy and time-consuming.* ▶ **clum·si·ly** /-zəli/ *adv.* **clum·si·ness** *noun* [U]

clung *pt, pp of* CLING

clunk /klʌŋk/ *noun* a dull sound made by two heavy objects hitting each other ▶ **clunk** *verb* [I]

clunk·er /ˈklʌŋkər/ *noun* (*informal*) **1** an old car in bad condition **2** a serious mistake

clunk·y /ˈklʌŋki/ *adj.* (*informal*) heavy and awkward: *clunky leather shoes*

clus·ter /ˈklʌstər/ *noun, verb*

- **noun** **1** a group of things of the same type that grow or appear close together: *a cluster of stars* ◆ *The plant bears its flowers in clusters.* ◆ *a leukemia cluster (= an area where there are more cases of the disease than you would expect)* **2** a group of people, animals, or things close together: *a cluster of spectators* ◆ *a little cluster of houses* **3** (*phonetics*) a group of consonants which come together in a word or phrase, for example /str/ at the beginning of *string: a consonant cluster*
- **verb** [I] to come together in a small group or groups: ~ **together** *The children clustered together in the corner of the room.* ◆ ~ **around sb/sth** *The doctors clustered anxiously around his bed.*

'cluster ,bomb *noun* a type of bomb that throws out smaller bombs when it explodes

clutch /klʌtʃ/ *verb, noun*

- **verb** **1** [T, I] to hold someone or something tightly **SYN** GRIP *v.:* ~ **sth** (+ *adv./prep.*) *He clutched the child to*

him. ◆ *She stood there, the flowers still clutched in her hand.* ◆ + *adv./prep. I clutched on to the chair for support* ⊃ thesaurus box at HOLD **2** [T, I] to take hold of something suddenly, because you are afraid or in pain: ~ **sth** *He gasped and clutched his stomach.* ◆ ~ **at sb/sth** (*figurative*) *Fear clutched at her heart.* **IDM** see STRAW ⊃ thesaurus box at HOLD **PHR V** **'clutch/'catch at sth/sb** to try to quickly get hold of something or someone **SYN** GRAB AT

- **noun** **1** [C] the PEDAL in a car or other vehicle that you press with your foot so that you can change gear: *Put your foot on the clutch.* ⊃ collocations at DRIVING **2** [C] a device in a machine that connects and DISCONNECTS working parts, especially the engine and the gears: *The car needs a new clutch.* **3** **a** ~ **of sth** [sing.] a group of people, animals, or things: *He's won a whole clutch of awards.* **4** **clutches** [pl.] (*informal*) power or control: *He managed to escape from their clutches.* ◆ *Now that she had him in her clutches, she wasn't going to let go.* **5** [C, usually sing.] a tight hold on someone or something **SYN** GRIP *n.:* (*figurative*) *She felt the sudden clutch of fear.* **6** [C] a group of eggs that a bird lays at one time; the young birds that come out of a group of eggs at the same time **7** [C] = CLUTCH BAG ⊃ picture at BAG

'clutch bag (also **clutch**) *noun* a small flat bag that women carry in their hands, especially on formal occasions

clut·ter /ˈklʌtər/ *verb, noun*

- **verb** ~ **sth (up) (with sth/sb)** to fill a place with too many things, so that it is messy: *Don't clutter the page with too many diagrams.* ◆ *I don't want all these files cluttering up my desk.* ◆ (*figurative*) *Try not to clutter your head with trivia.*
- **noun** [U, sing.] (*disapproving*) a lot of things in a messy state, especially things that are not necessary or are not being used; a state of confusion **SYN** MESS: *There's always so much clutter on your desk!* ◆ *There was a clutter of bottles and tubes on the shelf.*

clut·tered /ˈklʌtərd/ *adj.* ~ **(up) (with sb/sth)** covered with, or full of, a lot of things, in a way that is messy: *a cluttered room/desk* ◆ (*figurative*) *a cluttered mind* **ANT** UNCLUTTERED

cm ✍ *abbr.* (*pl.* **cm** *or* **cms**) CENTIMETER

CNN /ˌsi ɛn ˈɛn/ *abbr.* Cable News Network (a broadcasting company that sends television news programs all over the world)

CO /ˌsi ˈoʊ/ *abbr.* **1** Commanding Officer (an officer who commands a group of soldiers, sailors, etc.) **2** (in writing) Colorado

Co. *abbr.* **1** /koʊ; ˈkʌmpəni/ (*business*) company: *Pitt, Briggs & Co.* **2** /koʊ; ˈkʌmpəni/ **and co.** (*informal*) and other members of a group of people: *Were Jane and co. at the party?* **3** (in writing) county

co- /koʊ/ *prefix* (used in adjectives, adverbs, nouns, and verbs) together with: *co-produced* ◆ *cooperatively* ◆ *co-author* ◆ *coexist*

c/o /ˌsi ˈoʊ/ *abbr.* (used on letters to a person staying at someone else's house) care of: *Mr. P. Brown, c/o Ms. M. Jones*

coach ✍ /koʊtʃ/ *noun, verb*

- **noun** **1** [C] a person who trains a person or team in sports: *a basketball/football/tennis, etc. coach* ◆ *the head/assistant coach* **2** [U] the cheapest seats in a plane: *to fly coach* ◆ *coach fares/passengers/seats* **3** [C] a large closed vehicle with four wheels, pulled by horses, used in the past for carrying passengers ⊃ see also STAGECOACH **4** [C] (*formal*) a comfortable bus for carrying passengers over long distances: *They saw New England on a coach tour.*
- **verb** **1** to train someone to play a sport, to do a job better, or to improve a skill: ~ **sb (in/for sth)** *Her father coached her for the Olympics.* ◆ ~ **sb (to do sth)** *She has coached hundreds of young singers.* ◆ ~ **sth** *He coaches basketball and soccer.* **2** ~ **sb (in/on sth)** | ~ **sb (to do sth)** to give someone special instructions for what they should do or say in a particular situation: *They believed the witnesses had been coached on what to say.*

---

v **v**oice   θ **th**in   ð **th**en   s **s**o   z **z**oo   ʃ **sh**e   ʒ vi**s**ion   x **Ch**anukah

coach house *noun* a building where CARRIAGES pulled by horses are or were kept

coach·ing /ˈkoʊtʃɪŋ/ *noun* [U] the process of training someone to play a sport, to do a job better, or to improve a skill: *a coaching session*

coach·man /ˈkoʊtʃmən/ *noun* (*pl.* coach·men /-mən/) (in the past) a man who drove a COACH pulled by horses

co·ag·u·late /koʊˈægyəˌleɪt/ *verb* [I, T] ~ (sth) if a liquid **coagulates** or something **coagulates** it, it becomes thick and partly solid **SYN** CONGEAL: *Blood began to coagulate around the edges of the wound.* ▶ **co·ag·u·la·tion** /koʊˌægyəˈleɪʃn/ *noun* [U]

coal 🔑 /koʊl/ *noun*
1 [U] a hard black mineral that is found below the ground and burned to produce heat: *I put more coal on the fire.* ◆ *a lump of coal* ◆ *a coal fire* ◆ *a coal mine* ◆ *the coal industry* **2** [C] a piece of coal, especially one that is burning: *A hot coal fell out of the fire and burned the carpet.* **IDM** see RAKE

coal-black *adj.* very dark in color: *coal-black eyes*

co·a·lesce /ˌkoʊəˈlɛs/ *verb* [I] ~ (into/with sth) (*formal*) to come together to form one larger group, substance, etc. **SYN** AMALGAMATE: *The puddles had coalesced into a small stream.* ▶ **co·a·les·cence** /ˌkoʊəˈlɛsns/ *noun* [U]

coal·field /ˈkoʊlfild/ *noun* a large area where there is a lot of coal under the ground

coal-fired *adj.* using coal as fuel: *a coal-fired power station*

coal gas *noun* [U] a mixture of gases produced from coal, which can be used for electricity and heating

co·a·li·tion /ˌkoʊəˈlɪʃn/ *noun* **1** [C] a government formed by two or more political parties working together: *to form a coalition* ◆ *a two-party coalition* ◆ *a coalition government* **2** [C] a group formed by people from several different groups, especially political ones, agreeing to work together for a particular purpose: *a coalition of environmental and consumer groups* **3** [U] the act of two or more groups joining together: *They didn't rule out coalition with the Social Democrats.*

coal mine *noun* a place underground where coal is dug

coal miner *noun* a person whose job is digging coal in a coal mine

coal tar *noun* [U] a thick, black, sticky substance produced when gas is made from coal

coarse /kɔrs/ *adj.* (coars·er, coars·est) **1** (of skin or cloth) rough: *coarse hands/linen* **ANT** SMOOTH, SOFT **2** consisting of relatively large pieces: *coarse sand/salt/hair* **ANT** FINE **3** rude and offensive, especially about sex **SYN** VULGAR: *coarse manners/laughter* ▶ **coarse·ly** *adv.*: *coarsely chopped onions* (= cut into large pieces) ◆ *He laughed coarsely at her.* **coarse·ness** *noun* [U]

coars·en /ˈkɔrsn/ *verb* **1** [I, T] to become or make something become thicker and/or rougher: *Her hair gradually coarsened as she grew older.* ◆ ~ sth *His features had been coarsened by the weather.* **2** to become or make someone become less polite and often offensive in the way they behave: [T, I] ~ (sb) *The six long years in prison had coarsened him.*

coast 🔑 /koʊst/ *noun, verb*
● *noun* [C, U] the land beside or near to the ocean: *a town on the north coast of Nantucket* ◆ *islands off the east coast of Florida* ◆ *We walked along the coast for five miles.* ◆ *the California coast* ◆ *a pretty stretch of coast* ◆ *the coast road* **IDM** the coast is clear (*informal*) there is no danger of being seen or caught: *As soon as the coast was clear, he climbed in through the window.*
● *verb* **1** [I] (+ adv./prep.) (of a car or a bicycle) to move, especially down a hill, without using any power: *The car coasted along until it stopped.* ◆ *She took her feet off the pedals and coasted downhill.* **2** [I] (+ adv./prep.) (of a vehicle) to move quickly and smoothly, without using much power: *The plane coasted down the runway.* **3** [I] ~ (through/to sth) to be successful at something without having to try hard: *He coasted through his final exams.* **4** [I] ~ (along) (*disapproving*)

to put very little effort into something: *You're just coasting—it's time to work hard now.* **5** [I] (of a ship) to stay close to land while sailing around the coast

THESAURUS

coast

beach ◆ **shore** ◆ **coastline** ◆ **sand** ◆ **seashore**

These are all words for the land beside or near to the ocean, a river, or a lake.

coast the land beside or near to the ocean: *a town on the south coast of Georgia* **NOTE** It is nearly always **the coast**, except when it is uncountable: *That's a pretty stretch of coast.*

beach an area of sand, or small stones, beside the ocean or a lake: *She took the kids to the beach for the day.* ◆ *sandy beaches*

shore an area that is by the ocean or a lake, especially one where people go for a day or a vacation: *Let's go to the shore.* ◆ *The reef runs along the island's north shore.*

coastline the land along a coast, especially when you are thinking of its shape or appearance: *California's rugged coastline*

sand a large area of sand on a beach: *We went for a walk on the sand.* ◆ *a resort with miles of golden sands*

the seashore the land along the edge of the ocean, usually where there is sand and rocks: *He liked to look for shells on the seashore.*

BEACH OR SEASHORE?

Beach is usually used to talk about a sandy area next to the sea where people lie in the sun or play, for example when they are on vacation. **Seashore** is used more to talk about the area by the sea in terms of things such as waves, sea shells, rocks, etc., especially where people walk for pleasure. It is often used in formal or literary contexts.

PATTERNS
- **along** the coast/beach/shore/coastline/seashore
- **on** the coast/beach/shore/coastline/sands/ seashore
- **at** the coast/beach/shore/seashore
- **by** the coast/shore/seashore
- a(n) **rocky/unspoiled** coast/beach/shore/coastline
- to **go to** the coast/beach/shore/seashore

coast·al /ˈkoʊstl/ *adj.* [usually before noun] of or near a coast: *coastal waters/resorts/scenery* ◆ *a coastal path* (= one that follows the line of the coast) ⊃ compare INLAND

coast·er /ˈkoʊstər/ *noun* **1** a small flat object that you put under a glass to protect the top of a table **2** a ship that sails from port to port along a coast ⊃ see also ROLLER COASTER

the Coast Guard *noun* [sing.] a branch of the armed forces whose job is to watch the ocean near a coast in order to help ships and people in trouble, and to stop people from breaking the law: *The Coast Guard was alerted.* ◆ *They radioed the Cape Hatteras Coast Guard.* ◆ *a Coast Guard station*

coast·line /ˈkoʊstlaɪn/ *noun* the land along a coast, especially when you are thinking of its shape or appearance: *a rugged/rocky/beautiful coastline* ◆ *to protect the coastline from oil spillage* ⊃ thesaurus box at COAST

coat 🔑 /koʊt/ *noun, verb*
● *noun* **1** a piece of outdoor clothing that is worn over other clothes to keep warm or dry. Coats have sleeves and may be long or short: *a fur/leather coat* ◆ *a long winter coat* ◆ *to put on/take off your coat* ⊃ see also DUFFEL COAT, HOUSECOAT, OVERCOAT, PETTICOAT, RAINCOAT, TRENCH COAT **2** a jacket that is worn as part of a suit ⊃ see also FROCK COAT, MORNING COAT, TAILCOAT, WAISTCOAT ⊃ picture at CLOTHES **3** the fur, hair, or wool that covers an animal's

| h hat | m man | n no | ŋ sing | l leg | r red | y yes | w wet |

body: *a dog with a **smooth/shaggy coat*** ⊃ picture at ANIMAL **4** a layer of paint or some other substance that covers a surface: *to give the walls a second coat of paint* ⊃ see also TOPCOAT, UNDERCOAT

• **verb** [often passive] ~ sth (with/in sth) to cover something with a layer of a substance: *cookies thickly coated with chocolate* ♦ *A film of dust coated the table.* ⊃ see also SUGAR-COATED

'**coat check** noun = CHECKROOM

'**coat ,hanger** noun = HANGER

co·a·ti /koʊˈɑti/ (also **co·a·ti·mun·di** /koʊˌɑtiˈmʌndi/) noun a small animal with a long nose and a long tail with lines across it, which lives mainly in Central and S. America

coat·ing /ˈkoʊtɪŋ/ noun a thin layer of a substance covering a surface: *a thin coating of chocolate* ♦ *magnetic coating on a floppy disk*

'**coat of 'arms** noun (pl. coats of arms) (also **arms**) a design or a SHIELD that is a special symbol of a family, city, or other organization: *the royal coat of arms*

coat·room /ˈkoʊtrum; -rʊm/ noun = CHECKROOM

'**coat stand** noun a stand with hooks for hanging coats and hats on

coat·tails /ˈkoʊtteɪlz/ noun [pl.]
IDM **on sb's coattails** using the success and influence of another person to help yourself become successful: *She got where she is today on her brother's coattails.*

'**co-,author** noun a person who writes a book or an article with someone else ▶ **co-'author** verb [T] ~ sth
'**co-,authorship** noun [U]

coax /koʊks/ verb to persuade someone to do something by talking to them in a kind and gentle way **SYN** CAJOLE: ~ sb/sth (into doing sth) *She coaxed the horse into coming a little closer.* ♦ ~ sb/sth (into/out of sth) *He was coaxed out of retirement to help the failing company.* ♦ ~ sb/sth (+ adv./prep.) *She had to coax the car along.* ♦ ~ (sb/sth) + speech *"Nearly there," she coaxed.*
PHRV **coax sth out of/from sb** to gently persuade someone to do something or give you something: *The director coaxed a brilliant performance out of the cast.*

coax·ing /ˈkoʊksɪŋ/ noun [U] gentle attempts to persuade someone to do something or to get a machine to start: *No amount of coaxing will make me change my mind.* ▶ **coaxi·ng** adj. **coax·ing·ly** adv.

cob /kɑb/ noun **1** (also **corn·cob**) the long hard part of the corn plant that the rows of yellow grains grow on: *corn on the cob* **2** a strong horse with short legs

co·balt /ˈkoʊbɔlt/ noun [U] **1** (symb. **Co**) a chemical element. Cobalt is a hard silver-white metal, often mixed with other metals and used to give a deep blue-green color to glass. **2** (also ,cobalt 'blue) a deep blue-green color

cob·ble /ˈkɑbl/ verb ~ sth (old-fashioned) to make or repair shoes
PHRV ,**cobble sth↔to'gether** to produce something quickly and without great care or effort, so that it can be used but is not perfect: *The essay was cobbled together from some old notes.*

cob·bled /ˈkɑbld/ adj. (of streets and roads) having a surface that is made of COBBLES

cob·bler /ˈkɑblər/ noun **1** [C] a type of fruit PIE with thick PASTRY on top: *peach cobbler* **2** [C] (old-fashioned) a person who repairs shoes ⊃ compare SHOEMAKER

cobble·stones /ˈkɑblˌstoʊnz/ (also **cob·bles** /ˈkɑblz/) noun [pl.] small stones used to make the surfaces of roads, especially in the past: *a cart clattering over the cobblestones* ▶ **cob·ble·stone** adj.

COBOL /ˈkoʊbɔl/ noun [U] an early computer language used in business programs

co·bra /ˈkoʊbrə/ noun a poisonous snake that can spread the skin at the back of its neck to make itself look bigger. Cobras live in Asia and Africa. ⊃ picture at ANIMAL

,**co-'branding** noun [U] (business) a marketing strategy in which two companies work together to sell their products or services, using both company names

cob·web /ˈkɑbwɛb/ noun a fine net of threads made by a spider to catch insects; a single thread of this net (usually when it is old and covered with dirt): *Thick cobwebs hung in the dusty corners.* ♦ *He brushed a cobweb out of his hair.* ⊃ see also SPIDERWEB ▶ **cob·webbed** /ˈkɑbwɛbd/ adj.: *cob-webbed corners*
IDM **blow/clear the cobwebs away** to help someone start something in a fresh, lively state of mind: *A brisk walk should blow the cobwebs away.*

co·ca /ˈkoʊkə/ noun [U] a tropical bush whose leaves are used to make the drug COCAINE

Coca-Cola™ /ˌkoʊkə ˈkoʊlə/ (also informal **Coke**™) noun **1** [U, C] a popular type of COLA drink **2** [C] a glass, bottle, or can of Coca-Cola

co·caine /koʊˈkeɪn; ˈkoʊkeɪn/ (also informal **coke**) noun [U] a powerful drug that some people take illegally for pleasure and can become ADDICTED to. Doctors sometimes use it as an ANESTHETIC.

coc·cyx /ˈkɑksɪks/ noun (pl. **coc·cy·ges** /ˈkɑksədʒiz/ or **coc·cyx·es**) (anatomy) the small bone at the bottom of the SPINE **SYN** TAILBONE

coch·i·neal /ˈkɑtʃəˌnil/ noun [U] a bright red substance used to give color to food

coch·le·a /ˈkɑkliə; ˈkoʊ-/ noun (pl. **coch·le·ae** /-lii; -liaɪ/) (anatomy) a small curved tube inside the ear, which contains a small part that sends nerve signals to the brain when sounds cause it to VIBRATE

cock /kɑk/ noun, verb
• **noun 1** [C] = ROOSTER: *The cock crowed.* ⊃ compare HEN **2** [C] (especially in compounds) a male of the type of bird mentioned: *a cock pheasant* ⊃ see also PEACOCK **3** [C] = STOPCOCK ⊃ see also BALL COCK
• **verb 1** ~ sth to raise a part of your body so that it is vertical or at an angle: *The dog cocked its leg by every tree on our route* (= in order to URINATE). ♦ *He cocked an inquisitive eyebrow at her.* ♦ *She cocked her head to one side and looked at me.* ♦ *The dog stood listening, its ears cocked.* **2** ~ a gun/pistol/rifle to raise the HAMMER on a gun so that it is ready to fire ⊃ see also HALF-COCKED
IDM **cock an ear/eye at sth/sb** to look at or listen to someone or something carefully and with a lot of attention

cock·ade /kɑˈkeɪd/ noun a decorated BADGE or an arrangement of RIBBON, feathers, etc. that is worn in a hat to show military rank, membership of a political party, etc.

cock-a-doo·dle-doo /ˌkɑk ə ˌdudl ˈdu/ noun the word for the sound that a ROOSTER makes

cock·a·ma·mie (also **cock·a·ma·my**) /ˈkɑkəˌmeɪmi/ adj. (informal) (of an idea, a story, etc.) silly; not to be believed

,**cock and 'bull ,story** noun a story that is unlikely to be true but is used as an explanation or excuse

cock·a·tiel /ˈkɑkəˌtil/ noun an Australian PARROT with a gray body and a yellow and orange face

cock·a·too /ˈkɑkəˌtu/ noun (pl. **cock·a·toos**) an Australian bird of the PARROT family, with a large row of feathers (called a CREST) standing up on its head

cock·crow /ˈkɑkkroʊ/ noun [U] (literary) the time of the day when it is becoming light **SYN** DAWN

cock·er /ˈkɑkər/ (also ,cocker 'spaniel) noun a small SPANIEL (= type of dog) with soft hair

cock·er·el /ˈkɑkərəl/ noun a young male chicken

cock·eyed /ˈkɑkaɪd/ adj. (informal) **1** not level or straight **SYN** CROOKED: *Doesn't that picture look cockeyed to you?* **2** not practical; not likely to succeed: *a cockeyed policy to make people use less water*

cock·fight /ˈkɑkfaɪt/ noun a fight between two adult male chickens, watched as a sport and illegal in many countries ▶ **cock·fight·ing** noun [U]

cock·le /ˈkakl/ noun a small SHELLFISH that can be eaten

cock·le·shell /ˈkaklˌʃel/ noun **1** the shell of a cockle **2** a small light boat

cock·ney /ˈkakni/ noun **1** [C] a person from the East End of London **2** [U] the way of speaking that is typical of cockneys: *a cockney accent*

cock·pit /ˈkakpɪt/ noun the area in a plane, boat, or racing car where the pilot or driver sits ⊃ picture at BOAT, PLANE

cock·roach /ˈkakroʊtʃ/ (also informal **roach**) noun a large brown insect with wings, that lives in houses, especially where there is dirt

cock·sure /ˌkakˈʃʊr/ adj. (old-fashioned, informal) confident in a way that is annoying to other people and that they might find offensive

cock·tail /ˈkakteɪl/ noun **1** [C] a drink usually made from a mixture of one or more strong alcoholic drinks and fruit juice or SODA. It can also be made without alcohol: *a cocktail bar/lounge* ◆ *cocktail hour* **2** [C, U] a dish of small pieces of food, usually served cold: *a shrimp cocktail* ◆ *fruit cocktail* **3** [C] a mixture of different substances, usually ones that do not mix together well: *a lethal cocktail of drugs* ⊃ see also MOLOTOV COCKTAIL

cocktail dress noun a dress that is suitable for formal social occasions

cocktail party noun a formal social occasion, usually in the early evening, when people drink COCKTAILS or other alcoholic drinks

cocktail waitress noun a waitress who serves alcoholic drinks to people sitting at tables in a club or bar

cock·y /ˈkaki/ adj. (cock·i·er, cock·i·est) (informal) too confident about yourself in a way that annoys other people ▶ **cock·i·ness** noun [U]

co·coa /ˈkoʊkoʊ/ noun **1** [U] dark brown powder made from the crushed seeds (called **cocoa beans**) of a tropical tree **2** [U] a hot drink made by mixing cocoa powder with milk and/or water and usually sugar: *a mug of cocoa* **3** [C] a cup of cocoa ⊃ compare CHOCOLATE, DRINKING CHOCOLATE

cocoa butter noun [U] fat that is obtained from cocoa beans and used in making chocolate and COSMETICS

co·co·nut /ˈkoʊkənʌt/ noun **1** [C] the large nut of a tropical tree (called a **coconut palm**). It grows inside a hard shell and contains a soft white substance that can be eaten and juice that can be drunk. ⊃ picture at FRUIT **2** [U] the soft white substance inside a coconut, used in cooking: *coconut flakes* ◆ *coconut cookies* ◆ *coconut oil*

coconut butter noun [U] a solid substance inside COCONUT that is used to make soap, CANDLES, etc.

co·coon /kəˈkun/ noun, verb
● noun **1** a covering of silk threads that some insects make to protect themselves before they become adults **2** a soft covering that wraps all around a person or thing and forms a protection: (figurative) *the cocoon of a caring family*
● verb [usually passive] **~ sb/sth (in sth)** to protect someone or something by surrounding them or it completely with something: *We were warm and safe, cocooned in our sleeping bags.*

COD /ˌsi oʊ ˈdi/ abbr. cash on delivery or collect on delivery (payment for goods will be made when the goods are delivered)

cod /kad/ noun [C, U] (pl. **cod**) (also **cod·fish**) a large ocean fish with white flesh that is used for food: *fishing for cod* ◆ *cod fillets*

co·da /ˈkoʊdə/ noun the final passage of a piece of music: (figurative) *The final two months were a miserable coda to the President's first period in office.*

cod·dle /ˈkadl/ verb **1 ~ sb** (often disapproving) to treat someone with too much care and attention ⊃ compare MOLLYCODDLE **2 ~ sth** to cook eggs in water slightly below boiling point

code /koʊd/ AWL noun, verb
● noun **1** [C, U] (often in compounds) a system of words, letters, numbers, or symbols that represent a message or record information secretly or in a shorter form: *to break/crack a code* (= to understand and read the message) ◆ *It's written in code.* ◆ *Tap your code number into the machine.* ◆ *In the event of the machine not operating correctly, an error code will appear.* ⊃ see also AREA CODE, BAR CODE, MORSE CODE, SORT CODE, ZIP CODE **2** [U] (computing) a system of computer programming instructions ⊃ see also MACHINE CODE, SOURCE CODE **3** [C] a set of moral principles or rules of behavior that are generally accepted by society or a social group: *a strict code of conduct* ⊃ see also HONOR CODE **4** [C] a system of laws or written rules that state how people in an institution or a country should behave: *the penal code* ⊃ see also DRESS CODE
● verb **1 ~ sth** to write or print words, letters, numbers, etc. on something so that you know what it is, what group it belongs to, etc.: *Each order is coded separately.* **2** to put a message into code so that it can only be understood by a few people **3 ~ sth** (computing) to write a computer program by putting one system of numbers, words, and symbols into another system SYN ENCODE

co·ded AWL /ˈkoʊdəd/ adj. **1** [only before noun] a **coded** message or **coded** information is written or sent using a special system of words, letters, numbers, etc. that can only be understood by a few other people or by a computer: *a coded warning of a bomb at the airport* **2** expressed in an indirect way: *There was coded criticism of the government from some party members.*

co·deine /ˈkoʊdin/ noun [U] a drug used to reduce pain

code name noun a name used for a person or thing in order to keep the real name secret ▶ **code-named** adj. [not before noun]: *a drug investigation, code-named Snoopy*

code of practice noun (pl. **codes of practice**) a set of standards that members of a particular profession agree to follow in their work

co·de·pend·en·cy /ˌkoʊdɪˈpɛndənsi/ noun [U] (psychology) a situation in which two people have a close relationship in which they rely too much on each other emotionally, especially when one person is caring for the other one ▶ **co·de·pend·ent** adj., noun

code-sharing noun [U] (technical) an agreement between two or more AIRLINES to carry each other's passengers and use their own set of letters and numbers for flights provided by another airline

code switching noun [U] (linguistics) the practice of changing between languages when you are speaking

code word noun a word or phrase with a secret meaning, or one that is used instead of another, more direct word or phrase: *"Big bear" was their code word for the boss.* ◆ *"Inner city" is often used as a code word for poor black neighborhoods.*

co·dex /ˈkoʊdɛks/ noun (pl. **co·di·ces** /ˈkoʊdəsiz/ ˈkadə-/ or **co·dex·es**) **1** an ancient text in the form of a book **2** an official list of medicines or chemicals

cod·fish /ˈkadfɪʃ/ noun (pl. **cod·fish**) = COD

codg·er /ˈkadʒər/ noun (informal) **old ~** an informal way of referring to an old man that shows that you do not respect him

cod·i·cil /ˈkadəsl/ noun (law) an instruction that is added later to a WILL, usually to change a part of it

cod·i·fy /ˈkadəˌfaɪ, ˈkoʊ-/ verb (cod·i·fies, cod·i·fy·ing, cod·i·fied, cod·i·fied) **~ sth** (technical) to arrange laws, rules, etc. into a system ▶ **cod·i·fi·ca·tion** /ˌkadəfəˈkeɪʃn; ˌkoʊ-/ noun [U]

cod liver oil noun [U] a thick yellow oil from the LIVER of COD (= a type of fish), containing a lot of VITAMIN A and D and often given as a medicine

cod·piece /ˈkadpis/ noun a piece of cloth, especially a decorative one, attached to a man's lower clothing and covering his GENITALS, worn in Europe in the 15th and 16th centuries

co·ed /ˌkouˈɛd; ˈkouɛd/ noun (old-fashioned) a female student at a co-educational school or college

ˌco·eduˈcational (also informal co-ed) adj. (of a school or an EDUCATIONAL system) where girls and boys are taught together ▶ ˌco-eduˈcation noun [U]

co·ef·fi·cient /ˌkouəˈfɪʃnt/ noun **1** (mathematics) a number that is placed before another quantity and that multiplies it, for example 3 in the quantity 3[x] **2** (physics) a number that measures a particular property (= characteristic) of a substance: the coefficient of friction

coe·la·canth /ˈsiləˌkænθ/ noun a large fish found mainly in the ocean near Madagascar. It was thought to be EXTINCT until one was discovered in 1938.

co·erce /kouˈərs/ verb ~ sb (into sth/into doing sth) | ~ sb (to do sth) (formal) to force someone to do something by using threats: They were coerced into negotiating a settlement.

co·er·cion /kouˈərʃn; -ʒn/ noun [U] (formal) the action of making someone do something that they do not want to do, using force or threatening to use force: He claimed he had only acted under coercion.

co·er·cive /kouˈərsɪv/ adj. (formal) using force or the threat of force: coercive measures/powers

co·e·val /kouˈivl/ adj. (formal) ~ (with sth) (of two or more things) having the same age or date of origin: The industry is coeval with the construction of the first railroads.

co·ex·ist /ˌkouɪgˈzɪst/ verb [I] ~ (with sb/sth) (formal) to exist together in the same place or at the same time, especially in a peaceful way: The illness frequently coexists with other chronic diseases. ◆ English speakers now coexist peacefully with their Spanish-speaking neighbors. ◆ Different traditions coexist successfully side by side.

co·ex·ist·ence /ˌkouɪgˈzɪstəns/ noun [U] the state of being together in the same place at the same time: to live in **uneasy/peaceful coexistence** within one nation

coffee

pot — | — filter | plunger

coffee maker   French press

espresso machine   teakettle

cof·fee 🔊 /ˈkɔfi; ˈka-/ noun
1 [U, C] the ROAST seeds (called **coffee beans**) of a tropical bush; a powder made from them: decaffeinated/instant coffee ◆ ground/real coffee ◆ a jar of coffee ◆ a blend of Brazilian and Colombian coffees ◆ coffee ice cream **2** [U] a hot drink made from coffee powder and boiling water. It may be drunk with milk and/or sugar added: black/white coffee

(= without/with milk) ◆ Tea or coffee? ◆ I'll just make some coffee. ◆ Let's talk over coffee (= while drinking coffee). ◆ go out/meet for coffee **3** [C] a cup of coffee: Two strong black coffees, please. **4** [U] the color of coffee mixed with milk; light brown **IDM** see WAKE v.

coffee ˌbar noun a small restaurant that sells special kinds of coffee and cakes

coffee ˌbreak noun a short period of rest when you stop working and drink coffee: to have a coffee break

coffee ˌcake noun a type of cake with melted sugar on top that people eat with coffee

coffee ˌhouse noun **1** a restaurant serving coffee, etc. where people go to listen to music, poetry, etc. **2** a restaurant serving coffee, etc., especially one of a type popular in Central Europe: the coffee houses of Vienna

cof·fee klatch (also **cof·fee klatsch**) /ˈkɔfi ˌklatʃ; ˈkafi-; -ˌklætʃ/ noun an informal social occasion, often at someone's home, at which people drink coffee and talk

coffee maˌchine noun a machine that you put coins in to get a cup of coffee

coffee ˌmaker (also **cof·fee·mak·er**) noun a small machine for making cups of coffee ⊃ picture at COFFEE

coffee ˌshop noun a small restaurant, often in a store, hotel, etc., where coffee, tea, and other drinks without alcohol, and simple food are served

coffee ˌtable noun a small low table for putting magazines, cups, etc. on, usually in front of a SOFA

coffee-table ˌbook noun a large expensive book containing many pictures or photographs, that is designed for people to look through rather than to read carefully

cof·fer /ˈkɔfər; ˈka-/ noun **1** [C] a large strong box, used in the past for storing money or valuable objects **2** also **coffers** [pl.] a way of referring to the money that a government, an organization, etc. has available to spend: The nation's coffers are empty.

cof·fin /ˈkɔfən/ (also **cas·ket**) noun a box in which a dead body is buried or CREMATED **IDM** see NAIL

cog /kag; kɔg/ noun **1** one of a series of teeth on the edge of a wheel that fit between the teeth on the next wheel and cause it to move **2** = COGWHEEL ⊃ picture at COGWHEEL **IDM** a cog in the machine/wheel (informal) a person who is a small part of a large organization

co·gent /ˈkoudʒənt/ adj. (formal) strongly and clearly expressed in a way that influences what people believe **SYN** CONVINCING: She put forward some cogent reasons for abandoning the plan. ▶ co·gen·cy /ˈkoudʒənsi/ noun [U] co·gent·ly adv.

cog·i·tate /ˈkadʒəˌteɪt/ verb [I] ~ (about/on sth) (formal) to think carefully about something ▶ cog·i·ta·tion /ˌkadʒəˈteɪʃn/ noun [U, C]

co·gnac /ˈkounyæk; ˈkan-/ noun **1** [U, C] a type of fine BRANDY made in western France **2** [C] a glass of cognac

cog·nate /ˈkagneɪt/ adj., noun
● adj. **1** (linguistics) having the same origin as another word or language: "Haus" in German is cognate with "house" in English. ◆ German and Dutch are cognate languages. **2** (formal) related in some way and therefore similar: a cognate development
● noun (linguistics) a word that has the same origin as another: "Haus" and "house" are cognates.

cog·ni·tion /kagˈnɪʃn/ noun [U] (psychology) the process by which knowledge and understanding is developed in the mind

cog·ni·tive /ˈkagnətɪv/ adj. [usually before noun] connected with mental processes of understanding: a child's cognitive development ◆ cognitive psychology

cog·ni·zance /ˈkagnəzəns/ noun [U] (formal) knowledge or understanding of something ▶ **cog·ni·zant** adj. [not before noun]: cognizant of the importance of the case

IDM **take cognizance of sth** (*law*) to understand or consider something; to take notice of something

co·gno·scen·ti /ˌkɑnyəˈʃɛnti; ˌkɑgnə-/ *noun* [pl.] **the cognoscenti** (from *Italian, formal*) people with a lot of knowledge about a particular subject

cog·wheel /ˈkɑgwil/ (also **cog**) *noun* a wheel with a series of teeth on the edge that fit between the teeth on the next wheel and cause it to move

cogwheel

cog

co·hab·it /koʊˈhæbət/ *verb* [I] **~ (with sb)** (*formal*) (usually of a man and a woman) to live together and have a sexual relationship without being married ▸ **co·hab·i·ta·tion** /ˌkoʊˌhæbəˈteɪʃn/ *noun* [U]

co·here /koʊˈhɪr/ *verb* (*formal*) **1** [I] **~ (with sth)** (of different ideas, arguments, sentences, etc.) to have a clear logical connection so that together they make a whole: *This view does not cohere with their other beliefs.* **2** [I] (of people) to work closely together: *It can be difficult to get a group of people to cohere.*

co·her·ence **AWL** /koʊˈhɪrəns; -ˈhɛr-/ *noun* [U] the situation in which all the parts of something fit together well: *The points you make are fine, but the whole essay lacks coherence.* **ANT INCOHERENCE**

co·her·ent **AWL** /koʊˈhɪrənt; -ˈhɛr-/ *adj.* **1** (of ideas, thoughts, arguments, etc.) logical and well organized; easy to understand and clear: *a coherent narrative/account/explanation* ◆ *a coherent policy for the transport system* **2** (of a person) able to talk and express yourself clearly: *She only became coherent again two hours after the attack.* **ANT INCOHERENT** ▸ **co·her·ent·ly** **AWL** *adv.*

co·he·sion /koʊˈhiʒn/ *noun* [U] **1** (*formal*) the act or state of keeping together **SYN UNITY**: *the cohesion of the nuclear family* ◆ *social/political/economic cohesion* **2** (*physics, chemistry*) the force causing **MOLECULES** of the same substance to stick together

co·he·sive /koʊˈhisɪv; -zɪv/ *adj.* (*formal*) **1** forming a united whole: *a cohesive group* **2** causing people or things to become united: *the cohesive power of shared suffering* ◆ *well-structured sentences illustrating the use of cohesive markers such as "nevertheless" and "however"* ▸ **co·he·sive·ness** *noun* [U]

co·hort /ˈkoʊhɔrt/ *noun* **1** (*technical*) a group of people who share a common feature or aspect of behavior: *the 1999 birth cohort* (= all those born in 1999) **2** (*disapproving*) a member of a group of people who support another person: *Robinson and his cohorts were soon ejected from the meeting.*

coif·fure /kwɑˈfyʊr/ *noun* (from *French, formal* or *humorous*) the way in which a person's hair is arranged **SYN HAIRSTYLE**

coil /kɔɪl/ *verb, noun*
• *verb* [I, T] to wind into a series of circles; to make something do this: **~ up** *The snake coiled up, ready to strike.* ◆ **~ around sth** *Mist coiled around the tops of the hills.* ◆ **~ sth** (+ *adv./prep.*) *to coil a rope into a loop* ◆ *Her hair was coiled on top of her head.* ◆ *a coiled spring* ⊃ picture at **KNOT**
• *noun* **1** a series of circles formed by winding up a length of rope, wire, etc.: *a coil of wire* **2** one circle of rope, wire, etc. in a series: *Shake the rope and let the coils unwind.* ◆ *a snake's coils* **3** a length of wire, wound into circles, that can carry electricity **4** = IUD

coin /kɔɪn/ *noun, verb*
• *noun* **1** [C] a small flat piece of metal used as money: *a ten-cent coin* **2** [U] money made of metal: *paper money and coin* **IDM** see **SIDE, TWO**
• *verb* **1 ~ sth** to invent a new word or phrase that other people then begin to use: *Who coined the term "Generation X"?* **2 ~ sth** to make coins out of metal **IDM** **to coin a phrase 1** used to show that you are aware that you are using an expression that is not new: *Oh well, no news is good news, to coin a phrase.* **2** used to introduce a well-known expression that you have changed slightly in order to be funny

coin·age /ˈkɔɪnɪdʒ/ *noun* **1** [U] the coins used in a particular place or at a particular time; coins of a particular type: *Roman coinage* ◆ *gold/silver/bronze coinage* **2** [U] the system of money used in a particular country **3** [C, U] a word or phrase that has been invented recently; the process of inventing a word or phrase: *new coinages*

co·in·cide **AWL** /ˌkoʊɪnˈsaɪd/ *verb* **1** [I] (of two or more events) to take place at the same time: *It's a shame our trips to New York don't coincide.* ◆ **~ with sth** *The strike was timed to coincide with the party conference.* **2** [I] (of ideas, opinions, etc.) to be the same or very similar: *The interests of employers and employees do not always coincide.* ◆ **~ with sth** *Her story coincided exactly with her brother's.* **3** [I] (*formal*) (of objects or places) to meet; to share the same space: *At this point the two paths coincide briefly.* ◆ **~ with sth** *The present position of the house coincides with that of an earlier dwelling.*

co·in·ci·dence **AWL** /koʊˈɪnsədəns/ *noun* **1** [C, U] the fact of two things happening at the same time by chance, in a surprising way: *a strange/an extraordinary/a remarkable coincidence* ◆ *What a coincidence! I wasn't expecting to see you here.* ◆ *It's not a coincidence that none of the directors are women* (= it did not happen by chance). ◆ *By (sheer) coincidence, I met the person we'd been discussing the next day.* ⊃ thesaurus box at **LUCK 2** [sing.] (*formal*) the fact of things being present at the same time: *the coincidence of inflation and unemployment* **3** [sing.] (*formal*) the fact of two or more opinions, etc. being the same: *a coincidence of interests between the two partners*

co·in·ci·dent **AWL** /koʊˈɪnsədənt/ *adj.* **~ (with sth)** (*formal*) happening in the same place or at the same time

co·in·ci·den·tal **AWL** /koʊˌɪnsəˈdɛntl/ *adj.* [not usually before noun] happening by chance; not planned: *I suppose your presence here today is not entirely coincidental.* ◆ *It's purely coincidental that we both chose to name our daughters Emma.* ▸ **co·in·ci·den·tal·ly** /-ˈdɛntli; -ˈdɛntəli/ *adv.*: *Coincidentally, they had both studied in Paris.*

coir /ˈkɔɪər/ *noun* [U] rough material made from the shells of **COCONUTS**, used for making ropes, for covering floors, etc.

co·i·tus /ˈkoʊətəs/ *noun* [U] (*medical* or *formal*) = SEXUAL INTERCOURSE

Coke™ /koʊk/ *noun* [C, U] (*informal*) = COCA-COLA™: *Can I have a Diet Coke?*

coke /koʊk/ *noun* [U] **1** (*informal*) = COCAINE **2** a black substance that is produced from coal and burned to provide heat

col /kɑl/ *noun* (*technical*) a low point between two higher points in a mountain range **SYN PASS**

Col. *abbr.* (in writing) COLONEL: *Col. Stewart*

col. *abbr.* (in writing) COLUMN

co·la /ˈkoʊlə/ *noun* **1** [U, C] a sweet brown drink with bubbles that does not contain alcohol. Its flavor comes from the seeds of a W. African tree and other substances. **2** [C] a glass, can, or bottle of cola ⊃ see also COCA-COLA™

col·an·der /ˈkɑləndər/ *noun* a metal or plastic bowl with a lot of small holes in it, used for **DRAINING** water from vegetables, etc. after washing or cooking ⊃ picture at **KITCHEN**

cola nut (also **kola nut**) *noun* the seed of the cola tree, that can be chewed or made into a drink

cold /koʊld/ *adj., noun, adv.*
• *adj.* (**cold·er, cold·est**)
▸ **LOW TEMPERATURE 1** having a lower than usual temperature; having a temperature lower than the human body: *I'm cold. Turn the heat up.* ◆ *to feel/look cold* ◆ *cold hands and feet* ◆ *a cold room/house* ◆ *Isn't it cold today?* ◆ *It's freezing cold.* ◆ *to get/turn colder* ◆ *bitterly cold weather* ◆ *the coldest May on record*

t **tea**   ṭ **butter**   d **did**   k **cat**   g **got**   tʃ **chin**   dʒ **June**   f **fall**

> **FOOD/DRINKS 2** not heated; cooled after being cooked: *a cold drink* ◆ *Hot and cold food is available in the cafeteria.* ◆ *cold chicken for lunch*
> **UNFRIENDLY 3** (of a person) without emotion; unfriendly: *to give someone a **cold look/stare/welcome*** ◆ *Her manner was cold and distant.* ◆ *He was staring at her with **cold eyes.***
> **LIGHT/COLORS 4** seeming to lack warmth, in an unpleasant way: *clear cold light* ◆ *cold gray skies*
> **ROUTE 5** not easy to find: *The police followed the robbers to the airport but then the trail went cold.*
> **IN GAMES 6** used in children's games to say that the person playing is not close to finding a person or thing, or to guessing the correct answer
> **UNCONSCIOUS 7 out ~** [not before noun] (*informal*) unconscious: *He was knocked out cold in the second round.*
> **FACTS 8 the ~ facts/truth** facts with nothing added to make them more interesting or pleasant ⊃ see also COLDLY, COLDNESS

IDM a cold fish a person who seems unfriendly and without strong emotions **get/have cold feet** (*informal*) to suddenly become nervous about doing something that you had planned to do: *He was going to ask her but he got cold feet and said nothing.* **give sb the cold shoulder** (*informal*) to treat someone in an unfriendly way ⊃ see also COLD-SHOULDER **in cold blood** acting in a way that is deliberately cruel; with no feeling for someone else's suffering: *to kill someone in cold blood* **in the cold light of day** when you have had time to think calmly about something; in the morning when things are clearer: *These things always look different in the cold light of day.* **leave sb cold** to fail to affect or interest someone: *Most modern art leaves me cold.* **pour/throw cold water on sth** to give reasons for not being in favor of something; to criticize something ⊃ more at BLOOD, BLOW v., HOT

● **noun v.**
> **LOW TEMPERATURE 1** [U] a lack of heat or warmth; a low temperature, especially in the atmosphere: *He shivered with cold.* ◆ *Don't stand outside **in the cold**.* ◆ *She doesn't seem to **feel the cold**.*
> **ILLNESS 2** [C] (also *less frequent* the **common cold**) a common illness that affects the nose and/or throat, making you cough, SNEEZE, etc.: *I've got a cold.* ◆ *a bad/heavy/slight cold* ◆ *to catch a cold*

IDM come in from the cold to become accepted or included in a group, etc. after a period of being outside it **leave sb out in the cold** to not include someone in a group or an activity ⊃ more at CATCH

● **adv. 1** suddenly and completely: *His final request stopped her cold.* **2** without preparing: *I can't just walk in there cold and give a speech.*

THESAURUS

cold

cool • freezing • chilly • lukewarm • tepid

These words all describe a person or thing that has a low temperature.

cold having a temperature that is lower than usual or lower than the human body; (of food or drink) not heated; cooled after being cooked: *I'm cold.* ◆ *Turn the heat up.* ◆ *It was bitterly cold outside.* ◆ *a cold wind* ◆ *hot and cold water* ◆ *I often have cold pizza for breakfast.*

cool (*often approving*) fairly cold, especially in a pleasant way: *a long cool drink* ◆ *We found a cool place to sit.*

freezing extremely cold; having a temperature below 32°F: *It's absolutely freezing outside.* ◆ *I'm freezing!*

chilly (*somewhat informal*) too cold to be comfortable: *Bring a coat. It might get chilly later.*

lukewarm (*often disapproving*) slightly warm, sometimes in an unpleasant way: *Her coffee was now lukewarm.*

tepid (*often disapproving*) slightly warm, sometimes in an unpleasant way: *a glass of tepid water*

LUKEWARM OR TEPID?
There is really no difference in meaning or use between these words.

PATTERNS
- to feel/get cold/cool/chilly
- cold/cool/freezing/chilly **air/weather**
- a cold/cool/freezing/chilly **wind**
- cold/cool/freezing/lukewarm/tepid **water**
- a cold/cool/lukewarm/tepid **shower/bath**
- cold/lukewarm/tepid **tea/coffee/food**
- a cold/cool **drink**
- It's cold/chilly/freezing outside.

cold-blooded adj. **1** (of people and their actions) showing no feelings or sympathy for other people: *a cold-blooded killer* **2** (*biology*) (of animals, for example fish or snakes) having a body temperature that depends on the temperature of the surrounding air or water ⊃ compare WARM-BLOODED ▶ **cold-bloodedly** adv.

cold-calling noun [U] the practice of telephoning someone that you do not know, in order to sell them something ▶ **cold call** noun

cold cash (also **hard cash**) noun [U] money, especially in the form of coins and notes, that you can spend

cold comfort noun [U] the fact that something that would normally be good does not make you happy because the whole situation is bad: *A small drop in the inflation rate was cold comfort for the millions without a job.*

cold cream noun [U] a thick white cream that people use for cleaning their face or making their skin soft

cold cuts noun [pl.] slices of cooked meat that are served cold

cold frame (also **frame**) noun a small wooden or metal frame covered with glass that you grow seeds or small plants in to protect them from cold weather

cold fusion noun [U] (*physics*) FUSION that takes place at or near room temperature

cold-hearted adj. not showing any love or sympathy for other people; unkind ⊃ compare WARM-HEARTED

cold·ly /ˈkoʊldli/ adv. without any emotion or warm feelings; in an unfriendly way

cold·ness /ˈkoʊldnəs/ noun [U] **1** the lack of warm feelings; unfriendly behavior: *She was hurt by the coldness in his voice.* **2** the state of being cold: *the icy coldness of the water* **ANT** WARMTH

cold-shoulder verb **~ sb** to treat someone in an unfriendly way ⊃ see also GIVE SB THE COLD SHOULDER at COLD adj.

cold snap noun (*informal*) a sudden short period of very cold weather

cold sore (also **fever blister**) noun a small painful spot on the lips or inside the mouth that is caused by a virus

cold spell noun a period when the weather is colder than usual

cold storage noun [U] a place where food, etc. can be kept fresh or frozen until it is needed; the storing of something in such a place: (*figurative*) *I've had to **put** my plans **into cold storage*** (= I've decided not to carry them out immediately but to keep them for later).

cold store noun a room where food, etc. can be kept at a low temperature in order to keep it in good condition

cold sweat noun [usually sing.] a state when you have sweat on your face or body but still feel cold, usually because you are very frightened or anxious: *to break out into a cold sweat* ◆ *I woke up in a cold sweat about the interview.*

,cold 'turkey *noun* [U] the unpleasant state that drug ADDICTS experience when they suddenly stop taking a drug; a way of treating drug ADDICTS that makes them experience this state ▶ ,cold 'turkey *adv.*: *I quit smoking cold turkey.*

,cold 'war *noun* [sing., U] often **the Cold War** a very unfriendly relationship between two countries who are not actually fighting each other, usually used about the situation between the U.S. and the Soviet Union after World War II

cole·slaw /'koʊlslɔ/ *noun* [U] a salad of pieces of raw CABBAGE, carrot, onion, etc., mixed with MAYONNAISE

col·ic /'kɑlɪk/ *noun* [U] severe pain in the stomach and BOWEL, suffered especially by babies ▶ col·ick·y *adj.*

col·i·se·um /,kɑlə'siəm/ *noun* a large building used for sports events, entertainment, exhibitions, etc.

co·li·tis /kə'laɪtəs/ *noun* [U] (*medical*) a disease that causes pain and swelling in the COLON (= part of the BOWEL)

col·lab·o·rate /kə'læbə,reɪt/ *verb* **1** [I] to work together with someone in order to produce or achieve something: *Researchers around the world are collaborating to develop a new vaccine.* ◆ ~ **(with sb) (on sth)** *We have collaborated on many projects over the years.* ◆ ~ **(with sb) (in sth/in doing sth)** *She agreed to collaborate with him in writing her biography.* **2** [I] ~ **(with sb)** (*disapproving*) to help the enemy who has taken control of your country during a war

col·lab·o·ra·tion /kə,læbə'reɪʃn/ *noun* **1** [U, C] the act of working with another person or group of people to create or produce something: *It was a collaboration that produced extremely useful results.* ◆ ~ **(with sb) (on sth)** *She wrote the book in collaboration with one of her students.* ◆ *The administration worked in close collaboration with teachers on the new curriculum.* ◆ ~ **(between A and B)** *collaboration between the teachers and the administration* **2** [C] a piece of work produced by two or more people or groups working together **3** [U] (*disapproving*) the act of helping the enemy during a war when they have taken control of your country

col·lab·o·ra·tive /kə'læbrətɪv; -bərə-/ *adj.* [only before noun] involving, or done by, several people or groups of people working together: *collaborative projects/studies/ research* ◆ *a collaborative effort/venture* ▶ col·lab·o·ra·tive·ly *adv.*

col·lab·o·ra·tor /kə'læbə,reɪtər/ *noun* **1** a person who works with another person to create or produce something such as a book **2** (*disapproving*) a person who helps the enemy in a war, when they have taken control of the person's country

col·lage /kə'lɑʒ/ *noun* **1** [U, C] the art of making a picture by sticking pieces of colored paper, cloth, or photographs onto a surface; a picture that you make by doing this **2** [C] a collection of things, which may be similar or different: *an interesting collage of 1960s songs*

col·la·gen /'kɑlədʒən/ *noun* [U] a PROTEIN found in skin and bone, sometimes INJECTED into the body, especially the face, to improve its appearance: *collagen injections*

col·lapse AWL /kə'læps/ *verb, noun*

● *verb*
> OF BUILDING **1** [I] to fall down or fall in suddenly, often after breaking apart: *The roof collapsed under the weight of snow.*
> OF SICK PERSON **2** [I] to fall down (and usually become unconscious), especially because you are very sick: *He collapsed in the street and died two hours later.*
> RELAX **3** [I] (*informal*) to sit or lie down and relax, especially after working hard: *When I get home, I like to collapse on the sofa and listen to music.*
> FAIL **4** [I] to fail suddenly or completely **SYN** BREAK DOWN: *Talks between management and unions have collapsed.* ◆ *All opposition to the plan has collapsed.*
> OF PRICES/CURRENCIES **5** [I] to decrease suddenly in amount or value: *Share prices collapsed after the news.*
> FOLD **6** [I, T] ~ **(sth)** to fold something into a shape that uses

less space; to be able to be folded in this way **SYN** FOLD UP: *The table collapses for easy storage.*
> MEDICAL **7** [I, T] ~ **(sth)** if a lung or BLOOD VESSEL **collapses** or is **collapsed**, it falls in and becomes flat and empty
▶ col·lapsed **AWL** *adj.*: *collapsed buildings* ◆ *a collapsed investment bank* ◆ *a collapsed lung*

● *noun*
> FAILURE **1** [C, usually sing., U] a sudden failure of something, such as an institution, a business, or a course of action: *the collapse of law and order in the area* ◆ *The peace talks were on the verge of collapse.*
> OF BUILDING **2** [U] the action of a building suddenly falling: *The walls were strengthened to protect them from collapse.*
> ILLNESS **3** [U, C, usually sing.] a medical condition when a person suddenly becomes very sick, or when someone falls because they are sick or weak: *a state of mental/nervous collapse* ◆ *She was taken to hospital after her collapse at work.*
> OF PRICES/CURRENCIES **4** [C, usually sing.] a sudden fall in value: *the collapse of share prices/the dollar/the market*

col·laps·i·ble **AWL** /kə'læpsəbl/ *adj.* that can be folded flat or made into a smaller shape that uses less space: *a collapsible chair/boat/bicycle*

col·lar /'kɑlər/ *noun, verb*
● *noun* **1** the part around the neck of a shirt, jacket, or coat that usually folds down: *a coat with a fur collar* ◆ *I turned up my collar against the wind* (= to keep warm). ● picture at CLOTHES ⮕ see also BLUE-COLLAR, DOG COLLAR, WHITE-COLLAR, WING COLLAR **2** a band of leather or strong cloth put around the neck of an animal, especially a dog: *a collar and leash* ⮕ see also CHOKE COLLAR **3** (*technical*) a band made of a strong material that is put around something, such as a pipe or a piece of machinery, to make it stronger or to join two parts together **IDM** see HOT
● *verb* (*informal*) **1** ~ **sb** to capture someone and hold them tightly so that they cannot escape from you: *Police collared the culprit as he was leaving the premises.* **2** ~ **sb** to stop someone in order to talk to them: *I was collared in the street by a woman doing a survey.*

col·lar·bone /'kɑlər,boʊn/ *noun* either of the two bones that go from the base of the neck to the shoulders **SYN** CLAVICLE ● picture at BODY

col·lards /'kɑlərdz/ (also col·lard greens /'kɑlərd ,grinz/) *noun* [pl.] a dark green vegetable with broad flat leaves that grows in the southern U.S. and is eaten cooked

col·lar·less /'kɑlərləs/ *adj.* with no collar: *a collarless shirt*

col·late /kə'leɪt; 'koʊleɪt; 'kɑleɪt/ *verb* **1** ~ **sth** to collect information together from different sources in order to examine and compare it: *to collate data/information/ figures* **2** ~ **sth** to collect pieces of paper or the pages of a book, etc. and arrange them in the correct order
▶ col·la·tion /kə'leɪʃn/ *noun* [U]: *the collation of information*

col·lat·er·al /kə'lætərəl/ *noun, adj.*
● *noun* **1** (*finance*) property or something valuable that you promise to give to someone if you cannot pay back money that you borrow
● *adj.* (*formal*) connected with something else, but in addition to it and less important: *collateral benefits* ◆ *The government denied that there had been any collateral damage* (= injury to ordinary people or buildings) *during the bombing raid.*

col·league AWL /'kɑlig/ *noun*

a person that you work with, especially in a profession or a business: *a colleague of mine from work* ◆ *We were friends and colleagues for more than 20 years.* ◆ *the president and his Cabinet colleagues*

col·lect /kə'lɛkt/ *verb, adj., adv.*
● *verb*
> BRING TOGETHER **1** [T] to bring things together from different people or places **SYN** GATHER: ~ **sth** *to collect data/ evidence/information* ◆ *We're collecting signatures for a petition.* ◆ ~ **sth from sb/sth** *Samples were collected from over 200 patients.*

> **AS HOBBY 2** [T] ~ **sth** to buy or find things of a particular type and keep them as a hobby: *to collect stamps/postcards, etc.* ⊃ see also **STAMP COLLECTING**

> **OF PEOPLE 3** [I] to come together in one place to form a larger group **SYN GATHER**: *A crowd began to collect in front of the embassy.*

> **INCREASE IN AMOUNT 4** [I, T] to gradually increase in amount in a place; to gradually obtain more and more of something in a place **SYN ACCUMULATE**: *Dirt had collected in the corners of the room.* ♦ ~ **sth** *We seem to have collected an enormous number of boxes* (= without intending to). ♦ *That guitar's been sitting collecting dust* (= not being used) *for years now.*

> **MONEY 5** [I, T] to ask people to give you money for a particular purpose: ~ **(for sth)** *We're collecting for local charities.* ♦ ~ **sth (for sth)** *We collected over $300 for the fund-raising drive.* **6** [T] ~ **sth** to obtain the money, etc. that someone owes, for example by going to their house to get it: *to collect rent/debts/tax*

> **RECEIVE/WIN 7** to receive something; to win something: [T, I] ~ **(sth)** *She collected $25,000 in compensation.* ♦ *to collect a prize/a medal*

IDM **collect yourself/your thoughts 1** to try to control your emotions and become calm: *I'm fine—I just need a minute to collect myself.* **2** to prepare yourself mentally for something: *She paused to collect her thoughts before entering the interview room.*

● *adj.* (of a telephone call) paid for by the person who receives the call: *to make a collect call* ▶ **col·lect** *adv.*: *to call someone collect*

THESAURUS

collect

gather ♦ accumulate ♦ amass

These words all mean to get more of something over a period of time, or to increase in quantity over a period of time.

collect to bring things or information together from different people or places; to gradually increase in amount in a place: *We've been collecting data from various sources.* ♦ *Dirt had collected in the corners of the room.* **NOTE** People sometimes **collect** things of a particular type as a hobby: *to collect stamps*

gather to bring things together that have been spread around; to collect information from different sources: *I waited while he gathered up his papers.* ♦ *Detectives have spent months gathering evidence.*

COLLECT OR GATHER?
Both **collect** and **gather** can be used in the same way to talk about bringing together data, information, or evidence. When talking about things, **gather** is used with words like *things, belongings,* or *papers* when the things are spread around within a short distance. **Collect** is used for getting examples of something from different people or places that are physically separated.

accumulate (*somewhat formal*) to gradually get more and more of something over a period of time; to gradually increase in number or quantity over a period of time: *I seem to have accumulated a lot of books.* ♦ *Debts began to accumulate.*

amass (*somewhat formal*) to collect something in large quantities, especially money, debts, or information: *He amassed a fortune from silver mining.*

PATTERNS
- to collect/gather/accumulate/amass **data/ evidence/information**
- to accumulate/amass **a fortune/debts**
- **dirt/dust/debris** collects/accumulates
- to **gradually/slowly** collect/gather/accumulate (sth)

---

col·lect·ed /kəˈlɛktəd/ *adj.* **1** [not before noun] very calm and in control of yourself: *She always stays **calm, cool, and collected** in a crisis.* **2** ~ **works, papers, poems, etc.** all the books, etc. written by one author, published in one book or in a set

col·lect·i·ble /kəˈlɛktəbl/ *adj.* worth collecting because it is beautiful or may become valuable ▶ **col·lect·i·ble** *noun* [usually pl.]

col·lec·tion 🔑 /kəˈlɛkʃn/ *noun*

> **GROUP OF OBJECTS/PEOPLE 1** [C] a group of objects, often of the same sort, that have been collected: *a stamp/coin, etc. collection* ♦ *The painting comes from his private collection.* **2** [C] a group of objects or people: *There was a collection of books and shoes on the floor.* ♦ *There is always a strange collection of runners in the New York Marathon.*

> **TAKING AWAY/BRINGING TOGETHER 3** [C, U] an act of taking something away from a place; an act of bringing things together into one place: *garbage/trash collection* ♦ *The first stage in research is data collection.* ⊃ compare **PICKUP**

> **POEMS/STORIES/MUSIC 4** [C] a group of poems, stories, or pieces of music published together as one book or disk: *a collection of stories by women writers*

> **MONEY 5** [C] an act of collecting money to help a charity or during a church service; the money collected: *a house-to-house collection for youth organizations* ♦ *The total collection last week amounted to $250.*

> **NEW CLOTHES 6** [C] a line of new clothes or items for the home that are designed, made, and offered for sale, often for a particular season: *Armani's stunning new fall collection* ⊃ compare **FASHION**

col·lec·tive /kəˈlɛktɪv/ *adj., noun*

● *adj.* [usually before noun] **1** done or shared by all members of a group of people; involving a whole group or society: *collective leadership/decision-making/responsibility* ♦ *collective memory* (= things that a group of people or a community know or remember, that are often passed from parents to children) **2** used to refer to all members of a group: *The collective name for mast, boom, and sails on a boat is the "rig."* ▶ **col·lec·tive·ly** *adv.*: *the collectively agreed-on rate* ♦ *We have had a successful year, both collectively and individually.* ♦ *rain, snow, and hail, collectively known as "precipitation"* (= as a group)

● *noun* a group of people who own a business or a farm and run it together; the business that they run: *an independent collective making movies for television*

col·lective ˈbargaining *noun* [U] discussions between a **LABOR UNION** and an employer about the pay and working conditions of the union members

col·lective ˈfarm *noun* a large farm, or a group of farms, owned by the government and run by a group of people

col·lective ˈnoun *noun* (*grammar*) a singular noun, such as *committee* or *team*, that refers to a group of people, animals, or things and that is used with a singular verb

col·lective unˈconscious *noun* [sing.] (*psychology*) the part of the unconscious mind that is thought to be shared with other humans because it is passed from generation to generation

col·lec·tiv·ism /kəˈlɛktəˌvɪzəm/ *noun* [U] the political system in which all farms, businesses, and industries are owned by the government or by all the people ▶ **col·lec·tiv·ist** *adj.*

col·lec·ti·vize /kəˈlɛktəˌvaɪz/ *verb* [often passive] ~ **sth** to join several private farms, industries, etc. together so that they are controlled by the community or by the government ▶ **col·lec·ti·vi·za·tion** /kəˌlɛktəvəˈzeɪʃn/ *noun* [U]

col·lec·tor /kəˈlɛktər/ *noun* (especially in compounds) a person who collects things, either as a hobby or as a job: *a stamp collector* ♦ *ticket/tax/debt collectors*

col·lector's ˌitem *noun* a thing that is valued because it is very old or rare, or because it has some special interest

col·lege 🔑 /ˈkɑlɪdʒ/ *noun*

1 [C, U] (often in names) a place where students can study

---

for a degree after they have finished high school: *Carleton College* ◆ *a college campus/student* ◆ *a private college* ◆ *He got interested in politics when he was in college.* ◆ *She's away at college in California.* ◆ *He's hoping to go to college next year.* ⊃ collocations at EDUCATION ⊃ see also COMMUNITY COLLEGE **2** [C] one of the main divisions of some large universities: *The history department is part of the College of Arts and Sciences.* **3** [C] the teachers and/or students of a college **4** [C] (usually in names) an organized group of professional people with special interests, duties, or powers: *the National College of District Attorneys* ◆ *the American College of Cardiology* ⊃ see also ELECTORAL COLLEGE

col·le·giate /kəˈlidʒət/ *adj., noun*
● *adj.* relating to a college or its students: *collegiate life*
● *noun* (also **col‚legiate 'institute**) (in some parts of Canada) a public high school

col·lide /kəˈlaɪd/ *verb* **1** [I] if two people, vehicles, etc. **collide**, they crash into each other; if a person, vehicle, etc. **collides** with another, or with something that is not moving, they crash into it: *The car and the van collided head-on in thick fog.* ◆ **~ with sth/sb** *The car collided head-on with the van.* ◆ *As he fell, his head collided with the table.* ⊃ thesaurus box at CRASH **2** [I] **~ (with sb) (over sth)** (*formal*) (of people, their opinions, etc.) to disagree strongly: *They regularly collide over policy decisions.* ⊃ see also COLLISION

col·lid·er /kəˈlaɪdər/ *noun* (*physics*) a machine for making two streams of PARTICLE move at high speed and crash into each other

col·lie /ˈkɑli/ *noun* a dog, of which there are several types. Those with long pointed noses and long thick hair are popular as pets. Smaller collies with shorter hair are often trained to help control sheep on a farm.

col·lier /ˈkɑlyər/ *noun* **1** (*old-fashioned*) = COAL MINER **2** a ship that carries coal

col·lier·y /ˈkɑlyəri/ *noun* (*pl.* **col·lier·ies**) a coal mine with its buildings and equipment

col·li·gate /ˈkɑlə‚geɪt/ *verb* [I, T] **~ (with sth)** | **~ sth (with sth) 1** (*formal*) if two ideas, facts, etc. **colligate**, or are **colligated**, they are linked together by a single explanation or theory **2** (*linguistics*) if two words **colligate**, or are **colligated**, they occur together and are linked by grammar

col·li·sion /kəˈlɪʒn/ *noun* [C, U] **~ (with sb/sth)** | **~ (between/of A and B) 1** an accident in which two vehicles or people crash into each other: *a collision between two trains* ◆ *Stewart was injured in a collision with another player.* ◆ *a head-on collision* (= between two vehicles that are moving toward each other) ◆ *a mid-air collision* (= between two aircraft while they are flying) **2** (*formal*) a strong disagreement between two people or between opposing ideas, opinions, etc.; the meeting of two things that are very different: *a collision between two opposing points of view* ◆ *In his work, we see the collision of two different traditions.*
IDM **be on a collision course (with sb/sth) 1** to be in a situation that is almost certain to cause a disagreement or argument: *I was on a collision course with my boss over the sales figures.* **2** to be moving in a direction in which it is likely that you will crash into someone or something: *A giant iceberg was on a collision course with the ship.*

col·lo·cate /ˈkɑlə‚keɪt/ *verb* [I] **~ (with sth)** (*linguistics*) (of words) to be often used together in a language: *"Bitter" collocates with "tears" but "sour" does not.* ◆ *"Bitter" and "tears" collocate.* ▶ **col·lo·cate** /ˈkɑləkət/ *noun*: *"Bitter" and "tears" are collocates.*

col·lo·ca·tion /‚kɑləˈkeɪʃn/ *noun* (*linguistics*) **1** [C] a combination of words in a language, that happens very often and more frequently than would happen by chance: *"Resounding success" and "crying shame" are English collocations.* **2** [U] the fact of two or more words often being used together, in a way that happens more frequently than would happen by chance: *Advanced students need to be aware of the importance of collocation.*

col·lo·qui·al /kəˈloʊkwiəl/ *adj.* (of words and language) used in conversation but not in formal speech or writing **SYN** INFORMAL ▶ **col·lo·qui·al·ly** *adv.*

col·lo·qui·al·ism /kəˈloʊkwiə‚lɪzəm/ *noun* a word or phrase that is used in conversation but not in formal speech or writing

col·lo·qui·um /kəˈloʊkwiəm/ *noun* (*pl.* **col·lo·qui·a** /-kwiə/) a formal academic SEMINAR or conference

col·lo·quy /ˈkɑləkwi/ *noun* (*pl.* **col·lo·quies**) (*formal*) a conversation

col·lude /kəˈlud/ *verb* [I] (*formal, disapproving*) to work together secretly or illegally in order to trick other people: **~ (with sth) (in sth/in doing sth)** *Several people had colluded in the murder.* ◆ **~ (with sb) (to do sth)** *They colluded with terrorists to overthrow the government.*

col·lu·sion /kəˈluʒn/ *noun* [U] (*formal, disapproving*) secret agreement especially in order to do something dishonest or to trick people: *The police were corrupt and were operating in collusion with the drug dealers.* ◆ *There was collusion between the two witnesses* (= they gave the same false evidence). ▶ **col·lu·sive** /kəˈlusɪv/ *adj.*

col·o·bus /ˈkɑləbəs/ (also **'colobus ‚monkey**) *noun* a small African MONKEY with a long tail, that eats leaves

co·logne /kəˈloʊn/ (also **eau de co·logne**) *noun* [U] a type of light PERFUME

co·lon /ˈkoʊlən/ *noun* **1** the mark (:) used to introduce a list, a summary, an explanation, etc. or before reporting what someone has said ⊃ compare SEMICOLON **2** (*anatomy*) the main part of the large INTESTINE (= part of the BOWEL) ⊃ picture at BODY

colo·nel /ˈkɜrnl/ *noun* (*abbr.* **Col.**) an officer of high rank in the army, the MARINES, or the AIR FORCE: *Colonel Jim Edge*

co·lo·ni·al /kəˈloʊniəl/ *adj., noun*
● *adj.* **1** connected with or belonging to a country that controls another country: *a colonial power* ◆ *Tunisia achieved independence from French colonial rule in 1956.* ◆ *Western colonial attitudes* ⊃ see also COLONY **2** often **Colonial** typical of or connected with the U.S. at the time when it was still a British COLONY: *life in colonial times* ◆ *Colonial homes*
● *noun* a person who lives in a COLONY and who comes from the country that controls it: *British colonials in India*

co·lo·ni·al·ism /kəˈloʊniə‚lɪzəm/ *noun* [U] the practice by which a powerful country controls another country or other countries: *European colonialism* ▶ **co·lo·ni·al·ist** *adj., noun*: *colonialist laws*

co·lon·ic /kəˈlɑnɪk/ *adj.* (*anatomy*) connected with the COLON (= part of the BOWEL): *colonic irrigation* (= the process of washing out the COLON with water)

col·o·nist /ˈkɑlənɪst/ *noun* a person who settles in an area that has become a COLONY

col·o·nize /ˈkɑlə‚naɪz/ *verb* **1** **~ sth** to take control of an area or a country that is not your own, especially using force, and send people from your own country to live there: *The area was colonized by the Vikings.* **2** **~ sth** (*biology*) (of animals or plants) to live or grow in large numbers in a particular area: *The slopes are colonized by flowering plants.* ◆ *Bats had colonized the ruins.* ▶ **col·o·ni·za·tion** /‚kɑlənə-ˈzeɪʃn/ *noun* [U]: *the colonization of the "New World"* ◆ *plant colonization* **col·o·niz·er** /ˈkɑlə‚naɪzər/ *noun*

col·on·nade /‚kɑləˈneɪd/ *noun* a row of stone columns with equal spaces between them, usually supporting a roof ⊃ picture at ARCHITECTURE ▶ **col·on·nad·ed** /‚kɑlə-ˈneɪdəd/ *adj.*

col·o·ny /ˈkɑləni/ *noun* (*pl.* **col·o·nies**) **1** [C] a country or an area that is governed by people from another, more powerful, country: *former British colonies* **2** [sing.] a group of people who go to live permanently in a colony **3** [C] a group of people from the same place or with the same work or interests who live in a particular city or country or who live together: *an artists' colony* **4** [C] (*biology*) a group of plants or animals that live together or grow in the same place: *a colony of ants* ◆ *a bird colony*

color

shade ◆ hue ◆ tint ◆ tinge

These words all describe the appearance of things, resulting from the way in which they reflect light.

color the appearance that things have, resulting from the way in which they reflect light. Red, green, and blue are colors: *What's your favorite color?* ◆ *bright/dark/light colors*

shade a particular form of a color, especially when describing how light or dark it is. Lavender is a shade of purple.

hue (*literary* or *technical*) a color or a particular shade of a color: *His face took on an unhealthy, whitish hue.*

tint a shade or small amount of a particular color; a faint color covering a surface: *green leaves with red and gold tints*

tinge a small amount of a color: *Her hair is brown with just a tinge of red.*

TINT OR TINGE?

You can say *a reddish tint/tinge* or *a tinge of red* but not: *a tint of red.* **Tint** is more often used in the plural.

PATTERNS

- a **warm/rich** color/shade/hue/tint
- a **bright/vivid/vibrant/dark/deep** color/shade/hue
- a **pale/pastel/soft/subtle/delicate** color/shade/hue
- a **light/strong/neutral/natural** color/shade

col·or 🔑 (*CanE usually* **col·our**) /ˈkʌlər/ *noun, verb*

● *noun*

> RED, GREEN, ETC. **1** [C, U] the appearance that things have that results from the way in which they reflect light. Red, orange, and green are colors: *What's your favorite color?* ◆ *bright/dark/light colors* ◆ *available in 12 different colors* ◆ *the color of the sky* ◆ *Her hair is a reddish-brown color.* ◆ *Foods that go through a factory process lose much of their color, flavor, and texture.* ◆ *The garden was a mass of color.* **2** [U] (usually before another noun) the use of all the colors, not only black and white: *a color TV* ◆ *color photography/printing* ◆ *a full-color brochure* ◆ *Do you dream in color?*

> OF FACE **3** [U] a red or pink color in someone's face, especially when it shows that they look healthy or that they are embarrassed: *The fresh air brought color to their cheeks.* ◆ *Color flooded her face when she thought of what had happened.* ◆ *His face was drained of color* (= he looked pale and sick).

> OF SKIN **4** [U, C] the color of a person's skin, when it shows the race they belong to: *discrimination on the grounds of race, color, or religion* ◆ *a person/man/woman of color* (= who is not white)

> SUBSTANCE **5** [C, U] a substance that is used to give color to something: *a semi-permanent hair color that lasts six to eight weeks* ⊃ see also WATERCOLOR

> INTERESTING DETAILS **6** [U] interesting and exciting details or qualities: *The old town is full of color and attractions.* ◆ *Her acting added warmth and color to the production.* ◆ *to add/give/lend color to something* (= make it brighter, more interesting, etc.) ⊃ see also LOCAL COLOR

> OF TEAM/COUNTRY, ETC. **7** colors [pl.] the particular colors that are used on clothes, flags, etc. to represent a team, school, political party, or country: *Red and white are the team colors.* ◆ *Spain's national colors* ◆ (*figurative*) *There are people of different political colors on the committee.* **8** colors [pl.] a flag, BADGE, etc. that represents a team, country, ship, etc.: *Most buildings had a flagpole with the national colors flying.* ◆ *sailing under the French colors*

IDM **see the color of sb's money** (*informal*) to make sure that someone has enough money to pay for something ⊃ more at FLYING, HORSE, LEND, TRUE ⊃ see also OFF COLOR

● *verb*

> PUT COLOR ON SOMETHING **1** [I, T] to put color on something using paint, colored pencils, etc.: *The children love to draw and color.* ◆ *a coloring book* (= with pictures that you can add color to) ◆ ~ **sth** *How long have you been coloring* (= DYEING) *your hair?* ◆ ~ **sth + adj.** *He drew a monster and colored it green.*

> OF FACE **2** [I] ~ **(at sth)** (*formal*) (of a person or their face) to become red with embarrassment SYN BLUSH: *She colored at his remarks.*

> AFFECT **3** [T] ~ **sth** to affect something, especially in a negative way: *This incident colored her whole life.* ◆ *Don't let your judgment be colored by personal feelings.*

PHR V ,color sth↔'in to put color inside a particular area, shape, etc. using colored pencils, CRAYON, etc.: *I'll draw a tree and you can color it in.*

col·or·ant (*CanE usually* **col·our·ant**) /ˈkʌlərənt/ *noun* a substance that is used to put color in something, especially a person's hair

col·or·a·tion (*CanE usually* **col·our·a·tion**) /ˌkʌləˈreɪʃn/ *noun* [U] (*technical*) the natural colors and patterns on a plant or an animal

col·o·ra·tu·ra /ˌkʌlərəˈtʊrə/ *noun* [U] (*music*) complicated passages for a singer, for example in OPERA: *a coloratura soprano* (= one who often sings coloratura passages)

color ,bar (*CanE usually* **,colour ,bar**) (also **,color ,line,** *CanE usually* **,colour ,line**) *noun* [usually sing.] a social system that does not allow black people the same rights as white people

color–,blind (*CanE usually* **,colour–,blind**) *adj.* **1** unable to see the difference between some colors, especially red and green **2** treating people with different colored skin in exactly the same way ▶ **,color–,blindness** (*CanE usually* **,colour–,blindness**) *noun* [U]

color ,code (*CanE usually* **,colour ,code**) *noun* a system of marking things with different colors so that you can easily identify them ▶ **,color–,coded** (*CanE usually* **,colour–,coded**) *adj.*: *The files have labels that are color-coded according to subject.*

col·ored (*CanE usually* **col·oured**) /ˈkʌlərd/ *adj., noun*

● *adj.* **1** (often in compounds) having a particular color or different colors: *brightly colored balloons* ◆ *colored lights* ◆ *She was wearing a cream-colored suit.* **2** (*old-fashioned* or *offensive*) (of a person) from a race that does not have white skin

● *noun* (*old-fashioned* or *offensive*) a person who does not have white skin

color ,fast (*CanE usually* **,colour ,fast**) /ˈkʌlər ˌfæst/ *adj.* cloth that is **color fast** will not lose color when it is washed

col·or·ful (*CanE usually* **col·our·ful**) /ˈkʌlərfl/ *adj.* **1** full of bright colors or having a lot of different colors: *colorful shop windows* ◆ *The male birds are more colorful than the females.* **2** interesting or exciting; full of variety, sometimes in a way that is slightly shocking: *a colorful history/past/career* ◆ *one of the book's most colorful characters*

color ,guard (*CanE usually* **,colour ,guard**) *noun* a small group of people who carry official flags in a ceremony

col·or·ing (*CanE usually* **col·our·ing**) /ˈkʌlərɪŋ/ *noun* **1** [U, C] a substance that is used to give a particular color to food: *red food coloring* **2** [U] the color of a person's skin, eyes, and hair: *Blue looked good with her fair coloring.* **3** [U] the colors that exist in something, especially a plant or an animal: *insects with vivid yellow and black coloring*

coloring ,book *noun* a book for children with pictures that are drawn with a black outline so that they can be colored in

col·or·ist (*CanE usually* **col·our·ist**) /ˈkʌlərɪst/ *noun* a person who uses color, especially an artist or a hairdresser

col·or·is·tic (CanE usually **col·our·is·tic**) /ˌkʌləˈrɪstɪk/ adj. (technical) showing or relating to a special use of color: coloristic effects

col·or·ize (CanE usually **col·our·ize**) /ˈkʌləˌraɪz/ verb ~ sth (technical) to add color to a black and white movie, using a computer process

col·or·less (CanE usually **col·our·less**) /ˈkʌlərləs/ adj. **1** without color or very pale: a colorless liquid like water **2** not interesting **SYN** DULL: a colorless personality

color line noun = COLOR BAR

color scheme (CanE usually **colour scheme**) noun the way in which colors are arranged, especially in the furniture and decoration of a room

color sepa·ration (CanE usually **colour sepa·ration**) noun (technical) **1** [C] one of four images of something made using only the colors CYAN, MAGENTA, yellow, or black. The four images containing these colors are then used together to print an image in full color. **2** [U] the process that is used to do this

col·or·way (CanE usually **col·our·way**) /ˈkʌlərˌweɪ/ noun a color, or combination of colors, that a piece of clothing, etc. is available in: The designs are available in two colorways: red/gray or blue/gray.

co·los·sal /kəˈlɑsl/ adj. extremely large: a colossal statue ◆ The singer earns a colossal amount of money.

co·los·sus /kəˈlɑsəs/ noun **1** [sing.] (formal) a person or thing that is extremely important or large in size **2** [C] (pl. **co·los·si** /kəˈlɑsaɪ/) an extremely large statue

co·los·to·my /kəˈlɑstəmi/ noun (pl. **co·los·to·mies**) (medical) an operation in which part of a person's COLON (= the lower part of the BOWEL) is removed and an opening is made in the ABDOMEN through which the person can get rid of waste matter from the body

co·los·trum /kəˈlɑstrəm/ noun [U] the substance produced in the breasts of a new mother, which has a lot of antibodies (ANTIBODY) that help her baby to resist disease

col·our (CanE) = COLOR **HELP** You will find most words formed with **colour** at the spelling **color**.

col·our·ant (CanE) = COLORANT

col·our·a·tion (CanE) = COLORATION

col·oured (CanE) = COLORED

col·our·ful (CanE) = COLORFUL

col·our·ing (CanE) = COLORING

col·our·ist (CanE) = COLORIST

col·our·ize (CanE) = COLORIZE

col·our·less (CanE) = COLORLESS

col·our·way (CanE) = COLORWAY

colt /koʊlt/ noun **1** a young male horse up to the age of four or five ◆ compare FILLY, STALLION **2** Colt™ a type of small gun

colt·ish /ˈkoʊltɪʃ/ adj. (of a person) moving with a lot of energy but in an awkward way

co·lum·bine /ˈkɑləmˌbaɪn/ noun **1** [C, U] a garden plant with delicate leaves and pointed blue flowers that hang down **2 Columbine** [sing.] a female character in traditional Italian theater

Co·lum·bus Day /kəˈlʌmbəs ˌdeɪ/ noun [U, C] a national holiday on the second Monday in October when people celebrate the discovery of America by Christopher Columbus

col·umn 🖉 /ˈkɑləm/ noun
1 a tall, solid, vertical post, usually round and made of stone, that supports or decorates a building or stands alone as a MONUMENT: The temple is supported by marble columns. ◆ Nelson's Column in London ◆ picture at ARCHITECTURE **2** a thing shaped like a column: a column of smoke (= smoke rising straight up) ◆ see also SPINAL COLUMN, STEERING COLUMN **3** (abbr. col.) one of the vertical sections into which the printed page of a book, newspaper, etc. is divided: a

column of text ◆ a dictionary with two columns per page ◆ Put a mark in the appropriate column. ◆ Their divorce filled a lot of column inches in the local papers (= got a lot of attention). **4** a part of a newspaper or magazine that appears regularly and deals with a particular subject or is written by a particular writer: the gossip/financial column ◆ I always read her column in the local paper. **5** a series of numbers or words arranged one under the other down a page: to add up a column of figures **6** a long moving line of people or vehicles: a long column of troops and tanks ◆ see also FIFTH COLUMN

col·um·nist /ˈkɑləmnɪst; ˈkɑləmɪst/ noun a journalist who writes regular articles for a newspaper or magazine

com /kʌm/ abbr. (used in Internet addresses) commercial organization: The Internet address of Oxford University Press is www.oup.com.

co·ma /ˈkoʊmə/ noun a deep unconscious state, usually lasting a long time and caused by serious illness or injury: to go into/be in a coma

Co·man·che /kəˈmæntʃi/ noun (pl. **Co·man·che** or **Co·man·ches**) a member of a Native American people, many of whom live in the state of Oklahoma

com·a·tose /ˈkoʊməˌtoʊs; ˈkɑ-/ adj. **1** (medical) deeply unconscious; in a coma **2** (humorous) extremely tired and lacking in energy; sleeping deeply

comb /koʊm/ noun, verb
● **noun 1** [C] a flat piece of plastic or metal with a row of thin teeth along one side, used for making your hair neat; a smaller version of this worn by women in their hair to hold it in place or as a decoration **2** [C, usually sing.] the act of using a comb on your hair: Your hair needs a comb. **3** [C, U] = HONEYCOMB **4** [C] the soft red piece of flesh on the head of a male chicken **IDM** see FINE-TOOTH COMB

bristles

hairbrush

comb

● **verb 1** [T] ~ sth to pull a comb through your hair in order to make it neat: Don't forget to comb your hair! ◆ Her hair was combed back neatly. **2** [T, I] to search something carefully in order to find someone or something **SYN** SCOUR: ~ sth I combed the stores looking for something to wear. ◆ ~ sth for sb/sth The police combed the area for clues. ◆ ~ through sth (for sb/sth) They combed through the files for evidence of fraud. **3** [T] ~ sth (technical) to make wool, cotton, etc. clean and straight using a special comb so that it can be used to make cloth
PHR V ˌcomb sth↔ˈout to pull a comb through hair in order to make it neat or to remove knots from it

com·bat noun, verb
● **noun** /ˈkɑmbæt/ [U, C] fighting or a fight, especially during a time of war: He was killed in combat. ◆ armed/unarmed combat (= with/without weapons) ◆ combat troops ◆ combat boots ◆ see also SINGLE COMBAT
● **verb** /kəmˈbæt; ˈkɑmbæt/ (-t- or -tt-) **1** ~ sth to stop something unpleasant or harmful from happening or from getting worse: measures to combat crime/inflation/unemployment/disease **2** ~ sb (formal) to fight against an enemy

com·bat·ant /kəmˈbætnt/ noun a person or group involved in fighting in a war or battle ◆ compare NONCOMBATANT

combat fa·tigue (also **battle fa·tigue**) noun [U] mental problems caused by being in a war for a long period of time

combat fa·tigues (also **battle fa·tigues**) noun [pl.] clothes that soldiers wear for fighting that are covered in brown and green marks to make them difficult to see

com·bat·ive /kəmˈbætɪv/ adj. ready and willing to fight or argue: in a combative mood/spirit

com·bi·na·tion 🖉 /ˌkɑmbəˈneɪʃn/ noun
1 [C] two or more things joined or mixed together to form a single unit: His treatment was a combination of surgery,

radiation, and drugs. ◆ *What an unusual combination of flavors!* ◆ *Technology and good management. That's a **winning combination** (= one that will certainly be successful).* **2** [U] the act of joining or mixing together two or more things to form a single unit: *The firm is working on a new product **in combination with** several overseas partners.* ◆ *These paints can be used individually or **in combination**.* **3** [C] a series of numbers or letters used to open a combination lock: *I can't remember the combination.*

combi·nation ˌlock *noun* a type of lock that can only be opened by using a particular series of numbers or letters

com·bine 🔑 *verb, noun*

● *verb* /kəmˈbaɪn/ **1** [I, T] to come together to form a single thing or group; to join two or more things or groups together to form a single one: *Hydrogen and oxygen combine to form water.* ◆ *~ **with sth** Hydrogen combines with oxygen to form water.* ◆ *~ **to do sth** Several factors had combined to ruin our plans.* ◆ *~ **sth** Combine all the ingredients in a bowl.* ◆ *~ **sth with sth** Combine the eggs with a little flour.* ◆ *~ **A and B (together)** Combine the eggs and the flour.* ◆ *The German team scored a **combined total** of 652 points.* **2** [T] to have two or more different features or characteristics; to put two or more different things, features, or qualities together: *~ **sth** We are still looking for someone who combines all the necessary qualities.* ◆ *~ **A and/with B** The hotel combines comfort with convenience.* ◆ *This model combines a printer and fax machine.* ◆ *They have successfully combined the old with the new in this room.* ◆ *a kitchen and dining room combined* **3** [T] *~ **A and/with B** to do two or more things at the same time: *The trip will combine business with pleasure.* ◆ *She has successfully combined a career and bringing up a family.* **4** [I, T] to come together in order to work or act together; to put two things or groups together so that they work or act together: *They combined against a common enemy.* ◆ *~ **sth (with sth)** the combined effects of the two drugs* ◆ *You should try to combine exercise with a healthy diet.* **IDM** see **FORCE**

● *noun* /ˈkɒmbaɪn/ **1** a large farm machine that cuts a crop and separates the grains from the rest of the plant **2** a group of people or organizations acting together in business

com·bined /kəmˈbaɪnd/ *adj.* [only before noun] formed or achieved by putting several people or things together: *The project was completed through the **combined efforts** of the government and private organizations.* ◆ *The **combined total** of money raised from various sources was over $2 million.*

com·bining ˌform *noun* (*grammar*) a form of a word that can combine with another word or another combining form to make a new word, for example *techno-* and *-phobe* in *technophobe*

com·bo /ˈkɒmboʊ/ *noun* (*pl.* **com·bos**) **1** a small band that plays JAZZ or dance music **2** (*informal*) a number of different things combined together, especially different types of food: *I'll have the steak and chicken combo combo platter.*

com·bust /kəmˈbʌst/ *verb* [I, T] *~ **(sth)*** to start to burn; to start to burn something

com·bus·ti·ble /kəmˈbʌstəbl/ *adj.* able to begin burning easily **SYN** FLAMMABLE: *combustible material/gases*

com·bus·tion /kəmˈbʌstʃən/ *noun* [U] **1** the process of burning **2** (*technical*) a chemical process in which substances combine with the OXYGEN in the air to produce heat and light

com·bustion ˌchamber *noun* a space in which combustion takes place, for example in an engine

come 🔑 /kʌm/ *verb, exclamation*

● *verb* (**came** /keɪm/, **come**)

▷ **TO A PLACE 1** [I] to move to or toward a person or place: **(+ adv./prep.)** *He came into the room and shut the door.* ◆ *My son is coming home soon.* ◆ *Come here!* ◆ *Come and see us soon!* ◆ *Here comes Jo* (= Jo is coming)*!* ◆ *There's a storm coming.* ◆ *~ **to do sth** They're coming to stay with us for a week.* **HELP** In spoken English **come** can be used with **and** plus another verb, instead of with **to** and the infinitive, to show

purpose or to tell someone what to do: *When did she last come and see you?* ◆ *Come and have your dinner.* The **and** is sometimes left out: *Come have your dinner.* **2** [I] *~ **(to…)** to arrive at or reach a place: *They continued until they came to a river.* ◆ *What time did you come* (= to my house)*?* ◆ *Spring came late this year.* ◆ *Your breakfast is coming soon.* ◆ *Have any letters come for me?* ◆ *Help came at last.* ◆ *The CD **comes complete** with all the words of the songs.* ◆ *The time has come* (= now is the moment) *to act.* **3** [I] to arrive somewhere in order to do something or get something: *~ **for sth** I've come for my book.* ◆ *~ **about sth** I've come about my book.* ◆ *~ **to do sth** I've come to get my book.* ◆ *~ **doing sth** He came looking for me.* **4** [I] to move or travel, especially with someone else, to a particular place or in order to be present at an event: *I've only come for an hour.* ◆ *Thanks for coming* (= to my house, party, etc.)*.* ◆ *~ **(to sth) (with sb)** Are you coming to the club with us tonight?* ◆ *~ **doing sth** Why don't you come skating tonight?*

▷ **RUNNING/HURRYING ETC. 5** [I] *~ **doing sth** (+ adv./prep.) to move in a particular way or while doing something else: *The children came running into the room.*

▷ **TRAVEL 6** [I] + *noun* to travel a particular distance: *We've come 50 miles this morning.* ◆ (*figurative*) *The company has **come a long way*** (= made lot of progress) *in the last 5 years.*

▷ **HAPPEN 7** [I] to happen: *The agreement came after several hours of negotiations.* ◆ *The rains came too late to do any good.* ◆ *~ **as sth** Her death came as a terrible shock to us.* ◆ *His resignation came as no surprise.* **8** [T] *~ **to do sth** used in questions to talk about how or why something happened: *How did he come to break his leg?* ◆ *How do you come to be so late?*

▷ **TO A POSITION/STATE 9** [I] + *adv./prep.* (not used in the progressive tenses) to have a particular position: *That comes a long way down my list of priorities.* ◆ *His family **comes first*** (= is the most important thing in his life)*.* **10** [I] *~ **to/into sth** used in many expressions to show that something has reached a particular state: *At last winter **came to an end**.* ◆ *He **came to power** in 2006.* ◆ *When will they **come to a decision**?* ◆ *The trees are **coming into leaf**.* **11** [I] (not used in the progressive tenses) (of goods, products, etc.) to be available or to exist in a particular way: *~ **in sth** This dress comes in black and red.* ◆ + *adj.* (*informal*) *New cars don't **come cheap*** (= they are expensive)*.* **12** [I, T] to become: + *adj.* *The buttons had come undone.* ◆ *The handle came loose.* ◆ *~ **to do sth** This design came to be known as the Oriental style.* **13** [T] *~ **to do sth** to reach a point where you realize, understand, or believe something: *In time she came to love him.* ◆ *She had come to see the problem in a new light.* ◆ *I've come to expect this kind of behavior from him.*

▷ **TIME 14** come [T] *~ **sth** (*old-fashioned*, *informal*) when the time mentioned comes: *They would have been married forty years come this June.*

▷ **SEX 15** [I] (*slang*) to have an ORGASM

IDM Most idioms containing **come** are at the entries for the nouns or adjectives in the idioms. For example, **come to grief** is at **grief**. **be as handsome, stupid, etc. as they come** (*informal*) to be very HANDSOME, stupid, etc. **come again?** (*informal*) used to ask someone to repeat something: *"She's an entomologist." "Come again?" "An entomologist—she studies insects."* **come and go 1** to arrive and leave; to move freely: *They had a party next door—we heard people **coming and going** all night.* **2** to be present for a short time and then go away: *The pain in my leg comes and goes.* **come easily, naturally, etc. to sb** (of an activity, a skill, etc.) to be easy, natural, etc. for someone to do: *Acting comes naturally to her.* **come to nothing| not come to anything** to be unsuccessful; to have no successful result: *How sad that all his hard work should come to nothing.* ◆ *Her plans didn't come to anything.* **come to that| if it comes to that** (*informal*) used to introduce something extra that is connected with what has just been said: *I don't really trust him—nor his wife, come to that.* **come what may** despite any problems or difficulties you may have: *He promised to support her come what may.* **how come (…)?** used to say you do not understand how something can happen and would like an explanation: *If she spent five years in Paris, how come her*

French is so bad? **not come to much** to not be important or successful **to come** (used after a noun) in the future: *They may well regret the decision **in years to come**.* ◆ *This will be a problem **for some time to come*** (= for a period of time in the future). **when it comes to sth/to doing sth** when it is a question of something: *When it comes to getting things done, he's useless.* **where sb is coming from** (*informal*) somebody's ideas, beliefs, personality, etc. that makes them say what they have said: *I see where you're coming from* (= I understand what you mean). ◑ more at EAR

PHR V ,come a'bout (that…) to happen: *Can you tell me how the accident came about?*

,come a'cross **1** to be understood: *He spoke for a long time but his meaning didn't really come across.* **2** to make a particular impression: *She comes across well in interviews.* ◆ *He came across as a sympathetic person.* 'come across sb/ sth [no passive] to meet or find someone or something by chance: *I came across children sleeping under bridges.* ◆ *She came across some old photos in a drawer.* ,come a'cross (with sth) [no passive] to provide or supply something when you need it: *I hoped she'd come across with some more information.*

,come 'after sb [no passive] to chase or follow someone

,come a'long **1** to arrive; to appear: *When the right opportunity comes along, she'll take it.* **2** to go somewhere with someone: *I'm glad you came along.* **3** to improve or develop in the way that you want **SYN** PROGRESS: *Your French has come along a lot recently.*

,come a'part to break into pieces: *The book just came apart in my hands.* ◆ (*figurative*) *My whole life had **come apart at the seams**.*

,come a'round **1** (also ,come 'to) to become conscious again: *Your mother hasn't yet come around from the anesthetic.* **2** (of a date or a regular event) to happen again: *My birthday seems to come around quicker every year.* ,come a'round (to…) to come to a place, especially someone's house, to visit for a short time: *Please come around and see us some time.* ,come a'round (to sth) to change your mood or your opinion: *He'll never come around to our way of thinking.*

'come at sb [no passive] to move toward someone as though you are going to attack them: *She came at me with a knife.* ◆ (*figurative*) *The noise came at us from all sides.* 'come at sth to think about a problem, question, etc. in a particular way **SYN** APPROACH: *We're getting nowhere—let's come at it from another angle.*

,come a'way (from sth) to become separated from something: *The plaster had started to come away from the wall.* ,come a'way with sth [no passive] to leave a place with a particular feeling or impression: *We came away with the impression that all was not well with their marriage.*

,come 'back **1** to return: *You came back* (= came home) *very late last night.* ◆ *The color was coming back to her cheeks.* ◆ (*figurative*) *The Bruins came back from being two goals down to win 3–2.* ◑ thesaurus box at RETURN **2** to become popular or successful again: *Long hair for men seems to be coming back in.* ◑ related noun COMEBACK ,come 'back (at sb) (with sth) to reply to someone angrily or with force: *She came back at the speaker with some sharp questions.* ◑ related noun COMEBACK ,come 'back (to sb) to return to someone's memory: *It's all coming back to me now.* ◆ *Once you've been in France a few days, your French will come back.* ,come 'back to sth [no passive] to return to a subject, an idea, etc.: *Let's come back to the point at issue.* ◆ *It all comes back to a question of money.*

'come before sb/sth [no passive] (*formal*) to be presented to someone or something for discussion or a decision: *The case comes before the court next week.*

,come be'tween sb and sb [no passive] to damage a relationship between two people: *I'd hate for anything to come between us.*

,come 'by to make a short visit to a place, in order to see someone: *She came by the house.* 'come by sth **1** to manage to get something: *Jobs are hard to come by these days.* **2** to receive something: *How did you come by that scratch on your cheek?*

,come 'down **1** to break and fall to the ground: *The ceiling came down with a loud crash.* **2** (of rain, snow, etc.) to fall: *The*

rain came down in torrents. **3** (of an aircraft) to land or fall from the sky: *We were forced to come down in a field.* **4** if a price, a temperature, a rate, etc. **comes down**, it gets lower: *The price of gas is coming down.* ◆ *Gas is coming down (in price).* **5** to decide and say publicly that you support or oppose someone: *The committee came down in support of his application.* **6** to reach as far down as a particular point: *Her hair comes down to her waist.* ,come 'down (from…) (to…) to come from one place to another, usually from the north of a country to the south, or from a larger place to a smaller one ,come 'down on sb [no passive] (*informal*) to criticize someone severely or punish someone: *Don't come down too hard on her.* ◆ *The courts are coming down heavily on young offenders.* ,come 'down (to sb) to have come from a long time in the past: *The name has come down from the last century.* ,come 'down to sth [no passive] to be able to be explained by a single important point: *What it comes down to is, either I get more money or I leave.* ,come 'down with sth [no passive] to get an illness that is not very serious: *I think I'm coming down with the flu.*

,come 'forward to offer your help, services, etc.: *Several people came forward with information.* ◆ *Police have asked witnesses of the accident to come forward.*

'come from… (not used in the progressive tenses) to have as your place of birth or the place where you live: *She comes from Chicago.* ◆ *Where do you come from?* 'come from sth **1** to start in a particular place or be produced from a particular thing: *Much of our butter comes from Vermont.* ◆ *This wool comes from goats, not sheep.* ◆ *This poem comes from his new book.* ◆ *Where does her attitude come from?* ◆ *Where's that smell coming from?* ◆ *He comes from a family of actors.* **2** = COME OF STH

,come 'in **1** when the TIDE **comes in**, it moves toward the land **ANT** GO OUT **2** to finish a race in a particular position: *My horse came in last.* **3** to become fashionable: *Long hair for men came in in the sixties.* **ANT** GO OUT **4** to become available: *We're still waiting for copies of the book to come in.* **5** to have a part in something: *I understand the plan perfectly, but I can't see where I come in.* **6** to arrive somewhere; to be received: *The train is coming in now.* ◆ *News is coming in of a serious plane crash in Pennsylvania.* ◆ *She has over a thousand dollars a month coming in from her investments.* **7** to take part in a discussion: *Would you like to come in at this point, Susan?* **8** (of a law or rule) to be introduced; to begin to be used ,come 'in for sth [no passive] to receive something, especially something unpleasant: *The government's economic policies have come in for a lot of criticism.* ,come 'in (on sth) to become involved in something: *If you want to come in on the deal, you need to decide now.*

,come 'into sth [no passive] **1** to be left money by someone who has died: *She came into a fortune when her uncle died.* **2** to be important in a particular situation: *I've worked very hard to pass this exam—luck doesn't come into it.*

'come of/from sth to be the result of something: *I made a few inquiries, but nothing came of it.* ◆ + *doing sth That comes from eating too much!*

,come 'off **1** to be able to be removed: *Does this hood come off?* ◆ *That mark won't come off.* **2** (*informal*) to take place; to happen: *Did the trip to Las Vegas ever come off?* **3** (*informal*) (of a plan, etc.) to be successful; to have the intended effect or result: *They had wanted it to be a surprise but the plan didn't come off.* **4** ~ **well, badly, etc.** (*informal*) to be successful/ not successful in a fight, contest, etc.: *I thought they came off very well in the debate.* ,come 'off (sth) **1** to fall from something: *to come off your bicycle/horse* **2** to become separated from something: *When I tried to lift the jug, the handle came off in my hand.* ◆ *A button had come off my coat.* ,come 'off it (*informal*) used to disagree with someone rudely: *Come off it! We don't have a chance.* ,come 'off sth [no passive] to stop taking medicine, a drug, alcohol, etc.: *I've tried to get him to come off the tranquilizers.*

,come 'on **1** (of an actor) to walk onto the stage **2** (of a player) to join a team during a game: *Owen came on for Brown ten minutes before the end of the game.* **3** to improve or develop in the way you want: *The project is coming on fine.* **4** used in orders to tell someone to hurry or to try harder:

h hat   m man   n no   ŋ sing   l leg   r red   y yes   w wet

Come on! We don't have much time. ◆ *Come on! Try it again.* **5** used to show that you know what someone has said is not correct: *Oh, come on—you know that isn't true!* **6** (usually used in the progressive tenses) (of an illness or a mood) to begin: *I can feel a cold coming on.* ◆ *I think there's rain coming on.* **7** (of a TV program, etc.) to start: *What time does the news come on?* **8** to begin to operate: *Set the oven to come on at six.* ◆ *When does the heat come on?* **ˌcome ˈon/upon sb/sth** [no passive] (*formal*) to meet or find someone or something by chance **ˌcome ˈon to sb** (*informal*) to behave in a way that shows someone that you want to have a sexual relationship with them ➔ related noun COME-ON
ˌcome ˈout 1 when the sun, moon, or stars **come out**, they appear: *The rain stopped and the sun came out.* **2** (of flowers) to open: *The daffodils came out early this year.* **3** to be produced or published: *When is her new novel coming out?* **4** (of news, the truth, etc.) to become known: *The full story came out at the trial.* ◆ + *that*… *It came out that he'd been telling lies.* **5** if a photograph **comes out**, it is a clear picture when it is developed and printed: *The photos from our trip didn't come out.* **6** to be shown clearly: *Her best qualities come out in a crisis.* **7** when words **come out**, they are spoken: *I tried to say "I love you," but the words wouldn't come out.* **8** to say publicly whether you agree or disagree with something: *He came out against the plan.* ◆ *In her speech, the senator came out in favor of a change in the law.* **9** to no longer hide the fact that you are HOMOSEXUAL **10** (of a young UPPER-CLASS girl, especially in the past) to be formally introduced into society **ˌcome ˈout (of sth) 1** (of an object) to be removed from a place where it is fixed: *This nail won't come out.* **2** (of dirt, a mark, etc.) to be removed from something by washing or cleaning: *These ink stains won't come out of my dress.* ◆ *Will the color come out (= become faint or disappear) if I wash it?* **ˌcome ˈout of yourself** to relax and become more confident and friendly with other people: *It was when she started drama classes that she really came out of herself.* **ˌcome ˈout of sth** [no passive] to develop from something: *The book came out of his experiences in India.* ◆ *Rock music came out of the blues.* **ˌcome ˈout with sth** [no passive] **1** to say something, especially something surprising or rude: *He came out with a stream of abuse.* ◆ *She sometimes comes out with the most outrageous things.* **2** to make something available: *The company has just come out with a new line of cosmetics.*
ˌcome ˈover (to…) to come to a place, especially someone's house, to visit for a short time **ˌcome ˈover (to…) (from…)** to travel from one place to another, usually over a long distance: *Why don't you come over to the U.S. this summer?* ◆ *Her grandparents came over from Russia during the war.* **ˌcome ˈover (to sth)** to change from one side, opinion, etc. to another **ˌcome ˈover sb** [no passive] to affect someone: *A feeling of dizziness came over her.* ◆ *I can't think what came over me* (= I do not know what caused me to behave in that way).
ˌcome ˈthrough (of news or a message) to arrive by telephone, radio, etc. or through an official organization: *A message is just coming through.* **ˌcome ˈthrough (sth)** to get better after a serious illness or to avoid serious injury **SYN** SURVIVE: *With such a weak heart, she was lucky to come through the operation.* **ˌcome ˈthrough (for sb)** to prevent disaster for someone: *My sister really came through for me when I lost my job.* ➔ thesaurus box at SAVE **ˌcome ˈthrough (with sth)** to successfully do or complete something that you have promised to do: *We were worried she wouldn't be able to handle it, but she came through in the end.* ◆ *The bank finally came through with the money.*
ˌcome ˈto = COME AROUND (1) **ˈcome to sb** [no passive] (of an idea) to enter your mind: *The idea came to me in the shower.* ◆ ~ *that*… *It suddenly came to her that she had been wrong all along.* **ˈcome to sth** [no passive] **1** to add up to something: *The bill came to $30.* ◆ *I never expected those few items to come to so much.* **2** to reach a particular situation, especially a bad one: *The doctors will operate if necessary—but it may not come to that.* ◆ *Who'd have thought things would come to this* (= become so bad)?
ˌcome toˈgether if two or more different people or things

come together, they form a united group: *Three colleges have come together to create a new university.* ◆ *Bits and pieces of things he'd read and heard were coming together, and he began to understand.*
ˈcome under sth [no passive] **1** to be included in a particular group: *What heading does this come under?* **2** to be a person that others are attacking or criticizing: *The principal came under a lot of criticism from the parents.* **3** to be controlled or influenced by something: *All her students came under her spell.*
ˌcome ˈup 1 (of plants) to appear above the soil: *The daffodils are just beginning to come up.* **2** (of the sun) to rise: *We watched the sun come up.* **3** to happen: *I'm afraid something urgent has come up.* ◆ *We'll let you know if any job openings come up.* **4** to be mentioned or discussed: *The subject came up in conversation.* ◆ *The question is bound to come up at the meeting.* **5** (of an event or a time) to be going to happen very soon: *Her birthday is coming up soon.* **6** to be dealt with by a court: *Her divorce case comes up next month.* **7** if your number, name, ticket, etc. **comes up** in a betting game, it is chosen and you win something **8** (usually used in the progressive tenses) (*informal*) to arrive; to be ready soon: *"Is lunch ready?" "Coming up!"* **ˌcome ˈup (to…) (from…)** to come from one place to another, especially from the south of a country to the north or from a smaller place to a larger one: *Why don't you come up to Boston for a few days?* **ˌcome ˈup (to sb)** to move toward someone, in order to talk to them: *He came up to me and asked for a light.* **ˌcome ˈup against sb/sth** [no passive] to be faced with or opposed by someone or something: *We expect to come up against a lot of opposition to the plan.* **ˌcome ˈup for sth** [no passive] **1** to be considered for a job, an important position, etc.: *She comes up for reelection next year.* **2** to be reaching the time when something must be done: *His contract is coming up for renewal.* **ˌcome ˈup from/ through sth** to progress upward in rank or status through steps: *He started out in the mail room and came up through the ranks to become president of the company.* **ˌcome ˈup to sth** [no passive] **1** to reach as far as a particular point: *The water came up to my neck.* **2** to reach an acceptable level or standard: *His performance didn't really come up to his usual high standard.* ◆ *Their trip to Mexico didn't come up to expectations.* **ˌcome ˈup with sth** [no passive] to find or produce an answer, a sum of money, etc.: *She came up with a new idea for increasing sales.* ◆ *How soon can you come up with the money?*
ˈcome upon sb/sth = COME ON SB/STH
● *exclamation* (*old-fashioned*) used when encouraging someone to be sensible or reasonable, or when showing slight disapproval: *Oh come now, things aren't as bad as all that.* ◆ *Come, come, Miss Jones, you know perfectly well what I mean.*

come·back /ˈkʌmbæk/ *noun* **1** [usually sing.] if a person in public life makes a **comeback**, they start doing something again that they had stopped doing, or they become popular again: *an aging rock star trying to stage a comeback* **2** if a thing makes a **comeback**, it becomes popular and fashionable or successful again **3** (*informal*) a quick reply to a critical remark **SYN** RETORT

co·me·di·an /kəˈmidiən/ *noun* an entertainer who makes people laugh by telling jokes or funny stories

com·e·dic /kəˈmidɪk/ *adj.* [only before noun] of or relating to comedy: *a comedic actress/role*

co·me·di·enne /kəˌmidiˈɛn/ *noun* (*old-fashioned*) a female entertainer who makes people laugh by telling jokes or funny stories

come·down /ˈkʌmdaʊn/ *noun* [usually sing.] (*informal*) a situation in which a person is not as important as before, or does not get as much respect from other people

com·e·dy 🔑 /ˈkɑmədi/ *noun* (*pl.* **com·e·dies**)
1 [C, U] a play or movie that is intended to be funny, usually with a happy ending; plays and movies of this type: *a romantic comedy* ◆ *slapstick comedy* ➔ see also BLACK

⊃ compare TRAGEDY **2** [U] entertainment that is funny: *She does standup comedy at a comedy club.* **3** [U] an amusing aspect of something **SYN** HUMOR: *He didn't appreciate the comedy of the situation.*

ˌcomedy of ˈmanners *noun* an amusing play, movie, or book that shows the silly behavior of a group of people

ˌcome-ˈhither *adj.* [only before noun] (of someone's expression) appearing to be trying to attract someone sexually: *a come-hither look*

come·ly /ˈkʌmli/ *adj.* (*literary*) (especially of a woman) pleasant to look at **SYN** ATTRACTIVE

ˈcome-on *noun* [usually sing.] (*informal*) an object or action that is intended to attract someone or to persuade them to do something: *She was definitely giving him a come-on* (= trying to attract him sexually).

com·er /ˈkʌmər/ *noun* **1 all comers** [pl.] anyone who is interested in, or comes forward for, something, especially a competition: *The event is open to all comers.* **2** (with adjectives) a person who arrives somewhere ⊃ **see also** LATE-COMER, NEWCOMER **3** (*informal*) a person who is likely to be successful

co·mes·ti·ble /kəˈmɛstəbl/ *adj., noun* (*formal*)
• *adj.* that can be eaten **SYN** EDIBLE
• *noun* [usually pl.] an item of food

com·et /ˈkʌmət/ *noun* a mass of ice and dust that moves around the sun and looks like a bright star with a tail

come·up·pance /kʌmˈʌpəns/ *noun* [sing.] (*informal*) a punishment for something bad that you have done, that other people feel you really deserve: *I was glad to see that the bad guy got his comeuppance at the end of the movie.*

com·fort 🔑 /ˈkʌmfərt/
noun, verb

WORD FAMILY
comfort *noun*, *verb*
comfortable *adj.* (≠ uncomfortable)
comfortably *adv.* (≠ uncomfortably)
comforting *adj.*

• *noun* **1** [U] the state of being physically relaxed and free from pain; the state of having a pleasant life, with everything that you need: *These tennis shoes are designed for comfort and performance.* ◆ *With a DVD player, you can watch the latest movies in the comfort of your own home.* ◆ *The hotel offers a high standard of comfort and service.* ◆ *They had enough money to live in comfort in their old age.* **2** [U] a feeling of not suffering or worrying so much; a feeling of being less unhappy **SYN** CONSOLATION: *to take/draw comfort from someone's words* ◆ *I tried to offer a few words of comfort.* ◆ *The sound of gunfire was too close for comfort.* ◆ *If it's any comfort to you, I'm in the same situation.* ◆ *His words were of little comfort in the circumstances.* ◆ *comfort food* (= food that makes you feel better) **3** [sing.] a person or thing that helps you when you are suffering, worried, or unhappy: *The children have been a great comfort to me through all of this.* ◆ *It's a comfort to know that she is safe.* ⊃ **see also** COLD COMFORT **4** [C, usually pl.] a thing or situation that makes your life easier or more comfortable: *The hotel has all modern comforts/every modern comfort.* ◆ *material comforts* (= money and possessions) ⊃ **see also** CREATURE COMFORTS
• *verb* to make someone who is worried or unhappy feel better by being kind and sympathetic toward them: **~ sb** *The victim's widow was today being comforted by family and friends.* ◆ *She comforted herself with the thought that it would soon be spring.* ◆ **it comforts sb to do sth** *It comforted her to feel his arms around her.*

com·fort·a·ble 🔑 /ˈkʌmftərbl; ˈkʌmfərtəbl/ *adj.*
›CLOTHES/FURNITURE **1** (of clothes, furniture, etc.) making you feel physically relaxed; pleasant to wear, sit on, etc.: *It's such a comfortable bed.* ◆ *These new shoes are not very comfortable.* ◆ *a warm comfortable house*
ANT UNCOMFORTABLE
›PHYSICALLY RELAXED **2** feeling pleasantly physically relaxed; warm enough, without pain, etc.: *Are you comfortable?* ◆ *She shifted into a more comfortable position on the chair.* ◆ *Please make yourself comfortable while I get some coffee.*

◆ *The patient is comfortable* (= not in pain) *after his operation.*
ANT UNCOMFORTABLE
›CONFIDENT **3** confident and not worried or afraid: *He's more comfortable with computers than with people.*
ANT UNCOMFORTABLE
›HAVING MONEY **4** having enough money to buy what you want without worrying about the cost: *They're not millionaires, but they're certainly very comfortable.* ⊃ **thesaurus box at** RICH
›VICTORY **5** quite large; allowing you to win easily: *The party won with a comfortable majority.* ◆ *a comfortable 2–0 win*

com·fort·a·bly 🔑 /ˈkʌmftərbli; ˈkʌmfərtəbli/ *adv.*
1 in a comfortable way: *All the rooms were comfortably furnished.* ◆ *If you're all sitting comfortably, then I'll begin.* **2** with no problem **SYN** EASILY: *He can comfortably afford the extra expense.* ◆ *They are comfortably ahead in the opinion polls.*
IDM comfortably off having enough money to buy what you want without worrying too much about the cost

com·fort·er /ˈkʌmfərtər/ *noun* **1** a type of thick cover for a bed ⊃ **compare** QUILT **2** a person or thing that makes you feel calmer or less worried

com·fort·ing /ˈkʌmfərtɪŋ/ *adj.* making you feel calmer and less worried or unhappy: *her comforting words* ◆ *It's comforting to know that you'll be there.* ▶ com·fort·ing·ly *adv.*

com·fort·less /ˈkʌmfərtləs/ *adj.* (*formal*) without anything to make a place more comfortable

ˈcomfort ˌzone *noun* **1** (sometimes *disapproving*) a place or situation in which you feel safe or comfortable, especially when you choose to stay in this situation, instead of trying to work harder or achieve more: *Stepping outside your comfort zone and trying new things can be a great experience.* ◆ *We cannot afford to have anyone operating in a comfort zone.* **2** (*approving*) (especially in sports) a state in which you feel confident and are performing at your best: *I knew if I could find my comfort zone I would be difficult to beat.*

com·frey /ˈkʌmfri/ *noun* [U, C] a plant with large leaves covered with small hairs and small bell-shaped flowers

com·fy /ˈkʌmfi/ *adj.* (com·fi·er, com·fi·est) (*informal*) comfortable: *a comfy armchair/bed* **HELP** more comfy is also common as a comparative.

com·ic /ˈkʌmɪk/ *adj., noun*
• *adj.* **1** amusing and making you laugh: *a comic monologue/story* ◆ *The play is both comic and tragic.* ◆ *She can always be relied on to provide comic relief* (= something to make you laugh) *at a boring party.* **2** [only before noun] connected with comedy (= entertainment that is funny and that makes people laugh): *a comic opera* ◆ *a comic actor*
• *noun* **1** an entertainer who makes people laugh by telling jokes or funny stories **SYN** COMEDIAN **2** (also **comic book**) a magazine, especially for children, that tells stories through pictures **3 the comics** [pl.] the section of a newspaper that contains COMIC STRIP **SYN** FUNNIES

com·i·cal /ˈkʌmɪkl/ *adj.* funny or amusing, especially because of being strange or unexpected: *Many of the scenes in the book are truly comical.* ⊃ **thesaurus box at** FUNNY ▶ com·i·cal·ly /-kli/ *adv.*

ˈcomic ˌstrip (also car·toon, strip) *noun* a series of drawings inside boxes that tell a story and are often printed in newspapers

com·ing /ˈkʌmɪŋ/ *noun, adj.*
• *noun* [sing.] **the ~ of sth** the time when something new begins: *With the coming of modern technology, many jobs were lost.*
IDM comings and goings (*informal*) the movement of people arriving at and leaving a particular place: *It's hard to keep track of the kids' comings and goings.*
• *adj.* [only before noun] happening soon; next: *in the coming months* ◆ *This coming Sunday is her birthday.*

ˌcoming of ˈage *noun* [sing.] the time when a person reaches the age at which they have an adult's legal rights and responsibilities

ʌ cup   ə about   eɪ say   aɪ five   ɔɪ boy   aʊ now   oʊ go   ər bird

com·ma /'kɑmə/ *noun* the mark (,) used to separate the items in a list or to show where there is a slight pause in a sentence

com·mand 🖉 /kə'mænd/ *noun, verb*

● **noun**

> CONTROL **1** [U] control and authority over a situation or a group of people: *He has 1,200 men under his command.* ◆ *He has command of 1,200 men.* ◆ *The police arrived and took command of the situation.* ◆ *For the first time in years, she felt in command of her life.* ◆ *He looked relaxed and totally in command of himself.* ◆ *Who is in command here?* ⊃ see also SECOND IN COMMAND

> ORDER **2** [C] an order given to a person or an animal: *Begin when I give the command.* ◆ *You must obey the captain's commands.*

> FOR COMPUTER **3** [C] an instruction given to a computer

> IN ARMY **4** Command [C] a part of an army, AIR FORCE, etc. that is organized and controlled separately; a group of officers who give orders: *Strategic Air Command*

> KNOWLEDGE **5** [U, sing.] ~ (of sth) your knowledge of something; your ability to do or use something, especially a language: *Applicants will be expected to have (a) good command of English.*

IDM at your command if you have a skill or an amount of something at your command, you are able to use it well and completely be at sb's command (*formal*) to be ready to obey someone: *I'm at your command—what would you like me to do?* ⊃ more at WISH

● **verb**

> ORDER **1** [T] (of someone in a position of authority) to tell someone to do something ⊃ thesaurus box at ORDER: ~ sb to do sth *He commanded his men to retreat.* ◆ ~ sth *She commanded the release of the prisoners.* ◆ + speech *"Come here!" he commanded (them).* ◆ ~ that... (*formal*) *The commission intervened and commanded that work on the building cease.*

> IN ARMY **2** [T, I] ~ (sb/sth) to be in charge of a group of people in the army, navy, etc.: *The troops were commanded by General Haig.*

> DESERVE AND GET **3** [T, no passive] (not used in the progressive tenses) ~ sth to deserve and get something because of the special qualities you have: *to command sympathy/support* ◆ *She was able to command the respect of the class.* ◆ *The headlines commanded her attention.* ◆ *As a top lawyer, he can expect to command a six-figure salary.*

> VIEW **4** [T, no passive] (not used in the progressive tenses) ~ sth (*formal*) to be in a position from where you can see or control something: *The hotel commands a fine view of the valley.*

> CONTROL **5** [T, no passive] (not used in the progressive tenses) ~ sth (*formal*) to have control of something; to have something available for use: *The party was no longer able to command a majority in the Senate.* ◆ *the power commanded by the police*

com·man·dant /'kɑmən,dɑnt; -,dænt/ *noun* the officer in charge of a particular military group or institution

com·mand e·con·o·my *noun* = PLANNED ECONOMY

com·man·deer /,kɑmən'dɪr/ *verb* ~ sth to take control of a building, a vehicle, etc. for military purposes during a war, or by force for your own use SYN REQUISITION

com·mand·er /kə'mændər/ *noun* **1** a person who is in charge of something, especially an officer in charge of a particular group of soldiers or a military operation: *military/allied/field/flight commanders* ◆ *the commander of the expedition* **2** (*abbr.* Cdr) an officer of fairly high rank in the navy

com·mand·er-in-'chief (*abbr.* C-in-C) *noun* (*pl.* com·mand·ers-in-chief) the officer who commands all the armed forces of a country or all its forces in a particular area

com·mand·ing /kə'mændɪŋ/ *adj.* **1** [only before noun] in a position of authority that allows you to give formal orders: *Who is your commanding officer?* **2** [usually before noun] if you are in a **commanding position** or have a **commanding**

lead, you are likely to win a race or competition **3** [usually before noun] powerful and making people admire and obey you: *a commanding figure/presence/voice* **4** [only before noun] if a building is in a **commanding position** or has a **commanding view**, you can see the area around very well from it: *The castle occupies a commanding position on a hill.*

com·mand·ment /kə'mændmənt/ *noun* a law given by God, especially any of **the Ten Commandments** given to the Jews in the Bible ⊃ collocations at RELIGION

com'mand ,module *noun* the part of a SPACECRAFT that remains after the rest has separated from it, where the controls and the people that operate them are located

com·man·do /kə'mændoʊ/ *noun* (*pl.* com·man·dos) a soldier or a group of soldiers who are trained to make quick attacks in enemy areas

IDM go commando (*informal, humorous*) to not wear underwear under your clothes

com,mand per'formance *noun* [usually sing.] a special performance, for example at a theater, that is given for a head of state

com'mand post *noun* the place from which a military unit is commanded

com·me·dia dell'ar·te /kə,meɪdiə dɛl 'artei; -'arti/ *noun* [U] (from *Italian*) traditional Italian theater, in which the same characters appeared in different plays

com·mem·o·rate /kə'mɛmə,reɪt/ *verb* ~ sth to remind people of an important person or event from the past with a special action or object; to exist to remind people of a person or an event from the past: *A series of movies will be shown to commemorate the 30th anniversary of his death.* ◆ *A plaque commemorates the battle.*

com·mem·o·ra·tion /kə,mɛmə'reɪʃn/ *noun* [U, C] an action, or a ceremony, etc. that makes people remember and show respect for an important person or event in the past: *a commemoration service* ◆ *a statue in commemoration of a national hero*

com·mem·o·ra·tive /kə'mɛmrətɪv; -'mɛmərə-/ *adj.* intended to help people remember and respect an important person or event in the past: *commemorative stamps*

com·mence AWL /kə'mɛns/ *verb* [I, T] (*formal*) to begin to happen; to begin something: *The negotiations are scheduled to commence at noon.* ◆ *I will be on leave during the week commencing February 15th.* ◆ ~ with sth *The day commenced with a welcome from the principal.* ◆ ~ sth *She commenced her medical career in 1956.* ◆ ~ doing sth *We commence building next week.* ◆ ~ to do sth *Operators commenced to build pipelines in 1862.* ⊃ thesaurus box at START

com·mence·ment AWL /kə'mɛnsmənt/ *noun* [U, C, usually sing.] **1** (*formal*) beginning: *the commencement of the financial year* **2** a ceremony at which students receive their academic degrees or DIPLOMA SYN GRADUATION

com·mend /kə'mɛnd/ *verb* **1** ~ sb (for sth/for doing sth) | ~ sb (on sth/on doing sth) to praise someone or something, especially publicly: *She was commended on her handling of the situation.* ◆ *His designs were highly commended by the judges* (= they did not get a prize but they were especially praised). **2** ~ sb/sth (to sb) (*formal*) to recommend someone or something to someone: *She is an excellent worker and I commend her to you without reservation.* ◆ *The movie has little to commend it* (= it has few good qualities). **3** ~ itself to sb (*formal*) if something commends itself to someone, they approve of it: *His outspoken behavior did not commend itself to his colleagues.* **4** ~ sb/sth (to sb) (*formal*) to give someone or something to someone in order to be taken care of: *We commend her soul to God.*

com·mend·a·ble /kə'mɛndəbl/ *adj.* (*formal*) deserving praise and approval: *commendable behavior/honesty* ▶ **com·mend·a·bly** /-bli/ *adv.*

com·men·da·tion /,kɑmən'deɪʃn/ *noun* **1** [U] (*formal*) praise; approval **2** [C] ~ (for sth) an award or official statement giving public praise for someone or something: *a commendation for bravery*

com·men·sal /kəˈmensl/ *adj.* (*biology*) living on another animal or plant and getting food from the situation, but doing no harm: *commensal organisms* ▶ **com·men·sal·ism** /kəˈmensəˌlɪzəm/ *noun* [U]

com·men·su·rate /kəˈmensərət; -ʃərət/ *adj.* **~ (with sth)** (*formal*) matching something in size, importance, quality, etc.: *Salary will be commensurate with experience.* **ANT** INCOMMENSURATE ▶ **com·men·su·rate·ly** *adv.*

com·ment 🔑 **AWL** /ˈkament/ *noun, verb*

● *noun* **1** [C, U] **~ (about/on sth)** something that you say or write that gives an opinion on or explains someone or something: *Do you have any comments to make about the cause of the disaster?* ◆ *She made helpful comments on my essay.* ◆ *The director was not available for comment.* ◆ *He handed me the document without comment.* ◆ *What she said was a fair comment* (= a reasonable criticism). **2** [sing., U] criticism that shows the faults of something: *The results are a clear comment on government education policy.* ◆ *There was a lot of comment about his behavior.* **IDM** *no comment* (said in reply to a question, usually from a journalist) I have nothing to say about that: *"Will you resign, sir?" "No comment!"*

● *verb* [I, T] **~ (on/upon sth)** to express an opinion about something: *I don't feel I can comment on their decision.* ◆ *He refused to comment until after the trial.* ◆ **~ that...** *A spokesperson commented that levels of carbon dioxide were very high.* ◆ **+ speech** *"Not his best performance," she commented to the woman sitting next to her.*

THESAURUS

comment

note ◆ remark ◆ observe

These words all mean to say or write a fact or an opinion.

comment to express an opinion or give facts about something: *He refused to comment until after the trial.*

note (*somewhat formal*) to mention something because it is important or interesting: *He noted in passing that the company's record on safety issues was not good.*

remark to say or write what you have noticed about a situation: *He remarked that she had been looking tired lately.*

observe (*formal*) to say or write what you have noticed about a situation: *She observed that it was getting late.*

COMMENT, REMARK, OR OBSERVE?

If you **comment on** something, you say something about it; if you **remark on** something, or **observe** something, you say something about it that you have noticed: there is often not much difference between the three. However, while you can *refuse to comment* (*without on*), you cannot "refuse to remark" or "refuse to observe" (*without on*): ~~He refused to remark/observe until after the trial.~~

PATTERNS

▪ to comment/note/remark/observe **that**...
▪ to comment on/note/remark/observe **how**...
▪ to comment/remark **on** sth
▪ to comment/remark/observe **to** sb
▪ "It's long," he commented/noted/remarked/observed.

---

com·men·tar·y **AWL** /ˈkamənˌteri/ *noun* (*pl.* **commen·taries**) **~ (on sth)** **1** [C, U] a spoken description of an event that is given while it is happening, especially on the radio or television: *a sports commentary* ◆ *Our reporters will give a running commentary* (= a continuous one) *on the election results as they are announced.* ◆ *He kept up a running commentary on everyone who came in or went out.* **2** [C] a written explanation or discussion of something such as a book or a play: *a critical commentary on the final speech of the*

play **3** [C, U] a criticism or discussion of something: *The petty arguments were a sad commentary on the state of the government.* ◆ *political commentary*

com·men·tate /ˈkamənˌteɪt/ *verb* [I] **~ (on sth)** to give a spoken description of an event as it happens, especially on television or radio: *Who will be commentating on the game?*

com·men·ta·tor **AWL** /ˈkamənˌteɪtər/ *noun* **~ (on sth)** **1** a person who is an expert on a particular subject and talks or writes about it on television or radio, or in a newspaper: *a political commentator* **2** a person who describes an event while it is happening, especially on television or radio: *a television/sports commentator*

com·merce /ˈkamərs/ *noun* [U] trade, especially between countries; the buying and selling of goods and services: *leaders of industry and commerce* ➔ see also CHAMBER OF COMMERCE

com·mer·cial 🔑 /kəˈmərʃl/ *adj., noun*

● *adj.* **1** [usually before noun] connected with the buying and selling of goods and services: *the commercial heart of the city* ◆ *a commercial vehicle* (= one that is used for carrying goods or passengers who pay) ◆ *commercial baby foods* ◆ *the first commercial flights across the Atlantic* ➔ thesaurus box at ECONOMIC **2** [only before noun] making or intended to make a profit: *The movie was not a commercial success* (= did not make money). ➔ thesaurus box at SUCCESSFUL **3** (*disapproving*) more concerned with profit and being popular than with quality: *Their more recent music is far too commercial.* **4** (of television or radio) paid for by the money charged for broadcasting advertisements: *a commercial radio station/TV channel* ➔ collocations at TELEVISION ▶ **com·mer·cial·ly** /-ʃəli/ *adv.*: *commercially produced/grown/developed* ◆ *The product is not yet commercially available.* ◆ *His invention was not commercially successful.*

● *noun* an advertisement on the radio or on television ➔ thesaurus box at ADVERTISEMENT

com'mercial ˌbank *noun* a bank that offers services to the general public and to businesses

com·mercial ˈbreak *noun* a pause for advertisements in the middle of a television or radio program

com·mer·cial·ism /kəˈmərʃəˌlɪzəm/ *noun* [U] (*disapproving*) the fact of being more interested in making money than in the value or quality of things

com·mer·cial·ize /kəˈmərʃəˌlaɪz/ *verb* [often passive] **~ sth** to use something to try to make a profit, especially in a way that other people do not approve of: *Their music has become very commercialized in recent years.* ▶ **com·mer·cial·i·za·tion** /kəˌmərʃələˈzeɪʃn/ *noun* [U]

com·mie /ˈkami/ *noun* an insulting way of referring to someone that you think has ideas similar to those of COMMUNIST or SOCIALIST, or who is a member of a COMMUNIST or SOCIALIST party

com·min·gle /kəˈmɪŋgl/ *verb* [I, T] (*formal* or *technical*) to mix two or more things together or to be mixed, when it is impossible for the things to be separated afterward: **~ (with sth)** *The fluid must be prevented from commingling with other fluids.* ◆ **~ sth (with sth)** (*finance*) *Campaign funds must not be commingled with other money.*

com·mis·er·ate /kəˈmɪzəˌreɪt/ *verb* [I, T] **~ (with sb) (on/about/for/over sth)** | **+ speech** to show someone sympathy when they are upset or disappointed about something: *She commiserated with the losers on their defeat.*

com·mis·er·a·tion /kəˌmɪzəˈreɪʃn/ *noun* [U, C] (*formal*) an expression of sympathy for someone who has had something unpleasant happen to them, especially not winning a competition: *I offered him my commiseration.* ◆ *Commiserations to the losing team!*

com·mis·sar /ˈkaməˌsar/ *noun* an officer of the Communist Party, especially in the past in the Soviet Union

com·mis·sar·y /ˈkaməˌseri/ *noun* (*pl.* **com·mis·sar·ies**) **1** a store that sells food, etc. in a military base, a prison, etc. **2** a

---

t **tea**   t̬ **butter**   d **did**   k **cat**   ɡ **got**   tʃ **chin**   dʒ **June**   f **fall** restaurant for people working in a large organization, especially a movie studio

com·mis·sion `AWL` /kəˈmɪʃn/ noun, verb

● **noun**

> **OFFICIAL GROUP 1** often **Commission** [C] an official group of people who have been given responsibility to control something, or to find out about something, usually for the government: *the Public Service Commission* ♦ *a commission on human rights*

> **MONEY 2** [U, C] an amount of money that is paid to someone for selling goods and which increases with the amount of goods that are sold: *You get a 10% commission on everything you sell.* ♦ *He earned $2,000 in commission last month.* ♦ *In this job you work **on commission** (= are paid according to the amount you sell).* **3** [U] an amount of money that is charged by a bank, etc. for providing a particular service: *A 1% commission is charged for exchanging money.*

> **FOR ART/MUSIC, ETC. 4** [C] a formal request to someone to design or make a piece of work such as a building or a painting

> **IN ARMED FORCES 5** [C] an officer's position in the armed forces

> **OF CRIME 6** [U] (*formal*) the act of doing something wrong or illegal: *the commission of a crime*

IDM in/out of commission available/not available to be used: *Several of the airline's planes are temporarily out of commission and undergoing safety checks.*

● **verb**

> **PIECE OF ART/MUSIC, ETC. 1** to officially ask someone to write, make, or create something or to do a task for you: *~ sb to do sth She has been commissioned to write a new state song.* ♦ *~ sth Publishers have commissioned a French translation of the book.*

> **IN ARMED FORCES 2** [usually passive] to choose someone as an officer in one of the armed forces: *~ sb She was commissioned in 2007.* ♦ *~ sb (as sth) He has just been commissioned (as a naval officer).*

com·missioned ˈofficer noun an officer in the armed forces who has a higher rank, such as a captain or a **GENERAL** ◯ compare **NONCOMMISSIONED OFFICER**

com·mis·sion·er `AWL` /kəˈmɪʃənər/ noun **1** usually **Commissioner** a member of a **COMMISSION** (= an official group of people who are responsible for controlling something or finding out about something): *the Securities and Exchange Commissioner* ♦ *planning commissioners* **2** (also **poˈlice comˌmissioner**) the head of a particular police force in some countries **3** the head of a government department in some countries: *the **agriculture/health**, etc. commissioner* ♦ *Commissioner Rhodes was unavailable for comment.* ◯ see also **HIGH COMMISSIONER 4** an official chosen by a sports association to control it: *the baseball commissioner*

the Comˌmission on ˌCivil ˈRights noun [sing.] a government organization that works for equal rights for all Americans

com·mit `AWL` /kəˈmɪt/ verb (-tt-)

> **CRIME 1** [T] *~ a crime, etc.* to do something wrong or illegal: *to **commit murder/adultery**, etc.* ♦ *Most crimes are committed by young men.* ♦ *appalling crimes committed against innocent children*

> **SUICIDE 2** [T] *~ suicide* to kill yourself deliberately

> **PROMISE/SAY DEFINITELY 3** [T, often passive] to promise sincerely that you will definitely do something, keep to an agreement or arrangement, etc.: *~ sb/yourself (to sth/to doing sth) The President is committed to reforming health care.* ♦ *Borrowers should think carefully before committing themselves to taking out a loan.* ♦ *~ sb/yourself to do sth Both sides committed themselves to settle the dispute peacefully.* **4** [T] *~ yourself (to sth)* to give an opinion or make a decision openly so that it is then difficult to change it: *You don't have to commit yourself now, just think about it.* ◯ see also **NONCOMMITTAL**

> **BE LOYAL 5** [I] *~ (to sb/sth)* to be completely loyal to one

person, organization, etc. or give all your time and effort to your work, an activity, etc.: *Why are so many men scared to commit?* (= say they will be loyal to one person) ◯ see also **COMMITTED**

> **MONEY/TIME 6** [T] *~ sth* to spend money or time on something or someone: *The mayor has committed large amounts of money to housing projects.*

> **TO HOSPITAL/PRISON 7** [T, often passive] *~ sb to sth* to order someone to be sent to a hospital, prison, etc.: *She was committed to a psychiatric hospital.*

> **SOMETHING TO MEMORY 8** [T] *~ something to memory* to learn something well enough to remember it exactly: *She committed the instructions to memory.*

> **SOMETHING TO PAPER/WRITING 9** [T] *~ something to paper/writing* to write something down

com·mit·ment `AWL` /kəˈmɪtmənt/ noun

1 [C, U] a promise to do something or to behave in a particular way; a promise to support someone or something; the fact of committing yourself: *~ (to sb/sth) She doesn't want to **make a big emotional commitment** to Steve at the moment.* ♦ *the government's commitment to public services* ♦ *~ to do/doing sth The company's commitment to providing quality at a reasonable price has been vital to its success.* **2** [U] *~ (to sb/sth)* the willingness to work hard and give your energy and time to a job or an activity: *A career as an actor requires one hundred percent commitment.* **3** [C] a thing that you have promised or agreed to do, or that you have to do: *He's busy for the next month with professional commitments.* ♦ *Women very often have to juggle work with their family commitments.* **4** [U, C] *~ (of sth) (to sth)* agreeing to use money, time, or people in order to achieve something: *the commitment of resources to education* ♦ *Achieving success at this level requires a commitment of time and energy.*

com·mit·tal /kəˈmɪtl/ noun **1** [U] (*technical*) the official process of sending someone to prison or to a mental hospital: *He was released on bail pending committal proceedings.* **2** [C] (*formal*) the act or ceremony of burying a dead body in a grave

com·mit·ted `AWL` /kəˈmɪtəd/ adj. (*approving*) willing to work hard and give your time and energy to something; believing strongly in something: *a committed member of the team* ♦ *They are committed socialists.* **ANT UNCOMMITTED**

com·mit·tee /kəˈmɪti/ noun

a group of people who are chosen, usually by a larger group, to make decisions or to deal with a particular subject: *She's on the management committee.* ♦ *The committee has decided to close the restaurant.* ♦ *a committee member/a member of the committee* ♦ *a committee meeting* ◯ see also **CONFERENCE COMMITTEE**

com·mode /kəˈmoʊd/ noun **1** a piece of furniture that looks like a chair but has a toilet under the seat **2** a toilet. People say "commode" to avoid saying "toilet". **3** a piece of furniture, especially an old or **ANTIQUE** one, with drawers for storing things in

com·mo·di·ous /kəˈmoʊdiəs/ adj. (*formal*) having a lot of space

com·mod·i·ty `AWL` /kəˈmɑdəti/ noun (pl. **com·mod·i·ties**) **1** (*economics*) a product or a raw material that can be bought and sold: *rice, flour and other basic commodities* ♦ *a drop in commodity prices* ♦ *Crude oil is the world's most important commodity.* ◯ thesaurus box at **PRODUCT 2** a thing that is useful or has a useful quality: *Water is a precious commodity that is often taken for granted in the West.*

com·mo·dore /ˈkɑmədɔr/ noun (abbr. **Com.**) **1** an officer of high rank in the navy: *Commodore John Barry* **2** the head of a **YACHT** club **3** a captain of a group of ships carrying commercial goods

com·mon /ˈkɑmən/ adj., noun

● **adj.** (**com·mon·er**, **com·mon·est**) **HELP** more common and most common are more frequent **1** happening often; existing in large numbers or in many places: *Jackson is a common American name.* ♦ *Breast cancer is the most common*

form of cancer among women in this country. ◆ Some birds which were once a common sight are now becoming rare. ◆ a common spelling mistake ANT UNCOMMON 2 [usually before noun] ~ (to sb/sth) shared by or belonging to two or more people or by the people in a group: They share a common interest in photography. ◆ basic features which are common to all human languages ◆ We are working together for a common purpose. ◆ common ownership of the land ◆ This decision was made for the common good (= the advantage of everyone). ◆ It is, by common consent, Oregon's prettiest bay (= everyone agrees that it is). 3 [only before noun] ordinary; not unusual or special: the common garden frog ◆ Shakespeare's work was popular among the common people in his day. ◆ In most people's eyes she was nothing more than a common criminal. ◆ You'd think he'd have the common courtesy to apologize (= this would be the polite behavior that people would expect). ◆ It's only common decency to let her know what's happening (= people would expect it).
IDM the common touch the ability of a powerful or famous person to talk to and understand ordinary people make common cause with sb (formal) to be united with someone about something that you both agree on, believe in, or wish to achieve ⊃ more at KNOWLEDGE
● noun 1 [C] an area of open land in a town or village that anyone may use: We went for a walk on the common. ◆ Little Compton Common 2 commons [sing.] a large room where students can eat in a school, college, etc.: The commons is next to the gym.
IDM have sth in common (with sb) (of people) to have the same interests, ideas, etc. as someone else: Tim and I have nothing in common./I have nothing in common with Tim. have sth in common (with sth) (of things, places, etc.) to have the same features, characteristics, etc.: The two cultures have a lot in common. in common (technical) by everyone in a group: They hold the property as tenants in common. in common with sb/sth (formal) in the same way as someone or something: The U.S., in common with many other industrialized countries, has experienced major changes over the last 100 years.

the ˌcommon ˈcold noun [sing.] = COLD n. (2)

ˌcommon deˈnominator noun 1 (mathematics) a number that can be divided exactly by all the numbers below the line in a set of FRACTIONS ⊃ compare DENOMINATOR 2 an idea, attitude, or experience that is shared by all the members of a group ⊃ see also LOWEST COMMON DENOMINATOR

com·mon·er /ˈkɑmənər/ noun a person who does not come from a royal or NOBLE family ⊃ compare ARISTOCRAT

ˌCommon ˈEra noun [sing.] (abbr. C.E.) the period since the birth of Christ when the Christian CALENDAR starts counting years

ˌcommon ˈfraction noun a FRACTION (= a number less than one) that is shown as numbers above and below a line: ⅔ and ⅝ are common fractions. ⊃ compare DECIMAL FRACTION

ˌcommon ˈground noun [U] opinions, interests, and aims that you share with someone, although you may not agree with them about other things: Despite our disagreements, we have been able to find some common ground.

ˌcommon ˈlaw noun [U] a system of laws that have been developed from customs and from decisions made by judges, not created by Congress ⊃ compare CASE LAW, STATUTE LAW

ˌcommon-law ˈhusband, ˌcommon-law ˈwife noun a person that a woman or man has lived with for a long time and who is recognized as a husband or wife, without a formal marriage ceremony

com·mon·ly ✎ /ˈkɑmənli/ adv.
usually; very often; by most people: Christopher is commonly known as Kit. ◆ commonly held opinions ◆ This is one of the most commonly used methods.

ˌcommon ˈmarket noun [usually sing.] a group of countries that have agreed on low taxes on goods traded between countries in the group, and higher fixed taxes on goods imported from countries outside the group

ˌcommon ˈnoun noun (grammar) a word such as table, cat, or sea, that refers to an object or a thing but is not the name of a particular person, place, or thing ⊃ compare ABSTRACT NOUN, PROPER NOUN

com·mon·place /ˈkɑmənˌpleɪs/ adj., noun
● adj. done very often, or existing in many places, and therefore not unusual: Computers are now commonplace in elementary school classrooms.
● noun (formal) 1 [usually sing.] an event, etc. that happens very often and is not unusual 2 a remark, etc. that is not new or interesting SYN CLICHÉ

ˈcommonplace ˌbook noun (especially in the past) a book into which you copy parts of other books, poems, etc. and add your own comments

ˌcommon ˈrat noun = BROWN RAT

ˌcommon ˈroom noun a room used by the teachers or students of a school, college, etc. when they are not teaching or studying

ˌcommon ˈsense noun [U] the ability to think about things in a practical way and make sensible decisions: He may be academic, but he has no common sense! ◆ a common-sense approach to a problem

com·mon·wealth /ˈkɑmənˌwɛlθ/ noun [sing.] 1 usually the Commonwealth used in the official names of, and to refer to, some states (Kentucky, Massachusetts, Pennsylvania, and Virginia): the Commonwealth of Virginia ◆ The city and the Commonwealth have lost a great leader. 2 an independent area that is strongly connected to the U.S.: Puerto Rico remains a U.S. commonwealth, not a state. 3 usually Commonwealth used in the names of some groups of countries or states that have chosen to be politically linked with each other: the Commonwealth of Independent States (CIS) 4 the Commonwealth an organization consisting of the United Kingdom and most of the countries that used to be part of the British Empire: a member of the Commonwealth ◆ Commonwealth countries

com·mo·tion /kəˈmoʊʃn/ noun [C, usually sing., U] sudden noisy confusion or excitement: I heard a commotion and went to see what was happening. ◆ The crowd waiting outside was causing a commotion.

com·mu·nal /kəˈmyunl/ adj. 1 shared by, or for the use of, a number of people, especially people who live together: a communal kitchen/garden, etc. ◆ As a student he tried communal living for a few years. 2 involving different groups of people in a community: communal violence between religious groups ▶ com·mu·nal·ly /-nəli/ adv.: The property was owned communally.

com·mu·nal·ism /kəˈmyunəˌlɪzəm/ noun [U] the fact of living together and sharing possessions and responsibilities

com·mune noun, verb
● noun /ˈkɑmyun/ a group of people who live together and share responsibilities, possessions, etc.: a 1970s hippy commune
● verb /kəˈmyun/
PHR V comˈmune with sb/sth (formal) to share your emotions and feelings with someone or something without speaking; to be in close spiritual contact with someone or something: He spent much of this time communing with nature.

com·mu·ni·ca·ble AWL /kəˈmyunɪkəbl/ adj. 1 (of a disease) that someone can pass on to other people: communicable diseases such as measles and chicken pox 2 (formal) that someone can communicate to someone else

com·mu·ni·cant /kəˈmyunɪkənt/ noun a person who receives COMMUNION in a Christian church service

com·mu·ni·cate ✎ AWL /kəˈmyunəˌkeɪt/ verb
▷EXCHANGE INFORMATION 1 [I, T] to exchange information,

h hat　　m man　　n no　　ŋ sing　　l leg　　r red　　y yes　　w wet

news, ideas, etc. with someone: *We only communicate by e-mail.* ♦ *They communicated in sign language.* ♦ **~ with sb/sth** *Dolphins use sound to communicate with each other.* ♦ **~ sth (to sb)** *to communicate information/a message to someone* ⭢ **thesaurus box at** TALK

➤ **SHARE IDEAS/FEELINGS 2** [I, T] to make your ideas, feelings, thoughts, etc. known to other people so that they understand them: *Candidates must be able to communicate effectively.* ♦ **~ sth (to sb)** *He was eager to communicate his ideas to the group.* ♦ *Her nervousness was communicating itself to the children.* ♦ **~ how/what, etc...** *They failed to communicate what was happening and why.* **3** [I] **~ (with sb)** to have a good relationship because you are able to understand and talk about your own and other people's thoughts, feelings, etc.: *The novel is about a family who can't communicate with each other.*

➤ **DISEASE 4** [T, usually passive] **~ sth** to pass a disease from one person, animal, etc. to another: *The disease is communicated through dirty drinking water.*

com·mu·ni·ca·tion 🔑 **AWL** /kəˌmyunəˈkeɪʃn/ *noun*

1 [U] the activity or process of expressing ideas and feelings or of giving people information: *Speech is the fastest method of communication between people.* ♦ *All channels of communication need to be kept open.* ♦ *Doctors do not always have good **communication skills**.* ♦ *nonverbal communication* ♦ *We are in regular communication by mail.* **2** [U] also **communications** [pl.] methods of sending information, especially telephones, radio, computers, etc. or roads, and railroads: ***communication systems/links/technology*** ♦ *The new airport will improve communications between the islands.* ♦ *Snow has prevented communication with the outside world for three days.* **3** [C] (*formal*) a message, letter or telephone call: *a communication from the president of the company*

com·mu·ni·ca·tive **AWL** /kəˈmyunɪkətɪv; kəˈmyunəˌkeɪtɪv/ *adj.* **1** willing to talk and give information to other people: *I don't find him very communicative.* **ANT** UNCOMMUNICATIVE **2** connected with the ability to communicate in a language, especially a foreign language: *communicative skills*

the com·ˈmunicative apˌproach *noun* [sing.] (also **com·ˌmunicative ˈlanguage ˌteaching** [U]) a method of teaching a foreign language which stresses the importance of learning to communicate information and ideas in the language

com·ˌmunicative ˈcompetence *noun* [U] (*linguistics*) a person's ability to communicate information and ideas in a foreign language

com·mu·ni·ca·tor /kəˈmyunəˌkeɪtər/ *noun* a person who communicates something to others: *an effective/skilled/successful communicator* ♦ *a poor communicator* ⭢ **thesaurus box at** SPEAKER

com·mun·ion /kəˈmyunyən/ *noun* **1** (also **Com·mun·ion**, **ˌHoly Comˈmunion**) [U] a ceremony in the Christian Church during which people eat bread and drink wine in memory of the last meal that Christ had with his DISCIPLES: *to go to Communion* (= attend church for this celebration) ♦ *to take/receive communion* (= receive the bread and wine) ⭢ **see also** EUCHARIST, MASS **2** [U] **~ (with sb/sth)** (*formal*) the state of sharing or exchanging thoughts and feelings; the feeling of being part of something: *poets living in communion with nature* **3** [C] (*technical*) a group of people with the same religious beliefs: *the Anglican communion*

com·mu·ni·qué /kəˌmyunəˈkeɪ; kəˈmyunəˌkeɪ/ *noun* an official statement or report, especially to newspapers

com·mu·nism /ˈkɑmyəˌnɪzəm/ *noun* [U] **1** a political movement that believes in an economic system in which the state controls the means of producing everything on behalf of the people. It aims to create a society in which everyone is treated equally. **2 Communism** the system of government by a ruling Communist Party, such as in the former Soviet Union ⭢ **compare** CAPITALISM

com·mu·nist /ˈkɑmyənɪst/ *noun* **1** a person who believes in

or supports communism **2 Com·mu·nist** a member of a Communist Party ▶ **com·mu·nist** (also **Com·mu·nist**) *adj.*: *communist ideology* ♦ *a Communist country/government/leader*

the ˌCommunist ˈParty *noun* a political party that supports COMMUNISM or rules in a COMMUNIST country

com·mu·ni·ty 🔑 **AWL** /kəˈmyunəti/ *noun* (*pl.* **com·mu·ni·ties**) **1** [sing.] all the people who live in a particular area, country, etc. when talked about as a group: *The local community was shocked by the murders.* ♦ *health workers based in the community* (= working with people in a local area) ♦ ***the international community*** (= the countries of the world as a group) ♦ *good community relations with the police* ♦ ***community parks/libraries*** (= paid for by the local town/city) **2** [C] a group of people who share the same religion, race, job, etc.: *the Polish community in Chicago* ♦ *ethnic communities* ♦ *a farming community* **3** [U] the feeling of sharing things and belonging to a group in the place where you live: *There is a strong sense of community in this town.* ♦ ***community spirit*** ⭢ **collocations at** TOWN **4** [C] (*biology*) a group of plants and animals growing or living in the same place or environment

comˈmunity ˌcenter (*CanE usually* **comˈmunity ˌcentre**) *noun* a place where people from the same area can meet for social events or sports or to take classes

comˌmunity ˈcollege *noun* a college that is mainly for students from the local community and that offers programs that are two years long, including programs in practical skills

comˌmunity ˈgarden *noun* a large outdoor space where people have their own piece of land on which to grow flowers, vegetables, etc.

comˌmunity ˈproperty *noun* [U] (*law*) property that is considered to belong equally to a married couple

comˌmunity ˈservice *noun* [U] work helping people in the local community that someone does without being paid, because they want to, because it is part of their school work, or because they have been ordered to by a court as a punishment

comˌmunity ˈtheater *noun* [U] the activity of producing and acting in plays for the theater, by people who do it for enjoyment, not as a job: *Have you done community theater?*

com·mut·a·ble /kəˈmyutəbl/ *adj.* **1** (of a place or a distance) close enough or short enough to make traveling to work every day a possibility **2** (*law*) a **commutable** punishment can be made less severe **3** (*formal*) able to be changed

com·mu·ta·tion /ˌkɑmyəˈteɪʃn/ *noun* [C, U] **1** (*law*) the act of making a punishment less severe: *a commutation of the death sentence to life imprisonment* **2** (*finance*) the act of replacing one method of payment with another; a payment that is replaced with another

com·mu·ta·tive /ˈkɑmyəˌteɪtɪv; kəˈmyutətɪv/ *adj.* (*mathematics*) (of a calculation) giving the same result whatever the order in which the quantities are shown

com·mu·ta·tor /ˈkɑmyəˌteɪtər/ *noun* (*physics*) **1** a device that connects a motor to the electricity supply **2** a device for changing the direction in which electricity flows

com·mute /kəˈmyut/ *verb, noun*

● *verb* **1** [I, T] to travel regularly by bus, train, car, etc. between your place of work and your home: **~ (from A) (to B)** *She commutes from Palo Alto to San Francisco every day.* ♦ **~ between A and B** *He spent that year commuting between New York and Chicago.* ♦ *I live **within commuting distance** of Atlanta.* ♦ **~ sth** *People are prepared to commute long distances if they are desperate for work.* **2** [T] **~ sth (to sth)** (*law*) to replace one punishment with another that is less severe **3** [T] **~ sth (for/into sth)** (*finance*) to exchange one form of payment for something else

● *noun* the trip that a person makes when they commute to work: *a two-hour commute into downtown Washington* ♦ *I have only a short commute to work.* ⭢ **thesaurus box at** TRIP

| i **see** | ɪ **sit** | ɛ **ten** | æ **cat** | ɑ **hot** | ɔ **saw** | ʊ **put** | u **too** | 295 |

com·mut·er /kəˈmyutər/ noun a person who travels into a city to work each day

comp /kɑmp/ noun, verb
● **noun** (informal) **1** [C] a COMPLIMENTARY ticket, meal, etc. (= one that you do not have to pay for) **2** [U] = COMPEN-SATION: *comp time* (= time off work given for working extra hours)
● **verb** ~ **sb/sth** (informal) to give something away to someone for free: *The management did graciously comp our wine selection.* ◆ *The show's director asked us to comp several of his friends for this evening's performance.*

com·pact adj., noun, verb
● **adj.** /kəmˈpækt; ˈkɑmpækt/ **1** smaller than is usual for things of the same kind: *a compact camera* **2** using or filling only a small amount of space: *The kitchen was compact but well equipped.* **3** closely and firmly packed together: *a compact mass of earth* **4** (of a person or an animal) small and strong: *He had a compact and muscular body.* ▸ **com·pact·ly** adv. **com·pact·ness** noun [U]
● **noun** /ˈkɑmpækt/ **1** a small car ⊃ compare SUBCOMPACT **2** a small flat box with a mirror, containing powder that women use on their faces ⊃ picture at MAKEUP **3** (formal) a formal agreement between two or more people or countries
● **verb** /kəmˈpækt/ [usually passive] ~ **sth** to press something together firmly: *a layer of compacted snow*

ˌcompact ˈdisc noun = CD

com·pact·or (also **com·pact·er**) /kəmˈpæktər; ˈkɑm-/ noun a machine that crushes or presses trash together

com·pa·dre /kəmˈpɑdreɪ/ noun (from Spanish, informal) used as a friendly way of addressing someone

com·pan·ion /kəmˈpænyən/ noun **1** a person or an animal that travels with you or spends a lot of time with you: *traveling companions* ◆ (figurative) *Fear was the hostages' constant companion.* **2** a person who has similar tastes, interests, etc. to your own and whose company you enjoy: *She was a charming dinner companion.* ◆ *His younger brother is not much of a companion for him.* ◆ *They're drinking companions* (= they go out drinking together). **3** a person who shares in your work, pleasures, sadness, etc.: *We became companions in misfortune.* **4** a person, usually a woman, employed to live with and help someone, especially someone old or sick **5** one of a pair of things that go together or can be used together: *A companion volume is soon to be published.* **6** used in book titles to describe a book giving useful facts and information on a particular subject: *A Companion to French Literature* ⊃ see also BOON COM-PANION

com·pan·ion·a·ble /kəmˈpænyənəbl/ adj. friendly ▸ **com·pan·ion·a·bly** /-bli/ adv.

com·pan·ion·ship /kəmˈpænyənˌʃɪp/ noun [U] the pleasant feeling that you have when you have a friendly relationship with someone and are not alone: *They meet at the club for companionship and advice.* ◆ *She had only her cat for companionship.*

com·pan·ion·way /kəmˈpænyənˌweɪ/ noun (technical) a set of stairs on a ship

com·pa·ny 🔑 /ˈkʌmpəni/ noun (pl. **com·pan·ies**)
▷ BUSINESS **1** [C] (abbr. Co.) (often in names) a business organization that makes money by producing or selling goods or services: *the largest computer company in the world* ◆ *the National Bus Company* ◆ *She joined the company in 2009.* ◆ *Mike gets a company car with his new job* (= one that the company pays for). ◆ *Company profits were 5% lower than last year.* ⊃ collocations at BUSINESS
▷ THEATER/DANCE **2** (often in names) [C] a group of people who work or perform together: *a theater/dance, etc. company* ◆ *the Steppenwolf Theater Company*
▷ BEING WITH SOMEONE **3** [U] the fact of being with someone else and not alone: *I enjoy Jo's company* (= I enjoy being with her). ◆ *The children are very good company* (= pleasant to be

with) *at this age.* ◆ *a pleasant evening in the company of friends* ◆ *He's coming with me for company.*
▷ GUESTS **4** [U] guests in your house: *I didn't realize you had company.*
▷ GROUP OF PEOPLE **5** [U] (formal) a group of people together: *She told the assembled company what had happened.* ◆ *It is bad manners to whisper in company* (= in a group of people).
▷ SOLDIERS **6** [C] a group of soldiers that is part of a BAT-TALION
IDM **the company sb keeps** the people that someone spends time with: *Judging by the company he kept, Mark must have been a wealthy man.* **get into/keep bad company** to be friends with people that others disapprove of **in company with sb/sth** (formal) together with or at the same time as someone or something: *She arrived in company with the ship's captain.* ◆ *The U.S. dollar went through a difficult time, in company with the oil market.* **in good company** if you say that someone is **in good company**, you mean that they should not worry about a mistake, etc. because someone else, especially someone more important, has done the same thing **keep sb company** to stay with someone so that they are not alone: *I'll keep you company while you're waiting.* ⊃ more at PART, PRESENT, TWO

ˈcompany ˌcar noun a car that is provided by the company that you work for

ˈcompany ˌtown noun a town or city where most of the people work for one company, which supports the whole economy of the area

com·pa·ra·ble /ˈkɑmpərəbl/ adj. ~ **(to/with sb/sth)** similar to someone or something else and able to be compared: *A comparable house in the south of the city would cost twice as much.* ◆ *The situation in the U.S. is not directly comparable to that in the U.K.* ◆ *Inflation is now at a rate comparable with that in other developed countries.* ▸ **com·pa·ra·bil·i·ty** /ˌkɑmpərəˈbɪləti/ noun [U]: *Each group will have the same set of questions, in order to ensure comparability.*

com·par·a·tive /kəmˈpærətɪv/ adj., noun
● **adj.** **1** connected with studying things to find out how similar or different they are: *a comparative study of the educational systems of two countries* ◆ *comparative linguistics* **2** measured or judged by how similar or different it is to something else SYN RELATIVE: *Then he was living in comparative comfort* (= compared with others or with his own life at a previous time). ◆ *The company is a comparative newcomer to the software market* (= other companies have been in business much longer). **3** (grammar) relating to adjectives or adverbs that express more in amount, degree, or quality, for example *better, worse, slower,* and *more difficult* ⊃ compare SUPERLATIVE
● **noun** (grammar) the form of an adjective or adverb that expresses more in amount, degree, or quality: *"Better" is the comparative of "good" and "more difficult" is the comparative of "difficult".* ⊃ compare SUPERLATIVE

comˌparative ˈliterature noun [U] an area of study that involves reading books from different parts of the world, comparing their themes and styles, and focusing on the influence that one country's literature has on the others

com·par·a·tive·ly /kəmˈpærətɪvli/ adv. as compared to something or someone else SYN RELATIVELY: *The unit is comparatively easy to install and cheap to operate.* ◆ *He died comparatively young* (= at a younger age than most people die). ◆ *comparatively few/low/rare/recent*

com·pare 🔑 /kəmˈpɛr/ verb, noun
● **verb** **1** (abbr. cf., cp.) [T] to examine people or things to see how they are similar and how they are different: ~ **A and B** *It is interesting to compare their situation and ours.* ◆ *We compared the two reports carefully.* ◆ ~ **A with/to B** *We carefully compared the first report with the second.* ◆ *My own problems seem insignificant compared with other people's.* ◆ *Standards in health care have improved enormously compared to 40 years ago.* ⊃ language bank at CONTRAST, ILLUSTRATE **2** [I] ~ **with/to sb/sth** to be similar to someone or something else, either better or worse: *This school compares*

with the best in the country (= it is as good as them). ♦ *This house doesn't compare with our previous one* (= it is not as good). ♦ *I've had some difficulties, but they were **nothing compared to** yours* (= they were not nearly as bad as yours). ♦ *Their prices **compare favorably** with those of their competitors.* **3** [T] **~ A to B** to show or state that someone or something is similar to someone or something else: *The critics compared his work to that of Faulkner.*

IDM **compare notes (with sb)** if two or more people **compare notes**, they each say what they think about the same event, situation, etc. **you can't compare apples and oranges** it is impossible to say that one thing is better than another if the two are completely different: *They are both great but you can't compare apples and oranges.*

● *noun*
IDM **beyond/without compare** (*literary*) better than anything else of the same kind

com·par·i·son 🔑 /kəmˈpærəsn/ *noun*
1 [U] **~ (with sb/sth)** the process of comparing two or more people or things: *Comparison with other oil-producing countries is extremely interesting.* ♦ *I enclose the two plans **for comparison**.* ♦ *The education system **bears no comparison** with that in many European countries* (= it is not as good). **2** [C] an occasion when two or more people or things are compared: **~ of A and B** *A comparison of the rail systems in Japan and the U.S.* ♦ **~ of A with B** *A comparison of men's salaries with those of women* ♦ **~ between A and B** *comparisons between Connecticut and the rest of New England* ♦ **~ of A to B** *a comparison of the brain to a computer* (= showing what is similar) ♦ **~ (with sth)** *It is difficult to **make a comparison** with her previous book—they are completely different.* ♦ *You can **draw comparisons** with the situation in Texas* (= say how the two situations are similar). ⊃ language bank at SIMILARLY
IDM **by comparison** used especially at the beginning of a sentence when the next thing that is mentioned is compared with something in the previous sentence: *By comparison, expenditure on education increased last year.* **by/ in comparison (with sb/sth)** when compared with someone or something: *The second half of the game was dull by comparison with the first.* ♦ *The tallest buildings in Boston are small in comparison with New York's skyscrapers.* **there's no comparison** used to emphasize the difference between two people or things that are being compared: *In terms of price there's no comparison* (= one thing is much more expensive than the other). ⊃ more at PALE

com·parison-ˌshop *verb* (-pp-) [I] to go from one store to another and compare their prices on similar items, so that you can pay the least amount of money for something

com·part·ment /kəmˈpɑrtmənt/ *noun* **1** one of the separate sections that something such as a piece of furniture or equipment has for keeping things in: *The desk has a secret compartment.* ♦ *There is a handy storage compartment beneath the oven.* ⊃ see also GLOVE COMPARTMENT **2** one of the separate sections which a car on a train is divided into

com·part·men·tal·ize /kəmˌpɑrtˈmɛntlˌaɪz; ˌkɑmpɑrt-/ *verb* **~ sth (into sth)** to divide something into separate sections, especially so that one thing does not affect the other: *Life today is rigidly compartmentalized into work and leisure.*

com·pass /ˈkʌmpəs/ *noun* **1** (also **magˌnetic ˈcompass**) [C] an instrument for finding direction, with a needle that always points to the north: *a map and compass* ♦ *the **points of the compass*** (= N., S., E., W., etc.) **2** [C] (also **compasses** [pl.]) an instrument with two long thin parts joined together at the top, used for drawing circles and measuring distances on a map **3** [sing.] (*formal*) a range or an extent, especially of what can be achieved in a particular situation: *the compass of a singer's voice* (= the range from the lowest to the highest note that he or she can sing)

com·pas·sion /kəmˈpæʃn/ *noun* [U] **~ (for sb)** a strong

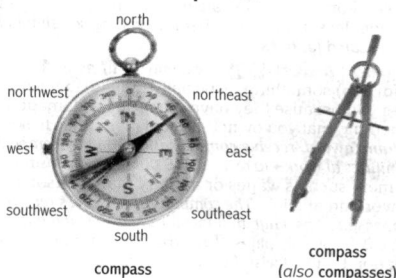

compasses

north
northwest   northeast
west   east
southwest   southeast
south

compass

compass
(*also* compasses)

feeling of sympathy for people who are suffering and a desire to help them: *to feel/show compassion*

com·pas·sion·ate /kəmˈpæʃənət/ *adj.* feeling or showing sympathy for people who are suffering: *He was allowed to go home on compassionate grounds* (= because he was suffering). ▶ **com·pas·sion·ate·ly** *adv.*

comˌpassionate ˈleave *noun* [U] time that you are allowed to be away from work because someone in your family is sick or has died

com·pat·i·bil·i·ty **AWL** /kəmˌpætəˈbɪləti/ *noun* [U] **~ (with sb/sth)** | **~ (between A and B) 1** the ability of people or things to live or exist together without problems **2** the ability of machines, especially computers, and computer programs to be used together

com·pat·i·ble **AWL** /kəmˈpætəbl/ *adj.* **1 ~ (with sth)** (of machines, especially computers) able to be used together: *compatible software* ♦ *The new system will be compatible with existing equipment.* **2 ~ (with sth)** (of ideas, methods, or things) able to exist or be used together without causing problems: *Are measures to protect the environment compatible with economic growth?* ♦ *compatible blood types* **3 ~ (with sb)** if two people are **compatible**, they can have a good relationship because they have similar ideas, interests, etc. **ANT** INCOMPATIBLE ▶ **com·pat·i·bly** /-bli/ *adv.*

com·pa·tri·ot /kəmˈpeɪtriət/ *noun* a person who was born in, or is a citizen of, the same country as someone else **SYN** COUNTRYMAN: *He played against one of his compatriots in the semi-final.*

com·pel /kəmˈpɛl/ *verb* (-ll-) (*formal*) **1** to force someone to do something; to make something necessary: **~ sb to do sth** *The law can compel fathers to make regular payments for their children.* ♦ *I feel compelled to write and tell you how much I enjoyed your book.* ♦ **~ sth** *Last year bad health compelled his retirement.* **2 ~ sth** (not used in the progressive tenses) to cause a particular reaction: *He spoke with an authority that compelled the attention of the whole crowd.* ⊃ see also COMPULSION

com·pel·ling /kəmˈpɛlɪŋ/ *adj.* **1** that makes you pay attention to it because it is so interesting and exciting: *Her latest book makes compelling reading.* ⊃ thesaurus box at INTERESTING **2** so strong that you must do something about it: *a compelling need/desire* **3** that makes you think it is true: *There is no compelling reason to believe him.* ♦ *compelling evidence* ▶ **com·pel·ling·ly** *adv.*: *compellingly attractive*

com·pen·di·ous /kəmˈpɛndiəs/ *adj.* (*formal*) containing all the necessary facts about something: *a compendious description*

com·pen·di·um /kəmˈpɛndiəm/ *noun* (*pl.* **com·pen·di·a** /-diə/ *or* **com·pen·di·ums**) a collection of facts, drawings, and photographs on a particular subject, especially in a book

com·pen·sate **AWL** /ˈkɑmpənˌseɪt/ *verb* **1** [I] **~ (for sth)** to provide something good to balance or reduce the bad effects of damage, loss, etc. **SYN** MAKE UP FOR: *Nothing can* compensate for the loss of a loved one. **2** [T] ~ **sb (for sth)** to pay someone money because they have suffered some damage, loss, injury, etc.: *Her lawyers say she should be compensated for her suffering.*

com·pen·sa·tion ![AWL] /ˌkɑmpənˈseɪʃn/ *noun* **1** [U, C] ~ **(for sth)** something, especially money, that someone gives you because they have hurt you, or damaged something that you own; the act of giving this to someone: *to claim/award/receive compensation* ◆ *to pay compensation for injuries at work* ◆ *to receive $10,000 in compensation.* **2** [U] payment such as wages or a salary that a person receives for working at a job: *The company's executives receive a compensation package that includes bonuses and many other perks.* **3** [C, usually pl.] ~ **(for sth)** things that make a bad situation better: *I wish I were young again, but getting older has its compensations.*

com·pen·sa·tor·y ![AWL] /kəmˈpɛnsəˌtɔri/ *adj.* [usually before noun] **1** intended to make up for something such as loss, suffering, or injury: *$50 million in compensatory damages* **2** reducing the unpleasant effect of something: *The government is taking compensatory action to keep interest rates constant.*

com·pete ![key] /kəmˈpit/ *verb* **1** [I, T] to try to be more successful or better than someone else who is trying to do the same as you: ~ **(with/against sb) (for sth)** *Several companies are competing for the contract.* ◆ *We can't compete with them on price.* ◆ *Young children will usually compete for their mother's attention.* ◆ *Small traders cannot compete in the face of cheap foreign imports.* ◆ ~ **to do sth** *There are too many magazines competing to attract readers.* **2** [I] ~ **(in sth) (against sb)** to take part in a contest or game: *He's hoping to compete in the Chicago marathon.*

com·pe·tence /ˈkɑmpətəns/ *noun* **1** (also less frequent **com·pe·ten·cy**) [U, C] ~ **(in sth)** | ~ **(in doing sth)** the ability to do something well: *to gain a high level of competence in English* ◆ *professional/technical competence* ![ANT] INCOMPETENCE **2** [U] (*law*) the power that a court, an organization or a person has to deal with something: *The judge has to act within the competence of the court.* ◆ *outside someone's area of competence* **3** [C] (also less frequent **com·pe·ten·cy** *technical*) a skill that you need in a particular job or for a particular task: *The syllabus lists the knowledge and competences required at this level.*

com·pe·ten·cy /ˈkɑmpətənsi/ *noun* (*pl.* **com·pe·ten·cies**) = COMPETENCE

com·pe·tent /ˈkɑmpətənt/ *adj.* **1** ~ **(to do sth)** having enough skill or knowledge to do something well or to the necessary standard: *Make sure the firm is competent to carry out the work.* ◆ *He's very competent in his work.* ![ANT] INCOMPETENT **2** of a good standard but not very good **3** having the power to decide something: *The case was referred to a competent authority.* **4** (*law*) (of someone charged with a crime) mentally able to understand the charges and to assist in defending themselves ▶ **com·pe·tent·ly** *adv.*: *to perform competently*

com·pet·ing /kəmˈpitɪŋ/ *adj.* [only before noun] **1** (of different ideas, interests, explanations, etc.) unable to exist comfortably or be true at the same time: *There were several competing accounts of what actually happened that night.* **2** (of different products, services, or businesses) each trying to get the attention of possible customers and be more successful than others: *competing brands of diet soda* **3** used to describe the different teams or players in a sports competition: *Five competing teams will vie for the trophy.*

com·pe·ti·tion ![key] /ˌkɑmpəˈtɪʃn/ *noun* **1** [U] ~ **(between/with sb) (for sth)** a situation in which people or organizations compete with each other for something that not everyone can have: *There is now intense competition between schools to attract students.* ◆ *We are in competition with four other companies for the contract.* ◆ *We won the contract in the face of stiff competition.* **2** [C] an event in which people compete with each other to find out who is

the best at something: *a music/photo, etc. competition* ◆ *to enter/win/lose a competition* **3** **the competition** [sing.] the people who are competing against someone: *We'll be able to assess the competition at the conference.*

com·pet·i·tive ![key] /kəmˈpɛtətɪv/ *adj.* **1** used to describe a situation in which people or organizations compete against each other: *competitive games/sports* ◆ *Graduates have to fight for jobs in a highly competitive market.* **2** ~ **(with sb/sth)** as good as or better than others: *a store selling clothes at competitive prices* (= as low as any other store) ◆ *We need to work harder to remain competitive with other companies.* ◆ *to gain a competitive advantage over rival companies* ⊃ thesaurus box at CHEAP **3** (of a person) trying very hard to be better than others: *You have to be highly competitive to do well in sports these days.* ![ANT] UNCOMPETITIVE ▶ **com·pet·i·tive·ly** *adv.*: *competitively priced goods* **com·pet·i·tive·ness** *noun*: *the competitiveness of U.S. industry*

com·pet·i·tor /kəmˈpɛtətər/ *noun* **1** a person or an organization that competes against others, especially in business: *our main/major competitor* **2** a person who takes part in a competition: *Over 200 competitors entered the race.*

com·pi·la·tion ![AWL] /ˌkɑmpəˈleɪʃn/ *noun* **1** [C] a collection of items, especially pieces of music or writing, taken from different places and put together: *Her latest CD is a compilation of all her best singles.* ◆ *a compilation album* **2** [U] the process of compiling something: *the compilation of a dictionary*

com·pile ![AWL] /kəmˈpaɪl/ *verb* **1** ~ **sth** to produce a book, list, report, etc. by bringing together different items, articles, songs, etc.: *We are trying to compile a list of suitable people for the job.* ◆ *The album was compiled from live recordings from last year's tour.* **2** ~ **sth** (*computing*) to translate instructions from one computer language into another so that a particular computer can understand them

com·pil·er /kəmˈpaɪlər/ *noun* **1** a person who compiles something **2** (*computing*) a program that translates instructions from one computer language into another for a computer to understand

com·pla·cen·cy /kəmˈpleɪsnsi/ *noun* [U] (usually *disapproving*) a feeling of satisfaction with yourself or with a situation, so that you do not think any change is necessary; the state of being complacent: *Despite signs of an improvement in the economy, there is no room for complacency.*

com·pla·cent /kəmˈpleɪsnt/ *adj.* ~ **(about sb/sth)** (usually *disapproving*) too satisfied with yourself or with a situation, so that you do not feel that any change is necessary; showing or feeling complacency: *a dangerously complacent attitude to the increase in unemployment* ◆ *We must not become complacent about progress.* ▶ **com·pla·cent·ly** *adv.*

com·plain ![key] /kəmˈpleɪn/ *verb* [I, T] to say that you are annoyed, unhappy, or not satisfied about someone or something: ~ **(to sb) (about/of sth)** *I'm going to complain to the manager about this.* ◆ *The defendant complained of intimidation during the investigation.* ◆ *She never complains, but she's obviously exhausted.* ◆ (*informal*) *"How are you?" "Oh, I can't complain* (= I'm all right)." ◆ ~ **(that)…** *He complained bitterly that he had been unfairly treated.* ◆ + **speech** *"It's not fair," she complained.* **PHR V** **com·plain of sth** to say that you feel sick or are suffering from a pain: *She left early, complaining of a headache.*

> **THESAURUS**
>
> **complain**
>
> **protest ◆ object ◆ grumble ◆ whine**
>
> These words all mean to say that you are annoyed, unhappy, or not satisfied about someone or something.
>
> **complain** to say that you are annoyed, unhappy, or not satisfied about someone or something: *I'm going to complain to the manager about this.*

t **tea**   ţ **butter**   d **did**   k **cat**   g **got**   tʃ **chin**   dʒ **June**   f **fall**

protest to say or do something to show that you disagree with or disapprove of something, especially publicly; to give something as a reason for protesting: *Students took to the streets to protest (against) the decision.*

object to say that you disagree with or disapprove of something; to give something as a reason for objecting: *Unless you object, we'll postpone the meeting till next week.* ◆ *He objected to being treated like a child.*

grumble (*somewhat informal, disapproving*) to complain about someone or something in a bad-tempered way: *They kept grumbling about the cold.*

whine (*somewhat informal, disapproving*) to complain in an annoying, crying voice: *Stop whining!* ◆ *What is he whining about now?* **NOTE** Whine is often used to talk about the way that young children complain.

PATTERNS
- to complain/protest/grumble/whine **about** sth
- to complain/protest/object/grumble/whine **to** sb
- to complain/protest/object/grumble/whine **that**…

com·plain·ant /kəmˈpleɪmənt/ *noun* = PLAINTIFF

com·plaint /kəmˈpleɪnt/ *noun* **1** [C] a reason for not being satisfied; a statement that someone makes saying that they are not satisfied: **~ (about sb/sth)** *The most common complaint is about poor service.* ◆ *We received a number of complaints from customers about the lack of parking facilities.* ◆ *I'd like to make a complaint about the noise.* ◆ **~ (against sb/sth)** *I believe you have a complaint against one of our nurses.* ◆ **~ (that…)** *a complaint that he had been unfairly treated* ◆ *a formal complaint* ◆ (*formal*) *to file/lodge* (= make) *a complaint* **2** [U] the act of complaining: *I can see no grounds for complaint.* ◆ *a letter of complaint* **3** [C] an illness, especially one that is not serious, and often one that affects a particular part of the body: *a skin complaint* **4** [C] (*law*) a formal charge brought against someone

com·plai·sant /kəmˈpleɪsnt; -znt/ *adj.* (*old-fashioned*) ready to accept other people's actions and opinions and to do what other people want ▶ **com·plai·sance** /-sns; -zns/ *noun* [U]

com·plect·ed /kəmˈplɛktəd/ *adj.* (*informal*) (used with adjectives) with skin and a COMPLEXION of the type mentioned: *fair/dark complected*

com·ple·ment **AWL** *verb, noun*
- *verb* /ˈkɑmpləˌmɛnt/ **~ sth** to add to something in a way that improves it or makes it more attractive: *The excellent menu is complemented by a good wine list.* ◆ *The team needs players who complement each other.* ➲ note at COMPLIMENT
- *noun* /ˈkɑmpləmənt/ **1 ~ (to sth)** a thing that adds new qualities to something in a way that improves it or makes it more attractive **2** the complete number or quantity needed or allowed: *We've taken our full complement of trainees this year.* **3** (*grammar*) a word or phrase, especially an adjective or a noun, that is used after linking verbs such as *be* and *become*, and describes the subject of the verb. In some descriptions of grammar it is used to refer to any word or phrase which is GOVERNED by a verb and usually comes after the verb in a sentence: *In the sentences "I'm angry" and "He became a politician," "angry" and "politician" are complements.*

com·ple·men·ta·ry **AWL** /ˌkɑmpləˈmɛntri; -ˈmɛntəri/ *adj.* **~ (to sth)** two people or things that are **complementary** are different but together form a useful or attractive combination of skills, qualities, or physical features: *The school's approach must be complementary to that of the parents.* ➲ note at COMPLIMENT

complementary ˈangle *noun* (*geometry*) either of two angles which together make 90° ➲ compare SUPPLEMENTARY ANGLE

complementary ˈcolor (*CanE usually* **complementary ˈcolour**) *noun* (*technical*) **1** a color that gives the greatest contrast when combined with a particular color: *The designer has chosen the complementary colors blue and* orange. **2** a color that, when mixed with another color, gives black or white

complementary ˈmedicine *noun* [U] medical treatment that is not part of the usual scientific treatment used in Western countries, for example ACUPUNCTURE

com·ple·men·ta·tion /ˌkɑmpləmənˈteɪʃn/ *noun* [U]
1 (*formal*) the fact of complementing something
2 (*grammar*) the complement of a verb in a clause

com·ple·men·tiz·er /ˈkɑmpləmənˌtaɪzər/ *noun* (*grammar*) a word or part of a word that shows a clause is being used as a complement

com·plete 🔑 /kəmˈplit/ *adj., verb*
- *adj.* **1** [usually before noun] used when you are emphasizing something, to mean "to the greatest degree possible" **SYN** TOTAL: *We were in complete agreement.* ◆ *a complete change* ◆ *in complete silence* ◆ *a complete stranger* ◆ *It came as a complete surprise.* ◆ *I felt like a complete idiot.* **2** including all the parts, etc. that are necessary; whole: *I've collected the complete set.* ◆ *a complete guide to events in Orlando* ◆ *the complete works of Tolstoy* ◆ *You will receive payment for each complete day that you work.* **ANT** INCOMPLETE **3 ~ with sth** [not before noun] including something as an extra part or feature: *The furniture comes complete with tools and instructions for assembly.* ◆ *The book, complete with CD, costs $35.* **4** [not before noun] finished: *Work on the office building will be complete at the end of the year.* **ANT** INCOMPLETE
  ▶ **com·plete·ness** *noun* [U]: *the accuracy and completeness of the information* ◆ *For the sake of completeness, all names are given in full.*
- *verb* **1** [often passive] **~ sth** to finish making or doing something: *She's just completed her law degree.* ◆ *The project should be completed within a year.* **2 ~ sth** to write all the information you are asked for on a form **SYN** FILL IN/OUT: *2,000 shoppers completed our questionnaire.* **3 ~ sth** to make something whole or perfect: *I only need one more card to complete the set.*

com·plete·ly 🔑 /kəmˈplitli/ *adv.*
(used to emphasize the following word or phrase) in every way possible **SYN** TOTALLY: *completely different* ◆ *completely and utterly broke* ◆ *I've completely forgotten her name.* ◆ *The explosion completely destroyed the building.*

com·ple·tion /kəmˈpliʃn/ *noun* [U] the act or process of finishing something; the state of being finished and complete: *the completion of the new hospital building* ◆ *Satisfactory completion of the course does not ensure you a job.* ◆ *The project is due for completion in the spring.* ◆ *The road is nearing completion* (= it is nearly finished). ◆ *the date of completion/the completion date*

com·plex 🔑 **AWL** *adj., noun*
- *adj.* /kəmˈplɛks; kɑmˈplɛks; ˈkɑmplɛks/ **1** made of many different things or parts that are connected; difficult to understand **SYN** COMPLICATED: *complex machinery* ◆ *the complex structure of the human brain* ◆ *a complex argument/problem/subject* **2** (*grammar*) (of a word or sentence) containing one main part (= the ROOT of a word or MAIN CLAUSE of a sentence) and one or more other parts (called AFFIX or SUBORDINATE CLAUSES) ➲ compare COMPOUND
- *noun* /ˈkɑmplɛks/ **1** a group of buildings of a similar type together in one place: *a sports complex* ◆ *an industrial complex* (= a site with many factories) ➲ thesaurus box at BUILDING **2** a group of things that are connected: *This is just one of a whole complex of issues.* **3** (especially in compounds) a mental state that is not normal: *to suffer from a guilt complex* ➲ see also INFERIORITY COMPLEX, OEDIPUS COMPLEX, PERSECUTION COMPLEX **4** if someone has a **complex** about something, they are worried about it in way that is not normal

com·plex·ion /kəmˈplɛkʃn/ *noun* **1** the natural color and condition of the skin on a person's face: *a pale/bad complexion* ➲ collocations at PHYSICAL **2** [usually sing.] the general character of something: *a move which changed the political complexion of the country*

IDM **put a new/different complexion on sth** to change the way that a situation appears

com·plex·i·ty AWL /kəmˈplɛksəti/ *noun* **1** [U] the state of being formed of many parts; the state of being difficult to understand: *the increasing complexity of modern telecommunication systems* ◆ *I was astonished by the size and complexity of the problem.* **2 complexities** [pl.] the features of a problem or situation that are difficult to understand: *the complexities of the system*

,**complex ˈnumber** *noun* (*mathematics*) a number containing both a REAL NUMBER and an IMAGINARY NUMBER

com·pli·ance /kəmˈplaɪəns/ *noun* [U] ~ **(with sth)** the practice of obeying rules or requests made by people in authority: *procedures that must be followed to ensure full compliance with the law* ◆ *Safety measures were carried out in compliance with paragraph 6 of the building regulations.* **ANT** NONCOMPLIANCE ➔ see also COMPLY

com·pli·ant /kəmˈplaɪənt/ *adj.* **1** willing to agree with other people or to obey rules: *Most of the patients were compliant with the diet.* **2** (*disapproving*) too willing to agree with other people or to obey rules: *By then, Henry seemed less compliant with his wife's wishes than he had six months before.* ◆ *We should not be producing compliant students who do not dare to criticize.* **3** in agreement with a set of rules: *This site is HTML compliant.* ➔ see also COMPLY

com·pli·cate /ˈkɑmpləˌkeɪt/ *verb* ~ **sth** to make something more difficult to do, understand, or deal with: *I do not want to complicate the task more than is necessary.* ◆ *To complicate matters further, there will be no transportation available till 8 o'clock.* ◆ *The issue is complicated by the fact that a vital document is missing.*

com·pli·cat·ed /ˈkɑmpləˌkeɪtəd/ *adj.* made of many different things or parts that are connected; difficult to understand **SYN** COMPLEX: *a complicated system* ◆ *The instructions look very complicated.* ◆ *It's all very complicated—but I'll try and explain.*

com·pli·ca·tion /ˌkɑmpləˈkeɪʃn/ *noun* **1** [C, U] a thing that makes a situation more complicated or difficult: *The bad weather added a further complication to our trip.* **2** [C, usually pl.] (*medical*) a new problem or illness that makes treatment of a previous one more complicated or difficult: *She developed complications after the surgery.*

com·plic·it /kəmˈplɪsət/ *adj.* ~ **(in/with sb/sth)** involved with other people in something wrong or illegal: *Several officers were complicit in the cover-up.*

com·plic·i·ty /kəmˈplɪsəti/ *noun* [U] ~ **(in sth)** (*formal*) the act of taking part with another person in a crime **SYN** COLLUSION: *to be guilty of complicity in the murder* ◆ *evident complicity between the two brothers*

WHICH WORD?

compliment ◆ complement

■ These words have similar spellings but completely different meanings. If you **compliment** someone, you say something very nice to them: *She complimented me on my English.* If one thing **complements** another, the two things work or look better because they are together: *The different flavors complement each other perfectly.*

■ The adjectives are also often confused. **Complimentary**: *She made some very complimentary remarks about my English.* It can also mean "free": *There was a complimentary basket of fruit in our room.* **Complementary**: *The team members have different but complementary skills.*

---

com·pli·ment *noun, verb*
● *noun* /ˈkɑmpləmənt/ **1** [C] a remark that expresses praise or admiration of someone: *to pay someone a compliment* (= to praise them for something) ◆ *"You understand the problem because you're so much older." "I'll take that as a*

---

compliment!" ◆ *It's a great compliment to be asked to do the job.* ◆ *to return the compliment* (= to treat someone in the same way as they have treated you) **2 compliments** [pl.] (*formal*) polite words or good wishes, especially when used to express praise and admiration: *My compliments to the chef!*
IDM **a backhanded/left-handed compliment** a remark that seems to express admiration but could also be understood as an insult
● *verb* /ˈkɑmpləˌmɛnt/ ~ **sb (on sth)** to tell someone that you like or admire something they have done, their appearance, etc.: *She complimented him on his excellent German.*

com·pli·men·ta·ry /ˌkɑmpləˈmɛntri; -ˈmɛntəri/ *adj.* **1** given free: *complimentary tickets for the show* **2** ~ **(about sth)** expressing admiration, praise, etc.: *a complimentary remark* ◆ *She was extremely complimentary about his work.* **ANT** UNCOMPLIMENTARY ➔ note at COMPLIMENT

com·ply /kəmˈplaɪ/ *verb* (**com·plies, com·ply·ing, com·plied**) [I] ~ **(with sth)** to obey a rule, an order, etc.: *They refused to comply with the U.N. resolution.* ➔ see also COMPLIANCE

com·po·nent /kəmˈpoʊnənt/ AWL *noun* one of several parts of which something is made: *the components of a machine* ◆ *the car component industry* ◆ *Key components of the government's plan are...* ◆ *Trust is a vital component in any relationship.* ▶ **com·po·nent** *adj.* [only before noun]: *Break the problem down into its component parts.*

com·po·nen·tial a·nal·y·sis /ˌkɑmpəˌnɛnʃl əˈnæləsɪs/ *noun* [U] (*linguistics*) the study of meaning by analyzing the different parts of words

com·port /kəmˈpɔrt/ *verb* ~ **yourself + adv./prep.** (*formal*) to behave in a particular way: *She always comports herself with great dignity.*

com·port·ment /kəmˈpɔrtmənt/ *noun* [U] (*formal*) the way in which someone or something behaves: *She won admiration for her comportment during the trial.*

com·pose /kəmˈpoʊz/ *verb* **1** [T, usually passive] (not used in the progressive tenses) ~ **sth** (*formal*) to combine together to form a whole **SYN** MAKE UP: *Ten men compose the committee.* ➔ see also COMPOSED **2** [T, I] ~ **(sth)** to write music: *Mozart composed his last opera shortly before he died.* **3** [T] ~ **a letter/speech/poem** to write a letter, etc. usually with a lot of care and thought: *She composed a letter of protest.* **4** [T, no passive] (*formal*) to manage to control your feelings or expression: ~ **yourself** *Emma frowned, making an effort to compose herself.* ◆ ~ **sth** *I was so confused that I could hardly compose my thoughts.* ➔ see also COMPOSURE

com·posed /kəmˈpoʊzd/ *adj.* **1 be composed of something** to be made or formed from several parts, things, or people: *The committee is composed mainly of lawyers.* ➔ thesaurus box at CONSIST OF **2** [not usually before noun] calm and in control of your feelings: *She seemed outwardly composed.*

com·pos·er /kəmˈpoʊzər/ *noun* a person who writes music, especially CLASSICAL music

com·pos·ite /kəmˈpɑzət/ *adj., noun*
● *adj.* [only before noun] made of different parts or materials: *a composite picture* (= one made from several pictures)
● *noun* **1** something made by putting together different parts or materials: *The document was a composite of information from various sources.* **2** (also **com·ˈposite sketch**) a set of drawings of different features that can be put together to form the face of a person, especially someone wanted by the police, using descriptions given by people who saw the person; a picture made in this way

com·po·si·tion /ˌkɑmpəˈzɪʃn/ *noun* **1** [U] the different parts that something is made of; the way in which the different parts are organized: *the chemical composition of the soil* ◆ *the composition of the board of directors* ➔ thesaurus box at STRUCTURE **2** [C] a piece of music or art, or a poem: *one of Beethoven's finest compositions* **3** [U] the act of composing (COMPOSE) something: *pieces performed in the order of their*

| h **hat** | m **man** | n **no** | ŋ **sing** | l **leg** | r **red** | y **yes** | w **wet** |

composition 4 [U] the art of writing music: *to study composition* **5** [C] a short text that is written as a school exercise; a short essay **6** [U] (*art*) the arrangement of people or objects in a painting or photograph

com·pos·i·tor /kəmˈpɑzətər/ *noun* a person who arranges text on a page before printing

com·pos men·tis /ˌkɑmpəs ˈmentəs/ *adj.* [not before noun] (from *Latin*, *formal* or *humorous*) having full control of your mind **ANT** NON COMPOS MENTIS

com·post /ˈkɑmpoʊst/ *noun*, *verb*
- *noun* [U, C] a mixture of decayed plants, food, etc. that can be added to soil to help plants grow
- *verb* **1** ~ sth to make something into compost **2** ~ sth to put compost on or in something

compost bin *noun* a container in the garden where leaves, plants, etc. are put, to make compost

compost heap *noun* (also **compost pile**) a place in the garden where leaves, plants, etc. are piled, to make compost

com·po·sure /kəmˈpoʊʒər/ *noun* [U] the state of being calm and in control of your feelings or behavior: *to keep/lose/recover/regain your composure*

com·pote /ˈkɑmpoʊt/ *noun* [C, U] a cold DESSERT (= a sweet dish) made of fruit that has been cooked slowly with sugar

com·pound **AWL** *noun*, *adj.*, *verb*
- *noun* /ˈkɑmpaʊnd/ **1** a thing consisting of two or more separate things combined together **2** (*chemistry*) a substance formed by a chemical reaction of two or more elements in fixed amounts relative to each other: *Table salt is a compound of sodium and chlorine.* ⊃ compare ELEMENT, MIXTURE **3** (*grammar*) a noun, an adjective, or a verb made of two or more words or parts of words, written as one or more words, or joined by a hyphen. *Travel agent*, *dark-haired*, and *bathroom* are all compounds. **4** an area surrounded by a fence or wall in which a factory or other group of buildings stands: *a prison compound*
- *adj.* /ˈkɑmpaʊnd/ /kɑmˈpaʊnd/ [only before noun] (*technical*) formed of two or more parts: *a compound adjective, such as "fair-skinned"* ◆ *A compound sentence contains two or more clauses.*
- *verb* /kəmˈpaʊnd; kɑm-; ˈkɑmpaʊnd/ **1** [often passive] ~ sth to make something bad become even worse by causing further damage or problems: *The problems were compounded by severe food shortages.* **2** be compounded of/from something (*formal*) to be formed from something: *The DNA molecule is compounded from many smaller molecules.* **3** [often passive] ~ sth (with sth) (*formal* or *technical*) to mix something together: *liquid soaps compounded with disinfectant* **4** ~ sth (*finance*) to pay or charge interest on an amount of money that includes any interest already earned or charged

compound eye *noun* (*biology*) an eye like that of most insects, made up of several parts that work separately: *the compound eye of a wasp*

compound fracture *noun* an injury in which a bone in the body is broken and part of the bone comes through the skin ⊃ compare SIMPLE FRACTURE

compound interest *noun* [U] interest that is paid both on the original amount of money saved and on the interest that has been added to it ⊃ compare SIMPLE INTEREST

com·pre·hend /ˌkɑmprɪˈhend/ *verb* [I, T] (often used in negative sentences) (*formal*) to understand something fully: *He stood staring at the dead body, unable to comprehend.* ◆ ~ sth *The infinite distances of space are too great for the human mind to comprehend.* ◆ ~ how/why, etc... *She could not comprehend how someone would risk people's lives in that way.* ◆ ~ that... *He simply could not comprehend that she could be guilty.* ⊃ thesaurus box at UNDERSTAND

com·pre·hen·si·ble /ˌkɑmprɪˈhensəbl/ *adj.* ~ (to sb) (*formal*) that can be understood by someone: *easily/readily*

comprehensible *to the average reader* **ANT** INCOMPREHENSIBLE ▸ **com·pre·hen·si·bil·i·ty** /ˌkɑmprɪˌhensəˈbɪləti/ *noun* [U]

com·pre·hen·sion /ˌkɑmprɪˈhenʃn/ *noun* [U] **1** the ability to understand: *speech and comprehension* ◆ *His behavior was completely beyond comprehension* (= impossible to understand). ◆ *She had no comprehension of what was involved.* **2** an exercise that trains students to understand a language: *listening comprehension* ◆ *reading comprehension*

com·pre·hen·sive **AWL** /ˌkɑmprɪˈhensɪv/ *adj.* including all, or almost all, the items, details, facts, information, etc., that may be concerned **SYN** COMPLETE, FULL: *a comprehensive list of addresses* ◆ *a comprehensive study* ◆ *comprehensive insurance* (= covering all risks) ▸ **com·pre·hen·sive·ness** *noun* [U]

com·pre·hen·sive·ly **AWL** /ˌkɑmprɪˈhensɪvli/ *adv.* completely; thoroughly: *They were comprehensively beaten in the final.*

com·press *verb*, *noun*
- *verb* /kəmˈpres/ **1** [T, I] to press or squeeze something together or into a smaller space; to be pressed or squeezed in this way: ~ sth (into sth) *compressed air/gas* ◆ ~ (into sth) *Her lips compressed into a thin line.* **2** [T] ~ sth (into sth) to reduce something and fit it into a smaller space or amount of time **SYN** CONDENSE: *The main arguments were compressed into one chapter.* **3** [T] ~ sth (*computing*) to make computer files, etc. smaller so that they use less space on a disk, etc. **ANT** DECOMPRESS ▸ **com·pres·sion** /kəmˈpreʃn/ *noun* [U]: *the compression of air* ◆ *data compression*
- *noun* /ˈkɑmpres/ a cloth that is pressed onto a part of the body to stop the loss of blood, reduce pain, etc.

com·pres·sor /kəmˈpresər/ *noun* a machine that compresses air or other gases

com·prise **AWL** /kəmˈpraɪz/ *verb* (not used in the progressive tenses) **1** also be comprised of ~ sth to have someone or something as parts or members **SYN** CONSIST OF: *The collection comprises 327 paintings.* ◆ *The committee is comprised of representatives from both the public and private sectors.* **2** ~ sth to be the parts or members that form something **SYN** MAKE STH UP: *Older people comprise a large proportion of those living in poverty.* ⊃ thesaurus box at CONSIST OF ⊃ language bank at PROPORTION

com·pro·mise /ˈkɑmprəˌmaɪz/ *noun*, *verb*
- *noun* **1** [C] an agreement made between two people or groups in which each side gives up some of the things they want so that both sides are happy at the end: *After lengthy talks the two sides finally reached a compromise.* ◆ *In any relationship, you have to make compromises.* ◆ *a compromise solution/agreement/candidate* **2** [C] ~ (between A and B) a solution to a problem in which two or more things cannot exist together as they are, in which each thing is reduced or changed slightly so that they can exist together: *This model represents the best compromise between price and quality.* **3** [U] the act of reaching a compromise: *Compromise is an inevitable part of life.* ◆ *There is no prospect of compromise in sight.*
- *verb* **1** [I] to give up some of your demands after a disagreement with someone, in order to reach an agreement: *Neither side is prepared to compromise.* ◆ ~ (with sb) (on sth) *After much argument, the judges finally compromised on* (= agreed to give the prize to) *the 18-year-old pianist.* ◆ *They were unwilling to compromise with the terrorists.* **2** [T, I] to do something that is against your principles or does not reach standards that you have set: ~ sth *I refuse to compromise my principles.* ◆ ~ (on sth) *We are not prepared to compromise on safety standards.* **3** [T] ~ sb/sth/yourself to bring someone or something/yourself into danger or under suspicion, especially by acting in a way that is not very sensible: *She had already compromised herself by accepting his invitation.* ◆ *Defeat at this stage would compromise their chances* (= reduce their chances) *of reaching the finals of the competition.*

computers

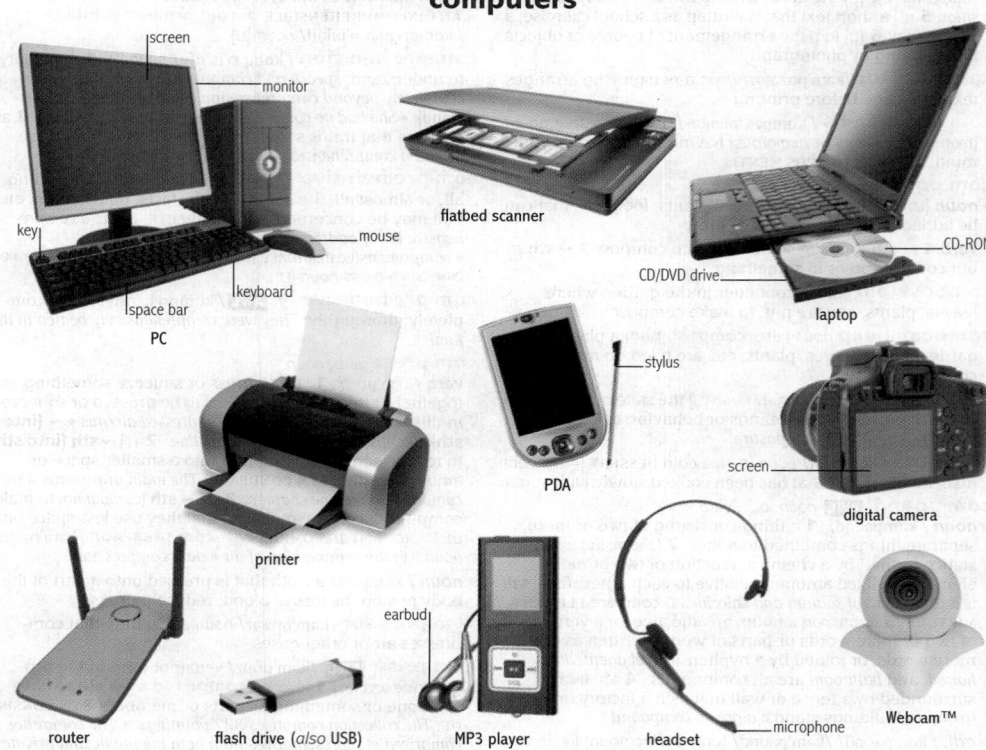

screen · monitor · flatbed scanner · key · mouse · keyboard · space bar · PC · CD-ROM · CD/DVD drive · laptop · stylus · PDA · screen · digital camera · printer · earbud · router · flash drive (also USB) · MP3 player · headset · microphone · Webcam™

com·pro·mis·ing /ˈkɑmprəˌmaɪzɪŋ/ *adj.* if something is **compromising**, it shows or tells people something that you want to keep secret, because it is wrong or embarrassing: *compromising photos* ◆ *They were discovered together in a compromising situation.*

comp·trol·ler /kənˈtroʊlər; kɑmpˈtroʊlər; ˈkɑmpˌ-/ *noun* = CONTROLLER

com·pul·sion /kəmˈpʌlʃn/ *noun* **1** [C] ~ **(to do sth)** a strong desire to do something, especially something that is wrong, silly, or dangerous SYN URGE: *He felt a great compulsion to tell her everything.* **2** [U, C] strong pressure that makes someone do something that they do not want to do: ~ **(to do sth)** *You are under no compulsion to pay immediately.* ◆ ~ **(on sb) to do sth** *There are no compulsions on students to attend classes.* ➔ see also COMPEL

com·pul·sive /kəmˈpʌlsɪv/ *adj.* **1** (of behavior) that is difficult to stop or control: *compulsive eating/spending/gambling* **2** (of people) not being able to control their behavior: *a compulsive drinker/gambler/liar* **3** that makes you pay attention to it because it is so interesting and exciting: *The program made compulsive viewing.* ▶ **com·pul·sive·ly** *adv.*: *She watched him compulsively.* ◆ *a compulsively readable book*

com·pul·so·ry /kəmˈpʌlsəri/ *adj.* that must be done because of a law or a rule SYN MANDATORY: *It is compulsory for all motorcyclists to wear helmets.* ◆ *English is a compulsory subject at this level.* ◆ *compulsory education/schooling* ◆ *compulsory lay-offs* ANT VOLUNTARY ▶ **com·pul·so·ri·ly** /kəmˈpʌlsərəli/ *adv.*: *Over 600 workers were compulsorily laid off.*

com·punc·tion /kəmˈpʌŋkʃn/ *noun* [U, C] ~ **(about doing sth)** (*formal*) a guilty feeling about doing something: *She felt no compunction about quitting her job.* ◆ *He had lied to her*

without compunction. ◆ *She has no compunctions about rejecting the plan.*

com·pu·ta·tion AWL /ˌkɑmpyuˈteɪʃn/ *noun* [C, U] (*formal*) an act or the process of calculating something: *All the statistical computations were performed by the new software system.* ◆ *an error in the computation*

com·pu·ta·tion·al AWL /ˌkɑmpyuˈteɪʃənl/ *adj.* [usually before noun] using or connected with computers: *computational methods* ◆ *a computational approach*

compu·tational lin·guistics *noun* [U] the study of language and speech using computers

com·pute AWL /kəmˈpyut/ *verb* ~ **sth** (*formal*) to calculate something: *The losses were computed at 5 million dollars.* ▶ **com·put·a·ble** AWL /kəmˈpyutəbl/ *adj.*

com·put·er ⚿ AWL /kəmˈpyutər/ *noun*
an electronic machine that can store, organize, and find information, do calculations, and control other machines: *a personal computer* ◆ *Our sales information is processed by computer.* ◆ *a computer program* ◆ **computer software/hardware/graphics** ◆ *a computer error* ◆ *computer-aided design* ➔ see also DESKTOP COMPUTER, MICROCOMPUTER, PERSONAL COMPUTER, SUPERCOMPUTER

com'puter ˌgame *noun* a game played on a computer

com·put·er·ize /kəmˈpyutəˌraɪz/ *verb* **1** ~ **sth** to provide a computer or computers to do the work of something: *The factory has been fully computerized.* **2** ~ **sth** to store information on a computer: *computerized databases* ◆ *The company has computerized its records.* ▶ **com·put·er·i·za·tion** /kəmˌpyutərəˈzeɪʃn/ *noun* [U]

com·puter–ˈliterate *adj.* able to use computers well ▶ **comˌputer ˈliteracy** *noun* [U]

com·puter 'science noun [U] the study of computers and how they can be used: *a degree in computer science* ▶ **com·puter 'scientist** noun

com·put·ing **AWL** /kəmˈpyuːtɪŋ/ noun [U] the fact of using computers: *to study computing* ◆ *educational/network/scientific computing* ◆ *computing power/services/skills/systems*

com·rade /ˈkɑmræd/ noun **1** a person who is a member of the same COMMUNIST or SOCIALIST political party as the person speaking **2** (also **comrade-in-'arms**) (*old-fashioned*) a friend or other person that you work with, especially as soldiers during a war: *They were old army comrades.* ▶ **com·rade·ly** /ˈkɑmrædli/ adj. **com·rade·ship** /ˈkɑmrædˌʃɪp/ noun [U]: *There was a sense of comradeship between them.*

con /kɑn/ noun, verb
● *noun* (*informal*) **1** [sing.] (also *formal* **'confidence game**) a trick; an act of cheating someone: *The so-called bargain was just a big con!* ◆ *a con game* ◆ *He's a real con artist* (= a person who regularly cheats others). ➔ see also CON MAN **2** [C] = CONVICT **IDM** see PRO
● *verb* (-nn-) (*informal*) to trick someone, especially in order to get money from them or persuade them to do something for you: *~ sb (into doing sth)* *I was conned into buying a useless car.* ◆ *~ sb (out of sth)* *They had been conned out of $100,000.* ◆ *~ your way into sth* *He conned his way into the job using false references.* ➔ thesaurus box at CHEAT

co·na·tion /koʊˈneɪʃn/ noun [U] (*philosophy, psychology*) a mental process that makes you want to do something or decide to do something ▶ **co·na·tive** /ˈkɑnətɪv; ˈkoʊ-/ adj.

con·cat·e·na·tion /kənˌkætəˈneɪʃn/ noun (*formal*) a series of things or events that are linked together: *a strange concatenation of events*

con·cave /kɑnˈkeɪv; ˈkɑnkeɪv/ adj. (of an outline or a surface) curving in: *a concave lens/mirror* ➔ picture at CONVEX **ANT** CONVEX

con·cav·i·ty /kɑnˈkævəṭi/ noun (*pl.* **con·cav·i·ties**) (*technical*) **1** [U] the quality of being concave (= curving in) **2** [C] a shape or place that curves in

con·ceal /kənˈsil/ verb (*formal*) to hide someone or something: *~ sb/sth* *The paintings were concealed beneath a thick layer of plaster.* ◆ *Tim could barely conceal his disappointment.* ◆ *She sat down to conceal the fact that she was trembling.* ◆ *~ sb/sth from sb/sth* *For a long time his death was concealed from her.* ➔ see also ILL-CONCEALED ➔ thesaurus box at HIDE

con·ceal·er /kənˈsilər/ noun [U, C] a skin-colored cream or powder used to cover marks or spots on the skin or dark circles under the eyes ➔ picture at MAKEUP

con·ceal·ment /kənˈsilmənt/ noun [U] (*formal*) the act of hiding something; the state of being hidden: *the concealment of crime* ◆ *Many animals rely on concealment for protection.*

con·cede /kənˈsid/ verb **1** [T] to admit that something is true, logical, etc.: *+ speech* *"Not bad," she conceded grudgingly.* ◆ *~ (that)...* *He was forced to concede (that) there might be difficulties.* ◆ *~ sth* *I had to concede the logic of this.* ◆ *~ sth to sb* *He reluctantly conceded the point to me.* ◆ *~ sb sth* *He reluctantly conceded me the point.* ◆ **it is conceded that...** *It must be conceded that different judges have different approaches to these cases.* ➔ thesaurus box at ADMIT **2** [T] to give something away, especially unwillingly; to allow someone to have something: *~ sth (to sb)* *The president was obliged to concede power to the army.* ◆ *The Packers conceded a field goal immediately after halftime.* ◆ *~ sb sth* *Women were only conceded full voting rights in 1920.* **3** [I, T] *~ (defeat)* to admit that you have lost a game, an election, etc.: *After losing this decisive battle, the general was forced to concede.* ◆ *Injury forced Hicks to concede defeat.* ➔ see also CONCESSION

con·ceit /kənˈsit/ noun **1** [U] (*disapproving*) too much pride in yourself and what you do **2** [C] (*formal*) an artistic effect or device, especially one that is very clever or tries to be very clever but does not succeed: *The ill-advised conceit of the*

guardian angel dooms the movie from the start. **3** (*technical*) a clever expression in writing or speech that involves a comparison between two things **SYN** METAPHOR: *The idea of the wind singing is a romantic conceit.*

con·ceit·ed /kənˈsiṭəd/ adj. (*disapproving*) having too much pride in yourself and what you do: *a very conceited person* ◆ *It's very conceited of you to assume that your work is always the best.* ▶ **con·ceit·ed·ly** adv.

con·ceiv·a·ble **AWL** /kənˈsivəbl/ adj. that you can imagine or believe **SYN** POSSIBLE: *It is conceivable that I'll see her tomorrow.* ◆ *a beautiful city with buildings of every conceivable age and style* **ANT** INCONCEIVABLE ▶ **con·ceiv·a·bly** **AWL** /-bli/ adv.: *The disease could conceivably be transferred to humans.*

con·ceive **AWL** /kənˈsiv/ verb **1** [T] (*formal*) to form an idea, a plan, etc. in your mind; to imagine something: *~ sth* *He conceived the idea of transforming the old power station into an arts center.* ◆ *~ of sth (as sth)* *God is often conceived of as male.* ◆ *~ (that)...* *I cannot conceive* (= I do not believe) *(that) he would wish to harm us.* ◆ *~ what/how, etc....* *I cannot conceive what it must be like.* **2** [I, T] when a woman **conceives** or **conceives a child**, she becomes pregnant: *She is unable to conceive.* ◆ *~ sth* *Their first child was conceived on their wedding night.* ➔ see also CONCEPTION

WORD FAMILY
conceive *verb*
conceivable *adj.* (≠ inconceivable)
conceivably *adv.*
concept *noun*
conception *noun*
conceptual *adj.*

con·cen·trate 🔑 **AWL** /ˈkɑnsnˌtreɪt/ verb, noun
● *verb* **1** [I, T] to give all your attention to something and not think about anything else: *~ (on sth/on doing sth)* *I can't concentrate with all that noise going on.* ◆ *~ sth* *Nothing concentrates the mind better than the knowledge that you could die tomorrow* (= it makes you think very clearly). ◆ *~ sth (on sth/on doing sth)* *I decided to concentrate all my efforts on finding somewhere to live.* **2** [T] *~ sth + adv./prep.* to bring something together in one place: *Power is largely concentrated in the hands of a small elite.* ◆ *We need to concentrate resources on the most run-down areas.* ◆ *Fighting was concentrated around the towns to the north.* **3** [T] *~ sth* (*technical*) to increase the strength of a substance by reducing its volume, for example by boiling it **SYN** REDUCE **PHR V** **'concentrate on sth** to spend more time doing one particular thing than others: *In this lecture I will concentrate on the early years of Charles's reign.*
● *noun* [C, U] a substance that is made stronger because water or other substances have been removed: *mineral concentrates found at the bottom of rivers* ◆ *jams made with fruit juice concentrate*

con·cen·trat·ed **AWL** /ˈkɑnsnˌtreɪṭəd/ adj. **1** showing determination to do something: *He made a concentrated effort to finish the work on time.* **2** (of a substance) made stronger because water or other substances have been removed: *concentrated orange juice* ◆ *a concentrated solution of salt in water* **3** if something exists or happens in a **concentrated** way, there is a lot of it in one place or at one time: *concentrated gunfire*

con·cen·tra·tion 🔑 **AWL** /ˌkɑnsnˈtreɪʃn/ noun **1** [U] the ability to direct all your effort and attention on one thing, without thinking of other things: *This book requires a great deal of concentration.* ◆ *Tiredness affects your powers of concentration.* **2** [U] *~ (on sth)* the process of people directing effort and attention on a particular thing: *a need for greater concentration on environmental issues* **3** [C] *~ (of sth)* a lot of something in one place: *a concentration of industry in the north of the country* **4** [C, U] the amount of a substance in a liquid or in another substance: *glucose concentrations in the blood*

concen'tration ˌcamp noun a type of prison, often consisting of a number of buildings inside a fence, where political prisoners are kept in extremely bad conditions: *a Nazi concentration camp*

con·cen·tric /kən'sentrɪk/ *adj.* (*geometry*) (of circles) having the same center: *concentric rings*

concentric circles

con·cept 🔑 **AWL** /'kɑnsept/ *noun*
an idea or a principle that is connected with something ABSTRACT: ~ **(of sth)** *the concept of social class* ♦ *concepts such as "civilization" and "government"* ♦ *He can't grasp the basic concepts of mathematics.* ♦ ~ **(that...)** *the concept that everyone should have equality of opportunity*

'concept ˌalbum *noun* a collection of pieces of popular music, all having the same theme and recorded on one CD, etc.

con·cep·tion **AWL** /kən'sepʃn/ *noun* **1** [U] the process of forming an idea or a plan: *The plan was brilliant in its conception but failed because of lack of money.* **2** [C, U] ~ **(of sth)** | ~ **(that...)** an understanding or a belief of what something is or what something should be: *Marx's conception of social justice* ♦ *He has no conception of how difficult life is if you're unemployed.* **3** [U, C] the process of an egg being FERTILIZED inside a woman's body so that she becomes pregnant: *the moment of conception* ⊃ see also CONCEIVE

con·cep·tu·al **AWL** /kən'septʃuəl/ *adj.* (*formal*) related to or based on ideas: *a conceptual framework within which children's needs are assessed* ♦ *a conceptual model* ▶ **con·cep·tu·al·ly** **AWL** *adv.*: *conceptually similar/distinct*

conˌceptual 'art *noun* [U] art in which the idea that the work of art represents is considered to be the most important thing about it

con·cep·tu·al·ism /kən'septʃuəˌlɪzəm/ *noun* [U] (*philosophy*) the theory that general ideas such as "beauty" and "red" exist only as ideas in the mind ▶ **con·cep·tu·al·ist** *noun*

con·cep·tu·al·ize **AWL** /kən'septʃuəˌlaɪz/ *verb* ~ **sth (as sth)** (*formal*) to form an idea of something in your mind

con·cern 🔑 /kən'sɜrn/ *verb, noun*

● **verb**
▷ AFFECT/INVOLVE **1** [often passive] ~ **sb** to affect someone; to involve someone: *Don't interfere in what doesn't concern you.* ♦ *The loss was a tragedy for all concerned* (= all those affected by it). ♦ *Where our children's education is concerned, no compromise is acceptable.* ♦ *The individuals concerned have some explaining to do.* ♦ *To whom it may concern:* ... (= used, for example, at the beginning of a public notice or of a job reference about someone's character and ability) ♦ *Everyone who was directly concerned in* (= had some responsibility for) *the incident has now resigned.*
▷ BE ABOUT **2** ~ **sth** also **be concerned with sth** to be about something: *The story concerns the prince's efforts to rescue Pamina.* ♦ *The book is primarily concerned with Soviet-American relations during the Cold War.* ♦ *This chapter concerns itself with the historical background.* ♦ *One major difference between these computers concerns the way in which they store information.*
▷ WORRY SOMEONE **3** to worry someone: ~ **sb** *What concerns me is our lack of preparation for the change.* ♦ ~ **sb that...** *It concerns me that you no longer seem to care.* ⊃ see also CONCERNED
▷ TAKE AN INTEREST **4** ~ **yourself with/about sth** to take an interest in something: *He didn't concern himself with the details.*
▷ CONSIDER IMPORTANT **5** **be concerned to do sth** (*formal*) to think it is important to do something: *She was concerned to write about situations that everyone could identify with.* **IDM** see FAR

● **noun**
▷ WORRY **1** [U, C] a feeling of worry, especially one that is shared by many people: ~ **(about sth/sb)** *There is growing concern about violence on television.* ♦ *In the meeting, voters raised concerns about health care.* ♦ ~ **(for sth/sb)** *She hasn't*

been seen for four days and there is concern for her safety. ♦ ~ **(over sth/sb)** *The report expressed concern over continuing high unemployment.* ♦ ~ **(that...)** *There is widespread concern that new houses will be built on protected land.* ♦ *Stress at work is a matter of concern to staff and management.* ♦ *The President's health was a serious cause for concern.* ⊃ compare UNCONCERN
▷ DESIRE TO PROTECT **2** [U] a desire to protect and help someone or something: *parents' concern for their children*
▷ SOMETHING IMPORTANT **3** [C] something that is important to a person, an organization, etc.: *What are your main concerns as a writer?* ♦ *The government's primary concern is to reduce crime.*
▷ RESPONSIBILITY **4** [C, usually sing.] (*formal*) something that is your responsibility or that you have a right to know about: *This matter is their concern.* ♦ *How much money I make is none of your concern.*
▷ COMPANY **5** [C] a company or business **SYN** FIRM: *a major publishing concern* **IDM** see GOING

con·cerned 🔑 /kən'sɜrnd/ *adj.*
1 worried and feeling concern about something: *Concerned parents held a meeting.* ♦ ~ **about/for sth** *The president is deeply concerned about this issue.* ♦ ~ **for sth** *He didn't seem in the least concerned for her safety.* ♦ ~ **(that)...** *She was concerned that she might miss the turn and get lost.* ⊃ thesaurus box at WORRIED **2** ~ **(about/with sth)** interested in something: *They were more concerned with how the others had dressed than with what the speaker was saying.* **ANT** UNCONCERNED **IDM** see FAR

con·cern·ing 🔑 /kən'sɜrnɪŋ/ *prep.* (*formal*)
about something; involving someone or something: *He asked several questions concerning the future of the company.* ♦ *All cases concerning children are dealt with in juvenile court.*

con·cert 🔑 /'kɑnsərt/ *noun*
a public performance of music: *a concert of music by Bach* ♦ *a classical/rock concert* ♦ *They're in concert at Madison Square Garden.* ♦ *a concert hall/pianist* ⊃ collocations at MUSIC **IDM** **in concert with sb/sth** (*formal*) working together with someone or something

con·cer·tan·te /ˌkɑntʃər'tɑnteɪ, -ti/ *adj.* [only before noun] (from *Italian, music*) related to a piece of music that contains an important part for a SOLO singer or player and that is similar to a CONCERTO in character

'concert ˌband *noun* a large group of people who play wind instruments together, and who perform in a concert hall ⊃ compare MILITARY BAND

con·cert·ed /kən'sɜrtəd/ *adj.* [only before noun] done in a planned and determined way, especially by more than one person, government, country, etc.: *a concerted approach/ attack/campaign* ♦ *She has begun to make a concerted effort to find a job.*

'concert-ˌgoer *noun* a person who regularly goes to concerts, especially of CLASSICAL music

ˌconcert 'grand *noun* a piano of the largest size, used especially for concerts

con·cer·ti·na /ˌkɑnsər'tinə/ *noun* a musical instrument like a small ACCORDION, that you hold in both hands. You press the ends together and pull them apart to produce sounds. ⊃ picture at ACCORDION

con·cert·mas·ter /'kɑnsərtˌmæstər/ *noun* the most important VIOLIN player in an ORCHESTRA

con·cer·to /kən'tʃɛrtoʊ/ *noun* (*pl.* **con·cer·tos**) a piece of music for one or more SOLO instruments playing with an ORCHESTRA: *a piano concerto* ♦ *a concerto for flute and harp*

con·ces·sion /kən'sɛʃn/ *noun* **1** [C, U] something that you allow or do, or allow someone to have, in order to end an argument or to make a situation less difficult: *The company will be forced to make concessions if it wants to avoid a strike.* ♦ *to win a concession from someone* ♦ *a major/an important concession* ♦ *She made no concession to his age; she expected him to work as hard as she did.* ⊃ see also CONCEDE **2** [U] the

t **tea**   ṭ **butter**   d **did**   k **cat**   g **got**   tʃ **chin**   dʒ **June**   f **fall**

act of giving something or allowing something; the act of conceding (CONCEDE): *McCain's concession speech* (= when he admitted that he had lost the election) **3** [C] a right or an advantage that is given to a group of people, an organization, etc., especially by a government or an employer: *The Bolivian government has granted logging concessions covering 22 million hectares.* **4** [C] the right to sell something in a particular place; the place where you sell it, sometimes an area that is part of a larger building or store: *the fast food concessions at the stadium*

con·ces·sion·aire /kənˌsɛʃəˈnɛr/ *noun* a person or a business that has been given a concession to sell something

con·ces·sive /kənˈsɛsɪv/ *adj.* (*grammar*) (of a preposition or conjunction) used at the beginning of a clause to say that the action of the main clause is in fact true or possible, despite the situation. "Despite" and "although" are concessive words.

conch /kɑŋk; kɑntʃ/ *noun* the shell of a sea creature that is also called a conch

con·cierge /kɑnˈsyɛrʒ; kɔn-/ *noun* (from *French*) a person in a hotel whose job is to help guests by giving them information, arranging theater tickets, etc.

con·cil·i·ate /kənˈsɪliˌeɪt/ *verb* ~ **sb** (*formal*) to make someone less angry or more friendly, especially by being kind and pleasant or by giving them something **SYN** PACIFY ▶ **con·cil·i·a·tion** /kənˌsɪliˈeɪʃn/ *noun* [U]: *A conciliation service helps to settle disputes between employers and workers.*

con·cil·i·a·tor /kənˈsɪliˌeɪtər/ *noun* a person or an organization that tries to make angry people calm so that they can discuss or solve their problems successfully

con·cil·i·a·to·ry /kənˈsɪliəˌtɔri/ *adj.* having the intention or effect of making angry people calm: *a conciliatory approach/attitude/gesture/move*

con·cise /kənˈsaɪs/ *adj.* **1** giving only the information that is necessary and important, using few words: *a concise summary* ◆ *clear concise instructions* **2** [only before noun] (of a book) shorter than the original book, on which it was based: *a concise dictionary* ▶ **con·cise·ly** *adv.* **con·cise·ness** (also less frequent **con·cis·ion** /kənˈsɪʒn/) *noun* [U]

con·clave /ˈkɑŋkleɪv/ *noun* (*formal*) a meeting to discuss something in private; the people at this meeting

---

AWL COLLOCATIONS

conclude

conclude *verb*

to reach a belief or an opinion as a result of thought or study

■ article, paper, report, study, survey | author, researcher, scientist | court

Lee's study concluded that rewarding employees who repeatedly try new things leads to more innovation.

■ reasonably, safely

Direct evidence is needed before safely concluding that the drug is not effective.

conclusion *noun*

a belief or an opinion that you reach after considering something carefully

■ arrive at, come to, draw, reach | reinforce, support

There are too many exceptions to draw any firm conclusions on this point.

The author supports his arguments well with many examples, and reaches convincing conclusions.

■ be based on, derive from

Their conclusion derives from a survey carried out in five countries.

■ definitive, firm | logical, valid | tentative | erroneous

Without careful examination, erroneous conclusions can result.

conclusive *adj.*

■ evidence, proof

Despite the lack of conclusive evidence, the claims were accepted.

■ far from

Despite years of study, the results from empirical research are far from conclusive.

inconclusive *adj.*

■ evidence, findings, result

The inconclusive findings of these studies indicate the need for additional research.

■ prove | remain

The experiment proved inconclusive.

The virus most likely originated from animals, but evidence remains inconclusive.

con·clude 🔑 **AWL** /kənˈklud/ *verb*

1 [T] (not used in the progressive tenses) to decide or believe something as a result of what you have heard or seen: ~ **sth (from sth)** *What do you conclude from that?* ◆ ~ **(that)...** *The report concluded (that) the cheapest option was to close the laboratory.* ◆ ~ **from sth that...** *He concluded from their remarks that they were not in favor of the plan.* ◆ **it is concluded that...** *It was concluded that the level of change necessary would be low.* ◆ + **speech** *"So it should be safe to continue," he concluded.* ⟳ language bank at CONCLUSION **2** [I, T] (*formal*) to come to an end; to bring something to an end: *Let me make just a few concluding remarks.* ◆ ~ **with sth** *The program concluded with Stravinsky's "Rite of Spring."* ◆ ~ **by doing sth** *He concluded by wishing everyone a safe trip home.* ◆ ~ **sth (with sth)** *The commission concluded its investigation last month.* ◆ + **speech** *"Anyway, she should be back soon," he concluded.* **3** [T] ~ **sth (with sb)** to arrange and settle an agreement with someone formally and finally: *They concluded a treaty with Turkey.* ◆ *A trade agreement was concluded between the two countries.*

con·clu·sion 🔑 **AWL** /kənˈkluʒn/ *noun*

1 [C] something that you decide when you have thought about all the information connected with the situation: *I've come to the conclusion that he's not the right person for the job.* ◆ *It took the jury some time to reach the conclusion that she was guilty.* ◆ *New evidence might lead to the conclusion that we are wrong.* ◆ *We can safely draw some conclusions from our discussion.* ⟳ collocations at SCIENTIFIC ⟳ collocations at CONCLUDE **2** [C, usually sing.] the end of something such as a speech or a piece of writing: *The conclusion of the book was disappointing.* ◆ *In conclusion,* (= finally) *I would like to thank...* ◆ *If we took this argument to its logical conclusion ...* **3** [U] the formal and final arrangement of something official **SYN** COMPLETION: *the successful conclusion of a trade treaty* **IDM** **jump/leap to conclusions**| **jump/leap to the conclusion that...** to make a decision about someone or something too quickly, before you know or have thought about all the facts: *There I go again—jumping to conclusions.* ⟳ more at FOREGONE

LANGUAGE BANK

conclusion

summing up an argument

■ **In conclusion,** the study has provided useful insights into the issues relating to people's perception of crime.

■ Based on this study, **it can be concluded that** the introduction of new street lighting did not reduce reported crime.

■ **To sum up,** no evidence can be found to support the

---

view that improved street lighting reduces reported crime.
- The available evidence clearly **leads to the conclusion that** the media do have an influence on the public perception of crime.
- **The main conclusion to be drawn from** this study is that the public perception of crime is significantly influenced by crime news reporting.
- **This study has shown that** people's fear of crime is out of all proportion to crime itself.
- Fear of crime is out of all proportion to the actual level of crime, and the reasons for this **can be summarized as follows**. First...
- **Overall/In general**, women are more likely than men to feel insecure walking alone after dark.
↪ Language Banks at EMPHASIS, FIRST, GENERALLY

con·clu·sive AWL /kənˈklusɪv/ adj. proving something, and allowing no doubt or confusion: *conclusive evidence/proof/results* **ANT** INCONCLUSIVE ↪ collocations at CONCLUDE ▸ **con·clu·sive·ly** AWL adv.: *to prove something conclusively*

con·coct /kənˈkɑkt/ verb **1** ~ sth to make something, especially food or a drink, by mixing different things: *The soup was concocted from up to a dozen different kinds of fish.* **2** ~ sth to invent a story, an excuse, etc. **SYN** COOK UP, MAKE UP: *She concocted some elaborate story to explain her absence.*

con·coc·tion /kənˈkɑkʃn/ noun a strange or unusual mixture of things, especially drinks or medicines: *a concoction of cream and rum*

con·com·i·tant /kənˈkɑmətənt/ adj., noun
- *adj.* (formal) happening at the same time as something else, especially because one thing is related to or causes the other
- *noun* (formal) a thing that happens at the same time as something else

con·cord /ˈkɑŋkɔrd/ noun [U] **1** ~ (with sb) (formal) peace and agreement **SYN** HARMONY: *living in concord with neighboring states* **ANT** DISCORD **2** ~ (with sth) (grammar) (of words in a phrase) the fact of having the same NUMBER, GENDER, or PERSON **SYN** AGREEMENT

con·cord·ance /kənˈkɔrdns/ noun **1** [C] an alphabetical list of the words used in a book, etc. showing where and how often they are used: *a Bible concordance* **2** [C] a list produced by a computer that shows all the examples of an individual word in a book, etc. **3** [U] (technical) the state of being similar to something or consistent with it: *There is reasonable concordance between the two sets of results.*

con·cord·ant /kənˈkɔrdnt/ adj. ~ with sth (formal) in agreement with something **SYN** CONSISTENT: *The results of the two studies were roughly concordant (with each other).*

con·cor·dat /kənˈkɔrdæt/ noun an agreement, especially between the Roman Catholic Church and the state

con·course /ˈkɑŋkɔrs/ noun a large, open part of a public building, especially an airport or a train station: *Your flight leaves from concourse B.*

con·crete 🔑 adj., noun
- *adj.* /ˈkɑŋkrit; ˈkɑŋkrit/ **1** made of concrete: *a concrete floor* **2** based on facts, not on ideas or guesses: *concrete evidence/proposals/proof* ◆ *"It's only a suspicion," she said, "nothing concrete."* ◆ *It is easier to think in concrete terms rather than in the abstract.* ↪ compare ABSTRACT **3** a concrete object is one that you can see and feel ▸ **con·crete·ly** /kənˈkritli/ adv.
- *noun* /kənˈkrit; ˈkɑŋ-/ [U] building material that is made by mixing together CEMENT, sand, small stones, and water: *a slab of concrete*

ˌ**concrete ˈjungle** noun [usually sing.] a way of describing a city or an area that is unpleasant because it has many large modern buildings and no trees or parks

ˌ**concrete ˌmixer** noun = CEMENT MIXER

ˌ**concrete ˈpoetry** noun [U] poetry in which the meaning or effect is communicated partly by using patterns of words or letters that are visible on the page

con·cu·bine /ˈkɑŋkyəˌbaɪn/ noun (especially in some societies in the past) a woman who lives with a man, often in addition to his wife or wives, but who is less important than they are

con·cu·pis·cence /kənˈkyupəsns/ noun [U] (formal, often disapproving) strong sexual desire **SYN** LUST

con·cur /kənˈkər/ verb (-rr-) [I, T] ~ (with sb) (in sth) | ~ (with sth) | ~ (that...) | (+ speech) (formal) to agree: *Historians have concurred with each other in this view.* ◆ *The coroner concurred with this assessment.*

con·cur·rence /kənˈkərəns/ noun (formal) **1** [U, sing.] agreement: *The doctor may seek the concurrence of a relative before carrying out the procedure.* **2** [sing.] an example of two or more things happening at the same time: *an unfortunate concurrence of events*

con·cur·rent AWL /kənˈkərənt/ adj. ~ (with sth) existing or happening at the same time: *He was imprisoned for two concurrent terms of 30 months and 18 months.* ▸ **con·cur·rent·ly** AWL adv.: *The prison sentences will run concurrently.*

con·cuss /kənˈkʌs/ verb ~ sb to hit someone on the head, making them become unconscious or confused for a short time ▸ **con·cussed** adj.: *She was concussed after the fall.*

con·cus·sion /kənˈkʌʃn/ noun a temporary loss of CONSCIOUSNESS caused by a blow to the head; the effects of a severe blow to the head such as confusion and temporary loss of physical and mental abilities: *He was taken to the hospital with a concussion.*

con·demn /kənˈdɛm/ verb
❯ EXPRESS DISAPPROVAL **1** ~ sb/sth (for/as sth) to express very strong disapproval of someone or something, usually for moral reasons: *The government issued a statement condemning the killings.* ◆ *The editor of the newspaper was condemned as lacking integrity.*
❯ SOMEONE TO PUNISHMENT **2** [usually passive] to say what someone's punishment will be **SYN** SENTENCE: ~ sb (to sth) *He was condemned to death for murder and later hanged.* ◆ ~ sb to do sth *She was condemned to hang for killing her husband.*
❯ SOMEONE TO DIFFICULT SITUATION **3** [usually passive] ~ sb to sth to force someone to accept a difficult or unpleasant situation **SYN** DOOM: *They were condemned to a life of hardship.* ◆ *He was condemned to spend the rest of the football season on the bench.*
❯ SOMETHING DANGEROUS **4** [usually passive] ~ sth (as sth) to say officially that something is not safe enough to be used: *a condemned building* ◆ *The old rollercoaster was condemned as a safety hazard.*
❯ SHOW GUILT **5** ~ sb to show or suggest that someone is guilty of something: *She is condemned out of her own mouth* (= her own words show that she is guilty).

con·dem·na·tion /ˌkɑndəmˈneɪʃn/ noun [U, C] ~ (of sb/sth) an expression of very strong disapproval: *There was widespread condemnation of the invasion.*

con·den·sa·tion /ˌkɑndənˈseɪʃn/ noun **1** [U] drops of water that form on a cold surface when warm water VAPOR becomes cool **2** [U] the process of a gas changing to a liquid **3** [C, usually sing., U] (formal) the process of making a book, etc. shorter by taking out anything that is not necessary

con·dense /kənˈdɛns/ verb **1** [I, T] to change from a gas into a liquid; to make a gas change into a liquid: ~ (into sth) *Steam condenses into water when it cools.* ◆ ~ sth (into sth) *The steam was condensed rapidly by injecting cold water into the cylinder.* **2** [I, T] ~ (sth) if a liquid **condenses** or you **condense** it, it becomes thicker and stronger because it has lost some of its water **SYN** REDUCE: *Condense the soup by boiling it for several minutes.* **3** [T] ~ sth (into sth) to put something such as a piece of writing into fewer words; to put a lot of information into a small space: *The article was*

h **hat**   m **man**   n **no**   ŋ **sing**   1 **leg**   r **red**   y **yes**   w **wet**

condensed into just two pages. ♦ *The author has condensed a great deal of material into just 100 pages.*

con·densed 'milk *noun* [U] a type of thick sweet milk that is sold in cans

con·dens·er /kənˈdɛnsər/ *noun* **1** a device that cools gas in order to change it into a liquid **2** a device that receives or stores electricity, especially in a car engine

con·de·scend /ˌkɑndəˈsɛnd/ *verb* **1** [I] ~ **to sb** to behave toward someone as though you are more important and more intelligent than they are: *When giving a talk, be careful not to condescend to your audience.* **2** [T] ~ **to do sth** (often *disapproving*) to do something that you think it is below your social or professional position to do **SYN** DEIGN: *We had to wait almost an hour before he condescended to see us.*
▶ **con·de·scen·sion** /ˌkɑndəˈsɛnʃn/ *noun* [U]: *Her smile was a mixture of pity and condescension.*

con·de·scend·ing /ˌkɑndəˈsɛndɪŋ/ *adj.* behaving as though you are more important and more intelligent than other people: *He has a condescending attitude toward women.*
▶ **con·de·scend·ing·ly** *adv.*

con·dign /kənˈdaɪn/ *adj.* (*formal*) (of a punishment) appropriate to the crime

con·di·ment /ˈkɑndəmənt/ *noun* [usually pl.] **1** a sauce, etc. that is used to give flavor to food, or that is eaten with food: *ketchup, mustard, and other condiments* **2** a substance such as salt or pepper that is used to give flavor to food

con·di·tion 🔎 /kənˈdɪʃn/ *noun, verb*

● *noun*
▷ **STATE OF SOMETHING 1** [U, sing.] the state that something is in: *to be in bad/good/excellent condition* ♦ *a used car in perfect condition*
▷ **CIRCUMSTANCES 2 conditions** [pl.] the circumstances or situation in which people live, work, or do things: *living/housing/working conditions* ♦ *changing economic conditions* ♦ *neglected children living under the most appalling conditions* ♦ *a strike to improve pay and conditions* ➔ thesaurus box at SITUATION **3 conditions** [pl.] the physical situation that affects how something happens: *The plants grow best in cool, damp conditions.* ♦ *freezing/icy/humid, etc. conditions* ♦ *Conditions are ideal* (= the weather is very good) *for sailing today.* ♦ *treacherous driving conditions*
▷ **MEDICAL 4** [U, sing.] the state of someone's health or how physically fit they are: *He is overweight and out of condition* (= not physically fit). ♦ *You are in no condition* (= too sick, etc.) *to go anywhere.* ♦ *The motorcyclist was in a critical condition in the hospital last night.* ➔ thesaurus box at ILLNESS **5** [C] an illness or a medical problem that you have for a long time because it is not possible to cure it: *a medical condition* ♦ *He suffers from a serious heart condition.* ➔ thesaurus box at DISEASE
▷ **RULE 6** [C] a rule or decision that you must agree to, sometimes forming part of a contract or an official agreement: *the terms and conditions of employment* ♦ *The offer is subject to certain conditions.* ♦ *They agreed to lend us the car on condition that* (= only if) *we returned it before the weekend.* ♦ *They will give us the money on one condition* —*that we pay it back within six months.* ♦ *They agreed under the condition that we give them regular progress reports.* ♦ *Congress can impose strict conditions on the bank.* ♦ *They have agreed to the ceasefire provided their conditions are met.*
▷ **NECESSARY SITUATION 7** [C] a situation that must exist in order for something else to happen: *a necessary condition for economic growth* ♦ *A good training program is one of the conditions for successful industry.*
▷ **STATE OF GROUP 8** [sing.] (*formal*) the state of a particular group of people because of their situation in life, their problems, etc.: *He spoke angrily about the condition of the urban poor.* ♦ *Work is basic to the human condition* (= the fact of being alive).
IDM **on/under no condition** (*formal*) not in any situation; never: *You must on no condition tell them what happened.* ➔ more at MINT

● *verb* **1** [usually passive] to train someone or something to behave in a particular way or to become used to a particular situation: ~ **sb/sth (to sth)** *the difference between inborn and conditioned reflexes* (= reactions that are learned/not natural) ♦ *Patients can become conditioned to particular forms of treatment.* ♦ ~ **sb/sth to do sth** *The rats had been conditioned to ring a bell when they wanted food.* **2** ~ **sb/sth** to have an important effect on someone or something; to influence the way that something happens: *Gender roles are often conditioned by cultural factors.* **3** ~ **sth** to keep something such as your hair or skin healthy: *a shampoo that cleans and conditions hair* ♦ *a polish for conditioning leather*

con·di·tion·al /kənˈdɪʃnl/ *adj., noun*
● *adj.* **1** ~ **(on/upon sth)** depending on something: *conditional approval/acceptance* ♦ *Payment is conditional upon delivery of the goods* (= if the goods are not delivered the money will not be paid) ♦ *He was found guilty and given a conditional discharge* (= allowed to go free on particular conditions). ♦ *a conditional offer* (= that depends on particular conditions being met) **ANT** UNCONDITIONAL **2** [only before noun] (*grammar*) expressing something that must happen or be true if another thing is to happen or be true: *a conditional sentence/clause* ▶ **con·di·tion·al·ly** /-ʃənəli/ *adv.*: *The offer was made conditionally.*
● *noun* (*grammar*) **1** [C] a sentence or clause that begins with *if* or *unless* and expresses a condition **2 the conditional** [sing.] the form of a verb that expresses a conditional action, for example *should* in *If I should die…*: *the present/past/perfect conditional* ♦ *the first/second/third conditional*

con·di·tion·er /kənˈdɪʃənər/ *noun* [C, U] a liquid that makes hair soft and shiny after washing: *shampoo and conditioner*

con·di·tion·ing /kənˈdɪʃənɪŋ/ *noun* [U] **1** the training or experience that an animal or a person has that makes them behave in a particular way in a particular situation: *Is personality the result of conditioning from parents and society, or are we born with it?* **2** the process of following a regular program of diet and exercise to become healthier and stronger: *Thanks to the efforts of the new coach, the team's conditioning had improved dramatically.* ➔ see also AIR CONDITIONING

con·do /ˈkɑndoʊ/ *noun* (*pl.* **con·dos**) (*informal*) = CONDOMINIUM

con·do·lence /kənˈdoʊləns/ *noun* [C, usually pl., U] sympathy that you feel for someone when a person in their family or that they know well has died; an expression of this

---

sympathy: *to give/offer/express* your *condolences* ◆ *Our condolences go to his wife and family.* ◆ *a letter of condolence*

con·dom /ˈkɑndəm/ *noun* **1** (*also formal or technical* **pro·phy·lac·tic**) a thin rubber covering that a man wears over his PENIS during sex to stop a woman from becoming pregnant or to protect against disease **2 female condom** a thin rubber device that a woman wears inside her VAGINA during sex to prevent herself from becoming pregnant

con·do·min·i·um /ˌkɑndəˈmɪniəm/ (*also informal* **con·do**) *noun* an apartment building in which each apartment is owned by the person living in it but the building and shared areas are owned by everyone together; a apartment in such a building

con·done /kənˈdoʊn/ *verb* ~ **sth** | ~ **(sb) doing sth** to accept behavior that is morally wrong or to treat it as if it were not serious: *Terrorism can never be condoned.*

con·dor /ˈkɑndɔr; -dər/ *noun* a large bird of the VULTURE family, that lives in S. America, Mexico, and the Western U.S.

con·du·cive /kənˈdusɪv/ *adj.* ~ **to sth** making it easy, possible, or likely for something to happen: *Chairs in rows are not as conducive to discussion as chairs arranged in a circle.*

con·duct ⚡ **AWL** *verb, noun*

● *verb* /kənˈdʌkt/ **1** [T] ~ **sth** to organize and/or do a particular activity: *to conduct an experiment/an investigation/a survey* ◆ *The negotiations have been conducted in a positive manner.* **2** [T, I] ~ **(sth)** to direct a group of people who are singing or playing music: *a concert by the San Francisco Symphony, conducted by Michael Tilson Thomas* **3** [T] ~ **sth** (*technical*) (of a substance) to allow heat or electricity to pass along or through it: *Copper conducts electricity well.* **4** [T] ~ **yourself + adv./prep.** (*formal*) to behave in a particular way: *He conducted himself far better than expected.* **5** [T] ~ **sb/sth + adv./prep.** to lead or guide someone through or around a place: *The guide conducted us around the ruins of the ancient city.*

● *noun* /ˈkɑndʌkt/ [U] (*formal*) **1** a person's behavior in a particular place or in a particular situation: *The sport has a strict code of conduct.* **2** ~ **of sth** the way in which a business or an activity is organized and managed: *There was growing criticism of the government's conduct of the war.* ⊃ see also SAFE CONDUCT

con·duct·ance /kənˈdʌktəns/ *noun* [U] (*physics*) the degree to which an object allows electricity or heat to pass through it

con·duc·tion /kənˈdʌkʃn/ *noun* [U] (*physics*) the process by which heat or electricity passes through a material

con·duc·tive /kənˈdʌktɪv/ *adj.* (*physics*) able to CONDUCT electricity, heat, etc. ▶ **con·duc·tiv·i·ty** /ˌkɑndʌkˈtɪvəti/ *noun* [U]

con·ductive edu·cation *noun* [U] a treatment for people with CEREBRAL PALSY that was developed in Hungary and that involves special physical exercises and learning methods

con·duc·tor /kənˈdʌktər/ *noun* **1** a person who stands in front of an ORCHESTRA, a group of singers etc., and directs their performance, especially someone who does this as a profession **2** a person who is in charge of a train and travels with it, but does not drive it **3** (*physics*) a substance that allows electricity or heat to pass along it or through it: *Wood is a poor conductor.* ⊃ see also LIGHTNING CONDUCTOR

con·duit /ˈkɑnduət/ *noun* **1** (*technical*) a pipe, channel, or tube through which liquid, gas, or electrical wire can pass **2** (*formal*) a person, an organization or a country that is used to pass things or information to other people or places: *The organization had acted as a conduit for money from the arms industry.*

cone /koʊn/ *noun* **1** a solid or hollow object with a round flat base and sides that slope up to a point ⊃ picture at SHAPE ⊃ see also CONIC, CONICAL **2** a solid or hollow object that is shaped like a cone: *a paper cone full of popcorn* ◆ *the cone of a volcano* ⊃ see also NOSE CONE, SNOW CONE **3** = TRAFFIC

CONE **4** a piece of thin crisp cookie shaped like a cone, which you can put ice cream in to eat it **5** the hard dry fruit of a PINE or FIR tree: *a pine cone* ⊃ picture at TREE

con·fab /ˈkɑnfæb/ *noun* (*informal*) **1** an informal private discussion or conversation **2** a meeting or conference of the members of a profession or group: *the annual movie confab in Cannes*

con·fab·u·la·tion /kənˌfæbyəˈleɪʃn/ *noun* [C, U] (*formal*) **1** a story that someone has invented in their mind; the act of inventing a story in your mind **2** a conversation; the activity of having a conversation

con·fec·tion /kənˈfɛkʃn/ *noun* **1** (*formal*) a cake or other sweet food that looks very attractive **2** a thing such as a building or piece of clothing, that is made in a skillful or complicated way **3** a book, movie, song, etc., that provides entertainment but is not very serious

con·fec·tion·er /kənˈfɛkʃənər/ *noun* a person or a business that makes or sells cakes and candy

con'fectioner's ˌsugar (*also* ˌpowdered ˈsugar) *noun* [U] fine white powder made from sugar, that is mixed with milk or water to make frosting

con·fec·tion·er·y /kənˈfɛkʃəˌnɛri/ *noun* [U] candy, chocolate, etc.

con·fed·er·a·cy /kənˈfɛdərəsi/ *noun* **1** [C] a union of states, groups of people, or political parties with the same aim **2 the Confederacy** [sing.] (*also* **the Conˌfederate ˈStates** [pl.]) the eleven southern states of the U.S. which left the United States in 1860-1, starting the American Civil War

con·fed·er·ate /kənˈfɛdərət/ *noun, adj.*

● *noun* **1 Confederate** a person who supported the confederacy in the American Civil War **2** a person who helps someone, especially to do something illegal or secret **SYN** ACCOMPLICE

● *adj.* **1 Confederate** belonging to the confederacy in the American Civil War: *a Confederate soldier* ◆ *the Confederate flag* **2** belonging to a confederacy

the Conˌfederate ˈStates *noun* [pl.] = CONFEDERACY (2)

con·fed·er·a·tion /kənˌfɛdəˈreɪʃn/ *noun* an organization consisting of countries, businesses, etc., that have joined together in order to help each other: *The New England Confederation existed from 1643 to 1684.*

con·fer **AWL** /kənˈfər/ *verb* (-rr-) (*formal*) **1** [I] ~ **(with sb) (on/about sth)** to discuss something with someone, in order to exchange opinions or get advice: *He wanted to confer with his colleagues before reaching a decision.* **2** [T] ~ **sth (on/upon sb)** to give someone an award, a degree, or a particular honor or right: *An honorary degree was conferred on him by Stanford University in 2009.*

con·fer·ence ⚡ **AWL** /ˈkɑnfrəns/ *noun*

1 a large official meeting, usually lasting for a few days, at which people with the same work or interests come together to discuss their views: *The hotel is used for exhibitions, conferences and social events.* ◆ *a conference room/center* ◆ *She is attending a three-day conference on AIDS education.* ◆ *The conference will be held in Orlando.* ◆ *delegates to the American Association of Pediatrics' annual conference* **2** a meeting at which people have formal discussions: *Representatives from all four countries involved will meet at the conference table this week.* ◆ *He was in conference with his lawyers all day.* ⊃ see also PRESS CONFERENCE **3** a group of sports teams that play against each other in a league: *Southeast Conference football champions*

ˈconference ˌcall *noun* a telephone call in which three or more people take part

ˈconference comˌmittee *noun* (*politics*) a temporary committee formed by members of the U.S. Congress (the House of Representatives and the Senate) to resolve differences between the two versions of a bill created by them

con·fer·en·cing /ˈkɑnfrənsɪŋ/ *noun* the activity of organizing or taking part in meetings, especially when people are in different places and use telephones, computers, or video to communicate: *video conferencing*

con·fer·ment /kənˈfɜrmənt/ *noun* [U, C] (*formal*) the action of giving someone an award, a university degree, or a particular honor or right

con·fess /kənˈfɛs/ *verb* **1** [I, T] to admit, especially formally or to the police, that you have done something wrong or illegal: *After hours of questioning, the suspect confessed.* ◆ **~ to sth/to doing sth** *She confessed to the murder.* ◆ **~ (that)...** *He confessed that he had stolen the money.* ◆ **~ sth** *We persuaded her to confess her crime.* **2** [I, T] to admit something that you feel ashamed or embarrassed about: **~ sth** *She was reluctant to confess her ignorance.* ◆ **~ to sth/to doing sth** *I must confess I know nothing about computers.* ◆ **~ (that)...** *I confess (that) I know nothing about computers.* ◆ **+ speech** *"I know nothing about them," he confessed.* ◆ **~ yourself + adj.** (*formal*) *I confess myself bewildered by their explanation.* ◆ see also SELF-CONFESSED ➔ thesaurus box at ADMIT **3** [I, T] **~ (sth) (to sb)** (especially in the Roman Catholic Church) to tell God or a priest about the bad things you have done so that you can say that you are sorry and be forgiven **4** [T] **~ sb** (of a priest) to hear someone confess their SINS (= the bad things they have done)

con·fes·sion /kənˈfɛʃn/ *noun* **1** [C, U] a statement that a person makes, admitting that they are guilty of a crime; the act of making such a statement: *After hours of questioning by police, she made a full confession.* **2** [C, U] a statement admitting something that you are ashamed or embarrassed about; the act of making such a statement **SYN** ADMISSION: *I have a confession to make—I lied about my age.* **3** [U, C] (especially in the Roman Catholic Church) a private statement to a priest about the bad things that you have done: *to go to confession* ◆ *to hear someone's confession* **4** [C] (*formal*) a statement of your religious beliefs, principles, etc.: *a confession of faith*

con·fes·sion·al /kənˈfɛʃnl/ *noun*
● *noun* a private place in a church where a priest listens to people making confessions
● *adj.* (of a speech or piece of writing) in which a person talks or writes about private thoughts or past events, especially ones that make the person feel ashamed or embarrassed: *his confessional outpourings*

con·fes·sor /kənˈfɛsər/ *noun* a Roman Catholic priest who listens to CONFESSIONS

con·fet·ti /kənˈfɛti/ *noun* [U] small pieces of colored paper that people often throw at weddings over people who have just been married, or at other special events

con·fi·dant (*feminine* also **con·fi·dante**) /ˈkɑnfəˌdɑnt/ *noun* a person that you trust and who you talk to about private or secret things: *a close/trusted confidant of the President*

con·fide /kənˈfaɪd/ *verb* to tell someone secrets and personal information that you do not want other people to know: **~ sth (to sb)** *She confided all her secrets to her best friend.* ◆ **~ (to sb) that...** *He confided to me that he had applied for another job.* ◆ **+ speech** *"It was a lie," he confided.*
PHR V **con·fide in sb** to tell someone secrets and personal information because you feel you can trust them: *It is important to have someone you can confide in.*

con·fi·dence 🔑 /ˈkɑnfədəns/ *noun*
> **BELIEF IN OTHERS 1** [U] **~ (in sb/sth)** the feeling that you can trust, believe in, and be sure about the abilities or good qualities of someone or something: *The players all have confidence in their manager.* ◆ *A fall in unemployment will help to restore consumer confidence.* ◆ *a lack of confidence in the government* ◆ *The new contracts have undermined the confidence of employees.* ◆ *She has every confidence in her students' abilities.* ➔ see also CONSUMER CONFIDENCE, VOTE OF CONFIDENCE, VOTE OF NO CONFIDENCE
> **BELIEF IN YOURSELF 2** [U] a belief in your own ability to do things and be successful: *He answered the questions with confidence.* ◆ *People often lose confidence when they are criticized.* ◆ *He gained confidence when he went to college.* ◆ *She*

suffers from a lack of confidence. ◆ *While girls sometimes lack confidence, boys often overestimate their abilities.* ◆ *I didn't have any confidence in myself at school.*
> **FEELING CERTAIN 3** [U] the feeling that you are certain about something: *They could not say with confidence that he would be able to walk again after the accident.* ◆ *He expressed his confidence that they would win.*
> **TRUST 4** [U] a feeling of trust that someone will keep information private: *Eva told me about their relationship in confidence.* ◆ *This is in the strictest confidence.* ◆ *It took a long time to gain her confidence* (= make her feel she could trust me).
> **A SECRET 5** [C] (*formal*) a secret that you tell someone: *The girls exchanged confidences.* ◆ *I could never forgive Mike for betraying a confidence.*
IDM **be in sb's confidence** to be trusted with someone's secrets: *He is said to be very much in the President's confidence.* **take sb into your confidence** to tell someone secrets and personal information about yourself: *She took me into her confidence and told me about the problems she was facing.*

con·fi·dent 🔑 /ˈkɑnfədənt/ *adj.*
1 feeling sure about your own ability to do things and be successful: *She was feeling relaxed and confident.* ◆ *The teacher wants the children to feel confident about asking questions when they don't understand.* ➔ see also SELF-CONFIDENT **2** feeling certain that something will happen in the way that you want or expect: **~ of sth/doing sth** *The team feels confident of winning.* ◆ **~ that...** *I'm confident that you will get the job.* ➔ thesaurus box at SURE ▶ **con·fi·dent·ly** *adv.*

con·fi·den·tial /ˌkɑnfəˈdɛnʃl/ *adj.* **1** meant to be kept secret and not told to or shared with other people: *confidential information/documents* ◆ *Your medical records are strictly confidential* (= completely secret). **2** (of a way of speaking) showing that what you are saying is private or secret: *He spoke in a confidential tone, his voice low.* **3** [only before noun] trusted with private or secret information: *a confidential secretary* ▶ **con·fi·den·tial·ly** /-ʃəli/ *adv.*: *She told me confidentially that she is going to retire early.*

con·fi·den·ti·al·i·ty /ˌkɑnfəˌdɛnʃiˈæləti/ *noun* [U] a situation in which you expect someone to keep information secret: *They signed a confidentiality agreement.* ◆ *All letters will be treated with complete confidentiality.*

con·fid·ing /kənˈfaɪdɪŋ/ *adj.* [usually before noun] showing trust; showing that you want to tell someone a secret: *a confiding relationship* ▶ **con·fid·ing·ly** *adv.*

con·fig·u·ra·tion /kənˌfɪgjəˈreɪʃn/ *noun* **1** (*formal* or *technical*) an arrangement of the parts of something or a group of things; the form or shape that this arrangement produces **2** (*computing*) the equipment and programs that form a computer system and the way that these are set up to run

con·fig·ure /kənˈfɪgjər/ *verb* [usually passive] **~ sth** (*technical*) to arrange something in a particular way, especially computer equipment; to make equipment or software work in the way that the user prefers

con·fine AWL /kənˈfaɪn/ *verb* **1 ~ sb/sth to sth** [often passive] to keep someone or something inside the limits of a particular activity, subject, area, etc. **SYN** RESTRICT: *The work will not be confined to the Cleveland area.* ◆ *I will confine myself to looking at the period from 1900 to 1916.* **2 ~ sb/sth (in sth)** [usually passive] to keep a person or an animal in a small or closed space: *Keep the dog confined in a suitable traveling cage.* ◆ *Here the river is confined in a narrow channel.* ◆ *The soldiers concerned were confined to barracks* (= had to stay in the BARRACKS, as a punishment) **3 be confined to bed, a wheelchair, etc.** to have to stay in bed, in a WHEELCHAIR, etc.: *She was confined to bed with the flu.* ◆ *He was confined to a wheelchair after the accident.*

con·fined AWL /kənˈfaɪnd/ *adj.* [usually before noun] (of a space or an area) small and surrounded by walls or sides: *It is cruel to keep animals in confined spaces.*

con·fine·ment /kənˈfaɪnmənt/ *noun* **1** [U] the state of being forced to stay in a closed space, prison, etc.; the act of putting someone there: *her confinement to a wheelchair*

♦ *years of confinement as a political prisoner* ➪ see also HOME CONFINEMENT, SOLITARY CONFINEMENT **2** [U, C] (*formal or old-fashioned*) the time when a woman gives birth to a baby: *the expected date of confinement*

con·fines **AWL** /'kɑnfaɪnz/ *noun* [pl.] (*formal*) limits or borders: *It is beyond the confines of human knowledge.* ♦ *the confines of family life*

con·firm 🔑 **AWL** /kən'fɚm/ *verb*
1 to state or show that something is definitely true or correct, especially by providing evidence: **~ sth** *Rumors of job losses were later confirmed.* ♦ *His guilty expression confirmed my suspicions.* ♦ *Please write to confirm your reservation* (= say that it is definite). ♦ **~ (that)…** *Has everyone confirmed (that) they're coming?* ♦ **~ what/when, etc.…** *Can you confirm what happened?* ♦ **it is confirmed that…** *It has been confirmed that the meeting will take place next week.* **2 ~ sth** | **~ sb (in sth)** to make someone feel or believe something even more strongly: *The walk in the mountains confirmed his fear of heights.* **3 ~ sth** to make a position, an agreement, etc. more definite or official; to establish someone or something firmly: *After a six-month probationary period, her position was confirmed.* ♦ *He was confirmed as captain for the rest of the season.* **4** [usually passive] **~ sb** to make someone a full member of the Christian Church: *She was baptized when she was a month old and confirmed when she was thirteen.* **5** [usually passive] **~ sb** to perform a ceremony when a young person has completed their high school Jewish studies

con·fir·ma·tion **AWL** /ˌkɑnfɚ'meɪʃn/ *noun* [U, C] **1** a statement, letter, etc. that shows that something is true, correct, or definite: *I'm still waiting for confirmation of the test results.* **2** a ceremony at which a person becomes a full member of the Christian Church **3** a Jewish ceremony similar to a BAR MITZVAH or BAT MITZVAH but usually for young people over the age of 16

con·firmed **AWL** /kən'fɚmd/ *adj.* [only before noun] having a particular habit or way of life and not likely to change: *a confirmed bachelor* (= a man who is not likely to get married, sometimes used in newspapers to refer to a HOMO-SEXUAL man)

con·fis·cate /'kɑnfəˌskeɪt/ *verb* **~ sth** to officially take something away from someone, especially as a punishment: *Their land was confiscated after the war.* ♦ *The teacher threatened to confiscate their phones if they kept using them in class.* ▶ **con·fis·ca·tion** /ˌkɑnfə'skeɪʃn/ *noun* [U, C]

con·fla·gra·tion /ˌkɑnflə'greɪʃn/ *noun* (*formal*) a very large fire that destroys a lot of land or buildings

con·flate /kən'fleɪt/ *verb* **~ A and/with B** (*formal*) to put two or more things together to make one new thing ▶ **con·fla·tion** /kən'fleɪʃn/ *noun* [U, C]

con·flict 🔑 **AWL** *noun, verb*
● *noun* /'kɑnflɪkt/ [C, U] **~ (between A and B)** | **~ (over sth)** **1** a situation in which people, groups, or countries are involved in a serious disagreement or argument: *a conflict between two cultures* ♦ *The violence was the result of political and ethnic conflicts.* ♦ *She found herself in conflict with her parents over her future career.* ♦ *John often comes into conflict with his boss.* ♦ *The government has done nothing to resolve the conflict over nurses' pay.* **2** a violent situation or period of fighting between two countries: *armed/military conflict* ➪ collocations at WAR **3** a situation in which there are opposing ideas, opinions, feelings, or wishes; a situation in which it is difficult to choose: *The story tells of a classic conflict between love and duty.* ♦ *Her diary was a record of her inner conflict.* ♦ *Many of these ideas appear to be in conflict with each other.*
IDM **conflict of interest(s)** a situation in which there are two jobs, aims, roles, etc., and it is not possible for both of them to be treated equally and fairly at the same time: *There was a conflict of interest between his business dealings and his political activities.*
● *verb* /kən'flɪkt/ [I] **~ (with sth)** if two ideas, beliefs, stories,

etc. **conflict**, it is not possible for them to exist together or for them both to be true **SYN** CLASH: *conflicting emotions/interests/loyalties* ♦ *These results conflict with earlier findings.* ♦ *Reports conflicted on how much of the aid was reaching the famine victims.*

con·flict·ed **AWL** /kən'flɪktəd/ *adj.* confused about what to do or choose because you have strong but opposing feelings

con·flu·ence /'kɑnfluəns/ *noun* [usually sing.] **1** (*technical*) the place where two rivers flow together and become one **2** (*formal*) the fact of two or more things becoming one: *a confluence of social factors*

con·form **AWL** /kən'fɔrm/ *verb* **1** [I] to behave and think in the same way as most other people in a group or society: *There is considerable pressure on teenagers to conform.* ♦ **~ to sth** *He refused to conform to the local customs.* **2** [I] **~ to/with sth** to obey a rule, law, etc. **SYN** COMPLY: *The building does not conform with safety regulations.* **3** [I] **~ to sth** to agree with or match something: *It did not conform to the usual stereotype of an industrial city.*

con·form·a·ble /kən'fɔrməbl/ *adj.* **~ to/with sth** (*formal*) similar in form or nature to something; in agreement with something **SYN** CONSISTENT: *What happens in cases where common law is not conformable to the Constitution?* ▶ **con·form·a·bil·i·ty** **AWL** /kənˌfɔrmə'bɪləti/ *noun* [U]

con·form·ance **AWL** /kən'fɔrməns/ *noun* [U] **~ (to/with sth)** (*formal*) the fact of following the rules or standards of something: *You need to ensure conformance to strict quality guidelines.* **SYN** CONFORMITY

con·for·ma·tion **AWL** /ˌkɑnfɔr'meɪʃn; -fɚ-/ *noun* [U, C] (*formal*) the way in which something is formed; the structure of something, especially an animal

con·form·ist **AWL** /kən'fɔrmɪst/ *noun* (often *disapproving*) a person who behaves and thinks in the same way as most other people and who does not want to be different ▶ **con·form·ist** *adj.* ➪ see also NONCONFORMIST

con·form·i·ty **AWL** /kən'fɔrməti/ *noun* [U] **~ (to/with sth)** (*formal*) behavior or actions that follow the accepted rules of society
IDM **in conformity with sth** following the rules of something; conforming to something: *regulations that are in conformity with local law*

con·found /kən'faʊnd/ *verb* (*formal*) **1 ~ sb** to confuse and surprise someone **SYN** BAFFLE: *The sudden rise in share prices has confounded economists.* **2 ~ sb/sth** to prove someone or something wrong: *to confound expectations* ♦ *She confounded her critics and proved she could do the job.* **3 ~ sb** (*old-fashioned*) to defeat an enemy
IDM **confound it/you!** (*old-fashioned*) used to show that you are angry about something/with someone

con·found·ed /kən'faʊndəd/ *adj.* [only before noun] (*old-fashioned*) used when describing something to show that you are annoyed

con·fra·ter·ni·ty /ˌkɑnfrə'tɜrnəti/ *noun* (pl. **con·fra·ter·ni·ties**) (*formal*) a group of people who join together especially for a religious purpose or to help other people

con·front 🔑 /kən'frʌnt/ *verb*
1 ~ sb/sth (of problems or a difficult situation) to appear and need to be dealt with by someone: *the economic problems confronting the country* ♦ *The government found itself confronted by massive opposition.* **2 ~ sth** to deal with a problem or difficult situation **SYN** FACE UP TO: *She knew that she had to confront her fears.* **3 ~ sb** to face someone so that they cannot avoid seeing and hearing you, especially in an unfriendly or dangerous situation: *This was the first time he had confronted an armed robber.* **4 ~ sb with sb/sth** to make someone face or deal with an unpleasant or difficult person or situation: *He confronted her with a choice between her career or their relationship.* **5 be confronted with sth** to have something in front of you that you have to deal with or react to: *When confronted with a bear, stop and stay calm.*

con·fron·ta·tion /ˌkɑnfrən'teɪʃn/ *noun* [U, C] **~ (with sb)** |

   t tea   **t̬** butter   **d** did   **k** cat   **g** got   **tʃ** chin   **dʒ** June   **f** fall

~ (between A and B) a situation in which there is an angry disagreement between people or groups who have different opinions: *She wanted to avoid another confrontation with her father.* ♦ *confrontation between employers and unions*

con·fron·ta·tion·al /ˌkɑnfrənˈteɪʃənl/ adj. tending to deal with people in an aggressive way that is likely to cause arguments, rather than discussing things with them

Con·fu·cian /kənˈfyuʃən/ adj. [usually before noun] based on or believing the teachings of the Chinese PHILOSOPHER Confucius ▶ **Con·fu·cian** noun **Con·fu·cian·ism** /kənˈfyuʃəˌnɪzəm/ noun [U]

con·fus·a·ble /kənˈfyuzəbl/ adj. if two things are **confusable**, it is easy to confuse them: *"Historic" and "historical" are easily confusable.* ♦ *The various types of owls are easily confusable with one another.* ▶ **con·fus·a·ble** noun: *confusables such as "principle" and "principal"*

con·fuse 🔑 /kənˈfyuz/ verb **~ sb**
1 to make someone unable to think clearly or understand something: *They confused me with conflicting accounts of what happened.* **2 ~ A and/with B** to think wrongly that someone or something is someone or something else **SYN** MIX UP: *People often confuse me and my twin sister.* ♦ *Be careful not to confuse quantity with quality.* **3 ~ sth** to make a subject more difficult to understand: *His comments only served to confuse the issue further.*

con·fused 🔑 /kənˈfyuzd/ adj.
1 unable to think clearly or to understand what is happening or what someone is saying: *People are confused about all the different labels on food these days.* ♦ *He was depressed and in a confused state of mind.* ♦ *I'm confused—say all that again.* **2** not clear or easy to understand: *The children gave a confused account of what had happened.* ▶ **con·fus·ed·ly** /kənˈfyuzədli/ adv.

con·fus·ing 🔑 /kənˈfyuzɪŋ/ adj.
difficult to understand; not clear: *The instructions on the box are very confusing.* ♦ *a very confusing experience* ▶ **con·fus·ing·ly** adv.

con·fu·sion 🔑 /kənˈfyuʒn/ noun
1 [U, C] **~ (about/over sth)** | **~ (as to sth)** a state of not being certain about what is happening, what you should do, what something means, etc.: *There is some confusion about what the correct procedure should be.* ♦ *a confusion as to what to do next* **2** [U, C] **~ (between A and B)** the fact of making a mistake about who someone is or what something is: *To avoid confusion, please write the children's names clearly on all their school clothes.* ♦ *confusion between letters of the alphabet like "o" and "a"* **3** [U] a feeling of embarrassment when you do not understand something and are not sure what to do in a situation: *He looked at me in confusion and did not answer the question.* **4** [U] a confused situation in which people do not know what action to take: *Fighting had broken out and all was chaos and confusion.* ♦ *Her unexpected arrival threw us into total confusion.*

con·fute /kənˈfyut/ verb **~ sb/sth** (formal) to prove a person or an argument to be wrong

con·ga /ˈkɑŋɡə/ noun **1** a fast dance in which the dancers follow a leader in a long winding line, with each person holding on to the person in front; a piece of music for this dance **2** (also **ˈconga drum**) a tall narrow drum that you play with your hands ⊃ picture at INSTRUMENT

con·geal /kənˈdʒil/ verb [I] (of blood, fat, etc.) to become thick or solid: *congealed blood* ♦ *The cold remains of supper had congealed on the plate.* ♦ (figurative) *The bitterness and tears had congealed into hatred.*

con·gen·ial /kənˈdʒinyəl/ adj. (formal) **1** (of a person) pleasant to spend time with because their interests and character are similar to your own: *a congenial colleague* **2 ~ (to sb)** (of a place, job, etc.) pleasant because it suits your character: *a congenial working environment* **3 ~ (to sth)** (formal) suitable for something: *a situation that was congenial to the expression of nationalist opinions*

con·gen·i·tal /kənˈdʒɛnətl/ adj. **1** (of a disease or medical condition) existing since or before birth: *congenital abnormalities* **2** [only before noun] existing as part of a person's character and not likely to change: *a congenital inability to tell the truth* **3** [only before noun] (of a person) born with a particular illness: (figurative) *a congenital liar* (= one who will not change) ▶ **con·gen·i·tal·ly** /-nətl·i/ adv.

con·ger /ˈkɑŋɡər/ (also ˌconger ˈeel) noun a large EEL (= a long thin fish) that lives in the ocean

con·gest·ed /kənˈdʒɛstəd/ adj. **1 ~ (with sth)** crowded; full of traffic: *congested city streets* ♦ *Many of the United States' airports are heavily congested.* **2** (medical) (of a part of the body) blocked with blood or MUCUS

con·ges·tion /kənˈdʒɛstʃən/ noun [U] **1** the state of being crowded and full of traffic: *traffic congestion and pollution* ⊃ collocations at TOWN **2** (medical) the state of part of the body being blocked with blood or MUCUS: *congestion of the lungs* ♦ *medicine to relieve nasal congestion*

con·glom·er·ate /kənˈɡlɑmərət/ noun **1** [C] (business) a large company formed by joining together different firms: *a media conglomerate* **2** [sing.] (formal) a number of things or parts that are put together to form a whole **3** [U] (geology) a type of rock made of small stones held together by dried CLAY

con·glom·er·a·tion /kənˌɡlɑməˈreɪʃn/ noun **1** [C, usually sing.] **a ~ (of sth)** (formal) a mixture of different things that are found all together: *a conglomeration of buildings of different sizes and styles* **2** [U] the process of forming a conglomerate or the state of being a conglomerate

con·grats /kənˈɡræts/ noun [pl.], exclamation (informal) = CONGRATULATION (2)

con·grat·u·late /kənˈɡrætʃəˌleɪt; -ˈɡrædʒə-/ verb **1** to tell someone that you are pleased about their success or achievements: **~ sb (on sth)** *I congratulated them all on their results.* ♦ **~ sb (for sth)** *The authors should be congratulated for producing such a clear and authoritative work.* **2 ~ yourself (on sth)** to feel pleased and proud because you have achieved something or been successful at something: *You can congratulate yourself on having done an excellent job.*

con·grat·u·la·tion 🔑 /kənˌɡrætʃəˈleɪʃn; -ˌɡrædʒə-/ noun
1 congratulations [pl.] a message congratulating someone (= saying that you are happy about their good luck or success): *to offer/send your congratulations to someone* **2 Congratulations!** used when you want to congratulate someone: *"We're getting married!" "Congratulations!"* ♦ *Congratulations on your exam results!* **3** [U] the act of congratulating someone: *a letter of congratulation*

con·grat·u·la·to·ry /kənˈɡrætʃələˌtɔri; -ˈɡrædʒə-/ adj. expressing congratulations: *a congratulatory message*

con·gre·gant /ˈkɑŋɡrəɡənt/ noun (formal) a member of a church or SYNAGOGUE

con·gre·gate /ˈkɑŋɡrəˌɡeɪt/ verb [I] to come together in a group: *Young people often congregate in the main square in the evenings.*

con·gre·ga·tion /ˌkɑŋɡrəˈɡeɪʃn/ noun **1** a group of people who are gathered together in a church or SYNAGOGUE to worship God, not including the priest or RABBI or the CHOIR: *The congregation stood to sing the hymn.* ⊃ collocations at RELIGION **2** the group of people who belong to a particular church and go there regularly to worship ▶ **con·gre·ga·tion·al** /-ʃənl/ adj.

Con·gre·ga·tion·al·ism /ˌkɑŋɡrəˈɡeɪʃənlˌɪzəm/ adj. a type of Christianity in which the congregation of each church is responsible for its own affairs ▶ **Con·gre·ga·tion·al** adj. **Con·gre·ga·tion·al·ist** noun

con·gress 🔑 /ˈkɑŋɡrəs/ noun
1 Congress the name of the group of people who are elected to make laws, in the U.S. consisting of the Senate and the HOUSE OF REPRESENTATIVES: *Congress will vote on the proposals tomorrow.* ⊃ collocations at POLITICS **2** a large

---

formal meeting or series of meetings where representatives from different groups discuss ideas, make decisions, etc.: *an international congress of trade unions* **3** used in the names of political parties in some countries: *the African National Congress*

con·gres·sion·al /kənˈgrɛʃənl; kən-/ *adj.* [only before noun] related to or belonging to a congress or the U.S. Congress: *a congressional committee/bill* ♦ *the midterm Congressional elections*

con·gressional ˈdistrict *noun* a district within a state that elects a member of the U.S. House of Representatives: *He represents the first congressional district of Massachusetts.*

con·gress·man /ˈkɑŋgrəsmən/, **con·gress·woman** /ˈkɑŋgrəsˌwʊmən/ *noun* often **Con·gress·man, Con·gress·woman** (*pl.* **con·gress·men** /-mən/, **con·gress·women** /-ˌwɪmən/) (also **con·gress·person** /-ˌpərsn/) a member of the U.S. Congress, especially the House of Representatives ⊃ **see also** SENATOR

con·gru·ent /kənˈgruənt; ˈkɑŋgruənt/ *adj.* **1** (*geometry*) having the same size and shape: *congruent triangles* **2** ~ **(with sth)** (*formal*) suitable for something; appropriate in a particular situation ▶ **con·gru·ence** /-əns/ *noun* [U]

con·ic /ˈkɑnɪk/ *adj.*, *noun* (*geometry*)
● *adj.* of or related to a CONE
● *noun* = CONIC SECTION

con·i·cal /ˈkɑnɪkl/ *adj.* shaped like a CONE

conic ˈsection (also **con·ic**) *noun* (*geometry*) a shape formed when a flat surface meets a CONE

co·ni·fer /ˈkɑnəfər/ *noun* any tree that produces hard dry fruit called CONE. Most conifers are EVERGREEN (= have leaves that stay on the tree all year). ▶ **co·nif·er·ous** /kəˈnɪfərəs/ *adj.*: *coniferous trees/forests*

con·jec·ture /kənˈdʒɛktʃər/ *noun*, *verb*
● *noun* (*formal*) **1** [C] an opinion or idea that is not based on definite knowledge and is formed by guessing **SYN** GUESS: *The truth of his conjecture was confirmed by the newspaper report.* **2** [U] the forming of an opinion or idea that is not based on definite knowledge **SYN** GUESS: *What was going through the killer's mind is a matter for conjecture.* ▶ **con·jec·tur·al** /-tʃərəl/ *adj.*
● *verb* [I, T] (*formal*) to form an opinion about something even though you do not have much information on it **SYN** GUESS: ~ **(about sth)** *We can only conjecture about what was in the killer's mind.* ♦ ~ **what/how, etc....** *We can only conjecture what was in the killer's mind* ♦ ~ **that...** *He conjectured that the population might double in ten years.* ♦ ~ **sth** *She conjectured the existence of a completely new species.* ♦ ~ **sth to do sth** *The remains are conjectured to be thousands of years old.*

con·join /kənˈdʒɔɪn/ *verb* [I, T] ~ **(sth)** (*formal*) to join together; to join two or more things together

con·joined ˈtwin *noun* (*technical*) (also **Siamese ˈtwin**) one of two people who are born with their bodies joined together in some way, sometimes sharing the same organs

con·joint /kənˈdʒɔɪnt/ *adj.* [usually before noun] (*formal*) combining all or both the people or things involved ▶ **con·joint·ly** *adv.*

con·ju·gal /ˈkɑndʒəgl/ *adj.* [only before noun] (*formal*) connected with marriage and the sexual relationship between a husband and wife: *conjugal love*

conjugal ˈrights *noun* [pl.] the rights that a husband and wife each has in a marriage, especially the right to have sex with their partner

con·ju·gate /ˈkɑndʒəˌgeɪt/ *verb* (*grammar*) **1** [T] ~ **sth** to give the different forms of a verb, as they vary according to NUMBER, PERSON, tense, etc. **2** [I] (of a verb) to have different forms, showing NUMBER, PERSON, tense, etc.: *How does this verb conjugate?* ⊃ **compare** DECLINE

con·ju·ga·tion /ˌkɑndʒəˈgeɪʃn/ *noun* (*grammar*) **1** [C, U] the way in which a verb conjugates: *a verb with an irregular conjugation* **2** [C] a group of verbs that conjugate in the same way: *Latin verbs of the second conjugation*

con·junc·tion /kənˈdʒʌŋkʃn/ *noun* **1** [C] (*grammar*) a word that joins words, phrases or sentences, for example "and," "but," and "or" **2** [C] (*formal*) a combination of events, etc., that causes a particular result: *The conjunction of low inflation and low unemployment came as a very pleasant surprise.* **3** [C, U] (*astronomy*) the fact of stars, planets, etc., passing close together as seen from the earth **IDM** **in conjunction with** (*formal*) together with: *The police are working in conjunction with tax officers on the investigation.* ♦ *The system is designed to be used in conjunction with a word processing program.*

con·junc·ti·vi·tis /kənˌdʒʌŋktɪˈvaɪtəs/ *noun* [U] (*medical*) an infectious eye disease that causes pain and swelling in part of the eye **SYN** PINKEYE

con·jure /ˈkɑndʒər/ *verb* [I, T] to do skillful tricks such as making things seem to appear or disappear as if by magic: *Her grandfather taught her to conjure.* ♦ ~ **sth + adv./prep.** *He could conjure coins from behind people's ears.* **IDM** see NAME *n.*
PHR V **ˌconjure sth↔ˈup 1** to make something appear as a picture in your mind **SYN** EVOKE: *That smell always conjures up memories of vacations in France.* **2** to make someone or something appear by using special magic words **conjure sth from/out of sth** to create something or make something appear in a surprising or unexpected way: *He conjured a delicious meal out of a few leftovers.*

con·jur·ing /ˈkɑndʒərɪŋ/ *noun* [U] entertainment in the form of magic tricks, especially ones which seem to make things appear or disappear: *a conjuring trick*

con·ju·ror (also **con·ju·rer**) /ˈkɑndʒərər/ *noun* a person who performs conjuring tricks

conk /kɑŋk; kɔŋk/ *verb* ~ **sb** (*informal*) to hit someone hard on their head
PHR V **ˌconk ˈout** (*informal*) **1** (of a machine, etc.) to stop working: *The car conked out halfway up the hill.* **2** (of a person) to go to sleep

ˈcon man *noun* (*informal*) a man who tricks others into giving him money, etc.

con·nect 🔑 /kəˈnɛkt/ *verb*
▷ **JOIN 1** [T, I] ~ **(A to/with/and B)** to join together two or more things; to be joined together: *The towns are connected by train and bus services.* ♦ *The canal was built to connect Lake Erie with the Hudson River.* ♦ *a connecting door* (= one that connects two rooms) ♦ *The rooms on this floor connect.*
▷ **ELECTRICITY/GAS/WATER 2** [T] ~ **sth (to sth)** to join something to the main supply of electricity, gas, water, etc., or to another piece of equipment: *First connect the printer to the computer.* ♦ *We're waiting for the telephone to be connected.* **ANT** DISCONNECT
▷ **INTERNET 3** [I, T] ~ **(sb) (to sth)** to join a computer to the Internet or a computer network: *Click "Continue" to connect to the Internet.* **ANT** DISCONNECT
▷ **LINK 4** [T] ~ **sb/sth (with sb/sth)** to notice or make a link between people, things, events, etc. **SYN** ASSOCIATE: *There was nothing to connect him with the crime.* ♦ *I was surprised to hear them mentioned together: I had never connected them before.*
▷ **OF TRAIN/BUS/PLANE 5** [I] ~ **(with sth)** to arrive just before another one leaves so that passengers can change from one to the other: *His flight to Chicago connects with an afternoon flight to New York.* ♦ *There's a connecting flight at noon.* **6** [I] to change from one train, bus, or plane to another: *There's an afternoon flight to Los Angeles but you have to connect in Chicago.*
▷ **TELEPHONE LINES 7** [T] ~ **sb** to join telephone lines so that people can speak to each other **SYN** PUT THROUGH: *Please hold while I try to connect you.* **ANT** DISCONNECT
▷ **FORM RELATIONSHIP 8** [I] ~ **(with sb)** to have a good relationship with someone so that you like and understand each other: *They met a couple of times but they didn't really connect.*
▷ **HIT 9** [I] ~ **(with sb/sth)** (*informal*) to hit someone or something: *The blow connected and she felt a surge of pain.*

   h **h**at   m **m**an   n **n**o   ŋ si**ng**   l **l**eg   r **r**ed   y **y**es   w **w**et

PHR V con·nect sth↔'up (to sth) | con·nect 'up (to sth) to join something to a supply of electricity, gas, etc., or to another piece of equipment; to be joined in this way: *She connected up the two computers.* **ANT** DISCONNECT

con·nect·ed /kəˈnɛktəd/ *adj.* **~ (with sb/sth)** (of two or more things or people) having a link between them: *market prices and other connected matters* ♦ *They are connected by marriage.* ♦ *jobs connected with the environment* ♦ *The two issues are closely connected.* **ANT** UNCONNECTED ⊃ see also WELL-CONNECTED

con·nect·ed·ness /kəˈnɛktədnəs/ *noun* [U] **~ (to/with sb/ sth)** a feeling that you have a link with someone or something or are part of a group: *the benefits of helping students feel a sense of connectedness to their school*

con·nec·tion ⚿ /kəˈnɛkʃn/ *noun*
> LINK **1** [C] something that connects two facts, ideas, etc. **SYN** LINK: **~ (between A and B)** *Scientists have established a connection between cholesterol levels and heart disease.* ♦ **~ (with sth)** *a direct/close/strong connection with something* ♦ *How did you make the connection* (= realize that there was a connection between two facts that did not seem to be related)?
> BEING CONNECTED **2** [U, C] **~ (to sth)** the act of connecting or the state of being connected: *Connection to the gas supply was delayed for three days.* ♦ *I'm having problems with my Internet connection.*
> IN ELECTRICAL SYSTEM **3** [C] a point, especially in an electrical system, where two parts connect: *A faulty connection caused the machine to stop.*
> TRAIN/BUS/PLANE **4** [C] a train, bus, or plane at a station or an airport that a passenger can take soon after getting off another in order to continue their trip: *We arrived in plenty of time for our connection to Denver.* **5** [C, usually pl.] a means of traveling to another place: *There are good bus and train connections between the resort and major cities.*
> PERSON/ORGANIZATION **6** [C, usually pl.] a person or an organization that you know and that can help or advise you in your social or professional life **SYN** CONTACT: *One of my business connections gave them my name.*
> RELATIONSHIP **7 connections** [pl.] people who are your relatives, but not members of your close family: *She is American but also has Cuban connections.* **8** [C] a friendly relationship between two or more people: *They had all been classmates at school and maintained a close connection over the years.*
IDM in connection with sb/sth for reasons connected with someone or something: *A man has been arrested in connection with the murder of the teenager.* ♦ *I am writing to you in connection with your recent job application.* in this/that connection (*formal*) for reasons connected with something recently mentioned

con·nec·tive /kəˈnɛktɪv/ *adj., noun*
● *adj.* (*medical*) that connects things: *connective tissue*
● *noun* (*grammar*) a word that connects two parts of a sentence: *Don't overuse a causal connective like "because."*

con·nec·tiv·i·ty /ˌkɑnɛkˈtɪvəti; kəˌnɛk-/ *noun* [U] (*technical*) the state of being connected or the degree to which two things are connected: *ISDN connectivity allows computers to communicate over a network.*

con·nec·tor /kəˈnɛktər/ *noun* a thing that links two or more things together: *a cable connector*

conn·ing tow·er /ˈkɑnɪŋ ˌtaʊər/ *noun* a raised structure on a SUBMARINE containing the PERISCOPE

con·nip·tion /kəˈnɪpʃn/ (*also* con'niption ˌfit) *noun* (*old-fashioned*) a sudden attack of anger or fear: *He had a conniption when he heard the news.*

con·niv·ance /kəˈnaɪvəns/ *noun* [U] (*disapproving*) help in doing something wrong; the failure to stop something wrong from happening: *The crime was committed with the connivance of a police officer.*

con·nive /kəˈnaɪv/ *verb* (*disapproving*) **1** [I] **~ (with sb) (to do sth)** to work together with someone to do something wrong or illegal **SYN** CONSPIRE: *The government was accused*

of having connived with the security forces to permit murder. **2** [I] **~ at/in sth** to seem to allow something wrong to happen: *She knew that if she said nothing she would be conniving in an injustice.*

con·niv·ing /kəˈnaɪvɪŋ/ *adj.* (*disapproving*) behaving in a way that secretly hurts others or deliberately fails to prevent others from being hurt

con·nois·seur /ˌkɑnəˈsər; -ˈsʊr/ *noun* an expert on matters involving the judgment of beauty, quality, or skill in art, food, or music: *a connoisseur of Italian painting* ♦ *a wine connoisseur*

con·no·ta·tion /ˌkɑnəˈteɪʃn/ *noun* an idea suggested by a word in addition to its main meaning: *The word "professional" has connotations of skill and excellence.* ♦ *negative connotations* ⊃ compare DENOTATION

con·note /kəˈnoʊt/ *verb* **~ sth** (*formal*) (of a word) to suggest a feeling, an idea, etc., as well as the main meaning ⊃ compare DENOTE

con·nu·bi·al /kəˈnubiəl/ *adj.* (*literary*) related to marriage, or the relationship between husband and wife

con·quer /ˈkɑŋkər/ *verb* **1 ~ sb/sth** to take control of a country or city and its people by force: *Cortés conquered Mexico in 1521.* ♦ *conquered peoples/races/territories* **2** [T, I] **~ sb** to defeat someone, especially in a competition, race, etc.: *The world champion conquered yet another challenger last night.* ♦ *The team members were greeted like* **conquering heroes. 3 ~ sth** to succeed in dealing with or controlling something: *The only way to conquer a fear is to face it.* ♦ *Mount Everest was conquered* (= successfully climbed) *in 1953.* **4 ~ sth** to become very popular or successful in a place: *The band is now setting out to conquer the world.* **IDM** see DIVIDE *v.*

con·quer·or /ˈkɑŋkərər/ *noun* a person who conquers: *William the Conqueror* (= King William I of England)

con·quest /ˈkɑŋkwɛst/ *noun* **1** (sing., U) the act of taking control of a country, city, etc., by force: *the Norman Conquest* (= of England in 1066) **2** [C] an area of land taken by force: *the Spanish conquests in South America* **3** [C] (usually *humorous*) a person that someone has persuaded to love them or to have sex with them: *I'm just one of his many conquests.* **4** [U] the act of gaining control over something that is difficult or dangerous: *the conquest of inflation*

con·quis·ta·dor /kɑnˈkistəˌdɔr/ *noun* (*pl.* con·quis·ta·dor·es /kɑnˌkistəˈdɔreɪz/ *or* con·quis·ta·dors) (from *Spanish*) one of the Spanish people who took control of Mexico and Peru by force in the 16th century

con·san·guin·i·ty /ˌkɑnsænˈgwɪnəti/ *noun* [U] (*formal*) relationship by birth in the same family

con·science /ˈkɑnʃəns/ *noun* **1** [C, U] the part of your mind that tells you whether your actions are right or wrong: *to have a* **clear/guilty conscience** (= to feel that you have done right/wrong) ♦ *This is a* **matter** *of individual conscience* (= everyone must make their own judgment about it). ♦ *He won't let it trouble his conscience.* ⊃ see also SOCIAL CONSCIENCE **2** [U, C] a guilty feeling about something you have done or failed to do: *She was seized by a sudden pang of conscience.* ♦ *I have a terrible conscience about it.* **3** [U] the fact of behaving in a way that you feel is right even though this may cause problems: *freedom of conscience* (= the freedom to do what you believe to be right) ♦ *Emilia is the voice of conscience in the play.* ⊃ see also PRISONER OF CONSCIENCE **IDM** in (all/good) conscience (*formal*) believing your actions to be fair **SYN** HONESTLY: *We cannot in all conscience refuse to help.* on your conscience making you feel guilty for doing or failing to do something: *I'll write and apologize. I've had it on my conscience for weeks.* ⊃ more at PRICK

'conscience-ˌstricken *adj.* feeling guilty about something you have done or failed to do

con·sci·en·tious /ˌkɑnʃiˈɛnʃəs/ *adj.* taking care to do things carefully and correctly: *a conscientious student/teacher/ worker* ▶ con·sci·en·tious·ly *adv.*: *She performed all her duties conscientiously.* con·sci·en·tious·ness *noun* [U]

conscientious ob'jector *noun* a person who refuses to serve in the armed forces for moral reasons ➔ compare DRAFT DODGER, PACIFIST

con·scious 🔑 /ˈkɒnʃəs/ *adj.*
1 [not before noun] aware of something; noticing something: ~ **of sth** *She's very conscious of the problems involved.* ◆ ~ **of doing sth** *He became acutely conscious of having failed his parents.* ◆ ~ **that…** *I was vaguely conscious that I was being watched.* **ANT** UNCONSCIOUS ➔ see also SELF-CONSCIOUS **2** able to use your senses and mental powers to understand what is happening: *A patient who is not fully conscious should never be left alone.* **ANT** UNCONSCIOUS **3** (of actions, feelings, etc.) deliberate or controlled: *to make a conscious decision* ◆ *I made a conscious effort to get there on time.* ◆ *a conscious act of cruelty* **ANT** UNCONSCIOUS ➔ compare SUBCONSCIOUS **4** being particularly interested in something: *environmentally conscious* ◆ *They have become increasingly health-conscious.* ▶ **con·scious·ly** *adv.*: *Consciously or unconsciously, you made a choice.*

con·scious·ness /ˈkɒnʃəsnəs/ *noun* [U] **1** the state of being able to use your senses and mental powers to understand what is happening: *I can't remember any more—I must have lost consciousness.* ◆ *She did not regain consciousness and died the next day.* **2** the state of being aware of something **SYN** AWARENESS: *his consciousness of the challenge facing him* ◆ *class-consciousness* (= consciousness of different classes in society) **3** the ideas and opinions of a person or group: *her newly-developed political consciousness* ➔ see also STREAM OF CONSCIOUSNESS

consciousness-raising *noun* [U] the process of making people aware of important social and political issues

con·script *verb, noun*
● *verb* /kənˈskrɪpt/ [usually passive] ~ **sb (into sth)** (*formal*) to make sb join the armed forces **SYN** DRAFT: *He was conscripted into the army in 1939.*
● *noun* /ˈkɒnskrɪpt/ (*formal*) = DRAFTEE ➔ compare VOLUNTEER

con·scrip·tion /kənˈskrɪpʃn/ *noun* [U] (*formal*) = DRAFT *n.*

con·se·crate /ˈkɒnsəˌkreɪt/ *verb* **1** ~ **sth** to state officially in a religious ceremony that something is holy and can be used for religious purposes: *The church was consecrated in 1853.* ◆ *consecrated ground* **2** ~ **sth** (in Christian belief) to make bread and wine into the body and blood of Christ **3** ~ **sb (as) (sth)** to state officially in a religious ceremony that someone is now a priest, etc.: *He was consecrated (as) bishop last year.* **4** ~ **sth/sb/yourself to sth** (*formal*) to give something or someone/yourself to a special purpose, especially a religious one ▶ **con·se·cra·tion** /ˌkɒnsəˈkreɪʃn/ *noun* [C, U]: *the consecration of a church/bishop*

con·sec·u·tive /kənˈsekyətɪv/ *adj.* [usually before noun] following one after another in a series, without interruption: *She was absent for nine consecutive days.* ◆ *He is beginning his fourth consecutive term of office.* ▶ **con·sec·u·tive·ly** *adv.*

con·sen·su·al /kənˈsenʃuəl/ *adj.* **1** (*formal*) that people in general agree with: *a consensual approach* **2** (of an activity) that the people taking part have agreed to: *consensual sex*

con·sen·sus **AWL** /kənˈsensəs/ *noun* [sing., U] an opinion that all members of a group agree with: ~ **(about/on sth)** *She is skilled at achieving consensus on sensitive issues.* ◆ *There is a growing consensus of opinion on this issue.* ◆ *an attempt to reach a consensus* ◆ ~ **(among sb) (about/on sth)** *There is a general consensus among teachers about the need for greater security in schools.* ◆ ~ **(that…)** *There seems to be a consensus that the plan should be rejected.*

con·sent **AWL** /kənˈsent/ *noun, verb*
● *noun* **1** [U] ~ **(to sth)** permission to do something, especially given by someone in authority: *Children under 16 cannot give consent to medical treatment.* ◆ *The written consent of a parent is required.* ◆ *to refuse/withhold your consent* ◆ *He is charged with taking a car without the owner's consent.* ➔ see also AGE OF CONSENT **2** [U] agreement about something: *She was chosen as leader by common consent* (= everyone

agreed to the choice). ◆ *By mutual consent they didn't go out* (= they both agreed not to). **3** [C] an official document giving permission for something
● *verb* [I] (*formal*) to agree to something or give your permission for something: *When she told them what she intended they readily consented.* ◆ ~ **to sth** *He reluctantly consented to his daughter's marriage.* ◆ ~ **to do sth** *She finally consented to be interviewed.* ➔ thesaurus box at AGREE

con·senting a'dult *noun* a person who is considered old enough, by law, to decide whether they should agree to have sex; a person who has agreed to have sex

con·se·quence 🔑 **AWL** /ˈkɒnsəˌkwens; -wəns/ *noun*
1 [C] ~ **(for sb/sth)** a result of something that has happened: *This decision could have serious consequences for the industry.* ◆ *Two hundred people lost their jobs as a direct consequence of the merger.* ◆ *He drove too fast, with tragic consequences.* ◆ *to suffer/face/take the consequences of your actions* ➔ thesaurus box at RESULT ➔ language bank at CONSEQUENTLY **2** [U] (*formal*) importance: *Don't worry. It's of no consequence.*
IDM in consequence (of sth) (*formal*) as a result of something: *The child was born deformed in consequence of an injury to its mother.*

con·se·quent **AWL** /ˈkɒnsəˌkwent; -wənt/ *adj.* (*formal*) happening as a result of something **SYN** RESULTANT: *the lowering of taxes and the consequent increase in spending* ◆ ~ **on/upon sth** *the responsibilities consequent upon the arrival of a new child*

con·se·quen·tial /ˌkɒnsəˈkwenʃl/ *adj.* (*formal*) **1** happening as a result or an effect of something **SYN** RESULTANT: *retirement and the consequential reduction in income* **2** important; that will have important results: *The report discusses a number of consequential matters that are yet to be decided.* **ANT** INCONSEQUENTIAL ▶ **con·se·quen·tial·ly** /-ʃəli/ *adv.*

con·se·quent·ly **AWL** /ˈkɒnsəˌkwentli; -wənt-/ *adv.* as a result; therefore: *This poses a threat to agriculture and the food chain, and consequently to human health.*

LANGUAGE BANK

consequently
describing the effect of something

- One **consequence** of changes in diet over recent years has been a dramatic increase in cases of childhood obesity.
- Many parents today do not have time to cook healthy meals for their children. **Consequently/As a consequence**, many children grow up eating too much junk food.
- Many children spend their free time watching TV instead of playing outside. **As a result**, more and more of them are becoming overweight.
- Last year, junk food was banned in schools. **The effect of this** has been to create a black market on the playground, with students bringing candy and snacks from home to sell to other students.
- ➔ note at AFFECT
- ➔ Language Banks at BECAUSE OF, CAUSE, THEREFORE

---

con·serv·an·cy /kənˈsɜːrvənsi/ *noun* **1 Conservancy** [sing.] a group of officials who control the use of a port, a river, an area of land, etc.: *the Central Park Conservancy* ◆ *Texas Nature Conservancy* **2** [U] (*formal*) the protection of the natural environment **SYN** CONSERVATION: *nature conservancy*

con·ser·va·tion /ˌkɒnsərˈveɪʃn/ *noun* [U] **1** the protection of the natural environment **SYN** CONSERVANCY: *to be interested in wildlife conservation* **2** the official protection of buildings that have historical or artistic importance **3** the act of preventing something from being lost, wasted, damaged, or destroyed: *to encourage the **conservation of water/fuel*** ◆ *energy conservation* ➔ see also CONSERVE

conser'vation ,area *noun* an area where the natural environment or the buildings are protected by law from being damaged or changed

con·ser·va·tion·ist /ˌkɑnsərˈveɪʃənɪst/ *noun* a person who takes an active part in the protection of the environment: *a meeting of local conservationists*

con·serv·a·tism /kənˈsɜrvəˌtɪzəm/ *noun* [U] **1** the tendency to resist great or sudden change: *the innate conservatism of older people* **2** also **Conservatism** the political belief that society should change as little as possible: *an examination of the political theories of conservatism and liberalism*

con·serv·a·tive 🔑 /kənˈsɜrvətɪv/ *adj., noun*
● *adj.* **1** opposed to great or sudden social change; showing that you prefer traditional styles and values: *the conservative views of his parents* ◆ *Her style of dress was never conservative.* ◆ *a conservative newspaper/talk show host/politician* **2** (of an estimate) lower than what is probably the real amount or number: *At a conservative estimate, he'll be earning $50,000.* **3** (CanE) connected with the Conservative Party, a political party in Canada ▶ **con·serv·a·tive·ly** *adv.*
● *noun* **1** a conservative person **2** (*politics*) a person with conservative political views who supports tradition and is often opposed to change: *Many conservatives in Congress voted against the health care bill.* ◆ *The candidate appeals to conservatives.*

the Con'servative Party *noun* [sing.] (CanE) one of the three main political parties in Canada, on the political right

con·ser·va·tor /kənˈsɜrvətər; -ˌtɔr/ *noun* a person who is responsible for repairing and preserving works of art, buildings, and other things of cultural interest

con·serv·a·to·ry /kənˈsɜrvəˌtɔri/ *noun* (*pl.* **con·serv·a·to·ries**) **1** a school or college at which people are trained in music and theater **2** a room with glass walls and a glass roof that is built on the side of a building. Conservatories are used for sitting in to enjoy the sun, and to protect plants from cold weather.

con·serve *verb, noun*
● *verb* /kənˈsɜrv/ **1** ~ sth to use as little of something as possible so that it lasts a long time: *Help to conserve energy by insulating your home.* **2** ~ sth to protect something and prevent it from being changed or destroyed: *new laws to conserve wildlife in the area* ➔ see also CONSERVATION
● *noun* /ˈkɑnsɜrv/ [C, U] jelly containing large or whole pieces of fruit

con·sid·er 🔑 /kənˈsɪdər/ *verb*
1 [I, T] to think about something carefully, especially in order to make a decision: *I'd like some time to consider.* ◆ ~ sth *She considered her options.* ◆ *a carefully considered response* ◆ *The company is being actively considered as a potential partner* (= it is thought possible that it could become one). ◆ ~ doing sth *We're considering buying a new car.* ◆ ~ how/what, etc.... *We need to consider how the law might be reformed.* ◆ *He was considering what to do next.* ➔ thesaurus box at EXAMINE ➔ language bank at ABOUT **2** [T] to think of someone or something in a particular way: ~ sb/sth + noun | ~ sb/sth (to be) sth | ~ sb/sth (as) sth *He considers himself an expert on the subject.* ◆ *This award is considered (to be) a great honor.* ◆ *These workers are considered (as) a high-risk group.* ◆ ~ sb/sth + adj. | ~ sb/sth (to be) sth *Consider yourself lucky you weren't fired.* ◆ *Whom do you consider (to be) responsible for the accident?* ◆ ~ sb/sth to do sth *He's generally considered to have the finest tenor voice in the country.* ◆ ~ (that)... *She considers that it is too early to form a definite conclusion.* ◆ **it is considered that...** *It is considered that the proposed development would create much-needed jobs.* ➔ thesaurus box at REGARD **3** [T] ~ sb/sth to think about something, especially the feelings of other people, and be influenced by it when making a decision, etc.: *You should consider other people before you act.* **4** [T] ~ sb/sth (*formal*) to

look carefully at someone or something: *He stood there, considering the painting.*
IDM **all things considered** thinking carefully about all the facts, especially the problems or difficulties, of a situation: *She's had a lot of problems since her husband died but she seems quite cheerful, all things considered.* **your considered opinion** your opinion that is the result of careful thought

con·sid·er·a·ble 🔑 **AWL** /kənˈsɪdərəbl/ *adj.* (*formal*)
great in amount, size, importance, etc. **SYN** SIGNIFICANT: *The project wasted a considerable amount of time and money.* ◆ *Damage to the building was considerable.*

con·sid·er·a·bly 🔑 **AWL** /kənˈsɪdərəbli/ *adv.* (*formal*)
much; a lot **SYN** SIGNIFICANTLY: *The need for sleep varies considerably from person to person.*

con·sid·er·ate /kənˈsɪdərət/ *adj.* always thinking of other people's wishes and feelings; careful not to hurt or upset others **SYN** THOUGHTFUL: *She is always polite and considerate toward her employees.* ◆ *It was very considerate of him to wait.* **ANT** INCONSIDERATE ▶ **con·sid·er·ate·ly** *adv.*

con·sid·er·a·tion 🔑 /kənˌsɪdəˈreɪʃn/ *noun*
1 [U, C] (*formal*) the act of thinking carefully about something: *Careful consideration should be given to issues of health and safety.* ◆ *The proposals are currently **under consideration*** (= being discussed). ◆ *After a few moments' consideration, he began to speak.* ◆ *a consideration of the legal issues involved* **2** [C] something that must be thought about when you are planning or deciding something: *economic/commercial/environmental/practical considerations* ◆ *Time is another important consideration.* **3** [U] ~ (for sb/sth) the quality of being sensitive toward others and thinking about their wishes and feelings: *They showed no consideration whatsoever for my feelings.* ◆ *Journalists stayed away from the funeral **out of consideration for** the bereaved family.* **4** [C] (*formal*) a reward or payment for a service
IDM **in consideration of sth** (*formal*) as payment for something: *a small sum in consideration of your services* **take sth into consideration** to think about and include a particular thing or fact when you are forming an opinion or making a decision: *The candidates' experience and qualifications will be taken into consideration when the decision is made.* ◆ *Taking everything into consideration, the event was a great success.* ➔ more at MATURE

con·sid·er·ing /kənˈsɪdərɪŋ/ *prep., conj., adv.* used to show that you are thinking about a particular fact, and are influenced by it, when you make a statement about something: *She's very active, considering her age.* ◆ *Considering he's only just started studying computer technology, he knows a lot about it.* ◆ (*informal*) *You've done very well, considering* (= in the difficult circumstances).

con·sign /kənˈsaɪn/ *verb* (*formal*) **1** ~ sb/sth to sth to put someone or something somewhere in order to get rid of them/it: *I consigned her letter to the waste basket.* ◆ *What I didn't want was to see my mother consigned to an old people's home.* **2** ~ sb/sth to sth to put someone or something in an unpleasant situation: *The decision to close the factory has consigned 6,000 people to the scrap heap.* ◆ *A car accident consigned him to a wheelchair for the rest of his life.* **3** ~ sth to sb to give or send something to someone **4** ~ sth to sb to sell old clothes, furniture, etc., through a consignment shop

con·sign·ment /kənˈsaɪnmənt/ *noun* **1** [C] a quantity of goods that are sent or delivered somewhere: *a consignment of medicines* **2** [U] the act of sending or delivering someone or something

con'signment ,shop (also **con'signment ,store**) *noun* a store where people take their old clothes, etc. to be sold to someone else. The consignment store keeps part of the money after an item is sold and gives the other part to the person who brought it in.

con·sist 🔑 **AWL** /kən'sɪst/ *verb* (not used in the progressive tenses)

PHR V **con·sist in sth** (*formal*) to have something as the main or only part or feature: *The beauty of the city consists in its magnificent buildings.* ◆ **+ doing sth** *True education does not consist in simply being taught facts.* **con·sist of sb/sth** to be formed from the things or people mentioned: *The committee consists of ten members.* ◆ *Their diet consisted largely of vegetables.* ◆ **+ doing sth** *Most of the fieldwork consisted of doing interviews.*

con·sist·en·cy **AWL** /kən'sɪstənsi/ *noun* (*pl.* **con·sist·en·cies**) **1** [U] (*approving*) the quality of always behaving in the same way or of having the same opinions, standard, etc.; the quality of being consistent: *She has played with great consistency all season.* ◆ *We need to ensure the consistency of service to our customers.* **ANT** INCONSISTENCY **2** [C, U] the consistency of a mixture or a liquid substance is how thick, smooth, etc. it is: *Beat the ingredients together to a creamy consistency.* ◆ *The cement should have the consistency of wet sand.*

con·sist·ent 🔑 **AWL** /kən'sɪstənt/ *adj.*
1 (*approving*) always behaving in the same way, or having the same opinions, standards, etc.: *She's not very consistent in the way she treats her children.* ◆ *He has been Nashville's most consistent player this season.* ◆ *We must be consistent in applying the rules.* ◆ *a consistent approach to the problem* **2** happening in the same way and continuing for a period of time: *the senator's consistent failure to come up with any new policies* ◆ *a pattern of consistent growth in the economy* **3** **~ with sth** in agreement with something; not CONTRA-DICTING something: *The results are entirely consistent with our earlier research.* ◆ *injuries consistent with a fall from an upper story* (= similar to those such a fall would have caused) **4** (of an argument or a set of ideas) having different parts that all

agree with each other: *a well-thought-out and consistent argument* **ANT** INCONSISTENT ▶ **con·sist·ent·ly** **AWL** *adv.*: *Her work has been consistently excellent.* ◆ *We have argued consistently for a change in the law.*

con·so·la·tion /ˌkɑnsə'leɪʃn/ *noun* [U, C] a person or thing that makes you feel better when you are unhappy or disappointed **SYN** COMFORT: *a few words of consolation* ◆ *If it's any consolation, she didn't get the job, either.* ◆ *The children were a great consolation to him when his wife died.*

conso'lation ˌprize *noun* a small prize given to someone who has not won a competition

con·sol·a·to·ry /kən'soʊləˌtɔri; -'sɑ-/ *adj.* (*formal*) intended to make someone who is unhappy or disappointed feel better

con·sole¹ /kən'soʊl/ *verb* to give comfort or sympathy to someone who is unhappy or disappointed **SYN** COMFORT: **~ sb/yourself** *Nothing could console him when his wife died.* ◆ *She put a consoling arm around his shoulders.* ◆ **~ sb/yourself with sth** *Console yourself with the thought that you did your best.* ◆ **~ sb/yourself that...** *I didn't like lying but I consoled myself that it was for a good cause.* ◆ **~ sb + speech** *"Never mind," Anne consoled her.*

con·sole² /'kɑnsoʊl/ *noun* **1** a flat surface that contains all the controls and switches for a machine, a piece of electronic equipment, etc.: *a video game console* **2** a cabinet for a television or STEREO that is designed to stand on the floor

con·sol·i·date /kən'sɑləˌdeɪt/ *verb* **1** [T, I] **~ (sth)** to make a position of power or success stronger so that it is more likely to continue: *With this new movie he has consolidated his position as the country's leading director.* ◆ *The Mets consolidated their lead with a second homerun.* **2** [T, I] **~ (sth)** (*finance*) to join things together into one; to be joined into one: *All the debts have been consolidated.* ◆ *consolidated accounts* ◆ *The two companies consolidated for greater efficiency.* ▶ **con·sol·i·da·tion** /kənˌsɑlə'deɪʃn/ *noun* [U]: *the consolidation of power* ◆ *the consolidation of Japan's banking industry*

con·som·mé /ˌkɑnsə'meɪ/ *noun* [U] a clear soup made with the juices from meat

con·so·nance /'kɑnsənəns/ *noun* **1** [U] **~ (with sth)** (*formal*) agreement: *a policy that is popular because of its consonance with traditional party doctrine* **2** [U, C] (*music*) a combination of musical notes that sound pleasing together **ANT** DISSONANCE

con·so·nant /'kɑnsənənt/ *noun, adj.*
● *noun* **1** a letter of the alphabet that represents a consonant sound, for example "b," "c," "d," "f," etc. **2** (*phonetics*) a speech sound made by completely or partly stopping the flow of air being breathed out through the mouth ⟳ compare VOWEL
● *adj.* **~ with sth** (*formal*) agreeing with or being the same as something else

con·so·nan·tal /ˌkɑnsə'næntl/ *adj.* (*phonetics*) relating to or consisting of a consonant or consonants ⟳ compare VOCALIC

con·sort *noun, verb*
● *noun* /'kɑnsɔrt/ **1** the husband or wife of a ruler: *the prince consort* (= the queen's husband) **2** a group of old-fashioned musical instruments, or a group of musicians who play music from several centuries ago
● *verb* /kən'sɔrt/ [I] **~ with sb** (*formal*) to spend time with someone that other people do not approve of: *He is known to have consorted with prostitutes.*

con·sor·ti·um /kən'sɔrtiəm; -ʃiəm/ *noun* (*pl.* **con·sor·ti·ums** or **con·sor·ti·a** /-tiə; -ʃiə/) a group of people, countries, companies, etc., who are working together on a particular project: *the Boston Consortium for Higher Education*

con·spic·u·ous /kən'spɪkyuəs/ *adj.* easy to see or notice; likely to attract attention: *Mary's red hair always made her conspicuous at school.* ◆ *I felt very conspicuous in my new car.* ◆ *The advertisements were all posted in a conspicuous place.*

t **t**ea   ṭ **butt**er   d **d**id   k **c**at   g **g**ot   tʃ **ch**in   dʒ **J**une   f **f**all

◆ *The event was a conspicuous success* (= a very great one). **ANT** INCONSPICUOUS ▶ **con·spic·u·ous·ly** *adv.*: *Women were conspicuously absent from the planning committee.* **con·spic·u·ous·ness** *noun* [U]

IDM **conspicuous by your absence** not present in a situation or place, when it is obvious that you should be there: *When it came to cleaning up afterward, Anne was conspicuous by her absence.*

con·spicuous con·sumption *noun* [U] the buying of expensive goods in order to impress people and show them how rich you are

con·spir·a·cy /kənˈspɪrəsi/ *noun* [C, U] (*pl.* **con·spir·a·cies**) a secret plan by a group of people to do something harmful or illegal: ~ **(to do sth)** *a conspiracy to overthrow the government* ◆ ~ **(against sb/sth)** *conspiracies against the president* ◆ ~ **(to sth)** *They were charged with conspiracy to murder.* ◆ *a conspiracy of silence* (= an agreement not to talk publicly about something which should be made public) ◆ *a conspiracy theory* (= the belief that a conspiracy is responsible for a particular event)

con·spir·a·tor /kənˈspɪrətər/ *noun* a person who is involved in a conspiracy

con·spir·a·to·ri·al /kənˌspɪrəˈtɔriəl/ *adj.* **1** connected with, or like, a conspiracy **2** (of a person's behavior) suggesting that a secret is being shared: *"I know you understand," he said, and gave a conspiratorial wink.* ▶ **con·spir·a·to·ri·al·ly** *adv.*

con·spire /kənˈspaɪr/ *verb* **1** [I] to secretly plan with other people to do something illegal or harmful: ~ **(with sb) (against sb)** *They were accused of conspiring against the government.* ◆ ~ **(together) (to do sth)** *They deny conspiring together to smuggle drugs.* ◆ ~ **(with sb) (to do sth)** *She admitted conspiring with her lover to murder her husband.* **2** [I] (of events) to seem to work together to make something bad happen: ~ **against sb/sth** *Circumstances had conspired against them.* ◆ ~ **to do sth** *Everything conspired to make her life a misery.*

con·sta·ble /ˈkɑnstəbl/ *noun* an official with some of the powers of a police officer, typically in a small town

con·stan·cy **AWL** /ˈkɑnstənsi/ *noun* [U] (*formal*) **1** the quality of staying the same and not changing **2** (*approving*) the quality of being faithful **SYN** FIDELITY: *He admired her courage and constancy.*

con·stant 🔑 **AWL** /ˈkɑnstənt/ *adj., noun*
• *adj.* **1** [usually before noun] happening all the time or repeatedly: *constant interruptions* ◆ *a constant stream of visitors all day* ◆ *Babies need constant attention.* ◆ *This entrance is in constant use.* **2** that does not change **SYN** FIXED: *traveling at a constant speed of 50 mph*
• *noun* (*technical*) a number or quantity that does not vary **ANT** VARIABLE

con·stant·ly 🔑 **AWL** /ˈkɑnstəntli/ *adv.*
all the time; repeatedly: *Fashion is constantly changing.* ◆ *Heat the sauce, stirring constantly.*

con·sta·tive /kənˈsteɪtɪv/ *adj.* (*grammar*) stating that something is real or true ⟶ see also PERFORMATIVE

con·stel·la·tion /ˌkɑnstəˈleɪʃn/ *noun* **1** a group of stars that forms a shape in the sky and has a name **2** (*formal*) a group of related ideas, things, or people: *a constellation of Hollywood talent*

con·ster·na·tion /ˌkɑnstərˈneɪʃn/ *noun* [U] (*formal*) a worried, sad feeling after you have received an unpleasant surprise **SYN** DISMAY: *The announcement of her retirement caused consternation among tennis fans.*

con·sti·pat·ed /ˈkɑnstəˌpeɪtəd/ *adj.* unable to get rid of waste material from the BOWELS easily

con·sti·pa·tion /ˌkɑnstəˈpeɪʃn/ *noun* [U] the condition of being being constipated

con·stit·u·en·cy **AWL** /kənˈstɪtʃuənsi/ (*pl.* **con·stit·u·en·cies**) *noun* [C] **1** a district that elects its own representative

to state or federal government: *Unemployment is high in her constituency.* **2** the people who live in and vote in a particular district: *constituency opinion* **3** a particular group of people in society who are likely to support a person, an idea, or a product

con·stit·u·ent **AWL** /kənˈstɪtʃuənt/ *noun, adj.*
• *noun* **1** a person who lives in, and can vote in a constituency: *She has the full support of her constituents.* **2** one of the parts of something that combine to form the whole
• *adj.* [only before noun] (*formal*) forming or helping to make a whole: *to break something up into its **constituent parts/ elements***

con·sti·tute **AWL** /ˈkɑnstəˌtut/ *verb* (*formal*) **1** linking verb + noun (not used in the progressive tenses) to be considered to be something: *Does such an activity constitute a criminal offense?* ◆ *The increase in racial tension constitutes a threat to our society.* **2** linking verb + noun (not used in the progressive tenses) to be the parts that together form something **SYN** MAKE UP: *Female workers constitute the majority of the labor force.* ⟶ note at COMPRISE ⟶ thesaurus box at CONSIST OF **3** [T, usually passive] ~ sth to form a group legally or officially **SYN** ESTABLISH, SET UP: *The committee was constituted in 1974 by the Senate.*

con·sti·tu·tion **AWL** /ˌkɑnstəˈtuʃn/ *noun* **1** [C] the system of laws and basic principles that a state, a country, or an organization is governed by: *your right to vote under the constitution* ◆ *According to the constitution...* ◆ *to propose a new amendment to the Constitution* **2** [C] the condition of a person's body and how healthy it is: *to have a **healthy/ strong/weak constitution*** **3** [U, C] (*formal*) the way something is formed or organized **SYN** STRUCTURE: *the genetic constitution of cells* **4** [U] (*formal*) the act of forming something **SYN** ESTABLISHMENT, SETTING UP: *He recommended the constitution of a review committee.*

con·sti·tu·tion·al **AWL** /ˌkɑnstəˈtuʃnl/ *adj., noun*
• *adj.* **1** [only before noun] connected with the constitution of a country or an organization: ***constitutional government/ reform*** ◆ *a constitutional amendment* **2** allowed or limited by the constitution of a country or an organization: *They can't pass this law. It's not constitutional.* ◆ ***constitutional rights*** ◆ *a **constitutional monarchy*** (= a country with a king or queen, whose power is controlled by a set of laws and basic principles) **ANT** UNCONSTITUTIONAL **3** [usually before noun] related to the body's ability to stay healthy, be strong, and fight illness: *constitutional remedies* ▶ **con·sti·tu·tion·al·ly** **AWL** /ˌkɑnstəˈtuʃnəli; -ˈtuʃnəli/ *adv.*: *constitutionally guaranteed rights* ◆ *He was much weakened constitutionally by the disease.*
• *noun* (*old-fashioned* or *humorous*) a short walk that people take because it is good for their health

con·sti·tu·tion·al·ism /ˌkɑnstəˈtuʃnlˌɪzəm/ *noun* [U] a belief in constitutional government

con·sti·tu·tion·al·i·ty /ˌkɑnstəˌtuʃəˈnæləti/ *noun* [U] (*technical*) the fact that something is acceptable according to a CONSTITUTION: *They questioned the constitutionality of the law.*

con·sti·tu·tive **AWL** /ˈkɑnstəˌtutɪv/ *adj.* (*formal*) ~ **(of sth)** forming a part, often an essential part, of something: *Memory is constitutive of identity.*

con·strain **AWL** /kənˈstreɪn/ *verb* (*formal*) **1** [usually passive] ~ **sb to do sth** to force someone to do something or behave in a particular way: *The evidence was so compelling that he felt constrained to accept it.* **2** [often passive] to restrict or limit someone or something: ~ **sth** *Research has been constrained by a lack of funds.* ◆ ~ **sb (from doing sth)** *She felt constrained from continuing by the threat of losing her job.*

con·strained **AWL** /kənˈstreɪnd/ *adj.* (*formal*) not natural; forced or too controlled: *constrained emotions*

con·straint **AWL** /kənˈstreɪnt/ *noun* **1** [C] a thing that limits or restricts something, or your freedom to do something **SYN** RESTRICTION: *constraints of time/money/space* ◆ ***financial/economic/legal/political constraints*** ◆ ~ **on sth** *This decision will impose serious constraints on all schools.* ⟶ thesaurus box at LIMIT **2** [U] strict control over the way that you behave or are allowed to behave: *At last we could relax and talk without constraint.*

con·strict /kənˈstrɪkt/ *verb* **1** [I, T] to become tighter or narrower; to make something tighter or narrower: *Her throat constricted and she swallowed hard.* ◆ **~ sth** *a drug that constricts the blood vessels.* **2 ~ sb** to limit or restrict what someone is able to do: *Movie directors of the time were constricted by the censors.* ◆ *constricting rules and regulations* ▶ **con·strict·ed** *adj.*: *Her throat felt dry and constricted.* ◆ *a constricted vision of the world* **con·stric·tion** /kənˈstrɪkʃn/ *noun* [U, C]: *a feeling of constriction in the chest* ◆ *political constrictions*

con·struct 🔑 **AWL** *verb, noun*

● *verb* /kənˈstrʌkt/ **1** [often passive] to build or make something such as a road, building, or machine: **~ sth** *When was the bridge constructed?* ◆ **~ sth from/out of/of sth** *They constructed a shelter out of fallen branches.* ➲ thesaurus box at BUILD **2 ~ sth** to form something by putting different things together: *You must learn how to construct a logical argument.* ◆ *to construct a theory* ◆ *a well-constructed novel* **3 ~ sth** (*geometry*) to draw a line or shape according to the rules of mathematics: *to construct a triangle*

● *noun* /ˈkɑnstrʌkt/ (*formal*) **1** an idea or a belief that is based on various pieces of evidence that are not always true: *a contrast between lived reality and the construct held in the mind* **2** (*linguistics*) a group of words that form a phrase **3** a thing that is built or made

construction vehicles

bulldozer

backhoe

dump truck

con·struc·tion 🔑 **AWL** /kənˈstrʌkʃn/ *noun*

> OF ROADS/BUILDINGS **1** [U] the process or method of building or making something, especially roads, buildings, bridges, etc.: *the construction industry* ◆ *road construction* ◆ *Work has begun on the construction of the new airport.* ◆ *Our new offices are still under construction* (= being built). ◆ *the construction of a new database* **2** [U] the way that something has been built or made: *strong in construction* ◆ *He blamed the accident on shoddy construction.* ➲ thesaurus box at STRUCTURE

> BUILDING/STRUCTURE **3** [C] (*formal*) a thing that has been built or made: *The summer house was a simple wooden construction.*

> GRAMMAR **4** [C] the way in which words are used together and arranged to form a sentence, phrase, etc.: *grammatical constructions*

> OF THEORY, ETC. **5** [U, C] the creating of something from ideas, opinions, and knowledge: *the construction of a new theory*

> MEANING **6** [C] (*formal*) the way in which words, actions, statements, etc., are understood by someone **SYN** INTERPRETATION: *What construction do you put on this letter* (= what do you think it means)?

con·struc·tion·al /kənˈstrʌkʃənl/ *adj.* connected with the making or building of things

con'struction ˌpaper *noun* [U] thick colored paper that people cut out to make designs, models, etc.

con'struction ˌsite (also **'building ˌsite**) *noun* an area of land where sth is being built

con·struc·tive **AWL** /kənˈstrʌktɪv/ *adj.* having a useful and helpful effect rather than being negative or with no purpose: *constructive criticism/suggestions/advice* ◆ *His work involved helping hyperactive children to use their energy in a constructive way.* ◆ *The government is encouraging all parties to play a constructive role in the reform process.* ➲ compare DESTRUCTIVE ▶ **con·struc·tive·ly** *adv.*

con·struc·tor /kənˈstrʌktər/ *noun* a person or company that builds things, especially cars or aircraft

con·strue /kənˈstru/ *verb* [usually passive] (*formal*) to understand the meaning of a word, a sentence, or an action in a particular way **SYN** INTERPRET: **~ sth** *He considered how the remark would be construed.* ◆ **~ sth as sth** *Her words could hardly be construed as an apology.*

con·sul /ˈkɑnsl/ *noun* a government official who is a representative of his or her country in a foreign city: *the American consul in Shanghai* ➲ see also AMBASSADOR ▶ **con·su·lar** /ˈkɑnsələr/ *adj.*: *consular officials*

con·su·late /ˈkɑnsələt/ *noun* the building where a consul works ➲ compare EMBASSY

con·sult 🔑 **AWL** /kənˈsʌlt/ *verb*

1 [T] to go to someone for information or advice: **~ sb** *If the pain continues, consult your doctor.* ◆ **~ sb about sth** *Have you consulted your lawyer about this?* ◆ **~ with sb (about/on sth)** *Consult with your physician about possible treatments.* **2** [T, I] to discuss something with someone to get their permission for something, or to help you make a decision: **~ sb** *You shouldn't have done it without consulting me.* ◆ **~ sb about/on sth** *I expect to be consulted about major issues.* ◆ **~ with sb (about/on sth)** *I need to consult with my colleagues on the proposals.* ➲ thesaurus box at TALK **3** [T] **~ sth** to look in or at something to get information **SYN** REFER TO: *He consulted the manual.*

con·sult·an·cy **AWL** /kənˈsʌltnsi/ *noun* (*pl.* **con·sult·an·cies**) **1** [C] a company that gives expert advice on a particular subject to other companies or organizations: *a management/design/computer, etc. consultancy* **2** [U] expert advice that a company or person is paid to provide on a particular subject: *consultancy fees*

con·sult·ant **AWL** /kənˈsʌltnt/ *noun* a person who knows a lot about a particular subject and is employed to give advice about it to other people: *a management consultant* ◆ **~ on sth** *the President's consultant on economic affairs*

con·sul·ta·tion **AWL** /ˌkɑnslˈteɪʃn/ *noun* **1** [U] the act of discussing something with someone or with a group of people before making a decision about it: *a consultation document/paper/period/process* ◆ *acting in consultation with all the departments involved* ◆ *The decision was made after close consultation with local residents.* ➲ thesaurus box at DISCUSSION **2** [C] a formal meeting to discuss something: *extensive consultations between the two countries* **3** [C] a meeting with an expert, such as a lawyer or doctor, to get advice or treatment ➲ thesaurus box at INTERVIEW **4** [U] the act of looking for information in a book, etc.: *There is a large collection of texts available for consultation on-screen.*

con·sul·ta·tive **AWL** /kənˈsʌltətɪv; ˈkɑnsl̩ˌteɪtɪv/ *adj.* giving advice or making suggestions **SYN** ADVISORY: *a consultative committee/body/document*

con'sulting ˌroom *noun* a room where a doctor talks to and examines patients

con·sum·a·ble /kənˈsuməbl/ *adj., noun* (*business*)

● *adj.* intended to be bought, used, and then replaced: *consumable electronic goods*

● *noun* **consumables** [pl.] goods that are intended to be used fairly quickly and then replaced: *computer consumables such as CD-Rs and printer cartridges*

con·sume **AWL** /kən'sum/ *verb* (*formal*) **1** ~ sth to use something, especially fuel, energy, or time: *The electricity industry consumes large amounts of fossil fuels.* **2** ~ sth to eat or drink something: *Before he died he had consumed a large quantity of alcohol.* **3** ~ sb (with sth) [usually passive] to fill someone with a strong feeling: *Carolyn was consumed with guilt.* ♦ *Rage consumed him.* **4** ~ sth (of fire) to completely destroy something: *The hotel was quickly consumed by fire.* ⊃ see also CONSUMING, CONSUMPTION, TIME-CONSUMING

con·sum·er 🔑 **AWL** /kən'sumər/ *noun* a person who buys goods or uses services: *consumer demand/choice/rights* ♦ *Health-conscious consumers want more information about the food they buy.* ♦ *a consumer society* (= one where buying and selling is considered very important) ♦ *Tax cuts will boost consumer confidence after the recession.* ⊃ compare PRODUCER

con·sumer con·fidence *noun* [U] a measure of the degree of confidence people have in the economy as a whole and in their own financial situation. If consumer confidence is high, people spend more and the economy expands; the opposite is true if consumer confidence is low: *Tax cuts will boost consumer confidence after the recession.*

con·sumer e·conomy *noun* an economic system that depends on people buying a lot of goods and services rather than on production

con·sumer goods *noun* [pl.] goods such as food, clothing, etc., bought by individual customers ⊃ compare CAPITAL GOODS

con·sumer group *noun* an organization that helps consumers by making sure that products are safe and that people are treated fairly in their dealings with banks, insurance companies, and other businesses

con·sum·er·ism /kən'sumə,rɪzəm/ *noun* [U] (sometimes *disapproving*) the buying and using of goods and services; the belief that it is good for a society or an individual person to buy and use a large quantity of goods and services ▶ **con·sum·er·ist** *adj.*: *consumerist values*

con·sumer price index *noun* [sing.] (*abbr.* CPI) a list of the prices of some ordinary goods and services that shows how much these prices change each month

con·sum·ing **AWL** /kən'sumɪŋ/ *adj.* [only before noun] (of a feeling, an interest, etc.) so strong or important that it takes up all your time and energy: *Basketball is his consuming passion.* ⊃ see also TIME-CONSUMING

con·sum·mate¹ /'kɑnsəmət; kən'sʌmət/ *adj.* [usually before noun] (*formal*) extremely skilled; perfect: *She was a consummate performer.* ♦ *He played the shot with consummate skill.* ♦ (*disapproving*) *a consummate liar* ▶ **con·sum·mate·ly** *adv.*

con·sum·mate² /'kɑnsə,meɪt/ *verb* (*formal*) **1** ~ sth to make a marriage or a relationship complete by having sex: *The marriage lasted only a week and was never consummated.* **2** ~ sth to make something complete or perfect

con·sum·ma·tion /,kɑnsə'meɪʃn/ *noun* [C, U] **1** the act of making a marriage or relationship complete by having sex **2** the fact of making something complete or perfect: *The paintings are the consummation of his life's work.*

con·sump·tion **AWL** /kən'sʌmpʃn/ *noun* [U] **1** (*formal*) the act of using energy, food, or materials; the amount used: *the production of fuel for domestic consumption* (= to be used in the country where it is produced) ♦ *Gas and oil consumption always increase in cold weather.* ♦ *The meat was declared unfit for human consumption.* ♦ *He was advised to reduce his alcohol consumption.* ♦ *Her speech to the town council was not intended for public consumption* (= to be heard by the public). ⊃ see also CONSUME **2** the act of buying and using products: *Consumption rather than saving has become the central feature of contemporary societies.* ⊃ see also CONSPICUOUS CONSUMPTION, CONSUME **3** (*old-fashioned*) a serious infectious disease of the lungs **SYN** TUBERCULOSIS

con·sump·tive /kən'sʌmptɪv/ *noun* (*old-fashioned*) a person

who suffers from consumption (= a disease of the lungs) ▶ **con·sump·tive** *adj.*

cont. (also **contd**) *abbr.* continued: *cont. on p.74*

con·tact 🔑 **AWL** /'kɑntækt/ *noun, verb*

● **noun**
> ACT OF COMMUNICATING **1** [U] ~ (with sb) | ~ (between A and B) the act of communicating with someone, especially regularly: *I don't have much contact with my uncle.* ♦ *There is little contact between the two organizations.* ♦ *Have you kept in contact with any of your friends from college* (= do you still see them or speak or write to them)? ♦ *She's lost contact with* (= no longer sees or writes to) *her son.* ♦ *I finally made contact with* (= succeeded in speaking to or meeting) *her in Paris.* ♦ *The organization put me in contact with other people in a similar position* (= gave me their addresses or telephone numbers). ♦ *two people avoiding eye contact* (= avoiding looking directly at each other) ♦ *Here's my contact number* (= temporary telephone number) *while I'm away.*
> TOUCHING SOMEONE OR SOMETHING **2** [U] the state of touching something: *His fingers were briefly in contact with the ball.* ♦ *This substance should not come into contact with food.* ♦ *a fear of physical contact* ♦ *This pesticide kills insects on contact* (= as soon as it touches them).
> MEETING SOMEONE OR SOMETHING **3** [U] the state of meeting someone or having to deal with something: *In her job she often comes into contact with* (= meets) *lawyers.* ♦ *Children should be brought into contact with poetry at an early age.*
> RELATIONSHIP **4** [C, usually pl.] an occasion on which you meet or communicate with someone; a relationship with someone: *We have good contacts with the local community.* ♦ *The company has maintained trade contacts with India.*
> PERSON **5** [C] a person that you know, especially someone who can be helpful to you in your work: *social/personal contacts* ♦ *I've made some useful contacts in journalism.*
> FOR EYES **6** **contacts** [pl.] (*informal*) = CONTACT LENS
> ELECTRICAL **7** [C] an electrical connection: *The switches close the contacts and complete the circuit.*
> MEDICAL **8** [C] a person who may be infectious because he or she has recently been near to someone with a CONTAGIOUS disease **IDM** see POINT

● **verb** ~ sb to communicate with someone, for example by telephone or letter: *I've been trying to contact you all day.* ▶ **con·tact·a·ble** **AWL** /'kɑn,tæktəbl/ *adj.*

contact lens (also *informal* **con·tact**, **lens**) *noun* a small round piece of thin plastic that you put on your eye to help you see better: *to wear contact lenses*

contact sport *noun* a sport in which players have physical contact with each other **ANT** NON-CONTACT SPORT

con·ta·gion /kən'teɪdʒən/ *noun* **1** [U] the spreading of a disease by people touching each other: *There is no risk of contagion.* **2** [C] (*old use*) a disease that can be spread by people touching each other. **3** [C] (*formal*) something bad that spreads quickly by being passed from person to person ⊃ compare INFECTION

con·ta·gious /kən'teɪdʒəs/ *adj.* **1** a contagious disease spreads by people touching each other: *Scarlet fever is highly contagious.* ♦ (*figurative*) *His enthusiasm was contagious* (= spread quickly to other people). ♦ *a contagious laugh* **2** [not usually before noun] if a person is contagious, they have a disease that can be spread to other people by touch ⊃ compare INFECTIOUS ▶ **con·ta·gious·ly** *adv.*

con·tain 🔑 /kən'teɪn/ *verb* (not used in the progressive tenses) **1** ~ sth if something contains something else, it has that thing inside it or as part of it: *This drink doesn't contain any alcohol.* ♦ *Her statement contained one or two inaccuracies.* ♦ *a brown envelope containing dollar bills* ♦ *The bottle contains* (= can hold) *two quarts.* **2** ~ sth to keep your feelings under control **SYN** RESTRAIN: *She was unable to contain her excitement.* ♦ *I was so furious I just couldn't contain myself* (= I had to express my feelings). **3** ~ sth to prevent something harmful from spreading or getting worse: *to contain an epidemic* ♦ *Government forces have failed to contain the rebellion.*

i see	**ɪ** sit	**ɛ** ten	**æ** cat	**ɑ** hot	**ɔ** saw	**ʊ** put	**u** too

4 ~ sth (*mathematics*) to be able to be divided exactly by a number: *Ten contains five and two, but not three.*

con·tain·er 🔑 /kənˈteɪnər/ *noun*
1 a box, bottle, etc., in which something can be stored or transported: *Food will last longer if kept in an airtight container.* **2** a large metal or wooden box of a standard size in which goods are packed so that they can easily be lifted onto a ship, train, etc., to be transported: *a container ship* (= one designed to transport such containers) ⊃ picture at BOAT

con·tain·er·ized /kənˈteɪnəˌraɪzd/ *adj.* packed and transported in CONTAINERS: *containerized cargo* ▶ **con·tain·er·i·za·tion** /kənˌteɪnərəˈzeɪʃn/ *noun* [U]

con·tain·ment /kənˈteɪnmənt/ *noun* [U] (*formal*) **1** the act of keeping something under control so that it cannot spread in a harmful way: *the containment of the epidemic* **2** the act of keeping another country's power within limits so that it does not become too powerful: *a policy of containment*

con·tam·i·nant /kənˈtæmənənt/ *noun* (*technical*) a substance that makes something IMPURE: *Filters do not remove all contaminants from water.*

con·tam·i·nate /kənˈtæməˌneɪt/ *verb* **1 ~ sth (with sth)** to make a substance or place dirty or no longer pure by adding a substance that is dangerous or carries disease **SYN** ADULTERATE: *The drinking water has become contaminated with lead.* ◆ *contaminated blood/food/soil* **2 ~ sth** (*formal*) to influence people's ideas or attitudes in a bad way: *They were accused of contaminating the minds of our young people.* ⊃ see also UNCONTAMINATED ▶ **con·tam·i·na·tion** /kənˌtæməˈneɪʃn/ *noun* [U]: *radioactive contamination* ⊃ see also CROSS-CONTAMINATION

contd *abbr.* = CONT.

con·tem·plate /ˈkɑntəmˌpleɪt/ *verb* **1** [T] to think about whether you should do something, or how you should do something **SYN** CONSIDER, THINK ABOUT/OF: **~ sth** *You're too young to be contemplating retirement.* ◆ **~ doing sth** *I have never contemplated living abroad.* ◆ **~ how/what, etc....** *He continued talking while she contemplated how to answer.* **2** [T] to think carefully about and accept the possibility of something happening: **~ sth** *The thought of war is too awful to contemplate.* ◆ **~ how/what, etc....** *I can't contemplate what it would be like to be alone.* ◆ **~ that...** *She contemplated that things might get even worse.* **3** [T, I] **~ (sth)** (*formal*) to think deeply about something for a long time: *to contemplate your future* ◆ *She lay in bed, contemplating.* **4** [T] **~ sb/sth** (*formal*) to look at someone or something in a careful way for a long time **SYN** STARE AT: *She contemplated him in silence.*

con·tem·pla·tion /ˌkɑntəmˈpleɪʃn/ *noun* [U] (*formal*) **1** the act of thinking deeply about something: *He sat there deep in contemplation.* ◆ *a few moments of quiet contemplation* ◆ *a life of prayer and contemplation* **2** the act of looking at something in a calm and careful way: *She turned from her contemplation of the photograph.*
IDM **in contemplation** (*formal*) being considered: *By 1613 even more desperate measures were in contemplation.*

con·tem·pla·tive /kənˈtɛmplətɪv/ *adj.*
● (*formal*) **1** thinking quietly and seriously about something: *She was in contemplative mood.* **2** spending time thinking deeply about religious matters: *the contemplative life* (= life in a religious community)

con·tem·po·ra·ne·ous /kənˌtɛmpəˈreɪniəs/ *adj.* **~ (with sb/sth)** (*formal*) happening or existing at the same time **SYN** CONTEMPORARY: *How do we know that the signature is contemporaneous with the document?* ◆ *contemporaneous events/accounts* ▶ **con·tem·po·ra·ne·ous·ly** *adv.*

con·tem·po·rar·y 🔑 **AWL** /kənˈtɛmpəˌrɛri/ *adj., noun*
● *adj.* **1** belonging to the present time **SYN** MODERN: *contemporary fiction/music/dance* **2 ~ (with sb/sth)** belonging to the same time: *We have no contemporary account of the battle* (= written near the time that it happened). ◆ *He was contemporary with the dramatist Congreve.*

● *noun* (*pl.* **con·tem·po·rar·ies**) a person who lives or lived at the same time as someone else, especially someone who is about the same age: *She and I were contemporaries in college.* ◆ *He was a contemporary of Freud and may have known him.*

con·tempt /kənˈtɛmpt/ *noun* [U, sing.] **1** the feeling that someone or something is without value and deserves no respect at all: *She looked at him with contempt.* ◆ *I will treat that suggestion with the contempt it deserves.* ◆ *His treatment of his children is beneath contempt* (= so unacceptable that it is not even worth feeling contempt for). ◆ *Politicians seem to be generally held in contempt by ordinary people.* ◆ **~ for sb/sth** *They had shown a contempt for the values she thought important.* **2 ~ for sth** a lack of worry or fear about rules, danger, etc.: *The firefighters showed a contempt for their own safety.* ◆ *His remarks betray a staggering contempt for the truth* (= are completely false). **3** = CONTEMPT OF COURT: *He could be jailed for two years for contempt.* ◆ *She was held in contempt for refusing to testify.* **IDM** see FAMILIARITY

con·tempt·i·ble /kənˈtɛmptəbl/ *adj.* (*formal*) not deserving any respect at all **SYN** DESPICABLE: *contemptible behavior*

con·tempt of ˈcourt (also **con·tempt**) *noun* [U] the crime of refusing to obey an order made by a court; not showing respect for a court or judge: *Any person who disregards this order will be in contempt of court.*

con·temp·tu·ous /kənˈtɛmptʃuəs/ *adj.* feeling or showing that you have no respect for someone or something **SYN** SCORNFUL: *She gave him a contemptuous look.* ◆ **~ of sb/sth** *He was contemptuous of everything I did.* ▶ **con·temp·tu·ous·ly** *adv.*: *to laugh contemptuously*

con·tend /kənˈtɛnd/ *verb* **1** [T] **~ that...** (*formal*) to say that something is true, especially in an argument **SYN** MAINTAIN: *I would contend that the senator's thinking is flawed on this point.* **2** [I] **~ (for sth)** to compete against someone in order to gain something: *Three armed groups were contending for power.*
PHR V **con'tend with sth** to have to deal with a problem or difficult situation: *Nurses often have to contend with violent or drunk patients.*

con·tend·er /kənˈtɛndər/ *noun* a person who takes part in a competition or tries to win something: *a contender for a gold medal in the Olympics* ◆ *a leading/serious/strong contender for the party leadership*

con·tent¹ 🔑 /ˈkɑntɛnt/ *noun*
⊃ see also CONTENT² **1 contents** [pl.] the things that are contained in something: *He tipped the contents of the bag onto the table.* ◆ *Fire has caused severe damage to the contents of the building.* ◆ *She hadn't read the letter and so was unaware of its contents.* **2 contents** [pl.] the different sections that are contained in a book: *a table of contents* (= the list at the front of a book) ◆ *a contents page* **3** [sing.] the subject matter of a book, speech, program, etc.: *Your tone of voice is as important as the content of what you have to say.* ◆ *The content of the course depends on what the students would like to study.* ◆ *Her poetry has a good deal of political content.* **4** [sing.] (following a noun) the amount of a substance that is contained in something else: *food with a high fat content* ◆ *the alcohol content of a drink* **5** [U] (*computing*) the information or other material contained on a Web site or CD-ROM: *online content providers*

con·tent² /kənˈtɛnt/ *adj., verb, noun* ⊃ see also CONTENT¹
● *adj.* [not before noun] **1 ~ (with sth)** happy and satisfied with what you have: *Not content with stealing my boyfriend* (= not thinking that this was enough), *she has turned all my friends against me.* ◆ *He seemed more content and less bitter.* ◆ *He had to be content with third place.* ⊃ thesaurus box at HAPPY **2 ~ to do sth** willing to do something: *I was content to wait.* ⊃ compare CONTENTED

● *verb* **1 ~ yourself with sth** to accept and be satisfied with something and not try to have or do something better: *Martina contented herself with a bowl of soup.* **2 ~ sb** (*formal*) to make someone feel happy or satisfied: *My apology seemed to content him.*

● *noun* = CONTENTMENT **IDM** see HEART

| ʌ **cup** | ə **about** | eɪ **say** | aɪ **five** | ɔɪ **boy** | aʊ **now** | oʊ **go** | ər **bird** |

con·tent·ed /kənˈtɛntəd/ *adj.* [usually before noun] showing or feeling happiness or satisfaction, especially because your life is good: *a contented smile ◆ He was a contented man.* ⊃ compare CONTENT¹ **ANT** DISCONTENTED ⊃ thesaurus box at HAPPY ▶ **con·tent·ed·ly** *adv.*: *She smiled contentedly.*

con·ten·tion /kənˈtɛnʃn/ *noun* (*formal*) **1** [U] angry disagreement between people **SYN** DISPUTE: *One area of contention is the availability of daycare. ◆ a point of contention* **2** [C] ~ **(that…)** a belief or an opinion that you express, especially in an argument: *It is our client's contention that the fire was an accident. ◆ I would reject that contention.*
IDM **in contention (for sth)** with a chance of winning something: *Only three teams are now in contention for the title.* **out of contention (for sth)** without a chance of winning something ⊃ more at BONE

con·ten·tious /kənˈtɛnʃəs/ *adj.* (*formal*) **1** likely to cause disagreement between people: *a contentious issue/topic/subject ◆ Both views are highly contentious.* **ANT** UNCONTENTIOUS **2** liking to argue; involving a lot of arguing: *a contentious meeting*

con·tent·ment /kənˈtɛntmənt/ (also *less frequent* **con·tent**) *noun* [U] a feeling of happiness or satisfaction: *He has found contentment at last. ◆ a sigh of contentment* ⊃ compare DISCONTENT ⊃ thesaurus box at SATISFACTION

content word *noun* (*linguistics*) a noun, verb, adjective, or adverb whose main function is to express meaning ⊃ compare FUNCTION WORD

con·test ♪ *noun, verb*
• *noun* /ˈkɑntɛst/ **1** a competition in which people try to win something: *a singing contest ◆ a talent contest ◆ to enter/win/lose a contest* ⊃ see also BEAUTY CONTEST **2** ~ **(for sth)** a struggle to gain control or power: *a contest for the leadership of the party*
IDM **be no contest** used to say that one side in a competition is so much stronger or better than the other that it is sure to win easily
• *verb* /kənˈtɛst/ **1** ~ **sth** to take part in a competition, election, etc., and try to win it: *Three candidates contested the leadership. ◆ a hotly/fiercely/keenly contested game* (= one in which the players try very hard to win and the scores are close) **2** ~ **sth** to formally oppose a decision or statement because you think it is wrong: *to contest a will* (= try to show that it was not correctly made in law) *◆ The divorce was not contested.*

con·test·ant /kənˈtɛstənt/ *noun* a person who takes part in a contest: *Please welcome our next contestant.*

con·text ♪ **AWL** /ˈkɑntɛkst/ *noun* [C, U]
1 the situation in which something happens and that helps you to understand it: *This speech needs to be set in the context of the U.S. in the 1960s. ◆ His decision can only be understood in context.* **2** the words that come just before and after a word, phrase, or statement, and help you to understand its meaning: *You should be able to guess the meaning of the word from the context. ◆ This quotation has been taken out of context* (= repeated without giving the circumstances in which it was said).

con·tex·tu·al **AWL** /kənˈtɛkstʃuəl/ *adj.* (*formal*) connected with a particular context: *contextual information ◆ contextual clues to the meaning* ▶ **con·tex·tu·al·ly** *adv.*

con·tex·tu·al·ize **AWL** /kənˈtɛkstʃuəˌlaɪz/ *verb* ~ **sth** (*formal*) to consider something in relation to the situation in which it happens or exists ▶ **con·tex·tu·al·i·za·tion** /kənˌtɛkstʃuələˈzeɪʃn/ *noun* [U]

con·tig·u·ous /kənˈtɪgyuəs/ *adj.* (*formal or technical*) touching or next to something: *The countries are contiguous. ◆ ~ with/to sth The bruising was not contiguous to the wound.* ▶ **con·ti·gu·i·ty** /ˌkɑntəˈgyuəti/ *noun* [U]

con·ti·nence /ˈkɑntənəns; ˈkɑntnæˌəns/ *noun* [U] **1** the ability to control the BLADDER and BOWELS **ANT** INCONTINENCE **2** (*formal*) the control of your feelings, especially your desire to have sex ▶ **con·ti·nent** *adj.* **ANT** INCONTINENT

con·ti·nent ♪ /ˈkɑntənənt; ˈkɑntnˌənt/ *noun* one of the large land masses of the earth such as Europe, Asia, or Africa: *the continent of Africa ◆ the African continent*

con·ti·nen·tal /ˌkɑntəˈnɛntl; ˌkɑntnˈɛntl/ *adj.* **1** [only before noun] connected with the main part of the N. American continent: *Prices are often higher in Hawaii than in the continental United States.* **2** [only before noun] forming part of, or typical of, any of the seven main land masses of the earth: *continental Antarctica/Asia/Europe ◆ to study continental geography* **3** typical of the main part of Europe: *The restaurant serves excellent continental fare. ◆ The shutters and balconies make New Orleans look continental.*

continental breakfast *noun* a light breakfast, usually consisting of coffee and rolls with butter and jelly

continental climate *noun* a fairly dry pattern of weather with very hot summers and very cold winters, that is typical of the central regions of the U.S., Canada, and Russia, for example

the Continental Di'vide (also the **Great Di'vide**) *noun* [sing.] an area along the Rocky Mountains in North America that separates the rivers flowing east into the Atlantic Ocean or the Gulf of Mexico from those flowing west into the Pacific Ocean

continental drift *noun* [U] (*geology*) the slow movement of the continents toward and away from each other during the history of the earth ⊃ see also PLATE TECTONICS

continental shelf *noun* [usually sing.] (*geology*) the area of land on the edge of a continent that slopes into the ocean

continental slope *noun* [sing.] (*geology*) the steep surface that goes down from the outer edge of the continental shelf to the ocean floor

con·tin·gen·cy /kənˈtɪndʒənsi/ *noun* (*pl.* **con·tin·gen·cies**) an event that may or may not happen **SYN** POSSIBILITY: *We must consider all possible contingencies. ◆ to make contingency plans* (= plans for what to do if a particular event happens or does not happen) *◆ a contingency fund* (= to pay for something that might happen in the future)

con'tingency fee *noun* an amount of money that is paid to a lawyer only if the person he or she is advising wins in court

con·tin·gent /kənˈtɪndʒənt/ *noun, adj.*
• *noun* **1** a group of people at a meeting or an event who have something in common, especially the place they come from, that is not shared by other people at the event: *The largest contingent was from the United States. ◆ A strong contingent of local residents was there to block the proposal.* **2** a group of soldiers that are part of a larger force: *the French contingent in the U.N. peacekeeping force*
• *adj.* **1** ~ **(on/upon sth)** (*formal*) depending on something that may or may not happen: *All payments are contingent upon satisfactory completion dates.* **2** ~ **worker/work/job** a person who does not have a permanent contract with a company, or work done by such a person: *the spread of contingent work throughout the economy* ▶ **con·tin·gent·ly** *adv.*

con·tin·u·al /kənˈtɪnyuəl/ *adj.* [only before noun] **1** repeated many times in a way that is annoying: *continual complaints/interruptions* **2** continuing without interruption **SYN** CONTINUOUS: *He was in a continual process of rewriting his material. ◆ We lived in continual fear of being discovered. ◆ Her daughter was a continual source of delight to her.* ⊃ note at CONTINUOUS ▶ **con·tin·u·al·ly** *adv.*: *They argue continually about money. ◆ the need to adapt to new and continually changing circumstances ◆ New products are continually being developed.*

con·tin·u·ance /kənˈtɪnyuəns/ *noun* **1** [U] (*formal*) the state of continuing to exist or function: *We can no longer support the President's continuance in office.* **2** [C] (*law*) a decision that a court case should be heard later: *The judge refused his motion for a continuance.*

con·tin·u·ant /kənˈtɪnyuənt/ *noun* (*phonetics*) a consonant that is pronounced with the breath passing through the throat, so that the sound can be continued. /f/, /l/, and /m/

are examples of continuants. ▶ **con·tin·u·ant** *adj.* [only before noun]: *continuant consonants*

con·tin·u·a·tion /kənˌtɪnyuˈeɪʃn/ *noun* **1** [U, sing.] an act or the state of continuing: *They are anxious to ensure the continuation of the economic reform program.* ♦ **~ in sth** *This year saw a continuation in the upward trend in sales.* **2** [C] something that continues or follows something else: *Her new book is a continuation of her autobiography.* **3** [C] something that is joined on to something else and forms a part of it: *There are plans to build a continuation of the by-pass next year.*

con·tin·ue /kənˈtɪnyu/ *verb*
1 [I, T] to keep existing or happening without stopping: *The exhibition continues until July 25th.* ♦ *The trial is expected to continue for three months.* ♦ **~ to do sth** *The rain continued to fall all afternoon.* ♦ **~ doing sth** *The rain continued falling all afternoon.* **2** [I, T] to keep doing something without stopping: **~ doing sth** *She wanted to continue working until she was 60.* ♦ **~ to do sth** *He continued to ignore everything I was saying.* ♦ **~ (with sth)** *Are you going to continue with the project?* ♦ **~ sth** *The FBI is continuing its investigations.* **3** [I] (**+ adv./prep.**) to go or move further in the same direction: *The path continued over rough, rocky ground.* ♦ *He continued on his way.* **4** [I] **~ (as sth)** to remain in a particular job or condition: *I want you to continue as project manager.* ♦ *She will continue in her present job until a replacement can be found.* **5** [I, T] to start or start something again after stopping for a time **SYN** RESUME: *The story continues in our next issue.* ♦ **~ sth** *The story will be continued in our next issue.* **6** [I, T] to start speaking again after stopping: *Please continue—I didn't mean to interrupt.* ♦ **+ speech** *"In fact," he continued, ""I'd like to congratulate you.*

con·tin·ued /kənˈtɪnyud/ (also **con·tin·u·ing** /kənˈtɪnyuɪŋ/) *adj.* [only before noun] existing in the same state without change or interruption: *We are grateful for your* **continued/continuing** *support.* ♦ *continued interest* ♦ *continuing involvement*

con·tinu·ing edu·ca·tion (also a·dult edu·ca·tion) *noun* [U] education for adults that is available outside the formal education system, for example at night classes or over the Internet

con·ti·nu·i·ty /ˌkɑntəˈnuəti/ *noun* (pl. **con·ti·nu·i·ties**) **1** [U] the fact of not stopping or not changing: *to ensure/provide/maintain continuity of fuel supplies* **ANT** DISCONTINUITY **2** [U, C] (*formal*) a logical connection between the parts of something, or between two things: *The novel fails to achieve narrative continuity.* ♦ *There are obvious continuities between diet and health.* **ANT** DISCONTINUITY **3** [U] (*technical*) the organization of a movie or television program, especially making sure that people's clothes, objects, etc., are the same from one scene to the next

con·tin·u·o /kənˈtɪnyuoʊ/ *noun* [U] (from *Italian*, *music*) a musical part played to accompany another instrument, in which a line of low notes is shown with figures to represent the higher notes to be played above them: *a trio for two violins and continuo*

con·tin·u·ous /kənˈtɪnyuəs/ *adj.*
1 happening or existing for a period of time without interruption: *She was in continuous employment until the age of sixty-five.* ♦ *The rain has been continuous since this morning.* **2** spreading in a line or over an area without any spaces: *a continuous line of traffic* **3** (*informal*) repeated many times **SYN** CONTINUAL: *For four days the town suffered continuous attacks.* **HELP** Continual is much more frequent in this meaning. **4** (*grammar*) = PROGRESSIVE: *the continuous tenses* ▶ **con·tin·u·ous·ly** *adv.*: *He has lived and worked in France almost continuously since 1990.*

con·tin·u·um /kənˈtɪnyuəm/ *noun* (pl. **con·tin·u·a** /-yuə/) a series of similar items in which each is almost the same as the ones next to it but the last is very different from the first **SYN** CLINE: *It is impossible to say at what point along the continuum a dialect becomes a separate language.*

WHICH WORD?

continuous ♦ continual

These adjectives are frequently used with the following nouns:

continuous ~	continual ~
process	change
employment	problems
flow	updating
line	questions
speech	pain
supply	fear

■ **Continuous** describes something that continues without stopping.
■ **Continual** usually describes an action that is repeated again and again.
■ The difference between these two words is now disappearing. In particular, **continual** can also mean the same as **continuous** and is used especially about undesirable things: *Life was a continual struggle for them.* However, **continuous** is much more frequent in this sense.

con·tort /kənˈtɔrt/ *verb* [I, T] to become twisted or make something twisted out of its natural or normal shape: *His face contorted with anger.* ♦ **~ sth** *Her mouth was contorted in a snarl.* ▶ **con·tort·ed** *adj.*: *contorted limbs/bodies* ♦ (*figurative*) *It was a contorted version of the truth.*

con·tor·tion /kənˈtɔrʃn/ *noun* **1** [U] the state of the face or body being twisted out of its natural shape: *Their bodies had suffered contortion as a result of malnutrition.* **2** [C] a movement which twists the body out of its natural shape: *His facial contortions amused the audience.* ♦ (*figurative*) *We had to go through all the usual contortions to get a ticket* (= a difficult series of actions).

con·tor·tion·ist /kənˈtɔrʃənɪst/ *noun* a performer who does contortions of their body to entertain others

con·tour /ˈkɑntʊr/ *noun* **1** the outer edges of something; the outline of its shape or form: *The road follows the natural contours of the coastline.* ♦ *She traced the contours of his face with her finger.* **2** (also ˈcontour line) a line on a map showing points that are the same height above sea level: *a contour map* (= a map that includes these lines)

con·toured /ˈkɑntʊrd/ *adj.* **1** with a specially designed outline that makes something attractive or comfortable: *It is smoothly contoured to look like a racing car.* **2** having or showing contours: *contoured hills/maps*

contra- /ˈkɑntrə/ *combining form* **1** (in nouns, verbs and adjectives) against; opposite: *contraflow* ♦ *contradict* **2** (in nouns) (*music*) having a PITCH an OCTAVE below: *a contrabassoon*

con·tra·band /ˈkɑntrəˌbænd/ *noun* [U] goods that are illegally taken into or out of a country: *contraband goods* ♦ *to smuggle contraband*

con·tra·cep·tion /ˌkɑntrəˈsɛpʃn/ *noun* [U] the practice of preventing a woman from becoming pregnant; the methods of doing this **SYN** BIRTH CONTROL: *to give advice about contraception*

con·tra·cep·tive /ˌkɑntrəˈsɛptɪv/ *noun* a drug, device, or practice used to prevent a woman from becoming pregnant: *oral contraceptives* ♦ **con·tra·cep·tive** *adj.* [only before noun]: *a contraceptive pill* ♦ *contraceptive advice/precautions/methods*

con·tract /ˈkɑntrækt/ **AWL** *noun, verb*
● *noun* /ˈkɑntrækt/ **1** an official written agreement: *a contract of employment* ♦ *a research contract* ♦ **~ with sb** *to enter into/make/sign a contract with the supplier* ♦ **~ between A and B** *These clauses form part of the contract between buyer and seller.* ♦ **~ for sth** *a contract for the supply of vehicles* ♦ **~ to do sth** *to win/be awarded a contract to build a new school* ♦ *a contract worker* (= one employed on a contract for a fixed period of time) ♦ *I was on a three-year contract that expired last*

t **tea**   ţ **butter**   d **did**   k **cat**   g **got**   tʃ **chin**   dʒ **June**   f **fall**

week. ◆ *Under the terms of the contract the job should have been finished yesterday.* ◆ *She is **under contract to** (= has a contract to work for) a major American computer firm.* ◆ *The offer has been accepted, **subject to contract** (= the agreement is not official until the contract is signed).* ◆ *They were sued for **breach of contract** (= not keeping to a contract).* **2** ~ **(on sb)** (*informal*) an agreement to kill someone for money: *to take out a contract on someone*

● **verb 1** /kənˈtrækt/ [I, T] to become less or smaller; to make something become less or smaller: *Glass contracts as it cools.* ◆ *a contracting market* ◆ *The heart muscles contract to expel the blood.* ◆ ~ **sth** *The exercise consists of stretching and contracting the leg muscles.* ◆ ~ **sth to sth** *"I'll"* is usually contracted to *"I'll"* (= made shorter). **ANT** EXPAND **2** /kənˈtrækt/ [T] ~ **sth** (*medical*) to get an illness: *to contract AIDS/a virus/a disease* **3** /ˈkɑntrækt; kənˈtrækt/ [T] to make a legal agreement with someone for them to work for you or provide you with a service: ~ **sb to do sth** *The player is contracted to play until August.* ◆ ~ **sb (to sth)** *Several computer engineers have been contracted to the finance department.* **4** /ˈkɑntrækt; kənˈtrækt/ [I] ~ **to do sth** to make a legal agreement to work for someone or provide them with a service: *She has contracted to work 20 hours a week.* **5** /ˈkɑntrækt; kənˈtrækt/ [T] ~ **a marriage/an alliance (with someone)** (*formal*) to formally agree to marry sb/form an ALLIANCE with someone **PHR V** con‧tract sth↔ **out (to sb)** to arrange for work to be done by another company rather than your own

contract ˈbridge *noun* [U] the standard form of the card game BRIDGE, in which points are given only for sets of cards that are BID[1] and won

con‧trac‧tile /kənˈtræktl; -taɪl/ *adj.* (*biology*) (of living TISSUE, organs, etc.) able to contract or, of an opening or a tube, become narrower

con‧trac‧tion /kənˈtrækʃn/ *noun* **1** [U] the process of becoming smaller: *the expansion and contraction of the metal* ◆ *The sudden contraction of the markets left them with a lot of unwanted stock.* **ANT** EXPANSION **2** [C, U] a sudden and painful contracting of muscles, especially of the muscles around a woman's WOMB that happens when she is giving birth to a child: *The contractions started coming every five minutes.* **3** [C] (*linguistics*) a short form of a word: *"He's"* may be a contraction of *"he is"* or *"he has."*

con‧trac‧tor **AWL** /ˈkɑnˌtræktər/ *noun* a person or company that has a contract to do work or provide goods or services for another company: *a building/landscaping, etc. contractor* ◆ *to employ an outside contractor*

con‧trac‧tu‧al /kənˈtræktʃuəl/ *adj.* connected with the conditions of a legal written agreement; agreed in a contract ▶ con‧trac‧tu‧al‧ly *adv.*

con‧tra‧dict **AWL** /ˌkɑntrəˈdɪkt/ *verb* **1** to say that something that someone else has said is wrong, and that the opposite is true: ~ **sth** *All evening her husband contradicted everything she said.* ◆ ~ **sb/yourself** *You've just contradicted yourself* (= said the opposite of what you said before). ◆ ~ **(sb) + speech** *"No, it's not,"* she contradicted (him). **2** ~ **sth** | ~ **each other** (of statements or pieces of evidence) to be so different from each other that one of them must be wrong: *The two stories contradict each other.* ⊃ language bank at EVIDENCE

con‧tra‧dic‧tion **AWL** /ˌkɑntrəˈdɪkʃn/ *noun* **1** [C, U] ~ **(between A and B)** a lack of agreement between facts, opinions, actions, etc.: *There is a contradiction between the two sets of figures.* ◆ *His public speeches are in direct contradiction to his personal lifestyle.* ◆ *How can we resolve this apparent contradiction?* **2** [U, C] the act of saying that something that someone else has said is wrong or not true; an example of this: *I think I can say, without fear of contradiction, that…* ◆ *Now you say you both left at ten—that's a contradiction of your last statement.*
IDM a contradiction in terms a statement containing words that contradict each other's meaning: *A "nomad settlement" is a contradiction in terms.*

con‧tra‧dic‧to‧ry **AWL** /ˌkɑntrəˈdɪktəri/ *adj.* containing or

showing a contradiction **SYN** CONFLICT: *We are faced with two apparently contradictory statements.* ◆ *The advice I received was often contradictory.*

con‧tra‧dis‧tinc‧tion /ˌkɑntrədɪˈstɪŋkʃn/ *noun*
IDM in contradistinction to sth/sb (*formal*) in contrast with something or someone

con‧trail /ˈkɑntreɪl/ *noun* a white trail of steam from an aircraft that is flying very high

con‧tra‧in‧di‧cate /ˌkɑntrəˈɪndəˌkeɪt/ *verb* ~ **sth** (*medical*) if a drug or treatment is **contraindicated**, there is a medical reason why it should not be used in a particular situation: *This drug is contraindicated in patients with asthma.*

con‧tra‧in‧di‧ca‧tion /ˌkɑntrəˌɪndəˈkeɪʃn/ *noun* (*medical*) a possible reason for not giving someone a particular drug or medical treatment

con‧tral‧to /kənˈtræltoʊ/ *noun* (*pl.* con‧tral‧tos) = ALTO

con‧trap‧tion /kənˈtræpʃn/ *noun* a machine or piece of equipment that looks strange: *She showed us a strange contraption that looked like a satellite dish.*

con‧tra‧pun‧tal /ˌkɑntrəˈpʌntl/ *adj.* (*music*) having two or more tunes played together to form a whole ⊃ see also COUNTERPOINT

con‧trar‧i‧wise /ˈkɑntreriˌwaɪz/ *adv.* (*formal*) **1** used at the beginning of a sentence or clause to introduce a contrast **2** in the opposite way: *It worked contrariwise—first you dialed the number, then you put the money in.*

con‧trar‧y[1] **AWL** /ˈkɑnˌtreri/ *adj., noun* ⊃ see also CONTRARY[2]

● *adj.* **1** ~ **to sth** different from something; against something: *Contrary to popular belief, many cats dislike milk.* ◆ *The government has decided that the publication of the report would be "contrary to the public interest."* **2** [only before noun] completely different in nature or direction **SYN** OPPOSITE: *contrary advice/opinions/arguments* ◆ *The contrary view is that prison provides an excellent education—in crime.*

● *noun* the contrary [sing.] the opposite fact, event, or situation: *In the end the contrary was proved true: he was innocent and she was guilty.*
IDM on the contrary used to introduce a statement that says the opposite of the last one: *"It must have been terrible." "On the contrary, I enjoyed every minute."* quite the contrary used to emphasize that the opposite of what has been said is true: *I don't find him funny at all. Quite the contrary.* to the contrary showing or proving the opposite: *Show me some evidence to the contrary* (= proving that something is not true). ◆ *I will expect to see you on Sunday unless I hear anything to the contrary* (= that you are not coming).

con‧trar‧y[2] **AWL** /ˈkɑnˌtreri; kənˈtreri/ *adj.* (*formal, disapproving*) (usually of children) behaving badly; choosing to do or say the opposite of what is expected: *She was such a contrary child—it was impossible to please her.* ⊃ see also CONTRARY[1] ▶ con‧trar‧i‧ly **AWL** /ˈkɑnˌtrerəli/ *adv.* con‧trar‧i‧ness /ˈkɑnˌtrerinəs; kənˈtreri-/ *noun* [U]

con‧trast ♪ **AWL** *noun, verb*

● *noun* /ˈkɑntræst/ **1** [C, U] a difference between two or more people or things that you can see clearly when they are compared or put close together; the fact of comparing two or more things in order to show the differences between them: ~ **(between A and B)** *There is an obvious contrast between the cultures of East and West.* ◆ ~ **(to sb/sth)** *The company lost $7 million this quarter in contrast to a profit of $6.2 million a year earlier.* ◆ *The situation when we arrived was in marked contrast to the news reports.* ◆ *The poverty of her childhood stands in total contrast to her life in Hollywood.* ◆ ~ **(with sb/sth)** to show a sharp/stark/striking contrast with something ◆ ~ **(in sth)** *A wool jacket complements the silk shirt and provides an interesting contrast in texture.* ◆ *When you look at their new system, ours seems very old-fashioned by contrast.* ◆ ~ **(of sth)** *Careful contrast of the two plans shows some important differences.* **2** [C] ~ **(to sb/sth)** a person or thing that is clearly different from someone or something else: *The work you did today is quite a contrast to (= very much* better/worse than) *what you did last week.* **3** [U] differences in color or in light and dark, used in photographs and paintings to create a special effect: *The artist's use of contrast is masterly.* **4** [U] the amount of difference between light and dark in a picture on a television, computer, etc., screen: *Use this button to adjust the contrast.*

● **verb** /kən'træst; 'kɑntræst/ **1** [T] ~ **(A and/with B)** to compare two things in order to show the differences between them: *It is interesting to contrast the British legal system with the American one.* ◆ *The poem contrasts youth and age.* **2** [I] ~ **(with sth)** to show a clear difference when close together or when compared: *Her actions contrasted sharply with her promises.* ◆ *Her actions and her promises contrasted sharply.*

contrast

highlighting differences

- This survey **highlights a number of differences in** the way that teenage boys and girls in the US spend their free time.
- **One of the main differences between** the girls **and** the boys who took part in the research was the way in which they use the Internet.
- **Unlike** the girls, who use the Internet mainly to keep in touch with friends, the boys questioned in this survey tend to use the Internet for playing computer games.
- The girls **differ from** the boys **in that** they tend to spend more time keeping in touch with friends on the telephone or on social networking websites.
- **Compared with** the boys, the girls spend much more time chatting to friends on the telephone.
- On average, the girls spend four hours a week chatting to friends on the phone. **In contrast,** very few of the boys spend more than five minutes a day talking to their friends in this way.
- The boys prefer competitive sports and computer games, **whereas/while** the girls seem to enjoy more cooperative activities, such as shopping with friends.
- When the girls go shopping, they mainly buy clothes and cosmetics. The boys, **on the other hand,** tend to purchase computer games or gadgets.
- ⊃ Language Banks at GENERALLY, ILLUSTRATE, PROPORTION, SIMILARLY, SURPRISING

con·trast·ing 🔊 AWL /kən'træstɪŋ; 'kɑnˌtræs-/ *adj.* [usually before noun]
very different in style, color, or attitude: *bright, contrasting colors* ◆ *The book explores contrasting views of the poet's early work.*

con·tras·tive AWL /kən'træstɪv/ *adj.* (*linguistics*) showing the differences between languages: *a contrastive analysis of American and Australian English*

con·tra·vene /ˌkɑntrə'vin/ *verb* ~ **sth** (*formal*) to do something that is not allowed by a law or rule SYN INFRINGE: *The company was found guilty of contravening safety regulations.* ▶ **con·tra·ven·tion** /ˌkɑntrə'vɛnʃn/ *noun* [U, C] SYN : *These actions are in contravention of Federal law.*

con·tre·temps /'kɑntrəˌtɑ/ *noun* (*pl.* **con·tre·temps** /'kɑntrəˌtɑ; 'kɑntrəˌtɑz/) (from *French, formal* or *humorous*)
1 an unexpected and unfortunate event **2** a minor argument or disagreement with another person

con·trib·ute 🔊 AWL /kən'trɪbyut/ *verb*
1 [T, I] to give something, especially money or goods, to help someone or something: ~ **sth (to/toward sth)** *We contributed $5,000 to the earthquake fund.* ◆ ~ **(to/toward sth)** *Would you like to contribute to our cause?* ◆ *Do you want to contribute?* **2** [I] ~ **(to sth)** to be one of the causes of something: *Medical negligence could have contributed to her death.* ⊃ language bank at CAUSE **3** [I, T] to increase,

improve, or add to something: ~ **to sth** *Immigrants have contributed to American culture in many ways.* ◆ ~ **sth to sth** *This book does not contribute much to our understanding of the subject.* **4** [T, I] to write things for a newspaper, magazine, or a radio or television program; to speak during a meeting or conversation, especially to give your opinion: ~ **sth (to sth)** *She contributed a number of articles to the magazine.* ◆ ~ **(to sth)** *He contributes regularly to the magazine "New Scientist."* ◆ *We hope everyone will contribute to the discussion.* ▶ **con·trib·ut·ing** AWL *adj.*: *Human error may have been a contributing factor*

AWL COLLOCATIONS

contribute

contribute *verb*
to give a part of the total, together with others
- **financially** | **greatly, significantly, substantially** | **positively** | **equally**
  Moreover, graduates can use their knowledge and skills in ways that contribute positively to their communities.

to help to produce something; to play a part in something
- **greatly, significantly, substantially** | **importantly** | **positively,** | **disproportionately** | **directly, indirectly**
  Relatively small areas of the city contribute disproportionately to the violent crime rate.
- **(most) likely, undoubtedly** | **significantly**
  Coral reefs in the oceans significantly contribute to the removal of atmospheric carbon dioxide.

contributing *adj.*
- **factor**
  The authors suggest that low proficiency in academic language is a contributing factor to academic failure.

contribution *noun*
- **important, significant** | **major, substantial** | **valuable** | **outstanding, seminal, unique** | **relative**
  Irving Fisher made seminal contributions to modern financial economics.

con·tri·bu·tion 🔊 AWL /ˌkɑntrə'byuʃn/ *noun*
1 [C] a sum of money that is given to a person or an organization in order to help pay for something SYN DONATION: ~ **(to sth)** *to make a contribution to charity* ◆ *a generous contribution* ◆ *All contributions will be gratefully received.* ◆ ~ **(toward(s) sth/doing sth)** *valuable contributions toward the maintenance of the cathedral* **2** [C] ~ **(to sth)** a sum of money that you pay regularly, often to your employer or the government, for benefits such as health insurance, a retirement plan, etc.: *monthly contributions to the retirement account* ⊃ thesaurus box at PAYMENT **3** [C, usually sing.] an action or a service that helps to cause or increase something: ~ **(to sth)** *He made a very positive contribution to the success of the project.* ◆ *the car's contribution to the greenhouse effect* ◆ ~ **(toward(s) sth/doing sth)** *These measures would make a valuable contribution toward reducing industrial accidents.* ⊃ collocations at CONTRIBUTE **4** [C] ~ **(to sth)** an item that forms part of a book, magazine, broadcast, discussion, etc.: *an important contribution to the debate* ◆ *All contributions for the May issue must be received by Friday.* **5** [U] ~ **(to sth)** the act of giving something, especially money, to help a person or an organization

con·trib·u·tor AWL /kən'trɪbyətər/ *noun* **1** ~ **(to sth)** a person who writes articles for a magazine or a book, or who talks on a radio or television program or at a meeting **2** ~ **(to sth)** a person or thing that provides money to help pay for something, or support something: *Older people are important contributors to the economy.* **3** ~ **(to sth)** something that helps to cause something: *sulfur dioxide is a pollutant and a major contributor to acid rain.*

con·trib·u·to·ry /kən'trɪbyəˌtɔri/ *adj.* [usually before noun]

h hat	**m man**	**n no**	**ŋ** sing	**l** leg	**r** red	**y yes**	**w wet**

1 helping to cause something: *Alcohol is a **contributory** factor in 10% of all traffic accidents.* **2** involving payments from the people who will benefit: *a **contributory** pension plan* (= paid for by both employers and employees) **ANT** NONCONTRIBUTORY

con·trite /kən'traɪt/ *adj.* (*formal*) very sorry for something bad that you have done ▶ **con·trite·ly** *adv.* **con·tri·tion** /kən'trɪʃn/ *noun* [U]: *a look of contrition*

con·triv·ance /kən'traɪvəns/ *noun* (*formal*) **1** [C, U] (usually *disapproving*) something that someone has done or written that does not seem natural; the fact of seeming artificial: *The novel is spoiled by unrealistic contrivances of plot.* ◆ *The story is told with a complete absence of contrivance.* **2** [C] a device or tool made for a particular purpose, using skill or imagination **3** [C, U] a smart plan or trick; the act of using a smart plan or trick: *an ingenious contrivance to get her to sign the document without reading it*

con·trive /kən'traɪv/ *verb* (*formal*) **1** ~ **to do sth** to manage to do something despite difficulties: *She contrived to spend a few hours with him every Sunday evening.* **2** ~ **sth** to succeed in making something happen despite difficulties: *I decided to contrive a meeting between the two of them.* **3** ~ **sth** to think of or make something, for example a plan or a machine, in a skillful way: *They contrived a plan to defraud the company.*

con·trived /kən'traɪvd/ *adj.* (*disapproving*) planned in advance and not natural or genuine; written or arranged in a way that is not natural or realistic: *a contrived situation* ◆ *The book's happy ending seemed contrived.*

con·trol 🔑 /kən'troʊl/ *noun, verb*

● **noun**
▷ POWER **1** [U] ~ **(of/over sb/sth)** the power to make decisions about how a country, an area, an organization, etc. is run: *The party is expecting to **gain control** of City Hall in the next election.* ◆ *The Democrats will probably **lose control** of Congress.* ◆ *A military junta **took control** of the country.* ◆ *The city is **in the control** of enemy forces.* ◆ *The city is **under enemy control**.* **2** [U] ~ **(of/over sb/sth)** the ability to make someone or something do what you want: *The teacher **had no control** over the children.* ◆ *She struggled to **keep control** of her voice.* ◆ *She **lost control** of her car on the ice.* ◆ *He got so angry he **lost control** (= shouted and said or did things he would not normally do).* ◆ *Due to **circumstances beyond our control**, the flight to Nashville has been canceled.* ◆ *The coach made the team work hard on ball control (= in a ball game).* ⊃ see also SELF-CONTROL
▷ LIMITING/MANAGING **3** [U, C] ~ **(of/on sth)** (often in compounds) the act of restricting, limiting, or managing something; a method of doing this: *traffic control* ◆ *gun control* ◆ *talks on arms control* ◆ *government controls on business and industry* ◆ *A new advance has been made in the control of malaria.* ◆ *Price controls on food were ended.* ◆ *a pest control officer* ⊃ see also BIRTH CONTROL, QUALITY CONTROL ⊃ thesaurus box at LIMIT
▷ IN MACHINE **4** [C, usually pl.] the switches and buttons, etc. that you use to operate a machine or a vehicle: *the controls of an aircraft* ◆ *the control panel* ◆ *the volume control of a CD player* ◆ *The co-pilot was **at the controls** when the plane landed.* ⊃ see also REMOTE CONTROL
▷ ON COMPUTER **5** [U] (also **con'trol key** [sing.]) (on a computer keyboard) a key that you press when you want to perform a particular operation
▷ IN EXPERIMENT **6** [C] (*technical*) a person, thing, or group used as a standard of comparison for checking the results of a scientific experiment; an experiment whose result is known, used for checking working methods: *One group was treated with the new drug, and the **control group** was given a sugar pill.*
▷ PLACE **7** [sing.] a place where orders are given or where checks are made; the people who work in this place: *air traffic control* ◆ *We went through passport control and into the departure lounge.* ◆ *This is Mission Control calling the space shuttle Discovery.*
IDM **be in control (of sth)** **1** to direct or manage an organization, an area, or a situation: *He's reached retiring*

age, but he's still firmly in control.* ◆ *There was some rioting, but the police are now in control.* **2** to be able to organize your life well and keep calm: *In spite of all her family problems, she's really in control.* **be/get/run/etc. out of control** to be or become impossible to manage or to control: *The children are completely out of control since their father left.* ◆ *A truck ran out of control on the hill.* **be under control** to be being dealt with successfully: *Don't worry—everything's under control!* **bring/ get/keep sth under control** to succeed in dealing with something so that it does not cause any damage or hurt anyone: *It took two hours to bring the fire under control.* ◆ *Please keep your dog under control!*

● **verb** (-ll-)
▷ HAVE POWER **1** ~ **sb/sth** to have power over a person, company, country, etc., so that you are able to decide what they must do or how it is run: *By the age of 21 he controlled the company.* ◆ *The whole territory is now controlled by the army.* ◆ *Can't you control your children?*
▷ LIMIT/MANAGE **2** to limit something or make it happen in a particular way: ~ **sth** *government attempts to control immigration* ◆ *Many biological processes are controlled by hormones.* ◆ ~ **what/how, etc.**... *Parents should control what their kids watch on television.* **3** ~ **sth** to stop something from spreading or getting worse: *Firefighters are still trying to control the blaze.* ◆ *She was given drugs to control the pain.*
▷ MACHINE **4** ~ **sth** to make something, such as a machine or system, work in the way that you want it to: *This knob controls the volume.* ◆ *The traffic lights are controlled by a central computer.*
▷ STAY CALM **5** to manage to make yourself remain calm, even though you are upset or angry: ~ **yourself** *I was so furious I couldn't control myself and I hit him.* ◆ ~ **sth** *He was finding it difficult to control his feelings.*

con'trol ˌfreak *noun* (*informal, disapproving*) a person who always wants to be in control of their own and others' lives, and to organize how things are done

con·trol·la·ble /kən'troʊləbl/ *adj.* that can be controlled

controlled 🔑 /kən'troʊld/ *adj.*
1 done or arranged in a very careful way: *a controlled explosion* ◆ *a controlled environment* **2** limited, or managed by law or by rules: *controlled airspace* **3** **-controlled** (in compounds) managed by a particular group, or in a particular way: *a U.S.-controlled company* ◆ *computer-controlled systems* **4** remaining calm and not getting angry or upset: *She remained quiet and controlled.* ⊃ compare UNCONTROLLED

con·trolled e'conomy *noun* (*economics*) a type of economic system in which a government controls its country's industries and decides what goods should be produced and in what amounts

con·trolled ex'periment *noun* a scientific experiment in which several tests are run, and only one condition is changed in each test, so that you can tell what effect that condition has on the results of the experiment

con·trolled 'substance (also **con·trolled 'drug**) *noun* (*technical*) an illegal drug: *to be arrested for possession of a controlled substance*

con·trol·ler /kən'troʊlər/ *noun* **1** a person who manages or directs something, especially a large organization or part of an organization ⊃ see also AIR TRAFFIC CONTROLLER **2** (*technical*) a device that controls or REGULATES a machine or part of a machine: *a temperature controller* **3** (also **comp·trol·ler**) a person who is in charge of the financial accounts of a business company, university, or hospital

con·trolling 'interest *noun* [usually sing.] the fact of owning enough shares in a company to be able to make decisions about what the company should do

con'trol room *noun* a room that is a center for the operation of a facility, a service, or a particular event: *a nuclear power plant's control room* ◆ *He works in the control room of a television station.* ◆ *the space shuttle control room*

---

con·trol ˌtower *noun* a building at an airport from which the movements of aircraft are controlled

con·tro·ver·sial **AWL** /ˌkɑntrəˈvərʃl/ *adj.* causing a lot of angry public discussion and disagreement: *a highly controversial topic* ♦ *a controversial plan to build a new road* ♦ *Malcolm X was a controversial figure.* **ANT** NONCONTROVERSIAL, UNCONTROVERSIAL ▶ **con·tro·ver·sial·ly** **AWL** /-ʃəli/ *adv.*

con·tro·ver·sy **AWL** /ˈkɑntrəˌvərsi/ *noun* [U, C] (*pl.* con·tro·ver·sies) **~ (over/about/surrounding sb/sth)** public discussion and argument about something that many people strongly disagree about, disapprove of, or are shocked by: *to arouse/cause controversy* ♦ *a bitter controversy over/about the site of the new airport* ♦ *the controversy surrounding his latest movie* ♦ *The president resigned amid considerable controversy.*

con·tro·vert /ˈkɑntrəˌvərt; ˌkɑntrəˈvərt/ *verb* **~ sth** (*formal*) to say or prove that something is not true **SYN** REFUTE ⊃ see also INCONTROVERTIBLE

con·tu·ma·cious /ˌkɑntuˈmeɪʃəs/ *adj.* (*old use* or *law*) lacking respect for authority

con·tu·sion /kənˈtuʒn/ *noun* [C, U] (*medical*) an injury to part of the body that does not break the skin **SYN** BRUISE

co·nun·drum /kəˈnʌndrəm/ *noun* **1** a confusing problem or question that is very difficult to solve **2** a question, usually involving a trick with words, that you ask for fun **SYN** RIDDLE

con·ur·ba·tion /ˌkɑnərˈbeɪʃn/ *noun* a large area where towns have grown and joined together, often around a city

con·va·lesce /ˌkɑnvəˈlɛs/ *verb* [I] to spend time getting your health and strength back after an illness **SYN** RECUPERATE: *She is convalescing at home after her operation.*

con·va·les·cence /ˌkɑnvəˈlɛsns/ *noun* [sing., U] a period of time when you get well again after an illness or a medical operation; the process of getting well: *You need four to six weeks' convalescence.*

con·va·les·cent /ˌkɑnvəˈlɛsnt/ *adj.* connected with convalescence; in the process of convalescence: *a convalescent home* (= a type of hospital where people go to get well after an illness) ♦ *a convalescent child* ▶ **con·va·les·cent** *noun*: *His therapist treated him as a convalescent, not as a sick man.*

con·vec·tion /kənˈvɛkʃn/ *noun* (*technical*) the process in which heat moves through a gas or a liquid as the hotter part rises and the cooler, heavier part sinks

con'vection ˌoven *noun* a cooking device with a fan that moves hot air around to heat food in an even way

con·vene **AWL** /kənˈvin/ *verb* (*formal*) **1** [T] **~ sth** to arrange for people to come together for a formal meeting: *to convene a meeting* ♦ *A Congressional committee was convened immediately after the tragedy.* **2** [I] to come together for a formal meeting: *The committee will officially convene at 11:30 next Thursday.*

con·ven·er (also **con·ven·or**) /kənˈvinər/ *noun* a person who arranges meetings of groups or committees

con·ven·ience /kənˈvinyəns/ *noun* **1** [U] the quality of being useful, easy, or suitable for someone: *We have provided seats for the convenience of our customers.* ♦ *For (the sake of) convenience, the two groups have been treated as one in this report.* ♦ *In this resort you can enjoy all the comfort and convenience of modern tourism.* ⊃ compare INCONVENIENCE ⊃ see also FLAG OF CONVENIENCE, MARRIAGE OF CONVENIENCE **2** [C] something that is useful and can make things easier or quicker to do, or more comfortable: *It was a great convenience to have the school so close to the house.*
IDM **at sb's convenience** (*formal*) at a time or a place which is suitable for someone: *Can you call me at your convenience to arrange a meeting?* ⊃ more at EARLY

con'venience ˌfood *noun* [C, U] food that you buy frozen or in a box or can, that you can prepare and cook very quickly and easily

con'venience ˌstore *noun* a store that sells food, newspapers, etc., and often stays open 24 hours a day

con·ven·ient 🔑 /kənˈvinyənt/ *adj.* **1 ~ (for sb/sth)** useful, easy, or quick to do; not causing problems: *It is very convenient to pay by credit card.* ♦ *You'll find these meals quick and convenient to prepare.* ♦ *Fruit is a convenient source of vitamins and energy.* ♦ *A bicycle is often more convenient than a car in cities.* ♦ *I can't see him now—it isn't convenient.* ♦ *I'll call back at a more convenient time.* ♦ (*disapproving*) *He used his wife's birthday as a convenient excuse for not going to the meeting.* **2 ~ (to sth)** near to a particular place; easy to get to: *The hotel is convenient to downtown.* **ANT** INCONVENIENT ▶ **con·ven·ient·ly** *adv.*: *The report can be conveniently divided into three main sections.* ♦ *The hotel is conveniently situated close to the beach.* ♦ *She conveniently forgot to mention that her husband would be at the party, too* (= because it suited her not to say).

con·ve·nor = CONVENER

con·vent /ˈkɑnvɛnt; -vənt/ *noun* **1** a building in which NUNS (= members of a female religious community) live together ⊃ collocations at RELIGION **2** (also ˈconvent school) a school run by NUNS

con·ven·tion 🔑 **AWL** /kənˈvɛnʃn/ *noun* **1** [C] a large meeting of the members of a profession, a political party, etc. **SYN** CONFERENCE: *to hold a convention* ♦ *the Democratic Party Convention* (= to elect a candidate for President) **2** [C, U] the way in which something is done that most people in a society expect and consider to be polite or the right way to do it: *social conventions* ♦ *By convention the co-chair was always a woman.* ♦ *She is a young woman who enjoys going against conventions.* **3** [C] an official agreement between countries or leaders: *the Geneva convention* ♦ *the United Nations convention on the rights of the child* **4** [C, U] a traditional method or style in literature, art, or the theater: *the conventions of Greek tragedy*

con·ven·tion·al 🔑 **AWL** /kənˈvɛnʃənl/ *adj.* **1** (often *disapproving*) tending to follow what is done or considered acceptable by society in general; normal and ordinary, and perhaps not very interesting: *conventional behavior/morality* ♦ *She's very conventional in her views.* **ANT** UNCONVENTIONAL **2** [usually before noun] following what is traditional or the way something has been done for a long time: *conventional methods/approaches* ♦ *It's not a hotel, in the conventional sense, but rather a whole village turned into a hotel.* **ANT** UNCONVENTIONAL **3** [usually before noun] (especially of weapons) not nuclear: *conventional forces/weapons* ♦ *a conventional power station* (= using oil or coal as fuel, rather than nuclear power) ▶ **con·ven·tion·al·i·ty** /kənˌvɛnʃəˈnæləti/ *noun* [U] **con·ven·tion·al·ly** **AWL** /kənˈvɛnʃənəli/ *adv.*: *conventionally dressed* ♦ *conventionally grown food* (= grown according to conventional methods) **IDM** see WISDOM

con·ven·tion·eer /kənˌvɛnʃəˈnɪr/ *noun* a person who is attending a convention

con·verge /kənˈvərdʒ/ *verb* **1** [I] **~ (on…)** (of people or vehicles) to move toward a place from different directions and meet: *Thousands of supporters converged on Washington, D.C. for the rally.* **2** [I] (of two or more lines, paths, etc.) to move toward each other and meet at a point: *There was a signpost where the two paths converged.* **3** [I] if ideas, policies, aims, etc., converge, they become very similar or the same **ANT** DIVERGE ▶ **con·ver·gent** /kənˈvərdʒənt/ *adj.*: *convergent lines/opinions* **con·ver·gence** /-dʒəns/ *noun* [U]

con·ver·sant /kənˈvərsnt/ *adj.* (*formal*) **~ with sth** knowing about something; familiar with something: *You need to become fully conversant with the company's procedures.*

con·ver·sa·tion 🔑 /ˌkɑnvərˈseɪʃn/ *noun* [C, U] **~ (with sb) (about sth)** an informal talk involving a small group of people or only two; the activity of talking in this way: *a telephone conversation* ♦ *I had a long conversation with her the other day.* ♦ *The*

ʌ **cup**   ə **about**   eɪ **say**   aɪ **five**   ɔɪ **boy**   aʊ **now**   oʊ **go**   ər **bird**

main *topic of conversation* was the probable outcome of the election. ♦ *Don was deep in conversation with the girl on his right.* ♦ *to get into a conversation with someone* ♦ *The conversation turned to gardening.* ♦ *I tried to make conversation* (= to speak in order to appear polite). ⊃ thesaurus box at DISCUSSION

con·ver·sa·tion·al /ˌkɑnvərˈseɪʃənl/ *adj.* **1** not formal; as used in conversation **SYN** COLLOQUIAL: *a casual and conversational tone* ♦ *I learned conversational Spanish at continuing education classes.* **2** [only before noun] connected with conversation: *Men have a more direct conversational style.* ▶ **con·ver·sa·tion·al·ly** /-ʃənəli/ *adv.*: "Have you been here long?" *he asked conversationally.*

con·ver·sa·tion·al·ist /ˌkɑnvərˈseɪʃənəlɪst/ *noun* a person who is good at talking to others, especially in an informal way

conver'sation ˌpiece *noun* **1** an object that is talked about a lot because it is unusual **2** (*art*) a type of painting in which a group of people are shown in the countryside or in a home

conver'sation ˌstopper *noun* (*informal*) an unexpected or shocking remark, that people do not know how to reply to

con·verse¹ /kənˈvərs/ *verb* [I] ~ **(with sb)** (*formal*) to have a conversation with someone

con·verse² **AWL** /ˈkɑnvərs/ *noun* **the converse** [sing.] (*formal*) the opposite or reverse of a fact or statement: *Building new roads increases traffic and the converse is equally true: reducing the number and size of roads means less traffic.* ▶ **con·verse** /ˈkɑnvərs; kənˈvərs/ *adj.*: *the converse effect*

con·verse·ly **AWL** /kənˈvərsli; ˈkɑnvərs-/ *adv.* (*formal*) in a way that is the opposite or reverse of something: *You can add the fluid to the powder, or, conversely, the powder to the fluid.*

con·ver·sion **AWL** /kənˈvərʒn; kənˈvərʃn/ *noun* **1** [U, C] ~ **(from sth) (into/to sth)** the act or process of changing something from one form, use, or system to another: *the conversion of farm buildings into family homes* ♦ *No conversion from analog to digital data is needed.* ♦ *a metric conversion table* (= showing how to change METRIC amounts into or out of another system) **2** [U, C] ~ **(from sth) (to sth)** the process or experience of changing your religion or beliefs: *the conversion of the Anglo-Saxons by Christian missionaries* ♦ *his conversion from Judaism to Christianity* **3** [C] (in football) a way of scoring extra points after scoring a TOUCHDOWN **4** [C] **loft ~** a room that has been changed so that it can be used for a different purpose, especially for living in

con'version ˌvan (also **'van con ˌversion**) *noun* a vehicle in which the back part behind the driver has been arranged as a living space

con·vert 🔑 **AWL** *verb, noun*

• *verb* /kənˈvərt/ **1** [T, I] to change or make something change from one form, purpose, system, etc., to another: ~ **sth (into sth)** *The hotel is going to be converted into a nursing home.* ♦ *What rate will I get if I convert my dollars into euros?* ♦ ~ **(from sth) (into/to sth)** *We converted from oil to gas central heating.* **2** [I] ~ **into/to sth** to be able to be changed from one form, purpose, or system to another: *a sofa that converts into a bed* **3** [I, T] to change or make someone change their religion or beliefs: ~ **(from sth) (to sth)** *He converted from Christianity to Islam.* ♦ ~ **sb (from sth) (to sth)** *She was soon converted to the socialist cause.* **4** [I, T] to change an opinion, a habit, etc.: ~ **(from sth) (to sth)** *I converted to organic food.* ♦ ~ **sb (from sth) (to sth)** *I didn't use to like opera but my husband has converted me.* **5** [T] ~ **sth** (in football) to score extra points after a TOUCHDOWN
IDM see PREACH

• *noun* /ˈkɑnvərt/ ~ **(from sth) (to sth)** a person who has changed their religion, beliefs, or opinions: *a convert to Islam* ♦ *converts from other faiths* ♦ *a convert to the cause*

con·vert·er (also **con·vert·or**) /kənˈvərtər/ *noun* **1** a person or thing that converts something: *a catalytic converter* **2** (*physics*) a device for converting ALTERNATING CURRENT

into DIRECT CURRENT or the other way around **3** (*physics*) a device for converting a radio signal from one FREQUENCY to another

con·vert·i·ble **AWL** /kənˈvərtəbl/ *adj., noun*
• *adj.* that can be changed to a different form or use: *a convertible sofa* (= one that can be used as a bed) ♦ *convertible currencies* (= ones that can be exchanged for those of other countries) ♦ ~ **into/to sth** *The bonds are convertible into ordinary shares.* ▶ **con·vert·i·bil·i·ty** /kənˌvərtəˈbɪləti/ *noun* [U]
• *noun* a car with a roof that can be folded down or taken off ⊃ picture at CAR

con·vex /kɑnˈvɛks; ˈkɑnvɛks/ *adj.* (of an outline or a surface) curving out: *a convex lens/mirror* **ANT** CONCAVE ▶ **con·vex·i·ty** /kɑnˈvɛksəti/ *noun* [U]

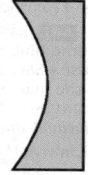

concave   convex

con·vey /kənˈveɪ/ *verb* **1** to make ideas, feelings, etc., known to someone **SYN** COMMUNICATE: ~ **sth** *Colors like red convey a sense of energy and strength.* ♦ ~ **sth to sb** (*formal*) *Please convey my apologies to your wife.* ♦ ~ **how, what, etc....** *He tried desperately to convey how urgent the situation was.* ♦ ~ **that...** *She did not wish to convey that they were all at fault.* **2** ~ **sb/sth (from...) (to...)** (*formal*) to take, carry, or transport someone or something from one place to another: *Pipes convey hot water from the boiler to the radiators.* **3** ~ **sth (to sb)** (*law*) to transfer property from one owner to another: *The house was conveyed to the new owners last week.*

con·vey·ance /kənˈveɪəns/ *noun* **1** [U] (*formal*) the process of taking someone or something from one place to another: *the conveyance of goods by rail* **2** [C] (*formal*) a vehicle: *horse-drawn conveyances* **3** [C] (*law*) a legal document that moves property from one owner to another

con·vey·anc·er /kənˈveɪənsər/ *noun* a lawyer who is an expert in conveyancing

con·vey·anc·ing /kənˈveɪənsɪŋ/ *noun* [U] (*law*) the branch of law concerned with moving property from one owner to another

con·vey·or /kənˈveɪər/ *noun* **1** = CONVEYOR BELT **2** (also **con·vey·er**) (*formal*) a person or thing that carries something or makes something known

con'veyor ˌbelt (also **con·vey·or**) *noun* a continuous moving band used for transporting goods from one part of a building to another, for example products in a factory or bags in an airport

con·vict *verb, noun*
• *verb* /kənˈvɪkt/ [often passive] ~ **sb (of sth)** to decide and state officially in court that someone is guilty of a crime: *a convicted murderer* ♦ *He was convicted of fraud.* ⊃ collocations at JUSTICE **ANT** ACQUIT
• *noun* /ˈkɑnvɪkt/ (also *informal* **con**) a person who has been found guilty of a crime and sent to prison: *an escaped convict*

con·vic·tion /kənˈvɪkʃn/ *noun* **1** [C, U] ~ **(for sth)** the act of finding someone guilty of a crime in court; the fact of having been found guilty: *She has six previous convictions for theft.* ♦ *He plans to appeal against his conviction.* ♦ *an offense which carries, on conviction, a sentence of not more than five years' imprisonment* ⊃ collocations at JUSTICE **ANT** ACQUITTAL **2** [C, U] ~ **(that...)** a strong opinion or belief: *strong political/moral convictions* ♦ *She was motivated by deep religious conviction.* ♦ *a conviction that all would be well in the end* **3** [U] the feeling or appearance of believing something strongly and of being sure about it: "Not true!" *she said with conviction.* ♦ *He said he agreed but his voice lacked conviction.* ♦ *The leader's speech in defense of the policy didn't carry much conviction.* **IDM** see COURAGE

con·vince 🔑 **AWL** /kənˈvɪns/ *verb*
1 to make someone/yourself believe that something is true: ~ **sb/yourself (of sth)** *You'll need to convince them of your enthusiasm for the job.* ◆ ~ **sb/yourself (that)...** *I'd convinced myself (that) I was right.* **2** ~ **sb to do sth** to persuade someone to do something: *I've been trying to convince him to see a doctor.* ➔ note at PERSUADE

con·vinced **AWL** /kənˈvɪnst/ *adj.* **1** [not before noun] completely sure about something: *Sam nodded but he didn't look convinced.* ◆ ~ **of sth** *I am convinced of her innocence.* ◆ ~ **that...** *I am convinced that she is innocent.* **ANT** UNCONVINCED ➔ thesaurus box at SURE **2** [only before noun] believing strongly in a particular religion or set of political ideas: *a convinced Christian*

con·vinc·ing **AWL** /kənˈvɪnsɪŋ/ *adj.* that makes someone believe that something is true: *a convincing argument/ explanation/case* ◆ *She sounded very convincing to me* (= I believed what she said). ◆ *a convincing victory/win* (= an easy one) **ANT** UNCONVINCING ▶ **con·vinc·ing·ly** **AWL** *adv.*: *Her case was convincingly argued.* ◆ *They won convincingly.*

con·viv·i·al /kənˈvɪviəl/ *adj.* cheerful and friendly in atmosphere or character: *a convivial evening/atmosphere* ◆ *convivial company* **SYN** SOCIABLE ▶ **con·viv·i·al·i·ty** /kənˌvɪviˈæləti/ *noun* [U]

con·vo·ca·tion /ˌkɑnvəˈkeɪʃn/ *noun* (*formal*) **1** [C] a large formal meeting, especially of church officials or members of a university **2** [U] the act of calling together a convocation **3** [C] a ceremony held in a university or college when students receive their degrees ➔ see also GRADUATION, COMMENCEMENT

con·voke /kənˈvoʊk/ *verb* ~ **sb/sth** (*formal*) to gather together a group of people for a formal meeting **SYN** CONVENE

con·vo·lut·ed /ˈkɑnvəˌlutəd; ˌkɑnvəˈlutəd/ *adj.* **1** extremely complicated and difficult to follow: *a convoluted argument/ explanation* ◆ *a book with a convoluted plot* **2** (*formal*) having many twists or curves: *a convoluted coastline*

con·vo·lu·tion /ˌkɑnvəˈluʃn/ *noun* [usually pl.] (*formal*) **1** a thing that is very complicated and difficult to follow: *the bizarre convolutions of the story* **2** a twist or curve, especially one of many: *the convolutions of the brain*

con·vol·vu·lus /kənˈvɑlvyələs/ *noun* [C, U] a plant with TRIANGULAR leaves and flowers that are shaped like TRUMPETS. It climbs up walls, fences, etc., and twists itself around other plants.

con·voy /ˈkɑnvɔɪ/ *noun* a group of vehicles or ships traveling together, especially when soldiers or other vehicles travel with them for protection: *a convoy of trucks/ freighters* ◆ *A United Nations aid convoy loaded with food and medicine finally got through to the besieged town.* **IDM** **in convoy** (of traveling vehicles) as a group; together: *We drove in convoy because I didn't know the way.*

con·vulse /kənˈvʌls/ *verb* **1** [T, I] ~ **(sb) (with sth)** to cause a sudden shaking movement in someone's body; to make this movement: *A violent shiver convulsed him.* ◆ *His whole body convulsed.* **2** [T] **be convulsed with laughter, anger, etc.** to be laughing so much, so angry, etc., that you cannot control your movements **3** [T, usually passive] to cause a lot of sudden, violent confusion in a place: *Many American cities were convulsed by violence in the 1960s and 70s.*

con·vul·sion /kənˈvʌlʃn/ *noun* [usually pl.] **1** a sudden shaking movement of the body that cannot be controlled: *The child went into convulsions.* **2** a sudden important change that happens to a country or an organization **SYN** UPHEAVAL

con·vul·sive /kənˈvʌlsɪv/ *adj.* (of movements or actions) sudden and impossible to control: *a convulsive movement/ attack/fit* ◆ *Her breath came in convulsive gasps.* ▶ **con·vul·sive·ly** *adv.*: *weeping convulsively*

coo /ku/ *verb* (**coo·ing, cooed, cooed**) **1** [I] when a DOVE¹ or a PIGEON **coos**, it makes a soft low sound **2** [I, T]

(**+ speech**) to say something in a soft quiet voice, especially to someone you love **IDM** see BILL v. ▶ **coo** *noun*

co-oc·cur *verb* [I] to occur together or at the same time: *The words "heavy" and "rain" co-occur frequently.* ▶ **co-oc·cur·rence** *noun* [U]

cook 🔑 /kʊk/ *verb, noun*
● *verb* **1** [I, T] to prepare food by heating it, for example by boiling, baking, or frying it: *Where did you learn to cook?* ◆ ~ **sth** *What's the best way to cook trout?* ◆ *Who's going to cook supper?* ◆ *He cooked lunch for me.* ◆ ~ **sb sth** *He cooked me lunch.* ➔ picture on page 329 ➔ collocations on page 330 **2** [I] (of food) to be prepared by boiling, baking, frying, etc.: *While the pasta is cooking, prepare the sauce.* **3** [I] be cooking (*informal*) to be planned secretly: *Everyone is being very secretive—there's something cooking.* **IDM** **cook the books** (*informal*) to change facts or figures dishonestly or illegally: *His accountant had been cooking the books for years.* **cook sb's goose** (*informal*) to ruin someone's chances of success **PHR V** **cook sth↔up** (*informal*) to invent something, especially in order to trick someone **SYN** CONCOCT: *to cook up a story*

● *noun* a person who cooks food or whose job is cooking: *John is a very good cook* (= he cooks well). ◆ *Who was the cook* (= who cooked the food)? ◆ *She was employed as a cook in a hotel.* ➔ compare CHEF **IDM** **too many cooks spoil the broth** (also **too many cooks in the kitchen**) (*saying*) if too many people are involved in doing something, it will not be done well

cook·book /ˈkʊkbʊk/ *noun* a book that gives instructions on cooking and how to cook individual dishes

cook·er·y /ˈkʊkəri/ *noun* [U] the art or activity of preparing and cooking food: *Italian cookery*

cook·house /ˈkʊkhaʊs/ *noun* an outdoor kitchen, for example in a military camp

cook·ie 🔑 /ˈkʊki/ *noun* (*pl.* **cook·ies**)
1 a small flat sweet cake for one person, usually baked until crisp: *chocolate chip cookies* ◆ *a cookie jar* ➔ see also FORTUNE COOKIE **2** **smart/tough** ~ (*informal*) a smart/tough person **3** (*computing*) a computer file with information in it that is sent to the central SERVER each time a particular person uses a NETWORK or the Internet **IDM** see TOSS v., WAY n.

cookie cutter *noun, adj.*
● *noun* an object used for cutting cookies in a particular shape
● *adj.* **cookie-cutter** [only before noun] (*disapproving*) having no special characteristics; not original in any way: *Handmade goods appeal to those who are tired of cookie-cutter products.*

cookie jar *noun* a container for cookies **IDM** **get caught/found with your hand in the cookie jar** (*informal*) to be discovered when doing something that is illegal or dishonest

cookie sheet (also **baking sheet**) *noun* a small sheet of metal used for baking food on

cook·ing 🔑 /ˈkʊkɪŋ/ *noun, adj.*
● *noun* [U] **1** the process of preparing food: *My husband does all the cooking.* ◆ *a book on Indian cooking* ➔ picture on page 329 ➔ collocations on page 330 **2** food that has been prepared in a particular way: *The restaurant offers traditional home cooking* (= food similar to that cooked at home). ◆ *They serve good French cooking.*
● *adj.* suitable for cooking rather than eating raw or drinking: *cooking sherry*

cooking apple *noun* any type of apple that is suitable for cooking, rather than eating raw ➔ compare EATING APPLE

cook·out /ˈkʊkaʊt/ *noun* (*informal*) a meal or party when food is cooked over an open fire outdoors, for example at a beach ➔ compare BARBECUE

Cooking

preparation

chop

dice

slice

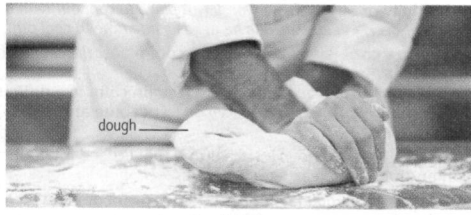

dough

knead

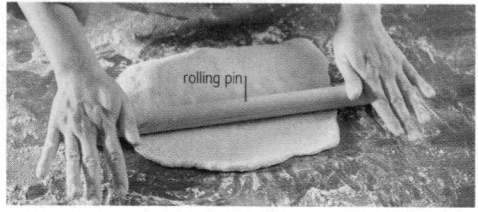

rolling pin

roll out

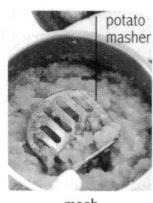

potato masher

mash

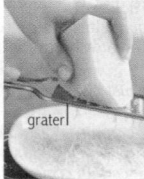

grater

grate

whisk

whisk (*also* whip)

cooking

flambé

wok

stir-fry

lid

steamer

steam

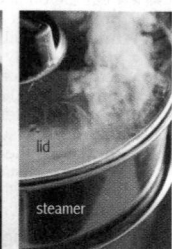

frying pan (*also* frypan, skillet)

fry

saucepan (*also* pot)

boil

pan

bake

tongs

barbecue

ladle

pot

stew

toast

toaster

toast

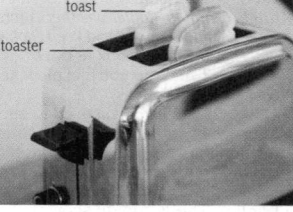

---

v **v**oice   θ **th**in   ð **th**en   s **s**o   z **z**oo   ʃ **sh**e   ʒ vi**s**ion   x **Ch**anukah

Cooking

preparing

- **prepare** a dish/a meal/a menu/dinner/the fish
- **weigh out** 4oz of sugar/the ingredients
- **wash/rinse** the lettuce/spinach
- **chop/slice/dice** the carrots/onions/potatoes
- **peel** the carrots/onion/potatoes/garlic/orange
- **grate** a carrot/the cheese/some nutmeg
- **remove/discard** the bones/seeds/skin/rind/peel
- **blend/combine/mix (together)** the flour and water/all the ingredients
- **beat/whisk** the cream/eggs/egg whites
- **knead/shape/roll (out)** the dough

cooking

- **heat** the oil in a frying pan
- **preheat/heat** the oven/the broiler
- **bring to** a boil
- **stir** constantly/gently with a wooden spoon
- **reduce** the heat
- **simmer** gently for 20 minutes/until reduced by half
- **melt** the butter/chocolate/cheese
- **dissolve** the sugar in water
- **brown** the meat for 8-10 minutes
- **drain** the pasta/the water from the pot/in a colander/in a strainer
- **mash** the potatoes/banana/avocado

ways of cooking

- **cook** food/fish/meat/rice/pasta/a Mexican dish
- **bake** (a loaf of) bread/a cake/a pie/potatoes/muffins/cookies/fish
- **boil** cabbage/potatoes/an egg/a hot dog/water
- **fry/deep-fry/stir-fry** the chicken/vegetables
- **broil** meat/steak/chicken/sausages
- **roast** potatoes/peppers/meat/chicken/beef
- **sauté** garlic/mushrooms/onions/potatoes/vegetables
- **steam** rice/vegetables/spinach/asparagus/dumplings
- **toast** bread/nuts
- **microwave** food/popcorn/a frozen dinner/a TV dinner

serving

- **serve** in a glass/on a bed of rice/with potatoes
- **arrange** the slices on a plate/in layers
- **carve** the meat/chicken/turkey
- **dress/toss** a salad
- **dress with/drizzle with** olive oil/vinaigrette
- **top with** a slice of lemon/a scoop of ice cream/whipped cream/syrup
- **garnish with** a sprig of parsley/fresh basil leaves/lemon wedges/a slice of lime/a twist of orange
- **sprinkle with** salt/sugar/herbs/parsley/freshly ground black pepper

cook·ware /ˈkʊkwer/ noun [U] pots and containers used in cooking

cool 🔑 /kul/ adj., verb, noun

● **adj.** (cool·er, cool·est)

▷ **FAIRLY COLD 1** fairly cold; not hot or warm: *a cool breeze/drink/climate* ◆ *Cooler weather is forecast for the weekend.* ◆ *Let's sit in the shade and keep cool.* ◆ *Store lemons in a cool dry place.* ⊃ **thesaurus box at** COLD

▷ **COLORS 2** making you feel pleasantly cool: *a room painted in cool greens and blues*

▷ **APPROVING 3** (*informal*) used to show that you admire or approve of something or someone because they are fashionable, attractive, and often different: *You look pretty cool with that new haircut.* ◆ *Dave's a really cool guy.* ◆ *It's a cool movie.* ⊃ **thesaurus box at** GREAT **4** (*informal*) people say **Cool!** or **That's cool** to show that they approve of something or agree to a suggestion: *"We're going to the beach this afternoon." "Cool!"* ◆ *"Can you come at 10:30 tomorrow?" "That's cool."* ◆ *I was surprised that she got the job, but I'm cool with it* (= it's not a problem for me).

▷ **CALM 5** calm; not excited, angry, or emotional: *Keep cool!* ◆ *She tried to remain cool, calm and collected* (= calm). ◆ *He has a cool head* (= he stays calm in an emergency).

▷ **NOT FRIENDLY/ENTHUSIASTIC 6** not friendly, interested, or enthusiastic: *She was decidedly cool about the proposal.* ◆ *They gave the Ambassador a cool reception.*

▷ **CONFIDENT 7** (*informal*) calm and confident in a way that lacks respect for other people, but makes people admire you as well as disapprove: *She just took his keys and walked out with them, cool as you please.*

▷ **MONEY 8** [only before noun] (*informal*) used about a sum of money to emphasize how large it is: *The car cost a cool thirty thousand.* ⊃ **see also** COOLLY, COOLNESS

IDM (as) cool as a cucumber very calm and controlled, especially in a difficult situation **play it cool** (*informal*) to deal with a situation in a calm way and not show what you are really feeling

● **verb**

▷ **BECOME COLDER 1** [I, T] to become or to make someone or something become cool or cooler: *Glass contracts as it cools.* ◆ **~ sth** *The cylinder is cooled by a jet of water.*

▷ **BECOME CALMER 2** [I] to become calmer, less excited, or less enthusiastic: *I think we should wait until tempers have cooled.* ◆ *Relations between them have definitely cooled* (= they are not as friendly with each other as they were).

IDM cool it! (*informal*) used to tell someone to be calmer and less excited or angry **cool your heels** (*informal*) to have to wait for someone or something

PHRV cool 'down/'off 1 to become cool or cooler: *We cooled off with a swim in the lake.* **2** to become calm, less excited, or less enthusiastic: *I think you should wait until she's cooled down a little.* **,cool sb↔'down/'off 1** to make someone feel cooler: *Drink plenty of cold water to cool yourself down.* **2** to make someone calm, less excited, or less enthusiastic: *A few hours in a police cell should cool him off.* **,cool sth↔'down/'off** to make something cool or cooler **,cool 'out** (*informal*) to relax and become calm after a period of activity or stress: *It's a wonderful place to cool out with a glass of beer.* ◆ *It sounds like he needs some time to cool out.*

● **noun the cool** [sing.] cool air or a cool place: *the cool of the evening*

IDM keep your cool (*informal*) to remain calm in a difficult situation **lose your cool** (*informal*) to become angry or excited

cool·ant /ˈkulənt/ noun [C, U] a liquid that is used for cooling an engine, a nuclear REACTOR, etc.

cool·er /ˈkulər/ noun **1** [C] a container or machine which cools things, especially drinks, or keeps them cold: *the office water cooler* ◆ *They took a cooler full of drinks to the beach.* **2** [C] a drink with ice and usually wine in it: *a wine cooler*

ˈcool-ˌheaded adj. calm; not showing excitement or nerves: *a cool-headed assessment of the situation*

coo·lie /ˈkuli/ noun (*old-fashioned*) an offensive word for a worker in Eastern countries with no special skills or training

ˌcooling-ˈoff ˌperiod noun **1** a period of time during which two sides in a disagreement try to reach an agreement before taking further action, for example by going on strike **2** a period of time after someone has bought a gun before they can take the gun out of the store

ˈcooling ˌtower noun a large high round building used in industry for cooling water before it is used again

cool·ly /ˈkuli/ adv. **1** in a way that is not friendly or enthusiastic: *"We're just good friends," she said coolly.* ◆ *He received my suggestion coolly.* **2** in a calm way

cool·ness /ˈkulnəs/ noun [U] the quality of being cool: *the delicious coolness of the water* ◆ *I admire her coolness under pressure.* ◆ *I noticed a certain coolness* (= lack of friendly feeling) *between them.*

| h **hat** | m **man** | n **no** | ŋ **sing** | l **leg** | r **red** | y **yes** | w **wet** |

coon·skin *noun* [U, C] the skin of a RACCOON: *a coonskin cap*

coop /kup/ *noun, verb*
* *noun* a CAGE for chickens, etc. **IDM** see FLY *v*.
* *verb*
  PHR V ,coop sb/sth 'up [usually passive] to keep a person or an animal inside a building or in a small space

co-op /'kouɑp/ *noun* (*informal*) a COOPERATIVE store, society or business: *a housing co-op*

coop·er /'kupər/ *noun* a person who makes BARRELS

co·op·er·ate **AWL** /kou'ɑpəˌreɪt/ *verb* **1** [I] ~ (with sb) (in/on sth) to work together with someone else in order to achieve something: *The two groups agreed to cooperate with each other.* ♦ *They had cooperated closely in the planning of the project.* **2** [I] ~ (with sb) (in/on sth) to be helpful by doing what someone asks you to do: *Their captors told them they would be killed unless they cooperated.*

co·op·er·a·tion 🔑 **AWL** /kouˌɑpə'reɪʃn/ *noun* [U]
1 the fact of doing something together or of working together toward a shared aim: ~ (with sb) (in doing sth) *a report produced by the government in cooperation with the chemical industry* ♦ ~ (between A and B) *We would like to see closer cooperation between parents and schools.* **2** ~ (in doing sth) willingness to be helpful and do as you are asked: *We would be grateful for your cooperation in vacating the theater as quickly as possible.*

co·op·er·a·tive **AWL** /kou'ɑprətɪv/ *adj., noun*
* *adj.* **1** [usually before noun] involving something together or working together with others toward a shared aim: *Cooperative activity is essential to effective community work.* **2** helpful by doing what you are asked to do: *Employees will usually be more cooperative if their opinions are taken seriously.* **ANT** UNCOOPERATIVE **3** [usually before noun] (*business*) owned and run by the people involved, with the profits shared by them: *a cooperative farm*
  ▶ **co·op·er·a·tive·ly** **AWL** *adv.*
* *noun* a cooperative business or other organization: *agricultural cooperatives in India* ♦ *The factory is now a workers' cooperative.*

co-opt /kou'ɑpt/ *verb* **1** ~ sb (onto/into sth) to include someone in something, often when they do not want to be part of it **2** ~ sb (onto/into sth) to make someone a member of a group, committee, etc., by the agreement of all the other members: *She was co-opted onto the board.* **3** ~ sth (*disapproving*) to take someone else's idea or policy for your own use: *Some of her best ideas had been co-opted by her supervisor and presented as his own.*

co·or·di·nate **AWL** *verb, noun*
* *verb* /kou'ɔrdnˌeɪt/ **1** [T] ~ sth to organize the different parts of an activity and the people involved in it so that it works well: *They appointed a new manager to coordinate the work of the team.* ♦ *We need to develop a coordinated approach to the problem.* **2** [T] ~ sth to make the different parts of your body work well together ⊃ see also UNCOORDINATED **3** [I, T] ~ (sth) (with sth) if you **coordinate** clothes, furniture, etc., or if they **coordinate**, they look nice together: *This shade coordinates with a wide range of other colors.* ▶ **co·or·di·na·tor** /kou'ɔrdnˌeɪtər/ *noun*: *The campaign needs an effective coordinator.*
* *noun* /kou'ɔrdn·ət/ **1** [C] either of two numbers or letters used to fix the position of a point on a map or GRAPH: *the x, y coordinates of any point on a line* **2 coordinates** [pl.] (used in stores etc.) pieces of clothing that can be worn together because, for example, the colors look good together

coordinate clause /kouˌɔrdn·ət 'klɔz/ *noun* (*grammar*) each of two or more parts of a sentence, often joined by *and*, *or*, *but*, etc., that make separate statements that each have an equal importance ⊃ compare SUBORDINATE CLAUSE

co,ordinating con'junction *noun* (*grammar*) a word such as *and*, *but*, or *or*, that connects clauses or sentences of equal importance ⊃ compare SUBORDINATING CONJUNCTION

co·or·di·na·tion **AWL** /kouˌɔrdn'eɪʃn/ *noun* [U] **1** the act of making parts of something, groups of people, etc., work together in an efficient and organized way: *a need for greater coordination between departments* ♦ *a lack of coordination in conservation policy* ♦ *a pamphlet produced by the government in coordination with* (= working together with) *the National Education Association* ♦ *advice on color coordination* (= choosing colors that look nice together, for example in clothes or furniture) **2** the ability to control your movements well: *You need good hand-eye coordination to play sports like tennis and baseball.*

coot /kut/ *noun* **1** a black bird with a white FOREHEAD and beak that lives on or near water **2** old ~ (*informal*) a strange or crazy old person **IDM** see BALD

cop /kɑp/ *noun, verb*
* *noun* (*informal*) a police officer: *Somebody call the cops!* ♦ *kids playing cops and robbers* ♦ *a TV cop show*
* *verb* (-pp-) ~ sth (*informal*) to receive or suffer something unpleasant: *He copped all the hassle after the accident.* **IDM** cop an attitude (*informal*) to show that you feel you are better or more important than someone else, especially by behaving rudely: *Joe always seemed to cop an attitude when he was called on in class.* cop a feel (*informal*) to touch someone in a sexual way, especially without their permission cop a plea (*informal*) to admit in court to being guilty of a small crime in the hope of receiving less severe punishment for a more serious crime ⊃ compare PLEA BARGAINING **PHR V** ,cop 'out (of sth) (*informal*) to avoid or stop doing something that you should do because you are afraid, lazy, etc.: *You're not going to cop out at the last minute, are you?* ⊃ related noun COP-OUT 'cop to sth (*informal*) to admit to something: *He copped to skipping school, but said he hadn't been anywhere near the scene of the crime.*

cope 🔑 /koup/ *verb, noun*
* *verb* [I] to deal successfully with something difficult **SYN** MANAGE: *I got to the stage where I wasn't coping any more.* ♦ ~ with sth *He wasn't able to cope with the stresses and strains of the job.* ♦ *Desert plants are adapted to cope with extreme heat.*
* *noun* a long loose piece of clothing worn by priests on special occasions

cop·i·er /'kɑpiər/ *noun* = PHOTOCOPIER

'co-,pilot *noun* a second pilot who helps the main pilot in an aircraft

cop·ing /'koupɪŋ/ *noun* (*architecture*) the top row of bricks or stones, usually sloping, on a wall

co·pi·ous /'koupiəs/ *adj.* in large amounts **SYN** ABUNDANT: *copious* (= large) *amounts of water* ♦ *I took copious notes.* ♦ *She supports her theory with copious evidence.* ▶ **co·pi·ous·ly** *adv.*: *bleeding copiously*

'cop-out *noun* (*informal, disapproving*) a way of avoiding doing something that you should do, or an excuse for not doing it: *Not turning up was just a cop-out.*

cop·per /'kɑpər/ *noun* [U] (*symb.* Cu) a chemical element. Copper is a soft reddish-brown metal used for making electric wires, pipes, and coins: *a copper mine* ♦ *copper pipes* ♦ *copper-colored hair*

,copper 'beech *noun* a tall type of BEECH tree with smooth BARK and reddish-brown leaves

cop·per·head /'kɑpərˌhɛd/ *noun* one of several types of poisonous snakes that are a brownish color

cop·per·plate /'kɑpərˌpleɪt/ *noun* [U] a neat old-fashioned way of writing with sloping letters joined together

cop·per·y /'kɑpəri/ *adj.* similar to or having the color of COPPER: *coppery hair*

cop·pice /'kɑpəs/ *verb, noun*
* *verb* [T, I] ~ (sth) (*technical*) to cut back young trees in order to make them grow faster
* *noun* = COPSE

cop·ra /ˈkoʊprə; ˈkɑprə/ noun [U] the dried white flesh of COCONUT

copse /kɑps/ (also **coppice**) noun a small area of trees or bushes growing together

cop·ter /ˈkɑptər/ noun (informal) = HELICOPTER

cop·u·la /ˈkɑpyələ/ noun (grammar) = LINKING VERB

cop·u·late /ˈkɑpyəˌleɪt/ verb [I] ~ (with sb/sth) (technical) to have sex ▶ **cop·u·la·tion** /ˌkɑpyəˈleɪʃn/ noun [U]

cop·y 🔑 /ˈkɑpi/ noun, verb

• **noun** (pl. **cop·ies**) **1** [C] ~ (of sth) a thing that is made to be the same as something else, especially a document or a work of art: *I will send you a copy of the report.* ◆ *The thieves replaced the original painting with a copy.* ◆ *You should make a copy of the disk as a backup.* ⊃ see also HARD COPY **2** [C] a single example of a book, newspaper, etc., of which many have been made: *a copy of "The New York Times"* ◆ *The book sold 20,000 copies within two weeks.* **3** [U] written material that is to be printed in a newspaper, magazine, etc.; news or information that can be used in a newspaper article or advertisement: *The copy editors prepare the reporters' copy for the paper and write the headlines.* ◆ *He writes copy for an online travel guide.* ◆ *This will make great copy for the advertisement.* **4** [C] = PHOTOCOPY: *Could I have ten copies of this page, please?*

• **verb** (**cop·ies**, **cop·y·ing**, **cop·ied**, **cop·ied**) **1** [T] ~ sth to make something that is exactly like something else: *They copied the designs from those on Greek vases.* ◆ *Everything in the computer's memory can be copied onto an external hard drive.* **2** [T] to write something exactly as it is written somewhere else: ~ sth (from sth) (into/onto sth) *She copied the phone number into her address book.* ◆ ~ sth (down/out) *I copied out several poems.* **3** [T] ~ sb/sth to behave or do something in the same way as someone else **SYN** IMITATE: *She copies everything her sister does.* ◆ *Their tactics have been copied by other terrorist organizations.* **4** [I] ~ (from/off sb) to cheat in an exam, school work, etc., by writing what someone else has written and pretending it is your own work **5** [T] ~ sth = PHOTOCOPY **6** [T] ~ sb (on sth) = COPY SB IN (ON STH) **PHR V** **copy sb ˈin (on sth)** to send someone a copy of a letter, e-mail message, etc., that you are sending to someone else: *Can you copy me in on your report?*

cop·y·book /ˈkɑpiˌbʊk/ noun a book, used in the past by children in school, containing examples of writing which school students had to copy

cop·y·cat /ˈkɑpiˌkæt/ noun, adj.

• **noun** (informal, disapproving) used especially by children about and to a person who copies what someone else does because they have no ideas of their own

• **adj.** [only before noun] (of crimes) similar to and seen as copying an earlier well-known crime

ˈcopy ˌeditor noun a person whose job is to correct and prepare a text for printing ▶ **ˈcopy-ˌedit** verb [T, I] ~ (sth)

cop·y·ist /ˈkɑpiɪst/ noun a person who makes copies of written documents or works of art

cop·y·right /ˈkɑpiˌraɪt/ noun, adj., verb

• **noun** [U, C] ~ (in/on sth) if a person or an organization holds the **copyright** on a piece of writing, music, etc., they are the only people who have the legal right to publish, broadcast, perform it, etc., and other people must ask their permission to use it or any part of it: *Who owns the copyright on this song?* ◆ *Copyright expires seventy years after the death of the author.* ◆ *They were sued for breach/infringement of copyright.*

• **adj.** (symb. ©) protected by copyright; not allowed to be copied without permission: *copyright material*

• **verb** ~ sth to get the copyright for something

cop·y·writ·er /ˈkɑpiˌraɪtər/ noun a person whose job is to write the words for advertising material

coq au vin /ˌkoʊk oʊ ˈvæ̃/ noun [U] (from French) a dish of chicken cooked in wine

co·quet·ry /ˈkoʊkətri; koʊˈkɛtri/ noun [U] (literary) behavior that is typical of a coquette

co·quette /koʊˈkɛt/ noun (literary, often disapproving) a woman who behaves in a way that is intended to attract men **SYN** FLIRT ▶ **co·quet·tish** /koʊˈkɛtɪʃ/ adj.: *a coquettish smile* **co·quet·tish·ly** adv.

cor·a·cle /ˈkɔrəkl; ˈkɑr-/ noun a small round boat with a wooden frame, used in Wales and Ireland

cor·al /ˈkɔrəl; ˈkɑrəl/ noun, adj.

• **noun 1** [U] a hard substance that is red, pink, or white in color, and that forms on the bottom of the ocean from the bones of very small creatures. Coral is often used in jewelry: *coral reefs/islands* ◆ *a coral necklace* **2** [C] a creature that produces coral

• **adj.** pink or red in color, like coral: *coral lipstick*

cor·bel /ˈkɔrbl/ noun (architecture) a piece of stone or wood that sticks out from a wall to support something, for example an ARCH

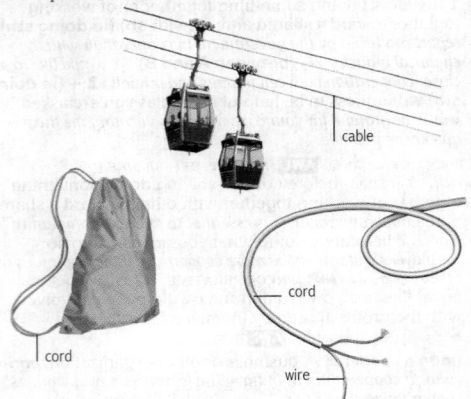

cable

cord

cord

wire

cord /kɔrd/ noun **1** [C, U] a piece of wire that is covered with plastic, used for carrying electricity to a piece of equipment: *an electrical cord* ◆ *telephone cord* ⊃ see also CORDLESS **2** [U, C] strong thick string or thin rope; a piece of this: *a piece/length of cord* ◆ *picture cord* (= used for hanging pictures) ◆ *a silk bag tied with a gold cord* **3** **cords** (also old-fashioned **cor·du·roys**) [pl.] pants made of CORDUROY: *a pair of cords* **4** [C] a measure of cut wood for burning in a fire, equal to 128 CUBIC feet ⊃ see also SPINAL CORD, UMBILICAL CORD, VOCAL CORDS

cord·ed /ˈkɔrdəd/ adj. **1** (of cloth) having raised lines **SYN** RIBBED **2** (of a muscle) TENSE and standing out so that it looks like a piece of cord **3** that has a cord attached: *a corded phone* **ANT** CORDLESS

cor·dial /ˈkɔrdʒəl/ adj., noun

• **adj.** (formal) pleasant and friendly: *a cordial atmosphere/meeting/relationship* ▶ **cor·dial·i·ty** /ˌkɔrdʒiˈæləti/ noun [U]: *I was greeted with a show of cordiality.*

• **noun 1** [U, C] = LIQUEUR **2** [C] a glass of cordial

cor·dial·ly /ˈkɔrdʒəli/ adv. (formal) **1** in a pleasant and friendly manner: *You are cordially invited to a celebration for Mr. Michael Brown on his retirement.* **2** (used with verbs showing dislike) very much: *They cordially detest each other.*

cord·ite /ˈkɔrdaɪt/ noun [U] an EXPLOSIVE used in bullets, bombs, etc.

cord·less /ˈkɔrdləs/ adj. (of a telephone or an electrical tool) not connected to its power supply by wires: *a cordless phone/drill* **ANT** CORDED

cor·don /ˈkɔrdn/ noun, verb

• **noun** a line or ring of police officers, soldiers, etc., guarding something or stopping people from entering or leaving a place: *Demonstrators broke through the police cordon.*

ʌ cup   ə about   eɪ say   aɪ five   ɔɪ boy   aʊ now   oʊ go   ər bird

• *verb*

PHR V ˌcordon sth↔ˈoff to stop people from getting into an area by surrounding it with police, soldiers, etc.: *Police cordoned off the area until the bomb was disabled.*

cor·don bleu /ˌkɔrdõ ˈblu/ *adj.* [usually before noun] (from French) of the highest standard of skill in cooking: *a cordon bleu chef* ♦ *cordon bleu cuisine*

cor·du·roy /ˈkɔrdəˌrɔɪ/ *noun* **1** [U] a type of strong soft cotton cloth with a pattern of raised parallel lines on it, used for making clothes: *a corduroy jacket* **2 corduroys** [pl.] (old-fashioned) = CORDS

core 🔑 **AWL** /kɔr/ *noun, adj., verb*
• *noun* **1** the hard central part of a fruit such as an apple, that contains the seeds ➔ picture at FRUIT **2** the central part of an object: *the earth's core* ♦ *the core of a nuclear reactor* **3** the most important or central part of something: *the core of the argument* ♦ *Concern for the environment is at the core of our policies.* **4** a small group of people who take part in a particular activity: *He gathered a small core of advisers around him.* ➔ see also HARD CORE

IDM **to the core** so that the whole of a thing or a person is affected: *She was shaken to the core by the news.* ♦ *He's a politician to the core* (= in all his attitudes and actions).
• *adj.* **1** most important; main or essential: *core subjects* (= subjects that all the students have to study) *such as English and mathematics* ♦ *the core curriculum* ♦ *We need to concentrate on our core business.* ♦ *The use of new technology is core to our strategy.* **2 ~ beliefs, values, principles, etc.** the most important or central beliefs, etc. of a person or group: *The party is losing touch with its core values.* **3** used to describe the most important members of a group: *The team is built around a core group of players.*
• *verb* ~ **sth** to take out the core of a fruit

co·ref·er·en·tial /ˌkoʊrɛfəˈrɛnʃl/ *adj.* (linguistics) if two words or expressions are **coreferential**, they refer to the same thing. For example, in the sentence "I had a camera but I lost it," "a camera" and "it" are coreferential.

ˌco·reˈspondent *noun* (law) a person who is said to have committed ADULTERY with the husband or wife of someone who is trying to get divorced

cor·gi /ˈkɔrgi/ *noun* a small dog with short legs and a pointed nose

co·ri·an·der /ˈkɔriˌændər/ *noun* [U] a plant whose leaves are used in cooking as an HERB and whose seeds are used in cooking as a spice ➔ compare CILANTRO

Co·rin·thi·an /kəˈrɪnθiən/ *adj.* [usually before noun] (architecture) used to describe a style of ARCHITECTURE in ancient Greece that has thin columns with decorations of leaves at the top: *Corinthian columns/capitals*

cork /kɔrk/ *noun, verb*
• *noun* **1** [U] a light, soft material that is the thick BARK of a type of Mediterranean OAK tree: *a cork mat* ♦ *cork tiles* **2** [C] a small round object made of cork or plastic, that is used for closing bottles, especially wine bottles. ➔ picture at PACKAGING ➔ thesaurus box at LID
• *verb* ~ **sth** to close a bottle with a cork **ANT** UNCORK

cork·age /ˈkɔrkɪdʒ/ *noun* [U] the money that a restaurant charges if you want to drink wine there that you have bought somewhere else

corked /kɔrkt/ *adj.* (of wine) with a bad taste because the cork has decayed

cork·screw /ˈkɔrkskru/ *noun, verb*
• *noun* a tool for pulling CORKS from bottles. Most corkscrews have a handle and a long twisted piece of metal for pushing into the cork. ➔ picture at KITCHEN
• *verb* [I] (+ adv./prep) to move in a particular direction while turning in circles

corm /kɔrm/ *noun* the small, round, underground part of some plants, from which the new plant grows every year

cor·mo·rant /ˈkɔrmərənt; -ˌrænt/ *noun* a large black bird

with a long neck that lives near the ocean or other areas of water

corn /kɔrn/ *noun* **1** [U] a tall plant grown for its large yellow grains that are used for making flour, eaten as a vegetable, or fed to animals: *a field of corn* ♦ **ears of corn** ♦ *corn-fed chicken* ➔ see also FIELD CORN ➔ picture at CEREAL ➔ collocations at FARMING **2** [U] the yellow seeds of a type of CORN plant, which grow on thick STEMS and are cooked and eaten as a vegetable ➔ see also CORNCOB, CORN ON THE COB, SWEET CORN ➔ picture at FRUIT **3** [C] a small area of hard skin on the foot, especially the toe, that is sometimes painful

the ˈCorn Belt *noun* the states of the Midwest where corn is an important crop

corn·bread /ˈkɔrnbrɛd/ *noun* [U] a kind of flat bread made with CORNFLOUR

ˈ**corn chip** *noun* a thin, crisp piece of food made from crushed corn that has been fried

corn·cob /ˈkɔrnkab/ *noun* = COB (1)

ˈ**corn dog** *noun* a HOT DOG that is covered with a mixture of CORNMEAL, fried, and served on a stick

cor·ne·a /ˈkɔrniə/ *noun* (anatomy) the transparent layer which covers and protects the outer part of the eye ➔ picture at BODY ▶ **cor·ne·al** /ˈkɔrniəl/ *adj.* [only before noun]: *a corneal transplant*

corned beef /ˌkɔrnd ˈbif; ˌkɔrn-/ *noun* [U] beef that has been cooked and preserved using salt, often sold in cans

cor·nel·ian /kɔrˈnilyən/ *noun* = CARNELIAN

cor·ner 🔑 /ˈkɔrnər/ *noun, verb*
• *noun*
▷ **OF BUILDING/OBJECT/SHAPE 1** a part of something where two or more sides, lines, or edges join: *the four corners of a square* ♦ *Write your name on the top right-hand corner of the paper.* ♦ *I hit my knee on the corner of the table.* ♦ *A smile lifted the corner of his mouth.* ♦ *a speck of dirt in the corner of her eye*
▷ **-CORNERED 2** (in adjectives) with the number of corners mentioned; involving the number of groups mentioned: *a three-cornered hat* ♦ *a three-cornered fight*
▷ **OF ROOM/BOX 3** the place inside a room or a box where two sides join; the area around this place: *There was a television in the far corner of the room.* ♦ *a corner table/seat/cupboard*
▷ **OF ROADS 4** a place where two streets join: *There was a group of youths standing on the street corner.* ♦ *Turn right at the corner of Sunset and Crescent Heights Boulevards.* ♦ *There's a hotel on/at the corner of my street.* ♦ *The wind hit me as he turned the corner.* **5** a sharp bend in a road: *The car was taking the corners too fast.*
▷ **AREA/REGION 6** a region or an area of a place (sometimes used for one that is far away or difficult to reach): *She lives in a quiet corner of rural Pennsylvania.* ♦ *Students come here from the four corners of the world.* ♦ *He knew every corner of the old town.*
▷ **DIFFICULT SITUATION 7** [usually sing.] a difficult situation: *to back/drive/force someone into a corner* ♦ *They had her in a corner, and there wasn't much she could do about it.* ♦ *He was used to talking his way out of tight corners.*
▷ **IN SPORTS 8** (in sports such as SOCCER and FIELD HOCKEY) a free kick or hit that you take from the corner of your opponent's end of the field: *to take a corner* ♦ *The referee awarded a corner.* ➔ see also CORNER KICK **9** (in boxing and WRESTLING) any of the four corners of a RING¹; the supporters who help in the corner

IDM **(just) around the corner** very near: *Her house is just around the corner.* ♦ (figurative) *There were good times around the corner* (= they would soon come). **cut corners** (disapproving) to do something in the easiest, cheapest, or quickest way, often by ignoring rules or leaving something out **cut the corner** to go across the corner of an area and not around the sides of it, because it is quicker **see sth out of the corner of your eye** to see something by accident or not very clearly because you see it from the side of your eye and are not looking straight at it: *Out of the corner of her eye, she saw him coming closer.* **turn the corner** to pass a very important point in an illness or a difficult situation and begin to improve ⊃ more at TIGHT

● **verb**

▸ **TRAP SOMEONE 1** [T, often passive] ~ **sb/sth** to get a person or an animal into a place or situation from which they cannot escape: *The man was finally cornered by police in a garage.* ◆ *If cornered, the snake will defend itself.* **2** [T] ~ **sb** to go toward someone in a determined way, because you want to speak to them: *I found myself cornered by her on the stairs.*

▸ **THE MARKET 3** [T] ~ **the market (in something)** to get control of the trade in a particular type of goods: *They've cornered the market in silver.*

▸ **OF VEHICLE/DRIVER 4** [I] to go around a corner: *The car has excellent cornering* (= it is easy to steer around corners).

cor·ner·back /ˈkɔrnərˌbæk/ *noun* (in football) a DEFENSIVE player whose position is outside and behind the LINE-BACKER

ˈcorner ˌkick (also **corˌner**) *noun* (in SOCCER) a free kick that you take from the corner of your opponent's end of the field

cor·ner·stone /ˈkɔrnərˌstoʊn/ *noun* **1** a stone at the corner of the base of a building, often laid in a special ceremony **2** the most important part of something that the rest depends on: *This study is the cornerstone of the whole research program.*

cor·net /kɔrˈnɛt/ *noun* a BRASS musical instrument like a small TRUMPET

cor·net·to /kɔrˈnɛtoʊ/ *noun* (*pl.* **cor·net·ti** /-ˈnɛti/) (from *Italian*) an early musical instrument consisting of a curved tube with holes in that you cover with your fingers while blowing into the end

ˈcorn-fed *adj.* [only before noun] typical of a people who come from the American Midwest, being strong and healthy, with good moral values, but not having a lot of knowledge about the world and things such as art and culture: *a healthy, corn-fed farm girl* ◆ *a backward, corn-fed Midwestern city*

corn·field /ˈkɔrnfild/ *noun* a field in which CORN is grown

corn·flakes /ˈkɔrnfleɪks/ *noun* [pl.] small, crisp, yellow pieces of crushed CORN, usually eaten with milk and sugar for breakfast

corn·flow·er /ˈkɔrnˌflaʊər/ *noun* a small wild plant with blue flowers

cor·nice /ˈkɔrnəs/ *noun* (*architecture*) a decorative border around the top of the walls in a room or on the outside walls of a building

corn·meal /ˈkɔrnmil/ *noun* [U] flour made from CORN

ˌcorn on the ˈcob *noun* [U] CORN that is cooked with all the grains still attached to the inner part and eaten as a vegetable ⊃ picture at FRUIT

ˈcorn pone (also **corn pone**) *noun* [U] a type of bread made from CORN and water

ˈcorn-pone *adj.* [only before noun] typical of people who live in rural areas and enjoy simple humor: *corn-pone humor* ◆ *a corn-pone way of talking*

corn·rows /ˈkɔrnroʊz/ *noun* [pl.] a HAIRSTYLE worn especially by black women, in which the hair is put into lines of BRAIDS along the head ⊃ picture at HAIR

corn·starch /ˈkɔrnstartʃ/ *noun* [U] fine white flour made from CORN, used especially for making sauces thicker

ˈcorn ˌsyrup *noun* [U] a thick sweet liquid made from CORN and used in cooking

cor·nu·co·pi·a /ˌkɔrnəˈkoʊpiə; -nyə-/ *noun* **1** (also **ˌhorn of ˈplenty**) a decorative object shaped like an animal's horn, shown in art as full of fruit and flowers **2** (*formal*) something that is or contains a large supply of good things: *The book is a cornucopia of good ideas.*

corn·y /ˈkɔrni/ *adj.* (**corn·i·er**, **corn·i·est**) (*informal*) not original; used too often to be interesting or to sound

sincere: *a corny joke/song* ◆ *I know it sounds corny, but it really was love at first sight!*

co·rol·la /kəˈroʊlə; -ˈrɑ-/ *noun* (*biology*) the ring of PETALS around the central part of a flower

cor·ol·lar·y /ˈkɔrəˌlɛri; ˈkɑr-/ *noun* (*pl.* **cor·ol·lar·ies**) ~ **(of/to sth)** (*formal* or *technical*) a situation, an argument, or a fact that is the natural and direct result of another one

co·ro·na /kəˈroʊnə/ *noun* (*pl.* **co·ro·nae** /-ni/) (*astronomy*) (also *informal* **ha·lo**) a ring of light seen around the sun or moon, especially during an ECLIPSE

cor·o·nar·y /ˈkɔrəˌnɛri; ˈkɑrəˌnɛri/ *adj.* (*medical*) connected with the heart, particularly the arteries (ARTERY) that take blood to the heart: *coronary disease* ◆ *a coronary patient* (= someone suffering from coronary disease)

ˌcoronary ˈartery *noun* (*anatomy*) either of the two arteries (ARTERY) that supply blood to the heart

ˌcoronary thromˈbosis (also *informal* **cor·o·nar·y**) *noun* (*medical*) a blocking of the flow of blood by a blood CLOT in an ARTERY supplying blood to the heart ⊃ compare HEART ATTACK

cor·o·na·tion /ˌkɔrəˈneɪʃn; ˌkɑr-/ *noun* a ceremony at which a crown is formally placed on the head of a new king or queen

cor·o·ner /ˈkɔrənər; ˈkɑr-/ *noun* an official whose job is to discover the cause of any sudden, violent, or suspicious death by holding an INQUEST

cor·o·net /ˌkɔrəˈnɛt; ˌkɑr-/ *noun* **1** a small crown worn on formal occasions by princes, princesses, lords, etc. **2** a round decoration for the head, especially one made of flowers

Corp. *abbr.* (in writing) CORPORATION

cor·po·ra *pl.* of CORPUS

cor·po·ral /ˈkɔrprəl; -pərəl/ *noun* (*abbr.* Cpl) a member of one of the lower ranks in the army or the MARINES: *Corporal Smith*

ˌcorporal ˈpunishment *noun* [U] the physical punishment of people, especially by hitting them

cor·po·rate 〔AWL〕 /ˈkɔrpərət; ˈkɔrprət/ *adj.* [only before noun] **1** connected with a corporation: *corporate finance/planning/strategy* ◆ *corporate identity* (= the image of a company, that all its members share) ◆ *corporate hospitality* (= when companies entertain customers to help develop good business relationships) **2** (*technical*) forming a CORPORATION: *The neighborhood association is a corporate body.* ◆ *The law applies to both individuals and corporate bodies.* **3** involving or shared by all the members of a group: *corporate responsibility*

ˌcorporate ˈraider *noun* (*business*) a person or company that regularly buys large numbers of shares in other companies against their wishes, either to control them or to sell them again for a large profit

ˌcorporate responˈsibility *noun* [U] the idea that a large company has a duty to treat its customers fairly and to provide good products or services

cor·po·ra·tion 〔AWL〕 /ˌkɔrpəˈreɪʃn/ *noun* **1** (*abbr.* Corp.) a large business company: *multinational corporations* ◆ *the Chrysler corporation* **2** an organization or a group of organizations that is recognized by law as a single unit: *urban development corporations*

cor·po·rat·ism /ˈkɔrpərəˌtɪzəm; ˈkɔrprə-/ *noun* [U] the control of a country, etc. by large groups, especially businesses

cor·po·re·al /kɔrˈpɔriəl/ *adj.* (*formal*) **1** that can be touched; physical rather than spiritual: *his corporeal presence* **2** of or for the body: *corporeal needs*

corps /kɔr/ *noun* (*pl.* **corps** /kɔrz/) **1** a large unit of an army, consisting of two or more DIVISIONS: *the commander of the third army corps* **2** one of the groups of an army with a special responsibility: *the U.S. Marine Corps* **3** a group of people involved in a particular job or activity: *a corps of* trained and experienced doctors ➲ see also DIPLOMATIC CORPS, PRESS CORPS

corps de bal·let /ˌkɔr də bæˈleɪ/ noun [C, pl.] (from French) dancers in a BALLET company who dance together as a group

corpse /kɔrps/ noun a dead body, especially of a human

corps·man /ˈkɔrmən/ noun (pl. **corps·men** /-mən/) a member of a military medical unit who is not an officer

cor·pu·lent /ˈkɔrpyələnt/ adj. (formal) (of a person) fat. People say "corpulent" to avoid saying "fat." ▸ **cor·pu·lence** /-ləns/ noun [U]

cor·pus /ˈkɔrpəs/ noun (pl. **cor·po·ra** /ˈkɔrpərə/ or **cor·pus·es** /-səz/) (technical) a collection of written or spoken texts: a corpus of 100 million words of spoken English ♦ the whole corpus of Renaissance poetry ➲ see also HABEAS CORPUS

cor·pus·cle /ˈkɔrˌpʌsl; -pəsl/ noun (anatomy) any of the red or white cells found in blood: red/white corpuscles

cor·ral /kəˈræl/ noun, verb
● noun a fenced area for horses, cows, etc. on a farm or RANCH: They drove the ponies into a corral.
● verb (-ll- or -l-) **1** ~ sth to force horses or cows into a corral **2** ~ sb to gather a group of people together and keep them in a particular place

cor·rect 🔑 /kəˈrekt/ adj., verb
● adj. **1** accurate or true, without any mistakes SYN RIGHT: Do you have the correct time? ♦ the correct answer ♦ Please check that this information is correct. ♦ "Are you in charge here?" "That's correct." ♦ Am I correct in saying that you know a lot about wine? ANT INCORRECT ➲ thesaurus box at TRUE **2** right and suitable, so that something is done as it should be done: Do you know the correct way to shut the machine down? ♦ I think you've made the correct decision. ➲ thesaurus box at RIGHT **3** taking care to speak or behave in a way that follows the accepted standards or rules: a correct young lady ♦ He is always very correct in his speech. ANT INCORRECT ➲ see also POLITICALLY CORRECT ▸ **cor·rect·ly** adv.: Have you spelled it correctly? ♦ They assumed, correctly, that she was away for the weekend. ♦ He was looking correctly grave. **cor·rect·ness** noun [U]: The correctness of this decision may be doubted. ➲ see also POLITICAL CORRECTNESS
● verb **1** ~ sth to make something right or accurate, for example by changing it or removing mistakes: Read through your work and correct any mistakes that you find. ♦ Their eyesight can be corrected in just a few minutes by the use of a laser. ♦ They issued a statement correcting the one they had made earlier. **2** ~ sth (of a teacher) to mark the mistakes in a piece of work (and sometimes give a grade to the work): I spent all evening correcting essays. **3** to tell someone that they have made a mistake: ~ sb Correct me if I'm wrong, but isn't this last year's brochure? ♦ Yes, you're right— **I stand corrected** (= I accept that I made a mistake). ♦ ~ (sb) + speech "It's Yates, not Wates," she corrected him.

cor·rec·tion /kəˈrekʃn/ noun, exclamation
● noun **1** [C] a change that makes something more accurate than it was before: I've made a few small corrections to your report. ♦ The paper had to publish a correction to the story. **2** [U] the act or process of correcting something: There are some programming errors that need correction. **3** [U] (old-fashioned) punishment: the correction of young offenders
● exclamation (informal) used when you want to correct something that you have just said: I don't know. Correction—I do know, but I'm not going to tell you.

cor·rec·tion·al /kəˈrekʃənl/ adj. [only before noun] concerned with improving the behavior of criminals, usually by punishing them: a correctional center/institution/facility (= a prison)

cor·rec·tion ˌfluid noun [U] a white liquid that you use to cover mistakes that you make when you are writing or typing, and that you can write on top of ➲ picture at STATIONERY ➲ see also WITEOUT™

cor·rec·tive /kəˈrektɪv/ adj., noun
● adj. (formal) designed to make something right that was wrong before: We need to take **corrective action** to halt this country's decline. ♦ corrective measures ♦ corrective surgery/glasses
● noun ~ (to sth) (formal) something that helps to give a more accurate or fairer view of someone or something: I would like to add a corrective to what I have written previously.

cor·re·late /ˈkɔrəˌleɪt; ˈkɑr-/ verb **1** [I] if two or more facts, figures, etc. correlate, or if a fact, figure, etc. correlates with another, the facts are closely connected and affect or depend on each other: The figures do not seem to correlate. ♦ ~ with sth A high-fat diet correlates with a greater risk of heart disease. **2** [T] ~ sth to show that there is a close connection between two or more facts, figures, etc.: Researchers are trying to correlate the two sets of figures. ▸ **cor·re·late** /ˈkɔrələt; ˈkɑr-/ noun

cor·re·la·tion /ˌkɔrəˈleɪʃn; ˌkɑr-/ noun [C, U] a connection between two things in which one thing changes as the other does: ~ (**between A and B**) There is a direct correlation between exposure to sun and skin cancer. ♦ ~ (**of A with B**) the correlation of social power with wealth

cor·rel·a·tive /kəˈrelətɪv/ noun (formal) a fact or an idea that is closely related to or depends on another fact or idea ▸ **cor·rel·a·tive** adj.

cor·re·spond AWL /ˌkɔrəˈspɑnd; ˌkɑr-/ verb **1** [I] to be the same as or match something SYN AGREE, TALLY: Your account and hers do not correspond. ♦ ~ with sth Your account of events does not correspond with hers. ♦ ~ to sth The written record of the conversation doesn't correspond to (= is different from) what was actually said. **2** [I] ~ (to sth) to be similar to or the same as something else SYN EQUIVALENT: The British job of Lecturer corresponds roughly to the U.S. job of Associate Professor. **3** [I] ~ (with sb) (formal) to write letters to someone and receive letters from them

cor·re·spond·ence AWL /ˌkɔrəˈspɑndəns; ˌkɑr-/ noun **1** [U] ~ (with sb) the letters a person sends and receives: personal/private correspondence ♦ The editor welcomes correspondence from readers on any subject. ♦ the correspondence column/page (= in a newspaper) **2** [U, C] ~ (with sb) the activity of writing letters: I refused to enter into any correspondence with him about it. ♦ We have been in correspondence for months. ♦ We kept up a correspondence for many years. **3** [C, U] ~ (between A and B) a connection between two things; the fact of two things being similar: There is a close correspondence between the two extracts.

corre·ˈspondence ˌcourse noun a course of study that you do at home, using books and exercises sent to you by mail or by e-mail

cor·re·spond·ent /ˌkɔrəˈspɑndənt; ˌkɑr-/ noun **1** a person who reports news from a particular country or on a particular subject for a newspaper or a television or radio station: NPR's political correspondent ♦ a foreign/war/business, etc. correspondent ♦ our London correspondent **2** (used with an adjective) a person who writes letters to another person: She's a poor correspondent (= she does not write regularly).

cor·re·spond·ing AWL /ˌkɔrəˈspɑndɪŋ; ˌkɑr-/ adj. matching or connected with something that you have just mentioned SYN EQUIVALENT: A change in the money supply brings a corresponding change in expenditure. ♦ Profits have risen by 15 percent compared with the corresponding period last year. ♦ The Redskins lost to the Cowboys in the corresponding game last year. ♦ ~ to sth Give each picture a number corresponding to its position on the page. ▸ **cor·re·spond·ing·ly** AWL adv.: a period of high demand and correspondingly high prices

ˌcorresponding ˈangles noun (geometry) equal angles formed on the same side of a line that crosses two parallel lines ➲ picture at SHAPE ➲ compare ALTERNATE ANGLES

cor·ri·dor /ˈkɔrəˌdɔr; -dər; ˈkɑr-/ noun **1** (also hall·way) a long narrow passage in a building, with doors that open into rooms on either side: *His room is along the corridor.* **2** a passage on a train **3** a long narrow strip of land belonging to one country that passes through the land of another country; a part of the sky over a country that planes, for example from another country, can fly through ⟹ **see also** AIR CORRIDOR **4** a long narrow strip of land that follows the course of an important road or river: *the technology industry in the Route 128 corridor*

IDM **the corridors of power** (sometimes *humorous*) the higher levels of government, where important decisions are made

cor·rie /ˈkɔri/ *noun* (*geology*) = CIRQUE

cor·rob·o·rate /kəˈrabəˌreɪt/ [I, T, often passive] **~ (sth)** (*formal*) to provide evidence or information that supports a statement, theory, etc. **SYN** CONFIRM: *The evidence was corroborated by two independent witnesses.* ◆ *corroborating evidence* ▶ **cor·rob·o·ra·tion** /kəˌrabəˈreɪʃn/ *noun* [U]

cor·rob·o·ra·tive /kəˈrabərətɪv; -əˌreɪtɪv/ *adj.* (*formal*) [usually before noun] giving support to a statement or theory: *Is there any corroborative evidence for this theory?*

cor·rode /kəˈroʊd/ *verb* [T, I] **~ (sth)** to destroy something slowly, especially by chemical action; to be destroyed in this way: *Acid corrodes metal.* ◆ *The copper pipework has corroded in places.* ◆ (*figurative*) *Corruption corrodes public confidence in a political system.* ▶ **cor·ro·sion** /kəˈroʊʒn/ *noun* [U]: *Look for signs of corrosion.* ◆ *Clean off any corrosion before applying the paint.*

cor·ro·sive /kəˈroʊsɪv/ *adj.* **1** tending to destroy something slowly by chemical action: *the corrosive effects of salt water* ◆ *corrosive acid* **2** (*formal*) tending to damage something gradually: *Unemployment is having a corrosive effect on our economy.*

cor·ru·gat·ed /ˈkɔrəˌgeɪtəd; ˈkɑr-/ *adj.* shaped into a series of regular folds that look like waves: *a corrugated metal roof* ◆ *corrugated cardboard*

corrugated

corrugated iron roof

cor·rupt /kəˈrʌpt/ *adj., verb*
● *adj.* **1** (of people) willing to use their power to do dishonest or illegal things in return for money or to get an advantage: *a corrupt regime* ◆ *corrupt officials accepting bribes* **2** (of behavior) dishonest or immoral: *corrupt practices* ◆ *The whole system is inefficient and corrupt.* **3** (*computing*) containing changes or faults, and no longer in the original state: *corrupt software* ◆ *The text on the disk seems to be corrupt.* ▶ **cor·rupt·ly** *adv.*

● *verb* **1** [T] **~ sb** to have a bad effect on someone and make them behave in an immoral or dishonest way: *He was corrupted by power and ambition.* ◆ *the corrupting effects of great wealth* **2** [T, often passive] **~ sth** to change the original form of something, so that it is damaged or spoiled in some way: *a corrupted form of Buddhism* **3** [T, I] **~ (sth)** (*computing*) to cause mistakes to appear in a computer file, etc. with the result that the information in it is no longer correct: *The program has somehow corrupted the system files.* ◆ *corrupted data* ◆ *The disk will corrupt if it is overloaded.*

cor·rupt·i·ble /kəˈrʌptəbl/ *adj.* that can be corrupted **ANT** INCORRUPTIBLE

cor·rup·tion /kəˈrʌpʃn/ *noun* **1** [U] dishonest or illegal behavior, especially of people in authority: *allegations of bribery and corruption* ◆ *The new district attorney has promised to fight police corruption.* ⟹ collocations at CRIME **2** [U] the act or effect of making someone change from moral to immoral standards of behavior: *He claimed that sex and violence on TV led to the corruption of young people.* **3** [C, usually sing.] the form of a word or phrase that has become changed from its original form in some way: *The word "holiday" is a corruption of "holy day."*

cor·sage /kɔrˈsaʒ/ *noun* a small bunch of flowers that is worn on a woman's dress, for example at a wedding

cor·set /ˈkɔrsət/ *noun* a piece of women's underwear, fitting the body tightly, worn especially in the past to make the waist look smaller

cor·tège (also **cor·tege**) /kɔrˈtɛʒ/ *noun* a line of cars or people moving along slowly at a funeral **SYN** FUNERAL PROCESSION

cor·tex /ˈkɔrtɛks/ *noun* (*pl.* **cor·ti·ces** /ˈkɔrtəsiz/) (*anatomy*) the outer layer of an organ in the body, especially the brain: *the cerebral/renal cortex* (= around the brain/ KIDNEY) ▶ **cor·ti·cal** /ˈkɔrtɪkl/ *adj.*

cor·ti·sone /ˈkɔrtəˌsoʊn; -ˌzoʊn/ *noun* [U] (*medical*) a HORMONE used in the treatment of diseases such as ARTHRITIS, to reduce swelling

cor·us·cate /ˈkɔrəˌskeɪt; ˈkar-/ *verb* (*literary*) **1** [I] (of light) to flash **2** [I] (of a person) to be full of life, enthusiasm, or humor ▶ **cor·us·cat·ing** *adj.*: *coruscating wit* **cor·us·cat·ing·ly** *adv.*: *coruscatingly brilliant*

cor·vette /kɔrˈvɛt/ *noun* a small fast ship used in war to protect other ships from attack

cos *abbr.* (in writing) COSINE

co·sign /ˈkoʊsaɪn/ *verb* [T, I] to sign a document in order to guarantee a loan or other legal commitment: **~ sth** *My sister will cosign the loan.* ◆ **~ (for sb)** *Since you don't have a job, someone must cosign for you.* ▶ **co·sign·er** /ˈkoʊˌsaɪnər/ *noun*: *Her dad is the cosigner on her apartment lease.*

co-ˈsignatory *noun* one of two or more people who sign a formal document: *co-signatories of/to the treaty*

co·sine /ˈkoʊsaɪn/ *noun* (*abbr.* cos) (*mathematics*) the RATIO of the length of the side next to an ACUTE ANGLE in a RIGHT TRIANGLE to the length of the longest side (= the HYPOTENUSE) ⟹ compare SINE, TANGENT

cos·met·ic /kazˈmɛtɪk/ *noun, adj.*
● *noun* [usually pl.] a substance that you put on your face or body to make it more attractive: *the cosmetics industry* ◆ *a cosmetic company* ◆ *cosmetic products* ⟹ collocations at FASHION
● *adj.* **1** improving only the outside appearance of something and not its basic character: *These reforms are not merely cosmetic.* ◆ *She dismissed the plan as a cosmetic exercise to win votes.* **2** connected with medical treatment that is intended to improve a person's appearance: *cosmetic surgery* ◆ *cosmetic dental work* ▶ **cos·met·i·cal·ly** /-kli/ *adv.*

cos·mic /ˈkazmɪk/ *adj.* [usually before noun] **1** connected with the whole universe: *Do you believe in a cosmic plan?* **2** very great and important: *This was disaster on a cosmic scale.*

cosmic ˈdust *noun* [U] (*astronomy*) very small pieces of matter floating in space

cosmic ˈrays *noun* [pl.] RAYS that reach the earth from outer space

cos·mol·o·gy /kazˈmalədʒi/ *noun* [U] the scientific study of the universe and its origin and development ▶ **cos·mo·log·i·cal** /ˌkazməˈladʒɪkl/ *adj.* **cos·mol·o·gist** /kazˈmaˌlədʒɪst/ *noun*

cos·mo·naut /ˈkazməˌnɔt; -ˌnat/ *noun* an ASTRONAUT from the former Soviet Union

cos·mo·pol·i·tan /ˌkazməˈpalətn; -tən/ *adj., noun*
● *adj.* (*approving*) **1** containing people of different types or from different countries, and influenced by their culture: *a cosmopolitan city/resort* ◆ *The club has a cosmopolitan atmosphere.* **2** having or showing a wide experience with people and things from many different countries: *people with a truly cosmopolitan outlook* ◆ *cosmopolitan young people*
● *noun* a person who has experienced many different parts of the world: *She's a real cosmopolitan.*

cos·mos /ˈkazmoʊs; ˈkazməs/ **the cosmos** *noun* [sing.] the universe, especially when it is thought of as an ordered system: *the structure of the cosmos* ◆ *our place in the cosmos*

cos·set /ˈkasət/ *verb* **~ sb** (often *disapproving*) to treat someone with a lot of care and give them a lot of attention, sometimes too much **SYN** PAMPER

cost 🔑 /kɔst/ noun, verb

• **noun 1** [C, U] the amount of money that you need in order to buy, make, or do something: *the high/low cost of housing* ♦ *A new computer system has been installed at a cost of $150,000.* ♦ *The plan had to be abandoned on grounds of cost.* ♦ *We did not even make enough money to cover the cost of the food.* ♦ *Consumers will have to bear the full cost of these pay increases.* ♦ *The total cost to you* (= the amount you have to pay) *is $3,000.* ⊃ thesaurus box at PRICE **2 costs** [pl.] the total amount of money that needs to be spent by a business: *The use of cheap labor helped to keep costs down.* ♦ *to cut/reduce costs* ♦ *running/operating/labor costs* ♦ *We have had to raise our prices because of rising costs.* ⊃ collocations at BUSINESS **3** [U, sing.] the effort, loss, or damage that is involved in order to do or achieve something: *the terrible cost of the war in death and suffering* ♦ *the environmental cost of nuclear power* ♦ *She saved him from the fire but at the cost of her own life* (= she died). ♦ *He worked non-stop for three months, at considerable cost to his health.* ♦ *I felt a need to please people, whatever the cost in time and energy.* **4 costs** (also **'court costs**) [pl.] the sum of money that someone is ordered to pay for lawyers, etc. in a legal case: *He was ordered to pay $2,000 costs.* **IDM** **at all costs** whatever is needed to achieve something: *You must stop the media from finding out at all costs.* **at any cost** under any circumstances: *He is determined to win at any cost.* **at cost** for only the amount of money that is needed to make or get something, without any profit being added on: *goods sold at cost* ⊃ more at COUNT v.

• **verb** (cost, cost) **HELP** In sense 4 **costed** is used for the past tense and past participle. **1** if something **costs** a particular amount of money, you need to pay that amount in order to buy, make, or do it: *~ sth How much did it cost?* ♦ *I didn't get it because it cost too much.* ♦ *Tickets cost ten dollars each.* ♦ *Calls to landlines cost 5 cents per minute.* ♦ *Don't use too much of it—it cost a lot of money.* ♦ *All these reforms will cost money* (= be expensive). ♦ *Good food need not cost a fortune* (= cost a lot of money). ♦ *~ sb sth The meal cost us about $40.* ♦ *This is costing the taxpayer $10 billion a year.* ♦ *~ sth to do sth The hospital will cost an estimated $3 million to build.* ♦ *It costs a fortune to fly first class.* **2** to cause the loss of something: *~ sb sth That one mistake almost cost him his life.* ♦ *A late penalty cost our team the game* (= meant that they did not win the game). ♦ *~ sth The closure of the factory is likely to cost 1,000 jobs.* **3 ~ sb sth** to involve you in making an effort or doing something unpleasant: *The accident cost me a visit to the doctor.* ♦ *Financial worries cost her many sleepless nights.* **4** (cost·ed, cost·ed) [usually passive] to estimate how much money will be needed for something or the price that should be charged for something: *~ sth The project needs to be costed in detail.* ♦ *Their accountants have costed the project at $8.1 million.* ♦ *~ sth out Have you costed out these proposals yet?* ⊃ see also COSTING **IDM** **cost sb dear/dearly** to make sb suffer a lot: *That one mistake has cost him dearly over the years.* **it will cost you** (*informal*) used to say that something will be expensive: *There is a deluxe model available, but it'll cost you.* ⊃ more at ARM

'cost ˌaccounting noun [U] (*business*) the process of recording and analyzing the costs involved in running a business

cos·tal /'kɔstl/ adj. (*anatomy*) connected with the RIBS

co·star (also **'co-star**) /'koʊstɑr/ noun, verb
• **noun** one of two or more famous actors who appear together in a movie or play
• **verb** (-rr-) **1** [I] *~* **(with sb)** to appear as one of the main actors with someone in a movie or play: *a new movie in which Johnny Depp costars with Angelina Jolie* **2** [T] *~* **sb** (of a movie or play) to have two or more famous actors acting in it: *a new movie costarring Johnny Depp and Angelina Jolie*

ˌcost-'benefit noun [U] (*economics*) the relationship between the cost of doing something and the value of the benefit that results from it: *cost-benefit analysis*

'cost-cutting noun [U] the reduction of the amount of money spent on something, especially because of financial difficulty: *Deliveries of mail could be delayed because of cost-cutting.* ♦ *a cost-cutting exercise/measure/program*

ˌcost-ef'fective adj. giving the best possible profit or benefits in comparison with the money that is spent
▶ **ˌcost-ef'fectiveness** noun [U]

costing /'kɔstɪŋ/ noun an estimate of how much money will be needed for something: *Here is a detailed costing of our proposals.* ♦ *You'd better do some costings.*

cost·ly /'kɔstli/ adj. (cost·li·er, cost·li·est) **HELP** You can also use **more costly** and **most costly**. **1** costing a lot of money, especially more than you want to pay **SYN** EXPENSIVE: *Buying new furniture may prove too costly.* ⊃ thesaurus box at EXPENSIVE **2** causing problems or the loss of something **SYN** EXPENSIVE: *a costly mistake/failure* ♦ *Mining can be costly in terms of lives* (= too many people can die). ▶ **cost·li·ness** noun [U]

the ˌcost of 'living noun [sing.] the amount of money that people need to pay for food, clothing, and somewhere to live: *a steady rise in the cost of living* ♦ *the high cost of living in New York*

cos·tume /'kɑstum/ noun **1** [C, U] the clothes worn by people from a particular place or during a particular historical period ⊃ see also NATIONAL COSTUME **2** [C, U] the clothes worn by actors in a play or movie, or worn by someone to make them look like something else: *The actors were still in costume and makeup.* ♦ *She has four costume* changes during the play. ◆ He went to the party in a giant chicken costume. ◆ a costume designer

cos·tumed /ˈkɑstumd/ adj. [usually before noun] wearing a costume

costume drama noun [C, U] a play or movie set in the past

costume jewelry noun [U] large heavy jewelry that can look expensive but is made with cheap materials

costume party noun a party where all the guests wear special clothes, in order to look like a different person, an animal, etc.

cos·tu·m·er /ˈkɑsˌtumər/ noun a person or company that makes COSTUMES or has COSTUMES to rent, especially for the theater: a company of theatrical costumers

cot /kɑt/ noun a light narrow bed that you can fold up and carry easily ➪ picture at BED

co·te·rie /ˈkoʊtəri/ noun (formal, often disapproving) a small group of people who have the same interests and do things together but do not like to include others

co·ter·mi·nous /koʊˈtɜrmənəs/ adj. [not usually before noun] (formal) **1** ~ (with sth) (of countries or areas) sharing a border **2** ~ (with sth) (of things or ideas) having so much in common that they are almost the same as each other

cot·tage 🔊 /ˈkɑtɪdʒ/ noun
1 a small house, especially in the country: a charming country cottage with roses around the door **2** (CanE) a second house that people have, usually near a lake, where they can go on weekends and for holidays

cottage cheese noun [U] soft white cheese with small lumps in it

cottage industry noun a small business in which the work is done by people in their homes: Weaving and knitting are traditional cottage industries.

cot·ton 🔊 /ˈkɑtn/ noun, verb
• noun [U] **1** a plant grown in warm countries for the soft white hairs around its seeds that are used to make cloth and thread: cotton fields/plants ◆ bales of cotton **2** the cloth made from the cotton plant: The sheets are 100% pure cotton. ◆ a cotton shirt/skirt ◆ printed cotton cloth ◆ the cotton industry ◆ a cotton mill **3** a soft mass of white material that is used for cleaning the skin or a wound: Use a cotton ball to apply the lotion.
• verb
PHR V cotton 'on (to sth) (informal) to begin to understand or realize something without being told: I suddenly cottoned on to what he was doing. 'cotton (up) to sb/sth (informal) to make an attempt to be friendly to someone

the 'Cotton Belt noun the states in the southern U.S. where cotton was the main crop

cotton candy noun [U] a type of candy in the form of a mass of sticky threads made from melted sugar and served on a stick, especially at FAIRGROUNDS

cotton gin (also gin) noun a machine for separating the seeds of a cotton plant from the cotton

cot·ton·mouth /ˈkɑtnˌmaʊθ/ (also cottonmouth 'moccasin, ˌwater 'moccasin) noun a poisonous snake which lives near water in the U.S.

cotton 'swab noun = Q-TIP™

cot·ton·tail /ˈkɑtnˌteɪl/ noun an American rabbit with gray or brown fur and a tail that is white underneath

cot·ton·wood /ˈkɑtnˌwʊd/ (also cottonwood tree) noun a type of N. American POPLAR tree, with seeds that are covered in hairs that look like white cotton

couch /kaʊtʃ/ noun, verb
• noun **1** a long comfortable seat for two or more people to sit on ➪ picture at CHAIR **SYN** SETTEE, SOFA **2** a long piece of furniture like a bed, especially in a doctor's office: on the psychiatrist's couch

• verb [usually passive] ~ sth (in sth) (formal) to say or write words in a particular style or manner: The letter was deliberately couched in very vague terms.

cou·chette /kuˈʃɛt/ noun a narrow bed on a train, that folds down from the wall

couch potato noun (informal, disapproving) a person who spends a lot of time sitting and watching television

cougar

cou·gar /ˈkugər/ (also 'mountain ˌlion, pan·ther, pu·ma) noun a large American wild animal of the cat family, with yellow-brown or grayish fur

cough 🔊 /kɔf/ verb, noun
• verb **1** [I] to force out air suddenly and noisily through your throat, for example when you have a cold: I couldn't stop coughing. ◆ to cough nervously/politely/discreetly **2** [T] ~ sth (up) to force something out of your throat or lungs by coughing: Sometimes she coughed (up) blood. **3** [I] (of an engine) to make a sudden unpleasant noise
PHR V cough 'up | ˌcough sth↔'up (informal) to give something, especially money, unwillingly: Steve finally coughed up the money he owed us.

• noun **1** an act or a sound of coughing: She gave a little cough to attract my attention. **2** an illness or infection that makes you cough often: to have a dry/persistent/hacking cough ◆ My cold's better, but I can't seem to shake off this cough. ➪ see also WHOOPING COUGH

coughing /ˈkɔfɪŋ/ noun [U] the action of coughing: Another fit of coughing seized him.

cough syrup (also 'cough medicine) noun [U] liquid medicine that you take for a cough

could 🔊 /kəd; strong form kʊd/ modal verb
(negative could not, short form could·n't /ˈkʊdnt/) **1** used as the past tense of "can": She said that she couldn't come. ◆ I couldn't hear what they were saying. ◆ Sorry, I couldn't get any more. ➪ note at CAN¹ **2** used to ask if you can do something: Could I use your phone, please? ◆ Could we stop by next week? **3** used to politely ask someone to do something for you: Could you babysit for us on Friday? **4** used to show that something is or might be possible: I could do it now, if you like. ◆ Don't worry—they could have just forgotten to call. ◆ You couldn't have left it on the bus, could you? ◆ "Have some more cake." "Oh, I couldn't, thank you (= I'm too full)." **5** used to suggest something: We could write a letter to the director. ◆ You could always try his home number. **6** used to show that you are annoyed that someone did not do something: They could have let me know they were going to be late! **7** (informal) used to emphasize how strongly you want to express your feelings: I'm so fed up I could scream! ➪ note at MODAL
IDM could do with sth (informal) used to say that you need or would like to have something: I could do with a drink! ◆ Her hair could have done with a wash.

cou·lis /kuˈli/ noun (pl. cou·lis) (from French) a thin fruit sauce

cou·lomb /ˈkulɑm; -loʊm/ noun (abbr. C) (physics) a unit for measuring electric charge

coun·cil 🔊 /ˈkaʊnsl/ noun
1 a group of people who are elected to govern an area such as a city or county: a city/town/county/borough/district council ◆ She's on the local council. ◆ a council meeting **2** a group of people chosen to give advice, make rules, do research, provide money, etc.: the Medical Research Council

ʌ cup   ə about   eɪ say   aɪ five   ɔɪ boy   aʊ now   oʊ go   ər bird

⊃ see also STUDENT COUNCIL **3** (*formal*) (especially in the past) a formal meeting to discuss what action to take in a particular situation: *The King held a council at Nottingham in mid-October 1330.*

coun·cil·man /ˈkaʊnslmən/ *noun* (*pl.* **coun·cil·men** /-mən/) a member of an elected council, especially a city council

coun·cil·or (*CanE usually* **coun·cil·lor**) /ˈkaʊnslər; ˈkaʊnsələr/ *noun* a member of a council ⊃ see also COUN-CILMAN, COUNCILWOMAN

coun·cil·wom·an /ˈkaʊnslˌwʊmən/ *noun* (*pl.* **coun·cil·wom·en** /-ˌwɪmɪn/) a woman who is a member of an elected council, especially a city council

coun·sel /ˈkaʊnsl/ *noun, verb*
● *noun* [U, C] **1** (*formal*) advice, especially given by older people or experts; a piece of advice: *Listen to the counsel of your elders.* ♦ *In the end, wiser counsels prevailed.* **2** (*law*) a lawyer or group of lawyers representing someone in court: *to be represented by counsel* ♦ *the* **counsel for the defense/prosecution** ♦ *defense/prosecuting counsel* ♦ *The court then heard counsel for the dead woman's father.* ⊃ collocations at JUSTICE ⊃ note at LAWYER
   IDM **keep your own counsel** (*formal*) to keep your opinions, plans, etc. secret
● *verb* **1** ~ **sb** to listen to and give support or professional advice to someone who needs help: *Therapists were brought in to counsel the bereaved.* **2** (*formal*) to advise someone to do something: ~ **sth** *Most experts counsel caution in such cases.* ♦ ~ **sb to do sth** *He counseled them to give up the plan.*

coun·sel·ing /ˈkaʊnslɪŋ; ˈkaʊnslɪŋ/ *noun* [U] professional advice about a problem: *a student counseling service* ⊃ see also MARRIAGE COUNSELING

coun·se·lor (*CanE usually* **coun·sel·lor**) /ˈkaʊnslər; ˈkaʊnsələr/ *noun* **1** a person who has been trained to advise people with problems, especially personal problems: *a marriage counselor* ⊃ see also GUIDANCE COUNSELOR **2** (*also* ˌcounselor-at-ˈlaw) a lawyer **3** a person who is in charge of young people at a summer camp

count 🔑 /kaʊnt/ *verb, noun*
● *verb*
❯ SAY NUMBERS **1** [I] to say numbers in the correct order: *Billy can't count yet.* ♦ ~ **to/up to sth** *She can count up to 10 in Italian.* ♦ ~ **(from sth) to/up to sth** *to count from 1 to 10*
❯ FIND TOTAL **2** [T, I] to calculate the total number of people, things, etc. in a particular group: ~ **sth (up)** *The diet is based on counting calories.* ♦ ~ **(up) how many…** *She began to count up how many guests they had to invite.* ♦ ~ **from…** *There are 12 weeks to go, counting from today.*
❯ INCLUDE **3** [T] ~ **sb/sth** to include someone or something when you calculate a total: *We have invited 50 people,* **not** *counting the children.*
❯ MATTER **4** [I] (not used in the progressive tenses) to be important **SYN** MATTER: *Every point in this game counts.* ♦ *It's the thought that counts* (= used about a small but kind action or gift). ♦ ~ **for sth** *The fact that she had apologized counted for nothing with him.*
❯ ACCEPT OFFICIALLY **5** [I, T] to be officially accepted; to accept something officially: *Don't go over that line or your throw won't count.* ♦ ~ **sth** *Applications received after July 1 will not be counted.*
❯ CONSIDER **6** [I, T] ~ **sb/sth (as) sb/sth** | ~ **as sb/sth** to consider someone or something in a particular way; to be considered in a particular way: ~ **(sb/sth) as sb/sth** *For tax purposes that money counts/is counted as income.* ♦ ~ **sb/sth/yourself + adv./prep.** *I count him among my closest friends.* ♦ ~ **sb/sth/yourself + adj.** *I count myself lucky to have known him.* ♦ ~ **sb/sth/yourself + noun** *She counts herself one of the lucky ones.*
   IDM **be able to count sb/sth on (the fingers of) one hand** used to say that the total number of someone or something is very small **…and counting** used to say that a total is continuing to increase: *The movie's ticket sales add up to $39 million and counting.* **count your blessings** to be grateful for the good things in your life **don't count your**

chickens (before they are hatched) (*saying*) you should not be too confident that something will be successful, because something may still go wrong **count the cost (of sth)** to feel the bad effects of a mistake, an accident, etc.: *The town is now counting the cost of its failure to provide adequate flood protection.* **count sheep** to imagine that sheep are jumping over a fence and to count them, as a way of getting to sleep **stand up and be counted** to say publicly that you support someone or you agree with something **who's counting?** (*informal*) used to say that you do not care how many times something happens
   PHR V ˌcount aˈgainst sb | ˌcount aˈgainst sb to be considered or to consider something as a disadvantage in someone: *For that job, her lack of experience may count against her.* ˌcount ˈdown (to sth) to think about a future event with pleasure or excitement and count the minutes, days, etc. until it happens: *She's already counting down to the big day.* ⊃ related noun COUNTDOWN ˌcount sb ˈin to include someone in an activity: *I hear you're planning a trip to the game next week. Count me in!* ˈcount on sb/sth to trust someone to do something or to be sure that something will happen **SYN** BANK ON STH: *"I'm sure he'll help." " Don't count on it."* ♦ *We can't count on the weather.* ♦ ~ **to do sth** *I'm counting on you to help me.* ♦ ~ **doing sth** *Few people can count on having a job for life.* ♦ ⊃ thesaurus box at TRUST ˌcount sb/sth↔ˈout to count things one after the other as you put them somewhere: *She counted out $70 in $10 bills.* ˌcount sb ˈout to not include someone in an activity: *If you're going out tonight, you'll have to count me out.* ˌcount toˈward sth to be included as part of something that you hope to achieve in the future: *Students gain college credits which count toward their degree.*

● *noun*
❯ TOTAL **1** [usually sing.] an act of counting to find the total number of something; the total number that you find: *The bus driver did a quick count of the empty seats.* ♦ *If the election result is close, there will be a second count.* ♦ *The body count* (= the total number of people who have died) *stands at 24.* ⊃ see also HEADCOUNT
❯ SAYING NUMBERS **2** [usually sing.] an act of saying numbers in order beginning with 1: *Raise your leg and hold for a count of ten.* ♦ *He was knocked to the ground and stayed down for a count of eight* (= in boxing).
❯ MEASUREMENT **3** [usually sing.] (*technical*) a measurement of the amount of something contained in a particular substance or area: *a raised white blood cell count* ⊃ see also BLOOD COUNT, POLLEN COUNT
❯ CRIME **4** (*law*) a crime that someone is accused of committing: *They were found guilty on all counts.* ♦ *She appeared in court on three counts of fraud.*
❯ IN DISCUSSION/ARGUMENT **5** [usually pl.] a point made during a discussion or an argument: *I disagree with you on both counts.*
❯ RANK/TITLE **6** (in some European countries) a NOBLEMAN of high rank, similar to an EARL in Britain: *Count Tolstoy* ⊃ see also COUNTESS
   IDM **at the last count** according to the latest information about the numbers of something: *She'd applied for 30 jobs at the last count.* **down for the count 1** (of a BOXER) unable to get up again within ten seconds after being knocked down **2** in a deep sleep **keep (a) count (of sth)** to remember or keep a record of numbers or amounts of something over a period of time: *Keep a count of your calorie intake for one week.* **lose count (of sth)** to forget the total of something before you have finished counting it: *I lost count and had to start again.* ♦ *She had lost count of the number of times she'd told him to be careful* (= she could not remember because there were so many).

count·a·ble /ˈkaʊntəbl/ *adj.* (*grammar*) a noun that is **countable** can be used in the plural or with *a* or *an*, for example *table*, *cat*, and *idea* **ANT** UNCOUNTABLE

count·down /ˈkaʊntdaʊn/ *noun* ~ **(to sth) 1** [sing., U] the action of counting seconds backward to zero, for example before a SPACECRAFT is launched **2** [sing.] the period of time just before something important happens: *the count-down to the wedding*

coun·te·nance /ˈkaʊntənəns/ *noun, verb*
- *noun* (*formal* or *literary*) a person's face or their expression
- *verb* ~ **sth** | ~ (**sb**) **doing sth** (*formal*) to support something or agree to something happening **SYN CONSENT TO**: *The committee refused to countenance his proposals.*

coun·ter 🔑 /ˈkaʊntər/ *noun, verb, adv.*
- *noun* **1** a long flat surface over which goods are sold or business is done in a store, bank, etc.: *I asked the woman behind the counter if they had any postcards.* **2** (also **coun·ter·top**) a flat surface in a kitchen for preparing food on **3** a small disk used for playing or scoring in some board games **4** (especially in compounds) an electronic device for counting something: *The needle on the rev counter soared.* ➔ see also **GEIGER COUNTER** ➔ compare **BEAN COUNTER 5** [usually sing.] ~ (**to sb/sth**) (*formal*) a response to someone or something that opposes their ideas, position, etc.: *The employers' association was seen as a counter to union power.*
- **IDM over the counter** goods, especially medicines, for sale **over the counter** can be bought without a **PRESCRIPTION** (= written permission from a doctor to buy a medicine) or special license: *These tablets are available over the counter.* ➔ see also **OVER-THE-COUNTER under the counter** goods that are bought or sold **under the counter** are sold secretly and sometimes illegally
- *verb* **1** [T, I] ~ (**sb/sth**) (**with sth**) to reply to someone by trying to prove that what they said is not true: ~ **sb/sth** *Such arguments are not easily countered.* ◆ ~ **that...** *I tried to argue but he countered that the plans were not yet finished.* ◆ ~ (**sb**) + speech *"But I was standing right here!" he countered.* ◆ ~ **with sth** *Butler had countered with a lawsuit against the firm.* **2** [T] ~ **sth** to do something to reduce or prevent the bad effects of something **SYN COUNTERACT**: *Businesses would like to see new laws to counter late payments of debts.*
- *adv.* ~ **to sth** in the opposite direction to something; in opposition to something: *The government's plans run counter to agreed European policy on this issue.*

counter- /ˈkaʊntər/ *combining form* (in nouns, verbs, adjectives, and adverbs) **1** against; opposite: *counterterrorism* ◆ *counterargument* **2 CORRESPONDING**: *counterpart*

coun·ter·act /ˌkaʊntəˈrækt/ *verb* ~ **sth** to do something to reduce or prevent the bad or harmful effects of something **SYN COUNTER**: *These exercises aim to counteract the effects of stress and tension.*

coun·ter·at·tack /ˈkaʊntərəˌtæk/ *noun, verb*
- *noun* an attack made in response to the attack of an enemy or opponent in war, sports, or an argument
- *verb* [I, T] ~ (**sb**) to make an attack in response to the attack of an enemy or opponent in war, sports, or an argument **SYN RETALIATE**

coun·ter·bal·ance *verb, noun*
- *verb* /ˌkaʊntərˈbæləns; ˈkaʊntərˌbæləns/ ~ **sth** (*formal*) to have an equal but opposite effect to something else **SYN OFFSET**: *Parents' natural desire to protect their children should be counterbalanced by the child's need for independence.*
- *noun* /ˈkaʊntərˌbæləns/ (also **counterweight**) [usually sing.] ~ (**to sth**) a thing that has an equal but opposite effect to something else and can be used to limit the bad effects of something: *The accused's right to silence was a vital counterbalance to the powers of the police.*

coun·ter·blast /ˈkaʊntərˌblæst/ *noun* ~ (**to sth**) a very strong spoken or written reply to something that has been said or written

coun·ter·claim /ˈkaʊntərˌkleɪm/ *noun* a claim made in reply to another claim and different from it

coun·ter·clock·wise /ˌkaʊntərˈklɑkwaɪz/ *adv., adj.* in the opposite direction to the movement of the hands of a clock: *Turn the key counterclockwise/in a counterclockwise direction.* **ANT CLOCKWISE**

coun·ter·cul·ture /ˈkaʊntərˌkʌltʃər/ *noun* [C, U] a way of life and set of ideas that are opposed to those accepted by most of society; a group of people who share such a way of life and such ideas

counter-ˈespionage *noun* [U] secret action taken by a country to prevent an enemy country from finding out its secrets

coun·ter·fac·tu·al /ˌkaʊntərˈfæktʃuəl/ *adj.* (*formal*) connected with what did not happen or what is not the case: *counterfactual questions such as "What if the President had not been assassinated?"* ◆ *an interesting exercise in counterfactual history* ▶ **coun·ter·fac·tu·al** *noun*: *"What if" questions involving counterfactuals are familiar in historical speculations.*

coun·ter·feit /ˈkaʊntərˌfɪt/ *adj., verb*
- *adj.* (of money and goods for sale) made to look exactly like something in order to trick people into thinking that they are getting the real thing **SYN FAKE**: *counterfeit watches* ◆ *Are you aware these notes are counterfeit?* **ANT GENUINE** ▶ **coun·ter·feit** *noun* ➔ compare **FORGERY**
- *verb* ~ **sth** to make an exact copy of something in order to trick people into thinking that it is the real thing ➔ compare **FORGE** ▶ **coun·ter·feit·ing** *noun* [U]

coun·ter·feit·er /ˈkaʊntərˌfɪtər/ *noun* a person who counterfeits money or goods ➔ compare **FORGER**

coun·ter·in·sur·gen·cy /ˌkaʊntərɪnˈsɜrdʒənsi/ *noun* [U, C] action taken against a group of people who are trying to take control of a country by force

coun·ter·in·tel·li·gence /ˌkaʊntərɪnˈtɛlədʒəns/ *noun* [U] secret action taken by a country to prevent an enemy country from finding out its secrets, for example by giving them false information; the department of a government, etc. that is responsible for this

coun·ter·in·tu·i·tive /ˌkaʊntərɪnˈtuətɪv/ *adj.* the opposite of what you would expect or what seems to be obvious: *These results seem counterintuitive.* ▶ **coun·ter·in·tu·i·tive·ly** *adv.*

coun·ter·mand /ˈkaʊntərˌmænd; ˌkaʊntərˈmænd/ *verb* ~ **sth** (*formal*) to cancel an order that has been given, especially by giving a different order

coun·ter·meas·ure /ˈkaʊntərˌmɛʒər/ *noun* a course of action taken to protect against something that is considered bad or dangerous

coun·ter·of·fen·sive /ˈkaʊntərəˌfɛnsɪv/ *noun* an attack made in order to defend against enemy attacks

coun·ter·part /ˈkaʊntərˌpɑrt/ *noun* a person or thing that has the same position or function as someone or something else in a different place or situation **SYN OPPOSITE NUMBER**: *The Secretary of State held talks with her Chinese counterpart.* ◆ *The women's shoe, like its male counterpart, is specifically designed for the serious tennis player.*

coun·ter·point /ˈkaʊntərˌpɔɪnt/ *noun, verb*
- *noun* **1** [U] (*music*) the combination of two or more tunes played together to form a single piece of music **SYN POLYPHONY**: *The two melodies are played in counterpoint.* ➔ see also **CONTRAPUNTAL 2** [C] ~ (**to sth**) (*music*) a tune played in combination with another one **3** [U, C] (*formal*) a pleasing or interesting contrast: *This work is in austere counterpoint to that of Gaudi.*
- *verb* ~ **sth** (**with/against sth**) (*formal*) to contrast something with something else; to form a contrast with something

coun·ter·pro·duc·tive /ˌkaʊntərprəˈdʌktɪv/ *adj.* [not usually before noun] having the opposite effect to the one that was intended ➔ compare **PRODUCTIVE**

coun·ter·rev·o·lu·tion /ˌkaʊntərˌrɛvəˈluʃn/ /ˌkaʊntərˌrɛvəˈluʃəˌneri/ *noun* [C, U] opposition to or violent action against a government that came to power as a result of a revolution, in order to destroy and replace it

coun·ter·rev·o·lu·tion·ar·y *noun* a person involved in a counterrevolution ▶ **coun·ter·rev·o·lu·tion·ar·y** *adj.*

t **tea** ţ **butter** d **did** k **cat** g **got** tʃ **chin** dʒ **June** f **fall**

coun·ter·sign /ˈkaʊntərˌsaɪn/ verb ~ sth (technical) to sign a document that has already been signed by another person, especially in order to show that it is valid

ˌcounter-ˈtenor noun a man who is trained to sing with a very high voice; a male ALTO ➔ compare ALTO

coun·ter·ter·ror·ism /ˌkaʊntərˈterəˌrɪzəm/ noun [U] action taken to prevent the activities of political groups who use violence to try to achieve their aims ▶ **coun·ter·ter·ror·ist** adj.

coun·ter·top /ˈkaʊntərˌtɑp/ noun = COUNTER

coun·ter·vail·ing /ˈkaʊntərˌveɪlɪŋ; ˌkaʊntərˈveɪlɪŋ/ adj. [only before noun] (formal) having an equal but opposite effect

coun·ter·weight /ˈkaʊntərˌweɪt/ noun [usually sing.] = COUNTERBALANCE

count·ess /ˈkaʊntəs/ noun **1** a woman who has the rank of a COUNT or an EARL **2** the wife of a COUNT or an EARL: the Earl and Countess of Rosebery

count·less /ˈkaʊntləs/ adj. [usually before noun] very many; too many to be counted or mentioned: I've warned her countless times. ◆ The new treatment could save Emma's life and the lives of countless others. ➔ compare UNCOUNTABLE

ˈcount noun noun (grammar) a countable noun

coun·tri·fied /ˈkʌntriˌfaɪd/ adj. (often disapproving) like the countryside or the people who live there

---

THESAURUS

country

landscape ◆ countryside ◆ terrain ◆ land ◆ scenery

These are all words for areas away from towns and cities, with fields, woods, and farms.

country (often the country) an area that is away from towns and cities, especially one with particular natural, social, or economic features: She lives in the country. ◆ Texas is cattle country.

landscape everything that you can see when you look across a large area of land, especially in the country: Iowa's landscape is mostly flat and grassy.

countryside land outside towns and cities, with fields, woods, and farms. **NOTE** Countryside is usually used when you are talking about the beauty or peacefulness of a country area: a little town in the Vermont countryside

terrain (formal) land **NOTE** Terrain is used when you are describing the natural features of an area, for example if it is rough, flat, etc: The truck bumped its way over the rough terrain.

land (usually the land) an area for farming: He has worked the land for twenty years. ◆ My parents grow all their own food and live off the land.

scenery the natural features of an area, such as mountains, valleys, rivers, and forests, especially when these are attractive to look at: We stopped on the mountain pass to admire the scenery.

PATTERNS

■ **mountainous/wild/rugged** country/landscape/ countryside/terrain/scenery
■ **beautiful/glorious/dramatic** country/landscape/ countryside/scenery
■ **open** country/landscape/countryside/terrain/land
■ **rolling** landscape/countryside
■ to **protect** the landscape/countryside/land

---

coun·try 🔊 /ˈkʌntri/ noun (pl. coun·tries)

1 [C] an area of land that has or used to have its own government and laws: European countries ◆ leading industrial countries ◆ She didn't know what life in a **foreign country** would be like. ◆ It's good to meet people from **different parts of the country. 2** [U] (often following an adjective) an area of land, especially with particular physical features, suitable for a particular purpose or connected with a particular person or

people: open/wooded, etc. country ◆ superb **walking country** ◆ Explore Eudora Welty country. ➔ see also BACKCOUNTRY **3 the country** [sing.] the people of a country; the nation as a whole: They have the support of most of the country. ◆ The rich benefited from the reforms, not the country as a whole. ➔ see also MOTHER COUNTRY, THE OLD COUNTRY, UPCOUNTRY **4 the country** [sing.] any area outside towns and cities, with fields, woods, farms, etc.: to live **in the country** ◆ We spent a pleasant day in the country. ◆ a country lane ➔ collocations at TOWN **5** [U] = COUNTRY MUSIC: pop, folk and country

IDM across country directly across fields, etc.; not by a main road: riding across country ➔ see also CROSS-COUNTRY ➔ more at FREE

WHICH WORD?

country ◆ state

■ **Country** is the most usual, neutral word for a geographical area that has or used to have its own central government.
■ **State** usually refers to one of the 50 states of the U.S.: the state of Alabama
■ **State** can also emphasize the political organization of an area under an independent government. It can also mean the government: the member states of the EU ◆ The state provides free education. ◆ heads of state (= leaders of various nations)

ˌcountry and ˈwestern (abbr. C & W) noun [U] = COUNTRY MUSIC: a country and western singer

ˌcountry ˈbumpkin (also bump·kin) noun (disapproving) a person from the countryside who seems stupid

ˈcountry club noun a club in the country, or on the edge of a town, where people can play sports and go to social events

ˌcountry ˈcousin noun a person from the country who does not know much about life in the city, and who dresses or behaves in a way that shows this

coun·try·man /ˈkʌntrimən/ noun (pl. coun·try·men /-mən/) a person born in or living in the same country as someone else **SYN** COMPATRIOT: The champion looks set to play his fellow countryman in the final.

ˌcountry ˈmusic (also ˈcoun·try, ˌcountry and ˈwestern) noun [U] a type of music in the style of the traditional music of the southern and western U.S.

coun·try·side 🔊 /ˈkʌntriˌsaɪd/ noun [U] land outside towns and cities, with fields, woods, etc.: The surrounding countryside is windswept and rocky. ◆ magnificent views over open countryside ◆ Everyone should enjoy the right of access to the countryside. ➔ collocations at TOWN ➔ thesaurus box at COUNTRY

coun·try·wide /ˌkʌntriˈwaɪd/ adj. over the whole of a country **SYN** NATIONWIDE: a countrywide mail-order service ▶ **coun·try·wide** adv.: The movie will be released in New York in March and countrywide in May.

coun·try·wom·an /ˈkʌntriˌwʊmən/ noun (pl. coun·try·wom·en /-ˌwɪmən/) **1** a woman living or born in the country, not in a city or town **2** a woman born or living in the same country as someone else

coun·ty 🔊 /ˈkaʊnti/ noun (pl. coun·ties; abbr. Co.) an area of a state or country that has its own government: county boundaries ◆ Orange County ◆ rural/urban counties

ˌcounty ˈclerk noun an elected county official who is responsible for elections and who keeps records of who owns buildings in the county, etc.

ˌcounty ˈseat noun the main town of a county, where its government is

coun·ty·wide /ˌkaʊntiˈwaɪd/ adj. over the whole of a county ▶ **coun·ty·wide** adv.

---

coup /kuː/ noun (pl. **coups** /kuːz/) **1** (also **coup d'état**) a sudden, illegal, and often violent change of government: *He seized power in a military coup in 2008.* ◆ *to stage/mount a coup* ◆ *an attempted coup* ◆ *a failed/an abortive coup* ◆ *She lost her position in a boardroom coup* (= a sudden change of power among senior managers in a company). **2** the fact of achieving something that was difficult to do: *Getting this contract has been quite a coup for us.*

coup de grâce /ˌkuː də ˈɡrɑːs/ noun [sing.] (from French, formal) **1** an action or event that finally ends something that has been getting weaker or worse: *My disastrous exam results dealt the coup de grâce to my college career.* **2** a hit or shot that finally kills a person or an animal, especially to put an end to their suffering **SYN** DEATH BLOW

coup d'é·tat /ˌkuː deɪˈtɑː/ noun (pl. **coups d'état** /ˌkuː deɪˈtɑː/ or **coup d'états**) = COUP

coup de thé·â·tre /ˌkuː də teɪˈɑːtrə; -teɪˈɑːt/ noun (pl. **coups de théâtre** /ˌkuː də teɪˈɑːtrə; -teɪˈɑːt/) (from French) **1** something very dramatic and surprising that happens, especially in a play **2** a play, show, etc. that is very successful

coupe /kuːp/ (also **coup·é** /ˈkuːpeɪ; kuːp/) noun a car with two doors and usually a sloping back

cou·ple 🔑 ■AWL /ˈkʌpl/ noun, verb

● **noun 1** [sing.] ~ **(of sth)** two people or things: *I saw a couple of men get out.* **2** [sing.] ~ **(of sth)** a small number of people or things **SYN** A FEW: *a couple of minutes* ◆ *We went there a couple of years ago.* ◆ *I've seen her a couple of times before.* ◆ *I'll be with you in a minute. There are a couple of things I have to do first.* ◆ *There are a couple more files to read first.* ◆ *We can do it in the **next couple of** weeks.* ◆ *The **last couple of** years have been difficult.* **3** [C] two people who are seen together, especially if they are married or in a romantic or sexual relationship: *married couples* ◆ *a young/an elderly couple* ◆ *Several couples were on the dance floor.* ◆ *The couple were/was married in 2006.* ⊃ collocations at MARRIAGE **IDM** see SHAKE *n.* ▶ **a couple** *pron.*: *Do you need any more glasses? I've got a couple I can lend you.* **couple** *det.*: *It's only a couple blocks away.*

● **verb 1** [T, usually passive] to join together two parts of something, for example two vehicles or pieces of equipment: ~ **A and B together** *The two train cars had been coupled together.* ◆ ~ **A (to B)** *CDTV uses a CD-ROM system that is coupled to a powerful computer.* **2** [I] (formal) (of two people or animals) to have sex **PHR V** **'couple sb/sth with sb/sth** [usually passive] to link one thing, situation, etc. to another **SYN** COMBINE WITH: *Overproduction, coupled with falling sales, has led to huge losses for the company.*

cou·plet /ˈkʌplət/ noun two lines of poetry of equal length, one after the other: *a poem written in rhyming couplets* ⊃ see also HEROIC COUPLET

cou·pling ■AWL /ˈkʌplɪŋ/ noun **1** [usually sing.] an action of joining or combining two things: *a coupling of Mozart's Prague Symphony and Schubert's Unfinished Symphony* (= for example, on the same CD) **2** (formal) an act of having sex: *illicit couplings* **3** (technical) a thing that joins together two parts of something, two vehicles, or two pieces of equipment

cou·pon /ˈkuːpɑːn; ˈkjuː-/ noun **1** a small piece of printed paper that you can exchange for something or that gives you the right to buy something at a cheaper price than normal: *cents-off coupons* ◆ *clothing coupons* **2** a printed form, often cut out from a newspaper, that is used to enter a competition, order goods, etc.: *Fill in and return the attached coupon.*

cour·age 🔑 /ˈkɜːrɪdʒ/ noun [U]

the ability to do something dangerous, or to face pain or opposition, without showing fear **SYN** BRAVERY: *He showed great courage and determination.* ◆ *I haven't yet had the courage to ask her.* ◆ *moral/physical courage* ◆ *courage in the face of danger* **IDM** **have/lack the courage of your convictions** to be/

not be brave enough to do what you feel to be right **take courage (from sth)** to begin to feel happier and more confident because of something ⊃ more at SCREW

cou·ra·geous /kəˈreɪdʒəs/ adj. showing courage **SYN** BRAVE: *a very courageous decision* ◆ *I hope people will be courageous enough to speak out against this injustice.* ▶ **cou·ra·geous·ly** adv.

cour·i·er /ˈkʊriər; ˈkʊr-/ noun a person or company whose job is to take packages or important papers somewhere: *We sent the documents by courier.* ▶ **cour·i·er** verb: ~ **sth** *Courier that letter—it needs to get there today* (= send it by courier).

course 🔑 /kɔːrs/ noun, verb

● **noun**
> **EDUCATION 1** [C] ~ **(in/on sth)** a series of lessons or lectures on a particular subject: *a French/chemistry, etc. course* ◆ *to take a course in art and design* ◆ *The college runs specialist language courses.* ⊃ collocations at EDUCATION ⊃ see also CORRESPONDENCE COURSE, REFRESHER COURSE
> **DIRECTION 2** [U, C, usually sing.] a direction or route followed by a ship or an aircraft: *The plane was on/off course* (= going/ not going in the right direction). ◆ *He radioed the pilot to change course.* ◆ *They set a course for the islands.* **3** [C, usually sing.] the general direction in which someone's ideas or actions are moving: *The president appears likely to change course on some key issues.* ◆ *Politicians are often obliged to steer a course between incompatible interests.*
> **ACTION 4** (also **course of 'action**) [C] a way of acting in or dealing with a particular situation: *There are various courses open to us.* ◆ *What course of action would you recommend?* ◆ *The wisest course would be to say nothing.*
> **DEVELOPMENT 5** [sing.] ~ **of sth** the way something develops or should develop: *an event that changed the course of history* ◆ *The unexpected course of events aroused considerable alarm.*
> **PART OF MEAL 6** [C] any of the separate parts of a meal: *a four-course dinner* ◆ *The main course was roast duck.* ⊃ collocations at RESTAURANT
> **FOR GOLF 7** [C] = GOLF COURSE: *He set a new course record.*
> **FOR RACES 8** [C] an area of land or water where races are held: *She was overtaken on the last stretch of the course.* ⊃ see also OBSTACLE COURSE, RACECOURSE
> **OF RIVER 9** [C, usually sing.] the direction a river moves in: *The path follows the course of the river.*
> **MEDICAL TREATMENT 10** [C] ~ **(of sth)** a series of medical treatments, pills, etc.: *to prescribe a course of antibiotics* **IDM** **in course of sth** (formal) going through a particular process: *The new textbook is in course of preparation.* **in/over the course of...** (used with expressions for periods of time) during: *He's seen many changes in the course of his long life.* ◆ *The company faces major challenges over the course of the next few years.* **in the course of time** when enough time has passed **SYN** EVENTUALLY: *It is possible that in the course of time a cure for cancer will be found.* **in the ordinary, normal, etc. course of events, things, etc.** as things usually happen **SYN** NORMALLY: *In the normal course of things we would not treat her disappearance as suspicious.* **of course 1** (also informal **course**) used to emphasize that what you are saying is true or correct: *"Don't you like my mother?" "Of course I do!"* ◆ *"Will you be there?" "Course I will."* **2** (also informal **course**) used as a polite way of giving someone permission to do something: *"Can I come, too?" "Course you can."* ◆ *"Can I have one of those pens?" "Of course—help yourself."* **3** (informal) used as a polite way of agreeing with what someone has just said: *"I did all I could to help." "Of course," he murmured gently.* **4** used to show that what you are saying is not surprising or is generally known or accepted: *Ben, of course, was the last to arrive.* ◆ *Of course, there are other ways of doing this.* ⊃ language bank at NEVERTHELESS **of course not** (also informal **'course not**) used to emphasize the fact that you are saying "no": *"Are you going?" "Of course not."* ◆ *"Do you mind?" "No, of course not."* **on course for sth/to do sth** likely to achieve or do something because you have already started to do it: *The American economy is on course for higher inflation than Britain*

by the end of the year. **run/take its course** to develop in the usual way and come to the usual end: *When her tears had run their course, she felt calmer and more in control.* ◆ *With minor ailments, the best thing is often to let nature take its course.* ⊃ more at COLLISION, DUE *adj.*, MATTER *n.*, MIDDLE *adj.*, PAR, STAY *v.*

● *verb* [I] + adv./prep. (*literary*) (of liquid) to move or flow quickly

---

MORE ABOUT

of course

- **Of course** is often used to show that what you are saying is not surprising or is generally known or accepted. For this reason, and because it can be difficult to get the right intonation, you may not sound polite if you use **of course** or **of course not** when you answer a request for information or permission. It can be safer to use a different word or phrase.
- "*Is this the right room for the English class?*" "*Yes, it is.*" ◆ "*Of course.*" or "*Of course it is.*"
- "*Can I borrow your dictionary?*" "*Certainly.*" (*formal*) ◆ "*Sure.*" (*informal*)
- "*Do you mind if I borrow your dictionary?*" "*Not at all.*" ◆ "*Go ahead.*" (*informal*).
- If you say **of course/of course not**, it may sound as though you think the answer to the question is obvious and that the person should not have asked. In the same way, **of course** should not be used as a reply to a statement of fact or when someone expresses an opinion: "*It's a lovely day.*" "*It certainly is.*" ◆ "*Of course it is.*" ◆ "*I think you'll enjoy that play.*" "*I'm sure I will.*"/"*Yes, it sounds really good.*" ◆ "*Of course.*"

---

course of 'action *noun* (*pl.* **courses of 'action**) = COURSE

course·ware /'kɔrswer/ *noun* [U] (*computing*) computer programs that are designed to be used to teach a subject

course·work /'kɔrswərk/ *noun* [U] work that students do during a course of study, not in exams, that is included in their final grade: *Coursework accounts for 40% of the final grades.*

cours·ing /'kɔrsɪŋ/ *noun* [U] the sport of hunting animals with dogs, using sight rather than smell

court 🔑 /kɔrt/ *noun, verb*
● *noun*
▷ LAW **1** [C, U] the place where legal trials take place and where crimes, etc. are judged: *the civil/criminal courts* ◆ *Her lawyer made a statement outside the court.* ◆ *She will appear in court tomorrow.* ◆ *They took their landlord to court for breaking the contract.* ◆ *The case took five years to come to court* (= to be heard by the court). ◆ *There wasn't enough evidence to bring the case to court* (= start a trial). ◆ *He won the court case and was awarded damages.* ◆ *She can't pay her tax and is facing court action.* ◆ *The case was settled out of court* (= a decision was reached without a trial). ⊃ collocations at JUSTICE ⊃ see also CIRCUIT COURT, COURTHOUSE, COURTROOM, FAMILY COURT ⊃ note at SCHOOL **2 the court** [sing.] the people in a court, especially those who make the decisions, such as the judge and jury: *Please tell the court what happened.* ⊃ see also CONTEMPT OF COURT, COUNTY COURT, HIGH COURT, FAMILY COURT, JUVENILE COURT, SUPREME COURT
▷ FOR SPORTS **3** [C] a place where games such as TENNIS are played: *a tennis/squash/badminton court* ◆ *He won after only 52 minutes on court.* ⊃ picture at SPORT ⊃ see also CLAY COURT, GRASS COURT
▷ BUILDINGS **4** [C] = COURTYARD **5** (*abbr.* Ct.) [C] used in the names of apartment buildings or of some short streets **6** [C] a large open section of a building, often with a glass roof: *the food court at the shopping mall*
▷ KINGS/QUEENS **7** [C, U] the official place where kings and queens live: *the court of Queen Victoria* **8 the court** [sing.] the king or queen, their family, and the people who work for them and/or give advice to them

---

IDM **hold court (with sb)** to entertain people by telling them interesting or funny things **throw sth out of court** to say that something is completely wrong or not worth considering, especially in a trial: *The charges were thrown out of court.* ⊃ more at BALL, LAUGH, PAY

● *verb*
▷ TRY TO PLEASE **1** [T] ~ **sb** to try to please someone in order to get something you want, especially the support of a person, an organization, etc. **SYN** CULTIVATE: *Both candidates have spent the last month courting the media.*
▷ TRY TO GET **2** [T] ~ **sth** (*formal*) to try to obtain something: *He has never courted popularity.*
▷ INVITE SOMETHING BAD **3** [T] ~ **sth** (*formal*) to do something that might result in something unpleasant happening: *to court danger/death/disaster* ◆ *As a politician he has often courted controversy.*
▷ HAVE RELATIONSHIP **4** [T] ~ **sb** (*old-fashioned*) if a man **courts** a woman, he spends time with her and tries to make her love him, so that they can get married **5 be courting** [I] (*old-fashioned*) (of a man and a woman) to have a romantic relationship before getting married: *At that time they had been courting for several years.* ⊃ see also COURTSHIP

WHICH WORD?

court ◆ court of law ◆ courthouse

- All these words can be used to refer to a place where legal trials take place. **Court** and (*formal*) **court of law** usually refer to the actual room where cases are judged. **Courtroom** is also used for this. **Courthouse** is more often used to refer to the building: *The prison is across the street from the courthouse.*

'court costs *noun* [pl.] = COST *n.* (4)

cour·te·ous /'kɜrtiəs/ *adj.* polite, especially in a way that shows respect: *a courteous young man* ◆ *The hotel staff are friendly and courteous.* **ANT** DISCOURTEOUS
▶ **cour·te·ous·ly** *adv.*

cour·te·san /'kɔrtəzn; -ˌzæn/ *noun* (in the past) a PROSTITUTE, especially one with rich customers

cour·te·sy /'kɜrtəsi/ *noun, adj.*
● *noun* (*pl.* **cour·te·sies**) **1** [U] polite behavior that shows respect for other people **SYN** : *I was treated with the utmost courtesy by the staff.* ◆ *It's only common courtesy to tell the neighbors that we'll be having a party* (= the kind of behavior that people would expect). **2** [C, usually pl.] (*formal*) a polite thing that you say or do when you meet people in formal situations: *an exchange of courtesies before the meeting*
IDM **courtesy of sb/sth 1** (also **by courtesy of sb/sth**) with the official permission of someone or something and as a favor: *The pictures have been reproduced by courtesy of the National Gallery of Art.* **2** given as a prize or provided free by a person or an organization: *Win a trip to New York, courtesy of Coast Airways.* **3** as the result of a particular thing or situation: *Viewers can see the stadium from the air, courtesy of a camera fastened to the plane.* **do sb the courtesy of doing sth** to be polite by doing the thing that is mentioned: *Please do me the courtesy of listening to what I'm saying.* **have the courtesy to do sth** to know when you should do something in order to be polite: *You think he'd at least have the courtesy to call to say he'd be late.*
● *adj.* [only before noun] (of a bus, car, etc.) provided free, at no cost to the person using it: *A courtesy bus operates between the hotel and the city center.* ◆ *The dealer will provide you with a courtesy car while your vehicle is being repaired.*

'courtesy call *noun* **1** (also **'courtesy visit**) a formal or official visit, usually by one important person to another, just to be polite, not to discuss important business **2** a telephone call from a company to one of its customers, for example to see if they are satisfied with the company's service

'courtesy light *noun* a small light inside a car which is automatically turned on when someone opens the door

---

courtesy ˌtitle *noun* a title that someone is allowed to use but which has no legal status

court·house /ˈkɔːrthaʊs/ *noun* **1** a building containing courts of law ⊃ note at COURT **2** a building containing the offices of a county government

cour·ti·er /ˈkɔːrtiər/ *noun* (especially in the past) a person who is part of the COURT of a king or queen

court·ly /ˈkɔːrtli/ *adj.* (*formal* or *literary*) extremely polite and full of respect, especially in an old-fashioned way

ˌcourtly ˈlove *noun* [U] a tradition in literature, especially in medieval times, involving the faithful love of a KNIGHT for his married LADY, with whom he can never have a relationship

ˈcourt ˌmartial *noun* [C, U] (*pl.* courts martial) a military court that deals with members of the armed forces who break military law; a trial at such a court: *He was convicted at a court martial.* ♦ *All the men now face court martial.*

ˈcourt-ˌmartial *verb* [often passive] ~ sb to hold a trial of someone in a military court: *He was court-martialed for desertion.*

ˌcourt of apˈpeals (also apˈpeals court) *noun* one of the courts in the U.S. that can change decisions made by a lower court ⊃ see also APPELLATE COURT

ˌcourt of ˈlaw *noun* (*pl.* courts of law) (also ˈlaw court) a room or building where legal cases are judged ⊃ note at COURT

ˌcourt ˈorder *noun* a decision that is made in court about what must happen in a particular situation

court·room /ˈkɔːrtrum; -rʊm/ *noun* a room in which trials or other legal cases are held ⊃ note at COURT

court·ship /ˈkɔːrtʃɪp/ *noun* **1** [C, U] (*old-fashioned*) the time when two people have a romantic relationship before they get married; the process of developing this relationship: *They married after a short courtship.* ♦ *Mr. Elton's courtship of Harriet* **2** [U] the special way animals behave in order to attract a mate for producing young animals: *courtship displays* **3** ~ (of sb/sth) (*formal*) the process or act of attracting a business partner, etc.: *the company's courtship by the government*

court·yard /ˈkɔːrtyɑːrd/ (also court) *noun* an open space that is partly or completely surrounded by buildings and is usually part of a castle, a large house, etc.: *the central/inner courtyard*

cous·cous /ˈkuskus/ *noun* [U] a type of N. African food made from crushed WHEAT; a dish of meat and/or vegetables with couscous

cous·in 🔑 /ˈkʌzn/ *noun*
1 (also ˌfirst ˈcousin) a child of your aunt or uncle: *She's my cousin.* ♦ *We're cousins.* ⊃ see also SECOND COUSIN **2** a person who is in your wider family but who is not closely related to you: *He's a distant cousin of mine.* **3** [usually pl.] a way of describing people from another country who are similar in some way to people in your own country: *our British cousins* **4** [usually pl.] a way of describing things that are similar or related in some way: *Asian elephants are smaller than their African cousins.* ⊃ see also COUNTRY COUSIN, KISSING COUSIN

cou·ture /kuˈtʊr/ *noun* [U] (from *French*) the design and production of expensive and fashionable clothes; these clothes: *a couture evening dress* ⊃ see also HAUTE COUTURE

cou·tu·ri·er /kuˈtʊriˌeɪ; -ˈtʊriər/ *noun* (from *French*) a person who designs, makes and sells expensive, fashionable clothes, especially for women SYN FASHION DESIGNER

co·va·lent /ˌkoʊˈveɪlənt/ *adj.* (*chemistry*) (of a chemical BOND) sharing a pair of ELECTRONS ⊃ compare IONIC

cove /koʊv/ *noun* a small bay: *a secluded cove*

cov·en /ˈkʌvn/ *noun* a group or meeting of WITCHES

cov·e·nant /ˈkʌvənənt/ *noun* a promise to someone, or a legal agreement, especially one to pay a regular amount of money to someone or something: *God's covenant with Abraham* ▶ **cov·e·nant** *verb* ~ sth

cov·er 🔑 /ˈkʌvər/ *verb, noun*
● *verb*
▷ HIDE/PROTECT **1** [T] ~ sth (with sth) to place something over or in front of something in order to hide or protect it: *Cover the chicken loosely with foil.* ♦ *She covered her face with her hands.* ♦ (*figurative*) *He laughed to cover* (= hide) *his nervousness.* ⊃ thesaurus box at HIDE
▷ SPREAD OVER SURFACE **2** [T] ~ sth to lie or spread over the surface of something: *Snow covered the ground.* ♦ *Much of the country is covered by forest.* **3** [T] to put or spread a layer of liquid, dust, etc. on someone or something: ~ sb/sth in sth *The players were soon covered in mud.* ♦ ~ sb/sth with sth *The wind blew in from the desert and covered everything with sand.*
▷ INCLUDE **4** [T] ~ sth to include something; to deal with something: *The survey covers all aspects of the business.* ♦ *The lectures covered a lot of ground* (= a lot of material, subjects, etc.). ♦ *the sales team covering the northern part of the country* (= selling to people in that area) ♦ *Do the rules cover* (= do they apply to) *a case like this?*
▷ MONEY **5** [T] ~ sth to be or provide enough money for something: *$100 should cover your expenses.* ♦ *Your parents will have to cover your tuition fees.* ♦ *The show barely covered its costs.*
▷ DISTANCE/AREA **6** [T] ~ sth to travel the distance mentioned: *By sunset we had covered thirty miles.* ♦ *They walked for a long time and covered a good deal of ground.* **7** [T] ~ sth to spread over the area mentioned: *The reserve covers an area of some 1,140 square miles.*
▷ REPORT NEWS **8** [T] ~ sth to report on an event for television, a newspaper, etc.; to show an event on television: *She's covering the party's annual conference.* ♦ *The station will cover all the major games of the tournament.*
▷ FOR SOMEONE **9** [I] ~ for sb to do someone's work or duties while they are away: *I'm covering for Jane while she's on leave.* **10** [I] ~ for sb to invent a lie or an excuse that will stop someone from getting into trouble: *I have to go out for a minute—will you cover for me if anyone asks where I am?*
▷ WITH INSURANCE **11** [T] to protect someone against loss, injury, etc. by insurance: ~ sb/sth (against/for sth) *Are you fully covered for fire and theft?* ♦ ~ sb/sth to do sth *Does this policy cover my husband to drive?*
▷ AGAINST BLAME **12** [T] ~ yourself (against sth) to take action in order to protect yourself against being blamed for something: *One reason doctors take temperatures is to cover themselves against negligence claims.*
▷ WITH GUN **13** [T] ~ sb to protect someone by threatening to shoot at anyone who tries to attack them: *Cover me while I move forward.* **14** [T] ~ sb/sth to aim a gun at a place or person so that no one can escape or shoot: *The police covered the exits to the building.* ♦ *Don't move—we've got you covered!*
▷ SONG **15** [T] ~ sth to record or perform a new version of a song that was originally recorded by another band or singer: *They've covered an old Rolling Stones number.*
IDM cover all the bases to consider and deal with all the things that could happen or could be needed when you are arranging something cover your back (*informal*) to realize that you may be blamed or criticized for something later and take action to avoid this: *Get everything in writing in order to cover your back.* cover your tracks to try and hide what you have done, because you do not want other people to find out about it: *He had attempted to cover his tracks by making her death appear like suicide.* ⊃ more at MULTITUDE
PHR V ˌcover sth↔ˈin to put a covering or roof over an open space ˌcover sth↔ˈover to cover something completely so that it cannot be seen: *The Roman remains are now covered over by office buildings.* ˌcover ˈup | ˌcover yourself ˈup to put on more clothes ˌcover sth↔ˈup **1** to cover something completely so that it cannot be seen: *He covered up the body with a sheet.* **2** (*disapproving*) to try to stop people from knowing the truth about a mistake, a crime, etc. ⊃ related noun COVER-UP
● *noun*
▷ PROTECTION/SHELTER **1** [C] a thing that is put over or on

another thing, usually to protect it or to decorate it: *a cushion cover* ♦ *a plastic waterproof cover for the stroller* ⟳ picture at LABORATORY ⟳ see also DUST COVER, SLIP COVER **2** [U] a place that provides shelter from bad weather or protection from an attack: *Everyone ran* **for cover** *when it started to rain.* ♦ *The climbers* **took cover** *from the storm in a cave.* ♦ *After the explosion the street was full of people* **running for cover**.
> OF BOOK **3** [C] the outside of a book or a magazine: *the front/back cover* ♦ *Her face was* **on the cover** (= the front cover) *of every magazine.* ♦ *He always reads the paper* **from cover to cover** (= everything in it).
> WITH WEAPONS **4** [U] support and protection that is provided when someone is attacking or in danger of being attacked: *The ships needed air cover* (= protection by military planes) *once they reached enemy waters.*
> TREES/PLANTS **5** [U] trees and plants that grow on an area of land: *The total forest cover of the earth is decreasing.*
> CLOUD/SNOW **6** [U] the fact of the sky being covered with cloud or the ground with snow: *Fog and low cloud cover are expected this afternoon.* ♦ *In this area there is snow cover for six months of the year.*
> ON BED **7 the covers** [pl.] the sheets, BLANKETS, etc. on a bed: *She threw back the covers and leapt out of bed.*
> SONG **8** [C] = COVER VERSION
> HIDING SOMETHING **9** [C, usually sing.] **~ (for sth)** activities or behavior that seem honest or true but that hide someone's real identity or feelings, or that hide something illegal: *His work as a civil servant was a cover for his activities as a spy.* ♦ *Her overconfident attitude was a cover for her nervousness.* ♦ *It would only take one phone call to* **blow their cover** (= make known their true identities and what they were really doing).
> FOR SOMEONE'S WORK **10** [U] the fact of someone doing another person's job when they are away or when there are not enough staff: *It's the manager's job to organize cover for staff who are absent.* ♦ *Ambulance drivers provided only emergency cover during the dispute.*
IDM **break cover** to leave a place that you have been hiding in, usually at a high speed **under cover 1** pretending to be someone else in order to do something secretly: *a police officer working under cover* **2** under a structure that gives protection from the weather **under (the) cover of sth** hidden or protected by something: *Later, under cover of darkness, they crept into the house.* **under separate cover** (*business*) in a separate envelope: *The information you requested is being forwarded to you under separate cover.* ⟳ more at JUDGE

cov·er·age /ˈkʌvrɪdʒ; ˈkʌvərɪdʒ/ *noun* [U] **1** the reporting of news and sports in newspapers and on the radio and television: *media/newspaper/press coverage* ♦ *tonight's* **live coverage** *of the hockey game* **2** the range or quality of information that is included in a book or course of study, on television, etc.: *magazines with extensive coverage of diet and health topics* **3** the amount of something that something provides; the amount or way that something covers an area: *Immunization coverage against fatal diseases has increased to 99% in some countries.* **4** protection that an insurance company provides by promising to pay you money if a particular event happens: *insurance coverage* ♦ *Medicaid health coverage for low-income families*

cov·er·alls /ˈkʌvərˌɔlz/ *noun* [pl.] a loose piece of clothing like a shirt and pants in one piece, made of heavy cloth and usually worn over other clothing by workers doing dirty work

ˈcover ˌcharge *noun* [usually sing.] an amount of money that you pay in some restaurants or clubs in addition to the cost of the food and drink

covered /ˈkʌvərd/ *adj.*
1 [not before noun] **~ in/with sth** having a layer or amount of something on it: *His face was covered in blood.* ♦ *The walls were covered with pictures.* **2** having a roof over it: *a covered area of the stadium with seats*

ˌcovered ˈwagon *noun* a large wooden vehicle with a

curved roof made of cloth, that is pulled by horses, used especially in the past in N. America by people traveling across the land to the west

ˈcover ˌgirl *noun* a young woman whose photograph is on the front of a magazine

cov·er·ing /ˈkʌvrɪŋ; ˈkʌvərɪŋ/ *noun*
1 a layer of something that covers something else: *a thick covering of snow on the ground* **2** a layer of material such as carpet or WALLPAPER, used to cover, decorate, and protect floors, walls, etc.: *floor/wall coverings* **3** a piece of material that covers something: *He pulled the plastic covering off the dead body.*

cov·er·let /ˈkʌvərlət/ *noun* (*old-fashioned*) a type of BED-SPREAD to cover a bed

ˈcover ˌletter *noun* a letter containing extra information that you send with something

ˈcover ˌstory *noun* **1** the main story in a magazine, that goes with the picture shown on the front cover **2** a story that is invented in order to hide something, especially a person's identity or their reasons for doing something

co·vert *adj., noun*
● *adj.* /ˈkoʊvərt; ˈkoʊˈvərt; ˈkʌvərt/ (*formal*) secret or hidden, making it difficult to notice: *covert operations/surveillance* ♦ *He stole a covert glance at her across the table.* ⟳ compare OVERT ▶ **co·vert·ly** *adv.*: *She watched him covertly in the mirror.*
● *noun* /ˈkʌvərt; ˈkoʊ-/ an area of thick low bushes and trees where animals can hide

ˈcover-ˌup *noun* [usually sing.] action that is taken to hide a mistake or illegal activity from the public: *Government sources denied there had been a deliberate cover-up.*

ˈcover ˌversion (also **cov·er**) *noun* a new recording or performance of an old song by a different band or singer

cov·et /ˈkʌvət/ *verb* **~ sth** (*formal*) to want something very much, especially something that belongs to someone else: *He had long coveted the chance to work with a famous musician.* ♦ *They are this year's winners of the coveted trophy* (= that everyone would like to win).

cov·et·ous /ˈkʌvətəs/ *adj.* (*formal*) having a strong desire for the things that other people have ▶ **cov·et·ous·ness** *noun* [U]

cov·ey /ˈkʌvi/ *noun* a small group of birds, especially PARTRIDGES

cow /kaʊ/ *noun, verb*
● *noun* **1** a large animal kept on farms to produce milk or beef: *cow's milk* ♦ *a herd of dairy cows* (= cows kept for their milk) ⟳ compare BULL, CALF, HEIFER ⟳ see also CATTLE **2** the female of the ELEPHANT, WHALE, and some other large animals ⟳ compare BULL **3** (*slang, disapproving*) an offensive word for a woman: *You stupid cow!* ⟳ see also CASH COW, SACRED COW
IDM **have a cow** (*informal*) to become very angry or anxious about something: *Don't have a cow—it's no big deal.* **till the cows come home** (*informal*) for a very long time; for ever
● *verb* [usually passive] **~ sb** to frighten someone in order to make them obey you **SYN** INTIMIDATE: *She was easily cowed by people in authority.*

cow·ard /ˈkaʊərd/ *noun* (*disapproving*) a person who is not brave or who does not have the courage to do things that other people do not think are especially difficult: *You coward! What are you afraid of?* ♦ *I'm a real coward when it comes to going to the dentist.* ▶ **cow·ard·ly** *adj.*: *a cowardly attack on a defenseless man*

cow·ard·ice /ˈkaʊərdəs/ *noun* [U] fear or lack of courage **ANT** BRAVERY, COURAGE

cow·bell /ˈkaʊbɛl/ *noun* a bell that is put around a cow's neck so that the cow can easily be found

cow·boy /ˈkaʊbɔɪ/ *noun* **1** a man who rides a horse and whose job is to take care of CATTLE in the western parts of the U.S. **2** a man like this as a character in a movie about the American West: *children playing a game of **cowboys and Indians***

cowboy boot *noun* [usually pl.] a style of boot with a pointed toe and a thick, somewhat high heel ➔ picture at SHOE

cowboy hat *noun* a hat with a wide BRIM, worn especially by American cowboys ➔ picture at HAT

cow·catch·er /ˈkaʊˌkætʃər/ *noun* a pointed metal structure at the front of a train that is used for pushing things off the track

cow chip (also **cow pie**) *noun* a round flat piece of solid waste from a cow

cowed /kaʊd/ *adj.* made to feel afraid and that you are not as good as someone else ➔ see also COW

cow·er /ˈkaʊər/ *verb* [I] to bend low and/or move backward because you are frightened: *A gun went off and people cowered behind walls and under tables.*

cow·girl /ˈkaʊɡərl/ *noun* a female COWBOY in the American West

cow·hand /ˈkaʊhænd/ *noun* a person whose job is taking care of cows

cow·hide /ˈkaʊhaɪd/ *noun* [U] strong leather made from the skin of a cow

cowl /kaʊl/ *noun* **1** a large loose covering for the head, worn especially by MONK **2** a cover for a CHIMNEY, etc., usually made of metal. Cowls often turn with the wind and are designed to improve the flow of air or smoke.

cow·lick /ˈkaʊlɪk/ *noun* a piece of hair that grows in a different direction from the rest of your hair and is difficult to make lie flat

cowl·ing /ˈkaʊlɪŋ/ *noun* (*technical*) a metal cover for an engine, especially on an aircraft ➔ picture at PLANE

cowl neck *noun* a COLLAR on a woman's sweater that hangs in several folds

co-worker *noun* a person that someone works with, doing the same kind of job SYN COLLEAGUE

cow·pea /ˈkaʊpi/ (also **black-eyed pea**) *noun* a type of BEAN that is white with a black spot and is grown for food: *Cowpeas are an important crop in many African countries.*

cow pie *noun* = COW CHIP

cow·poke /ˈkaʊpoʊk/ *noun* (*old-fashioned* or *humorous*) = COWBOY

cow·rie /ˈkaʊri/ *noun* a small shiny shell that was used as money in the past in parts of Africa and Asia

cow·shed /ˈkaʊʃɛd/ *noun* a farm building in which cows are kept

cow·slip /ˈkaʊslɪp/ *noun* a small wild plant with yellow flowers with a sweet smell

cox /kɑks/ *noun, verb*
• *noun* = COXSWAIN
• *verb* [T, I] ~ **(sth)** to control the direction of a racing boat while other people are ROWING; to act as a coxswain

cox·swain /ˈkɑksn/ *noun* **1** (also **cox**) the person who controls the direction of a racing boat while other people are ROWING **2** the person who is in charge of a LIFEBOAT and who controls its direction

coy /kɔɪ/ *adj.* **1** shy or pretending to be shy and innocent, especially about love or sex, and sometimes in order to make people more interested in you: *She gave me a coy smile.* **2** ~ **(about sth)** not willing to give information about something, or answer questions that tell people too much about you SYN RETICENT: *She was a little coy about how much her dress cost.* ▶ **coy·ly** *adv.* **coy·ness** *noun* [U]

coy·o·te /kaɪˈoʊti; ˈkaɪoʊt/ (also **prairie wolf**) *noun* a N. American wild animal of the dog family

coy·pu /ˈkɔɪpu/ *noun* a large S. American animal, like a BEAVER, that lives near water

co·zy /ˈkoʊzi/ *adj., verb*
• *adj.* (co·zi·er, co·zi·est) **1** warm, comfortable, and safe,

especially because of being small SYN SNUG: *a cozy little room* ◆ *a cozy feeling* ◆ *I felt warm and cozy sitting by the fire.* **2** friendly and private: *a cozy chat with a friend* **3** (often *disapproving*) easy and convenient, but not always honest or right: *The company has a cozy relationship with the Department of Defense.* ◆ *The danger is that things get too cozy.* ▶ **co·zi·ly** *adv.*: *sitting cozily by the fire* **co·zi·ness** *noun* [U]: *the warmth and coziness of the kitchen*

coyote

• *verb* (co·zies, co·zy·ing, co·zied, co·zied)
PHR V **cozy 'up to sb** (*informal*) to act in a friendly way toward someone, especially someone who will be useful to you

cp. *abbr.* (in writing) compare

CPA /ˌsi pi ˈeɪ/ *abbr.* certified public accountant (a member of an officially approved professional organization of ACCOUNTANTS)

CPI /ˌsi pi ˈaɪ/ *abbr.* CONSUMER PRICE INDEX

Cpl. *abbr.* (in writing) CORPORAL

CPP /ˌsi pi ˈpi/ *abbr.* (*CanE*) = CANADA PENSION PLAN

CPR /ˌsi pi ˈɑr/ *noun* [U] the abbreviation for "cardiopulmonary resuscitation" (breathing air into the mouth of an unconscious person and pressing on their chest to keep them alive by sending air around their body)

CPU /ˌsi pi ˈyu/ *abbr.* (*computing*) central processing unit (the part of a computer that controls all the other parts of the system)

CRA /ˌsi ɑr ˈeɪ/ *abbr.* (*CanE*) CANADA REVENUE AGENCY (the department of the Canadian government that deals with personal INCOME TAX)

crab /kræb/ *noun* **1** [C] a sea creature with a hard shell, eight legs, and two PINCERS (= curved and pointed arms for catching and holding things). Crabs move sideways on land. ➔ picture at ANIMAL ➔ see also HERMIT CRAB **2** [U] meat from a crab, used for food: *dressed crab* **3** crabs (*informal*) the condition caused by having LICE (called **crab lice**) in the hair around the GENITALS

crab apple *noun* a tree that produces fruit like small hard sour apples, also called crab apples

crab·bed /ˈkræbəd; kræbd/ *adj.* **1** (*literary*) (of someone's writing) small and difficult to read **2** (*old-fashioned*) = CRABBY

crab·by /ˈkræbi/ *adj.* (*informal*) (of people) bad-tempered and unpleasant

crab·grass /ˈkræbɡræs/ *noun* [U] a type of grass that grows where it is not wanted, spreads quickly, and is hard to get rid of

crab stick *noun* a small pink stick made from pressed pieces of fish that have been flavored to taste like CRAB

crab·wise /ˈkræbwaɪz/ *adv.* (of a movement) in a sideways direction, like a CRAB

crack 🔊 /kræk/ *verb, noun, adj.*
• *verb*
> BREAK **1** [I, T] to break without dividing into separate parts; to break something in this way: *The ice cracked as I stepped onto it.* ◆ ~ **sth** *He has cracked a bone in his arm.* ◆ *Her lips were dry and cracked.* ➔ picture at BROKEN **2** [I, T] to break open or into pieces; to break something in this way: + **adv./prep.** *A chunk of the cliff had cracked off in a storm.* ◆ (*figurative*) *His face cracked into a smile.* ◆ ~ **sth** *to crack a nut* ◆ ~ **sth** + **adv./prep.** *She cracked an egg into the pan.*
> HIT **3** [T] ~ **sth/sb (on/against sth)** to hit something or someone with a short hard blow: *I cracked my head on the low ceiling.* ◆ *He cracked me on the head with a ruler.*
> MAKE SOUND **4** [I, T] to make a sharp sound; to make

t tea   ṭ butter   d did   k cat   g got   tʃ chin   dʒ June   f fall

something do this: *A shot cracked across the ridge.* [no passive]: ~ **sth** *He cracked his whip and galloped away.*
> **OF VOICE 5** [I] if your voice **cracks**, it changes in depth, volume, etc. suddenly and in a way that you cannot control: *In a voice cracking with emotion, he told us of his son's death.*
> **UNDER PRESSURE 6** [I] to no longer be able to function normally because of pressure: *Things are terrible at work and people are cracking under the strain.* ◆ *They questioned him for days before he cracked.* ◆ *The old institutions are cracking.*
> **FIND SOLUTION 7** [T] ~ **sth** to find the solution to a problem, etc.; to find the way to do something difficult: *to crack the enemy's code* ◆ *(informal) After a year in this job I think I've got it cracked!*
> **STOP SOMEONE OR SOMETHING 8** [T] ~ **sth** to find a way of stopping or defeating a criminal or an enemy: *Police have cracked a major drug ring.*
> **BREAK INTO SOMETHING 9** [T,I] to break into something illegally: ~ **sth** *At the age of sixteen, Johnny was already cracking safes.* ◆ ~ **into sth** *They cracked into the computer network and stole a lot of information.*
> **OPEN BOTTLE 10** [T] ~ **(open) a bottle** *(informal)* to open a bottle, especially of wine, and drink it
> **A JOKE 11** [T] ~ **a joke** to tell a joke
> **A SMILE 12** [T] ~ **a smile** to smile slightly or suddenly: *She was trying to appear very serious, but I saw her crack a smile.*
> **IDM get cracking** *(informal)* to begin immediately and work quickly **SYN** GET GOING: *There's a lot to do, so let's get cracking.* **not all, everything, etc. sb's cracked up to be** *(informal)* not as good as people say: *He's not nearly as good a writer as he's cracked up to be.* **crack the whip** to use your authority or power to make someone work very hard, usually by treating them in a strict way
> **PHR V crack 'down (on sb/sth)** to try harder to prevent an illegal activity and deal more severely with those who are caught doing it: *Police are cracking down on drug dealers.* ⊃ related noun CRACKDOWN **crack into sth** *(informal)* to succeed at getting into a particular job or profession: *She was able to crack into fashion design at just the right time.* **crack 'up** *(informal)* **1** to become ill, either physically or mentally, because of pressure: *You'll crack up if you keep on working like this.* **2** to start laughing a lot: *He walked in and everyone just cracked up.* **crack sb 'up** *(informal)* to make someone laugh a lot: *Jill's so funny, she just cracks me up.*

● **noun**
> **BREAK 1** [C] ~ **(in sth)** a line on the surface of something where it has broken but not split into separate parts: *This cup has a crack in it.* ◆ *Cracks began to appear in the walls.* ◆ *(figurative) The cracks (= faults) in the government's economic policy are already beginning to show.*
> **NARROW OPENING 2** [C] a narrow space or opening: *She peeped through the crack in the curtains.* ◆ *The door opened a crack (= a small amount).*
> **SOUND 3** [C] a sudden loud noise: *a crack of thunder* ◆ *the sharp crack of a rifle shot*
> **HIT 4** [C] ~ **(on sth)** a sharp blow that can be heard: *She fell over and got a nasty crack on the head.*
> **ATTEMPT 5** [C] ~ **(at sth)** | ~ **(at doing sth)** *(informal)* an occasion when you try to do something **SYN** ATTEMPT: *She hopes to have another crack at the world record this year.*
> **DRUG 6** (also **crack co'caine**) [U] a powerful, illegal drug that is a form of COCAINE: *a crack addict*
> **JOKE 7** [C] *(informal)* a joke, especially a critical one: *He made a very unfair crack about his looks.*
> **CONVERSATION**
> **IDM at the crack of dawn** *(informal)* very early in the morning **fall/slip through the cracks** to be forgotten or missed by a system or program that was organized to deal with a particular situation: *Fatherless kids were not allowed to fall through the cracks.* ◆ *In spite of excellent quality control, some faulty goods always manage to slip through the cracks.*
● **adj.** [only before noun] expert and highly trained; excellent at something: *crack troops* ◆ *He's a crack shot (= accurate and skilled at shooting).*
crack·brained /'krækbreɪnd/ *adj. (informal)* crazy and unlikely to succeed: *a crackbrained idea*

crack·down /'krækdaʊn/ *noun* ~ **(on sb/sth)** severe action taken to restrict the activities of criminals or of people opposed to the government or someone in authority: *a military crackdown on student protesters* ◆ *a crackdown on crime*

cracked /krækt/ *adj.*
1 damaged with lines in its surface but not completely broken: *a cracked mirror/mug* ◆ *He suffered cracked ribs and bruising.* ◆ *She passed her tongue over her cracked lips and tried to speak.* ⊃ picture at BROKEN **2** (of someone's voice) sounding rough with sudden changes in how loud or high it is, because the person is upset: *"I'm just fine," she said in a cracked voice.* **3** [not before noun] *(informal)* crazy: *I think he must be cracked, don't you?*

crack·er /'krækər/ *noun* **1** food like a thin dry piece of bread, that is often salty and usually eaten with cheese ⊃ see also GRAHAM CRACKER, SODA CRACKER **2** *(informal)* a person who illegally finds a way of looking at or stealing information on someone else's computer system ⊃ see also FIRECRACKER

crack·er·jack /'krækərˌdʒæk/ *noun (informal)* an excellent person or thing ▶ **crack·er·jack** *adj.*

crack·head /'krækhɛd/ *noun (slang)* a person who uses the illegal drug CRACK

crack house *noun* a place where people sell the illegal drug CRACK

crack·ing /'krækɪŋ/ *noun* [U] **1** lines on a surface where it is damaged or beginning to break: *All planes are being inspected for possible cracking and corrosion.* **2** the sound of something cracking: *the cracking of thunder/twigs*

crack·le /'krækl/ *verb, noun*
● **verb** [I] to make short sharp sounds like something that is burning in a fire: *A log fire crackled in the hearth.* ◆ *The radio crackled into life.* ◆ *(figurative) The atmosphere crackled with tension.*
● **noun** [U, C] a series of short sharp sounds: *the distant crackle of machine-gun fire* ▶ **crack·ly** /'krækli/ *adj.*: *She picked up the phone and heard a crackly voice saying: "Hi, this is Sue."*

crack·ling /'kræklɪŋ/ *noun* **1** [U, sing.] a series of sharp sounds: *He could hear the crackling of burning trees.* **2 cracklings** [pl.] the hard skin of PORK (= meat from a pig) that has been cooked in the oven

crack·pot /'krækpɑt/ *noun (informal)* a person with strange or crazy ideas ▶ **crack·pot** *adj.* [only before noun]: *crackpot ideas/theories*

–cracy *combining form* (in nouns) the government or rule of: *democracy* ◆ *bureaucracy*

cra·dle /'kreɪdl/ *noun, verb*
● **noun** **1** a small bed for a baby that can be pushed gently from side to side: *She rocked the baby to sleep in his cradle.* ⊃ picture at BED **2** [usually sing.] ~ **of sth** the place where something important began: *Greece, the cradle of Western civilization* **3** the part of a telephone on which the RECEIVER rests
IDM from the cradle to the grave a way of referring to the whole of a person's life, from birth until death ⊃ more at ROB
● **verb** ~ **sb/sth** to hold someone or something gently in your arms or hands: *The old man cradled the tiny baby in his arms.*

cradle ˌcap *noun* [U] a skin condition that causes dry rough yellow areas on top of a baby's head

cradle-ˌrobber *noun (disapproving)* a person who has a sexual relationship with a much younger person ▶ **cradle-ˌrob** *verb* (-bb-) [I]

craft /kræft/ *noun, verb*
● **noun** **1** [C, U] an activity involving a special skill at making things with your hands: *traditional crafts like basket-weaving* ◆ *a craft fair/workshop* ⊃ see also ARTS AND CRAFTS **2** [sing.] all the skills needed for a particular activity: *chefs who learned their craft in five-star hotels* ◆ *the writer's craft* **3** [U] *(formal, disapproving)* skill in making people believe

what you want them to believe: *He knew how to win by craft and diplomacy what he could not gain by force.* **4** [C] (*pl.* **craft**) a boat or ship: *Hundreds of small craft bobbed around the liner as it steamed into the harbor.* ♦ *a landing/pleasure craft* **5** [C] (*pl.* **craft**) an aircraft or SPACECRAFT

● *verb* [usually passive] ~ **sth** to make something using special skills, especially with your hands SYN FASHION: *All the furniture is crafted from natural materials.* ♦ *a carefully crafted speech* ➔ see also HANDCRAFTED

crafts·man /ˈkræftsmən/ (*also* **crafts·per·son**) *noun* (*pl.* **crafts·men** /-mən/) a skilled person, especially one who makes beautiful things by hand: *rugs handmade by local craftsmen* ♦ *It is clearly the work of a master craftsman.* ➔ see also CRAFTSWOMAN

crafts·man·ship /ˈkræftsmənˌʃɪp/ *noun* [U] **1** the level of skill shown by someone in making something beautiful with their hands: *The whole house is a monument to her craftsmanship.* **2** the quality of design and work shown by something that has been made by hand: *the superb craftsmanship of the carvings*

crafts·per·son /ˈkræftsˌpɜrsn/ *noun* (*pl.* **crafts·peo·ple** /-ˌpipl/) = CRAFTSMAN

crafts·wom·an /ˈkræftsˌwʊmən/ *noun* (*pl.* **crafts·wom·en** /-ˌwɪmən/) a skilled woman, especially one who makes beautiful things by hand

craft·work /ˈkræftwɜrk/ *noun* [U] work done by a CRAFTSMAN

craft·y /ˈkræfti/ *adj.* (**craft·i·er**, **craft·i·est**) (usually *disapproving*) skilled at getting what you want, especially by indirect or dishonest methods SYN CUNNING, WILY: *He's a crafty old devil.* ♦ *one of the party's craftiest political strategists* ▶ **craft·i·ly** /-təli/ *adv.* **craft·i·ness** *noun* [U]

crag /kræg/ *noun* a high, steep, rough mass of rock: *a castle set on a crag above the village*

crag·gy /ˈkrægi/ *adj.* **1** having many crags: *a craggy coastline* **2** (usually *approving*) (of a man's face) having strong features and deep lines

cram /kræm/ *verb* (**-mm-**) **1** [T, I] to push or force someone or something into a small space; to move into a small space with the result that it is full: ~ **sb/sth into/onto sth** *He crammed eight people into his car.* ♦ ~ **sth in** *I could never cram in all that she does in a day.* ♦ ~ **sth + adv./prep.** *I managed to cram down a few mouthfuls of food.* ♦ ~ **sth** *Supporters crammed the streets.* ♦ ~ **sth full** *I bought a large basket and crammed it full of presents.* ♦ ~ **into/onto sth** *We all managed to cram into his car.* **2** [I] ~ **(for sth)** to learn a lot of things in a short time, in preparation for an exam: *He's been cramming for his exams all week.*

crammed /kræmd/ *adj.* **1** ~ **(with sb/sth)** full of things or people: *All the shelves were crammed with books.* ♦ *The room was crammed full of people.* SYN PACKED: *The article was crammed full of ideas.* **2** [not before noun] ~ **(with sb/sth)** if people are crammed into a place, there is not much room for them in it SYN PACKED: *We were crammed four to an office.*

cramp /kræmp/ *noun*, *verb*
● *noun* **1** [C] (*also* **char·ley horse**) a sudden pain that you get when the muscles in a particular part of your body contract, usually caused by cold or too much exercise: *to get a cramp in your leg* ➔ see also WRITER'S CRAMP **2 cramps** [pl.] severe pain in the stomach

● *verb* ~ **sth** to prevent the development or progress of someone or something SYN RESTRICT: *Tighter trade restrictions might cramp economic growth.*
IDM **cramp sb's style** (*informal*) to stop someone from behaving in the way they want to

cramped /kræmpt/ *adj.* **1** a cramped room, etc. does not have enough space for the people in it: *working in cramped conditions* **2** (of people) not having room to move freely **3** (of someone's writing) with small letters close together and therefore difficult to read

cram·pon /ˈkræmpɑn/ *noun* [usually pl.] a metal plate with pointed pieces of metal underneath, worn on someone's shoes when they are walking or climbing on ice and snow

cran·ber·ry /ˈkrænˌbɛri/ *noun* (*pl.* **cran·ber·ries**) a small sour red BERRY that grows on a small bush and is used in cooking: *cranberry sauce* ➔ picture at FRUIT

crane /kreɪn/ *noun*, *verb*
● *noun* **1** a tall machine with a long arm, used to lift and move building materials and other heavy objects **2** a large bird with long legs and a long neck

● *verb* [I, T] to lean or stretch over something in order to see something better; to stretch your neck: **(+ adv./prep.)** *People were craning out of the windows and waving.* ♦ ~ **sth** *She craned her neck to get a better view of the stage.*

cra·ni·um /ˈkreɪniəm/ *noun* (*pl.* **cra·ni·ums** or **cra·nia** /-niə/) (*anatomy*) the bone structure that forms the head and surrounds and protects the brain ➔ picture at BODY SYN SKULL ▶ **cra·ni·al** /ˈkreɪniəl/ *adj.* [only before noun]: *cranial nerves/injuries*

crank /kræŋk/ *noun*, *verb*
● *noun* **1** a bar and handle in the shape of an L that you pull or turn to produce movement in a machine, etc. ➔ picture at BICYCLE **2** a person who easily gets angry or annoyed **3** (*disapproving*) a person with ideas that other people find strange SYN ECCENTRIC: *Vegetarians are no longer dismissed as cranks.*

● *verb* ~ **sth (up)** to make something turn or move by using a crank: *to crank an engine* ♦ (*figurative*) *He has a limited time to crank the reforms into action.*
PHR V **crank sth↔'out** (*informal*) to produce a lot of something quickly, especially things of low quality SYN TURN OUT **crank sth↔'up** (*informal*) **1** to make a machine, etc. work or work at a higher level **2** to make music, etc. louder SYN TURN UP: *Crank up the volume!*

crank·shaft /ˈkræŋkʃæft/ *noun* (*technical*) a long straight piece of metal in a vehicle that connects the engine to the wheels and helps turn the engine's power into movement

crank·y /ˈkræŋki/ *adj.* (*informal*) bad-tempered: *The kids were getting tired and a little cranky.* SYN GROUCHY

cran·ny /ˈkræni/ *noun* (*pl.* **cran·nies**) a very small hole or opening, especially in a wall IDM see NOOK

craps /kræps/ *noun* [U] a gambling game played with two DICE: *to shoot craps* (= play this game) ▶ **crap** *adj.* [only before noun]: *a crap game*

crap·shoot /ˈkræpʃut/ *noun* **1** a game of craps **2** (*informal*) a situation whose success or result is based on luck rather than on effort or careful organization

crash 🔑 /kræʃ/ *noun*, *verb*, *adj.*
● *noun*
❯ **VEHICLE ACCIDENT 1** (*also* wreck) an accident in which a vehicle hits something, for example another vehicle, usually causing damage and often injuring or killing the passengers: *A girl was killed yesterday in a crash involving a stolen car.* ♦ *a car/plane crash* ➔ collocations at DRIVING
❯ **LOUD NOISE 2** [usually sing.] a sudden loud noise made, for example, by something falling or breaking: *The tree fell with a great crash.* ♦ *The first distant crash of thunder shook the air.*
❯ **IN FINANCE/BUSINESS 3** a sudden serious fall in the price or value of something; the occasion when a business, etc. fails SYN COLLAPSE: *the 1987 stock market crash*
❯ **COMPUTING 4** a sudden failure of a machine or system, especially of a computer or computer system

● *verb*
❯ **OF VEHICLE 1** [I, T] if a vehicle **crashes** or the driver **crashes** it, it hits an object or another vehicle, causing damage: *I was terrified that the plane would crash.* ♦ *We're going to crash, aren't we?* ♦ ~ **into sth** *A truck went out of control and crashed into the back of a bus.* ♦ ~ **sth (into sth)** *He crashed his car into a wall.*
❯ **HIT HARD/LOUD NOISE 2** [I, T] to hit something hard while moving, causing noise and/or damage; to make something hit someone or something in this way: **+ adv./prep.** *A brick crashed through the window.* ♦ *With a sweep of his hand he*

sent the glasses crashing to the floor. ✦ + *adj. The door crashed open.* ✦ **~** *sth* + *adj. She stormed out of the room and crashed the door shut behind her.* **3** [I] to make a loud noise: *Thunder crashed overhead.*

> IN FINANCE/BUSINESS **4** [I] (of prices, a business, shares, etc.) to lose value or fail suddenly and quickly: *Share prices crashed to an all-time low yesterday.* ✦ *The company crashed with debts of $50 million.*

> COMPUTING **5** [I, T] **~** **(sth)** if a computer **crashes** or you **crash** a computer, it stops working suddenly: *Files can be lost if the system suddenly crashes.*

> PARTY **6** [T] (*informal*) (also 'gate-crash) **~** *sth* to go to a party or social event without being invited

> SLEEP **7** [I] **~** **(out)** (*informal*) to fall asleep; to sleep somewhere you do not usually sleep: *I was so tired I crashed out on the sofa.* ✦ *I've come to crash on your floor for a couple of nights.*

> MEDICAL **8** [I] if someone **crashes**, their heart stops beating **IDM** **crash and burn** (*informal*) to fail suddenly and completely: *His grand plan to make a million dollars crashed and burned, leaving him not only broke but deeply in debt.*

• *adj.* [only before noun] involving hard work or a lot of effort over a short period of time in order to achieve quick results: *a crash course in computer programming* ✦ *a crash diet*

THESAURUS

crash

slam • collide • smash • wreck

These are all words that can be used when something, especially a vehicle, hits something else very hard and is damaged or destroyed.

crash (*somewhat informal*) to hit an object or another vehicle, causing damage; to make a vehicle do this: *I was terrified that the plane would crash.*

slam (*sth*) **into/against** *sb/sth* to crash into something with a lot of force; to make something do this: *The car skidded and slammed into a tree.*

collide (*somewhat formal*) (of two vehicles or people) to crash into each other; (of a vehicle or person) to crash into someone or something else: *The car and the van collided head-on in thick fog.*

smash (*somewhat informal*) to crash into something with a lot of force; to make something do this; to crash a car: *The thieves smashed a stolen car through the store's display.*

CRASH, SLAM, OR SMASH?

Crash is used especially to talk about vehicles and can be used without a preposition: *We're going to crash, aren't we?* In this meaning **slam** and **smash** always take a preposition: ~~We're going to slam/smash, aren't we?~~ They are used for a much wider range of things than just vehicles. **Crash** can also be used for other things, if used with a preposition: *She turned the corner in the hallway and crashed into the soda machine.*

wreck to crash a vehicle and damage it very badly

PATTERNS

▪ **two vehicles** crash/collide
▪ **two vehicles/people/things** crash/slam/smash **into each other**
▪ to crash/smash/wreck **a car**

---

crash·er *noun* (*informal*) = GATE-CRASHER

'**crash** ˌhelmet *noun* a hat made of very strong material and worn when riding a motorcycle to protect the head ⊃ picture at BICYCLE

ˌ**crash-'land** *verb* [I, T] **~** **(sth)** if a plane **crash-lands** or a pilot **crash-lands** it, the pilot lands it roughly in an emergency, usually because it is damaged and cannot land normally ▶ ˌ**crash** '**landing** *noun*: *to make a crash landing*

'**crash-test** *verb* **~** *sth* to deliberately crash a new vehicle

under controlled conditions in order to test how it reacts or to improve its safety ▶ '**crash test** *noun*

'**crash-test** ˌ**dummy** *noun* a model of a person used in crash tests to see what would happen to a driver or passenger in a real crash

crass /kræs/ *adj.* very stupid and showing no sympathy or understanding **SYN** INSENSITIVE: *the crass questions all disabled people get asked* ✦ *an act of crass* (= great) *stupidity* ▶ **crass·ly** *adv.* **crass·ness** *noun* [U]

-crat *combining form* (in nouns) a member or supporter of a particular type of government or system: *democrat* ✦ *bureaucrat* ▶ **-cratic** (in adjectives): *aristocratic*

crate /kreɪt/ *noun, verb*
• *noun* **1** a large wooden container for transporting goods: *a crate of bananas* **2** a container made of plastic or metal divided into small sections, for transporting or storing bottles: *a beer crate* **3** the amount of something contained in a crate: *They drank two crates of beer.*
• *verb* **~** *sth* **(up)** to pack something in a crate

cra·ter /'kreɪtər/ *noun* **1** a large hole in the top of a VOLCANO ⊃ picture at VOLCANO **2** a large hole in the ground caused by the explosion of a bomb or by something large hitting it: *a meteorite crater*

cra·vat /krə'væt/ (also **as·cot**) *noun* a short wide strip of silk, etc. worn by men around the neck, folded inside the COLLAR of a shirt

crave /kreɪv/ *verb* [T, I] **~** **(for)** *sth* | **~** **to do sth** to have a very strong desire for something **SYN** LONG FOR: *She has always craved excitement.*

cra·ven /'kreɪvn/ *adj.* (*formal, disapproving*) lacking courage **ANT** BRAVE ▶ **cra·ven·ly** *adv.*

crav·ing /'kreɪvɪŋ/ *noun* a strong desire for something: **~** **(for sth)** *a craving for chocolate* ✦ **~** **(to do sth)** *a desperate craving to be loved*

craw /krɔ/ *noun* the part of a bird's throat where food is kept **IDM** see STICK

craw·fish /'krɔfɪʃ/ *noun* = CRAYFISH

crawl /krɔl/ *verb, noun*
• *verb* **1** [I] (+ adv./prep.) to move forward on your hands and knees, with your body close to the ground: *Our baby is just starting to crawl.* ✦ *A man was crawling away from the burning wreckage.* **2** [I] (+ adv./prep.) when an insect **crawls**, it moves forward on its legs: *There's a spider crawling up your leg.* **3** [I] (+ adv./prep.) to move forward very slowly: *The traffic was crawling along.* ✦ *The weeks crawled by.* **IDM** **come crawling back (to sb)** (*disapproving*) to behave in a way that shows you are sorry for something you have done to someone and that you would now like their approval: *Don't come crawling back to me later when you realize what a mistake you've made.* ⊃ more at FLESH, SKIN, WOODWORK **PHR V** be '**crawling with sth** (*informal*) to be full of or completely covered with people, insects, or animals, in a way that is unpleasant: *The place was crawling with journalists.* ✦ *Her hair was crawling with lice.*
• *noun* **1** [sing.] a very slow speed: *The traffic slowed to a crawl.* **2** often **the crawl** [sing., U] a fast swimming stroke that you do lying on your front moving one arm over your head, and then the other, while kicking with your feet: *a swimmer doing the crawl* ⊃ picture at SPORT

cray·fish /'kreɪfɪʃ/ (also **craw·fish**) *noun* [C, U] (*pl.* **cray·fish, craw·fish**) an animal like a small LOBSTER, that lives in rivers and lakes and can be eaten, or one like a large LOBSTER, that lives in the ocean and can be eaten

cray·on /'kreɪən; -ɑn/ *noun* a stick of colored WAX, used for drawing ▶ **cray·on** *verb* [I, T] **~** **(sth)**

craze /kreɪz/ *noun* **~** **(for sth)** an enthusiastic interest in something that is shared by many people but that usually does not last very long; a thing that people have a craze for **SYN** FAD: *the latest fitness craze to sweep the country*

crazed /kreɪzd/ *adj.* **~** **(with sth)** (*formal*) full of strong

---

feelings and lacking control: *crazed with fear/grief/jealousy* ♦ *a crazed killer roaming the streets*

cra·zy 🔊 /'kreɪzi/ *adj., noun*
- *adj.* (**cra·zi·er, cra·zi·est**) (*informal*) **1** not sensible; stupid: *Are you crazy? We could get killed doing that.* ♦ *She must be crazy to lend him money.* ♦ *He drove like an idiot, passing in the craziest places.* ♦ *What a crazy idea!* ♦ *I know it sounds crazy but it just might work.* **2** very angry: *That noise is driving me crazy.* ♦ *Marie says he went crazy, and smashed the room up.* **3** ~ (**about sth**) (often in compounds) very enthusiastic or excited about something: *Rick is crazy about football.* ♦ *He's football-crazy.* ♦ *I'm not crazy about Chinese food* (= I don't like it very much). ♦ *The crowd went crazy when the band came on stage.* ♦ *You're so beautiful you're driving me crazy.* ⊃ thesaurus box at LIKE **4** ~ **about sb** liking someone very much; in love with someone: *I've been crazy about him since the first time I saw him.* **5** mentally ill; INSANE: *She's crazy—she ought to be locked up.* ▶ **cra·zi·ly** /-zəli/ *adv.* **cra·zi·ness** *noun* [U]
  IDM **like crazy/mad** (*informal*) very fast, hard, much, etc.: *We worked like crazy to get it done on time.*

- *noun* (*pl.* **cra·zies**) (*informal*) a crazy person

crazy quilt *noun* **1** [C] a type of QUILT in which small pieces of cloth of different shape, color, design, and size are sewn together ⊃ compare PATCHWORK **2** [sing.] a confusing mixture: *The new tax laws are a crazy quilt of rules and regulations.*

creak /krik/ *verb, noun*
- *verb* [I] to make the sound that a door sometimes makes when you open it or that a wooden floor sometimes makes when you step on it: *She heard a floorboard creak upstairs.* ♦ *a creaking bed/gate/stair* ♦ *The table creaked and groaned under the weight.* ♦ + **adj.** *The door creaked open.*
- *noun* [C] (also **creak·ing** [U, C]) a sound, for example that sometimes made by a door when it opens or shuts, or by a wooden floor when you step on it: *the creak/creaking of the door* ♦ *Distant creaks and groans echoed eerily along the dark corridors.*

creak·y /'kriki/ *adj.* (**creak·i·er, creak·i·est**) **1** making creaks: *a creaky old chair* **2** old-fashioned and no longer working well: *the country's creaky legal machinery*

cream 🔊 /krim/ *noun, adj., verb*
- *noun* **1** [U] the thick, pale yellow-white, FATTY liquid that rises to the top of milk, used in cooking or as a type of sauce to put on fruit, etc.: *strawberries and cream* ♦ *Would you like milk or cream in your coffee?* ♦ *fresh/whipped cream* ⊃ see also ICE CREAM, SOUR CREAM, WHIPPING CREAM **2** [C] (in compounds) a candy that has a soft substance like cream inside: *chocolate lemon cream candies* **3** [U, C] a soft substance or thick liquid used on your skin to protect it or make it feel soft; a similar substance used for cleaning things: *hand/ moisturizing cream* ♦ *antiseptic cream* ♦ *a cream cleaner* ⊃ see also COLD CREAM, FACE CREAM, SHAVING CREAM **4** [U] a pale yellow-white color **5 the ~ of sth** the best people or things in a particular group: *the cream of New York society* ♦ *the cream of the crop* of this season's movies **IDM** see PEACH
- *adj.* pale yellow-white in color: *a cream linen suit*
- *verb* **1** ~ **sth (together)** to mix things together into a soft smooth mixture: *Cream the butter and sugar together.* **2** ~ **sb** (*informal*) to completely defeat someone: *We got creamed in the first round.*
  PHR V **cream sb/sth↔'off** to take something away, usually the best people or things or an amount of money, in order to get an advantage for yourself: *The best students were creamed off by the top-ranked schools.*

cream cheese *noun* [U, C] soft white cheese containing a lot of cream

cream·er /'krimər/ *noun* **1** [U] a liquid or powder that you can put in coffee, etc. instead of cream or milk: *nondairy creamer* **2** [C] a small container for holding and pouring cream

cream·er·y /'krimmri/ *noun* (*pl.* **cream·er·ies**) a place where milk and cream are made into butter and cheese

cream puff *noun* **1** (also **pro·fit·er·ole**) a small cake in the shape of a ball, made of light PASTRY, filled with cream, and usually with chocolate on top **2** (*slang, disapproving*) a person who is not strong or brave **SYN** WIMP

cream 'soda *noun* [U, C] a CARBONATED drink (= one with bubbles) that tastes of VANILLA

cream·y /'krimi/ *adj.* (**cream·i·er, cream·i·est**) **1** thick and smooth like cream; containing a lot of cream: *a creamy sauce/soup* **2** pale yellow-white in color: *creamy skin*

crease /kris/ *noun, verb*
- *noun* **1** a line that is made in cloth or paper when it is pressed or crushed **SYN** WRINKLE *n.*: *She smoothed the creases out of her skirt.* ♦ *a shirt made of crease-resistant material* ⊃ picture at CLOTHES **2** a neat line that you make in something, for example when you fold it: *pants with a sharp crease in the legs* **3** a line in the skin, especially on the face **SYN** WRINKLE *n.*: *creases around the eyes*
- *verb* **1** [T, I] ~ **(sth)** to make lines on cloth or paper by folding or crushing it; to develop lines in this way: *Pack your suit carefully so that you don't crease it.* **2** [T, I] ~ **(sth)** to make lines in the skin; to develop lines in the skin: *A frown creased her forehead.* ♦ *Her face creased into a smile.* ▶ **creased** *adj.*: *I can't wear this blouse. It's creased.*

cre·ate 🔊 **AWL** /kri'eɪt/ *verb*
  1 ~ **sth** to make something happen or exist: *Scientists disagree about how the universe was created.* ♦ *The main purpose of industry is to create wealth.* ♦ *The government plans to create more jobs for young people.* ♦ *Create a new directory and put all your files into it.* ♦ *The table, created by our head chef.* ⊃ thesaurus box at MAKE **2** ~ **sth** to produce a particular feeling or impression: *The company is trying to*

create a young energetic image. ◆ The announcement only succeeded in creating confusion. ◆ They've painted it red to create a feeling of warmth.

create

create verb

■ **an/the ability to**
E-commerce advocates were overly optimistic about the ability of new technology to create more efficient markets.

■ **attempt to**, **strive to**, **try to** | **be able to** | **combine to**
Through her analysis, Vickery attempts to create an understanding of the 18th century home.

■ **job** | **atmosphere**, **environment** | **opportunity** | **illusion**, **image**, **impression** | **sense** | **condition** | **problem**
Firms have to create an atmosphere of trust in order to produce effectively.

■ **newly** | **artificially**
Hoffman Island and Swinburne Island are two artificially created islands in New York harbor.

creation noun

■ **wealth** | **job**
Creativity, knowledge, and agility are the catalysts of wealth creation.
The study found that only a small proportion of firms are able to expand sufficiently to provide job creation.

■ **spur** | **oversee** | **facilitate** | **foster**
Within three years, however, Truman had overseen the creation of a central intelligence service.
The evolution of communication technology has facilitated the creation of a global society.

creative adj.

■ **genuinely**, **truly** | **highly**
Research suggests that highly creative boys are more communicative than their peers.

■ **thinking** | **genius** | **process** | **solution** | **people**
Melville had a singular admiration for Milton as a poet and creative genius.

creativity noun

■ **artistic**, **intellectual**, **musical** | **human**
Researchers have unearthed engravings created more than 70,000 years ago, which are the earliest evidence of human creativity.

■ **stifle** | **nurture** | **foster**
The most effective way to stifle creativity is to make people feel that they have no discretion and autonomy.
The organization design of the corporation has to remain flexible to foster creativity.

cre·a·tion 🔑 **AWL** /kriˈeɪʃn/ noun
1 [U] the act or process of making something that is new, or of causing something to exist that did not exist before: the process of database creation ◆ wealth creation ◆ He had been with the company since its creation in 1989. ⊃ see also JOB CREATION ⊃ collocations at CREATE **2** [C] (often humorous) a thing that someone has made, especially something that shows ability or imagination: a literary creation ◆ The dessert was a delicious creation of sponge cake, cream and fruit. **3** usually **the Creation** [sing.] the making of the world, especially by God as described in the Bible **4** often **Creation** [U] the world and all the living things in it

cre·a·tion·ism /kriˈeɪʃəˌnɪzəm/ noun [U] the belief that the universe was made by God exactly as described in the Bible ► **cre·a·tion·ist** adj., noun

creˈation ˌscience noun [U] science that tries to find proof that God created the world

cre·a·tive 🔑 **AWL** /kriˈeɪtɪv/ adj., noun
● adj. **1** [only before noun] involving the use of skill and the imagination to produce something new or a work of art: a course on **creative writing** (= writing stories, plays and poems) ◆ the creative and performing arts ◆ **creative thinking** (= thinking about problems in a new way or thinking of new ideas) ◆ the company's creative team ◆ the creative process **2** having the skill and ability to produce something new, especially a work of art; showing this ability: She's very creative—she writes poetry and paints. ◆ Do you have any ideas? You're the creative one. ⊃ collocations at CREATE ► **cre·a·tive·ly** **AWL** adv. **cre·a·tiv·i·ty** **AWL** /ˌkriːeɪˈtɪvəti/ noun [U]: Creativity and originality are more important than technical skill.
● noun **1** [C] a person who is creative: The exhibition features the paintings of local creatives. **2** [U] creative ideas or material: We need to produce better creative if we want to attract big clients.

creˌative acˈcounting noun [U] (disapproving) a way of doing or presenting the accounts of a business that might not show what the true situation really is

cre·a·tor **AWL** /kriˈeɪtər/ noun **1** [C] a person who has made or invented a particular thing: Walt Disney, the creator of Mickey Mouse **2** **the Creator** [sing.] God

crea·ture 🔑 /ˈkriːtʃər/ noun
1 a living thing, real or imaginary, that can move around, such as an animal: The dormouse is a shy, nocturnal creature. ◆ respect for all **living creatures** ◆ strange creatures from outer space **2** (especially following an adjective) a person, considered in a particular way: You pathetic creature! ◆ She was an exotic creature with long red hair and brilliant green eyes. ◆ He always goes to bed at ten—he's **a creature of habit** (= he likes to do the same things at the same time every day).
IDM **a/the creature of sb** | **sb's creature** (formal, disapproving) a person or thing that depends completely on someone else and is controlled by them

creature ˈcomforts noun [pl.] all the things that make life, or a particular place, comfortable, such as good food, comfortable furniture, or modern equipment

crèche (also **creche**) /krɛʃ/ noun a model of the scene of Jesus Christ's birth, placed in churches and homes at Christmas

cred /krɛd/ noun [U] = STREET CRED

cre·dence /ˈkriːdns/ noun [U] (formal) **1** a quality that an idea or a story has that makes you believe it is true: Historical evidence **lends credence** to his theory. **2** belief in something as true: They could **give** no **credence** to the findings of the survey. ◆ Alternative medicine has been **gaining credence** (= becoming more widely accepted) recently.

cre·den·tial /krəˈdɛnʃl/ verb ~ **sb** to provide someone with credentials

cre·den·tials /krəˈdɛnʃlz/ noun [pl.] **1** ~ (**as/for sth**) the qualities, training, or experience that make you suitable to do something: He has all the credentials for the job. ◆ She will first have to establish her leadership credentials. **2** documents such as letters that prove that you are who you claim to be, and can therefore be trusted

cred·i·bil·i·ty /ˌkrɛdəˈbɪləti/ noun [U] the quality that someone or something has that makes people believe or trust them: to **gain/lack/lose credibility** ◆ The prosecution did its best to **undermine the credibility** of the witness. ◆ Newspapers were talking of a **credibility gap** between what he said and what he did. ⊃ see also STREET CRED

cred·i·ble /ˈkrɛdəbl/ adj. **1** that can be believed or trusted **SYN** CONVINCING: a credible explanation/witness ◆ It is just not credible that she would cheat. **2** that can be accepted, because it seems possible that it could be successful **SYN** VIABLE: Community service is seen as the only credible alternative to imprisonment. ► **cred·i·bly** /-bli/ adv.: We can credibly describe the band's latest album as their best yet.

cred·it 🔑 AWL /ˈkrɛdət/ noun, verb

• **noun**

> BUY NOW–PAY LATER **1** [U] an arrangement that you make, with a store for example, to pay later for something you buy: *to get/refuse credit* ◆ *We bought the dishwasher on credit.* ◆ *to offer interest-free credit* (= allow someone to pay later, without any extra charge) ◆ *a credit agreement* ◆ *credit terms* ◆ *Your credit limit is now $2,000.* ◆ *He's a bad credit risk* (= he is unlikely to pay the money later).

> MONEY BORROWED **2** [U, C] money that you borrow from a bank; a loan: *The bank refused further credit to the company.* ◆ *The company president applied for a $10,000 credit line/line of credit* (= an amount of money that you can borrow over a period of time). **3** [U] the status of being trusted to pay back money to someone who lends it to you: *Her credit isn't good anywhere now.*

> MONEY IN BANK **4** [U] the amount of money you have in your bank account: *You have a credit balance of $250.* **5** [C, U] a sum of money paid into a bank account; a record of the payment: *a credit of $50* ◆ *You'll be paid by direct credit into your bank account.* ANT DEBIT

> MONEY BACK **6** [C, U] (*technical*) a payment that someone has a right to for a particular reason: *a tax credit*

> PRAISE **7** [U] **~ (for sth)** praise or approval because you are responsible for something good that has happened: *He's a player who rarely seems to get the credit he deserves.* ◆ *I can't take all the credit for the show's success—it was a team effort.* ◆ *We did all the work and she gets all the credit!* ◆ *Credit will be given on the exam for good spelling and grammar.* ◆ *At least give him credit for trying* (= praise him because he tried, even if he did not succeed). ⊃ compare BLAME, DISCREDIT **8** [sing.] **~ to sb/sth** a person or thing whose qualities or achievements are praised and who therefore earns respect for someone or something else: *She is a credit to the school.*

> ON MOVIE/TV PROGRAM **9** [C, usually pl.] the act of mentioning someone who worked on a project such as a movie or a television program: *She was given a program credit for her work on the costumes for the play.* ◆ *The credits* (= the list of all the people involved) *seemed to last almost as long as the film!*

> UNIT OF STUDY **10** [C] a unit of study at a college, university or school; the fact of having successfully completed a unit of study: *My math class is worth three credits.*

IDM **do sb credit | do credit to sb/sth** if something **does credit** to a person or an organization, they deserve to be praised for it: *Your honesty does you great credit.* **have sth to your credit** to have achieved something: *He's only 30, and he already has four novels to his credit.* **on the credit side** used to introduce the good points about someone or something, especially after the bad points have been mentioned **to sb's credit** making someone deserve praise or respect: *To his credit, Jack never told anyone exactly what had happened.*

• **verb**

> PUT MONEY IN BANK **1** to add an amount of money to someone's bank account: **~ A (with B)** *Your account has been credited with $50,000.* ◆ **~ B (to A)** *$50,000 has been credited to your account.* ANT DEBIT

> WITH ACHIEVEMENT **2** [usually passive] to believe or say that someone is responsible for doing something, especially something good: **~ sb** *All the contributors are credited on the title page.* ◆ **~ A with B** *The company is credited with inventing the industrial robot.* ◆ **~ B to A** *The invention of the industrial robot is credited to the company.* ⊃ compare ACCREDIT

> WITH QUALITY **3 ~ A with B** to believe that someone or something has a particular good quality or feature: *I credited you with a little more sense.* **4** [usually passive] **~ sb/sth as sth** to believe that someone or something is of a particular type or quality: *The cheetah is generally credited as the world's fastest animal.*

cred·it·a·ble /ˈkrɛdətəbl/ *adj.* (*formal*) **1** of a good standard and deserving praise or approval SYN PRAISEWORTHY: *It was a very creditable result for the team.* **2** morally good SYN ADMIRABLE: *There was nothing very creditable in what he did.* ▶ **cred·it·a·bly** /-bli/ *adv.*

credit bureau *noun* (*pl.* credit bureaus *or* credit bureaux

/-ouz/) a company that collects information about people's CREDIT RATINGS and makes it available to credit card companies, financial institutions, etc.

credit card 🔑 *noun* a small plastic card that you can use to buy goods and services and pay for them later: *All major credit cards are accepted at our hotels.* ⊃ picture at MONEY ⊃ see also CHARGE CARD, CHECK CARD, DEBIT CARD, STORE CARD

credit crunch *noun* [usually sing.] (*economics*) an economic condition in which it suddenly becomes difficult and expensive to borrow money

cred·i·tor AWL /ˈkrɛdətər/ *noun* a person, company, etc. that someone owes money to ⊃ compare DEBTOR

credit rating *noun* a judgment made by a bank, etc. about how likely someone is to pay back money that they borrow, and how safe it is to lend money to them

credit union *noun* an organization that lends money to its members at low rates of interest

cred·it·worth·y /ˈkrɛdətˌwərði/ *adj.* able to be trusted to pay back money that is owed; safe to lend money to ▶ **cred·it·wor·thi·ness** *noun* [U]

cre·do /ˈkridou; ˈkrei-/ *noun* (*pl.* cre·dos) (*formal*) a set of beliefs SYN CREED

cre·du·li·ty /krəˈduləti; -ˈdʒu-/ *noun* [U] (*formal*) the ability or willingness to believe that something is real or true: *The plot of the novel stretches credulity to the limit* (= it is almost impossible to believe).

cred·u·lous /ˈkrɛdʒələs/ *adj.* (*formal*) too ready to believe things and therefore easy to trick SYN ⊃ compare IN-CREDULOUS

Cree /kri/ *noun* (*pl.* Cree *or* Crees) a member of a Native American people, living in Canada east of the Rocky Mountains

creed /krid/ *noun* **1** a set of principles or religious beliefs: *people of all races, colors and creeds* ◆ *What is his political creed?* **2 the Creed** [sing.] a statement of Christian belief that is spoken as part of some church services

Creek /krik/ *noun* (*pl.* Creek *or* Creeks) a member of a Native American people, many of whom now live in the state of Oklahoma

creek /krik; krɪk/ *noun* a small river or stream IDM **up the creek (without a paddle)** (*informal*) in a difficult or bad situation: *I was really up the creek without my car.*

creel /kril/ *noun* a BASKET for holding fish that have just been caught

creep /krip/ *verb, noun*

• **verb** (crept, crept /krɛpt/) HELP In the phrasal verb **creep someone out**, creeped is used for the past simple and past participle. **1** [I] (+ adv./prep.) (of people or animals) to move slowly, quietly, and carefully, because you do not want to be seen or heard: *I crept up the stairs, trying not to wake my parents.* **2** [I] (+ adv./prep.) to move with your body close to the ground; to move slowly on your hands and knees SYN CRAWL **3** [I] (+ adv./prep.) to move or develop very slowly: *Her arms crept around his neck.* ◆ *A slight feeling of suspicion crept over me.* **4** [I] (+ adv./prep.) (of plants) to grow along the ground or up walls using long STEMS or roots ⊃ see also CREEPER IDM see FLESH PHRV **creep 'in/into sth** to begin to happen or affect something: *As she became more tired, errors began to creep into her work.* **creep sb 'out** (creeped, creeped) (*informal*) to make someone feel afraid, uncomfortable or disgusted: *He said the empty streets creeped him out.* **creep 'up** to gradually increase in amount, price, etc.: *House prices are creeping up again.* **creep 'up on sb 1** to move slowly nearer to someone, usually from behind, without being seen or heard: *Don't creep up on me like that!* **2** to begin to affect someone, especially before they realize it: *Tiredness can easily creep up on you while you're driving.*

• **noun 1** [C] (*informal*) a person that you dislike very much

t **tea**   ţ **butter**   d **did**   k **cat**   g **got**   tʃ **chin**   dʒ **June**   f **fall**

and find very unpleasant: *He's a nasty little creep!* **2** [U] (in compounds) (often *disapproving*) the development of a project beyond the goal that was originally agreed: *The World Bank has been accused of **mission creep** when seeking to address these concerns.*

IDM give sb the creeps (*informal*) to make someone feel nervous and slightly frightened, especially because someone or something is unpleasant or strange

creep·er /ˈkripər/ *noun* a plant that grows along the ground, up walls, etc., often winding itself around other plants

creep·ing /ˈkripɪŋ/ *adj.* [only before noun] (of something bad) happening or moving gradually, and not easily noticed: *creeping inflation*

creep·y /ˈkripi/ *adj.* (creep·i·er, creep·i·est) (*informal*) **1** causing an unpleasant feeling of fear or slight horror **SYN** SCARY: *a creepy ghost story* ◆ *It's kind of creepy down in the cellar!* **2** strange in a way that makes you feel nervous: *What a creepy coincidence.* **SYN** SPOOKY

creep·y-crawl·y /ˌkripi ˈkrɔli/ *noun* (*pl.* creep·y-crawl·ies) (*informal*) an insect, a WORM, etc. when you think of it as unpleasant

cre·mains /krɪˈmeɪnz/ *noun* [pl.] the powder that is left after a dead person's body has been CREMATED (= burned) **SYN** ASHES

cre·mate /ˈkrimeɪt; krɪˈmeɪt/ *verb* [often passive] *~ sb/sth* to burn a dead body, especially as part of a funeral ceremony

cre·ma·tion /krɪˈmeɪʃn/ *noun* **1** [U] the act of cremating someone **2** [C] a funeral at which the dead person is cremated

cre·ma·to·ri·um /ˌkriməˈtɔriəm/ *noun* (*pl.* cre·ma·to·ri·a /-ˈtɔriə/ or cre·ma·to·ri·ums) (also cre·ma·to·ry /ˈkriməˌtɔri/ *pl.* cre·ma·to·ries) a building in which the bodies of dead people are burned

crème brû·lée /ˌkrɛm bru·ˈleɪ/ *noun* [C, U] (*pl.* crèmes brû·lées /ˌkrɛm bru·ˈleɪ/) (from *French*) a cold DESSERT (= a sweet dish) made from cream, with burnt sugar on top

crème car·a·mel /ˌkrɛm kærəˈmɛl/ *noun* [C, U] (*pl.* crèmes car·a·mels /ˌkrɛm kærəˈmɛl/) (from *French*) = FLAN

crème de la crème /ˌkrɛm də lɑ ˈkrɛm; -lə-/ *noun* [sing.] (from *French*, *formal* or *humorous*) the best people or things of their kind: *This school takes only the crème de la crème.*

crème de menthe /ˌkrɛm də ˈmɛnθ; -ˈmɪnt/ *noun* [U, C] (*pl.* crèmes de menthe /ˌkrɛm də ˈmɛnθ; -ˈmɪnt/) (from *French*) a strong, sweet, alcoholic drink made with MINT

crème fraiche /ˌkrɛm ˈfrɛʃ/ *noun* [U] (from *French*) thick cream with a slightly sour taste

cren·el·lated (also cren·e·lated) /ˈkrɛnlˌeɪtɪd/ *adj.* (*technical*) (of a tower, castle, etc.) having BATTLEMENTS

Cre·ole (also cre·ole) /ˈkrioʊl/ *noun, adj.*
• *noun* **1** [C] a person whose ANCESTORS were among the first Europeans who settled in the West Indies or S. America, or one of the French or Spanish people who settled in the southern states of the U.S. **2** [C] a person of mixed European and African race, especially one who lives in the West Indies **3** [U] a language formed when a mixture of a European language with a local language (especially an African language spoken by SLAVES in the West Indies) is spoken as a first language ⊃ compare PIDGIN
• *adj.* **1** of or relating to Creoles or their languages **2** usually **creole** in the traditional style of cooking of the Creoles in the southern states of the U.S., using lots of spices and strong flavors: *Creole cuisine is hot and spicy.* ◆ *shrimp creole*

cre·o·lize /ˈkriəˌlaɪz/ *verb* *~ sth* (*linguistics*) to change a language by combining it with a language from another place: *Creolized forms of Latin were spoken in various parts of Europe.* ▸ **cre·o·li·za·tion** /ˌkriəlɑrˈzeɪʃn/ *noun* [U, C]

cre·o·sote /ˈkriəˌsoʊt/ *noun, verb*
• *noun* [U] a thick brown liquid that is made from COAL TAR, used to preserve wood
• *verb* *~ sth* to paint or preserve something with creosote

crepe (also **crêpe**) *noun* **1** /kreɪp/ [U] a type of light thin cloth, made especially from cotton or silk, with a surface that is covered in lines and folds: *a black crêpe dress* ◆ *a crêpe bandage* **2** /kreɪp/ [U] a type of strong rubber with a rough surface, used for making the SOLES of shoes: *crêpe-soled shoes* **3** /kreɪp; krɛp/ [C] a thin PANCAKE

crepe paper /ˈkreɪp ˌpeɪpər/ *noun* [U] a type of thin brightly colored paper that stretches and has a surface covered in lines and folds, used especially for making decorations

crept *pt, pp of* CREEP

cre·pus·cu·lar /krɪˈpʌskyələr/ *adj.* (*literary*) related to the period of the evening when the sun has just gone down but there is still some light in the sky

cre·scen·do /krəˈʃɛndoʊ/ *noun* (*pl.* cre·scen·dos) [C, U] **1** (*music*) a gradual increase in how loudly a piece of music is played or sung **ANT** DIMINUENDO **2** a gradual increase in noise; the loudest point of a period of continuous noise **SYN** SWELL: *Voices rose in a crescendo and drowned him out.* ◆ (*figurative*) *The advertising campaign reached a crescendo just before Christmas.*

cres·cent /ˈkrɛsnt/ *noun* **1** [C] a curved shape that is wide in the middle and pointed at each end: *a crescent moon* **2** [C] (often used in street names) a curved street with a row of houses on it: *I live at 7 Park Crescent.* **3** the Crescent [sing.] the curved shape that is used as a symbol of Islam ⊃ see also THE RED CRESCENT

cress /krɛs/ *noun* [U] a small plant with thin STEMS and very small leaves, often eaten in salads and SANDWICHES ⊃ see also WATERCRESS

crest /krɛst/ *noun, verb*
• *noun* **1** [usually sing.] *~ (of sth)* the top part of a hill or wave: *surfers riding the crest of the wave* **2** a design used as the symbol of a particular family, organization, etc., especially one that has a long history: *the university crest* **3** a group of feathers that stand up on top of a bird's head ⊃ picture at ANIMAL
IDM the crest of a/the wave a situation in which someone is very successful, happy, etc. ⊃ more at RIDE *v.*
• *verb* **1** [T] *~ sth* (*formal*) to reach the top of a hill, mountain, or wave: *He slowed the pace as they crested the ridge.* **2** [I] (of a flood, wave, etc.) to reach its highest level before it falls again: (*figurative*) *The level of debt crested at a massive $920 billion in 2009.*

crest·ed /ˈkrɛstəd/ *adj.* **1** marked with a crest: *crested note-paper* **2** used especially in names of birds or animals that have a crest: *crested newts*

crest·fal·len /ˈkrɛstˌfɔlən/ *adj.* sad and disappointed because you have failed and you did not expect to

Cre·ta·ceous /krɪˈteɪʃəs/ *adj.* (*geology*) of the PERIOD between around 146 to 65 million years ago, when dinosaurs lived (until they died out); of the rocks formed during this time ▸ **the Cre·ta·ceous** *noun* [sing.]

cre·tin /ˈkritn/ *noun* (*informal*, *offensive*) a very stupid person: *Why did you do that, you cretin?* ▸ **cre·tin·ous** /ˈkritn·əs/ *adj.*

Creutz·feldt-Ja·kob dis·ease /ˌkrɔɪtsfɛlt ˈyækəb dɪˌziz/ *noun* [U] (*abbr.* CJD) a brain disease that causes gradual loss of control of the mind and body and, finally, death. It is linked to BSE in cows.

cre·vasse /krəˈvæs/ *noun* a deep open crack, especially in ice, for example in a GLACIER

crev·ice /ˈkrɛvəs/ *noun* a narrow crack in a rock or wall

crew /kru/ *noun, verb*
• *noun* **1** [C] all the people working on a ship, plane, etc.: *None of the passengers and crew were injured.* ◆ *crew members* ⊃ see also AIRCREW, CABIN CREW, FLIGHT CREW **2** [C] all the people working on a ship, plane, etc. except the officers who are in charge: *the officers and crew* **3** [C] a group of people with special skills working together: *a film/camera crew* ◆ *an ambulance crew* ⊃ see also GROUND CREW **4** [sing.] (usually *disapproving*) a group of people: *The people she invited were a pretty **motley crew*** (= a strange mix of types of people). **5** [C] a team of people who ROW boats in races: *a*

member of the German crew **6** [U] the sport of ROWING with other people in a boat: *I'm thinking of going out for crew this semester* (= joining the ROWING team).

- **verb** [T, I] to be part of a crew, especially on a ship: **~ (sth)** *Normally the boat is crewed by five people.* ◆ **~ (for sb)** *I crewed for him on his yacht last summer.*

crew cut *noun* a HAIRSTYLE for men in which the hair is cut very short ⊃ picture at HAIR

crew·man /ˈkruːmən/ *noun* (*pl.* **crew·men** /-mən/) a member of a crew, usually a man

crew neck *noun* a round neck on a sweater, etc.

crib /krɪb/ *noun, verb*
- **noun 1** a small bed with high sides for a baby or young child ⊃ picture at BED **2** a long open box that horses and cows can eat from **SYN** MANGER **3** (*informal*) written information such as answers to questions, often used dishonestly by students in tests: *a crib sheet* **4** (*informal*) the house, apartment, etc. where someone lives
- **verb** (-bb-) [I, T] **~ (sth) (from sb)** (*old-fashioned*) to dishonestly copy work from another student or from a book

crib·bage /ˈkrɪbɪdʒ/ *noun* [U] a card game in which players score points by collecting different combinations of cards. The score is kept by putting small PEGS in holes in a board.

crib death *noun* [U, C] the sudden death while sleeping of a baby that appears to be healthy

crick /krɪk/ (*also* **kink**) *noun* [usually sing.] a sudden painful stiff feeling in the muscles of your neck or back ▶ **crick** *verb*: **~ sth** *I suffered a cricked neck during a game of tennis.*

crick·et /ˈkrɪkət/ *noun* **1** [C] a small, brown, jumping insect that makes a loud high sound by rubbing its wings together: *the chirping of crickets* **2** [U] a game played on grass by two teams of 11 players. Players score points (called RUNS) by hitting the ball with a wooden BAT and running between two sets of vertical wooden sticks, called STUMPS: *a cricket match/team/club/ball*

cri de cœur /ˌkriː də ˈkɜːr/ *noun* (*pl.* **cris de cœur** /ˌkriː də ˈkɜːr/) (from *French*) an act of asking for something, or protesting, in a way that shows you care deeply about something

cried pt, pp of CRY

cri·er /ˈkraɪər/ *noun* = TOWN CRIER

crime 🔊 /kraɪm/ *noun*
1 [U] activities that involve breaking the law: *an increase in violent crime* ◆ *the fight against crime* ◆ *Stores spend more and more on* **crime prevention** *every year.* ◆ *petty/serious crime* ◆ *the connection between drugs and* **organized crime** ◆ *He turned to crime when he dropped out of school.* ◆ *The crime rate is rising.* ◆ *crime fiction/novels* (= stories about crime) ◆ *crime figures/statistics* ◆ *She's a crime writer* (= she writes stories about crime). ⊃ collocations at JUSTICE **2** [C] **~ (against sb)** an illegal act or activity that can be punished by law: *to commit a crime* (= do something illegal) ◆ *The massacre was a crime against humanity.* ⊃ see also WAR CRIME **3** a crime [sing.] an act that you think is immoral or is a big mistake: *It's a crime to waste so much money.*

TOPIC COLLOCATIONS

Crime

committing a crime
- **commit** a crime/a murder/a violent assault/a brutal killing/an armed robbery/fraud/perjury
- **be involved in** terrorism/a suspected arson attack/ human smuggling/human trafficking
- **engage/participate in** criminal activity/illegal practices/acts of mindless vandalism
- **steal** sb's wallet/purse/watch/cell phone
- **rob** a bank/a person/a tourist
- **break into/burglarize** a house/a home/an apartment/an office
- **hijack** a plane/ship/bus

- **smuggle** drugs/weapons/arms/people/immigrants
- **launder** (drug) money (through sth)
- **forge** documents/certificates/passports
- **take/accept/pay sb/offer (sb)** a bribe
- **run** a phishing scam/an e-mail scam/an Internet scam

fighting crime
- **combat/fight** crime/terrorism/drug trafficking/ corruption
- **prevent/stop** credit-card fraud/child abuse/software piracy
- **deter/stop** criminals/burglars/thieves/shoplifters/ vandals
- **reduce/tackle/crack down on** gun/violent/street/ property crime
- **foil** a bank robbery/a terrorist plot
- **help/support/protect** the victims of crime

investigating crime
- **report** a crime/a theft/a rape/an attack/an incident to the police
- **witness** a crime/an attack/a murder/an incident
- **investigate** a murder/a homicide/a burglary/a robbery/the alleged incident
- **conduct/launch/pursue/open** an investigation (into…)
- **investigate/reopen** a criminal/murder case
- **examine/investigate/find fingerprints at** the crime scene/the scene of crime
- **collect/gather** forensic evidence/physical evidence
- **uncover/discover** new evidence/a fraud/a scam/a plot/a conspiracy/political corruption/a cache of weapons
- **describe/identify** a suspect/the culprit/the perpetrator/the assailant/the attacker
- **question/interrogate** a suspect/witness
- **solve/crack** the case
- more collocations at JUSTICE

crime wave *noun* [sing.] a situation in which there is a sudden increase in the number of crimes that are committed

crim·i·nal 🔊 /ˈkrɪmənl/ *adj., noun*
- **adj. 1** [usually before noun] connected with or involving crime: *criminal offenses/behavior* ◆ *criminal damage* (= the crime of damaging someone's property deliberately) ◆ *criminal negligence* (= the illegal act of someone failing to do something that they should do, with the result that someone else is harmed) **2** [only before noun] connected to the laws that deal with crime: *criminal law* ◆ *the criminal justice system* ◆ *a criminal lawyer* ◆ *to bring criminal charges against someone* ⊃ compare CIVIL **3** morally wrong: *This is a criminal waste of resources.*
- **noun** a person who commits a crime: *Society does not know how to deal with* **hardened criminals** (= people who regularly commit crimes and are not sorry for what they do). ◆ *a career criminal* ⊃ collocations at CRIME

crim·i·nal·i·ty /ˌkrɪməˈnæləti/ *noun* [U] the fact of people being involved in crime; criminal acts

crim·i·nal·ize /ˈkrɪmənəˌlaɪz/ *verb* **1 ~ sth** to make something illegal by passing a new law: *The use of opium was not criminalized until fairly recently.* **2 ~ sb** to treat someone as a criminal ▶ **crim·i·nal·i·za·tion** /ˌkrɪmənələˈzeɪʃn/ *noun* [U]

criminal law *noun* [U, C] a system of law that deals with the punishment of people who commit crimes; a law belonging to this system ⊃ compare CIVIL LAW

crim·i·nal·ly /ˈkrɪmənəli/ *adv.* according to the laws that deal with crime: *criminally insane*

criminal record *noun* = RECORD

crim·i·nol·o·gy /ˌkrɪməˈnɑlədʒi/ *noun* [U] the scientific study of crime and criminals ▶ **crim·i·no·log·i·cal** /ˌkrɪmənəˈlɑdʒɪkl/ *adj.* **crim·i·nol·o·gist** /ˌkrɪməˈnɑlədʒɪst/ *noun*

crimp /krɪmp/ *verb, noun*
- *verb* **1** ~ sth to press cloth or paper into small folds **2** ~ sth (*informal*) to restrict the growth or development of something **3** ~ sth to make curls in someone's hair by pressing it with a heated tool
- *noun*
  IDM **put a crimp in/on sth** (*informal*) to have a bad or negative effect on something

crim·son /ˈkrɪmzn/ *adj.* dark red in color: *She went crimson* (= her face became very red because she was embarrassed). ► **crim·son** *noun* [U]

cringe /krɪndʒ/ *verb* **1** [I] to move back and/or away from someone because you are afraid **SYN** **COWER**: *a child cringing in terror* **2** [I] to feel very embarrassed and uncomfortable about something: *I cringe when I think of the poems I wrote then.*

cringe·wor·thy /ˈkrɪndʒˌwərði/ *adj.* (*informal*) making you feel embarrassed or uncomfortable: *It was a cringeworthy performance from start to finish.*

crin·kle /ˈkrɪŋkl/ *verb, noun*
- *verb* [I, T] ~ (sth) to become covered with or to form a lot of thin folds or lines, especially in skin, cloth, or paper: *He smiled, his eyes crinkling.* ◆ *Her face crinkled up in a smile.* ◆ *The pages crinkled and curled and turned to ashes in the fire.*
- *noun* a very thin fold or line made on paper, cloth, or skin

crin·kly /ˈkrɪŋkli/ *adj.* **1** having a lot of thin folds or lines: *crinkly aluminum foil* **2** (of hair) having a lot of small curls or waves

crin·o·line /ˈkrɪnl·ən/ *noun* a frame that was worn under a skirt by some women in the past in order to give the skirt a very round full shape

crip·ple /ˈkrɪpl/ *verb, noun*
- *verb* **1** [usually passive] ~ sb to damage someone's body so that they are no longer able to walk or move normally **SYN** **DISABLE**: *He was crippled by polio as a child.* ◆ *to be crippled with arthritis* **2** [usually passive] ~ sb/sth to seriously damage or harm someone or something: *The pilot tried to land his crippled plane.* ► **crip·pling** *adj.*: *a crippling disease* ◆ *crippling debts*
- *noun* (*old-fashioned* or *offensive*) a person who is unable to walk or move normally because of a disease or injury: *(figurative) He's an emotional cripple* (= he cannot express his feelings). **HELP** People now use **disabled person** or **person with a disability** instead of "cripple."

cri·sis /ˈkraɪsəs/ *noun* [C, U] (*pl.* **cri·ses** /-siz/) **1** a time of great danger, difficulty, or confusion when problems must be solved or important decisions must be made: *a political/financial crisis* ◆ *the government's latest economic crisis* ◆ *The business is still in crisis but it has survived the worst of the recession.* ◆ *The party was facing an identity crisis.* ◆ *an expert in crisis management* ◆ *We provide help to families in crisis situations.* ◆ *In times of crisis I know which friends I can turn to.* ◆ *The party was suffering a crisis of confidence among its supporters* (= they did not trust it any longer). ⊃ see also **MIDLIFE CRISIS** **2** a time when a problem, a bad situation, or an illness is at its worst point: *Their marriage has reached a crisis point.* ◆ *The fever has passed its crisis.* ⊃ see also **CRITICAL**

crisp /krɪsp/ *adj., noun, verb*
- *adj.* (**crisp·er, crisp·est**) (usually *approving*) **1** (of food) (also **crisp·y**) (*approving*) pleasantly hard and dry: *Bake until the pastry is golden and crisp.* **2** (of fruit and vegetables) (also **crisp·y**) firm and fresh: *a crisp apple/lettuce* **3** (of paper or cloth) fresh and clean; new and slightly stiff without any folds in it: *a crisp new $5 bill* ◆ *a crisp white shirt* **4** (of the air or the weather) pleasantly dry and cold: *a crisp winter morning* ◆ *The air was crisp and clear and the sky was blue.* **5** (of snow, leaves, etc.) firm or dry, and making a pleasant noise when crushed: *deep, crisp snow* **6** (of sounds, images, etc.) pleasantly clear and sharp: *The recording sounds very*

crisp, considering its age. **7** (sometimes *disapproving*) (of a person's way of speaking) quick and confident in a way that suggests that the person is busy or is not being friendly: *Her answer was crisp, and she gave no details.* ► **crisp·ly** *adv.*: *crisply fried potatoes* ◆ *"Take a seat," she said crisply.* **crisp·ness** *noun* [U]: *The salad had lost its crispness.*
- *noun* [U, C] a **DESSERT** (= a sweet dish) made from fruit that is covered with a rough mixture of flour, butter, and sugar, cooked in the oven and usually served hot: *apple crisp*
  IDM see **BURN**
- *verb* [I, T] ~ (sth) to become or make something crisp

crisp·y /ˈkrɪspi/ *adj.* (*approving*) = **CRISP**: *crispy batter*

criss-cross /ˈkrɪs krɔs/ *adj., verb*
- *adj.* [usually before noun] with many straight lines that cross each other: *a criss-cross pattern* ► **criss-cross** *noun* [sing.]: *a criss-cross of streets*
- *verb* [T, I] ~ (sth) | ~ sth (with sth) to make a pattern on something with many straight lines that cross each other: *The city is criss-crossed with canals.*

cri·te·ri·on /kraɪˈtɪriən/ *noun* **AWL**
(*pl.* **cri·te·ri·a** /-ˈtɪriə/)
a standard or principle by which something is judged, or with the help of which a decision is made: *The main criterion is value for money.* ◆ *What criteria are used for assessing a student's ability?*

crit·ic /ˈkrɪtɪk/ *noun* **1** a person who expresses opinions about the good and bad qualities of books, music, etc.: *a music/theater/literary, etc. critic* ◆ *The critics loved the movie.* **2** a person who expresses disapproval of someone or something and talks about their bad qualities, especially publicly: *She is one of the ruling party's most outspoken critics.* ◆ *a critic of private health care*

crit·i·cal /ˈkrɪtɪkl/ *adj.*
> **EXPRESSING DISAPPROVAL 1** expressing disapproval of someone or something and saying what you think is bad about them: *a critical comment/report* ◆ *The supervisor is always very critical.* ◆ ~ **of sb/sth** *Tom's parents were highly critical of the school.*
> **IMPORTANT 2** extremely important because a future situation will be affected by it **SYN** **CRUCIAL**: *a critical factor in the election campaign* ◆ *Reducing levels of carbon dioxide in the atmosphere is of critical importance.* ◆ *Your decision is critical to our future.* ⊃ thesaurus box at **ESSENTIAL**
> **SERIOUS/DANGEROUS 3** serious, uncertain, and possibly dangerous: *The first 24 hours after the operation are the most critical.* ◆ *a critical moment in our country's history* ◆ *One of the victims of the fire remains in critical condition.* ⊃ see also **CRISIS**
> **MAKING CAREFUL JUDGMENTS 4** involving making fair, careful judgments about the good and bad qualities of someone or something: *Students are encouraged to develop critical thinking instead of accepting opinions without questioning them.*
> **OF ART/MUSIC/BOOKS, ETC. 5** [only before noun] according to the judgment of critics of art, music, literature, etc.: *the film director's greatest critical success* ◆ *In her day, she never received the critical acclaim* (= praise from the critics) *she deserved.*
  ► **crit·i·cal·ly** /-kli/ *adv.*: *She spoke critically of her father.* ◆ *He is critically ill in intensive care.* ◆ *I looked at myself critically in the mirror.*

critical 'mass *noun* [C, U] **1** (*physics*) the smallest amount of a substance that is needed for a nuclear **CHAIN REACTION** to take place **2** the smallest size or amount of something that is needed for an effect or action to take place: *The new device already has a critical mass of users.* ◆ *I don't think we've reached critical mass for this particular law yet.*

critical 'path *noun* [sing.] (*technical*) the order of work that should be followed to complete a project as fast and as cheaply as possible

---

| i see | ɪ sit | ɛ ten | æ cat | ɑ hot | ɔ saw | ʊ put | u too | 355 |

critical 'theory *noun* [U] a way of thinking about and examining culture and literature by considering the social, historical, and ideological (IDEOLOGY) forces that affect it and make it the way it is

crit·i·cism 🔑 /ˈkrɪtəˌsɪzəm/ *noun*
1 [U, C] the act of expressing disapproval of someone or something and opinions about their faults or bad qualities; a statement showing disapproval: *The plan has attracted criticism from consumer groups.* ◆ *People in public life must always be **open to criticism** (= willing to accept being criticized).* ◆ *Ben is very sensitive, he just can't **take criticism**.* ◆ *to offer someone **constructive criticism** (= that is meant to be helpful)* ◆ *I didn't mean it as a criticism.* ◆ *criticisms **leveled at** (= aimed at) journalists* ◆ *~ **of sb/sth** There was widespread criticism of the government's handling of the disaster.* ◆ *~ **that**... My only criticism of the house is that it is on a main road.* **ANT** PRAISE **2** [U] the work or activity of making fair, careful judgments about the good and bad qualities of someone or something, especially books, music, etc.: *literary criticism*

crit·i·cize 🔑 /ˈkrɪtəˌsaɪz/ *verb*
1 [I, T] to say that you disapprove of someone or something; to say what you do not like or think is wrong about someone or something: *All you ever do is criticize!* ◆ *~ **sb/sth** The decision was criticized by environmental groups.* ◆ *~ **sb/sth for sth** The government has been criticized for not taking the problem seriously.* **ANT** PRAISE **2** [T] *~* **sth** to judge the good and bad qualities of something: *We were taught how to criticize poems.*

cri·tique /krɪˈtik/ *noun, verb*
● *noun* a piece of written criticism of a set of ideas, a work of art, etc.: *a feminist critique of Freud's theories*
● *verb ~* **sth** to write or give your opinion of, or reaction to, a set of ideas, a work of art, etc.: *Her job involves critiquing designs by fashion students.*

crit·ter /ˈkrɪtər/ *noun* (*informal*) a living creature: *wild critters*

croak /krouk/ *verb, noun*
● *verb* **1** [I] to make a rough low sound, like the sound a FROG makes **2** [I, T] to speak or say something with a rough low voice: *I had a sore throat and could only croak.* ◆ *~* **sth** *He managed to croak a greeting.* ◆ *+ speech* "*I'm fine,*" *she croaked.* **3** [I] (*slang*) to die
● *noun* a rough low sound made in the throat, like the sound made by a FROG

croc /krak/ *noun* (*informal*) = CROCODILE

cro·chet /krouˈʃeɪ/ *noun, verb*
● *noun* [U] a way of making clothes, etc. from wool or cotton using a special thick needle with a hook at the end to make a pattern of connected threads ➔ picture at HOBBY
● *verb* (cro·chet·ing, cro·cheted) [T, I] *~* (**sth**) to make something using crochet: *a crocheted shawl*

crock /krak/ *noun* (*old use*) a large pot made of baked CLAY
IDM see GOLD

crocked /krakt/ *adj.* [not before noun] (*slang*) drunk

crock·er·y /ˈkrakəri/ *noun* [U] dishes, etc. that you use in the oven

croc·o·dile /ˈkrakəˌdaɪl/ (also *informal* **croc**) *noun* **1** [C] a large REPTILE with a long tail, hard skin, and very big JAW. Crocodiles live in rivers and lakes in hot countries. ➔ picture at ANIMAL **2** [U] crocodile skin made into leather: *crocodile shoes*
IDM **crocodile tears** if someone SHEDS (= cries) **crocodile tears**, they pretend to be sad about something, but they are not really sad at all

cro·cus /ˈkroukəs/ *noun* a small yellow, purple, or white flower that appears in early spring

Crohn's dis·ease /ˈkrounz dɪˌziz/ *noun* [U] a disease affecting the lower INTESTINES, in which they develop many sore areas. The disease lasts for many years and is difficult to cure.

crois·sant /krəˈsɑnt; kwɑ-/ *noun* (from *French*) a small sweet roll with a curved shape, eaten especially at breakfast

crone /kroun/ *noun* (*literary*) an ugly old woman

cro·ny /ˈkrouni/ *noun* [usually pl.] (*pl.* **cro·nies**) (often *disapproving*) a person that someone spends a lot of time with: *He was playing cards with his cronies.*

cro·ny·ism /ˈkrouniˌɪzəm/ *noun* [U] (*disapproving*) the situation in which people in power give jobs to their friends

crook /krʊk/ *noun, verb, adj.*
● *noun* **1** (*informal*) a dishonest person **SYN** CRIMINAL: *That salesman is a real crook.* **2** *~* **of your arm/elbow** the place where your arm bends at the elbow **3** a long stick with a hook at one end, used especially in the past by SHEPHERDS for catching sheep **IDM** see HOOK
● *verb ~* **sth** to bend your finger or arm

crook·ed /ˈkrʊkəd/ *adj.* **1** not in a straight line; bent or twisted: *a crooked nose/smile* ◆ *a village of crooked streets* ◆ *Your glasses are on crooked.* **2** dishonest: *a crooked businessman/deal* ▶ **crook·ed·ly** *adv.*

croon /krun/ *verb* [T, I] *~* (**sth**) to sing something quietly and gently: *She gently crooned a lullaby.*

croon·er /ˈkrunər/ *noun* (*old-fashioned*) a male singer who sings slow romantic songs

crop 🔑 /krɑp/ *noun, verb*
● *noun*
▷ PLANTS FOR FOOD **1** [C] a plant that is grown in large quantities, especially as food: *Sugar is an important crop on the island.* ◆ *crop rotation/production/yield* ◆ *The crops are regularly sprayed with pesticides.* ➔ collocations at FARMING ➔ see also CASH CROP **2** [C] the amount of grain, fruit, etc. that is grown in one season **SYN** HARVEST: *a fall in this year's coffee crop* ◆ *We are looking forward to a **bumper crop** (= a very large one).*
▷ GROUP OF PEOPLE **3** [sing.] **a *~* of sth** a group of people who do something at the same time; a number of things that happen at the same time: *the current crop of trainees* ◆ *She is really the cream of the crop (= the best in her group).* ◆ *a crop of disasters/injuries*
▷ WHIP **4** [C] a short WHIP used by horse riders: *a riding crop*
▷ HAIR **5** [C] a very short HAIRSTYLE **6** [sing.] **a *~* of dark, fair, etc. hair/curls** hair that is short and thick: *He had a thick crop of black curly hair.*
▷ OF BIRD **7** (*technical*) a part of a bird's throat shaped like a bag where food is stored before it passes into the stomach
● *verb* (-pp-)
▷ HAIR **1** [T] *~* **sth** (+ *adj.*) to cut someone's hair very short: *closely cropped hair*
▷ PHOTOGRAPH **2** [T] *~* **sth** (*technical*) to cut off part of a photograph or picture
▷ OF ANIMALS **3** [T] *~* **sth** to bite off and eat the tops of plants, especially grass
▷ PLANTS **4** [I] (of plants) to produce a crop: *The potatoes cropped well this year.* **5** [T] *~* **sth** to use land to grow crops: *The river valley is intensively cropped.*
PHR V **crop 'up** to appear or happen, especially when it is not expected **SYN** COME UP: *His name just cropped up in conversation.* ◆ *I'll be late—something's cropped up at home.*

crop ˌdusting *noun* [U] the practice of spraying crops with chemicals such as PESTICIDES from a plane

crop top *noun* a woman's informal piece of clothing for the upper body, cut short so that the stomach can be seen

cro·quet /krouˈkeɪ/ *noun* [U] a game played on grass in which players use wooden hammers (called MALLETS) to knock wooden balls through a series of HOOPS (= curved wires)

cro·quette /krouˈkɛt/ *noun* a small amount of MASHED potato, fish, etc., shaped into a ball or tube, covered with BREADCRUMBS and fried

cro·sier (also **cro·zier**) /ˈkrouʒər/ *noun* a long stick, usually curved at one end, carried by a BISHOP (= a Christian priest of high rank) at religious ceremonies

ʌ **cup**   ə **about**   eɪ **say**   aɪ **five**   ɔɪ **boy**   aʊ **now**   oʊ **go**   ər **bird**

cross /krɔs/ noun, verb, adj.

● **noun**
> **FOR PUNISHMENT 1** [C] a long vertical piece of wood with a shorter piece across it near the top. In the past people were hung on crosses and left to die as a punishment.
> **CHRISTIAN SYMBOL 2 the Cross** [sing.] the cross that Jesus Christ died on, used as a symbol of Christianity **3** [C] an object, a design, a piece of jewelry, etc. in the shape of a cross, used as a symbol of Christianity: *She wore a small gold cross on a chain around her neck.*
> **MEDAL 4** usually **Cross** [C] a small decoration in the shape of a cross that is given to someone as an honor for doing something very brave
> **MARK ON PAPER 5** [C] a mark or an object formed by two lines crossing each other (X or +); the mark (X) is often used on paper to show something: *I've put a cross on the map to show where the hotel is.* ◆ *Put a check if the answer is correct and a cross if it's wrong.* ◆ *Sign your name on the form where I've put a cross.* ◆ *Those who could not write signed with a cross.* ◆ compare CHECK
> **MIXTURE 6** [C, usually sing.] ~ **(between A and B)** a mixture of two different things, breeds of animal, etc.: *The play was a cross between a farce and a tragedy.* ◆ *A mule is a cross between a horse and a donkey.* ◆ see also HYBRID
> **IN SPORTS 7** [C] (in SOCCER or FIELD HOCKEY) a kick or hit of the ball across the field rather than up or down it ◆ see also THE RED CROSS
> **IDM** **have a cross to bear** to have a difficult problem that makes you worried or unhappy but that you have to deal with: *We all have our crosses to bear.*

● **verb**
> **GO/PUT ACROSS 1** [I, T] to go across; to pass or stretch from one side to the other: ~ **(over)** *I waved and she crossed over* (= crossed the road toward me). ◆ ~ **(over) (from…) (to/into…)** *We crossed from Maine to New Brunswick.* ◆ ~ **sth** *to cross a/the road* ◆ *to cross the ocean/mountains* ◆ *to cross France by train* ◆ *The bridge crosses the Hudson River.* ◆ *A look of annoyance crossed her face.* ◆ *They crossed the finish line together* (= in a race). ◆ ~ **over sth** *He crossed over the road and joined me.* **2** [I] to pass across each other: *The roads cross just outside the town.* ◆ *The straps cross over at the back and are tied at the waist.* ◆ *Our letters must have crossed in the mail* (= each was sent before the other was received). **3** [T] ~ **sth** to put or place something across or over something else: *to cross your arms/legs* (= place one arm or leg over the other) ◆ *She sat with her legs crossed.* ◆ *a flag with a design of two crossed keys*
> **OPPOSE 4** [T] ~ **sb** to oppose someone or speak against them or their plans or wishes: *She's really nice until you cross her.* ◆ (*literary*) *He had been crossed in love* (= the person he loved was not faithful to him).
> **MIX ANIMALS/PLANTS 5** [T] ~ **A with B** | ~ **A and B** to make two different types of animal breed together; to mix two types of plant to form a new one: *A mule is the product of a horse crossed with a donkey.* ◆ (*figurative*) *He behaved like an army officer crossed with a professor.*
> **IN SPORTS 6** [I] (in SOCCER, etc.) to kick or pass a ball sideways across the field
> **DRAW LINE 7** [T] ~ **sth** to draw a line across something: *to cross your t's* (= the letters in writing)
> **MAKE CHRISTIAN SYMBOL 8** [T] ~ **yourself** to make the sign of the cross (= the Christian symbol) on your chest
> **IDM** **cross that bridge when you come to it** to worry about a problem when it actually happens and not before **cross your fingers** to hope that your plans will be successful (sometimes putting one finger across another as a sign of hoping for good luck): *I'm crossing my fingers that my proposal will be accepted.* ◆ *Keep your fingers crossed!* **cross my heart (and hope to die)** (*informal*) used to emphasize that you are telling the truth or will do what you promise: *I saw him do it—cross my heart.* **cross your mind** (of thoughts, etc.) to come into your mind: *It never crossed my mind that she might lose* (= I was sure that she would win). **cross sb's path** | **people's paths cross** if someone **crosses someone's path** or **their paths cross**, they meet by chance: *I hope I never cross her path again.* ◆ *Our paths were to cross again many years*

later. **cross swords (with sb)** to fight or argue with someone ◆ more at DOT, WIRE
> **PHR V** ,**cross sb/sth↔'off** | ,**cross sb/sth 'off sth** to draw a line through a person's name or an item on a list because they/it is no longer required or involved: *We can cross his name off; he's not coming.* ,**cross sth↔'out/'through** to draw a line through a word, usually because it is wrong ,**cross 'over (to/into sth)** to move or change from one type of culture, music, political party, etc. to another: *a cult movie that has crossed over to mass appeal* ◆ related noun CROSSOVER

● **adj.** (**cross·er**, **cross·est**) ~ **(with sb)** (*old-fashioned*) annoyed or quite angry: *I was cross with him for being late.* ▶ **cross·ly** adv. (*old-fashioned*): *"Well what did you expect?" she said crossly.*

cross- /krɔs/ combining form (in nouns, verbs, adjectives, and adverbs) involving movement or action from one thing to another or between two things: *cross-river ferries* ◆ *cross-fertilize* ◆ *crossfire*

cross·bar /'krɔsbɑr/ noun **1** the bar joining the two vertical posts of a goal ◆ picture at SPORT **2** the bar between the seat and the HANDLEBARS of a man's bicycle ◆ picture at BICYCLE, BAR

cross·bones /'krɔsbounz/ noun [pl.] ◆ SKULL AND CROSS-BONES

'**cross-,border** adj. [only before noun] involving activity across a border between two countries: *a cross-border raid by guerrillas*

cross·bow /'krɔsbou/ noun a weapon which consists of a BOW ¹ that is fixed onto a larger piece of wood, and that shoots short heavy arrows (called BOLTS)

'**cross-breed** verb, noun
● **verb** [T, I] ~ **(sth)** to make an animal or a plant breed with a different breed; to breed with an animal or a plant of a different breed: *cross-bred sheep* ▶ '**cross-,breeding** noun [U]
● **noun** an animal or a plant that is a result of cross-breeding ◆ compare HYBRID

'**cross-check** verb to make sure that information, figures etc. are correct by using a different method or system to check them: ~ **sth** *Cross-check your answers with a calculator.* ◆ ~ **against sth** *Baggage should be cross-checked against the names of individual passengers.* ▶ '**cross-check** noun

,**cross-contami'nation** noun [U] the process by which harmful bacteria spread from one substance to another

,**cross-'country** adj., adv., noun
● **adj.** [usually before noun], **adv. 1** across fields or open country rather than on roads or a track: *cross-country running* ◆ *We rode cross-country.* **2** from one part of a country to the other, especially not using main roads or routes: *cross-country train trips*
● **noun 1 the cross-country** [sing.] a cross-country running or SKIING race **2** [U] the sport of running or SKIING across country ◆ compare DOWNHILL

,**cross-country 'skiing** noun [U] the sport of SKIING across the countryside, rather than down mountains ◆ picture at SPORT

,**cross-'cultural** adj. involving or containing ideas from two or more different countries or cultures

'**cross-,current** noun **1** a current of water in a river or in the ocean that flows across the main current **2** [usually pl.] (*formal*) a set of beliefs or ideas that are different from others, especially from those that most people hold

'**cross-,dressing** noun [U] the practice of wearing clothes usually worn by a person of the opposite sex, especially for sexual pleasure ▶ '**cross-,dresser** noun

,**cross-ex'amine** verb ~ **sb** to question someone carefully and in a lot of detail about answers that they have already given, especially in court: *The witness was cross-examined for over two hours.* ◆ collocations at JUSTICE ▶ ,**cross-exami-'nation** noun [U, C]: *He broke down under cross-examination*

(= while he was being cross-examined) *and admitted his part in the assault.*

cross-eyed *adj.* having one or both eyes looking toward the nose

cross-fertilize *verb* **1** ~ sth *(biology)* to FERTILIZE a plant using POLLEN from a different plant of the same SPECIES **2** ~ sth to help something develop in a useful or positive way by mixing ideas from a different area: *The study of psychology has recently been widely cross-fertilized by new discoveries in genetics.* ▶ **cross-fertilization** *noun* [U, sing.]

cross-fire /ˈkrɔsˌfaɪər/ *noun* [U] the firing of guns from two or more directions at the same time, so that the bullets cross: *The doctor was killed in crossfire as he went to help the wounded.* ◆ *(figurative) When two industrial giants clash, small companies can get caught in the crossfire* (= become involved and suffer as a result).

cross-hatch *verb* ~ sth *(technical)* to mark or color something with two sets of parallel lines crossing each other ▶ **cross-hatching** *noun* [U]

cross-ing /ˈkrɔsɪŋ/ *noun* **1** a place where you can safely cross a road, a river, etc., or from one country to another: *The child was killed when a car failed to stop at the crossing.* ◆ *The next crossing point is a long way downstream.* ◆ *He was arrested by guards at the border crossing.* ➔ **see also** LEVEL CROSSING, PEDESTRIAN CROSSING **2** a place where two lines, two roads, or two tracks cross **SYN** INTERSECTION **3** a journey across an ocean or a wide river: *a three-hour ferry crossing* ◆ *the first Atlantic crossing* **4** an act of going from one side to another: *attempted crossings of the border*

cross-leg-ged /ˈkrɔs ˌlɛgəd; -ˌlɛgd/ *adv.* sitting on the floor with your legs pulled up in front of you and with one leg or foot over the other ▶ **cross-leg-ged** *adj.*: *the cross-legged figure of the Hindu god*

cross-o-ver /ˈkrɔsˌoʊvər/ *noun* the process or result of changing from one area of activity or style of doing something to another: *The album was an exciting jazz-pop crossover.*

cross-piece /ˈkrɔspis/ *noun* *(technical)* a piece of a structure or a tool that lies or is fixed across another piece

cross-platform *adj.* (of a computer program or an electronic device) that can be used with different types of computers or programs

cross-pollinate *verb* ~ sth *(biology)* to move POLLEN from a flower or plant onto another flower or plant so that it produces seeds ▶ **cross-pollination** *noun* [U]

cross-promotion *noun* [C, U] *(business)* a set of advertisements or other activities that are designed to help a company sell two different products, or to help two companies sell their products or services together

cross purposes *noun* [pl.] if two people are at cross purposes, they do not understand each other because they are talking about or aiming at different things, without realizing it: *I think we're talking at cross purposes; that's not what I meant at all.*

cross-question *verb* ~ sb to question someone thoroughly and often in a way that seems aggressive

cross-re-fer *verb* (-rr-) [T, I] ~ (sth) to sth to refer to another text or part of a text, especially to give more information about something: *The entry for "polygraph" is cross-referred to the entry for "lie detector."*

cross reference *noun* ~ (to sth) a note that tells a reader to look in another part of a book or file for further information

cross-roads /ˈkrɔsroʊdz/ *noun* (pl. **cross-roads**) a place where two roads meet and cross each other: *At the next crossroads, turn right.* ◆ *(figurative) He has reached a career crossroads* (= he must decide which way to go next in his career). ➔ **see also** INTERSECTION, JUNCTION **IDM** **at a/the crossroads** at an important point in someone's life or development

cross section *noun* **1** [C, U] what you see when you cut

through the middle of something so that you can see the different layers it is made of; a drawing of this view: *a diagram representing a cross section of the human eye* ◆ *the human eye in cross section* **2** [C, usually sing.] a group of people or things that are typical of a larger group: *a representative cross section of society*

cross-selling *noun* [U] *(business)* the activity of selling a different extra product to a customer who is already buying a product from a company

cross street *noun* a street that crosses another street

cross-talk /ˈkrɔstɔk/ *noun* [U] *(technical)* a situation in which a communications system is picking up the wrong signals

cross-town /ˈkrɔstaʊn/ *adj., adv.* going from one side to another of a town or city to the other: *a crosstown bus*

cross-trainer *noun* a piece of exercise equipment that you use standing up, with parts that you push up and down with your feet and parts that you hold onto and push with your arms

cross-training *noun* [U] the activity of training in sports other than your main sport in order to make yourself fitter and able to do your main sport better

cross-walk /ˈkrɔswɔk/ (also pe·destrian 'crossing) *noun* a part of a road where vehicles must stop to allow people to cross

cross-wind /ˈkrɔswɪnd/ *noun* a wind that is blowing across the direction that you are moving in

cross-wise /ˈkrɔswaɪz/ *adv.* **1** across, especially from one corner to the opposite one: *Cut the fabric crosswise.* **2** in the form of a cross

cross-word /ˈkrɔswərd/ (also 'crossword ˌpuzzle) *noun* a game in which you have to fit words across and downward into spaces with numbers in a square diagram. You find the words by solving CLUES: *to do a/the crossword* ◆ *I've finished the crossword except for 3 across and 10 down.*

crotch /krɑtʃ/ *noun* **1** the part of the body where the legs join at the top, including the area around the GENITALS **2** the part of a pair of pants, etc. that covers the crotch: *There's a hole in the crotch.*

crotch·et·y /ˈkrɑtʃəti/ *adj.* *(informal)* bad-tempered; easily made angry: *He was tired and crotchety.*

crotch·less /ˈkrɑtʃləs/ *adj.* (of underwear) having a hole at the CROTCH

crouch /kraʊtʃ/ *verb, noun*
● *verb* [I] (+ adv./prep.) to put your body close to the ground by bending your legs under you **SYN** SQUAT: *He crouched down beside her.* ◆ *Doyle crouched behind a hedge.* ▶ **crouched** *adj.*: *She sat crouched in a corner.* **PHR V** **crouch over sb/sth** to bend over someone or something so that you are very close to them or it: *He crouched over the papers on his desk.*
● *noun* [sing.] a crouching position: *She dropped to a crouch.*

croup /krup/ *noun* [U] a disease of children that makes them cough a lot and have difficulty breathing

croup·i·er /ˈkrupiˌeɪ; -piər/ *noun* a person whose job is to be in charge of a gambling table and collect and pay out money, give out cards, etc.

crou·ton /ˈkrutɑn/ *noun* a small piece of cold, crisp, fried bread served in soup or as part of a salad

Crow /kroʊ/ *noun* (pl. **Crow** or **Crows**) a member of a Native American people, many of whom live in Montana

crow /kroʊ/ *noun, verb*
● *noun* **1** a large bird, completely or mostly black, with a rough unpleasant cry **2** a sound like that of a ROOSTER: *She gave a little crow of triumph.* **IDM** **as the crow flies** in a straight line: *The villages are no more than a mile apart as the crow flies.* ➔ **more at** EAT
● *verb* **1** [I] (of a ROOSTER) to make repeated loud high sounds, especially early in the morning **2** [I, T] *(disapproving)* to talk too proudly about something you have achieved, especially when someone else has been unsuccessful

t tea   ṭ butter   d did   k cat   g got   tʃ chin   dʒ June   f fall

SYN BOAST, GLOAT: ~ **(about/over sth)** *He won't stop crowing about his victory.* ♦ + **speech** *"I've won, I've won!" she crowed.* ♦ ~ **that…** *He crowed that they had sold out in one day.*

crow·bar /ˈkrəʊbɑːr/ *noun* a straight iron bar, usually with a curved end, used for forcing open boxes and moving heavy objects

crowd 🅰 /kraʊd/ *noun, verb*

● **noun 1** [C] a large number of people gathered together in a public place, for example in the streets or at a sports game: *He pushed his way through the crowd.* ♦ *A small crowd had gathered outside the church.* ♦ *Police had to break up the crowd.* ♦ *Crowds of people poured into the street.* ♦ *I want to get there early to avoid the crowds.* ♦ *The match attracted a capacity crowd of 80,000.* ♦ *The crowd cheered the winning hit.* ♦ *crowd control* ♦ *crowd trouble* ♦ *A whole crowd of us are going to the club* (= a lot of us). ♦ *He left the hotel surrounded by crowds of journalists.* **2** [C] (*informal*, often *disapproving*) a particular group of people: *Bob introduced her to some of his usual crowd* (= people who often meet each other). **3 the crowd** [sing.] (sometimes *disapproving*) ordinary people, not special or unusual in any way: *We all like to think we **stand out from the crowd*** (= are different from and better than other people). ♦ *He prefers to be **one of the crowd**.* ♦ *She's quite happy to **follow the crowd**.* **IDM** see TWO

● **verb 1** ~ **sth** to fill a place so there is little room to move: *Thousands of people crowded the narrow streets.* **2** ~ **sth** to fill your mind so that you can think of nothing else: *Memories crowded his mind.* **3** ~ **sb** (*informal*) to stand very close to someone so that they feel uncomfortable or nervous **PHR V** ,**crowd a'round (sb/sth)** to gather in large numbers around someone or something: *We all crowded around the stove to keep warm.* ♦ *Photographers were crowding around outside.* ,**crowd 'in (on sb)** | ,**crowd 'into sth** (of thoughts, questions etc.) to fill your mind so that you can think of nothing else: *Too many uncomfortable thoughts were crowding in on her.* ♦ *Memories came crowding into her mind.* ,**crowd 'into/'onto sth** | ,**crowd 'in** to move in large numbers into a small space: *We all crowded into her office to sing "Happy Birthday."* ,**crowd sb/sth 'into/'onto sth** | ,**crowd sb/sth 'in** to put many people or things into a small space: *Guests were crowded into the few remaining rooms.* ,**crowd sb/sth 'out** to fill a place so that other people or things are kept out

crowd·ed 🅰 /ˈkraʊdəd/ *adj.* ~ **(with sth) 1** having a lot of people or too many people: *crowded streets* ♦ *a crowded bar* ♦ *In the spring the place is crowded with skiers.* ♦ *London was very crowded.* ➲ compare UNCROWDED **2** full of something: *a room crowded with books* ♦ *We have a very crowded schedule.*

ˈcrowd-ˌpleaser *noun* (*informal*) a person or performance that always pleases an audience

crown 🅰 /kraʊn/ *noun, verb*

● **noun**
▷ OF KING/QUEEN **1** [C] an object in the shape of a circle, usually made of gold and PRECIOUS STONES, that a king or queen wears on his or her head on official occasions **2 the crown** [sing.] the position or power of a king or queen: *She refused the crown* (= refused to become queen). ♦ *his claim to the French crown* **3 the Crown** [sing.] the government of a country, thought of as being represented by a king or queen: *land owned by the Crown*
▷ OF FLOWERS/LEAVES **4** [C] a circle of flowers, leaves, etc. that is worn on someone's head, sometimes as a sign of victory
▷ IN SPORTS COMPETITION **5** [C, usually sing.] (*informal*) the position of winning a sports competition: *She is determined to retain her Wimbledon crown.*
▷ OF HEAD/HAT **6** usually **the crown** [sing.] the top part of the head or a hat
▷ HIGHEST PART **7** usually **the crown** [sing.] the highest part of something: *the crown of a hill*
▷ ON TOOTH **8** [C] an artificial cover for a damaged tooth
▷ SHAPE **9** [C] anything in the shape of a crown, especially as a decoration or a BADGE

▷ MONEY **10** [C] a unit of money in several European countries: *Czech crowns* **11** [C] an old British coin worth five SHILLINGS (= now 25 pence) **IDM** see JEWEL

● **verb**
▷ KING/QUEEN **1** to put a crown on the head of a new king or queen as a sign of royal power: ~ **sb** *Queen Elizabeth was crowned in 1953.* ♦ ~ **sb** + **noun** *The prince was soon to be crowned King of England.*
▷ COVER TOP **2** [usually passive] ~ **sth (with sth)** to form or cover the top of something: *His head was crowned with a mop of brown curls.*
▷ MAKE COMPLETE **3** [often passive] ~ **sth (with sth)** to make something complete or perfect, especially by adding an achievement, a success, etc.: *The award of the Nobel Prize has crowned a glorious career in physics.* ♦ *Their efforts were finally crowned with success.*
▷ HIT ON HEAD **4** ~ **sb** (*old-fashioned, informal*) to hit someone on the head
▷ TOOTH **5** ~ **sth** to put an artificial cover on a tooth **SYN** CAP: *I've had one of my teeth crowned.*

crowning /ˈkraʊnɪŋ/ *adj.* [only before noun] making something perfect or complete: *The cathedral is the **crowning glory** of the city.* ♦ *His "Beethoven" sculpture is seen as the **crowning achievement** of his career.*

,**crown ˈjewels** *noun* [pl.] the crown and other objects worn or carried by a king or queen on formal occasions

,**crown ˈprince** *noun* (in some countries) a prince who will become king when the present king or queen dies

,**crown prinˈcess** *noun* **1** the wife of a crown prince **2** (in some countries), a princess who will become queen when the present king or queen dies

ˈ**crow's feet** *noun* [pl.] lines in the skin around the outer corner of a person's eye

ˈ**crow's nest** *noun* a platform at the top of a ship's MAST (= the post that supports the sails) from which someone can see a long way and watch for land, danger, etc.

cro·zier = CROSIER

cru·cial 🅰 **AWL** /ˈkruːʃl/ *adj.* extremely important, because it will affect other things **SYN** CRITICAL, ESSENTIAL: *a crucial factor/issue/decision* ♦ *topics of crucial importance* ♦ *The next few weeks are going to be crucial.* ♦ ~ **to/for sth** *Winning this contract is crucial to the success of the company.* ♦ ~ **that…** *It is crucial that we get this right.* ♦ *Parents **play a crucial role** in preparing their children for school.* ♦ *He wasn't there **at the crucial moment*** (= when he was needed most). ➲ thesaurus box at ESSENTIAL ➲ language bank at EMPHASIS, VITAL ▶ **cru·cial·ly** **AWL** /-ʃəli/ *adv.*: *crucially important*

cru·ci·ble /ˈkruːsəbl/ *noun* **1** a pot in which substances are heated to high temperatures, metals are melted, etc. ➲ picture at LABORATORY **2** (*formal* or *literary*) a place or situation in which people or ideas are tested severely, often creating something new or exciting in the process

cru·ci·fix /ˈkruːsəfɪks/ *noun* a model of a cross with a figure of Jesus Christ on it, as a symbol of the Christian religion

cru·ci·fix·ion /ˌkruːsəˈfɪkʃn/ *noun* sometimes **Crucifixion 1** [C, U] the act of killing someone by fastening them to a cross: *the Crucifixion* (= of Jesus) **2** [C] a painting or other work of art representing the crucifixion of Jesus Christ

cru·ci·form /ˈkruːsəfɔːrm/ *adj.* (*technical*) (especially of buildings) in the shape of a cross

cru·ci·fy /ˈkruːsəfaɪ/ *verb* (**cru·ci·fies, cru·ci·fy·ing, cru·ci·fied, cru·ci·fied**) **1** ~ **sb** to kill someone as a punishment by fastening them to a wooden cross **2** ~ **sb** (*informal*) to criticize or punish someone very severely: *The senator was crucified in the press for his handling of the affair.*

crud /krʌd/ *noun* [U] (*informal*) any dirty or unpleasant substance

crud·dy /ˈkrʌdi/ *adj.* (**crud·di·er, crud·di·est**) (*informal*) bad, dirty, or of low quality: *We got really cruddy service in that restaurant last time.*

crude /kruːd/ *adj., noun*

● *adj.* (**crud·er, crud·est**) **1** simple and not very accurate but giving a general idea of something: *In crude terms, the causes of mental illness seem to be of three main kinds.* **2** (of objects or works of art) simply made, not showing much skill or attention to detail: *a crude drawing of a face* **3** (of people or the way they behave) offensive or rude, especially about sex **SYN** VULGAR: *crude jokes/language* **4** [usually before noun] (of oil and other natural substances) in its natural state, before it has been treated with chemicals: *crude oil/metal* ▶ **crude·ly** *adv.*: *a crudely drawn ship* ◆ *To put it crudely, the poor are going without food so that the rich can drive cars.* **crude·ness** *noun* [U]

● *noun* (also ˌcrude ˈoil) [U] oil in its natural state, before it has been treated with chemicals: *50,000 barrels of crude*

cru·di·tés /ˌkruːdɪˈteɪ/ *noun* [pl.] (from *French*) pieces of raw vegetables that are eaten at the beginning of a meal

cru·di·ty /ˈkruːdəti/ *noun* [U, C] (*pl.* **cru·di·ties**) the fact of being CRUDE; an example of something CRUDE: *Despite the crudity of their methods and equipment, the experiment was a considerable success.* ◆ *the novel's structural crudities* ◆ *The crudity of her language shocked him.*

cru·el 🔊 /ˈkruːəl; krʊl/ *adj.* (**cru·el·er, cru·el·est,** CanE usually **cru·el·ler, cru·el·lest**) **1** ~ (**to sb/sth**) having a desire to cause pain and suffering: *a cruel dictator* ◆ *I can't stand people who are cruel to animals.* ◆ *Her eyes were cruel and hard.* ◆ *Sometimes you have to be cruel to be kind* (= make someone suffer because it will be good for them later). **ANT** KIND **2** causing pain or suffering: *a cruel punishment/ joke* ◆ *Her father's death was a cruel blow.* ▶ **cru·el·ly** *adv.*: *The dog had been cruelly treated.* ◆ *I was cruelly deceived.*

cru·el·ty /ˈkruːəlti; ˈkrʊlti/ *noun* (*pl.* **cru·el·ties**) **1** [U] ~ (**to sb/sth**) behavior that causes pain or suffering to others, especially deliberately: *cruelty to animals* ◆ *The deliberate cruelty of his words cut her like a knife.* **ANT** KINDNESS **2** [C, usually pl.] a cruel action **3** [C, U] something that happens that seems unfair: *the cruelties of life*

cru·et /ˈkruːət/ *noun* a small container, or set of containers, for salt, pepper, oil, etc. for use on the table at meals

cruise /kruːz/ *noun, verb*

● *noun* a journey by ocean, visiting different places, especially as a vacation: *I'd love to go on a round-the-world cruise.* ◆ *a luxury cruise ship* ⊃ collocations at TRAVEL

● *verb* **1** [I, T] to travel in a ship or boat visiting different places, especially as a vacation: (+ **adv./prep.**) *They cruised down the Nile.* ◆ *We spent two weeks cruising the Bahamas.* **2** [I] (+ **adv./prep.**) (of a car, plane, etc.) to travel at a steady speed: *a light aircraft cruising at 4,000 feet* ◆ *a cruising speed of 50 miles an hour* **3** [I, T] (of a car, etc. or its driver) to drive along slowly, especially when you are looking at or for something: + **adv./prep.** *She cruised around the block looking for a parking space.* ◆ ~ **sth** *Taxis cruised the streets, looking for fares.* **4** [I] + **adv./prep.** to win or achieve something easily: *The home team cruised to victory.* **5** [I, T] ~ (**sth**) (*slang*) to go around in public places looking for a sexual partner

ˈcruise conˌtrol *noun* [U] a device in a vehicle that allows it to stay at the speed that the driver has chosen

ˈcruise ˌmissile *noun* a large weapon with a WARHEAD that flies close to the ground and is guided by its own computer to an exact place

cruis·er /ˈkruːzər/ *noun* **1** a large fast ship used in war **2** (also ˈcabin ˌcruiser) a boat with a motor and room for people to sleep, used for pleasure trips **3** a police car

crumb /krʌm/ *noun* **1** a very small piece of food, especially of bread or cake, that has fallen off a larger piece: *She stood up and brushed the crumbs from her sweater.* **2** a small piece or amount: *a few crumbs of useful information* ◆ *The president's only crumb of comfort is that his opponents are as confused as he is.*

crum·ble /ˈkrʌmbl/ *verb* **1** [I, T] to break or break something into very small pieces: *Rice flour makes the cake less likely to crumble.* ◆ ~ **sth** *Crumble the cheese over the salad.* **2** [I] if a building or piece of land **is crumbling**, parts of it are breaking off: *buildings crumbling into dust* ◆ *crumbling stonework* ◆ *The cliff is gradually crumbling away.* **3** [I] to begin to fail or get weaker or to come to an end: *a crumbling business/ relationship* ◆ ~ **away** *All his hopes began to crumble away.* ◆ ~ **into/to sth** *The empire finally crumbled into dust.* **IDM** see WAY

crum·bly /ˈkrʌmbli/ *adj.* that easily breaks into very small pieces: *crumbly soil/cheese*

crum·my /ˈkrʌmi/ *adj.* (*informal*) of very bad quality: *Most of his songs are pretty crummy.*

crum·ple /ˈkrʌmpl/ *verb* **1** [T, I] ~ (**sth**) (**up**) (**into sth**) to crush something into folds; to become crushed into folds: *She crumpled the letter up into a ball and threw it on the fire.* ◆ *This material crumples very easily.* ⊃ picture at SQUEEZE **2** [I] ~ (**up**) if your face **crumples**, you look sad and disappointed, as if you might cry **3** [I] ~ (**up**) to fall down in an uncontrolled way because you are injured, unconscious, drunk, etc. **SYN** COLLAPSE: *He crumpled up in agony.* ▶ **crum·pled** *adj.*: *crumpled clothes/papers* ◆ *A crumpled figure lay motionless in the doorway.*

ˈcrumple ˌzone *noun* the part of a car that is designed to crumple easily if there is an accident, to protect the people in the car

crunch /krʌntʃ/ *noun, verb, adj.*

● *noun* **1** [C, usually sing.] a noise like the sound of something firm being crushed: *the crunch of feet on snow* ◆ *The car drove up with a crunch of gravel.* **2** **the crunch** [sing.] (*informal*) an important and often unpleasant situation: *The crunch came when she returned from England.* ◆ *He always says he'll help but when it comes to the crunch* (= when it is time for action) *he does nothing.* **3** [C, usually sing.] a situation in which there is suddenly not enough of something, especially money: *a budget/energy/housing crunch* **4** [C] an exercise for making your muscles strong, in which you lie on your back on the floor and raise your head and shoulders off the floor ⊃ compare SIT-UP

● *verb* **1** [T, I] ~ (**on**) **sth** to crush something noisily between your teeth when you are eating: *She crunched her apple noisily.* **2** [I, T] ~ (**sth**) to make or cause something to make a noise like something hard being crushed: *The snow crunched under our feet.* **3** [I] + **adv./prep.** to move over a surface, making a loud crushing noise: *I crunched across the gravel to the front door.* **4** [T] ~ **sth** (*computing*) to deal with large amounts of data very quickly ⊃ see also NUMBER CRUNCHING

PHR V ˌcrunch sth↔ˈup to crush something completely: *He crunched up the empty pack and threw it out of the window.*

● *adj.* [only before noun] (*informal*) a **crunch** meeting, sports game, etc. is very important and may be the last chance to succeed: *Sunday's crunch game against San Francisco*

ˈcrunch time *noun* [U] (*informal*) an extremely important moment or period of time when you must make a decision or take action; a crucial time: *It's crunch time for students who want to graduate early.*

crunch·y /ˈkrʌntʃi/ *adj.* (*approving*) (especially of food) firm and crisp and making a sharp sound when you bite or crush it: *a crunchy salad*

cru·sade /kruːˈseɪd/ *noun, verb*

● *noun* **1** ~ (**for/against sth**) | ~ (**to do sth**) a long and determined effort to achieve something that you believe to be right or to stop something that you believe to be wrong **SYN** CAMPAIGN: *to lead a crusade against crime* ◆ *a moral crusade* **2** sometimes **Crusade** any of the wars fought in Palestine by European Christian countries against the Muslims in the Middle Ages

● *verb* [I] to make a long and determined effort to achieve something that you believe to be right or to stop something you believe to be wrong **SYN** CAMPAIGN

h **hat**　　m **man**　　n **no**　　ŋ **sing**　　l **leg**　　r **red**　　y **yes**　　w **wet**

cru·sad·er /kruˈseɪdər/ noun a person who takes part in a crusade: *moral crusaders*

crush /krʌʃ/ verb, noun

• **verb 1** ~ sb/sth to press or squeeze something so hard that it is damaged or injured, or loses its shape: *The car was completely crushed under the truck.* ◆ *They crush the olives with a heavy wooden press.* ◆ *Several people were crushed to death in the accident.* ⊃ picture at SQUEEZE **2** ~ sb/sth + adv./prep. to push or press someone or something into a small space: *Over twenty prisoners were crushed into a small dark cell.* **3** ~ sth to break something into small pieces or into a powder by pressing hard: *Add two cloves of crushed garlic.* **4** ~ sth to become or make something full of folds or lines **5** ~ sb to use violent methods to defeat people who are opposing you **SYN** QUASH: *The army was sent in to crush the rebellion.* **6** ~ sb to destroy someone's confidence or happiness: *She felt completely crushed by the teacher's criticism.*

• **noun 1** [C, usually sing.] a crowd of people pressed close together in a small space: *a big crush in the theater bar* ◆ *I couldn't find a way through the crush.* **2** [C] ~ (on sb) a strong feeling of love that usually does not last very long and often is not expressed. It is usually young people that have crushes, especially on people they do not know very well: *a schoolgirl crush* ◆ *I had a huge crush on her.*

crush·er /ˈkrʌʃər/ noun (often in compounds) a machine or tool for crushing something

crush·ing /ˈkrʌʃɪŋ/ adj. [usually before noun] used to emphasize how bad or severe something is: *a crushing defeat in the election* ◆ *The shipyard has been dealt another crushing blow with the failure to win this contract.* ▶ **crush·ing·ly** adv.

crust /krʌst/ noun **1** [C, U] the hard outer surface of bread: *sandwiches with the crusts cut off* **2** [C, usually sing.] a layer of PASTRY, especially on top of a PIE: *Bake until the crust is golden.* **3** [C, U] a hard layer or surface, especially above or around something soft or liquid: *a thin crust of ice* ◆ *Earth's crust* ⊃ see also THE UPPER CRUST

crus·ta·cean /krʌˈsteɪʃn/ noun (technical) any creature with a soft body that is divided into sections, and a hard outer shell. Most crustaceans live in water. CRAB, LOBSTER, and SHRIMP are all crustaceans. ⊃ compare SHELLFISH

crust·ed /ˈkrʌstəd/ adj. [not usually before noun] ~ (with sth) having a hard layer or covering of something

crust·y /ˈkrʌsti/ adj. (crust·i·er, crust·i·est) **1** (of food) having a hard outer layer: *fresh crusty bread* **2** (informal) (especially of older people) bad-tempered; easily irritated: *a crusty old man*

crutch /krʌtʃ/ noun **1** one of two long sticks that you put under your arms to help you walk after you have injured your leg or foot: *After the accident I spent six months on crutches.* **2** (usually disapproving) a person or thing that gives you help or support but often makes you depend on it too much

crux /krʌks/ noun [sing.] **the** ~ **(of sth)** the most important or difficult part of a problem or an issue **SYN** HEART (5): *Now we come to the crux of the matter.*

cry /kraɪ/ verb, noun

• **verb** (cries, cry·ing, cried, cried) **1** [I, T] to produce tears from your eyes because you are unhappy or hurt: *It's all right. Don't cry.* ◆ *I just couldn't stop crying.* ◆ ~ for sb/sth *The baby was crying for* (= because it wanted) *its mother.* ◆ ~ about/over sth *There's nothing to cry about.* ◆ ~ with sth *He felt like crying with rage.* ◆ + **speech** *"Waaa!" she cried.* ◆ *I found him crying his eyes out* (= crying very much). ◆ *That night she cried herself to sleep.* **2** [I, T] to shout loudly: ~ for sth *She ran to the window and cried for help.* ◆ + **speech** *"You're safe!" Tom cried in delight.* ⊃ thesaurus box at SHOUT **3** [I] (of a bird or an animal) to make a loud unpleasant noise: *Seagulls followed the boat, crying loudly.*

IDM **cry foul** (informal) to complain that someone else has done something wrong or unfair **cry over spilled milk** to waste time worrying about something that has happened that you cannot do anything about: *As the saying goes — it's no use crying over spilled milk.* **cry wolf** to call for help when you do not need it, with the result that when you do need it people do not believe you **for crying out loud** (informal) used to show you are angry or surprised: *For crying out loud! Why did you have to do that?* ⊃ more at LAUGH, SHOULDER, UNCLE

PHR V ,cry 'out to make a loud sound without words because you are hurt, afraid, surprised, etc.: *She tried to stop herself from crying out.* ◆ *to cry out in fear/alarm/pain* ,cry 'out/,cry 'out sth to shout something loudly: *She cried out for help.* ◆ *She cried out his name.* ◆ + **speech** *"Help!" he cried out.* ⊃ thesaurus box at CALL ,cry 'out for sth (usually used in the progressive tenses) to need something very much: *The company is crying out for fresh new talent.*

• **noun** (pl. **cries**) **1** [C] a loud sound without words that expresses a strong feeling: *to give a cry of anguish/despair/relief/surprise/terror, etc.* **2** [C] a loud shout: *With a cry of "Stop thief!" he ran after the boy.* ◆ *Her answer was greeted with cries of outrage.* **3** [C] the sound made by a bird or an animal: *the cry of gulls circling overhead* **4** [sing.] an action or a period of crying: *I felt a lot better after a good long cry.* **5** [C] ~ **(for sth)** an urgent demand or request for something: *Her suicide attempt was really a cry for help.* **6** [C] (especially in compounds) a word or phrase that expresses a group's beliefs and calls people to action: *a battle cry* **IDM** see FAR, HUE

cry·ba·by /ˈkraɪˌbeɪbi/ noun (pl. **cry·ba·bies**) (informal, disapproving) a person, especially a child, who cries too often or without good reason: *Don't be such a crybaby.*

cry·ing /ˈkraɪɪŋ/ adj., noun

• **adj.** [only before noun] **IDM** **be a crying shame** (informal) used to emphasize that you think something is extremely bad or shocking: *It's a crying shame to waste all that food.* **a crying need (for sth)** a great and urgent need for something

• **noun** [U] the sound or act of crying: *the crying of terrified children*

cry·o·gen·ic /ˌkraɪəˈdʒenɪk/ adj. (physics) involving the use of very low temperatures: *a cryogenic storage system*

cry·o·gen·ics /ˌkraɪəˈdʒenɪks/ noun [U] (physics) the scientific study of the production and effects of very low temperatures ⊃ compare CRYONICS

cry·on·ics /kraɪˈɑnɪks/ noun [U] (medical) the process of freezing a body at the moment of its death with the hope that it will be brought back to life at some future time ⊃ compare CRYOGENICS

crypt /krɪpt/ noun a room under the floor of a church, used especially in the past as a place for burying people

cryp·tic /ˈkrɪptɪk/ adj. with a meaning that is hidden or not easily understood **SYN** MYSTERIOUS: *a cryptic message/*

remark/smile ♦ *a cryptic crossword clue* ▶ **cryp·ti·cally** /-kli/ *adv.*: "Yes and no," she replied cryptically.

crypto- /ˈkrɪptoʊ/ *combining form* (in nouns) secret: *a crypto-communist*

cryp·tog·ra·phy /krɪpˈtɑɡrəfi/ *noun* [U] the art of writing or solving codes

cryp·to·spor·i·di·um /ˌkrɪptoʊspəˈrɪdiəm/ *noun* a PARASITE found in water that causes infections inside the body

crys·tal /ˈkrɪstl/ *noun* **1** [C] a small piece of a substance with many even sides, that is formed naturally when the substance becomes solid: *ice/salt crystals* **2** [U, C] a clear mineral, such as QUARTZ, used in making jewelry and decorative objects: *a pair of crystal earrings* **3** [U] glass of very high quality: *a crystal chandelier/vase* **4** [C] a piece of glass or plastic that covers the face of a watch ⊃ see also LIQUID CRYSTAL DISPLAY **5** = METH

ˌcrystal ˈball *noun* a clear glass ball used by people who claim they can predict what will happen in the future by looking into it: *Without a crystal ball, it's impossible to say where we'll be next year.*

ˌcrystal ˈclear *adj.* **1** (of glass, water, etc.) completely clear and bright **2** very easy to understand; completely obvious: *I want to make my meaning crystal clear.*

crys·tal·line /ˈkrɪstələn/ *adj.* **1** (*technical*) made of or similar to CRYSTAL: *crystalline structure/rocks* **2** (*formal*) very clear **SYN** TRANSPARENT: *water of crystalline purity*

crys·tal·lize /ˈkrɪstəˌlaɪz/ *verb* **1** [I, T] (of thoughts, plans, beliefs, etc.) to become clear and fixed; to make thoughts, beliefs, etc. clear and fixed: *Our ideas began to crystallize into a definite plan.* ♦ ~ **sth** *The final chapter crystallizes all the main issues.* **2** [I, T] ~ (**sth**) (*technical*) to form or make something form into CRYSTAL: *The salt crystallizes as the water evaporates.* ▶ **crys·tal·li·za·tion** /ˌkrɪstələˈzeɪʃn/ *noun* [U, sing.]

crystallized /ˈkrɪstəˌlaɪzd/ *adj.* (especially of fruit) preserved in and covered with sugar

crys·tal·log·ra·phy /ˌkrɪstəˈlɑɡrəfi/ *noun* [U] the branch of science that deals with CRYSTALS ▶ **crys·tal·log·ra·pher** /-fər/ *noun*

ˌcrystal ˈmeth /ˌkrɪstl ˈmɛθ/ *noun* = METH

ˈcrystal ˌset (also ˌcrystal ˈradio) *noun* a simple early radio which was listened to wearing HEADPHONES

C-section /ˈsi ˌsɛkʃn/ *noun* = CESAREAN

CS gas /ˌsi ɛs ˈɡæs/ *noun* [U] a gas that stings the eyes, producing tears and making it difficult to breathe. CS gas is sometimes used to control crowds. ⊃ see also TEAR GAS

CSIS /ˈsɪsɪs/ *noun* (CanE) a service of the Canadian government that investigates TERRORISM and similar threats to Canadian society (the abbreviation for "Canadian Security Intelligence Service")

CST /ˌsi ɛs ˈti/ *abbr.* CENTRAL STANDARD TIME

CT *abbr.* (in writing) Connecticut

Ct. (also **Ct.**) *abbr.* (used in written addresses) COURT: *30 Willow Ct.*

ct. ✍ (also **ct.**) *abbr.* (in writing) CARAT: *a 2-ct. diamond*

CT scan /ˌsi ˈti skæn/ *noun* = CAT SCAN

cu. *abbr.* (in writing) CUBIC: *a volume of 2 cu. m* (= 2 cubic meters)

cub /kʌb/ *noun* **1** [C] a young animal, such as a young BEAR, LION, FOX, etc.: *a lioness guarding her cubs* **2** the Cubs [pl.] a branch of the SCOUTS organization in Canada, for boys and girls between the ages of eight and ten **3** Cub [C] a member of the Cubs ⊃ compare BROWNIE (3), CUB SCOUT, SCOUT *n.*

Cu·ban /ˈkyubən/ *adj., noun*
● *adj.* from or connected with Cuba
● *noun* a person from Cuba

cub·by·hole /ˈkʌbiˌhoʊl/ (also **cub·by** /ˈkʌbi/) *noun* a small room or a small space: *My office is a cubbyhole in the basement.*

cube /kyub/ *noun, verb*
● *noun* **1** a solid or hollow figure with six equal square sides ⊃ picture at SHAPE **2** a piece of something, especially food, with six sides: *Cut the meat into cubes.* ⊃ see also BOUILLON CUBE, ICE CUBE, SUGAR CUBE **3** (*mathematics*) the number that you get when you multiply a number by itself twice: *The cube of 5 (5^3) is 125 (5×5×5).*
● *verb* **1** [usually passive] ~ **sth** (*mathematics*) to multiply a number by itself twice: *10 cubed is 1,000.* **2** ~ **sth** to cut food into cubes **SYN** DICE

ˌcube ˈroot *noun* (*mathematics*) a number that, when multiplied by itself twice, produces a particular number: *The cube root of 64 ($\sqrt[3]{64}$) is 4.* ⊃ compare SQUARE ROOT

cu·bic /ˈkyubɪk/ *adj.* **1** (*abbr.* cu) [only before noun] used to show that a measurement is the volume of something, that is the height multiplied by the length and the width: *cubic centimeters/inches/meters* **2** measured or expressed in cubic units: *the cubic capacity of a car's engine* **3** having the shape of a cube: *a cubic figure*

cu·bi·cle /ˈkyubɪkl/ *noun* a small room that is made by separating off part of a larger room: *a shower cubicle* ♦ *an office cubicle*

cub·ism /ˈkyuˌbɪzəm/ also **Cubism** *noun* [U] a style and movement in early 20th-century art in which objects and people are represented as GEOMETRIC shapes, often shown from many different angles at the same time ▶ **cub·ist** also **Cubist** *noun*: *The exhibit includes works by the Cubists.* **cub·ist** also **Cubist** *adj.* [usually before noun]: *cubist paintings*

cu·bit /ˈkyubət/ *noun* an ancient measurement of length, about 18 inches or the length from the elbow to the end of the fingers

cu·boid /ˈkyubɔɪd/ *noun, adj.*
● *noun* (*geometry*) a solid object which has six rectangular (RECTANGLE) sides at RIGHT ANGLES to each other
● *adj.* shaped approximately like a CUBE

ˌcub reˈporter *noun* a young newspaper REPORTER without much experience

Cub Scout *noun* **1** the Cub Scouts [pl.] a branch of the BOY SCOUTS organization in the U.S., for boys between the ages of eight and ten: *to join the Cub Scouts* **2** [C] a member of the Cub Scouts ⊃ compare BROWNIE (3), CUB (2), SCOUT *n.*

cuck·old /ˈkʌkəld; -koʊld/ *noun, verb*
● *noun* (*old use, disapproving*) a man whose wife has sex with another man
● *verb* (*old use*) **1** ~ **sb** (of a man) to make another man a cuckold by having sex with his wife **2** ~ **sb** (of a woman) to make her husband a cuckold by having sex with another man

cuck·oo /ˈkuku; ˈkʊku/ *noun, adj.*
● *noun* (*pl.* cuck·oos) a bird with a call that sounds like its name. Cuckoos leave their eggs in the nests of other birds.
● *adj.* [not before noun] (*old-fashioned, informal*) crazy

ˈcuckoo ˌclock *noun* a clock that has a small toy bird inside that comes out every hour and marks the hours with a sound like that of a cuckoo

cu·cum·ber /ˈkyukʌmbər/ *noun* [C, U] a long vegetable with dark green skin and light green flesh, that is usually eaten raw ⊃ picture at FRUIT ⊃ see also SEA CUCUMBER **IDM** see COOL *adj.*

cud /kʌd/ *noun* [U] the food that cows and similar animals bring back from the stomach into the mouth to chew again: *cows chewing the cud*

cud·dle /ˈkʌdl/ *verb, noun*
● *verb* [I, T] to hold someone or something close in your arms to show love or affection **SYN** HUG: *A couple of teenagers were kissing and cuddling on the doorstep.* ♦ ~ **sth** (+ *adj.*) *The little boy cuddled the teddy bear close.*
PHR V ˌcuddle ˈup (to/against sb/sth) | ˌcuddle ˈup

ʌ cup   ə about   eɪ say   aɪ five   ɔɪ boy   aʊ now   oʊ go   ər bird

(together) to sit or lie very close to someone or something: *She cuddled up against him.* ◆ *We cuddled up together under the blanket.*

● **noun** [usually sing.] the action of holding someone close in your arms to show love or affection **SYN** HUG: *to give someone a cuddle*

cud·dly /ˈkʌdli/ adj. (informal) (**cud·dli·er, cud·dli·est**) **1** (approving) if a person is **cuddly**, they make you want to cuddle them **2** [only before noun] (of a child's toy) soft and designed to be cuddled: *a cuddly rabbit*

cudg·el /ˈkʌdʒl/ noun, verb
● **noun** a short thick stick that is used as a weapon
IDM **take up (the) cudgels on behalf of sb/sth** (old-fashioned) to defend or support someone or something strongly
● **verb** ~ **sb** to hit someone with a cudgel

cue /kyu/ noun, verb
● **noun** **1** an action or event that is a signal for someone to do something: ~ **(for sth)** *Jon's arrival was a cue for more champagne.* ◆ ~ **(to do sth)** *I think that's my cue to explain why I'm here.* **2** a few words or an action in a play that is a signal for another actor to do something: *She stood in the wings and waited for her cue to go on.* **3** a long wooden stick with a leather tip, used for hitting the ball in the games of BILLIARDS and POOL ⊃ picture at HOBBY
IDM **(right) on cue** at exactly the moment you expect or that is appropriate: *"Where is that boy?" As if on cue, Simon appeared in the doorway.* **take your cue from sb/sth** to copy what someone else does as an example of how to behave or what to do: *Investors are taking their cue from the big banks and selling dollars.*
● **verb** (**cue·ing, cued, cued**) ~ **sb** to give someone a signal so they know when to start doing something: *Can you cue me when you want me to begin speaking?*

cue ball noun the ball that is hit with the cue in games such as BILLIARDS and POOL ⊃ picture at HOBBY

cue card noun a large card held up behind a television camera so that it can be read by actors or television PRESENTERS but cannot be seen on television

cuff /kʌf/ noun, verb
● **noun** **1** [C] the end of a coat or shirt sleeve at the wrist: *a collar and cuffs of white lace* ⊃ picture at CLOTHES **2 cuffs** [pl.] (informal) = HANDCUFFS **3** [C] the bottom of the leg of a pair of pants that are folded over on the outside **4** [C] a light hit with an open hand: *to give someone a friendly cuff*
IDM **off the cuff** (of speaking, remarks, etc.) without previous thought or preparation: *I'm just speaking off the cuff here—I haven't seen the results yet.* ◆ *an off-the-cuff remark*
● **verb** ~ **sb** to hit someone quickly and lightly with your hand, especially in a way that is not serious: *She cuffed him lightly on his head.*

cuff link noun [usually pl.] one of a pair of small decorative objects used for fastening shirt cuffs together: *a pair of gold cuff links* ⊃ picture at JEWELRY

cui·sine /kwɪˈzin/ noun [U, C] (from French) **1** a style of cooking: *Italian cuisine* **2** the food served in a restaurant (usually an expensive one): *The hotel restaurant is noted for its excellent cuisine.* ⊃ see also HAUTE CUISINE, NOUVELLE CUISINE

cul-de-sac /ˈkʌl də ˌsæk; ˈkʊl-/ noun (pl. **cul-de-sacs** or **culs-de-sac**) (from French) a street that is closed at one end

cu·li·nar·y /ˈkʌləˌneri; ˈkyu-/ adj. [only before noun] (formal) connected with cooking or food: *culinary skills* ◆ *Savor the culinary delights of Mexico.*

cull /kʌl/ verb, noun
● **verb** ~ **sth** to kill a particular number of animals of a group in order to prevent the group from getting too large
PHR V **'cull sth from sth** to choose or collect something from a source or several different sources: *an exhibition of paintings culled from regional art galleries*
● **noun** the act of killing some animals (usually the weakest

ones) of a group in order to prevent the group from getting too large: *the annual seal cull*

cul·mi·nate /ˈkʌlməˌneɪt/ verb [I] ~ **(in/with sth)** (formal) to end with a particular result, or at a particular point: *a gun battle which culminated in the death of two police officers* ◆ *Months of hard work culminated in success.* ◆ *Their summer tour will culminate at a spectacular concert in New York.*

cul·mi·na·tion /ˌkʌlməˈneɪʃn/ noun [sing.] (formal) the highest point or end of something, usually happening after a long time: *The reforms marked the successful culmination of a long campaign.*

cu·lottes /ˈkulɑts; kuˈlɑts/ noun [pl.] women's wide short pants that are made to look like a skirt: *a pair of culottes*

cul·pa·ble /ˈkʌlpəbl/ adj. (formal) responsible and deserving blame for having done something wrong ▶ **cul·pa·bil·i·ty** /ˌkʌlpəˈbɪləti/ noun [U] **cul·pa·bly** /ˈkʌlpəbli/ adv.

ˌculpable ˈhomicide noun [U] (law) in some countries, the crime of killing someone illegally but not deliberately ⊃ compare JUSTIFIABLE HOMICIDE

cul·prit /ˈkʌlprət/ noun **1** a person who has done something wrong or against the law: *The police quickly identified the real culprits.* **2** a person or thing responsible for causing a problem: *The main culprit in the current crisis seems to be modern farming techniques.*

cult /kʌlt/ noun, adj.
● **noun** **1** [usually sing.] ~ **(of sth)** a way of life, an attitude, an idea, etc. that has become very popular: *the cult of physical fitness* ◆ *An extraordinary personality cult/cult of personality had been created around the leader.* **2** a small group of people who have extreme religious beliefs and who are not part of any established religion: *Their son ran away from home and joined a cult.* **3** (formal) a system of religious beliefs and practices: *the Chinese cult of ancestor worship*
● **adj.** [only before noun] very popular with a particular group of people; treating someone or something as a cult figure, etc.: *a cult movie/book* ◆ *The singer has become a cult figure among college students.* ◆ *The cartoon has achieved cult status.* ◆ *The TV series has a cult following among young people.*

cul·ti·va·ble /ˈkʌltəvəbl/ adj. (of land) that can be used to grow crops

cul·ti·var /ˈkʌltəˌvar/ noun (technical) a type of plant that has been deliberately developed to have particular features

cul·ti·vate /ˈkʌltəˌveɪt/ verb **1** ~ **sth** to prepare and use land for growing plants or crops **SYN** GROW: *The land around here has never been cultivated.* **2** ~ **sth** to grow plants or crops: *The people cultivate mainly rice and beans.* **3** ~ **sb/sth** (sometimes disapproving) to try to get someone's friendship or support: *He purposely tried to cultivate good relations with the press.* ◆ *It helps if you go out of your way to cultivate the local people.* **4** ~ **sth** to develop an attitude, a way of talking or behaving, etc.: *She cultivated an air of sophistication.*

cul·ti·vat·ed /ˈkʌltəˌveɪtəd/ adj. **1** (of people) having a high level of education and showing good manners **SYN** CULTURED **2** (of land) used to grow crops: *cultivated fields* **3** (of plants that are also wild) grown on a farm, etc. in order to be sold: *cultivated mushrooms* **ANT** WILD

cul·ti·va·tion /ˌkʌltəˈveɪʃn/ noun [U] **1** the preparation and use of land for growing plants or crops: *fertile land that is under cultivation* (= being CULTIVATED) ◆ *rice/wheat, etc. cultivation* ⊃ see also SHIFTING CULTIVATION **2** the deliberate development of a particular relationship, quality or skill: *the cultivation of a good relationship with local firms*

cul·ti·va·tor /ˈkʌltəˌveɪtər/ noun **1** a person who CULTIVATES (= grows crops on) the land **2** a machine for breaking up soil and destroying WEEDS (= plants growing where they are not wanted)

ˌcult of ˈperson'ality noun = PERSONALITY CULT

cul·tur·al 🔑 **AWL** /ˈkʌltʃərəl/ adj. [usually before noun] **1** connected with the culture of a particular society or group, its customs, beliefs, etc.: *cultural differences between*

the two communities ◆ *economic, social and cultural factors*
2 connected with art, literature, music, etc.: *a cultural event*
◆ *Europe's cultural heritage* ◆ *The orchestra is very important for
the cultural life of the city.* ▶ **cul·tur·al·ly** **AWL** *adv.*

cul·ture 🔑 **AWL** /ˈkʌltʃər/ *noun, verb*

● *noun*
> **WAY OF LIFE 1** [U] the customs and beliefs, art, way of life,
and social organization of a particular country or group:
European/Islamic/African/American, etc. culture ◆ *working-
class culture* **2** [C] a country, group, etc. with its own beliefs,
etc.: *The children are taught to respect different cultures.* ◆ *the
effect of technology on traditional cultures*
> **ART/MUSIC/LITERATURE 3** [U] art, music, literature, etc.,
thought of as a group: *Venice is a beautiful city full of culture
and history.* ◆ *popular culture* (= that is enjoyed by a lot of
people)
> **BELIEFS/ATTITUDES 4** [C, U] the beliefs and attitudes about
something that people in a particular group or organization
share: *The political cultures of the United States and Europe are
very different.* ◆ *A culture of failure exists in some schools.*
◆ *company culture* ◆ *We are living in a consumer culture.*
> **GROWING/BREEDING 5** [U] (*technical*) the growing of plants or
breeding of particular animals in order to get a particular
substance or crop from them: *the culture of silkworms* (= for
silk)
> **CELLS/BACTERIA 6** [C] (*biology, medical*) a group of cells or
bacteria, especially one taken from a person or an animal
and grown for medical or scientific study, or to produce
food; the process of obtaining and growing these cells: *a
culture of cells from the tumor* ◆ *Yogurt is made from active
cultures.* ◆ *to do/take a throat culture*

● *verb* ~ sth (*biology, medical*) to grow a group of cells or
bacteria for medical or scientific study

cul·tured **AWL** /ˈkʌltʃərd/ *adj.* **1** (of people) well educated
and able to understand and enjoy art, literature, etc.
SYN CULTIVATED **ANT** UNCULTURED **2** (of cells or bacteria)
grown for medical or scientific study **3** (of a PEARL) grown
artificially

'**culture ,shock** *noun* [C, U] a feeling of confusion and
anxiety that someone may feel when they live in or visit
another country

'**culture ,vulture** *noun* (*humorous*) a person who is very
interested in serious art, music, literature, etc.

cul·vert /ˈkʌlvərt/ *noun* a tunnel that carries a river or a pipe
for water under a road

cum /kʌm; kʊm/ *prep.* (used for linking two nouns) and; as
well as: *a bedroom-cum-study*

cum·ber·some /ˈkʌmbərsəm/ *adj.* **1** large and heavy; difficult to carry **SYN** BULKY: *cumbersome machinery* **2** slow
and complicated: *cumbersome legal procedures* **3** (of words
or phrases) long or complicated: *The organization changed
its cumbersome title to something easier to remember.*

cum·in /ˈkʌmən; ˈkyu-; ˈku-/ *noun* [U] the dried seeds of the
cumin plant, used in cooking as a spice: *cumin seeds*

cum lau·de /kʊm ˈlaʊdə; kʌm ˈlɔːdə; -di/ *adv., adj.* (from *Latin*)
at the third of the three highest levels of achievement that
students can reach when they finish their studies at
college: *He graduated cum laude.* ↪ compare MAGNA CUM
LAUDE, SUMMA CUM LAUDE

cum·mer·bund /ˈkʌmərˌbʌnd/ *noun* a wide band of silk,
etc. worn around the waist, especially under a DINNER
JACKET

cu·mu·la·tive /ˈkyumyələtɪv/ *adj.* **1** having a result that
increases in strength or importance each time more of
something is added: *the cumulative effect of human activity
on the world environment* **2** including all the amounts that
have been added previously: *the monthly sales figures and the
cumulative total for the past six months* ▶ **cu·mu·la·tive·ly**
adv.

cu·mu·lo·nim·bus /ˌkyumyəloʊˈnɪmbəs/ *noun* [U] (*technical*)
a high mass of thick cloud with a flat base, often seen
during THUNDERSTORMS

cu·mu·lus /ˈkyumyələs/ *noun* [U] (*technical*) a type of thick
white cloud

cu·ne·i·form /kyuˈniəˌfɔrm; ˈkyuniə-/ *noun* [U] an ancient
system of writing used in Persia and Assyria

cun·ning /ˈkʌnɪŋ/ *adj., noun*
● *adj.* **1** (*disapproving*) able to get what you want in a skillful
way, especially by tricking or cheating someone
SYN CRAFTY, WILY: *a cunning liar* ◆ *He was as cunning as a
fox.* **2** skillful and creative **SYN** INGENIOUS: *It was a cunning
piece of detective work.* ▶ **cun·ning·ly** *adv.*: *The microphone
was cunningly concealed in the bookcase.*
● *noun* [U] the ability to achieve something by tricking or
cheating other people in a skillful way **SYN** : *It took energy
and cunning just to survive.* ◆ *She used low cunning* (= dishonest
behavior) *to get what she wanted.*

cups and glasses

cup and saucer   mug   sippy cup

beer mug   wine glass   champagne flute   tumbler

cup 🔑 /kʌp/ *noun, verb*
● *noun* **1** [C] a small container shaped like a bowl, usually
with a handle, used for drinking tea, coffee, etc.: *a teacup* ◆ *a
coffee cup* ◆ *a cup and saucer* ◆ *a paper cup* **2** [C] the contents
of a cup: *She drank the whole cup.* ◆ *Would you like a cup of
tea?* **3** [C] a unit for measuring quantity used in cooking; a
metal or plastic container used to measure this quantity:
two cups of flour and half a cup of butter **4** [C] a thing shaped
like a cup: *an egg cup* **5** [C] a gold or silver cup on a STEM,
often with two handles, that is given as a prize in a
competition: *She's won several cups for skating.* ◆ *He lifted the
cup for the fifth time this year* (= it was the fifth time he had
won). **6** [sing.] usually **Cup** a sports competition in which a
cup is given as a prize: *the World Cup* **7** [C] one of the two
parts of a BRA that cover the breast: *a C cup* **8** [C] (in GOLF) a
hole in the ground that you must get the ball into **9** [C] a
piece of plastic that a man wears over his sex organs to
protect them while he is playing a sport
IDM **a cup of joe** (*informal*): *a cup of coffee* **not sb's cup of
tea** (*informal*) not what someone likes or is interested in: *An
evening at the opera isn't everyone's cup of tea.* ◆ *He's nice
enough but not really my cup of tea.* ↪ more at SLIP
● *verb* (-pp-) **1** ~ your hand(s) (around/over something)
to make your hands into the shape of a bowl: *She held the
bird gently in cupped hands.* **2** ~ something (in your hands)
to hold something, making your hands into a round shape:
He cupped her face in his hands and kissed her.

cup·board 🔑 /ˈkʌbərd/ *noun*
a piece of furniture with doors and shelves used for storing
dishes, food, clothes, etc.: *kitchen cupboards*

cup·cake /ˈkʌpkeɪk/ *noun* a small cake, baked in a paper
container shaped like a cup and often with ICING on top

cup·ful /ˈkʌpfʊl/ *noun* the amount that a cup will hold:
3 cupfuls of water ↪ see also CUP

Cu·pid /ˈkyupəd/ *noun* **1** the Roman god of love who is
shown as a beautiful baby boy with wings, carrying a BOW²
and arrow **2 cupid** [C] a picture or statue of a baby boy who
looks like Cupid
IDM **play Cupid** to try to start a romantic relationship
between two people

cu·pid·i·ty /kyuˈpɪdəti/ *noun* [U] (*formal*) a strong desire for more wealth, possessions, power, etc. than a person needs **SYN** GREED

cu·po·la /ˈkyupələ/ *noun* a round part on top of a building (like a small DOME) ⊃ picture at ARCHITECTURE

cup·ping /ˈkʌpɪŋ/ *noun* [U] a way of treating pain by putting special cups on the skin and heating them so that the flow of blood to the skin increases

cur /kər/ *noun* (*old-fashioned*, *disapproving*) an aggressive dog, especially a MONGREL

cur·a·ble /ˈkyʊrəbl/ *adj.* (of an illness) that can be cured: *Most skin cancers are curable if treated early.* **ANT** INCURABLE

cu·ra·çao /ˈkyʊrəˌsaʊ; -ˌsoʊ; ˈkʊrə-/ *noun* [U, C] a strong alcoholic drink made from the skin of bitter oranges

cu·ra·cy /ˈkyʊrəsi/ *noun* (*pl.* **cu·ra·cies**) the position of a curate, the time that someone is a curate

cu·rate¹ /ˈkyʊrət/ *noun* (in the Anglican Church) an assistant to a VICAR (= a priest who is in charge of the church or churches in a particular area)

cu·rate² /ˈkyʊreɪt; kyuˈreɪt/ *verb* ~ sth to select, organize, and look after the objects or works of art in a museum or ART GALLERY, etc.

cur·a·tive /ˈkyʊrətɪv/ *adj.* (*formal*) able to cure illness **SYN** HEALING: *the curative properties of herbs* ⊃ compare PREVENTIVE

cu·ra·tor /ˈkyʊrˌeɪtər; kyuˈreɪtər; ˈkyʊrətər/ *noun* a person whose job is to be in charge of the objects or works of art in a museum or art gallery, etc.

curb /kərb/ *verb, noun*
• *verb* ~ sth to control or limit something, especially something bad **SYN** CHECK: *He needs to learn to curb his temper.* ◆ *A range of policies have been introduced aimed at curbing inflation.*
• *noun* 1 the edge of the raised path at the side of a road, usually made of long pieces of stone: *The bus mounted the curb (= went onto the SIDEWALK) and hit a tree.* 2 ~ (on sth) something that controls and puts limits on something: *curbs on government spending*

curb·side /ˈkərbsaɪd/ *noun* [U] the side of the street or path near the curb

curb·stone /ˈkərbstoʊn/ *noun* a block of stone or concrete in a curb

curd /kərd/ *noun* [U] (also **curds**) [pl.] a thick soft substance that is formed when milk turns sour

cur·dle /ˈkərdl/ *verb* 1 [I, T] ~ (sth) when a liquid, especially milk, **curdles** or something **curdles** it, it separates into solid and liquid parts 2 [I, T] ~ (sth) if something **curdles** your blood or makes your blood **curdle**, it makes you extremely frightened or shocked ⊃ see also BLOOD-CURDLING

cure /kyʊr/ *verb, noun*
• *verb* 1 ~ sb (of sth) to make a person or an animal healthy again after an illness: *Will you be able to cure him, doctor?* 2 ~ sth to make an illness go away: *TB is a serious illness, but it can be cured.* 3 ~ sth to deal with a problem successfully: *I finally managed to cure the rattling noise in my car.* 4 ~ sb of sth to stop someone from behaving in a particular way, especially a way that is bad or annoying 5 ~ sth to treat food or TOBACCO with smoke, salt, etc. in order to preserve it
• *noun* 1 ~ (for sth) a medicine or medical treatment that cures an illness: *the search for a cure for cancer* ◆ *There is no known cure but the illness can be treated.* 2 the act of curing someone of an illness or the process of being cured: *Doctors cannot effect a cure if the disease has spread too far.* ◆ *The cure took six weeks.* 3 ~ (for sth) something that will solve a problem, improve a bad situation, etc.: *a cure for poverty* **IDM** see OUNCE

ˈcure-all *noun* something that people believe can cure any problem or any disease **SYN** PANACEA

cur·few /ˈkərfyu/ *noun* [C, U] 1 a law that says that people must not go outside after a particular time at night until the morning; the time after which nobody must go outside: *The army imposed a dusk-to-dawn curfew.* ◆ *You must get home before curfew.* ⊃ collocations at WAR 2 a time when children must be home in the evening: *I have a 10 o'clock curfew.*

cu·rie /ˈkyʊri; kyuˈri/ *noun* (*abbr.* Ci) (*physics*) a unit for measuring radioactivity (RADIOACTIVE)

cu·ri·o /ˈkyʊrioʊ/ *noun* (*pl.* **cu·ri·os**) a small object that is rare or unusual, often something that people collect

cu·ri·os·i·ty /ˌkyʊriˈɑsəti/ *noun* (*pl.* **cu·ri·os·i·ties**)
1 [U, sing.] ~ (about sth) | ~ (to do sth) a strong desire to know about something: *Children show curiosity about everything.* ◆ *a certain curiosity to see what would happen next* ◆ *The letter wasn't addressed to me but I opened it out of curiosity.* ◆ *His answer did not satisfy my curiosity at all.* ◆ *Sophie's curiosity was aroused by the mysterious phone call.* ◆ *intellectual curiosity* ◆ *"Why do you ask?" "Oh, just idle curiosity."* (= no particular reason) 2 [C] an unusual and interesting thing: *The museum is full of historical curiosities.* **IDM** **curiosity killed the cat** (*saying*) used to tell someone not to ask questions or try to find out about things that do not concern them

cu·ri·ous /ˈkyʊriəs/ *adj.*
1 ~ (about sth) | ~ (to do sth) having a strong desire to know about something **SYN** INQUISITIVE: *They were very curious about the people who lived upstairs.* ◆ *I was curious to find out what she had said.* ◆ *Everyone was curious as to why Mark was leaving.* ◆ *He is such a curious boy, always asking questions.* 2 ~ (that...) strange and unusual: *There was a curious mixture of people in the audience.* ◆ *It was a curious feeling, as though we were floating on air.* ◆ *It was curious that she didn't tell anyone.* ▶ **cu·ri·ous·ly** *adv.*: *"Are you really an artist?" Sara asked curiously.* ◆ *His clothes were curiously old-fashioned.* ◆ *Curiously enough, a year later exactly the same thing happened again.*

cu·ri·um /ˈkyʊriəm/ *noun* [U] (*symb.* Cm) a chemical element. Curium is a RADIOACTIVE metal produced artificially from PLUTONIUM.

curl /kərl/ *verb, noun*
• *verb* 1 [I, T] ~ (sth) to form or make something form into a curl or curls: *His hair curls naturally.* 2 [I, T] to form or make something form into a curved shape: (+ adv./prep.) *The cat curled into a ball and went to sleep.* ◆ ~ sth (+ adv./prep.) *She curled her legs up under her.* 3 [I, T] to move while forming into a twisted or curved shape; to make something do this: (+ adv./prep.) *The smoke curled steadily upward.* ◆ ~ sth (+ adv./prep.) *He turned and curled the ball around the goalkeeper.* 4 [T, I] ~ (sth) if you curl your lip or your lip curls, you move your lip upward and sideways to show that you think someone or something is stupid or that you are better than they are **IDM** see TOE **PHR V** **curl 'up** | **be ˌcurled 'up** to lie or sit with your back curved and your arms and legs bent close to your body: *She curled up and closed her eyes.* **ˌcurl 'up** | **ˌcurl sth↔'up** to form or make something form into a tightly curled shape: *The paper started to shrivel and curl up in the heat.* ⊃ picture at CURVED
• *noun* 1 [C] a small bunch of hair that forms a curved or round shape: *Her hair was a mass of curls.* ◆ *The baby had dark eyes and dark curls.* 2 [C, U] the tendency of hair to form curls: *His hair had a natural curl.* 3 [C] a thing that forms a curved or round shape: *a curl of smoke* ◆ *Decorate the cake with curls of chocolate.* ◆ *a contemptuous curl of the lip* (= an expression showing disapproval)

curl·er /ˈkərlər/ *noun* [usually pl.] a small plastic or metal tube which you can wrap wet hair around in order to make it curl **SYN** ROLLER

cur·lew /ˈkərlu/ *noun* a bird with a long thin beak that curves downward and that lives near water

curl·i·cue /ˈkərliˌkyu/ *noun* (*technical*) a decorative curl or twist in writing or in a design

curl·ing /ˈkərlɪŋ/ *noun* [U] a game played on ice, especially in Canada, in which players slide heavy flat stones toward a mark

'curling ,iron *noun* a tool that is heated and used for curling hair

curl·y /'kərli/ *adj.*
(curl·i·er, curl·i·est)
having a lot of curls or a curved shape: *short curly hair* ◆ *a dog with a curly tail* **ANT** STRAIGHT ⊃ picture at HAIR, CURVED

,curly 'endive *noun* [C, U] = ENDIVE

cur·mudg·eon /kər'mʌdʒən/ *noun* (*old-fashioned*) a bad-tempered person, often an old one ▶ **cur·mudg·eon·ly** *adj.*

cur·rant /'kərənt/ *noun* **1** a small dried GRAPE, used in cakes, etc.: *a currant bun* **2** (usually in compounds) a small black, red, or white BERRY that grows in bunches on bushes: *blackcurrants* ◆ *currant bushes*

cur·ren·cy **AWL** /'kərənsi/ *noun* (*pl.* **cur·ren·cies**) **1** [C, U] the system of money that a country uses: *trading in foreign currencies* ◆ *a single European currency* ◆ *You'll need some cash in local currency but you can also use your credit card.* ⊃ see also HARD CURRENCY **2** [U] the fact that something is used or accepted by a lot of people: *The term "post-industrial" now has wide currency.* ◆ *The qualification has gained currency all over the world.*

cur·rent /'kərənt/ *adj., noun*
● *adj.* **1** [only before noun] happening now; of the present time: *current prices* ◆ *a budget for the current year* ◆ *your current employer* ⊃ note at ACTUAL **2** being used by or accepted by most people: *words that are no longer current*
● *noun* **1** the movement of water in the ocean or a river; the movement of air in a particular direction: *He swam to the shore against a strong current.* ◆ *Birds use warm air currents to help their flight.* **2** the flow of electricity through a wire, etc.: *a 15 amp electrical current* ⊃ see also ALTERNATING CURRENT, DIRECT CURRENT **3** the fact of particular ideas, opinions, or feelings being present in a group of people: *Ministers are worried by this current of antigovernment feeling.*

,current e'vents (also **,current af'fairs**) *noun* [pl.] events of political or social importance that are happening now

cur·rent·ly /'kərəntli/ *adv.*
at the present time: *The hourly charge is currently $35.* ◆ *Currently, over 500 students are enrolled in the course.* ◆ *All the options are currently available.* ◆ *This matter is currently being discussed.*

cur·ric·u·lar /kə'rɪkyələr/ *adj.* connected with the curriculum of a school, etc. ⊃ see also EXTRACURRICULAR

cur·ric·u·lum /kə'rɪkyələm/ *noun* (*pl.* **cur·ric·u·la** /-lə/ or **cur·ric·u·lums**) the subjects that are included in a course of study or taught in a school, college, etc.: *the school curriculum* ◆ *Spanish is in the curriculum.* ⊃ collocations at EDUCATION ⊃ compare SYLLABUS

cur·ric·u·lum vi·tae /kə,rɪkyələm 'vitar; -'vaɪti/ (*abbr.* CV) *noun* (also **vi·ta**) a record of a university/college teacher's education and where they have worked, also including a list of books and articles that they have published and courses that they have taught, used when they are applying for a job ⊃ compare RESUME

curried /'kərid/ *adj.* [only before noun] cooked with hot spices: *curried chicken/beef/eggs, etc.*

cur·ry /'kəri/ *noun, verb*
● *noun* [C, U] a S. Asian dish of meat, vegetables, etc. cooked with hot spices, often served with rice: *a chicken curry* ◆ *Would you like some more curry?*
● *verb* (**cur·ries, cur·ry·ing, cur·ried, cur·ried**) ~ **sth** to make curry out of meat or vegetables
IDM **curry favor (with sb)** (*disapproving*) to try to get someone to like or support you by praising or helping them a lot

'curry ,powder *noun* [U] a powder made from a mixture of spices, used to give a hot flavor to food, especially curry

curse /kərs/ *noun, verb*
● *noun* **1** (also **cuss**) [C] a rude or offensive word or phrase that some people use when they are very angry **SYN** OATH, SWEAR WORD: *He muttered a curse at the other driver.* **2** [C] a word or phrase that has a magic power to make something bad happen: *The family thought that they were under a curse.* ⊃ compare HEX **3** [C] something that causes harm or evil: *the curse of drug addiction* ◆ *Noise is a curse of modern city life.* **4 the curse** [sing.] (*old-fashioned, informal*) MENSTRUATION
IDM see BLESSING
● *verb* **1** [I] to swear: *He hit his head as he stood up and cursed loudly.* **2** [T] to say rude things to someone or think rude things about someone or something: ~ **sb/sth/yourself** *She cursed her bad luck.* ◆ ~ **sb/sth/yourself for sth** *He cursed himself for his stupidity.* **3** [T] ~ **sb/sth** to use a magic word or phrase against someone in order to harm them: *Legend has it that the whole village had been cursed by a witch.* ⊃ compare HEX
PHR V **be 'cursed with sth** to continuously suffer from or be affected by something bad: *She seems cursed with bad luck.*

curs·ed *adj.* **1** /kərst/ having a curse on it; suffering from a curse: *The necklace was cursed.* ◆ *The whole family seemed cursed.* **2** /'kərsɪd/ [only before noun] (*old-fashioned*) unpleasant; annoying

cur·sive /'kərsɪv/ *adj.* (*technical*) (of HANDWRITING) with the letters joined together

cur·sor /'kərsər/ *noun* a small mark on a computer screen that can be moved and that shows the position on the screen where, for example, text will be added

cur·so·ry /'kərsəri/ *adj.* (often *disapproving*) done quickly and without giving enough attention to details **SYN** BRIEF, PERFUNCTORY: *a cursory glance/examination/inspection* ▶ **cur·so·ri·ly** /-rəli/ *adv.*

curt /kərt/ *adj.* (of a person's manner or behavior) appearing rude because very few words are used, or because something is done in a very quick way **SYN** ABRUPT, BRUSQUE: *a curt reply* ◆ *a curt nod* ◆ *His tone was curt and unfriendly.* ▶ **curt·ly** *adv.* **curt·ness** *noun* [U]

cur·tail /kər'teɪl/ *verb* ~ **sth** (*formal*) to limit something or make it last for a shorter time: *Spending on books has been severely curtailed.* ◆ *The lecture was curtailed by the fire alarm going off.* ▶ **cur·tail·ment** *noun* [U]: *the curtailment of civil liberties*

cur·tain /'kərtn/ *noun, verb*
● *noun* **1** [C] a piece of cloth that is hung to cover a window: *to draw/pull/close the curtains* (= to pull them across the window so they cover it) ◆ *to draw/draw back/pull back the curtains* (= to open them, so that the window is no longer covered) ◆ *It was ten in the morning but the curtains were still drawn* (= closed). ◆ *a pair of curtains* ⊃ see also DRAPE **2** [C] a very thin piece of cloth that you hang at a window, that allows light to enter but stops people outside from being able to see inside **3** [C] a piece of cloth that is hung up as a screen in a room or around a bed, for example: *a shower curtain* **4** [sing.] a piece of thick, heavy cloth that hangs in front of the stage in the theater: *The audience was waiting for the curtain to rise* (= for the play to begin). ◆ *There was tremendous applause when the curtain came down* (= the play ended). ◆ *We left just before the final curtain.* ◆ (*figurative*) *The curtain has fallen on her long and distinguished career* (= her career has ended). ◆ (*figurative*) *It's time to face the final curtain* (= the end; death). ⊃ see also THE IRON CURTAIN **5** [C, usually sing.] a thing that covers, hides, or protects something: *a curtain of rain/smoke* ◆ *She pushed back the curtain of brown hair from her eyes.*
IDM **be curtains (for sb)** (*informal*) to be a situation without hope or that you cannot escape from: *When I saw he had a gun, I thought it was curtains for me.* **bring down the curtain on sth | bring the curtain down on sth** to finish or mark the end of something: *His sudden decision to retire brought down the curtain on a distinguished career.*
● *verb* ~ **sth** to provide curtains for a window or a room

PHR V ,curtain sth↔'off to separate an area of a room with a curtain or curtains

'curtain ,call noun the time in the theater when the actors come to the front of the stage at the end of a play to receive the APPLAUSE of the audience

'curtain ,raiser noun 1 ~ (to sth) a small event that prepares for a more important one 2 ~ (to sth) a short performance before the main performance in a theater, etc.

curt·sy (also curt·sey) /'kɜrtsi/ noun (pl. curt·sies or curt·seys) a formal sign made by a woman in a dance or to say hello or goodbye to an important person, in which she bends her knees with one foot in front of the other ▶ curt·sy verb (curt·sies, curt·sy·ing, curt·sied, curt·sied) (also curt·sey) [I]: ~ (to sb) She curtsied to the President.

cur·va·ceous /kər'veɪʃəs/ adj. (informal) used in newspapers, etc. to describe a woman whose body has attractive curves

cur·va·ture /'kɜrvətʃər; -,tʃʊr/ noun [U] (technical) the state of being curved; the amount that something is curved: the curvature of the earth ◆ curvature of the spine

curve 🔊 /kɜrv/ noun, verb

● noun 1 a line or surface that bends gradually; a smooth bend: the delicate curve of her ear ◆ a pattern of straight lines and curves ◆ a curve in the road ◆ The driver lost control on a curve and the vehicle hit a tree. ◆ to plot a curve on a graph ◆ (technical) the unemployment-income curve (= a line on a GRAPH showing the relationship between the number of unemployed people and national income) ⊃ see also LEARNING CURVE 2 (also 'curve ball) (in baseball) a ball that moves in a curve when it is thrown to the BATTER: (figurative) One of the journalists threw the senator a curve (= surprised him by asking a difficult question).

IDM ahead of/behind the curve (business) in advance of or behind a particular trend: Our expert advice will help you stay ahead of the curve. ◆ We've fallen behind the curve when it comes to developing new digital products.

● verb [I, T] ~ (sth) (+ adv./prep.) to move or make something move in the shape of a curve; to be in the shape of a curve: The road curved around the bay. ◆ The ball curved through the air. ◆ His lips curved in a smile.

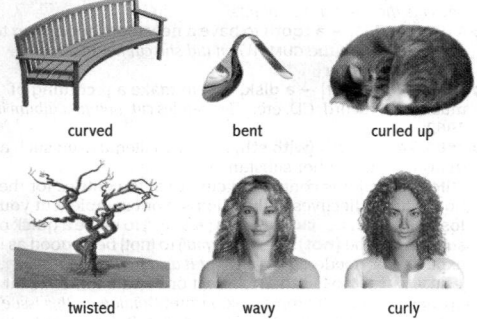

curved   bent   curled up

twisted   wavy   curly

curved 🔊 /kɜrvd/ adj. having a round shape: a curved path/roof/blade ⊃ picture at LINE

cur·vi·lin·e·ar /ˌkɜrvə'lɪniər/ adj. (formal) consisting of a curved line or lines

curv·y /'kɜrvi/ adj. (informal) having curves: a curvy body ◆ curvy lines

cush·ion /'kʊʃn/ noun, verb

● noun 1 (also pil·low) a cloth bag filled with soft material or feathers that is used, for example, to make a seat more comfortable: matching curtains and cushions ◆ a floor cushion (= a large cushion that you put on the floor to sit on) ◆ (figurative) a cushion of moss on a rock ⊃ picture at CHAIR 2 a layer of something between two surfaces that

keeps them apart: A hovercraft rides on a cushion of air. 3 [usually sing.] ~ (against sth) something that protects you against something unpleasant that might happen: His savings were a comfortable cushion against financial problems. ◆ The team built up a safe cushion of twenty points in the first half. 4 (in the game of BILLIARDS, etc.) the soft inside edge along each side of the table that the balls BOUNCE off ⊃ picture at HOBBY

● verb 1 ~ sth to make the effect of a fall or hit less severe: My fall was cushioned by the deep snow. 2 ~ sb/sth (against/from sth) to protect someone or something from being hurt or damaged, or from the unpleasant effects of something: The south of the country has been cushioned from the worst effects of the recession. ◆ He broke the news of my brother's death to me, making no effort to cushion the blow (= make the news less shocking). 3 [usually passive] ~ sth to make something soft with a cushion

cush·y /'kʊʃi/ adj. (cush·i·er, cush·i·est) (informal, often disapproving) very easy and pleasant; needing little or no effort: a cushy job

cusp /kʌsp/ noun 1 (technical) a pointed end where two curves meet: the cusp of a leaf 2 the time when one sign of the ZODIAC ends and the next begins: I was born on the cusp between Virgo and Libra. ◆ (figurative) He was on the cusp between small acting roles and moderate fame.

cuss /kʌs/ verb, noun

● verb [I, T] ~ (sb/sth) (old-fashioned, informal) to swear at someone: My dad used to come home drunk, shouting and cussing.

● noun (old-fashioned, informal) 1 used with a negative adjective to describe a person: He's an awkward cuss. 2 = CURSE: cuss words

cuss·ed /'kʌsɪd/ adj. (old-fashioned, informal) (of people) not willing to be helpful SYN STUBBORN ▶ cuss·ed·ly adv. cuss·ed·ness noun [U]

cus·tard /'kʌstərd/ noun 1 [C, U] a mixture of eggs, milk, and sugar baked until it is firm 2 [U] (also ,custard 'sauce) a sweet yellow sauce made from milk, sugar, eggs, and flour, usually served hot with cooked fruit, PUDDING, etc.: apple pie and custard

,custard 'pie noun a flat PIE filled with something soft and wet that looks like custard, that performers throw at each other to make people laugh

cus·to·di·al /kʌ'stoʊdiəl/ adj. [usually before noun] 1 (law) connected with the right or duty of taking care of someone; having CUSTODY: The mother is usually the custodial parent after a divorce. ANT NONCUSTODIAL 2 relating to work done by a custodian: The custodial staff cleans the building at night.

cus·to·di·an /kʌ'stoʊdiən/ noun 1 a person who takes responsibility for taking care of or protecting something: the museum's custodians ◆ a self-appointed custodian of public morals 2 a person whose job is to take care of a building such as a school or an apartment building SYN JANITOR ⊃ see also CARETAKER

cus·to·dy /'kʌstədi/ noun [U] 1 the legal right or duty to take care of or keep someone or something; the act of taking care of something or someone: Who will have custody of the children? ◆ The divorce court awarded custody to the child's mother. ◆ The parents were locked in a bitter battle for custody. ◆ He and his former wife share joint custody of their 10-year-old daughter. ◆ The bank provides safe custody for valuables. ◆ The castle is now in the custody of the state. ⊃ collocations at MARRIAGE 2 the state of being in prison, especially while waiting for trial: After the riot, 32 people were taken into police custody.

cus·tom 🔊 /'kʌstəm/ noun, adj.

● noun ⊃ see also CUSTOMS 1 [C, U] ~ (of doing sth) an accepted way of behaving or of doing things in a society or a community: an old/ancient custom ◆ the custom of giving presents at Christmas ◆ It's a local custom. ◆ It is the custom in that country for women to marry young. 2 [sing.] (formal or literary) the way a person always behaves SYN HABIT,

PRACTICE: *It was her custom to rise early.* ◆ *As was his custom, he knocked three times.*

● *adj.* [only before noun] = CUSTOM-BUILT, CUSTOM-MADE: *a custom motorcycle*

cus·tom·ar·y /ˈkʌstəˌmɛri/ *adj.* **1** if something is **custom-ary**, it is what people usually do in a particular place or situation **SYN** USUAL: *Is it customary to tip hairdressers in this country?* **2** typical of a particular person **SYN** HABITUAL: *She arranged everything with her customary efficiency.* ▶ **cus·tom·ar·i·ly** /ˌkʌstəˈmɛrəli/ *adv.*

ˌcustom-ˈbuilt (also **cus·tom**) *adj.* designed and built for a particular person

cus·tom·er 🔑 /ˈkʌstəmər/ *noun*
1 a person or an organization that buys something from a store or business: *one of the shop's **best/biggest customers*** ◆ *They know me—I'm a **regular customer**.* ◆ *the **customer service** department* ◆ *The firm has excellent customer relations.* ⊃ collocations at SHOPPING **2** (*old-fashioned, informal*) used after an adjective to describe a particular type of person: *a tough customer*

ˈcustomer ˌbase *noun* [usually sing.] (*business*) all the people who buy or use a particular product or service: *We need to appeal to a wider customer base.*

ˈcustomer-ˌfacing *adj.* [only before noun] (*business*) dealing directly with customers or used by customers: *customer-facing operations such as call centers* ◆ *customer-facing software applications*

cus·tom·ize /ˈkʌstəˌmaɪz/ *verb* ~ sth to make or change something to suit the needs of the owner: *You can customize the software in several ways.* ▶ **cus·tom·ized** *adj.*: *a custom-ized car*

ˌcustom-ˈmade (also **cus·tom**) *adj.* designed and made for a particular person ⊃ see also BESPOKE

cus·toms 🔑 /ˈkʌstəmz/ *noun* [pl.]
1 usually **Customs** the government department that collects taxes on goods bought and sold and on goods brought into the country, and that checks what is brought in: *Customs seized large quantities of smuggled heroin.* ◆ *a customs officer* **HELP** Use a singular verb with **customs** in this meaning. **2** the place at a port or an airport where your bags are checked as you come into a country: *to go through customs and passport control* **3** the taxes that must be paid to the government when goods are brought in from other countries: *to pay customs on something* ◆ *customs duty/duties* ⊃ thesaurus box at TAX ⊃ compare EXCISE¹

ˈcustoms ˌunion *noun* a group of states that agree to have the same taxes on imported goods

cut 🔑 /kʌt/ *verb, noun*
● *verb* (cut·ting, cut, cut)
▷ **WOUND/HOLE 1** [T, I] to make an opening or a wound in something, especially with a sharp tool such as a knife or scissors: ~ sth *She cut her finger on a piece of glass.* ◆ ~ **yourself** *He cut himself* (= his face) *shaving.* ◆ ~ sth + adj. *She had fallen and cut her head open.* ◆ ~ **through sth** *You need a powerful saw to cut through metal.* ◆ (*figurative*) *The canoe cut through the water.*
▷ **REMOVE WITH KNIFE 2** [T] to remove something or a part of something, using a knife, etc.: ~ **sth (from sth)** *He cut four thick slices from the loaf.* ◆ *a bunch of cut flowers* ◆ ~ **sb sth** *I cut them all a piece of birthday cake.* ◆ ~ **sth for sb** *I cut a piece of birthday cake for them all.*
▷ **DIVIDE 3** [T] to divide something into two or more pieces with a knife, etc.: ~ sth *Don't cut the string; untie the knots.* ◆ ~ **sth in/into sth** *He cut the loaf into thick slices.* ◆ *The bus was cut in two by the train.* ◆ *Now cut the tomatoes in half.*
▷ **SHAPE/FORM 4** [T] ~ **sth (in sth)** to make or form something by removing material with a knife, etc.: *The climbers cut steps in the ice.* ◆ *Workmen cut a hole in the pipe.*
▷ **HAIR/NAILS/GRASS, ETC. 5** [T] to make something shorter by cutting: ~ **sth** *to cut your hair/nails* ◆ *to cut the grass/lawn/hedge* ◆ ~ **sth + adj.** *He's had his hair cut really short.*

▷ **RELEASE 6** [T] to allow someone to escape from somewhere by cutting the rope, object, etc., that is holding them: ~ **sb (from sth)** *The injured driver had to be cut from the wreckage.* ◆ + **sb + adj.** *Two survivors were **cut free** after being trapped for twenty minutes.*
▷ **CLOTHING 7** [T, usually passive] ~ **sth + adj.** to design and make a piece of clothing in a particular way: *The swimsuit was cut high in the leg.*
▷ **ABLE TO CUT/BE CUT 8** [I] to be capable of cutting: *This knife won't cut.* **9** [I] to be capable of being cut: *Sandstone cuts easily.*
▷ **REDUCE 10** [T] to reduce something by removing a part of it: ~ **sth** *to cut prices/taxes/spending/production* ◆ *Buyers will bargain hard to **cut the cost** of the house they want.* ◆ ~ **sth by...** *His salary has been cut by ten percent.* ◆ ~ **sth (from...) (to...)** *Could you cut your essay from 5,000 to 3,000 words?*
▷ **REMOVE 11** [T] ~ **sth (from sth)** to remove something from something: *This scene was cut from the final version of the movie.*
▷ **COMPUTING 12** [I, T] ~ **(sth)** to DELETE (= remove) part of a text on a computer screen in order to place it somewhere else: *You can **cut and paste** between different programs.*
▷ **STOP 13** [T] ~ **sth** (*informal*) used to tell someone to stop doing something: *Cut the chatter and get on with your work!*
▷ **END 14** [T] ~ **sth** to completely end a relationship or all communication with someone **SYN** SEVER: *She has cut all ties with her family.*
▷ **IN MOVIE/TV 15** [T] ~ **sth** to prepare a movie or tape by removing parts of it or putting them in a different order **SYN** EDIT ⊃ see also DIRECTOR'S CUT **16** [I] (usually used in orders) to stop filming or recording: *The director shouted "Cut!"* **17** [I] ~ **(from sth) to sth** (in movies, radio, or television) to move quickly from one scene to another: *The scene cuts from the bedroom to the street.*
▷ **MISS CLASS 18** [T] ~ **sth** (*informal*) to stay away from a class that you should go to: *He's always **cutting class**.* **SYN** SKIP *v.* (2)
▷ **UPSET 19** [T] ~ **sb** to hurt someone emotionally: *His cruel remarks cut her deeply.*
▷ **IN CARD GAMES 20** [I, T] ~ **(sth)** to lift and turn up a DECK of PLAYING CARDS in order to decide who is to play first, etc.: *Let's cut for dealer.*
▷ **GEOMETRY 21** [T] ~ **sth** (of a line) to cross another line: *The line cuts the circle at two points.*
▷ **A TOOTH 22** [T] ~ **a tooth** to have a new tooth beginning to appear through the GUM: *When did she cut her first tooth?* ⊃ see also TOOTH
▷ **A DISK, ETC. 23** [T] ~ **a disk, etc.** to make a recording of music on a record, CD, etc.: *The Beatles cut their first album in 1962.*
▷ **DRUG 24** [T] ~ **sth (with sth)** to mix an illegal drug such as HEROIN with another substance

IDM Most idioms containing **cut** are at the entries for the nouns and adjectives in the idioms. For example, **cut your losses** is at LOSS. **cut and run** (*informal*) to make a quick or sudden escape **(not) cut it** (*informal*) to (not) be as good as is expected or needed: *He won't cut it as a professional singer.*
PHR V ˌcut aˈcross sth **1** to affect or be true for different groups that usually remain separate: *Opinion on this issue cuts across traditional political boundaries.* **2** (also ˌcut ˈthrough sth) to go across something in order to make your route shorter: *I usually cut across the park on my way home.*
PHR V ˌcut sth↔aˈway (from sth) to remove something from something by cutting: *They cut away all the dead branches from the tree.*
ˌcut sth↔ˈback **1** (also ˌcut ˈback (on sth)) to reduce something: *If we don't sell more, we'll have to cut back production.* ◆ *to cut back on spending* ⊃ related noun CUTBACK ⊃ thesaurus box at CUT **2** to make a bush, etc. smaller by cutting branches off **SYN** PRUNE: *to cut back a rose bush* ˌcut sb↔ˈdown (*formal*) to kill someone: *He was cut down by an assassin's bullet.* ˌcut sth↔ˈdown to make something fall down by cutting it at the base: *to cut down a tree* ˌcut sth↔ˈdown (to...) | ˌcut ˈdown (on sth) to reduce the size, amount, or number of something: *We need to cut the article down to 1,000 words.* ◆ *The doctor told him to cut down*

ʌ cup   ə about   eɪ say   aɪ five   ɔɪ boy   aʊ now   oʊ go   ər bird

on his drinking. ◆ *I won't have a cigarette, thanks—I'm trying to cut down* (= smoke fewer).

,cut 'in 1 if a motor or an engine **cuts in**, it starts working: *Emergency generators cut in.* 2 to go in front of other people who are waiting 3 to begin dancing with sb who had until then been dancing with another person: *"Mind if I cut in?"* ,cut 'in (on sb/sth) 1 to interrupt someone when they are speaking **SYN** BUTT IN: *She kept cutting in on our conversation.* ◆ [+ **speech**] *"Forget it!" she cut in.* 2 (of a vehicle or its driver) to move suddenly in front of another vehicle, leaving little space between the two vehicles ,cut sb 'in (on sth) (*informal*) to give someone a share of the profit in a business or an activity

,cut sb↔'off 1 [often passive] to interrupt someone who is speaking on the telephone by breaking the connection: *We were cut off in the middle of our conversation.* 2 to refuse to let someone receive any of your property after you die **SYN** DISINHERIT: *He cut his son off without a penny.* ,cut sb/ sth↔'off 1 to interrupt someone and stop them from speaking: *My explanation was cut off by loud protests.* 2 [often passive] to stop the supply of something to someone: *Our water supply has been cut off.* ◆ *They were cut off for not paying their phone bill.* 3 to suddenly drive in front of another vehicle in a dangerous way ,cut sth↔'off 1 (also ,cut sth 'off sth) to remove something from something larger by cutting: *He had his finger cut off in an accident at work.* ◆ (*figurative*) *The winner cut ten seconds off* (= ran the distance ten seconds faster than) *the world record.* ⊃ see also CUT-OFF 2 to block or get in the way of something: *They cut off the enemy's retreat.* ◆ *The new factory cuts off our view of the hills.* ,cut sb/sth 'off (from sb/sth) [often passive] to prevent someone or something from leaving or reaching a place or communicating with people outside a place: *The army was cut off from its base.* ◆ *She feels very cut off living in the country.* ◆ *He cut himself off from all human contact.*

,cut 'out if a motor or an engine **cuts out**, it suddenly stops working ⊃ related noun CUTOUT ,cut sb↔'out (of sth) to not allow someone to be involved in something: *Don't cut your parents out of your lives.* ◆ *Furious, his mother cut him out of her will* (= refused to let him receive any of her property after she died). ,cut sth↔'out 1 to make something by cutting: *She cut the dress out of some old material.* ◆ (*figurative*) *He's cut out a niche for himself* (= found a suitable job) *in journalism.* ⊃ related noun CUTOUT 2 (*informal*) used to tell someone to stop doing or saying something annoying: *I'm sick of you two arguing—just cut it out!* 3 to leave something out of a piece of writing, etc. **SYN** OMIT: *I would cut out the part about working as a waitress.* 4 to block something, especially light: *Tall trees cut out the sunlight.* ,cut sth↔'out (of sth) 1 to remove something from something larger by cutting, usually with scissors: *I cut this article out of the newspaper.* 2 to stop doing, using, or eating something: *I've been advised to cut sugar out of my diet.* be ,cut 'out for sth | be ,cut 'out to be sth (*informal*) to have the qualities and abilities needed for something: *He's not cut out for teaching.* ◆ *He's not cut out to be a teacher.*

,cut 'through sth 1 = CUT ACROSS STH 2 (also ,cut sth 'through sth) to make a path or passage through something by cutting: *They used a machete to cut through the bush.* ◆ *The prisoners cut their way through the barbed wire.*

,cut 'up (*informal*) to behave in a noisy and silly way ,cut sb↔'up (*informal*) 1 to injure someone badly by cutting or hitting them: *He was very badly cut up in the fight.* 2 [usually passive] to upset someone emotionally: *She was pretty cut up about them leaving.* ,cut sth↔'up to divide something into small pieces with a knife, etc.: *He cut up the meat on his plate.*

● **noun**
▷WOUND 1 a wound caused by something sharp: *cuts and bruises on the face* ◆ *Blood poured from the deep cut on his arm.*
▷HOLE 2 a hole or an opening in something, made with something sharp: *Using sharp scissors, make a small cut in the material.*
▷REDUCTION 3 ~ (in sth) a reduction in amount, size, supply, etc.: *price/tax/job cuts* ◆ *They had to take a 20 percent cut in pay.* ◆ *They announced cuts in public spending.* ⊃ see also POWER CUT, SHORTCUT

▷OF HAIR 4 [usually sing.] an act of cutting someone's hair; the style in which it is cut: *Your hair could use a cut* (= it is too long). ◆ *a cut and blow-dry* ⊃ see also BUZZ CUT
▷OF CLOTHING 5 [usually sing.] the shape and style that a piece of clothing has because of the way the cloth is cut: *the elegant cut of her dress*
▷SHARE OF MONEY 6 a share in something, especially money: *They were rewarded with a cut of 5 percent from the profits.*
▷OF MOVIE/PLAY, ETC. 7 ~ (in sth) an act of removing part of a movie, play, piece of writing, etc.: *The director objected to the cuts ordered by the censor.* ◆ *She made some cuts before handing over the finished novel.*
▷MEAT 8 a piece of meat cut from an animal: *a lean cut of pork* ◆ *cheap cuts of stewing lamb* ⊃ see also COLD CUTS
IDM a cut above sb/sth better than someone or something: *His latest novel is a cut above the rest.*

THESAURUS

cut

slash • cut sth back • scale sth back • streamline • downsize

These words all mean to reduce the amount or size of something, especially of an amount of money or a business.

cut to reduce something, especially an amount of money that is demanded, spent, earned, etc. or the size of a business: *The President has promised to cut taxes significantly.* ◆ *Most small business owners work hard to cut costs.* ◆ *His salary has been cut by ten percent.* ◆ *Could you cut your essay from 5,000 to 3,000 words?*

slash [often passive] (*somewhat informal*) (often used in newspapers) to reduce something by a large amount: *Prices have been slashed in the clearance sale.*

cut sth back/cut back on sth to reduce something, especially an amount of money or business: *We had to cut back on production.*

scale sth back (*especially business*) to reduce something, especially an amount of money or business: *The IMF has scaled back its growth forecasts for the next decade.*

streamline (*business*) to make changes to a business or system, in order to make it more efficient, especially by spending less money.

downsize (*business*) to make a company or organization smaller by reducing the number of jobs in it, in order to reduce costs. **NOTE Downsize** is often used by people who want to avoid saying more obvious words like "fire" or "lay off" because they sound too negative.

PATTERNS
- to cut/slash/cut back on/scale back/streamline **production**
- to cut/slash/cut back on/scale back **spending**
- to cut/slash/cut back on **jobs**
- to cut/slash/downsize **the workforce**
- to cut/slash **prices/taxes/the budget/the cost of sth**
- to cut sth/slash sth/cut sth back **drastically**

,cut and 'dried *adj.* [not usually before noun] decided in a way that cannot be changed or argued about: *The inquiry is by no means cut and dried.*

cu·ta·ne·ous /kyuˈteɪniəs/ *adj.* (*anatomy*) connected with the skin

cut·a·way /ˈkʌtəˌweɪ/ *adj., noun*
● *adj.* [only before noun] (of a model or diagram) with some outside parts left out, in order to show what the inside looks like: *a cutaway picture of the inside of a nuclear reactor*
● *noun* 1 ~ (to sb/sth) (on television, in a movie, etc.) a picture that shows something different from the main thing that is being shown: *There was a cutaway to Jackson's guest on*

---

the podium. **2** a model or diagram with some outside parts left out, in order to show what the inside looks like

cut·back /ˈkʌtbæk/ noun [usually pl.] **~ (in sth)** a reduction in something: cutbacks in public spending ♦ staff cutbacks

ˈcut-down adj. [only before noun] reduced in length, size, or range: a cut-down version of the program

cute 🔑 /kyut/ adj. (**cut·er, cut·est**)
1 pretty and attractive: a cute little baby ♦ an unbearably cute picture of two kittens (= it seems SENTIMENTAL) **2** (informal) sexually attractive: Check out those cute guys over there! **3** (informal) showing intelligence, but often in an annoying way because a person is trying to get an advantage for him or herself: She had a really cute idea. ♦ Don't get cute with me! ▶ **cute·ly** adv.: to smile cutely **cute·ness** noun [U]

cute·sy /ˈkyutsi/ adj. (informal) too pretty or attractive in a way that is annoying or not realistic

ˌcut ˈglass noun [U] glass with patterns cut in it: a cut-glass vase

cu·ti·cle /ˈkyutɪkl/ noun an area of hard skin at the base of the nails on the fingers and toes ⊃ picture at BODY

cut·ie /ˈkyuti/ noun (informal) a person who is attractive or kind: He's a real cutie.

cut·lass /ˈkʌtləs/ noun a short SWORD with a curved blade that was used as a weapon by sailors and PIRATES in the past

cut·ler·y /ˈkʌtləri/ noun [U] **1** knives, forks, and spoons, used for eating and serving food **SYN** FLATWARE **2** knives, etc. that are sharp

cut·let /ˈkʌtlət/ noun a slice of meat that is fried or BROILED, often covered in BREADCRUMBS

ˈcut-off noun, adj.
● **noun 1** a point or limit when you stop something: The government announced a cut-off in overseas aid. ♦ Is there a cut-off point between childhood and adulthood? **2** cut-offs [pl.] cut-off pants: wearing frayed cut-offs
● **adj.** [only before noun] (of pants) made shorter by cutting off part of the legs: cut-off jeans

cut·out /ˈkʌtaʊt/ noun **1** a shape cut out of paper, wood, etc.: a cardboard cutout **2** a piece of safety equipment that stops an electric current from flowing through something: A cutout stops the kettle boiling dry.

ˌcut-ˈrate adj. [only before noun] **1** sold at a reduced price: cut-rate tickets **2** selling goods at a reduced price: a cut-rate store

cut·ter /ˈkʌtər/ noun **1** (usually in compounds) a person or thing that cuts: a pastry cutter **2** cutters [pl.] (usually in compounds) a tool for cutting: a pair of wire-cutters **3** a small fast ship **4** a ship's boat, used for traveling between the ship and land

cut·throat /ˈkʌtθroʊt/ adj. [usually before noun] (of an activity) in which people compete with each other in aggressive and unfair ways: the cutthroat world of politics

cut·ting /ˈkʌtɪŋ/ noun, adj.
● **noun** a piece cut off a plant that will be used to grow a new plant
● **adj.** [usually before noun] **1** unkind and likely to hurt someone's feelings **SYN** BITING: a cutting remark **2** (of winds) cold in a sharp and unpleasant way **SYN** BITING

ˈcutting ˌboard noun a board made of wood or plastic used for cutting meat or vegetables on ⊃ picture at KITCHEN **SYN** CHOPPING BLOCK

ˌcutting ˈedge noun [sing.] **1** the **~ (of sth)** the newest, most advanced stage in the development of something: working **at the cutting edge** of computer technology ⊃ compare BLEEDING EDGE **2** an aspect of something that gives it an advantage: We're relying on him to give the team a cutting edge.

ˈcutting ˌroom noun a room in which the different parts of a movie are cut and put into order

cut·tle·fish /ˈkʌtlˌfɪʃ/ noun (pl. **cut·tle·fish**) a sea creature with eight arms, two TENTACLES (= long thin parts like arms), and a wide flat shell inside its body, that produces a black substance like ink when it is attacked

ˈcut-up /ˈkʌtʌp/ noun (informal) a person who behaves in a silly way in order to attract attention and make people laugh

CV /ˌsi ˈvi/ noun the abbreviation for "curriculum vitae" (a record of a university/college teacher's education and where they have worked, also including a list of books and articles that they have published and courses that they have taught, used when they are applying for a job): Send a full CV with your job application. ⊃ compare RÉSUMÉ

cwm /kʊm/ noun (geology) = CIRQUE

cwt. abbr. (pl. **cwt.**) (in writing) HUNDREDWEIGHT

-cy /si/, **-acy** suffix (in nouns) **1** the state or quality of: infancy ♦ accuracy **2** the status or position of: chaplaincy

cy·an /ˈsaɪæn; ˈsaɪən/ noun [U] (technical) a green-blue color, used in printing

cy·a·nide /ˈsaɪəˌnaɪd/ noun [U] a highly poisonous chemical

cyber- /ˈsaɪbər/ combining form (in nouns and adjectives) connected with electronic communication networks, especially the Internet: cybernetics ♦ cybercafé

cy·ber·ca·fé /ˈsaɪbərkæˌfeɪ/ noun a CAFÉ with computers on which customers can use the Internet, send e-mail, etc.

cy·ber·crime /ˈsaɪbərˌkraɪm/ noun [U, C] crime that is committed using the Internet, for example by stealing someone's personal or bank details or infecting their computer with a virus

cy·ber·naut /ˈsaɪbərˌnɔt; -ˌnɑt/ noun (computing) **1** a person who wears special devices in order to experience VIRTUAL REALITY **2** a person who uses the Internet

cy·ber·net·ics /ˌsaɪbərˈnɛtɪks/ noun [U] the scientific study of communication and control, especially concerned with comparing human and animal brains with machines and electronic devices ▶ **cy·ber·net·ic** adj.

cy·ber·punk /ˈsaɪbərˌpʌŋk/ noun [U] stories set in an imaginary future world controlled by technology and computers

cy·ber·sex /ˈsaɪbərˌsɛks/ noun [U] communication between people using the Internet which makes them sexually excited

cy·ber·space /ˈsaɪbərˌspeɪs/ noun [U] the imaginary place where electronic messages, etc. exist while they are being sent between computers

cy·ber·squat·ting /ˈsaɪbərˌskwɑtɪŋ/ noun [U] the illegal activity of buying and officially recording an address on the Internet that is the name of an existing company or a well-known person, with the intention of selling it to the owner in order to make money ▶ **cy·ber·squat·ter** noun

cy·borg /ˈsaɪbɔrg/ noun (in SCIENCE FICTION stories) a creature that is part human, part machine

cy·cla·men /ˈsaɪkləmən/ noun (pl. **cy·cla·men** or **cy·cla·mens**) a plant with pink, purple, or white flowers that grow on long STEMS pointing downward, often grown indoors

cy·cle 🔑 **AWL** /ˈsaɪkl/ noun, verb
● **noun 1** the fact of a series of events being repeated many times, always in the same order: the cycle of the seasons ⊃ see also LIFE CYCLE **2** a complete set or series, for example of movements in a machine: eight cycles per second ♦ the rinse cycle (= in a washing machine) **3** a bicycle or motorcycle ⊃ see also BIKE
● **verb 1** [I] (+adv./prep.) to ride a bicycle; to travel by bicycle: I usually cycle home through the park. ⊃ compare BICYCLE, BIKE **2** [I, T] to move in, follow, or put something through a regularly repeated series of events or actions: + adv./prep. Economies cycle regularly between boom and slump. ♦ **~ sth** Our computer network cycles data 24 hours a day.

cycle-rickshaw *noun* a vehicle like a bicycle with three wheels, with a covered seat for passengers behind the driver, used especially in some Asian countries

cy·clic **AWL** /'saɪklɪk; 'sɪk-/ (also **cy·clic·al** /'saɪklɪkl; 'sɪk-/) *adj.* [usually before noun] repeated many times and always happening in the same order: *the cyclic processes of nature* ◆ *Economic activity often follows a cyclical pattern.* ▶ **cy·cli·cally** /-kli/ *adv.*: *events that occur cyclically*

cy·cling 🚲 **AWL** /'saɪklɪŋ/ *noun* [U] the sport or activity of riding a bicycle: *to go cycling* ◆ *Cycling is Europe's second most popular sport.* ◆ *cycling shorts* ⊃ **picture at** SPORT

cy·clist /'saɪklɪst/ *noun* a person who rides a bicycle ⊃ **compare** BICYCLIST

cy·clone /'saɪkloʊn/ *noun* a violent tropical storm in which strong winds move in a circle ⊃ **compare** HURRICANE, TYPHOON ▶ **cy·clon·ic** /saɪ'klɑnɪk/ *adj.*

Cy·clops /'saɪklɑps/ *noun* (in ancient Greek stories) a giant with only one eye in the middle of his face

cy·clo·tron /'saɪklə,trɑn/ *noun* (*physics*) a machine which makes atoms or ELECTRONS move more quickly, using electrical and MAGNETIC FIELD

cyg·net /'sɪgnət/ *noun* a young SWAN (= a large white bird with a long neck that lives on or near water)

cyl·in·der /'sɪləndər/ *noun* **1** a solid or hollow figure with round ends and long straight sides ⊃ **picture at** SHAPE **2** an object shaped like a cylinder, especially one used as a container: *a gas/oxygen cylinder* **3** the hollow tube in an engine, shaped like a cylinder, inside which the PISTON moves: *a six-cylinder engine* **IDM** **working/firing on all cylinders** (*informal*) using all your energy to do something; working as well as possible

cy·lin·dri·cal /sə'lɪndrɪkl/ *adj.* shaped like a cylinder: *huge cylindrical gas tanks*

cym·bal /'sɪmbl/ *noun* a musical instrument in the form of a round metal plate. It is hit with a stick, or two cymbals are hit against each other: *a clash/crash of cymbals* ⊃ **picture at** INSTRUMENT

cyn·ic /'sɪnɪk/ *noun* **1** a person who believes that people only do things to help themselves, rather than for good or sincere reasons **2** a person who does not believe that something good will happen or that something is important: *Cynics will say that there is not the slightest chance of success.* ▶ **cyn·i·cism** /'sɪnə,sɪzəm/ *noun* [U]: *In a world full of cynicism she was the one person I felt I could trust.*

cyn·i·cal /'sɪnɪkl/ *adj.* **1** believing that people only do things to help themselves rather than for good or honest reasons: *Do you have to be so cynical about everything?* ◆ *a cynical view/smile* **2** not believing that something good will happen or that something is important: *I'm a bit cynical about the benefits of the plan.* **3** not caring that something might hurt other people, if there is some advantage for you: *a cynical disregard for the safety of others* ▶ **cyn·i·cally** /-kli/ *adv.*

cy·no·sure /'saɪnəʃʊr; 'sɪ-/ *noun* [sing.] (*formal*) a person or thing that is the center of attention: *Ruth was the cynosure of all eyes.*

cy·pher = CIPHER

cy·press /'saɪprəs/ *noun* a tall, straight, EVERGREEN tree

Cy·ril·lic /sə'rɪlɪk/ *adj.* the **Cyrillic** alphabet is used to write Russian, Bulgarian, and some other Central European languages ▶ **Cy·ril·lic** *noun* [U]

cyst /sɪst/ *noun* a GROWTH containing liquid that forms in or on a person's or an animal's body and may need to be removed

cys·tic fi·bro·sis /,sɪstɪk faɪ'broʊsəs/ *noun* [U] a serious medical condition that some people are born with, in which GLANDS in the lungs and other organs do not work correctly. It often leads to infections and can result in early death.

cys·ti·tis /sɪ'staɪtəs/ *noun* [U] an infection of the BLADDER, especially in women, that causes frequent, painful urination (URINATE)

cy·tol·o·gy /saɪ'tɑlədʒi/ *noun* [U] the scientific study of the structure and function of cells from living things

cy·to·meg·a·lo·vi·rus /,saɪtoʊ'mɛgəloʊ,vaɪrəs/ *noun* (*medical*) a virus that usually causes mild infections, but that can be serious for people with AIDS or for new babies

cy·to·plasm /'saɪtə,plæzəm/ *noun* [U] (*biology*) all the living material in a cell, not including the NUCLEUS ▶ **cy·to·plas·mic** /,saɪtə'plæzmɪk/ *adj.* ⊃ **compare** PROTOPLASM

czar (also **tsar, tzar**) /zɑr; tsɑr/ *noun* **1** the title of the EMPEROR of Russia in the past: *Czar Nicholas II* **2** (in compounds) an official whose job is to advise the government on policy in a particular area: *a drug czar*

cza·ri·na (also **tsa·ri·na, tza·ri·na**) /zɑ'rinə; tsɑ-/ *noun* the title of the EMPRESS of Russia in the past

czar·ism (also **tsar·ism, tzar·ism**) /'zɑrɪzəm; 'tsɑr-/ *noun* [U] the Russian system of government by a czar, which existed before 1917 ▶ **czar·ist** (also **tsar·ist, tzar·ist**) /-ɪst/ *noun, adj.*

Dd

D /di/ noun, abbr., symbol
- **noun** [C, U] (pl. **Ds, D's** /diz/) **1** also **d** (pl. **d's**) the fourth letter of the English alphabet: *"Dog" begins with (a) D/"D."* **2** (music) the second note in the SCALE of C MAJOR **3** the fourth highest grade that a student can get for a course, test, or piece of work, showing that it is not very good: *He got a D in geography.* ➔ see also D-DAY
- **abbr.** (also **D.**) DEMOCRAT; Democratic
- **symbol** also **d** the number 500 in ROMAN NUMERALS

d. abbr. (in writing) died: *Emily Clifton, d. 1865*

-d suffix ➔ -ED

D.A. /ˌdi ˈeɪ/ abbr. DISTRICT ATTORNEY

dab /dæb/ verb, noun
- **verb** (-bb-) **1** to touch something lightly, usually several times: ~ **sth** *She dabbed her eyes and blew her nose.* ◆ ~ **at sth** *He dabbed at the cut with his handkerchief.* **2** ~ **sth** + **adv./prep.** to put something on a surface with quick light movements: *She dabbed a little perfume behind her ears.*
- **noun 1** a small amount of a liquid, cream, or powder that is put on a surface in a quick gentle movement: *She put a dab of perfume behind her ears.* **2** an act of gently touching or pressing something without rubbing: *He gave the cut a quick dab with a towel.* **3** a small flat fish

dab·ble /ˈdæbl/ verb **1** [I] ~ **(in/with sth)** to take part in a sport, an activity, etc., but not very seriously: *He dabbles in local politics.* **2** [T] ~ **sth (in sth)** to move your hands, feet, etc. around in water: *She dabbled her toes in the stream.*
▶ **dab·bler** noun [C]

da·cha /ˈdɑtʃə/ noun a Russian country house

dachs·hund /ˈdɑkshʊnt; -hʊnd/ noun a small dog with a long body, long ears, and very short legs

dac·tyl /ˈdæktl/ noun (technical) a unit of sound in poetry consisting of one strong or long syllable followed by two weak or short syllables

dad 🔑 /dæd/ noun (informal)
(often used as a name) father: *That's my dad over there.* ◆ *Do you live with your mom or your dad?* ◆ *Is it OK if I borrow the car, Dad?*

Da·da /ˈdɑdɑ/ noun [U] an early 20th century movement in art, literature, music, and film that made fun of social and artistic conventions ▶ **Da·da·ism** /ˈdɑdɑˌɪzəm/ noun [U] **Da·da·ist** /ˈdɑdɑɪst/ noun

dad·dy /ˈdædi/ noun (pl. **dad·dies**) used especially by and to young children, and often as a name, to mean "father": *What does your daddy look like?* ◆ *Daddy, where are you?* ◆ *Come to Daddy.*

dad·dy ˈlong·legs /ˌdædi ˈlɔŋlegz/ noun (pl. **dad·dy long·legs**) (informal) a small creature like a spider with very long legs

da·do /ˈdeɪdoʊ/ noun (pl. **da·dos** or **da·does**) the lower part of the wall of a room when it is a different color or material from the top part

dae·mon /ˈdimən/ noun a creature in stories from ancient Greece that is half man and half god

daf·fo·dil /ˈdæfədɪl/ noun a tall, yellow, spring flower shaped like a TRUMPET ➔ picture at PLANT

daf·fy /ˈdæfi/ adj. (**daf·fi·er, daf·fi·est**) (informal) silly

daft /dæft/ adj. (**daft·er, daft·est**) (informal) silly, often in a way that is amusing: *Don't be so daft!* ▶ **daft·ness** noun [U]

dag·ger /ˈdægər/ noun a short pointed knife that is used as a weapon ➔ picture at SWORD ➔ see also CLOAK-AND-DAGGER

da·guerre·o·type (also **da·guer·ro·type**) /dəˈgɛrəˌtaɪp/

noun a photograph taken using an early process that used a silver plate and MERCURY gas

dahl·ia /ˈdɑlyə; ˈdæl-/ noun a large, brightly colored, garden flower, often shaped like a ball

dai·kon /ˈdaɪkən/ noun [U, C] a long, white, root vegetable that you can eat

dai·ly 🔑 /ˈdeɪli/ adj., adv., noun
- **adj.** [only before noun] **1** happening, done, or produced every day: *a daily routine/visit/newspaper* ◆ *events affecting the daily lives of millions of people* ◆ *Invoices are signed on a daily basis.* **2** connected with one day's work: *They charge a daily rate.*
IDM your daily bread the basic things that you need to live, especially food
- **adv.** every day: *The machines are inspected twice daily.*
- **noun** (pl. **dai·lies**) a newspaper published every day, or every day except Sunday: *The story was in all the dailies.*

dain·ty /ˈdeɪnti/ adj. (**dain·ti·er, dain·ti·est**) **1** (of people and things) small and delicate in a way that people find attractive SYN DELICATE: *dainty feet* ◆ *a dainty porcelain cup* **2** (of movements) careful, often in a way that suggests good manners SYN DELICATE: *She took a dainty little bite of the apple.* ▶ **dain·ti·ly** /-təli/ adv.: *She blew her nose as daintily as possible.* **dain·ti·ness** noun [U]

dai·qui·ri /ˈdækəri/ noun an alcoholic drink made from RUM mixed with fruit juice, sugar, etc.

dairy /ˈdɛri/ noun, adj.
- **noun** (pl. **dair·ies**) **1** [C] a company that sells milk, eggs, cheese, and other milk products **2** [C] a place on a farm where milk is kept and where butter and cheese are made **3** [U] milk, eggs, cheese, and other milk products: *The doctor told me to eat less red meat and dairy.*
- **adj.** [only before noun] **1** made from milk: *dairy products/produce* **2** connected with the production of milk rather than meat: *the dairy industry* ◆ *dairy cattle/farmers* ◆ *a dairy cow/farm*

dairy·maid /ˈdɛriˌmeɪd/ noun (old-fashioned) a woman who works in a dairy

dairy·man /ˈdɛrimən; -ˌmæn/ noun (pl. **dairy·men** /-mən; -ˌmɛn/) **1** a man who works in a dairy **2** a man who owns or manages a dairy and sells the products

da·is /ˈdeɪɪs/ noun a stage, especially at one end of a room, on which people stand to make speeches to an audience

dai·sy /ˈdeɪzi/ noun (pl. **dai·sies**) a small wild flower with white PETALS around a yellow center; a taller plant with similar but larger flowers ➔ picture at PLANT ➔ see also MICHAELMAS DAISY **IDM** see PUSH v.

ˈdaisy ˌchain noun a string of daisies tied together to wear around the neck, etc.

ˈdaisy-ˌcutter noun a very powerful bomb dropped from an aircraft that explodes close to the ground and causes a lot of destruction over a large area

ˈdaisy ˌwheel noun a small disk, used in some printers and TYPEWRITERS, with metal letters around the edge which print onto paper: *a daisy wheel printer*

the Da·lai La·ma /ˌdɑlaɪ ˈlɑmə; ˌdaɪleɪ-/ noun [sing.] the leader of Tibetan Buddhism and, in former times, the ruler of Tibet

dale /deɪl/ noun (old-fashioned) a valley

dal·li·ance /ˈdæliəns/ noun [U, C] (old-fashioned or humorous) **1** the behavior of someone who is dallying with someone or something: *It turned out to be his last dalliance with the education system.* **2** a sexual relationship that is not serious

dal·ly /ˈdæli/ verb (**dal·lies, dal·ly·ing, dal·lied, dal·lied**) (old-fashioned) to do something too slowly; to take too much time making a decision
PHRV dally with sb/sth (old-fashioned) to treat someone or something in a way that is not serious enough ➔ see also DILLY-DALLY

Dal·ma·tian /dælˈmeɪʃn/ noun a large dog that has short white hair with black spots

| h hat | m man | n no | ŋ sing | l leg | r red | y yes | w wet |

dam /dæm/ noun, verb

• **noun** **1** a barrier that is built across a river in order to stop the water from flowing, used especially to make a RESER-VOIR (= a lake for storing water) or to produce electricity **2** (technical) the mother of some animals, especially horses ⊃ compare SIRE **3** = DENTAL DAM

• **verb** (-mm-) ~ sth (up) to build a dam across a river, especially in order to make an artificial lake for use as a water supply, etc.

dam·age 🔊 /'dæmɪdʒ/ noun, verb

• **noun** **1** [U] ~ (to sth) physical harm caused to something that makes it less attractive, useful, or valuable: *serious/severe/extensive/permanent/minor damage* ◆ *brain/liver, etc. damage* ◆ *fire/smoke/storm damage* ◆ *The earthquake caused property damage estimated at $6 million.* ◆ *The storm didn't do much damage.* ◆ *Let's take a look at the damage.* ◆ *I insist on paying for the damage.* ◆ *Make sure you insure your camera against loss or damage.* **2** [U] ~ (to sb/sth) harmful effects on someone or something: *emotional damage resulting from divorce* ◆ *damage to a person's reputation* ◆ *This could cause serious damage to the country's economy.* ◆ *I'm going—I've done enough damage here already.* **3** damages [pl.] an amount of money that a court decides should be paid to someone by the person, company, etc., that has caused them harm or injury: *He was ordered to pay damages totalling $30,000.* ◆ *They intend to sue for damages.* ◆ *Ann was awarded $6,000 in damages.*
IDM what's the damage? (*informal*) a way of asking how much something costs

• **verb** ~ sth/sb to harm or spoil something or someone: *The fire badly damaged the town hall.* ◆ *Several vehicles were damaged in the crash.* ◆ *Smoking seriously damages your health.* ◆ *The allegations are likely to damage his political career.* ◆ *emotionally damaged children* ⊃ collocations at INJURY

THESAURUS

damage

hurt ◆ harm ◆ impair

These words all mean to have a bad effect on someone or something.

damage to cause physical harm to something, making it less attractive, useful, or valuable; to have a bad effect on someone or something's health, happiness, or chances of success: *The fire badly damaged the town hall.* ◆ *emotionally damaged children*

hurt (*somewhat informal*) to have a bad effect on someone or something's life, health, happiness, or chances of success: *Hard work never hurt anyone.*

harm to have a bad effect on someone or something's life, health, happiness, or chances of success: *Pollution can harm marine life.*

DAMAGE, HURT, OR HARM?

Hurt is slightly less formal than **damage** or **harm**, especially when it is used in negative statements: *It won't hurt him to have to wait a bit.* ◆ It won't damage/harm him to have to wait a bit. **Harm** is also often used to talk about ways in which things in the natural world, such as *wildlife* and the *environment*, are affected by human activity.

impair (*somewhat formal*) to damage someone's health, abilities, or chances: *Even one drink can impair driving performance.*

PATTERNS

▪ to damage/hurt/harm/impair sb's **chances**
▪ to damage/hurt/harm sb's **interests/reputation**
▪ to damage/harm/impair sb's **health**
▪ to **seriously/greatly** damage/hurt/harm/impair sb/sth
▪ to **badly/severely** damage/hurt/impair sb/sth

'damage con₁trol noun [U] the process of trying to limit the amount of damage that is caused by something

dam·ag·ing /'dæmɪdʒɪŋ/ adj. causing damage; having a bad effect on someone or something: *damaging consequences/effects* ◆ ~ to sb/sth *Lead is potentially damaging to children's health.*

Da·mas·cus /də'mæskəs/ noun
IDM the road to Damascus an experience that results in a great change in a person's attitudes or beliefs: *Spending a night in jail was his road to Damascus.* **ORIGIN** From the story in the Bible in which St. Paul hears the voice of God on the road to Damascus and becomes a Christian.

dam·ask /'dæməsk/ noun [U] a type of thick cloth, usually made from silk or LINEN, with a pattern that is visible on both sides: *a damask tablecloth*

dame /deɪm/ noun **1 Dame** (in Britain) a title given to a woman as a special honor because of the work she has done: *Dame Maggie Smith* **2** (old-fashioned, informal) a woman

damn /dæm/ exclamation, adj., verb, adv., noun

• **exclamation** (also dam·mit /'dæmɪt/, 'damn it) (*informal, offensive*) a swear word that people use to show that they are annoyed, disappointed, etc.: *Oh damn! I forgot he was coming.*

• **adj.** (also damn·ed) [only before noun] (*informal, offensive*) **1** a swear word that people use to show that they are annoyed with someone or something: *Where's that damn book!* ◆ *The damned thing won't start!* ◆ *It's none of your damn business!* ◆ *He's a damn nuisance!* **2** a swear word that people use to emphasize what they are saying: *What a damn shame!*

• **verb** **1** ~ sb/sth (*informal, offensive*) used when swearing at someone or something to show that you are angry: *Damn you! I'm not going to let you bully me.* ◆ *Damn this machine! Why won't it work?* **2** ~ sb (of God) to decide that someone must suffer in hell **3** ~ sb/sth to criticize someone or something very strongly: *The film was damned by the critics for its mindless violence.*
IDM damn the consequences, expense, etc. (*informal*) used to say that you are going to do something even though you know it may be expensive, have bad results, etc.: *Let's celebrate and damn the expense!* damn sb/sth with faint praise to praise someone or something only a little, in order to show that you do not really like them/it: *I'll be damned!* (old-fashioned, informal) used to show that you are very surprised about something: *I'm damned if...* (*informal*) used to show that you refuse to do something or do not know something: *I'm damned if I'll apologize!* ◆ *I'm damned if I know who he is.*

• **adv.** (also damned) (*informal, offensive*) **1** a swear word that people use to show that they are annoyed with someone or something: *Don't be so damn silly!* ◆ *What a damn stupid question!* ◆ *You know damn well* (= you know very well) *what I mean!* ◆ *I'll damn well leave tonight* (= I am determined to). **2** a swear word that people use to emphasize what they are saying: *damn good* ◆ *We got out pretty damned fast!* ◆ *I'm damn sure she had no idea.*

• **noun**
IDM not give a damn (about sb/sth) (*informal, offensive*) to not care at all about someone or something

dam·na·ble /'dæmnəbl/ adj. (old-fashioned) bad or annoying ▸ dam·na·bly /-bli/ adv.

dam·na·tion /dæm'neɪʃn/ noun [U] the state of being in hell; the act of sending someone to hell: *eternal damnation*

damned /dæmd/ adj., adv., noun
• **adj., adv.** = DAMN
• **noun the damned** [pl.] people who are forced to live in hell after they die

damned·est /'dæmdəst/ noun, adj. (*informal*)
IDM the damnedest... the most surprising...: *It's the damnedest thing I ever saw.* do/try your damnedest (to do

---

sth) to try as hard as you can (to do something): *She did her damnedest to get it done on time.*

damn·ing /ˈdæmɪŋ/ *adj.* critical of someone or something; suggesting that someone is guilty: *damning criticism/ evidence* ✦ *a damning conclusion/report* ✦ *Her report is expected to deliver a damning indictment of education standards.*

Dam·o·cles /ˈdæməkliz/ *noun* **IDM** see SWORD

damp 🔑 /dæmp/ *adj., verb*
● *adj.* **(damp·er, damp·est)** slightly wet, often in a way that is unpleasant: *The cottage was cold and damp.* ✦ *It feels damp in here.* ✦ *damp clothes* ✦ *Wipe the surface with a damp cloth.* ⊃ thesaurus box at WET ▶ **damp·ly** *adv.*: *The blouse clung damply to her skin.*
● *verb*
PHRV **damp ˈdown sth** to make an emotion or a feeling less strong ˌdamp sth↔ˈdown to make a fire burn more slowly or stop burning

damp·en /ˈdæmpən/ *verb* **1** ~ **sth** to make something slightly wet: *Perspiration dampened her face and neck.* ✦ *He dampened his hair to make it lie flat.* **2** ~ **sth** to make something such as a feeling or a reaction less strong: *None of the setbacks could dampen his enthusiasm for the project.* ✦ *She wasn't going to let anything dampen her spirits today.*

damp·er /ˈdæmpər/ *noun* **1** a piece of metal that can be moved to allow more or less air into a fire so that the fire burns more or less strongly **2** a device in a piano that is used to reduce the level of the sound produced **IDM** **put a damper on sth** *(informal)* to make something less enjoyable, successful, etc.

damp·ness /ˈdæmpnəs/ *noun* [U] the fact or state of being damp: *To avoid dampness, air the room regularly.*

dam·sel /ˈdæmzl/ *noun* *(old use)* a young woman who is not married **IDM** **a damsel in distress** *(humorous)* a woman who needs help

dam·sel·fly /ˈdæmzlˌflaɪ/ *noun* *(pl.* **dam·sel·flies)** an insect with a long thin body and two pairs of wings

dam·son /ˈdæmzn/ *noun* a small purple fruit, like a PLUM: *a damson tree*

dan /dɑn; dæn/ *noun* **1** one of the levels in KARATE or JUDO **2** a person who has reached a particular level in KARATE or JUDO

dance 🔑 /dæns/ *noun, verb*
● *noun* **1** [C] a series of movements and steps that are usually performed to music; a particular example of these movements and steps: *a dance class/routine* ✦ *Find a partner and practice these new dance steps.* ✦ *Do you know any other Latin American dances?* ✦ *The next dance will be a waltz.* ⊃ see also RAIN DANCE **2** [U] the art of dancing, especially for entertainment: *an evening of drama, music and dance* ✦ *modern/classical dance* ✦ *a dance company/troupe* **3** [C] an act of dancing: *He did a little dance of triumph.* **4** [C] a social event at which people dance: *We hold a dance every year to raise money for charity.* **5** [C] a piece of music for dancing to: *The band finished with a few slow dances.* **IDM** see SONG
● *verb* **1** [I] to move your body to the sound and rhythm of music: *Do you want to dance?* ✦ *He asked me to dance.* ✦ *They stayed up all night singing and dancing.* ✦ *They danced to the music of a string quartet.* ✦ *Ruth danced all evening with Richard.* ✦ *Ruth and Richard danced together all evening.* **2** [T] ~ **sth** to do a particular type of dance: *to dance the tango* ✦ *to dance a waltz* **3** [I] to move in a lively way: *The children danced around her.* ✦ *The sun shone on the ocean and the waves danced and sparkled.* ✦ *The words danced before her tired eyes.* **IDM** **dance the night away** to dance for the whole evening or night **dance to sb's tune** to do whatever someone tells you to

ˈdance band *noun* a group of musicians who play music at dances

ˈdance floor *noun* an area where people can dance in a hotel, restaurant, etc.

ˈdance hall *noun* a large public room where people pay to go and dance (more common in the past than now) ⊃ compare BALLROOM

danc·er 🔑 /ˈdænsər/ *noun* a person who dances or whose job is dancing: *She's a fantastic dancer.* ✦ *He's a dancer with the National Ballet.*

dancing 🔑 /ˈdænsɪŋ/ *noun* [U] moving your body to music: *dancing classes* ✦ *There was music and dancing until two in the morning.*

ˈD and ˈC *abbr.* DILATATION AND CURETTAGE

dan·de·li·on /ˈdændəˌlaɪən/ *noun* a small wild plant with a bright yellow flower that becomes a soft white ball of seeds called a **dandelion clock** ⊃ picture at PLANT

dan·di·fied /ˈdændɪˌfaɪd/ *adj.* *(old-fashioned, disapproving)* (of a man) caring a lot about his clothes and appearance

dan·dle /ˈdændl/ *verb* ~ **sb** *(old-fashioned)* to play with a baby or young child by moving them up and down on your knee

dan·druff /ˈdændrəf/ *noun* [U] very small pieces of dead skin, seen as a white dust in a person's hair

dan·dy /ˈdændi/ *noun, adj.*
● *noun* *(pl.* **dan·dies)** *(old-fashioned)* a man who cares a lot about his clothes and appearance
● *adj.* *(old-fashioned)* very good

dang /dæŋ/ *adj., exclamation* *(informal)* a mild swear word, used instead of DAMN: *It's just dang stupid!*

dan·ger 🔑 /ˈdeɪndʒər/ *noun*
1 [U] ~ **(of sth)** the possibility of something happening that will injure, harm, or kill someone, or damage or destroy something: *Danger! Keep Out!* ✦ *Children's lives are in danger every time they cross this road.* ✦ *Doctors said she is now out of danger* (= not likely to die). **2** [C, U] the possibility of something bad or unpleasant happening: *There is no danger of a bush fire now.* ✦ ~ **of sth** *The building is in danger of collapsing.* ✦ *How many factory workers are in danger of losing their jobs?* ✦ *"Nicky won't find out, will she?" "Oh, no, there's no danger of that."* ✦ ~ **that…** *There is a danger that the political disorder of the past will return.* **3** [C] ~ **(to sb/sth)** a person or thing that may cause damage, or harm someone: *Smoking is a serious danger to health.* ✦ *Police said the man was a danger to the public.* ✦ *the hidden dangers in your home* ⊃ see also ENDANGER

dan·ger·ous 🔑 /ˈdeɪndʒərəs/ *adj.* likely to injure or harm someone, or to damage or destroy something: *a dangerous road/illness/sport* ✦ *dangerous levels of carbon monoxide* ✦ *The prisoners who escaped are violent and dangerous.* ✦ *The situation is highly dangerous.* ✦ ~ **for sb** *The traffic here is very dangerous for children.* ✦ ~ **for sb to do sth** *It would be dangerous for you to stay here.* ▶ **dan·ger·ous·ly** *adv.*: *She was standing dangerously close to the fire.* ✦ *His father is dangerously ill* (= so ill that he might die). ✦ *Mel enjoys living dangerously* (= doing things that involve risk or danger). **IDM** **dangerous ground** a situation or subject that is likely to make someone angry, or that involves risk: *We'd be on dangerous ground if we asked about race or religion.*

ˈdanger ˌpay *noun* [U] = HAZARD PAY

dan·gle /ˈdæŋgl/ *verb* **1** [I] **(+adv./prep.)** to hang or swing freely: *Gold charms dangled from her bracelet.* ✦ *A single light bulb dangled from the ceiling.* ✦ *He sat on the edge with his legs dangling over the side.* **2** [T] ~ **sth** to hold something so that it hangs or swings freely: *She dangled her car keys nervously as she spoke.* ▶ **dan·gly** /ˈdæŋgli/ *adj.*: *a pair of dangly earrings* **IDM** **keep/leave sb dangling** *(informal)* to keep someone in an uncertain state by not telling them something that they want to know: *She kept him dangling for a week before making her decision.* **PHRV** ˌdangle sth beˈfore/in ˈfront of sb to offer

ʌ **cup**   ə **about**   eɪ **say**   aɪ **five**   ɔɪ **boy**   aʊ **now**   oʊ **go**   ər **bird**

someone something good in order to persuade them to do something

dangling 'participle *noun* (*grammar*) a participle that relates to a noun that is not mentioned **HELP** "Dangling participles" are not considered correct. In the sentence "While walking home, my phone rang," "walking" is a dangling participle. A correct form of the sentence would be "While I was walking home, my phone rang."

Dan·ish /'deɪnɪʃ/ *adj.*, *noun*
- *adj.* from or connected with Denmark
- *noun* **1** [U] the language of Denmark **2** [C] (also ,Danish 'pastry) *noun* a sweet cake made of light PASTRY, often containing apple, nuts, etc., and/or covered with ICING

,Danish 'blue *noun* [U] a type of soft cheese with blue parts in it and a strong flavor

dank /dæŋk/ *adj.* (especially of a place) damp, cold, and unpleasant: *a dark dank cave* ▶ **dank·ness** /'dæŋknəs/ *noun* [U]

dap·per /'dæpər/ *adj.* (*old-fashioned*) (of a man) small with a neat appearance and nice clothes

dap·pled /'dæpld/ *adj.* marked with spots of color, or shade: *the cool dappled light under the trees*

dap·ple gray /,dæpl 'greɪ/ *adj.* (of a horse) gray or white with darker round marks ▶ **dap·ple gray** *noun*

DAR *abbr.* Daughters of the American Revolution (a politically conservative organization of women who had relatives who fought in the American Revolution)

dare 🔑 /dɛr/ *verb*, *noun*
- *verb* **1** (not usually used in the progressive tenses) to be brave enough to do something: *She said it as loudly as she dared.* ◆ *~ (to) do sth He didn't dare (to) say what he thought.* ◆ *They dare not ask for any more money.* ◆ (*literary*) *She dared not breathe a word of it to anybody.* ◆ *There was something, dare I say it, a little unusual about him.* **2** [T] to persuade someone to do something dangerous, difficult, or embarrassing so that they can show that they are not afraid: *~ sb Go on! Take it! I dare you.* ◆ *~ sb to do sth Some of the older boys had dared him to do it.* ⊃ note at MODAL
  IDM **don't you dare!** (*informal*) used to tell someone strongly not to do something: *"I'll tell her about it." "Don't you dare!"* ◆ *Don't you dare say anything to anybody.* **how dare you, etc.** used to show that you are angry about something that someone has done: *How dare you talk to me like that?* ◆ *How dare she imply that I was lying?* **I dare say** (*formal* or *old-fashioned*) used when you are saying that something is likely: *I dare say you know about it already.*
- *noun* [usually sing.] something dangerous, difficult, or embarrassing that you try to persuade someone to do, to see if they will do it: *She learned to fly on a dare.*

GRAMMAR

dare

- Dare (sense 1) usually forms negatives and questions like an ordinary verb and is often followed by an infinitive with *to*. It is most common in the negative: *I didn't dare to ask.* ◆ *He won't dare to break his promise.* ◆ *You told him? How did you dare?* ◆ *I hardly dared to hope that she'd remember me.* In positive sentences, a phrase like **not be afraid** is often used instead: *She wasn't afraid* (= she dared) *to tell him the truth.*
- It can also be used like a modal verb, especially in present tense negative forms, and is followed by an infinitive without *to*: *I dare not tell her the truth.*
- In spoken English, the forms of the ordinary verb are often used with an infinitive without *to*: *Don't you dare tell her what I said!* ◆ *I didn't dare look at him.*

---

dare·dev·il /'dɛr,dɛvl/ *noun* a person who enjoys doing dangerous things, in a way that other people may think is stupid: *a reckless daredevil* ▶ **dare·dev·il** *adj.* [only before noun]: *Don't try any daredevil stunts.*

dar·ing /'dɛrɪŋ/ *adj.*, *noun*
- *adj.* brave; willing to do dangerous or unusual things; involving danger or taking risks: *a daring walk in space* ◆ *There are plenty of activities at the resort for the less daring.* ◆ *The gallery was known for putting on daring exhibitions.* ◆ *a daring strapless dress in black silk* ▶ **dar·ing·ly** *adv.*
- *noun* [U] courage and the willingness to take risks: *the skill and daring of the mountain climbers*

dark 🔑 /dɑrk/ *adj.*, *noun*
- *adj.* (**dark·er**, **dark·est**)
- › WITH LITTLE LIGHT **1** with no or very little light, especially because it is night: *a dark room/street/forest* ◆ *What time does it get dark in summer?* ◆ *It was dark outside and I couldn't see much.* **ANT** LIGHT
- › COLORS **2** not light; closer in shade to black than to white: *dark blue/green/red, etc.* ◆ *Darker colors are more practical and don't show stains.* **ANT** LIGHT, PALE **3** having a color that is close to black: *a dark suit* ◆ *dark-colored wood* ◆ *The dark clouds in the sky meant that a storm was coming.*
- › HAIR/SKIN/EYES **4** brown or black in color: *Sue has long dark hair.* ◆ *Even if you have dark skin, you still need protection from the sun.* **5** (of a person) having dark hair, eyes, etc.: *a dark handsome stranger* **ANT** FAIR
- › MYSTERIOUS **6** mysterious; hidden and not known about: *There are no dark secrets in our family.*
- › EVIL **7** evil or frightening: *There was a darker side to his nature.* ◆ *the dark forces of the imagination*
- › WITHOUT HOPE **8** unpleasant and without any hope that something good will happen: *the darkest days of Fascism* ◆ *The film is a dark vision of the future.*
- › PHONETICS **9** (of a speech sound) produced with the back part of the tongue close to the back of the mouth. In many accents of English, dark /l/ is used after a vowel, as in *ball.* **ANT** CLEAR
  IDM **a dark horse** a person taking part in a race, etc. who surprises everyone by winning
- *noun*
- › NO LIGHT **1** the dark [sing.] the lack of light in a place, especially because it is night: *All the lights went out and we were left in the dark.* ◆ *Are the children afraid of the dark?* ◆ *animals that can see in the dark*
- › COLOR **2** [U] an amount of something that is dark in color: *patterns of light and dark*
  IDM **after/before dark** after/before the sun goes down and it is night: *Try to get home before dark.* ◆ *Don't go out alone after dark.* **in the dark (about sth)** knowing nothing about something: *Workers were kept in the dark about the plans to sell the company.* ◆ *She arrived at the meeting as much in the dark as everyone else.* **a shot/stab in the dark** a guess; something you do without knowing what the result will be: *The figure he came up with was really just a shot in the dark.* ⊃ more at LEAP *n.*

the 'dark ,ages *noun* [pl.] **1 the Dark Ages** the period of European history between the end of the Roman Empire and the 10th century A.D. **2** (often *humorous*) a period of history or a time when something was not developed or modern: *Back in the dark ages of computing, in about 1980, they started a software company.*

,dark 'chocolate *noun* [U] dark brown chocolate with a slightly bitter taste, made without milk being added ⊃ compare MILK CHOCOLATE, WHITE CHOCOLATE

dark·en /'dɑrkən/ *verb* **1** [I, T] to become dark; to make something dark: *The sky began to darken as the storm approached.* ◆ *~ sth We walked quickly through the darkened streets.* ◆ *a darkened room* **2** [I, T] to become unhappy or angry; to make someone unhappy or angry: *Her mood darkened at the news.* ◆ *Luke's face darkened* (= he looked angry). ◆ *~ sth It was a tragedy that darkened his later life.* **IDM** **never darken my door again** (*old-fashioned*, *humorous*) used to tell someone never to come to your home again

,dark 'glasses *noun* [pl.] glasses that have dark-colored LENSES ⊃ see also SUNGLASSES

---

dark·ling /'dɑrklɪŋ/ adj. (literary) becoming dark or connected with the dark: the darkling sky

dark·ly /'dɑrkli/ adv. **1** in a threatening or unpleasant way: He hinted darkly that all was not well. **2** showing a dark color: Her eyes burned darkly.

dark ˌmatter noun [U] (astronomy) according to some theories, material that exists in space that does not produce any light

dark meat noun [U] darker-colored meat from the legs of a chicken or other bird that has been cooked ⊃ compare WHITE MEAT (2)

dark·ness /'dɑrknəs/ noun [U] **1** the state of being dark, without any light: After a few minutes our eyes got used to the darkness. ◆ The house was plunged into total darkness when the electricity was cut off. ◆ The sun went down and darkness fell n. (= it became night). ◆ There is an extra hour of darkness on winter mornings. ◆ Her face was in darkness. ◆ They managed to escape under cover of darkness. **2** the quality or state of being dark in color: It depends on the darkness of your skin. **3** (literary) evil: the forces of darkness

dark·room /'dɑrkrum; -rʊm/ noun a room that can be made completely dark, where you can take film out of a camera and develop photographs

dark ˈstar noun (astronomy) an object in space similar to a star, that produces no light or very little light

dar·ling /'dɑrlɪŋ/ noun, adj.
● noun **1** (informal) a way of addressing someone that you love: What's the matter, darling? **2** a person who is very friendly and kind: You are a darling, Hugo. **3 the ~ of sb/sth** a person who is especially liked and very popular: She is the darling of the newspapers and can do no wrong.
● adj. [only before noun] (informal) much loved; very attractive, special, etc.: My darling daughter. ◆ "Darling Henry," the letter began.

darm·stadt·i·um /,dɑrm'stætiəm; -'ʃtætiəm/ noun [U] (symb. Ds) a chemical element. Darmstadtium is a RADIOACTIVE element that is produced artificially.

darn /dɑrn/ verb, noun, adj., adv.
● verb [T, I] ~ (sth) to repair a hole in a piece of clothing by sewing STITCHES across the hole: to darn socks
   IDM darn it! (informal) used as a mild swear word to show that you are angry or annoyed about something, to avoid saying "damn": Darn it! I lost my keys! **I'll be darned!** (informal) used to show that you are surprised about something
● noun a place on a piece of clothing that has been repaired by darning
● adj. (also darned) (informal) used as a mild swear word, to emphasize something: Why don't you switch the darn thing off and listen to me!
● adv. (also darned) (informal) used as a mild swear word, instead of saying DAMN, to mean "extremely" or "very": You had a darn good try. ◆ It's darn cold tonight.

darned /dɑrnd/ adj., adv. = DARN: That's a darned good idea! ▸ **darned·est** adj.

dart /dɑrt/ noun, verb
● noun **1** [C] a small pointed object, sometimes with feathers to help it fly, that is shot as a weapon or thrown in the game of darts: a poisoned dart ⊃ picture at HOBBY **2 darts** [U] a game in which darts are thrown at a round board marked with numbers for scoring: a darts match ⊃ picture at HOBBY **3** [sing.] a sudden quick movement SYN DASH: She made a dart for the door. **4** [sing.] (literary) a sudden feeling of a strong emotion: Nina felt a sudden dart of panic. **5** [C] a pointed fold that is sewn in a piece of clothing to make it fit better
● verb **1** [I] + adv./prep. to move suddenly and quickly in a particular direction: A dog darted across the road in front of me. ◆ Her eyes darted around the room, looking for Greg. **2** [T] to look at someone suddenly and quickly ~ a glance/look (at sb): He darted an impatient look at Vicky. ◆ ~ sb a glance/look He darted Vicky an impatient look.

dart·board /'dɑrtbɔrd/ noun a round board used in the game of darts ⊃ picture at HOBBY

Dar·win·ism /'dɑrwɪnɪzəm/ noun [U] (biology) the theory that living things EVOLVE by NATURAL SELECTION, developed by Charles Darwin in the 19th century ⊃ see also SOCIAL DARWINISM ▸ **Dar·win·i·an** /dɑr'wɪniən/ adj.: Darwinian ideas

dash /dæʃ/ noun, verb
● noun
> SMALL AMOUNT **1** [C, usually sing.] ~ (of sth) a small amount of something that is added to something else: Add a dash of lemon juice. ◆ The rug adds a dash of color to the room. ⊃ compare SPLASH
> SOMETHING DONE QUICKLY **2** [sing.] a ~ (for sth) an act of going somewhere suddenly and/or quickly: When the doors opened, there was a mad dash for seats. ◆ a 60-mile dash to safety ◆ He jumped off the bus and made a dash for the nearest bar. ◆ We waited for the police to leave, then made a dash for it (= left quickly in order to escape). **3** [sing.] an act of doing something quickly because you do not have enough time: a last-minute dash to buy presents
> SYMBOL **4** [C] the mark (—) used to separate parts of a sentence, often instead of a colon or in pairs instead of parentheses ⊃ compare HYPHEN
> RACE **5** [C, usually sing.] a race in which the people taking part run very fast over a short distance SYN SPRINT: the 100-meter dash
> PART OF CAR **6** [C] (informal) = DASHBOARD
> WAY OF BEHAVING **7** [U] (old-fashioned, approving) a way of behaving that combines style, enthusiasm, and confidence
● verb
> GO QUICKLY **1** [I] to go somewhere very quickly SYN RUSH: I have to dash (= leave quickly), I'm late. ◆ + adv./prep. She dashed off to keep an appointment. ◆ He dashed along the platform and jumped on the train.
> THROW/BEAT **2** [T, I] to throw something or make something fall violently onto a hard surface; to beat against a surface: ~ sth + adv./prep. The boat was dashed repeatedly against the rocks. ◆ + adv./prep. The waves were dashing against the harbor wall.
   IDM dash sb's hopes to destroy someone's hopes by making what they were hoping for impossible
   PHRV ˌdash sth↔'off to write or draw something very quickly: I dashed off a note to my brother.

dash·board /'dæʃbɔrd/ (also informal dash) noun the part of a car in front of the driver that has instruments and controls in it ⊃ picture at CAR

da·shi·ki /dɑ'ʃiki/ noun a loose shirt or longer piece of clothing worn by men in W. Africa, often made from cloth with brightly colored patterns

dash·ing /'dæʃɪŋ/ adj. (old-fashioned) **1** (usually of a man) attractive, confident, and elegant: a dashing young officer ◆ his dashing good looks **2** (of a thing) attractive and fashionable: his dashing red bow tie

das·tard·ly /'dæstərdli/ adj. (old-fashioned) evil and cruel: My first acting role was Captain O'Hagarty, a dastardly villain.

DAT /dæt; ˌdi eɪ 'ti/ abbr. DIGITAL AUDIOTAPE

da·ta 🔑 **AWL** /'deɪtə; 'dætə/ noun
(used as a plural noun in technical English, when the singular is datum) **1** [U, pl.] facts or information, especially when examined and used to find out things or to make decisions: This data was collected from 69 countries. ◆ the analysis/interpretation of the data ◆ raw data (= that has not been analyzed) ◆ demographical/historical/personal data ◆ (technical) These data show that many cancers are detected during medical checkups. ⊃ collocations at SCIENTIFIC **2** [U] information that is stored by a computer: data retrieval (= ways of storing or finding information on a computer)

data ˌbank noun a large amount of data on a particular subject that is stored in a computer

da·ta·base /'deɪtəbeɪs; 'dætə-/ noun an organized set of data that is stored in a computer and can be looked at and used in various ways

| t tea | ṱ butter | d did | k cat | g got | tʃ chin | dʒ June | f fall |

database 'management ,system *noun* (*abbr.* DBMS) (*computing*) a system for organizing and managing a large amount of data

dat·a·ble /'deɪtəbl/ *adj.* that can be dated to a particular time: *pottery that is datable to the second century*

'data ,capture *noun* [U] the action or process of collecting data, especially using computers

'data ,mining *noun* [U] (*computing*) looking at large amounts of information that has been collected on a computer and using it to provide new information

,data 'processing *noun* [U] (*computing*) a series of actions that a computer performs on data to produce an output

'data pro,jector (also **pro·jec·tor**) *noun* a piece of equipment that takes data and images from a computer and shows them on a wall or large screen ➔ compare OVERHEAD PROJECTOR, SLIDE PROJECTOR

,data pro'tection *noun* [U] legal restrictions that keep information stored on computers private and that control who can read it or use it

'data ,set *noun* (*computing*) a collection of data that is treated as a single unit by a computer

'data ,warehouse *noun* a large amount of data that comes from different parts of a business and that is stored together ▶ **'data ,warehousing** *noun* [U]: *We use data warehousing to analyze long-term trends.*

date 🖉 /deɪt/ *noun, verb*

● *noun*
▷ **PARTICULAR DAY 1** [C] a particular day of the month, sometimes in a particular year, given in numbers and words: *"What's the date today?" "The 10th."* ◆ *Write today's date at the top of the page.* ◆ *They haven't set a date for the wedding yet.* ◆ *I can't come on that date.* ◆ *Please give your name, address and date of birth.* ◆ *name, address and birth date* ◆ *There's no date on this letter.* ➔ see also CLOSING DATE, SELL-BY DATE
▷ **PAST TIME/FUTURE 2** [sing., U] a time in the past or future that is not a particular day: *The details can be added at a later date.* ◆ *The work will be carried out at a future date.* ◆ *a building of late Roman date*
▷ **ROMANTIC MEETING 3** [C] a meeting that you have arranged with a boyfriend or girlfriend or with someone who might become a boyfriend or girlfriend: *I have a date with Lacey tomorrow night.* ◆ *Paul's not coming. He's got a hot date* (= an exciting one). ➔ collocations at MARRIAGE ➔ see also BLIND DATE, DOUBLE DATE **4** [C] a boyfriend or girlfriend with whom you have arranged a date: *My date is meeting me at seven.*
▷ **ARRANGEMENT TO MEET 5** [C] an arrangement to meet someone at a particular time: *Call me next week and we'll try and make a date.* ◆ *I have a lunch date with Sue at 12:30.* ◆ *Last Sunday Jimmy and Steve had a play date* (= an arrangement made by parents for children to play together). ◆ *an Internet/online date* (= an arrangement that you make on the Internet to meet someone that you have not seen before)
▷ **FRUIT 6** [C] a sweet, sticky, brown fruit that grows on a tree called a **date palm**, common in N. Africa and W. Asia **IDM** **to date** until now: *To date, we have received over 200 replies.* ◆ *The exhibit contains some of his best work to date.* ➔ see also OUT OF DATE, UP TO DATE

● *verb*
▷ **WRITE DATE 1** [T] ~ sth to write or print the date on something: *Thank you for your letter dated March 24th.*
▷ **FIND AGE 2** [T] ~ sth (at/to sth) to say when something old existed or was made: *The skeleton has been dated at about 2000 B.C.*
▷ **OF CLOTHES/WORDS 3** [I] to become old-fashioned: *She designs classic clothes which do not date.*
▷ **PERSON 4** [T] ~ sb if something **dates** you, it shows that you are fairly old or older than the people you are with: *I was at the Woodstock festival—that dates me, doesn't it?*
▷ **HAVE RELATIONSHIP 5** [T, I] ~ (sb) to have a romantic relationship with someone: *She's been dating Ron for several months.*

PHR V **,date 'back (to…)** | **'date from…** to have existed since a particular time in the past or for the length of time mentioned: *The college dates back to medieval times.* ◆ *The custom dates back hundreds of years.* ◆ *a law dating from the 17th century*

date·book /'deɪtbʊk/ *noun* = APPOINTMENT BOOK

dat·ed /'deɪtəd/ *adj.* old-fashioned; belonging to a time in the past ➔ compare UNDATED

'Date Line *noun* = INTERNATIONAL DATE LINE

'date rape *noun* [U] the crime of raping (RAPE) someone, committed by a person the victim has gone out with on a DATE

'dating ,service *noun* a business or an organization that arranges meetings between single people who want to begin a romantic relationship: *He met his wife through an online dating service.*

da·tive /'deɪtɪv/ *noun* (*grammar*) (in some languages) the form of a noun, a pronoun, or an adjective when it is the INDIRECT OBJECT of a verb or is connected with the INDIRECT OBJECT: *In the sentence "I sent her a postcard," the word "her" is in the dative.* ➔ compare ABLATIVE, ACCUSATIVE, GENITIVE, LOCATIVE, NOMINATIVE, VOCATIVE ▶ **da·tive** *adj.*

da·tum /'deɪtəm; 'dætəm/ *noun* (*pl.* da·ta) (*technical*) a fact or piece of information ➔ see also DATA

daub /dɔb/ *verb, noun*
● *verb* ~ A on, etc. B | ~ B with A | + adv./prep. to spread a substance such as paint, mud, etc., thickly and/or carelessly onto something: *The walls of the building were daubed with red paint.*
● *noun* **1** [U] a mixture of CLAY, etc. that was used in the past for making walls: *walls made of wattle and daub* **2** [C] a small amount of a substance such as paint that has been spread carelessly: *a daub of lipstick* **3** [C] a badly painted picture

daugh·ter 🖉 /'dɔtər/ *noun*
1 a person's female child: *We have two sons and a daughter.* ◆ *They have three grown-up daughters.* ◆ *She's the daughter of a Harvard professor.* ➔ collocations at CHILD ➔ see also GOD-DAUGHTER, GRANDDAUGHTER, STEPDAUGHTER **2** (*literary*) a woman who belongs to a particular place or country, etc.: *one of the town's most famous daughters*

daughter-in-,law *noun* (*pl.* daughters-in-law) the wife of your son ➔ compare SON-IN-LAW

daunt /dɔnt/ *verb* [usually passive] ~ sb to make someone feel nervous and less confident about doing something **SYN** INTIMIDATE: *She was a brave woman but she felt daunted by the task ahead.* ▶ **daunt·ing** *adj.* **SYN** INTIMIDATING: *She has the daunting task of cooking for 20 people every day.* ◆ *Starting a new job can be a daunting prospect.* **daunt·ing·ly** *adv.*

daunt·less /'dɔntləs/ *adj.* (*literary*) not easily frightened or stopped from doing something difficult **SYN** RESOLUTE

dau·phin /'doʊfən; doʊ'fæ/ *noun* (*old use*) the oldest son of the king of France

Da·vid and Go·li·ath /,deɪvəd ən gə'laɪəθ/ *adj.* used to describe a situation in which a small or weak person or organization tries to defeat another much larger or stronger opponent: *The game looks like it will be a David and Goliath contest.* **ORIGIN** From the Bible story in which Goliath, a giant, is killed by the boy David with a stone.

daw·dle /'dɔdl/ *verb* [I] to take a long time to do something or go somewhere: *Stop dawdling! We're going to be late!* ◆ + adv./prep. *They dawdled around by the river, laughing and talking.*

dawn /dɔn/ *noun, verb*
● *noun* **1** [U, C] the time of day when light first appears **SYN** DAYBREAK, SUNRISE: *They start work at dawn.* ◆ *It's almost dawn.* ◆ *We arrived in New York as dawn broke* (= as the first light could be seen). ◆ *I woke up just before dawn.* ◆ *summer's early dawns* ◆ *He works from dawn to dusk* (= from

morning to night). ⟳ compare DUSK **2** [sing.] ~ **(of sth)** the beginning or first signs of something: *the **dawn** of civilization/time/history* ♦ *Peace marked a new **dawn** in the country's history.* **IDM** see BREAK *n.*, CRACK *n.*

● *verb* **1** [I] (of a day or a period of time) to begin: *The following morning dawned bright and warm.* ♦ *A new technological age had dawned.* **2** [I] to become obvious or easy to understand: *Slowly the awful truth dawned.* **IDM** see LIGHT **PHR V** '**dawn on sb** [no passive] if something **dawns on you**, you begin to realize it for the first time: [+ **that**] *Suddenly it dawned on me that they couldn't possibly have met before.*

the ˌdawn ˈchorus *noun* [sing.] the sound of birds singing very early in the morning

day 🔑 /deɪ/ *noun*

1 [C] a period of 24 hours: *I saw Tom three **days** ago.* ♦ *"What day is it today?" "Monday."* ♦ *We're going away **in a few days**.* ♦ *They left **the day before yesterday** (= two days ago).* ♦ *We're meeting **the day after tomorrow** (= in two days).* ♦ *New Year's Day* ♦ *Take the medicine three times **a day**.* ♦ *We can't go there today. You can go **another day**.* ⟳ see also FIELD DAY, OFF DAY, RED-LETTER DAY **2** [U] the time between when it becomes light in the morning and when it becomes dark in the evening: *The sun was shining **all day**.* ♦ *I could sit and watch the river **all day long**.* ♦ *He works at night and sleeps **during the day**.* ♦ *Nocturnal animals sleep **by day** and hunt by night.* **3** [C, usually sing.] the hours of the day when you are awake, working, etc.: *a seven-hour **working day*** ♦ *It's been a **long day** (= I've been very busy).* ♦ *Did you have a good **day**?* ♦ *She didn't do a full **day's work**.* ♦ *I took a half **day** off yesterday.* ♦ *Have a nice **day**!* ⟳ see also WORKDAY **4** [C, usually pl.] a particular period of time or history: *in George Washington's **day*** ♦ *the **early days** of computers* ♦ *Most women stayed at home **in those days**.* ♦ *(informal)* **in the old days** (= in the past) ⟳ see also GLORY DAYS, HEYDAY, NOWADAYS, THE PRESENT DAY **HELP** There are many other compounds ending in **day**. You will find them at their place in the alphabet. **IDM all in a day's work** part of your normal working life and not unusual **any day (now)** *(informal)* very soon: *The letter should arrive any day now.* **back in the day** in the past: *My dad's always talking about how great everything was back in the day.* **back in the days** at a particular time in the past: *I was a fan back in the days when the band wasn't yet famous.* **carry/win the day** *(formal)* to be successful against someone or something: *Despite strong opposition, the ruling party carried the day.* **day after day** each day repeatedly (used especially when something is boring or annoying): *She hates doing the same work day after day.* **day by day** all the time; a little at a time and gradually: *Day by day his condition improved.* **day in, day out | day in and day out** every day for a long period of time **a day of reckoning** the time when someone will have to deal with the result of something that they have done wrong, or be punished for something bad that they have done **sb's/sth's days are numbered** a person or thing will not continue to live, exist, or be successful for much longer: *His days as leader of the party are numbered.* **from day one** *(informal)* from the beginning: *It's never worked from day one.* **from day to day 1** with no thoughts or plans for the future: *They live from day to day, taking care of their sick daughter.* **2** if a situation changes **from day to day**, it changes often: *A baby's need for food can vary from day to day.* **from one day to the next** if a situation changes **from one day to the next**, it is uncertain and not likely to stay the same each day: *I never know what to expect from one day to the next.* **have had your day** to no longer be successful, powerful, etc.: *She's had her day as a supermodel.* **have seen/known better days** *(humorous)* to be in poor condition: *Our car has seen better days!* **if he's, she's, etc. a day** *(informal)* (used when talking about someone's age) at least: *He must be 70 if he's a day!* **in sb's day 1** during the part of someone's life when they were most successful, famous, etc.: *She was a great dancer in her day.* **2** when someone was young: *In my day, there were*

plenty of jobs when you left school. **in this day and age** now, in the modern world **it's not every day (that...)** used when something unusual happens, especially something good or enjoyable: *It's not every day that I have such an expensive lunch!* **it's not sb's day** *(informal)* used when several unfortunate or unpleasant things happen on the same day: *My car broke down and then I locked myself out—it's just not my day!* **make sb's day** to make someone feel very happy on a particular day: *The phone call from Mike really made my day.* **make a day of it** *(informal)* to make a particular enjoyable activity last for a whole day instead of only part of it **not have all day** to not have much time: *Come on! We don't have all day!* **of sb's day** during a particular period of time when someone lived: *the best player of his day* ♦ *Bessie Smith was the Madonna of her day.* **of the day** that is served on a particular day in a restaurant: *soup of the day* **one day** at some time in the future, or on a particular day in the past: *One day, I want to leave the city and move to the country.* ♦ *One day, he walked out of the house with a small bag and never came back.* **one of these days** before a long time has passed: *One of these days you'll come back and ask me to forgive you.* **one of those days** *(informal)* a day when there are a lot of mistakes and a lot of things go wrong: *It's been one of those days!* **take it/things one day at a time** *(informal)* to not think about what will happen in the future: *I don't know if he'll get better. We're just taking it one day at a time.* **that'll be the day** *(informal, ironic)* used when you are saying that something is very unlikely to happen: *Paul? Apologize? That'll be the day!* **these days** *(informal)* used to talk about the present, especially when you are comparing it with the past: *These days kids grow up so quickly.* **those were the days** *(informal)* used to suggest that a time in the past was happier or better than now **to the day** exactly: *It's been three years to the day since we met.* **to this day** even now, when a lot of time has passed: *To this day, I still don't understand why he did it.* ⟳ more at BORN *adj.*, BREAK *n.*, CALL *v.*, CLEAR *adj.*, COLD *adj.*, DEED, DOG *n.*, END *n.*, END *v.*, FORTH, GIVE *v.*, LATE *adv.*, LIVE¹, LIVELONG, NICE, NIGHT, OLD, ORDER *n.*, OTHER, PASS *v.*, RAINY, ROME, SALAD, SAVE *v.*, TIME *n.*

day·break /ˈdeɪbreɪk/ *noun* [U] the time of day when light first appears **SYN** DAWN: *We left before daybreak.*

ˈday camp *noun* [C, U] a place where young people go during the day in summer and take part in sports and other activities: *My son is learning to swim in day camp.*

ˈday care (also **day·care**) /ˈdeɪker/ *noun* [U] care for small children, or for old or sick people, away from home, during the day: *Day care is provided by the company she works for.* ♦ *a day care center*

ˈday ˌcenter (CanE usually **ˈday ˌcentre**) *noun* a place that provides care for old or sick people during the day

day·dream /ˈdeɪdriːm/ *noun* pleasant thoughts that make you forget about the present: *She stared out of the window, lost in a daydream.* ▶ **day·dream** *verb* [I]: ~ **(about sb/sth)** *I would spend hours daydreaming about a house of my own.*

Day-Glo™ /ˈdeɪ gloʊ/ *adj.* having a very bright orange, yellow, green, or pink color: *Day-Glo cycling shorts*

ˈday job *noun* [sing.] the paid work that someone normally does **IDM don't give up the/your day job** *(informal, humorous)* used to tell someone that they should continue doing what they are used to, rather than trying something new that they are likely to fail at: *So you want to be a writer? Well my advice is, don't give up your day job.*

ˈday ˌlabor *noun* [U] work that does not require much skill and for which you are paid every day ▶ **ˈday ˌlaborer** *noun*: *Day laborers help with the fall harvest.*

day·light /ˈdeɪlaɪt/ *noun* [U] the light that comes from the sun during the day: *They emerged from the church into the bright daylight.* ♦ *The street looks very different **in daylight**.* ♦ *They left **before daylight** (= before the sun had risen).* **IDM** see BROAD *adj.*

day·lights /'deɪlaɪts/ noun [pl.]

IDM **beat/knock the (living) daylights out of sb** (*informal*) to hit someone very hard several times and hurt them very much **scare/frighten the (living) daylights out of sb** (*informal*) to scare someone very much

daylight 'saving time (also daylight 'savings time) (*abbr.* DST) *noun* [U] the period during which in some countries the clocks are put forward one hour, so that it is light for an extra hour in the evening

day·lil·y (also **day lily**) /'deɪ,lɪli/ *noun* a lily with large yellow, red, or orange flowers, each flower lasting only one day

day·long /'deɪlɔŋ/ *adj.* [only before noun] lasting for a whole day: *a daylong meeting*

the Day of 'Atonement *noun* [sing.] = YOM KIPPUR

day 'off *noun* (*pl.* days 'off) a day on which you do not have to work: *Most weeks, Sunday is my only day off.* ♦ *Why not take a few days off?*

the Day of 'Judgment *noun* [sing.] = JUDGMENT DAY

day·pack /'deɪpæk/ *noun* a small BACKPACK in which you carry the things you need for one day

day room *noun* a room in a hospital or other institution where people can sit, relax, watch television, etc. during the day

day school *noun* a private school with students who live at home and only go to school during the day ➔ compare BOARDING SCHOOL

day student *noun* a school student who goes to a BOARDING SCHOOL or college but lives at home

day·time /'deɪtaɪm/ *noun* [U] the period during the day between the time when it gets light and the time when it gets dark: *You don't often see this bird* **in the daytime.** ♦ *The park is open* **during the daytime.** ♦ *Daytime temperatures never fell below 80°F.* ♦ *Please give me your name and daytime phone number.* **ANT** NIGHTTIME

day-to-'day *adj.* [only before noun] **1** planning for only one day at a time: *I have organized the cleaning* **on a day-to-day basis** *until our usual housekeeper returns.* **2** involving the usual events or tasks of each day: *She has been responsible for the* **day-to-day running** *of the school.*

day trading *noun* [U] (*finance*) buying and selling shares very quickly on the same day using the Internet in order to make a profit from small price changes ▶ **day trader** *noun*

day trip *noun* a trip or visit completed in one day: *a day trip to the beach* ▶ **day tripper** *noun*

day·wear /'deɪwɛr/ *noun* [U] clothes for wearing every day, for example for working or shopping, not for special occasions ➔ see also NIGHTWEAR

daze /deɪz/ *noun*

IDM **in a daze** in a confused state: *I've been in a complete daze since I heard the news.*

dazed /deɪzd/ *adj.* unable to think clearly, especially because of a shock or because you have been hit on the head: *Survivors waited for the rescue boats, dazed and scared.* ♦ *Jimmy was still dazed by the blow to his head.*

daz·zle /'dæzl/ *verb, noun*

● *verb* [often passive] **1** [T, I] ~ **(sb)** if a strong light **dazzles** you, it is so bright that you cannot see for a short time **SYN** BLIND: *He was momentarily dazzled by the strong sunlight.* **2** [T] ~ **sb** to impress someone a lot with your beauty, skill, etc.: *He was dazzled by the warmth of her smile.* ▶ **daz·zling** *adj.*: *a dazzling display of Japanese dance* **daz·zling·ly** *adv.*: *She was dazzlingly beautiful.*

● *noun* [U, sing.] **1** the quality that bright light has that stops you from seeing clearly **2** a thing or quality that impresses you but may prevent you from understanding or thinking clearly

d.b.a. /,di bi 'eɪ/ *abbr.* doing business as: *Philip Smith, d.b.a. Phil's Signs*

DBMS /,di bi ɛm 'ɛs/ *abbr.* DATABASE MANAGEMENT SYSTEM

DC /,di 'si/ *abbr.* **1** DIRECT CURRENT ➔ compare ALTERNATING CURRENT **2** D.C. District of Columbia: *Washington, D.C.*

D-Day /'di deɪ/ *noun* [U] a date on which something important is expected to happen **ORIGIN** From the name given to June 6, 1944, the day on which the U.S., British, and other armies landed on the beaches of northern France in the Second World War.

DDT /,di di 'ti/ *noun* [U] a chemical used, especially in the past, for killing insects that harm crops

DE *abbr.* (in writing) Delaware

de- /di; dɪ/ *prefix* (in verbs and related nouns, adjectives, and adverbs) **1** the opposite of: *decentralization* **2** removing something: *to defrost the refrigerator* (= remove layers of ice from it)

dea·con /'dikən/ *noun* **1** (in the Roman Catholic, Anglican, and Orthodox Churches) a religious leader just below the rank of a priest **2** (in some Nonconformist Churches) a person who is not a member of the CLERGY, but who helps a minister with church business affairs

dea·con·ess /'dikənəs/ *noun* (in some Christian Churches) a woman who has duties that are similar to those of a deacon

de·ac·ti·vate /,di'æktə,veɪt/ *verb* ~ **sth** to make something such as a device or chemical process stop working: *Do you know how to deactivate the alarm?*

dead 🔑 /dɛd/ *adj., noun, adv.*

● *adj.*

▷ **NOT ALIVE 1** no longer alive: *My mother's dead; she died in 1987.* ♦ *a dead person/animal* ♦ *He was shot dead by a gunman outside his home.* ♦ *Catherine's dead body lay peacefully on the bed.* ♦ *He dropped dead* (= died suddenly) *last week.* ♦ *The poor child looks* **more dead than alive.** ♦ (*figurative*) *In ten years he'll be* **dead and buried** *as a politician.*

▷ **IDEA/BELIEF/PLAN 2** [not before noun] no longer believed in or aimed for: *Many believe the peace plan is dead.* ♦ *Unfortunately racism is not yet dead.* ♦ *Though the idea may be dead, it is far from being buried* (= people still talk about it, even though there is nothing new to say).

▷ **NOT USED 3** belonging to the past; no longer practiced or fashionable: *Is the Western a dead art form?* ♦ *a dead language* (= one that is no longer spoken, for example Latin)

▷ **FINISHED 4** (*informal*) finished; not able to be used any more: *dead matches* ♦ *There were two dead bottles of wine on the table.*

▷ **MACHINE 5** (of machines or equipment) not working because of a lack of power: *a dead battery* ♦ *The hard disk is dead.* ♦ *Suddenly the phone* **went dead.**

▷ **PLACE 6** (*informal, disapproving*) very quiet, without activity or interest: *There were no theaters, no clubs, and no coffee bars. It was dead as anything.*

▷ **BUSINESS 7** (*informal, disapproving*) without activity; with no one buying or selling anything: *"The market is absolutely dead this morning," said one foreign exchange trader.* ♦ *Winter is traditionally the dead season for the housing market.*

▷ **TIRED 8** [not usually before noun] (*informal*) extremely tired; not well: *half dead with cold and hunger* ♦ *She felt* **dead on her feet** *and didn't have the energy to question them further.*

▷ **WITHOUT FEELING 9** [not before noun] (of a part of the body) unable to feel because of cold, etc. **SYN** NUMB: *My left arm had gone dead.* **10** ~ **to sth** unable to feel or understand emotions **SYN** INSENSITIVE: *He was dead to all feelings of pity.* **11** (especially of someone's voice, eyes, or face) showing no emotion **SYN** EXPRESSIONLESS: *She said, "I'm sorry, too," in a quiet, dead voice.* ♦ *His usually dead gray eyes were sparkling.*

▷ **COMPLETE/EXACT 12** [only before noun] complete or exact: *a dead silence/calm* ♦ *the dead center of the target* ♦ *The car gave a sudden jerk and came to a dead stop.* ♦ *She crumpled to the floor in a dead faint* (= completely unconscious).

▷ **NEVER ALIVE 13** never having been alive: *dead matter* (= for example rock) ♦ *a dead planet* (= one with no life on it)

▷ **IN SPORTS 14** used to describe the ball at a time when play must stop during a game: *The ball is dead when it's out of bounds.* **ANT** LIVE² *adj.* (9)

IDM **be a dead ringer for sb** (*informal*) to look very like someone: *She's a dead ringer for a girl I used to know.* **beat/flog a dead horse** (*informal*) to waste your effort by trying to do something that is no longer possible **(as) dead as a doornail** (*informal*) completely dead **a dead duck** (*informal*) a plan, an event, etc., that has failed or is certain to fail and that is therefore not worth discussing **be dead and gone** (*informal*) to be dead: *You'll be sorry you said that when I'm dead and gone.* **the dead hand of sth** an influence that controls or restricts something: *We need to free business from the dead hand of bureaucracy.* **dead in the water** a person or plan that **is dead in the water** has failed and has little hope of succeeding in the future: *His leadership campaign is dead in the water.* **dead meat** (*informal*) in serious trouble: *If anyone finds out, you're dead meat.* **dead on arrival** (*abbr.* DOA) **1** (of an accident victim or other patient) already dead when arriving at the hospital: *She was pronounced dead on arrival.* **2** (*informal*) very unlikely to be successful; not working when it is delivered: *The bill was dead on arrival in the Senate.* ◆ *The software was DOA.* **dead to rights** (*informal*) with definite proof of having committed a crime, so that you cannot claim to be innocent: *We've got you dead to rights handling stolen property.* **dead to the world** fast asleep **over my dead body** (*informal*) used to show you are strongly opposed to something: *She moves into our home over my dead body.* **sb wouldn't be seen/caught dead…** (*informal*) used to say that you would not like to wear particular clothes, or to be in a particular situation: *She wouldn't be seen dead in a hat.* ◆ *He wouldn't be caught dead going to a club with his mother.* ⊃ more at KNOCK *v.*

● *noun* **the dead 1** [pl.] people who have died: *The dead and wounded in that one attack amounted to 5,000.* **2** [sing.] the state of being dead: *Christians believe that God raised Jesus from the dead.* ◆ (*figurative*) *In nine years he has brought his party back from the dead almost to the brink of power.*
IDM **in the dead of night** in the quietest part of the night: *I crept out of bed in the dead of night and sneaked downstairs.* **in the dead of winter** in the coldest part of winter

● *adv.* (*informal*)
▷ COMPLETELY completely; exactly: *You're dead right!* ◆ *He's dead against the idea.* ◆ *The sight made him stop dead in his tracks* (= stop suddenly). ◆ *She's dead set on getting* (= determined to get) *this new job.* ◆ *Her office is dead ahead at the end of the hallway.*
IDM **dead on** exactly right: *Her judgment is dead on.* ⊃ more at RIGHT

dead·beat /ˈdɛdbit/ *noun* (*informal*) **1** a lazy person; a person with no job and no money, who is not part of normal society **2** a person or company that tries to avoid paying their debts **3** (*also* ˌdeadbeat ˈdad) a father who does not live with his children and does not pay their mother any money to take care of them

dead·bolt /ˈdɛdboʊlt/ *noun* a type of strong lock on a door that needs a key or handle to open or close it

dead·en /ˈdɛdn/ *verb* ~ sth to make something such as a sound, a feeling, etc., less strong **SYN** DULL: *He was given drugs to deaden the pain.* ▶ **dead·en·ing** *adj.* [only before noun]: *the deadening effect of alcohol on your reactions*

ˌdead ˈend *noun* **1** a road, passage, etc. that is closed at one end: *The first street we tried turned out to be a dead end.* **2** a point at which you can make no further progress in what you are doing: *We came to a dead end in our research.* ◆ *He's in a dead-end job in the local factory* (= one with low pay and no hope of promotion). ◆ *These negotiations are a dead-end street* (= they have reached a point where no further progress is possible).

dead·head /ˈdɛdhɛd/ *verb* ~ sth to remove dead flowers from a plant

ˌdead ˈheat *noun* **1** a result in a race when two of those taking part finish at exactly the same time **2** a situation during a race or competition, etc. when two or more people

are at the same level: *The two candidates are in a dead heat in the polls.*

ˌdead ˈletter *noun* **1** [usually sing.] a law or an agreement that still exists but that is ignored **2** a letter that cannot be delivered to an address or to the person who sent it

dead·line /ˈdɛdlaɪn/ *noun* ~ (for sth) a point in time by which something must be done: *I prefer to work under a deadline.* ◆ *a reporter on a deadline* (= who has work that must be finished by a certain time) ◆ *The deadline for applications is April 30.* ◆ *the January 15 deadline set by the United Nations* ◆ *The project has a tight deadline* (= it must be finished very soon).

dead·lock /ˈdɛdlɑk/ *noun* [sing., U] a complete failure to reach agreement or settle an argument **SYN** STALEMATE: *Senate subcommittee members failed to break the deadlock over farm subsidies.* ◆ *The strike has reached a deadlock.* ▶ **dead·locked** *adj.* [not before noun]: *Despite months of discussion the negotiations remained deadlocked.*

dead·ly /ˈdɛdli/ *adj., adv.*
● *adj.* (dead·li·er, dead·li·est) **HELP** More deadly and deadliest are the usual forms. You can also use most deadly. **1** causing or likely to cause death **SYN** LETHAL: *a deadly weapon/disease* ◆ *deadly poison* ◆ *The cobra is one of the world's deadliest snakes.* ◆ *The terrorists have chosen to play a deadly game with the civilian population.* **2** [only before noun] extreme; complete: *We sat in deadly silence.* ◆ *They are deadly enemies* (= are full of hatred for each other). **3** extremely effective, so that no defense is possible: *His aim is deadly* (= so accurate that he can kill easily). ◆ *Snipers can shoot with deadly accuracy.* **4** (*informal*) very boring: *The lecture was absolutely deadly.*
● *adv.* **1** (*informal*) extremely: *deadly serious/calm* **2** = DEATHLY: *deadly pale/cold*

dead·ly night·shade /ˌdɛdli ˈnaɪtʃeɪd/ (*also* bel·la·don·na) *noun* [U] a very poisonous plant with purple flowers and black berries (BERRY)

ˌdeadly ˈsin *noun* one of the seven actions for which you can go to hell, in Christian tradition: *Greed is one of the seven deadly sins.*

dead·pan /ˈdɛdpæn/ *adj.* without any expression or emotion; often pretending to be serious when you are joking: *deadpan humor*

ˌdead ˈweight *noun* [usually sing.] **1** a thing that is very heavy and difficult to lift or move **2** a person or thing that makes it difficult for something to succeed or change

dead·wood /ˈdɛdwʊd/ *noun* [U] **1** people or things that have become useless or unnecessary in an organization **2** dead branches or wood on a tree

ˈdead zone *noun* **1** a place or a period of time in which nothing happens: *The town is a cultural dead zone.* **2** an area that separates two places, groups of people, etc.: *The UN is trying to maintain a dead zone between the warring groups.* **3** a place where a cell phone does not work because no signal can be received **4** (*biology*) an area of water in which animals cannot live because there is not enough OXYGEN

deaf 🔊 /dɛf/ *adj.* (deaf·er, deaf·est)
1 unable to hear anything or unable to hear very well: *to become/go deaf* ◆ *She was born deaf.* ⊃ see also STONE DEAF, TONE-DEAF **2** the deaf *noun* [pl.] people who cannot hear: *television subtitles for the deaf and hard of hearing* **3** [not before noun] ~ to sth not willing to listen or pay attention to something: *He was deaf to my requests for help.* ▶ **deaf·ness** *noun* [U]
IDM **(as) deaf as a post** (*informal*) very deaf **fall on deaf ears** to be ignored or not noticed by other people: *Her advice fell on deaf ears.* **turn a deaf ear (to sb/sth)** to ignore or refuse to listen to someone or something: *He turned a deaf ear to the rumors.*

deaf·en /ˈdɛfn/ *verb* [usually passive] **1** ~ sb to make someone unable to hear the sounds around them because there is too much noise: *The noise of the siren was deafening her.* **2** ~ sb to make someone deaf

ʌ **cup**   ə **about**   eɪ **say**   aɪ **five**   ɔɪ **boy**   aʊ **now**   oʊ **go**   ər **bird**

deaf·en·ing /ˈdɛfənɪŋ/ *adj.* very loud: *deafening applause* ◆ *The noise of the machine was deafening.* ◆ *The government's response to the report has been a deafening silence* (= it was very noticeable that nothing was said or done). ▶ **deaf·en·ing·ly** *adv.*

ˌdeaf ˈmute *noun* (usually *offensive*) a person who is unable to hear or speak

deal /dil/ *verb, noun*

● *verb* (**dealt**, **dealt** /dɛlt/)

> CARDS **1** [I, T] to give cards to each player in a game of cards: *Whose turn is it to deal?* ◆ **~ (sth) (out) (to sb)** *Start by dealing out ten cards to each player.* ◆ **~ sb sth** *He dealt me two aces.*

> DRUGS **2** [I, T] **~ (sth)** to buy and sell illegal drugs: *You can often see people dealing openly on the streets.*

IDM **deal sb/sth a blow** | **deal a blow to sb/sth** (*formal*) **1** to be very shocking or harmful to someone or something: *Her sudden death dealt a blow to the whole country.* **2** to hit someone or something ⊃ more at WHEEL

PHR V **ˈdeal in sth 1** to buy and sell a particular product SYN TRADE IN: *The company deals in computer software.* **2** to accept something as a basis for your decisions, attitudes, or actions: *We don't deal in rumors or guesswork.* ˌdeal sb ˈin (*informal*) to include someone in an activity: *That sounds great. Deal me in!* ˌdeal sthↄˈout **1** to share something out among a group of people SYN DISTRIBUTE: *The profits were dealt out among the investors.* **2** to say what punishment someone should have: *Many judges deal out harsher sentences to men than to women.* ˈdeal with sb to take appropriate action in a particular situation or according to the person you are talking to, managing, etc. SYN HANDLE: *She is used to dealing with all kinds of people in her job.* ˈdeal with sb/sth to do business with a person, a company, or an organization ˈdeal with sth **1** to solve a problem, perform a task, etc.: *to deal with inquiries/issues/complaints* ◆ *Have you dealt with these letters yet?* ◆ *He's good at dealing with pressure.* **2** to be about something: *Her poems often deal with the subject of death.* ⊃ language bank at ABOUT

● *noun*

> A LOT **1** [sing.] **a good/great ~** much; a lot: *They spent a great deal of money.* ◆ *It took a great deal of time.* ◆ *I'm feeling a good deal better.* ◆ *We see them a great deal* (= often). ⊃ see also BIG DEAL

> BUSINESS AGREEMENT **2** [C] an agreement, especially in business, on particular conditions for buying or doing something: *to make/sign/conclude/close a deal (with someone)* ◆ (*informal*) *Did you cut a deal* (= make one)? ◆ *We did a deal with the management on overtime.* ◆ *They were hoping for a better pay deal.* ◆ *A deal was struck after lengthy negotiations.* ◆ *The deal fell through* (= no agreement was reached). ◆ *I got a good deal on the car* (= bought it cheaply). ◆ *It's a deal!* (= I agree to your terms) ◆ *Listen. This is the deal* (= this is what we have agreed and are going to do). ⊃ see also PACKAGE ⊃ collocations at BUSINESS

> TREATMENT **3** [C, usually sing.] the way that someone or something is treated: *If elected, the governor has promised a new deal* (= better and fairer treatment) *for teachers.* ◆ *They knew they'd been given a raw/rough deal* (= been treated unfairly). ◆ *We tried to ensure that everyone got a fair deal.* ◆ *It was a square deal for everyone.*

> IN CARD GAMES **4** [C, usually sing.] the action of giving out cards to the players: *It's your deal.*

IDM **what's the deal?** (*informal*) what is happening in the present situation?: *What's the deal? Do you want to go out or not?* ⊃ more at DONE *adj.*, STRIKE *v.*

ˈdeal-ˌbreaker (also ˈdeal ˌbreaker) *noun* something that causes someone to reject a deal in politics or business: *The candidate's support for the war is the deal-breaker* (= people will not vote for the candidate because of it).

deal·er /ˈdilər/ *noun* **1** a person whose business is buying and selling a particular product: *an art/antique dealer* ◆ **~ in sth** *He's a dealer in used cars.* ⊃ see also DOUBLE-DEALER, WHEELER-DEALER **2** a person who sells illegal drugs **3** the person who gives out the cards in a card game

deal·er·ship /ˈdilərˌʃɪp/ *noun* a business that buys and sells products, especially cars, for a particular company; the position of being a dealer who can buy and sell something: *a Ford dealership*

deal·ing /ˈdilɪŋ/ *noun* **1 dealings** [pl.] business activities; the relations that you have with someone in business: *Have you had any previous dealings with this company?* ◆ *I knew nothing of his business dealings.* ◆ *She has always been very polite in her dealings with me.* **2** [U] a way of doing business with someone: *a reputation for fair/honest dealing* **3** [U, C] buying and selling: *drug dealing* ◆ *dealings in shares*

dealt pt, pp of DEAL

dean /din/ *noun* **1** a person in a university who is in charge of a department of studies **2** a person who is responsible for the discipline of students in a college or university: *the dean of students* **3** a priest who is in charge of several priests or churches in an area **4** the most respected or most experienced member of a group or profession SYN DOYEN

dean·er·y /ˈdinəri/ *noun* (*pl.* **dean·er·ies**) **1** a group of PARISHES controlled by a dean **2** the office or house of a dean

ˈdean's list *noun* a list that is published of the best students in a college or university ⊃ compare HONOR ROLL

dear /dɪr/ *adj., exclamation, noun, adv.*

● *adj.* (**dear·er**, **dear·est**) **1** loved by or important to someone: *He's one of my dearest friends.* ◆ **~ to sb** *Her daughter is very dear to her.* **2 Dear** used at the beginning of a letter before the name or title of the person that you are writing to: *Dear Sir or Madam* ◆ *Dear Mrs. Jones*

IDM **dear old/little…** used to describe someone in a way that shows affection: *Dear old Sue! I knew she'd help.* ◆ *Their baby's a dear little thing.* **hold sb/sth dear** (*formal*) to care very much for someone or something; to value someone or something highly: *He had destroyed everything we held dear.* ⊃ more at HEART, LIFE, NEAR *adj.*

● *exclamation* used in expressions that show that you are surprised, upset, annoyed, or worried: *Oh dear! I think I lost my purse!* ◆ *Oh dear! What a shame.* ◆ *Dear me! What a mess!* ◆ *Dear oh dear! What are you going to do now?*

● *noun* **1** (*informal*) a kind person: *Isn't he a dear?* ◆ *Be a dear and fetch me my coat.* **2** used when speaking to someone you love: *Would you like a drink, dear?* ◆ *Come here, my dear.* **3** used when speaking to someone in a friendly way, for example by an older person to a young person or a child: *What's your name, dear?*

● *adv.* IDM see COST

dear·est /ˈdɪrəst/ *adj., noun*

● *adj.* (*old-fashioned*) **1** used when writing to someone you love: *"Dearest Nina," the letter began.* **2** [usually before noun] that you feel deeply: *It was her dearest wish to have a family.*

● *noun* (*old-fashioned*) used when speaking to someone you love: *Come (my) dearest, let's go home.* IDM see NEAR *adj.*

dear·ie /ˈdɪri/ *noun* (*old-fashioned, informal*) used to address someone in a friendly way: *Sit down, dearie.*

dear·ly /ˈdɪrli/ *adv.* **1** very much: *She loves him dearly.* ◆ *I would dearly like/love to know what he was thinking.* ◆ *dearly beloved* (= used by a minister at a Christian church service to address people) **2** in a way that causes a lot of suffering or damage, or that costs a lot of money: *Success has cost him dearly.* ◆ *She paid dearly for her mistake.*

dearth /dərθ/ *noun* [sing.] **~ (of sth)** a lack of something; the fact of there not being enough of something SYN SCARCITY: *There was a dearth of reliable information on the subject.*

death /dɛθ/ *noun*

1 [C] the fact of someone dying or being killed: *a sudden/violent/peaceful, etc. death* ◆ *the anniversary of his wife's death* ◆ *an increase in deaths from cancer* ◆ *He died a slow and painful death.* **2** [U] the end of life; the state of being dead: *The victim bled to death before the ambulance arrived* (= he died as a result of bleeding). ◆ *He's drinking himself to death* (= so that it will kill him). ◆ *Police are trying to establish the **cause of death**.* ◆ *Do you believe in **life after death**?* ◆ *a **death camp*** (= a place where prisoners are killed, usually in a war) ◆ *He was **sentenced to death*** (= to be EXECUTED). **3** [U] **~ of sth** the permanent end or destruction of something: *the death of all my plans* ◆ *the death of fascism* **4** also **Death** [U] (*literary*) the power that destroys life, imagined as human in form: *Death is often shown in paintings as a human skeleton.* ➔ see also SUDDEN DEATH

IDM **at death's door** (*often humorous*) so sick that you may die **be the death of sb** (*informal*) to worry or upset someone very much: *Those kids will be the death of me.* **do sth to death** to do or perform something so often that people become tired of seeing or hearing it: *That joke's been done to death.* **scare/frighten sb to death** to frighten someone very much **look/feel like death warmed over** (*informal*) to look or feel very sick or tired **put sb to death** to kill someone as a punishment **SYN** EXECUTE: *The prisoner will be put to death at dawn.* **to death** extremely; very much: *to be bored to death* ◆ *I'm sick to death of your endless criticism.* **to the death** until someone is dead: *a fight to the death* ➔ more at CATCH *v.*, CHEAT *v.*, DIE *v.*, FATE, FIGHT *v.*, KISS *n.*, LIFE, MATTER *n.*

death·bed /'dεθbεd/ *noun* [usually sing.] the bed in which someone is dying or dies: *a deathbed confession/conversion* ◆ *He told me the truth **on his deathbed*** (= as he lay dying). ◆ *She was **on her deathbed*** (= going to die very soon). ◆ (*humorous*) *You'd have to be practically on your deathbed before the doctor would come and see you!*

death blow *noun* an event that destroys or puts an end to something: *They thought the arrival of television would **deal a death blow** to mass movie audiences.*

death cer·tificate *noun* an official document, signed by a doctor, that states the cause and time of someone's death

death knell (also **death knell**) *noun* [sing.] an event that means that the end or destruction of something will come soon

death·less /'dεθləs/ *adj.* never dying or forgotten **SYN** IMMORTAL: (*ironic*) *written in his usual deathless prose* (= very bad)

death·ly /'dεθli/ (also *less frequent* **dead·ly**) *adv.* like a dead person; suggesting death: *Her face was deathly pale.* ◆ *The house was deathly still.* ▶ **death·ly** *adj.*: *A deathly hush fell over the room as he walked in.*

death mask *noun* a model of the face of a person who has just died, made by pressing a soft substance over his or her face and removing it when it becomes hard

the 'death penalty *noun* [sing.] the punishment of being killed that is used in some countries for very serious crimes **SYN** CAPITAL PUNISHMENT: *the abolition/return of the death penalty* ◆ *The two men are **facing the death penalty**.* ➔ collocations at JUSTICE

death rate *noun* **1** the number of deaths every year for every 1,000 people in the population of a place: *a high/low death rate* **2** the number of deaths every year from a particular disease or in a particular group: *Death rates from heart disease have risen considerably in recent years.*

death rattle *noun* [sing.] **1** a sound sometimes heard in the throat of a dying person **2** the signs that something is failing or coming to an end: *the death rattle of outdated technology*

death row *noun* [U] the cells in a prison for prisoners who are waiting to be killed as punishment for a serious crime: *prisoners on death row* ➔ collocations at JUSTICE

death sentence *noun* the legal punishment of being killed for a serious crime: *to be given/to receive the death sentence* for murder

death's head *noun* a human SKULL (= the bone structure of the head) used as a symbol of death

death squad *noun* a group of people who are ordered by a government to kill other people, especially the government's political opponents

death throes *noun* [pl.] **1** the final stages of something

just before it comes to an end: *The regime is now in its death throes.* **2** violent pains and movements at the moment of death

death toll *noun* the number of people killed in an accident, a war, a disaster, etc.

death trap *noun* (*informal*) a building, vehicle, etc. that is dangerous and could cause someone's death: *The cars blocking the exits could turn this place into a death trap.*

death warrant *noun* an official document stating that someone should receive the punishment of being killed for a crime that they have committed: *The president **signed the death warrant**.* ◆ *If you pay the ransom, you may be signing your son's death warrant.* ◆ (*figurative*) *By withdrawing the funding, the government signed the project's death warrant.*

death·watch bee·tle /'dεθwɑtʃ ˌbitl/ *noun* a small insect that eats into old wood, making sounds like a watch TICKING

death wish *noun* [sing.] a desire to die, often that someone is not aware of

de·ba·cle /dɪ'bɑkl; deɪ-; -'bækl/ *noun* an event or a situation that is a complete failure and causes embarrassment

de·bar /di'bɑr/ *verb* (-rr-) [usually passive] **~ sb (from sth/ from doing sth)** (*formal*) to officially prevent someone from doing something, joining something, etc.: *He was debarred from holding public office.*

de·bark /dɪ'bɑrk/ *verb* [I] = DISEMBARK ▶ **de·bar·ka·tion** /ˌdibɑr'keɪʃn/ *noun* [U]

de·base /dɪ'beɪs/ *verb* **1 ~ sb/sth** to make someone or something less valuable or respected **SYN** DEVALUE: *Professional sports are being debased by commercial sponsorship.* **2 ~ sth** to lower the value of a country's coins by reducing the quantity of valuable metal in them ▶ **de·base·ment** *noun* [U]

de·bat·a·ble **AWL** /dɪ'beɪtəbl/ *adj.* not certain because people can have different ideas and opinions about the thing being discussed **SYN** ARGUABLE, QUESTIONABLE: *a debatable point* ◆ *It is highly debatable whether conditions have improved for low-income families.*

de·bate ✏ **AWL** /dɪ'beɪt/ *noun, verb*

● *noun* [C, U] **~ (on/about/over sth)** **1** an argument or discussion expressing different opinions: *a heated/wide-ranging/lively debate* ◆ *the current debate about taxes* ◆ *There had been much debate on the issue of childcare.* ◆ *Whether he deserves what has happened to him is **open to debate/a matter of/for debate*** (= cannot be certain or decided yet). ◆ *The theater's future is a subject of considerable debate.* **2** a formal discussion of an issue at a public meeting or in government. In a debate, two or more speakers express opposing views and then there is often a vote on the issue: *a debate on abortion* ◆ *The senator **opened the debate*** (= was the first to speak). ◆ *The motion **under debate*** (= being discussed) *was put to a vote.* ◆ *After a long debate, Congress approved the proposal.* ➔ collocations at POLITICS ➔ thesaurus box at DISCUSSION

● *verb* **1** [T, I] to discuss something, especially formally, before making a decision or finding a solution **SYN** DISCUSS: **~ (sth)** *Politicians will be debating the bill later this week.* ◆ *The question of the origin of the universe is still **hotly debated*** (= strongly argued about) *by scientists.* ◆ **~ whether, what, etc....** *The committee will debate whether to lower the age of club membership to 16.* ➔ thesaurus box at TALK **2** [I, T] to think carefully about something before making a decision: **~ (with yourself)** *She debated with herself for a while, and then picked up the phone.* ◆ **~ whether, what, etc....** *We're debating whether or not to go skiing this winter.* ◆ **~ doing sth** *For a moment he debated going after her.* ▶ **de·bat·ing** **AWL** *noun* [U]: *a debating club at a school*

de·bat·er /dɪ'beɪtər/ *noun* a person who is involved in a debate

de·bauched /dɪ'bɔtʃt/ *adj.* a **debauched** person is immoral in their sexual behavior, drinks a lot of alcohol, takes drugs, etc. **SYN** DEPRAVED, DISSOLUTE

de·bauch·er·y /dɪˈbɔtʃəri/ noun [U] immoral behavior involving sex, alcohol, or drugs

de·ben·ture /dɪˈbɛntʃər/ noun (finance) an official document that is given by a company, showing it has borrowed money from a person and stating the INTEREST payments that it will make to them

de·bil·i·tate /dɪˈbɪləˌteɪt/ verb (formal) **1** ~ sb/sth to make someone's body or mind weaker: a debilitating disease **2** ~ sth to make a country, an organization, etc., weaker: Prolonged strikes debilitated the industry.

de·bil·i·ty /dɪˈbɪləti/ noun [U, C] (pl. de·bil·i·ties) (formal) physical weakness, especially as a result of illness ⊃ compare DISABILITY

deb·it /ˈdɛbət/ noun, verb
• **noun 1** a sum of money taken from a bank account **2** a written note in a bank account or other financial record of a sum of money owed or spent: on the debit side of an account ◆ (figurative) On the debit side (= a negative result will be that), the new shopping center will increase traffic problems. **ANT** CREDIT ⊃ see also DIRECT DEBIT
• **verb** ~ sth when a bank **debits** an account, it takes money from it: The money will be debited from your account each month. **ANT** CREDIT

debit ˌcard (also ˈcheck card) noun a plastic card that can be used to take money directly from your bank account when you pay for something ⊃ compare CREDIT CARD

deb·o·nair /ˌdɛbəˈnɛr/ adj. (old-fashioned) (usually of men) fashionable and confident

de·brief /ˌdiˈbrif/ verb ~ sb (on sth) to ask someone questions officially, in order to get information about the task that they have just completed: He was taken to an American air base to be debriefed on the mission. ⊃ compare BRIEF ▸ de·brief·ing noun [U, C]: a debriefing session

de·bris /dəˈbri; deɪ-/ noun [U] **1** pieces of wood, metal, brick, etc., that are left after something has been destroyed: Emergency teams are still clearing the debris from the plane crash. **2** (formal) pieces of material that are not wanted and trash that is left somewhere: Clear away leaves and other garden debris from the pond.

debt /dɛt/ noun
1 [C] a sum of money that someone owes: I need to pay off all my **debts** before I leave the country. ◆ an outstanding debt of $300 ◆ He had run up credit card debts of thousands of dollars. **2** [U] the situation of owing money, especially when you cannot pay: He died heavily **in debt**. ◆ The club is $4 million **in debt**. ◆ We were poor but we never **got into debt**. ◆ It's hard to stay **out of debt** when you are a student. ◆ a country's foreign debt burden ⊃ see also BAD DEBT **3** [C, usually sing.] the fact that you should feel grateful to someone because they have helped you or been kind to you: to owe a debt of gratitude to someone ◆ I would like to acknowledge my debt to my teachers. **IDM** be in sb's debt (formal) to feel grateful to someone for their help, kindness, etc. ⊃ more at PAY

debt·or /ˈdɛtər/ noun a person, a country, or an organization that owes money **ANT** CREDITOR

de·bug /ˌdiˈbʌg/ verb (-gg-) ~ sth (computing) to look for and remove the faults in a computer program

de·bug·ger /ˌdiˈbʌgər/ noun a computer program that helps to find and correct mistakes in other programs

de·bunk /ˌdiˈbʌŋk/ verb ~ sth to show that an idea, a belief, etc., is false; to show that something is not as good as people think it is: His theories have been debunked by recent research.

de·but (also **dé·but**) /deɪˈbyu; ˈdeɪbyu/ noun, verb
• **noun** the first public appearance of a performer or sports player: He will **make his debut** in the major leagues this week. ◆ the band's debut album
• **verb 1** [I] (of a performer or show) to make a first public appearance: The ballet will debut next month in New York.
2 [T] ~ sth (business) to present a new product or advertising campaign to the market: They will debut the products at the trade show.

deb·u·tante /ˈdɛbyuˌtɑnt/ (also informal **deb**) noun a young, rich woman who is going to UPPER-CLASS social events for the first time

deca- /ˈdɛkə/ combining form (in nouns) ten; having ten: decathlon ⊃ compare DECI-

dec·ade /ˈdɛkeɪd/ noun
a period of ten years, especially a period such as 1910–1919 or 1990–1999

dec·a·dence /ˈdɛkədəns/ noun [U] (disapproving) behavior, attitudes, etc., that show a fall in standards, especially moral ones, and an interest in pleasure and enjoyment rather than more serious things: the decadence of modern Western society

dec·a·dent /ˈdɛkədənt/ adj. (disapproving) having or showing low standards, especially moral ones, and an interest only in pleasure and enjoyment rather than serious things: the decadent rich ◆ a decadent lifestyle/society

de·caf /ˈdikæf/ noun [U, C] (informal) decaffeinated coffee: Regular or decaf coffee? ◆ I'll have a decaf, please.

de·caf·fein·at·ed /ˌdiˈkæfəˌneɪtəd/ adj. (of coffee or tea) with most or all of the CAFFEINE removed ▸ de·caf·fein·at·ed noun [U, C]

dec·a·gon /ˈdɛkəˌgɑn/ noun (geometry) a flat shape with ten straight sides and ten angles ▸ de·cag·o·nal /dəˈkægənl/ adj.

de·cal /ˈdikæl/ noun a picture or design that can be removed from a piece of paper and stuck onto a surface, for example by being pressed or heated

dec·a·li·ter (also **dek·a·li·ter**, CanE usually **dec·a·li·tre**) /ˈdɛkəˌlitər/ noun a unit for measuring volume, equal to 10 liters

dec·a·me·ter (also **dek·a·me·ter**, CanE usually **dec·a·me·tre**) /ˈdɛkəˌmitər/ noun a unit for measuring length, equal to 10 meters

de·camp /dɪˈkæmp/ verb [I] ~ (from…) (to…) to leave a place suddenly, often secretly

de·cant /dɪˈkænt/ verb ~ sth (into sth) to pour liquid, especially wine, from one container into another

de·cant·er /dɪˈkæntər/ noun a glass bottle, often decorated, that wine and other alcoholic drinks are poured into from an ordinary bottle before serving

de·cap·i·tate /dɪˈkæpəˌteɪt/ verb ~ sb/sth to cut off someone's head **SYN** BEHEAD: His decapitated body was found floating in a canal. ▸ de·cap·i·ta·tion /dɪˌkæpəˈteɪʃn/ noun [U, C]

de·cath·lete /dɪˈkæθlit/ noun a person who competes in a decathlon

de·cath·lon /dɪˈkæθlɑn; -lən/ noun a sporting event in which people compete in ten different sports ⊃ compare BIATHLON, HEPTATHLON, PENTATHLON, TETRATHLON, TRIATHLON

de·cay /dɪˈkeɪ/ noun, verb
• **noun** [U] **1** the process or result of being destroyed by natural causes or by not being cared for (= of decaying): tooth decay ◆ The landlord had let the building **fall into decay**. ◆ The smell of death and decay hung over the town. **2** the gradual destruction of a society, an institution, a system, etc.: economic/moral/urban decay ◆ the decay of the steel industry
• **verb 1** [I, T] ~ (sth) to be destroyed gradually by natural processes; to destroy something in this way **SYN** ROT: decaying leaves/teeth/food **2** [I] if a building or an area decays, its condition slowly becomes worse: decaying areas of the inner city **3** [I] to become less powerful and lose influence over people, society, etc.: decaying standards of morality

---

de·cease /dɪ'siːs/ noun [U] (law or formal) the death of a person

de·ceased /dɪ'siːst/ adj. (law or formal) **1** dead: *her deceased parents* **2 the deceased** noun (pl. the de·ceased) a person who has died, especially recently

de·ceit /dɪ'siːt/ noun [U, C] dishonest behavior that is intended to make someone believe something that is not true; an example of this behavior **SYN DECEPTION**: *He was accused of lies and deceit.* ♦ *Everyone was involved in this web of deceit.* ♦ *Their marriage was an illusion and a deceit.*

de·ceit·ful /dɪ'siːtfl/ adj. behaving in a dishonest way by telling lies and making people believe things that are not true **SYN DISHONEST** ▶ **de·ceit·ful·ly** /-fəli/ adv. **de·ceit·ful·ness** noun [U]

de·ceive /dɪ'siːv/ verb **1** [T] to make someone believe something that is not true: ~ **sb** *Her husband had been deceiving her for years.* ♦ ~ **sb into doing sth** *She deceived him into handing over all his savings.* ⊃ thesaurus box at CHEAT **2** [T] ~ **yourself (that…)** to refuse to admit to yourself that something unpleasant is true: *You're deceiving yourself if you think he'll change his mind.* **3** [T, I] ~ **(sb)** to make someone have a wrong idea about someone or something **SYN MISLEAD**: *Unless my eyes are deceiving me, that's his wife.* ⊃ see also DECEPTIVE ▶ **de·ceiv·er** noun

WORD FAMILY
deceive verb
deceit noun
deceitful adj.
deception noun
deceptive adj.

de·cel·er·ate /ˌdiː'seləˌreɪt/ verb (formal) **1** [I, T] ~ **(sth)** to reduce the speed at which something, especially a vehicle, is traveling **2** [I, T] ~ **(sth)** to become or make something become slower **SYN SLOW DOWN**: *Economic growth decelerated sharply in June.* **ANT ACCELERATE** ▶ **de·cel·er·a·tion** /ˌdiːseləˈreɪʃn/ noun [U]

De·cem·ber 🔑 /dɪ'sembər/ noun [U, C] (abbr. **Dec.**) the 12th and last month of the year **HELP** To see how **December** is used, look at the examples at **April**.

de·cen·cy /'diːsnsi/ noun **1** [U] honest, polite behavior that follows accepted moral standards and shows respect for others: *Her behavior showed a total lack of **common decency**.* ♦ *Have you no **sense of decency**?* ♦ *He might **have had the decency to** apologize.* **2 the decencies** [pl.] (formal) standards of behavior in society that people think are acceptable: *the basic decencies of civilized society*

de·cent 🔑 /'diːsnt/ adj. **1** of a good enough standard or quality: (informal) *a decent meal/job/place to live* ♦ *I need a decent night's sleep.* **2** (of people or behavior) honest and fair; treating people with respect: *ordinary, decent, hard-working people* ♦ *Everyone said he was a pretty decent guy.* **3** acceptable to people in a particular situation: *a decent burial* ♦ *That dress isn't decent.* ♦ *She should have waited for a decent amount of time before getting married again.* **4** (informal) wearing enough clothes to allow someone to see you: *I can't go to the door—I'm not decent.* ⊃ compare INDECENT ▶ **de·cent·ly** adv.
IDM **do the decent thing** to do what people or society expect, especially in a difficult situation: *He did the decent thing and resigned.*

de·cen·tral·ize /ˌdiː'sentrəˌlaɪz/ verb [T, I] ~ **(sth)** to give some of the power of a central government, organization, etc., to smaller parts or organizations around the country: *decentralized authority/administration* **ANT CENTRALIZE** ▶ **de·cen·tral·i·za·tion** /ˌdiːsentrələˈzeɪʃn/ noun [U, sing.]

de·cep·tion /dɪ'sepʃn/ noun **1** [U] the act of deliberately making someone believe something that is not true (= of deceiving (DECEIVE) them) **SYN DECEIT**: *a drama full of lies and deception* ♦ *He was accused of obtaining property by deception.* **2** [C] a trick intended to make someone believe something that is not true **SYN DECEIT**: *The whole episode had been a cruel deception.*

de·cep·tive /dɪ'septɪv/ adj. likely to make you believe something that is not true **SYN MISLEADING**: *a deceptive advertisement* ♦ *Appearances can often be deceptive* (= things are not always what they seem to be). ♦ *the deceptive simplicity of her writing style* (= it seems simple but is not really) ▶ **de·cep·tive·ly** adv.: *a deceptively simple idea*

deci- /'desɪ/ combining form (in nouns; often used in units of measurement) one tenth: *deciliter* ⊃ compare DECA-

dec·i·bel /'desəbl; -ˌbel/ noun a unit for measuring how loud a sound is

de·cide 🔑 /dɪ'saɪd/ verb
1 [I, T] to think carefully about the different possibilities that are available and choose one of them: *It's up to you to decide.* ♦ ~ **between A and B** *It was difficult to decide between the two candidates.* ♦ ~ **against sth** *They decided against taking legal action.* ♦ ~ **what, whether, etc.…** *I can't decide what to wear.* ♦ ~ **(that)…** *She decided (that) she wanted to live in France.* ♦ ~ **to do sth** *We decided not to go away after all.* ♦ ~ **sth** *We might be hiring more people, but nothing has been decided yet.* ♦ **it is decided (that)…** *It was decided (that) the school should purchase new software.* ⊃ thesaurus box at CHOOSE **2** [T, I] (law) to make an official or legal judgment: ~ **sth** *The case will be decided by a jury.* ♦ ~ **for/in favor of sb** | ~ **in sb's favor** *The court of appeals decided in their favor.* ♦ ~ **against sb** *It is always possible that the judge may decide against you.* **3** [T, I] to affect the result of something: ~ **(sth)** *A mixture of skill and good luck decided the outcome of the game.* ♦ ~ **if, whether, etc.…** *A number of factors decide whether a movie will be successful or not.* **4** [T] to be the reason why someone does something: *For most customers, price is **the deciding factor**.*
PHRV **de·cide on/upon sth** to choose something from a number of possibilities: *We're still trying to decide on a venue.*

WORD FAMILY
decide verb
decision noun (≠ indecision)
decisive adj. (≠ indecisive)
undecided adj.

de·cid·ed /dɪ'saɪdəd/ adj. [only before noun] obvious and definite: *His height was a decided advantage in the job.* ⊃ compare UNDECIDED

de·cid·ed·ly /dɪ'saɪdədli/ adv. **1** (used with an adjective or adverb) definitely and in an obvious way: *Amy was looking decidedly worried.* **2** in a way that shows that you are sure and determined about something: *"I won't go," she said decidedly.*

de·cid·er /dɪ'saɪdər/ noun [usually sing.] the game, race, etc., that will decide who the winner is in a competition

de·cid·u·ous /dɪ'sɪdʒuəs/ adj. (of a tree, bush, etc.) that loses its leaves every year ⊃ compare EVERGREEN

dec·ile /'desaɪl; 'desl/ noun (statistics) one of ten equal groups into which a collection of things or people can be divided according to the DISTRIBUTION of a particular VARIABLE: *families in the top decile of income* (= the 10% of families with the highest income)

dec·i·li·ter (CanE usually **dec·i·li·tre**) /'desəˌliːtər/ noun a unit for measuring liquids. There are 10 deciliters in a liter.

dec·i·mal /'desəml/ adj., noun
• adj. based on or counted in tens or tenths: *the decimal system*
• noun (also **decimal fraction**) a FRACTION (= a number less than one) that is shown as a dot or point followed by the number of tenths, HUNDREDTHS, etc.: *The decimal 0.61 stands for 61 hundredths.* ⊃ see also REPEATING DECIMAL

dec·i·mal·ize /'desəməˌlaɪz/ verb **1** ~ **sth** to change a system of coins or weights and measurements to a decimal system **2** ~ **sth** to express an amount using the decimal system instead of the system it is already expressed in: *The question asks you to decimalize the fraction ⅞.* ▶ **dec·i·mal·i·za·tion** /ˌdesəmələˈzeɪʃn/ noun [U]

ˈdecimal ˌplace noun the position of a number after a decimal point: *The figure is **accurate to two decimal places**.*

ˈdecimal ˌpoint noun a dot or point used to separate the whole number from the tenths, HUNDREDTHS, etc., of a decimal, for example in 0.61

h **h**at   m **m**an   n **n**o   ŋ si**ng**   l **l**eg   r **r**ed   y **y**es   w **w**et

dec·i·mate /ˈdesəˌmeɪt/ verb **1** [usually passive] ~ sth to kill large numbers of animals, plants, or people in a particular area: *The rabbit population was decimated by the disease.* **2** ~ sth (*informal*) to severely damage something or make something weaker: *Cheap imports decimated the American auto industry.* ▶ **dec·i·ma·tion** /ˌdesəˈmeɪʃn/ noun [U]

de·ci·pher /dɪˈsaɪfər/ verb ~ sth to succeed in finding the meaning of something that is difficult to read or understand **SYN** DECODE (1): *to decipher a code* ◆ *Can anyone decipher his handwriting?* ⟳ see also INDECIPHERABLE

de·ci·sion 🔑 /dɪˈsɪʒn/ noun
1 [C] ~ (on/about sth) | ~ (to do sth) a choice or judgment that you make after thinking and talking about what is the best thing to do: *to make a decision* (= to decide) ◆ *We need a decision on this by next week.* ◆ *Who made the decision to go ahead with the project?* ◆ *He is really bad at making decisions.* ◆ *We finally reached a decision* (= decided after some difficulty). ◆ *We must come to a decision about what to do next by tomorrow.* ◆ *a big* (= an important) *decision* ◆ *The final decision is yours.* ◆ *It's a difficult decision for any doctor.* ◆ *The editor's decision is final.* ◆ *Mary is the decision-maker in the house.* **2** (also **de·ci·sive·ness**) [U] the ability to decide something clearly and quickly: *This is not a job for someone who lacks decision.* **ANT** INDECISION **3** [U] the process of deciding something: *The moment of decision had arrived.*

de·cision-ˌmaking noun [U] the process of deciding about something important, especially in a group of people or in an organization ▶ **de·cision-ˌmaker** noun

de·ci·sive /dɪˈsaɪsɪv/ adj. **1** very important for the final result of a particular situation: *a decisive factor/victory/battle/action* ◆ *She has played a decisive role in the peace negotiations.* ◆ *a decisive step* (= an important action that will change a situation) *toward a cleaner environment* ⟳ thesaurus box at ESSENTIAL **2** able to decide something quickly and with confidence: *decisive management* ◆ *The government must take decisive action on gun control.* **ANT** INDECISIVE ▶ **de·ci·sive·ly** adv.

de·ci·sive·ness /dɪˈsaɪsɪvnəs/ noun [U] = DECISION

deck /dek/ noun, verb
● **noun 1** the top outside floor of a ship or boat: *I was the only person on deck at that time of night.* ◆ *As the storm began, everyone disappeared below deck(s).* **2** one of the floors of a ship, bus, plane, or sports STADIUM: *the upper/lower/main deck of a ship* ◆ *We sat on the top deck of the bus.* ◆ *the upper deck of Yankee Stadium* ⟳ see also DOUBLE-DECKER, FLIGHT DECK, SINGLE-DECKER **3** (also ˌdeck of ˈcards) (also pack) a complete set of 52 PLAYING CARDS **4** a wooden floor that is built outside the back of a house where you can sit and relax **5** a part of a SOUND SYSTEM that records and/or plays sounds on a disk or tape: *a cassette/tape deck* **IDM** see CLEAR v., HAND n., HIT v.
● **verb 1** [often passive] ~ sb/sth (out) (in/with sth) to decorate someone or something with something: *The room was decked out in flowers and balloons.* **2** ~ sb (*informal*) to hit someone very hard so that they fall to the ground **IDM** on deck (in baseball) next in line to hit the ball: *One of their best batters is on deck.*

ˈdeck chair noun a folding chair with a seat made from a long strip of material on a wooden or metal frame, used for example on a beach ⟳ picture at CHAIR

deck·hand /ˈdekhænd/ noun a worker on a ship who does work that is not skilled

deck·ing /ˈdekɪŋ/ noun [U] wood used to build a deck

ˈdeck shoe noun a flat shoe made of strong cloth or soft leather, with a soft SOLE that does not slip

de·claim /dɪˈkleɪm/ verb [T, I] ~ (against) sth | ~ that... | + speech (*formal*) to say something loudly; to speak loudly and with force about something you feel strongly about, especially in public: *She declaimed the famous opening speech of the play.* ◆ *He declaimed against the evils of alcohol.*

dec·la·ma·tion /ˌdekləˈmeɪʃn/ noun (*formal*) **1** [U] the act of speaking or expressing something to an audience in a

formal way **2** [C] a speech or piece of writing that strongly expresses feelings and opinions

de·clam·a·to·ry /dɪˈklæməˌtɔri/ adj. (*formal*) expressing feelings or opinions in a strong way in a speech or a piece of writing

dec·la·ra·tion /ˌdekləˈreɪʃn/ noun **1** [C, U] an official or formal statement, especially about the plans of a government or an organization; the act of making such a statement: *to issue/sign a declaration* ◆ *the declaration of war* ◆ *the Declaration of Independence* **2** [C] a written or spoken statement, especially about what people feel or believe: *a declaration of love/faith/guilt* **3** [C] an official written statement giving information: *a declaration of income* ◆ *customs declarations* (= giving details of goods that have been brought into a country)

the Decla·ra·tion of Inde·pendence noun [sing.] the document that stated that the thirteen British COLONIES in America were independent of Britain. It was adopted on July 4, 1776.

de·clar·a·tive /dɪˈklærətɪv/ adj. (*grammar*) (of a sentence) in the form of a simple statement ⟳ compare EXCLAMATORY, INTERROGATIVE adj.

THESAURUS

declare

state ◆ indicate ◆ announce

These words all mean to say something, usually firmly and clearly and often in public.

declare (*somewhat formal*) to say something officially or publicly; to state something firmly and clearly: *to declare war* ◆ *The painting was declared (to be) a forgery.*

state (*somewhat formal*) to formally write or say something, especially in a careful and clear way: *He has already stated his intention to run for re-election.*

indicate (*somewhat formal*) to state something, sometimes in a way that is slightly indirect: *During our meeting, he indicated his willingness to cooperate.*

announce to tell people officially about a decision or plans; to give information about something in a public place, especially through a loudspeaker; to say something in a loud and/or serious way: *They haven't formally announced their engagement yet.* ◆ *Has our flight been announced yet?*

DECLARE OR ANNOUNCE?

Declare is used more often for giving judgments; **announce** is used more often for giving facts: ~~The painting was announced to be a forgery.~~ ◆ ~~They haven't formally declared their engagement yet.~~

PATTERNS

- to declare/state/indicate/announce **that...**
- to declare/state/indicate/announce **your intention** to do sth
- to declare/state/announce sth **formally/publicly/officially**
- to declare/state/announce sth **firmly/confidently**

---

de·clare 🔑 /dɪˈkler/ verb
1 [T] to say something officially or publicly: ~ sth *The government has declared a state of emergency.* ◆ *Germany declared war on France on August 3, 1914.* ◆ *The government has declared war on* (= officially stated its intention to stop) *illiteracy.* ◆ ~ **that...** *The court declared that the strike was illegal.* ◆ ~ **sth + noun** *The area has been declared a national park.* ◆ ~ **sth to be sth** *The painting was declared to be a forgery.* ◆ ~ **sth + adj.** *The contract was declared void.* ◆ *I declare this bridge open.* **2** [T] to state something firmly and clearly: + **speech** *"I'll do it!" Tom declared.* ◆ ~ **that...** *He declared that he was in love with her.* ◆ ~ **sth** *Few people dared to declare their opposition to the regime.* ◆ ~ **yourself + adj./noun** *She declared herself extremely hurt by his lack of support.*

---

3 [T] ~ **sth** to tell the tax authorities how much money you have earned: *All income must be declared.* **4** [T] ~ **sth** to tell customs officers (= at the border of a country) that you are carrying goods on which you should pay tax: *Do you have anything to declare?*

PHR V declare a·gainst sb/sth (*formal*) to say publicly that you do not support someone or something de·clare for sb/sth (*formal*) to say publicly that you support someone or something

de·clared /dɪˈklɛrd/ *adj.* [only before noun] stated in an open way so that people know about it **SYN** PROFESSED: *the government's declared intention to reduce crime*

de·clas·si·fy /ˌdiˈklæsəˌfaɪ/ *verb* (de·clas·si·fies, de·clas·si·fy·ing, de·clas·si·fied, de·clas·si·fied) ~ **sth** to state officially that secret government information is no longer secret **ANT** CLASSIFY: *declassified information/documents* **ANT** CLASSIFY ▶ de·clas·si·fi·ca·tion /ˌdiˌklæsəfəˈkeɪʃn/ *noun* [U]

de·clen·sion /dɪˈklɛnʃn/ *noun* (*grammar*) **1** [C] a set of nouns, adjectives, or pronouns that change in the same way to show CASE, number, and GENDER **2** [U] the way in which some sets of nouns, adjectives, and pronouns change their form or endings to show CASE, number, or GENDER

de·cline 🔑 **AWL** /dɪˈklaɪn/ *noun, verb*

● **noun** [C, usually sing., U] ~ **(in sth)** | ~ **(of sth)** a continuous decrease in the number, value, quality, etc. of something: *a rapid/sharp/gradual decline* ◆ *urban/economic decline* ◆ *The company reported a small decline in its profits.* ◆ *An increase in cars on the roads has resulted in the decline of public transport.* ◆ *The town fell into (a) decline* (= started to be less busy, important, etc.) *after the mine closed.* ◆ *The steel industry in the United States has been in decline since the 1970s.*

● **verb 1** [I] to become smaller, fewer, weaker, etc.: *Support for the candidate continues to decline.* ◆ *The number of tourists going to the resort declined by 10% last year.* ◆ *Her health was declining rapidly.* **2** [I, T] (*formal*) to refuse politely to accept or to do something **SYN** REFUSE¹: *I offered to give them a ride but they declined.* ◆ ~ **sth** *to decline an offer/invitation* ◆ ~ **to do sth** *Their spokesman declined to comment on the allegations.* **3** [I, T] ~ **(sth)** (*grammar*) if a noun, an adjective, or a pronoun **declines**, it has different forms according to whether it is the subject or the object of a verb, whether it is in the singular or plural, etc. When you **decline** a noun, etc., you list these forms. ➲ compare CONJUGATE

IDM sb's declining years (*literary*) the last years of someone's life

de·clut·ter /ˌdiˈklʌtər/ *verb* [I, T] to remove things that you do not use so that you have more space and can easily find things when you need them: *Moving is a good opportunity to declutter.* ◆ ~ **sth** *a 7-step plan to help you declutter your home*

de·code /diˈkoʊd/ *verb* **1** ~ **sth** to find the meaning of something, especially something that has been written in code **SYN** DECIPHER **2** ~ **sth** to receive an electronic signal and change it into pictures that can be shown on a television screen: *decoding equipment* **3** ~ **sth** (*linguistics*) to understand the meaning of something in a foreign language ➲ compare ENCODE

de·cod·er /diˈkoʊdər/ *noun* a device that changes an electronic signal into a form that people can understand, such as sound and pictures: *a satellite/video decoder*

dé·colle·tage /ˌdeɪkɑləˈtɑʒ; ˌdeɪkɔlˈtɑʒ; ˌdekələ-/ *noun* (from French) the top edge of a woman's dress, etc. that is designed to be very low in order to show her shoulders and the top part of her breasts ▶ dé·colle·té /-ˈteɪ/ *adj.*

de·col·o·ni·za·tion /ˌdiˌkɑlənəˈzeɪʃn/ *noun* [U] the process of a COLONY or colonies becoming independent

de·com·mis·sion /ˌdikəˈmɪʃn/ *verb* ~ **sth** to officially stop using weapons, a nuclear power station, etc.

de·com·pose /ˌdikəmˈpoʊz/ *verb* **1** [I, T] to be destroyed gradually by natural chemical processes **SYN** DECAY, ROT: *a decomposing corpse* ◆ *As the waste materials decompose, they*

produce methane gas. ◆ ~ **sth** *a decomposed body* **2** [T, I] ~ **(sth) (into sth)** (*technical*) to divide something into smaller parts; to divide into smaller parts ▶ de·com·po·si·tion /ˌdiˌkɑmpəˈzɪʃn/ *noun* [U]: *the decomposition of organic waste*

de·com·press /ˌdikəmˈprɛs/ *verb* **1** [I, T] ~ **(sth)** to have the air pressure in something reduced to a normal level or to reduce it to its normal level **2** ~ **sth** (*computing*) to return files, etc. to their original size after they have been COMPRESSED **ANT** COMPRESS

de·com·pres·sion /ˌdikəmˈprɛʃn/ *noun* [U] **1** a reduction in air pressure; the act of reducing the pressure of the air: *a decompression chamber* (= a piece of equipment that DIVERS sit in so that they can return slowly to normal air pressure after being deep in the ocean) ◆ *decompression sickness* (= severe pain and difficulty in breathing experienced by DIVERS who come back to the surface of deep water too quickly) ➲ see also BEND *n.* (2) **2** (*technical*) the act or process of allowing something that has been compressed (= made smaller) to fill the space that it originally took up

de·com·pres·sor /ˌdikəmˈprɛsər/ *noun* (*computing*) a computer program that returns files, etc. to their original size after they have been COMPRESSED

de·con·ges·tant /ˌdikənˈdʒɛstənt/ *noun* a medicine that helps someone with a cold to breathe more easily: *a nasal decongestant*

de·con·se·crate /ˌdiˈkɑnsəˌkreɪt/ *verb* ~ **sth** (*religion*) to stop using something, especially a building, for a religious purpose: *a deconsecrated church* ▶ de·con·se·cra·tion /ˌdiˌkɑnsəˈkreɪʃn/ *noun* [U]

de·con·struct /ˌdikənˈstrʌkt/ *verb* ~ **sth** (*technical*) (in literature and philosophy) to analyze a text in order to show that there is no fixed meaning within the text but that the meaning is created each time in the act of reading

de·con·struc·tion /ˌdikənˈstrʌkʃn/ *noun* [U] (*technical*) (in literature and philosophy) a theory that states that it is impossible for a text to have one fixed meaning, and emphasizes the role of the reader in the production of meaning ➲ compare STRUCTURALISM ▶ de·con·struc·tion·ist /-ˈʃənɪst/ *noun, adj.*: *a deconstructionist critic/approach*

de·con·tam·i·nate /ˌdikənˈtæməˌneɪt/ *verb* ~ **sth** to remove harmful substances from a place or thing: *the process of decontaminating areas exposed to radioactivity* ▶ de·con·tam·i·na·tion /ˌdikənˌtæməˈneɪʃn/ *noun* [U]

de·con·trol /ˌdikənˈtroʊl/ *verb* (-ll-) ~ **sth** (*formal*) if a government **decontrols** something, it removes legal controls from it **SYN** DEREGULATE ▶ de·con·trol *noun* [U]

de·cor (also dé·cor) /deɪˈkɔr; dɪ-/ *noun* [U, C, usually sing.] the style in which the inside of a building is decorated: *interior decor* ◆ *the restaurant's elegant new decor*

dec·o·rate 🔑 /ˈdɛkəˌreɪt/ *verb*

1 [T] ~ **sth (with sth)** to make something look more attractive by putting things on it: *They decorated the room with flowers and balloons.* ◆ *The cake was decorated to look like a car.* **2** [T] ~ **sth** to be placed on something in order to make it look more attractive **SYN** ADORN: *Photographs of actors decorated the walls of the restaurant.* **3** [I, T] to put paint, WALLPAPER, etc. on the walls and ceilings of a room or house: ~ **sth** *We need to decorate the living room.* ◆ *The living room needs decorating.* **4** [T, usually passive] ~ **sb (for sth)** to give someone a MEDAL as a sign of respect for something they have done

TOPIC COLLOCATIONS

Decorating and Home Improvement

houses

- **refurbish/renovate** a building/a house
- **convert** a building/house/room into homes/offices/apartments/condominiums/condos
- **extend/enlarge** a house/building/room/kitchen
- **build** an addition (on/to sth)/a sunroom/a deck

ʌ **cup**   ə **about**   eɪ **say**   aɪ **five**   ɔɪ **boy**   aʊ **now**   oʊ **go**   ər **bird**

- **knock down/demolish** a house/home/building/wall
- **knock out/down** the wall separating two rooms

decoration

- **furnish/paint/repaint** a home/house/apartment/room
- **be decorated** in bright colors/in a traditional style/with flowers/with paintings
- **paint/plaster** the walls/ceiling
- **hang/put up/strip off/remove** (the) wallpaper
- **install/replace/remove** the bathroom fixtures
- **build/put up** shelves
- **lay** wooden flooring/timber decking/floor tiles/a carpet/a patio floor
- **put up/hang/take down** a picture/painting/poster/curtain

home improvement

- **do** carpentry/the plumbing/the wiring (yourself)
- **make** home improvements
- **add/install** central heating/underfloor heating/insulation
- **install** double-glazing/a smoke alarm
- **insulate** your house/your home/the walls/the pipes/the tanks/the attic
- **fix/repair** a roof/a leak/a pipe/the plumbing/a leaking faucet
- **block/clog (up)/unblock/unclog** a pipe/sink/drain
- **make/drill/fill** a hole
- **hammer (in)/pull out/remove** a nail
- **tighten/loosen/remove** a screw
- **saw/cut/treat/stain/varnish/paint** wood

dec·o·ra·tion ✐ /ˌdekəˈreɪʃn/ noun
1 [C, usually pl.] a thing that makes something look more attractive on special occasions: *Christmas decorations* ◆ *a table decoration* **2** [U, C] a pattern, etc. that is added to something and that stops it from being plain: *the elaborate decoration on the carved wooden door* **3** [U] the style in which something is decorated: *a Chinese theme in the interior decoration* **4** [C] a MEDAL that is given to someone as an honor

dec·o·ra·tive ✐ /ˈdekrətɪv; ˈdekərə-/ adj.
(of an object or a building) decorated in a way that makes it attractive; intended to look attractive or pretty: *The mirror is functional yet decorative.* ◆ *purely decorative arches*

decorative ˈarts noun [pl.] artistic activities that produce objects which are useful and beautiful at the same time

dec·o·ra·tor /ˈdekəˌreɪtər/ noun a person whose job is decorating the inside of a building: *an interior decorator*

dec·o·rous /ˈdekərəs/ adj. (formal) polite and appropriate in a particular social situation; not shocking **SYN** PROPER: *a decorous kiss* ▶ **dec·o·rous·ly** adv.

de·co·rum /dɪˈkɔrəm/ noun [U] (formal) polite behavior that is appropriate in a social situation **SYN** PROPRIETY

de·cou·page /ˌdeɪkuˈpɑʒ/ noun [U] (art) the art of decorating furniture or other objects by cutting out pictures or designs on paper and sticking them onto the surface

de·cou·ple /diˈkʌpl/ verb ~ **sth (from sth)** (formal) to end the connection or relationship between two things

de·coy /ˈdikɔɪ/ noun [C] **1** an animal or a bird, or a model of one, that attracts other animals or birds, especially so that they can be shot by people who are hunting them **2** a thing or a person that is used to trick someone into doing what you want them to do; going where you want them to go, etc. ▶ **de·coy** /dɪˈkɔɪ/ verb ~ **sth**

de·crease ✐ verb, noun
- *verb* /dɪˈkris; ˈdikris/ [I, T] to become or make something become smaller in size, number, etc.: ~ **(from sth) (to sth)** *The number of new students decreased from 210 to 160 this year.* ◆ *a decreasing population* ◆ ~ **by sth** *The price of wheat*

has decreased by 5%. ◆ ~ **in sth** *This species of bird is decreasing in numbers every year.* ◆ ~ **sth** *People should decrease the amount of fat they eat.* **ANT** INCREASE
- *noun* /ˈdikris; dɪˈkris/ [C, U] the process of reducing something or the amount that something is reduced by **SYN** REDUCTION: ~ **(in sth)** *There has been some decrease in military spending this year.* ◆ ~ **(of sth)** *a decrease of nearly 6% in the number of visitors to the museum* **ANT** INCREASE

de·cree /dɪˈkri/ noun, verb
- *noun* **1** [C, U] an official order from a ruler or a government that becomes the law: *to issue/sign a decree* ◆ *a leader who rules by decree* (= not in a democratic way) **2** [C] a decision that is made in court
- *verb* (**de·cree·ing, de·creed, de·creed**) [T, I] to decide, judge, or order something officially: ~ **(sth)** *The government decreed a state of emergency.* ◆ ~ **what, how, etc....** *We cannot decree what the committee should do.* ◆ **it is decreed that...** *It was decreed that the following day would be a holiday.*

de·crep·it /dɪˈkrepɪt/ adj. (of a thing or person) very old and not in good condition or health

de·crep·i·tude /dɪˈkrepəˌtud/ noun [U] (formal) the state of being old and in poor condition or health

de·crim·i·nal·ize /ˌdiˈkrɪmənəˌlaɪz/ verb ~ **sth** to change the law so that something is no longer illegal: *There are moves to decriminalize some soft drugs.* **ANT** CRIMINALIZE ▶ **de·crim·i·nal·i·za·tion** /ˌdiˌkrɪmənələˈzeɪʃn/ noun [U]

de·cry /dɪˈkraɪ/ verb (**de·cries, de·cry·ing, de·cried, de·cried**) ~ **sb/sth (as sth)** (formal) to strongly criticize someone or something, especially publicly **SYN** CONDEMN: *The measures were decried as useless.*

de·crypt /diˈkrɪpt/ verb ~ **sth** (computing) to change information that is in code into ordinary language so that it can be understood by anyone **ANT** ENCRYPT ▶ **de·cryp·tion** /diˈkrɪpʃn/ noun [U] **ANT** ENCRYPTION

ded·i·cate /ˈdedəˌkeɪt/ verb **1** to give a lot of your time and effort to a particular activity or purpose because you think it is important **SYN** DEVOTE: ~ **yourself/sth to sth** *She dedicates herself to her work.* ◆ ~ **yourself/sth to doing sth** *He dedicated his life to helping the poor.* **2** ~ **sth to sb** to say at the beginning of a book, a piece of music, or a performance that you are doing it for someone, as a way of thanking them or showing respect: *This book is dedicated to my parents.* **3** to hold an official ceremony to say that a building or an object has a special purpose or is special to the memory of a particular person: ~ **sth** *The chapel was dedicated in 1880.* ◆ ~ **sth to sb/sth** *A memorial stone was dedicated to those who were killed in the war.*

ded·i·cat·ed /ˈdedəˌkeɪtəd/ adj. **1** working hard at something because it is very important to you **SYN** COMMITTED: *a dedicated teacher* ◆ ~ **to sth** *She is dedicated to her job.* **2** [only before noun] designed to do only one particular type of work; used for one particular purpose only: *Software is exported through a dedicated satellite link.*

ded·i·ca·tion /ˌdedəˈkeɪʃn/ noun **1** [U] ~ **(to sth)** (approving) the hard work and effort that someone puts into an activity or purpose because they think it is important **SYN** COMMITMENT: *hard work and dedication* **2** [C] a ceremony that is held to show that a building or an object has a special purpose or is special to the memory of a particular person **3** [C] the words that are used at the beginning of a book, piece of music, a performance, etc., to offer it to someone as a sign of thanks or respect

de·duce **AWL** /dɪˈdus/ verb (formal) to form an opinion about something based on the information or evidence that is available **SYN** INFER: ~ **sth (from sth)** *We can deduce a lot from what people choose to buy.* ◆ ~ **(from sth) that, what, how, etc....** *Can we deduce from your silence that you do not approve?* ⊃ see also DEDUCTION ▶ **de·duc·i·ble** /dɪˈdusəbl/ adj.

de·duct /dɪˈdʌkt/ verb [often passive] to take away money, points, etc., from a total amount **SYN** SUBTRACT: ~ **sth** *Ten* *points will be deducted for a wrong answer.* ◆ ~ **sth from sth** *The cost of your uniform will be deducted from your wages.*

de·duct·i·ble /dɪˈdʌktəbl/ *adj., noun*
- *adj.* that can be taken away from an amount of money you earn, from tax, etc.: *These costs are deductible from profits.* ◆ *tax-deductible expenses* (= that you do not have to pay tax on)
- *noun* the part of an insurance claim that a person has to pay while the insurance company pays the rest: *a policy with a very high deductible*

de·duc·tion AWL /dɪˈdʌkʃn/ *noun* **1** [U, C] the process of using information you have in order to understand a particular situation or to find the answer to a problem: *He arrived at the solution by a simple process of deduction.* ◆ *If my deductions are correct, I can tell you who the killer was.* ⊃ see also DEDUCE ⊃ compare INDUCTION **2** [U, C] the process of taking a certain amount of something, especially money, away from a total; the amount that is taken away: *deductions from your pay for taxes, etc.* ◆ *tax deductions*

de·duc·tive /dɪˈdʌktɪv/ *adj.* [usually before noun] using knowledge about things that are generally true in order to think about and understand particular situations or problems: *deductive logic/reasoning* ⊃ compare INDUCTIVE

deed /diːd/ *noun* **1** (*formal, literary*) a thing that someone does that is usually very good or very bad SYN ACT: *a brave/charitable/evil/good deed* ◆ *a tale of heroic deeds* **2** a legal document that you sign, especially one that proves that you own a house or a building: *the deed to the house* ⊃ see also TITLE DEED
IDM **your good deed for the day** a helpful, kind thing that you do

dee·jay /ˈdiːdʒeɪ/ *noun, verb*
- *noun* (*informal*) = DISC JOCKEY
- *verb* [I] to perform as a DISC JOCKEY, especially in a club

deem /diːm/ *verb* ~ **sth** + **noun/adj.** | ~ **sth to be sth** | ~ **(that)…** (*formal*) (not usually used in the progressive tenses) to have a particular opinion about something SYN CONSIDER: *The evening was deemed a great success.* ◆ *She deemed it prudent not to say anything.* ◆ *They would take any action deemed necessary.*

deep 🔑 /diːp/ *adj., adv., noun*
- *adj.* (**deep·er, deep·est**)
> TOP TO BOTTOM **1** having a large distance from the top or surface to the bottom: *a deep hole/well/river* ◆ *deep water/snow* ANT SHALLOW

WORD FAMILY
deep *adj., adv.*
deeply *adv.*
deepen *verb*
depth *noun*

> FRONT TO BACK **2** having a large distance from the front edge to the farthest point inside: *a deep cut/wound* ◆ *a deep space* ANT SHALLOW
> MEASUREMENT **3** used to describe or ask about the depth of something: *The water is only a few inches deep.* ◆ *How deep is the wound?*
> -DEEP **4** (in adjectives) as far up or down as the point mentioned: *The water was only waist-deep so I walked ashore.* **5** (in adjectives) in the number of rows mentioned, one behind the other: *They were standing three-deep at the bar.*
> BREATH/SIGH **6** [usually before noun] taking in or giving out a lot of air: *She took a deep breath.* ◆ *He gave a deep sigh.*
> SOUNDS **7** low: *I heard his deep warm voice filling the room.* ◆ *a deep roar/groan*
> COLORS **8** strong and dark: *a rich deep red* ANT PALE
> SLEEP **9** a person in a **deep** sleep is difficult to wake: *to be in a deep sleep/trance/coma* ANT LIGHT
> SERIOUS **10** extreme or serious: *He's in deep trouble.* ◆ *a deep economic recession* ◆ *The affair had exposed deep divisions within the party.* ◆ *a place of great power and of deep significance*
> EMOTIONS **11** strongly felt SYN SINCERE: *deep respect* ◆ *a deep sense of loss*
> KNOWLEDGE **12** showing great knowledge or understanding: *a deep understanding*
> DIFFICULT TO UNDERSTAND **13** difficult to understand

SYN PROFOUND: *This discussion's getting too deep for me.* ◆ *He pondered, as if over some deep philosophical point.*
> PERSON **14** serious and thinking hard about complex issues: *She's a very deep person, extremely intelligent.* ANT SHALLOW
> INVOLVED **15** ~ **in sth** fully involved in an activity or a state: *to be deep in thought/conversation* ◆ *He is often so deep in his books that he forgets to eat.* ◆ *The firm ended up deep in debt.*
> IN SPORTS **16** a deep ball is hit, thrown, or kicked to or from a position far down or across the field: *Fiedler throws a good deep ball.* ⊃ see also DEPTH
IDM **go off the deep end** (*informal*) to suddenly become very angry or emotional **in deep water(s)** (*informal*) in trouble or difficulty **jump/be thrown in/into the deep end** (*informal*) to start or be made to start a new and difficult activity that you are not prepared for: *Medical interns are thrown in the deep end in their first jobs.* ⊃ more at DEVIL
- *adv.* (**deep·er, deep·est**) ~ **(below, into, under, etc.)** a long way below the surface of something or a long way inside or into something: *Dig deeper!* ◆ *The miners were trapped deep underground.* ◆ *whales that feed deep beneath the waves* ◆ *He gazed deep into her eyes.* ◆ *They sat and talked deep into the night* (= until very late). ◆ *deep in the forest* ◆ *He stood with his hands deep in his pockets.*
IDM **deep down 1** if you know something **deep down**, you know your true feelings about something, although you may not admit them to yourself: *Deep down I still loved him.* **2** if something is true **deep down**, it is really like that, although it may not be obvious to people: *He seems confident but deep down he's quite insecure.* **go/run deep** (of emotions, beliefs, etc.) to be felt in a strong way, especially for a long time: *Dignity and pride run deep in this community.* **in (too) deep** very involved in a situation: *He knew he was in deep when his new girlfriend got him an expensive birthday gift.* ⊃ more at DIG *v.*, STILL *adj.*
- *noun* [sing.] **the deep** (*literary*) the ocean

WHICH WORD?

deep ◦ deeply
■ The adverbs **deep** and **deeply** can both mean "a long way down or into something." **Deep** can mean only this and is more common than **deeply** in this sense. It is usually followed by a word like *into* or *below*: *We decided to go deeper into the jungle.*
■ **Deeply** usually means "very much": *deeply in love* ◆ *deeply hurt.* You can use **deep down** (but not **deeply**) to talk about a person's real nature: *She can seem stern, but deep down she's a very kind person.* ◆ ~~She can seem stern, but deeply she's a very kind person.~~

deep-'dyed *adj.* having a particular characteristic or opinion very strongly: *a deep-dyed socialist*

deep·en /ˈdiːpən/ *verb* **1** [I, T] ~ **(sth) (into sth)** if an emotion or a feeling **deepens**, or if something **deepens** it, it becomes stronger: *Their friendship soon deepened into love.* **2** [I, T] ~ **(sth)** to become worse; to make something worse: *Warships were sent in as the crisis deepened.* ◆ *a deepening economic recession* **3** [I, T] to become deeper; to make something deeper: *The water deepened gradually.* ◆ *His frown deepened.* ◆ ~ **sth** *There were plans to deepen a stretch of the river.* **4** [T] ~ **sth** to improve your knowledge or understanding of something: *an opportunity for students to deepen their understanding of different cultures* **5** [I, T] ~ **(sth)** if color or light **deepens** or if something **deepens** it, it becomes darker: *deepening shadows* **6** [I, T] ~ **(sth) (to sth)** if a sound or voice **deepens** or if you **deepen** it, it becomes lower or you make it lower: *His voice deepened to a growl.* **7** [I] if your breathing **deepens**, you breathe more air into your lungs than before

deep-'frozen *adj.* preserved at an extremely low temperature

deep-'fry *verb* [usually passive] ~ **sth** to cook food in oil that covers it completely: *deep-fried chicken*

t **t**ea   ţ bu**tt**er   d **d**id   k **c**at   g **g**ot   tʃ **ch**in   dʒ **J**une   f **f**all

deep·ly 🔑 /ˈdiːpli/ adv.
1 very; very much: *She is deeply religious.* ◆ *They were deeply disturbed by the accident.* ◆ *Opinion is deeply divided on this issue.* ◆ *deeply rooted customs/ideas* ◆ *deeply held beliefs/convictions/views* (= that someone feels very strongly) **2** used with some verbs to show that something is done in a very complete way: *to breathe/sigh/exhale deeply* (= using all of the air in your lungs) ◆ *sleep deeply* (= in a way that makes it difficult for you to wake up) ◆ *to think deeply* (= about all the aspects of something) **3** to a depth that is quite a long way from the surface of something: *to drill deeply into the wood* ⊃ note at DEEP

deep ˈpockets noun [pl.] a large amount of money that can be spent; great financial resources: *The Foundation is reputed to have very deep pockets.* ▶ **deep-ˈpock·et·ed** adj.: *deep-pocketed companies*

deep-ˈrooted, deep-ˈseated adj. [usually before noun] (of feelings and beliefs) very fixed and strong; difficult to change or to destroy: *a deep-rooted desire* ◆ *The country's political divisions are deep-seated.*

deep-sea (also *less frequent* **deep-ˈwater**) adj. [only before noun] of or in the deeper parts of the ocean: *a deep-sea diver* ◆ *deep-sea fishing/diving*

deep-ˈset adj. (formal) eyes that are **deep-set** seem to be quite far back in a person's face

deep-ˈsix verb [usually passive] **~ sth** (informal) to decide not to do or use something that you had planned to do or use: *Plans to build a new mall were deep-sixed after protests from local residents.*

the ˌDeep ˈSouth noun [sing.] the southern states of the U.S., especially Georgia, Alabama, Mississippi, Louisiana, and South Carolina

deep vein throm'bosis noun [U, C] (abbr. DVT) (medical) a serious condition caused by a blood CLOT (= a thick mass of blood) forming in a VEIN: *Passengers on long-distance flights are being warned about the risks of deep vein thrombosis.*

deer /dɪr/ noun (pl. **deer**) an animal with long legs that eats grass, leaves, etc. and can run fast. Most male deer have ANTLERS (= horns shaped like branches). There are many types of deer: *a herd of deer* ◆ *a deer park* ⊃ picture at ANIMAL ⊃ see also RED DEER, REINDEER, DOE, FAWN, STAG

deer·stalk·er /ˈdɪrˌstɔkər/ noun a cap with two PEAKS, one in front and one behind, and two pieces of cloth that are usually tied together on top but can be folded down to cover the ears

def /dɛf/ adj. (slang) excellent: *a def band*

de·face /dɪˈfeɪs/ verb **~ sth** to damage the appearance of something, especially by drawing or writing on it ▶ **de·face·ment** noun [U]

de fac·to /di ˈfæktoʊ; deɪ-/ adj. [usually before noun] (from Latin, formal) existing as a fact although it may not be legally accepted as existing: *The general took de facto control of the country.* ▶ **de fac·to** adv.: *He continued to rule the country de facto.* ⊃ compare DE JURE

def·a·ma·tion /ˌdɛfəˈmeɪʃn/ noun [U, C] (formal) the act of damaging someone's reputation by saying or writing bad or false things about them: *The company sued for defamation.*

de·fam·a·to·ry /dɪˈfæməˌtɔri/ adj. (formal) (of speech or writing) intended to harm someone by saying or writing bad or false things about them

de·fame /dɪˈfeɪm/ verb **~ sb/sth** (formal) to harm someone by saying or writing bad or false things about them

de·fault /dɪˈfɔlt/ noun, verb
● **noun 1** [U, C] failure to do something that must be done by law, especially paying a debt: *The company is in default on the loan.* ◆ *Mortgage defaults have risen in the last year.* **2** [U, C, usually sing.] (computing) what happens or appears if you do not make any other choice or change: *The default option is to save your work every five minutes.* ◆ *On this screen, 256 colors is the default.*
IDM by default 1 a game or competition can be won by

default if there are no other people, teams, etc. taking part **2** if something happens **by default**, it happens because you have not made any other decision or choice that would make things happen in a different way **in default of sth** (formal) because of a lack of something: *They accepted what he had said in default of any evidence to disprove it.*
● **verb 1** [I] **~ (on sth)** to fail to do something that you legally have to do, especially by not paying a debt: *to default on a loan/debt* ◆ *defaulting borrowers/tenants* **2** [I] **~ (to sth)** (computing) to happen when you do not make any other choice or change ▶ **de·fault·er** noun: *mortgage defaulters*

de·feat 🔑 /dɪˈfit/ verb, noun
● **verb 1 ~ sb/sth** to win against someone in a war, competition, sports game, etc. SYN BEAT : *He defeated the champion in three sets.* ◆ *a defeated army* **2 ~ sb** (formal) if something **defeats** you, you cannot understand it: *The instruction manual completely defeated me.* **3 ~ sth** to stop something from being successful: *The motion was defeated by 19 votes.* ◆ *Staying late at the office to discuss shorter working hours rather defeats the object of the exercise!*
● **noun 1** [U, C] failure to win or to be successful: *The party faces defeat in the election.* ◆ *a narrow/heavy defeat* ◆ *The world champion has only had two defeats in 20 fights.* ◆ *They finally had to admit defeat* (= stop trying to be successful). **2** [C, usually sing.] the act of winning a victory over someone or something: *the defeat of fascism*

de·feat·ist /dɪˈfitɪst/ adj. expecting not to succeed, and showing it in a particular situation: *a defeatist attitude/view* ▶ **de·feat·ist** noun: *He is a pessimist and a defeatist.* **de·feat·ism** /dɪˈfitɪzəm/ noun [U]

def·e·cate /ˈdɛfəˌkeɪt/ verb [I] (formal) to get rid of solid waste from your body through your BOWELS ▶ **def·e·ca·tion** /ˌdɛfəˈkeɪʃn/ noun [U]

de·fect noun, verb
● **noun** /ˈdifɛkt; dɪˈfɛkt/ a fault in something or in the way it has been made that means that it is not perfect: *a speech defect* ◆ *a defect in the glass*
● **verb** /dɪˈfɛkt/ [I] **~ (from sth) (to sth)** to leave a political party, country, etc. to join another that is considered to be an enemy ▶ **de·fec·tion** /dɪˈfɛkʃn/ noun [U, C]: **~ (from sth) (to sth)** *There have been several defections from the ruling party.* **de·fec·tor** /dɪˈfɛktər/ noun [U]

de·fec·tive /dɪˈfɛktɪv/ adj. having a fault or faults; not perfect or complete SYN FAULTY: *defective goods* ◆ *Her hearing was found to be slightly defective.* ▶ **de·fec·tive·ly** adv. **de·fec·tive·ness** noun [U]

de·fend 🔑 /dɪˈfɛnd/ verb
> PROTECT AGAINST ATTACK **1** [T, I] to protect someone or something from attack: **~ sb/yourself/sth** *Troops have been sent to defend the borders.* ◆ **~ sb/yourself/sth from/against sb/sth** *All our officers are trained to defend themselves against knife attacks.* ◆ **~ against sb/sth** *It is impossible to defend against an all-out attack.*
> SUPPORT **2** [T] to say or write something in support of someone or something that has been criticized: **~ sth** *How can you defend such behavior?* ◆ **~ sb/yourself/sth from/against sb/sth** *Politicians are skilled at defending themselves against their critics.*
> IN SPORTS **3** [I, T] **~ (sth)** (in sports) to protect your own goal to stop your opponents from scoring ANT ATTACK
> IN COMPETITIONS **4** [T] **~ sth** to take part in a competition that you won the last time and try to win it again: *He is defending champion.* ◆ *She will be defending her title at next month's championships.* ◆ (politics) *He intends to defend his seat in the next election.*
> LAW **5** [T, I] **~ (sb/yourself)** to act as a lawyer for someone who has been charged with a crime: *He has employed one of the country's top lawyers to defend him.* ⊃ compare PROSECUTE

de·fend·ant /dɪˈfɛndənt/ noun the person in a trial who is accused of committing a crime, or who is being SUED by another person ⊃ collocations at JUSTICE ⊃ compare ACCUSED, PLAINTIFF

de·fend·er /dɪˈfɛndər/ *noun* **1** a person who defends and believes in protecting something: *a passionate defender of human rights* **2** a player who must stop the other team from scoring in games such as SOCCER, HOCKEY, etc.

de·fense 🔑 /dɪˈfɛns/ *noun*
> PROTECTION AGAINST ATTACK **1** [U] the act of protecting someone or something from attack, criticism, etc.: *soldiers who died in defense of their country* ◆ *When her brother was criticized she leapt to his defense.* ◆ *What points can be raised in defense of this argument?* ◆ *I have to say in her defense that she knew nothing about it beforehand.* ⊃ see also SELF-DEFENSE **2** [C, U] ~ (against sth) something that provides protection against attack from enemies, the weather, illness, etc.: *The town walls were built as a defense against enemy attacks.* ◆ *The harbor's sea defenses are in poor condition.* ◆ *The body has natural defense mechanisms to protect it from disease.* ◆ *Humor is a more effective defense than violence.* **3** [U] the organization of the people and systems that are used by a government to protect a country from attack: *the Department of Defense* ◆ *Further cuts in defense spending are being considered.*
> SUPPORT **4** [C] something that is said or written in order to support something: *a defense of Marxism*
> LAW **5** [C] what is said in court to prove that a person did not commit a crime; the act of presenting this argument in court: *Her defense was that she was somewhere completely different at the time of the crime.* ◆ *He wanted to conduct his own defense.* **6** the defense [sing.] the lawyer or lawyers whose job is to prove in court that a person did not commit a crime ⊃ compare PROSECUTION
> IN SPORTS **7** /ˈdifɛns/ [sing., U] the players who must prevent the other team from scoring; the position of these players on the sports field: *The Lakers broke through the defense to score the winning basket.* ◆ *He plays on defense.* ⊃ compare OFFENSE **8** [C] a contest, game, etc. in which the previous winner or winners compete in order to try to win again: *New England's defense of the Super Bowl title*

de·fense·less /dɪˈfɛnsləs/ *adj.* weak; not able to protect yourself; having no protection: *defenseless children* ◆ *The village is defenseless against attack.* ▶ **de·fense·less·ness** *noun* [U]

de·fen·si·ble /dɪˈfɛnsəbl/ *adj.* **1** able to be supported by reasons or arguments that show that it is right or should be allowed: *Is abortion morally defensible?* **ANT** INDEFENSIBLE **2** (of a place) able to be defended from an attack

de·fen·sive /dɪˈfɛnsɪv/ *adj., noun*
• *adj.* **1** protecting someone or something against attack: *a defensive measure* ◆ *Troops took up a defensive position around the town.* ⊃ compare OFFENSIVE **2** behaving in a way that shows that you feel that people are criticizing you: *Don't ask him about his plans—he just gets defensive.* **3** (*sports*) connected with trying to prevent the other team or player from scoring points or goals: *defensive play* ⊃ compare OFFENSIVE ▶ **de·fen·sive·ly** *adv.* **de·fen·sive·ness** *noun* [U]
• *noun*
IDM on the defensive acting in a way that shows that you expect to be attacked or criticized; having to defend yourself: *Their questions about the money put her on the defensive.* ◆ *Warnings of an enemy attack forced the troops to go on the defensive.*

de·fensive 'medicine *noun* [U] medical treatment that involves more tests, operations, etc. than a person really needs because a doctor is worried that a claim or complaint may be made against them in court if they make a mistake in the treatment they give

de·fer /dɪˈfər/ *verb* (-rr-) ~ (doing) sth to delay something until a later time **SYN** PUT OFF: *The department deferred the decision for six months.* ◆ *She had applied for deferred admission to college.* ▶ **de·fer·ment, de·fer·ral** /dɪˈfərəl/ *noun* [U, C] **PHR V** de'fer to sb/sth (*formal*) to agree to accept what someone has decided or what they think about someone or

something because you respect him or her: *We will defer to whatever the committee decides.*

def·er·ence /ˈdɛfərəns; ˈdɛfrəns/ *noun* [U] behavior that shows that you respect someone or something: *The women wore veils in deference to the customs of the country.* ◆ *The flags were lowered out of deference to the bereaved family.* ▶ **def·er·en·tial** /ˌdɛfəˈrɛnʃl/ *adj.* **def·er·en·tial·ly** /-ʃəli/ *adv.*

de·fi·ance /dɪˈfaɪəns/ *noun* [U] open refusal to obey someone or something: *a look/an act/a gesture of defiance* ◆ *Nuclear testing was resumed in defiance of an international ban.*

de·fi·ant /dɪˈfaɪənt/ *adj.* openly refusing to obey someone or something, sometimes in an aggressive way: *a defiant teenager* ◆ *The terrorists sent a defiant message to the government.* ▶ **de·fi·ant·ly** *adv.*

de·fib·ril·la·tion /ˌdiˌfɪbrəˈleɪʃn/ *noun* [U] (*medical*) the use of a controlled electric shock from a defibrillator to return the heart to its natural rhythm

de·fib·ril·la·tor /diˈfɪbrəˌleɪtər/ *noun* (*medical*) a piece of equipment used to control the movements of the heart muscles by giving the heart a controlled electric shock

de·fi·cien·cy /dɪˈfɪʃnsi/ *noun* (*pl.* de·fi·cien·cies) **1** [U, C] ~ (in/of sth) the state of not having, or not having enough of, something that is essential **SYN** SHORTAGE: *Vitamin deficiency in the diet can cause illness.* ◆ *a deficiency of Vitamin B* **2** [C] ~ (in/of sth) a fault or a weakness in something or someone that makes it or them less successful: *deficiencies in the computer system*

de·fi·cient /dɪˈfɪʃnt/ *adj.* **1** ~ (in sth) not having enough of something, especially something that is essential: *a diet that is deficient in vitamin A* **2** (*formal*) not good enough: *Deaf people are sometimes treated as being mentally deficient.*

def·i·cit /ˈdɛfəsət/ *noun* **1** (*economics*) the amount by which money spent or owed is greater than money earned in a particular period of time: *a budget/trade deficit* ◆ *The trade balance has been in deficit for the past five years.* ⊃ collocations at INTERNATIONAL ⊃ compare SURPLUS **2** the amount by which something, especially an amount of money, is too small or smaller than something else: *There's a deficit of $3 million in the total needed to complete the project.* ◆ *The team has to come back from a 2–0 deficit in the first half.*

ˌdeficit 'spending *noun* [U] (*economics*) government spending of money that was obtained from borrowing rather than from taxes

de·fied *pt, pp* of DEFY

de·file¹ /dɪˈfaɪl/ *verb* ~ sth (*formal* or *literary*) to make something dirty or no longer pure, especially something that people consider important or holy: *Many victims of burglary feel their homes have been defiled.* ◆ *The altar had been defiled by vandals.* ▶ **de·file·ment** *noun* [U, C]

de·file² /dɪˈfaɪl; ˈdifaɪl/ *noun* (*formal*) a narrow way through mountains

de·fine 🔑 **AWL** /dɪˈfaɪn/ *verb*
1 to say or explain what the meaning of a word or phrase is: ~ sth *The term "mental illness" is difficult to define.* ◆ ~ sth as sth *Life imprisonment is defined as 60 years under state law.* **2** to describe or show something accurately: ~ sth *We need to define the task ahead very clearly.* ◆ *The difficulty of a problem was defined in terms of how long it took to complete.* ◆ ~ what, how, etc. ... *It is difficult to define what makes him so popular.* **3** ~ sth to show clearly a line, shape, or edge: *The mountain was sharply defined against the sky.*
▶ **de·fin·a·ble** **AWL** /dɪˈfaɪnəbl/ *adj.*

LANGUAGE BANK

define
defining terms
■ It is important to clarify what is meant by climate change.
■ Climate change can/may be defined as "the long-term

h **h**at   m **m**an   n **n**o   ŋ si**ng**   l **l**eg   r **r**ed   y **y**es   w **w**et

fluctuations in temperature, precipitation, wind, and other aspects of the earth's climate."

- **A generally accepted definition of** global warming **is** the gradual increase in the overall temperature of the earth's atmosphere due to the greenhouse effect.
- The greenhouse effect **is defined** by the author **as** the process by which heat from the sun is trapped in the earth's atmosphere, causing the temperature of the earth to rise.
- The author **uses the term** "climate change" **to refer to** any significant change in measures of climate lasting for an extended period.
- **The term** "carbon footprint" **refers to** the amount of carbon dioxide released into the atmosphere as a result of the activities of an individual or organization.
- Scientists suggest that increased carbon dioxide in the atmosphere will result in an increase in global temperatures, and the term "global warming" **is used** to describe this phenomenon.
- ⟳ Language Bank at FIRST

de·fined 'benefit noun a fixed amount of money that will be paid by a PENSION PLAN, especially when this amount is based on your salary at the end of your working life and the number of years you worked

de·fined contri'bution noun fixed payments that are made to a PENSION PLAN, where the amount that will be paid out can change

de'fin·ing /dɪˈfaɪnɪŋ/ adj. = RESTRICTIVE

de'fining vo,cabulary noun a set of carefully chosen words used to write the explanations in some dictionaries

def·i·nite 🔑 **AWL** /ˈdɛfənət/ adj., noun

● **adj. 1 ~ (that…)** sure or certain; unlikely to change: *Can you give me a definite answer by tomorrow?* ◆ *Is it definite that he's leaving?* ◆ *I heard rumors, but nothing definite.* ◆ *a definite offer of a job* ◆ *That's definite then?* ◆ *They have very definite ideas on how to bring up children.* ⟳ thesaurus box at CERTAIN **2** easily or clearly seen or understood; obvious **SYN** CLEAR: *The look on her face was a definite sign that something was wrong.* ◆ *There was a definite feeling that things were getting worse.* **3** [not before noun] **~ (about sth)** | **~ (that…)** (of a person) sure that something is true or that something is going to happen and stating it to other people: *I'm definite about this.*

● **noun** [sing.] (*informal*) something that you are certain about or that you know will happen; someone who is sure to do something: *"Is Sarah coming to the party?" "Yes, she's a definite."*

,definite 'article noun (*grammar*) the word *the* in English, or a similar word in another language ⟳ compare INDEFINITE ARTICLE

def·i·nite·ly 🔑 **AWL** /ˈdɛfənətli/ adv.
1 (*informal*) a way of emphasizing that something is true and that there is no doubt about it: *I definitely remember sending the letter.* ◆ *"Was it what you expected?" "Yes, definitely."* ◆ *"Do you plan to have children?" "Definitely not!"* ◆ *Some old people want help; others most definitely do not.* **2** in a way that is certain or that shows that you are certain: *The date of the move has not been definitely decided yet* (= it may change). ◆ *Please say definitely whether you will be coming or not.*

def·i·ni·tion 🔑 **AWL** /ˌdɛfəˈnɪʃn/ noun
1 [C, U] an explanation of the meaning of a word or phrase, especially in a dictionary; the act of stating the meanings of words and phrases: *clear simple definitions* ◆ *Neighbors by definition live close by* (= this is what being a neighbor means). ⟳ language bank at DEFINE **2** [C] what an idea, etc. means: *What's your definition of happiness?* **3** [U] the quality of being clear and easy to see: *Digital TV screens have excellent definition.* ⟳ see also HD

de·fin·i·tive **AWL** /dɪˈfɪnətɪv/ adj. **1** final; not able to be changed: *a definitive agreement/answer/statement* ◆ *The definitive version of the text is ready to be published.* **2** [usually before noun] considered to be the best of its kind and almost impossible to improve: *the definitive biography of Einstein* ▶ **de·fin·i·tive·ly** adv.

de·flate verb **1** /dɪˈfleɪt, ˌdi-/ [T, I] **~ (sth)** to let air or gas out of a tire, BALLOON, etc.; to become smaller because of air or gas coming out **2** /dɪˈfleɪt/ [T, often passive] **~ sb/sth** to make someone feel less confident; to make someone or something feel or seem less important: *All the criticism had left her feeling totally deflated.* **3** /ˌdiˈfleɪt; dɪ-/ [T] **~ sth** (*economics*) to reduce the amount of money being used in a country so that prices fall or stay steady ⟳ compare INFLATE, REFLATE

de·fla·tion /dɪˈfleɪʃn, ˌdi-/ noun [U] **1** (*economics*) a reduction in the amount of money in a country's economy so that prices fall or remain the same ⟳ collocations at ECONOMY **2** the action of air being removed from something **ANT** INFLATION ▶ **de·fla·tion·ar·y** /-ʃəˌnɛri/ adj.: *deflationary policies*

de·flect /dɪˈflɛkt/ verb **1** [I, T] to change direction or make something change direction, especially after hitting something: *The puck deflected off Lemieux's stick into the goal.* ◆ **~ sth** *He raised his arm to try to deflect the blow.* **2** [T] **~ sth** to succeed in preventing something from being directed toward you **SYN** DIVERT: *All attempts to deflect attention from his private life have failed.* ◆ *She sought to deflect criticism by blaming her family.* **3** [T] **~ sb (from sth)** to prevent someone from doing something that they are determined to do: *The government will not be deflected from its commitments.*

de·flec·tion /dɪˈflɛkʃn/ noun [U, C, usually sing.] a sudden change in the direction that something is moving in, usually after it has hit something; the act of causing something to change direction: *the angle of deflection* ◆ *the deflection of the missile away from its target* ◆ *The goal was scored with a deflection off the goalkeeper.*

de·flow·er /ˌdiˈflaʊər/ verb **~ sb** (*old-fashioned, literary*) to have sex with a woman who has not had sex before

de·fog /ˌdiˈfɔg; -ˈfag/ verb (**-gg-**) [T, I] **~ (sth)** to remove the CONDENSATION from a car's windows so that you can see clearly

de·fo·li·ant /ˌdiˈfoʊliənt/ noun [C, U] a chemical that removes the leaves from plants, sometimes used as a weapon in war

de·fo·li·ate /ˌdiˈfoʊliˌeɪt/ verb **~ sth** (*technical*) to destroy the leaves of trees or plants, especially with chemicals ▶ **de·fo·li·a·tion** /ˌdiˌfoʊliˈeɪʃn/ noun [U]

de·for·est /ˌdiˈfɔrəst; -ˈfar-/ verb [usually passive] **~ sth** to cut down and destroy all the trees in a place: *Two thirds of the region has been deforested in the past decade.*

de·for·est·a·tion /ˌdiˌfɔrəˈsteɪʃn; -ˌfar-/ noun [U] the act of cutting down or burning the trees in an area ⟳ collocations at ENVIRONMENT ⟳ compare AFFORESTATION, REFORESTATION

de·form /dɪˈfɔrm/ verb **~ sth** to change or spoil the usual or natural shape of something: *The disease had deformed his spine.*

de·for·ma·tion /ˌdifɔrˈmeɪʃn; ˌdɛfər-/ noun **1** [U] the process or result of changing and spoiling the normal shape of something **2** [C] a change in the normal shape of something as a result of injury or illness: *a deformation of the spine*

de·formed /dɪˈfɔrmd/ adj. (of a person or a part of the body) having a shape that is not normal because it has grown wrongly: *She was born with deformed hands.*

de·form·i·ty /dɪˈfɔrməti/ noun (pl. **de·form·i·ties**) [C, U] a condition in which a part of the body is not the normal shape because of injury, illness, or because it has grown wrongly **SYN** MALFORMATION: *Drugs taken during pregnancy may cause physical deformity in babies.*

---

de·frag·ment /ˌdiˈfræɡmɛnt/ (also informal **de·frag** /ˌdiˈfræɡ/) verb ~ **sth** (computing) to organize the files on a computer so that information relating to each file is stored in the same area, so the computer works faster

de·fraud /dɪˈfrɔd/ verb [I, T] to get money illegally from a person or an organization by tricking them: *All three men were charged with conspiracy to defraud.* ◆ ~ **sb (of sth)** *They were accused of defrauding the company of $14,000.*

de·fray /dɪˈfreɪ/ verb ~ **costs/expenses** (formal) to give someone back the money that they have spent on something

de·frock /ˌdiˈfrɑk/ verb [usually passive] ~ **sb** to officially remove a priest from his or her job, because he or she has done something wrong: *a defrocked priest*

de·frost /dɪˈfrɔst/ verb **1** [I, T] to become or make something warmer, especially food, so that it is no longer frozen: *It will take about four hours to defrost.* ◆ ~ **sth** *Make sure you defrost the chicken completely before cooking.* **2** [T, I] ~ **(sth)** when you **defrost** a refrigerator or FREEZER, or when it **defrosts**, you remove the ice from it ➲ compare DE-ICE, MELT, THAW, UNFREEZE **3** [T] ~ **sth** to remove ice from the surface of a car's windows ▶ **de·frost·er** noun

deft /dɛft/ adj. **1** (of a person's movements) skillful and quick: *deft hands/fingers/footwork* ◆ *He finished off the painting with a few deft strokes of the brush.* **2** skillful: *her deft command of the language* ◆ **deft·ly** adv.: *I threw her a towel which she deftly caught.* ◆ *They deftly avoided answering my questions.* **deft·ness** noun [U]

de·funct /dɪˈfʌŋkt/ adj. (formal) no longer existing, operating, or being used

de·fuse /ˌdiˈfyuz; dɪ-/ verb **1** ~ **sth** to stop a possibly dangerous or difficult situation from developing, especially by making people less angry or nervous: *Local police are trying to defuse racial tension in the community.* **2** ~ **sth** to remove the FUSE from a bomb so that it cannot explode

de·fy /dɪˈfaɪ/ verb (de·fies, de·fy·ing, de·fied, de·fied)

WORD FAMILY
defy verb
defiance noun
defiant adj.

1 ~ **sb/sth** to refuse to obey or show respect for someone in authority, a law, a rule, etc.: *I wouldn't have dared to defy my teachers.* ◆ *Hundreds of people today defied the ban on political gatherings.* **2** ~ **belief, explanation, description, etc.** to be impossible or almost impossible to believe, explain, describe, etc.: *a political move that defies explanation* ◆ *The beauty of the scene defies description.* **3** ~ **sth** to successfully resist something to a very unusual degree: *The baby boy defied all the odds and survived* (= stayed alive when it seemed certain that he would die).

IDM **I defy you/anyone to do sth** used to say that someone should try to do something, as a way of emphasizing that you think it is impossible to do it: *I defy anyone not to cry at the end of the movie.*

deg. abbr. DEGREE(S): 76 deg. F

de·gen·er·ate verb, adj., noun
● **verb** /dɪˈdʒɛnəˌreɪt/ [I] to become worse, for example by becoming lower in quality or weaker **SYN** DETERIORATE: *Her health degenerated quickly.* ◆ ~ **into sth** *The march degenerated into a riot.*
● **adj.** /dɪˈdʒɛnərət/ **1** having moral standards that have fallen to a level that is very low and unacceptable to most people: *a degenerate popular culture* **2** (technical) having returned to a simple structure; lacking something that is usually present ▶ **de·gen·er·a·cy** /dɪˈdʒɛnərəsi/ noun [U]
● **noun** /dɪˈdʒɛnərət/ a person whose behavior shows moral standards that have fallen to a very low level

de·gen·er·a·tion /dɪˌdʒɛnəˈreɪʃn/ noun [U] the process of becoming worse or less acceptable in quality or condition: *social/moral degeneration* ◆ *Intensive farming in the area has caused severe degeneration of the land.*

de·gen·er·a·tive /dɪˈdʒɛnərətɪv/ adj. (technical) (of an

illness) getting or likely to get worse as time passes: *degenerative diseases such as arthritis*

de·grad·a·ble /dɪˈɡreɪdəbl/ adj. (technical) that can be changed to a simpler form ➲ see also BIODEGRADABLE

deg·ra·da·tion /ˌdɛɡrəˈdeɪʃn/ noun [U] **1** a situation in which someone has lost all SELF-RESPECT and the respect of other people: *the degradation of being sent to prison* **2** (technical) the process of something being damaged or made worse: *environmental degradation*

de·grade /dɪˈɡreɪd/ verb **1** [T] ~ **sb** to show or treat someone in a way that makes them seem not worth any respect or not worth taking seriously: *This poster is offensive and degrades women.* **2** [I, T] (technical) to change or make something change to a simpler chemical form **3** [T] ~ **sth** (technical) to make something become worse, especially in quality

de·grad·ing /dɪˈɡreɪdɪŋ/ adj. treating someone as if they have no value, so that they lose their SELF-RESPECT and the respect of other people: *the inhuman and degrading treatment of prisoners*

de·grease /ˌdiˈɡris/ verb ~ **sth** to remove GREASE or oil from something

de·gree 🔑 /dɪˈɡri/ noun
1 [C] a unit for measuring angles: *an angle of ninety degrees (90°)* **2** [C] (abbr. **deg.**) a unit for measuring temperature: *Water freezes at 32 degrees Fahrenheit (32°F) or zero degrees Celsius (0°C).* **3** [C, U] the amount or level of something: *Her job demands a high degree of skill.* ◆ *I agree with you **to a certain degree**.* ◆ *To what degree can parents be held responsible for a child's behavior?* ◆ *Most pop music is influenced, to a greater or lesser degree, by the blues.* **4** [C] the qualification obtained by students who successfully complete a university or college course: *My brother has a master's degree from Harvard.* ◆ *She has a degree in Biochemistry from the University of Virginia.* ◆ *a four-year degree course* ➲ collocations at EDUCATION **5** [C] a level in a scale of how serious something is: *murder in the first degree* (= of the most serious kind) ◆ *first-degree murder* ◆ *third-degree* (= very serious) *burns*
IDM **by degrees** slowly and gradually: *By degrees their friendship grew into love.* ➲ more at NTH

de·hu·man·ize /ˌdiˈhyumənaɪz/ verb ~ **sb** to make someone lose their human qualities such as kindness, understanding, etc.: *the dehumanizing effects of poverty and squalor* ▶ **de·hu·man·i·za·tion** /ˌdiˌhyumənəˈzeɪʃn/ noun [U]

de·hu·mid·i·fi·er /ˌdihyuˈmɪdəˌfaɪər; ˌdiyu-/ noun an electrical machine for removing water from the air ➲ see also HUMIDIFIER

de·hy·drate /diˈhaɪdreɪt/ verb **1** [T, usually passive] ~ **sth** to remove the water from something, especially food, in order to preserve it **2** [I, T] to lose too much water from your body; to make a person's body lose too much water: *Runners can dehydrate very quickly in this heat.* ◆ ~ **sb** *the dehydrating effects of alcohol* ▶ **de·hy·dra·tion** /ˌdihaɪˈdreɪʃn/ noun [U]: *to suffer from dehydration* **de·hy·drat·ed** /ˌdiˈhaɪdreɪtəd/ adj.: *Drink lots of water to avoid becoming dehydrated.*

de·ice /ˌdiˈaɪs/ verb ~ **sth** to remove the ice from something ➲ compare DEFROST, MELT, THAW, UNFREEZE

de·ic·er /ˌdiˈaɪsər/ noun [C, U] a substance that is put on a surface to remove ice or to stop it from forming

deic·tic /ˈdaɪktɪk/ adj. (linguistics) relating to a word or expression whose meaning depends on who says it, where they are, who they are talking to, etc., for example "you," "me," "here," "next week." ➲ see also DEIXIS

de·i·fy /ˈdiəˌfaɪ; ˈdeɪə-/ verb (de·i·fies, de·i·fy·ing, de·i·fied, de·i·fied) ~ **sb** (formal) to treat or worship someone as a god ▶ **de·i·fi·ca·tion** /ˌdiəfəˈkeɪʃn; ˌdeɪə-/ noun [U]: *the deification of medieval kings*

deign /deɪn/ verb ~ **to do sth** (formal, disapproving) to do something in a way that shows you think you are too important to do it **SYN** CONDESCEND: *She just grunted, not deigning to look up from the page.*

ʌ **cup**   ə **about**   eɪ **say**   aɪ **five**   ɔɪ **boy**   aʊ **now**   oʊ **go**   ər **bird**

de·ism /ˈdiːɪzəm; ˈdeɪɪzəm/ *noun* [U] belief in God, especially a God that created the universe but does not take part in it ▸ **de·ist** /ˈdiːɪst; ˈdeɪ-/ *noun* **de·is·tic** /diˈɪstɪk/ *adj.*

de·i·ty /ˈdiːəti; ˈdeɪə-/ *noun* (*pl.* **de·i·ties**) **1** [C] a god or GODDESS: *Greek/Roman/Hindu deities* **2 the Deity** [sing.] (*formal*) God

deix·is /ˈdaɪksɪs/ *noun* [U] (*linguistics*) the function or use of DEICTIC words or expressions (= ones whose meaning depends on where, when, or by whom they are used)

dé·jà vu /ˌdeɪʒɑ ˈvuː/ *noun* [U] (from *French*) the feeling that you have previously experienced something that is happening to you now: *I had a strong sense of déjà vu as I entered the room.*

de·ject·ed /dɪˈdʒɛktəd/ *adj.* unhappy and disappointed **SYN** DESPONDENT: *She looked so dejected when she lost the game.* ▸ **de·ject·ed·ly** *adv.*

de·jec·tion /dɪˈdʒɛkʃn/ *noun* [U] a feeling of unhappiness and disappointment

de ju·re /dɪ ˈdʒʊri; deɪ ˈjʊreɪ/ *adj., adv.* (from *Latin, law*) according to the law: *He held power de jure and de facto* (= both according to the law and in reality). ⊃ **compare DE FACTO**

de·lay 🔑 /dɪˈleɪ/ *noun, verb*
• *noun* **1** [C] a period of time when someone or something has to wait because of a problem that makes something slow or late: *Commuters will face long delays on the roads today.* ◆ *We apologize for the delay in answering your letter.* ◆ *a delay of two hours/a two-hour delay* ⊃ collocations at TRAVEL **2** [C, U] a situation in which something does not happen when it should; the act of delaying: *There's no time for delay.* ◆ *Report it to the police without delay* (= immediately).
• *verb* **1** [I, T] to not do something until a later time or to make something happen at a later time **SYN** DEFER: *Don't delay—call us today!* ◆ *~ sth The judge will delay his verdict until he receives medical reports on the suspect.* ◆ *She's suffering a delayed reaction* (= a reaction that did not happen immediately) *to the shock.* ◆ *~ doing sth He delayed telling her the news, waiting for the right moment.* **2** [T] *~ sb* to make someone late or cause them to do something more slowly **SYN** HOLD UP: *Thousands of commuters were delayed for over an hour.* ◆ *The government is accused of using delaying tactics* (= deliberately doing something to delay a process, decision, etc.).

de·lec·ta·ble /dɪˈlɛktəbl/ *adj.* **1** (of food and drink) extremely pleasant to taste, smell, or look at **SYN** DELICIOUS: *the delectable smell of freshly baked bread* **2** (*humorous*) (of a person) very attractive: *his delectable body*

de·lec·ta·tion /ˌdiːlɛkˈteɪʃn/ *noun* [U] (*formal or humorous*) enjoyment or entertainment **SYN** DELIGHT

del·e·gate *noun, verb*
• *noun* /ˈdɛləɡət/ a person who is chosen or elected to represent the views of a group of people and vote and make decisions for them: *The conference was attended by delegates from 56 countries.*
• *verb* /ˈdɛləˌɡeɪt/ **1** [I, T] to give part of your work, power, or authority to someone in a lower position than you: *Some managers find it difficult to delegate.* ◆ *~ (sth) (to sb) The job had to be delegated to an assistant.* **2** [T] *~ sb to do sth* [usually passive] to choose someone to do something: *I've been delegated to organize the Christmas party.*

del·e·ga·tion /ˌdɛləˈɡeɪʃn/ *noun* **1** [C] a group of people who represent the views of an organization, a country, etc.: *the Dutch delegation to the United Nations* ◆ *a delegation of teachers* ⊃ collocations at INTERNATIONAL **2** [U] the process of giving someone work or responsibilities that would usually be yours: *delegation of authority/decision-making*

de·lete /dɪˈliːt/ *verb ~ sth (from sth)* to remove something that has been written or printed, or that has been stored on a computer: *Your name has been deleted from the list.* ◆ *This command deletes files from the directory.* ⊃ collocations at E-MAIL ▸ **de·le·tion** /dɪˈliːʃn/ *noun* [U, C]: *He made several deletions to the manuscript.*

de·le·te·ri·ous /ˌdɛləˈtɪriəs/ *adj.* (*formal*) harmful and damaging

del·i /ˈdɛli/ *noun* = DELICATESSEN

de·lib·er·ate 🔑 *adj., verb*
• *adj.* /dɪˈlɪbrət; -bərət/ **1** done on purpose rather than by accident **SYN** INTENTIONAL, PLAN: *a deliberate act of vandalism* ◆ *The speech was a deliberate attempt to embarrass the government.* **ANT** UNINTENTIONAL **2** (of a movement or an action) done slowly and carefully: *She spoke in a slow and deliberate way.*
• *verb* /dɪˈlɪbəˌreɪt/ [I, T] to think very carefully about something, usually before making a decision: *The jury deliberated for five days before finding him guilty.* ◆ *~ (on) whether, what, etc.... They deliberated (on) whether to continue with the talks.*

de·lib·er·ate·ly 🔑 /dɪˈlɪbrətli; -bərət-/ *adv.* **1** done in a way that was planned, not by chance **SYN** INTENTIONALLY: *She's been deliberately ignoring him all day.* **2** slowly and carefully: *He packed up his possessions slowly and deliberately.*

de·lib·er·a·tion /dɪˌlɪbəˈreɪʃn/ *noun* **1** [U, C, usually pl.] the process of carefully considering or discussing something: *After ten hours of deliberation, the jury returned a verdict of "not guilty."* ◆ *The deliberations of the committee are completely confidential.* **2** [U] the quality of being slow and careful in what you say or do: *She signed her name with great deliberation.*

de·lib·er·a·tive /dɪˈlɪbrətɪv; dɪˈlɪbəˌreɪtɪv/ *adj.* (*formal*) relating to careful consideration or discussion: *A deliberative assembly will make the final decision.*

del·i·ca·cy /ˈdɛlɪkəsi/ *noun* (*pl.* **del·i·ca·cies**) **1** [U] the quality of being, or appearing to be, easy to damage or break **SYN** FRAGILE: *the delicacy of the fabric* **2** [U] the quality of being done carefully and gently **SYN** TENDER *adj.*: *the delicacy of his touch* **3** [U] very careful behavior in a difficult situation so that nobody is offended **SYN** TACT: *She handled the situation with great sensitivity and delicacy.* **4** [U] the fact that a situation is difficult and someone may be easily offended: *I need to talk to you about a matter of some delicacy.* **5** [C] a type of food considered to be very special in a particular place **SYN** SPECIALITY: *local delicacies*

del·i·cate 🔑 /ˈdɛlɪkət/ *adj.*
1 easily damaged or broken **SYN** FRAGILE: *delicate china teacups* ◆ *The eye is one of the most delicate organs of the body.* ◆ *the delicate ecological balance of the rainforest* ◆ *Babies have very delicate skin.* ◆ *a cool wash cycle for delicate fabrics* **2** (of a person) not strong and easily becoming sick: *a delicate child/constitution* **3** small and having a beautiful shape or appearance: *his delicate hands* **4** made or formed in a very careful and detailed way: *the delicate mechanisms of a clock* **5** showing or needing skillful, careful, or sensitive treatment: *I admired your delicate handling of the situation.* ◆ *a delicate problem* ◆ *The delicate surgical operation took five hours.* **6** (of colors, flavors, and smells) light and pleasant; not strong **SYN** SUBTLE: *a delicate fragrance/flavor* ◆ *a river scene painted in delicate watercolors* ▸ **del·i·cate·ly** *adv.*: *He stepped delicately over the broken glass.* ◆ *delicately balanced flavors*

del·i·ca·tes·sen /ˌdɛlɪkəˈtɛsn/ (also **de·li**) *noun* a store or part of one that sells cooked meats and cheeses, and special or unusual foods that come from other countries

de·li·cious /dɪˈlɪʃəs/ *adj.* **1** having a very pleasant taste or smell: *Who cooked this? It's delicious.* **2** (*literary*) extremely pleasant or enjoyable: *the delicious coolness of the breeze* ▸ **de·li·cious·ly** *adv.*: *deliciously creamy soup*

de·lic·to ⊃ IN FLAGRANTE

de·light 🔑 /dɪˈlaɪt/ *noun, verb*
• *noun* **1** [U] a feeling of great pleasure **SYN** JOY: *a feeling of sheer/pure delight* ◆ *The children squealed with delight when they saw the puppy.* ◆ *She won the game easily, to the delight of*

all her fans. ◆ He **takes (great) delight in** (= enjoys) *proving others wrong.* ➔ thesaurus box at PLEASURE **2** [C] something that gives you great pleasure **SYN** JOY: *This guitar is a delight to play.* ◆ *the delights of living in the country*

● **verb ~ sb** to give someone a lot of pleasure and enjoyment: *This news will delight his fans all over the world.*
PHR V de'light in sth/doing sth [no passive] to enjoy doing something very much, especially something that makes other people feel embarrassed, uncomfortable, etc.

de·light·ed /dɪˈlaɪtəd/ *adj.*
very pleased: *a delighted smile* ◆ **~ to do sth** *I'd be absolutely delighted to come.* ◆ **~ that…** *I was delighted that you could stay.* ◆ **~ by/at sth** *She was delighted by/at the news of the wedding.* ◆ **~ with sth** *I was delighted with my presents.* ➔ thesaurus box at GLAD ▶ de'light·ed·ly *adv.*

de·light·ful /dɪˈlaɪtfl/ *adj.* very pleasant **SYN** CHARMING: *a delightful book/restaurant/town* ◆ *a delightful child* ▶ de·light·ful·ly /-fəli/ *adv.*

de·lim·it /dɪˈlɪmət/ *verb* **~ sth** (*formal*) to decide what the limits of something are

de·lin·e·ate /dɪˈlɪniˌeɪt/ *verb* **~ sth** (*formal*) to describe, draw, or explain something in detail: *Our objectives need to be precisely delineated.* ◆ *The ship's route is clearly delineated on the map.* ▶ de·lin·e·a·tion /dɪˌlɪniˈeɪʃn/ *noun* [U, C]

de·lin·quen·cy /dɪˈlɪŋkwənsi/ *noun* [U, C] (*pl.* de·lin·quen·cies) **1** bad or criminal behavior, usually of young people: *an increase in juvenile delinquency* **2** (*formal*) a failure to pay a debt

de·lin·quent /dɪˈlɪŋkwənt/ *adj.* **1** (especially of young people or their behavior) showing a tendency to commit crimes: *delinquent teenagers* **2** (*finance*) having failed to pay money that is owed: *a delinquent borrower* **3** (*finance*) (of a sum of money) not having been paid in time: *a delinquent loan* ▶ de·lin·quent *noun* ➔ see also JUVENILE DELINQUENT

del·i·quesce /ˌdɛlɪˈkwɛs/ *verb* (*formal*) **1** [I] to become liquid as a result of decaying **2** [I] (*chemistry*) to become liquid as a result of absorbing water from the air ▶ del·i·ques·cence /-ˈkwɛsns/ *noun* [U]

de·lir·i·ous /dɪˈlɪriəs/ *adj.* **1** in an excited state and not able to think or speak clearly, usually because of fever: *He became delirious and couldn't recognize people.* **2** extremely excited and happy: *The crowd was delirious with joy.* ▶ de·lir·i·ous·ly *adv.*

de·lir·i·um /dɪˈlɪriəm/ *noun* [U] a mental state where someone becomes delirious, usually because of illness: *fits of delirium*

de·lir·i·um tre·mens /dɪˌlɪriəm ˈtrimənz; -ˈtrɛmənz/ *noun* [U] (*medical*) = DTs

de·liv·er 🔑 /dɪˈlɪvər/ *verb*
▷ **TAKE GOODS/LETTERS 1** [T, I] to take goods, letters, etc. to the person or people they have been sent to; to take someone somewhere: **~ sth** *Do you have your groceries delivered?* ◆ **~ (sth) to sb** *Leaflets have been delivered to every household.* ◆ **~ (to sb/sth)** *We promise to deliver within 48 hours.*
▷ **GIVE SPEECH 2** [T] **~ sth** to give a speech, talk, etc. or other official statement: *She is due to deliver a lecture on genetic engineering.* ◆ *He delivered his lines confidently.* ◆ *The jury finally delivered its verdict.*
▷ **KEEP PROMISE 3** [I, T] to do what you promised to do or what you are expected to do; to produce or provide what people expect you to: *He has promised to finish the job by June and I am sure he will deliver.* ◆ **~ on sth** *She always delivers on her promises.* ◆ **~ sth** *If you can't deliver improved sales figures, you're fired.* ◆ *The team delivered a stunning victory last night.*
▷ **GIVE TO SOMEONE'S CONTROL 4** [T] **~ sb/sth (up/over) (to sb)** (*formal*) to give someone or something to someone else so that they are under this person's control: *They delivered their prisoner over to the invading army.*
▷ **BABY 5** [T] **~ a baby** to help a woman to give birth to a baby: *The baby was delivered by Caesarean section.* **6** [T] be

delivered of a baby (*formal*) to give birth to a baby: *She was delivered of a healthy boy.*
▷ **THROW 7** [T] **~ sth** to throw or aim something: *He delivered the blow* (= hit someone hard) *with all his force.*
▷ **RESCUE 8** [T] **~ sb (from sth)** (*old use*) to rescue someone from something bad **SYN** SAVE **IDM** see GOODS, SIGN *v.*

de·liv·er·a·ble /dɪˈlɪvərəbl/ *noun* [usually pl.] a product that a company promises to have ready for a customer: *computer software deliverables*

de·liv·er·ance /dɪˈlɪvrəns; -ˈlɪvrəns/ *noun* [U] **~ (from sth)** (*formal*) the state of being rescued from danger, evil, or pain

de·liv·er·y 🔑 /dɪˈlɪvəri; -ˈlɪvri/ *noun*
(*pl.* de·liv·er·ies) **1** [U, C] the act of taking goods, letters, etc. to the people they have been sent to: *a delivery van* ◆ *Please pay for goods on delivery* (= when you receive them). ◆ *Allow 28 days for delivery.* ◆ *Is there mail delivery on Saturdays?* ◆ (*formal*) *When can you take delivery of* (= be available to receive) *the car?* ◆ (*figurative*) *the delivery of public services* **2** [C, U] the process of giving birth to a baby: *an easy/difficult delivery* ◆ *a delivery room/ward* (= in a hospital, etc.) **3** [sing.] the way in which someone speaks, sings a song, etc. in public: *The beautiful poetry was ruined by her poor delivery.* **4** [C] the way a ball is thrown, especially in baseball: *a fast delivery* **IDM** see CASH *n.*

de·liv·er·y·man (also **de'livery ˌman**) /dɪˈlɪvəriˌmæn; dɪˈlɪvri-; -mən/ *noun* (*pl.* de·liv·er·y·men /-mɛn; -mən/) a man whose job is to deliver goods to the people they have been sent to

dell /dɛl/ *noun* (*literary*) a small valley with trees growing in or around it

de·louse /ˌdiˈlaʊs/ *verb* **~ sb/sth** to remove LICE (= small insects) from someone's hair or from an animal's coat

Del·phic /ˈdɛlfɪk/ *adj.* **1** relating to the ancient Greek ORACLE at Delphi (= the place where people went to ask the gods for advice or information about the future) **2** often **delphic** (*formal*) with a meaning that is deliberately hidden or difficult to understand: *a delphic utterance*

del·phin·i·um /dɛlˈfɪniəm/ *noun* a tall garden plant with blue or white flowers growing up its STEM

del·ta /ˈdɛltə/ *noun* **1** the fourth letter of the Greek alphabet (Δ, δ) **2** an area of land, shaped like a triangle, where a river has split into several smaller rivers before entering the ocean: *the Nile Delta*

del·toids /ˈdɛltɔɪdz/ (also *informal* **delts** /dɛlts/) *noun* [pl.] (*anatomy*) thick muscles in the shape of triangles that cover the shoulder joints

de·lude /dɪˈlud/ *verb* to make someone believe something that is not true **SYN** DECEIVE: **~ sb** *You poor deluded creature.* ◆ **~ yourself** *He's deluding himself if he thinks it's going to be easy.* ◆ **~ sb/yourself into doing sth** *Don't be deluded into thinking that we are out of danger yet.* ◆ **~ yourself that…** *She had been deluding herself that he loved her.* ➔ see also DELUSION

del·uge /ˈdɛljudʒ; -juʒ; ˈdeɪluʒ/ *noun, verb*
● *noun* [usually sing.] **1** a sudden, very heavy fall of rain **SYN** FLOOD **2** a large number of things that happen or arrive at the same time: *a deluge of calls/complaints/letters*
● *verb* **1** **~ sb/sth (with sth)** [usually passive] to send or give someone or something a large number of things at the same time **SYN** FLOOD, INUNDATE: *We have been deluged with applications for the job.* **2** [often passive] **~ sth** (*formal*) to flood a place with water: *The campsite was deluged by a flash flood.*

de·lu·sion /dɪˈluʒn/ *noun* **1** [C] a false belief or opinion about yourself or your situation: *the delusions of the mentally ill* ◆ *Don't go getting delusions of grandeur* (= a belief that you are more important than you actually are). **2** [U] the act of believing or making yourself believe something that is not true

de·lu·sion·al /dɪˈluʒənl/ *adj.* having ideas or beliefs that are not based in reality: *Delusional thinking led him to believe*

| t **t**ea | ţ bu**tt**er | d **d**id | k **c**at | g **g**ot | tʃ **ch**in | dʒ **J**une | f **f**all |

they were plotting against him. ◆ *Her plan to become a famous movie star turned out to be completely delusional.*

de·lu·sive /dɪˈlusɪv/ (also **de·lu·so·ry** /dɪˈlusəri; -zəri/) *adj.* (*formal*) not real or true **SYN** DECEPTIVE

de·luxe /dəˈlʌks/ *adj.* [usually before noun] of a higher quality and more expensive than usual **SYN** LUXURY: *a deluxe hotel*

delve /dɛlv/ *verb* **1** [I] + **adv./prep.** to search for something inside a bag, container, etc. **SYN** DIG: *She delved into her handbag for a pen.* **2** [I] + **adv./prep.** to try hard to find out more information about something: *She had started to delve into her father's distant past.*

Dem. *abbr.* DEMOCRAT; DEMOCRATIC

dem·a·gogue /ˈdɛməˌɡɑɡ/ *noun* (*disapproving*) a political leader who tries to win support by using arguments based on emotion rather than reason ▶ **dem·a·gog·ic** /ˌdɛməˈɡɑɡɪk; -ˈɡɑdʒɪk/ *adj.* **dem·a·gogu·er·y** /ˈdɛməˌɡɑɡəri/, **dem·a·go·gy** /ˈdɛməˌɡɑɡi; -ˌɡɑdʒi; -ˌɡoʊdʒi/ *noun* [U]

de·mand 🔊 /dɪˈmænd/ *noun, verb*

● *noun* **1** [C] ~ **(for sth/that...)** a very firm request for something; something that someone needs: *a demand for higher pay* ◆ *demands that the law on gun ownership should be changed* ◆ *firms attempting to* **meet/satisfy** *their customers'* **demands** (= to give them what they are asking for) **2** demands [pl.] ~ **(of sth)** | ~ **(on sb)** things that someone or something makes you do, especially things that are difficult, make you tired, worried, etc.: *the demands of children/work* ◆ *Flying* **makes** *enormous* **demands** *on pilots.* **3** [U,C] ~ **(for sth/sb)** the desire or need of customers for goods or services that they want to buy or use: *to meet the demand for a product* ◆ *There's an increased demand for organic produce these days.* ◆ *Demand is exceeding supply.* ◔ collocations at ECONOMY

IDM **by popular demand** because a lot of people have asked for something: *By popular demand, the play will run for another week.* **in demand** wanted by a lot of people: *Good nurses are always in demand.* **on demand** done or happening whenever someone asks: *Feed the baby on demand.* ◆ *on-demand printing of books* ◔ see also SUPPLY AND DEMAND

● *verb* **1** to ask for something very firmly: ~ **sth** *She demanded an immediate explanation.* ◆ ~ **that...** *The U.N. has demanded that all troops be withdrawn.* ◆ ~ **to do sth** *I demand to see the manager.* ◆ ~ + **speech** *"Who the hell are you?" he demanded angrily.* ◔ thesaurus box at ASK **2** ~ **sth** to need something in order to be done successfully: *This sport demands both speed and strength.*

THESAURUS

demand

expect ◆ **insist** ◆ **ask** ◆ **require**

These words all mean to say that someone should do or have something.

demand to ask for something very firmly; to say very firmly that someone should have or do something: *She demanded an immediate explanation.*

expect to demand that someone should do, have, or be something, especially because it is their duty or responsibility: *I expect to be paid promptly for the work.*

insist to demand that something happens or that someone agrees to do something: *She insisted that I go with her.* ◆ *We insist on the highest standards at all times.*

ask to expect or demand something: *You're asking too much of him.*

DEMAND, EXPECT, OR ASK?

Ask is not as strong as **demand** or **expect**, both of which can be more like a command.

require [often passive] (*somewhat formal*) to make someone do or have something, especially because it is necessary according to a law or set of rules or standards: *All candidates will be required to take a short test.*

PATTERNS

■ to demand/expect/ask/require sth **of/from** sb
■ to demand/expect/insist/ask/require **that...**
■ to expect/ask/require sb **to do** sth
■ to demand/expect/ask/require **a lot/too much/a great deal**
■ to **be too much to** expect/ask

de·mand·ing /dɪˈmændɪŋ/ *adj.* **1** (of a piece of work) needing a lot of skill, patience, effort, etc.: *The work is physically demanding.* ◔ thesaurus box at DIFFICULT **2** (of a person) expecting a lot of work or attention from others; not easily satisfied: *a demanding boss/child* **ANT** UNDEMANDING

de·mar·cate /dɪˈmɑrkeɪt; ˈdimɑrˌkeɪt/ *verb* ~ **sth** (*formal*) to mark or establish the limits of something: *Plots of land have been demarcated by barbed wire.*

de·mar·ca·tion /ˌdimɑrˈkeɪʃn/ *noun* [U,C] a border or line that separates two things, such as types of work, groups of people, or areas of land: *It was hard to draw clear lines of demarcation between work and leisure.* ◆ *social demarcations*

de·mean /dɪˈmin/ *verb* **1** ~ **yourself** to do something that makes people have less respect for you: *I wouldn't demean myself by asking for charity.* **2** ~ **sb/sth** to make people have less respect for someone or something **SYN** DEGRADE: *Such images demean women.*

de·mean·ing /dɪˈminɪŋ/ *adj.* putting someone in a position that does not give them the respect that they should have: *He found it demeaning to work for his former employee.*

de·mean·or /dɪˈminər/ *noun* [U] (*formal*) the way that someone looks or behaves: *He maintained a professional demeanor throughout.*

de·ment·ed /dɪˈmɛntəd/ *adj.* **1** behaving or thinking in a crazy way, especially because you are extremely upset or worried: *He was crashing about the house like a demented animal.* ◆ *a dark and demented sense of humor* **2** (*old-fashioned* or *medical*) having a mental illness ▶ **de·ment·ed·ly** *adv.*

de·men·tia /dɪˈmɛnʃə/ *noun* [U] (*medical*) a serious mental DISORDER caused by brain disease or injury that affects the ability to think, remember, and behave normally ◔ see also SENILE DEMENTIA

de·mer·it /dɪˈmɛrət/ *noun* (*formal*) **1** [usually pl.] a fault in something or a disadvantage of something: *the merits and demerits of the scheme* **2** a mark on someone's school record showing that they have done something wrong: *You'll get three demerits if you're caught smoking on school grounds.*

de·mesne /dɪˈmeɪn; dɪˈmin/ *noun* **1** (in the past) land attached to a MANOR (= large house) that was kept by the owners for their own use **2** (*old use*) a region or large area of land

demi- /ˈdɛmi/ *prefix* (in nouns) half; partly: *demigod*

dem·i·god /ˈdɛmiˌɡɑd/ *noun* **1** a minor god, or a BEING that is partly or fully human **2** a ruler or other person who is treated like a god

dem·i·john /ˈdɛmiˌdʒɑn/ *noun* a very large bottle with a narrow opening at the top, for holding and transporting water, wine, etc.

de·mil·i·ta·rize /ˌdiˈmɪlətəˌraɪz/ *verb* [usually passive] ~ **sth** to remove military forces from an area: *a demilitarized zone* **ANT** MILITARIZE ▶ **de·mil·i·ta·ri·za·tion** /ˌdiˌmɪlətərəˈzeɪʃn/ *noun* [U]

dem·i·monde /ˈdɛmiˌmɑnd/ *noun* [sing.] (from *French*) people whose behavior or beliefs prevent them from being fully accepted as part of the main group in society

de·mise /dɪˈmaɪz/ *noun* [sing.] **1** the end or failure of an institution, an idea, a company, etc. **2** (*formal* or *humorous*) death: *his imminent/sudden/sad demise*

dem·i·urge /ˈdɛmiˌərdʒ/ *noun* (*literary*) **1** a BEING that is responsible for creating the world **2** a BEING that controls the part of the world which is not spiritual

---

dem·o /ˈdɛmoʊ/ *noun, verb*

● ***noun*** (*pl.* de·mos) (*informal*) **1** = DEMONSTRATION: *I'll give you a demo.* **2** a recording with an example of someone's music on it: *a demo CD*

● ***verb*** ~ **sth** to use something, especially a piece of software, to show someone or to see for yourself how it works: *He demoed the new program he had just created.* ◆ *Can I demo the software before I buy it?*

demo- /ˈdɛmə/ *prefix* (in nouns, adjectives, and adverbs) connected with people or population: *democracy* ◆ *democratic*

de·mo·bi·lize /diˈmoʊbəˌlaɪz/ *verb* ~ **sb** to release someone from military service, especially at the end of a war ⟳ compare MOBILIZE ▶ **de·mo·bi·li·za·tion** /diˌmoʊbələˈzeɪʃn/ *noun* [U]

de·moc·ra·cy 🔑 /dɪˈmɑkrəsi/ *noun* (*pl.* de·moc·ra·cies) **1** [U] a system of government in which all the people of a country can vote to elect their representatives: *representative democracy* ◆ *the principles of democracy* **2** [C] a country which has this system of government: *Western democracies* ◆ *I thought we were supposed to be living in a democracy.* **3** [U] fair and equal treatment of everyone in an organization, etc., and their right to take part in making decisions: *the fight for justice and democracy*

dem·o·crat /ˈdɛməˌkræt/ *noun* **1** a person who believes in or supports democracy **2** Democrat (*abbr.* D, Dem.) a member or supporter of the Democratic Party ⟳ compare REPUBLICAN

dem·o·crat·ic 🔑 /ˌdɛməˈkrætɪk/ *adj.* **1** (of a country, state, system, etc.) controlled by representatives who are elected by the people of a country; connected with this system: *a democratic country* ◆ *a democratic system* ◆ *democratic government* **2** based on the principle that all members have an equal right to be involved in running an organization, etc.: *democratic participation* ◆ *a democratic decision* **3** based on the principle that all members of society are equal rather than divided by money or social class: *a democratic society* ◆ *democratic reforms* **4** Democratic (*abbr.* Dem., D) connected with the Democratic Party: *the Democratic senator from Oregon* ▶ **dem·o·crat·i·cally** /-kli/ *adv.*: *a democratically elected government* ◆ *democratically controlled* ◆ *The decision was made democratically.*

the Democratic Party *noun* [sing.] one of the two main political parties in the U.S., usually considered to be in favor of social reform ⟳ compare THE REPUBLICAN PARTY

de·moc·ra·tize /dɪˈmɑkrəˌtaɪz/ *verb* ~ **sth** (*formal*) to make a country or an institution more democratic ▶ **de·moc·ra·ti·za·tion** /dɪˌmɑkrətəˈzeɪʃn/ *noun* [U]

dem·o·graph·ic /ˌdɛməˈgræfɪk/ *noun, adj.*

● ***noun*** **1** demographics [pl.] (*statistics*) data relating to the population and different groups within it: *the demographics of radio listeners* **2** [sing.] (*business*) a group of customers who are of a similar age, the same sex, etc.: *The products are designed to appeal to a young demographic.* ◆ *the 18–30 demographic*

● ***adj.*** relating to the population and different groups within it: *demographic changes/trends/factors* ▶ **dem·o·graph·i·cally** /-kli/ *adv.*

de·mog·ra·phy /dɪˈmɑgrəfi/ *noun* [U] the changing number of births, deaths, diseases, etc. in a community over a period of time; the scientific study of these changes: *the social demography of Africa* ▶ **de·mog·ra·pher** /-fər/ *noun*

de·mol·ish /dɪˈmɑlɪʃ/ *verb* **1** ~ **sth** to pull or knock down a building: *The factory is due to be demolished next year.* **2** ~ **sth** to destroy something accidentally: *The car had skidded across the road and demolished part of the wall.* **3** ~ **sth** to show that an idea or theory is completely wrong: *A recent book has demolished this theory.* **4** ~ **sb/sth** to defeat someone easily and completely: *The Yankees demolished the Red Sox 12–1.* ▶ **dem·o·li·tion** /ˌdɛməˈlɪʃn/ *noun* [U, C]: *The*

whole row of houses is scheduled for demolition.* ◆ *His speech did a very effective **demolition job** on the government's proposals.*

demolition derby *noun* a type of race in which drivers crash old cars into each other until only one car is left in the race

de·mon /ˈdimən/ *noun* **1** an evil spirit: *demons torturing the sinners in Hell* **2** (*informal*) a person who does something very well or with a lot of energy: *He skis like a demon.* **3** something that causes a person to worry and makes them unhappy: *the demons of jealousy*

de·mon·ic /dɪˈmɑnɪk/ *adj.* connected with, or like, a demon: *demonic forces* ◆ *a demonic appearance*

de·mon·ize /ˈdiməˌnaɪz/ *verb* ~ **sb/sth** to describe someone or something in a way that is intended to make other people think of them or it as evil or dangerous: *He was demonized by the right-wing press.* ▶ **de·mon·i·za·tion** /ˌdimənəˈzeɪʃn/ *noun* [U]

de·mon·stra·ble AWL /dɪˈmɑnstrəbl/ *adj.* (*formal*) that can be shown or proved: *a demonstrable need* ▶ **de·mon·stra·bly** AWL /-bli/ *adv.*: *demonstrably unfair*

dem·on·strate 🔑 AWL /ˈdɛmənˌstreɪt/ *verb* **1** [T] to show something clearly by giving proof or evidence: ~ **that...** *These results demonstrate convincingly that our campaign is working.* ◆ ~ **sth (to sb)** *Let me demonstrate to you some of the difficulties we are facing.* ◆ ~ **how, what, etc....** *His sudden departure had demonstrated how unreliable he was.* ◆ ~ **sb/sth to be sth** *The theories were demonstrated to be false.* ◆ **it is demonstrated that...** *It has been demonstrated that this drug is effective.* ⟳ language bank at EVIDENCE **2** [T] ~ **sth** to show by your actions that you have a particular quality, feeling or opinion SYN DISPLAY: *You need to demonstrate more self-control.* ◆ *We want to demonstrate our commitment to human rights.* **3** [T] to show and explain how something works or how to do something: ~ **sth (to sb)** *Her job involves demonstrating new educational software.* ◆ ~ **(to sb) how, what, etc....** *Let me demonstrate to you how it works.* **4** [I] to take part in a public meeting or march, usually as a protest or to show support for something SYN PROTEST: ~ **(against sth)** *students demonstrating against the war* ◆ ~ **(in favor/support of sth)** *They are demonstrating in favor of free higher education.*

dem·on·stra·tion 🔑 AWL /ˌdɛmənˈstreɪʃn/ *noun* **1** [C] ~ **(against sb/sth)** a public meeting or march at which people show that they are protesting against or supporting someone or something: *to take part in/go on a demonstration* ◆ *to hold/stage a demonstration* ◆ *mass demonstrations in support of the exiled leader* ◆ *anti-government demonstrations* ◆ *a peaceful/violent demonstration* ⟳ compare MARCH **2** (*also informal* de·mo) [C, U] an act of showing or explaining how something works or is done: *We were given a brief demonstration of the computer's functions.* ◆ *a practical demonstration* ◆ *We provide demonstrations of videoconferencing over the Internet.* **3** [C, U] an act of giving proof or evidence for something: *a demonstration of the connection between the two sets of figures* ◆ *a demonstration of how something that seems simple can turn out to be very complicated* **4** [C] an act of showing a feeling or an opinion: *a public demonstration of affection* ◆ *a demonstration of support for the reforms*

de·mon·stra·tive AWL /dəˈmɑnstrətɪv/ *adj., noun*

● ***adj.*** **1** showing feelings openly, especially feelings of affection: *Some people are more demonstrative than others.* ◆ *a demonstrative greeting* **2** (*grammar*) used to identify the person or thing that is being referred to: *"This" and "that" are demonstrative pronouns.* ▶ **de·mon·stra·tive·ly** AWL *adv.*

● ***noun*** (*grammar*) a demonstrative pronoun or determiner

dem·on·stra·tor AWL /ˈdɛmənˌstreɪtər/ *noun* **1** a person who takes part in a public meeting or march in order to protest against someone or something or to show support for someone or something **2** a person whose job is to show or explain how something works or is done

de·mor·al·ize /dɪˈmɔrəˌlaɪz; -ˈmɑr-/ *verb* [usually passive]

~ sb to make someone lose confidence or hope **SYN** DISHEARTEN: *Constant criticism is enough to demoralize anyone.* ▶ **de·mor·al·ized** *adj.*: *The workers here seem very demoralized.* **de·mor·al·iz·ing** *adj.*: *the demoralizing effects of unemployment* **de·mor·al·i·za·tion** /dɪˌmɔrələˈzeɪʃn; -ˌmɑr-/ *noun* [U]

de·mote /dɪˈmoʊt/ *verb* [often passive] **~ sb (from sth) (to sth)** to move someone to a lower position or rank, often as a punishment **ANT** PROMOTE ▶ **de·mo·tion** /dɪˈmoʊʃn/ *noun* [C, U]

de·mot·ic /dɪˈmɑtɪk/ *adj.* (*formal*) used by or typical of ordinary people

de·mo·ti·vate /ˌdiˈmoʊtəˌveɪt/ *verb* **~ sb** to make someone feel that it is not worth making an effort: *Failure can demotivate students.* ▶ **de·mo·ti·vat·ing** *adj.* **de·mo·tivat·ed** *adj.* **de·mo·ti·va·tion** /ˌdiˌmoʊtəˈveɪʃn/ *noun* [U]

de·mur /dɪˈmər/ *verb, noun*
● *verb* (-rr-) [I] (**+ speech**) (*formal*) to say that you do not agree with something or that you refuse to do something: *At first she demurred, but then finally agreed.*
● *noun*
  IDM **without demur** (*formal*) without objecting or hesitating: *They accepted without demur.*

de·mure /dɪˈmyʊr/ *adj.* **1** (of a woman or a girl) behaving in a way that does not attract attention to herself or her body; quiet and serious **SYN** MODEST: *a demure young lady* **2** suggesting that a woman or girl is demure **SYN** MODEST: *a demure smile* ◆ *a demure navy blouse with a white collar* ▶ **de·mure·ly** *adv.*

de·mys·ti·fy /ˌdiˈmɪstəˌfaɪ/ *verb* (**de·mys·ti·fies, de·mys·tify·ing, de·mys·ti·fied, de·mys·ti·fied**) **~ sth** to make something easier to understand and less complicated by explaining it in a clear and simple way ▶ **de·mys·ti·fica·tion** /ˌdiˌmɪstəfəˈkeɪʃn/ *noun* [U]

den /dɛn/ *noun* **1** a room in a house where people go to relax, watch television, etc. **2** the hidden home of some types of wild animals: *a bear's/lion's den* **3** (*disapproving*) a place where people meet in secret, especially for some illegal or immoral activity: *a den of thieves* ◆ *a drinking/ gambling den* ◆ *He thought of New York as a den of iniquity.* **4** a group of Cub Scouts **IDM** see LION

de·na·tion·al·ize /ˌdiˈnæʃənəˌlaɪz; -ˈnæʃnəˌlaɪz/ *verb* **~ sth** to sell a company or an industry so that it is no longer owned by the government **SYN** PRIVATIZE **ANT** NATIONALIZE ▶ **de·na·tion·al·i·za·tion** /ˌdiˌnæʃənələˈzeɪʃn; -ˌnæʃnələ-/ *noun* [U]

den·drite /ˈdɛndraɪt/ (also **den·dron** /ˈdɛndrɑn/) *noun* (*biology*) a short branch at the end of a nerve cell, that receives signals from other cells ⊃ compare AXON ▶ **den·drit·ic** /dɛnˈdrɪtɪk/ *adj.*: *dendritic cells*

den·gue /ˈdɛŋgi; -geɪ/ (also **dengue fever, breakbone fever**) *noun* [U] a disease caused by a virus carried by MOSQUITOES, that is found in tropical areas and causes fever and severe pain in the joints

de·ni·a·ble **AWL** /dɪˈnaɪəbl/ *adj.* that can be denied **ANT** UNDENIABLE

de·ni·al **AWL** /dɪˈnaɪəl/ *noun* **1** [C] **~ (of sth/that...)** a statement that says something is not true or does not exist: *the prisoner's repeated denials of the charges against him* ◆ *The terrorists issued a denial of responsibility for the attack.* **2** [C, U] **(a) ~ of sth** a refusal to allow someone to have something they have a right to expect: *the denial of basic human rights* **3** [U] (*psychology*) a refusal to accept that something unpleasant or painful is true: *The patient is still in denial.*

de·ni·er /ˈdɛnyər/ *noun* a unit for measuring how fine threads of NYLON, silk, etc. are: *840 denier nylon*

den·i·grate /ˈdɛnɪˌgreɪt/ *verb* **~ sb/sth** (*formal*) to criticize someone or something unfairly; to say someone or something does not have any value or is not important **SYN** BELITTLE: *I didn't intend to denigrate her achievements.* ▶ **den·i·gra·tion** /ˌdɛnɪˈgreɪʃn/ *noun* [U]

den·im /ˈdɛnəm/ *noun* **1** [U] a type of strong cotton cloth that

is usually blue and is used for making clothes, especially jeans: *a denim jacket* **ORIGIN** From the French *serge de Nîmes,* meaning serge (a type of cloth) from the town of Nîmes. **2 denims** [pl.] (*old-fashioned*) pants made of denim **SYN** JEANS

den·i·zen /ˈdɛnəzn/ *noun* (*formal* or *humorous*) a person, an animal, or a plant that lives, grows, or is often found in a particular place **SYN** INHABITANT: *polar bears, denizens of the frozen north* ◆ *the denizens of the local bar*

den mother *noun* the female leader of a DEN of Cub Scouts

de·nom·i·nate /dɪˈnɑməˌneɪt/ *verb* **1 ~ sth (in sth)** to express an amount of money using a particular unit: *The loan was denominated in pounds sterling.* **2 ~ sb (as) sth** (*formal*) to give something a particular name or description: *These payments are denominated as "fees" rather than "salary."*

de·nom·i·na·tion /dɪˌnɑməˈneɪʃn/ *noun* (*formal*) **1** a branch of the Christian Church: *Christians of all denominations attended the conference.* **2** a unit of value, especially of money: *coins and bills of various denominations*

de·nom·i·na·tion·al /dɪˌnɑməˈneɪʃənl/ *adj.* belonging to a particular branch of a religious group, especially in the Christian Church **ANT** NONDENOMINATIONAL

de·nom·i·na·tor /dɪˈnɑməˌneɪtər/ *noun* (*mathematics*) the number below the line in a FRACTION showing how many parts the whole is divided into, for example 4 in $\frac{3}{4}$ ⊃ compare NUMERATOR, COMMON DENOMINATOR

de·no·ta·tion **AWL** /ˌdinoʊˈteɪʃn/ *noun* (*technical*) the act of naming something with a word; the actual object or idea to which the word refers ⊃ compare CONNOTATION ▶ **de·no·ta·tion·al** /-ʃənl/ *adj.*

de·note **AWL** /dɪˈnoʊt/ *verb* (*formal*) **1 ~ sth** | **~ that...** to be a sign of something **SYN** INDICATE: *A very high temperature often denotes a serious illness.* **2 ~ sth** | **~ what, when, etc....** to mean something **SYN** REPRESENT: *In this example "X" denotes the time taken and "Y" denotes the distance covered.* ◆ *The red sign denotes danger.* ◆ *Here "family" denotes mother, father, and children.* ⊃ compare CONNOTE

de·noue·ment (also **dé·noue·ment**) /ˌdeɪnuˈmɑ̃/ *noun* (from French) the end of a play, book, etc., in which everything is explained or settled; the end result of a situation

de·nounce /dɪˈnaʊns/ *verb* **1** to strongly criticize someone or something that you think is wrong, illegal, etc.: **~ sb/sth** *She publicly denounced the government's handling of the crisis.* ◆ **~ sb/sth as sth** *The project was denounced as a scandalous waste of public money.* **2** to tell the police, the authorities, etc. about someone's illegal political activities: **~ sb as sth** *They were denounced as spies.* ◆ **~ sb (to sb)** *Many people denounced their neighbors to the secret police.* ⊃ see also DENUNCIATION

dense /dɛns/ *adj.* (**dens·er, dens·est**) **1** containing a lot of people, things, plants, etc. with little space between them: *a dense crowd/forest* ◆ *areas of dense population* **2** difficult to see through **SYN** THICK: *dense fog/smoke/fumes* **3** (*informal*) stupid: *How can you be so dense?* **4** difficult to understand because it contains a lot of information: *a dense piece of writing* **5** (*technical*) heavy in relation to its size: *Less dense substances move upward to form a crust.* ▶ **dense·ly** *adv.*: *a densely populated area* ◆ *densely covered/packed*

den·si·ty /ˈdɛnsəti/ *noun* (*pl.* **den·si·ties**) **1** [U, C] the quality of being dense; the degree to which something is dense: *population density* ◆ *low density forest* **2** [C, U] (*physics*) the thickness of a solid, liquid, or gas measured by its mass per unit of volume: *the density of a gas* **3** [U] (*computing*) the amount of space available on a disk for recording data: *a high/double density disk*

dent /dɛnt/ *verb, noun*
● *verb* **1 ~ sth** to make a hollow place in a hard surface, usually by hitting it: *The back of the car was badly dented in the accident.* **2 ~ sth** to damage someone's confidence, reputation, etc.: *It seemed that nothing could dent his confidence.*

---

i **see**   ɪ **sit**   ɛ **ten**   æ **cat**   ɑ **hot**   ɔ **saw**   ʊ **put**   u **too**   **397**

• **noun** a hollow place in a hard surface, usually caused by something hitting it: *a large dent in the car door* **IDM** **make, etc. a dent in sth** to reduce the amount of something, especially money: *The lawyer's fees will make a big dent in our finances.*

den·tal /ˈdɛntl/ *adj.* [only before noun] **1** connected with teeth: *dental disease/care/treatment/health* ◆ *dental school* ◆ *dental records* **2** (*phonetics*) (of a consonant) produced with the tongue against the upper front teeth, for example /θ/ and /ð/ in *thin* and *this*

dental ˌdam (also **dam**) *noun* a small rubber sheet used by dentists to keep a tooth separate from the other teeth

dental ˌfloss (also **floss**) *noun* [U] a type of thread that is used for cleaning between the teeth

dental hyˈgienist (also **hy·gien·ist**) *noun* a person who works with a dentist and whose job is to clean people's teeth and give them advice about keeping them clean

dental ˌsurgeon *noun* = ORAL SURGEON

den·tine /ˈdɛntin/ (also **den·tin** /ˈdɛntən/) *noun* [U] (*biology*) the hard substance that forms the main part of a tooth under the ENAMEL

den·tist /ˈdɛntɪst/ *noun*
1 a person whose job is to take care of people's teeth ⊃ see also DENTAL SURGEON, ORTHODONTIST **2** the dentist/dentist's a place where a dentist sees patients: *an appointment at the dentist's*

den·tist·ry /ˈdɛntəstri/ *noun* [U] **1** the medical study of the teeth and mouth **2** the work of a dentist: *preventive dentistry*

den·ti·tion /dɛnˈtɪʃn/ *noun* [U, C] (*technical*) the arrangement or condition of a person's or animal's teeth

den·tures /ˈdɛntʃərz/ *noun* [pl.] artificial teeth on a thin piece of plastic worn by someone who no longer has all their own teeth ▶ **den·ture** *adj.*: *denture adhesive* ⊃ compare FALSE TEETH

de·nude /dɪˈnud/ *verb* [usually passive] **~ sth (of sth)** (*formal*) to remove the covering, features, etc. from something, so that it is exposed: *hillsides denuded of trees*

de·nun·ci·a·tion /dɪˌnʌnsiˈeɪʃn/ *noun* [C, U] **~ (of sb/sth)** an act of criticizing someone or something strongly in public: *an angry denunciation of the government's policies* ◆ *All parties joined in bitter denunciation of the terrorists.* ⊃ see also DENOUNCE

Den·ver boot /ˌdɛnvər ˈbut/ (also **boot**) *noun* a device that is attached to the wheel of a car that has been parked illegally, so that it cannot be driven away

de·ny 🔑 **AWL** /dɪˈnaɪ/ *verb*
(de·nies, de·ny·ing, de·nied, de·nied) **1** to say that something is not true: **~ sth** *to deny a claim/a charge/an accusation* ◆ *to flatly/categorically/vehemently*

WORD FAMILY
deny *verb*
denial *noun*
undeniable *adj.*
undeniably *adv.*

deny (= deny strongly) *the rumors* ◆ *The spokesman refused either to confirm or deny the reports.* ◆ **~ (that)…** *She denied (that) there had been any cover-up.* ◆ **There's no denying (the fact) that** *quicker action could have saved them.* ◆ **it is denied that…** *It can't be denied that we need to devote more resources to this problem.* ◆ **~ doing sth** *He denies attempting to murder his wife.* **2 ~ sth** to refuse to admit or accept something: *She denied all knowledge of the incident.* ◆ *The department denies responsibility for what occurred.* **3** (*formal*) to refuse to allow someone to have something that they want or ask for: **~ sb sth** *They were denied access to the information.* ◆ **~ sth to sb** *Access to the information was denied to them.* **4 ~ yourself (sth)** (*formal*) to refuse to let yourself have something that you would like to have, especially for moral or religious reasons

de·o·dor·ant /diˈoʊdərənt/ *noun* [C, U] a substance that people put on their bodies to prevent or hide unpleasant smells: *(a) roll-on deodorant* ⊃ see also ANTIPERSPIRANT

de·o·dor·ize /diˈoʊdəˌraɪz/ *verb* **~ sth** to remove or hide an unpleasant smell in a place: *You can use dried flowers to deodorize your home.* ▶ **de·o·dor·iz·er** /diˈoʊdəˌraɪzər/ *noun*: *Room deodorizers come in many different scents.*

de·oxy·ribo·nucle·ic ac·id /diˌɑksiˌraɪboʊnuˌkliɪk ˈæsɪd; -ˌkleɪk-/ *noun* [U] = DNA

dep. *abbr.* (in writing) DEPART; DEPARTURE ⊃ compare ARR.

de·part /dɪˈpɑrt/ *verb* (somewhat *formal*) **1** [I, T] to leave a place, especially to start a trip **ANT** ARRIVE: **~ (for…) (from…)** *Flights for Rome depart from Terminal 3.* ◆ *She waited until the last of the guests had departed.* ◆ **~ sth** *The train departed Baltimore at 6:15 p.m.* **2** [I, T] to leave your job: *the departing president* ◆ **~ sth** *He departed his job on December 16.* ⊃ see also DEPARTURE
IDM **depart this life** to die. People say "depart this life" to avoid saying "die."
PHRV **deˈpart from sth** to behave in a way that is different from usual: *Departing from her usual routine, she took the bus to work.*

de·part·ed /dɪˈpɑrtəd/ *adj.* [only before noun] (*formal*) **1** dead. People say "departed" to avoid saying "dead": *your dear departed brother* **2 the departed** *noun* (*pl.* the de-part·ed) the person who has died

de·part·ment 🔑 /dɪˈpɑrtmənt/ *noun* (*abbr.* Dept.)
1 a section of a large organization such as a government, business, university, etc.: *the Department of Defense* ◆ *the Treasury Department* ◆ *a government/university, etc. depart-ment* ◆ *the marketing/sales, etc. department* ◆ *the English department* ⊃ see also POLICE DEPARTMENT, THE STATE DEPARTMENT **2** a section of a large store that sells a particular type of goods: *the children's department*
IDM **be sb's department** (*informal*) to be something that someone is responsible for or knows a lot about: *Don't ask me about it—that's her department.*

de·part·men·tal /ˌdipɑrtˈmɛntl/ *adj.* [only before noun] connected with a department rather than with the whole organization: *a departmental manager*

deˈpartment ˌstore *noun* a large store that is divided into several parts, each part selling a different type of goods

de·par·ture 🔑 /dɪˈpɑrtʃər/ *noun*
1 [C, U] **~ (from…)** the act of leaving a place; an example of this: *His sudden departure threw the office into chaos.* ◆ *Flights should be confirmed 48 hours before departure.* ◆ *They had received no news of him since his departure from the island.* **ANT** ARRIVAL **2** [C] a plane, train, etc. leaving a place at a particular time: *arrivals and departures* ◆ *All departures are from Terminal B.* ◆ *the departure lounge/time/gate* ◆ *the departures board* **ANT** ARRIVAL **3** [C] **~ (from sth)** an action that is different from what is usual or expected: *It was a radical departure from tradition.* ◆ *Their latest single represents a significant departure for the band.* **IDM** see POINT *n.*

de·pend 🔑 /dɪˈpɛnd/ *verb*
IDM **depending on/upon** according to: *Starting salary varies from $26,000 to $30,500, depending on experience.* ◆ *He either resigned or was fired, depending on whom you talk to.* **that depends| it (all) depends** used to say that you are not certain about something because other things have to be considered: *"Is he coming?" "That depends. He may not have the time."* ◆ *I don't know if we can help—it all depends.* ◆ *I might not go. It depends how tired I am.* ◆ *"Your job sounds fun." "It depends what you mean by 'fun.'"* ◆ *I shouldn't be too late. But it depends if the traffic's bad.*
PHRV **deˈpend on/upon sb/sth 1** to rely on someone or something and be able to trust them: *He was the sort of person you could depend on.* ◆ **~ sb/sth to do sth** *He knew he could depend upon her to deal with the situation.* ⊃ thesaurus box at TRUST **2** to be sure or expect that something will happen **SYN** COUNT ON: *Depend on it* (= you can be sure) *we won't give up.* ◆ **~ sb/sth doing sth** *Can we depend on you coming in on Sunday?* ◆ (*formal*) *You can depend on him coming in on Sunday.* ◆ **~ sb/sth to do sth** (*ironic*) *You can depend on her to be* (= she always is) *late.* **deˈpend on/upon sb/sth**

ʌ **cup**   ə **about**   eɪ **say**   aɪ **five**   ɔɪ **boy**   aʊ **now**   oʊ **go**   ər **bird**

(for sth) (not usually used in the progressive tenses) to need money, help, etc. from someone or something else for a particular purpose: *The community depends on the shipping industry for its survival.* ◆ *I don't want to depend too much on my parents.* **de'pend on/upon sth** (not used in the progressive tenses) to be affected or decided by something: *Does the quality of teaching depend on class size?* ◆ *It would depend on the circumstances.* ◆ **~ how, what, etc.…** *Whether we need more food depends on how many people show up.*

de·pend·a·ble /dɪˈpɛndəbl/ *adj.* that can be relied on to do what you want or need **SYN** RELIABLE ▶ **de·pend·a·bil·i·ty** /dɪˌpɛndəˈbɪləti/ *noun* [U]

de·pend·ence /dɪˈpɛndəns/ *noun* [U] **1 ~ (on/upon sb/sth)** the state of needing the help and support of someone or something in order to survive or be successful: *his dependence on his parents* ◆ *Our relationship was based on mutual dependence.* ◆ *the dependence of Europe on imported foods* ◆ *financial/economic dependence* **ANT** INDEPENDENCE **2** (also **de·pend·en·cy**) the state of being ADDICTED to something (= unable to stop taking or using it): *drug/alcohol dependence* **3 ~ of A and B** (*technical*) the fact of one thing being affected by another: *the close dependence of soil and landforms*

de·pend·en·cy /dɪˈpɛndənsi/ *noun* (*pl.* **de·pend·en·cies**) **1** [U] **~ (on/upon sb/sth)** the state of relying on someone or something for something, especially when this is not normal or necessary: *financial dependency* ◆ *Their aim is to reduce people's dependency on welfare.* ◆ *the* **dependency culture** (= a way of life in which people depend too much on money from the government) ⊃ compare CODEPENDENCY **2** [C] a country, an area, etc. that is controlled by another country **3** = DEPENDENCE

de·pend·ent /dɪˈpɛndənt/ *adj., noun*
● *adj.* **1** needing someone or something in order to survive or be successful: *a woman with several dependent children* ◆ **~ on/upon sb/sth** *You can't be dependent on your parents all your life.* ◆ **~ on/upon sb/sth for sth** *The festival is heavily dependent on sponsorship for its success.* **2 ~ on/upon sth** ADDICTED to something (= unable to stop taking or using it): *to be dependent on drugs* **3 ~ on/upon sth** (*formal*) affected or decided by something: *A child's development is dependent on many factors.* ◆ *The price is dependent on how many extras you choose.*
● *noun* a person, especially a child, who depends on another person for a home, food, money, etc.

de·pend·ent ˈclause *noun* (*grammar*) = SUBORDINATE CLAUSE

de·pend·ent ˈvariable *noun* (*mathematics*) a VARIABLE whose value depends on another variable

de·per·son·al·ize /diˈpərsənəˌlaɪz/ *verb* **~ sth** [often passive] to make something less personal so that it does not seem as if humans with feelings and personality are involved

de·pict /dɪˈpɪkt/ *verb* (somewhat *formal*) **1** to show an image of someone or something in a picture: **~ sb/sth (as sb/sth)** *a painting depicting the Virgin and Child* ◆ **~ sb/sth doing sth** *The artist had depicted her lying on a bed.* **2** to describe something in words, or give an impression of something in words or with a picture: **~ sb/sth** *The novel depicts French society in the 1930s.* ◆ **~ sb/sth as sb/sth** *The advertisements depict smoking as glamorous and attractive.*

▶ **de·pic·tion** /dɪˈpɪkʃn/ *noun* [U, C]: *They object to the movie's depiction of gay people.*

dep·i·la·tor /ˈdɛpəˌleɪtər/ *noun* a device that removes hair from your body by pulling it out

de·pil·a·to·ry /dɪˈpɪləˌtɔri/ *noun* (*pl.* **de·pil·a·to·ries**) a substance used for removing body hair ▶ **de·pil·a·to·ry** *adj.* [only before noun]: *depilatory creams*

de·plane /diˈpleɪn/ *verb* [I] to get off a plane **SYN** DISEMBARK

de·plete /dɪˈplit/ *verb* [usually passive] **~ sth** to reduce something by a large amount so that there is not enough left: *Food supplies were severely depleted.* ▶ **de·ple·tion** /dɪˈpliʃn/ *noun* [U]: *ozone depletion* ◆ *the depletion of fish stocks*

de·plor·a·ble /dɪˈplɔrəbl/ *adj.* (*formal*) very bad and unacceptable, often in a way that shocks people **SYN** APPALLING: *a deplorable incident* ◆ *They were living in the most deplorable conditions.* ◆ *The acting was deplorable.* ▶ **de·plor·a·bly** /-bli/ *adv.*: *They behaved deplorably.* ◆ *deplorably high/low/bad*

de·plore /dɪˈplɔr/ *verb* **~ sth** (*formal*) to strongly disapprove of something and criticize it, especially publicly: *Like everyone else, I deplore and condemn this killing.*

de·ploy /dɪˈplɔɪ/ *verb* **1 ~ sb/sth** (*technical*) to move soldiers or weapons into a position where they are ready for military action: *2,000 troops were deployed in the area.* ◆ *At least 5,000 missiles were deployed along the border.* **2 ~ sth** (*formal*) to use something effectively: *to deploy arguments/resources* ▶ **de·ploy·ment** *noun* [U, C]

de·po·lit·i·cize /ˌdipəˈlɪtəˌsaɪz/ *verb* **~ sth** to remove something from political activity or influence: *to depoliticize the teaching of certain subjects in school*

de·pop·u·late /ˌdiˈpɑpyəˌleɪt/ *verb* [usually passive] **~ sth** to reduce the number of people living in a place: *Whole stretches of land were laid waste and depopulated.* ▶ **de·pop·u·la·tion** /ˌdiˌpɑpyəˈleɪʃn/ *noun* [U]

de·port /dɪˈpɔrt/ *verb* **~ sb** to force someone to leave a country, usually because they have broken the law or because they have no legal right to be there ▶ **de·por·ta·tion** /ˌdipɔrˈteɪʃn/ *noun* [C, U]: *Several of the asylum seekers now face deportation.* ◆ *a deportation order*

de·por·tee /ˌdipɔrˈti/ *noun* a person who has been DEPORTED or is going to be deported

de·port·ment /dɪˈpɔrtmənt/ *noun* [U] (*formal, old-fashioned*) the way in which a person behaves

de·pose /dɪˈpoʊz/ *verb* **~ sb** to remove someone, especially a ruler, from power: *The president was deposed in a military coup.*

de·pos·it 🔑 /dɪˈpɑzət/ *noun, verb*
● *noun*
▷ MONEY **1** [usually sing.] **a ~ (on sth)** a sum of money that is given as the first part of a larger payment: *We've put down a 5% deposit on the house.* ◆ *They normally ask you to pay a $100 deposit.* ⊃ thesaurus box at PAYMENT **2** [usually sing.] a sum of money that is paid by someone when they rent something and that is returned to them if they do not lose or damage the thing they are renting: *to pay a deposit* ⊃ see also SECURITY DEPOSIT **3** a sum of money that is paid into a bank account: *Deposits can be made at any branch.* **ANT** WITHDRAWAL
▷ SUBSTANCE **4** a layer of a substance that has formed naturally underground: *mineral/gold/coal deposits* **5** a layer of a substance that has been left somewhere, especially by a river, flood, etc., or is found at the bottom of a liquid: *The rain left a deposit of mud on the windows.* ◆ *fatty deposits in the arteries of the heart*
● *verb*
▷ PUT DOWN **1 ~ sb/sth + adv./prep.** to put or lay someone or something down in a particular place: *She deposited a pile of books on my desk.* ◆ (*informal*) *I was whisked off in a taxi and deposited outside the hotel.*

> **LEAVE SUBSTANCE 2** ~ sth (especially of a river or a liquid) to leave a layer of something on the surface of something, especially gradually and over a period of time: *Sand was deposited, which hardened into sandstone.*

> **MONEY 3** ~ sth to put money into a bank account: *Millions were deposited in Swiss bank accounts.* **4** ~ sth to pay a sum of money as the first part of a larger payment; to pay a sum of money that you will get back if you return in good condition something that you have rented

> **PUT IN SAFE PLACE 5** ~ sth (in sth) | ~ sth (with sb/sth) to put something valuable or important in a place where it will be safe: *Guests may deposit their valuables in the hotel safe.*

dep·o·si·tion /ˌdepəˈzɪʃn/ *noun* **1** [C] (*law*) a formal statement, taken from someone and used in court **2** [U, C] (*technical*) the natural process of leaving a layer of a substance on rocks or soil; a substance left in this way: *marine/river deposition* **3** [U, C] the act of removing someone, especially a ruler, from power: *the deposition of the king*

de·pos·i·tor /dɪˈpɑzətər/ *noun* a person who puts money in a bank account

de·pos·i·to·ry /dɪˈpɑzəˌtɔri/ *noun* (*pl.* de·pos·i·to·ries) a place where things can be stored

de·pot /ˈdipoʊ/ *noun* **1** a place where large amounts of food, goods, or equipment are stored: *an arms depot* **2** a small station where trains or buses stop

de·prave /dɪˈpreɪv/ *verb* ~ sb (*formal*) to make someone morally bad **SYN CORRUPT**: *In my view, this book would deprave young children.*

de·praved /dɪˈpreɪvd/ *adj.* (*formal*) morally bad **SYN WICKED, EVIL**: *This is the work of a depraved mind.*

de·prav·i·ty /dɪˈprævəti/ *noun* [U] (*formal*) the state of being morally bad **SYN WICKEDNESS**: *a life of depravity*

dep·re·cate /ˈdeprəˌkeɪt/ *verb* ~ sth (*formal*) to feel and express strong disapproval of something or someone, often yourself ▶ **dep·re·cat·ing** (also *less frequent* dep·re·ca·to·ry /ˈdeprəkəˌtɔri/) *adj.*: *a deprecating comment* ♦ *He delivered the speech with typical self-deprecating humor.* **dep·re·cat·ing·ly** *adv.*

de·pre·ci·ate /dɪˈpriʃiˌeɪt/ *verb* **1** [I] to become less valuable over a period of time: *New cars start to depreciate as soon as they are on the road.* ♦ *Shares continued to depreciate on the stock markets today.* **ANT APPRECIATE 2** [T] ~ sth (*business*) to reduce the value, as stated in the company's accounts, of a particular **ASSET** over a particular period of time: *The bank depreciates PCs over a period of five years.* **3** [T] ~ sth (*formal*) to make something seem unimportant or of no value: *I had no intention of depreciating your contribution.* ▶ **de·pre·ci·a·tion** /dɪˌpriʃiˈeɪʃn/ *noun* [U]: *currency depreciation* ♦ *the depreciation of fixed assets*

dep·re·da·tion /ˌdeprəˈdeɪʃn/ *noun* [usually pl.] (*formal*) acts that cause damage to people's property, lives, etc.

de·press 🔑 **AWL** /dɪˈpres/ *verb*

1 to make someone sad and without enthusiasm or hope: ~ sb *Wet weather always depresses me.* ♦ it depresses sb to do sth *It depresses me to see so many teenagers smoking.* **2** ~ sth to make trade, business, etc. less active: *The recession has depressed the housing market.* **3** ~ sth to make the value of prices or wages lower: *to depress wages/prices* **4** ~ sth (*formal*) to press or push something down, especially part of a machine: *to depress the gas pedal* (= when driving).

de·pres·sant /dɪˈpresnt/ *noun* (*medical*) a drug that slows the rate of the body's functions

de·pressed 🔑 **AWL** /dɪˈprest/ *adj.*

1 very sad and without hope: *She felt very depressed about the future.* **2** suffering from the medical condition of **DEPRESSION** ⮕ thesaurus box at **MENTALLY 3** (of a place or an industry) without enough economic activity or jobs for people: *an attempt to bring jobs to depressed areas* **4** having a lower amount or level than usual: *depressed prices*

de·press·ing 🔑 **AWL** /dɪˈpresɪŋ/ *adj.*
making you feel very sad and without enthusiasm: *a depressing sight/thought/experience* ♦ *Looking for a job these days can be very depressing.* ▶ **de·press·ing·ly** *adv.*: *a depressingly familiar experience*

de·pres·sion **AWL** /dɪˈpreʃn/ *noun* **1** [U] a medical condition in which a person feels very sad and anxious and often has physical **SYMPTOMS** such as being unable to sleep, etc.: *clinical depression* ♦ *She suffered from severe depression after losing her job.* ⮕ see also **POSTPARTUM DEPRESSION 2** [U, C] the state of feeling very sad and without hope: *There was a feeling of gloom and depression in the office when the news of the job cuts was announced.* **3** [C, U] a period when there is little economic activity and many people are poor or without jobs: *The country was in the grip of (an) economic depression.* ♦ *the Great Depression of the 1930s* **4** [C] (*formal*) a part of a surface that is lower than the parts around it **SYN HOLLOW**: *Rainwater collects in shallow depressions on the ground.* **5** [C] (*technical*) a weather condition in which the pressure of the air becomes lower, often causing rain ⮕ compare **ANTICYCLONE**

de·pres·sive /dɪˈpresɪv/ *adj., noun*
- *adj.* connected with the medical condition of depression: *depressive illness*
- *noun* a person who is suffering from the medical condition of depression

de·pres·sor /dɪˈpresər/ *noun* ⮕ **TONGUE DEPRESSOR**

dep·ri·va·tion /ˌdeprəˈveɪʃn/ *noun* [U] the fact of not having something that you need, like enough food, money, or a home; the process that causes this: *neglected children suffering from social deprivation* ♦ *sleep deprivation* ♦ *the deprivation of war* (= the suffering caused by not having enough of some things)

de·prive /dɪˈpraɪv/ *verb*
PHR V de'prive sb/sth of sth to prevent someone from having or doing something, especially something important: *They were imprisoned and deprived of their basic rights.* ♦ *Why should you deprive yourself of such simple pleasures?*

de·prived /dɪˈpraɪvd/ *adj.* without enough food, education, and all the things that are necessary for people to live a happy and comfortable life: *a deprived childhood/background/area* ♦ *economically/emotionally/socially deprived* ⮕ thesaurus box at **POOR**

Dept. (also **dept.**) *abbr.* (in writing) department

depth 🔑 /depθ/ *noun*

> **MEASUREMENT 1** [C, U] the distance from the top or surface to the bottom of something: *What's the depth of the water here?* ♦ *Water was found at a depth of 30 feet.* ♦ *They dug down to a depth of 10 feet.* ♦ *Many dolphins can dive to depths of 500 feet.* ♦ *The oil well extended several hundreds of feet in depth.* ♦ *the depth of a cut/wound/crack* ⮕ picture at **DIMENSION 2** [C, U] the distance from the front to the back of something: *The depth of the shelves is 15 inches.*

> **OF FEELINGS 3** [U] the strength and power of feelings: *the depth of her love*

> **OF KNOWLEDGE 4** [U] (*approving*) the quality of knowing or understanding a lot of details about something; the ability to provide and explain these details: *a writer of great wisdom and depth* ♦ *a job that doesn't require any great depth of knowledge* ♦ *His ideas lack depth.*

> **DEEPEST PART 5** [C, usually pl.] the deepest, most extreme or serious part of something: *the depths of the ocean* ♦ *to live in the depths of the country* (= a long way from a town) ♦ *in the depths of winter* (= when it is coldest) ♦ *She was in the depths of despair.* ♦ *He gazed into the depths of her eyes.* ♦ *Her paintings reveal hidden depths* (= unknown and interesting things about her character).

> **OF COLOR 6** [U] the strength of a color: *Strong light will affect the depth of color of your carpets and curtains.*

> **PICTURE/PHOTOGRAPH 7** [U] (*technical*) the quality in a work of art or a photograph that makes it appear not to be flat ⮕ see also **DEEP**

IDM in depth in a detailed and thorough way: *I haven't* looked at the report in depth yet. ♦ an in-depth study **be out of your depth** to be unable to understand something because it is too difficult; to be in a situation that you cannot control: He felt totally out of his depth in his new job. ⟳ more at PLUMB v.

ˈdepth charge noun a bomb that is set to explode underwater, used to destroy SUBMARINES.

ˌdepth of ˈfield (also ˌdepth of ˈfocus) noun (technical) the distance between the nearest and the furthest objects that a camera can produce a clear image of at the same time

dep·u·ta·tion /ˌdepjəˈteɪʃn/ noun a small group of people who are asked or allowed to act or speak for others

de·pute /dɪˈpjuːt/ verb ~ **sb to do sth** [often passive] (formal) to give someone else the authority to represent you or do something for you SYN DELEGATE: He was deputed to put our views to the committee.

dep·u·tize /ˈdepjəˌtaɪz/ verb ~ **sb to do sth** to give someone the power to do something that someone in a higher position would usually do: Ms. Green deputized me to manage the office while she was on vacation.

dep·u·ty /ˈdepjəti/ noun (pl. dep·u·ties) **1** a person who is the next most important person below a business manager, a head of a school, a political leader, etc. and who does the person's job when he or she is away: I'm acting as deputy until the manager returns. ♦ the deputy editor of a magazine **2** a police officer who helps the SHERIFF of an area

de·rac·in·ate /dɪˈræsəˌneɪt/ verb ~ **sb** (formal) to force someone to leave the place or situation in which they feel comfortable ▶ **de·rac·i·nat·ed** /dɪˈræsəˌneɪtəd/ adj.

de·rail /dɪˈreɪl/ verb [I, T] (of a train) to leave the track; to make a train do this: The train derailed and plunged into the river. ♦ ~ **sth** (figurative) This latest incident could derail the peace process. ▶ **de·rail·ment** noun [C, U]

de·rail·leur /dɪˈreɪlər/ noun (technical) a type of gear on a bicycle that works by lifting the chain from one gear wheel to another larger or smaller one

de·ranged /dɪˈreɪndʒd/ adj. unable to behave and think normally, especially because of mental illness: mentally deranged ♦ a deranged attacker ▶ **de·range·ment** noun [U]: He seemed to be on the verge of total derangement.

der·by /ˈdɜːrbi/ noun (pl. der·bies) **1** Derby used in the name of several horse races which happen every year: the Kentucky Derby **2** a race or sports competition: a motorcycle derby ⟳ see also DEMOLITION DERBY **3** (also bow·ler, ˌbowler ˈhat) a hard black hat with a curved BRIM and round top, worn in the past

de·reg·u·late /ˌdiːˈregjəˌleɪt/ verb [often passive] ~ **sth** to free a trade, a business activity, etc. from rules and controls SYN DECONTROL: deregulated financial markets ▶ **de·reg·u·la·tion** AWL /ˌdiːˌregjəˈleɪʃn/ noun [U] **de·reg·u·la·to·ry** /ˌdiːˈregjələˌtɔːri/ adj. [only before noun]: deregulatory reforms

der·e·lict /ˈderəlɪkt/ adj., noun
• **adj.** (especially of land or buildings) not used or cared for and in bad condition: derelict land/buildings/sites
• **noun** (formal, disapproving) a person without a home, a job, or property: derelicts living on the streets SYN VAGRANT ⟳ compare HOMELESS

der·e·lic·tion /ˌderəˈlɪkʃn/ noun (formal) **1** [U] the state of being derelict: industrial/urban dereliction ♦ a house in a state of dereliction **2** [U, sing.] ~ **of duty** (formal or law) the fact of deliberately not doing what you ought to do, especially when it is part of your job: The police officers were found guilty of serious dereliction of duty.

de·ride /dɪˈraɪd/ verb [often passive] ~ **sb/sth (as sth)** (formal) to treat someone or something as ridiculous and not worth considering seriously SYN MOCK: His views were derided as old-fashioned.

de ri·gueur /də rɪˈɡɜːr/ adj. [not before noun] (from French) considered necessary if you wish to be accepted socially: Evening dress is de rigueur at the casino.

de·ri·sion /dəˈrɪʒn/ noun [U] a strong feeling that someone or something is ridiculous and not worth considering seriously, shown by laughing in an unkind way or by making unkind remarks SYN SCORN: Her speech was greeted with howls of derision. ♦ He became an object of universal derision.

de·ri·sive /dɪˈraɪsɪv/ (also less frequent de·ri·so·ry) adj. unkind and showing that you think someone or something is ridiculous: She gave a short, derisive laugh. ▶ **de·ri·sive·ly** adv.

de·ri·so·ry /dɪˈraɪsəri; -zə-/ adj. (formal) **1** too small or of too little value to be considered seriously SYN LAUGHABLE: They offered us a derisory $10 a week. **2** = DERISIVE

der·i·va·tion AWL /ˌderəˈveɪʃn/ noun [U, C] the origin or development of something, especially a word: a word of Greek derivation

de·riv·a·tive AWL /dəˈrɪvətɪv/ noun, adj.
• **noun** a word or thing that has been developed or produced from another word or thing: "Happiness" is a derivative of "happy." ♦ Crack is a highly potent and addictive derivative of cocaine.
• **adj.** (usually disapproving) copied from something else; not having new or original ideas: a derivative design/style

de·rive 🔑 AWL /dɪˈraɪv/ verb
PHR V **deˈrive from sth** | **be deˈrived from sth** to come or develop from something: The word "politics" is derived from a Greek word meaning "city." **deˈrive sth from sth 1** (formal) to get something from something: He derived great pleasure from painting. **2** (technical) to obtain a substance from something: The new drug is derived from fish oil.

der·ma·ti·tis /ˌdɜːrməˈtaɪtəs/ noun [U] (medical) a skin condition in which the skin becomes red, swollen, and sore

der·ma·tol·o·gist /ˌdɜːrməˈtɑːlədʒɪst/ noun a doctor who studies and treats skin diseases

der·ma·tol·o·gy /ˌdɜːrməˈtɑːlədʒi/ noun [U] the scientific study of skin diseases ▶ **der·ma·to·log·i·cal** /ˌdɜːrmətlˈɑːdʒɪkl/ adj.

der·mis /ˈdɜːrməs/ noun [U] (biology) the thick layer of living TISSUE beneath the EPIDERMIS (= the outer layer of the skin)

de·ro·gate /ˈderəˌɡeɪt/ verb ~ **sth** (formal) to state that something or someone is without worth
PHR V **ˈderogate from sth** to ignore a responsibility or duty

de·ro·ga·tion /ˌderəˈɡeɪʃn/ noun [U, C] (formal) **1** an occasion when a rule or law is allowed to be ignored **2** words or actions that show that someone or something is considered to have no worth

de·rog·a·to·ry /dəˈrɑːɡəˌtɔːri/ adj. showing a critical attitude toward someone SYN INSULTING: derogatory remarks/comments

der·rick /ˈderɪk/ noun **1** a tall machine used for moving or lifting heavy weights, especially on a ship; a type of CRANE **2** a tall structure over an OIL WELL for holding the DRILL (= the machine that makes the hole in the ground for getting the oil out)

der·ring-do /ˌderɪŋ ˈduː/ noun [U] (old-fashioned, humorous) brave actions, like those in adventure stories

der·vish /ˈdɜːrvɪʃ/ noun a member of a Muslim religious group whose members make a promise to stay poor and live without comforts or pleasures. They perform a fast lively dance as part of their worship: He threw himself around the stage like a whirling dervish.

de·sal·i·na·tion /ˌdiːˌsæləˈneɪʃn/ noun [U] the process of removing salt from ocean water: a desalination plant

des·cant /ˈdeskænt/ noun (music) a tune that is sung or played at the same time as, and usually higher than, the main tune

de·scend /dɪˈsend/ verb **1** [I, T] (formal) to come or go down from a higher to a lower level: The plane began to descend. ♦ The results, ranked in descending order (= from the highest to the lowest) are as follows: ♦ ~ **sth** She descended the stairs slowly. **ANT** ASCEND **2** [I] (*formal*) (of a hill, etc.) to slope downward: *At this point the path descends steeply.* **ANT** ASCEND **3** [I] (*literary*) (of night, DARKNESS, a mood, etc.) to arrive and begin to affect someone or something **SYN** FALL: *Night descends quickly in the tropics.* ◆ *~ **on/upon sb/sth** Calm descended on the crowd.*

PHR V **be des'cended from sb** to be related to someone who lived a long time ago: *He claims to be descended from a Spanish prince.* **des'cend into sth** [no passive] (*formal*) to gradually get into a bad state: *The country was descending into chaos.* **des'cend on/upon sb/sth** to visit someone or something in large numbers, sometimes unexpectedly: *Hundreds of football fans descended on the city.* **des'cend to sth** [no passive] to do something that makes people stop respecting you: *They descended to the level of personal insults.*

de·scend·ant /dɪˈsɛndənt/ *noun* **1** a person's **descendants** are their children, their children's children, and all the people who live after them who are related to them: *He was an Adams and a **direct descendant** of the second President of the United States.* ◆ *Many of them are descendants of the original settlers.* **2** something that has developed from something similar in the past

de·scent /dɪˈsɛnt/ *noun* **1** [C, usually sing.] an action of coming or going down: *The plane began its descent to JFK.* ◆ (*figurative*) *the country's swift descent into anarchy* **ANT** ASCENT **2** [C] a slope going downward: *There is a gradual descent to the ocean.* **ANT** ASCENT **3** [U] a person's family origins **SYN** ANCESTRY: *to be of Scottish descent* ◆ *~ **from sb** He traces his line of descent from the Mayflower Pilgrims.*

de·scribe 🔑 /dɪˈskraɪb/ *verb*
1 to say what someone or something is like: *~ **sb/sth (to/for sb)** Can you describe him to me?* ◆ *~ **sb/sth as sth** The man was described as tall and dark, and aged about 20.* ◆ *Jim was described by his colleagues as "unusual."* ◆ *~ **how, what, etc.** ... Describe how you did it.* ◆ *~ **(sb/sth) doing sth** Several people described seeing strange lights in the sky.* **2** *~ **sth*** (*formal* or *technical*) to make a movement that has a particular shape; to form a particular shape: *The shark described a circle around the shoal of fish.* ► **de·scrib·a·ble** /dɪˈskraɪbəbl/ *adj.*

de·scrip·tion 🔑 /dɪˈskrɪpʃn/ *noun*
1 [C, U] *~ **(of sb/sth)*** a piece of writing or speech that says what someone or something is like; the act of writing or saying in words what someone or something is like: *to give a detailed/full description of the procedure* ◆ *a brief/general description of the software* ◆ *Police have issued a description of the gunman.* ◆ *"Scared stiff" is an apt description of how I felt at that moment.* ◆ *a personal pain that goes beyond description* (= is too great to express in words) ◆ *the novelist's powers of description* **2** [C] **of some, all, every, etc.** *~* of some, etc. type: *boats of every description/all descriptions* ◆ *Their money came from trade of some description.* ◆ *medals, coins, and things of that description*
IDM **answer (to)/fit a description (of sb/sth)** to be like a particular person or thing: *A child answering the description of the missing boy was found safe and well in Chicago yesterday.* ⊃ more at BEGGAR *v.*

de·scrip·tive /dɪˈskrɪptɪv/ *adj.* **1** saying what someone or something is like; describing something: *the descriptive passages in the novel* ◆ *The term I used was meant to be purely descriptive* (= not judging). **2** (*linguistics*) saying how language is actually used, without giving rules for how it should be used **ANT** PRESCRIPTIVE ► **de·scrip·tive·ly** *adv.*

de·scrip·tor /dɪˈskrɪptər/ *noun* (*linguistics*) a word or expression used to describe or identify something

de·scry /dɪˈskraɪ/ *verb* (de·scries, de·scry·ing, de·scried, de·scried) *~ **sb/sth*** (*literary*) to suddenly see someone or something

des·e·crate /ˈdɛsəˌkreɪt/ *verb* *~ **sth*** to damage a holy thing or place or treat it without respect: *desecrated graves* ► **des·e·cra·tion** /ˌdɛsəˈkreɪʃn/ *noun* [U]: *the desecration of a*

cemetery ◆ (*figurative*) *the desecration of the countryside by new roads*

de·seg·re·gate /ˌdiˈsɛgrəˌɡeɪt/ *verb* *~ **sth*** to end the policy of SEGREGATION in a place in which people of different races are kept separate in public places, etc. ► **de·seg·re·ga·tion** /ˌdiˌsɛɡrəˈɡeɪʃn/ *noun* [U]

de·se·lect /ˌdiˈsɪˈlɛkt/ *verb* *~ **sth*** (*computing*) to remove something from the list of possible choices on a computer menu ► **de·se·lec·tion** /ˌdiˈsɪˈlɛkʃn/ *noun* [U]

de·sen·si·tize /ˌdiˈsɛnsəˌtaɪz/ *verb* [usually passive] **1** *~ **sb/sth (to sth)*** to make someone or something less aware of something, especially a problem or something bad, by making them become used to it: *People are increasingly becoming desensitized to violence on television.* **2** *~ **sb/sth*** (*technical*) to treat someone or something so that they will stop being sensitive to physical or chemical changes, or to a particular substance ► **de·sen·si·ti·za·tion** /ˌdiˌsɛnsətə-ˈzeɪʃn/ *noun* [U]

de·sert 🔑 *noun, verb*
● *noun* /ˈdɛzərt/ ⊃ see also DESERTS [C, U] a large area of land that has very little water and very few plants growing on it. Many deserts are covered by sand: *the Sahara Desert* ◆ *Somalia is mostly desert.* ◆ *burning desert sands* ◆ (*figurative*) *a cultural desert* (= a place without any culture)
● *verb* /dɪˈzɜrt/ **1** [T] *~ **sb*** to leave someone without help or support **SYN** ABANDON: *She was deserted by her husband.* **2** [T, often passive] *~ **sth*** to go away from a place and leave it empty **SYN** ABANDON: *The villages have been deserted.* ◆ *The owl seems to have deserted its nest.* **3** [I, T] *~ **(sth)*** to leave the armed forces without permission: *Large numbers of soldiers deserted as defeat became inevitable.* **4** [T] *~ **sth (for sth)*** to stop using, buying, or supporting something: *Why did you desert teaching for politics?* **5** [T] *~ **sb*** if a particular quality **deserts** you, it is not there when you need it: *Her courage seemed to desert her for a moment.* **IDM** see SINK *v.* ► **de·ser·tion** /dɪˈzɜrʃn/ *noun* [U, C]: *She felt betrayed by her husband's desertion.* ◆ *The army was badly affected by desertions.*

desert ˌboot *noun* a SUEDE boot that just covers the ankle

de·sert·ed /dɪˈzɜrtəd/ *adj.* **1** (of a place) with no people in it: *deserted streets* **2** left by a person or people who do not intend to return **SYN** ABANDONED: *a deserted village* ◆ *deserted wives*

de·sert·er /dɪˈzɜrtər/ *noun* a person who leaves the army, navy, etc. without permission (= DESERTS)

de·sert·i·fi·ca·tion /dɪˌzɜrtəfəˈkeɪʃn/ *noun* [U] (*technical*) the process of becoming or making something a desert

ˌdesert ˈisland *noun* a tropical island where no people live

deserts /dɪˈzɜrts/ *noun* [pl.]
IDM **sb's (just) deserts** what someone deserves, especially when it is something bad: *The family of the victim said that the killer had **got his just deserts** when he was jailed for life.*

de·serve 🔑 /dɪˈzɜrv/ *verb* (not used in the progressive tenses)
if someone or something **deserves** something, it is right that they should have it, because of the way they have behaved or because of what they are: *~ **sth** You deserve a rest after all that hard work.* ◆ *The report deserves careful consideration.* ◆ *One player in particular deserves a mention.* ◆ *What have I done to deserve this?* ◆ *~ **to do sth** They didn't deserve to win.* ◆ *He deserves to be locked up forever for what he did.* ◆ *~ **doing sth** Several other points deserve mentioning.*
IDM **sb deserves a medal** (*informal*) used to say that you admire someone because they have done something difficult or unpleasant **get what you deserve** | **deserve all/everything you get** (*informal*) used to say that you think someone has earned the bad things that happen to them ⊃ more at TURN *n.*

de·serv·ed·ly /dɪˈzɜrvədli/ *adv.* in the way that is deserved; correctly: *The restaurant is deservedly popular.* ◆ *He has just been chosen for the top job, and **deservedly so**.*

de·serv·ing /dɪˈzɜrvɪŋ/ *adj.* *~ **(of sth)*** (*formal*) that deserves help, praise, a reward, etc.: *to give money to a deserving cause* ◆ *This family is one of the most deserving cases.* ◆ *an issue deserving of attention* **ANT** UNDESERVING

dés·ha·billé /ˌdɛzæbiˈyeɪ/ (also **dis·ha·bille** /ˌdɪsəˈbil; -ˈbi/) *noun* [U] (*formal or humorous*) the state of wearing no clothes or very few clothes: *in a state of déshabillé*

desiccated /ˈdɛsɪˌkeɪtəd/ *adj.* **1** (of food) dried in order to preserve it: *desiccated coconut* **2** (*technical*) completely dry: *treeless and desiccated soil*

des·ic·ca·tion /ˌdɛsɪˈkeɪʃn/ *noun* [U] (*technical*) the process of becoming completely dry

de·sid·er·a·tum /dɪˌsɪdəˈrɑtəm; -ˈreɪ-/ *noun* (*pl.* **de·sid·er·a·ta** /-ˈtə/) (from Latin, *formal*) a thing that is wanted or needed

de·sign ✒ **AWL** /dɪˈzaɪn/ *noun, verb*

● **noun**
> ARRANGEMENT **1** [U, C] the general arrangement of the different parts of something that is made, such as a building, book, machine, etc.: *The basic design of the car is very similar to that of earlier models.* ◆ *special new design features* ◆ *The magazine will appear in a new design from next month.*
> DRAWING/PLAN/MODEL **2** [U] the art or process of deciding how something will look, work, etc. by drawing plans, making models, etc.: *a course in art and design* ◆ *a design studio* ◆ *computer-aided design* ◆ *the design and development of new products* ⊃ see also INTERIOR DESIGN **3** [C] ~ **(for sth)** a drawing or plan from which something may be made: *designs for aircraft* ◆ *new and original designs*
> PATTERN **4** [C] an arrangement of lines and shapes as a decoration **SYN** PATTERN: *floral/abstract/geometric designs* ◆ *The tiles come in a huge range of colors and designs.*
> INTENTION **5** [U, C] a plan or an intention: *It happened—whether by accident or design—that the two of them were left alone after all the others had gone.* ◆ *It is all part of his grand design.*
> **IDM** **have designs on sb** (*formal or humorous*) to want to start a sexual relationship with someone **have designs on sth** (*formal*) to be planning to get something for yourself, often in a way that other people do not approve of: *Rumors spread that the Duke had designs on the crown* (= wanted to make himself king).

● **verb**
> DRAW PLANS **1** to decide how something will look, work, etc., especially by drawing plans or making models: ~ **sth** *to design a car/a dress/an office* ◆ *a badly designed kitchen* ◆ ~ **sth for sb/sth** *They asked me to design a poster for the campaign.* ◆ ~ **sth** *Could you design us a poster?*
> PLAN SOMETHING **2** ~ **sth** to think of and plan a system, a way of doing something, etc.: *The teacher had to design a brand-new syllabus for the class.*
> FOR SPECIAL PURPOSE **3** [usually passive] to make, plan, or intend something for a particular purpose or use: ~ **sth (for sth)** *The method is specifically designed for use in small groups.* ◆ ~ **sth (as sth)** *This course is primarily designed as an introduction to the subject.* ◆ ~ **sth to do sth** *The program is designed to help people who have been out of work for a long time.*

des·ig·nate *verb, adj.*
● **verb** /ˈdɛzɪɡˌneɪt/ [often passive] **1** to say officially that someone or something has a particular character or name; to describe someone or something in a particular way: ~ **sb/sth (as) sth** *This area has been designated (as) a national park.* ◆ ~ **sb/sth (as being/having sth)** *Several students were designated as having moderate or severe learning difficulties.* ◆ *a designated nature reserve* ◆ *designated seats for the elderly* **2** to choose or name someone for a particular job or position: ~ **sb/sth** *The director is allowed to designate his or her successor.* ◆ ~ **sb (as) sth** *Who has she designated (as) her deputy?* ◆ ~ **sb to do sth** *the man designated to succeed the president* **3** ~ **sth (by sth)** to show something using a particular mark or sign: *The different types are designated by the letters A, B, and C.*

● **adj.** /ˈdɛzɪɡnət; ˈdɛzɪɡˌneɪt/ [after noun] (*formal*) chosen to do a job but not yet having officially started it: *an interview with the director designate*

ι**designated 'driver** *noun* (*informal*) the person who agrees to drive and not drink alcohol when people go to a party, a bar, etc.

ι**designated 'hitter** *noun* (in baseball) a player who is named at the start of the game as the person who will hit the ball in place of the PITCHER

des·ig·na·tion /ˌdɛzɪɡˈneɪʃn/ *noun* (*formal*) **1** [U] ~ **(as sth)** the action of choosing a person or thing for a particular purpose, or of giving them or it a particular status: *The district is under consideration for designation as a conservation area.* **2** [C] a name, title, or description: *Her official designation is Financial Controller.*

de·sign·er ✒ **AWL** /dɪˈzaɪnər/ *noun, adj.*
● **noun** a person whose job is to decide how things such as clothes, furniture, tools, etc. will look or work by making drawings, plans, or patterns: *a fashion/jewelry/etc. designer* ◆ *an industrial designer*
● **adj.** [only before noun] made by a famous designer; expensive and having a famous brand name: *designer jeans* ◆ *designer labels* ◆ *designer water* ⊃ collocations at FASHION

de·signer 'baby *noun* (used especially in newspapers) a baby that is born from an EMBRYO that was selected from a number of embryos produced using IVF, for example because the parents want a baby that can provide cells to treat a brother's or sister's medical condition

de·signer 'drug *noun* a drug produced artificially, usually one that is illegal

de·sir·a·ble /dɪˈzaɪrəbl/ *adj.* **1** (*formal*) that you would like to have or do; worth having or doing: *She chatted for a few minutes about the qualities she considered desirable in a secretary.* ◆ *Such measures are desirable, if not essential.* ◆ *The house has many desirable features.* ◆ *highly desirable* ◆ ~ **that** *It is desirable that interest rates be reduced.* ◆ ~ **(for sb) to do sth** *It is no longer desirable for adult children to live with their parents.* **ANT** UNDESIRABLE **2** (of a person) causing other people to feel sexual desire ▶ **de·sir·a·bil·i·ty** /dɪˌzaɪrəˈbɪləti/ *noun* [U] (*formal*): *No one questions the desirability of cheaper fares.*

de·sire ✒ /dɪˈzaɪər/ *noun, verb*
● **noun 1** [C, U] a strong wish to have or do something: *enough money to satisfy all your desires* ◆ ~ **for sth** *a strong desire for power* ◆ ~ **to do sth** *She felt an overwhelming desire to return home.* ◆ (*formal*) *I have no desire* (= I do not want) *to discuss the matter further.* ◆ (*formal*) *He has expressed a desire to see you.* **2** [U, C] ~ **(for sb)** a strong wish to have sex with someone: *She felt a surge of love and desire for him.* **3** [C, usually sing.] a person or thing that is wished for: *When she agreed to marry him he felt he had achieved his heart's desire.*
● **verb** (not used in the progressive tenses) **1** (*formal*) to want something; to wish for something: ~ **sth** *We all desire health and happiness.* ◆ *The house had everything you could desire.* ◆ *The medicine did not achieve the desired effect.* ◆ ~ **(sb/sth) to do sth** *Fewer people desire to live in the north of the country.* **2** ~ **sb** to be sexually attracted to someone: *He still desired her.*
> **IDM** **leave a lot, much, something, etc. to be desired** to be bad or unacceptable

de·sir·ous /dɪˈzaɪrəs/ *adj.* [not before noun] ~ **(of sth / of doing sth)** | ~ **(to do sth)** (*formal*) having a wish for something; wanting something: *At that point Franco was desirous of prolonging the war.*

de·sist /dɪˈzɪst; dɪˈsɪst/ *verb* [I] ~ **(from sth/from doing sth)** (*formal*) to stop doing something: *They agreed to desist from the bombing campaign.* **IDM** see CEASE

desk ✒ /dɛsk/ *noun*
1 a piece of furniture like a table, usually with drawers in it, that you sit at to read, write, work, etc.: *He used to be a pilot*

but now he has **a desk job. 2** a place where you can get information or be served at an airport, a hotel, etc.: *the check-in desk* ◆ *the reception desk* ➔ see also FRONT DESK **3** an office at a newspaper, television company, etc. that deals with a particular subject: *the sports desk* ➔ see also CITY DESK, NEWS DESK

'**desk clerk** *noun* = CLERK *n.* (4)

de·skill /ˌdiˈskɪl/ *verb* ~ **sth** (*technical*) to reduce the amount of skill that is needed to do a particular job ▶ **de·skill·ing** *noun* [U]

desk·top /ˈdɛsktɑp/ *noun* **1** the top of a desk **2** a screen on a computer that shows the ICONS of the programs that can be used **3** = DESKTOP COMPUTER

ˌ**desktop com'puter** (also **desk·top**) *noun* a computer with a keyboard, screen, and main processing unit, that sits on a desk ➔ compare LAPTOP, NOTEBOOK

ˌ**desktop 'publishing** *noun* [U] (*abbr.* DTP) the use of a small computer and a printer to produce a small book, a magazine, or other printed material

des·o·late *adj., verb*

● *adj.* /ˈdɛsələt/ **1** (of a place) empty and without people, making you feel sad or frightened: *a bleak and desolate landscape* **2** very lonely and unhappy SYN FORLORN

● *verb* /ˈdɛsəˌleɪt/ [usually passive] ~ **sb** (*literary*) to make someone feel sad and without hope: *She had been desolated by the death of her friend.*

des·o·la·tion /ˌdɛsəˈleɪʃn/ *noun* [U] (*formal*) **1** the feeling of being very lonely and unhappy **2** the state of a place that is ruined or destroyed and offers no joy or hope to people: *a scene of utter desolation*

de·spair /dɪˈspɛr/ *noun, verb*

● *noun* [U] the feeling of having lost all hope: *She uttered a cry of despair.* ◆ *A deep sense of despair overwhelmed him.* ◆ *He gave up the struggle in despair.* ◆ *One harsh word would send her into the depths of despair.* ◆ *Eventually, driven to despair, he threw himself under a train.* ➔ see also DESPERATE IDM **be the despair of sb** to make someone worried or unhappy, because they cannot help: *My handwriting was the despair of my teachers.*

● *verb* [I] to stop having any hope that a situation will change or improve: *Don't despair! We'll think of a way out of this.* ◆ ~ **of sth/sb** *I despair of him; he can't keep a job for more than six months.* ◆ ~ **of doing sth** *They'd almost despaired of ever having children.*

des·pair·ing /dɪˈspɛrɪŋ/ *adj.* showing or feeling the loss of all hope: *a despairing cry/look/sigh* ◆ *With every day that passed he became more despairing.* ▶ **des·pair·ing·ly** *adv.*: *She looked despairingly at the mess.*

des·per·a·do /ˌdɛspəˈrɑdoʊ/ *noun* (*pl.* **des·per·a·does** or **des·per·a·dos**) (*old-fashioned*) a man who does dangerous and criminal things without caring about himself or other people

des·per·ate 🔑 /ˈdɛsprət; -pərət/ *adj.*
1 feeling or showing that you have little hope and are ready to do anything without worrying about danger to yourself or others: *The prisoners grew increasingly desperate.* ◆ *Stores are getting desperate after two years of poor sales.* ◆ *Somewhere out there was a desperate man, cold, hungry, hunted.* ◆ *I heard sounds of a desperate struggle in the next room.* **2** [usually before noun] (of an action) giving little hope of success; tried when everything else has failed: *a desperate bid for freedom* ◆ *She clung to the edge in a desperate attempt to save herself.* ◆ *His increasing financial difficulties forced him to take desperate measures.* ◆ *Doctors were fighting a desperate battle to save the little girl's life.* **3** [not usually before noun] needing or wanting something very much: ~ **(for sth)** *He was so desperate for a job he would have done anything.* ◆ (*informal*) *I'm desperate for a cigarette.* ◆ ~ **(to do sth)** *I was absolutely desperate to see her.* **4** (of a situation) extremely serious or dangerous: *The children are in desperate need of love and attention.* ◆ *They face a desperate shortage of clean water.* ▶ **des·per·ate·ly** *adv.*: *desperately ill/unhappy/*

lonely ◆ *He took a deep breath, desperately trying to keep calm.* ◆ *They desperately wanted a child.* ◆ *She looked desperately around for a weapon.*

des·per·a·tion /ˌdɛspəˈreɪʃn/ *noun* [U] the state of being desperate: *In desperation, she called Louise and asked for her help.* ◆ *There was a note of desperation in his voice.* ◆ *an act of sheer desperation*

des·pi·ca·ble /dɪˈspɪkəbl/ *adj.* (*formal*) very unpleasant or evil: *a despicable act/crime* ◆ *I hate you! You're despicable.*

de·spise /dɪˈspaɪz/ *verb* ~ **sb/sth** (not used in the progressive tenses) to dislike and have no respect for someone or something: *She despised gossip in any form.* ◆ *He despised himself for being so cowardly.* ➔ thesaurus box at HATE

de·spite 🔑 AWL /dɪˈspaɪt/ *prep.*
1 used to show that something happened or is true although something else might have happened to prevent it SYN IN SPITE OF: *Her voice was shaking despite all her efforts to control it.* ◆ *Despite applying for hundreds of jobs, he is still out of work.* ◆ *She was good at physics despite the fact that she found it boring.* ➔ language bank at HOWEVER **2 despite yourself** used to show that someone did not intend to do the thing mentioned SYN IN SPITE OF: *He had to laugh despite himself.*

de·spoil /dɪˈspɔɪl/ *verb* ~ **sth (of sth)** (*literary*) to steal something valuable from a place; to make a place less attractive by damaging or destroying it SYN PLUNDER

de·spond·ent /dɪˈspɑndənt/ *adj.* ~ **(about/over sth)** sad, without much hope SYN DEJECTED: *She was becoming increasingly despondent about the way things were going.* ▶ **de·spond·en·cy** /-dənsi/ *noun* [U]: *a mood of despondency* ◆ *Life's not all gloom and despondency.* ◆ **de·spond·ent·ly** *adv.*

des·pot /ˈdɛspət; -pɑt/ *noun* a ruler with great power, especially one who uses it in a cruel way: *an enlightened despot* (= one who tries to use his/her power in a good way) ▶ **des·pot·ic** /dɛˈspɑtɪk; dɪ-/ *adj.*: *despotic power/rule*

des·pot·ism /ˈdɛspəˌtɪzəm/ *noun* [U] the rule of a despot

des·sert /dɪˈzərt/ *noun* [U, C] sweet food eaten at the end of a meal: *What's for dessert?* ◆ *a rich chocolate dessert* ◆ *a dessert wine* ◆ *the dessert cart* (= a table on wheels from which you choose your dessert in a restaurant) ➔ collocations at RESTAURANT

des·sert·spoon /dɪˈzərtspun/ *noun* **1** a spoon of medium size **2** (also **des·sert·spoon·ful** /dɪˈzərtspunfʊl/) the amount a dessertspoon can hold

de·sta·bi·lize /ˌdiˈsteɪbəˌlaɪz/ *verb* ~ **sth** to make a system, country, government, etc. become less firmly established or successful: *Terrorist attacks were threatening to destabilize the government.* ◆ *The news had a destabilizing effect on the stock market.* ➔ compare STABILIZE ▶ **de·sta·bi·li·za·tion** /ˌdiˌsteɪbələˈzeɪʃn/ *noun* [U]

des·ti·na·tion /ˌdɛstəˈneɪʃn/ *noun, adj.*

● *noun* a place to which someone or something is going or being sent: *popular holiday destinations like the Bahamas* ◆ *arrive at/reach your destination* ◆ *Our luggage was checked all the way through to our final destination.*

● *adj.* ~ **hotel/store/restaurant, etc.** a hotel, store, etc. that people will make a special trip to visit

des·tined /ˈdɛstənd/ *adj.* (*formal*) **1** having a future that has been decided or planned at an earlier time, especially by FATE: ~ **for sth** *He was destined for a military career, like his father before him.* ◆ ~ **to do sth** *We seem destined never to meet.* **2** ~ **for...** on the way to or intended for a place SYN BOUND FOR: *goods destined for Poland*

des·ti·ny /ˈdɛstəni/ *noun* (*pl.* **des·ti·nies**) **1** [C] what happens to someone or what will happen to them in the future, especially things that they cannot change or avoid: *the destinies of nations* ◆ *He wants to be in control of his own destiny.* **2** [U] the power believed to control events SYN FATE: *I believe there's some force guiding us—call it God, destiny or fate.* ➔ thesaurus box at LUCK

des·ti·tute /ˈdɛstəˌtut/ *adj.* **1** without money, food, and the other things necessary for life: *When he died, his family was* *left completely destitute.* **2 the destitute** *noun* [pl.] people who are destitute **3 ~ of sth** (*formal*) lacking something: *They seem destitute of ordinary human feelings.* ▶ **des·ti·tu·tion** /ˌdɛstəˈtuʃn/ *noun* [U]: *homelessness and destitution*

de·stress /ˌdiˈstrɛs/ *verb* [I, T] **~ (sb/yourself)** to relax after working hard or experiencing stress; to reduce the amount of stress that you experience: *De-stress yourself with a relaxing bath.*

de·stroy /dɪˈstrɔɪ/ *verb*
1 ~ sth/sb to damage something so badly that it no longer exists, works, etc.: *The building was completely destroyed by fire.* ◆ *They've destroyed all the evidence.* ◆ *Heat gradually destroys vitamin C.* ◆ *You have destroyed my hopes of happiness.* ◆ *Failure was slowly destroying him* (= making him less and less confident and happy). **2 ~ sth** to kill an animal deliberately, usually because it is sick or not wanted: *The injured horse had to be destroyed.* **3 ~ sb** (*informal*) to defeat someone completely: *The Tigers destroyed the Padres in five games.* ⭢ see also SOUL-DESTROYING

WORD FAMILY
destroy *verb*
destroyer *noun*
destruction *noun*
destructive *adj.*
indestructible *adj.*

de·stroy·er /dɪˈstrɔɪər/ *noun* **1** a small fast ship used in war, for example to protect larger ships **2** a person or thing that destroys: *Sugar is the destroyer of healthy teeth.*

de·struc·tion /dɪˈstrʌkʃn/ *noun* [U]
the act of destroying something; the process of being destroyed: *the destruction of the rainforests* ◆ *weapons of mass destruction* ◆ *a tidal wave bringing death and destruction in its wake* ◆ *The central argument is that capitalism sows the seeds of its own destruction* (= creates the forces that destroy it).

de·struc·tive /dɪˈstrʌktɪv/ *adj.* causing destruction or damage: *the destructive power of modern weapons* ◆ *the destructive effects of anxiety* ⭢ compare CONSTRUCTIVE ▶ **de·struc·tive·ly** *adv.* **de·struc·tive·ness** *noun* [U]

des·ul·to·ry /ˈdɛsəlˌtɔri/ *adj.* (*formal*) going from one thing to another, without a definite plan and without enthusiasm: *I wandered about in a desultory fashion.* ◆ *a desultory conversation* ▶ **des·ul·to·ri·ly** /ˈdɛsəlˈtɔrəli/ *adv.*

Det. *abbr.* (in writing) DETECTIVE: *Det. Cox*

de·tach /dɪˈtætʃ/ *verb* **1** [T, I] to remove something from something larger; to become separated from something: **~ sth** *Detach the coupon and return it as soon as possible* ◆ **~ sth from sth** *One of the panels had become detached from the main structure.* ◆ **~ (from sth)** *The skis should detach from the boot if you fall.* ⭢ compare ATTACH **2** [T] **~ yourself (from sb/sth)** (*formal*) to leave or separate yourself from someone or something: *She detached herself from his embrace.* ◆ (*figurative*) *I tried to detach myself from the reality of these terrible events.* **3** [T] **~ sb/sth** (*technical*) to send a group of soldiers, etc. away from the main group, especially to do special duties

de·tach·a·ble /dɪˈtætʃəbl/ *adj.* that can be taken off **SYN** REMOVABLE: *a coat with a detachable hood*

de·tached /dɪˈtætʃt/ *adj.* **1** showing a lack of feeling **SYN** INDIFFERENT: *She wanted him to stop being so cool, so detached, so cynical.* **2** (*approving*) not influenced by other people or by your own feelings **SYN** IMPARTIAL: *a detached observer* **3** (of a house) not joined to another house on either side ⭢ compare SEMI-DETACHED

de·tach·ment /dɪˈtætʃmənt/ *noun* **1** [U] the state of not being involved in something in an emotional or personal way: *He answered with an air of detachment.* ◆ *She felt a sense of detachment from what was going on.* **ANT** INVOLVEMENT **2** [U] (*approving*) the state of not being influenced by other people or by your own feelings: *In judging these issues a degree of critical detachment is required.* **3** [C] a group of soldiers, ships, etc. sent away from a larger group, especially to do special duties: *a detachment of artillery* **4** [U] the act of detaching something; the process of being detached from something: *to suffer detachment of the retina*

de·tail /ˈditeɪl; dɪˈteɪl/ *noun, verb*
● *noun* /ˈditeɪl; dɪˈteɪl/
▷ FACTS/INFORMATION **1** [C] a small individual fact or item; a less important fact or item: *an expedition planned down to the last detail* ◆ *He stood still, absorbing every detail of the street.* ◆ *Tell me the main points now; leave the details until later.* **2** [U] the small facts or features of something, when you consider them all together: *This issue will be discussed in more detail in the next chapter.* ◆ *The research has been carried out with scrupulous attention to detail.* ◆ *He had an eye for detail* (= noticed and remembered small details). ◆ *The fine detail of the plan has yet to be worked out.* **3** details [pl.] information about something: *Please supply the following details: name, age, and sex.* ◆ *Further details and forms are available on request.* ◆ *They didn't give any details about the game.* ◆ *"We had a terrible time—" "Oh, spare me the details* (= don't tell me any more)."
▷ SMALL PARTS **4** [C, U] a small part of a picture or painting; the smaller or less important parts of a picture, pattern, etc. when you consider them all together: *This is a detail from the 1844 Turner painting.* ◆ *a huge picture with a lot of detail in it*
▷ SOLDIERS **5** [C] a group of soldiers given special duties
IDM **go into detail(s)** to explain something fully: *I can't go into details now; it would take too long.*
● *verb* /dɪˈteɪl; ˈditeɪl/
▷ GIVE FACTS/INFORMATION **1 ~ sth** to give a list of facts or all the available information about something: *The brochure details all the hotels in the area and their facilities.*
▷ ORDER SOLDIER **2** [often passive] **~ sb (to do sth)** to give an official order to someone, especially a soldier, to do a particular task: *Several of the men were detailed to form a search party.*
▷ CLEAN CAR **3** /ˈditeɪl/ **~ sth** to clean a car extremely thoroughly: *He got work for a while detailing cars.*

de·tailed /dɪˈteɪld; ˈditeɪld/ *adj.*
giving many details and a lot of information; paying great attention to details: *a detailed description/analysis/study* ◆ *He gave me detailed instructions on how to get there.*

de·tail·ing /ˈditeɪlɪŋ/ *noun* [U] small details put on a building, piece of clothing, etc., especially for decoration

de·tain /dɪˈteɪn/ *verb* **1 ~ sb** to keep someone in an official place, such as a police station, a prison, or a hospital, and prevent them from leaving: *One man has been detained for questioning.* **2 ~ sb** (*formal*) to delay someone or prevent them from going somewhere: *I'm sorry—he'll be late; he's been detained at a meeting.* ⭢ see also DETENTION

de·tain·ee /ˌditeɪˈni; dɪˌteɪˈni/ *noun* a person who is kept in prison, usually because of his or her political opinions

de·tect AWL /dɪˈtɛkt/ *verb* **~ sth** to discover or notice something, especially something that is not easy to see, hear, etc.: *The tests are designed to detect the disease early.* ◆ *an instrument that can detect small amounts of radiation* ◆ *Do I detect a note of criticism?* ⭢ thesaurus box at NOTICE ▶ **de·tect·a·ble** AWL /dɪˈtɛktəbl/ *adj.*: *The noise is barely detectable by the human ear.* **ANT** UNDETECTABLE

de·tec·tion AWL /dɪˈtɛkʃn/ *noun* [U] the process of detecting something; the fact of being detected: *crime prevention and detection* ◆ *Last year the detection rate for car theft was just 13%.* ◆ *Many problems, however, escape detection.* ◆ *Early detection of cancer is vitally important.*

de·tec·tive AWL /dɪˈtɛktɪv/ *noun* (*abbr.* Det.) **1** a person, especially a police officer, whose job is to examine crimes and catch criminals: *Detective (Roger) Brown* ◆ *detectives from the anti-terrorist squad* ◆ *a detective story/novel* ⭢ see also STORE DETECTIVE **2** a person employed by someone to find out information about someone or something ⭢ see also PRIVATE DETECTIVE

de·tec·tor AWL /dɪˈtɛktər/ *noun* a piece of equipment for discovering the presence of something, such as metal, smoke, EXPLOSIVES, or changes in pressure or temperature: *a smoke detector*

dé·tente (also **de·tente**) /deɪˈtɑnt/ *noun* [U] (from *French*, *formal*) an improvement in the relationship between two or more countries that have been unfriendly toward each other in the past

de·ten·tion /dɪˈtɛnʃn/ *noun* **1** [U] the state of being kept in a place, especially a prison, and prevented from leaving: *a sentence of 12 months' detention in a juvenile detention center* ◆ *police powers of arrest and detention* ◆ *allegations of torture and detention without trial* ◆ *a detention camp* **2** [U, C] the punishment of being kept at school for a time after other students have gone home: *They can't give me (a) detention for this.* ⊃ see also DETAIN

de·ten·tion ˌcenter (*CanE usually* **de·ten·tion ˌcentre**) *noun* **1** a place where young people who have committed offenses are kept in detention **2** a place where people are kept in detention, especially people who have entered a country illegally

de·ter /dɪˈtɜr/ *verb* (**-rr-**) [T, I] **~ (sb) (from sth/from doing sth)** to make someone decide not to do something or continue doing something, especially by making them understand the difficulties and unpleasant results of their actions: *I told him I wasn't interested, but he wasn't deterred.* ◆ *The high price of the service could deter people from seeking advice.* ⊃ see also DETERRENT

de·ter·gent /dɪˈtɜrdʒənt/ *noun* [U, C] a liquid or powder that helps remove dirt, for example from clothes or dishes

de·te·ri·o·rate /dɪˈtɪriəˌreɪt/ *verb* [I] to become worse: *Her health deteriorated rapidly, and she died shortly afterward.* ◆ *deteriorating weather conditions* ◆ **~ into sth** *The discussion quickly deteriorated into an angry argument.* ▶ **de·te·ri·o·ra·tion** /dɪˌtɪriəˈreɪʃn/ *noun* [U, C]: *a serious deterioration in relations between the two countries*

de·ter·mi·na·ble /dɪˈtɜrmɪnəbl/ *adj.* (*formal*) that can be found out or calculated: *During the third month of pregnancy the sex of the child becomes determinable.*

de·ter·mi·nant /dɪˈtɜrmənənt/ *noun* (*formal*) a thing that decides whether or how something happens

de·ter·mi·nate /dɪˈtɜrmənət/ *adj.* (*formal*) fixed and definite: *a sentence with a determinate meaning* **ANT** INDETERMINATE

de·ter·mi·na·tion 🔑 /dɪˌtɜrməˈneɪʃn/ *noun*
1 [U] the quality that makes you continue trying to do something even when this is difficult: *fierce/grim/dogged determination* ◆ *He fought the illness with courage and determination.* ◆ *They had survived by sheer determination.* ◆ **~ to do sth** *I admire her determination to get it right.* **2** [U] (*formal*) the process of deciding something officially: *factors influencing the determination of future policy* **3** [U, C] (*technical*) the act of finding out or calculating something: *Both methods rely on the accurate determination of the pressure of the gas.*

de·ter·mine 🔑 /dɪˈtɜrmən/ *verb* (*formal*)
1 [T] to discover the facts about something; to calculate something exactly **SYN** ESTABLISH: **~ sth** *An inquiry was set up to determine the cause of the accident.* ◆ **~ what, whether, etc.…** *We set out to determine exactly what happened that night.* ◆ **it is determined that…** *It was determined that she had died of natural causes.* **2** [T] **~ sth** | **~ what, whether, etc.…** to make something happen in a particular way or be of a particular type: *Age and experience will be determining factors in our choice of candidate.* ◆ *Upbringing plays an important part in determining a person's character.* **3** [T] to officially decide and/or arrange something: **~ sth** *A date for the meeting has yet to be determined.* ◆ **~ (that)…** *The court determined (that) the defendant should pay the legal costs.* **4** [T, I] **~ to do sth** | **~ (that)…** | **~ on sth** to decide definitely to do something: *They determined to start early.*

de·ter·mined 🔑 /dɪˈtɜrmənd/ *adj.*
1 [not before noun] **~ (to do sth)** if you are **determined** to do something, you have made a firm decision to do it and you will not let anyone prevent you: *I'm determined to succeed.* **2** showing a person's determination to do some-

thing: *a determined effort to stop smoking* ◆ *The proposal had been dropped in the face of determined opposition.* **IDM** see BOUND *adj.* ▶ **de·ter·mined·ly** /dɪˈtɜrməndli; -mənədli/ *adv.*

de·ter·min·er /dɪˈtɜrmənər/ *noun* (*grammar*) (abbreviation *det.* in this dictionary) a word such as *the, some, my*, etc. that comes before a noun to show how the noun is being used

de·ter·min·ism /dɪˈtɜrməˌnɪzəm/ *noun* [U] (*philosophy*) the belief that people are not free to choose what they are like or how they behave, because these things are decided by their surroundings and other things over which they have no control ▶ **de·ter·min·is·tic** /dɪˌtɜrməˈnɪstɪk/ *adj.*

de·ter·rent /dɪˈtɜrənt/ *noun* **~ (to sb/sth)** a thing that makes someone less likely to do something (= that deters them): *Hopefully his punishment will act as a deterrent to others.* ◆ *the country's nuclear deterrents* (= nuclear weapons that are intended to stop an enemy from attacking) ▶ **de·ter·rence** /dɪˈtɜrəns/ *noun* [U] (*formal*) **de·ter·rent** *adj.*: *a deterrent effect*

de·test /dɪˈtɛst/ *verb* (not used in the progressive tenses) **~ sb/sth** | **~ doing sth** to hate someone or something very much **SYN** LOATHE: *They detested each other on sight.* ⊃ thesaurus box at HATE ▶ **de·tes·ta·tion** /ˌditɛˈsteɪʃn/ *noun* [U]

de·test·a·ble /dɪˈtɛstəbl/ *adj.* that deserves to be hated: *All terrorist crime is detestable, whoever the victims.*

de·throne /ˌdiˈθroʊn/ *verb* **~ sb** to remove a king or queen from power; to remove someone from a position of authority or power

det·o·nate /ˈdɛtnˌeɪt/ *verb* [I, T] **~ (sth)** to explode, or to make a bomb or other device explode: *Two other bombs failed to detonate.* ⊃ thesaurus box at EXPLODE

det·o·na·tion /ˌdɛtnˈeɪʃn/ *noun* [C, U] an explosion; the action of making something explode

det·o·na·tor /ˈdɛtnˌeɪtər/ *noun* a device for making something, especially a bomb, explode

de·tour /ˈditʊr/ *noun, verb*
● *noun* **1** a longer route that you take in order to avoid a problem or to visit a place: *We had to make a detour around the flooded fields.* ◆ *It's well worth making a detour to see the village.* **2** a road or route that is used when the usual one is closed
● *verb* [I, T] **~ (sb/sth) (to…)** to take a longer route in order to avoid a problem or to visit a place; to make someone or something take a longer route: *The president detoured to Chicago for a special meeting.*

de·tox /ˈditɑks/ *noun, verb* (*informal*)
● *noun* [U] **1** = DETOXIFICATION: *a detox clinic* ◆ *He's gone into detox.* **2** the process of removing harmful substances from your body by only eating and drinking particular things
● *verb* [T, I] **1** **~ (sb)** = DETOXIFY: *He was detoxed from painkillers.* **2** **~ (sb)** to remove harmful substances from your body by following a special diet: *I detoxed by eating mostly protein and vegetables.*

de·tox·i·fi·ca·tion /ˌditɑksəfəˈkeɪʃn/ (also *informal* **de·tox**) *noun* [U] treatment given to people to help them stop drinking alcohol or taking drugs: *a detoxification unit*

de·tox·i·fy /dɪˈtɑksəˌfaɪ/ *verb* (**de·tox·i·fies**, **de·tox·i·fy·ing**, **de·tox·i·fied**, **de·tox·i·fied**) **1** **~ sth** to remove harmful substances or poisons from something **2** **~ sb** to treat someone in order to help them stop drinking too much alcohol or taking drugs

de·tract /dɪˈtrækt/ *verb*
PHR V **deˈtract from sth** | **deˈtract sth from sth** (not used in the progressive tenses) to make something seem less good or enjoyable **SYN** TAKE AWAY FROM: *He was determined not to let anything detract from his enjoyment of the trip.*

de·trac·tor /dɪˈtræktər/ *noun* [usually pl.] (especially *formal*) a person who tries to make someone or something seem less good or valuable by criticizing it

de·train /dɪˈtreɪn/ *verb* [I, T] **~ (sb)** (*formal*) to leave a train or make someone leave a train

t tea   ṭ butter   d did   k cat   g got   tʃ chin   dʒ June   f fall

det·ri·ment /ˈdɛtrəmənt/ *noun* [U, C, usually sing.] (*formal*) the act of causing harm or damage; something that causes harm or damage
IDM to the detriment of sb/sth | to sb/sth's detriment resulting in harm or damage to someone or something: *He was engrossed in his job to the detriment of his health.* **without detriment (to sb/sth)** not resulting in harm or damage to someone or something

det·ri·men·tal /ˌdɛtrəˈmɛntl/ *adj.* ~ **(to sb/sth)** harmful **SYN** DAMAGING: *the sun's detrimental effect on skin* ◆ *The policy will be detrimental to the peace process.* ▶ **det·ri·men·tal·ly** /-ˈmɛntl·i/ *adv.*

de·tri·tus /dɪˈtraɪtəs/ *noun* [U] **1** (*technical*) natural waste material that is left after something has been used or broken up: *organic detritus from fish and plants* **2** (*formal*) any kind of garbage that is left after an event or when something has been used **SYN** DEBRIS: *the detritus of everyday life*

de trop /də ˈtroʊ/ *adj.* [not before noun] (from *French*, *formal*) not wanted, especially in a social situation with other people

deuce /dus/ *noun* **1** [C] a PLAYING CARD with two dots on it: *the deuce of clubs* **2** [U, C] (in TENNIS) the situation when both players have 40 as a score, after which one player must win two points one after the other in order to win the game **3 the deuce** [sing.] (*old-fashioned*, *informal*) used in questions to show that you are annoyed: *What the deuce is he doing?*

deuc·ed /ˈdusəd/ *adj.* [only before noun] (*old use*) used for emphasizing feelings, especially anger, disappointment, or surprise: *The man's a deuced fool!* ▶ **deuc·ed** *adv.*: *It's deuced awkward.*

de·us ex ma·chi·na /ˌdeɪəs ɛks ˈmɑkɪnə; -ˈmæ-/ *noun* [sing.] (*literary*) an unexpected power or event that saves a situation that seems without hope, especially in a play or novel

deu·te·ri·um /duˈtɪriəm/ *noun* [U] (*symb.* D) (*chemistry*) an ISOTOPE (= a different form) of HYDROGEN with twice the mass of the usual isotope

Deutsch·mark /ˈdɔɪtʃmɑrk/ (also **mark**) *noun* (*abbr.* DM) the former unit of money in Germany (replaced in 2002 by the EURO)

de·val·ue /ˌdiˈvælyu/ *verb* **1** [I, T] ~ **(sth) (against sth)** (*finance*) to reduce the value of the money of one country when it is exchanged for the money of another country **ANT** REVALUE **2** [T] ~ **sth** to give a lower value to something, making it seem less important than it really is: *Work in the home is often ignored and devalued.* ▶ **de·val·u·a·tion** /ˌdiˌvælyuˈeɪʃn/ *noun* [C, U]: *There has been a further small devaluation against the dollar.*

De·va·na·ga·ri /ˌdeɪvəˈnɑgəri/ *noun* [U] the alphabet used to write Sanskrit, Hindi, and some other Indian languages

dev·as·tate /ˈdɛvəˌsteɪt/ *verb* **1** ~ **sth** to completely destroy a place or an area: *The bomb devastated much of the old part of the city.* **2** [often passive] ~ **sb** to make someone feel very shocked and sad

dev·as·tat·ed /ˈdɛvəˌsteɪtəd/ *adj.* extremely upset and shocked: *His family is absolutely devastated by his death.*

dev·as·tat·ing /ˈdɛvəˌsteɪtɪŋ/ *adj.* **1** causing a lot of damage and destruction **SYN** DISASTROUS: *a devastating explosion/fire/cyclone* ◆ *Oil spills are having a devastating effect on coral reefs in the ocean.* ◆ *He received devastating injuries in the accident.* ◆ *It will be a devastating blow to the local community if the factory closes.* **2** extremely shocking to a person: *the devastating news that her father was dead* **3** impressive and powerful: *his devastating performance in the 100 meter relay* ◆ *Her smile was devastating.* ◆ *a devastating attack on the president's economic record* ▶ **dev·as·tat·ing·ly** *adv.*: *a devastatingly handsome man*

dev·as·ta·tion /ˌdɛvəˈsteɪʃn/ *noun* [U] great destruction or damage, especially over a wide area: *The bomb caused widespread devastation.*

de·vel·op 🔑 /dɪˈvɛləp/ *verb*
> **GROW BIGGER/STRONGER 1** [I, T] to gradually grow or become bigger, more advanced, stronger, etc.; to make something do this: *The child is developing normally.* ◆ ~ **(from sth) (into sth)** *The place has rapidly developed from a small fishing community into a thriving tourist resort.* ◆ ~ **sth (from sth)** *She developed the company from nothing.*
> **NEW IDEA/PRODUCT 2** [T] ~ **sth** to think of or produce a new idea, product, etc. and make it successful: *The company develops and markets new software.* ⊃ **thesaurus box at** MAKE
> **DISEASE/PROBLEM 3** [I, T] ~ **(sth)** to begin to have something such as a disease or a problem; to start to affect someone or something: *Her son developed asthma when he was two.* ◆ *The car developed engine trouble and we had to stop.*
> **HAPPEN/CHANGE 4** [I] to start to happen or change, especially in a bad way: *A crisis was rapidly developing in the Gulf.* ◆ *We need more time to see how things develop before we take action.*
> **BECOME BETTER 5** [T, I] ~ **(sth)** to start to have a skill, ability, quality, etc. that becomes better and stronger; to become better and stronger: *He's developed a real flair for management.* ◆ *Their relationship has developed over a number of years.*
> **BUILD HOUSES 6** [T] ~ **sth** to build new houses, factories, etc. on an area of land, especially land that was not being used effectively before: *The site is being developed by a French company.*
> **IDEA/STORY 7** [T] ~ **sth** to make an idea, a story, etc. clearer by explaining it further **SYN** ELABORATE ON: *She develops the theme more fully in her later books.*
> **PHOTOGRAPHS 8** [T] ~ **sth** to treat film that has been used to take photographs with chemicals so that the pictures can be seen: *I had the film developed yesterday.*

de·vel·oped /dɪˈvɛləpt/ *adj.* **1** (of a country, society, etc.) having many industries and a complicated economic system: *financial aid to less developed countries* ◆ *The average citizen in the **developed world** uses over 155 kg of paper per year.* ⊃ compare UNDERDEVELOPED **2** in an advanced state: *children with highly developed problem-solving skills* ⊃ see also WELL DEVELOPED

de·vel·op·er /dɪˈvɛləpər/ *noun* **1** [C] a person or company that buys land or buildings in order to build new houses, stores, etc., or to improve the old ones, and makes a profit from doing this: *property developers* **2** [C] a person or a company that designs and creates new products: *a software developer* **3** [U] a chemical substance that is used for developing photographs from a film

de·vel·op·ing /dɪˈvɛləpɪŋ/ *adj.* [only before noun] (of a country, society, etc.) poor, and trying to make its industry and economic system more advanced: *developing countries/nations/economies* ⊃ compare UNDERDEVELOPED

de·vel·op·ment 🔑 /dɪˈvɛləpmənt/ *noun*
> **GROWTH 1** [U] the gradual growth of something so that it becomes more advanced, stronger, etc.: *a baby's development in the womb* ◆ *the development of basic skills such as literacy and numeracy* ◆ *career development*
> **NEW PRODUCT 2** [U, C] the process of producing or creating something new or more advanced; a new or advanced product: *the development of vaccines against tropical diseases* ◆ *developments in aviation technology* ◆ *This piece of equipment is an exciting new development.* ⊃ see also RESEARCH AND DEVELOPMENT
> **NEW EVENT 3** [C] a new event or stage that is likely to affect what happens in a continuing situation: *the latest developments in the war* ◆ *Are there further developments in the investigation?*
> **NEW BUILDINGS 4** [C] a piece of land with new buildings on it: *a commercial/business/housing development* **5** [U] the process of using an area of land, especially to make a profit by building on it, etc.: *He bought the land for development.*

de·vel·op·men·tal /dɪˌvɛləpˈmɛntl/ *adj.* **1** in a state of developing or being developed: *The product is still at a developmental stage.* **2** connected with the development of someone or something: *developmental psychology* ▶ **de·vel·op·men·tal·ly** /-ˈmɛntl·i/ *adv.*

---

de·vi·ant /ˈdiviənt/ *adj.* different from what most people consider to be normal and acceptable: *deviant behavior/ sexuality* ▶ **de·vi·ant** *noun*: *sexual deviants* **de·vi·ance** /-əns/, **de·vi·an·cy** /-ənsi/ *noun* [U]: *a study of social deviance and crime*

de·vi·ate **AWL** /ˈdiviˌeɪt/ *verb* [I] ~ **(from sth)** to be different from something; to do something in a different way from what is usual or expected: *The bus had to deviate from its usual route because of a road closure.* ◆ *He never deviated from his original plan.*

de·vi·a·tion **AWL** /ˌdiviˈeɪʃn/ *noun* **1** [U, C] ~ **(from sth)** the act of moving away from what is normal or acceptable; a difference from what is expected or acceptable: *deviation from the previously accepted norms* ◆ *sexual deviation* ◆ *a deviation from the plan* **2** [C] ~ **(from sth)** (*technical*) the amount by which a single measurement is different from the average: *a compass deviation of 5°* (= from true north) ⊃ see also STANDARD DEVIATION

de·vice 🔑 **AWL** /dɪˈvaɪs/ *noun*

1 an object or a piece of equipment that has been designed to do a particular job: *a water-saving device* ◆ *electronic labor-saving devices around the home* **2** a bomb or weapon that will explode: *A powerful device exploded outside the station.* ◆ *the world's first atomic device* **3** a method of doing something that produces a particular result or effect: *Sending advertising by e-mail is very successful as a marketing device.* **4** a plan or trick that is used to get something that someone wants: *The report was a device used to hide rather than reveal problems.* **IDM** **leave sb to their own devices** to leave someone alone to do as they wish, and not tell them what to do

dev·il /ˈdɛvl/ *noun* **1 the Devil** [sing.] (in the Christian, Jewish, and Muslim religions) the most powerful evil BEING **SYN** SATAN **2** [C] an evil spirit: *They believed she was possessed by devils.* **3** [C] (*informal*) a person who behaves badly, especially a child: *a naughty little devil* **4** [C, usually sing.] (*informal*) used to talk about someone and to emphasize an opinion that you have of them: *I miss the old devil, now that he's gone.* ◆ *She's off to Greece for a month—lucky devil!* **IDM** **better the devil you know (than the devil you don't)** (*saying*) used to say that it is easier and wiser to stay in a bad situation that you know and can deal with rather than change to a new situation that may be much worse **between the devil and the deep blue sea** in a difficult situation where there are two equally unpleasant or unacceptable choices **the devil** (*old-fashioned*) very difficult or unpleasant: *These berries are the devil to pick because they're so small.* **the devil looks after his own** (*saying*) bad people often seem to have good luck **the devil makes work for idle hands** (*saying*) people who do not have enough to do often start to do wrong: *She blamed the crimes on the local jobless teenagers. "The devil makes work for idle hands," she would say.* **a devil of a time** (*old-fashioned*) a very difficult or unpleasant time: *I've had a devil of a time finding you.* **like the devil** (*old-fashioned, informal*) very hard, fast, etc.: *We ran like the devil.* **speak/talk of the devil** (*informal*) people say **speak/talk of the devil** when someone they have been talking about appears unexpectedly: *Well, speak of the devil—here's Alice now!* **what, where, who, why, etc. the devil…** (*old-fashioned*) used in questions to show that you are annoyed or surprised: *What the devil do you think you're doing?* ⊃ more at PAY *v.*

dev·iled /ˈdɛvld/ *adj.* cooked with hot spices: *deviled eggs*

dev·il·ish /ˈdɛvəlɪʃ/ *adj.* **1** cruel or evil: *a devilish conspiracy* **2** morally bad, but in a way that people find attractive: *He was handsome, with a devilish charm.*

dev·il·ish·ly /ˈdɛvəlɪʃli/ *adv.* (*old-fashioned*) extremely; very: *a devilishly hot day*

devil-may-ˈcare *adj.* [usually before noun] cheerful and not worrying about the future

dev·il·ment /ˈdɛvlmənt/ (also **dev·il·ry** /ˈdɛvlri/) *noun* (*formal*) wild behavior that causes trouble **SYN** MISCHIEF

devil's ˈadvocate *noun* a person who expresses an opinion that they do not really hold in order to encourage a discussion about a subject: *Often the interviewer will need to play devil's advocate in order to get a discussion going.*

devil's food ˌcake *noun* [U, C] a type of chocolate cake made with a lot of fat

de·vi·ous /ˈdiviəs/ *adj.* **1** behaving in a dishonest or indirect way, or tricking people, in order to get something **SYN** DECEITFUL, UNDERHAND: *a devious politician* ◆ *He got rich by devious means.* **2** ~ **route/path** a route or path that is not straight but has many changes in direction; not direct: *a devious route from the airport* ▶ **de·vi·ous·ly** *adv.* **de·vi·ous·ness** *noun* [U]

de·vise /dɪˈvaɪz/ *verb* ~ **sth** to invent something new or a new way of doing something **SYN** THINK UP: *A new system has been devised to control traffic in the city.*

de·voice /ˌdiˈvɔɪs/ *verb* ~ **sth** (*phonetics*) to make a speech sound, usually a consonant, VOICELESS

de·void /dɪˈvɔɪd/ *adj.* ~ **of sth** completely lacking in something: *The letter was devoid of warmth and feeling.*

dev·o·lu·tion /ˌdɛvəˈluʃn/ *noun* [U] the act of giving power from a central authority or government to an authority or a government in a local region

de·volve /dɪˈvɑlv/ *verb* **PHR V** **de'volve on/upon sb/sth** (*formal*) **1** if a duty, responsibility, etc. **devolves on/upon** you, it is given to you by someone at a higher level of authority **2** if property, money, etc. **devolves on/upon** you, you receive it after someone else dies **de'volve sth to/on/upon sb** to give a duty, responsibility, power, etc. to someone who has less authority than you: *The central government devolved most tax-raising powers to the regional authorities.*

de·volved /dɪˈvɑlvd/ *adj.* if power or authority is **devolved**, it has passed to someone who has less power: *devolved responsibility* ◆ *a system of devolved government*

de·vote 🔑 **AWL** /dɪˈvoʊt/ *verb* **PHR V** **de'vote yourself to sb/sth** to give most of your time, energy, attention, etc. to someone or something: *She devoted herself to her career.* **de'vote sth to sth** to give an amount of time, attention, etc. to something: *I could only devote two hours a day to the work.*

de·vot·ed 🔑 **AWL** /dɪˈvoʊtəd/ *adj.* ~ **(to sb/sth)** having great love for someone or something and being loyal to them: *They are devoted to their children.* ◆ *a devoted son/friend/fan* ▶ **de·vot·ed·ly** **AWL** *adv.*

dev·o·tee /ˌdɛvoʊˈti; -ˈteɪ/ *noun* **1** ~ **(of sb/sth)** a person who admires and is very enthusiastic about someone or something: *a devotee of science fiction* **2** ~ **(of sb/sth)** a very religious person who belongs to a particular group: *devotees of Krishna*

de·vo·tion **AWL** /dɪˈvoʊʃn/ *noun* **1** [U, sing.] ~ **(to sb/sth)** great love, care, and support for someone or something: *His devotion to his wife and family is touching.* **2** [U, sing.] ~ **(to sb/sth)** the action of spending a lot of time or energy on something **SYN** DEDICATION: *her devotion to duty* ◆ *Her devotion to the job left her with very little free time.* **3 devotions** [pl.] prayers and other religious practices

de·vo·tion·al /dɪˈvoʊʃənl/ *adj.* (of music, etc.) connected with or used in religious services

de·vour /dɪˈvaʊər/ *verb* **1** ~ **sth** to eat all of something quickly, especially because you are very hungry **SYN** GOBBLE UP **2** to read or look at something with great interest and enthusiasm: *She devoured everything she could lay her hands on: books, magazines, and newspapers.* **3** ~ **sb/sth** (*formal*) to destroy someone or something **SYN** ENGULF: *Flames devoured the house.* **IDM** **be devoured by sth** to be filled with a strong emotion that seems to control you: *She was devoured by envy and hatred.*

de·vout /dɪˈvaʊt/ *adj.* (of a person) believing strongly in a particular religion and obeying its laws and practices: *a devout Christian/Muslim* ▶ **de·vout·ly** *adv.*: *a devoutly*

| h hat | m man | n no | ŋ sing | l leg | r red | y yes | w wet |

Catholic region ♦ She devoutly (= very strongly) hoped he was telling the truth.

dew /du/ *noun* [U] the very small drops of water that form on the ground, etc. during the night: *The grass was wet with early morning dew.*

dew·ber·ry /'du,bɛri/ *noun* (*pl.* **dew·ber·ries**) a small soft black or blue-black fruit like a BLACKBERRY, or the bush that it grows on

dew·drop /'dudrɑp/ *noun* a small drop of dew or other liquid

Dew·ey dec·i·mal clas·si·fi·ca·tion /ˌdui 'dɛsəml klæsəfə,keɪʃn/ (also **Dewey ˌsystem**) *noun* [sing.] an international system for arranging books in a library

'dew point *noun* [sing.] (*technical*) the temperature at which air can hold no more water. Below this temperature the water comes out of the air in the form of drops.

dew·y /'dui/ *adj.* wet with DEW

'dewy-ˌeyed *adj.* (*disapproving*) showing emotion about something, perhaps with a few tears in the eyes **SYN** SENTIMENTAL

dex·ter·i·ty /dɛkˈstɛrəti/ *noun* [U] skill in using your hands or your mind: *You need manual dexterity to be good at video games.* ♦ *mental/verbal dexterity*

dex·ter·ous (also **dex·trous**) /'dɛkstrəs/ *adj.* (*formal*) skillful with your hands; skillfully done ▶ **dex·ter·ous·ly** (also **dex·trous·ly**) *adv.*

dex·trose /'dɛkstroʊs/ *noun* [U] (*chemistry*) a form of GLUCOSE (= a type of natural sugar)

dhar·ma /'dɑrmə/ *noun* [U] (in Indian religion) truth or law that affects the whole universe

dho·ti /'douti/ *noun* a long piece of cloth worn by Hindu men. It is sometimes tied around the waist, with the lower part passed between the legs and put into the cloth at the back, so that the knees are usually covered.

dhow /daʊ/ *noun* an Arab ship with one large sail in the shape of a triangle

DHS /ˌdi eɪtʃ 'ɛs/ *abbr.* Department of Homeland Security (the U.S. government department whose aim is to prevent TERRORIST attacks)

dhur·rie (also **dur·rie**) /'dəri/ *noun* a heavy cotton RUG (= small carpet) from S. Asia

di- /daɪ/ *combining form* (*chemistry*) (in nouns that are names of chemical COMPOUNDS) containing two atoms or groups of the type mentioned: *carbon dioxide*

di·a·be·tes /ˌdaɪəˈbitiz; -ˈbitəs/ *noun* [U] a medical condition that makes the patient produce a lot of URINE and feel very thirsty. There are several types of diabetes.

di·a·be·tic /ˌdaɪəˈbɛtɪk/ *adj., noun*
● *adj.* **1** having or connected with diabetes: *She's diabetic.* ♦ *a diabetic patient* ♦ *diabetic complications* **2** suitable for or used by someone who has diabetes: *a diabetic diet*
● *noun* a person who suffers from DIABETES

di·a·bol·i·cal /ˌdaɪəˈbɑlɪkl/ *adj.* **1** (also *less frequent* **di·a·bol·ic** /ˌdaɪəˈbɑlɪk/) morally bad and evil; like a DEVIL **2** (*informal*) extremely bad or annoying **SYN** TERRIBLE: *The traffic was diabolical.* ▶ **di·a·bol·i·cally** /-kli/ *adv.*

di·a·chron·ic /ˌdaɪəˈkrɑnɪk/ *adj.* (*technical*) relating to the way something, especially a language, has developed over time ⊃ compare SYNCHRONIC

di·a·crit·ic /ˌdaɪəˈkrɪtɪk/ *noun* (*linguistics*) a mark such as an accent, placed over, under, or through a letter in some languages, to show that the letter should be pronounced in a different way from the same letter without a mark ▶ **di·a·crit·i·cal** /-ˈkrɪtɪkl/ *adj.*: *diacritical marks*

di·a·dem /'daɪə,dɛm/ *noun* a crown, worn especially as a sign of royal power

di·ag·nose /'daɪəg,noʊs; ,daɪəgˈnoʊs/ *verb* [T, I] to say exactly what an illness or the cause of a problem is: **~ (sth)** *The test is used to diagnose a variety of diseases.* ♦ **~ sth as sth** *The*

illness was diagnosed as cancer. ♦ **~ sb with sth** *He has recently been diagnosed with angina.* ♦ **~ sb as sth** *He was diagnosed as a diabetic when he was 64.*

di·ag·no·sis /ˌdaɪəgˈnoʊsəs/ *noun* [C, U] (*pl.* **di·ag·no·ses** /-ˈsiz/) **~ (of sth)** the act of discovering or identifying the exact cause of an illness or a problem: *a diagnosis of lung cancer* ♦ *They are waiting for the doctor's diagnosis.* ♦ *An accurate diagnosis was made after a series of tests.*

di·ag·nos·tic /ˌdaɪəgˈnɑstɪk/ *adj., noun*
● *adj.* [usually before noun] (*technical*) connected with identifying something, especially an illness: *to carry out diagnostic tests/tools/procedures* ♦ *specific conditions that are diagnostic of AIDS*
● *noun* (*computing*) **1** (also **ˌdiagˈnostic program**) [C] a program used for identifying a computer fault **2** [C] a message on a computer screen giving information about a fault **3** **diagnostics** [U] the practice or methods of DIAGNOSIS (= finding out what is wrong with a person who is sick)

di·ag·o·nal /daɪˈæɡənl; -ˈæɡnəl/ *adj., noun*
● *adj.* (of a straight line) at an angle; joining two opposite sides of something at an angle: *diagonal stripes* ⊃ picture at LINE ▶ **di·ag·o·nal·ly** /daɪˈæɡnəli; -ˈæɡnəli/ *adv.*: *Walk diagonally across the field to the far corner and then turn left.*
● *noun* a straight line that joins two opposite sides of something at an angle; a straight line that is at an angle

di·a·gram /'daɪə,ɡræm/ *noun*
a simple drawing using lines to explain where something is, how something works, etc.: *a diagram of the wiring system* ♦ *The results are shown in diagram 2.* ▶ **di·a·gram·mat·ic** /ˌdaɪəɡrəˈmætɪk/ *adj.* **di·a·gram·mat·i·cally** /-kli/ *adv.*

di·al /'daɪəl; daɪl/ *noun, verb*
● *noun* **1** the face of a clock or watch, or a similar control on a machine, piece of equipment, or vehicle that shows a measurement of time, amount, speed, temperature, etc.: *an alarm clock with a luminous dial* ♦ *Check the tire pressure on the dial.* ⊃ see also SUNDIAL **2** the round control on a radio, stove, etc. that you turn in order to adjust something, for example to choose a particular station or to choose a particular temperature **3** the round part on some older telephones, with holes for the fingers, that you move around to call a particular number ⊃ see also SPEED DIAL
● *verb* [T, I] (-l-, CanE also -ll-) **~ (sth)** to use a telephone by pushing buttons or turning the dial to call a number: *He dialed the number and waited.* ♦ *Dial 212 for Manhattan.* ⊃ collocations at PHONE

di·a·lect /'daɪə,lɛkt/ *noun* [C, U] the form of a language that is spoken in one area with grammar, words, and pronunciation that may be different from other forms of the same language: *a Southern dialect* ⊃ compare ACCENT, IDIOLECT ▶ **di·a·lec·tal** /ˌdaɪəˈlɛktl/ *adj.*

di·a·lec·tic /ˌdaɪəˈlɛktɪk/ *noun* [sing.] (also *less frequent* **di·a·lec·tics** [U]) **1** (*philosophy*) a method of discovering the truth of ideas by discussion and logical argument, and by considering ideas that are opposed to each other **2** (*formal*) the way in which two aspects of a situation affect each other ▶ **di·a·lec·ti·cal** /-tɪkl/ *adj.*

diaˌlectical maˈterialism *noun* [U] (*philosophy*) the Marxist theory that all change results from opposing social forces, which come into conflict because of material needs

di·al·er /'daɪələr; 'daɪlər/ *noun* a computer program or piece of equipment that calls telephone numbers automatically

'dialog ˌbox (CanE usually **'dialogue ˌbox**) *noun* a box that appears on a computer screen asking the user to choose what they want to do next

di·a·logue (also **di·a·log**) /'daɪə,lɔɡ; -,lɑɡ/ *noun* [C, U]
1 conversations in a book, play, or movie: *The novel has long descriptions and not much dialogue.* ♦ *dialogues for language learners* ⊃ thesaurus box at DISCUSSION **2** a formal discussion between two groups or countries, especially when

they are trying to solve a problem, end a disagreement, etc.: *The president told waiting reporters there had been a constructive dialogue.* ➲ compare MONOLOGUE

'dial ˌtone *noun* the sound that you hear when you pick up a telephone that means you can make a call

'dial-ˌup *adj.* [only before noun] using a telephone line and a MODEM to connect your computer to the Internet ▶ **'dial-up** *noun* [U]: *I still have dial-up at home.*

di·al·y·sis /daɪˈæləsəs/ *noun* [U] (*technical*) a process for separating substances from a liquid, especially for taking waste substances out of the blood of people with damaged KIDNEYS: *kidney/renal dialysis* ♦ *a dialysis machine*

di·a·man·té /ˌdiːəmɑːnˈteɪ/ *adj.* decorated with glass that is cut to look like diamonds: *diamanté earrings*

di·a·man·tine /ˌdaɪəˈmæntin/ *adj.* (*technical*) **1** made from, or looking like, diamonds **2** very hard or strong

di·am·e·ter /daɪˈæmətər/ *noun* **1** a straight line going from one side of a circle or any other round object to the other side, passing through the center: *the diameter of a tree trunk* ♦ *The dome is 120 feet in diameter.* ➲ picture at SHAPE ➲ compare RADIUS **2** (*technical*) a measurement of the power of an instrument to MAGNIFY something: *a lens magnifying 300 diameters* (= making something look 300 times larger than it really is).

di·a·met·ri·cal /ˌdaɪəˈmɛtrɪkl/ *adj.* [usually before noun] **1** used to emphasize that people or things are completely different: *He's the diametrical opposite of his brother.* **2** relating to the DIAMETER of something

di·a·met·ri·cally /ˌdaɪəˈmɛtrɪkli/ *adv.* ~ **opposed/opposite** completely different: *We hold diametrically opposed views.*

dia·mond 🔑 /ˈdaɪmənd; ˈdaɪə-/ *noun* **1** [U, C] a clear PRECIOUS STONE of pure CARBON, the hardest substance known. Diamonds are used in jewelry and also in industry, especially for cutting glass.: *a ring with a diamond in it* ♦ *a diamond ring/necklace* ♦ *She was wearing her diamonds* (= jewelry with diamonds in it). ♦ *The lights shone like diamonds.* **2** [C] a shape with four straight sides of equal length and with angles that are not RIGHT ANGLES **3** diamonds [pl.] one of the four SUITS (= sets) in a DECK of cards. The cards are marked with red diamond shapes: *the ten of diamonds* ➲ picture at PLAYING CARD **4** [C] a card of this SUIT: *You must play a diamond if you have one.* **5** [C] (in baseball) the space inside the lines that connect the four BASES; also used to mean the whole baseball field ➲ picture at BASEBALL
    IDM diamond in the rough a person who has many good qualities even though they do not seem to be very polite, educated, etc.

ˌdiamond anniˈversary *noun* the 60th anniversary of a wedding or other important event ➲ compare GOLDEN ANNIVERSARY, SILVER ANNIVERSARY

dia·per /ˈdaɪpər/ *noun* a piece of soft cloth or other thick material that is folded around a baby's bottom and between its legs to absorb and hold its body waste ▶ **dia·per** *verb*: ~ **sb** *to diaper a baby*

'diaper ˌrash *noun* [U] an area of red spots on a baby's bottom and between its legs, caused by a wet diaper

di·aph·a·nous /daɪˈæfənəs/ *adj.* (*formal*) (of cloth) so light and fine that you can almost see through it

di·a·phragm /ˈdaɪəfræm/ *noun* **1** (*anatomy*) the layer of muscle between the lungs and the stomach, used especially to control breathing **2** a rubber or plastic device that a woman places inside her VAGINA before having sex to prevent SPERM from entering the WOMB and making her pregnant **3** a device that controls the amount of light that enters a camera **4** (*technical*) a thin disk used to turn electronic signals into sound, and sound into electronic signals in telephones, LOUDSPEAKERS, etc.

di·a·rist /ˈdaɪərɪst/ *noun* a person who writes a diary,

especially one that is later published: *Samuel Pepys, the famous 17th century diarist*

di·ar·rhe·a /ˌdaɪəˈriə/ (also *informal* the runs) *noun* [U] an illness in which waste matter is emptied from the BOWELS much more frequently than normal, and in liquid form: *Symptoms include diarrhea and vomiting.*

di·a·ry 🔑 /ˈdaɪəri/ *noun*
    (*pl.* di·a·ries) a book in which you can write down the experiences you have each day, your private thoughts, etc.: *Do you keep a diary* (= write in one regularly)*?* ➲ see also JOURNAL, VIDEO DIARY ➲ note at AGENDA

di·as·po·ra /daɪˈæspərə/ *noun* [sing.] (*formal*) **1** the Diaspora the movement of the Jewish people away from their own country to live and work in other countries **2** the movement of people from any nation or group away from their own country

di·a·tom·ic /ˌdaɪəˈtɑmɪk/ *adj.* (*chemistry*) consisting of two atoms

di·a·ton·ic /ˌdaɪəˈtɑnɪk/ *adj.* (*music*) using only the notes of the appropriate MAJOR or MINOR SCALE ➲ compare CHROMATIC

di·a·tribe /ˈdaɪətraɪb/ *noun* ~ **(against sb/sth)** (*formal*) a long and angry speech or piece of writing attacking and criticizing someone or something: *He launched a bitter diatribe against the younger generation.*

di·az·e·pam /daɪˈæzəˌpæm/ *noun* [U] (*medical*) a drug that is used to make people feel less anxious and more relaxed

dibs /dɪbz/
    IDM have (first) dibs on… (*informal*) used to claim something as yours before someone else can claim it: *I've got dibs on the last piece of cake!*

dice /daɪs/ *noun*, *verb*
● *noun* **1** [pl.] (*sing.* die) small CUBES of wood, plastic, etc., with a different number of spots on each of their sides, used in games of chance: *a pair of dice* ♦ *to roll/throw/shake the dice* ➲ picture at TOY **2** [U] a game played with dice: *We played dice all night.* **3** [pl.] small square pieces of meat, vegetables, etc.: *The recipe says to use two onions, small dice.* ➲ picture at COOKING
    IDM no dice (*informal*) used to show that you refuse to do something, or that something cannot be done: *"Did you get that job?" "No dice."* ➲ more at LOAD *v.*
● *verb* ~ **sth** to cut meat, vegetables, etc. into small square pieces: *diced carrots*

dic·ey /ˈdaɪsi/ *adj.* (*informal*) uncertain and dangerous SYN RISKY

di·chot·o·my /daɪˈkɑtəmi/ *noun* [usually sing.] (*pl.* di·chot·o·mies) ~ **(between A and B)** (*formal*) the separation that exists between two groups or things that are completely opposite to and different from each other

dick·ens /ˈdɪkənz/ *noun* the dickens (*old-fashioned, informal*) **1** used in questions instead of "devil" to show that you are annoyed or surprised: *Where the dickens did he go?* **2** used when you are emphasizing something: *cute as the dickens* ♦ *He worked like the dickens.*

Dick·en·si·an /dɪˈkenziən/ *adj.* connected with or typical of the novels of Charles Dickens, which often describe social problems and bad social conditions: *a Dickensian slum*

dick·er /ˈdɪkər/ *verb* [I] ~ **(with sb) (over sth)** to argue about or discuss something with someone, especially in order to agree on a price SYN BARGAIN

di·cot·y·le·don /ˌdaɪˌkɑtlˈidn/ (also di·cot /ˈdaɪkɑt/) *noun* (*biology*) a plant whose seeds form EMBRYOS that each produce two leaves ➲ compare MONOCOTYLEDON

Dic·ta·phone™ /ˈdɪktəˌfoʊn/ *noun* a small machine used to record on tape people speaking, so that their words can be played back later and written down

dic·tate *verb*, *noun*
● *verb* /ˈdɪkteɪt/ **1** [T, I] ~ **(sth) (to sb)** to say words for someone else to write down: *He dictated a letter to his*

ʌ cup   ə about   eɪ say   ɪə here   aɪ five   ɔɪ boy   aʊ now   oʊ go   ər bird assistant. **2** [T] to tell someone what to do, especially in an annoying way: ~ **sth (to sb)** *They are in no position to **dictate** terms* (= tell other people what to do). ◆ ~ **how, what, etc....**/ **that...** *What right do they have to dictate how we live our lives?* **3** [T, I] to control or influence how something happens **SYN** DETERMINE: ~ **(sth)** *When we take our vacations is very much dictated by Greg's work schedule.* ◆ ~ **where, what, etc....** *It's generally your job that dictates where you live now.* ◆ ~ **that...** *The social conventions of the day dictated that she should remain at home with her parents.* **PHR V** **dictate to sb** [often passive] to give orders to someone, often in a rude or aggressive way: *She refused to be dictated to by anyone.*

● **noun** [usually pl.] (*formal*) an order or a rule that you must obey: *to follow the dictates of fashion*

dic·ta·tion /dɪkˈteɪʃn/ *noun* **1** [U] the act of speaking or reading so that someone can write down the words **2** [C, U] a test in which students write down what is being read to them, especially in language lessons

dic·ta·tor /ˈdɪkteɪtər/ *noun* (*disapproving*) **1** a ruler who has complete power over a country, especially one who has gained it using military force **2** a person who behaves as if they have complete power over other people, and tells them what to do

dic·ta·to·ri·al /ˌdɪktəˈtɔriəl/ *adj.* (*disapproving*) **1** connected with or controlled by a dictator: *a dictatorial ruler* ◆ *a dictatorial regime* **2** using power in an unreasonable way by telling people what to do and not listening to their views or wishes: *dictatorial behavior* ▶ **dic·ta·to·ri·al·ly** *adv.*

dic·ta·tor·ship /dɪkˈteɪtər ʃɪp, ˈdɪkteɪtər-/ *noun* **1** [C, U] government by a dictator ➔ **collocations** at POLITICS **2** [C] a country that is ruled by a dictator

dic·tion /ˈdɪkʃn/ *noun* [U] **1** the way that someone pronounces words: *clear diction* **2** (*technical*) the choice and use of words in literature

dic·tion·ar·y 🔑 /ˈdɪkʃəˌneri/ *noun* (*pl.* **dic·tion·ar·ies**) **1** a book that gives a list of the words of a language in alphabetical order and explains what they mean, or gives a word for them in a foreign language: *a Spanish-English dictionary* **2** a book that explains the words that are used in a particular subject: *a dictionary of mathematics* **3** a list of words in electronic form, for example stored in a computer's SPELL-CHECKER

dic·tum /ˈdɪktəm/ *noun* (*pl.* **dic·ta** /-tə/ or **dic·tums**) (*formal*) a statement that expresses something that people believe is always true or should be followed

did /dɪd/ ➔ DO¹

di·dac·tic /daɪˈdæktɪk/ *adj.* (*formal*) **1** designed to teach people something, especially a moral lesson: *didactic art* **2** (usually *disapproving*) telling people things rather than letting them find out for themselves ▶ **di·dac·ti·cal·ly** /-kli/ *adv.*

did·dle /ˈdɪdl/ *verb* (*informal*) **1** [I] ~ **(around)** to waste time without having a purpose: *Sometimes I just diddle around all day.* **2** [I] ~ **(with sth)** to play with something carelessly or without thinking: *He diddled with the graphics on his computer.*

did·dly /ˈdɪdli/ (also **diddly-ˌsquat**) *noun* (*informal*) (used in negative sentences) not anything; nothing: *She doesn't know diddly about it.*

didg·er·i·doo /ˌdɪdʒəriˈdu/ *noun* (*pl.* **didg·er·i·doos**) an Australian musical instrument consisting of a long wooden tube that you blow through to produce a variety of deep sounds

did·n't /ˈdɪdnt/ *short form* did not

die 🔑 /daɪ/ *verb, noun*
● **verb** (**dies, dy·ing, died, died**) **1** [I, T] to stop living: *Her husband died suddenly last week.* ◆ *The plants died within a week.* ◆ ~ **of/from sth** *to die of/from cancer* ◆ ~ **for sth** *He died for his beliefs.* ◆ *I'll never forget it to my dying day* (= until I die). ◆ (*informal*) *I nearly died when I saw him there* (= it was

very embarrassing). ◆ ~ **sth** *to die a violent/painful/natural, etc. death* ◆ + **adj.** *She died young.* ◆ *At least they died happy.* ◆ + **noun** *He died a poor man.* **2** [I] to stop existing; to disappear: *The old customs are dying.* ◆ *His secret died with him* (= he never told anyone). ◆ *The words died on my lips* (= I stopped speaking). **3** [I] (of a machine) to stop working: *The engine spluttered and died.* ◆ *My car just died on me.*
IDM **be dying for sth/to do sth** (*informal*) to want something or want to do something very much: *I'm dying for a glass of water.* ◆ *I'm dying to know what happened.* **die in your bed** to die because you are old or sick **die laughing** to find something extremely funny: *I almost died laughing when she said that.* **old habits, traditions, etc. die hard** used to say that things change very slowly **to die for** (*informal*) if you think something is **to die for**, you really want it, and would do anything to get it: *She was wearing a dress to die for.* ➔ more at CROSS *v.*, FLY *n.*, SAY *v.*
PHR V **die aˈway** to become gradually weaker or fainter and finally disappear: *The sound of their laughter died away.* **die back** if a plant **dies back**, it loses its leaves but remains alive **die ˈdown** to become gradually less strong, loud, noticeable, etc.: *The flames finally died down.* ◆ *When the applause had died down, she began her speech.* **die ˈoff** to die one after the other until there are none left **die ˈout** to stop existing: *This species has nearly died out because its habitat is being destroyed.*

● **noun** **1** a block of metal with a special shape, or with a pattern cut into it, that is used for shaping other pieces of metal such as coins, or for making patterns on paper or leather **2** (*pl.* **dice**) a small CUBE of wood, plastic, etc., with a different number of spots on each of its sides, used in games of chance ➔ see also DICE *n.*
IDM **the die is cast** (*saying*) used to say that an event has happened or a decision has been made that cannot be changed

ˈdie-cast *adj.* (of a metal object) made by pouring liquid metal into a MOLD and allowing it to cool

die·hard /ˈdaɪhɑrd/ *adj.* **1** strongly opposing change and new ideas: *diehard conservatives* **2** continuing to support something in spite of opposition: *She's a diehard Yankees fan.* ▶ **die·hard** *noun*: *A few diehards are trying to stop the reforms.*

di·er·e·sis /daɪˈɛrəsəs/ (*pl.* **di·er·e·ses** /-siz/) *noun* (*technical*) the mark placed over a vowel to show that it is pronounced separately, as in *naïve*

die·sel /ˈdizl, ˈdisl/ *noun* **1** (also **ˈdiesel fuel**) [U] a type of heavy oil used as a fuel instead of gas: *a diesel engine* (= one that burns diesel) ◆ *diesel cars/locomotives/trains* ➔ compare GAS **2** [C] a vehicle that uses diesel fuel: *Our new car is a diesel.*

di·et 🔑 /ˈdaɪət/ *noun, verb*
● **noun** **1** [C, U] the food that you eat and drink regularly: *to have a healthy, balanced diet* ◆ *The Japanese diet of rice, vegetables, and fish* ◆ *to receive advice on diet and nutrition* **2** [C] a limited variety or amount of food that you eat for medical reasons or because you want to lose weight; a time when you only eat this limited variety or amount: *a low-fat, salt-free diet* ◆ *diet soda* (= with fewer CALORIES than normal) ◆ *I decided to go on a diet* (= to lose weight) *before my vacation.* **3** [sing.] **a ~ of sth** (*disapproving*) a large amount of a restricted range of activities: *Children today are brought up on a diet of television cartoons and reality shows.*
▶ **di·e·tary** /ˈdaɪəˌteri/ *adj.* [usually before noun]: *dietary advice/changes/habits* ◆ *dietary fiber* ◆ *special dietary needs*
● **verb** [I] to eat less food or only food of a particular type in order to lose weight **SYN** BE ON A DIET: *She's always dieting, but she never seems to lose any weight.*

di·et·er /ˈdaɪətər/ *noun* a person who is trying to lose weight on a diet

di·e·tet·ics /ˌdaɪəˈtɛtɪks/ *noun* [U] the scientific study of diet and healthy eating ▶ **di·e·tet·ic** *adj.*: *dietetic advice*

Diet and Exercise

weight
- put on/gain/lose weight/a few pounds
- watch/control/struggle with your weight
- be/become seriously overweight/underweight
- be/become clinically/morbidly obese
- achieve/facilitate/promote/stimulate weight loss
- slim down to 160 pounds
- combat/prevent/tackle/treat obesity
- develop/have/suffer from/struggle with/recover from anorexia/bulimia/an eating disorder
- be on/go on/follow a crash/strict diet
- have/suffer from a negative/distorted body image
- have/develop a positive/healthy/realistic body image

healthy eating
- eat a balanced diet/healthily/well
- get/provide/receive adequate/proper nutrition
- contain/get/provide essential nutrients/vitamins/minerals
- be high/low in calories/fat/fiber/protein/vitamin D/Omega-3 fatty acids/trans-fats
- contain (no)/use/be full of/be free from additives/chemical preservatives/artificial sweeteners/high-fructose corn syrup
- avoid/cut down on/cut out alcohol/caffeine/fatty foods
- stop/quit smoking

exercise
- get regular exercise
- do moderate/strenuous/vigorous exercise
- play football/hockey/tennis/soccer
- go jogging/running
- go to/visit/hit/work out at the gym
- strengthen/tone/train your stomach muscles
- contract/relax/stretch/use/work your lower-body muscles
- build (up)/gain muscle
- improve/increase your stamina/energy levels/physical fitness
- burn/consume/expend calories

staying healthy
- be/get/keep/stay healthy/in shape
- lower your cholesterol/blood pressure
- boost/stimulate/strengthen your immune system
- prevent/reduce the risk of heart disease/high blood pressure/diabetes/osteoporosis
- reduce/relieve/manage/combat stress
- enhance/promote relaxation/physical and mental well-being

di·e·ti·tian (also **di·e·ti·cian**) /ˌdaɪəˈtɪʃn/ *noun* a person whose job is to advise people on what kind of food they should eat to keep healthy

dif·fer /ˈdɪfər/ *verb* **1** [I] to be different from someone or something: *They hold differing views.* ◆ **A ~ from B** *French differs from English in this respect.* ◆ **A and B ~ (from each other)** *French and English differ in this respect.* ◆ **~ between A and B** *Ideas on childcare may differ considerably between the parents.* ⊃ language bank at CONTRAST **2** [I] to disagree with someone: **~ (with sb) (about/on/over sth)** *I have to differ with you on that.* ◆ **~ (as to sth)** *Medical opinion differs as to how to treat the disease.* **IDM** see AGREE, BEG

dif·fer·ence ♪ /ˈdɪfrəns/ *noun*
1 [C, U] **~ (between A and B)** | **~ (in sth)** the way in which two people or things are not like each other; the way in which someone or something has changed: *There are no significant differences between the education systems of the two countries.* ◆ *He was studying the complex similarities and differences between humans and animals.* ◆ *There's no differ-*
ence in the results. ◆ *I can never **tell the difference** (= distinguish) between the twins* ◆ *She noticed a **marked difference** in the children on her second visit.* ◆ *There's **a world of difference** between liking someone and loving them.* ◆ *What a difference! You look great with your hair like that.* ⊃ language bank at CONTRAST **ANT** SIMILARITY **2** [sing., U] **~ (in sth) (between A and B)** the amount that something is greater or smaller than something else: *There's not much difference in price between the two computers.* ◆ *There's an age difference of six years between the boys* (= one is six years older than the other). ◆ *I'll lend you $500 and you'll have to find the difference* (= the rest of the money that you need). ◆ *We measured the difference in temperature.* **3** [C] a disagreement between people: *We have our differences, but she's still my sister.* ◆ *Why don't you settle your differences and be friends again?* ◆ *There was a difference of opinion over who had won.*
IDM **make a, no, some, etc. difference (to/in sb/sth)** to have an effect/no effect on someone or something: *The rain didn't make much difference to the game.* ◆ *Your age shouldn't make any difference to whether you get the job or not.* ◆ *Changing schools made a **big difference** in my life.* ◆ *What difference will it make if he knows or not?* ◆ *I don't think it makes a **lot of difference** what color it is* (= it is not important). ◆ *"Should we go on Friday or Saturday?" "It makes no difference (to me)."* **make all the difference (to sb/sth)** to have an important effect on someone or something; to make someone feel better: *A few kind words at the right time make all the difference.* **same difference** (*informal*) used to say that you think the differences between two things are not important: *"That's not a xylophone, it's a glockenspiel." "Same difference." * **with a difference** (*informal*) (after nouns) used to show that something is interesting or unusual: *The traditional backpack with a difference—it's waterproof.* ⊃ more at BURY, SINK *v.*, SPLIT *v.*, WORLD

dif·fer·ent ♪ /ˈdɪfrənt/ *adj.*
1 **~ (from/than sb/sth)** not the same as someone or something; not like someone or something else: *American English is significantly different from British English.* ◆ *He saw he was no different than anyone else.* ◆ *It's different now than it was a year ago.* ◆ *People often give very different accounts of the same event.* ◆ *My son is really messy; my daughter is **no different**.* **ANT** SIMILAR **2** [only before noun] separate and individual: *She offered us five different kinds of cake.* ◆ *The program was about customs in different parts of the country.* ◆ *They are sold in many different colors.* ◆ *I looked it up in three different dictionaries.* **3** [not usually before noun] (*informal*) unusual; not like other people or things: *"Did you enjoy the play?" "Well, it was certainly different!"* ▶ **dif·fer·ent·ly** *adv.*: *Boys and girls may behave differently.* ◆ *The male bird has a differently shaped head.*
IDM **a different kettle of fish** (*informal*) a completely different situation or person from the one previously mentioned ⊃ more at COMPLEXION, HORSE *n.*, KNOW *v.*, MATTER *n.*, PULL *v.*, SING, TELL

dif·fer·en·tial /ˌdɪfəˈrenʃl/ *noun, adj.*
• *noun* **1** **~ (between A and B)** a difference in the amount, value, or size of something, especially the difference in rates of pay for people doing different work in the same industry or profession: *wage/pay/income differentials* **2** (also **differential 'gear**) a gear that makes it possible for a vehicle's back wheels to turn at different speeds when going around corners
• *adj.* [only before noun] (*formal*) showing or depending on a difference; not equal: *the differential treatment of prisoners based on sex and social class* ◆ *differential rates of pay*

differential 'calculus *noun* [U] (*mathematics*) a type of mathematics that deals with quantities that change in time. It is used to calculate a quantity at a particular moment. ⊃ compare INTEGRAL CALCULUS

differ,ential e'quation *noun* (*mathematics*) an EQUATION that involves FUNCTIONS (= quantities that can vary) and their rates of change

dif·fer·en·ti·ate **AWL** /ˌdɪfəˈrɛnʃiˌeɪt/ *verb* **1** [I, T] to recognize or show that two things are not the same **SYN** DISTINGUISH: ~ **(between) A and B** *It's difficult to differentiate between the two varieties.* ◆ ~ **A (from B)** *I can't differentiate one variety from another.* **2** [T] ~ **sth (from sth)** to be the particular thing that shows that things or people are not the same **SYN** DISTINGUISH: *The male's yellow beak differentiates it from the female.* **3** [I] ~ **between A and B** to treat people or things in a different way, especially in an unfair way **SYN** DISCRIMINATE ▶ **dif·fer·en·ti·a·tion** **AWL** /ˌdɪfəˌrɛnʃiˈeɪʃn/ *noun* [U]

dif·fi·cult 🔊 /ˈdɪfɪˌkʌlt; -kəlt/ *adj.*

1 ~ **(for sb) (to do sth)** not easy; needing effort or skill to do or to understand: *a difficult problem/task/exam* ◆ *It's difficult for them to get here much before seven.* ◆ *It's really difficult to read your writing.* ◆ *Your writing is really difficult to read.* ◆ *She finds it very difficult to get up early.* **2** full of problems; causing a lot of trouble: *to be in a difficult position/situation* ◆ *My boss is making life very difficult for me.* ◆ *Thirteen is a difficult age.* **3** (of people) not easy to please; not helpful **SYN** AWKWARD: *a difficult child/customer/boss* ◆ *Don't pay any attention to her—she's just being difficult.* **IDM** see LIFE

dif·fi·cul·ty 🔊 /ˈdɪfɪˌkʌlti; -kəlti/ *noun* (*pl.* **dif·fi·cul·ties**)

1 [C, usually pl., U] a problem; a thing or situation that causes problems: *the difficulties of English syntax* ◆ *children with severe learning difficulties* ◆ *We've run into difficulties/ difficulty with the new project.* ◆ *He got into difficulties while swimming and had to be rescued.* ◆ *The bank is in difficulty/ difficulties.* ◆ *It was a time fraught with difficulties and frustration.* **2** [U] the state or quality of being hard to do or to understand; the effort that something involves: *I had considerable difficulty (in) persuading her to leave.* ◆ *I had no difficulty (in) making myself understood.* ◆ *The changes were made with surprisingly little difficulty.* ◆ *He spoke slowly and*

with great difficulty. ◆ *We found the house without difficulty.* ◆ *They discussed the difficulty of studying abroad.* **HELP** You cannot say "have difficulty to do sth": ~~I had difficulty to persuade her to leave.~~ **3** [U] how hard something is: *varying levels of difficulty* ◆ *questions of increasing difficulty*

dif·fi·dent /ˈdɪfɪdənt/ *adj.* ~ **(about sth)** not having much confidence in yourself; not wanting to talk about yourself **SYN** SHY: *a diffident manner/smile* ◆ *He was modest and diffident about his own success.* ▶ **dif·fi·dence** /-dəns/ *noun* [U]: *She overcame her natural diffidence and spoke with great frankness.* **dif·fi·dent·ly** *adv.*

dif·fract /dɪˈfrækt/ *verb* ~ **sth** (*physics*) to break up a stream of light into a series of dark and light bands or into the different colors of the SPECTRUM ▶ **dif·frac·tion** /dɪˈfrækʃn/ *noun* [U]

dif·fuse *adj., verb*

● *adj.* /dɪˈfyus/ **1** spread over a wide area: *diffuse light* ◆ *a diffuse community* **2** not clear or easy to understand; using a lot of words: *a diffuse style of writing* ▶ **dif·fuse·ly** *adv.* **dif·fuse·ness** *noun* [U]

● *verb* /dɪˈfyuz/ **1** [T, I] ~ **(sth)** (*formal*) to spread something or become spread widely in all directions: *The problem is how to diffuse power without creating anarchy.* ◆ *Technologies diffuse rapidly.* **2** [I, T] ~ **(sth)** (*technical*) if a gas or liquid diffuses or is diffused in a substance, it becomes slowly mixed with that substance **3** [T] ~ **sth** (*formal*) to make light shine less brightly by spreading it in many directions: *The moon was fuller than the night before, but the light was diffused by clouds.* ▶ **dif·fu·sion** /dɪˈfyuʒn/ *noun* [U]

dif·fus·er /dɪˈfyuzər/ *noun* **1** a device used in photography to avoid dark shadows or areas that are too bright **2** a part that is attached to a HAIR DRYER to spread the hot air around the head and dry the hair more gently

dig 🔊 /dɪɡ/ *verb, noun*

● *verb* (**dig·ging**, **dug**, **dug** /dʌɡ/) **1** [I, T] to make a hole in the ground or to move soil from one place to another using your hands, a tool, or a machine: ~ **(for sth)** *to dig for coal/ gold/Roman remains* ◆ *They dug deeper and deeper but still found nothing.* ◆ *I think I'll do some digging in the garden.* ◆ ~ **sth** *to dig a ditch/grave/hole/tunnel* **2** [T] ~ **sth** to remove something from the ground with a tool: *I'll dig some potatoes for lunch.* **3** [I] (+ *adv./prep.*) to search in something in order to find an object in something: *I dug around in my bag for a pen.* **4** [T] ~ **sth** (*old-fashioned, slang*) to approve of or like something very much

IDM **dig deep (into sth)** **1** to search thoroughly for information: *You'll need to dig deep into the records to find the figures you want.* **2** to try hard to provide the money, equipment, etc. that is needed: *We're asking you to dig deep for the earthquake victims.* **dig your heels/toes in** to refuse to do something or to change your mind about something: *They dug in their heels and would not lower the price.* **dig (deep) in/into your pocket(s), savings, etc.** to spend a lot of your own money on something **dig sb in the ribs** to push your finger or your elbow into someone's side, especially to attract their attention **dig yourself into a hole** to put yourself into a bad situation that will be very difficult to get out of **dig your own grave | dig a grave for yourself** to do something that will have very harmful results for you

PHR V **dig** ˈin (*informal*) **1** used to tell someone to start to eat: *Help yourselves, everybody! Dig in!* **2** to wait, or deal with a difficult situation, with great patience: *There is nothing we can do except dig in and wait.* **dig sth⇔ˈin 1** to mix soil into another substance by digging the two substances together: *The manure should be well dug in.* **2** to push something into something else: *He dug his fork into the steak.* **dig yourself ˈin** (of soldiers) to protect yourself against an attack by making a safe place in the ground **dig ˈinto sth 1** (*informal*) to start to eat food with enthusiasm: *She dug into her bowl of pasta.* **2** to push or rub against your body in a painful or uncomfortable way: *His fingers dug painfully into my arm.* **3** to find out information by searching or asking questions:

Will you dig a little into his past and see what you find? **,dig sth 'into sth 1** to mix soil with another substance by digging the two substances together **2** to push or press something into something else: *She dug her hands deeper into her pockets.* **,dig sb/sth↔'out (of sth) 1** to remove someone or something from somewhere by digging the ground around them or it: *More than a dozen people were dug out of the avalanche alive.* **2** to find something that has been hidden or forgotten for a long time: *I went to the attic and dug out Grandpa's medals.* **,dig sth↔'over** to prepare ground by digging the soil to remove stones, etc. **,dig sth↔'up 1** to break the ground into small pieces before planting seeds, building something, etc.: *They are digging up the football field to lay a new surface.* **2** to remove something from the ground by digging: *An old Roman vase was dug up here last month.* **3** to discover information about someone or something **SYN** UNEARTH: *Tabloid newspapers love to dig up scandal.*

• *noun* ⊃ see also DIGS **1** a small push with your finger or elbow: *She gave him a dig in the ribs.* **2 ~ (at sb/sth)** a remark that is intended to annoy or upset someone: *He kept making sly little digs at me.* ✦ *to have a dig at someone or something* **3** an occasion when an organized group of people dig in the ground to discover old buildings or objects, in order to find out more about their history **SYN** EXCAVATION: *to go on a dig* ✦ *an archaeological dig*

the di·ge·ra·ti /ˌdɪdʒəˈrɑti/ *noun* [pl.] (*humorous*) people who are very good at using computers or who use computers a lot

di·gest *verb, noun*
• *verb* /daɪˈdʒɛst; dɪ-/ **1** [T, I] **~ (sth)** when you **digest** food, or it **digests**, it is changed into substances that your body can use: *Humans cannot digest plants such as grass.* ✦ *You should allow a little time after a meal for the food to digest.* **2** [T] **~ sth** to think about something so that you fully understand it: *He paused, waiting for her to digest the information.*
• *noun* /ˈdaɪdʒɛst/ a short report containing the most important facts of a longer report or piece of writing; a collection of short reports: *a monthly news digest*

di·gest·i·ble /daɪˈdʒɛstəbl/ *adj.* easy to digest; pleasant to eat or easy to understand **ANT** INDIGESTIBLE

di·ges·tion /daɪˈdʒɛstʃən; dɪ-/ *noun* [U] **1** the process of digesting food ⊃ compare INDIGESTION **2** the ability to digest food: *to have good/poor digestion*

di·ges·tive /daɪˈdʒɛstɪv; dɪ-/ *adj.* [only before noun] connected with the digestion of food: *the digestive system/tract* ✦ *digestive problems*

di'gestive ,system *noun* the series of organs inside the body that digest food

dig·ger /ˈdɪgər/ *noun* **1** a large machine that is used for digging up the ground **2** a person or an animal that digs ⊃ see also GOLD DIGGER

dig·it /ˈdɪdʒət/ *noun* **1** any of the numbers from 0 to 9: *The number 57306 contains five digits.* ✦ *a four-digit number* **2** (*anatomy*) a finger, thumb, or toe

dig·it·al 🔑 /ˈdɪdʒətl/ *adj., noun*
• *adj.* **1** using a system of receiving and sending information as a series of the numbers one and zero, showing that an electronic signal is there or is not there: *a digital camera* ✦ *digital terrestrial and digital satellite broadcasting* **2** (of clocks, watches, etc.) showing information by using figures, rather than with HANDS that point to numbers: *a digital clock/watch* ⊃ compare ANALOG ► **dig·it·al·ly** /-tl.i/ *adv.*: *digitally remastered tapes*
• *noun* [U] digital television: *How long have you had digital?* ✦ *With digital you can choose the camera angle you want.*

dig·it·al·is /ˌdɪdʒəˈtæləs/ *noun* [U] (*medical*) a drug made from the FOXGLOVE plant, that helps the heart muscle to work

dig·it·al·ize /ˈdɪdʒətlˌaɪz/ *verb* **~ sth** = DIGITIZE

,digital re'cording *noun* [C, U] a recording in which sounds or pictures are represented by a series of numbers showing that an electronic signal is there or is not there; the process of making a recording in this way

,digital 'signature *noun* (*computing*) a way of securely adding someone's name to an electronic message or document to prove the identity of the person who is sending it and show that the data has not been changed at all

,digital 'television *noun* **1** [U] the system of broadcasting television using digital signals **2** [C] a television set that can receive digital signals

dig·i·tize /ˈdɪdʒəˌtaɪz/ (also **dig·i·tal·ize**) *verb* **~ sth** to change data into a DIGITAL form that can be easily read and processed by a computer: *a digitized map*

di·glos·si·a /daɪˈɡlɒsiə; -ˈɡlɑ-/ *noun* [U] (*linguistics*) a situation in which two languages or two forms of a language are used under different conditions in a community ► **di·glos·sic** /daɪˈɡlɒsɪk; -ˈɡlɑ-/ *adj.*

dig·ni·fied /ˈdɪgnəˌfaɪd/ *adj.* calm and serious and deserving respect: *a dignified person/manner/voice* ✦ *Throughout his trial he maintained a dignified silence.* **ANT** UNDIGNIFIED

dig·ni·fy /ˈdɪgnəˌfaɪ/ *verb* (dig·ni·fies, dig·ni·fy·ing, dig·ni·fied) (*formal*) **1 ~ sb/sth** to make someone or something seem impressive: *The mayor was there to dignify the celebrations.* **2 ~ sth** to make something appear important when it is not really: *I'm not going to dignify his comments by reacting to them.*

dig·ni·tar·y /ˈdɪgnəˌteri/ *noun* (*pl.* dig·ni·tar·ies) a person who has an important official position **SYN** VIP

dig·ni·ty /ˈdɪgnəti/ *noun* [U] **1** a calm and serious manner that deserves respect: *She accepted the criticism with quiet dignity.* **2** the fact of being given honor and respect by people: *the dignity of work* ✦ *The terminally ill should be allowed to die with dignity.* **3** a sense of your own importance and value: *It's difficult to preserve your dignity when you have no job and no home.*
IDM beneath your dignity below what you see as your own importance or worth **stand on your dignity** (*formal*) to demand to be treated with the respect that you think that you deserve

di·graph /ˈdaɪgræf/ *noun* a combination of two letters representing one sound, for example "ph" and "sh" in English

di·gress /daɪˈgres; dɪ-/ *verb* [I] (*formal*) to start to talk about something that is not connected with the main point of what you are saying ► **di·gres·sion** /daɪˈgreʃn; dɪ-/ *noun* [C, U]: *After several digressions, he finally got to the point.*

digs /dɪgz/ *noun* [pl.] (*old-fashioned, informal*) a room or rooms that you rent to live in

dike (also **dyke**) /daɪk/ *noun* a long thick wall that is built to stop water flooding onto a low area of land, especially from the ocean

dik·tat /dɪkˈtɑt/ *noun* [C, U] (*disapproving*) an order given by a government, for example, that people must obey: *an EU diktat from Brussels* ✦ *government by diktat*

di·lap·i·dat·ed /dəˈlæpəˌdeɪtəd/ *adj.* (of furniture and buildings) old and in very bad condition **SYN** RAMSHACKLE ► **di·lap·i·da·tion** /dəˌlæpəˈdeɪʃn/ *noun* [U]: *in a state of dilapidation*

dil·a·ta·tion /ˌdaɪləˈteɪʃn; ˌdaɪ-/ *noun* [U] (*medical*) the process of becoming wider (= of becoming dilated), or the action of making something become wider

dila,tation and curet'tage (also **di,lation and curet-'tage**, **D** and **C**) *noun* (*medical*) an operation in which the CERVIX is opened and material is removed from the UTERUS, for example after a MISCARRIAGE

di·late /ˈdaɪleɪt; daɪˈleɪt/ *verb* [I, T] to become or to make something larger, wider, or more open: *Her eyes dilated with fear.* ✦ **~ sth** *dilated pupils/nostrils* ✦ *Red wine can help to dilate* blood vessels. **ANT** CONTRACT ▶ **di·la·tion** /daɪˈleɪʃn/ *noun* [U, C]

dil·a·to·ry /ˈdɪləˌtɔri/ *adj.* **~ (in doing sth)** (*formal*) not acting quickly enough; causing delay: *The government has been dilatory in dealing with the problem of unemployment.*

di·lem·ma /dɪˈlɛmə/ *noun* a situation that makes problems, often one in which you have to make a very difficult choice between things of equal importance **SYN** PREDICAMENT: *to face a dilemma ♦ to be in a dilemma* **IDM** see HORN

dil·et·tante /ˈdɪləˌtɑnt; ˌdɪləˈtɑnt/ *noun* (*pl.* **dil·et·tan·ti** /-ˈtɑnti/ or **dil·et·tantes**) (*disapproving*) a person who does or studies something but is not serious about it and does not have much knowledge ▶ **dil·et·tante** *adj.*: *a dilettante artist*

dil·i·gence /ˈdɪlədʒəns/ *noun* [U] (*formal*) careful and thorough work or effort: *She shows great diligence in her schoolwork.*

dil·i·gent /ˈdɪlədʒənt/ *adj.* (*formal*) showing care and effort in your work or duties: *a diligent student/worker* ▶ **dil·i·gent·ly** *adv.*

dill /dɪl/ *noun* [U] a plant with yellow flowers whose leaves and seeds have a strong taste and are used in cooking as an HERB. Dill is often used to flavor PICKLES: *dill pickles* ⊃ picture at HERB

dil·ly-dal·ly /ˈdɪli ˌdæli/ *verb* (dil·ly-dal·lies, dil·ly-dal·ly·ing, dil·ly-dal·lied, dil·ly-dal·lied) [I] (*old-fashioned, informal*) to take too long to do something, go somewhere, or make a decision **SYN** DAWDLE

di·lute *verb, adj.* /daɪˈlut; dɪ-/
• *verb* **1 ~ sth (with sth)** to make a liquid weaker by adding water or another liquid to it **SYN** WATER DOWN: *The paint can be diluted with water to make a lighter shade.* **2 ~ sth** to make something weaker or less effective **SYN** WATER DOWN: *Large classes dilute the quality of education that children receive.* ▶ **di·lu·tion** /daɪˈluʃn; dɪ-/ *noun* [U]: *the dilution of sewage ♦ This is a serious dilution of their election promises.*
• *adj.* (also **di·lu·ted**) (of a liquid) made weaker by adding water or another substance: *a dilute acid/solution*

dim /dɪm/ *adj., verb*
• *adj.* (dim·mer, dim·mest)
> LIGHT **1** not bright: *the dim glow of the fire in the grate ♦ This light is too dim to read by.*
> PLACE **2** where you cannot see well because there is not much light: *a dim room/street*
> SHAPE **3** that you cannot see well because there is not much light: *the dim outline of a house in the moonlight ♦ I could see a dim shape in the doorway.*
> EYES **4** not able to see well: *His eyesight is getting dim.*
> MEMORIES **5** that you cannot remember or imagine clearly **SYN** VAGUE: *dim memories ♦ She had a dim recollection of meeting him. ♦* (*humorous*) *in the **dim and distant** past*
> PERSON **6** (*informal*) not intelligent: *He's very dim.*
> SITUATION **7** not giving any reason to have hope; not good: *Her future career prospects look dim.*
▶ **dim·ness** *noun* [U]: *It took a while for his eyes to adjust to the dimness.* ⊃ see also DIMLY
IDM **take a dim view of sb/sth** to disapprove of someone or something; to not have a good opinion of someone or something: *She took a dim view of my suggestion.*
• *verb* (-mm-)
> LIGHT **1** [I, T] **~ (sth)** if a light dims, or if you dim it, it becomes or you make it less bright: *The lights in the theater dimmed as the curtain rose.*
> FEELING/QUALITY **2** [I, T] **~ (sth)** if a feeling or quality dims, or if something dims it, it becomes less strong: *Her passion for dancing never dimmed over the years.*

dime /daɪm/ *noun* a coin of the U.S. and Canada worth ten cents ⊃ picture at MONEY
IDM **a dime a dozen** very common and therefore not valuable

dime novel *noun* (*old-fashioned*) a cheap popular novel, usually an exciting adventure or romantic story

dimensions

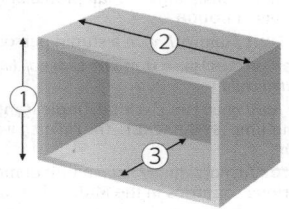

① height
② width
③ depth

di·men·sion **AWL** /dɪˈmɛnʃn/ *noun* **1** a measurement in space, for example the height, width, or length of something: *We measured the dimensions of the kitchen. ♦ computer design tools that work in three dimensions* ⊃ see also THE FOURTH DIMENSION **2** [usually pl.] the size and extent of a situation: *a problem of considerable dimensions* **3** an aspect, or way of looking at or thinking about something: *Her job added a new dimension to her life. ♦ the social dimension of unemployment*

-dimensional **AWL** /dɪˈmɛnʃənl/ *combining form* (in adjectives) having the number of dimensions mentioned: *a multi-dimensional model* ⊃ see also MULTIDIMENSIONAL, THREE-DIMENSIONAL, TWO-DIMENSIONAL

dime store *noun* (*old-fashioned*) = FIVE-AND-DIME

di·min·ish **AWL** /dɪˈmɪnɪʃ/ *verb* **1** [I, T] **~ (sth)** to become or to make something become smaller, weaker, etc. **SYN** DECREASE: *The world's resources are rapidly diminishing. ♦ His influence has diminished with time. ♦ Our efforts were producing diminishing returns* (= we achieved less although we spent more time or money). **2** [T] **~ sb/sth** to make someone or something seem less important than they really are **SYN** BELITTLE: *I don't wish to diminish the importance of their contribution.*

diminished ca·pac·i·ty *noun* [U] (*law*) a state in which a person who is accused of a crime is not considered to be responsible for their actions, because they are mentally ill: *He was found not guilty of murder on the grounds of diminished capacity.*

di·min·u·en·do /dɪˌmɪnyuˈɛndoʊ/ *noun* (*pl.* **di·min·u·en·dos**) [C, U] (*music*) a gradual decrease in how loudly a piece of music is played or sung **ANT** CRESCENDO

dim·i·nu·tion **AWL** /ˌdɪməˈnuʃn/ *noun* **~ (of/in sth)** (*formal*) **1** [U] the act of reducing something or of being reduced: *the diminution of political power* **2** [C, usually sing.] a reduction; an amount reduced: *a diminution in population growth*

di·min·u·tive /dɪˈmɪnyətɪv/ *adj., noun*
• *adj.* (*formal*) very small: *She was a diminutive figure beside her husband.*
• *noun* **1** a word or an ending of a word that shows that someone or something is small, for example *piglet* (= a young pig), *kitchenette* (= a small kitchen) **2** a short, informal form of a word, especially a name: *"Nick" is a common diminutive of "Nicholas."*

dim·ly /ˈdɪmli/ *adv.* not very brightly or clearly: *a dimly lit room ♦ I was dimly aware* (= only just aware) *of the sound of a car in the distance. ♦ I did remember, but only dimly.*

dim·mer switch /ˈdɪmər ˌswɪtʃ/ (also **dim·mer**) *noun* **1** a switch that allows you to make an electric light brighter or less bright **2** a switch that allows you to make the front lights on a car point downward

dim·ple /ˈdɪmpl/ *noun, verb*
• *noun* **1** a small hollow place in the skin, especially in the cheek or chin: *She had a dimple that appeared when she smiled.* **2** any small hollow place in a surface: *a pane of glass with a dimple pattern* ▶ **dim·pled** /ˈdɪmpld/ *adj.*: *a dimpled chin*
• *verb* [I] to make a hollow place appear on each of your cheeks, especially by smiling

dim sum /ˌdɪm ˈsʌm/ *noun* [U] (from *Chinese*) a Chinese dish or meal consisting of small pieces of food wrapped in sheets of DOUGH

dim·wit /ˈdɪmwɪt/ *noun* a stupid person

dim-ˈwitted (also **dim·wit·ted**) *adj.* (*informal*) stupid: *a dim-witted child*

din /dɪn/ *noun* [sing.] a loud, unpleasant noise that lasts for a long time **SYN** RACKET: *The children were making an awful din.*

di·nar /dɪˈnɑr; ˈdinɑr/ *noun* a unit of money in Serbia and various countries in the Middle East and N. Africa

din-din /ˈdɪndɪn/ *noun* [U] (*humorous*) (used when talking to a baby or a pet) food

dine /daɪn/ *verb* [I] (*formal*) to eat dinner: *We dined with my parents at a restaurant in town.* ➔ collocations at RESTAURANT **IDM** see WINE *v.* **PHR V** ˌdine ˈon sth to have a particular type of food for dinner ˌdine ˈout to eat dinner in a restaurant or someone else's home ˌdine ˈout on sth (*informal*) to regularly entertain friends with a humorous story, in order to make them interested in you

din·er /ˈdaɪnər/ *noun* **1** a person eating a meal, especially in a restaurant: *a restaurant capable of seating 100 diners* **2** a small, usually cheap, restaurant: *a roadside diner*

di·ne·ro /dɪˈnɛroʊ/ *noun* [U] (*informal*, from *Spanish*) money

di·nette /daɪˈnɛt/ *noun* a small room or part of a room for eating meals

ding /dɪŋ/ *noun, verb*
● *noun* **1** a blow, especially one that causes slight damage to a car, etc.: *I got a ding in my rear fender.* **2** used to represent the sound made by a bell: *The lift came to a halt with a loud "ding."*
● *verb* **1** [I] to make a sound like a bell: *The computer just dings when I press a key.* **2** [T] ~ sth to cause slight damage to a car, etc.: *I dinged my passenger door.* **3** [T] ~ sb to hit someone: (*figurative*) *My department got dinged by the budget cuts.*

ding·bat /ˈdɪŋbæt/ *noun* (*slang*) a stupid person

ding-dong /ˈdɪŋ dɔŋ; -dɑŋ/ *noun* **1** [U] used to represent the sound made by a bell: *I rang the doorbell. Ding-dong! No answer.* **2** [C] (*informal*) a silly or stupid person

din·ghy /ˈdɪŋi; ˈdɪŋgi/ *noun* (*pl.* **din·ghies**) **1** a small open boat that you sail or ROW: *a sailing dinghy* ➔ compare YACHT **2** a small boat made of rubber that is filled with air, used especially for rescuing people from ships and planes

din·go /ˈdɪŋgoʊ/ *noun* (*pl.* **din·goes**) a wild Australian dog

din·gy /ˈdɪndʒi/ *adj.* (**din·gi·er, din·gi·est**) dark and dirty: *a dingy room/hotel* ◆ *dingy curtains/clothes* ▶ **din·gi·ness** *noun* [U]

ˈdining ˌcar *noun* a car on a train in which meals are served

ˈdining ˌroom *noun* a room that is used mainly for eating meals in

ˈdining ˌtable *noun* a table for having meals on ➔ compare DINNER TABLE

dink /dɪŋk/ *noun* **1** (*informal, humorous*) one of a couple who have a lot of money because both partners work and they have no children **ORIGIN** Formed from the first letters of "double income, no kids." **2** = DROP SHOT ▶ **dink** *verb* ~ sth

dink·y /ˈdɪŋki/ *adj.* (*informal, disapproving*) too small: *I grew up in a dinky little town that didn't even have a movie theater.*

din·ner 🖉 /ˈdɪnər/ *noun*
1 [U, C] the main meal of the day, eaten either in the middle of the day or in the evening: *It's time for dinner.* ◆ *When do you have dinner?* ◆ *What time do you serve dinner?* ◆ *Let's invite them to dinner tomorrow.* ◆ *What should we have for dinner tonight?* ◆ *It's your turn to cook dinner.* ◆ *She didn't eat much dinner.* ◆ *I never eat a big dinner.* ◆ *Christmas dinner* ◆ *a three-course dinner* ◆ *I'd like to take you out to dinner tonight.* ➔ collocations at RESTAURANT **2** [C] a large formal social

gathering at which dinner is eaten: *The club's annual dinner will be held on June 3.* ➔ see also DINNER PARTY

ˈdinner ˌdance *noun* a social event in the evening that includes a formal meal and dancing

ˈdinner ˌjacket *noun* a black or white jacket worn with a BOW TIE at formal occasions in the evening ➔ compare TUXEDO, TAILCOAT

ˈdinner ˌparty *noun* a social event at which a small group of people eat dinner at someone's house

ˈdinner ˌservice (also **ˈdinner ˌset**) *noun* a set of matching plates, dishes, etc. for serving a meal

ˈdinner ˌtable *noun* often **the dinner table** [usually sing.] the table at which people are eating dinner; an occasion when people are eating together: *conversation at the dinner table* ➔ compare DINING TABLE

ˈdinner ˌtheater (*CanE usually* **ˈdinner ˌtheatre**) *noun* a restaurant where you see a play after your meal

din·ner·time /ˈdɪnərˌtaɪm/ (also **ˈdinner ˌtime**) *noun* the time at which dinner is normally eaten

din·ner·ware /ˈdɪnərˌwɛr/ *noun* [U] plates, dishes, etc. used for serving a meal

di·no·saur /ˈdaɪnəˌsɔr/ *noun* **1** an animal that lived millions of years ago but is now EXTINCT (= it no longer exists). There were many types of dinosaurs, some of which were very large. **2** (*disapproving*) a person or thing that is old-fashioned and cannot change in the changing conditions of modern life

dint /dɪnt/ *noun*
IDM **by dint of sth/of doing sth** (*formal*) by means of something: *He succeeded by dint of hard work.*

di·o·cese /ˈdaɪəsəs; -siz; -sis/ *noun* (*pl.* **di·o·ces·es** /ˈdaɪəsəsəz; ˈdaɪəsizəz; ˈdaɪəsiz/) (in the Christian Church) a district for which a BISHOP is responsible ▶ **di·oc·e·san** /daɪˈɑsəsn/ *adj.*

di·ode /ˈdaɪoʊd/ *noun* (*technical*) an electronic device in which the electric current passes in one direction only, for example a SILICON CHIP

Di·o·ny·si·ac /ˌdaɪəˈnɪziˌæk; -ˈnɪsi-/ (also **Di·o·ny·si·an**) /ˌdaɪəˈnɪʒən; -ˈniʒən; -ˈnɪʃən; -ˈnaɪsiən/ *adj.* (*formal*) **1** relating to the ancient Greek god Dionysus **2** relating to the physical senses and the emotions, especially when they are expressed without control ➔ compare APOLLONIAN

di·op·ter (*CanE usually* **di·op·tre**) /daɪˈɑptər/ *noun* (*physics*) a unit for measuring the power of a LENS to REFRACT light (= make it change direction)

di·op·trics /daɪˈɑptrɪks/ *noun* [U] (*physics*) the scientific study of REFRACTION (= the way light changes direction when it goes through glass, etc.) ▶ **di·op·tric** *adj.*

di·o·ram·a /ˌdaɪəˈræmə; -ˈrɑmə/ *noun* a model representing a scene with figures, especially in a museum

di·ox·ide /daɪˈɑksaɪd/ *noun* [U, C] (*chemistry*) a substance formed by combining two atoms of OXYGEN and one atom of another chemical element ➔ see also CARBON DIOXIDE

di·ox·in /daɪˈɑksən/ *noun* a chemical used in industry and farming. Most dioxins are poisonous.

dip /dɪp/ *verb, noun*
● *verb* (-pp-) **1** [T] to put something quickly into a liquid and take it out again: ~ sth (into sth) *He dipped the brush into the paint.* ◆ ~ sth (in) *Dip your hand in to see how hot the water is.* ◆ *The fruit had been dipped in chocolate.* **2** [I, T] to go downward or to a lower level; to make something do this **SYN** FALL: (+ adv./prep.) *The sun dipped below the horizon.* ◆ *Sales for this quarter have dipped from 38.7 million to 33 million.* ◆ *The road dipped suddenly as we approached the town.* ◆ ~ sth (+ adv./prep.) *The plane dipped its wings.* **3** [T] ~ sth when farmers **dip** animals, especially sheep, they put them in a bath of a liquid containing chemicals in order to kill insects, etc.
IDM **dip into your pocket** (*informal*) to spend some of your own money on something **dip a toe in/into sth | dip a toe**

ʌ **cup**   ə **about**   eɪ **say**   aɪ **five**   ɔɪ **boy**   aʊ **now**   oʊ **go**   ər **bird**

in/into the water (*informal*) to start doing something very carefully to see if it will be successful or not

PHR V ˌdip ˈinto sth **1** to put your hand into a container to take something out: *She dipped into her purse and took out some coins.* **2** to take an amount from money that you have saved: *We took out a loan for the car because we didn't want to dip into our savings.* **3** to read or watch only parts of something: *I have only had time to dip into the report.*

• **noun 1** [C] (*informal*) a quick swim: *Let's go for a dip before breakfast.* **2** [C, U] a thick mixture into which pieces of food are dipped before being eaten **3** [C] a decrease in the amount or success of something, usually for only a short period **SYN** FALL: *a sharp dip in profits* **4** [C] a place where a surface suddenly drops to a lower level and then rises again: *a dip in the road* ♦ *Puddles had formed in the dips.* **5** [U, C] a liquid containing a chemical into which sheep and other animals can be dipped in order to kill insects on them **6** [sing.] **~ into sth** a quick look at something: *A brief dip into history serves to confirm this view.* **7** [C, usually sing.] a quick movement of something down and up: *He gave a dip of his head.* **8** [C] (*informal*) a stupid person

diph·the·ri·a /dɪfˈθɪriə; dɪp-/ *noun* [U] a serious infectious disease of the throat that causes difficulty in breathing

diph·thong /ˈdɪfθɔŋ; -θɑŋ; ˈdɪp-/ *noun* (*phonetics*) a combination of two vowel sounds or vowel letters, for example the sounds /aɪ/ in *pipe* /paɪp/ or the letters *ou* in *doubt*
➔ compare MONOPHTHONG, TRIPHTHONG ▶ **diph·thong·al** /dɪfˈθɔŋgl; -ˈθɑŋgl; dɪp-/ *adj.*

di·plod·o·cus /dɪˈplɑdəkəs/ *noun* a very large DINOSAUR with a long thin neck and tail

dip·loid /ˈdɪplɔɪd/ *adj.* (*biology*) (of a cell) containing two complete sets of CHROMOSOMES, one from each parent
➔ compare HAPLOID

di·plo·ma /dəˈploʊmə/ *noun* a document showing that you have completed a course of study or part of your education: *a high school diploma*

di·plo·ma·cy /dəˈploʊməsi/ *noun* [U] **1** the activity of managing relations between different countries; the skill in doing this: *international diplomacy* ♦ *Diplomacy is better than war.* ➔ collocations at INTERNATIONAL **2** skill in dealing with people in difficult situations without upsetting or offending them **SYN** TACT ➔ see also SHUTTLE DIPLOMACY

dip·lo·mat /ˈdɪpləmæt/ *noun* **1** (also *old-fashioned* di·plo·ma·tist) a person whose job is to represent his or her country in a foreign country, for example, in an EMBASSY ➔ see also CHIEF DIPLOMAT **2** a person who is skilled at dealing with other people

dip·lo·mat·ic /ˌdɪpləˈmætɪk/ *adj.* **1** connected with managing relations between countries (= DIPLOMACY): *a diplomatic crisis* ♦ *Attempts are being made to settle the dispute by diplomatic means.* ♦ *to break off/establish/restore diplomatic relations with a country* **2** having or showing skill in dealing with people in difficult situations **SYN** TACTFUL: *a diplomatic answer* ▶ **dip·lo·mat·i·cally** /-kli/ *adv.*: *The country remained diplomatically isolated.* ♦ *"Why don't we take a break for coffee?" she suggested diplomatically.*

diploˈmatic ˌcorps *noun* usually **the diplomatic corps** [usually sing.] (*pl.* dip·lo·mat·ic corps) all the diplomats who work in a particular city or country

ˌdiplomatic imˈmunity *noun* [U] special rights given to diplomats working in a foreign country that mean they cannot be arrested, taxed, etc. in that country

ˌdiplomatic ˈpouch *noun* a container that is used for sending official letters and documents between a government and its representatives in another country and that cannot be opened by customs officers

the Diploˈmatic ˌService *noun* = FOREIGN SERVICE

di·plo·ma·tist /dɪˈploʊmətɪst/ *noun* (*old-fashioned*) = DIPLOMAT

di·pole /ˈdaɪpoʊl/ *noun* (*physics*) a pair of separated POLES, one positive and one negative

dip·per /ˈdɪpər/ *noun* **1** a bird that lives near rivers **2** a

large deep spoon, used to take up an amount of liquid
➔ see also BIG DIPPER

dip·py /ˈdɪpi/ *adj.* (*informal*) stupid; crazy

dip·so·ma·ni·ac /ˌdɪpsəˈmeɪniæk/ *noun* a person who has a strong desire for alcoholic drink that they cannot control **SYN** ALCOHOLIC

dip·stick /ˈdɪpstɪk/ *noun* **1** a long straight piece of metal used for measuring the amount of liquid in a container, especially the amount of oil in an engine **2** (*informal*) a stupid person

dip·tych /ˈdɪptɪk/ *noun* (*technical*) a painting, especially a religious one, with two wooden panels that can be closed like a book

dire /ˈdaɪər/ *adj.* (dir·er, dir·est) **1** [usually before noun] (*formal*) very serious: *living in dire poverty* ♦ *Such action may have dire consequences.* ♦ *We're in dire need of your help.* ♦ *The firm is in dire straits* (= in a very difficult situation) *and may go bankrupt.* **2** (*informal*) (of a warning or threat) predicting disaster: *dire warnings about breathing the fumes*

di·rect 🔑 /dəˈrɛkt; daɪ-/ *adj., verb, adv.*

• **adj.**

> NO ONE/NOTHING IN BETWEEN **1** [usually before noun] happening or done without involving other people, actions, etc. in between: *They are in direct contact with the hijackers.* ♦ *His death was a direct result of your actions.* ♦ *We are looking for somebody with direct experience of this type of work.* ♦ *This information has a direct bearing on* (= it is closely connected with) *the case.* **ANT** INDIRECT

> TRIP/ROUTE **2** going in the straightest line between two places without stopping or changing direction: *the most direct route/course* ♦ *a direct flight* (= a flight that does not stop) ♦ *There's a direct train to Boston* (= it may stop at other stations but you do not have to change trains). ♦ *a direct hit* (= a hit that is accurate and does not touch something else first) **ANT** INDIRECT

> HEAT/LIGHT **3** [only before noun] with nothing between something and the source of the heat or light: *Protect your child from direct sunlight by using a sunscreen.*

> EXACT **4** [only before noun] exact: *That's the direct opposite of what you told me yesterday.* ♦ *a direct quote* (= one using a person's exact words)

> SAYING WHAT YOU MEAN **5** saying exactly what you mean in a way that no one can pretend not to understand: *a direct answer/question* ♦ *You'll have to get used to his direct manner.* **ANT** INDIRECT ➔ thesaurus box at HONEST

> RELATIONSHIP **6** [only before noun] related through parents and children rather than brothers, sisters, aunts, etc.: *a direct descendant of the country's first president* **ANT** INDIRECT

• **verb**

> AIM **1** [T] to aim something in a particular direction or at a particular person: **~ sth at sth/sb** *The machine directs a powerful beam at the affected part of the body.* ♦ *Was that remark directed at me?* ♦ **~ sth to/toward sth/sb** *There are three main issues that we need to direct our attention to.* ♦ **~ sth against sth/sb** *Most of his anger was directed against himself.*

> CONTROL **2** [T] **~ sb/sth** to control or be in charge of someone or something: *A new manager has been appointed to direct the project.* ♦ *He was asked to take command and direct operations.*

> MOVIE/PLAY/MUSIC **3** [I, T] to be in charge of actors in a play or a movie, or musicians in an ORCHESTRA, etc.: *She prefers to act rather than direct.* ♦ **~ sb/sth** *The movie was directed by Steven Spielberg.* ♦ *She now directs a large choir.*

> SHOW THE WAY **4** [T] **~ sb (to...)** to tell or show someone how to get to somewhere or where to go: *Could you direct me to the station?* ♦ *A police officer was directing (the) traffic.*
➔ thesaurus box at TAKE

> GIVE ORDERS **5** [T] (*formal*) to give an official order **SYN** ORDER: **~ sb to do sth** *The police officers had been directed to search the building.* ♦ **~ that...** *The judge directed that the mother be given custody of the children.* ➔ thesaurus box at ORDER

> LETTER/COMMENT **6** [T] **~ sth to...** (*formal*) to send a letter,

etc. to a particular place or to a particular person: *Direct any complaints to the Customer Service department.*

● *adv.*

> TRIP/ROUTE **1** without stopping or changing direction: *We flew direct to Hong Kong.* ◆ *The 10:40 goes direct to Philadelphia.*

> NO ONE IN BETWEEN **2** without involving other people: *I prefer to deal with him direct.*

di·rect 'access *noun* [U] (*computing*) the ability to get data immediately from any part of a computer file

di·rect 'action *noun* [U, C] the use of strikes, protests, etc. instead of discussion in order to get what you want

di·rect 'current *noun* [C, U] (*abbr.* DC) an electric current that flows in one direction only ⊃ compare ALTERNATING CURRENT

di·rect 'debit *noun* [U, C] an instruction to your bank to allow someone else to take an amount of money from your account on a particular date, especially to pay bills: *We pay all our bills by direct debit.*

di·rect de'posit *noun* [U] the system of paying someone's wages straight into their bank account

di·rec·tion 🔑 /dəˈrɛkʃn; daɪ-/ *noun*

> WHERE TO **1** [C, U] the general position a person or thing moves or points toward: *Tom went off in the direction of home.* ◆ *She glanced in his direction.* ◆ *The aircraft was flying in a northerly direction.* ◆ *The road was blocked in both directions.* ◆ *They hit a truck coming from the opposite direction.* ◆ *Has the wind changed direction?* ◆ *When the police arrived, the crowd scattered in all directions.* ◆ *I lost all sense of direction* (= I didn't know which way to go).

> DEVELOPMENT **2** [C, U] the general way in which a person or thing develops: *The exhibition provides evidence of several new directions in her work.* ◆ *I am very unhappy with the direction the club is taking.* ◆ *It's only a small improvement, but at least it's a step in the right direction.*

> WHERE FROM **3** [C] the general position a person or thing comes or develops from: *Support came from an unexpected direction.* ◆ *Let us approach the subject from a different direction.*

> PURPOSE **4** [U] a purpose; an aim: *We are looking for somebody with a clear sense of direction.* ◆ *Once again her life felt lacking in direction.*

> INSTRUCTIONS **5** [C, usually pl.] instructions about how to do something, where to go, etc.: *Let's stop and ask for directions.* ◆ *Simple directions for assembling the model are printed on the box.*

> CONTROL **6** [U] the art of managing or guiding someone or something: *All work was produced by the students under the direction of John Williams.*

> MOVIE **7** [U] the instructions given by someone directing a movie: *There is some clever direction and the film is very well shot.* **IDM** see PULL *v.*

di·rec·tion·al /dəˈrɛkʃənl/ *adj.* (*technical*) **1** producing or receiving signals, sound, etc. better in one particular direction: *a directional microphone/aerial* **2** connected with the direction in which something is moving: *directional stability*

di·rec·tion·less /dəˈrɛkʃənləs/ *adj.* (*formal*) without a direction or purpose

di·rec·tive /dəˈrɛktɪv; daɪ-/ *noun, adj.*

● *noun* an official instruction: *The Environmental Protection Agency has issued a new set of directives on pollution.*

● *adj.* (*formal*) giving instructions: *They are seeking a central, directive role in national energy policy.*

di·rect·ly 🔑 /dəˈrɛktli; daɪ-/ *adv.*

1 in a direct line or manner: *He drove her directly to her hotel.* ◆ *She looked directly at us.* ◆ *He's directly responsible to the boss.* ◆ *We have not been directly affected by the budget cuts.* **ANT** **2** exactly in a particular position: *directly opposite/below/ahead* ◆ *They remain directly opposed to these new plans.* **3** immediately: *She left directly after the show.*

di·rect 'mail *noun* [U] advertisements that are sent to people through the mail

di·rect 'marketing *noun* [U] the business of selling products or services directly to customers who order by mail or by telephone instead of going to a store

the di·rect 'method *noun* [sing.] a way of teaching a foreign language using only that language and not treating the study of grammar as the most important thing

di·rect·ness /dəˈrɛktnəs/ *noun* [U] the quality of being simple and clear, so that it is impossible not to understand: *"What's that?" she asked with her usual directness.*

di·rect 'object *noun* (*grammar*) a noun, noun phrase, or pronoun that refers to a person or thing that is directly affected by the action of a verb: *In "I met him in town," the word "him" is the direct object.* ⊃ compare INDIRECT OBJECT

di·rec·tor 🔑 /dəˈrɛktər; daɪ-/ *noun*

1 a person in charge of a movie or play who tells the actors and staff what to do ⊃ compare PRODUCER **2** one of a group of senior managers who run a company: *He's on the board of directors.* ◆ *the sales director* ◆ *an executive director* **3** a person who is in charge of a particular activity or department in a company, a college, etc.: *the musical director* ◆ *a regional director* ◆ *the director of education*

di·rec·to·rate /dəˈrɛktərət/ *noun* **1** a section of a government department in charge of one particular activity: *the environmental directorate* **2** the group of directors who run a company **SYN** BOARD OF DIRECTORS

di·rec·to·ri·al /dəˌrɛkˈtɔriəl; ˌdaɪrɛk-/ *adj.* [only before noun] connected with the position or work of a director, especially of a director of movies: *The film marks her directorial debut.*

di·rector's 'chair *noun* a folding wooden chair with the seat and back made of cloth, sides on which you can rest your arms, and crossed legs ⊃ picture at CHAIR

di·rector's 'cut *noun* a version of a movie, usually released some time after the original is first shown, that is exactly how the director wanted it to be

di·rec·tor·ship /dəˈrɛktərˌʃɪp; daɪ-/ *noun* the position of a company director; the period during which this is held

di·rec·to·ry /dəˈrɛktəri; daɪ-/ *noun* (*pl.* di·rec·to·ries) **1** a book containing lists of information, usually in alphabetical order, for example people's telephone numbers or the names and addresses of businesses in a particular area: *a telephone/trade directory* ◆ *a directory of restaurants in the city* **2** a file containing a group of other files or programs in a computer

di·rectory as'sistance (also *informal* in·for·ma·tion) *noun* [U] a telephone service that you can use to find out a person's telephone number

di·rect 'rule *noun* [U] government of a region by a central government, when that region has had its own government in the past

di·rect 'speech *noun* [U] (*grammar*) a speaker's actual words; the use of these in writing: *Only direct speech should go inside quotation marks.* ⊃ compare INDIRECT SPEECH, REPORTED SPEECH

di·rect 'tax *noun* (*technical*) a tax, such as income tax, that is collected directly from the person who pays it, rather than being added to the price of goods and services ⊃ compare INDIRECT TAX ▶ **di·rect tax'ation** *noun* [U]

dirge /dərdʒ/ *noun* **1** a song sung in the past at a funeral or for a dead person **2** (*informal, disapproving*) any song or piece of music that is too slow and sad

dir·i·gi·ble /ˈdɪrədʒəbl; dəˈrɪdʒəbl/ *adj., noun*

● *adj.* (*formal*) able to be guided or steered: *a dirigible balloon*

● *noun* an AIRSHIP ⊃ see also BLIMP

dirk /dərk/ *noun* a long, heavy, pointed knife that was used as a weapon in Scotland in the past

dirn·dl /ˈdərndl/ *noun* (from *German*) a very full wide skirt,

t tea ţ butter d did k cat g got tʃ chin dʒ June f fall

pulled in tightly at the waist; a dress with a skirt like this and a closely fitting top

dirt 🔑 /dərt/ *noun* [U]
1 any substance that makes something dirty, for example dust, soil, or mud: *His clothes were covered in dirt.* ◆ *First remove any grease or dirt from the surface.* **2** loose earth or soil: *He picked up a handful of dirt and threw it at them.* ◆ *Pack the dirt firmly around the plants.* ◆ *They lived in a shack with a dirt floor.* ➔ thesaurus box at SOIL **3** (*informal*) unpleasant or harmful information about someone that could be used to damage their reputation, career, etc.: *Do you have any dirt on the new guy?* **4** (*informal*) = EXCREMENT: *dog dirt* **IDM** see DISH *v.*, DRAG *v.*, HIT *v.*, PAY DIRT, TREAT *v.*

dirt·bag /'dərtbæg/ *noun* (*informal*) a dirty or very unpleasant person

dirt bike *noun* a small motorcycle designed for riding on rough ground ➔ compare MOUNTAIN BIKE ➔ picture at BICYCLE

dirt 'cheap *adj., adv.* (*informal*) very cheap: *It was dirt cheap.* ◆ *I got it dirt cheap.*

dirt 'farmer *noun* a farmer who has poor land and does not make much money, and who does not pay anyone else to work on the farm

dirt 'poor *adj.* (*informal*) extremely poor

dirt 'road (also **dirt 'track**) *noun* a rough road in the country that is made from hard earth

dirt 'track *noun* **1** = DIRT ROAD **2** a track made of CINDERS, soil, etc. used for motorcycle racing: *a dirt-track race*

dirt·y 🔑 /'dərti/ *adj., verb, adv.*
● *adj.* (dirt·i·er, dirt·i·est)
▸ NOT CLEAN **1** not clean: *dirty hands/clothes* ◆ *a dirty mark* ◆ *Try not to get too dirty!* ◆ *I always get the dirty jobs* (= jobs that make you become dirty).
▸ OFFENSIVE **2** [usually before noun] connected with sex in an offensive way: *a dirty joke/book* ◆ *He's got a dirty mind* (= he often thinks about sex).

▸ UNPLEASANT/DISHONEST **3** [usually before noun] unpleasant or dishonest: *a dirty lie* ◆ *She's a dirty player.* ◆ *He's a great man for doing the dirty jobs* (= jobs which are unpleasant because they involve being dishonest or mean to people).
▸ COLORS **4** [only before noun] dull: *a dirty brown carpet*
▸ DRUGS **5** (*slang*) using illegal drugs
IDM **be a dirty word** to be a subject or an idea that people think is bad or immoral: *Profit is not a dirty word around here.* **(do sb's) dirty work** (to do) the unpleasant or dishonest jobs that someone else does not want to do **down and dirty** (*informal*) **1** behaving in an unfair or aggressive way, especially because you want to win: *The candidate got down and dirty again with his rival.* **2** rude and shocking: *The singer got down and dirty at the club last night and made headlines again.* **give sb a dirty look** to look at someone in a way that shows you are annoyed with them ➔ more at AIR *v.*, HAND *n.*
● *verb* (dirt·ies, dirt·y·ing, dirt·ied, dirt·ied) ~ sth to make something dirty
IDM **dirty your hands** = GET YOUR HANDS DIRTY at HAND *n.*
● *adv.*
IDM **play dirty** (*informal*) to behave or play a game in an unfair way

dirty 'blond *adj.* (of hair) dull and light brown in color

dirty 'bomb *noun* a bomb that contains RADIOACTIVE material

dirty old 'man *noun* (*informal*) an older man whose interest in sex or in sexually attractive young people is considered to be offensive or not natural for someone of his age

dirty 'trick *noun* **1** [usually pl.] dishonest, secret, and often illegal activity by a political group or other organization that is intended to harm the reputation or success of an opponent: *a dirty tricks campaign* **2** an unpleasant and dishonest act: *What a dirty trick to play!*

dis (also **diss**) /dɪs/ *verb* (-ss-) ~ sb (*informal*) to show a lack of respect for someone, especially by saying insulting things to them

dis- /dɪs/ *prefix* (in adjectives, adverbs, nouns, and verbs) not; the opposite of: *dishonest* ◆ *disagreeably* ◆ *disadvantage* ◆ *disappear*

dis·a·bil·i·ty 🔑 /ˌdɪsə'bɪləti/ *noun*
(*pl.* dis·a·bil·i·ties) **1** [C] a physical or mental condition that means you cannot use a part of your body completely or easily, or that you cannot learn easily: *a physical/mental disability* ◆ *people with severe learning disabilities* ➔ thesaurus box at ILLNESS **2** [U] the state of not being able to use a part of your body completely or easily; the state of not being able to learn easily: *He qualifies for help on the grounds of disability.* ◆ *Since I'm self-employed I have to pay for my own disability insurance.* ➔ note at DISABLED
IDM **on disability** used to refer to the pay that you receive if you are not able to work because of health problems: *After the accident, I was on disability for two weeks.*

dis·a·ble /dɪs'eɪbl/ *verb* **1** ~ sb to injure or affect someone permanently so that, for example, they cannot walk or cannot use a part of their body: *He was disabled in a car accident.* ◆ *a disabling condition* **2** ~ sth to make something unable to work so that it cannot be used: *The burglars gained entry to the building after disabling the alarm.*

dis·a·bled /dɪs'eɪbld/ *adj.* **1** unable to use a part of your body completely or easily because of a physical condition, illness, injury, etc.; unable to learn easily: *physically/ mentally disabled* ◆ *severely disabled* ◆ *He was born disabled.* ◆ *facilities for disabled people* **2** **the disabled** *noun* [pl.] people who are disabled: *caring for the sick, elderly, and disabled*

completely or easily. **Handicapped** is slightly old-fashioned and many people now think it is offensive. People also now prefer to use the word **disability** rather than **handicap**. The expression **people with disabilities** is often preferred to **the disabled** or **disabled people** because it focuses more on the person and less on the disability.

- **Disabled** and **disability** can be used with other words to talk about a mental condition: *mentally disabled ◆ learning disabilities*

- If someone's ability to hear, speak, or see has been damaged but not destroyed completely, they have **impaired hearing/speech/sight** (or **vision**). They can be described as **visually/hearing impaired** or **partially sighted**: *The museum has special facilities for blind and partially sighted visitors.*

dis'abled ˌlist *noun* a list of players on a sports team who are not able to play because of an injury

dis·a·ble·ment /dɪsˈeɪblmənt/ *noun* [U] (*formal*) the state of being disabled or the process of becoming disabled: *The insurance policy covers sudden death or disablement.*

dis·a·buse /ˌdɪsəˈbyuz/ *verb* ~ **sb** (of sth) (*formal*) to tell someone that what they think is true is, in fact, not true

dis·ad·van·tage 🔑 /ˌdɪsədˈvæntɪdʒ/ *noun* [C, U] something that causes problems and tends to stop someone or something from succeeding or making progress: *a serious/severe/considerable disadvantage ◆ ~ (of sth) One major disadvantage of the area is the lack of public transportation. ◆ ~ (to sth) There are disadvantages to the plan. ◆ What's the main disadvantage? ◆ I was at a disadvantage compared to the younger members of the team. ◆ The fact that he didn't speak a foreign language put him at a distinct disadvantage. ◆ I hope my lack of experience won't be to my disadvantage. ◆ The advantages of the plan far outweighed the disadvantages. ◆ Many children in the class suffered severe social and economic disadvantages.* **ANT** ADVANTAGE
▶ dis·ad·van·tage *verb* ~ **sb/sth**

dis·ad·van·taged /ˌdɪsədˈvæntɪdʒd/ *adj.* **1** not having the things, such as education, or enough money, that people need in order to succeed in life **SYN** DEPRIVED: *disadvantaged groups/children ◆ a severely disadvantaged area* **ANT** ADVANTAGED ⊃ thesaurus box at POOR **2** the disadvantaged *noun* [pl.] people who are disadvantaged

dis·ad·van·ta·geous /ˌdɪsˌædvənˈteɪdʒəs; -væn-/ *adj.* ~ **(to/for sb)** (*formal*) causing someone to be in a worse situation compared to other people: *The deal will not be disadvantageous to your company.* **ANT** ADVANTAGEOUS

dis·af·fect·ed /ˌdɪsəˈfɛktəd/ *adj.* no longer satisfied with your situation, organization, belief, etc. and therefore not loyal to it: *Some disaffected members left to form a new party.*
▶ dis·af·fec·tion /ˌdɪsəˈfɛkʃn/ *noun* [U]: *There are signs of growing disaffection amongst voters.*

dis·af·fil·i·ate /ˌdɪsəˈfɪliˌeɪt/ *verb* [I, T] ~ (sth) (from sth) to end the link between a group, a company, or an organization and a larger one: *The team has disaffiliated from the National Collegiate Athletic Association.* ▶ dis·af·fil·i·a·tion /ˌdɪsəˌfɪliˈeɪʃn/ *noun* [U]

dis·a·gree 🔑 /ˌdɪsəˈɡri/ *verb*
1 [I] if two people **disagree** or one person **disagrees** with another about something, they have a different opinion about it: *Even friends disagree sometimes. ◆ No, I disagree. I don't think it would be the right thing to do. ◆ ~ (with sb) (about/on/over sth) He disagreed with his parents on most things. ◆ Some people disagree with this argument. ◆ ~ that... Few would disagree that students learn best when they are interested in the topic.* **2** [I] if statements or reports **disagree**, they give different information **ANT** AGREE
PHR V disa'gree with sb if something, especially food, disagrees with you, it has a bad effect on you and makes you feel sick disa'gree with sth/with doing sth to believe

that something is bad or wrong; to disapprove of something: *I disagree with violent protests.*

dis·a·gree·a·ble /ˌdɪsəˈɡriəbl/ *adj.* (*formal*) **1** not nice or enjoyable **SYN** UNPLEASANT: *a disagreeable smell/experience/job* **2** (of a person) rude and unfriendly **SYN** UNPLEASANT: *a disagreeable, grumpy old man* **ANT** AGREEABLE ▶ dis·a·gree·a·bly /-bli/ *adv.*

dis·a·gree·ment 🔑 /ˌdɪsəˈɡrimənt/ *noun*
1 [U, C] a situation where people have different opinions about something and often argue: *~ (about/on/over/as to sth) Disagreement arose about exactly how to plan the show. ◆ disagreement on the method to be used ◆ There is considerable disagreement over the safety of the treatment. ◆ ~ (between A and B) It was a source of disagreement between the two states. ◆ ~ (among...) There is disagreement among archaeologists as to the age of the sculpture. ◆ ~ (with sb) They have had several disagreements with their neighbors.* **ANT** AGREEMENT **2** [U, C] ~ **between A and B** a difference between two things that should be the same: *The comparison shows considerable disagreement between theory and practice.*

dis·al·low /ˌdɪsəˈlaʊ/ *verb* ~ **sth** [often passive] to officially refuse to accept something because it is not valid: *to disallow a claim/an appeal ◆ The second goal was disallowed.* ⊃ compare ALLOW

dis·am·big·u·ate /ˌdɪsæmˈbɪɡyuˌeɪt/ *verb* ~ **sth** (*technical*) to show clearly the difference between two or more words, phrases, etc. that are similar in meaning

dis·ap·pear 🔑 /ˌdɪsəˈpɪr/ *verb*
1 [I] (+ adv./prep.) to become impossible to see **SYN** VANISH: *The plane disappeared behind a cloud. ◆ Lisa watched until the train disappeared from view.* **2** [I] to stop existing **SYN** VANISH: *Her nervousness quickly disappeared once she was on stage. ◆ The problem won't just disappear. ◆ Our forests are disappearing at an alarming rate.* **3** [I] to be lost or impossible to find **SYN** VANISH: *I can never find a pen in this house. They disappear as soon as I buy them. ◆ ~ from sth The child disappeared from his home some time after four.*
▶ dis·ap·pear·ance /ˌdɪsəˈpɪrəns/ *noun* [U, C]: *the disappearance of many species of plants and animals from our planet ◆ Police are investigating the disappearance of a young woman.* **IDM** see ACT *n.*, FACE *n.*

dis·ap·point 🔑 /ˌdɪsəˈpɔɪnt/ *verb*
1 [T, I] ~ (sb) | (it disappoints sb that...) to make someone feel sad because something that they hope for or expect to happen does not happen or is not as good as they hoped: *Her decision to cancel the concert is bound to disappoint her fans. ◆ I hate to disappoint you, but I'm just not interested. ◆ The movie had disappointed her* (= it wasn't as good as she had expected). *◆ His latest novel does not disappoint.* **2** [T] ~ **sth** to prevent something that someone hopes for from becoming a reality: *The new government had soon disappointed the hopes of many of its supporters.*

dis·ap·point·ed 🔑 /ˌdɪsəˈpɔɪntəd/ *adj.*
upset because something you hoped for has not happened or been as good, successful, etc. as you expected: *~ (at/by sth) They were bitterly disappointed at the result of the game. ◆ I was disappointed by the quality of the wine. ◆ ~ (in/with sb/sth) I'm disappointed in you—I really thought I could trust you! ◆ I was very disappointed with myself. ◆ ~ (to see, hear, etc.) He was disappointed to see she wasn't at the party. ◆ ~ (that...) I'm disappointed (that) it was sold out. ◆ ~ (not) to be... She was disappointed not to be chosen for the team.*

dis·ap·point·ing 🔑 /ˌdɪsəˈpɔɪntɪŋ/ *adj.*
not as good, successful, etc. as you had hoped; making you feel disappointed: *a disappointing result/performance ◆ The outcome of the court case was disappointing for the family involved.* ▶ dis·ap·point·ing·ly *adv.*: *The room was disappointingly small.*

dis·ap·point·ment 🔑 /ˌdɪsəˈpɔɪntmənt/ *noun*
1 [U] sadness because something has not happened or

h **hat**   m **man**   n **no**   ŋ **sing**   l **leg**   r **red**   y **yes**   w **wet**

been as good, successful, etc. as you expected or hoped: *Reserve early for the show to avoid disappointment.* ◆ *To our great disappointment, it rained every day of the trip.* ◆ *He found it difficult to hide his disappointment when she didn't arrive.* **2** [C] a person or thing that is disappointing: *a bitter/major disappointment* ◆ *That new restaurant was a big disappointment.* ◆ *~ to sb I always felt I was a disappointment to my father.*

dis·ap·pro·ba·tion /ˌdɪsˌæprəˈbeɪʃn/ *noun* [U] (*formal*) disapproval of someone or something that you think is morally wrong

dis·ap·prov·al 🔑 /ˌdɪsəˈpruːvl/ *noun* [U]
~ **(of sb/sth)** a feeling that you do not like an idea, an action, or someone's behavior because you think it is bad, not suitable, or going to have a bad effect on someone else: *disapproval of his methods* ◆ *to show/express disapproval* ◆ *He shook his head in disapproval.* ◆ *She looked at my clothes with disapproval.* **ANT** APPROVAL

dis·ap·prove 🔑 /ˌdɪsəˈpruːv/ *verb*
[I, T] to think that someone or something is not good or suitable; to not approve of someone or something: *She wants to be an actress, but her parents disapprove.* ◆ *~ of sb/sth He strongly disapproved of the changes that had been made.* ◆ *~ sth A solid majority disapproves the way the president is handling the controversy.* **ANT** APPROVE

dis·ap·prov·ing 🔑 /ˌdɪsəˈpruːvɪŋ/ *adj.*
showing that you do not approve of someone or something: *a disapproving glance/tone/look* **ANT** APPROVING
▶ **dis·ap·prov·ing·ly** *adv.*: *He looked disapprovingly at the row of empty wine bottles.*

dis·arm /dɪsˈɑːrm/ *verb* **1** [T] ~ **sb** to take a weapon or weapons away from someone: *Most of the rebels were captured and disarmed.* **2** [I] (of a country or a group of people) to reduce the size of an army or to give up some or all weapons, especially nuclear weapons **3** [T] ~ **sb** to make someone feel less angry or critical: *He disarmed her immediately by apologizing profusely.* ⊃ compare ARM

dis·ar·ma·ment /dɪsˈɑːrməmənt/ *noun* [U] the fact of a country reducing the size of its armed forces or the number of weapons, especially nuclear weapons, that it has: *nuclear disarmament* ◆ *disarmament talks* ⊃ compare ARMAMENT

dis·arm·ing /dɪsˈɑːrmɪŋ/ *adj.* making people feel less angry or suspicious than they were before: *a disarming smile*
▶ **dis·arm·ing·ly** *adv.*: *disarmingly frank*

dis·ar·range /ˌdɪsəˈreɪndʒ/ *verb* [usually passive] ~ **sth** (*formal*) to make something messy

dis·ar·ray /ˌdɪsəˈreɪ/ *noun* [U] a state of confusion and lack of organization in a situation or a place: *The peace talks broke up in disarray.* ◆ *Our plans were thrown into disarray by her arrival.*

dis·as·sem·ble /ˌdɪsəˈsɛmbl/ *verb* **1** [T] ~ **sth** to take apart a machine or structure so that it is in separate pieces: *We had to completely disassemble the engine to find the problem.* **ANT** ASSEMBLE **2** [T] ~ **sth** (*computing*) to translate something from computer code into a language that can be read by humans **3** [I] (*formal*) (of a group of people) to move apart and go away in different directions: *The concert ended and the crowd disassembled.*

dis·as·sem·bler /ˌdɪsəˈsɛmblər/ *noun* (*computing*) a program used to disassemble computer code

dis·as·so·ci·ate /ˌdɪsəˈsoʊʃieɪt; -siˌeɪt/ *verb* = DISSOCIATE

dis·as·ter 🔑 /dɪˈzæstər/ *noun*
1 [C] an unexpected event, such as a very bad accident, a flood, or a fire, that kills a lot of people or causes a lot of damage **SYN** CATASTROPHE: *an air disaster* ◆ *environmental disasters* ◆ *Thousands died in the disaster.* ⊃ see also NATURAL DISASTER **2** [C, U] a very bad situation that causes problems: *Losing your job doesn't have to be such a disaster.* ◆ *Disaster struck when the wheel came off.* ◆ *financial disaster*

◆ *Letting her organize the party is a recipe for disaster* (= something that is likely to go badly wrong). **3** [C, U] (*informal*) a complete failure: *As a teacher, he's a disaster.* ◆ *The play's first night was a total disaster.* **IDM** see WAIT *v.*

di·saster ˌarea *noun* **1** a place where a disaster has happened and that needs special help **2** (*informal*) a place or situation that has a lot of problems, is a failure, or is badly organized

dis·as·trous /dɪˈzæstrəs/ *adj.* very bad, harmful, or unsuccessful **SYN** DEVASTATING: *a disastrous harvest/fire/result*
◆ *Lowering interest rates could have disastrous consequences for the economy.* ▶ **dis·as·trous·ly** *adv.*: *How could everything go so disastrously wrong?*

dis·a·vow /ˌdɪsəˈvaʊ/ *verb* ~ **sth** (*formal*) to state publicly that you have no knowledge of something or that you are not responsible for something or someone: *The coach disavowed responsibility for the player's behavior.* ▶ **dis·a·vow·al** /-ˈvaʊəl/ *noun* [C, U]

dis·band /dɪsˈbænd/ *verb* [T, I] ~ **(sb/sth)** to stop someone or something from operating as a group; to separate or no longer operate as a group: *They set about disbanding the terrorist groups.* ◆ *The committee formally disbanded in August.* ▶ **dis·band·ment** *noun* [U]

dis·bar /dɪsˈbɑːr/ *verb* (-rr-) [usually passive] ~ **sb (from sth/ from doing sth)** to stop a lawyer from working in the legal profession, especially because he or she has done something illegal

dis·be·lief /ˌdɪsbɪˈliːf/ *noun* [U] the feeling of not being able to believe something: *He stared at me in disbelief.* ◆ *To enjoy the movie you have to suspend your disbelief* (= pretend to believe something, even if it seems very unlikely). ⊃ compare BELIEF, UNBELIEF

dis·be·lieve /ˌdɪsbɪˈliːv/ *verb* [T, I] (not used in the progressive tenses) ~ **(sth)** (*formal*) to not believe that something is true or that someone is telling the truth: *Why should I disbelieve her story?* ▶ **dis·be·liev·ing** *adj.*: *a disbelieving look/smile/laugh* **dis·be·liev·ing·ly** *adv.*
PHR V disbe'lieve in sth to not believe that something exists

dis·burse /dɪsˈbɜːrs/ *verb* ~ **sth** (*formal*) to pay money to someone from a large amount that has been collected for a purpose ▶ **dis·burse·ment** *noun* [U, C]: *the disbursement of funds* ◆ *aid disbursements*

disc 🔑 /dɪsk/ *noun*
= DISK ⊃ see also CD, DISC JOCKEY

dis·card *verb, noun*
● *verb* /dɪˈskɑːrd/ **1** [T] to get rid of something that you no longer want or need: *~ sb/sth The room was littered with discarded newspapers.* ◆ *He had discarded his jacket because of the heat.* ◆ *(figurative) She could now discard all thought of promotion.* ◆ *~ sb/sth as sth 10% of the data was discarded as unreliable* **2** [T, I] ~ **(sth)** (in card games) to get rid of a card that you do not want
● *noun* /ˈdɪskɑːrd/ a person or thing that is not wanted or that is thrown away, especially a card in a card game

'disc brake *noun* [usually pl.] a BRAKE that works by two surfaces pressing onto a disk in the center of a wheel

dis·cern /dɪˈsɜːrn/ *verb* (not used in the progressive tenses) (*formal*) **1** to know, recognize, or understand something, especially something that is not obvious **SYN** DETECT: ~ **sth** *It is possible to discern a number of different techniques in her work.* ◆ *He discerned a certain coldness in their welcome.* ◆ ~ **how, whether, etc....** *It is often difficult to discern how widespread public support is.* ◆ ~ **that...** *I quickly discerned that something was wrong.* **2** ~ **sth** to see or hear something, but not very clearly **SYN** MAKE OUT: *We could just discern the house in the distance.* ▶ **dis·cern·i·ble** /dɪˈsɜːrnəbl/ *adj.* **SYN** PERCEPTIBLE: *There is often no discernible difference between rival brands.* ◆ *His face was barely discernible in the gloom.*

dis·cern·ing /dɪˈsɜrnɪŋ/ adj. (approving) able to show good judgment about the quality of someone or something

dis·cern·ment /dɪˈsɜrnmənt/ noun [U] (formal, approving) the ability to show good judgment about the quality of someone or something SYN DISCRIMINATION: He shows great discernment in his choice of friends.

dis·charge verb, noun
● **verb** /dɪsˈtʃɑrdʒ; ˈdɪstʃɑrdʒ/
> FROM HOSPITAL/JOB **1** [T, usually passive] ~ sb (from sth) to give someone official permission to leave a place or job; to make sb leave a job: Patients were being discharged from the hospital too early. ♦ She had discharged herself against medical advice. ♦ He was discharged from the army following his injury. ♦ She was discharged from the police force for bad conduct.
> FROM PRISON/COURT **2** [T, often passive] ~ sb to allow someone to leave prison or court: He was conditionally discharged after admitting to the theft.
> GAS/LIQUID **3** [I, T] when a gas or a liquid discharges or is discharged, or someone discharges it, it flows somewhere: ~ (into sth) The river is diverted through the power station before discharging into the sea. ♦ ~ sth (into sth) The factory was fined for discharging chemicals into the river.
> FORCE/POWER **4** [T, I] ~ (sth) (technical) to release force or power: Lightning is caused by clouds discharging electricity.
> DUTY **5** [T] ~ sth (formal) to do everything that is necessary to perform and complete a particular duty: to discharge your duties/ responsibilities/obligations ♦ to discharge a debt (= to pay it)
> GUN **6** [T] ~ sth (formal) to fire a gun, etc.
● **noun** /ˈdɪstʃɑrdʒ/
> OF LIQUID/GAS **1** [U, C] the action of releasing a substance such as a liquid or gas; a substance that comes out from inside somewhere: a ban on the discharge of toxic waste ♦ thunder and lightning caused by electrical discharges ♦ nasal discharge (= from the nose)
> FROM HOSPITAL/JOB **2** [U, C] ~ (from sth) the act of officially allowing someone, or of telling someone, to leave somewhere, especially someone in a hospital or the army
> OF DUTY **3** [U] (formal) the act of performing a task or a duty or of paying money that is owed: the discharge of debts/ obligations

dis·ci·ple /dɪˈsaɪpl/ noun **1** a person who believes in and follows the teachings of a religious or political leader SYN FOLLOWER: a disciple of the economist John Maynard Keynes **2** (according to the Bible) one of the people who followed Jesus Christ and his teachings when he was living on earth, especially one of the twelve APOSTLES

dis·ci·pli·nar·i·an /ˌdɪsəpləˈnɛriən/ noun a person who believes in using rules and punishments for controlling people: She's a very strict disciplinarian.

dis·ci·pli·nar·y /ˈdɪsəpləˌnɛri/ adj. connected with the punishment of people who break rules: a disciplinary hearing (= to decide if someone has done something wrong) ♦ The company will be taking disciplinary action against him.

dis·ci·pline 🔑 /ˈdɪsəplən/ noun, verb
● **noun 1** [U] the practice of training people to obey rules and orders and punishing them if they do not; the controlled behavior or situation that results from this training: The school has a reputation for high standards of discipline. ♦ Strict discipline is imposed on army recruits. ♦ She keeps good discipline in class. **2** [C] a method of training your mind or body or of controlling your behavior; an area of activity where this is necessary: Yoga is a good discipline for learning to relax. **3** [U] the ability to control your behavior or the way you live, work, etc.: He'll never get anywhere working for himself—he's got no discipline. ⊃ see also SELF-DISCIPLINE **4** [C] an area of knowledge; a subject that people study or are taught, especially in a university
● **verb 1** ~ sb (for sth) to punish someone for something they have done: The officers were disciplined for using racist language. **2** ~ sb to train someone, especially a child, to obey particular rules and control the way they behave: a guide to the best ways of disciplining your child **3** to control the

way you behave and make yourself do things that you believe you should do: ~ yourself Dieting is a matter of disciplining yourself. ♦ ~ yourself to do sth He disciplined himself to exercise at least three times a week. ▶ **dis·ci·plined** adj.: a disciplined army/team ♦ a disciplined approach to work

'disc ˌjockey (also 'disk jockey) noun (abbr. DJ) (also informal dee·jay) a person whose job is to introduce and play recorded popular music, on radio or television or at a club

dis·claim /dɪsˈkleɪm/ verb (formal) **1** ~ sth to state publicly that you have no knowledge of something, or that you are not responsible for something SYN DENY: She disclaimed any knowledge of her husband's whereabouts. ♦ The rebels disclaimed all responsibility for the explosion. **2** ~ sth to give up your right to something, such as property or a title SYN RENOUNCE

dis·claim·er /dɪsˈkleɪmər/ noun **1** (formal) a statement in which someone says that they are not connected with or responsible for something, or that they do not have any knowledge of it **2** (law) a statement in which a person says officially that they do not claim the right to do something

dis·close /dɪsˈkloʊz/ verb **1** to give someone information about something, especially something that was previously secret SYN REVEAL: ~ sth (to sb) The spokesman refused to disclose details of the takeover to the press. ♦ ~ that... The report discloses that human error was to blame for the accident. ♦ **it is disclosed that...** It was disclosed that two women were being interviewed by the police. ♦ ~ what, whether, etc. ... I cannot disclose what we discussed. **2** ~ sth (formal) to allow something that was hidden to be seen SYN REVEAL: The door swung open, disclosing a long, dark passage.

dis·clo·sure /dɪsˈkloʊʒər/ noun (formal) **1** [U] the act of making something known or public that was previously secret or private SYN REVELATION: the newspaper's disclosure of defense secrets **2** [C] information or a fact that is made known or public that was previously secret or private SYN REVELATION: startling disclosures about his private life

dis·co /ˈdɪskoʊ/ (pl. dis·cos) noun **1** (also old-fashioned dis·co·theque) [C] a club or party where people dance to recorded pop music: disco dancing **2** (also 'disco ˌmusic) [U] pop music with a strong beat, intended for discos and popular in the 1970s

dis·cog·ra·phy /dɪsˈkɑgrəfi/ noun (pl. dis·cog·ra·phies) **1** [C] all of the music that has been performed, written or collected by a particular person or group; a list of this music **2** [U] the study of musical recordings or collections

dis·col·or (CanE usually dis·col·our) /dɪsˈkʌlər/ verb [I, T] to change color, or to make the color of something change, in a way that makes it look less attractive: Plastic tends to discolor with age. ♦ ~ sth The pipes were beginning to rust, discoloring the water.

dis·col·or·a·tion (CanE usually dis·col·our·a·tion) /ˌdɪsˌkʌləˈreɪʃn/ noun **1** [U] the process of becoming discolor ed: discoloration caused by the sun **2** [C] a place where something has become discolored

dis·com·fit /dɪsˈkʌmfət/ verb [often passive] ~ sb (literary) to make someone feel confused or embarrassed ▶ **dis·com·fi·ture** /dɪsˈkʌmfətʃər/ noun [U]: He was clearly taking delight in her discomfiture.

dis·com·fort /dɪsˈkʌmfərt/ noun, verb
● **noun 1** [U] a feeling of slight pain or of being physically uncomfortable: You will experience some minor discomfort during the treatment. ♦ abdominal discomfort **2** [U] a feeling of worry or embarrassment SYN UNEASE: John's presence caused her considerable discomfort. **3** [C] (formal) something that makes you feel uncomfortable or causes you a slight feeling of pain
● **verb** [often passive] ~ sb (formal) to make someone feel anxious or embarrassed

dis·com·pose /ˌdɪskəmˈpoʊz/ verb ~ sb (formal) to disturb someone and make them feel anxious SYN DISCONCERT, DISTURB ▶ **dis·com·po·sure** /ˌdɪskəmˈpoʊʒər/ noun [U]

dis·con·cert /ˌdɪskən'sərt/ *verb* ~ **sb** to make someone feel anxious, confused, or embarrassed **SYN** DISTURB: *His answer really disconcerted her.* ▶ **dis·con·cert·ed** *adj.*: *I was disconcerted to find that everyone else already knew it.* **dis·con·cert·ing** *adj.*: *She had the disconcerting habit of saying exactly what she thought.* **dis·con·cert·ing·ly** *adv.*

dis·con·nect /ˌdɪskə'nɛkt/ *verb* **1** [T] ~ **sth (from sth)** to remove a piece of equipment from a supply of gas, water, or electricity: *First, disconnect the boiler from the water mains.* **2** [T] ~ **sb/sth** [usually passive] to officially stop the supply of telephone lines, water, electricity, or gas to a building: *You may be disconnected if you do not pay the bill.* **3** [T] ~ **sth (from sth)** to separate something from something: *The ski had become disconnected from the boot.* **4** [T] ~ **sb** [usually passive] to break the contact between two people who are talking on the telephone: *We were suddenly disconnected.* **5** [T, I, often passive] to end a connection to the Internet: ~ **sb (from sth)** *I keep getting disconnected when I'm online.* ◆ ~ **(from sth)** *My computer crashes every time I disconnect from the Internet.* **ANT** CONNECT ▶ **dis·con·nec·tion** /ˌdɪskə'nɛkʃn/ *noun* [U, C]

dis·con·nect·ed /ˌdɪskə'nɛktəd/ *adj.* **1** not related to or connected with the things or people around: *disconnected images/thoughts/ideas* ◆ *I felt disconnected from the world around me.* **2** (of speech or writing) with the parts not connected in a logical order **SYN** DISJOINTED, INCOHERENT

dis·con·so·late /dɪs'kɑnsələt/ *adj.* (*formal*) very unhappy and disappointed **SYN** DEJECTED ▶ **dis·con·so·late·ly** *adv.*

dis·con·tent /ˌdɪskən'tɛnt/ (also **dis·con·tent·ment** /ˌdɪskən'tɛntmənt/) *noun* [U, C] ~ **(at/over/with sth)** a feeling of being unhappy because you are not satisfied with a particular situation; something that makes you have this feeling **SYN** DISSATISFACTION: *There is widespread discontent among the staff at the proposed changes to pay and conditions.* ⊃ compare CONTENTMENT

dis·con·tent·ed /ˌdɪskən'tɛntəd/ *adj.* ~ **(with sth)** unhappy because you are not satisfied with your situation **SYN** DIS-SATISFIED **ANT** CONTENTED ▶ **dis·con·tent·ed·ly** *adv.*

dis·con·tin·ue /ˌdɪskən'tɪnyu/ *verb* **1** ~ **(doing) sth** to stop doing, using, or providing something, especially something that you have been doing, using, or providing regularly: *The doctor decided to discontinue the treatment after three months.* **2** [usually passive] ~ **sth** to stop making a product: *a sale of discontinued china* ▶ **dis·con·tin·u·ance** *noun* **dis·con·tin·u·a·tion** *noun* [U]

dis·con·ti·nu·i·ty /ˌdɪsˌkɑntə'nuəti/ *noun* (*pl.* **dis·con·ti·nu·i·ties**) (*formal*) **1** [U] the state of not being continuous: *discontinuity in the children's education* **2** [C] a break or change in a continuous process: *Changes in government led to discontinuities in policy.* **ANT** CONTINUITY

dis·con·tin·u·ous /ˌdɪskən'tɪnyuəs/ *adj.* (*formal*) not continuous; stopping and starting again **SYN** INTERMITTENT

dis·cord /'dɪskɔrd/ *noun* **1** [U] (*formal*) disagreement; arguing: *marital/family discord* ◆ *A note of discord surfaced during the proceedings.* **ANT** CONCORD ⊃ compare HARMONY **2** [C, U] (*music*) a combination of musical notes that do not sound pleasant together

dis·cord·ant /dɪs'kɔrdnt/ *adj.* **1** [usually before noun] (*formal*) not in agreement; combining with other things in a way that is strange or unpleasant: *discordant views* **2** (of sounds) not sounding pleasant together **ANT** HARMONIOUS

dis·co·theque /'dɪskəˌtɛk/ *noun* (*old-fashioned*) = DISCO

dis·count 🔑 *noun, verb*

● *noun* /'dɪskaʊnt/ an amount of money that is taken off the usual cost of something **SYN** REDUCTION: *to get/give/offer a discount* ◆ *discount rates/prices* ◆ ~ **(on/off sth)** *They're offering a 10% discount on all sofas this month.* ◆ *They were selling everything at a discount* (= at reduced prices). ◆ *a discount store* (= one that regularly sells goods at reduced prices) ◆ *Do you give any discounts?* ⊃ collocations at SHOPPING

● *verb* **1** /dɪs'kaʊnt/ (*formal*) to think or say that something is not important or not true **SYN** DISMISS: ~ **sth** *We cannot discount the possibility of further strikes.* ◆ ~ **sth as sth** *The news reports were being discounted as propaganda.* **2** /'dɪskaʊnt; dɪs'kaʊnt/ ~ **sth** to take an amount of money off the usual cost of something; to sell something at a discount **SYN** REDUCE: *discounted prices/fares*

dis·count·er /'dɪskaʊntər/ (also 'discount ˌstore) *noun* a store that sells things very cheaply, often in large quantities or from a limited range of goods

'**discount ˌrate** *noun* (*finance*) **1** the minimum rate of interest that banks must pay when they borrow money from other banks **2** the amount that the price of a BILL OF EXCHANGE is reduced by when it is bought before it reaches its full value **3** the rate at which an investment increases in value each year

dis·cour·age /dɪ'skɜrɪdʒ/ *verb* **1** to try to prevent something or to prevent someone from doing something, especially by making it difficult to do or by showing that you do not approve of it: ~ **(doing) sth** *a campaign to discourage smoking among teenagers* ◆ ~ **sb** *I leave a light on when I'm out to discourage burglars.* ◆ ~ **sb from doing sth** *His parents tried to discourage him from being an actor.* **2** to make someone feel less confident or enthusiastic about doing something **SYN** DISHEARTEN: ~ **sb** *Don't be discouraged by the first failure—try again!* ◆ ~ **sb from doing sth** *The weather discouraged people from attending.* **ANT** ENCOURAGE ▶ **dis·cour·aged** *adj.* [not usually before noun] *Learners can feel very discouraged if an exercise is too difficult.* **dis·cour·ag·ing** *adj.*: *a discouraging experience/response/ result* **dis·cour·ag·ing·ly** *adv.*

dis·cour·age·ment /dɪ'skɜrɪdʒmənt/ *noun* **1** [U] a feeling that you no longer have the confidence or enthusiasm to do something: *an atmosphere of discouragement and despair* **2** [U] the action of trying to stop something: *the government's discouragement of political protest* **3** [C] a thing that discourages someone from doing something: *Despite all these discouragements, she refused to give up.*

dis·course *noun, verb*
● *noun* /'dɪskɔrs/ **1** [C, U] (*formal*) a long and serious treatment or discussion of a subject in speech or writing: *a discourse on issues of gender and sexuality* ◆ *He was hoping for some lively political discourse at the meeting.* **2** [U] (*linguistics*) the use of language in speech and writing in order to produce meaning; language that is studied, usually in order to see how the different parts of a text are connected: *spoken/written discourse* ◆ *discourse analysis*
● *verb* /dɪs'kɔrs; 'dɪskɔrs/
PHR V dis'course on/upon sth (*formal*) to talk or give a long speech about something that you know a lot about

'**discourse ˌmarker** *noun* (*grammar*) a word or phrase that organizes spoken language into different parts, for example "Well…" or "On the other hand…"

dis·cour·te·ous /dɪs'kɜrtiəs/ *adj.* (*formal*) having bad manners and not showing respect for other people **SYN** IMPOLITE **ANT** COURTEOUS ⊃ thesaurus box at RUDE

dis·cour·te·sy /dɪs'kɜrtəsi/ *noun* [U, C] (*pl.* **dis·cour·te·sies**) (*formal*) behavior or an action that is not polite

dis·cov·er 🔑 /dɪ'skʌvər/ *verb*

1 ~ **sth** to be the first person to become aware that a particular place or thing exists: *Cook is credited with discovering Hawaii.* ◆ *Scientists around the world are working to discover a cure for AIDS.* **2** to find someone or something that was hidden or that you did not expect to find: ~ **sb/sth** *Police discovered a large stash of drugs while searching the house.* ◆ *We discovered this beach while we were sailing around the island.* ◆ ~ **sb/sth doing sth** *He was discovered hiding in a shed.* ◆ ~ **sb/sth + adj.** *She was discovered dead at her home in Portland.* **3** to find out about something: ~ **sth** *I've just discovered hang gliding!* ◆ ~ **(that)…** *It was a shock to discover (that) he couldn' read.* ◆ ~ **why, how, etc.…** *We never did discover why she gave up her job.* ◆ **it is discovered that…** *It was later* discovered that the diaries were a fraud. ◆ **sb/sth is discovered to be/have…** *He was later discovered to be seriously ill.* **4** [often passive] **~ sb** to be the first person to realize that someone is very good at singing, acting, etc. and help them to become successful and famous: *The singer was discovered while still in school.* ▶ **dis·cov·er·er** *noun: the discoverer of penicillin*

dis·cov·er·y 🔊 /dɪˈskʌvəri; -ˈskʌvri/ *noun* (*pl.* **dis·cov·er·ies**)

1 [C, U] an act or the process of finding someone or something, or learning about something that was not known about before: **~ (of sth)** *the discovery of antibiotics in the 20th century* ◆ *The discovery of a child's body in the river has shocked the community.* ◆ *the discovery of new talent in the art world* ◆ *Researchers in this field have* **made** *some important new* **discoveries.** ◆ *He saw life as a voyage of discovery.* ◆ **~ (that…)** *She was shocked by the discovery that he had been unfaithful.* **2** [C] a thing, fact, or person that is found or learned about for the first time: *The drug is not a new discovery—it's been known about for years.*

dis·cred·it /dɪsˈkrɛdət/ *verb, noun*

• *verb* **1 ~ sb/sth** to make people stop respecting someone or something: *The photos were deliberately taken to discredit the president.* ◆ *a discredited* **government/policy 2 ~ sth** to make people stop believing that something is true; to make something appear unlikely to be true: *These theories are now largely discredited among scientists.*

• *noun* [U] (*formal*) damage to someone's reputation; loss of respect: *Their actions* **brought discredit to** *the college.* ◆ *The mayor,* **to his discredit,** *did not speak out against these atrocities.* ⊃ compare CREDIT

dis·cred·it·a·ble /dɪsˈkrɛdətəbl/ *adj.* (*formal*) bad and unacceptable; causing people to lose respect

dis·creet /dɪˈskrit/ *adj.* careful in what you say or do, in order to keep something secret or to avoid causing embarrassment or difficulty for someone

WORD FAMILY
discreet *adj.* (≠ indiscreet)
discretion *noun* (≠ indiscretion)

SYN TACTFUL: *He was always very discreet about his love affairs.* ◆ *You should ask a few discreet questions before you sign anything.* ▶ **dis·creet·ly** *adv.: She coughed discreetly to announce her presence.*

dis·crep·an·cy /dɪsˈkrɛpənsi/ *noun* (*pl.* **dis·crep·an·cies**) [C, U] a difference between two or more things that should be the same: **~ (in sth)** *large discrepancies in prices quoted for the work* ◆ **~ (between A and B)** *What are the reasons for the discrepancy between girls' and boys' performance in school?*

dis·crete AWL /dɪˈskrit/ *adj.* (*formal* or *technical*) independent of other things of the same type **SYN** SEPARATE: *The organisms can be divided into discrete categories.* ▶ **dis·crete·ly** AWL *adv.* **dis·crete·ness** *noun* [U]

dis·cre·tion /dɪˈskrɛʃn/ *noun* [U] **1** the freedom or power to decide what should be done in a particular situation: *I'll leave it up to you to* **use your discretion.** ◆ *How much to tell terminally ill patients is* **left to the discretion of** *the doctor.* **2** care in what you say or do, in order to keep something secret or to avoid causing embarrassment to, or difficulty for, someone; the quality of being DISCREET: *This is confidential, but I know that I can rely on your discretion.* ⊃ compare INDISCRETION

IDM **at sb's discretion** according to what someone decides or wishes to do: *Bail is granted at the discretion of the court.* ◆ *There is no service charge and tipping is at your discretion.* **discretion is the better part of valor** (*saying*) you should avoid danger and not take unnecessary risks

dis·cre·tion·ar·y /dɪˈskrɛʃəˌnɛri/ *adj.* [usually before noun] (*formal*) decided according to the judgment of a person in authority about what is necessary in each particular situation; not decided by rules: *You may be eligible for a discretionary grant for your college tuition.*

dis·crim·i·nate AWL /dɪˈskrɪməˌneɪt/ *verb* **1** [I, T] to recognize that there is a difference between people or things; to show a difference between people or things

SYN DIFFERENTIATE, DISTINGUISH: **~ (between A and B)** *The computer program was unable to discriminate between letters and numbers.* ◆ **~ sth** *When do babies learn to discriminate voices?* ◆ **~ A from B** *A number of features discriminate this species from others.* **2** [I] to treat one person or group worse/better than another in an unfair way: **~ (against sb)** | **~ (in favor of sb)** *practices that discriminate against women and in favor of men* ◆ **~ (on the grounds of sth)** *It is illegal to discriminate on grounds of race, sex, or religion.*

dis·crim·i·nat·ing AWL /dɪˈskrɪməˌneɪtɪŋ/ *adj.* (*approving*) able to judge the good quality of something **SYN** DISCERNING: *a discriminating audience/customer*

dis·crim·i·na·tion AWL /dɪˌskrɪməˈneɪʃn/ *noun* **1** [U] the practice of treating someone or a particular group in society less fairly than others: *age/racial/sex/sexual discrimination* (= because of someone's age, race, or sex) ◆ **~ against sb** *discrimination against the elderly* ◆ **~ in favor of sb** *discrimination in favor of the young* ◆ **~ on the grounds of sth** *discrimination on the grounds of race, gender, or sexual orientation* **2** [U] (*approving*) the ability to judge what is good, true, etc. **SYN** DISCERNMENT: *He showed great discrimination in his choice of friends.* **3** (*formal*) [U, C] the ability to recognize a difference between one thing and another; a difference that is recognized: *to learn discrimination between right and wrong* ◆ *fine discriminations*

dis·crim·i·na·to·ry /dɪˈskrɪmənəˌtɔri/ *adj.* unfair; treating someone or one group of people worse than others: *discriminatory practices/rules/measures* ◆ *sexually/racially discriminatory laws*

dis·cur·sive /dɪsˈkərsɪv/ *adj.* (of a style of writing or speaking) moving from one point to another without any strict structure: *the discursive style of the novel* ▶ **dis·cur·sive·ly** *adv.* **dis·cur·sive·ness** *noun* [U]

dis·cus /ˈdɪskəs/ *noun* **1** [C] a heavy, flat, round object thrown in a sporting event **2 the discus** [sing.] the event or sport of throwing a discus as far as possible ⊃ picture at SPORT

dis·cuss 🔊 /dɪˈskʌs/ *verb*

1 to talk about something with someone, especially in order to decide something: **~ sth with sb** *Have you discussed the problem with anyone?* ◆ **~ sth** *I'm not prepared to discuss this on the phone.* ◆ **~ when, what, etc.…** *We need to discuss when we should go.* ◆ **~ (sb/sth) doing sth** *We briefly discussed buying a second car.* **HELP** You cannot say "discuss about sth": *I discussed about my problem with my parents.* Look also at **discussion.** ⊃ thesaurus box at TALK **2 ~ sth** | **~ what, how, etc.…** to write or talk about something in detail, showing the different ideas and opinions about it: *This topic will be discussed at greater length in the next chapter.* ⊃ thesaurus box at EXAMINE ⊃ language bank at ABOUT

dis·cus·sion 🔊 /dɪˈskʌʃn/ *noun* [U, C]

1 the process of discussing someone or something; a conversation about someone or something: *a topic/subject for discussion* ◆ *After considerable discussion, they decided to accept our offer.* ◆ *The plans have been* **under discussion** (= being talked about) *for a year now.* ◆ *Discussions are still taking place between the two leaders.* ◆ **~ (with sb) (about/on sb/sth)** *We had a discussion with them about the differences between Britain and the U.S.* **2 ~ (of sth)** a speech or a piece of writing that discusses many different aspects of a subject: *Her article is a discussion of the methods used in research.*

> **THESAURUS**
>
> **discussion**
>
> conversation ◆ dialogue ◆ talk ◆ debate ◆ consultation ◆ chat ◆ gossip
>
> These are all words for an occasion when people talk about something.

t **tea** t̬ **butter** d **did** k **cat** g **got** tʃ **chin** dʒ **June** f **fall**

discussion a detailed conversation about something that is considered to be important: *Discussions are still taking place between the two countries.*

conversation a talk, usually a private or informal one, involving two people or a small group; the activity of talking in this way: *a telephone conversation*

dialogue conversations in a book, play, or movie: *The novel has long descriptions and not much dialogue.* A **dialogue** is also a formal discussion between two groups, especially when they are trying to solve a problem or end a dispute: *The leaders engaged in a constructive dialogue about climate change.*

talk a conversation or discussion, often one about a problem or something important for the people involved: *I had a long talk with my boss about my career prospects.*

debate a formal discussion of an issue at a public meeting or in Congress. In a debate, two or more speakers express opposing views and then there is often a vote on the issue: *a debate over prison reform*

consultation a formal discussion between groups of people before a decision is made about something: *The proposal was based on extensive consultations with leading scientists.*

chat a friendly, informal conversation; informal talking: *Could I have a quick chat with you?*

gossip talk about other people and their private lives, that is often unkind or not true: *Office gossip can be nasty and cruel.*

PATTERNS

- (a) discussion/conversation/dialogue/talk/debate/consultation/chat/gossip **about** sth
- a discussion/conversation/dialogue/debate/consultation **on** sth
- **in (close)** discussion/conversation/dialogue/debate/consultation **with** sb
- to **have** a discussion/conversation/dialogue/talk/debate/consultation/chat **with** sb
- to **hold** a discussion/conversation/debate/consultation

dis·dain /dɪsˈdeɪn/ *noun, verb*
- *noun* [U, sing.] the feeling that someone or something is not good enough to deserve your respect or attention **SYN** CONTEMPT: *to treat someone with disdain* ◆ ~ **for sb/sth** *a disdain for the law*
- *verb* (*formal*) **1** ~ **sb/sth** to think that someone or something is not good enough to deserve your respect: *She disdained his offer of help.* **2** ~ **to do sth** to refuse to do something because you think that you are too important to do it: *He disdained to turn to his son for advice.*

dis·dain·ful /dɪsˈdeɪnfl/ *adj.* ~ **(of sb/sth)** showing disdain **SYN** CONTEMPTUOUS, DISMISSIVE: *She's always been disdainful of people who didn't go to college.* ▶ **dis·dain·ful·ly** /-fəli/ *adv.*

dis·ease /dɪˈziz/ *noun* [U, C]
1 an illness affecting humans, animals, or plants, often caused by infection: **heart/liver/kidney, etc. disease** ◆ *health measures to prevent the* **spread of disease** ◆ *an* **infectious/contagious disease** (= one that can be passed to someone very easily) ◆ *It is not known what causes the disease.* ◆ *protection against sexually transmitted diseases* ◆ *He suffers from a rare blood disease.* **2** [C] (*formal*) something that is very wrong with people's attitudes or way of life, or with society: *Greed is a disease of modern society.*

dis·eased /dɪˈzizd/ *adj.* suffering from a disease: *diseased tissue* ◆ *the diseased social system*

dis·em·bark /ˌdɪsɪmˈbɑrk/ (*also* de·bark) *verb* [I] ~ **(from sth)** (*formal*) to leave a vehicle, especially a ship or an aircraft, at the end of a journey **ANT** EMBARK ▶ **dis·em·bar·ka·tion** /ˌdɪsˌɛmbɑrˈkeɪʃn/ (*also* de·bar·ka·tion) *noun* [U]

THESAURUS

disease

illness ◆ disorder ◆ infection ◆ condition ◆ ailment ◆ bug

These are all words for a medical problem.

disease a medical problem affecting humans, animals, or plants, often caused by infection: *He suffers from a rare blood disease.*

illness a medical problem, or a period of suffering from one: *She died after a long illness.*

DISEASE OR ILLNESS?

Disease is used to talk about more severe physical medical problems, especially those that affect the organs. **Illness** is used to talk about both more severe and more minor medical problems, and, more commonly, those that affect mental health: *heart/kidney/liver illness* ◆ *mental disease.* **Disease** is not used about a period of illness: *She died after a long disease.*

disorder (*somewhat formal*) an illness that causes a part of the body to stop functioning correctly: *a rare disorder of the liver* **NOTE** A disorder is generally not infectious. **Disorder** is used most frequently with words relating to mental problems, for example *psychiatric, personality, mental,* and *eating.* When it is used to talk about physical problems, it is most often used with *blood, bowel,* and *kidney,* and these are commonly *serious, severe,* or *rare.*

infection an illness that is caused by bacteria or a virus: *a sinus infection* ◆ *an ear infection*

condition a medical problem that you have for a long time because it is not possible to cure it: *a heart condition*

ailment (*somewhat formal*) an illness that is not very serious: *childhood ailments*

bug (*informal*) an infectious illness that is usually fairly mild: *a nasty flu bug*

PATTERNS

- to **have/suffer from** a(n) disease/illness/disorder/infection/condition/ailment/bug
- to **catch/contract/get/pick up** a(n) disease/illness/infection/bug

dis·em·bod·ied /ˌdɪsɪmˈbɑdid/ *adj.* [usually before noun] **1** (of sounds) coming from a person or place that cannot be seen or identified: *a disembodied voice* **2** separated from the body: *disembodied spirits*

dis·em·bow·el /ˌdɪsɪmˈbaʊəl/ *verb* ~ **sb/sth** to take the stomach, BOWELS, and other organs out of a person or an animal

dis·en·chant·ed /ˌdɪsɪnˈtʃæntəd/ *adj.* ~ **(with sb/sth)** no longer feeling enthusiasm for someone or something; not believing something is good or worth doing **SYN** DISILLUSIONED: *He was becoming disenchanted with his job as a lawyer.* ▶ **dis·en·chant·ment** *noun* [U]: *a growing sense/feeling of disenchantment with his job*

dis·en·fran·chise /ˌdɪsɪnˈfræntʃaɪz/ *verb* ~ **sb** to take away someone's rights, especially their right to vote **ANT** ENFRANCHISE

dis·en·gage /ˌdɪsɪnˈgeɪdʒ/ *verb* **1** [T, I] to free someone or something from the person or thing that is holding them or it; to become free: ~ **yourself (from sb/sth)** *She gently disengaged herself from her sleeping son.* ◆ (*figurative*) *They wished to disengage themselves from these policies.* ◆ ~ **(sth/sb) (from sth/sb)** *to disengage the clutch* (= when driving a car) ◆ *We saw the booster rockets disengage and fall into the ocean.* **2** [I, T] (*technical*) if an army **disengages** or someone **disengages** it, it stops fighting and moves away ⊃ compare ENGAGE ▶ **dis·en·gage·ment** *noun* [U]

---

dis·en·tan·gle /ˌdɪsɪnˈtæŋgl/ verb **1 ~ sth (from sth)** to separate different arguments, ideas, etc. that have become confused: *It's not easy to disentangle the truth from the official statistics.* **2 ~ sth/sb (from sth)** to free someone or something that has become wrapped or twisted around it or them: *He tried to disentangle his fingers from her hair.* ◆ (figurative) *She has just disentangled herself from a painful relationship.* **3 ~ sth** to get rid of the twists and knots in something: *He was sitting on the deck disentangling a coil of rope.* ⊃ compare ENTANGLE

dis·e·qui·lib·ri·um /ˌdɪsˌiːkwəˈlɪbriəm/ noun [U] (formal or technical) a loss or lack of balance in a situation

dis·es·tab·lish **AWL** /ˌdɪsɪˈstæblɪʃ/ verb **~ sth** (formal) to end the official status of an organization, especially a church: *In 1924, Turkey was the first country to disestablish Islam.* ▶ **dis·es·tab·lish·ment** **AWL** noun [U]

dis·fa·vor (CanE usually **dis·fa·vour**) /dɪsˈfeɪvər/ noun [U] (formal) the feeling that you do not like or approve of someone or something

dis·fig·ure /dɪsˈfɪgyər/ verb **~ sb/sth** to spoil the appearance of a person, thing, or place: *Her face was disfigured by a long red scar.* ▶ **dis·fig·ure·ment** noun [U, C]: *He suffered permanent disfigurement in the fire.*

dis·gorge /dɪsˈgɔrdʒ/ verb (formal) **1 ~ sth** to pour something out in large quantities: *The pipe disgorges sewage into the ocean.* **2 ~ sb/sth** if a vehicle or building **disgorges** people, they come out of it in large numbers: *The bus disgorged a crowd of noisy children.*

dis·grace /dɪsˈgreɪs/ noun, verb
• **noun 1** [U] the loss of other people's respect and approval because of the bad way someone has behaved **SYN** SHAME: *Her behavior has brought disgrace on her family.* ◆ *The swimmer was sent home from the Olympics in disgrace.* ◆ *There is no disgrace in being poor.* ◆ *Sam was in disgrace with his parents.* **2** [sing.] **a ~ (to sb/sth)** a person or thing that is so bad that people connected with them or it feel or should feel ashamed: *Your homework is an absolute disgrace.* ◆ *That sort of behavior is a disgrace to the legal profession.* ◆ *The state of our roads is a national disgrace.* ◆ *It's a disgrace that* (= it is very wrong that) *they are paid so little.*
• **verb 1** to behave badly in a way that makes you or other people feel ashamed: **~ yourself** *I disgraced myself by drinking far too much.* ◆ **~ sb/sth** *He had disgraced the family name.* **2 be disgraced** to lose the respect of people, usually so that you lose a position of power: *He was publicly disgraced and sent into exile.* ◆ *a disgraced politician/leader*

dis·grace·ful /dɪsˈgreɪsfl/ adj. very bad or unacceptable; that people should feel ashamed about: *His behavior was absolutely disgraceful!* ◆ *It's disgraceful that no one in the family tried to help her.* ◆ *a disgraceful waste of money* ▶ **dis·grace·ful·ly** /-fəli/ adv.

dis·grun·tled /dɪsˈgrʌntld/ adj. annoyed or disappointed because something has happened to upset you: *disgruntled employees* ◆ **~ at sb/sth** *I left feeling disgruntled at the way I was treated.*

dis·guise /dɪsˈgaɪz/ verb, noun
• **verb 1** to change your appearance so that people cannot recognize you: **~ sb** *The hijackers were heavily disguised.* ◆ **~ sb as sb/sth** *They got in disguised as security guards.* ◆ **~ yourself (as sb/sth)** *She disguised herself as a boy.* **2 ~ sth** to hide something or change it, so that it cannot be recognized **SYN** CONCEAL: *She made no attempt to disguise her surprise.* ◆ *It was a thinly disguised attack on the President.* ◆ *She couldn't disguise the fact that she felt uncomfortable.* ⊃ thesaurus box at HIDE
• **noun 1** [C, U] a thing that you wear or use to change your appearance so that people do not recognize you: *She wore glasses and a wig as a disguise.* ◆ *The star traveled in disguise* (= wearing a disguise). ◆ (figurative) *Don't be fooled—a chocolate chip muffin is just a cupcake in disguise.* **2** [U] the art of changing your appearance so that people do not recognize you: *He is a master of disguise.* **IDM** see BLESSING

dis·gust /dɪsˈgʌst/ noun, verb
• **noun** [U] a strong feeling of dislike or disapproval for someone or something that you feel is unacceptable, or for something that looks, smells, etc. unpleasant: **~ (at/with sth)** *She expressed her disgust at the program by writing a letter of complaint.* ◆ **~ (for sb)** *I can only feel disgust for these criminals.* ◆ *The idea fills me with disgust.* ◆ *He walked away in disgust.* ◆ *Much to my disgust, they refused to help.* ◆ *She wrinkled her nose in disgust at the smell.* ⊃ thesaurus box at SHOCK
• **verb ~ sb** if something **disgusts** you, it makes you feel shocked and almost sick because it is so unpleasant: *The level of violence in the film really disgusted me.*

dis·gust·ed /dɪsˈgʌstəd/ adj. feeling or showing disgust: **~ (at/by sb/sth)** *I was disgusted at/by the sight.* ◆ **~ (with sb/sth/yourself)** *I was disgusted with myself for eating so much.* ◆ **~ (to see, hear, etc. …)** *He was disgusted to see such awful living conditions.* ▶ **dis·gust·ed·ly** adv.: *"This champagne is warm!" he said disgustedly.*

dis·gust·ing /dɪsˈgʌstɪŋ/ adj. **1** extremely unpleasant **SYN** REVOLTING: *The kitchen was in a disgusting state when she left.* ◆ *What a disgusting smell!* **2** unacceptable and shocking **SYN** DESPICABLE, OUTRAGEOUS: *I think it's disgusting that they're closing the local hospital.* ◆ *His language is disgusting* (= he uses a lot of offensive words).

THESAURUS

disgusting

foul ◆ **revolting** ◆ **repulsive** ◆ **offensive** ◆ **gross**

These words all describe something, especially a smell, taste, or habit, that is extremely unpleasant and often makes you feel slightly ill.

disgusting extremely unpleasant and making you feel slightly ill: *What a disgusting smell!*

foul dirty, and tasting or smelling bad: *She could smell his foul breath.*

revolting extremely unpleasant and making you feel slightly ill: *The stew looked revolting.*

DISGUSTING OR REVOLTING?

Both of these words are used to describe things that smell and taste unpleasant, and unpleasant personal habits and people who have them. There is no real difference in meaning, but **disgusting** is more frequent, especially in spoken English.

repulsive (somewhat formal) extremely unpleasant in a way that offends you or makes you feel slightly ill **NOTE** Repulsive usually describes people, their behavior, or their habits, that you may find offensive for physical or moral reasons.

offensive (formal) (especially of smells) extremely unpleasant.

gross (informal) (of a smell, taste, or personal habit) extremely unpleasant.

PATTERNS

■ disgusting/revolting/repulsive/offensive **to** sb
■ to **find** sb/sth disgusting/revolting/repulsive/offensive
■ to **smell/taste** disgusting/foul/revolting/gross
■ a(n) disgusting/foul/revolting/offensive/gross **smell/odor**
■ a disgusting/foul/revolting/repulsive/gross **habit**
■ disgusting/repulsive/offensive/gross **behavior**
■ a disgusting/revolting/repulsive **man/woman/person**

h hat	m man	n no	ŋ sing	l leg	r red	y yes	w wet

dis·gust·ing·ly /dɪsˈɡʌstɪŋli/ adv. **1** (sometimes humorous) extremely (in a way that other people feel jealous of): *He looked disgustingly healthy when he got back from the Bahamas.* **2** in a disgusting way: *disgustingly dirty*

dish /dɪʃ/ noun, verb
• noun **1** [C] a flat shallow container for cooking food in or serving it from: *a glass dish* ◆ *a casserole dish* ◆ *a baking/serving dish* ◆ *They helped themselves from a large dish of pasta.* **2 the dishes** [pl.] the plates, bowls, cups, etc. that have been used for a meal and need to be washed: *I'll do the dishes* (= wash them). **3** [C] food prepared in a particular way as part of a meal: *a vegetarian/fish dish* ◆ *This makes an excellent hot main dish.* ◆ *I can recommend the chef's dish of the day.* ⊃ see also SIDE DISH **4** [C] any object that is shaped like a dish or bowl: *a soap dish* ⊃ see also SATELLITE DISH **5** [C] (informal, old-fashioned) a sexually attractive person: *What a dish!*
• verb
  IDM **dish the dirt (on sb)** (informal) to tell people unkind or unpleasant things about someone, especially about their private life **dish it out** (disapproving) to criticize other people: *He enjoys dishing it out, but he really can't take it* (= cannot accept criticism from other people).
  PHRV **dish sth↔out** (informal) to give something, often to a lot of people or in large amounts: *Students dished out leaflets to passers-by.* ◆ *She's always dishing out advice, even when you don't want it.* **2** to serve food onto plates for a meal: *Can you dish out the potatoes, please?* **dish 'up** | **dish sth↔'up** to serve food onto plates for a meal **dish 'up sth** to offer something to someone, especially something that is not very good

dis·ha·bille /ˌdɪsəˈbil/ adj. = DESHABILLE

dis·har·mo·ny /dɪsˈhɑrməni/ noun [U] (formal) a lack of agreement about important things, that causes bad feelings between people or groups of people: *marital/racial/social disharmony* **ANT** HARMONY

dish·cloth /ˈdɪʃklɔθ/ (also dish·rag) noun a cloth for washing dishes

dis·heart·en /dɪsˈhɑrtn/ verb ~ sb to make someone lose hope or confidence **SYN** DISCOURAGE: *Don't let this defeat dishearten you.* ▶ **dis·heart·ened** adj.: *a disheartened team* **dis·heart·en·ing** /dɪsˈhɑrtn·ɪŋ/ adj.: *a disheartening experience*

di·shev·eled /dɪˈʃɛvld/ adj. (of hair, clothes, or someone's general appearance) very messy **SYN** UNKEMPT: *He looked tired and disheveled.*

dis·hon·est /dɪsˈɑnəst/ adj.
not honest; intending to trick people: *Beware of dishonest traders in the tourist areas.* ◆ *I don't like him, and it would be dishonest of me to pretend otherwise.* **ANT** HONEST ▶ **dis·hon·est·ly** adv. **dis·hon·es·ty** /dɪsˈɑnəsti/ noun [U]

dis·hon·or (CanE usually **dis·hon·our**) /dɪsˈɑnər/ noun, verb
• noun [U] (formal) a loss of honor or respect because you have done something immoral or unacceptable
• verb (formal) **1** ~ sb/sth to make someone or something lose the respect of other people: *You have dishonored the name of the school.* **2** ~ sth to refuse to keep an agreement or promise: *He had dishonored nearly all of his election pledges.* **ANT** HONOR

dis·hon·or·a·ble /dɪsˈɑnərəbl/ adj. not deserving respect; immoral or unacceptable: *It would have been dishonorable of her not to keep her promise.* ◆ *He was given a dishonorable discharge* (= an order to leave the army for unacceptable behavior). **ANT** HONORABLE ▶ **dis·hon·or·a·bly** /-bli/ adv.

dish·pan /ˈdɪʃpæn/ noun a bowl for washing plates, etc. in

dish·rag /ˈdɪʃræg/ noun = DISHCLOTH

dish towel noun (CanE **'tea towel**) a small towel used for drying cups, plates, knives, etc. after they have been washed ⊃ picture at CLEANING

dish·ware /ˈdɪʃwɛr/ noun [U] dishes and bowls used for serving food

dish·wash·er /ˈdɪʃwɑʃər; -ˌwɔʃər/ noun **1** a machine for washing plates, cups, etc.: *to load the dishwasher* **2** a person whose job is to wash plates, etc., for example in a restaurant

'dishwashing de,tergent noun [U] soap used to wash dishes in a dishwasher

'dishwashing ,liquid noun [U] liquid soap used to wash dishes ⊃ picture at CLEANING

dish·wa·ter /ˈdɪʃˌwɔtər; -ˌwɑtər/ noun [U] water that someone has used to wash dirty plates, etc. **IDM** see DULL adj.

dish·y /ˈdɪʃi/ adj. (informal) (dish·i·er, dish·i·est) **1** (old-fashioned) (of a person) physically attractive **2** containing a lot of information and stories about the private lives of famous people: *a dishy new magazine*

dis·il·lu·sion /ˌdɪsəˈluʒn/ verb ~ sb to destroy someone's belief in, or good opinion of, someone or something: *I hate to disillusion you, but not everyone is as honest as you.* ▶ **disillusion** noun [U] = DISILLUSIONMENT

dis·il·lu·sioned /ˌdɪsəˈluʒnd/ adj. ~ (by/with sb/sth) disappointed because the person you admired or the idea you believed to be good and true now seems without value **SYN** DISENCHANTED: *I soon became disillusioned with the job.*

dis·il·lu·sion·ment /ˌdɪsəˈluʒnmənt/ (also **dis·il·lu·sion**) noun [U, sing.] ~ (with sth) the state of being disillusioned **SYN** : *There is widespread disillusionment with the present government.*

dis·in·cen·tive /ˌdɪsɪnˈsɛntɪv/ noun [C] a thing that makes someone less willing to do something **ANT** INCENTIVE

dis·in·cli·na·tion /ˌdɪsˌɪnkləˈneɪʃn; -ˌɪŋklə-/ noun [sing., U] (formal) a lack of willingness to do something; a lack of enthusiasm for something: *There was a general disinclination to return to the office after lunch.*

dis·in·clined /ˌdɪsɪnˈklaɪnd/ adj. [not before noun] ~ (to do sth) (formal) not willing **SYN** RELUCTANT: *He was strongly disinclined to believe anything that she said.*

dis·in·fect /ˌdɪsɪnˈfɛkt/ verb **1** ~ sth to clean something using a substance that kills bacteria: *to disinfect a surface/room/wound* **2** ~ sth to run a computer program to get rid of a computer virus ▶ **dis·in·fec·tion** /ˌdɪsɪnˈfɛkʃn/ noun [U]

dis·in·fec·tant /ˌdɪsɪnˈfɛktənt/ noun [U, C] a substance that disinfects: *a strong smell of disinfectant*

dis·in·for·ma·tion /ˌdɪsˌɪnfərˈmeɪʃn/ noun [U] false information that is given deliberately, especially by government organizations

dis·in·gen·u·ous /ˌdɪsɪnˈdʒɛnyuəs/ adj. [not usually before noun] (formal) not sincere, especially when you pretend to know less about something than you really do: *It would be disingenuous of me to claim I had never seen it.* ⊃ compare INGENUOUS ▶ **dis·in·gen·u·ous·ly** adv.

dis·in·her·it /ˌdɪsɪnˈhɛrət/ verb ~ sb to prevent someone, especially your son or daughter, from receiving your money or property after your death ⊃ compare INHERIT

dis·in·hib·it /ˌdɪsɪnˈhɪbət/ verb ~ sb (formal) to help someone to stop feeling shy so that they can relax and show their feelings ▶ **dis·in·hi·bi·tion** /ˌdɪsˌɪnhəˈbɪʃn; -ˌɪnə-/ noun [U]

dis·in·te·grate /dɪsˈɪntəˌɡreɪt/ verb **1** [I] to break into small parts or pieces and be destroyed: *The plane disintegrated as it fell into the sea.* **2** [I] to become much less strong or united and be gradually destroyed **SYN** FALL APART: *The authority of the central government was rapidly disintegrating.* ▶ **dis·in·te·gra·tion** /dɪsˌɪntəˈɡreɪʃn/ noun [U]: *the gradual disintegration of traditional values*

dis·in·ter /ˌdɪsɪnˈtər/ verb (-rr-) (formal) **1** ~ sth to dig up something, especially a dead body, from the ground **ANT** INTER **2** ~ sth (from sth) to find something that has been hidden or lost for a long time

---

i see   ɪ sit   ɛ ten   æ cat   ɑ hot   ɔ saw   ʊ put   u too

dis·in·ter·est /dɪsˈɪntrəst; -trɛst/ *noun* [U] **1 ~ (in sth)** lack of interest: *His total disinterest in money puzzled his family.* **2** the fact of not being involved in something

dis·in·ter·est·ed /dɪsˈɪntrəstəd; -ˈɪntəˌrɛstəd; -ˈɪntrɛstəd/ *adj.* **1** not influenced by personal feelings, or by the chance of getting some advantage for yourself **SYN** IMPARTIAL, OBJECTIVE, UNBIASED: *a disinterested onlooker/spectator* ◆ *Her advice appeared to be disinterested.* **2** (*informal*) not interested ⊃ note at INTERESTED ▶ **dis·in·ter·est·ed·ly** *adv.*

dis·in·vest /ˌdɪsɪnˈvɛst/ *verb* [I] **~ (from sth)** (*business*) to stop investing money in a company, industry, or country; to reduce the amount of money invested

dis·in·vest·ment /ˌdɪsɪnˈvɛstmənt/ *noun* [U] (*finance*) the process of reducing the amount of money that you have invested in a particular company, industry, etc.

dis·joint·ed /dɪsˈdʒɔɪntəd/ *adj.* not communicated or described in a clear or logical way; not connected **SYN** DISCONNECTED, INCOHERENT

dis·junc·tion /dɪsˈdʒʌŋkʃn/ (also *less frequent* **dis·junc·ture** /dɪsˈdʒʌŋktʃər/) *noun* **~ (between A and B)** (*formal*) a difference between two things that you would expect to be in agreement with each other

disk 🔑 (also **disc**) /dɪsk/ *noun* **1** (also **mag·netic ˈdisk**) (*computing*) a device for storing information on a computer, with a MAGNETIC surface that records information received in electronic form ⊃ see also FLOPPY DISK, HARD DISK **2** a thin, flat, round object: *Red blood cells are roughly the shape of a disk.* ◆ *He wears an identity disk around his neck.* **3** = CD: *This recording is available online or on disk.* **4** a structure made of CARTILAGE between the bones of the back: *He's been out of work with a **slipped disk** (= one that has moved from its correct position, causing pain).* **5** (*old-fashioned*) = RECORD

ˈdisk drive *noun* a device that passes data between a disk and the memory of a computer or from one disk or computer to another

disk·ette /dɪsˈkɛt/ *noun* = FLOPPY DISK

ˈdisk ˌjockey *noun* = DISC JOCKEY

dis·like 🔑 /dɪsˈlaɪk/ *verb, noun*
● *verb* (somewhat *formal*) to not like someone or something: *~ sb/sth Why do you dislike him so much?* ◆ *He **disliked** it when she behaved badly in front of his mother.* ◆ *~ doing sth I dislike being away from my family.* ◆ *Much as she disliked going to funerals (= although she did not like it at all), she knew she had to be there.* ◆ *~ sb/sth doing sth He disliked her staying away from home.* ◆ thesaurus box at HATE **ANT** LIKE
● *noun* **1** [U, sing.] **~ (of/for sb/sth)** a feeling of not liking someone or something: *He did not try to hide his dislike of his boss.* ◆ *She took an **instant dislike** to the house and the neighborhood.* **2** [C, usually pl.] a thing that you do not like: *I've told you all my **likes and dislikes.***

dis·lo·cate /dɪsˈloʊkeɪt; ˈdɪsloʊˌkeɪt/ *verb* **1 ~ sth** to put a bone out of its normal position in a joint: *He dislocated his shoulder in the accident.* ◆ *a dislocated finger* ⊃ collocations at INJURY **2 ~ sth** to stop a system, plan, etc. from working or continuing in the normal way **SYN** DISRUPT ▶ **dis·lo·ca·tion** /ˌdɪsloʊˈkeɪʃn/ *noun* [C, U]: *a dislocation of the shoulder* ◆ *These policies could cause severe economic and social dislocation.*

dis·lodge /dɪsˈlɑdʒ/ *verb* **1 ~ sth (from sth)** to force or knock something out of its position: *The wind dislodged one or two tiles from the roof.* **2 ~ sb (from sth)** to force someone to leave a place, position, or job: *The rebels have so far failed to dislodge the president.*

dis·loy·al /dɪsˈlɔɪəl/ *adj.* **~ (to sb/sth)** not loyal or faithful to your friends, family, country, etc.: *He was accused of being disloyal to the government.* ▶ **dis·loy·al·ty** /-ˈlɔɪəlti/ *noun* [U]

dis·mal /ˈdɪzməl/ *adj.* **1** causing or showing sadness **SYN** GLOOMY, MISERABLE: *dismal conditions/surroundings/*

weather **2** (*informal*) not skillful or successful; of very low quality: *The singer gave a dismal performance of some old songs.* ◆ *Their recent attempt to increase sales has been a **dismal failure**.* ▶ **dis·mal·ly** *adv.*: *I tried not to laugh but failed dismally (= was completely unsuccessful).*

dis·man·tle /dɪsˈmæntl/ *verb* **1 ~ sth** to take apart a machine or structure so that it is in separate pieces: *I had to dismantle the engine in order to repair it.* ◆ *The steel mill was dismantled piece by piece.* **2 ~ sth** to end an organization or system gradually in an organized way: *The government was in the process of dismantling the state-owned industries.* ▶ **dis·man·tling** *noun* [U]

dis·may /dɪsˈmeɪ/ *noun, verb*
● *noun* [U] a worried, sad feeling after you have received an unpleasant surprise: *She could not hide her dismay at the result.* ◆ *He looked at her **in dismay**.* ◆ *To her dismay, her name was not on the list.* ◆ *The news has been greeted **with dismay** by local business leaders.*
● *verb* **~ sb** to make someone feel shocked and disappointed: *Their reaction dismayed him.* ▶ **dis·mayed** *adj.*: ◆ **~ (at/by sth)** *He was dismayed at the change in his old friend.* ◆ *The suggestion was greeted by a dismayed silence.* ◆ **~ (to find, hear, see, etc....)** *They were dismayed to find that the ferry had already left.*

dis·mem·ber /dɪsˈmɛmbər/ *verb* **1 ~ sth** to cut or tear the dead body of a person or an animal into pieces **2 ~ sth** (*formal*) to divide a country, an organization, etc. into smaller parts ▶ **dis·mem·ber·ment** *noun* [U]

dis·miss 🔑 /dɪsˈmɪs/ *verb*
1 to decide that someone or something is not important and not worth thinking or talking about **SYN** WAVE ASIDE: **~ sb/sth** *I think we can safely dismiss their objections.* ◆ **~ sb/sth as sth** *Vegetarians are no longer dismissed as eccentrics.* ◆ *He dismissed the opinion polls as worthless.* ◆ *The suggestion should not be **dismissed out of hand** (= without thinking about it).* **2** to put thoughts or feelings out of your mind: **~ sth** *Dismissing her fears, she climbed higher.* ◆ **~ sb/sth from sth** *He dismissed her from his mind.* **3 ~ sb (from sth)** (*formal*) to officially remove someone from their job **SYN** FIRE: *She claims she was unfairly dismissed from her post.* **4 ~ sb** to send someone away or allow them to leave: *At 12 o'clock the class was dismissed.* **5 ~ sth** (*law*) to say that a trial or legal case should not continue, usually because there is not enough evidence: *The case was dismissed.*

dis·miss·al /dɪsˈmɪsl/ *noun* **1** [U, C] (*formal*) the act of dismissing someone from their job; an example of this: *He still hopes to win his claim against **unfair dismissal**.* ◆ *The dismissals followed the resignation of the chairman.* **2** [U] the failure to consider something as important: *Her casual dismissal of the threats seemed irresponsible.* **3** [U, C] (*law*) the act of not allowing a trial or legal case to continue, usually because there is not enough evidence: *the dismissal of the appeal* **4** [U, C] the act of sending someone away or allowing them to leave

dis·mis·sive /dɪsˈmɪsɪv/ *adj.* **~ (of sb/sth)** showing that you do not believe a person or thing to be important or worth considering **SYN** DISDAINFUL: *a dismissive gesture/tone* ▶ **dis·mis·sive·ly** *adv.*: *to shrug/wave dismissively*

dis·mount /dɪsˈmaʊnt/ *verb* [I] **~ (from sth)** to get off a horse, bicycle, or motorcycle **ANT** MOUNT

Dis·ney·land /ˈdɪzniˌlænd/ *noun* [usually sing.] a place that is full of interesting or exciting things: *They're trying to turn this unfashionable winter resort town into a snowy Disneyland.* **ORIGIN** From Disneyland™, the name of an amusement park in California based on the characters in the movies of Walt Disney.

dis·o·be·di·ence /ˌdɪsəˈbidiəns/ *noun* [U] failure or refusal to obey ⊃ see also CIVIL DISOBEDIENCE

dis·o·be·di·ent /ˌdɪsəˈbidiənt/ *adj.* failing or refusing to obey: *a disobedient child* **ANT** OBEDIENT

dis·o·bey /ˌdɪsəˈbeɪ/ *verb* [T, I] **~ (sb/sth)** to refuse to do what a person, law, order, etc. tells you to do; to refuse to obey: *He was punished for disobeying orders.* **ANT** OBEY

dis·o·blig·ing /ˌdɪsəˈblaɪdʒɪŋ/ *adj.* deliberately not helpful: *a disobliging manner*

dis·or·der /dɪsˈɔrdər/ *noun* **1** [U] a messy state; a lack of order or organization: *His financial affairs were in complete disorder.* ♦ *The room was in a state of disorder.* **ANT** ORDER **2** [U] violent behavior of large groups of people: *an outbreak of rioting and public disorder* ⊃ compare ORDER **3** [C] an illness that causes a part of the body to stop functioning correctly: *a blood/bowel, etc. disorder* ♦ *eating disorders* ♦ *He was suffering from some form of psychiatric disorder.* ⊃ thesaurus box at DISEASE

dis·or·dered /dɪsˈɔrdərd/ *adj.* **1** showing a lack of order or control: *disordered hair* ♦ *a disordered state* **ANT** ORDERED **2** (*technical*) suffering from a mental or physical disorder: *emotionally disordered children*

dis·or·der·ly /dɪsˈɔrdərli/ *adj.* [usually before noun] (*formal*) **1** (of people or behavior) showing lack of control; publicly violent or noisy: *disorderly conduct* ♦ *They were arrested for being drunk and disorderly.* **2** messy: *newspapers in a disorderly pile by the door* **ANT** ORDERLY

dis·or·gan·ized /dɪsˈɔrgəˌnaɪzd/ (also *less frequent* **un·or·gan·ized**) *adj.* badly planned; not able to plan or organize well: *It was a hectic, disorganized weekend.* ♦ *She's so disorganized.* ⊃ compare ORGANIZED ▶ **dis·or·gan·i·za·tion** /dɪsˌɔrgənəˈzeɪʃn/ *noun* [U]

dis·o·ri·ent /dɪsˈɔriənt/ (also **dis·o·ri·en·tate** /dɪsˈɔriənˌteɪt/) *verb* **1** ~ sb to make someone unable to recognize where they are or where they should go: *The darkness had disoriented him.* **2** ~ sb to make someone feel confused: *Ex-soldiers can be disoriented by the transition to civilian life.* ⊃ compare ORIENT ▶ **dis·o·ri·ent·ed** *adj.*: *She felt shocked and totally disoriented.* **dis·o·ri·en·ta·tion** /dɪsˌɔriənˈteɪʃn/ *noun* [U]

dis·own /dɪsˈoʊn/ *verb* ~ sb/sth to decide that you no longer want to be connected with or responsible for someone or something: *Her family disowned her for marrying a foreigner.*

dis·par·age /dɪˈspærɪdʒ/ *verb* ~ sb/sth (*formal*) to suggest that someone or something is not important or valuable **SYN** BELITTLE: *I don't mean to disparage your achievements.* ▶ **dis·par·age·ment** *noun* [U] **dis·par·ag·ing** *adj.*: *disparaging remarks* **dis·par·ag·ing·ly** *adv.*: *He spoke disparagingly of his colleagues.*

dis·pa·rate /ˈdɪspərət/ *adj.* (*formal*) **1** made up of parts or people that are very different from each other: *a disparate group of individuals* **2** (of two or more things) so different from each other that they cannot be compared or cannot work together

dis·par·i·ty /dɪˈspærəti/ *noun* [U, C] (*pl.* **dis·par·i·ties**) (*formal*) a difference, especially one connected with unfair treatment: *the wide disparity between rich and poor*

dis·pas·sion·ate /dɪsˈpæʃənət/ *adj.* (*approving*) not influenced by emotion **SYN** IMPARTIAL: *taking a calm, dispassionate view of the situation* ♦ *a dispassionate observer* ▶ **dis·pas·sion·ate·ly** *adv.*

dis·patch /dɪˈspætʃ/ *verb, noun*
● *verb* **1** ~ sb/sth (to…) (*formal*) to send someone or something somewhere, especially for a special purpose: *Troops have been dispatched to the area.* ♦ *A courier was dispatched to collect the documents.* **2** ~ sth (to sb/sth) (*formal*) to send a letter, package, or message somewhere: *Goods are dispatched within 24 hours of your order reaching us.* **3** ~ sb/sth (*formal*) to deal or finish with someone or something quickly and completely: *He dispatched the younger player in straight sets.* **4** ~ sb/sth (*old-fashioned*) to kill a person or an animal
● *noun* **1** [U] (*formal*) the act of sending someone or something somewhere: *More food supplies are ready for immediate dispatch.* **2** [C] a message or report sent quickly from one military officer to another or between government officials

3 [C] a report sent to a newspaper by a journalist who is working in a foreign country: *dispatches from the war zone* **IDM with dispatch** (*formal*) quickly and efficiently

dis·patch box (also **dis·patch case**) *noun* [C] a container for carrying official documents

dis·patch·er /dɪˈspætʃər/ *noun* **1** a person whose job is to see that trains, buses, planes, etc. leave on time **2** a person whose job is to send emergency vehicles to where they are needed

dis·pel /dɪˈspɛl/ *verb* (-ll-) ~ sth to make something, especially a feeling or belief, go away or disappear: *His speech dispelled any fears about his health.*

dis·pen·sa·ble /dɪˈspɛnsəbl/ *adj.* [not usually before noun] not necessary; that can be gotten rid of: *They looked on music and art lessons as dispensable.* **ANT** ESSENTIAL, INDISPENSABLE

dis·pen·sa·ry /dɪˈspɛnsəri/ *noun* (*pl.* **dis·pen·sa·ries**) **1** a place in a hospital, store, etc. where medicines are prepared for patients **2** (*old-fashioned*) a place where patients are treated, especially one run by a charity

dis·pen·sa·tion /ˌdɪspənˈseɪʃn; -pɛn-/ *noun* **1** [C, U] special permission, especially from a religious leader, to do something that is not usually allowed or legal: *She needed a special dispensation to remarry.* ♦ *The sport's ruling body gave him dispensation to compete in national competitions.* **2** [U] (*formal*) the act or process of providing something, especially by someone in authority: *the dispensation of justice* **3** [C] (*technical*) a political or religious system that operates in a country at a particular time

dis·pense /dɪˈspɛns/ *verb* **1** ~ sth (to sb) to give out something to people: *The machine dispenses a variety of drinks and snacks.* **2** ~ sth (to sb) (*formal*) to provide something, especially a service, for people: *The organization dispenses free healthcare to the poor.* ♦ *to dispense justice/advice* **3** ~ sth to prepare medicine and give it to people, as a job: *to dispense a prescription*
PHR V di'spense with sb/sth to stop using someone or something because you no longer need them or it **SYN** DO AWAY WITH: *Debit cards dispense with the need for cash altogether.* ♦ *I think we can dispense with the formalities* (= speak openly and naturally to each other).

dis·pens·er /dɪˈspɛnsər/ *noun* a machine or container holding money, drinks, paper towels, etc. that you can obtain quickly, for example by pulling a handle or pressing buttons: *a soap dispenser* ♦ *a tape dispenser* ⊃ picture at STATIONERY

dis·per·sal /dɪˈspɜrsl/ *noun* [U, C] (*formal*) the process of sending someone or something in different directions; the process of spreading something over a wide area: *police trained in crowd dispersal* ♦ *the dispersal of seeds*

dis·perse /dɪˈspɜrs/ *verb* **1** [I, T] to move apart and go away in different directions; to make someone or something do this: *The fog began to disperse.* ♦ *The crowd dispersed quickly.* ♦ ~ sb/sth *Police dispersed the protesters with tear gas.* **2** [T, I] ~ (sth) to spread or to make something spread over a wide area **SYN** SCATTER: *The seeds are dispersed by the wind.*

dis·per·sion /dɪˈspɜrʒn; -ʃn/ *noun* [U] (*technical*) the process by which people or things are spread over a wide area

dis·pir·it·ed /dɪˈspɪrətəd/ *adj.* having no hope or enthusiasm: *She looked tired and dispirited.* ⊃ compare SPIRITED

dis·pir·it·ing /dɪˈspɪrətɪŋ/ *adj.* making someone lose their hope or enthusiasm: *a dispiriting experience/failure*

dis·place **AWL** /dɪsˈpleɪs/ *verb* [often passive] **1** ~ sb/sth to take the place of someone or something **SYN** REPLACE: *Gradually factory workers have been displaced by machines.* ♦ (*technical*) *The ship displaces 58,000 tons* (= as a way of measuring its size). **2** ~ sb to force people to move away from their home to another place: *Around 10,000 people have been displaced by the fighting.* **3** ~ sth to move something from its usual position: *Check for roof tiles that have been displaced by the wind.* **4** ~ sb to remove someone from a job or position: *displaced workers*

displaced 'person noun (pl. di,splaced 'persons) (technical) a REFUGEE

dis·place·ment ⬛AWL /dɪs'pleɪsmənt/ noun [U] **1** (formal) the act of displacing someone or something; the process of being displaced: *the largest displacement of civilian population since World War Two* **2** [C] (physics) the amount of a liquid moved out of place by something floating or put in it, especially a ship floating in water: *a ship with a displacement of 10,000 tons*

dis'placement ac,tivity noun **1** [U] things that you do in order to avoid doing what you are supposed to be doing **2** (biology, psychology) [U, C] behavior in animals or humans that seems to have no connection with the situation in which it is performed, resulting from two conflicting urges

dis·play 🔑 ⬛AWL /dɪ'spleɪ/ verb, noun

• **verb 1** [T] ~ sth (to sb) to put something in a place where people can see it easily; to show something to people **SYN** EXHIBIT: *The exhibition gives local artists an opportunity to display their work.* ◆ *She displayed her bruises for all to see.* **2** [T] ~ sth to show signs of something, especially a quality or feeling: *I have rarely seen her display any sign of emotion.* ◆ *These statistics display a definite trend.* **3** [T] ~ sth (of a computer, etc.) to show information: *The screen will display the username in the top right-hand corner.* ◆ *This column displays the title of the mail message.* **4** [I] (technical) (of male birds and animals) to show a special pattern of behavior that is intended to attract a female bird or animal

• **noun 1** an arrangement of things in a public place to inform or entertain people or advertise something for sale: *a beautiful floral display outside the Town Hall* ◆ *a window display* ◆ *a display cabinet* **2** an act of performing a skill or of showing something happening, in order to entertain: *a fireworks display* ◆ *a breathtaking display of acrobatics* **3** an occasion when you show a particular quality, feeling, or ability by the way that you behave: *a display of affection/strength/wealth* **4** the words, pictures, etc. shown on a computer screen: *a high resolution color display* ⊃ see also LIQUID CRYSTAL DISPLAY, VDT
  IDM **on display** put in a place where people can look at it **SYN** ON SHOW: *Designs for the new sports complex are on display in the library.* ◆ *to put something on temporary/permanent display*

dis·please /dɪs'pliz/ verb ~ sb (formal) to make someone feel upset, annoyed, or not satisfied **ANT** PLEASE ▶ **dis·pleased** adj.: ~ (with sb/sth) *Are you displeased with my work?* ◆ ~ (at sth) *She was not displeased at the effect she was having on the young man.* **dis·pleas·ing** adj.: ~ (to sb/sth) *His remarks were clearly not displeasing to her.*

dis·pleas·ure /dɪs'plɛʒər/ noun [U] ~ (at/with sb/sth) (formal) the feeling of being upset and annoyed **SYN** ANNOYANCE: *She made no attempt to hide her displeasure at the prospect.* ⊃ compare PLEASURE

dis·port /dɪ'spɔrt/ verb ~ yourself (old-fashioned or humorous) to enjoy yourself by doing something active

dis·pos·a·ble ⬛AWL /dɪ'spoʊzəbl/ adj. [usually before noun] **1** made to be thrown away after use: *disposable gloves/razors* ◆ *disposable diapers* **2** (finance) available for use: *disposable assets/capital/resources* ◆ *a person's disposable income* (= the money that you have left to spend after tax, food, housing, etc.)

dis·pos·a·bles /dɪ'spoʊzəblz/ noun [pl.] items such as DIAPERS and CONTACT LENSES that are designed to be thrown away after use

dis·pos·al ⬛AWL /dɪ'spoʊzl/ noun **1** [U] the act of getting rid of something: *a bomb disposal squad* ◆ *sewage disposal systems* ◆ *the disposal of nuclear waste* **2** [C] (business) the sale of part of a business, property, etc. **3** [C] = GARBAGE DISPOSAL
  IDM **at your/sb's disposal** available for use as you prefer/someone prefers: *He will have a car at his disposal for the whole month.* ◆ *Well, I'm at your disposal* (= I am ready to help you in any way I can).

dis·pose ⬛AWL /dɪ'spoʊz/ verb (formal) **1** + adv./prep. to arrange things or people in a particular way or position **2** ~ sb to/toward sth | ~ sb to do sth to make someone behave in a particular way: *a drug that disposes the patient toward sleep*
  PHRV **di'spose of sb/sth 1** to get rid of someone or something that you do not want or cannot keep: *the difficulties of disposing of nuclear waste* ◆ *to dispose of stolen property* **2** to deal with a problem, question, or threat successfully: *That seems to have disposed of most of their arguments.* **3** to defeat or kill someone: *It took her a mere 20 minutes to dispose of her opponent.*

dis·posed ⬛AWL /dɪ'spoʊzd/ adj. [not before noun] (formal) **1** ~ (to do sth) willing or prepared to do something: *I'm not disposed to argue.* ◆ *You're most welcome to join us if you feel so disposed.* **2** (following an adverb) ~ to/toward sb/sth having a good/bad opinion of a person or thing: *She seems favorably disposed to the move.* ⊃ see also ILL-DISPOSED, WELL DISPOSED

dis·po·si·tion /ˌdɪspə'zɪʃn/ noun **1** [C, usually sing.] the natural qualities of a person's character **SYN** TEMPERAMENT: *to have a cheerful disposition* ◆ *people with a nervous disposition* **2** [C, usually sing.] ~ to/toward sth | ~ to do sth (formal) a tendency to behave in a particular way: *to have/show a disposition toward violence* **3** [C, usually sing.] (formal) the way something is placed or arranged **SYN** ARRANGEMENT **4** [C, U] (law) a formal act of giving property or money to someone

dis·pos·sess /ˌdɪspə'zɛs/ verb [usually passive] ~ sb (of sth) (formal) to take someone's property, land, or house away from them ▶ **dis·pos·ses·sion** /ˌdɪspə'zɛʃn/ noun [U]

the dis·pos·sessed /ˌdɪspə'zɛst/ noun [pl.] people who have had property taken away from them

dis·pro·por·tion ⬛AWL /ˌdɪsprə'pɔrʃn/ noun [U, C] (formal) the state of two things not being at an equally high or low level; an example of this: ~ (between A and B) *the disproportion between the extra responsibilities and the small salary increase* ◆ ~ (of A to B) *a profession with a high disproportion of male to female employees*

dis·pro·por·tion·ate ⬛AWL /ˌdɪsprə'pɔrʃənət/ adj. ~ (to sth) too large or too small when compared with something else: *The area contains a disproportionate number of young middle-class families.* ⊃ compare PROPORTIONATE ▶ **dis·pro·por·tion·ate·ly** ⬛AWL adv.: *The lower-paid spend a disproportionately large amount of their earnings on food.*

dis·prove /ˌdɪs'pruv/ verb ~ sth to show that something is wrong or false: *The theory has now been disproved.* **ANT** PROVE

dis·put·a·ble /dɪ'spyutəbl/ adj. (formal) that can or should be questioned or argued about ⊃ compare INDISPUTABLE

dis·pu·ta·tion /ˌdɪspyu'teɪʃn/ noun [C, U] (formal) a discussion about something that people cannot agree on

dis·pute /dɪ'spyut/ noun, verb

• **noun** [C, U] an argument or a disagreement between two people, groups, or countries; discussion about a subject where there is disagreement: ~ (between A and B) *a dispute between the two countries about the border* ◆ ~ (over/about sth) *the latest dispute over fishing rights* ◆ *industrial/pay disputes* ◆ *The union is in dispute with management over working hours.* ◆ *The cause of the accident was still in dispute* (= being argued about). ◆ *The matter was settled beyond dispute by the court judgment* (= it could no longer be argued about). ◆ *His theories are open to dispute* (= can be disagreed with).

• **verb 1** [T] to question whether something is true and valid: ~ sth *These figures have been disputed.* ◆ *to dispute a decision/claim* ◆ *The family wanted to dispute the will.* ◆ ~ that... *No one is disputing that there is a problem.* ◆ ~ whether, how, etc.... | *it is disputed whether, how, etc.... It is disputed whether the law applies in this case.* **2** [T, I] ~ (sth) to argue or disagree strongly with someone about something, especially about who owns something: *disputed territory* ◆ *The issue remains hotly disputed.* **3** [T] ~ sth to fight to get

t tea   ț butter   d did   k cat   g got   tʃ chin   dʒ June   f fall control of something or to win something: *On the last lap, three runners were disputing the lead.*

dis·qual·i·fy /dɪsˈkwɑləˌfaɪ/ *verb* (dis·qual·i·fies, dis·qual·i·fy·ing, dis·qual·i·fied, dis·qual·i·fied) to prevent someone from doing something because they have broken a rule or are not suitable **SYN** BAR: ~ **sb (from sth)** *He was disqualified from the competition for using drugs.* ♦ ~ **sb (from doing sth)** *They were disqualified from voting.* ♦ ~ **sb (for sth)** *A heart condition disqualified him for military service.* ▸ **dis·qual·i·fi·ca·tion** /dɪsˌkwɑləfəˈkeɪʃn/ *noun* [C, U]: *Any form of cheating means automatic disqualification.*

dis·qui·et /dɪsˈkwaɪət/ *noun* [U] ~ **(about/over sth)** (*formal*) feelings of worry and unhappiness about something **SYN** UNEASE: *There is considerable public disquiet about the safety of the new trains.*

dis·qui·et·ing /dɪsˈkwaɪətɪŋ/ *adj.* (*formal*) causing worry and unhappiness

dis·qui·si·tion /ˌdɪskwəˈzɪʃn/ *noun* (*formal*) a long complicated speech or written report on a particular subject

dis·re·gard /ˌdɪsrɪˈɡɑrd/ *verb, noun*
● *verb* ~ **sth** to not consider something; to treat something as unimportant **SYN** IGNORE: *The board completely disregarded my recommendations.* ♦ *Safety rules were disregarded.*
● *noun* [U] ~ **(for/of sb/sth)** the act of treating someone or something as unimportant and not caring about them/it: *She shows a total disregard for other people's feelings.*

dis·re·pair /ˌdɪsrɪˈper/ *noun* [U] a building, road, etc. that is in a state of **disrepair** has not been taken care of and is broken or in bad condition: *The station quickly fell into disrepair after it was closed.*

dis·rep·u·ta·ble /dɪsˈrepyətəbl/ *adj.* that people consider to be dishonest and bad: *She spent the evening with her disreputable brother Steve.* ♦ *a disreputable area of the city* **ANT** RESPECTABLE ⊃ compare REPUTABLE

dis·re·pute /ˌdɪsrɪˈpyut/ *noun* [U] the fact that someone or something loses the respect of other people: *The scandal brought the military into disrepute.*

dis·re·spect /ˌdɪsrɪˈspekt/ *noun, verb*
● *noun* [U, C] ~ **(for/to sb/sth)** a lack of respect for someone or something: *disrespect for the law/the dead* ♦ *No disrespect intended, sir. It was just a joke.* ▸ **dis·re·spect·ful** /ˌdɪsrɪˈspektfl/ *adj.* ⊃ thesaurus box at RUDE **dis·re·spect·ful·ly** /-fəli/ *adv.*
● *verb* ~ **sb/sth** (*informal*) to speak about or treat someone or something without respect: *They were accused of disrespecting the country's flag.* **HELP** Some people consider that it is not correct to use **disrespect** as a verb, and that you should use the noun instead, especially in formal and written English: *They were accused of treating the country's flag with disrespect.*

dis·robe /dɪsˈroʊb/ *verb* [I, T] ~ **(sb)** (*formal or humorous*) to take off your or someone else's clothes; to take off clothes worn for an official ceremony: *She went behind the screen to disrobe.*

dis·rupt /dɪsˈrʌpt/ *verb* ~ **sth** to make it difficult for something to continue in the normal way: *Demonstrators succeeded in disrupting the meeting.* ♦ *Bus services will be disrupted tomorrow because of the bridge closure.* ▸ **dis·rup·tion** /dɪsˈrʌpʃn/ *noun* [U, C]: *We aim to help you move house with minimum disruption to your life.* ♦ *disruptions to rail services* ♦ *The strike caused serious disruptions.*

dis·rup·tive /dɪsˈrʌptɪv/ *adj.* causing problems, noise, etc. so that something cannot continue normally: *She had a disruptive influence on the rest of the class.*

diss /dɪs/ = DIS

dis·sat·is·fac·tion /dɪsˌsætəsˈfækʃn; ˌdɪsˌsætəs-/ *noun* [U] ~ **(with/at sb/sth)** a feeling that you are not pleased and satisfied: *Many people have expressed their dissatisfaction with the arrangement.* **ANT** SATISFACTION

dis·sat·is·fied /dɪˈsætəsˌfaɪd; dɪsˈsætəs-/ *adj.* not happy or satisfied with someone or something: *dissatisfied customers*

♦ ~ **with sb/sth** *If you are dissatisfied with our service, please write to the manager.* **ANT** SATISFIED ⊃ compare UNSATISFIED

dis·sect /dɪˈsekt; daɪ-/ *verb* **1** ~ **sth** to cut up a dead person, an animal, or a plant in order to study it **2** ~ **sth** to study something closely and/or discuss it in great detail: *Her latest novel was dissected by the critics.* **3** ~ **sth** to divide something into smaller pieces, areas, etc.: *The city is dissected by a network of old canals.* ▸ **dis·sec·tion** /dɪˈsekʃn; daɪ-/ *noun* [U, C]: *anatomical dissection* ♦ *Your enjoyment of a novel can suffer from too much analysis and dissection.*

dis·sem·ble /dɪˈsembl/ *verb* [I, T] (*formal*) to hide your real feelings or intentions, often by pretending to have different ones: *She was a very honest person who was incapable of dissembling.*

dis·sem·i·nate /dɪˈseməˌneɪt/ *verb* ~ **sth** (*formal*) to spread information, knowledge, etc. so that it reaches many people: *Their findings have been widely disseminated.* ▸ **dis·sem·i·na·tion** /dɪˌseməˈneɪʃn/ *noun* [U]

dis·sen·sion /dɪˈsenʃn/ *noun* [U] (*formal*) disagreement between people or within a group: *dissension within the government*

dis·sent /dɪˈsent/ *noun, verb*
● *noun* **1** [U] the fact of having or expressing opinions that are different from those that are officially accepted: *political/religious dissent* **2** [C] a judge's statement giving reasons why he or she disagrees with a decision made by the other judges in a court case
● *verb* [I] ~ **(from sth)** (*formal*) to have or express opinions that are different from those that are officially accepted: *Only two ministers dissented from the official view.* ▸ **dis·sent·ing** *adj.*: *dissenting groups/voices/views/opinion*

dis·sent·er /dɪˈsentər/ *noun* a person who does not agree with opinions that are officially or generally accepted

dis·ser·ta·tion /ˌdɪsərˈteɪʃn/ *noun* ~ **(on sth)** a long piece of writing on a particular subject, especially one written for a university degree

dis·serv·ice /dɪˈsɜrvəs; dɪsˈsər-/ *noun* [sing.] **IDM do sb a disservice** to do something that harms someone and the opinion that other people have of them

dis·si·dent /ˈdɪsədənt/ *noun* a person who strongly disagrees with and criticizes their government, especially in a country where this kind of action is dangerous ▸ **dis·si·dence** /ˈdɪsədəns/ *noun* [U] **dis·si·dent** *adj.*

dis·sim·i·lar **AWL** /dɪˈsɪmələr; dɪsˈsɪ-/ *adj.* ~ **(from/to sb/sth)** (*formal*) not the same: *These wines are not dissimilar* (= are similar). **ANT** SIMILAR ⊃ collocations at SIMILAR ▸ **dis·sim·i·lar·i·ty** /ˌdɪsɪməˈlærəti; ˌdɪsˌsɪ-/ *noun* [C, U]

dis·sim·u·late /dɪˈsɪmyəˌleɪt/ *verb* [T, I] ~ **(sth)** (*formal*) to hide your real feelings or intentions, often by pretending to have different ones **SYN** DISSEMBLE ▸ **dis·sim·u·la·tion** /dɪˌsɪmyəˈleɪʃn/ *noun* [U]

dis·si·pate /ˈdɪsəˌpeɪt/ *verb* (*formal*) **1** [I, T] to gradually become or make something become weaker until it disappears: *Eventually, his anger dissipated.* ♦ ~ **sth** *Her laughter soon dissipated the tension in the air.* **2** [T] ~ **sth** to waste something, such as time or money, especially by not planning the best way of using it **SYN** SQUANDER

dis·si·pat·ed /ˈdɪsəˌpeɪtəd/ *adj.* (*disapproving*) enjoying activities that are harmful such as drinking too much alcohol

dis·si·pa·tion /ˌdɪsəˈpeɪʃn/ *noun* [U] (*formal*) **1** the process of disappearing or of making something disappear: *the dissipation of energy in the form of heat* **2** the act of wasting money or spending money until there is none left: *concerns about the dissipation of the country's wealth* **3** (*disapproving*) behavior which is enjoyable but has a harmful effect on you

dis·so·ci·ate /dɪˈsoʊʃiˌeɪt; -siˌeɪt/ *verb* **1** (also **dis·as·so·ci·ate**) ~ **yourself/sb from sb/sth** to say or do something to show that you are not connected with or do not support someone or something; to make it clear that something is not connected with a particular plan, action, etc.: *He tried to* dissociate himself from the party's more extreme views. ◆ They were determined to dissociate the UN from any agreement to impose sanctions. **2** ~ **sb/sth (from sth)** (formal) to think of two people or things as separate and not connected with each other: She tried to dissociate the two events in her mind. **ANT** ASSOCIATE ▶ **dis·so·ci·a·tion** /dɪˌsoʊsiˈeɪʃn; -ʃiˈeɪ-/ noun [U]

dis·so·lute /ˈdɪsəˌlut/ adj. (formal, disapproving) enjoying immoral activities and not caring about behaving in a morally acceptable way

dis·so·lu·tion /ˌdɪsəˈluʃn/ noun [U] ~ **(of sth) 1** the act of officially ending a marriage, a business agreement, or a parliament **2** the process in which something gradually disappears: the dissolution of barriers of class and race **3** the act of breaking up an organization, etc.

dis·solve 🔑 /dɪˈzɑlv/ verb
1 [I] ~ **(in sth)** (of a solid) to mix with a liquid and become part of it: Salt dissolves in water. ◆ Heat gently until the sugar dissolves. **2** [T] ~ **sth (in sth)** to make a solid become part of a liquid: Dissolve the tablet in water. **3** [T] ~ **sth** to officially end a marriage, business agreement, or parliament: Their marriage was dissolved in 1999. **4** [T, I] ~ **(sth)** to officially close a company or other organization; to be officially closed: My brothers have decided to dissolve their business. **5** [I, T] to disappear; to make something disappear: When the ambulance left, the crowd dissolved. ◆ ~ **sth** His calm response dissolved her anger. **6** [I] ~ **into laughter, tears, etc.** to suddenly start laughing, crying, etc.: When the teacher looked up, the children dissolved into giggles. ◆ Every time she heard his name, she dissolved into tears. **7** [T, I] to remove or destroy something, especially by a chemical process; to be destroyed in this way: ~ **sth (away)** a new detergent that dissolves stains ◆ ~ **(away)** All the original calcium had dissolved away.

dis·so·nance /ˈdɪsənəns/ noun **1** [C, U] (music) a combination of musical notes that do not sound pleasant together **ANT** CONSONANCE **2** [U] (formal) lack of agreement ▶ **dis·so·nant** /ˈdɪsənənt/ adj.: dissonant voices/notes

dis·suade /dɪˈsweɪd/ verb ~ **sb (from sth/from doing sth)** to persuade someone not to do something: I tried to dissuade him from giving up his job. ◆ They were going to set off in the fog, but were dissuaded.

dis·taff /ˈdɪstæf/ noun a stick that was used in the past for holding wool when it was spun by hand
IDM **on the distaff side** (old-fashioned) on the woman's side of the family

dis·tal /ˈdɪstl/ adj. (anatomy) located away from the center of the body or at the far end of something: the distal end of the tibia

dis·tance 🔑 /ˈdɪstəns/ noun, verb
● **noun 1** [C, U] the amount of space between two places or things: a **short/long distance** ◆ the distance of the earth from the sun ◆ **a distance** of 200 miles ◆ What's the distance between New York City and Boston/from New York City to Boston? ◆ In the U.S., distance is measured in miles. ◆ The beach is **within walking distance** of my house (= you can walk there easily). ◆ Paul has to drive very long distances as part of his job. ◆ Our parents live some **distance away** (= quite far away). ⊃ see also LONG-DISTANCE, MIDDLE DISTANCE, OUTDISTANCE **2** [U] being far away in space or in time: Distance is no problem on the Internet. **3** [sing.] a point that is a particular amount of space away from something else: You'll never get the ball in from that distance. **4** [C, usually sing., U] a difference or lack of a connection between two things: The distance between fashion and art remains as great as ever. ◆ The government is eager to **put some distance between** itself and these events (= show that there is no connection between them). **5** [U, C] a situation in which there is a lack of friendly feelings or of a close relationship between two people or groups of people: The coldness and distance in her voice took me by surprise.
IDM **at/from a distance** from a place or time that is not near; from far away: She had loved him at a distance for years. **go the (full) distance** to continue playing in a competition

or sports contest until the end: Nobody thought he would last 15 rounds, but he went the full distance. **in/into the distance** far away but still able to be seen or heard: We saw lights in the distance. ◆ Alice stood staring into the distance. **keep sb at a distance** to refuse to be friendly with someone; to not let someone be friendly toward you **keep your distance (from sb/sth) 1** to make sure you are not too near someone or something **2** to avoid getting too friendly or involved with a person, group, etc.: She was warned to keep her distance from Charles if she didn't want to get hurt. ⊃ **more** at SHOUTING, STRIKE v.
● **verb** ~ **yourself/sb/sth (from sb/sth)** to become, or to make someone or something become, less involved or connected with someone or something: When he retired, he tried to distance himself from politics. ◆ It's not always easy for nurses to distance themselves emotionally.

distance ˌlearning noun [U] a system of education in which people study at home with the help of special Internet sites and television and radio programs, and send or e-mail work to their teachers

dis·tant 🔑 /ˈdɪstənt/ adj.
1 far away in space or time: the distant sound of music ◆ distant stars/planets ◆ The time we spent together is now a distant memory. ◆ (formal) The airport was about 20 miles distant. ◆ a star 30,000 light years distant from the Earth ◆ (figurative) Peace was just a distant hope (= not very likely). **2** ~ **(from sth)** not like something else **SYN** REMOTE: Their life seemed utterly distant from his own. **3** [only before noun] (of a person) related to you but not closely: a distant cousin/aunt/relative **4** not friendly; not wanting a close relationship with someone: Pat sounded very cold and distant on the phone. **5** not paying attention to something but thinking about something completely different: There was a distant look in her eyes; her mind was obviously on something else. ▶ **dis·tant·ly** adv.: Somewhere, distantly, he could hear the sound of the ocean. ◆ We're distantly related. ◆ Holly smiled distantly.
IDM **the (dim and) distant past** a long time ago: stories from the distant past **in the not too distant future** not a long time in the future but fairly soon

dis·taste /dɪsˈteɪst/ noun [U, sing.] a feeling that someone or something is unpleasant or offensive: He looked around the filthy room in distaste. ◆ ~ **for sb/sth** a distaste for politics of any sort

dis·taste·ful /dɪsˈteɪstfl/ adj. unpleasant or offensive

dis·tem·per /dɪsˈtɛmpər/ noun [U] an infectious disease of animals, especially cats and dogs, that causes fever and coughing

dis·tend /dɪˈstɛnd/ verb [T, I] ~ **(sth)** (formal or medical) to swell or make something swell because of pressure from inside: starving children with huge distended bellies ▶ **dis·ten·sion** /dɪˈstɛnʃn/ noun [U]: distension of the stomach

dis·till /dɪˈstɪl/ verb **1** ~ **sth (from sth)** to make a liquid pure by heating it until it becomes a gas, then cooling it and collecting the drops of liquid that form: to distill fresh water from sea water ◆ distilled water **2** ~ **sth** to make something such as a strong alcoholic drink in this way: The factory distills and bottles whiskey. **3** ~ **sth (from/into sth)** (formal) to get the essential meaning or ideas from thoughts, information, experiences, etc.: The notes I made on my travels were distilled into a book. ▶ **dis·til·la·tion** /ˌdɪstəˈleɪʃn/ noun [C, U]: the distillation process

dis·til·late /ˈdɪstəˌleɪt; -lət; dɪˈstɪlət/ noun [U, C] (technical) a substance which is formed by distilling a liquid

dis·till·er /dɪˈstɪlər/ noun a person or company that produces LIQUOR (= strong alcoholic drinks) such as WHISKEY by distilling them

dis·till·er·y /dɪˈstɪləri/ noun (pl. **dis·till·er·ies**) a factory where strong alcoholic drinks are made by the process of distillation

dis·tinct **AWL** /dɪˈstɪŋkt/ adj. **1** easily or clearly heard, seen, felt, etc.: There was a distinct smell of gas. ◆ His voice was quiet but every word was distinct. **2** clearly different or of a different kind: *The results of the survey fell into two distinct groups.* ◆ **~ from sth** *Jamaican reggae music is quite distinct from North American jazz or blues.* ◆ *rural areas,* **as distinct from** *major cities* **3** [only before noun] used to emphasize that you think an idea or situation definitely exists and is important **SYN** DEFINITE: *Being tall gave Tony a distinct advantage.* ◆ *I had the distinct impression I was being watched.* ◆ *A strike is now a distinct possibility.* ▶ **dis·tinct·ly** **AWL** *adv.*: *I distinctly heard someone calling me.* ◆ *a distinctly Australian accent* ◆ *He could remember everything very distinctly.* **dis·tinct·ness** *noun* [U]

AWL COLLOCATIONS

distinct

distinct *adj.*

clearly different or of a different kind
- sufficiently | clearly | fundamentally, radically | wholly

  Mexican culture is sufficiently distinct in ethnic, religious, and linguistic terms to retain its individuality.
- functionally | structurally | geographically | culturally | analytically, logically

  Single-subject research will likely be the best way to extend our research into culturally distinct populations.
- remain | become | appear

  These factors suggest that Dominicans probably will remain distinct from the American population as a whole into the twenty-first century.
- **~ from one another, ~ from each other**

  Overall, the two extreme groups were found to be distinct from each other in nearly every characteristic considered.
- **~ from something**

  Art that is appreciated for its beauty is distinct from art that produces items for practical use, such as furniture.

distinction *noun*

a clear difference or contrast, especially between two things that are similar or related
- clear, sharp | subtle | crucial, fundamental, important | conceptual

  However, subtle distinctions can generally be made between these species.
- blur | clarify | collapse, elide

  Both books elide distinctions between nature and human society.
- draw, make

  The authors note that respondents make a sharp distinction between religion and spirituality.

distinctive *adj.*

having a quality or characteristic that makes something different and easily noticed
- highly, particularly, truly | sufficiently | individually | culturally

  We marked each bird with an individually distinctive combination of colored leg bands.
- feature, characteristic

  The most distinctive feature of these costumes is the striped, fringed skirt, woven from flax.

---

dis·tinc·tion **AWL** /dɪˈstɪŋkʃn/ *noun* **1** [C] **~ (between A and B)** a clear difference or contrast especially between people or things that are similar or related: *distinctions between traditional and modern societies* ◆ *Philosophers did not use to* **make a distinction** *between arts and science.* ◆ *We need to* **draw a distinction** *between the two events.* ⊃ collocations at DISTINCT **2** [U] the quality of being excellent or important: *a writer of distinction* **3** [sing.] the quality of being something that is special: *She* **had the distinction** *of being the first woman to fly the Atlantic.* **4** [U] **~ (between A and B)** the separation of people or things into different groups: *The new law makes*

no distinction between adults and children (= treats them equally). ◆ *All groups are entitled to this money* **without distinction.** **5** [C, U] a special grade or award that is given to someone, especially a student, for excellent work: *He graduated* **with distinction.**

dis·tinc·tive **AWL** /dɪˈstɪŋktɪv/ *adj.* having a quality or characteristic that makes something different and easily noticed **SYN** CHARACTERISTIC ⊃ collocations at DISTINCT: *clothes with a distinctive style* ◆ *The male bird has distinctive white markings on its head.* ▶ **dis·tinc·tive·ly** **AWL** *adv.*: *a distinctively nutty flavor*

dis·tin·guish 🔑 /dɪˈstɪŋgwɪʃ/ *verb*
1 [I, T] to recognize the difference between two people or things **SYN** DIFFERENTIATE: **~ between A and B** *At what age are children able to distinguish between right and wrong?* ◆ **~ A from B** *It was hard to distinguish one twin from the other.* ◆ **~ A and B** *Sometimes reality and fantasy are hard to distinguish.* **2** [T] (not used in the progressive tenses) **~ A (from B)** to be a characteristic that makes two people, animals, or things different: *What was it that distinguished her from her classmates?* ◆ *The male bird is distinguished from the female by its red beak.* ◆ *Does your cat have any distinguishing marks?* **3** [T] (not used in the progressive tenses) **~ sth** to be able to see or hear something **SYN** DIFFERENTIATE, MAKE OUT: *I could not distinguish her words, but she sounded agitated.* **4** [T] **~ yourself (as sth)** to do something so well that people notice and admire you: *She has already distinguished herself as an athlete.* ▶ **dis·tin·guish·a·ble** /dɪˈstɪŋgwɪʃəbl/ *adj.*: **~ (from sb/sth)** *The male bird is easily distinguishable from the female.* ◆ *The coast was barely distinguishable in the mist.*

dis·tin·guished /dɪˈstɪŋgwɪʃt/ *adj.* **1** very successful and admired by other people: *a distinguished career in medicine* **2** having an appearance that makes someone look important or that makes people admire or respect them: *I think gray hair makes you look very distinguished.*

dis·tort **AWL** /dɪˈstɔrt/ *verb* **1** **~ sth** to change the shape, appearance, or sound of something so that it is strange or not clear: *a fairground mirror that distorts your shape* ◆ *The loudspeaker seemed to distort his voice.* **2** **~ sth** to twist or change facts, ideas, etc. so that they are no longer correct or true: *Newspapers are often guilty of distorting the truth.* ◆ *The article gave a distorted picture of his childhood.* ▶ **dis·tor·tion** **AWL** /dɪˈstɔrʃn/ *noun* [C, U]: *modern alloys that are resistant to wear and distortion* ◆ *a distortion of the facts*

dis·tract /dɪˈstrækt/ *verb* **~ sb/sth (from sth)** to take someone's attention away from what they are trying to do **SYN** DIVERT: *You're distracting me from my work.* ◆ *Don't talk to her—she's very easily distracted.* ◆ *It was another attempt to* **distract attention** *from the truth.* ▶ **dis·tract·ing** *adj.*: *distracting thoughts* ◆ *a distracting noise*

dis·tract·ed /dɪˈstræktəd/ *adj.* **~ (by sb/sth)** unable to pay attention to someone or something because you are worried or thinking about something else ▶ **dis·tract·ed·ly** *adv.*

dis·trac·tion /dɪˈstrækʃn/ *noun* **1** [C, U] a thing that takes your attention away from what you are doing or thinking about: *I find it hard to work at home because there are too many distractions.* ◆ *movie audiences looking for distraction* **2** [C] an activity that amuses or entertains you **IDM** **to distraction** so that you become upset, excited, or angry and not able to think clearly: *The children are* **driving me to distraction** *today.*

dis·trac·tor /dɪˈstræktər/ *noun* **1** a person or thing that takes your attention away from what you should be doing **2** one of the wrong answers in a MULTIPLE-CHOICE test

dis·traught /dɪˈstrɔt/ *adj.* extremely upset and anxious so that you cannot think clearly

dis·tress /dɪˈstrɛs/ *noun, verb*
● *noun* [U] **1** a feeling of great worry or unhappiness; great suffering: *The newspaper article caused the actor considerable distress.* ◆ *She was obviously* **in distress** *after the attack.* ◆ *deep emotional distress* **2** suffering and problems caused by not

---

having enough money, food, etc. **SYN** HARDSHIP: *economic/financial distress* **3** a situation in which a ship, plane, etc. is in danger or difficulty and needs help: *a distress signal* (= a message asking for help) ◆ *It is a rule of the sea to help another boat in distress.* **IDM** see DAMSEL

• *verb* to make someone feel very worried or unhappy: *~ sb It was clear that the letter had deeply distressed her.* ◆ *~ yourself Don't distress yourself* (= don't worry).

dis·tressed /dɪˈstrɛst/ *adj.* **1** upset and anxious: *He was too distressed and confused to answer their questions.* **2** suffering pain; in a poor physical condition: *When the baby was born, it was blue and distressed.* **3** (of a piece of clothing or furniture) made to look older and more worn than it really is: *a distressed leather jacket* **4** (*formal* or *business*) having problems caused by lack of money: *They buy up financially distressed companies.* ◆ *The charity helps kids in distressed situations.*

dis·tress·ing /dɪˈstrɛsɪŋ/ *adj.* making you feel extremely upset, especially because of someone's suffering ▶ **dis·tress·ing·ly** *adv.*

dis·trib·ute 🔑 **AWL** /dɪˈstrɪbjut; -yət/ *verb* **1** to give things to a large number of people; to share something between a number of people: *~ sth The newspaper is distributed free.* ◆ *~ sth to sb/sth The organization distributed food to the earthquake victims.* ◆ *~ sth among sb/sth The money was distributed among schools in the area.* **2** *~ sth* to send goods to stores and businesses so that they can be sold: *Who distributes our products in the U.K.?* **3** [often passive] *~ sth* to spread something, or different parts of something, over an area: *Make sure that your weight is evenly distributed.*

dis·tri·bu·tion 🔑 **AWL** /ˌdɪstrəˈbyuʃn/ *noun* **1** [U, C] the way that something is shared or exists over a particular area or among a particular group of people: *the unfair distribution of wealth* ◆ *The map shows the distribution of this species across the world.* ◆ *They studied the geographical distribution of the disease.* **2** [U] the act of giving or delivering something to a number of people: *the distribution of food and medicines to the flood victims* ◆ *He was arrested on drug distribution charges.* **3** [U] (*business*) the system of transporting and delivering goods: *distribution costs* ◆ *worldwide distribution systems* ◆ *marketing, sales and distribution* **4** [C] (*mathematics*) an arrangement of numbers that shows how frequently each number appears in a set of data ▶ **dis·tri·bu·tion·al** **AWL** /-ʃənl/ *adj.*

dis·tri·bu·tive **AWL** /dɪˈstrɪbyətɪv/ *adj.* [usually before noun] (*business*) connected with distribution of goods

dis·trib·u·tor **AWL** /dɪˈstrɪbyətər/ *noun* **1** a person or company that supplies goods to stores, etc.: *Japan's largest software distributor* **2** a device in an engine that sends electric current to the SPARK PLUG

dis·trict 🔑 /ˈdɪstrɪkt/ *noun* **1** an area of a country or city, especially one that has particular features: *New York's financial district* **2** one of the areas which a country, city, or state is divided into for purposes of organization, with official boundaries (= borders): *a school district* ◆ *congressional districts* ◆ *district councils*

ˌdistrict atˈtorney *noun* (*abbr.* D.A.) a government lawyer who is responsible for bringing criminal charges against someone in a particular area or state

ˌdistrict ˈcourt *noun* a court that deals with cases in a particular area that involve national law rather than state law

dis·trust /dɪsˈtrʌst/ *noun, verb*
• *noun* [U, sing.] a feeling of not being able to trust someone or something: *They looked at each other with distrust.* ◆ *~ of sb/sth He has a deep distrust of all modern technology.* ▶ **dis·trust·ful** /dɪsˈtrʌstfl/ *adj.*: *distrustful of authority*
• *verb ~ sb/sth* to feel that you cannot trust or believe

someone or something: *She distrusted his motives for wanting to see her again.* ⊃ compare MISTRUST

WHICH WORD?

distrust ◆ **mistrust**

- There is very little difference between these two words, but **distrust** is more common and perhaps slightly stronger. If you are sure that someone is acting dishonestly or cannot be relied on, you are more likely to say that you **distrust** them. If you are expressing doubts and suspicions, on the other hand, you would probably use **mistrust**.

dis·turb 🔑 /dɪˈstərb/ *verb* **1** *~ sb/sth* to interrupt someone when they are trying to work, sleep, etc.: *I'm sorry to disturb you, but can I talk to you for a moment?* ◆ *If you get up early, try not to disturb everyone else.* ◆ *Do not disturb* (= a sign placed on the outside of the door of a hotel room, office, etc.) ◆ *She awoke early after a disturbed night.* **2** *~ sth* to move something or change its position: *Don't disturb the papers on my desk.* **3** to make someone worry: *~ sb The letter shocked and disturbed me.* ◆ *it disturbs sb to do sth It disturbed her to realize that she was alone.*

dis·tur·bance /dɪˈstərbəns/ *noun* **1** [U, C, usually sing.] actions that make you stop what you are doing, or that upset the normal state that something is in; the act of disturbing someone or something or the fact of being disturbed: *The building work is creating constant noise, dust and disturbance.* ◆ *a disturbance in the usual pattern of events* ◆ *the disturbance of the local wildlife by tourists* **2** [C] a situation in which people behave violently in a public place: *serious disturbances in the streets* ◆ *He was charged with causing a disturbance after the game.* **3** [U, C] a state in which someone's mind or a function of the body is upset and not working normally: *emotional disturbance*

dis·turbed /dɪˈstərbd/ *adj.* **1** mentally ill, especially because of very unhappy or shocking experiences: *a special school for emotionally disturbed children* ⊃ thesaurus box at MENTALLY ILL **2** unhappy and full of bad or shocking experiences: *The killer had a disturbed family background.* **3** very anxious and unhappy about something: *I was deeply disturbed and depressed by the news.* ⊃ compare UNDISTURBED

dis·turb·ing 🔑 /dɪˈstərbɪŋ/ *adj.* making you feel anxious and upset or shocked: *a disturbing piece of news* ▶ **dis·turb·ing·ly** *adv.*

dis·u·nite /ˌdɪsyuˈnaɪt/ *verb* [usually passive] *~ sb/sth* (*formal*) to make a group of people unable to agree with each other or work together: *a disunited political party*

dis·u·ni·ty /dɪsˈyunəti/ *noun* [U] (*formal*) a lack of agreement between people: *disunity within the Democratic party* **ANT** UNITY

dis·use /dɪsˈyus/ *noun* [U] a situation in which something is no longer being used: *The factory fell into disuse twenty years ago.*

dis·used /ˌdɪsˈyuzd/ *adj.* [usually before noun] no longer used: *a disused station* ⊃ compare UNUSED[1]

ditch /dɪtʃ/ *noun, verb*
• *noun* a long channel dug at the side of a field or road, to hold or take away water
• *verb* **1** [T] *~ sth/sb* (*informal*) to get rid of something or someone because you no longer want or need it/them: *The new road building program has been ditched.* ◆ *He ditched his girlfriend.* **2** [T, I] *~ (sth)* if a pilot **ditches** an aircraft, or if it **ditches**, it lands in the ocean in an emergency **3** [T] *~ school* (*informal*) to stay away from school without permission

dith·er /ˈdɪðər/ *verb, noun*
• *verb* [I] to hesitate about what to do because you are unable to decide: *Stop dithering and get on with it.* ◆ *~ over sth She was dithering over what to wear.*

● **noun** [sing.] (*informal*) **1** a state of not being able to decide what you should do: *I'm **in a dither** about who to invite.* **2** a state of excitement or worry: *Don't get yourself **in a dither** over everything.*

di·tran·si·tive /daɪˈtrænsətɪv; -ˈtrænzə-/ *adj.* (*grammar*) (of verbs) used with two objects. In the sentence "I gave her the book", for example, the verb "give" is ditransitive and "her" and "the books" are both objects.

dit·sy = DITZY

dit·to /ˈdɪtoʊ/ *noun, adv.*
● *noun* (*abbr.* **do.**) (*symb.* **"**) used, especially in a list, underneath a particular word or phrase, to show that it is repeated and to avoid having to write it again
● *adv.* (*informal*) **1** used instead of a particular word or phrase, to avoid repeating it: *The waiters were rude and unhelpful, the manager ditto.* **2** used to say that you agree with someone or feel the same way: *"I'm in the mood for a good movie." "Ditto."*

dit·ty /ˈdɪti/ *noun* (*pl.* **dit·ties**) (often *humorous*) a short simple song

ditz /dɪts/ *noun* (*pl.* **ditz·es**) (*slang*) a person who does not think clearly or who forgets things: *She's very creative, but a real ditz when it comes to organizing her life.*

dit·zy (also **dit·sy**) /ˈdɪtsi/ *adj.* (*informal*) (usually of a woman) silly; not able to be trusted to remember things or to think in an organized way

di·u·ret·ic /ˌdaɪyəˈrɛtɪk/ *noun* (*medical*) a substance that causes an increase in the flow of URINE ▶ **di·u·ret·ic** *adj.*: *diuretic drugs/effects*

di·ur·nal /daɪˈɜrnl/ *adj.* **1** (*biology*) (of animals) active during the day **ANT** NOCTURNAL **2** (*astronomy*) taking one day: *the diurnal rotation of the earth*

Div. *abbr.* (in writing) DIVISION: *League Div. 1* (= in SOCCER)

di·va /ˈdivə/ *noun* **1** a famous woman singer, especially an OPERA singer **2** an attractive and famous woman, especially a performer or singer: *the greatest living pop diva of the 1960s*

Di·va·li /dɪˈvɑli/ = DIWALI

di·van /dɪˈvæn; ˈdaɪvæn/ *noun* a long, low, soft seat without a back or arms

dive /daɪv/ *verb, noun*
● *verb* (**dived**, **dived** or **dove** /doʊv/, **dived**)
➤ **JUMP INTO WATER 1** [I] **~ (from/off sth) (into sth)** | **~ (in)** to jump into water with your head and arms going in first: *We dove into the river to cool off.*
➤ **UNDERWATER 2** usually **go diving** [I] to swim underwater wearing breathing equipment, collecting or looking at things: *to dive for pearls* ♦ *The main purpose of his vacation to Greece was to go diving.* ⊃ see also DIVING **3** [I] to go to a deeper level underwater: *The whale dove as the harpoon struck it.*
➤ **OF BIRDS/AIRCRAFT 4** [I] to go steeply down through the air: *The seagulls soared then dived.* ⊃ see also NOSEDIVE
➤ **OF PRICES 5** [I] to fall suddenly **SYN** PLUNGE: *The share price dove from 49 cents to an all-time low of 40 cents.*
➤ **MOVE/JUMP/FALL 6** [I] (*informal*) to move or jump quickly in a particular direction, especially to avoid something, to try to catch a ball, etc.: **~ for sth** *We heard an explosion and dove for cover* (= got into a place where we would be protected). ♦ *The goalie dove for the ball, but missed it.* ♦ **+ adv./prep.** *It started to rain so we dove into the nearest store.* **7** [I] (in SOCCER, FIELD HOCKEY, etc.) to fall deliberately when someone TACKLES you, so that the REFEREE awards a FOUL
PHR V **dive ˈin 1** to start doing something fully, with a lot of energy and enthusiasm: *The only way to learn a new language is to just dive in and not be afraid of making mistakes.* **2** (also **dive ˈinto sth**) to start eating in an eager way without hesitating: *They were very hungry and dove into the meal with gusto.* **ˈdive into sth** (*informal*) to put your hand quickly into something such as a bag or pocket: *She dove into her bag and took out a couple of coins.*

● *noun*
➤ **JUMP INTO WATER 1** a jump into deep water with your head first and your arms in front of you: *a spectacular high dive* (= from high above the water)
➤ **UNDERWATER 2** an act of going underwater and swimming there with special equipment: *a dive to a depth of 120 feet*
➤ **OF BIRDS/AIRCRAFT 3** an act of suddenly flying downward
➤ **BAR/CLUB 4** (*informal*) a bar, music club, etc. that is cheap, and perhaps dark or dirty
➤ **FALL 5** (in SOCCER, FIELD HOCKEY, etc.) a deliberate fall that a player makes when someone TACKLES them, so that the REFEREE awards a FOUL
IDM **make a dive (for sth)** to suddenly move or jump forward to do something or reach someone or something: *The goalkeeper made a dive for the ball.* **take a dive** (*informal*) to suddenly get worse: *Profits really took a dive last year.*

ˈdive-bomb *verb* **~ sb/sth** (of an aircraft, a bird, etc.) to dive steeply through the air and attack someone or something

div·er /ˈdaɪvər/ *noun* **1** a person who works underwater, usually with special equipment: *a deep-sea diver* ⊃ see also FROGMAN **2** a person who jumps into the water with their head first and their arms in front of them

di·verge /dəˈvɜrdʒ; daɪ-/ *verb* (*formal*) **1** [I] to separate and go in different directions: *The parallel lines appear to diverge.* ♦ *We went through high school and college together, but then our paths diverged.* ♦ **~ from sth** *The coastal road diverges from the freeway just north of Santa Monica.* ♦ *Many species have diverged from a single ancestor.* **2** [I] **~ (from sth)** (*formal*) (of opinions, views, etc.) to be different: *Opinions diverge greatly on this issue.* **3** [I] **~ from sth** to be or become different from what is expected, planned, etc.: *to diverge from the norm* ♦ *He diverged from established procedure.* **ANT** CONVERGE ▶ **di·ver·gence** /dəˈvɜrdʒəns; daɪ-/ *noun* [C, U]: *a wide divergence of opinion* **di·ver·gent** /-dʒənt; daɪˈvɜrdʒənt/ *adj.*: *divergent paths/opinions*

di·vers /ˈdaɪvɜrz/ *adj.* [only before noun] (*old use*) of many different kinds

di·verse **AWL** /dəˈvɜrs; daɪ-/ *adj.* very different from each other and of various kinds: *people from diverse cultures* ♦ *My interests are very diverse.*

di·ver·si·fy **AWL** /dəˈvɜrsəˌfaɪ; daɪ-/ *verb* (**di·ver·si·fies**, **di·ver·si·fy·ing**, **di·ver·si·fied**, **di·ver·si·fied**) **1** [I, T] **~ (sth) (into sth)** (especially of a business or company) to develop a wider range of products, interests, skills, etc. in order to be more successful or reduce risk **SYN** BRANCH OUT: *Farmers are being encouraged to diversify into new crops.* **2** [I, T] to change or to make something change so that there is greater variety: *Patterns of family life are diversifying.* ♦ **~ sth** *The culture has been diversified with the arrival of immigrants.* ▶ **di·ver·si·fi·ca·tion** **AWL** /dəˌvɜrsəfəˈkeɪʃn; daɪ-/ *noun* [U]

di·ver·sion /dəˈvɜrʒn; daɪ-/ *noun* **1** [C, U] the act of changing the direction that someone or something is following, or what something is used for: *a river diversion project* ♦ *We made a short diversion to go and look at the church.* ♦ *the diversion of funds from the public to the private sector of industry* **2** [C] something that takes your attention away from someone or something while something else is happening: *For the government, the war was a welcome diversion from the country's economic problems.* ♦ *A smoke bomb **created a diversion** while the robbery took place.* **3** [C] (*formal*) an activity that is done for pleasure, especially because it takes your attention away from something else **SYN** DISTRACTION: *The party will make a pleasant diversion.* ♦ *The city is full of diversions.*

di·ver·sion·ar·y /dəˈvɜrʒəˌnɛri; daɪ-/ *adj.* intended to take someone's attention away from something

di·ver·si·ty **AWL** /dəˈvɜrsəti; daɪ-/ *noun* **1** [U, C, usually sing.] a range of many people or things that are very different from each other **SYN** VARIETY: *the biological diversity of the rainforests* ♦ *a great/wide/rich diversity of opinion* **2** [U] the quality or fact of including a range of many people or things: *There is a need for greater diversity and choice in education.*

di·vert /dəˈvərt; daɪ-/ verb ~ sb/sth (from sth) (to sth) **1** to make someone or something change direction: *Northbound traffic will have to be diverted onto minor roads.* **2** ~ sth to use money, materials, etc. for a different purpose from their original purpose **3** ~ sth to take someone's thoughts or attention away from something **SYN** DISTRACT: *The war diverted people's attention away from the economic situation.* **4** ~ sb (formal) to entertain people: *Children are easily diverted.*

di·vert·ing /dəˈvərtɪŋ; daɪ-/ adj. (formal) entertaining and amusing

di·vest /dəˈvest; daɪ-/ verb (formal) **1** ~ yourself of sth to get rid of something: *The company is divesting itself of some of its assets.* **2** ~ sb/sth of sth to take something away from someone or something: *After her illness she was divested of much of her responsibility.* **3** ~ sb/yourself of sth to remove clothes: *He divested himself of his jacket.*

di·vest·iture /dəˈvestətʃər; daɪ-/ noun [C, U] (economics) the act of selling part of a business or investment

di·vest·ment /dəˈvestmənt; daɪ-/ noun [U, C] (finance) the act of selling the shares you have bought in a company or of taking money away from where you have invested it

di·vide 🔑 /dəˈvaɪd/ verb, noun

● **verb**

> SEPARATE **1** [I, T] to separate or make something separate into parts **SYN** SPLIT UP: ~ (up) (into sth) *The cells began to divide rapidly.* ◆ ~ sth (up) (into sth) *A sentence can be divided up into meaningful segments.* **2** [T] to separate something into parts and give a share to each of a number of different people, etc. **SYN** SHARE: ~ sth (up) *Jack divided up the rest of the cash.* ◆ ~ sth (up) between/among sb *We divided the work between us.* **3** [T] ~ sth (between A and B) to use different parts of your time, energy, etc. for different activities, etc.: *He divides his energies between politics and business.* **4** [T] ~ A from B (formal) to separate two people or things: *Can it ever be right to divide a mother from her child?* **5** [T] ~ sth (off) | ~ A from B to be the real or imaginary line or barrier that separates two people or things **SYN** SEPARATE (OFF): *A fence divides off the western side of the grounds.* **6** [I] (of a road) to separate into two parts that lead in different directions: *Where the path divides, keep right.*
> CAUSE DISAGREEMENT **7** [T] ~ sb/sth to make two or more people disagree **SYN** SPLIT: *The issue has divided the government.*
> MATHEMATICS **8** [T, I] ~ (sth) by sth to find out how many times one number is contained in another: *30 divided by 6 is 5 (30÷6=5).* **9** [I, T] ~ (sth) into sth to be able to be multiplied to give another number: *5 divides into 30 6 times.*
> **IDM** **divide and conquer/rule** to gain or keep control over people by making them disagree with and fight each other, therefore not giving them the chance to unite and oppose you together: *a policy of divide and rule*

● **noun** [usually sing.]
> DIFFERENCE **1** a difference between two groups of people that separates them from each other: *the North/South divide* ◆ ~ between A and B *the divide between liberals and conservatives*
> BETWEEN RIVERS **2** a line of high land that separates two systems of rivers **SYN** WATERSHED ➔ see also CONTINENTAL DIVIDE **IDM** see BRIDGE v.

di·vid·ed /dəˈvaɪdəd/ adj. (of a group or an organization) split by disagreements or different opinions: *The government is divided on this issue.* ◆ *a deeply divided society* ◆ *The regime is profoundly divided against itself.*

di·vided 'highway noun a road with a strip of land in the middle that divides the lines of traffic moving in opposite directions

div·i·dend /ˈdɪvɪdɛnd/ noun **1** an amount of the profits that a company pays to people who own shares in the company: *dividend payments of 50 cents a share* **2** (mathematics) a number that is divided by another number

di·vid·er /dəˈvaɪdər/ noun **1** [C] a thing that divides something: *a room divider* (= a screen or door that divides a room into two parts) **2** dividers [pl.] an instrument made of two long, thin, metal parts joined together at the top, used for measuring lines and angles: *a pair of dividers*

di'viding ˌline noun [usually sing.] **1** something that marks the separation between two things or ideas: *There is no clear dividing line between what is good and what is bad.* **2** a place that separates two areas: *The river was chosen as a dividing line between the two districts.*

div·i·na·tion /ˌdɪvəˈneɪʃn/ noun [U] the act of finding out and saying what will happen in the future

di·vine /dəˈvaɪn/ adj., verb
● **adj.** **1** [usually before noun] coming from or connected with God or a god: *divine law/love/will* ◆ *divine intervention* (= help from God to change a situation) **2** (old-fashioned) wonderful; beautiful ▶ **di·vine·ly** adv.
● **verb** **1** [T] ~ what, whether, etc. ... | ~ sth (formal) to find out something by guessing: *She could divine what he was thinking just by looking at him.* **2** [T, I] ~ (sth) to search for underground water using a stick in the shape of a Y, called a **divining rod**

di·vine 'right noun [U, sing.] **1** (in the past) the belief that the right of a king or queen to rule comes directly from God rather than from the agreement of the people **2** a right that someone thinks they have to do something, without needing to ask anyone else: *No player has a divine right to be on this team.*

div·ing /ˈdaɪvɪŋ/ noun [U] **1** the sport or activity of diving into water with your head and arms first: *a diving competition* **2** the activity of swimming underwater using special breathing equipment: *I'd love to go diving in the Aegean.* ◆ *a diving suit* ➔ see also SCUBA DIVING, SKIN-DIVING

'diving ˌbell noun a container that has a supply of air and that is open at the bottom, in which a person can be carried down to the deep ocean

'diving ˌboard noun a board at the side of or above a swimming pool from which people can jump or DIVE into the water

di·vin·i·ty /dəˈvɪnəti/ noun (pl. di·vin·i·ties) **1** [U] the quality of being a god or like God: *the divinity of Christ* **2** [C] a god or GODDESS: *Roman/Greek/Egyptian divinities* **3** [U] the study of the nature of God and religious belief **SYN** THEOLOGY: *a Doctor of Divinity*

di·vis·i·ble /dəˈvɪzəbl/ adj. [not before noun] ~ (by sth) that can be divided, usually with nothing remaining: *8 is divisible by 2 and 4, but not by 3.* **ANT** INDIVISIBLE ▶ **di·vis·i·bility** /dəˌvɪzəˈbɪləti/ noun [U]

di·vi·sion 🔑 /dəˈvɪʒn/ noun
> INTO SEPARATE PARTS **1** [U, sing.] the process or result of dividing into separate parts; the process or result of dividing something up or sharing it between people or things: *cell division* ◆ ~ of sth *a fair division of time and resources* ◆ ~ of sth between A and B *the division of labor between the sexes* ◆ ~ (of sth) into sth *the division of the population into age groups*
> MATHEMATICS **2** [U] the process of dividing one number by another: *the division sign (÷)* ➔ compare MULTIPLICATION ➔ see also LONG DIVISION
> DISAGREEMENT/DIFFERENCE **3** [C, U] a disagreement or difference in opinion, way of life, etc., especially between members of a society or an organization: ~ (in/within sth) *There are deep divisions in the party over the war.* ◆ *the work of healing the divisions within society* ◆ ~ (between A and B) *divisions between rich and poor* ◆ *social/class divisions*
> PART OF ORGANIZATION **4** [C] (abbr. Div.) a large and important unit or section of an organization: *the company's sales division*
> IN SPORTS **5** [C] (abbr. Div.) one of several groups of teams

| t tea | ţ butter | d did | k cat | g got | tʃ chin | dʒ June | f fall |

that a sports competition is divided into: *the **first division**/* ***division one*** ♦ *a first-division team*
> **PART OF ARMY** **6** [C] (*abbr.* **Div.**) a unit of an army, consisting of several **BRIGADES** or **REGIMENTS**: *the 4th Infantry Division*
> **BORDER** **7** [C] a line that divides something: *A hedge forms the division between their land and ours.*

di·vi·sion·al /də'vɪʒənl/ *adj.* [only before noun] belonging to or connected with a **DIVISION** (= a section of the army or department of an organization): *the **divisional** commander/ headquarters*

di·vi·sive /də'vaɪsɪv/ *adj.* (*disapproving*) causing people to be split into groups that disagree with or oppose each other: *He believes that unemployment is socially divisive.* ⊃ see also **DIVIDE** ▶ **di·vi·sive·ly** *adv.* **di·vi·sive·ness** *noun* [U]

di·vi·sor /də'vaɪzər/ *noun* (*mathematics*) a number by which another number is divided

di·vorce 🔑 /də'vɔrs/ *noun, verb*
● *noun* **1** [U, C] the legal ending of a marriage: *The marriage **ended in divorce** in 1996.* ♦ *an increase in the **divorce rate** (= the number of divorces in a year)* ♦ *They have agreed to **get a divorce**.* ♦ ***Divorce proceedings** (= the legal process of divorce) started today.* ⊃ collocations at MARRIAGE ⊃ compare SE-PARATION **2** [C, usually sing.] ~ **(between A and B)** (*formal*) a separation; the ending of a relationship between two things: *the divorce between religion and science*
● *verb* **1** [T, I] ~ **(sb)** to end your marriage to someone legally: *They're **getting divorced**.* ♦ *She's divorcing her husband.* ♦ *I'd heard they're divorcing.* **2** [T, often passive] ~ **sb/sth from sth** (*formal*) to separate, a person, an idea, a subject, etc. from something; to keep two things separate: *They believed that art should be divorced from politics.* ♦ *When he was depressed, he felt utterly divorced from reality.*

di·vor·cé /də,vɔr'seɪ; -'si/ *noun* a man whose marriage has been legally ended

di·vorced 🔑 /də'vɔrst/ *adj.*
1 no longer married: *Many **divorced** men remarry and have second families.* ♦ *My parents are divorced.* ♦ *Are they going to **get divorced**?* ⊃ collocations at MARRIAGE **2** ~ **from sth** (*formal*) appearing not to be affected by something; separate from something: *He seems completely divorced from reality.*

di·vor·cée (also **di·vor·cee**) /də,vɔr'seɪ; -'si/ *noun* a woman whose marriage has been legally ended

div·ot /'dɪvət/ *noun* a piece of grass and earth that is dug out by accident, for example by a **CLUB** when someone is playing **GOLF**

di·vulge /də'vʌldʒ; daɪ-/ *verb* ~ **sth (to sb)** | ~ **what, whether, etc....** (*formal*) to give someone information that is supposed to be secret **SYN** REVEAL: *Police refused to divulge the identity of the suspect.*

div·vy /'dɪvi/ *verb* (**div·vies, div·vy·ing, div·vied, div·vied**) **PHR V** ,**divvy sth**↔'**up** (*informal*) to divide something, especially money, into two or more parts

Di·wa·li /dɪ'vɑli; dɪ'wɑli/ (also **Di·va·li**) *noun* [U] a Hindu festival that is held in the fall, celebrated by lighting CANDLES and CLAY lamps, and with FIREWORKS

Dix·ie /'dɪksi/ *noun* [U] an informal name for the SOUTHEASTERN states of the U.S.

'**Dixie Cup**™ *noun* a small paper cup

Dix·ie·land /'dɪksi,lænd/ *noun* [U] a type of traditional JAZZ

DIY /,di aɪ 'waɪ/ *noun* [U] the abbreviation for "do-it-yourself" (the activity of making, repairing or decorating things in the home yourself, instead of paying someone to do it): *a DIY store*

,**dizy·gotic** '**twin** /,daɪzaɪ,gɑtɪk 'twɪn/ (also **dizygous twin** /daɪ,zaɪgəs 'twɪn/) *adj.* (*technical*) = FRATERNAL TWIN ⊃ compare IDENTICAL TWIN

diz·zy /'dɪzi/ *adj.* (**diz·zi·er, diz·zi·est**) **1** feeling as if everything is spinning around you and that you are not able to

balance **SYN** GIDDY: *Climbing so high made me **feel dizzy**.* ♦ *I suffer from **dizzy spells** (= short periods when I am dizzy).* **2** making you feel dizzy; making you feel that a situation is changing very fast **SYN** GIDDY: *the dizzy descent from the summit* ♦ *the dizzy pace of life in Hong Kong* **3** (*informal*) silly or stupid: *a dizzy blonde* ▶ **diz·zi·ly** /'dɪzəli/ *adv.* **diz·zi·ness** *noun* [U]
IDM **the dizzy heights (of sth)** (*informal*) an important or impressive position

diz·zy·ing /'dɪziɪŋ/ *adj.* making you feel dizzy: *The car drove past at a dizzying speed.*

DJ /'di dʒeɪ/ *noun, verb*
● *noun* the abbreviation for DISC JOCKEY
● *verb* (**DJ's, DJ'ing, DJ'd, DJ'd**) [I] to perform as a DISC JOCKEY, especially in a club

djinn /dʒɪn/ *noun* (in Arabian stories) a spirit with magic powers **SYN** GENIE

DMA /,di ɛm 'eɪ/ *noun* [U] the abbreviation for "direct memory access" (a system that allows a device attached to a computer to take data from the computer's memory without using the CENTRAL PROCESSING UNIT)

DNA /,di ɛn 'eɪ/ *noun* [U] (*chemistry*) deoxyribonucleic acid (the chemical in the cells of animals and plants that carries GENETIC information and is a type of NUCLEIC ACID): *a DNA test*

,**DNA** '**fingerprinting** *noun* [U] = GENETIC FINGERPRINT-ING

do[1] 🔑 *verb, auxiliary verb, noun* ⊃ IRREGULAR VERBS on page R5 ⊃ see also DO[2]
● *verb* /du/
> **ACTION** **1** [T] ~ **sth** used to refer to actions that you do not mention by name or that you do not know about: *What are you doing this evening?* ♦ *We will do what we can to help.* ♦ *Are you doing anything tomorrow evening?* ♦ *The company ought to do something about the poor service.* ♦ *What have you done to your hair?* ♦ *There's **nothing to do** (= no means of passing the time in an enjoyable way) in this place.* ♦ *There's **nothing we can do** about it (= we can't change the situation).* ♦ *What can I do for you (= how can I help)?*
> **BEHAVE** **2** [I] to act or behave in the way mentioned: ~ **as...** *Do as you're told!* ♦ *They are free to do as they please.* ♦ + **adv./ prep.** *You would **do well to** (= I advise you to) consider all the options before buying.*
> **SUCCEED/PROGRESS** **3** [I] + **adv./prep.** used to ask or talk about the success or progress of someone or something: *How is the business doing?* ♦ *He's **doing very well** at school (= his work is good).* ♦ *Both mother and baby are **doing well** (= after the birth of the baby).* ♦ (*informal*) *How are you doing (= how are you)?*
> **TASK/ACTIVITY** **4** [T] ~ **sth** to work at or perform an activity or a task: *I'm doing some research on the subject.* ♦ *I have a number of things to do today.* ♦ *I do aerobics once a week.* ♦ (*informal*) *Let's do (= meet for) lunch.* ♦ *Sorry. I don't do funny (= I can't be funny).* **5** [T] ~ **sth** used with nouns to talk about tasks such as cleaning, washing, arranging, etc.: *to do (= wash) the dishes* ♦ *to do (= arrange) the flowers* ♦ *I like the way you've done your hair.* **6** [T] to perform the activity or task mentioned ~ **the ironing, cooking, shopping, etc.**: *I like listening to the radio when I'm doing the ironing.* ♦ ~ **some, a little, etc. acting, writing, etc.** *She did a lot of acting when she was at college.*
> **JOB** **7** [T] ~ **sth** (usually used in questions) to work at something as a job: *What do you do (= what is your job)?* ♦ *What does she want to do when she leaves school?* ♦ *What did she do for a living?* ♦ *What's Tom doing these days?*
> **SOLVE** **8** [T] ~ **sth** to find the answer to something; to solve something: *I can't do this math problem.* ♦ *Are you good at doing crosswords?*
> **MAKE** **9** [T] to produce or make something: ~ **sth** *to do a drawing/painting/sketch* ♦ *Who's doing (= organizing and preparing) the food for the wedding reception?* ⊃ thesaurus box at MAKE

PERFORM 10 [T] ~ sth to perform or produce a play, an OPERA, etc.: *The local dramatic society is doing "Hamlet" next month.*

COPY SOMEONE 11 [T] ~ sb/sth to copy someone's behavior or the way someone speaks, sings, etc., especially in order to make people laugh: *He does a great Elvis Presley.* ♦ *Can you do a Southern accent?*

FINISH 12 [I, T] to finish something **be/have done** *Sit there and wait till I'm done.* ♦ **be/have done doing sth** *I'm done talking—let's get started.* ♦ **get sth done** *Did you get your article done in time?*

TRAVEL 13 [T] ~ sth to travel a particular distance: *How many miles did you do during your tour?* **14** [T] ~ sth to complete a trip: *We did the round trip in two hours.*

SPEED 15 [T] ~ sth to travel at or reach a particular speed: *The car was doing 90 miles an hour.*

VISIT 16 [T] ~ sth (*informal*) to visit a place as a tourist: *We did Tokyo in three days.*

SPEND TIME 17 [T] ~ sth to spend a period of time doing something: *She did a year at college, but then dropped out.* ♦ *He did six years* (= in prison) *for armed robbery.*

DEAL WITH 18 [T] ~ sb/sth to deal with or attend to someone or something: *The hairdresser said she could do me* (= cut my hair) *at three.*

BE SUITABLE/ENOUGH 19 [I, T] to be suitable or be enough for someone or something: *"Can you lend me some money?" "Sure— will $20 do?"* ♦ ~ **for sb/sth** *These shoes won't do for the party.* ♦ ~ **as sth** *The box will do fine as a table.* ♦ ~ **sb (+ adv./prep.)** *This room will do me nicely, thank you* (= it has everything I need).

COOK 20 [T] ~ sth to cook something: *How would you like your steak done?*

STEAL 21 [T] ~ sth (*informal*) to steal from a place: *The gang did a warehouse and a supermarket.*

TAKE DRUGS 22 [T] ~ sth (*informal*) to take an illegal drug: *He doesn't smoke, drink or do drugs.*

HAVE SEX 23 [T] ~ **it** (*slang*) to have sex

IDM Most idioms containing **do** are at the entries for the nouns and adjectives in the idioms. For example, **do sth to death** is at **death**. **be/have to do with sb/sth** to be about or connected with someone or something: *"What do you want to see me about?" "It's to do with that letter you sent me."* **have (got) something, nothing, a lot, etc. to do with sb/sth** to talk about how much someone or something is connected with someone or something else: *Her job has something to do with computers.* ♦ *"How much do you earn?" "What's it got to do with you?"* ♦ *Hard work has a lot to do with* (= is an important reason for) *her success.* ♦ *We don't have very much to do with our neighbors* (= we do not speak to them very often). ♦ *I'd have nothing to do with him, if I were you.* **it won't do** used to say that a situation is not acceptable and should be changed or improved: *This is the third time you've been late this week; it simply won't do.* **not do anything/a lot/much for sb** (*informal*) used to say that something does not make someone look attractive: *That hairstyle doesn't do anything for her.* **nothing doing** (*informal*) used to refuse a request: *"Can you lend me ten dollars?" "Nothing doing!"* **no you don't** (*informal*) used to show that you intend to stop someone from doing something that they were going to do: *Sharon went to get into the taxi. "Oh no you don't," said Steve.* **that does it** (*informal*) used to show that you will not accept something any longer: *That does it, I'm out of here. You can't talk to me like that.* **that will do** used to order someone to stop doing or saying something: *That'll do, children—you're getting much too noisy.* **what do you do for sth?** used to ask how someone manages to obtain the thing mentioned: *What do you do for entertainment out here?* **what is sb/sth doing…?** used to ask why someone or something is in the place mentioned: *What are these shoes doing on my desk?*

PHR V **do a way with sb/yourself** (*informal*) to kill someone/yourself **do a way with sth** (*informal*) to stop doing or having something; to make something end **SYN** ABOLISH: *He thinks it's time we did away with the $50 fine.* **do sb/yourself 'in** (*informal*) **1** to kill someone/yourself **2** [usually passive] to make someone very tired: *The long*

hike really did me in. **do sb 'out of sth** (*informal*) to unfairly prevent someone from having what they ought to have: *She was done out of her promotion.* **do sth↔'over 1** to clean or decorate something again: *The paintwork will need to be done over soon.* **2** to do something again: *She insisted that everything be done over.* **do 'up** to be fastened: *The skirt does up at the back.* **do sth↔'up 1** to fasten a coat, skirt, etc.: *He never bothers to do his jacket up.* **ANT** UNDO **2** to make something into a package **SYN** WRAP: *She was carrying a package done up in brown paper.* **3** to repair and decorate a house, etc.: *He makes money by buying old houses and doing them up.* **do yourself 'up** (*informal*) to make yourself more attractive by putting on MAKEUP, attractive clothes, etc. **'do sth with sb/sth** (used in negative sentences and questions with *what*): *I don't know what to do with* (= how to use) *all the food that's left over.* ♦ *What have you done with* (= where have you put) *my umbrella?* ♦ *What have you been doing with yourselves* (= how have you been passing the time)? ⊃ see also COULD DO WITH **do with'out (sb/sth)** to manage without someone or something: *She can't do without an assistant.* ♦ *If they can't get it to us in time, we'll just have to do without.* ♦ ~ **doing sth** (*ironic*) *I could have done without being* (= I wish I had not been) *woken up at three in the morning.*

VOCABULARY BUILDING

household jobs: do or make?

- To write or talk about jobs in the home, you can use such phrases as **wash the dishes**, **clean the kitchen floor**, **set the table**, etc. In conversation, the verb **do** is often used instead: *Let me do the dishes.* ♦ *Michael said he would do the kitchen floor.* ♦ *It's your turn to do the bathroom.* **Do** is often used with nouns ending *-ing*: *to do the shopping/cleaning/ironing/vacuuming*
- The verb **make** is used especially in the phrase **make the beds** and when you are talking about preparing or cooking food: *He makes a great lasagna.* ♦ *I'll make breakfast while you take a shower.* You can also say **get ready** and **fix** for preparing meals: *Can you get dinner ready while I put the kids to bed?* ♦ *Sit down — I'll fix supper for you.*

● **auxiliary verb** /də; dʊ; *strong form* du/ **1** used before a full verb to form negative sentences and questions: *I don't like fish.* ♦ *They didn't go to Paris.* ♦ *Don't forget to write.* ♦ *Does she speak French?* **2** used to make QUESTION TAGS (= short questions at the end of statements): *You live in New York, don't you?* ♦ *She doesn't work here, does she?* **3** used to avoid repeating a full verb: *He plays better than he did a year ago.* ♦ *She works harder than he does.* ♦ *"Who won?" "I did." ♦ "I love peaches." "So do I." ♦ "I don't want to go back." "Neither do I."* **4** used when no other auxiliary verb is present, to emphasize what you are saying: *He does look tired.* ♦ *She did at least write to say thank you.* ♦ *Do shut up!* **5** used to change the order of the subject and verb when an adverb is moved to the front: *Not only does she speak Spanish, she's also good with computers.*

● **noun** /du/ (*pl.* **dos** or **do's** /duz/) (*informal*) a party; a social event: *Are you having a big do for your birthday?* **IDM** **dos and don'ts** (also **do's and don'ts**) (*informal*) rules that you should follow: *Here are some dos and don'ts for exercise during pregnancy.* ⊃ more at FAIR *adj.*

do² /dou/ *noun* (*music*) the 1st and 8th note of a MAJOR SCALE ⊃ see also DO¹

do. *abbr.* DITTO

DOA /ˌdi oʊ ˈeɪ/ *abbr.* = DEAD ON ARRIVAL at DEAD, *adj.*

do·a·ble /ˈduəbl/ *adj.* [not usually before noun] (*informal*) able to be done: *It's not doable by Friday.* ⊃ compare FEASIBLE

D.O.B. *abbr.* date of birth

Do·ber·man /ˈdoʊbərmən/ (also **Do·ber·man 'pin·scher** /ˌdoʊbərmən ˈpɪnʃər/) *noun* a large dog with short dark hair, often used for guarding buildings

h **h**at   m **m**an   n **n**o   ŋ si**ng**   l **l**eg   r **r**ed   y **y**es   w **w**et

doc /dɑk/ noun (informal) a way of addressing or talking about a doctor

do·cent /'doʊsnt/ noun a person whose job is to show tourists around a museum, etc. and talk to them about it

doc·ile /'dɑsl/ adj. quiet and easy to control: a docile child/horse ▶ **doc·ile·ly** /'dɑsəli/ adv. **do·cil·i·ty** /dɑ'sɪləti/ noun [U]

dock /dɑk/ noun, verb
- **noun 1** [C] a part of a port where ships are repaired, or where goods are put onto or taken off them: dock workers ◆ The ship was **in dock**. ➔ see also DRY DOCK **2 docks** [pl.] a group of docks in a port and the buildings around them that are used for repairing ships, storing goods, etc. **3** [C] a long low structure built along, or out from, the shore of a lake, river, or the ocean, used by boats to allow passengers to get on and off SYN WHARF, PIER **4** [C] a raised platform for loading vehicles or trains **5** [C] the part of a court where the person who has been accused of a crime stands or sits during a trial: He's been **in the dock** (= on trial for a crime) several times already.
- **verb 1** [I, T] ~ (sth) if a ship **docks** or you **dock** a ship, it sails into a HARBOR and stays there: The ferry is expected to dock at 6. **2** [I, T] ~ (sth) if two SPACECRAFT dock, or are docked, they are joined together in space: Next year, a technology module will be docked on the space station. **3** [T] to take away part of someone's pay, etc.: ~ sth If you're late, your pay will be docked. ◆ ~ sth **from/off** sth They've docked 15% off my pay for this week. **4** [T] ~ sth (computing) to connect a computer to a DOCKING STATION ANT UNDOCK **5** [T] ~ sth to cut an animal's tail short

dock·er /'dɑkər/ noun a person whose job is moving goods on and off ships

dock·et /'dɑkət/ noun **1** (also 'docket sheet) a list of cases to be dealt with in a particular court **2** a list of items to be discussed at a meeting

'**docking** ¡station noun (computing) a device to which a LAPTOP computer can be connected so that it can be used like a DESKTOP computer

dock·side /'dɑksaɪd/ noun [sing.] the area around the DOCK (= the place where ships are loaded and unloaded) in a port

dock·yard /'dɑkyɑrd/ noun an area with DOCKS (= the place where ships are loaded and unloaded in a port) and equipment for building and repairing ships

doc·tor 🖉 /'dɑktər/ noun, verb
- **noun** (abbr. **Dr.**) **1** a person who has been trained in medical science, whose job is to treat people who are sick or injured: You'd better **see a doctor** about that cough. ◆ Doctor Staples (= as a title/form of address) **2** a person who has received the highest university degree: a Doctor of Philosophy/Law ◆ Doctor Franks (= as a title/form of address) **3** used as a title or form of address for a dentist **IDM just what the doctor ordered** (humorous) exactly what someone wants or needs
- **verb 1** [T] ~ sth to change something in order to trick someone SYN FALSIFY: He was accused of doctoring the figures. **2** [T] ~ sth to add something harmful to food or drink: The wine had been doctored. **3** [I, T] ~ (sb) to treat people who are sick or injured: He's been doctoring in a small town.

doc·tor·al /'dɑktərəl/ adj. [only before noun] connected with a doctorate: a doctoral dissertation

doc·tor·ate /'dɑktərət/ noun the highest university degree: She's studying for her doctorate.

doc·tri·naire /ˌdɑktrə'ner/ adj. (disapproving) strictly following a theory in all circumstances, even if there are practical problems or disagreement: a doctrinaire communist ◆ doctrinaire attitudes/beliefs/policies

doc·tri·nal /'dɑktrənl/ adj. (formal) relating to a doctrine or doctrines: the doctrinal position of the English Church ◆ (disapproving) a rigidly doctrinal approach ▶ **doc·tri·nal·ly** /-nəli/ adv.

doc·trine /'dɑktrən/ noun **1** [C, U] a belief or set of beliefs held and taught by a Church, a political party, etc.: Christian doctrine **2 Doctrine** [C] a statement of government policy: the Monroe Doctrine

doc·u·dra·ma /'dɑkyəˌdrɑmə/ noun a movie, usually made for television, in which real events are shown in the form of a story

doc·u·ment 🖉 **AWL** noun, verb
- **noun** /'dɑkyəmənt/ **1** an official paper or book that gives information about something, or that can be used as evidence or proof of something: legal documents ◆ travel documents ◆ Copies of the relevant documents must be filed in court. ◆ One of the documents leaked to the press was a memorandum written by the chief of police. **2** a computer file that contains text that has a name that identifies it: Save the document before closing.
- **verb** /'dɑkyəˌmɛnt/ **1** ~ sth to record the details of something: Causes of the disease have been well documented. **2** ~ sth to prove or support something with documents: documented evidence

doc·u·men·ta·ry /ˌdɑkyə'mɛntəri; -'mɛntri/ noun, adj.
- **noun** (pl. **doc·u·men·ta·ries**) a film or a radio or television program giving facts about something: a television documentary about/on the future of nuclear power ➔ collocations at TELEVISION
- **adj.** [only before noun] **1** consisting of documents: documentary evidence/sources/material **2** giving a record of or report on the facts about something, especially by using pictures, recordings, etc. of people involved: a documentary film about the war

doc·u·men·ta·tion **AWL** /ˌdɑkyəmən'teɪʃn; -mɛn-/ noun [U] **1** the documents that are required for something, or that give evidence or proof of something: I couldn't enter the country because I didn't have all the necessary documentation. **2** the act of recording something in a document; the state of being recorded in a document: the documentation of an agreement

'**document** ¡case noun a soft flat case without a handle, usually made from leather, plastic, etc., and used for holding and carrying documents

DOD /ˌdi oʊ 'di/ abbr. Department of Defense (the government department in the U.S. that is responsible for defense)

dod·der·ing /'dɑdərɪŋ/ adj. weak, slow, and not able to walk in a steady way, especially because you are old

do·dec·a·he·dron /ˌdoʊdɛkə'hidrən/ noun (geometry) a solid figure with twelve flat sides

do·dec·a·phon·ic /ˌdoʊdɛkə'fɑnɪk/ adj. (music) = TWELVE-NOTE

dodge /dɑdʒ/ verb, noun
- **verb 1** [T, I] to move quickly and suddenly to one side in order to avoid someone or something: He ran across the road, dodging the traffic. ◆ **(+ adv./prep.)** The girl dodged behind a tree to hide from the other children. **2** [T] to avoid doing something, especially in a dishonest way: ~ sth He dodged his military service. ◆ ~ **doing** sth She tried to dodge paying her taxes. ◆ He tried to **dodge the question/issue** (= avoid giving an answer) by changing the subject.
- **noun** a dishonest trick, played in order to avoid something: a tax dodge ◆ When it comes to getting off work, he knows all the dodges.

dodge·ball /'dɑdʒbɔl/ noun [U] a game in which teams of players try to hit other teams with a large ball

dodg·er /'dɑdʒər/ noun (informal) a person who dishonestly avoids doing something: tax dodgers ◆ a crackdown on fare dodgers on trains ➔ see also DRAFT DODGER

do·do /'doʊdoʊ/ noun (pl. **do·dos**) **1** a large bird that could not fly and that is now EXTINCT (= no longer exists) **2** a stupid person

DOE /ˌdi oʊ 'i/ abbr. Department of Energy (the U.S.

| i see | ɪ sit | ɛ ten | æ cat | ɑ hot | ɔ saw | ʊ put | u too | 439 |

government department that plans and controls the development of the country's sources of energy)

doe /doʊ/ *noun* a female DEER, RABBIT or HARE ⊃ compare BUCK, HIND, STAG

do·er /'duər/ *noun* (*approving*) a person who does things rather than thinking or talking about them: *We need fewer organizers and more doers.*

does /dəz; *strong form* dʌz/ ⊃ DO[1]

does·n't /'dʌznt/ *short form* does not

doff /dɑf; dɔf/ *verb* ~ **sth** (*old-fashioned*) to take off your hat, especially to show respect for someone or something

dog 🐕 /dɔg; dɑg/ *noun, verb*
● *noun* **1** [C] an animal with four legs and a tail, often kept as a pet or trained for work, for example hunting or guarding buildings. There are many types of dogs, some of which are wild: *I took the dog for a walk.* ◆ *I could hear a dog barking.* ◆ *dog food* ◆ *guard dogs* ◆ *a dog and her puppies* ⊃ see also GUIDE DOG, GUN DOG, HEARING DOG, LAPDOG, PRAIRIE DOG, SHEEPDOG **2** [C] a male dog, FOX or WOLF ⊃ compare BITCH **3** [C] (*informal*) a thing of low quality; a failure: *Her last movie was an absolute dog.* **4** [C] (*informal*) an offensive way of describing a woman who is not considered attractive **5** [C] (*informal, disapproving*) used, especially after an adjective, to describe a man who has done something bad: *You dirty dog!* ⊃ see also HOT DOG, SHAGGY-DOG STORY, TOP DOG, WATCHDOG
IDM **a dog and pony show** (*informal, disapproving*) an event that is planned only in order to impress people so that they will support or buy something **(a case of) dog eat dog** a situation in business, politics, etc. where there is a lot of competition and people are willing to harm each other in order to succeed: *I'm afraid in this line of work it's a case of dog eat dog.* ◆ *We're operating in a dog-eat-dog world.* **a dog in the manger** a person who stops other people from enjoying what he or she cannot use or does not want **a dog's life** an unhappy life, full of problems or unfair treatment **every dog has his/its day** (*saying*) everyone has good luck or success at some point in their life **go to the dogs** (*informal*) to get into a very bad state: *This company's gone to the dogs since the new management took over.* ⊃ more at FIGHT *v.*, HAIR, RAIN, SICK *adj.*, SLEEP *v.*, TAIL, TEACH
● *verb* (-gg-) **1** ~ **sb/sth** (of a problem or bad luck) to cause you trouble for a long time: *He had been dogged by bad health all his life.* **2** ~ **sb/sth** to follow someone closely: *She had the impression that someone was dogging her steps.*

'**dog** ˌ**biscuit** *noun* a small hard cookie fed to dogs

dog·catch·er /'dɔgˌkætʃər; 'dɑg-/ (*becoming old-fashioned*) (also *formal* ˌ**animal conˈtrol ˌofficer**) *noun* a person whose job is to catch dogs and cats that are walking freely in the streets and do not seem to have a home

'**dog** ˌ**collar** *noun* **1** a COLLAR for a dog **2** (*informal*) a stiff white COLLAR fastened at the back and worn by some Christian priests

'**dog days** *noun* [pl.] the hottest period of the year

'**dog-eared** /'dɔgɪrd/ *adj.* (of a book) used so much that the corners of many of the pages are turned down

dog·fight /'dɔgfaɪt; 'dɑg-/ *noun* **1** a fight between aircraft in which they fly around close to each other **2** a struggle between two people or groups in order to win something **3** dog fight a fight between dogs, especially one that is arranged illegally, for entertainment ▶ **dog·fight·ing** *noun* [U]

dog·fish /'dɔgfɪʃ; 'dɑg-/ *noun* (*pl.* **dog·fish**) a small SHARK (= an aggressive sea fish with very sharp teeth)

dog·ged /'dɔgəd; 'dɑ-/ *adj.* [usually before noun] (*approving*) showing determination; not giving up easily **SYN** TENACIOUS: *dogged determination/persistence* ◆ *their dogged defense of the city* ▶ **dog·ged·ly** *adv.* **SYN** TENACIOUSLY **dog·ged·ness** *noun* [U] **SYN** TENACITY

dog·ger·el /'dɔgərəl; 'dɑg-/ *noun* [U] poetry that is badly

written or ridiculous, sometimes because the writer has not intended to be serious

dog·gone /'dɔggɔn; -gɑn/ *adj.* [only before noun], *adv.*, *exclamation* (*informal*) used to show that you are annoyed or surprised: *Where's the doggone key?* ◆ *Don't drive so doggone fast.* ◆ *Well, doggone it!*

dog·gy /'dɔgi; 'dɑ-/ *noun, adj.*
● *noun* (also **dog·gie**) (*pl.* **dog·gies**) (*informal*) a child's word for a dog
● *adj.* [only before noun] of or like a dog: *a doggy smell*

'**doggy** ˌ**bag** (also ˈ**doggie bag**) *noun* (*informal*) a bag for taking home any food that is left after a meal in a restaurant

'**doggy-ˌpaddle** *noun* = DOG-PADDLE

'**dog** ˌ**handler** *noun* a police officer who works with a trained dog

dog·house /'dɔghaʊs; 'dɑg-/ *noun* a small shelter for a dog to sleep in **SYN** KENNEL
IDM **be in the doghouse** (*informal*) if you are **in the doghouse**, someone is annoyed with you because of something that you have done

do·gie /'doʊgi/ *noun* a young cow that has lost its mother

dog·leg /'dɔglɛg; 'dɑg-/ *noun* a sharp bend, especially in a road or on a GOLF COURSE

dog·ma /'dɔgmə; 'dɑg-/ *noun* [U, C] (often *disapproving*) a belief or set of beliefs held by a group or organization, that others are expected to accept without argument: *political/ religious/party dogma* ◆ *one of the central dogmas of the Church*

dog·mat·ic /dɔg'mætɪk; dɑg-/ *adj.* (*disapproving*) being certain that your beliefs are right and that others should accept them, without paying attention to evidence or other opinions: *a dogmatic approach* ◆ *There is a danger of becoming too dogmatic about teaching methods.* ▶ **dog·mat·i·cally** /-kli/ *adv.*

dog·ma·tism /'dɔgmətɪzəm; 'dɑg-/ *noun* [U] (*disapproving*) behavior and attitudes that are dogmatic

do-good·er /'du ˌgʊdər/ *noun* (*informal, disapproving*) a person who tries to help other people but who does it in a way that is annoying

'**dog-ˌpaddle** (also ˈ**doggy-ˌpaddle**) *noun* [U] a simple swimming stroke, with short quick movements like those of a dog in the water

dog·sled /'dɔgslɛd; 'dɑg-/ *noun* a SLED (= a vehicle that slides over snow) pulled by dogs, used especially in Canada and Alaska

'**dog tag** *noun* (*slang*) a small piece of metal that U.S. soldiers wear around their necks with their name and number on it

ˌ**dog-ˈtired** *adj.* [not usually before noun] (*informal*) very tired **SYN** EXHAUSTED

dog·wood /'dɔgwʊd; 'dɑg-/ *noun* [U, C] a bush or small tree with red or pink berries (BERRY) and red STEMS, that grows in northern regions; the hard wood of this tree

d'oh /doʊ/ *exclamation* (*informal*) used when you have just said or done something that you know is stupid: *D'oh! That was the biggest mistake ever.* **ORIGIN** Used by Homer Simpson in *The Simpsons* television series.

DOI /ˌdi oʊ 'aɪ/ *abbr.* **1** (*computing*) digital object identifier (a series of numbers and letters that identifies a particular text or document published in electronic form on the Internet) **2** Department of the Interior (the U.S. government department responsible for protecting the country's environment)

doi·ly /'dɔɪli/ *noun* (*pl.* **doi·lies**) **1** a small circle of paper or cloth with a pattern of very small holes in it, that you put on a plate under a cake or SANDWICH **2** a small decorative MAT that you put on top of a piece of furniture

do·ing /'duɪŋ/ *noun* [C, usually pl., U] a thing done or caused by someone: *I've been hearing a lot about your doings recently.* ◆ *I promise you this was not my doing* (= I didn't do it).
IDM **take some doing | take a lot of doing** to be hard

ʌ **cup**   ə **about**   eɪ **say**   aɪ **five**   ɔɪ **boy**   aʊ **now**   oʊ **go**   ər **bird**

work; to be difficult: *Getting it finished by tomorrow will take some doing.*

do-it-your·self *noun* [U] = DIY: *The materials you need are available from any good do-it-yourself store.*

do·jo /ˈdoʊdʒoʊ/ *noun* (*pl.* -os) (from *Japanese*) a hall or school where JUDO or other similar MARTIAL ARTS (= fighting sports) are practiced

Dol·by™ /ˈdoʊlbi/ *noun* [U] a system for reducing background noise in sound recordings

dol·drums /ˈdoʊldrəmz; ˈdɔl-; ˈdɑl-/ *noun* [pl.] usually **the doldrums 1** the state of feeling sad or depressed: *He's been in the doldrums ever since she left him.* **2** a lack of activity or improvement: *The bond market normally revives after the summer doldrums.* ◆ *Despite these measures, the economy remains in the doldrums.* **ORIGIN** From the place in the ocean near the equator where there are sudden periods of calm. A sailing ship caught in this area can be stuck there because of a lack of wind.

dole /doʊl/ *noun, verb*
● *noun* [sing.] usually **the dole** (*informal*) payments or goods given by the government or a charity to people who are poor or unemployed
● *verb*
PHR V ˌdole sth↔ˈout (to sb) to give out an amount of food, money, etc. to a number of people in a group

dole·ful /ˈdoʊlfl/ *adj.* very sad **SYN** MOURNFUL: *a doleful expression/face/song* ◆ *a doleful looking man* ▶ **dole·ful·ly** /-fəli/ *adv.*

doll /dɑl/ *noun, verb*
● *noun* **1** a child's toy in the shape of a person, especially a baby or a child: *a rag doll* (= one made out of cloth) ⊃ see also PAPER DOLL **2** (*informal*) a very nice or generous person: *Would you be a doll and bring me my purse?* **3** (*old-fashioned, informal*) a word used to describe a pretty or attractive woman, now often considered offensive: *She's quite a doll.*
● *verb*
PHR V ˌdoll sb/yourself ˈup (*old-fashioned, informal*) to make someone/yourself look attractive for a party, etc., with fashionable clothes: *Are you getting dolled up for the party?*

dol·lar 🔑 /ˈdɑlər/ *noun*
1 [C] (*symb.* **$**) the unit of money in the U.S., Canada, Australia and several other countries: *You will be paid in American dollars.* ⊃ compare BUCK ⊃ see also DOLLAR SIGN, TOP DOLLAR [C] a BANKNOTE or coin worth one dollar: *Do you have a dollar?* ◆ *a dollar bill* ⊃ see also SILVER DOLLAR **3 the dollar** [sing.] (*finance*) the value of the U.S. dollar compared with the value of the money of other countries: *The dollar closed two cents down.* **IDM** see BET *v.*, DOLLAR SIGN, MILLION

dol·lar·ize /ˈdɑləˌraɪz/ *verb* [T, I] ~ **(sth)** (of a country) to start using the U.S. dollar as its own CURRENCY ▶ **dol·lar·i·za·tion** /ˌdɑlərəˈzeɪʃn/ *noun* [U]

ˈdollar ˌsign *noun* (*symb.* **$**) the sign that you put before a number to show that it represents an amount in dollars **IDM** (see) **dollar signs** (*informal*) to think about how you can make a lot of money from a situation or person: *She looked at the wealthy widower and saw only dollar signs.* ◆ *Many inventors with dollar signs in their eyes are eager to come up with the latest gadget.*

doll·house /ˈdɑlhaʊs/ *noun* a toy house with small furniture and sometimes DOLLS in it for children to play with ⊃ picture at TOY

dol·lop /ˈdɑləp/ *noun* (*informal*) **1** a lump of soft food, often dropped from a spoon: *a dollop of whipped cream* **2** an amount of something: *A dollop of romance now and then is good for everyone.*

dol·ly /ˈdɑli/ *noun* (*pl.* dol·lies) **1** a child's word for a DOLL **2** a low platform on wheels for moving heavy objects

dol·men /ˈdoʊlmən; ˈdɔl-; ˈdɑl-/ *noun* a pair or group of

vertical stones with a large flat stone on top, built in ancient times to mark a place where someone was buried

dol·or·ous /ˈdoʊlərəs/ *adj.* [usually before noun] (*literary*) feeling or showing great sadness

dol·phin /ˈdɑlfən; ˈdɔl-/ *noun* a sea animal (a MAMMAL) that looks like a large fish with a pointed mouth. Dolphins are very intelligent and often friendly toward humans. There are several types of dolphins: *a school of dolphins* ⊃ compare PORPOISE

dolphin

dol·phi·nar·i·um /ˌdɑlfəˈnɛriəm; ˌdɔl-/ *noun* (*pl.* dol·phi·nar·i·ums or dol·phi·nar·ia /-ˈnɛriə/) a building with a pool where people can go to see dolphins, especially ones who have been trained to do tricks

dolt /doʊlt/ *noun* (*disapproving*) a stupid person **SYN** IDIOT ▶ **dolt·ish** /ˈdoʊltɪʃ/ *adj.*

-dom /dəm/ *suffix* (in nouns) **1** the condition or state of: *freedom* ◆ *martyrdom* **2** the rank of; an area ruled by: *kingdom* **3** the group of: *officialdom*

do·main **AWL** /doʊˈmeɪn; də-/ *noun* **1** an area of knowledge or activity; especially one that someone is responsible for: *The care of older people is being placed firmly within the domain of the family.* ◆ *Physics used to be very much a male domain.* ⊃ see also PUBLIC DOMAIN **2** lands owned or ruled by a particular person, government, etc., especially in the past: *The Spice Islands were within the Spanish domains.* **3** (*computing*) a set of Web sites on the Internet which end with the same group of letters, for example ".com" or ".org" **4** (*mathematics*) the range of possible values of a particular VARIABLE

doˈmain name *noun* (*computing*) a name that identifies a Web site or group of Web sites on the Internet

dome /doʊm/ *noun* **1** a round roof with a CIRCULAR base: *the dome of St. Paul's Cathedral* ⊃ picture at ARCHITECTURE **2** a thing or a building shaped like a dome: *his bald dome of a head* **3** (in names) a sports STADIUM with a roof shaped like a dome: *the Houston Astrodome*

domed /doʊmd/ *adj.* [usually before noun] having or shaped like a dome: *a domed forehead/ceiling*

do·mes·tic 🔑 **AWL** /dəˈmɛstɪk/ *adj., noun*
● *adj.* **1** [usually before noun] of or inside a particular country; not foreign or international: *domestic affairs/politics* ◆ *domestic flights* (= to and from places within a country) ◆ *Output consists of both exports and sales on the domestic market.* **ANT** FOREIGN **2** [only before noun] used in the home; connected with the home or family: *domestic appliances* ◆ *domestic chores* ◆ *the growing problem of domestic violence* (= violence between members of the same family) ◆ *domestic service* (= the work of a servant in a large house) ◆ *domestic help* (= help with the work in a house; the person or people who do this work) **3** liking home life; enjoying or good at cooking, cleaning the house, etc.: *I'm not a very domestic sort of person.* **4** (of animals) kept on farms or as pets; not wild ▶ **do·mes·ti·cal·ly** **AWL** /-kli/ *adv.*: *domestically produced goods*
● *noun* (also ˌdomestic ˈworker) (*old-fashioned*) a servant who works in someone's house, doing the cleaning and other jobs

do·mes·ti·cate **AWL** /dəˈmɛstəˌkeɪt/ *verb* **1** ~ **sth** to make a wild animal used to living with or working for humans **2** ~ **sth** to grow plants or crops for human use **SYN** CULTIVATE **3** ~ **sb** (often *humorous*) to make someone good at cooking, caring for a house, etc.; to make someone enjoy home life: *Some men are very hard to domesticate.* ▶ **do·mes·ti·cated** **AWL** *adj.*: *domesticated animals* ◆ *They've become a lot more domesticated since they got married.* **do·mes·ti·ca·tion** /dəˌmɛstəˈkeɪʃn/ *noun* [U]: *the domestication of cattle*

do·mes·tic·i·ty /ˌdoʊmɛˈstɪsəti/ *noun* [U] home or family life: *an atmosphere of happy domesticity*

do·mestic ˈpartner *noun* used to describe the sexual partner that someone lives with, especially when they are not married

ˈdome tent *noun* a tent which forms the shape of a dome ⊃ compare A-FRAME TENT, WALL TENT

dom·i·cile /ˈdaməˌsaɪl; ˈdoʊ-/ *noun* (*formal* or *law*) the place where someone lives, especially when it is stated for official or legal purposes

dom·i·ciled /ˈdaməˌsaɪld; ˈdoʊ-/ *adj.* [not before noun] (*formal* or *law*) living in a particular place: *to be domiciled in the United States*

dom·i·cil·i·ar·y /ˌdaməˈsɪliˌɛri/ *adj.* [only before noun] (*formal*) in someone's home: *a domiciliary visit* (= for example, by a doctor) ♦ *domiciliary care/services/treatment*

dom·i·nant AWL /ˈdamənənt/ *adj.* **1** more important, powerful or noticeable than other things: *The company has achieved a dominant position in the world market.* ♦ *The dominant feature of the room was the large fireplace.* **2** (*biology*) a **dominant** GENE causes a person to have a particular physical characteristic, for example brown eyes, even if only one of their parents has passed on this GENE ⊃ compare RECESSIVE ▶ **dom·i·nance** AWL /-nəns/ *noun* [U]: *to achieve/assert dominance over someone* ♦ *political/economic dominance*

dom·i·nate 🔑 AWL /ˈdaməˌneɪt/ *verb* **1** [T, I] ~ (sb/sth) to control or have a lot of influence over someone or something, especially in an unpleasant way: *As a child he was dominated by his father.* ♦ *He tended to dominate the conversation.* ♦ *She always says a lot in meetings, but she doesn't dominate.* **2** [T] ~ sth to be the most important or noticeable feature of something: *The train crash dominated the news.* **3** [T] ~ sth to be the largest, highest, or most obvious thing in a place: *The cathedral dominates the city.* **4** [T, I] ~ (sth) (*sports*) to play much better than your opponent in a game: *He dominated in the first game of the chess match.* ▶ **dom·i·na·tion** AWL /ˌdaməˈneɪʃn/ *noun* [U]: *political domination* ♦ *companies fighting for domination of the software market*

dom·i·na·trix /ˌdaməˈneɪtrɪks/ *noun* (*pl.* **dom·i·na·tri·ces** /-trəsiz/, **dom·i·na·trix·es**) a woman who controls a man during sex, often using violence to give sexual pleasure

dom·i·neer·ing /ˌdaməˈnɪrɪŋ/ *adj.* (*disapproving*) trying to control other people without considering their opinions or feelings: *a cold and domineering father* ♦ *a domineering manner*

Do·min·i·can /dəˈmɪnɪkən/ *noun* a member of a Christian group of MONKS or NUNS following the rules of St. Dominic ▶ **Do·min·i·can** *adj.*

do·min·ion /dəˈmɪnyən/ *noun* **1** [U] ~ (over sb/sth) (*literary*) authority to rule; control: *Man has dominion over the natural world.* ♦ *Soon the whole country was under his sole dominion.* **2** [C] (*formal*) an area controlled by one ruler: *the vast dominions of the Roman Empire* **3** often **Dominion** [C] (in the past) any of the countries of the British Commonwealth that had their own government ⊃ compare COLONY, PROTECTORATE

dom·i·no /ˈdaməˌnoʊ/ *noun* (*pl.* **dom·i·noes**) **1** [C] a small flat block, often made of wood, marked on one side with two groups of dots representing numbers, used for playing games ⊃ picture at TOY **2 dominoes** [U] a game played with a set of dominoes, in which players take turns to put them onto a table

ˈdomino efˌfect *noun* [usually sing.] a situation in which one event causes a series of similar events to happen one after the other

don /dan/ *noun, verb*
● *noun* (*informal*) the leader of a group of criminals involved with the Mafia

● *verb* (-nn-) ~ sth (*formal*) to put clothes, etc. on: *He donned his jacket and went out.*

do·nate /ˈdoʊneɪt; doʊˈneɪt/ *verb* **1** ~ sth (to sb/sth) to give money, food, clothes, etc. to someone or something, especially a charity: *He donated thousands of dollars to charity.* **2** ~ sth (to sb/sth) to allow doctors to remove blood or a body organ in order to help someone who needs it: *All donated blood is tested for HIV and other infections.*

do·na·tion /doʊˈneɪʃn/ *noun* [C, U] something that is given to a person or an organization such as a charity, in order to help them; the act of giving something in this way: ~ (to sb/sth) *to make a donation to charity* ♦ *a generous/large/small donation* ♦ ~ (of...) *a donation of $200/a $200 donation* ♦ *The work of the charity is funded by voluntary donations.* ♦ *organ donation* (= allowing doctors to use an organ from your body after your death in order to save a sick person's life)

done /dʌn/ *adj., exclamation* ⊃ see also DO[1]
● *adj.* [not before noun] **1** finished; completed: *When you're done, perhaps I can say something.* ♦ ~ **with** *I'll be glad when this job is over and done with.* ♦ **be done with sth** *If you're done with that magazine, can I have a look at it?* **2** (of food) cooked enough: *The meat isn't quite done yet.* **3** socially acceptable, especially among people who have a strict set of social rules: *At school, it simply wasn't done to show interest in anything but sports.*
IDM **be done for** (*informal*) to be in a very bad situation; to be certain to fail: *Unless we start making some sales, we're done for.* ♦ *When he pointed the gun at me, I thought I was done for* (= about to die). **be done in** (*informal*) to be extremely tired SYN BE EXHAUSTED **be done with it** to do something unpleasant as quickly as possible, so that it is finished: *Why not tell her you're quitting and be done with it?* **a done deal** an agreement or a plan that has been finally completed or agreed: *The merger is by no means a done deal yet.* ⊃ more at EASY, SOON
● *exclamation* used to show that you accept an offer: *"I'll give you $800 for it." "Done!"*

don·gle /ˈdaŋgl; ˈdɔŋ-/ *noun* (*computing*) **1** a cable that is used to attach a computer to a telephone system or to another computer **2** a device or code that is needed in order to use protected software

Don Juan /ˌdan ˈwan; -ˈhwan/ *noun* (*informal*) a man who has sex with a lot of women ORIGIN From the name of a character from Spanish legend who was skilled at persuading women to have sex with him.

don·key /ˈdaŋki; ˈdɔŋ-; ˈdʌŋ-/ *noun* an animal of the horse family, with short legs and long ears. People ride donkeys or use them to carry heavy loads.

donkey

ˈdonkey ˌwork *noun* [U] (*informal*) the hard, boring part of a job or task

do·nor /ˈdoʊnər/ *noun* **1** a person or an organization that makes a gift of money, clothes, food, etc. to a charity, etc.: *international aid donors* (= countries which give money, etc. to help other countries) ♦ *She is one of the charity's main donors.* **2** a person who gives blood or a part of his or her body to be used by doctors in medical treatment: *a blood donor* ♦ *The heart transplant will take place as soon as a suitable donor can be found.* ♦ *donor organs* ♦ *a donor card* (= a card that you carry giving permission for doctors to use parts of your body after your death)

ˈdo-ˌnothing *adj., noun*
● *adj.* [only before noun] (*slang*) lazy or not effective: *He's just a no-good, do-nothing loafer.* ♦ *Their do-nothing policies have only made things worse.*
● *noun* (*slang*) a person who is lazy or lacks ambition: *If you keep hanging out with those do-nothings, you'll never amount to anything.*

don't /doʊnt/ *short form* do not

do·nut = DOUGHNUT

doo·dad /ˈduːdæd/ *noun* (*informal*) a small object whose name you have forgotten or do not know

doo·dle /ˈduːdl/ *verb* [I] to draw lines, shapes, etc., especially when you are bored or thinking about something else: *I often doodle when I'm on the phone.* ▶ **doo·dle** *noun*

doo·fus /ˈduːfəs/ *noun* (*informal*) a stupid person

doo·hick·ey /ˈduːˌhɪki/ *noun* (*informal*) a small object the name of which you have forgotten or do not know, especially part of a machine

doom /duːm/ *noun, verb*
• *noun* [U] death or destruction; any terrible event that you cannot avoid: *to meet your doom* ♦ *She had a sense of impending doom* (= felt that something very bad was going to happen).
   IDM **doom and gloom | gloom and doom** a general feeling of having lost all hope, and of PESSIMISM (= expecting things to go badly): *Despite the obvious setbacks, it is not all doom and gloom for our team.* **prophet of doom | doom merchant** a person who predicts that things will go very badly: *The prophets of doom who said television would kill off the book were wrong.*
• *verb* [usually passive] ~ **sb/sth (to sth)** | ~ **sb/sth to do sth** to make someone or something certain to fail, suffer, die, etc.: *The plan was doomed to failure.* ♦ *The marriage was doomed from the start.*

doom-laden *adj.* [usually before noun] predicting or leading to death or destruction: *doom-laden economic forecasts*

doom·say·er /ˈduːmˌseɪər/ *noun* a person who says that something very bad is going to happen

dooms·day /ˈduːmzdeɪ/ *noun* [sing.] the last day of the world when Christians believe that everyone will be judged by God
   IDM **till doomsday** (*informal*) a very long time; forever: *This job's going to take me till doomsday.*

doom·y /ˈduːmi/ *adj.* (**doom·i·er, doom·i·est**) suggesting disaster and unhappiness: *doomy predictions* ♦ *Their new album is their doomiest.*

door 🔊 /dɔːr/ *noun*
1 a piece of wood, glass, etc. that is opened and closed so that people can get in and out of a room, building, car, etc.; a similar thing in a closet: *a knock on the door* ♦ *to open/shut/close/slam/lock/bolt the door* ♦ *to answer the door* (= to go and open it because someone has knocked on it or rung the bell) ♦ *the front/back door* (= at the entrance at the front/back of a building) ♦ *the bedroom door* ♦ *the door frame* ♦ *a four-door sedan* ♦ *the fridge door* ♦ *Shut the door!* ♦ *Close the door behind you, please.* ♦ *The door closed behind him.* ⊃ see also BACK DOOR, FIRE DOOR, FRENCH DOOR, OPEN DOOR, REVOLVING DOOR, SCREEN DOOR, SLIDING DOOR, STABLE DOOR, STAGE DOOR, SWING DOOR, TRAPDOOR **2** the space when a door is open: *Marc appeared through a door at the far end of the room.* ♦ (*informal*) *She just arrived—she just came in the door.* ♦ (*informal*) *He walked out the door.* **3** the area close to the entrance of a building: *There's someone at the door* (= at the front door of a house). ♦ *"Can I help you?" asked the man at the door.* ⊃ see also DOORWAY **4** a house, room, etc. that is a particular number of houses, rooms, etc. away from another: *the family that lives three doors up from us* ♦ *Our other branch is just a few doors down the road.* ⊃ see also NEXT DOOR
   IDM **close/shut the door on sth** to make it unlikely that something will happen: *She was careful not to close the door on the possibility of further talks.* **(from) door to door** from building to building: *The trip takes about an hour door to door.* ♦ *a door-to-door salesman* **(open) the door to sth** (to provide) the means of getting or reaching something; (to create) the opportunity for something: *The agreement will open the door to increased international trade.* ♦ *Our courses are the door to success in English.* **lay sth at sb's door** (*formal*) to say that someone is responsible for something that has gone wrong **leave the door open (for sth)** to make sure

that there is still the possibility of doing something **out of doors** not inside a building: *You should spend more time out of doors in the fresh air.* **shut/slam the door in sb's face 1** to shut a door hard when someone is trying to come in **2** to refuse to talk to someone or meet them, in a rude way **to sb's door** directly to someone's house: *We promise to deliver to your door within 48 hours of your call.* ⊃ more at BACK DOOR, BARN, BEAT *v.*, CLOSE¹ *v.*, CLOSED, DARKEN, DEATH, FOOT *n.*, OPEN *v.*, SHOW *v.*, STABLE DOOR, WOLF *n.*

door·bell /ˈdɔːrbɛl/ *noun* a bell with a button outside a house that you push to let the people inside know that you are there: *to ring the doorbell* ⊃ picture at HOUSE

do-or-die *adj.* having or needing great determination: *a do-or-die attitude*

door·keep·er /ˈdɔːrˌkiːpər/ *noun* a person who guards the entrance to a large building, especially to check on people going in

door·knob /ˈdɔːrnɑb/ *noun* a type of round handle for a door, that you turn in order to open the door ⊃ picture at KNOB

door knocker *noun* = KNOCKER

door·man /ˈdɔːrmæn; -mən/ *noun* (*pl.* **doormen** /-mɛn; -mən/) a man, often in uniform, whose job is to stand at the entrance to a large building, such as an apartment house or hotel, and open the door for people, find them taxis, etc.

door·mat /ˈdɔːrmæt/ *noun* **1** a small piece of strong material near a door that people can clean their shoes on **2** (*informal*) a person who allows other people to treat them badly but usually does not complain

door·nail /ˈdɔːrneɪl/ *noun* **IDM** see DEAD *adj.*

door prize *noun* a prize awarded to the person holding the winning ticket purchased or distributed at the beginning of a party or other social event: *The door prize turned out to be the group's latest CD.*

door·step /ˈdɔːrstɛp/ *noun* a step outside a door of a building, or the area that is very close to the door: *The police turned up on their doorstep at 3 o'clock this morning.* ⊃ picture at HOUSE
   IDM **on the/your doorstep** very close to where a person lives: *The nightlife is great, with bars and clubs right on the doorstep.*

door·stop /ˈdɔːrstɑp/ *noun* a thing that is used to stop a door from closing or to prevent it from hitting and damaging a wall when it is opened

door·way /ˈdɔːrweɪ/ *noun* an opening into a building or a room, where the door is: *She stood in the doorway for a moment before going in.* ♦ *homeless people sleeping in store doorways*

doo·zy (also **doo·zie**) /ˈduːzi/ *noun* (*pl.* **doo·zies**) (*informal*) something that is very special or unusual

do·pa·mine /ˈdoʊpəˌmiːn/ *noun* [U] a chemical produced by nerve cells that has an effect on other cells

dope /doʊp/ *noun, verb*
• *noun* **1** [U] (*informal*) a drug that is taken illegally for pleasure, especially CANNABIS **2** [U] a drug that is taken by a person or given to an animal to affect their performance in a race or sport: *The athlete failed a dope test* (= a medical test showed that he had taken such drugs). **3** [C] (*informal*) a stupid person **SYN** IDIOT **4** [U] **the ~ (on sb/sth)** (*informal*) information on someone or something, especially details that are not generally known: *Give me the dope on the new boss.*
• *verb* **1** ~ **sb/sth** to give a drug to a person or an animal in order to affect their performance in a race or sport **2** ~ **sb/sth** to give someone a drug, often in their food or drink, in order to make them unconscious; to put a drug in food, etc.: *Thieves doped a guard dog and stole $10,000 worth of goods.* ♦ *The wine was doped.* **3** [usually passive] ~ **sb (up)** (*informal*) if someone is **doped** or **doped up**, they cannot think clearly or act normally because they are under the influence of drugs

dope·y /ˈdoʊpi/ adj. (informal) (dop·i·er, dop·i·est) **1** stupid or silly: a dopey grin **2** not fully awake or thinking clearly, sometimes because you have taken a drug: I felt dopey and drowsy after the operation.

dop·pel·gäng·er /ˈdɑplˌɡæŋər; -ˌɡɛŋər/ noun (from German) a person's **doppelgänger** is another person who looks exactly like them

the Dop·pler ef·fect /ˈdɑplər ɪˌfɛkt/ noun [sing.] (physics) the way that sound waves, light waves, etc. change according to the direction that the source is moving in with relation to the person who is observing

'Doppler ˌshift noun (physics) the change in sound, color, etc. caused by the Doppler effect

Dor·ic /ˈdɔrɪk/ adj. [usually before noun] (architecture) used to describe the oldest style of ARCHITECTURE in ancient Greece that has thick plain columns and no decoration at the top: a Doric column/temple

dork /dɔrk/ noun (informal) a stupid or boring person that other people laugh at ▶ **dork·y** adj.

dorm /dɔrm/ noun (informal) = DORMITORY

dor·mant /ˈdɔrmənt/ adj. not active or growing now but able to become active or to grow in the future **SYN** INACTIVE: a dormant volcano ♦ During the winter the seeds lie dormant in the soil. **ANT** ACTIVE ▶ **dor·man·cy** /ˈdɔrmənsi/ noun [U]

dor·mer /ˈdɔrmər/ (also **'dormer ˌwindow**) noun a vertical window in a room that is built into a sloping roof

dor·mi·to·ry /ˈdɔrməˌtɔri/ noun (pl. **dor·mi·to·ries**) (also informal **dorm**) **1** (also **'residence ˌhall**) a building for university or college students to live in **2** a room for several people to sleep in, especially in a prison or other institution

dor·mouse /ˈdɔrmaʊs/ noun (pl. **dor·mice** /-maɪs/) a small animal like a mouse, with a tail covered in fur

dor·sal /ˈdɔrsl/ adj. [only before noun] (technical) on or connected with the back of a fish or an animal: a shark's dorsal fin ⊃ picture at ANIMAL

do·ry /ˈdɔri/ noun (pl. **do·ries**) a narrow fish that has a deep body and that can open its mouth very wide

DOS /dɑs; dɔs/ abbr. (computing) disk operating system

dos·age /ˈdoʊsɪdʒ/ noun [usually sing.] an amount of something, usually a medicine or a drug, that is taken regularly over a particular period of time: a high/low dosage ♦ to increase/reduce the dosage ♦ Do not exceed the recommended dosage.

dos and don'ts ⊃ DO[1] n.

dose /doʊs/ noun, verb
● noun **1** an amount of a medicine or a drug that is taken once, or regularly over a period of time: a high/low/lethal dose ♦ Repeat the dose after 12 hours if necessary. **2** (informal) an amount of something: A dose of flu kept me off work. ♦ Workers at the nuclear plant were exposed to high doses of radiation. ♦ I can cope with her in small doses (= for short amounts of time). **IDM** see MEDICINE
● verb ~ sb/yourself (up) (with sth) to give someone/yourself a medicine or drug: She dosed herself up with vitamin pills. ♦ He was heavily dosed with painkillers.

dos·si·er /ˈdɑsiˌer; ˈdɔ-/ noun a collection of documents that contain information about a person, an event, or a subject **SYN** FILE: to assemble/compile a dossier ♦ ~ on sb/sth We have a dossier on him.

dot 🔑 /dɑt/ noun, verb
● noun **1** a small round mark, especially one that is printed: There are dots above the letters i and j. ♦ Text and graphics are printed at 300 dots per inch. ♦ The helicopters appeared as two black dots on the horizon. ⊃ thesaurus box at PATCH **2** (computing) a symbol like a period used to separate parts of a DOMAIN NAME, a URL or an e-mail address **IDM** on the dot (informal) exactly on time or at the exact time mentioned: The taxi showed up on the dot. ♦ Breakfast is served at 8 on the dot.

● verb (-tt-) **1** ~ sth to put a dot above or next to a letter or word: Why do you never dot your i's? **2** [usually passive] ~ sth to spread things or people over an area; to be spread over an area: The countryside was dotted with small villages. ♦ Small villages dot the countryside. ♦ There are lots of Italian restaurants dotted around the city. **3** to put very small amounts of something in a number of places on a surface: ~ A on/over B Dot the cream all over your face. ♦ ~ B with A Dot your face with the cream. **IDM** dot your i's and cross your t's to pay attention to the small details when you are finishing a task

dot·age /ˈdoʊtɪdʒ/ noun **IDM** be in your dotage to be old and not always able to think clearly

dot-com (also **dot·com**) /ˌdɑt ˈkɑm/ noun a company that sells goods and services on the Internet, especially one whose address ends ".com": The weaker dot-coms have collapsed. ♦ a dot-com millionaire

dote /doʊt/ verb **PHR V 'dote on/upon sb** to feel and show great love for someone, ignoring their faults: He dotes on his children.

dot·ing /ˈdoʊtɪŋ/ adj. [only before noun] showing a lot of love for someone, often ignoring their faults

ˌdot ˈmatrix ˌprinter noun a machine that prints letters, numbers, etc. formed from very small dots

dot·ted /ˈdɑtəd/ adj. **1** covered in dots **2** [only before noun] (music) (of a musical note) followed by a dot to show that it is one and a half times the length of the same note without the dot

ˌdotted ˈline noun a line made of dots: Country boundaries are shown on this map as dotted lines. ♦ Fold along the dotted line. ♦ Write your name on the dotted line. **IDM** see SIGN v.

dou·ble 🔑 /ˈdʌbl/ adj., det., adv., noun, verb
● adj. [usually before noun]
▷ TWICE AS MUCH/MANY **1** twice as much or as many as usual: a double helping ♦ two double whiskies
▷ WITH TWO PARTS **2** having or made of two things or parts that are equal or similar: double doors ♦ a double-page advertisement ♦ "Otter" is spelled with a double t. ♦ My extension is two four double 0 (2400).
▷ FOR TWO PEOPLE **3** made for two people or things: a double bed/room ⊃ compare SINGLE adj. (4)
▷ COMBINING TWO THINGS **4** combining two things or qualities: a double meaning/purpose/aim ♦ It has the double advantage of being both easy and cheap.

WHICH WORD?

double ▪ dual

These adjectives are frequently used with the following nouns:

double ~	dual ~
bed	purpose
doors	function
figures	role
standards	approach
thickness	citizenship

▪ **Dual** describes something that has two parts, uses, or aspects.
▪ **Double** can be used with a similar meaning, but when it is used to describe something that has two parts, the two parts are usually the same or very similar.
▪ **Double**, but not **dual**, can describe something that is made for two people or things, or is twice as big as usual.

● det.
▷ TWICE AS MUCH/MANY twice as much or as many as: His income is double hers. ♦ He earns double what she does. ♦ We need double the amount we already have.

| h **hat** | m **man** | n **no** | ŋ **sing** | l **leg** | r **red** | y **yes** | w **wet** |

• adv.
> **IN TWO PARTS** in twos or in two parts: *I thought I was seeing double* (= seeing two of something). ♦ *Fold the blanket double.* ♦ *I was bent over double, trying to get under the table.*

• noun
> **TWICE AS MUCH/MANY 1** [U] twice the number or amount: *He gets paid double for doing the same job I do.*
> **ALCOHOLIC DRINK 2** [C] a glass of strong alcoholic drink containing twice the usual amount: *Two Scotches, please— and make those doubles, will you?*
> **PERSON/THING 3** [C] a person or thing that looks exactly like another: *She's the double of her mother.* **4** [C] an actor who replaces another actor in a movie to do dangerous or other special things ⊃ see also BODY DOUBLE
> **BEDROOM 5** [C] = DOUBLE ROOM: *Is that a single or a double you want?* ⊃ compare SINGLE n. (2)
> **IN SPORTS 6 doubles** [U] a game, especially in TENNIS, in which one pair plays another: *mixed doubles* (= in which each pair consists of a man and a woman) ⊃ compare SINGLE n. (5)
IDM double or nothing (in gambling) a risk in which you could win twice the amount you pay, or you could lose all your money **on the double** (*informal*) quickly; hurrying

• verb
> **BECOME TWICE AS MUCH/MANY 1** [I, T] to become, or make something become, twice as much or as many: *Membership almost doubled in two years.* ♦ *~ sth Double all the quantities in the recipe to make enough for eight people.*
> **FOLD 2** [T] *~ sth (over)* to bend or fold something so that there are two layers: *She doubled the blanket and put it under his head.*
> **IN BASEBALL 3** [I] to hit the ball far enough for you to get to second BASE: *He doubled to left field.*
PHR V double as sth | double up as sth to have another use or function as well as the main one: *The kitchen doubles as a dining room.* **double back** to turn back and go in the direction you have come from **double up (on sth/with sb)** (*informal*) to form a pair in order to do something or to share something: *We'll have to double up on books; there aren't enough to go around.* ♦ *They only have one room left: you'll have to double up with Peter.* **double up/over | double sb up/over** to bend or to make your body bend over quickly, for example because you are in pain: *Jo doubled up with laughter.* ♦ *I was doubled over with pain.*

'double ,act *noun* two people who work together, usually to entertain an audience

double-'action *adj.* [usually before noun] **1** working in two ways: *double-action tablets* **2** (of a gun) needing two separate actions for preparing to fire and firing

double 'agent *noun* a person who is a SPY for a particular country, and also for another country which is an enemy of the first one

double 'bar *noun* (*music*) a pair of vertical lines at the end of a piece of music

double-'barreled *adj.* [usually before noun] **1** (of a gun) having two BARRELS (= places where the bullets come out) **2** (of a plan, etc.) having two parts, and therefore likely to be effective

double 'bass (also **bass**) *noun* the largest musical instrument in the VIOLIN family, that plays very low notes ⊃ picture at INSTRUMENT

double 'bill *noun* two movies, television programs, performances, etc. that are shown or performed one after the other

double 'bind *noun* [usually sing.] a situation in which it is difficult to choose what to do because whatever you choose will have negative results

double-'blind *adj.* [only before noun] (of a test) conducted so that none of the people involved know any information which might influence the results: *A randomized double-blind study was carried out to test the drug's effectiveness.*

double 'bluff *noun* a way of trying to trick someone by telling them the truth while hoping that they think you are lying

double 'boiler *noun* a cooking pot consisting of two pans, one inside the other. The upper pan is heated by boiling water in the lower pan: *Melt the chocolate in a double boiler.*

double 'book *verb* [often passive] *~ sth* to promise the same room, seat, table, etc. to two different people at the same time ⊃ compare OVERBOOK ▶ **double-'booking** *noun* [C, U]

double-'breasted *adj.* a double-breasted jacket or coat has two front parts so that one part covers the other, and two rows of buttons can be seen ⊃ compare SINGLE-BREASTED

double-'check *verb* [T, I] *~ (sth)* | *~ (that)...* to check something for a second time or with great care: *I'll double-check the figures.* ▶ **double-'check** *noun*

double 'chin *noun* a fold of fat under a person's chin, that looks like another chin

double-'click *verb* [I, T] *~ (on) sth* (*computing*) to choose a particular function or item on a computer screen, etc. by pressing one of the buttons on a mouse twice quickly

double-'cross *verb* *~ sb* to cheat or trick someone who trusts you (usually in connection with something illegal or dishonest): *He double-crossed the rest of the gang and disappeared with all the money.* ▶ **double-'cross** *noun* [usually sing.] **double-'crosser** *noun*

double 'date *noun* an occasion when two couples go out together on a DATE ▶ **double-'date** *verb* [I]

double-'dealer *noun* (*informal*) a dishonest person who cheats other people ▶ **double-'dealing** *noun* [U]

double-'decker *noun* **1** a bus with two floors, one on top of the other **2** a SANDWICH made from three pieces of bread with two layers of food between them

double-'density *adj.* (*computing*) (of a computer disk) able to hold twice the amount of data as other older disks of the same size

double 'digits *noun* [pl.] used to describe a number that is not less than 10 and not more than 99: *Inflation is in double digits.* ▶ **double-'digit** *adj.* [only before noun]: *a double-digit pay raise*

double-'dip *noun, verb*
• noun an ice-cream CONE with two balls of ice cream
• verb (-pp-) [I] (*informal*) to get an income from two different sources in an illegal way

double-double *noun* (*CanE*) a cup of coffee with a double amount of both cream and sugar

double 'Dutch (also **double 'dutch**) *noun* [U] a game in which a child jumps over two long ropes that two other children swing in opposite directions

double-'edged *adj.* **1** (of a knife, etc.) having two cutting edges **2** (of a remark, comment, etc.) having two possible meanings SYN AMBIGUOUS **3** having two different parts or uses, often parts that contrast with each other: *the double-edged quality of life in a small town—security and boredom* **IDM be a double-edged sword/weapon** to be something that has both advantages and disadvantages

dou·ble en·ten·dre /ˌdʌbl ɑnˈtɑndrə; ˌdubl-/ *noun* (from *French*) a word or phrase that can be understood in two different ways, one of which usually refers to sex

double-entry 'bookkeeping *noun* [U] (*business*) a system of keeping financial records in which each piece of business is recorded as a CREDIT in one account and a DEBIT in another

double 'fault *noun* (in TENNIS) the loss of a point caused by a player not SERVING correctly twice ▶ **double-'fault** *verb* [I]

double 'feature *noun* two movies that are shown one after the other

double 'glazing *noun* [U] windows that have two layers of glass with a space between them, designed to make the room warmer and to reduce noise ⊃ collocations at

DECORATE ▶ ¦double-¦glaze verb ~ sth ¦double-¦glazed adj.: double-glazed windows

¦double-¦header noun (in baseball) two games that are played on the same day, traditionally on a Sunday, and usually by the same two teams

¦double ¦helix noun (biology) the structure of DNA, consisting of two connected long thin pieces that form a SPIRAL shape

¦double ¦jeopardy noun (law) the fact of taking someone to court twice for the same crime, or punishing someone twice for the same reason

¦double-¦jointed adj. having joints in your fingers, arms, etc. that allow you to bend them both backward and forward

¦double ¦life noun the life of a person who leads two different lives which are kept separate from each other, usually because one of them involves secret, often illegal or immoral, activities: to live/lead a double life

¦double ¦negative noun (grammar) a negative statement containing two negative words. "I didn't say nothing" is a double negative because it contains two negative words, "n't" and "nothing". This use is not considered correct in standard English.

¦double-¦park verb [T, I, usually passive] ~ (sth) to park a car or other vehicle beside one that is already parked in a street: A car stood double-parked almost in the middle of the road. ◆ I'll have to rush—I'm double-parked.

¦double ¦play noun (in baseball) a situation in which two players are put out (= made to finish their attempt at scoring)

¦double ¦rhyme noun [U] (in poetry) a pair of words which have two parts ending with the same sounds, for example "reading" and "speeding"

¦double ¦room (also dou·ble) noun a bedroom for two people

dou·ble·speak /ˈdʌblˌspik/ (also dou·ble·talk) noun [U] language that is intended to make people believe something that is not true, or that can be understood in two different ways

¦double ¦standard noun a rule or moral principle that is unfair because it is used in one situation, but not in another, or because it treats one group of people in a way that is different from the treatment of another

dou·blet /ˈdʌblət/ noun a short, tightly fitting jacket worn by men from the 14th to the 17th century: dressed in doublet and hose

¦double ¦take noun if you do a double take, you wait for a moment before you react to something that has happened, because it is very surprising

dou·ble·talk /ˈdʌblˌtɔk/ noun [U] = DOUBLESPEAK

dou·ble·think /ˈdʌblˌθɪŋk/ noun [U] the act of holding two opposite opinions or beliefs at the same time; the ability to do this

¦double ¦time noun [U] twice someone's normal pay, that they earn for working at times which are not normal working hours

¦double ¦vision noun [U] if you have double vision, you can see two things where there is actually only one

dou·bloon /dʌˈblun/ noun (in the past) a Spanish gold coin

dou·bly /ˈdʌbli/ adv. (used before adjectives) 1 more than usual: doubly difficult/hard/important ◆ I made doubly sure I locked all the doors when I went out. 2 in two ways; for two reasons: I was doubly attracted to the house—by its size and its location.

doubt 🔑 /daʊt/ noun, verb
• noun [U, C] a feeling of being uncertain about something or not believing something: a feeling of doubt and uncertainty ◆ ~ (about sth) There is some doubt about the best way to do it. ◆ The article raised doubts about how effective the new drug really was. ◆ ~ (that…) There is no doubt at all that we did the

right thing. ◆ ~ (as to sth) If you are in any doubt as to whether you should be doing these exercises, consult your doctor. ◆ New evidence has cast doubt on the guilt of the man jailed for the crime. ◆ She knew without a shadow of a doubt that he was lying to her. ◆ Whether he will continue to be successful in the future is open to doubt. ⊃ language bank at IMPERSONAL
IDM beyond (any) doubt in a way that shows that something is completely certain: The research showed beyond doubt that smoking contributes to heart disease. ◆ (law) The prosecution was able to establish beyond a reasonable doubt that the woman had been lying. be in doubt to be uncertain: The success of the system is not in doubt. have your doubts (about sth) to have reasons why you are not certain about whether something is good or whether something good will happen: I've had my doubts about his work since he joined our department. ◆ It may be all right. Personally, I have my doubts. if in doubt used to give advice to someone who cannot decide what to do: If in doubt, wear black. no doubt 1 used when you are saying that something is likely: No doubt she'll call us when she gets there. 2 used when you are saying that something is certainly true: He's made some great movies. There's no doubt about it. without/beyond doubt used when you are giving your opinion and emphasizing the point that you are making: This meeting has been, without doubt, one of the most useful we have had so far. ⊃ more at BENEFIT n.

• verb 1 to feel uncertain about something; to feel that something is not true, will probably not happen, etc.: ~ sth There seems no reason to doubt her story. ◆ "Do you think we will win?"—" I doubt it." ◆ ~ (that)… I never doubted (that) she would come. ◆ ~ whether, if, etc.… I doubt whether/if the new one will be any better. 2 ~ sb/sth to not trust someone or something; to not believe someone: I had no reason to doubt him. ▶ doubt·er noun

doubt·ful /ˈdaʊtfl/ adj. 1 (of a person) not sure; uncertain and feeling doubt SYN DUBIOUS: ~ (about sth) Rose was doubtful about the whole idea. ◆ ~ (about doing sth) He was doubtful about accepting extra work. 2 unlikely: ~ (if…) It's doubtful if this painting is a Picasso. ◆ ~ (that…) With her injuries, it's doubtful that she'll ever walk again. ◆ ~ (whether…) It's doubtful whether the car will last another year. ◆ ~ (for sth) He is injured and is doubtful for the game tomorrow (= unlikely to play). 3 [not usually before noun] (of a thing) uncertain and likely to get worse: At the beginning of the war things were looking very doubtful. 4 [only before noun] of low value; probably not genuine or of a quality that you can rely on SYN DUBIOUS: This wine is of doubtful quality. ▶ doubt·ful·ly /-fəli/ adv.

doubt·ing Thom·as /ˌdaʊtɪŋ ˈtaməs/ noun [sing.] (old-fashioned) a person who is unlikely to believe something until they see proof of it ORIGIN From St. Thomas in the Bible, who did not believe that Jesus Christ had risen from the dead until he saw and touched his wounds.

doubt·less /ˈdaʊtləs/ adv. (also less frequent doubt·less·ly) almost certainly SYN WITHOUT DOUBT: He would doubtless disapprove of what Kelly was doing.

douche /duʃ/ noun a method of washing inside a woman's VAGINA using a stream of water ▶ douche verb [I, T] ~ (sth)

dough /doʊ/ noun 1 [U, sing.] a mixture of flour, water, etc. that is made into bread and PASTRY: Knead the dough on a floured surface. ⊃ picture at COOKING 2 [U] (old-fashioned, slang) money

dough·nut (also do·nut) /ˈdoʊnʌt/ noun a small cake made of fried dough, usually in the shape of a ring, or round and filled with jelly, fruit, cream, etc.

dough·ty /ˈdaʊti/ adj. (old-fashioned) brave and strong

dou·la /ˈdulə/ noun a woman whose role is to provide emotional support to a woman who is giving birth ⊃ compare MIDWIFE

dour /ˈdaʊər; dʊr/ adj. 1 (of a person) giving the impression of being unfriendly and severe 2 (of a thing, a place, or a situation) not pleasant; with no features that make it lively or interesting: The city, drab and dour by day, is transformed at night. ◆ *The game proved to be a dour struggle, with both men determined to win.* ▶ **dour·ly** *adv.*

douse (also **dowse**) /daʊs/ *verb* **1** ~ **sth (with sth)** to stop a fire from burning by pouring water over it; to put out a light **2** ~ **sb/sth (in/with sth)** to pour a lot of liquid over someone or something; to SOAK someone or something in liquid: *The car was doused in gasoline and set alight.*

dove¹ /dʌv/ /doʊv/ *noun* **1** a bird of the PIGEON family. The white dove is often used as a symbol of peace: *A dove cooed softly.* ◆ *He wore a dove-gray suit.* ⊃ see also TURTLE DOVE **2** a person, especially a politician, who prefers peace and discussion to war **ANT** HAWK

dove² /doʊv/ *pt of* DIVE

dove·cote /ˈdʌvkoʊt/ (also **dove·cot** /ˈdʌvkɑt/) *noun* a small building for doves or PIGEONS to live in

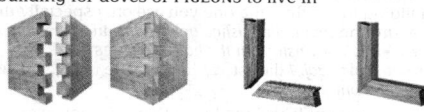

dovetail joint   miter joint

dove·tail /ˈdʌvteɪl/ *verb, noun*
- *verb* [I, T] *(formal)* ~ **(sth) (with/into sth)** if two things **dovetail** or if one thing **dovetails** with another, they fit together well: *My plans dovetailed nicely with hers.*
- *noun* (also ˌdovetail ˈjoint) a joint for fixing two pieces of wood together

dov·ish /ˈdʌvɪʃ/ *adj.* preferring to use peaceful discussion rather than military action in order to solve a political problem **ANT** HAWKISH

dow·a·ger /ˈdaʊədʒər/ *noun* **1** a woman of high social rank who has a title from her dead husband: *the dowager Duchess of Norfolk* **2** *(informal)* an impressive, usually rich, old woman

dow·dy /ˈdaʊdi/ *adj.* (dowd·i·er, dowd·i·est) **1** (of a woman) not attractive or fashionable **2** (of a thing) dull or boring and not attractive **SYN** DRAB: *a dowdy dress*

dow·el /ˈdaʊəl/ (also ˈdowel ˌrod) *noun* a small piece of wood, plastic, etc. in the shape of a CYLINDER, used to hold larger pieces of wood, plastic, etc. together

dow·el·ing /ˈdaʊəlɪŋ/ *noun* [U] short RODS of wood, metal, or plastic that are used for holding parts of something together

the Dow Jones Index /ˌdaʊ ˈdʒoʊnz ˌɪndɛks/ (also ˌDow ˈJones ˌaverage, the ˈDow) *noun* [sing.] a list of the share prices of 30 U.S. industrial companies that can be used to compare the prices to previous levels

down /daʊn/ *adv., prep., verb, adj., noun*
- *adv.* **HELP** For the special uses of **down** in phrasal verbs, look at the entries for the verbs. For example, **climb down** is in the phrasal verb section at **climb**. **1** to or at a lower place or position: *She jumped down off the chair.* ◆ *He looked down at her.* ◆ *We watched as the sun went down.* ◆ *She bent down to pick up her glove.* ◆ *Mary's not down yet* (= she is still upstairs). ◆ *The baby can't keep any food down* (= in her body). **2** from a standing or vertical position to a sitting or horizontal one: *Please sit down.* ◆ *He had to go and lie down for a while.* **3** at a lower level or rate: *Prices have gone down recently.* ◆ *We're already two goals down* (= the other team has two goals more). ⊃ language bank at FALL **4** used to show that the amount or strength of something is lower, or that there is less activity: *Turn the music down!* ◆ *The class settled down and she began the lesson.* **5** (in a CROSSWORD) reading from top to bottom, not from side to side: *I can't do 3 down.* **6** to or in the south of a country: *They flew down to Texas.* ◆ *Houses are less expensive down south.* **7** on paper; on a list: *Did you get that down?* ◆ *I always write everything down.* ◆ *Do you have me down for the trip?* **8** used to show the limits in a range or an order: *Everyone will be there, from the Principal down.* **9** having lost the amount of money mentioned: *At*

the end of the day we were $20 down. **10** if you pay an amount of money **down**, you pay that to start with, and the rest later **11** *(informal)* used to say how far you have gotten in a list of things you have to do: *Well, I've seen six apartments so far. That's six down and four to go!* **12** *(informal)* to or at a local place such as a store: *I'm just going down to the post office.* ◆ *I saw him down at the mall.*
IDM **be down to sb** *(informal)* to be the responsibility of someone: *It's down to you to check the door.* **be down to sb/sth** to be caused by a particular person or thing: *She claimed her problems were down to the media.* **be down to sth** to have only a little money left: *I'm down to my last dollar.* **be/go down with sth** to have or catch an illness **down through sth** *(formal)* during a long period of time: *Down through the years this town has seen many changes.* **down to the last, smallest, final, etc. sth** including every small part or detail of something: *She organized everything down to the last detail.* **down under** *(informal)* to or in Australia and/or New Zealand **down with sb/sth** used to say that you are opposed to something, or to a person: *The crowds chanted "Down with NATO!"* ⊃ more at MAN *n.*
- *prep.* **1** from a high or higher point on something to a lower one: *The stone rolled down the hill.* ◆ *Tears ran down her face.* ◆ *Her hair hung down her back to her waist.* **2** along; toward the direction in which you are facing: *He lives just down the street.* ◆ *Go down the road till you reach the traffic lights.* ◆ *There's a bridge a mile down the river from here.* **3** all through a period of time: *an exhibition of costumes down the ages* (= from all periods of history)
- *verb* *(informal)* **1** ~ **sth** to finish a drink or eat something quickly: *We downed our coffees and left.* **2** ~ **sb/sth** to force someone or something down to the ground: *to down a plane*
- *adj.* [not before noun] **1** *(informal)* sad or depressed: *I feel a little down today.* **2** (of a computer or computer system) not working: *The system was down all morning.* ⊃ see also DOWNTIME **3** ~ **with sth** *(slang)* to support or agree with someone or something: *"You going to the movies?" "Yeah, I'm down with that."* **IDM** see HIT *v.*, KICK *v.*, LUCK *n.*, MOUTH *n.*
- *noun* **1** [U] the very fine, soft feathers of a bird: *duck/goose down* **2** [U] fine, soft hair ⊃ see also DOWNY **3** [C] (in football) one of a series of four chances to carry the ball forward ten yards that a team is allowed. These series continue until the team loses the ball or fails to go forward ten yards in four downs. **IDM** see UP *n.*

ˌdown and ˈout *adj.* (of a person) **1** without money, a home, or a job, and living on the streets: *a novel about being down and out in a big city* **2** certain to be defeated

ˌdown-and-ˈout (also ˌdown-and-ˈouter) *noun* a person without money, a home, or a job, who lives on the streets

ˌdown at ˈheel *adj.* looking less attractive and fashionable than before, usually because of a lack of money: *The town has become very down at heel.* ◆ *a down-at-heel hotel*

down·beat /ˈdaʊnbit/ *adj.* *(informal)* **1** dull or depressing; not having much hope for the future: *The overall mood of the meeting was downbeat.* **ANT** UPBEAT **2** not showing strong feelings or enthusiasm

down·cast /ˈdaʊnkæst/ *adj.* **1** (of eyes) looking down: *Eyes downcast, she continued eating.* **2** (of a person or an expression) sad or depressed **SYN** DEJECTED: *A group of downcast men stood waiting for food.*

down·draft /ˈdaʊndræft/ *noun* a downward movement of air, for example down a CHIMNEY **ANT** UPDRAFT

down·er /ˈdaʊnər/ *noun* *(informal)* **1** [usually pl.] a drug, especially a BARBITURATE, that relaxes you or makes you want to sleep ⊃ compare UPPER **2** an experience that makes you feel sad or depressed: *Not getting the promotion was a real downer.* ◆ *He's really on a downer* (= very depressed).

down·fall /ˈdaʊnfɔl/ *noun* [sing.] the loss of a person's money, power, social position, etc.; the thing that causes this: *The sex scandal finally led to his downfall.* ◆ *Greed was her downfall.*

down·grade /ˈdaʊngreɪd/ *verb* **1** ~ **sb/sth (from sth) (to**

sth) to move someone or something down to a lower rank or level: *She's been downgraded from principal to vice-principal.* **2 ~ sth/sb** to make something or someone seem less important or valuable than it/they really are ➲ compare UPGRADE ▶ **down·grad·ing** *noun* [U, C]: *a downgrading of diplomatic relations*

down·heart·ed /ˌdaʊnˈhɑrtəd/ *adj.* [not before noun] feeling depressed or sad: *We're disappointed by these results but we're not downhearted.*

down·hill *adv., adj., noun*
- *adv.* /ˌdaʊnˈhɪl/ toward the bottom of a hill; in a direction that goes down: *to run/walk downhill* **ANT** UPHILL
  IDM **go downhill** to get worse in quality, health, etc. **SYN** DETERIORATE: *Their marriage went downhill after the first child was born.*
- *adj.* /ˈdaʊnˈhɪl; ˈdaʊnhɪl/ going or sloping toward the bottom of a hill: *a downhill path* **ANT** UPHILL
  IDM **be (all) downhill | be downhill all the way** (*informal*) **1** to be easy compared to what came before: *It's all downhill from here. We'll soon be finished.* **2** to become worse or less successful: *It's been all downhill for his career since then, with four defeats in five games.* ♦ *I started work as a journalist and it was downhill all the way for my health.*
- *noun* /ˈdaʊnhɪl/ [U] the type of SKIING in which you go directly down a mountain; a race in which people ski down a mountain ➲ compare CROSS-COUNTRY

down-ˈhome *adj.* used to describe a person or thing that reminds you of a simple way of life, typical of the country, not the city

down·light /ˈdaʊnlaɪt/ *noun* a light on a wall that shines downward ➲ compare UPLIGHT

down·link /ˈdaʊnlɪŋk/ *noun* a communications link by which information is received from space or from an aircraft ▶ **down·link** *verb*: *~ sth Any organization can downlink the program without charge.*

down·load *verb, noun*
- *verb* /ˈdaʊnloʊd/ *~ sth* (*computing*) to move data to a smaller computer system from a larger one ➲ collocations at E-MAIL ➲ compare LOAD **ANT** UPLOAD
- *noun* (*computing*) data which is downloaded from another computer system ▶ **down·load·a·ble** /ˈdaʊnˌloʊdəbl/ *adj.*

down-low *noun, adj.*
- *noun*
  IDM **on the down-low** secretly; not wanting other people to discover what you are doing
- *adj.* [only before noun] (*slang*) used to refer to a man who appears to be HETEROSEXUAL, but secretly has sex with men

down ˈpayment *noun* a sum of money that is given as the first part of a larger payment: *We are saving for a down payment on a house.*

down·play /ˈdaʊnpleɪ/ *verb ~ sth* to make people think that something is less important than it really is **SYN** PLAY DOWN: *The coach is downplaying the team's poor performance.*

down·pour /ˈdaʊnpɔr/ *noun* [usually sing.] a heavy fall of rain that often starts suddenly

down·right /ˈdaʊnraɪt/ *adj.* [only before noun] used as a way of emphasizing something negative or unpleasant: *There was suspicion and even downright hatred between them.* ▶ **down·right** *adv.*: *She couldn't think of anything to say that wasn't downright rude.* ♦ *It's not just stupid—it's downright dangerous.*

down·riv·er /ˌdaʊnˈrɪvər/ *adv.* = DOWNSTREAM

down·scale /ˈdaʊnskeɪl/ (also down·mar·ket) *adj.* (*disapproving*) cheap and of poor quality **ANT** UPSCALE ▶ **down·scale** (also down·mar·ket) *adv.*

down·shift /ˈdaʊnʃɪft/ *verb* **1** [I] to change to a lower gear in a vehicle **2** [I] to change to a job or style of life where you may earn less but which puts less pressure on you and involves less stress ➲ collocations at TOWN ▶ **down·shift** *noun* [C, U] **down·shift·er** *noun*

down·side /ˈdaʊnsaɪd/ *noun* [sing.] the disadvantages or less positive aspects of something **ANT** UPSIDE

down·size /ˈdaʊnsaɪz/ *verb* [I, T] *~ (sth)* (*business*) to reduce the number of people who work in a company, business, etc. in order to reduce costs ➲ thesaurus box at CUT ▶ **down·siz·ing** *noun* [U] ➲ compare DELAYERING

down·spout /ˈdaʊnspaʊt/ *noun* = DRAINPIPE ➲ picture at HOUSE

Down's syn·drome /ˈdaʊnz ˌsɪndroʊm/ *noun* [U] = DOWN SYNDROME

down·stage /ˌdaʊnˈsteɪdʒ/ *adv.* toward the front of the stage in a theater ▶ **down·stage** *adj.* **ANT** UPSTAGE

down·stairs *adv., noun*
- *adv.* /ˌdaʊnˈsterz/ down the stairs; on or to a floor of a house or building lower than the one you are on, especially the one at ground level: *She rushed downstairs and burst into the kitchen.* ♦ *Wait downstairs in the hall.* **ANT** UPSTAIRS ▶ **down·stairs** *adj.* /ˈdaʊnsterz/ [only before noun]: *a downstairs bathroom*
- *noun* /ˌdaʊnˈsterz/ [sing.] the lower floor of a house or building, especially the one at ground level: *We're painting the downstairs.* **ANT** UPSTAIRS

down·stream /ˌdaʊnˈstrim/ *adv., adj.*
- (also less frequent down·riv·er) *adv. ~ (of/from sth)* in the direction in which a river flows: *to drift/float downstream* ♦ *downstream of/from the bridge* **ANT** UPSTREAM
- *adj.* **1** (also less frequent down·riv·er) in a position along a river which is nearer the ocean: *downstream areas* **ANT** UPSTREAM **2** happening as a consequence of something that has happened earlier: *downstream effects*

down·swing /ˈdaʊnswɪŋ/ *noun* [usually sing.] **1 ~ (in sth)** a situation in which something gets worse or decreases over a period of time: *the current downswing in the airline industry* ♦ *He is on a career downswing.* **ANT** UPSWING **2** (in GOLF) the downward movement of a CLUB when a player is about to hit the ball

Down syn·drome /ˈdaʊn ˌsɪndroʊm/ (also Down's syn·drome) *noun* [U] a medical condition, caused by a fault with one CHROMOSOME, in which a person is born with particular physical characteristics and a mental ability that is below average

down·tick /ˈdaʊntɪk/ *noun* [C, usually sing.] (*economics*) a small decrease in the level or value of something, especially in the price of shares: *The shares were bought on a downtick.* **ANT** UPTICK

down·time /ˈdaʊntaɪm/ *noun* [U] **1** the time during which a machine, especially a computer, is not working ➲ compare UPTIME **2** the time when someone stops working and is able to relax: *Everyone needs a little downtime.*

down to ˈearth *adj.* (*approving*) sensible and practical, in a way that is helpful and friendly

down·town *adv., noun*
- *adv.* /ˌdaʊnˈtaʊn/ in or toward the center of a city, especially its main business area: *to go/work downtown* ➲ collocations at TOWN ➲ compare MIDTOWN, UPTOWN ▶ **down·town** /ˈdaʊnˌtaʊn/ *adj.*: *a downtown store*
- *noun* /ˌdaʊnˈtaʊn/ [U, C] (also cen·ter [C]) the main part of a town or city where there are a lot of stores and offices: *a hotel in the heart of downtown*

down·trend /ˈdaʊntrend/ *noun* [sing.] a situation in which business activity or performance decreases or becomes worse over a period of time **ANT** UPTREND

down·trod·den /ˈdaʊnˌtrɑdn/ *adj.* downtrodden people are treated so badly by the people with authority and power that they no longer have the energy or ability to fight back

down·turn /ˈdaʊntɜrn/ *noun* [usually sing.] *~ (in sth)* a fall in the amount of business that is done; a time when the economy becomes weaker: *a downturn in sales/trade/business* ♦ *the economic downturn of the late 1990s* **ANT** UPTURN

t tea   t̬ butter   d did   k cat   g got   tʃ chin   dʒ June   f fall

down·ward /ˈdaʊnwərd/ adj., adv.
- **adj.** [usually before noun] moving or pointing toward a lower level: *the downward slope of a hill* ◆ *the downward trend in inflation* ◆ *She was trapped in a **downward spiral** of personal unhappiness.* **ANT** UPWARD ▶ **down·ward·ly** adv.
- **adv.** (also **down·wards** /ˈdaʊnwərdz/) toward the ground or toward a lower level: *She was lying **face downward** on the grass.* ◆ *The garden sloped gently downward to the river.* ◆ *It was a move welcomed by politicans from the president downward.* **ANT** UPWARD ⊃ language bank at FALL

down·wind /ˌdaʊnˈwɪnd/ adv. in the direction in which the wind is blowing: *sailing downwind* ◆ **~ of sth** *Warnings were issued to people living downwind of the fire to stay indoors.* **ANT** UPWIND ▶ **down·wind** adj.

down·y /ˈdaʊni/ adj. covered in something very soft, especially hair or feathers ⊃ see also DOWN n.

dow·ry /ˈdaʊri/ noun (pl. **dow·ries**) **1** money and/or property that, in some societies, a wife or her family must give to her husband when they get married **2** money and/or property that, in some societies, a husband must give to his wife's family when they get married

dowse /daʊz/ verb **1** [I] to look for underground water or minerals by using a special stick or long piece of metal that moves when it comes near water, etc. **2** = DOUSE ▶ **dows·er** noun

dowsing rod noun a stick used when looking for water or minerals underground

dox·y /ˈdɑksi/ noun (pl. **dox·ies**) (old use) **1** a woman who is someone's lover **2** = PROSTITUTE

doy·en /ˈdɔɪɛn; -ən/ noun the most respected or most experienced member of a group or profession **SYN** DEAN: *Robert Frost, the doyen of American poets*

doy·enne /dɔɪˈɛn/ noun the most respected or most experienced woman member of a group or profession: *Martha Graham, the doyenne of American modern dance*

doz. abbr. (in writing) DOZEN: *2 doz. eggs*

doze /doʊz/ verb [I] to sleep lightly for a short time ⊃ thesaurus box at SLEEP
PHR V **doze 'off** to go to sleep, especially during the day: *She dozed off in front of the fire.*

doz·en /ˈdʌzn/ noun, det.
(pl. **doz·en**) **1** [C] (abbr. **doz.**) a group of twelve of the same thing: *Give me a dozen, please.* ◆ *two dozen eggs* ◆ *three dozen red roses* ⊃ see also BAKER'S DOZEN **2** [C] a group of approximately twelve people or things: *several dozen/a few dozen people* ◆ *The company employs no more than a **couple of dozen** people.* ◆ *Only about **half a dozen** people turned up.* ◆ *There was only space for a **half-dozen** tables.* **3** **dozens** [pl.] (informal) a lot of people or things: *They arrived **in dozens** (= in large numbers).* ◆ **~ of sth** *I've been there dozens of times.* **IDM** see DIME, SIX

dpi /ˌdi pi ˈaɪ/ abbr. (computing) dots per inch (a measure of how clear the images produced by a printer, SCANNER, etc. are)

Dr. abbr.
1 (in writing) Doctor: *Dr. (Jane) Walker* **2** (in street names) DRIVE

drab /dræb/ adj. (**drab·ber**, **drab·best**) without interest or color; dull and boring: *a cold drab little office* ◆ *drab women, dressed in browns and grays* ▶ **drab·ness** noun [U]

drabs /dræbz/ noun **IDM** see DRIBS

drach·ma /ˈdrækmə; ˈdrɑk-/ noun (pl. **drach·mas** or **drach·mae** /-mi/) the former unit of money in Greece (replaced in 2002 by the EURO)

dra·co·ni·an /drəˈkoʊniən/ adj. (formal) (of a law, punishment, etc.) extremely cruel and severe **ORIGIN** From **Draco**, a legislator in ancient Athens who gave severe punishments for crimes, especially the punishment of being killed.

Drac·u·la /ˈdrækyələ/ noun a character in many horror films who is a VAMPIRE. Vampires appear at night and suck the blood of their victims. **ORIGIN** From the novel *Dracula* by Bram Stoker.

draft **AWL** /dræft/ noun, adj., verb
- **noun** **1** [C] a rough written version of something that is not yet in its final form: *I've made a **rough draft** of the letter.* ◆ *This is only the first draft of my speech.* ◆ *the **final draft** (= the final version)* ◆ *The legislation is still in **draft form**.* ◆ *a draft constitution/treaty/agreement* **2** [C] (finance) a written order to a bank to pay money to someone: *Payment must be made by **bank draft** drawn on a U.S. bank.* **3** **the draft** [sing.] (also formal **con·scrip·tion**) the practice of ordering people by law to serve in the armed forces **4** [sing.] a process of picking players for professional sports teams from college or other teams **5** [C] a flow of cool air in a room: *Can you shut the door? There's a draft in here.* ◆ *A cold draft of air blew in from the open window.* ◆ *I was sitting **in a draft**.* **6** [C] (formal) one continuous action of swallowing liquid; the amount swallowed: *He took a deep draft of his beer.* **7** [C] (old use or literary) medicine in a liquid form: *a sleeping draft (= one that makes you sleep)*
IDM **on draft** (of beer) taken from a BARREL (= a large container): *This beer is not available on draft (= it is available only in bottles or cans).*
- **adj.** **1** [usually before noun] served from a large container (= a BARREL) rather than in a bottle: *draft beer* **2** [only before noun] used for pulling heavy loads: *a draft horse*
- **verb** **1** **~ sth** to write the first rough version of something such as a letter, speech, or book: *to draft a constitution/contract/bill* ◆ *I'll draft a letter for you.* **2** **~ sb + adv./prep.** to choose people and send them somewhere for a special task: *Extra police are being drafted into controlling the crowds.* **3** [usually passive] **~ sb** to make sb join the armed forces **SYN** ENLIST, CONSCRIPT: *They were drafted into the army.*

draft board noun an official group whose job is to select and register people for the armed forces

draft card noun a card that someone gets from the government, telling them that they have been selected to serve in the armed forces

draft dodger noun (disapproving) a person who illegally tries to avoid doing military service ⊃ compare CONSCIENTIOUS OBJECTOR

draft·ee /ˌdræfˈti/ noun (also formal **con·script**) a person who has been drafted into the armed forces ⊃ compare VOLUNTEER

draft·er /ˈdræftər/ noun **1** a person who prepares a rough version of a plan, document, etc. **2** = DRAFTSMAN (3)

drafts·man /ˈdræftsmən/ noun (pl. **drafts·men** /-mən/) **1** a person whose job is to draw detailed plans of machinery, buildings, etc. **2** a person who draws: *He's a poor draftsman.* **3** (also **draft·er**) a person who writes official or legal documents: *the draftsmen of the Constitution* ⊃ see also DRAFTSWOMAN, DRAFTSPERSON

drafts·man·ship /ˈdræftsmənˌʃɪp/ noun [U] the ability to draw well: *You have to admire her superb draftsmanship.*

drafts·per·son /ˈdræftsˌpərsn/ noun a draftsman or draftswoman

drafts·wom·an /ˈdræftsˌwʊmən/ noun (pl. **drafts·wom·en** /-ˌwɪmən/) **1** a woman whose job is to draw detailed plans of machinery, buildings, etc. **2** a woman who draws ⊃ see also DRAFTSMAN

draft·y /ˈdræfti/ adj. (**draft·i·er**, **draft·i·est**) (of a room, etc.) uncomfortable because cold air is blowing through: *a drafty room/corridor*

drag /dræg/ verb, noun
- **verb** (-gg-)
▷ **PULL** **1** [T] (+ adv./prep.) to pull someone or something along with effort and difficulty: *I dragged the chair over to the window.* ◆ *They dragged her from her bed.* ⊃ thesaurus box at PULL

> MOVE SLOWLY **2** [T, I] to move yourself slowly and with effort: ~ **yourself** + **adv./prep.** *I managed to drag myself out of bed.* ◆ + **adv./prep.** *She always drags behind when we walk anywhere.*

> PERSUADE SOMEONE TO GO **3** [T] ~ **sb/yourself** + **adv./prep.** to persuade someone to come or go somewhere they do not really want to come or go to: *I'm sorry to drag you all this way in the heat.* ◆ *The party was so good I couldn't drag myself away.*

> OF TIME **4** [I] (of time or an event) to pass very slowly: *Time dragged terribly.* ◆ *The meeting really dragged.* ⊃ see also DRAG ON

> TOUCH GROUND **5** [I, T] to move, or make something move, partly touching the ground: *This dress is too long—it drags on the ground when I walk.* ◆ ~ **sth** *He was dragging his coat in the mud.*

> SEARCH RIVER **6** [T] ~ **sth (for sb/sth)** to search the bottom of a river, lake, etc. with nets or hooks: *They dragged the canal for the missing children.*

> COMPUTING **7** [T] ~ **sth** + **adv./prep.** to move some text, an ICON, etc. across the screen of a computer using the mouse **IDM** **drag your feet/heels** to be deliberately slow in doing something or in making a decision **drag sb's name through the dirt/mud** to harm someone's reputation by saying bad things about them **PHR V** ,drag **'by** (of time) to pass very slowly: *The last few weeks of the summer really dragged by.* ,drag **sb↔'down** to make someone feel weak or unhappy ,drag **sb/ sth↔'down (to sth)** to bring someone or something to a lower social or economic level, a lower standard of behavior, etc.: *If he fails, he'll drag us all down with him.* ,drag **sth/sb 'into sth** | ,drag **sth/sb↔'in 1** to start to talk about something or someone that has nothing to do with what is being discussed: *Do you have to drag politics into everything?* **2** to try to get someone who is not connected with a situation involved in it: *Don't drag the children into our argument.* ,drag **'on** (disapproving) to go on for too long: *The dispute has dragged on for months.* ,drag **sth↔'out** to make something last longer than necessary **SYN** PROLONG: *Let's not drag out this discussion; we need to reach a decision.* ,drag **sth 'out of sb** to make someone say something they do not want to say: *We dragged a confession out of him.* ,drag **sth↔'up** to mention an unpleasant story, fact, etc. that people do not want to remember or talk about: *Why do you have to keep dragging up my divorce?*

● *noun*

> BORING PERSON/THING **1** [sing.] (informal) a boring person or thing; something that is annoying: *He's such a drag.* ◆ *Walking's a drag—let's drive there.* ◆ *Having to work late every day is a drag.*

> SOMEONE OR SOMETHING STOPPING PROGRESS **2** [sing.] a ~ **on sb/sth** (informal) a person or thing that makes progress difficult: *He came to be seen as a drag on his own party's prospects.*

> ON CIGARETTE **3** [C] (informal) an act of breathing in smoke from a cigarette, etc. **SYN** DRAW: *She took a long drag on her cigarette.*

> WOMEN'S CLOTHES **4** [U] (informal) clothes that are usually worn by the opposite sex (usually women's clothes worn by men): *He performed in drag.* ◆ *a drag queen* (= a man who dresses in women's clothes, usually in order to entertain people)

> PHYSICS **5** [U] the force of the air that acts against the movement of an aircraft or other vehicle ⊃ see also MAIN DRAG ⊃ compare LIFT

,drag-and-'drop *adj.* (computing) relating to the moving of ICONS, etc. on a computer screen using the mouse

drag·net /'drægnɛt/ *noun* **1** a net that is pulled through water to catch fish, or along the ground to catch animals **2** a thorough search, especially for a criminal

drag·on /'drægən/ *noun* (in stories) a large aggressive animal with wings and a long tail, that can breathe out fire

'dragon ,boat *noun* a long narrow boat of traditional Chinese design that is used for racing and that is moved through the water by a lot of people using PADDLES. It is decorated to look like a dragon.

drag·on·fly /'drægən,flaɪ/ *noun* (pl. drag·on·flies) an insect with a long, thin body, often brightly colored, and two pairs of large, transparent wings. Dragonflies are often seen over water. ⊃ picture at ANIMAL

'dragon ,lady *noun* (informal, disapproving) a woman who behaves in an aggressive and frightening way

dra·goon /drə'gun/ *noun, verb*
● *noun* a soldier in the past who rode a horse and carried a gun
● *verb*
PHR V dra'goon **sb into sth/into doing sth** (formal) to force or persuade someone to do something that they do not want to do **SYN** COERCE

'drag race *noun* a race between specially adapted cars over a short distance ▶ 'drag ,racing *noun* [U]

drag·ster /'drægstər/ *noun* a car that is used in a drag race

drain /dreɪn/ *verb, noun*
● *verb* **1** [T, I] ~ **(sth)** to make something empty or dry by removing all the liquid from it; to become empty or dry in this way: *Drain and rinse the pasta.* ◆ *The marshes have been drained.* ◆ *You will need to drain the central heating system before you replace the radiator.* ◆ *The swimming pool drains very slowly.* ◆ *Leave the dishes to drain.* ⊃ collocations at COOKING **2** [T, I] to make liquid flow away from something; to flow away: ~ **sth (from/out of sth)** *We had to drain the oil out of the engine.* ◆ ~ **sth away/off** *Drain off the excess fat from the meat.* ◆ ~ **away/off** *She pulled out the plug and the water drained away.* ◆ (figurative) *My anger slowly drained away.* ◆ ~ **into sth** *The river drains into a lake.* ◆ ~ **from/out of sth** *All the color drained from his face when I told him the news* ◆ ~ **of sth** *His face was drained of color.* **3** [T] ~ **sth** to empty a cup or glass by drinking everything in it: *In one gulp, he drained the glass.* ◆ *She quickly drained the last of her drink.* **4** [T] to make someone or something weaker, poorer, etc. by using up their/its strength, money, etc.: ~ **sb/sth** *My mother's hospital expenses were slowly draining my income.* ◆ *an exhausting and draining experience* ◆ ~ **sb/sth of sth** *I felt drained of energy.*

● *noun* **1** [C] a pipe that carries away dirty water or other liquid waste: *We had to call in a plumber to unblock the drain.* ◆ *The drains* (= the system of pipes) *date from the beginning of the century.* **2** [C] a hole in a BATHTUB, SINK, etc. where the water flows away and into which a plug fits **3** [sing.] **a ~ on sb/sth** a thing that uses a lot of the time, money, etc. that could be used for something else: *Military spending is a huge drain on the country's resources.* ⊃ see also BRAIN DRAIN **IDM** **(go) down the drain** (informal) (to be) wasted; (to get) very much worse: *It's just money down the drain, you know.* ◆ *Safety standards have gone down the drain.*

drain·age /'dreɪnɪdʒ/ *noun* [U] **1** the process by which water or liquid waste is drained from an area: *a drainage system/channel/ditch* ◆ *The area has good natural drainage.* **2** a system of drains

drain·board *noun* the area next to a kitchen SINK where cups, plates, etc. are put for the water to run off, after they have been washed

drained /dreɪnd/ *adj.* [not usually before noun] very tired and without energy: *She suddenly felt totally drained.* ◆ *The experience left her emotionally drained.*

drain·pipe /'dreɪnpaɪp/ *noun* **1** (also down·spout) a pipe that carries RAINWATER from the roof of a building to a DRAIN ⊃ picture at HOUSE **2** a pipe that carries dirty water or other liquid waste away from a building

drake /dreɪk/ *noun* a male DUCK

dram /dræm/ *noun* a small amount of an alcoholic drink, especially WHISKEY

dra·ma 🔑 **AWL** /ˈdrɑmə/ *noun*
1 [C] a play for the theater, television, or radio: *a costume/historical, etc. drama* **2** [U] plays considered as a form of literature: *classical/Elizabethan/modern, etc. drama* ◆ *a drama critic* ◆ *drama school* ◆ *a drama student* ◆ *I studied English and Drama at college.* **3** [C] an exciting event: *A powerful human drama was unfolding before our eyes.* **4** [U] the fact of being exciting: *You couldn't help being thrilled by the drama of the situation.*
IDM **make a drama out of sth** to make a small problem or event seem more important or serious than it really is

ˈdrama ˌqueen *noun* (*informal, disapproving*) a person who behaves as if a small problem or event is more important or serious than it really is

dra·mat·ic 🔑 **AWL** /drəˈmætɪk/ *adj.*
1 (of a change, an event, etc.) sudden, very great, and often surprising: *a dramatic increase/fall/change/improvement* ◆ *dramatic results/developments/news* ◆ *The announcement had a dramatic effect on house prices.* **2** exciting and impressive: *a dramatic victory* ◆ *They watched dramatic pictures of the police raid on TV.* ⊃ thesaurus box at EXCITING **3** [usually before noun] connected with the theater or plays: *a local dramatic society* **4** exaggerated in order to create a special effect and attract people's attention: *He flung out his arms in a dramatic gesture.* ◆ *Don't be so dramatic!*
▶ **dra·mat·i·cally** **AWL** /-kli/ *adv.*: *Prices have fallen dramatically.* ◆ *Events could have developed in a dramatically different way.* ◆ *"At last!" she cried dramatically.*

draˌmatic ˈirony *noun* [U] a situation in a play when a character's words carry an extra meaning to the audience because they know more than the character, especially about what is going to happen

dra·mat·ics /drəˈmætɪks/ *noun* [pl.] behavior that does not seem sincere because it is exaggerated or too emotional

dram·a·tis per·so·nae /ˌdræmətəs pərˈsouni; ˌdrɑ-; -naɪ/ *noun* [pl.] (from *Latin, formal*) all the characters in a play in the theater

dram·a·tist **AWL** /ˈdrɑmətɪst; ˈdræ-/ *noun* a person who writes plays for the theater, television, or radio
SYN PLAYWRIGHT: *a TV dramatist*

dram·a·tize **AWL** /ˈdrɑməˌtaɪz; ˈdræ-/ *verb* **1** [T] ~ **sth** to present a book, an event, etc. as a play or a movie **2** [T, I] ~ **(sth)** to make something seem more exciting or important than it really is: *Don't worry too much about what she said —she tends to dramatize things.* ▶ **dram·a·ti·za·tion** **AWL** /ˌdrɑmətəˈzeɪʃn; ˌdræ-/ *noun* [U, C]: *a television dramatization of the trial*

dram·a·tur·gy /ˈdrɑməˌtərdʒi; ˈdræ-/ *noun* [U] (*formal*) the study or activity of writing dramatic texts

dra·me·dy /ˈdrɑmədi/ *noun* (*pl.* **dra·me·dies**) a television program that is intended to be both humorous and serious

drank pt of DRINK

drape /dreɪp/ *verb, noun*
● *verb* **1** ~ **sth around/over/across, etc. sth** to hang clothes, materials, etc. loosely on someone or something: *She had a shawl draped around her shoulders.* ◆ *He draped his coat over the back of the chair.* ◆ *She draped a cover over the old sofa.* **2** ~ **sb/sth in/with sth** to cover or decorate someone or something with material: *walls draped in ivy* **3** ~ **sth around/over**, etc. to allow part of your body to rest on something in a relaxed way: *His arm was draped casually around her shoulders.*
● *noun* (also **dra·per·y**) [usually pl.] a long, thick curtain: *blue velvet drapes*

dra·per·y /ˈdreɪpəri/ *noun* (*pl.* **dra·per·ies**) **1** [U] (also **dra·per·ies** [pl.]) cloth or clothing hanging in loose folds: *a cradle swathed in draperies and blue ribbon* **2** [C, usually pl.] = DRAPE

dras·tic /ˈdræstɪk/ *adj.* extreme in a way that has a sudden, serious, or violent effect on something: *drastic measures/changes* ◆ *The government is threatening to take drastic action.* ◆ *a drastic shortage of food* ◆ *Talk to me before you do anything*

drastic. ▶ **dras·ti·cally** /-kli/ *adv.*: *Output has been drastically reduced.* ◆ *Things have started to go drastically wrong.*

drat /dræt/ *exclamation* (*old-fashioned, informal*) used to show that you are annoyed: *Drat! I forgot my key.*

Dra·vid·i·an /drəˈvɪdiən/ *adj.* connected with a group of languages spoken in southern India and in Sri Lanka, or with the people who speak these languages

draw 🔑 /drɔ/ *verb, noun*
● *verb* (drew /dru/, drawn /drɔn/)
❯ **MAKE PICTURES 1** [I, T] to make pictures, or a picture of something, with a pencil, pen, or CHALK (but not paint): *You draw beautifully.* ◆ ~ **sth** *to draw a picture/diagram/graph* ◆ *She drew a house.* ◆ *He drew a circle in the sand with a stick.* ◆ (*figurative*) *The report drew a grim picture of inefficiency and corruption.* ⊃ collocations at ART
❯ **PULL 2** [T] ~ **sth/sb + adv./prep.** to move something or someone by pulling it or them gently: *He drew the cork out of the bottle.* ◆ *I drew my chair up closer to the fire.* ◆ *She drew me onto the balcony.* ◆ *I tried to draw him aside* (= for example where I could talk to him privately). ◆ (*figurative*) *My eyes were drawn to the man in the corner.* ⊃ thesaurus box at PULL **3** [T] ~ **sth** (of horses, etc.) to pull a vehicle such as a CARRIAGE: *The Queen's coach was drawn by six horses.* ◆ *a horse-drawn carriage*
❯ **CURTAINS 4** [T] ~ **sth** to open or close curtains, etc.: *The blinds were drawn.* ◆ *It was getting dark so I switched on the light and drew the curtains.* ◆ *She drew back the curtains and let the sunlight in.*
❯ **MOVE 5** [I] **+ adv./prep.** to move in the direction mentioned: *The train drew into the station.* ◆ *The train drew in.* ◆ *The figures in the distance seemed to be drawing closer.* ◆ *Their car drew alongside ours.* ◆ (*figurative*) *Her retirement is drawing near.* ◆ (*figurative*) *The meeting was drawing to a close.*
❯ **WEAPON 6** [T, I] ~ **(sth) (on sb)** to take out a weapon, such as a gun or a SWORD, in order to attack someone: *She drew a revolver on me.* ◆ *He came toward them with his sword drawn.*
❯ **ATTRACT 7** [T] to attract or interest someone: ~ **sb** *The movie is drawing large audiences.* ◆ *The course draws students from all over the country.* ◆ ~ **sb to sth** *Her screams drew passers-by to the scene.*
❯ **GET REACTION 8** [T] to produce a reaction or response: ~ **sth** *The plan has drawn a lot of criticism.* ◆ ~ **sth from sb** *The announcement drew loud applause from the audience.*
❯ **CONCLUSION 9** [T] ~ **sth (from sth)** to have a particular idea after you have studied something or thought about it: *What conclusions did you draw from the report?* ◆ *We can draw some lessons for the future from this accident.*
❯ **COMPARISON 10** [T] ~ **sth** to express a comparison or a contrast: *to draw an analogy/a comparison/a parallel/a distinction between two events*
❯ **CHOOSE 11** [I, T] ~ **sth** to decide something by picking cards, tickets, or numbers by chance: *We drew for partners.* ◆ *They had to draw lots to decide who would go.* ◆ *He drew the winning ticket.* ◆ *Names were drawn from a hat for the last few places.*
❯ **MONEY 12** [T] to take money from a bank account **SYN** WITHDRAW: ~ **sth out (of sth)** *I drew out $200.* ◆ *Can I draw $80 out of my account?* ◆ ~ **sth on sth** *The check was drawn on his personal account.* **13** [T] ~ **sth** to receive a regular payment from your employer or the government: *She draws a salary of $120,000.* ◆ *He lost his job and is now drawing unemployment.*
❯ **LIQUID/GAS 14** [T] ~ **sth (+adv./prep.)** to take or pull liquid or gas from somewhere: *to draw water from a well* ◆ *The device draws gas along the pipe.*
❯ **SMOKE/AIR 15** [I, T] to breathe in smoke or air: ~ **at/on sth** *He drew thoughtfully on his pipe.* ◆ ~ **sth in** *She breathed deeply, drawing in the fresh mountain air.*
IDM **draw a blank** to get no response or result: *So far, the police investigation has drawn a blank.* **draw blood** to make someone BLEED **draw (a)breath 1** to stop doing something and rest: *She talks all the time and hardly stops to draw breath.* **2** (*literary*) to live; to be alive: *He was as kind a man as ever drew breath.* **draw the line (at sth/at doing sth)** to

refuse to do something; to set a limit: *I don't mind helping, but I draw the line at doing everything myself.* ◆ *We would have liked to invite all our relatives, but you have to draw the line somewhere.* **draw the line (between sth and sth)** to distinguish between two closely related ideas: *Where do you draw the line between genius and madness?* **draw straws (for sth)** to decide on someone to do or have something, by choosing pieces of paper, etc.: *We drew straws for who went first.* ➔ more at BATTLE *n.*, BEAD *n.*, FIRE *n.*, HEIGHT, HORN, LOT *n.*, SIDE *n.*

PHR V **draw 'back** to move away from someone or something: *He came close but she drew back.* **,draw 'back (from sth/from doing sth)** to choose not to take action, especially because you feel nervous: *We drew back from taking our neighbors to court.* **,draw sth↔'down** | **,draw 'down** to reduce a supply of something that has been created over a period of time; to be reduced: *There are many life events that can unexpectedly draw down savings.* ◆ *If we don't cut costs, our reserves will draw down.* ➔ related noun DRAWDOWN **,draw sth↔'down (from sth)** | **,draw 'down on sth** (*finance*) to take money from a fund that a bank, etc. has made available: *The company has already drawn down £600 million of its £725 million credit line.* ◆ *They can draw down on the loan at any time.* ➔ related noun DRAWDOWN **'draw sth from sb/sth** to take or obtain something from a particular source: *to draw support/comfort/strength from your family* ◆ *She drew her inspiration from her childhood experiences.* **,draw 'in** to become dark earlier in the evening as winter gets nearer: *The nights/days are drawing in.* **'draw sb into sth/into doing sth** | **,draw sb↔'in** to involve someone or make someone take part in something, although they may not want to take part at first: *youngsters drawn into a life of crime* ◆ *The book starts slowly, but it gradually draws you in.* **,draw 'off** to remove some liquid from a larger supply: *The doctor drew off some fluid to relieve the pressure.* **,draw 'on** (*formal*) if a time or a season draws on, it passes: *Night was drawing on.* **'draw on/upon sth** to use a supply of something that is available to you: *I'll have to draw on my savings.* ◆ *The novelist draws heavily on her personal experiences.* **,draw 'out** to become lighter in the evening as summer gets nearer: *The days/evenings are drawing out.* **,draw sb↔'out** to encourage someone to talk or express themselves freely **,draw sth↔'out** to make something last longer than usual or necessary: *She drew the interview out to over an hour.* ➔ see also LONG-DRAWN-OUT **,draw 'up** if a vehicle draws up, it arrives and stops: *The cab drew up outside the house.* **,draw sth↔'up** to make or write something that needs careful thought or planning: *to draw up a contract/list*

● *noun*
> CHOOSING **1** = DRAWING (3, 4)
> SPORTS/GAMES **2** a game in which both teams or players finish with the same number of points: *He managed to hold Smith to a draw* (= to stop him from winning when he seemed likely to do so). ➔ compare TIE *n.* (5)
> ATTRACTION **3** a person, a thing, or an event that attracts a lot of people **SYN** ATTRACTION: *She is currently one of the biggest draws on the music scene.*
> SMOKE **4** an act of breathing in the smoke from a cigarette **SYN** DRAG
IDM **be quick/fast on the draw 1** (*informal*) to be quick to understand or react in a new situation: *You can't fool him—he's always quick on the draw.* **2** to be quick at pulling out a gun in order to shoot it ➔ more at LUCK *n.*

draw·back /'drɔːbæk/ *noun* ~ **(of/to sth)** | ~ **(of/to doing sth)** a disadvantage or problem that makes something a less attractive idea **SYN** DISADVANTAGE, SNAG: *The main drawback to it is the cost.* ◆ *This is the one major drawback of the new system.*

draw·bridge /'drɔːbrɪdʒ/ *noun* a bridge that can be pulled up, for example to stop people from entering a castle or to allow ships to pass under it

draw·down /'drɔːdaʊn/ *noun* [C, U] ~ **(on sth) 1** the act of reducing a supply of something that has been created over a period of time; the amount used: *The cold winter has led to a*

larger-than-expected drawdown on oil stocks.* **2** (*finance*) the act of using money that is available to you; the amount used: *a drawdown of cash from the company's reserves*

drawer 🔊 *noun*
1 /drɔːr/ a part of a piece of furniture such as a desk, used for keeping things in. It is shaped like a box and has a handle on the front for pulling it out.: *in the top/middle/bottom drawer* of the desk ➔ see also CHEST OF DRAWERS, TOP DRAWER **2** /'drɔːər/ (*formal*) a person who writes a check

drawers /drɔːz/ *noun* [pl.] (*old-fashioned*) UNDERPANTS, especially ones that cover the upper parts of the legs

draw·ing 🔊 /'drɔːɪŋ/ *noun*
1 [C] a picture made using a pencil or pen rather than paint: *a pencil/charcoal drawing* ◆ *a drawing of a yacht* ◆ *He did/made a drawing of the old farmhouse.* ➔ thesaurus box at PICTURE ➔ collocations at ART **2** [U] the art or skill of making pictures, plans, etc. using a pen or pencil: *I'm not very good at drawing.* ➔ technical drawing **3** (*also* draw) [C, usually sing.] ~ **(for sth)** the act of choosing something, for example the winner of a prize or the teams who play each other in a competition, usually by taking pieces of paper, etc. out of a container without being able to see what is written on them: *The drawing for the raffle takes place on Saturday.* **4** (*also* draw) [C] a competition in which the winners are chosen in a drawing: *a prize drawing* ➔ compare LOTTERY

'drawing ,board *noun* a large flat board used for holding a piece of paper while a drawing or plan is being made **IDM** **(go) back to the drawing board** to start thinking about a new way of doing something after a previous plan or idea has failed **on the drawing board** being prepared or considered: *It's one of several projects on the drawing board.*

'drawing ,power *noun* [U] the ability of someone or something to attract people

'drawing ,room *noun* (*formal* or *old-fashioned*) a room in a large house in which people relax and guests are entertained ➔ compare LIVING ROOM

drawl /drɔːl/ *verb* [T, I] ~ **+ speech** | ~ **(sth)** to speak or say something slowly with vowel sounds that are longer than usual: *"Hi there!" she drawled lazily.* ◆ *He had a smooth, drawling voice.* ► **drawl** *noun* [sing.]: *She spoke in a slow Southern drawl.*

drawn /drɔːn/ *adj.* (of a person or their face) looking pale and thin because the person is sick, tired, or worried ➔ see also DRAW *v.*

,drawn-'out *adj.* = LONG-DRAWN-OUT

draw·string /'drɔːstrɪŋ/ *noun* a piece of string sewn inside the material at the top of a bag, pair of pants, etc. that can be pulled tighter in order to make the opening smaller: *They fasten with a drawstring.* ➔ picture at CLOTHES

dray /dreɪ/ *noun* a low, flat vehicle pulled by horses and used in the past for carrying heavy loads, especially BARRELS of beer

dread /drɛd/ *verb, noun*
● *verb* to be very afraid of something; to fear that something bad is going to happen: ~ **sth** *This was the moment he had been dreading.* ◆ ~ **doing sth** *I dread being sick.* ◆ ~ **sb doing sth** *She dreads her husband finding out.* ◆ ~ **to do sth** *I dread to think what would happen if there really was a fire here.*
● *noun* [U, C, usually sing.] a feeling of great fear about something that might or will happen in the future; a thing that causes this feeling: *The prospect of growing old fills me with dread.* ◆ *She has an irrational dread of hospitals.* ◆ *The committee members live in dread of* (= are always worried about) *anything that may cause a scandal.* ◆ *My greatest dread is that my parents will find out.*

dread·ed /'drɛdəd/ (*also formal* dread) *adj.* [only before noun] causing fear: *The dreaded moment had finally arrived.* ◆ (*humorous*) *Did I hear the dreaded word "homework"?*

dread·ful /'drɛdfl/ *adj.* **1** [usually before noun] causing fear or suffering **SYN** TERRIBLE: *a dreadful accident* ◆ *They*

ʌ cup ə about eɪ say aɪ five ɔɪ boy aʊ now oʊ go ər bird

suffered dreadful injuries. **2** very bad or unpleasant: *What a dreadful thing to say!* ◆ *It's dreadful the way they treat their staff.* ◆ *How dreadful!* ◆ *Jane looked dreadful* (= looked sick or tired). ⊃ thesaurus box at TERRIBLE **3** [only before noun] used to emphasize how bad something is **SYN** TERRIBLE: *She's making a dreadful mess of things.* ◆ *I'm afraid there's been a dreadful mistake.*

dread·ful·ly /'drɛdfəli/ adv. **1** extremely; very much: *I'm dreadfully sorry.* ◆ *I miss you dreadfully.* **2** very badly: *They suffered dreadfully during the war.*

dread·locks /'drɛdlɑks/ (also informal **dreads** /drɛdz/) noun [pl.] hair that is twisted into long thick pieces that hang down from the head, worn especially by RASTAFARIANS ⊃ picture at HAIR

dread·nought /'drɛdnɔt/ noun a type of ship used in war in the early 20th century

dream /drim/ noun, verb

• **noun 1** [C] a series of images, events, and feelings that happen in your mind while you are asleep: *I had a vivid dream about my old school.* ◆ *I thought someone came into the bedroom, but it was just a dream.* ◆ *"Goodnight. Sweet dreams."* ⊃ compare NIGHTMARE ⊃ see also WET DREAM **2** [C] a wish to have or be something, especially one that seems difficult to achieve: *Her lifelong dream was to be a famous writer.* ◆ *He wanted to be rich but it was an impossible dream.* ◆ *If I win, it will be a dream come true.* ◆ *She tried to turn her dream of running her own business into reality.* ◆ *a dream car/house/job, etc.* ◆ *I've finally found the man of my dreams.* ◆ *a chance to fulfill a childhood dream* ◆ *It was the end of all my hopes and dreams.* ⊃ see also PIPE DREAM **3** [sing.] a state of mind or a situation in which things do not seem real or part of normal life: *She walked around in a dream all day.* ⊃ see also DAYDREAM **4** [sing.] (informal) a beautiful or wonderful person or thing: *That meal was an absolute dream.*
IDM go/work like a dream 1 to work very well: *My new car goes like a dream.* **2** to happen without problems, in the way that you had planned **in your dreams** (informal) used to tell someone that something they are hoping for is not likely to happen: *"I'll be a manager before I'm 30." "In your dreams."* **like a bad dream** (of a situation) so unpleasant that you cannot believe it is true: *In broad daylight the events of the night before seemed like a bad dream.* ⊃ more at WILD adj.

• **verb** (**dreamed** or **dreamt** /drɛmt/) **1** [I, T] to experience a series of images, events, and feelings in your mind while you are asleep: *There must have been dreaming.* ◆ *~ of/about sb/sth I dreamed about you last night.* ◆ *~ sth Did it really happen or did I just dream it?* ◆ *~ (that)… I dreamt (that) I got the job.* **2** [I, T] to imagine and think about something that you would like to happen: *~ of/about sth She dreams of running her own business.* ◆ *It was the kind of trip most of us only dream about.* ◆ *~ of/about doing sth* (informal) *I wouldn't dream of going without you* (= I would never go without you). ◆ *~ sth Who'd have dreamt it? They're getting married.* ◆ *~ (that)… I never dreamt (that) I'd actually get the job.*
PHR V dream sth a'way to waste time just thinking about things you would like to do without actually doing anything **dream 'on** (informal) you say **dream on** to tell someone that an idea is not practical or likely to happen **dream sth↔'up** (informal) to have an idea, especially a very unusual or silly one **SYN** THINK UP: *Trust you to dream up a crazy idea like this!*

dream·boat /'drimboʊt/ noun (old-fashioned, informal) a man who is very attractive

dream·catch·er /'drim,kætʃər/ noun a ring containing a decorated net, originally made by Native Americans, and thought to give its owner good dreams

dream·er /'drimər/ noun **1** (sometimes disapproving) a person who has ideas or plans that are not practical or realistic **2** (usually disapproving) a person who does not pay attention to what is happening around them, but thinks about other things instead **3** a person who dreams: *Dreamers do not always remember their dreams.*

dream·land /'drimlænd/ noun [U] (disapproving) a pleasant but not very realistic situation that only exists in your mind: *You must be living in dreamland if you think he'll change his mind.*

dream·less /'drimləs/ adj. (of sleep) without dreams; deep and peaceful

dream·like /'drimlaɪk/ adj. as if existing or happening in a dream

dream team noun the best possible combination of people for a particular competition or activity

dream ,ticket noun [sing.] (used especially in newspapers about candidates for an election) a combination of people who, together, are considered to be the best

dream·world /'drimwərld/ noun a world that is not like the real world; a person's idea of reality that is not realistic: *If he thinks it's easy to get a job, he's living in a dreamworld.*

dream·y /'drimi/ adj. (**dream·i·er, dream·i·est**) **1** looking as though you are thinking about other things and not paying attention to what is happening around you: *She had a dreamy look in her eyes.* **2** (of a person or an idea) having a lot of imagination, but not very realistic: *Paul was dreamy and not very practical.* **3** as if you are in a dream or asleep: *He moved in the dreamy way of a man in a state of shock.* **4** (informal) pleasant and gentle; that makes you feel relaxed: *a slow, dreamy melody* **5** (informal) beautiful; wonderful: *What's he like? I bet he's really dreamy.* ▶ **dream·i·ly** /-məli/ adv. **dream·i·ness** noun [U]

drear·y /'drɪri/ adj. (**drear·i·er, drear·i·est**) that makes you feel sad; dull and not interesting **SYN** DULL: *a dreary winter's day* ◆ *a dreary film* ◆ *a long and dreary journey on the train* ▶ **drear·i·ly** /'drɪrəli/ adv. **drear·i·ness** noun [U]

dreck /drɛk/ noun [U] (slang) something that you think is of very bad quality: *The movie is utter dreck.*

dredge /drɛdʒ/ verb **1** [T, I] ~ (sth) (for sth) to remove mud, stones, etc. from the bottom of a river, CANAL, etc. using a boat or special machine, to make it deeper or to search for something: *They're dredging the harbor so that larger ships can use it.* ◆ *They dredge the bay for gravel.* **2** [T] ~ sth (up) (from sth) to bring something up from the bottom of a river, etc. using a boat or special machine: *waste dredged (up) from the seabed* **3** [T] ~ sth in/with sth to cover food lightly with sugar, flour, etc.: *Dredge the top of the cake with confectioner's sugar.*
PHR V ,dredge sth↔'up 1 (usually disapproving) to mention something that has been forgotten, especially something unpleasant or embarrassing: *The papers keep trying to dredge up details of his past love life.* **2** to manage to remember something, especially something that happened a long time ago: *Now she was dredging up memories from the depths of her mind.*

dredg·er /'drɛdʒər/ noun a boat or machine that is used to clear mud, etc. from the bottom of a river, or to make the river wider

dregs /drɛgz/ noun [pl.] **1** the last drops of a liquid, mixed with little pieces of solid material that are left in the bottom of a container: *coffee dregs* **2** the worst and most useless parts of something: *the dregs of society* **3** (literary) the last parts of something: *the last dregs of daylight*

drei·del /'dreɪdl/ noun a small TOP (= a toy that you spin) with a Hebrew letter on each of its four sides, used in a game that children play during the Jewish festival of Hanukkah

drench /drɛntʃ/ verb [often passive] to make someone or something completely wet **SYN** SOAK: *~ sb/sth We were caught in the storm and got drenched to the skin.* ◆ *~ sb/sth in/*

dreamcatcher

with sth *His face was drenched with sweat.* ♦ (*figurative*) *She drenched herself in perfume.* ⊃ thesaurus box at WET

dress ⚷ /dres/ *noun, verb*

● **noun**

> CLOTHES **1** [C] a piece of women's clothing that is made in one piece and covers the body down to the legs, sometimes reaching to below the knees, or to the ankles: *a long white dress* ♦ *a wedding dress* ⊃ picture at CLOTHES ⊃ see also COCKTAIL DRESS, EVENING DRESS, SUNDRESS **2** [U] clothes for either men or women: *to wear casual/formal dress* ♦ *He has no dress sense* (= no idea of how to dress well). ⊃ see also EVENING DRESS, HEADDRESS, MORNING DRESS

● **verb**

> CLOTHES **1** [I, T] to put clothes on yourself/someone: *~ (in sth) I dressed quickly.* ♦ *~ sb (in sth) She dressed the children in their best clothes.* ♦ *Get up and get dressed!* ⊃ collocations at FASHION ANT UNDRESS **2** [I, T] to wear a particular type or style of clothes: *to dress well/badly/fashionably/comfortably* ♦ *~ for/in/as sth You should dress for cold weather today.* ♦ *~ sb (for/in/as sth) She always dressed entirely in black.* ♦ *He was dressed as a woman* (= he was wearing women's clothes). ⊃ collocations at FASHION ⊃ thesaurus box at CLOTHES **3** [I] to put on formal clothes: *Do they expect us to dress for dinner?* **4** [T] *~ sb* to provide clothes for someone: *He dresses many of Hollywood's most famous young stars.*

> WOUND **5** [T] *~ sth* to clean, treat, and cover a wound: *The nurse will dress that cut for you.*

> FOOD **6** [T] *~ sth* to prepare food for cooking or eating: *to dress a salad* (= put oil or VINEGAR, etc. on it) ♦ *to dress a chicken* (= take out the parts you cannot eat)

> DECORATE **7** [T] *~ sth* (*formal*) to decorate or arrange something: *to dress a store window* (= arrange a display of clothes or goods in it)

> STONE/WOOD/LEATHER **8** [T] *~ sth* to prepare a material such as stone, wood, leather, etc. for use IDM see PART *n.*

PHR V **dress 'down** to wear clothes that are more informal than those you usually wear, for example in an office **,dress sb 'down** to criticize or speak angrily to someone because they have done something wrong **,dress 'up** to wear clothes that are more formal than those you usually wear **,dress 'up | ,dress sb 'up** to put on special clothes, especially to pretend to be someone or something different; to help sb do this: *Kids love dressing up.* ♦ *dress-up clothes* **,dress sth 'up** to present something in a way that makes it seem better or different: *However much you try to dress it up, office work is not glamorous.*

dres·sage /drə'sɑʒ/ *noun* [U] a set of controlled movements that a rider trains a horse to perform; a competition in which these movements are performed

'dress ,circle (also **,first 'balcony**) *noun* the first level of seats above the ground floor in a theater

'dress code *noun* rules about what clothes people should wear at work, for a special occasion, etc.: *The company has a strict dress code—all male employees are expected to wear suits.*

dressed ⚷ /drest/ *adj.* [not before noun]
1 wearing clothes and not naked or wearing clothes for sleeping: *Hurry up and get dressed.* ♦ *fully dressed* ♦ *I can't go to the door—I'm not dressed yet.* **2** wearing clothes of a particular type: *fashionably dressed* ♦ *~ in... The bride was dressed in white.* ♦ *He was casually dressed in jeans and a T-shirt.*
IDM **dressed to kill** (*informal*) wearing the kind of clothes that will make people notice and admire you **dressed to the nines** (*informal*) wearing very elegant or formal clothes

dres·ser /'dresər/ *noun* **1** = CHEST OF DRAWERS **2** (used with an adjective) a person who dresses in the way mentioned: *a snappy dresser* **3** (in a theater) a person whose job is to take care of an actor's clothes for a play and help him/her to get dressed

dress·ing /'dresɪŋ/ *noun* **1** (also **'salad dressing**) [C, U] a thin sauce used to add flavor to salads, usually made from oil, VINEGAR, salt, pepper, etc. ⊃ see also FRENCH DRESSING, RANCH DRESSING **2** [U] = STUFFING **3** [C] a piece

of soft material placed over a wound in order to protect it **4** [U] the act of putting on clothes: *Many of our patients need help with dressing.* ⊃ see also CROSS-DRESSING, POWER DRESSING, WINDOW DRESSING

,dressing-'down *noun* [sing.] (*old-fashioned, informal*) an occasion when someone speaks angrily to a person because they have done something wrong

'dressing ,gown *noun* (*formal*) a BATHROBE

'dressing ,room *noun* **1** a room in a store where you can put on clothes to see how they look **SYN** FITTING ROOM **2** a room for changing your clothes in, especially one for actors **3** a small room next to a bedroom in some large houses, in which clothes are kept and people get dressed

'dressing ,table (also **van·i·ty**) *noun* a piece of bedroom furniture like a table with drawers and a mirror on top

dress·mak·er /'dres,meɪkər/ *noun* a person who makes women's clothes, especially as a job ▶ **dress·mak·ing** *noun* [U]

'dress re,hearsal *noun* the final practice of a play in the theater, using the clothes and lights that will be used for the real performance: (*figurative*) *The earlier protests had just been dress rehearsals for full-scale revolution.*

'dress shirt *noun* **1** a white shirt worn on formal occasions with a BOW TIE and suit **2** a shirt with long sleeves, which can be worn with a tie

'dress ,uniform *noun* [U] a uniform that army, navy, etc. officers wear for formal occasions and ceremonies

dress·y /'dresi/ *adj.* (**dress·i·er, dress·i·est**) **1** (of clothes) elegant and formal **2** (of people) liking to wear elegant or formal clothes

drew *pt of* DRAW

drib·ble /'drɪbl/ *verb, noun*
● **verb** **1** [I, T] *~ (sth)* to let SALIVA or another liquid come out of your mouth and run down your chin **SYN** DROOL **2** [I] + adv./prep. to fall in small drops or in a thin stream: *Melted wax dribbled down the side of the candle.* **3** [T] *~ sth (into/over/onto sth)* to pour something slowly, in drops or a thin stream **SYN** DRIZZLE, TRICKLE: *Dribble a little olive oil over the salad.* **4** [T, I] *~ (sth)* (+ adv.prep.) (in basketball, SOCCER and some other sports) to move the ball along with several short kicks, hits, or BOUNCES: *She dribbled the ball the length of the field.* ♦ *He dribbled past two defenders and scored a magnificent goal.*
● **noun** **1** [C] a very small amount of liquid, in a thin stream: *a dribble of blood* ♦ *Add just a dribble of oil.* **2** [U] SALIVA (= liquid) from a person's mouth: *There was dribble all down the baby's front.* **3** [C] the act of dribbling in a sport

dribs /drɪbz/ *noun* [pl.]
IDM **in dribs and drabs** (*informal*) in small amounts or numbers over a period of time: *She paid me in dribs and drabs, not all at once.*

dried *pt, pp of* DRY

,dried 'fruit *noun* [U, C] fruit (for example, CURRANTS or RAISINS) that has been dried to be used in cooking or eaten on its own

dri·er = DRYER ⊃ see also DRY *adj.*

driest ⊃ DRY *adj.*

drift /drɪft/ *noun, verb*
● **noun**
> SLOW MOVEMENT **1** [sing., U] a slow steady movement from one place to another; a gradual change or development from one situation to another, especially to something bad: *a population drift away from rural areas* ♦ *attempts to halt the drift toward war*
> OF SHIP **2** [U] the movement of a ship or plane away from its direction because of currents or wind
> OF OCEAN/AIR **3** [U, C] the movement of the ocean or air **SYN** CURRENT: *the general direction of drift on the east coast* ♦ *He knew the hidden drifts in that part of the river.*
> OF SNOW **4** [C] a large pile of something, especially snow,

| t tea | t̬ butter | d did | k cat | g got | tʃ chin | dʒ June | f fall |

made by the wind: *The road was blocked by deep drifts of snow.* ⊃ see also SNOWDRIFT

▷ OF FLOWERS **5** [C] a large mass of something, especially flowers: *Plant daffodils in informal drifts.*

▷ MEANING **6** [sing.] the general meaning of what someone says or writes **SYN** GIST: *Do you catch my drift?* ◆ *My German isn't very good, but I got the drift of what she said.* ⊃ see also CONTINENTAL DRIFT

● *verb*

▷ MOVE SLOWLY **1** [I] (+ **adv./prep.**) to move along smoothly and slowly in water or air: *Clouds drifted across the sky.* ◆ *The empty boat drifted out to sea.* **2** [I] + **adv./prep.** to move or go somewhere slowly: *The crowd drifted away from the scene of the accident.* ◆ *Her gaze drifted around the room.*

▷ WITHOUT PURPOSE **3** [I] (+ **adv./prep.**) to happen or change, or to do something without a particular plan or purpose: *I didn't intend to be a teacher—I just drifted into it.* ◆ *He hasn't decided what to do yet—he's just drifting.* ◆ *The conversation drifted onto politics.*

▷ INTO STATE/SITUATION **4** [I] ~ **in/into sth** to go from one situation or state to another without realizing it: *Finally she drifted into sleep.* ◆ *The injured man tried to speak but soon drifted into unconsciousness.*

▷ OF SNOW/SAND **5** [I] to be blown into large piles by the wind: *drifting sand* ◆ *Some roads are closed because of drifting.*

▷ FLOAT **6** [T] + **adv./prep.** to make something float somewhere: *The logs are drifted downstream to the mill.*

PHR V ˌdrift a'part to become less friendly or close to someone: *As children we were very close, but as we grew up we just drifted apart.* ˌdrift 'off (to sleep) to fall asleep: *I didn't hear the storm. I must have drifted off by then.*

drift·er /ˈdrɪftər/ *noun* (*disapproving*) a person who moves from one job or place to another with no real purpose

'**drift net** *noun* a very large net used by fishing boats. The net has weights at the bottom and FLOATS at the top and is allowed to hang in the ocean.

drift·wood /ˈdrɪftwʊd/ *noun* [U] wood that the ocean carries up onto land, or that floats on the water

drill /drɪl/ *noun, verb*

● *noun* **1** [C] a tool or machine with a pointed end for making holes: *an electric drill* ◆ *a pneumatic drill* ◆ *a hand drill* ◆ *a dentist's drill* ◆ *a drill bit* (= the pointed part at the end of the drill) ⊃ picture at TOOL **2** [C, U] a way of learning something by means of repeated exercises **3** [C, U] a practice of what to do in an emergency, for example if there is a fire: *a fire drill* **4** [U] military training in marching, the use of weapons, etc.: *rifle drill* **5 the drill** [sing.] the correct or usual way to do something **SYN** PROCEDURE: *What's the drill for claiming expenses?* **6** [U] a type of strong cotton cloth **7** [C] a machine for planting seeds in rows

● *verb* **1** [T, I] to make a hole in something, using a drill: ~ **sth** *Drill a series of holes in the frame.* ◆ ~ **(for sth)** *They're drilling for oil off the Irish coast.* ◆ ~ **(through sth)** *He drilled through the wall by mistake.* **2** [T] to teach someone to do something by making them repeat it a lot of times: ~ **sb to do sth** *The children were drilled to leave the classroom quickly when the fire bell rang.* ◆ ~ **sb (in sth)** *a well-drilled team* **3** [T] ~ **sb** to train soldiers to perform military actions

PHR V ˌdrill 'down (*computing*) to go to deeper levels of an organized set of data on a computer or a Web site in order to find more detail: *Navigation is good and there's a display to show how far you've drilled down.* '**drill sth into sb** to make someone remember or learn something by repeating it often: *It was drilled into us at an early age never to drop litter.*

dri·ly = DRYLY

drink 🔑 /drɪŋk/ *noun, verb*

● *noun* **1** [C, U] a liquid for drinking; an amount of a liquid that you drink: *Can I have a drink?* ◆ *soft drinks* (= cold drinks without alcohol) ◆ *a drink of water* ◆ *food and drink* ◆ *She took a drink from the glass and then put it down.* **2** [C, U] alcohol or an alcoholic drink; something that you drink on a social occasion: *They went for a drink.* ◆ *The drinks are on me* (= I'll pay for them). ◆ *I need a stiff drink* (= a very strong drink). ◆ *He*

has a drinking problem. ◆ (*humorous*) *The kids are enough to drive me to drink.* ◆ *She took to drink* (= drank too much alcohol) *after her marriage broke up.* **3 drinks** [pl.] a social occasion where you have alcoholic drinks: *Would you like to come for drinks on Sunday?*

● *verb* (**drank** /dræŋk/, **drunk** /drʌŋk/) **1** [T, I] ~ **(sth)** to take liquid into your mouth and swallow it: *What would you like to drink?* ◆ *In hot weather, drink plenty of water.* ◆ *I don't drink coffee.* ◆ *He was drinking straight from the bottle.* **2** [I, T] to drink alcohol, especially when it is done regularly: *He doesn't drink.* ◆ *Don't drink and drive* (= drive a car after drinking alcohol). ◆ *She's been drinking heavily since she lost her job.* ◆ ~ **sth** *I drank far too much last night.* ◆ ~ **yourself** + **adj.** *He had drunk himself unconscious on vodka.* ⊃ see also DRUNK

IDM **drink like a fish** to drink a lot of alcohol regularly **drink to sb's health** to wish someone good health as you lift your glass, and then drink from it **drink sb under the table** (*informal*) to drink more alcohol than someone else without becoming as drunk as they are ⊃ more at EAT, LEAD v.

PHR V ˌdrink sth↔'in to look at or listen to something with great interest and enjoyment: *We just stood there drinking in the scenery.* 'drink to sb/sth to wish someone good luck, health, or success as you lift your glass and then drink from it **SYN** TOAST: *All raise your glasses and drink to Katie and Tom!* ˌdrink 'up | ˌdrink (sth)↔'up to drink all of something: *Drink up and let's go.* ◆ *Come on, drink up your juice.*

drink·a·ble /ˈdrɪŋkəbl/ *adj.* **1** clean and safe to drink **2** pleasant to drink: *a very drinkable wine*

drink·er /ˈdrɪŋkər/ *noun* **1** a person who drinks alcohol regularly, especially someone who drinks too much: *a heavy/moderate drinker* **2** (after a noun) a person who regularly drinks the particular drink mentioned: *a coffee drinker*

drink·ing /ˈdrɪŋkɪŋ/ *noun* [U] the act of drinking alcohol: *Drinking is not advised during pregnancy.* ◆ *There are tough penalties for drinking and driving.*

'**drinking box** *noun* (*CanE*) a small paper box of juice, etc. that has a STRAW with it that can be pushed through a small hole in the top

'**drinking ˌfountain** *noun* = WATER FOUNTAIN

'**drinking ˌstraw** *noun* = STRAW

'**drinking ˌwater** *noun* [U] water that is safe for drinking

drip /drɪp/ *verb, noun*

● *verb* (-pp-) **1** [I] (+ **adv./prep.**) (of liquid) to fall in small drops: *She was hot and sweat dripped into her eyes.* ◆ *Water was dripping down the walls.* **2** [I, T] to produce drops of liquid: *The tap was dripping.* ◆ + **adv./prep.** *Her hair dripped down her back.* ◆ ~ **sth** (+adv./prep.) *Be careful, you're dripping paint everywhere!* **3** [I, T] to contain or hold a lot of something: ~ **with sth** *The trees were dripping with fruit.* ◆ ~ **sth** (*figurative*) *His voice dripped sarcasm.*

● *noun* **1** [sing.] the sound or action of small drops of liquid falling continuously: *The silence was broken only by the steady drip, drip of water from the roof.* **2** [C] a small drop of liquid that falls from something: *We put a bucket under the hole in the roof to catch the drips.* **3** [C] (*medical*) = IV: *She's been put on a drip.* **4** [C] (*informal, old-fashioned*) a boring or stupid person with a weak personality **SYN** WIMP: *Don't be such a drip—come and join in the fun!*

ˌdrip-'dry *adj.* made of a type of cloth that will dry quickly without CREASES when you hang it up wet

'**drip-feed** *verb* (**drip-fed, drip-fed**) ~ **sb/sth** to give someone something in separate small amounts ▶ '**drip feed** *noun* [U, C]: *the steady drip feed of leaked documents in the papers*

drip·ping /ˈdrɪpɪŋ/ *adj.* (also ˌdripping 'wet) very wet: *His clothes were still dripping wet.*

drip·pings /ˈdrɪpɪŋz/ *noun* [pl.] fat that comes out of meat when it is cooked, often kept for frying other food in

drip·py /ˈdrɪpi/ *adj.* (**drip·pi·er, drip·pi·est**) (*informal*)

1 (*disapproving*) too emotional in a silly way
SYN SENTIMENTAL (2): *a drippy love story* **2** (*old-fashioned, disapproving*) (of a person) boring, stupid, and weak: *her drippy boyfriend* **3** in a liquid state, and likely to fall in drops: *drippy paint* ◆ *a drippy nose* (= with drops of liquid falling from it) ▶ **drip·pi·ly** /-pəli/ *adv.* **drip·pi·ness** *noun* [U]

drive ✎ /draɪv/ *verb, noun*

● **verb** (**drove** /droʊv/, **driv·en** /ˈdrɪvn/)

> VEHICLE **1** [I, T] to operate a vehicle so that it goes in a particular direction: *Can you drive?* ◆ *Don't drive so fast!* ◆ *I drove to work this morning.* ◆ *Should we drive* (= go there by car) *or go by train?* ◆ *He drives a taxi* (= that is his job). ⊃ collocations at DRIVING **2** [T] ~ sb (+ adv./prep.) to take someone somewhere in a car, taxi, etc.: *Could you drive me home?* ⊃ thesaurus box at TAKE **3** [T] ~ sth to own or use a particular type of vehicle: *What car do you drive?*

> MACHINE **4** [T, usually passive] ~ sth to provide the power that makes a machine work: *a steam-driven locomotive*

> MAKE SOMEONE DO SOMETHING **5** [T] ~ sb/yourself (+ adv./prep.) to force someone/yourself to act in a particular way: *The urge to survive drove them on.* ◆ *You're driving yourself too hard.* **6** [T] to make someone very angry, crazy, etc. or to make them do something extreme: ~ sb + adj. *to drive someone crazy/mad/insane* ◆ ~ sb to do sth *Hunger drove her to steal.* ◆ ~ sb to sth *Those kids are driving me to despair.* ◆ (*humorous*) *It's enough to drive you to drink* (= to make you start drinking too much alcohol).

> MAKE SOMEONE OR SOMETHING MOVE **7** [T] ~ sb/sth + adv./prep. to force someone or something to move in a particular direction: *to drive sheep into a field* ◆ *The enemy was driven back.*

> CAUSE SOMETHING TO MAKE PROGRESS **8** [T] ~ sth to influence something or cause it to make progress: *This is the main factor driving investment in the area.*

> HIT/PUSH **9** [T] ~ sth + adv./prep. to force something to go in a particular direction or into a particular position by pushing it, hitting it, etc.: *to drive a nail into a piece of wood*

> MAKE A HOLE **10** [T] ~ sth + adv./prep. to make an opening in or through something by using force: *They drove a tunnel through the solid rock.*

> IN SPORTS **11** [T, I] ~ (sth) (+ adv./prep.) to hit a ball with force, sending it forward: *to drive the ball into the rough* (= in GOLF)

> WIND/WATER **12** [T] ~ sth (+ adv./prep.) to carry something along: *Huge waves drove the yacht onto the rocks.* **13** [I] (+ adv./prep.) to fall or move rapidly and with great force: *The waves drove against the shore.*

IDM **drive sth home (to sb)** to make someone understand or accept something by saying it often, loudly, angrily, etc.: *You will really need to drive your point home.* **what sb is driving at** the thing that someone is trying to say: *I wish I knew what they were driving at.* ⊃ more at GROUND *n.*, HARD *adj.*, SNOW *n.*

PHRV **drive a'way** | **drive sb/sth a'way** to leave in a vehicle; to take someone away in a vehicle: *We heard him drive away.* ◆ *Someone drove the car away in the night.* **drive sb a'way** to make someone not want to stay or not want to go somewhere: *Her constant nagging drove him away.* ◆ *Terrorist threats are driving away tourists.* **drive 'off 1** (of a driver, car, etc.) to leave: *The robbers drove off in a stolen vehicle.* **2** (in GOLF) to hit the ball to begin a game **drive sb/sth↔'off** to force someone or something to go back or away: *The defenders drove off each attack.* **drive 'on** to continue driving: *Don't stop—drive on!* **drive sb/sth↔'out (of sth)** to make someone or something disappear or stop doing something: *New fashions drive out old ones.* **drive sth↔'up/'down** to make something such as prices rise or fall quickly

● **noun**

> IN/OF VEHICLE **1** [C] a trip in a car or other vehicle: *Let's go for a drive.* ◆ *It's a three-hour drive to their house.* **2** [C, U] the equipment in a vehicle that takes power from the engine to the wheels: *the drive shaft* ◆ *a car with four-wheel drive* **3** [U] the position of the gears in which the vehicle will move forward: *He threw the car into drive.* ⊃ compare PARK *n.* (5)

> OUTSIDE HOUSE **4** = DRIVEWAY: [C] *There were two cars parked in/on the drive.* ⊃ picture at HOUSE

> EFFORT **5** [C] an organized effort by a group of people to achieve something: *a recruitment drive* ◆ ~ for sth *a drive for greater efficiency* ◆ ~ to do sth *the government's drive to reduce energy consumption* ⊃ see also BLOOD DRIVE ⊃ thesaurus box at CAMPAIGN

> ATTACK **6** [C] a major military attack: *a drive into enemy territory*

> DESIRE/ENERGY **7** [C, U] a strong desire or need in people: *a strong sex drive* **8** [U] (*approving*) a strong desire to do things and achieve something; great energy: *He'll do very well—he has tremendous drive.*

> IN SPORTS **9** [C] a long, hard hit or kick: *She has a strong forehand drive* (= in TENNIS). ◆ *He scored with a brilliant 25-yard drive.*

> COMPUTING **10** [C] the part of a computer that reads and stores information on disks or tapes: *a 750GB hard drive* ◆ *a CD drive* ⊃ see also DISK DRIVE

> ANIMALS **11** [C] an act of chasing animals and making them go into a smaller area, especially in order to kill or capture them

> ROAD **12** Drive (*abbr.* Dr.) used in the names of roads: *21 Island Heights Drive*

'**drive bay** *noun* (*computing*) a space inside a computer for a DISK DRIVE

'**drive-by** *adj.* [only before noun] a **drive-by** shooting, etc. is done from a moving car: *a drive-by killing* ▶ '**drive-by** *noun*

'**drive-in** *noun* a place where you can watch movies, eat, etc. without leaving your car: *We stopped at a drive-in for a hamburger.* ◆ *drive-in movies*

driv·el /ˈdrɪvl/ *noun, verb*

● *noun* [U] (*informal, disapproving*) silly nonsense: *How can you watch that drivel on TV?*

● *verb* [I] ~ (on) (about sth) (usually used in the progressive tenses) to keep talking about silly or unimportant things

driv·en /ˈdrɪvn/ *adj.* **1** (of a person) determined to succeed, and working very hard to do so **2 -driven** (in compounds) influenced or caused by a particular thing: *a market-driven economy* ◆ *a character-driven movie* ⊃ see also DRIVE *v.*

driv·er ✎ /ˈdraɪvər/ *noun*

1 a person who drives a vehicle: *a bus/train/ambulance/taxi driver* ◆ *She climbed into the driver's seat.* ◆ *a student driver* ◆ *The car comes equipped with a driver's airbag.* ⊃ see also BACKSEAT DRIVER **2** one of the main things that influence something or cause it to make progress: *Housing is a key driver of the economy.* **3** (in GOLF) a CLUB with a wooden head **4** (*computing*) software that controls the sending of data between a computer and a piece of equipment that is attached to it, such as a printer **IDM** see SEAT *n.*

'**driver's ,license** (also '**driver ,license**, *CanE* '**driver's licence**) *noun* an official document that shows that you are qualified to drive

drive·shaft /ˈdraɪvʃæft/ *noun* a long, thin part of a machine that turns around and around and sends power from the engine to another part of the machine

'**drive-through** (also '**drive-thru**) *noun* a restaurant, bank, etc. where you can be served without having to get out of your car

'**drive time** *noun* [U] a time during the day when many people are driving their cars, for example to or from work ▶ '**drive-time** *adj.*: *a drive-time radio show*

drive·way /ˈdraɪvweɪ/ (also **drive**) *noun* [C] a wide, hard path or a private road that leads from the street to a house: *There was a car parked in/on the driveway.* ⊃ picture at HOUSE

driv·ing ✎ /ˈdraɪvɪŋ/ *noun, adj.*

● *noun* [U] the way that someone drives a vehicle; the act of driving: *dangerous driving* ◆ *driving lessons*

● *adj.* [only before noun] **1** strong and powerful; having a strong influence in making something happen: *Who was the driving force* (= the person with the strongest influence) in

| h hat | m man | n no | ŋ sing | l leg | r red | y yes | w wet |

the band? **2** (of rain, snow, etc.) falling very fast and at an angle

Driving

having a car
- **have/own** a car
- **ride** a motorcycle/moped/scooter
- **drive/use/prefer** an automatic/a manual/a stick shift
- **have/get** your car **fixed/repaired/looked at**
- **buy/sell** a used car
- **take/pass/fail** a driver's test/road test/knowledge test
- **get/obtain/have/lose/carry** a/your driver's license/learner's permit

driving
- **put on/fasten/buckle/wear/undo** your seat belt
- **put/turn/leave** the key in the ignition
- **start** the car/engine
- **change/shift** gears
- **shift/put** the car into gear/neutral/drive/park
- **press/put your foot on** the brake pedal/clutch/accelerator
- **release** the clutch/the emergency brake/the parking brake
- **drive/park/reverse** the car
- **signal** that you are turning left/right
- **take/miss** the turn
- **apply/hit/slam on** the brake(s)
- **beep/honk** your horn

problems and accidents
- a car **skids/crashes (into sth)/collides (with sth)**
- **swerve to avoid** an oncoming car/a pedestrian
- **crash/lose control of** the car
- **have/be in/be killed in/survive** a (car) crash/a (car) wreck/an accident/a hit-and-run
- **be run over/hit** by a car/bus/truck
- **dent/hit** the hood/trunk/door/side panel/bumper/fender
- **break/crack/shatter** the windshield
- **blow/puncture** a tire
- **get/have** a flat tire
- **inflate/change/replace/check** a tire

traffic and driving regulations
- **be caught in/get stuck in/sit in** a traffic jam
- **cause** congestion/traffic jams/gridlock/backups
- **experience/face** lengthy delays
- **beat/avoid** the traffic/the rush hour
- **exceed/observe/drive** the speed limit
- **be caught by** a speed camera
- **stop sb for/pull sb over for** speeding
- (*informal*) **run** a red light/the lights
- **be arrested for/charged with** drunk driving/driving under the influence (DUI)/driving while intoxicated (DWI)
- **be banned** from driving
- **have your license** suspended/taken away/(*informal*) pulled

ˈdriving ˌrange *noun* a place where people can practice hitting GOLF balls

ˈdriving ˌschool *noun* a business that gives people lessons in how to drive a car, etc.

ˈdriving ˌtest *noun* a test that must be passed before you are qualified to drive a car, etc. ⟳ see also ROAD TEST

driz·zle /ˈdrɪzl/ *verb, noun*
- *verb* **1** [I] when it is drizzling, it is raining lightly **2** [T] **~ sth (over sth)** to pour a small amount of liquid over the surface of something **SYN** DRIBBLE

- *noun* [U, sing.] light, fine rain ▶ **driz·zly** /ˈdrɪzli/ *adj.*: *a dull, drizzly morning*

DRM /ˌdi ɑr ˈɛm/ *abbr.* (*computing*) digital rights management (actions and devices that are used by the owners of software or information to prevent people from copying it from the Internet)

drogue /droʊg/ *noun* a small PARACHUTE, used to pull a larger one from its bag

droit de sei·gneur /ˌdrwɑ də sɛnˈyər/ *noun* [U] (from *French*) the right of a lord to have sex with a woman of lower social rank on her wedding night, said to exist in the Middle Ages

droll /droʊl/ *adj.* (*old-fashioned* or *ironic*) amusing, but not in a way that you expect

drom·e·dar·y /ˈdrɑməˌdɛri/ *noun* (*pl.* drom·e·dar·ies) an animal of the CAMEL family, with only one HUMP, that lives in desert countries

drone /droʊn/ *noun, verb*
- *noun* **1** [usually sing.] a continuous low noise: *the distant drone of traffic* **2** a male BEE that does not work ⟳ compare QUEEN BEE, WORKER **3** a person who is lazy and gives nothing to society while others work **4** an aircraft without a pilot, controlled from the ground
- *verb* [I] to make a continuous low noise: *A plane was droning in the distance.* ◆ *a droning voice*
PHR V ˌdrone ˈon (about sth) to talk for a long time in a boring way

drool /drul/ *verb* **1** [I] to let SALIVA (= liquid) come out of your mouth **SYN** DRIBBLE: *The dog was drooling at the mouth.* **2** [I] **~ (over sb/sth)** (*disapproving*) to show in a silly or exaggerated way that you want or admire someone or something very much: *teenagers drooling over photos of movie stars*

droop /drup/ *verb* **1** [I] to bend, hang, or move downward, especially because of being weak or tired: *She was so tired, her eyelids were beginning to droop.* **2** [I] to become sad or depressed: *Our spirits drooped when we heard the news.* ▶ **droop** *noun* [sing.]: *the slight droop of her mouth* **droop·y** *adj.*: *a droopy mustache*

drop ✏ /drɑp/ *verb, noun*
- *verb* (-pp-)
> **FALL 1** [I, T] to fall or allow something to fall by accident: *The climber slipped and dropped to his death.* ◆ **~ sth** *Be careful not to drop that plate.* **2** [I, T] to fall or make something fall deliberately: + **adv./prep.** *He staggered in and dropped into a chair.* ◆ **~ sth (+ adv./prep.)** *Medical supplies are being dropped into the stricken area.* ◆ *He dropped his pants.* **3** [I] to fall down or be no longer able to stand because you are extremely tired: *I feel ready to drop.* ◆ *She expects everyone to work till they drop.*
> **BECOME WEAKER/LESS 4** [I, T] to become or make something weaker, lower, or less **SYN** FALL: *The temperature has dropped considerably.* ◆ *At last the wind dropped.* ◆ *His voice dropped to a whisper.* ◆ *The Dutch team has dropped to fifth place.* ◆ *The price of shares dropped by 14 cents.* ◆ *Shares dropped in price by 14 cents.* ◆ **~ sth** *She dropped her voice dramatically.* ◆ *You must drop your speed in built-up areas.* ⟳ language bank at FALL
> **EYES 5** [I, T] **your eyes/gaze ~ | ~ your eyes/gaze** (*formal*) to look down: *Her eyes dropped to her book.*
> **SLOPE DOWNWARD 6** [I] **~ (away) (from sth)** to slope steeply downward: *In front of them the valley dropped sharply away from the road.*
> **DELIVER/SEND 7** [T] to deliver something, often on the way to somewhere else; to stop so that someone can get out of a car, etc.: **~ sb/sth off** *You left your jacket, but I can drop it off on my way to work tomorrow.* ◆ **~ sb/sth** *Can you drop me near the bank?* ⟳ related noun DROP-OFF *n.* (3) **8** [T] **~ someone a line/note** to send a short letter to someone: *Drop me a line when you get there.*
> **LEAVE OUT 9** [T] **~ sb/sth (from sth)** to leave someone or something out by accident or deliberately: *She's been dropped from the team because of injury.*

> FRIENDS **10** [T] **~ sb** to stop seeing someone socially: *She's dropped most of her old friends.*
> STOP **11** [T] **~ sth** to stop doing or discussing something; to not continue with something: *I dropped German* (= stopped studying it) *when I was 14.* ◆ *I can't just drop everything every time you need a ride.* ◆ *Look, can we just drop it* (= stop talking about it)? ◆ *I think we'd better drop the subject.* ◆ *Let's drop the formalities—please call me Mike.* ◆ *The police decided to drop the charges against her.*
> HINT **12** [T] **~ a hint** to say or do something in order to show someone, in an indirect way, what you are thinking
> IN KNITTING **13** [T] **~ a stitch** to let a STITCH go off the needle

IDM **drop the ball** (*informal*) to make a mistake and spoil something that you are responsible for **drop dead 1** (*informal*) to die suddenly and unexpectedly **2** (*informal*) used to tell someone, rudely, to stop annoying you, INTERFERING, etc. ➔ see also DROP-DEAD **drop names** to mention famous people you know or have met in order to impress others ➔ related noun NAME-DROPPING **let sb/sth drop 1** to do or say nothing more about someone or something: *I suggest we let the matter drop.* **2** to mention someone or something in a conversation, by accident or as if by accident: *He let it drop that the actor was a close friend of his.* ➔ more at BOTTOM *n.*, FLY *n.*, HEAR, JAW *n.*, LAP *n.*
PHR V **drop a'way** to become weaker or less: *She could feel the tension drop away.* **,drop 'back/be'hind | ,drop be'hind sb** to move or fall into position behind someone else: *We cannot afford to drop behind our competitors.* **,drop 'by/'in | ,drop in on sb | ,drop 'into sth** to pay an informal visit to a person or a place: *Drop by sometime.* ◆ *I thought I'd drop in on you while I was passing.* ◆ *Sorry we're late—we dropped into a store on the way.* **,drop 'off** (*informal*) **1** to fall into a light sleep **SYN** FALL ASLEEP: *I dropped off and missed the end of the movie.* **2** to become fewer or less: *Traffic in the town has dropped off since the bypass opened.* ➔ related noun DROP-OFF *n.* (1) **,drop 'out (of sth) 1** to no longer take part in or be part of something: *He has dropped out of active politics.* ◆ *a word that has dropped out of the language* ➔ language bank at FALL **2** to leave school, college, etc. without finishing your studies: *She dropped out after only a year of college.* ➔ related noun DROPOUT **3** to reject the ideas and ways of behaving that are accepted by the rest of society ➔ related noun DROPOUT

● **noun**
> OF LIQUID **1** [C] a very small amount of liquid that forms a round shape: *drops of rain* ◆ *a drop of blood* ➔ see also RAINDROP, TEARDROP **2** [C, usually sing.] a small quantity of a liquid: *Could I have just a drop more milk in my coffee, please?* ◆ *I haven't touched a drop* (= drunk any alcohol) *all evening.*
> FALL **3** [C, usually sing.] **~ (in sth)** a fall or reduction in the amount, level, or number of something: *a drop in prices/temperature, etc.* ◆ *a dramatic/sharp drop in profits* ◆ *a five-percent drop* ➔ language bank at FALL
> DISTANCE **4** [sing.] a distance down from a high point to a lower point: *There was a sheer drop of fifty yards to the rocks below.* ◆ *a twenty-foot drop*
> MEDICINE **5** **drops** [pl.] a liquid medicine that you put one drop at a time into your eyes, ears, or nose: *eye drops*
> DELIVERING **6** [C] the act of delivering someone or something in a vehicle or by plane; the act of dropping something: *Aid agencies are organizing food drops to civilians in the war zone.* ◆ *a parachute drop*
> CANDY **7** [C] a small round candy of the type mentioned: *fruit drops* ◆ *cough drops* (= candy to help a cough)
IDM **at the drop of a hat** immediately; without hesitating: *The company can't expect me to move my home and family at the drop of a hat.* **a drop in the bucket** an amount of something that is too small or unimportant to make any real difference to a situation

'drop cloth *noun* a large sheet that is used to protect floors, furniture, etc. from dust or paint

,drop-'dead *adv.* (*informal*) used before an adjective to emphasize that someone or something is attractive in a very noticeable way: *a drop-dead gorgeous Hollywood star*

'drop-down ,menu *noun* (*computing*) a menu that appears on a computer screen when you choose it, and that stays there until you choose one of the functions on it

'drop-in *adj.* [only before noun] able to be visited without arranging a fixed time first: *a drop-in center*

drop·let /'drɑplət/ *noun* a small drop of a liquid

'drop-off *noun, adj.*
● **noun 1** [C] a decline or decrease in something: *There has been a steady drop-off in tourism.* **2** [C] a downward slope: *The hill has a very steep drop-off.* **3** [U, C] an occasion when someone or something is delivered: *Drop-offs are on Tuesdays.* **4** [C] a place where something is delivered: *The drop-off is near my office.*
● **adj.** [only before noun] connected with the delivery of something: *The bags will be left at two drop-off points.*

drop·out /'drɑpaʊt/ *noun* **1** a person who leaves school or college before they have finished their studies: *high school dropouts* ◆ *a college with a high dropout rate* **2** a person who rejects the ideas and ways of behaving that are accepted by the rest of society

drop·per /'drɑpər/ *noun* a short glass or plastic tube with a hollow rubber end used for measuring medicine or other liquids in drops ➔ picture at LABORATORY

drop·pings /'drɑpɪŋz/ *noun* [pl.] the solid waste matter of birds and animals (usually small animals)

'drop shot *noun* (also **dink**) (in TENNIS) a soft hit that makes the ball just go over the net and land on the ground without bouncing (BOUNCE) much

drop·sy /'drɑpsi/ *noun* [U] (*old-fashioned*) = EDEMA

'drop zone *noun* the area in which someone or something should land after being dropped from an aircraft

dro·soph·i·la /drə'sɑfələ/ (*pl.* **dro·soph·i·la**) *noun* a small fly that feeds on fruit and is often used in scientific research

dross /drɔs; drɑs/ *noun* [U] **1** something of very low quality; the least valuable part of something: *mass-produced dross* **2** (*technical*) a waste substance, especially that separated from a metal when it is melted

drought /draʊt/ *noun* [U, C] a long period of time when there is little or no rain: *two years of severe drought* ◆ *one of the worst droughts on record*

drove /droʊv/ *noun* [usually pl.] a large number of people or animals, often moving or doing something as a group: *droves of tourists* ◆ *People were leaving the countryside in droves to look for work in the cities.* ➔ see also DRIVE *v.*

dro·ver /'droʊvər/ *noun* a person who moves groups of cows or sheep from one place to another, especially to market

drown /draʊn/ *verb* **1** [I, T] to die because you have been underwater too long and you cannot breathe; to kill someone in this way: *Two children drowned after falling into the river.* ◆ *He had attempted to rescue the drowning man.* ◆ **~ sb/sth/yourself** *She tried to drown herself.* ◆ *He was drowned at sea.* ◆ *They had drowned the unwanted kittens.* **2** [T] **~ sth (in sth)** to make something very wet; to completely cover something in water or another liquid **SYN** DRENCH: *The fruit was drowned in cream.* **3** [T] **~ sb/sth (out)** (of a sound) to be louder than other sounds so that you cannot hear them: *She turned up the radio to drown out the noise from next door.* ▶ **drown·ing** *noun* [U, C]: *death by drowning* ◆ *Alcohol plays a part in an estimated 30% of drownings.* **IDM** **drown your fears/loneliness/sorrows, etc.** (especially *humorous*) to get drunk in order to forget your problems **like a drowned rat** (especially *humorous*) very wet and messy: *Come inside—you look like a drowned rat!*

drowse /draʊz/ *verb* [I] to be in a light sleep or almost asleep

drow·sy /'draʊzi/ *adj.* (**drow·si·er**, **drow·si·est**) **1** tired and almost asleep **SYN** SLEEPY: *The medicine may make you feel drowsy.* **2** making you feel relaxed and tired: *a drowsy afternoon in the sunshine* ▶ **drow·si·ly** /-zəli/ *adv.* **drow·si·ness** *noun* [U]: *The drugs tend to cause drowsiness.*

drub·bing /'drʌbɪŋ/ *noun* (*informal*) (in a sport) a situation where one team easily beats another: *We gave them a drubbing in the game on Saturday.*

drudge /drʌdʒ/ *noun* a person who has to do long, hard, boring jobs

drudg·er·y /ˈdrʌdʒəri/ *noun* [U] hard boring work

drug /drʌg/ *noun, verb*
- *noun* **1** an illegal substance that some people smoke, INJECT, etc. for the physical and mental effects it has: *He does not smoke or take drugs.* ◆ *teenagers experimenting with drugs* ◆ *I found out Steve was on drugs* (= regularly used drugs). ◆ *drug and alcohol abuse* ◆ *a hard* (= very harmful) *drug such as heroin* ◆ *a soft drug* (= one that is not considered very harmful) ◆ *Drugs have been seized with a street value of two million dollars.* ◆ *She was a drug addict* (= could not stop using drugs). ◆ *He was charged with pushing drugs* (= selling them). ◆ *(informal) I don't do drugs* (= use them). ◆ *drug rehabilitation* **2** a substance used as a medicine or used in a medicine: *prescribed drugs* ◆ *The doctor put me on a course of pain-killing drugs.* ◆ *drug companies* ◆ *The drug has some bad side effects.* ⊃ see also DESIGNER DRUG
- *verb* (-gg-) **1** ~ sb/sth to give a person or an animal a drug, especially to make them unconscious, or to affect their performance in a race or competition: *He was drugged and bundled into the back of the car.* ◆ *It's illegal to drug horses before a race.* **2** ~ sth to add a drug to someone's food or drink to make them unconscious or SLEEPY: *Her drink must have been drugged.*

drug dealer *noun* a person who sells illegal drugs

drug·gie /ˈdrʌgi/ *noun* (pl. drug·gies) (informal) a person who takes illegal drugs regularly

drug·gist /ˈdrʌgɪst/ *noun* (old-fashioned) = PHARMACIST

drug·gy /ˈdrʌgi/ *adj.* (drug·gi·er, drug·gi·est) (informal) using or involving illegal drugs

drug lord *noun* a powerful leader of a group of people who buy and sell large quantities of illegal drugs

drug peddler *noun* = PEDDLER

drug·store /ˈdrʌgstɔr/ *noun*
a store that sells medicines and also other types of goods, for example COSMETICS ⊃ compare PHARMACY

Dru·id /ˈdruɪd/ *noun* a priest of an ancient Celtic religion

drum /drʌm/ *noun, verb*
- *noun* **1** a musical instrument made of a hollow round frame with plastic or skin stretched tightly across one or both ends. You play it by hitting it with sticks or with your hands.: *a bass drum* ◆ *Tony Hill on drums* ◆ *to play the drums* ◆ *a regular drum beat* **2** a large container for oil or chemicals, shaped like a CYLINDER: *a 50 gallon drum* ◆ *an oil drum* **3** a thing shaped like a drum, especially part of a machine: *The mixture flows to a revolving drum where the water is filtered out.* **IDM** beat/bang the drum (for sb/sth) to speak with enthusiasm in support of someone or something ⊃ more at MARCH v.
- *verb* (-mm-) **1** [I] to play a drum **2** [T, I] ~ (sth) on sth to make a sound by hitting a surface again and again: *Impatiently, he drummed his fingers on the table.* **IDM** drum sth into sb's head = DRUM STH INTO SB **PHRV** drum sth into sb to make someone remember something by repeating it a lot of times: *We had it drummed into us that we should never talk to strangers.* drum sb out (of sth) [usually passive] to force someone to leave an organization as a punishment for doing something wrong drum sth↔up to try hard to get support or business: *He flew to the north of the country to drum up support for the campaign.*

drum and bass (also drum 'n' bass) *noun* [U] a type of electronic dance music developed in Britain in the early 1990s, which has a fast drum beat and a strong, slower BASS¹ beat

drum·beat /ˈdrʌmbɪt/ *noun* the sound that a beat on a drum makes

drum kit *noun* a set of drums ⊃ picture at INSTRUMENT

drum·lin /ˈdrʌmlən/ *noun* (geology) a very small hill formed by the movement of a GLACIER (= a large moving mass of ice)

drum ma·chine *noun* an electronic musical instrument that produces the sound of drums

drum major *noun* the leader of a marching band of musicians, especially in the army

drum major·ette *noun* = MAJORETTE

drum·mer /ˈdrʌmer/ *noun* a person who plays a drum or drums **IDM** see MARCH v.

drum·ming /ˈdrʌmɪŋ/ *noun* [U, sing.] **1** the act of playing a drum; the sound of a drum being played **2** a continuous sound or feeling like the beats of a drum: *the steady drumming of the rain on the tin roof*

drum 'n' bass *noun* = DRUM AND BASS

drum·stick /ˈdrʌmstɪk/ *noun* **1** a stick used for playing a drum ⊃ picture at INSTRUMENT **2** the lower part of the leg of a chicken or other bird that is cooked and eaten as food: *a chicken/turkey drumstick*

drunk /drʌŋk/ *adj., noun* ⊃ see also DRINK v.
- *adj.* **1** [not usually before noun] having drunk so much alcohol that it is impossible to think or speak clearly: *She was too drunk to remember anything about the party.* ◆ *His only way of dealing with his problems was to go out and get drunk.* ◆ *They got drunk on vodka.* **ANT** SOBER **2** ~ with sth in a great state of excitement because of a particular emotion or situation: *drunk with success* **IDM** (as) drunk as a skunk (informal) very drunk ⊃ more at BLIND adv., ROARING
- *noun* a person who is drunk or who often gets drunk

drunk·ard /ˈdrʌŋkərd/ *noun* (old-fashioned) a person who gets drunk very often **SYN** ALCOHOLIC

drunk driver *noun* a person who drives a vehicle after drinking too much alcohol

drunk driving *noun* [U] driving a vehicle after drinking too much alcohol

drunk·en /ˈdrʌŋkən/ *adj.* [only before noun] **1** drunk or often getting drunk: *a drunken driver* ◆ *She was often beaten by her drunken husband.* **2** showing the effects of too much alcohol; involving people who are drunk: *He came home to find her in a drunken stupor.* ◆ *a drunken brawl* ▶ **drunk·en·ly** *adv.*: *He staggered drunkenly to his feet.* **drunk·en·ness** *noun* [U]

drunk tank *noun* (informal, humorous) a place where people are put by the police because they are drunk: *He spent the night in the drunk tank at the local police station.*

druth·ers /ˈdrʌðərz/ *noun* [pl.] (informal) used to say what you would prefer if you could choose: *If I had my druthers I wouldn't be going to this meeting.*

dry /draɪ/ *adj., verb*
- *adj.* (dri·er, dri·est)
  ⊳ NOT WET **1** not wet, damp, or sticky; without water or MOISTURE: *Is my shirt dry yet?* ◆ *Store onions in a cool dry place.* ◆ *I'm afraid this cake has turned out very dry.* ◆ *Her mouth felt as dry as a bone* (= completely dry). ◆ *When the paint is completely dry, apply another coat.* ◆ *It was high summer and the rivers were dry* (= had no water in them). ⊃ see also BONE DRY **ANT** WET
  ⊳ LITTLE RAIN **2** with very little rain: *weeks of hot dry weather* ◆ *the dry season* ◆ *I hope it stays dry for our picnic.* ◆ *Rattlesnakes live in the warmer, drier parts of North America.* **ANT** WET
  ⊳ SKIN/HAIR **3** without the natural oils that makes it soft and healthy: *a shampoo for dry hair*
  ⊳ COUGH **4** that does not produce any PHLEGM (= the thick liquid that forms in the nose and throat): *a dry hacking cough*
  ⊳ BREAD **5** eaten on its own without any butter, etc.: *Breakfast consisted of dry bread and a cup of coffee.*
  ⊳ WINE **6** not sweet: *a crisp, dry white wine* ◆ *a dry sherry* **ANT** SWEET
  ⊳ HUMOR **7** (approving) amusing but expressed in a quiet way

---

that is not obvious, often using IRONY: *He was a man of few words with a dry sense of humor.*
> WITHOUT EMOTION **8** not showing emotion: *a dry voice*
> BORING **9** not interesting: *Government reports tend to make dry reading.*
> WITHOUT ALCOHOL **10** without alcohol; where it is illegal to buy, sell, or drink alcohol: *The state was dry on Sundays.* ◆ *a dry county/state* ⊃ see also DRYLY ▸ **dry·ness** *noun* [U]
   IDM **milk/suck sb/sth dry** to get from someone or something all the money, help, information, etc. they have, usually giving nothing in return **not a dry eye in the house** (*humorous*) used to say that everyone was very emotional about something: *There wasn't a dry eye in the house when they announced their engagement.* **run dry** to stop supplying water; to be all used so that none is left: *The wells in most villages in the region have run dry.* ◆ *Vaccine supplies started to run dry as the flu outbreak reached epidemic proportions.* ⊃ more at BLEED, HIGH *adj.*, POWDER *n.*, SQUEEZE *v.*
• **verb** (dries, dry·ing, dried, dried) [I, T] to become dry; to make something dry: *Be careful. The paint hasn't dried yet.* ◆ *You wash the dishes and I'll dry.* ◆ *~ sth Use this towel to dry your hands.* ◆ *dry your hair* ◆ *to dry your eyes/tears* (= stop crying)
   PHR V ,dry 'off | ,dry sb/sth↔'off to become dry or make something dry: *We went swimming, then lay in the sun to dry off.* ◆ *We dried our boots off by the fire.* ,dry 'out | ,dry sb↔'out (*informal*) to stop drinking alcohol after you have continuously been drinking too much; to cure someone of drinking too much alcohol: *He went to an expensive clinic to dry out.* ,dry 'out | ,dry sth↔'out to become or to allow something to become dry, in a way that is not wanted: *Water the plant regularly, never letting the soil dry out.* ◆ *Hot sun and cold winds can soon dry out your skin.* ,dry 'up **1** (of rivers, lakes, etc.) to become completely dry: *During the drought the river dried up.* **2** if a supply of something **dries up**, there is gradually less of it until there is none left: *As she got older, offers of modeling work began to dry up.*

dry·ad /'draɪæd/ *noun* (in stories) a female spirit who lives in a tree

'dry cell *noun* the type of cell in a **dry battery** which contains chemicals only in solid form

'dry-clean (also clean) *verb* ~ sth to clean clothes using chemicals instead of water: *This garment must be dry-cleaned only.* ⊃ thesaurus box at CLEAN ▸ dry- cleaning *noun* [U]

'dry ,cleaners *noun* = CLEANER (3)

'dry dock *noun* [C, U] an area in a port from which the water can be removed, used for building or repairing ships

dry·er (also dri·er) /'draɪər/ *noun* (especially in compounds) a machine for drying something: *a hair dryer*

'dry-eyed *adj.* [not before noun] not crying: *She remained dry-eyed throughout the trial.*

'dry ,farming *noun* [U] = DRY-LAND FARMING

'dry goods *noun* [pl.] (*old-fashioned*) cloth and things that are made out of cloth, such as clothes and sheets: *a dry goods store* ⊃ compare DRAPERY

,dry 'ice *noun* [U] solid CARBON DIOXIDE used for keeping food, etc. cold and producing special effects in the theater

,dry 'land *noun* [U] land, rather than the ocean SYN TERRA FIRMA: *It was a great relief to be back on dry land after such a rough crossing.*

dry·ly (also dri·ly) /'draɪli/ *adv.* ⊃ see also DRY **1** if someone speaks **dryly**, they are being humorous, but not in an obvious way: *"Well, at least it's not purple," she commented dryly.* **2** in a way that shows no emotion: *He smiled dryly and leaned back in his chair.* **3** in a way that shows that there is no liquid present: *She coughed dryly.*

,dry 'milk (also ,powdered 'milk) *noun* [U] milk in the form of a powder

,dry-'roasted *adj.* cooked in an oven without adding oil or fat: *dry-roasted peanuts*

'dry rot *noun* [U] **1** wood that has decayed and turned to powder **2** any FUNGUS that causes this decay

,dry 'run *noun* [usually sing.] a complete practice of a performance or way of doing something, before the real one

'dry slope (also 'dry-ski ,slope) *noun* a steep slope with a special surface for practicing SKIING

'dry·suit /'draɪsut/ *noun* a piece of clothing that fits the whole body closely and keeps water out, worn by people swimming underwater or sailing ⊃ see also WETSUIT

'dry·wall /'draɪwɔl/ *noun* [U] **1** = PLASTERBOARD **2** a stone wall built without MORTAR (= a substance usually used to hold bricks or stones together in building) between the stones

DSL /,di ɛs 'ɛl/ *abbr.* (*computing*) digital subscriber line (a way of sending electronic data at high speed along ordinary telephone lines, used for supplying the Internet to homes, businesses, etc.)

DST /,di ɛs 'ti/ *abbr.* DAYLIGHT SAVING TIME

DTP /,di ti 'pi/ *abbr.* DESKTOP PUBLISHING

DTs (also D.T.'s) /,di 'tiz/ *noun* usually **the DTs** [pl.] the abbreviation for "delirium tremens" (a physical condition in which people who drink too much alcohol feel their body shaking and imagine that they are seeing things that are not really there)

du·al /'duəl/ *adj.* [only before noun] having two parts or aspects: *his dual role as composer and conductor* ◆ *She has dual nationality* (= is a citizen of two different countries). ◆ *The piece of furniture serves a dual purpose as a cabinet and as a table.* ⊃ see also DUAL-PURPOSE ⊃ note at DOUBLE

,dual con'trols *noun* [pl.] two sets of instruments for controlling a vehicle or aircraft, so that a teacher, for example, can take control from the driver ▸ ,dual con'trol *adj.*: *a dual-control vehicle*

du·al·ism /'duə,lɪzəm/ *noun* [U] **1** (*philosophy*) the theory that there are two opposite principles in everything, for example good and evil **2** (*formal*) the state of having two parts ▸ du·al·ist /'duəlɪst/, du·al·is·tic /,duə'lɪstɪk/ *adj.* du·al·ist *noun*

du·al·i·ty /du'æləti/ *noun* [U, C] (*pl.* du·al·i·ties) (*formal*) the state of having two parts or aspects

,dual-'purpose *adj.* that can be used for two different purposes: *a dual-purpose vehicle* (= for carrying passengers or goods)

dub /dʌb/ *verb* (-bb-) **1** ~ sb + noun to give someone or something a particular name, often in a humorous or critical way: *The Belgian actor Jean Claude Van Damme has been dubbed "Muscles from Brussels."* **2** ~ sth (into sth) to replace the original speech in a movie or television program with words in another language: *an American movie dubbed into Italian* ⊃ compare SUBTITLE

du·bi·e·ty /du'baɪəti/ *noun* [U] (*formal*) the fact of being uncertain

du·bi·ous /'dubiəs/ *adj.* **1** [not usually before noun] ~ (about sth)/(about doing sth) (of a person) not certain and slightly suspicious about something; not knowing whether something is good or bad SYN DOUBTFUL: *I was pretty dubious about the whole idea.* **2** (*disapproving*) probably not honest SYN SUSPICIOUS: *They indulged in some highly dubious business practices to obtain their current position in the market.* **3** that you cannot be sure about; that is probably not good: *They consider the plan to be of dubious benefit to most families.* ◆ (*ironic*) *She had the dubious honor of being chosen to head a failing company* (= it was not an honor at all). ▸ du·bi·ous·ly *adv.*

dub·ni·um /'dubniəm/ *noun* [U] (*symb.* Db) a RADIOACTIVE chemical element. Dubnium is produced when atoms COLLIDE (= crash into each other).

du·cal /'dukl/ *adj.* [only before noun] of or belonging to a DUKE

t tea   ʈ butter   d did   k cat   g got   tʃ chin   dʒ June   f fall

duc·at /ˈdʌkət/ noun (in the past) a gold coin used in many European countries

duch·ess /ˈdʌtʃəs/ noun **1** the wife of a DUKE: *the Duchess of York* **2** a woman who has the rank of a DUKE

duch·y /ˈdʌtʃi/ noun (pl. **duch·ies**) (also **duke·dom**) an area of land that is owned and controlled by a DUKE or DUCHESS

duck /dʌk/ noun, verb
• noun **1** (pl. **ducks** or **duck**) [C] a common bird that lives on or near water and has short legs, WEBBED feet (= feet with thin pieces of skin between the toes), and a wide beak. There are many types of ducks, some of which are kept for their meat or eggs: *wild ducks* ◆ *duck eggs* ⟳ picture at ANIMAL **2** [C] a female duck ⟳ compare DRAKE **3** [U] meat from a duck: *roast duck* ⟳ see also LAME DUCK, SITTING DUCK **IDM get/have (all) your ducks in a row** to have made all the preparations needed to do something; to be well organized **(take to sth) like a duck to water** (to become used to something) very easily, without any problems or fears: *She has taken to teaching like a duck to water.* ⟳ more at DEAD *adj.*, WATER *n.*
• verb **1** [I, T] to move your head or body downward to avoid being hit or seen: *He had to duck as he came through the door.* ◆ ~ **(down) (behind/under sth)** *We ducked down behind the wall so they wouldn't see us.* ◆ *He just managed to duck out of sight.* ◆ ~ **sth** *She ducked her head and got into the car.* **2** [T] ~ **sth** to avoid something by moving your head or body out of the way **SYN DODGE**: *He ducked the first few blows, then started to fight back.* **3** [I] + *adv./prep.* to move somewhere quickly, especially in order to avoid being seen: *She ducked into the adjoining room as we came in.* **4** [I] + *adv./prep.* to visit somewhere, especially for a short time: *I think he ducked into the grocery store for a few minutes.* **5** [I, T] (*informal*) to avoid a difficult or unpleasant duty or responsibility: ~ **out of sth** *It's his turn to cook dinner, but I bet he'll try to duck out of it.* ◆ ~ **sth** *The government is ducking the issue.*

duck–billed ˈplatypus noun = PLATYPUS

duck·boards /ˈdʌkbɔrdz/ noun [pl.] long narrow wooden boards used to make a path over wet ground

duck·ling /ˈdʌklɪŋ/ noun [C, U] a young duck; the meat of a young duck ⟳ see also UGLY DUCKLING

duck ˈsoup noun [U] (*informal*) a problem that is easy to deal with, or an opponent who is easy to defeat

duck·weed /ˈdʌkwid/ noun [U] a very small plant that grows on the surface of still water

duck·y /ˈdʌki/ adj. (**duck·i·er**, **duck·i·est**) (*old-fashioned* or *humorous*) very pleasant: *Everything is just ducky.*

duct /dʌkt/ noun **1** a pipe or tube carrying liquid, gas, electric or telephone wires, etc.: *a heating/ventilation duct* **2** a tube in the body or in plants through which liquid passes: *the bile duct*

duc·tile /ˈdʌktl; -taɪl/ adj. (*technical*) (of a metal) that can be made into a thin wire

duct·ing /ˈdʌktɪŋ/ noun [U] **1** a system of ducts **2** material in the form of a duct or ducts: *a short piece of ducting*

duct tape noun [U] very strong cloth tape that is sticky on one side, often used for repairing things or covering holes in pipes

dud /dʌd/ noun **1** [C] (*informal*) a thing that is useless, especially because it does not work correctly: *Two of the fireworks in the box were duds.* **2 duds** [pl.] (*old-fashioned*, *slang*) clothes

dude /dud/ noun (*slang*) a man: *He's a cool dude.* ◆ *Hey, dude, what's up?*

dude ranch noun a RANCH (= a large farm) where people can go on vacation and do the types of activities that COWBOYS do **ORIGIN** From an old meaning of the word *dude*, a man from the city who wears fashionable clothes.

dudg·eon /ˈdʌdʒən/ noun **IDM** see HIGH *adj.*

due /du/ adj., noun, adv.
• adj.
▸ CAUSED BY **1** [not before noun] ~ **to sth/sb** caused by someone or something; because of someone or something: *The team's success was largely due to her efforts.* ◆ *Most of the problems were due to human error.* ◆ *The project had to be abandoned due to a lack of government funding.* ⟳ language bank at BECAUSE **HELP** Some people think that it is more correct to use **owing to** to mean "because of" after a verb or at the beginning of a clause, as **due** is an adjective.
▸ EXPECTED **2** [not before noun] arranged or expected: *When's the baby due?* ◆ *The next train is due in five minutes.* ◆ *My essay's due next Friday* (= it has to be given to the teacher by then). ◆ ~ **to do sth** *Rose is due to start school in January.* ◆ ~ **for sth** *The band's first album is due for release later this month.*
▸ OWED **3** [not usually before noun] when a sum of money is **due**, it must be paid immediately: *Payment is due on October 2.* **4** [not before noun] ~ **(to sb)** owed to someone as a debt, because it is their right or because they have done something to deserve it: *Have they been paid the money that is due to them?* ◆ *Our thanks are due to the whole team.* **5** [not before noun] owed something; deserving something: ~ **sth** *I'm still due 15 days' vacation.* ◆ ~ **for sth** *She's due for promotion soon.*
▸ SUITABLE/RIGHT **6** [only before noun] (*formal*) that is suitable or right in the circumstances: *After due consideration, we have decided to appoint Mr. Davis to the job.* ◆ *to make due allowance for something* ⟳ compare UNDUE
IDM in due course at the right time and not before: *Your request will be dealt with in due course.* ⟳ more at RESPECT *n.*
• noun **1 your/someone's** ~ [U] a thing that should be given to someone by right: *He received a large reward, which was no more than his due* (= than what he deserved). ◆ *She's a slow worker, but to give her her due* (= to be fair to her), *she does try very hard.* **2 dues** [pl.] charges, for example to be a member of a club: *to pay your dues* **IDM** see PAY *v.*
• adv. ~ **north/south/east/west** exactly; in a straight line: *to sail due east* ◆ *The town is five miles due north of here.*

due date noun [usually sing.] **1** the date or day that something is supposed to be paid, returned, completed, etc.: *Tomorrow is the due date for the rent.* ◆ *The two library books have different due dates.* ◆ *The due date for your final paper is next Thursday.* **2** the date on which a woman is expected to give birth: *Her due date and mine are just two weeks apart.*

du·el /ˈduəl/ noun **1** a formal fight with weapons between two people, used in the past to settle a disagreement, especially over a matter of honor: *to fight/win a duel* ◆ *to challenge someone to a duel* **2** a competition or struggle between two people or groups: *a verbal duel* ▸ **duel** verb (-**l**- or -**ll**-) [I]: *The two men dueled to the death.*

duel·ing /ˈduəlɪŋ/ (also **duel·ling**) noun [U] the practice of fighting duels

due ˌprocess of ˈlaw (also **ˌdue ˈprocess**) noun [U] (*law*) the right of a citizen to be treated fairly, especially the right to a fair trial

du·et /duˈɛt/ (also *less frequent* **duo**) noun a piece of music for two players or singers: *a piano duet* ⟳ compare SOLO, TRIO

duff /dʌf/ noun (*informal*) a person's bottom

duf·fel bag (also **duf·fle bag**) /ˈdʌfl ˌbæg/ noun **1** a large bag made of strong cloth or soft leather, used when you are traveling for carrying clothes, etc. ⟳ picture at BAG **2** a bag made out of cloth, shaped like a tube and closed by a string around the top. It is usually carried over the shoulder.

duf·fel coat (also **duf·fle coat**) /ˈdʌfl ˌkout/ noun a heavy coat made of wool, that usually has a HOOD, and is fastened with TOGGLE

dug pt, pp of DIG

dug·out /ˈdʌɡaʊt/ noun **1** a shelter by the side of a baseball or SOCCER field where a team's manager, etc. can sit and watch the game **2** a rough shelter made by digging a hole in the ground and covering it, used by soldiers **3** (also ˌdugout ca'noe) a CANOE (= a type of light narrow boat) made by cutting out the inside of a tree TRUNK

duh /dʌ/ *exclamation* (*informal*) used to comment on a statement you think is stupid or obvious: *"You should always lock up your bike." "Well, duh!"*

DUI /ˌdi yu 'aɪ/ *noun* [U, C] the crime of driving a vehicle after drinking too much alcohol. It is the abbreviation for "driving under the influence" and is a less serious crime than DWI (= driving while intoxicated).

du jour /də 'ʒʊr; duː-; də 'ʒɜr/ *adj.* [after noun] (*informal, humorous*) very popular or important now: *This age group is the target group du jour.* **ORIGIN** From French, meaning "of the day".

duke /duk/ *noun* **1** a NOBLEMAN of the highest rank: *the Duke of Edinburgh* **2** (in some parts of Europe, especially in the past) a male ruler of a small independent state ⊃ see also DUCHESS, DUCHY

duke·dom /'dukdəm/ *noun* **1** the rank or position of a duke **2** = DUCHY

dul·cet /'dʌlsət/ *adj.* [only before noun] (*humorous* or *ironic*) sounding sweet and pleasant: *I thought I recognized the dulcet tones of the kids* (= the sound of their voices).

dul·ci·mer /'dʌlsəmər/ *noun* **1** a musical instrument that you play by hitting the metal strings with two HAMMERS **2** a musical instrument with strings, popular in American traditional music, that you lay on your knee and play with your fingers

dull 🔑 /dʌl/ *adj., verb*
● *adj.* (**dull·er, dull·est**)
▷ BORING **1** not interesting or exciting **SYN** DREARY: *Life in a small town could be really dull.* ◆ *The first half of the game was pretty dull.* ◆ *There's never a dull moment when John's around.* ⊃ thesaurus box at BORING
▷ LIGHT/COLORS **2** not bright or shiny: *a dull gray color* ◆ *dull, lifeless hair* ◆ *Her eyes were dull.*
▷ SOUNDS **3** not clear or loud: *The gates shut behind him with a dull thud.*
▷ WEATHER **4** not bright, with a lot of clouds **SYN** OVERCAST: *It was a dull, gray day.*
▷ BLADES **5** not sharp: *dull knives*
▷ PAIN **6** not very severe, but continuous: *a dull ache/pain*
▷ PERSON **7** slow in understanding **SYN** STUPID: *a dull student*
▷ TRADE **8** not busy; slow: *Don't sell in a dull market.*
  ▶ **dull·ness** *noun* [U] **dul·ly** /'dʌlli/ *adv.*: *"I suppose so," she said dully.* ◆ *His leg ached dully.*
  IDM (**as**) **dull as dishwater** extremely boring ⊃ more at WORK *n.*
● *verb*
▷ PAIN **1** [T, I] **~ (sth)** (of pain or an emotion) to become or be made weaker or less severe: *The pills they gave him dulled the pain for a while.*
▷ PERSON **2** [T] **~ sb** to make a person slower or less lively: *He felt dulled and stupid with sleep.*
▷ COLORS, SOUNDS **3** [I, T] to become or to make something less bright, clean, or sharp: *His eyes dulled and he slumped to the ground.* ◆ **~ sth** *The endless rain seemed to dull all sound.*

dull·ard /'dʌlərd/ *noun* (*old-fashioned*) a stupid person with no imagination

dulls·ville /'dʌlzvɪl/ *noun* [U] (*informal*) a place or situation that is extremely boring

dull-'witted *adj.* (*old-fashioned*) not understanding quickly or easily **SYN** STUPID

du·ly /'duli/ *adv.* **1** (*formal*) in the correct or expected manner: *The document was duly signed by the inspector.* **2** at the expected and correct time: *They duly arrived at 9:30 in spite of torrential rain.* ⊃ compare UNDULY

dumb /dʌm/ *adj., verb*
● *adj.* (**dumb·er, dumb·est**) **1** (*informal*) stupid: *That was a pretty dumb thing to do.* ◆ *If the police question you, act dumb* (= pretend you do not know anything). ◆ *In her early movies she*
played a *dumb blonde.* **2** temporarily not speaking or refusing to speak: *We were all struck dumb with amazement.* ◆ *We sat there in dumb silence.* **3** unable to speak: *She was born deaf and dumb.* **HELP** Dumb used in this meaning is old-fashioned and can be offensive. It is better to use **speech-impaired** instead. ▶ **dumb·ly** *adv.*: *"Are you all right?" Laura nodded dumbly.* **dumb·ness** *noun* [U]
● *verb*
  PHR V ˌdumb 'down | ˌdumb sth↔'down (*disapproving*) to make something less accurate or EDUCATIONAL, and of worse quality, by trying to make it easier for people to understand

dumb·bell /'dʌmbɛl/ *noun* **1** a short bar with a weight at each end, used for making the arm and shoulder muscles stronger ⊃ picture at EXERCISE **2** (*informal*) a stupid person

dumb·found /'dʌmfaʊnd; dʌm'faʊnd/ *verb* **~ sb** to surprise or shock someone so much that they are unable to speak: *His reply dumbfounded me.*

dumbfounded /'dʌm faʊndəd; dʌm'faʊndəd/ (also less frequent **dumb·struck** /'dʌmstrʌk/) *adj.* unable to speak because of surprise: *The news left her dumbfounded.*

dum·bo /'dʌmboʊ/ *noun* (*pl.* **dum·boes**) (*informal*) a stupid person

'**dumb ˌwaiter** *noun* a small elevator for carrying food and plates from one floor to another in a restaurant

dum·dum /'dʌmdʌm/ (also '**dumdum ˌbullet**) *noun* a bullet that spreads out and breaks into many pieces when it hits someone **ORIGIN** It is named after the factory at Dumdum near Calcutta in India, where such bullets were originally made. They are now illegal.

dum·my /'dʌmi/ *noun, adj., verb*
● *noun* (*pl.* **dum·mies**) **1** [C] a model of a person, used especially when making clothes or for showing them in a store window: *a tailor's dummy* **2** [C] a thing that seems to be real but is only a copy of the real thing **3** [C] (*informal*) a stupid person: *Don't just stand there, you dummy.* **4** [C] (in some sports) an occasion when you pretend to pass the ball to another player and then do not do so **5** [U] (in card games, especially BRIDGE) the cards that are placed facing upward on the table and that can be seen by all the players
● *adj.* [only before noun] made to look real, although it is actually a copy which does not work **SYN** REPLICA: *a dummy bomb*
● *verb* [T, I] (in soccer) to pretend to make a particular move in order to confuse your opponent: **~ sth** *She dummied a shot that brought the goalie to her knees.* ◆ **+ adv./prep.** *He dummied past three defenders, then scored.* ⊃ compare JUKE

dump 🔑 /dʌmp/ *verb, noun*
● *verb*
▷ GET RID OF **1** **~ sth** to get rid of something you do not want, especially in a place which is not suitable: *Too much toxic waste is being dumped in the ocean.* ◆ *The dead body was just dumped by the roadside.* **2** **~ sb/sth (on sb)** (*informal*) to get rid of someone or something or leave them for someone else to deal with: *He's got no right to keep dumping his problems on me.* **3** **~ sth** (*business*) to get rid of goods by selling them at a very low price, often in another country
▷ PUT DOWN **4** **~ sth** to put something down in a careless or messy way: *Just dump your stuff over there—we'll sort it out later.*
▷ END RELATIONSHIP **5** **~ sb** (*informal*) to end a romantic relationship with someone: *Did you hear he dumped his girlfriend?*
▷ COMPUTING **6** **~ sth** to copy information and move it somewhere to store it **IDM** see LAP *n.*
  PHR V '**dump on sb** (*informal*) to criticize someone severely or treat them badly
● *noun* ⊃ see also DUMPS
▷ FOR WASTE **1** a place where waste or garbage is taken and left: *a garbage dump* ◆ *the municipal dump* ◆ *a toxic/nuclear waste dump*

> **DIRTY PLACE** **2** (*informal*, *disapproving*) a dirty or unpleasant place: *How can you live in this dump?*

> **FOR WEAPONS** **3** a temporary store for military supplies: *an ammunition dump*

> **COMPUTING** **4** an act of copying data stored in a computer; a copy or list of the contents of this data ➜ see also SCREEN DUMP

> **WASTE FROM BODY** **5** [C] (*slang*) an act of passing waste matter from the body through the BOWEL: *to take a dump*

dump·er /ˈdʌmpər/ *noun* a person who throws away dangerous or harmful things, especially in the wrong place

dumping /ˈdʌmpɪŋ/ *noun* [U] the act or practice of dumping something, especially dangerous substances: *a ban on the dumping of radioactive waste in the ocean*

ˈdumping ˌground *noun* [usually sing.] a place where something that is not wanted is dumped

dump·ling /ˈdʌmplɪŋ/ *noun* **1** a small ball of DOUGH (= a mixture of flour, fat, and water) that is cooked and served with meat dishes: *chicken with herb dumplings* **2** a small ball of PASTRY, often with fruit in it, eaten as a DESSERT: *apple dumplings*

dumps /dʌmps/ *noun* [pl.]
IDM **down in the dumps** (*informal*) feeling unhappy **SYN** DEPRESSED

Dump·ster™ /ˈdʌmpstər/ *noun* a large open container for putting garbage, etc. in. The Dumpster is then loaded on a truck and taken away.

ˈdump truck *noun* a vehicle for carrying earth, stones, etc. in a container which can be lifted up for the load to fall out ➜ picture at CONSTRUCTION

dump·y /ˈdʌmpi/ *adj.* (especially of a person) short and fat

dun /dʌn/ *adj.* gray brown in color ▶ **dun** *noun* [U]

dunce /dʌns/ *noun* (*old-fashioned*) a person, especially a child at school, who is stupid or slow to learn

ˈdunce's ˌcap *noun* a pointed hat that was sometimes given in the past to a child in a class at school who was slow to learn

dun·der·head /ˈdʌndərˌhɛd/ *noun* (*informal*) a silly or stupid person

dune /dun/ (also **ˈsand dune**) *noun* a small hill of sand formed by the wind, near the ocean or in a desert

ˈdune ˌbuggy (also **ˈbeach ˌbuggy**) *noun* a small car used for driving on sand

dung /dʌŋ/ *noun* [U] solid waste from animals, especially from large ones **SYN** MANURE: *cow dung*

dun·ga·rees /ˌdʌŋɡəˈriz/ *noun* [pl.] (*old-fashioned*) heavy cotton pants for working in

dun·geon /ˈdʌndʒən/ *noun* a dark underground room used as a prison, especially in a castle

dung·heap /ˈdʌŋhip/ (also **dung·hill** /ˈdʌŋhɪl/) *noun* a large pile of dung, especially on a farm

dunk /dʌŋk/ *verb* **1** [T] ~ sth (in/into sth) to put food quickly into liquid before eating it: *She sat reading a magazine, dunking cookies in her coffee.* **2** [T] ~ sb/sth to push someone underwater for a short time, as a joke; to put something into water: *The camera survived being dunked in the river.* **3** [I, T] ~ (sth) (in BASKETBALL) to jump very high and put the ball through the BASKET with great force from above

dun·no /dəˈnoʊ/ (*non-standard*) a way of writing the informal spoken form of "I don't know"

du·o /ˈduoʊ/ *noun* (pl. **du·os**) **1** two people who perform together or are often seen or thought of together: *the comedy duo Laurel and Hardy* ➜ compare TRIO **2** = DUET

du·o·de·num /ˌduəˈdinəm; duˈɑdn-əm/ *noun* (pl. **du·o·de-nums** or **du·o·de·na** /ˌduəˈdinə; duˈɑdn-ə/) (*anatomy*) the first part of the small INTESTINE, next to the stomach ➜ picture at BODY ➜ compare ILEUM, JEJUNUM ▶ **du·o·de·nal** /ˌduəˈdinl; duˈɑdn-əl/ *adj.*: *a duodenal ulcer*

du·op·o·ly /duˈɑpəli/ *noun* (pl. **du·op·o·lies**) (*business*) **1** a right to trade in a particular product or service, held by only

two companies or organizations **2** a group of two companies or organizations who hold a duopoly ➜ compare MONOPOLY

dupe /dup/ *verb*, *noun*
• *verb* to trick or cheat someone: ~ sb *They soon realized they had been duped.* ♦ ~ sb into doing sth *He was duped into giving them his credit card.*
• *noun* (*formal*) a person who is tricked or cheated

du·plex /ˈdupleks/ *noun* **1** a building divided into two separate homes ➜ picture at HOUSE **2** an apartment with rooms on two floors

du·pli·cate *verb*, *adj.*, *noun*
• *verb* /ˈdupləˌkeɪt/ **1** [often passive] ~ sth to make an exact copy of something: *a duplicated form* **2** ~ sth to do something again, especially when it is unnecessary: *There's no point in duplicating work already done.* ▶ **du·pli·ca·tion** /ˌdupləˈkeɪʃn/ *noun* [U, C]
• *adj.* /ˈdupləkət/ [only before noun] exactly like something else; made as a copy of something else: *a duplicate invoice*
• *noun* /ˈdupləkət/ one of two or more things that are the same in every detail **SYN** COPY: *Is this a duplicate or the original?*
IDM **in duplicate** (of documents, etc.) as two copies that are exactly the same in every detail: *to prepare a contract in duplicate* ➜ compare TRIPLICATE

du·plic·i·ty /duˈplɪsəti/ *noun* [U] (*formal*) dishonest behavior that is intended to make someone believe something that is not true **SYN** DECEIT ▶ **du·plic·i·tous** /duˈplɪsəṭəs/ *adj.*

du·ra·ble /ˈdʊrəbl/ *adj.* likely to last for a long time without breaking or getting weaker: *durable plastics* ♦ *negotiations for a durable peace* ▶ **du·ra·bil·i·ty** /ˌdʊrəˈbɪləti/ *noun* [U]: *the durability of gold*

ˌdurable ˈgoods (also **du·ra·bles**) *noun* [pl.] (*business*) goods that are expected to last for a long time after they have been bought, such as cars, televisions, etc.

du·ra·tion **AWL** /dʊˈreɪʃn/ *noun* [U] (*formal*) the length of time that something lasts or continues: *The school was used as a hospital for the duration of the war.* ♦ *a contract of three years' duration*
IDM **for the duration** (*informal*) until the end of a particular situation

dur·a·tive /ˈdʊrəṭɪv/ *adj.* (*grammar*) (of a verb tense, a word, etc.) describing an action that continues for some time

du·ress /dʊˈrɛs/ *noun* [U] (*formal*) threats or force that are used to make someone do something: *He signed the confession under duress.*

dur·ing 🔑 /ˈdʊrɪŋ/ *prep.*
1 all through a period of time: *during the 1990s* ♦ *There are extra flights to Colorado during the winter.* ♦ *Please remain seated during the performance.* **2** at some point in a period of time: *He was taken to the hospital during the night.* ♦ *I only saw her once during my stay in Rome.* **HELP** *During* is used to say when something happens; *for* answers the question "how long?": *I stayed in Minneapolis for a week.* ♦ I stayed in Minneapolis during a week.

dur·rie *noun* = DHURRIE

du·rum /ˈdʊrəm/ (also **ˌdurum ˈwheat**) *noun* [U] a type of hard WHEAT, used to make PASTA

dusk /dʌsk/ *noun* [U] the time of day when the light has almost gone, but it is not yet dark **SYN** TWILIGHT: *The street lights go on at dusk.* ➜ compare DAWN

dusk·y /ˈdʌski/ *adj.* (*literary*) not very bright; dark or soft in color: *the dusky light inside the cave* ♦ *dusky pink*

dust 🔑 /dʌst/ *noun*, *verb*
• *noun* **1** [U] a fine powder that consists of very small pieces of sand, earth, etc.: *A cloud of dust rose as the truck pulled away.* ♦ *The workers wear masks to avoid inhaling the dust.* ➜ see also COSMIC DUST ➜ thesaurus box at SOIL **2** the fine powder of dirt that forms in buildings, on furniture, floors, etc.: *The books were all covered with dust.* ♦ *There wasn't a*

speck of dust anywhere in the room. ♦ *That guitar's been sitting gathering dust* (= not being used) *for years now.* **3** a fine powder that consists of very small pieces of a particular substance: *coal/gold dust* ⊃ see also DUSTY

IDM **leave sb in the dust** to leave someone far behind **let the dust settle | wait for the dust to settle** to wait for a situation to become clear or certain ⊃ more at BITE *v.*

● *verb* **1** [I, T] to clean furniture, a room, etc. by removing dust from surfaces with a cloth: *I broke the vase while I was dusting.* ♦ ~ *sth Could you dust the living room?* **2** [T] ~ *sth* (+ *adv./prep.*) to remove dirt from someone or something/yourself with your hands or a brush: *She dusted some ash from her sleeve.* **3** [T] ~ *sth* (**with sth**) to cover something with fine powder: *Dust the cake with sugar.*

PHR V **dust sb/sth↔'off** to remove dust, dirt, etc. from someone or something: (*figurative*) *For the concert, he dusted off some of his old hits.*

dust·ball /'dʌstbɔl/ (also *informal* '**dust ‚bunny**) *noun* a mass of dust and small pieces of thread, hair, material, etc.

'**dust bowl** *noun* an area of land that has been turned into desert by lack of rain or too much farming

'**dust ‚bunny** *noun* (*informal*) a DUSTBALL

'**dust ‚cover** *noun* **1** = DUST JACKET **2** a hard or soft plastic cover on a piece of equipment, etc. that protects it when it is not being used

'**dust ‚devil** *noun* a small column of dust over land, caused by the wind

dust·er /'dʌstər/ *noun* **1** a cloth for removing dust from furniture **2** (*old-fashioned*) a piece of clothing that you wear over your other clothes when you are cleaning the house, etc. ⊃ picture at CLEANING **3** a long coat that was worn by COWBOYS

'**dust ‚jacket** (also '**dust ‚cover**) *noun* a paper cover on a book that protects it but that can be removed

'**dust mite** (also '**house dust ‚mite**) *noun* a very small creature that lives in houses and can cause ALLERGIES

dust·pan /'dʌstpæn/ *noun* a small flat container with a handle into which dust is brushed from the floor ⊃ picture at CLEANING

'**dust storm** *noun* a storm that carries clouds of dust in the wind over a wide area

dust·y /'dʌsti/ *adj.* (**dust·i·er**, **dust·i·est**) **1** full of dust; covered with dust: *a dusty road* ♦ *piles of dusty books* ⊃ thesaurus box at DIRTY **2** (of a color) not bright; dull: *dusty pink*

Dutch /dʌtʃ/ *adj.* of or connected with the Netherlands, its people or its language

IDM **go Dutch (with sb)** to share the cost of something with someone

‚**Dutch 'auction** *noun* a sale in which the price of an item is reduced until someone offers to buy it

‚**Dutch 'door** *noun* a door which is divided into two parts so that the top part can be left open while the bottom part is kept shut

‚**Dutch 'elm dis‚ease** *noun* [U] a disease that kills ELM trees

dut·i·ful /'dutɪfl/ *adj.* doing everything that you are expected to do; willing to obey and to show respect **SYN** OBEDIENT: *a dutiful daughter/son/wife* ▸ **du·ti·ful·ly** /-fli/ *adv.*

du·ty 🔑 /'duti/ *noun* (*pl.* **du·ties**)
1 [C, U] something that you feel you have to do because it is your moral or legal responsibility: *It is my duty to report it to the police.* ♦ *Local officials have a duty to serve the community.* ♦ *I don't want you to visit me simply out of a sense of duty.* ♦ *your duties as a parent* ♦ *to do your duty for your country* **2** [U] the work that is your job: *Report for duty at 8 a.m.* ⊃ see also NIGHT DUTY **3** **duties** [pl.] tasks that are part of your job: *I spend a lot of my time on administrative duties.* ♦ *Your duties include data entry and record keeping.* ⊃ see also HEAVY-DUTY

⊃ thesaurus box at TASK **4** [U] (in compounds) a job that you have to do in the place where you live: *The kids are on bathroom duty tomorrow.* **5** [C, U] a tax that you pay on things that you buy, especially those that you bring into a country: *customs/excise/import duties* ♦ ~ *on sth duty on wine and beer* ⊃ thesaurus box at TAX

IDM **do duty as/for sth** to serve or act as a substitute for something else: *A drinking glass can do duty as a flower vase.* **on/off duty** (of nurses, police officers, etc.) working/not working at a particular time: *Who's on duty today?* ♦ *What time do you go off duty?* ⊃ see also OFF-DUTY ⊃ more at BOUNDEN, LINE *n.*

‚**duty-'bound** *adj.* [not before noun] (*formal*) having to do something because it is your duty: *I felt duty-bound to help.*

‚**duty-'free** *adj.* (of goods) that you can bring into a country without paying tax on them: *duty-free cigarettes* ▸ ‚**duty-'free** *adv.*

‚**duty-'free ‚shop** (also ‚**duty-'free**) *noun* a shop in an airport or on a ship, etc. that sells goods such as cigarettes, alcohol, PERFUME, etc. without tax on them

'**duty ‚officer** *noun* the officer, for example in the police, army, etc., who is on duty at a particular time in a particular place

du·vet /du'veɪ/ *noun* a large cloth bag that is filled with feathers or other soft material and that you have on top of you in bed to keep yourself warm: *a duvet cover* (= a cover that you can wash, that you put over a duvet) ⊃ see also COMFORTER

DVD 🔑 /‚di vi 'di/ *noun*
the abbreviation for "digital videodisc" or "digital versatile disk" (a disk on which large amounts of information, especially photographs and video, can be stored, for use with a computer or **DVD player**): *a DVD drive* ♦ *Is it available on DVD yet?*

DVD-A /‚di vi di 'eɪ/ *noun* the abbreviation for "digital versatile disk audio" (a type of DVD that stores sound of very high quality)

‚**DV'D ‚burner** (also ‚**DV'D ‚writer**) *noun* a piece of equipment used for recording from a computer onto a DVD

DVD-R /‚di vi vi 'ɑr/ *noun* the abbreviation for "digital versatile disk recordable" (a type of DVD that you can use only once to record data)

DVD-ROM /‚di vi di 'rɑm/ *noun* the abbreviation for "digital versatile disk read-only memory" (a type of DVD that allows you to store data but not to record it)

DVD-RW /‚di vi ‚di ɑr 'dʌblyu/ *noun* the abbreviation for "digital versatile disk rewritable" (a type of DVD that you can use many times to record data)

DVR /‚di vi 'ɑr/ *noun* the abbreviation for digital video recorder (a device that records video onto a hard disk or other memory device, using digital technology) **SYN** PVR

DVT /‚di vi 'ti/ *abbr.* DEEP VEIN THROMBOSIS

dwarf /dwɔrf/ *noun, adj., verb*
● *noun* (*pl.* **dwarfs** or **dwarves** /dwɔrvz/) **1** (in stories) a creature like a small man, who has magic powers and who is usually described as living and working under the ground, especially working with metal **2** (sometimes *offensive*) an extremely small person, who will never grow to a normal size because of a physical problem; a person suffering from DWARFISM **HELP** There is no other word that is generally considered more acceptable.
● *adj.* [only before noun] (of a plant or an animal) much smaller than the normal size: *dwarf conifers*
● *verb* ~ *sth* to make something seem small or unimportant compared with something else: *The old houses were dwarfed by the huge new apartment buildings.*

dwarf·ism /'dwɔrfɪzəm/ *noun* the medical condition of being a dwarf. People who suffer from this condition are very short and often have short arms and legs.

ʌ **cup**   ə **about**   eɪ **say**   aɪ **five**   ɔɪ **boy**   aʊ **now**   oʊ **go**   ər **bird**

dwarf 'planet noun a round object in space that goes around the sun but is not as large as a planet and does not clear other objects from its path: *the dwarf planets Pluto and Ceres* ➜ compare PLUTOID

dweeb /dwib/ noun (*slang*) a person who does not have good social skills and is not fashionable

dwell /dwɛl/ verb (**dwelled** or **dwelt**) /dwɛlt/ [I] **+ adv./ prep.** (*formal* or *literary*) to live somewhere: *For ten years she dwelled among the nomads of North America.*
PHR V '**dwell on/upon sth 1** to think or talk a lot about something, especially something it would be better to forget: *So you made a mistake, but there's no need to dwell on it.* **2** to look at something for a long time

dwell·er /'dwɛlər/ noun (especially in compounds) a person or an animal that lives in the particular place that is mentioned: *apartment dwellers*

dwell·ing /'dwɛlɪŋ/ noun (*formal*) a house, apartment, etc. where a person lives: *The development will consist of 66 dwellings and a number of offices.*

'**dwelling** ˌ**place** noun (*old-fashioned*) the place where someone lives

DWI /ˌdi dʌblyu 'aɪ/ noun [U, C] the crime of driving a vehicle after drinking too much alcohol. It is the abbreviation for "driving while intoxicated" and is a more serious crime than DUI (= driving under the influence).

dwin·dle /'dwɪndl/ verb [I] to become gradually less or smaller: *dwindling audiences* ◆ ~ **(away) (to sth)** *Support for the party has dwindled away to nothing.* ◆ ~ **(from sth) (to sth)** *Membership of the club has dwindled from 70 to 20.*

dy·ad /'daɪæd/ noun **1** (*technical*) something that consists of two parts: *the mother-child dyad* **2** (*mathematics*) an OPERATOR that is the combination of two VECTORS ▶ **dy·ad·ic** /daɪ'ædɪk/ adj.

dye /daɪ/ verb, noun
● *verb* (**dyes, dye·ing, dyed, dyed**) to change the color of something, using a special liquid or substance: ~ **sth** *to dye fabric* ◆ ~ **sth + adj.** *She dyed her hair blonde.* ➜ see also TIE-DYE
● *noun* [C, U] a substance that is used to change the color of things such as cloth or hair: *black dye* ◆ *hair dye* ◆ *natural/chemical/vegetable dyes*

ˌ**dyed in the** '**wool** adj. [usually before noun] (usually *disapproving*) having strong beliefs or opinions that are never going to change: *dyed-in-the-wool traditionalists*
ORIGIN From the idea that wool which was dyed in its raw state gave a more even and lasting color.

dy·ing 🔊 /'daɪɪŋ/ adj.
1 [only before noun] connected with or happening at the time of someone's death: *I will remember it to my dying day.* ◆ *her dying wishes/words* **2** **the dying** noun [pl.] people who are dying: *doctors who care for the dying* **IDM** see BREATH ➜ see also DIE v.

dyke = DIKE

dy·nam·ic **AWL** /daɪ'næmɪk/ noun, adj.
● *noun* **1 dynamics** [pl.] the way in which people or things behave and react to each other in a particular situation: *the dynamics of political change* ◆ *group dynamics* (= the way in which members of a group react to each other) **2 dynamics** [U] the science of the forces involved in movement: *fluid dynamics* ➜ compare STATIC **3** [sing.] (*formal*) a force that produces change, action, or effects **4 dynamics** [pl.] (*music*) changes in volume in music
● *adj.* **1** (*approving*) (of a person) having a lot of energy and a strong personality: *a dynamic personality* **2** (of a process) always changing and making progress **ANT** STATIC **3** (*physics*) (of a force or power) producing movement

ANT STATIC **4** (*linguistics*) (of verbs) describing an action rather than a state. **Dynamic** verbs (for example *eat, grow, knock, die*) can be used in the progressive tenses. ➜ compare STATIVE ▶ **dy·nam·i·cally** **AWL** /-kli/ adv.

dy·na·mism /'daɪnəˌmɪzəm/ noun [U] energy and enthusiasm to make new things happen or to make things succeed

dy·na·mite /'daɪnəˌmaɪt/ noun, verb
● *noun* [U] **1** a powerful EXPLOSIVE: *a stick of dynamite* **2** a thing that is likely to cause a violent reaction or a lot of trouble: *The abortion issue is political dynamite.* **3** (*informal, approving*) an extremely impressive or exciting person or thing: *Their new album is dynamite.*
● *verb* ~ **sth** to destroy or damage something using dynamite

dy·na·mo /'daɪnəmoʊ/ noun (pl. **dy·na·mos**) **1** a device for turning MECHANICAL energy (= energy from movement) into electricity; a GENERATOR **2** (*informal*) a person with a lot of energy: *the team's midfield dynamo* ◆ *She's a human dynamo.*

dy·nas·ty /'daɪnəsti/ noun (pl. **dy·nas·ties**) **1** a series of rulers of a country who all belong to the same family: *the Nehru-Gandhi dynasty* **2** a period of years during which members of a particular family rule a country **3** a series of people from the same family who play an important role in business, politics, or another field: *the Rothschild banking dynasty* ▶ **dy·nas·tic** /daɪ'næstɪk/ adj. [usually before noun]: *dynastic history*

dys·en·ter·y /'dɪsənˌtɛri/ noun [U] an infection of the BOWEL that causes severe DIARRHEA with loss of blood

dys·func·tion /dɪs'fʌŋkʃn/ noun [U, C] **1** (*medical*) the fact of a part of the body not working normally: *He's suffering from sexual dysfunction caused by depression.* **2** the situation when the relationships within a society, family, etc. are not working normally: *a tale of loneliness and family dysfunction*

dys·func·tion·al /dɪs'fʌŋkʃənl/ adj. (*technical*) not working normally: *children from dysfunctional families*

dys·lex·i·a /dɪs'lɛksiə/ noun [U] a slight DISORDER of the brain that causes difficulty in reading and spelling, for example, but does not affect intelligence ▶ **dys·lex·ic** /dɪs'lɛksɪk/ adj.: *He's dyslexic.* **dys·lex·ic** noun: *writing courses for dyslexics*

dys·mor·phi·a /dɪs'mɔrfiə/ noun [U] (*medical*) a condition in which a part of the body grows larger than normal ▶ **dys·mor·phic** /dɪs'mɔrfɪk/ adj.

dys·pep·sia /dɪs'pɛpsiə; -'pɛpʃə/ noun [U] (*medical*) pain caused by difficulty in DIGESTING food **SYN** INDIGESTION

dys·pep·tic /dɪs'pɛptɪk/ adj. **1** (*medical*) connected with or suffering from dyspepsia **2** (*formal*) bad-tempered

dys·pho·ri·a /dɪs'fɔriə/ noun [U] (*medical*) a state of worry or general unhappiness ➜ compare EUPHORIA ▶ **dys·phor·ic** /dɪs'fɔrɪk/ adj.

dys·pla·sia /dɪs'pleɪʒə/ noun [U] (*medical*) a condition in which cells multiply in a way that is not normal, sometimes leading to cancer or another serious medical problem

dys·prax·i·a /dɪs'præksiə/ noun [U] a condition of the brain which causes children to have difficulties, for example with physical movement, with writing neatly, and with organizing themselves

dys·pro·si·um /dɪs'proʊziəm/ noun [U] (*symb.* **Dy**) a chemical element. Dysprosium is a soft silver-white metal used in nuclear research.

dys·to·pi·a /dɪs'toʊpiə/ noun an imaginary place or state in which everything is extremely bad or unpleasant ➜ compare UTOPIA ▶ **dys·to·pi·an** /dɪs'toʊpiən/ (also **dys·top·ic** /dɪs'tɑpɪk/) adj.

dys·tro·phy ➜ MUSCULAR DYSTROPHY

Ee

E /i/ noun, abbr.
- **noun** [C, U] (pl. **Es, E's** /iz/) **1** also **e** (pl. **e's**) the fifth letter of the English alphabet: *"Egg" begins with (an) E/"E."* **2** (*music*) the third note in the SCALE OF C MAJOR
- **abbr. 1** usually **E.** (in writing) east; eastern: *E. Asia* **2** (*slang*) the drug ECSTASY: *She had taken some E.*

e- /i/ *combining form* (in nouns and verbs) connected with the use of electronic communication, especially the Internet, for sending information, doing business, etc.: *e-commerce* ◆ *e-business* ⊃ see also E-MAIL

each 🔑 /itʃ/ *det., pron.*
used to refer to every one of two or more people or things, when you are thinking about them separately: *Each answer is worth 20 points.* ◆ *Each of the answers is worth 20 points.* ◆ *The answers are worth 20 points each.* ◆ *"Red or blue?" "I'll take one of each, please."* ◆ *We each have our own car.* ◆ *There aren't enough books for everyone to have one each.* ◆ *They lost $40 each.* ◆ *Each day that passed he grew more and more desperate.*

> **GRAMMAR**
>
> **each ◆ every**
> - **Each** is used in front of a singular noun and is followed by a singular verb: *Each book is labeled with a price.* It is usually preferable to use *their* instead of *his or her*, even in the singular: *Each student will be given their own e-mail address.*
> - ⊃ note at GENDER
> - When **each** is used after a plural subject, it has a plural verb: *They each have their own e-mail address.*
> - **Every** is always followed by a singular verb: *Every student in the class is capable of passing the exam.*
> - **Each of, each one of,** and **every one of** are followed by a plural noun or pronoun, but the verb is singular: *Each (one) of the houses was slightly different.* ◆ *I bought a dozen eggs and every one of them was bad.*

each ˈother 🔑 *pron.*
used as the object of a verb or preposition to show that each member of a group does something to or for the other members: *Don and Susie really loved each other* (= he loved her and she loved him). ◆ *They looked at each other and laughed.* ◆ *We can wear each other's clothes.*

ea·ger 🔑 /ˈigər/ *adj.*
very interested and excited by something that is going to happen or about something that you want to do: *eager crowds outside the stadium* ◆ **~ for sth** *She is eager for* (= wants very much to get) *her parents' approval.* ◆ **~ to do sth** *Everyone in the class seemed eager to learn.* ◆ *They're **eager to please*** (= wanting to be helpful). ► **ea·ger·ly** *adv.*: *the band's eagerly awaited new CD* **ea·ger·ness** *noun* [U, sing.]: *I couldn't hide my eagerness to get back home.*

ˌeager ˈbeaver *noun* (*informal*) an enthusiastic person who works very hard

ea·gle /ˈigl/ *noun* **1** a large BIRD OF PREY (= a bird that kills other creatures for food) with a sharp, curved beak and very good sight: *eagles soaring overhead* ⊃ see also BALD EAGLE, GOLDEN EAGLE **2** (in GOLF) a score of two strokes less than the standard score for a hole (= two under PAR) ⊃ compare BIRDIE, BOGEY

ˌeagle ˈeye *noun* [usually sing.] if someone has an **eagle eye**, they watch things carefully and are good at noticing things: *Nothing escaped our teacher's eagle eye.* ► **ˈeagle-ˌeyed** *adj.*

SYN HAWK-EYED: *An eagle-eyed tourist found the suspicious package.*

ea·glet /ˈiglət/ *noun* a young eagle

EAP /ˌi eɪ ˈpi/ *abbr.* ENGLISH FOR ACADEMIC PURPOSES

ear 🔑 /ɪr/ *noun*
1 [C] either of the organs on the sides of the head that you hear with: *an ear infection* ◆ *the **inner/outer ear*** ◆ *She whispered something in his ear.* ◆ *He put his hands over his ears.* ◆ *She had her ears pierced.* ◆ *The elephant flapped its ears.* ◆ *He was always there with a sympathetic ear* (= a willingness to listen to people). ⊃ picture at BODY ⊃ see also CAULIFLOWER EAR, MIDDLE EAR **2** **-eared** (in adjectives) having the type of ears mentioned: *a long-eared owl* **3** [sing.] an ability to recognize and copy sounds well: *You need a good ear to master the piano.* **4** [C] the top part of a grain plant, such as WHEAT, that contains the seeds: *ears of corn* ⊃ picture at CEREAL
IDM **be all ears** (*informal*) to be waiting with interest to hear what someone has to say: *"Do you know what he said?" "Go on—I'm all ears."* **be out on your ear** (*informal*) to be forced to leave (a job, etc.) **be up to your ears in sth** to have a lot of something to deal with: *We're up to our ears in work.* **sth comes to/reaches sb's ears** someone hears about something, especially when other people already know about it: *News of his affair eventually reached her ears.* **sb's ears are burning** a person thinks that other people are talking about them, especially in an unkind way: *"I bumped into your ex-wife last night." "I thought I could feel my ears burning!"* **go in one ear and out the other** (of information, etc.) to be forgotten quickly: *Everything I tell them just goes in one ear and out the other.* **have sth coming out of your ears** (*informal*) to have a lot of something, especially more than you need **have sb's ear | have the ear of sb** to be able to give someone advice, influence them, etc. because they trust you: *He had the ear of the president.* **keep/have your ear to the ground** to make sure that you always find out about the most recent developments in a particular situation **play (sth) by ear** to play music by remembering how it sounds rather than by reading it **play it by ear** (*informal*) to decide how to deal with a situation as it develops rather than by having a plan to follow: *I don't know what they'll want when they arrive—we'll have to play it by ear.* **shut/close your ears to sth** to refuse to listen to something: *She decided to shut her ears to all the rumors.* **smile/grin/beam from ear to ear** to be smiling, etc. a lot because you are very pleased about something **with half an ear** without giving your full attention to what is being said, etc. ⊃ more at BELIEVE, BEND *v.*, BOX *v.*, COCK *v.*, DEAF *adj.*, EASY *adj.*, FEEL *v.*, LEND, MUSIC, OPEN *adj.*, PRICK *v.*, RING² *v.*, SILK, WALL *n.*, WET *adj.*

ear·ache /ˈɪreɪk/ *noun* [U, C] pain inside the ear: *to have an earache*

ear·bud /ˈɪrbʌd/ *noun* [usually pl.] a very small HEADPHONE that is worn inside the ear ⊃ picture at COMPUTER

ˈear drops *noun* [pl.] liquid medicine that can be put into the ears

ear·drum /ˈɪrdrʌm/ *noun* the piece of thin, tightly stretched skin inside the ear which is moved by sound waves, making you able to hear: *a perforated eardrum*

ear·ful /ˈɪrfʊl/ *noun* [sing.] (*informal*) if someone gives you an **earful**, they tell you for a long time how angry they are about something

ear·hole /ˈɪrhoʊl/ *noun* (*informal*) the outer opening of the ear

earl /ərl/ *noun* (in Britain) a NOBLEMAN of high rank: *the Earl of Essex* ⊃ see also COUNTESS

ˌEarl ˈGrey *noun* [U] a type of tea flavored with BERGAMOT

ear·li·est /ˈərliəst/ *noun* [sing.] **the earliest** the time before which something cannot happen: *The earliest we can finish is next Friday.* ◆ *We could finish next Friday at the earliest.*

ear·lobe /ˈɪrloʊb/ (also **lobe**) *noun* the soft part at the bottom of the ear

ear·ly /ˈərli/ adj., adv.

● **adj.** (ear·li·er, ear·li·est) **1** near the beginning of a period of time, an event, etc.: *the early morning* ◆ *my earliest memories* ◆ *The project is still in the early stages.* ◆ *the early 1990s* ◆ in **the early days of** *space exploration* (= when it was just beginning) ◆ *He's in his early twenties.* ◆ *Mozart's early works* (= those written at the beginning of his career) **2** arriving or done before the usual, expected, or planned time: *You're early! I wasn't expecting you till seven.* ◆ *The bus was ten minutes early.* ◆ *an early breakfast* ◆ *Let's* **get/make an early start** *tomorrow.* ◆ *She's an early riser* (= she gets up early in the morning). ◆ *He learned to play the piano at an early age.* ◆ *early potatoes* (= that are ready to eat at the beginning of the season) **ANT** LATE ▶ **ear·li·ness** noun [U]
IDM an early bird (*humorous*) a person who gets up, arrives, etc. very early **at your earliest convenience** (*business*) as soon as possible: *Please call at your earliest convenience.* **the early bird catches the worm** (*saying*) a person who takes the opportunity to do something before other people will have an advantage over them ➔ **more at** BRIGHT adj., HOUR, NIGHT

● **adv.** (ear·li·er, ear·li·est) **1** near the beginning of a period of time, an event, a piece of work, etc.: *early in the week/year/season/morning* ◆ *The best rooms go to those who reserve earliest.* ◆ *We arrived early the next day.* ◆ *He started writing music as early as 1989.* **ANT** LATE **2** before the usual, expected, or planned time: *The bus came five minutes early.* ◆ *I woke up early this morning.* ◆ *The baby arrived earlier than expected.* **ANT** LATE **3** **earlier** before the present time or the time mentioned: *As I mentioned earlier…* ◆ *a week earlier* ◆ *She had seen him earlier in the day.* **ANT** LATER
IDM early on at an early stage of a situation, relationship, period of time, etc.: *I knew early on that I wanted to marry her.*

ˌearly ˈwarning noun [U, sing.] a thing that tells you in advance that something serious or dangerous is going to happen: *an early warning of heart disease* ◆ *an early warning system* (= of enemy attack)

ear·mark /ˈɪrmɑrk/ verb, noun

● **verb** [usually passive] to decide that something will be used for a particular purpose, or to state that something will happen to someone or something in the future: **~ sth (for sb/sth)** *The money had been earmarked to be spent on new school buildings.* ◆ *The factory has been earmarked for closure.* ◆ **~ sb/sth (as sb/sth)** *She was earmarked early as a possible champion.*

● **noun** [usually pl.] a feature or quality that is typical of someone or something: *The incident has all the earmarks of a terrorist attack.*

ear·muffs /ˈɪrmʌfs/ noun [pl.] a pair of coverings for the ears connected by a band across the top of the head, and worn to protect the ears, especially from cold: *a pair of earmuffs*

earn /ərn/ verb

1 [T] to get money for work that you do: **~ sth** *He earns about $40,000 a year.* ◆ *She earned a living as a part-time bookkeeper.* ◆ *She must earn a fortune* (= earn a lot of money). ◆ **~ sb sth** *His victory in the tournament earned him $50,000.* **2** [T] **~ sth** to get money as profit or interest on money you lend, have in a bank, etc.: *Your money would earn more in a high-interest account.* **3** [T] to get something that you deserve, usually because of something good you have done or because of the good qualities you have: **~ sth** *He earned a reputation as an expert on tax law.* ◆ *As a teacher, she had earned the respect of her students.* ◆ *I need a rest. I think I've earned it, don't you?* ◆ *She's having a well-earned rest this week.* ◆ **~ sb sth** *His outstanding ability earned him a place on the team.*
IDM earn your keep 1 to do useful or helpful things in return for being allowed to live or stay somewhere **2** to be worth the amount of time or money that is being spent: *He felt he no longer deserved such a high salary. He just wasn't earning his keep.* ➔ **more at** PENNY, SPUR n.

ˌearned ˈrun noun (in baseball) a RUN scored without the help of errors by the opposing team

earn·er /ˈərnər/ noun **1** a person who earns money for a job

that they do: *high/low earners* ➔ **see also** WAGE EARNER **2** an activity or a business that makes a profit: *Tourism is the country's biggest foreign currency earner.*

ear·nest /ˈərnəst/ adj. very serious and sincere: *an earnest young man* ◆ *Despite her most earnest efforts, she could not find a job.* ▶ **ear·nest·ly** adv. **ear·nest·ness** noun [U]
IDM in earnest 1 more seriously and with more force or effort than before: *The work on the house will begin in earnest on Monday.* **2** very serious and sincere about what you are saying and about your intentions; in a way that shows that you are serious: *I could tell she spoke in earnest.* ➔ **thesaurus box at** SERIOUS

earn·ings /ˈərnɪŋz/ noun [pl.] (*business*) **1** the money that you earn for the work that you do: *a rise in average earnings* ◆ *compensation for loss of earnings caused by the accident* ➔ **thesaurus box at** INCOME **2** the profit that a company makes: *earnings per share* ◆ *export earnings* ➔ **collocations at** BUSINESS

ear·phones /ˈɪrfoʊnz/ noun [pl.] = HEADPHONES

ear·piece /ˈɪrpis/ noun the part of a telephone or piece of electrical equipment that you hold next to or put into your ear so that you can listen

ˈear-ˌpiercing adj., noun
● **adj.** [only before noun] very high, loud, and unpleasant: *an ear-piercing scream*
● **noun** [U] the practice of making small holes in someone's ears so jewelry can be put in them

ear·plug /ˈɪrplʌg/ noun [usually pl.] a piece of soft material that you put into your ear to keep out noise or water

ear·ring /ˈɪrɪŋ/ noun a piece of jewelry that you fasten in or on your ear: *a pair of earrings*

ear·shot /ˈɪrʃɑt/ noun
IDM out of earshot (of sb/sth) too far away to hear someone or something or to be heard: *We waited until Ted was safely out of earshot before discussing it.* **within earshot (of sb/sth)** near enough to hear someone or something or to be heard: *As she came within earshot of the group, she heard her name mentioned.*

ˈear-ˌsplitting adj. extremely loud

earth /ərθ/ noun

1 also **Earth, the Earth** [U, sing.] the world; the planet that we live on: *the planet Earth* ◆ *the history of life on earth* ◆ *the earth's ozone layer* ◆ *The earth revolves around the sun.* ◆ *I must be the happiest person on earth!* ➔ **picture on page 468 2** [U, sing.] land; the hard surface of the world that is not the ocean or the sky; the ground: *After a week at sea, it was good to feel the earth beneath our feet again.* ◆ *You could feel the earth shake as the truck came closer.* ➔ **thesaurus box at** FLOOR **3** [U] the substance that plants grow in: *a clod/lump/mound of earth* ➔ **thesaurus box at** SOIL **4** [C] the hole where an animal, especially a FOX, lives
IDM come back/down to earth (with a bang/bump) | bring sb (back) down to earth (with a bang/bump) (*informal*) to return, or to make someone return, to a normal way of thinking or behaving after a time when they have been very excited, not very practical, etc. ➔ **see also** DOWN TO EARTH **how, why, where, who, etc. on earth** (*informal*) used to emphasize the question you are asking when you are surprised or angry or cannot think of an obvious answer: *What on earth are you doing?* ◆ *How on earth can she afford that?* **be, feel, look, taste, etc. like nothing on earth** (*informal*) to be, feel, look, taste, etc. very bad **on earth** used after negative nouns or pronouns to emphasize what you are saying: *Nothing on earth would persuade me to go with him.* ➔ **more at** END n., MOVE v., PROMISE v., SALT n., WIPE v.

earth·bound /ˈərθbaʊnd/ adj. **1** unable to leave the surface of the earth: *birds and their earthbound predators* **2** (*literary*) not spiritual or having much imagination

earth·en /ˈərθən/ adj. [only before noun] **1** (of floors or walls) made of earth **2** (of objects) made of baked CLAY: *earthen pots*

The Earth and the Solar System

the earth

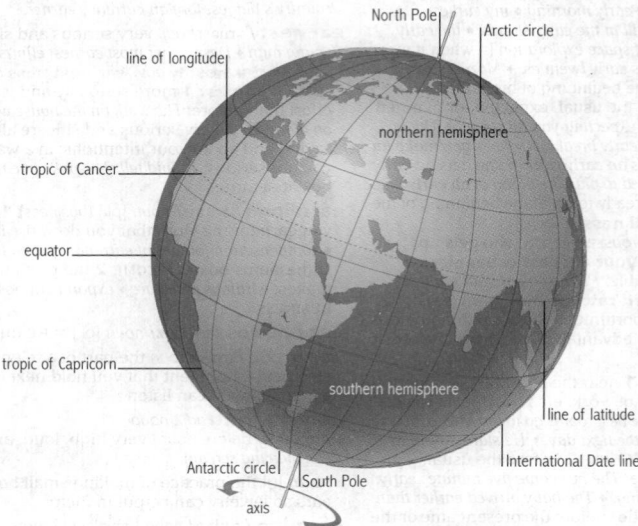

North Pole
Arctic circle
line of longitude
northern hemisphere
tropic of Cancer
equator
tropic of Capricorn
southern hemisphere
line of latitude
Antarctic circle
South Pole
International Date line
axis

the seasons

earth's orbit around the sun

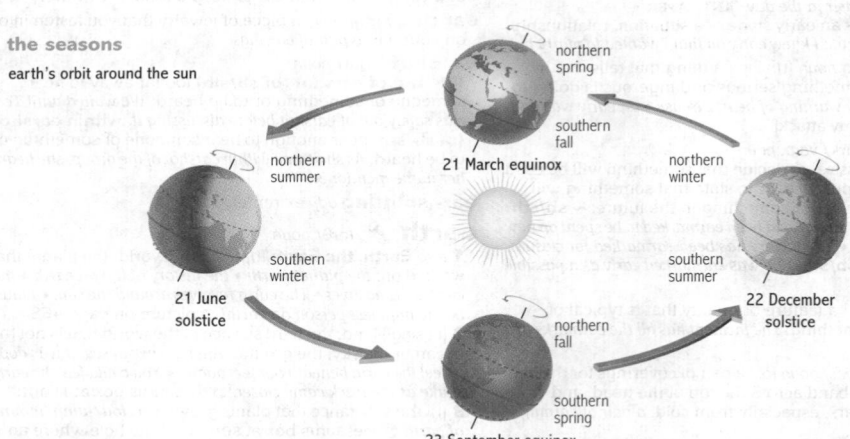

northern
spring
southern
fall
21 March equinox
northern
summer
southern
winter
21 June
solstice
northern
winter
southern
summer
22 December
solstice
northern
fall
southern
spring
23 September equinox

the solar system

orbit
the Sun
Mercury Venus Earth Mars Jupiter Saturn Uranus Neptune

h **hat**   m **man**   n **no**   ŋ **sing**   l **leg**   r **red**   y **yes**   w **wet**

earth·en·ware /'ɔrθn,wɛr/ adj. made of very hard baked CLAY: an earthenware bowl ▶ **earth·en·ware** noun [U]

earth·ling /'ɔrθlɪŋ/ noun a word used in SCIENCE FICTION stories by creatures from other planets to refer to a person living on the earth

earth·ly /'ɔrθli/ adj. [usually before noun] **1** (literary) connected with life on earth and not with any spiritual life: the sorrows of this earthly life **2** (often used in questions and negatives for emphasis) possible: There's **no earthly reason** why you shouldn't go. ◆ What earthly difference is my opinion going to make? ◆ He didn't have an earthly chance of getting the job.

earth ‚mother noun **1** also **Earth Mother** a GODDESS who represents the earth as the source of life; a GODDESS of FERTILITY **2** (informal) a woman who seems very suited to being a mother

earth ‚mover noun a vehicle or machine that digs up large quantities of soil

earth·quake /'ɔrθkweɪk/ (also informal **quake**) noun a sudden, violent shaking of the earth's surface

earth ‚science noun [C, U] a science concerned with studying the earth or part of it. Geography and GEOLOGY are both earth sciences. ⊃ **compare** LIFE SCIENCES, NATURAL SCIENCE

earth-‚shattering (also ‚earth-shaking) adj. having a very great effect and of great importance: an earth-shattering discovery

earth tone noun a color that has some shade of brown in it: The hotel rooms are decorated in earth tones.

earth·work /'ɔrθwɔrk/ noun [usually pl.] a large bank of earth that was built long ago and used as a defense in the past

earth·worm /'ɔrθwɔrm/ noun a common long, thin WORM that lives in soil

earth·y /'ɔrθi/ adj. (earth·i·er, earth·i·est) **1** concerned with the body, sex, etc. in an open and direct way that some people find rude or embarrassing: an earthy sense of humor **2** of like earth or soil: earthy colors **3** natural, plain, or simple: Her pottery has an earthy quality that many people like. **4** (of a person) practical, direct, and open: It's hard not to fall in love with her earthy charm. ▶ **earth·i·ness** noun [U]

ear ‚trumpet noun a device shaped like a TRUMPET, used in the past by people who could not hear well

ear·wax /'ɪrwæks/ noun [U] the yellow substance produced inside the ear to protect it

ear·wig /'ɪrwɪg/ noun a small brown insect with a long body and two curved, pointed parts (called **pincers**) that stick out at the back end of its body

ease 🔑 /iz/ noun, verb
• **noun** [U] **1** lack of difficulty: He passed the exam **with ease**. ◆ The ease with which she learns languages is astonishing. ◆ This computer is popular for its good design and **ease of use**. ◆ All important points are numbered **for ease of** reference (= so that you can find them easily). **2** the state of feeling relaxed or comfortable without worries, problems, or pain: In his retirement, he lived a life of ease.
IDM **(stand) at ease** used as a command to soldiers to tell them to stand with their feet apart and their hands behind their backs ⊃ **compare** ATTENTION **at (your) ease** relaxed and confident and not nervous or embarrassed: I never feel completely at ease with him. **put sb at (their) ease** to make someone feel relaxed and confident, not nervous or embarrassed ⊃ more at ILL adj., MIND n.
• **verb 1** [I, T] to become or to make something less unpleasant, painful, severe, etc. **SYN** ALLEVIATE: The pain immediately eased. ◆ ~ sth This should help ease the pain. ◆ The plan should ease traffic congestion in the city. ◆ It would **ease my mind** (= make me less worried) to know that she was happy. **2** [I, T] to move, or to move someone or something, slowly and carefully: + adv./prep. He eased slowly forward. ◆ ~ sb/

sth + adv./prep. She eased herself into a chair. ◆ He eased off the brakes. **3** [T] ~ sth to make something easier: Ramps have been built to ease access for the disabled. **4** [T, I] ~ (sth) to make something or to become less tight and more relaxed **SYN** RELAX: Ease your grip on the wheel a little. **5** [I, T] ~ (sth) to become or make something lower in price or value **SYN** REDUCE: Share prices eased back from yesterday's levels.
PHR V ‚ease **into sth** | ‚ease **yourself/sb into sth** to become or help someone to become familiar with something new, especially a new job ‚ease 'off | ‚ease 'off sth to become or make something become less strong, unpleasant, etc.: We waited until the traffic had eased off. ◆ Ease off the training a few days before the race. ‚ease sb↔'out (of sth) to force someone to leave a job or position of authority, especially by making it difficult or unpleasant for them over a period of time ‚ease 'up **1** to reduce the speed at which you are traveling **2** to become less strong, unpleasant, etc.

ease·ful /'izfl/ adj. (literary) that provides comfort or peace

ea·sel /'izl/ noun a wooden frame to hold a picture while it is being painted, boards with information or advertising on them, or (in the past) a BLACKBOARD ⊃ **picture at** HOBBY

ease·ment /'izmənt/ noun [U] **1** (law) the right to cross or use someone's land for a particular purpose **2** (literary) a state or feeling of peace or happiness

eas·i·ly 🔑 /'izəli/ adv.
1 without problems or difficulty: I can easily finish it tonight. ◆ The museum is easily accessible by car. **2** very probably; very likely: Are you sure you locked the gate? You could easily have forgotten. ◆ The situation might **all too easily** have become a disaster. **3** ~ the best, nicest, etc. without doubt; definitely: It's easily the best play I've seen this year. **4** quickly; more quickly than is usual: I get bored easily. ◆ He's easily distracted.

east 🔑 /ist/ noun, adj., adv.
• **noun** [U, sing.] (abbr. E., E) **1** also **the east** the direction that you look toward to see the sun rise; one of the four main points of the COMPASS: Which way is east? ◆ A gale was blowing from the east. ◆ a town **to the east of** (= further east than) Las Vegas ⊃ **picture at** COMPASS ⊃ **compare** NORTH, SOUTH, WEST **2** **the east** the eastern part of a country, region, or city: His store is in the east of the town. **3** **the East** the part of the United States that is further east than the Mississippi River and further north than Washington, D.C.: I was born in the East, but now live in San Francisco. **4** **the East** the countries of Asia, especially China, Japan, and India **5** **the East** (in the past) the Communist countries of Eastern Europe: East-West relations
• **adj.** [only before noun] **1** (abbr. E., E) in or toward the east: East Africa ◆ They live on the east coast of the island. **2** an **east wind** blows from the east ⊃ **compare** EASTERLY
• **adv.** toward the east: The house faces east.

east·bound /'istbaʊnd/ adj. traveling or leading toward the east: eastbound traffic ◆ the eastbound lane of the highway

Eas·ter /'istər/ noun **1** [U, C] (also ‚Easter 'Sunday) (in the Christian religion) a Sunday in March or April when Christians remember the death of Christ and his return to life **2** the period that includes Easter Sunday and the days close to it: the Easter holiday/Easter vacation

'Easter ‚egg noun **1** an egg that is colored and decorated at Easter **2** an egg made of chocolate that is eaten at Easter

east·er·ly /'istərli/ adj., noun
• **adj.** [only before noun] **1** in or toward the east: traveling in an easterly direction **2** [usually before noun] (of winds) blowing from the east: a cold easterly wind ⊃ **compare** EAST
• **noun** (pl. east·er·lies) a wind that blows from the east

east·ern 🔑 /'istərn/ adj.
1 also **Eastern** [only before noun] (abbr. E., E) located in the east or facing east: eastern Spain ◆ Eastern Europe ◆ the eastern slopes of the mountain **2** usually **Eastern** connected

with the part of the world that is to the east of Europe: *Eastern cookery*

East·ern·er /ˈiːstərnər/ *noun* a person who comes from or lives in the eastern part of a country, especially the U.S.

east·ern·most /ˈiːstərnˌmoʊst/ *adj.* furthest east: *the eastermost city in Europe*

the ˌEastern ˌOrthodox ˈChurch *noun* = THE ORTHODOX CHURCH

ˌEastern ˌtime *noun* [U] the standard time system that is used in the eastern U.S. and parts of Canada ⊃ compare ATLANTIC TIME, CENTRAL TIME, MOUNTAIN TIME, PACIFIC TIME

ˌeast-northˈeast *noun* [sing.] (*abbr.* ENE) the direction at an equal distance between east and northeast ▸ ˌeast-northˈeast *adv.*

ˌeast-southˈeast *noun* [sing.] (*abbr.* ESE) the direction at an equal distance between east and southeast ▸ ˌeast-southˈeast *adv.*

east·ward /ˈiːstwərd/ (also **east·wards**) *adv.* toward the east: *to go/look/turn eastward* ▸ **east·ward** *adj.*: *in an eastward direction*

eas·y /ˈiːzi/ *adj., adv.*
● *adj.* (**eas·i·er**, **eas·i·est**) **1** not difficult; done or obtained without a lot of effort or problems: *an easy exam/job* ◆ *He didn't make it easy for me to leave.* ◆ *Their house isn't the easiest place to get to.* ◆ *vegetables that are easy to grow* ◆ *Several schools are within easy reach* (= not far away). ◆ *It can't be easy for her, by herself with the kids.* ◆ *It's easy for you to tell me to keep calm, but you're not in my position.* **ANT HARD**
2 comfortable, relaxed, and not worried: *I'll agree to anything for an easy life.* **ANT UNEASY 3** [only before noun] open to attack; not able to defend yourself: *She's an easy target for their criticisms.* ◆ *The baby fish are easy prey for birds.* **4** [only before noun] pleasant and friendly **SYN EASYGOING**: *He had a very easy manner.* **ANT AWKWARD 5** [not usually before noun] (*informal, disapproving*) (of women) willing to have sex with many different people ⊃ see also EASILY ▸ **eas·i·ness** *noun* [U]
IDM as easy as anything/as pie/as ABC/as falling off a log (*informal*) very easy or very easily **easy money** money that you get without having to work very hard for it **easy on the ear/eye** (*informal*) pleasant to listen to or look at **have an easy time (of it)** to have no difficulties or problems **I'm easy** (*informal*) used to say that you do not have a strong opinion when someone has offered you a choice: *"Do you want to watch this or the news?" "Oh, I'm easy. It's up to you."* **of easy virtue** (*old-fashioned*) (of a woman) willing to have sex with anyone **on easy street** enjoying a comfortable way of life with plenty of money **take the easy way out** to end a difficult situation by choosing the simplest solution even if it is not the best one ⊃ more at FREE *adj.*, OPTION, REACH *n.*, RIDE *n.*, TOUCH *n.*
● *adv.* (**eas·i·er**, **eas·i·est**) used to tell someone to be careful when doing something: *Easy with that chair—one of its legs is loose.*
IDM breathe/rest easy to relax and stop worrying: *You can rest easy—I'm not going to tell anyone.* **be easier said than done** (*saying*) to be much more difficult to do than to talk about: *"Why don't you get yourself a job?" "That's easier said than done."* **easy come, easy go** (*saying*) used to mean that someone does not care very much about money or possessions, especially if they spend it or lose something **easy does it** (*informal*) used to tell someone to do something, or move something, slowly and carefully **go easy on sb** (*informal*) used to tell someone to treat a person in a gentle way and not to be too angry or severe: *Go easy on her —she's having a really hard time at the moment.* **go easy on/ with sth** (*informal*) used to tell someone not to use too much of something: *Go easy on the sugar.* **not come easy (to sb)** to be difficult for someone to do: *Talking about my problems doesn't come easy to me.* **stand easy** used as a command to soldiers who are already standing AT EASE to tell them that they can stand in an even more relaxed way **take it easy**

(*informal*) used to tell someone not to be worried or angry: *Take it easy! Don't panic.* **take it/things easy** to relax and avoid working too hard or doing too much: *The doctor told me to take it easy for a few weeks.*

ˌeasy-ˈcare *adj.* (of clothes or cloth) not needing to be ironed after washing

ˈeasy ˌchair *noun* a large comfortable chair: *to sit in an easy chair*

eas·y·go·ing /ˌiːziˈɡoʊɪŋ/ *adj.* relaxed and happy to accept things without worrying or getting angry

ˈeasy ˈlistening *noun* [U] music that is pleasant and relaxing but that some people think is not very interesting

eat /iːt/ *verb* (**ate** /eɪt/, **eat·en** /ˈiːtn/)
1 [I, T] to put food in your mouth, chew it, and swallow it: *I was too nervous to eat.* ◆ *She doesn't eat healthily* (= doesn't eat food that is good for her). ◆ *~ sth I don't eat meat.* ◆ *Would you like something to eat?* ◆ *I couldn't eat another thing* (= I have had enough food). ⊃ collocations at DIET **2** [I] to have a meal: *Where should we eat tonight?* ◆ *We ate at a pizzeria in town.*
IDM eat sb alive (*informal*) **1** [usually passive] (of insects, etc.) to bite someone many times: *I was being eaten alive by mosquitoes.* **2** to defeat someone completely in an argument, a competition, etc.: *The defense lawyers are going to eat you alive tomorrow.* **3** to criticize or punish someone severely because you are extremely angry with them **eat crow** (also **eat humble pie**) to say and show that you are sorry for a mistake that you made **eat, drink, and be merry** (*saying*) said to encourage someone to enjoy life now, while they can, and not to think of the future **eat your heart out!** (*informal*) used to compare two things and say that one of them is better: *Look at him dance! Eat your heart out, Fred Astaire* (= he dances even better than Fred Astaire). **eat your heart out (for sb/sth)** to feel very unhappy, especially because you want someone or something you cannot have **eat like a horse** (*informal*) to eat a lot: *She may be thin, but she eats like a horse.* **eat out of your/sb's hand** to trust someone and be willing to do what they say: *She'll have them eating out of her hand in no time.* **eat sb out of house and home** (*informal, often humorous*) to eat a lot of someone else's food **eat your words** to admit that what you said was wrong **I could eat a horse** (*informal*) used to say that you are very hungry **I'll eat my hat** (*informal*) used to say that you think something is very unlikely to happen: *If he's here on time, I'll eat my hat!* **what's eating him, her, etc.?** (*informal*) used to ask what someone is annoyed or worried about ⊃ more at CAKE *n.*, DOG *n.*
PHR V eat sth↔aˈway to reduce or destroy something gradually **SYN ERODE**: *The coastline is being eaten away year by year.* ˌeat aˈway at sth/sb **1** to reduce or destroy something gradually: *Woodworm had eaten away at the door frame.* ◆ *His constant criticism ate away at her self-confidence.* **2** to worry someone over a period of time ˈeat into sth **1** to use up a part of something, especially someone's money or time: *Those repair bills have really eaten into my savings.* **2** to destroy or damage the surface of something: *Rust had eaten into the metal.* ˌeat ˈout to have a meal in a restaurant, etc. rather than at home: *Do you feel like eating out tonight?* ˌeat ˈup | ˌeat sth↔ˈup to eat all of something: *Eat up! We have to go out soon.* ◆ *Come on. Eat up your potatoes.* ˌeat sb ˈup [usually passive] to fill someone with a particular emotion so that they cannot think of anything else: *She was eaten up by regrets.* ˌeat sth↔ˈup to use something in large quantities: *Legal costs had eaten up all the savings she had.*

eat·a·ble /ˈiːtəbl/ *adj.* good enough to be eaten ⊃ see also EDIBLE

eat·er /ˈiːtər/ *noun* (usually after an adjective or a noun) a person or an animal that eats a particular thing or in a particular way: *We're not great meat eaters.* ◆ *He's a big eater* (= he eats a lot).

eat·er·y /ˈiːtəri/ *noun* (*pl.* **eat·er·ies**) (*informal*) a restaurant or other place that serves food

ʌ cup ə about eɪ say aɪ five ɔɪ boy aʊ now oʊ go ər bird

eat-in *adj.* [only before noun] (of a kitchen) big enough for eating in as well as cooking in

eat·ing /'itɪŋ/ *noun* [U] the act of eating something: *healthy eating* **IDM** see PROOF

eating apple *noun* any type of apple that can be eaten raw ⊃ compare COOKING APPLE

eating dis·order *noun* an emotional DISORDER that causes eating habits that are not normal, for example ANOREXIA ⊃ see also BULIMIA

eats /its/ *noun* [pl.] (*informal*) food, especially at a party

eau de co·logne /ˌoʊ də kəˈloʊn/ *noun* [U] = COLOGNE

eau de toi·lette /ˌoʊ də twaˈlɛt/ *noun* [C, U] PERFUME that contains a lot of water and does not smell very strong

eaves /ivz/ *noun* [pl.] the lower edges of a roof that stick out over the walls: *birds nesting under the eaves*

eaves·drop /'ivzdrɑp/ *verb* (-pp-) [I] **~ (on sb/sth)** to listen secretly to what other people are saying: *We caught him eavesdropping outside the window.* ▶ **eaves·drop·per** *noun*

eaves·trough /'ivztrɔf/ *noun* (*CanE*) = GUTTER *n.* (1)

e·Bay™ /'ibeɪ/ *noun* [U] a Web site on the Internet where people can AUCTION goods (= sell them to the person who offers the most money for them): *He buys rare baseball cards on eBay.* ▶ **e·Bay sth ~ sth**

ebb /ɛb/ *noun, verb*
• *noun* the ebb [usually sing.] the period of time when the ocean flows away from the land: *the ebb tide*
IDM the ebb and flow (of sth/sb) the repeated, often regular, movement from one state to another; the repeated change in level, numbers, or amount: *the ebb and flow of the seasons* ♦ *She sat in silence enjoying the ebb and flow of conversation.* ⊃ more at LOW *adj.*
• *verb* **1** [I] (*formal*) (of the TIDE in the ocean) to move away from the land **SYN** GO OUT **ANT** FLOW **2** [I] **~ (away)** to become gradually weaker or less **SYN** DECREASE: *The pain was ebbing.* ♦ *As night fell, our enthusiasm began to ebb away.*

Eb·o·la vi·rus /i'boulə ˌvaɪrəs/ *noun* [U] a virus that causes a very serious disease called **Ebola fever**, which causes internal parts of the body to lose blood and usually ends in death

E·bon·ics /i'bɑnɪks/ *noun* [U] a type of English spoken by many African Americans that has been considered by some people to be a separate language ⊃ compare BLACK ENGLISH

eb·on·y /'ɛbəni/ *noun, adj.*
• *noun* [U] the hard black wood of various tropical trees: *an ebony carving*
• *adj.* black in color: *an ebony sky*

e-book *noun* a book that is displayed on a computer screen or on an electronic device that is held in the hand, instead of being printed on paper (an electronic book)

e·bul·lient /i'bʌlyənt/ *adj.* (*formal*) full of confidence, energy, and good humor: *The boss was in ebullient mood.* ▶ **e·bul·lience** /-yəns/ *noun* [U] **e·bul·lient·ly** *adv.*

e-busi·ness *noun* = E-COMMERCE

e-cash *noun* [U] a system for sending and receiving payments using the Internet

ec·cen·tric /ɪk'sɛntrɪk/ *adj.* considered by other people to be strange or unusual: *eccentric behavior/clothes* ♦ *an eccentric aunt* ▶ **ec·cen·tric** *noun*: *Most people considered him a harmless eccentric.* **ec·cen·tri·cally** /-kli/ *adv.*

ec·cen·tri·ci·ty /ˌɛksɛn'trɪsəti/ (*pl.* **ec·cen·tric·i·ties**) *noun* **1** [U] behavior that people think is strange or unusual; the quality of being unusual and different from other people: *As a teacher, she had a reputation for eccentricity.* ♦ *Arthur was noted for the eccentricity of his clothes.* **2** [C, usually pl.] an unusual act or habit: *We all have our little eccentricities.*

ec·cle·si·as·tic /ɪˌklizi'æstɪk/ *noun* (*formal*) a priest or minister in the Christian Church

ec·cle·si·as·ti·cal /ɪˌklizi'æstɪkl/ *adj.* [usually before noun] connected with the Christian Church

ECG /ˌi si 'dʒi/ *abbr.* = EKG

ech·e·lon /'ɛʃəˌlɑn/ *noun* **1** [usually pl.] a rank or position of authority in an organization or a society: *the lower/upper/top/higher echelons of the Pentagon* **2** an arrangement of soldiers, planes, etc. in which each one is behind and to the side of the one in front

e·chid·na /ɪ'kɪdnə/ (also ˌspiny 'anteater) *noun* an Australasian animal with a long nose, sharp CLAWS on its feet, and sharp SPINES on its body, that eats insects

ech·i·na·cea /ˌɛkə'neɪʃə; -'neɪsiə/ *noun* [U, C] a plant similar to a DAISY, that is thought to help the body heal itself and fight infection

ech·o /'ɛkoʊ/ *noun, verb*
• *noun* (*pl.* **ech·oes**) **1** the reflecting of sound off a wall or inside a space so that a noise appears to be repeated; a sound that is reflected back in this way: *There was an echo on the line and I couldn't hear clearly.* ♦ *The hills sent back a faint echo.* ♦ *the echo of footsteps running down the corridor* **2** the fact of an idea, event, etc. being like another and reminding you of it; something that reminds you of something else: *Yesterday's crash has grim echoes of previous disasters.* **3** an opinion or attitude that agrees with or repeats one already expressed or thought: *His words were an echo of what she had heard many times before.* ♦ *The speech found an echo in the hearts of many in the audience* (= they agreed with it).
• *verb* (**ech·oes**, **ech·o·ing**, **ech·oed**, **ech·oed**) **1** [I] if a sound **echoes**, it is reflected off a wall, the side of a mountain, etc. so that you can hear it again **SYN** REVERBERATE: *Her footsteps echoed in the empty room.* ♦ *The gunshot echoed through the forest.* **2** [I, T] to send back and repeat a sound; to be full of a sound **SYN** REVERBERATE: *The whole house echoed.* ♦ **~ to/with sth** *The street echoed with the shouts of children.* ♦ **~ sth (back)** *The valley echoed back his voice.* **3** [T] **~ sth** to repeat an idea or opinion because you agree with it: *This is a view echoed by many conservative politicians.* **4** [T] **+ speech | ~ sth** to repeat what someone else has just said, especially because you find it surprising: *"He's gone!" Viv echoed.*

ech·o·lo·ca·tion /ˌɛkoʊloʊ'keɪʃn/ *noun* [U] the use of reflected sound waves to find things, especially by creatures such as DOLPHINS and BATS

é·clair /eɪ'klɛr; ɪ'klɛr/ (also **e·clair**) *noun* a long thin cake for one person, made of light PASTRY, filled with cream and usually with chocolate on top

ec·lamp·si·a /ɪ'klæmpsiə/ *noun* [U] a condition in which a pregnant woman has high blood pressure and CONVULSIONS, which can be dangerous to the woman and the baby ⊃ compare PREECLAMPSIA

ec·lec·tic /ɪ'klɛktɪk/ *adj.* (*formal*) not following one style or set of ideas but choosing from or using a wide variety: *She has very eclectic tastes in literature.* ▶ **ec·lec·ti·cally** /-kli/ *adv.* **ec·lec·ti·cism** /ɪ'klɛktəˌsɪzəm/ *noun* [U]

e·clipse /ɪ'klɪps/ *noun, verb*
• *noun* **1** [C] an occasion when the moon passes between the earth and the sun so that you cannot see all or part of the sun for a time; an occasion when the earth passes between the moon and the sun so that you cannot see all or part of the moon for a time: *an eclipse of the sun/moon* ♦ *a total/partial eclipse* **2** [sing., U] a loss of importance, power, etc. especially because someone or something else has become more important, powerful, etc.: *The election result marked the eclipse of the right wing.* ♦ *Her work was in eclipse for most of the 20th century.*
• *verb* **1** [often passive] **~ sth** (of the moon, the earth, etc.) to cause an eclipse **2** **~ sb/sth** to make someone or something seem dull or unimportant by comparison **SYN** OUTSHINE, OVERSHADOW: *Though a talented player, he was completely eclipsed by his brother.*

eco- /'ikoʊ/ *combining form* (in nouns, adjectives, and adverbs) connected with the environment: *eco-friendly*

◆ *eco-warriors* (= people who protest about damage to the environment) ◆ *eco-terrorism* (= the use of force or violent action in order to protest about damage to the environment)

ec·o·cide /ˈikouˌsaɪd/ *noun* [U] the destruction of the natural environment, especially when this is deliberate

ˌeco-ˈfriendly *adj.* not harmful to the environment: *eco-friendly products*

E. coli /ˌi ˈkoʊlaɪ/ *noun* [U] a type of bacteria that lives inside humans and some animals, some forms of which can cause FOOD POISONING

ec·o·log·i·cal /ˌikəˈlɑdʒɪkl; ˌɛkə-/ *adj.* **1** connected with the relation of plants and living creatures to each other and to their environment: *We risk upsetting the ecological balance of the area.* ◆ *an ecological disaster* (= one that alters the whole balance of ecology in an area) **2** interested in and concerned about the ecology of a place: *the ecological movement* ▶ **ec·o·log·i·cal·ly** /-kli/ *adv.*: *The system is both practical and ecologically sound.*

ˌeco·logical ˈfootprint *noun* a measure of the amount of the earth's resources used by a person or a population that lives in a particular way: *the ecological footprint of the average Canadian* ➔ **see also** CARBON FOOTPRINT

e·col·o·gist /ɪˈkɑlədʒɪst/ *noun* **1** a scientist who studies ecology **2** a person who is interested in ecology and believes the environment should be protected

e·col·o·gy /ɪˈkɑlədʒi/ *noun* [U] the relation of plants and living creatures to each other and to their environment; the study of this: *plant/animal/human ecology* ◆ *the ecology movement* ◆ *Oil pollution could damage the fragile ecology of the coral reefs.*

e-com·merce (also **e-busi·ness**) *noun* [U] business that is conducted on the Internet.

ec·o·nom·ic 🔑 **AWL** /ˌɛkəˈnɑmɪk; ˌikə-/ *adj.* **1** [only before noun] connected with the trade, industry, and development of wealth of a country, an area, or a society: *social, economic and political issues* ◆ *economic growth/ cooperation/development/reform* ◆ *the government's economic policy* ◆ *economic history* ◆ *the current economic climate* **2** (of a process, a business, or an activity) producing enough profit to continue **SYN** PROFITABLE **ANT** UNECONOMIC

THESAURUS

economic

financial ◆ commercial ◆ monetary ◆ fiscal

These words all describe activities or situations that are connected with the use of money, especially by a business or country.

economic connected with the trade, industry, and development of wealth of a country, an area, or a society: *This book deals with the social, economic, and political issues of the period.*

financial connected with money and finance: *She had gotten into financial difficulties.* ◆ *Tokyo is a major financial center.*

commercial connected with the buying and selling of goods and services: *We rent both commercial and residential properties.*

monetary (*formal* or *finance*) connected with money, especially all the money in a country: *The Federal Reserve Bank controls monetary policy in the U.S.*

fiscal (*finance*) connected with government or public money, especially taxes: *The fiscal year begins in July.*

PATTERNS
- economic/financial/commercial/monetary/fiscal **affairs/decisions**
- the economic/financial/commercial/fiscal **climate**
- the economic/financial/commercial **side** of sth
- an economic/financial/commercial **center**

WHICH WORD?

economic ◆ economical

- **Economic** means "connected with the economy of a country or an area, or with the money that a society or an individual has": *the government's economic policy* ◆ *the economic impact of having children*
  ➔ see also ECONOMY 1
- **Economical** means "spending money or using something in a careful way that avoids waste": *It is usually more economical to buy washing powder in large quantities.*
  ➔ see also ECONOMY 3

ec·o·nom·i·cal **AWL** /ˌɛkəˈnɑmɪkl; ˌikə-/ *adj.* **1** providing good service or value in relation to the amount of time or money spent: *an economical car to run* (= one that does not use too much gas) ◆ *It would be more economical to buy the bigger size.* **ANT** UNECONOMICAL ➔ note at ECONOMIC **2** using no more of something than is necessary: *an economical use of space* ◆ *an economical prose style* (= one that uses no unnecessary words) **ANT** UNECONOMICAL **3** not spending more money than necessary: *He was economical in all areas of his life.* **SYN** FRUGAL
IDM **economical with the truth** a way of saying that someone has left out some important facts, when you do not want to say that they are lying

ec·o·nom·i·cal·ly **AWL** /ˌɛkəˈnɑmɪkli; ˌikə-/ *adv.* **1** in a way connected with the trade, industry, and development of wealth of a country, an area, or a society: *The factory is no longer economically viable.* ◆ *Economically, the center of Spain has lost its dominant role.* **2** in a way that provides good service or value in relation to the amount of time or money spent: *I'll do the job as economically as possible.* **3** in a way that uses no more of something than is necessary: *The design is intended to use space as economically as possible.* ◆ *She writes elegantly and economically.*

ˌeconomic ˈmigrant *noun* a person who moves from their own country to a new country in order to find work or have a better standard of living: *They claimed they were political refugees and not economic migrants.*

ec·o·nom·ics 🔑 **AWL** /ˌɛkəˈnɑmɪks; ˌikə-/ *noun* **1** [U] the study of how a society organizes its money, trade, and industry: *He studied politics and economics at Yale.* ◆ *Keynesian/Marxist economics* ➔ **see also** HOME ECONOMICS **2** [pl., U] the way in which money influences, or is organized within an area of business or society: *The economics of the project are very encouraging.*

e·con·o·mist **AWL** /ɪˈkɑnəmɪst/ *noun* a person who studies or writes about economics

e·con·o·mize /ɪˈkɑnəˌmaɪz/ *verb* [I] **~ (on sth)** to use less money, time, etc. than you normally use: *Old people often try to economize on heating, thus endangering their health.*
➔ thesaurus box at SAVE

e·con·o·my 🔑 **AWL** /ɪˈkɑnəmi/ *noun* (*pl.* e·con·o-mies)
1 often **the economy** [C] the relationship between production, trade, and the supply of money in a particular country or region: *The economy is in a recession.* ◆ *the world economy* ◆ *a market economy* (= one in which the price is fixed according to both cost and demand) ➔ **see also** CONSUMER ECONOMY **2** [C] a country, when you are thinking about its economic system: *Ireland was one of the fastest-growing economies in Western Europe in the 1990s.* **3** [C, U] the use of the time, money, etc. that is available in a way that avoids waste: *We need to make substantial economies.* ◆ *It's a false economy to buy cheap clothes* (= it seems cheaper but it is not really since they do not last very long). ◆ *She writes with a great economy of words* (= using only the necessary words). ◆ *Buy the large economy pack!* (= the one that gives you better value for

money) ♦ *to fly economy (class)* (= by the cheapest class of air travel) ♦ *an economy fare* (= the cheapest)

TOPIC COLLOCATIONS

The Economy

managing the economy
- handle/run/manage the economy
- boost investment/spending/employment/growth
- stimulate demand/the economy/industry
- cut/reduce investment/spending/borrowing
- reduce/curb/control/keep down inflation
- create/fuel growth/demand/a boom/a bubble
- encourage/foster/promote/stimulate/stifle innovation/competition
- encourage/work with/compete with the private sector
- increase/boost/promote U.S./agricultural exports
- ban/restrict/block cheap/foreign imports
- the economy grows/expands/shrinks/contracts/slows (down)/recovers/improves/is booming
- enjoy an economic/housing/property boom

economic problems
- push up/drive up prices/costs/inflation
- damage/hurt/destroy industry/the economy
- cause/lead to/go into/avoid/escape recession
- experience/suffer a recession/downturn
- fight/combat inflation/deflation/unemployment
- cause/create inflation/poverty/unemployment
- create/burst a housing/stock market bubble
- cause/trigger a stock market crash/the collapse of the banking system
- face/be plunged into a financial/an economic crisis
- be caught in/experience cycles of boom and bust

public finance
- cut/reduce/slash/increase/double the defense/education budget
- increase/boost/slash/cut public spending
- increase/raise/cut/lower/reduce taxes
- raise/cut/lower/reduce interest rates
- ease/loosen/tighten monetary policy
- balance the (state/federal) budget
- achieve/maintain a balanced budget
- run a ($4 trillion) budget deficit/surplus
⊃ more collocations at POLITICS, VOTE

e'conomy class ˌsyndrome *noun* [U] the fact of a person suffering from DEEP VEIN THROMBOSIS after they have traveled on a plane. This condition is thought to be more common among people who travel in the cheapest seats because they do not have space to move their legs much.

ec·o·sys·tem /'ikou̯ˌsɪstəm/ *noun* all the plants and living creatures in a particular area considered in relation to their physical environment ⊃ collocations at ENVIRONMENT

ec·o·ter·ror·ism /ˌikou̯'tɛrərɪzəm/ *noun* [U] **1** violent activities which are done in order to draw attention to issues relating to the environment **2** deliberate damage to the environment, done in order to draw attention to a political issue ► e·co·ter·ror·ist /-rɪst/ *noun*

ec·o·tour·ism /ˌikou̯'tʊrɪzəm; 'ikou̯ˌtʊrɪzəm/ *noun* [U] organized vacations that are designed so that the tourists damage the environment as little as possible, especially when some of the money they pay is used to protect the local environment and animals ► ec·o·tour·ist /'ikou̯ˌtʊrɪst/ *noun*

ec·o·type /'ikou̯ˌtaɪp/ *noun* (*biology*) the type or race of a plant or animal species that has adapted to live in particular local conditions

ec·ru /'ɛkru; 'eɪkru/ *noun* a light brown or cream color

ec·sta·sy /'ɛkstəsi/ *noun* (*pl.* ec·sta·sies) **1** [U, C] a feeling or state of very great happiness **SYN** BLISS **2 Ecstasy** [U]

(*abbr.* E) an illegal drug, taken especially by young people at parties, clubs, etc.

ec·stat·ic /ɪk'stætɪk/ *adj.* very happy, excited, and enthusiastic; feeling or showing great enthusiasm **SYN** DELIGHTED: *Sally was ecstatic about her new job.* ♦ *ecstatic applause/praise/reviews* ⊃ thesaurus box at EXCITED ► ec·stat·i·cal·ly /-kli/ *adv.*

ECT /ˌi si 'ti/ *abbr.* ELECTROCONVULSIVE THERAPY

-ectomy /'ɛktəmi/ *combining form* (in nouns) a medical operation in which part of the body is removed: *appendectomy* (= removal of the APPENDIX)

ec·top·ic /ɛk'tɑpɪk/ *adj.* (*medical*) in an ectopic PREGNANCY, the baby starts to develop outside the mother's WOMB

ec·to·plasm /'ɛktəˌplæzəm/ *noun* [U] **1** (*biology*) the outer layer of the thick substance inside cells ⊃ compare ENDOPLASM **2** a substance which is said to come from the body of someone who is communicating with the spirit of a dead person, allowing the spirit to have a form

ec·u·men·i·cal /ˌɛkyə'mɛnɪkl/ *adj.* involving or uniting members of different branches of the Christian Church

ec·u·me·nism /ɪ'kyumə̯ˌnɪzəm; 'ɛkyəmə-/ *noun* [U] the principle or aim of uniting different branches of the Christian Church

ec·ze·ma /'ɛgzəmə; 'ɛksəmə; ɪg'zimə/ *noun* [U] a skin condition in which areas of skin become red, rough, and ITCHY

-ed, -d /d; t; əd/ *suffix* **1** (in adjectives) having; having the characteristics of: *talented* ♦ *bearded* ♦ *diseased* **2** (makes the past tense and past participle of regular verbs): *hated* ♦ *walked* ♦ *loved*

ed. also **Ed.** *abbr.* EDITed by, EDITION, EDITOR: *"Eighteenth Century Women Poets," Ed. Lonsdale* ♦ *7th ed.*

E·dam /'idam; 'idæm/ *noun* [U, C] a type of round yellow Dutch cheese that is covered with red WAX

ed·a·ma·me /ˌɛdə'mɑmeɪ/ *noun* [pl.] fresh green SOYBEANS, usually eaten in their PODS

Ed.D. /ˌi di 'di/ *noun* a second university degree (the abbreviation for "Doctor of Education"): *to be/have/do an Ed.D.* ♦ *John McDonald, Ed.D.*

ed·dy /'ɛdi/ *noun, verb*
• *noun* (*pl.* ed·dies) a movement of air, dust, or water in a circle
• *verb* (ed·dies, ed·dy·ing, ed·died, ed·died) [I] (of air, dust, water, etc.) to move around in a circle **SYN** SWIRL: *The waves swirled and eddied around the rocks.*

e·de·ma /ɪ'dimə/ *noun* [U] (*medical*) a condition in which liquid collects in the spaces inside the body and makes it swell

E·den /'idn/ (also the ˌGarden of 'Eden) *noun* [sing.] (in the Bible) the beautiful garden where Adam and Eve, the first humans, lived before they did something God had told them not to and were sent away, often seen as a place of happiness and INNOCENCE

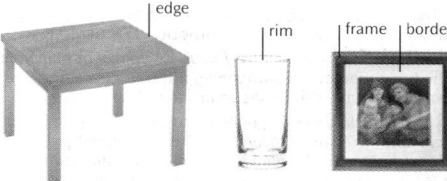

edge · rim · frame · border

edge /ɛdʒ/ *noun, verb*
• *noun* **1** [C] the outside limit of an object, a surface, or an area; the part farthest from the center: *He stood on the edge of the cliff.* ♦ *a big house on/at the edge of town* ♦ *Don't put that glass so near the edge of the table.* ♦ *I sat down at the water's edge.* ♦ *Stand the coin on its edge.* ⊃ picture at SHAPE ⊃ see also LEADING EDGE, TRAILING EDGE **2** [C] the sharp part of a blade, knife, or SWORD that is used for cutting: *Be careful—it*

has a sharp edge. ⊃ picture at KITCHEN ⊃ see also CUTTING EDGE, KNIFE EDGE **3** usually **the edge** [sing.] the point at which something, especially something bad, may begin to happen **SYN** BRINK, VERGE: *They had brought the country to the edge of disaster.* **4** [sing.] a slight advantage over someone or something: *The company needs to improve its competitive edge.* ◆ **~ on/over sb/sth** *They have the edge on us.* **5** [sing.] a strong, often exciting, quality: *Her show now has a hard political edge to it.* **6** [sing.] a sharp tone of voice, often showing anger: *He did his best to remain calm, but there was a distinct edge to his voice.* **7 -edged** (in adjectives) having the type of edge or edges mentioned: *a lace-edged handkerchief* ⊃ see also GILT-EDGED

IDM **be on edge** to be nervous, excited, or bad-tempered ⊃ thesaurus box at NERVOUS **on the edge of your seat** very excited and giving your full attention to something: *The game had the crowd on the edge of their seats.* **take the edge off sth** to make something less strong, less bad, etc.: *The sandwich took the edge off my appetite.* ⊃ more at FRAY v., RAZOR, ROUGH adj., TEETER, TOOTH

● **verb 1** [I, T] to move or to move something slowly and carefully in a particular direction: + **adv./prep.** *She edged a little closer to me.* ◆ *I edged nervously past the dog.* ◆ **~ sth** + **adv./prep.** *Emily edged her chair forward.* **2** [T, usually passive] **~ sth (with/in sth)** to put something around the edge of something: *The handkerchief is edged with lace.* **3** [I] + **adv./prep.** to increase or decrease slightly: *Prices edged up 2% in 2010.*

PHR V **,edge sb/sth↔'out (of sth)** to move someone from their position or job gradually, especially when they are not fully aware of what is happening: *She was edged out of the company by the new director.*

,edge 'city *noun* a large area of buildings on the edge of a city, usually near a main road: *an edge city full of office parks and shopping centers*

edge·wise /'ɛdʒwaɪz/ *adv.* with the edge upward or forward; on one side: *You'll only get the desk through the door if you turn it edgewise.* **IDM** see WORD n.

edg·ing /'ɛdʒɪŋ/ *noun* [U, C] something that forms the border or edge of something, added to make it more attractive, etc.

edg·y /'ɛdʒi/ *adj.* (**edg·i·er, edg·i·est**) (*informal*) **1** nervous, especially about what might happen: *She's been very edgy lately.* ◆ *After the recent unrest there is an edgy calm in the capital.* **2** (of a movie, book, piece of music, etc.) having a sharp, exciting quality: *an edgy film about street gangs* ▶ **edg·i·ly** /'ɛdʒəli/ *adv.*: *"I'm not sure I can make it tomorrow,"* he said edgily. **edg·i·ness** *noun* [U, sing.]

EDI /ˌi di 'aɪ/ *noun* [U] (*computing*) the abbreviation for "electronic data interchange" (a system that is used in business for sending information between different companies' computer systems)

ed·i·ble /'ɛdəbl/ *adj.* fit or suitable to be eaten; not poisonous: *The food at the hotel was barely edible.* ◆ *edible fungi/snails/flowers*

e·dict /'idɪkt/ *noun* [U, C] (*formal*) an official order or statement given by someone in authority **SYN** DECREE

ed·i·fi·ca·tion /ˌɛdəfɪ'keɪʃn/ *noun* [U] (*formal* or *humorous*) the improvement of someone's mind or character: *The books were intended for the edification of the masses.*

ed·i·fice /'ɛdəfəs/ *noun* (*formal*) **1** a large, impressive building: *an imposing edifice* ◆ (*figurative*) *Their new manifesto hardly threatens to bring the whole edifice of capitalism crashing down.* ◆ (*figurative*) *an edifice of lies* ⊃ note at BUILDING

ed·i·fy /'ɛdəˌfaɪ/ *verb* (**ed·i·fies, ed·i·fy·ing, ed·i·fied, ed·i·fied**) [I, T] **~ sb** (*formal*) to improve people's minds or character by teaching them about something

ed·i·fy·ing /'ɛdəˌfaɪɪŋ/ *adj.* (*formal* or *humorous*) likely to improve your mind or your character

ed·it **AWL** /'ɛdət/ *verb* **1** [T, I] **~ (sth)** to prepare a piece of writing, a book, etc. to be published by correcting the mistakes, making improvements to it, etc.: *I know that this*

rough draft will need to be edited. ◆ *This is the edited version of my speech* (= some parts have been taken out). **2** [T] **~ sth** to prepare a book to be published by collecting together and arranging pieces of writing by one or more authors: *He's editing a book of essays by Gore Vidal.* **3** [T, I] **~ (sth)** (*computing*) to make changes to text or data on a screen: *You can download the file and edit it on your computer.* **4** [T] **~ sth** when someone **edits** a movie, television program, etc. they take what has been filmed or recorded and decide which parts to include and in which order: *They're showing the edited highlights of last month's game.* **5** [T] **~ sth** to be responsible for planning and publishing a newspaper, magazine, etc. (= to be the editor): *She used to edit a women's magazine.* ▶ **ed·it** *noun*: *I had time to do a quick edit of my essay before handing it in.*

PHR V **,edit sth↔'out (of sth)** to remove words, phrases, or scenes from a book, program, etc. before it is published or shown **SYN** CUT OUT: *They edited out references to her father in the interview.*

ed·it·a·ble /'ɛdətəbl/ *adj.* (*computing*) (of text or software) that can be edited by the user: *an editable document*

e·di·tion ♪ **AWL** /ɪ'dɪʃn/ *noun*
1 the form in which a book is published: *a paperback/hardcover edition* ◆ *She collects first editions of famous children's books.* ◆ *the electronic edition of "Newsweek"* **2** a particular newspaper or magazine, or radio or television program, especially one in a regular series: *Tonight's edition of "Nightline" looks at unemployment.* **3** (*abbr.* **ed.**) the total number of copies of a book, newspaper, or magazine, etc. published at one time: *The dictionary is now in its sixth edition.* ◆ *The article appeared in the evening edition of the "Tribune."* ⊃ see also LIMITED EDITION ⊃ compare IMPRESSION

ed·i·tor ♪ **AWL** /'ɛdətər/ *noun*
1 a person who is in charge of a newspaper, magazine, etc., or part of one, and who decides what should be included: *the editor of "The Washington Post"* ◆ *the sports/financial/fashion editor* **2** a person who prepares a book to be published, for example by checking and correcting the text, making improvements, etc. ⊃ see also COPY EDITOR, MANAGING EDITOR **3** a person who prepares a movie, radio, or television program for being shown or broadcast by deciding what to include, and what order it should be in **4** a person who works as a journalist for radio or television reporting on a particular area of news: *our economics editor* **5** a person who chooses texts written by one or by several writers and prepares them to be published in a book: *She's the editor of a new collection of ghost stories.* **6** (*computing*) a program that allows you to change stored text or data ▶ **ed·i·tor·ship** /'ɛdətərˌʃɪp/ *noun* [U]: *the editorship of "The Denver Post"*

ed·i·to·ri·al **AWL** /ˌɛdə'tɔriəl/ *adj., noun*
● **adj.** [usually before noun] connected with the task of preparing something such as a newspaper, a book, or a television or radio program, to be published or broadcast: *the magazine's editorial staff* ◆ *an editorial decision*
● **noun** an important article in a newspaper that expresses the editor's opinion about an item of news or an issue, or a comment on radio or television that expresses the opinion of the station or network

ed·i·to·ri·al·ize /ˌɛdə'tɔriəˌlaɪz/ *verb* **1** [I] to express your opinions rather than just reporting the news or giving the facts: *He accused the magazine of editorializing in its handling of the story.* **2** [I] to express an opinion in an editorial: *Yesterday the "Washington Post" editorialized on this subject.*

'edit ,suite *noun* a room containing electronic equipment for EDITING material recorded on video

ed·u·cate ♪ /'ɛdʒəˌkeɪt/ *verb*
1 [often passive] **~ sb** to teach someone over a period of time at a school, college, etc.: *She was educated in the U.S.* ◆ *He was educated at his local high school and then at Yale.* **2** to teach someone about something or how to do something:

~ **sb (in/on sth)** *Children need to be educated on the dangers of taking drugs.* ♦ ~ **sb to do sth** *The campaign is intended to educate the public to respect the environment.*

ed·u·cat·ed 🔊 /ˈɛdʒəˌkeɪtəd/ *adj.*

1 –**educated** having had the kind of education mentioned; having been to the school or college mentioned: *privately educated children* ♦ *a British-educated lawyer* ♦ *He's a Princeton-educated Texan.* **2** having had a high standard of education; showing a high standard of education: *an educated and articulate person* ♦ *the educated elite* ♦ *He spoke in an educated voice.*

IDM **an educated guess** a guess that is based on some degree of knowledge, and is therefore likely to be correct

ed·u·ca·tion 🔊 /ˌɛdʒəˈkeɪʃn/ *noun*

1 [U, sing.] a process of teaching, training, and learning, especially in schools or colleges, to improve knowledge and develop skills: *elementary education* ♦ *secondary education* ♦ *higher education* ♦ *adult education classes* ♦ *a college education* ♦ *the state education system* ♦ *a man of little education* ♦ *She completed her formal education in 1995.* **2** [U, sing.] a particular kind of teaching or training: *health education* **3** also **Education** [U] the institutions or people involved in teaching and training: *the Education Department* ♦ *the Board of Education* ♦ *There should be closer links between education and industry.* **4** usually **Education** [U] the subject of study that deals with how to teach: *a College of Education* ♦ *a Bachelor of Education degree* ♦ *She's an education major.* **5** [sing.] (often *humorous*) an interesting experience that teaches you something: *The rock concert was quite an education for my parents!*

TOPIC COLLOCATIONS

Education

learning
- acquire/get/lack experience/training/(an) education
- receive/provide sb with training
- develop/design/plan a curriculum/course/program/syllabus
- give/go to/attend a class/lesson/lecture/seminar
- hold/run/conduct a class/seminar/workshop
- moderate/lead/facilitate a discussion
- sign up for/take a course/classes/lessons

school
- go to/start preschool/kindergarten/nursery school
- be in the first, second, etc. grade (at school)
- study/take/drop history/chemistry/German, etc.
- finish/drop out of/quit school
- graduate from high school/college

problems at school
- be the victim/target of bullying/teasing
- skip/cut/(informal) ditch class/school
- cheat on an exam/a test
- get/be given a detention (for doing sth)
- be expelled from/be suspended from school

work and exams
- do your homework/a project on sth
- work on/write/do/submit an essay/a dissertation/a thesis/an assignment/a paper
- finish/complete your dissertation/thesis/studies
- hand in/turn in your homework/essay/assignment/paper
- study/prepare/review/(informal) cram for a test/an exam
- take/(formal) sit for a test/an exam
- grade homework/a test
- do well on/(informal) ace a test/an exam
- pass/fail/(informal) flunk a test/an exam/a class/a course/a subject

college
- apply to/get into/go to/start college
- leave/graduate from college (with a degree in computer science)/law school
- study for/work towards a law degree/a degree in physics
- major/minor in biology/philosophy
- earn/receive/be awarded/get/have/hold a master's degree/a bachelor's degree/a Ph.D. in economics

ed·u·ca·tion·al 🔊 /ˌɛdʒəˈkeɪʃənl/ *adj.*
connected with education; providing education: *children with special educational needs* ♦ *an educational psychologist* ♦ *an educational visit* ♦ ***educational games/toys*** (= that teach you something as well as amusing you) ♦ *Watching television can be very educational.* ▶ **ed·u·ca·tion·al·ly** /-ʃənəli/ *adv.*: *Children living in inner-city areas may be educationally disadvantaged.*

ed·u·ca·tion·al·ist /ˌɛdʒəˈkeɪʃənəlɪst/ (also **ed·u·ca·tion·ist** /ˌɛdʒəˈkeɪʃənɪst/) *noun* a specialist in theories and methods of teaching

ed·u·ca·tive /ˈɛdʒəˌkeɪtɪv/ *adj.* (*formal*) that teaches something: *the educative role of the community*

ed·u·ca·tor /ˈɛdʒəˌkeɪtər/ *noun* (*formal*) **1** a person whose job is to teach or educate people: *adult educators* (= who teach adults) **2** a person who is an expert in the theories and methods of education ⊃ see also EDUCATIONALIST

ed·u·tain·ment /ˌɛdʒuˈteɪnmənt/ *noun* [U] products such as books, television programs, and especially computer software that both educate and entertain

Ed·ward·i·an /ɛdˈwɑrdiən; -ˈwɔr-/ *adj.* from the time of the British king Edward VII (1901–1910): *Edwardian architecture* ▶ **Ed·ward·i·an** *noun*

-ee /i/ *suffix* **1** (in nouns) a person affected by an action: *employee* ⊃ compare -ER, -OR **2** a person described as or concerned with a particular thing: *absentee* ♦ *refugee*

EEG /ˌi i ˈdʒi/ *noun* the abbreviation for "electroencephalogram" (a medical test that measures and records electrical activity in the brain)

eek /ik/ *exclamation* used to express fear or surprise: *Eek! It moved!*

eel /il/ *noun* [C, U] a long, thin, ocean or FRESHWATER fish that looks like a snake. There are several types of eels, some of which are used for food: *electric eels*

e'en /in/ *adv.* (*literary*) = EVEN

e'er /ɛr/ *adv.* (*literary*) = EVER

-eer /ɪr/ *suffix* **1** (in nouns) a person concerned with a particular thing: *auctioneer* ♦ *mountaineer* **2** (in verbs) (often *disapproving*) to be concerned with a particular thing: *profiteer* ♦ *commandeer*

ee·rie /ˈɪri/ *adj.* strange, mysterious, and frightening **SYN** UNCANNY: *an eerie yellow light* ♦ *I found the silence underwater really eerie.* ▶ **ee·ri·ly** /ˈɪrəli/ *adv.* **ee·ri·ness** *noun* [U]

ef·face /ɪˈfeɪs/ *verb* ~ **sth** (*formal*) to make something disappear; to remove something ⊃ see also SELF-EFFACING

ef·fect 🔊 /ɪˈfɛkt/ *noun, verb*

● *noun* **1** [C, U] ~ **(on sb/sth)** a change that someone or something causes in someone or something else; a result: *the effect of heat on metal* ♦ *dramatic/long-term effects* ♦ *to learn to distinguish between cause and effect* ♦ *the beneficial effects of exercise* ♦ *Modern farming methods can have an adverse effect on the environment.* ♦ *Her criticisms had the effect of discouraging him completely.* ♦ *Despite her ordeal, she seems to have suffered no ill effects.* ♦ *I can certainly feel the effects of too many late nights.* ♦ *"I'm feeling really depressed." "The winter here has that effect sometimes."* ♦ *I tried to persuade him, but with little or no effect.* ⊃ language bank at CONSEQUENTLY ⊃ see also GREENHOUSE EFFECT, SIDE EFFECT ⊃ note at

AFFECT **2** [C, U] a particular look, sound, or impression that someone, such as an artist or a writer, wants to create: *The overall effect of the painting is overwhelming.* ◆ *The stage lighting gives the effect of a moonlight scene.* ◆ *Add a scarf for a casual effect.* ◆ *He only behaves like that **for effect** (= in order to impress people).* ⊃ see also **SPECIAL EFFECTS, SOUND EFFECT** **3** **effects** [pl.] *(formal)* your personal possessions **SYN** BELONGINGS: *The insurance policy covers all baggage and personal effects.* **IDM** **come into effect** to come into use; to begin to apply: *New controls come into effect next month.* **in effect** **1** used when you are stating what the facts of a situation are: *In effect, the two systems are identical.* ◆ *His wife had, in effect, run the government for the past six months.* **2** (of a law or rule) in use: *These laws are in effect in twenty states.* **put/bring sth into effect** to cause something to come into use: *The recommendations will soon be put into effect.* **take effect** **1** to start to produce the results that are intended: *The aspirin will soon take effect.* **2** to come into use; to begin to apply: *The new law takes effect tomorrow.* **to the effect that… | to this/ that effect** used to show that you are giving the general meaning of what someone has said or written rather than the exact words: *He left a note to the effect that he would not be coming back.* ◆ *She told me to get out—or **words to that effect**.* **to good, great, dramatic, etc. effect** producing a good, successful, dramatic, etc. result or impression **to no effect** not producing the result you intend or hope for: *We warned them, but to no effect.* **with immediate effect** *(formal)* starting now; starting from…: *The government has cut interest rates with immediate effect.*
• *verb* ~ sth *(formal)* to make something happen: *to effect a cure/change/recovery* ⊃ note at AFFECT

ef·fec·tive 🔊 /ɪˈfɛktɪv/ *adj.*
1 producing the result that is wanted or intended; producing a successful result: *Long prison sentences can be a very effective deterrent for offenders.* ◆ *Aspirin is a simple but highly effective treatment.* ◆ *drugs that are effective against cancer* ◆ *I admire the effective use of color in her paintings.* **ANT** INEFFECTIVE ⊃ see also COST-EFFECTIVE **2** [only before noun] in reality, although not officially intended: *the effective, if not the actual, leader of the party* ◆ *He has now taken effective control of the country.* **3** *(formal)* (of laws and rules) coming into use: *The new speed limit on this road is effective June 1.* ▶ **ef·fec·tive·ness** (also less frequent **ef·fec·tiv·i·ty** /ˌɪfɛkˈtɪvəti/) *noun* [U]: *to check the effectiveness of the security system*

ef·fec·tive·ly 🔊 /ɪˈfɛktɪvli/ *adv.*
1 in a way that produces the intended result or a successful result: *The company must reduce costs to compete effectively.* ◆ *You dealt with the situation very effectively.* **2** used when you are saying what the facts of a situation are: *He was very polite but effectively he was telling me that I had no chance of getting the job.*

ef·fec·tor /ɪˈfɛktər/ *noun* (biology) an organ or a cell in the body that is made to react by something outside the body

ef·fec·tu·al /ɪˈfɛktʃuəl/ *adj.* *(formal)* (of things, not people) producing the result that was intended **SYN** EFFECTIVE: *an effectual remedy* ⊃ compare INEFFECTUAL ▶ **ef·fec·tu·al·ly** *adv.*

ef·fec·tu·ate /ɪˈfɛktʃuˌeɪt/ *verb* ~ sth *(formal)* to make something happen **SYN** CAUSE

ef·fem·i·nate /ɪˈfɛmənət/ *adj.* *(disapproving)* (of a man or a boy) looking, behaving, or sounding like a woman or a girl ▶ **ef·fem·i·na·cy** /ɪˈfɛmənəsi/ *noun* [U]

ef·fer·ves·cent /ˌɛfərˈvɛsnt/ *adj.* **1** *(approving)* (of people and their behavior) excited, enthusiastic, and full of energy **SYN** BUBBLY **2** (of a liquid) having or producing small bubbles of gas ⊃ compare SPARKLING ▶ **ef·fer·ves·cence** /-ˈvɛsns/ *noun* [U]

ef·fete /ɪˈfit/ *adj.* *(disapproving)* **1** (of a man) without strength; looking or behaving like a woman **2** weak; without the power that it once had

ef·fi·ca·cious /ˌɛfəˈkeɪʃəs/ *adj.* *(formal)* (of things, not of people) producing the result that was wanted or intended **SYN** EFFECTIVE: *They hope the new drug will prove especially efficacious in the relief of pain.*

ef·fi·ca·cy /ˈɛfɪkəsi/ *noun* [U] *(formal)* the ability of something, especially a drug or a medical treatment, to produce the results that are wanted

ef·fi·cien·cy /ɪˈfɪʃnsi/ *noun* **1** [U] the quality of doing something well with no waste of time or money: *improvements in efficiency at the factory* ◆ *I was impressed by the efficiency with which she handled the crisis.* **2** **ef·fi·cien·cies** [pl.] ways of wasting less time and money or of saving time or money: *We are looking at our business to see where savings and efficiencies can be made.* **3** [U] *(technical)* the relationship between the amount of energy that goes into a machine or an engine, and the amount that it produces **4** [C] = EFFICIENCY APARTMENT

ef'ficiency a,partment (also **ef·fi·cien·cy**) *noun* a small apartment with one main room for living, cooking, and sleeping in and a separate bathroom ⊃ compare STUDIO

ef·fi·cient 🔊 /ɪˈfɪʃnt/ *adj.*
doing something well and thoroughly with no waste of time, money, or energy: *an efficient worker* ◆ *efficient heating equipment* ◆ *the efficient use of energy* ◆ *As we get older, our bodies become less efficient at burning up calories.* ◆ *fuel-efficient cars* (= that do not use much fuel) **ANT** INEFFICIENT ▶ **ef·fi·cient·ly** *adv.*: *a very efficiently organized event*

ef·fi·gy /ˈɛfədʒi/ *noun* (pl. **ef·fi·gies**) **1** a statue of a famous person, a SAINT or a god: *stone effigies in the church* **2** a model of a person that makes them look ugly: *The demonstrators burned a crude effigy of the President.*

ef·flo·res·cence /ˌɛfləˈrɛsns/ *noun* [U, C] **1** *(formal)* the most developed stage of something **2** *(chemistry)* the powder which appears on the surface of bricks, rocks, etc. when water EVAPORATES

ef·flu·ent /ˈɛfluənt/ *noun* [U, C] *(formal)* liquid waste, especially chemicals produced by factories, or SEWAGE

ef·fort 🔊 /ˈɛfərt/ *noun*
1 [U, C] the physical or mental energy that you need to do something; something that takes a lot of energy: *You should put more effort into your work.* ◆ *A lot of effort has gone into making this event a success.* ◆ *It's a long climb to the top, but well worth the effort.* ◆ *Getting up this morning was quite an effort* (= it was difficult). ◆ *With some effort* (= with difficulty) *she managed to stop herself from laughing.* **2** [C] an attempt to do something, especially when it is difficult to do: *a determined/real/special effort* ◆ *to make an effort* ◆ *I didn't really feel like going out, but I am glad I made the effort.* ◆ *~ (to do sth) The company has laid off 150 workers in an effort to save money.* ◆ *The sports clubs are making every effort to interest more young people.* ◆ *We need to make a concerted effort to finish on time.* ◆ *I spent hours cleaning the house, but there isn't much to show for all my efforts.* ◆ *With an effort of will, he resisted the temptation.* ◆ *The project was a joint/group effort.* **3** [C] (usually after a noun) a particular activity that a group of people organize in order to achieve something: *the Russian space effort* ◆ *the United Nations' peacekeeping effort* **4** [C] the result of an attempt to do something: *I think this essay is a poor effort.* **IDM** See BEND v.

ef·fort·less /ˈɛfərtləs/ *adj.* needing little or no effort, so that it seems easy: *She dances with effortless grace.* ◆ *He made playing the guitar look effortless.* ▶ **ef·fort·less·ly** *adv.* **ef·fort·less·ness** *noun* [U]

ef·fron·ter·y /ɪˈfrʌntəri/ *noun* [U] *(formal)* behavior that is confident and very rude, without any feeling of shame **SYN** NERVE

ef·ful·gent /ɪˈfʌldʒənt/ *adj.* *(literary)* shining brightly ▶ **ef·ful·gence** /-dʒəns/ *noun* [U]

ef·fu·sion /ɪˈfyuʒn/ *noun* [C, U] **1** *(technical)* something, especially a liquid, that flows out of someone or something; the act of flowing out **2** *(formal)* the expression of feelings in

ʌ **cup**   ə **about**   eɪ **say**   aɪ **five**   ɔɪ **boy**   aʊ **now**   oʊ **go**   ər **bird**

an exaggerated way; feelings that are expressed in this way

ef·fu·sive /ɪˈfyusɪv/ adj. showing much or too much emotion: *an effusive welcome* ♦ *He was effusive in his praise.* ▶ **ef·fu·sive·ly** adv.

EFL /ˌi ɛf ˈɛl/ abbr. English as a foreign language (refers to the teaching of English to people for whom it is not the first language)

EFTA /ˈɛftə/ abbr. European Free Trade Association (an economic association of some European countries)

e.g. 🖉 /ˌi ˈdʒi/ abbr.
for example (from Latin "exempli gratia"): *popular pets (e.g., cats and dogs)*

LANGUAGE BANK

e.g.

giving examples

■ The Web site has a variety of interactive exercises (**e.g.**, matching games, crosswords, and quizzes).

■ The Web site has a variety of interactive exercises, **including** matching games, crosswords, and quizzes.

■ Web 2.0 technologies, **such as** wikis, blogs, and social networking sites, have changed the way that people use the Internet.

■ Many Web sites now allow users to contribute information. **A good example of this is** the "wiki," a type of Web site that anyone can edit.

■ Wikis vary in how open they are. **For example**, some wikis allow anybody to edit content, while others only allow registered users to do this.

■ Wikis vary in how open they are. Some wikis, **for example/for instance**, allow anybody to edit content, while others only allow registered users to do this.

■ More and more people read their news on the Internet. **To take one example**, over 18 million people visited the "New York Times" Web site in December.

■ Online newspapers are now more popular than paper ones. The "Los Angeles Times" **is a case in point**. Its print circulation has fallen in recent years, while its Web site attracts millions of users every month.

⊃ note at EXAMPLE
⊃ Language Banks at ADDITION, ARGUE, EVIDENCE, ILLUSTRATE

---

e·gal·i·tar·i·an /ɪˌgæləˈtɛriən/ adj. based on, or holding, the belief that everyone is equal and should have the same rights and opportunities ▶ **e·gal·i·tar·i·an** noun: *He described himself as an egalitarian.* **e·gal·i·tar·i·an·ism** /-iəˌnɪzəm/ noun [U]

egg 🖉 /ɛg/ noun, verb
● **noun 1** [C] a small OVAL object with a thin hard shell produced by a female bird and containing a young bird; a similar object produced by a female fish, insect, etc.: *The female sits on the eggs until they hatch.* ♦ *The fish lay thousands of eggs at one time.* ♦ *crocodile eggs* ⊃ picture at ANIMAL ⊃ collocations at LIFE **2** [C, U] a bird's egg, especially one from a chicken, that is eaten as food: *a hard-boiled egg* ♦ *bacon and eggs* ♦ *fried/poached/scrambled eggs* ♦ *Bind the mixture together with a little beaten egg.* ♦ *You have egg on your shirt.* ♦ *egg yolks/whites* ♦ *egg noodles* ♦ *duck/quail eggs* ♦ *a chocolate egg* (= made from chocolate in the shape of an egg) ⊃ see also EASTER EGG **3** [C] (in women and female animals) a cell that combines with a SPERM to create a baby or young animal **SYN** OVUM: *The male sperm fertilizes the female egg.* ♦ *an egg donor* ⊃ see also NEST EGG
IDM **a good egg** (old-fashioned, informal) a person who you can rely on to behave well **have egg on your face** (informal) to be made to look stupid: *They were left with egg on their faces when only ten people showed up.* **put all your eggs in one basket** to rely on one particular course of action for

success rather than giving yourself several different possibilities ⊃ more at CHICKEN n., KILL v., OMELET
● **verb**
PHR V **,egg sb↔'on** to encourage someone to do something, especially something that they should not do: *He hit the other boy again and again as his friends egged him on.*

'egg cup noun a small cup for holding a boiled egg

egg·head /ˈɛghɛd/ noun (informal, disapproving, or humorous) a person who is very intelligent and is only interested in books and learning

egg·nog /ˈɛgnɑg/ noun [U, C] an alcoholic drink made by mixing eggs with milk and often alcohol such as RUM

egg·plant /ˈɛgplænt/ noun [C, U] a vegetable with shiny, dark purple skin and soft white flesh ⊃ picture at FRUIT

'egg roll noun a type of Asian food consisting of a tube of thin DOUGH, filled with vegetables and/or meat and fried until it is crisp ⊃ see also SPRING ROLL

eggs Ben·e·dict /ˌɛgz ˈbɛnədɪkt/ noun [pl.] a dish consisting of eggs and HAM served on an ENGLISH MUFFIN (= a small round flat bread) with a white sauce

egg·shell /ˈɛgʃɛl/ noun **1** [C, U] the hard thin outside of an egg **2** (also **'eggshell ˌpaint**) [U] a type of paint that is smooth but not shiny when it dries

'egg ˌtimer noun a device that you use to measure the time needed to boil an egg

e·go /ˈigoʊ/ noun (pl. e·gos) **1** your sense of your own value and importance: *He has the biggest ego of anyone I've ever met.* ♦ *Winning the prize really boosted her ego.* **2** (psychology) the part of the mind that is responsible for your sense of who you are (= your identity) ⊃ see also ALTER EGO ⊃ compare SUPEREGO,

e·go·cen·tric /ˌigoʊˈsɛntrɪk/ adj. thinking only about yourself and not about what other people need or want **SYN** SELFISH

e·go·ism /ˈigoʊˌɪzəm/ noun [U] = EGOTISM ▶ **e·go·ist** /ˈigoʊɪst/ noun **e·go·is·tic** /ˌigoʊˈɪstɪk/ adj.

e·go·ma·ni·a /ˌigoʊˈmeɪniə/ noun [U] a mental condition in which you are very interested in yourself or concerned about yourself in a way that is not normal ▶ **e·go·ma·ni·ac** /-ˈmeɪniæk/ noun **e·go·ma·ni·a·cal** /-məˈnaɪəkl/ adj.

e·go·surf·ing /ˈigoʊˌsərfɪŋ/ noun [U] (informal) the activity of searching the Internet to find places where your own name has been mentioned

e·go·tism /ˈigəˌtɪzəm/ (also **e·go·ism**) noun [U] (disapproving) the fact of thinking that you are better or more important than anyone else ▶ **e·go·tis·tic** /ˌigəˈtɪstɪk/ (also **e·go·tis·ti·cal** /ˌigəˈtɪstɪkl/) adj. **e·go·tis·ti·cally** /-kli/ adv.

e·go·tist /ˈigətɪst/ /ˈigətɪst/ (also **e·go·ist**) noun (disapproving) a person who thinks that he or she is better than other people and who thinks and talks too much about himself or herself

'ego ˌtrip noun (usually disapproving) an activity that someone does because it makes them feel good and important

e·gre·gious /ɪˈgridʒəs/ adj. (formal) extremely bad

e·gress /ˈigrɛs/ noun [U] (formal) the act of leaving a place ⊃ compare ACCESS, INGRESS

e·gret /ˈigrət/ /ˈigrɛt/ noun a bird of the HERON family, with long legs and long white tail feathers

E·gyp·tol·o·gy /ˌidʒɪpˈtɑlədʒi/ noun [U] the study of the language, history, and culture of ancient Egypt ▶ **E·gyp·tol·o·gist** /-dʒɪst/ noun

eh /eɪ/ (especially CanE) exclamation **1** the sound that people make when they want someone to agree or reply: *Good party, eh?* **2** the sound people make when they are surprised: *Another new dress, eh!* **3** the sound that people make when they want someone to repeat something: *"I'm not hungry." "Eh?" "I said I'm not hungry."*

EI /ˌi ˈaɪ/ abbr. (CanE) = EMPLOYMENT INSURANCE

Eid (also **Id**) /id/ *noun* one of the two main Muslim festivals, either **Eid ul-Fitr** /ˌid ʊl ˈfitrə/ at the end of Ramadan, or **Eid ul-Adha** /ˌid ʊl ˈɑdə/ that celebrates the end of the PILGRIMAGE to Mecca and Abraham's SACRIFICE of a sheep

eight /eɪt/ **1** *number* 8 **HELP** There are examples of how to use numbers at the entry for **five**. **2** *noun* a team of eight people who ROW a long narrow boat in races; the boat they row ⤳ see also FIGURE EIGHT

the ˌEighteenth Aˈmendment *noun* [sing.] the statement in the U.S. Constitution that made it illegal to make and sell alcoholic drinks

eight·fold /ˈeɪtfoʊld; ˌeɪtˈfoʊld/ *adj., adv.* ⤳ -FOLD

eighth /eɪtθ; eɪθ/ *ordinal number, noun*
● *ordinal number* 8th **HELP** There are examples of how to use ordinal numbers at the entry for **fifth**.
● *noun* each of eight equal parts of something

ˈeighth note *noun* (*music*) a note that lasts half as long as a QUARTER NOTE ⤳ picture at MUSIC

eight·y /ˈeɪti/ **1** *number* 80 **2** *noun* **the eighties** [pl.] numbers, years, or temperatures from 80 to 89 ▶ **eight·i·eth** /ˈeɪtiəθ/ *ordinal number, noun* **HELP** There are examples of how to use ordinal numbers at the entry for fifth.
IDM **in your eighties** between the ages of 80 and 89

ein·stein·i·um /aɪnˈstaɪniəm/ *noun* [U] (*symb.* **Es**) a chemical element. Einsteinium is a RADIOACTIVE element produced artificially from PLUTONIUM and other elements.

ei·ther 🔑 /ˈiðər; ˈaɪðər/ *det., pron., adv.*
● *det., pron.* **1** one or the other of two; it does not matter which: *You can park on either side of the street.* ◆ *You can keep one of the photos. Either of them—whichever you like.* ◆ *There are two types of application—either is acceptable.* ⤳ note at NEITHER **2** each of two: *The offices on either side were empty.* ◆ *There's a door at either end of the hallway.*
● *adv.* **1** used after negative phrases to state that a feeling or situation is similar to one already mentioned: *Pete can't go and I can't either.* ◆ (*informal*) *"I don't like it." "Me either."* (= Neither do I). **2** used to add extra information to a statement: *I know a good Italian restaurant. It's not far from here, either.* **3 either… or…** used to show a choice of two things: *Well, I think she's either Czech or Slovak.* ◆ *I'm going to buy either a camera or a DVD player with the money.* ◆ *Either he could not come, or he did not want to.* ⤳ compare OR ⤳ note at NEITHER

e·jac·u·late /ɪˈdʒækyəˌleɪt/ *verb* **1** [I, T] **~ (sth)** when a man or a male animal **ejaculates**, SEMEN comes out through the PENIS **2** + **speech** (*old-fashioned*) to say or shout something suddenly **SYN** EXCLAIM

e·jac·u·la·tion /ɪˌdʒækyəˈleɪʃn/ *noun* **1** [C, U] the act of ejaculating; the moment when SPERM comes out of a man's PENIS: *premature ejaculation* **2** [C] (*formal*) a sudden shout or sound that you make when you are angry or surprised **SYN** EXCLAMATION

e·ject /ɪˈdʒɛkt/ *verb* **1** [T] **~ sb (from sth)** (*formal*) to force someone to leave a place **SYN** THROW OUT: *Police ejected a crowd of violent protesters from the hall.* **2** [T] **~ sth (from sth)** to push something out suddenly and with a lot of force: *Used cartridges are ejected from the gun after firing.* **3** [T, I] **~ (sth)** when you eject a disk, etc., or when it **ejects**, it comes out of the machine after you have pressed a button **4** [I] (of a pilot) to escape from an aircraft that is going to crash, sometimes using an ejection seat ▶ **e·jec·tion** /ɪˈdʒɛkʃn/ *noun* [U, C]

eˈjection ˌseat *noun* a seat that allows a pilot to be thrown out of an aircraft in an emergency

eke /ik/ *verb*
PHRV ˌeke sth↔ˈout **1** to make a small supply of something such as food or money last longer by using only small amounts of it: *She managed to eke out her student loan till the end of the year.* **2 ~ a living, etc.** to manage to live with very little money

EKG /ˌi keɪ ˈdʒi/ (also **ECG**) *noun* the abbreviation for "electrocardiogram" (a medical test that measures and records electrical activity of the heart)

e·lab·o·rate *adj., verb*
● *adj.* /ɪˈlæbrət; -bərət/ [usually before noun] very complicated and detailed; carefully prepared and organized: *elaborate designs* ◆ *She had prepared a very elaborate meal.* ◆ *an elaborate computer system* ▶ **e·lab·o·rate·ly** *adv.*: *an elaborately decorated room* **e·lab·o·rate·ness** *noun* [U]
● *verb* /ɪˈlæbəˌreɪt/ **1** [I, T] to explain or describe something in a more detailed way: **~ (on/upon sth)** *He said he was resigning but did not elaborate on his reasons.* ◆ **~ sth** *She went on to elaborate her argument.* **2** [T] **~ sth** to develop a plan, an idea, etc. and make it complicated or detailed: *In his plays, he takes simple traditional tales and elaborates them.* ▶ **e·lab·o·ra·tion** /ɪˌlæbəˈreɪʃn/ *noun* [U, C]: *The importance of the plan needs no further elaboration.*

é·lan /eɪˈlɑn; eɪˈlɑ̃/ *noun* [U] (from French, *literary*) great enthusiasm, energy, style, and confidence

e·land /ˈilənd/ *noun* (*pl.* **e·land** or **e·lands**) a large African ANTELOPE with curled horns

e·lapse /ɪˈlæps/ *verb* [I] (not usually used in the progressive tenses) (*formal*) if a period of time **elapses**, it passes **SYN** GO BY: *Many years elapsed before they met again.*

e·lapsed ˈtime *noun* [U] (*technical*) used to describe the time that passes between the start and end of a project or a computer operation, in contrast to the actual time needed to do a particular task that is part of the project

e·las·tic /ɪˈlæstɪk/ *noun, adj.*
● *noun* [U] **1** material made with rubber, that can stretch and then return to its original size: *This skirt needs some new elastic in the waist.* **2** [C] a narrow band that stretches **SYN** RUBBER BAND: *Her ponytail was held in place with an elastic.*
● *adj.* **1** made with elastic: *an elastic headband* **2** able to stretch and return to its original size and shape: *elastic materials* **3** that can change or be changed: *Our plans are fairly elastic.*

e·las·tic·i·ty /ɪˌlæˈstɪsəti; ˌilæ-/ *noun* [U] **1** the quality that something has of being able to stretch and return to its original size and shape (= of being elastic) **2 ~ of supply/ demand** (*economics*) the degree to which the supply of or demand for a product or service changes when the price changes

e·las·ti·cized /ɪˈlæstəˌsaɪzd/ *adj.* (of clothing, or part of a piece of clothing) made using elastic material that can stretch: *a skirt with an elasticized waist*

e·las·tin /ɪˈlæstən/ *noun* [U] (*biology*) a natural substance that stretches easily, found in the skin, the heart, and other body TISSUES

e·las·to·mer /ɪˈlæstəmər/ *noun* (*chemistry*) a natural or artificial chemical that behaves like rubber

e·lat·ed /ɪˈleɪtəd/ *adj.* **~ (at/by sth)** very happy and excited because of something good that has happened, or will happen: *They were elated at the result.* ◆ *I was elated by the prospect of the new job ahead.* ⤳ thesaurus box at EXCITED

e·la·tion /ɪˈleɪʃn/ *noun* [U] a feeling of great happiness and excitement

el·bow 🔑 /ˈɛlboʊ/ *noun, verb*
● *noun* **1** the joint between the upper and lower parts of the arm where it bends in the middle: *She jabbed him with her elbow.* ◆ *He fractured his elbow.* ⤳ picture at BODY **2** the part of a piece of clothing that covers the elbow: *The jacket was worn at the elbows.* **3** a part of a pipe, CHIMNEY, etc. where it bends at a sharp angle **IDM** see RUB *v.*
● *verb* **~ sb/sth (+adv./prep.)** to push someone with your elbow, usually in order to get past them: *She elbowed me out of the way to get to the front of the line.* ◆ *He elbowed his way through the crowd.*

ˈelbow ˌgrease *noun* [U] (*informal*) the effort used in physical work, especially in cleaning or polishing something

---

   t **tea**   ţ **butter**   d **did**   k **cat**   g **got**   tʃ **chin**   dʒ **June**   f **fall**

'elbow ,room *noun* [U] (*informal*) enough space to move or walk in

eld·er /ˈɛldər/ *adj., noun*

● *adj.* **1** [only before noun] (*old-fashioned* or *formal*) (of people, especially two members of the same family) older: *my elder brother* ◆ *his elder sister* **2 the elder** (*old-fashioned* or *formal*) used without a noun immediately after it to show who is the older of two people: *the elder of their two sons* **3 the Elder** used before or after someone's name to show that they are the older of two people who have the same name: *the Elder Pitt* ◆ *Pitt the Elder* ⮁ compare THE YOUNGER at YOUNG *adj.* (6) ⮁ note at OLD

● *noun* **1 elders** [pl.] people of greater age, experience, and authority: *Children have no respect for their elders nowadays.* ◆ *the village elders* (= the old and respected people of the village) **2 my, etc. elder** [sing.] (*formal*) a person older than you, etc.: *He is her elder by several years.* **3** [C] an official in some Christian churches **4** [C] a small tree with white flowers with a sweet smell (**elderflowers**) and bunches of small black berries (**elderberries**)

'elder a,buse *noun* [U] the crime of harming or stealing from an old person, committed by someone who is trusted to care for or help them

el·der·ber·ry /ˈɛldərˌbɛri/ *noun* (*pl.* **el·der·ber·ries**) a small black BERRY that grows in bunches on an elder tree

el·der·care /ˈɛldərˌkɛr/ *noun* [U] help for old people, especially services such as special homes and medical care: *nursing homes and other eldercare facilities*

eld·er·ly /ˈɛldərli/ *adj.*

1 (of people) used as a polite word for "old": *an elderly couple* ◆ *elderly relatives* ⮁ thesaurus box at OLD **2 the elderly** *noun* [pl.] people who are old

,elder 'statesman *noun* **1** an old and respected politician or former politician whose advice is still valued because of his or her long experience **2** any experienced and respected person whose advice or work is valued: *an elder statesman of golf*

eld·est /ˈɛldəst/ *adj.* (*old-fashioned* or *formal*) **1** (of people, especially of three or more members of the same family) oldest: *Tom is my eldest son.* **2 the eldest** used without a noun immediately after it to show who is the oldest of three or more people: *the eldest of their three children* ⮁ note at OLD

e·lect /ɪˈlɛkt/ *verb, adj.*

● *verb* **1** to choose someone to do a particular job by voting for them: *~ sb/sth an elected assembly/leader/representative* ◆ *the newly elected government* ◆ *~ sb to sth She became the first black woman to be elected to the Senate.* ◆ *~ sb (as) sth* | *~ sb + noun He was elected (as) mayor of Baltimore.* ⮁ collocations at VOTE **2 ~ to do sth** (*formal*) to choose to do something: *Increasing numbers of people elect to work from home nowadays.*

● *adj.* **1 -elect** used after nouns to show that someone has been chosen for a job, but is not yet doing that job: *the president-elect* **2 the elect** *noun* [pl.] (*religion*) people who have been chosen to be saved from punishment after death

e·lec·tion /ɪˈlɛkʃn/ *noun*

1 [U, C] the process of choosing a person or a group of people for a position, especially a political position, by voting: *election campaigns/results* ◆ *to win/lose an election* ◆ *to vote in an election* ◆ *Presidential elections are held every four years.* ◆ *to run for election* ⮁ collocations at VOTE **2** [U] the fact of having been chosen by election: *~ (as sth) We welcome his election as president.* ◆ *~ (to sth) a year after her election to the committee* ⮁ see also GENERAL ELECTION

e·lec·tion·eer·ing /ɪˌlɛkʃəˈnɪrɪŋ/ *noun* [U] the activity of making speeches and visiting people to try to persuade them to vote for a particular politician or political party in an election

e·lec·tive /ɪˈlɛktɪv/ *adj., noun*

● *adj.* [usually before noun] (*formal*) **1** using or chosen by election: *an elective democracy* ◆ *an elective assembly* ◆ *an elective member* ◆ *He had never held elective office* (= a position that is filled by election). **2** having the power to elect: *an elective body* **3** (of medical treatment) that you choose to have; that is not urgent **SYN** OPTIONAL: *elective surgery* **4** (of a course or subject) that a student can choose **SYN** OPTIONAL

● *noun* a course or subject at a college or school that a student can choose to take

e·lec·tor /ɪˈlɛktər; -tɔr/ *noun* **1** a person who has the right to vote in an election **2** a member of the U.S. electoral college

e·lec·tor·al /ɪˈlɛktərəl/ *adj.* [only before noun] connected with elections: *electoral systems/reforms* ▶ **e·lec·tor·al·ly** *adv.*: *an electorally effective campaign*

e,lectoral 'college *noun* **1 the Electoral College** a group of people who come together to elect the president and vice president of the United States, based on the votes of people in each state **2** (in some other countries) a group of people who are chosen to represent the members of a political party, etc. in the election of a leader

e·lec·tor·ate /ɪˈlɛktərət/ *noun* [C] the people in a country or an area who have the right to vote, thought of as a group: *Only 60% of the electorate voted in the last election.* ⮁ collocations at VOTE

e·lec·tric /ɪˈlɛktrɪk/ *adj., noun*

● *adj.* **1** [usually before noun] connected with electricity; using, produced by, or producing electricity: *an electric motor* ◆ *an electric guitar* ◆ *an electric current/charge* ◆ *an electric generator* ◆ *an electric plug/outlet/switch* (= that carries electricity) ⮁ note on page 480 ⮁ see also ELECTRIC SHOCK **2** full of excitement; making people excited **SYN** ELECTRIFYING: *The atmosphere was electric.*

● *noun* [U] (*informal*) used to refer to the supply of electricity to a building: *The electric will be off tomorrow.* ◆ *I paid the electric* (= the bill for the supply of electricity).

e·lec·tri·cal /ɪˈlɛktrɪkl/ *adj.*

connected with electricity; using or producing electricity: *an electrical fault in the engine* ◆ *electrical equipment/ appliances* ◆ *electrical power/energy* ▶ **e·lec·tri·cally** /-kli/ *adv.*: *electrically charged particles* ⮁ note on page 480

---

e‧lectrical engi'neering *noun* [U] the design and building of machines and systems that use or produce electricity; the study of this subject ▶ **e‧lectrical engi'neer** *noun*

e'lectrical ˌstorm *noun* a violent storm in which electricity is produced in the atmosphere

e‧lectric 'blanket *noun* a BLANKET for a bed that is heated by electricity passing through the wires inside it

e‧lectric 'blue *noun* [U] a bright or METALLIC blue color

e'lectric ˌchair usually **the electric chair** (also *informal* **the chair**) *noun* [sing.] a chair in which criminals are killed by passing a powerful electric current through their bodies; the method of EXECUTION which uses this chair: *He was sent to the electric chair.* ◆ *They face death by the electric chair.*

e‧lectric 'fence *noun* a wire fence through which an electric current can be passed

e‧lec‧tri‧cian /ɪˌlɛkˈtrɪʃn/ *noun* a person whose job is to connect, repair, etc. electrical equipment

e‧lec‧tric‧i‧ty 🔑 /ɪˌlɛkˈtrɪsəti/ *noun*
1 [U] a form of energy from charged ELEMENTARY PARTICLES, usually supplied as electric current through cables, wires, etc. for lighting, heating, driving machines, etc.: *a waste of electricity* ◆ *The electricity is off* (= there is no electric power supply). **2** [U, sing.] a feeling of great emotion, excitement, etc.

e‧lectric 'razor *noun* = SHAVER

e‧lectric 'shock (also **shock**) *noun* a sudden painful feeling that you get when electricity passes through your body

e‧lec‧tri‧fi‧ca‧tion /ɪˌlɛktrəfəˈkeɪʃn/ *noun* [U] the process of changing something so that it works by electricity

e‧lec‧tri‧fy /ɪˈlɛktrəˌfaɪ/ *verb* (**e‧lec‧tri‧fies**, **e‧lec‧tri‧fy‧ing**, **e‧lec‧tri‧fied**, **e‧lec‧tri‧fied**) **1** [usually passive] ~ **sth** to make something work by using electricity; to pass an electrical current through something: *The railroad line was electrified in the 1950s.* ◆ *He had all the fences around his home electrified.* **2** ~ **sb** to make someone feel very excited and enthusiastic about something: *Her performance electrified the audience.*

e‧lec‧tri‧fy‧ing /ɪˈlɛktrəˌfaɪɪŋ/ *adj.* very exciting: *The dancers gave an electrifying performance.*

electro– /ɪˈlɛktroʊ/ *combining form* (in nouns, adjectives, verbs, and adverbs) connected with electricity: *electromagnetism*

e‧lec‧tro‧car‧di‧o‧gram /ɪˌlɛktroʊˈkɑrdiəˌgræm/ *noun* = EKG

e‧lectrocon‧vulsive 'therapy /ɪˌlɛktroʊkənˈvʌlsɪv ˈθɛrəpi/ *noun* [U] (*abbr.* ECT) (*technical*) = ELECTROSHOCK

e‧lec‧tro‧cute /ɪˈlɛktrəˌkyut/ *verb* [usually passive] ~ **sb** to injure or kill someone by passing electricity through their body: *The boy was electrocuted when he wandered onto a railroad track.* ◆ *James Roach was electrocuted in South Carolina in 1986* (= punished by being killed in the electric chair). ▶ **e‧lec‧tro‧cu‧tion** /ɪˌlɛktrəˈkyuʃn/ *noun* [U]: *Six people were drowned; five died from electrocution.* ◆ *He was sentenced to death by electrocution.*

e‧lec‧trode /ɪˈlɛktroʊd/ *noun* either of two points (TERMINALS) by which an electric current enters or leaves a battery or other electrical device ⟳ see also ANODE, CATHODE

e‧lec‧tro‧dy‧nam‧ics /ɪˌlɛktroʊdaɪˈnæmɪks/ *noun* [U] (*physics*) the study of the way that electric currents and MAGNETIC FIELDS affect each other

e‧lec‧tro‧en‧ceph‧a‧lo‧gram /ɪˌlɛktroʊɪnˈsɛfələˌgræm/ *noun* = EEG

e‧lec‧trol‧y‧sis /ɪˌlɛkˈtrɑləsəs/ *noun* [U] **1** the destruction of the roots of hairs by means of an electric current, as a beauty treatment **2** (*chemistry*) the separation of a liquid (an **electrolyte**) into its chemical parts by passing an electric current through it

e‧lec‧tro‧lyte /ɪˈlɛktrəˌlaɪt/ *noun* (*chemistry*) a liquid that an electric current can pass through, especially in an electric cell or battery ▶ **e‧lec‧tro‧lyt‧ic** /ɪˌlɛktrəˈlɪtɪk/ *adj.*

e‧lec‧tro‧mag‧net /ɪˈlɛktroʊˌmægnət/ *noun* (*physics*) a piece of metal that becomes MAGNETIC when electricity is passed through it

e‧lec‧tro‧mag‧net‧ic /ɪˌlɛktroʊmægˈnɛtɪk/ *adj.* (*physics*) having both electrical and MAGNETIC characteristics or properties (PROPERTY): *an electromagnetic wave/field*

e‧lec‧tro‧mag‧net‧ism /ɪˌlɛktroʊˈmægnəˌtɪzəm/ *noun* [U] (*physics*) the production of a MAGNETIC FIELD by means of an electric current, or of an electric current by means of a MAGNETIC FIELD

e‧lec‧tron /ɪˈlɛktrɑn/ *noun* (*physics*) a very small piece of matter (= a substance) with a negative electric charge, found in all atoms ⟳ picture at ATOM ⟳ see also NEUTRON, PROTON

e‧lec‧tron‧ic 🔑 /ɪˌlɛkˈtrɑnɪk/ *adj.* [usually before noun] **1** (of a device) having or using many small parts, such as MICROCHIPS, that control and direct a small electric current: *an electronic calculator* ◆ *electronic music* ◆ *This dictionary is available in electronic form.* **2** concerned with electronic equipment: *an electronic engineer*

e‧lec‧tron‧i‧cally /ɪˌlɛkˈtrɑnɪkli/ *adv.* in an electronic way, or using a device that works in an electronic way: *to process data electronically* (= using a computer)

elec‧tronic 'mail *noun* [U] (*formal*) = E-MAIL

elec‧tronic 'organizer *noun* a very small computer that can be carried around, used for storing information such as addresses and important dates ⟳ see also PDA

elec‧tronic 'publishing *noun* [U] the business of publishing books, etc. in a form that can be read on a computer

e‧lec‧tron‧ics /ɪˌlɛkˈtrɑnɪks/ *noun* **1** [U] the branch of science and technology that studies electric currents in electronic equipment **2** [U] the use of electronic technology, especially in developing new equipment: *the electronics industry* **3** [pl.] the electronic CIRCUITS and COMPONENTS (= parts) used in electronic equipment: *a fault in the electronics*

e'lectron ˌmicroscope *noun* a very powerful MICROSCOPE that uses ELECTRONS instead of light

e‧lec‧tro‧plate /ɪˈlɛktrəˌpleɪt/ *verb* [usually passive] ~ **sth** to cover something with a thin layer of metal using ELECTROLYSIS

e‧lec‧tro‧shock /ɪˈlɛktroʊˌʃɑk/ (also **e‧lectroshock 'therapy**, **e‧lectrocon‧vulsive 'therapy**) *noun* a medical treatment of mental illness that passes electricity through the patient's brain

e·lec·tro·stat·ic /ɪˌlɛktroʊˈstætɪk/ *adj.* (*physics*) used to talk about electric charges that are not moving, rather than electric currents

el·e·gant 🔑 /ˈɛləɡənt/ *adj.*
1 (of people or their behavior) attractive and showing a good sense of style **SYN** STYLISH: *She was tall and elegant.* **2** (of clothes, places, and things) attractive and designed well **SYN** STYLISH: *an elegant dress ◆ an elegant room/ restaurant* **3** (of a plan or an idea) showing skill and imagination, but simple: *an elegant solution to the problem* ▶ **el·e·gance** /-ɡəns/ *noun* [U]: *She dresses with casual elegance. ◆ His writing combines elegance and wit.* **el·e·gant·ly** *adv.*: *elegantly dressed ◆ elegantly furnished*

el·e·gi·ac /ˌɛləˈdʒaɪæk/ *adj.* (*formal* or *literary*) expressing sadness, especially about the past or people who have died

el·e·gy /ˈɛlədʒi/ *noun* (*pl.* **el·e·gies**) a poem or song that expresses sadness, especially for someone who has died

el·e·ment 🔑 **AWL** /ˈɛləmənt/ *noun*
> PART/AMOUNT **1** [C] **~ (in/of sth)** a necessary or typical part of something: *Cost was a key element in our decision. ◆ The story has all the elements of a soap opera. ◆ Customer relations is an important element of the job.* **2** [C, usually sing.] **~ of surprise, risk, truth, etc.** a small amount of a quality or feeling: *We need to preserve the element of surprise. ◆ There appears to be an element of truth in his story.*
> GROUP OF PEOPLE **3** [C, usually pl.] a group of people who form a part of a larger group or society: *moderate/radical elements within the party ◆ unruly elements in the school*
> CHEMISTRY **4** [C] a simple chemical substance that consists of atoms of only one type and cannot be split by chemical means into a simpler substance. Gold, OXYGEN, and CARBON are all elements. ⊃ compare COMPOUND
> EARTH/AIR/FIRE/WATER **5** [C] one of the four substances: earth, air, fire, and water, that people used to believe everything else was made of
> WEATHER **6 the elements** [pl.] the weather, especially bad weather: *Are we going to brave the elements and go for a walk? ◆ to be exposed to the elements*
> BASIC PRINCIPLES **7 elements** [pl.] the basic principles of a subject that you have to learn first **SYN** BASICS: *He taught me the elements of map-reading.*
> ENVIRONMENT **8** [C, usually sing.] a natural or suitable environment, especially for an animal: *Water is a fish's natural element.*
> ELECTRICAL PART **9** [C] the part of a piece of electrical equipment that gives out heat: *The broiler needs a new element.*
IDM **in your element** doing what you are good at and enjoy: *She's really in her element at parties.* **out of your element** in a situation that you are not used to and that makes you feel uncomfortable

el·e·men·tal /ˌɛləˈmɛntl/ *adj.* [usually before noun] (*formal*)
1 wild and powerful; like the forces of nature: *the elemental fury of the storm* **2** basic and important: *an elemental truth*

el·e·men·ta·ry /ˌɛləˈmɛntri; -ˈmɛntəri/ *adj.* **1** in or connected with the first stages of a course of study: *an elementary English course ◆ at an elementary level* **2** connected with the education of children between the ages of about 5 and 12: *a book for elementary students* **3** of the most basic kind: *the elementary laws of economics ◆ an elementary mistake* **4** very simple and easy: *elementary questions*

ˌelementary **'particle** *noun* (*physics*) any of the different types of very small pieces of matter (= a substance) smaller than an atom

eleˈmentary ˌschool (also *informal* 'grade school) *noun* a school for children between the ages of about 5 and 12 ⊃ see also MIDDLE SCHOOL, HIGH SCHOOL

el·e·phant /ˈɛləfənt/ *noun* a very large animal with thick gray skin, large ears, two curved outer teeth (called TUSKS) and a long nose (called a TRUNK). There are two types of elephants, the African and the Asian: *herds of elephants/*

elephant herds ◆ *a baby elephant* ⊃ picture at ANIMAL ⊃ see also WHITE ELEPHANT
IDM **the elephant in the room** a problem or question that everyone knows about but does not mention because it is easier not to discuss it: *The elephant in the room was the money that had to be paid in bribes.*

el·e·phan·ti·a·sis /ˌɛləfənˈtaɪəsəs/ *noun* [U] (*medical*) a condition in which part of the body swells and becomes very large because the lymphatic (LYMPH) system is blocked

el·e·phan·tine /ˌɛləˈfæntin; ˈɛləfənˌtin/ *adj.* (*formal* or *humorous*) very large and CLUMSY; like an elephant

el·e·vate /ˈɛləˌveɪt/ *verb* **1** (*formal*) to give someone or something a higher position or rank, often more important than they deserve **SYN** RAISE, PROMOTE: **~ sb/sth (to sth)** *He elevated many of his friends to powerful positions within the government. ◆ ~ sth (into sth) He was a great writer who elevated travel writing into an art.* **2 ~ sth** (*technical* or *formal*) to lift something up or put something in a higher position: *It is important to elevate the injured leg.* **3 ~ sth** (*technical*) to make the level of something increase: *Smoking often elevates blood pressure.* **4 ~ sth** (*formal*) to improve a person's mood, so that they feel happy: *The song never failed to elevate his spirits.*

el·e·vat·ed /ˈɛləˌveɪtəd/ *adj.* [usually before noun] **1** high in rank: *an elevated status* **2** (*formal*) having a high moral or intellectual level: *elevated language/sentiments/thoughts* **3** higher than the area around; above the level of the ground: *The house is in an elevated position, overlooking the town. ◆ an elevated highway/railroad/road* (= one that runs on a bridge above the ground or street) **4** (*technical*) higher than normal: *elevated blood pressure*

el·e·va·tion /ˌɛləˈveɪʃn/ *noun* **1** [U] (*formal*) the process of someone getting a higher or more important rank: *his elevation to the presidency* **2** [C, usually sing.] (*technical*) the height of a place, especially its height above sea level: *The city is at an elevation of about 5,000 feet.* **3** [C] (*formal*) a piece of ground that is higher than the area around **4** [C] (*architecture*) one side of a building, or a drawing of this by an ARCHITECT: *the front/rear/side elevation of a house* ⊃ compare GROUND PLAN (1), PLAN **5** [U, sing.] (*technical*) an increase in the level or amount of something: *elevation of blood sugar levels*

el·e·va·tor 🔑 /ˈɛləˌveɪtər/ *noun*
1 a machine that carries people or goods up and down to different levels in a building or a mine: *It's on the fifth floor, so we'd better take the elevator.* **2** a place for storing large quantities of grain **3** a part in the tail of an aircraft that is moved to make it go up or down ⊃ picture at PLANE

e·lev·en /ɪˈlɛvn/ *number* 11 ▶ **e·lev·enth** /ɪˈlɛvnθ/ *ordinal number, noun* **HELP** There are examples of how to use ordinal numbers at the entry for **fifth**.
IDM **at the eleventh hour** at the last possible moment; just in time

elf /ɛlf/ *noun* (*pl.* **elves** /ɛlvz/) (in stories) a creature like a small person with pointed ears, who has magic powers

elf·in /ˈɛlfən/ *adj.* (of a person or their features) small and delicate: *an elfin face*

e·lic·it /ɪˈlɪsət/ *verb* **~ sth (from sb)** (*formal*) to get information or a reaction from someone, often with difficulty: *I could elicit no response from him. ◆ Her tears elicited great sympathy from her audience.* ▶ **e·lic·i·ta·tion** /ɪˌlɪsəˈteɪʃn/ *noun* [U]

e·lide /ɪˈlaɪd/ *verb* **~ sth** (*phonetics*) to leave out the sound of part of a word when you are pronouncing it: *The "t" in "often" may be elided.* ⊃ see also ELISION

el·i·gi·ble /ˈɛlədʒəbl/ *adj.* **1** a person who is **eligible** for something or to do something is able to have or do it because they have the right qualifications, are the right age, etc.: **~ (for sth)** *Only those over 70 are eligible for the special payment. ◆ ~ (to do sth) When are you eligible to vote in your country?* **ANT** INELIGIBLE **2** an **eligible** young man or woman is thought to be a good choice as a husband/

| i **see** | ɪ **sit** | ɛ **ten** | æ **cat** | ɑ **hot** | ɔ **saw** | ʊ **put** | u **too** | **481** |

wife, usually because they are rich or attractive ▶ **el·i·gi·bil·i·ty** /ˌɛlədʒəˈbɪləti/ *noun* [U]

e·lim·i·nate 🔑 **AWL** /ɪˈlɪməˌneɪt/ *verb*
1 to remove or get rid of something or someone: ~ sth/sb *Credit cards eliminate the need to carry a lot of cash.* ♦ ~ sth/sb **from sth** *The police have eliminated two suspects from their investigation.* ♦ *This diet claims to eliminate toxins from the body.* **2** ~ sb (from sth) [usually passive] to defeat a person or a team so that they no longer take part in a competition, etc. **SYN** KNOCK OUT: *Her team was eliminated in the early stages of the competition.* **3** ~ sb (formal) to kill someone, especially an enemy or opponent: *Most of the regime's left-wing opponents were eliminated.* ▶ **e·lim·i·na·tion** **AWL** /ɪˌlɪməˈneɪʃn/ *noun* [U, C]: *the elimination of disease/poverty/crime* ♦ *There were three eliminations in the first round of the competition.* ♦ *the elimination of toxins from the body*

elimiˈnation reˌaction *noun* (chemistry) a chemical reaction that involves the separation of a substance from other substances ➔ compare ADDITION REACTION

e·li·sion /ɪˈlɪʒn/ *noun* [U, C] (phonetics) the act of leaving out the sound of part of a word when you are pronouncing it, as in *we'll, don't* and *let's* ➔ see also ELIDE

e·lite /ɪˈlit; eɪˈlit/ *noun* a group of people in a society, etc. who are powerful and have a lot of influence, because they are rich, intelligent, etc.: *a member of the ruling/intellectual elite* ♦ *Public opinion is influenced by the small elite who control the media.* ♦ *In these countries, only the elite can afford an education for their children.* ▶ **e·lite** *adj.* [only before noun]: *an elite group of senior officials* ♦ *an elite military academy*

e·lit·ism /ɪˈliˌtɪzəm; eɪ-/ *noun* [U] (often disapproving) **1** a way of organizing a system, society, etc. so that only a few people (an elite) have power or influence: *Many people believe that private education encourages elitism.* **2** the feeling of being better than other people that being part of an elite encourages ▶ **e·lit·ist** /ɪˈlitɪst; eɪ-/ *adj.*: *an elitist model of society* ♦ *She accused him of being elitist.* **e·lit·ist** *noun*

e·lix·ir /ɪˈlɪksər/ *noun* (literary) a magic liquid that is believed to cure illnesses or to make people live forever: *the elixir of life/youth*

E·liz·a·be·than /ɪˌlɪzəˈbiθn/ *adj.* connected with the time when Queen Elizabeth I was queen of England (1558–1603) ▶ **E·liz·a·be·than** *noun*: *Shakespeare was an Elizabethan.*

elk /ɛlk/ *noun* (pl. **elk** or **elks**) **1** (also **wap·i·ti**) a very large N. American DEER **2** **Elk** a member of the Benevolent and Protective Order of Elks, a social organization that gives money to charity

el·lipse /ɪˈlɪps/ *noun* (technical) a regular OVAL shape, like a circle that has been squeezed on two sides ➔ picture at SHAPE

el·lip·sis /ɪˈlɪpsəs/ *noun* (pl. **el·lip·ses** /-siz/) [C, U] **1** (grammar) the act of leaving out a word or words from a sentence deliberately, when the meaning can be understood without them **2** three dots (…) used to show that a word or words have been left out

el·lip·ti·cal /ɪˈlɪptɪkl/ *adj.* **1** (grammar) with a word or words left out of a sentence deliberately: *an elliptical remark* (= one that suggests more than is actually said) **2** (also less frequent **el·lip·tic** /ɪˈlɪptɪk/) (geometry) connected with or in the form of an ellipse ▶ **el·lip·ti·cally** /-kli/ *adv.*: *to speak/write elliptically*

El·lis Is·land /ˌɛləs ˈaɪlənd/ *noun* a small island near New York City that from 1892 to 1943 was the official place of entry for people coming to live in the U.S. from other countries

elm /ɛlm/ *noun* **1** [C, U] (also **'elm tree**) a tall tree with broad leaves: *a line of stately elms* ♦ *The avenues were planted with elm.* **2** [U] the hard wood of the elm tree

El Ni·ño /ɛl ˈninyoʊ/ *noun* [U] a set of changes in the weather system near the coast of northern Peru and Ecuador that happens every few years, causing the surface of the Pacific Ocean there to become warmer and having severe effects on the weather in many parts of the world ➔ compare LA NIÑA

el·o·cu·tion /ˌɛləˈkyuʃn/ *noun* [U] the ability to speak clearly and correctly, especially in public, and pronouncing words in a way that is considered to be socially acceptable

e·lon·gate /ɪˈlɔŋɡeɪt/ *verb* [I, T] ~ (sth) to become longer; to make something longer **SYN** LENGTHEN ▶ **e·lon·ga·tion** /ˌilɔŋˈɡeɪʃn/ *noun* [U]: *the elongation of vowel sounds*

e·lon·gat·ed /ɪˈlɔŋɡeɪtəd/ *adj.* long and thin, often in a way that is not normal: *The women in Modigliani's portraits have strangely elongated faces.*

e·lope /ɪˈloʊp/ *verb* [I] ~ (with sb) to run away with someone in order to marry them secretly ▶ **e·lope·ment** *noun* [C, U]

el·o·quent /ˈɛləkwənt/ *adj.* **1** able to use language and express your opinions well, especially when you are speaking in public: *an eloquent speech/speaker* **2** (of a look or movement) able to express a feeling: *His eyes were eloquent.* ▶ **el·o·quence** /-kwəns/ *noun* [U]: *a speech of passionate eloquence* ♦ *the eloquence of his smile* **el·o·quent·ly** *His face expressed his grief more eloquently than any words.*

else 🔑 /ɛls/ *adv.*
(used in questions or after nothing, nobody, something, anything, etc.) **1** in addition to something already mentioned: *What else did he say?* ♦ *I don't want anything else, thanks.* ♦ *I'm taking a few clothes and some books, not much else.* **2** different: *Ask somebody else to help you.* ♦ *Don't you have anything else to wear?* ♦ *Why didn't you come? Everybody else was there.* ♦ *Yes I did give it to her. What else could I do?* **IDM or else 1** if not **SYN** OTHERWISE: *Hurry up or else you'll be late.* ♦ *They can't be coming or else they'd have called.* **2** used to introduce the second of two possibilities: *He either forgot or else decided not to come.* **3** (informal) used to threaten or warn someone: *Just shut up, or else!*

else·where 🔑 /ˈɛlswɛr/ *adv.*
in, at, or to another place: *The answer to the problem must be sought elsewhere.* ♦ *Our favorite restaurant was closed, so we had to go elsewhere.* ♦ *Elsewhere, the weather today has been fairly sunny.* ♦ *Prices are higher here than elsewhere.*

e·lu·ci·date /ɪˈlusəˌdeɪt/ *verb* [T, I] (formal) to make something clearer by explaining it more fully **SYN** EXPLAIN: ~ (sth) *He elucidated a point of grammar.* ♦ *Let me elucidate.* ♦ ~ what, how, etc. … *I will try to elucidate what I think the problems are.* ▶ **e·lu·ci·da·tion** /ɪˌlusəˈdeɪʃn/ *noun* [U, C]: *Their objectives and methods require further elucidation.*

e·lude /ɪˈlud/ *verb* **1** ~ sb/sth to manage to avoid or escape from someone or something, especially in a skillful way: *The two men managed to elude the police for six weeks.* **2** ~ sb if something **eludes** you, you are not able to achieve it, or not able to remember or understand it: *He was extremely tired but sleep eluded him.* ♦ *They're a popular band but worldwide success has eluded them so far.* ♦ *Finally he remembered the tiny detail that had eluded him the night before.*

e·lu·sive /ɪˈlusɪv/ *adj.* difficult to find, define, or achieve: *Eric, as elusive as ever, was nowhere to be found.* ♦ *the elusive concept of "literature"* ♦ *A solution to the problem of toxic waste is proving elusive.* ▶ **e·lu·sive·ly** *adv.* **e·lu·sive·ness** *noun* [U]

elves pl. of ELF

E·ly·sian /ɪˈlɪʒən; ɪˈli-/ *adj.* (literary) relating to heaven or to a place of perfect happiness **IDM the Elysian Fields** (in ancient Greek stories) a wonderful place where some people were taken by the gods after death

em- /ɪm; ɛm/ ➔ EN-

'em /əm/ *pron.* (informal) = THEM: *Don't let 'em get away.*

e·ma·ci·at·ed /ɪˈmeɪʃiˌeɪtəd/ *adj.* thin and weak, usually because of illness or lack of food ▶ **e·ma·ci·a·tion** /ɪˌmeɪʃiˈeɪʃn/ *noun* [U]: *She was very thin, almost to the point of emaciation.*

ʌ cup   ə about   eɪ say   aɪ five   ɔɪ boy   aʊ now   oʊ go   ər bird

e-mail 🔑 (also **e·mail**) /'imeɪl/ noun, verb

- **noun 1** (also formal **elec·tronic 'mail**) [U] a way of sending messages and data to other people by means of computers connected together in a network: *to send a message by e-mail* **2** [C, U] a message sent by e-mail
- **verb** [T, I] to send a message to someone by e-mail: ~ **(sb)** *Patrick e-mailed me yesterday.* ♦ ~ **sth (to sb)** *I'll e-mail the documents to her.* ♦ ~ **sb sth** *I'll e-mail her the documents.*

em·a·nate /'ɛmə,neɪt/ verb ~ **sth** (formal) to produce or show something: *He emanates power and confidence.* ▶ **em·a·na·tion** /,ɛmə'neɪʃn/ noun [C, U]
PHR V **'emanate from sth** to come from something or somewhere **SYN** ISSUE FROM: *The sound of loud music emanated from the building.* ♦ *The proposal originally emanated from the U.N.*

e·man·ci·pate /ɪ'mænsə,peɪt/ verb [often passive] ~ **sb (from sth)** to free someone, especially from legal, political, or social restrictions **SYN** SET FREE: *Slaves were not emancipated until 1863 in the United States.* ▶ **e·man·ci·pat·ed** adj.: *Are women now fully emancipated (= with the same rights and opportunities as men)?* ♦ *an emancipated young woman (= one with modern ideas about women's place in society)* **e·man·ci·pa·tion** /ɪ,mænsə'peɪʃn/ noun [U]: *the emancipation of slaves*

e·mas·cu·late /i'mæskyə,leɪt/ verb [often passive] (formal) **1** ~ **sb/sth** to make someone or something less powerful or less effective **2** ~ **sb** to make a man feel that he has lost his male role or qualities ▶ **e·mas·cu·la·tion** /i,mæskyə-'leɪʃn/ noun [U]

em·balm /ɪm'bɑm/ verb ~ **sth** to prevent a dead body from decaying by treating it with special substances to preserve it ▶ **em·balm·er** noun

em·bank·ment /ɪm'bæŋkmənt/ noun **1** a wall of stone or earth made to keep water back or to carry a road or railroad over low ground **2** a slope made of earth or stone that rises up from either side of a road or railroad

em·bar·go /ɪm'bɑrgoʊ/ noun, verb
- **noun** (pl. **em·bar·goes**) an official order that bans trade with another country **SYN** BOYCOTT: *an arms embargo* ♦ ~ **(on sth)** *an embargo on arms sales to certain countries* ♦ *a trade embargo against certain countries* ♦ *to* **impose/enforce/lift an embargo** ⊃ collocations at INTERNATIONAL
- **verb** (em·bar·goes, em·bar·go·ing, em·bar·goed, em·bar·goed) ~ **sth** to place an embargo on something **SYN** BOYCOTT: *There have been calls to embargo all arms shipments to the region.*

em·bark /ɪm'bɑrk/ verb [I, T] to get onto a ship; to put something onto a ship: *We stood on the pier and watched as they embarked.* ♦ ~ **sb/sth** *They embarked the troops by night.* **ANT** DISEMBARK ▶ **em·bar·ka·tion** /,ɛmbɑr'keɪʃn/ noun [U, C]: *Embarkation will be at 4:00 p.m.*
PHR V **em'bark on/upon sth** to start to do something new or difficult: *She is about to embark on a diplomatic career.*

em·bar·rass 🔑 /ɪm'bærəs/ verb
1 to make someone feel shy, awkward, or ashamed, especially in a social situation: ~ **sb** *Her questions about my private life embarrassed me.* ♦ *I didn't want to embarrass him by kissing him in front of his friends.* ♦ **it embarrasses sb to do sth** *It embarrassed her to talk about her weight problem.* **2** to cause problems or difficulties for someone: *The speech was deliberately designed to embarrass the mayor.*

em·bar·rassed 🔑 /ɪm'bærəst/ adj.
(of a person or their behavior) shy, awkward, or ashamed, especially in a social situation: *I've never felt so embarrassed in my life!* ♦ *Her remark was followed by an embarrassed silence.* ♦ ~ **about sth** *She's embarrassed about her height.* ♦ ~ **at sth** *He felt embarrassed at being the center of attention.* ♦ ~ **to do sth** *Some women are too embarrassed to consult their doctor about the problem.* ⊃ note at ASHAMED

em·bar·rass·ing 🔑 /ɪm'bærəsɪŋ/ adj.
1 making you feel shy, awkward, or ashamed: *an embarrassing mistake/question/situation* ♦ *It can be embarrassing for children to tell complete strangers about such incidents.* ♦ *It was so embarrassing having to sing in public.* **2** causing someone to look stupid, dishonest, etc.: *The report is likely to prove highly embarrassing to the government.* ▶ **em·bar·rass·ing·ly** adv.: *The play was embarrassingly bad.*

em·bar·rass·ment 🔑 /ɪm'bærəsmənt/ noun
1 [U] shy, awkward, or guilty feelings; a feeling of being embarrassed: *I nearly died of embarrassment when he said that.* ♦ *I'm glad you offered—it saved me the embarrassment of having to ask.* ♦ *Much to her embarrassment, she realized that everybody had been listening to her singing.* **2** [C] ~ **(to/for sb)** a situation that causes problems for someone: *Her resignation will be a severe embarrassment to the party.* **3** [C] ~ **(to sb)** a person who causes problems for another person or other people and makes them feel embarrassed
IDM **an embarrassment of riches** so many good things that it is difficult to choose just one

em·bas·sy /'ɛmbəsi/ noun (pl. **em·bas·sies**) **1** a group of officials led by an AMBASSADOR who represent their government in a foreign country: *embassy officials* ♦ *to inform the embassy of the situation* **2** the building in which an embassy works: *a demonstration outside the Russian Embassy* ⊃ compare CONSULATE

em·bat·tled /ɪmˈbætld/ adj. **1** surrounded by problems and difficulties: *the embattled party leader* **2** (of an army, a city, etc.) involved in war; surrounded by the enemy

em·bed (also **im·bed**) /ɪmˈbɛd/ verb (-dd-) [usually passive] **1** ~ sth (in sth) to fix something firmly into a substance or solid object: *an operation to remove glass that was embedded in his leg* ◆ *The bullet embedded itself in the wall.* ◆ (figurative) *These attitudes are deeply embedded in our society* (= felt very strongly and difficult to change). **2** ~ sb to send a journalist, photographer, etc. to an area where there is fighting, so that he or she can travel with the army and report what is happening: *embedded reporters in the war zone* **3** ~ sth (linguistics) to place a sentence inside another sentence. In the sentence "I'm aware that she knows", *she knows* is an embedded sentence.

em·bel·lish /ɪmˈbɛlɪʃ/ verb (formal) **1** ~ sth to make something more beautiful by adding decorations to it **SYN** DECORATE **2** ~ sth to make a story more interesting by adding details that are not always true **SYN** EMBROIDER ▶ **em·bel·lish·ment** noun [U, C]: *a 16th century church with 18th century embellishments*

em·ber /ˈɛmbər/ noun [usually pl.] a piece of wood or coal that is not burning but is still red and hot after a fire has died

em·bez·zle /ɪmˈbɛzl/ verb [T, I] ~ (sth) to steal money that you are responsible for or that belongs to your employer: *He was found guilty of embezzling $150,000 of public funds.* ▶ **em·bez·zle·ment** noun [U]: *She was found guilty of embezzlement.* **em·bez·zler** /ɪmˈbɛzlər/ noun

em·bit·ter /ɪmˈbɪtər/ verb ~ sb to make someone feel angry or disappointed about something over a long period of time ▶ **em·bit·tered** adj.: *a sick and embittered old man* ◆ *an embittered laugh*

em·bla·zon /ɪmˈbleɪzn/ (also **bla·zon**) verb [usually passive] to decorate something with a design, a symbol, or words so that people will notice it easily: ~ A with B *baseball caps emblazoned with the team's logo* ◆ ~ B on, across, etc. A *The team's logo was emblazoned on the baseball caps.*

em·blem /ˈɛmbləm/ noun ~ (of sth) **1** a design or picture that represents a country or an organization: *America's national emblem, the bald eagle* ◆ *the club emblem* **2** something that represents a perfect example or a principle: *The dove is an emblem of peace.*

em·blem·at·ic /ˌɛmbləˈmætɪk/ adj. ~ (of sth) (formal) **1** that represents or is a symbol of something **SYN** REPRESENTATIVE **2** that is considered typical of a situation, an area of work, etc. **SYN** TYPICAL: *The violence is emblematic of what is happening in our inner cities.*

em·bod·i·ment /ɪmˈbɑdimənt/ noun [usually sing.] ~ of sth (formal) a person or thing that represents or is a typical example of an idea or a quality **SYN** EPITOME: *He is the embodiment of the young successful businessman.*

em·body /ɪmˈbɑdi/ verb (em·bod·ies, em·bod·y·ing, em·bod·ied, em·bod·ied) **1** to express or represent an idea or a quality **SYN** REPRESENT: ~ sth *a politician who embodied the hopes of black youth* ◆ **be embodied in sth** *the principles embodied in the Declaration of Human Rights* **2** ~ sth (formal) to include or contain something: *This model embodies many new features.*

em·bold·en /ɪmˈbouldən/ verb **1** [usually passive] (formal) to make someone feel braver or more confident: ~ sb *Emboldened by the wine, he went over to introduce himself to her.* ◆ ~ sb to do sth *With such a majority, the administration was emboldened to introduce radical new policies.* **2** ~ sth (technical) to make a piece of text appear in BOLD print

em·bo·lism /ˈɛmbəˌlɪzəm/ noun (medical) a condition in which a BLOOD CLOT or air bubble blocks an ARTERY in the body

em·bo·lus /ˈɛmbələs/ noun (pl. **em·bo·li** /-ˌlaɪ; -li/) (medical) a BLOOD CLOT, air bubble, or small object that causes an embolism

em·boss /ɪmˈbɔs; -ˈbɑs/ verb [usually passive] to put a raised design or piece of writing on paper, leather, etc.: ~ A with B

stationery embossed with the hotel's name ◆ ~ B on A *The hotel's name was embossed on the stationery.* ▶ **em·bossed** adj.: *embossed stationery*

em·bou·chure /ˈɑmbəˌʃʊr/ noun (music) **1** the shape of the mouth when playing a WIND INSTRUMENT **2** the MOUTH-PIECE of a FLUTE

em·brace /ɪmˈbreɪs/ verb **1** [I, T] (formal) to put your arms around someone as a sign of love or friendship **SYN** HUG: *They embraced and promised to keep in touch.* ◆ ~ sb *She embraced her son warmly.* **2** ~ sth (formal) to accept an idea, a proposal, a set of beliefs, etc., especially when it is done with enthusiasm: *to embrace democracy/feminism/Islam* **3** ~ sth (formal) to include something: *The talks embraced a wide range of issues.* ▶ **em·brace** noun [C, U]: *He held her in a warm embrace.* ◆ *There were tears and embraces as they said goodbye.* ◆ *the country's eager embrace of modern technology*

em·bra·sure /ɪmˈbreɪʒər/ noun (architecture) an opening in a wall for a door or window, wider on the inside than on the outside

em·broi·der /ɪmˈbrɔɪdər/ verb **1** [T, I] to decorate cloth with a pattern of STITCHES, usually using colored thread: ~ A on B *She embroidered flowers on the cushion covers.* ◆ ~ B with A *She embroidered the cushion cover with flowers.* ◆ ~ (sth) *an embroidered blouse* ◆ *She sat in the window, embroidering.* **2** [T] ~ sth to make a story more interesting by adding details that are not always true **SYN** EMBELLISH

em·broi·der·y /ɪmˈbrɔɪdəri/ noun **1** [U, C] patterns that are sewn onto cloth using threads of various colors; cloth that is decorated in this way: *a beautiful piece of embroidery* ◆ *Indian embroideries* ⊃ picture at HOBBY **2** [U] the skill or activity of decorating cloth in this way

em·broil /ɪmˈbrɔɪl/ verb [often passive] ~ sb/yourself (in sth) (formal) to involve someone/yourself in an argument or a difficult situation: *He became embroiled in a dispute with his neighbors.* ◆ *I was reluctant to embroil myself in his problems.*

em·bry·o /ˈɛmbriou/ noun (pl. **em·bry·os**) a young animal or plant in the very early stages of development before birth, or before coming out of its egg or seed, especially a human egg in the first eight weeks after FERTILIZATION: *human embryos* ◆ (figurative) *the embryo of an idea*
IDM in embryo existing but not yet fully developed: *The idea already existed in embryo in his earlier novels.*

em·bry·ol·o·gy /ˌɛmbriˈɑlədʒi/ noun [U] the scientific study of the development of embryos ▶ **em·bry·o·log·i·cal** /ˌɛmbriəˈlɑdʒɪkl/ adj. **em·bry·ol·o·gist** /ˌɛmbriˈɑlədʒɪst/ noun

em·bry·on·ic /ˌɛmbriˈɑnɪk/ adj. [usually before noun] **1** (formal) in an early stage of development: *The plan, as yet, only exists in embryonic form.* **2** (technical) of an embryo: *embryonic cells*

em·cee /ˌɛmˈsi/ noun (informal) a person who introduces guests or entertainers at a formal dinner, party, etc. or on television **SYN** MASTER OF CEREMONIES ▶ **em·cee** verb [I, T] ~ (sth)

e·mend /iˈmɛnd/ verb ~ sth (formal) to remove the mistakes in a piece of writing, especially before it is printed **SYN** CORRECT

e·men·da·tion /ˌimɛnˈdeɪʃn/ noun [C, U] (formal) a letter or word that has been changed or corrected in a text; the act of making changes to a text

em·er·ald /ˈɛmərəld/ noun **1** [C, U] a bright green PRECIOUS STONE: *an emerald ring* **2** (also ˌemerald ˈgreen) [U] a bright green color ▶ **em·er·ald** (also ˌemerald ˈgreen) adj.

e·merg /iˈmərdʒ/ noun (CanE, informal) = EMERGENCY ROOM

e·merge 🔑 **AWL** /iˈmərdʒ/ verb
1 [I] to come out of a dark or hidden place: ~ (from sth) *The swimmer emerged from the lake.* ◆ *She finally emerged from her room at noon.* ◆ ~ (into sth) *We emerged into bright sunlight.* **2** [I, T] (of facts, ideas, etc.) to become known **SYN** TRANSPIRE: *No new evidence emerged during the investigation.* ◆ **it emerges that...** *It emerged that the company was*

| t tea | ʧ butter | d did | k cat | g got | tʃ chin | dʒ June | f fall |

going to be sold. **3** [I] to start to exist; to appear or become known: *After the election, protest groups began to emerge.* ◆ **~ as sth** *He emerged as a key figure in the campaign* **4** [I] **~ (from sth)** to survive a difficult situation or experience: *She emerged from the scandal with her reputation intact.*
▶ **e·mer·gence** **AWL** /ɪ'mərdʒəns/ *noun* [U]: *the emergence of new technologies*

e·mer·gen·cy 🔑 /ɪ'mərdʒənsi/ *noun* (*pl.* **e·mer·gen·cies**) [C, U]
a sudden serious and dangerous event or situation that needs immediate action to deal with it: *The government has declared a* **state of emergency** *following the earthquake.* ◆ *This door should only be used* **in an emergency**. ◆ *the emergency exit* (= to be used in an emergency) ◆ *The government had to take emergency action.* ◆ *The pilot made an emergency landing in a field.* ◆ *I always have some extra cash with me* **for emergencies**. ◆ *The government has been granted emergency powers* (= to deal with an emergency).

e'mergency ˌbrake *noun* **1** (also **'parking ˌbrake**, **hand·ˌbrake**) a BRAKE in a vehicle that is is used to stop the vehicle moving, especially when it is parked: *to put the emergency brake on* ◆ *to take the emergency brake off* ◆ *Is the emergency brake on?* ⊃ picture at CAR ⊃ collocations at DRIVING **2** a BRAKE on a train that can be pulled in an emergency

e'mergency ˌroom (*CanE, informal* **e·merg**) *noun* (*abbr.* ER) the part of a hospital where people who need urgent treatment are taken

e·mer·gent **AWL** /ɪ'mərdʒənt/ *adj.* [usually before noun] new and still developing: *emergent nations/states*

e·merg·ing *adj.* [only before noun] starting to exist, grow, or become known: *the emerging markets of South Asia*

e·mer·i·tus /ɪ'mɛrətəs/ *adj.* often **Emeritus** used with a title to show that a person, usually a college teacher, keeps the title as an honor, although he or she has stopped working: *the Emeritus Professor of Biology* **HELP** The form **Emerita** /ɪ'mɛrətə/ is used for women: *Professor Emerita Mary Judd*

em·er·y /'ɛmari; 'ɛmri/ *noun* [U] a hard mineral used especially in powder form for polishing things and making them smooth

'emery ˌboard *noun* a small strip of wood or thick paper covered in emery, used for shaping your nails

e·met·ic /ɪ'mɛtɪk/ *noun* (*medical*) a substance that makes you VOMIT (= bring up food from the stomach) ▶ **e·met·ic** *adj.*

em·i·grant /'ɛməgrənt/ *noun* a person who leaves their country to live in another: *emigrant workers* ◆ *emigrants to Canada* ⊃ compare IMMIGRANT

em·i·grate /'ɛmə,greɪt/ *verb* [I] **~ (from…) (to…)** to leave your own country to go and live permanently in another country ⊃ compare IMMIGRATE ▶ **em·i·gra·tion** /ˌɛmə-'greɪʃn/ *noun* [U, C]: *the mass emigration of Jews from Eastern Europe* ⊃ compare IMMIGRATION

é·mi·gré /'ɛmɪˌgreɪ/ *noun* (from *French*) a person who has left their own country, usually for political reasons SYN EXILE

em·i·nence /'ɛmənəns/ *noun* **1** [U] (*formal*) the quality of being famous and respected, especially in a profession: *a man of political eminence* **2** [C] **His/Your Eminence** a title used in speaking to or about a CARDINAL (= a priest of the highest rank in the Roman Catholic Church): *Their Eminences will see you now.* **3** [C] (*old-fashioned* or *formal*) an area of high ground

em·i·nent /'ɛmənənt/ *adj.* [usually before noun] **1** (of people) famous and respected, especially in a particular profession: *an eminent architect* **2** (of good qualities) unusual; excellent: *a man of eminent good sense*

ˌeminent doˈmain *noun* [U] (*law*) the right to force someone to sell land or a building if it is needed by the government

em·i·nent·ly /'ɛmənəntli/ *adv.* (*formal*) (used to emphasize a positive quality) very; extremely: *She seems eminently suitable for the job.*

e·mir (also **a·mir**) /ə'mɪr; eɪ'mɪr/ *noun* the title given to some Muslim rulers: *the Emir of Kuwait*

e·mir·ate /'ɛmərət/ *noun* **1** an area of land that is ruled over by an emir: *the United Arab Emirates* **2** the position of an emir **3** the period of time that an emir rules

em·is·sar·y /'ɛmə,sɛri/ *noun* (*pl.* **em·is·sar·ies**) (*formal*) a person who is sent to deliver an official message, especially from one country to another, or to perform a special task SYN ENVOY

e·mis·sion /ɪ'mɪʃn/ *noun* **1** [U] (*formal*) the production or sending out of light, heat, gas, etc.: *the emission of carbon dioxide into the atmosphere* ◆ *emission controls* **2** [C] gas, etc. that is sent out into the air: *The government has pledged to clean up industrial emissions.* ⊃ collocations at ENVIRONMENT

e'missions ˌtrading *noun* = CARBON TRADING

e·mit /ɪ'mɪt/ *verb* (-tt-) **~ sth** (*formal*) to send out something such as light, heat, sound, gas, etc.: *The metal container began to emit a clicking sound.* ◆ *Sulfur gases were emitted by the volcano.*

Em·my /'ɛmi/ *noun* (*pl.* **Em·mys**) one of the awards given every year to the best actors and programs on television

e·mo /'imoʊ/ *noun* (*pl.* **e·mos**) **1** [U] a style of rock music that developed from PUNK, but has more complicated musical arrangements and deals with more emotional subjects **2** [U] a person who likes emo music and often follows emo fashion, wearing tight jeans and having long black hair. Emos are typically supposed to be emotional and sensitive and full of ANGST.

e·mol·lient /ɪ'malyənt/ *adj., noun*
● *adj.* (*formal*) **1** (*technical*) used for making your skin soft or less painful SYN : *an emollient cream* **2** making a person or situation calmer in the hope of keeping relations peaceful SYN : *an emollient reply*
● *noun* [C, U] (*technical*) a liquid or cream that is used to make the skin soft

e·mol·u·ment /ɪ'malyəmənt/ *noun* [usually pl.] (*formal*) money paid to someone for work they have done, especially to someone who earns a lot of money

e·mote /ɪ'moʊt/ *verb* [I] to show emotion in a very obvious way

e·mo·ti·con /ɪ'moʊtɪ,kan/ *noun* (*computing*) a short set of keyboard symbols that represents the expression on someone's face, used in e-mail, etc. to show the feelings of the person sending the message. For example :-) represents a smiling face (when you look at it sideways).

e·mo·tion 🔑 /ɪ'moʊʃn/ *noun* [C, U]
a strong feeling such as love, fear, or anger; the part of a person's character that consists of feelings: *He lost control of his emotions.* ◆ *They expressed mixed emotions at the news.* ◆ *Emotions are running high* (= people are feeling very excited, angry, etc.). ◆ *The decision was based on emotion rather than rational thought.* ◆ *She showed no emotion at the verdict.* ◆ *Mary was overcome with emotion.*

e·mo·tion·al 🔑 /ɪ'moʊʃənl/ *adj.*
1 [usually before noun] connected with people's feelings (= with the emotions): *emotional problems/needs* ◆ *emotional stress* ◆ *a child's emotional and intellectual development* ◆ *Mothers are often the ones who provide emotional support for the family.* **2** causing people to feel strong emotions SYN EMOTIVE: *emotional language* ◆ *abortion and other emotional issues* **3** (sometimes *disapproving*) showing strong emotions, sometimes in a way that other people think is unnecessary: *an emotional outburst/response/reaction* ◆ *They made an emotional appeal for help.* ◆ *He tends to get emotional on these occasions.* ▶ **e·mo·tion·al·ly** /-ʃənəli/ *adv.*: *emotionally disturbed children* ◆ *I try not to become emotionally involved.* ◆ *They have suffered physically and emotionally.* ◆ *an emotionally charged atmosphere*

eˌmotional inˈtelligence *noun* [U] the ability to understand your emotions and those of other people and to behave in an appropriate way in different situations

e·mo·tion·less /ɪˈmoʊʃənləs/ adj. not showing any emotion: an emotionless voice

e·mo·tive /ɪˈmoʊtɪv/ adj. causing people to feel strong emotions **SYN** EMOTIONAL: emotive language/words ◆ Capital punishment is a highly emotive issue.

em·pa·na·da /ˌɛmpəˈnɑdə/ noun a Spanish or Latin American PASTRY filled with meat, vegetables, etc. and baked or fried

em·pan·el /ɪmˈpænl/ = IMPANEL

em·pa·thize /ˈɛmpəˌθaɪz/ verb [I] ~ (with sb/sth) to understand another person's feelings and experiences, especially because you have been in a similar situation

em·pa·thy /ˈɛmpəθi/ noun [U] the ability to understand another person's feelings, experience, etc.: ~ (with sb/sth) the writer's imaginative empathy with his subject ◆ ~ (for sb/sth) empathy for other people's situations ◆ ~ (between A and B) The empathy between the two women was obvious. ▶ **em·pa·thet·ic** /ˌɛmpəˈθɛtɪk/ (also **em·path·ic** /ɛmˈpæθɪk/) adj.

em·per·or /ˈɛmpərər/ noun the ruler of an empire: the Roman emperors ◆ the Emperor Napoleon ⊃ see also EMPRESS **IDM** **the emperor has no clothes** used to describe a situation in which everyone suddenly realizes that they were mistaken in believing that someone or something was very good, important, etc.: Soon investors will realize that the emperor has no clothes, and there will be a big sell-off in stocks. **ORIGIN** From the story of The Emperor's New Clothes by Hans Christian Andersen, in which the emperor is tricked into thinking he is wearing beautiful new clothes and everyone pretends to admire them, until a little boy points out that he is naked.

em·pha·sis 🖉 **AWL** /ˈɛmfəsəs/ noun (pl. **em·pha·ses** /-siz/) [U, C]
1 special importance that is given to something **SYN** STRESS: ~ (on/upon sth) The emphasis is very much on learning the spoken language. ◆ to put/lay/place emphasis on something ◆ We provide all types of information, with an emphasis on legal advice. ◆ There has been a shift of emphasis from manufacturing to service industries. ◆ The course has a vocational emphasis. ◆ The examples we will look at have quite different emphases. **2** the extra force given to a word or phrase when spoken, especially in order to show that it is important; a way of writing a word (for example drawing a line underneath it) to show that it is important **SYN** STRESS: "I can assure you," she added with emphasis, "the figures are correct."

em·pha·size 🖉 **AWL** /ˈɛmfəˌsaɪz/ verb
1 to give special importance to something **SYN** STRESS: ~ sth His speech emphasized the importance of attracting industry to the town. ◆ ~ that... She emphasized that their plan would mean sacrifices and hard work. ◆ ~ how, what, etc.... He emphasized how little was known about the disease. ◆ it must/should be emphasized that... It should be emphasized that this is only one possible explanation. ◆ + speech "This must be our top priority," he emphasized. ⊃ language bank at EMPHASIS **2** ~ sth to make something more noticeable: She swept her hair back from her face to emphasize her high cheekbones. **3** ~ sth to give extra force to a word or phrase when you are speaking, especially to show that it is important ⊃ thesaurus box at STRESS

em·phat·ic **AWL** /ɪmˈfætɪk/ adj. **1** an **emphatic** statement, answer, etc. is given with force to show that it is important: an emphatic denial/rejection **2** (of a person) making it very clear what you mean by speaking with force: He was emphatic that he could not work with her. **3** an **emphatic** victory, win, or defeat is one in which one team or player wins by a large amount ▶ **em·phat·i·cally** **AWL** /-kli/ adv.: "Certainly not," he replied emphatically. ◆ She is emphatically opposed to the proposals. ◆ He has always emphatically denied the allegations. ◆ The proposal was emphatically defeated.

em·phy·se·ma /ˌɛmfəˈzimə; -ˈsimə/ noun [U] (medical) a condition that affects the lungs, making it difficult to breathe

em·pire 🖉 /ˈɛmpaɪər/ noun
1 a group of countries or states that are controlled by one ruler or government: the Roman empire **2** a group of commercial organizations controlled by one person or company: a business empire

empire-building noun [U] (usually disapproving) the process of obtaining extra land, authority, etc. in order to increase your own power or position

em·pir·i·cal **AWL** /ɪmˈpɪrɪkl/ adj. [usually before noun] based on experiments or experience rather than ideas or theories: empirical evidence/knowledge/research ◆ an empirical study **ANT** THEORETICAL ▶ **em·pir·i·cally** **AWL** /-kli/ adv.: Such claims need to be tested empirically.

em·pir·i·cism `AWL` /ɪmˈpɪrəˌsɪzəm/ noun [U] (philosophy) the use of experiments or experience as the basis for your ideas; the belief in these methods ▶ **em·pir·i·cist** /-sɪst/ adj.: an empiricist theory **em·pir·i·cist** noun: the English empiricist John Locke

em·place·ment /ɪmˈpleɪsmənt/ noun (technical) a position that has been specially prepared so that a large gun can be fired from it

em·ploy /ɪmˈplɔɪ/ verb, noun
- **verb 1** to give someone a job to do for payment: ~ **sb** How many people does the company employ? ◆ ~ **sb as sth** For the past three years he has been employed as a firefighter. ◆ ~ **sb to do sth** A number of people have been employed to deal with the backlog of work. ⊃ collocations at JOB ⊃ see also SELF-EMPLOYED, UNEMPLOYED **2** ~ **sth** (formal) to use something such as a skill, method, etc. for a particular purpose: He criticized the repressive methods employed by the country's government. ◆ The police had to employ force to enter the building.
  IDM be employed in doing sth if a person or their time is **employed in doing something**, the person spends time doing that thing: She was employed in making a list of all the jobs to be done.
- **noun** [U]
  IDM in sb's employ | in the employ of sb (formal) working for someone; employed by someone

em·ploy·a·ble /ɪmˈplɔɪəbl/ adj. having the skills and qualifications that will make someone want to employ you

em·ploy·ee /ɪmˈplɔɪiː; ɪmˌplɔɪˈiː; ˌemplɔɪˈiː/ noun a person who is paid to work for someone: The company has over 500 employees. ◆ government employees ◆ **employee rights/relations**

em·ploy·er /ɪmˈplɔɪər/ noun a person or company that pays people to work for them: They're very good employers (= they treat the people that work for them well). ◆ one of the largest employers in the area

em·ploy·ment /ɪmˈplɔɪmənt/ noun
1 [U, C] work, especially when it is done to earn money; the state of being employed: to be in **paid employment** ◆ full-time/part-time employment ◆ conditions/terms of employment ◆ Graduates are finding it more and more difficult to find employment. ◆ pensions from previous employments ⊃ collocations at JOB, UNEMPLOYMENT ⊃ thesaurus box at WORK **2** [U] the situation in which people have work: The government is aiming at **full employment**. ◆ Changes in farming methods have badly affected employment in the area. **ANT** UNEMPLOYMENT **3** [U] the act of employing someone: The law prevented the employment of children under ten in the cotton mills. **4** [U] ~ **(of sth)** (formal) the use of something: the employment of artillery in the capture of the town

em·ploy·ment ˌagency noun a business that helps people to find work and employers to find workers

em·ploy·ment inˌsurance noun [U] (abbr. EI) (CanE, business) a type of insurance system that is run by the Canadian Government, that pays money regularly to people who are out of work

em·po·ri·um /emˈpɔːriəm/ noun (pl. **em·por·i·ums** or **em·por·ia** /-iə/) **1** (old-fashioned) a large store **2** a store that sells a particular type of goods: an arts and crafts emporium

em·pow·er /ɪmˈpaʊər/ verb [often passive] **1** ~ **sb (to do sth)** (formal) to give someone the power or authority to do something **SYN** AUTHORIZE: The courts were empowered to impose the death sentence for certain crimes. **2** ~ **sb (to do sth)** to give someone more control over their own life or the situation they are in: The movement actively empowered women and gave them confidence in themselves. ▶ **em·pow·er·ment** noun [U]: the empowerment of the individual

em·press /ˈemprəs/ noun **1** a woman who is the ruler of an empire: the Empress of Japan **2** the wife of an EMPEROR

emp·ties /ˈemptiz/ noun [pl.] empty bottles or glasses

emp·ti·ness /ˈemptinəs/ noun [U, sing.] **1** a feeling of being sad because nothing seems to have any value: There was an aching emptiness in her heart. **2** the fact that there is nothing or no one in a place: The silence and emptiness of the house did not scare her. **3** (formal) a place that is empty: He stared out at the vast emptiness that was the ocean.

emp·ty /ˈempti/ adj., verb
- **adj.** (**emp·ti·er**, **emp·ti·est**) **1** with no people or things inside: an empty box/glass ◆ empty hands (= not holding anything) ◆ an empty plate (= with no food on it) ◆ The theater was **half empty**. ◆ an empty house/room/bus ◆ Is this an empty chair (= not one that another person will be using)? ◆ The house had been **standing empty** (= without people living in it) for some time. ◆ It's not good to drink alcohol **on an empty stomach** (= without having eaten something). ◆ ~ **of sth** (formal) The room was empty of furniture. **2** [usually before noun] (of something that someone says or does) with no meaning; not meaning what is said **SYN** HOLLOW: empty words ◆ an empty promise ◆ an empty gesture aimed at pleasing the crowds **3** (of a person, or a person's life) unhappy because life does not seem to have a purpose, usually after something sad has happened: Three months after his death, she still felt empty. ◆ My life seems empty without you. **4** ~ **of sth** without a quality that you would expect to be there: words that were empty of meaning ▶ **emp·ti·ly** /-təli/ adv.: She stood staring emptily into space.
- **verb** (**emp·ties**, **emp·ty·ing**, **emp·tied**, **emp·tied**) **1** [T] to remove everything that is in a container, etc.: ~ **sth** He emptied the ashtrays, washed the glasses, and went to bed. ◆ He emptied his glass and asked for a refill. ◆ ~ **sth out** I emptied out my pockets but could not find my keys. ◆ ~ **sth out of sth** She emptied the water out of the vase. ◆ ~ **sth of sth** The room had been emptied of all furniture. ◆ (figurative) She emptied her mind of all thoughts of home. **2** [I] to become empty: The streets soon emptied when the rain started. ◆ ~ **out** The tank empties out in five minutes. **3** [T] ~ **sth (out)** to take out the contents of something and put them somewhere else: She emptied the contents of her bag onto the table. ◆ Many factories emptied their waste into the river. **4** [T] ~ **sth** to make sure that everyone leaves a room, building, etc. **SYN** EVACUATE: Police had instructions to empty the building because of a bomb threat. **5** [I] to flow or move out from one place to another: ~ **into/onto sth** The Rhine empties into the North Sea. ◆ ~ **out into/onto sth** Fans emptied out onto the streets after the concert.

ˌempty-ˈhanded adj. [not usually before noun] without getting what you wanted; without taking something to someone: The robbers fled empty-handed. ◆ She visited every Sunday and never arrived empty-handed.

ˌempty-ˈheaded adj. (disapproving) unable to think or behave in an intelligent way

ˌempty ˈnest noun [sing.] the situation that parents are in when their children have grown up and left home

emp·ty ˈnest·er /ˌempti ˈnestər/ noun [usually pl.] a parent whose children have grown up and left home

EMS /ˌi em ˈes/ noun **1** [U] the abbreviation for "enhanced message service" (a system for sending pictures, music, and long written messages from one cell phone to another) **2** [C] a message sent by EMS **3** [U] the abbreviation for "emergency medical services" (an organization that provides emergency medical treatment to people who are not in a hospital)

EMT /ˌi em ˈti/ noun the abbreviation for "emergency medical technician" (a person who is trained to provide emergency medical treatment to people who are not in a hospital): The EMTs arrived less than ten minutes after the highway accident.

e·mu /ˈiːmjuː/ noun a large Australian bird that can run fast but cannot fly

em·u·late /ˈemyəˌleɪt/ verb **1** ~ **sb/sth** (formal) to try to do something as well as someone else because you admire them: She hopes to emulate her sister's athletic achievements. **2** ~ **sth** (computing) (of a computer program, etc.) to work in the same way as another computer, etc. and perform the same tasks ▶ **em·u·la·tion** /ˌɛmyəˈleɪʃn/ noun [U, C]

em·u·la·tor /ˈɛmyəˌleɪtər/ noun (computing) a device or piece of software that makes it possible to use programs, etc. on one type of computer even though they have been designed for a different type

e·mul·si·fi·er /ɪˈmʌlsəˌfaɪər/ noun (chemistry) a substance that is added to food to make the different substances in them combine to form a smooth mixture

e·mul·si·fy /ɪˈmʌlsəˌfaɪ/ verb (e·mul·si·fies, e·mul·si·fy·ing, e·mul·si·fied, e·mul·si·fied) [I, T] ~ (sth) (technical) if two liquids of different thicknesses **emulsify** or **are emulsified**, they combine to form a smooth mixture

e·mul·sion /ɪˈmʌlʃn/ noun [C, U] **1** any mixture of liquids that do not normally mix together, such as oil and water **2** (technical) a substance on the surface of PHOTOGRAPHIC film that makes it sensitive to light

en- /ɪn; ɛn/ (also **em-** before b, m, or p) prefix (in verbs) **1** to put into the thing or condition mentioned: encase ♦ endanger **2** to cause to be: enlarge ♦ embolden

-en /ən/ suffix **1** (in verbs) to make or become: blacken **2** (in adjectives) made of; looking like: wooden ♦ golden

en·a·ble 🔑 ⟨AWL⟩ /ɪˈneɪbl/ verb

1 ~ sb to do sth to make it possible for someone to do something SYN ALLOW: The software enables you to create your own DVDs. ♦ a new program to enable older people to get a college degree **2** to make it possible for something to happen or exist by creating the necessary conditions SYN ALLOW: ~ sth to do sth Insulin enables the body to use and store sugar. ♦ ~ sth a new subway line to enable easier access to the stadium ⊃ language bank at PROCESS¹

-en·abled /ɪˈneɪbld/ adj. (in compound adjectives) (computing) that can be used with a particular system or technology, especially the Internet: web-enabled phones

en·abling ˌact noun a law that allows a person or an organization to do something, especially to make rules

en·act /ɪˈnækt/ verb **1** [often passive] ~ sth (law) to pass a law: legislation enacted by Congress **2** [often passive] ~ sth (formal) to perform a play or act a part in a play: scenes from history enacted by local residents **3 be enacted** (formal) to take place SYN BE PLAYED OUT: They seemed unaware of the drama being enacted a few feet away from them.

en·act·ment /ɪˈnæktmənt/ noun [U, C] (law) the process of a law becoming official; a law that has been made official

e·nam·el /ɪˈnæml/ noun **1** [U, C] a substance that is melted onto metal, pots, etc. and forms a hard shiny surface to protect or decorate them; an object made from enamel: a chipped enamel bowl ♦ a handle inlaid with enamel ♦ an exhibition of enamels and jewelry **2** [U] the hard white outer layer of a tooth **3** (also eˌnamel ˈpaint) [U, C] a type of paint that dries to leave a hard shiny surface

e·nam·eled /ɪˈnæmld/ adj. [usually before noun] covered or decorated with enamel

en·am·ored /ɪˈnæmərd/ adj. **1** (formal) (often in negative sentences) liking something a lot: ~ of sth He was less than enamored of the music. ♦ ~ with sth (humorous) I'm not exactly enamored with the idea of spending a whole day with them. **2** ~ of/with sb (literary) in love with someone

enc. = ENCL.

en·camp /ɪnˈkæmp/ verb [I, T] (formal) if a group of people **encamp** or **are encamped** somewhere, they set up a camp or have set up a camp there

en·camp·ment /ɪnˈkæmpmənt/ noun a group of tents, HUTS, etc. where people live together, usually for only a short period of time: a military encampment

en·cap·su·late /ɪnˈkæpsəˌleɪt/ verb ~ sth (in sth) (formal) to express the most important parts of something in a few words, a small space, or a single object SYN SUM UP: The poem encapsulates many of the central themes of her writing. ▶ **en·cap·su·la·tion** /ɪnˌkæpsəˈleɪʃn/ noun [U, C]

en·case /ɪnˈkeɪs/ verb [often passive] ~ sth (in sth) (formal) to surround or cover something completely, especially to protect it: The reactor is encased in concrete and steel.

-ence ⊃ -ANCE

en·ceph·a·li·tis /ɪnˌsɛfəˈlaɪtəs/ noun [U] (medical) a condition in which the brain becomes swollen, caused by an infection or ALLERGIC reaction

en·ceph·a·lop·a·thy /ɪnˌsɛfəˈlɑpəθi/ noun [U] (medical) a disease in which the functioning of the brain is affected by infection, BLOOD POISONING, etc. ⊃ see also BSE

en·chant /ɪnˈtʃænt/ verb **1** ~ sb (formal) to attract someone strongly and make them feel very interested, excited, etc. SYN DELIGHT **2** ~ sb/sth to place someone or something under a magic SPELL (= words that have special powers) SYN BEWITCH

en·chant·ed /ɪnˈtʃæntəd/ adj. **1** placed under a magic SPELL (= words that have special powers): an enchanted forest/kingdom **2** (formal) filled with great pleasure SYN DELIGHTED: He was enchanted to see her again after so long.

en·chant·er /ɪnˈtʃæntər/ noun (in stories) a man who has magic powers that he uses to control people

en·chant·ing /ɪnˈtʃæntɪŋ/ adj. attractive and pleasing SYN DELIGHTFUL: an enchanting view ▶ **en·chant·ing·ly** adv.

en·chant·ment /ɪnˈtʃæntmənt/ noun **1** [U] (formal) a feeling of great pleasure **2** [U] the state of being under a magic SPELL (= words that have special powers): It was a place of deep mystery and enchantment. **3** [C] (literary) = SPELL: They had been turned to stone by an enchantment.

en·chant·ress /ɪnˈtʃæntrəs/ noun **1** (in stories) a woman who has magic powers that she uses to control people **2** (literary) a woman that men find very attractive and interesting

en·chi·la·da /ˌɛntʃəˈlɑdə/ noun (from Spanish) a Mexican dish consisting of a TORTILLA filled with meat and covered with a spicy sauce

IDM **the whole enchilada** (informal) the whole thing; everything ⊃ more at BIG

en·cir·cle /ɪnˈsərkl/ verb ~ sb/sth (formal) to surround someone or something completely in a circle: Jack's arms encircled her waist. ♦ The island is encircled by a coral reef. ▶ **en·cir·cle·ment** noun [U]

encl. (also **enc.**) abbr. (business) (in writing) enclosed or enclosure (used on business letters to show that another document is being sent in the same envelope)

en·clave /ˈɛnkleɪv; ˈɑn-/ noun a small area of a city or country where the people have a different religion, culture, or NATIONALITY from those who live in the city or country that surrounds it

en·close /ɪnˈkloʊz/ verb **1** [usually passive] ~ sth (in/with sth) to build a wall, fence, etc. around something: The yard had been enclosed with iron railings. ♦ (figurative) All translated words should be enclosed in brackets. **2** ~ sth (especially of a wall, fence, etc.) to surround something: Low hedges enclosed the flower beds. ♦ She felt his arms enclose her. **3** ~ sth (with sth) to put something in the same envelope, package, etc. as something else: Please return the completed form, enclosing a recent photograph.

en·closed /ɪnˈkloʊzd/ adj. **1** with walls, etc. all around: Do not use this substance in an enclosed space. **2** (abbr. **encl.**) sent with a letter, etc.: Please complete the enclosed application form. ♦ Please **find enclosed** a check for $100. **3** (of religious communities) having little contact with the outside world

en·clo·sure /ɪnˈkloʊʒər/ noun **1** [C] a piece of land that is surrounded by a fence or wall and is used for a particular purpose: a wildlife enclosure **2** [U, C] the act of placing a fence or wall around a piece of land: the enclosure of pastures **3** (abbr. **encl.**) [C] something that is placed in an envelope with a letter

ʌ **cup**   ə **about**   eɪ **say**   aɪ **five**   ɔɪ **boy**   aʊ **now**   oʊ **go**   ər **bird**

en·code /ɪnˈkoʊd/ verb **1** ~ sth to change ordinary language into letters, symbols, etc. in order to send secret messages **2** ~ sth (computing) to change information into a form that can be processed by a computer **3** ~ sth (linguistics) to express the meaning of something in a foreign language ⊃ compare DECODE

en·co·mi·um /ɛnˈkoʊmiəm/ noun (pl. en·co·mi·ums or en·co·mi·a /-miə/) (formal) a speech or piece of writing that praises someone or something highly

en·com·pass /ɪnˈkʌmpəs/ verb (formal) **1** ~ sth to include a large number or range of things: The job encompasses a wide range of responsibilities. ◆ The group encompasses all ages. **2** ~ sth to surround or cover something completely: The fog soon encompassed the whole valley.

en·core /ˈɑŋkɔr; ˈɑn-/ noun, exclamation
• noun an extra short performance given at the end of a concert or other performance; a request for this made by an audience calling out: She played a Chopin waltz as an encore. ◆ The group got three encores.
• exclamation an audience calls out encore! at the end of a concert to ask the performer to play or sing another piece of music

en·coun·ter 🔑 **AWL** /ɪnˈkaʊntər/ verb, noun
• verb **1** ~ sth to experience something, especially something unpleasant or difficult, while you are trying to do something else **SYN** MEET WITH, RUN INTO: We encountered a number of difficulties in the first week. ◆ I had never encountered such resistance before. **2** ~ sb/sth (formal) to meet someone, or discover or experience something, especially someone or something new, unusual, or unexpected **SYN** COME ACROSS: She was the most remarkable woman he had ever encountered.
• noun **1** a meeting, especially one that is sudden, unexpected, or violent: ~ (with sb/sth) Three of them were killed in the subsequent encounter with the police. ◆ ~ (between A and B) The story describes the extraordinary encounter between a man and a dolphin. ◆ a chance encounter ◆ I've had a number of close encounters (= situations that could have been dangerous) with bad drivers. **2** a sports competition against a particular player or team: She has beaten her opponent in all of their previous encounters.

en·counter ˌgroup noun a group of people who meet regularly in order to help each other with emotional and PSYCHOLOGICAL problems

en·cour·age 🔑 /ɪnˈkɜrɪdʒ/ verb
1 to give someone support, courage, or hope: ~ sb in sth My parents have always encouraged me in my choice of career. ◆ ~ sb We were greatly encouraged by the positive response of the public. **2** ~ sb to do sth | ~ doing sth to persuade someone to do something by making it easier for them and making them believe it is a good thing to do: Banks actively encourage people to borrow money. **3** to make something more likely to happen or develop: ~ sth (in sb/sth) They claim that some computer games encourage violent behavior in young children. ◆ ~ sb to do sth Music and lighting are used to encourage shoppers to buy more. ◆ ~ doing sth Technology encourages multitasking. **ANT** DISCOURAGE ▶ en·cour·ag·ing adj. [not usually before noun]: This month's unemployment figures are not very encouraging. You could try being a little more encouraging. en·cour·ag·ing·ly adv.: to smile encouragingly ◆ The attendance was encouragingly high.

en·cour·age·ment 🔑 /ɪnˈkɜrɪdʒmənt/ noun
[U, C, usually sing.]
the act of encouraging someone to do something; something that encourages someone: a few words of encouragement ◆ He needs all the support and encouragement he can get. ◆ With a little encouragement from his parents he should do well. ◆ ~ (to sb) (to do sth) She was given every encouragement to try something new. ◆ Her words were a great encouragement to them. **ANT** DISCOURAGEMENT

en·croach /ɪnˈkroʊtʃ/ verb (formal) **1** [I] ~ (on/upon sth) (disapproving) to begin to affect or use up too much of someone's time, rights, personal life, etc.: I won't encroach on your time any longer. ◆ He never allows work to encroach upon his family life. **2** [I] ~ (on/upon sth) to slowly begin to cover more and more of an area: The growing town soon encroached on the surrounding countryside. ▶ en·croach·ment noun [U, C]: ~ (on/upon sth) the regime's many encroachments on human rights

en·crus·ta·tion /ˌɛnkrʌˈsteɪʃn/ noun = INCRUSTATION

en·crusted /ɪnˈkrʌstəd/ adj. ~ (with/in sth) covered with a thin hard layer of something; forming a thin hard layer on something: a crown encrusted with diamonds ◆ encrusted blood

en·crypt /ɪnˈkrɪpt/ verb ~ sth (computing) to put information into a special code, especially in order to prevent people from looking at it without authority ▶ en·cryp·tion /ɪnˈkrɪpʃn/ noun [U] **ANT** DECRYPT

en·cum·ber /ɪnˈkʌmbər/ verb [usually passive] (formal) **1** ~ sb/sth (with sth) to make it difficult for someone to do something or for something to happen: The police operation was encumbered by crowds of reporters. **2** ~ sb/sth (with sth) to be large and/or heavy and make it difficult for someone to move: The divers were encumbered by their equipment.

en·cum·brance /ɪnˈkʌmbrəns/ noun (formal) a person or thing that prevents someone from moving easily or from doing what they want **SYN** BURDEN: I felt I was an encumbrance to them.

-ency ⊃ -ANCY

en·cyc·li·cal /ɪnˈsɪklɪkl/ noun an official letter written by the Pope and sent to all Roman Catholic BISHOPS

en·cy·clo·pe·di·a /ɪnˌsaɪkləˈpidiə/ noun a book or set of books giving information about all areas of knowledge or about different areas of one particular subject, usually arranged in alphabetical order; a similar collection of information on a CD-ROM or on the Internet

en·cy·clo·pe·dic /ɪnˌsaɪkləˈpidɪk/ adj. **1** connected with encyclopedias or the type of information found in them: encyclopedic information ◆ an encyclopedic dictionary **2** having a lot of information about a wide variety of subjects; containing complete information about a particular subject: She has an encyclopedic knowledge of natural history.

end 🔑 /ɛnd/ noun, verb
• noun
> FINAL PART **1** the final part of a period of time, an event, an activity, or a story: at the end of the week ◆ We didn't leave until the very end. ◆ the end of the book ◆ We had to hear about the whole trip from beginning to end. ◆ It's the end of an era.
> FARTHEST PART **2** the part of an object or a place that is the farthest away from its center: Turn right at the end of the road. ◆ I went to the end of the line. ◆ Go to the end of the line! ◆ You have something on the end of your nose. ◆ Tie the ends of the string together. ◆ That's his wife sitting at the far end of the table. ◆ These two products are from opposite ends of the price range. ◆ We've traveled from one end of Mexico to the other. ◆ They live in the end house. ⊃ see also DEAD END, SPLIT END, TAIL END
> FINISH **3** a situation in which something does not exist anymore: the end of all his dreams ◆ The meeting came to an end (= finished). ◆ The war was finally at an end. ◆ The coup brought his corrupt regime to an end. ◆ There's no end in sight to the present crisis. ◆ They have called for an end to violence. ◆ That was by no means the end of the matter.
> AIM **4** an aim or a purpose: They are prepared to use violence in pursuit of their ends. ◆ He is exploiting the current situation for his own ends. ◆ With this end in view (= in order to achieve this) they employed 50 new staff members. ◆ We are willing to make any concessions necessary to this end (= in order to achieve this). ⊃ thesaurus box at TARGET
> PART OF ACTIVITY **5** [usually sing.] a part of an activity with which someone is concerned, especially in business: We need someone to handle the marketing end of the business. ◆ Are there any problems at your end? ◆ I have kept my end of the bargain.

> **OF TELEPHONE LINE/TRIP 6** [usually sing.] either of two places connected by a telephone call, a trip, etc.: *I answered the phone but there was no one at the other end.* ♦ *Jean is going to meet me at the other end.*

> **OF SPORTS FIELD 7** one of the two halves of a sports field: *The teams changed ends at half-time.*

> **DEATH 8** [usually sing.] a person's death. People say "end" to avoid saying "death": *She came to an untimely end* (= died young). ♦ *I was with him at the end* (= when he died). ♦ (*literary*) *He met his end* (= died) *at the Battle of Waterloo.* ⊃ see also LOOSE END, ODDS AND ENDS

IDM **at the end of the day** (*informal*) used to introduce the most important fact after everything has been considered: *At the end of the day, he'll still have to make his own decision.* **be at the end of sth** to have almost nothing left of something: *I'm at the end of my patience.* ♦ *They are at the end of their food supply.* **be at the end of your rope** to feel that you cannot deal with a difficult situation any more because you are too tired, worried, etc. **an end in itself** a thing that is itself important and not just a part of something more important **the end justifies the means** (*saying*) bad or unfair methods of doing something are acceptable if the result of that action is good or positive **(reach) the end of the line/road** (to reach) the point at which something can no longer continue in the same way: *A defeat in the second round marked the end of the line for last year's champion.* **end of story** (*informal*) used when you are stating that there is nothing more that can be said or done about something **end to end** in a line, with the ends touching: *They arranged the tables end to end.* **go to the ends of the earth** to do everything possible, even if it is difficult, in order to get or achieve something: *I'd go to the ends of the earth to see her again.* **in the end** after a long period of time or series of events: *He tried various jobs and in the end became an accountant.* **2** after everything has been considered: *You can try your best to impress the interviewers but in the end it's often just a question of luck.* **make ends meet** to earn just enough money to be able to buy the things you need: *Many families struggle to make ends meet.* **(to) no end** (*informal*) very much: *It upset me to no end to hear they'd split up.* **no end of sth** (*informal*) a lot of something: *We had no end of trouble getting them to agree.* **not the end of the world** (*informal*) not the worst thing that could happen to someone: *Failing one exam is not the end of the world.* **on end 1** in a vertical position: *It'll fit if you stand it on end.* **2** for the stated length of time, without stopping: *He would disappear for weeks on end.* **put an end to it all** to kill yourself ⊃ more at BEGINNING, BITTER, BURN *v.*, DEEP *adj.*, HAIR, HEAR, LIGHT *n.*, LOOSE END, MEANS, RECEIVE, SHARP *adj.*, SHORT *adj.*, WIT, WRONG *adj.*

● *verb* [I, T] to finish; to make something finish: *The road ends here.* ♦ *How does the story end?* ♦ *The speaker ended by suggesting some topics for discussion.* ♦ *~ with sth Her note ended with the words: "See you soon."* ♦ *~ sth They decided to end their relationship.* ♦ *~ sth with sth They ended the play with a song.* ♦ *+ speech "And that was that," she ended.*

IDM **a/the sth to end all sths** used to emphasize how large, important, exciting, etc. you think something is: *The movie has a car chase to end all car chases.* **end your days/life (in sth)** to spend the last part of your life in a particular state or place: *He ended his days in poverty.* **end it all | end your life** to kill yourself

PHR V **'end in sth** [no passive] **1** to have something as an ending: *The word I'm thinking of ends in "-ous."* **2** to have something as a result: *Their long struggle ended in failure.* ♦ *The debate ended in uproar.* **,end 'up** to find yourself in a place or situation that you did not intend or expect to be in: *~ doing sth I ended up doing all the work myself.* ♦ *+ adv./prep. If you go on like this, you'll end up in prison.* ♦ *+ adj. If he continues driving like that, he'll end up dead.*

en·dan·ger /ɪnˈdeɪndʒər/ *verb* *~ sb/sth* to put someone or something in a situation in which they could be harmed or damaged: *The health of our children is being endangered by exhaust fumes.* ♦ *That one mistake seriously endangered the*

future of the company. ♦ *The sea turtle is an endangered species* (= it may soon no longer exist).

en·dear /ɪnˈdɪr/ *verb*
PHR V **en'dear sb/yourself to sb** to make someone/yourself popular: *Their policies on taxation didn't endear them to voters.* ♦ *She was a talented teacher who endeared herself to all who worked with her.*

en·dear·ing /ɪnˈdɪrɪŋ/ *adj.* causing people to feel affection **SYN** LOVABLE: *an endearing habit* ▶ **en·dear·ing·ly** *adv.*

en·dear·ment /ɪnˈdɪrmənt/ *noun* [C, U] a word or an expression that is used to show affection: *They were whispering endearments to each other.* ♦ *"Darling" is a term of endearment.*

en·deav·or (*CanE usually* **en·deav·our**) /ɪnˈdɛvər/ *noun*, *verb*
● *noun* [U, C] (*formal*) an attempt to do something, especially something new or difficult: *Please make every endeavor to arrive on time.* ♦ *advances in the field of scientific endeavor* ♦ *The manager is expected to use his or her best endeavors to promote the artist's career.*
● *verb* *~ to do sth* (*formal*) to try very hard to do something **SYN** STRIVE: *I will endeavor to do my best for my country.*

en·dem·ic /ɛnˈdɛmɪk/ *adj.* regularly found in a particular place or among a particular group of people and difficult to get rid of: *~ (in...) Malaria is endemic in many hot countries.* ♦ *Corruption is endemic in the system.* ♦ *~ (among...) an attitude endemic among senior members of the profession* ♦ *~ (to...) species endemic to* (= only found in) *Madagascar* ♦ *the endemic problem of racism* ⊃ compare PANDEMIC

end·game /ˈɛndɡeɪm/ *noun* **1** the final stage of a game of CHESS **2** the final stage of a political process

end·ing /ˈɛndɪŋ/ *noun*
1 the last part of a story, movie, etc.: *His stories usually have a happy ending.* **ANT** OPENING **2** the act of finishing something; the last part of something: *the anniversary of the ending of the Pacific War* ♦ *It was the perfect ending to the perfect day.* **3** the last part of a word, that is added to a main part: *verb endings* ♦ *a masculine/feminine ending*

en·dive /ˈɛndaɪv; ˌɑnˈdiv/ *noun* [C, U] **1** (*also* ˌcurly ˈendive, frisée, chicory [U]) a plant with green curly leaves that are eaten raw as a vegetable **2** (*also* Bel·gian en·dive) a young CHICORY plant (= a pale green plant with bitter leaves), eaten as a cooked vegetable or in salads

end·less /ˈɛndləs/ *adj.* **1** very large in size or amount and seeming to have no end **SYN** LIMITLESS: *endless patience* ♦ *endless opportunities for making money* ♦ *The possibilities are endless.* ♦ *an endless list of things to do* ♦ *We don't have an endless supply of money, you know.* **2** continuing for a long time and seeming to have no end: *an endless round of parties and visits* ♦ *The journey seemed endless.* ♦ *I've had enough of their endless arguing.* **3** (*technical*) (of a LOOP, etc.) having the ends joined together so it forms one piece: *an endless loop of tape* ▶ **end·less·ly** *adv.*: *She talks endlessly about her problems.* ♦ *an endlessly repeated pattern*

end·note /ˈɛndnoʊt/ *noun* a note printed at the end of a book or section of a book

en·do·crine /ˈɛndəkrən/ *adj.* (*biology*) connected with GLANDS that put HORMONES and other products directly into the blood: *the endocrine system* ⊃ compare EXOCRINE

en·do·cri·nol·o·gy /ˌɛndəkrəˈnɑlədʒi/ *noun* [U] (*medical*) the part of medicine concerning the endocrine system and HORMONES ▶ **en·do·cri·nol·o·gist** /-dʒɪst/ *noun*

en·dog·a·my /ɛnˈdɑɡəmi/ *noun* [U] (*technical*) the custom of marrying only people from your local community ⊃ compare EXOGAMY

en·dog·e·nous /ɛnˈdɑdʒənəs/ *adj.* (*medical*) (of a disease or SYMPTOM) having no obvious cause ⊃ compare EXOGENOUS

en·do·plasm /ˈɛndəˌplæzəm/ *noun* [U] (*biology*) (*old-fashioned*) the more liquid inner layer of the substance like jelly inside cells ⊃ compare ECTOPLASM

---

en·dor·phin /ɛnˈdɔrfən/ noun (biology) a HORMONE produced in the brain that reduces the feeling of pain

en·dorse /ɪnˈdɔrs/ verb **1 ~ sth** to say publicly that you support a person, statement, or course of action: *I whole-heartedly endorse his remarks.* ◆ *The world leaders endorsed a ban on land mines.* **2 ~ sth** to say in an advertisement that you use and like a particular product so that other people will want to buy it **3 ~ sth** to write your name on the back of a check so that it can be paid into a bank account

en·dorse·ment /ɪnˈdɔrsmənt/ noun [C, U] **1** a public statement or action showing that you support someone or something: *The election victory is a clear endorsement of their policies.* ◆ *a letter of endorsement* **2** a statement made in an advertisement, usually by someone famous or important, saying that they use and like a particular product

en·do·scope /ˈɛndəˌskoʊp/ noun an instrument used in medical operations that consists of a very small camera on a long thin tube, that can be put into a person's body so that the parts inside can be seen

en·dos·co·py /ɛnˈdɑskəpi/ noun (pl. **en·dos·co·pies**) [C, U] (medical) a medical operation in which an endoscope is put into a person's body so that the parts inside can be seen

en·do·skel·e·ton /ˈɛndoʊˌskɛlətn/ noun (anatomy) the bones inside the body of an animal that give it shape and support ⊃ compare EXOSKELETON

en·do·sperm /ˈɛndoʊˌspɜrm/ noun [U] (biology) the part of the plant seed that provides food for the EMBRYO

en·do·ther·mic /ˌɛndoʊˈθɜrmɪk/ adj. (chemistry) (of a chemical reaction) needing heat in order to take place ⊃ compare EXOTHERMIC

en·dow /ɪnˈdaʊ/ verb **~ sth** to give a large sum of money to a school, a college, or another institution to provide it with an income
PHR V **be en'dowed with sth** to naturally have a particular feature, quality, etc.: *She was endowed with intelligence and beauty.* ⊃ see also WELL-ENDOWED **en'dow sb/sth with sth 1** to believe or imagine that someone or something has a particular quality: *She had endowed Marcus with the qualities she wanted him to possess.* **2** (formal) to give something to someone or something: *to endow someone with a responsibility*

en·dow·ment /ɪnˈdaʊmənt/ noun **1** [C, U] money that is given to a school, a college, or another institution to provide it with an income; the act of giving this money **2** [C, usually pl.] (formal) a quality or an ability that you are born with

end·pa·per /ˈɛndˌpeɪpər/ noun (technical) a blank or decorated page stuck inside the front or back cover of a book

ʹend ˌproduct noun something that is produced by a particular activity or process

ˌend reˈsult noun [usually sing.] the final result of a particular activity or process

ʹend run noun (in football) an attempt by the person carrying the ball to run around the end of the line of DEFENSIVE players

ʹend ˌtable noun a small table beside a SOFA

en·dur·ance /ɪnˈdʊrəns/ noun [U] the ability to continue doing something painful or difficult for a long period of time without complaining: *They were humiliated **beyond endurance**.* ◆ *This event tests both physical and mental endurance.* ◆ *powers of endurance* ◆ *The party turned out to be more of an **endurance test** than a pleasure.*

en·dure /ɪnˈdʊr/ verb **1** [T] to experience and deal with something that is painful or unpleasant, especially without complaining **SYN** BEAR: **~ sth** *They had to endure a long wait before the case came to trial.* ◆ *She could not endure the thought of leaving him.* ◆ *The pain was almost too great to endure.* ◆ (formal) *a love that endures all things and never fails* ◆ **~ doing sth** *He can't endure being defeated.* **2** [I] (formal) to continue to exist for a long time **SYN** LAST¹: *a success that will endure* ▶ **en·dur·a·ble** /ɪnˈdʊrəbl/ adj.: *I felt that life was no longer endurable.* **ANT** UNENDURABLE

en·dur·ing /ɪnˈdʊrɪŋ/ adj. lasting for a long time: *enduring memories* ◆ *What is the reason for the game's enduring appeal?* ▶ **en·dur·ing·ly** adv.: *an enduringly popular style*

ʹend-ˌuser noun a person who actually uses a product rather than one who makes or sells it, especially a person who uses a product connected with computers

end·ways /ˈɛndweɪz/ (also **end·wise** /ˈɛndwaɪz/) adv. **1** (of an object) with one end facing up, forward, or toward the person who is looking at it: *We turned the table endways to get it through the doors.* **2** with the end of one thing touching the end of another: *The stones are laid down endways to make a path.*

ʹend zone noun the area at the end of a football field into which the ball must be carried or passed in order to score points ⊃ picture at FOOTBALL

en·e·ma /ˈɛnəmə/ noun a liquid that is put into a person's RECTUM (= the opening through which solid waste leaves the body) in order to clean out the BOWELS, especially before a medical operation; the act of cleaning out the bowels in this way

en·e·my /ˈɛnəmi/ noun (pl. **en·e·mies**)
1 [C] a person who hates someone or who acts or speaks against someone or something: *He has a lot of enemies in the company.* ◆ *After just one day, she had already **made an enemy** of her manager.* ◆ *It is rare to find a prominent politician with few **political enemies**.* ◆ *The state has a duty to protect its citizens against external enemies.* ◆ *Birds are the **natural enemies** of many insect pests* (= they kill them). ⊃ see also ENMITY **2 the enemy** [sing.] a country that you are fighting a war against; the soldiers, etc. of this country: *The enemy was forced to retreat.* ◆ *enemy **forces/aircraft/territory*** ◆ *behind enemy lines* (= the area controlled by the enemy) ⊃ collocations at WAR **3** [C] **~ (of sth)** (formal) anything that harms something or prevents it from being successful: *Poverty and ignorance are the enemies of progress.* **IDM** see WORST

en·er·get·ic **AWL** /ˌɛnərˈdʒɛtɪk/ adj. having or needing a lot of energy and enthusiasm: *He knew I was energetic and dynamic and would get things done.* ◆ *an energetic supporter* ◆ *I'm not feeling very energetic today* ◆ *For the more energetic* (= people who prefer physical activities), *we offer windsurfing and diving.* ◆ *I think I'd prefer something a little less energetic.* ▶ **en·er·get·i·cally** **AWL** /-kli/ adv.

en·er·gize /ˈɛnərˌdʒaɪz/ verb **1 ~ sb** to make someone enthusiastic about something **2 ~ sb** to give someone more energy, strength, etc.: *a refreshing and energizing fruit drink* **3 ~ sth** (technical) to supply power or energy to a machine, an atom, etc.

en·er·gy **AWL** /ˈɛnərdʒi/ noun
1 [U] the ability to put effort and enthusiasm into an activity, work, etc.: *It's a waste of time and energy.* ◆ *She's always **full of energy**.* ◆ ***nervous energy*** (= energy produced by feeling nervous) **2 energies** [pl.] the physical and mental effort that you use to do something: *She put all her energies into her work.* ◆ ***creative/destructive energies*** **3** [U] a source of power, used as fuel, used for driving machines, providing heat, etc.: ***solar/nuclear energy*** ◆ *It is important to conserve energy.* ◆ *an energy crisis* (= for example when fuel is not freely available) ⊃ collocations at ENVIRONMENT **4** [U] (physics) the ability of matter or RADIATION to work because of its mass, movement, electric charge, etc.: ***kinetic/potential, etc. energy*** **5** [U] a force that some people believe is present in a place and can affect your mood or thoughts: *Let's use the **positive energy** in the room to help relax our minds and bodies.*

en·er·vate /ˈɛnərˌveɪt/ verb **~ sb** (formal) to make someone feel weak and tired: *an enervating disease/climate* ▶ **en·er·va·tion** /ˌɛnərˈveɪʃn/ noun [U]

en·fant ter·ri·ble /ˌɑ̃fɑ̃ tɛˈriblə/ noun (pl. **en·fants ter·ri·bles** /ˌɑ̃fɑ̃ tɛˈriblə/) (from French) a person who is young and successful and whose behavior and ideas may be unusual and may shock or embarrass other people

en·fee·ble /ɪnˈfibl/ verb **~ sb/sth** (formal) to make someone or something weak ▶ **en·fee·bled** adj.

en·fold /ɪnˈfoʊld/ verb (*literary*) **1** ~ **sb/sth (in sth)** to hold someone in your arms in a way that shows affection **SYN** EMBRACE: *She lay quietly, enfolded in his arms.* **2** ~ **sb/ sth (in sth)** to surround or cover someone or something completely: *Darkness spread and enfolded him.*

en·force **AWL** /ɪnˈfɔrs/ verb **1** to make sure that people obey a particular law or rule: ~ **sth** *It's the job of the police to enforce the law.* ♦ *The legislation will be difficult to enforce.* ♦ *United Nations troops enforced a ceasefire in the area.* ♦ ~ **sth on/against sb/sth** *to enforce a ban on smoking* **2** ~ **sth (on sb)** to make something happen or force someone to do something: *You can't enforce cooperation between the players.* ▶ **en·force·a·ble** /ɪnˈfɔrsəbl/ adj.: *A gambling debt is not legally enforceable.* **en·force·ment** **AWL** noun [U]: *strict enforcement of regulations* ♦ *law enforcement officers* **en·forc·er** noun: *They will be tough enforcers of the law.*

en·forced **AWL** /ɪnˈfɔrst/ adj. that someone is forced to do or experience without being able to control it: *a period of enforced absence*

en·fran·chise /ɪnˈfræntʃaɪz/ verb [usually passive] ~ **sb** (*formal*) to give someone the right to vote in an election **ANT** DISENFRANCHISE ▶ **en·fran·chise·ment** noun [U]

en·gage 🔑 /ɪnˈgeɪdʒ/ verb
1 [T] ~ **sth** (*formal*) to succeed in attracting and keeping someone's attention and interest: *It is a movie that engages both the mind and the eye.* **2** [T] ~ **sb (as sth)** | ~ **sth** | ~ **sb to do sth** (*formal*) to employ someone to do a particular job: *They engaged a consultant to review their business plan.* **3** [I] ~ **(with sth/sb)** to become involved with and try to understand something or someone: *She has the ability to engage with young minds.* **4** [T, I] ~ **(sb)** (*formal*) to begin fighting with someone: *to engage the enemy* **5** [I, T] when a part of a machine **engages**, or when you **engage** it, it fits together with another part of the machine and the machine begins to work: *The cogwheels are not engaging.* ♦ ~ **with sth** *One cogwheel engages with the next.* ♦ ~ **sth** *Engage the clutch before selecting a gear.* **ANT** DISENGAGE
PHR V **en·gage in sth** | **en·gage sb in sth** to take part in something; to make someone take part in something: *Even in prison, he continued to engage in criminal activities.* ♦ *She tried desperately to engage him in conversation.*

en·gaged 🔑 /ɪnˈgeɪdʒd/ adj.
1 having agreed to marry someone: *When did you get engaged?* ♦ *an engaged couple* ♦ ~ **to sb** *She's engaged to Peter.* ♦ *They are engaged to be married* (= to each other). ⊃ collocations at MARRIAGE **2** (*formal*) busy doing something: ~ **(in sth)** *They are engaged in talks with the Chinese government.* ♦ *They were engaged in conversation.* ♦ ~ **(on sth)** *He is now engaged on his second novel.* ♦ (*old-fashioned or formal*) *I can't come to dinner on Tuesday—I'm otherwise engaged* (= I have already arranged to do something else).

en·gage·ment /ɪnˈgeɪdʒmənt/ noun
❯ BEFORE MARRIAGE **1** [C] an agreement to marry someone; the period during which two people are engaged: *Their engagement was announced in the local paper.* ♦ ~ **(to sb)** *She broke off her engagement to Charles.* ♦ *an engagement party* ♦ *a long/short engagement*
❯ ARRANGEMENT TO DO SOMETHING **2** [C] (*formal*) an arrangement to do something at a particular time, especially something official or something connected with your job: *an engagement book/diary* ♦ *He has a number of social engagements next week.* ♦ *It was her first official engagement.* ♦ *I had to refuse because of a prior engagement.*
❯ FIGHTING **3** [C, U] (*technical*) fighting between two armies, etc.: *The general tried to avoid an engagement with the enemy.*
❯ BEING INVOLVED **4** [U] ~ **(with sb/sth)** (*formal*) being involved with someone or something in an attempt to understand them/it: *Her views are based on years of engagement with the problems of the inner city.*

en'gagement ˌring noun a ring that a man gives to a woman when they agree to get married ⊃ picture at JEWELRY

en·gag·ing /ɪnˈgeɪdʒɪŋ/ adj. interesting or pleasant in a way that attracts your attention: *an engaging smile* ▶ **en·gag·ing·ly** adv.

en·gen·der /ɪnˈdʒɛndər/ verb ~ **sth** (*formal*) to make a feeling or situation exist: *The issue engendered controversy.*

en·gine 🔑 /ˈɛndʒən/ noun
1 the part of a vehicle that produces power to make the vehicle move: *a diesel/gasoline engine* ♦ *My car had to have a new engine.* ♦ *engine trouble* ♦ *I turned the engine off.* ⊃ picture at BICYCLE ⊃ see also INTERNAL-COMBUSTION ENGINE, JET ENGINE, TRACTION ENGINE **2** (also lo·co·mo·tive) a vehicle that pulls a train ⊃ picture at TRAIN **3** -engined (in adjectives) having the type or number of engines mentioned: *a twin-engined speedboat* ⊃ see also FIRE ENGINE, SEARCH ENGINE **4** ~ **of sth** something that causes a particular process to start and keep going: *Exports used to be the engine of growth.*

en·gi·neer 🔑 /ˌɛndʒəˈnɪr/ noun, verb
● **noun 1** a person whose job involves designing and building engines, machines, roads, bridges, etc. ⊃ see also LIGHTING ENGINEER, RECORDING ENGINEER, SOFTWARE ENGINEER, SOUND ENGINEER **2** a person who is trained to repair machines and electrical equipment: *They're sending an engineer to fix the cable.* **3** a person whose job is to control and repair engines, especially on a ship or an aircraft: *a flight engineer* ♦ *the chief engineer on a cruise ship* **4** a person whose job is driving a railroad engine **5** a soldier trained to design and build military structures
● **verb 1** ~ **sth** (often *disapproving*) to arrange for something to happen or take place, especially when this is done secretly in order to give yourself an advantage **SYN** CONTRIVE: *She engineered a further meeting with him.* **2** [usually passive] ~ **sth** to design and build something: *The car is beautifully engineered and a pleasure to drive.* **3** ~ **sth** to change the GENETIC structure of something **SYN** GENETICALLY MODIFY: *genetically engineered crops*

en·gi·neer·ing 🔑 /ˌɛndʒəˈnɪrɪŋ/ noun [U]
1 the activity of applying scientific knowledge to the design, building, and control of machines, roads, bridges, electrical equipment, etc.: *The bridge is a triumph of modern engineering.* ⊃ compare REVERSE ENGINEERING **2** (also ˌengineering 'science) the study of engineering as a subject: *a degree in engineering* ⊃ see also CHEMICAL ENGINEERING, CIVIL ENGINEERING, ELECTRICAL ENGINEERING, GENETIC ENGINEERING, MECHANICAL ENGINEERING, SOCIAL ENGINEERING

'engine ˌroom noun **1** the part of a ship where the engines are **2** the part of an organization where most of the important activity takes place or important decisions are made

Eng·lish /ˈɪŋglɪʃ/ noun, adj.
● **noun 1** [U, C] the language, originally of England, now spoken in many other countries and used as a language of international communication throughout the world: *She speaks good English.* ♦ *I need to improve my English.* ♦ *world Englishes* **2** [U] English language or literature as a subject of study: *a degree in English* ♦ *English is my best subject.* **3** the English [pl.] the people of England (sometimes wrongly used to mean the British, including the Scots, the Welsh, and the Northern Irish) **IDM** see PLAIN adj.
● **adj.** connected with England, its people or its language: *the English countryside* ♦ *an English man/woman* ♦ *typically English attitudes* ♦ *an English dictionary* ⊃ note at BRITISH

ˌEnglish for ˌAcademic 'Purposes noun (*abbr.* EAP) [U] the teaching of English for people who are using English for study, but whose first language is not English

ˌEnglish 'horn noun a musical instrument of the WOODWIND group, like an OBOE but larger and playing lower notes

Eng·lish·man /ˈɪŋglɪʃmən/ noun (*pl.* Eng·lish·men /-mən/) a man from England

ˌEnglish 'muffin noun a type of round flat bread roll,

usually TOASTED and eaten hot with butter ⊃ compare MUFFIN

Eng·lish·wom·an /'ɪŋglɪʃ,wʊmən/ *noun* (*pl.* **Eng·lish-wom·en** /-,wɪmən/) a woman from England

en·gorge /ɪn'gɔrdʒ/ *verb* [often passive] **~ sth** (*technical*) to cause something to become filled with blood or another liquid and to swell

en·grave /ɪn'greɪv/ *verb* [often passive] to cut words or designs on wood, stone, metal, etc.: **~ A (with B)** *The silver cup was engraved with his name.* ◆ **~ B on A** *His name was engraved on the silver cup.*
  IDM **be engraved on/in your heart, memory, mind, etc.** to be something that you will never forget because it affected you so strongly

en·grav·er /ɪn'greɪvər/ *noun* a person whose job is to cut words or designs on wood, stone, metal, etc.

en·grav·ing /ɪn'greɪvɪŋ/ *noun* **1** [C] a picture made by cutting a design on a piece of metal and then printing the design on paper **2** [U] the art or process of cutting designs on wood, stone, metal, etc. ⊃ collocations at ART

en·gross /ɪn'groʊs/ *verb* **~ sb** if something **engrosses** you, it is so interesting that you give it all your attention and time ▶ **en·gross·ing** *adj.*: *an engrossing problem*

en·grossed /ɪn'groʊst/ *adj.* **~ (in/with sth)** so interested or involved in something that you give it all your attention: *She was engrossed in conversation.*

en·gulf /ɪn'gʌlf/ *verb* (*formal*) **1 ~ sb/sth** to surround or to cover someone or something completely: *He was engulfed by a crowd of reporters.* ◆ *The vehicle was engulfed in flames.* **2 ~ sb/sth** to affect someone or something very strongly: *Fear engulfed her.*

en·hance **AWL** /ɪn'hæns/ *verb* **~ sth** to increase or further improve the good quality, value, or status of someone or something: *This is an opportunity to enhance the reputation of the company.* ◆ *the skilled use of makeup to enhance your best features* ▶ **en·hanced** **AWL** *adj.*: *enhanced efficiency* **en·hance·ment** **AWL** *noun* [U, C]: *equipment for the en-hancement of sound quality* ◆ *software enhancements*

en·hanc·er /ɪn'hænsər/ *noun* (*technical*) a substance or device that is designed to improve something: *flavor enhancers*

e·nig·ma /ɪ'nɪgmə/ *noun* a person, thing, or situation that is mysterious and difficult to understand **SYN** MYSTERY, PUZZLE

en·ig·mat·ic /,enɪg'mæt̮ɪk/ *adj.* mysterious and difficult to understand: *an enigmatic smile* ▶ **en·ig·mat·i·cally** /-kli/ *adv.*: *"I might," he said enigmatically.*

en·jambe·ment (also **en·jamb·ment**) /ɪn'dʒæmmənt/ *noun* [U, C] (from *French*, *technical*) the fact of a sentence continuing beyond the end of a line of poetry ⊃ compare CAESURA

en·join /ɪn'dʒɔɪn/ *verb* **1** [often passive] **~ sb to do sth** | **~ sth** (*formal*) to order or strongly advise someone to do something; to say that a particular action or quality is necessary **2 ~ sb from doing sth** (*law*) to legally prevent someone from doing something, for example with an INJUNCTION (= official order)

en·joy 🔑 /ɪn'dʒɔɪ/ *verb*

1 [T] to get pleasure from something: **~ sth** *We thoroughly enjoyed our time in New York.* ◆ *Thanks for a great evening. I really enjoyed it.* ◆ **~ doing sth** *I enjoy playing tennis and squash.* **2** [T] **~ yourself** to be happy and get pleasure from what you are doing: *They all enjoyed themselves at the party.* **3** [T] **~ sth** (*formal*) to have something good that is an advantage to you: *People in this country enjoy a high standard of living.* ◆ *He's always enjoyed good health.* **4** [I] **enjoy!** (*informal*) used to say that you hope someone gets pleasure from something that you are giving them or recommend-ing to them: *Here's that book I promised you. Enjoy!*

GRAMMAR

enjoy

Note the following patterns:
- I enjoyed myself at the party. ◆ ~~I enjoyed at the party.~~
- Thanks. I really enjoyed it. ◆ ~~Thanks. I really enjoyed.~~
- I enjoy playing basketball. ◆ ~~I enjoy to play basketball.~~
- I enjoy reading very much. ◆ ~~I enjoy very much reading.~~
- I hope you enjoy your trip. ◆ ~~I hope you enjoy with your trip.~~

en·joy·a·ble 🔑 /ɪn'dʒɔɪəbl/ *adj.* giving pleasure: *an enjoyable weekend/experience* ◆ **highly/ really/thoroughly/very enjoyable** ▶ **en·joy·a·bly** /-bli/ *adv.*: *The evening passed enjoyably.*

en·joy·ment 🔑 /ɪn'dʒɔɪmənt/ *noun* **1** [U] the pleasure that you get from something: *He spoiled my enjoyment of the game by talking all through it.* ◆ *The rules are there to ensure everyone's safety and enjoyment.* ◆ *Children seem to have lost their enjoyment of reading.* ◆ *I get a lot of enjoyment from my grandchildren.* ⊃ note at FUN **2** [C] (*formal*) something that gives you pleasure: *He was a stranger to the pleasures and enjoyments that most of us take for granted.* **3** [U] **~ of sth** (*formal*) the fact of having and using something: *the enjoyment of equal rights*

en·large /ɪn'lɑrdʒ/ *verb* **1** [T, I] **~ (sth)** to make something bigger; to become bigger: *There are plans to enlarge the recreation area.* ◆ *Reading will enlarge your vocabulary.* **2** [T, usually passive] **~ sth** to make a bigger copy of a photograph or document: *We're going to have this picture enlarged.* ▶ **en·larged** *adj.*: *an enlarged heart*
  PHR V **en'large on/upon sth** (*formal*) to say or write more about something that has been mentioned **SYN** ELABORATE

en·large·ment /ɪn'lɑrdʒmənt/ *noun* **1** [U, sing.] **~ (of sth)** the process or result of something becoming or being made larger: *the enlargement of the company's overseas business activities* ◆ *There was widespread support for NATO enlargement* (= the fact of more countries joining). **2** [C] something that has been made larger, especially a photo-graph: *If you like the picture, I can send you an enlargement of it.* **ANT** REDUCTION

en·larg·er /ɪn'lɑrdʒər/ *noun* a piece of equipment for making photographs larger or smaller

en·light·en /ɪn'laɪtn/ *verb* **~ sb** (*formal*) to give someone information so that they understand something better: *She didn't enlighten him about her background.* ▶ **en·light·en·ing** *adj.*: *It was a very enlightening interview.*

en·light·ened /ɪn'laɪtnd/ *adj.* [usually before noun] (*ap-proving*) having or showing an understanding of people's needs, a situation, etc. that is not based on old-fashioned attitudes and PREJUDICE: *enlightened opinions/attitudes/ ideas*

en·light·en·ment /ɪn'laɪtnmənt/ *noun* **1** [U] knowledge about and understanding of something; the process of understanding something or making someone understand it: *The newspapers provided little enlightenment about the cause of the accident.* ◆ *spiritual enlightenment* ⊃ collocations at RELIGION **2 the Enlightenment** [sing.] the period in the 18th century when many writers and scientists began to argue that science and reason were more important than religion and tradition

en·list /ɪn'lɪst/ *verb* **1** [I, T] to join or to make someone join the armed forces **SYN** DRAFT: *They both enlisted in 1915.* ◆ **~ as sth** to enlist as a soldier ◆ **~ sb (in/into/for/as sth)** *He was enlisted into the U.S. Navy.* **2** [T] to persuade someone to help you or to join you in doing something: **~ sth/sb (in sth)** *They hoped to enlist the help of the public in solving the crime.* ◆ **~ sb (as sth)** *We were enlisted as helpers.* ◆ **~ sb to do sth** *We were enlisted to help.* ▶ **en·list·ment** *noun* [U]: *the enlistment of expert help* ◆ *his enlistment in the U.S. Air Force*

---

en·list·ed /ɪnˈlɪstəd/ adj. (of a member of the army, etc.) having a rank that is below that of an officer: *enlisted men and women* ◆ *enlisted personnel*

en·liv·en /ɪnˈlaɪvn/ verb ~ **sth** (formal) to make something more interesting or more fun

en masse /ˌɑn ˈmæs/ adv. (from French) all together, and usually in large numbers

en·mesh /ɪnˈmɛʃ/ verb [usually passive] ~ **sb/sth (in sth)** (formal) to involve someone or something in a bad situation that it is not easy to escape from

en·mi·ty /ˈɛnməti/ noun (pl. **en·mi·ties**) [U, C] (formal) feelings of hatred toward someone: *personal enmities and political conflicts* ◆ *Her action earned her the enmity of two or three colleagues.* ◆ ~ **between A and B** the traditional problem of the enmity between Protestants and Catholics ➔ see also ENEMY

en·no·ble /ɪˈnoʊbl; ɛ-/ verb (formal) **1** ~ **sb/sth** to give someone or something a better moral character: *In a strange way she seemed ennobled by her grief.* **2** [usually passive] ~ **sb** to make someone a member of the NOBILITY ▶ **en·no·ble·ment** /ɪˈnoʊblmənt/ noun [U]

en·nui /ˌɑnˈwi/ noun [U] (from French, literary) feelings of being bored and not satisfied because nothing interesting is happening

e·nol·o·gy (also **oe·nol·o·gy**) /iˈnɑlədʒi/ noun [U] (technical) the study of wine

e·no·phile (also **oe·no·phile**) /ˈinəˌfaɪl/ noun (formal) a person who knows a lot about wine

e·nor·mi·ty **AWL** /ɪˈnɔrməti/ noun (pl. **en·or·mi·ties**) **1** [U] **the ~ of sth** (of a problem, etc.) the very great size, effect, etc. of something; the fact of something being very serious: *the enormity of the task* ◆ *People are still coming to terms with the enormity of the disaster.* ◆ *The full enormity of the crime has not yet been revealed.* **HELP** Some people think that **enormity** should only be used about something morally bad such as a crime, but in fact it is commonly used about the great size or seriousness of something, without any moral judgment being made. **2** [C, usually pl.] (formal) a very serious crime: *the enormities of the Hitler regime*

e·nor·mous 🔑 **AWL** /ɪˈnɔrməs/ adj. extremely large **SYN** HUGE, IMMENSE: *an enormous house/dog* ◆ *an enormous amount of time* ◆ *enormous interest* ◆ *The problems facing the president are enormous.*

e·nor·mous·ly **AWL** /ɪˈnɔrməsli/ adv. very; very much: *enormously rich/powerful/grateful* ◆ *The price of wine varies enormously depending on where it comes from.* ◆ *She was looking forward to the meeting enormously.*

e·nough 🔑 /ɪˈnʌf/ det., pron., adv.
● **det.** used with plural or uncountable nouns to mean "as many or as much as someone needs or wants" **SYN** SUFFICIENT: *Have you made enough copies?* ◆ *Is there enough room for me?* ◆ *I didn't have enough clothes to last a week.* ◆ *Don't ask me to do it. I have enough problems as it is.* ◆ *(old-fashioned) There was food enough for all.* **HELP** Although **enough** after a noun now sounds old-fashioned, **time enough** is still fairly common: *There'll be time enough to relax when you've finished your work.*
● **pron.** as many or as much as someone needs or wants: *Six bottles should be enough.* ◆ *Have you had enough (= to eat)?* ◆ *If enough of you are interested, we'll organize a trip to the theater.* ◆ *There was nowhere near enough for everyone.* ◆ *We've nearly run out of paper. Do you think there's enough for today?* **IDM** **enough already** (informal) used to say that something is annoying or boring and that you want it to stop **enough is enough** (saying) used when you think that something should not continue any longer **enough said** used to say that you understand a situation and there is no need to say any more: *"He's a politician, remember." "Enough said."* **have had enough (of sth/sb)** used when something or someone is annoying you and you no longer want to do,

have or see it or them: *I've had enough of driving the kids around.*
● **adv.** (used after verbs, adjectives, and adverbs) **1** to the necessary degree: *I haven't trained enough for the game.* ◆ *This house isn't big enough for us.* ◆ *She's old enough to decide for herself.* ◆ *We didn't leave early enough.* ◆ *Tell them it's just not good enough.* ◆ *Who on earth would be stupid enough to believe that?* ◆ *Two years ago I was lucky enough to visit some friends in Japan.* **2** to an acceptable degree, but not to a very great degree: *He seemed pleasant enough to me.* **3** to a degree that you do not wish to get any greater: *I hope my job's safe. Life is hard enough as it is.* **IDM** **oddly, strangely, curiously, etc. enough** used to show that something is surprising: *Oddly enough, I said the same thing myself only yesterday.* ➔ more at FAIR adj., FAR adv., LIKE adv., MAN n., SURE adv.

en·quire, en·quir·er, en·quir·ing, en·quir·y = INQUIRE, INQUIRER, INQUIRING, INQUIRY

en·rage /ɪnˈreɪdʒ/ verb [usually passive] ~ **sb** to make someone very angry **SYN** INFURIATE

en·rap·ture /ɪnˈræptʃər/ verb [usually passive] ~ **sb** (formal) to give someone great pleasure or joy **SYN** ENCHANT

en·rap·tured /ɪnˈræptʃərd/ adj. (formal) filled with great pleasure or joy **SYN** ENCHANTED

en·rich /ɪnˈrɪtʃ/ verb **1** to improve the quality of something, often by adding something to it: ~ **sth** *The study of science has enriched all of our lives.* ◆ ~ **sth with sth** *Most breakfast cereals are enriched with vitamins.* **2** ~ **sb/sth** to make someone or something rich or richer: *a nation enriched by oil revenues* ◆ *He used his position to enrich himself.* ▶ **en·rich·ment** noun [U]

en·roll /ɪnˈroʊl/ verb [I, T] to arrange for yourself or for someone else to officially join a school, start a program of study, etc. **SYN** REGISTER v. (2): *You need to enroll before the end of August.* ◆ *to enroll in a course* ◆ ~ **sb** *The center will soon be ready to enroll candidates for the new program.*

en·roll·ee /ɪnˌroʊˈli/ noun a person who has officially joined an organization, started a program of study, etc.

en·roll·ment /ɪnˈroʊlmənt/ noun [U, C] the act of officially joining a school, starting a program of study, etc.; the number of people who do this: *Enrollment is the first week of September.* ◆ *School enrollments are currently falling.*

en route /ˌɑn ˈrut; ˌɛn-/ adv. (from French) on the way; while traveling from/to a particular place: *We stopped for a picnic en route.* ◆ ~ **(from…) (to…)** *The bus broke down en route from Boston to New York.*

en·sconce /ɪnˈskɑns/ verb **be ensconced (+adv./prep.)** | ~ **yourself (+adv./prep.)** (formal) if you **are ensconced** or **ensconce yourself** somewhere, you are made or make yourself comfortable and safe in that place or position

en·sem·ble /ɑnˈsɑmbl/ noun **1** a small group of musicians, dancers, or actors who perform together: *a brass/wind/string, etc. ensemble* ◆ *The ensemble is based in Chicago.* **2** [usually sing.] (formal) a number of things considered as a group **3** [usually sing.] a set of clothes that are worn together

en·shrine /ɪnˈʃraɪn/ verb [usually passive] ~ **sth (in sth)** (formal) to make a law, right, etc. respected or official, especially by stating it in an important written document: *These rights are enshrined in the country's constitution.*

en·shroud /ɪnˈʃraʊd/ verb ~ **sth** (literary) to cover or surround something completely so that it cannot be seen or understood

en·sign noun **1** /ˈɛnsən; ˈɛnsaɪn/ a flag flown on a ship to show which country it belongs to: *the United States Ensign* **2** /ˈɛnsən/ an officer of low rank in the U.S. Navy: *Ensign Marshall*

en·slave /ɪnˈsleɪv/ verb [usually passive] **1** ~ **sb** to make someone a SLAVE **2** ~ **sb/sth (to sth)** (formal) to make someone or something completely depend on something so that they cannot manage without it ▶ **en·slave·ment** noun [U]

en·snare /ɪnˈsnɛr/ verb ~ sb/sth (formal) to make someone or something unable to escape from a difficult situation or from a person who wants to control them **SYN** TRAP: *young homeless people who become ensnared in a life of crime*

en·sue /ɪnˈsu/ verb [I] (formal) to happen after or as a result of another event **SYN** FOLLOW: *An argument ensued.* ▶ **en·su·ing** adj.: *He had become separated from his parents in the ensuing panic.*

en·sure 🔑 **AWL** (also **in·sure**) /ɪnˈʃʊr/ verb
to make sure that something happens or is definite: ~ *sth The book ensured his success.* ♦ ~ *sb sth Victory ensured them a place in the final.* ♦ ~ *(that)... Please ensure (that) all lights are switched off.*

ENT /ˌi ɛn ˈti/ abbr. ear, nose, and throat (used to talk about doctors who work in this branch of medicine)

-ent ⊃ -ANT

en·tail /ɪnˈteɪl/ verb to involve something that cannot be avoided **SYN** INVOLVE: ~ *sth The job entails a lot of hard work.* ♦ **be entailed in sth** *The girls learn exactly what is entailed in caring for a newborn baby.* ♦ ~ **(sb) doing sth** *It will entail driving a long distance every day.*

en·tan·gle /ɪnˈtæŋgl/ verb [usually passive] **1** ~ sb/sth (in/with sth) to make someone or something become caught or twisted in something: *The bird had become entangled in the wire netting.* **2** to involve someone in a difficult or complicated situation: ~ **sb in sth** *He became entangled in a series of conflicts with the management.* ♦ ~ **sb with sb** *She didn't want to get entangled* (= emotionally involved) *with him.*

en·tan·gle·ment /ɪnˈtæŋglmənt/ noun **1** [C] a difficult or complicated relationship with another person or country **2** [U] the act of becoming entangled in something; the state of being entangled: *Many dolphins die each year from entanglement in fishing nets.*

en·tente /ɑnˈtɑnt/ noun [U, sing.] (from French) a friendly relationship between two countries: *the Franco-Russian entente*

en·ter 🔑 /ˈɛntər/ verb
‣ COME/GO IN **1** [I, T] (not usually in the passive) (formal) to come or go into something: *Knock before you enter.* ♦ ~ **sth** *Someone entered the room behind me.* ♦ *Where did the bullet enter the body?* ♦ (figurative) *A note of defiance entered her voice.* ♦ (figurative) *It never entered my head* (= I never thought) *that she would tell him about me.*
‣ JOIN INSTITUTION/START WORK **2** [T, no passive] ~ **sth** to become a member of an institution; to start working in an organization or a profession: *to enter a school/college/university* ♦ *to enter politics*
‣ BEGIN ACTIVITY **3** [T] ~ **sth** to begin or become involved in an activity, a situation, etc.: *to enter a relationship/conflict/war* ♦ *Several new companies have now entered the market.* ♦ *The investigation has entered a new phase.* ♦ *The strike is entering its fourth week.*
‣ EXAM/COMPETITION **4** [T] to put your name on the list for a race, competition, etc.; to do this for someone: ~ **sth** *1,000 children entered the competition.* ♦ ~ **sb/sth in sth** *An experienced trainer, he has entered several horses in the race.* ♦ ~ **sb/sth for sth** *How many cars have been entered for the race?*
‣ WRITE INFORMATION **5** [T] to put names, numbers, details, etc. in a list, book, or computer: ~ **sth (in sth)** *Enter your name and occupation in the boxes* (= on a form). ♦ ~ **sth (into sth)** *to enter data into a computer* ♦ ~ **sth (on sth)** *to enter figures on a spreadsheet*
‣ SAY OFFICIALLY **6** [T] ~ **sth** (formal) to say something officially so that it can be recorded: *to enter a plea of not guilty* (= at the beginning of a court case) ♦ *to enter an offer* ⊃ see also ENTRANCE¹, ENTRY **IDM** see FORCE v.
PHR V **'enter into sth** (formal) **1** to begin to discuss or deal with something: *Let's not enter into details at this stage.* **2** to take an active part in something: *They entered into the spirit of the occasion* (= began to enjoy and feel part of it). **3** [no passive] to form part of something or have an influence on

something: *This possibility never entered into our calculations.* ♦ *Your personal feelings shouldn't enter into this at all.* **'enter into sth (with sb)** to begin something or become involved in something: *to enter into an agreement* ♦ *to enter into negotiations* **'enter on/upon sth** (formal) to start to do something or become involved in it: *to enter on a new career*

en·ter·ic /ɛnˈtɛrɪk/ adj. (medical) connected with the INTESTINES

en·ter·itis /ˌɛntəˈraɪtəs/ noun [U] (medical) a painful infection in the INTESTINES that usually causes DIARRHEA ⊃ see also GASTROENTERITIS

en·ter·prise /ˈɛntərˌpraɪz/ noun **1** [C] a company or business: *an enterprise with a turnover of $26 billion* ♦ *state-owned/public enterprises* ♦ *small and medium-sized enterprises* **2** [C] a large project, especially one that is difficult **SYN** VENTURE: *his latest business enterprise* ♦ *a joint enterprise* **3** [U] the development of businesses by the people of a country rather than by the government: *grants to encourage enterprise in the region* ♦ *an enterprise culture* (= in which people are encouraged to develop small businesses) ⊃ see also FREE ENTERPRISE, PRIVATE ENTERPRISE **4** [U] (approving) the ability to think of new projects and make them successful **SYN** INITIATIVE: *a job in which enterprise is rewarded*

en·ter·pris·ing /ˈɛntərˌpraɪzɪŋ/ adj. (approving) having or showing the ability to think of new projects or new ways of doing things and make them successful

en·ter·tain 🔑 /ˌɛntərˈteɪn/ verb
1 [I, T] to invite people to eat or drink with you as your guests, especially in your home: *The job involves a lot of entertaining.* ♦ ~ **sb** *Barbecues are a favorite way of entertaining friends.* **2** [T, I] ~ **(sb) (with sth)** to interest and amuse someone in order to please them: *He entertained us for hours with his stories and jokes.* ♦ *The aim of the series is both to entertain and inform.* **3** [T] (not used in the progressive tenses) ~ **sth** (formal) to consider or allow yourself to think about an idea, a hope, a feeling, etc.: *He had entertained hopes of a reconciliation.* ♦ *to entertain a doubt/suspicion*

en·ter·tain·er 🔑 /ˌɛntərˈteɪnər/ noun
a person whose job is amusing or interesting people, for example by singing, telling jokes, or dancing

en·ter·tain·ing 🔑 /ˌɛntərˈteɪnɪŋ/ adj.
interesting and amusing: *an entertaining speech/evening* ♦ *I found the talk both informative and entertaining.* ♦ *She was always so funny and entertaining.* ⊃ thesaurus box at FUNNY ▶ **en·ter·tain·ing·ly** adv.

en·ter·tain·ment 🔑 /ˌɛntərˈteɪnmənt/ noun
1 [U, C] movies, music, etc. used to entertain people; an example of this: *radio, television, and other forms of entertainment* ♦ *There will be live entertainment at the party.* ♦ *It was typical family entertainment.* ♦ *The entertainment was provided by a folk band.* ♦ *Local entertainments are listed in the newspaper.* ♦ *The show was good entertainment value.* **2** [U] the act of entertaining someone: *a budget for the entertainment of clients*

THESAURUS

entertainment

fun ♦ **recreation** ♦ **relaxation** ♦ **play** ♦ **pleasure** ♦ **amusement**

These are all words for things or activities used to entertain people when they are not working.

entertainment movies, television, music, etc. used to entertain people: *The club offers live entertainment seven nights a week.*

fun (somewhat informal) behavior or activities that are not serious but come from a sense of enjoyment: *I took an art class just for the fun of it.* ♦ *The lottery provides harmless fun for millions.*

recreation (*somewhat formal*) things people do for enjoyment when they are not working: *His only form of recreation is playing basketball.*

relaxation (*somewhat formal*) things people do to rest and enjoy themselves when they are not working; the ability to relax: *I go hiking for relaxation.*

RECREATION OR RELAXATION?

Both these words can be used for a wide range of activities, physical and mental, but **relaxation** is sometimes used for gentler activities than **recreation**: *I play the flute in a wind band for recreation. ◆ I listen to music for relaxation.*

play things that people, especially children, do for enjoyment rather than as work: *the importance of learning through play*

pleasure the activity of enjoying yourself, especially in contrast to working: *Are you in Paris for business or pleasure?*

amusement (*somewhat formal*) the fact of being entertained by something: *What do you do for amusement around here?*

PATTERNS

- to do sth **for** entertainment/fun/recreation/relaxation/pleasure/amusement
- to **provide** entertainment/fun/recreation/relaxation/amusement

en·thrall /ɪnˈθrɔl/ *verb* [T, I, usually passive] ~ **(sb)** if something **enthralls** you, it is so interesting, beautiful, etc. that you give it all your attention **SYN** ENTRANCE²: *The child watched, enthralled by the bright moving images.* ▶ **en·thral·ling** *adj.*: *an enthralling performance*

en·throne /ɪnˈθroʊn/ *verb* [usually passive] ~ **sb** when a king, queen, or important member of a Church is **enthroned**, they sit on a THRONE (= a special chair) in a ceremony to mark the beginning of their rule ▶ **en·throne·ment** *noun* [U, C]

en·thuse /ɪnˈθuz/ *verb* **1** [I, T] to talk in an enthusiastic and excited way about something: ~ **(about/over sth/sb)** *The article enthused about the benefits that the new system would bring.* ◆ **+ speech** *"It's a wonderful idea," he enthused.* ◆ ~ **that…** *The organizers enthused that it was their most successful event yet.* **2** [usually passive] ~ **sb (with sth)** to make someone feel very interested and excited: *Everyone present was enthused by the idea.*

en·thu·si·asm /ɪnˈθuziˌæzəm/ *noun*
1 [U] a strong feeling of excitement and interest in something, and a desire to become involved in it: ~ **(for sth)** *I can't say I share your enthusiasm for the idea. ◆ He had a real enthusiasm for the work. ◆* ~ **(for doing sth)** *She never lost her enthusiasm for teaching. ◆ The news was greeted with a lack of enthusiasm by those at the meeting. ◆ "I don't mind," she said, without much enthusiasm. ◆ full of enthusiasm ◆ Wet weather did not dampen the enthusiasm of the participants in the event.* **2** [C] (*formal*) something that you are very interested in and spend a lot of time doing

en·thu·si·ast /ɪnˈθuziˌæst/ *noun* **1** ~ **(for/of sth)** a person who is very interested in something and spends a lot of time doing, watching, etc. it: *a soccer enthusiast ◆ an enthusiast of jazz* **2** ~ **(for/of sth)** a person who approves of something and shows enthusiasm for it: *enthusiasts for national health insurance*

en·thu·si·as·tic /ɪnˌθuziˈæstɪk/ *adj.*
feeling or showing a lot of excitement and interest about someone or something: *an enthusiastic supporter ◆ an enthusiastic welcome ◆* ~ **about sb/sth** *You don't sound very enthusiastic about the idea. ◆* ~ **about doing sth** *She was even less enthusiastic about going to Spain.* ▶ **en·thu·si·as·ti·cally** /-kli/ *adv.*

en·tice /ɪnˈtaɪs/ *verb* to persuade someone or something to go somewhere or to do something, usually by offering them something **SYN** PERSUADE: ~ **sb/sth (+ adv./prep.)** *The bargain prices are expected to entice customers away from other stores. ◆ The animal refused to be enticed from its hole. ◆* ~ **sb into doing sth** *He was not enticed into parting with his cash. ◆* ~ **sb to do sth** *Try to entice your son to eat by offering small portions of his favorite food.* ▶ **en·tice·ment** *noun* [C, U]: *The party is offering low taxation as its main enticement.*

en·tic·ing /ɪnˈtaɪsɪŋ/ *adj.* something that is **enticing** is so attractive and interesting that you want to have it or know more about it: *The offer was too enticing to refuse.* ▶ **en·tic·ing·ly** *adv.*

en·tire 🔑 /ɪnˈtaɪər/ *adj.* [only before noun]
(used when you are emphasizing that the whole of something is involved) including everything, everyone, or every part **SYN** WHOLE: *The entire village was destroyed. ◆ I wasted an entire day on it. ◆ I have never in my entire life heard such nonsense! ◆ The disease threatens to wipe out the entire population.*

en·tire·ly 🔑 /ɪnˈtaɪərli/ *adv.*
in every way possible; completely: *I entirely agree with you. ◆ I'm not entirely happy about the proposal. ◆ That's an entirely different matter. ◆ The audience was almost entirely female.*

en·tire·ty /ɪnˈtaɪərti; -ˈtaɪrəti/ *noun* [sing.] (*formal*) **the ~ of sth** the whole of something
IDM **in its/their entirety** as a whole, rather than in parts: *The poem is too long to quote in its entirety.*

en·ti·tle 🔑 /ɪnˈtaɪtl/ *verb*
1 [often passive] to give someone the right to have or to do something: ~ **sb to sth** *You will be entitled to your pension when you reach 65. ◆ Everyone's entitled to their own opinion. ◆* ~ **sb to do sth** *This ticket does not entitle you to travel first class.* **2** [usually passive] ~ **sth + noun** to give a title to a book, play, etc.: *He read a poem entitled "Salt."*

en·ti·tled /ɪnˈtaɪtld/ *adj.* (usually *disapproving*) feeling that you have a right to the good things in life without necessarily having to work for them: *He's so entitled! ◆ The college attracts both the entitled children of wealthy parents and a large number of scholarship students.*

en·ti·tle·ment /ɪnˈtaɪtlmənt/ *noun* (*formal*) **1** [U] ~ **(to sth)** the official right to have or do something: *This may affect your entitlement to compensation.* **2** [C] something that you have an official right to; the amount that you have the right to receive: *Your contributions will affect your healthcare entitlements.* **3** [C] a government system that provides financial support to a particular group of people: *a reform of entitlements ◆ Medicare and other entitlement programs* **4** [U] (usually *disapproving*) the feeling of having a right to the good things in life without necessarily having to work for them: *I can't stand the sense of entitlement among these kids.*

en·ti·ty 🅰🆆🅻 /ˈɛntəti/ *noun* (*pl.* **en·ti·ties**) (*formal*) something that exists separately from other things and has its own identity: *The unit has become part of a larger department and no longer exists as a separate entity. ◆ These countries can no longer be viewed as a single entity.*

en·tomb /ɪnˈtum/ *verb* [usually passive] (*formal*) **1** ~ **sb/sth (in sth)** to bury or completely cover someone or something so that they cannot get out, be seen, etc. **2** ~ **sb/sth (in sth)** to put a dead body in a TOMB

en·to·mol·o·gy /ˌɛntəˈmɑlədʒi/ *noun* [U] the scientific study of insects ▶ **en·to·mo·log·i·cal** /ˌɛntəməˈlɑdʒɪkl/ *adj.* **en·to·mol·o·gist** /ˌɛntəˈmɑlədʒɪst/ *noun*

en·tou·rage /ˈɑntʊrɑʒ/ *noun* a group of people who travel with an important person

en·tr'acte /ˈɑntrækt; ɑnˈtrækt/ *noun* (from French) **1** (*formal*) the time between the different parts of a play, show, etc. **SYN** INTERMISSION **2** a short performance between the different parts of a play, show, etc.

en·trails /ˈɛntreɪlz/ *noun* [pl.] the organs inside the body of a

t **tea**   ț **butter**   d **did**   k **cat**   g **got**   tʃ **chin**   dʒ **June**   f **fall**

person or an animal, especially their INTESTINES **SYN** INNARDS, INSIDES

en·trance¹ 🔊 /ˈɛntrəns/ *noun*
➔ see also ENTRANCE²
› **DOOR/GATE 1** [C] ~ **(to sth)** a door, gate, passage, etc. used for entering a room, building, or place: *the entrance to the museum/the museum entrance* ◆ *A lighthouse marks the entrance to the harbor.* ◆ *the front/back/side entrance of the house* ◆ *I'll meet you at the main entrance.* ➔ compare EXIT
› **GOING IN 2** [C, usually sing.] the act of entering a room, building, or place, especially in a way that attracts the attention of other people: *His sudden entrance took everyone by surprise.* ◆ *A fanfare signaled the entrance of the king.* ◆ *She made her entrance after all the other guests had arrived.* ◆ *The hero makes his entrance* (= walks onto the stage) *in Scene 2.* **3** [U] ~ **(to sth)** the right or opportunity to enter a building or place: *They were refused entrance to the exhibition.* ◆ *The police were unable to gain entrance to the house.* ◆ *an entrance fee* (= money paid to go into a museum, etc.)
› **BECOMING INVOLVED 4** [C] ~ **(into sth)** the act of becoming involved in something: *The company made a dramatic entrance into the export market.*
› **TO CLUB/INSTITUTION 5** [U] permission to become a member of a club or society, a student at a college, etc.: *a college entrance exam* ◆ *entrance requirements* ◆ ~ **(to sth)** *Entrance to the golf club is by sponsorship only.* ➔ compare ENTRY

en·trance² /ɪnˈtræns/ *verb* [usually passive] ~ **sb** (*formal*) to make someone feel great pleasure and admiration so that they give someone or something all their attention **SYN** ENTHRALL: *He listened to her, entranced.* ➔ see also ENTRANCE¹ ▸ **en·tranc·ing** *adj.*: *entrancing music*

en·trant /ˈɛntrənt/ *noun* **1** ~ **(to sth)** a person or an animal that enters a race, competition, etc. **2** ~ **(to sth)** a person who has recently joined a profession, started at a college, etc.: *new women entrants to the police force* ◆ *college entrants*

en·trap /ɪnˈtræp/ *verb* (-pp-) [often passive] (*formal*) **1** ~ **sb/ sth** to put or catch someone or something in a place or situation from which they cannot escape **SYN** TRAP **2** ~ **sb (into doing sth)** to trick someone, and encourage them to do something, especially to commit a crime, so that they can be arrested for it

en·trap·ment /ɪnˈtræpmənt/ *noun* [U] (*law*) the illegal act of tricking someone into committing a crime so that they can be arrested for it

en·treat /ɪnˈtrit/ *verb* (*formal*) to ask someone to do something in a serious and often emotional way **SYN** BEG, IMPLORE: *~ sb Please help me, I entreat you.* ◆ ~ **sb to do sth** *She entreated him not to go.* ◆ ~ **(sb) + speech** *"Please don't go," she entreated (him).*

en·treaty /ɪnˈtriti/ *noun* (*pl.* **en·treat·ies**) [C, U] (*formal*) a serious and often emotional request

en·trée (also **en·tree**) /ˈɑntreɪ/ *noun* (from *French*) **1** [C] (in a restaurant or at a formal meal) the main course of the meal **2** [U, C] ~ **(into/to sth)** (*formal*) the right or ability to enter a social group or institution

en·trench /ɪnˈtrɛntʃ/ *verb* [usually passive] ~ **sth** (sometimes *disapproving*) to establish something very firmly so that it is very difficult to change: *Sexism is deeply entrenched in our society.* ◆ *entrenched attitudes/interests/opposition*

en·trench·ment /ɪnˈtrɛntʃmənt/ *noun* **1** [U] the fact of something being firmly established **2** [C, usually pl.] a system of TRENCHES (= long narrow holes dug in the ground by soldiers to provide defense)

en·tre·pôt /ˈɑntrəˌpou/ *noun* (from *French*) a port or other place where goods are brought for import and export

en·tre·pre·neur /ˌɑntrəprəˈnɚr; -ˈnʊr/ *noun* a person who makes money by starting or running businesses, especially when this involves taking financial risks
▸ **en·tre·pre·neur·i·al** /-ˈnɚriəl; -ˈnʊriəl/ *adj.*: *entrepreneurial skills* **en·tre·pre·neur·ship** *noun* [U]

en·tro·py /ˈɛntrəpi/ *noun* [U] **1** (*technical*) a way of measuring the lack of order that exists in a system **2** (*physics*) (*symb.*

S.) a measurement of the energy that is present in a system or process but is not available to do work **3** a complete lack of order: *In the business world, entropy rules.* ▸ **en·tro·pic** /ɛnˈtrɑpɪk; -ˈtrou-/ *adj.* **en·tro·pi·cally** /-kli/ *adv.*

en·trust /ɪnˈtrʌst/ *verb* to make someone responsible for doing something or taking care of someone: *~ A to B He entrusted the task to his nephew.* ◆ ~ **B with A** *He entrusted his nephew with the task.*

en·try 🔊 /ˈɛntri/ *noun* (*pl.* **en·tries**)
› **GOING IN 1** [C, U] an act of going into or getting into a place: *She made her entry to the sound of thunderous applause.* ◆ *The children were surprised by the sudden entry of their teacher.* ◆ ~ **(into sth)** *How did the thieves gain entry into the building?* **2** [U] the right or opportunity to enter a place: *No Entry* (= for example, on a sign) ◆ ~ **(to/into sth)** *Entry to the museum is free.* ◆ *to be granted/refused entry into the country*
› **JOINING GROUP 3** [U] ~ **(into sth)** the right or opportunity to take part in something or become a member of a group: *countries seeking entry into NATO* ◆ *the entry of women into the workforce*
› **IN COMPETITION 4** [C] something that you do, write, or make to take part in a competition, for example answering a set of questions: *There have been some impressive entries in the wildlife photography section* (= impressive photographs). ◆ *The closing date for entries is March 31.* ◆ *The sender of the first correct entry drawn will win a weekend for two in Venice.* **5** [U] the act of taking part in a competition, race, etc.: *Entry is open to anyone over the age of 18.* ◆ *an entry form* **6** [sing.] the total number of people who are taking part in a competition, race, etc.: *There's a record entry for this year's marathon.*
› **WRITTEN INFORMATION 7** [C] an item, for example a piece of information, that is written or printed in a dictionary, an account book, a diary, etc.: *an encyclopedia entry* ◆ ~ **(in sth)** *There is no entry in his diary for that day.* **8** [U] the act of recording information into a computer, book, etc.: *More keyboarders are required for data entry.*
› **DOOR/GATE 9** (also **en·try·way** /ˈɛntriˌweɪ/) [C] a door, gate, or passage where you enter a building: *You can leave your umbrella in the entry.*

entry-·level *adj.* [usually before noun] **1** (of a job) at the lowest level in a company **2** (of a product) basic and suitable for new users who may later move on to a more advanced product: *an entry-level computer*

en·twine /ɪnˈtwaɪn/ *verb* [usually passive] **1** ~ **sth (with/in/ around sth)** to twist or wind something around something else: *They strolled through the park, with arms entwined.* **2** be **entwined (with something)** to be very closely involved or connected with something: *Her destiny was entwined with his.*

e·nu·mer·ate /ɪˈnuməˌreɪt/ *verb* ~ **sth** (*formal*) to name things on a list one by one ▸ **e·nu·mer·a·tion** /ɪˌnuməˈreɪʃn/ *noun* [U, C]

e·nun·ci·ate /ɪˈnʌnsiˌeɪt/ *verb* **1** [T, I] ~ **(sth)** | **+ speech** to say or pronounce words clearly: *She enunciated each word slowly and carefully.* **2** [T] ~ **sth** (*formal*) to express an idea clearly and exactly: *He enunciated his vision of the future.* ▸ **e·nun·ci·a·tion** /ɪˌnʌnsiˈeɪʃn/ *noun* [U]

en·ure·sis /ˌɛnyuˈrisəs/ *noun* [U] (*medical*) urination (URINATE) (= letting waste liquid flow from the body) that is not under someone's control, especially in the case of a child who is asleep ➔ see also BED-WETTING

en·vel·op /ɪnˈvɛləp/ *verb* ~ **sb/sth (in sth)** (*formal*) to wrap someone or something up or cover them or it completely: *She was enveloped in a huge white towel.* ◆ *Clouds enveloped the mountaintops.* ▸ **en·vel·op·ment** *noun* [U]

en·vel·ope 🔊 /ˈɛnvəˌloup; ˈɑn-/ *noun* a flat paper container used for sending letters in: *an airmail/padded/prepaid envelope* ➔ picture at STATIONERY ➔ see also PAY ENVELOPE, SASE **IDM** see PUSH *v.*

en·vi·a·ble /ˈɛnviəbl/ *adj.* something that is enviable is the kind of thing that is good and that other people want to have too: *He is in the enviable position of having two job offers* *to choose from.* **ANT** UNENVIABLE ► **en·vi·a·bly** /-bli/ *adv.*: *an enviably mild climate*

en·vi·ous /ˈɛnviəs/ *adj.* **~ (of sb/sth)** wanting to be in the same situation as someone else; wanting something that someone else has: *Everyone is so envious of her.* ◆ *They were envious of his success.* ◆ *He saw the envious look in the other boy's eyes.* ► **en·vi·ous·ly** *adv.*: *They look enviously at the success of their competitors.* ⊃ see also ENVY

en·vi·ron·ment 🔑 **AWL** /ɪnˈvaɪərnmənt; -ˈvaɪrən-/ *noun*
1 [C, U] the conditions that affect the behavior and development of someone or something; the physical conditions that someone or something exists in: *a pleasant **working/ learning environment*** ◆ *An unhappy **home environment** can affect a child's behavior.* ◆ *They have created an environment in which productivity should flourish.* ◆ *the political environment* ◆ *tests carried out in a controlled environment* **2 the environment** [sing.] the natural world in which people, animals, and plants live: *measures to protect the environment* ◆ *pollution of the environment* ◆ *damage to the environment* **3** [C] (*computing*) the complete structure within which a user, computer, or program operates: *a user-friendly desktop development environment*

THESAURUS

environment

setting ◆ surroundings ◆ background

These are all words for the type of place in which someone or something exists or is situated.

environment the conditions in a place that affect the behavior and development of someone or something: *An unhappy **home environment** can affect children's behavior.* ◆ *a pleasant **working environment***

setting a place or situation of a particular type, in which something happens or exists: *The island provided an exotic setting for the concert.*

surroundings everything that is around or near someone or something: *The cabins blend in perfectly with their surroundings.*

background the things or area behind or around the main objects or people that are in a place or picture: *The mountains in the background were capped with snow.*

PATTERNS

- **in (a/an) ... environment/setting/surroundings**
- **(a/an) new/unfamiliar environment/setting/surroundings**
- **sb/sth's immediate environment/surroundings**
- **(a) dramatic setting/background**

TOPIC COLLOCATIONS

The Environment

environmental damage

- **cause/contribute to** climate change/global warming
- **produce** pollution/CO_2/greenhouse (gas) emissions
- **damage/destroy** the environment/a marine ecosystem/the ozone layer/coral reefs
- **degrade** ecosystems/habitats/the environment
- **harm** the environment/wildlife/marine life
- **threaten** natural habitats/coastal ecosystems/a species with extinction
- **deplete** natural resources/the ozone layer
- **pollute** rivers and lakes/waterways/the air/the atmosphere/the environment/oceans
- **contaminate** groundwater/the soil/food/crops
- **log** forests/rainforests/trees

protecting the environment

- **address/combat/tackle** the threat/effects/impact of climate change

- **fight/take action on/reduce/stop** global warming
- **limit/curb/control** air/water/atmospheric/environmental pollution
- **cut/reduce** pollution/greenhouse (gas) emissions
- **offset** carbon/CO_2 emissions
- **reduce** (the size of) your carbon footprint
- **achieve/promote** sustainable development
- **preserve/conserve** biodiversity/natural resources
- **protect** endangered species/a coastal ecosystem
- **prevent/stop** soil erosion/overfishing/massive deforestation/damage to ecosystems
- **raise** awareness of environmental issues
- **save** the planet/the rainforests/an endangered species

energy and resources

- **conserve/save/consume/waste** energy
- **manage/exploit/be rich in** natural resources
- **dump/dispose of** hazardous/toxic/nuclear waste/sewage
- **dispose of/throw away** litter/garbage/trash
- **use/be made from** recycled/recyclable/biodegradable material
- **recycle** bottles/packaging/paper/plastic/waste
- **promote/encourage** recycling/sustainable development/the use of renewable energy
- **develop/invest in/promote** renewable energy
- **reduce** your dependence/reliance on fossil fuels
- **get/obtain/generate/produce** electricity from wind, solar, and wave power/renewable sources
- **build/develop** a (50-megawatt/offshore) wind farm
- **install/be powered by** solar panels

en·vi·ron·men·tal 🔑 **AWL** /ɪnˌvaɪərnˈmɛntl; -ˌvaɪrən-/ *adj.* [usually before noun]
1 connected with the natural conditions in which people, animals, and plants live; connected with the environment: *the environmental impact of pollution* ◆ *environmental issues/problems* ◆ *an environmental group/movement* (= that aims to improve or protect the natural environment) ◆ *environmental damage* **2** connected with the conditions that affect the behavior and development of someone or something: *environmental influences* ◆ *an environmental health officer* ► **en·vi·ron·men·tal·ly** **AWL** /-ˈmɛntl-i/ *adv.*: *an environmentally sensitive area* (= one that is easily damaged or that contains rare animals, plants, etc.) ◆ *environmentally damaging*

en·vi·ron·men·tal·ist **AWL** /ɪnˌvaɪərnˈmɛntlɪst; -ˌvaɪrən-/ *noun* a person who is concerned about the natural environment and wants to improve and protect it ► **en·vi·ron·men·tal·ism** /-ˈmɛntlˌɪzəm/ *noun* [U]

en·vi·ron·men·tal·ly 'friendly (also en·vironment-'friendly) *adj.* (of products) not harming the environment: *environmentally friendly packaging*

en·vi·rons /ɪnˈvaɪərənz; -ˈvaɪərnz/ *noun* [pl.] (*formal*) the area surrounding a place: *Boston and its environs* ◆ *people living in the immediate environs of a nuclear plant*

en·vis·age /ɪnˈvɪzɪdʒ/ *verb* **~ sth** (*formal*) to imagine what will happen in the future: *What level of profit do you envisage?*

en·vi·sion /ɪnˈvɪʒən/ *verb* to imagine what will happen or what a situation will be like in the future: **~ sth** *They envision an equal society, free of poverty and disease.* ◆ *They didn't envision any problems with the new building.* ◆ **~ (sb) doing sth** *I can't envision her coping with this job.* ◆ **~ that...** *I envision that the work will be completed next year.* ◆ **~ how, where, etc.** *It is difficult to envision how people will react.* ⊃ thesaurus box at IMAGINE

en·voy /ˈɛnvɔɪ; ˈɑn-/ *noun* a person who represents a government or an organization and is sent as a representative to talk to other governments and organizations **SYN** EMISSARY

en·vy /ˈɛnvi/ *noun*, *verb*
● *noun* [U] the feeling of wanting to be in the same situation

h hat   m man   n no   ŋ sing   1 leg   r red   y yes   w wet

as someone else; the feeling of wanting something that someone else has: ~ **(of sb)** *He couldn't conceal his envy of me.* ✦ ~ **(at/of sth)** *She felt a pang of envy at the thought of his success.* ✦ *They looked* **with envy** *at her latest purchase.* ✦ *Her colleagues were* **green with envy** (= they had very strong feelings of envy).

IDM **be the envy of sb/sth** to be a person or thing that other people admire and that causes feelings of envy: *Our universities are the envy of the world.* ➔ see also ENVIABLE, ENVIOUS

● *verb* (en·vies, en·vy·ing, en·vied, en·vied) **1** to wish you had the same qualities, possessions, opportunities, etc. as someone else: ~ **sb** *He envied her—she seemed to have everything she could possibly want.* ✦ ~ **sth** *She has always envied my success.* ✦ ~ **sb sth** *I envied him his good looks.* ✦ ~ **sb doing sth** *I envy you having such a close family.* **2** to be glad that you do not have to do what someone else has to do: **not** ~ **sb** *It's a difficult situation you're in. I don't envy you.* ✦ **not** ~ **sb sth** *I don't envy her that job.*

en·zyme /ˈɛnzaɪm/ *noun* (*biology*) a substance, produced by all living things, that helps a chemical change happen or happen more quickly, without being changed itself

e·o·li·an (also **ae·o·li·an**) /iˈoʊliən/ *adj.* (*technical*) connected with or caused by the action of the wind

e·on /ˈiən; ˈiɑn/ *noun* **1** an extremely long period of time; thousands of years **2** (*geology*) a major division of time, divided into ERAS: *eons of geological history*

ep·au·let (also **ep·au·lette**) /ˈɛpəˌlɛt; ˌɛpəˈlɛt/ *noun* a decoration on the shoulder of a coat, jacket, etc., especially when part of a military uniform

é·pée /ˈɛpeɪ; ɛˈpeɪ/ *noun* **1** [C] a SWORD used in the sport of FENCING **2** [U] the sport of FENCING with an épée

e·phem·er·a /ɪˈfɛmərə/ *noun* [pl.] things that are important or used for only a short period of time: *a collection of postcards, tickets, and other ephemera*

e·phem·er·al /ɪˈfɛmərəl/ *adj.* (*formal*) lasting or used for only a short period of time **SYN** SHORT-LIVED

ep·ic /ˈɛpɪk/ *noun, adj.*

● *noun* **1** [C,U] a long poem about the actions of great men and women or about a nation's history; this style of poetry: *one of the great Hindu epics* ✦ *the creative genius of Greek epic* ➔ compare LYRIC **2** [C] a long movie or book that contains a lot of action, usually about a historical subject **3** [C] (sometimes *humorous*) a long and difficult job or activity that you think people should admire: *Their four-hour match was really an epic.*

● *adj.* [usually before noun] **1** having the features of an epic: *an epic poem* ➔ compare LYRIC **2** taking place over a long period of time and involving a lot of difficulties: *an epic journey/struggle* **3** very great and impressive: *a tragedy of epic proportions*

ep·i·cene /ˈɛpəˌsin/ *adj.* **1** (*formal*) having characteristics of both the male and female sex or of neither sex in particular: *epicene beauty* **2** (*grammar*) (of a word) having one form to represent male and female: *You can write "s/he" as an epicene pronoun when you are not referring to men or women in particular.*

ep·i·cen·ter (CanE usually **ep·i·cen·tre**) /ˈɛpəˌsɛntər/ *noun* **1** the point on the earth's surface where the effects of an EARTHQUAKE are felt most strongly **2** (*formal*) the central point of something

ep·i·cure /ˈɛpɪˌkyʊr/ *noun* (*formal*) a person who enjoys food and drink of high quality and knows a lot about it

ep·i·cu·re·an /ˌɛpɪkyʊˈriən; ˌɛpɪˈkyʊriən/ *adj.* (*formal*) devoted to pleasure and enjoying yourself
▶ **ep·i·cu·re·an·ism** /ˌɛpɪkyʊˈriəˌnɪzəm; ˌɛpɪˈkyʊriə-/ *noun* [U]

ep·i·dem·ic /ˌɛpəˈdɛmɪk/ *noun* **1** a large number of cases of a particular disease happening at the same time in a particular community: *the outbreak of a flu epidemic* ✦ *an epidemic of measles* **2** a sudden rapid increase in how often something bad happens: *an epidemic of crime in the inner*

cities ▶ **ep·i·dem·ic** *adj.*: *Car theft is now reaching* **epidemic proportions.** ➔ compare PANDEMIC

ep·i·de·mi·ol·o·gy /ˌɛpəˌdimiˈɑlədʒi/ *noun* [U] the scientific study of the spread and control of diseases
▶ **ep·i·de·mi·o·log·i·cal** /ˌɛpəˌdimiəˈlɑdʒɪkl/ *adj.*
ep·i·de·mi·ol·o·gist /ˌɛpəˌdimiˈɑlədʒɪst/ *noun*

ep·i·der·mis /ˌɛpəˈdərmɪs/ *noun* [sing., U] (*anatomy*) the outer layer of the skin ➔ compare DERMIS

ep·i·du·ral /ˌɛpəˈdʊrəl/ *noun* (*medical*) an ANESTHETIC that is put into the lower part of the back so that no pain is felt below the waist: *Some mothers choose to have an epidural when giving birth.*

ep·i·glot·tis /ˌɛpəˈglɑtəs/ *noun* (*anatomy*) a thin piece of TISSUE behind the tongue that prevents food or drinks from entering the lungs

ep·i·gram /ˈɛpəˌgræm/ *noun* a short poem or phrase that expresses an idea in an amusing way ▶ **ep·i·gram·mat·ic** /ˌɛpəgrəˈmætɪk/ *adj.*

ep·i·graph /ˈɛpəˌgræf/ *noun* a line of writing, short phrase, etc. on a building or statue, or as an introduction to part of a book

ep·i·lep·sy /ˈɛpəˌlɛpsi/ *noun* [U] a DISORDER of the nervous system that causes a person to become unconscious suddenly, often with violent movements of the body
▶ **ep·i·lep·tic** /ˌɛpəˈlɛptɪk/ *adj.*: *an epileptic fit* **ep·i·lep·tic** *noun*: *Is she an epileptic?*

ep·i·logue /ˈɛpəˌlɔg; -ˌlɑg/ *noun* a speech, etc. at the end of a play, book, or movie that comments on or acts as a conclusion to what has happened ➔ compare PROLOGUE

E·piph·a·ny /ɪˈpɪfəni/ *noun* [U] a Christian festival, held on January 6, in memory of the time when the MAGI came to see the baby Jesus at Bethlehem

e·pis·co·pa·cy /ɪˈpɪskəpəsi/ *noun* [U] government of a church by BISHOPS

e·pis·co·pal /ɪˈpɪskəpl/ *adj.* **1** connected with a BISHOP or BISHOPS: *episcopal power* **2** usually **Episcopal** (also E·pis·co·pa·lian) (of a Christian Church) that is governed by BISHOPS: *the Episcopal Church* (= the church in the U.S. that developed from the Church of England)

E·pis·co·pa·lian /ɪˌpɪskəˈpeɪliən/ *noun* a member of the Episcopal Church

e·pis·co·pate /ɪˈpɪskəpət/ *noun* [usually sing.] (*religion*) **1** the episcopate the BISHOPS of a particular church or area **2** the job of BISHOP or the period of time during which someone is bishop

ep·i·si·ot·o·my /ɪˌpiziˈɑtəmi/ *noun* (*pl.* **e·pi·si·ot·o·mies**) (*medical*) a cut that is sometimes made at the opening of a woman's VAGINA to make the birth of a baby easier or safer

ep·i·sode /ˈɛpəˌsoʊd/ *noun* **1** an event, a situation, or a period of time in someone's life, a novel, etc. that is important or interesting in some way **SYN** INCIDENT: *I'd like to try and forget the whole episode.* ✦ *One of the funniest episodes in the book occurs in Chapter 6.* **2** one part of a story that is broadcast on television or radio in several parts

ep·i·sod·ic /ˌɛpəˈsɑdɪk/ *adj.* (*formal*) **1** happening occasionally and not at regular intervals **2** (of a story, etc.) containing or consisting of many separate and different events: *My memories of childhood are hazy and episodic.*

ep·i·ste·mic /ˌɛpəˈstimɪk; -ˈstɛ-/ *adj.* (*formal*) relating to knowledge

ep·is·te·mol·o·gy /ɪˌpɪstəˈmɑlədʒi/ *noun* [U] the part of philosophy that deals with knowledge

e·pis·tle /ɪˈpɪsl/ *noun* **1 Epistle** any of the letters in the New Testament of the Bible, written by the first people who followed Christ: *the Epistles of St. Paul* **2** (*formal* or *humorous*) a long, serious letter on an important subject

e·pis·to·lar·y /ɪˈpɪstəˌlɛri/ *adj.* (*formal*) written or expressed in the form of letters: *an epistolary novel*

ep·i·taph /ˈɛpəˌtæf/ *noun* **1** words that are written or said about a dead person, especially words on a GRAVESTONE

2 ~ (to sb/sth) something which is left to remind people of a particular person, a period of time, or an event: *These slums are an epitaph to the housing policy of the 1960s.*

ep·i·thet /ˈɛpəˌθɛt/ *noun* **1** an adjective or a phrase that is used to describe someone's/something's character or most important quality, especially in order to give praise or criticism: *The movie is long and dramatic but does not quite earn the epithet "epic."* **2** an offensive word or phrase that is used about a person or group of people: *Racial epithets were scrawled on the walls.*

e·pit·o·me /ɪˈpɪtəmi/ *noun* [sing.] **the ~ of sth** a perfect example of something **SYN** EMBODIMENT: *He is the epitome of a modern young man.* ◆ *clothes that are the epitome of good taste*

e·pit·o·mize /ɪˈpɪtəˌmaɪz/ *verb* **~ sth** to be a perfect example of something: *The fighting qualities of the team are epitomized by the captain.* ◆ *These movies seem to epitomize the 1950s.*

ep·och /ˈɛpək/ *noun* (*formal* or *literary*) **1** a period of time in history, especially one during which important events or changes happen **SYN** ERA: *The death of the emperor marked the end of an epoch in the country's history.* **2** (*geology*) a length of time that is a division of a PERIOD: *geological epochs*

epoch-making *adj.* (*formal*) having a very important effect on people's lives and on history

ep·o·nym /ˈɛpənɪm/ *noun* (*technical*) a person or thing, or the name of a person or thing, from which a place, an invention, a discovery, etc. gets its name

e·pon·y·mous /ɪˈpɑnəməs/ *adj.* [only before noun] the **eponymous** character of a book, play, movie, etc. is the one mentioned in the title **SYN** TITULAR: *Don Quixote, eponymous hero of the great novel by Cervantes*

ep·ox·y /ɪˈpɑksi/ *noun* (*pl.* **ep·ox·ies**) (also **ep'oxy ˌresin**) [U, C] a type of strong glue

ep·si·lon /ˈɛpsəˌlɑn/ *noun* the fifth letter of the Greek alphabet (E., ε)

Ep·som salts /ˈɛpsəm ˌsɔlts/ *noun* [pl.] a white powder that can be mixed with water and used as a medicine or LAXATIVE

eq·ua·ble /ˈɛkwəbl/ *adj.* (*formal*) **1** calm and not easily upset or annoyed: *an equable temperament* **2** (of weather) keeping a steady temperature with no sudden changes
▸ **eq·ua·bly** /-bli/ *adv.*

e·qual 🔑 /ˈikwəl/ *adj., noun, verb*

● *adj.* **1** the same in size, quantity, value, etc. as something else: *There is an equal number of boys and girls in the class.* ◆ *two pieces of wood equal in length/of equal length* ◆ **~ to sb/ sth** *One unit of alcohol is equal to one glass of wine.* **HELP** You can use **exactly, precisely, approximately,** etc. with **equal** in this meaning. **2** having the same rights or being treated the same as other people, without differences such as race, religion, or sex being considered: *equal rights/pay* ◆ *The company is an equal opportunity employer* (= gives the same chances of employment to everyone). ◆ *the desire for a more equal society* (= in which everyone has the same rights and chances) **HELP** You can use **more** with **equal** in this meaning. **3 ~ to sth** (*formal*) having the necessary strength, courage, and ability to deal with something successfully: *I hope that he proves equal to the challenge.* ⊃ see also EQUALLY
IDM on equal terms (with sb) having the same advantages and disadvantages as someone else: *Can our industry compete on equal terms with its overseas rivals?* **some (people, members, etc.) are more equal than others** (*saying*) although the members of a society, group, etc. appear to be equal, some, in fact, get better treatment than others **ORIGIN** This phrase is used by one of the pigs in the book "Animal Farm" by George Orwell: "All animals are equal but some animals are more equal than others." ⊃ more at THING

● *noun* a person or thing of the same quality or with the same status, rights, etc. as another: *She treats the people who work*

for her as her equals. ◆ *Our cars are the equal of those produced anywhere in the world.*
IDM be without equal | have no equal (*formal*) to be better than anything else or anyone else of the same type: *He is a player without equal.* ⊃ more at FIRST *n.*

● *verb* (-l-, *CanE usually* -ll-) **1** linking verb **+ noun** to be the same in size, quantity, value, etc. as something else: *2x plus y equals 7* (2x+y=7) ◆ *A yard equals 36 inches.* **2 ~ sth** to be as good as something else or do something to the same standard as someone else: *This achievement is unlikely ever to be equaled.* ◆ *Her hatred of religion is equaled only by her loathing for politicians.* ◆ *With his last jump he equaled the world record.* **3 ~ sth** to lead to or result in something: *Cooperation equals success.*

e·qual·i·ty /ɪˈkwɑləti/ *noun* [U] the fact of being equal in rights, status, advantages, etc.: *racial/social/sexual equality* ◆ *equality of opportunity* ◆ *the principle of equality before the law* (= the law treats everyone the same) ◆ *Don't you believe in equality between men and women?* **ANT** INEQUALITY

e·qual·ize /ˈikwəˌlaɪz/ *verb* **1** [T] **~ sth** to make things equal in size, quantity, value, etc. in the whole of a place or group: *a policy to equalize the distribution of resources throughout the country* **2** [I] (especially in soccer) to score a goal that makes the score of both teams equal ▸ **e·qual·i·za·tion** /ˌikwə-ləˈzeɪʃn/ *noun* [U]

e·qual·iz·er /ˈikwəˌlaɪzər/ *noun* [usually sing.] (especially in soccer) a goal that makes the score of both teams equal

e·qual·ly 🔑 /ˈikwəli/ *adv.*
1 to the same degree; in the same or in a similar way: *Diet and exercise are equally important.* ◆ *This job could be done equally well by a computer.* ◆ *We try to treat every member of staff equally.* **2** in equal parts, amounts, etc.: *The money was divided equally among her four children.* ◆ *They share the housework equally.* **3** used to introduce another phrase or idea that adds to, and is as important as, what you have just said: *I'm trying to do what is best, but equally I have to consider the cost.*

equals sign (also **equal ˌsign**) *noun* the symbol (=), used in mathematics

e·qua·nim·i·ty /ˌikwəˈnɪməti; ˌɛkwə-/ *noun* [U] (*formal*) a calm state of mind that means that you do not become angry or upset, especially in difficult situations: *She accepted the prospect of her operation with equanimity.*

e·quate **AWL** /ɪˈkweɪt/ *verb* **~ sth (with sth)** to think that something is the same as something else or is as important: *Some parents equate education with exam success.* ◆ *I don't see how you can equate the two things.*
PHR V e'quate to sth to be equal to something else: *A $5,000 raise equates to 25%.*

e·qua·tion **AWL** /ɪˈkweɪʒn/ *noun* **1** [C] (*mathematics*) a statement showing that two amounts or values are equal, for example 2x+y = 54 **2** [U, sing.] the act of making something equal or considering something as equal (= of equating them): *The equation of wealth with happiness can be dangerous.* **3** [C, usually sing.] a problem or situation in which several things must be considered and dealt with: *When children enter the equation, further tensions may arise within a marriage.*

e·qua·tor /ɪˈkweɪtər/ usually **the equator** *noun* [sing.] an imaginary line around the earth at an equal distance from the North and South Poles ⊃ picture at EARTH

e·qua·to·ri·al /ˌikwəˈtɔriəl; ˌɛkwə-/ *adj.* near the equator, or typical of a country that is near the equator: *equatorial rainforests* ◆ *an equatorial climate*

eq·uer·ry /ˈɛkwəri; ɪˈkwɛri/ *noun* (*pl.* **eq·uer·ries**) a male officer who acts as an assistant to a member of a royal family

e·ques·tri·an /ɪˈkwɛstriən/ *adj.* [usually before noun] connected with riding horses, especially as a sport: *equestrian events at the Olympic Games*

e·ques·tri·an·ism /ɪˈkwɛstriəˌnɪzəm/ *noun* [U] **1** the skill or sport of riding horses **2** an Olympic sport consisting of SHOW JUMPING, DRESSAGE, and EVENTING

ʌ **cup**   ə **about**   eɪ **say**   aɪ **five**   ɔɪ **boy**   aʊ **now**   oʊ **go**   ər **bird**

equi- /ˈikwə; ˈɛkwə/ *combining form* (in nouns, adjectives, and adverbs) equal; equally: *equidistant* ♦ *equilibrium*

e·qui·dis·tant /ˌikwəˈdɪstənt; ˌɛkwə-/ *adj.* [not before noun] **~ (from sth)** (*formal*) equally far from two or more places: *All points on a circle are equidistant from the center.*

e·qui·lat·er·al tri·an·gle /ˌikwəˌlætərəl ˈtraɪæŋgl/ *noun* (*geometry*) a triangle whose three sides are all the same length ⊃ picture at SHAPE

e·qui·lib·ri·um /ˌikwəˈlɪbriəm/ *noun* [U, sing.] **1** a state of balance, especially between opposing forces or influences: *The point at which the solid and the liquid are in equilibrium is called the freezing point.* ♦ *Any disturbance to the body's state of equilibrium can produce stress.* ♦ *We have achieved an equilibrium in the economy.* **2** a calm state of mind and a balance of emotions: *He sat down to try and recover his equilibrium.*

e·quine /ˈikwaɪn/ /ˈɛ-/ *adj.* (*formal*) connected with horses; like a horse

e·qui·noc·tial /ˌikwəˈnɑkʃl; ˌɛkwə-/ *adj.* connected with an equinox

e·qui·nox /ˈikwənɑks; ˈɛkwə-/ *noun* one of the two times in the year (around March 20 and September 22) when the sun is above the EQUATOR and day and night are of equal length: *the spring/fall equinox* ⊃ picture at EARTH

e·quip AWL /ɪˈkwɪp/ *verb* (-pp-) **1** to provide yourself/ someone or something with the things that are needed for a particular purpose or activity: **~ sth** *to be fully/poorly equipped* ♦ *She got a bank loan to rent and equip a small workshop.* ♦ **~ yourself/sb/sth (with sth) (for sth)** *He equipped himself with a street map.* ♦ *The center is well equipped for canoeing and mountaineering.* **2 ~ sb (for sth)** | **~ sb (to do sth)** to prepare someone for an activity or a task, especially by teaching them what they need to know: *The course is designed to equip students for a career in nursing.*

e·quip·ment 🔑 AWL /ɪˈkwɪpmənt/ *noun* [U]
1 the things that are needed for a particular purpose or activity: *a useful piece of equipment for the kitchen* ♦ *office equipment* ♦ *new equipment for the sports club* **2** the process of providing a place or person with necessary things: *The equipment of the photographic studio was expensive.*

THESAURUS

equipment

material ♦ gear ♦ kit ♦ apparatus

These are all words for the things that you need for a particular purpose or activity.

equipment the things that are needed for a particular purpose or activity: *camping equipment* ♦ *a piece of laboratory/medical equipment*

material things that are needed for a particular activity: *household cleaning materials* ♦ *teaching material*

EQUIPMENT OR MATERIAL?

Equipment is usually solid things, especially large ones. **Materials** may be liquids, powders, or books, CDs, etc. containing information, as well as small solid items.

gear the equipment or clothes needed for a particular activity: *Camping gear can be expensive.*

kit a set of tools or equipment that you use for a particular purpose: *a first-aid kit* ♦ *a sewing kit*

apparatus (*formal*) the tools or other pieces of equipment that are needed for a particular activity or task: *breathing apparatus for firefighters* ♦ *laboratory apparatus* **NOTE** Apparatus is used especially for scientific, medical, or technical purposes.

PATTERNS
- **electrical/electronic** equipment/gear/apparatus
- **sports** equipment/gear
- **camping** equipment/gear
- a **piece of** equipment/apparatus

---

e·qui·poise /ˈikwəˌpɔɪz/ *noun* [U] (*formal*) a state of balance

eq·ui·ta·ble /ˈɛkwətəbl/ *adj.* (*formal*) fair and reasonable; treating everyone in an equal way **SYN** FAIR **ANT** INEQUITABLE ▸ **eq·ui·ta·bly** /-bli/ *adv.*

Eq·ui·ty /ˈɛkwəti/ *noun* [U] the LABOR UNION for actors in the U.S. and some other countries

eq·ui·ty /ˈɛkwəti/ *noun* **1** [U] (*finance*) the value of a company's shares; the value of a property after all charges and debts have been paid ⊃ see also NEGATIVE EQUITY **2 equities** [pl.] (*finance*) shares in a company which do not pay a fixed amount of interest **3** [U] (*formal*) a situation in which everyone is treated equally **SYN** FAIRNESS **ANT** INEQUITY **4** [U] (*law*) a system of natural justice allowing a fair judgment in a situation that is not covered by the existing laws

e·quiv·a·len·cy /ɪˈkwɪvələnsi/ *noun* [U] **1** = EQUIVALENCE **2** short for "General Equivalency Diploma" (an official certificate that people who did not finish high school can get, after taking classes and passing a test) ⊃ see also GED

e·quiv·a·lent 🔑 AWL /ɪˈkwɪvələnt/ *adj., noun*
• *adj.* equal in value, amount, meaning, importance, etc.: *250 grams or an equivalent amount in ounces* ♦ **~ to sth** *Eight kilometers is roughly equivalent to five miles.* ▸ **e·quiv·a·lence** AWL /-ləns/ *noun* [U] (*formal*): *There is no straightforward equivalence between economic progress and social well-being.*
• *noun* a thing, an amount, a word, etc. that is equivalent to something else: *Send $20 or the equivalent in your own currency.* ♦ **~ of/to sth** *Creutzfeldt-Jakob disease, the human equivalent of BSE* ♦ *Breathing such polluted air is the equivalent of* (= has the same effect as) *smoking ten cigarettes a day.* ♦ *The German "Gymnasium" is the closest equivalent to a U.S. prep school.*

e·quiv·o·cal /ɪˈkwɪvəkl/ *adj.* (*formal*) **1** (of words or statements) not having one clear or definite meaning or intention; able to be understood in more than one way **SYN** AMBIGUOUS: *She gave an equivocal answer, typical of a politician.* **2** (of actions or behavior) difficult to understand or explain clearly or easily: *The experiments produced equivocal results.* ⊃ see also UNEQUIVOCAL

e·quiv·o·cate /ɪˈkwɪvəˌkeɪt/ *verb* [I, T] **(+ speech)** (*formal*) to talk about something in a way that is deliberately not clear in order to avoid or hide the truth

e·quiv·o·ca·tion /ɪˌkwɪvəˈkeɪʃn/ *noun* [C, U] (*formal*) a way of behaving or speaking that is not clear or definite and is intended to avoid or hide the truth

ER /ˌi ˈɑr/ (CanE, informal **e·merg**) *abbr.* EMERGENCY ROOM

er /ə; ər/ *exclamation* the sound that people make when they are deciding what to say next: *"Will you do it?" "Er, yes, I suppose so."*

-er /ər/ *suffix* **1** (in nouns) a person or thing that: *lover* ♦ *computer* ⊃ compare -AR, -EE, -OR **2** (in nouns) a person or thing that has the thing or quality mentioned: *three-wheeler* ♦ *foreigner* **3** (in nouns) a person concerned with: *astronomer* ♦ *philosopher* **4** (in nouns) a person belonging to: *New Yorker* **5** (makes comparative adjectives and adverbs): *wider* ♦ *bigger* ♦ *happier* ♦ *sooner* ⊃ compare -EST

e·ra 🔑 /ˈɪrə; ˈɛrə/ *noun*
1 a period of time, usually in history, that is different from other periods because of particular characteristics or events: *the colonial/modern/post-war era* ♦ *When she left the company, it was the end of an era* (= things were different after that). **2** (*geology*) a length of time that is a division of an EON

e·rad·i·cate /ɪˈrædəˌkeɪt/ *verb* to destroy or get rid of something completely, especially something bad **SYN** WIPE OUT: **~ sth** *Diphtheria has been virtually eradicated in the United States.* ♦ **~ sth from sth** *We are determined to eradicate racism from our sport.* ▸ **e·rad·i·ca·tion** /ɪˌrædəˈkeɪʃn/ *noun* [U]

e·rase /ɪˈreɪs/ *verb* **1** to remove something completely: **~ sth** *She tried to erase the memory of that evening.* ♦ **~ sth**

---

from sth *All doubts were suddenly **erased from** his mind.* ◆ *You cannot erase injustice from the world.* **2** ~ **sth** to make a mark or something you have written disappear, for example by rubbing it, especially in order to correct it: *He erased the wrong word.* **3** ~ **sth** to remove a recording from a tape or information from a computer's memory: *Parts of the recording have been erased.*

e·ras·er /ɪˈreɪsər/ *noun* a small piece of rubber or a similar substance, used for removing pencil marks from paper; a piece of soft material used for removing CHALK marks from a BLACKBOARD or ink from a WHITEBOARD ➡ **picture at STATIONERY**

e·ra·sure /ɪˈreɪʃər/ *noun* [U] (*formal*) the act of removing or destroying something: *the accidental erasure of important computer files*

er·bi·um /ˈɜrbiəm/ *noun* [U] (*symb.* **Er**) a chemical element. Erbium is a soft silver-white metal.

ere /ɛr/ *conj., prep.* (*old use* or *literary*) before: *Ere long* (= soon) *they returned.*

e·rect /ɪˈrɛkt/ *adj., verb*
- *adj.* **1** (*formal*) in a vertical position: *Stand with your arms by your side and your head erect.* **2** (of the PENIS or NIPPLES) stiff and larger than usual because of sexual excitement
- *verb* (*formal*) **1** ~ **sth** to build something: *The church was erected in 1582.* ➡ thesaurus box at **BUILD 2** ~ **sth** to put something in position and make it stand vertical **SYN** PUT: *Police had to erect barriers to keep crowds back.* ◆ *to erect a tent* ➡ **note at BUILD 3** ~ **sth** to create or establish something: *to erect trade barriers*

e·rec·tile /ɪˈrɛktaɪl; -tl/ *adj.* (*biology*) (of a part of the body) able to become stiff: *erectile tissue*

e·rec·tion /ɪˈrɛkʃn/ *noun* **1** [C] if a man has an **erection**, his PENIS is stiff because he is sexually excited: *to **get/have an erection*** **2** [U] (*formal*) the act of building something or putting it in a vertical position: *the erection of scaffolding around the building* **3** [C] (*formal*) a structure or building, especially a large one

erg /ɜrg/ *noun* a unit of work or energy

er·ga·tive /ˈɜrɡətɪv/ *adj.* (*grammar*) (of verbs) able to be used in both a TRANSITIVE and an INTRANSITIVE way with the same meaning, where the object of the transitive verb is the same as the subject of the intransitive verb: *The verb "grow" is ergative because you can say "She grew flowers in her garden" or "Flowers grew in her garden."* ➡ compare **CAUSATIVE, INCHOATIVE** ▶ **er·ga·tive·ly** *adv.*

er·go /ˈɜrɡoʊ; ˈɛrɡoʊ/ *adv.* (from *Latin, formal* or *humorous*) therefore

er·go·nom·ic /ˌɜrɡəˈnɑmɪk/ *adj.* designed to improve people's working conditions and to help them work more efficiently: *ergonomic design* ▶ **er·go·nom·i·cally** /-kli/ *adv.*: *The layout is hard to fault ergonomically.*

er·go·nom·ics /ˌɜrɡəˈnɑmɪks/ *noun* [U] the study of working conditions, especially the design of equipment and furniture, in order to help people work more efficiently

er·mine /ˈɜrmən/ *noun* [U] the white winter fur of the STOAT, used especially to decorate the formal clothes of judges, kings, etc.

e·rode **AWL** /ɪˈroʊd/ *verb* [often passive] **1** [T, I] to gradually destroy the surface of something through the action of wind, rain, etc.; to be gradually destroyed in this way **SYN** WEAR AWAY: ~ **sth (away)** *The cliff face has been steadily eroded by the ocean.* ◆ ~ **(away)** *The rocks have eroded away over time.* **2** [T, I] ~ **(sth)** to gradually destroy something or make it weaker over a period of time; to be destroyed or made weaker in this way: *Her confidence has been slowly eroded by repeated failures.* ◆ *Mortgage payments have been eroded* (= decreased in value) *by inflation.*

e·rog·e·nous zone /ɪˈrɑdʒənəs ˌzoʊn/ *noun* an area of the body that gives sexual pleasure when it is touched

E·ros /ˈɛrɑs; ˈɛroʊs; ˈɪr-/ *noun* [U] (*formal*) sexual love or desire

e·ro·sion /ɪˈroʊʒn/ *noun* [U] **1** the process by which the surface of something is gradually destroyed through the action of wind, rain, etc.: *the erosion of the coastline by the ocean* ◆ *soil erosion* **2** the process of gradually destroying something or making it weaker over a period of time: *the erosion of her confidence*

e·rot·ic /ɪˈrɑtɪk/ *adj.* showing or involving sexual desire and pleasure; intended to make someone feel sexual desire: *erotic art* ◆ *an erotic fantasy* ▶ **e·rot·i·cally** /-kli/ *adv.*

e·rot·i·ca /ɪˈrɑtɪkə/ *noun* [U] books, pictures, etc. that are intended to make someone feel sexual desire

e·rot·i·cism /ɪˈrɑtəˌsɪzəm/ *noun* [U] the fact of expressing or describing sexual feelings and desire, especially in art, literature, etc.

err /ɛr; ər/ *verb* [I] (*old-fashioned, formal*) to make a mistake: *To err is human…*
IDM **err on the side of sth** to show too much of a good quality: *I thought it was better **to err on the side of caution*** (= to be too careful rather than take a risk).

er·rand /ˈɛrənd/ *noun* a job that you do, often for someone else, that involves going somewhere to buy something, deliver goods, etc.: *He often **runs errands** for his grandmother.* ◆ *Her boss sent her **on an errand** into town.* ➡ see also **FOOL'S ERRAND**

er·rant /ˈɛrənt/ *adj.* [only before noun] (*formal* or *humorous*) **1** doing something that is wrong; not behaving in an acceptable way **2** (of a husband or wife) not sexually faithful

er·rat·ic /ɪˈrætɪk/ *adj., noun*
- *adj.* (often *disapproving*) not happening at regular times; not following any plan or regular pattern; that you cannot rely on **SYN** UNPREDICTABLE: *The electricity supply here is quite erratic.* ◆ *She had learned to live with his sudden changes of mood and erratic behavior.* ◆ *Mary is a gifted but erratic player* (= she does not always play well). ▶ **er·rat·i·cally** /-kli/ *adv.*: *He was obviously upset and was driving erratically.*
- *noun* (also **er·ratic ˈblock, er·ratic ˈboulder**) (*geology*) a large rock that is different from the rock around and was left behind when a large mass of ice melted

er·ra·tum /ɛˈrɑtəm/ *noun* (*pl.* **er·ra·ta** /-tə/) [usually pl.] (*technical*) a mistake in a book (shown in a list at the back or front)

er·ro·ne·ous **AWL** /ɪˈroʊniəs/ *adj.* (*formal*) not correct; based on wrong information: *erroneous conclusions/assumptions* ▶ **er·ro·ne·ous·ly** **AWL** *adv.*

er·ror 🔑 **AWL** /ˈɛrər/ *noun* [C, U] a mistake, especially one that causes problems or affects the result of something: *No payments were made last week because of a computer error.* ◆ ~ **in sth** *There are too many errors in your work.* ◆ ~ **in doing sth** *I think you have made an error in calculating the total.* ◆ *A simple **error of judgment** meant that there was not enough food to go around.* ◆ *a **grave error*** (= a very serious mistake) ◆ *a **glaring error*** (= a mistake that is very obvious) ◆ *The delay was due to **human error*** (= a mistake made by a person rather than by a machine). ◆ *The computer system was turned off **in error*** (= by mistake). ◆ *There is no **room for error** in this job.* ➡ see also **MARGIN OF ERROR** ➡ thesaurus box at **MISTAKE**
IDM **see, realize, etc. the error of your ways** (*formal* or *humorous*) to realize or admit that you have done something wrong and decide to change your behavior ➡ more at **TRIAL**

ˈerror ˌmessage *noun* (*computing*) a message that appears on a computer screen that tells you that you have done something wrong or that the program cannot do what you want it to do

er·satz /ˈɛrzɑts; -sɑts/ *adj.* artificial and not as good as the real thing or product: *ersatz coffee*

erst·while /ˈɜrstwaɪl/ *adj.* [only before noun] (*formal*) former; that until recently was the type of person or thing described but is not anymore: *an erstwhile opponent* ◆ *His erstwhile friends turned against him.*

er·u·dite /ˈɛrjəˌdaɪt; ˈɛrə-/ adj. (formal) having or showing great knowledge that is gained from academic study **SYN** LEARNED

er·u·di·tion /ˌɛrjəˈdɪʃn; ˌɛrə-/ noun [U] (formal) great academic knowledge

e·rupt /ɪˈrʌpt/ verb **1** [I, T] when a VOLCANO **erupts** or burning rocks, smoke, etc. **erupt** or **are erupted**, the burning rocks, etc. are thrown out from the volcano: *The volcano could erupt at any time.* ◆ ~ **from sth** *Ash began to erupt from the crater.* ◆ ~ **sth** *An immense volume of rocks and molten lava was erupted.* ⊃ thesaurus box at EXPLODE **2** [I] to start happening, suddenly and violently **SYN** BREAK OUT: *Violence erupted outside the embassy gates.* ◆ ~ **into sth** *The unrest erupted into revolution.* **3** [I, T] to suddenly express your feelings very strongly, especially by shouting loudly: *When Davis scored for the third time the crowd erupted.* ◆ ~ **in /into sth** *My father just erupted into fury.* ◆ + **speech** *"How dare you?" she erupted.* **4** [I] (of spots, etc.) to suddenly appear on your skin: *A rash had erupted all over his chest.* ▶ **e·rup·tion** /ɪˈrʌpʃn/ noun [C, U]: *a major volcanic eruption* ◆ *an eruption of violent protest* ◆ *skin rashes and eruptions*

e·rup·tive /ɪˈrʌptɪv/ adj. relating to or produced by the eruption of a VOLCANO

-ery /əri/, **-ry** suffix (in nouns) **1** the group or class of: *greenery* ◆ *gadgetry* **2** the state or character of: *bravery* ◆ *rivalry* **3** the art or practice of: *cookery* ◆ *archery* **4** a place where something is made, grows, lives, etc.: *bakery* ◆ *orangery*

e·ryth·ro·cyte /ɪˈrɪθrəˌsaɪt/ noun (biology) = RED BLOOD CELL

es·ca·late /ˈɛskəˌleɪt/ verb [I, T] to become or make something greater, worse, more serious, etc.: ~ **(into sth)** *The fighting escalated into a full-scale war.* ◆ *the escalating costs of health care* ◆ ~ **sth (into sth)** *We do not want to escalate the war.* ▶ **es·ca·la·tion** /ˌɛskəˈleɪʃn/ noun [C, U]: *an escalation in food prices* ◆ *further escalation of the conflict*

es·ca·la·tor /ˈɛskəˌleɪtər/ noun moving stairs that carry people between different floors of a large building

es·ca·pade /ˈɛskəˌpeɪd/ noun an exciting adventure (often one that people think is dangerous or stupid): *Isabel's latest romantic escapade*

es·cape 🔑 /ɪˈskeɪp/ verb, noun
● **verb 1** [I] to get away from a place where you have been kept as a prisoner or not allowed to leave: *Two prisoners have escaped.* ◆ ~ **from sb/sth** *He escaped from prison this morning.* **2** [I, T] to get away from an unpleasant or dangerous situation: ~ **(from sth)** *She managed to escape from the burning car.* ◆ ~ **(into sth)** (figurative) *As a child, he would often escape into a dream world of his own.* ◆ ~ **sth** *They were glad to have escaped the clutches of winter for another year.* **3** [T, no passive] to avoid something unpleasant or dangerous: ~ **sth** *She was lucky to escape punishment.* ◆ *The pilot escaped death by seconds.* ◆ *There was no escaping the fact that he was overweight.* ◆ ~ **doing sth** *He narrowly escaped being killed.* **4** [I] to suffer no harm or less harm than you would expect: ~ **(with sth)** *I was lucky to escape with minor injuries.* ◆ + **adj.** *Both drivers escaped unhurt.* **5** [T, no passive] ~ **sb/sth** to be forgotten or not noticed: *Her name escapes me* (= I can't remember it). ◆ *It might have escaped your notice, but I'm very busy at the moment.* **6** [I] (of gases, liquids, etc.) to get out of a container, especially through a hole or crack: *Put a lid on to prevent heat from escaping.* ◆ *toxic waste escaping into the ocean* **7** [T, I] ~ **(sth)** (of a sound) to come out from your mouth without your intending it to: *A groan escaped her lips.*
● **noun 1** [C, U] ~ **(from sth)** the act or a method of escaping from a place or an unpleasant or dangerous situation: *an escape from a prisoner of war camp* ◆ *I had a narrow escape* (= I was lucky to have escaped). ◆ *There was no hope of escape from her disastrous marriage.* ◆ *He took an elaborate escape route from South Africa to Britain.* ◆ *As soon as he turned his back, she would make her escape.* ⊃ see also FIRE ESCAPE **2** [sing., U] a way of forgetting something unpleasant or difficult for a short time: *For her, travel was an escape from the boredom of*

her everyday life. **3** [C] the fact of a liquid, gas, etc. coming out of a pipe or container by accident; the amount that comes out: *an escape of gas* **4** [U] (also **es'cape key** [C]) (computing) a button on a computer keyboard that you press to stop a particular operation or leave a program: *Press escape to get back to the menu.*
IDM **make good your escape** (formal) to manage to escape completely ⊃ more at BARN

es'cape clause noun a part of a contract that states the conditions under which the contract may be broken

es'caped /ɪˈskeɪpt/ adj. [only before noun] having escaped from a place: *an escaped prisoner/lion*

es·cap·ee /ɪˌskeɪˈpi; ˌɛskeɪˈpi/ noun (formal) a person or an animal that has escaped from somewhere, especially someone who has escaped from prison

es'cape key noun = ESCAPE n. (4)

es·cap·ism /ɪˈskeɪpɪzəm/ noun [U] an activity, a form of entertainment, etc. that helps you avoid or forget unpleasant or boring things: *the pure escapism of adventure movies* ◆ *For John, books are a form of escapism.* ▶ **es·cap·ist** /-pɪst/ adj.

es·cap·ol·o·gist /ˌɛskeɪˈpɑlədʒɪst; ˌɪˌskeɪ-/ noun a performer who escapes from ropes, chains, boxes, etc.

es·ca·role /ˈɛskəˌroʊl/ noun [C, U] a type of LETTUCE with a slightly bitter flavor

es·carp·ment /ɪˈskɑrpmənt/ noun a steep slope that separates an area of high ground from an area of lower ground

ES cell /ˌi ˈɛs sɛl/ noun (biology) the abbreviation for "embryonic stem cell" (a STEM CELL taken from an EMBRYO soon after it is formed)

es·cha·tol·o·gy /ˌɛskəˈtɑlədʒi/ noun [U] (religion) the part of THEOLOGY concerned with death and judgment ▶ **es·cha·to·log·i·cal** /ɛˌskætlˈɑdʒɪkl/ adj.

es·chew /ɪsˈtʃu/ verb ~ **sth** (formal) to deliberately avoid or keep away from something

es·cort noun, verb
● **noun** /ˈɛskɔrt/ **1** [C, U] a person or group of people or vehicles that travels with someone or something in order to protect or guard them: *Armed escorts are provided for visiting heads of state.* ◆ *Prisoners are taken to court under police escort.* **2** [C] (formal or old-fashioned) a person, especially a man, who takes someone to a particular social event **3** [C] a person, especially a woman, who is paid to go out socially with someone: *an escort service/agency*
● **verb** /ɪˈskɔrt/ ~ **sb** (+ adv./prep.) to go with someone to protect or guard them or to show them the way: *The president was escorted by twelve soldiers.* ⊃ thesaurus box at TAKE

es·cu·do /ɛˈskudoʊ/ noun (pl. **es·cu·dos**) the unit of money in Cape Verde, and formerly in Portugal (replaced in 2002 by the EURO)

es·cutch·eon /ɪˈskʌtʃən/ noun **1** a SHIELD that has a COAT OF ARMS on it **2** a flat piece of metal around a KEYHOLE, door handle, or light switch

-ese /iz; is/ suffix **1** (in adjectives and nouns) of a country or city; a person who lives in a country or city; the language spoken there: *Chinese* ◆ *Viennese* **2** (in nouns) (often disapproving) the style or language of: *journalese* ◆ *officialese* ◆ *legalese*

es·ker /ˈɛskər/ noun (geology) a long narrow area of small stones and earth that has been left by a large mass of ice that has melted

Es·ki·mo /ˈɛskəmoʊ/ noun (pl. **Es·ki·mo** or **Es·ki·mos**) (sometimes offensive) a member of a race of people from parts of Alaska, northern Canada, Greenland, and Siberia. Some of these people prefer to use the name Inuit. ⊃ compare INUIT

ESL /ˌi ɛs ˈɛl/ abbr. English as a second language (refers to the teaching of English as a foreign language to people who are living in a country in which English is either the first or second language)

e·soph·a·gus /ɪˈsɑfəgəs/ *noun* (*pl.* **e·soph·a·gi** /-ˌgaɪ; -ˌdʒaɪ/ or **e·soph·a·gus·es**) (*anatomy*) the tube through which food passes from the mouth to the stomach **SYN** GULLET ➔ picture at BODY

es·o·ter·ic /ˌɛsəˈtɛrɪk/ *adj.* (*formal*) likely to be understood or enjoyed by only a few people with a special knowledge or interest

ESP /ˌi ɛs ˈpi/ *abbr.* **1** extrasensory perception (the ability to know things without using the senses of sight, hearing, etc., for example to know what people are thinking or what will happen in the future) **2** English for specific/special purposes (the teaching of English for scientific, technical, etc. purposes to people whose first language is not English)

esp. *abbr.* (in writing) especially

es·pa·drille /ˈɛspəˌdrɪl/ *noun* a light shoe made of strong cloth with a SOLE made of rope

es·pal·ier /ɪˈspælyɚ; -yɚ/ *noun* **1** a tree or SHRUB that is grown flat along a wooden or wire frame on a wall **2** the frame that such a tree grows along

es·pe·cial /ɪˈspɛʃl/ *adj.* [only before noun] (*formal*) greater or better than usual; special in some way or for a particular group: *a matter of especial importance* ◆ *The lecture will be of especial interest to history students.* ➔ compare SPECIAL

es·pe·cial·ly 🔊 /ɪˈspɛʃəli; ɪˈspɛʃli/ *adv.* (*abbr.* **esp.**) **1** more with one person, thing, etc. than with others, or more in particular circumstances than in others **SYN** PARTICULARLY: *The car feels really small, especially if you have children.* ◆ *Teenagers are very fashion conscious, especially girls.* ◆ *I love Rome, especially in the spring.* ➔ language bank at EMPHASIS **2** for a particular purpose, person, etc.: *I made it especially for you.* **3** very much; to a particular degree: *I wasn't feeling especially happy that day.* ◆ *"Do you like his novels?" "Not especially."*

WHICH WORD?

especially ◆ specially

- Especially usually means "particularly": *She loves all sports, especially swimming.* It is not placed first in a sentence: *I especially like sweet things.* ◆ ~~Especially I like sweet things.~~

- Specially usually means "for a particular purpose" and is often followed by a past participle, such as *designed*, *developed*, or *made*: *a course specially designed to meet your needs* ◆ *She has her clothes specially made in New York.*

- In informal spoken English, especially and specially are often used in the same way and it can be hard to hear the difference when people speak: *I bought this especially/specially for you.* ◆ *It is especially/specially important to remember this.*

- The adjective for both especially and specially is usually special.

Es·pe·ran·to /ˌɛspəˈrɑntoʊ/ *noun* [U] an artificial language invented in 1887 as a means of international communication, based on the main European languages but with easy grammar and pronunciation

es·pi·o·nage /ˈɛspiəˌnɑʒ; -ˌnɑdʒ/ *noun* [U] the activity of secretly getting important political or military information about another country or of finding out another company's secrets by using SPIES **SYN** SPYING: *Some of the commercial activities were a cover for espionage.* ◆ *She may call it research; I call it industrial espionage.* ➔ see also COUNTER-ESPIONAGE

es·pla·nade /ˈɛspləˌnɑd; -ˌneɪd/ *noun* a level area of open ground in a town for people to walk along, often by the ocean or a river

es·pouse /ɪˈspaʊz; ɪˈspaʊs/ *verb* ~ sth (*formal*) to give your support to a belief, policy, etc.: *They espoused the notion of equal opportunity for all in education.* ▶ **es·pous·al** /ɪˈspaʊzl; -sl/ *noun* [U, sing.]: *~ of sth his recent espousal of populism*

---

es·pres·so /ɛˈsprɛsoʊ/ *noun* (*pl.* **es·pres·sos**) **1** [U] strong black coffee made by forcing steam or boiling water through ground coffee **2** [C] a cup of espresso

es·prit de corps /ɛˌspri də ˈkɔr/ *noun* [U] (from *French*) feelings of pride, care, and support for each other, etc. that are shared by the members of a group

es·py /ɛˈspaɪ/ *verb* (**es·pies, es·py·ing, es·pied, es·pied**) ~ sb/sth (*literary*) to see someone or something suddenly **SYN** CATCH SIGHT OF, SPY

Esq. /ˈɛskwaɪɚ/ *abbr.* **1** used as a title after the name of a male or female lawyer **2** (*old-fashioned*) Esquire (a polite title written after a man's name, especially on an official letter addressed to him. If Esq. is used, Mr. is not then used): *Edward Smith, Esq.*

-esque /ɛsk/ *suffix* (in adjectives) in the style of: *statuesque* ◆ *Kafkaesque*

-ess /əs; ɛs/ *suffix* (in nouns) female: *lioness* ◆ *actress*

es·say 🔊 *noun, verb*

● *noun* /ˈɛseɪ/ **1** ~ (on sth) a short piece of writing by a student as part of a course of study: *an essay on the causes of the First World War* **2** ~ (on sth) a short piece of writing on a particular subject, written in order to be published **3** ~ (in sth) (*formal*) an attempt to do something: *His first essay in politics was a complete disaster.*

● *verb* /ɛˈseɪ/ ~ sth (*literary*) to try to do something

es·say·ist /ˈɛseɪɪst/ *noun* a person who writes essays to be published

es·sence /ˈɛsns/ *noun* **1** [U] ~ (of sth) the most important quality or feature of something, that makes it what it is: *His paintings capture the essence of France.* ◆ *In essence* (= when you consider the most important points), *your situation isn't so different from mine.* **2** [U, C] a liquid taken from a plant, etc. that contains its smell and taste in a very strong form: *essence of rosewood* ➔ see also EXTRACT

 IDM **of the essence** necessary and very important: *In this situation time is of the essence* (= we must do things as quickly as possible).

es·sen·tial 🔊 /ɪˈsɛnʃl/ *adj., noun*

● *adj.* **1** completely necessary; extremely important in a particular situation or for a particular activity **SYN** VITAL: *an essential part/ingredient/component of something* ◆ *essential services such as gas, water, and electricity* ◆ *Even in small companies, computers are an essential tool.* ◆ ~ to sth *Money is not essential to happiness.* ◆ ~ for sth *Experience is essential for this job.* ◆ it is essential to do sth *It is essential to keep the two groups separate.* ◆ it is essential that… *It is essential that you have some experience.* ➔ compare INESSENTIAL, NONESSENTIAL **ANT** DISPENSABLE ➔ language bank at EMPHASIS, VITAL **2** [only before noun] connected with the most important aspect or basic nature of someone or something **SYN** FUNDAMENTAL: *The essential difference between Sara and me is in our attitude to money.* ◆ *The essential character of the town has been destroyed by the new road.*

● *noun* [usually pl.] **1** something that is needed in a particular situation or in order to do a particular thing: *I only had time to pack the bare essentials* (= the most necessary things). ◆ *The studio had all the essentials like heating and running water.* **2** an important basic fact or piece of knowledge about a subject: *the essentials of English grammar*

THESAURUS

essential

vital ◆ crucial ◆ critical ◆ decisive ◆ indispensable

These words all describe someone or something that is extremely important and completely necessary because a particular situation or activity depends on them.

essential extremely important and completely necessary, because without it something cannot exist, be made, or be successful: *Experience is essential for this job.*

vital essential: *The police play a vital role in our society.*

---

h hat   m man   n no   ŋ sing   l leg   r red   y yes   w wet

ESSENTIAL OR VITAL?

These words have the same meaning but there can be a slight difference in tone. **Essential** is used to state a fact or an opinion with authority. **Vital** is often used when there is some anxiety felt about something, or a need to persuade someone that a fact or an opinion is true, right, or important. **Vital** is less often used in negative statements: *It was vital to show that he was not afraid.* ◆ *Money is not vital to happiness.*

crucial extremely important because a particular situation or activity depends on it: *It is crucial that we get this right.*

critical extremely important because a particular situation or activity depends on it: *Your decision is critical to our future.*

CRUCIAL OR CRITICAL?

These words have the same meaning but there can be a slight difference in context. **Critical** is often used in technical matters of business or science; **crucial** is often used to talk about matters that may cause anxiety or other emotions.

decisive of the greatest importance in affecting the final result of a particular situation: *She played a decisive role in the peace negotiations.*

indispensable essential; too important to be without: *This database has become an indispensable resource in our research.*

PATTERNS

- essential/vital/crucial/critical/decisive/indispensable **for** sth
- essential/vital/crucial/critical/indispensable **to** sth
- essential/vital/crucial/critical **that**...
- essential/vital/crucial/critical **to do** sth
- a(n) essential/vital/crucial/critical/decisive/indispensable **part/role/factor**
- of vital/crucial/critical/decisive **importance**
- **absolutely** essential/vital/crucial/critical/decisive/indispensable

es·sen·tial·ly 🔑 /ɪˈsɛnʃəli/ *adv.*
when you think about the true, important, or basic nature of someone or something **SYN** BASICALLY, FUNDAMEN-TALLY: *There are three **essentially** different ways of tackling the problem.* ◆ *The pattern is **essentially the same** in all cases.* ◆ *Essentially, what we are suggesting is that the organization needs to change.* ◆ *He was, essentially, a teacher, not a manager.* ◆ *The article was essentially concerned with her relationship with her parents* (= it dealt with other things, but this was the most important).

es,sential ¦oil *noun* an oil taken from a plant, used because of its strong smell for making PERFUME and in AROMATHERAPY

-est /əst/ *suffix* (makes superlative adjectives and adverbs): *widest* ◆ *biggest* ◆ *happiest* ◆ *soonest* ⊃ compare -ER

es·tab·lish 🔑 **AWL** /ɪˈstæblɪʃ/ *verb*
1 ~ sth to start or create an organization, a system, a place, etc. that is meant to last for a long time **SYN** SET UP: *The committee was established in 1912.* ◆ *The new treaty establishes a free trade zone.* ◆ *to establish a park/forest/nature preserve* ⊃ thesaurus box at BUILD **2** ~ sth to start having a relationship, especially a formal one, with another person, group, or country: *The school has established a successful relationship with the local community.* **3** ~ sb/sth/yourself **(in sth) (as sth)** to hold a position for long enough to succeed in something well enough to make people accept and respect you: *By then she was established as a star.* ◆ *He has just set up his own business but it will take him a while to get*

established. **4** ~ sth to make people accept a belief, claim, custom, etc.: *It was this campaign that established the paper's reputation.* ◆ *Traditions get established over time.* **5** to discover or prove the facts of a situation **SYN** ASCERTAIN: ~ sth *Police are still trying to establish the cause of the accident.* ◆ ~ that... *They have established that his injuries were caused by a fall.* ◆ ~ where, what, etc.... *We need to establish where she was at the time of the shooting.* ◆ it is established that... *It has since been established that the horse was drugged.*

es·tab·lished **AWL** /ɪˈstæblɪʃt/ *adj.* [only before noun]
1 respected or given official status because it has existed or been used for a long time: *They are an established company with a good reputation.* ◆ *This unit is now an established part of the course.* ⊃ see also WELL ESTABLISHED **2** (of a person) well known and respected in a job, etc. that they have been doing for a long time: *an established actor* **3** (of a Church or a religion) made official for a country

es·tab·lish·ment **AWL** /ɪˈstæblɪʃmənt/ *noun* **1** [C] (*formal*) an organization, a large institution, or a hotel: *an educational establishment* ◆ *a research establishment* ◆ *The hotel is a comfortable and well-run establishment.* **2** usually **the Es-tablishment** [sing.] (often *disapproving*) the people in a society or a profession who have influence and power and who usually do not support change: *the medical/military/political, etc. establishment* ◆ *young people rebelling against the Establishment* **3** [U] the act of starting or creating something that is meant to last for a long time: *The speaker announced the establishment of a new college.* ◆ *the establishment of diplomatic relations between the countries*

es·tate 🔑 **AWL** /ɪˈsteɪt/ *noun*
1 (*law*) [C, U] all the money and property that a person owns, especially everything that is left when they die: *Her estate was left to her daughter.* **2** [C] a large area of land, usually in the country, that is owned by one person or family

es'tate sale *noun* a sale of someone's possessions, usually after they have died

es'tate tax *noun* [U] tax that must be paid on the money or property of sb who dies ⊃ compare INHERITANCE TAX

es·teem /ɪˈstim/ *noun, verb*
● *noun* [U] (*formal*) great respect and admiration; a good opinion of someone: *She is held in high esteem by her colleagues.* ◆ *Please accept this small gift as a token of our esteem.* ⊃ see also SELF-ESTEEM
● *verb* (*formal*) (not used in the progressive tenses) **1** [usually passive] ~ sb/sth to respect and admire someone or something very much: *a highly esteemed scientist* **2** ~ sb/sth + *noun* (*old-fashioned, formal*) to think of someone or something in a particular way: *She was esteemed the perfect novelist.*

es·ter /ˈɛstər/ *noun* (*chemistry*) a sweet-smelling substance that is formed from an ORGANIC acid and an alcohol

es·thete, es·thet·ic = AESTHETE, AESTHETIC

es·ti·ma·ble /ˈɛstɪməbl/ *adj.* (*old-fashioned* or *formal*) deserving respect and admiration

es·ti·mate 🔑 **AWL** *noun, verb*
● *noun* /ˈɛstəmət/ **1** a judgment that you make without having the exact details or figures about the size, amount, cost, etc. of something: *I can give you a rough estimate of the amount of wood you will need.* ◆ *a ballpark estimate* (= an approximate estimate) ◆ *official government estimates of traffic growth over the next decade* ◆ *At least 5,000 people were killed, and that's a conservative estimate* (= the real figure will be higher). **2** a statement of how much a piece of work will probably cost
● *verb* /ˈɛstəˌmeɪt/ [often passive] to form an idea of the cost, size, value, etc. of something, but without calculating it exactly: ~ sth (at sth) *Police estimate the crowd at 30,000.* ◆ ~ sth to do sth *The deal is estimated to be worth around $1.5 million.* ◆ ~ (that)... *We estimated (that) it would cost about $5,000.* ◆ it is estimated (that)... *It is estimated (that) the*

project will last four years. ◆ ~ **how many, large, etc.**... *It is hard to estimate how many children have dyslexia.*
▶ **es·ti·ma·ted** **AWL** *adj.*: *The satellite will cost an estimated $400 million.*

estimate

estimate *verb*
■ accurately, correctly, reliably | conservatively | roughly | empirically, quantitatively | separately
These models were estimated separately for the 2000, 2004, and 2007 data sets.
■ difficult to | possible to | impossible to
Population figures are difficult to estimate, with figures ranging from 10 to 16 million.
■ distance, size | frequency, rate | likelihood, probability | abundance, prevalence | variance
Measuring risk means estimating the probability of an occurrence as a result of a specific event.

overestimate *verb*
■ greatly, grossly | consistently | systematically
Forecasters tended to systematically overestimate inflation.
■ tend to
People tend to overestimate their activity levels, so Wyatt asked participants in the study to wear pedometers.

underestimate *verb*
■ grossly | systematically | likely
These statistics grossly underestimate the number of unemployed.

estimated *adj.*
■ probability | percent | prevalence | variance | cost
Table 2 reports the estimated prevalence of work-related asthma.

estimate *noun*
■ accurate, precise, reliable | reasonable | unbiased | biased | conservative | rough
Sufficient information exists to support reasonable estimates of life expectancy.
■ calculate, compute | derive | obtain | revise
Estimates are calculated using the method of maximum likelihood.
■ be based on
Most available demographic estimates are based on one or two years of data.
■ differ, range, vary | indicate, suggest
Estimates of the number of species range between 3.6 million and 100 million.
■ according to
Bangladesh is approximately the size of Wisconsin, yet it has a population of more than 130 million, according to a 1996 estimate.

es·ti·ma·tion **AWL** /ˌɛstəˈmeɪʃn/ *noun* (*formal*) **1** [sing.] a judgment or an opinion about the value or quality of someone or something: *Who is the best candidate in your estimation?* ◆ *Since he left his wife he's certainly gone down in my estimation* (= I have less respect for him). ◆ *She went up in my estimation* (= I have more respect for her) *when I discovered how much charity work she does.* **2** [C] a judgment about the levels or quantity of something: *Estimations of our total world sales are around 50 million.*

es·tranged /ɪˈstreɪndʒd/ *adj.* (*formal*) **1** [usually before noun] no longer living with your husband or wife: *his estranged wife Emma* **2** ~ **(from sb)** no longer friendly, loyal, or in contact with someone: *He became estranged from his family after the argument.* **3** ~ **(from sth)** no longer involved in or connected with something, especially something that used

to be important to you: *She felt estranged from her former existence.*

es·trange·ment /ɪˈstreɪndʒmənt/ *noun* [U, C] the state of being estranged; a period of being estranged: ~ **(from sb/sth)** *a period of estrangement from his wife* ◆ ~ **(between A and B)** *The misunderstanding had caused a seven-year estrangement between them.*

es·tro·gen /ˈɛstrədʒən/ *noun* [U] a HORMONE produced in women's ovaries (OVARY) that causes them to develop the physical and sexual features that are characteristic of females, and that causes them to prepare their body to have babies ➲ compare PROGESTERONE, TESTOSTERONE

es·trus /ˈɛstrəs/ *noun* [U] (*technical*) a period of time in which a female animal is ready to have sex

es·tu·ar·y /ˈɛstʃuˌɛri/ (*pl.* es·tu·ar·ies) *noun* the wide part of a river where it flows into the ocean: *the Hudson River estuary*

ETA /ˌi ti ˈeɪ/ *abbr.* estimated time of arrival (the time at which an aircraft, a ship, etc. is expected to arrive) ➲ compare ETD

e·ta /ˈeɪtə/ *noun* the 7th letter of the Greek alphabet (H, η)

e-tail·ing /ˈiˌteɪlɪŋ/ *noun* [U] the business of selling goods to the public over the Internet: *E-tailing in the U.S. broke all records last year.* **ORIGIN** shortened form of **electronic retailing** ▶ **e-tail·er** *noun*: *America's leading e-tailers*

et al. /ˌɛt ˈɑl; -ˈæl/ *abbr.* (used especially after names) and other people or things (from Latin "et alii/alia"): *research by West et al., 1996*

etc. 🔑 /ˌɛt ˈsɛtərə; -ˈsɛtrə; ɪt-/ *abbr.*
used after a list to show that there are other things that you could have mentioned (the abbreviation for "et cetera"): *Remember to take some paper, a pen, etc.* ◆ *We talked about the contract, pay, etc.*

et cet·er·a /ˌɛt ˈsɛtərə; -ˈsɛtrə; ɪt-/ = ETC.

etch /ɛtʃ/ *verb* **1** to cut lines into a piece of glass, metal, etc. in order to make words or a picture: ~ **A (in/into/on B)** *a glass tankard with his initials etched on it* ◆ ~ **B (with A)** *a glass tankard etched with his initials* **2** [usually passive] (*literary*) if a feeling is etched on someone's face, or someone's face is etched with a feeling, that feeling can be seen very clearly: ~ **A in/into/on B** *Tiredness was etched on his face.* ◆ ~ **B with A** *His face was etched with tiredness.* **3** [usually passive] ~ **sth** (+ *adv./prep.*) to make a strong clear mark or pattern on something: *a mountain etched* (= having a clear outline) *against the sky*
IDM **be etched on your heart/memory/mind** if something is etched on your memory, you remember it because it has made a strong impression on you

etch·ing /ˈɛtʃɪŋ/ *noun* [C, U] a picture that is printed from an etched piece of metal; the art of making these pictures

ETD /ˌi ti ˈdi/ *abbr.* estimated time of departure (the time at which an aircraft, a ship, etc. is expected to leave) ➲ compare ETA

e·ter·nal /ɪˈtɜrnl/ *adj.* **1** without an end; existing or continuing forever: *the promise of eternal life in heaven* ◆ *She's an eternal optimist* (= she always expects that the best will happen). ◆ *eternal truths* (= ideas that are always true and never change) **2** [only before noun] (*disapproving*) happening often and seeming never to stop **SYN** CONSTANT: *I'm tired of your eternal arguments.* ▶ **e·ter·nal·ly** /-nəli/ *adv.*: *I'll be eternally grateful to you for this.* ◆ *women trying to look eternally young* **IDM** see HOPE *n.*

e·ternal 'triangle *noun* a situation where two people are in love with or having a sexual relationship with the same person

e·ternal 'verity *noun* [usually pl.] (*formal*) an essential, basic, moral principle

e·ter·ni·ty /ɪˈtɜrnəti/ *noun* **1** [U] (*formal*) time without end, especially life continuing without end after death: *There will be rich and poor for all eternity.* ◆ *They believed that their souls would be condemned to burn in hell for eternity.* **2** an eternity [sing.] (*informal*) a period of time that seems to be very long or to never end: *After what seemed like an eternity, the nurse returned with the results of the test.*

eth /εð/ noun (*phonetics*) the letter ð that was used in Old English to represent the sounds /θ/ and /ð/, and later written as *th*. This letter is now used as a PHONETIC symbol for the sound /ð/, as in *this*.

eth·ane /'εθeɪn/ noun [U] (*symb.* C_2H_6) (*chemistry*) a gas that has no color or smell and that can burn. Ethane is found in natural gas and mineral oil.

eth·a·nol /'εθə,nɔl; -,nɑl/ (also ,ethyl 'alcohol) noun [U] (*chemistry*) the type of alcohol in alcoholic drinks, also used as a fuel or SOLVENT

eth·ene /'εθin/ noun [U] = ETHYLENE

e·ther /'iθər/ noun [U] **1** a clear liquid made from alcohol, used in industry as a SOLVENT and, in the past, in medicine to make people unconscious before an operation **2 the ether** (*old use* or *literary*) the upper part of the sky: *Her words disappeared into the ether.* **3 the ether** the air, when it is thought of as the place in which radio or electronic communication takes place

e·the·re·al /ɪ'θɪriəl/ adj. (*formal*) extremely delicate and light; seeming to belong to another, more spiritual, world: *ethereal music* ♦ *her ethereal beauty*

E·ther·net /'iθər,nεt/ noun [sing.] (*computing*) a system for connecting a number of computer systems to form a network

eth·ic AWL /'εθɪk/ noun **1** ethics [pl.] moral principles that control or influence a person's behavior: *professional/business/medical ethics* ♦ *to draw up a code of ethics* ♦ *He began to question the ethics of his position.* **2** [sing.] a system of moral principles or rules of behavior: *a strongly defined work ethic* ♦ *the Protestant ethic* **3** ethics [U] the branch of philosophy that deals with moral principles

eth·i·cal AWL /'εθɪkl/ adj. **1** connected with beliefs and principles about what is right and wrong: *ethical issues/standards/questions* ♦ *the ethical problems of human embryo research* **2** morally correct or acceptable: *Is it ethical to promote cigarettes through advertising?* ♦ *ethical investment* (= investing money in businesses that are considered morally acceptable) ▸ **eth·i·cal·ly** AWL /-kli/ adv.: *The committee judged that he had not behaved ethically.*

eth·nic 🔑 AWL /'εθnɪk/ adj., noun
● **adj.** **1** connected with or belonging to a nation, race, or people that shares a cultural tradition: *ethnic groups/communities* ♦ *ethnic strife/tensions/violence* (= between people from different races or peoples) ♦ *ethnic Albanians living in Germany* **2** typical of a country or culture that is very different from modern Western culture and therefore interesting for people in Western countries: *ethnic clothes/jewelry/cooking* ▸ **eth·ni·cally** /-kli/ adv.: *an ethnically divided region*
● **noun** a person from an ETHNIC MINORITY

ethnic 'cleansing noun [U] (used especially in news reports) the policy of forcing the people of a particular race or religion to leave an area or a country, or killing them ⊃ collocations at WAR

eth·nic·i·ty AWL /εθ'nɪsəti/ noun (*pl.* eth·nic·i·ties) (*technical*) **1** [U] the fact of belonging to a particular race or culture: *Many factors are important, for example class, gender, age, and ethnicity.* **2** [C, usually pl.] (*formal*) a group of people with a common cultural or national tradition: *We're trying to recruit people of different races and ethnicities.*

ethnic mi'nority noun a group of people from a particular culture or of a particular race living in a country where the main group is of a different culture or race

eth·no·cen·tric /,εθnoʊ'sεntrɪk/ adj. based on the ideas and beliefs of one particular culture and using these to judge other cultures: *a white, ethnocentric school curriculum* ▸ **eth·no·cen·trism** /-'sεntrɪzəm/ noun [U]

eth·nog·ra·pher /εθ'nɑgrəfər/ noun a person who studies different races and cultures

eth·nog·ra·phy /εθ'nɑgrəfi/ noun [U] the scientific description of different races and cultures ▸ **eth·no·graph·ic** /,εθnə'græfɪk/ adj.: *ethnographic research*

eth·nol·o·gy /εθ'nɑlədʒi/ noun [U] the scientific study and comparison of human races ▸ **eth·no·log·i·cal** /,εθnə'lɑdʒɪkl/ adj. **eth·nol·o·gist** /εθ'nɑlədʒɪst/ noun

e·thos /'iθɑs; 'iθoʊs/ noun [sing.] (*formal*) the moral ideas and attitudes that belong to a particular group or society: *an ethos of public service*

eth·yl /'εθl/ adj. [only before noun] (*chemistry*) containing the group of atoms C_2H_5, formed from ETHANE: *ethyl acetate*

,**ethyl 'alcohol** noun [U] (*chemistry*) = ETHANOL

eth·yl·ene /'εθə,lin/ (also eth·ene) noun [U] (*symb.* C_2H_4) (*chemistry*) a gas that is present in coal, CRUDE OIL, and NATURAL GAS

eth·yne /'εθaɪn/ noun [U] (*symb.* C_2H_2) the chemical name for ACETYLENE

'**e-,ticket** (also 'E-,ticket) noun a ticket, for example a plane ticket, that you buy over the Internet and receive by e-mail. Your purchase details are stored on a computer so you do not need a paper ticket.

e·ti·o·lat·ed /'itiə,leɪtəd/ adj. **1** (*biology*) if a plant is etiolated, it is pale because it does not receive enough light **2** (*formal*) lacking force and energy

e·ti·ol·o·gy /,iti'ɑlədʒi/ noun [U] (*medical*) the scientific study of the causes of disease

et·i·quette /'εtəkət/ noun [U] the formal rules of correct or polite behavior in society or among members of a particular profession: *advice on etiquette* ♦ *medical/legal/professional etiquette* ⊃ see also NETIQUETTE

–**ette** /εt/ suffix (in nouns) **1** small: *kitchenette* **2** female: *usherette*

é·tude /'eɪtud/ noun (*music from French*) (also stud·y) a piece of music designed to give a player practice in technical skills

et·y·mol·o·gy /,εtə'mɑlədʒi/ noun (*pl.* et·y·mol·o·gies) **1** [U] the study of the origin and history of words and their meanings **2** [C] the origin and history of a particular word ▸ **et·y·mo·log·i·cal** /,εtəmə'lɑdʒɪkl/ adj.: *an etymological dictionary* **et·y·mol·o·gist** /,εtə'mɑlədʒɪst/ noun

EU /,i 'yu/ abbr. EUROPEAN UNION

eu·ca·lyp·tus /,yukə'lɪptəs/ noun (*pl.* eu·ca·lyp·tus·es or eu·ca·lyp·ti /-taɪ/) [C, U] (also euca'lyptus ,tree, 'gum tree [C]) a tall straight tree with leaves that produce an oil with a strong smell that is used in medicine. There are several types of eucalyptuses and they grow especially in Australasia.

Eu·cha·rist /'yukərɪst/ noun [sing.] a ceremony in the Christian Church during which people eat bread and drink wine in memory of the last meal that Christ had with his DISCIPLES; the bread and wine used at this ceremony ⊃ see also COMMUNION, MASS

Eu·clid·e·an ge·om·e·try /yu,klɪdiən dʒi'ɑmətri/ noun [U] the system of GEOMETRY based on the work of the Greek MATHEMATICIAN Euclid

eu·gen·ics /yu'dʒεnɪks/ noun [U] the study of methods to improve the mental and physical characteristics of the human race by choosing who may become parents ▸ **eu·gen·ic** adj. **eu·gen·ist** /'yudʒənɪst; 'yudʒənɪst/ (also eu·gen·i·cist /yu'dʒεnəsɪst/) noun

eu·lo·gize /'yulə,dʒaɪz/ verb ~ **sb/sth (as sth)** (*formal*) to praise someone or something very highly: *He was eulogized as a hero.* ▸ **eu·lo·gis·tic** /,yulə'dʒɪstɪk/ adj.

eu·lo·gy /'yulədʒi/ noun (*pl.* eu·lo·gies) [C, U] **1** ~ **(for/to sb)** a speech given at a funeral praising the person who has died **2** (*formal*) ~ **(of/to sb/sth)** a speech or piece of writing praising someone or something very much: *a eulogy to marriage*

eu·nuch /'yunək/ noun **1** a man who has been CASTRATED, especially one who guarded women in some Asian countries in the past **2** (*formal*) a person without power or influence: *a political eunuch*

eu·phe·mism /ˈyufəˌmɪzəm/ *noun* ~ **(for sth)** an indirect word or phrase that people often use to refer to something embarrassing or unpleasant, sometimes to make it seem more acceptable than it really is: *"Pass away" is a euphemism for "die."* ◆ *"User fees" is just a politician's euphemism for taxes.* ▸ **eu·phe·mis·tic** /ˌyufəˈmɪstɪk/ *adj.*: *euphemistic language* **eu·phe·mis·ti·cal·ly** /-kli/ *adv.*: *The prison camps were euphemistically called "retraining centers."*

eu·pho·ni·ous /yuˈfouniəs/ *adj.* (*formal*) (of a sound, word, etc.) pleasant to listen to ▸ **eu·pho·ny** /ˈyufəni/ *noun* [U]

eu·pho·ni·um /yuˈfouniəm/ *noun* a large **BRASS** musical instrument like a TUBA

eu·pho·ri·a /yuˈfɔriə/ *noun* [U] an extremely strong feeling of happiness and excitement that usually lasts only a short time ▸ **eu·phor·ic** /yuˈfɔrɪk; -ˈfar-/ *adj.*: *My euphoric mood could not last.* ⊃ **thesaurus box at** EXCITED

Eur·a·sian /yʊˈreɪʒn; yə-/ *adj., noun*
● *adj.* **1** of or connected with both Europe and Asia: *the center for Russian and Eurasian Studies* **2** having one Asian parent and one parent who is white or from Europe
● *noun* a person with one Asian parent and one parent who is white or from Europe

eu·re·ka /yʊˈrikə/ *exclamation* used to show pleasure at having found something, especially the answer to a problem

eu·ˈreka ˌmoment *noun* the moment when you suddenly understand something important, have a great idea, or find the answer to a problem

eu·ro /ˈyʊrou; ˈyərou/ *noun* (*pl.* **eu·ros** or **eu·ro**) (*symb.* €) the unit of money of some countries of the European Union: *The price is given in dollars or euros.* ◆ *I paid five euros for it.* ◆ *a 30-million-euro deal* ◆ *the value of the euro against the dollar*

Euro- /ˈyʊrou; ˈyərou/ *combining form* (in nouns and adjectives) connected with Europe or the European Union: *Euro-elections*

Eu·ro·cen·tric /ˌyʊrouˈsɛntrɪk/ *adj.* focusing on European culture or history and regarding it as more important than the culture or history of other regions: *The description represents a Eurocentric view of Native Americans.* ▸ **Eu·ro·cen·trism** /ˌyʊrouˈsɛntrɪzəm/ *noun* [U]

Eu·ro·land /ˈyʊrouˌlænd; ˈyər-/ *noun* [U] = EUROZONE

Eu·ro·pe·an /ˌyʊrəˈpiən; ˌyər-/ *adj., noun*
● *adj.* of or connected with Europe: *European languages*
● *noun* a person from Europe, or whose ANCESTORS came from Europe

Eu·ro·pe·an·ize /ˌyʊrəˈpiəˌnaɪz; ˌyər-/ *verb* ~ **sb/sth** to make someone or something feel or seem European: *a Europeanized American* ▸ **Eu·ro·pe·an·i·za·tion** /ˌyʊrə-ˌpiənəˈzeɪʃn; ˌyər-/ *noun* [U]

Euro·ˈpean ˌplan *noun* [U] a system of charging for a hotel room only, without meals ⊃ **compare** AMERICAN PLAN

the ˌEuropean ˈUnion *noun* [sing.] (*abbr.* EU) an economic and political organization that many European countries belong to

eu·ro·pi·um /yʊˈroupiəm/ *noun* [U] (*symb.* **Eu**) a chemical element. Europium is a silver-white metal used in television screens.

Eu·ro·trash /ˈyʊrouˌtræʃ/ *noun* [U, pl.] (*informal, disapproving*) rich, fashionable Europeans, especially those living in the U.S., who go to a lot of parties and don't have to work very hard

the Eu·ro·zone /ˈyʊrouˌzoun; ˈyər-/ *noun* [sing.] (also Eu·ro·land [U]) the countries in the European Union that use the EURO as a unit of money

eu·ryth·mics (also **eu·rhyth·mics**) /yʊˈrɪðmɪks/ *noun* [U] a form of exercise that combines physical movement with music and speech

Eu·sta·chian tube /yuˈsteɪʃn ˌtub/ *noun* (*anatomy*) a narrow tube that joins the throat to the middle ear

eu·tha·na·sia /ˌyuθəˈneɪʒə/ *noun* [U] the practice (illegal in most countries) of killing without pain a person who is suffering from a disease that cannot be cured **SYN** MERCY KILLING: *They argued in favor of legalizing voluntary euthanasia* (= people being able to ask for euthanasia themselves).

eu·tha·nize /ˈyuθəˌnaɪz/ *verb* ~ **sb/sth** (*formal*) to kill a sick or injured animal or person by giving them drugs so that they die without pain **SYN** PUT STH TO SLEEP

eu·troph·ic /yuˈtrafɪk; -ˈtrou-/ *adj.* (*technical*) (of a lake, river, etc.) containing too many food substances that encourage plants to grow, which then kill animal life by using too much OXYGEN from the water

eu·troph·i·ca·tion /ˌyutrəfəˈkeɪʃn; yuˌtrafə-; yuˌtroufə-/ *noun* [U] (*technical*) the process of too many plants growing on the surface of a river, lake, etc., often because chemicals that are used to help crops grow have been carried there by rain

e·vac·u·ate /ɪˈvækyuˌeɪt/ *verb* **1** [T] to move people from a place of danger to a safer place: ~ **sth** *Police evacuated nearby buildings.* ◆ ~ **sb (from…) (to…)** *Children were evacuated from the area to escape the bombing.* **2** [T, I] ~ **(sth)** to move out of a place because of danger, and leave the place empty: *Employees were urged to evacuate their offices immediately.* ◆ *Locals were told to evacuate.* **3** [T] ~ **sth** (*formal*) to empty your BOWELS ▸ **e·vac·u·a·tion** /ɪˌvækyuˈeɪʃn/ *noun* [U, C]: *the emergency evacuation of thousands of people after the earthquake*

e·vac·u·ee /ɪˌvækyuˈi/ *noun* a person who is sent away from a place because it is dangerous, especially during a war

e·vade /ɪˈveɪd/ *verb* **1** ~ **(doing) sth** to escape from someone or something or avoid meeting someone: *For two weeks they evaded the press.* ◆ *He managed to evade capture.* **2** ~ **(doing) sth** to find a way of not doing something, especially something that legally or morally you should do: *to evade payment of taxes* ◆ *She is trying to evade all responsibility for her behavior.* **3** to avoid dealing with or talking about something: ~ **sth** *Come on, don't you think you're evading the issue?* ◆ ~ **doing sth** *to evade answering a question* **4** ~ **sb** (*formal*) to not come or happen to someone **SYN** ELUDE: *The answer evaded him* (= he could not think of it). ⊃ **see also** EVASION, EVASIVE

e·val·u·ate **AWL** /ɪˈvælyuˌeɪt/ *verb* to form an opinion of the amount, value, or quality of something after thinking about it carefully **SYN** ASSESS: ~ **sth** *Our research attempts to evaluate the effectiveness of the different drugs.* ◆ ~ **how, whether, etc.…** *We need to evaluate how well the policy is working.* ▸ **e·val·u·a·tion** **AWL** /ɪˌvælyuˈeɪʃn/ *noun* [C, U]: *an evaluation of the health care system* **e·val·u·a·tive** **AWL** /ɪˈvælyuˌeɪtɪv/ *adj.*

AWL COLLOCATIONS

evaluate
evaluate *verb*
■ critically | objectively | quantitatively | carefully, rigorously | thoroughly | empirically | scientifically, systematically
This article critically evaluates the results of the two approaches.
These probabilities can be evaluated empirically.
■ effectiveness | effect | accuracy | hypothesis | usefulness | significance | performance | outcome
Although numerous statistical approaches can be used to evaluate the hypothesis, we will consider three here.
■ designed to
This study is designed to evaluate two methods of teaching economics.
■ difficult to
The evidence is difficult to evaluate and, in some respects, inconsistent.

ev·a·nes·cent /ˌɛvəˈnɛsnt/ *adj.* (*literary*) disappearing quickly from sight or memory ▶ **ev·a·nes·cence** /-ˈnɛsns/ *noun* [U]

e·van·gel·i·cal /ˌivænˈdʒɛlɪkl; ˌɛvən-/ *adj., noun*
- *adj.* **1** of or belonging to a Christian group that emphasizes the authority of the Bible and the importance of people being saved through faith: *They're evangelical Christians.* **2** wanting very much to persuade people to accept your views and opinions: *He delivered his speech with evangelical fervor.* ▶ **e·van·gel·i·cal·ism** /-kəˌlɪzəm/ *noun* [U]
- *noun* a member of the evangelical branch of the Christian Church

e·van·ge·list /ɪˈvændʒəlɪst/ *noun* **1** a person who tries to persuade people to become Christians, especially by traveling around the country holding religious meetings or speaking on radio or television ⊃ see also TELEVANGELIST **2 Evangelist** one of the four writers (Matthew, Mark, Luke, John) of the books called the GOSPELS in the Bible ▶ **e·van·ge·lism** /ɪˈvændʒəˌlɪzəm/ *noun* [U] **e·van·ge·lis·tic** /ɪˌvændʒəˈlɪstɪk/ *adj.*: *an evangelistic meeting*

e·van·ge·lize /ɪˈvændʒəˌlaɪz/ *verb* ~ **sb** to try to persuade people to become Christians

e·vap·o·rate /ɪˈvæpəˌreɪt/ *verb* **1** [I, T] if a liquid **evaporates** or if something **evaporates** it, it changes into a gas, especially steam: *Heat until all the water has evaporated.* ◆ ~ **sth** *The sun is constantly evaporating the earth's moisture.* **2** [I] to disappear, especially by gradually becoming less and less: *Her confidence completely evaporated.* ▶ **e·vap·o·ra·tion** /ɪˌvæpəˈreɪʃn/ *noun* [U]

eˌ**vaporated ˈmilk** *noun* [U] thick sweet milk sold in cans, used in cooking

eˈ**vaporating** ˌ**dish** *noun* (*technical*) a dish in which scientists heat a liquid, so that it leaves a solid when it has disappeared ⊃ picture at LABORATORY

e·va·sion /ɪˈveɪʒn/ *noun* [C, U] **1** the act of avoiding someone or of avoiding something that you are supposed to do: *His behavior was an evasion of his responsibilities as a father.* ◆ *She's been charged with* **tax evasion. 2** a statement that someone makes that avoids dealing with something or talking about something honestly and directly: *His speech was full of evasions and half-truths.* ⊃ see also EVADE

e·va·sive /ɪˈveɪsɪv/ *adj.* not willing to give answers to a question **SYN** CAGEY: *evasive answers/comments/replies* ◆ *Tess was evasive about why she had not been at home that night.* ▶ **e·va·sive·ly** *adv.*: *"I'm not sure," she replied evasively.* **e·va·sive·ness** *noun* [U]
IDM **take evasive action** to act in order to avoid danger or an unpleasant situation

eve /iv/ *noun* **1** the day or evening before an event, especially a religious festival or holiday: *Christmas Eve* (= December 24) ◆ *a New Year's Eve party* (= on December 31) ◆ *on the eve of the election* **2** (*old use* or *literary*) evening

e·ven 🔑 /ˈivən/ *adv., adj., verb*
- *adv.* **1** used to emphasize something unexpected or surprising: *He never even opened the letter* (= so he certainly didn't read it). ◆ *It was cold there even in summer* (= so it must have been very cold in winter). ◆ *Even a child can understand it* (= so adults certainly can). ◆ *She didn't even call to say she wasn't coming.* **2** used when you are comparing things, to make the comparison stronger: *You know even less about it than I do.* ◆ *She's even more intelligent than her sister.* **3** used to introduce a more exact description of someone or something: *It's an unattractive building, ugly even.* ⊃ note at ALTHOUGH
IDM **even as** (*formal*) just at the same time as someone does something or as something else happens: *Even as he shouted the warning, the car skidded.* **even if/though** despite the fact or belief that; no matter whether: *I'll get there, even if I have to walk.* ◆ *I like her, even though she can be annoying at times.* ⊃ note at ALTHOUGH **even now/then 1** despite what has/had happened: *I've shown him the photos, but even now he won't believe me.* ◆ *Even then she would not admit her mistake.* **2** (*formal*) at this or that exact moment: *The troops are even now preparing to march into the city.* **even so** despite that: *There are a lot of spelling mistakes; even so, it's a very good essay.*
- *adj.*
- ⊳ SMOOTH/LEVEL **1** smooth, level, and flat: *You need an even surface to work on.* **ANT** UNEVEN
- ⊳ NOT CHANGING **2** not changing very much in amount, speed, etc.: *an even temperature all year* ◆ *Children do not learn at an even pace.* **ANT** UNEVEN
- ⊳ EQUAL **3** (of an amount of something) equal or the same for each person, team, place, etc.: *Our scores are now even.* ◆ *the even distribution of food* **ANT** UNEVEN **4** (of two people or teams) equally balanced or of an equal standard: *an even contest* ◆ *The two players were pretty even.* **ANT** UNEVEN
- ⊳ NUMBERS **5** that can be divided exactly by two: *4, 6, 8, 10 are all even numbers.* **ANT** ODD
- ⊳ SAME SIZE **6** equally spaced and the same size: *even features/teeth* **ANT** UNEVEN
- ⊳ CALM **7** calm; not changing or becoming upset: *She has a very even temperament.* ◆ *He spoke in a steady, even voice.*
  ▶ **e·ven·ness** /ˈivənnəs/ *noun* [U]
IDM **be even** (*informal*) to no longer owe someone money or a favor **be/get even (with sb)** (*informal*) to cause someone the same amount of trouble or harm as they have caused you: *I'll get even with you for this, just you wait.* **break even** to complete a piece of business, etc. without either losing money or making a profit: *The company just about broke even last year.* **have an even chance (of doing sth)** to be equally likely to do or not do something: *She has more than an even chance of winning tomorrow.* **on an even keel** living, working, or happening in a calm way, with no sudden changes, especially after a difficult time
- *verb*
IDM **even the score** to harm or punish someone who has harmed or cheated you in the past
PHR V ˌ**even ˈout** to become level or steady, usually after varying a lot: *House prices keep rising and falling but they should eventually even out.* ˌ**even sth**↔ˈ**out** to spread things equally over a period of time or among a number of people: *He tried to even out the distribution of work among his employees.* ˌ**even sth**↔ˈ**up** to make a situation or a competition more equal

ˌ**even-ˈhanded** *adj.* completely fair, especially when dealing with different groups of people

eve·ning 🔑 /ˈivnɪŋ/ *noun*
1 [C, U] the part of the day between the afternoon and the time you go to bed: *I'll see you tomorrow evening.* ◆ *Come over on Thursday evening.* ◆ *What do you usually do in the evening?* ◆ *She's going to her sister's for the evening.* ◆ *the long winter evenings* ◆ *the evening performance* ⊃ see also GOOD EVENING **2** [C] an event of a particular type happening in the evening: *a musical evening at school* (= when music is performed) ▶ **eve·nings** *adv.*: *He works evenings.* **IDM** see OTHER *adj.*

ˈ**evening** ˌ**dress** *noun* **1** [U] elegant clothes worn for formal occasions in the evening: *Everyone was in evening dress.* **2** [C] a woman's long formal dress

evening ˈprimrose noun [C, U] a plant with yellow flowers that open in the evening, sometimes used as a medicine

the ˌevening ˈstar noun [sing.] the planet Venus, when it is seen in the western sky after the sun has set

e·ven·ly /ˈivənli/ adv. **1** in a smooth, regular, or equal way: *Make sure the paint covers the surface evenly.* ◆ *She was fast asleep, breathing evenly.* ◆ ***evenly spaced** at four inches apart* **2** with equal amounts for each person or in each place: ***evenly distributed/divided*** ◆ *Incidence of the disease is fairly **evenly spread** across Europe.* ◆ *The two teams are very **evenly matched** (= are equally likely to win).* **3** calmly; without showing any emotion: *"I warned you not to call me," he said evenly.*

even ˈmoney noun (in betting) ODDS that give an equal chance of winning or losing and that mean a person has the chance of winning the same amount of money that he or she has bet

e·vent 🔑 /ɪˈvɛnt/ noun
1 a thing that happens, especially something important: *The election was the main event of 2008.* ◆ *In the light of later events the decision was proved right.* ◆ *The decisions we make now may influence **the course of events** (= the way things happen) in the future.* ◆ *Everyone was shocked by the strange **sequence of events**.* ◆ *In the **normal course of events** (= if things had happened as expected) she would have gone with him.* **2** a planned public or social occasion: *a fund-raising event* ◆ *the social event of the year* **3** one of the races or competitions in a sports program: *The 800 meters is the fourth event of the afternoon.* ⊃ see also FIELD EVENT, TRACK EVENT
IDM **in any event** used to emphasize or show that something is true or will happen in spite of other circumstances **SYN** IN ANY CASE: *I think she'll agree to do it, but in any event, all she can say is "no."* **in the event of sth | in the event that sth happens** if something happens: *In the event of an accident, call this number.* ◆ *Sheila will inherit everything in the event of his death.* **in that event** if that happens: *In that event, we will have to reconsider our offer.* ⊃ more at HAPPY, WISE adj.

even-ˈtempered adj. not easily made angry or upset

e·vent·ful /ɪˈvɛntfl/ adj. full of things that happen, especially exciting, important, or dangerous things: *an eventful day/life/trip*

e·ven·tide /ˈivənˌtaɪd/ noun [U] (old use or literary) evening

e·vent·ing /ɪˈvɛntɪŋ/ noun [U] the sport of taking part in competitions riding horses. These are often held over three days and include riding across country, jumping, and DRESSAGE.

e·ven·tu·al **AWL** /ɪˈvɛntʃuəl/ adj. [only before noun] happening at the end of a period of time or of a process: *the eventual winner of the tournament* ◆ *It is impossible to predict what the eventual outcome will be.* ◆ *The hospital may face eventual closure.*

e·ven·tu·al·i·ty **AWL** /ɪˌvɛntʃuˈæləti/ noun (pl. **e·ven·tu·al·i·ties**) (formal) something that may possibly happen, especially something unpleasant: *We were prepared for **every eventuality**.* ◆ *The money had been saved **for just such an eventuality**.*

e·ven·tu·al·ly 🔑 **AWL** /ɪˈvɛntʃəli; -tʃuəli/ adv. at the end of a period of time or a series of events: *Our flight eventually left five hours late.* ◆ *I'll get around to repairing it eventually.* ◆ *She hopes to get a job on the local newspaper and eventually work for "The New York Times."* **HELP** Use **finally** for the last in a list of things.

e·ven·tu·ate /ɪˈvɛntʃuˌeɪt/ verb [I] (formal) to happen as a result of something

ev·er 🔑 /ˈɛvər/ adv.
1 used in negative sentences and questions, or sentences with *if*, to mean "at any time": *Nothing ever happens here.* ◆ *Don't you ever get tired?* ◆ *If you're ever in Miami, come and see us.* ◆ *"Have you ever thought of a career change?" "No, never/No I haven't."* ◆ *"Have you ever been to Rome?" "Yes, I have, actually. Not long ago."* ◆ *She **hardly ever** (= almost never) goes out.* ◆ *We see them very seldom, **if ever**.* ◆ *(informal) I'll **never ever** do that again!* **2** used for emphasis when you are comparing things: *It was raining harder than ever.* ◆ *It's my **best ever** score.* **3** (somewhat formal) all the time or every time; always: *Paul, ever the optimist, agreed to try again.* ◆ *She married the prince and they **lived happily ever after**.* ◆ *He said he would love her **for ever and ever**.* ◆ *Their debts grew **ever** larger (= kept increasing).* ◆ *the **ever-growing** problem* ◆ *an ever-present danger* **4** used after *when, why,* etc. to show that you are surprised or shocked: *Why ever did you agree?*
IDM **all sb ever does is …** used to emphasize that someone does the same thing very often, usually in an annoying way: *All he ever does is grumble about things.* **did you ever (…)!** (old-fashioned, informal) used to show that you are surprised or shocked: *Did you ever hear anything like it?* **ever since (…)** continuously since the time mentioned: *He's had a car ever since he was 18.* ◆ *I was bitten by a dog once and I've been afraid of them ever since.* **if ever there was (one)** (informal) used to emphasize that something is certainly true: *That was a disaster if ever there was one!* **was/is/does, etc. sb ever!** (informal) used to emphasize something you are talking about: *"You must have been upset by that." "Was I ever!"*

ev·er·green /ˈɛvərˌgrin/ noun a tree or bush that has green leaves all through the year ⊃ compare CONIFER, DECIDUOUS ▶ **ev·er·green** adj.: *evergreen shrubs* ◆ *(figurative) a new production of Rossini's evergreen (= always popular) opera*

ev·er·last·ing /ˌɛvərˈlæstɪŋ/ adj. **1** continuing forever; never changing **SYN** ETERNAL: *everlasting life/love* ◆ *an everlasting memory of her smile* ◆ *To his **everlasting credit**, he never told anyone what I'd done.* **2** (disapproving) continuing too long; repeated too often **SYN** CONSTANT, INTERMINABLE, NEVER-ENDING: *I'm tired of your everlasting complaints.* ▶ **ev·er·last·ing·ly** adv.

ev·er·more /ˌɛvərˈmɔr/ (also **for ˌever·ˈmore**) adv. (literary) always

eve·ry 🔑 /ˈɛvri/ det.
1 used with singular nouns to refer to all the members of a group of things or people: *She knows every student in the school.* ◆ *I could hear every word they said.* ◆ *We enjoyed every minute of our stay.* ◆ *Every day seemed the same to him.* ◆ ***Every single** time he calls, I'm out.* ◆ *I read **every last** article in the newspaper (= all of them).* ◆ *They were watching her every movement.* ◆ *Every one of their CDs has been a hit.* ⊃ note at EACH **2** all possible: *We wish you every success.* ◆ *He had every reason to be angry.* **3** used to say how often something happens or is done: *The buses go every 10 minutes.* ◆ *We had to stop every few miles.* ◆ *One in every three marriages ends in divorce.* ◆ *He has every third day off (= he works for two days, then has one day off, then works for two days, and so on).* ◆ *We see each other **every now and again**.* ◆ ***Every now and then** he regretted his decision.*
IDM **every other** each ALTERNATE one (= the first, third, fifth, etc. one, but not the second, fourth, sixth, etc.): *They visit us every other week.*

eve·ry·bod·y /ˈɛvriˌbɑdi; -ˌbʌdi; -bədi/ pron. = EVERYONE: *Everybody knows Tom.* ◆ *Have you asked everybody?* ◆ *Didn't you like it? Everybody else did.*

eve·ry·day /ˈɛvriˌdeɪ/ adj. [only before noun] used or happening every day or regularly; ordinary: *everyday objects* ◆ *The Internet has become part of everyday life.* ◆ *a small dictionary for everyday use*

Eve·ry·man /ˈɛvriˌmæn/ noun [sing.] an ordinary or typical person: *a story of Everyman*

eve·ry·one 🔑 /ˈɛvriˌwʌn; -wən/ (also **eve·ry·bod·y**) pron.
every person; all people: *Everyone cheered and clapped.* ◆ *Everyone has a chance to win.* ◆ *Everyone brought their partner to the party.* ◆ *(formal) Everyone brought his or her partner to the party.* ◆ *The police questioned everyone in the room.* ◆ *The*

| h hat | m man | n no | ŋ sing | l leg | r red | y yes | w wet |

teacher commented on everyone's work. ◆ *Everyone else was there.*

eve·ry·place /'ɛvriˌpleɪs/ *adv.* = EVERYWHERE

eve·ry·thing 🔑 /'ɛvriˌθɪŋ/ *pron.*
(with a singular verb) **1** all things: *Everything was gone.* ◆ *When we confronted him, he denied everything.* ◆ *Take this bag, and leave everything else to me.* ◆ *She seemed to have everything* —looks, money, intelligence. **2** the situation now; life generally: *Everything in the capital is now quiet.* ◆ *"How's everything with you?" "Fine, thanks."* **3** the most important thing: *Money isn't everything.* ◆ *My family means everything to me.*
IDM **and everything** (*informal*) and so on; and other similar things: *Do you have his name and address and everything?* ◆ *She told me about the baby and everything.*

eve·ry·where 🔑 /'ɛvriˌwɛr/ (also **eve·ry·place**) *adv., pron., conj.*
in, to, or at every place; all places: *I've looked everywhere.* ◆ *He follows me everywhere.* ◆ *We'll have to eat here— everywhere else is full.* ◆ *Everywhere we went was full of tourists.*

e·vict /ɪ'vɪkt/ *verb* **~ sb (from sth)** to force someone to leave a house or land, especially when you have the legal right to do so: *A number of tenants have been evicted for not paying the rent.* ▶ **e·vic·tion** /ɪ'vɪkʃn/ *noun* [U, C]: *to face eviction from your home*

ev·i·dence 🔑 **AWL** /'ɛvədəns/ *noun, verb*
● *noun* **1** [U, C] the facts, signs, or objects that make you believe that something is true: **~ (of sth)** *There is convincing evidence of a link between exposure to sun and skin cancer.* ◆ *The room bore evidence of a struggle.* ◆ **~ (for sth)** *We found further scientific evidence for this theory.* ◆ **~ (that…)** *There is not a shred of evidence that the meeting actually took place.* ◆ **~ (to suggest, show, etc.)** *Do you have any evidence to support this allegation?* ⊃ collocations at EVIDENT **2** [U] the information that is used in court to try to prove something: *I was asked to give evidence* (= to say what I knew, describe what I had seen, etc.) *at the trial.* ◆ *He was released when the judge ruled there was no evidence against him.* ⊃ see also CIRCUMSTANTIAL, STATE'S EVIDENCE ⊃ collocations at JUSTICE
IDM **(be) in evidence** present and clearly seen: *The police were much in evidence at today's demonstration.* ⊃ more at BALANCE
● *verb* [usually passive] **~ sth** (*formal*) to prove or show something; to be evidence of something **SYN** TESTIFY TO: *Investment banking is still a largely male world, as evidenced by the small number of women in senior roles.*

LANGUAGE BANK

evidence
giving proof
■ New evidence has been found that/Studies have shown that TV advertising influences what children buy.
■ It is clear from numerous studies that TV advertising influences what children buy.
■ Recent research demonstrates that TV advertising influences children's spending habits.
■ Many parents think that TV advertising influences their children. This view is supported by the findings of a recent study, which show a clear link between television advertisements and children's spending habits.
■ The findings also reveal that most children are unaware of the persuasive purpose of advertising.
■ Little evidence has been found that children understand the persuasive intent of advertising.
■ The results contradict claims that advertising is unrelated to children's spending habits.
■ Manufacturers argue that it is difficult to prove that advertising alone influences what children buy.
⊃ Language Banks at ARGUE, E.G., ILLUSTRATE

ev·i·dent **AWL** /'ɛvədənt/ *adj.* clear; easily seen **SYN** OBVIOUS: *The orchestra played with evident enjoyment.* ◆ **~ (to sb) (that…)** *It has now become evident to us that a mistake has been made.* ◆ **~ in/from sth** *The growing interest in history is clearly evident in the number of people visiting museums and historic houses.* ⊃ see also SELF-EVIDENT ⊃ thesaurus box at CLEAR

AWL COLLOCATIONS

evident
evident *adj.*
■ appear, seem | become | remain
Several trends become evident from the results.
■ clearly, plainly | especially, particularly | increasingly
A regional pattern is clearly evident in the data.

evidence *noun*
■ anecdotal | circumstantial | empirical, experimental | scientific | theoretical | compelling, convincing
There is extensive theoretical and empirical evidence. This experimental evidence is based on clinical observations of patients.
■ based on
These observations are based on the evidence provided by numerous surveys.
■ find, gather | present, provide
Evidence was gathered from a number of sources. In this paper, I have provided evidence for two major assumptions of the theory.
■ indicate, suggest | back, support | justify, prove, substantiate
Empirical evidence suggests that being married and being employed are frequently associated with better health.
■ body of ~
As the body of scientific evidence grows, the speed of climatic change is proving greater than predicted.

ev·i·den·tial /ˌɛvə'dɛnʃl/ *adj.* [usually before noun] (*formal*) providing or connected with evidence: *The necessary evidential basis for her claim is lacking.*

ev·i·dent·ly **AWL** /ˌɛvə'dɛntli; 'ɛvədəntli/ *adv.* **1** clearly; that can be seen or understood easily **SYN** OBVIOUSLY: *She walked slowly down the road, evidently in pain.* ◆ *"I'm afraid I couldn't finish the work last night." "Evidently not."* **2** according to what people say **SYN** APPARENTLY: *Evidently, she had nothing to do with the whole affair.*

e·vil 🔑 /'ivl/ *adj., noun*
● *adj.* **1** (of people) enjoying harming others; morally bad and cruel: *an evil man* ◆ *an evil grin* **2** having a harmful effect on people; morally bad: *evil deeds* ◆ *the evil effects of racism* **3** connected with the DEVIL and with what is bad in the world: *evil spirits* **4** extremely unpleasant: *an evil smell*
● *noun* (*formal*) **1** [U] a force that causes bad things to happen; morally bad behavior: *the eternal struggle between good and evil* ◆ *the forces of evil* ◆ *You can't pretend there's no evil in the world.* **ANT** GOOD **2** [C, usually pl.] a bad or harmful thing; the bad effect of something: *the evils of drugs/alcohol* ◆ *social evils* **IDM** see LESSER, NECESSARY

'evil-ˌdoer *noun* (*formal*) a person who does very bad things

the ˌevil 'eye *noun* [sing.] the magic power to harm someone by looking at them

e·vil·ly /'ivəli/ *adv.* in a morally bad or very unpleasant way: *to grin evilly* ◆ *to look evilly at someone*

e·vince /ɪ'vɪns/ *verb* **~ sth** (*formal*) to show clearly that you have a feeling or quality: *He evinced a strong desire to be reconciled with his family.*

e·vis·cer·ate /ɪ'vɪsəˌreɪt/ *verb* **~ sth** (*formal*) to remove the inner organs of a body **SYN** DISEMBOWEL

e·voc·a·tive /ɪ'vɑkətɪv/ adj. making you think of or remember a strong image or feeling, in a pleasant way: *evocative smells/sounds/music* ♦ **~ of sth** *Her new book is wonderfully evocative of small town life.*

e·voke /ɪ'vouk/ verb **~ sth** (formal) to bring a feeling, a memory, or an image into your mind: *The music evoked memories of her youth.* ♦ *His case is unlikely to evoke public sympathy.* ▶ **ev·o·ca·tion** /ˌivou'keɪʃn; ˌɛvə-/ noun [C, U]: *a brilliant evocation of childhood in the 1940s*

ev·o·lu·tion AWL /ˌɛvə'luʃn/ noun [U] **1** (biology) the gradual development of plants, animals, etc. over many years as they adapt to changes in their environment: *the evolution of the human species* ♦ *Darwin's theory of evolution* **2** the gradual development of something: *In politics he preferred evolution to revolution* (= gradual development to sudden violent change).

ev·o·lu·tion·ar·y AWL /ˌɛvə'luʃəˌnɛri/ adj. connected with evolution; connected with gradual development and change: *evolutionary theory* ♦ *evolutionary change* ▶ **ev·o·lu·tion·ar·i·ly** /ˌɛvəˌluʃə'nɛrəli/ adv.

ev·o·lu·tion·ist AWL /ˌɛvə'luʃənɪst/ noun, adj.
● **noun** a person who believes in the theories of evolution and NATURAL SELECTION
● **adj.** relating to the theories of evolution and NATURAL SELECTION ▶ **ev·o·lu·tion·ism** /-ʃəˌnɪzəm/ noun

e·volve AWL /ɪ'vɑlv/ verb **1** [I, T] to develop gradually, especially from a simple to a more complicated form; to develop something in this way: **~ (from sth) (into sth)** *The idea evolved from a drawing I discovered in the attic.* ♦ *The company has evolved into a major chemical manufacturer.* ♦ **~ sth** *Each school must evolve its own way of working.* **2** [I, T] (biology) (of plants, animals, etc.) to develop over time, often many generations, into forms that are better adapted to survive changes in their environment: **~ (from sth)** *The three species evolved from a single ancestor.* ♦ **~ sth** *The dolphin has evolved a highly developed jaw.*

ewe /yu/ noun a female sheep ⊃ compare RAM n. (1)

ew·er /'yuər/ noun a large JUG used in the past for carrying water

ex /ɛks/ noun (pl. **ex·es**) (informal) a person's former wife, husband, or partner: *The kids are spending the weekend with my ex and his new wife.*

ex- /ɛks/ prefix (in nouns) former: *ex-wife* ♦ *ex-president*

ex·ac·er·bate /ɪg'zæsərˌbeɪt/ verb **~ sth** (formal) to make something worse, especially a disease or problem SYN AGGRAVATE: *The symptoms may be exacerbated by certain drugs.* ▶ **ex·ac·er·ba·tion** /ɪgˌzæsər'beɪʃn/ noun [U, C]

ex·act 🖉 /ɪg'zækt/ adj., verb
● **adj. 1** correct in every detail SYN PRECISE: *She gave an exact description of the attacker.* ♦ *an exact copy/replica of the painting* ♦ *We need to know the exact time the incident occurred.* ♦ *What were his exact words?* ♦ *She's in her mid-thirties—thirty-six to be exact.* ♦ *The colors were an exact match.* ♦ *He started to call me at the exact moment I started to call him* (= at the same time). ♦ *Her second husband was the exact opposite of her first* (= completely different). **2** (of people) very accurate and careful about details SYN METICULOUS, PRECISE **3** (of a science) using accurate measurements and following set rules SYN PRECISE: *Assessing insurance risk can never be an exact science.* ▶ **ex·act·ness** noun [U]
● **verb** (formal) **1 ~ sth (from sb)** to demand and get something from someone: *She was determined to exact a promise from him.* **2** to make something bad happen to someone: **~ sth** *He exacted* (= took) *terrible revenge for their treatment of him.* ♦ **~ sth from sb** *Stress can exact a high price from workers* (= can affect them badly). ▶ **ex·ac·tion** /ɪg'zækʃn/ noun [C, U] (formal)

ex·act·ing /ɪg'zæktɪŋ/ adj. needing or demanding a lot of effort and care about details SYN DEMANDING: *exacting work* ♦ *products designed to meet the exacting standards of today's marketplace* ♦ *He was an exacting man to work for.*

ex·ac·ti·tude /ɪg'zæktəˌtud/ noun [U] (formal) the quality of being very accurate and exact

ex·act·ly 🖉 /ɪg'zæktli; -'zækli/ adv.
1 used to emphasize that something is correct in every way or in every detail SYN PRECISELY: *I know exactly how she felt.* ♦ *Do exactly as I tell you.* ♦ *It happened almost exactly a year ago.* ♦ *It's exactly nine o'clock.* ♦ *You haven't changed at all—you still look exactly the same.* ♦ *His words had exactly the opposite effect.* ♦ *Your answer is exactly right.* ♦ *It was a warm day, if not exactly hot.* **2** (informal) used to ask for more information about something: *Where exactly did you stay in France?* ♦ (disapproving) *Exactly what are you trying to tell me?* **3** used as a reply, agreeing with what someone has just said, or emphasizing that it is correct: *"You mean someone in this room must be the murderer?" "Exactly."*
IDM **not exactly** (informal) **1** used when you are saying the opposite of what you really mean: *He wasn't exactly pleased to see us—in fact he refused to open the door.* ♦ *It's not exactly beautiful, is it?* (= it's ugly) **2** used when you are correcting something that someone has said: *"So he told you you'd get the job?" "Not exactly, but he said they were impressed with me."*

ex·ag·ger·ate 🖉 /ɪg'zædʒəˌreɪt/ verb [I, T] to make something seem larger, better, worse, or more important than it really is: *The hotel was really filthy, and I'm not exaggerating.* ♦ **~ sth** *He tends to exaggerate the difficulties.* ♦ *I'm sure he exaggerates his British accent* (= tries to sound more British than he really is). ♦ *Demand for the product has been greatly exaggerated.*

ex·ag·ger·at·ed 🖉 /ɪg'zædʒəˌreɪtəd/ adj.
1 made to seem larger, better, worse, or more important than it really is or needs to be: *to make greatly/grossly/wildly exaggerated claims* ♦ *She has an exaggerated sense of her own importance.* **2** (of an action) done in a way that makes people notice it: *He looked at me with exaggerated surprise.* ▶ **ex·ag·ger·at·ed·ly** adv.

ex·ag·ger·a·tion /ɪgˌzædʒə'reɪʃn/ noun [C, usually sing., U] a statement or description that makes something seem larger, better, worse, or more important than it really is; the act of making a statement like this: *a slight/gross/wild exaggeration* ♦ *It would be an exaggeration to say I knew her well—I only met her twice.* ♦ *It's no exaggeration to say that most students have never read a complete Shakespeare play.* ♦ *He told his story simply and without exaggeration.*

ex·alt /ɪg'zɔlt/ verb (formal) **1 ~ sb (to sth)** to make someone rise to a higher rank or position, sometimes to one that they do not deserve **2 ~ sb/sth** to praise someone or something very much

ex·al·ta·tion /ˌɛgzɔl'teɪʃn; ˌɛksɔl-/ noun [U] (formal) **1** a feeling of very great joy or happiness **2** an act of raising something or someone to a high position or rank: *the exaltation of emotion above logical reasoning*

ex·alt·ed /ɪg'zɔltəd/ adj. **1** (formal or humorous) of high rank or position, or of great importance: *She was the only woman to rise to such an exalted position.* **2** (formal) full of great joy and happiness: *I felt exalted and newly alive.*

ex·am 🔊 /ɪɡˈzæm/ (also formal ex·am·i·na·tion) noun
1 a formal written, spoken, or practical test, especially in school or college, to see how much you know about a subject, or what you can do: *to take an exam* ◆ *to pass/fail an exam* ◆ *an exam paper* ◆ *I got my exam results today.* ◆ *A lot of students suffer from exam nerves.* ◆ *to grade an exam* ◆ *She did well on her exams.* ◆ *I got an 86% on my chemistry exam.* ⬧ collocations at EDUCATION **2** a medical test of a particular part of the body: *an eye exam*

ex·am·i·na·tion 🔊 /ɪɡˌzæməˈneɪʃn/ noun
1 [C] (formal) = EXAM: *to take an examination in mathematics* ◆ *an entrance examination* ◆ *Applicants are selected on the results of a competitive examination.* **HELP** Use: *take an examination* not ~~write an examination~~. **2** [U,C] the act of looking at or considering something very carefully: *Careful examination of the ruins revealed an even earlier temple.* ◆ *On closer examination, they found that the signature was not genuine.* ◆ *Your proposals are still under examination.* ◆ *The issue needs further examination.* ◆ *The chapter concludes with a brief examination of some of the factors causing family breakup.* **3** [C] a close look at something or someone, especially to see if there is anything wrong or to find the cause of a problem: *a complete physical examination* ◆ *a postmortem examination*

examine

consider ◆ **look at sth** ◆ **analyze** ◆ **review** ◆ **study** ◆ **discuss**

These words all mean to think about, study, or describe someone or something carefully, especially in order to understand them, form an opinion of them, or make a decision about them.

examine to think about, study, or describe an idea, subject, or piece of work very carefully: *These ideas will be examined in more detail in Chapter 10.*

consider to think carefully about something, especially in order to make a decision: *She carefully considered her options.*

look at sth (somewhat informal) to consider, think about, or study something, especially in order to learn something useful or important: *I'm going to look at the budget estimates on the weekend.*

analyze to examine the nature or structure of something, especially by separating it into its parts, in order to understand or explain it: *The job involves gathering and analyzing data.* ◆ *He tried to analyze his feelings.*

review to examine something again, especially so that you can decide whether any changes need to be made: *The government will review the situation later in the year.*

study to examine someone or something in order to understand them or it: *We will study the report carefully before making a decision.*

EXAMINE OR STUDY?

You **examine** something in order to understand it or to help other people understand it, for example by describing it in a book; you **study** something in order to understand it yourself.

discuss to write or talk about something in detail, showing the different ideas and opinions about it: *This topic will be discussed at greater length in the next chapter.*

PATTERNS

■ to examine/consider/look at/analyze/review/ study/discuss **what/how/whether…**
■ to examine/consider/look at/analyze/review/ study/discuss the **situation/evidence/implications**
■ to examine/consider/look at/analyze/review/ study/discuss sth **carefully/critically/systematically/briefly**

ex·am·ine 🔊 /ɪɡˈzæmən/ verb
1 to consider or study an idea, a subject, etc. very carefully: ~ **sth** *These ideas will be examined in more detail in Chapter 10.* ◆ ~ **how, what, etc....** *It is necessary to examine how the proposals can be carried out.* ⬧ language bank at ABOUT **2** to look at someone or something closely, to see if there is anything wrong or to find the cause of a problem: ~ **sb/sth** *The doctor examined her but could find nothing wrong.* ◆ ~ **sth/sb for sth** *The goods were examined for damage on arrival.* ⬧ thesaurus box at CHECK **3** ~ **sb (in/on sth)** (formal) to give someone a test to see how much they know about a subject or what they can do: *The students will be examined in all subjects at the end of the year.* ◆ *You are only being examined on this semester's work.* **4** ~ **sb** (law) to ask someone questions formally, especially in court ⬧ see also CROSS-EXAMINE **IDM** see NEED *v.*

ex·am·i·nee /ɪɡˌzæməˈniː/ noun a person who is being tested to see how much they know about a subject or what they can do; a person who is taking an exam

ex·am·in·er /ɪɡˈzæmənər/ noun **1** a person who writes the questions for, or grades, a test of knowledge or ability: *The papers are sent to external examiners* (= ones not connected with the students' school or college). **2** a person who has the official duty to check that things are being done correctly and according to the rules of an organization; a person who officially examines something ⬧ see also MEDICAL EXAMINER

ex·am·ple 🔊 /ɪɡˈzæmpl/ noun
1 ~ **(of sth)** something such as an object, a fact, or a situation that shows, explains, or supports what you say: *Can you give me an example of what you mean?* ◆ *This dictionary has many examples of how words are used.* ◆ *Just to give you an example of his generosity—he gave me his old car and wouldn't take any money for it.* ◆ *It is important to cite examples to support your argument.* ⬧ language bank at E.G. **2** ~ **(of sth)** a thing that is typical of or represents a particular group or set: *This is a good example of the artist's early work.* ◆ *It is a perfect example of a medieval castle.* ◆ *Japan is often quoted as the prime example of a modern industrial nation.* ◆ *It is a classic example of how not to design a new downtown area.* **3** a person or their behavior that is thought to be a good model for others to copy: ~ **(to sb)** *Her courage is an example to us all.* ◆ ~ **(for sb)** *He sets an example for the other students.* ◆ ~ **(of sth)** *She is a shining example of what people with disabilities can achieve.* ◆ *He is a captain who leads by example.* **4** a person's behavior, either good or bad, that other people copy: *It would be a mistake to follow his example.* **IDM for example** (abbr. **e.g.**) used to emphasize something that explains or supports what you are saying; used to give an example of what you are saying: *There is a similar word in many languages, for example in French and Italian.* ◆ *The report is incomplete; it does not include sales in France, for example.* ◆ *It is possible to combine Computer Science with other subjects, for example Physics.* ⬧ language bank at E.G. **make an example of sb** to punish someone as a warning to others not to do the same thing

example

case ◆ **instance** ◆ **specimen** ◆ **illustration**

These are all words for a thing or situation that is typical of a particular group or set, and is sometimes used to support an argument.

example something such as an object, a fact, or a situation that shows, explains, or supports what you say; a thing that is typical of or represents a particular group or set: *Can you give me an example of what you mean?*

case a particular situation or a situation of a particular type; a situation that relates to a particular person or thing: *In some cases people have had to wait several weeks for an appointment.*

instance (*somewhat formal*) a particular situation or a situation of a particular type: *The report highlights a number of instances of injustice.*

specimen an example of something, especially an animal or a plant: *The aquarium has some interesting specimens of tropical fish.*

illustration (*somewhat formal*) a story, an event, or an example that clearly shows the truth about something: *The statistics are a clear illustration of the point I am trying to make.*

EXAMPLE OR ILLUSTRATION?

An **illustration** is often used to show that something is true. An **example** is used to help to explain something.

PATTERNS

- a(n) example/case/instance/specimen/illustration **of** sth
- **in** a particular case/instance
- **for** example/instance

ex·as·per·ate /ɪɡˈzæspəˌreɪt/ *verb* ~ **sb** to annoy or irritate someone very much **SYN** INFURIATE ▶ **ex·as·per·a·tion** /ɪɡˌzæspəˈreɪʃn/ *noun* [U]: *He shook his head in exasperation.* ◆ *a groan/look/sigh of exasperation*

ex·as·per·at·ed /ɪɡˈzæspəˌreɪtəd/ *adj.* extremely annoyed, especially if you cannot do anything to improve the situation **SYN** INFURIATE: *"Why won't you answer me?" he asked in an exasperated voice.* ◆ *She was becoming exasperated with all the questions they were asking.* ▶ **ex·as·per·at·ed·ly** *adv.*

ex·as·per·at·ing /ɪɡˈzæspəˌreɪtɪŋ/ *adj.* extremely annoying **SYN** INFURIATING

ex·ca·vate /ˈɛkskəˌveɪt/ *verb* **1** to dig in the ground to look for old buildings or objects that have been buried for a long time; to find something by digging in this way: ~ **sth** *The site has been excavated by archaeologists.* ◆ ~ **sth from sth** *pottery and weapons excavated from the burial site* **2** ~ **sth** (*formal*) to make a hole, etc. in the ground by digging: *The body was discovered when builders excavated the area.*

ex·ca·va·tion /ˌɛkskəˈveɪʃn/ *noun* **1** [C, U] the activity of digging in the ground to look for old buildings or objects that have been buried for a long time **2** [C, usually pl.] a place where people are digging to look for old buildings or objects: *The excavations are open to the public.* **3** [U] the act of digging, especially with a machine

ex·ca·va·tor /ˈɛkskəˌveɪtər/ *noun* **1** a large machine that is used for digging and moving earth **2** a person who digs in the ground to look for old buildings and objects

ex·ceed **AWL** /ɪkˈsid/ *verb* (*formal*) **1** ~ **sth** to be greater than a particular number or amount: *The price will not exceed $100.* ◆ *His achievements have exceeded expectations.* **2** ~ **sth** to do more than the law or an order, etc. allows you to do: *She was exceeding the speed limit* (= driving faster than is allowed). ◆ *The officers had exceeded their authority.* ➔ see also EXCESS

ex·ceed·ing·ly /ɪkˈsidɪŋli/ *adv.* (*formal*) extremely; very; very much **SYN** EXCEPTIONALLY

ex·cel /ɪkˈsɛl/ *verb* (-ll-) [I] to be very good at doing something: ~ **(in/at sth)** *She has always excelled in foreign languages.* ◆ *As a child he excelled at music and art.* ◆ ~ **(at doing sth)** *The Badgers excel at generating turnovers.*

ex·cel·lence /ˈɛksələns/ *noun* [U] the quality of being extremely good: *a reputation for academic excellence* ◆ ~ **in sth** *The hospital is recognized as a center of excellence in research and teaching.* ➔ see also PAR EXCELLENCE

Ex·cel·len·cy /ˈɛksələnsi/ *noun* **His/Her/Your Excellency** (*pl.* **Ex·cel·len·cies**) a title used when talking to or about someone who has a very important official position, especially an AMBASSADOR: *Good evening, your Excellency.* ◆ *their Excellencies the French and Spanish Ambassadors*

ex·cel·lent 🔑 /ˈɛksələnt/ *adj.*

1 extremely good: *an excellent meal* ◆ *excellent service* ◆ *At $300 the bike is an excellent value.* ◆ *She speaks excellent French.* ◆ (*informal*) *It was absolutely excellent.* **2** used to show that you are very pleased about something or that you approve of something: *You can all come? Excellent!* ▶ **ex·cel·lent·ly** *adv.*

THESAURUS

excellent

outstanding ◆ **perfect** ◆ **superb**

These words all describe something that is extremely good.

excellent extremely good. **NOTE** Excellent is used especially about standards of service or of something that someone has worked to produce: *The rooms are excellent value at $20 a night.* ◆ *He speaks excellent English.* **NOTE** Excellent is also used to show that you are very pleased about something or that you approve of something: *You can all come? Excellent!*

outstanding extremely good. **NOTE** Outstanding is used especially about how well someone does something or how good someone is at something: *an outstanding achievement* ◆ *She's an outstanding dancer.*

perfect extremely good. **NOTE** Perfect is used especially about conditions or how suitable something is for a purpose: *Conditions were perfect for walking.* ◆ *She came up with the perfect excuse.*

superb (*formal*) extremely good or impressive: *The facilities at the hotel are superb.*

PATTERNS

- a(n) excellent/outstanding/perfect/superb **job/ performance**
- a(n) excellent/outstanding/superb **achievement**
- **absolutely** excellent/outstanding/perfect/superb

ex·cept 🔑 /ɪkˈsɛpt/ *prep., conj., verb*

- **prep.** (also **ex·cept for**) used before you mention the only thing or person about which a statement is not true **SYN** APART FROM: *We work every day except Sunday.* ◆ *They all came except Matt.* ◆ *I had nothing on except for my socks.* ◆ *This door should remain locked except in an emergency.* ➔ note at BESIDES

- **conj.** used before you mention something that makes a statement not completely true **SYN** APART FROM THE FACT THAT: ~ **(that)…** *I didn't tell him anything except that I needed the money.* ◆ *Our dresses were the same, except mine was red.* ◆ ~ **to do sth** *I had no choice except to continue.* ◆ ~ **do sth** *I could do nothing except watch it all happen.* ◆ ~ **when, where, etc.…** *He's never happy, except when he's out on his tractor.*

- **verb** [usually passive] (*formal*) to not include someone or something: ~ **sb/sth** *The sanctions ban the sale of any products excepting medical supplies and food.* ◆ *Tours are arranged year round (January excepted).* ◆ ~ **sb/sth from sth** *Children under five are excepted from the survey.* **IDM** see PRESENT *adj.*

LANGUAGE BANK

except

making an exception

- She wrote all of the songs on the album **except for** the final track.
- **Apart from/Aside from** the final track, all of the songs on the album were written by her.
- The songwriting — **with a few minor exceptions** — is of a very high quality.
- **With only one or two exceptions**, the songwriting is of a very high quality.

t tea   ţ butter   d did   k cat   g got   tʃ chin   dʒ June   f fall

- The majority of the compositions are less than three minutes long, **with the notable exception of** the title track.
- **With the exception of** the title track, this album is a huge disappointment.
- Here is a list of all the band's CDs, **excluding** unofficial "bootleg" recordings.

ex·cep·tion 🔑 /ɪk'sɛpʃn/ noun

1 a person or thing that is not included in a general statement: *Most of the buildings in the town are modern, but the church is an exception.* ◆ *With very few exceptions, private schools get the best exam results.* ◆ *Nobody had much money at the time and I was no exception.* ⊃ language bank at EXCEPT
2 a thing that does not follow a rule: *Good writing is unfortunately the exception rather than the rule* (= it is unusual). ◆ *There are always a lot of exceptions to grammar rules.*
IDM **make an exception** to allow someone not to follow the usual rule on one occasion: *Children are not usually allowed in, but I'm prepared to make an exception in this case.* **take exception to sth** to object strongly to something; to be angry about something: *I take great exception to the fact that you told my wife before you told me.* ◆ *No one could possibly take exception to his comments.* **with the exception of** except; not including: *All his novels are set in Italy with the exception of his last.* ⊃ language bank at EXCEPT **without exception** used to emphasize that the statement you are making is always true and everyone or everything is included: *All students without exception must take the English examination.*

ex·cep·tion·al /ɪk'sɛpʃənl/ adj. **1** unusually good **SYN** OUTSTANDING: *At the age of five he showed exceptional talent as a musician.* ◆ *The quality of the recording is exceptional.* **2** very unusual: *This deadline will be extended only in exceptional circumstances.* **ANT** UNEXCEPTIONAL **3** (of a child) having a physical or mental disability: *The program helps parents of exceptional children.*

ex·cep·tion·al·ly /ɪk'sɛpʃənəli/ adv. **1** used before an adjective or adverb to emphasize how strong or unusual the quality is: *The weather, even for January, was exceptionally cold.* ◆ *I thought Bill played exceptionally well.* **2** (formal) only in unusual circumstances: *Exceptionally, students may be accepted without formal qualifications.*

ex·cerpt noun /'ɛksərpt/ ~ **(from sth)** a short piece of writing, music, film, etc. taken from a longer whole ▶ **ex·cerpt** /ɛk'sərpt; 'ɛksərpt/ verb: ~ **sth (from sth)** *The document was excerpted from an unidentified FBI file.*

ex·cess noun, adj.
● *noun* /ɪk'sɛs; 'ɛksɛs/ **1** [sing., U] more than is necessary, reasonable, or acceptable: *You can throw away any excess.* ◆ ~ **of sth** *Are you suffering from an excess of stress in your life?* ◆ *In an excess of enthusiasm I agreed to work late.* ◆ *He started drinking to excess after losing his job.* ◆ *The increase will not be in excess of* (= more than) *two percent.* **2** [C, U] an amount by which something is larger than something else: *We cover costs up to $600 and then you pay the excess.* **3** **excesses** [pl.] extreme behavior that is unacceptable, illegal, or immoral: *We need a free press to curb government excesses.*
● *adj.* /'ɛksɛs/ [only before noun] in addition to an amount that is necessary, usual, or legal: *Excess food is stored as fat.* ◆ *Driving with excess alcohol in the blood is a serious offense.*

excess 'baggage noun [U] bags, cases, etc. taken on to a plane that weigh more than the amount each passenger is allowed to carry without paying extra

ex·ces·sive /ɪk'sɛsɪv/ adj. greater than what seems reasonable or appropriate: *They complained about the excessive noise coming from the upstairs apartment.* ◆ *The amounts she borrowed were not excessive.* ◆ *Excessive drinking can lead to stomach disorders.* ▶ **ex·ces·sive·ly** adv.: *excessively high prices*

ex·change 🔑 /ɪks'tʃeɪndʒ/ noun, verb
● *noun*
⟩ GIVING AND RECEIVING **1** [C, U] an act of giving something to someone or doing something for someone and receiving something in return: *The exchange of prisoners took place this morning.* ◆ *We need to promote an open exchange of ideas and information.* ◆ *an exchange of glances/insults* ◆ *an exchange of fire* (= between enemy soldiers) ◆ *I buy you lunch and you fix my computer. Is that a fair exchange?* ◆ *Would you like my old TV in exchange for this camera?* ◆ *I'll edit your report if you'll babysit in exchange.* ◆ *This shirt is an exchange. I just need a larger size.*
⟩ CONVERSATION/ARGUMENT **2** [C] a conversation or an argument: *There was only time for a brief exchange.* ◆ *The senator was involved in a heated exchange with two of his colleagues.* ◆ *After a harsh exchange of words, Owen stormed off.*
⟩ OF MONEY **3** [U] the process of changing an amount of one CURRENCY (= the money used in one country) for an equal value of another: *currency exchange facilities* ◆ *Where can I find the best exchange rate / rate of exchange?* ⊃ see also FOREIGN EXCHANGE
⟩ BETWEEN TWO COUNTRIES **4** [C] an arrangement when two people or groups from different countries visit each other's homes or do each other's jobs for a short time: *Our school does an exchange with a school in France.* ◆ *Nick went on the French exchange.* ◆ *trade and cultural exchanges with China*
⟩ BUILDING **5** often **Exchange** [C] (in compounds) a building where business people met in the past to buy and sell a particular type of goods: *the old Corn Exchange* ⊃ see also STOCK EXCHANGE
⟩ TELEPHONE **6** [C] = TELEPHONE EXCHANGE
● *verb*
⟩ GIVE AND RECEIVE **1** to give something to someone and at the same time receive the same type of thing from them: ~ **sth** *to exchange ideas/news/information* ◆ *Juliet and David exchanged glances* (= they looked at each other). ◆ *Everyone in the group exchanged e-mail addresses.* ◆ *The two men exchanged blows* (= hit each other). ◆ ~ **sth with sb** *I shook hands and exchanged a few words with the manager.*
⟩ MONEY/GOODS **2** to give or return something that you have and get something different or better instead: ~ **sth** *If it doesn't fit, take it back and the store will exchange it.* ◆ ~ **A for B** *You can exchange your currency for dollars in the hotel.* **IDM** see WORD n.

ex·change·a·ble /ɪks'tʃeɪndʒəbl/ adj. that can be exchanged: *These tokens are exchangeable for DVDs only.*

ex·cheq·uer /ɪks'tʃɛkər; 'ɛkstʃɛkər/ noun [sing.] often **the Exchequer** (in Britain) the government department that controls public money **SYN** TREASURY

ex·cise¹ /'ɛksaɪz/ noun [U] a government tax on some goods made, sold, or used within a country: *new excise duties on low-alcohol drinks* ◆ *a sharp increase in vehicle excise* ◆ *an excise officer* (= an official whose job is to collect excise) ⊃ compare CUSTOMS

ex·cise² /ɪk'saɪz/ verb ~ **sth (from sth)** (formal) to remove something completely: *Certain passages were excised from the book.*

ex·ci·sion /ɪk'sɪʒn/ noun [U, C] (formal or technical) the act of removing something completely from something; the thing removed

ex·cit·a·ble /ɪk'saɪtəbl/ adj. (of people or animals) likely to become easily excited: *a class of excitable ten-year-olds* ▶ **ex·cit·a·bil·i·ty** /ɪkˌsaɪtə'bɪləti/ noun [U]

ex·cite 🔑 /ɪk'saɪt/ verb
1 ~ **sb** to make someone feel very pleased, interested, or enthusiastic, especially about something that is going to happen: *The prospect of a year in India really excited her.* **2** to make someone nervous or upset and unable to relax: ~ **sb** *Try not to excite your baby too much before bedtime.* ◆ ~ **yourself** *Don't excite yourself* (= keep calm). **3** to make someone feel a particular emotion or react in a particular way **SYN** AROUSE: ~ **sth** *to excite attention/criticism/curiosity* ◆ *The news has certainly excited comment* (= made people

talk about it). ◆ **~ sth in sb** *Economic issues generally excite great interest in voters.* **4 ~ sb** to make someone feel sexual desire **SYN** AROUSE **5 ~ sth** (*formal*) to make a part of the body or part of a physical system more active **SYN** STIMULATE

ex·cit·ed 🔊 /ɪkˈsaɪtəd/ *adj.*

1 feeling or showing happiness and enthusiasm: **~ (about sth)** *The kids were excited about opening their gifts.* ◆ **~ (at sth)** *I'm really excited at the prospect of working abroad.* ◆ **~ (by sth)** *Don't get too excited by the sight of your name in print.* ◆ **~ (to do sth)** *He was very excited to be asked to play for the team.* ◆ *The new restaurant is **nothing to get excited about** (= not particularly good).* ◆ *An excited crowd of people gathered around her.* **2** nervous or upset and unable to relax: *Some horses become excited when they're in traffic.* **3** feeling sexual desire ▶ **ex·cit·ed·ly** *adv.*: *She waved excitedly as the car approached.*

THESAURUS

excited

ecstatic ◆ elated ◆ euphoric ◆ rapturous ◆ exhilarated

These words all describe feeling or showing happiness and enthusiasm.

excited feeling or showing happiness and enthusiasm: *The kids were excited about their vacation plans.*

ecstatic very happy, excited, and enthusiastic; showing this enthusiasm: *Sally was ecstatic about her new job.*

elated happy and excited because of something good that has happened or will happen: *I was elated to learn of their engagement.*

euphoric very happy and excited, but usually only for a short time: *I was euphoric after hearing the news.*

rapturous expressing extreme pleasure or enthusiasm: *He was greeted with rapturous applause.*

exhilarated happy and excited, especially after physical activity: *I felt exhilarated after a morning of skiing.*

PATTERNS
- to **be/feel** excited/elated/euphoric/exhilarated
- to be excited/ecstatic/elated/euphoric **at** sth
- to be excited/ecstatic/elated **about** sth
- to be excited/elated/exhilarated **by** sth
- to be ecstatic/elated/exhilarated **with** sth

---

ex·cite·ment 🔊 /ɪkˈsaɪtmənt/ *noun*

1 [U] the state of feeling excited: *The news caused great excitement among her friends.* ◆ *to feel a **surge/thrill/shiver of excitement*** ◆ *He was flushed **with excitement** at the thought.* ◆ *The dog leapt and wagged its tail **in excitement**.* ◆ *In her excitement she dropped her glass.* **2** [C] (*formal*) something that you find exciting: *The new job was not without its excitements.*

ex·cit·ing 🔊 /ɪkˈsaɪtɪŋ/ *adj.*

causing great interest or excitement: *This is just one of the many exciting projects we are working on.* ◆ *They waited and waited for something exciting to happen.* ◆ *an **exciting prospect/possibility*** ◆ *an **exciting story/discovery*** ▶ **ex·cit·ing·ly** *adv.*

THESAURUS

exciting

dramatic ◆ thrilling ◆ exhilarating

These words all describe an event, an experience, or a feeling that causes excitement.

exciting causing great interest or excitement: *This is one of the most exciting developments in biology in recent years.*

dramatic (of events or scenes) exciting and impressive: *They saw dramatic pictures of the hurricane on TV.*

---

thrilling exciting and enjoyable: *Don't miss next week's thrilling episode!*

exhilarating very exciting and enjoyable: *My first parachute jump was an exhilarating experience.*

EXCITING, THRILLING, OR EXHILARATING?

Exhilarating is the strongest of these words and **exciting** the least strong. **Exciting** is the most general and can be used to talk about any activity, experience, feeling, or event that excites you. **Thrilling** is used especially for contests and stories where the ending is uncertain. **Exhilarating** is used especially for physical activities that involve speed and/or danger.

PATTERNS
- a(n) exciting/dramatic/thrilling/exhilarating **experience/moment**
- a(n) exciting/dramatic **atmosphere**
- a(n) exciting/dramatic/thrilling **finish/finale/victory/win**

---

ex·claim /ɪkˈskleɪm/ *verb* [I, T] to say something suddenly and loudly, especially because of strong emotion or pain: *She opened her eyes and exclaimed in delight at the scene.* ◆ **+ speech** *"It isn't fair!" he exclaimed angrily.* ◆ **~ that...** *She exclaimed that it was useless.* ➲ thesaurus box at CALL

ex·cla·ma·tion /ˌekskləˈmeɪʃn/ *noun* a short sound, word, or phrase spoken suddenly to express an emotion. *Oh!*, *Look out!* and *Ow!* are exclamations: *He gave an exclamation of surprise.*

excla'mation ˌpoint (also **excla'mation ˌmark**) *noun* the mark (!) that is written after an exclamation

ex·clam·a·to·ry /ɪkˈsklæməˌtɔri/ *adj.* (*formal*) (of language) expressing surprise or strong feelings

ex·clude 🔊 **AWL** /ɪkˈsklud/ *verb*

1 ~ sth (from sth) to deliberately not include something in what you are doing or considering: *The cost of borrowing has been excluded from the inflation figures.* ◆ *Try excluding fat from your diet.* ◆ *Buses run every hour, Sundays excluded.* **ANT** INCLUDE **2 ~ sb/sth (from sth)** to prevent someone or something from entering a place or taking part in something: *Women are still excluded from some clubs.* ◆ *She felt excluded by the other girls* (= they did not let her join in what they were doing). **3 ~ sth** to decide that something is not possible: *We should not **exclude the possibility** of negotiation.* ◆ *The police have excluded theft as a motive for the murder.* **ANT** INCLUDE

ex·clud·ing 🔊 **AWL** /ɪkˈskludɪŋ/ *prep.*

not including: *Lunch costs $10 per person, excluding drinks.* ➲ language bank at EXCEPT

ex·clu·sion **AWL** /ɪkˈskluʒn/ *noun* **1** [U] **~ (of sb/sth) (from sth)** the act of preventing someone or something from entering a place or taking part in something: *He was disappointed with his exclusion from the squad.* ◆ *Exclusion of air creates a vacuum in the bottle.* ◆ *Memories of the past filled her mind **to the exclusion of** all else.* **2** [C] a person or thing that is not included in something: *Check the list of exclusions in the insurance policy.* **3** [U] **~ (of sth)** the act of deciding that something is not possible: *the exclusion of robbery as a motive* **ANT** INCLUSION

ex·clu·sion·ar·y **AWL** /ɪkˈskluʒəˌneri/ *adj.* (*formal*) designed to prevent a particular person or group of people from taking part in something or doing something

ex'clusion ˌzone *noun* an area where people are not allowed to enter because it is dangerous or is used for secret activities

ex·clu·sive **AWL** /ɪkˈsklusɪv/ *adj., noun*

● *adj.* **1** only to be used by one particular person or group; only given to one particular person or group: *The hotel has exclusive access to the beach.* ◆ *exclusive rights to televise the World Series* ◆ *His mother has told "People" magazine about his death in an exclusive interview* (= not given to any other

h **hat**   m **man**   n **no**   ŋ **sing**   l **leg**   r **red**   y **yes**   w **wet**

newspaper). **2** (of a group, society, etc.) not very willing to allow new people to become members, especially if they are from a lower social class: *He belongs to an exclusive club.* **3** of a high quality and expensive, and therefore not often bought or used by most people: *an exclusive hotel* ◆ *exclusive designer clothes* **4** not able to exist or be a true statement at the same time as something else: *The two options are not **mutually exclusive** (= you can have them both).* **5** (*formal*) **~ of sb/sth** not including someone or something: *The price is for room only, exclusive of meals.* **ANT** INCLUSIVE ▶ **ex·clu·sive·ly** **AWL** *adv.*: *a charity that relies almost exclusively on voluntary contributions*

● **noun** an item of news or a story about famous people that is published in only one newspaper or magazine

ex·clu·siv·i·ty /ˌɛkskluˈsɪvəti/ (also **ex·clu·sive·ness** /ɪkˈsklusɪvnəs/) *noun* [U] the quality of being exclusive: *The resort still preserves a feeling of exclusivity.* ◆ *a designer whose clothes have not lost their exclusiveness*

ex·com·mu·ni·cate /ˌɛkskəˈmyunəˌkeɪt/ *verb* **~ sb (for sth)** to punish someone by officially stating that they can no longer be a member of a Christian Church, especially the Roman Catholic Church ▶ **ex·com·mu·ni·ca·tion** /ˌɛkskə-ˌmyunəˈkeɪʃn/ *noun* [U, C]

ex·co·ri·ate /ɪkˈskɔriˌeɪt/ *verb* **1 ~ sth** (*medical*) to irritate a person's skin so that it starts to come off **2 ~ sb/sth** (*formal*) to criticize someone or something severely ▶ **ex·co·ri·a·tion** /ɪkˌskɔriˈeɪʃn/ *noun* [U, C]

ex·cre·ment /ˈɛkskrəmənt/ *noun* [U] (*formal*) solid waste matter that is passed from the body through the BOWELS **SYN** FECES: *the pollution of drinking water by untreated human excrement* ▶ **ex·cre·men·tal** /ˌɛkskrəˈmɛntl/ *adj.*

ex·cres·cence /ɪkˈskrɛsns/ *noun* (*formal*) an ugly lump that has grown on a part of an animal's body or on a plant: (*figurative*) *The new office building is an excrescence* (= it is very ugly).

ex·cre·ta /ɪkˈskritə/ *noun* [U] (*formal*) solid and liquid waste matter passed from the body: *human excreta*

ex·crete /ɪkˈskrit/ *verb* [I, T] **~ (sth)** (*technical*) to pass solid or liquid waste matter from the body ▶ **ex·cre·tion** /ɪkˈskriʃn/ *noun* [U, C]

ex·cre·to·ry /ˈɛkskrəˌtɔri/ *adj.* (*biology*) connected with getting rid of waste matter from the body: *the excretory organs*

ex·cru·ci·at·ing /ɪkˈskruʃiˌeɪtɪŋ/ *adj.* extremely painful or bad: *The pain in my back was excruciating.* ◆ *She groaned at the memory, suffering all over again the excruciating embarrassment of those moments.* ⮞ thesaurus box at PAINFUL ▶ **ex·cru·ci·at·ing·ly** *adv.*: *excruciatingly uncomfortable* ◆ *excruciatingly painful/boring/embarrassing*

ex·cul·pate /ˈɛkskʌlˌpeɪt/ *verb* **~ sb** (*formal*) to prove or state officially that someone is not guilty of something ▶ **ex·cul·pa·tion** /ˌɛkskʌlˈpeɪʃn/ *noun* [U]

ex·cur·sion /ɪkˈskərʒn/ *noun* **1** a short trip made for pleasure, especially one that has been organized for a group of people: *They've gone **on an excursion** to New York.* ⮞ thesaurus box at TRIP **2 ~ into sth** (*formal*) a short period of trying a new or different activity: *After a brief excursion into drama, he concentrated on his main interest, which was poetry.*

ex·cus·a·ble /ɪkˈskyuzəbl/ *adj.* [not usually before noun] that can be excused **SYN** FORGIVABLE: *Doing it once was just about excusable — doing it twice was certainly not.* **ANT** INEXCUSABLE

ex·cuse 🔑 *noun, verb*

● **noun** /ɪkˈskyus/ **1** a reason, either true or invented, that you give to explain or defend your behavior: *Late again! What's your excuse this time?* ◆ **~ (for sth)** *There's no excuse for such behavior.* ◆ **~ (for doing sth)** *His excuse for forgetting her birthday was that he had lost his calendar.* ◆ *You don't have to **make excuses** for her* (= try to think of reasons for her behavior). ◆ *It's late. I'm afraid I'll have to **make my excuses*** (= say I'm sorry, give my reasons, and leave). ⮞ thesaurus box at REASON **2** a good reason that you give for doing some-

thing that you want to do for other reasons: **~ (for sth/for doing sth)** *It's just an excuse for a party.* ◆ **~ (to do sth)** *It gave me an excuse to drive instead of walking.* **3** a very bad example of something: *Why get involved with that pathetic excuse for a human being?* **4** a note written by a parent or doctor to explain why a student cannot go to school or someone cannot go to work

● **verb** /ɪkˈskyuz/ **1** to forgive someone for something that they have done, for example not being polite or making a small mistake: **~ sth** *Please excuse the mess.* ◆ **~ sb** *You must excuse my father—he's not always that rude.* ◆ **~ sb for sth/for doing sth** *I hope you'll excuse me for being so late.* ◆ *You can be excused for thinking that Ben is in charge* (= he is not, but it is an easy mistake to make). ◆ **~ sb doing sth** (*formal*) *Excuse my interrupting you.* **2 ~ sth** | **~ sb/yourself (for sth/for doing sth)** to make your or someone else's behavior seem less offensive by finding reasons for it **SYN** JUSTIFY: *Nothing can excuse such rudeness.* **3 ~ sb/yourself (from sth)** to allow someone to leave; to say in a polite way that you are leaving: *Now if you'll excuse me, I'm a very busy man.* ◆ *She excused herself and left the meeting early.* **4** [usually passive] **~ sb (from sth/from doing sth)** | **~ sb sth** to allow someone to not do something that they should normally do: *She was excused from giving evidence because of her age.* **IDM** **excuse me 1** used to politely get someone's attention, especially someone you do not know: *Excuse me, is this the way to the train station?* **2** used to politely ask someone to move so that you can get past them: *Excuse me, could you let me through?* **3** used to say that you are sorry for interrupting someone or behaving in a slightly rude way: *Guy sneezed loudly. "Excuse me," he said.* **4** used to disagree politely with someone: *Excuse me, but I don't think that's true.* **5** used to politely tell someone that you are going to leave or talk to someone else: *"Excuse me for a moment," she said and left the room.* **6** used to say sorry for pushing someone or doing something wrong: *Oh, excuse me. I didn't see you there.* **7 excuse me?** used when you did not hear what someone said and you want them to repeat it ⮞ more at FRENCH *n.*

ex·ec /ɪgˈzɛk/ *noun* (*informal*) an executive in a business

ex·e·cra·ble /ˈɛksəkrəbl/ *adj.* (*formal*) very bad **SYN** TERRIBLE

ex·e·cut·a·ble /ˈɛksəˌkyutəbl/ *adj.* (*computing*) (of a file or program) that can be run by a computer

ex·e·cute /ˈɛksəˌkyut/ *verb* **1** [usually passive] **~ sb (for sth)** to kill someone, especially as a legal punishment: *He was executed for treason.* ◆ *The prisoners were executed by firing squad.* **2 ~ sth** (*formal*) to do a piece of work, perform a duty, put a plan into action, etc.: *They drew up and executed a plan to reduce fuel consumption.* ◆ *The crime was very cleverly executed.* ◆ *Check that the computer has executed your commands.* **3 ~ sth** (*formal*) to successfully perform a skillful action or movement: *The pilot executed a perfect landing.* **4 ~ sth** (*formal*) to make or produce a work of art: *Picasso also executed several landscapes at Horta de San Juan.* **5 ~ sth** (*law*) to follow the instructions in a legal document; to make a document legally valid

ex·e·cu·tion /ˌɛksəˈkyuʃn/ *noun* **1** [U, C] the act of killing someone, especially as a legal punishment: *He faced execution by hanging for murder.* ◆ *Over 200 executions were carried out last year.* **2** [U] (*formal*) the act of doing a piece of work, performing a duty, or putting a plan into action: *He had failed in the execution of his duty.* ◆ *The idea was good, but the execution was poor.* **3** [U] (*formal*) skill in performing or making something, such as a piece of music or work of art: *Her execution of the piano piece was perfect.* **4** [U] (*law*) the act of following the instructions in a legal document, especially those in someone's WILL **IDM** see STAY *n.*

ex·e·cu·tion·er /ˌɛksəˈkyuʃənər/ *noun* a public official whose job is to execute criminals

ex·ec·u·tive 🔑 /ɪgˈzɛkyətɪv/ *noun, adj.*

● **noun 1** [C] a person who has an important job as a manager of a company or an organization: *advertising/*

business/sales, etc. executives ♦ a chief/senior executive in a computer company **2** [C] a group of people who run a company or an organization: *The union's executive has yet to reach a decision.* **3 the executive** [sing.] the part of a government responsible for putting laws into effect **SYN** EXECUTIVE BRANCH ⊃ compare JUDICIARY, LEGISLATURE

● *adj.* [only before noun] **1** connected with managing a business or an organization, and with making plans and decisions: *She has an executive position in a finance company.* ♦ *executive decisions/duties/jobs/positions* ♦ *the executive producer of a TV show* **2** having the power to put important laws and decisions into effect: *executive authority* ♦ *an executive board/body/committee/officer* ♦ *Executive power is held by the president.* **3** expensive; for the use of someone who is considered important: *an executive car/home* ♦ *an executive suite* (= in a hotel) ♦ *an executive lounge* (= at an airport)

the ex'ecutive 'branch *noun* [sing.] the part of the U.S. government that is controlled by the president ⊃ compare JUDICIAL BRANCH, LEGISLATIVE BRANCH

ex,ecutive 'privilege *noun* [U] the right of the U.S. president and the executive part of the government to keep official documents secret

ex,ecutive 'secretary *noun* a secretary who manages the business activities of an executive or an organization

ex·ec·u·tor /ɪɡˈzɛkyətər/ *noun* (*technical*) a person, bank, etc. that is chosen by someone who is making their WILL to follow the instructions in it

ex·e·ge·sis /ˌɛksəˈdʒisəs/ *noun* (*pl.* **ex·e·ge·ses** /-siz/) [C, U] (*formal*) the detailed explanation of a piece of writing, especially religious writing

ex·em·plar /ɪɡˈzɛmplɑr; -plər/ *noun* (*formal*) a person or thing that is a good or typical example of something **SYN** MODEL

ex·em·pla·ry /ɪɡˈzɛmpləri/ *adj.* (*formal*) **1** providing a good example for people to copy: *Her behavior was exemplary.* ♦ *a man of exemplary character* **2** [usually before noun] (*law* or *formal*) (of punishment) severe; used especially as a warning to others

ex·em·pli·fy /ɪɡˈzɛmpləˌfaɪ/ *verb* (**ex·em·pli·fies, ex·em·pli·fy·ing, ex·em·pli·fied, ex·em·pli·fied**) [often passive] (*formal*) **1** ~ *sth* to be a typical example of something: *Her early work is exemplified in her book, "A Study of Children's Minds."* ♦ *His food exemplifies Italian cooking at its best.* **2** ~ *sth* to give an example in order to make something clearer **SYN** ILLUSTRATE: *She exemplified each of the points she was making with an amusing anecdote.* ▶ **ex·em·pli·fi·ca·tion** /ɪɡˌzɛmpləfəˈkeɪʃn/ *noun* [U, C]

ex·empt /ɪɡˈzɛmpt/ *adj., verb*
● *adj.* [not before noun] ~ **(from sth)** if someone or something is **exempt** from something, they are not affected by it, do not have to do it or pay it, etc.: *The interest on the money is exempt from tax.* ♦ *Some students are exempt from certain exams.* ▶ **-exempt** (in compounds, forming adjectives): *tax-exempt organizations such as churches*

● *verb* ~ sb/sth **(from sth/from doing sth)** (*formal*) to give or get someone's official permission not to do something or not to pay something they would normally have to do or pay: *His bad eyesight exempted him from military service.* ♦ *In 1983, charities were exempted from paying the tax.*

ex·emp·tion /ɪɡˈzɛmpʃn/ *noun* **1** [U, C] ~ **(from sth)** official permission not to do something or pay something that you would normally have to do or pay: *She was given an exemption from the final examination.* **2** [C] a part of your income that you do not have to pay tax on: *a tax exemption for college students*

ex·er·cise ♪ /ˈɛksərˌsaɪz/ *noun, verb*
● *noun*
> ACTIVITY/MOVEMENTS **1** [U] physical or mental activity that you do to stay healthy or become stronger: *Swimming is good exercise.* ♦ *I don't get much exercise sitting in the office all day.* ♦ *The mind needs exercise as well as the body.* ♦ *vigorous/gentle exercise* ⊃ collocations at DIET **2** [C] a set of movements or activities that you do to stay healthy or develop a skill: *breathing/relaxation/stretching exercises* ♦ *exercises for the piano* ♦ *Repeat the exercise ten times on each leg.*
> QUESTIONS **3** [C] a set of questions in a book that tests your knowledge or practices a skill: *grammar exercises* ♦ *Do exercise one for homework.*
> USE OF POWER/RIGHT/QUALITY **4** [U] ~ **of sth** (*formal*) the use of power, a skill, a quality, or a right to make something happen: *the exercise of power by the government* ♦ *the exercise of discretion*
> FOR PARTICULAR RESULT **5** [C] an activity that is designed to achieve a particular result: *a communications exercise* ♦ *In the end it proved a pointless exercise.* ♦ ~ **in sth** *an exercise in public relations* ♦ *Staying calm was an exercise in self-control.*
> FOR SOLDIERS **6** [C, usually pl.] a set of activities for training soldiers: *military exercises*
> CEREMONIES **7 exercises** [pl.] ceremonies: *college graduation exercises*
● *verb*
> DO PHYSICAL ACTIVITY **1** [I, T] to do sports or other physical activities in order to stay healthy or become stronger; to make an animal do this: *I exercise every morning before work.* ♦ *How often do you exercise?* ♦ ~ *sth* *Horses need to be exercised regularly.* **2** [T] ~ *sth* to give a part of the body the movement and activity it needs to keep strong and healthy: *These movements will exercise your arms and shoulders.*

exercise

push-up   sit-up   barbell   dumbbell

jogging   yoga   exercise bike   rowing machine   treadmill

> USE POWER/RIGHT/QUALITY **3** [T] ~ **sth** (formal) to use your power, rights, or personal qualities in order to achieve something: *When she appeared in court, she exercised her right to remain silent.* ◆ *He was a man who exercised considerable influence over people.*
> BE ANXIOUS **4** [usually passive] ~ **sb/sth (about sth)** (formal) if someone is **exercised** about something, they are very anxious about it

'**exercise** ˌ**ball** (also sta'bility ˌball) *noun* a large ball that you can sit on when doing exercises to make your muscles work in a different way

'**exercise** ˌ**bike** *noun* a bicycle that does not move forward but is used for getting exercise indoors ⊃ picture at EXERCISE

'**exercise** ˌ**book** *noun* = WORKBOOK

ex·ert /ɪgˈzɜrt/ *verb* **1** ~ **sth** to use power or influence to affect someone or something: *He exerted all his authority to make them accept the plan.* ◆ *The moon exerts a force on the earth that causes the tides.* **2** ~ **yourself** to make a big physical or mental effort: *In order to be successful, he would have to exert himself.*

ex·er·tion /ɪgˈzɜrʃn/ *noun* **1** [U] also **exertions** [pl.] physical or mental effort; the act of making an effort: *She was hot and breathless from the exertion of riding her bike uphill.* ◆ *He needed to relax after the exertions of a busy day at work.* **2** [sing.] the use of power to make something happen: *the exertion of force/strength/authority*

ex·e·unt /ˈɛksiˌʌnt; -ˌʊnt/ *verb* [I] (from *Latin*) used in a play as a written instruction that tells two or more actors to leave the stage ⊃ compare EXIT

ex·fo·li·ate /eksˈfouliˌeɪt/ *verb* [I, T] ~ **(sth)** to remove dead cells from the surface of the skin in order to make it smoother ► **ex·fo·li·a·tion** /eksˌfouliˈeɪʃn/ *noun* [U]

ex gra·ti·a /ˌeks ˈgreɪʃiə/ *adj.* (from *Latin*) given or done as a gift or favor, not because there is a legal duty to do it: *ex gratia payments* ► **ex gra·ti·a** *adv.*: *The sum was paid ex gratia.*

ex·hale /eksˈheɪl; ˈeksheɪl/ *verb* [I, T] to breathe out the air or smoke, etc. in your lungs: *He sat back and exhaled deeply.* ◆ ~ **sth** *She exhaled the smoke through her nose.* **ANT** INHALE ► **ex·ha·la·tion** /ˌekshəˈleɪʃn; ˌeksə-/ *noun* [U, C]

ex·haust /ɪgˈzɔst/ *noun, verb*
● *noun* **1** [U] waste gases that come out of a vehicle, an engine, or a machine: *car exhaust fumes* **2** (also ex'haust pipe, tail·pipe) [C] a pipe through which exhaust gases come out: *My car needs a new exhaust.* ⊃ picture at CAR
● *verb* **1** to make someone feel very tired **SYN** WEAR OUT: ~ **sb** *Even a short walk exhausted her.* ◆ ~ **yourself** *Don't exhaust yourself. We'll clean up for you.* **2** ~ **sth** to use all of something so that there is none left: *Within three days they had exhausted their supply of food.* ◆ *Don't give up until you have exhausted all the possibilities.* **3** ~ **sth** to talk about or study a subject until there is nothing else to say about it: *I think we've exhausted that particular topic.*

ex·haust·ed /ɪgˈzɔstəd/ *adj.* **1** very tired: *I'm exhausted!* ◆ *to feel completely/totally exhausted* ◆ *The exhausted climbers were rescued by helicopter.* **2** completely used or finished: *You cannot grow crops on exhausted land.*

ex·haust·ing /ɪgˈzɔstɪŋ/ *adj.* making you feel very tired: *an exhausting day at work* ◆ *I find her exhausting—she never stops talking.*

ex·haus·tion /ɪgˈzɔstʃən/ *noun* [U] **1** the state of being very tired: *suffering from physical/mental/nervous exhaustion* ◆ *Her face was gray with exhaustion.* ⊃ see also HEAT EX-HAUSTION **2** (formal) the act of using something until it is completely finished: *the exhaustion of natural resources*

ex·haus·tive /ɪgˈzɔstɪv/ *adj.* including everything possible; very thorough or complete: *exhaustive research/tests* ◆ *This list is not intended to be exhaustive.* ► **ex·haus·tive·ly** *adv.*: *Every product is exhaustively tested before being sold.*

ex'haust pipe *noun* = EXHAUST

ex·hib·it 🔑 **AWL** /ɪgˈzɪbət/ *verb, noun*
● *verb* **1** [T, I] to show something in a public place for people to enjoy or to give them information: ~ **sth (at/in…)** *They will be exhibiting their new designs at the trade fairs.* ◆ ~ **(at/in…)** *He exhibits regularly in local art galleries.* **2** [T] ~ **sth** (formal) to show clearly that you have or feel a particular feeling, quality, or ability **SYN** DISPLAY: *The patient exhibited signs of fatigue and memory loss.*
● *noun* **1** an object or a collection of objects shown in a public place, for example a museum: *The new exhibit will tour a dozen European cities next year.* **2** a thing that is used in court to prove that someone is guilty or not guilty: *The first exhibit was a knife that the prosecution claimed was the murder weapon.*

ex·hi·bi·tion 🔑 **AWL** /ˌeksəˈbɪʃn/ *noun*
1 [C] a collection of things, for example works of art, that are shown to the public **SYN** EXHIBIT *n.* (1): *Have you seen the Picasso exhibition?* ◆ *an exhibition of old photographs* ⊃ collocations at ART **2** (CanE) [C] a large regional fair, where you can ride on machines, look at farm animals, buy products people have made, etc. **3** [U] ~ **of sth** the act of showing something, for example works of art, to the public: *She refused to allow the exhibition of her husband's work.* **4** [sing.] **an ~ of sth** the act of showing a skill, a feeling, or a kind of behavior: *We were treated to an exhibition of the athlete's speed and skill.* ◆ *an appalling exhibition of cruelty* **IDM** **make an exhibition of yourself** (disapproving) to behave in a bad or stupid way in public

ex·hi·bi·tion·ism /ˌeksəˈbɪʃəˌnɪzəm/ *noun* [U] **1** (disapproving) behavior that is intended to make people notice or admire you **2** (psychology) the mental condition that makes someone want to show their sexual organs in public

ex·hi·bi·tion·ist /ˌeksəˈbɪʃənɪst/ *noun* (usually disapproving) a person who likes to make other people notice him or her: *Children are natural exhibitionists.*

ex·hib·i·tor /ɪgˈzɪbətər/ *noun* a person or a company that shows their work or products to the public

ex·hil·a·rate /ɪgˈzɪləˌreɪt/ *verb* ~ **sb** to make someone feel very happy and excited: *Speed had always exhilarated him.* ► **ex·hil·a·rat·ed** *adj.*: *I felt exhilarated after a morning of skiing.* ⊃ thesaurus box at EXCITED **ex·hil·a·ra·tion** /ɪgˌzɪləˈreɪʃn/ *noun* [U]: *the exhilaration of performing on stage*

ex·hil·a·rat·ing /ɪgˈzɪləˌreɪtɪŋ/ *adj.* very exciting and enjoyable: *My first parachute jump was an exhilarating experience.* ⊃ thesaurus box at EXCITING

ex·hort /ɪgˈzɔrt/ *verb* (formal) to try hard to persuade someone to do something **SYN** URGE: ~ **sb to do sth** *The media have been exhorting people to come to the demonstration.* ◆ ~ **sb to sth** *They had been exhorted to action.* ◆ ~ **(sb) + speech** *"Come on!" he exhorted (them).* ► **ex·hor·ta·tion** /ˌegzɔrˈteɪʃn; ˌeksɔr-/ *noun* [C, U]

ex·hume /ɪgˈzum/ *verb* [usually passive] ~ **sth** (formal) to remove a dead body from the ground especially in order to examine how the person died **SYN** DIG UP ► **ex·hu·ma·tion** /ˌegzuˈmeɪʃn; ˌekshyu-/ *noun* [U]

ex·i·gen·cy /ˈeksədʒənsi/ *noun* (pl. **ex·i·gen·cies**) [C, usually pl., U] (formal) an urgent need or demand that you must deal with **SYN** DEMAND

ex·ig·u·ous /egˈzɪgyuəs/ *adj.* (formal) very small in size or amount; hardly enough

ex·ile /ˈegzaɪl; ˈeksaɪl/ *noun, verb*
● *noun* **1** [U, sing.] the state of being sent to live in another country that is not your own, especially for political reasons or as a punishment: *to be/live in exile* ◆ *to be forced/sent into exile* ◆ *to go into exile* ◆ *a place of exile* ◆ *He returned after 40 years of exile.* **2** [C] a person who chooses or is forced to live away from his or her own country: *political exiles* ◆ *a tax exile* (= rich person who moves to another country where taxes are lower)
● *verb* [usually passive] ~ **sb (from…)** to force someone to leave their country, especially for political reasons or as a

punishment; to send someone into exile: *the party's exiled leaders*

ex·ist 🔑 /ɪgˈzɪst/ *verb*
1 [I] (not used in the progressive tenses) to be real; to be present in a place or situation: *Does life exist on other planets?* ♦ *The problem only exists in your head, Jen.* ♦ *Few of these monkeys still exist in the wild.* ♦ *When he retires, his position will cease to exist.* ♦ *The charity exists to support victims of crime.* **2** [I] ~ **(on sth)** to live, especially in a difficult situation or with very little money: *We existed on a diet of rice.* ♦ *They can't exist on the money he's earning.*

ex·ist·ence 🔑 /ɪgˈzɪstəns/ *noun*
1 [U] the state or fact of being real or living. or of being present: *I was unaware of his existence until today.* ♦ *This is the oldest Hebrew manuscript in existence.* ♦ *Pakistan came into existence as an independent country in 1947.* ♦ *a crisis that threatens the industry's continued existence* **2** [C] a way of living, especially when this is difficult or boring: *The family endured a miserable existence in a cramped apartment.* ♦ *We led a poor but happy enough existence as children.* ♦ *They eke out a precarious existence* (= they have hardly enough money to live on). ♦ *The peasants depend on a good harvest for their very existence* (= in order to continue to live).

ex·ist·ent /ɪgˈzɪstənt/ *adj., noun*
● *adj.* (*formal*) existing; real: *creatures existent in nature* **ANT** NONEXISTENT
● *noun* (*philosophy*) a thing that is real and exists: *The self is the only knowable existent.*

ex·is·ten·tial /ˌɛgzɪˈstɛnʃəl/ *adj.* [only before noun] **1** (*formal*) connected with human existence **2** (*philosophy*) connected with the theory of existentialism

ex·is·ten·tial·ism /ˌɛgzɪˈstɛnʃəˌlɪzəm/ *noun* [U] (*philosophy*) the theory that humans are free and responsible for their own actions in a world without meaning
▶ **ex·is·ten·tial·ist** /-ʃəlɪst/ *noun*: *Sartre was an existentialist.* **ex·is·ten·tial·ist** *adj.*: *existentialist theory*

ex·ist·ing /ɪgˈzɪstɪŋ/ *adj.* [only before noun] found or used now: *New laws will soon replace existing legislation.*

ex·it 🔑 /ˈɛgzət; ˈɛksət/ *noun, verb*
● *noun* **1** a way out of a public building or vehicle: *Where's the exit?* ♦ *There is a fire exit on each floor of the building.* ♦ *The emergency exit is at the back of the bus.* ⊃ compare ENTRANCE[1] **2** an act of leaving, especially of an actor from the stage: *The heroine made her exit to great applause.* ♦ *He made a quick exit to avoid meeting her.* ♦ *an exit visa* (= a stamp in a passport giving someone permission to leave a particular country) **3** a place where vehicles can leave a road to join another road: *Leave the traffic circle at the second exit.* ♦ *Take the exit for Pennsylvania Avenue.*
● *verb* **1** [I, T] (*formal*) to go out; to leave a building, stage, vehicle, etc.: *(+ adv./prep.) The bullet entered her back and exited through her chest.* ♦ *We exited via a fire door.* ♦ *As the actors exited the stage the lights went on.* **2** [I, T] to finish using a computer program: ~ **(from sth)** *To exit from this page, press the return key.* ♦ ~ **sth** *I exited the database and turned off the computer.* **3** [I] **exit…** used in the instructions printed in a play to say that an actor must leave the stage ⊃ compare EXEUNT

ˈexit ex·am (also *formal* **ˈexit ex·amination**) *noun* an exam that students in some states take at the end of the last year in school or at the end of a period of training: *a high school exit exam*

ˈexit ·poll *noun* in an **exit poll** immediately after an election, people are asked how they voted, in order to predict the result of the election

ex li·bris /ˌɛks ˈlibrɪs/ *adv.* written in the front of a book before the name of the person the book belongs to: *ex libris David Harris*

ex·o·crine /ˈɛksəkrən/ *adj.* (*biology*) connected with GLANDS that do not put substances directly into the blood, but

export their product through tubes for use outside the body: *exocrine glands* ⊃ compare ENDOCRINE

ex·o·dus /ˈɛksədəs/ *noun* [sing.] ~ **(from…) (to…)** (*formal* or *humorous*) a situation in which many people leave a place at the same time: *the mass exodus from New York City to the beach in the summer*

ex of·fi·ci·o /ˌɛks əˈfɪʃioʊ/ *adj.* (from Latin, *formal*) included or allowed because of your job, position, or rank: *an ex officio member of the committee* ▶ **ex of·fi·ci·o** *adv.*

ex·og·a·my /ɛkˈsɑgəmi/ *noun* [U] (*technical*) marriage outside your family or CASTE (= division of society) ⊃ compare ENDOGAMY ▶ **ex·og·a·mous** /-məs/ *adj.*

ex·og·e·nous /ɛkˈsɑdʒənəs/ *adj.* (*medical*) (of a disease or SYMPTOM) having a cause that is outside the body ⊃ compare ENDOGENOUS

ex·on·er·ate /ɪgˈzɑnəˌreɪt/ *verb* ~ **sb (from sth)** (*formal*) to officially state that someone is not responsible for something that they have been blamed for: *The police report exonerated Lewis from all charges of corruption.*
▶ **ex·on·er·a·tion** /ɪgˌzɑnəˈreɪʃn/ *noun* [U]

ex·or·bi·tant /ɪgˈzɔrbətənt/ *adj.* (*formal*) (of a price) much too high: *exorbitant costs/fares/fees/prices/rents*
▶ **ex·or·bi·tant·ly** *adv.*: *Prices are exorbitantly high in this store.*

ex·or·cise (also **ex·or·cize**) /ˈɛksɔrˌsaɪz; -sər-/ *verb* **1** ~ **sth (from sb/sth)** to make an evil spirit leave a place or someone's body by special prayers or magic **2** ~ **sth (from sth)** (*formal*) to remove something that is bad or painful from your mind: *She had managed to exorcise these unhappy memories from her mind.* ♦ *to exorcise the demons/ghosts of your past*

ex·or·cism /ˈɛksɔrˌsɪzəm; -sər-/ *noun* [C, U] **1** the act of getting rid of an evil spirit from a place or a person's body by prayers or magic; a ceremony where this is done **2** (*formal*) the act of making yourself forget a bad experience or memory

ex·or·cist /ˈɛksɔrsɪst; -sər-/ *noun* a person who makes evil spirits leave a place or a person's body by prayers or magic

ex·o·skel·e·ton /ˈɛksoʊˌskɛlətn/ *noun* (*biology*) a hard outer covering that protects the bodies of certain animals, such as insects ⊃ compare ENDOSKELETON

ex·o·ther·mic /ˌɛksoʊˈθərmɪk/ *adj.* (*chemistry*) (of a chemical reaction) producing heat ⊃ compare ENDOTHERMIC

ex·ot·ic /ɪgˈzɑtɪk/ *adj.* from or in another country, especially a tropical one; seeming exciting and unusual because it is connected with foreign countries: *brightly-colored exotic flowers/plants/birds* ♦ *She travels to all kinds of exotic locations all over the world.* ▶ **ex·ot·i·cally** /-kli/ *adv.*: *rainbows of exotically colored blooms*

ex·ot·i·ca /ɪgˈzɑtɪkə/ *noun* [U] unusual and exciting things, especially from other countries

ex·otic ·dancer *noun* an entertainer who dances with very few clothes on, or who removes clothes while dancing ⊃ see also STRIPPER

ex·ot·i·cism /ɪgˈzɑtəˌsɪzəm/ *noun* [U] (*formal*) the quality of being exciting and unusual because it is connected with foreign countries

ex·pand 🔑 **AWL** /ɪkˈspænd/ *verb*
1 [I, T] to become greater in size, number, or importance; to make something greater in size, number, or importance: *Metals expand when they are heated.* ♦ *Student numbers are expanding rapidly.* ♦ *A child's vocabulary expands through reading.* ♦ *The waist expands to fit all sizes.* ♦ ~ **sth** *In breathing, the chest muscles expand the rib cage and allow air to be sucked into the lungs.* ♦ *The new system expanded the role of social workers.* ♦ *There are no plans to expand the local airport.* **ANT** CONTRACT **2** [I, T] if a business **expands** or **is expanded**, new branches are opened, it makes more money, etc.: *an expanding economy* (= with more businesses starting and growing) ♦ ~ **sth** *We've expanded the business by opening two more stores.* **3** [I] to talk more; to add details to

t **t**ea   ţ bu**tt**er   d **d**id   k **c**at   g **g**ot   tʃ **ch**in   dʒ **J**une   f **f**all

what you are saying: *I repeated the question and waited for her to expand.*
PHR V **ex'pand on/upon sth** to say more about something and add some details: *Could you expand on that point, please?*

ex·pand·a·ble /ɪkˈspændəbl/ *adj.* (*technical*) that can be expanded: *an expandable briefcase* ◆ **~ to sth** *The system has 1GB RAM, expandable to 4GB.*

ex·panse /ɪkˈspæns/ *noun* **~ (of sth)** a wide and open area of something, especially land or water: *a wide/vast expanse of blue sky* ◆ *flat expanses of open farmland*

ex·pan·sion **AWL** /ɪkˈspænʃn/ *noun* [U, C] an act of increasing, or making something increase, in size, amount, or importance: *a period of rapid economic expansion* ◆ *Despite the recession, the company is confident of further expansion.* ◆ *The book is an expansion of a series of lectures given last year.*

ex·pan·sion·ary /ɪkˈspænʃəˌnɛri/ *adj.* (*formal*) encouraging economic expansion: *This budget will have a net expansionary effect on the economy.*

ex'pansion ˌcard (also **ˈadd-in**) *noun* (*computing*) a CIRCUIT BOARD that can be put into a computer to give it more memory or make it able to do more things

ex·pan·sion·ism **AWL** /ɪkˈspænʃəˌnɪzəm/ *noun* [U] (sometimes *disapproving*) the belief in and process of increasing the size and importance of something, especially in a country or a business: *the economic expansionism of America* ◆ *military/territorial expansionism* ▶ **ex·pan·sion·ist** /-ʃənɪst/ *adj.*: *expansionist policies* **ex·pan·sion·ist** *noun*: *He was a ruthless expansionist.*

ex·pan·sive **AWL** /ɪkˈspænsɪv/ *adj.* **1** covering a large amount of space: *She opened her arms wide in an expansive gesture of welcome.* ◆ *landscape with expansive skies* **2** covering a large subject area, rather than trying to be exact and use few words: *We need to look at a more expansive definition of the term.* ◆ *The piece is written in his usual expansive style.* **3** friendly and willing to talk a lot: *She was clearly relaxed and in an expansive mood.* **4** (especially of a period of time) encouraging economic EXPANSION: *In the creative 1990s bright graduates could advance rapidly.* ▶ **ex·pan·sive·ly** *adv.*: *He waved his arms expansively.* **ex·pan·sive·ness** *noun* [U]

ex·pa·ti·ate /ɪkˈspeɪʃiˌeɪt/ *verb*
PHR V **ex'patiate on/upon sth** (*formal*) to write or speak in detail about a subject

ex·pa·tri·ate /ˌɛksˈpeɪtriət/ (also *informal* **ex·pat** /ˌɛksˈpæt/) *noun* a person living in a country that is not their own: *American expatriates in Paris* ▶ **ex·pa·tri·ate** *adj.* [only before noun]: *expatriate Americans in Spain* ◆ *expatriate workers*

ex·pect 🔑 /ɪkˈspɛkt/ *verb*
1 [T] to think or believe that something will happen or that someone will do something: **~ sth** *We are expecting a rise in food prices this month.* ◆ **~ sth from sb/sth** *Don't expect sympathy from me!* ◆ **~ sth of sb/sth** *That's not the sort of behavior I expect of you!* ◆ **~ to do sth** *You can't expect to learn a foreign language in a few months.* ◆ *I looked back, half expecting to see someone following me.* ◆ **~ sb/sth to do sth** *House prices are expected to rise sharply.* ◆ *Do you really expect me to believe you?* ◆ **~ (that)…** *Many people were expecting (that) the peace talks would break down.* ◆ **it is expected that…** *It is expected that the report will suggest some major reforms.* **2** [T] (often used in the progressive tenses) to be waiting for someone or something to arrive, as this has been arranged: **~ sb/sth** *to expect a visit/call/letter from someone* ◆ *Are you expecting visitors?* ◆ *We were expecting him yesterday.* ◆ **~ sb to do sth** *We were expecting him to arrive yesterday.* **3** [T] to demand that someone will do something because it is their duty or responsibility: **~ sth (from sb)** *Her parents expected high standards from her.* ◆ *He's still getting over the flu, so don't expect too much from him.* ◆ **~ sth (of sb)** *Are you clear what is expected of you?* ◆ **~ sb to do sth** *They expected all their children to be high achievers.* ◆ **~ to do sth** *I expect to be paid promptly for the work.* ⊃ thesaurus box at

DEMAND **4** [I, T] (*informal*) (not used in the progressive tenses) used when you think something is probably true: *"Will you be late?" "I expect so."* ◆ *"Are you going out tonight?" "I don't expect so."* ◆ **~ (that…)** *"Who's eaten all the cake?" "Tom, I expect/I expect it was Tom."* **HELP** "That" is nearly always left out. ⊃ compare UNEXPECTED
IDM **be expecting (a baby/child)** (*informal*) to be pregnant: *Ann's expecting a baby in June.* **be (only) to be expected** to be likely to happen; to be normal: *A little tiredness after taking these drugs is to be expected.* **what (else) do you expect?** (*informal*) used to tell someone not to be surprised by something: *She swore at you? What do you expect when you treat her like that?*

LANGUAGE BANK

expect
discussing predictions

- The number of people using cell phones to purchase goods and services is **expected/likely** to more than double by the end of 2015.
- Experts have **predicted/forecast** that the number of people using their cell phones to pay for goods and services should exceed 190 million in 2015.
- This figure **is set to** reach 200 million by 2016.
- **By** 2015, 800 million cell phone users worldwide **will** be participating in social networks via their phone.
- Sales of cell phones in 2010 were lower **than expected**.
- The company's announcement of 1.26 billion handsets sold for the year is **in line with predictions**.
⊃ Language Banks at FALL, ILLUSTRATE, INCREASE, PROPORTION

---

ex·pect·an·cy /ɪkˈspɛktənsi/ *noun* [U] the state of expecting or hoping that something, especially something good or exciting, will happen: *There was an air of expectancy in the waiting crowd.* ⊃ see also LIFE EXPECTANCY

ex·pect·ant /ɪkˈspɛktənt/ *adj.* **1** hoping for something, especially something good and exciting: *children with expectant faces waiting for the fireworks to begin* ◆ *A sudden roar came from the expectant crowd.* **2 ~ mother/father/parent** used to describe someone who is going to have a baby soon or become a father ▶ **ex·pect·ant·ly** *adv.*: *She looked at him expectantly.* ◆ *waiting expectantly*

ex·pec·ta·tion 🔑 /ˌɛkspɛkˈteɪʃn/ *noun*
1 [U, C] a belief that something will happen because it is likely: **~ (of sth)** *We are confident in our expectation of a full recovery.* ◆ **~ (that…)** *There was a general expectation that he would win.* ◆ *The expectation is that property prices will rise.* ◆ *I applied for the position more in hope than expectation.* ◆ *Contrary to expectations, interest rates did not rise.* ◆ *Against all expectations, she was enjoying herself.* **2** [C, usually pl.] a hope that something good will happen: *She went to college with great expectations.* ◆ *There was an air of expectation.* ◆ *The results exceeded our expectations.* ◆ *The numbers attending fell short of expectations.* ◆ *The event did not live up to expectations.* **3** [C, usually pl.] a strong belief about the way something should happen or how someone should behave: *Some parents have unrealistic expectations of their children.* ◆ *Unfortunately the new software has failed to meet expectations.*

expecˌtation of ˈlife *noun* [U] = LIFE EXPECTANCY

ex·pect·ed 🔑 /ɪkˈspɛktəd/ *adj.*
that you think will happen: *Double the expected number of people came to the meeting.* ◆ *this year's expected earnings* ⊃ compare UNEXPECTED

ex·pec·to·rant /ɪkˈspɛktərənt/ *noun* (*medical*) a cough medicine that helps you to get rid of PHLEGM (= thick liquid) from the lungs

ex·pec·to·rate /ɪkˈspɛktəˌreɪt/ *verb* [I] (*formal*) to cough and make PHLEGM come up from your lungs into your mouth so

---

you can SPIT it out ▸ **ex·pec·to·ra·tion** /ɪkˌspɛktəˈreɪʃn/ *noun* [U]

ex·pe·di·ent /ɪkˈspidiənt/ *noun, adj.*

● *noun* (*formal*) an action that is useful or necessary for a particular purpose, but not always fair or right: *The disease was controlled by the simple expedient of not allowing anyone to leave the city.*

● *adj.* (*formal*) [not usually before noun] (of an action) useful or necessary for a particular purpose, but not always fair or right: *The government has clearly decided that a cut in interest rates would be politically expedient.* **ANT** INEXPEDIENT
▸ **ex·pe·di·en·cy** /-ənsi/ *noun* [U]: *He acted out of expediency, not principle.* **ex·pe·di·ent·ly** *adv.*

ex·pe·dite /ˈɛkspəˌdaɪt/ *verb* ~ **sth** (*formal*) to make a process happen more quickly **SYN** SPEED UP: *We have developed rapid order processing to expedite deliveries to customers.*

ex·pe·di·tion /ˌɛkspəˈdɪʃn/ *noun* **1** an organized trip with a particular purpose, especially to find out about a place that is not well known: *to plan/lead/go on an expedition to the North Pole* **2** the people who go on an expedition: *Three members of the Everest expedition were killed.* **3** (sometimes humorous) a short trip that you make when you want or need something: *a shopping expedition* ⟳ thesaurus box at TRIP

ex·pe·di·tion·ar·y force /ˌɛkspəˈdɪʃəneri ˌfɔrs/ *noun* a group of soldiers who are sent to another country to fight in a war

ex·pe·di·tious /ˌɛkspəˈdɪʃəs/ *adj.* (*formal*) that works well without wasting time, money, etc. **SYN** EFFICIENT
▸ **ex·pe·di·tious·ly** *adv.*

ex·pel /ɪkˈspɛl/ *verb* (-ll-) **1** ~ **sb** (**from sth**) to officially make someone leave a school or an organization: *She was expelled from school at 15.* ◆ *Olympic athletes expelled for taking drugs* ⟳ collocations at EDUCATION **2** ~ **sb** (**from sth**) to force someone to leave a country: *Foreign journalists are being expelled.* **3** ~ **sth** (**from sth**) (*technical*) to force air or water out of a part of the body or from a container: *to expel air from the lungs* ⟳ see also EXPULSION

ex·pend /ɪkˈspɛnd/ *verb* ~ **sth** (**in/on sth**) | ~ **sth** (**in/on/doing sth**) (*formal*) to use or spend a lot of time, money, energy, etc.: *She expended all her efforts on the care of her home and children.*

ex·pend·a·ble /ɪkˈspɛndəbl/ *adj.* (*formal*) if you consider people or things to be **expendable**, you think that you can get rid of them when they are no longer needed, or think it is acceptable if they are killed or destroyed **SYN** DISPENSABLE

ex·pend·i·ture /ɪkˈspɛndətʃər/ *noun* [U, C] **1** the act of spending or using money; an amount of money spent: *a reduction in public/government/military expenditure* ◆ *plans to increase expenditure on health* ◆ *The budget provided for a total expenditure of $27 billion.* ⟳ thesaurus box at COST **2** (*formal*) the use of energy, time, materials, etc.: *the expenditure of emotion* ◆ *This study represents a major expenditure of time and effort.* ⟳ compare INCOME

ex·pense /ɪkˈspɛns/ *noun*

1 [U] the money that you spend on something: *The yard was landscaped at great expense.* ◆ *No expense was spared* (= they spent as much money as was needed) *to make the wedding perfect.* ◆ *He's arranged everything, no expense spared.* ◆ *She always travels first-class, regardless of expense.* ◆ *The results are well worth the expense.* ⟳ thesaurus box at PRICE **2** [C, usually sing.] something that makes you spend money: *Having a car is a big expense.* **3 expenses** [pl.] money spent in doing a particular job, or for a particular purpose: *living/household/medical/legal, etc. expenses* ◆ *Can I give you something toward expenses?* ◆ *financial help to meet the expenses of an emergency* ◆ *The payments he gets barely cover his expenses.* ⟳ thesaurus box at COST **4 expenses** [pl.] money that you spend while you are working that your employer will pay back to you

later: *You can claim back your travel/entertainment expenses.* ◆ *an all-expenses-paid trip* ⟳ note at COST
IDM **at sb's expense 1** paid for by someone: *We were taken out for dinner at the company's expense.* **2** if you make a joke **at someone's expense**, you laugh at them and make them feel silly **at the expense of sb/sth** with loss or damage to someone or something: *He built up the business at the expense of his health.* **go to the expense of sth/of doing sth | go to a lot of, etc. expense** to spend money on something: *They went to a lot of expense to renovate the house, and then they moved.* **put sb to the expense of sth/of doing sth | put sb to a lot of, etc. expense** to make someone spend money on something: *Their visit put us to a lot of expense.* ⟳ more at OBJECT *n.*

ex·pense ac·count *noun* an arrangement by which money spent by someone while they are at work is later paid back to them by their employer; a record of money spent in this way

ex·pen·sive /ɪkˈspɛnsɪv/ *adj.*

costing a lot of money: *an expensive car/restaurant/vacation* ◆ *Art books are expensive to produce.* ◆ *I can't afford it—it's too expensive.* ◆ *Making the wrong decision could prove expensive.* ◆ *That dress was an expensive mistake.* **ANT** INEXPENSIVE
▸ **ex·pen·sive·ly** *adv.*: *expensively dressed/furnished* ◆ *There are other restaurants where you can eat less expensively.*

THESAURUS

expensive

costly ◆ overpriced ◆ pricey

These words all describe something that costs a lot of money.

expensive costing a lot of money; charging high prices: *I can't afford it—it's just too expensive for me.* ◆ *an expensive restaurant*

costly (*somewhat formal*) costing a lot of money, especially more than you want to pay: *You want to avoid costly legal proceedings if you can.*

overpriced too expensive; costing more than it is worth: *ridiculously overpriced designer clothes*

pricey (*informal*) expensive: *Condos downtown are now too pricey for local people to afford.*

PATTERNS
- expensive/costly/pricey for sb/sth
- expensive/costly to do sth
- very/too/fairly/quite/pretty expensive/costly/pricey

---

ex·pe·ri·ence /ɪkˈspɪriəns/ *noun, verb*

● *noun* **1** [U] the knowledge and skill that you have gained through doing something for a period of time; the process of gaining this: *to have more than ten years of teaching experience* ◆ *Do you have any previous experience with this type of work?* ◆ *a doctor with experience in dealing with patients suffering from stress* ◆ *My lack of practical experience was a disadvantage.* ◆ *She didn't get paid much, but it was all good experience.* ◆ *He gained valuable experience while working on the project.* ◆ *We all learn by experience.* ⟳ see also WORK EXPERIENCE **2** [U] the things that have happened to you that influence the way you think and behave: *Experience has taught me that life can be very unfair.* ◆ *It is important to try and learn from experience.* ◆ *In my experience, very few people really understand the problem.* ◆ *She knew from past experience that Ann would not give up easily.* ◆ *The book is based on personal experience.* ◆ *direct/first-hand experience of poverty* **3** [C] an event or activity that affects you in some way: *an enjoyable/exciting/unusual/unforgettable, etc. experience* ◆ ~ **(of sth)** *It was her first experience of living alone.* ◆ *Living in Africa was very different from home and quite an experience* (= unusual for us). ◆ *I had a bad experience with fireworks once.* ◆ *He seems to have had some sort of religious experience.* **4 the… experience** [sing.] events or knowledge shared by

---

| h hat | m man | n no | ŋ sing | l leg | r red | y yes | w wet |

all the members of a particular group in society, that influences the way they think and behave: *musical forms like jazz that emerged out of the Black American experience* **IDM put sth down to experience** (also **chalk sth up to experience**) used to say that someone should think of a failure as being something that they can learn from: *We lost a lot of money, but we just chalked it up to experience.*
- *verb* **1** ~ **sth** to have a particular situation affect you or happen to you: *The country experienced a foreign currency shortage for several months.* ♦ *Everyone experiences these problems at some time in their lives.* **2** ~ **sth** to have and be aware of a particular emotion or physical feeling: *to experience pain/pleasure/unhappiness* ♦ *I experienced a moment of panic as I boarded the plane.*

ex·pe·ri·enced ♪ /ɪkˈspɪriənst/ *adj.*
1 having knowledge or skill in a particular job or activity: *an experienced teacher* ♦ ~ **in sth/in doing sth** *He's very experienced in taking care of animals.* **2** having knowledge as a result of doing something for a long time, or having had a lot of different experiences: *She's very young and not very experienced.* ♦ *an experienced traveler* (= someone who has traveled a lot) **ANT INEXPERIENCED**

ex·pe·ri·en·tial /ɪkˌspɪriˈenʃl/ *adj.* (*formal* or *technical*) based on or involving experience: *experiential knowledge* ♦ *experiential learning methods*

ex·per·i·ment ♪ *noun, verb*
- *noun* /ɪkˈspɛrəmənt/ [C, U] **1** a scientific test that is done in order to study what happens and to gain new knowledge: *to do/perform/conduct an experiment* ♦ *proved by experiment* ♦ *laboratory experiments* ♦ *Many people do not like the idea of experiments on animals.* ⇨ collocations at **SCIENTIFIC** ⇨ see also **CONTROLLED EXPERIMENT 2** a new activity, idea, or method that you try out to see what happens or what effect it has: *I've never cooked this before so it's an experiment.* ♦ ~ **in sth** *the country's brief experiment in democracy*
- *verb* /ɪkˈspɛrəˌmɛnt/ **1** ~ **(on sb/sth)** | ~ **(with sth)** to do a scientific experiment or experiments: *Some people feel that experimenting on animals is wrong.* **2** ~ **(on sb/sth)** | ~ **(with sth)** to try or test new ideas, methods, etc. to find out what effect they have: *He wanted to experiment more with different textures in his paintings.* ♦ *I experimented until I got the recipe just right.* **3** [I] ~ **with sth** to try something such as drugs or sex to find out what it is like: *He experimented with drugs when he was in college.* ▶ **ex·per·i·ment·er** *noun*

ex·per·i·men·tal /ɪkˌspɛrəˈmɛntl/ *adj.* **1** based on new ideas, forms, or methods that are used to find out what effect they have: *experimental teaching methods* ♦ *experimental theater/art/music* ♦ *The equipment is still at the experimental stage.* **2** connected with scientific experiments: *experimental conditions/data/evidence* ▶ **ex·per·i·men·tal·ly** /-ˈmɛntl-i/ *adv.*: *This theory can be confirmed experimentally.* ♦ *The new drug is being used experimentally on some patients.* ♦ *He moved his shoulder experimentally to see if it still hurt.*

ex·per·i·men·ta·tion /ɪkˌspɛrəmɛnˈteɪʃn; -mən-/ *noun* [U] (*formal*) the activity or process of experimenting: *experimentation with new teaching methods* ♦ *Many people object to experimentation on embryos.*

ex·pert ♪ **AWL** /ˈɛkspərt/ *noun, adj.*
- *noun* a person with special knowledge, skill, or training in something: *a computer/medical expert* ♦ ~ **(at/in/on sth)** *an expert in child psychology* ♦ *an expert on modern literature* ♦ ~ **(at/in doing sth)** *He's an expert at getting his own way.* ♦ *Don't ask me—I'm no expert!*
- *adj.* done with, having, or involving great knowledge or skill: *to seek expert advice/an expert opinion* ♦ *an expert driver* ♦ *We need some expert help.* ♦ ~ **(at/in sth)** *They are all expert in this field.* ♦ ~ **(at/in doing sth)** *She's expert at making cheap but stylish clothes.* ⇨ compare **INEXPERT** ▶ **ex·pert·ly** **AWL** *adv.*: *The roads were icy, but she stopped the car expertly.* ♦ *The music was expertly performed.*

ex·per·tise **AWL** /ˌɛkspərˈtiz/ *noun* [U] expert knowledge or skill in a particular subject, activity, or job: *professional/ scientific/technical, etc. expertise* ♦ *We have the expertise to help you run your business.* ♦ ~ **in sth/in doing sth** *They have considerable expertise in dealing with oil spills.*

ˌexpert ˈsystem *noun* (*computing*) a computer system that can provide information and expert advice on a particular subject. The program asks users a series of questions about their problem and gives them advice based on its store of knowledge.

ex·pi·ate /ˈɛkspiˌeɪt/ *verb* ~ **sth** (*formal*) to accept punishment for something that you have done wrong in order to show that you are sorry: *He had a chance to confess and expiate his guilt.* ▶ **ex·pi·a·tion** /ˌɛkspiˈeɪʃn/ *noun* [U, sing.]

ex·pi·ra·tion /ˌɛkspəˈreɪʃn/ *noun* [U] an ending of the period of time when an official document can be used, or when an agreement is valid: *the expiration of a fixed-term contract* ♦ *The license can be renewed on expiration.*

expiˈration ˌdate *noun* **1** the date after which an official document, agreement, etc. is no longer valid, or after which something cannot legally be used: *Check the expiration date on your passport.* **2** the date by which an item of food should be eaten: *The expiration date on this yogurt was November 20.*

ex·pire /ɪkˈspaɪər/ *verb* **1** [I] (of a document, an agreement, etc.) to be no longer valid because the period of time for which it could be used has ended **SYN RUN OUT**: *When does your driver's license expire?* **2** [I] (of a period of time, especially one during which someone holds a position of authority) to end: *His term of office expires at the end of June.* **3** [I] (*literary*) to die ⇨ see also **UNEXPIRED** ▶ **ex·pired** *adj.*: *an expired passport*

ex·plain ♪ /ɪkˈspleɪn/ *verb* **1** [T, I] to tell someone about something in a way that makes it easy to understand: ~ **(sth) (to sb)** *First, I'll explain the rules of the game.* ♦ *It was difficult to explain the problem to beginners.*
- *"I'll be happy to explain," he added helpfully.* ♦ ~ **that…** *I explained that an ambulance would be coming soon.* ♦ ~ **who, how, etc.…** *He explained who each person in the photo was.* ♦ ~ **to sb who, how, etc.…** *She explained to them what to do in an emergency.* ♦ + **speech** *"It works like this," she explained.* **2** [I, T] to give a reason, or be a reason, for something: *She tried to explain but he wouldn't listen.* ♦ ~ **that…** *Alex explained that his car had broken down.* ♦ ~ **why, how, etc.…** *Well, that doesn't explain why you didn't call.* ♦ ~ **sth (to sb)** *scientific findings that help explain the origins of the universe* ♦ *The government now has to explain its decision to the public.* ♦ (*informal*) *Oh well then, that explains it* (= I understand now why something happened). **HELP** You cannot say "explain me, him, her, etc.": *Can you explain the situation to me?* ♦ ~~Can you explain me the situation?~~ ♦ *I'll explain to you why I like it.* ♦ ~~I'll explain you why I like it.~~ **IDM explain yourself 1** to give someone reasons for your behavior, especially when they are angry or upset because of it: *I really don't see why I should have to explain myself to you.* **2** to say what you mean in a clear way: *Could you explain yourself a little more—I didn't understand.* **PHR V ex·plain sth↔aˈway** to give reasons why something is not your fault, or why something is not important

WORD FAMILY
explain *verb*
explanation *noun*
explanatory *adj.*
explicable *adj.* (≠ inexplicable)

ex·pla·na·tion ♪ /ˌɛkspləˈneɪʃn/ *noun*
1 [C, U] a statement, fact, or situation that tells you why something happened; a reason given for something: *The most likely explanation is that his plane was delayed.* ♦ *to offer/ provide an explanation* ♦ ~ **(for sth)** *I can't think of any possible explanation for his absence.* ♦ ~ **(for doing sth)** *She didn't give an adequate explanation for being late.* ♦ ~ **(of sth)** *The book opens with an explanation of why some drugs are banned.* ♦ ~ **(as to why…)** *an explanation as to why he had left early* ♦ *She left the room abruptly without explanation.* ♦ *"I had to see you," he said, by way of explanation.* ⇨ thesaurus box at **REASON 2** [C] a statement or piece of writing that tells you

how something works, or that makes something easier to understand: *For a full explanation of how the machine works, turn to page 5.*

ex·plan·a·to·ry /ɪkˈsplænəˌtɔri/ *adj.* [usually before noun] giving the reasons for something; intended to describe how something works, or to make something easier to understand: *There are explanatory notes at the back of the book.* ➔ see also SELF-EXPLANATORY

ex·ple·tive /ˈɛksplətɪv/ *noun* (*formal*) a word, especially an offensive word, that you use when you are angry or in pain **SYN** SWEAR WORD

ex·pli·ca·ble /ɪkˈsplɪkəbl; ˈɛksplɪkəbl/ *adj.* [not usually before noun] (*formal*) that can be explained or understood: *His behavior is only explicable in terms of* (= because of) *his recent illness.* **ANT** INEXPLICABLE

ex·pli·cate /ˈɛkspləˌkeɪt/ *verb* ~ **sth** (*formal*) to explain an idea or a work of literature in a lot of detail ▸ **ex·pli·ca·tion** /ˌɛkspləˈkeɪʃn/ *noun* [C, U]

ex·plic·it **AWL** /ɪkˈsplɪsət/ *adj.* **1** (of a statement or piece of writing) clear and easy to understand: *He gave me very explicit directions on how to get there.* **2** (of a person) saying something clearly, exactly, and openly **SYN** FRANK: *She was very explicit about why she had left.* **3** said, done, or shown in an open or direct way, so that you have no doubt about what is happening: *The reasons for the decision should be made explicit.* ♦ *She made some very explicit references to my personal life.* ➔ compare IMPLICIT ▸ **ex·plic·it·ly** **AWL** *adv.*: *The report states explicitly that the system was to blame.* **ex·plic·it·ness** *noun* [U]: *He didn't like the degree of sexual explicitness in the movie.*

ex·plode 𝄞 /ɪkˈsploʊd/
verb

	WORD FAMILY
	explode *verb*
	explosion *noun*
	explosive *adj., noun*
	unexploded *adj.*

▸ **BURST VIOLENTLY 1** [I, T] to burst, or to make something burst, loudly and violently, causing damage **SYN** BLOW UP: *Bombs were exploding all over the city.* ♦ ~ **sth** *There was a huge bang as if someone had exploded a rocket outside.* ♦ *Bomb disposal experts exploded the device under controlled conditions.* ➔ compare IMPLODE

▸ **GET ANGRY/DANGEROUS 2** [I, T] (of a person or situation) to suddenly become very angry or dangerous: ~ **(with sth)** *Suddenly Charles exploded with rage.* ♦ ~ **(into sth)** *The protest exploded into a riot.* ♦ + **speech** *"Of course there's something wrong!" Jim exploded.*

▸ **EXPRESS EMOTION 3** [I] ~ **(into/with sth)** to suddenly express an emotion: *We all exploded into wild laughter.*

▸ **MOVE SUDDENLY 4** [I] ~ **(into sth)** to suddenly and quickly do something; to move suddenly with a lot of force: *After ten minutes, the game exploded into life.*

▸ **MAKE LOUD NOISE 5** [I] to make a sudden very loud noise: *Thunder exploded overhead.*

▸ **INCREASE QUICKLY 6** [I] to increase suddenly and very quickly in number: *the exploding world population*

▸ **SHOW SOMETHING IS NOT TRUE 7** [T] ~ **sth** to show that something is not true, especially something that people believe: *At last, here is a women's magazine to explode the myth that thin equals beautiful.*

go off (of a bomb) to explode; (of a gun) to be fired: *The bomb went off in a crowded street.* **NOTE** When used about guns, the choice of **go off** (instead of "be fired") can suggest that the gun was fired by accident.

burst to break open or apart, especially because of pressure from inside; to make something break in this way: *A water pipe burst and flooded the kitchen.*

erupt (of a volcano) to throw out burning rocks and smoke; (of burning rocks and smoke) to be thrown out of a volcano: *Mount St. Helens erupted in 1980.*

detonate (*somewhat formal*) (of a bomb) to explode; to make a bomb explode: *Two other bombs failed to detonate.*

PATTERNS
- a **bomb** explodes/blows up/goes off/bursts/detonates
- a **car/plane/vehicle** explodes/blows up
- a **firework/rocket** explodes/goes off

ex·plod·ed /ɪkˈsploʊdəd/ *adj.* (*technical*) (of a drawing or diagram) showing the parts of something separately, but also showing how they are connected to each other ➔ compare UNEXPLODED

ex·ploit **AWL** *verb, noun*
- *verb* /ɪkˈsplɔɪt/ **1** ~ **sth** (*disapproving*) to treat a person or situation as an opportunity to gain an advantage for yourself: *He exploited his father's name to get himself a job.* ♦ *She realized that her youth and inexperience were being exploited.* **2** ~ **sb** (*disapproving*) to treat someone unfairly by making them work and not giving them much in return: *What is being done to stop employers from exploiting young people?* **3** ~ **sth** to use something well in order to gain as much from it as possible: *She fully exploits the humor of her role in the play.* **4** to develop or use something for business or industry: ~ **sth** *Minerals have been exploited in this area.* ♦ ~ **sth for sth** *countries exploiting the rainforests for hardwood* ▸ **ex·ploit·er** *noun* [C]
- *noun* /ˈɛksplɔɪt/ [usually pl.] a brave, exciting, or interesting act: *the daring exploits of Roman heroes*

ex·ploi·ta·tion **AWL** /ˌɛksplɔɪˈteɪʃn/ *noun* [U] **1** (*disapproving*) a situation in which someone treats someone else in an unfair way, especially in order to make money from their work: *the exploitation of children* **2** the use of land, oil, minerals, etc.: *commercial exploitation of the mineral resources in Antarctica* **3** (*disapproving*) the fact of using a situation in order to get an advantage for yourself: *exploitation of the situation for his own purposes*

ex·ploit·a·tive /ɪkˈsplɔɪtətɪv/ (also **ex·ploit·ive** /ɪkˈsplɔɪtɪv/) *adj.* treating someone unfairly in order to gain an advantage or to make money

ex·plo·ra·tion /ˌɛkspləˈreɪʃn/ *noun* [C, U] **1** the act of traveling through a place in order to find out about it or look for something in it: *the exploration of space* ♦ *oil exploration* (= searching for oil in the ground) **2** an examination of something in order to find out about it: *the book's explorations of the human mind*

ex·plor·a·to·ry /ɪkˈsplɔrəˌtɔri/ *adj.* done with the intention of examining something in order to find out more about it: *exploratory surgery* ♦ *exploratory drilling for oil*

ex·plore 𝄞 /ɪkˈsplɔr/ *verb*

1 [T, I] to travel to or around an area or a country in order to learn about it: ~ **sth (for sth)** *The city is best explored on foot.* ♦ *They explored the land to the south of the Murray River.* ♦ ~ **(for sth)** *As soon as we arrived on the island we were eager to explore.* ♦ *companies exploring for* (= searching for) *oil* **2** [T] ~ **sth** to examine something completely or carefully in order to find out more about it **SYN** ANALYZE: *These ideas will be explored in more detail in chapter 7.* ➔ language bank at ABOUT **3** [T] ~ **sth** to feel something with your hands or another part of the body: *She explored the sand with her toes.* ➔ see also UNEXPLORED

ex·plor·er /ɪkˈsplɔrər/ *noun* a person who travels to unknown places in order to find out more about them

ex·plo·sion 🔑 /ɪkˈsploʊʒn/ *noun*
1 [C, U] the sudden violent bursting and loud noise of something such as a bomb exploding; the act of deliberately causing something to explode: *a bomb/nuclear/gas explosion* ◆ *There were two loud explosions and then the building burst into flames.* ◆ *Bomb Squad officers carried out a controlled explosion of the device.* ◆ *300 people were injured in the explosion.* **2** [C] a large, sudden, or rapid increase in the amount or number of something: *a population explosion* ◆ *an explosion of interest in learning Japanese* **3** [C] (*formal*) a sudden, violent expression of emotion, especially anger **SYN** OUTBURST

ex·plo·sive /ɪkˈsploʊsɪv/ *adj., noun*
● *adj.* **1** easily able or likely to explode: *an explosive device* (= a bomb) ◆ *an explosive mixture of chemicals* **2** likely to cause violence or strong feelings of anger or hatred: *a potentially explosive situation* **3** often having sudden violent or angry feelings: *an explosive temper* **4** increasing suddenly and rapidly: *the explosive growth of the export market* **5** (of a sound) sudden and loud ▶ **ex·plo·sive·ly** *adv.*
● *noun* [C, U] a substance that is able or likely to cause an explosion: *plastic explosives* ⮞ **see also** HIGH EXPLOSIVE

ex·po /ˈɛkspoʊ/ *noun* (*pl.* **ex·pos**) a large exhibition

ex·po·nent /ɪkˈspoʊnənt; ˈɛkspoʊnənt/ *noun* **1** a person who supports an idea, a theory, etc. and persuades others that it is good **SYN** PROPONENT: *She was a leading exponent of free trade during her political career.* **2** a person who is able to perform a particular activity with skill: *the most famous exponent of the art of mime* **3** (*mathematics*) a raised figure or symbol that shows how many times a quantity must be multiplied by itself, for example the figure 4 in a^4

ex·po·nen·tial /ˌɛkspəˈnɛnʃl/ *adj.* **1** (*mathematics*) of or shown by an exponent: 2^4 *is an exponential expression.* ◆ *an exponential curve/function* **2** (*formal*) (of a rate of increase) becoming faster and faster: *exponential growth/increase* ▶ **ex·po·nen·tial·ly** /-ʃəli/ *adv.: to increase exponentially*

ex·port 🔑 **AWL** *verb, noun*
● *verb* /ɪkˈspɔrt; ˈɛkspɔrt/ **1** [T, I] ~ (sth) (to sb) to sell and send goods to another country: *The islands export sugar and fruit.* ◆ *90% of the engines are exported to Europe.* ⮞ collocations at ECONOMY **2** [T] ~ sth (+ adv./prep.) to introduce an idea or activity to another country or area: *American rock music has been exported around the world.* **3** [T] ~ sth (*computing*) to send data to another program, changing its form so that the other program can read it **ANT** IMPORT
● *noun* /ˈɛkspɔrt/ **1** [U] the selling and transporting of goods to another country: *a ban on the export of live cattle* ◆ *Then the fruit is packaged for export.* ◆ *export earnings* ◆ *an export license* **2** [C, usually pl.] a product that is sold to another country: *the country's major exports* ◆ *a fall in the value of exports* **ANT** IMPORT

ex·por·ta·tion /ˌɛkspɔrˈteɪʃn/ *noun* [U] the process of sending goods to another country for sale **ANT** IMPORTATION

ex·port·er **AWL** /ɪkˈspɔrtər; ˈɛkspɔrtər/ *noun* a person, company, or country that sells goods to another country: *the world's largest/major/leading exporter of cars* ◆ *The country is now a net exporter of fuel* (= it exports more than it imports). **ANT** IMPORTER

ex·pose 🔑 **AWL** /ɪkˈspoʊz/ *verb*
⟩ **SHOW SOMETHING HIDDEN** **1** to show something that is usually hidden **SYN** REVEAL: ~ **sth** *He smiled suddenly, exposing a set of amazingly white teeth.* ◆ *Miles of sand are exposed at low tide.* ◆ *My job as a journalist is to expose the truth.* ◆ ~ **sth to sb** *He did not want to expose his fears and insecurity to anyone.*
⟩ **SHOW TRUTH** **2** ~ sb/sth (as sth) to tell the true facts about a person or a situation, and show them/it to be immoral, illegal, etc.: *She was exposed as a liar and a fraud.* ◆ *He*

threatened to expose the racism that existed within the police force.
⟩ **TO SOMETHING HARMFUL** **3** ~ sb/sth/yourself (to sth) to put someone or something in a place or situation where they are not protected from something harmful or unpleasant: *to expose yourself to ridicule* ◆ *Do not expose babies to strong sunlight.*
⟩ **GIVE EXPERIENCE** **4** ~ sb to sth to let someone find out about something by letting them experience it or showing them what it is like: *We want to expose the kids to as much art and culture as possible.*
⟩ **FILM IN CAMERA** **5** ~ sth to allow light onto the film inside a camera when taking a photograph
⟩ **YOURSELF** **6** ~ yourself a man who **exposes** himself shows his sexual organs in public in a way that is offensive to other people ⮞ **see also** EXPOSURE

ex·po·sé /ˌɛkspoʊˈzeɪ/ *noun* an account of the facts of a situation, especially when these are shocking or have deliberately been kept secret

ex·posed **AWL** /ɪkˈspoʊzd/ *adj.* **1** (of a place) not protected from the weather by trees, buildings, or high ground **2** (of a person) not protected from attack or criticism: *She was left feeling exposed and vulnerable.* **3** (*finance*) likely to experience financial losses

ex·po·si·tion /ˌɛkspəˈzɪʃn/ *noun* **1** [C, U] (*formal*) a full explanation of a theory, plan, etc.: *a clear and detailed exposition of their legal position* **2** [C] an event at which people, businesses, etc. show and sell their goods; a TRADE FAIR

ex·pos·i·to·ry /ɪkˈspɑzəˌtɔri/ *adj.* (*formal*) intended to explain or describe something: *The movie suffers from too much expository dialogue.* ◆ *expository writing*

ex·pos·tu·late /ɪkˈspɑstʃəˌleɪt/ *verb* [I, T] (+ speech) (*formal*) to argue, disagree, or protest about something ▶ **ex·pos·tu·la·tion** /ɪkˌspɑstʃəˈleɪʃn/ *noun* [U, C]

ex·po·sure **AWL** /ɪkˈspoʊʒər/ *noun*
⟩ **TO SOMETHING HARMFUL** **1** [U] ~ (to sth) the state of being in a place or situation where there is no protection from something harmful or unpleasant: *prolonged exposure to harmful radiation* ◆ (*finance*) *the company's exposure on the foreign exchange markets* (= to the risk of experiencing financial losses)
⟩ **SHOWING TRUTH** **2** [U] the state of having the true facts about someone or something told, after they have been hidden because they are bad, immoral, or illegal: *exposure as a liar and a fraud* ◆ *the exposure of illegal currency deals*
⟩ **ON TV/IN NEWSPAPERS, ETC.** **3** [U] the fact of being discussed or mentioned on television, in newspapers, etc. **SYN** PUBLICITY: *Her new movie has had a lot of exposure in the media.*
⟩ **MEDICAL CONDITION** **4** [U] a medical condition caused by being out in very cold weather for too long without protection: *Two climbers were brought in suffering from exposure.*
⟩ **FILM IN CAMERA** **5** [C] a length of film in a camera that is used to take a photograph: *There are three exposures left on this roll of film.* **6** [C] the length of time for which light is allowed to reach the film when taking a photograph: *I used a long exposure for this one.*
⟩ **SHOWING SOMETHING HIDDEN** **7** [U] the act of showing something that is usually hidden ⮞ **see also** INDECENT EXPOSURE
⟩ **DIRECTION FACED** **8** [C, usually sing.] the direction in which something such as a building faces: *Our living room has a southern exposure.*

ex·pound /ɪkˈspaʊnd/ *verb* [T, I] (*formal*) to explain something by talking about it in detail: ~ **sth (to sb)** *He expounded his views on the subject to me at great length.* ◆ ~ **on sth** *We listened as she expounded on the government's new policies.*

ex·press 🔑 /ɪkˈsprɛs/ *verb, adj., adv., noun*
● *verb* **1** to show or make known a feeling, an opinion, etc. by words, looks, or actions: ~ **sth** *Teachers have expressed*

concern about the changes. ♦ *His views have been expressed in numerous speeches.* ♦ *to express fears/doubts/reservations* ♦ *to express interest/regret/surprise* ♦ *~ how, what, etc....* *Words cannot express how pleased I am.* ⊃ see also UNEX-PRESSED **2** to speak, write, or communicate in some other way, what you think or feel: *~ yourself Teenagers often have difficulty expressing themselves.* ♦ *~ yourself + adv./prep. Perhaps I have not expressed myself very well.* ♦ *She expresses herself most fully in her paintings.* **3** *~ itself (+ adv./prep.)* (*formal*) (of a feeling) to become obvious in a particular way: *Their pleasure expressed itself in a burst of applause.* **4** (*mathematics*) to represent something in a particular way, for example by symbols: *~ sth as sth The figures are expressed as percentages.* ♦ *~ sth in sth Educational expenditure is often expressed in terms of the amount spent per student.* **5** *~ sth (from sth)* to remove air or liquid from something by pressing it: *Coconut milk is expressed from grated coconuts.* **6** *~ sth (to sb/sth)* to send something by a special, very quick system of delivery: *As soon as I receive payment I will express the book to you.*

● *adj.* [only before noun] **1** traveling very fast; operating very quickly: *an express bus/train* ♦ *express delivery services* **2** (of a letter, package, etc.) sent by a special, very quick system of delivery **3** (of a company that delivers packages) providing a special, very quick delivery service: *an air express company* **4** (*formal*) (of a wish or an aim) clearly and openly stated **SYN** DEFINITE: *It was his express wish that you should have his gold watch after he died.* ♦ *I came here with the express purpose of speaking with the manager.*

● *adv.* using a special, very quick delivery service: *I'd like to send this express, please.*

● *noun* **1** (also ex'press train) [C] a fast train that does not stop at many places: *the 9:07 express* ♦ *the Trans-Siberian Express* **2** [U] a service for sending or transporting things quickly

ex·pres·sion 🔑 /ɪkˈsprɛʃn/ noun

>SHOWING FEELINGS/IDEAS **1** [U, C] things that people say, write, or do in order to show their feelings, opinions, and ideas: *an expression of support* ♦ *Expressions of sympathy flooded in from all over the country.* ♦ *Freedom of expression* (= freedom to say what you think) *is a basic human right.* ♦ (*formal*) *The poet's anger finds expression in* (= is shown in) *the last verse of the poem.* ♦ *Only in his dreams does he give expression to his fears.*

>ON FACE **2** [C] a look on a person's face that shows their thoughts or feelings **SYN** LOOK: *There was a worried expression on her face.* ♦ *an expression of amazement/disbelief/ horror* ♦ *His expression changed from surprise to one of amusement.* ♦ *The expression in her eyes told me something was wrong.* ♦ *facial expressions*

>WORDS **3** [C] a word or phrase: *an old-fashioned expression* ♦ (*informal*) *He's a pain in the butt, if you'll pardon the expression.* ⊃ thesaurus box at WORD

>IN MUSIC/ACTING **4** [U] a strong show of feeling when you are playing music, speaking, acting, etc.: *Try to put a little more expression into it!*

>MATHEMATICS **5** [C] a group of signs that represent an idea or a quantity

ex·pres·sion·ism /ɪkˈsprɛʃəˌnɪzəm/ also **Expressionism** *noun* [U] a style and movement in early 20th century art, theater, and the movies that tries to express people's feelings and emotions rather than showing events or objects in a realistic way ▶ ex·pres·sion·ist /-ʃənɪst/ also **Expressionist** *noun, adj.*

ex·pres·sion·less /ɪkˈsprɛʃənləs/ *adj.* not showing feelings, thoughts, etc.: *an expressionless face/tone/voice* ⊃ compare EXPRESSIVE

ex·pres·sive /ɪkˈsprɛsɪv/ *adj.* **1** showing or able to show your thoughts and feelings: *She has wonderfully expressive eyes.* ♦ *the expressive power of his music* ⊃ compare EXPRESSIONLESS **2** [not before noun] *~ of sth* (*formal*) showing something; existing as an expression of something: *Every*

word and gesture is expressive of the artist's sincerity. ▶ ex·pres·sive·ly *adv.* ex·pres·sive·ness *noun* [U]

ex'press lane *noun* part of a road on which certain vehicles can go to travel faster because there is less traffic there

ex·press·ly /ɪkˈsprɛsli/ *adv.* (*formal*) **1** clearly; definitely: *She was expressly forbidden to touch my papers.* **2** for a special and deliberate purpose **SYN** ESPECIALLY: *The rule was introduced expressly for this purpose.*

ex·press·way /ɪkˈsprɛsweɪ/ *noun* a wide road that allows traffic to travel fast through a city or other area where many people live

ex·pro·pri·ate /ɛksˈproʊprɪˌeɪt/ *verb* **1** *~ sth* (*formal or law*) (of a government or an authority) to officially take away private property from its owner for public use **2** *~ sth* (*formal*) to take someone's property and use it without permission ▶ ex·pro·pri·a·tion /ɛksˌproʊprɪˈeɪʃn/ *noun* [U]

ex·pul·sion /ɪkˈspʌlʃn/ *noun* **1** [U, C] *~ (from...)* the act of forcing someone to leave a place; the act of EXPELLING someone: *These events led to the expulsion of senior diplomats from the country.* **2** [U, C] *~ (from...)* the act of sending someone away from a school or an organization, so that they can no longer attend it or belong to it; the act of EXPELLING someone: *The principal threatened the three girls with expulsion.* ♦ *The team faces expulsion from the football league.* **3** [U] *~ (from...)* (*formal*) the act of sending or driving a substance out of your body or a container

ex·punge /ɪkˈspʌndʒ/ *verb* *~ sth (from sth)* (*formal*) to remove or get rid of something such as a name or memory from a book or list or from your mind **SYN** ERASE: *Details of his criminal activities were expunged from the file.* ♦ *What happened just before the accident was expunged from his memory.*

ex·pur·gate /ˈɛkspərˌgeɪt/ *verb* *~ sth* [usually passive] (*formal*) to remove or leave out parts of a piece of writing or a conversation when printing or reporting it, because you think those parts could offend people

ex·quis·ite /ɪkˈskwɪzɪt; ˈɛkskwɪzət/ *adj.* **1** extremely beautiful or carefully made: *exquisite craftsmanship* **2** (*formal*) (of a feeling) strongly felt **SYN** ACUTE: *exquisite pain/pleasure* **3** (*formal*) delicate and sensitive: *The room was decorated in exquisite taste.* ♦ *an exquisite sense of timing* ▶ ex·quis·ite·ly *adv.*

ext. *abbr.* (used as part of a telephone number) EXTENSION: *ext. 4299*

ex·tant /ˈɛkstənt; ɛkˈstænt/ *adj.* (*formal*) (of something very old) still in existence: *extant remains of the ancient wall*

ex·tem·po·ra·ne·ous /ɪkˌstɛmpəˈreɪniəs/ *adj.* spoken or done without any previous thought or preparation **SYN** IMPROMPTU: *extemporaneous speaking* ▶ ex·tem·po·ra·ne·ous·ly *adv.*

ex·tem·po·re /ɛkˈstɛmpəri/ *adj.* (*formal*) = EXTEMPORANEOUS ▶ ex·tem·po·re *adv.*

ex·tem·po·rize /ɪkˈstɛmpəˌraɪz/ *verb* [I] (*formal*) to speak or perform without preparing or practicing **SYN** IMPROVISE ▶ ex·tem·po·ri·za·tion /ɪkˌstɛmpərəˈzeɪʃn/ *noun* [U]

ex·tend 🔑 /ɪkˈstɛnd/ *verb*

>MAKE LONGER/LARGER/WIDER **1** *~ sth* to make something longer or larger: *to extend a fence/road* ♦ *There are plans to extend the subway line.* **2** [T] *~ sth* to make something last longer: *to extend a deadline/visa* ♦ *The show has been extended for another six weeks.* ♦ *Careful maintenance can extend the life of your car.* **3** [T] *~ sth* to make a business, an idea, an influence, etc. cover more areas or operate in more places: *The company plans to extend its operations into Europe.* ♦ *The school is extending the range of subjects taught.*

>INCLUDE **4** [I] *+ adv./prep.* to relate to or include someone or something: *The offer does not extend to employees' partners.* ♦ *His willingness to help did not extend beyond making a few phone calls.*

>COVER AREA/TIME/DISTANCE **5** [I] *+ adv./prep.* to cover a particular area, distance, or length of time: *Our land extends*

t tea	ṭ butter	d did	k cat	g got	tʃ chin	dʒ June	f fall

as far as the river. ♦ *His writing career extended over a period of 40 years.* **6** [T] **~ sth + adv./prep.** to make something reach something or stretch: *to extend a rope between two posts*
> **PART OF BODY 7** [T] **~ sth** to stretch part of your body, especially an arm or a leg, away from yourself: *He extended his hand to* (= offered to shake hands with) *the new employee.* ♦ *(figurative) to extend the hand of friendship to* (= try to have good relations with) *another country*
> **OFFER/GIVE 8** [T] *(formal)* to offer or give something to someone: **~ sth to sb** *I'm sure you will join me in extending a very warm welcome to our visitors.* ♦ *to extend hospitality to overseas students* ♦ *The bank refused to extend credit to them* (= to lend them money). ♦ **~ sb sth** *to extend someone an invitation*
> **USE EFFORT/ABILITY 9** [T, often passive] **~sb/sth/yourself** to make someone or something use all their effort, abilities, supplies, etc.: *Jim didn't really have to extend himself on the exam.* ♦ *Hospitals were already fully extended because of the epidemic.* ⊃ see also EXTENSION, EXTENSIVE

ex·tend·a·ble (also **ex·tend·i·ble**) /ɪkˈstɛndəbl/ *adj.* that can be made longer, or made valid for a longer time: *an extendable ladder* ♦ *The visa is for 14 days, extendable to one month.*

ex·tend·ed /ɪkˈstɛndəd/ *adj.* [only before noun] long, or longer than usual or expected: *an extended lunch hour*

ex,tended 'family *noun* a family group that includes not only parents and children but also uncles, aunts, grandparents, etc. ⊃ compare NUCLEAR FAMILY

ex·ten·sion 🔑 /ɪkˈstɛnʃn/ *noun*
> **INCREASING INFLUENCE 1** [U, C] **~ (of sth)** the act of increasing the area of activity, group of people, etc. that is affected by something: *the extension of new technology into developing countries* ♦ *a gradual extension of the powers of central government* ♦ *The bank plans various extensions to its credit facilities.*
> **EXTRA TIME 2** [C] **~ (of sth)** an extra period of time allowed for something: *He's been granted an extension of the contract for another year.* ♦ *a visa extension*
> **TELEPHONE 3** [C] *(abbr. ext.)* an extra telephone line connected to a central telephone in a house or to a SWITCHBOARD in a large building. In a large building, each extension usually has its own number: *We have an extension in the bedroom.* ♦ *What's your extension number?* ♦ *Can I have extension 4332 please?*
> **MAKING SOMETHING LONGER/LARGER 4** [U, C] the act of making something longer or larger; the thing that is made longer and larger: *The extension of the subway will take several months.* ♦ *extensions to the original railroad track* ♦ *hair extensions* (= pieces of artificial hair that are added to your hair to make it longer)
> **OF BUILDING 5** [C] a new room or rooms that are added to a house
> **COLLEGE/UNIVERSITY 6** [C] a part of a college or university that offers courses to students who are not studying FULL-TIME; a program of study for these students: *extension courses*
> **COMPUTING 7** the set of three letters that are placed after a dot at the end of the name of a file and that show what type of file it is
IDM **by extension** *(formal)* taking the argument or situation one stage further: *The blame lies with the teachers and, by extension, with the Board of Education.*

ex'tension ,agent *noun* a person who works for a state university in a country area, and whose job is to give advice to farmers, do research into farming, etc.

ex'tension ,cord *noun* an extra length of electric wire, used when the wire on an electrical device is not long enough

ex·ten·sive 🔑 /ɪkˈstɛnsɪv/ *adj.*
1 covering a large area; great in amount: *The house has extensive grounds.* ♦ *The fire caused extensive damage.* ♦ *She suffered extensive injuries in the accident.* ♦ *Extensive repair*

work is being carried out. ♦ *an extensive range of wines* **2** including or dealing with a wide range of information **SYN** FAR-REACHING: *Extensive research has been done into this disease.* ♦ *His knowledge of music is extensive.*
▶ **ex·ten·sive·ly** *adv.*: *a spice used extensively in Eastern cooking* ♦ *She has traveled extensively.*

ex·ten·sor /ɪkˈstɛnsər; -sɔr/ (also **ex'tensor ,muscle**) *noun* *(anatomy)* a muscle that allows you to make part of your body straight or stretched out ⊃ compare FLEXOR

ex·tent 🔑 /ɪkˈstɛnt/ *noun* [sing., U]
1 how large, important, serious, etc. something is: *It is difficult to assess the full extent of the damage.* ♦ *She was exaggerating the true extent of the problem.* ♦ *I was amazed at the extent of his knowledge.* **2** the physical size of an area: *You can't see the full extent of the beach from here.*
IDM **to... extent** used to show how far something is true or how great an effect it has: *To a certain extent, we are all responsible for this tragic situation.* ♦ *He had changed to such an extent* (= so much) *that I no longer recognized him.* ♦ *To some extent, what she argues is true.* ♦ *The pollution of the forest has seriously affected plant life and, to a lesser extent, wildlife.* ♦ *To what extent is this true of all schools?* ♦ *The book discusses the extent to which* (= how much) *family life has changed over the past 50 years.* ⊃ language bank at GENERALLY

ex·ten·u·at·ing /ɪkˈstɛnyuˌeɪtɪŋ/ *adj.* [only before noun] *(formal)* showing reasons why a wrong or illegal act, or a bad situation, should be judged less seriously or excused: *There were extenuating circumstances and the defendant did not receive a prison sentence.*

ex·te·ri·or /ɪkˈstɪriər/ *noun, adj.*
●*noun* **1** [C] the outside of something, especially a building: *The exterior of the house needs painting.* **ANT** INTERIOR **2** [sing.] the way that someone appears or behaves, especially when this is very different from their real feelings or character: *Beneath his confident exterior, he was desperately nervous.*
●*adj.* [usually before noun] on the outside of something; done or happening outdoors: *exterior walls/surfaces* ♦ *The filming of the exterior scenes was done on the mountains.* **ANT** INTERIOR

ex·ter·mi·nate /ɪkˈstərməˌneɪt/ *verb* **~ sb/sth** to kill all the members of a group of people or animals **SYN** WIPE OUT
▶ **ex·ter·mi·na·tion** /ɪkˌstərməˈneɪʃn/ *noun* [U]

ex·ter·mi·nat·or /ɪkˈstərməˌneɪtər/ *noun* a person whose job is to kill particular types of insects and small animals that bother people in a building: *We had mice in our house and had to hire an exterminator.*

ex·ter·nal **AWL** /ɪkˈstərnl/ *adj.* **1** connected with or located on the outside of something or someone: *the external walls of the building* ♦ *The lotion is for external use only* (= only for the skin and must not be swallowed). **2** happening or coming from outside a place, an organization, your particular situation, etc.: *A combination of internal and external factors caused the company to close down.* ♦ *external pressures on the economy* ♦ *Many external influences can affect your state of mind.* **3** coming from or arranged by someone from outside a school, a university, or an organization: *An external auditor will verify the accounts.* **4** connected with foreign countries: *The government is committed to reducing the country's external debt.* ♦ *external affairs* **ANT** INTERNAL
▶ **ex·ter·nal·ly** **AWL** /-nəli/ *adv.*: *The building has been restored externally and internally.* ♦ *The university has many externally funded research projects.*

ex,ternal 'ear *noun* *(anatomy)* the parts of the ear outside the EARDRUM

ex·ter·nal·ize **AWL** /ɪkˈstərnəˌlaɪz/ *verb* **~ sth** *(formal)* to show what you are thinking and feeling by what you say or do ⊃ compare INTERNALIZE ▶ **ex·ter·nal·iza·tion** **AWL** /ɪkˌstərnələˈzeɪʃn/ *noun* [U]

ex·ter·nals /ɪkˈstərnlz/ *noun* [pl.] *(formal)* the outer appearance of something

ex·tinct /ɪkˈstɪŋkt/ *adj.* **1** (of a type of plant, animal, etc.) no longer in existence: *an extinct species* ◆ *to become extinct* **2** (of a type of person, job, or way of life) no longer in existence in society: *Servants are now almost extinct in modern society.* **3** (of a VOLCANO) no longer active **ANT** ACTIVE

ex·tinc·tion /ɪkˈstɪŋkʃn/ *noun* [U] a situation in which a plant, an animal, a way of life, etc. stops existing: *a tribe threatened with extinction/in danger of extinction* ◆ *The mountain gorilla is on the verge of extinction.*

ex·tin·guish /ɪkˈstɪŋɡwɪʃ/ *verb* **1 ~ sth** to make a fire stop burning or a light stop shining **SYN** PUT OUT: *Firefighters tried to extinguish the flames.* ◆ (*formal*) *All lights had been extinguished.* **2 ~ sth** to destroy something: *News of the bombing extinguished all hope of peace.*

ex·tin·guish·er /ɪkˈstɪŋɡwɪʃər/ *noun* = FIRE EXTINGUISHER

ex·tir·pate /ˈɛkstərˌpeɪt/ *verb* **~ sth** (*formal*) to destroy or get rid of something that is bad or not wanted ▶ **ex·tir·pa·tion** /ˌɛkstərˈpeɪʃn/ *noun* [U]

ex·tol /ɪkˈstoʊl/ *verb* (-ll-) (*formal*) to praise someone or something very much: **~ sb/sth** *Doctors often extol the virtues of eating less fat.* ◆ **~ sb/sth as sth** *She was extolled as a genius.*

ex·tort /ɪkˈstɔrt/ *verb* **~ sth (from sb)** to make someone give you something by threatening them: *The gang extorted money from over 30 local businesses.* ▶ **ex·tor·tion** /ɪkˈstɔrʃn/ *noun* [U, C]: *He was arrested and charged with extortion.*

ex·tor·tion·ate /ɪkˈstɔrʃənət/ *adj.* (*disapproving*) (of prices, etc.) much too high **SYN** EXCESSIVE, OUTRAGEOUS: *They are offering loans at extortionate rates of interest.* ▶ **ex·tor·tion·ate·ly** *adv.*: *extortionately priced*

ex·tra 🔑 /ˈɛkstrə/ *adj., noun, adv.*

● *adj.* more than is usual or expected, or than exists already **SYN** ADDITIONAL: *Breakfast is provided at no extra charge.* ◆ *The conference is going to be a lot of extra work.* ◆ *an extra pint of milk* ◆ *The government has promised an extra $1 billion for the program.* ◆ *Take extra care on the roads this evening.*

● *noun* **1** a thing that is added to something that is not usual, standard, or necessary and that costs more: *The monthly fee is fixed and there are no hidden extras* (= unexpected costs). **2** a person who is employed to play a very small part in a movie, usually as a member of a crowd

● *adv.* **1** in addition; more than is usual or expected, or than exists already: *to charge/pay/cost extra* ◆ *I need to earn a little extra this month.* ◆ *The rate for a room is $75, but breakfast is extra.* **2** (with an adjective or adverb) more than usually: *You need to be extra careful not to make any mistakes.* ◆ *an extra large T-shirt* ◆ *She tried extra hard.*

extra- /ˈɛkstrə/ *prefix* (in adjectives) **1** outside; beyond: *extramarital sex* ◆ *extraterrestrial beings* **2** (*informal*) very; more than usual: *extra-thin* ◆ *extra-special*

ex·tract **AWL** *noun, verb*

● *noun* /ˈɛkstrækt/ **1** [C] **~ (from sth)** a short passage from a book, piece of music, etc. that gives you an idea of what the whole thing is like: *The following extract is taken from her new novel.* **2** [U, C] a substance that has been obtained from something else using a particular process: *moisturizer containing natural plant extracts* ◆ *vanilla extract* ⊃ see also ESSENCE

● *verb* /ɪkˈstrækt/ **1 ~ sth (from sb/sth)** to remove or obtain a substance from something, for example by using an industrial or a chemical process: *a machine that extracts excess moisture from the air* ◆ *to extract essential oils from plants* **2 ~ sth (from sb/sth)** to obtain information, money, etc., often by taking it from someone who is unwilling to give it: *Journalists managed to extract all kinds of information about her private life.* **3 ~ sth (from sth)** to choose information, etc. from a book, a computer, etc. to be used for a particular purpose: *This article is extracted from his new book.* **4 ~ sth (from sb/sth)** (*formal* or *technical*) to take or pull something out, especially when this needs force or effort: *The dentist may decide that the wisdom teeth need to be extracted.* ◆ *He rifled through his briefcase and extracted a file.* **5 ~ sth (from sb/sth)** (*formal*) to get a particular feeling or

quality from a situation **SYN** DERIVE: *They are unlikely to extract much benefit from the trip.*

ex·trac·tion **AWL** /ɪkˈstrækʃn/ *noun* **1** [U, C] the act or process of removing or obtaining something from something else: *oil/mineral/coal, etc. extraction* ◆ *the extraction of salt from the ocean* **2** [U] **of… extraction** (*formal*) having a particular family origin: *an American of Hungarian extraction* **3** [C] (*technical*) the removal of a tooth

ex·trac·tive /ɪkˈstræktɪv/ *adj.* (*technical*) relating to the process of removing or obtaining something, especially minerals: *extractive industries*

ex·trac·tor /ɪkˈstræktər/ *noun* a device or machine that removes something from something else: *a juice extractor*

ex·tra·cur·ric·u·lar /ˌɛkstrəkəˈrɪkyələr/ *adj.* [usually before noun] not part of the usual course of work or studies at a school or college: *She's involved in a lot of extracurricular activities.*

ex·tra·dite /ˈɛkstrəˌdaɪt/ *verb* **~ sb (to…) (from…)** to officially send back someone who has been accused or found guilty of a crime to the country where the crime was committed: *The government attempted to extradite the suspect from Canada to the U.S.* ▶ **ex·tra·di·tion** /ˌɛkstrəˈdɪʃn/ *noun* [U, C]: *the extradition of terrorist suspects* ◆ *an extradition treaty* ◆ *to start extradition proceedings*

ex·tra·ju·di·cial /ˌɛkstrədʒuˈdɪʃl/ *adj.* happening outside the normal power of the law

ex·tra·mar·i·tal /ˌɛkstrəˈmærətl/ *adj.* happening outside marriage: *an extramarital affair*

ex·tra·mu·ral /ˌɛkstrəˈmyʊrəl/ *adj.* [usually before noun] **1** involving students at more than one school or college: *extramural athletics* **2** (*formal*) happening or existing outside or separate from a place, an organization, etc.: *The hospital provides extramural care to patients who do not need to be admitted.*

ex·tra·ne·ous /ɪkˈstreɪniəs/ *adj.* (*formal*) not directly connected with the particular situation you are in or the subject you are dealing with **SYN** IRRELEVANT: *We do not want any extraneous information on the page.* ◆ **~ to sth** *We shall ignore factors extraneous to the problem.*

ext·ra·net /ˈɛkstrəˌnɛt/ *noun* (*computing*) an INTRANET (= a private computer network) that is partly available to some outside users, so that businesses and customers can exchange information

ex·tra·or·di·naire /ɪkˌstrɔrdnˈɛr/ *adj.* (from *French, approving, often humorous*) used after nouns to say that someone is a good example of a particular kind of person: *Houdini, escape artist extraordinaire*

ex·traor·di·nar·y 🔑 /ɪkˈstrɔrdnˌɛri/ *adj.*

1 unexpected, surprising, or strange **SYN** INCREDIBLE: *It's extraordinary that he managed to sleep through the party.* ◆ *What an extraordinary thing to say!* **2** not normal or ordinary; greater or better than usual: *an extraordinary achievement* ◆ *She was a truly extraordinary woman.* ◆ *They went to extraordinary lengths to explain their behavior.* ⊃ compare ORDINARY **3** [only before noun] (*formal*) (of a meeting, etc.) arranged for a special purpose and happening in addition to what normally or regularly happens: *An extraordinary meeting was held to discuss the problem.* **4** (following nouns) (*technical*) (of an official) employed for a special purpose in addition to the usual staff: *an envoy extraordinary* ▶ **ex·traor·di·nar·i·ly** /ɪkˈstrɔrdnˈɛrəli/ *adv.*: *He behaves extraordinarily for someone in his position.* ◆ *extraordinarily difficult* ◆ *She did extraordinarily well.*

ex,traordinary ren'dition *noun* the practice of sending foreign suspects to be questioned in another country where the laws about the treatment of prisoners are less strict ⊃ compare RENDITION (2)

ex·trap·o·late /ɪkˈstræpəˌleɪt/ *verb* [I, T] (*formal*) to estimate something or form an opinion about something, using the facts that you have now and that are valid for one situation and supposing that they will be valid for the new one: **~ (from/to sth)** *The figures were obtained by extrapolating*

from past trends. ◆ **~ sth (from/to sth)** *We have extrapolated these results from research done in other countries.*
▶ **ex·trap·o·la·tion** /ɪkˌstræpəˈleɪʃn/ *noun* [U, C]: *Their age can be determined by extrapolation from their growth rate.*

ex·tra·sen·so·ry per·cep·tion /ˌɛkstrəˌsensəri pərˈsepʃn/ *noun* [U] = ESP

ex·tra·so·lar /ˌɛkstrəˈsoʊlər/ *adj.* [usually before noun] (*technical*) (of a planet, etc.) located outside our SOLAR SYSTEM

ex·tra·ter·res·tri·al /ˌɛkstrətəˈrestriəl/ *noun, adj.*
● *noun* (in stories) a creature that comes from another planet; a creature that may exist on another planet
● *adj.* connected with life existing outside the planet Earth: *extraterrestrial beings/life*

ex·tra·ter·ri·to·ri·al /ˌɛkstrəˌterəˈtɔriəl/ *adj.* (of a law) valid outside the country where the law was made

ex·trav·a·gance /ɪkˈstrævəgəns/ *noun* **1** [U] the act or habit of spending more money than you can afford or than is necessary **2** [C] something that you buy although it costs a lot of money, perhaps more than you can afford or than is necessary: *Going to the theater is our only extravagance.* **3** [C, U] something that is impressive or noticeable because it is unusual or extreme: *the extravagance of Strauss's music*

ex·trav·a·gant /ɪkˈstrævəgənt/ *adj.* **1** spending a lot more money, or using a lot more of something, than you can afford or than is necessary: *I felt very extravagant spending $200 on a dress.* ◆ *She has very extravagant tastes.* ◆ *Residents were warned not to be extravagant with water, in view of the low rainfall this year.* **2** costing a lot more money than you can afford or than is necessary: *an extravagant present* **3** (of ideas, speech, or behavior) very extreme or impressive but not reasonable or practical **SYN** EXAGGERATED: *the extravagant claims/promises of politicians* ▶ **ex·trav·a·gant·ly** *adv.*: *extravagantly expensive* ◆ *extravagantly high hopes*

ex·trav·a·gan·za /ɪkˌstrævəˈɡænzə/ *noun* a large, expensive, and impressive entertainment

ex·tra·vert = EXTROVERT

ˌextra ˈvirgin *adj.* used to describe good quality oil obtained the first time that OLIVES are pressed: *extra virgin olive oil*

ex·treme 🖉 /ɪkˈstrim/ *adj., noun*
● *adj.* **1** [usually before noun] very great in degree: *We are working under extreme pressure at the moment.* ◆ *people living in extreme poverty* ◆ *The heat in the desert was extreme.* **2** not ordinary or usual; serious or severe: *Children will be removed from their parents only in extreme circumstances.* ◆ *Don't go doing anything extreme like leaving the country.* ◆ *It was the most extreme example of cruelty to animals I had ever seen.* ◆ *extreme weather conditions* **3** (of people, political organizations, opinions, etc.) far from what most people consider to be normal, reasonable, or acceptable: *extreme left-wing/right-wing views* **ANT** MODERATE **4** [only before noun] as far as possible from the center, from the beginning, or in the direction mentioned: *She lives in the extreme west of Tennessee.* ◆ *She sat on the extreme edge of her seat.*
● *noun* **1** a feeling, situation, way of behaving, etc. that is as different as possible from another or is opposite to it: *extremes of love and hate* ◆ *He used to be very shy, but now he's gone to the opposite extreme* (= changed from one extreme kind of behavior to another). **2** the greatest or highest degree of something: *extremes of cold, wind, or rain* **IDM** **go, etc. to extremes| take sth to extremes** to act or be forced to act in a way that is far from normal or reasonable: *It's embarrassing the extremes he'll go to in order to impress his boss.* ◆ *Taken to extremes, this kind of behavior can be dangerous.* **in the extreme** (*formal*) to a great degree: *The journey would be dangerous in the extreme.*

ex·treme ˈfighting *noun* [U] = ULTIMATE FIGHTING

ex·treme·ly 🖉 /ɪkˈstrimli/ *adv.*
(usually with adjectives and adverbs) to a very high degree:

extremely important/useful/complicated ◆ *She found it extremely difficult to get a job.*

ex·treme ˈsports *noun* [pl.] sports that are extremely exciting to do and often dangerous, for example SKYDIVING and BUNGEE JUMPING

ex·treme ˈunction *noun* [U] (*religion*) (*old use*) in the Catholic Church, the ceremony of BLESSING sick or dying people: *He was given extreme unction.*

extremis ⊃ IN EXTREMIS

ex·trem·ism /ɪkˈstrimɪzəm/ *noun* [U] political, religious, etc. ideas or actions that are extreme and not normal, reasonable, or acceptable to most people: *political extremism*

ex·trem·ist /ɪkˈstrimɪst/ *noun* (usually *disapproving*) a person whose opinions, especially about religion or politics, are extreme, and who may do things that are violent, illegal, etc. for what they believe: *left-wing/right-wing/political/religious extremists* ▶ **ex·trem·ist** *adj.* [usually before noun]: *extremist attacks/groups/policies*

ex·trem·i·ty /ɪkˈstreməti/ *noun* (*pl.* **ex·trem·i·ties**) **1** [C] the furthest point, end, or limit of something: *The lake is situated at the eastern extremity of the mountain range.* **2** [C, U] the degree to which a situation, a feeling, an action, etc. is extreme, difficult, or unusual: *the extremities/extremity of pain* **3 extremities** [pl.] (*formal*) the parts of your body that are furthest from the center, especially your hands and feet

ex·tri·cate /ˈɛkstrəˌkeɪt/ *verb* (*formal*) **1** **~ sb/sth/yourself (from sth)** to escape or enable someone to escape from a difficult situation: *He had managed to extricate himself from most of his official duties.* **2** **~ sb/sth/yourself (from sth)** to free someone or something or yourself from a place where they/it or you are trapped: *They managed to extricate the pilot from the tangled control panel.*

ex·trin·sic /ɛksˈtrɪnzɪk; -sɪk/ *adj.* (*formal*) not belonging naturally to someone or something; coming from or existing outside someone or something rather than within them: *extrinsic factors* ⊃ compare INTRINSIC

ex·tro·vert (also less frequent **ex·tra·vert**) /ˈɛkstrəˌvərt/ *noun* a lively and confident person who enjoys being with other people **ANT** INTROVERT ▶ **ex·tro·vert·ed** *adj.*

ex·trude /ɪkˈstrud/ *verb* **1** [T, I] **~ (sth) (from sth)** (*formal*) to force or push something out of something; to be forced or pushed in this way: *Lava is extruded from the volcano.* **2** [T] **~ sth** (*technical*) to shape metal or plastic by forcing it through a hole ▶ **ex·tru·sion** /ɪkˈstruʒn/ *noun* [U]

ex·tru·sive /ɪkˈstrusɪv/ *adj.* (*geology*) (of rock) that has been pushed out of the earth by a VOLCANO

ex·u·ber·ant /ɪgˈzubərənt/ *adj.* **1** full of energy, excitement, and happiness: *She gave an exuberant performance.* ◆ *an exuberant personality/imagination* ◆ *a picture painted in exuberant reds and yellows* **2** (of plants, etc.) strong and healthy; growing quickly and well ▶ **ex·u·ber·ance** /-rəns/ *noun* [U]: *We can excuse his behavior as youthful exuberance.* **ex·u·ber·ant·ly** *adv.*

ex·ude /ɪgˈzud/ *verb* **1** [T, I] **~ sth | ~ (from sb)** if you **exude** a particular feeling or quality, or it **exudes** from you, people can easily see that you have it: *She exuded confidence.* **2** [T, I] if something **exudes** a liquid or smell, or a liquid or smell **exudes** from somewhere, the liquid, etc. comes out slowly: **~ sth** *The plant exudes a sticky fluid.* ◆ **~ (from sth)** *An awful smell exuded from the creature's body.*

ex·ult /ɪgˈzʌlt/ *verb* [I, T] (*formal*) to feel and show that you are very excited and happy because of something that has happened: **~ (at/in sth)** *He leaned back, exulting at the success of his plan.* ◆ **+ speech** *"We won!" she exulted.*

ex·ult·ant /ɪgˈzʌltənt/ *adj.* **~ (at sth)** (*formal*) feeling or showing great pride or happiness, especially because of something exciting that has happened **SYN** TRIUMPHANT ▶ **ex·ult·ant·ly** *adv.*

ex·ul·ta·tion /ˌɛgzʌlˈteɪʃn; ˌɛksʌl-/ *noun* [U] (*formal*) great pride or happiness, especially because of something exciting that has happened

eye 🔑 /aɪ/ *noun, verb*

● **noun**

> PART OF BODY **1** [C] either of the two organs on the face that you see with: *The suspect has dark hair and green eyes.* ◆ *to close/open your eyes* ◆ *to drop/lower your eyes* (= to look down) ◆ *There were tears in his eyes.* ◆ *I have something in my eye.* ◆ *to make/avoid eye contact with someone* (= to look/avoid looking at them at the same time as they look at you) ◆ *All eyes were on him* (= everyone was looking at him) *as he walked onto the stage.* ⊃ picture at BODY ⊃ collocations at PHYSICAL ⊃ see also BLACK EYE, COMPOUND EYE, LAZY EYE, SHUT-EYE
2 -eyed (in adjectives) having the type or number of eyes mentioned: *a blue-eyed blonde* ◆ *a one-eyed monster*

> ABILITY TO SEE **3** [sing.] the ability to see: *A surgeon needs a good eye and a steady hand.* ⊃ see also EAGLE EYE

> WAY OF SEEING **4** [C, usually sing.] a particular way of seeing something: *He looked at the design with the eye of an engineer.* ◆ *She viewed the findings with a critical eye.* ◆ *To my eye, the windows seem out of proportion.* ◆ *She has a good eye for color.*

> OF NEEDLE **5** [C] the hole in the end of a needle that you put the thread through

> ON CLOTHES **6** [C] a small metal ring that a small hook fits into, used for fastening clothes: *It fastens with a hook and eye.* ⊃ picture at CLOTHES

> OF STORM **7** [sing.] **an/the ~ of a/the storm, tornado, hurricane, etc.** a calm area at the center of a storm, etc.

> ON POTATO **8** [C] a dark mark on a potato from which another plant will grow ⊃ see also BULL'S-EYE, THE EVIL EYE, FISHEYE LENS, GOOGLY EYES, RED-EYE

IDM **be all eyes** to be watching someone or something carefully and with a lot of interest **before/in front of sb's (very) eyes** in someone's presence; in front of someone: *He had seen his life's work destroyed before his very eyes.* **be up to your eyes in sth** to have a lot of something to deal with: *We're up to our eyes in work.* **an eye for an eye (and a tooth for a tooth)** (*saying*) used to say that you should punish someone by doing to them what they have done to you or to someone else **sb's eyes are bigger than their stomach** used to say that someone has been GREEDY by taking more food than they can eat **for sb's eyes only** to be seen only by a particular person: *I'll lend you the letters but they're for your eyes only.* **have an eye for sth** to be able to judge if things look attractive, valuable, etc.: *I've never had much of an eye for fashion.* ◆ *She has an eye for a bargain.* **have eyes in the back of your head** to be aware of everything that is happening around you, even things that seem difficult or impossible to see **have eyes like a hawk** to be able to notice or see everything: *She's bound to notice that chipped glass. The woman has eyes like a hawk!* **have one eye/half an eye on sth** to look at or watch something while doing something else, especially in a secret way so that other people do not notice: *During his talk, most of the delegates had one eye on the clock.* **have your eye on sb 1** to be watching someone carefully, especially to check that they do not do anything wrong **2** to be thinking about asking someone out, offering someone a job, etc. because you think they are attractive, good at their job, etc.: *He has his eye on the new girl in your class.* **have your eye on sth** to be thinking about buying something **in the eyes of the law, world, etc.** according to the law, most people in the world, etc. **in sb's eyes** in someone's opinion or according to the way that they see the situation: *She can do no wrong in her father's eyes.* **keep an eye on sb/sth** to take care of someone or something and make sure that they are not harmed, damaged, etc.: *We've asked the neighbors to keep an eye on the house for us while we're away.* **keep an/your eye open/out (for sb/sth)** to look for someone or something while you are doing other things: *Police have asked residents to keep an eye out for anything suspicious.* **keep your eye on the ball** to continue to give your attention to what is most important **keep your eyes peeled (for sb/sth)** to look carefully for someone or something: *We kept our eyes peeled for any signs of life.* **lay/set eyes on sb/sth** (*informal*) (usually used in negative sentences) to see someone or something: *I hope I never set eyes on this place again!* **look sb in the eye(s)/face** (usually used in negative sentences and questions) to look straight at someone without feeling embarrassed or ashamed: *Can you look me in the eye and tell me you're not lying?* ◆ *I'll never be able to look her in the face again!* **make eyes at sb | give sb the eye** to look at someone in a way that shows that you find them sexually attractive: *He's definitely giving you the eye!* **my eye!** (*old-fashioned, informal*) used to show that you do not believe someone or something: *"It's an antique." "An antique, my eye!"* **not see eye to eye with sb (on sth)** to not share the same views as someone about something **not (be able to) take your eyes off sb/sth** to find someone or something so interesting, attractive, etc. that you watch them all the time **only have eyes for/have eyes only for sb** to be in love with only one particular person: *He's only ever had eyes for his wife.* **run/cast an eye/your eyes over sth** to look at or examine something quickly: *Could you just run your eyes over this report?* **see, look at, etc. sth through sb's eyes** to think about or see something the way that another person sees it: *Try looking at it through her eyes for a change.* **shut/close your eyes to sth** to pretend that you have not noticed something so that you do not have to deal with it **take your eye off the ball** to stop giving your attention to what is most important **under the (watchful) eye of sb** being watched carefully by someone: *The children played under the watchful eye of their father.* **with an eye to sth/to doing sth** with the intention of doing something: *He bought the warehouse with an eye to converting it into a hotel.* **with your eyes open** fully aware of the possible problems or results of a particular course of action: *I went into this with my eyes open so I guess I only have myself to blame.* **with your eyes shut/closed** having enough experience to be able to do something easily: *I've made this trip so often, I could do it with my eyes shut.* ⊃ more at APPLE, BAT *v.*, BEAUTY, BELIEVE, BIRD, BLIND *adj.*, BLINK *n.*, BLUE *adj.*, CATCH *v.*, CLOSE[1], COCK *v.*, CORNER *n.*, DRY *adj.*, EASY *adj.*, FAR *adv.*, FEAST *v.*, MEET *v.*, MIND *n.*, NAKED, OPEN *adj.*, OPEN *v.*, PLEASE *v.*, PUBLIC *adj.*, PULL *v.*, ROVING, SIGHT *n.*, TWINKLING, WEATHER *n.*

● **verb** (eye-ing or ey·ing, eyed, eyed) **~ sb/sth (+ adv./prep.)** to look at someone or something carefully, especially because you want something or you are suspicious of something: *to eye someone suspiciously* ◆ *He couldn't help eyeing the cakes hungrily.* ◆ *They eyed us with alarm.*

eye·ball /'aɪbɔl/ *noun, verb*

● **noun** the whole of the eye, including the part inside the head that cannot be seen
IDM **eyeball to eyeball (with sb)** very close to someone and looking at them, especially during an angry conversation, meeting, etc.: *The protesters and police stood eyeball to eyeball.* ◆ *an eyeball-to-eyeball confrontation* **be up to your eyeballs in sth** to have a lot of something to deal with: *They're up to their eyeballs in work.*

● **verb ~ sb/sth** (*informal*) to look at someone or something in a way that is very direct and not always polite or friendly

eye·brow /'aɪbraʊ/ (also **brow**) *noun* [usually pl.] the line of hair above the eye ⊃ picture at BODY ⊃ collocations at PHYSICAL
IDM **be up to your eyebrows in sth** to have a lot of something to deal with: *He's in it* (= trouble) *up to his eyebrows.* ⊃ more at RAISE *v.*

'eyebrow ˌpencil *noun* a type of makeup in the form of a pencil, used for emphasizing or improving the shape of the eyebrow

'eye ˌcandy *noun* [U] (*informal*) a person or thing that is attractive but not intelligent or useful

'eye-ˌcatching *adj.* (of a thing) immediately noticeable because it is particularly interesting, bright, or attractive: *an eye-catching advertisement*

eye·cup /'aɪkʌp/ *noun* a small container that you put a liquid in to wash your eye with

eye·ful /'aɪfʊl/ *noun* **1** an amount of something, such as

| ʌ cup | ə about | eɪ say | aɪ five | ɔɪ boy | aʊ now | oʊ go | ər bird |

liquid or dust, that has been thrown or blown into your eye **2** (*informal*) a person or thing that is beautiful or interesting to look at

eye·glass /ˈaɪɡlæs/ *noun* **1** a LENS for one eye, used to help you see more clearly with that eye **2** eye·glass·es = GLASSES

eye·lash /ˈaɪlæʃ/ (also **lash**) *noun* [usually pl.] one of the hairs growing on the edge of the EYELID: *false eyelashes* ◆ *She just bats her eyelashes and the men come running!* ⊃ picture at BODY ⊃ collocations at PHYSICAL

eye·let /ˈaɪlət/ *noun* **1** a hole with a metal ring around it in a piece of cloth or leather, normally used for passing a rope or string through **2** a type of cloth decorated with little holes: *white eyelet curtains*

eye ˌlevel *noun* [U] the height of a person's eyes: *Computer screens should be at eye level.* ◆ *an eye-level oven*

eye·lid /ˈaɪlɪd/ (also **lid**) *noun* either of the pieces of skin above and below the eye that cover it when you BLINK or close the eye ⊃ picture at BODY

eye·line /ˈaɪlaɪn/ *noun* the direction that someone is looking in

eye·lin·er /ˈaɪˌlaɪnər/ (also **lin·er**) *noun* [U] a type of makeup that is put around the edge of the eyelids to make them more noticeable and attractive ⊃ picture at MAKEUP

eye-ˌopener *noun* [usually sing.] an event, experience, etc. that is surprising and shows you something that you did not already know: *Traveling around India was a real eye-opener for me.*

eye·patch /ˈaɪpætʃ/ *noun* a piece of material worn over one eye, usually because the eye is damaged

eye·piece /ˈaɪpis/ *noun* the piece of glass (= the LENS) at the end of a TELESCOPE or MICROSCOPE that you look through ⊃ picture at LABORATORY

eye·shad·ow /ˈaɪˌʃædoʊ/ *noun* [C, U] a type of colored makeup that is put on the skin above the eyes (= the EYELIDS) to make them look more attractive ⊃ picture at MAKEUP

eye·sight /ˈaɪsaɪt/ *noun* [U] the ability to see: *to have good/bad/poor eyesight*

eye·sore /ˈaɪsɔr/ *noun* a building, an object, etc. that is unpleasant to look at: *That old factory is a real eyesore!*

ˈeye strain *noun* [U] a condition of the eyes caused, for example, by a long period of reading or looking at a computer screen

eye·teeth /ˈaɪtiθ/ *noun* [pl.]
IDM **give your eyeteeth for sth/to do sth** (*informal*) used when you are saying that you want something very much: *I'd give my eyeteeth to own a car like that.*

eye·wall /ˈaɪwɔl/ *noun* (*technical*) a thick ring of cloud around the EYE (= calm area at the center) of a HURRICANE

eye·wear /ˈaɪwɛr/ *noun* [U] (*formal*) things worn on the eyes, such as glasses or CONTACT LENSES

eye·wit·ness /ˌaɪˈwɪtnəs; ˈaɪˌwɪtnəs/ *noun* a person who has seen a crime, an accident, etc. and can describe it afterward: *an eyewitness account of the suffering of the refugees* ⊃ thesaurus box at WITNESS ⊃ see also WITNESS

ey·rie = AERIE

e-zine /ˈi zin/ *noun* a magazine published in electronic form on the Internet

Ff

F /ɛf/ *noun, abbr.*
● *noun* [C, U] (*pl.* Fs, F's /ɛfs/) **1** also **f** (*pl.* f's) the 6th letter of the English alphabet: *"Fox" begins with (an) F/"F."* **2** (*music*) the fourth note in the SCALE of C MAJOR **3** the lowest grade that a student can get for a course, test, or piece of work, showing that it is very bad and the student has failed: *He got an F in Chemistry.*
● *abbr.* **1** FAHRENHEIT: *Water freezes at 32°F.* **2** FARAD

f (also **f.**) *abbr.* **1** female **2** (*grammar*) feminine **3** (*music*) loudly (from Italian "forte")

F-1 visa /ˌɛf wʌn ˈvizə/ *noun* a document that allows someone from another country to enter the U.S. as a student

fa /fɑ/ *noun* (*music*) the fourth note of a MAJOR SCALE

fa·ble /ˈfeɪbl/ *noun* **1** [C, U] a traditional short story that teaches a moral lesson, especially one with animals as characters; these stories considered as a group: *Aesop's Fables* ◆ *a land rich in fable* **2** [U, C] a statement, or an account of something, that is not true

fa·bled /ˈfeɪbld/ *adj.* (*literary* or *humorous*) famous and often talked about, but rarely seen **SYN** LEGENDARY: *a fabled monster* ◆ *For the first week he never actually saw the fabled Jack.*

THESAURUS

fabric

cloth ◆ material ◆ textile

These are all words for woven or knitted cotton, silk, wool, etc., used for making things such as clothes and curtains, and for covering furniture.

fabric woven or knitted cotton, silk, wool, etc., used for making things such as clothes and curtains, and for covering furniture: *cotton fabric* ◆ *upholstery fabrics* **NOTE** Fabric is often fairly strong material, and is often used when talking about covering furniture or making curtains.

cloth fabric made by weaving or knitting cotton, wool, silk, etc.: *His bandages had been made from strips of cloth.* **NOTE** Cloth is often fairly light material. **Cloth** is frequently used in talking about clothing material, or buying and selling woven material.

material fabric used for making clothes, curtains, etc: *The material was dyed with natural ingredients.* **NOTE** Material is a more general word than **fabric** or **cloth** as it has the related meaning of "a substance that things can be made from." It is not used when it might not be clear which type of material is meant: ~~upholstery material~~ ◆ ~~the material industry~~

textile any type of fabric made by weaving or knitting: *She owns a factory producing a range of textiles.* ◆ *the textile industry* **NOTE** Textile is used mostly when talking about the business of making woven materials. The industry of making textiles is called **textiles**: *He works in textiles.*

PATTERNS
- **woven/cotton/woolen** fabric/cloth/material/textiles
- **synthetic** fabric/material/textiles
- **dyed/printed** fabric/cloth/textiles
- **curtain/dress/clothing/upholstery** fabric/material

---

fab·ric /ˈfæbrɪk/ *noun* **1** [U, C] material made by weaving (WEAVE) wool, cotton, silk, etc., used for making clothes, curtains, etc. and for covering furniture: *cotton fabric* **2** [sing.] **the ~ (of sth)** (*formal*) the basic structure of a society, an organization, etc. that enables it to function successfully: *a trend which threatens the very fabric of society* ⟳ thesaurus box at STRUCTURE **3** [sing.] **the ~ (of sth)** the basic structure of a building, such as the walls, floor, and roof

fab·ri·cate /ˈfæbrɪˌkeɪt/ *verb* [often passive] **1 ~ sth** to invent false information in order to trick people **SYN** MAKE UP: *The evidence was totally fabricated.* **2 ~ sth** (*technical*) to make or produce goods, equipment, etc. from various different materials **SYN** MANUFACTURE ▶ **fab·ri·ca·tion** /ˌfæbrɪˈkeɪʃn/ *noun* [C, U]: *Her story was a complete fabrication from start to finish.*

fab·u·list /ˈfæbyəlɪst/ *noun* (*formal*) a person who invents or tells stories

fab·u·lous /ˈfæbyələs/ *adj.* **1** (*informal*) extremely good: *a fabulous performance* ◆ *Jane is a fabulous cook.* ⟳ thesaurus box at GREAT **2** (*formal*) very great: *fabulous wealth/riches/beauty* **3** [only before noun] (*literary*) appearing in FABLES: *fabulous beasts*

fab·u·lous·ly /ˈfæbyələsli/ *adv.* (*formal*) extremely: *fabulously wealthy/rich*

fa·cade (also **fa·çade**) /fəˈsɑd/ *noun* **1** the front of a building **2** [usually sing.] the way that someone or something appears to be, which is different from the way someone or something really is: *She managed to maintain a facade of indifference.* ◆ *Squalor and poverty lay behind the city's glittering facade.*

face /feɪs/ *noun, verb*
● *noun*
▷ FRONT OF HEAD **1** the front part of the head between the FOREHEAD and the chin: *a pretty/round/freckled face* ◆ *He buried his face in his hands.* ◆ *You should have seen the look on her face when I told her!* ◆ *The expression on his face never changed.* ⟳ picture at BODY
▷ EXPRESSION **2** an expression that is shown on someone's face: *a sad/happy/smiling face* ◆ *Her face lit up* (= showed happiness) *when she spoke of the past.* ◆ *His face fell* (= showed disappointment, sadness, etc.) *when he read the headlines.*
▷ -FACED **3** (in adjectives) having the type of face or expression mentioned: *pale-faced* ◆ *grim-faced*
▷ PERSON **4** (in compounds) used to refer to a person of the type mentioned: *She looked around for a familiar face.* ◆ *a well-known face on our television screens* ◆ *It's nice to see some new faces here this evening.* ◆ *I'm tired of seeing the same old faces every time we go out!*
▷ SIDE/SURFACE **5** a side or surface of something: *the north face of the mountain* ◆ *The birds build their nests in the rock face.* ◆ *How many faces does a cube have?* ⟳ picture at SHAPE
▷ FRONT OF CLOCK **6** the front part of a clock or watch ⟳ picture at CLOCK
▷ CHARACTER/ASPECT **7 ~ of sth** the particular character of something: *the changing face of our city* **8 ~ of sth** a particular aspect of something: *the unacceptable face of capitalism* ⟳ see also IN-YOUR-FACE, TYPEFACE, VOLTE-FACE
IDM **disappear/vanish off the face of the earth** to disappear completely: *Keep looking—they can't just have vanished off the face of the earth.* **face to face (with sb)** close to and looking at someone: *The two have never met face to face before.* **face to face with sth** in a situation where you have to accept that something is true and deal with it: *She was at an early age brought face to face with the horrors of war.* **face up/down 1** (of a person) with your face and stomach facing upward/downward: *She lay face down on the bed.* **2** with the front part or surface facing upward/downward: *Place the card face up on the pile.* **in sb's face** (*informal*) annoying someone by criticizing them or telling them what to do all the time **in the face of sth 1** despite problems, difficulties, etc.: *She showed great courage in the face of danger.* **2** as a result of something: *He was unable to deny the charges in the face of new evidence.* **lose face** to be less

---

t tea　　　ţ butter　　　d did　　　k cat　　　g got　　　tʃ chin　　　dʒ June　　　f fall

respected or look stupid because of something you have done **SYN** BE HUMILIATED **make faces/a face (at sb)** to produce an expression on your face to show that you do not like someone or something, or in order to make someone laugh **on the face of it** (*informal*) used to say that something seems to be good, true, etc. but that this opinion may need to be changed when you know more about it: *On the face of it, it seems like a great deal.* **put your face on** (*informal*, *old-fashioned*) to put on MAKEUP **stuff/feed your face** (*informal*, usually *disapproving*) to eat a lot of food or too much food **to sb's face** if you say something **to someone's face**, you say it to them directly rather than to other people ➔ compare BEHIND SB'S BACK **what's his/her face** (*informal*) used to refer to a person whose name you cannot remember: *Are you still working for what's her face?* ➔ more at BLOW *v.*, BLUE *adj.*, BRAVE *adj.*, DOOR, EGG *n.*, EYE *n.*, FLAT *adv.*, FLY *v.*, LAUGH *v.*, LONG *adj.*, NOSE *n.*, PLAIN *adj.*, PRETTY *adj.*, SAVE *v.*, SHOW *v.*, SHUT *v.*, SLAP *n.*, STARE *v.*, STRAIGHT *adj.*, WIPE *v.*, WRITE

VOCABULARY BUILDING

expressions on your face

- To **beam** is to have a big happy smile on your face.
- To **frown** is to make a serious, angry, or worried expression by bringing your eyebrows closer together so that lines appear on your forehead.
- To **glare** or **glower** is to look in an angry, aggressive way.
- To **grimace** is to make an ugly expression with your face to show pain, disgust, etc.
- To **scowl** is to look at someone in an angry or annoyed way.
- To **smirk** is to smile in a silly or unpleasant way that shows that you are pleased with yourself, know something that other people do not know, etc.
- To **sneer** is to show that you have no respect for someone by turning your upper lip upward.

These words can also be used as nouns: *She looked up with a puzzled frown.* ♦ *He gave me an icy glare.* ♦ *a grimace of pain*

• *verb*

▷ BE OPPOSITE **1** [T, I] to be opposite someone or something; to have your face or front pointing toward someone or something, or in a particular direction: **~ sb/sth** *She turned and faced him.* ♦ *Most of the rooms face the ocean.* ♦ **+ adv./prep.** *The terrace faces south.* ♦ *a north-facing wall* ♦ *Stand with your feet apart and your hands facing upward.* ♦ *Which direction are you facing?*

▷ SOMEONE OR SOMETHING DIFFICULT **2** [T] if you **face** a particular situation, or it **faces** you, you have to deal with it: **~ sth** *the problems faced by one-parent families* ♦ *The company is facing a financial crisis.* ♦ **be faced with sth** *She's faced with a difficult decision.* **3** [T] **~ sth** to accept that a difficult situation exists, although you would prefer not to: *It's not always easy to face the truth.* ♦ *She had to face the fact that her life had changed forever.* ♦ *Face facts —she isn't coming back.* ♦ *Let's face it, we're not going to win.* **4** [T] if you **can't face** something unpleasant, you feel unable or unwilling to deal with it: **~ sth** *I just can't face work today.* ♦ **~ doing sth** *I can't face seeing them.* **5** [T] **~ sb** to talk to or deal with someone, even though this is difficult or unpleasant: *How can I face Tom? He'll be so disappointed.*

▷ COVER SURFACE **6** [T, usually passive] **~ sth with sth** to cover a surface with another material: *a brick building faced with stone*

IDM **face the music** (*informal*) to accept and deal with criticism or punishment for something you have done: *The others all ran off, leaving me to face the music.* **PHR V** **face sb↔down** to oppose or beat someone by dealing with them directly and confidently ,**face 'off 1** to start a game such as HOCKEY: *Both teams are ready to face off.* **2** to get ready to argue, fight, or compete with someone: *The candidates are preparing to face off on TV tonight.* ➔ **related noun** FACE-OFF ,**face 'up to sth** to accept and deal

with something that is difficult or unpleasant: *She had to face up to the fact that she would never walk again.*

Face·book™ /ˈfeɪsbʊk/ *noun* a SOCIAL NETWORKING Web site

'face card *noun* a PLAYING CARD with a picture of a king, a queen, or a JACK on it ➔ picture at SUIT

'face cream *noun* [U, C] a thick cream that you put on your face to clean the skin or keep it soft

face·less /ˈfeɪsləs/ *adj.* [usually before noun] (*disapproving*) having no noticeable characteristics or identity: *faceless bureaucrats* ♦ *faceless high-rise apartment buildings*

face·lift /ˈfeɪslɪft/ *noun* [usually sing.] **1** a medical operation in which the skin on a person's face is made tighter in order to make them look younger: *to have a facelift* **2** changes made to a building or place to make it look more attractive: *The town has recently been given a facelift.*

'face-off *noun* **1** (*informal*) an argument or a fight: *a face-off between the presidential candidates* **2** the way of starting play in a game of HOCKEY

'face ˌpowder *noun* [U] powder that you put on your face to make it look less shiny

'face-ˌsaving *adj.* [only before noun] intended to protect someone's reputation and to avoid embarrassment: *a face-saving compromise*

fac·et /ˈfæsət/ *noun* **1 ~ (of sth)** a particular part or aspect of something: *Now let's look at another facet of the problem.* **2** one of the flat sides of a JEWEL

'face time *noun* [U] (*informal*) time that you spend talking in person to people you work with, rather than speaking on the phone or sending e-mails

fa·ce·tious /fəˈsiːʃəs/ *adj.* trying to appear amusing and intelligent at a time when other people do not think it is appropriate, and when it would be better to be serious **SYN** FLIPPANT: *a facetious comment/remark* ♦ *Stop being facetious; this is serious.* ▶ **fa·ce·tious·ly** *adv.* **fa·ce·tious·ness** *noun* [U]

'face-to-ˌface *adj.* [only before noun] involving people who are close together and looking at each other: *a face-to-face conversation* ▶ ˌ**face to 'face** *adv.*: *He opened the door and came face to face with a burglar.* ♦ *I deal with customers on the phone and rarely meet them face to face.* ♦ (*figurative*) *She was brought face to face with the horrors of war.*

ˌ**face 'value** *noun* [U, sing.] the value of a stamp, coin, ticket, etc. that is shown on the front of it **IDM** **take sth at face value** to believe that something is what it appears to be, without questioning it: *Taken at face value, the figures look very encouraging.* ♦ *You shouldn't take anything she says at face value.*

fa·cial /ˈfeɪʃl/ *adj.*, *noun*

• *adj.* [usually before noun] connected with a person's face; on a person's face: *a facial expression* ♦ *facial hair* ▶ **fa·cial·ly** /-ʃəli/ *adv.*: *Facially, the two men were very different.*

• *noun* a beauty treatment in which a person's face is cleaned using creams, steam, etc. in order to improve the quality of the skin

fac·ile /ˈfæsl/ *adj.* (*disapproving*) **1** produced without effort or careful thought **SYN** GLIB: *a facile remark/generalization* **2** [only before noun] (*formal*) obtained too easily and having little value: *a facile victory*

fa·cil·i·tate **AWL** /fəˈsɪləteɪt/ *verb* **~ sth** (*formal*) to make an action or a process possible or easier: *The new trade agreement should facilitate more rapid economic growth.* ♦ *Structured teaching facilitates learning.* ▶ **fa·cil·i·ta·tion** **AWL** /fəˌsɪləˈteɪʃn/ *noun* [U, sing.]

fa·cil·i·ta·tor **AWL** /fəˈsɪləteɪtər/ *noun* **1** a person who helps someone do something more easily by discussing problems, giving advice, etc. rather than telling them what to do: *The teacher acts as a facilitator of learning.* **2** (*formal*) a thing that helps a process take place

---

| v **v**oice | θ **th**in | ð **th**en | s **s**o | z **z**oo | ʃ **sh**e | ʒ vi**s**ion | x **Ch**anukah | 533 |

fa·cil·i·ty 🔑 〚AWL〛/fəˈsɪləti/ noun (pl. fa·cil·i·ties)
1 facilities [pl.] buildings, services, equipment, etc. that are provided for a particular purpose: *sports/leisure facilities* ◆ *conference facilities* ◆ *shopping/banking/cooking facilities* ◆ *The hotel has special facilities for disabled people.* ◆ *All rooms have private facilities* (= a private bathroom). **2** [C] a special feature of a machine, service, etc. that makes it possible to do something extra: *a bank account with an overdraft facility* ◆ *a facility for checking spelling* **3** [C] a place, usually including buildings, used for a particular purpose or activity: *the world's largest nuclear waste facility* ◆ *a new healthcare facility* **4** [sing., U] ~ **(for sth)** a natural ability to learn or do something easily: *She has a facility for languages.*

fac·ing /ˈfeɪsɪŋ/ noun **1** [C, U] a layer of brick, stone, etc. that covers the surface of a wall to make it look more attractive **2** [C, U] a layer of stiff material sewn around the inside of the neck, ARMHOLES, etc. of a piece of clothing to make them stronger **3** facings [pl.] the COLLAR, CUFFS, etc. of a piece of clothing that are made in a different color or material

fac·sim·i·le /fækˈsɪməli/ noun **1** [C] an exact copy of something: *a facsimile edition* ◆ *a manuscript reproduced in facsimile* **2** [C, U] (*formal*) = FAX: *a facsimile machine*

fact 🔑 /fækt/ noun
1 [sing.] ~ **(that…)** used to refer to a particular situation that exists: *I could no longer ignore the fact that he was deeply unhappy.* ◆ *Despite the fact that she was wearing a seat belt, she was thrown sharply forward.* ◆ *Due to the fact that they did not read English, the prisoners were unaware of what they were signing.* ◆ *She was happy apart from the fact that she could not return home.* ◆ *Voluntary work was particularly important in view of the fact that women were often forced to give up paid work on marriage.* ◆ *How do you account for the fact that unemployment is still rising?* ◆ *The fact remains that we are still two teachers short.* ◆ *The mere fact of being poor makes such children criminals in the eyes of the police.* ⊃ language bank at HOWEVER **2** [C] a thing that is known to be true, especially when it can be proved: *Isn't it a fact that the company is losing money?* ◆ (*informal*) *I haven't spoken to anyone in English for days and that's a fact.* ◆ *I know for a fact* (= I am certain) *that she's involved in something illegal.* ◆ *The judge instructed both lawyers to stick to the facts of the case.* ◆ *First, some basic facts about healthy eating!* ◆ *The report is based on hard facts* (= information that can be proved to be true). ◆ *If you're going to make accusations, you'd better get your facts right* (= make sure your information is correct). ◆ *It's about time you learned to face (the) facts* (= accepted the truth about the situation). **3** [U] things that are true rather than things that have been invented: *The story is based on fact.* ◆ *It's important to distinguish fact from fiction.*
IDM **after the fact** after something has happened or been done when it is too late to prevent it or change it: *On some vital decisions employees were only informed after the fact.* **the fact (of the matter) is (that)…** used to emphasize a statement, especially one that is the opposite of what has just been mentioned: *A new car would be wonderful, but the fact of the matter is that we can't afford one.* **a fact of life** a situation that cannot be changed, especially one that is unpleasant **facts and figures** accurate and detailed information: *I've asked to see all the facts and figures before I make a decision.* **the facts of life** the details about sex and about how babies are born, especially as told to children **the facts speak for themselves** it is not necessary to give any further explanation about something because the information that is available already proves that it is true **in (actual) fact 1** used to give extra details about something that has just been mentioned: *I used to live in France; in fact, not far from where you're going.* **2** used to emphasize a statement, especially one that is the opposite of what has just been mentioned: *I thought the work would be difficult. In actual fact, it's very easy.* ⊃ language bank at HOWEVER **Is that a fact?** (*informal*) used to reply to a statement that you find interesting or surprising, or that you do not believe: *"She says I'm one of the best students she's ever taught." "Is that a fact?"* ⊃ more at MATTER *n.*, POINT *n.*

fact-find·ing adj. [only before noun] done in order to find out information about a country, an organization, a situation, etc.: *a fact-finding mission/visit*

fac·tion /ˈfækʃn/ noun **1** [C] a small group of people within a larger one, whose members have some different aims and beliefs to those of the larger group: *rival factions within the administration* ⊃ collocations at POLITICS **2** [U] opposition, disagreement, etc. that exists between small groups of people within an organization or political party: *a party divided by faction and intrigue* **3** [U] movies, books, etc. that combine fact with FICTION (= imaginary events)

fac·tion·al /ˈfækʃənl/ adj. [only before noun] connected with a faction of an organization or political party: *factional conflict* ▶ **fac·tion·al·ism** /-nəˌlɪzəm/ noun [U]

fac·ti·tious /fækˈtɪʃəs/ adj. (*formal*) not genuine but created deliberately and made to appear to be true

fac·toid /ˈfæktɔɪd/ noun **1** something that is widely accepted as a fact, although it is probably not true **2** a small piece of interesting information, especially about something that is not very important: *Here's a pop factoid for you.*

fac·tor 🔑 〚AWL〛/ˈfæktər/ noun, verb
● noun **1** [C] one of several things that cause or influence something: *economic factors* ◆ *The closure of the mine was the single most important factor in the town's decline.* ◆ *the key/crucial/deciding factor* ⊃ language bank at CAUSE **2** [C] (*mathematics*) a number that divides into another number exactly: *1, 2, 3, 4, 6, and 12 are the factors of 12.* **3** [C] the amount by which something increases or decreases: *The real wage of the average worker has increased by a factor of over ten in the last 70 years.* **4** [C] a particular level on a scale of measurement: *The wind chill factor will make it seem colder.* ◆ *a sunblock with a sun protection factor of 30* **5** [U] (*medical*) a substance in the blood that helps the CLOTTING process. There are several types of this substance: *Hemophiliacs have no factor 8 in their blood*
● verb
PHR V **factor sth↩'in** | **factor sth↩into sth** (*technical*) to include a particular fact or situation when you are thinking about or planning something: *Remember to factor in staffing costs when you are planning the project.*

fac·tor VIII (also **fac·tor 8, fac·tor eight**) /ˌfæktər ˈeɪt/ noun [U] (*biology*) a substance in the blood that helps it to CLOT (= become thick)

fac·to·ri·al /fækˈtɔriəl/ noun (*mathematics*) the result when you multiply a whole number by all the numbers below it: *factorial 5 (represented as 5!) =5×4×3×2×1*

fac·tor·ize /ˈfæktəˌraɪz/ verb ~ sth (*mathematics*) to express a number in terms of its FACTORS ▶ **fac·tor·i·za·tion** /ˌfæktərəˈzeɪʃn/ noun [U, sing.]

fac·to·ry 🔑 /ˈfæktəri; -tri/ noun (pl. fac·to·ries) a building or group of buildings where goods are made: *a car factory* ◆ *factory workers*

THESAURUS

factory

plant ◆ mill ◆ works ◆ yard ◆ workshop/shop ◆ foundry

These are all words for buildings or places where things are made or where industrial processes take place.

factory a building or group of buildings where goods are made: *a chocolate/cigarette/clothing factory*

plant a factory or place where power is produced or an industrial process takes place: *a nuclear power plant* ◆ *a manufacturing plant* ◆ *a bottling plant*

mill a factory that produces a particular type of material: *a steel/cotton/paper/textile/woolen mill*

works (often in compounds) a place where things are made or an industrial process takes place: *a brickworks* ◆ *a steelworks* ◆ *Raw materials were carried to the works by rail.*

h hat   m man   n no   ŋ sing   l leg   r red   y yes   w wet

yard (usually in compounds) an area of land used for building something: *a shipyard*

workshop/shop a room or building in which things are made or repaired using tools or machinery: *a car repair shop* ◆ *a sheet metal workshop*

foundry a factory where metal or glass is melted and made into different shapes or objects: *an iron foundry*

PATTERNS

- a **car/chemical/munitions** factory/plant
- an **engineering** plant/(work)shop
- to **manage/run** a factory/plant/mill/works/yard/ workshop/foundry
- to **work in/at** a factory/plant/mill/yard/workshop/ foundry
- factory/mill/foundry **owners/managers/workers**

'factory ˌfarm *noun* a type of farm in which animals are kept inside in small spaces and are fed special food so that a large amount of meat, milk, etc. is produced as quickly and cheaply as possible ▶ **'factory ˌfarming** *noun* [U]

ˌfactory 'floor *noun* often **the factory floor** [sing.] the part of a factory where the goods are actually produced: *Jobs are at risk, not just* **on the factory floor** (= among the workers, rather than the managers) *but throughout the business.*

'factory ˌship *noun* a large ship used for catching fish, that has equipment for cleaning and freezing the fish on board

fac·to·tum /fæk'toʊtəm/ *noun* (*formal* or *humorous*) a person employed to do a wide variety of jobs for someone

'fact sheet *noun* a piece of paper giving information about a subject

fac·tu·al /'fæktʃuəl/ *adj.* based on or containing facts: *a factual account of events* ◆ *factual information* ◆ *The essay contains a number of factual errors.* ▶ **fac·tu·al·ly** *adv.*: *factually correct*

fac·ul·ty /'fæklti/ *noun* (*pl.* **fac·ul·ties**) **1** [C, usually pl.] any of the physical or mental abilities that a person is born with: *the faculty of sight* ◆ *She retained her mental faculties* (= the ability to think and understand) *until the day she died.* ◆ *to be in* **full possession of your faculties** (= be able to speak, hear, see, understand, etc.) **2** [sing.] **~ of/for (doing) sth** (*formal*) a particular ability for doing something: *the faculty of understanding complex issues* ◆ *He had a faculty for seeing his own mistakes.* **3** [C, U] often **the faculty** all the teachers of a particular university, college, or school: *faculty members* **4** [C] a department or group of related departments in a college or university: *the Faculty of Law* ◆ *the Arts Faculty* **5** [C] all the teachers in a faculty of a college or university: *the Law School faculty*

fad /fæd/ *noun* something that people are interested in for only a short period of time **SYN** CRAZE: *the latest/current fad* ◆ *a fad for physical fitness* ◆ *Rap music proved to be more than just a* **passing fad.**

fade /feɪd/ *verb* **1** [I, T] to become, or to make something become, paler or less bright: *The curtains had faded in the sun.* ◆ **~ from sth** *All color had faded from her face.* ◆ **~ sth** *The sun had faded the curtains.* ◆ *He was wearing faded blue jeans.* **2** [I] to disappear gradually: *Her smile faded.* ◆ **~ away** *Hopes of reaching an agreement seem to be fading away.* ◆ *The laughter faded away.* ◆ **~ to/into sth** *His voice faded to a whisper* (= gradually became quieter). ◆ *All other issues* **fade into insignificance** *compared with the struggle for survival.* **3** [I] if a sports player, team, actor, etc. **fades**, they stop playing or performing as well as they did before: *Black faded on the final bend.* **IDM** see WOODWORK
PHR V ˌfade a'way (of a person) to become very weak or sick and die: *In the last weeks of her life she simply faded away.* ˌfade 'in/'out to become clearer or louder / less clear or quieter: *George saw the monitor black out and then a few words faded in.* ˌfade sth 'in/'out to make a picture or a sound clearer or louder / less clear or quieter: *Fade out the music at the end of the scene.*

'fade-out *noun* [U, C] (in movies, broadcasting, etc.) the process of making a sound or an image gradually disappear; an occasion when this happens

fad·er /'feɪdər/ *noun* (*technical*) a piece of equipment used to make sounds or images gradually appear or disappear

Fahr·en·heit /'færənˌhaɪt/ *adj.* (*abbr.* F) of or using a scale of temperature in which water freezes at 32° and boils at 212°: *fifty degrees Fahrenheit* ▶ **Fahr·en·heit** *noun* [U]: *to give the temperature in Fahrenheit*

fail /feɪl/ *verb, noun*

● *verb*
> **NOT SUCCEED 1** [I, T] to not be successful in achieving something: *Many diets fail because they are boring.* ◆ *a failing business* ◆ **~ in sth** *I failed in my attempt to persuade her.* ◆ **~ to do sth** *She failed to get into law school.* ◆ *The song can't fail to be a hit* (= definitely will be a hit).
> **NOT DO SOMETHING 2** [I] to not do something: **~ to do sth** *He failed to keep the appointment.* ◆ *She never fails to e-mail every week.* ◆ *I fail to see* (= I don't understand) *why you won't even try it.* ◆ **~ in sth** *He felt he would be failing in his duty if he did not report it.*
> **TEST/EXAM 3** [T, I] to not pass a test or an exam; to decide that someone or something has not passed a test or an exam: **~ (sth)** *He failed his driving test.* ◆ *She was disqualified after failing a drug test.* ◆ *What will you do if you fail?* ◆ **~ sb** *The professor failed several students last semester.* **ANT** PASS
> **OF MACHINES/PARTS OF BODY 4** [I] to stop working: *The brakes on my bike failed halfway down the hill.*
> **OF HEALTH/SIGHT 5** [I] (especially in the progressive tenses) to become weak: *Her eyesight is failing.* ◆ *His last months in office were marred by failing health.*
> **DISAPPOINT SOMEONE 6** [T] **~ sb** to disappoint someone; to be unable to help when needed: *When he lost his job, he felt he had failed his family.* ◆ *She tried to be brave, but her courage failed her.* ◆ (*figurative*) *Words fail me* (= I cannot express how I feel).
> **NOT BE ENOUGH 7** [I] to not be enough when needed or expected: *The crops failed again last summer.* ◆ *The rains had failed and the rivers were dry.*
> **OF COMPANY/BUSINESS 8** [I] to be unable to continue: *Several banks failed during the recession.*
IDM if all else 'fails used to suggest something that someone can do if nothing else works: *If all else fails, you can always sell your motorcycle.*

● *noun*
IDM without 'fail **1** when you tell someone to do something **without fail**, you are telling them that they must do it: *I want you here by two o'clock without fail.* **2** always: *He e-mails every week without fail.*

failed /feɪld/ *adj.* [only before noun] not successful: *a failed writer* ◆ *a failed coup*

ˌfailed 'state *noun* a country in which the government is so weak that it has lost control of the structures of the state and other groups have more power

fail·ing /'feɪlɪŋ/ *noun, prep.*
● *noun* [usually pl.] a weakness or fault in someone or something: *She is aware of her own failings.* ◆ *The investigation acknowledges failings in the judicial system.*
● *prep.* used to introduce a suggestion that could be considered if the one just mentioned is not possible: *Ask a friend to recommend a doctor or,* **failing that,** *look on the Internet.*

'fail-safe *adj.* [usually before noun] (of machinery or equipment) designed to stop working if anything goes wrong: *a fail-safe device/mechanism/system*

fail·ure /'feɪlyər/ *noun*
> **NOT SUCCESSFUL 1** [U] lack of success in doing or achieving something: *The success or failure of the plan depends on you.* ◆ *The attempt was* **doomed to failure.** ◆ *All my efforts* **ended in failure.** ◆ *the problems of economic failure and increasing unemployment* ◆ *She is still coming to terms with the failure of*

her marriage. **ANT** SUCCESS **2** [C] a person or thing that is not successful: *The whole thing was a complete failure.* ◆ *He was a failure as a teacher.* **ANT** SUCCESS
> NOT DOING SOMETHING **3** [U, C] ~ **to do sth** an act of not doing something, especially something that you are expected to do: *the failure of the United Nations to maintain food supplies* ◆ *Failure to comply with the regulations will result in prosecution.*
> OF MACHINE/PART OF BODY **4** [U, C] the state of not working correctly or as expected; an occasion when this happens: *patients suffering from heart/kidney, etc. failure* ◆ *A power failure plunged everything into darkness.* ◆ *The cause of the crash was given as engine failure.*
> OF BUSINESS **5** [C, U] **business/bank ~** a situation in which a business or bank has to close because it is not successful
> OF CROPS **6** [U, C] **crop ~** a situation in which crops do not grow correctly and do not produce food

fain /feɪn/ *adv.* (*old use*) willingly or with pleasure: *I would fain do as you ask.*

faint 🔑 /feɪnt/ *adj., verb, noun*
● *adj.* (faint·er, faint·est) **1** that cannot be clearly seen, heard, or smelled: *a faint glow/glimmer/light* ◆ *a faint smell of perfume* ◆ *We could hear their voices growing fainter as they walked down the road.* ◆ *His breathing became faint.* **2** very small; possible but unlikely **SYN** SLIGHT: *There is still a faint hope that she may be cured.* ◆ *They don't have the faintest chance of winning.* **3** not enthusiastic: *a faint show of resistance* ◆ *a faint smile* **4** [not before noun] feeling weak and tired and likely to become unconscious: *She suddenly felt faint.* ◆ *The walkers were faint from hunger.* ▶ **faint·ly** *adv.*: *She smiled faintly.* ◆ *He looked faintly embarrassed.*
IDM **not have the faintest (idea)** (*informal*) to not know anything at all about something: *I didn't have the faintest idea what you meant.* ⊃ more at DAMN *v.*
● *verb* [I] to become unconscious when not enough blood is going to your brain, usually because of the heat, a shock, etc. **SYN** PASS OUT: *to faint from hunger* ◆ *Suddenly the woman in front of me fainted.* ◆ (*informal*) *I almost fainted* (= I was very surprised) *when she told me.*
● *noun* [sing.] the state of becoming unconscious: *He fell to the ground in a dead faint.*

faint-'hearted *adj.* lacking confidence and not brave; afraid of failing **SYN** COWARDLY ▶ **the faint-'hearted** *noun* [pl.]: *The climb is not for the faint-hearted* (= people who are not brave).

faint·ness /'feɪntnəs/ *noun* [U] the state of feeling weak and tired and likely to become unconscious

fair 🔑 /fer/ *adj., adv., noun*
● *adj.* (fair·er, fair·est)
> ACCEPTABLE/APPROPRIATE **1** acceptable and appropriate in a particular situation: *a fair deal/price/question* ◆ *The punishment was very fair.* ◆ **~ to sb (to do sth)** *Was it really fair to him to ask him to do all the work?* ◆ **~ to do sth** *It's only fair to add that they were not told about the problem until the last minute.* ◆ *I think it is fair to say that they are pleased with the latest offer.* ◆ **~ that…** *It seems only fair that they give us something in return.* ◆ **To be fair**, *she behaved better than we expected.* **ANT** UNFAIR
> TREATING PEOPLE EQUALLY **2** treating everyone equally and according to the rules or law: *She has always been scrupulously fair.* ◆ *demands for a fairer distribution of wealth* ◆ **~ (to sb)** *We have to be fair to both players.* ◆ *to receive a fair trial* ◆ *free and fair elections* ◆ *It's not fair! He always gets more than me.* ◆ *The new tax is fairer than the old system.* **ANT** UNFAIR
> FAIRLY LARGE **3** [only before noun] fairly large in number, size, or amount: *A fair number of people came along.* ◆ *a fair-sized town* ◆ *We've still got a fair amount* (= some more things) *to do.*
> FAIRLY GOOD **4** fairly good: *There's a fair chance that we might win this time.* ◆ *It's a fair bet that they won't turn up.* ◆ *I have a fair idea of what happened.* ◆ *His knowledge of French is only fair.*

> HAIR/SKIN **5** pale in color: *a fair complexion* ◆ *She has long, fair hair.* ◆ *All her children are fair* (= they all have pale hair or skin). **ANT** DARK
> WEATHER **6** bright and not raining: *a fair and breezy day*
7 (*literary*) (of winds) not too strong and blowing in the right direction: *They set sail with the first fair wind.*
> BEAUTIFUL **8** (*literary* or *old use*) beautiful: *a fair maiden*
IDM **all's fair in love and war** (*saying*) in some situations any type of behavior is acceptable to get what you want **be fair!** (*informal*) used to tell someone to be reasonable in their judgment of someone or something: *Be fair! She didn't know you were coming.* **by fair means or foul** using dishonest methods if honest ones do not work **fair enough** (*informal*) used to say that an idea or a suggestion seems reasonable: *"We'll meet at 8." "Fair enough." ◆ If you don't want to come, fair enough, but let Bill know.* **fair's fair** (*informal*) used, especially as an exclamation, to say that you think that an action, a decision, etc. is acceptable and appropriate because it means that everyone will be treated fairly: *Fair's fair—you can't expect them to cancel everything just because you can't make it.* **(give sb/get) a fair shake** (*informal*) (to give sb/get) fair treatment that gives you the same chance as someone else **(more than) your fair share of sth** (more than) an amount of something that is considered to be reasonable or acceptable: *He has more than his fair share of problems.* ◆ *I've had my fair share of success in the past.* **fair to middling** (*old-fashioned*) not particularly good or bad **(give sb) a fair trial/hearing** (to allow someone) the opportunity to give their opinion of something before deciding if they have done something wrong, often in court: *I'll make sure that you get a fair trial.*
● *adv.* according to the rules; in a way that is considered to be acceptable and appropriate: *Come on, you two, fight fair!* ◆ *They'll respect you as long as you play fair* (= behave honestly).
IDM **fair and square** honestly and according to the rules: *We won the election fair and square.*
● *noun*
> ENTERTAINMENT **1** a type of entertainment in a field, park, or street at which people can ride on large machines, play games to win prizes, watch performers, etc. **SYN** CARNIVAL: *Let's take the kids to the fair.* ◆ *all the fun of the fair* ◆ *She performs regularly at street fairs, malls, festivals, and the like.* **2** a type of entertainment in a field or park at which farm animals and products are shown and take part in competitions: *the county/state fair*
> BUSINESS **3** an event at which people, businesses, etc. show and sell their goods: *a world trade fair* ◆ *a craft/a book/an antique fair*
> JOBS **4** **job/career ~** an event at which people who are looking for jobs can get information about companies who might employ them

the 'fairer ˌsex *noun* = THE FAIR SEX

ˌfair 'game *noun* [U] if a person or thing is said to be **fair game**, it is considered acceptable to play jokes on them, criticize them, etc.: *The younger teachers were considered fair game by most of the kids.*

fair·ground /'fergraʊnd/ *noun* **1** an outdoor area where a FAIR is held **2** [usually pl.] a place where a FAIR showing farm animals, farm products, etc. is held: *the Ohio State Fairgrounds* **3** [usually pl.] a place where companies and businesses hold a FAIR to show their products: *the Miami trade fairgrounds*

'fair-haired *adj.* with light or blond hair

fair·ly 🔑 /'ferli/ *adv.*
1 (before adjectives and adverbs) to some extent but not very: *a fairly easy book* ◆ *a fairly typical reaction* ◆ *I know him fairly well, but I wouldn't say we were really close friends.* ◆ *I go jogging fairly regularly.* ◆ *We'll have to leave fairly soon* (= before very long). ◆ *I'm fairly certain I can do the job.* ◆ *I think you'll find it fairly difficult* (= you do not want to say that it is very difficult). **2** in a fair and reasonable way; honestly: *He has always treated me very fairly.* ◆ *Her attitude could fairly be*

ʌ **cup**   ə **about**   eɪ **say**   aɪ **five**   ɔɪ **boy**   aʊ **now**   oʊ **go**   ər **bird**

described as hostile. **3** (*old-fashioned*) used to emphasize something that you are saying: *The time fairly raced by.*

ˈfair-ˌminded *adj.* (of people) looking at and judging things in a fair and open way

fairˈness /ˈfɛrnəs/ *noun* [U] **1** the quality of treating people equally or in a way that is reasonable: *the fairness of the judicial system* **2** (of skin or hair) a pale color: *A tan emphasized the fairness of her hair.*
IDM **in (all) fairness (to sb)** used to introduce a statement that defends someone who has just been criticized, or that explains another statement that may seem unreasonable: *In all fairness to him, he did try to stop her from leaving.*

ˌfair ˈplay *noun* [U] the fact of playing a game or acting honestly, fairly, and according to the rules: *a player admired for his sense of fair play* ♦ *The task of the organization is to ensure fair play when food is distributed to the refugees.*

the ˈfair sex (also **the ˈfairer ˌsex**) *noun* [sing.] (*old-fashioned*) women

ˌfair-ˈtrade *adj.* involving trade that supports producers in developing countries by paying fair prices and making sure that workers have good working conditions and fair pay

ˈfair·way /ˈfɛrweɪ/ *noun* (in GOLF) the long strip of short grass that you must hit the ball along before you get to the GREEN and the hole ⊃ picture at SPORT ⊃ compare THE ROUGH

ˈfair-ˌweather *adj.* [only before noun] (*disapproving*) (of people) behaving in a particular way or doing a particular activity only when it is pleasant for them: *a fair-weather friend* (= someone who stops being a friend when you are in trouble)

fair·y /ˈfɛri/ *noun* (*pl.* **fair·ies**) (in stories) a creature like a small person, who has magic powers: *a good/wicked fairy* ⊃ see also TOOTH FAIRY

ˌfairy ˈgodmother *noun* a person who rescues you when you most need help

ˈfair·y·land /ˈfɛriˌlænd/ *noun* **1** [U] the home of fairies (FAIRY) **2** [sing.] a beautiful, special, or unusual place: *The toy store is a fairyland for young children.*

ˈfairy ˌtale *noun* **1** a story about magic or fairies, usually for children **2** a story that someone tells that is not true; a lie: *Now tell me the truth: I don't want any more of your fairy tales.*

ˈfairy-ˌtale *adj.* typical of something in a fairy tale: *a fairy-tale castle on an island* ♦ *a fairy-tale wedding in the cathedral*

fait ac·com·pli /ˌfeɪt əkɑmˈpli; ˌfɛt-/ *noun* [usually sing.] (*pl.* **faits ac·com·plis** /ˌfeɪt əkɑmˈpli; -ˈpliz; ˌfɛt-/) (from *French*) something that has already happened or been done and that you cannot change

faith 🔑 /feɪθ/ *noun*
1 [U] ~ **(in sb/sth)** trust in someone's ability or knowledge; trust that someone or something will do what has been promised: *I have great faith in you—I know you'll do well.* ♦ *We've lost faith in the government's promises.* ♦ *Her friend's kindness has restored her faith in human nature.* ♦ *He has blind faith* (= unreasonable trust) *in the doctor's ability to find a cure.* **2** [U, sing.] strong religious belief: *to lose your faith* ♦ *Faith is stronger than reason.* ⊃ collocations at RELIGION **3** [C] a particular religion: *the Christian faith* ♦ *The children are learning to understand people of different faiths.* **4** [U] **good ~** the intention to do something right: *They handed over the weapons as a gesture of good faith.*
IDM **break/keep faith with sb** to break/keep a promise that you have made to someone; to stop/continue being loyal to someone **in bad faith** knowing that what you are doing is wrong **in good faith** believing that what you are doing is right; believing that something is correct: *We printed the report in good faith but have now learned that it was incorrect.* ⊃ more at PIN v.

faith·ful 🔑 /ˈfeɪθfl/ *adj.*
1 staying with or supporting a particular person, organization, or belief **SYN** LOYAL: *a faithful friend/dog/servant* ♦ *She was rewarded for 40 years of faithful service to the*

company. ♦ *I have been a faithful reader of your newspaper for many years.* ♦ ~ **to sb/sth** *He remained faithful to the ideals of the party.* **2** **the faithful** *noun* [pl.] people who believe in a religion; the loyal supporters of a political party: *The president will keep the support of the party faithful.* **3** (of a wife, husband, or partner) ~ **(to sb)** not having a sexual relationship with anyone else **ANT** UNFAITHFUL **4** true and accurate; not changing anything: *a faithful copy/account/ description* ♦ ~ **to sth** *His translation manages to be faithful to the spirit of the original.* **5** [only before noun] able to be trusted; that you can rely on: *my faithful old car*
▶ **faith·ful·ness** *noun* [U]: *faithfulness to tradition* ♦ *She had doubts about his faithfulness.*

faith·ful·ly 🔑 /ˈfeɪθfəli/ *adv.*
1 accurately; carefully: *to follow instructions faithfully* ♦ *The events were faithfully recorded in her diary.* **2** in a loyal way; in a way that you can rely on: *He had supported the local team faithfully for 30 years.* ♦ *She promised faithfully not to tell anyone my secret.*

ˈfaith ˌhealing *noun* [U] a method of treating a sick person through the power of belief and prayer ▶ **ˈfaith ˌhealer** *noun*

faith·less /ˈfeɪθləs/ *adj.* (*formal*) not loyal; that you cannot rely on or trust: *a faithless friend*

fa·ji·tas /fəˈhitəz; fɑ-/ *noun* [pl.] (from *Spanish*) a Mexican dish of strips of meat and/or vegetables wrapped in a soft TORTILLA and often served with sour cream

fake /feɪk/ *adj., noun, verb*
• *adj.* **1** (*disapproving*) not genuine; appearing to be something it is not **SYN** COUNTERFEIT: *a fake designer watch* ♦ *a fake British accent* **2** made to look like something else **SYN** IMITATION: *a jacket made of fake fur* ♦ *Don't go out in the sun—use a cream to get a fake tan.* ⊃ thesaurus box at ARTIFICIAL
• *noun* **1** an object such as a work of art, a coin, or a piece of jewelry that is not genuine but has been made to look as if it is: *All the paintings proved to be fakes.* **2** a person who pretends to be what they are not in order to cheat people
• *verb* **1** [T] ~ **sth** to make something false appear to be genuine, especially in order to cheat someone: *She faked her mother's signature on the document.* ♦ *He arranged the accident in order to fake his own death.* **2** [T, I] ~ **(sth)** to pretend to have a particular feeling, illness, etc.: *She's not really sick—she's just faking it.* ♦ *He faked a yawn.* ▶ **fak·er** *noun*

fak·ie /ˈfeɪki/ *noun* (*informal*) a movement backward on a SKATEBOARD or SNOWBOARD

fa·kir (also **fa·quir**) /fəˈkɪr; ˈfeɪkər/ *noun* a Muslim (or sometimes a Hindu) who lives a strict religious life without physical pleasures, and who survives by receiving food and money from other people

fa·la·fel (also **fe·la·fel**) /fəˈlɑfl/ *noun* (*pl.* **fa·la·felor fa·la·fels**) [U, C] a Middle Eastern dish consisting of small balls formed from crushed CHICKPEAS and fried, usually eaten with flat bread; one of these balls

fal·con /ˈfælkən; ˈfɔl-/ *noun* a BIRD OF PREY (= a bird that kills other creatures for food) with long pointed wings

fal·con·er /ˈfælkənər; ˈfɔl-/ *noun* a person who keeps and trains falcons, often for hunting

fal·con·ry /ˈfælkənri; ˈfɔl-/ *noun* [U] the art or sport of breeding falcons and training them to hunt other birds or animals

fall 🔑 /fɔl/ *verb, noun*
• *verb* (**fell** /fɛl/, **fall·en** /ˈfɔlən/)
> DROP DOWN **1** [I] to drop down from a higher level to a lower level: *September had come and the leaves were starting to fall.* ♦ *They were injured by falling rocks.* ♦ + **adv./prep.** *Several of the books had fallen onto the floor.* ♦ *One of the kids fell into the river.* ♦ *The handle had fallen off the drawer.* ♦ *He fell 20 feet onto the rocks below.* ♦ *The rain was falling steadily.*
> STOP STANDING **2** [I] to suddenly stop standing: *She slipped on the ice and fell.* ♦ + **adv./prep.** *I fell down and cut my knee.*

◆ *The house looked like it was about to fall down.* ➲ **see also** FALLEN

❯ **OF HAIR/MATERIAL 3** [I] + **adv./prep.** to hang down: *Her hair fell over her shoulders in a mass of curls.*

❯ **SLOPE DOWNWARD 4** [I] **~ (away/off)** to slope downward: *The land falls away sharply toward the river.*

❯ **DECREASE 5** [I] to decrease in amount, number, or strength: *Their profits have fallen by 30 percent.* ◆ *Prices continued to fall on the stock market today.* ◆ *The temperature fell sharply during the night.* ◆ *falling birth rates* ◆ *Her voice fell to a whisper.* ◆ + **noun** *The company's share price fell 30 cents.* **ANT** RISE

❯ **BE DEFEATED 6** [I] to be defeated or captured: *The coup failed but the government fell shortly afterward.* ◆ **~ to sb** *Troy finally fell to the Greeks.*

❯ **DIE IN BATTLE 7** [I] (*literary*) to die in battle; to be shot: *a memorial to those who fell in the two world wars*

❯ **BECOME 8** [I] to pass into a particular state; to begin to be something: + **adj.** *He had fallen asleep on the sofa.* ◆ *The book fell open at a page of illustrations.* ◆ *The room had fallen silent.* ◆ *She fell ill soon after and did not recover.* ◆ **~ into sth** *I had fallen into conversation with a man on the train.* ◆ *The house had fallen into disrepair.* ◆ + **noun** *She knew she must not fall prey to his charm.*

❯ **HAPPEN/OCCUR 9** [I] (*literary*) to come quickly and suddenly **SYN** DESCEND: *A sudden silence fell.* ◆ *Darkness falls quickly in the tropics.* **10** [I] + **adv./prep.** to happen or take place: *My birthday falls on a Monday this year.* **11** [I] + **adv./prep.** to move in a particular direction or come in a particular position: *Which syllable does the stress fall on?* ◆ *My eye fell on (= I suddenly saw) a strange object.* ◆ *A shadow fell across her face.*

❯ **BELONG TO GROUP 12** [I] + **adv./prep.** to belong to a particular class, group, or area of responsibility: *Out of more than 400 staff, there are just seven that fall into this category.* ◆ *This case falls outside my jurisdiction.* ◆ *This falls under the heading of scientific research.*

IDM Idioms containing **fall** are at the entries for the nouns and adjectives in the idioms. For example, **fall by the wayside** is at **wayside**.

PHRV ˌfall aˈpart **1** to be in very bad condition so that parts are breaking off: *My car is falling apart.* **2** to have so many problems that it is not possible to exist or function anymore: *Their marriage finally fell apart.* ◆ *The deal fell apart when we failed to agree on a price.*

ˌfall aˈway to become gradually fewer or smaller; to disappear: *His supporters fell away as his popularity declined.* ◆ *The market for their products fell away to almost nothing.* ◆ *All our doubts fell away.*

ˌfall ˈback **1** to move or turn back **SYN** RETREAT: *The enemy fell back as our troops advanced.* **2** to decrease in value or amount ˌfall ˈback on sb/sth [no passive] to go to someone for support; to have something to use when you are in difficulty: *I have a little money in the bank to fall back on.* ◆ *She fell back on her usual excuse of having no time.* ➲ **related noun** FALLBACK

ˌfall beˈhind (sb/sth) to fail to keep level with someone or something: *She soon fell behind the leaders.* ˌfall beˈhind with/on sth to not pay or do something at the right time: *They had fallen behind with their mortgage repayments.* ◆ *He's fallen behind on his school work again.*

ˌfall ˈdown to be shown to be not true or not good enough: *And that's where the theory falls down.* ➲ **see also** FALL v. (2)

ˈfall for sb [no passive] (*informal*) to be strongly attracted to someone; to fall in love with someone: *They fell for each other instantly.* ˈfall for sth [no passive] (*informal*) to be tricked into believing something that is not true: *I'm surprised you fell for that trick.*

ˌfall ˈin if soldiers **fall in**, they form lines: *The sergeant ordered his men to fall in.*

ˈfall into sth to be able to be divided into something: *My talk falls naturally into three parts.*

ˌfall ˈoff to decrease in quantity or quality: *Attendance at my lectures has fallen off considerably.* **ANT** RISE

ˌfall on/upon sb/sth [no passive] **1** to be the responsibility of someone: *The full cost of the wedding fell on us.* **2** to attack or take hold of someone or something with a lot of energy

and enthusiasm: *They fell on him with sticks.* ◆ *The children fell on the food and ate it greedily.*

ˌfall ˈout **1** to become loose and drop: *His hair is falling out.* **2** if soldiers **fall out**, they leave their lines and move away ˌfall ˈout (with sb) to have an argument with someone so that you are not friendly with them anymore

ˌfall ˈover sb/sth [no passive] to hit your foot against something when you are walking and fall, or almost fall **SYN** TRIP OVER: *I rushed for the door and fell over the cat in the hallway.* ➲ **see also** FALL v. (2) ˌfall (all) ˈover yourself to do sth (*informal*) to try very hard or want very much to do something: *He was falling over himself to be nice to me.*

ˌfall ˈthrough to not be completed, or not happen: *Our plans fell through because of lack of money.*

ˈfall to sb to become the duty or responsibility of someone: *With his partner away, all the work fell to him.* ◆ **it falls to sb to do sth** *It fell to me to inform her of her son's death.* ˈfall to sth (*literary*) to begin to do something: **~ doing something** *She fell to brooding about what had happened to her.*

● **noun**

❯ **SEASON 1** [C] the season of the year between summer and winter, when leaves change color and the weather becomes colder **SYN** AUTUMN: *She starts college in the fall of 2012.* ◆ *in early/late fall* ◆ *fall colors/leaves/air* ◆ *We spent a crisp fall day raking leaves.*

❯ **ACT OF FALLING 2** [C] an act of falling: *I had a bad fall and broke my arm.* ◆ *She was injured in a fall from a horse.*

❯ **DECREASE 3** [C] **~ (in sth)** a decrease in size, number, rate, or level: *a steep fall in profits* ◆ *a big fall in unemployment* **ANT** RISE

❯ **WAY SOMETHING FALLS/HAPPENS 4** [sing.] **~ of sth** the way in which something falls or happens: *the fall of the dice* ◆ *the dark fall of her hair* (= the way her hair hangs down)

❯ **OF WATER 5 falls** [pl.] (especially in names) a large amount of water falling down from a height **SYN** WATERFALL: *The falls upstream are full of salmon.* ◆ *Niagara Falls*

❯ **DEFEAT 6** [sing.] **~ (of sth)** a loss of political, economic, etc. power or success; the loss or defeat of a city, country, etc. in war: *the fall of the Roman Empire* ◆ *the rise and fall of the American automobile industry* ◆ *the fall of Atlanta to Union troops*

❯ **LOSS OF RESPECT 7** [sing.] a situation in which a person, an organization, etc. loses the respect of other people because they have done something wrong: *the governor's spectacular fall from grace*

❯ **IN BIBLE 8 the Fall** [sing.] the occasion when Adam and Eve did not obey God and had to leave the Garden of Eden **IDM** break sb's ˈfall to stop someone from falling onto something hard: *Luckily, a bush broke his fall.* take the fall (for sb/sth) (*informal*) to accept responsibility or punishment for something that you did not do, or did not do alone: *He took the fall for his boss and resigned.* ➲ **more at** PRIDE *n.*, RIDE *v.*

LANGUAGE BANK

fall

describing a decrease

■ Car crime in Greenville **fell significantly** last year.
■ Car crime **fell** by about a quarter over a 12-month period.
■ The number of stolen vehicles **dropped** from 1,013 to 780, **a fall of** 26 percent.
■ According to these data, 780 vehicles were stolen, **down** 26% from the previous year.
■ The city saw an 11% **drop** in reported thefts from motor vehicles from 1,871 to 1,737.
■ These figures show that, as far as car crime is concerned, **the main trend is downward**.

➲ Language Banks at EXPECT, ILLUSTRATE, INCREASE, PROPORTION

fal·la·cious /fəˈleɪʃəs/ *adj.* (*formal*) wrong; based on a false idea: *a fallacious argument*

| t tea | ṱ butter | d did | k cat | g got | tʃ chin | dʒ June | f fall |

fal·la·cy /ˈfæləsi/ noun (pl. **fal·la·cies**) **1** [C] a false idea that many people believe is true: *It is a fallacy to say that the camera never lies.* **2** [U, C] a false way of thinking about something: *He detected the fallacy of her argument.* ⊃ see also PATHETIC FALLACY

fall·back /ˈfɔlbæk/ noun a plan or course of action that is ready to be used in an emergency if other things fail: *What's our fallback if they don't come up with the money?* ◆ *We need a fallback position if they won't do the job.*

fall·en /ˈfɔlən/ adj. [only before noun] **1** lying on the ground, after falling: *a fallen tree* **2** (formal) (of a soldier) killed in a war ⊃ see also FALL v.

fallen ˈwoman noun (old-fashioned) a way of describing a woman in the past who had a sexual relationship with someone who was not her husband

fall guy noun a person who is blamed or punished for something wrong that another person has done SYN SCAPEGOAT

fal·li·ble /ˈfæləbl/ adj. able to make mistakes or be wrong: *Memory is selective and fallible.* ◆ *All human beings are fallible.* ANT INFALLIBLE ▶ **fal·li·bil·i·ty** /ˌfæləˈbɪləti/ noun [U]: *human fallibility*

falling-ˈout noun (informal) [sing.] a situation where people are not friends anymore, caused by a disagreement or an argument: *Dave and I had a falling-out.*

falling ˈstar noun = SHOOTING STAR

fall·off /ˈfɔlɔf/ noun [sing.] **~ (in sth)** a reduction in the number, amount, or quality of something: *a recent falloff in sales*

fal·lo·pi·an tube (also **Fal·lo·pi·an tube**) /fəˈloʊpiən ˌtub/ noun (anatomy) one of the two tubes in the body of a woman or female animal along which eggs pass from the ovaries (OVARY) to the UTERUS

fall·out /ˈfɔlaʊt/ noun [U] **1** dangerous RADIOACTIVE dust that is in the air after a nuclear explosion **2** the bad results of a situation or an action

fal·low /ˈfæloʊ/ adj. **1** (of farm land) not used for growing crops, especially so that the quality of the land will improve: *Farmers are now paid to let their land lie fallow.* **2** (of a period of time) when nothing is created or produced; not successful: *Contemporary dance is coming onto the arts scene again after a long fallow period.*

false 🔑 /fɔls/ adj.
> NOT TRUE **1** wrong; not correct or true: *A whale is a fish. True or false?* ◆ *Predictions of an early improvement in the housing market proved false.* ◆ *She gave false information to the insurance company.* ◆ *He used a false name to get the job.* ⊃ thesaurus box at WRONG
> NOT NATURAL **2** not natural: *false teeth/eyelashes* ◆ *a false beard* ⊃ thesaurus box at ARTIFICIAL
> NOT GENUINE **3** not genuine, but made to look real to cheat people: *a false passport*
> NOT SINCERE **4** (of people's behavior) not real or sincere: *false modesty* ◆ *She flashed him a false smile of congratulation.*
> WRONG/MISTAKEN **5** [usually before noun] wrong or mistaken, because it is based on something that is not true or correct: *a false argument/assumption/belief* ◆ *to give a false impression of wealth* ◆ *to lull someone into a false sense of security* (= make someone feel safe when they are really in danger) ◆ *They didn't want to raise any false hopes, but they believed her husband had escaped capture.* ◆ *Buying a cheap computer is a false economy* (= will not actually save you money).
> NOT FAITHFUL **6** (literary) (of people) not faithful: *a false lover*
> ▶ **false·ly** adv.: *to be falsely accused of something* ◆ *She smiled falsely at his joke.*
> IDM **by/under/on false pretenses** by pretending to be something that you are not, in order to gain some advantage for yourself: *She was accused of obtaining money under false pretenses.* ⊃ more at RING¹

false aˈlarm noun a warning about a danger that does not happen; a belief that something bad is going to happen,

when it is not: *The fire department was called out but it was a false alarm.* ◆ *Analysts predicted a stock market crash, but it was just a false alarm.*

false beˈginner noun a person who has a basic knowledge of a language, but has started to study it again from the beginning

false ˈdawn noun [usually sing.] (formal) a situation in which you think that something is going to happen but it does not: *a false dawn for the economy*

false ˈfriend noun a word in a foreign language that looks similar to a word in your own language, but has a different meaning: *The English word "sensible" and the French word "sensible" are false friends.*

false·hood /ˈfɔlshʊd/ noun (formal) **1** [U] the state of not being true; the act of telling a lie: *to test the truth or falsehood of her claims* **2** [C] a statement that is not true SYN LIE¹

false imˈprisonment noun [U] (law) the crime of illegally keeping someone as a prisoner somewhere

false ˈmemory noun (psychology) a memory of something that did not actually happen

false ˈmove noun [usually sing.] an action that is not allowed or not recommended and that may cause a bad result: *One false move and the bomb might blow up.*

false ˈrib noun = FLOATING RIB

false ˈstart noun **1** an attempt to begin something that is not successful: *After a number of false starts, she finally found a job she liked.* **2** (sports) a situation in which someone taking part in a race starts before the official signal has been given

false ˈteeth noun [pl.] a set of artificial teeth used by someone who has lost their natural teeth ⊃ compare DENTURES

fal·set·to /fɔlˈsɛtoʊ/ noun (pl. **fal·set·tos**) an unusually high voice, especially the voice that men use to sing very high notes

fals·ies /ˈfɔlsiz/ noun [pl.] (informal) pieces of material used inside a BRA to make a woman's breasts seem larger

fal·si·fy /ˈfɔlsəˌfaɪ/ verb (**fal·si·fies**, **fal·si·fy·ing**, **fal·si·fied**, **fal·si·fied**) **~ sth** to change a written record or information so that it is not true anymore ▶ **fal·si·fi·ca·tion** /ˌfɔlsəfəˈkeɪʃn/ noun [U, C]: *the deliberate falsification of the company's records*

fal·si·ty /ˈfɔlsəti/ noun [U] (formal) the state of not being true or genuine ANT TRUTH

Fal·staff·i·an /fɔlˈstæfiən/ adj. (literary) fat, cheerful, and eating and drinking a lot: *My uncle was a Falstaffian figure.* ORIGIN From Sir John Falstaff, a character in several plays by William Shakespeare.

fal·ter /ˈfɔltər/ verb **1** [I] to become weaker or less effective SYN WAVER: *The economy shows no signs of faltering.* ◆ *Her courage never faltered.* **2** [I, T] (+ speech) to speak in a way that shows that you are not confident: *His voice faltered as he began his speech.* **3** [I] to walk or behave in a way that shows that you are not confident: *She walked up to the platform without faltering.* ◆ *He never faltered in his commitment to the party.* ▶ **fal·ter·ing** adj.: *the faltering peace talks* ◆ *the baby's first faltering steps*

fame 🔑 /feɪm/ noun [U]
the state of being known and talked about by many people: *to achieve/win instant fame* ◆ *to rise/shoot to fame overnight* ◆ *Kelly Clarkson of "American Idol" fame* (= famous for "American Idol") ◆ *The town's only claim to fame is that there was once a riot there.* ◆ *She went to Hollywood in search of fame and fortune.* ⊃ see also FAMOUS

famed /feɪmd/ adj. **~ (for sth)** very well known SYN RENOWNED: *Las Vegas, famed for its casinos* ◆ *a famed poet and musician* ⊃ see also FAMOUS

fa·mil·ial /fəˈmɪlyəl/ adj. [only before noun] (formal) **1** related to or typical of a family **2** (medical) (of diseases, conditions, etc.) affecting several members of a family: *familial left-handedness*

fa·mil·iar 🔊 /fəˈmɪlyər/ *adj.*
1 well known to you; often seen or heard and therefore easy to recognize: *to look/sound/taste familiar* ◆ *He's a familiar figure in the neighborhood.* ◆ *Something about her voice was vaguely familiar.* ◆ **~ to sb** *The smell is very familiar to anyone who lives near a bakery.* ◆ *Violent attacks are becoming all too familiar* (= sadly familiar). **ANT UNFAMILIAR 2 ~ with sth** knowing something very well: *an area I had been familiar with since childhood* ◆ *Are you familiar with the computer software they use?* **ANT UNFAMILIAR 3 ~ (with sb)** (of a person's behavior) very informal, sometimes in a way that is unpleasant: *You seem to be on very familiar terms with your teacher.* ◆ *After a few drinks her boss started getting a little too familiar.*

fa·mil·iar·i·ty /fəˌmɪliˈærəti; -ˌmɪlˈyær-/ *noun* [U] **1 ~ (with sth)** | **~ (to sb)** the state of knowing someone or something well; the state of recognizing someone or something: *His familiarity with the language helped him enjoy his stay.* ◆ *When she saw the house, she had a feeling of familiarity.* **2** a friendly, informal manner: *She addressed me with an easy familiarity that made me feel at home.*
IDM familiarity breeds contempt (*saying*) knowing someone or something very well may cause you to lose admiration and respect for them/it

fa·mil·iar·ize /fəˈmɪlyəˌraɪz/ *verb* **~ yourself/sb (with sth)** to learn about something or teach someone about something, so that you/they start to understand it **SYN** ACQUAINT: *You'll need time to familiarize yourself with our procedures.* ▶ **fa·mil·iar·i·za·tion** /fəˌmɪlyərəˈzeɪʃn/ *noun* [U]

fa·mil·iar·ly /fəˈmɪlyərli/ *adv.* **1** in a friendly and informal manner, sometimes in a way that is too informal to be pleasant: *John Hunt, familiarly known to his friends as Jack* ◆ *He touched her cheek familiarly.* **2** in the way that is well known to people: *The elephant's nose or, more familiarly, trunk, is the most versatile organ in the animal kingdom.*

fam·i·ly 🔊 /ˈfæmli; ˈfæməli/ *noun, adj.*
● *noun* (*pl.* **fam·i·lies**) **1** [sing.] a group consisting of one or two parents and their children: *the other members of my family* ◆ *Almost every family in the country owns a television.* ◆ *My whole family enjoys skiing.* ◆ *one-parent/single-parent families* ◆ *a family of four* ◆ *families with young children* ⊃ see also BLENDED FAMILY, NUCLEAR FAMILY **2** [sing., U] a group consisting of one or two parents, their children and close relations: *The whole family came to Grandpa's eightieth birthday party.* ◆ *The support of family and friends is vital.* ◆ *We've only told the immediate family* (= the closest relations). ◆ *I always think of you as one of the family.* ◆ (*informal*) *She's family* (= she is a relation). ⊃ see also EXTENDED FAMILY **3** [C] all the people who are related to each other, including those who are now dead: *Some families have farmed in this area for hundreds of years.* ◆ *This painting has been in our family for generations.* **4** [C, U] a couple's or a person's children, especially young children: *They have a large family.* ◆ *I addressed it to Mr. and Mrs. Jones and family.* ◆ *Do they plan to start a family* (= have children)? ◆ *to bring up/raise a family* ⊃ collocations at CHILD **5** [C] a group of related animals and plants; a group of related things, especially languages: *Lions belong to the cat family.* ◆ *the Germanic family of languages*
IDM (be/get) in the family way (*old-fashioned, informal*) (to be/become) pregnant **run in the family** to be a common feature in a particular family: *Heart disease runs in the family.*
● *adj.* [only before noun] **1** connected with the family or a particular family: *family life* ◆ *your family background* **2** owned by a family: *a family business* **3** suitable for all members of a family, both adults and children: *a family movie*

family ˌcourt *noun* a court that deals with cases that affect families, for example when people get divorced

family ˈdoctor *noun* (*informal*) = GENERAL PRACTITIONER

family ˌman *noun* a man who has a wife or partner and children; a man who enjoys being at home with his wife or partner and children: *I see he's become a family man.* ◆ *a devoted family man*

family ˈmedicine *noun* [U] the branch of medicine that is designed to provide general health care to families and people of all ages

family ˌname *noun* the part of your name that shows which family you belong to ⊃ compare LAST NAME

family ˈplanning *noun* [U] the process of controlling the number of children you have by using CONTRACEPTION

family ˈpractice *noun* a group of doctors that provide general health care to families and people of all ages: *Dr. Simon is part of a family practice in our neighborhood.*

family pracˈtitioner *noun* = GENERAL PRACTITIONER

family ˌroom *noun* **1** a room in a house where the family can relax, watch television, etc. **2** a room in a hotel for three or four people to sleep in, especially parents and children

family ˈtree *noun* a diagram that shows the relationship between members of a family over a long period of time: *How far back can you trace your family tree?*

fam·ine /ˈfæmən/ *noun* [C, U] a lack of food during a long period of time in a region: *a severe famine* ◆ *disasters such as floods and famine* ◆ *the threat of widespread famine in the area* ◆ *to raise money for famine relief*

fam·ished /ˈfæmɪʃt/ *adj.* [not usually before noun] (*informal*) very hungry **SYN** STARVING: *When's lunch? I'm famished!*

fa·mous 🔊 /ˈfeɪməs/ *adj.*
known about by many people: *a famous artist/hotel* ◆ *famous landmarks in San Francisco* ◆ *One day, I'll be rich and famous.* ◆ **~ for sth** *He became internationally famous for his novels.* ◆ **~ as sth** *She was more famous as an actress than as a singer.* ⊃ see also FAME, INFAMOUS, NOTORIOUS, WORLD-FAMOUS
IDM famous last words (*saying*) people sometimes say **Famous last words!** when they think someone is being too confident about something that is going to happen: *"Everything's under control." "Famous last words!"* **ORIGIN** This phrase refers to a collection of quotations of the dying words of famous people.

fa·mous·ly /ˈfeɪməsli/ *adv.* in a way that is famous: *Arizona has some spectacular scenery, most famously the Grand Canyon.*
IDM get along famously (*informal*, becoming *old-fashioned*) to have a very good relationship

fan 🔊 /fæn/ *noun, verb*
● *noun* **1** a person who admires someone or something or enjoys watching or listening to someone or something very much: *movie fans* ◆ *crowds of football fans* ◆ *a big fan of Madonna* ◆ *fan mail* (= letters from fans to the person they admire) **2** a machine with blades that go around to create a current of air: *to switch on the electric fan* ◆ *a ceiling fan* ⊃ see also EXTRACTOR **3** a flat object that you hold in your hand and wave to create a current of cool air

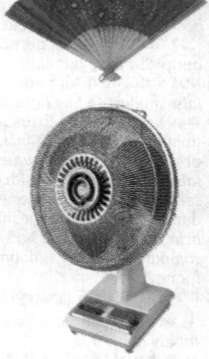
fans

● *verb* (**-nn-**) **1 ~ sb/sth/ yourself** to make air blow onto someone or something by waving a fan, your hand, etc.: *He fanned himself with a newspaper to cool down.* **2 ~ sth** to make a fire burn more strongly by blowing on it: *Fanned by a westerly wind, the fire spread rapidly through the city.* **3 ~ sth** (*literary*) to make a feeling, an attitude, etc.

stronger **SYN** FUEL: *His reluctance to answer her questions simply fanned her curiosity.*

IDM **fan the flames (of sth)** to make a feeling such as anger, hatred, etc. worse: *His writings fanned the flames of racism.*

PHR V **fan 'out | ,fan sth⟷'out** to spread out, or spread something out, over an area: *The police fanned out to surround the house.* ◆ *The bird fanned out its tail feathers.*

fa·nat·ic /fəˈnætɪk/ *noun* **1** (*informal*) a person who is extremely enthusiastic about something **SYN** ENTHUSIAST: *a fitness/crossword, etc. fanatic* **2** (*disapproving*) a person who holds extreme or dangerous opinions **SYN** EXTREMIST: *religious fanatics* ▶ **fa·nat·i·cal** /-kl/ *adj.*: *a fanatical supporter* ◆ *the fanatical anti-communists* ◆ *a fanatical interest in baseball* ◆ *She's fanatical about healthy eating.* **fa·nat·i·cally** /-kli/ *adv.*: *fanatically organized*

fa·nat·i·cism /fəˈnætəˌsɪzəm/ *noun* [U] (*disapproving*) extreme beliefs or behavior, especially in connection with religion or politics **SYN** EXTREMISM

'fan belt *noun* a belt that operates the machinery that cools a car engine

fan·boy /ˈfænbɔɪ/ *noun* (*informal*) a person, especially a boy or young man, who is extremely interested in something such as a particular type of music or software: *a Nintendo fanboy* ◆ *Linux fanboys*

fan·ci·er /ˈfænsiər/ *noun* (usually in compounds) a person who has a special interest in something, especially someone who keeps or breeds birds, animals, or plants: *an orchid fancier*

fan·ci·ful /ˈfænsɪfl/ *adj.* **1** (*disapproving*) based on imagination and not facts or reason: *a fanciful children's story* **2** (of things) decorated in an unusual style that shows imagination: *a fanciful gold border* ▶ **fan·ci·fully** /-fli/ *adv.*

'fan club *noun* an organization that the fans of a person, band, team, etc. belong to, and that sends them information, etc. about that person

fan·cy ✎ /ˈfænsi/ *adj., noun, verb*
• *adj.* (**fan·ci·er, fan·ci·est**) **1** (sometimes *disapproving*) expensive or connected with an expensive way of life: *fancy restaurants with fancy prices* ◆ *a big, fancy house* **2** unusually complicated, often in an unnecessary way; intended to impress other people: *a kitchen full of fancy gadgets* ◆ *They added a lot of fancy footwork to the dance.* ◆ *He's always using fancy legal words.* **ANT** SIMPLE **3** [only before noun] (especially of small things) with a lot of decorations or bright colors: *fancy pastries shaped like swans* ⊃ compare PLAIN **4** (of food) of high quality
• *noun* (*pl.* **fan·cies**) **1** [C, U] something that you imagine; your imagination **SYN** FANTASY: *a child's wild flights of fancy* **2** [sing.] a feeling that you would like to have or to do something **SYN** WHIM: *She said she wanted a dog, but it was only a passing fancy.*
IDM **as/whenever, etc. the fancy takes you** as/whenever, etc. you feel like doing something: *We bought an RV so we could go away whenever the fancy took us.* **catch/take/strike sb's fancy** to attract or please someone: *She looked through the hotel ads until one of them caught her fancy.* **take a fancy to sb/sth** (*old-fashioned*) to start liking someone or something, often without an obvious reason ⊃ more at TICKLE *v.*
• *verb* (**fan·cies, fan·cy·ing, fan·cied, fan·cied**) **1** [I, T] (*informal*) used to show that you are surprised or shocked by something: **~ doing sth** *Fancy meeting you here!* ◆ **~ sth** *"She remembered my name after all those years." " Fancy that!* " **2** [T] **~ (that)...** (*literary*) to believe or imagine something: *She fancied (that) she could hear footsteps.*

,fancy-'free *adj.* free to do what you like because you are not emotionally involved with anyone: *I was still footloose and fancy-free* (= free to enjoy myself) *in those days.*

'fancy ,man, 'fancy ,woman *noun* (*old-fashioned, informal, disapproving*) the man/woman with whom a person is having a romantic relationship, especially when one or both of them is married to someone else

fan·dan·go /fænˈdæŋgoʊ/ *noun* (*pl.* **fan·dan·goes** or **fan·dan·gos**) [C] a lively Spanish dance; a piece of music for this dance

fan·fare /ˈfænfɛr/ *noun* **1** [C] a short loud piece of music that is played to celebrate someone or something important arriving **2** [U, C] a large amount of activity and discussion on television, in newspapers, etc. to celebrate someone or something: *The product was launched amid much fanfare worldwide.*

'fan ,fiction *noun* [U] a type of literature, usually written on the Internet, by people who admire a particular novel, movie, etc., with characters taken from these stories

fang /fæŋ/ *noun* [usually pl.] either of two long sharp teeth at the front of the mouths of some animals, such as a snake or dog ⊃ picture at ANIMAL

fan·light /ˈfænlaɪt/ (also **tran·som**) *noun* a small window above a door or another window

fan·ny /ˈfæni/ *noun* (*pl.* **fan·nies**) (*informal*) a person's bottom

'fanny ,pack *noun* (*informal*) a small bag attached to a belt and worn around the waist, to keep money, etc. in ⊃ picture at BAG

fan·ta·sia /fænˈteɪʒə/ *noun* a piece of music in a free form, often based on familiar tunes

fan·ta·size /ˈfæntəˌsaɪz/ *verb* [I, T] **~ (about sth)** | **~ (that...)** to imagine that you are doing something that you would like to do, or that something that you would like to happen is happening, even though this is very unlikely: *He sometimes fantasized about winning the gold medal.* ▶ **fan·ta·sist** /ˈfæntəsɪst/ *noun*

fan·tas·tic /fænˈtæstɪk/ *adj.* **1** (*informal*) extremely good; excellent **SYN** GREAT: *a fantastic beach in California* ◆ *a fantastic achievement* ◆ *The weather was absolutely fantastic.* ◆ *You got the job? Fantastic!* ⊃ thesaurus box at GREAT **2** (*informal*) very large; larger than you expected **SYN** AMAZING, ENORMOUS: *The response to our fundraiser was fantastic.* ◆ *The car costs a fantastic amount of money.* **3** (also less frequent **fan·tas·tic·al** /fænˈtæstɪkl/) [usually before noun] strange and showing a lot of imagination **SYN** WEIRD: *fantastic dreams of forests and jungles* **4** impossible to put into practice: *a fantastic idea/project* ▶ **fan·tas·ti·cally** /-kli/ *adv.*: *fantastically successful* ◆ *a fantastically shaped piece of stone*

fan·ta·sy /ˈfæntəsi/ *noun* (*pl.* **fan·ta·sies**) **1** [C] a pleasant situation that you imagine but that is unlikely to happen: *his childhood fantasies about becoming a famous football player* **2** [C] a product of your imagination: *Her books are usually escapist fantasies.* **3** [U] the act of imagining things; a person's imagination: *a work of fantasy* ◆ *Stop living in a fantasy world.*

,fantasy 'football *noun* [U] a competition in which you choose players to make your own imaginary team, and score points according to the performance of the real players

fan·zine /ˈfænzin/ *noun* a magazine that is written and read by fans of a musician, sports team, etc.

FAQ /fæk; ˌɛf eɪ ˈkyu/ *abbr.* used in writing to mean "frequently asked questions"

fa·quir = FAKIR

far ✎ /fɑr/ *adv., adj.*
• *adv.* (**far·ther, far·thest** or **fur·ther, fur·thest**)
▷ DISTANCE **1** a long distance away: *We didn't go far.* ◆ *Have you come far?* ◆ *It's not far to the beach.* ◆ *There's not far to go now.* ◆ **~ (from, away, below, etc.)** *The restaurant is not far from here.* ◆ *countries as far apart as Japan and Brazil* ◆ *He looked down at the traffic far below.* ◆ *Far away in the distance, a train whistled.* ◆ *The farther north they went, the colder it became.* ◆ *a concert of music from near and far* **HELP** In positive sentences it is more usual to use **a long way**: *We*

went a long way. ◆ ~~We went far.~~ ◆ *The restaurant is a long way from here.* **2** used when you are asking or talking about the distance between two places, or the distance that has been traveled or is to be traveled: *How far is it to your house from here?* ◆ *How much farther is it?* ◆ *We'll go by train as far as Boston, and then take a bus.* ◆ *We didn't go as far as the others.* ◆ *I'm not sure I can walk so far.*

> **TIME 3** a long time from the present; for a large part of a particular period of time: ~ **back** *The band made their first record as far back as 1990.* ◆ ~ **ahead** *Let's try to plan farther ahead.* ◆ ~ **into sth** *We worked far into the night.*

> **DEGREE 4** very much; to a great degree: *That's a far better idea.* ◆ *There are far more opportunities for young people than there used to be.* ◆ *It had been a success far beyond their expectations.* ◆ *He's fallen far behind in his work.* ◆ *She always gives us far too much homework.* **5** used when you are asking or talking about whether sth is true or possible: *How far can we trust him?* ◆ *His parents supported him as far as they could.* ◆ *Plan your route in advance, using main roads as far as possible.*

> **PROGRESS 6** used to talk about how much progress has been made in doing or achieving something: *How far have you gotten with that report?* ◆ *I read as far as the third chapter.* ⊃ note at FARTHER

IDM **as far as the eye can/could see** to the HORIZON (= where the sky meets the land or ocean): *The cornfields stretched on all sides as far as the eye could see.* **as far as I know | as far as I can remember, see, tell, etc.** used to say that you think you know, remember, understand, etc. something but you cannot be completely sure, especially because you do not know all the facts: *As far as we knew, there was no cause for concern.* ◆ *As far as I can see, you haven't done anything wrong.* ◆ *She lived in Chicago, as far as I can remember.* **as/so far as I am/I'm concerned** used to give your personal opinion on something: *As far as I'm concerned, you can do whatever you want.* **as/so far as sb/sth is concerned | as/so far as sb/sth goes** used to give facts or an opinion about a particular aspect of something **as/so far as it goes** to a limited degree, usually less than is sufficient: *It's a good plan as far as it goes, but there are a lot of things they haven't thought of.* **by far** (used with comparative or superlative adjectives or adverbs) by a great amount: *The last of these reasons is by far the most important.* ◆ *Amy is the smartest by far.* **carry/take sth too far** to continue doing something beyond reasonable limits **far and away** (followed by comparative or superlative adjectives) by a very great amount: *She's far and away the best player.* **far and wide** over a large area: *They searched far and wide for the missing child.* **far be it from me to do sth (but…)** (*informal*) used when you are just about to disagree with someone or to criticize them and you would like them to think that you do not really want to do this: *Far be it from me to interfere in your plans, but I would like to give you just one piece of advice.* **far from sth/from doing sth** almost the opposite of something or of what is expected: *It is far from clear (= it is not clear) what he intends to do.* ◆ *Computers, far from destroying jobs, can create employment.* **far from it** (*informal*) used to say that the opposite of what someone says is true: *"You're not angry, then?" "Far from it. I've never laughed so much in my life."* **go far** (of people) to be very successful in the future: *She is very talented and should go far.* **go far enough** (used in questions and negative sentences) to achieve all that is wanted: *The new legislation is welcome but does not go far enough.* ◆ *Do these measures go far enough?* ◆ (*disapproving*) *Stop it now. The joke has gone far enough (= it has continued too long).* **go so/as far as to…** to be willing to go to extreme or surprising limits in dealing with something: *I wouldn't go as far as to say that he's a liar (= but I think he may be slightly dishonest).* **go too far | go this/that far** to behave in an extreme way that is not acceptable: *He's always been kind of crude, but this time he's gone too far.* ◆ *I never thought she'd go this far.* **in so/as far as | in so far as** to the degree that: *That's the truth, in so far as I know it.* **not far off/wrong** (*informal*) almost correct: *Your guess wasn't far off at all.* **not go far 1** (of money) to not be enough to buy a lot of things: *Twenty dollars doesn't go very far these days.* **2** (of a supply of

something) to not be enough for what is needed: *Four bottles of wine won't go far among twenty people.* **so far | thus far** until now; up to this point: *What do you think of the book so far?* ◆ *Detectives are so far at a loss to explain the reason for his death.* **so far** (*informal*) only to a limited degree: *I trust him only so far.* **so far, so good** (*saying*) used to say that things have been successful until now and you hope they will continue to do so, but you know the task, etc. is not finished yet ⊃ more at AFIELD, FEW *det.*, NEAR *adv.*

● **adj.** (**far·ther**, **far·thest** or **fur·ther**, **fur·thest**) [only before noun]

> **DISTANT 1** at a greater distance away from you: *I saw her on the far side of the road.* ◆ *at the far end of the room* ◆ *They made for an empty table in the far corner.* **2** at the farthest point in a particular direction: *the far north of Alaska* ◆ *Who is that on the far left of the photo?* ◆ *She is on the far right of the party (= holds extreme RIGHT-WING political views).* **3** (*old-fashioned* or *literary*) a long distance away: *a far country*

IDM **a far cry from sth** a very different experience from something

far·ad /ˈfærəd; -əd/ *noun* (*abbr.* F) (*physics*) a unit for measuring CAPACITANCE

far·a·way /ˈfɑːrəˌweɪ/ *adj.* [only before noun] **1** a long distance away **SYN** DISTANT: *a war in a faraway country* **2** a ~ **look/expression** an expression on your face that shows that your thoughts are far away from your present surroundings **SYN** DISTANT

farce /fɑːrs/ *noun* **1** [C, U] a funny play for the theater that is based on ridiculous and unlikely situations and events; this type of writing or performance: *a bedroom farce (= a funny play about sex)* **2** [C] a situation or an event that is so unfair or badly organized that it becomes ridiculous: *The trial was a complete farce.*

far·ci·cal /ˈfɑːrsɪkl/ *adj.* ridiculous and not worth taking seriously: *It was a farcical trial.* ◆ *a situation verging on the farcical*

fare /fer/ *noun*, *verb*

● **noun 1** [C, U] the money that you pay to travel by bus, plane, taxi, etc.: *bus/taxi fares* ◆ *train fares* ◆ *I need some cash for taxi fare.* ◆ *When do the kids start paying the full fare?* ⊃ see also AIRFARE, ROUND TRIP ⊃ thesaurus box at RATE **2** [C] a passenger in a taxi: *The taxi driver picked up a fare at the airport.* **3** [U] (*old-fashioned* or *formal*) food that is offered as a meal: *The restaurant provides traditional Italian fare.*

● **verb** [I] ~ **well, badly, better, etc.** to be successful/unsuccessful in a particular situation: *The party fared very badly in the last election.*

the ˌFar ˈEast *noun* China, Japan, and other countries of E. and S.E. Asia ⊃ compare THE MIDDLE EAST ▶ ˌFar ˈEastern *adj.*

fare·well /ˌferˈwel/ *noun*, *exclamation*

● **noun** [C, U] the act of saying goodbye to someone: *She bade them a fond farewell.* ◆ *a farewell party/drink, etc.*

● **exclamation** (*old use* or *formal*) goodbye

ˌfar-ˈfetched *adj.* very difficult to believe: *The whole story sounds very far-fetched.*

ˌfar-ˈflung *adj.* [usually before noun] (*literary*) **1** a long distance away: *expeditions to the far-flung corners of the world* **2** spread over a wide area: *a newsletter that helps to keep all our far-flung alumni in touch*

ˌfar ˈgone *adj.* [not before noun] (*informal*) very sick, crazy, or drunk: *She was too far gone to understand anything we said to her.*

farm /fɑːrm/ *noun*, *verb*

● **noun 1** an area of land, and the buildings on it, used for growing crops and/or keeping animals: *a 400-acre farm* ◆ *a farm worker/laborer* ◆ *farm buildings/machinery* ◆ *to live/work on a farm* ⊃ collocations at FARMING **2** (especially in compounds) a place where particular fish or animals are bred: *a trout/mink/pig farm* ⊃ see also COLLECTIVE FARM, DAIRY FARM, FACTORY FARM, FUNNY FARM, TRUCK FARM, WIND FARM **IDM** see BUY *v.*

ʌ **cup**   ə **about**   eɪ **say**   aɪ **five**   ɔɪ **boy**   aʊ **now**   oʊ **go**   ɚ **bird**

- **verb** [I, T] to use land for growing crops and/or keeping animals: *The family has farmed in Kansas for over 100 years.* ◆ **~ sth** *They farm dairy cattle.* ◆ *He farmed 200 acres of prime arable land.* ◆ *organically farmed produce*
PHR V ˌfarm sb↔'out (to sb) (*disapproving*) to arrange for someone to be taken care of by other people ˌfarm sb/sth↔'out to sb to send out work for other people to do: *The company farms out a lot of work to freelancers.*

'farm belt *noun* an area where there are a lot of farms

farm·er 🔊 /ˈfɑrmər/ *noun*
a person who owns or manages a farm

'farmers' ˌmarket *noun* a place where farmers sell food directly to the public

'farm·hand /ˈfɑrmhænd/ (also 'field hand) *noun* a person who works for a farmer

'farm·house /ˈfɑrmhaʊs/ *noun* the main house on a farm, where the farmer lives

farm·ing 🔊 /ˈfɑrmɪŋ/ *noun* [U]
the business of managing or working on a farm: *dairy/fish, etc. farming* ◆ *organic farming* ◆ *modern farming methods* ◆ *a farming community*

TOPIC COLLOCATIONS

Farming

growing food and raising animals
- plant trees/seeds/crops/vines/barley
- grow/produce corn/wheat/rice/fruit
- plow land/a field
- sow/harvest seeds/crops/fields
- spread manure/fertilizer on sth
- cultivate/irrigate/water/contaminate crops/plants/fields/land
- damage/destroy/lose your crop
- ripen/pick fruit/berries/grapes
- press/dry/ferment grapes
- grind/thresh grain/corn/wheat
- raise/rear/keep chickens/poultry/cattle/pigs
- raise/breed/feed/graze livestock/cattle/sheep
- butcher/kill/slaughter livestock
- preserve/smoke/cure/salt meat

modern farming
- run a fish farm/an organic dairy farm
- engage in/be involved in intensive (pig/fish) farming
- use/apply (chemical/organic) fertilizer/insecticides/pesticides
- begin/do/conduct field trials of GM (= genetically modified) crops
- grow/develop GM crops/seeds/plants/foods
- fund/invest in genetic engineering/research
- improve/increase crop yields
- face/suffer from/alleviate food shortages
- label food that contains GMOs (= genetically modified organisms)
- eliminate/reduce farm subsidies
- oppose/be against factory farming/GM food
- promote/encourage/support organic/sustainable farming

'farm·land /ˈfɑrmlænd/ *noun* [U, pl.] land that is used for farming: *250 acres of farmland* ◆ *the prosperous farmlands of Iowa*

'farm·stead /ˈfɑrmstɛd/ *noun* a FARMHOUSE and the buildings near it

'farm team *noun* a minor league team, especially in baseball, that provides players to a particular major league team

'farm·yard /ˈfɑrmyɑrd/ *noun* an area that is surrounded by farm buildings

'far-off *adj.* [only before noun] **1** a long distance away

SYN DISTANT, FARAWAY, REMOTE: *a far-off land* **2** a long time ago **SYN** DISTANT: *memories of those far-off days*

ˌfar-'out *adj.* (*informal*) **1** very strange: *He showed us one of his far-out inventions.* **2** (*old-fashioned*) very good or enjoyable: *Wow! That band is far-out!*

far·ra·go /fəˈrɑgou; -ˈreɪ-/ *noun* (*pl.* **far·ra·goes** or **far·ra·gos**) [usually sing.] (*formal, disapproving*) a confused mixture of different things **SYN** HODGEPODGE

ˌfar-'reaching *adj.* likely to have a lot of influence or many effects: *far-reaching consequences/implications* ◆ *far-reaching changes/reforms*

far·ri·er /ˈfæriər/ *noun* a person whose job is making and fitting HORSESHOES for horses' feet

far·row /ˈfærou/ *noun, verb*
- **noun 1** a group of baby pigs that are born together to the same mother **SYN** LITTER **2** an act of giving birth to pigs
- **verb** [I] (of a female pig) to give birth

Far·si /ˈfɑrsi/ *noun* [U] = PERSIAN

far·sight·ed *adj.* **1** not able to see things that are close to you clearly: *She's farsighted and needs glasses to read.* **ANT** NEARSIGHTED **2** having or showing an understanding of the effects in the future of actions that you take now, and being able to plan for them: *the most farsighted of politicians* ◆ *a farsighted decision* ▶ **far·sight·ed·ness** *noun* [U]

fart /fɑrt/ *verb, noun*
- **verb** [I] (*informal, impolite*) to let air from the BOWELS come out through the ANUS, especially when it happens loudly **HELP** A more polite way of expressing this is "to break wind."
PHR V ˌfart a'round (*informal, impolite*) to waste time by behaving in a silly way
- **noun** (*informal, impolite*) **1** an act of letting air from the BOWELS come out through the ANUS, especially when it happens loudly **2** an unpleasant, boring, or stupid person

far·ther 🔊 /ˈfɑrðər/ *adv., adj.*
- *adv.* (comparative of *far*) at or to a greater distance in space or time: *farther north/south* ◆ *farther along the road* ◆ *I can't go any farther.* ◆ *As a family we grew farther and farther apart.* ◆ *We watched their ship moving gradually farther away.* ◆ *How much farther is it?* ◆ *They haven't gotten any farther with the work* (= they have made no progress). **IDM** see AFIELD ➔ note at FURTHER
- *adj.* (comparative of *far*) at a greater distance in space, direction, or time: *the farther shore of the lake*

far·thest 🔊 /ˈfɑrðəst/ (also **fur·thest**) *adv., adj.*
- *adv.* (superlative of *far*) at or to the greatest distance in space or time: *the house farthest away from the road* ◆ *a competition to see who could throw (the) farthest*
- *adj.* (superlative of *far*) at the greatest distance in space, direction, or time: *the farthest point of the journey* ◆ *the part of the lawn farthest from the house* ➔ note at FURTHER

far·thin·gale /ˈfɑrðɪnˌgeɪl/ *noun* in the past, a thick piece of material or set of large rings worn under a woman's skirt to give it a wide round shape

fas·cia¹ /ˈfeɪʃə/ *noun* (also 'fascia ˌboard) a board on the roof of a house, at the end of the RAFTERS

fas·cia² /ˈfæʃə/ *noun* (*pl.* **fas·cia** or **fas·ciae** /ˈfæʃii/) (*anatomy*) a thin band of TISSUE in the body that encloses a muscle or other organ

fas·ci·nate /ˈfæsəˌneɪt/ *verb* [T, I] **~ (sb)** to attract or interest someone very much: *China has always fascinated me.* ◆ *It was a question that had fascinated him since he was a boy.* ◆ *The private lives of movie stars never fail to fascinate.*

fas·ci·nat·ed /ˈfæsəˌneɪtəd/ *adj.* very interested: *The children watched, fascinated, as the picture began to appear.* ◆ **~ by sth** *I've always been fascinated by his ideas.* ◆ **~ to see, learn, etc.** *They were fascinated to see that it was similar to one they had at home.*

fas·ci·nat·ing /ˈfæsəˌneɪtɪŋ/ *adj.* extremely interesting and attractive: *a fascinating story/subject* ♦ *The results of the survey made fascinating reading.* ♦ *It's **fascinating to see** how different people approach the problem.* ♦ *I don't understand what women find so fascinating about him.* ➔ thesaurus box at INTEREST-ING ▶ **fas·ci·nat·ing·ly** *adv.*

fas·ci·na·tion /ˌfæsəˈneɪʃn/ *noun* **1** [C, usually sing.] a very strong attraction that makes something very interesting: *Water **holds a fascination** for most children.* ♦ *The fascination of the game lies in trying to guess what your opponent is thinking.* **2** [U, sing.] the state of being very attracted to and interested in someone or something: *The girls listened **in fascination** as the story unfolded.* ♦ **~ for/with sb/sth** *the public's enduring fascination with movie stars*

fas·cism (also **Fas·cism**) /ˈfæʃɪzəm/ *noun* [U] an extreme RIGHT-WING political system or attitude that is in favor of strong central government and that does not allow any opposition

fas·cist (also **Fas·cist**) /ˈfæʃɪst/ *noun* **1** a person who supports fascism **2** a way of referring to someone that you disapprove of because they have RIGHT-WING attitudes ▶ **fas·cist** *adj.*: *a fascist state* ♦ *fascist sympathies*

Clothes and Fashion

clothes

- be wearing a new outfit/bright colors/fur/a uniform/a costume
- be (dressed) in black/red/jeans and a T-shirt/your best suit/leather/silk/rags (= very old torn clothes)
- be dressed for work/school/dinner/a special occasion
- be dressed as a man/woman/clown/pirate
- wear/dress in casual/designer/second-hand clothes
- wear jewelry/accessories/a watch/glasses/contact lenses/perfume
- have a cowboy hat/red dress/blue suit on
- put on/take off your clothes/coat/shoes/gloves/socks/helmet
- change into/get changed into a pair of jeans/your pajamas

appearance

- change/enhance/improve your appearance
- create/get/have/give sth a new/contemporary/retro look
- brush/comb/shampoo/wash/blow-dry your hair
- have/get a haircut/your hair cut/a new hairstyle
- have/get a piercing/your nose pierced
- have/get a tattoo/a tattoo done (on your arm)/a tattoo removed
- have/get a makeover/plastic surgery/cosmetic surgery/Botox™ treatment
- use/wear/apply/put on makeup/cosmetics

fashion

- follow/keep up with fashion/the latest fashions
- spend/waste money on designer clothes
- be fashionably/stylishly/well dressed
- have good/great/terrible/awful taste in clothes
- update/revamp your wardrobe
- be in/come into/go out of fashion
- be (back/very much) in vogue
- create a style/trend for sth
- organize/put on a fashion show
- show/unveil a designer's spring/summer collection
- sashay/strut down the catwalk/runway
- be on/do a photo/fashion shoot

fash·ion /ˈfæʃn/ *noun, verb*
- *noun* **1** [U, C] a popular style of clothes, hair, etc. at a particular time or place; the state of being popular: *dressed in the latest fashion* ♦ *the new season's fashions* ♦ *Long skirts*

have **come into fashion** again. ♦ *Jeans are still **in fashion**.* ♦ *Some styles never **go out of fashion**.* **2** [C] a popular way of behaving, doing an activity, etc.: *The fashion at the time was for teaching mainly the written language.* ♦ *Fashions in art and literature come and go.* **3** [U] the business of making or selling clothes in new and different styles: *a **fashion designer/magazine/show*** ♦ *the world of fashion* ♦ *the fashion industry*

IDM **after a fashion** to some extent, but not very well: *I can play the piano, after a fashion.* **after the fashion of sb/sth** (*formal*) in the style of someone or something: *Many homes of that period were built after the fashion of Frank Lloyd Wright.* **in (a)… fashion** (*formal*) in a particular way: *How could they behave in such a fashion?* ♦ *She was proved right, in dramatic fashion, when the whole department resigned.* **like it's going out of fashion** (*informal*) used to emphasize that someone is doing something or using something a lot: *She's been spending money like it's going out of fashion.*

- *verb* to make or shape something, especially with your hands: **~ A (from/out of B)** *She fashioned a pot from the clay.* ♦ **~ B (into A)** *She fashioned the clay into a pot.*

fash·ion·a·ble /ˈfæʃənəbl/ *adj.*

1 following a style that is popular at a particular time: *fashionable clothes/furniture/ideas* ♦ *It's becoming fashionable to have long hair again.* ♦ *Such thinking is fashionable among right-wing politicians.* **2** used or visited by people following a current fashion, especially by rich people: *a fashionable address/resort/restaurant* ♦ *She lives in a very fashionable part of Chicago.* **ANT** UNFASHIONABLE ➔ compare OLD-FASHIONED ▶ **fash·ion·a·bly** /-bli/ *adv.*: *fashionably dressed* ♦ *His wife was blonde and fashionably thin.*

ˈfashion-ˌconscious *adj.* aware of the latest fashions and wanting to follow them: *fashion-conscious teenagers*

ˈfashion deˌsigner *noun* a person who designs fashionable clothes

ˈfashion-ˈforward *adj.* more modern than the current fashion: *We tend to be traditional rather than fashion-forward in our designs.*

fash·ion·is·ta /ˌfæʃəˈnistə/ *noun* (used especially in newspapers) a fashion DESIGNER, or a person who is always dressed in a fashionable way

ˈfashion ˌshow *noun* an occasion where people can see new designs of clothes being worn by fashion models

ˈfashion ˌstatement *noun* something that you wear or own that is new or unusual and is meant to draw attention to you: *This shirt is great for anyone who wants to **make a fashion statement**.*

ˈfashion ˌvictim *noun* a person who always wears the newest fashions even if they do not suit him or her

fast /fæst/ *adj., adv., verb, noun*
- *adj.* (**fast·er, fast·est**)
- ▷ QUICK **1** moving or able to move quickly: *a fast car/horse* ♦ *the world's fastest runner* **2** happening in a short time or without delay: *the fastest rate of increase for years* ♦ *a fast response time* **3** able to do something quickly: *a fast learner*
- ▷ SURFACE **4** producing or allowing quick movement: *a fast road/track* ➔ see also FAST LANE
- ▷ WATCH/CLOCK **5** [not before noun] showing a time later than the true time: *I'm early—my watch must be fast.* ♦ *That clock is ten minutes fast.*
- ▷ FIRMLY FASTENED **6** (of a boat, etc.) firmly fastened or attached: *He made the boat fast.*
- ▷ COLORS IN CLOTHES **7** not likely to change or to come out when washed
- ▷ PHOTOGRAPHIC FILM **8** (*technical*) very sensitive to light, and therefore useful when taking photographs in poor light or of something that is moving very quickly **HELP** There is no noun related to *fast*. Use **speed** in connection with vehicles, actions, etc.; **quickness** is used about thinking.

IDM **fast and furious** (of films/movies, shows, etc.) full of rapid action and sudden changes: *In his latest movie, the action is fast and furious.* **a fast talker** a person who can talk

| t **t**ea | ṭ bu**tt**er | d **d**id | k **c**at | g **g**ot | tʃ **ch**in | dʒ **J**une | f **f**all

very quickly and easily, but who cannot always be trusted ⟳ more at BUCK n., HARD adj., PULL v.

● *adv.* (fast·er, fast·est)
> QUICKLY **1** quickly: *Don't drive so fast!* ◆ *How fast were you going?* ◆ *I can't go any faster.* ◆ *The water was rising fast.* ◆ *Her heart beat faster.* ◆ *(formal) Night was fast approaching.* ◆ *a fast-flowing stream* ⟳ note at QUICK **2** in a short time; without delay: *Children grow up so fast these days.* ◆ *The United States is fast becoming a nation of fatties.* ◆ *The police said that they reacted as fast as they could.*
> FIRMLY **3** firmly; completely: *Within a few minutes she was fast asleep* (= sleeping deeply). ◆ *The boat was stuck fast* (= unable to move) *in the mud.* **HELP** There is no noun related to fast. Use **speed** in connection with vehicles, actions, etc.; **quickness** is used about thinking.
IDM as fast as your legs can carry you as quickly as you can hold fast to sth (*formal*) to continue to believe in an idea, etc. despite difficulties play fast and loose (with sb/sth) (*old-fashioned*) to treat someone or something in a way that shows that you feel no responsibility or respect for them stand fast/firm to refuse to move back; to refuse to change your opinions ⟳ more at THICK adv.

● *verb* [I] to eat little or no food for a period of time, especially for religious or health reasons: *Muslims fast during Ramadan.*

● *noun* a period during which you do not eat food, especially for religious or health reasons: *to go on a fast* ◆ *to break* (= end) *your fast*

WHICH WORD?

fast • quick • rapid

These adjectives are frequently used with the following nouns:

fast ~	quick ~	rapid ~
car	glance	change
train	look	growth
runner	reply	increase
pace	decision	decline
lane	way	progress

- **Fast** is used especially to describe a person or thing that moves or is able to move at great speed.
- **Quick** is more often used to describe something that is done in a short time or without delay.
- **Rapid**, **swift**, and **speedy** are more formal words.
- **Rapid** is most commonly used to describe the speed at which something changes. It is not used to describe the speed at which something moves or is done: *a rapid train* ◆ *We had a rapid coffee.*
- **Swift** usually describes something that happens or is done quickly and immediately: *a swift decision* ◆ *The government took swift action.*
- **Speedy** has a similar meaning: *a speedy recovery*. It is used less often to talk about the speed at which something moves: *a speedy car*

For the use of **fast** and **quick** as adverbs, see the usage note at QUICK.

---

fast·ball /ˈfæstbɔl/ *noun* **1** (in baseball) a ball that is thrown at the PITCHER 's fastest speed **2** = FAST-PITCH SOFTBALL

ˌfast ˈbreeder (also ˌfast ˌbreeder reˈactor) *noun* a REACTOR in a nuclear power station in which the reaction that produces energy is not made slower

fas·ten 🔊 /ˈfæsn/ *verb*
1 [T, I] to close or join together the two parts of something; to become closed or joined together **SYN** DO UP: ~ **sth** *Fasten your seat belts, please.* ◆ ~ **sth up** *She fastened up her coat and hurried out.* ◆ ~ **(up)** *The dress fastens at the back.* **ANT** UNFASTEN **2** [T, I] ~ **(sth)** to close something firmly so that it will not open; to be closed in this way: *Fasten the gates*

securely so that they do not blow open. ◆ *The window wouldn't fasten.* **ANT** UNFASTEN **3** [T] ~ **sth** + **adv./prep.** to fix or place something in a particular position, so that it will not move: *He fastened back the shutters.* **4** [T] ~ **A to B** | ~ **A and B (together)** to attach or tie one thing to another thing: *She fastened the papers together with a paper clip.* **5** [T, I] if you **fasten** your arms around someone, your teeth into something, etc., or if your arms, teeth, etc. **fasten** around, into, etc. someone or something, you hold the person/thing firmly with your arms, etc.: ~ **sth** + **adv./prep.** *The dog fastened its teeth in his leg.* ◆ + **adv./prep.** *His hand fastened on her arm.* **6** [T, I] ~ **(sth) (on sb/sth)** if you **fasten** your eyes on someone or something, or your eyes **fasten** on someone or something, you look at them for a long time: *He fastened his gaze on her face.*
PHR V ˈfasten on(to) sb/sth to choose or follow someone or something in a determined way

fas·ten·er /ˈfæsənər/ (also fas·ten·ing) *noun* a device, such as a button or a ZIPPER, used to close a piece of clothing; a device used to close a window, bag, etc. tightly

fast·en·ing /ˈfæsənɪŋ/ *noun* **1** = FASTENER **2** the place where something, especially a piece of clothing, fastens; the way something fastens: *The pants have a fly fastening.*

ˌfast ˈfood *noun* [U] hot food that is served very quickly in special restaurants, and often taken away to be eaten in the street ⟳ compare SLOW FOOD

ˌfast-ˈforward *verb* [T, I] ~ **(sth)** to wind a tape or video forward without playing it ► ˌfast ˈforward *noun* [U]: *Press fast forward to advance the tape.* ◆ *the fast-forward button*

fas·tid·i·ous /fæˈstɪdiəs; fə-/ *adj.* **1** being careful that every detail of something is correct **SYN** METICULOUS: *Everything was planned in fastidious detail.* ◆ *He was fastidious in his preparation for the big day.* **2** (sometimes *disapproving*) not liking things to be dirty or messy: *She wasn't very fastidious about personal hygiene.* ► **fas·tid·i·ous·ly** *adv.* **fas·tid·i·ous·ness** *noun* [U]

ˈfast lane *noun* [sing.] the part of a major road such as a highway or INTERSTATE where vehicles drive fastest
IDM in the fast lane where things are most exciting and where a lot is happening: *He had a good job, plenty of money, and he was enjoying life in the fast lane.*

fast·ness /ˈfæstnəs/ *noun* (*literary*) a place that is thought to be safe because it is difficult to get to or easy to defend **SYN** STRONGHOLD

ˈfast track *noun* [sing.] a quick way to achieve something, for example a high position in a job ► ˈfast-track *adj.*: *the fast-track route to promotion* ◆ *fast-track graduates*

ˈfast-track *verb* ~ **sb/sth** to make someone's progress in achieving something, for example in a job, quicker than usual

fat 🔊 /fæt/ *adj., noun*
● *adj.* (fat·ter, fat·test) **1** (of a person's or an animal's body) having too much flesh on it and weighing too much: *a big, fat man/woman* ◆ *You'll get fat if you keep eating so much junk food.* ◆ *He grew fatter and fatter.* ◆ *fat, flabby legs* **ANT** THIN ⟳ note on page 546 **2** thick or wide: *a fat volume on American history* **3** [only before noun] (*informal*) large in quantity; worth a lot of money: *a fat sum/profit* ◆ *He gave me a nice fat check.* ► **fat·ness** *noun* [U]: *Fatness tends to run in families.*

WORD FAMILY
fat *adj.*
fatty *adj.*
fatten *verb*
fattening *adj.*

IDM (a) fat chance (of sth/doing sth) (*informal*) used for saying that you do not believe something is likely to happen: *"They might let us in without tickets." "Fat chance of that!"* a fat lot of good, use, etc. (*informal*) not at all good or useful: *Paul can't drive, so he was a fat lot of good when I broke my arm.* it's not over until the fat lady sings (*saying*) used for saying that a situation may still change, for example that a contest, an election, etc. is not finished yet, and someone still has a chance to win it

---

saying that someone is fat

- **Fat** is the most common and direct word, but it is not polite to say to someone that they are fat: *Does this dress make me look fat?* ◆ ~~You're looking fat now.~~
- **Overweight** is a more neutral word: *I'm a little overweight.* It can also mean too fat, especially so that you are not fit.
- **Large** or **heavy** is less offensive than **fat**: *He's a fairly large man.* **Big** describes someone who is tall as well as fat: *Her sister is a big girl, isn't she?*
- **Plump** means slightly fat in an attractive way, often used to describe women.
- **Chubby** is used mainly to describe babies and children who are fat in a pleasant, healthy-looking way: *the baby's chubby cheeks*
- **Tubby** (*informal*) is used in a friendly way to describe people who are short and round, especially around the stomach.
- **Stocky** is a neutral word and means fairly short, broad, and strong.
- **Stout** is often used to describe older people who have a round and heavy appearance: *a short, stout man with a bald head*
- **Flabby** describes flesh that is fat and loose: *exercises to firm up flabby thighs*
- **Obese** is used by doctors to describe people who are so fat that they are unhealthy. It is also used in a general way to mean "really fat."

Note that although people talk a lot about their own size or weight, it is generally not considered polite to refer to a person's large size or their weight when you talk to them or about them.
⊃ note at THIN

- **noun 1** [U] a white or yellow substance in the bodies of animals and humans, stored under the skin: *excess body fat* ◆ *This ham has too much fat on it.* ⊃ collocations at DIET **2** [C, U] a solid or liquid substance from animals or plants, treated so that it becomes pure for use in cooking: *Saute the onions in bacon fat or butter.* **3** [C, U] animal and vegetable fats, when you are thinking of them as part of what a person eats: *You should cut down on fats and carbohydrates.* ◆ *foods that are low in fat* ◆ *reduced-fat margarine* **IDM** see CHEW *v.*, LIVE[1]

fa·tal /ˈfeɪtl/ *adj.* **1** causing or ending in death: *a fatal accident/blow/illness* ◆ *a potentially fatal form of cancer* ◆ *If she gets sick again, it could prove fatal.* ⊃ compare MORTAL **2** causing disaster or failure: *a fatal error/mistake* ◆ *Any delay would be fatal.* ◆ *There was a fatal flaw in the plan.* ◆ *It would be fatal to try and rush things now.* ▶ **fa·tal·ly** /ˈfeɪtl·i/ *adv.*: *fatally injured/wounded* ◆ *The plan was fatally flawed from the start.*

fa·tal·ism /ˈfeɪtlˌɪzəm/ *noun* [U] the belief that events are decided by FATE and that you cannot control them; the fact of accepting that you cannot prevent something from happening ▶ **fa·tal·ist** /ˈfeɪtlɪst/ *noun*: *I'm a fatalist.*

fa·tal·is·tic /ˌfeɪtlˈɪstɪk/ *adj.* showing a belief in FATE and feeling that you cannot control events or stop them from happening ▶ **fa·tal·is·ti·cally** /-kli/ *adv.*

fa·tal·i·ty /feɪˈtæləti; fə-/ *noun* (*pl.* **fa·tal·i·ties**) **1** [C] a death that is caused in an accident or a war, or by violence or disease: *Several people were injured, but there were no fatalities.* **2** [U] the fact that a particular disease will result in death: *to reduce the fatality of certain types of cancer* ◆ *Different forms of cancer have different fatality rates.* **3** [U] the belief or feeling that we have no control over what happens to us: *A sense of fatality gripped her.*

ˈfat camp *noun* [U, C] an organized vacation for fat children during which they are helped to lose weight

ˈfat cat *noun* (*informal*, *disapproving*) a person who earns, or

who has, a lot of money (especially when compared to people who do not earn so much)

fate /feɪt/ *noun* **1** [C] the things, especially bad things, that will happen or have happened to someone or something: *The fate of the three men is unknown.* ◆ *She sat outside, waiting to find out her fate.* ◆ *The court will decide our fate/fates.* ◆ *Each of the managers suffered the same fate.* ◆ *The government had abandoned the refugees to their fate.* ◆ *From that moment, our fate was sealed* (= our future was decided). **2** [U] the power that is believed to control everything that happens and that cannot be stopped or changed: *Fate was kind to me that day.* ◆ *By a strange twist of fate, Andy and I were on the same plane.* ⊃ thesaurus box at LUCK
IDM a fate worse than death (often *humorous*) a terrible thing that could happen ⊃ more at TEMPT

fat·ed /ˈfeɪtəd/ *adj.* **1** ~ (to do sth) unable to escape a particular fate; certain to happen because everything is controlled by fate **SYN** DESTINED: *We were fated never to meet again.* ◆ *He believes that everything in life is fated.* **2** = ILL-FATED

fate·ful /ˈfeɪtfl/ *adj.* [usually before noun] having an important, often very bad, effect on future events: *She looked back now to that fateful day in December.*

ˌfat-ˈfree *adj.* not containing any fat: *fat-free yogurt*

fa·ther 🔊 /ˈfɑðər/ *noun, verb*

- **noun 1** a male parent of a child or an animal; a person who is acting as the father to a child: *Ben is a wonderful father.* ◆ *You've been like a father to me.* ◆ *Our new boss is a father of three* (= he has three children). ◆ *He was a wonderful father to both his natural and adopted children.* ◆ (*old-fashioned*) *Father, I cannot lie to you.* ⊃ see also GODFATHER, GRANDFATHER, STEPFATHER **2 fathers** [pl.] (*literary*) a person's ANCESTORS (= people who are related to you who lived in the past): *the land of our fathers* ⊃ see also FOREFATHER **3** ~ (of sth) the first man to introduce a new way of thinking about something or of doing something: *Pablo Picasso is considered the father of modern art.* ⊃ see also FOUNDING FATHER **4 Father** used by Christians to refer to God: *Father, forgive us.* ◆ *God the Father* **5 Father** (abbr. Fr.) the title of a priest, especially in the Roman Catholic Church and the Orthodox Church: *Father Dominic* ⊃ see also HOLY FATHER
IDM from father to son from one generation of a family to the next **like father, like son** (*saying*) used to say that a son's character or behavior is similar to that of his father ⊃ more at OLD, WISH *n.*
- **verb 1** ~ sb to become the father of a child by making a woman pregnant: *He fathered 3 children with his first wife and 2 with his second wife.* **2** ~ sth to create new ideas or a new way of doing something

ˈfather ˌfigure *noun* an older man that someone respects because he will advise and help them like a father

fa·ther·hood /ˈfɑðərˌhʊd/ *noun* [U] the state of being a father

ˈfather-in-ˌlaw *noun* (*pl.* **ˈfathers-in-law**) the father of your husband or wife ⊃ compare MOTHER-IN-LAW

fa·ther·land /ˈfɑðərˌlænd/ *noun* [usually sing.] (*old-fashioned*) the country where a person, or their family, was born, especially when they feel very loyal toward it

fa·ther·less /ˈfɑðərləs/ *adj.* [usually before noun] without a father, either because he has died or because he does not live with his children: *fatherless families*

fa·ther·ly /ˈfɑðərli/ *adj.* typical of a good father: *fatherly advice* ◆ *He keeps a fatherly eye on his players.*

ˈFather's ˌDay *noun* a day when fathers receive cards and gifts from their children, usually the third Sunday in June

ˌFather ˈTime *noun* an imaginary figure who represents time and looks like an old man carrying a SCYTHE and an HOURGLASS

fath·om /ˈfæðəm/ *verb, noun*
- **verb** to understand or find an explanation for something:

~ sb/sth *It is hard to fathom the pain felt at the death of a child.* ◆ **~ what, where, etc....** *He couldn't fathom what the man could possibly mean.*

● **noun** a unit for measuring the depth of water, equal to 6 feet or 1.8 meters: *The ship sank in 20 fathoms.* ◆ *(figurative) She kept her feelings hidden fathoms deep.*

fath·om·less /ˈfæðəmləs/ *adj.* (*literary*) too deep to be measured: *the fathomless ocean* ◆ *fathomless sorrow*

fa·tigue /fəˈtig/ *noun* **1** [U] a feeling of being extremely tired, usually because of hard work or exercise **SYN** EXHAUSTION: *physical and mental fatigue* ◆ *Driver fatigue was to blame for the accident.* ◆ *I was heavy with fatigue and could not keep my eyes open.* **2** [U] (usually after another noun) a feeling of not wanting to do a particular activity any longer because you have done too much of it: *battle fatigue* **3** [U] weakness in metal or wood caused by repeated bending or stretching: *The wing of the plane showed signs of metal fatigue.* **4 fatigues** [pl.] loose clothes worn by soldiers **5** (also **fa·tigue detail**) [U] duties, such as cleaning and cooking, that soldiers have to do, especially as a punishment

fa·tigued /fəˈtigd/ *adj.* [not usually before noun] (*formal*) very tired, both physically and mentally **SYN** EXHAUSTED

fa·ti·guing /fəˈtigɪŋ/ *adj.* (*formal*) very tiring, both physically and mentally **SYN** EXHAUSTING

fat·so /ˈfætsoʊ/ *noun* (*pl.* **fat·sos**) (*informal*) = FATTY

fat·ten /ˈfætn/ *verb* [T, I] **~ (sb/sth) (up)** to make someone or something fatter, especially an animal before killing it for food; to become fatter: *The piglets are taken from the sow to be fattened for market.* ◆ *She's very thin after her illness—but we'll soon fatten her up.*

fat·ten·ing /ˈfætn-ɪŋ/ *adj.* (of food) likely to make you fat: *fattening snacks*

fat·tism /ˈfætɪzəm/ *noun* [U] unfair treatment of people because of their large body size ▸ **fat·tist** /ˈfætɪst/ *adj.*

fat·ty /ˈfæti/ *adj.*, *noun*
● **adj.** (**fat·ti·er**, **fat·ti·est**) containing a lot of fat; consisting of fat: *fatty foods* ◆ *fatty tissue*
● **noun** (*pl.* **fat·ties**) (also **fat·so**) (*informal, disapproving*) a fat person: *The United States has become a nation of fatties.*

fatty acid *noun* (*chemistry*) an acid that is found in fats and oils

fat·u·ous /ˈfætʃuəs/ *adj.* (*formal*) silly or stupid: *a fatuous comment/grin* ▸ **fat·u·ous·ly** *adv.*

fat·wa /ˈfatwɑ/ *noun* a decision or an order made under Islamic law

fau·cet /ˈfɔsət/ (also **tap**) *noun* a device that controls the flow of water from a pipe: *the hot/cold water faucet* ◆ *to turn a faucet on/off* ⊃ picture at PLUG

fault 🔑 /fɔlt/ *noun*, *verb*
● **noun**
> RESPONSIBILITY **1** [U] the responsibility for something wrong that has happened or been done: *Why should I say sorry when it's not my fault?* ◆ *It's nobody's fault.* ◆ **~ (that...)** *It was his fault that we were late.* ◆ **~ (for doing sth)** *It's your own fault for being careless.* ◆ *Many people live in poverty through no fault of their own.* ◆ *I think the owners are at fault* (= responsible) *for not warning us.*
> IN SOMEONE'S CHARACTER **2** [C] a bad or weak aspect of someone's character **SYN** SHORTCOMING: *He's proud of his children and blind to their faults.* ◆ *I love her for all her faults* (= in spite of them).
> SOMETHING WRONG **3** [C] something that is wrong or not perfect with something; something that is wrong with a machine or system that stops it from working correctly **SYN** DEFECT: *The book's virtues far outweigh its faults.* ◆ *The system, for all its faults, is the best available at the present time.* ◆ *a major fault in the design* ◆ *a structural fault* ◆ *an electrical fault*
> IN TENNIS **4** [C] a mistake made when SERVING: *He has served a number of double faults in this set.*

> GEOLOGY **5** [C] a place where there is a break that is longer than usual in the layers of rock in the earth's CRUST: *the San Andreas fault* ◆ *a fault line*
  IDM **to a fault** used to say that someone has a lot, or even too much, of a particular good quality: *She is generous to a fault.* ⊃ more at FIND v.
● **verb** **~ sb/sth** (often used in negative sentences with *can* and *could*) to find a mistake or a weakness in someone or something **SYN** CRITICIZE: *Her colleagues could not fault her dedication to the job.* ◆ *He had always been polite—she couldn't fault him on that.*

fault-finding *noun* [U] the act of looking for faults in someone or something

fault·less /ˈfɔltləs/ *adj.* having no mistakes **SYN** PERFECT: *faultless English* ▸ **fault·less·ly** *adv.*

fault·y /ˈfɔlti/ *adj.* **1** not perfect; not working or made correctly **SYN** DEFECTIVE: *Ask for a refund if the product is faulty.* ◆ *faulty workmanship* ◆ *an accident caused by a faulty signal* **2** (of a way of thinking) wrong or containing mistakes, often resulting in bad decisions: *faulty reasoning*

faun /fɔn/ *noun* (in ancient Roman stories) a god of the woods, with a man's face and body and a GOAT's legs and horns

fau·na /ˈfɔnə/ *noun* [U, C] all the animals living in an area or in a particular period of history: *the local flora and fauna* (= plants and animals) ◆ *(technical)* *land and marine faunas*

Faus·ti·an /ˈfaʊstiən/ *adj.* (*formal*) **~ bargain/pact/agreement** an agreement in which someone agrees to do something bad or dishonest, in return for money, success, or power **ORIGIN** From Faust, who, according to the German legend, sold his soul to the Devil in return for many years of power and pleasure.

Fauve (also **fauve**) /foʊv/ *noun* a member of a group of French painters who were important in Fauvism

Fauv·ism (also **fauv·ism**) /ˈfoʊvɪzəm/ *noun* (*art*) a style of painting that uses bright colors and in which objects and people are represented in a non-realistic way. It was popular in Paris for a short period from 1905.

faux /foʊ/ *adj.* artificial, but intended to look or seem real: *The chairs were covered in faux animal skin.* ◆ *His accent was so faux.*

faux pas /ˌfoʊ ˈpɑ/ *noun* (*pl.* **faux pas** /ˌfoʊ ˈpɑz; -ˈpɑ/) (from French) an action or a remark that causes embarrassment because it is not socially correct

fa·va bean /ˈfavə ˌbin/ (also **broad bean**) *noun* a type of round, pale green BEAN. Several fava beans grow together inside a fat POD.

fave /feɪv/ *noun* (*informal*) a favorite person or thing: *That song is one of my faves.* ▸ **fave** *adj.*: *her fave TV show*

fa·ve·la /fəˈvɛlə/ *noun* (from *Portuguese*) a poor area in or near a Brazilian city, with many small houses that are close together and in bad condition ⊃ compare SHANTY TOWN

fa·vor 🔑 (*CanE usually* **fa·vour**) /ˈfeɪvər/ *noun*, *verb*
● **noun**
> HELP **1** [C] a thing that you do to help someone: *Could you do me a favor and pick up Sam from school today?* ◆ *Can I ask a favor?* ◆ *I would never ask for any favors from her.* ◆ *I'm going as a favor to Ann, not because I want to.* ◆ *I'll ask Steve to take it. He owes me a favor.* ◆ *Thanks for helping me out. I'll return the favor* (= help you because you have helped me) *sometime.* ◆ *Do yourself a favor* (= help yourself) *and wear a helmet on your bike.*
> APPROVAL **2** [U] approval or support for someone or something: *The suggestion to close the road has found favor with* (= been supported by) *local people.* ◆ *The program has lost favor with viewers recently.* ◆ *an athlete who fell out of favor after a drug scandal* ◆ *(formal)* *The government looks with favor on* (= approves of) *the report's recommendations.* ◆ *She's not in favor with* (= supported or liked by) *the media right now.* ◆ *It seems Tim has come back into favor with the boss* (= the boss likes him again).

> BETTER TREATMENT **3** [U] treatment that is generous to one person or group in a way that seems unfair to others **SYN** BIAS: *As a coach, she showed no favor to any of the girls on the softball team.*
> PARTY GIFT **4** favors [pl.] = PARTY FAVORS
> SEX **5** favors [pl.] (*old-fashioned*) agreement to have sex with someone: *demands for sexual favors*
> **IDM** **do sb no favors** to do something that is not helpful to someone, or that gives a bad impression of them: *You're not doing yourself any favors, working for nothing.* ◆ *The orchestra did Beethoven no favors.* **do me a favor** (*informal*) used to angrily tell someone that you want them to do something: *Do me a favor and leave before you break anything else.* **in favor (of sb/sth)** **1** if you are **in favor** of someone or something, you support and agree with them/it: *He argued in favor of a strike.* ◆ *There were 247 votes in favor (of the motion) and 2 against.* ◆ *I'm all in favor of* (= completely support) *equal pay for equal work.* ◆ *Most of the "don't knows" in the opinion polls came down in favor of* (= eventually chose to support) *the Democrats.* **2** in exchange for another thing (because the other thing is better or you want it more): *He abandoned teaching in favor of a career as a musician.* **in sb's favor** **1** if something is **in someone's favor**, it gives them an advantage or helps them: *The exchange rate is in our favor right now.* ◆ *She was willing to bend the rules in Mary's favor.* **2** a decision or judgment that is **in someone's favor** benefits that person or says that they were right ➔ more at CURRY *v.*, FEAR *n.*, STACKED
● *verb*
> PREFER **1** ~ sth | ~ (sb) doing sth to prefer one system, plan, way of doing something, etc. to another: *Many countries favor a presidential system of government.*
> TREAT BETTER **2** ~ sb to treat someone better than you treat other people, especially in an unfair way: *The treaty seems to favor the U.S.*
> HELP **3** ~ sth to provide suitable conditions for a particular person, group, etc.: *The warm climate favors many types of tropical plants.*
> LOOK LIKE PARENT **4** ~ sb (*old-fashioned*) to look like one of your parents or older relations: *She definitely favors her father.*

fa·vor·a·ble (*CanE usually* **fa·vour·a·ble**) /'feɪvərəbl; 'feɪvrəbl/ *adj.* **1** making people have a good opinion of someone or something: *She made a favorable impression on his parents.* ◆ *The biography shows him in a favorable light.* **2** positive and showing your good opinion of someone or something: *favorable comments* **3** ~ (to/for sb/sth) good for something and making it likely to be successful or have an advantage **SYN** ADVANTAGEOUS: *The terms of the agreement are favorable to both sides.* ◆ *favorable economic conditions* **4** fairly good and not too expensive: *They offered me a loan on very favorable terms.* **ANT** UNFAVORABLE
▶ **fa·vor·a·bil·i·ty** (*CanE usually* **fa·vour·a·bil·i·ty**) /ˌfeɪvərə-'bɪləti; ˌfeɪvrə-/ *noun* [U] **fa·vor·a·bly** (*CanE usually* **fa·vour·a·bly**) /'feɪvərəbli; 'feɪvrə-/ *adv.*: *He speaks very favorably of your work.* ◆ *These figures compare favorably with last year's.* ◆ *I was very favorably impressed with her work.*

fa·vored (*CanE usually* **fa·voured**) /'feɪvərd/ *adj.* **1** treated in a special way, or receiving special help or advantages in a way that may seem unfair: *a member of the president's favored circle of advisers* **2** preferred by most people: *the favored candidate* **3** (*formal*) particularly pleasant and worth having: *Their house is in a very favored position near the park.*

fa·vor·ite 🔊 (*CanE usually* **fa·vour·ite**) /'feɪvrət; -vərət/ *adj.*, *noun*
● *adj.* liked more than others of the same kind: *It's one of my favorite movies.* ◆ *Who is your favorite writer?* ◆ *January is my least favorite month.* ➔ thesaurus box at CHOICE
IDM **sb's favorite son** **1** a performer, politician, sports player, etc., who is popular where they were born **2** a candidate for president who is supported by his or her own state in the first part of a campaign
● *noun* **1** a person or thing that you like more than the others of the same type: *These cookies are great favorites with the*

children. ◆ *This song is a personal favorite of mine.* ◆ *The band played all my old favorites.* ◆ *Which one's your favorite?* ◆ *The program has become a fan favorite with young audiences.* **2** a person who is liked better by someone and receives better treatment than others: *She loved all her grandchildren, but Ann was her favorite.* **3** the horse, runner, team, etc. that is expected to win: *The favorite came third.* ◆ ~ (for sth) *Her horse is the runaway favorite for the race.* ◆ ~ (to do sth) *The Penguins are the favorite to win the Stanley Cup.* **4** the person who is expected by most people to get a particular job or position: ~ (for sth) *She's the favorite for the job.* ◆ ~ (to do sth) *She's the favorite to succeed him as leader.* **5** a page on the Internet that you like and whose address you save so that you can return to it easily **SYN** BOOKMARK: *The library's home page is in my favorites.*

fa·vor·it·ism (*CanE usually* **fa·vour·it·ism**) /'feɪvrəˌtɪzəm; -vərə-/ *noun* [U] (*disapproving*) the act of unfairly treating one person better than others because you like them more: *The students accused the teacher of favoritism.*

fa·vour (*CanE*) = FAVOR

fawn /fɔn/ *adj.*, *noun*, *verb*
● *adj.* light yellowish-brown in color: *a fawn coat*
● *noun* **1** [C] a DEER less than one year old **2** [U] a light yellowish-brown color
● *verb* [I] ~ (on/over sb) (*disapproving*) to try to please someone by praising them or paying them too much attention

fax /fæks/ *noun*, *verb*
● *noun* (also *formal* **fac·sim·i·le**) **1** (also 'fax machine') [C] a machine that sends and receives documents in an electronic form along telephone wires and then prints them: *Do you have a fax?* **2** [U] a system for sending documents using a fax machine: *Can you send it to me by fax?* ◆ *What is your fax number?* **3** [C] a letter or message sent by fax: *Did you get my fax?* ◆ *You can send faxes by e-mail from your computer.* ➔ collocations at PHONE
● *verb* to send someone a document, message, etc. by fax: ~ sb sth *Could you fax me the latest version?* ◆ ~ sth (to sb) *Could you fax it to me?* ◆ *I faxed the list of hotels to them.*

faze /feɪz/ *verb* ~ sb [often passive] (*informal*) to make you feel confused or shocked, so that you do not know what to do **SYN** DISCONCERT: *She wasn't fazed by his comments.* ◆ *He looked as if nothing could faze him.*

FBI /ˌɛf bi 'aɪ/ *abbr.* Federal Bureau of Investigation (the police department in the U.S. that is controlled by the national government and that is responsible for dealing with crimes that affect more than one state)

FCC /ˌɛf si 'si/ *abbr.* Federal Communications Commission (the U.S. government department that controls radio, television, telephone, and other communications)

FDA /ˌɛf di 'eɪ/ *abbr.* Food and Drug Administration (the U.S. government department that is responsible for making sure that food and drugs are safe to be sold)

FDIC /ˌɛf di aɪ 'si/ *abbr.* Federal Deposit Insurance Corporation (the U.S. government department that provides insurance for most private bank deposits)

fe·al·ty /'fiəlti/ *noun* [U] (*old use*) a promise to be loyal to someone, especially a king or queen

fear 🔊 /fɪr/ *noun*, *verb*
● *noun* [U, C] the bad feeling that you have when you are in danger, when something bad might happen, or when a particular thing frightens you: *Her eyes showed no fear.* ◆ *The child was shaking with fear.* ◆ ~ (of sb/sth) *(a) fear of the dark/spiders/flying, etc.* ◆ *We lived in constant fear of losing our jobs.* ◆ ~ (for sb/sth) *her fears for her son's safety* ◆ *Alan spoke of his fears for the future.* ◆ ~ (that…) *the fear that he had cancer* ◆ *The doctor's report confirmed our worst fears.*
IDM **for fear of sth/of doing sth | for fear (that)…** to avoid the danger of something happening: *We spoke quietly for fear of waking the guards.* ◆ *I had to run away for fear (that) he might one day kill me.* **in fear of/for your life** feeling frightened that you might be killed **put the fear of God**

ʌ cup   ə about   eɪ say   aɪ five   ɔɪ boy   aʊ now   oʊ go   ɚ bird

into sb to make someone very frightened, especially in order to make them do something **without fear or favor** (*formal*) in a fair way ⊃ more at STRIKE *v*.
● ***verb* 1** [T] to be frightened of someone or something, or frightened of doing something: *~ sb/sth All his employees fear him.* ◆ *to fear death/persecution/the unknown* ◆ *Don't worry, you have nothing to fear from us.* ◆ *~ **to do sth** (formal) He feared to tell them the truth.* ◆ *~ **doing sth** (formal) She feared going out at night.* **2** [T,I] to feel that something bad might have happened or might happen in the future: *~ sth She has been missing for three days now and police are beginning to fear the worst* (= think that she is dead). ◆ *~ sb/ sth + adj. Hundreds of people are feared dead.* ◆ **be feared to be/have sth** *Women and children are feared to be among the victims.* ◆ **it is feared (that)...** *It is feared (that) he may have been kidnapped.* ◆ *~ **(that)...** She feared (that) he might be dead.* ◆ (*formal or humorous*) *Never fear/Fear not* (= Don't worry), *I shall return.* **3 I fear** [I] (*formal*) used to tell someone that you think that something bad has happened or is true: *They are unlikely to get here on time, I fear.* ◆ *"He must be dead then." "I fear so."* ◆ *"She's not coming back?" "I fear not."*
PHR V 'fear for sb/sth to be worried about someone or something: *We fear for his safety.* ◆ *He feared for his mother, left alone on the farm.*

THESAURUS

fear

terror ◆ panic ◆ alarm ◆ fright

These are all words for the bad feeling you have when you are afraid.
fear the bad feeling that you have when you are in danger, when something bad might happen, or when a particular thing frightens you: *(a) fear of flying* ◆ *She showed no fear.*
terror a feeling of extreme fear: *His eyes were wild with terror.*
panic a sudden feeling of great fear that cannot be controlled and prevents you from thinking clearly: *I had a sudden moment of panic.*
alarm fear or worry that someone feels when something dangerous or unpleasant might happen: *The doctor said there was no cause for alarm.*
fright a feeling of fear, usually sudden: *I cried out in fright.*

FEAR OR FRIGHT?

Fright is a reaction to something that has just happened or is happening now. Use **fear**, but not **fright**, to talk about things that always frighten you and things that may happen in the future: ~~I have a fright of spiders.~~ ◆ ~~his fright of what might happen~~

PATTERNS
▪ a fear/terror **of** sth
▪ **in** fear/terror/panic/alarm/fright
▪ fear/terror/panic/alarm **that...**
▪ to be **filled with** fear/terror/panic/alarm
▪ a **feeling of** fear/terror/panic/alarm

fear·ful /ˈfɪrfl/ *adj.* **1** (*formal*) nervous and afraid: *~ (for sb) Parents are always fearful for their children.* ◆ *~ (of sth/of doing sth) fearful of an attack* ◆ *~ (that...) She was fearful that she would fail.* **2** [only before noun] (*formal*) terrible and frightening ▶ **fear·ful·ly** /-fəli/ *adv.*: *We watched fearfully.* **fear·ful·ness** noun [U]

fear·less /ˈfɪrləs/ *adj.* (*approving*) not afraid, in a way that people admire: *a fearless mountaineer* ▶ **fear·less·ly** *adv.* **fear·less·ness** noun [U]

fear·some /ˈfɪrsəm/ *adj.* (*formal*) making people feel very frightened

fea·si·ble /ˈfizəbl/ *adj.* that is possible and likely to be achieved **SYN** PRACTICABLE: *a feasible plan/suggestion/idea*

◆ *It's just not feasible to manage the business on a part-time basis.* **ANT** UNFEASIBLE ▶ **fea·si·bil·i·ty** /ˌfizəˈbɪləti/ *noun* [U]: *a feasibility study on the proposed new airport* ◆ *I doubt the feasibility of the plan.*

feast /fist/ *noun, verb*
● ***noun* 1** a large or special meal, especially for a lot of people and to celebrate something: *a wedding feast* **2** a day or period of time when there is a religious festival: *the feast of Christmas* ◆ *a feast day* **3** [usually sing.] a thing or an event that brings great pleasure: *a feast of colors* ◆ *The evening was a real feast for music lovers.*
● ***verb*** [I] *~ (on sth)* to eat a large amount of food, with great enjoyment
IDM **feast your eyes (on sb/sth)** to look at someone or something and get great pleasure

ˌFeast of 'Tabernacles *noun* [U] = SUKKOT
ˌFeast of 'Weeks *noun* [U] = SHAVUOTH

feat /fit/ *noun* (*approving*) an action or a piece of work that needs skill, strength, or courage: *The tunnel is a brilliant feat of engineering.* ◆ *to perform/attempt/achieve astonishing feats* ◆ *That was no mean feat* (= it was difficult to do).

feath·er 🔑 /ˈfɛðər/ *noun, verb*
● ***noun*** one of the many soft, light parts covering a bird's body: *a peacock feather* ◆ *a feather pillow* (= one containing feathers) ⊃ picture at ANIMAL
IDM **a feather in your cap** an action that you can be proud of **ORIGIN** This idiom comes from the Native American custom of giving a feather to someone who has been very brave in battle. ⊃ more at BIRD, KNOCK *v.*, RUFFLE *v.*, SMOOTH *v.*
● ***verb***
IDM **feather your (own) nest** to make yourself richer, especially by spending money on yourself that should be spent on something else ⊃ more at TAR *v.*

ˌfeather 'boa (also bo·a) *noun* a long, thin piece of clothing like a SCARF, made of feathers and worn over the shoulders by women, especially in the past

feath·er·brained /ˈfɛðərˌbreɪnd/ *adj.* (*informal, disapproving*) very silly

'feather ˌduster *noun* a stick with feathers on the end of it that is used for cleaning ⊃ picture at CLEANING

feath·ered /ˈfɛðərd/ *adj.* covered with feathers or having feathers

feath·er·weight /ˈfɛðərˌweɪt/ *noun* a BOXER weighing between 118 and 126 pounds (53.5–57 kg), heavier than a BANTAMWEIGHT

feath·er·y /ˈfɛðəri/ *adj.* light and soft; like feathers

fea·ture 🔑 **AWL** /ˈfitʃər/ *noun, verb*
● ***noun*** [C] **1** something important, interesting, or typical of a place or thing: *An interesting feature of the city is the old market.* ◆ *Teamwork is a key feature of the training program.* ◆ *Which features do you look for when choosing a car?* ◆ *The software has no particular distinguishing features.* ◆ *geographical features* ⊃ see also WATER FEATURE **2** [usually pl.] a part of someone's face such as their nose, mouth, and eyes: *his strong, handsome features* ◆ *Her eyes are her most striking feature.* **3** *~ (on sb/sth)* (in newspapers, on television, etc.) a special article or program about someone or something: *a special feature on education* **4** the main movie shown at a theater ⊃ see also DOUBLE FEATURE
● ***verb* 1** [T] to include a particular person or thing as a special feature: *~ sb/sth as sb/sth The movie features Cary Grant as a professor.* ◆ *~ sb/sth The latest model features alloy wheels and an electronic alarm.* ◆ *Many of the hotels featured in the brochure offer special deals on the weekend.* **2** [I] *~ (in sth)* to have an important part in something: *Olive oil and garlic feature prominently in his recipes.*

ˌfeature 'film *noun* a main movie with a story, rather than a DOCUMENTARY, etc.

feature-length *adj.* [usually before noun] of the same length as a typical movie

fea·ture·less /ˈfiːtʃərləs/ *adj.* without any qualities or noticeable characteristics: *The countryside is flat and featureless.*

fe·brile /ˈfebraɪl/ ˈfiː-/ *adj.* **1** (*formal*) nervous, excited, and very active: *a product of her febrile imagination* **2** (*medical*) (of an illness) caused by fever

Feb·ru·ar·y 🔑 /ˈfebjuˌeri; ˈfebru-/ *noun* [U, C] (*abbr.* Feb.)
the 2nd month of the year, between January and March
HELP To see how **February** is used, look at the examples at **April.**

fe·ces /ˈfiːsiz/ *noun* [pl.] (*formal*) solid waste material that leaves the body through the ANUS **SYN** EXCREMENT ▶ **fe·cal** /ˈfiːkl/ *adj.* [only before noun]

feck·less /ˈfekləs/ *adj.* having a weak character; not behaving in a responsible way: *Her husband was a charming, but lazy and feckless man.* ▶ **feck·less·ness** *noun* [U]

fe·cund /ˈfiːkənd/ *adj.* (*formal*) **1** able to produce a lot of children, crops, etc. **SYN** FERTILE **2** producing new and useful things, especially ideas ▶ **fe·cun·di·ty** /fɪˈkʌndəti/ *noun* [U]

Fed /fed/ *noun* (*informal*) **1** often **fed** [C, usually pl.] an officer of the FBI or another federal organization: *The feds were after him for armed robbery.* **2 the Fed** [sing.] = FEDERAL RESERVE SYSTEM **3 the feds** [pl.] (*CanE*) the federal government

fed pt, pp of FEED

fed·er·al 🔑 **AWL** /ˈfedərəl/ *adj.*
1 having a system of government in which the individual states of a country have control over their own affairs, but are controlled by a central government for national decisions, etc.: *a federal republic* **2** connected with national government rather than the local government of an individual state or PROVINCE: *a federal law* ◆ *state and federal income taxes* ▶ **fed·er·al·ly** *adv.*: *federally funded health care*

the Federal Bureau of Investigation *noun* [sing.] = FBI

fed·er·al·ist /ˈfedərəlɪst/ *noun* a supporter of a federal system of government ▶ **fed·er·al·ism** /ˈfedərəˌlɪzəm/ *noun* [U]: *The founders of the U.S. Constitution were strong believers in federalism.* **fed·er·al·ist** *adj.*: *a federalist government*

the Federal Reserve System (also the **Federal Reserve**) *noun* (*abbr.* the FRS) (also *informal* the Fed) [sing.] the organization that controls the supply of money in the U.S.

fed·er·ate /ˈfedəˌreɪt/ *verb* [I] (*technical*) (of states, organizations, etc.) to unite under a central government or organization while keeping some local control

fed·er·a·tion **AWL** /ˌfedəˈreɪʃn/ *noun* **1** [C] a country consisting of a group of individual states that have control over their own affairs but are controlled by a central government for national decisions, etc.: *the Russian Federation* **2** [C] a group of clubs, LABOR UNIONS, etc. that have joined together to form an organization: *the World Wrestling Federation* **3** [U] the act of forming a federation: *Some of the unions are against federation.*

fe·do·ra /fɪˈdɔːrə/ *noun* a low soft hat with a curled BRIM

fed up *adj.* [not before noun] (*informal*) bored or unhappy, especially with a situation that has continued for too long: *You look fed up. What's the matter?* ◆ **~ with sb/sth** *People are fed up with all these traffic jams.* ◆ *In the end, I just got fed up with his constant complaining.* ◆ *This noise has got to stop. I'm fed up with it.* ◆ **~ with doing sth** *I'm fed up with waiting for her.*

fee 🔑 **AWL** /fiː/ *noun*
1 an amount of money that you pay for professional advice or services: *legal fees* ◆ *Does the bank charge a fee for setting up the account?* ◆ *Some phone companies charge you for each call*

you make and some charge a **flat fee** (= an amount of money that allows you to make as many calls as you want).
➔ thesaurus box at RATE **2** an amount of money that you pay to join an organization, or to do something: *membership fees* ◆ *Is there an entrance fee to the park?*

fee·ble /ˈfiːbl/ *adj.* (**fee·bler** /ˈfiːblər/, **fee·blest** /ˈfiːbləst/)
1 very weak: *a feeble old man* ◆ *The heartbeat was feeble and irregular.* **2** not effective; not showing determination or energy: *a feeble argument/excuse/joke* ◆ *a feeble attempt to explain* ▶ **fee·ble·ness** *noun* [U] **fee·bly** /-bli/ *adv.*

feeble-minded *adj.* **1** (*old use*) having less than usual intelligence **2** weak and unable to make decisions

feed 🔑 /fiːd/ *verb, noun*
● *verb* (**fed**, **fed** /fed/)
▷ **GIVE/EAT FOOD 1** [T] to give food to a person or an animal: **~ sb/sth/yourself** *Have you fed the cat yet?* ◆ *The baby can't feed itself yet* (= can't put food into its own mouth). ◆ **~ sb/sth (on) sth** *The cattle are fed (on) barley.* ◆ **~ sth to sb/sth** *The barley is fed to the cattle.* **2** [I] (of a baby or an animal) to eat food: *Slugs and snails feed at night.* ➔ see also FEED ON/OFF STH **3** [T] **~ sb** to provide food for a family or group of people: *They have a large family to feed.* ◆ *There's enough here to feed an army.*
▷ **PLANT 4** [T] **~ sth** to give a plant a special substance to make it grow: *Feed the plants once a week.*
▷ **GIVE ADVICE/INFORMATION 5** [T] to give advice, information, etc. to someone or something: **~ sb (with) sth** *The media constantly feeds us (with) gossip and speculation.* ◆ **~ sth to sb** *Gossip and speculation are constantly fed to us by the media.*
▷ **SUPPLY 6** [T] to supply something to someone or something: **~ A (with B)** *The electricity line is fed with power through an underground cable.* ◆ **~ B into A** *Power is fed into the electricity line through an underground cable.*
▷ **PUT INTO MACHINE 7** [T] to put or push something into or through a machine: **~ A (with B)** *He fed the meter with coins.* ◆ **~ B into A** *He fed coins into the meter.* ◆ **~ sth into/through sth** *The fabric is fed through the machine.*
▷ **SATISFY NEED 8** [T] **~ sth** to satisfy a need, desire, etc. and keep it strong: *For drug addicts, the need to feed the addiction takes priority over everything else.* **IDM** see BITE *v.*, FACE *n.*
PHR V ˌfeed ˈback (into/to sth) to have an influence on the development of something by reacting to it in some way: *What the audience tells me feeds back into my work.* ˌfeed (sth)↔ˈback (to sb) to give information or opinions about something, especially so that it can be improved: *Test results will be fed back to the schools.* ˈfeed into sth to have an influence on the development of something: *The report's findings will feed into company policy.* ˈfeed on/off sth **1** (of an animal) to eat something: *Butterflies feed on the flowers of garden plants.* **2** (often *disapproving*) to become stronger because of something else: *Racism feeds on fear.* ˌfeed ˈthrough (to sb/sth) to reach someone or something after going through a process or system: *It will take time for the higher rates to feed through to investors.*

● *noun*
▷ **FOR ANIMALS/PLANTS 1** [U, C] food for animals or birds: *winter feed for the horses*
▷ **FOR MACHINE 2** [U] material supplied to a machine **3** [C] a pipe, device, etc. that supplies a machine with something: *the cold feed to the water tank* ◆ *The printer has an automatic paper feed.*
▷ **LARGE MEAL 4** [C] (*informal*) a large meal: *They needed a bath and a good feed.*
▷ **TELEVISION PROGRAMS 5** [U] television programs that are sent from a central station to other stations in a network; the system of sending out these programs: *network feed*
▷ **INTERNET 6** [C] = WEB FEED

feed·back /ˈfiːdbæk/ *noun* [U] **1** advice, criticism, or information about how good or useful something or someone's work is: *I'd appreciate some feedback on my work.* ◆ *The teacher will give you feedback on the test.* ◆ *We need both positive and negative feedback from our customers.* **2** the unpleasant noise produced by electrical equipment such as an AMPLIFIER when some of the power returns to the system

t **tea**   ţ **butter**   d **did**   k **cat**   g **got**   tʃ **chin**   dʒ **June**   f **fall**

feed·bag /'fidbæg/ *noun* a bag containing food for a horse, that you hang from its head

feed·er /'fidər/ *noun, adj.*

- *noun* **1** (used with an adjective or a noun) an animal or plant that eats a particular thing or eats in a particular way: *plankton feeders* **2** a part of a machine that supplies something to another part of the machine **3** a container filled with food for birds or animals
- *adj.* [only before noun] **1** (of roads, rivers, etc.) leading to a bigger road, etc.: *a feeder road to the freeway* **2** supplying goods, services, etc. to a large organization **3** (of animals on a farm) kept to be killed and used for meat

feed·ing /'fidɪŋ/ *noun* **1** [U] the act of giving food to a person, an animal, or a plant: *breast/bottle feeding* **2** [C] a meal of milk for a young baby; a meal for an animal: *her 11 o'clock feeding*

'feeding ,frenzy *noun* **1** an occasion when a group of SHARKS or other fish attack something **2** a situation in which a lot of people compete with each other in an excited way because they want to get something

feel /fil/ *verb, noun*

- *verb* (felt, felt /fɛlt/)
> WELL/SICK/HAPPY/SAD, ETC. **1** linking verb, [T] to experience a particular feeling or emotion: **+ adj.** *The heat made him feel faint.* ◆ *She sounded more confident than she felt.* ◆ *I was feeling guilty.* ◆ *You'll feel better after a good night's sleep.* ◆ *She felt betrayed.* ◆ *I feel sorry for him.* ◆ **+ adv./prep.** *How are you feeling today?* ◆ *I know exactly how you feel* (= I feel sympathy for you). ◆ **~ sth** *He seemed to feel no remorse at all.* ◆ **~ like sth** *I felt like a complete idiot.*
> BE/BECOME AWARE **2** [T] (not usually used in the progressive tenses) to notice or be aware of something because it is touching you or having a physical effect on you: **SYN** SENSE: **~ sth** *I could feel the warm sun on my back.* ◆ *She could not feel her legs.* ◆ *He felt a hand on his shoulder.* ◆ **~ sb/sth/yourself doing sth** *He felt a hand touching his shoulder.* ◆ *She could feel herself blushing.* ◆ **~ sb/sth/yourself do sth** *I felt something crawl up my arm.* ◆ *We felt the ground give way under our feet.* **3** [T] (not usually used in the progressive tenses) **~ sth** to become aware of something even though you cannot see it, hear it, etc. **SYN** SENSE: *Can you feel the tension in this room?*
> GIVE IMPRESSION **4** linking verb (not used in the progressive tenses) to give you a particular feeling or impression: **+ adj.** *It felt strange to be back in my old school.* ◆ *My mouth felt completely dry.* ◆ **~ like sth** *The interview only took ten minutes, but it felt like hours.* ◆ *It feels like rain* (= seems likely to rain). ◆ **~ as if/though…** *Her head felt as if it would burst.* ◆ *It felt as though he had run a marathon.* ◆ *How does it feel to be alone all day?* **HELP** In spoken English people often use like instead of as if or as though in this meaning: *He felt like he'd run a marathon.*
> TOUCH **5** linking verb (not used in the progressive tenses) to have a particular physical quality that you become aware of by touching: **+ adj.** *The water feels warm.* ◆ *Its skin feels really smooth.* ◆ **~ like sth** *This wallet feels like leather.* **6** [T] to deliberately move your fingers over something in order to find out what it is like: **~ sth** *Can you feel the bump on my head?* ◆ *Try to tell what this is just by feeling it.* ◆ **~ how, what, etc.…** *Feel how rough this is.*
> THINK/BELIEVE **7** [T, I] (not usually used in the progressive tenses) to think or believe that something is the case; to have a particular opinion or attitude: **~ (that)…** *We all felt (that) we had been cheated.* ◆ *I felt (that) I had to apologize.* ◆ **~ it to be sth** *She felt it to be her duty to tell the police.* ◆ **~ it + noun** *She felt it her duty to tell the police.* ◆ **~ it + adj.** *I felt it advisable to do nothing.* ◆ **(+ adv./prep.)** *This is something I feel strongly about.* ◆ *This decision is, I feel, a huge mistake.* ⊃ thesaurus box at THINK
> BE STRONGLY AFFECTED **8** [T] **~ sth** to experience the effects or results of something, often strongly: *He feels the cold a lot.* ◆ *Cathy was really feeling the heat.* ◆ *She felt her mother's death very deeply.* ◆ *The effects of the recession are being felt everywhere.* ◆ *We all felt the force of her arguments.*
> SEARCH WITH HANDS **9** [I] **~ (in sth/around, etc.) (for sth)**

to search for something with your hands, feet, etc.: *He felt in his pockets for some money.* ◆ *I had to feel around in the dark for the light switch.*

IDM **feel your age** to realize that you are getting old, especially compared with people you are with who are younger than you **feel your ears burning** to think or imagine that other people are talking about you **feel free (to do sth)** (*informal*) used to tell someone that they are allowed to do something: *Feel free to ask questions if you don't understand.* ◆ *"Can I use your phone?" "Feel free."* **feel good** to feel happy, confident, etc.: *It makes me feel good to know my work is appreciated.* **feel (it) in your bones (that…)** to be certain about something even though you do not have any direct proof and cannot explain why you are certain: *I know I'm going to fail this exam—I can feel it in my bones.* **feel like sth/like doing sth** to want to have or do something: *I feel like a drink.* ◆ *We all felt like celebrating.* ◆ *We'll go for a walk if you feel like it.* **feel the pinch** (*informal*) to not have enough money: *Lots of people who have lost their jobs are starting to feel the pinch.* **feel sick to your stomach** to feel as though you will VOMIT soon **feel your way 1** to move along carefully, for example when it is dark, by touching walls, objects, etc. **2** to be cautious about how you do things, usually because you are in a situation that you are not familiar with: *She was new to the job, still feeling her way.* **not feel yourself** to not feel healthy and well ⊃ more at DEATH, FLATTER, HONOR *n.*, HONOR *v.*, JELLY, MARK *n.*, MILLION, PRESENCE, SMALL *adj.*

PHR V **'feel for sb** to have sympathy for someone: *I really felt for her when her husband died.* ◆ *I do feel for you, honestly.* **,feel sb↔'up** (*informal*) to touch someone sexually, especially when they do not want you to **SYN** GROPE **,feel 'up to sth** to have the strength and energy to do or deal with something: *Do we have to go to the party? I really don't feel up to it.* ◆ **~ doing sth** *After the accident she didn't feel up to driving.*

- *noun* [sing.]
> TOUCH **1** the feel the feeling you get when you touch something or are touched: *You can tell it's silk by the feel.* ◆ *She loved the feel of the sun on her skin.* **2** an act of feeling or touching: *I had a feel of the material.*
> IMPRESSION **3** the impression that is created by a place, situation, etc.; atmosphere: *It's a big city but it has the feel of a small town.* ◆ *The room has a comfortable feel to it.*

IDM **get the feel of sth/of doing sth** to become familiar with something or with doing something: *I haven't got the feel of the brakes in this car yet.* **have a feel for sth** to have an understanding of something or be naturally good at doing it: *She has a real feel for languages.* ⊃ more at COP *v.*

feel·er /'filər/ *noun* [usually pl.] either of the two long, thin parts on the heads of some insects, and some animals that live in shells, that they use to feel and touch things with **SYN** ANTENNA

IDM **put out feelers** (*informal*) to try to find out what people think about a particular course of action before you do it

'feel-good *adj.* making you feel happy and pleased about life: *a feel-good movie*

feel·ing /'filɪŋ/ *noun*

> SOMETHING THAT YOU FEEL **1** [C] **~ (of sth)** something that you feel through the mind or through the senses: *a feeling of hunger/excitement/sadness, etc.* ◆ *guilty feelings* ◆ *I've got a tight feeling in my stomach.* ◆ (*informal*) *"I really resent the way he treated me." "I know the feeling."* (= I know how you feel) ◆ *"I'm going to miss you." "The feeling's mutual"* (= I feel exactly the same)."
> IDEA/BELIEF **2** [sing.] the idea or belief that a particular thing is true or a particular situation is likely to happen **SYN** IMPRESSION: **~ (of sth)** *He suddenly had the feeling of being followed.* ◆ **~ (that…)** *I got the feeling that he didn't like me much.* ◆ *I had a nasty feeling that we were lost.*
> ATTITUDE/OPINION **3** [U, C] an attitude or opinion about something: *The general feeling of the meeting was against the decision.* ◆ **~ (about/on sth)** *I don't have any strong feelings about it one way or the other.* ◆ *She had mixed feelings about*

giving up her job. ◆ My own feeling is that we should buy the cheaper one. ◆ Public feeling is being ignored by the government. **> EMOTIONS 4 feelings** [pl.] a person's emotions rather than their thoughts or ideas: He hates talking about his feelings. ◆ I didn't mean to **hurt your feelings** (= offend you). **5** [U, C] strong emotion: She spoke **with feeling** about the plight of the homeless. ◆ **Feelings are running high** (= people are very angry or excited).
> UNDERSTANDING 6 [U] the ability to understand someone or something, or to do something in a sensitive way: He played the piano with great feeling. ◆ **~ for sb/sth** She has a wonderful feeling for color.
> SYMPATHY/LOVE 7 [U, pl.] **~ (for sb/sth)** sympathy or love for someone or something: You have no feeling for the sufferings of others. ◆ I still **have feelings** for her (= feel attracted to her in a romantic way).
> PHYSICAL 8 [U] the ability to feel physically: I've lost all feeling in my legs.
> ATMOSPHERE 9 [sing.] the atmosphere of a place, situation, etc.: They managed to recreate the feeling of the original theater. **IDM bad/ill feeling** (also **bad/ill feelings**) anger between people, especially after an argument or a disagreement: There was a lot of bad feeling between the two groups of students. ⊃ more at HARD adj., SINK v., SPARE

feel·ing·ly /ˈfiːlɪŋli/ adv. with strong emotion
  SYN EMOTIONALLY: He spoke feelingly about his dead father.

feet pl. of FOOT

feign /feɪn/ verb **~ sth | ~ to do sth** to pretend that you have a particular feeling or that you are sick, tired, etc.: He survived the massacre by feigning death. ◆ "Who cares?" said Alex, feigning indifference.

feint /feɪnt/ noun, verb
● **noun** (especially in sports) a movement that is intended to make your opponent think you are going to do one thing when you are really going to do something else
● **verb** [I] (especially in sports) to confuse your opponent by making them think you are going to do one thing when you are really going to do something else

feist·y /ˈfaɪsti/ adj. (feist·i·er, feist·i·est) (informal, approving) (of people) strong, determined, and not afraid of arguing with people

fe·la·fel = FALAFEL

feld·spar /ˈfeldspɑːr; ˈfelspɑːr/ noun [U, C] a type of white or red rock

fe·lic·i·tous /fəˈlɪsətəs/ adj. (formal or literary) (especially of words) chosen well; very suitable; giving a good result
  SYN APT, HAPPY: a felicitous turn of phrase ▶ **fe·lic·i·tous·ly** adv.

fe·lic·i·ty /fəˈlɪsəti/ noun (pl. fe·lic·i·ties) (formal or literary) **1** [U] great happiness **2** [U] the quality of being well chosen or suitable **3 felicities** [pl.] well-chosen or successful features, especially in a speech or piece of writing

fe·line /ˈfiːlaɪn/ adj., noun
● **adj.** (formal) like a cat; connected with an animal of the cat family: She walks with feline grace.
● **noun** (formal) a cat; an animal of the cat family

fell /fel/ verb, adj. ⊃ see also FALL
● **verb 1 ~ sth** to cut down a tree **2 ~ sb** (literary) to make someone fall to the ground: He felled his opponent with a single blow.
● **adj.** (literary) very evil or violent
  IDM at/in one fell swoop all at the same time; in a single action, especially a sudden or violent one

fel·la (also **fell·er**) /ˈfelər/ noun (informal) **1** an informal way of referring to a man **2** an informal way of referring to someone's boyfriend: Have you met her new fella?

fel·low 🔊 /ˈfeloʊ/ noun, adj.
● **noun 1** (informal, becoming old-fashioned) a way of referring to a man or boy: He's a nice fellow. ⊃ see also FELLA **2** [usually pl.] (formal) a person that you work with or who is like you; a thing that is similar to the one mentioned: She

has a very good reputation among her fellows. ◆ Many caged birds live longer than their fellows in the wild. **3** a graduate student who holds a FELLOWSHIP: a graduate fellow ◆ a teaching fellow **4** a member of an academic or professional organization
● **adj.** [only before noun] used to describe someone who is the same as you in some way, or in the same situation: fellow members/citizens/workers ◆ my fellow passengers on the train

fellow 'feeling noun [U, C] a feeling of sympathy for someone because you have shared similar experiences

fel·low·ship /ˈfeloʊʃɪp; ˈfelə-/ noun **1** [U] a feeling of friendship between people who do things together or share an interest **2** [C] an organized group of people who share an interest, an aim, or a belief **3** [C] an award of money to a graduate student to allow them to continue their studies or to do research

fellow 'traveler noun **1** a person who is traveling to the same place as another person **2** a person who agrees with the aims of a political party, especially the Communist party, but is not a member of it

fel·on /ˈfelən/ noun (law) a person who has committed a felony

fe·lo·ni·ous /fəˈloʊniəs/ adj. (formal) relating to or involved in crime

fel·ony /ˈfeləni/ noun (pl. fel·o·nies) [C, U] (law) the act of committing a serious crime such as murder or RAPE; a crime of this type: a charge of felony ⊃ compare MISDE-MEANOR

felt /felt/ noun [U] a type of soft, thick cloth made from wool or hair that has been pressed tightly together: a felt hat ⊃ see also FEEL v.

felt-tip 'pen (also **'felt tip, 'felt-tipped 'pen**) noun a pen that has a point made of felt ⊃ picture at STATIONERY

fe·male 🔊 /ˈfiːmeɪl/ adj., noun
● **adj. 1** being a woman or a girl: a female student/employee/artist ◆ Two of the candidates must be female. **2** of the sex that can lay eggs or give birth to babies: a female cat **3** of women; typical of women; affecting women: female characteristics ◆ the female role ⊃ compare FEMININE **4** (biology) (of plants and flowers) that can produce fruit **5** (technical) (of electrical equipment) having a hole that another part fits into: a female plug **ANT** MALE
● **noun 1** an animal that can lay eggs or give birth to babies; a plant that can produce fruit **2** a woman or a girl: More females than males are employed in the factory. **ANT** MALE

fem·i·nine /ˈfemənən/ adj., noun
● **adj. 1** having the qualities or appearance considered to be typical of women; connected with women: That dress makes you look very feminine. ◆ He had delicate, almost feminine, features. ◆ the traditional feminine role ⊃ compare FEMALE, MASCULINE **2** (grammar) belonging to a class of words that refer to female people or animals and often have a special form: Some people prefer not to use the feminine form "actress" and use the word "actor" for both sexes. **3** (grammar) (in some languages) belonging to a class of nouns, pronouns, or adjectives that have feminine GENDER not MASCULINE or NEUTER: The French word for "table" is feminine.
● **noun** (grammar) **1 the feminine** [sing.] the feminine GENDER (= form of nouns, adjectives, and pronouns) **2** [C] a feminine word or word form ⊃ compare MASCULINE, NEUTER

fem·i·nin·i·ty /ˌfeməˈnɪnəti/ noun [U] the fact of being a woman; the qualities that are considered to be typical of women

fem·i·nism /ˈfeməˌnɪzəm/ noun [U] the belief and aim that women should have the same rights and opportunities as men; the struggle to achieve this aim

fem·i·nist /ˈfemənɪst/ noun a person who supports the belief that women should have the same rights and opportunities as men ▶ **fem·i·nist** adj. [usually before noun]: feminist demands/ideas/theories ◆ the feminist movement

fem·i·nize /'fɛmə,naɪz/ verb **1** ~ sb to make someone more like a woman **2** ~ sth to make something involve more women: *Offices became increasingly feminized during the 1960s.*

femme fa·tale /,fɛm fə'tæl; -'tɑl/ noun (pl. **femmes fa·tales** /,fɛm fə'tælz; -'tɑlz; -'tæl; -'tɑl/) (from *French*) a very beautiful woman that men find sexually attractive but who brings them trouble or unhappiness

femto- /'fɛmtoʊ/ combining form (technical) (in units of measurement) 10⁻¹⁵: *a femtosecond*

fe·mur /'fimər/ noun (pl. **fe·murs** or **fem·o·ra** /'fɛmərə/) (anatomy) the THIGH BONE ⊃ picture at BODY ▸ **fem·o·ral** /'fɛmərəl/ adj. [only before noun]

fen /fɛn/ noun an area of low, flat, wet land

fence 🔑 /fɛns/ noun, verb
• **noun 1** a structure made of wood or wire supported with posts that is put between two areas of land as a BOUNDARY, or around a yard, field, etc. to keep animals in, or to keep people and animals out **2** a structure that horses must jump over in a race or a competition **3** (informal) a criminal who buys and sells stolen goods **IDM** see GRASS n., MEND v., SIDE n., SIT
• **verb 1** [T] ~ sth to surround or divide an area with a fence: *His property is fenced with barbed wire.* ⊃ see also UNFENCED **2** [I] to take part in the sport of FENCING **3** [I] ~ (with sb) to speak to someone in a such a way as to gain an advantage in the conversation
PHRV ,fence sb/sth↔'in [often passive] **1** to surround someone or something with a fence **2** to restrict someone's freedom **SYN** HEM SB IN: *She felt fenced in by domestic routine.* ,fence sth↔'off [often passive] to divide one area from another with a fence

fence-,mending noun [U] an attempt to improve relations between two people or groups and to try to find a solution to a disagreement between them

fenc·er /'fɛnsər/ noun a person who takes part in the sport of FENCING

fenc·ing /'fɛnsɪŋ/ noun [U] **1** the sport of fighting with long, thin SWORDS ⊃ picture at SPORT **2** fences; wood, wire, or other material used for making fences: *The factory is surrounded by electric fencing.*

fend /fɛnd/ verb
PHRV ,fend for your'self to take care of yourself without help from anyone else: *His parents agreed to pay the rent on his apartment but otherwise left him to fend for himself.* ,fend sth/sb↔'off **1** to defend or protect yourself from something or someone that is attacking you **SYN** FIGHT OFF, WARD OFF: *The police officer fended off the blows with his riot shield.* **2** to protect yourself from difficult questions, criticisms, etc., especially by avoiding them **SYN** WARD OFF: *She managed to fend off questions about new tax increases.*

fend·er /'fɛndər/ noun **1** a part of a car that is above a wheel ⊃ picture at CAR **2** a curved cover over a wheel of a bicycle **3** a frame around a FIREPLACE to prevent burning coal or wood from falling out **4** a soft, solid object, such as an old tire or a piece of rope, that is hung over the side of a boat so that the boat is not damaged if it touches another boat, a wall, etc.

fender ,bender noun (informal) a car accident in which there is not a lot of damage

feng shui /,fʌŋ 'ʃweɪ/ noun [U] (from Chinese) a Chinese system for deciding the right position for a building and for placing objects inside a building in order to make people feel comfortable and happy

Fe·ni·an /'finiən/ noun a member of an organization formed in the 1850s in the U.S. and Ireland in order to end British rule in Ireland

fen·nel /'fɛnl/ noun [U] a vegetable that has a thick round STEM with a strong taste. The seeds and leaves are also used in cooking. ⊃ picture at FRUIT

fen·u·greek /'fɛnyə,grik; 'fɛnə-/ noun [U] a plant with hard yellow-brown seeds that are used in S. Asian cooking as a spice

fe·ral /'fɛrəl; 'fɪrəl/ adj. (of animals) living wild, especially after escaping from life as a pet or on a farm: *feral cats*

fer·ma·ta /fər'mɑtə; fɛr-/ noun (music) = PAUSE

fer·ment verb, noun
• **verb** /fər'mɛnt/ [I, T] to experience a chemical change because of the action of YEAST or bacteria, often changing sugar to alcohol; to make something change in this way: *Fruit juices ferment if they are kept for too long.* ♦ (figurative) A blend of emotions fermented inside her. ♦ ~ sth Red wine is fermented at a higher temperature than white. ▸ **fer·men·ta·tion** /,fərmɛn'teɪʃn; -mən-/ noun [U]
• **noun** /'fərmɛnt/ [U, sing.] (formal) a state of political or social excitement and confusion: *The country is in ferment.*

fer·mi·um /'fərmiəm/ noun [U] (symb. **Fm**) a chemical element. Fermium is a very rare RADIOACTIVE metal.

fern /fərn/ noun [C, U] a plant with large delicate leaves and no flowers that grows in wet areas or is grown in a pot. There are many types of ferns. ⊃ picture at PLANT ▸ **fern·y** adj.

fe·ro·cious /fə'roʊʃəs/ adj. very aggressive or violent; very strong **SYN** SAVAGE: *a ferocious beast/attack/storm* ♦ *a man driven by ferocious determination* ♦ *ferocious opposition to the plan* ♦ **fe·ro·cious·ly** adv.

fe·roc·i·ty /fə'rɑsəti/ noun [U] violence; aggressive behavior: *The police were shocked by the ferocity of the attack.*

fer·ret /'fɛrət/ noun, verb
• **noun** a small aggressive animal with a long, thin body, kept for chasing RABBITS from their holes, killing RATS, etc.
• **verb 1** [I] ~ (around) (for sth) (informal) to search for something that is lost or hidden among a lot of things: *She opened the drawer and ferreted around for her keys.* **2** [I] to hunt RABBITS, RATS, etc. using ferrets
PHRV ,ferret sb/sth↔'out (informal) to discover information or to find someone or something by searching thoroughly, asking a lot of questions, etc.

Fer·ris wheel /'fɛrəs ,wil/ noun a large wheel that stands in a vertical position at an AMUSEMENT PARK, with seats hanging at its edge for people to ride in

fer·rite /'fɛraɪt/ noun [U] **1** a chemical containing iron, used in electrical devices such as ANTENNAS **2** a form of pure iron found in steel that contains low amounts of CARBON

fer·ro·mag·net·ic /,fɛroʊmæg'nɛtɪk/ adj. (physics) having the kind of MAGNETISM that iron has

fer·rous /'fɛrəs/ adj. [only before noun] (technical) containing iron; connected with iron

fer·rule /'fɛrəl; -ul/ noun a piece of metal or rubber that covers the end of an umbrella or a stick to protect it

fer·ry /'fɛri/ noun, verb
• **noun** (pl. **fer·ries**) a boat or ship that carries people, vehicles, and goods across a river or across a narrow part of the ocean: *the Washington State ferry service* ♦ *We caught the ferry at Ludington, Michigan.* ♦ *the Port Angeles-Victoria, BC ferry crossing* ♦ *the Staten Island ferry* ♦ *a car/bike/pedestrian ferry* ⊃ picture at BOAT ⊃ collocations at TRAVEL
• **verb** (**fer·ries, fer·ry·ing, fer·ried, fer·ried**) [T, I] ~ **sb/sth** (+ adv./prep.) to carry people or goods in a boat or other vehicle from one place to another, often for a short distance and as a regular service: *He offered to ferry us across the river in his boat.* ♦ *The children need to be ferried to and from school.*

fer·ry·boat /'fɛri,boʊt/ noun a boat that is used as a ferry

fer·ry·man /'fɛrimən/ noun (pl. **fer·ry·men** /-mən/) a person in charge of a ferry across a river

fer·tile /'fərtl/ adj. **1** (of land or soil) that plants grow well in: *a fertile region* **ANT** INFERTILE **2** (of people, animals, or plants) that can produce babies, young animals, fruit, or new plants: *The treatment has been tested on healthy fertile women under the age of 35.* **ANT** INFERTILE **3** [usually before

---

i **see**   ɪ **sit**   ɛ **ten**   æ **cat**   ɑ **hot**   ɔ **saw**   ʊ **put**   u **too**

noun] that produces good results; that encourages activity: *a fertile partnership* ◆ *The region at the time was fertile ground for revolutionary movements* (= there were the necessary conditions for them to develop easily). **4** [usually before noun] (of a person's mind or imagination) that produces a lot of new ideas: *the product of a fertile imagination* ⊃ compare STERILE

fer·til·i·ty /fərˈtɪləti/ *noun* [U] the state of being fertile: *the fertility of the soil/land* ◆ *a god of fertility* ◆ *fertility treatment* (= medical help given to a person to help them have a baby) **ANT** INFERTILITY

fer·ti·lize /ˈfərtḷˌaɪz/ *verb* **1** ~ sth to put POLLEN into a plant so that a seed develops; to join SPERM with an egg so that a baby or young animal develops: *Flowers are often fertilized by bees as they gather nectar.* ◆ *a fertilized egg* **2** ~ sth to add a substance to soil to make plants grow more successfully ▸ **fer·til·i·za·tion** /ˌfərtḷəˈzeɪʃn/ *noun* [U]: *Immediately after fertilization, the cells of the egg divide.* ◆ *the fertilization of soil with artificial chemicals*

fer·ti·liz·er /ˈfərtḷˌaɪzər/ *noun* [C, U] a substance added to soil to make plants grow more successfully: *artificial/chemical fertilizers* ⊃ collocations at FARMING

fer·vent /ˈfərvənt/ *adj.* [usually before noun] having or showing very strong and sincere feelings about something **SYN** ARDENT: *a fervent admirer/believer/supporter* ◆ *a fervent belief/hope/desire* ▸ **fer·vent·ly** *adv.*

fer·vid /ˈfərvɪd/ *adj.* (*formal*) feeling something too strongly; showing feelings that are too strong ▸ **fer·vid·ly** *adv.*

fer·vor (*CanE usually* **fer·vour**) /ˈfərvər/ *noun* [U] very strong feelings about something **SYN** ENTHUSIASM: *She greeted them with unusual fervor.* ◆ *religious/patriotic fervor*

fess /fɛs/ *verb*
　PHR V ˌfess ˈup (*informal*) to admit that you have done something wrong **SYN** OWN UP

-fest /fɛst/ *combining form* (in nouns) a festival or large meeting involving a particular activity, or with a particular atmosphere: *a jazzfest* ◆ *a talkfest* (= a session involving long discussions) ◆ (usually *disapproving*) *a lovefest* (= an event in which people show too much affection for each other that may not be genuine)

fes·ter /ˈfɛstər/ *verb* **1** [I] (of a wound or cut) to become badly infected: *festering sores/wounds* **2** [I] (of bad feelings or thoughts) to become much worse because you do not deal with them successfully

fes·ti·val 🔑 /ˈfɛstəvl/ *noun*
1 a series of performances of music, plays, movies, etc., usually organized in the same place once a year; a series of public events connected with a particular activity or idea: *the Ravinia Festival* ◆ *the Cannes film festival* ◆ *a beer festival* ◆ *a rock festival* (= where bands perform, often outdoors and over a period of several days) **2** a day or period of the year when people stop working to celebrate a special event, often a religious one ⊃ see also HARVEST FESTIVAL

fes·tive /ˈfɛstɪv/ *adj.* typical of a special event or celebration: *a festive occasion* ◆ *The whole town is in a festive mood.*

fes·tiv·i·ty /fɛˈstɪvəti/ *noun* **1** festivities [pl.] the activities that are organized to celebrate a special event **2** [U] the happiness and enjoyment that exist when people celebrate something: *The wedding was an occasion of great festivity.* ◆ *an air of festivity*

fes·toon /fɛˈstun/ *verb, noun*
● *verb* [usually passive] ~ sb/sth (with sth) to decorate someone or something with flowers, colored paper, etc., often as part of a celebration
● *noun* a chain of lights, colored paper, flowers, etc., used to decorate something

Fest·schrift /ˈfɛstʃrɪft/ *noun* (from *German*) a collection of articles published in honor of a SCHOLAR

fet·a cheese /ˌfɛtə ˈtʃiz/ (also **fet·a**) *noun* [U] a type of Greek cheese made from sheep's milk

fe·tal /ˈfitl/ *adj.* [only before noun] connected with a fetus; typical of a fetus: *fetal abnormalities* ◆ *She lay curled up in a fetal position.*

ˌfetal ˈalcohol ˌsyndrome *noun* [U] (*medical*) a condition in which a child's mental and physical development are damaged because the mother drank too much alcohol while she was pregnant

fetch /fɛtʃ/ *verb* **1** [T] ~ sb/sth (*old-fashioned*) to go to where someone or something is and bring them/it back: *to fetch help / a doctor* ◆ *The inhabitants have to walk a mile to fetch water.* **2** [I, T] (of a dog) to bring back an object that someone has thrown: *Many dogs need to be trained to fetch.* ◆ ~ sth *Go fetch the bone!* **3** [T] ~ sth to be sold for a particular price **SYN** SELL FOR: *The painting is expected to fetch $10,000 at auction.*
　IDM fetch and carry (for sb) (*old-fashioned*) to do a lot of little jobs for someone as if you were their servant

fetch·ing /ˈfɛtʃɪŋ/ *adj.* (*old-fashioned*) (especially of a person or their clothes) attractive ▸ **fetch·ing·ly** *adv.*

fête (also **fete**) /feɪt; fɛt/ *noun, verb*
● *noun* a special occasion held to celebrate something: *a harvest fête*
● *verb* [usually passive] ~ sb (*formal*) to welcome, praise, or entertain someone publicly

fet·id /ˈfɛtəd/ *adj.* [usually before noun] (*formal*) smelling very unpleasant **SYN** STINKING

fet·ish /ˈfɛtɪʃ/ *noun* **1** (usually *disapproving*) the fact that a person spends too much time doing or thinking about a particular thing: *She has a fetish about cleanliness.* ◆ *He makes a fetish of his work.* **2** the fact of getting sexual pleasure from a particular object: *to have a leather fetish* **3** an object that some people worship because they believe that it has magic powers ▸ **fet·ish·ism** /ˈfɛtɪˌʃɪzəm/ *noun* [U] **fet·ish·ist** /-ˌʃɪst/ *noun* **fet·ish·is·tic** /ˌfɛtɪˈʃɪstɪk/ *adj.*

fet·ish·ize /ˈfɛtɪˌʃaɪz/ *verb* **1** ~ sth to spend too much time thinking about or doing something **2** ~ sth to get sexual pleasure from thinking about or looking at a particular thing

fet·lock /ˈfɛtlɑk/ *noun* the part at the back of a horse's leg, just above its HOOF, where long hair grows

fet·ter /ˈfɛtər/ *verb, noun*
● *verb* [usually passive] **1** ~ sb (*literary*) to restrict someone's freedom to do what they want **2** ~ sb to put chains around a prisoner's feet **SYN** SHACKLE
● *noun* **1** [usually pl.] (*literary*) something that stops someone from doing what they want: *They were at last freed from the fetters of ignorance.* **2** fetters [pl.] chains that are put around a prisoner's feet **SYN** CHAIN, SHACKLES

fet·tle /ˈfɛtl/ *noun* **IDM** see FINE *adj.*

fe·tus /ˈfitəs/ *noun* a young human or animal before it is born, especially a human more than eight weeks after FERTILIZATION

feud /fyud/ *noun, verb*
● *noun* an angry and bitter argument between two people or groups of people that continues over a long period of time: ~ (between A and B) *a long-running feud between the two artists* ◆ ~ (with sb) *a feud with the neighbors* ◆ *a family feud* (= within a family or between two families) ◆ ~ (over sb/sth) *a feud over money*
● *verb* [I] ~ (with sb) to have an angry and bitter argument with someone over a long period of time ▸ **feud·ing** *noun* [U]: *stories of bitter feuding between rival drug dealers*

feu·dal /ˈfyudl/ *adj.* [usually before noun] connected with or similar to feudalism: *the feudal system*

feu·dal·ism /ˈfyudlˌɪzəm/ *noun* [U] the social system that existed during the Middle Ages in Europe, in which people were given land and protection by a NOBLEMAN, and had to work and fight for him in return ▸ **feu·dal·is·tic** /ˌfyudlˈɪstɪk/ *adj.*

fe·ver /ˈfivər/ noun
1 [C, U] a medical condition in which a person has a temperature that is higher than normal: *He has a high fever.* ♦ *Aspirin should help reduce the fever.* ⊃ compare TEMPERA-TURE **2** [C, U] (old-fashioned) (used mainly in compounds) a particular type of disease in which someone has a high temperature: *She caught a fever on her travels in Africa, and died.* ⊃ see also HAY FEVER, RHEUMATIC FEVER, SCARLET FEVER, YELLOW FEVER **3** [sing.] ~ (of sth) a state of nervous excitement: *He waited for her arrival in a fever of impatience.* **4** [U] (especially in compounds) great interest or excite-ment about something: *election fever* ⊃ see also SPRING FEVER

fever blister noun = COLD SORE

fe·vered /ˈfivərd/ adj. [only before noun] **1** showing great excitement or worry: *fevered excitement/speculation* ♦ *a fevered imagination/mind* (= that imagines strange things) **2** (formal) suffering from a fever: *She mopped his fevered brow.*

fe·ver·few /ˈfivərfyu/ noun [U] a plant of the DAISY family, sometimes used as a medicine

fe·ver·ish /ˈfivərɪʃ/ adj. **1** [usually before noun] showing strong feelings of excitement or worry, often with a lot of activity or quick movements: *The whole place was a scene of feverish activity.* ♦ *a state of feverish excitement* ♦ *feverish with longing* **2** suffering from a fever; caused by a fever: *She was aching and feverish.* ♦ *a feverish cold/dream* ▶ **fe·ver·ish·ly** adv.: *The team worked feverishly up to the November deadline.* ♦ *Her mind raced feverishly.*

fever pitch noun [U, C] a very high level of excitement or activity: *Speculation about his future had reached fever pitch.* ♦ *Excitement has been at fever pitch for days.*

few /fyu/ det., adj., pron.
● **det., adj.** (few·er, few·est) **1** used with plural nouns and a plural verb to mean "not many": *Few people understand the difference.* ♦ *There seem to be fewer tourists around this year.* ♦ *Very few students learn Latin now.* **2** usually **a few** used with plural nouns and a plural verb to mean "a small number," "some": *We've had a few replies.* ♦ *I need a few things from the store.* ♦ *I try to visit my parents every few weeks.*
IDM few and far between not frequent; not happening often
● **pron. 1** not many people, things, or places: *Very few of his books are worth reading.* ♦ *You can pass with as few as 25 points.* ♦ (formal) *Few will argue with this conclusion.* **2** a few a small number of people, things, or places; some: *I recognized a few of the other people.* ♦ *I've seen most of his movies. Only a few are as good as his first one.* ♦ *Could you give me a few more details?* **3** fewer not as many as: *Fewer than 20 students passed all their courses.* ♦ *There are no fewer than 100 different species in the area.* **HELP** Look at the note at **less**. **4** the few used with a plural verb to mean "a small group of people": *Real power belongs to the few.* ♦ *She was one of the chosen few* (= the small group with special rights).
IDM quite a few a fairly large number: *I've been there quite a few times.* ♦ *Quite a few people are going to arrive early.* **have had a few (too many)** (informal) to have had enough alcohol to make you drunk

fey /feɪ/ adj. (literary, sometimes disapproving) (usually of a person) sensitive and rather mysterious or strange; not acting in a very practical way

fez /fez/ noun (pl. fez·zes) a round red hat with a flat top and a TASSEL but no BRIM, worn by men in some Muslim countries

ff abbr. (music) very loudly (from Italian "fortissimo")

ff. abbr. written after the number of a page or line to mean "and the following pages or lines": *See pp. 96 ff.*

fi·an·cé /ˌfiɑnˈseɪ; fiˈɑnseɪ/ noun the man that a woman is engaged to: *Linda and her fiancé were there.* ⊃ collocations at MARRIAGE

fi·an·cée /ˌfiɑnˈseɪ; fiˈɑnseɪ/ noun the woman that a man is engaged to: *Paul and his fiancée were there.* ⊃ collocations at MARRIAGE

fi·as·co /fiˈæskoʊ/ noun (pl. fias·cos or fias·coes) something that does not succeed, often in a way that causes embar-rassment **SYN** DISASTER: *What a fiasco!*

fi·at /ˈfiæt; -æt; -ət/ noun [C, U] (formal) an official order given by someone in authority **SYN** DECREE

fib /fɪb/ noun, verb
● **noun** (informal) a statement that is not true; a lie about something that is not important: *Stop telling fibs.*
● **verb** (-bb-) [I] (informal) to tell a lie, usually about something that is not important: *Come on, don't fib! Where were you really last night?* ▶ **fib·ber** noun: *You fibber!*

fi·ber /ˈfaɪbər/ noun **1** [U] the part of food that helps to keep a person healthy by keeping the BOWELS working and moving other food quickly through the body **SYN** ROUGHAGE: *dietary fiber* ♦ *Dried fruits are especially high in fiber.* ♦ *a high-/low-fiber diet* **2** [C, U] a material such as cloth or rope that is made from a mass of natural or artificial threads: *nylon and other man-made fibers* **3** [C] one of the many thin threads that form body TISSUE, such as muscle, and natural materials, such as wood and cotton: *cotton/wood/nerve/muscle fibers* ♦ (literary) *She loved him with every fiber of her being.* ⊃ see also MORAL FIBER, OPTICAL FIBER

fi·ber·board /ˈfaɪbərbɔrd/ noun [U] a building material made of wood or other plant fibers pressed together to form boards

fi·ber·glass /ˈfaɪbərˌglæs/ noun [U] a strong light material made from glass fibers and plastic, used for making boats, etc.

fiber optics noun [U] the use of thin fibers of glass, etc. for sending information in the form of light signals ▶ **fiber-optic** adj.: *fiber-optic cables*

Fi·bo·nac·ci se·ries /ˌfibəˈnɑtʃi ˈsɪriz; ˌfibə-/ noun (mathe-matics) a series of numbers in which each number is equal to the two numbers before it added together. Starting from 1, the series is 1,1,2,3,5,8,13, etc.

fi·brin /ˈfaɪbrən/ noun [U] (biology) a PROTEIN that stops blood from flowing or being lost from a wound

fi·brin·o·gen /faɪˈbrɪnədʒən/ noun [U] (biology) a PROTEIN in the blood from which fibrin is produced

fi·broid /ˈfaɪbrɔɪd/ noun (medical) a mass of cells that form a lump, usually found in the wall of a woman's UTERUS

fi·bro·ma /faɪˈbroʊmə/ noun (medical) a harmless lump that grows inside the body

fi·brous /ˈfaɪbrəs/ adj. [usually before noun] (technical) made of many fibers; looking like fibers: *fibrous tissue*

fib·u·la /ˈfɪbyələ/ noun (pl. fib·u·lae or fib·u·las) (anatomy) the outer bone of the two bones in the lower part of the leg between the knee and the ankle ⊃ picture at BODY ⊃ see also TIBIA

FICA /ˈfaɪkə/ abbr. Federal Insurance Contributions Act (a tax paid by employees and employers to provide money for SOCIAL SECURITY and MEDICARE)

fick·le /ˈfɪkl/ adj. (disapproving) **1** changing often and suddenly: *The weather here is notoriously fickle.* ♦ *the fickle world of fashion* **2** (of a person) often changing their mind in an unreasonable way so that you cannot rely on them: *a fickle friend* ▶ **fick·le·ness** noun [U]: *the fickleness of the New England climate*

fic·tion /ˈfɪkʃn/ noun **1** [U] a type of literature that describes imaginary people and events, not real ones: *a work of popular fiction* ♦ *historical/romantic fiction* **ANT** NONFICTION ⊃ collocations at LITERATURE ⊃ see also SCIENCE FICTION **2** [C, U] a thing that is invented or imagined and is not true: *For years he managed to keep up the fiction that he was not married.* **IDM** see TRUTH

fic·tion·al /ˈfɪkʃənl/ adj. not real or true; existing only in stories; connected with fiction: *fictional characters* ♦ *a fic-tional account of life on a desert island* ♦ *fictional techniques* **ANT** REAL-LIFE

fic·tion·al·ize /ˈfɪkʃənəˌlaɪz/ verb [usually passive] ~ sth to write a book or make a movie about a true story, but changing some of the details, characters, etc.: *a fictionalized account of his childhood*

fic·ti·tious /fɪkˈtɪʃəs/ *adj.* invented by someone rather than true: *All the places and characters in my novel are fictitious* (= they do not exist in real life).

fic·tive /ˈfɪktɪv/ *adj.* created by imagination **SYN** IMAGINARY: *the novel's fictive universe*

fid·dle /ˈfɪdl/ *noun, verb*
● *noun* [C] (*informal*) = VIOLIN
IDM **play second fiddle (to sb/sth)** to be treated as less important than someone or something; to have a less important position than someone or something else ➲ more at FIT *adj.*
● *verb* **1** [I] (*informal*) to play music on the VIOLIN **2** [I] **~ (with sth)** to keep touching or moving something with your hands, especially because you are bored or nervous: *He was fiddling with his keys while he talked to me.*
PHR V **fiddle aˈround** to spend your time doing things that are not important **fiddle aˈround with sth** | **ˈfiddle with sth 1** to keep touching something, or making small changes to something, because you are not satisfied with it: *I've been fiddling around with this design for ages.* **2** to touch or move the parts of something in order to try to change it or repair it: *Who's been fiddling with the TV again?*

fid·dler /ˈfɪdlər/ *noun* a person who plays the VIOLIN, especially to play FOLK MUSIC

fid·dle·sticks /ˈfɪdlˌstɪks/ *exclamation* (*old-fashioned*, *informal*) used to say that you disagree with someone

fid·dling /ˈfɪdlɪŋ/ *adj.* [usually before noun] (*informal*) small, unimportant, and often annoying

fi·del·i·ty /fɪˈdɛləti/ *noun* [U] **1 ~ (to sth)** (*formal*) the quality of being loyal to someone or something: *fidelity to your principles* **2 ~ (to sb)** the quality of being faithful to your husband, wife, or partner by not having a sexual relationship with anyone else: *marital/sexual fidelity* **ANT** INFIDELITY **3 ~ (of sth) (to sth)** (*formal*) the quality of being accurate: *the fidelity of the translation to the original text* ➲ see also HIGH FIDELITY

fidg·et /ˈfɪdʒət/ *verb, noun*
● *verb* [I] **~ (with sth)** to keep moving your body, your hands, or your feet because you are nervous, bored, excited, etc.: *Sit still and stop fidgeting!*
● *noun* a person who is always fidgeting

fidg·et·y /ˈfɪdʒəti/ *adj.* (*informal*) (of a person) unable to remain still or quiet, usually because of being bored or nervous **SYN** RESTLESS

fi·du·ci·ar·y /fɪˈduʃɪˌɛri/ *adj., noun* (*law*)
● *adj.* involving trust, especially in a situation where a person or company controls money or property belonging to others: *the company's fiduciary duty to its shareholders*
● *noun* (*pl.* fi·du·ci·ar·ies) a person or company that is in a position of trust, especially when it involves controlling money or property belonging to others

fief /fif/ (*also* fief·dom /ˈfifdəm/) *noun* **1** (*law*) (*old use*) an area of land, especially a rented area for which the payment is work, not money **2** an area or a situation in which someone has control or influence: *She considers the office as her own private fiefdom.*

field 🔑 /fild/ *noun, verb*
● *noun*
> AREA OF LAND **1** [C] an area of land in the country used for growing crops or keeping animals in, usually surrounded by a fence, etc.: *People were working in the fields.* ◆ *a plowed field* ◆ *a field of wheat* ◆ *We camped in a field near the town.* ➲ collocations at FARMING **2** [C] (usually in compounds) an area of land used for the purpose mentioned: *a landing field* ◆ *a medal for bravery in the field (of battle)* ➲ see also AIRFIELD, BATTLEFIELD, MINEFIELD **3** [C] (usually in compounds) a large area of land covered with the thing mentioned; an area from which the thing mentioned is obtained: *ice fields*

◆ *gas fields* ➲ see also COALFIELD, GOLDFIELD, OIL FIELD, SNOWFIELD
> SUBJECT/ACTIVITY **4** [C] a particular subject or activity that someone works in or is interested in **SYN** AREA: *famous in the field of music* ◆ *All of them are experts in their chosen field.* ◆ *This discovery has opened up a whole new field of research.*
> PRACTICAL WORK **5** [C] (usually used as an adjective) the fact of people doing practical work or study, rather than working in a library or laboratory: *a field study/investigation* ◆ *field research/methods* ◆ *essential reading for those working in the field* ➲ see also FIELD TRIP, FIELDWORK
> IN SPORTS **6** [C] (usually in compounds) an area of land used for playing a sport on: *a football, soccer, etc. field* ◆ *a sports field* ◆ *Today they take the field* (= go on to the field to play a game) *against Notre Dame.* ➲ picture at FOOTBALL ➲ see also PLAYING FIELD **7** [sing.] (in baseball) the team that is trying to catch the ball rather than hit it **8** [sing.] all the people or animals competing in a particular sports event: *The field includes three world-record holders.*
> IN BUSINESS **9** [sing.] all the people or products competing in a particular area of business: *They lead the field in home entertainment systems.*
> PHYSICS **10** [C] (usually in compounds) an area within which the force mentioned has an effect: *the earth's gravitational field* ◆ *an electro-magnetic field*
> COMPUTING **11** [C] part of a record that is a separate item of data: *You will need to create separate fields for first name, last name, and address.*
IDM **leave the field clear for sb** | **leave sb in possession of the field** to enable someone to be successful in a particular area of activity because other people or groups have given up competing with them **play the field** (*informal*) to have romantic relationships with a lot of different people
● *verb*
> CANDIDATE/TEAM **1** [T] **~ sb/sth** to provide a candidate, speaker, team, etc. to represent you in an election, a competition, etc.: *Each of the main parties fielded more than 300 candidates.* ◆ *This year the United States is fielding a very strong group of swimmers.*
> IN BASEBALL **2** [I] to be the person or the team that catches the ball and throws it back after someone has hit it: *Our team will field first.* **3** [T] **~ sth** to catch the ball and throw it back: *He expertly fielded the ball.*
> QUESTIONS **4** [T] **~ sth** to receive and deal with questions or comments: *The network had to field more than 300 phone calls after last night's program.*

ˈfield corn *noun* [U] CORN that is grown to feed animals

ˈfield day *noun* a special day at school when there are no classes and children compete in sports events
IDM **have a field day** to be given the opportunity to do something that you enjoy, especially something that other people do not approve of: *The media had a field day with the latest insider trading scandal.*

field·er /ˈfildər/ *noun* (in baseball) a member of the team that is trying to catch the ball rather than hit it ➲ picture at BASEBALL

ˈfield eˌvent *noun* [usually pl.] a sport done by ATHLETES that is not a race, for example jumping or throwing the JAVELIN ➲ compare TRACK EVENT

ˈfield ˌglasses *noun* [pl.] = BINOCULARS

ˈfield goal *noun* **1** (in football) a goal scored by kicking the ball over the bar of the goal **2** (in basketball) a goal scored by throwing the ball through the net during normal play

ˈfield hand *noun* = FARMHAND

ˈfield ˌhockey (*also* hock·ey) *noun* [U] a game played on a field by two teams of 11 players, with curved sticks and a small hard ball. Teams try to hit the ball into the other team's goal. ➲ picture at SPORT

ˈfield ˌhospital *noun* a temporary hospital near a BATTLEFIELD

ˈfield house *noun* **1** a building where sports events are held, with seats for people to watch **2** a building at a sports

t **tea**	ṭ **butter**	d **did**	k **cat**	g **got**	tʃ **chin**	dʒ **June**	f **fall**

field where people can change their clothes, take a shower, etc.

field·ing /ˈfildɪŋ/ noun [U] (in baseball) the activity of catching and returning the ball

field marshal noun (abbr. FM) an officer of the highest rank in the British army: *Field Marshal Montgomery*

field mouse noun a dark brown mouse with a long tail and large eyes

field of vision (also **field of view** or technical **visual field**) noun (pl. **fields of vision/view, visual fields**) the total amount of space that you can see from a particular point without moving your head

field–test verb ~ sth to test something, such as a piece of equipment, in the place where it will be used ▶ **field test** noun: *Laboratory and field tests have been conducted.*

field trip noun a trip made by a group of people, often students, to learn about something: *We went on a geology field trip.*

field·work /ˈfildwərk/ noun [U] research or study that is done in the real world rather than in a library or laboratory ▶ **field·work·er** noun

fiend /find/ noun **1** a very cruel or unpleasant person **2** (informal) (used after another noun) a person who is very interested in the thing mentioned **SYN** FANATIC: *a cross-word puzzle fiend* **3** an evil spirit

fiend·ish /ˈfindɪʃ/ adj. [usually before noun] **1** cruel and unpleasant: *a fiendish act* ◆ *shrieks of fiendish laughter* **2** (informal) extremely complicated, often in an unpleasant way: *a puzzle of fiendish complexity* ◆ *a fiendish plan* **3** (informal) extremely difficult: *a fiendish problem*

fiend·ish·ly /ˈfindɪʃli/ adv. (informal) very; extremely: *fiend-ishly clever/complicated*

fierce /fɪrs/ adj. (**fierc·er, fierc·est**) **1** (especially of people or animals) angry and aggressive in a way that is frightening: *a fierce dog* ◆ *Two fierce eyes glared at them.* ◆ *He suddenly looked fierce.* ◆ *She spoke in a fierce whisper.* **2** (especially of actions or emotions) showing strong feelings or a lot of activity, often in a way that is violent: *fierce loyalty* ◆ *the scene of fierce fighting* ◆ *He launched a fierce attack on the Democrats.* ◆ *Competition from abroad became fiercer in the 1990s.* **3** (of weather conditions or temperatures) very strong in a way that could cause damage: *fierce wind* ◆ *the fierce heat of the flames* ▶ **fierce·ly** adv.: *"Let go of that," she said fiercely.* ◆ *fiercely competitive* ◆ *The aircraft was burning fiercely.* **fierce·ness** noun [U]
IDM something fierce (informal) very much; more than usual: *I sure do miss you something fierce!*

fier·y /ˈfaɪəri/ adj. (**fier·i·er, fier·i·est**) [usually before noun] **1** looking like fire; consisting of fire: *fiery red hair* ◆ *The sun was now sinking, a fiery ball of light in the west.* **2** quickly or easily becoming angry: *She has a fiery temper.* ◆ *a fiery young man* **3** showing strong emotions, especially anger **SYN** PASSIONATE: *a fiery look* **4** (of food or drinks) causing a part of your body to feel as if it is burning: *a fiery Mexican dish*

fi·es·ta /fiˈɛstə/ noun (from Spanish) a public event when people celebrate and are entertained with music and dancing, usually connected with a religious festival in countries where the people speak Spanish

fife /faɪf/ noun a musical instrument like a small FLUTE that plays high notes and is used with drums in military music

fif·teen /ˌfɪfˈtin/ number 15 ▶ **fif·teenth** /ˌfɪfˈtinθ/ ordinal number, noun **HELP** There are examples of how to use ordinal numbers at the entry for **fifteen**.

fifth /fɪfθ/ ordinal number, noun
● ordinal number 5th: *Today is the fifth (of May).* ◆ *the fifth century B.C.* ◆ *It's her fifth birthday.* ◆ *My office is on the fifth floor.* ◆ *It's the fifth time that I've been to Mexico.* ◆ *Her mother had just given birth to another child, her fifth.* ◆ *the world's fifth-largest oil exporter* ◆ *He finished fifth in the race.* ◆ *Edward V (= Edward the fifth)*

● noun each of five equal parts of something: *She cut the cake into fifths.* ◆ *He gave her a fifth of the total amount.*
IDM take/plead the fifth to make use of the right to refuse to answer questions in court about a crime, because you may give information that will make it seem that you are guilty **ORIGIN** From the **Fifth Amendment** of the U.S. Constitution, which guarantees this right.

fifth column noun a group of people working secretly to help the enemy of the country or organization they are in ▶ **fifth columnist** noun

fifth generation adj. (computing) relating to a type of computer that is starting to be developed that uses ARTIFICIAL INTELLIGENCE

fifth·ly /ˈfɪfθli/ adv. used to introduce the fifth of a list of points you want to make in a speech or piece of writing: *Fifthly, we need to consider the effect on the local population.*

fif·ty /ˈfɪfti/ **1** number 50 **2** noun **the fifties** [pl.] numbers, years, or temperatures from 50 to 59: *She was born in the fifties.* ▶ **fif·ti·eth** /ˈfɪftiəθ/ ordinal number, noun **HELP** There are examples of how to use ordinal numbers at the entry for **fifth**.
IDM in your fifties between the ages of 50 and 59: *He retired when he was in his fifties.*

fifty–fifty adj., adv. (informal) divided equally between two people, groups, or possibilities: *Costs will be shared on a fifty-fifty basis between state and local governments.* ◆ *She has a fifty-fifty chance of winning* (= an equal chance of winning or losing). ◆ *Let's split this fifty-fifty.*

fig /fɪg/ noun a soft sweet fruit that is full of small seeds and often eaten dried: *a fig tree* ➔ picture at FRUIT

fig. abbr. **1** (in writing) FIGURE: *See fig. 3.* **2** (in writing) FIGURATIVE(LY)

fight 🔑 /faɪt/ verb, noun
● verb (**fought, fought** /fɔt/)
▷ IN WAR/BATTLE **1** [I, T] to take part in a war or battle against an enemy: *soldiers trained to fight* ◆ *He fought in Vietnam.* ◆ ~ **against sb** *My grandfather fought against them in World War II.* ◆ ~ **sb/sth to fight a war/battle** ◆ *They gathered soldiers to fight the invading army.* ➔ collocations at WAR
▷ STRUGGLE/HIT **2** [I, T] ~ (**sb**) to struggle physically with someone: *My little brothers are always fighting.*
▷ ARGUE **3** [I] ~ (**with sb**) (**about/over sth**) to have an argument with someone about something: *It's a trivial matter and not worth fighting about.*
▷ OPPOSE **4** [T, I] ~ (**sth**) to try hard to stop, deal with, or oppose something bad: *to fight racism/corruption/poverty, etc.* ◆ *Workers are fighting the decision to close the factory.* ◆ *The fire crews had problems fighting the blaze.* ◆ *He fought a long battle with cancer.* ◆ *We will fight for as long as it takes.*
▷ TRY TO GET/DO SOMETHING **5** [I, T] to try very hard to get something or to achieve something: ~ (**for sth**) *He's still fighting for compensation after the accident.* ◆ ~ **your way...** *She gradually fought her way to the top of the company.* ◆ ~ **to do sth** *Doctors fought for more than six hours to save his life.* ◆ *She'll fight like a tiger to protect her children.* ➔ thesaurus box at CAMPAIGN
▷ IN CONTEST **6** [I, T] to take part in a contest against someone: ~ **for sth** *She's fighting for a place on the national team.* ◆ ~ **sb/sth** *It was a hard-fought presidential campaign.*
▷ IN BOXING **7** [I, T] ~ (**sb**) to take part in a BOXING match: *Doctors fear he may never fight again.*
▷ LAW **8** [T, I] to try to get what you want in court: ~ (**sb**) **for sth** *He fought his wife for custody of the children.* ◆ ~ **sth** *I'm determined to fight the case.*

▶ **fight·ing** noun [U]: *Fighting broke out in three areas of the city last night.* ◆ *outbreaks of street fighting*
IDM fight fire with fire to use similar methods in a fight or an argument to those your opponent is using **fight for (your) life** to make a great effort to stay alive, especially when you are badly injured or seriously ill **a fighting chance** a small chance of being successful if a great effort is made **fighting spirit** a feeling that you are ready to fight very hard for something or to try something difficult

fighting words angry words that insult or challenge someone **fight like cats and dogs** to argue in a very angry way, especially regularly over a period of time: *We fought like cats and dogs when we were younger.* **fight a losing battle** to try to do something that you will probably never succeed in doing **fight to the death/finish** to fight until one of the two people or groups is dead, or until one person or group defeats the other **fight tooth and nail** to fight in a very determined way for what you want: *The residents are fighting tooth and nail to stop the new development.* **fight your own battles** to be able to win an argument or get what you want without anyone's help: *I wouldn't get involved—he's old enough to fight his own battles.* ⟳ more at LIVE¹, TOE *n.*

PHR V ,fight 'back (against sb/sth) to resist strongly or attack someone who has attacked you: *Don't let them bully you. Fight back!* ◆ *It is time to fight back against street crime.* ,fight sth↔'back to try hard not to do or show something, especially not to show your feelings: *I was fighting back the tears.* ,fight sb/sth↔'off to resist someone or something by fighting against them/it: *The jeweler was stabbed as he tried to fight the robbers off.* ,fight 'out sth | ,fight it 'out to fight or argue until an argument has been settled: *The conflict is still being fought out.* ◆ *They hadn't reached any agreement so we left them to fight it out.*

● **noun**
> **STRUGGLE 1** [C] a struggle against someone or something using physical force: **~ (with sb/sth)** *He got into a fight with a guy at the bar.* ◆ *a street/gang fight* ◆ **~ (between A and B)** *A fight broke out between rival groups of fans.* ◆ *a world title fight* (= fighting as a sport)
> **ARGUMENT 2** [C] **~ (with sb) (over/about sth)** an argument about something: *Did you have a fight with him?* ◆ *We had a fight over money.*
> **TRYING TO GET/DO SOMETHING 3** [sing.] the work of trying to destroy, prevent, or achieve something: **~ (against sth)** *the fight against crime* ◆ **~ (for sth)** *a fight for survival* ◆ **~ (to do sth)** *Workers won their fight to stop compulsory layoffs.*
> **COMPETITION 4** [sing.] a competition or an act of competing, especially in a sport: *The team put up a good fight* (= they played well) *but were finally beaten.* ◆ *She now has a fight on her hands* (= will have to play very well) *to make it through to the next round.* ⟳ note at CAMPAIGN
> **BATTLE/WAR 5** [C] a battle, especially for a particular place or position: *In the fight for control of Canada, the French were defeated.*
> **DESIRE TO FIGHT 6** [U] the desire or ability to keep fighting for something: *In spite of many defeats, they still had plenty of fight left in them.*

IDM a fight to the finish a sports competition, an election, etc. between sides that are so equal in ability that they continue fighting very hard until the end ⟳ more at PICK *v.*, SPOIL *v.*

THESAURUS

fight

clash ◆ brawl ◆ struggle ◆ scuffle

These are all words for a situation in which people try to defeat each other using physical force.

fight a situation in which two or more people try to defeat each other using physical force: *He got into a fight with a man in the parking lot.*

clash (*journalism*) a short fight between two groups of people: *Clashes broke out between police and demonstrators.*

brawl a noisy and violent fight involving a group of people, usually in a public place: *a drunken brawl in a bar*

struggle a fight between two people or groups of people, especially when one of them is trying to escape, or to get something from the other: *There were no signs of a struggle at the murder scene.*

scuffle a short and not very violent fight or struggle: *He was involved in a scuffle with a photographer.*

PATTERNS
- a fight/clash/brawl/struggle/scuffle **over** sth
- **in** a fight/brawl/struggle/scuffle
- a **violent** fight/clash/struggle
- to **be in/get into/be involved in** a fight/clash/brawl/scuffle
- a fight/clash/brawl/scuffle **breaks out**

fight·er /ˈfaɪtər/ *noun* **1** (also ˈfighter plane) a fast military plane designed to attack other aircraft: *a jet fighter* ◆ *a fighter pilot* ◆ *fighter bases* ⟳ picture at PLANE **2** a person who fights ⟳ see also FIREFIGHTER, FREEDOM FIGHTER, PRIZEFIGHT **3** (*approving*) a person who does not give up hope or admit that they are defeated

fighter-'bomber *noun* a military plane that can fight other planes in the air and also drop bombs

'fig leaf *noun* **1** a leaf of a FIG tree, traditionally used for covering the sex organs of naked bodies in paintings and on statues **2** a thing that is used to hide an embarrassing fact or situation

fig·ment /ˈfɪgmənt/ *noun*
IDM a figment of sb's imagination something that someone has imagined and that does not really exist

fig·ur·a·tive /ˈfɪgjərətɪv/ *adj.* [usually before noun] **1** (of language, words, phrases, etc.) used in a way that is different from the usual meaning, in order to create a particular mental picture. For example, "He exploded with rage" shows a figurative use of the verb "explode" ⟳ compare LITERAL, METAPHORICAL **2** (of paintings, art, etc.) showing people, animals, or objects as they really look: *a figurative artist* ⟳ compare ABSTRACT ▶ **fig·ur·a·tive·ly** *adv.*: *She is, figuratively speaking, holding a gun to his head.*

fig·ure 🔑 /ˈfɪgjər/ *noun, verb*
● **noun**
> **NUMBERS 1** [C, usually pl.] a number representing a particular amount, especially one given in official information: *the latest trade/sales/unemployment, etc. figures* ◆ *By 2009, this figure had risen to 14 million.* ◆ *Experts put the real figure at closer to 75%.* **2** [C] a symbol rather than a word representing one of the numbers between 0 and 9: *Write the figure "7" on the board.* ◆ *a six-figure salary* (= over 100,000 dollars) ◆ *His salary is now in six figures.* ⟳ see also DOUBLE FIGURES, SINGLE FIGURES **3** figures [pl.] (*informal*) the area of mathematics that deals with adding, multiplying, etc. numbers **SYN** ARITHMETIC: *Are you any good at figures?* ◆ *I'm afraid I don't have a head for figures* (= I am not good at adding, etc.).
> **PERSON 4** [C] a person of the type mentioned: *a leading figure in the music industry* ◆ *a political figure* ◆ *an authority figure* ⟳ see also FATHER FIGURE, MOTHER FIGURE **5** [C] the shape of a person seen from a distance or not clearly: *a tall figure in black*
> **SHAPE OF BODY 6** [C] the shape of the human body, especially a woman's body that is attractive: *She's always had a good figure.* ◆ *I'm watching my figure* (= trying not to get fat). ⟳ collocations at PHYSICAL
> **IN PAINTING/STORY 7** [C] a person or an animal in a drawing, painting, etc., or in a story: *The central figure in the painting is the artist's daughter.*
> **STATUE 8** [C] a statue of a person or an animal: *a bronze figure of a horse*
> **PICTURE/DIAGRAM 9** [C] (*abbr.* fig.) a picture, diagram, etc. in a book, that is referred to by a number: *The results are illustrated in figure 3 opposite.*
> **GEOMETRY 10** [C] a particular shape formed by lines or surfaces: *a five-sided figure* ◆ *a solid figure*
> **MOVEMENT ON ICE 11** [C] a pattern or series of movements performed on ice

IDM be/become a figure of fun to be/become someone that other people laugh at cut a... figure (of a person) to have a particular appearance: *He cut a striking figure in his*

---

h hat   m man   n no   ŋ sing   l leg   r red   y yes   w wet

white dinner jacket. **put a figure on sth** to say the exact price or number of something ⇨ more at FACT

• *verb*

> **BE IMPORTANT 1** [I] to be part of a process, situation, etc., especially an important part **SYN FEATURE:** *My feelings about the matter didn't seem to figure at all.* ♦ **~ (as sth) (in/on/ among sth)** *Do I still figure in your plans?* ♦ *The question of the peace settlement is likely to **figure** prominently in the talks.* ♦ *It did not figure high on her list of priorities.*

> **THINK/DECIDE 2** [T] (*informal*) to think or decide that something will happen or is true: **~ (that)**... *I figured (that) if I took a late plane from Seattle, I'd be in Miami by morning.* ♦ *We figured the sensible thing to do was to wait.* ♦ **~ sth** *That's what I figured.* ♦ **~ why, whether, etc....** *He tried to figure why she had come.*

> **CALCULATE 3** [T] **~ sth (at sth)** to calculate an amount or the cost of something: *We figured the attendance at 150,000.*

IDM **go figure** (*informal*) used to say that you do not understand the reason for something, or that you do not want to give an explanation for something because you think it is obvious: *People are more aware of the risks of smoking nowadays, but more young women are smoking than ever. Go figure!* **it/that figures** used to say that something was expected or seems logical: *"John called in sick." "That figures; he wasn't feeling well yesterday."* ♦ (*disapproving*) *"She was late again." "Yes, that figures."*

PHR V **'figure on sth** | **'figure on (sb/sth) doing sth** to plan something or to do something; to expect something (to happen) **SYN PLAN ON:** *I hadn't figured on getting home so late.* **,figure sb/sth↔'out 1** to think about someone or something until you understand them/it: *We couldn't figure her out.* ♦ **~ how, what, etc....** *I can't figure out how to do this.* **2** to calculate an amount or the cost of something **SYN WORK OUT: ~ how, what, etc....** *Have you figured out how much the trip will cost?*

fig·ured /ˈfɪɡyərd/ *adj.* [only before noun] (*technical*) decorated with a small pattern: *figured pottery*

,figure 'eight *noun* (*pl.* **figure eights**) a pattern or movement that looks like the shape of the number 8

fig·ure·head /ˈfɪɡyərˌhed/ *noun* **1** a person who is in a high position in a country or an organization but who has no real power or authority **2** a large wooden statue, usually representing a woman, that used to be fixed to the front end of a ship

'figure-,hugging *adj.* [usually before noun] (of a piece of clothing) tight in an attractive way that shows the shape of a woman's body

,figure of 'speech *noun* (*pl.* **figures of speech**) a word or phrase used in a different way from its usual meaning in order to create a particular mental picture or effect

'figure ,skating *noun* [U] a type of ICE SKATING in which you cut patterns in the ice and do jumps and spins ⇨ compare SPEED SKATING

fig·ur·ine /ˌfɪɡyəˈrin/ *noun* a small statue of a person or an animal, used as a decorative object

fil·a·ment /ˈfɪləmənt/ *noun* **1** a thin wire in a LIGHT BULB that produces light when electricity is passed through it **2** (*technical*) a long, thin piece of something that looks like a thread: *glass/metal filaments*

fil·bert /ˈfɪlbərt/ *noun* = HAZELNUT

filch /fɪltʃ/ *verb* **~ sth** (*informal*) to steal something, especially something small or not very valuable

file 🔑 **AWL** /faɪl/ *noun, verb*

• *noun* **1** a box or folded piece of thick paper for keeping loose papers together and in order: *a hanging file* ♦ *A stack of files awaited me on my desk.* ⇨ picture at STATIONERY **2** a collection of information stored together in a computer, under a particular name: *to access/copy/create/delete/ download/save a file* ♦ *Every file in the same folder must have a different name.* ⇨ see also PDF **3** a file and the information it contains, for example about a particular person or subject: *secret police files* ♦ *Your application will be kept on file*

(= in a file, to be used later). ♦ **~ on sb** to have/open/keep a confidential **file** on someone ♦ *Police have reopened the file* (= have started collecting information again) *on the missing girl.* **4** a metal tool with a rough surface for cutting or shaping hard substances or for making them smooth ⇨ picture at TOOL ⇨ see also NAIL FILE **5** a line of people or things, one behind the other: *They set off in file behind the teacher.* **IDM** see SINGLE *adj.*

• *verb* **1** [T] to put and keep documents, etc. in a particular place and in a particular order so that you can find them easily; to put a document into a file: **~ sth (+ adv./prep.)** *The forms should be filed alphabetically.* ♦ *Please file it in my "Research" file.* ♦ **~ sth away** *I filed the letters away in a drawer.* **2** [I, T] (*law*) to present something so that it can be officially recorded and dealt with: **~ for sth** *to file for divorce* ♦ **~ sth** *to file a claim/complaint/petition/lawsuit* ♦ **~ to do sth** *He filed to divorce his wife.* **3** [T] **~ sth** (of a journalist) to send a report or a story to your employer **4** [I] **+ adv./prep.** to walk in a line of people, one after the other, in a particular direction: *The doors of the museum opened and the visitors began to file in.* **5** [T] **~ sth (away/down, etc.)** to cut or shape something, or make something smooth, using a file: *to file your nails*

'file ,cabinet (also **'filing ,cabinet**) *noun* a piece of office furniture with deep drawers for storing files

'file clerk *noun* a person whose job is to FILE letters, etc. and do general office tasks

file·name /ˈfaɪlneɪm/ *noun* (*computing*) a name given to a computer file in order to identify it

'file ,sharing *noun* [U] the practice of sharing computer files with other people over the Internet or another computer network: *Illegal music file-sharing sites have spread through the Net.*

fi·let *noun* = FILLET

fil·i·al /ˈfɪliəl/ *adj.* [usually before noun] (*formal*) connected with the way children behave toward their parents: *filial affection/duty*

fil·i·bus·ter /ˈfɪləˌbʌstər/ *noun* (*politics*) a long speech made in Congress in order to delay a vote ▶ **filibuster** *verb* [I]

fil·i·gree /ˈfɪləɡri/ *noun* [U] delicate decoration made from gold or silver wire

fil·ing **AWL** /ˈfaɪlɪŋ/ *noun* **1** [U] the act of putting documents, letters, etc. into a file **2** [C] something that is placed in an official record: *a bankruptcy filing* **3 filings** [pl.] very small pieces of metal, made when a larger piece of metal is filed: *iron filings*

'filing ,cabinet *noun* = FILE CABINET

Fil·i·pi·no /ˌfɪləˈpinoʊ/ *noun, adj.*

• *noun* (*pl.* **Fil·i·pi·nos**) **1** [C] a person from the Philippines **2** [U] the language of the Philippines

• *adj.* connected with the Philippines, its people, or their language

fill 🔑 /fɪl/ *verb, noun*

• *verb*

> **MAKE FULL 1** [T, I] to make something full of something; to become full of something: **~ sth** *Please fill this glass for me.* ♦ *to fill a vacuum/void* ♦ *The school is filled to capacity.* ♦ *Smoke filled the room.* ♦ *The wind filled the sails.* ♦ *A Disney movie can always fill theaters* (= attract a lot of people to see it). ♦ **~ sth with sth** *to fill a hole with earth/a bucket with water* ♦ **~ sth + adj.** *Fill a pan half full of water.* ♦ **~ (with sth)** *The room was filling quickly.* ♦ *Her eyes suddenly filled with tears.* ♦ *The sails filled with wind.*

> **BLOCK HOLE 2** [T] **~ sth (with sth)** to block a hole with a substance: *The crack in the wall had been filled with plaster.* ♦ *I need to have two teeth filled* (= have FILLINGS put in them). ♦ (*figurative*) *The product has filled a gap in the market.*

> **WITH FEELING 3** [T] **~ sb (with sth)** to make someone have a strong feeling: *We were all filled with admiration for his achievements.*

> **WITH SMELL/SOUND/LIGHT 4** [T] **~ sth (with sth)** if a smell,

---

sound, or light **fills** a place, it is very strong, loud, or bright and easy to notice

> **-FILLED 5** (in adjectives) full of the thing mentioned: *a smoke-filled room ♦ a fun-filled day*

> **A NEED 6** [T] **~ sth** to stop people from continuing to want or need something: *More preschools will be built to fill the need for high-quality child care.*

> **JOB 7** [T] **~ sth** to do a job, have a role or position, etc.: *He fills the position satisfactorily* (= performs his duties well). *♦ The team needs someone to fill the role of manager very soon.* **8** [T] **~ sth** to appoint someone to a job: *The vacancy has already been filled.*

> **TIME 9** [T] **~ sth (up)** to use up a particular period of time doing something: *How do you fill your days now that you're retired?*

> **WITH FOOD 10** [T] **~ sb/yourself (up) (with sth)** (*informal*) to make someone/yourself feel unable to eat any more: *The kids filled themselves up with snacks.*

> **AN ORDER 11** [T] **~ sth** if someone **fills** an order or a **PRESCRIPTION**, they give the customer what they asked for ⊃ see also **UNFILLED**

IDM **fill sb's shoes** to do someone's job in an acceptable way when they are not there ⊃ more at **BILL** *n.*

PHRV ,fill 'in (for sb) to do someone's job for a short time while they are not there ,fill sth↔'in **1** to fill something completely: *The hole was filled in.* **2** to spend time doing something while waiting for something more important: *He filled in the rest of the day watching television.* **3** to complete a drawing, etc. by covering the space inside the outline with color ,fill sb 'in (on sth) to tell someone about something that has happened ,fill 'out to become larger, rounder, or fatter ,fill sth↔'out to complete a form, etc. by writing information on it: *to fill out an application form ♦ To order, fill out the coupon on p54.* ,fill 'up (with sth) | ,fill sth↔'up (with sth) to become completely full; to make something completely full: *The ditches had filled up with mud. ♦ to fill up the tank with oil*

● *noun* [sing.] **1 your ~ (of sth/sb)** as much of something or someone as you are willing to accept: *I've had my fill of entertaining for one week.* **2 your ~ (of food/drinks)** as much as you can eat/drink

fill·er /'fɪlər/ *noun* **1** [U, C] a substance used to fill holes or cracks, especially in walls before painting them **2** [C] (*informal*) something that is not important or not of good quality, but is used to complete something else because nothing better is available: *The song was originally a filler on their first album. ♦ pure beef burgers without any fillers* ⊃ see also **STOCKING STUFFER**

fil·let /'fɪleɪ/ *noun, verb*
● *noun* (also **fi·let**) [C, U] a piece of meat or fish that has no bones in it: *perch fillets ♦ a fillet of cod ♦ fillet of beef tenderloin*
● *verb* (fil·let·ing /-'leɪd/, fil·leted /-'leɪŋ/) **~ sth** to remove the bones from a piece of fish or meat; to cut fish or meat into fillets

fill·ing /'fɪlɪŋ/ *noun, adj.*
● *noun* **1** [C] a small amount of metal or other material used to fill a hole in a tooth: *I had to have two fillings at the dentist's today.* **2** [C, U] food put inside a **SANDWICH**, cake, **PIE**, etc.: *a pie with a mixed berry filling ♦ a wide range of sandwich fillings* **3** [C, U] soft material used to fill **CUSHIONS**, **PILLOWS**, etc.
● *adj.* (of food) making your stomach feel full: *This cake is very filling.*

'filling ,station *noun* (*old-fashioned*) = **GAS STATION**

fil·lip /'fɪləp/ *noun* [usually sing.] **~ (to/for sth)** (*formal*) a thing or person that causes something to improve suddenly **SYN** **BOOST**: *A drop in interest rates gave a welcome fillip to the housing market.*

'fill-up *noun* an occasion when a car is completely filled up with gas

fil·ly /'fɪli/ *noun* (*pl.* fil·ies) a young female horse ⊃ compare **COLT, MARE**

film 🔑 /fɪlm/ *noun, verb*
● *noun*
> **MOVING PICTURES 1** [C] a movie, especially a more serious or artistic one: *a documentary/feature film ♦ a silent film* (= one recorded without sound) *♦ an international film festival ♦ a film crew/critic ♦ the film version of the novel* **2** [U] the art or business of making movies: *to study film and photography ♦ the film industry* **3** [U] moving pictures of real events, shown for example on television **SYN** **FOOTAGE**: *television news film of the riots ♦ The accident was captured/caught on film.*

> **IN CAMERAS 4** [U] thin plastic that is sensitive to light, used for taking photographs and making movies; a roll of this plastic, used in cameras: *a roll of film ♦ 35 mm film ♦ to have film developed*

> **THIN LAYER 5** [C, usually sing.] **~ (of sth)** a thin layer of something, usually on the surface of something else **SYN** **COAT, COATING, LAYER**: *Everything was covered in a film of dust.*

● *verb* [I, T] to make a movie of a story or a real event: *They are filming in Utah right now. ♦ ~ sth The show was filmed on location in New York. ♦ ~ sb/sth doing sth Two young boys were filmed stealing CDs on the security video.* ▶ **film·ing** *noun* [U]: *Filming was delayed because of bad weather.*

film·ic /'fɪlmɪk/ *adj.* [only before noun] (*formal*) connected with movies

film·mak·er /'fɪlm,meɪkər/ *noun* a person who makes movies ▶ **film·mak·ing** *noun* [U]

film noir /,fɪlm 'nwɑr/ *noun* (from *French*) **1** [U] a style of making movies in which there are strong feelings of fear or evil; movies made in this style **2** [C] (*pl.* films noirs /,fɪlm 'nwɑr/) a movie made in this style

film·og·ra·phy /,fɪl'mɑgrəfi/ *noun* (*pl.* film·og·ra·phies) a list of movies made by a particular actor or director, or a list of movies that deal with a particular subject

film·strip /'fɪlmstrɪp/ *noun* a series of images on a film, through which light is shone to show them on a screen

film·y /'fɪlmi/ *adj.* [usually before noun] thin and almost transparent **SYN** **SHEER**: *filmy fabric/material*

filo pas·try /,fiːloʊ 'peɪstri/ (also **filo**) *noun* [U] a type of thin **PASTRY**, used in layers

fil·ter /'fɪltər/ *noun, verb*
● *noun* **1** a device containing paper, sand, chemicals, etc. that a liquid or gas is passed through in order to remove any materials that are not wanted: *an air/oil filter ♦ a coffee/water filter ♦ He smokes cigarettes without filters.* ⊃ picture at **COFFEE** **2** a device that allows only particular types of light or sound to pass through it **3** (*computing*) a program that stops particular types of electronic information, e-mail, etc. from being sent to a computer
● *verb* **1** [T] **~ sth** to pass liquid, light, etc. through a special device, especially to remove something that is not wanted: *All drinking water must be filtered. ♦ Use a sun block that filters UVA effectively.* ⊃ see also **FILTRATION** **2** [T] **~ sth** to use a special program to check the content of e-mails or websites before they are sent to your computer **3** [I] **+ adv./prep.** (of people) to move slowly in a particular direction: *The doors opened and people started filtering in.* **4** [I] **+ adv./prep.** (of information, news, etc.) to slowly become known: *More details about the crash are filtering through.* **5** [I] **+ adv./prep.** (of light or sound) to come into a place slowly or in small amounts: *Sunlight filtered in through the curtains.*
PHRV ,filter sth↔'out **1** to remove something that you do not want from a liquid, light, etc. by using a special device or substance: *to filter out dust particles/light/impurities* **2** to remove someone or something that you do not want from a large number of people or things using a special system, device, etc.: *The software filters out Internet sites whose content is not suitable for children.*

'filter ,tip *noun* a filter at the end of a cigarette that removes some of the harmful substances from the smoke; a cigarette that has this filter

ʌ cup   ə about   eɪ say   aɪ five   ɔɪ boy   aʊ now   oʊ go   ər bird

filth /fɪlθ/ *noun* [U] **1** any very dirty and unpleasant substance: *The floor was covered in grease and filth.* **2** words, magazines, etc. that are connected with sex and that are considered very offensive: *How can you read such filth?*

filth·y /ˈfɪlθi/ *adj., adv.*
• *adj.* (filth·i·er, filth·i·est) **1** very dirty and unpleasant: *filthy rags/streets* ♦ *It's filthy in here!* ⊃ thesaurus box at DIRTY **2** very rude and offensive and usually connected with sex: *filthy language/words* ♦ *He's got a filthy mind* (= is always thinking about sex). ▶ **filth·i·ly** /-θəli/ *adv.* **filth·i·ness** /-θinəs/ *noun* [U]
• *adv.* (*informal*) **1** ~ **dirty** extremely dirty **2** ~ **rich** so rich that you think the person is too rich and you find it offensive

fil·trate /ˈfɪltreɪt/ *noun* (*chemistry*) a liquid that has passed through a FILTER

fil·tra·tion /fɪlˈtreɪʃn/ *noun* [U] (*chemistry*) the process of FILTERING a liquid or gas

fin /fɪn/ *noun* **1** a thin, flat part that sticks out from the body of a fish, used for swimming and maintaining balance ⊃ picture at ANIMAL **2** a thin, flat part that sticks out from the body of a vehicle, an aircraft, etc., used for improving its balance and movement: *tail fins* ⊃ picture at PLANE

fi·na·gle /fɪˈneɪgl/ *verb* [T, I] ~ (sth) (*informal*) to behave dishonestly or to obtain something in an indirect or dishonest way: *He finagled some tickets for tonight's big game.*

fi·nal 🔑 **AWL** /ˈfaɪnl/ *adj., noun*
• *adj.* **1** [only before noun] being or happening at the end of a series of events, actions, statements, etc.: *his final act as senator* ♦ *The referee blew the final whistle.* ♦ *The project is in its final stages.* ♦ *I'd like to return to the final point you made.* ⊃ language bank at PROCESS[1] **2** [only before noun] being the result of a particular process: *the final product* ♦ *No one could have predicted the final outcome.* **3** that cannot be argued with or changed: *The judge's decision is final.* ♦ *Who has the final say around here?* ♦ *I'll give you $500 for it, and that's my final offer!* ♦ *I'm not coming, and that's final!* (= I will not change my mind) **IDM** see ANALYSIS, STRAW, WORD
• *noun* **1** the last of a series of games or competitions in which the winner is decided: *She reached the final of the 100m hurdles.* ♦ *the 2010 NBA Finals* (= the last few games in the competition) ⊃ see also QUARTER-FINAL, SEMIFINAL **2** an exam taken by school or college students at the end of a SEMESTER or school year on everything they have learned during the course: *I got an "A" on my American history final.*

final ˈclause *noun* (*grammar*) a CLAUSE that expresses purpose or intention, for example one that follows "in order that" or "so that"

fi·na·le /fɪˈnæli; -ˈnɑli/ *noun* **1** the last part of a show or a piece of music: *the rousing finale of Beethoven's Ninth Symphony* ♦ *The festival ended with a grand finale in Golden Gate Park.* **2** ~ (to sth) (after an adjective) an ending to something of the type mentioned: *a fitting finale to the day's events*

Final ˈFour *noun* [pl.] the four basketball teams that remain to compete in the last part of the annual college CHAMPIONSHIP

fi·nal·ist /ˈfaɪnl-ɪst/ *noun* a person who takes part in the final of a game or competition: *an Olympic finalist*

fi·nal·i·ty **AWL** /faɪˈnæləti; fɪ-/ *noun* [U] the quality of being final and impossible to change: *the finality of death* ♦ *There was a note of finality in his voice.*

fi·nal·ize **AWL** /ˈfaɪnl·aɪz/ *verb* ~ sth to complete the last part of a plan, trip, project, etc.: *to finalize your plans/arrangements* ♦ *They met to finalize the terms of the treaty.* ▶ **fi·nal·i·za·tion** /ˌfaɪnl·əˈzeɪʃn/ *noun* [U]

fi·nal·ly 🔑 **AWL** /ˈfaɪnl·i/ *adv.*
1 after a long time, especially when there has been some difficulty or delay **SYN** EVENTUALLY: *The performance finally started half an hour late.* ♦ *I finally managed to get her attention.* ♦ *When they finally arrived, it was well past midnight.* **2** used to introduce the last in a list of things **SYN** LASTLY: *And finally, I*

would like to thank you all for coming here today. ⊃ language bank at FIRST, PROCESS[1] **3** in a way that ends all discussion about something: *The matter was not finally settled until later.*

TOPIC COLLOCATIONS

Finance

income
- earn money/cash/(*informal*) a fortune
- make money/a fortune/(*informal*) a killing in the stock market
- acquire/inherit/amass wealth/a fortune
- build up funds/savings/principal/equity
- receive/leave (sb) an inheritance/a legacy
- live on a low wage/a fixed income/a pension
- get/receive/draw/collect a pension
- depend/be dependent on welfare/social security/food stamps

expenditure
- spend money/your savings/(*informal*) a fortune on…
- invest/put your savings in…/into…
- throw away/waste/(*informal*) shell out money on…
- lose your money/inheritance/pension/retirement savings
- use up/(*informal*) wipe out all your savings
- pay (in) cash
- pay by/use a credit/debit card
- pay by/use a/make out a/write sb a/accept a check
- change/exchange money/currency/traveler's checks
- give/pay/leave (sb) a deposit

banks
- have/hold/open/close/freeze a bank account/an account
- credit/debit/deposit sth into/take money out of your account
- deposit money/funds into your account
- withdraw money/cash/$50 from an ATM, etc.
- make a deposit/withdrawal
- find/go to/use an ATM
- be in debit/in the black/in good standing (= have money in the bank)/in the red/overdrawn (= owe money to the bank)

personal finance
- manage/handle/plan/run/organize your finances
- plan out/manage/work out/stick to a budget
- offer/extend credit (to sb)
- arrange for/take out a loan/overdraft protection
- pay back/repay money/a loan/a debt
- pay for sth in installments
- make weekly/monthly payments

financial difficulties
- get into debt/financial difficulties
- be short on/ (*informal*) be strapped for cash
- run out of/owe money
- face/get/ (*informal*) be slapped with a bill for $…
- can't afford the cost of…/payments/rent
- fall behind on the mortgage/payments/rent

- incur/run up/accumulate debts
- declare/file for bankruptcy
- tackle/reduce/settle your debts

fi·nance 🔑 **AWL** /ˈfaɪnæns; fəˈnæns/ *noun, verb*
• *noun* **1** [U] the activity of managing money, especially by a government or commercial organization: *the finance director/department/committee* ♦ *a specialization in banking and finance* ♦ *the world of high finance* (= finance involving large companies or countries) **2** finances [pl.] the money available to a person, an organization, or a country; the way this money is managed: *government/public/personal finances* ♦ *It's about time you got your finances in order.*

♦ *Buying a house put a severe strain on our finances.*
● **verb** ~ **sth** to provide money for a project **SYN** FUND: *The new bridge will be financed by the state government.* ♦ *He took a job to finance his stay in Brazil.*

'finance ˌcompany *noun* a company that lends money to people or businesses

fi·nan·cial 🔑 **AWL** /fəˈnænʃl; faɪ-/ *adj.* [usually before noun]
connected with money and finance: *financial services* ♦ *to give financial advice* ♦ *to be in **financial difficulties*** ♦ *an independent financial adviser* ♦ *Tokyo and New York are major financial centers.* ⊃ thesaurus box at ECONOMIC ▶ **fi·nan·cial·ly** **AWL** /-ʃəli/ *adv.*: *She is still **financially dependent** on her parents.* ♦ *Financially, I'm much better off than before.* ♦ *Such projects are not **financially viable** without government funding.*

fiˌnancial 'aid *noun* [U] money that is given or lent to students at an independent school, a college, or a graduate school who cannot pay the full cost of their education: *to apply for financial aid*

fin·an·cier **AWL** /ˌfaɪmænˈsɪr; ˌfɪnæn-; ˌfɪnənˈ/ *noun* a person who lends large amounts of money to businesses

fi·nanc·ing /ˈfaɪmænsɪŋ; fəˈnæn-/ *noun* [U] ~ **(for sth)** money used to run a business, an activity, or a project: *The project will only go ahead if they can raise the necessary financing.*

finch /fɪntʃ/ *noun* (often in compounds) a small bird with a short beak. There are several types of finches. ⊃ see also GOLDFINCH

find 🔑 /faɪnd/ *verb, noun*
● **verb** (found, found /faʊnd/)
▷ BY CHANCE **1** [T] to discover someone or something unexpectedly or by chance: ~ **sth** *Look what I found!* ♦ *We found a great new restaurant near the office.* ♦ ~ **sb/sth + adj.** *A whale was found washed up on the shore.*
▷ BY SEARCHING **2** [T] to get back something or someone that was lost after searching for it/them: ~ **sth for sb** *Can you find my bag for me?* ♦ ~ **sb sth** *Can you find me my bag?* ♦ ~ **sb/sth** *I wanted to talk to him but he was **nowhere to be found**.* ♦ ~ **sb/sth + adj.** *The child was found safe and well.*
▷ BY STUDYING/THINKING **3** [T] to discover something or someone by searching, studying, or thinking carefully: ~ **sth/sb** *scientists trying to find a cure for cancer* ♦ *I finally found a solution to the problem.* ♦ *I'm having trouble finding anything new to say on this subject.* ♦ *Have they found anyone to replace her yet?* ♦ ~ **sth for sb** *Can you find a hotel for me?* ♦ ~ **sb sth** *Can you find me a hotel?*
▷ BY EXPERIENCE/TESTING **4** [T] to discover that something is true after you have tried it, tested it, or experienced it: ~ **(that)…** *I find (that) it pays to be honest.* ♦ *The report found that 30% of the businesses studied had failed within a year.* ♦ ~ **sb/sth + adj./noun** *We found the beds very comfortable.* ♦ ~ **sb/sth to be/do sth** *They found him to be charming.* ♦ *Her blood was found to contain poison.* ♦ **it is found that…** *It was found that her blood contained poison.*
▷ HAVE OPINION/FEELING **5** [T] to have a particular feeling or opinion about something: ~ **sth + adj.** *You may find his story hard to believe.* ♦ *You may **find it hard** to believe his story.* ♦ *I find it amazing that they're still together.* ♦ ~ **sth + noun** *She finds it a strain to meet new people.* ⊃ thesaurus box at REGARD
▷ HAVE/MAKE AVAILABLE **6** [T] ~ **sth** to have something available so that you can use it: *I keep meaning to write, but never seem to find (the) time.* ♦ *How are we going to find $10,000 for a car?*
▷ IN UNEXPECTED SITUATIONS **7** [T] to discover someone or something/yourself doing something or in a particular situation, especially when this is unexpected: ~ **sb/sth/ yourself + adv./prep.** *She woke up and found herself in a hospital bed.* ♦ ~ **sb/sth/yourself + adj.** *We came home and found him asleep on the sofa.* ♦ ~ **sb/sth/yourself doing sth** *I suddenly found myself running down the street.* ♦ ~ **(that)…** *I was disappointed to find that they had already left.*
▷ REACH **8** [T] ~ **sth** (of things) to arrive at something naturally; to reach something: *Most of the money finds its way*

to the people who need it. ♦ *The criticism found its mark* (= had the intended effect).
▷ EXIST/GROW **9** [T] ~ **sth + adv./prep.** used to say that something exists, grows, etc. somewhere: *These cacti are found only in the Southwest.* ♦ *You'll find this style of architecture all over New Orleans.*
▷ IN COURT **10** [T, I] (*formal*) to make a particular decision in a court case: ~ **sb + adj.** *The jury found him guilty.* ♦ *How do you find the accused?* ♦ ~ **in sb's favor** *The court found in her favor.*
IDM **find fault (with sb/sth)** to look for and discover mistakes in someone or something; to complain about someone or something **find it in your heart/yourself to do sth** to be able or willing to do something: *Can you find it in your heart to forgive her?* ♦ *He couldn't find it in himself to trust anyone again.* **find your voice/tongue** to be able to speak or express your opinion **find your way (around)** to become able to act independently and with confidence: *I only recently joined the company so I'm still finding my way.* **find your way (to…)** to discover the right route (to a place): *I hope you can find your way home.* **find your/its way (to/into…)** to come to a place or a situation by chance or without intending to: *He eventually found his way into acting.* **take sb as you find them** to accept someone as they are without expecting them to behave in a special way or have special qualities ⊃ more at BEARING, MATCH *n.*, NOWHERE
PHRV **'find for/against sb** [no passive] (*law*) to make a decision in favor of/against someone in a court case: *The jury found for the defendant.* **ˌfind 'out (about sth/sb)** | **ˌfind 'out sth (about sth/sb)** to get some information about something or someone by asking, reading, etc.: *She'd been seeing him for a while, but didn't want her parents to find out.* ♦ *I haven't found anything out about him yet.* ♦ ~ **what, when, etc.…** *Can you find out what time the meeting starts?* ♦ ~ **that…** *We found out later that we had gone to the same school.* **ˌfind sb 'out** to discover that someone has done something wrong: *He had been cheating on his taxes, but it was years before he was found out.*
● **noun** a thing or person that has been found, especially one that is interesting, valuable, or useful: *an important archaeological find* ♦ *Our new babysitter is **a real find**.*

find·er /ˈfaɪndər/ *noun* a person who finds something ⊃ see also VIEWFINDER
IDM **finders keepers** (*saying*) (often used by children) anyone who finds something has a right to keep it

fin de siècle /ˌfæ̃ də ˈsyɛkl/ *adj.* (from *French*) typical of the end of the 19th century, especially of its art, literature, and attitudes

find·ing /ˈfaɪndɪŋ/ *noun* **1** [usually pl.] information that is discovered as the result of research into something: *The findings of the commission will be published today.* ⊃ collocations at SCIENTIFIC **2** (*law*) a decision made by the judge or jury in a court case

fine 🔑 /faɪn/ *adj., adv., noun, verb*
● **adj.** (fin·er, fin·est)
▷ VERY GOOD **1** [usually before noun] of high quality; good: *a very fine performance* ♦ *fine clothes/wines/workmanship* ♦ *a particularly fine example of Spanish colonial architecture* ♦ *people who enjoy the **finer things** in life* (= for example art, good food, etc.) ♦ *He tried to appeal to their **finer feelings*** (= feelings of duty, love, etc.). ♦ *It was his **finest hour*** (= most successful period) *as manager of the American team.*
▷ VERY WELL **2** (of a person) in good health: *"How are you?" "Fine, thanks."* ♦ *I was **feeling fine** when I got up this morning.* ⊃ thesaurus box at WELL
▷ ACCEPTABLE/GOOD ENOUGH **3** (also used as an exclamation) used to tell someone that an action, a suggestion, or a decision is acceptable: *"I'll leave this here, OK?" "Fine."* ♦ *"Bob wants to know if he can come too." "That's fine with me."* **4** used to say you are satisfied with something: *Don't worry. Your speech was fine.* ♦ *"What did you think of the restaurant?" "It was fine, but not as good as everyone says."* ♦ *You go on without me. I'll be fine.* ♦ *"Can I get you another drink?" "No, thanks. I'm fine."* ♦ (*ironic*) *This is a **fine** (= terrible) **mess** we're in!*

t **tea**   ţ **butter**   d **did**   k **cat**   g **got**   tʃ **chin**   dʒ **June**   f **fall**

♦ (*ironic*) *You're a fine one to talk!* (= you are not in a position to criticize, give advice, etc.)
> **ATTRACTIVE 5** [usually before noun] pleasing to look at: *a fine view* ♦ *a fine-looking woman* ♦ *a fine figure of a man*
> **DELICATE 6** [usually before noun] attractive and delicate: *fine bone china* ♦ *She has inherited her mother's fine features* (= a small nose, mouth, etc.).
> **WEATHER 7** bright and not raining: *a fine day/evening*
> **VERY THIN 8** very thin or narrow: *fine blond hair* ♦ *a fine thread* ♦ *a brush with a fine tip*
> **DETAIL/DISTINCTIONS 9** [usually before noun] difficult to see or describe **SYN** SUBTLE: *You really need a magnifying glass to appreciate all the fine detail.* ♦ *You don't need to make such fine distinctions.* ♦ *There's a fine line between love and hate* (= it is easy for one to become the other).
> **WITH SMALL GRAINS 10** made of very small grains: *fine sand* ♦ *Use a finer piece of sandpaper to finish.* **ANT** COARSE
> **PERSON 11** [only before noun] that you have a lot of respect for: *He was a fine man.*
> **WORDS/SPEECHES 12** sounding important and impressive but unlikely to have any effect: *Her speech was full of fine words that meant nothing.*
> **METALS 13** (*technical*) containing only a particular metal and no other substances that reduce the quality: *fine gold*
IDM **get sth down to a fine art** (*informal*) to learn to do something well and efficiently: *I spend so much time traveling that I've got packing down to a fine art.* **in fine fettle** (*old-fashioned, informal*) healthy; in good condition **not to put too fine a point on it** used to emphasize something that is expressed clearly and directly, especially a criticism: *Not to put too fine a point on it, I think you are lying.* ➔ more at LINE
● **adv.** (*informal*) in a way that is acceptable or good enough: *Keep going like that—you're doing fine.* ♦ *Things were going fine until you showed up.* ♦ *That arrangement suits me fine.*
IDM **cut it/things fine** (*informal*) to leave yourself just enough time to do something: *If we don't leave till after lunch we'll be cutting it very fine.*
● **noun** a sum of money that must be paid as punishment for breaking a law or rule: *a parking fine* ♦ *Offenders will be liable for a heavy fine* (= one that costs a lot of money). ♦ *She has already paid over $2,000 in fines.* ➔ collocations at JUSTICE ➔ thesaurus box at RATE
● **verb** [often passive] to make someone pay money as an official punishment: **~ sb (for sth/for doing sth)** *She was fined for speeding.* ♦ **~ sb sth (for sth/for doing sth)** *The company was fined $50,000 for breaching safety regulations.*

ˌfine ˈart *noun* [U] (also ˌfine ˈarts [pl.]) forms of art, especially painting, drawing, and SCULPTURE, that are created to be beautiful rather than useful

fine·ly /ˈfaɪnli/ *adv.*
1 into very small grains or pieces: *finely chopped herbs* **2** in a beautiful or impressive way: *a finely furnished room* **3** in a very delicate or exact way: *a finely tuned engine* ♦ *The competition was finely balanced throughout.*

fine·ness /ˈfaɪnnəs/ *noun* [U] **1** the quality of being made of thin threads or lines very close together: *fineness of detail* **2** (*technical*) the quality of something: *the fineness of the gold*

the ˌfine ˈprint (also the ˌsmall ˈprint) *noun* [U] the important details of an agreement or a legal document that are usually printed in small type and are therefore easy to miss: *Read all the fine print before signing.*

fin·er·y /ˈfaɪnəri/ *noun* [U] (*formal*) brightly colored and elegant clothes and jewelry, especially those that are worn for a special occasion

fi·nesse /fɪˈnɛs/ *noun, verb*
● **noun** [U] great skill in dealing with people or situations, especially in a delicate way
● **verb 1 ~ sth** to deal with something in a way that is skillful but slightly dishonest: *to finesse a deal* **2 ~ sth** to do something with a lot of skill or style

ˌfine-tooth ˈcomb (also ˌfine-toothed ˈcomb) *noun* a

COMB in which the pointed parts are thin and very close together
IDM **go over/through sth with a fine-tooth/fine-toothed comb** to examine or search something very carefully

ˌfine-ˈtune *verb* **~ sth** to make very small changes to something so that it is as good as it can possibly be ▶ **fine-ˈtuning** *noun* [U]: *The system is set up but it needs some fine-tuning.*

fin·ger /ˈfɪŋɡər/ *noun, verb*
● **noun 1** one of the four long, thin parts that stick out from the hand (or five, if the thumb is included): *She ran her fingers through her hair.* ♦ *Hold the material between finger and thumb.* ♦ *He was about to speak but she raised a finger to her lips.* ➔ collocations at PHYSICAL ➔ see also BUTTERFINGERS, FOREFINGER, INDEX FINGER, LITTLE FINGER, MIDDLE FINGER, RING FINGER **2** -**fingered** (in adjectives) having the type of fingers mentioned; having or using the number of fingers mentioned: *long-fingered* ♦ *nimble-fingered* ♦ *a four-fingered chord* ➔ see also LIGHT-FINGERED **3** the part of a glove that covers the finger **4 ~ (of sth)** a long, narrow piece of bread, cake, land, etc.: *The peninsula is a thin finger of farmland.* ➔ see also LADYFINGER
IDM **the finger of suspicion** if **the finger of suspicion** points or is pointed at someone, they are suspected of having committed a crime, being responsible for something, etc. **give sb the finger** (*informal*) to raise your middle finger in the air with the back part of your hand facing someone, done to be rude to someone or to show them that you are angry **have a finger in every pie** (*informal*) to be involved in a lot of different activities and have influence over them, especially when other people think that this is annoying **have/keep your finger on the pulse (of sth)** to always be aware of the most recent developments in a particular situation **lay a finger on sb** (usually used in negative sentences) to touch someone with the intention of hurting them physically: *I never laid a finger on her.* **not put your finger on sth** to not be able to identify what is wrong or different about a particular situation: *There was something odd about him but I couldn't put my finger on it.* **work your fingers to the bone** to work very hard ➔ more at BURN *v.*, COUNT *v.*, CROSS *v.*, LIFT *v.*, POINT *v.*, SLIP *v.*, SNAP *v.*, STICKY
● **verb 1 ~ sth** to touch or feel something with your fingers: *Gary sat fingering his beard, saying nothing.* **2 ~ sb (for sth)** | **~ sb (as sth)** (*informal*) to accuse someone of doing something illegal and tell the police about it: *Who fingered him for the burglaries?*

fin·ger·board /ˈfɪŋɡərbɔrd/ *noun* a flat strip on the neck of a musical instrument such as a GUITAR or VIOLIN, against which the strings are pressed to play different notes

ˈfinger ˌbowl *noun* a small bowl of water for washing your fingers during a meal

ˈfinger ˌfood *noun* [U, C] pieces of food that you can easily eat with your fingers

fin·ger·ing /ˈfɪŋɡərɪŋ/ *noun* [U, C] the positions in which you put your fingers when playing a musical instrument

fin·ger·nail /ˈfɪŋɡərneɪl/ *noun* the thin hard layer that covers the outer tip of each finger ➔ picture at BODY

fin·ger·print /ˈfɪŋɡərprɪnt/ *noun* a mark made by the pattern of lines on the tip of a person's finger, often used by the police to identify criminals ➔ see also GENETIC FINGERPRINTING ➔ thesaurus box at MARK ▶ **fingerprint** *verb* **~ sb**

fin·ger·print·ing /ˈfɪŋɡərprɪntɪŋ/ *noun* [U] the practice of recording someone's fingerprint, often used by the police to identify criminals ➔ see also DNA FINGERPRINTING, GENETIC FINGERPRINTING

fin·ger·tip /ˈfɪŋɡərtɪp/ *noun* [usually pl.] the end of the finger that is furthest from the hand
IDM **have sth at your fingertips** to have the information, knowledge, etc. that is needed in a particular situation and be able to find it easily and use it quickly

fin·i·al /ˈfɪniəl/ *noun* **1** (*architecture*) a decorative part at the top of a roof, wall, etc. **2** a decorative part that fits on the end of a curtain ROD (= pole)

fin·ick·y /ˈfɪnɪki/ *adj.* **1** (*disapproving*) too worried about what you eat, wear, etc.; disliking many things **SYN** FUSSY: *a finicky eater* **2** needing great care and attention to detail: *It's a very finicky job.*

fin·ish ⚿ /ˈfɪnɪʃ/ *verb, noun*

● *verb* **1** [T, I] to stop doing something or making something because it is complete: **~ (sth)** *Haven't you finished your homework yet?* ◆ *She finished law school last year.* ◆ *I thought you'd never finish!* ◆ *a beautifully finished piece of furniture* ◆ *He put the finishing touches on his painting* (= did the things that made it complete). ◆ **~ doing sth** *Be quiet! He hasn't finished speaking.* ◆ **+ speech** *"And that was all," she finished.* **2** [I, T] to come to an end; to bring something to an end: *The play finished at 10:30.* ◆ **~ with sth** *The symphony finishes with a flourish.* ◆ **~ sth** *A cup of coffee finished the meal perfectly.* **3** [T] **~ sth (off/up)** to eat, drink, or use what remains of something: *He finished off his drink with one large gulp.* ◆ *We might as well finish up the cake.* **4** [I] to be in a particular state or position at the end of a race or a competition: **+ adj.** *She was delighted to finish second.* ◆ *The dollar finished the day slightly down.* ◆ **+ noun** *She was delighted to finish a close second.* ◆ **+ adv./prep.** *He finished 12 seconds ahead of his closest rival.* **5** [T] **~ sb (off)** (*informal*) to make someone so tired or impatient that they cannot do any more: *Climbing that hill really finished me off.* ◆ *A lecture from my parents now would just finish me.* **PHR V** ˌfinish sb/sth↔ˈoff (*informal*) to destroy someone or something, especially someone or something that is badly injured or damaged: *The hunter moved in to finish the animal off.* ˌfinish sth↔ˈoff to do the last part of something; to make something end by doing one last thing: *I need about an hour to finish off this report.* ◆ *They finished off the show with one of their most famous songs.* ˈfinish with sth **1** to no longer need to use something: *When you're finished with the book, can I see it?* **2** (*informal*) to stop doing something: *I'm finished with gambling.* ˌfinish (up) with sth to have something at the end: *We had a five-course lunch and finished up with coffee and mints.* ◆ *We'll finish with a few songs.*

● *noun* **1** [C, usually sing.] the last part or the end of something: *a dramatic finish to the race* ◆ *It was a close finish, as they had predicted.* ◆ *They won in the end, but it was a tight finish.* ◆ *The story was a lie from start to finish.* ◆ *I want to see the job through to the finish.* ⊃ see also PHOTO FINISH **2** [C, U] the last covering of paint, polish, etc. that is put onto the surface of something; the condition of the surface: *a gloss/matte finish* ◆ *furniture available in a range of finishes* **3** [C, U] the final details that are added to something to make it complete: *The bows will give a feminine finish to the curtains.* **IDM** see FIGHT *n.*

fin·ished ⚿ /ˈfɪnɪʃt/ *adj.* **1** [not before noun] no longer doing something or dealing with someone or something: *I won't be finished for another hour.* ◆ **~ with sb/sth** *I'm not finished with you yet.* **2** [not before noun] no longer powerful, effective, or able to continue: *If the media find out, he's finished in politics.* ◆ *Their marriage was finished.* **3** [usually before noun] fully completed, especially in a particular way: *the finished product/article* ◆ *a beautifully finished suit*

fin·ish·er /ˈfɪnɪʃər/ *noun* a person or an animal that finishes a race, etc.

ˈfinishing ˌschool *noun* (*old-fashioned*) a private school for young women that teaches them how to behave in fashionable society

ˈfinish ˌline *noun* the line across a sports track, etc. that marks the end of a race: *The two horses crossed the finish line together.*

fi·nite **AWL** /ˈfaɪnaɪt/ *adj.* **1** having a definite limit or fixed size: *a finite number of possibilities* ◆ *The world's resources are finite.* **ANT** INFINITE **2** (*grammar*) a finite verb form or CLAUSE shows a particular tense, PERSON, and NUMBER:

"Am," "is," "are," "was," and "were" are the finite forms of "be"; "being" and "been" are the non-finite forms. **ANT** NONFINITE

fink /fɪŋk/ *noun* (*informal*) an unpleasant person

fiord = FJORD

fir /fər/ (also ˈfir tree) *noun* an EVERGREEN forest tree with leaves like needles ⊃ picture at TREE

fire ⚿ /ˈfaɪər/ *noun, verb*

● *noun*
▷ **SOMETHING BURNING 1** [U] the flames, light, and heat, and often smoke, that are produced when something burns: *Most animals are afraid of fire.* **2** [U, C] flames that are out of control and destroy buildings, trees, etc.: *The car was on fire.* ◆ *The warehouse has been badly damaged by fire.* ◆ *Several youths had set fire to the police car* (= had made it start burning). ◆ *A candle had set the curtains on fire.* ◆ *These thatched roofs frequently catch fire* (= start to burn). ◆ *forest fires* ◆ *Five people died in a house fire last night.* ◆ *A small fire started in the kitchen.* ◆ *Fires were breaking out everywhere.* ◆ *It took two hours to put out the fire* (= stop it from burning).
▷ **FOR HEATING/COOKING 3** [C] a pile of burning fuel, such as wood or coal, used for cooking food or heating a room: *to make/build a fire* ◆ *a log/charcoal fire* ◆ *Sam lit a fire to welcome us home.* ◆ *Come and get warm by the fire.* ◆ *We sat in front of a roaring fire.* ⊃ see also BONFIRE, CAMPFIRE
▷ **FROM GUNS 4** [U] shots from guns: *a burst of machine-gun fire* ◆ *to return fire* (= to fire back at someone who is shooting at you) ◆ *The gunmen opened fire on* (= started shooting at) *the police.* ◆ *Their vehicle came under fire* (= was being shot at). ◆ *He ordered his men to hold their fire* (= not to shoot). ◆ *A young girl was in the line of fire* (= between the person shooting and what he/she was shooting at).
▷ **ANGER/ENTHUSIASM 5** [U] very strong emotion, especially anger or enthusiasm: *Her eyes were full of fire.*
IDM be/come under/draw ˈfire to be criticized severely for something you have done: *The bank president has come under fire from all sides.* hang/hold ˈfire to delay or be delayed in taking action: *The project had hung fire for several years for lack of funds.* on ˈfire giving you a painful burning feeling: *He couldn't breathe. His chest was on fire.* play with ˈfire to act in a way that is not sensible and take dangerous risks ⊃ more at BALL, BAPTISM, FIGHT *v.*, FRYING PAN, HOUSE *n.*, IRON *n.*, SMOKE *n.*, WORLD

● *verb*
▷ **SHOOT 1** [I, T] to shoot bullets from a gun: *The officer ordered his men to fire.* ◆ **~ on sb/sth** *Soldiers fired on the crowd.* ◆ **~ sth** *They ran away as soon as the first shot was fired.* ◆ **~ (sth) (into sth)** *He fired the gun into the air.* ◆ **~ (sth) (at sb/sth)** *Missiles were fired at the enemy.* ⊃ collocations at WAR **2** [I, T] (of a gun) to shoot bullets out: *We heard the sound of guns firing.* ◆ **~ sth** *A starter's pistol fires only blanks.* **3** [T] **~ sth** to shoot an arrow: *She fired an arrow at the target.*
▷ **FROM JOB 4** [T] **~ sb** to force someone to leave their job **SYN** DISMISS: *We had to fire him for dishonesty.* ◆ *She got fired from her first job.* ◆ *He was responsible for hiring and firing staff.* ⊃ collocations at UNEMPLOYMENT
▷ **MAKE SOMEONE ENTHUSIASTIC 5** [T] **~ sb (with sth)** to make someone feel very excited about something or interested in something: *The talk had fired her with enthusiasm for the project.* ◆ *His imagination was fired by the film.*
▷ **OF ENGINE 6** [I] when an engine fires, an electrical SPARK is produced that makes the fuel burn and the engine start to work
▷ **-FIRED 7** (in adjectives) using the fuel mentioned in order to operate: *a gas-fired heating system*
▷ **CLAY OBJECTS 8** [T] **~ sth** to heat a CLAY object to make it hard and strong: *to fire pottery* ◆ *to fire bricks in a kiln*
IDM fire questions, insults, etc. at sb to ask someone a lot of questions one after another or make a lot of comments very quickly: *The room was full of journalists, all firing questions at them.* ⊃ more at CYLINDER
PHR V ˌfire aˈway (*informal*) used to tell someone to begin to speak or ask a question: *"I've got a few questions." "OK then, fire away."* ˌfire sth↔ˈoff **1** to shoot a bullet from a gun: *They fired off a volley of shots.* **2** to write or say something to

h hat   m man   n no   ŋ sing   1 leg   r red   y yes   w wet

someone very quickly, often when you are angry: *He fired off a letter of complaint.* ♦ *She spent an hour firing off e-mails to all concerned.* ˌfire sb↔'up to make someone excited or interested in something: *She's all fired up about her new job.* ˌfire sth↔'up (*informal*) to start a machine, piece of equipment, etc.: *We need to fire up one of the generators.*

'fire aˌlarm *noun* a bell or other device that gives people warning of a fire in a building: *Who set off the fire alarm?*

'fire ant *noun* a type of ANT (= a type of insect) that has a painful sting that is sometimes dangerous

fire·arm /'faɪərˌɑrm/ *noun* (*formal*) a gun that can be carried: *The police were issued with firearms.*

fire·ball /'faɪərˌbɔl/ *noun* a bright ball of fire, especially one at the center of an explosion

fire·bomb /'faɪərˌbɑm/ *noun* a bomb that causes a fire to start burning after it explodes ▸ fire·bomb *verb* ~ sth

fire·brand /'faɪərˌbrænd/ *noun* a person who is always encouraging other people to take strong political action, often causing trouble

fire·break /'faɪərˌbreɪk/ *noun* a thing that stops a fire from spreading, for example a special door or a strip of land in a forest that has been cleared of trees

fire·brick /'faɪərˌbrɪk/ *noun* [U, C] (*technical*) brick that is not destroyed by very strong heat; an individual block of this

fire·bug /'faɪərˌbʌɡ/ *noun* (*informal*) a person who deliberately starts fires

fire·crack·er /'faɪərˌkrækər/ *noun* a small FIREWORK that explodes with a loud noise

'fire deˌpartment *noun* [usually sing.] an organization of people who are trained and employed to put out fires and to rescue people from fires; the people who belong to this organization

'fire ˌdoor *noun* a heavy door that is used to prevent a fire from spreading in a building

'fire ˌdrill *noun* [C, U] a practice of what people must do in order to escape safely from a fire in a building

'fire-ˌeater *noun* an entertainer who pretends to eat fire

'fire ˌengine (also 'fire ˌtruck) *noun* a special vehicle that carries equipment for fighting large fires

'fire esˌcape *noun* metal stairs or a LADDER on the outside of a building, which people can use to escape from a fire ⊃ picture at HOUSE

'fire exˌtinguisher (also ex·tin·guish·er) *noun* a metal container with water or chemicals inside for putting out small fires

fire·fight /'faɪərˌfaɪt/ *noun* (*technical*) a battle where guns are used, involving soldiers or the police

fire·fight·er /'faɪərˌfaɪtər/ *noun* a person whose job is to put out fires ⊃ see also FIREMAN ▸ fire·fight·ing *noun* [U]: *firefighting equipment/vehicles*

fire·fly /'faɪərˌflaɪ/ *noun* (*pl.* fire·flies) (also 'lightning ˌbug) a flying insect with a tail that shines in the dark

'fire ˌhose *noun* a long tube that is used for directing water onto fires

fire·house /'faɪərˌhaʊs/ *noun* a FIRE STATION in a small town

'fire ˌhydrant (also hy·drant) *noun* a pipe in the street through which water can be sent using a PUMP in order to put out fires or to clean the streets

fire·light /'faɪərˌlaɪt/ *noun* [U] the light that comes from a fire in a room

fire·man /'faɪərmən/ *noun* (*pl.* fire·men /-mən/) a person, usually a man, whose job is to put out fires ⊃ see also FIREFIGHTER ⊃ note at GENDER

fire·place /'faɪərˌpleɪs/ *noun* an open space for a fire in the wall of a room

fire·pow·er /'faɪərˌpaʊər/ *noun* [U] the number and size of guns that an army, a ship, etc. has available: (*figurative*) *The company has enormous financial firepower.*

fire·proof /'faɪərˌpruf/ *adj.* able to resist great heat without burning or being badly damaged: *a fireproof door*

fire-retardant /'faɪər rɪˌtɑrdnt/ (also 'flame-reˌtardant) *adj.* [usually before noun] that makes a fire burn more slowly

'fire ˌsale *noun* 1 a sale of goods at low prices because they have been damaged by a fire or because they cannot be stored after a fire 2 a sale at low prices of things that a company or person owns, usually in order to pay debts: *The company was forced to have a fire sale of its assets.*

'fire ˌscreen *noun* 1 a metal frame that is put in front of a fire in a room to prevent people from burning themselves 2 a screen, often decorative, that is put in front of an open fire in a room to protect people from the heat or from SPARKS, or to hide it when it is not lit

fire·side /'faɪərˌsaɪd/ *noun* [usually sing.] the part of a room beside the fire: *sitting by the fireside*

'fire ˌstation *noun* a building for a FIRE DEPARTMENT and its equipment

fire·storm /'faɪərˌstɔrm/ *noun* 1 a very large fire, usually started by bombs, that is not under control and is made worse by the winds that it causes 2 an expression of intense anger or criticism: *The incident ignited a firestorm of controversy.*

fire·trap /'faɪərˌtræp/ *noun* a building that would be very dangerous if a fire started there, especially because it would be difficult for people to escape

'fire ˌtruck *noun* = FIRE ENGINE ⊃ picture at TRUCK

fire·wall /'faɪərˌwɔl/ *noun* (*computing*) a part of a computer system that is designed to prevent people from getting at information without authority but still allows them to receive information that is sent to them ⊃ collocations at E-MAIL

fire·wa·ter /'faɪərˌwɔtər; -ˌwɑtər/ *noun* [U] (*informal*) strong alcoholic drink

fire·wood /'faɪərˌwʊd/ *noun* [U] wood that has been cut into pieces to be used for burning in fires

fire·work /'faɪərˌwərk/ *noun* 1 [C] a small device containing powder that burns or explodes and produces bright colored lights and loud noises, used especially at celebrations: *to set off a few fireworks* ♦ *a firework(s) display* 2 fireworks [pl.] a display of fireworks: *When do the fireworks start?* 3 fireworks [pl.] (*informal*) strong or angry words; exciting actions: *There'll be fireworks when he finds out!*

fir·ing /'faɪərɪŋ/ *noun* 1 [U] the action of firing guns: *There was continuous firing throughout the night.* 2 [U, C] the action of forcing someone to leave their job: *teachers protesting against the firing of a colleague* ♦ *She's responsible for the hirings and firings.*

'firing ˌline *noun*
IDM be on the firing line 1 to be in a position where you can be shot at 2 to be in a position where people can criticize or blame you: *The labor secretary found himself on the firing line over recent job cuts.*

'firing ˌsquad *noun* [C, U] a group of soldiers who are ordered to shoot and kill someone who is found guilty of a crime: *He was executed by (a) firing squad.*

firm 🔑 /fərm/ *adj., adv., verb, noun*
● *adj.* (firm·er, firm·est) 1 fairly hard; not easy to press into a different shape: *a firm bed/mattress* ♦ *These peaches are still firm.* ♦ *Bake the cakes until they are firm to the touch.* 2 not likely to change: *a firm believer in free enterprise* ♦ *a firm agreement/date/decision/offer/promise* ♦ *firm beliefs/conclusions/convictions/principles* ♦ *We have no firm evidence to support the case.* ♦ *They remained firm friends.* 3 strongly fixed in place **SYN** SECURE: *Stand the fish tank on a firm base.* ♦ *No building can stand without firm foundations, and neither can a marriage.* 4 (of someone's voice or hand movements) strong and steady: *"No," she repeated, her voice firmer this time.* ♦ *With a firm grip on my hand, he pulled me away.* ♦ *Her handshake was cool and firm.* 5 (of someone's behavior,*

position, or understanding of something) strong and in control: *to exercise firm control/discipline/leadership* ◆ *Parents must be firm with their children.* ◆ *The company now has a firm footing in the marketplace.* ◆ *This book will give your students a firm grasp of English grammar.* ◆ *We need to keep a firm grip on the situation.* **6** [usually before noun] **~ (against sth)** (of a country's money, etc.) not lower than another: *The dollar remained firm against the pound, but fell against the yen.* ⊃ see also FIRMLY ▶ **firm·ness** *noun* [U]
IDM **be on firm ground** to be in a strong position in an argument, etc. because you know the facts: *Everyone agreed with me, so I knew I was on firm ground.* **a firm hand** strong control or discipline: *Those children need a firm hand to make them behave.* **take a firm stand (on/against sth)** to make your beliefs known and to try to make others follow them: *They took a firm stand against drugs in the school.*

● *adv.*
IDM **hold firm (to sth)** (*formal*) to believe something strongly and not change your mind: *She held firm to her principles.* **stand fast/firm** to refuse to move back; to refuse to change your opinions

● *verb* **1** [T] **~ sth** to make something become stronger or harder: *Firm the soil around the plant.* ◆ *This product claims to firm your body in six weeks.* **2** [I] **~ (to/at...)** (*finance*) (of shares, prices, etc.) to become steady or rise steadily: *The company's share price has firmed in recent days.*
PHR V **firm 'up** to become harder or more solid: *Put the mixture somewhere cool to firm up.* **firm 'up sth 1** to make arrangements more final and fixed: *The company has not yet firmed up its plans for expansion.* ◆ *The precise details still have to be firmed up.* **2** to make something harder or more solid: *A few weeks of Pilates will firm up that flabby stomach.*

● *noun* a business or company: *an engineering firm* ◆ *a firm of accountants* ⊃ collocations at BUSINESS

fir·ma·ment /'fɜrməmənt/ *noun* **the firmament** [sing.] (*old use* or *literary*) the sky: (*figurative*) *a rising star in the literary firmament*

firm·ly 🔑 /'fɜrmli/ *adv.*
in a strong or definite way: *"I can manage," she said firmly.* ◆ *It is now firmly established as one of the leading brands in the country.* ◆ *Keep your eyes firmly fixed on the road ahead.*

firm·ware /'fɜrmwɛr/ *noun* [U] (*computing*) a type of computer software that is stored in such a way that it cannot be changed or lost

first 🔑 /fɜrst/ *det., ordinal number, adv., noun*
● *det., ordinal number* **1** happening or coming before all other similar things or people; 1st: *his first wife* ◆ *It was the first time they had ever met.* ◆ *I didn't take the first bus.* ◆ *students in their first year of college* ◆ *your first impressions* ◆ *She resolved to do it at the first* (= earliest) *opportunity.* ◆ *King Edward I* (= said as "King Edward the First") ◆ *May 1st/the first of May* ◆ *His second book is better than his first.* **2** the most important or best: *Your first duty is to your family.* ◆ *She won first prize in the competition.* ◆ *an issue of the first importance*
IDM **there's a first time for everything** (*saying, humorous*) the fact that something has not happened before does not mean that it will never happen

● *adv.* **1** before anyone or anything else; at the beginning: *"Do you want a drink?" "I'll finish my work first."* ◆ *First I had to decide what to wear.* ◆ *Who came first in the race* (= who won)? ◆ *She plunged head first into the river to try and save the little boy.* **2** for the first time: *When did you first meet him?* **3** used to introduce the first of a list of points you want to make in a speech or piece of writing **SYN** FIRSTLY: *This method has two advantages: first it is cheaper and second it is quicker.* ⊃ language bank at PROCESS¹ **4** used to emphasize that you are determined not to do something: *She swore that she wouldn't apologize—she'd die first!*
IDM **at first** at or in the beginning: *I didn't like the job much at first.* ◆ *At first I thought he was shy, but then I discovered he was just not interested in other people.* ◆ (*saying*) *If at first you don't succeed, try, try again.* **come first** to be considered more important than anything else: *In any decision he*

makes, his family always comes first. **first and foremost** more than anything else: *He does a little teaching, but first and foremost he's a writer.* **first and last** in every way that is important; completely: *She regarded herself, first and last, as a musician.* **first come, first served** (*saying*) people will be dealt with, seen, etc. strictly in the order in which they arrive: *Tickets are available on a first come, first served basis.* **first of all 1** before doing anything else; at the beginning: *First of all, let me ask you something.* **2** as the most important thing: *The content of any article needs, first of all, to be relevant to the reader.* ⊃ language bank at PROCESS¹ **put sb/sth first** to consider someone or something to be more important than anyone/anything else: *She always puts her children first.* ⊃ more at FOOT *n.*, HEAD *n.*, SAFETY

━━━━━━━━━━━━━━━━━━━━━━━━
WHICH WORD?

first (of all) ◆ firstly ◆ at first
■ **First (of all)** and **firstly** are used to introduce a series of facts, reasons, opinions, etc: *The brochure is divided into two sections, dealing first of all/firstly with basic courses and second/secondly with advanced ones.* **First (of all)** is more common than **firstly**.
■ **At first** is used to talk about the situation at the beginning of a period of time, especially when you are comparing it with a different situation at a later period: *Maggie had seen him nearly every day at first. Now she saw him much less often.*

● *noun* **1 the first** [C] (*pl.* **the first**) the first person or thing mentioned; the first person or thing to do a particular thing: *I was the first in my family to go to college.* ◆ *Sheila and Jim were the first to arrive.* ◆ *I'd be the first to admit* (= I willingly admit) *I might be wrong.* ◆ *The first I heard about the wedding* (= the first time I became aware of it) *was when I saw it in the local paper.* **2** [C, usually sing.] an achievement, event, etc., never done or experienced before: *We went on a cruise, a first for both of us.* **3** (also **first 'gear**) [U] the lowest gear on a car, bicycle, etc. that you use when you are moving slowly: *He put the car in first and revved it.*
IDM **first among equals** the person or thing with the highest status in a group **from the (very) first** from the beginning: *They were attracted to each other from the first.* **from first to last** from beginning to end; during the whole time: *It's a fine performance that commands attention from first to last.*

━━━━━━━━━━━━━━━━━━━━━━━━
LANGUAGE BANK

first
ordering your points
■ This study has **the following** aims: **first**, to investigate how international students in America use humor; **second**, to examine how jokes can help to establish social relationships; and, **third**, to explore the role that humor plays in helping overseas students adjust to life in the U.S.
■ **Let us begin by** identifying some of the popular joke genres in the U.S.
■ **Next, let us turn to/Next, let us consider** the question of gender differences in the use of humor.
■ **Finally/Lastly**, let us briefly examine the role of humor in defining a nation's culture.
⊃ note LASTLY
⊃ Language Banks at CONCLUSION, PROCESS

first 'aid *noun* [U] simple medical treatment that is given to someone before a doctor comes or before the person can be taken to a hospital: *to give first aid* ◆ *a first-aid course* ◆ *a first-aid kit*

the ,First A'mendment *noun* [sing.] the statement in the U.S. Constitution that protects freedom of speech and religion and the right to meet in peaceful groups

ʌ **cup**   ə **about**   eɪ **say**   aɪ **five**   ɔɪ **boy**   aʊ **now**   oʊ **go**   ər **bird**

first 'balcony *noun* = DRESS CIRCLE

first 'base *noun* [sing.] (in baseball) the first of the BASES that players must touch: *He didn't make it past first base.* ⊃ picture at BASEBALL
IDM **not get to first base (with sth/sb)** (*informal*) to fail to make a successful start in a project, relationship, etc.; to fail to get through the first stage

first·born /ˈfɜːrstbɔːrn/ *noun* a person's first child ▸ **first-born** *adj.* [only before noun]: *their firstborn son*

first 'class *noun, adv.*
● *noun* [U] **1** the best and most expensive seats or rooms on a plane, train, or ship: *There is more room in first class.* **2** the class of mail that is used for letters
● *adv.* **1** using the best and most expensive seats or rooms in a plane, train, or ship: *to travel first class* **2** by the class of mail that is used for letters

first-'class *adj.* **1** [usually before noun] in the best group; of the highest standard **SYN** EXCELLENT: *a first-class novel* ◆ *a first-class writer* ◆ *The car was in first-class condition.* ◆ *I know a place where the food is first-class.* **2** [only before noun] connected with the best and most expensive way of traveling on a plane, train, or ship: *first-class plane travel* ◆ *a first-class cabin/seat/ticket* **3** [only before noun] connected with mail that costs the most to send: *first-class mail/ postage/stamps*

first 'cousin *noun* = COUSIN

first-de'gree *adj.* [only before noun] **1** ~ **murder, assault, robbery, etc.** murder, etc. of the most serious kind **2** ~ **burns** burns of the least serious of three kinds, affecting only the surface of the skin ⊃ compare SECOND-DEGREE, THIRD-DEGREE

first 'down *noun* (in football) **1** the first of a series of four DOWNS (= chances to move the ball forward ten yards) **2** the chance to start a new series of four DOWNS because your team has succeeded in going forward ten yards

first e'dition *noun* one of the copies of a book that was produced the first time the book was printed

first-'ever *adj.* [only before noun] never having happened or been experienced before: *his first-ever visit to Los Angeles* ◆ *the first-ever woman vice president*

the ˌfirst 'family *noun* [sing.] the family of the President of the United States

first 'finger *noun* = INDEX FINGER ⊃ picture at BODY

first 'floor *noun* usually **the first floor** [sing.] the floor of a building that is at the same level as the ground outside **SYN** GROUND FLOOR ▸ **first-'floor** *adj.* [only before noun]: *a first-floor apartment* ⊃ note at FLOOR

first 'fruit *noun* [usually pl.] the first result of someone's work or effort

first genˌer'ation *noun* [sing.] **1** people who have left their country to go and live in a new country; the children of these people **2** the first type of a machine to be developed: *the first generation of personal computers* ▸ **first-gener-'ation** *adj.*: *first-generation Korean-Americans*

first·hand /ˌfɜːrstˈhænd/ *adj.* [only before noun] obtained or experienced yourself: *to have firsthand experience of poverty* ⊃ compare SECONDHAND ▸ **first·hand** *adv.*: *to experience poverty firsthand*

first 'lady *noun* [usually sing.] **1 the First Lady** the wife of the President of the United States **2** the wife of the governor of a state **3** the woman who is thought to be the best in a particular profession, sport, etc.: *the first lady of country music*

first 'language *noun* the language that you learn to speak first as a child; the language that you speak best: *His first language is Spanish.* ⊃ compare SECOND LANGUAGE

first lieu'tenant *noun* **1** an officer in the U.S. army, AIR FORCE, or MARINE CORPS, just below the rank of a captain **2** an officer in the navy with responsibility for managing a ship, etc. **3** (*informal*) a person who is the next most important to someone

first 'light *noun* [U] the time when light first appears in the morning **SYN** DAWN, DAYBREAK: *We left at first light.*

first·ly /ˈfɜːrstli/ *adv.* used to introduce the first of a list of points you want to make in a speech or piece of writing: *There are two reasons for this decision: firstly…* ⊃ note at FIRST ⊃ language bank at FIRST

first 'mate (also ˌfirst 'officer) *noun* the officer on a commercial ship just below the rank of captain

first 'name (also 'given ˌname) *noun* a name that was given to you when you were born, that comes before your family name: *His first name is Tom and his last name is Green.* ◆ *The children all know each other by their first names.* ◆ *to be on a first-name basis with someone* (= to call them by their first name as a sign of a friendly, informal relationship)

First 'Nations *noun* [pl.] (*CanE*) the Aboriginal peoples of Canada, not including the Inuit or Métis ⊃ note at NATIVE AMERICAN

first 'night *noun* **1** the first public performance of a play, movie, etc. **2** a public celebration of NEW YEAR'S EVE

first of'fender *noun* a person who has been found guilty of a crime for the first time

first 'officer *noun* = FIRST MATE

the ˌfirst 'person *noun* [sing.] **1** (*grammar*) a set of pronouns and verb forms used by a speaker to refer to himself or herself, or to a group including himself or herself: *"I am" is the first person singular of the present tense of the verb "to be."* ◆ *"I," "me," "we," and "us" are first-person pronouns.* **2** a way of writing a novel, etc. as if one of the characters is telling the story using the word *I*: *a novel written in the first person* ⊃ compare THE SECOND PERSON, THE THIRD PERSON

first 'principles *noun* [pl.] the basic ideas on which a theory, system, or method is based: *I think we should go back to first principles.*

first-'rate *adj.* of the highest quality **SYN** EXCELLENT: *a first-rate swimmer* ◆ *The food here is absolutely first-rate.*

first re'fusal *noun* [U] the right to decide whether to accept or refuse something before it is offered to others: *Will you give me first refusal on the car, if you decide to sell it?*

first re·spond·er /ˌfɜːrst rɪˈspɑːndər/ *noun* a person such as a member of the police or fire department in a position to arrive first at an emergency, who has been trained to give basic medical treatment

first 'strike *noun* an attack on an enemy made before they attack you

first-string *adj.* [only before noun] (usually of a player on a sports team) very good and used regularly: *a first-string pitcher* ◆ *He's the first-string critic for our local paper.*

first-time *adj.* [only before noun] doing or experiencing something for the first time: *homes for first-time buyers* ◆ *a computer program designed for first-time users*

first-'timer *noun* a person who does something for the first time: *conference first-timers*

First 'World *noun* [sing.] the rich industrial countries of the world ⊃ compare THE THIRD WORLD

the ˌFirst World 'War *noun* [sing.] = WORLD WAR I

firth /fɜːrθ/ *noun* (especially in Scottish place names) a narrow strip of the ocean that runs a long way into the land, or a part of a river where it flows into the ocean: *the Moray Firth* ◆ *the Firth of Clyde*

fis·cal /ˈfɪskl/ *adj.* (*finance*) connected with government or public money, especially taxes: *fiscal policies/reforms* ⊃ thesaurus box at ECONOMIC ▸ **fis·cal·ly** /-kəli/ *adv.*

fiscal 'year (also 'tax year) *noun* [usually sing.] a period of twelve months over which the accounts and taxes of a company or a person are calculated

fish 🔊 /fɪʃ/ *noun, verb*
● *noun* (*pl.* **fish** or **fish·es**) **HELP** Fish is the usual plural form. The older form, **fishes**, can be used to refer to different

kinds of fish. **1** [C] a creature that lives in water, breathes through gills (GILL¹), and uses FINS and a tail for swimming: *They caught several fish.* ◆ *tropical/marine/ freshwater fish* ◆ **shoals** (= groups) *of fish* ◆ *a fish tank/pond* ◆ *There are about 30,000 species of fish in the world.* ◆ *The list of endangered species includes nearly 600 fishes.* ◆ *Fish stocks in the North Atlantic are in decline.* ⟳ *collocations at* LIFE ⟳ *see also* FLATFISH, SEA FISH, SHELLFISH **2** [U] the flesh of fish eaten as food: *frozen/smoked/fresh fish* ◆ *fish stew*
IDM **a fish out of water** a person who feels uncomfortable or awkward because he or she is in surroundings that are not familiar **have bigger/other fish to fry** to have more important or more interesting things to do **neither fish nor fowl** neither one thing nor another **there are plenty of other/more fish in the sea** there are many other people or things that are as good as the one someone has failed to get ⟳ *more at* BIG, COLD *adj.,* DIFFERENT, DRINK *v.,* SHOOT *v.*

• **verb** **1** [I] to try to catch fish with a hook, nets, etc.: *The trawler was fishing off the coast of Alaska.* ◆ **~ for sth** *You can fish for trout in this stream.* **2** [I] **go fishing** to spend time fishing for pleasure: *Let's go fishing this weekend.* **3** [T] **~ sth (for sth)** to try to catch fish in the area of water mentioned: *They fished the coastal waters for salmon.* **4** [I] **+ adv./prep.** to search for something, using your hands: *She fished around in her bag for her keys.*
PHR V **'fish for sth** to try to get something, or to find out something, although you are pretending not to: *to fish for compliments/information* **,fish sth/sb↔'out (of sth)** to take or pull something or someone out of a place: *She fished a piece of paper out of the pile on her desk.* ◆ *They fished a dead body out of the river.*

,fish and 'chips *noun* [U] a dish of fish that has been fried in BATTER, served with French fries (FRENCH FRY): *Three orders of fish and chips, please.*

'fish·bowl /'fɪʃboʊl/ *noun* = GOLDFISH BOWL

'fish cake *noun* pieces of fish mixed with MASHED potatoes made into a flat round shape, covered with BREADCRUMBS and fried

fish·er·man /'fɪʃərmən/ *noun* (*pl.* fish·er·men /-mən/) a person who catches fish, either as a job or as a sport ⟳ *compare* ANGLER

fish·er·wom·an /'fɪʃər,wʊmən/ *noun* (*pl.* fish·er·wom·en /-,wɪmən/) a woman who catches fish, either as a job or as a sport ⟳ *compare* ANGLER

fish·er·y /'fɪʃəri/ *noun* (*pl.* fish·er·ies) **1** a part of the ocean or a river where fish are caught in large quantities: *a herring fishery* ◆ *coastal/freshwater fisheries* **2** = FISH FARM: *a trout fishery*

'fish·eye lens /'fɪʃaɪ ˌlɛnz/ *noun* a camera LENS with a wide angle that gives the view a curved shape

'fish farm (also fishery) *noun* a place where fish are bred as a business

'fish hook *noun* a sharp metal hook for catching fish, with a point that curves backward to make it difficult to pull out ⟳ *picture at* HOOK

fish·ing /'fɪʃɪŋ/ *noun* [U] the sport or business of catching fish: *They often go fishing.* ◆ *deep-sea fishing* ◆ *a fishing boat* ◆ *fishing grounds* ◆ *We enjoyed a day of fishing by the river.*

'fishing ,line *noun* [C, U] a long thread with a sharp hook attached to it, which is used for catching fish

'fishing ,rod (also 'fishing ,pole, rod) *noun* a long wooden or plastic stick with a fishing line and hook attached to it, which is used for catching fish

'fishing ,tackle *noun* [U] equipment used for catching fish

'fish knife *noun* a knife with a broad blade and without a sharp edge, used for eating fish

fish·mon·ger /'fɪʃ,mʌŋgər; -,mɑŋ-/ *noun* (*old-fashioned*) **1** a person whose job is to sell fish in a store **2** a store that sells fish

fish·net /'fɪʃnɛt/ *noun* [U] a type of cloth made of threads that produce a pattern of small holes like a net: *fishnet stockings*

'fish stick *noun* a long, narrow piece of fish covered with BREADCRUMBS or BATTER, usually frozen and sold in packs

fish·tail /'fɪʃteɪl/ *verb* [I] if a vehicle **fishtails**, the back end slides from side to side

fish·wife /'fɪʃwaɪf/ *noun* (*pl.* fish·wives /-waɪvz/) (*old-fashioned, disapproving*) a woman with a loud voice and bad manners

fish·y /'fɪʃi/ *adj.* (fish·i·er, fish·i·est) **1** (*informal*) that makes you suspicious because it seems dishonest **SYN** SUSPICIOUS: *There's something fishy going on here.* **2** smelling or tasting like a fish: *What's that fishy smell?*

fis·sile /'fɪsl; 'fɪsaɪl/ *adj.* (*physics*) capable of nuclear FISSION: *fissile material*

fis·sion /'fɪʃn/ *noun* [U] **1** (also ,nuclear 'fission) (*physics*) the act or process of splitting the NUCLEUS (= central part) of an atom, when a large amount of energy is released ⟳ *compare* FUSION **2** (*biology*) the division of cells into new cells as a method of reproducing cells **3** (*chemistry*) the breaking of a chemical BOND between two atoms

fis·sure /'fɪʃər/ *noun* (*technical*) a long, deep crack in something, especially in rock or in the earth ▶ **fis·sured** /-ʃərd/ *adj.*

fist /fɪst/ *noun* a hand when it is tightly closed with the fingers bent into the PALM: *He punched me with his fist.* ◆ *She clenched her fists to stop herself from trembling.* ◆ *He got into a fist fight in the bar.* ⟳ *see also* HAM-FISTED, TIGHT-FISTED
IDM *see* IRON, MONEY

fist·ful /'fɪstfʊl/ *noun* a number or an amount of something that can be held in a fist: *a fistful of coins*

fist·i·cuffs /'fɪstɪˌkʌfs/ *noun* [pl.] (*old-fashioned* or *humorous*) a fight in which people hit each other with their FISTS

fis·tu·la /'fɪstʃələ/ *noun* (*medical*) an opening between two organs of the body, or between an organ and the skin, that would not normally exist, caused by injury, disease, etc.

fit /fɪt/ *verb, adj., noun*
• **verb** (fit·ting, fit·ted, fit·ted or fit·ting, fit, fit , except in the passive)
▷ RIGHT SIZE/TYPE **1** [I, T] (not used in the progressive tenses) to be the right shape and size for someone or something: *I tried the dress on but it didn't fit.* ◆ *That jacket fits well.* ◆ *a close-fitting dress* ◆ **~ sb/sth** *I can't find clothes to fit me.* ◆ *The key doesn't fit the lock.* **2** [I] to be of the right size, type, or number to go somewhere: *I'd like to have a desk in the room but it won't fit.* ◆ **+ adv./prep.** *All the kids will fit in the back of the car.* **3** [T, often passive] **~ sb (for sth)** to put clothes on someone and make them the right size and shape: *I'm going to be fitted for my wedding dress today.*
▷ PUT SOMETHING SOMEWHERE **4** [T] to put or attach something somewhere: **~ sth + adv./prep.** *They fit a smoke alarm to the ceiling.* ◆ **~ sth with sth** *The rooms have all been fitted with smoke alarms.* **5** [I, T] to put or join something in the right place: **~ + adv./prep.** *The glass fits on top of the jug to form a lid.* ◆ *How do these two parts fit together?* ◆ **~ sth + adv./prep.** *We fit together the pieces of the puzzle.*
▷ AGREE/MATCH **6** [I, T] (not used in the progressive tenses) to agree with, match, or be suitable for something; to make something do this: *Something doesn't quite fit here.* ◆ **~ into sth** *His pictures don't fit into any category.* ◆ **~ sth** *The facts certainly fit your theory.* ◆ *The punishment ought to fit the crime.* ◆ **~ sth to sth** *We should fit the punishment to the crime.* ⟳ *see also* FITTED
IDM **fit (sb) like a glove** to be the perfect size or shape for someone ⟳ *more at* BILL *n.,* DESCRIPTION, SHOE
PHR V **,fit sb/sth↔'in** | **,fit sb/sth 'in/'into sth 1** to find time to see someone or to do something: *I'll try and fit you in after lunch.* ◆ *I had to fit ten appointments into one morning.* **2** to find or have enough space for someone or something in a place: *We can't fit in any more chairs.* **,fit 'in (with sb/sth)** to live, work, etc. in an easy and natural way with someone or something: *He's never done this type of work before; I'm not*

t **tea**	ṭ **butter**	d **did**	k **cat**	g **got**	tʃ **chin**	dʒ **June**	f **fall**

sure how he'll *fit in* with the other people. ◆ *Where do I fit in?* ◆ *Do these plans fit in with your arrangements?* **fit sb/sth↔ 'out/ 'up (with sth)** to supply someone or something with all the equipment, clothes, food, etc. they need **SYN** EQUIP: *to fit out a ship before a long voyage* ◆ *The room has been fitted out with a stove and a sink.*

● **adj. (fit·ter, fit·test)**
▷ **SUITABLE 1** suitable; of the right quality; with the right qualities or skills: **~ for sb/sth** *The food was not fit for human consumption.* ◆ *It was a meal **fit for a king** (= of very good quality).* ◆ *The kids seem to think I'm only fit for cooking and cleaning!* ◆ **~ to do sth** *Your car isn't fit to be on the road!* ◆ *He's so angry he's **in no fit state** to see anyone.* **ANT** UNFIT
▷ **HEALTHY 2** healthy and strong, especially because you do regular physical exercise: *Top athletes have to be extremely **physically fit.*** ◆ **~ (to do sth)** *He won't be fit to play in the game on Saturday.* ◆ *She tries to **keep fit** by jogging every day.* **ANT** UNFIT
IDM (as) fit as a fiddle (*informal*) in very good physical condition fit to be tied (*informal*) very angry or annoyed: *I was fit to be tied when I saw the mess.* see/think fit (to do sth) (*formal*) to consider it right or acceptable to do something; to decide or choose to do something: *You must do as you think fit* (= but I don't agree with your decision). ◆ *The newspaper did not see fit to publish my letter* (= and I criticize it for that). ◆ more at SURVIVAL

● **noun**
▷ **OF STRONG FEELING 1** [C] a short period of very strong feeling: *to act in a fit of anger/rage/temper/pique* ◆ *When I came home an hour late, my mom had a complete fit* (= of anger). ◆ see also HISSY FIT
▷ **OF COUGHING/LAUGHTER 2** [C] a sudden short period of coughing or of laughing, that you cannot control **SYN** BOUT: *a fit of coughing* ◆ *He had us all **in fits of laughter** with his jokes.*
▷ **ILLNESS 3** [C] (*old-fashioned*) a sudden attack of an illness, such as EPILEPSY, in which someone becomes unconscious and their body may make violent movements **SYN** SEIZURE: *to have an epileptic fit*
▷ **OF CLOTHING 4** [C, U] (often with an adjective) the way that something, especially a piece of clothing, fits: *a good/bad/close/perfect fit*
▷ **MATCH 5** [C] **~ (between A and B)** the way that two things match each other or are suitable for each other: *We need to work out the best fit between the staff required and the staff available.*
IDM by/in fits and starts frequently starting and stopping again; not continuously: *Because of other commitments I can only write my book in fits and starts.* have/throw a fit (*informal*) to be very shocked, upset, or angry: *Your mother would have a fit if she knew you'd been drinking!*

fit·ful /'fɪtfl/ *adj.* happening only for short periods; not continuous or regular: *a fitful night's sleep* ▸ **fit·ful·ly** /-fəli/ *adv.*: *to sleep fitfully*

fit·ness /'fɪtnəs/ *noun* [U] **1** the state of being physically healthy and strong: *a magazine on health and fitness* ◆ *a **fitness instructor/class*** ◆ *a high level of physical fitness* ◆ collocations at DIET **2** the state of being suitable or good enough for something: **~ for sth** *He convinced us of his fitness for the task.* ◆ **~ to do sth** *There were doubts about her fitness to hold office.*

fit·ted /'fɪtəd/ *adj.* [only before noun] (of clothes) made to follow the shape of the body: *a fitted jacket* **ANT** LOOSE

fit·ter /'fɪtər/ *noun* a person whose job is to cut and fit clothes or carpets, etc.

fit·ting /'fɪtɪŋ/ *adj., noun*
● **adj. 1** (*formal*) suitable or right for the occasion **SYN** APPROPRIATE: *The award was a fitting tribute to her years of devoted work.* ◆ *A fitting end to the meal would be strawberry shortcake.* ◆ *It is fitting that we hold this memorial service on the grounds of the school he helped build.* **2** **-fitting** (in adjectives) having a particular FIT: *a tight-fitting dress*
● **noun 1** [usually pl.] a small part on a piece of equipment or furniture: *a pine cabinet with brass fittings* **2** an occasion

when you try on a piece of clothing that is being made for you to see if it fits

'fitting ˌroom *noun* a room in a store where you can put on clothes to see how they look **SYN** DRESSING ROOM

five /faɪv/ *number*
5: *There are only five cookies left.* ◆ *five of the country's top financial experts* ◆ *Ten people were invited but only five turned up.* ◆ *Do you have change for five dollars?* ◆ *a five-month contract* ◆ *Look at page five.* ◆ *Five and four is nine.* ◆ *Three times five is fifteen.* ◆ *I can't read your writing—is this supposed to be a five?* ◆ *The bulbs are planted in threes* (= groups of three or five). ◆ *We moved to America when I was five* (= five years old). ◆ *Shall we meet at five* (= at five o'clock), *then?* ◆ see also HIGH FIVE
IDM give sb five (*informal*) to hit the inside of someone's hand with your hand as a way of saying hello or to celebrate a victory: *Give me five!* ◆ more at NINE

ˌfive-and-'dime (also **ˌfive-and-'ten**, **'dime store**) *noun* (*old-fashioned*) a store that sells a range of cheap goods

five·fold /'faɪvfoʊld; ˌfaɪv'foʊld/ *adj., adv.* ◆ -FOLD

ˌfive o'clock 'shadow *noun* [sing.] (*informal*) the dark color that appears on a man's chin and face when the hair has grown a little during the day

fiv·er /'faɪvər/ *noun* (*informal, old-fashioned*) $5 or a five-dollar bill

'five-star *adj.* [usually before noun] **1** having five stars in a system that measures quality. Five stars usually represents the highest quality: *a five-star hotel* **2** having the highest military rank, and wearing a uniform which has five stars on it: *a five-star general*

fix /fɪks/ *verb, noun*
● **verb**
▷ **REPAIR 1** **~ sth** to repair or correct something: *The car won't start—can you fix it?* ◆ *I've fixed the problem.*
▷ **ARRANGE 2** **~ sth** to decide on a date, a time, an amount, etc. for something **SYN** SET: *Has the date of the next meeting been fixed?* ◆ *They fixed the rent at $600 a month.* ◆ *Their prices are fixed until the end of the year* (= will not change before then). **3** to arrange or organize something: **~ sth (for sb)** *I'll fix a meeting for all of you next week.* ◆ **~ sth up (for sb)** *You have to fix up visits up in advance with the museum.* ◆ **~ sth with sth** (*informal*) *Don't worry, I'll fix it with Sarah.* ◆ **~ it up (for sb) to do sth** *I've fixed it up (for us) to go to the theater next week.*
4 be fixing to do sth [I] (*somewhat old-fashioned, informal*) (used in the Southern U.S.) to be preparing to do something or to be thinking about doing something: *We were fixing to go to the party on Saturday night.*
▷ **FOOD/DRINK 5** to provide or prepare something, especially food: **~ sb sth** *Can I fix you a drink?* ◆ **~ sth for sb** *Can I fix a drink for you?* ◆ **~ sth** *I'll fix supper.*
▷ **HAIR/FACE 6** **~ sth** to make something such as your hair or face neat and attractive: *I'll fix my hair and then I'll be ready.*
▷ **RESULT 7** [often passive] **~ sth** (*informal*) to arrange the result of something in a way that is not honest or fair: *I'm sure the race was fixed.*
▷ **ANIMAL 8** **~ sth** (*informal*) to make an animal unable to have young, by means of an operation ◆ see also NEUTER
▷ **PUNISH 9** **~ sb** (*informal*) to punish someone who has harmed you and stop them from doing you any more harm: *Don't worry—I'll fix him.*
▷ **POSITION/TIME 10** **~ sth** to discover or say the exact position, time, etc. of something: *We can fix the ship's exact position at the time the fire broke out.*
▷ **ATTACH 11** **~ sth (+ adv./prep.)** to put something firmly in a place so that it will not move: *to fix a shelf to the wall* ◆ *to fix a post in the ground*
▷ **IN PHOTOGRAPHY 12** **~ sth** (*technical*) to treat film for cameras, etc. with a chemical so that the colors do not change or become less bright
IDM fix sb with a look, stare, gaze, etc. to look directly at someone for a long time: *He fixed her with an angry stare.* ◆ more at AIN'T
PHR V 'fix on sb/sth to choose someone or something:

| v **v**oice | θ **th**in | ð **th**en | s **s**o | z **z**oo | ʃ **sh**e | ʒ vi**s**ion | x **Ch**anukah | 569 |

They've fixed on Bermuda for their honeymoon. **'fix sth on sb/sth** [often passive] if your eyes or your mind are **fixed on** something, you are looking at or thinking about something with great attention .**fix sth↔'up** to repair, decorate, or make something ready: *They fixed up the house before they moved in.* .**fix sb 'up (with sb)** (*informal*) to arrange for someone to have a meeting with someone who might become a boyfriend or girlfriend .**fix sb 'up (with sth)** (*informal*) to arrange for someone to have something; to provide someone with something: *I'll fix you up with a place to stay.*

● **noun**
> SOLUTION **1** [C] (*informal*) a solution to a problem, especially an easy or temporary one: *There is no quick fix for the steel industry.*
> DRUG **2** [sing.] (*informal*) an amount of something that you need and want frequently, especially an illegal drug such as HEROIN: *to get yourself a fix* ◆ *I need a coffee fix before I can face the day.*
> DIFFICULT SITUATION **3** [sing.] a difficult situation **SYN** MESS: *We've really gotten ourselves into a fix this time.*
> ON POSITION **4** [sing.] the act of finding the position of a ship or an aircraft: *They managed to get a fix on the yacht's position.*
> UNDERSTANDING **5** [sing.] (*informal*) an act of understanding something: *He tried to get a fix on the young man's motives, but he just couldn't understand him.*

fixated /ˈfɪkseɪtəd/ *adj.* [not before noun] **~ (on sb/sth)** always thinking and talking about someone or something in a way that is not normal

fix·a·tion /fɪkˈseɪʃn/ *noun* **1** [C] a very strong interest in someone or something, that is not normal or natural: *a mother fixation* ◆ **~ with/on sb/sth** *He's got this fixation with cleanliness.* **2** [U] (*technical*) the process of a gas becoming solid: *nitrogen fixation*

fix·a·tive /ˈfɪksətɪv/ *noun* [C, U] **1** a substance that is used to prevent colors or smells from changing or becoming weaker, for example in photography, art, or the making of PERFUME **2** a substance that is used to stick things together or keep things in position

fixed /fɪkst/ *adj.*
1 staying the same; not changing or able to be changed: *fixed prices* ◆ *a fixed rate of interest* ◆ *people living on fixed incomes* ◆ *The money has been invested for a fixed period.* **2** (often *disapproving*) (of ideas and wishes) held very firmly; not easily changed: *My parents had fixed ideas about what I should become.* **3** [only before noun] (of expressions on someone's face) not changing and not sincere: *He greeted all his guests with a fixed smile on his face.*
IDM how are you, etc. fixed (for sth)? (*informal*) used to ask how much of something a person has, or to ask about arrangements: *How are you fixed for cash?* ◆ *How are we fixed for Saturday* (= have we arranged to do anything)?

,**fixed 'assets** *noun* [pl.] (*business*) land, buildings, and equipment that are owned and used by a company

,**fixed 'costs** *noun* [pl.] (*business*) the costs that a business must pay that do not change even if the amount of work produced changes

fix·ed·ly /ˈfɪksədli/ *adv.* continuously, without looking away, but often with no real interest: *to stare/gaze fixedly at someone or something*

,**fixed-'term** *adj.* [only before noun] a **fixed-term** contract, etc. is one that only lasts for the agreed period of time

,**fixed-'wing** *adj.* [only before noun] used to describe aircraft with wings that remain in the same position, rather than HELICOPTERS, etc.

fix·er /ˈfɪksər/ *noun* (*informal*) a person who arranges things for other people, sometimes dishonestly: *a great political fixer*

fix·er-up·per /ˌfɪksər ˈʌpər/ *noun* (*informal*) a house or an apartment that is cheap because it needs a lot of repair work when you buy it

fix·ings /ˈfɪksɪŋz; -sənz/ *noun* [pl.] = TRIMMINGS: *a hamburger with all the fixings*

fix·i·ty /ˈfɪksəti/ *noun* [U] (*formal*) the quality of being firm and not changing

fix·ture /ˈfɪkstʃər/ *noun* a thing such as a BATHTUB or toilet that is fixed in a house and that you do not take with you when you move: *We're going to be putting in new bathroom fixtures.* ◆ (*figurative*) *He has stayed with us so long he seems to have become a permanent fixture.* ⊃ collocations at DECORATE

fizz /fɪz/ *verb, noun*
● **verb** [I] when a liquid **fizzes**, it produces a lot of bubbles and makes a long sound like an "s": *Champagne was fizzing in the glass.* ◆ **~ with sth** (*figurative*) *He started to fizz with enthusiasm.*
● **noun** [U, sing.] **1** the small bubbles of gas in a liquid: (*figurative*) *There is plenty of fizz and sparkle in the show.* ◆ (*figurative*) *The fizz has gone out of the market.* **2** the sound that is made by bubbles of gas in a liquid, or a sound similar to this: *the fizz of fireworks before they explode* ▶ **fizz·y** *adj.* (fizz·i·er, fizz·i·est)

fiz·zle /ˈfɪzl/ *verb* [I] when something, especially something that is burning, **fizzles**, it makes a sound like a long "s" **SYN** HISS
PHRV fizzle 'out (*informal*) to gradually become less successful and end in a disappointing way

fjord (also **fiord**) /fjɔrd/ *noun* a long narrow strip of ocean between high CLIFFS, especially in Norway

FL *abbr.* (in writing) Florida

flab /flæb/ *noun* [U] (*informal, disapproving*) soft, loose flesh on a person's body

flab·ber·gast·ed /ˈflæbərˌgæstəd/ *adj.* [not usually before noun] (*informal*) extremely surprised and/or shocked **SYN** ASTONISHED

flab·by /ˈflæbi/ *adj.* (*informal, disapproving*) (flab·bi·er, flab·bi·est) **1** having soft, loose flesh; fat: *flabby thighs* **2** weak; with no strength or force: *a flabby grip* ◆ *a flabby argument*

flac·cid /ˈflæksəd; ˈflæsəd/ *adj.* (*formal*) soft and weak; not firm and hard: *flaccid breasts*

flack /flæk/ *noun* **1** [U] = FLAK **2** [C] (*informal*) = PRESS AGENT

flag /flæg/ *noun, verb*
● **noun** **1** a piece of cloth with a special colored design on it that may be the symbol of a particular country or organization, or may have a particular meaning. A flag can be attached to a pole or held in the hand: *the American flag* ◆ *the flag of the United States* ◆ *The hotel flies the Canadian flag.* ◆ *The Mexican flag was flying.* ◆ *All the flags were at half mast* (= in honor of a famous person who has died). ◆ *The black and white flag went down, and the race began.* **2** used to refer to a particular country or organization and its beliefs and values: *to swear allegiance to the flag* ◆ *He was working under the flag of the United Nations.* **3** a piece of cloth that is attached to a pole and used as a signal or MARKER in various sports **4** a flower that is a type of IRIS and that grows near water: *yellow flags* **5** = FLAGSTONE
IDM fly/show/wave the flag to show your support for your country, an organization, or an idea to encourage or persuade others to do the same **keep the flag flying** to represent your country or organization: *Our exporters keep the flag flying at international trade exhibitions.* ⊃ more at WAVE v.
● **verb** (-gg-) **1** [T] **~ sth** to put a special mark next to information that you think is important: *I've flagged the paragraphs that we need to look at in more detail.* **2** [I] to become tired, weaker, or less enthusiastic: *It had been a long day and the children were beginning to flag.* ◆ *Her confidence never flagged.* ◆ *flagging support/enthusiasm*
PHRV flag sb/sth↔'down to signal to the driver of a vehicle to stop by waving at them

,**'Flag Day** *noun* June 14, the anniversary of the day in 1777 when the Stars and Stripes became the national flag of the United States

flag·el·late /ˈflædʒəˌleɪt/ *verb* ~ **sb/yourself** (*formal*) to WHIP yourself or someone else, especially as a religious punishment ▶ **flag·el·la·tion** /ˌflædʒəˈleɪʃn/ *noun* [U]

flag 'football *noun* [U] a type of football played without the usual form of tackling (TACKLE). A tackle is made, instead, by pulling a piece of cloth from an opponent's WAISTBAND. ⊃ compare TOUCH FOOTBALL

flag of con'venience *noun* a flag of a foreign country that is used by a ship from another country for legal or financial reasons

flag·on /ˈflæɡən/ *noun* a large bottle or similar container, often with a handle, in which wine, etc. is sold or served

flag·pole /ˈflæɡpoʊl/ (also **flag·staff**) *noun* a tall pole on which a flag is hung

fla·grant /ˈfleɪɡrənt/ *adj.* (of an action) shocking because it is done in a very obvious way and shows no respect for people, laws, etc. **SYN** BLATANT: *a flagrant abuse of human rights* ◆ *He showed a flagrant disregard for anyone else's feelings.* ▶ **fla·grant·ly** *adv.*

flagrante ⊃ IN FLAGRANTE

flag·ship /ˈflæɡʃɪp/ *noun* **1** the main ship in a FLEET of ships in the navy **2** [usually sing.] the most important product, service, building, etc. that an organization owns or produces: *The company is opening a new flagship store in New Orleans.*

flag·staff /ˈflæɡstæf/ *noun* = FLAGPOLE

flag·stone /ˈflæɡstoʊn/ (also **flag**) *noun* a large, flat, square piece of stone that is used for floors, paths, etc.

flag-ˌwaving *noun* [U] the expression of strong national feelings, especially in a way that people disapprove of

flail /fleɪl/ *verb, noun*
- *verb* **1** [I, T] ~ **(sth) (around)** to move around without control; to move your arms and legs around without control: *The boys flailed around on the floor.* ◆ *He was running along, his arms flailing wildly.* **2** [T] ~ **sb/sth** to hit someone or something very hard, especially with a stick
- *noun* a tool that has a long handle with a stick swinging from it, used especially in the past to separate grains of WHEAT from their dry outer covering, by beating the WHEAT

flair /fler/ *noun* **1** [sing., U] ~ **for sth** a natural ability to do something well **SYN** TALENT: *He has a flair for languages.* **2** [U] a quality showing the ability to do things in an interesting way that shows imagination: *artistic flair* ◆ *She dresses with real flair.*

flak (also **flack**) /flæk/ *noun* [U] **1** guns on the ground that are shooting at enemy aircraft; bullets from these guns **2** (*informal*) severe criticism: *He's taken a lot of flak for his left-wing views.* ◆ *She came in for a lot of flak from the press.*

flake /fleɪk/ *noun, verb*
- *noun* **1** a small, very thin layer or piece of something, especially one that has broken off from something larger: *flakes of snow/paint* ◆ *dried onion flakes* ⊃ see also CORN-FLAKES, SNOWFLAKE **2** (*informal*) a person who is strange or unusual or who forgets things easily
- *verb* **1** [I] ~ **(off)** to fall off in small thin pieces: *You could see bare wood where the paint had flaked off.* ◆ *His skin was dry and flaking.* **2** [T, I] ~ **(sth)** to break something, especially fish or other food into small thin pieces; to fall into small thin pieces: *Flake the tuna and add to the sauce.* ◆ *flaked coconut*
PHRV **flake 'out 1** (*informal*) to lie down or fall asleep because you are extremely tired: *As soon as I got home I flaked out on the bed.* **2** (*informal*) to begin to behave in a strange way

flak jacket *noun* a heavy jacket without sleeves that has metal inside it to make it stronger, and is worn by soldiers and police officers to protect them from bullets

flak·y /ˈfleɪki/ *adj.* **1** tending to break into small, thin pieces: *flaky pastry* ◆ *dry flaky skin* **2** (*informal*) (of a person) behaving

in a strange or unusual way; tending to forget things ▶ **flak·i·ness** *noun* [U]

flam·bé /flɑmˈbeɪ/ *adj.* [after noun] (from *French*) (of food) covered with alcohol, especially BRANDY and allowed to burn for a short time ⊃ picture at COOKING ▶ **flambé** *verb* ~ **sth**

flam·boy·ant /flæmˈbɔɪənt/ *adj.* **1** (of people or their behavior) different, confident, and exciting in a way that attracts attention: *a flamboyant gesture/style/personality* **2** brightly colored and noticeable: *flamboyant clothes/designs* ▶ **flam·boy·ance** /-ˈbɔɪəns/ *noun* [U] **flam·boy·ant·ly** *adv.*

flame /fleɪm/ *noun, verb*
- *noun* **1** [C, U] a hot bright stream of burning gas that comes from something that is on fire: *the tiny yellow flame of a match* ◆ *The flames were growing higher and higher.* ◆ *The building was in flames* (= was burning). ◆ *The plane burst into flame(s)* (= suddenly began burning strongly). ◆ *Everything went up in flames* (= was destroyed by fire). ⊃ picture at LABORATORY **2** [U] a bright red or orange color: *a flame-red car* **3** [C] (*literary*) a very strong feeling: *a flame of passion* ⊃ see also OLD FLAME **4** [C] (*informal*) an angry or insulting message sent to someone by e-mail or on the Internet **IDM** see FAN *v.*
- *verb* **1** [I] (+ *adj.*) (*literary*) to burn with a bright flame: *The logs flamed on the hearth.* ◆ (*figurative*) *Hope flamed in her.* **2** [I, T] (+ *adj.*) | ~ **(sth)** (*literary*) (of a person's face) to become red as a result of a strong emotion; to make something become red: *Her cheeks flamed with rage.* **3** [T] ~ **sb** (*informal*) to send someone an angry or insulting message by e-mail or on the Internet

fla·men·co /fləˈmɛŋkoʊ/ *noun* (*pl.* **fla·men·cos**) **1** [U, C] a fast exciting Spanish dance that is usually danced to music played on a GUITAR: *flamenco dancing* ◆ *to dance the flamenco* **2** [U] the GUITAR music that is played for this dance

flame·proof /ˈfleɪmpruf/ *adj.* made of or covered with a special material that will not burn easily

flame-retardant /ˈfleɪm rɪˌtɑrdnt/ *adj.* = FIRE-RETARDANT

flame·throw·er /ˈfleɪm θroʊər/ *noun* a weapon like a gun that shoots out burning liquid or flames and is often used for clearing plants from land

flam·ing /ˈfleɪmɪŋ/ *adj.* [only before noun] **1** full of anger: *a flaming argument/temper* **2** burning and covered in flames: *Flaming fragments were still falling from the sky.* **3** bright red or orange in color: *flaming red hair* ◆ *a flaming sunset* **4** (*slang*) used to make a statement of anger or criticism more intense: *He's a flaming hypocrite, talking that way about his students when he doesn't treat them with any respect.*

fla·min·go /fləˈmɪŋɡoʊ/ *noun* (*pl.* **fla·min·gos** or **fla·min·goes**) a large pink bird with long thin legs and a long neck, that lives near water in warm countries

flam·ma·ble /ˈflæməbl/ (also **in·flam·ma·ble**) *adj.* that can burn easily: *highly flammable liquids* **ANT** NONFLAMMABLE **HELP** Flammable and inflammable have the same meaning, but it is usually better to use **flammable** to avoid confusion. The opposite of both words is **nonflammable**.

flan /flɑn; flæn/ *noun* [C, U] (also **crème caramel**) a cold DESSERT (= a sweet dish) made from milk, eggs, and sugar

flange /flændʒ/ *noun* an edge that sticks out from an object and makes it stronger or (as in a wheel of a train) keeps it in the correct position

flank /flæŋk/ *noun, verb*
- *noun* **1** the side of something such as a building or mountain **2** the left or right side of an army during a battle, or a sports team during a game **3** the side of an animal between the RIB and the hip ⊃ picture at HORSE
- *verb* **1** be flanked by sb or sth to have someone or something on one or both sides: *She left the courtroom flanked by armed guards.* **2** ~ **sth** to be placed on one or both

sides of something: *They drove through the cotton fields that flanked Highway 17.*

flank·er /'flæŋkər/ *noun* an offensive player in football

flan·nel /'flænl/ *noun* **1** [U] a type of soft light cloth, containing cotton or wool, used for making clothes: *a flannel shirt* ◆ *a gray flannel suit* **2 flannels** [pl.] pants made of flannel

flap /flæp/ *noun, verb*
● *noun*
▷ FLAT PIECE OF PAPER, ETC. **1** [C] a flat piece of paper, cloth, metal, etc. that is attached to something along one side and that hangs down or covers an opening: *the flap of an envelope* ◆ *I zipped the tent flaps shut.* ⊃ picture at STATIONERY
▷ MOVEMENT **2** [C, usually sing.] a quick, often noisy, movement of something up and down or from side to side: *With a flap of its wings, the bird was gone.* ◆ *the flap of the sails*
▷ PUBLIC DISAGREEMENT **3** [sing.] public disagreement, anger, or criticism caused by something a public figure has said or done: *the flap about the President's business affairs*
▷ PART OF AIRCRAFT **4** [C] a part of the wing of an aircraft that can be moved up or down to control upward or downward movement ⊃ picture at PLANE
▷ PHONETICS **5** [C] = TAP *n.*
● *verb* (-pp-)
▷ MOVE QUICKLY **1** [T, I] ~ **(sth)** if a bird **flaps** its wings, or if its wings **flap**, they move quickly up and down **SYN** BEAT : *The bird flapped its wings and flew away.* ◆ *The gulls flew off, wings flapping.* **2** [I, T] to move, or to make something move, up and down or from side to side, often making a noise: **(+ adv./prep.)** *The sails flapped in the breeze.* ◆ *Two large birds flapped* (= flew) *slowly across the water.* ◆ ~ **sth** *She walked up and down, flapping her arms to keep warm.* ◆ *A gust of wind flapped the tents.*
▷ PHONETICS **3** [T] ~ **sth** = TAP *v.*

flap·jack /'flæpdʒæk/ *noun* a thick PANCAKE

flap·per /'flæpər/ *noun* a fashionable young woman in the 1920s who was interested in modern ideas and was determined to enjoy herself

flare /flɛr/ *verb, noun*
● *verb* **1** [I] to burn brightly, but usually for only a short time or not steadily: *The match flared and went out.* ◆ *The fire flared into life.* ◆ *(figurative) Color flared in her cheeks.* **2** [I] ~ **(up)** (especially of anger and violence) to suddenly start or become much stronger **SYN** ERUPT: *Violence flared when the police moved in.* ◆ *Tempers flared toward the end of the meeting.* ⊃ related noun FLARE-UP **3** [T, I] **(+ speech)** to say something in an angry and aggressive way: *"You should have told me!" she flared at him.* **4** [I] (of clothes) to become wider toward the bottom: *The sleeves are tight to the elbow, then flare out.* **5** [T, I] ~ **(sth)** if a person or an animal **flares** its NOSTRILS (= the openings at the end of the nose) or if their nostrils **flare**, their nostrils become wider, especially as a sign of anger: *The horse backed away, its nostrils flaring with fear.*
PHR V ,flare 'up **1** (of flames, a fire, etc.) to suddenly start burning more brightly ⊃ related noun FLARE-UP **2** (of a person) to suddenly become angry ⊃ related noun FLARE-UP **3** (of an illness, injury, etc.) to suddenly start again or become worse ⊃ related noun FLARE-UP
● *noun* **1** [usually sing.] a bright but unsteady light or flame that does not last long: *The flare of the match lit up his face.* **2** a device that produces a bright flame, used especially as a signal; a flame produced in this way: *The ship sent up distress flares to attract the attention of the coastguard.* **3** a shape that becomes gradually wider: *a skirt with a slight flare*

flared /flɛrd/ *adj.* (of clothes) wider at the bottom edge than at the top

ˈ**flare-up** *noun* [usually sing.] **1** a sudden expression of angry or violent feeling **SYN** OUTBURST: *a flare-up of tension between the two sides* **2** (of an illness) a sudden painful attack, especially after a period without any problems or pain **3** the fact of a fire suddenly starting to burn again more strongly than before: *a flare-up of the brushfires*

flash /flæʃ/ *verb, noun, adj.*
● *verb*
▷ SHINE BRIGHTLY **1** [I, T] to shine very brightly for a short time; to make something shine in this way: *Lightning flashed in the distance.* ◆ *the flashing blue lights of a police car* ◆ + **adv./prep.** *A neon sign flashed on and off above the door.* ◆ ~ **sth** *The guide flashed a light into the cave.*
▷ GIVE SIGNAL **2** [T, I] to use a light to give someone a signal: ~ **sth (at sb)** *Red lights flashed a warning at them.* ◆ ~ **sb (sth)** *Red lights flashed them a warning.* ◆ ~ **(sth at) sb** *Why is that driver flashing his lights at us?*
▷ SHOW QUICKLY **3** [T] ~ **sth at sb** to show something to someone quickly: *He flashed his pass at the security officer.*
▷ MOVE QUICKLY **4** [I] + **adv./prep.** to move or pass very quickly: *The countryside flashed past the train windows.* ◆ *A look of terror flashed across his face.*
▷ OF THOUGHTS/MEMORIES **5** [I] + **adv./prep.** to come into your mind suddenly: *A terrible thought flashed through my mind.*
▷ ON SCREEN **6** [I, T] to appear on a television screen, computer screen, etc. for a short time; to make something do this: *A message was flashing on his pager.* ◆ ~ **(sth) (up)** *His name was flashed up on the screen.*
▷ SEND NEWS **7** [T] ~ **sth** + **adv./prep.** to send information quickly by radio, computer, etc.: *News of their triumph was flashed around the world.*
▷ SHOW EMOTION **8** [I] **(+ adv./prep.)** (*literary*) to show a strong emotion suddenly and quickly: *Her eyes flashed with anger.*
▷ OF A MAN **9** [I, T] (*informal*) if a man **flashes**, he shows his sexual organs in public
IDM **flash sb a smile, look, etc.** to smile, look, etc. at someone suddenly and quickly
PHR V ,flash sth a'round (*disapproving*) to show something to other people in order to impress them: *He's always flashing his money around.* ,flash 'back (to sth) **1** if your mind **flashes back** to something, you remember something that happened in the past: *Her thoughts flashed back to their wedding day.* ⊃ related noun FLASHBACK **2** if a movie **flashes back** to something, it shows things that happened at an earlier time, for example at an earlier part of someone's life ⊃ related noun FLASHBACK **3** to reply very quickly and/or angrily ,flash 'by/'past (of time) to go very quickly: *The morning just flashed by.* 'flash on sth (*informal*) to suddenly remember or think of something: *I flashed on an argument I had with my sister when we were kids.* 'flash on sb [no passive] if something **flashes on you**, you suddenly realize it: *It flashed on me that he was the man I saw in the hotel.*
● *noun*
▷ LIGHT **1** [C] a sudden bright light that shines for a moment and then disappears: *a flash of lightning* ◆ *Flashes of light were followed by an explosion.* ◆ *There was a blinding flash and the whole building shuddered.*
▷ SIGNAL **2** [C] the act of shining a light on something, especially as a signal
▷ SUDDEN IDEA/EMOTION **3** [C] ~ **of sth** a particular feeling or idea that suddenly comes into your mind or shows on your face: *a flash of anger/inspiration, etc.*
▷ OF BRIGHT COLOR **4** [C] ~ **of sth** the sudden appearance for a short time of something bright: *a flash of white teeth* ◆ *On the horizon, she saw a flash of silver—the sea!*
▷ IN PHOTOGRAPHY **5** [C, U] a piece of equipment that produces a bright light for a very short time, used for taking photographs indoors, when it is dark, etc.; the use of this when taking a photograph: *a camera with a built-in flash* ◆ *I'll need flash for this shot.* ◆ *flash photography* ⊃ picture at HOBBY
▷ NEWS **6** [C] = NEWS FLASH
▷ COMPUTING **7** Flash™ [U] a program that creates moving images for websites ⊃ see also HOT FLASH
IDM **a flash in the pan** a sudden success that lasts only a short time and is not likely to be repeated **in/like a flash** very quickly and suddenly ⊃ more at QUICK *adv.*
● *adj.* [only before noun] happening suddenly or done quickly: *flash freezing of food such as fish* ⊃ see also FLASH FLOOD

ʌ cup   ə about   eɪ say   aɪ five   ɔɪ boy   aʊ now   oʊ go   ər bird

flash·back /'flæʃbæk/ *noun* **1** [C, U] a part of a movie, play, etc. that shows a scene that happened earlier in time than the main story: *The events that led up to the murder were shown in a series of flashbacks.* ◆ *The reader is told the story* **in flashback.** ⊃ compare FLASH-FORWARD **2** [C] a sudden, very clear, strong memory of something that happened in the past that is so real you feel that you are living through the experience again

flash·bulb /'flæʃbʌlb/ *noun* a small electric BULB that can be attached to a camera to take photographs indoors or when it is dark

flash·card /'flæʃkɑrd/ *noun* a card with a word or picture on it, that teachers use during class

flash drive (also US **B drive**, **pen drive**, **thumb drive**, **memory stick**) *noun* (*computing*) a small memory device that can be used to store data from a computer and to move it from one computer to another ⊃ picture at COMPUTER

flash·er /'flæʃər/ *noun* **1** (*informal*) a man who shows his sexual organs in public, especially in order to shock or frighten women **2** a device that turns a light on and off quickly **3** a light on a vehicle that you can turn on and off quickly as a signal: *four-way flashers* (= four lights that flash together to warn other drivers of possible danger)

flash flood *noun* a sudden flood of water caused by heavy rain

flash-forward *noun* [C, U] a part of a movie, play, etc. that shows a scene or an event that will happen later in the story; the technique of using this type of scene in a movie, etc.: *The director uses flash-forward to show us that the hero's future life will be tragic.*

flash·gun /'flæʃgʌn/ *noun* a piece of equipment that holds and operates a bright light that is used to take photographs indoors or when it is dark

flash·ing /'flæʃɪŋ/ *noun* [U] also **flashings** [pl.] a strip of metal put on a roof where it joins a wall to prevent water from getting through

flash·light /'flæʃlaɪt/ *noun* a small electric lamp that uses batteries and that you can hold in your hand

flashlight

flashlight   battery

flash memory *noun* [U] (*computing*) computer memory that does not lose data when the power supply is lost

flash·mob /'flæʃmɑb/ *noun* a large group of people who arrange (by cell phone or e-mail) to gather together in a public place at exactly the same time, spend a short time doing something there, and then quickly all leave at the same time ▶ **flash·mob·ber** *noun* **flash·mob·bing** *noun* [U]

flash·point /'flæʃpɔɪnt/ *noun* [C, U] a situation or place in which violence or anger starts and cannot be controlled: *Tension in the city is rapidly reaching flashpoint.* ◆ *potential flashpoints in the suburbs*

flash·y /'flæʃi/ *adj.* (**flash·i·er**, **flash·i·est**) (*informal*, usually *disapproving*) **1** (of things) attracting attention by being bright, expensive, large, etc.: *a flashy hotel* ◆ *I just want a good reliable car, nothing flashy.* **2** (of people) attracting attention by wearing expensive clothes, etc. **3** intended to impress by looking very skillful: *He specializes in flashy technique, without much depth.* ▶ **flash·i·ly** /-ʃəli/ *adv.*: *flashily dressed*

flask /flæsk/ *noun* **1** a bottle with a narrow top, used in scientific work for mixing or storing chemicals ⊃ picture at LABORATORY **2** (also **hip flask**) a small flat bottle made of metal or glass and often covered with leather, used for carrying alcohol

flat 🔊 /flæt/ *adj., adv., noun*

● *adj.* (**flat·ter**, **flat·test**)

> LEVEL **1** having a level surface, not curved or sloping: *low buildings with flat roofs* ◆ *People used to think the earth was flat.*

◆ *Exercise is the only way to get a flat stomach after having a baby.* ◆ *The sails hung limply in the flat calm* (= conditions at sea when there is no wind and the water is completely level). **2** (of land) without any slopes or hills: *The road stretched ahead across the flat landscape.* **3** (of surfaces) smooth and even; without lumps or holes: *I need a flat surface to write on.* ◆ *We found a large flat rock to sit on.*

> NOT HIGH **4** broad but not very high: *Tortillas are a kind of flat Mexican bread.* ◆ *flat shoes* (= with no heels or very low ones)

> DULL **5** dull; lacking interest or enthusiasm: *He felt very flat after his friends went home.*

> VOICE **6** not showing much emotion; not changing much in tone: *Her voice was flat and expressionless.*

> COLORS/PICTURES **7** very smooth, with no contrast between light and dark, and giving no impression of depth: *Acrylic paints can be used to create large, flat blocks of color.*

> BUSINESS **8** not very successful because very little is being sold: *The housing market has been flat for months.*

> REFUSAL/DENIAL **9** [only before noun] not allowing discussion or argument; definite: *Her request was met with a flat refusal.* ◆ *He gave a flat "No!" to one reporter's question.*

> IN MUSIC **10** used after the name of a note to mean a note a HALF STEP lower: *That note should be B flat, not B.* ⊃ picture at MUSIC **ANT** SHARP ⊃ compare NATURAL **11** below the correct PITCH (= how high or low a note sounds): *The high notes were slightly flat.* **ANT** SHARP

> DRINK **12** no longer having bubbles in it; not fresh: *The soda was warm and had gotten flat.*

> TIRE **13** not containing enough air, usually because of a hole

> FEET **14** with no natural raised curves underneath ⊃ see also FLAT-FOOTED

▶ **flat·ness** *noun* [U]

IDM **as flat as a pancake** completely flat ⊃ more at BACK *n.*

● *adv.* (*comparative* **flat·ter**, no *superlative*)

> LEVEL **1** spread out in a level, straight position, especially against another surface: *Lie flat and breathe deeply.* ◆ *They pressed themselves flat against the tunnel wall as the train approached.*

> REFUSING/DENYING **2** (*informal*) in a definite and direct way: *I made them a reasonable offer, but they turned it down flat.*

> IN MUSIC **3** lower than the correct PITCH (= how high or low a note sounds): *He sings flat all the time.* **ANT** SHARP

IDM **fall flat** if a joke, a story, or an event **falls flat**, it completely fails to amuse people or to have the effect that was intended **fall flat on your face 1** to fall so that you are lying on your front **2** to fail completely, usually causing embarrassment: *His next television venture fell flat on its face.* **flat broke** (*informal*) completely BROKE (= having no money) **flat out** (*informal*) **1** as fast or as hard as possible: *Workers are working flat out to meet the increase in demand for new cars.* **2** in a definite and direct way; completely: *I told him flat out "No."* ◆ *We had lost all our money and were flat out broke.* ⊃ see also FLAT-OUT **in... flat** (*informal*) used with an expression of time to say that something happened or was done very quickly, in no more than the time stated: *They changed the tire in three minutes flat* (= in only three minutes).

● *noun*

> IN MUSIC **1** [C] a note played a HALF STEP lower than the note that is named. The written symbol is (♭): *There are no sharps or flats in the key of C major.* **ANT** SHARP ⊃ compare NATURAL

> TIRE **2** [C] a tire that has lost air, usually because of a hole: *We got a flat on the way home.* ◆ *We had to stop to change a flat.*

> SHOES **3** **flats** [pl.] shoes with a very low heel: *a pair of flats* ⊃ picture at SHOE

> LAND **4** [C, usually pl.] an area of low flat land, especially near water: *salt flats* ⊃ see also MUDFLAT

> LEVEL PART **5** [sing.] **the ~ of sth** the flat level part of something: *He beat on the door with the flat of his hand.* ◆ *the flat of a sword*

> IN THEATER **6** [C] (*technical*) a vertical section of SCENERY used on a theater stage

flat·bed /ˈflætbed/ noun **1** (computing) = FLATBED SCANNER **2** (also ˌflatbed ˈtruck, ˌflatbed ˈtrailer) an open truck or TRAILER without high sides, used for carrying large objects

ˌflatbed ˈscanner (also flat·bed) noun (computing) a SCANNER (= device for copying pictures and documents so that they can be stored on a computer) on which the picture or document can be laid flat for copying ⊃ picture at COMPUTER

flat·car /ˈflætkɑr/ noun a car on a train without a roof or sides, used for carrying goods

ˈflat-ˌchested adj. (of a woman) having small breasts

flat·fish /ˈflætfɪʃ/ noun (pl. flat·fish) any sea fish with a flat body, for example a FLOUNDER

ˈflat-ˌfooted adj. **1** without naturally raised curves (= ARCHES) under the feet **2** not prepared for what is going to happen: *They were caught flat-footed by the attack.*

flat·line /ˈflætlaɪn/ verb (informal) **1** [I] to die **2** [I] to be at a low level and fail to improve or increase

flat·ly /ˈflætli/ adv. **1** in a way that is very definite and will not be changed SYN ABSOLUTELY: *to flatly deny/reject/oppose something* ◆ *I flatly refused to spend any more time helping him.* **2** in a dull way with very little interest or emotion: *"Oh, it's you," she said flatly.*

ˌflat-ˈout adj. [only before noun] definite and direct; complete: *His story was full of contradictions and flat-out lies.* ▶ ˌflat-ˈout adv.: *She just flat-out hated me.* ⊃ see also FLAT adv.

ˌflat-ˈpanel adj. = FLAT-SCREEN

ˌflat ˈrate noun a price that is the same for everyone and in all situations: *Interest is charged at a flat rate of 11%.*

ˌflat-ˈscreen (also ˌflat-ˈpanel) adj. [only before noun] ~ television/TV/computer/monitor, etc. a type of television or computer monitor that is very thin when compared with the traditional type

flat·ten /ˈflætn/ verb **1** [I, T] to become or make something become flat or flatter: *The cookies will flatten slightly while cooking.* ◆ ~ sth *These exercises will help to flatten your stomach.* ◆ *He flattened his hair down with gel.* **2** [T] ~ sth to destroy or knock down a building, tree, etc.: *Most of the factory was flattened by the explosion.* **3** [T] ~ sb (informal) to defeat someone easily in a competition, an argument, etc.: *Our team got flattened last night!* **4** [T] ~ sb (informal) to hit someone very hard so that they fall down: *He flattened the intruder with a single punch.* ◆ *I'll flatten you if you do that again!* **PHRV** flatten sth/yourself aˈgainst sb/sth to press sth/your body against someone or something: *She flattened her nose against the window and looked in.* ◆ *Greg flattened himself against the wall to let me pass.* ˌflatten ˈout **1** to gradually become completely flat: *The hills first rose steeply then flattened out toward the water.* **2** to stop growing or going up: *Export growth has started to flatten out.* ˌflatten sth↔ˈout to make something completely flat

flat·ter /ˈflætər/ verb **1** ~ sb to say nice things about someone, often in a way that is not sincere, because you want them to do something for you or you want to please them: *Are you trying to flatter me?* **2** ~ yourself (that…) to choose to believe something good about yourself and your abilities, especially when other people do not share this opinion: *"How will you manage without me?" "Don't flatter yourself."* **3** ~ sb to make someone seem more attractive or better than they really are: *That color doesn't flatter many people.* ◆ *The scorecard flattered him* (= he did not deserve to get such a high score). ▶ flat·ter·er noun **IDM** be/feel flattered to be pleased because someone has made you feel important or special: *He was flattered by her attention.* ◆ *I felt flattered at being asked to give a lecture.*

flat·ter·ing /ˈflætərɪŋ/ adj. **1** making someone look more attractive: *a flattering dress* **2** saying nice things about someone or something: *flattering remarks* **3** making someone feel pleased and special: *I found it flattering that he still recognized me after all these years.*

flat·ter·y /ˈflætəri/ noun [U] praise that is not sincere, especially in order to obtain something from someone: *You're too intelligent to fall for his flattery.* **IDM** flattery will get you everywhere/nowhere (informal, humorous) praise that is not sincere will/will not get you what you want

flat·top /ˈflættɑp/ noun a HAIRSTYLE in which the hair is cut short and flat across the top ⊃ picture at HAIR

flat·u·lence /ˈflætʃələns/ noun [U] an uncomfortable feeling caused by having too much gas in the stomach

flat·u·lent /ˈflætʃələnt/ adj. **1** suffering from too much gas in the stomach **2** (disapproving) sounding important and impressive in a way that exaggerates the truth or facts

flat·ware /ˈflætwer/ noun [U] **1** knives, forks, and spoons, used for eating and serving food SYN CUTLERY, SILVERWARE **2** flat dishes such as plates and SAUCERS

flat·worm /ˈflætwɜrm/ noun a very simple WORM with a flat body

flaunt /flɔnt/ verb (disapproving) ~ sth to show something you are proud of to other people, in order to impress them: *He did not believe in flaunting his wealth.* ◆ *She openly flaunted her affair with the senator.* **IDM** if you've got it, flaunt it (humorous, saying) used to tell someone that they should not be afraid of allowing other people to see their qualities and abilities or their beauty

flau·tist /ˈflaʊtɪst/ noun = FLUTIST

fla·vo·noid /ˈfleɪvəˌnɔɪd/ noun (chemistry) a type of substance that is found in some plants such as tomatoes, and is thought to protect against some types of cancer and heart disease

fla·vor 🔑 (CanE usually fla·vour) /ˈfleɪvər/ noun, verb
● noun **1** [U] how food or drink tastes SYN TASTE: *The tomatoes give extra flavor to the sauce.* ◆ *It is stronger in flavor than many other aged cheeses.* **2** [C] a particular type of taste: *This yogurt comes in ten different flavors.* ◆ *a wine with a delicate fruit flavor* **3** = FLAVORING **4** [sing.] a particular quality or atmosphere SYN AMBIENCE: *the distinctive flavor of South Florida* ◆ *Foreign visitors help to give a truly international flavor to the occasion.* **5** [sing.] a/the ~ of sth an idea of what something is like: *I have tried to convey something of the flavor of the argument.* **6** [C] (computing) a particular type of something, especially computer software **IDM** flavor of the month a person or thing that is very popular at a particular time
● verb ~ sth (with sth) to add something to food or drink to give it more flavor or a particular flavor

fla·vored (CanE usually fla·voured) /ˈfleɪvərd/ adj. **1** -flavored having the type of flavor mentioned: *lemon-flavored candy* **2** having had flavor added to it: *flavored coffee*

fla·vor·ful (CanE usually fla·vour·ful) /ˈfleɪvərfl/ adj. having a lot of flavor

fla·vor·ing (CanE usually fla·vour·ing) /ˈfleɪvərɪŋ/ (also fla·vor) noun [U, C] a substance added to food or drink to give it a particular flavor: *orange/vanilla flavoring* ◆ *This food contains no artificial flavorings.*

fla·vor·less (CanE usually fla·vour·less) /ˈfleɪvərləs/ adj. having no flavor: *The meat was tough and flavorless.*

flaw /flɔ/ noun **1** a mistake in something that means that it is not correct or does not work correctly SYN DEFECT, FAULT: *The argument is full of fundamental flaws.* ◆ ~ in sth *The report reveals fatal flaws in security at the airport.* **2** ~ (in sth) a crack or fault in something that makes it less attractive or valuable **3** ~ (in sb/sth) a weakness in someone's character: *There is always a flaw in the character of a tragic hero.*

flawed /flɔd/ adj. having a flaw; damaged or spoiled: *seriously/fundamentally/fatally flawed* ◆ *a flawed argument* ◆ *the book's flawed heroine*

flaw·less /ˈflɔləs/ adj. without FLAWS and therefore perfect

| t tea | ṭ butter | d did | k cat | g got | tʃ chin | dʒ June | f fall

SYN PERFECT: *a flawless complexion/performance* ♦ *Her English is almost flawless.* ▶ **flaw·less·ly** *adv.*

flax /flæks/ *noun* [U] **1** a plant with blue flowers, grown for its STEMS which are used to make thread, and its seeds which are used to make LINSEED OIL **2** threads from the STEM of the flax plant, used to make LINEN

flax·en /'flæksn/ *adj.* (*literary*) (of hair) pale yellow **SYN** BLOND

flax·seed /'flæksid; 'flæksid/ *noun* [U, C] the seeds of the flax plant, eaten as a health food or used to make LINSEED OIL

flaxseed oil *noun* [U] = LINSEED OIL

flay /fleɪ/ *verb* **1** ~ sth/sb to remove the skin from an animal or person, usually when they are dead **2** ~ sb to hit or WHIP someone very hard so that some of their skin comes off **3** ~ sb/yourself (*formal*) to criticize someone/yourself severely

flea /fli/ *noun* a very small jumping insect without wings, which bites animals and humans and sucks their blood: *The dog has fleas.* ⊃ **picture at** ANIMAL

flea·bag /'flibæg/ *noun* (usually before another noun) (*informal*) a hotel that is cheap and dirty: *a fleabag motel*

flea-bitten *adj.* (*informal*) in poor condition and with an unpleasant appearance

flea market *noun* an outdoor market that sells SECOND-HAND (= old or used) goods at low prices

fleck /flɛk/ *noun, verb*
● *noun* [usually pl.] ~ (of sth) **1** a very small area of a particular color: *His hair was dark, with flecks of gray.* **2** a very small piece of something: *flecks of dust/foam/dandruff*
● *verb* [usually passive] ~ sth (with sth) to cover or mark something with small areas of a particular color or with small pieces of something: *The fabric was red, flecked with gold.* ♦ *His hair was flecked with paint.*

flec·tion = FLEXION

fled pt, pp of FLEE

fledged /flɛdʒd/ *adj.* (of birds) able to fly ⊃ see also FULL-FLEDGED

fledg·ling /'flɛdʒlɪŋ/ *noun* **1** a young bird that has just learned to fly **2** (usually before another noun) a person, an organization, or a system that is new and without experience: *fledgling democracies*

flee /fli/ *verb* (fled, fled /flɛd/) [I, T, no passive] to leave a person or place very quickly, especially because you are afraid of possible danger: *She burst into tears and fled.* ♦ ~ from sb/sth *a camp for refugees fleeing from the war* ♦ ~ to.../into... *He fled to Los Angeles after an argument with his family.* ♦ ~ sth *He was caught trying to flee the country.* ⊃ compare FLY

fleece /flis/ *noun, verb*
● *noun* **1** [C] the wool coat of a sheep; this coat when it has been removed from a sheep (by SHEARING) **2** [U, C] a type of soft warm cloth that feels like sheep's wool; a jacket or SWEATSHIRT that is made from this cloth: *a fleece lining* ♦ *a bright red fleece* ⊃ **picture at** CLOTHES
● *verb* ~ sb (*informal*) to take a lot of money from someone by charging them too much: *Some local stores have been fleecing tourists.*

fleecy /'flisi/ *adj.* [usually before noun] made of soft material, like the wool coat of a sheep; looking like this: *a fleecy sweatshirt* ♦ *a blue sky with fleecy clouds*

fleet /flit/ *noun, adj.*
● *noun* **1** [C] a group of military ships commanded by the same person **2** [C] a group of ships fishing together: *a fishing/whaling fleet* **3** the fleet [sing.] all the military ships of a particular country: *a reduction in the size of the American fleet* **4** [C] ~ (of sth) a group of planes, buses, taxis, etc. traveling together or owned by the same organization: *the company's new fleet of vans*
● *adj.* (*literary*) able to run fast: *fleet of foot* ♦ *fleet-footed*

Fleet Admiral *noun* an admiral of the highest rank in the navy: *Fleet Admiral William Leahy*

fleet·ing /'flitɪŋ/ *adj.* [usually before noun] lasting only a short time **SYN** BRIEF: *a fleeting glimpse/smile* ♦ *a fleeting moment of happiness* ♦ *We paid a fleeting visit to San Antonio.* ▶ **fleet·ing·ly** *adv.*

Flem·ish /'flɛmɪʃ/ *noun* [U] the Dutch language as spoken in northern Belgium

flesh /flɛʃ/ *noun, verb*
● *noun* **1** [U] the soft substance between the skin and bones of animal or human bodies: *The trap had cut deeply into the rabbit's flesh.* ♦ *Tigers are flesh-eating animals.* ♦ *the smell of rotting flesh* **2** [U] the skin of the human body: *She gently stroked the soft flesh of the baby's arm.* ♦ *flesh-colored* (= the color of white people's skin) **3** [U] the soft part of fruit and vegetables, especially when it is eaten **4** the flesh [sing.] (*literary*) the human body when considering its physical and sexual needs, rather than the mind or soul: *the pleasures/sins of the flesh*
IDM **flesh and blood** when you say that someone is **flesh and blood**, you mean that they are a normal human with needs, emotions, and weaknesses: *Listening to the cries was more than flesh and blood could stand.* **your (own) flesh and blood** a person that you are related to **in the flesh** if you see someone **in the flesh**, you are in the same place as them and actually see them rather than just seeing a picture of them **make your flesh crawl/creep** to make you feel afraid or full of disgust **put flesh on (the bones of) sth** to develop a basic idea, etc. by giving more details to make it more complete: *The strength of the book is that it puts flesh on the bare bones of this argument.* ⊃ **more at** POUND *n.*, PRESS *v.*, SPIRIT *n.*, WAY *n.*
● *verb*
PHR V **flesh sth↔'out** to add more information or details to a plan, an argument, etc.: *These points were fleshed out in the later parts of the speech.*

flesh·ly /'flɛʃli/ *adj.* [only before noun] (*literary*) connected with physical and sexual desires: *fleshly temptations/pleasures*

flesh·pots /'flɛʃpats/ *noun* [pl.] (*humorous*) places supplying food, drinks, and sexual entertainment

flesh wound *noun* an injury in which the skin is cut but the bones and organs inside the body are not damaged

flesh·y /'flɛʃi/ *adj.* **1** (of parts of the body or people) having a lot of flesh: *fleshy arms/lips* ♦ *a large fleshy man* **2** (of plants or fruit) thick and soft: *fleshy fruit/leaves*

fleur-de-lis (also **fleur-de-lys**) /ˌflɜr də 'li; ˌflʊr-/ *noun* (*pl.* fleurs-de-lis /ˌflɜr də 'li; -'liz; ˌflʊr-/) (from *French*) a design representing a flower with three PETALS joined together at the bottom, often used in coats of arms (COAT OF ARMS)

flew pt of FLY

flex /flɛks/ *verb* [T, I] ~ (sth) to bend, move, or stretch an arm or a leg, or contract a muscle, especially in order to prepare for a physical activity: *to flex your fingers/feet/legs* ♦ *He stood on the side of the pool flexing his muscles.*
IDM **flex your muscles** to show someone how powerful you are, especially as a warning or threat

flex·i·ble **AWL** /'flɛksəbl/ *adj.* **1** (*approving*) able to change to suit new conditions or situations: *a more flexible approach* ♦ *flexible working hours* ♦ *Our plans need to be flexible enough to accommodate everyone.* ♦ *You need to be more flexible and imaginative in your approach.* **2** able to bend easily without breaking: *flexible plastic tubing* **ANT** INFLEXIBLE ▶ **flex·i·bil·i·ty** **AWL** /ˌflɛksə'bɪləti/ *noun* [U]: *Computers offer a much greater degree of flexibility in the way work is organized.* ♦ *exercises to develop the flexibility of dancers' bodies* **flex·i·bly** /'flɛksəbli/ *adv.*

flex·ion (also **flec·tion**) /'flɛkʃn/ *noun* [U] (*technical*) the action of bending something

flex·or /'flɛksər; -sɔr/ (also **flexor muscle**) *noun* (*anatomy*) a muscle that allows you to bend part of your body ⊃ compare EXTENSOR

flex·time /'flɛkstaɪm/ *noun* [U] a system in which employees work a particular number of hours each week or month but can choose when they start and finish work each day: *She works flextime.*

flib·ber·ti·gib·bet /ˈflɪbərtiˌdʒɪbət; ˌflɪbərtiˈdʒɪbət/ *noun* (*old-fashioned, informal*) a person who is not serious enough or talks a lot about silly things

flick /flɪk/ *verb, noun*
• *verb* **1** [T] ~ sth + adv./prep. to hit something with a sudden quick movement, especially using your finger and thumb together, or your hand: *She flicked the dust off her collar.* ◆ *The horse was flicking flies away with its tail.* ◆ *James flicked a peanut at her.* ◆ *Please don't flick ash on the carpet!* **2** [I, T] to move or make something move with sudden quick movements: + adv./prep. *The snake's tongue flicked out.* ◆ *Her eyes flicked from face to face.* ◆ ~ sth (+ adv./prep.) *He flicked his head, flicking his hair off his face.* ◆ *The horse moved off, flicking its tail.* **3** [T] to smile or look at someone suddenly and quickly: ~ a smile/look, etc. at sb *She flicked a nervous glance at him.* ◆ ~ sb a smile/look, etc. *She flicked him a nervous glance.* **4** [T] to press a button or switch quickly in order to turn a machine, etc. on or off SYN FLIP: ~ sth a switch and all the lights went out. ◆ ~ sth on/off *She flicked the TV on.* **5** [T] to move something up and down with a sudden movement so that the end of it hits something: ~ A (with B) *He flicked me with a wet towel.* ◆ ~ B (at A) *He flicked a wet towel at me.* ◆ *to flick a whip*
PHR V flick 'through sth **1** to turn the pages of a book, etc. quickly and look at them without reading everything SYN FLIP THROUGH **2** to keep changing television channels quickly to see what programs are on SYN FLIP THROUGH
• *noun* **1** [C, usually sing.] a small, sudden, quick movement or hit, for example with a WHIP or part of the body: *He threw the ball back with a quick flick of the wrist.* ◆ *All this information is available at the flick of a switch* (= by simply turning on a machine). **2** [C] (*old-fashioned, informal*) a movie

flick·er /ˈflɪkər/ *verb, noun*
• *verb* **1** [I] (of a light or a flame) to keep going on and off as it shines or burns: *The lights flickered and went out.* ◆ *the flickering screen of the television* **2** [I] + adv./prep. (of an emotion, a thought, etc.) to be expressed or appear somewhere for a short time: *Anger flickered in his eyes.* **3** [I] to move with small, quick movements: *Her eyelids flickered as she slept.*
• *noun* [usually sing.] ~ (of sth) **1** a light that shines in an unsteady way: *the flicker of a television screen/candle* **2** a small sudden movement with part of the body: *the flicker of an eyelid* **3** a feeling or an emotion that lasts for only a very short time: *a flicker of hope/doubt/interest* ◆ *A flicker of a smile crossed her face.*

fli·er (also **fly·er**) /ˈflaɪər/ *noun* **1** (*informal*) a person who flies an aircraft (usually a small one, not a passenger plane) **2** a person who travels in a plane as a passenger: *frequent fliers* **3** a person who operates something such as a model aircraft or a KITE from the ground **4** a thing, especially a bird or an insect, that flies in a particular way: *Butterflies can be strong fliers.* **5** a sheet of paper that advertises a product or an event and is given to a large number of people

flies /flaɪz/ *noun* [pl.] **1** pl. of FLY **2 the flies** the space above the stage in a theater, used for lights and for storing SCENERY

flight ✎ /flaɪt/ *noun*
> JOURNEY BY AIR **1** [C] a trip made by air, especially in a plane: *a smooth/comfortable/bumpy flight* ◆ *a domestic/an international flight* ◆ *a hot-air balloon flight* ◆ *We met on a flight from Las Vegas to Kansas City.* ⊃ see also IN-FLIGHT
> PLANE **2** [C] a plane making a particular journey: *We're on the same flight.* ◆ *Flight 4793 is now boarding at Gate 17.* ◆ *If we leave now, I can catch the earlier flight.* ◆ *mercy/relief flights* (= planes taking help to countries where there is a war) ⊃ collocations at TRAVEL
> FLYING **3** [U] the act of flying: *the age of supersonic flight* ◆ *flight safety* ◆ *The bird is easily recognized in flight* (= when it is flying) *by the black band at the end of its tail.*

> MOVEMENT OF OBJECT **4** [U] the movement or direction of an object as it travels through the air: *the flight of a ball*
> OF STEPS **5** [C] a series of steps between two floors or levels: *She fell down a flight of stairs/steps and hurt her back.*
> RUNNING AWAY **6** [U, sing.] the act of running away from a dangerous or difficult situation: *the flight of refugees from the advancing forces* ◆ *The main character is a journalist in flight from a failed marriage.*
> OF FANCY/IMAGINATION **7** [C] ~ of fancy/imagination an idea or a statement that shows a lot of imagination but is not practical or sensible
> GROUP OF BIRDS/AIRCRAFT **8** [C] a group of birds or aircraft flying together: *a flight of geese*
IDM put sb to flight (*old-fashioned*) to force someone to run away take flight to run away: *The gang took flight when they heard the police car.* ⊃ more at TOP adj.

flight at·tendant *noun* a person whose job is to serve and take care of passengers on an aircraft

flight crew *noun* the people who work on a plane during a flight

flight deck *noun* **1** an area at the front of a large plane where the pilot sits to use the controls and fly the plane ⊃ picture at PLANE **2** a long flat surface on top of a ship that carries aircraft (= an AIRCRAFT CARRIER) where they take off and land

flight jacket *noun* a short leather jacket with a warm LINING and COLLAR, originally worn by pilots

flight·less /ˈflaɪtləs/ *adj.* [usually before noun] (of birds or insects) unable to fly

flight officer *noun* an officer of low rank in the U.S. AIR FORCE

flight path *noun* the route taken by an aircraft through the air

flight re·corder *noun* = BLACK BOX

flight simulator *noun* a device that reproduces the conditions that exist when flying an aircraft, used for training pilots

flight suit *noun* a piece of clothing that covers the whole body, worn by the pilot and CREW of a military or light aircraft

flight·y /ˈflaɪti/ *adj.* (*informal*) someone who is **flighty** cannot be relied on because he or she is always changing activities, ideas, or partners without treating them seriously

flim·flam /ˈflɪmflæm/ *noun* (*old-fashioned, informal*) **1** [U] nonsense **2** [C] an attempt to trick someone, usually to get money

flim·sy /ˈflɪmzi/ *adj.* (flim·si·er, flim·si·est) **1** badly made and not strong enough for the purpose for which it is used SYN RICKETY: *a flimsy table* **2** (of material) thin and easily torn: *a flimsy piece of paper/fabric/plastic* **3** difficult to believe SYN FEEBLE: *a flimsy excuse/explanation* ◆ *The evidence against him is pretty flimsy.* ▶ flim·si·ly /-zəli/ *adv.* flim·si·ness /-zinəs/ *noun* [U]

flinch /flɪntʃ/ *verb* [I] to make a sudden movement with your face or body as a result of pain, fear, surprise, etc.: *He met my gaze without flinching.* ◆ ~ at sth *He flinched at the sight of the blood.* ◆ ~ away *She flinched away from the dog.* ⊃ see also UNFLINCHING
PHR V 'flinch from sth | 'flinch from doing sth (often used in negative sentences) to avoid thinking about or doing something unpleasant: *He never flinched from facing up to his responsibilities.*

fling /flɪŋ/ *verb, noun*
• *verb* (flung, flung /flʌŋ/) **1** ~ sb/sth + adv./prep. to throw someone or something somewhere with force, especially because you are angry SYN HURL: *Someone had flung a brick through the window.* ◆ *She flung the bag to the ground.* ◆ *The door was suddenly flung open.* ◆ *He had his enemies flung into prison.* ⊃ thesaurus box at THROW **2** ~ yourself/sth + adv./prep. to move yourself or part of your body suddenly and with a lot of force: *She flung herself*

onto the bed. ♦ *He flung out an arm to stop her from falling.*
3 ~ sth (at sb) | + speech to say something to someone in an aggressive way **SYN** HURL: *They were flinging insults at each other.* ⊃ **see also** FAR-FLUNG
PHR V **'fling yourself into sth** to start to do something with a lot of energy and enthusiasm: *They flung themselves into the preparations for the party.* **,fling sth↔'off/'on** (*informal*) to take off or put on clothing in a quick and careless way: *He flung off his coat and collapsed on the sofa.*
● *noun* [usually sing.] (*informal*) **1 ~ (with sb)** a short romantic relationship with someone **2** a short period of enjoyment when you do not allow yourself to worry or think seriously about anything: *He was determined to have one last fling before returning to work.* ⊃ **see also** HIGHLAND FLING

flint /flɪnt/ *noun* **1** [U, C] a type of very hard gray stone that can produce a SPARK when it is hit against steel: *prehistoric flint tools* ♦ *His eyes were as hard as flint.* **2** [C] a piece of flint or hard metal that is used to produce a SPARK

flint·lock /'flɪntlɑk/ *noun* a gun used in the past that produced a SPARK from a flint when the TRIGGER was pressed

flint·y /'flɪnti/ *adj.* **1** showing no emotion: *a flinty look/gaze/stare* **2** containing flint: *flinty pebbles/soil*

flip /flɪp/ *verb, noun, adj.*
● *verb* (-pp-) **1** [I, T] to turn over into a different position with a sudden quick movement; to make something do this: *The plane flipped and crashed.* ♦ (*figurative*) *She felt her heart flip* (= with excitement, etc.). ♦ **~ sth (+ adj.)** *He flipped the lid open and looked inside the case.* ⊃ **see also** FLIP OVER **2** [T] to press a button or switch in order to turn a machine, etc. on or off **SYN** FLICK: **~ sth** *to flip a switch* ♦ **~ sth on/off** *She reached over and flipped off the light.* **3** [T] to throw something somewhere using your thumb and fingers **SYN** TOSS: **~ a coin:** *They flipped a coin to decide who would get the ticket.* ♦ **~ sth + adv./prep.** *He flipped the keys onto the desk.* **4** [I] **~ (out)** (*informal*) to become very angry, excited, or unable to think clearly: *My mom flipped when she found out I failed my math test.*
IDM **flip your lid** (*informal*) to become very angry and lose control of what you are saying or doing
PHR V **,flip 'over** to turn onto the other side or upside down: *The car hit a tree and flipped over.* ♦ *He flipped over and sat up.* **,flip sth↔'over** to turn something onto the other side or upside down: *The tornado flipped over several cars.* **'flip through sth 1** to turn the pages of a book, etc. quickly and look at them without reading everything **SYN** FLICK THROUGH: *She flipped through the magazine looking for the advice column.* **2** to keep changing television channels quickly to see what programs are on **SYN** FLICK THROUGH
IDM see BIRD
● *noun* **1** a small quick hit with a part of the body that causes something to turn over: *The whole thing was decided on the flip of a coin.* **2** a movement in which the body turns over in the air: *The handstand was followed by a back flip.* ♦ (*figurative*) *Her heart did a flip.*
● *adj.* (*informal*) = FLIPPANT: *a flip answer/comment* ♦ *Don't be flip with me.*

'flip chart *noun* large sheets of paper fixed at the top to a stand so that they can be turned over, used for presenting information at a talk or meeting

'flip-flop *noun, verb*
● *noun* (also **thong**) a type of SANDAL (= open shoe) that has a piece of rubber, leather, etc. that goes between the big toe and the toe next to it: *a pair of flip-flops* ⊃ **picture at** SHOE
● *verb* (-pp-) [I] **~ (on sth)** (*informal*) to change your opinion about something, especially when you then hold the opposite opinion: *The vice president was accused of flip-flopping on several major issues.*

flip-flop·per /'flɪp ˌflɑpər/ *noun* (*informal*) a person, especially a politician, who suddenly changes his or her opinion or policy ⊃ **see also** U-TURN

flip·pant /'flɪpənt/ (also *informal* **flip**) *adj.* showing that you do not take something as seriously as other people think

you should: *a flippant answer/attitude* ♦ *Sorry, I didn't mean to sound flippant.* ▶ **flip·pan·cy** /-pənsi/ *noun* [U] **flip·pant·ly** *adv.*

flip·per /'flɪpər/ *noun* [usually pl.] **1** a flat part of the body of some sea animals such as SEALS and TURTLES, used for swimming **2** a long flat piece of rubber or plastic that you wear on your foot to help you swim more quickly, especially below the surface of the water ⊃ **picture at** HOBBY

'flip phone *noun* a small cell phone with a cover that opens upward

'flip side *noun* [usually sing.] **~ (of/to sth) 1** a different way of looking at an idea, argument, or action **2** (*old-fashioned*) the side of a record that does not have the main song or piece of music on it

flirt /flərt/ *verb, noun*
● *verb* [I] **~ (with sb)** to behave toward someone as if you find them sexually attractive, without seriously wanting to have a relationship with them
PHR V **'flirt with sth 1** to think about or be interested in something for a short time but not very seriously: *She flirted with the idea of becoming an actress when she was younger.* **2** to take risks or not worry about a dangerous situation that may happen: *to flirt with danger/death/disaster*
● *noun* [usually sing.] a person who flirts with a lot of people: *She's a real flirt.*

flir·ta·tion /flər'teɪʃn/ *noun* **1** [C, U] **~ with sth** a short period of time during which someone is involved or interested in something, often not seriously: *a brief and unsuccessful flirtation with the property market* **2** [U] behavior that shows you find someone sexually attractive but are not serious about them: *Frank's efforts at flirtation had become annoying to her.* **3** [C] **~ (with sb)** a short romantic relationship with someone that is not taken seriously

flir·ta·tious /flər'teɪʃəs/ (also *informal* **flirt·y**) *adj.* behaving in a way that shows a sexual attraction to someone that is not serious: *a flirtatious young woman* ♦ *a flirtatious smile* ▶ **flir·ta·tious·ly** *adv.* **flir·ta·tious·ness** *noun* [U]

flit /flɪt/ *verb* (-tt-) [I] to move lightly and quickly from one place or thing to another: **~ from A to B** *Butterflies flitted from flower to flower.* ♦ *He flits from one job to another.* ♦ **+ adv./prep.** *A smile flitted across his face.* ♦ *A thought flitted through my mind.*

float ♪ /floʊt/ *verb, noun*
● *verb*
⟩ ON WATER/IN AIR **1** [I] **+ adv./prep.** to move slowly on water or in the air **SYN** DRIFT: *A group of swans floated by.* ♦ *The smell of freshly baked bread floated up from the kitchen.* ♦ *Beautiful music came floating out of the window.* ♦ (*figurative*) *An idea suddenly floated into my mind.* ♦ (*figurative*) *People seem to float in and out of my life.* **2** [I] to stay on or near the surface of a liquid and not sink: *Wood floats.* ♦ **~ in/on sth** *A plastic bag was floating in the water.* ♦ *Can you float on your back?* **3** [T] to make something move on or near the surface of a liquid: **~ sth** *There wasn't enough water to float the ship.* ♦ **~ sth + adv./prep.** *They float the logs down the river to the sawmill.*
⟩ WALK LIGHTLY **4** [I] **+ adv./prep.** (*literary*) to walk or move in a smooth and easy way **SYN** GLIDE: *She floated down the steps to greet us.*
⟩ SUGGEST IDEA **5** [T] **~ sth** to suggest an idea or a plan for other people to consider: *They floated the idea of increasing taxes on alcohol.*
⟩ BUSINESS/ECONOMICS **6** [T] **~ sth** (*business*) to sell shares in a company or business to the public for the first time: *The company was floated on the stock market in 2007.* ♦ *Shares were floated at $35.00.* **7** [T, I] **~ (sth)** (*economics*) if a government **floats** its country's money or allows it to **float**, it allows its value to change freely according to the value of the money of other countries
IDM **float sb's boat** (*informal*) to be what someone likes: *You can listen to whatever kind of music floats your boat.* ⊃ **more at** AIR *n.*
PHR V **,float a'round** (usually used in the progressive

tenses) if an idea, etc. **is floating around**, it is talked about by a number of people or passed from one person to another

● *noun*
> VEHICLE **1** a large vehicle on which people dressed in special COSTUMES are carried in a PARADE: *a carnival float*
> IN FISHING **2** a small light object attached to a FISHING LINE that stays on the surface of the water and moves when a fish has been caught
> FOR SWIMMING **3** a light object that floats in the water and is held by a person who is learning to swim to stop them from sinking
> DRINK **4** a drink with ice cream floating in it: *a root beer float*
> BUSINESS **5** = FLOTATION

float·er /ˈfloʊtər/ *noun* (*medical*) a very small object inside a person's eye that they see moving up and down

float·ing /ˈfloʊtɪŋ/ *adj.* [usually before noun] not fixed permanently in one particular position or place: *floating exchange rates* ◆ *a floating population* (= one in which people frequently move from one place to another) ◆ (*medical*) *a floating kidney*

,floating 'rib *noun* (*anatomy*) any of the lower RIBS that are not attached to the BREASTBONE

float·y /ˈfloʊti/ *adj.* (of cloth or clothing) very light and thin

flock /flɑk/ *noun, verb*
● *noun* **1** [C] ~ (of sth) a group of sheep, GOATS, or birds of the same type ⊃ compare HERD **2** [C] ~ (of sb) a large group of people, especially of the same type: *a flock of reporters* ◆ *They came in flocks to see the procession.* **3** [C] (*literary*) the group of people who regularly attend the church of a particular priest, etc. **4** [U] small pieces of soft material used for filling CUSHIONS, chairs, etc. **5** [U] small pieces of soft material on the surface of paper or cloth that produce a raised pattern: *flock wallpaper*
● *verb* [I] to go or gather together somewhere in large numbers: + adv./prep. *Thousands of people flocked to the beach this weekend.* ◆ *Huge numbers of birds had flocked together by the lake.* ◆ ~ to do sth *People flocked to hear him speak.* IDM see BIRD

floe /floʊ/ *noun* = ICE FLOE

flog /flɑg; flɔg/ *verb* (-gg-) [often passive] ~ sb to punish someone by hitting them many times with a WHIP or stick: *He was publicly flogged for breaking the country's alcohol laws.* IDM see DEAD

flog·ging /ˈflɑgɪŋ; ˈflɔ-/ *noun* [C, U] a punishment in which someone is hit many times with a WHIP or stick: *a public flogging*

flood 🔊 /flʌd/ *noun, verb*
● *noun*
> WATER **1** [C, U] a large amount of water covering an area that is usually dry: *The heavy rain caused floods in many parts of the country.* ◆ *flood damage* ◆ *Police have issued flood warnings for Nevada.* ⊃ see also FLASH FLOOD
> LARGE NUMBER **2** [C] ~ (of sth) a very large number of things or people that appear at the same time: *a flood of complaints* ◆ *a flood of refugees* ◆ *My son came home in a flood of tears* (= was crying a lot).
● *verb*
> FILL WITH WATER **1** [I, T] if a place **floods** or something **floods** it, it becomes filled or covered with water: *The basement floods whenever it rains heavily.* ◆ ~ sth *If the pipe bursts it could flood the whole house.*
> OF RIVER **2** [I, T] to become so full that it spreads out onto the land around it: *When the Ohio River floods, it causes considerable damage.* ◆ ~ sth *The river flooded the valley.*
> LARGE NUMBERS **3** [I] ~ in/into/out of sth to arrive or go somewhere in large numbers SYN POUR: *Refugees continue to flood into neighboring countries.* ◆ *Telephone calls came flooding in from all over the country.* **4** [T, usually passive] ~ sth/sb with sth to send something somewhere in large numbers: *The office was flooded with applications for the job.* **5** [T] to become or make something become available in a

place in large numbers: ~ sth *Cheap imported goods are flooding the market.* ◆ ~ sth with sth *A man who planned to flood the country with cocaine was jailed for 15 years.*
> OF FEELING/THOUGHT **6** [I, T] to affect someone suddenly and strongly: + adv./prep. *A great sense of relief flooded over him.* ◆ *Memories of her childhood came flooding back.* ◆ ~ sb with sth *The words flooded him with self-pity.*
> OF LIGHT/COLOR **7** [I, T] to spread suddenly into something; to cover something: + adv./prep. *She drew the curtains and the sunlight flooded in.* ◆ ~ sth *She looked away as color flooded her cheeks.* ◆ be flooded with sth *The room was flooded with light.*
> ENGINE **8** [I, T] ~ (sth) if an engine **floods** or if you **flood** it, it becomes so full of gas that it will not start
  ▶ **flood·ed** *adj.*: *flooded fields* **flood·ing** *noun* [U]: *There will be heavy rain with flooding in some areas.*
  PHR V ,flood sb↔'out [usually passive] to force someone to leave their home because of a flood

flood·gate /ˈflʌdgeɪt/ *noun* [usually pl.] a gate that can be opened or closed to control the flow of water on a river: (*figurative*) *If the case is successful, it may* **open the floodgates** *to more damages claims against the industry* (= start something that will be difficult to stop).

flood·light /ˈflʌdlaɪt/ *noun, verb*
● *noun* [usually pl.] a large powerful lamp, used for lighting sports fields, theater stages, and the outside of buildings: *a game played* **under floodlights**
● *verb* (flood·lit, flood·lit /-lɪt/) [usually passive] ~ sth to light a place or a building using floodlights: *The swimming pool is floodlit in the evenings.* ◆ *floodlit tennis courts*

'flood plain *noun* an area of flat land beside a river that regularly becomes flooded when there is too much water in the river

'flood tide *noun* a very high rise in the level of the ocean as it moves in toward the coast ⊃ compare HIGH TIDE

flood·wa·ter /ˈflʌd,wɔtər; -,wɑtər/ *noun* [U] (also **flood-waters** [pl.]) water that covers land after there has been a flood: *The floodwaters have now receded.*

floor 🔊 /flɔr/ *noun, verb*
● *noun*
> OF ROOM **1** [C, usually sing.] the surface of a room that you walk on: *a wooden/concrete/marble, etc. floor* ◆ *ceramic floor tiles* ◆ *The body was lying on the kitchen floor.* ◆ *The alterations should give us extra floor space.*
> OF VEHICLE **2** (also floor·board) [C, usually sing.] the bottom surface of a vehicle: *The floor of the car was covered in cigarette butts.*
> LEVEL OF BUILDING **3** [C] all the rooms that are on the same level of a building: *Her office is* **on the second floor**. ◆ *The young couple who live two floors above* ◆ *There is an elevator to all the floors.* ◆ *Their house is* **on three floors** (= it has three floors). ⊃ see also GROUND FLOOR
> OF THE OCEAN/FORESTS **4** [C, usually sing.] the ground at the bottom of the ocean, a forest, etc.: *the ocean/valley/cave/forest floor*
> IN CONGRESS, ETC. **5** the floor [sing.] the part of a building where discussions or debates are held; the people who attend a discussion or debate: *Opposition politicians registered their protest on the floor of the House.* ◆ *We will now take any questions from the floor.*
> AREA FOR WORK **6** [C, usually sing.] an area in a building that is used for a particular activity: *on the floor of the Stock Exchange* (= where trading takes place) ⊃ see also DANCE FLOOR, FACTORY FLOOR, SHOP FLOOR
> FOR WAGES/PRICES **7** [C, usually sing.] the lowest level allowed for wages or prices: *Prices have gone through the floor* (= fallen to a very low level). ⊃ compare CEILING
  IDM be/be given/have the floor to get/be given/have the right to speak during a discussion or debate hold the floor to speak during a discussion or debate, especially for a long time so that nobody else is able to say anything take (to) the floor to start dancing on a DANCE FLOOR: *Couples took the floor for the last dance of the evening.* wipe/mop the

ʌ **cup**   ə **about**   eɪ **say**   aɪ **five**   ɔɪ **boy**   aʊ **now**   oʊ **go**   ər **bird**

floor with sb (*informal*) to defeat someone completely in an argument or a competition ⊃ **more at** GROUND FLOOR

● **verb**

▸SURPRISE/CONFUSE **1** ~ **sb** to surprise or confuse someone so that they are not sure what to say or do

▸HIT **2** [usually passive] ~ **sb** to make someone fall down by hitting them, especially in a sport

▸BUILDING/ROOM **3** [usually passive] ~ **sth** to provide a building or room with a floor

▸DRIVING **4** ~ **sth** to press the ACCELERATOR pedal of a car hard: *She floored it and sped up the hill.*

THESAURUS

floor

ground ◆ land ◆ earth

These are all words for the surface that you walk on.

floor the surface of a room that you walk on: *She was sitting on the floor watching TV.*

ground (often **the ground**) the solid surface of the earth that you walk on: *I found her lying on the ground.* ◆ *The rocket crashed a few seconds after it left the ground.*

land the surface of the earth that is not sea: *It was good to be back on dry land again.* ◆ *They fought both on land and at sea.*

earth (often **the earth**) the solid surface of the world that is made of rock, soil, sand, etc.: *You could feel the earth shake as the truck came closer.*

GROUND, LAND, OR EARTH?

Ground is the normal word for the solid surface that you walk on when you are not in a building or vehicle. You can use **earth** if you want to draw attention to the rock, soil, etc. that the ground is made of. **Land** is used only when you want to contrast it with the sea: *the land beneath our feet* ◆ *feel the land shake* ◆ *travel by ground/earth*

PATTERNS

- **on/under** the floor/ground/earth
- **bare** floor/ground/earth
- to **drop to/fall to** the floor/the ground/(the) earth
- to **reach** the floor/the ground/land

floor·board /ˈflɔːbɔːd/ *noun* **1** a long flat piece of wood in a wooden floor: *bare/polished floorboards* **2** [usually sing.] = FLOOR: *a car floorboard* ◆ *He had his foot to the floorboard* (= was going very fast).

floor·ing /ˈflɔːrɪŋ/ *noun* [U] material used to make the floor of a room: *vinyl/wooden/tile flooring* ◆ *kitchen/bathroom flooring*

floor lamp *noun* a tall lamp that stands on the floor ⊃ picture at LIGHT

floor plan *noun* (*technical*) a drawing of the shape of a room or building, as seen from above, showing entrances and exits and sometimes the position of the furniture

floor show *noun* a series of performances by singers, dancers, etc. at a restaurant or club

floo·zy (also **floo·zie**) /ˈfluːzi/ *noun* (pl. **floo·zies**) (*old-fashioned, informal, disapproving*) a woman who has sexual relationships with many different men

flop /flɒp/ *verb, noun*
● **verb** (-pp-) **1** [I] ~ **(down/back) (into/on sth)** to sit or lie down in a heavy and sudden way because you are very tired: *Exhausted, he flopped down into a chair.* **2** [I] + **adv./prep.** to fall, move, or hang in a heavy or awkward way, without control: *Her hair flopped over her eyes.* ◆ *The fish were flopping around in the bottom of the boat.* **3** [I] (*informal*) to be a complete failure: *The play flopped on Broadway.*
● **noun** a movie, play, party, etc. that is not successful ANT HIT ⊃ see also BELLYFLOP

flop·house /ˈflɒphaʊs/ *noun* (*informal*) a cheap place to stay for people who have no home

flop·py /ˈflɒpi/ *adj.* (**flop·pi·er, flop·pi·est**) hanging or falling loosely; not hard and stiff: *a floppy hat*

floppy 'disk (also **flop·py**, pl. **flop·pies**) (also **disk·ette**) *noun* a flat disk inside a plastic cover, that is used to store data in the form that a computer can read, and that can be removed from the computer ⊃ **compare** HARD DISK

flo·ra /ˈflɔːrə/ *noun* [U] (*technical*) the plants of a particular area, type of environment, or period of time: *alpine flora* ◆ *rare species of flora and fauna* (= plants and animals)

flo·ral /ˈflɔːrəl/ *adj.* [usually before noun] **1** consisting of pictures of flowers; decorated with pictures of flowers: *wallpaper with a floral design/pattern* ◆ *a floral dress* **2** made of flowers: *a floral arrangement/display* ◆ *Floral tributes were sent to the church.*

florentine /ˈflɒrəntiːn; ˈflɑːr-/ *adj.* (of food) served on SPINACH: *eggs florentine*

flo·ret /ˈflɒrət; fləˈret/ *noun* a flower part of some vegetables, for example BROCCOLI and CAULIFLOWER. Each vegetable has several florets coming from one main STEM.

flo·ri·bun·da /ˌflɒrəˈbʌndə/ *noun* (*technical*) a plant, especially a ROSE, with flowers that grow very close together in groups

flor·id /ˈflɒrəd; ˈflɑːr-/ *adj.* **1** (usually *disapproving*) having too much decoration or detail: *florid language* **2** (of a person's face) red: *a florid complexion* ▸ **flor·id·ly** *adv.*

flo·rist /ˈflɒrɪst; ˈflɑːr-/ *noun* **1** a person who owns or works in a store that sells flowers and plants **2** a store that sells flowers and plants: *I ordered some flowers from the florist's.*

floss /flɒs; flɑs/ *noun, verb*
● **noun** [U] **1** = DENTAL FLOSS **2** thin silk thread
● **verb** [I, T] ~ **(sth)** to clean between your teeth with DENTAL FLOSS

flo·ta·tion /floʊˈteɪʃn/ *noun* **1** [U] the act of floating on or in water: *a flotation device* (= a LIFE PRESERVER, used to help someone float in water) **2** (also **float**) [C, U] (*business*) the process of selling shares in a company to the public for the first time in order to raise money: *plans for (a) flotation on the stock exchange* ◆ *a stock-market flotation*

flo'tation ˌtank *noun* a container filled with salt water in which people float in the dark as a way of relaxing

flo·til·la /floʊˈtɪlə/ *noun* a group of boats or small ships sailing together

flot·sam /ˈflɒtsəm/ *noun* [U] **1** parts of boats, pieces of wood or garbage, etc. that are found on land near the ocean or floating on the ocean; any kind of garbage: *The beaches are wide and filled with interesting flotsam and jetsam.* ⊃ compare JETSAM **2** people who have no home or job and who move from place to place, often rejected by society: *the human flotsam of inner cities*

flounce /flaʊns/ *verb, noun*
● **verb** [I] (+ **adv./prep.**) to move somewhere in a way that draws attention to yourself, for example because you are angry or upset: *She flounced out of the room.*
● **noun** **1** a strip of cloth that is sewn around the edge of a skirt, dress, curtain, etc. **2** a quick and exaggerated movement that you make when you are angry or want people to notice you: *She left the room with a flounce.* ▸ **flounced** *adj.*: *a flounced skirt*

floun·der /ˈflaʊndər/ *verb, noun*
● **verb** **1** [I] to have a lot of problems and to be in danger of failing completely: *At that time the industry was floundering.* **2** [I] (+ **adv./prep.**) to struggle to move or get somewhere in water, mud, etc.: *She was floundering around in the deep end of the swimming pool.* **3** [I] to struggle to know what to say or do or how to continue with something: *His abrupt change of subject left her floundering helplessly.*
● **noun** (pl. **floun·der** or **floun·ders**) a small, flat, ocean fish that is used for food

---

flour 🔑 /'flaʊər/ *noun, verb*
- *noun* [U] a fine white or brown powder made from grain, especially WHEAT, and used in cooking for making bread, cakes, etc. ⮕ see also ALL-PURPOSE FLOUR, SELF-RISING FLOUR
- *verb* [usually passive] ~ sth to cover something with a layer of flour: *Roll the dough on a lightly floured surface.*

flour·ish /'flɜːrɪʃ/ *verb, noun*
- *verb* **1** [I] to develop quickly and be successful or common **SYN** THRIVE: *Few businesses are flourishing in the present economic climate.* **2** [I] to grow well; to be healthy and happy **SYN** THRIVE: *These plants flourish in a damp climate.* ◆ *Peter is really flourishing in his new school.* **3** [T] ~ sth to wave something around in a way that makes people look at it
- *noun* **1** [usually sing.] an exaggerated movement that you make when you want someone to notice you: *He opened the door for her with a flourish.* **2** [usually sing.] an impressive act or way of doing something: *The playoffs ended with a flourish for Kobe, when he scored the winning basket in the final second of the game.* **3** details and decoration that are used in speech or writing: *a speech full of rhetorical flourishes* **4** a curved line that is used as decoration, especially in writing **5** [usually sing.] a loud short piece of music, that is usually played to announce an important person or event: *a flourish of trumpets*

flour·y /'flaʊəri/ *adj.* **1** covered with flour: *floury hands* **2** like flour; tasting of flour: *a floury texture* **3** (of potatoes) soft and light when they are cooked

flout /flaʊt/ *verb* ~ sth to show that you have no respect for a law, etc. by openly not obeying it **SYN** DEFY: *Motorists regularly flout the law.* ◆ *to flout authority/convention*

flow 🔑 /floʊ/ *verb, noun*
- *verb*
> MOVE CONTINUOUSLY **1** [I] (of liquid, gas, or electricity) to move steadily and continuously in one direction: *She lost control and the tears began to flow.* ◆ + adv./prep. *It's here that the river flows down into the ocean.* ◆ *Blood flowed from a cut on her head.* ◆ *This can prevent air from flowing freely to the lungs.* **2** [I] (+ adv./prep.) (of people or things) to move or pass continuously from one place or person to another, especially in large numbers or amounts: *Constant streams of traffic flowed past.* ◆ *Election results flowed in throughout the night.*
> OF IDEAS/CONVERSATION **3** [I] to develop or be produced in an easy and natural way: *Conversation flowed freely throughout the meal.*
> BE AVAILABLE EASILY **4** [I] to be available easily and in large amounts: *It was obvious that money flowed freely in their family.* ◆ *The party got livelier as the wine began to flow.*
> OF FEELING **5** [I] + adv./prep. to be felt strongly by someone: *Fear and excitement suddenly flowed over me.*
> OF CLOTHES/HAIR **6** [I] ~ (down/over sth) to hang loosely and freely: *Her hair flowed down over her shoulders.* ◆ *long flowing skirts*
> OF THE OCEAN **7** [I] (of the TIDE in the ocean) to come in toward the land **ANT** EBB
  PHR V 'flow from sth (*formal*) to come or result from something
- *noun* [C, usually sing., U]
> CONTINUOUS MOVEMENT **1** ~ (of sth/sb) the steady and continuous movement of something or someone in one direction: *She tried to stop the flow of blood from the wound.* ◆ *an endless flow of refugees into the country* ◆ *to improve traffic flow* (= make it move faster) ◆ *to control the direction of flow*
> PRODUCTION/SUPPLY **2** ~ (of sth) the continuous production or supply of something: *the flow of goods and services to remote areas* ◆ *to encourage the free flow of information* ◆ *data flow* ⮕ see also CASH FLOW
> OF SPEECH/WRITING **3** continuous talk by someone: *You interrupted my flow—I can't remember what I was saying.* **4** ~ of sth the way that words and ideas are linked together

in speech or writing: *Too many examples can interrupt the smooth flow of the text.*
> OF THE OCEAN **5** the movement of the ocean toward the land: *the ebb and flow of the tide*
  IDM go with the 'flow (*informal*) to be relaxed and not worry about what you should do ⮕ more at EBB *n.*

'flow chart (also **'flow ˌdiagram**) *noun* a diagram that shows the connections between the different stages of a process or parts of a system ⮕ picture at GRAPH

flow·er 🔑 /'flaʊər/ *noun, verb*
- *noun* **1** the colored part of a plant from which the seed or fruit develops. Flowers usually grow at the end of a STEM and last only a short time: *The plant has a beautiful bright red flower.* ◆ *The roses are in flower early this year.* ◆ *The crocuses are late coming into flower.* ⮕ picture at PLANT ⮕ collocations at LIFE **2** a plant grown for the beauty of its flowers: *a garden full of flowers* ◆ *a flower garden/show* ⮕ picture at PLANT **3** a flower with its STEM that has been picked as a decoration: *I picked some flowers.* ◆ *a bunch of flowers* ◆ *a flower arrangement* ⮕ see also BOUQUET
  IDM the flower of sth (*literary*) the finest or best part of something
- *verb* **1** [I] (of a plant or tree) to produce flowers **SYN** BLOOM: *This particular variety flowers in July.* ◆ *early-flowering spring bulbs* **2** [I] (*literary*) to develop and become successful **SYN** BLOSSOM

'flower arˌranging *noun* [U] the art of arranging cut flowers in an attractive way

'flower ˌbed *noun* a piece of ground in a yard or park where flowers are grown

flow·ered /'flaʊərd/ *adj.* [usually before noun] decorated with patterns of flowers

'flower ˌgirl *noun* a young girl who carries flowers in front of the BRIDE at a wedding

flow·er·ing /'flaʊərɪŋ/ *noun* **1** [U] the time when a plant has flowers **2** [C, usually sing.] ~ of sth the time when something, especially a period of new ideas in art, music, science, etc., reaches its most complete and successful stage of development

flow·er·pot /'flaʊərˌpɑt/ *noun* a container made of plastic or CLAY for growing plants in

'flower ˌpower *noun* [U] the culture connected with young people of the 1960s and early 1970s who believed in love and peace and were against war

flow·er·y /'flaʊəri/ *adj.* [usually before noun] **1** covered with flowers or decorated with pictures of flowers **2** smelling or tasting of flowers **3** (usually *disapproving*) (of speech or writing) too complicated; not expressed in a clear and simple way

flown pp of FLY

fl. oz. *abbr.* (*pl.* **fl. oz.**) (in writing) FLUID OUNCE: *Add 8 fl. oz. water.*

flu 🔑 /flu/ often **the flu** (also *formal* in·flu·en·za) *noun* [U] an infectious disease like a very bad cold, which causes fever, pains, and weakness: *The whole family has the flu.*

flub /flʌb/ *verb* (-bb-) [T, I] ~ (sth) (*informal*) to do something badly or make a mistake: *She flubbed the first line of the song.* ▶ **flub** *noun*

fluc·tu·ate **AWL** /'flʌktʃuˌeɪt/ *verb* [I] to change frequently in size, amount, quality, etc., especially from one extreme to another **SYN** VARY: *fluctuating prices* ◆ ~ **between A and B** *During the crisis, oil prices fluctuated between $40 and $80 a barrel.* ◆ + adv./prep. *Temperatures can fluctuate by as much as 10 degrees.* ◆ *My mood seems to fluctuate from day to day.* ▶ **fluc·tu·a·tion** **AWL** /ˌflʌktʃuˈeɪʃn/ *noun* [C, U]: ~ (in/of sth) *wild fluctuations in interest rates*

flue /flu/ *noun* a pipe or tube that takes smoke, gas, or hot air away from a FIREPLACE, a FURNACE, or an oven

flu·en·cy /'fluənsi/ *noun* [U, sing.] **1** the quality of being able to speak or write a language, especially a foreign

| t tea | ţ butter | d did | k cat | g got | tʃ chin | dʒ June | f fall |

language, easily and well: *Fluency in French is required for this job.* **2** the quality of moving in a smooth and skillful way: *The dancers lacked fluency during the first half of the program.*

flu·ent /ˈfluənt/ *adj.* **1** ~ **(in sth)** able to speak, read, or write a language, especially a foreign language, easily and well: *She's fluent in Polish.* ◆ *a fluent speaker/reader* **2** (of a language, especially a foreign language) expressed easily and well: *He speaks fluent Italian.* **3** (of an action) done in a smooth and skillful way: *fluent handwriting* ◆ *fluent movements* ▶ **flu·ent·ly** *adv.*

fluff /flʌf/ *noun, verb*
● *noun* [U] **1** (also lint) small pieces of wool, cotton, etc. that gather on clothes and other surfaces **2** soft animal fur or bird feathers, that is found especially on young animals or birds **3** (*informal*) entertainment that is not serious and is not considered to have great value
● *verb* **1** ~ **sth** (*informal*) to do something badly or to fail at something **SYN** BUNGLE: *He completely fluffed an easy shot* (= in sports). ◆ *Most actors fluff their lines occasionally.* **2** ~ **sth (out/up)** to shake or brush something so that it looks larger and/or softer: *The female sat on the eggs, fluffing out her feathers.* ◆ *Let me fluff up your pillows for you.*

fluff·y /ˈflʌfi/ *adj.* (fluff·i·er, fluff·i·est) **1** like fluff; covered in fluff: *a fluffy little kitten* **2** (of food) soft, light, and containing air: *Beat the butter and sugar until soft and fluffy.* **3** looking as if it is soft and light: *fluffy white clouds*

flu·gel·horn /ˈfluɡlˌhɔrn/ *noun* a BRASS musical instrument like a small TRUMPET

flu·id /ˈfluəd/ *noun, adj.*
● *noun* [C, U] a liquid; a substance that can flow: *bodily fluids* (= for example, blood) ◆ *The doctor told him to drink plenty of fluids.* ◆ *cleaning fluid*
● *adj.* **1** (*formal*) (of movements, designs, music, etc.) smooth and elegant **SYN** FLOW: *a loose, fluid style of dancing* ◆ *fluid guitar playing* ◆ *the fluid lines of the drawing* **2** (*formal*) (of a situation) likely to change; not fixed: *a fluid political situation* **3** (*technical*) that can flow freely, as gases and liquids do: *a fluid consistency*

flu·id·i·ty /fluˈɪdəti/ *noun* [U] **1** (*formal*) the quality of being smooth and elegant: *She danced with great fluidity of movement.* **2** (*formal*) the quality of being likely to change: *the fluidity of human behavior* ◆ *social fluidity* **3** (*technical*) the quality of being able to flow freely, as gases and liquids do

ˌfluid ˈounce *noun* (*abbr.* fl. oz.) a unit for measuring liquids. There are 16 fluid ounces in an American pint.

fluke /fluk/ *noun* [usually sing.] (*informal*) a lucky or unusual thing that happens by accident, not because of planning or skill: *They are determined to show that their last win wasn't just a fluke.* ◆ *a fluke goal* ▶ **fluk·y** (also **fluk·ey**) /ˈfluki/ *adj.*

flume /flum/ *noun* **1** a narrow channel made to carry water for use in industry **2** a water CHUTE (= a tube for sliding down) at an AMUSEMENT PARK or a swimming pool

flum·mer·y /ˈflʌməri/ *noun* [U] nonsense, especially praise that is silly or not sincere: *She hated the flummery of public relations.*

flum·mox /ˈflʌməks/ *verb* [usually passive] (not used in the progressive tenses) ~ **sb** (*informal*) to confuse someone so that they do not know what to say or do: *I was flummoxed by her question.* ▶ **flum·moxed** *adj.*

flung pt, pp of FLING

flunk /flʌŋk/ *verb* (*informal*) **1** [T, I] ~ **(sth)** to fail an exam, a test, or a course: *I flunked math in fourth grade.* **2** [T] ~ **sb** to make someone fail an exam, a test, or a course by giving them a low grade: *She's flunked 13 of the 18 students.*
PHRV ˌflunk ˈout (of sth) (*informal*) to have to leave a school or college because your grades are not good enough

flun·ky (also **flun·key**) /ˈflʌŋki/ *noun* (*pl.* flun·kies or flun·keys) **1** (*disapproving*) a person who tries to please someone who is important and powerful by doing small jobs for them **2** (*old-fashioned*) a servant in uniform

fluo·res·cent /flɔˈrɛsnt; flʊ-/ *adj.* **1** (of substances) producing bright light by using some forms of RADIATION: *a fluorescent lamp* (= one that uses such a substance) ◆ *fluorescent lighting* **2** (of a color, material, etc.) appearing very bright when light shines on it; that can be seen in the dark: *fluorescent armbands worn by cyclists* ⊃ compare PHOSPHORESCENT ⊃ note at BRIGHT ▶ **fluo·res·cence** /-ˈrɛsns/ *noun* [U]

fluor·i·da·tion /ˌflɔrəˈdeɪʃn; ˌflʊr-/ *noun* [U] the practice of adding fluoride to drinking water to prevent tooth decay

fluor·ide /ˈflɔraɪd; ˈflʊr-/ *noun* [U] a chemical containing fluorine that protects teeth from decay and is often added to TOOTHPASTE and sometimes to drinking water

fluor·ine /ˈflɔrin; ˈflʊr-/ *noun* [U] (*symb.* F) a chemical element. Fluorine is a poisonous, pale yellow gas and is very REACTIVE.

flur·ried /ˈflɜrid/ *adj.* nervous and confused, especially because there is too much to do

flur·ry /ˈflɜri/ *noun* (*pl.* flur·ries) **1** [usually sing.] an occasion when there is a lot of activity, interest, excitement, etc. within a short period of time: *a sudden flurry of activity* ◆ *Her arrival caused a flurry of excitement.* ◆ *A flurry of shots rang out in the darkness.* **2** a small amount of snow that falls for a short time and then stops: *snow flurries* **3** a sudden short movement of paper or cloth, especially clothes: *The ladies departed in a flurry of silks and satins.*

flush /flʌʃ/ *verb, noun, adj.*
● *verb* **1** [I, T] (of a person or their face) to become red, especially because you are embarrassed, angry, or hot: *She flushed with anger.* ◆ + *adj.*: *Sam felt her cheeks flush red.* ◆ ~ **sth** *A rosy blush flushed her cheeks.* **2** [I, T] ~ **(sth)** when a toilet **flushes** or you **flush** it, water passes through it to clean it, after a handle, etc. has been pressed **3** [T] to clean something by causing water to pass through it: ~ **sth out (with sth)** *Flush the pipe out with clean water.* ◆ ~ **sth through sth** *Flush clean water through the pipe.* **4** [T] ~ **sth** + **adv./prep.** to get rid of something with a sudden flow of water: *They flushed the drugs down the toilet.* ◆ *Drinking lots of water will help to flush toxins out of the body.*
PHRV ˌflush sb/sth ˈout (of sth) | ˌflush sb/sth↔ˈout to force a person or an animal to leave the place where they are hiding
● *noun* **1** [C, usually sing.] a red color that appears on your face or body because you are embarrassed, excited, or hot: *A pink flush spread over his cheeks.* **2** [C, usually sing.] a sudden strong feeling; the hot feeling on your face or body caused by this: *a flush of anger/embarrassment/enthusiasm/guilt* **3** [sing.] the act of cleaning a toilet with a sudden flow of water: *Give the toilet another flush.* **4** [C] (in card games) a set of cards that a player has that are all of the same SUIT ⊃ see also ROYAL FLUSH
IDM (in) the first flush of sth (*formal*) (at) a time when something is new, exciting, and strong: *in the first flush of youth/enthusiasm/romance*
● *adj.* [not before noun] **1** (*informal*) having a lot of money, usually for a short time **2** ~ **with sth** (of two surfaces) completely level with each other: *Make sure the paving stones are flush with the lawn.*

flushed /flʌʃt/ *adj.* (of a person) red; with a red face: *flushed cheeks* ◆ *Her face was flushed with anger.* ◆ (*figurative*) *He was flushed with success* (= very excited and pleased) *after his first novel was published.*

flust·er /ˈflʌstər/ *verb* [often passive] ~ **sb** to make someone nervous and/or confused, especially by giving them a lot to do or by making them hurry ▶ **flust·ered** *adj.*: *She arrived late, looking hot and flustered.*

flute /flut/ *noun* **1** a musical instrument of the WOODWIND group, shaped like a thin pipe. The player holds it sideways and blows across a hole at one end. ⊃ picture at INSTRUMENT, KEY **2** champagne ~ a tall narrow glass used for drinking CHAMPAGNE ⊃ picture at GLASS

flut·ed /ˈflutəd/ *adj.* (especially of a round object) with a pattern of curves cut around the outside: *fluted columns* ▶ **flut·ing** *noun* [U]

flut·ist /'flutɪst/ (also **flaut·ist**) *noun* a person who plays the FLUTE

flut·ter /'flʌtər/ *verb, noun*
● *verb* **1** [I, T] to move lightly and quickly; to make something move in this way: *Flags fluttered in the breeze.* ◆ *Her eyelids fluttered but did not open.* ◆ *~ sth He fluttered his hands around wildly.* ◆ (*figurative*) *She fluttered her eyelashes at him* (= tried to attract him in order to persuade him to do something). **2** [I, T] **~ (sth)** when a bird or an insect **flutters** its wings, or its wings **flutter**, the wings move lightly and quickly up and down **3** [I] **+ adv./prep.** (of a bird or an insect) to fly somewhere moving the wings quickly and lightly: *The butterfly fluttered from flower to flower.* **4** [I] (of your heart, etc.) to beat very quickly and not regularly: *I could feel a fluttering pulse.* ◆ (*figurative*) *The sound of her voice in the hall made his heart flutter.*
● *noun* **1** [C, usually sing.] a quick, light movement: *the flutter of wings* ◆ *with a flutter of her long, dark eyelashes* ◆ (*figurative*) *to feel a flutter of panic in your stomach* **2** [sing.] a state of nervous or confused excitement: *Her sudden arrival caused quite a flutter.* ◆ *to be in a flutter* **3** [C] a very fast HEARTBEAT, caused when someone is nervous or excited: *Her heart gave a flutter as she went out on stage.* **4** [U] (*medical*) a medical condition in which you have a fast, unsteady HEARTBEAT **5** [U] (*technical*) rapid changes in the PITCH or volume of recorded sound ⊃ compare WOW

flu·vi·al /'fluviəl/ *adj.* (*technical*) relating to rivers

flux /flʌks/ *noun* **1** [U] continuous movement and change: *Our society is in a state of flux.* **2** [C, usually sing., U] (*technical*) a flow; an act of flowing: *a flux of neutrons*

fly 🪰 /flaɪ/ *verb, noun, adj.*
● *verb* (**flies, fly·ing, flew** /flu/, **flown** /floʊn/) **HELP** In sense 15 **flied** is used for the past tense and past participle.
▷ OF BIRD/INSECT **1** [I] **(+ adv./prep.)** to move through the air, using wings: *A hawk flew in circles above the field.* ◆ *A wasp had flown in through the window.*
▷ AIRCRAFT/SPACECRAFT **2** [I] **(+ adv./prep.)** (of an aircraft or a SPACECRAFT) to move through air or space: *They were on a plane flying from Washington to New York.* ◆ *to fly at the speed of sound* ◆ *Northwest flies from Minneapolis to Seattle.* **3** [I] to travel in an aircraft or a SPACECRAFT: *Is this the first time that you've flown?* ◆ **(from…) (to…)** *I'm flying to Hong Kong tomorrow.* ◆ **+ noun** *I always fly business class.* ◆ *We're flying Delta.* **4** [T, I] **~ (sth)** to control an aircraft, etc. in the air: *a pilot trained to fly large passenger planes* ◆ *children flying kites* ◆ *He's learning to fly.* **5** [T] **+ adv./prep.** to transport goods or passengers in a plane: *The stranded tourists were finally flown home.* ◆ *He had flowers specially flown in for the ceremony.* **6** [T] **~ sth** to travel over an ocean or area of land in an aircraft: *to fly the Atlantic*
▷ MOVE QUICKLY/SUDDENLY **7** [I] **(+ adv./prep.)** to go or move quickly: *The train was flying along.* ◆ *She gasped and her hand flew to her mouth.* ◆ *It's late—I've got to fly.* **8** [I] to move suddenly and with force: **(+ adv./prep.)** *A large stone came flying in through the window.* ◆ *Several people were hit by flying glass.* ◆ **+ adj.** *David gave the door a kick and it flew open.*
▷ OF TIME **9** [I] to seem to pass very quickly: *Doesn't time fly?* ◆ **~ by/past** *This summer just flew by.*
▷ FLAG **10** [I, T] if a flag **flies**, or if you **fly** it, it is displayed, for example on a long pole: *Flags were flying at half mast on all public buildings.* ◆ **~ sth** *to fly the Stars and Stripes*
▷ MOVE FREELY **11** [I] to move around freely: *hair flying in the wind*
▷ OF STORIES/RUMORS **12** [I] to be talked about by many people
▷ ESCAPE **13** [T, I] **~ (sth)** (*formal*) to escape from someone or something: *Both suspects have flown the country.* ⊃ compare FLEE
▷ OF PLAN **14** [I] (*informal*) to be successful: *It remains to be seen whether his project will fly.*
▷ IN BASEBALL **15** (**flies, fly·ing, flied, flied**) [I, T] **~ (sth)** to hit a ball high into the air

IDM **fly the coop** (*informal*) to escape from a place **fly high** to be successful **fly in the face of sth** to oppose or be the opposite of something that is usual or expected: *Such a proposal flies in the face of common sense.* **fly into a rage, temper, etc.** to become suddenly very angry **go fly a kite** (*informal*) used to tell someone to go away and stop annoying you or INTERFERING **fly off the handle** (*informal*) to suddenly become very angry **go flying** (*informal*) to fall, especially as a result of not seeing something under your feet: *She tripped over the rug and went flying.* **let fly (at sb/ sth) (with sth)** to attack someone by hitting them or speaking angrily to them: *He let fly at me with his fist.* ◆ *She let fly with a stream of abuse.* ⊃ more at CROW n., FLAG n., PIG n., SEAT n., TIME n., WINDOW
PHR V **'fly at sb** (of a person or an animal) to attack someone suddenly
● *noun* (*pl.* **flies**)
▷ INSECT **1** [C] a small flying insect with two wings. There are many different types of flies: *A fly was buzzing against the window.* ◆ *Flies rose in thick black swarms.* ⊃ picture at ANIMAL
▷ IN FISHING **2** [C] a fly or something made to look like a fly, that is put on a hook and used as BAIT to catch fish: *fly-fishing*
▷ ON PANTS **3** [sing.] an opening down the front of a pair of pants that fastens with a ZIPPER or buttons and is usually covered over by a strip of material: *Your fly is open!* ⊃ picture at CLOTHES
▷ ON TENT **4** [C] a piece of material that covers the entrance to a tent ⊃ see also FLIES
IDM **die/drop/fall like flies** (*informal*) to die or fall down in very large numbers: *People were dropping like flies in the intense heat.* **a/the fly in the ointment** a person or thing that spoils a situation or an occasion that is fine in all other ways **a fly on the wall** a person who watches others without being noticed: *I'd love to be a fly on the wall when he tells her the news.* ◆ *fly-on-the-wall documentaries* (= in which people are filmed going about their normal lives as if the camera were not there) **(there are) no flies on sb** (*informal*) the person mentioned is smart and not easily tricked ⊃ more at HURT v.
IDM **on the fly** (*informal*) if you do something **on the fly**, you do it quickly while something else is happening, and without thinking about it very much
● *adj.* (*informal*) fashionable and attractive

fly a'garic (also **fly 'agaric**) *noun* a poisonous MUSHROOM with a red top with white spots

fly·a·way /'flaɪəweɪ/ *adj.* (especially of hair) soft and fine; difficult to keep neat

fly 'ball *noun* (in baseball) a ball that is hit high into the air

fly·boy /'flaɪbɔɪ/ *noun* (*old-fashioned, informal*) a pilot, especially one in the AIR FORCE

fly·by /'flaɪbaɪ/ *noun* (*pl.* **fly·bys**) **1** (also **fly·over**) a special flight by a group of aircraft, for people to watch at an important ceremony **2** the flight of a SPACECRAFT near a planet to record data

'fly-by-'night *adj.* [only before noun] (of a person or business) dishonest and only interested in making money quickly ▶ **'fly-by-night** *noun*

fly·catch·er /'flaɪˌkætʃər/ *noun* a small bird that catches insects while it is flying

fly·er = FLIER

'fly-fishing *noun* [U] the sport of fishing in a river or lake using an artificial fly to attract and catch the fish

fly·ing 🪰 /'flaɪɪŋ/ *adj., noun*
● *adj.* [only before noun] able to fly: *flying insects*
IDM **with flying colors** very well; with a very high grade: *She passed the course with flying colors.* **ORIGIN** In the past, a ship returned to port after a victory in battle decorated with flags (= colors).
● *noun* [U] **1** traveling in an aircraft: *I'm terrified of flying.* **2** operating the controls of an aircraft: *flying lessons*

flying 'buttress *noun* (*architecture*) a half ARCH of brick or

| h **hat** | m **man** | n **no** | ŋ **sing** | l **leg** | r **red** | y **yes** | w **wet** |

stone that supports the outside wall of a large building such as a church

flying 'fish noun a tropical sea fish that can rise and move forward above the surface of the water, using its FINS (= flat parts that stick out from its body) as wings

flying 'fox noun a large BAT (= an animal like a mouse with wings) that lives in hot countries and eats fruit

flying 'leap noun a long high jump made while you are running quickly: *to take a flying leap into the air*

'flying ma,chine noun an aircraft, especially one that is unusual or was built a long time ago

flying 'saucer noun a round SPACECRAFT that some people claim to have seen and that some people believe comes from another planet ⟳ compare UFO

flying 'squirrel noun a small animal like a SQUIRREL that travels through the air between trees, spreading out the skin between its front and back legs to stop itself from falling too quickly

flying 'start noun [sing.] a very fast start to a race, competition, etc.
IDM **get off to a flying start** to make a very good start; to begin something well

fly·leaf /'flaɪlif/ noun (pl. **fly·leaves**) an empty page at the beginning or end of a book

fly·o·ver /'flaɪˌoʊvər/ noun = FLYBY

'flyover ,country noun [U] (also the **'flyover ,states** [pl.]) (informal, disapproving) the area in the middle of the United States between the states on the coasts: *It's an area most New Yorkers know as flyover country.*

fly·pa·per /'flaɪˌpeɪpər/ noun [C, U] a strip of sticky paper that you hang in a room to catch flies

'fly ,swatter (also **fly·swat·ter**) /'flaɪˌswɑtər/ noun a plastic tool with a handle, used to SWAT (= hit) insects

fly·weight /'flaɪweɪt/ noun a BOXER, WRESTLER, etc. of the lightest class, usually weighing no more than 112 pounds (51 kg) ⟳ compare BANTAMWEIGHT

fly·wheel /'flaɪwil/ noun a heavy wheel in a machine or an engine that helps to keep it working smoothly and at a steady speed

FM /ˌɛf 'ɛm/ abbr. frequency modulation (a method of broadcasting high-quality sound by radio): *You're listening to 96.5 FM.*

foal /foʊl/ noun, verb
• noun a very young horse or DONKEY
IDM **in foal** (of a female horse) pregnant
• verb [I] to give birth to a foal

foam /foʊm/ noun, verb
• noun **1** (also ,foam 'rubber) [U] a soft, light, rubber material, full of small holes, that is used for seats, MATTRESSES, etc.: *a foam mattress ♦ foam packaging* **2** [U] a mass of very small air bubbles on the surface of a liquid **SYN** FROTH: *a glass of beer with a good head of foam ♦ The breaking waves left the beach covered with foam.* ⟳ picture at FROTH **3** [U, C] a chemical substance that forms or produces a soft mass of very small bubbles, used for washing, shaving, or putting out fires, for example: *shaving foam*
• verb [I] (of a liquid) to have or produce a mass of small bubbles **SYN** FROTH
IDM **foam at the mouth 1** (especially of an animal) to have a mass of small bubbles in and around its mouth, especially because it is sick or angry **2** (informal) (of a person) to be very angry

foam·y /'foʊmi/ adj. consisting of or producing a mass of small bubbles; like foam

fob /fɑb/ verb, noun
• verb (-bb-)
PHR V **fob sb↔'off (with sth) 1** to try to stop someone from asking questions or complaining by telling them something that is not true: *Don't let him fob you off with any more excuses. ♦ She wouldn't be fobbed off this time.* **2** to give

someone something that is not what they want or is of worse quality than they want: *He was unaware that he was being fobbed off with out-of-date stock.*
• noun **1** a small decorative object that is attached to a KEY RING, etc. **2** a short chain that is attached to a watch that is carried in a pocket **3** (also 'fob watch) a watch that is attached to a fob

f.o.b. abbr. (in writing) FREE ON BOARD

fo·cac·cia /foʊˈkɑtʃə/ noun [U, C] a type of flat Italian bread, often baked with vegetables or other ingredients on the top

fo·cal /'foʊkl/ adj. [only before noun] central; very important; connected with or providing a focus

fo·cal·ize /'foʊkəˌlaɪz/ verb ~ sth (formal) to make something focus or concentrate on a particular thing ▶ **fo·cal·i·za·tion** /ˌfoʊkələ'zeɪʃn/ noun [U, C]

'focal ,length noun (physics) the distance between the center of a mirror or a LENS and its FOCUS

'focal ,point noun **1** a thing or person that is the center of interest or activity: *In rural areas, the church is often the focal point for the local community. ♦ He quickly became the focal point for those who disagreed with government policy.* **2** (technical) = FOCUS

fo'c's'le = FORECASTLE

fo·cus ⚘ **AWL** /'foʊkəs/ verb, noun
• verb (-s- or -ss-) **1** [I, T] to give attention, effort, etc. to one particular subject, situation, or person rather than another: ~ **(on sb/sth)** *The discussion focused on three main problems. ♦ Each exercise focuses on a different grammar point. ♦ ~ sth* **(on sb/sth)** *The visit helped to focus world attention on the plight of the refugees.* **2** [I, T] (of your eyes, a camera, etc.) to adapt or be adjusted so that things can be seen clearly; to adjust something so that you can see things clearly: *It took a few moments for her eyes to focus in the dark. ♦ ~ on sb/sth Let your eyes focus on objects that are farther away from you. ♦ In this scene, the camera focuses on the actor's face. ♦ ~ sth* **(on sb/sth)** *He focused his blue eyes on her. ♦ I quickly focused the camera on the children.* **3** [T] ~ **sth (on sth)** (technical) to aim light onto a particular point using a LENS
• noun (pl. **fo·cus·es** or **fo·ci** /'foʊsaɪ/) **1** [U, C, usually sing.] the thing or person that people are most interested in; the act of paying special attention to something and making people interested in it: *It was the main focus of attention at the meeting. ♦ ~ for sth His comments provided a focus for debate. ♦ ~ on sth We will keep our focus on the needs of the customer. ♦ In today's lecture the focus will be on recent changes in corporate tax structure. ♦ The incident brought the problem of violence in schools into sharp focus. ♦ What we need now is a change of focus* (= to look at things in a different way). **2** [U] a point or distance at which the outline of an object is clearly seen by the eye or through a LENS: *The children's faces are badly out of focus in the photo. ♦ The binoculars were not in focus* (= were not showing things clearly). **3** (also 'focal ,point) [C] (physics) a point at which waves of light, sound, etc. meet after REFLECTION or refraction (REFRACT); the point from which waves of light, sound, etc. seem to come **4** [C] (geology) the point at which an EARTHQUAKE starts to happen

fo·cused (also **fo·cussed**) /'foʊkəst/ adj. with your attention directed to what you want to do; with very clear aims: *She should do well at college this year—she's very focused.*

'focus ,group noun a small group of people, specially chosen to represent different social classes, ethnic backgrounds, etc., who are asked to discuss and give their opinions about a particular subject. The information obtained is used by people doing MARKET RESEARCH, for example about new products or for a political party.

fod·der /'fɑdər/ noun [U] **1** food for horses and farm animals **2** (disapproving) (often after a noun) people or things that are considered to have only one use: *Without education, these children will end up as factory fodder* (= only able to work in a factory). *♦ This story will be more fodder for the gossip columnists.* ⟳ see also CANNON FODDER

foe /fəʊ/ noun (old use or formal) an enemy

fog /fɒg; fɑːg/ noun, verb
- **noun** [U, C] **1** a thick cloud of very small drops of water in the air close to the land or ocean, that is very difficult to see through: *Dense/thick fog is affecting traffic in the north and visibility is poor.* ◆ *freezing fog* ◆ *Patches of fog will clear by mid-morning.* ◆ *We get heavy fogs on this coast in winter.* ◆ *The town was covered in a thick blanket of fog.* ◆ *The fog finally lifted* (= disappeared). ⊃ collocations at WEATHER ⊃ compare MIST **2** a state of confusion, in which things are not clear: *He went through the day with his mind in a fog.*
- **verb** (-gg-) **1** [I, T] ~ (sth) (up) if a glass surface fogs or is fogged up, it becomes covered in steam or small drops of water so that you cannot see through **2** [T] ~ sth to make someone or something confused or less clear: *I tried to clear the confusion that was fogging my brain.* ◆ *The mayor was trying to fog the real issues before the election.*

fog·bound /'fɒgbaʊnd; 'fɑːg-/ adj. unable to operate because of fog; unable to travel or to leave a place because of fog: *a fogbound airport* ◆ *fogbound passengers* ◆ *She spent hours fogbound in San Francisco.*

fo·gey (also **fo·gy**) /'fəʊgi/ noun (pl. **fo·geys** or **fo·gies**) (usually disapproving) a person with old-fashioned ideas that he or she is unwilling to change: *He sounds like such an old fogey!*

fog·gy /'fɒgi; 'fɑːgi/ adj. (**fog·gi·er**, **fog·gi·est**) not clear because of FOG: *foggy conditions* ◆ *a foggy road*
- **IDM** **not have the foggiest (idea)** (informal) to not know anything at all about something: *"Do you know where she is?" "Sorry, I don't have the foggiest idea."*

fog·horn /'fɒghɔːn; 'fɑːg-/ noun an instrument that makes a loud noise to warn ships of danger in FOG: *He's got a voice like a foghorn* (= a loud unpleasant voice).

'fog light noun [usually pl.] a very bright light on the front or back of a car to help the driver to see or be seen in FOG

fo·gy = FOGEY

foi·ble /'fɔɪbl/ noun a silly habit or a strange or weak aspect of a person's character, that is considered harmless by other people **SYN** IDIOSYNCRASY ◆ *We have to tolerate each other's little foibles.*

foie gras /ˌfwɑː 'grɑː/ noun [U] = PATE DE FOIE GRAS

foil /fɔɪl/ noun, verb
- **noun 1** [U] metal made into very thin sheets that is used for covering or wrapping things, especially food: *aluminum foil* ◆ *Cover the fish loosely with foil and bake for 30 minutes.* ⊃ see also TINFOIL **2** [U] paper that is covered in very thin sheets of metal: *The chocolates are individually wrapped in gold foil.* **3** [C] ~ (for sb/sth) a person or thing that contrasts with, and therefore emphasizes, the qualities of another person or thing: *The pale walls provide a perfect foil for the furniture.* **4** [C] a long, thin, light SWORD used in the sport of FENCING
- **verb** [often passive] to stop something from happening, especially something illegal; to prevent someone from doing something **SYN** THWART: ~ sth *to foil a plan/crime/plot* ◆ *Customs officials foiled an attempt to smuggle the paintings out of the country.* ◆ ~ sb (in sth) *They were foiled in their attempt to smuggle the paintings.*

foist /fɔɪst/ verb
- **PHR V** **'foist sb/sth on sb** to force someone to accept someone or something that they do not want: *The title for her novel was foisted on her by the publishers.*

fold /fəʊld/ verb, noun
- **verb 1** [T] to bend something, especially paper or cloth, so that one part lies on top of another part: ~ sth (up) *He folded the map up and put it in his pocket.* ◆ *First, fold the paper in half/in two.* ◆ ~ sth (back, down, over, etc.) *The blankets had been folded down.* ◆ *a pile of neatly folded clothes* ◆ *The bird folded its wings.* **ANT** UNFOLD ⊃ see also FOLDUP **2** [T, I] to bend something so that it becomes smaller or flatter and can be stored or carried more easily; to bend or be able to bend in this way: ~ sth (away/down/up) *The bed can be folded away during the day.* ◆ ~ (away/up) *The table folds up*

when not in use. ◆ (figurative) *When she heard the news, her legs just folded under her* (= she fell). ◆ + adj. *The ironing board folds flat for easy storage.* **3** [T] to wrap something around someone or something: ~ A in B *She gently folded the baby in a blanket.* ◆ ~ B around/over A *She folded a blanket around the baby.* **4** [I] (of a company, a play, etc.) to close because it is not successful
- **IDM** **fold sb in your arms** (literary) to put your arms around someone and hold them against your body **fold your arms** to put one of your arms over the other one and hold them against your body **fold your hands** to bring or hold your hands together with the fingers bent: *She kept her hands folded in her lap.*
- **PHR V** **fold sth↔in** | **fold sth 'into sth** (in cooking) to add one substance to another and gently mix them together: *Fold in the beaten egg whites.*
- **noun 1** [C] a part of something, especially cloth, that is folded or hangs as if it had been folded: *the folds of her dress* ◆ *loose folds of skin* **2** [C] a mark or line made by folding something, or showing where something should be folded **3** [C] an area in a field surrounded by a fence or wall where sheep are kept for safety ◆ **the fold** [sing.] a group of people with whom you feel you belong or who share the same ideas or beliefs: *He called on former Republican voters to return to the fold.* **5** [C] (geology) a curve or bend in the line of the layers of rock in the earth's CRUST
- **IDM** **above/below the fold** in/not in a position where you see it first, for example in the top/bottom part of a newspaper page or web page: *Your ad will be placed above the fold for prominent exposure.* ⊃ see also ABOVE-THE-FOLD, BELOW-THE-FOLD

-fold /fəʊld/ suffix (in adjectives and adverbs) multiplied by; having the number of parts mentioned: *to increase tenfold*

fold·a·way /'fəʊldəˌweɪ/ adj. = FOLDING

fold·er /'fəʊldər/ noun **1** a thick paper or plastic cover for holding loose papers, etc. ⊃ picture at STATIONERY **2** (in some computer systems) a way of organizing and storing computer files

fold·ing /'fəʊldɪŋ/ (also less frequent **fold·a·way**) adj. [only before noun]
(of a piece of furniture, a bicycle, etc.) that can be folded, so that it can be carried or stored in a small space: *a folding chair* ◆ *a foldaway bed*

folding 'money noun [U] (informal) paper money

fold·up /'fəʊldʌp/ adj. [only before noun] (of an object) that can be made smaller by closing or folding so that it takes up less space

fo·li·age /'fəʊliɪdʒ/ noun [U] the leaves of a tree or plant; leaves and branches together: *dense green foliage*

fo·li·ar /'fəʊliər/ adj. (technical) relating to leaves: *foliar color*

fo·lic ac·id /ˌfəʊlɪk 'æsɪd/ noun [U] a VITAMIN found in green vegetables, LIVER, and KIDNEYS, needed by the body for the production of red blood cells

fo·li·o /'fəʊliəʊ/ noun (pl. **fo·li·os**) **1** a book made with large sheets of paper, especially as used in early printing **2** (technical) a single sheet of paper from a book

folk /fəʊk/ noun, adj.
- **noun 1** (also **folks**) [pl.] (informal) people in general: *ordinary working-class folk* ◆ *an old folks' home* ◆ *the folks back home* (= from the place where you come from) **2 folks** [pl.] (informal) a friendly way of addressing more than one person: *Well, folks, what are we going to do today?* **3 folks** [pl.] (informal) the members of your family, especially your parents: *How are your folks?* **4** [pl.] people from a particular country or region, or who have a particular way of life: *country folk* ◆ *townsfolk* ◆ *farming folk* **5** [U] = FOLK MUSIC
- **adj.** [only before noun] **1** (of art, culture, etc.) traditional and typical of the ordinary people of a country or community: *folk art* ◆ *a folk museum* **2** based on the beliefs of ordinary people: *folk wisdom* ◆ *Garlic is widely used in Chinese folk medicine.*

ʌ cup   ə about   eɪ say   aɪ five   ɔɪ boy   aʊ now   əʊ go   ər bird

'folk dance noun [C, U] a traditional dance of a particular area or country; a piece of music for such a dance

'folk ety,mology (also ,popular ety'mology) noun [U, C] a process by which a word is changed, for example because of a mistaken belief that it is related to another word, or to make a foreign word sound more familiar: *Folk etymology has created the cheeseburger and the veggieburger, but the first hamburgers were in fact named after the city of Hamburg.*

'folk ,hero noun a person that people in a particular place admire because of something special he or she has done

folk·lore /'foʊklɔr/ noun [U] the traditions and stories of a country or community: *Irish/African folklore* ◆ *The story rapidly became part of family folklore.*

folk·lor·ist /'foʊk,lɔrɪst/ noun a person who studies folklore, especially as an academic subject

,folk 'memory noun [C, U] a memory of something in the past that the people of a country or community never forget

'folk ,music (also **folk**) noun [U] **1** music in the traditional style of a country or community: *traditional Irish folk music* **2** a type of music that developed from traditional folk music and became popular in the U.S. in the 1960s. The songs were often about political topics, and were played on a GUITAR, without electronic equipment: *a folk festival/concert*

,folk 'rock noun [U] a style of music that combines elements of folk music and ROCK

'folk ,singer noun a person who sings folk songs

'folk song noun **1** a song in the traditional style of a country or community **2** a type of song that became popular in the U.S. in the 1960s, played on a GUITAR and often about political topics

folk·sy /'foʊksi/ adj. **1** simple, friendly, and informal: *They wanted the store to have a folksy small-town image.* **2** (sometimes *disapproving*) done or made in a traditional style that is typical of simple customs in the past: *a folksy ballad*

'folk tale noun a very old traditional story from a particular place that was originally passed on to people in a spoken form

folk·ways /'foʊkweɪz/ noun [pl.] the traditional behavior or customs of a particular community or group of people: *a study of Native American folkways*

fol·li·cle /'fɑlɪkl/ noun one of the very small holes in the skin that hair grows from

fol·low 🔑 /'fɑloʊ/ verb
> GO AFTER **1** [T, I] ~ (sb/sth) to come or go after or behind someone or something: *He followed her into the house.* ◆ *Follow me please. I'll show you the way.* ◆ *I think we're being followed.* ◆ (*figurative*) *She followed her mother into the medical profession.* ◆ *Wherever she led, they followed.* ◆ *Sam walked in, with the rest of the boys following closely behind.*
> HAPPEN/DO AFTER **2** [T, I] ~ (sth/sb) to come after something or someone else in time or order; to happen as a result of something else: *The first two classes will be followed by a break of ten minutes.* ◆ *I remember little of the days that followed the accident.* ◆ *A period of unrest followed the president's resignation.* ◆ *A detailed news report will follow shortly.* ◆ *There followed a short silence.* ◆ *The opening hours are as follows…* ◆ *A new proposal followed on from the discussions.* **3** [T] to do something after something else: ~ sth with sth *Follow your treatment with plenty of rest.* ◆ ~ sth up with sth *They follow up their March show with four more dates next summer.*
> BE RESULT **4** [I, T] (not usually used in the progressive tenses) to be the logical result of something: ~ (from sth) *I don't see how that follows from what you just said.* ◆ it follows that… *If a=b and b=c, it follows that a=c.*
> OF PART OF MEAL **5** [T, I] ~ (sth) to come or be eaten after another part: *The main course was followed by fresh fruit.* **HELP** This pattern is usually used in the passive.
> ROAD/PATH **6** [T] ~ sth to go along a road, path, etc.: *Follow this road until you get to the school, then turn left.* **7** [T] ~ sth (of a road, path, etc.) to go in the same direction as something

or parallel to something: *The path follows the edge of the woods for about a mile.*
> ADVICE/INSTRUCTIONS **8** [T] ~ sth to accept advice, instructions, etc. and do what you have been told or shown to do: *to follow a diet/recipe* ◆ *He has trouble following simple instructions.* ◆ *Why didn't you follow my advice?*
> ACCEPT/COPY **9** [T] ~ sth to accept someone or something as a guide, a leader, or an example; to copy someone or something: *They followed the teachings of Buddha.* ◆ *He always followed the latest fashions* (= dressed in fashionable clothes). ◆ *I don't want you to follow my example and rush into marriage.* ◆ *The movie follows the book faithfully.*
> UNDERSTAND **10** [I, T] to understand an explanation or the meaning of something: ~ (sb) *Sorry, I don't follow.* ◆ *Could you repeat that? I'm not following you.* ◆ ~ sth *The plot is almost impossible to follow.* ⊃ thesaurus box at UNDERSTAND
> WATCH/LISTEN **11** [T] ~ sb/sth to watch or listen to someone or something very carefully: *The children were following every word of the story intently.* ◆ *Her eyes followed him everywhere* (= she was looking at him all the time).
> BE INTERESTED IN **12** [T] ~ sth to take an active interest in something and be aware of what is happening: *Have you been following the basketball championships?* ◆ *Millions of people followed the trial on TV.*
> OF BOOK/MOVIE **13** [T] ~ sth to be concerned with the life or development of someone or something: *The novel follows the fortunes of a small farming community in North Dakota.*
> PATTERN/COURSE **14** [T] ~ sth to develop or happen in a particular way: *The day followed the usual pattern.*
IDM **follow in sb's footsteps** to do the same job, have the same style of life, etc. as someone else, especially someone in your family: *She works in television, following in her father's footsteps.* **follow your nose 1** to be guided by your sense of smell **2** to go straight forward: *The garage is a mile up the hill—just follow your nose.* **3** to act according to what seems right or reasonable, rather than following any particular rules **follow suit 1** (in card games) to play a card of the same SUIT that has just been played **2** to act or behave in the way that someone else has just done ⊃ more at ACT n.
PHR V **,follow sb a'round** to keep going with someone wherever they go: *Will you stop following me around!* **,follow 'through** (in TENNIS, GOLF, etc.) to complete a stroke by continuing to move the club, RACKET, etc. after hitting the ball ⊃ related noun FOLLOW-THROUGH **,follow 'through (with sth)** | **,follow sth⟷'through** to finish something that you have started ⊃ related noun FOLLOW-THROUGH **,follow sth⟷'up 1** to add to something that you have just done by doing something else: *You should follow up your phone call with an e-mail or a letter.* **2** to find out more about something that someone has told you or suggested to you **SYN** INVESTIGATE: *The police are following up several leads after their TV appeal for information.* ⊃ related noun FOLLOW-UP

fol·low·er /'fɑloʊər/ noun **1** a person who supports and admires a particular person or set of ideas: *the followers of Mahatma Gandhi* **2** a person who is very interested in a particular activity and follows all the recent news about it: *enthusiastic followers of horse racing* ◆ *a follower of fashion* **3** a person who does things after someone else has done them first: *She is a leader, not a follower.*

fol·low·ing 🔑 /'fɑloʊɪŋ/ adj., noun, prep.
● *adj.* **the following… 1** next in time: *the following afternoon/month/year/week* ◆ *They arrived on Monday night and we got there the following day.* **2** that is/are going to be mentioned next: *Answer the following questions.* ⊃ language bank at FIRST
IDM **a following wind** a wind blowing in the same direction as a ship or other vehicle that helps it move faster
● *noun* **1** [usually sing.] a group of supporters: *The band has a huge following on the West Coast.* **2 the following** (used with either a singular or a plural verb, depending on whether you are talking about one thing or person or several things or people) the thing or things that you will mention next;

the person or people that you will mention next: *The following is a summary of events.* ◆ *The following have been chosen to take part: Megan, Christy, and Amanda.*

● **prep.** after or as a result of a particular event: *He took charge of the family business following his father's death.*

follow-the-'leader *noun* [U] a children's game in which people copy the actions and words of a person who has been chosen as leader

follow-,through *noun* **1** [U, sing.] (in TENNIS, GOLF, etc.) the final part of a stroke after the ball has been hit **2** [U] the actions that someone takes in order to complete a plan: *The project could fail if there isn't any follow-through.*

follow-,up *noun* [C, U] an action or a thing that continues something that has already started or comes after something similar that was done earlier: *The book is a follow-up to her excellent television series.* ▶ **follow-up** *adj.* [only before noun]: *a follow-up study* ◆ *We need to schedule a follow-up appointment.*

fol·ly /ˈfɑli/ *noun* (*pl.* **fol·lies**) **1** [U, C] a lack of good judgment; the fact of doing something stupid; an activity or idea that shows a lack of judgment **SYN** STUPIDITY: *an act of sheer folly* ◆ *Giving up a secure job seems to be the height of folly.* ◆ ~ **(to do sth)** *It would be folly to turn the offer down.* ◆ *the follies of youth* **2** [C] a building that has no practical purpose but was built in the past for decoration, often in the garden of a large country house

fo·ment /ˈfoʊment; foʊˈment/ *verb* ~ **sth** (*formal*) to create trouble or violence or make it worse **SYN** INCITE: *They accused him of fomenting political unrest.*

fond /fɑnd/ *adj.* (**fond·er, fond·est**) **1** ~ **of sb** feeling affection for someone, especially someone you have known for a long time: *Over the years, I have grown quite fond of her.* **2** ~ **of (doing) sth** finding something pleasant or enjoyable, especially something you have liked or enjoyed for a long time: *fond of music/cooking* ◆ *We had grown fond of the house and didn't want to leave.* ⊃ **thesaurus box at** LIKE **3** ~ **of (doing) sth** liking to do something that other people find annoying or unpleasant, and doing it often: *Sheila's very fond of telling other people what to do.* ◆ *He's a little too fond of the sound of his own voice* (= he talks too much). **4** [only before noun] kind and loving **SYN** AFFECTIONATE: *a fond look/embrace/farewell* ◆ *I have very fond memories of my time in Mexico* (= I remember it with affection and pleasure). **5** [only before noun] ~ **hope** a hope about something that is not likely to happen: *I waited all day in the fond hope that she would change her mind.* ▶ **fond·ness** *noun* [U, sing.]: *He will be remembered by the staff with great fondness.* ◆ ~ **for sb/sth** *a fondness for animals* **IDM** **see** ABSENCE

fon·dant /ˈfɑndənt/ *noun* **1** [U] a thick, sweet, soft mixture made from sugar and water, used especially to cover cakes: *fondant icing* **2** [C] a soft candy that melts in the mouth, made of fondant

fon·dle /ˈfɑndl/ *verb* ~ **sb/sth** to touch and move your hand gently over someone or something, especially in a sexual way **SYN** CARESS

fond·ly /ˈfɑndli/ *adv.* **1** in a way that shows great affection **SYN** AFFECTIONATELY: *He looked at her fondly.* ◆ *I fondly remember my first job as a reporter.* **2** in a way that shows hope that is not reasonable or realistic: *I fondly imagined that you cared for me.*

fon·due /fɑnˈdu/ *noun* [C, U] **1** a hot dish of melted cheese into which pieces of bread are DIPPED **2** a dish of hot oil into which small pieces of meat, vegetables, etc. are DIPPED

font /fɑnt/ *noun* **1** a large stone bowl in a church that holds water for the ceremony of BAPTISM **2** (*technical*) the particular size and style of a set of letters that are used in printing, etc.

fon·ta·nel (*especially CanE* **fon·ta·nelle**) /ˌfɑntəˈnɛl; ˈfɑntəˌnɛl/ *noun* (*anatomy*) a space between the bones of a baby's SKULL, which makes a soft area on the top of the baby's head

food /fud/ *noun* **1** [U] things that people or animals eat: *a shortage of food/food shortages* ◆ *food and drinks* ◆ *the food industry* **2** [C, U] a particular type of food: *Do you like Italian food?* ◆ *frozen foods* ◆ *a can of dog food* (= for a dog to eat) ⊃ **see also** CONVENIENCE FOOD, FAST FOOD, HEALTH FOOD, JUNK FOOD, SEAFOOD, SOUL FOOD, WHOLE FOOD

IDM **food for thought** an idea that makes you think seriously and carefully

'food bank *noun* a place where poor people can go to get free food

'food chain *noun* usually **the food chain** a series of living creatures in which each type of creature feeds on the one below it in the series: *Insects are fairly low down (on) the food chain.*

'food court *noun* an area in a shopping mall where there are several small restaurants around a central area with tables and chairs

food·ie /ˈfudi/ *noun* (*informal*) a person who is very interested in cooking and eating different kinds of food

'food mile *noun* a measurement of the distance food has to be transported from the producer to the consumer and the fuel that this uses: *We keep food miles to a minimum by sourcing products locally.*

'food ,poisoning *noun* [U] an illness of the stomach caused by eating food that contains harmful bacteria

'food ,processor *noun* a piece of equipment that is used to mix or cut up food ⊃ **picture at** KITCHEN

'food ,science *noun* [U] the scientific study of food, for example what it is made of, the effects it has on our body, and how to prepare it and store it safely

'food stamp *noun* a piece of paper that is given by the government to poor people, for them to buy food with

food·stuff /ˈfudstʌf/ *noun* [usually pl.] (*technical*) any substance that is used as food: *basic foodstuffs*

'food web *noun* (*technical*) a system of FOOD CHAINS that are related to and depend on each other

fool /ful/ *noun, verb, adj.*

● **noun** **1** a person who you think behaves or speaks in a way that lacks intelligence or good judgment **SYN** IDIOT: *Don't be such a fool!* ◆ *I felt like a fool when I realized my mistake.* ◆ *He told me he was an actor and I was fool enough to believe him.* **2** (in the past) a man employed by a king or queen to entertain people by telling jokes, singing songs, etc. **SYN** JESTER

IDM **act/play the fool** to behave in a stupid way in order to make people laugh, especially in a way that may also annoy them: *Quit playing the fool and get to work!* **any fool can/could…** (*informal*) used to say that something is very easy to do: *Any fool could tell she was lying.* **be no/nobody's fool** to be too intelligent or know too much about something to be tricked by other people: *She's nobody's fool when it comes to dealing with difficult patients.* **a fool and his money are soon parted** (*saying*) a person who is not sensible usually spends money too quickly or carelessly, or is cheated by others **fools rush in (where angels fear to tread)** (*saying*) people with little experience try to do the difficult or dangerous things that more experienced people would not consider doing **make a fool of sb** to say or do something deliberately so that people will think that someone is stupid: *Can't you see she's making a fool of you?* **make a fool of yourself** to do something stupid that makes other people think that you are a fool: *I made a complete fool of myself in front of everyone!* **(there's) no fool like an old fool** (*saying*) an older person who behaves in a stupid way is worse than a younger person who does the same thing, because experience should have taught him or her not to do it ⊃ **more at** SUFFER

● **verb** **1** [T] to trick someone into believing something that is not true: ~ **sb** *You don't fool me!* ◆ *She certainly had me fooled —I really believed her!* ◆ ~ **yourself** *You're fooling yourself if you think none of this will affect you.* ◆ ~ **sb into doing sth**

t **tea**   ţ **butter**   d **did**   k **cat**   g **got**   tʃ **chin**   dʒ **June**   f **fall**

Don't be fooled into thinking they're going to change anything. ⊃ **thesaurus box at** CHEAT **2** [I] to say or do stupid or silly things, often in order to make people laugh: ~ **around** *Stop fooling around and sit down!* ◆ ~ **(around) with sth** *If you fool around with matches, you'll end up getting burned.*

IDM you could have fooled me (*informal*) used to say that you do not believe something that someone has just told you: *"I'm trying as hard as I can!" "You could have fooled me!"* **PHR V** **fool a'round 1** to waste time instead of doing something that you should be doing **SYN** MESS AROUND **2 ~ (with sb)** to have a sexual relationship with another person's partner; to have a sexual relationship with someone who is not your partner **SYN** MESS AROUND

• *adj.* [only before noun] (*informal*) showing a lack of intelligence or good judgment **SYN** SILLY, STUPID, FOOLISH: *That was a damn fool thing to do!*

fool·har·dy /ˈfʊlˌhɑrdi/ *adj.* (*disapproving*) taking unnecessary risks **SYN** RECKLESS: *It would be foolhardy to sail in weather like this.* ▶ **fool·har·di·ness** *noun* [U]

fool·ish /ˈfulɪʃ/ *adj.* **1** (of actions or behavior) not showing good sense or judgment **SYN** SILLY, STUPID: *She's just a vain, foolish woman.* ◆ *I was foolish enough to believe what Jeff told me.* ◆ *The accident was my fault— it would be foolish to pretend otherwise.* ◆ *How could she have been so foolish as to fall in love with him?* ◆ *a foolish idea/dream/mistake* ◆ *It was a very foolish thing to do.* **2** [not usually before noun] made to feel or look silly and embarrassed **SYN** SILLY, STUPID: *I felt foolish.* ◆ *He's afraid of looking foolish in front of his friends.* ▶ **fool·ish·ly** *adv.*: *We foolishly thought that everyone would speak English.* ◆ *Foolishly, I allowed myself to be persuaded to enter the contest.* **fool·ish·ness** *noun* [U]: *Jenny had to laugh at her own foolishness.*

fool·proof /ˈfulpruf/ *adj.* (of a plan, machine, method, etc.) very well designed and easy to use so that it cannot fail and you cannot use it wrongly **SYN** INFALLIBLE: *This recipe is foolproof—it works every time.*

fool's 'errand *noun* [sing.] a task that has no hope of being done successfully: *He sent me on a fool's errand.*

fool's 'gold *noun* [U] **1** a yellow mineral found in rock, which looks like gold but is not valuable, also called **iron pyrites** ⊃ see also PYRITE **2** something that you think is valuable or will earn you a lot of money, but which has no chance of succeeding

fool's 'paradise *noun* [usually sing.] a state of happiness that is based on something that is false or cannot last although the happy person does not realize it

foos·ball™ /ˈfuzbɔl/ *noun* [U] an indoor game for two people or teams, played by moving rows of small models of SOCCER players in order to move a ball on a board that has marks like a SOCCER field

foot /fʊt/ *noun, verb*

• *noun* (*pl.* **feet** /fit/)
▸ PART OF BODY **1** [C] the lowest part of the leg, below the ankle, on which a person or an animal stands: *My feet are aching.* ◆ *to get/rise to your feet* (= stand up) ◆ *I've been on my feet* (= standing or walking around) *all day.* ◆ *We came on foot* (= we walked). ◆ *walking around the house in bare feet* (= not wearing shoes or socks) ◆ *Please wipe your feet* (= your shoes) *on the mat.* ◆ *a foot pump* (= operated using your foot, not your hand) ◆ *a foot passenger* (= one who travels on a FERRY without a car) ⊃ picture at BODY ⊃ collocations at PHYSICAL ⊃ see also ATHLETE'S FOOT, BAREFOOT, CLUB FOOT, UNDERFOOT ⊃ thesaurus box at STAND
▸ -FOOTED **2** (in adjectives and adverbs) having or using the type or number of foot/feet mentioned: *bare-footed* ◆ *four-footed* ◆ *a left-footed kick* ⊃ see also FLAT-FOOTED, SURE-FOOTED
▸ PART OF SOCK **3** [C, usually sing.] the part of a sock, etc. that covers the foot
▸ BASE/BOTTOM **4** [sing.] **the ~ of sth** the lowest part of something; the base or bottom of something: *the foot of the*

stairs/cliff/mountain ◆ *The nurse hung a chart at the foot of the bed* (= the part of the bed where your feet normally are when you are lying in it). ⊃ **thesaurus box at** BOTTOM
▸ MEASUREMENT **5** (*pl.* **feet** or **foot**) [C] (*abbr.* **ft.**) a unit for measuring length equal to 12 inches or 30.48 centimeters: *a 6-foot high wall* ◆ *We're flying at 35,000 feet.* ◆ *"How tall are you?" "Five foot nine"* (= five feet and nine inches).*
▸ -FOOTER **6** (in compound nouns) a person or thing that is a particular number of feet tall or long: *His boat is an eighteen-footer.*
▸ IN POETRY **7** [sing.] (*technical*) a unit of rhythm in a line of poetry containing one stressed syllable and one or more syllables without stress. Each of the four divisions in the following line is a foot: *For 'men / may 'come / and 'men / may 'go.*

IDM **be rushed/run off your feet** to be extremely busy; to have too many things to do **feet first 1** with your feet touching the ground before any other part of your body: *He landed feet first.* **2** (*humorous*) if you leave a place **feet first**, you are carried out after you are dead: *You'll have to carry me out feet first!* **get/have a/your foot in the door** to succeed in entering an organization, a field of business, etc. that could bring you success: *I always wanted to work in TV but it took me two years to get a foot in the door.* **get/put sb/sth on their/its feet** to make someone or something independent or successful: *His business sense helped get the organization on its feet again.* **get/start off on the right/wrong foot (with sb)** (*informal*) to start a relationship well/badly: *I seem to have gotten off on the wrong foot with the new boss.* **get your feet wet** (*informal*) to start doing something that is new for you: *At that time he was a young actor, just getting his feet wet.* **have feet of clay** to have a fault or weakness in your character **have/keep your feet on the ground** to have a sensible and realistic attitude to life **have/keep a foot in both camps** to be involved in or connected with two different or opposing groups **have one foot in the grave** (*informal*) to be so old or sick that you are not likely to live much longer **...my foot!** (*informal, humorous*) a strong way of saying that you disagree completely with what has just been said: *"David can't come because he's tired." "Tired my foot! Lazy's more like it!"* **on your feet** completely well or in a normal state again after an illness or a time of trouble: *Sue's back on her feet again after her operation.* ◆ *The new chairman hopes to get the company back on its feet within six months.* ⊃ note at STAND **put your best foot forward** to make a great effort to do something, especially if it is difficult or you are feeling tired **put your feet up** to sit down and relax, especially with your feet raised and supported: *After a hard day's work, it's nice to get home and put your feet up.* **put your foot down** to be very strict in opposing what someone wishes to do: *You've got to put your foot down and make him stop seeing her.* **put your foot in your mouth** to say or do something that upsets, offends, or embarrasses someone: *I really put my foot in my mouth with Ella—I didn't know she and Tom broke up.* **set foot in/on sth** to enter or visit a place: *the first man to set foot on the moon* ◆ *I vowed never to set foot in the place again.* **stand on your own (two) feet** to be independent and able to take care of yourself: *When his parents died he had to learn to stand on his own two feet.* ⊃ more at COLD *adj.*, DRAG *v.*, GRASS *n.*, HAND *n.*, HEAD *n.*, ITCHY, JUMP *v.*, LAND *v.*, LEFT *adj.*, PATTER *n.*, PULL *v.*, SHOE *n.*, SHOOT *v.*, SIT, STOCKING, SWEEP *v.*, THINK *v.*, VOTE *v.*, WAIT *v.*, WALK *v.*, WORLD

• *verb*
IDM **foot the bill** (*informal*) to be responsible for paying the cost of something: *Once again it will be the taxpayer who has to foot the bill.*

foot·age /ˈfʊtɪdʒ/ *noun* [U] part of a film showing a particular event: *old film footage of the moon landing*

foot-and-'mouth dis·ease (also ,hoof-and-'mouth dis,ease) *noun* [U] a disease of cows, sheep, etc., which causes sore places on the mouth and feet

football

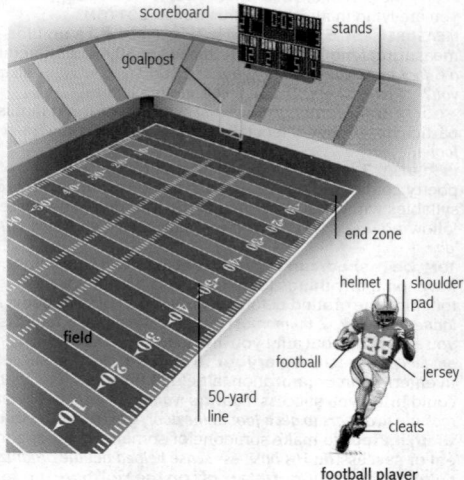

scoreboard
stands
goalpost
end zone
helmet | shoulder pad
field
football | jersey
50-yard line
cleats

football player

foot·ball /ˈfʊtbɔl/ *noun*
1 [U] a game played by two teams of 11 players each, using an OVAL ball that players kick, throw, or carry. Teams try to put the ball over the other team's goal line: *to play football* ♦ *a football game/team/stadium* **2** [C] a large OVAL ball made of leather or plastic and filled with air **3** [U] (outside the U.S.) = SOCCER **4** [C] (always used with an adjective) an issue or a problem that frequently causes argument and disagreement: *Health care should not become a political football.*

MORE ABOUT

football

- Football is played by two teams of 11 players wearing **helmets** and **pads** to protect themselves. Each football game is divided into four **quarters**, usually of 12 or 15 minutes each.
- Players try to get the ball into the other team's **end zone**, either by carrying it or **passing** (= throwing) it to other players on their team. If the player carries the ball, this is a **run play** or **running play**; if the ball is passed, this is called a **pass play** or **passing play**.
- The team that has the ball is called the **offense** and the other team is the **defense**. The offense has a series of four chances, called **downs**, to get the ball forward ten yards. When they move the ball forward at least ten yards, they receive a new set of four downs. The downs continue until the team loses the ball or fails to go forward ten yards in four downs. The defense tries to stop the offense from moving forward by **intercepting** the ball (= catching it when it is thrown to an opponent) or by causing a **fumble** (= when a player drops the ball).
- The most important player is the **quarterback**, who directs the team's offensive play and passes the ball or gives it to another player at the start of each play. If the ball is given to another player, this is called a **handoff**.
- Players try to score **touchdowns** by catching the ball in the other team's end zone or by carrying it into the end zone. A touchdown is worth six points. They can also score **field goals** by kicking the ball over the bar of the goal from anywhere on the field. A field goal is worth three points.

foot·brake /ˈfʊtbreɪk/ *noun* a BRAKE in a vehicle that is operated using your foot

foot·bridge /ˈfʊtbrɪdʒ/ *noun* a narrow bridge used only by people who are walking

foot·er /ˈfʊtər/ *noun* **1** a line or block of text that is automatically added to the bottom of every page that is printed from a computer ⊃ compare HEADER **2** a line at the bottom of a page on the Internet: *a Web site footer*

foot·fall /ˈfʊtfɔl/ *noun* (*literary*) the sound of the steps made by someone walking

foot fault *noun* (in TENNIS) a mistake that is made by not keeping behind the line when SERVING

foot·hill /ˈfʊthɪl/ *noun* [usually pl.] a hill or low mountain at the base of a higher mountain or range of mountains: *the foothills of the Rockies*

foot·hold /ˈfʊthoʊld/ *noun* **1** a crack, hole, or branch where your foot can be safely supported when climbing **2** [usually sing.] a strong position in a business, profession, etc. from which someone can make progress and achieve success: *The company is eager to gain a foothold in South America.*

foot·ing /ˈfʊtɪŋ/ *noun* [sing.] **1** the position of your feet when they are safely on the ground or some other surface: *She lost her footing* (= she slipped or lost her balance) *and fell backward into the water.* ♦ *I slipped and struggled to regain my footing.* **2** the basis on which something is established or organized: *The company is now on a sound financial footing.* ♦ *The country has been on a war footing* (= prepared for war) *since March.* **3** the position or status of someone or something in relation to others; the relationship between two or more people or groups: *The two groups must meet on an equal footing.* ♦ *They were demanding to be treated on the same footing as the rest of the teachers.*

foot·lights /ˈfʊtlaɪts/ *noun* [pl.] a row of lights along the front of the stage in a theater

foot·lock·er /ˈfʊtlɑkər/ *noun* a large metal box used especially by soldiers to store things in and often kept at the end of a bed

foot·loose /ˈfʊtlus/ *adj.* free to go where you like or do what you want because you have no responsibilities: *Bert was a footloose, unemployed actor.* ♦ *Ah, I was still footloose and fancy-free* (= free to enjoy myself) *in those days.*

foot·man /ˈfʊtmən/ *noun* (*pl.* foot·men /-mən/) a male servant in a house in the past, who opened the door to visitors, served food at the table, etc.

foot·note /ˈfʊtnoʊt/ *noun* **1** an extra piece of information that is printed at the bottom of a page in a book **2** (of an event or a person) that may be remembered but only as something or someone that is not important

foot·path /ˈfʊtpæθ/ *noun* a path that is made for people to walk along, especially in the country SYN TRAIL: *a public footpath*

foot·print /ˈfʊtprɪnt/ *noun* **1** [usually pl.] a mark left on a surface by a person's foot or shoe or by an animal's foot: *footprints in the sand* ♦ *muddy footprints on the kitchen floor* **2** the amount of space that something fills, for example the amount of space that a computer takes up on a desk **3** the area on the earth in which a signal from a communications SATELLITE can be received ⊃ see also CARBON FOOTPRINT

foot·rest /ˈfʊtrɛst/ *noun* a support for your foot or feet, for example on a motorcycle or when you are sitting down

foot·sie /ˈfʊtsi/ *noun* (*informal*)
IDM **play footsie with sb** to touch someone's feet lightly with your own feet, especially under a table, as an expression of affection or sexual interest

foot soldier *noun* **1** a soldier who fights on foot, not on a horse or in a vehicle **2** a person in an organization who does work that is important but boring, and who has no power or responsibility

foot·sore /ˈfʊtsɔr/ *adj.* (*formal*) having sore or tired feet, especially after walking a long way

foot·step /ˈfʊtstɛp/ *noun* [usually pl.] the sound or mark made each time your foot touches the ground when you are

h **hat**   m **man**   n **no**   ŋ **sing**   l **leg**   r **red**   y **yes**   w **wet**

walking or running: *the sound of footsteps on the stairs* **IDM** see FOLLOW

foot·stool /ˈfʊtstuːl/ *noun* a low piece of furniture used for resting your feet on when you are sitting

foot·wear /ˈfʊtwɛr/ *noun* [U] things that people wear on their feet, for example shoes and boots: *Be sure to wear the correct footwear to prevent injuries to your feet.*

foot·work /ˈfʊtwɜːrk/ *noun* [U] **1** the way in which a person moves their feet when playing a sport or dancing **2** the ability to react quickly and skillfully to a difficult situation: *It was going to take some deft political footwork to save the situation.*

fop /fɑːp/ *noun* (*old-fashioned*) a man who is too interested in his clothes and the way he looks ▶ **fop·pish** /ˈfɑːpɪʃ/ *adj.*

for ♪ /fər; *strong form* fɔːr/ *prep.*, *conj.*

● **prep.** **HELP** For the special uses of **for** in phrasal verbs, look at the entries for the verbs. For example, **fall for someone** is in the phrasal verb section at **fall**. **1** used to show who is intended to have or use something or where something is intended to be put: *There's a letter for you.* ◆ *It's a book for children.* ◆ *We got a new table for the dining room.* ◆ *This is the place for me* (= I like it very much). **2** in order to help someone or something: *What can I do for you* (= how can I help you)? ◆ *Can you translate this letter for me?* ◆ *I taught her classes for her while she was sick.* ◆ *soldiers fighting for their country* **3** concerning someone or something: *They are anxious for her safety.* ◆ *Fortunately for us, the weather changed.* **4** as a representative of: *I am speaking for everyone in this department.* **5** employed by: *She's been working for IBM for over a year.* **6** meaning: *Shaking your head for "No" is not universal.* **7** in support of someone or something: *Are you for or against the proposal?* ◆ *They voted for independence in a referendum.* ◆ *There's a strong case for postponing the trip.* ◆ *I'm all for people having fun.* ⊃ compare AGAINST **8** used to show purpose or function: *a machine for slicing bread* ◆ *Let's go for a walk.* ◆ *Are you learning English for pleasure or for your work?* ◆ *What did you do that for* (= Why did you do that)? **9** used to show a reason or cause: *The town is famous for its cathedral.* ◆ *She gave me a watch for my birthday.* ◆ *He got an award for bravery.* **10** in order to obtain something: *He came to me for advice.* ◆ *For more information, call this number.* ◆ *There were over fifty applicants for the job.* **11** in exchange for something: *Copies are available for two dollars each.* ◆ *I'll swap these two bottles for that one.* **12** considering what can be expected from someone or something: *The weather was warm for the time of year.* ◆ *She's tall for her age.* ◆ *That's too much responsibility for a child.* **13** better, happier, etc. ~ **something** better, happier, etc. following something: *You'll feel better for a good night's sleep.* ◆ *He was happier now for having given up the idea of making it on Broadway.* **14** used to show where someone or something is going: *Is this the bus for Chicago?* ◆ *She knew she was destined for a great future.* **15** used to show a length of time: *I'm going away for a few days.* ◆ *That's all the news there is for now.* **16** used to show that something is arranged or intended to happen at a particular time: *an appointment for May 12* ◆ *We're invited for 7:30.* **17** used to show the occasion when something happens: *I'm warning you for the last time—stop talking!* **18** used to show a distance: *The road went on for miles and miles.* **19** used to say how difficult, necessary, pleasant, etc. something is that someone might do or has done: *It's useless for us to continue.* ◆ *There's no need for you to go.* ◆ *For her to have survived such an ordeal was remarkable.* ◆ *The box is too heavy for me to lift.* ◆ *Is it clear enough for you to read?* **20** used to show who can or should do something: *It's not for me to say why he left.* ◆ *How to spend the money is for you to decide.*
IDM **be in for it** (*informal*) to be going to get into trouble or be punished: *We'd better hurry or we'll be in for it.* **for all 1** despite: *For all its clarity of style, the book is not easy reading.* **2** used to say that something is not important or is of no interest or value to you/someone: *For all I know she's still living in Boston.* ◆ *You can do what you like, for all I care.* ◆ *For all the good it's done we might as well not have bothered.*

there's/that's… for you (*often ironic*) used to say that something is a typical example of its kind: *She might at least have called to explain. There's gratitude for you.*

● **conj.** (*old-fashioned* or *literary*) used to introduce the reason for something mentioned in the previous statement: *We listened eagerly, for he brought news of our families.* ◆ *I believed her—for surely she would not lie to me.*

for·age /ˈfɔːrɪdʒ; ˈfɑːr-/ *verb*, *noun*
● **verb 1** [I] ~ (**for sth**) (especially of an animal) to search for food **2** [I] ~ (**for sth**) (of a person) to search for something, especially using the hands **SYN** RUMMAGE
● **noun** [U] food for horses and cows: *forage crops/grass*

for·ay /ˈfɔːreɪ; ˈfɑːr-/ *noun* **1** ~ (**into sth**) an attempt to become involved in a different activity or profession: *the company's first foray into the computer market* **2** ~ (**into sth**) a short sudden attack made by a group of soldiers **3** ~ (**to/into…**) a short journey to find a particular thing or to visit a new place **SYN** EXPEDITION: *weekend shopping forays to Dallas*

for·bade *pt of* FORBID

for·bear *verb*, *noun*
● **verb** /fɔːrˈbɛr; fər-/ (**for·bore** /fɔːrˈbɔːr; fər-/, **for·borne** /fɔːrˈbɔːrn; fər ˈbɔːrn /) [I, T] (*formal*) to stop yourself from saying or doing something that you could or would like to say or do: ~ (**from sth/from doing sth**) *He wanted to answer back, but he forbore from doing so.* ◆ ~ **to do sth** *She forbore to ask any further questions.*
● **noun** = FOREBEAR

for·bear·ance /fɔːrˈbɛrəns; fər-/ *noun* [U] (*formal*) the quality of being patient and sympathetic toward other people, especially when they have done something wrong

for·bear·ing /fɔːrˈbɛrɪŋ; fər-/ *adj.* (*formal*) showing forbearance **SYN** PATIENT: *Thank you for being so forbearing.*

for·bid /fərˈbɪd/ *verb* (**for·bade** /fərˈbeɪd; -ˈbæd/, **for·bid·den** /fərˈbɪdn/) **1** to order someone not to do something; to order that something must not be done: ~ **sb** (**from doing sth**) *He forbade them from mentioning the subject again.* ◆ ~ **sth** *Her father forbade the marriage.* ◆ ~ **sb to do sth** *You are all forbidden to leave.* ◆ ~ **sb sth** *My doctor has forbidden me sugar.* ◆ ~ (**sb**) **doing sth** *She knew her mother would forbid her going.* **ANT** ALLOW, PERMIT **2** ~ **sth** | ~ **sb to do sth** (*formal*) to make it difficult or impossible to do something **SYN** PROHIBIT: *Lack of space forbids further treatment of the topic here.*
IDM **God/Heaven forbid (that…)** (*informal*) used to say that you hope that something will not happen: *"Maybe you'll end up as a lawyer, like me." "God forbid!"* **HELP** Some people find this use offensive.

for·bid·den /fərˈbɪdn/ *adj.* not allowed: *Photography is strictly forbidden in the museum.* ◆ *The conversation was in danger of wandering into forbidden territory* (= topics that they were not allowed to talk about).
IDM **forbidden fruit** a thing that is not allowed and that therefore seems very attractive

for·bid·ding /fərˈbɪdɪŋ/ *adj.* seeming unfriendly and frightening and likely to cause harm or danger: *a forbidding appearance/look/manner* ◆ *The house looked dark and forbidding.* ▶ **for·bid·ding·ly** *adv.*

for·bore *pt of* FORBEAR

for·borne *pp of* FORBEAR

force ♪ /fɔːrs/ *noun*, *verb*
● **noun**
> VIOLENT ACTION **1** [U] violent physical action used to obtain or achieve something: *The release of the hostages could not be achieved without the use of force.* ◆ *The rioters were taken away by force.* ◆ *The ultimatum contained the threat of military force.* ◆ *We will achieve much more by persuasion than by brute force.*

WORD FAMILY
force *noun, verb*
forceful *adj.*
forcefully *adv.*
forced *adj.* (≠ unforced)
forcible *adj.*
forcibly *adv.*
enforce *verb*

> **PHYSICAL STRENGTH 2** [U] the physical strength of something that is shown as it hits something else: *the force of the blow/explosion/collision* ◆ *The shopping mall took the full force of the blast.*

> **STRONG EFFECT 3** [U] the strong effect or influence of something: *They realized the force of her argument.* ◆ *He controlled himself by sheer force of will.* ◆ *She spoke with force and deliberation.*

> **SOMEONE OR SOMETHING WITH POWER 4** [C] a person or thing that has a lot of power or influence: *economic/market forces* ◆ *the forces of good/evil* ◆ *Ron is the driving force* (= the person who has the most influence) *behind the project.* ◆ *She's a force to be reckoned with* (= a person who has a lot of power and influence and should therefore be treated seriously). ◆ *The expansion of higher education should be a powerful force for change.*

> **AUTHORITY 5** [U] the authority of something: *These guidelines do not have the force of law.* ◆ *The court ruled that these standards have force in civil law.*

> **GROUP OF PEOPLE 6** [C] a group of people who have been organized for a particular purpose: *a member of the sales force* ◆ *A large proportion of the labor force* (= all the people who work in a particular company, area, etc.) *is unskilled.* ⊃ see also WORKFORCE

> **MILITARY 7** [C] a group of people who have been trained to protect other people, usually by using weapons: *a member of the security forces* ◆ *rebel/government forces* ◆ *a peace-keeping force* ⊃ see also AIR FORCE, POLICE FORCE, TASK FORCE **8 forces** [pl.] the weapons and soldiers that an army, etc. has, considered as things that may be used: *strategic nuclear forces.*

> **POLICE 9 the force** [sing.] the police force: *He joined the force twenty years ago.*

> **PHYSICS 10** [C, U] an effect that causes things to move in a particular way: *The moon exerts a force on the earth.* ◆ *the force of gravity* ◆ *magnetic/centrifugal force*

> **OF WIND 11** [C, usually sing.] a unit for measuring the strength of the wind: *a force 9 gale* ◆ *a gale force wind* ⊃ see also TOUR DE FORCE

IDM bring sth into force to cause a law, rule, etc. to start being used: *They are hoping to bring the new legislation into force before the end of the year.* **come/enter into force** (of a law, rule, etc.) to start being used: *When do the new regulations come into force?* **force of habit** if you do something from or out of **force of habit**, you do it automatically and in a particular way because you have always done it that way in the past **the forces of nature** the power of the wind, rain, etc., especially when it causes damage or harm **in force 1** (of people) in large numbers: *Protesters turned out in force.* **2** (of a law, rule, etc.) being used: *The new regulations are now in force.* **join/combine forces (with sb)** to work together in order to achieve a shared aim: *The two firms joined forces to win the contract.* ⊃ more at SPENT

● *verb*

> **MAKE SOMEONE DO SOMETHING 1** [often passive] to make someone do something that they do not want to do **SYN** COMPEL: **~ sb into doing sth** *The President was forced into resigning.* ◆ **~ sb/yourself to do sth** *The President was forced to resign.* ◆ *I was forced to take a taxi because the last bus had left.* ◆ *She forced herself to be polite to them.* ◆ **~ sb into sth** *Health problems forced him into early retirement.* ◆ **~ sb** *He didn't force me—I wanted to go.* ◆ **~ yourself** (*informal, humorous*) *"I shouldn't really have any more." "I guess I could force myself to have another piece of pie."* ◆ **~ sth** *Public pressure managed to force a change in the administration's position.*

> **USE PHYSICAL STRENGTH 2** to use physical strength to move someone or something into a particular position: **~ sth into/against/onto sth** *to force a lock/window/door* (= to break it open using force) ◆ *to force an entry* (= to enter a building using force) ◆ **~ sth + adv./prep.** *She forced her way through the crowd of reporters.* ◆ *He tried to force a copy of his book into my hand.* ◆ **~ sth + adj.** *The door had been forced open.*

> **MAKE SOMETHING HAPPEN 3** to make something happen, especially before other people are ready: **~ sth** *He was in a position where he had to force a decision.* ◆ **~ sth + adv./prep.** *Building a new road here will force home prices down.*

> **A SMILE/LAUGH 4 ~ sth** to make yourself smile, laugh, etc. rather than doing it naturally: *She managed to force a smile.*

> **FRUIT/PLANTS 5 ~ sth** to make fruit, plants, etc. grow or develop faster than normal by keeping them in special conditions: *forced spring bulbs* ◆ (*figurative*) *It is unwise to force a child's talent.*

IDM force sb's hand to make someone do something that they do not want to do or make them do it sooner than they had intended **force the issue** to do something to make people take a decision quickly **force the pace 1** to run very fast in a race in order to make the other people taking part run faster **2** to make someone do something faster than they want to: *The demonstrations have succeeded in forcing the pace of change.* ⊃ more at THROAT

PHR V force sth↔'back to make yourself hide an emotion: *She swallowed hard and forced back her tears.* **force sth↔'down 1** to make yourself eat or drink something that you do not really want **2** to make a plane, etc. land, especially by threatening to attack it **'force sb/sth on sb** to make someone accept something that they do not want: *to force your attentions/opinions/company on someone* **force sth 'out of sb** to make someone tell you something, especially by threatening them: *I managed to force the truth out of him.*

forced /fɔrst/ *adj.* **1** happening or done against someone's will: *forced relocation to a job in another city* ◆ *a forced sale of his property* **2** not sincere; not the result of genuine emotions: *She said she was enjoying herself but her smile was forced.* ⊃ see also UNFORCED

forced 'entry *noun* [U, C] an occasion when someone enters a building illegally, using force

forced 'labor *noun* [U] **1** hard physical work that someone, often a prisoner or SLAVE, is forced to do **2** prisoners or SLAVES who are forced to work: *The mines were manned by forced labor from conquered countries.*

forced 'landing *noun* an act of having to land an aircraft unexpectedly in order to avoid a crash: *to make a forced landing*

forced 'march *noun* a long march, usually made by soldiers in difficult conditions

force-'feed *verb* **~ sb** to use force to make someone, especially a prisoner, eat or drink, by putting food or drink down their throat

'force field *noun* (often used in stories about space travel) a barrier that you cannot see

force-ful /'fɔrsfl/ *adj.* **1** (of people) expressing opinions firmly and clearly in a way that persuades other people to believe them **SYN** ASSERTIVE: *a forceful woman/speaker* ◆ *a forceful personality* **2** (of opinions, etc.) expressed firmly and clearly so that other people believe them: *a forceful argument/speech* **3** using force: *the forceful suppression of minorities* ▶ **force-ful-ly** /-fəli/ *adv.*: *He argued his case forcefully.* **force-ful-ness** *noun* [U]

force ma-jeure /ˌfɔrs mɑ'ʒər/ *noun* [U] (from *French*, *law*) unexpected circumstances, such as war, that can be used as an excuse when they prevent someone from doing something that is written in a contract

'force-out *noun* (in baseball) a situation in which a player is forced to run to the next BASE and is out because a FIELDER is holding the ball at the base

'force play *noun* (in baseball) a situation in which a player is forced to run to the next BASE and is out because the BATTER is running toward the previous BASE. This situation can lead to a force-out.

for-ceps /'fɔrsɛps; -səps/ *noun* [pl.] an instrument used by doctors, with two long thin parts for picking up and holding things: *a pair of forceps* ◆ *a forceps delivery* (= a birth in which the baby is delivered with the help of forceps)

for-ci-ble /'fɔrsəbl/ *adj.* [only before noun] involving the use

ʌ cup   ə about   eɪ say   aɪ five   ɔɪ boy   aʊ now   oʊ go   ər bird

of physical force: *forcible repatriation* ♦ *The police checked all windows and doors for signs of forcible entry.*

for·ci·bly /'fɔrsəbli/ *adv.* **1** in a way that involves the use of physical force: *Supporters were forcibly removed from the court.* **2** in a way that makes something very clear: *It struck me forcibly how honest he was.*

ford /fɔrd/ *noun, verb*
• *noun* a shallow place in a river where it is possible to drive or walk across
• *verb* ~ sth to walk or drive across a river or stream

fore /fɔr/ *noun, adj., adv.*
• *noun*
  IDM **come to/be at the fore** to be/become important and noticed by people; to play an important part: *She has always been at the fore at moments of crisis.* ♦ *The problem has come to the fore again in recent months.* **bring sth to the fore** to make something become noticed by people
• *adj.* [only before noun] (*technical*) located at the front of a ship, an aircraft, or an animal ⊃ compare AFT, HIND
• *adv.* **1** at or toward the front of a ship or an aircraft ⊃ compare AFT **2** **Fore!** used in the game of GOLF to warn people that they are in the path of a ball that you are hitting

fore- /fɔr/ *combining form* (in nouns and verbs) **1** before; in advance: *foreword* ♦ *foretell* **2** in the front of: *the foreground of the picture*

fore·arm¹ /'fɔrɑrm/ *noun* the part of the arm between the elbow and the wrist ⊃ picture at BODY

fore·arm² /ˌfɔr'ɑrm/ *verb* **IDM** see FOREWARN

fore·bear (also **forbear**) /'fɔrbɛr/ *noun* [usually pl.] (*formal* or *literary*) a person in your family who lived a long time ago **SYN** ANCESTORS

fore·bod·ing /fɔr'boudɪŋ/ *noun* [U, C] a strong feeling that something unpleasant or dangerous is going to happen: *She had **a sense of foreboding** that the news would be bad.* ♦ *He knew from her face that his forebodings had been justified.* ▶ **fore·bod·ing** *adj.*: *a foreboding feeling that something was wrong*

fore·brain /'fɔrbreɪn/ *noun* (*anatomy*) the front part of the brain

fore·cast /'fɔrkæst/ *noun, verb*
• *noun* a statement about what will happen in the future, based on information that is available now: *sales forecasts* ♦ *The forecast said there would be sunny intervals and showers.* ⊃ see also WEATHER FORECAST
• *verb* (fore·cast, fore·cast or fore·cast·ed, fore·cast·ed) to say what you think will happen in the future based on information that you have now **SYN** PREDICT: ~ sth *Experts are forecasting a recovery in the economy.* ♦ *Snow is forecast for tomorrow.* ♦ ~ to do sth *Temperatures were forecast to reach 95°F.* ♦ ~ that... *The report forecasts that prices will rise by 3% next month.* ♦ ~ how, what, etc.... *It is difficult to forecast how the markets will react.* ⊃ collocations at WEATHER ⊃ language bank at EXPECT

fore·cast·er /'fɔrˌkæstər/ *noun* a person who says what is expected to happen, especially someone whose job is to forecast the weather: *a weather forecaster* ♦ *an economic forecaster*

fore·cas·tle (also **fo'c's'le**) /'foʊksl; 'fɔrˌkæsl/ *noun* the front part of a ship below the DECK, where the sailors live

fore·close /fɔr'kloʊz/ *verb* **1** [I, T] ~ (on sb/sth) | ~ sth (*finance*) (especially of a bank) to take control of someone's property because they have not paid back money that they borrowed to buy it **2** [T] ~ sth (*formal*) to reject something as a possibility **SYN** EXCLUDE

fore·clo·sure /fɔr'kloʊʒər/ *noun* [U, C] (*finance*) the act of foreclosing on money that has been borrowed; an example of this

fore·doomed /fɔr'dumd/ *adj.* ~ (to sth) (*formal*) that will not be successful, as if FATE has decided this from the

beginning: *Any attempt to construct an ideal society is foredoomed to failure.*

fore·fa·ther /'fɔrˌfɑðər/ *noun* [usually pl.] (*formal* or *literary*) a person (especially a man) in your family who lived a long time ago **SYN** ANCESTORS

fore·fin·ger /'fɔrˌfɪŋɡər/ *noun* the finger next to the thumb **SYN** INDEX FINGER

fore·foot /'fɔrfʊt/ *noun* (*pl.* **fore·feet** /-fit/) either of the two front feet of an animal that has four feet

fore·front /'fɔrfrʌnt/ *noun* [sing.]
  IDM **at/in/to the forefront (of sth)** in or into an important or leading position in a particular group or activity: *Women have always been at the forefront of the Green movement.* ♦ *The new product took the company to the forefront of the computer software field.*

fore·gath·er = FORGATHER

fore·go = FORGO

fore·go·ing /'fɔrˌɡoʊɪŋ/ *adj.* [only before noun] (*formal*) **1** used to refer to something that has just been mentioned: *the foregoing discussion* **2** **the foregoing** *noun* [sing.] what has just been mentioned **ANT** FOLLOWING

fore·gone /'fɔrɡɔn; -ɡɑn/ *adj.*
  IDM **a foregone conclusion** if you say that something is **a foregone conclusion**, you mean that it is a result that is certain to happen

fore·ground /'fɔrɡraʊnd/ *noun, verb*
• *noun* **the foreground** **1** [C, usually sing.] the part of a view, picture, etc. that is nearest to you when you look at it: *The figure **in the foreground** is the artist's mother.* **2** [sing.] an important position that is noticed by people: *Inflation and interest rates will be very much **in the foreground** of their election campaign.* ⊃ compare BACKGROUND
  IDM **in the foreground** (*computing*) (of a computer program) being used at the present time and appearing in front of any other programs on the screen ⊃ compare BACKGROUND
• *verb* ~ sth to give particular importance to something: *The play foregrounds the relationship between father and daughter.*

fore·hand /'fɔrhænd/ *noun* [usually sing.] (in TENNIS, etc.) a way of hitting a ball in which the inner part of the hand (= the PALM) faces the ball as it is hit: *She has a strong forehand.* ♦ *a forehand volley* ♦ *He served to his opponent's forehand.* ⊃ compare BACKHAND

fore·head /'fɔrhɛd; 'fɔrəd; 'fɑrəd/ *noun* the part of the face above the eyes and below the hair **SYN** BROW ⊃ picture at BODY ⊃ collocations at PHYSICAL

for·eign /'fɔrən; 'fɑr-/ *adj.*
  1 in or from a country that is not your own: *a foreign accent/language/student* ♦ *a foreign-owned company* ♦ *foreign vacations* ♦ *You could tell she was foreign by the way she dressed.* **2** [only before noun] dealing with or involving other countries: *foreign affairs/news/policy/trade* ♦ *foreign aid* ♦ *a foreign correspondent* (= one who reports on foreign countries in newspapers or on television) **ANT** DOMESTIC, HOME **3** ~ to sb/sth (*formal*) not typical of someone or something; not known to someone or something and therefore seeming strange: *Dishonesty is foreign to his nature.* **4** ~ object/body (*formal*) an object that has entered something by accident and should not be there: *Tears help to protect the eye from potentially harmful foreign bodies.*

for·eign·er /'fɔrənər; 'fɑr-/ *noun* (sometimes *offensive*) **1** a person who comes from a different country: *The fact that I was a foreigner was a big disadvantage.* **2** a person who does not belong in a particular place: *I have always been regarded as a foreigner by the local folk.*

foreign ex'change *noun* **1** [U, C] the system of exchanging the money of one country for that of another country; the place where money is exchanged: *The dollar fell on the foreign exchanges yesterday.* **2** [U] money that is obtained using this system: *our largest source of foreign exchange*

Foreign 'Service (also **the Diplo'matic ˌService**) *noun* [sing.] the government department concerned with representing a country in foreign countries

fore·knowl·edge /ˈfɔrˌnɑlɪdʒ/ *noun* [U] (*formal*) knowledge of something before it happens

fore·leg /ˈfɔrleg/ (also **fore·limb** /ˈfɔrlɪm/) *noun* either of the two front legs of an animal that has four legs

fore·lock /ˈfɔrlɑk/ *noun* **1** (*literary*) a piece of hair that grows at the front of the head and hangs down over the FOREHEAD **2** a part of a horse's MANE that grows forward between its ears

fore·man /ˈfɔrmən/, **fore·wom·an** /ˈfɔrˌwumən/ *noun* (*pl.* fore·men /-mən/, fore·wom·en /-ˌwɪmən/) **1** a worker who is in charge of a group of other factory or building workers **2** a person who acts as the leader of a jury in court

fore·most /ˈfɔrmoʊst/ *adj., adv.*
• *adj.* the most important or famous; in a position at the front: *the world's foremost authority on the subject* ♦ *The governor was foremost among those who condemned the violence.* ♦ *This question has been foremost in our minds recently.*

• *adv.* **IDM** see FIRST

fore·noon /ˈfɔrnun/ *noun* (*old-fashioned*) the morning

fo·ren·sic /fəˈrɛnsɪk; -zɪk/ *adj.* [only before noun] **1** connected with the scientific tests used by the police when trying to solve a crime: *forensic evidence/medicine/science/tests* ♦ *the forensic laboratory* ♦ *a forensic pathologist* ⊃ collocations at CRIME **2** connected with or used in court: *a forensic psychiatrist* (= one who examines people who have been accused of a crime)

fore·play /ˈfɔrpleɪ/ *noun* [U] sexual activity, such as touching the sexual organs and kissing, that takes place before people have sex

fore·run·ner /ˈfɔrˌrʌnər/ *noun* ~ (of sb/sth) a person or thing that came before and influenced someone or something else that is similar; a sign of what is going to happen: *Rhythm and blues was undoubtedly one of the forerunners of rock and roll.*

fore·sail /ˈfɔrseɪl; ˈfɔrsl/ *noun* [usually sing.] the main sail on the MAST of a ship that is nearest the front (called the **foremast**)

fore·see /fɔrˈsi/ *verb* (fore·saw /-ˈsɔ/, fore·seen /-ˈsin/) to think something is going to happen in the future; to know about something before it happens **SYN** PREDICT: ~ sth *We do not foresee any problems.* ♦ *The extent of the damage could not have been foreseen.* ♦ ~ (that)... *No one could have foreseen that things would turn out this way.* ♦ ~ how, what, etc.... *It is impossible to foresee how life will work out.* ♦ ~ sb/sth doing sth *I just didn't foresee that happening.* ⊃ compare UNFORESEEN

fore·see·a·ble /fɔrˈsiəbl/ *adj.* that you can predict will happen; that can be foreseen: *foreseeable risks/consequences* **ANT** UNFORESEEABLE
IDM for/in the foreseeable future for/in the period of time when you can predict what is going to happen, based on the present circumstances: *The statue will remain in the museum for the foreseeable future.* ♦ *It's unlikely that the hospital will be closed in the foreseeable future* (= soon).

fore·shad·ow /fɔrˈʃædoʊ/ *verb* ~ sth (*formal*) to be a sign of something that will happen in the future

fore·short·en /fɔrˈʃɔrtn/ *verb* **1** ~ sth/sb (*technical*) to draw, photograph, etc. objects or people so that they look smaller or closer together than they really are **2** ~ sth (*formal*) to end something before it would normally finish **SYN** CURTAIL: *a foreshortened education*

fore·sight /ˈfɔrsaɪt/ *noun* [U] (*approving*) the ability to predict what is likely to happen and to use this to prepare for the future: *She had the foresight to prepare herself financially in case of an accident.* ⊃ compare HINDSIGHT

fore·skin /ˈfɔrskɪn/ *noun* the loose piece of skin that covers the end of a man's PENIS

for·est 🔑 /ˈfɔrəst; ˈfɑr-/ *noun* **1** [C, U] a large area of land that is thickly covered with trees: *a tropical forest* ♦ *a forest fire* ♦ *Thousands of acres of forest are destroyed each year.* ⊃ see also CLOUD FOREST, RAINFOREST **2** [C] ~ (of sth) a mass of tall narrow objects that are close together: *a forest of television antennas* **IDM** not see the forest for the trees to not see or understand the main point about something, because you are paying too much attention to small details

fore·stall /fɔrˈstɔl/ *verb* ~ sth/sb to prevent something from happening or someone from doing something by doing something first: *Try to anticipate what your child will do and forestall problems.*

for·est·ed /ˈfɔrəstəd; ˈfɑr-/ *adj.* covered in forest: *thickly forested hills* ♦ *The area is heavily forested and sparsely populated.*

for·est·er /ˈfɔrəstər; ˈfɑr-/ *noun* a person who works in a forest, taking care of the trees, planting new ones, etc.

for·est·ry /ˈfɔrəstri; ˈfɑr-/ *noun* [U] the science or practice of planting and taking care of trees and forests

fore·taste /ˈfɔrteɪst/ *noun* [sing.] a ~ (of sth) a small amount of a particular experience or situation that shows you what it will be like when the same thing happens on a larger scale in the future: *They were unaware that the street violence was just a foretaste of what was to come.*

fore·tell /fɔrˈtɛl/ *verb* (fore·told, fore·told /-ˈtoʊld/) (*literary*) to know or say what will happen in the future, especially by using magic powers: ~ sth *to foretell the future* ♦ ~ that... *The witch foretold that she would marry a prince.* ♦ ~ what, when, etc.... *None of us can foretell what lies ahead.*

fore·thought /ˈfɔrθɔt/ *noun* [U] careful thought to make sure that things are successful in the future: *Some forethought and preparation is necessary before you embark on the project.* **IDM** see MALICE

fore·told pt, pp of FORETELL

for·ev·er 🔑 /fəˈrɛvər; fɔ-/ *adv.* **1** used to say that a particular situation or state will always exist: *I'll love you forever!* ♦ *After her death, their lives changed forever.* ♦ *Just keep telling yourself that it won't last forever.* **2** (*informal*) a very long time: *It takes her forever to get dressed.* **3** used with verbs in the progressive tenses to say that someone does something very often and in a way that is annoying to other people: *As a kid he was forever asking questions.*

fore·warn /fɔrˈwɔrn/ *verb* [often passive] ~ sb (of sth) | ~ sb that... (*formal*) to warn someone about something bad or unpleasant before it happens: *The commander had been forewarned of the attack.* ▶ **fore·warn·ing** *noun* [U, C] **IDM** forewarned is forearmed (*saying*) if you know about problems, dangers, etc. before they happen, you can be better prepared for them

fore·wom·an *noun* ⊃ FOREMAN

fore·word /ˈfɔrwərd/ *noun* a short introduction at the beginning of a book ⊃ compare PREFACE

for·feit /ˈfɔrfət/ *verb, noun, adj.*
• *verb* ~ sth to lose something or have something taken away from you because you have done something wrong: *If you cancel your flight, you will forfeit your deposit.* ♦ *He has forfeited his right to be taken seriously.*

• *noun* something that a person has to pay, or something that is taken from them, because they have done something wrong

• *adj.* [not before noun] (*formal*) taken away from someone as a punishment

for·fei·ture /ˈfɔrfətʃər/ *noun* [U] (*law*) the act of forfeiting something: *the forfeiture of property*

for·fend /fɔrˈfɛnd/ *verb* **IDM** see HEAVEN

for·gath·er (also **fore·gath·er**) /fɔrˈgæðər/ *verb* [I] (*formal*) to meet together in a group

for·gave pt of FORGIVE

t tea	t̬ butter	d did	k cat	g got	tʃ chin	dʒ June	f fall

forge /fɔrdʒ/ *verb, noun*

● *verb* **1** [T] ~ **sth** to put a lot of effort into making something successful or strong so that it will last: *a move to forge new links between management and workers* ◆ *Strategic alliances are being forged with major European companies.* ◆ *She forged a new career in the music business.* **2** [T] ~ **sth** to make an illegal copy of something in order to cheat people: *to forge a passport/banknote/check* ◆ *He's getting good at forging his mother's signature.* ⊃ collocations at CRIME ⊃ compare COUNTERFEIT **3** [T] ~ **sth (from sth)** to shape metal by heating it in a fire and hitting it with a hammer; to make an object in this way: *swords forged from steel* **4** [I] + adv./prep. (*formal*) to move forward in a steady but powerful way: *He forged through the crowds to the front of the stage.* ◆ *She forged into the lead* (= in a competition, race, etc.). PHR V ,forge a'head (with sth) to move forward quickly; to make a lot of progress quickly: *The company is forging ahead with its plans for expansion.*

● *noun* **1** a place where objects are made by heating and shaping pieces of metal, especially one where a BLACK-SMITH works **2** a large piece of equipment used for heating metals in; a building or part of a factory where this is found

forg·er /ˈfɔrdʒər/ *noun* a person who makes illegal copies of money, documents, etc. in order to cheat people ⊃ compare COUNTERFEITER

for·ger·y /ˈfɔrdʒəri/ *noun* (**for·ger·ies**) **1** [U] the crime of copying money, documents, etc. in order to cheat people SYN FAKE **2** [C] something, for example a document, piece of paper money, etc., that has been copied in order to cheat people: *Experts are dismissing claims that the painting is a forgery.* ⊃ compare COUNTERFEIT

for·get 🔊 /fərˈgɛt/ *verb* (**for·got** /-ˈgɑt/, **for·got·ten** /-ˈgɑtn/)

> EVENTS/FACTS **1** [I, T] (not usually used in the progressive tenses) to be unable to remember something that has happened in the past or information that you knew in the past: ~ **(about sth)** *I'd completely forgotten about the money he owed me.* ◆ *Before I forget, there was a call from your bank for you.* ◆ ~ **sth** *I never forget a face.* ◆ *Who could forget his speech at last year's party?* ◆ *She keeps forgetting (that) I'm not a child any more.* ◆ *I was forgetting* (= I had forgotten) *(that) you've been here before.* ◆ ~ **where, how, etc.**... *I've forgotten where they live exactly.* ◆ *I forget how much they paid for it.* ◆ ~ **(sb) doing sth** *I'll never forget hearing this piece of music for the first time.* ◆ **it is forgotten that...** *It should not be forgotten that people used to get much more exercise.*

> TO DO SOMETHING **2** [I, T] to not remember to do something that you ought to do, or to bring or buy something that you ought to bring or buy: ~ **(about sth)** *"Why weren't you at the meeting?" "Sorry—I forgot."* ◆ ~ **to do sth** *Take care, and don't forget to write.* ◆ *I forgot to ask him for his address.* ◆ ~ **sth/sb** *I forgot my purse* (= I did not remember to bring it). ◆ *"Hey, don't forget me* (= don't leave without me)*!"* ◆ *Aren't you forgetting something?* (= I think you have forgotten to do something)

> STOP THINKING ABOUT SOMETHING **3** [I, T] to deliberately stop thinking about someone or something: ~ **(about sb/sth)** *Try to forget about what happened.* ◆ *Could you possibly forget about work for five minutes?* ◆ ~ **sb/sth** *Forget him!* ◆ *Let's forget our differences and be friends.* ◆ ~ **(that)**... *Forget (that) I said anything!* **4** [I, T] to stop thinking that something is a possibility: ~ **about sth** *If I lose this job, we can forget about buying a new car.* ◆ ~ **sth** *"I was hoping you might be able to lend me the money." "You can forget that!"*

> YOURSELF **5** [T] ~ **yourself** to behave in a way that is not socially acceptable: *I'm forgetting myself. I haven't offered you a drink yet!*

IDM **and don't (you) forget it** (*informal*) used to tell someone how they should behave, especially when they have been behaving in a way you do not like: *You're a suspect, not a detective, and don't you forget it.* **forget it** (*informal*) **1** used to tell someone that something is not important and that they should not worry about it: *"I still owe you for lunch yesterday." "Forget it."* **2** used to tell someone that you are not going to repeat what you said:

"Now, what were you saying about John?" "Forget it, it doesn't matter." **3** used to emphasize that you are saying "no" to something: *"Any chance of you helping out here?" "Forget it, I've got too much to do."* **4** used to tell someone to stop talking about something because they are annoying you: *Just forget it.* ⊃ more at FORGIVE

for·get·ful /fərˈgɛtfl/ *adj.* **1** often forgetting things SYN ABSENTMINDED: *She has become very forgetful in recent years.* **2** ~ **of sb/sth** (*formal*) not thinking about someone or something that you should be thinking about ▶ **for·get·ful·ly** /-fəli/ *adv.* **for·get·ful·ness** *noun* [U]

for'get-me-ˌnot *noun* a small wild plant with light blue flowers

for·get·ta·ble /fərˈgɛtəbl/ *adj.* not interesting or special and therefore easily forgotten: *an instantly forgettable tune* ANT UNFORGETTABLE

for·giv·a·ble /fərˈgɪvəbl/ *adj.* that you can understand and forgive SYN EXCUSABLE: *His rudeness was forgivable under the circumstances.* ANT UNFORGIVABLE

for·give 🔊 /fərˈgɪv/ *verb* (**for·gave** /-ˈgeɪv/, **forgiven** /-ˈgɪvn/)

1 [T, I] to stop feeling angry with someone who has done something to harm, annoy, or upset you; to stop feeling angry with yourself: ~ **sb/yourself (for sth/for doing sth)** *I'll never forgive her for what she did.* ◆ *I'd never forgive myself if she heard the truth from someone else.* ◆ ~ **(sth)** *I can't forgive that type of behavior.* ◆ *We all have to learn to forgive.* ◆ ~ **sb sth** *She'd forgive him anything.* **2** [T] used to say in a polite way that you are sorry if what you are doing or saying seems rude or silly: ~ **me** *Forgive me, but I don't see that any of this concerns me.* ◆ ~ **me for doing sth** *Forgive me for interrupting, but I really don't agree with that.* ◆ ~ **my ...** *Forgive my ignorance, but what exactly does the company do?* ◆ ~ **my doing sth** *Forgive my interrupting but I really don't agree with that.* **3** [T] ~ **(sb) sth** (*formal*) (of a bank, country, etc.) to say that someone does not need to pay back money that they have borrowed: *The government has agreed to forgive a large part of the debt.*

IDM **sb could/might be forgiven for doing sth** used to say that it is easy to understand why someone does or thinks something, although they may be wrong: *Looking at the crowds out shopping, you could be forgiven for thinking that everyone has plenty of money.* **forgive and forget** to stop feeling angry with someone for something they have done to you and to behave as if it had not happened

for·give·ness /fərˈgɪvnəs/ *noun* [U] the act of forgiving someone; willingness to forgive someone: *to pray for God's forgiveness* ◆ *the forgiveness of sins* ◆ *He begged forgiveness for what he had done.*

for·giv·ing /fərˈgɪvɪŋ/ *adj.* **1** willing to forgive: *She had not inherited her mother's forgiving nature.* ◆ ~ **of sth** *The public was more forgiving of the president's difficulties than the press and fellow politicians.* **2** ~ **(of sth)** (of a method, tool, or material) that works well, even when you do not follow it perfectly or treat it very well: *These flooring planks are more durable and forgiving of heavy traffic than real wood.*

for·go (also **fore·go**) /fərˈgoʊ/ *verb* (**for·went** /-ˈwɛnt/, **for·gone** /-ˈgɔn; -ˈgɑn/) ~ **sth** (*formal*) to decide not to have or do something that you would like to have or do: *No one was prepared to forgo their lunch hour to attend the meeting.*

for·got *pt of* FORGET

for·got·ten *pp of* FORGET

fork 🔊 /fɔrk/ *noun, verb*

● *noun* **1** a tool with a handle and three or four sharp points (called PRONGS), used for picking up and eating food: *to eat with a knife and fork* **2** a garden tool with a long or short handle and three or four sharp metal points, used for digging ⊃ picture at TOOL ⊃ see also PITCHFORK **3** a place where a road, river, etc. divides into two parts; either of these two parts: *Shortly before dusk they reached a fork and took the left-hand track.* ◆ *Take the right fork.* **4** a thing shaped like a fork, with two or more long parts: *a jagged fork of* *lightning* ➲ see also TUNING FORK **5** either of two metal supporting pieces into which a wheel on a bicycle or motorcycle is fitted ➲ picture at BICYCLE

• ***verb* 1** [I] (not used in the progressive tenses) **(+ adv./prep.)** (of a road, river, etc.) to divide into two parts that lead in different directions: *The path forks at the bottom of the hill.* ◆ *The road forks right after the bridge.* **2** [I] **+ adv./prep.** (not used in the progressive tenses) (of a person) to turn left or right where a road, etc. divides into two: *Fork right after the bridge.* **3** [T] **(+ adv./prep.)** to move, carry, or dig something using a fork: *Clear the soil of weeds and fork in plenty of compost.*

PHR V **ˌfork ˈout (for sth)** | **ˌfork ˈout sth (for/on sth)** (*informal*) to spend a lot of money on something, especially unwillingly: *Why fork out for a taxi when there's a perfectly good bus service?* ◆ *We've forked out a small fortune on their education.*

forked /fɔrkt/ *adj.* with one end divided into two parts, like the shape of the letter "Y": *a bird with a forked tail* ◆ *the forked tongue of a snake*

ˌforked ˈlightning *noun* [U] the type of LIGHTNING that is like a line that divides into smaller lines near the ground ➲ compare SHEET LIGHTNING

fork·ful /ˈfɔrkfʊl/ *noun* the amount that a fork holds

fork·lift /ˈfɔrklɪft/ (also **ˌforklift ˈtruck**) *noun* a vehicle with special equipment on the front for moving and lifting heavy objects ➲ picture at TRUCK

for·lorn /fərˈlɔrn; fɔr-/ *adj.* **1** (of a person) appearing lonely and unhappy: *She looked so forlorn, standing there in the rain.* **2** (of a place) not cared for and with no people in it: *Empty houses quickly take on a forlorn look.* **3** unlikely to succeed, come true, etc.: *She waited* ***in the forlorn hope*** *that he would one day come back to her.* ◆ *His father smiled weakly* ***in a forlorn attempt*** *to reassure him that everything was all right.* ▶ **for·lorn·ly** *adv.*

form 🔑 /fɔrm/ *noun, verb*

• ***noun***

› TYPE **1** [C] a type or variety of something: *forms of transportation/government/energy* ◆ *one of the most common forms of cancer* ◆ *all the millions of different life forms on the planet today* ➲ see also ART FORM

› WAY SOMETHING IS/LOOKS **2** [C, U] the particular way something is, seems, looks, or is presented: *The disease can take several different forms.* ◆ *Help* ***in the form of*** *money will be very welcome.* ◆ *Help arrived* ***in the form of*** *two police officers.* ◆ *The training program* ***takes the form of*** *a series of workshops.* ◆ *Most political questions involve morality* ***in some form or other.*** ◆ *We need to come to* ***some form of*** *agreement.* ◆ *I'm opposed to censorship* ***in any way, shape, or form.*** ◆ *This dictionary is also available in electronic form.*

› DOCUMENT **3** [C] an official document containing questions and spaces for answers: *an* ***application/entry/order form*** ◆ *to* ***fill out a form*** ◆ *I filled out a form on their Web site.* ◆ *to complete a form* ◆ *a* ***reservation form***

› SHAPE **4** [C] the shape of someone or something; a person or thing of which only the shape can be seen: *her slender form* ◆ *The human form has changed little over the last 30,000 years.* ◆ *They made out a shadowy form in front of them.*

› ARRANGEMENT OF PARTS **5** [U] the arrangement of parts in a whole, especially in a work of art or piece of writing: *In a novel, form and content are equally important.* ➲ thesaurus box at STRUCTURE

› PERFORMANCE **6** [U] how well someone or something is performing; the fact that someone or something is performing well: *The new quarterback shows disappointing form so far this season.* ◆ *She signaled her return to form with a convincing victory.* ◆ *She was* ***in great form*** (= happy and cheerful and full of energy) *at the wedding party.*

› WAY OF DOING THINGS **7** [U, C] the usual way of doing something: *conventional social forms* ◆ ***True to form*** (= as he usually does) *he arrived an hour late.* ◆ *Partners of employees are invited* ***as a matter of form.***

› OF WORD **8** [C] a way of writing or saying a word that shows, for example, if it is plural or in a particular tense: *the infinitive form of the verb*

IDM **take form** (*formal*) to gradually form into a particular shape; to gradually develop: *In her body a new life was taking form.* ➲ more at SHAPE *n.*

• ***verb***

› START TO EXIST **1** [I, T] (especially of natural things) to begin to exist and gradually develop into a particular shape; to make something begin to exist in a particular shape: *Flowers appeared, but fruits failed to form.* ◆ *Storm clouds are forming on the horizon.* ◆ **~ sth** *These hills were formed by glaciation.* **2** [I, T] to start to exist and develop; to make something start to exist and develop: *A plan formed in my head.* ◆ **~ sth** *I formed many close friendships in college.* ◆ *I didn't see enough of the play to form an opinion about it.* ➲ thesaurus box at MAKE

› MAKE SHAPE/FORM **3** [T, often passive] to produce something in a particular way or make it have a particular shape: **~ sth** *Bend the wire so that it forms a "V."* ◆ *Rearrange the letters to form a new word.* ◆ *Games can help children learn to form letters.* ◆ *Do you know how to form the past tense?* ◆ **~ sth into sth** *Form the dough into balls with your hands.* ◆ **~ sth from/of sth** *The chain is formed from 136 links.* **4** [T, I] to move or arrange objects or people so that they are in a group with a particular shape; to become arranged in a group like this: **~ sb/sth (into sth)** *to* ***form a line/circle*** ◆ *First get students to form groups of four.* ◆ **~ (into sth)** *Lines were already forming outside the theater.* ◆ *The teams formed into two lines.*

› HAVE FUNCTION/ROLE **5** [T] **~ sth** to have a particular function or pattern: *The trees form a natural protection from the sun's rays.* **6** ***linking verb*** **+ noun** to be something: *The college forms the focal point of the town.* ◆ *The survey* ***formed part of*** *a larger program of research.* ◆ *These drawings will* ***form the basis of*** *the exhibition.*

› ORGANIZATION **7** [T, I] **~ (sth)** to start a group of people, such as an organization, a committee, etc.; to come together in a group of this kind: *They hope to form a grassroots political movement.* ◆ *He formed a band with some friends from school.* ◆ *a newly-formed political party* ◆ *The band formed in 2007.*

› HAVE INFLUENCE ON **8** [T] **~ sth** to have an influence on the way that something develops **SYN** MOLD: *Positive and negative experiences form a child's character.*

for·mal 🔑 /ˈfɔrml/ *adj.*

1 (of a style of dress, speech, writing, behavior, etc.) very correct and suitable for official or important occasions: *formal evening wear* ◆ *The dinner was very formal.* ◆ *He kept the tone of the letter formal and businesslike.* ◆ *She has a very formal manner, which can seem unfriendly.* **ANT** INFORMAL
2 official; following an agreed or official way of doing things: *formal legal processes* ◆ *to make a* ***formal apology/complaint/request*** ◆ *Formal diplomatic relations between the two countries were re-established in December.* ◆ *It is time to put these arrangements on a slightly more formal basis.* **3** (of education or training) received in a school, college, or university, with classes, exams, etc., rather than gained just through practical experience: *He has no formal teaching qualifications.* ◆ *Young children are beginning their formal education sometimes as early as four years old.* **4** concerned with the way something is done rather than what is done: *Getting approval for the plan is a purely formal matter; nobody will seriously oppose it.* ◆ *Critics have concentrated too much on the formal elements of her poetry, without really looking at what it is saying.* **5** (of a garden, room, or building) arranged in a regular manner, according to a clear, exact plan: *stately formal gardens, with terraced lawns and an avenue of trees* **ANT** INFORMAL ▶ **for·mal·ly** /-məli/ *adv.*: *"How do you do?" she said formally.* ◆ *The accounts were formally approved by the board.* ◆ *Although not formally trained as an art historian, he is widely respected for his knowledge of the period.*

form·al·de·hyde /fɔrˈmældəˌhaɪd; fər-/ *noun* [U] **1** (*symb.* CH_2O) a gas with a strong smell **2** (also *technical* **for·ma·lin** /ˈfɔrməlɪn/) a liquid made by mixing formaldehyde and water, used for preserving BIOLOGICAL SPECIMENS, making plastics, and as a DISINFECTANT

for·mal·ism /ˈfɔrməˌlɪzəm/ *noun* [U] a style or method in art, music, literature, science, etc. that pays more attention to the rules and the correct arrangement and appearance of things than to inner meaning and feelings ▶ **for·mal·ist** /-lɪst/ *noun* **for·mal·ist** *adj.* [usually before noun]: *formalist theory*

for·mal·i·ty /fɔrˈmæləti/ *noun* (*pl.* **for·mal·i·ties**)
1 [C, usually pl.] a thing that you must do as a formal or official part of a legal process, a social situation, etc.: *to go through all the formalities necessary in order to get a gun license* ◆ *Let's skip the formalities and get down to business.*
2 [C, usually sing.] a thing that you must do as part of an official process, but that has little meaning and will not affect what happens: *He already knows he has the job, so the interview is a mere formality.* **3** [U] correct and formal behavior: *Different levels of formality are appropriate in different situations.* ◆ *She greeted him with stiff formality.*

for·mal·ize /ˈfɔrməˌlaɪz/ *verb* **1** ~ **sth** to make an arrangement, a plan, or a relationship official: *They decided to formalize their relationship by getting married.* **2** ~ **sth** to give something a fixed structure or form by introducing rules: *The college has a highly formalized system of assessment.* ▶ **for·mal·i·za·tion** /ˌfɔrmələˈzeɪʃn/ *noun* [U]

for·mat AWL /ˈfɔrmæt/ *noun, verb*
● *noun* **1** the general arrangement, plan, design, etc. of something: *The format of the new quiz show has proved popular.* **2** the shape and size of a book, magazine, etc.: *They brought out the magazine in a new format last month.* **3** (*computing*) the way in which data is stored or held to be worked on by a computer
● *verb* (-tt-) **1** ~ **sth** to arrange text in a particular way on a page or a screen **2** ~ **sth** to prepare a computer disk so that data can be recorded on it

for·ma·tion /fɔrˈmeɪʃn/ *noun* **1** [U] the action of forming something; the process of being formed: *the formation of a new corporate structure* ◆ *evidence of recent star formation in the galaxy* **2** [C] a thing that has been formed, especially in a particular place or in a particular way: *rock formations* **3** [U, C] a particular arrangement or pattern: *aircraft flying in formation* ◆ *formation flying* ◆ *The team usually plays in an irregular formation.*

for·ma·tive /ˈfɔrmətɪv/ *adj.* [only before noun] having an important and lasting influence on the development of something or or someone's character: *the formative years of childhood*

form·er /ˈfɔrmər/ *adj.* [only before noun]
1 that used to exist in earlier times: *in former times* ◆ *the countries of the former Soviet Union* ◆ *This beautiful old building has been restored to its former glory.* **2** that used to have a particular position or status in the past: *the former world champion* ◆ *my former boss/colleague/wife* **3** **the former…** used to refer to the first of two things or people mentioned: *The former option would be much more sensible.* ⊃ compare LATTER **4** **the former** *pron.* the first of two things or people mentioned: *He had to choose between giving up his job and giving up his principles. He chose the former.* ⊃ compare LATTER
IDM **be a shadow/ghost of your former self** to not have the strength, influence, etc. that you used to have

for·mer·ly /ˈfɔrmərli/ *adv.*
in earlier times: *Namibia, formerly known as South-West Africa* ◆ *I learned that the house had formerly been an inn.* ◆ *Paul Peterson, formerly of Duluth, now living in Sarasota*

form-fitting *adj.* (of clothing) fitting your body tightly, so that the shape of your body is clearly visible: *She wore a form-fitting dress.*

For·mi·ca™ /fɔrˈmaɪkə/ *noun* [U] a hard plastic that can resist heat, used for covering work surfaces, etc.

for·mic ac·id /ˌfɔrmɪk ˈæsɪd/ *noun* [U] (*chemistry*) an acid

made from CARBON MONOXIDE and steam. It is also present in a liquid produced by some ANTS.

for·mi·da·ble /ˈfɔrmɪdəbl; fərˈmɪdəbl/ *adj.* if people, things, or situations are **formidable**, you feel fear and/or respect for them, because they are impressive or powerful, or because they seem very difficult: *In debate he was a formidable opponent.* ◆ *She has a formidable list of qualifications.* ◆ *The two players together make a formidable combination.* ◆ *The task was a formidable one.* ◆ *They had to overcome formidable obstacles.* ▶ **for·mi·da·bly** /-bli/ *adv.*: *He now has the chance to prove himself in a formidably difficult role.* ◆ *She's formidably intelligent.*

form·less /ˈfɔrmləs/ *adj.* without a clear or definite shape or structure: *formless dreams* ▶ **form·less·ness** *noun* [U]

form letter *noun* a letter that is sent to a large number of people, often to answer a common complaint or question

for·mu·la AWL /ˈfɔrmyələ/ *noun*
(*pl.* **for·mu·las** or, especially in scientific use, **for·mu·lae** /-li/) **1** [C] (*mathematics*) a series of letters, numbers, or symbols that represent a rule or law: *This formula is used to calculate the area of a circle.* **2** [C] (*chemistry*) letters and symbols that show the parts of a chemical COMPOUND, etc.: *CO is the formula for carbon monoxide.* **3** [C] a particular method of doing or achieving something: *They're trying to work out a **peace formula** acceptable to both sides in the dispute.* ◆ ~ **for sth/for doing sth** *There's no **magic formula** for a perfect marriage.* **4** [C] a list of the things that something is made from, giving the amount of each substance to use: *the secret formula for the blending of the whiskey* **5** (also **formula milk**) [U, C] a type of liquid food for babies, given instead of breast milk **6** [C] a class of racing car, based on engine size, etc.: *Formula One racing*™ **7** [C] a fixed form of words used in a particular situation: *legal formulae* ◆ *The minister keeps coming out with the same tired formulas.*

for·mu·la·ic /ˌfɔrmyəˈleɪk/ *adj.* (*formal*) made up of fixed patterns of words or ideas: *Traditional stories make use of formulaic expressions like "Once upon a time…"*

for·mu·late AWL /ˈfɔrmyəˌleɪt/ *verb* **1** to create or prepare something carefully, giving particular attention to the details: ~ **sth** *to formulate a policy/theory/plan/proposal* ◆ *The compost is specially formulated for potted plants.* ◆ ~ **sth to do sth** *This new kitchen cleaner is formulated to cut through grease and dirt.* **2** ~ **sth** to express your ideas in carefully chosen words: *She has lots of good ideas, but she has difficulty formulating them.* ▶ **for·mu·la·tion** AWL /ˌfɔrmyəˈleɪʃn/ *noun* [U, C]: *the formulation of new policies*

for·ni·cate /ˈfɔrnəˌkeɪt/ *verb* [I] (*formal, disapproving*) to have sex with someone that you are not married to ▶ **for·ni·ca·tion** /ˌfɔrnəˈkeɪʃn/ *noun* [U] **for·ni·ca·tor** /ˈfɔrnəˌkeɪtər/ *noun*

for·sake /fərˈseɪk/ *verb* (**for·sook** /-ˈsʊk/, **for·sak·en** /-ˈseɪkən/) (*literary*) **1** ~ **sb/sth (for sb/sth)** to leave someone or something, especially when you have a responsibility to stay SYN ABANDON: *He had made it clear to his wife that he would never forsake her.* **2** ~ **sth (for sb/sth)** to stop doing something, or leave something, especially something that you enjoy SYN RENOUNCE: *She forsook the glamor of the city and went to live in the wilds of Montana.* ⊃ see also GODFORSAKEN

for·sooth /fərˈsuːθ/ *adv.* (*old use or humorous*) used to emphasize a statement, especially in order to show surprise

for·swear /fɔrˈswɛr/ *verb* (**for·swore** /-ˈswɔr/, **for·sworn** /-ˈswɔrn/) ~ **sth** (*formal or literary*) to stop doing or using something; to make a promise that you will stop doing or using something SYN RENOUNCE: *The group forswears all worldly possessions.* ◆ *The country has not forsworn the use of chemical weapons.*

for·syth·i·a /fərˈsɪθiə/ *noun* [U, C] a bush that has small, bright yellow flowers in the early spring

fort /fɔrt/ *noun* **1** a building or buildings built in order to defend an area against attack ⊃ picture at BUILDING **2** a place where soldiers live and have their training: *Fort Drum* **IDM** **hold down the fort** (*informal*) to have the responsibility for something or care of someone while other people are away or out: *You should take a day off. I'll hold down the fort for you.*

for·te *noun, adv.*
● *noun* /ˈfɔrteɪ; fɔrt/ [sing.] a thing that someone does particularly well: *Languages were never my forte.*
● *adv.* /ˈfɔrteɪ/ (*music*) played or sung loudly **ANT** PIANO ▶ **for·te** /ˈfɔrteɪ/ *adj.*

forth /fɔrθ/ *adv.* (*literary except in particular idioms and phrasal verbs*) **1** away from a place; out: *They set forth at dawn.* ◆ *Huge chimneys belched forth smoke and grime.* **2** toward a place; forward: *Water gushed forth from a hole in the rock.* ⊃ see also BRING FORTH
IDM **from that day/time forth** (*literary*) beginning on that day; from that time ⊃ more at BACK, SO

forth·com·ing **AWL** /ˌfɔrθˈkʌmɪŋ; ˈfɔrθˌkʌmɪŋ/ *adj.* **1** [only before noun] going to happen, be published, etc. very soon: *the forthcoming elections* ◆ *a list of forthcoming books* ◆ *the band's forthcoming U.S. tour* **2** [not before noun] ready or made available when needed: *Financial support was not forthcoming.* **3** [not before noun] willing to give information about something: *She's never very forthcoming about her plans.* **ANT** UNFORTHCOMING

forth·right /ˈfɔrθraɪt/ *adj.* direct and honest in manner and speech **SYN** FRANK: *a woman of forthright views* ▶ **forth·right·ly** *adv.* **forth·right·ness** *noun* [U]

forth·with /ˌfɔrθˈwɪθ; -ˈwɪð/ *adv.* (*formal*) immediately; at once: *The agreement between us is terminated forthwith.*

for·ti·eth /ˈfɔrtiəθ/ ⊃ FORTY

for·ti·fi·ca·tion /ˌfɔrtəfəˈkeɪʃn/ *noun* **1** [C, usually pl.] a tower, wall, gun position, etc. built to defend a place against attack: *the ramparts and fortifications of the Old Town* **2** [U] the act of fortifying or making something stronger: *plans for the fortification of the city*

for·ti·fy /ˈfɔrtəfaɪ/ *verb* (**for·ti·fies, for·ti·fy·ing, for·ti·fied, for·ti·fied**) **1 ~ sth (against sb/sth)** to make a place more able to resist attack, especially by building high walls: *a fortified town* **2 ~ sb/yourself (against sb/sth)** to make someone/yourself feel stronger, braver, etc.: *He fortified himself against the cold with a hot drink.* **3** to make a feeling or an attitude stronger: *The news merely fortified their determination.* **4 ~ sth (with sth)** to increase the strength or quality of food or drink by adding something to it: *cereal fortified with extra vitamins*

for·ti·o·ri ⊃ A FORTIORI

for·tis·si·mo /fɔrˈtɪsəmoʊ/ *adv.* (*abbr.* ff) (*music*) played or sung very loudly **ANT** PIANISSIMO

for·ti·tude /ˈfɔrtətud/ *noun* [U] (*formal*) courage shown by someone who is suffering great pain or facing great difficulties **SYN** BRAVERY, COURAGE

Fort Knox /ˌfɔrt ˈnɑks/ *noun*
IDM **be like/as safe as Fort Knox** (of a building) to be strongly built, often with many locks, strong doors, guards, etc., so that it is difficult for people to enter and the things kept there are safe: *This home of yours is like Fort Knox.*
ORIGIN From the name of the military base in Kentucky where most of the U.S.'s store of gold is kept.

for·tress /ˈfɔrtrəs/ *noun* a building or place that has been made stronger and protected against attack: *a fortress town enclosed by four miles of ramparts* ◆ *Fear of terrorist attack has turned the conference center into a fortress.*

for·tu·i·tous /fɔrˈtuətəs/ *adj.* (*formal*) happening by chance, especially a lucky chance that brings a good result ▶ **for·tu·i·tous·ly** *adv.*

for·tu·nate /ˈfɔrtʃənət/ *adj.* having or bringing an advantage, an opportunity, a piece of good luck, etc. **SYN** LUCKY: **~ (to do sth)** *I have been fortunate enough to visit many parts of the world as a lecturer.* ◆ **~ (in having...)** *I was fortunate in having a good teacher.* ◆ *Remember those less fortunate than yourselves.* ◆ **~ (for sb)(that...)** *It was very fortunate for him that I arrived on time.* **ANT** UNFORTUNATE

for·tu·nate·ly /ˈfɔrtʃənətli/ *adv.* by good luck **SYN** LUCKY: *I was late, but fortunately the meeting hadn't started.* ◆ *Fortunately for him, he was very soon offered another job.* **ANT** UNFORTUNATELY

for·tune 🔑 /ˈfɔrtʃən/ *noun* **1** [U] chance or luck, especially in the way it affects people's lives: *I have had the good fortune to work with some brilliant directors.* ◆ *By a stroke of fortune, she found work almost immediately.* ◆ *Fortune smiled on me* (= I had good luck). **2** [C] a large amount of money: *He made a fortune in real estate.* ◆ *She inherited a share of the family fortune.* ◆ *A car like that costs a small fortune.* ◆ *You don't have to spend a fortune to give your family tasty, healthy meals.* ◆ *She is hoping her New York debut will be the first step on the road to fame and fortune.* ◆ *That ring must be worth a fortune.* **3** [C, usually pl., U] the good and bad things that happen to a person, family, country, etc.: *the changing fortunes of the movie industry* ◆ *the fortunes of war* ◆ *a reversal of fortune(s)* **4** [C] a person's FATE or future: *She can tell your fortune by looking at the lines on your hand.* **IDM** see SEEK ⊃ see also SOLDIER OF FORTUNE

ˈfortune ˌcookie *noun* a thin hollow cookie, served in Chinese restaurants, containing a short message that predicts what will happen to you in the future

ˈfortune ˌhunter *noun* a person who tries to become rich by marrying someone with a lot of money

ˈfortune-ˌteller *noun* a person who claims to have magic powers and who tells people what will happen to them in the future

for·ty /ˈfɔrti/ *number* **1** number 40 **2** *noun* **the forties** [pl.] numbers, years, or temperatures from 40 to 49 ▶ **for·ti·eth** /ˈfɔrtiəθ/ *ordinal number, noun* **HELP** There are examples of how to use ordinal numbers at the entry for **fifth**.
IDM **in your forties** between the ages of 40 and 49

the ˌforty-ninth ˈparallel *noun* the line on a map that is 49° north of the EQUATOR, thought of as forming the border between western Canada and the U.S.

ˌforty ˈwinks *noun* [pl.] (*informal*) a short sleep, especially during the day: *I'll feel a lot better once I've had forty winks.*

fo·rum /ˈfɔrəm/ *noun* **1 ~ (for sth)** a place where people can exchange opinions and ideas on a particular issue; a meeting organized for this purpose: *Television is now an important forum for political debate.* ◆ *an Internet forum* ◆ *to hold an international forum on drug abuse* ⊃ collocations at E-MAIL **2** (in ancient Rome) a public place where meetings were held

for·ward 🔑 /ˈfɔrwərd/ *adv., adj., verb, noun*
● *adv.* **1** (also **for·wards**) toward a place or position that is in front: *She leaned forward and kissed him on the cheek.* ◆ *He took two steps forward.* ◆ *They ran forward to welcome her.* **ANT** BACK, BACKWARD **2** toward a good result: *We consider this agreement to be an important step forward.* ◆ *Cutting our costs is the only way forward.* ◆ *We are not getting any further forward with the discussion.* ◆ *The project will go forward* (= continue) *as planned.* **ANT** BACKWARD **3** toward the future; ahead in time: *Looking forward, we hope to expand our operations in several of our overseas branches.* ◆ *The next scene takes the story forward five years.* ◆ (*old use*) *from this day forward* **4** earlier; sooner: *It was decided to bring the meeting forward two weeks.* **5** (*technical*) in or toward the front part of a ship or plane: *The main cabin is situated forward of* (= in front of) *the mast.* ⊃ see also LOOK FORWARD, PUT FORWARD **IDM** **going/moving forward** (*formal* or *business*) in the future, starting from now: *We have a very solid financial position going forward.* ⊃ more at BACKWARD, CLOCK, FOOT
● *adj.* **1** [only before noun] directed or moving toward the front: *The door opened, blocking his forward movement.* ◆ *a forward pass* (= in a sports game) **2** [only before noun] (*technical*) located in front, especially on a ship, plane, or other vehicle: *the forward cabins* ◆ *A bolt may have fallen off the plane's forward door.* **3** relating to the future: *the forward*

ʌ cup ə about eɪ say eɪ ɪə ˈaɪ five ɔɪ boy aʊ now oʊ go ər bird

movement of history ◆ *A little **forward planning** at the outset can save you a lot of expense.* ◆ *The plans are still **no further forward** than they were last month.* **4** behaving toward someone in a manner that is too confident or too informal: *I hope you don't think I'm being too forward.* ⊃ compare BACKWARD

● **verb 1** to send or pass goods or information to someone: *~ sth to sb We will be forwarding our new catalog to you next week.* ◆ *~ sb sth We will be forwarding you our new catalog next week.* ◆ *~ sth to forward a request/complaint/proposal* **2** to send a letter, etc. received at the address a person used to live at to their new address SYN SEND ON: *~ sth (to sb) Could you forward any mail to us in New York?* ◆ *~ (sth) I put "please forward" on the envelope.* **3** *~ (sb) sth* to send an e-mail that you have received on to someone else: *I'll forward you that e-mail about the sales conference.* **4** *~ sth (formal)* to help to improve or develop something SYN FURTHER: *He saw the assignment as a way to forward his career.* ⊃ see also FAST-FORWARD

● **noun** an attacking player whose position is near the front of a team in some sports ⊃ compare BACK

ˌforwarding adˈdress *noun* a new address to which letters should be sent on from an old address that someone has moved away from

ˈforward-ˌlooking *adj.* (*approving*) planning for the future; willing to consider modern ideas and methods

for·ward·ness /ˈfɔrwərdnəs/ *noun* [U] behavior that is too confident or too informal

ˈforward ˌslash *noun* the symbol (/) used in computer commands and in Internet addresses to separate the different parts SYN SLASH *n.* ⊃ compare BACKSLASH

for·went pt of FORGO

fos·sil /ˈfɑsl/ *noun* **1** the remains of an animal or a plant that have become hard and turned into rock: *fossils over two million years old* **2** (*informal, disapproving*) an old person, especially one who is unable to accept new ideas or adapt to changes

ˈfossil ˌfuel *noun* [C, U] fuel such as coal or oil, that formed over millions of years from the remains of animals or plants ⊃ compare BIOMASS

fos·sil·ize /ˈfɑsəˌlaɪz/ *verb* **1** [T, usually passive, I] *~ (sth)* to become, or make something become, a fossil: *fossilized bones* **2** [I, T] *~ (sb/sth)* (*disapproving*) to become, or make someone or something become, fixed and unable to change or develop ▸ fos·sil·i·za·tion /ˌfɑsələˈzeɪʃn/ *noun* [U]

fos·ter /ˈfɔstər; ˈfɑs-/ *verb, adj.*
● **verb 1** *~ sth* to encourage something to develop SYN ENCOURAGE, PROMOTE: *The organization's aim is to foster better relations within the community.* **2** *~ sb* to take another person's child into your home for a period of time, without becoming his or her legal parents: *They have fostered over 60 children during the past ten years.* ⊃ collocations at CHILD ⊃ compare ADOPT
● **adj.** [only before noun] used with some nouns in connection with the fostering of a child: *a **foster mother/father/family*** ◆ *foster parents* ◆ *a **foster child*** ◆ *foster home* ◆ *foster care*

fought pt, pp of FIGHT

foul /faʊl/ *adj., verb, noun*
● **adj.** (foul·er, foul·est) **1** dirty and smelling bad: *foul air/breath* ◆ *a **foul-smelling** prison* ⊃ thesaurus box at DISGUSTING **2** very unpleasant; very bad: *She's in a **foul mood**.* ◆ *His boss has a **foul temper**.* ◆ *This tastes foul.* ⊃ thesaurus box at TERRIBLE **3** (of language) including rude words and swearing SYN OFFENSIVE: *foul language* ◆ *I'm sick of her **foul mouth*** (= habit of swearing). ◆ *He called her the foulest names imaginable.* **4** (of weather) very bad, with strong winds and rain: *a foul night* **5** (*literary*) very evil or cruel SYN ABOMINABLE: *a foul crime/murder* ▸ foul·ly /ˈfaʊlli/ *adv.*: *He swore foully.* ◆ *She had been foully murdered during the night.* foul·ness *noun* [U]: *The foulness of the air* IDM **fall foul of sb/sth** to get into trouble with a person or

an organization because of doing something wrong or illegal: *to **fall foul of the law*** ⊃ more at FAIR *adj.*, CRY *v.*

● **verb 1** [T] *~ sb* (in sports) to do something to another player that is against the rules of the game: *He was fouled as he tried to make a shot.* **2** [I, T] *~ (sth)* (in baseball) to hit the ball outside the playing area **3** [T] *~ sth* to make something dirty, usually with waste material: *Do not permit your dog to foul the grass.* **4** [T, I] to become caught or twisted in something and stop it from working or moving: *~ sth (up) The rope fouled the propeller.* ◆ *~ (up) A rope fouled up* (= became twisted) *as we pulled the sail down.*
PHR V ˌfoul ˈout (in baseball) to hit a ball that goes outside the allowed area that is then caught, causing you to be out, ˌfoul ˈup (*informal*) to make a lot of mistakes; to do something badly: *I fouled up badly again, didn't I?* ⊃ related noun FOUL-UP, ˌfoul sth↔ˈup (*informal*) to spoil something, especially by doing something wrong ⊃ related noun FOUL-UP

● **noun** (in sports) an action that is against the rules of the game: *It was a clear foul by James on the point guard.* ◆ *to hit a foul* (= in baseball, a ball that is too far left or right, outside the lines that mark the side of the field)

ˌfoul ˈball *noun* (in baseball) a hit that goes outside the allowed area

ˈfoul line *noun* **1** (in baseball) either of two lines that show the area inside which the ball must be hit **2** (in basketball) a line from which a player is allowed to try to throw the ball into the BASKET after a foul

foul-mouthed /ˈfaʊl maʊðd; -maʊθt/ *adj.* using rude, offensive language: *a foul-mouthed racist*

ˌfoul ˈplay *noun* [U] criminal or violent activity that causes someone's death: *Police immediately began an investigation, but did not suspect foul play* (= did not suspect that the person had been murdered).

ˈfoul-up *noun* (*informal*) a problem caused by bad organization or a stupid mistake

found 🔑 **AWL** /faʊnd/ *verb*
1 *~ sth* to start something, such as an organization or an institution, especially by providing money SYN ESTABLISH: *to found a museum/company* ◆ *Her family founded the college in 1895.* **2** *~ sth* to be the first to start building and living in a town or country: *The town was founded by English settlers in 1790.* **3** [usually passive] *~ sth (on sth)* to base something on something: *Their marriage was founded on love and mutual respect.* ⊃ see also ILL-FOUNDED, UNFOUNDED, WELL-FOUNDED **4** *~ sth* (*technical*) to melt metal and pour it into a MOLD; to make objects using this process ⊃ see also FIND

foun·da·tion 🔑 **AWL** /faʊnˈdeɪʃn/ *noun*
1 [C, usually pl.] a layer of bricks, concrete, etc. that forms the solid underground base of a building: *The builders are now beginning to **lay the foundations** of the new school.* ◆ *The explosion shook the foundations of the houses nearby.* ⊃ thesaurus box at BOTTOM **2** [C, U] a principle, an idea, or a fact that something is based on and that it grows from: *Respect and friendship provide a **solid foundation** for marriage.* ◆ *The rumor is totally **without foundation*** (= not based on any facts). ◆ *These stories **have no foundation*** (= are not based on any facts). ⊃ thesaurus box at BASIS **3** [C] an organization that is established to provide money for a particular purpose, for example for scientific research or charity: *The money will go to the San Francisco AIDS Foundation.* **4** [U] the act of starting a new institution or organization SYN ESTABLISHMENT: *The organization has grown enormously since its foundation in 1955.* **5** [U] a skin-colored cream that is put on the face underneath other makeup ⊃ picture at MAKEUP
IDM **shake/rock the foundations of sth| shake/rock sth to its foundations** to cause people to question their basic beliefs about something: *This issue has shaken the foundations of Louisiana politics.*

founˈdation ˌstone *noun* a large block of stone that is put at the base of an important new public building in a special ceremony: *to lay the foundation stone of the new museum*

found·er /ˈfaʊndər/ *noun, verb*
- *noun* a person who starts an organization, institution, etc. or causes something to be built: *the founder and president of the company*
- *verb* (*formal*) **1** [I] ~ **(on sth)** (of a plan, etc.) to fail because of a particular problem or difficulty: *The peace talks foundered on a basic lack of trust.* **2** [I] ~ **(on sth)** (of a ship) to fill with water and sink: *Our boat foundered on a reef.*

ˌfounding ˈfather *noun* **1** (*formal*) a person who starts or develops a new movement, institution, or idea **2** Founding Father a member of the group of people who wrote the U.S. Constitution in 1787

ˌfounding ˈmember *noun* = CHARTER MEMBER

found·ling /ˈfaʊndlɪŋ/ *noun* (*old-fashioned*) a baby who has been left by its parents and who is found and taken care of by someone else

found·ry /ˈfaʊndri/ *noun* (*pl.* **found·ries**) a factory where metal or glass is melted and made into different shapes or objects: *an iron foundry* ♦ *foundry workers* ➔ note at FACTORY

fount /faʊnt/ *noun* ~ **(of sth)** (*literary* or *humorous*) the place where something important comes from SYN SOURCE: *She treats him as if he were the fount of all knowledge.*

foun·tain /ˈfaʊntn/ *noun* **1** a structure from which water is sent up into the air by a PUMP, used to decorate parks, etc. ➔ see also WATER FOUNTAIN **2** a strong flow of liquid or of another substance that is forced into the air: *The amplifier exploded in a fountain of sparks.* **3** a rich source or supply of something: *Tourism is a fountain of wealth for the city.*

foun·tain·head /ˈfaʊntn hɛd/ *noun* (*literary*) a source or origin

ˈfountain ˌpen *noun* a pen with a container that you fill with ink that flows to a NIB ➔ picture at STATIONERY

four /fɔr/ *number, noun*
- *number* **4** HELP There are examples of how to use numbers at the entry for **five**.
  IDM **these four walls** used when you are talking about keeping something secret: *Don't let this go further than these four walls* (= Don't tell anyone else who is not in the room now).
- *noun* a team of four people who ROW a long narrow boat in races; the boat that they row
  IDM **on all fours** (of a person) bent over with hands and knees on the ground: *We were crawling around on all fours.*

ˈfour-byˌfour (also **4x4**) *noun* a vehicle with FOUR-WHEEL DRIVE (= a system in which power is applied to all four wheels, making it easier to control)

ˌfour-color ˈprocess (CanE usually ˌfour-colour ˈprocess) *noun* (*technical*) a way of reproducing natural colors in photographs and printing using COLOR SEPARATION

ˌfour-diˈmensional *adj.* having four DIMENSIONS, usually length, width, depth, and time

four·fold /ˈfɔrfoʊld; ˌfɔrˈfoʊld/ *adj., adv.* ➔ -FOLD

ˌfour-letter ˈword *noun* a short word that is considered offensive, especially because it refers to sex or other functions of the body SYN SWEAR WORD

ˌfour-poster ˈbed (also ˌfour-ˈposter) *noun* a large bed with a tall post at each of the four corners, and sometimes a cover over the top and curtains around the sides ➔ picture at BED

four·some /ˈfɔrsəm/ *noun* a group of four people taking part in a social activity or sport together: *Can you make up a foursome for tennis tomorrow?*

ˌfour-ˈsquare *adj.* **1** (of a building) square in shape, solid, and strong **2** (of a person) firm, steady, and determined ► four-ˈsquare *adv.*: *I stand four-square with the President on this issue.*

ˈfour-star *adj.* [usually before noun] **1** having four stars in a system that measures quality. The highest quality is shown

by either four or five stars: *a four-star hotel* **2** having the second-highest military rank, and wearing a uniform that has four stars on it: *a four-star general*

ˈfour-stroke *adj.* (*technical*) (of an engine or vehicle) with a PISTON that makes four up and down movements in each power CYCLE ➔ compare TWO-STROKE

four·teen /ˌfɔrˈtin/ *number* 14 ▶ **four·teenth** /ˌfɔrˈtinθ/ *ordinal number, noun* HELP There are examples of how to use ordinal numbers at the entry for **fifth**.

the ˌFourteenth Aˈmendment *noun* [sing.] a change made to the U.S. Constitution in 1866 that gave all Americans equal rights and allowed former SLAVES to become citizens

fourth /fɔrθ/ *ordinal number, noun*
- *ordinal number* **4th** HELP There are examples of how to use ordinal numbers at the entry for **fifth**.
- *noun* = QUARTER

the ˌfourth diˈmension *noun* [sing.] **1** (used by scientists and writers of SCIENCE FICTION) time **2** an experience that is outside normal human experience

the ˌfourth esˈtate *noun* [sing.] newspapers and journalists in general and the political influence that they have SYN THE PRESS

fourth·ly /ˈfɔrθli/ *adv.* used to introduce the fourth of a list of points you want to make in a speech or piece of writing

the ˌFourth of Juˈly *noun* [sing.] a national holiday in the U.S. when people celebrate the anniversary of the Declaration of Independence in 1776 ➔ see also INDEPENDENCE DAY

ˌfour-way ˈstop *noun* a place where two streets cross each other, at which there are signs indicating that vehicles must stop before continuing

ˌfour-wheel ˈdrive *noun* [U, C] (*abbr.* **4WD**) a system in which power is applied to all four wheels of a vehicle, making it easier to control; a vehicle with this system: *a car with four-wheel drive* ♦ *We rented a four-wheel drive to get around the island.* ➔ see also FOUR-BY-FOUR

ˌfour-ˈwheeler *noun* a motorcycle with four large wheels, used for riding over rough ground, often for fun ➔ see also ATV

fowl /faʊl/ *noun* (*pl.* **fowl** or **fowls**) **1** [C, U] a bird that is kept for its meat and eggs, for example a chicken: *fowl such as turkeys and ducks* **2** [C] (*old use*) any bird ➔ see also GUINEA FOWL, WATERFOWL, WILDFOWL IDM see FISH

fox /faks/ *noun* **1** [C] a wild animal of the dog family, with red-brown fur, a pointed face and a thick heavy tail ➔ see also FLYING FOX, VIXEN **2** [U] the skin and fur of the fox, used to make coats, etc. **3** [C] (*often disapproving*) a person who is smart and able to get what they want by influencing or tricking other people: *He's a wily old fox.* **4** [C] (*informal*) a sexually attractive person

fox

fox·glove /ˈfaksglʌv/ *noun* a tall plant with purple or white flowers shaped like bells growing up its STEM

fox·hole /ˈfakshoʊl/ *noun* a hole in the ground that soldiers use as a shelter against the enemy or as a place to fire back from ➔ compare HOLE

fox·hound /ˈfakshaʊnd/ *noun* a dog with a very good sense of smell, which is trained to hunt FOXES

ˈfox ˌhunting *noun* [U] a sport in which FOXES are hunted by specially trained dogs and by people on horses: *to go fox hunting* ► ˈfox hunt *noun*: *a ban on fox hunts*

ˌfox ˈterrier *noun* a small dog with short hair

fox·trot /ˈfakstrat/ *noun* a formal dance for two people

t tea   t̬ butter   d did   k cat   g got   tʃ chin   dʒ June   f fall

together, with both small fast steps and longer slow ones; a piece of music for this dance

fox·y /'fɑksi/ adj. **1** like a FOX in appearance **2** (informal) (especially of a woman) sexually attractive **SYN** SEXY **3** skillful at tricking others **SYN** CUNNING

foy·er /'fɔɪər; 'fɔɪeɪ/ noun **1** a large open space inside the entrance of a theater or hotel where people can meet or wait **SYN** LOBBY **2** an entrance hall in a private house or apartment

Fr. abbr. Father (used in front of the name of some Christian priests): Fr. (Paul) O'Connor

fra·cas /'fræ:kəs; 'freɪ-/ noun [usually sing.] a noisy argument or fight, usually involving several people

frac·tal /'fræktl/ noun (mathematics, physics) a curve or pattern that includes a smaller curve or pattern that has exactly the same shape

frac·tion /'frækʃn/ noun **1** a small part or amount of something: Only a small fraction of a bank's total deposits will be withdrawn at any one time. ◆ She hesitated for the merest fraction of a second. **HELP** If fraction is used with a plural noun, the verb is usually plural: Only a fraction of cars in the U.S. use leaded gasoline. If it is used with a singular noun that represents a group of people, the verb is usually singular: A tiny fraction of the population never votes. **2** a division of a number, for example ½ ⊃ see also COMMON FRACTION ⊃ compare INTEGER

frac·tion·al /'frækʃənl/ adj. **1** (formal) very small; not important **SYN** MINIMAL: a fractional decline in earnings **2** (mathematics) of or in fractions: a fractional equation

fractional distil'lation noun [U] (chemistry) the process of separating the parts of a liquid mixture by heating it. As the temperature goes up, each part in turn becomes a gas, which then cools as it moves up a tube and can be collected as a liquid.

frac·tion·al·ly /'frækʃənəli/ adv. to a very small degree: He was just fractionally ahead at the finishing line.

frac·tious /'frækʃəs/ adj. **1** bad-tempered or easily upset, especially by small things **SYN** IRRITABLE: Children often get fractious when they're tired. **2** (formal) making trouble and complaining: The six fractious republics are demanding autonomy.

frac·ture /'fræktʃər/ noun, verb
● noun **1** [C] a break in a bone or other hard material: a fracture of the leg/skull ◆ a compound/simple fracture (= one in which the broken bone comes/does not come through the skin) ⊃ collocations at INJURY ⊃ see also GREENSTICK FRACTURE **2** [U] the fact of something breaking, especially a bone: Elderly people's bones are more prone to fracture.
● verb **1** [I, T] to break or crack; to make something break or crack: His leg fractured in two places. ◆ ~ sth She fell and fractured her skull. ◆ a fractured pipeline **2** [I, T] (formal) (of a society, an organization, etc.) to split into several parts so that it no longer functions or exists; to split a society or an organization, etc. in this way: Many people predicted that the party would fracture and split. ◆ ~ sth (into sth) The company fractured into several smaller groups. ▶ **frac·tured** adj. [usually before noun]: He suffered a badly fractured arm. ◆ (figurative) They spoke a sort of fractured German.

frag·ile /'frædʒl/ adj. **1** easily broken or damaged: fragile china/glass/bones **2** weak and uncertain; easily destroyed or spoiled: a fragile alliance/ceasefire/relationship ◆ The economy remains extremely fragile. **3** delicate and often beautiful: fragile beauty ◆ The woman's fragile face broke into a smile. **4** not strong and likely to become sick: Her father is now 86 and in fragile health. ▶ **fra·gil·i·ty** /frə'dʒɪləti/ noun [U]: the fragility of the human body

frag·ment noun, verb
● noun /'frægmənt/ a small part of something that has broken off or comes from something larger: Police found fragments of glass near the scene. ◆ The shattered vase lay in fragments on the floor. ◆ I overheard a fragment of their conversation.
● verb /'frægmɛnt/ [I, T] ~ (sth) to break or make something

break into small pieces or parts ▶ **frag·men·ta·tion** /ˌfrægmən'teɪʃn/ noun [U]: the fragmentation of the country into small independent states **frag·men·ted** /'frægmɛntəd/ adj.: a fragmented society

frag·men·tar·y /'frægmən,tɛri/ adj. made of small parts that are not connected or complete: There is only fragmentary evidence to support this theory.

fragmen'tation gre,nade (also **fragmen'tation ,bomb**) noun a bomb that breaks into very small pieces when it explodes

fra·grance /'freɪgrəns/ noun **1** [C, U] a pleasant smell: The bath oil comes in various fragrances. **2** [C] a liquid that you put on your skin in order to make yourself smell nice **SYN** PERFUME: an exciting new fragrance from Dior

fra·grant /'freɪgrənt/ adj. having a pleasant smell: fragrant herbs/flowers/oils ◆ The air was fragrant with scents from the ocean and the hills. ▶ **fra·grant·ly** adv.

fraid·y cat /'freɪdi ˌkæt/ noun (informal, disapproving) = SCAREDY-CAT

frail /freɪl/ adj. (**frail·er**, **frail·est**) **1** (especially of an old person) physically weak and thin: Mother was becoming too frail to live alone. **2** weak; easily damaged or broken: the frail stems of the flowers ◆ Human nature is frail.

frail·ty /'freɪlti/ noun (pl. **frail·ties**) **1** [U] weakness and poor health: Increasing frailty meant that she was more and more confined to bed. **2** [U, C] weakness in a person's character or moral standards: human frailty ◆ the frailties of human nature

frames

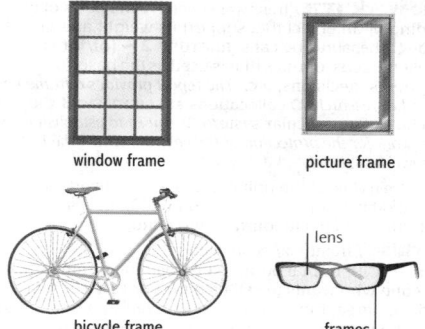

window frame   picture frame

bicycle frame   lens   frames

frame 🔑 /freɪm/ noun, verb
● noun
> **BORDER 1** [C] a strong border or structure of wood, metal, etc. that holds a picture, door, piece of glass, etc. in position: a picture frame ◆ aluminum window frames ⊃ picture at EDGE
> **STRUCTURE 2** [C] the supporting structure of a piece of furniture, a building, a vehicle, etc. that gives it its shape: the frame of an aircraft/a car/a bicycle ⊃ picture at BICYCLE ⊃ see also CLIMBING FRAME
> **OF GLASSES 3** [C, usually pl.] a structure of plastic or metal that holds the LENSES in a pair of glasses: gold-rimmed frames
> **PERSON/ANIMAL'S BODY 4** [C, usually sing.] the form or structure of a person or animal's body: to have a small/ slender/large frame
> **GENERAL IDEAS 5** [sing.] the general ideas or structure that form the background to something: In this course we hope to look at literature in the frame of its social and historical context. ⊃ see also TIME FRAME
> **OF MOVIE/VIDEO 6** [C] one of the single photographs that a movie or video is made of
> **OF PICTURE STORY 7** [C] a single picture in a COMIC STRIP
> **COMPUTING 8** [C] one of the separate areas on an Internet page that you can SCROLL through (= read by using the mouse to move the text up or down)

> IN GARDEN **9** [C] = COLD FRAME
> IN BOWLING/POOL **10** [C] a single section of play in the game of BOWLING or POOL
• **verb**
> MAKE BORDER **1** [usually passive] ~ sth to put or make a frame or border around something: *The photograph had been framed.* ♦ *Her blonde hair framed her face.* ♦ *He stood there, head back, framed against the blue sky.*
> PRODUCE FALSE EVIDENCE **2** [usually passive] ~ sb (for sth) to produce false evidence against an innocent person so that people think he or she is guilty: *He says he was framed.*
> DEVELOP PLAN/SYSTEM **3** ~ sth (formal) to create and develop something such as a plan, a system, or a set of rules
> EXPRESS SOMETHING **4** ~ sth to express something in a particular way: *You'll have to be careful how you frame the question.*
  ▶ **framed** adj. (often in compounds): *a framed photograph*

ˌframe ˈhouse noun a house that is built on a wooden frame: *a typical frame house from the mid-19th century*

ˌframe of ˈmind noun [sing.] the way you feel or the mood you are in at a particular time: *We'll discuss this when you're in a better frame of mind.*

ˌframe of ˈreference noun (pl. frames of reference) a particular set of beliefs, ideas, or experiences that affects how a person understands or judges something

ˈframe-up noun (informal) a situation in which false evidence is produced in order to make people think that an innocent person is guilty of a crime

frame·work [AWL] /ˈfreɪmwɜrk/ noun **1** the parts of a building or an object that support its weight and give it shape ⊃ thesaurus box at STRUCTURE **2** ~ (of/for sth) a set of beliefs, ideas, or rules that is used as the basis for making judgments, decisions, etc.: *The report provides a framework for further research.* ⊃ collocations at SCIENTIFIC **3** the structure of a particular system: *We need to establish a legal framework for the protection of the environment.* ♦ *the basic framework of society*

franc /fræŋk/ noun the unit of money in Switzerland and several other countries (replaced in 2002 in France, Belgium, and Luxembourg by the EURO)

fran·chise /ˈfræntʃaɪz/ noun, verb
• **noun 1** [C, U] formal permission given by a company to someone who wants to sell its goods or services in a particular area; formal permission given by a government to someone who wants to operate a service such as television or radio broadcasting: *a franchise agreement/company* ♦ *a television franchise* ♦ *In the reorganization, part of the former corporation lost its franchise.* ♦ *to operate a business under franchise* ⊃ collocations at BUSINESS **2** [C] a business or service run under franchise: *They operate franchises throughout the United States and Canada.* ♦ *a fast-food franchise* **3** [U] (formal) the right to vote in a country's elections: *universal adult franchise* SYN SUFFRAGE ⊃ see also ENFRANCHISE **4** [C] a professional sports team
• **verb** [usually passive] ~ sth to give or sell a franchise to someone: *The company has franchised several new units in the past year.* ♦ *franchised restaurants* ▶ **fran·chis·ing** noun [U]

fran·chi·see /ˌfræntʃaɪˈziː/ noun a person or company that has been given a franchise

ˈfranchise ˈplayer noun the best or most valuable player on a professional sports team

fran·chis·er (also **fran·chi·sor**) /ˈfræntʃaɪzər/ noun a company or an organization that gives someone a franchise

Fran·cis·can /frænˈsɪskən/ noun, adj.
• **noun** a member of a religious organization started in 1209 by St. Francis of Assisi in Italy ⊃ see also MONK
• **adj.** relating to St. Francis or to this organization: *a Franciscan monk*

fran·ci·um /ˈfrænsiəm/ noun [U] (symb. **Fr.**) a chemical element. Francium is a RADIOACTIVE metal.

Franco- /ˈfræŋkoʊ; -kə/ combining form (in nouns and adjectives) French; France: *the Franco-Prussian War* ♦ *Francophile*

fran·co·phone /ˈfræŋkəˌfoʊn/ adj. [only before noun] speaking French as the main language ▶ **fran·co·phone** noun: *Canadian francophones*

fran·gi·pan·i /ˌfrændʒəˈpæni; -ˈpɑːni/ noun **1** [U, C] a tropical American tree or bush with groups of white, pink, or yellow flowers **2** [U] a PERFUME that is made from the frangipani plant

fran·glais /ˌfrɑːŋˈɡleɪ/ noun [U] (informal) language that is a mixture of French and English, used in a humorous way

frank /fræŋk/ adj., verb
• **adj.** (frank·er, frank·est HELP more frank is also common) honest and direct in what you say, sometimes in a way that other people might not like: *a full and frank discussion* ♦ *a frank admission of guilt* ♦ *He was very frank about his relationship with the actress.* ♦ *To be frank with you, I think your son has little chance of passing the course.* ⊃ thesaurus box at HONEST ▶ **frank·ness** noun [U]: *They outlined their aims with disarming frankness.*
• **verb** [often passive] ~ sth to stamp a mark on an envelope, etc. to show that the cost of mailing it has been paid or does not need to be paid

Frank·en·food /ˈfræŋkənˌfud/ (also ˈFrankenstein ˌfood) noun [C, U] (informal, disapproving) food that has been GENETICALLY MODIFIED

Frank·en·stein /ˈfræŋkənˌstaɪn/ noun (also ˌFranken- stein's ˈmonster, ˈFrankenstein ˌmonster) used to talk about something that someone creates or invents that goes out of control and becomes dangerous, often destroying the person who created it ORIGIN From the novel *Frankenstein* by Mary Shelley in which a scientist called Frankenstein makes a creature from pieces of dead bodies and brings it to life.

frank·furt·er /ˈfræŋkfɔrtər; -fətər/ (also wie·ner, informal wee·nie) noun a long, thin, smoked SAUSAGE, often eaten in a long bread roll

frank·in·cense /ˈfræŋkɪnˌsɛns/ noun [U] a substance that is burned to give a sweet smell, especially during religious ceremonies

frank·ly /ˈfræŋkli/ adv. **1** in an honest and direct way that people might not like: *He spoke frankly about the ordeal.* ♦ *They frankly admitted their responsibility.* **2** used to show that you are being honest about something, even though people might not like what you are saying: *Frankly, I couldn't care less what happens to him.* ♦ *Quite frankly, I'm not surprised you failed.*

fran·tic /ˈfræntɪk/ adj. **1** done quickly and with a lot of activity, but in a way that is not very well organized SYN HECTIC: *a frantic dash/search/struggle* ♦ *They made frantic attempts to revive him.* ♦ *Things are frantic at the office right now.* **2** unable to control your emotions because you are extremely frightened or worried about something SYN BESIDE YOURSELF: *frantic with worry* ♦ *Let's go back. Your parents must be getting frantic by now.* ♦ *The kids are making me frantic* (= making me very annoyed). ▶ **fran·ti·cally** /-kli/ adv.: *They worked frantically to finish on time.*

frap·pé /fræˈpeɪ/ adj., noun (from French)
• **adj.** [after noun] (of drinks) served cold with a lot of ice: *mixed-fruit frappé*
• **noun** a sweet drink served cold with very small pieces of ice

frat /fræt/ noun (informal) = FRATERNITY: *a frat boy* (= a member of a fraternity)

fra·ter·nal /frəˈtɜrnl/ adj. [usually before noun] **1** connected with the relationship that exists between people or groups that share the same ideas or interests: *a fraternal organiza- tion/society* **2** connected with the relationship that exists between brothers: *fraternal rivalry* ▶ **fra·ter·nal·ly** /-nəli/ adv.

fra·ternal ˈtwin (also ˌdizy·gotic ˈtwin technical) noun either of two children or animals born from the same mother at the same time but not from the same egg ⊃ compare IDENTICAL TWIN.

fra·ter·ni·ty /frəˈtərnəti/ *noun* (*pl.* **fra·ter·ni·ties**) **1** [C] a group of people sharing the same profession, interests, or beliefs: *members of the medical/banking/racing, etc. fraternity* **2** (*also informal* **frat**) [C] a club for a group of male students at an American college or university ⊃ compare SORORITY **3** [U] (*formal*) a feeling of friendship and support that exists between the members of a group: *the ideals of liberty, equality, and fraternity*

frat·er·nize /ˈfrætərˌnaɪz/ *verb* [I] ~ **(with sb)** to behave in a friendly manner, especially toward someone that you are not supposed to be friendly with: *She was accused of fraternizing with the enemy.* ▶ **frat·er·ni·za·tion** /ˌfrætərnəˈzeɪʃn/ *noun* [U]

frat·ri·cide /ˈfrætrəˌsaɪd/ *noun* [U, C] **1** (*formal*) the crime of killing your brother or sister; a person who is guilty of this crime ⊃ compare MATRICIDE, PARRICIDE, PATRICIDE **2** the crime of killing people of your own country or group; a person who is guilty of this crime ▶ **frat·ri·cid·al** /ˌfrætrəˈsaɪdl/ *adj.*: *to be engaged in a fratricidal struggle*

fraud /frɔd/ *noun* **1** [U, C] the crime of cheating someone in order to get money or goods illegally: *She was charged with credit card fraud.* ◆ *property that has been obtained by fraud* ◆ *a $100 million fraud* ⊃ collocations at CRIME **2** [C] a person who pretends to have qualities, abilities, etc. that they do not really have in order to cheat other people: *He's nothing but a liar and a fraud.* ◆ *She felt like a fraud accepting their sympathy* (= because she was not really sad). **3** [C] something that is not so good, useful, etc. as people claim it is

fraud·u·lent /ˈfrɔdʒələnt/ *adj.* intended to cheat someone, usually in order to make money illegally: *fraudulent advertising* ◆ *fraudulent insurance claims* ▶ **fraud·u·lence** /-ləns/ *noun* [U] **fraud·u·lent·ly** *adv.*

fraught /frɔt/ *adj.* **1** ~ **with sth** filled with something unpleasant: *a situation fraught with danger/difficulty/problems* **2** causing or feeling worry and anxiety **SYN** TENSE: *There was a fraught silence.*

fray /freɪ/ *verb, noun*
• *verb* **1** [I, T] if cloth frays or something frays it, the threads in it start to come apart: *The cuffs of his shirt were fraying.* ◆ *This material frays easily.* ◆ ~ **sth** *It was fashionable to fray the bottoms of your jeans.* **2** [I, T] ~ **(sth)** if someone's nerves or TEMPER frays or something frays them, the person starts to get irritated or annoyed: *As the debate went on, tempers began to fray.* ▶ **frayed** *adj.*: *frayed denim shorts* ◆ *Tempers were getting very frayed.*
IDM **fray around/at the edges** to start to come apart or to fail: *Support for the governor was fraying around the edges.*
• *noun* **the fray** [sing.] a fight, a competition, or an argument, especially one that is exciting or seen as a test of your ability: *They were ready for the fray.* ◆ *to enter/join the fray* ◆ *At 71, he has now retired from the political fray.*

fraz·zle /ˈfræzl/ *noun* **IDM** see WORN

fraz·zled /ˈfræzld/ *adj.* (*informal*) tired and easily annoyed: *They finally arrived home, hot and frazzled.* ◆ *I need someone to soothe my poor frazzled nerves.*

freak /frik/ *noun, adj., verb*
• *noun* **1** (*informal*) a person with a very strong interest in a particular subject: *a health/fitness/jazz, etc. freak* ⊃ see also CONTROL FREAK **2** (*disapproving*) a person who is considered to be unusual because of the way they behave, look, or think: *She was treated like a freak because she didn't want children.* ◆ *He's going out with a real freak.* **3** (*also* **freak of nature**) (*sometimes offensive*) a person, an animal, a plant, or a thing that is not physically normal **4** a very unusual and unexpected event: *By some freak of fate they all escaped without injury.*
• *adj.* [only before noun] (of an event or the weather) very unusual and unexpected: *a freak accident/storm/occurrence* ◆ *freak weather conditions*
• *verb* [I, T] (*informal*) if someone freaks or if something freaks

them, they react very strongly to something that makes them suddenly feel shocked, surprised, frightened, etc.: ~ **(out)** *My parents really freaked when they saw my hair.* ◆ ~ **sb (out)** *Snakes really freak me out.*

freak·ish /ˈfrikɪʃ/ *adj.* very strange, unusual, or unexpected: *freakish weather/behavior* ▶ **freak·ish·ly** *adv.*

freak show *noun* **1** a small show at a FAIR, where people pay to see people or animals with strange physical characteristics **2** (*disapproving*) an event that people watch because it is very strange

freak·y /ˈfriki/ *adj.* (*informal*) very strange or unusual

freck·le /ˈfrɛkl/ *noun* [usually pl.] a small, pale brown spot on a person's skin, especially on their face, caused by the sun ⊃ compare MOLE[1] ▶ **freck·led** /ˈfrɛkld/ *adj.*: *a freckled face/schoolgirl*

free 🔑 /fri/ *adj., verb, adv.*
• *adj.* (**fre·er** /ˈfriər/ **fre·est** /ˈfriəst/)
> NOT CONTROLLED **1** not under the control or in the power of someone else; able to do what you want: *I have no ambitions other than to have a happy life and be free.* ◆ ~ **to do sth** *You are free to come and go as you please.* ◆ (*informal*) "*Can I use the phone?*" "*Please, feel free*" (= of course you can use it)." **2** not restricted or controlled by anyone else; able to do or say what you want: *A true democracy complete with free speech and a free press was called for.* ◆ *the country's first free election* ◆ *They gave me free access to all the files.*
> NOT PRISONER **3** (of a person) not a prisoner or SLAVE: *He walked out of jail a free man.*
> ANIMAL/BIRD **4** not tied up or in a CAGE: *The researchers set the birds free.*
> NO PAYMENT **5** costing nothing: *Admission is free.* ◆ *free samples/tickets/advice* ◆ *We're offering a fabulous free gift with each copy you buy.* ◆ *You can't expect people to work for free* (= without payment).
> NOT BLOCKED **6** clear; not blocked: *Ensure that there is a free flow of air around the machine.*
> WITHOUT SOMETHING **7** ~ **from/of sth** not containing or affected by something harmful or unpleasant: *free from difficulty/doubt/fear* ◆ *free from artificial colors and flavorings* ◆ *It was several weeks before he was completely free of pain.* **8** **–free** (in adjectives) without the thing mentioned: *a virtually fat-free meal* ◆ *tax-free earnings* ◆ *a trouble-free life*
> NOT ATTACHED/TRAPPED **9** ~ **(of sth)** not attached to something or trapped by something: *Pull gently on the free end of the rope.* ◆ *They had to be cut free from their car after the accident.* ◆ *She finally managed to pull herself free.*
> NOT BEING USED **10** not being used: *He held out his free hand and I took it.* ◆ *Is this seat free?*
> NOT BUSY **11** ~ **(for sth)** (of a person or time) without particular plans or arrangements; not busy: *If Sarah is free for lunch I'll take her out.* ◆ *Keep Friday night free for my party.* ◆ *What do you like to do in your free time* (= when you are not working)?
> READY TO GIVE **12** ~ **with sth** (often *disapproving*) ready to give something, especially when it is not wanted: *He's too free with his opinions.*
> TRANSLATION **13** a free translation is not exact but gives the general meaning ⊃ compare LITERAL
IDM **free and easy** informal; relaxed: *Life was never going to be so free and easy again.* **get, have, etc. a free hand** to get, have, etc. the opportunity to do what you want to do and to make your own decisions: *I was given a free hand in designing the syllabus.* **get, take, etc. a free ride** to get or take something without paying because someone else is paying for it **it's a free country** (*informal*) used as a reply when someone suggests that you should not do something: *It's a free country; I'll say whatever I want!* **there's no such thing as a free lunch** (*informal*) used to say that it is not possible to get something for nothing ⊃ more at HOME *adv.*, REIN *n.*
• *verb*
> PRISONER **1** ~ **sb (from sth)** to allow someone to leave prison or somewhere they have been kept against their will

SYN RELEASE: *By the end of May nearly 100 of an estimated 2,000 political prisoners had been freed.* ◆ *The hijackers agreed to free a further ten hostages.*
> **SOMEONE OR SOMETHING TRAPPED** **2** ~ sb/sth/yourself **(from sth)** to move someone or something that is caught or fixed on something **SYN** RELEASE: *Three people were freed from the wreckage.* ◆ *She struggled to free herself.*
> **REMOVE SOMETHING** **3** ~ sb/sth of/from sb/sth to remove something that is unpleasant or not wanted from someone or something **SYN** RID: *These exercises help free the body of tension.* ◆ *The police are determined to free the town of violent crime.* ◆ *The organization aims to free young people from dependency on drugs.*
> **MAKE AVAILABLE** **4** ~ sb/sth **(up)** to make someone or something available for a particular purpose: *We freed time each week for a project meeting.* ◆ *The government has promised to free up more resources for education.* **5** ~ sb **to do sth** to give someone the extra time to do something that they want to do: *Winning the prize freed him to paint full-time.*

● *adv.*
> **WITHOUT PAYMENT** **1** (also ,free of 'charge) without payment: *Children under five travel free.*
> **NOT TRAPPED** **2** away from or out of a position in which someone or something is stuck or trapped: *The wagon broke free from the train.* ⊃ see also SCOT-FREE

IDM **make free with sth** (*disapproving*) to use something a lot or in a careless way, even though it does not belong to you **run free** (of an animal) to be allowed to go where it likes; not tied to anything or kept in a CAGE ⊃ more at HOME *adv.*, WALK *v.*

,free 'agent *noun* a person who can do whatever they want because they are not responsible to or for anyone else

,free associ'ation *noun* [U] **1** the mental process by which one word or image may suggest another without any obvious connection **2** a method of treating a patient by asking them to use the mental process of free association ▶ ,free as'sociate *verb* [I]: *Patients were encouraged to free associate as a way of revealing negative thoughts.*

free·base /ˈfriːbeɪs/ *noun* [U] (*slang*) a specially prepared form of the powerful illegal drug COCAINE

free·bas·ing /ˈfriːbeɪsɪŋ/ *noun* [U] (*slang*) the activity of smoking freebase

free·bie /ˈfriːbi/ *noun* (*informal*) something that is given to someone without payment, usually by a company: *He took all the freebies that were offered.* ◆ *a freebie vacation*

free·boot·er /ˈfriːbuːtər/ *noun* a person who takes part in a war in order to steal goods and money ▶ free·boot·ing *adj.*, *noun* [U]

free·born /ˈfriːbɔːrn/ *adj.* [only before noun] (*formal*) not born as a SLAVE

free·dom 🔑 /ˈfriːdəm/ *noun*

1 [U, C] ~ **(of sth)** the right to do or say what you want without anyone stopping you: *freedom of speech/thought/expression/worship* ◆ *a threat to press/academic, etc. freedom* ◆ *rights and freedoms guaranteed by the constitution* **2** [U, sing.] the state of being able to do what you want, without anything stopping you: ~ **(of sth)** *freedom of movement/choice* ◆ *Thanks to the automobile, Americans soon had a freedom of movement previously unknown.* ◆ ~ **(to do sth)** *complete freedom to do whatever you want* **3** [U] the state of not being a prisoner or SLAVE: *He finally won his freedom after twenty years in jail.* **4** [U] ~ **from sth** the state of not being affected by the thing mentioned: *freedom from fear/pain/hunger, etc.* ⊃ see also FREEMAN

'freedom ˌfighter *noun* a name used to describe a person who uses violence to try to remove a government from power, by people who support this ⊃ compare GUERRILLA

ˌfreedom of as'sembly *noun* [U] the right to have public meetings, which is guaranteed by law in the U.S.

ˌfreedom of associ'ation *noun* [U] the right to meet people and to form organizations without needing permission from the government

ˌfreedom of infor'mation *noun* [U] the right to see any information that a government has about people and organizations

ˌfree 'enterprise *noun* [U] an economic system in which private businesses compete with each other without much government control ⊃ compare PRIVATE ENTERPRISE

'free fall *noun* [U] **1** the movement of an object or a person falling through the air without engine power or a PARACHUTE: *a free fall display* **2** a sudden drop in the value of something that cannot be stopped: *Share prices have gone into free fall.*

ˌfree-'floating *adj.* not attached to or controlled by anything: *a free-floating exchange rate*

'free-for-ˌall *noun* [sing.] **1** a noisy fight or argument in which a lot of people take part: *Prompt action by prison staff prevented a violent free-for-all.* **2** a situation in which there are no rules or controls and everyone acts for their own advantage: *The lowering of trade barriers has led to a free-for-all among exporters.*

'free form (also ˌfree 'morpheme) *noun* (*linguistics*) a unit of language that can be used by itself: *The plural "s" is not a free form, as it must always be attached to a noun.*

'free-form *adj.* [only before noun] (of art or music) not created according to standard forms or structures: *a free-form jazz improvisation*

free·gan /ˈfriːɡən/ *noun* a person who only eats food that they can get for free and that would otherwise be thrown out or wasted

free·hand /ˈfriːhænd/ *adj.* [only before noun] drawn without using a ruler or other instruments: *a freehand drawing* ▶ free·hand *adv.*: *to draw freehand*

ˌfree 'kick *noun* (in SOCCER) an opportunity to kick the ball without any opposition, which is given to one team when the other team does something wrong: *to take a free kick*

free·lance /ˈfriːlæns/ *adj.*, *verb*
● *adj.* earning money by selling your work or services to several different organizations rather than being employed by one particular organization: *a freelance writer/editor* ◆ *freelance work* ⊃ collocations at JOB ▶ free·lance *adv.*: *I work freelance from home.*
● *verb* [I] to earn money by selling your work to several different organizations

free·lanc·er /ˈfriːlænsər/ (also free·lance) *noun* a person who works freelance

free·load·er /ˈfriːloʊdər/ *noun* (*informal, disapproving*) a person who is always accepting free food and housing from other people without giving them anything in exchange ▶ free·load *verb* [I] free·load·ing *adj.*, *noun* [U]

ˌfree 'love *noun* [U] (*old-fashioned*) the practice of having sex without being married or having several sexual relationships at the same time

free·ly 🔑 /ˈfriːli/ *adv.*

1 without anyone trying to prevent or control something: *the country's first freely elected president* ◆ *Workers were allowed to travel freely between the two countries.* **2** without anything stopping the movement or flow of something: *When the gate is raised, the water can flow freely.* ◆ *Traffic is now moving more freely following an earlier accident.* ◆ *The book is now freely available in the stores* (= it is not difficult to get a copy). ◆ (*figurative*) *The wine flowed freely* (= there was a lot of it to drink). **3** without trying to avoid the truth even though it might be unpleasant or embarrassing: *I freely admit that I made a mistake.* **4** in an honest way without worrying about what people will say or do: *For the first time he was able to speak freely without the fear of reprisals against his family.* **5** in a willing and generous way: *Millions of people gave freely in response to the appeal for the victims of the earthquake.* **6** a piece of writing that is translated **freely** is not translated exactly but the general meaning is given

free·man /ˈfriːmən/ *noun* (*pl.* free·men /-mən/) a person who is not a SLAVE

free ˈmarket *noun* an economic system in which the price of goods and services is affected by supply and demand rather than controlled by a government: *She was a supporter of the free market economy.*

free marketˈeer *noun* a person who believes that prices should be allowed to rise and fall according to supply and demand and not be controlled by the government

Free·ma·son /ˈfriːˌmeɪsn/ (also **Ma·son**) *noun* a man belonging to a secret society whose members help each other and communicate using secret signs

Free·ma·son·ry /ˈfriːˌmeɪsnri/ *noun* [U] **1** the system and practices of Freemasons **2** **freemasonry** (*formal*) the friendship that exists between people who have the same profession or interests: *the freemasonry of actors*

free ˈmorpheme *noun* (*linguistics*) = FREE FORM

free on ˈboard *adj.* (*abbr.* **f.o.b.**) (*business*) including putting goods onto a ship in the price

free ˈperiod *noun* a period of time in a school day when a student or teacher does not have a class

free ˈport *noun* a port at which tax is not paid on goods that have been brought there temporarily before being sent to a different country

free ˈradical *noun* (*chemistry*) an atom or group of atoms that has an ELECTRON that is not part of a pair, causing it to take part easily in chemical reactions. Free radicals in the body are thought to be one of the causes of diseases such as cancer. ⊃ see also ANTIOXIDANT

ˈfree-range *adj.* [usually before noun] connected with a system of farming in which animals are kept in natural conditions and can move around freely: *free-range chickens* ♦ *free-range eggs*

free·ride /ˈfriːraɪd/ (also **ˈfreeride ˌboard**) *noun* a type of SNOWBOARD used for riding on all types of snow

free ˈsafety *noun* (in football) a DEFENSIVE player who can try to stop any offensive player rather than one particular offensive player

free·sia /ˈfriːʒə/ *noun* a plant with yellow, pink, white, or purple flowers with a sweet smell, which are also called freesias

free ˈspirit *noun* a person who is independent and does what they want instead of doing what other people do

free-ˈstanding *adj.* **1** not supported by or attached to anything: *a free-standing sculpture* **2** not a part of something else: *a free-standing clinic*

free·style /ˈfriːstaɪl/ *noun, verb*
● *noun* [U] **1** a swimming race in which people taking part can use any stroke they want (usually CRAWL): *the men's 400m freestyle* **2** (often used as an adjective) a sports competition in which people taking part can use any style that they want: *freestyle skiing*
● *verb* [I] to RAP, play music, dance, etc. by inventing it as you do it, rather than by planning it in advance or following fixed patterns **SYN** IMPROVISE

free·think·er /ˌfriːˈθɪŋkər/ *noun* a person who forms their own ideas and opinions rather than accepting those of other people, especially in religious teaching ▶ **free-think·ing** *adj.* [only before noun]

free ˈthrow *noun* (in basketball) an attempt to throw a ball into the BASKET without any player trying to stop you, that you are allowed after a FOUL

free ˈtrade *noun* [U] a system of international trade in which there are no restrictions or taxes on imports and exports ⊃ collocations at INTERNATIONAL

free ˈverse *noun* [U] (*technical*) poetry without a regular rhythm or RHYME ⊃ compare BLANK VERSE

free·ware /ˈfriːwɛr/ *noun* [U] (*computing*) computer software that is offered free for anyone to use ⊃ compare SHARE-WARE

free·way /ˈfriːweɪ/ (also **ex·press·way**) *noun* a wide road, where traffic can travel fast for long distances. You can only

enter and leave freeways at special RAMPS: *a freeway exit* ♦ *an accident on the freeway*

free·wheel·ing /ˌfriːˈwiːlɪŋ/ *adj.* [only before noun] (*informal*) not concerned about rules or the possible results of what you do: *a freewheeling lifestyle*

free ˈwill *noun* [U] the power to make your own decisions without being controlled by God or FATE
IDM **of your own free will** because you want to do something rather than because someone has told or forced you to do it: *She left of her own free will.*

freeze 🔑 /friːz/ *verb, noun*
● *verb* (froze /froʊz/, fro·zen /ˈfroʊzn/)
‣ BECOME ICE **1** [I, T] to become hard, and often turn to ice, as a result of extreme cold; to make something do this: *Water freezes at 32°F.* ♦ *It's so cold that even the river has frozen.* ♦ ~ **sth** *The cold weather had frozen the ground.* ♦ + **adj.** *The clothes froze solid on the clothesline.* **ANT** THAW
‣ OF PIPE/LOCK/MACHINE **2** [I, T] if a pipe, lock, or machine freezes, or something freezes it, it becomes blocked with frozen liquid and therefore cannot be used: ~ **(up)** *The pipes froze up last night, so we don't have any water.* ♦ ~ **sth (up)** *Ten degrees of frost had frozen the lock on the car.*
‣ OF WEATHER **3** [I] when **it** freezes, the weather is at or below 32° Fahrenheit or 0° Celsius: *It may freeze tonight, so bring those plants inside.*
‣ BE VERY COLD **4** [I, T] to be very cold; to be so cold that you die: *Every time she opens the window we all freeze.* ♦ *Two men froze to death on the mountain.* ♦ ~ **sb** *Two men were frozen to death on the mountain.*
‣ FOOD **5** [T] ~ **sth** to keep food at a very low temperature in order to preserve it: *Can you freeze this cake?* ♦ *These meals are ideal for home freezing.* **6** [I] to be able to be kept at a very low temperature: *Some fruits freeze better than others.*
‣ STOP MOVING **7** [I] to stop moving suddenly because of fear, etc.: *I froze with terror as the door slowly opened.* ♦ (*figurative*) *The smile froze on her lips.* ♦ *The police officer shouted "Freeze!" and the man dropped the gun.*
‣ COMPUTER **8** [I] when a computer screen **freezes**, you cannot move any of the images, etc. on it, because there is a problem with the system
‣ MOVIE **9** [T] ~ **sth** to stop a movie or video in order to look at a particular picture: *Freeze the action there!* ⊃ see also FREEZE-FRAME
‣ SALARIES/PRICES **10** [T] ~ **sth** to hold salaries, prices, etc. at a fixed level for a period of time: *Salaries have been frozen for the current year.*
‣ MONEY/BANK ACCOUNT **11** [T] ~ **sth** to prevent money, a bank account, etc. from being used by getting a court order which bans it: *The company's assets have been frozen.*
IDM **freeze your blood| make your blood freeze** to make you extremely frightened or shocked ⊃ more at TRACK *n.*
PHR V **ˌfreeze sb↔ˈout (of sth)** (*informal*) to be deliberately unfriendly to someone, creating difficulties, etc. in order to stop or DISCOURAGE them from doing something or taking part in something **ˌfreeze ˈover** to become completely covered by ice: *The lake freezes over in winter.*
● *noun*
‣ OF WAGES/PRICES **1** the act of keeping wages, prices, etc. at a particular level for a period of time: *a salary/price freeze*
‣ STOPPING SOMETHING **2** [usually sing.] ~ **(on sth)** the act of stopping something: *a freeze on imports*
‣ COLD WEATHER **3** a short period of time, especially at night, when the temperature is below 32° Fahrenheit or 0° Celsius: *A freeze warning was posted for Thursday night.* ⊃ see also DEEP FREEZE (1)

ˈfreeze-dry *verb* [usually passive] ~ **sth** to preserve something such as food by freezing and drying it very quickly

ˈfreeze-frame *noun* [U] the act of stopping a movie at one particular FRAME (= picture)

freez·er /ˈfriːzər/ *noun* **1** a large piece of electrical equipment in which you can store food for a long time at a low temperature so that it stays frozen **2** the part of a REFRIGERATOR that is very cold and keeps food frozen

freez·ing /ˈfriːzɪŋ/ *adj.* **1** extremely cold: *It's freezing in here!* ◆ *I'm freezing!* ⊃ thesaurus box at COLD **2** [only before noun] having temperatures that are below 32° Fahrenheit or 0° Celsius: *freezing rain* ◆ *freezing temperatures* ⊃ note at COLD ▶ **freez·ing** *adv.* (*informal*): *It's freezing cold outside.*

ˈfreezing ˌpoint *noun* **1** (also **freez·ing**) [U] 32° Fahrenheit or 0° Celsius, the temperature at which water freezes: *Tonight temperatures will fall well below freezing.* **2** [C, usually sing.] the temperature at which a particular liquid freezes: *the freezing point of polar sea water*

freight /freɪt/ *noun*, *verb*
• *noun* [U] goods that are transported by ships, planes, trains, or trucks; the system of transporting goods in this way: *to send goods by air freight* ◆ *a freight business* ◆ *passenger and freight transportation services*
• *verb* **1** ~ sth to send or carry goods by air, sea, truck, or train **2** [usually passive] ~ sth with sth (*literary*) to fill something with a particular mood or tone: *Each word was freighted with anger.*

ˈfreight car a railroad car for carrying goods

freight·er /ˈfreɪtər/ *noun* a large ship or plane that carries goods

ˈfreight train *noun* a train that carries only goods ⊃ picture at TRAIN

French /frɛntʃ/ *adj.*, *noun*
• *adj.* of or connected with France, its people, or its language
• *noun* the language of France and some other countries
IDM **excuse/pardon my French** (*informal*) used to say that you are sorry for swearing

ˌFrench ˈbraid a HAIRSTYLE for women in which all the hair is gathered into a flat BRAID against the head ⊃ picture at HAIR

ˌFrench ˈbread *noun* [U] white bread in the shape of a long thick stick

ˌFrench ˈdoor *noun* a glass door, often one of a pair, that leads to a room, a yard, or a BALCONY ⊃ picture at HOUSE

ˌFrench ˈdressing *noun* [U, C] a thick orange-red sauce made from oil, tomatoes, etc., used to add flavor to a salad

ˈFrench fry (also **fry**) *noun* [usually pl.] a long thin piece of potato fried in oil or fat

ˌFrench ˈhorn *noun* a BRASS musical instrument that consists of a long tube curled around in a circle with a wide opening at the end ⊃ picture at INSTRUMENT

ˌFrench ˈkiss *noun* a kiss during which people's mouths are open and their tongues touch

ˌFrench ˈpress *noun* a special glass container for making coffee with a metal FILTER that you push down ⊃ picture at COFFEE

ˌFrench ˈtoast *noun* [U] slices of bread that have been covered with a mixture of egg and milk and then fried

ˌFrench ˈtwist *noun* a HAIRSTYLE for women in which all the hair is lifted up at the back of the head, twisted and held in place ⊃ picture at HAIR

fre·net·ic /frəˈnɛtɪk/ *adj.* involving a lot of energy and activity in a way that is not organized: *a scene of frenetic activity* ▶ **fre·net·i·cally** /-kli/ *adv.*

fren·u·lum /ˈfrɛnyələm/ *noun* (*anatomy*) a small fold of skin that prevents an organ from moving too much, for example the fold of skin under the tongue

fren·zied /ˈfrɛnzid/ *adj.* [usually before noun] involving a lot of activity and strong emotions in a way that is often violent or frightening and not under control: *a frenzied attack* ◆ *frenzied activity* ▶ **fren·zied·ly** *adv.*

fren·zy /ˈfrɛnzi/ *noun* (*pl.* **fren·zies**) [C, usually sing., U] ~ (of sth) a state of great activity and strong emotion that is often violent or frightening and not under control: *in a frenzy of*

activity/excitement/violence ◆ *The speaker worked the crowd up into a frenzy.* ◆ *an outbreak of patriotic frenzy* ◆ *a killing frenzy* ⊃ see also FEEDING FRENZY

fre·quen·cy /ˈfrikwənsi/ *noun* (*pl.* **fre·quen·cies**) **1** [U, C] the rate at which something happens or is repeated: *Fatal road accidents have decreased in frequency over recent years.* ◆ *a society with a high/low frequency* (= happening often/not very often) *of stable marriages* ◆ *The program can show us word frequency* (= how often words occur in a language). **2** [U] the fact of something happening often: *the alarming frequency of computer errors* ◆ *Objects like this turn up at sales with surprising frequency.* **3** [C, U] (*technical*) the rate at which a sound or ELECTROMAGNETIC wave VIBRATES (= moves up and down): *a high/low frequency* **4** [C, U] (*technical*) the number of radio waves for every second of a radio signal: *a frequency band* ◆ *There are only a limited number of broadcasting frequencies.*

fre·quent /ˈfrikwənt/ *adj.*, *verb*
• *adj.* /ˈfrikwənt/ happening or doing something often: *He is a frequent visitor to this country.* ◆ *Her calls became less frequent.* ◆ *There is frequent bus service into the center of town.* ◆ *How frequent is this word* (= how often does it occur in the language)? **ANT** INFREQUENT
• *verb* /ˈfrikwənt; friˈkwɛnt/ ~ sth (*formal*) to visit a particular place often: *We met in a local bar much frequented by students.*

fre·quent·ly /ˈfrikwəntli/ *adv.*
often: *Buses run frequently between the city and the airport.* ◆ *some of the most frequently asked questions about the Internet* **ANT** INFREQUENTLY

fres·co /ˈfrɛskoʊ/ *noun* (*pl.* **fres·coes** or **fres·cos**) [C, U] a picture that is painted on a wall while the PLASTER is still wet; the method of painting in this way ⊃ see also ALFRESCO ⊃ collocations at ART

fresh /frɛʃ/ *adj.*, *adv.*
• *adj.* (**fresh·er**, **fresh·est**)
▷ FOOD **1** (usually of food) recently produced or picked and not frozen, dried, or preserved in cans: *Is this milk fresh?* ◆ *fresh bread/flowers* ◆ *Eat plenty of fresh fruit and vegetables.* ◆ *vegetables fresh from the garden* ◆ *Our chefs use only the freshest produce available.*
▷ NEW **2** made or experienced recently: *fresh tracks in the snow* ◆ *Let me write it down while it's still fresh in my mind.* **3** [usually before noun] new or different in a way that adds to or replaces something: *fresh evidence* ◆ *I think it's time we tried a fresh approach.* ◆ *a fresh coat of paint* ◆ *Could we order some fresh coffee?* ◆ *This is the opportunity he needs to make a fresh start* (= to try something new after not being successful at something else).
▷ CLEAN/COOL **4** [usually before noun] pleasantly clean, pure, or cool: *a toothpaste that leaves a nice fresh taste in your mouth* ◆ *Let's go and get some fresh air* (= go outside where the air is cooler).
▷ WATER **5** [usually before noun] containing no salt: *There is a shortage of fresh water on the island.* ⊃ see also FRESHWATER
▷ WIND **6** quite strong and cold **SYN** BRISK: *a fresh breeze*
▷ CLEAR/BRIGHT **7** looking clear, bright, and attractive: *He looked fresh and neat in a clean white shirt.* ◆ *a collection of summer dresses in fresh colors* ◆ *a fresh complexion*
▷ FULL OF ENERGY **8** [not usually before noun] full of energy: *I was able to sleep on the plane and arrived feeling as fresh as a daisy.*
▷ JUST FINISHED **9** ~ from sth having just come from a particular place; having just had a particular experience: *students fresh from college* ◆ *fresh from her success at the Olympic Games*
▷ RUDE/CONFIDENT **10** [not before noun] ~ (with sb) (*informal*) rude and too confident in a way that shows a lack of respect for someone or a sexual interest in someone: *Don't get fresh with me!*
IDM see BLOOD, BREATH
▶ **fresh·ness** *noun* [U]: *We guarantee the freshness of all our produce.* ◆ *the cool freshness of the water* ◆ *I like the freshness of his approach to the problem.*

t **tea**   ţ **butter**   d **did**   k **cat**   g **got**   tʃ **chin**   dʒ **June**   f **fall**

● *adv.*

IDM **fresh out of sth** (*informal*) having recently finished a supply of something: *Sorry, we're fresh out of milk.*

fresh·en /ˈfrɛʃn/ *verb* **1** [T] **~ sth (up)** to make something cleaner, cooler, newer, or more pleasant: *The walls need freshening up with white paint.* ◆ *The rain had freshened the air.* ◆ *Use a mouthwash to freshen your breath.* **2** [T] **~ sth (up)** to add more liquid to a drink, especially an alcoholic one **3** [I] (of the wind) to become stronger and colder: *The wind will freshen tonight.*

PHR V ˌfreshen ˈup | ˌfreshen yourself ˈup to wash and make yourself look clean and neat: *I'll just go and freshen up before supper.*

fresh·en·er /ˈfrɛʃənər/ *noun* [U, C] (often in compounds) a thing that makes something cleaner, purer, or more pleasant: *air freshener*

ˈfresh-faced *adj.* having a young, healthy-looking face: *fresh-faced kids*

fresh·ly /ˈfrɛʃli/ *adv.*
usually followed by a past participle showing that something has been made, prepared, etc. recently: *freshly brewed coffee*

fresh·man /ˈfrɛʃmən/ *noun* (*pl.* **fresh·men** /-mən/) a student who is in his or her first year of college, or in ninth grade of school: *high school/college freshmen* ◆ *during my freshman year* ⊃ compare JUNIOR *n.*, SENIOR *n.*, SOPHOMORE

fresh·wa·ter /ˈfrɛʃˌwɔtər; -ˌwɑtər/ *adj.* [only before noun] **1** living in water that is not the ocean and is not salty: *freshwater fish* **2** having water that is not salty: *freshwater lakes* ⊃ compare SALT WATER

fret /frɛt/ *verb, noun*
● *verb* (-tt-) [I, T] **~ (about/over sth)** | **~ (that…)** to be worried or unhappy and not able to relax: *Fretting about it won't help.* ◆ *Her baby starts to fret as soon as she goes out of the room.*
● *noun* one of the bars on the long thin part of a GUITAR, etc. Frets show you where to press the strings with your fingers to produce particular sounds.

fret·ful /ˈfrɛtfl/ *adj.* behaving in a way that shows you are unhappy or uncomfortable **SYN** RESTLESS ▶ **fret·ful·ly** /-fəli/ *adv.*

fret·saw /ˈfrɛtsɔ/ *noun* a SAW with a thin blade that is used for cutting patterns in wood, metal, etc.

fret·ted /ˈfrɛtəd/ *adj.* (*technical*) (especially of wood or stone) decorated with patterns

fret·work /ˈfrɛtwərk/ *noun* [U] patterns cut into wood, metal, etc. to decorate it; the process of making these patterns

Freud·i·an /ˈfrɔɪdiən/ *adj.* **1** connected with the ideas of Sigmund Freud about the way the human mind works, especially his theories of unconscious sexual feelings **2** (of someone's speech or behavior) showing your secret thoughts or feelings, especially those connected with sex

ˌFreudian ˈslip *noun* something you say by mistake but that is believed to show your true thoughts **ORIGIN** This expression is named after Sigmund Freud and his theories of unconscious thought.

fri·a·ble /ˈfraɪəbl/ *adj.* (*technical*) easily broken up into small pieces: *friable soil*

fri·ar /ˈfraɪər/ *noun* a member of one of several Roman Catholic religious communities of men who in the past traveled around teaching people about Christianity and lived by asking other people for food (= by BEGGING) ⊃ compare MONK

fri·ar·y /ˈfraɪəri/ *noun* (*pl.* **fri·ar·ies**) a building in which friars live

fric·as·sée /ˌfrɪkəˈsi; ˈfrɪkəsi/ *noun* [C, U] a hot dish consisting of small pieces of meat and vegetables that are cooked and served in a thick white sauce

fric·a·tive /ˈfrɪkətɪv/ (also **spi·rant**) *noun* (*phonetics*) a speech

sound made by forcing breath out through a narrow space in the mouth with the lips, teeth, or tongue in a particular position, for example /f/ and /ʃ/ in *fee* and *she* ▶ **fric·a·tive** (also **spi·rant**) *adj.* ⊃ compare PLOSIVE

fric·tion /ˈfrɪkʃn/ *noun* **1** [U] the action of one object or surface moving against another: *Friction between moving parts had caused the engine to overheat.* **2** [U] (*physics*) the RESISTANCE (= the force that stops something moving) of one surface to another surface or substance moving over or through it: *The force of friction slows the spacecraft down as it re-enters the earth's atmosphere.* **3** [U, C] **~ (between A and B)** disagreement or a lack of friendship among people who have different opinions about something **SYN** TENSION: *conflicts and frictions that have still to be resolved*

ˈfriction ˌtape *noun* [U] = INSULATING TAPE

Fri·day /ˈfraɪdeɪ; -di/ *noun* [C, U] (*abbr.* **Fri.**)
the day of the week after Thursday and before Saturday **HELP** To see how **Friday** is used, look at the examples at **Monday**. **ORIGIN** Originally translated from the Latin for "day of the planet Venus" *Veneris dies* and named after the Germanic goddess *Frigga*.

fridge /frɪdʒ/ *noun* (*informal*) = REFRIGERATOR: *This dessert can be served straight from the fridge.*

fried *pt, pp* of FRY

friend /frɛnd/ *noun*
> **PERSON YOU LIKE 1** a person you know well and like, and who is not usually a member of your family: *This is my friend Tom.* ◆ *Is he a friend of yours?* ◆ *She's an old friend* (= I have known her a long time). ◆ *He's one of my best friends.* ◆ *a close/good friend* ◆ *a childhood/family/lifelong friend* ◆ *I heard about it through a friend of a friend.* ◆ *She has a wide circle of friends.* ⊃ see also BEFRIEND, BOYFRIEND, FAIR-WEATHER, FALSE FRIEND, GIRLFRIEND, SCHOOL FRIEND
> **SUPPORTER 2** a person who supports an organization, a charity, etc., especially by giving or raising money; a person who supports a particular idea, etc.: *the Friends of the Jones Library* ◆ *a friend of democracy*
> **NOT ENEMY 3** a person who has the same interests and opinions as yourself, and will help and support you: *You're among friends here—you can speak freely.*
> **SILLY/ANNOYING PERSON 4** (*ironic*) used to talk about someone you do not know who has done something silly or annoying: *I wish our friend at the next table would shut up.*
> **IN RELIGION 5** **Friend** a member of the Society of Friends **SYN** QUAKER
IDM **be/make friends (with sb)** to be/become a friend of someone: *We've been friends for years.* ◆ *They had a fight, but they're friends again now.* ◆ *Samantha finds it hard to make friends with other children.* **be (just) good friends** used to say that two friends are not having a romantic relationship with each other **a friend in need (is a friend indeed)** (*saying*) a friend who gives you help when you need it (is a true friend) **have friends in high places** to know important people who can help you ⊃ more at MAN *n.*

friend·less /ˈfrɛndləs/ *adj.* without any friends

friend·ly /ˈfrɛndli/ *adj.*
(**friend·li·er**, **friend·li·est**) **1** behaving in a kind and pleasant way because you like someone or want to help them: *a warm and friendly person* ◆ *~ to/toward(s) sb Everyone was very friendly toward me.* **ANT** UNFRIENDLY **2** showing kindness; making you feel relaxed and as though you are among friends: *a friendly smile/welcome* ◆ *a small hotel with a friendly atmosphere* **ANT** UNFRIENDLY **3** **~ (with sb)** treating someone as a friend: *We soon became friendly with the couple next door.* ◆ *She was on friendly terms with most of the hospital staff.* **4** (especially of the relationship between countries) not treating someone or something as an enemy: *to maintain friendly relations with all countries* **ANT** HOSTILE **5** (often in compound adjectives) that is helpful and easy to use; that helps someone or something do something or does not harm it: *This software is much friendlier than the previous version.* ◆ *environmentally friendly*

farming methods ◆ *ozone-friendly cleaning materials* ⟳ **see also USER-FRIENDLY 6** in which the people, teams, etc. taking part are not seriously competing against each other: *a friendly argument* ◆ *friendly rivalry* ◆ *It was only a friendly game.* ▶ **friend·li·ness** *noun* [U]

ˌfriendly ˈfire *noun* [U] in a war, if people are killed or injured by **friendly fire**, they are hit by a bomb or weapon that is fired by their own side

friend·ship 🔑 /ˈfrɛndʃɪp/ *noun*

1 [C] a relationship between friends: *a close/lasting/lifelong friendship* ◆ *friendships formed while she was in college* ◆ *~ with sb He seemed to have already struck up* (= begun) *a friendship with Jo.* ◆ *~ between A and B It's the story of an extraordinary friendship between a boy and a seal.* **2** [U] the feeling or relationship that friends have; the state of being friends: *Your friendship is very important to me.* ◆ *a conference to promote international friendship*

fri·er = FRYER

frieze /friz/ *noun* a border that goes around the top of a room or building with pictures or CARVINGS on it

frig·ate /ˈfrɪɡət/ *noun* a small fast ship in the navy that travels with other ships in order to protect them

fright /fraɪt/ *noun* **1** [U] a feeling of fear: *to cry out in fright* ◆ *He was shaking with fright.* ⟳ **see also STAGE FRIGHT** ⟳ **thesaurus box at FEAR 2** [C] an experience that makes you feel fear: *I got the fright of my life.*

fright·en 🔑 /ˈfraɪtn/ *verb* [T, I] *~ (sb)* | *~ sb to do sth*

to make someone suddenly feel afraid: *Sorry, I didn't mean to frighten you.* ◆ *She's not easily frightened.* ◆ *She doesn't frighten easily* (= it is not easy to make her afraid). **IDM** see DAYLIGHTS, DEATH, LIFE

PHR V ˌfrighten sb/sth↔aˈway/ˈoff | ˌfrighten sb/sth aˈway from sth **1** to make a person or an animal go away by making them feel afraid: *He threatened the intruders with a gun and frightened them off.* **2** to make someone afraid or nervous so that they no longer want to do sth: *The high prices frightened off many customers.* ˈfrighten sb into sth/ into doing sth to make someone do something by making them afraid ⟳ thesaurus box at SCARE

fright·ened 🔑 /ˈfraɪtnd/ *adj.*

afraid; feeling fear: *a frightened child* ◆ *Don't be frightened.* ◆ *He sounded frightened.* ◆ *~ of sth What are you frightened of?* ◆ *~ of doing sth I'm frightened of walking home alone in the dark.* ◆ *~ to do sth I'm too frightened to ask him now.* ◆ *~ that… She was frightened that the plane would crash.* ◆ *~ for sb I'm frightened for him* (= that he will be hurt, etc.). ◆ *(informal) I'd never do that. I'd be frightened to death.* **IDM** see SHADOW *n.*, WIT ⟳ thesaurus box at AFRAID

fright·en·ing 🔑 /ˈfraɪtn·ɪŋ; ˈfraɪtnɪŋ/ *adj.*

making you feel afraid: *a frightening experience/prospect/thought* ◆ *It's frightening to think it could happen again.* ▶ **fright·en·ing·ly** *adv.*

fright·ful /ˈfraɪtfl/ *adj.* (*old-fashioned*) **1** (*informal*) used to emphasize how bad something is **SYN AWFUL, TERRIBLE**: *It was absolutely frightful!* **2** very serious or unpleasant **SYN AWFUL, TERRIBLE**: *a frightful accident*

fright·ful·ly /ˈfraɪtfəli/ *adv.* (*old-fashioned*) very; extremely **SYN AWFULLY, TERRIBLY**: *I'm frightfully sorry.*

ˈfright wig *noun* a WIG with the hair standing up or sticking out, especially worn by a CLOWN

frig·id /ˈfrɪdʒəd/ *adj.* **1** very cold: *frigid air* **2** not showing any feelings of friendship or kindness **SYN FROSTY**: *a frigid voice* ◆ *There was a frigid atmosphere in the room.* **3** (of a woman) not able to enjoy sex ▶ **frig·id·ly** *adv.*

fri·gid·i·ty /frɪˈdʒɪdəti/ *noun* [U] (in a woman) the lack of the ability to enjoy sex

ˈfrigid ˌzone *noun* [C, usually sing.] (*technical*) the area inside the Arctic Circle or Antarctic Circle ⟳ compare TEMPERATE ZONE, TORRID ZONE

frill /frɪl/ *noun* **1** [C] a narrow strip of cloth with a lot of folds that is attached to the edge of a dress, curtain, etc. to decorate it: *a white blouse with frills at the cuffs* **SYN RUFFLE 2** **frills** [pl.] things that are not necessary but are added to make something more attractive or interesting: *a simple meal with no frills* ⟳ **see also NO-FRILLS**

frill·y /ˈfrɪli/ *adj.* having a lot of frills: *a frilly blouse*

fringe /frɪndʒ/ *noun*, *verb*

● *noun* **1** [C] a strip of hanging threads attached to the edge of something to decorate it **2** [C] the outer edge of an area or a group: *on the northern fringe of the city* ◆ *the urban/rural fringe* ◆ *the fringes of society* ◆ *Nina remained on the fringe of the crowd.* **3** [sing.] usually **the fringe** groups of people, events, and activities that are not part of the main group or activity: *Street musicians have been gathering as part of the festival fringe.* ◆ *fringe meetings at the party conference* **IDM** see LUNATIC

● *verb* [usually passive] *~ sth* to form a border around something: *The beach was fringed by coconut palms.* ▶ **fringed** *adj.*: *a rug with a fringed edge*

ˈfringe ˌbenefit *noun* [usually pl.] extra things that an employer gives you as well as your pay: *The fringe benefits include free health insurance.*

frip·per·y /ˈfrɪpəri/ *noun* (*pl.* frip·per·ies) [C, usually pl., U] (*old-fashioned, disapproving*) objects, decorations, and other items that are considered unnecessary and expensive

Fris·bee™ /ˈfrɪzbi/ *noun* a light plastic object, shaped like a plate, that is thrown from one player to another in a game ⟳ **see also ULTIMATE FRISBEE** ⟳ picture at TOY

fri·sée /friˈzeɪ/ *noun* = ENDIVE

frisk /frɪsk/ *verb* **1** [T] *~ sb* to pass your hands over someone's body to search them for hidden weapons, drugs, etc. **2** [I] *~ (around)* (of animals) to run and jump in a lively and happy way **SYN GAMBOL, SKIP**: *Lambs frisked in the fields.*

frisk·y /ˈfrɪski/ *adj.* (frisk·i·er, frisk·i·est) **1** (of people or animals) full of energy; wanting to play: *a frisky puppy* **2** (*informal*) wanting to enjoy yourself in a sexual way ▶ **frisk·i·ness** *noun* [U]

fris·son /friˈsoʊ/ *noun* [usually sing.] (from *French*) a sudden strong feeling, especially of excitement or fear

frit·il·lar·y /ˈfrɪtˌɛri/ *noun* (*pl.* frit·il·lar·ies) **1** a plant with flowers shaped like bells **2** a BUTTERFLY with orange-brown and black wings

frit·ter /ˈfrɪtər/ *verb*, *noun*

● *verb*
PHR V ˌfritter sth↔aˈway (on sth) to waste time or money on things that are not important: *He frittered away the millions his father had left him.*

● *noun* (usually in compounds) a piece of fruit, meat, or vegetable that is covered with BATTER and fried

fritz /frɪts/ *noun*
IDM on the fritz (*informal*) not working: *The TV is on the fritz again.*

fri·vol·i·ty /frɪˈvɑləti/ *noun* (*pl.* fri·vol·i·ties) (often *disapproving*) [U, C] behavior that is silly or amusing, especially when this is not suitable: *It was just a piece of harmless frivolity.* ◆ *I can't waste time on such frivolities.*

friv·o·lous /ˈfrɪvələs/ *adj.* (*disapproving*) **1** (of people or their behavior) silly or amusing, especially when such behavior is not suitable: *frivolous comments/suggestions* ◆ *Sorry, I was being frivolous.* **2** having no useful or serious purpose: *frivolous pastimes/pleasures* ▶ **friv·o·lous·ly** *adv.*

frizz /frɪz/ *verb*, *noun*

● *verb* [I, T] *~ (sth)* (*informal*) (of hair) to curl very tightly; to make hair do this ▶ **friz·zy** /ˈfrɪzi/ *adj.* (friz·zi·er, friz·zi·est): *frizzy hair*

● *noun* [U] hair that is very tightly curled

friz·zle /ˈfrɪzl/ *verb* **1** *~ sth* to fry something until it is crisp or burns: *frizzled bacon* **2** *~ sth* to cause hair to curl tightly: *frizzled hair*

fro /froʊ/ adv. **IDM** see TO adv.

frock /frɑk/ noun (old-fashioned) a dress: a party frock

'**frock coat** noun a long coat worn in the past by men, now worn only for special ceremonies

frog /frɔg; frɑg/ noun **1** a small animal with smooth skin, that lives both on land and in water (= is an AMPHIBIAN). Frogs have very long back legs for jumping, and no tail: the croaking of frogs ➲ picture at ANIMAL **2** a decorative fastening on a coat consisting of a long wooden button and a LOOP
IDM have, etc. a frog in your throat to lose your voice or be unable to speak clearly for a short time

frog·man /'frɔgmæn; 'frɑg-; -mən/ noun (pl. **frog·men** /-mɛn; -mən/) a person who works underwater, wearing a rubber suit, FLIPPERS, and special equipment to help them breathe: Navy frogmen searched the lake for the murder weapon. ➲ compare DIVER

frog·spawn /'frɔgspɔn; 'frɑg-/ noun [U] an almost transparent substance that looks like jelly and contains the eggs of a FROG ➲ picture at ANIMAL

frol·ic /'frɑlɪk/ verb, noun
● verb (-ck-) [I] (old-fashioned) to play and move around in a lively, happy way: children frolicking on the beach
● noun [C, U] (old-fashioned) a lively and enjoyable activity during which people forget their problems and responsibilities: It was just a harmless frolic.

frol·ic·some /'frɑlɪksəm/ adj. (especially literary) playing in a lively, happy way: frolicsome lambs

from /frəm; frʌm; frɑm/ prep.
HELP For the special uses of **from** in phrasal verbs, look at the entries for the verbs. For example, **keep something from someone** is in the phrasal verb section at **keep**.
1 used to show where someone or something starts: She began to walk away from him. ◆ Has the train from New Haven arrived? **2** used to show when something starts: We're open from 8 to 7 every day. ◆ He was blind from birth. **3** used to show who sent or gave something or someone: a letter from my brother ◆ information from witnesses ◆ the man from (= representing) the insurance company **4** used to show what the origin of someone or something is: I'm from Kansas. ◆ documents from the sixteenth century ◆ quotations from Shakespeare ◆ heat from the sun **5** used to show the material that something is made of: Steel is made from iron. **6** used to show how far apart two places are: 100 yards from the scene of the accident **7** used to show someone's position or point of view: You can see the island from here. ◆ From a financial point of view, the project was a disaster. **8** ~ sth (to sth) used to show the range of something: The temperature varies from 80 degrees to minus 10. ◆ The store sells everything from shoelaces to computers. ◆ Conditions vary from school to school. **9** ~ sth (to sth) used to show the state or form of something or someone before a change: Things went from bad to worse. ◆ translating from English to Spanish ◆ You need a break from routine. **10** used to show that someone or something is separated or removed: The Democrats were ousted from power after eight years. **11** used to show that something is prevented: She saved him from drowning. **12** used to show the reason for something: She felt sick from tiredness. **13** used to show the reason for making a judgment: You can tell a lot about a person from their handwriting. ◆ From what I heard the company's in deep trouble. **14** used when distinguishing between two people or things: Is Portuguese very different from Spanish? ◆ I can't tell one twin from the other.
IDM from... on starting at the time mentioned and continuously after that: From now on you can work on your own. ◆ She never spoke to him again from that day on.

frond /frɑnd/ noun **1** a long leaf of some plants or trees, especially PALMS or FERNS. Fronds are often divided into parts along the edge. **2** a long piece of SEAWEED that looks like one of these leaves

front /frʌnt/ noun, adj., verb
● **noun**
> FORWARD PART/POSITION **1** usually **the front** [C, usually sing.] the part or side of something that faces forward; the side of something that you look at first: The front of the building was covered with ivy. ◆ The book has a picture of Rome on the front. ◆ The front of the car was badly damaged. ➲ see also STOREFRONT **2 the front** [sing.] the position that is in the direction that someone or something is facing: Keep your eyes to the front and walk straight ahead. ◆ There's a big yard at the front of the house. **3 the front** [sing.] the part of something that is farthest forward: I prefer to travel in the front of the car (= next to the driver). ◆ The teacher made me move my seat to the front of the classroom. ◆ Write your name in the front of the book (= the first few pages).
> CHEST **4 someone's front** [sing.] the part of someone's body that faces forward; someone's chest: She was lying on her front. ◆ I spilled coffee down my front.
> IN WAR **5** [C, usually sing.] an area where fighting takes place during a war: More troops were sent to the front last month. ◆ to serve at the front ◆ fighting a war on two fronts ➲ see also FRONT LINE, HOME FRONT
> AREA OF ACTIVITY **6** [C] a particular area of activity: Things are looking unsettled on the economic front. ◆ Progress has been made on all fronts.
> HIDING TRUE FEELINGS **7** [sing.] behavior that is not genuine, done in order to hide your true feelings or opinions: Rudeness is just a front for her shyness. ◆ It's not always easy to put on a brave front for the family. ◆ The senator stressed the need to present a united front (= show people that all members of the group have the same opinion about things).
> HIDING SOMETHING ILLEGAL **8** [C, usually sing.] **~ (for sth)** a person or an organization that is used to hide an illegal or secret activity: The travel agency is just a front for drug trafficking.
> POLITICAL ORGANIZATION **9 Front** [sing.] used in the names of some political organizations: the Animal Liberation Front ➲ see also POPULAR FRONT
> WEATHER **10** [C] the line where a mass of cold air meets a mass of warm air: a cold/warm front
IDM front and center in or into the most important position **in front** adv. **1** in a position that is further forward than someone or something but not very far away: Their house is the one with the big oak tree in front. **2** in first place in a race or competition: The blue team is currently in front with a lead of six points. **in front of** prep. **1** in a position that is further forward than someone or something but not very far away: The car in front of me stopped suddenly and I had to brake. ◆ The bus stops right in front of our house. ◆ He was standing in front of me in the line. ◆ She spends all day sitting in front of (= working at) her computer. **2** if you do something in front of someone, you do it when they are there: Please don't talk about it in front of the children. **3 ~ sb** (of time) still to come; not yet passed: Don't give up. You still have your whole life in front of you. **out front 1** in the part of a theater, restaurant, etc. where the public sits: There's only a small audience out front tonight. **2** in the area near to the entrance to a building: I'll wait for you out front. **up front** (informal) **1** as payment in advance: We'll pay you half up front and the other half when you're finished with the job. **2** (in sports) in a forward position: to play up front ➲ see also UPFRONT ➲ more at CASH n., LEAD[1] v.
● **adj.** [only before noun] **1** on or at the front of something: front teeth ◆ the front wheels of the car ◆ We had seats in the front row. ◆ an animal's front legs ◆ a front-seat passenger ➲ compare BACK, HIND **2** (phonetics) (of a vowel) produced with the front of the tongue in a higher position than the back, for example /i/ in English ➲ compare BACK, CENTRAL
IDM on the front burner (informal) (of an issue, a plan, etc.) being given a lot of attention because it is considered important: Anything that keeps education on the front burner is good. ➲ compare ON THE BACK BURNER at BACK adj.

● **verb**

▷ **FACE SOMETHING 1** [T, I] to face something or be in front of something; to have the front pointing toward something: ~ **sth** *The cathedral fronts the city's main square.* ◆ ~ **onto sth** *The line of houses fronted straight onto the road.*

▷ **COVER FRONT 2** [T, usually passive] ~ **sth** to have the front covered with something: *a glass-fronted bookcase*

▷ **LEAD GROUP 3** [T] ~ **sth** to lead or represent an organization, a group, etc.: *He fronts a multinational company.* ◆ *A former art student fronted the band* (= was the main singer).

PHR V ˌfront **for sb/sth** to represent a group or an organization and try to hide its secret or illegal activities: *He fronted for them in several illegal property deals.*

WHICH WORD?

in front of • in the front of

■ **In front of** can mean the same as **outside**, but not **across from**: *I'll meet you in front of/outside your hotel.* ◆ *There's a bus stop in front of the house* on the same side of the road. ◆ *There's a bus stop across the street from the house* on the other side of the road.

■ **In/at the front (of sth)** means "in the most forward part of something": *The driver sits at the front of the bus.* ◆ *Put the shortest flowers in the front (of the bunch).*

---

front·age /ˈfrʌntɪdʒ/ *noun* **1** [C, U] the front of a building, especially when this faces a street or river: *the baroque frontage of Milan Cathedral* **2** [U] land that is next to a building, a street, or an area of water: *They bought two miles of river frontage along the Colorado.*

ˈ**frontage** ˌ**road** *noun* = SERVICE ROAD

fron·tal /ˈfrʌntl/ *adj.* [only before noun] **1** connected with the front of something: *Airbags protect the driver in the event of a severe frontal impact.* ⊃ see also FULL-FRONTAL **2** (also ˌfull-ˈfrontal) a **frontal** attack or a criticism is very strong and direct: *They launched a frontal attack on company directors.* **3** connected with a weather FRONT: *a cold frontal system* **4** (*medical*) connected with the front part of the head: *the frontal lobes of the brain* ▶ **fron·tal·ly** /ˈfrʌntl·i/ *adv.*

ˌfrontal ˈlobe *noun* (*anatomy*) either of the two parts at the front of the brain that are concerned with behavior, learning, and personality

ˌfront ˈdesk *noun* the desk inside the entrance of a hotel, an office building, etc. where guests or visitors go when they first arrive ⊃ compare RECEPTION

ˌfront ˈdoor *noun* the main entrance to a house, usually at the front: *There's someone at the front door.* ⊃ picture at HOUSE

ˈfront-end *adj.* [only before noun] (*computing*) (of a device or program) directly used by a user, and allowing the user to use other devices or programs ⊃ compare BACK-END

ˌfront-end ˈload·er /ˈfrʌnt end ˌloʊdər/ *noun* a large vehicle with machinery for digging worked by a system of HYDRAULICS

fron·tier /frʌnˈtɪr/ *noun* **1** [C] a line that separates two countries, etc.; the land near this line: ~ **(between A and B)** *the frontier between Guatemala and Mexico* ◆ ~ **(with sth)** *a customs station on the frontier with Brazil* ◆ *a frontier town/zone* ⊃ thesaurus box at BORDER **2** **the frontier** [sing.] the edge of land where people live and have built towns, beyond which the country is wild and unknown, especially in the western U.S. in the 19th century: *a remote frontier settlement* **3** [C, usually pl.] ~ **(of sth)** the limit of something, especially the limit of what is known about a particular subject or activity: *to push back the frontiers of science* (= to increase knowledge of science)

fron·tiers·man /frʌnˈtɪrzmən/ *noun* (*pl.* fron·tiers·men /-mən/) a man living on the frontier, especially one who lived in the western U.S. during the 19th century

fron·tis·piece /ˈfrʌntəsˌpis/ *noun* [usually sing.] a picture at the beginning of a book, on the page opposite the page with the title on it

---

the ˌfront ˈline *noun* [sing.] an area where the enemies are facing each other during a war and where fighting takes place: *Tanks have been deployed all along the front line.* ◆ *front-line troops*

IDM **on the front line (of sth)** doing work that will have an important effect on something: *a life spent on the front line of research*

ˌfront-ˈload *verb* **1** ~ **sth** (*business*) to spread the costs of a project so that more of the money is spent in the earlier stages: *a need to front-load budget spending* ◆ *the positive effects of front-loading funds* **2** ~ **sth** to organize work on a project or information in a document so that the more important work or information is done or placed first: *Teach your students to front-load their research.*

front·man /ˈfrʌntmæn/ *noun* (*pl.* front·men /-mɛn/) **1** a person who represents an organization and tries to make its activities seem acceptable to the public, although in fact they may be illegal: *He acted as a frontman for a drug cartel.* **2** the leader of a group of musicians

ˌfront ˈoffice *noun* [sing.] the part of a business or organization concerned with managing things

ˌfront ˈpage *noun* the first page of a newspaper, where the most important news is printed: *The story was on the front pages of all the tabloids.* ▶ ˈfront-page *adj.* [only before noun]: *The divorce made front-page news.*

ˈfront ˌrunner *noun* a person, an animal, or an organization that seems most likely to win a race or competition

ˌfront-wheel ˈdrive *noun* [U] a system in which power from the engine is sent to the front wheels of a vehicle ⊃ compare FOUR-WHEEL DRIVE, REAR-WHEEL DRIVE

frost /frɔst/ *noun, verb*
● *noun* **1** [U, C] a weather condition in which the temperature drops below 32°F or 0°C (= FREEZING POINT) so that a thin white layer of ice forms on the ground and other surfaces, especially at night: *It will be a clear night with some* **ground frost.** ◆ *a light/heavy/hard frost* ◆ *frost damage* **2** [U] the thin white layer of ice that forms when the temperature drops below 32°F or 0°C: *The car windows were covered with frost.* ⊃ see also HOARFROST
● *verb* **1** [T, I] to cover something, or to become covered, with a thin white layer of ice: ~ **sth (over/up)** *The mirror was frosted up.* ◆ ~ **(over/up)** *The windows had frosted over.* **2** [T] ~ **sth** to cover a cake, etc with FROSTING

frost·bite /ˈfrɔstbaɪt/ *noun* [U] a medical condition in which parts of the body, especially the fingers and toes, become damaged as a result of extremely cold temperatures ▶ **frost·bit·ten** /-ˌbɪtn/ *adj.*

frost·ed /ˈfrɔstəd/ *adj.* **1** [only before noun] (of glass) that has been given a rough surface, so that it is difficult to see through **2** (of cakes, etc.) covered with frosting **3** covered with FROST: *the frosted lawn* **4** containing very small shiny pieces: *frosted eyeshadow*

frost·ing /ˈfrɔstɪŋ/ *noun* [U] a sweet mixture of sugar and water, milk, butter, or egg white that is used to cover, decorate, and fill cakes, etc. **SYN** ICING **IDM** see CAKE *n.*

frost·y /ˈfrɔsti/ *adj.* (frost·i·er, frost·i·est) **1** (of the weather) extremely cold; cold with FROST: *a frosty morning* ◆ *He breathed in the frosty air.* **2** covered with FROST: *frosty fields* **3** unfriendly, in a way that suggests that someone does not approve of something: *a frosty look/reply* ◆ *The latest proposals were given a frosty reception.* ▶ **frost·i·ly** /-stəli/ *adv.*: *"No, thank you," she said frostily.*

froth /frɔθ/ *noun, verb*
● *noun* **1** [U] a mass of small bubbles, especially on the surface of a liquid **SYN** FOAM: *a glass of beer with thick froth on top* **2** [U] ideas, activities, etc. that seem attractive and enjoyable but have no real value **3** [sing.] ~ **of sth** something that looks like a mass of small bubbles on liquid: *a froth of black lace*
● *verb* **1** [I, T] ~ **(sth)** if a liquid **froths**, or if someone or something **froths** it, a mass of small bubbles appears on the surface: *a cup of frothing coffee* **2** [I] to produce a lot of SALIVA

ʌ **cup**   ə **about**   eɪ **say**   aɪ **five**   ɔɪ **boy**   aʊ **now**   oʊ **go**   ər **bird**

froth

bubbles

(= liquid in your mouth): *The dog was **frothing at the mouth**.* ◆ (*figurative*) *He **frothed at the mouth** (= was very angry) when I asked for more money.*

froth·y /ˈfrɔːθi/ *adj.* **1** (of liquids) having a mass of small bubbles on the surface: *frothy coffee* **2** seeming attractive and enjoyable but having no real value: *frothy romantic novels* **3** (of clothes or cloth) light and delicate

frown /fraʊn/ *verb, noun*
● *verb* [I, T] to make a serious, angry, or worried expression by bringing your EYEBROWS closer together so that lines appear on your FOREHEAD: **~ (at sb/sth)** *What are you frowning at me for?* ◆ **+ speech** *"I don't understand," she frowned.*
PHR V **ˈfrown on/upon sb/sth** to disapprove of someone or something: *In her family, any expression of feeling was frowned upon.*
● *noun* [usually sing.] a serious, angry, or worried expression on a person's face that causes lines on their FOREHEAD: *She looked up with a puzzled frown on her face.* ◆ *a slight frown of disapproval/concentration, etc.*

froze *pt of* FREEZE

fro·zen 🔑 /ˈfroʊzn/ *adj.*
1 [usually before noun] (of food) kept at a very low temperature in order to preserve it: *frozen peas* **2** [not usually before noun] (of people or parts of the body) extremely cold: *I'm absolutely frozen!* ◆ *You look like you're frozen stiff.* **3** (of rivers, lakes, etc.) with a layer of ice on the surface **4** (especially of ground) so cold that it has become very hard: *The ground was frozen solid.* **5** **~ with/in sth** unable to move because of a strong emotion such as fear or horror: *She stared at him, frozen with shock.* ➔ see also FREEZE

FRS /ˌɛf ɑr ˈɛs/ *abbr.* FEDERAL RESERVE SYSTEM

fruc·tose /ˈfrʌktoʊs; ˈfrʊk-; ˈfruːk-/ *noun* [U] (*chemistry*) a type of sugar found in fruit juice and HONEY

fru·gal /ˈfruːgl/ *adj.* **1** using only as much money or food as is necessary: *a frugal existence/life* **ANT** EXTRAVAGANT **2** (of meals) small, plain, and not costing very much **SYN** MEAGER: *a frugal lunch of bread and cheese* ▶ **fru·gal·i·ty** /fruˈgæləti/ *noun* [U] **fru·gal·ly** /ˈfruːgəli/ *adv.*: *to live/eat frugally*

fruit 🔑 /fruːt/ *noun, verb*
● *noun* **1** [C, U] the part of a plant that consists of one or more seeds and flesh, can be eaten as food and usually tastes sweet: *tropical fruits, such as bananas and pineapples* ◆ *Eat plenty of fresh fruit and vegetables.* ◆ *a piece of fruit* (= an apple, an orange, etc.) ◆ *fruit juice* ◆ *fruit trees* ➔ see also DRIED FRUIT, FIRST FRUIT ➔ compare VEGETABLE ➔ picture at FRUIT **2** [C] (*technical*) a part of a plant or tree that is formed after the flowers have died and in which seeds develop **3** [C, usually pl.] (*literary*) all the natural things that the earth produces
IDM **the fruit/fruits of sth** the good results of an activity or a situation: *to enjoy the fruits of your labors* (= the rewards for your hard work) ◆ *The book is the fruit of years of research.* ➔ more at BEAR, FORBIDDEN
● *verb* [I] (*technical*) (of a tree or plant) to produce fruit

fruit·ar·i·an /fruˈtɛriən/ *noun* a person who eats only fruit ➔ compare VEGETARIAN

ˈfruit bat *noun* a BAT (= an animal like a mouse with wings) that lives in hot countries and eats fruit

ˈfruit cake /ˈfruːtkeɪk/ *noun* **1** [C, U] a cake containing dried

fruit **2** **fruitcake** [C] (*informal*) a person who behaves in a strange or crazy way: *She's nutty as a fruitcake.*

ˌfruit ˈcocktail (also **ˈfruit cup**) *noun* [U] a mixture of small pieces of fruit, often sold in cans

ˈfruit fly *noun* a small fly that eats plants that are decaying, especially fruit

fruit·ful /ˈfruːtfl/ *adj.* **1** producing many useful results **SYN** PRODUCTIVE: *a fruitful collaboration/discussion* **ANT** FRUITLESS **2** (*literary*) (of land or trees) producing a lot of crops ▶ **fruit·ful·ly** /-fəli/ *adv.* **fruit·ful·ness** *noun* [U]

fruit·i·ness /ˈfruːtinəs/ *noun* [U] (especially of wine) the quality of tasting or smelling strongly of fruit

fru·i·tion /fruˈɪʃn/ *noun* [U] (*formal*) the successful result of a plan, a process, or an activity: *After months of hard work, our plans finally came to fruition.* ◆ *His extravagant ideas were never brought to fruition.*

fruit·less /ˈfruːtləs/ *adj.* producing no useful results **SYN** UNPRODUCTIVE: *a fruitless attempt/search* ◆ *Our efforts to persuade her proved fruitless.* **ANT** FRUITFUL ▶ **fruit·less·ly** *adv.*

ˈfruit ˌsalad *noun* [U, C] a mixture of different types of chopped fruit, served as a DESSERT (= a sweet dish) or a salad

fruit·y /ˈfruːti/ *adj.* (**fruit·i·er**, **fruit·i·est**) **1** smelling or tasting strongly of fruit: *The wine from this region is rich and fruity.* **2** (*informal*) (of people) slightly crazy

frump /frʌmp/ *noun* (*disapproving*) a woman who wears clothes that are not fashionable ▶ **frump·y** (also *less frequent* **frump·ish**) *adj.*: *frumpy clothes* ◆ *a frumpy housewife*

frus·trate /ˈfrʌstreɪt/ *verb* **1** **~ sb** to make someone feel annoyed or impatient because they cannot do or achieve what they want: *What frustrates him is that there's too little money to spend on the project.* **2** **~ sb/sth** to prevent someone from doing something; to prevent something from happening or succeeding **SYN** THWART: *The rescue attempt was frustrated by bad weather.*

frus·trat·ed /ˈfrʌstreɪtəd/ *adj.* **1** feeling annoyed and impatient because you cannot do or achieve what you want: *It's very easy to get frustrated in this job.* ◆ **~ at/with sth** *They felt frustrated at the lack of progress.* **2** (of an emotion) having no effect; not being satisfied: *He stamped his foot in frustrated rage.* ◆ *frustrated desires* **3** [only before noun] unable to be successful in a particular career: *a frustrated artist* **4** not satisfied sexually

frus·trat·ing /ˈfrʌstreɪtɪŋ/ *adj.* causing you to feel annoyed and impatient because you cannot do or achieve what you want: *It's frustrating to have to wait so long.* ▶ **frus·trat·ing·ly** *adv.*: *Progress was frustratingly slow.*

frus·tra·tion /frʌˈstreɪʃn/ *noun* **1** [U] the feeling of being frustrated: *Dave thumped the table in frustration.* ◆ *She couldn't stand the frustration of not being able to help.* ◆ *sexual frustration* **2** [C, usually pl.] something that causes you to feel frustrated: *Every job has its difficulties and frustrations.* ◆ *Inevitably she took out her frustrations on the children.* **3** [U] **~ of sth** (*formal*) the fact that something is preventing something or someone from succeeding: *the frustration of all his ambitions*

fry 🔑 /fraɪ/ *verb, noun*
● *verb* (**fries**, **fry·ing**, **fried**, **fried**) **1** [T, I] **~ (sth)** to cook something in hot fat or oil; to be cooked in hot fat or oil: *fried fish* ◆ *the smell of bacon frying* ➔ picture at COOKING ➔ collocations at COOKING ➔ see also STIR-FRY **2** [I] (*informal*) to be burned by the sun: *You'll fry on the beach if you're not careful.* **IDM** see FISH
● *noun* **1** [pl.] very small young fish ➔ see also SMALL FRY **2** [C] usually **fries** [pl.] = FRENCH FRY: *Would you like ketchup with your fries?* ➔ see also HOME FRIES

fry·er (also **fri·er**) /ˈfraɪər/ *noun* **1** a large deep pan used for frying food in: *a deep-fat fryer* **2** a young chicken that is suitable for frying

Fruit and Vegetables

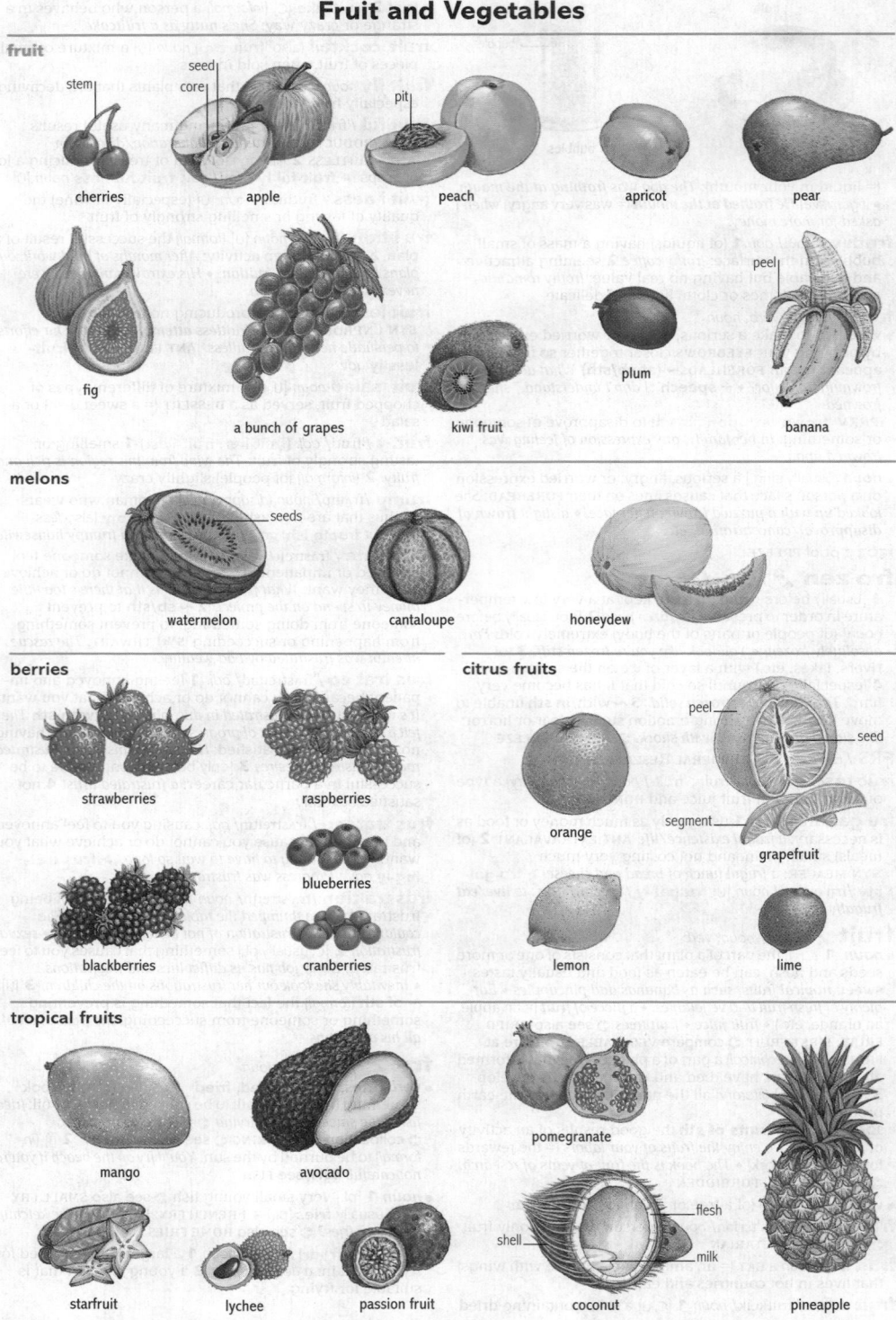

fruit

stem

seed

core

pit

cherries

apple

peach

apricot

pear

peel

fig

a bunch of grapes

kiwi fruit

plum

banana

melons

seeds

watermelon

cantaloupe

honeydew

berries

strawberries

raspberries

blueberries

blackberries

cranberries

citrus fruits

peel

seed

orange

segment

grapefruit

lemon

lime

tropical fruits

mango

avocado

pomegranate

starfruit

lychee

passion fruit

flesh

shell

milk

coconut

pineapple

t tea   ṭ butter   d did   k cat   g got   tʃ chin   dʒ June   f fall

vegetables

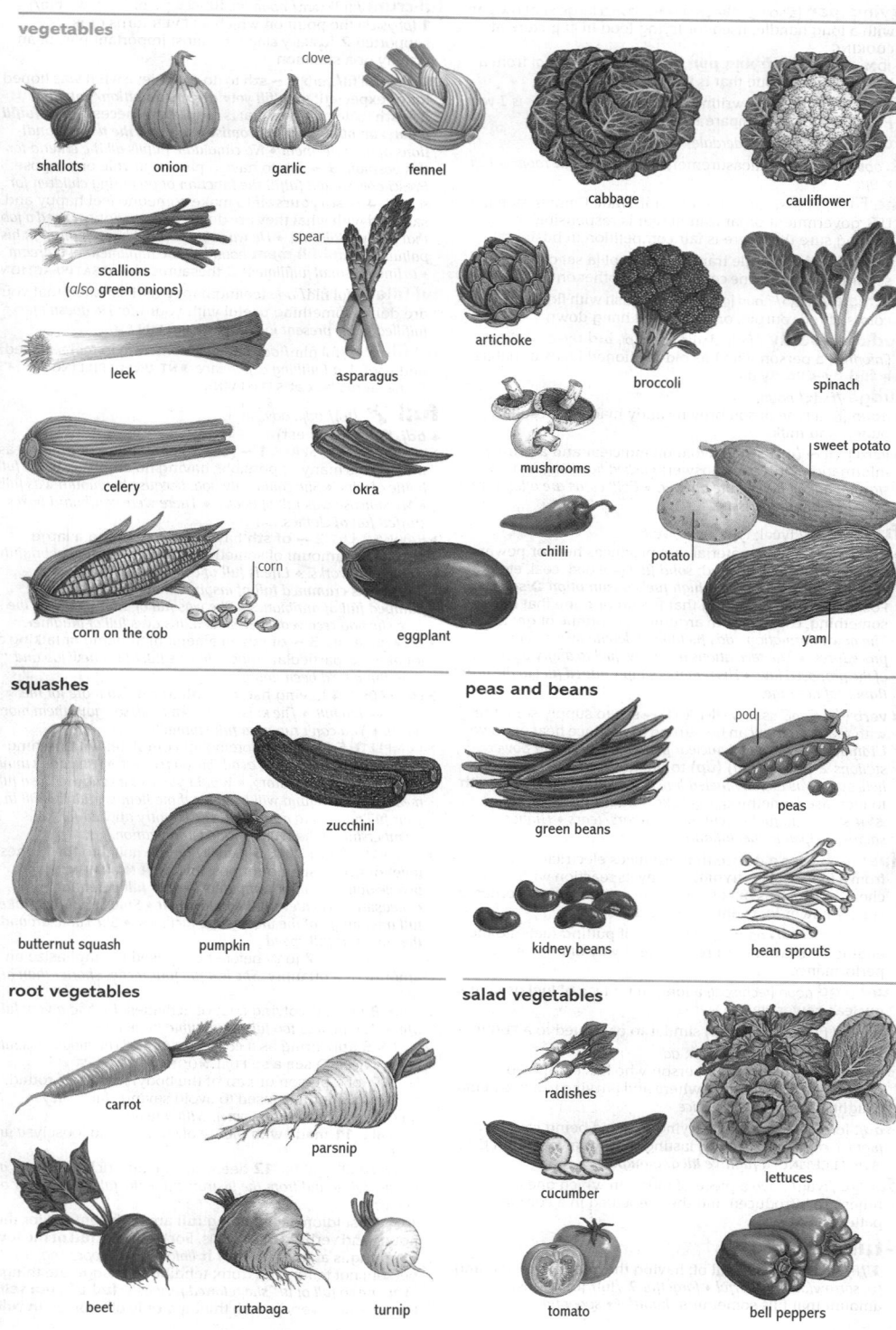

shallots

onion

clove

garlic

fennel

cabbage

cauliflower

scallions
(*also* green onions)

spear

asparagus

artichoke

broccoli

spinach

leek

celery

okra

mushrooms

sweet potato

chilli

potato

yam

corn

corn on the cob

eggplant

squashes

zucchini

butternut squash

pumpkin

peas and beans

pod

peas

green beans

kidney beans

bean sprouts

root vegetables

carrot

parsnip

beet

rutabaga

turnip

salad vegetables

radishes

cucumber

lettuces

tomato

bell peppers

frying pan (also **fry·pan**, **skil·let**) *noun* a large shallow pan with a long handle, used for frying food in ⊃ **picture at** COOKING
IDM **out of the frying pan into the fire** (*saying*) from a bad situation to one that is worse

FT (also **F/T**) *abbr.* (in writing) FULL-TIME: *The course is 1 year FT, 2 years PT.* ⊃ **compare** PT

Ft. *abbr.* FORT: *Ft. Lauderdale*

ft. *abbr.* (in writing measurements) feet; foot: *The room is 12ft. × 9ft.*

the FTC /ˌɛf ti ˈsi/ *abbr.* the Federal Trade Commission (the U.S. government organization that is responsible for making sure that there is fair competition in business)

FTP /ˌɛf ti ˈpi/ *abbr.* file transfer protocol (a set of rules for sending files from one computer to another on the Internet)

fuch·sia /ˈfyuʃə/ *noun* [C, U] a small bush with flowers in two colors of red, purple, or white, that hang down

fud·dy-dud·dy /ˈfʌdi ˌdʌdi/ *noun* (*pl.* **fud·dy-dud·dies**) (*informal*) a person who has old-fashioned ideas or habits ▶ **fud·dy-dud·dy** *adj.*

fudge /fʌdʒ/ *noun, verb*
• *noun* [U] a type of soft brown candy made from sugar, butter, and milk
• *verb* [T, I] **~ (on) sth** to avoid giving clear and accurate information, or a clear answer: *I asked how long he was staying, but he fudged the answer.* ◆ *Politicians are often very good at* **fudging the issue.**

fu·el 🔑 /ˈfyuəl; fyul/ *noun, verb*
• *noun* **1** [U, C] any material that produces heat or power, usually when it is burned: *solid fuel* (= wood, coal, etc.) ◆ *nuclear fuels* ◆ *a car with high fuel consumption* ⊃ **see also** FOSSIL FUEL **2** [U] a thing that is said or done that makes something, especially an argument, continue or get worse: *The new information adds fuel to the debate over safety procedures.* ◆ *The revelations gave new fuel to angry opponents of the proposed law.* ◆ *His remarks simply added fuel to the fire/flames of her rage.*
• *verb* (**-l-**, CanE usually **-ll-**) **1** [T] **~ sth** to supply something with material that can be burned to produce heat or power: *Uranium is used to fuel nuclear plants.* ◆ *coal-fueled power stations* **2** [T, I] **~ (sth) (up)** to put gas into a vehicle: *The helicopter was already fueled (up) and ready to go.* **3** [T] **~ sth** to increase something; to make something stronger **SYN** STOKE: *to fuel speculation/rumors/fears* ◆ *Higher salaries helped to fuel inflation.*

fuel cell *noun* a device that produces electricity directly from a fuel, such as HYDROGEN, by its reaction with another chemical, such as OXYGEN, without any burning, in order to supply power to a vehicle or machine

fuel in·jection *noun* [U] a system of putting fuel into the engine of a car under pressure as a way of improving its performance

fuel rod *noun* (*technical*) a long thin piece of fuel used in a nuclear power station

fu·gal /ˈfyugl/ *adj.* (*music*) similar to or related to a FUGUE

fu·gi·tive /ˈfyudʒətɪv/ *noun, adj.*
• *noun* **~ (from sb/sth)** a person who has escaped or is running away from somewhere and is trying to avoid being caught: *a fugitive from justice*
• *adj.* [only before noun] **1** trying to avoid being caught: *a fugitive criminal* **2** (*literary*) lasting only for a very short time **SYN** FLEETING: *a fugitive idea/thought*

fugue /fyug/ *noun* a piece of music in which one or more tunes are introduced and then repeated in a complicated pattern

-ful 🔑 *suffix*
1 /fl/ (in adjectives) full of; having the qualities of; tending to: *sorrowful* ◆ *masterful* ◆ *forgetful* **2** /fʊl/ (in nouns) an amount that fills something: *handful* ◆ *spoonful*

ful·crum /ˈfʊlkrəm/ *noun* (*pl.* **ful·crums** or **ful·cra** /-krə/)
1 (*physics*) the point on which a LEVER turns or is supported **2** [usually sing.] the most important part of an activity or a situation

ful·fill /fʊlˈfɪl/ *verb* **1** **~ sth** to do or achieve what was hoped for or expected: *to fulfill your dream/ambition/potential* **2** **~ sth** to do or have what is required or necessary: *to fulfill a duty/an obligation/a promise* ◆ *to fulfill the terms/conditions of an agreement* ◆ *No candidate fulfills all the criteria for this position.* **3** **~ sth** to have a particular role or purpose: *Preschools should fulfill the function of preparing children for school.* **4** **~ sb/yourself** to make someone feel happy and satisfied with what they are doing or have done: *I need a job that really fulfills me.* ◆ *He was able to fulfill himself through his painting.* ▶ **ful·fill·ment** *noun* [U]: *the fulfillment of a dream* ◆ *to find personal fulfillment* ⊃ **thesaurus box at** SATISFACTION

ful·filled /fʊlˈfɪld/ *adj.* feeling happy and satisfied that you are doing something useful with your life: *He doesn't feel fulfilled in his present job.* **ANT** UNFULFILLED

ful·fill·ing /fʊlˈfɪlɪŋ/ *adj.* causing someone to feel satisfied and useful: *a fulfilling experience* **ANT** UNFULFILLING ⊃ **thesaurus box at** SATISFYING

full 🔑 /fʊl/ *adj., adv.*
• *adj.* (**full·er**, **full·est**)
▷ WITH NO EMPTY SPACE **1** **~ (of sth)** containing or holding as much or as many as possible; having no empty space: *a full bottle of wine* ◆ *She could only nod, because her mouth was full.* ◆ *My suitcase was full of books.* ◆ *There were cardboard boxes stuffed full of clothes.*
▷ HAVING A LOT **2** **~ of sth** having or containing a large number or amount of something: *The sky was full of brightly colored fireworks.* ◆ *Life is full of coincidences.* ◆ *Our new brochure is crammed full of inspirational ideas.* ◆ *animals pumped full of antibiotics* ◆ *She was full of admiration for the care she had received.* ◆ *He smiled, his eyes full of laughter.*
▷ TALKING A LOT **3** **~ of sth** (of a person) thinking or talking a lot about a particular thing: *He was full of his new job and everything he'd been doing.*
▷ WITH FOOD **4** having had enough to eat: *No more for me, thanks—I'm full.* ◆ *The kids still weren't full, so I gave them more pasta.* ◆ *You can't run on a full stomach.*
▷ COMPLETE **5** [usually before noun] complete; with nothing missing: *Full details are available on request.* ◆ *I still don't think we've heard the full story.* ◆ *Would you like a sandwich or a full meal?* ◆ *A full refund will be given if the item is faulty.* ◆ *Fill in your full name and address.* ◆ *The country applied for full membership in the World Trade Organization.*
▷ AS MUCH AS POSSIBLE **6** [usually before noun] to the highest level or greatest amount possible **SYN** MAXIMUM: *Many people don't use their computers to their full potential.* ◆ *measures to achieve full employment* ◆ *Students should take full advantage of the university's facilities.* ◆ *She came around the corner at full speed.*
▷ FOR EMPHASIS **7** [only before noun] used to emphasize an amount or a quantity: *She is a full four inches shorter than her sister.*
▷ BUSY **8** busy; involving a lot of activities: *He had a very full life.* ◆ *Her life was too full to find time for hobbies.*
▷ MOON **9** appearing as a complete circle: *The moon was full, the sky clear.* ⊃ **see also** FULL MOON
▷ FAT **10** (of a person or part of the body) large and round. "Full" is sometimes used to avoid saying "fat": *They specialize in clothes for women with a fuller figure.*
▷ CLOTHES **11** made with plenty of cloth; fitting loosely: *a full skirt*
▷ TONE/VOICE/FLAVOR **12** deep, strong, and rich: *He draws a unique full sound from the instrument.* ◆ *the full fruity flavor of the wine*
IDM Most idioms containing **full** are at the entries for the nouns and verbs in the idioms. For example, **full of the joys of spring** is at *joy*. **full of it** (*informal, disapproving*) (of a person) not telling the truth; tending to exaggerate things: *"You are so full of it!" she retorted furiously.* **full of yourself** (*disapproving*) very proud; thinking only of yourself **in full**

h **hat**   m **man**   n **no**   ŋ **sing**   l **leg**   r **red**   y **yes**   w **wet**

including the whole of something: *The address must be printed in full.* **to the fullest** to the greatest possible degree: *I've always believed in living life to the fullest.*

• *adv.* ~ **in/on sth** directly: *She looked him full in the face.*

full·back /'fʊlbæk/ *noun* **1** [C] the offensive player in football whose position is behind the QUARTERBACK and beside the HALFBACK **2** [C] one of the defending players in HOCKEY or SOCCER, whose position is near the goal they are defending **3** [U] the position a fullback plays

full-,blooded *adj.* [only before noun] **1** involving very strong feelings or actions; done in an enthusiastic way: *a full-blooded attack* **2** having parents, grandparents, etc. from only one race or country: *a full-blooded Scotsman*

full-'blown *adj.* [only before noun] having all the characteristics of someone or something; fully developed: *full-blown AIDS* ♦ *The border dispute turned into a full-blown crisis.*

full-,bodied *adj.* having a pleasantly strong taste or sound: *a full-bodied red wine* ♦ *a full-bodied string section*

full-'color (*CanE usually* **full-'colour**) *adj.* [only before noun] printed using colors rather than just black and white

full-court 'press *noun* [sing.] **1** (in basketball) a way of attacking in which the members of a team stay close to their opponents over the whole area of play **2** (*informal*) a strong effort to influence someone or a group of people by putting pressure on them

ful·ler's earth /,fʊlərz 'ərθ/ *noun* [U] a type of CLAY used for cleaning cloth and making it thicker

full-'face *adj.* [only before noun] showing the whole of someone's face; not in PROFILE: *a full-face view/portrait* ▶ **full 'face** *adv.*: *She is seen full face and then from the other side as the camera circles her.*

full-'fledged *adj.* completely developed; with all the qualifications necessary for something

full-'frontal *adj., noun*
• *adj.* [only before noun] **1** showing the whole of the front of a person's body: *full-frontal nudity* **2** = FRONTAL
• *noun* a picture or a scene in a movie that shows the naked body of a person from the front

full-'grown *adj.* (of people, animals, or plants) having reached the greatest size to which they can grow and stopped growing

full 'house *noun* **1** an occasion in a theater, concert hall, etc. when there are no empty seats: *They played to a full house.* **2** (in the card game of POKER) three cards of one kind and two of another kind

full-'length *adj., adv.*
• *adj.* [only before noun] **1** (of a mirror or picture) showing the whole of a person's body: *a full-length portrait* **2** (of clothing) reaching a person's ankles: *a full-length skirt* **3** (of a book, play, etc.) not made shorter; of the usual length: *a full-length novel* **4** (of curtains or a window) reaching the ground
• *adv.* a person who is lying **full-length** is lying flat with their legs straight: *He was sprawled full-length across the bed.*

full 'moon *noun* [C, usually sing., U] the moon when it appears as a full circle; a time when this happens ᕲ compare HALF-MOON, HARVEST MOON, NEW MOON

full·ness /'fʊlnəs/ *noun* [U, sing.] **1** (of the body or part of the body) the quality of being large and round: *the fullness of her lips* **2** (of colors, sounds, and flavors) the quality of being deep and rich **3** the quality of being complete and satisfying: *the fullness of life*
IDM **in the fullness of time** when the time is appropriate, usually after a long period

full-'on *adj.* (*informal*) used to say that something is done to the greatest possible degree: *It was a full-on party that lasted all night.*

full-page *adj.* [only before noun] filling a complete page of a newspaper or magazine: *a full-page ad*

full pro'fessor *noun* a college or university teacher of the highest rank

full-scale *adj.* [only before noun] **1** that is as complete and thorough as possible: *a full-scale attack* **2** that is the same size as something that is being copied: *a full-scale model*

full-size (also **full-sized**) *adj.* [usually before noun] not made smaller; of the usual size: *a full-size model* ♦ *a full-size pool table* ♦ *a full-size bed* ᕲ picture at BED

full 'stop *noun*
IDM **come to a full stop** to stop completely

full-'term *adj.* (*technical*) **1** (of a PREGNANCY) lasting the normal length of time **2** (of a baby) born after a PREGNANCY lasting the normal length of time

full-'time *adj., adv.* (*abbr.* FT) for all the hours of a week during which people normally work or study, rather than just for a part of it: *a full-time employee* ♦ *a full-time job* ♦ *Taking care of a baby is a full-time job* (= hard work that takes a lot of time). ♦ *students in school full-time* ♦ *She works full-time and still manages to run a home.* ᕲ compare PART-TIME

full-'timer *noun* a person who works full-time

ful·ly 🔑 /'fʊli/ *adv.*
1 completely: *She had fully recovered from the accident.* ♦ *We are fully aware of the dangers.* ♦ *I fully understand your motives.* **2** (*formal*) (used to emphasize an amount) the whole of; as much as: *The disease affects fully 30 percent of the population.*

ful·mar /'fʊlmər/ *noun* a gray and white bird that lives near the ocean

ful·mi·nate /'fʊlmə,neɪt/ *verb* [I] ~ **against (sb/sth)** (*formal*) to criticize someone or something angrily ▶ **ful·mi·na-tion** /,fʊlmə'neɪʃn/ *noun* [C, U]

ful·some /'fʊlsəm/ *adj.* (*disapproving*) too generous in praising or thanking someone, or in saying that you are sorry, so that you do not sound sincere: *a fulsome apology* ♦ *He was fulsome in his praise of the governor.* ▶ **ful·some·ly** *adv.*

fum·ble /'fʌmbl/ *verb, noun*
• *verb* **1** [I] to use your hands in an awkward way when you are doing something or looking for something: ~ **(at/with/in sth) (for sth)** *She fumbled in her pocket for a tissue.* ♦ *He fumbled with the buttons on his shirt.* ♦ ~ **around** *She was fumbling around in the dark looking for the light switch.* ♦ ~ **to do sth** *I fumbled to zip up my jacket.* **2** [I, T] to express yourself or deal with something in an awkward or nervous way: ~ **(for sth)** *During the interview, she fumbled helplessly for words.* ♦ ~ **sth** *The company fumbled the marketing campaign.* **3** [T] ~ **sth** (especially in sports) to drop a ball or to fail to stop or kick it
• *noun* **1** [sing.] an awkward action using the hands **2** [C] (in football) the action of dropping the ball while it is in play **3** [C] (in baseball) the action of failing to pick up a ball that is rolling on the ground

fum·bling /'fʌmblɪŋ/ *adj.* awkward, uncertain, or hesitating: *She made a fumbling attempt to explain why she had missed the deadline.*

fume /fyum/ *verb* **1** [I, T] to be very angry about something: ~ **(at/over/about sb/sth)** *She sat in the car, silently fuming at the traffic jam.* ♦ ~ **(with sth)** *He was fuming with indignation.* ♦ + *speech* "*This is intolerable!*" *she fumed.* **2** [I] to produce smoke or fumes

fumes /fyumz/ *noun* [pl.] (also *less frequent* **fume** [U]) smoke, gas, or something similar that smells strongly or is dangerous to breathe in: *diesel/gas/exhaust fumes* ♦ *to be overcome by smoke and fumes* ♦ *Clouds of toxic fumes escaped in a huge chemical factory blaze.* ♦ *The body of a man was found in a fume-filled car yesterday.*

fu·mi·gate /'fyumə,geɪt/ *verb* ~ **sth** to use special chemicals, smoke, or gas to destroy the harmful insects or bacteria in a place: *to fumigate a room* ▶ **fu·mi·ga·tion** /,fyumə'geɪʃn/ *noun* [U, C]

fun /fʌn/ noun, adj.

- **noun** [U] **1** enjoyment; pleasure; a thing that gives enjoyment or pleasure and makes you feel happy: *We had a lot of fun at Sarah's party.* ♦ *Sailing is **great fun**.* ♦ ***Have fun** (= Enjoy yourself)!* ♦ *I decided to learn Spanish, **just for fun**.* ♦ *I didn't do all that work **just for the fun of it**.* ♦ *It's not much fun going to a party by yourself.* ♦ *"**What fun!**" she said with a laugh.* ♦ *Walking three miles in the pouring rain is **not my idea of fun**.* ♦ *"What do you say to a weekend in New York?" "Sounds like fun."* **2** behavior or activities that are not serious but come from a sense of enjoyment: *She's very lively and **full of fun**.* ♦ *We didn't mean to hurt him. We were just **having a little fun**.* ♦ *It wasn't serious—it was all done **in fun**.* ⊃ thesaurus box at ENTERTAINMENT
  IDM fun and games (*informal*) activities that are not serious and that other people may disapprove of **make fun of sb/sth** to laugh at someone or something or make other people laugh at them, usually in an unkind way: *It's cruel to make fun of people who stutter.* ⊃ more at FIGURE *n.*, POKE *v.*
- **adj.** amusing or enjoyable: *She's really fun to be with.* ♦ *This game looks like fun!* ♦ *There are lots of fun things for young people to do here.*

THESAURUS

fun

pleasure ♦ a good time ♦ enjoyment ♦ a great time

These are all words for the feeling of enjoying yourself, or activities or times that you enjoy.

fun (*somewhat informal*) the feeling of enjoying yourself; activities that you enjoy: *We had a lot of fun at Sarah's party.* ♦ *Sailing is **great fun**.*

pleasure (*somewhat formal*) the feeling of enjoying yourself or being satisfied: *Reading for pleasure and reading for work are not the same.*

a good time (*somewhat informal*) a time that you spend enjoying yourself: *We had a good time in Spain.*

enjoyment (*somewhat formal*) the feeling of enjoying yourself: *I get a lot of enjoyment from music.*

PLEASURE OR ENJOYMENT?

Enjoyment usually comes from an activity that you do; **pleasure** can come from something that you do or something that happens: *He beamed with pleasure at seeing her.* ♦ *He beamed with enjoyment at seeing her.*

a great time (*somewhat informal*) a time that you spend enjoying yourself very much: *We had a really great time together.*

PATTERNS

- to do sth **for** fun/pleasure/your own enjoyment
- **great** fun/pleasure/enjoyment
- to **have** fun/a good time/a great time
- to **get** pleasure/enjoyment **from** sth
- to **spoil** the fun/sb's pleasure/sb's enjoyment

---

func·tion /ˈfʌŋkʃn/ AWL noun, verb

- **noun** **1** [C, U] a special activity or purpose of a person or thing: *to fulfill/perform a function* ♦ *bodily functions* (= for example eating, sex, going to the bathroom) ♦ *The function of the heart is to pump blood through the body.* ♦ *This design aims for harmony of form and function.* **2** [C] a social event or official ceremony: *The hall provided a venue for weddings and other functions.* **3** [C] (*mathematics*) a quantity whose value depends on the varying values of others. In the statement $2x = y$, y is a function of x: (*figurative*) *Salary is **a function of** age and experience.* **4** [C] (*computing*) a part of a program, etc. that performs a basic operation
- **verb** [I] (+ *adv./prep.*) to work in the correct way **SYN** OPERATE: *Despite the power cuts, the hospital continued to function normally.* ♦ *We now have a functioning shower.* ♦ *Many children can't function effectively in large classes.*

PHR V 'function as sb/sth to perform the action or the job of the thing or person mentioned: *The couch also functions as a bed.*

func·tion·al AWL /ˈfʌŋkʃənl/ adj. **1** practical and useful; with little or no decoration **SYN** UTILITARIAN: *Bathrooms don't have to be purely functional.* ♦ *The office was large and functional rather than welcoming.* **2** having a special purpose; making it possible for someone to do something or for something to happen: *a functional disorder* (= an illness caused when an organ of the body fails to perform its function) ♦ *a functional approach to language learning* ♦ *These units played a key functional role in the military operation.* **3** (especially of a machine, an organization, or a system) working; able to work: *The hospital will soon be fully functional.* ▶ **func·tion·al·ly** AWL /-ʃənəli/ adv.

ˌfunctional ˈgrammar noun [U] (*linguistics*) grammar that analyzes how language is used to communicate

func·tion·al·ism /ˈfʌŋkʃənə,lɪzəm/ noun [U] the idea or belief that the most important thing about the style or design of a building or object is how it is going to be used, not how it will look ▶ **func·tion·al·ist** /-ʃənəlɪst/ noun **func·tion·al·ist** adj. [usually before noun]

func·tion·al·i·ty /ˌfʌŋkʃəˈnæləti/ noun (pl. **func·tion·al·i·ties**) **1** [U] the quality in something of being very suitable for the purpose it was designed for **SYN** PRACTICALITY **2** [U] the purpose that something is designed for or expected to perform: *Manufacturing processes may be affected by the functionality of the product.* **3** [U, C] (*computing*) the range of functions that a computer or other electronic system can perform: *new software with additional functionality*

func·tion·ar·y /ˈfʌŋkʃə,neri/ noun (pl. **func·tion·ar·ies**) (often *disapproving*) a person with official duties **SYN** OFFICIAL: *party/state/government functionaries*

ˈfunction ˌkey noun (*computing*) one of several keys on a computer keyboard, each marked with "F" and a number, that can be used to do something, such as save a file or get to the "help" function in a program

ˈfunction ˌword (also **func·tor**) noun (*grammar*) a word that is important to the grammar of a sentence rather than its meaning, for example "do" in "we do not live here" ⊃ compare CONTENT WORD

func·tor /ˈfʌŋktər/ noun **1** (*mathematics*) a FUNCTION or a symbol such as + or × **2** (*grammar*) = FUNCTION WORD

fund AWL /fʌnd/ noun, verb

- **noun** **1** [C] an amount of money that has been saved or has been made available for a particular purpose: *a disaster relief fund* ♦ *the company's retirement fund* ♦ *the International Monetary Fund* **2 funds** [pl.] money that is available to be spent: *government funds* ♦ *The hospital is trying to **raise funds** for a new kidney machine.* ♦ *The project has been canceled because of lack of funds* ♦ *I'm **short of funds** right now—can I pay you back next week?* **3** [sing.] **~ of sth** an amount or a supply of something: *a fund of knowledge*
- **verb** **~ sth** to provide money for something, usually something official: *a poetry festival funded by the Mabel Dodge Foundation* ♦ *The museum is privately funded.* ♦ *a government-funded program*

fun·da·men·tal /ˌfʌndəˈmɛntl/ AWL adj., noun

- **adj.** **1** serious and very important; affecting the most central and important parts of something **SYN** BASIC: *There is a **fundamental difference** between the two points of view.* ♦ *A fundamental change in the organization of health services was required.* ♦ *a question of fundamental importance* **2 ~ (to sth)** central; forming the necessary basis of something **SYN** ESSENTIAL: *Hard work is fundamental to success.* **3** [only before noun] (*physics*) forming the source or base from which everything else is made; not able to be divided any further: *a fundamental particle*
- **noun** [usually pl.] a basic rule or principle; an essential part: *the fundamentals of modern physics* ♦ *He taught me the fundamentals of the job.*

ʌ **cup**   ə **about**   eɪ **say**   aɪ **five**   ɔɪ **boy**   aʊ **now**   oʊ **go**   ər **bird**

fundamental 'force *noun* (*technical*) a force that is a property (= characteristic) of everything in the universe. There are four fundamental forces including GRAVITY and ELECTROMAGNETISM.

fun·da·men·tal·ism /ˌfʌndəˈmɛntlˌɪzəm/ *noun* [U] **1** the practice of following very strictly the basic rules and teachings of any religion **2** (in Christianity) the belief that everything that is written in the Bible is completely true ▶ **fun·da·men·tal·ist** /-ˈmɛntl·ɪst/ *noun* **fun·da·men·tal·ist** *adj.*

fun·da·men·tal·ly AWL /ˌfʌndəˈmɛntl·i/ *adv.* **1** in every way that is important; completely: *The two approaches are fundamentally different.* ◆ *By the 1960s, the situation had changed fundamentally.* ◆ *They remained fundamentally opposed to the plan.* **2** used when you are introducing a topic and stating something important about it SYN BASICALLY: *Fundamentally, there are two different approaches to the problem.* **3** used when you are saying what is the most important thing about someone or something SYN BASICALLY: *She is fundamentally a nice person, but she finds it difficult to communicate.*

fund·er AWL /ˈfʌndər/ *noun* a person or an organization that provides money for a particular purpose

fund·ing AWL /ˈfʌndɪŋ/ *noun* [U] money for a particular purpose; the act of providing money for such a purpose: *There have been large cuts in government funding for scientific research.*

fund-rais·er /ˈfʌnd ˌreɪzər/ *noun* **1** a person who collects money for a charity or an organization **2** a social event or an entertainment held in order to collect money for an organization ▶ **'fund-ˌraising** *noun* [U]

fu·ner·al 🎵 /ˈfyunərəl/ *noun* a ceremony, usually a religious one, for burying or cremating (= burning) a dead person: *Hundreds of people attended the funeral.* ◆ *a funeral procession* ◆ *a funeral march* (= a sad piece of music suitable for funerals) IDM **it's your funeral** (*informal*) used to tell someone that they, and nobody else, will have to deal with the unpleasant results of their own actions

funeral di'rector *noun* (also **un·der·tak·er, mor·ti·cian**) a person whose job is to prepare the bodies of dead people to be buried or CREMATED, and to arrange funerals

funeral ˌhome (also **mor·tu·ar·y, funeral parlor**, *CanE* usually **funeral parlour**) *noun* a place where a body is kept before the funeral, where visitors can see the body, and where the funeral is sometimes held

fu·ner·ary /ˈfyunəˌrɛri/ *adj.* [only before noun] (*formal*) of or used at a funeral: *funerary monuments/rites*

fu·ne·re·al /fyuˈnɪriəl/ *adj.* (*formal*) suitable for a funeral; sad: *a funereal atmosphere*

fun·gal /ˈfʌŋgl/ *adj.* of or caused by FUNGUS: *a fungal infection*

fun·gi·cide /ˈfʌndʒəˌsaɪd/ *noun* [C, U] a substance that kills fungus

fun·goid /ˈfʌŋgɔɪd/ *adj.* (*technical*) like a FUNGUS: *a fungoid growth*

fun·gus /ˈfʌŋgəs/ *noun* (*pl.* **fun·gi** /ˈfʌndʒaɪ; ˈfʌŋgaɪ/) **1** [C] any plant without leaves, flowers, or green coloring, usually growing on other plants or on decaying matter. MUSHROOMS and MILDEW are both fungi. ⊃ collocations at LIFE **2** [U, C] a covering of MOLD or a similar fungus, for example on a plant or wall: *fungus infections*

fun·house /ˈfʌnhaʊs/ *noun* a building at an AMUSEMENT PARK containing mirrors that make strange images, moving floors, and other devices for scaring and amusing people

fu·nic·u·lar /fyuˈnɪkyələr; fə-/ (also **fu·nicular ˈrailway**) *noun* a track with rails up a steep slope, with special cars that transport passengers up and down by means of a moving cable ⊃ picture at TRAIN

funk /fʌŋk/ *noun* **1** [U] a type of dance music with a strong rhythm, developed by African American musicians in the 1960s **2** (also **blue ˈfunk**) [sing.] (*old-fashioned, informal*) a state of fear or anxiety: *She was in a funk for months after her best friend moved away.* **3** [C, usually sing.] a strong unpleasant smell

funk·y /ˈfʌŋki/ *adj.* (**funk·i·er, funk·i·est**) (*informal*) **1** (of pop music) with a strong rhythm that is easy to dance to: *a funky disco beat* **2** (*approving*) fashionable and unusual: *She wears really funky clothes.* **3** having a strong unpleasant smell

ˈfun-ˌloving *adj.* (of people) liking to enjoy themselves

fun·nel /ˈfʌnl/ *noun, verb*

● *noun* **1** a device that is wide at the top and narrow at the bottom, used for pouring liquids or powders into a small opening ⊃ picture at LABORATORY **2** a metal CHIMNEY, for example on a ship or an engine, through which smoke comes out SYN SMOKESTACK

● *verb* (-l-, *CanE* usually -ll-) [I, U] to move or make something move through a narrow space, or as if through a funnel: (+ *adv./prep.*) *Wind was funneling through the gorge.* ◆ ~ **sth** (+ *adv./prep.*) *Huge pipes funnel the water down the mountainside.* ◆ *Barricades funneled the crowds toward the square.* ◆ (*figurative*) *Some $10 million in aid was funneled into the country through government agencies.*

the fun·nies /ˈfʌniz/ *noun* [pl.] (*informal*) the part of a newspaper where there are several COMIC STRIPS (= series of drawings that tell a funny story) SYN COMIC

fun·ni·ly /ˈfʌnl·i/ *adv.* in a strange way IDM **funnily enough** used to show that you expect people to find a particular fact surprising: *Funnily enough, I met her just yesterday.*

fun·ny 🎵 /ˈfʌni/ *adj.* (**fun·ni·er, fun·ni·est**)

▷ AMUSING **1** making you laugh; amusing: *a funny story* ◆ *That's the funniest thing I ever heard.* ◆ *It's not funny! Someone could have been hurt.* ◆ *I was really embarrassed, but then I saw the funny side of it.* ◆ (*ironic*) *Oh very funny! You expect me to believe that?* ◆ "*What's so funny?*" *she demanded.* HELP Note that **funny** does not mean "enjoyable": *The party was great fun.* ◆ The party was very funny.

▷ STRANGE **2** difficult to explain or understand SYN STRANGE, PECULIAR: *A funny thing happened to me today.* ◆ *It's funny how things never happen the way you expect them to.* ◆ *That's funny —he was here a minute ago and now he's gone.* ◆ *The funny thing is it never happened again after that.* ◆ *The engine's making a very funny noise.* ◆ *I'm glad I didn't get that job, in a funny sort of way.*

▷ SUSPICIOUS/ILLEGAL **3** (*informal*) suspicious and probably illegal or dishonest: *I suspect there may be something funny going on.* ◆ *If there has been any funny business, we'll soon find out.*

▷ ILL/SICK **4** (*informal*) slightly ill/sick: *I feel a little funny today —I don't think I'll go to work.*

▷ MACHINE **5** (*informal*) not working as it should: *My computer is acting funny.* IDM **funny ha-ha** (*informal*) used to show that "funny" is being used with the meaning of "amusing" **funny weird/strange** (*informal*) used to show that "funny" is being used with the meaning of "strange"

THESAURUS

funny

amusing ◆ entertaining ◆ witty ◆ humorous ◆ comical ◆ hilarious

These words all describe someone or something that makes you laugh or smile.

funny that makes you laugh: *a funny story* ◆ *She was a very funny lady.*

amusing (*somewhat formal*) funny and enjoyable: *It's a very amusing game to play.*

entertaining amusing and interesting: *It was a very entertaining evening.*

witty smart and amusing; able to say or write smart and amusing things: *a witty remark* ◆ *a witty public speaker*

humorous funny and entertaining; showing a sense of humor: *a humorous look at the world of fashion*

comical funny, especially because of being strange or unexpected: *Many of the scenes in the book are truly comical.*

hilarious extremely funny

FUNNY, AMUSING, HUMOROUS, OR COMICAL?

Amusing is the most general of these words because it includes the idea of being enjoyable as well as making people laugh, and can be used to describe events, activities, and occasions: *an amusing party/evening* ◆ *a funny/humorous/comic party/evening*. **Humorous** is more about showing that you see the humor in a situation than actually making people laugh out loud. **Comical** is used especially to talk about things that are funny in an unexpected way. It is not used to describe people. **Funny** can describe people, jokes and stories, things that happen, or anything that makes people laugh. It can also mean "odd" in a somewhat comical way: *He's a funny old man.*

PATTERNS

- a(n) funny/amusing/entertaining/witty/humorous/comical **story**
- a(n) funny/amusing/entertaining/witty/humorous **speech**
- a(n) funny/entertaining/witty/humorous **writer**
- a(n) funny/amusing/hilarious **joke**
- to **find sth** funny/amusing/entertaining/witty/humorous/comical/hilarious

ˈfunny ˌbone *noun* [usually sing.] (*informal*) the part of the elbow containing a very sensitive nerve that is painful if you hit it against something

ˈfunny ˌfarm *noun* (*informal, offensive*) a hospital for people who are mentally ill

ˈfunny ˌmoney *noun* [U] (*informal, disapproving*) **1** a CURRENCY (= the money used in one country) that is not worth much value and whose value can change quickly **2** money that has been FORGED (= is not real), or stolen, or that has come from illegal activities

fur 🔑 /fər/ *noun*
1 [U] the soft thick mass of hair that grows on the body of some animals: *The cat carefully licked its fur.* **2** [U] the skin of an animal with the fur still on it, used especially for making clothes: *a fur coat* ◆ *the fur trade* ◆ *a fur farm* (= where animals are bred and killed for their fur) ◆ *The animal is hunted for its fur.* ◆ *fur-lined gloves* **3** [U] an artificial material that looks and feels like fur **4** [C] a piece of clothing, especially a coat or jacket, made of real or artificial fur: *elegant ladies in furs* **5** [U] a white layer that forms on a person's tongue, especially when they are sick ⊃ see also FURRED

fu·ri·ous /ˈfyuriəs/ *adj.* **1** very angry: ~ **(at sth/sb)** *She was absolutely furious at having been deceived.* ◆ ~ **(with sb/yourself)** *He was furious with himself for letting things get so out of control.* ◆ ~ **(that…)** *I'm furious that I wasn't told about it.* ⊃ thesaurus box at ANGRY **2** with great energy, speed, or anger: *a furious debate* ◆ *She drove off at a furious pace.* ◆ *a furious denunciation of the president's economic reforms* ⊃ see also FURY ▶ **fu·ri·ous·ly** *adv.*: *furiously angry* ◆ *"Damn!" he said furiously.* ◆ *They worked furiously all weekend, trying to get it finished on time.* **IDM** see FAST *adj.*

furl /fərl/ *verb* ~ **sth** to roll and fasten something such as a sail, a flag, or an umbrella

fur·long /ˈfərlɔŋ/ *noun* (especially in horse racing) a unit for measuring distance, equal to 220 yards; one eighth of a mile

fur·lough /ˈfərloʊ/ *noun* [U, C] **1** permission to leave your duties for a period of time, especially for soldiers working in a foreign country **2** a period of time during which workers are told not to come to work, usually because there is not enough money to pay them **3** permission for a prisoner to leave prison for a period of time ▶ **fur·lough** *verb* ~ **sb**

fur·nace /ˈfərnəs/ *noun* **1** a piece of equipment that is used to heat a building, in which air or water is heated by burning gas or oil, and then PUMPED around the building **2** a space surrounded on all sides by walls and a roof for heating metal or glass to very high temperatures: *It's like a furnace* (= very hot) *in here!* ⊃ see also BLAST FURNACE

fur·nish /ˈfərnɪʃ/ *verb* **1** ~ **sth** to put furniture in a house, room, etc.: *The room was furnished with antiques.* ⊃ collocations at DECORATE **2** ~ **sb/sth with sth** | ~ **sth** (*formal*) to supply or provide someone or something with something; to supply something to someone: *She furnished him with the facts surrounding the case.*

fur·nished /ˈfərnɪʃt/ *adj.* (of a house, room, etc.) containing furniture: *a furnished apartment* (= for rent complete with furniture) ◆ *The house was simply furnished.*

fur·nish·ings /ˈfərnɪʃɪŋz/ *noun* [pl.] the furniture, curtains, etc. in a room or house: *The wallpaper should match the furnishings.*

fur·ni·ture 🔑 /ˈfərnɪtʃər/ *noun* [U]
objects that can be moved, such as tables, chairs, and beds, that are put into a house or an office to make it suitable for living or working in: *a piece of furniture* ◆ *patio/office, etc. furniture* ◆ *We need to buy some new furniture.* **IDM** see PART *n.*

fu·ror /ˈfyurɔr; -ər/ *noun* [sing.] great anger or excitement shown by a number of people, usually caused by a public event: ~ **(among sb)** *His novel about Jesus caused a furor among Christians.* ◆ ~ **(about/over sth)** *the recent furor over tax increases* **SYN** UPROAR

furred /fərd/ *adj.* covered with fur or with something that looks like fur: *a furred tongue*

fur·ri·er /ˈfəriər/ *noun* a person who prepares or sells clothes made from fur

fur·row /ˈfəroʊ/ *noun, verb*
- *noun* **1** a long, narrow cut in the ground, especially one made by a PLOW for planting seeds in **2** a deep line in the skin of the face
- *verb* **1** [T] ~ **sth** to make a furrow in the earth: *furrowed fields* **2** [I, T] ~ **(sth)** (*formal*) if your BROWS or EYEBROWS **furrow** or **are furrowed**, you pull them together, usually because you are worried, and so produce lines on your face

fur·ry /ˈfəri/ *adj.* (**fur·ri·er**, **fur·ri·est**) **1** covered with fur: *small furry animals* **2** like fur: *The moss was soft and furry to the touch.*

fur·ther 🔑 /ˈfərðər/ *adv., adj., verb*
- *adv.* **1** to a greater degree or extent: *The police decided to investigate further.* ◆ *My life is further complicated by having to work such long hours.* ◆ *Nothing could be further from the truth.* **2** (*formal*) in addition to what has just been said **SYN** FURTHERMORE: *Further, it is important to consider the cost of repairs.* **3** (comparative of *far*) at or to a greater distance in space or time **SYN** FARTHER: *We had walked further than I realized.* ◆ *Think further back into your childhood.* ◆ *Two miles further on we came to a small town.* **IDM** **go further 1** to say more about something, or make a more extreme point about it: *I would go even further and suggest that the entire industry is corrupt.* **2** to last longer; to serve more people: *They watered down the soup to make it go further.* **go no further** | **not go any further** if you tell someone that a secret will **go no further**, you promise not to tell it to anyone else **take sth further** to take more serious action about something or speak to someone at a higher level about it: *I am not satisfied with your explanation and intend to take the matter further.* ⊃ **more at** AFIELD

adj. (comparative of *far*) (*formal*) more; additional: *Cook for a further 2 minutes.* ◆ *Have you any further questions?* ◆ *For further details call this number.* ◆ *We have decided to take no further action.* ◆ *The museum is closed **until further notice** (= until we say that it is open again).* ➲ language bank at ACCORDING TO

verb ~ sth to help something to develop or be successful: *They hoped the new venture would further the cause of cultural cooperation throughout the Americas.* ◆ *She took the new job to further her career.*

WHICH WORD?

further ◆ farther ◆ farthest ◆ furthest

- These are the comparative and superlative forms of **far**.
- To talk about distance, **further** and **farthest** are the most common: *I have to travel further to work now.* ◆ *the house farthest away from the road*
- To talk about the degree or extent of something, **further/furthest** are usually preferred: *Let's consider this point further.*
- **Further**, but not **farther**, can also be used in formal situations to mean "more" or "additional": *Are there any further/more/additional questions?*

---

fur·ther·ance /'fərðərəns/ *noun* [U] (*formal*) the process of helping something to develop or to be successful **SYN** ADVANCEMENT: *He took these actions purely in (the) furtherance of his own career.*

fur·ther·more **AWL** /'fərðər‚mɔr/ *adv.* (*formal*) in addition to what has just been stated. Furthermore is used especially to add a point to an argument. **SYN** MOREOVER: *He said he had not discussed the matter with her. Furthermore, he had not even contacted her.* ➲ language bank at ACCORDING TO

fur·ther·most /'fərðər‚moust/ *adj.* (*formal*) located at the greatest distance from something: *at the furthermost end of the street*

fur·thest 🔊 /'fərðəst/ *adj., adv.*
= FARTHEST ➲ note at FURTHER

fur·tive /'fərtɪv/ *adj.* (*disapproving*) behaving in a way that shows that you want to keep something secret and do not want to be noticed **SYN** STEALTHY: *She cast a furtive glance over her shoulder.* ◆ *He looked sly and furtive.* ▶ **fur·tive·ly** *adv.* **fur·tive·ness** *noun* [U]

fu·ry /'fyuri/ *noun* **1** [U] extreme anger that often includes violent behavior **SYN** RAGE: *Her eyes blazed with fury.* ◆ *Fury over tax increases* (= as a newspaper HEADLINE). ◆ (*figurative*) *There was no shelter from the fury of the storm.* **2** [sing.] a state of being extremely angry about something **SYN** RAGE: *He flew into a fury when I refused.* **3 the Furies** [pl.] (in ancient Greek stories) three GODDESSES who punish people for their crimes ➲ see also FURIOUS **IDM** see HELL

fuse /fyuz/ *noun, verb*
● **noun 1** a small wire or device inside a piece of electrical equipment that breaks and stops the current if the flow of electricity is too strong: *to change a fuse* ◆ *Check whether a fuse has blown.* **2** a long piece of string or paper which is lit to make a bomb or a FIRECRACKER explode **3** (also **fuze**) a device that makes a bomb explode when it hits something or at a particular time: *He set the fuse for three minutes.* ◆ *The bombs inside were on a one-hour fuse.* **IDM** see BLOW v., SHORT adj.
● **verb 1** [I, T] when one thing **fuses** with another, or two things **fuse** or **are fused**, they are joined together to form a single thing: *~* **(together)** *As they heal, the bones will fuse together.* ◆ *~* **(into sth)** *Our different ideas fused into a plan.* ◆ *~* **with sth** *The sperm fuses with the egg to begin the process of fertilization.* ◆ *~* **sth** **(into sth)** *The two companies were fused into a single organization.* ◆ *Atoms of hydrogen are fused to make helium.* **2** [I, T] *~* **(sth)** (*technical*) when a substance,

---

especially metal, **fuses**, or you **fuse** it, it is heated until it melts **3** [T, usually passive] *~* **(sth)** to put a FUSE in a CIRCUIT or in a piece of equipment: *Is this plug fused?*

'fuse box *noun* a small box or cabinet that contains the fuses of the electrical system of a building

fu·se·lage /'fyusə‚laʒ/ *noun* the main part of an aircraft in which passengers and goods are carried ➲ picture at PLANE

fu·sil·ier /‚fyuzə'lɪr/ *noun* (in the past) a soldier who carried a light gun

fu·sil·lade /'fyusə‚lɑd; -‚leɪd/ *noun* a rapid series of shots fired from one or more guns; a rapid series of objects that are thrown **SYN** BARRAGE: *a fusillade of bullets/stones* ◆ (*figurative*) *He faced a fusillade of questions from the waiting journalists.*

fu·sion /'fyuʒn/ *noun* **1** [U, sing.] the process or result of joining two or more things together to form one: *the fusion of copper and zinc to produce brass* ◆ *The movie displayed a perfect fusion of image and sound.* **2** (also ‚nuclear 'fusion) [U] (*physics*) the act or process of combining the NUCLEUS (= central parts) of atoms to form a heavier NUCLEUS, with energy being released ➲ compare FISSION **3** [U] music that is a mixture of different styles, especially JAZZ and ROCK **4** [U] cooking that is a mixture of different styles: *French–Thai fusion*

'fusion ‚bomb *noun* a bomb that gets its energy from nuclear fusion, especially a HYDROGEN BOMB

fu·sion·ist /'fyuʒənɪst/ *noun* a musician who plays fusion music

fuss /fʌs/ *noun, verb*
● **noun 1** [U, sing.] unnecessary excitement, worry, or activity: *He does what he's told without any fuss.* ◆ *All that fuss over a few dollars!* ◆ *It's a very ordinary movie—I don't know what all the fuss is about* (= why other people think it is so good). ◆ *It was all a lot of fuss about nothing.* ◆ *We'd like a quiet wedding without any fuss.* **2** [sing.] anger or complaints about something, especially something that is not important: *I'm sorry for making such a fuss about the noise.* ◆ *Steve kicks up a fuss every time I even suggest seeing you.*
IDM **make a fuss over sb** to pay a lot of attention to someone, usually to show how much you like them: *They made a big fuss over the baby.* ◆ *The dog loves being made a fuss over.*
● **verb 1** [I] *~* **(about sth)** to worry about things that are not very important: *Don't fuss, mom, everything is all right.* **2** [I] to show that you are annoyed or not happy: *A bored baby is more likely to fuss and cry.*
PHR V **'fuss over sb** to pay a lot of attention to someone **'fuss with sth** to keep touching or moving something around in a nervous way: *Don't fuss with your hair!*

fuss·budg·et /'fʌs‚bʌdʒət/ *noun* (*informal*) a person who is often worried about unimportant things and is difficult to please

fuss·y /'fʌsi/ *adj.* (fuss·i·er, fuss·i·est) **1** too concerned or worried about details or standards, especially unimportant ones: *fussy parents* ◆ *~* **(about sth)** *Our teacher is very fussy about punctuation.* ◆ *She's such a fussy eater.* ◆ *"Where do you want to go for lunch?" "I'm not fussy* (= I don't mind)*."* **2** having too much detail or decoration: *The costume designs are too fussy.* **3** doing something with small, quick, nervous movements: *a fussy manner* ◆ *the quick, fussy movements of her small hands* ▶ **fuss·i·ly** /-səli/ *adv.* **fuss·i·ness** /-sinəs/ *noun* [U]

fus·tian /'fʌstʃən/ *noun* [U] **1** a thick strong cotton cloth with a slightly rough surface, used in the past for making clothes **2** (*literary*) language that sounds impressive but does not mean much

fus·ty /'fʌsti/ *adj.* (*disapproving*) **1** smelling old, damp, or not fresh **SYN** MUSTY: *a dark fusty room* **2** old-fashioned: *fusty ideas* ◆ *a fusty old professor*

fu·tile /'fyutl/ *adj.* having no purpose because there is no chance of success **SYN** POINTLESS: *a futile attempt/exercise/*

---

gesture ◆ *Their efforts to revive him were futile.* ◆ *It would be futile to protest.* ◆ *My appeal proved futile.* ▶ **fu·tile·ly** /ˈfyutl·i/ *adv.* **fu·til·i·ty** /fyuˈtɪləti/ *noun* [U]: *a sense of futility* ◆ *the futility of war*

fu·ton /ˈfutɑn/ *noun* (from *Japanese*) a MATTRESS, usually filled with cotton or FOAM and often on a wooden frame, that can be used for sitting on or opened out to make a bed ⊃ picture at BED

fu·ture 🖉 /ˈfyutʃər/ *noun, adj.*

• *noun* **1 the future** [sing.] the time that will come after the present or the events that will happen then: *We need to plan for the future.* ◆ *What will the cities of the future look like?* ◆ *The movie is set in the future.* ◆ *The exchange rate is likely to fall in the near future* (= soon). ◆ *What does the future hold?* **2** [C] what will happen to someone or something at a later time: *Her future is uncertain.* ◆ *This deal could safeguard the futures of the 2,000 employees.* **3** [sing., U] the possibility of being successful or surviving at a later time: *She has a great future ahead of her.* ◆ *I can't see any future in this relationship.* **4 futures** [pl.] (*finance*) goods or shares that are bought at agreed prices but that will be delivered and paid for at a later time: *oil futures* ◆ *the futures market* **5 the future** (also **the ˌfuture ˈtense**) [sing.] (*grammar*) the form of a verb that expresses what will happen after the present
IDM **in the future** from now on: *Please be more careful in the future.* ◆ *In the future, make sure the door is never left unlocked.* ⊃ more at DISTANT, FORESEEABLE

• *adj.* [only before noun] taking place or existing at a time after the present: *future generations* ◆ *at a future date* ◆ *future developments in computer software* ◆ *He met his future wife at law school.*

the ˌfuture ˈperfect (also **the ˌfuture ˌperfect ˈtense**) *noun* [sing.] (*grammar*) the form of a verb that expresses an action completed before a particular point in the future, formed in English with *will have* or *shall have* and the past participle

fu·tur·ism /ˈfyutʃəˌrɪzəm/ *noun* [U] a movement in art and literature in the 1920s and 30s that did not try to show realistic figures and scenes but aimed to express confidence in the modern world, particularly in modern machines ▶ **fu·tur·ist** /-rɪst/ *noun* **fu·tur·ist** *adj.*: *futurist poets*

fu·tur·is·tic /ˌfyutʃəˈrɪstɪk/ *adj.* **1** extremely modern and unusual in appearance, as if belonging to a future time: *futuristic design* **2** imagining what the future will be like: *a futuristic novel*

fu·tu·ri·ty /fyuˈtʊrəti; -ˈtʃʊr-/ *noun* [U] (*formal*) the time that will come after the present and what will happen then: *a vision of futurity*

fu·tur·ol·o·gist /ˌfyutʃəˈrɑlədʒɪst/ *noun* a person who is an expert in futurology

fu·tur·ol·o·gy /ˌfyutʃəˈrɑlədʒi/ *noun* [U] the study of how people will live in the future

fuze = FUSE

fuzz /fʌz/ *noun* **1** [U] short soft fine hair or fur that covers something, especially a person's face or arms **SYN** DOWN **2** [U] small pieces of wool, cotton, etc. that gather on clothes and other surfaces: *There's (a piece of) fuzz on your shirt.* **3** [sing.] a mass of hair in tight curls: *a fuzz of blonde hair* **4 the fuzz** [sing.] (*old-fashioned, slang*) the police **5** something that you cannot see clearly **SYN** BLUR: *I saw it as a dim fuzz through the binoculars.*

fuzz·box /ˈfʌzbɑks/ *noun* a device that is used to change the sound of an electric GUITAR or other instrument by making the notes sound noisier and less clear

fuzz·y /ˈfʌzi/ *adj.* (fuzz·i·er, fuzz·i·est) **1** covered with short, soft, fine hair or fur **SYN** DOWNY **2** (of hair) in a mass of tight curls **3** not clear in shape or sound **SYN** BLURRED: *a fuzzy image* ◆ *The soundtrack is fuzzy in places.* **4** confused and not expressed clearly: *fuzzy ideas/thinking* ▶ **fuzz·i·ly** /-zəli/ *adv.* **fuzz·i·ness** /-zinəs/ *noun* [U]

ˌfuzzy ˈlogic *noun* [U] (*computing*) a type of logic that is used to try to make computers behave like the human brain

FWIW *abbr.* (*informal*) used in writing to mean "for what it's worth"

FX /ˌɛf ˈɛks/ *abbr.* **1** a short way of writing SPECIAL EFFECTS **2** a short way of writing FOREIGN EXCHANGE

-fy ⊃ -IFY

FYI *abbr.* used in writing to mean "for your information"

| h **hat** | m **man** | n **no** | ŋ **sing** | l **leg** | r **red** | y **yes** | w **wet** |

Gg

G /dʒi/ *noun, abbr.*
- *noun* [C, U] (*pl.* **Gs, G's** /dʒiz/) **1** also **g** (*pl.* **g's**) the 7th letter of the English alphabet: *"Gold" begins with (a) G/"G."* **2** (*music*) the fifth note in the SCALE of C MAJOR ➔ see also G AND T, G-STRING
- *abbr.* **1** used to show that a particular movie is suitable for anyone, including children (the abbreviation for general audience ➔ compare NC-17, PG, PG-13 , R *abbr.* (3) **2** (*informal*) $1,000

g *abbr.*
1 gram(s): *3g vitamin C* **2** /dʒi/ (*technical*) GRAVITY or a measurement of the force with which something moves faster through space because of GRAVITY: *Spacecraft that are re-entering the earth's atmosphere are affected by g forces.*

GA *abbr.* (in writing) Georgia

gab /gæb/ *verb, noun*
- *verb* (-bb-) (*informal*) [I] to talk for a long time about things that are not important
- *noun* **IDM** see GIFT

gab·ar·dine (also **gab·er·dine**) /ˈgæbərˌdin/ *noun* [U] a strong cloth, usually of cotton or wool, used especially for making coats and suits

gab·ble /ˈgæbl/ *verb, noun*
- *verb* [I, T] **~ (sth)** (*informal*) to talk quickly so that people cannot hear you clearly or understand you: *She was nervous and started to gabble.*
- *noun* [sing.] fast speech that is difficult to understand, especially when a lot of people are talking at the same time

gab·by /ˈgæbi/ *adj.* (*informal, disapproving*) talking a lot, especially about things that are not important

gab·fest /ˈgæbfɛst/ *noun* (*informal*) an informal meeting to talk and exchange news; a long conversation

ga·bi·on /ˈgeɪbiən/ *noun* a large container made of wire, filled with earth, rocks, or other material, used in road building and other outdoor construction work

ga·ble /ˈgeɪbl/ *noun* the upper part of the end wall of a building, between the two sloping sides of the roof, that is shaped like a triangle

ga·bled /ˈgeɪbld/ *adj.* having one or more gables: *a gabled house/roof*

gad·a·bout /ˈgædəˌbaʊt/ *noun* (*informal often humorous*) a person who is always going out socially or traveling for pleasure

gad·fly /ˈgædflaɪ/ *noun* (*pl.* **gad·flies**) (usually *disapproving*) a person who annoys or criticizes other people in order to make them do something

gadg·et /ˈgædʒət/ *noun* a small tool or device that does something useful

gadg·et·ry /ˈgædʒətri/ *noun* [U] (sometimes *disapproving*) a collection of modern tools and devices: *His desk is covered with electronic gadgetry.*

gad·o·lin·i·um /ˌgædlˈɪniəm/ *noun* [U] (*symb.* **Gd**) a chemical element. Gadolinium is a soft silver-white metal.

gad·zooks /gædˈzuks/ *exclamation* (*old use*) used in the past to show that someone is surprised or annoyed

Gael·ic *noun* [U] **1** /ˈgeɪlɪk; ˈgælɪk/ the Celtic language of Scotland ➔ compare SCOTS **2** /ˈgeɪlɪk/ (also ˌIrish ˈGaelic) the Celtic language of Ireland ➔ compare IRISH ▶ **Gael·ic** *adj.*

gaff /gæf/ *noun* a pole with a hook on the end used to pull large fish out of the water

gaffe /gæf/ *noun* a mistake that a person makes in public or in a social situation, especially something embarrassing **SYN** FAUX PAS

gaf·fer /ˈgæfər/ *noun* the person who is in charge of the lights when a movie or television program is being made

gag /gæg/ *noun, verb*
- *noun* **1** a piece of cloth that is put over or in someone's mouth to stop the person from speaking **2** (*informal*) a joke or action that makes people laugh, especially in a show or movie **SYN** JOKE: *a running gag* (= one that is regularly repeated during a performance) ◆ *a sight gag* (= one that does not involve speaking) **3** a trick you play on someone: *It was just a gag—we didn't mean to upset anyone.*
- *verb* (-gg-) **1** [T] **~ sb** to put a piece of cloth in or over someone's mouth to prevent them from speaking or shouting: *The hostages were bound and gagged.* **2** [T] **~ sb/sth** to prevent someone from speaking freely or expressing their opinion: *The new laws are seen as an attempt to gag the press.* **3** [I] **~ (on sth)** to have the unpleasant feeling in your mouth and stomach as if you are going to VOMIT **SYN** RETCH: *She gagged on the blood that filled her mouth.*

ga·ga /ˈgɑgɑ/ *adj.* [not usually before noun] (*informal*) **1** slightly crazy because you are very excited about someone or something, or very much in love: *The fans went totally gaga over the band.* **2** (*offensive*) slightly crazy or silly: *Don't listen to him; he's a little gaga.*

gage = GAUGE

gag·gle /ˈgægl/ *noun* **1** a group of noisy people: *a gaggle of tourists/photographers* **2** a group of GEESE

gag order *noun* an order by a court that prevents people from talking or writing about what is happening in a particular court case

gag rule *noun* a rule that prevents people from discussing a particular topic at a particular time or place

Gai·a /ˈgaɪə/ *noun* [sing.] the Earth, considered as a great natural system that organizes and controls itself

gai·e·ty /ˈgeɪəti/ *noun* [U] (*old-fashioned*) the state of being cheerful and full of fun: *The colorful flags added to the gaiety of the occasion.* ➔ see also GAILY, GAY ➔ compare GAYNESS

gai·ly /ˈgeɪli/ *adv.* **1** in a bright and attractive way: *a gaily decorated room* **2** in a cheerful way: *gaily laughing children* ◆ *She waved gaily to the little crowd.* **3** without thinking or caring about the effect of your actions on other people: *She gaily announced that she was leaving the next day.* ➔ see also GAIETY, GAY

gain /geɪn/ *verb, noun*
- *verb*
> OBTAIN/WIN **1** [T] to obtain or win something, especially something that you need or want: **~ sth** *to gain entrance/entry/access to something* ◆ *The country gained its independence ten years ago.* ◆ *The party gained over 50% of the vote.* ◆ **~ sb sth** *Her unusual talent gained her worldwide recognition.* **2** [T, I] to obtain an advantage or benefit from something or from doing something: **~ sth (by/from sth)** *There is nothing to be gained from delaying the decision.* ◆ **~ (by/from sth)** *Who stands to gain from this decision?*
> GET MORE **3** [T] **~ sth** to gradually get more of something: *to gain confidence/strength/experience* ◆ *I've gained weight recently.* **ANT** LOSE
> OF WATCH/CLOCK **4** [T, I] **~ (sth)** to go too fast: *My watch gains two minutes every 24 hours.* **ANT** LOSE
> OF CURRENCIES/SHARES **5** [T, I] to increase in value: **~ sth** *The shares gained 14 cents.* ◆ **~ against sth** *The euro gained against the dollar again today.*
> REACH PLACE **6** [T] **~ sth** (*formal*) to reach a place, usually after a lot of effort: *At last she gained the shelter of an old barn.* **IDM** **gain ground** to become more powerful or successful: *The Republican candidate appears to be gaining ground this week.* **gain time** to delay something so that you can have more time to make a decision, deal with a problem, etc. ➔ more at VENTURE *v.*
PHRV **ˈgain in sth** to get more of a particular quality: *to gain in confidence* ◆ *His books have gained in popularity in*

recent years. **'gain on sb/sth** to get closer to someone or something that you are chasing

● **noun**

➤INCREASE **1** [C, U] an increase in the amount of something, especially in wealth or weight: *a $3,000 gain from our investment* ◆ *Regular exercise helps prevent weight gain.*

➤ADVANTAGE **2** [C] an advantage or improvement: *recent economic gains* ◆ *These policies resulted in significant gains in public health.* ◆ *Our loss is their gain.* **ANT** LOSS

➤PROFIT **3** [U] (often *disapproving*) financial profit: *He only seems to be interested in personal gain.* ◆ *It's amazing what some people will do for gain.* ➜ see also CAPITAL GAIN **IDM** see PAIN *n.*

gain·ful /'geɪnfl/ *adj.* (*formal*) used to describe useful work that you are paid for: *gainful employment* ▶ **gain·ful·ly** /-fəli/ *adv.*: *gainfully employed*

gain·say /ˌgeɪn'seɪ; 'geɪnseɪ/ *verb* (gain·says /ˌgeɪn'sɛz; 'geɪnsɛz/, gain·said, gain·said /ˌgeɪn'sɛd; 'geɪnsɛd/) ~ **sth** (*formal*) (often used in negative sentences) to say that something is not true; to disagree with or deny something **SYN** DENY: *Nobody can gainsay his claims.*

gait /geɪt/ *noun* [sing.] a way of walking: *He walked with a rolling gait.*

gait·er /'geɪtər/ *noun* [usually pl.] a cloth or leather covering for the leg between the knee and the foot. Gaiters were worn by men in the past and are now mainly worn by people who go walking or climbing: *a pair of gaiters*

gal /gæl/ *noun* (*informal*) a girl or woman

gal. *abbr.* (in writing) gallon(s)

ga·la /'geɪlə; 'gælə; 'gɑlə/ *noun* a special public celebration or entertainment: *a gala fund-raiser to benefit the museum* ◆ *a gala dinner/night*

ga·lac·tic /gə'læktɪk/ *adj.* relating to a galaxy

gal·ax·y /'gæləksi/ *noun* (*pl.* gal·ax·ies) **1** [C] any of the large systems of stars, each far away in outer space **2 the Galaxy** (also the ˌMilky ˈWay) [sing.] the system of stars that contains our sun and its planets, seen as a bright band in the night sky **3** [C] (*informal*) a group of famous people, or people with a particular skill: *a galaxy of Hollywood stars*

gale /geɪl/ *noun* an extremely strong wind: *The gale blew down hundreds of trees.* ➜ collocations at WEATHER: *gale-force winds*
IDM **gale(s) of laughter** the sound of people laughing very loudly: *His speech was greeted with gales of laughter.*

gall /gɔl/ *noun, verb*

● **noun 1** rude behavior showing a lack of respect that is surprising because the person doing it is not embarrassed **SYN** : *Then they had the gall to complain!* **2** (*formal*) a bitter feeling full of hatred **SYN** RESENTMENT **3** a swelling on plants and trees caused by insects, disease, etc. **4** (*old-fashioned*) = BILE

● **verb ~ sb | it galls sb to do sth | it galls sb that…** to make someone feel upset and angry, especially because something is unfair: *It galls me to have to apologize to her.* ➜ see also GALLING

gal·lant *adj., noun*

● **adj. 1** /'gælənt/ (*old-fashioned* or *literary*) brave, especially in a very difficult situation **SYN** HEROIC: *gallant soldiers* ◆ *She made a gallant attempt to hide her tears.* **2** /'gælənt; gə'lænt; -'lɑnt/ (of a man) giving polite attention to women ▶ **gal·lant·ly** *adv.*: *She gallantly battled on alone.* ◆ *He bowed and gallantly kissed my hand.*

● **noun** (*old-fashioned*) a fashionable young man, especially one who gives polite attention to women

gal·lant·ry /'gæləntri/ *noun* [U] (*formal*) **1** courage, especially in a battle: *a medal for gallantry* **2** polite attention given by men to women

'gall ˌbladder *noun* an organ attached to the LIVER in which BILE is stored ➜ picture at BODY

gal·le·on /'gæliən/ *noun* a large Spanish sailing ship, used between the 15th and the 17th centuries

gal·ler·ied /'gælərid/ *adj.* (of a building) having a gallery

gal·ler·y /'gæləri/ *noun* (*pl.* gal·ler·ies) **1** a room or building for showing works of art, especially to the public: *an art gallery* ◆ *the National Gallery* ➜ see also ART GALLERY ➜ collocations at ART **2** a small private store where you can see and buy works of art **3** an upstairs area at the back or sides of a large hall where people can sit: *Relatives of the victim watched from the public gallery as the murder charge was read out in court.* ➜ see also PRESS GALLERY **4** the highest level in a theater where the cheapest seats are ➜ see also PEANUT GALLERY **5** a long, narrow room, especially one used for a particular purpose ➜ see also SHOOTING GALLERY **6** a level passage under the ground in a mine or CAVE
IDM **play to the gallery** to behave in an exaggerated way to attract people's attention

gal·ley /'gæli/ *noun* **1** the kitchen on a ship or plane **2** a long flat ship with sails, usually ROWED by SLAVES or criminals, especially one used by the ancient Greeks or Romans in war

Gal·lic /'gælɪk/ *adj.* connected with or considered typical of France or its people: *Gallic charm*

gall·ing /'gɔlɪŋ/ *adj.* [not usually before noun] (of a situation or fact) making you angry because it is unfair: *It was galling to have to apologize to a man she hated.*

gal·li·um /'gæliəm/ *noun* [U] (*symb.* **Ga**) a chemical element. Gallium is a soft silver-white metal.

gal·li·vant /'gælə,vænt/ *verb* [I] (usually used in the progressive tenses) ~ **(around)** (*old-fashioned, informal*) to go from place to place enjoying yourself: *You're too old to go gallivanting around Europe.*

gal·lon 🔑 /'gælən/ *noun* (*abbr.* **gal.**)
a unit for measuring liquid. In the U.S. it is equal to about 3.8 liters. In Canada, the U.K., and other countries it is equal to about 4.5 liters. There are four QUARTS in a gallon.

gal·lop /'gæləp/ *verb, noun*

● **verb 1** [I] (+ *adv./prep.*) when a horse or similar animal gallops, it moves very fast and each STRIDE includes a stage when all four feet are off the ground together ➜ compare CANTER **2** [I, T] to ride a horse very fast, usually at a gallop: (+ *adv./prep.*) *Jo galloped across the field toward him.* ◆ ~ **sth (+ adv./prep.)** *He galloped his horse home.* ➜ compare CANTER **3** [I] (+ *adv./prep.*) (*informal*) (of a person) to run very quickly **SYN** CHARGE: *She came galloping down the street.*

● **noun 1** [sing.] the fastest speed at which a horse can run, with a stage in which all four feet are off the ground together: *He rode off at a gallop.* ◆ *My horse suddenly broke into a gallop.* **2** [C] a ride on a horse at its fastest speed: *to go for a gallop* **3** [sing.] an unusually fast speed

gal·lop·ing /'gæləpɪŋ/ *adj.* [only before noun] increasing or spreading rapidly: *galloping inflation*

gal·lows /'gæloʊz/ *noun* (*pl.* gal·lows) a structure on which people, for example criminals, are killed by hanging: *to send a man to the gallows* (= to send him to his death by hanging)

ˈgallows ˌhumor (*CanE* usually **ˈgallows ˌhumour**) (also) *noun* [U] jokes about unpleasant things like death

gall·stone /'gɔlstoʊn/ *noun* a hard painful mass that can form in the GALL BLADDER

Gal·lup poll™ /'gæləp ˌpoʊl/ *noun* a way of finding out public opinion by asking a typical group of people questions **ORIGIN** From G. H. Gallup, who invented it.

ga·lore /gə'lɔr/ *adj.* [after noun] (*informal*) in large quantities: *There will be games and prizes galore.*

ga·losh·es /gə'lɑʃəz/ *noun* [pl.] rubber shoes (no longer very common) that are worn over normal shoes in wet weather: *a pair of galoshes*

ga·lumph /gə'lʌmf/ *verb* [I] + **adv./prep.** (*informal*) to move in an awkward, careless, or noisy way

ʌ **cup**   ə **about**   eɪ **say**   aɪ **five**   ɔɪ **boy**   aʊ **now**   oʊ **go**   ər **bird**

gal·van·ic /gælˈvænɪk/ *adj.* **1** (*technical*) producing an electric current by the action of a chemical on metal **2** (*formal*) making people react in a sudden and dramatic way

gal·va·nize /ˈgælvəˌnaɪz/ *verb* **1** ~ **sb (into sth/into doing sth)** to make someone take action by shocking them or by making them excited: *The urgency of his voice galvanized them into action.* **2** ~ **sth** (*technical*) to cover metal with ZINC in order to protect it from RUST: *a galvanized bucket* ♦ *galvanized steel*

gam·bit /ˈgæmbət/ *noun* **1** a thing that someone does, or something that someone says at the beginning of a situation or conversation, that is intended to give them some advantage: *an opening gambit* (= the first thing you say) **2** a move or moves made at the beginning of a game of CHESS in order to gain an advantage later

gam·ble 🔊 /ˈgæmbl/ *verb, noun*
• *verb* **1** [I, T] to risk money on a card game, horse race, etc.: ~ **(on sth)** *to gamble on the horses* ♦ ~ **sth (on sth)** *I gambled all my winnings on the last race.* **2** [T, I] to risk losing something in the hope of being successful: ~ **sth (on sth)** *He's gambling his reputation on this deal.* ♦ ~ **with/on sth** *It was wrong to gamble with our children's future.* ▶ **gam·bler** /ˈgæmblər/ *noun*: *He was a compulsive gambler* (= found it difficult to stop).
PHR V **gamble sth↔aˈway** to lose something such as money, possessions, etc. by gambling **ˈgamble on sth/on doing sth** to take a risk with something, hoping that you will be successful: *He gambled on being able to buy a ticket at the last minute.*
• *noun* [sing.] an action that you take when you know there is a risk but when you hope that the result will be a success: *She knew she was taking a gamble but decided it was worth it.* ♦ *They invested money in the company right at the start and the gamble paid off* (= brought them success).

gam·bling 🔊 /ˈgæmblɪŋ/ *noun* [U]
the activity of playing games of chance for money and of betting on horses, etc.: *heavy gambling debts*

gam·bol /ˈgæmbl/ *verb* (-l- or -ll-) [I] (+ adv./prep.) to jump or run about in a lively way: *lambs gamboling in the meadow*

game 🔊 /ɡeɪm/ *noun, adj.*
• *noun*
> **ACTIVITY/SPORT** **1** [C] an activity or a sport with rules in which individuals or teams compete against each other: *card games* ♦ *board games* ♦ *a game of chance/skill* ♦ *ball games*, such as football or tennis ♦ *We're going to the ball game* (= baseball game). **See also** WAR GAME **2** [C] an occasion of playing a game: *to play a game of chess* ♦ *Saturday's Little League game against St. Francis* ♦ *Let's play a game of ping-pong.* ♦ *They're in training for the big game.* **3** [sing.] **sb's** ~ the way in which someone plays a game: *Jones raised his game to collect the $50,000 first prize.* ♦ *Stretching exercises can help you avoid injury and improve your game.*
> **SPORTS** **4 games** [pl.] a large organized sports event: *the Olympic Games*
> **PART OF SPORTS MATCH** **5** [C] a section of some games, such as TENNIS, which forms a unit in scoring: *two games all* (= both players have won two games)
> **CHILDREN'S ACTIVITY** **6** [C] a children's activity when they play with toys, pretend to be someone else, etc.: *a game of cops and robbers*
> **FUN** **7** [C] an activity that you do to have fun: *He was playing games with the dog.*
> **COMPUTER/VIDEO GAMES** **8** [C] an activity that you do for fun on a computer or television in which you press controls to move images on the screen: *a new computer/video game*
> **ACTIVITY, BUSINESS** **9** [C] a type of activity or business: *How long have you been in this game?* ♦ *the game of politics* ♦ *I'm new to this game myself.* ♦ *Getting dirty was all part of the game to the kids.* ➔ **see also** WAITING GAME
> **SECRET PLAN** **10** [C] (*informal*) a secret and usually dishonest plan; a trick: *So that's his game* (= now I know what he has been planning).
> **WILD ANIMALS/BIRDS** **11** [U] wild animals or birds that people hunt for sport or food ➔ **see also** BIG GAME, FAIR GAME
IDM **be ahead of the game** to be more successful than the people you are competing with in an activity: *Claire found that she was ahead of the game in her new job since she already had experience with marketing.* **be a game** to not be considered to be serious: *For her the whole project was just a game.* **be out of the game** to no longer have a chance of winning a game or succeeding in an activity that you are taking part in **be still/back in the game** to still/once again have a good chance of winning a game or succeeding in an activity that you are taking part in: *The team was still in the game, just one run down.* **the game/jig is up** (*informal*) said when someone who has done something wrong is caught and the crime or trick is discovered **give the game away** to tell a secret, especially by accident; to show something that should be kept hidden **the only game in town** (*informal*) the most important thing of a particular type, or the only thing that is available **play the game** to respect the rules or conditions set for a particular situation, especially in order to gain an advantage for yourself: *In politics, you need to play the game to get the support you need.* **play games (with sb)** not to treat a situation seriously, especially in order to cheat someone: *Don't play games with me; I know you did it.* **what's sb's/your game?** (*informal*) used to ask why someone is behaving as they are ➔ **more at** BEAT *v.*, CAT, FUN *n.*, LATE *adv.*, NAME *n.*, NUMBER *n.*, RULE *n.*, TALK *v.*, TOP *n.*, TWO
• *adj.* ~ **(for sth/to do sth)** ready and willing to do something new, difficult, or dangerous: *She's game for anything.* ♦ *We need a volunteer for this exercise. Who's game to try?*

ˈgame bird *noun* a bird that people hunt for sport or food

ˈgame-ˌchanger *noun* a person, an idea, or an event that completely changes the way a situation develops

game·keep·er /ˈɡeɪmˌkipər/ *noun* a person whose job is to take care of and breed wild animals and birds that are kept on private land in order to be hunted

gam·e·lan /ˈɡæməˌlæn; -ˌlɑn/ *noun* a traditional group of Indonesian musicians, playing instruments such as XYLOPHONES and GONGS

game·ly /ˈɡeɪmli/ *adv.* in a way that seems brave, although a lot of effort is involved: *She tried gamely to finish the race.*

ˈgame plan *noun* a plan for success in the future, especially in sports, politics, or business

game·play /ˈɡeɪmpleɪ/ *noun* [U] the features of a computer game, such as its story or the way it is played, rather than the images or sounds it uses

ˈgame point *noun* (especially in TENNIS) a point that, if won by a player, will win them the GAME

ˈgame preˌserve *noun* a large area of land where wild animals can live in safety

gam·er /ˈɡeɪmər/ *noun* (*informal*) **1** a person who likes playing computer games **2** (in sports) a player who is enthusiastic and works hard

ˈgame show *noun* a television program in which people play games or answer questions to win prizes **SYN** QUIZ SHOW

games·man·ship /ˈɡeɪmzmənˌʃɪp/ *noun* [U] the ability to win games by making your opponent less confident and using rules to your advantage

gam·ete /ˈɡæmit/ *noun* (*biology*) a male or female cell that joins with a cell of the opposite sex to form a ZYGOTE (= a single cell that develops into a person, animal, or plant)

ˈgame ˌtheory *noun* [U] the part of mathematics that deals with situations in which people compete with each other, for example war or business

ˈgame ˌwarden *noun* a person whose job is to manage and take care of the wild animals in a GAME PRESERVE

gam·ey (also **gam·y**) /ˈɡeɪmi/ adj. (of meat that has been hunted) having a strong flavor or smell as a result of being kept for some time before cooking

gam·ine /ˈɡæmin; ɡæˈmin/ adj. (formal) (of a young woman) thin and attractive; looking like a boy ▶ **gam·ine** noun

gam·ing /ˈɡeɪmɪŋ/ noun [U] **1** (old-fashioned or law) = GAMBLING: *He spent all night at the gaming tables.* **2** playing computer games ⊃ see also WAR GAMING

gam·ma /ˈɡæmə/ noun the third letter of the Greek alphabet (Γ, γ)

gam·ma glob·u·lin /ˌɡæmə ˈɡlɑbyələn/ noun [U] (biology) a type of PROTEIN in the blood that gives protection against some types of diseases

gamma radi·ation noun [U] (also ˈgamma ˌrays [pl.]) (physics) high-energy RAYS of very short WAVELENGTH sent out by some RADIOACTIVE substances ⊃ compare ALPHA RADIATION

the gam·ut /ˈɡæmət/ noun [sing.] the complete range of a particular kind of thing: *The network will provide the gamut of computer services to your home.* ◆ *She felt she had* **run the (whole) gamut** *of human emotions from joy to despair.*

gan·der /ˈɡændər/ noun a male GOOSE (= a bird like a large DUCK)
  IDM **have/take a gander (at sth)** (informal) to look at something ⊃ more at SAUCE

G and T /ˌdʒi ən ˈti/ noun a drink consisting of GIN mixed with TONIC

gang /ɡæŋ/ noun, verb
● noun **1** an organized group of criminals: *criminal gang members and drug dealers* ◆ *a gang of pickpockets* ◆ *An armed gang robbed the bank.* **2** a group of young people who spend a lot of time together and often cause trouble or fight against other groups: *gang violence* ◆ *a street gang* **3** (informal) a group of friends who meet regularly: *The whole gang will be there.* **4** an organized group of workers or prisoners doing work together ⊃ see also CHAIN GANG
● verb
  PHR V **gang to·gether** (informal) to join together in a group in order to have more power or strength **gang ˈup (on/against sb)** (informal) to join together in a group to hurt, frighten, or oppose someone: *At school the older boys ganged up on him and called him names.*

gang·bust·ers /ˈɡæŋˌbʌstərz/ noun
  IDM **like gangbusters** (informal) with a lot of energy and enthusiasm

gang·land /ˈɡæŋlænd/ noun [sing.] the world of organized and violent crime: *gangland killings*

gan·gling /ˈɡæŋɡlɪŋ/ (also **gan·gly** /ˈɡæŋɡli/) adj. (of a person) tall, thin, and awkward in their movements
  SYN LANKY: *a gangling youth/adolescent*

gan·gli·on /ˈɡæŋɡliən/ noun (pl. **gan·gli·a** /-ɡliə/) (medical) **1** a mass of nerve cells **2** a swelling in a TENDON, often at the back of the hand

gang·plank /ˈɡæŋplæŋk/ noun a board for people to walk on between the side of a boat and land

gang rape noun [U, C] the RAPE of a person by a number of people one after the other ▶ **gang-rape** verb ~ sb

gan·grene /ˈɡæŋɡrin; ɡæŋˈɡrin/ noun [U] the decay that takes place in a part of the body when the blood supply to it has been stopped because of an illness or injury: *Gangrene set in and he had to have his leg amputated.* ▶ **gan·gre·nous** /ˈɡæŋɡrənəs/ adj.

gang·sta /ˈɡæŋstə/ noun **1** [C] (slang) a member of a street GANG **2** (also **ˈgangsta ˌrap**) [U] a type of RAP music, typically with words about violence, guns, drugs, and sex

gang·ster /ˈɡæŋstər/ noun a member of a group of violent criminals: *Chicago gangsters*

gang·way /ˈɡæŋweɪ/ noun a bridge placed between the side of a ship and land so people can get on and off; a large GANGPLANK

gan·ja /ˈɡɑndʒə; ˈɡæn-/ noun [U] (slang) = MARIJUANA

gan·net /ˈɡænət/ noun a large bird that lives near the ocean and catches fish by DIVING

gan·try /ˈɡæntri/ noun (pl. **gan·tries**) a tall metal frame that is used to support a CRANE, a SPACECRAFT while it is still on the ground, etc.

Gantt chart /ˈɡænt tʃɑrt/ noun (business) a chart used for managing the tasks involved in a project that shows when each stage should start and end and compares the amount of work done with the amount planned

gap /ɡæp/ noun
~ (in/between sth)
1 a space between two things or in the middle of something, especially because there is a part missing: *a gap in a hedge* ◆ *She had a gap between her two front teeth.* **2** a period of time when something stops, or between two events: *a gap in the conversation* ◆ *They met again after a gap of twenty years.* ◆ *There's a big* **age gap** *between them* (= a big difference in their ages). **3** a difference that separates people, or their opinions, situation, etc.: *the gap between rich and poor* ◆ *the gap between theory and practice* ⊃ see also CREDIBILITY, GENERATION GAP **4** a space where something is missing: *His death left an enormous gap in my life.* ◆ *There were several gaps in my education.* ◆ *We think we've identified* **a gap in the market** (= a business opportunity to make or sell something that is not yet available). **IDM** see BRIDGE v.

gape /ɡeɪp/ verb **1** [I] ~ (at sb/sth) to stare at someone or something with your mouth open because you are shocked or surprised **2** [I] to be or become wide open: *a gaping hole/mouth/wound* ◆ *~ open* He stood yawning, his pajama jacket gaping open. ▶ **gape** noun

gap-toothed adj. [usually before noun] having wide spaces between your teeth

gap year noun (in some countries, such as Britain and Australia) a year that a young person spends working and/or traveling, often between high school and college: *I'm planning to take a gap year and go backpacking in South America.*

ga·rage /ɡəˈrɑʒ; -ˈrɑdʒ/ noun, verb
● noun **1** a building for keeping one or more cars or other vehicles in: *a house with an attached garage* ◆ *a two-car garage* ◆ *a parking garage* ◆ *an underground garage* (= for example under an office building) ⊃ picture at HOUSE **2** a place where vehicles are repaired and where you can buy a car or buy gas and oil: *a garage mechanic* ⊃ see also GAS STATION
● verb ~ sth to put or keep a vehicle in a garage

ga·rage ˌband noun a group of people who play rock music together and practice in a garage or similar place

ga·rage ˌrock noun [U] a type of rock music played with a lot of energy, often by musicians who are not professionals

ga·rage ˌsale noun a sale of used clothes, furniture, etc., held in the garage or yard of someone's house ⊃ see also RUMMAGE SALE, TAG SALE, YARD SALE

garb /ɡɑrb/ noun [U] (formal or humorous) clothes, especially unusual clothes or those worn by a particular type of person: *prison garb*

gar·bage /ˈɡɑrbɪdʒ/ noun [U]
1 waste food, paper, etc. that you throw away: *garbage collection* ◆ *Don't forget to take out the garbage.* ⊃ collocations at ENVIRONMENT **2** a place or container where waste food, paper, etc. can be placed: *Throw it in the garbage.* **3** (informal) something stupid or not true
  IDM **garbage in, garbage out** (abbr. GIGO) used to express the idea that if wrong or poor quality data is put into a computer, wrong or poor quality data will come out of it

garbage ˌcan (also **ˈtrash can**) noun a large container with a lid, used for putting garbage in, usually kept outside the house

garbage dis·pos·al (also **dis·pos·al**) noun a machine

connected to the waste pipe of a kitchen SINK, for cutting food waste into small pieces

garbage man (also *formal* **garbage col·lector**) *noun* a person whose job is to remove waste from outside houses, etc. **SYN** SANITATION WORKER

garbage truck *noun* a vehicle for collecting garbage from outside houses, etc.

gar·ban·zo /gɑrˈbɑnzoʊ/ (also **gar·banzo bean**) *noun* (*pl.* **gar·ban·zos**) = CHICKPEA

garbed /gɑrbd/ *adj.* [not before noun] (*formal*) ~ **(in sth)** dressed in a particular way: *brightly garbed*

gar·bled /ˈgɑrbld/ *adj.* (of a message or story) told in a way that confuses the person listening, usually by someone who is shocked or in a hurry **SYN** CONFUSED: *He gave a garbled account of what happened.* ♦ *There was a garbled message from her on my voice mail.*

gar·den 🔑 /ˈgɑrdn/ *noun, verb*
• *noun* **1** [C] a small piece of land (usually near a house) where vegetables or plants are grown: *This is a good time to plant a garden.* ♦ *a vegetable/flower garden* ♦ *a rose garden* (= where only ROSES are grown) ⊃ see also COMMUNITY GARDEN, ROOF GARDEN **2** [C] often **gardens** a public place with flowers, trees, and other plants: *the Missouri Botanical Garden in St. Louis* ⊃ see also ZOOLOGICAL GARDEN **IDM** see LEAD¹ v.
• *verb* [I] to work in a garden ► **gar·den·er** /ˈgɑrdnər; ˈgɑrdn‑ər/ *noun*: *My wife's an avid gardener.* ♦ *We employ a gardener two days a week.* **gar·den·ing** *noun* [U] *organic gardening* ♦ *gardening gloves* ♦ *a gardening program on TV* ⊃ picture at HOBBY

garden center (*CanE usually* **garden centre**) *noun* a place that sells plants, seeds, garden equipment, etc.

gar·de·nia /gɑrˈdinyə/ *noun* a bush with shiny leaves and large white or yellow flowers with a sweet smell, also called gardenias

the Garden of Eden *noun* [sing.] = EDEN

garden party *noun* a formal social event that takes place outdoors in a large garden

garden salad [U, C] a salad containing a variety of raw vegetables, especially LETTUCE

garden-va·riety *adj.* [only before noun] ordinary; with no special features: *He is not one of your garden-variety criminals.*

gar·gan·tu·an /gɑrˈgæntʃuən/ *adj.* [usually before noun] extremely large **SYN** ENORMOUS: *a gargantuan appetite/meal*

gar·gle /ˈgɑrgl/ *verb, noun*
• *verb* [I] ~ **(with sth)** to wash inside your mouth and throat by moving a liquid around at the back of your throat and then SPITTING it out
• *noun* **1** [C, U] a liquid used for gargling (gargle): *an antiseptic gargle* **2** [sing.] an act of gargling (gargle) or a sound like that made when gargling (gargle): *to have a gargle with salt water*

gar·goyle /ˈgɑrgɔɪl/ *noun* an ugly figure of a person or an animal that is made of stone and through which water is carried away from the roof of a building, especially a church ⊃ picture at ARCHITECTURE

gar·ish /ˈgɛrɪʃ; ˈgær‑/ *adj.* very brightly colored in an unpleasant way **SYN** GAUDY: *garish clothes/colors* ► **gar·ish·ly** *adv.*: *garishly decorated/lit/painted*

gar·land /ˈgɑrlənd/ *noun, verb*
• *noun* a circle of flowers and leaves that is worn on the head or around the neck or is hung in a room as decoration
• *verb* [usually passive] ~ **sb/sth** (*literary*) to decorate someone or something with a garland or garlands

gar·lic /ˈgɑrlɪk/ *noun* [U] a vegetable of the onion family with a very strong taste and smell, used in cooking to give flavor to food: *a clove of garlic* (= one section of it) ⊃ picture at FRUIT ► **gar·lick·y** /ˈgɑrlɪki/ *adj.*: *garlicky breath/food*

garlic bread *noun* [U] bread containing melted butter or oil and garlic

garlic press *noun* a small kitchen tool used to crush garlic ⊃ picture at KITCHEN

gar·ment /ˈgɑrmənt/ *noun* (*formal*) a piece of clothing: *a strange shapeless garment* ♦ **woolen/winter/outer garments** ⊃ see also UNDERGARMENT ⊃ thesaurus box at CLOTHES

garment bag *noun* a large plastic bag in which clothes are hung to keep them clean and safe

gar·ner /ˈgɑrnər/ *verb* ~ **sth** (*formal*) to obtain or collect something such as information, support, etc. **SYN** ACQUIRE, GATHER

gar·net /ˈgɑrnət/ *noun* a clear, dark red SEMI-PRECIOUS STONE that is fairly valuable

gar·nish /ˈgɑrnɪʃ/ *verb, noun*
• *verb* ~ **sth (with sth)** to decorate a dish of food with a small amount of another food ⊃ collocations at COOKING
• *noun* [C, U] a small amount of food that is used to decorate a larger dish of food

gar·ret /ˈgærət/ *noun* a room, often small, dark, unpleasant one, at the top of a house, especially in the roof ⊃ compare ATTIC ⊃ see also LOFT

gar·ri·son /ˈgærəsn/ *noun, verb*
• *noun* a group of soldiers living in a town or FORT to defend it; the buildings these soldiers live in: *a garrison of 5,000 troops* ♦ *a garrison town*
• *verb* to put soldiers in a place in order to defend it from attack: ~ **sth** *Two regiments were sent to garrison the town.* ♦ ~ **sb + adv./prep.** *100 soldiers were garrisoned in the town.*

gar·rote (also **gar·rotte, ga·rotte**) /gəˈrɑt; ‑ˈroʊt/ *verb, noun*
• *verb* ~ **sb** to kill someone by putting a piece of wire, etc. around their neck and pulling it tight
• *noun* a piece of wire, etc. used for garroting someone

gar·ru·lous /ˈgærələs/ *adj.* talking a lot, especially about unimportant things **SYN** TALKATIVE ► **gar·ru·lous·ly** *adv.*

gar·ter /ˈgɑrtər/ *noun* **1** a band, usually made of ELASTIC, that is worn around the leg to keep up a sock **2** one of the pieces of ELASTIC material that are attached to women's underwear or to a garter belt, and to the tops of her STOCKINGS, in order to keep the stockings up

garter belt *noun* a piece of women's underwear like a belt, worn around the waist, used for holding STOCKINGS up

garter snake *noun* a harmless American snake with colored lines along its back

gas 🔑 /gæs/ *noun, verb*
• *noun* (*pl.* **gas·es** or *less frequent* **gas·ses**)
> IN VEHICLE **1** (also **gas·o·line**) [U] a liquid obtained from PETROLEUM, used as fuel in car engines, etc.: *We need to stop for gas.* ♦ *a gas station* ♦ *a gas pump* ♦ *to fill up the gas tank* **2** the gas [sing.] = GAS PEDAL: *Step on the gas, we're late.*
> NOT SOLID/LIQUID **3** [C, U] any substance like air that is neither a solid nor a liquid; for example, HYDROGEN and OXYGEN are both gases: *Air is a mixture of gases.* ♦ *CFC gases* ♦ *a gas bottle/cylinder* (= for storing gas) ⊃ see also GREENHOUSE GAS **4** [U] a particular type of gas or mixture of gases used as fuel for heating and cooking: *a gas stove/furnace* ♦ *a gas explosion/leak* ♦ *gas heat* ⊃ see also COAL GAS, NATURAL GAS **5** [U] a particular type of gas used during a medical operation, to make the patient sleep or to make the pain less: *an anesthetic gas* ⊃ see also LAUGHING GAS **6** [U] a particular type of gas used in war to kill or injure people, or used by the police to control people: *a gas attack* ⊃ see also CS GAS, NERVE GAS, TEAR GAS
> FUN **7** [sing.] a person or an event that is fun: *The party was a real gas.*
> IN STOMACH **8** [U] air that you swallow with food or drink; gas that is produced in your stomach or INTESTINES that makes you feel uncomfortable
IDM **run out of gas** (*informal*) to lose energy and enthusiasm and stop doing something, or do it less well

- **verb** (-ss-)
 > KILL/HARM WITH GAS **1** [T] ~ **sb/yourself** to kill or harm someone by making them breathe poisonous gas
 > TALK **2** [I] (usually used in the progressive tenses) (*old-fashioned, informal*) to talk for a long time about things that are not important **SYN** CHAT

gas·bag /'gæsbæg/ *noun* (*informal, humorous*) a person who talks a lot

'**gas cap** *noun* a lid for covering the end of the pipe through which gas is put into a vehicle

'**gas ‚chamber** *noun* a room that can be filled with poisonous gas for killing animals or people

'**gas-cooled** *adj.* [only before noun] using gas to keep the temperature cool: *gas-cooled nuclear reactors*

gas·e·ous /'gæsiəs; 'gæʃəs/ *adj.* [usually before noun] like or containing gas: *a gaseous mixture* ♦ *in gaseous form*

‚**gas 'giant** *noun* (*astronomy*) a large planet made mostly of the gases HYDROGEN and HELIUM, for example Jupiter or Saturn

'**gas ‚guzzler** (also **guz·zler**) *noun* (*informal*) a car that uses a lot of gas ▶ '**gas-‚guzzling** *adj.* [only before noun]

gash /gæʃ/ *noun, verb*
- **noun** ~ (**in/on sth**) a long, deep cut in the surface of something, especially a person's skin
- **verb** ~ **sth/sb** to make a long, deep cut in something, especially a person's skin: *He gashed his hand on a sharp piece of rock.*

gas·ket /'gæskət/ *noun* a flat piece of rubber, etc. placed between two metal surfaces in a pipe or an engine to prevent steam, gas, or oil from escaping: *The engine had* **blown a gasket** (= had allowed steam, etc. to escape). ♦ (*figurative, informal*) *He blew a gasket* at the news (= became very angry).

'**gas lamp** (also **gas‚light**) *noun* a lamp in the street or in a house, that produces light from burning gas

gas·light /'gæslaɪt/ *noun* **1** [U] light produced from burning gas: *In the gaslight she looked paler than ever.* **2** [C] = GAS LAMP

gas·man /'gæsmæn/ *noun* (*pl.* **gas·men** /-mɛn/) (*informal*) a person whose job is to visit people's houses to see how much gas they have used, or to fit and check gas equipment

'**gas ‚mantle** *noun* = MANTLE

'**gas mask** *noun* a piece of equipment worn over the face as protection against poisonous gas

gas·o·hol /'gæsə,hɔl; -,hɑl/ *noun* [U] a mixture of gas and alcohol that can be used in cars

'**gas oil** *noun* [U] a type of oil obtained from PETROLEUM that is used as a fuel

gas·o·line 🔑 (also **gas·o·lene**) /'gæsə'lin; 'gæsə,lin/ *noun* [U]
= GAS *n.* (1): *I fill up the tank* **with gasoline** about once a week. ♦ *leaded/unleaded gasoline*

gasp /gæsp/ *verb, noun*
- **verb 1** [I, T] to take a quick deep breath with your mouth open, especially because you are surprised or in pain: ~ (**at sth**) *She gasped at the wonderful view.* ♦ *They gasped in astonishment at the news.* ♦ + **speech** *"What was that noise?" he gasped.* **2** [I, T] to have difficulty breathing or speaking: ~ (**for sth**) *He came to the surface of the water gasping for air.* ♦ ~ (**sth**) (**out**) *She managed to gasp out her name.* ♦ + **speech** *"Can't breathe," he gasped.*
- **noun** a quick deep breath, usually caused by a strong emotion: *to give a* **gasp of horror/surprise/relief** ♦ *His breath came in short gasps.* **IDM** see LAST¹

'**gas ‚pedal** *noun* the PEDAL in a car or other vehicle that you press with your foot to control the speed of the engine ⊃ picture at CAR

‚**gas-'permeable** *adj.* allowing gases to pass through: *gas-permeable contact lenses*

'**gas ‚station** (also '**service ‚station**) *noun* a place at the side of a road where you take your car to buy gas, oil, etc.

gas·sy /'gæsi/ *adj.* (of people) having a lot of gas in your stomach, etc.

gas·tric /'gæstrɪk/ *adj.* [only before noun] (*medical*) connected with the stomach: *a gastric ulcer* ♦ *gastric juices* (= the acids in your stomach that help you to DIGEST food)

‚**gastric 'bypass** *noun* surgery that reduces the size of someone's stomach so they will eat less food

gas·tri·tis /gæ'straɪtəs/ *noun* [U] (*medical*) an illness in which the inside of the stomach becomes swollen and painful

gas·tro·en·ter·i·tis /,gæstrou,entə'raɪtəs/ *noun* [U] (*medical*) an illness of the stomach and other food passages that causes DIARRHEA and VOMITING

gas·tro·in·tes·ti·nal /,gæstrouɪn'testənl/ *adj.* (*medical*) of or related to the stomach and INTESTINES

gas·tro·nom·ic /,gæstrə'namɪk/ *adj.* [only before noun] connected with cooking and eating good food ▶ **gas·tro·nom·i·cally** /-kli/ *adv.*

gas·tron·o·my /gæ'stranəmi/ *noun* [U] (*formal*) the art and practice of cooking and eating good food

gas·tro·pod /'gæstrə,pad/ *noun* (*biology*) a MOLLUSK such as a SNAIL or SLUG, that moves on one large foot

gas·works /'gæswərks/ *noun* (*pl.* **gas·works**) a factory where gas for lighting and heating is made from coal

gate 🔑 /geɪt/ *noun*
1 [C] a barrier like a door that is used to close an opening in a fence or a wall outside a building: *an iron gate* ♦ *He pushed open the garden gate.* ♦ *A crowd gathered at the factory gates.* ♦ *the gates of the city* ⊃ see also LYCHGATE, STARTING GATE **2** [C] an opening that can be closed by a gate or gates: *We drove through the gate and onto the grounds of the estate.* **3** [C] a barrier that is used to control the flow of water on a river or CANAL: *a lock/sluice gate* **4** [C] a way out of an airport through which passengers go to get on their plane: *The flight to Houston is now boarding at gate 16.* **5** [C] the number of people who attend a sports event: *Tonight's game has attracted the largest gate of the season.* **6** (also '**gate ‚money**) [U] the amount of money made by selling tickets for a sports event: *Today's gate will be given to charity.* **7** -**gate** (forming nouns from the names of people or places; used especially in newspapers) a political SCANDAL connected with the person or place mentioned **ORIGIN** From **Watergate**, the scandal in the United States that brought about the resignation of President Nixon in 1974. **8** [C] (*computing*) = LOGIC GATE

'**gate-‚crasher** (also *informal* **crash·er**) *noun* a person who goes to a party or social event without being invited ▶ '**gate-crash** (also *informal* **crash**) *verb* [T, I] ~ (**sth**)

gat·ed /'geɪtəd/ *adj.* [usually before noun] (of a road) having gates that need to be opened and closed by drivers

‚**gated com'munity** *noun* a group of houses surrounded by a wall or fence, with an entrance that is guarded

gate·fold /'geɪtfould/ *noun* a large page folded to fit a book or magazine that can be opened out for reading

gate·house /'geɪthaus/ *noun* a house built at or over a gate, for example at the entrance to a park or castle

gate·keep·er /'geɪt,kipər/ *noun* **1** a person whose job is to check and control who is allowed to go through a gate **2** a person, system, etc. that decides whether someone or something will be allowed, or allowed to reach a particular place or person: *His secretary acts as a gatekeeper, reading all mail before it reaches her boss.*

gate·leg ta·ble /,geɪtleg 'teɪbl/ *noun* a table with extra sections that can be folded out to make it larger, supported on legs that swing out from the center

'**gate ‚money** *noun* [U] = GATE

gate·post /ˈgeɪtpoʊst/ noun a post to which a gate is attached or against which it is closed

gate·way /ˈgeɪtweɪ/ noun **1** an opening in a wall or fence that can be closed by a gate: *They turned through the gateway on the left.* **2** [usually sing.] ~ **to/into…** a place through which you can go to reach another larger place: *St. Louis is called The Gateway to the West.* **3** [usually sing.] ~ **to sth** a means of getting or achieving something: *A good education is the gateway to success.* **4** (*computing*) a device that connects two computer networks that cannot be connected in any other way

gath·er 🔊 /ˈgæðər/ verb

> COME/BRING TOGETHER **1** [I, T] to come together, or bring people together, in one place to form a group: *A crowd soon gathered.* ◆ **+ adv./prep.** *His supporters gathered in the hotel ballroom.* ◆ *Can you all **gather around**? I've got something to tell you.* ◆ *The whole family **gathered together** at Ray's home.* ◆ **be gathered + adv./prep.** *They were all **gathered around** the TV.* ◆ *A large crowd was gathered outside the studio.* ◆ *The kids were **gathered together** in one room.* **2** [T] to bring things together that have been spread around: ~ **sth** *People slowly gathered their belongings and left the hall.* ◆ ~ **sth together/ up** *I waited while he gathered up his papers.* ⊃ thesaurus box at COLLECT

> COLLECT **3** [T] ~ **sth** to collect information from different sources: *Detectives have spent months gathering evidence.* ⊃ thesaurus box at COLLECT **4** [T] ~ **sth** to collect plants, fruit, etc. from a wide area: *to gather wild flowers*

> CROPS/HARVEST **5** [T] ~ **sth (in)** to pick or cut and collect crops to be stored: *It was late August and the harvest had been safely gathered in.*

> BELIEVE/UNDERSTAND **6** [T, I] (not used in the progressive tenses) to believe or understand that something is true because of information or evidence you have: ~ **(that)…** *I gather (that) you wanted to see me.* ◆ *I gather from your letter that you're not enjoying your job.* ◆ ~ **(sth)** *"There's been a delay." "I gathered that." ◆ "She won't be coming." "So I gather."* ◆ *You're self-employed, I gather.* ◆ *As far as I can gather, he got involved in a fight.* ◆ *From what I can gather, there's been some kind of problem.*

> INCREASE **7** [T] ~ **sth** to increase in speed, force, etc.: *The truck gathered speed.* ◆ *During the 1980s the green movement gathered momentum.* ◆ *Thousands of these machines were gathering dust* (= not being used) *in stockrooms.*

> OF CLOUDS/DARKNESS **8** [I] to gradually increase in number or amount: *The storm clouds were gathering.* ◆ *the gathering gloom of a winter's afternoon*

> CLOTHING **9** [T] to pull a piece of clothing tighter to your body: ~ **sth around you/sth** *He gathered his cloak around him.* ◆ ~ **sth up** *She gathered up her skirts and ran.* **10** [T] ~ **sth (in)** to pull parts of a piece of clothing together in folds and sew them in place: *She wore a skirt gathered (in) at the waist.*

> HOLD SOMEONE **11** [T] ~ **sb + adv./prep.** to pull someone toward you and put your arms around them: *She gathered the child in her arms and held him close.* ◆ *He gathered her to him.*

> PREPARE YOURSELF **12** [T] ~ **sth/yourself** to prepare yourself to do something that requires effort: *I sat down for a minute to gather my strength.* ◆ *She was still trying to gather her thoughts when the door opened.* **IDM** see ROLL v.

gath·er·er /ˈgæðərər/ noun a person who collects something: *prehistoric hunters and gatherers*

gath·er·ing /ˈgæðərɪŋ/ noun **1** [C] a meeting of people for a particular purpose: *a social/family gathering* ◆ *a gathering of religious leaders* **2** [U] the process of collecting something: *methods of information gathering*

gath·ers /ˈgæðərz/ noun [pl.] small folds that are sewn into a piece of clothing

ga·tor /ˈgeɪtər/ noun (*informal*) = ALLIGATOR

GATT /gæt/ noun the General Agreement on Tariffs and Trade (in the past, an international organization that tried to encourage international trade and reduce taxes on imports; the agreement by which this organization was created. GATT was replaced by the WTO in 1994.)

gauche /goʊʃ/ adj. awkward when dealing with people and often saying or doing the wrong thing: *a gauche teenager/ manner* ▶ **gauche·ness** (also **gau·che·rie** /ˌgoʊʃəˈri/) noun [U]: *the gaucheness of youth*

gau·cho /ˈgautʃoʊ/ noun (*pl.* **gau·chos**) a S. American COWBOY

gaud·y /ˈgɔdi/ adj. (**gaud·i·er**, **gaud·i·est**) (*disapproving*) too brightly colored in a way that lacks taste **SYN** GARISH: *gaudy clothes/colors* ▶ **gaud·i·ly** /ˈgɔdli/ adv.: *gaudily dressed/painted* **gaud·i·ness** /ˈgɔdinəs/ noun [U]

gauge (also **gage**) /geɪdʒ/ noun, verb

● **noun 1** (often in compounds) an instrument for measuring the amount or level of something: *a fuel/gas/tempera-ture, etc. gauge* ⊃ picture at CAR **2** a measurement of the width or thickness of something: *What gauge of wire do we need?* **3** the distance between the rails of a railroad track or the wheels of a train: *standard gauge* (= 56½ inches in the U.S.) ◆ *a narrow gauge* (= narrower than standard) *railroad* **4** a measurement of the width of the BARREL of a gun **SYN** BORE: *a 12-gauge shotgun* **5** [usually sing.] ~ **(of sth)** a fact or an event that can be used to estimate or judge something: *Tomorrow's game against the defending champions will be a good gauge of their strength.*

● **verb 1** to make a judgment about something, especially people's feelings or attitudes: ~ **sth** *They interviewed employees to gauge their reaction to the changes.* ◆ *He tried to gauge her mood.* ◆ ~ **whether, how, etc.…** *It was difficult to gauge whether he was angry or not.* **2** ~ **sth** to measure something accurately using a special instrument: *precision instruments that can gauge the diameter to a fraction of a millimeter* **3** ~ **sth** | ~ **how, what, etc.…** to calculate something approximately: *We were able to gauge the strength of the wind from the movement of the trees.*

gaunt /gɔnt/ adj. **1** (of a person) very thin, usually because of illness, not having enough food, or worry: *a gaunt face* **2** (of a building) not attractive and without any decoration ▶ **gaunt·ness** noun [U]

gaunt·let /ˈgɔntlət/ noun **1** a metal glove worn as part of a suit of ARMOR by soldiers in the Middle Ages **2** a strong glove with a wide covering for the wrist, used for example when driving: *motorcyclists with leather gauntlets* **IDM run the gauntlet** to be criticized or attacked by a lot of people, especially a group of people that you have to walk through: *Some of the witnesses had to run the gauntlet of television cameras and reporters.* **ORIGIN** This phrase refers to an old army punishment where a man was forced to run between two lines of soldiers hitting him. **take up the gauntlet** to accept someone's invitation to fight or compete **ORIGIN** In the Middle Ages, a KNIGHT threw his gauntlet at the feet of another KNIGHT as a challenge to fight. If he accepted the challenge, the other KNIGHT would pick up the glove. **throw down the gauntlet** to invite someone to fight or compete with you

gauze /gɔz/ noun **1** [U] a type of light transparent cloth, usually made of cotton or silk **2** [U] a type of thin cotton cloth used for covering and protecting wounds: *a gauze dressing* **3** [U, C] material made of a network of wire; a piece of this: *wire gauze* ⊃ picture at LABORATORY ▶ **gauz·y** adj. [usually before noun]: *a gauzy material*

gave pt of GIVE

gav·el /ˈgævl/ noun a small hammer used by a person in charge of a meeting or an AUCTION, or by a judge in court, in order to get people's attention

ga·votte /gəˈvat/ noun a French dance that was popular in the past; a piece of music for this dance

Gawd /gɔd/ noun, exclamation (*informal*) used in written English to show that the word "God" is being pronounced in a particular way to express surprise, anger, or fear: *For Gawd's sake hurry up!*

gawk /gɔk/ *verb* [I] ~ **(at sb/sth)** (*informal*) to stare at someone or something in a rude or stupid way **SYN** GAPE

gawk·y /'gɔki/ *adj.* (especially of a tall young person) awkward in the way they move or behave ▶ **gawk·i·ly** /-kəli/ *adv.* **gawk·i·ness** /-kinəs/ *noun* [U]

gay /geɪ/ *adj., noun*
● *adj.* **1** (of people, especially men) sexually attracted to people of the same sex **SYN** HOMOSEXUAL: *gay men* ◆ *I didn't know he was gay.* ◆ *Is she gay?* **ANT** STRAIGHT **2** [only before noun] connected with people who are gay: *a gay club/bar* ◆ *the lesbian and gay community* **3** [not before noun] (*slang, disapproving*) (used especially by young people) boring and not fashionable or attractive: *That ringtone is so gay!* **4** (**gay·er, gay·est**) (*old-fashioned*) happy and full of fun: *gay laughter* **5** (*old-fashioned*) brightly colored: *The garden was gay with red geraniums.* ➔ see also GAIETY, GAILY
● *noun* a person who is HOMOSEXUAL, especially a man

gay·dar /'geɪdɑr/ *noun* [U] (*informal*) the ability that someone has to recognize whether other people are homosexual

gay·ness /'geɪnəs/ *noun* [U] the state of being HOMOSEXUAL ➔ compare GAIETY

gay 'pride *noun* [U] the feeling that HOMOSEXUAL people should not be ashamed of telling people that they are homosexual and should feel proud of themselves

gaze /geɪz/ *verb, noun*
● *verb* [I] + **adv./prep.** to look steadily at someone or something for a long time, either because you are very interested or surprised, or because you are thinking of something else **SYN** STARE: *She gazed at him in amazement.* ◆ *He sat for hours just gazing into space.* ➔ thesaurus box at STARE
● *noun* [usually sing.] a long steady look at someone or something: *He met her gaze* (= looked at her while she looked at him). ◆ *She dropped her gaze* (= stopped looking). ➔ thesaurus box at LOOK

ga·ze·bo /gə'zibou/ *noun* (*pl.* **ga·ze·bos**) a small building with open sides in a garden or yard, especially one with a view

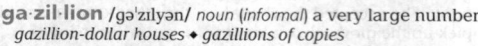
gazebo

ga·zelle /gə'zɛl/ *noun* (*pl.* **ga·zelle** or **ga·zelles**) a small ANTELOPE

ga·zette /gə'zɛt/ *noun* used in the titles of some newspapers: *the Evening Gazette*

gaz·et·teer /ˌgæzə'tɪr/ *noun* a list of place names published as a book or at the end of a book

ga·zil·lion /gə'zɪlyən/ *noun* (*informal*) a very large number: *gazillion-dollar houses* ◆ *gazillions of copies*

gaz·pa·cho /gə'spɑtʃou; gɑ-/ *noun* [U] a cold Spanish soup made with tomatoes, peppers, CUCUMBER, etc.

GB *abbr.* **1** GIGABYTE: *a 750GB hard drive* **2** (also **G.B.**) /ˌdʒi 'bi/ Great Britain

GDP /ˌdʒi di 'pi/ *noun* the abbreviation for "gross domestic product" (the total value of all the goods and services produced by a country in one year) ➔ compare GNP

GDR /ˌdʒi di 'ɑr/ *abbr.* German Democratic Republic

gear /gɪr/ *noun, verb*
● *noun*
▷ IN VEHICLE **1** [C, usually pl.] machinery in a vehicle that turns engine power (or power on a bicycle) into movement forward or backward: *Careless use of the clutch may damage the gears.* ➔ picture at BICYCLE **2** [U, C] a particular position of the gears in a vehicle that gives a particular range of speed and power: *first/second, etc. gear* ◆ *reverse gear* ◆ *low/ high gear* ◆ *to shift gear* ◆ *When parking on a hill, leave the car in gear.* ◆ *What gear are you in?* ◆ *He drove wildly, crashing through the gears like a maniac.* ➔ see also HIGH GEAR, TOP GEAR ➔ collocations at DRIVING
▷ EQUIPMENT/CLOTHES **3** [U] the equipment or clothing needed for a particular activity: *climbing/fishing/sports, etc. gear* ➔ see also HEADGEAR, RIOT GEAR ➔ thesaurus box at EQUIPMENT **4** [U] (*informal*) clothes: *wearing the latest gear* ➔ thesaurus box at CLOTHES
▷ POSSESSIONS **5** [U] (*informal*) the things that a person owns: *I left all my gear at Dave's house.*
▷ MACHINERY **6** [U] (often in compounds) a piece of machinery used for a particular purpose: *lifting/towing/winding, etc. gear* ➔ see also LANDING GEAR
▷ SPEED/EFFORT **7** [U, C] used to talk about the speed or effort involved in doing something: *The wedding preparations moved into high gear as the day approached.* ◆ *Coming out of the final turn, the runner stepped up a gear to overtake the rest of the pack.*
IDM **change/shift gears 1** to put a motor vehicle or a bicycle into a different gear **2** to move from one activity or interest to another: *After giving an intense performance it was difficult for the actress to change gears and become herself again.* **get into gear | get sth into gear** to start working, or to start something working, in an efficient way **IDM** see HIGH GEAR
● *verb*
PHR V **'gear sth to/toward sth** [usually passive] to make, change, or prepare something so that it is suitable for a particular purpose: *The course was geared to the needs of the community.* **,gear 'up (for/to sth) | ,gear sb/sth↔'up (for/to sth)** to prepare yourself/someone or something to do something: *Gamers are gearing up for the latest version of the video game.* ➔ see also GEARED

gear·box /'gɪrbɑks/ *noun* the part containing the gears of a vehicle

geared /gɪrd/ *adj.* [not before noun] **1** ~ **to/toward sth** | ~ **to do sth** designed or organized to achieve a particular purpose, or to be suitable for a particular group of people: *The program is geared to students for the world of work.* ◆ *The resort is geared toward families with children.* **2** ~ **up (for sth) | ~ up (to do sth)** prepared and ready for something: *We have people on board geared up to help with any problems.*

gear·head /'gɪrhɛd/ *noun* (*informal*) a person who is very enthusiastic about cars or new technical devices and equipment: *He's a total gearhead—can't keep away from the racetrack.*

gear·ing /'gɪrɪŋ/ *noun* [U] a particular set or arrangement of gears in a machine or vehicle

gear·shift /'gɪrʃɪft/ (also **'stick shift**) *noun* a handle used to change the gears of a vehicle ➔ picture at CAR

geck·o /'gɛkou/ *noun* (*pl.* **geck·os** or **geck·oes**) a small LIZARD (= a type of REPTILE) that lives in warm countries

GED /ˌdʒi i 'di/ *noun* **1** the abbreviation for "General Equivalency Diploma" (an official certificate that people who did not finish high school can get, after taking classes and passing a test) **2** the abbreviation for "General Educational Development" (the test that people take in order to get the GED certificate)

gee /dʒi/ *exclamation* a word that some people use to show that they are surprised, impressed, or annoyed: *Gee, what a great idea!*

geek /gik/ *noun* (*informal*) **1** a person who is boring, wears clothes that are not fashionable, does not know how to behave in social situations, etc. **2** a person who is very interested in computers or science: *a computer geek* **SYN** NERD ▶ **geek·y** *adj.*

geese pl. of GOOSE

gee whiz /ˌdʒi 'wɪz/ *exclamation* (*old-fashioned*) = GEE

gee·zer /'gizər/ *noun* (*informal*) an old man, especially one who is rather strange: *Some old geezer keeps coming around asking for money.*

ʌ **cup**   ə **about**   eɪ **say**   aɪ **five**   ɔɪ **boy**   aʊ **now**   oʊ **go**   ər **bird**

Gei·ger count·er /ˈɡaɪɡər ˌkaʊntər/ *noun* a device used for finding and measuring RADIOACTIVITY

gei·sha /ˈɡeɪʃə/ (also **ˈgeisha ˌgirl**) *noun* a Japanese woman who is trained to entertain men with conversation, dancing, and singing

gel /dʒel/ *noun, verb*
● *noun* [U, C] a thick substance like jelly, especially one used in products for the hair or skin: *hair/shower gel*
● *verb* (-ll-) **1** = JELL (1) **2** = JELL (2) **3** [I] (also **jell**) *(technical)* (of a liquid) to become thicker and more solid; to form a gel **4** [T] ~ sth to put gel on your hair

gel·a·tin /ˈdʒelətn; -tən/ *noun* [U] a clear substance without any taste that is made from boiling animal bones and is used to make Jell-O™ etc.

ge·lat·i·nous /dʒəˈlætn.əs/ *adj.* thick and sticky, like jelly: *a gelatinous substance*

geld /ɡeld/ *verb* ~ sth *(technical)* to remove the TESTICLES of a male animal, especially a horse **SYN** CASTRATE

geld·ing /ˈɡeldɪŋ/ *noun* a horse that has been CASTRATED ⊃ compare STALLION

gel·ig·nite /ˈdʒelɪɡˌnaɪt/ *noun* [U] a powerful EXPLOSIVE

gem /dʒem/ *noun* **1** (also *less frequent* **gem·stone** /ˈdʒemstoʊn/) a PRECIOUS STONE that has been cut and polished and is used in jewelry **SYN** JEWEL, PRECIOUS STONE: *a crown studded with gems* **2** a person, place, or thing that is especially good: *This picture is the gem* (= the best) *of the collection.* ◆ *a gem of a place* ◆ *She's a real gem!* ⊃ compare JEWEL

gem·i·nate /ˈdʒemənət; -ˌneɪt/ *adj.* *(phonetics)* (of a speech sound) consisting of the same consonant pronounced twice, for example /kk/ in the middle of the word *backcomb*

Gem·i·ni /ˈdʒeməˌnaɪ; -ni/ *noun* **1** [U] the third sign of the ZODIAC, the TWINS **2** [C] a person born under the influence of this sign, that is between May 22 and June 21

Gen. *abbr.* (in writing) GENERAL: *Gen. (Stanley) Armstrong*

gen·darme /ˈʒɑndɑrm/ *noun* (from *French*) a member of the French police force

gen·der **AWL** /ˈdʒendər/ *noun* **1** [C, U] the fact of being male or female, especially when considered with reference to social and cultural differences, not differences in biology: *issues of class, race and gender* ◆ *traditional concepts of gender* ◆ **gender differences/relations/roles** ⊃ compare SEX **2** [C, U] *(grammar)* (in some languages) each of the classes (MASCULINE, FEMININE, and sometimes NEUTER) into which nouns, pronouns, and adjectives are divided; the division of nouns, pronouns, and adjectives into these different genders. Different genders may have different endings, etc.: *In French the adjective must agree with the noun in number and gender.*

MORE ABOUT

gender

ways of talking about men and women

■ When you are writing or speaking English, it is important to use language that includes both men and women equally. Some people may be very offended if you do not.

the human race

■ Man and mankind have traditionally been used to mean "all men and women." Many people now prefer to use humanity, the human race, human beings, or people.

jobs

■ The suffix -ess in names of occupations such as actress, hostess, and waitress shows that the person doing the job is a woman. Many people now avoid these. Instead, you can use actor or host, (although actress and hostess are still very common) or a

---

neutral word, such as **server** for *waiter* and *waitress*.
■ Neutral words like **assistant, worker, person**, or **officer** are now often used instead of *-man* or *-woman* in the names of jobs. For example, you can use **police officer** instead of *policeman* or *policewoman*, and **spokesperson** instead of *spokesman* or *spokeswoman*. Neutral words are very common in newspapers, on television and radio, and in official writing.
■ When talking about jobs that are traditionally done by the other sex, some people say: **a male secretary/ nurse/model** or **a female doctor/scientist/driver**. However, this is now not usually used unless you need to emphasize which sex the person is or it is still unusual for the job to be done by a man/woman: *My daughter prefers to see a female doctor.* ◆ *They have a male nanny for their sons.*

pronouns

■ He used to be considered to cover both men and women: *Everyone needs to feel he is loved.* This is not now acceptable. Instead, after **everyone, everybody, anyone, anybody, someone, somebody**, etc. one of the plural pronouns **they, them**, and **their** is often used: *Does everybody know what they want?* ◆ *Somebody's left their coat here.* ◆ *I hope nobody's forgotten to bring their passport with them.*
■ Some people prefer to use **he or she, his or her**, or **him or her** in speech and writing: *Everyone knows what's best for him or herself.* **He/she** or **(s)he** can also be used in writing: *If in doubt, ask your doctor. He/she can give you more information.* (You may find that some writers just use "she" or alternate between "he" and "she.") These uses can seem awkward when they are used a lot. It is better to try to change the sentence, using a plural noun. Instead of saying: *A baby cries when he or she is tired*, you can say *Babies cry when they are tired.*

ˈgender ˌbender *noun* *(informal)* a person who dresses and behaves like a member of the opposite sex

ˌgender-ˈneutral *adj.* used to describe words or language that do not refer specifically to men or women, and so can be understood to include both sexes: *The consistent use of gender-neutral language can be a problem, even for native speakers.*

ˈgender reasˌsignment *noun* [U] the act of changing a person's sex by a medical operation in which parts of their body are changed so that they become like a person of the opposite sex

ˌgender-speˈcific *adj.* connected with women only or with men only: *The report was redrafted to remove gender-specific language.*

gene /dʒin/ *noun* *(biology)* a unit inside a cell that controls a particular quality in a living thing that has been passed on from its parents: *a dominant/recessive gene* ◆ *genes that code for the color of the eyes* ⊃ see also GENETIC
IDM be in the genes to be a quality that your parents have passed on to you: *I've always enjoyed music—it's in the genes.*

ge·ne·al·o·gist /ˌdʒiniˈɑlədʒɪst; -ˈælə-/ *noun* a person who studies family history

ge·ne·al·o·gy /ˌdʒiniˈɑlədʒi; -ˈælə-/ *noun* (*pl.* **ge·ne·al·o·gies**) **1** [U] the study of family history, including the study of who the ANCESTORS of a particular person were **2** [C] a particular person's line of ANCESTORS; a diagram that shows this ▶ **ge·ne·a·log·i·cal** /ˌdʒiniəˈlɑdʒɪkl/ *adj.* [only before noun]: *a genealogical chart/table/tree* (= a chart with branches that shows a person's ANCESTORS)

ˈgene pool *noun* *(biology)* all of the GENES that are available within breeding populations of a particular SPECIES of animal or plant

gen·er·a *pl.* of GENUS

---

gen·er·al 🔊 /ˈdʒɛnərəl; ˈdʒɛnrəl/ *adj.*, *noun*

● *adj.*

▸ **AFFECTING ALL 1** affecting all or most people, places, or things: *The **general** opinion is that the conference was a success.* ◆ *the **general** belief/consensus* ◆ *books of **general** interest* (= of interest to most people)

▸ **USUAL 2** [usually before noun] normal; usual: *There is one exception to this **general** principle.* ◆ *As a **general** rule* (= usually) *he did what he could to be helpful.* ◆ *This opinion is common among the **general** population* (= ordinary people).

▸ **NOT DETAILED 3** including the most important aspects of something; not exact or detailed **SYN** OVERALL: *I checked the weather forecast to get a **general** idea of what activities to plan.* ◆ *I know how it works **in general** terms.* ◆ *They gave a **general** description of the man.*

▸ **DIRECTION/AREA 4** the ~ **direction/area** approximately, but not exactly, the direction/area mentioned: *They fired in the **general** direction of the enemy.*

▸ **NOT LIMITED 5** not limited to a particular subject, use, or activity: *a **general** hospital* ◆ ***general** education* ◆ *We will at this stage keep the discussion fairly **general**.* **6** not limited to one part or aspect of a person or thing: *a **general** anesthetic* ◆ *The building was in a **general** state of disrepair.* ⊃ compare LOCAL *adj.* (2)

▸ **HIGHEST IN RANK 7** [only before noun] also **General** [after noun] highest in rank; chief: *the **general** manager* ◆ *the Inspector **General*** ⊃ see also ATTORNEY GENERAL, GOVERNOR GENERAL, SECRETARY GENERAL, SOLICITOR GENERAL, SURGEON GENERAL

IDM in **general 1** usually; mainly: *In **general**, Japanese cars are very reliable and breakdowns are rare.* ⊃ language bank at CONCLUSION, GENERALLY **2** as a whole: *This is a crucial year for your relationships **in general** and your love life in particular.*

● *noun* (*abbr.* Gen.) an officer of very high rank in the army and the U.S. AIR FORCE; the officer with the highest rank in the MARINES: *a four-star **general*** ◆ *General Tom Parker* ⊃ see also BRIGADIER GENERAL, MAJOR GENERAL

ˌGeneral Aˈmerican *noun* [U] the way people speak English in most parts of the U.S., not including New England, New York, and the South

ˌgeneral ˈcounsel *noun* the main lawyer who gives legal advice to a company

ˌgeneral deˈlivery *noun* [U] an arrangement in which a post office keeps a person's mail until they come to collect it

ˌgeneral eˈlection *noun* an election in which all the people of a state or country vote to choose a government

ˌgeneral ˈheadquarters *noun* [U] = GHQ

gen·er·al·ist /ˈdʒɛnərəlɪst; ˈdʒɛnrə-/ *noun* a person who has knowledge of several different subjects or activities **ANT** SPECIALIST

gen·er·al·i·ty /ˌdʒɛnəˈræləti/ *noun* (*pl.* gen·er·al·i·ties) **1** [C, usually pl.] a statement that discusses general principles or issues rather than details or particular examples: *to speak in broad **generalities*** ◆ *As usual, he confined his comments to **generalities**.* **2** the **generality** [sing.] (*formal*) most of a group of people or things: *This view is held by the **generality** of leading scholars.* **3** [U] (*formal*) the quality of being general rather than detailed or exact: *An account of such **generality** is of little value.*

gen·er·al·i·za·tion /ˌdʒɛnərələˈzeɪʃn; ˈdʒɛnrə-/ *noun* [C, U] a general statement that is based on only a few facts or examples; the act of making such statements: *a speech full of **broad/sweeping generalizations*** ◆ *to make **generalizations** about something* ◆ *Try to avoid **generalization**.*

gen·er·al·ize /ˈdʒɛnərəˌlaɪz; ˈdʒɛnrə-/ *verb* **1** [I] ~ (**from sth**) to use a particular set of facts or ideas in order to form an opinion that is considered valid for a different situation: *It would be foolish to **generalize** from a single example.* **2** [I] ~ (**about sth**) to make a general statement about something and not look at the details: *It is dangerous to **generalize** about the poor.* **3** [T, often passive] ~ **sth** (**to sth**) (*formal*) to apply a theory, idea, etc. to a wider group or situation than

the original one: *These conclusions cannot be **generalized** to the whole country.*

generalized /ˈdʒɛnərəˌlaɪzd; ˈdʒɛnrə-/ *adj.* [usually before noun] not detailed; not limited to one particular area: *a **generalized** discussion* ◆ *a **generalized** disease/rash* (= affecting the whole body)

ˌgeneral ˈknowledge *noun* [U] knowledge of facts about a lot of different subjects: *a **general knowledge** quiz*

gen·er·al·ly 🔊 /ˈdʒɛnərəli; ˈdʒɛnrəli/ *adv.*

1 by or to most people: *The plan was **generally** welcomed.* ◆ *It is now **generally** accepted that…* ◆ *The new drug will be **generally** available in January.* ◆ *He was a **generally** unpopular choice for captain.* **2** in most cases **SYN** AS A RULE: *I **generally** get up at six.* ◆ *The male is **generally** larger with a shorter beak.* **3** without discussing the details of something: *Let's talk just about investment **generally**.*

LANGUAGE BANK

generally

ways of saying "in general"

- Women **generally** earn less than men.
- **Generally speaking**, jobs traditionally done by women are paid at a lower rate than those traditionally done by men.
- **In general/By and large**, women do not earn as much as men.
- Certain jobs, like nursing and cleaning, are still **mainly** carried out by women.
- Senior management posts are held **predominantly** by men.
- Most senior management posts **tend to** be held by men.
- Women are, **for the most part**, still paid less than men.
- Economic and social factors are, **to a large extent**, responsible for women being concentrated in low-paid jobs.

⊃ Language Banks at CONCLUSION, EXCEPT, SIMILARLY

ˌgeneral ˈpractice *noun* [U, C] **1** the work of a doctor who treats people in the community rather than at a hospital and who is not a specialist in one particular area of medicine; a place where a doctor like this works: *to be in **general practice*** ◆ *She runs a **general practice** in Milwaukee.* **2** the work of a lawyer who deals with all kinds of legal cases and who is not a specialist in one particular area of law; the place where a lawyer like this works

ˌgeneral pracˈtitioner (*abbr.* G.P.) (also ˌfamily pracˈtitioner) (also *informal* ˌfamily ˈdoctor) *noun* a doctor who is trained in general medicine and who treats patients in a local community rather than at a hospital

the ˌgeneral ˈpublic *noun* ordinary people who are not members of a particular group or organization: *At that time, the **general public** was not aware of the health risks.* ◆ *The exhibition is not open to the **general public**.*

ˌgeneral-ˈpurpose *adj.* [only before noun] having a wide range of different uses: *a **general-purpose** farm vehicle*

gen·er·al·ship /ˈdʒɛnərəlˌʃɪp; ˈdʒɛnrəl-/ *noun* [U] the skill or practice of leading an army during a battle

ˌgeneral ˈstaff often the general staff *noun* [sing.] officers who advise a military leader and help to plan a military operation ⊃ note at STAFF

ˌgeneral ˈstore *noun* a store that sells a wide variety of goods, especially one in a small town

ˌgeneral ˈstrike *noun* a period of time when most or all of the workers in a country go on strike

gen·er·ate 🔊 **AWL** /ˈdʒɛnəˌreɪt/ *verb* ~ **sth** to produce or create something: *to **generate** electricity/heat/power* ◆ *to **generate** income/profit* ◆ *We need someone to **generate** new ideas.* ◆ *The proposal has **generated** a lot of interest.* ⊃ thesaurus box at MAKE

---

t tea   ṱ butter   d did   k cat   g got   tʃ chin   dʒ June   f fall

gen·er·a·tion 🔑 **AWL** /ˌdʒɛnəˈreɪʃn/ noun
1 [C] all the people who were born at about the same time: *the younger/older generation* ◆ *My generation has grown up without the experience of a world war.* ◆ *I often wonder what future generations will make of our efforts.* **2** [C] the average time in which children grow up, become adults, and have children of their own (usually considered to be about 30 years): *a generation ago* ◆ *My family has lived in this house for generations.* **3** [C, U] a single stage in the history of a family: *stories passed down from generation to generation* ◆ *a first-/second-generation American* (= a person whose family has lived in America for one/two generations) **4** [C, usually sing.] a group of people of similar age involved in a particular activity: *She has inspired a whole generation of fashion school graduates.* **5** [C, usually sing.] a stage in the development of a product, usually a technical one: *fifth-generation computing* ◆ *a new generation of vehicle* **6** [U] the production of something, especially electricity, heat, etc.: *the generation of electricity* ◆ *methods of income generation*

gen·er·a·tion·al /ˌdʒɛnəˈreɪʃənl/ adj. [usually before noun] connected with a particular generation or with the relationship between different generations: *generational conflict*

the gener'ation ˌgap noun [sing.] the difference in attitude or behavior between younger and older people that causes a lack of understanding: *a movie that is sure to bridge the generation gap*

Generˌation 'X noun [U] the group of people who were born between the early 1960s and the middle of the 1970s, who seemed when they were young to lack a sense of direction in life and to feel that they had no part to play in society

gen·er·a·tive /ˈdʒɛnərətɪv/ adj. (formal) that can produce something: *generative processes*

ˌgenerative 'grammar noun [C, U] (linguistics) a type of grammar that describes a language by giving a set of rules that can be used to produce all the possible sentences in that language

gen·er·a·tor /ˈdʒɛnəˌreɪtər/ noun **1** a machine for producing electricity: *The factory's emergency generators were used during the power cut.* ◆ *a wind generator* (= a machine that uses the power of the wind to produce electricity) **2** a machine for producing a particular substance: *The museum uses smells and smoke generators to create atmosphere.* ◆ (figurative) *The company is a major generator of jobs.*

ge·ner·ic /dʒəˈnɛrɪk/ adj. **1** shared by, including, or typical of a whole group of things; not specific: *"Broadband" is a generic term for any high-speed connection to the Internet.* **2** (of a product, especially a drug) not using the name of the company that made it: *The doctor offered me a choice of a branded or a generic drug.* ▶ **ge·ner·i·cally** /-kli/ adv.

gen·er·os·i·ty /ˌdʒɛnəˈrɑsəti/ noun [U, sing.] **~ (to/toward sb)** the fact of being generous (= willing to give someone money, gifts, time, or kindness freely): *He treated them with generosity and thoughtfulness.*

gen·er·ous 🔑 /ˈdʒɛnərəs/ adj. (approving)
1 giving or willing to give freely; given freely: *a generous benefactor* ◆ **~ (with sth)** *to be generous with your time* ◆ *to be generous in giving help* ◆ *a generous gift/offer* ◆ *It was generous of him to offer to pay for us both.* **ANT** STINGY **2** more than is necessary; large **SYN** LAVISH: *a generous helping of meat* ◆ *The car has a generous amount of space.* **3** kind in the way you treat people; willing to see what is good about someone or something: *a generous mind* ◆ *He wrote a very generous assessment of my work.* ▶ **gen·er·ous·ly** adv.: *Please give generously.* ◆ *a dress that is generously cut* (= uses plenty of material)

gen·e·sis /ˈdʒɛnəsəs/ noun [sing.] (formal) the beginning or origin of something

ˈgene ˌtherapy noun [U] (medical) a treatment in which normal GENES are put into cells to replace ones that are missing or not normal

ge·net·ic /dʒəˈnɛtɪk/ adj. connected with GENES (= the units in the cells of a living thing that control its physical characteristics) or GENETICS (= the study of genes): *genetic and environmental factors* ◆ *genetic abnormalities* ▶ **ge·net·i·cally** /-kli/ adv.: *genetically engineered/determined/transmitted*

geˌnetically 'modified adj. (abbr. **GM**) (of a plant, etc.) having had its genetic structure changed artificially, so that it will produce more fruit or not be affected by disease: *genetically modified foods* (= made from plants that have been changed in this way) ⊃ collocations at FARMING

geˌnetic 'code noun the arrangement of GENES that controls how each living thing will develop

geˌnetic engiˈneering noun [U] the science of changing how a living creature or plant develops by changing the information in its GENES

geˌnetic 'fingerprinting (also ˌDNA 'fingerprinting) noun [U] the method of finding the particular pattern of GENES in an individual person, particularly to identify someone or find out if someone has committed a crime ▶ **geˌnetic 'fingerprint** noun

ge·net·i·cist /dʒəˈnɛtəsɪst/ noun a scientist who studies genetics

ge·net·ics /dʒəˈnɛtɪks/ noun [U] the scientific study of the ways in which different characteristics are passed from each generation of living things to the next

Ge·ne·va Con·ven·tion /dʒəˌnivə kənˈvɛnʃn/ noun [sing.] an international agreement that states how prisoners of war should be treated

ge·ni·al /ˈdʒinyəl; ˈdʒiniəl/ adj. friendly and cheerful **SYN** AFFABLE: *a genial person* ◆ *a genial smile* ▶ **ge·ni·al·i·ty** /ˌdʒiniˈæləti/ noun [U]: *an atmosphere of warmth and geniality* **ge·ni·al·ly** /ˈdʒinyəli/ adv.: *to smile genially*

ge·nie /ˈdʒini/ noun (pl. ge·nies or ge·ni·i /ˈdʒiniˌaɪ/) (in Arabian stories) a spirit with magic powers, especially one that lives in a bottle or a lamp **SYN** DJINN

gen·i·tal /ˈdʒɛnətl/ adj. [only before noun] connected with the outer sexual organs of a person or an animal: *the genital area* ◆ *genital infections*

gen·i·tals /ˈdʒɛnətlz/ (also gen·i·ta·li·a /ˌdʒɛnəˈteɪlyə/) noun [pl.] a person's sex organs that are outside their body

gen·i·tive /ˈdʒɛnətɪv/ noun (grammar) (in some languages) the special form of a noun, a pronoun, or an adjective that is used to show possession or close connection between two things ⊃ compare ABLATIVE, ACCUSATIVE, DATIVE, NOMINATIVE, POSSESSIVE, VOCATIVE ▶ **gen·i·tive** adj.

gen·ius /ˈdʒinyəs/ noun (pl. gen·ius·es) **1** [U] unusually great intelligence, skill, or artistic ability: *the genius of Shakespeare* ◆ *a statesman of genius* ◆ *Her idea was a stroke of genius.* **2** [C] a person who is unusually intelligent or artistic, or who has a very high level of skill, especially in one area: *a mathematical/comic, etc. genius* ◆ *He's a genius at organizing people.* ◆ *You don't have to be a genius to see that they are in love!* **3** [sing.] **~ for sth/for doing sth** a special skill or ability: *He had a genius for making people feel at home.*

gen·o·cide /ˈdʒɛnəˌsaɪd/ noun [U] the murder of a whole race or group of people ⊃ collocations at WAR ▶ **gen·o·cid·al** /ˌdʒɛnəˈsaɪdl/ adj.

ge·nome /ˈdʒinoʊm/ noun (biology) the complete set of GENES in a cell or living thing: *the human genome*

gen·o·type /ˈdʒinəˌtaɪp/ noun (biology) the combination of GENES that a particular living thing carries, some of which may not be noticed from its appearance ⊃ compare PHENOTYPE

gen·re /ˈʒɑnrə/ noun (formal) a particular type or style of literature, art, film, or music that you can recognize because of its special features

ˈgenre ˌpainting noun [U, C] (art) a style of painting showing scenes from ordinary life that is associated with 17th century Dutch and Flemish artists; a painting done in this style

gent /dʒɛnt/ *noun* (*old-fashioned*, *informal*) a man; a gentleman: *This way please, ladies and gents!*

gen·teel /dʒɛnˈtil/ *adj.* **1** (of people and their way of life) quiet and polite, often in an exaggerated way; from, or pretending to be from, a high social class: *a genteel manner* ◆ *Her genteel accent irritated me.* ◆ *He lived in genteel poverty* (= trying to keep the style of a high social class, but with little money). **2** (of places) quiet and old-fashioned and perhaps slightly boring ▶ **gen·teel·ly** /-ˈtilli/ *adv.*

gen·tian /ˈdʒɛnʃn/ *noun* [C, U] a small plant with bright blue flowers that grows in mountain areas

gen·tile /ˈdʒɛntaɪl/ also **Gentile** *noun* a person who is not Jewish ◆ **gen·tile** also **Gentile** *adj.* [only before noun]

gen·til·i·ty /dʒɛnˈtɪləti/ *noun* [U] (*formal*) **1** very good manners and behavior; the fact of belonging to a high social class: *He took her hand with discreet gentility.* ◆ *She thinks expensive clothes are a mark of gentility.* **2** the fact of being quiet and old-fashioned: *the faded gentility of the town*

gen·tle 🔑 /ˈdʒɛntl/ *adj.* (**gen·tler** /ˈdʒɛntlər/, **gen·tlest** /ˈdʒɛntləst/)
1 calm and kind; doing things in a quiet and careful way: *a quiet and gentle man* ◆ *a gentle voice/laugh/touch* ◆ *She was the gentlest of nurses.* ◆ *He lived in a gentler age than ours.* ◆ *Be gentle with her!* ◆ *She agreed to come, after a little gentle persuasion.* ◆ *He looks scary but he's really a gentle giant.* **2** (of weather, temperature, etc.) not strong or extreme: *a gentle breeze* ◆ *the gentle swell of the ocean* ◆ *Cook over a gentle heat.* **3** having only a small effect; not strong or violent: *We went for a gentle stroll.* ◆ *a little gentle exercise* ◆ *This soap is very gentle on the hands.* **4** not steep or sharp: *a gentle slope/curve/angle* ⊃ see also GENTLY ▶ **gen·tle·ness** *noun* [U]

gent·le·folk /ˈdʒɛntlˌfoʊk/ *noun* [pl.] (*old-fashioned*) (in the past) people belonging to respected families of the higher social classes

gent·le·man 🔑 /ˈdʒɛntlmən/ *noun* (*pl.* **gent·le·men** /-mən/)
1 [C] a man who is polite and well educated, who has excellent manners and always behaves well: *Thank you— you're a real gentleman.* ◆ *He's no gentleman!* ⊃ compare LADY **2** [C, usually pl.] (*formal*) used to address or refer to a man, especially someone you do not know: *Ladies and gentlemen! Can I have your attention, please?* ◆ *Gentlemen of the jury! Can I help you, gentlemen?* ◆ *There's a gentleman to see you.* **HELP** In more informal speech, you could say: *Can I help you?* ◆ *There's someone to see you.* **3** used to address or refer to a male member of a LEGISLATURE, for example the House of Representatives **4** (*old-fashioned*) a man from a high social class, especially one who does not need to work: *a country gentleman* ◆ *a gentleman farmer* (= one who owns a farm for pleasure, not as his main job) **IDM** see LEISURE

gen·tle·man·ly /ˈdʒɛntlmənli/ *adj.* (*approving*) behaving very well and showing very good manners; like a gentleman: *gentlemanly behavior* ◆ *So far, the election campaign has been very gentlemanly.*

gentleman's aˈgreement (also ˌgentlemen's aˈgreement) *noun* an agreement made between people who trust each other, that is not written down and that has no legal force

gen·tle·wom·an /ˈdʒɛntlˌwʊmən/ *noun* (*pl.* **gen·tle·wom·en** /-ˌwɪmən/) **1** (*old use*) a woman who belongs to a high social class; a woman who is well educated and has excellent manners **2** used to address or refer to a female member of a LEGISLATURE, for example the House of Representatives

gen·tly 🔑 /ˈdʒɛntli/ *adv.*
in a gentle way: *She held the baby gently.* ◆ *"You miss them, don't you?" he asked gently.* ◆ *Simmer the soup gently for 30 minutes.* ◆ *Massage the area gently but firmly.* ◆ *leaves moving gently in the breeze* ◆ *The path ran gently down to the ocean.*

gen·tri·fy /ˈdʒɛntrəˌfaɪ/ *verb* (**gen·tri·fies, gen·tri·fying,**

gen·tri·fied, gen·tri·fied) [usually passive] **~ sth/sb** to change an area, a person, etc. so that they are suitable for, or can mix with, people of a higher social class than before: *Old working-class areas of the city are being gentrified.* ▶ **gen·tri·fi·ca·tion** /ˌdʒɛntrəfəˈkeɪʃn/ *noun* [U]

gen·try /ˈdʒɛntri/ *noun* [pl.] usually **the gentry** (*old-fashioned*) people belonging to a high social class: *the local gentry* ◆ *the landed gentry* (= those who own a lot of land)

gen·u·flect /ˈdʒɛnyəˌflɛkt/ *verb* (*formal*) **1** [I] to move your body into a lower position by bending one or both knees, as a sign of respect during worship in a church **2** [I] **~ (to sth)** (*disapproving*) to show too much respect to someone or something ▶ **gen·u·flec·tion** /ˌdʒɛnyəˈflɛkʃn/ *noun* [C, U]

gen·u·ine 🔑 /ˈdʒɛnyuən/ *adj.*
1 real; exactly what it appears to be; not artificial **SYN** AUTHENTIC: *Is the painting a genuine Picasso?* ◆ *Fake designer watches are sold at a fraction of the price of the genuine article.* ◆ *Only genuine refugees can apply for asylum.* **2** sincere and honest; that can be trusted: *He made a genuine attempt to improve conditions.* ◆ *genuine concern for others* ◆ *a very genuine person* ▶ **gen·u·ine·ly** *adv.*: *genuinely sorry* **gen·u·ine·ness** *noun* [U]

ge·nus /ˈdʒinəs/ *noun* (*pl.* **gen·er·a** /ˈdʒɛnərə/) (*biology*) a group into which animals, plants, etc. that have similar characteristics are divided, smaller than a family and larger than a SPECIES ⊃ compare CLASS, KINGDOM, ORDER, PHYLUM ⊃ see also GENERIC

geo- /ˈdʒioʊ/ *combining form* (in nouns, adjectives, and adverbs) of the earth: *geochemical* ◆ *geoscience*

ge·o·cen·tric /ˌdʒioʊˈsɛntrɪk/ *adj.* (*technical*) with the earth as the center

ge·o·des·ic /ˌdʒiəˈdɛsɪk; -ˈdisɪk/ *adj.* (*technical*) relating to the shortest possible line between two points on a curved surface

ˌgeo·desic ˈdome *noun* (*architecture*) a DOME that is built from panels whose edges form geodesic lines ⊃ picture at ARCHITECTURE

ge·og·ra·pher /dʒiˈɑgrəfər/ *noun* a person who studies geography; an expert in geography

ge·og·ra·phy 🔑 /dʒiˈɑgrəfi/ *noun*
1 [U] the scientific study of the earth's surface, physical features, divisions, products, population, etc.: *human/physical/economic/social geography* ◆ *a geography class/department/teacher/textbook* ◆ *a degree in geography* **2** [sing.] the way in which the physical features of a place are arranged: *the geography of New York City* ◆ *Kim knew the geography of the building and strode along the corridor.* **3** [sing.] the way in which a particular aspect of life or society is influenced by geography or varies according to geography: *The geography of poverty and the geography of voting are connected.* ▶ **ge·o·graph·ic** /ˌdʒiəˈgræfik/ (*CanE* usually **ge·o·graph·i·cal** /-ˈgræfikl/) *adj.*: *The survey covers a wide geographic area.* ◆ *The importance of the town is due to its geographic location.* **ge·o·graph·i·cally** /-ˈgræfikli/ *adv.*: *geographically remote areas*

ge·ol·o·gist /dʒiˈɑlədʒɪst/ *noun* a scientist who studies geology

ge·ol·o·gy /dʒiˈɑlədʒi/ *noun* **1** [U] the scientific study of the earth, including the origin and history of the rocks and soil of which the earth is made **2** [sing.] the origin and history of the rocks and soil of a particular area: *the geology of the Rocky Mountains* ▶ **ge·o·log·i·cal** /ˌdʒiəˈlɑdʒɪkl/ (also **ge·o·log·ic** /-ˈlɑdʒɪk/) *adj.*: *a geological survey* **ge·o·log·i·cally** /-ˈlɑdʒɪkli/ *adv.*

ge·o·mag·net·ism /ˌdʒioʊˈmægnəˌtɪzəm/ *noun* [U] (*geology*) the study of the MAGNETIC characteristics of the earth ▶ **ge·o·mag·net·ic** /ˌdʒioʊmægˈnɛtɪk/ *adj.*

ge·o·man·cy /ˈdʒiəˌmænsi/ *noun* [U] **1** the art of arranging buildings and areas in a good or lucky position **2** a method of saying what will happen in the future using patterns on the ground

h **hat**   m **man**   n **no**   ŋ **sing**   1 **leg**   r **red**   y **yes**   w **wet**

ge·o·met·ric /ˌdʒiəˈmɛtrɪk/ (also *less frequent* ge·o·met·ri·cal /ˌdʒiəˈmɛtrɪkl/) *adj.* of GEOMETRY; of or like the lines, shapes, etc. used in GEOMETRY, especially because of having regular shapes or lines: *a geometric design* ▶ ge·o·met·ri·cal·ly /-kli/ *adv.*

ˌ**geometric ˈmean** *noun* the central number in a geometric progression

ˌ**geometric proˈgression** (also ˌgeometric ˈseries) *noun* a series of numbers in which each is multiplied or divided by a fixed number to produce the next, for example 1, 3, 9, 27, 81 ⊃ compare ARITHMETIC PROGRESSION

ge·om·e·try /dʒiˈɑmətri/ *noun* **1** [U] the branch of mathematics that deals with the measurements and relationships of lines, angles, surfaces, and solids **2** [sing.] the measurements and relationships of lines, angles, etc. in a particular object or shape: *the geometry of a spiderweb*

ge·o·phys·ics /ˌdʒiouˈfɪzɪks/ *noun* [U] the scientific study of the earth's atmosphere, oceans, and climate ▶ ge·o·phys·i·cal /-ˈfɪzɪkl/ *adj.*: *geophysical data* ge·o·phys·i·cist /-ˈfɪzəsɪst/ *noun*

ge·o·pol·i·tics /ˌdʒiouˈpɑlətɪks/ *noun* [U] the political relations between countries and groups of countries in the world; the study of these relations ▶ ge·o·po·lit·i·cal /ˌdʒioupəˈlɪtɪkl/ *adj.*

geor·gette /dʒɔrˈdʒɛt/ *noun* [U] a type of thin silk or cotton cloth, used for making clothes

Geor·gian /ˈdʒɔrdʒən/ *adj.* (especially ARCHITECTURE and furniture) from the time of the British kings George I–IV (1714–1830): *a Georgian house*

ge·o·ther·mal /ˌdʒiouˈθɜrml/ *adj.* (*geology*) connected with the natural heat of rock deep in the ground: *geothermal energy*

ge·ra·ni·um /dʒəˈreɪniəm/ *noun* a garden plant with a mass of red, pink, or white flowers on the end of each STEM

ger·bil /ˈdʒɜrbl/ *noun* a small desert animal like a mouse, that is often kept as a pet

ger·i·at·ric /ˌdʒɛriˈætrɪk; ˌdʒɪr-/ *noun* **1** ger·i·at·rics [U] the branch of medicine concerned with the diseases and care of old people **2** [C] (*informal*, *offensive*) an old person, especially one with poor physical or mental health: *I'm not a geriatric yet, you know!* ▶ ger·i·at·ric *adj.*: *geriatric patients* ♦ *a geriatric vehicle* (= old and in bad condition)

ger·i·a·tri·cian /ˌdʒɛriəˈtrɪʃn; ˌdʒɪr-/ *noun* a doctor who studies and treats the diseases of old people

germ /dʒɜrm/ *noun* **1** [C, usually pl.] a very small living thing that can cause infection and disease: *Disinfectant kills germs.* ♦ *Dirty hands can be a breeding ground for germs.* **2** [sing.] **~ of sth** an early stage of the development of something: *Here was the germ of a brilliant idea.* **3** [C] (*biology*) the part of a plant or an animal that can develop into a new one ⊃ see also WHEAT GERM

Ger·man /ˈdʒɜrmən/ *adj.*, *noun*
● *adj.* from or connected with Germany
● *noun* **1** [C] a person from Germany **2** [U] the language of Germany, Austria, and parts of Switzerland

ger·mane /dʒɜrˈmeɪn/ *adj.* [not usually before noun] **~ (to sth)** (*formal*) (of ideas, remarks, etc.) connected with something in an important or appropriate way **SYN** RELEVANT: *remarks that are germane to the discussion*

Ger·man·ic /dʒərˈmænɪk/ *adj.* **1** connected with or considered typical of Germany or its people: *She had an almost Germanic regard for order.* **2** connected with the language family that includes German, English, Dutch, and Swedish among others

ger·ma·ni·um /dʒərˈmeɪniəm/ *noun* [U] (*symb.* **Ge**) a chemical element. Germanium is a shiny gray element that is a METALLOID (= is similar to a metal).

ˌ**German ˈmeasles** (also ru·bel·la) *noun* [U] a mild infectious disease that causes a sore throat and red spots all over the body. It can seriously affect babies born to women who catch it soon after they become pregnant.

ˌ**German ˈshepherd** *noun* a large dog, often trained to help the police, to guard buildings, or to help blind people find their way

ger·mi·cide /ˈdʒɜrməˌsaɪd/ *noun* [C, U] a substance that destroys bacteria, etc. ▶ ger·mi·cid·al /ˌdʒɜrməˈsaɪdl/ *adj.*

ger·mi·nate /ˈdʒɜrməˌneɪt/ *verb* [I, T] **~ (sth)** when the seed of a plant **germinates** or **is germinated**, it starts to grow: (*figurative*) *An idea for a novel began to germinate in her mind.* ▶ ger·mi·na·tion /ˌdʒɜrməˈneɪʃn/ *noun* [U]

ˌ**germ ˈwarfare** *noun* [U] = BIOLOGICAL WARFARE

ger·on·toc·ra·cy /ˌdʒɛrənˈtɑkrəsi/ *noun* (*pl.* ger·on·toc·ra·cies) [C, U] a state, society, or group governed by old people; government by old people ▶ ge·ron·to·crat·ic /dʒəˌrɑntəˈkrætɪk/ *adj.*

ger·on·tol·o·gist /ˌdʒɛrənˈtɑlədʒɪst/ *noun* a person who studies the process of people growing old

ger·on·tol·o·gy /ˌdʒɛrənˈtɑlədʒi/ *noun* [U] the scientific study of OLD AGE and the process of growing old

ger·ry·man·der /ˈdʒɛriˌmændər/ *verb* **~ (sth)** (*disapproving*) to change the size and borders of an area for voting in order to give an unfair advantage to one party or group in an election ▶ ger·ry·man·der·ing *noun* [U]

ger·und /ˈdʒɛrənd/ *noun* (*grammar*) a noun in the form of the present participle of a verb (that is, ending in *-ing*) for example *traveling* in the sentence *I preferred traveling alone.*

ge·stalt /ɡəˈʃtɑlt; -ˈʃtɔlt/ *noun* (from *German*, *psychology*) a set of things, such as a person's thoughts or experiences, that is considered as a single system that is different from the individual thoughts, experiences, etc. within it

ges·tate /ˈdʒɛsteɪt/ *verb* **~ sth** (*biology* or *medical*) to carry a young human or animal inside the WOMB until it is born

ges·ta·tion /dʒɛˈsteɪʃn/ *noun* **1** [U, sing.] the time that the young of a person or an animal develops inside its mother's body until it is born; the process of developing inside the mother's body: *a baby born at 38 weeks' gestation* ♦ *The **gestation period** of a horse is about eleven months.* **2** [U] (*formal*) the process by which an idea or a plan develops **SYN** DEVELOPMENT

ges·tic·u·late /dʒɛˈstɪkyəˌleɪt/ *verb* [I] to move your hands and arms about in order to attract attention or make someone understand what you are saying: *He gesticulated wildly at the clock.* ▶ ges·tic·u·la·tion /dʒɛˌstɪkyəˈleɪʃn/ *noun* [C, U]: *wild/frantic gesticulations*

ges·ture /ˈdʒɛstʃər; ˈdʒɛʃtʃər/ *noun*, *verb*
● *noun* **1** [C, U] a movement that you make with your hands, your head, or your face to show a particular meaning: *He made a rude gesture at the driver of the other car.* ♦ *She finished what she had to say with a gesture of despair.* ♦ *They communicated entirely by gesture.* **2** [C] something that you do or say to show a particular feeling or intention: *They sent some flowers as a gesture of sympathy to the parents of the child.* ♦ *It was a nice gesture* (= it was kind) *to invite his wife too.* ♦ *We do not accept responsibility but we will refund the money as a **gesture of goodwill**.* ♦ *The mayor has made a gesture toward public opinion* (= has tried to do something that the public will like). ⊃ note at ACTION
● *verb* [I, T] to move your hands, head, face, etc. as a way of expressing what you mean or want: (+ adv./prep.) *"I see you read a lot," he said, gesturing at the wall of books.* ♦ **~ to sb (to do sth)** | **~ for sb to do sth** *She gestured for them to come in.* ♦ **~ (to sb) (that)…** *He gestured (to me) that it was time to go.* ♦ *They gestured that I should follow.*

ge·sund·heit /ɡəˈzʊnthaɪt/ *exclamation* (from *German*) used when someone has SNEEZED to wish them good health

get /ɡɛt/ *verb* (get·ting, got /ɡɑt/, got or got·ten /ˈɡɑtn/)

HELP The past participle **gotten** is almost always used.

> RECEIVE/OBTAIN **1** [T, no passive] **~ sth** to receive something: *I got a letter from Dave this morning.* ♦ *What* (= What presents) *did you get for your birthday?* ♦ *He gets* (= earns) *about $40,000 a year.* ♦ *My car gets 40 miles to the gallon* (= uses one

gallon of gas to travel 40 miles). ◆ *This room gets very little sunshine.* ◆ *I got a shock when I saw the bill.* ◆ *I get the impression that he is bored with his job.* **2** [T, no passive] to obtain something: ~ **sth** *Where did you get* (= buy) *that skirt?* ◆ *Were you able to get tickets for the concert?* ◆ *She opened the door wider to get a better look.* ◆ *Try to get some sleep.* ◆ *He just got a new job.* ◆ ~ **sth for sb** *Did you get a present for your mother?* ◆ ~ **sb/yourself sth** *Did you get your mother a present?* ◆ *Why don't you get yourself a car?* **3** [T, no passive] ~ **sth (for sth)** to obtain or receive an amount of money by selling something: *How much did you get for your car?*

▷ **BRING 4** [T] to go to a place and bring someone or something back: ~ **sb/sth** *Quick— go get a cloth!* ◆ *Somebody get a doctor!* ◆ *I have to go get my mother from the airport* (= pick her up). ◆ ~ **sth for sb** *Get a drink for John.* ◆ ~ **sb/yourself sth** *Get John a drink.*

▷ **PUNISHMENT 5** [T, no passive] ~ **sth** to receive something as a punishment: *He got ten years* (= was sent to prison for ten years) *for armed robbery.*

▷ **BROADCASTS 6** [T, no passive] ~ **sth** to receive broadcasts from a particular television or radio station: *We can't get the Sci-Fi Channel in our area.*

▷ **BUY 7** [T, no passive] ~ **sth** to buy something, for example a newspaper or magazine, regularly: *Which newspaper do you get?*

▷ **GRADE 8** [T, no passive] ~ **sth** to achieve or be given a particular grade in a course or an exam: *He got a "C" in Chemistry and a "B" in English.*

▷ **ILLNESS 9** [T, no passive] ~ **sth** to become infected with an illness; to suffer from a pain, etc.: *I got this cold from you!* ◆ *She gets* (= often suffers from) *really bad headaches.*

▷ **CONTACT 10** [T, no passive] ~ **sb** to be connected with someone by telephone: *I wanted to speak to the manager but I got his assistant instead.*

▷ **STATE/CONDITION 11** *linking verb* to reach a particular state or condition; to make someone or something/yourself reach a particular state or condition: **+ adj.** *to get angry/ bored/hungry/fat* ◆ *You'll get used to the climate here.* ◆ *We should go; it's getting late.* ◆ *to get dressed/undressed* (= to put your clothes on/take your clothes off) ◆ *They plan to get married in the summer.* ◆ *She's upstairs getting ready.* ◆ *I wouldn't go there alone; you might get* (= be) *mugged.* ◆ *My car got* (= was) *stolen over the weekend.* ◆ ~ **sb/sth + adj.** *Don't get your dress dirty!* ◆ *He got his fingers caught in the door.* ◆ *She got the kids ready for school.* ⊃ *note at* BECOME **12** [I] ~ **to do sth** to reach the point at which you feel, know, are, etc. something: *After a while, you get to realize that these things don't matter.* ◆ *You'll like her once you get to know her.* ◆ *His drinking is getting to be a problem.* ◆ *She's getting to be an old lady now.*

▷ **MAKE/PERSUADE 13** [T] to make, persuade, etc. someone or something to do something: ~ **sb/sth to do sth** *I couldn't get the car to start this morning.* ◆ *He got his sister to help him with his homework.* ◆ *You'll never get him to understand.* ◆ ~ **sb/ sth doing sth** *Can you really get that old car going again?* ◆ *It's not hard to get him talking—the problem is stopping him!*

▷ **GET SOMETHING DONE 14** [T] ~ **sth done** to cause something to happen or be done: *I need to get my hair cut.* ◆ *I'll never get all this work finished.*

▷ **START 15** [T] ~ **doing sth** to start doing something: *I got talking to her.* ◆ *We need to get going soon.*

▷ **OPPORTUNITY 16** [I] ~ **to do sth** (*informal*) to have the opportunity to do something: *He got to try out all the new software.* ◆ *It's not fair—I never get to go first.*

▷ **ARRIVE 17** [I] **+ adv./prep.** to arrive at or reach a place or point: *We got to San Diego at 7 o'clock.* ◆ *You got in very late last night.* ◆ *What time did you get here?* ◆ *I haven't gotten very far with the book I'm reading.*

▷ **MOVE/TRAVEL 18** [I, T] to move to or from a particular place or in a particular direction, sometimes with difficulty; to make someone or something do this: **+ adv./prep.** *The bridge was destroyed so we couldn't get across the river.* ◆ *She got into bed.* ◆ *He got down from the ladder.* ◆ *We didn't get* (= go) *to bed until 3 a.m.* ◆ *Where do we get on the bus?* ◆ *I'm getting off* (= leaving the train) *at the next station.* ◆ *We should be getting home; it's past midnight.* ◆ ~ **sb/sth + adv./prep.** *The general*

had to get his troops across the river. ◆ *We couldn't get the piano through the door.* ◆ *We'd better call a taxi and get you home.* ◆ *I can't get the lid off.* **19** [T, no passive] ~ **sth** to use a bus, taxi, plane, etc.: *We're going to be late—let's get a taxi.* ◆ *I usually get the bus to work.*

▷ **MEAL 20** [T] to prepare a meal: ~ **sth** *Who's getting dinner?* ◆ ~ **sth for sb/yourself** *I should go home and get lunch for the kids.* ◆ ~ **sb/yourself sth** *I should go home and get the kids their lunch.*

▷ **TELEPHONE/DOOR 21** [T] ~ **sth** (*informal*) to answer the telephone or a door when someone calls, knocks, etc.: *Will you get the phone?*

▷ **CATCH/HIT 22** [T] ~ **sb** to catch or take hold of someone, especially in order to harm or punish them: *He was on the run for a week before the police got him.* ◆ *to get someone by the arm/wrist/throat* ◆ *She fell overboard and the sharks got her.* ◆ *He thinks everybody is out to get him* (= trying to harm him). ◆ (*informal*) *I'll get you for that!* **23** [T] ~ **sb + adv./prep.** to hit or wound someone: *The bullet got him in the neck.*

▷ **UNDERSTAND 24** [T, no passive] ~ **sb/sth** (*informal*) to understand someone or something: *I don't get you.* ◆ *She didn't get the joke.* ◆ *I don't get it—why would she do a thing like that?* ◆ *I got the message—you don't want me to come.* ⊃ thesaurus box at UNDERSTAND

▷ **HAPPEN/EXIST 25** [T, no passive] ~ **sth** (*informal*) used to say that something happens or exists: *You get* (= There are) *all these kids hanging around in the street.* ◆ *They still get cases of typhoid there.*

▷ **CONFUSE/ANNOY 26** [T, no passive] ~ **sb** (*informal*) to make someone feel confused because they do not understand something **SYN** PUZZLE: *"What's the capital of Bulgaria?" "You've got me there!"* (= I don't know). **27** [T, no passive] ~ **sb** (*informal*) to annoy someone: *What gets me is having to do the same thing all day long.* **HELP** Get is one of the most common words in English, but some people try to avoid it in formal writing.

IDM Most idioms containing **get** are at the entries for the nouns and adjectives in the idioms. For example, **get someone's goat** is at **goat**. **be getting on** (*informal*) (of a person) to be becoming old **can't get over sth** (*informal*) used to say that you are shocked, surprised, amused, etc. by something: *I can't get over how rude she was.* **get away from it all** (*informal*) to have a short vacation in a place where you can relax **get it on (with sb)** (*slang*) to have sex with someone **get it** (also **catch hell**) (*informal*) to be punished or spoken to angrily about something: *If Mom catches you, you'll really get it.* **get sb going** (*informal*) to make someone angry, worried, or excited **get sb nowhere/not get sb anywhere** to not help someone make progress or succeed: *This line of investigation is getting us nowhere.* ◆ *Being rude to me won't get you anywhere.* **get somewhere/anywhere/nowhere** to make some progress/no progress: *After six months of work on the project, I finally feel like I'm getting somewhere.* ◆ *I don't seem to be getting anywhere with this letter.* **get there** to achieve your aim or complete a task: *I'm sure you'll get there in the end.* ◆ *It's not perfect, but we're getting there* (= making progress). **get this!** (*informal*) used to say that you are going to tell someone something that they will find surprising or interesting: *OK, get this guys—there are only two left!* **how selfish, stupid, ungrateful, etc. can you get?** (*informal*) used to express surprise or disapproval that someone has been so stupid, etc. **there's no getting away from sth | you can't get away from sth** you have to admit that something unpleasant is true **what are you, was he, etc. getting at?** (*informal*) used to ask, especially in an angry way, what someone is/was suggesting: *I'm partly to blame? What exactly are you getting at?* **what has gotten into sb?** (*informal*) used to say that someone has suddenly started to behave in a strange or different way: *What's gotten into Alex? He never used to worry like that.*

PHR V ,get a'cross (to sb) | ,get sth↔a'cross (to sb) to be communicated or understood; to succeed in communicating something: *Your meaning didn't really get across.* ◆ *He's not very good at getting his ideas across.*

,get a'head (of sb) to make progress (further than others

have done): *She wants to get ahead in her career.* ♦ *He soon got ahead of the others in his class.*

get a'long 1 (usually used in the progressive tenses) to leave a place: *It's late — we should be getting along.* **2** to manage or survive: *We can get along perfectly well without her.* ♦ *I just can't get along without an assistant.* **3** used to talk or ask about how well someone is doing in a particular situation: *He's getting along very well at school.* ♦ *How did you get along at the interview?*

get a'long with sb | **get a'long (together)** to have a friendly relationship with someone: *She never really got along with her sister.* ♦ *She and her sister have never really gotten along.* ♦ *We get along just fine together.*

get a'round to move from place to place or from person to person: *She gets around with the help of a cane.* ♦ *News soon got around that he had resigned.* **get a'round sb** to persuade someone to agree or to do what you want, usually by doing nice things for them: *She knows how to get around her dad.* **get a'round sth** to deal with a problem successfully **SYN** OVERCOME: *A smart lawyer might find a way of getting around that clause.* **get a'round to sth** to find the time to do something: *I meant to do the laundry but I didn't get around to it.* ♦ [+ **-ing**] *I hope to get around to answering your letter next week.*

'get at sb/sth to reach someone or something; to gain access to someone or something: *The files are locked up and I can't get at them.* **'get at sth** to learn or find out something: *The truth is sometimes difficult to get at.*

get a'way to have a vacation: *We're hoping to get away for a few days in April.* ◑ related noun GETAWAY **get a'way (from…)** to succeed in leaving a place: *I won't be able to get away from the office before 7.* **get a'way (from sb/…)** to escape from someone or a place **get a'way with sth 1** to steal something and escape with it: *Thieves got away with computer equipment worth $30,000.* ◑ related noun GETAWAY **2** to receive a relatively light punishment: *He was lucky to get away with only a fine.* **3** to do something wrong and not be punished for it: *Don't be tempted to cheat—you'll never get away with it.* ♦ **~ doing sth** *Nobody gets away with insulting me like that.* **4** to manage with less of something than you might expect to need: *After the first month, you should be able to get away with one lesson a week.*

get 'back to return, especially to your home: *What time did you get back last night?* ◑ thesaurus box at RETURN **get sth↔'back** to obtain something again after having lost it: *She got her old job back.* ♦ *I never lend books—you never get them back.* **get 'back (in)** (of a political party) to win an election after having lost the previous one **get 'back at sb** (*informal*) to do something bad to someone who has done something bad to you; to get REVENGE on someone: *I'll find a way of getting back at him!* **get 'back to sb** to speak or write to someone again later, especially in order to give a reply: *I'll find out and get back to you.* **get 'back to sth** to return to something: *Could we get back to the question of funding?* **get back to'gether (with sb)** to start a relationship with someone again, especially a romantic relationship, after having ended a previous relationship with the same person: *I just got back together with my ex-girlfriend.*

get be'hind (with sth) to fail to make enough progress or to produce something at the right time: *I'm getting behind with my work.* ♦ *He got behind with his car payments.*

get 'by (on/in/with sth) to manage to live or do a particular thing using the money, knowledge, equipment, etc. that you have: *How does she get by on such a small salary?* ♦ *I can just about get by in German* (= I can speak basic German).

get sb 'down (*informal*) to make someone feel sad or depressed **get sth↔'down 1** to swallow something, usually with difficulty **2** to make a note of something **SYN** WRITE DOWN: *Did you get his number down?* **get 'down to sth** to begin to do something; to give serious attention to something: *Let's get down to business.* ♦ *I like to get down to work by 9.* ♦ **~ doing sth** *It's time I got down to thinking about that essay.*

get 'in | **get 'into sth 1** to arrive at a place: *The train got in late.* ♦ *What time do you get into Kennedy?* **2** to win an election: *The Republican candidate stands a good chance of*

getting in. ♦ *She first got into the Senate* (= became a senator) *in 2004.* **3** to be admitted to a school, university, etc.: *She got into law school at Duke.* **get sb↔'in** to call someone to your house to do a job **get sth↔'in 1** to collect or gather something: *to get the crops/harvest in* **2** to manage to do or say something: *I got in an hour of work while the baby was asleep.* ♦ *She talks so much that it's impossible to get a word in.* **get 'in on sth** to take part in an activity: *He's hoping to get in on any discussions about the new project.* **get 'in with sb** (*informal*) to become friendly with someone, especially in order to gain an advantage

get 'into sth 1 to put on a piece of clothing, especially with difficulty: *I can't get into these shoes—they're too small.* **2** to start a career in a particular profession: *What's the best way to get into journalism?* **3** to become involved in something; to start something: *I got into conversation with an Italian student.* ♦ *to get into a fight* **4** to develop a particular habit: *Don't let yourself get into bad habits.* ♦ *You should get into the routine of saving the document you are working on every ten minutes.* ♦ *How did she get into* (= start taking) *drugs?* **5** (*informal*) to become interested in something: *I'm really getting into jazz these days.* **6** to become familiar with something; to learn something: *I haven't really gotten into my new job yet.* **get 'into sth** | **get yourself/sb 'into sth** to reach a particular state or condition; to make someone reach a particular state or condition: *He got into trouble with the police while he was still at school.* ♦ *Three people were rescued from a yacht that got into difficulties.* ♦ *She got herself into a real state* (= became very anxious) *before the interview.*

get 'off | **get 'off sb** used especially to tell someone to stop touching you or another person: *Get off me, that hurts!* **get 'off** | **get sb 'off** to leave a place or start a journey; to help someone do this: *We got off right after breakfast.* ♦ *He got the children off to school.* **get 'off** | **get 'off sth** to leave work with permission: *Could you get off (work) early tomorrow?* **get 'off sth** | **get sb 'off sth** to stop discussing a particular subject; to make someone do this: *Please can we get off the subject of dieting?* ♦ *I couldn't get him off politics once he got started.* **get sth 'off** to send something by mail: *I need to get these letters off first thing tomorrow.* **get 'off on sth** (*informal*) to be excited by something, especially in a sexual way **get 'off (with sth)** to have no or almost no injuries in an accident: *She was lucky to get off with just a few bruises.* **get 'off (with sth)** | **get sb 'off (with sth)** to receive no or almost no punishment; to help someone do this: *He was lucky to get off with a small fine.* ♦ *A good lawyer might be able to get you off.*

get 'on to sb to become aware of someone's activities, especially when they have been doing something bad or illegal: *He had been stealing money from the company for years before they got on to him.* **get 'on to sth** to begin to talk about a new subject: *It's time we got on to the question of costs.* **get 'on with sth** to continue doing something, especially after an interruption: *Be quiet and get on with your work.* ♦ (*informal*) *Get on with it! We haven't got all day.*

get 'out to become known: *If this gets out there'll be trouble.* **get sth↔'out 1** to produce or publish something: *Will we get the book out by the end of the year?* **2** to say something with difficulty: *She managed to get out a few words of thanks.* **get 'out (of sth)** to leave or go out of a place: *You ought to get out of the house more.* ♦ *She screamed at me to get out.* **get 'out of sth 1** to avoid a responsibility or duty: *We promised we'd go—we can't get out of it now.* ♦ **~ doing sth** *I wish I could get out of going to that meeting.* **2** to stop having a particular habit: *I can't get out of the habit of waking up at six in the morning.* **get sth 'out of sth** to persuade someone to tell or give you something, especially by force: *The police finally got a confession out of her.* **get sth 'out of sb/sth** to gain or obtain something good from someone or something: *She seems to get a lot out of life.* ♦ *He always gets the best out of people.*

get 'over sth to deal with or gain control of something **SYN** OVERCOME: *She can't get over her shyness.* ♦ *I think the problem can be gotten over without too much difficulty.* **get 'over sth/sb** to return to your usual state of health, happiness, etc. after an illness, a shock, the end of a relationship, etc.: *He was disappointed at not getting the job, but he'll get over it.* ,get 'over yourself (*informal*) to stop thinking that you are so important; to stop being so serious: *Just get over yourself and stop complaining!* ◆ *He needs to grow up a little and get over himself.* ,get sth↔'over (to sb) to make something clear to someone: *He didn't really get his meaning over to the audience.* ,get sth 'over (with) (*informal*) to complete something unpleasant but necessary: *I'll be glad to get the exam over and done with.*

'get through sth to manage to do or complete something: *Let's start—there's a lot to get through.* ,get sb 'through sth to help someone to be successful in an exam: *She got all her students through the finals.* ,get 'through (sth) | ,get sth 'through (sth) to be officially accepted; to make something be officially accepted: *They got the bill through Congress.* ,get 'through (to sb) 1 to reach someone: *Thousands of refugees will die if these supplies don't get through to them.* 2 to make contact with someone by telephone: *I tried calling you several times but I couldn't get through.* ,get 'through (to sth) (of a player or team) to reach the next stage of a competition: *Moya got through to the final.* ,get 'through to sb to make someone understand or accept what you say, especially when you are trying to help them: *I find it impossible to get through to her.* ,get 'through with sth to finish or complete a task

'get to sb (*informal*) to annoy or affect someone: *The pressure of work is beginning to get to him.*

,get sb/sth to'gether to collect people or things in one place: *I'm trying to get a team together for Saturday.* ,get to'gether (with sb) to meet with someone socially or in order to discuss something: *We must get together for a drink sometime.* ◆ *Management should get together with the union.* ➲ related noun GET-TOGETHER

,get 'up 1 to stand up after sitting, lying, etc. SYN RISE: *The class got up when the teacher came in.* ➲ thesaurus box at STAND 2 if the ocean or wind gets up, it increases in strength and becomes violent ,get 'up | ,get sb 'up to get out of bed; to make someone get out of bed: *He always gets up early.* ◆ *Could you get me up at 6:30 tomorrow?* ,get 'up to sth 1 to reach a particular point: *We got up to page 72 last time.* 2 to be busy with something, especially something surprising or unpleasant: *She's been getting up to her old tricks again!*

get·a·way /'gɛtə,weɪ/ noun [usually sing.] 1 an escape from a difficult situation, especially after committing a crime: *to make a quick getaway* ◆ *a getaway car* 2 a short vacation; a place that is suitable for a vacation: *a romantic weekend getaway in New York* ◆ *the popular island getaway of Santa Catalina*

get·ting /'gɛtɪŋ/ noun [sing.]
   IDM while the getting/going is good before a situation changes and it is no longer possible to do something

'get-to,gether noun (*informal*) an informal meeting; a party

get·up /'gɛtʌp/ noun (*old-fashioned*, *informal*) a set of clothes, especially strange or unusual ones

,get-up-and-'go noun [U] (*informal*) energy and determination to get things done

gew·gaw /'gyugɔ; 'gu-/ noun an object that attracts attention but has no value or use

gey·ser /'gaɪzər/ noun a natural SPRING that sometimes sends hot water or steam up into the air ➲ picture at VOLCANO

ghast·ly /'gæstli/ adj. (ghast·li·er, ghast·li·est) 1 (of an event) very frightening and unpleasant, because it involves pain, death, etc. SYN HORRIBLE: *a ghastly crime/murder* 2 (*informal*) (of an experience or a situation) very bad; unpleasant SYN TERRIBLE: *The weather was ghastly.* ◆ *It's all been a ghastly mistake.* 3 (*informal*) (of a person or thing) that you find unpleasant and dislike very much SYN HORRIBLE: *her ghastly husband* ◆ *This lipstick is a ghastly color.* 4 [not usually before noun] sick or upset SYN TERRIBLE: *I felt ghastly the next day.* 5 (*literary*) very pale in appearance, like a dead person: *His face was ghastly white.*

gher·kin /'gərkən/ noun a small CUCUMBER

ghet·to /'gɛtoʊ/ noun (pl. ghet·tos or ghet·toes) 1 an area of a city where many people of the same race or background live, separately from the rest of the population. Ghettos are often crowded, with bad living conditions: *a poor kid growing up in the ghetto* ◆ *Niagara Falls has become something of a tourist ghetto.* 2 the area of a town where Jews were forced to live in the past: *the Warsaw ghetto*

ghet·to blast·er /'gɛtoʊ ,blæstər/ noun (*old-fashioned*, *offensive*) = BOOM BOX

ghost /goʊst/ noun, verb
● noun 1 [C] the spirit of a dead person that a living person believes they can see or hear: *Do you believe in ghosts?* (= believe that they exist)? ◆ *the ghost of her father that had come back to haunt her* ◆ *He looked as if he had seen a ghost* (= looked very frightened). 2 [C] the memory of something, especially something bad: *The ghost of anti-Semitism still haunts Europe.* 3 [sing.] ~ of sth a very slight amount of something that is left behind or that you are not sure really exists: *There was a ghost of a smile on his face.* ◆ *You don't have a ghost of a chance* (= you have no chance). 4 [sing.] a second image on a television screen that is not as clear as the first, caused by a fault
   IDM give up the ghost 1 to die 2 (*humorous*) (of a machine) to stop working: *My car finally gave up the ghost.* ➲ more at FORMER
● verb 1 = GHOSTWRITE 2 [I] + adv./prep. (*literary*) to move without making a sound: *They ghosted up the smooth waters of the river.*

ghost·ing /'goʊstɪŋ/ noun [U] the appearance of a faint second image next to an image on a television screen, computer screen, etc.

ghost·ly /'goʊstli/ adj. (ghost·li·er, ghost·li·est) looking or sounding like a ghost; full of ghosts: *a ghostly figure* ◆ *ghostly footsteps* ◆ *the ghostly churchyard*

'ghost ,story noun a story about ghosts that is intended to frighten you

'ghost town noun a town that used to be busy and have a lot of people living in it, but is now empty

ghost·write /'goʊstraɪt/ (also ghost) verb [T, often passive, I] ~ (sth) to write a book, an article, etc. for another person who publishes it as their own work: *Her memoirs were ghostwritten.*

ghost·writ·er /'goʊst,raɪtər/ noun a person who writes a book, etc. for another person, under whose name it is then published

ghoul /gul/ noun 1 (in stories) an evil spirit that opens graves and eats the dead bodies in them 2 (*disapproving*) a person who is too interested in unpleasant things such as death and disaster ▶ ghoul·ish /'gulɪʃ/ adj.: *ghoulish laughter*

GHQ /,dʒi eɪtʃ 'kyu/ noun [U] the abbreviation for "general headquarters" (the main center of a military organization)

GHz abbr. (in writing) GIGAHERTZ

GI /,dʒi 'aɪ/ noun, abbr.
● noun (pl. GIs) a soldier in the U.S. armed forces
● abbr. GLYCEMIC INDEX(= a system for measuring the effect of foods containing CARBOHYDRATES on the level of sugar in the blood): *The diet is based mainly on low GI foods.*

gi·ant /'dʒaɪənt/ noun, adj.
● noun 1 (in stories) a very large, strong person who is often cruel and stupid ➲ see also GIANTESS 2 an unusually large person, animal, or plant: *He's a giant of a man.* 3 a very large and powerful organization: *the multinational oil giants* 4 a person who is very good at something: *literary giants*
● adj. [only before noun] very large; much larger or more important than similar things usually are: *a giant crab* ◆ *a giant-size box of tissues* ◆ *a giant step toward achieving independence*

gi·ant·ess /ˈdʒaɪəntəs/ *noun* (in stories) a female giant

gi·ant·ism /ˈdʒaɪənˌtɪzəm/ *noun* [U] = GIGANTISM

ˌgiant ˈpanda *noun* = PANDA

ˌgiant ˈslalom *noun* a SLALOM SKIING competition over a long distance, with wide fast turns

gib·ber /ˈdʒɪbər/ *verb* [I, T] (+ **speech**) to speak quickly in a way that is difficult to understand, often because of fear: *He cowered in the corner, gibbering with terror.* ♦ *By this time I was a gibbering wreck.*

gib·ber·ish /ˈdʒɪbərɪʃ/ *noun* [U] (*informal*) words that have no meaning or are impossible to understand **SYN** NONSENSE: *You were talking gibberish in your sleep.*

gib·bet /ˈdʒɪbət/ *noun* (*old-fashioned*) a vertical wooden structure on which criminals used to be hanged **SYN** GALLOWS

gib·bon /ˈgɪbən/ *noun* a small APE (= an animal like a large MONKEY without a tail) with long arms, that lives in S.E. Asia

gib·bous /ˈgɪbəs/ *adj.* (*technical*) (of the moon) with the bright part bigger than a SEMICIRCLE and smaller than a circle

gibe (also **jibe**) /dʒaɪb/ *noun, verb*
• *noun* ~ (**at sb/sth**) an unkind or insulting remark about someone: *He made several cheap gibes at his opponent during the interview.*
• *verb* [I, T] ~ (**at sth**) | ~ **that…** | + **speech** to say something that is intended to embarrass someone or make them look silly: *He gibed repeatedly at the errors they had made.*

gib·lets /ˈdʒɪbləts/ *noun* [pl.] the inside parts of a chicken or other bird, including the heart and LIVER, that are usually removed before it is cooked

GIC /ˌdʒi aɪ ˈsi/ *abbr.* (*CanE*) GUARANTEED INVESTMENT CER-TIFICATE (= an investment giving a fixed interest rate on a sum of money deposited with a bank for a certain length of time)

gid·dy /ˈgɪdi/ *adj.* (**gid·di·er, gid·di·est**) **1** [not usually before noun] ~ (**with sth**) so happy and excited that you cannot behave normally: *She was giddy with happiness.* **2** [not usually before noun] feeling that everything is moving and that you are going to fall **SYN** DIZZY: *When I looked down from the top floor, I felt giddy.* **3** [usually before noun] making you feel as if you were about to fall: *The kids were pushing the merry-go-round at a giddy speed.* ♦ (*figurative*) *the giddy heights of success* **4** (*old-fashioned*) (of people) not serious **SYN** SILLY: *Isabel's giddy young sister* ▶ **gid·di·ly** /ˈgɪdl-i/ *adv.*: *She swayed giddily across the dance floor.* **gid·di·ness** /ˈgɪdinəs/ *noun* [U]: *teenage giddiness*

ˌgiddy-ˈup *exclamation* used as a command to a horse to make it go faster

GIF™ /gɪf; dʒɪf/ *noun* (*computing*) the abbreviation for "Graphic Interchange Format" (a type of computer file that contains images and is used a lot on the Internet).

gift 🖉 /gɪft/ *noun, verb*
• *noun* **1** a thing that you give to someone, especially on a special occasion or to say thank you **SYN** PRESENT: *The watch was a gift from my mother.* ♦ *Thank you for your generous gift.* ♦ *a free gift for every reader* ♦ *the gift of life* ♦ (*formal*) *The family made a gift of his paintings to the museum.* ♦ *gifts of toys for the children* **2** a natural ability **SYN** TALENT: ~ (**for sth**) *She has a great gift for music.* ♦ ~ (**for doing sth**) *He has a gift for making friends easily.* ♦ *She can pick up a tune instantly on the piano. It's a gift.* **3** [usually sing.] (*informal*) a thing that is very easy to do or cheap to buy: *That home run was an absolute gift.* ♦ *At $500, it's a gift.*
  IDM **the gift of gab** (also **a gift for gab**) (*informal, sometimes disapproving*) the ability to speak easily and to persuade other people with your words **look a gift horse in the mouth** (usually with negatives) (*informal*) to refuse to criticize something that is given to you for nothing ⊃ more at GOD
• *verb* (used especially in JOURNALISM) to give something to

someone as a gift: *An anonymous donor has gifted the library with his collection of rare books.*

ˈgift card *noun* a card that is worth a particular amount of money that can be exchanged for goods in a store

ˈgift cerˌtificate *noun* a piece of paper that is worth a particular amount of money and that can be exchanged for goods in a store

gift·ed /ˈgɪftəd/ *adj.* **1** having a lot of natural ability or intelligence: *a gifted musician/player, etc.* ♦ *gifted children* **2** ~ **with sth** having something pleasant: *He was gifted with a charming smile.*

ˈgift shop *noun* a store that sells goods that are suitable for giving as presents

ˈgift wrap *noun* [U] attractive colored or patterned paper used for wrapping presents in

ˈgift-wrap *verb* (**-pp-**) [often passive] ~ **sth** to wrap something as a present for someone, especially in a store: *Would you like the chocolates gift-wrapped?* ♦ *The store offers a gift-wrapping service.*

gig /gɪg/ *noun* **1** a performance by musicians playing popular music in front of an audience; a similar performance by a COMEDIAN: *We're doing a gig in the park tomorrow night.* ♦ *Do you have any gigs lined up for next month?* ⊃ collocations at MUSIC **2** (*informal*) a job, especially a temporary one: *a summer gig as a basketball coach* **3** (*informal*) = GIGABYTE **4** a small light CARRIAGE with two wheels, pulled by one horse

giga- /ˈgɪgə/ *combining form* (in nouns; used in units of measurement) 10^9 or 2^{30}: *gigahertz*

gig·a·byte /ˈgɪgəˌbaɪt/ (also *informal* **gig**) *noun* (*abbr.* GB) (*computing*) a unit of computer memory, equal to 2^{30} (or about a billion) BYTES

gig·a·hertz /ˈgɪgəˌhɜrts/ *noun* (*pl.* **gig·a·hertz**) (*abbr.* GHz) (*computing, physics*) a unit for measuring radio waves and the speed at which a computer operates; 1,000,000,000 HERTZ

gi·gan·tic /dʒaɪˈgæntɪk/ *adj.* extremely large **SYN** ENORMOUS, HUGE

gi·gan·tism /dʒaɪˈgæntɪzəm; ˈdʒaɪgænˌtɪzəm/ (also **gi·ant·ism**) *noun* [U] (*medical*) a condition in which someone grows to an unusually large size

gig·gle /ˈgɪgl/ *verb, noun*
• *verb* [I] ~ (**at/about sb/sth**) to laugh in a silly way because you are amused, embarrassed, or nervous: *The girls giggled at the joke.* ♦ *They giggled nervously as they waited for their turn.*
• *noun* **1** [C] a slight, silly, repeated laugh: *She gave a nervous giggle.* ♦ *Matt collapsed into giggles and hung up the phone.* **2 the giggles** [pl.] (*informal*) continuous giggling that you cannot control or stop: *I get the giggles when I'm nervous.* ♦ *She had an attack of the giggles and had to leave the room.*

gig·gly /ˈgɪgli/ *adj.* laughing a lot in a silly, nervous way

GIGO /ˈgaɪgoʊ/ ⊃ GARBAGE

gig·o·lo /ˈdʒɪgəˌloʊ; ˈʒɪ-/ *noun* (*pl.* **gig·o·los**) a man who is paid to be the lover of an older woman, usually one who is rich

gild /gɪld/ *verb* **1** ~ **sth** (*literary*) to make something look bright, as if covered with gold: *The golden light gilded the sea.* **2** ~ **sth** to cover something with a thin layer of gold or gold paint
  IDM **gild the lily** to spoil something that is already good or beautiful by trying to improve it

gild·ed /ˈgɪldəd/ *adj.* [only before noun] **1** covered with a thin layer of gold or gold paint **2** (*literary*) rich and belonging to the upper class: *the gilded youth* (= rich, upper-class, young people) *of the Edwardian era* ♦ *a gilded age* (= time of success and wealth) *of industrial expansion*

gild·ing /ˈgɪldɪŋ/ *noun* [U] a layer of gold or gold paint; the surface that this makes

gill[1] /gɪl/ *noun* [usually pl.] one of the openings on the side of a fish's head that it breathes through ⊃ picture at ANIMAL

IDM **to the gills** (*informal*) completely full: *I was stuffed to the gills with chocolate cake.*

gill² /dʒɪl/ *noun* a unit for measuring liquids. There are four gills in a pint.

gilt /gɪlt/ *noun* **1** [U] a thin layer of gold, or something like gold that is used on a surface for decoration: *gilt lettering* **2** [C] a young female pig

gilt-edged *adj.* (*finance*) (especially of investments) very safe: *gilt-edged securities/shares/stocks*

gim·crack /'dʒɪmkræk/ *adj.* [only before noun] badly made and of little value **SYN** SHODDY

gim·let /'gɪmlət/ *noun* a small tool for making holes in wood to put screws in: (*figurative*) *eyes like gimlets* (= looking very hard at things and noticing every detail)

gim·me /'gɪmi/ (*non-standard*)
● a way of writing the way that the words "give me" are sometimes spoken: *Gimme back my bike!*
● *noun* [usually sing.] something that is very easy to do or achieve

gim·mick /'gɪmɪk/ *noun* (often *disapproving*) an unusual trick or unnecessary device that is intended to attract attention or to persuade people to buy something: *a promotional/publicity/sales gimmick* ▶ **gim·mick·y** /'gɪmɪki/ *adj.*: *a gimmicky idea*

gim·mick·ry /'gɪmɪkri/ *noun* [U] (*disapproving*) the use of gimmicks in selling, etc.

gin /dʒɪn/ *noun* **1** [U] an alcoholic drink made from grain and flavored with JUNIPER **2** [C] a glass of gin: *I'll have a gin and tonic, please.* **3** [C] = COTTON GIN

gin·ger /'dʒɪndʒər/ *noun* [U] the root of a plant originally from S.E. Asia, used in cooking as a spice: *a teaspoon of ground ginger* ⟳ picture at HERB

ginger 'ale *noun* **1** [U] a clear drink with bubbles that does not contain alcohol, flavored with ginger **2** [C] a bottle or glass of ginger ale

gin·ger·bread /'dʒɪndʒər‚brɛd/ *noun* [U] a sweet cake or soft cookie flavored with GINGER: *a gingerbread man* (= a gingerbread cookie in the shape of a person)

gin·ger·ly /'dʒɪndʒərli/ *adv.* in a careful way, because you are afraid of being hurt, of making a noise, etc.: *He opened the box gingerly and looked inside.*

ginger ‚snap *noun* a hard sweet cookie flavored with GINGER

gin·ger·y /'dʒɪndʒəri/ *adj.* like GINGER in color or flavor

ging·ham /'gɪŋəm/ *noun* [U] a type of cotton cloth with a pattern of white and colored squares: *a blue and white gingham dress*

gin·gi·vi·tis /‚dʒɪndʒə'vaɪtəs/ *noun* [U] (*medical*) a condition in which the GUMS around the teeth become painful, red, and swollen

gink·go (also ging·ko) /'gɪŋkoʊ/ *noun* (*pl.* gink·gos or gink·goes) a Chinese tree with yellow flowers **SYN** MAIDENHAIR TREE

gin ‚rummy *noun* [U] a card game in which players try to get sets of cards that add up to ten

gin·seng /'dʒɪnsɛŋ/ *noun* [U] a medicine obtained from a plant root that some people believe helps you stay young and healthy

gip·sy = GYPSY

gi·raffe /dʒə'ræf/ *noun* (*pl.* gi·raffe or gi·raffes) a tall African animal with a very long neck, long legs, and dark marks on its coat

gird /gərd/ *verb* **~ sth (with sth)** to surround something with something; to fasten something around someone or something
  IDM **gird (up) your loins** (*literary* or *humorous*) to get ready to do something difficult: *The company is girding its loins for a plunge into the overseas market.*
  PHR V **gird (yourself/sb/sth) (up) for sth** (*literary*) to

prepare for something difficult, especially a fight, contest, etc.

gird·er /'gərdər/ *noun* a long, strong, iron or steel bar used for building bridges and the FRAMEWORK of large buildings

gir·dle /'gərdl/ *noun, verb*
● *noun* **1** a piece of women's underwear that fits closely around the body from the waist to the top of the legs, designed to make a woman look thinner **2** (*literary*) a thing that surrounds something else: *carefully tended lawns set in a girdle of trees*
● *verb* **~ sth** (*literary*) to surround something: *A chain of volcanoes girdles the Pacific.*

girl 🔑 /gərl/ *noun*
1 [C] a female child: *a baby girl* ◆ *a little girl of six* ◆ *Hello, girls and boys!* ⟳ see also POSTER CHILD **2** [C] a daughter: *Our youngest girl is in college.* **3** [C] (sometimes *offensive*) a young woman: *Alex is not interested in girls yet.* ◆ *He married the girl next door.* **4** [C] (usually in compounds) (*old-fashioned, offensive*) a female worker: *an office girl* **5** [C] (*old-fashioned*) a man's girlfriend **6** girls [pl.] (used especially as a form of address by women) a woman's female friends: *I'm going out with the girls tonight.* ◆ *Good morning, girls!*

girl band *noun* a group of attractive young women who sing pop music and dance

girl 'Friday *noun* a girl or a woman who is employed in an office to do several different jobs, helping other people

girl·friend 🔑 /'gərlfrɛnd/ *noun*
1 a girl or a woman that someone is having a romantic relationship with **2** a woman's female friend: *I had lunch with a girlfriend.* ◆ *Hey girlfriend, how's it going?*

girl·hood /'gərlhʊd/ *noun* [U] the time when someone is a girl; the fact of being a girl: *She spent her girlhood on a farm in Missouri.*

girl·ie /'gərli/ *adj., noun* (*informal*)
● *adj.* (also girl·y) [only before noun] **1** containing photographs of naked or nearly naked women: *girlie magazines* **2** (*disapproving*) suitable for or like girls, not boys: *She likes girlie dresses with lots of ruffles.*
● *noun* an offensive way of referring to a girl or young woman

girl·ish /'gərlɪʃ/ *adj.* like a girl; of a girl: *a girlish giggle* ◆ *a girlish figure*

girl ‚power *noun* [U] the idea that women should take control of their careers and lives

Girl Scout *noun* a member of an organization (called **Girl Scouts of the USA**) that trains girls in practical skills and does a lot of activities with them, for example camping ⟳ compare BOY SCOUT

girth /gərθ/ *noun* **1** [U, C] the measurement around something, especially a person's waist: *a man of enormous girth* ◆ *a tree one yard in girth/with a girth of one yard* **2** [C] a narrow piece of leather or cloth that is fastened around the middle of a horse to keep the seat (called a SADDLE) or a load in place

gis·mo = GIZMO

gist /dʒɪst/ *noun* usually **the gist** [sing.] **~ (of sth)** the main or general meaning of a piece of writing, a speech, or a conversation: *to get* (= understand) *the gist of an argument* ◆ *I missed the beginning of the lecture—can you give me the gist of what he said?*

give 🔑 /gɪv/ *verb, noun*
● *verb* (gave /geɪv/, giv·en /'gɪvn/)
> HAND/PROVIDE **1** [T] to hand something to someone so that they can look at it, use it, or keep it for a time: **~ sth to sb** *Give the letter to your mother after you read it.* ◆ *She gave her ticket to the usher.* ◆ **~ sb sth** *Give your mother the letter.* ◆ *They were all given a box to carry.* **2** [T, I] to hand something to someone as a present; to allow someone to have something as a present: **~ sb sth** *What are you giving your father for his birthday?* ◆ *We gave her a huge bunch of flowers.* ◆ *Did you give*

the waiter a tip? ♦ **~ sth to sb** *We don't usually give presents to people at work.* ♦ **~ (sth)** *They say it's better to give than to receive.* **3** [T] to provide someone with something: **~ sb sth** *They were all thirsty so I gave them a drink.* ♦ *Give me your name and address.* ♦ *We've been given a 2% pay increase.* ♦ *I was hoping you would give me a job.* ♦ *He was given a new heart in a five-hour operation.* ♦ *She wants a job that gives her more responsibility.* ♦ *Can I give you a ride to the airport?* ♦ *They couldn't give me any more information.* ♦ *I'll give you* (= allow you to have) *ten minutes to prepare your answer.* ♦ *Don't give me any of that back talk* (= don't be rude). ♦ **~ sth to sb** *He gives Italian lessons to his colleagues.* ♦ *The reforms should give a better chance to the less able children.*

> MONEY **4** [I, T] to pay money to a charity, etc., to help people: *We need your help—please give generously.* ♦ **~ to sth** *They both gave regularly to charity.* ♦ **~ sth (to sth)** *I gave a small donation.* **5** [T] to pay in order to have or do something: **~ sb sth (for sth)** *How much will you give me for the car?* ♦ **~ sth** *I'd give anything to see him again.*

> TREAT AS IMPORTANT **6** [T] to use time, energy, etc. for someone or something: **~ sb/sth sth** *I gave the matter a lot of thought.* ♦ **~ sth to sb/sth** *I gave a lot of thought to the matter.* ♦ *The government has given top priority to reforming the tax system.*

> PUNISHMENT **7** [T] to make someone suffer a particular punishment: **~ sb sth** *The judge gave him a nine-month suspended sentence.* ♦ **~ sth to sb** *We discussed what punishment should be given to the boys.*

> ILLNESS **8** [T] to infect someone with an illness: **~ sb sth** *You've given me your cold.* ♦ **~ sth to sb** *She gave the bug to all her colleagues.*

> PARTY/EVENT **9** [T] **~ sth** if you **give** a party, you organize it and invite people **10** [T] **~ sth** to perform something in public: *She gave a reading from her latest volume of poetry.* ♦ *The President will be giving a press conference this afternoon.*

> DO/PRODUCE SOMETHING **11** [T] used with a noun to describe a particular action, giving the same meaning as the related verb: **~ sth** *She gave a shrug of her shoulders* (= she shrugged). ♦ *He turned to us and gave a big smile* (= smiled broadly). ♦ *She looked up from her work and gave a yawn* (= yawned). ♦ *He gave a loud cry* (= cried out loudly) *and fell to the floor.* ♦ *Her work has given pleasure to* (= pleased) *millions of readers.* ♦ **~ sb sth** *He gave her a kiss* (= kissed her). ♦ *I have to admit that the news gave us a shock* (= shocked us). ♦ *We'll give you all the help we can* (= help you in every way we can). **HELP** For other similar expressions, look up the nouns in each. For example, you will find **give your approval** at **approval. 12** [T] **~ sb sth** to produce a particular feeling in someone: *All that driving has given me a headache.* ♦ *Go for a walk. It'll give you an appetite.*

> TELEPHONE CALL **13** [T] **~ sb sth** to make a telephone call to someone: *Give me a call tomorrow.* ♦ *I'll give you a ring in the morning.*

> GRADE **14** [T] **~ sb/sth sth | ~ sth (to sb/sth)** to judge someone or something to be of a particular standard: *She gave me an A on my essay.* ♦ *I give it ten out of ten for originality.* ♦ *I'm giving a failing grade to anyone who doesn't complete this assignment.*

> PREDICT HOW LONG **15** [T] **~ sb/sth sth** to predict that something will last a particular length of time: *That marriage won't last. I'll give them two years, at the most.*

> BEND **16** [I] to bend or stretch under pressure: *The branch began to give under his weight.* ♦ (*figurative*) *We can't go on like this— something's got to give.* **17** [I] to agree to change your mind or give up some of your demands: *You're going to have to give a little.*

IDM Most idioms containing **give** are at the entries for the nouns and adjectives in the idioms. For example, **give rise to something** is at **rise** *n.* **don't give me that** (*informal*) used to tell someone that you do not accept what they say: *"I didn't have time to do it." "Oh, don't give me that!"* **give and take** to be willing, in a relationship, to accept what someone else wants and to give up some of what you want: *You're going to have to learn to give and take.* **give as good as you get** to react with equal force when someone attacks or criticizes you: *She can give as good as she gets.* **give it up (for**

sb) (*informal*) to show your approval of someone by clapping your hands: *Give it up for Eddie Murphy!* **give me sth/sb (any day/time)** (*informal*) used to say that you prefer a particular thing or person to the one that has just been mentioned: *We don't go out much. Give me a quiet night in front of the TV any day!* **give or take (sth)** if something is correct **give or take** a particular amount, it is approximately correct: *It'll take about three weeks, give or take a day or so.* **give sb to believe/understand (that)...** [often passive] (*formal*) to make someone believe/understand something: *I was given to understand that she had resigned.* **I give you...** used to ask people to drink a TOAST to someone: *Ladies and gentlemen, I give you Hal Goodwin!* **I/I'll give you that** (*informal*) used when you are admitting that something is true **what gives?** (*informal*) what is happening?; what is the news?; what is the problem?

PHR V **give sb a'way** (in a marriage ceremony) to lead the BRIDE to the BRIDEGROOM and formally allow her to marry him: *The bride was given away by her father.* **give sth↔a'way 1** to give something as a gift: *He gave away most of his money to charity.* ♦ (*informal*) *Check out the prices of our pizzas—we're virtually giving them away!* ↗ related noun GIVEAWAY **2** to present something: *The mayor gave away the prizes at the community fair.* **3** to carelessly allow someone to have an advantage: *They've given away two baskets already.* **give sth/sb↔a'way** to make known something that someone wants to keep secret **SYN** BETRAY: *She gave away state secrets to the enemy.* ♦ *It was supposed to be a surprise but the children gave it away.* ♦ *His voice gave him away* (= showed who he really was). ↗ related noun GIVEAWAY **give sb 'back sth | give sth↔'back (to sb) 1** to return something to its owner: *Could you give me back my pen?* ♦ *Could you give me my pen back?* ♦ *I picked it up and gave it back to him.* **2** to allow someone to have something again: *The operation gave him back the use of his legs.* **give 'in (to sb/sth) 1** to admit that you have been defeated by someone or something: *The rebels were forced to give in.* **2** to agree to do something that you do not want to do: *The authorities have shown no signs of giving in to the kidnappers' demands.* **give 'off sth** to produce something such as a smell, heat, light, etc.: *The flowers gave off a fragrant perfume.* **give 'out 1** to come to an end; to be completely used up: *After a month their food supplies gave out.* ♦ *Her patience finally gave out.* **2** to stop working: *One of the plane's engines gave out shortly after takeoff.* ♦ *Her legs gave out and she collapsed.* **give sth↔'out** to give something to a lot of people: *The teacher gave out the test.* **give 'out sth** to produce something such as heat, light, etc.: *The radiator gives out a lot of heat.* **give yourself 'over to sth** (also **give yourself 'up to sth**) to spend all your time doing something or thinking about something; to allow something to completely control your life **give sth↔'over to sth** [usually passive] to use something for one particular purpose: *This gallery is given over to early American furniture.* **give 'up** to stop trying to do something: *They gave up without a fight.* ♦ *She doesn't give up easily.* ♦ *I give up—tell me the answer.* **give sb 'up 1** (also **give 'up on sb**) to believe that someone is never going to arrive, get better, be found, etc.: *We hadn't heard from him for so long, we'd given him up for dead.* ♦ *There you are at last! We'd given up on you.* **2** to stop having a relationship with someone: *Why don't you give him up?* **give sth↔'up 1** [no passive] to stop doing or having something: *We'd given up hope of ever having children.* ♦ **~ doing sth** *You ought to give up smoking.* **2** to spend time on a task that you would normally spend on something else: *I gave up my weekend to help him paint his apartment.* **give sth↔'up (to sb)** to hand something over to someone else: *We had to give our passports up to the authorities.* ♦ *He gave up his seat to a pregnant woman* (= stood up to allow her to sit down). **give yourself/sb 'up (to sb)** to offer yourself/someone to be captured: *After a week on the run he gave himself up to the police.* **give yourself 'up to sth** = GIVE YOURSELF OVER TO STH **give 'up on sb 1** to stop hoping or believing that someone will change, get better, etc.: *His teachers seem to have given up on him.* **2** = GIVE SB UP

● **noun** [U] the ability of something to bend or stretch under pressure: *The shoes may seem tight at first, but the leather has plenty of give in it.*

IDM **give and take 1** willingness in a relationship to accept what someone else wants and give up some of what you want **2** an exchange of words or ideas: *to encourage a lively give and take*

give·a·way /ˈɡɪvəˌweɪ/ *noun, adj.*

● **noun** (*informal*) **1** something that a company gives for free, usually with something else that is for sale **2** something that makes you guess the real truth about something or someone: *She pretended she wasn't excited but the expression on her face was a dead* (= obvious) *giveaway.*

● **adj.** [only before noun] (*informal*) (of prices) very low

give·back /ˈɡɪvbæk/ *noun* a situation in which workers agree to accept lower pay or fewer benefits at a particular time, in return for more money or benefits later

giv·en /ˈɡɪvn/ *adj., prep., noun*

● **adj.** [usually before noun] **1** already arranged: *They were to meet at a given time and place.* **2** that you have stated and are discussing; particular: *We can find out how much money is spent on food in any given period.*

IDM **be given to sth/to doing sth** (*formal*) to do something often or regularly: *He's given to going for long walks on his own.*

● **prep.** when you consider something: *Given his age,* (= considering how old he is) *he's remarkably active.* ◆ *Given her interest in children, teaching seems the right job for her.* ▶ **given that** *conj.*: *It was surprising the governor was re-elected, given that she had raised taxes so much.*

● **noun** something that is accepted as true, for example when you are discussing something, or planning something: *It's a given that some time will be wasted.*

'given ˌname *noun* = FIRST NAME

giv·er /ˈɡɪvər/ *noun* (often in compounds) a person or an organization that gives: *They are very generous givers to charity.*

giz·mo (also **gis·mo**) /ˈɡɪzmoʊ/ *noun* (*pl.* **giz·mos**) (*informal*) a general word for a small piece of equipment, especially an electronic one that does something in a new and clever way

giz·zard /ˈɡɪzərd/ *noun* the part of a bird's stomach in which food is broken up into smaller pieces before being DIGESTED

gla·cé /ɡlæˈseɪ/ *adj.* [only before noun] (of fruit) preserved in sugar: *glacé fruits* ◆ *glacé cherries*

gla·cial /ˈɡleɪʃl/ *adj.* **1** [usually before noun] (*geology*) connected with the Ice Age: *the glacial period* (= the time when much of the northern half of the world was covered by ice) **2** (*technical*) caused or made by glaciers; connected with glaciers: *a glacial landscape* ◆ *glacial deposits/erosion* **3** (*formal*) very cold; like ice **SYN** ICY: *glacial winds/temperatures* **4** (*formal*) (of people) cold and unfriendly; not showing feelings **SYN** ICY: *Her expression was glacial.* ◆ *Relations between the two countries had always been glacial.* **5** very slow: *The workers were making progress on the new house, but it was at a glacial pace.*

gla·ci·a·tion /ˌɡleɪʃiˈeɪʃn; -si-/ *noun* [U] (*geology*) the process or result of land being covered by glaciers

gla·cier /ˈɡleɪʃər/ *noun* a large mass of ice, formed by snow on mountains, that moves very slowly down a valley

glad 🔑 /ɡlæd/ *adj.*

1 [not before noun] pleased; happy: *"I passed the test!" "I'm so glad (for you)."* ◆ *She was glad when the meeting was over.* ◆ **~ about sth** *"He doesn't need the pills any more." "I'm glad about that."* ◆ **~ to know, hear, see…** *I'm glad to hear you're feeling better.* ◆ **~ (that)…** *I'm glad (that) you're feeling better.* ◆ *He was glad he'd come.* ◆ *I'm so glad (that) you're safe!* ◆ **~ to do sth** *I'm glad to meet you. I've heard a lot about you.* ◆ *I've*

never been so glad to see anyone in my life! **2** grateful for something: **~ for sth** *She was very glad for her warm coat in the biting wind.* ◆ *I'd be glad for your help.* ◆ **~ if…** *I'd be glad if you could help me.* **3 ~ to do sth** very willing to do something: *I'd be glad to lend you the money.* ◆ *If you'd like me to help you, I'd be only too glad to.* **4** [only before noun] (*old-fashioned*) bringing joy; full of joy: *glad news/tidings*

IDM **I'm glad to say (that…)** (*informal*) used when you are commenting on a situation and saying that you are happy about it: *Most teachers, I'm glad to say, take their jobs very seriously.*

THESAURUS

glad
happy ● pleased ● delighted ● proud ● relieved ● thrilled

These words all describe people feeling happy about something that has happened or is going to happen.

glad [not usually before noun] happy about something or grateful for it: *He was glad that she had won.* ◆ *She was glad when the meeting was over.*

happy pleased about something nice that you have to do or something that has happened to someone: *We are happy to announce the winner of our talent contest.*

pleased [not before noun] (*somewhat formal*) happy about something that has happened or something that you have to do: *She was pleased with her exam results.* ◆ *You're coming? I'm so pleased.*

GLAD, HAPPY, OR PLEASED?

Feeling **pleased** can suggest that you have judged someone or something and approve of them. Feeling **glad** can be more about feeling grateful for something. You cannot be "glad with someone": ~~The boss should be glad with you.~~ **Happy** can mean glad, pleased, or satisfied.

delighted very pleased about something; very happy to do something; showing your delight: *I'm delighted with the progress you've made.* **NOTE** Delighted is often used to accept an invitation: *"Can you stay for dinner?" "I'd be delighted (to)."*

proud pleased and satisfied about something that you own, have done, or are connected with: *proud parents* ◆ *He was proud of himself for not giving up.*

relieved feeling happy because something unpleasant has stopped or has not happened; showing this: *You'll be relieved to know that your jobs are safe.*

thrilled [not before noun] extremely pleased and excited about something: *I was thrilled to be invited.*

DELIGHTED OR THRILLED?

Thrilled may express a stronger feeling than **delighted**, but **delighted** can be made stronger with *absolutely*, *more than*, or *only too*. **Thrilled** can be made negative and ironic with *not exactly* or *less than*: *She was not exactly thrilled at the prospect of babysitting her niece.*

PATTERNS
- glad/happy/pleased/delighted/relieved/thrilled **about** sth
- pleased/delighted/relieved/thrilled **at** sth
- glad/happy/pleased/delighted/thrilled **for** sb
- glad/happy/pleased/delighted/proud/relieved/thrilled **that…/to see/to hear/to find/to know…**
- **very** glad/happy/pleased/proud/delighted
- **absolutely** delighted/thrilled

glad·den /ˈɡlædn/ *verb* (*old-fashioned*) to make someone feel pleased or happy: *The sight of the flowers gladdened her heart.* ◆ **it gladdens sb to do sth** *It gladdened him to see them all enjoying themselves.*

glade /gleɪd/ noun (literary) a small open area of grass in a wood or a forest

glad-hand verb [I, T] ~ (sb) (especially of a politician) to say hello to someone in a friendly way, especially when this is not sincere ▶ **'glad-handing** noun [U]

glad·i·a·tor /'glædiˌeɪtər/ noun (in ancient Rome) a man trained to fight other men or animals in order to entertain the public ▶ **glad·i·a·to·ri·al** /ˌglædiə'tɔriəl/ adj.: gladiatorial combat

glad·i·o·lus /ˌglædi'oʊləs/ noun (pl. **glad·i·o·li** /-laɪ/) a tall garden plant with long, thin leaves and brightly colored flowers growing up the STEM

glad·ly /'glædli/ adv. **1** willingly: I would gladly pay extra for a good seat. **2** happily; with thanks: When I offered her my seat, she accepted it gladly. **IDM** see SUFFER

glad·ness /'glædnəs/ noun [U] (literary) joy; happiness

glad rags noun [pl.] (old-fashioned, informal) a person's best clothes, worn on a special occasion

glam·or·ize (also **glam·our·ize**) /'glæməˌraɪz/ verb ~ sth (usually disapproving) to make something bad appear attractive or exciting: Television tends to glamorize violence.

glam·or·ous /'glæmərəs/ (also informal **glam** /glæm/) adj. especially attractive and exciting, and different from ordinary things or people: glamorous movie stars ◆ a glamorous job **ANT** UNGLAMOROUS ▶ **glam·or·ous·ly** adv.: glamorously dressed

glam·our (also **glam·or**) /'glæmər/ noun [U] **1** the attractive and exciting quality that makes a person, a job, or a place seem special, often because of wealth or status: hopeful young actors and actresses dazzled by the glamour of Hollywood ◆ Now that she's a flight attendant, foreign travel has lost its glamour for her. **2** physical beauty that also suggests wealth or success: Add a cashmere scarf under your jacket for a touch of glamour.

glam rock /ˌglæm 'rɑk/ noun [U] a style of music popular in the 1970s, in which male singers wore unusual clothes and makeup

glance /glæns/ verb, noun
• verb **1** [I] + adv./prep. to look quickly at something or someone: She glanced at her watch. ◆ He glanced around the room. ◆ I glanced up quickly to see who had come in. **2** [I] ~ at/down/over/through sth to read something quickly and not thoroughly **SYN** SCAN: I only had time to glance at the newspapers. ◆ He glanced briefly down the list of names. ◆ She glanced through the report.
PHR V **'glance on/off sth** (of light) to flash on a surface or be reflected off it **,glance 'off (sth)** to hit something at an angle and move off it in a different direction: The ball glanced off the rim into the net.
• noun ~ (at sb/sth) a quick look: to take a glance at the newspaper headlines ◆ a cursory/brief/casual/furtive glance ◆ The sisters exchanged glances (= looked at each other). ◆ She shot him a sideways glance. ◆ He walked away without a backward glance. ◆ She stole a glance (= looked secretly) at her watch. ➔ thesaurus box at LOOK
IDM **at a (single) glance** immediately; with only a quick look: He could tell at a glance what was wrong. **at first glance** when you first look at or think about something, often fairly quickly: At first glance the problem seemed easy.

glanc·ing /'glænsɪŋ/ adj. [only before noun] hitting something or someone at an angle, not with full force: to strike somebody a glancing blow

gland /glænd/ noun an organ in a person's or an animal's body that produces a substance for the body to use. There are many different glands in the body: a snake's poison glands ◆ Her glands are swollen. ➔ see also PITUITARY ▶ **glan·du·lar** /'glændʒələr/ adj. [usually before noun]: glandular tissue

glans /glænz/ (pl. **glan·des** /'glændiz/) noun (anatomy) the round part at the end of a man's PENIS or a woman's CLITORIS

glare /glɛr/ verb, noun
• verb **1** [I] ~ (at sb/sth) to look at someone or something in an angry way **SYN** GLOWER: He didn't shout, he just glared at me silently. ➔ thesaurus box at STARE **2** [I] to shine with a very bright, unpleasant light
• noun **1** [U, sing.] a very bright, unpleasant light: the glare of the sun ◆ The rabbit was caught in the glare of the car's headlights. ◆ These sunglasses are designed to reduce glare. ◆ (figurative) The divorce was conducted in the full glare of publicity (= with continuous attention from newspapers and television). **2** [C] a long, angry look: to give someone a hostile glare ➔ thesaurus box at LOOK

glar·ing /'glɛrɪŋ/ adj. **1** [usually before noun] (of something bad) very easily seen **SYN** BLATANT: a glaring error/omission/inconsistency/injustice ◆ the most glaring example of this problem **2** (of a light) very bright and unpleasant **3** angry; aggressive: glaring eyes ▶ **glar·ing·ly** adv.: glaringly obvious

glass 🔊 /glæs/ noun, verb
• noun
❯ **TRANSPARENT SUBSTANCE 1** [U] a hard, usually transparent, substance used, for example, for making windows and bottles: a sheet/pane of glass ◆ frosted/tinted glass ◆ a glass bottle/dish/roof ◆ I cut myself on a piece of broken glass. ◆ The vegetables are grown under glass (= in a GREENHOUSE). ➔ see also CUT GLASS, PLATE GLASS, STAINED GLASS, GLAZIER
❯ **FOR DRINKING 2** [C] (often in compounds) a container, usually made of glass, used for drinking out of: a water glass ◆ a wine glass ◆ Do you have a plastic glass for the little girl? ➔ picture at CUP **3** [C] the contents of a glass: a glass of juice/wine/water, etc. ◆ He drank three whole glasses.
❯ **GLASS OBJECTS 4** [U] objects made of glass: We keep all our glass and china in this cabinet. ◆ She has a fine collection of Bohemian glass.
❯ **ON WATCH/PICTURE 5** [sing.] a protecting cover made of glass on a watch, picture or photograph frame, FIRE ALARM, etc.: In case of emergency, break the glass and press the button.
❯ **FOR EYES 6 glasses** (also **eyeglasses**) (also old-fashioned **spectacles**) [pl.] two LENSES in a frame that rests on the nose and ears. People wear glasses in order to be able to see better or to protect their eyes from bright light: a pair of glasses ◆ dark glasses ◆ I wear glasses for driving. ➔ see also FIELD GLASSES, MAGNIFYING GLASS, SUNGLASSES **IDM** see PEOPLE n., RAISE v.
• verb
PHR V **,glass sth 'in/'over** [usually passive] to cover something with a roof or wall made of glass: a glassed-in pool ➔ compare GLAZE

'glass-,blowing noun [U] the art or activity of blowing hot glass into shapes using a special tube ▶ **'glass-,blower** noun

,glass 'ceiling noun [usually sing.] the imaginary barrier that stops women, or other groups, from getting the best jobs in a company, etc. although there are no official rules to prevent them from getting these jobs

glass·ful /'glæsfʊl/ noun the amount that a drinking glass will hold

glass·ware /'glæswɛr/ noun [U] objects made of glass

glass·y /'glæsi/ adj. (**glass·i·er**, **glass·i·est**) **1** like glass; smooth and shiny: a glassy lake ◆ a glassy material **2** showing no feeling or emotion: glassy eyes ◆ a glassy look/stare ◆ He looked flushed and glassy-eyed.

glau·co·ma /glaʊ'koʊmə; glɔ-/ noun [U] an eye disease that causes gradual loss of sight

glaze /gleɪz/ verb, noun
• verb **1** [I] ~ (over) if a person's eyes glaze or glaze over, the person begins to look bored or tired: Her eyes glazed over when he started to describe his job writing computer code. ◆ "I'm feeling a little tired," he said, his eyes glazing. **2** [T] ~ sth to fit sheets of glass into something: to glaze a window/house ◆ a glazed door ➔ compare GLASS **3** [T] ~ sth (with sth) to cover something with a glaze to give it a shiny surface:

Glaze the pie with beaten egg. ◆ *glazed tiles* ◆ *a glazed doughnut*
- **noun** [C, U] **1** a thin clear liquid put on CLAY objects such as cups and plates before they are finished, to give them a hard shiny surface **2** a thin liquid, made of egg, milk, or sugar, for example, that is put on cake, bread, etc. to make it look shiny

glazed /ɡleɪzd/ *adj.* (especially of the eyes) showing no feeling or emotion; dull: *eyes glazed with boredom*

gla·zier /ˈɡleɪʒər/ *noun* a person whose job is to fit glass into the frames of windows, etc.

gleam /ɡlim/ *verb, noun*
- **verb** **1** [I] to shine with a pale clear light: *The moonlight gleamed on the water.* ◆ *Her eyes gleamed in the dark.* ➔ thesaurus box at SHINE **2** [I] to look very clean or bright: **~ (with sth)** *The house was gleaming with fresh white paint.* ◆ **+ adj.** *Her teeth gleamed white against the tanned skin of her face.* **3** [I] if a person's eyes **gleam** with a particular emotion, or an emotion **gleams** in a person's eyes, the person shows that emotion: **~ (with sth)** *His eyes gleamed with amusement.* ◆ **~ (in sth)** *Amusement gleamed in his eyes.*
- **noun** [usually sing.] **1** a pale clear light, often reflected from something: *the gleam of moonlight on the water* ◆ *I saw the gleam of the knife as it flashed through the air.* **2** a small amount of something: *a faint gleam of hope* ◆ *a serious book with an occasional gleam of humor* **3** an expression of a particular feeling or emotion that shows in someone's eyes **SYN** GLINT: *a gleam of triumph in her eyes* ◆ *a mischievous gleam in his eye* ◆ *The gleam in his eye made her uncomfortable* (= as if he was planning something secret or unpleasant).

gleam·ing /ˈɡlimɪŋ/ *adj.* shining brightly: *gleaming white teeth*

glean /ɡlin/ *verb* **~ sth (from sb/sth)** to obtain information, knowledge, etc., sometimes with difficulty and often from various different places: *These figures were gleaned from a number of studies.*

glean·ings /ˈɡlinɪŋz/ *noun* [pl.] information, knowledge, etc., that you obtain from various different places, often with difficulty

glebe /ɡlib/ *noun* (*old use*) **1** [C] a piece of land that provided an income for a priest **2** [U] land; fields

glee /ɡli/ *noun* [U] a feeling of happiness, usually because something good has happened to you but without much thought, and usually not sincere: *He rubbed his hands in glee as he thought of all the money he would make.* ◆ *She couldn't disguise her glee at their embarrassment.*

glee club *noun* a group of people, usually students, who sing and perform short songs together

glee·ful /ˈɡlifl/ *adj.* happy because of something good you have done or something bad that has happened to someone else: *a gleeful laugh* ▶ **glee·ful·ly** /-fəli/ *adv.*

glen /ɡlɛn/ *noun* a deep narrow valley, especially in Scotland or Ireland

glib /ɡlɪb/ *adj.* (*disapproving*) (of speakers and speech) using words in an easy and smooth way but without much thought, and usually not sincere: *a glib salesman* ◆ *glib answers* ▶ **glib·ly** *adv.*

glide /ɡlaɪd/ *verb, noun*
- **verb** **1** [I] (+ adv./prep.) to move smoothly and quietly, especially as though it takes no effort: *Swans went gliding past.* ◆ *The skaters were gliding over the ice.* **2** [I] (+ adv./prep.) (of birds or aircraft) to fly using air currents, without the birds moving their wings or the aircraft using the engine: *An eagle was gliding high overhead.* ◆ *The plane managed to glide down to the runway.*
- **noun** **1** [sing.] a continuous smooth movement: *the graceful glide of a skater* **2** [C] (*phonetics*) a speech sound made while moving the tongue from one position to another ➔ compare DIPHTHONG

glid·er /ˈɡlaɪdər/ *noun* a light aircraft that flies without an engine ➔ picture at PLANE

glid·ing /ˈɡlaɪdɪŋ/ *noun* [U] the sport of flying in a glider

glim·mer /ˈɡlɪmər/ *noun, verb*
- **noun** **1** a faint unsteady light: *We could see a glimmer of light on the far shore.* **2** (also **glim·mer·ing**) a small sign of something: *a glimmer of hope* ◆ *I caught the glimmer of a smile in his eyes.* ◆ *the glimmering of an idea*
- **verb** [I] to shine with a faint unsteady light: *The candles glimmered in the corner.* ◆ (*figurative*) *Amusement glimmered in his eyes.*

glimpse /ɡlɪmps/ *noun, verb*
- **noun** [usually sing.] **1 ~ (of sb/sth)** | **~ (at sb/sth)** a look at someone or something for a very short time, when you do not see the person or thing completely: *He caught a glimpse of her in the crowd.* ◆ *I came up on deck to get my first glimpse of the island.* ➔ thesaurus box at LOOK **2** a short experience of something that helps you to understand it: **~ (into sth)** *a fascinating glimpse into life in the ocean* ◆ **~ (of sth)** *The program gives us a rare glimpse of a great artist at work.*
- **verb** **1 ~ sb/sth** to see someone or something for a moment, but not very clearly **SYN** CATCH SIGHT OF, SPOT: *He glimpsed her through the window as he passed.* **2 ~ sth** to start to understand something: *Suddenly she glimpsed the truth about her sister.*

glint /ɡlɪnt/ *verb, noun*
- **verb** **1** [I] (+ adv./prep.) to produce small bright flashes of light: *The sea glinted in the moonlight.* ◆ *The sun glinted on the windows.* ➔ thesaurus box at SHINE **2** [I] + adv./prep. if a person's eyes **glint** with a particular emotion, or an emotion **glints** in a person's eyes, the person shows that emotion, which is usually a strong one: *Her eyes glinted angrily.* ◆ *Hostility glinted in his eyes.*
- **noun** **1** a sudden flash of light or color shining from a bright surface: *the glint of the sun on the water* ◆ *golden glints in her red hair* ◆ *She saw a glint of silver in the grass.* **2** an expression in someone's eyes showing a particular emotion, often a negative one: *He had a wicked glint in his eye.* ◆ *a glint of anger*

glis·san·do /ɡlɪˈsɑndoʊ/ *noun* (*pl.* **glis·san·dos** or **glis·san·di** /-di/) (from *Italian*) a way of playing a series of notes so that each one slides into the next, making a smooth continuous sound

glis·ten /ˈɡlɪsn/ *verb* [I] (of something wet) to shine: *Her eyes were glistening with tears.* ◆ *Sweat glistened on his forehead.* ◆ **+ adj.** *The road glistened wet after the rain.* ➔ thesaurus box at SHINE

glitch /ɡlɪtʃ/ *noun* (*informal*) a small problem or fault that stops something from working successfully

glit·ter /ˈɡlɪtər/ *verb, noun*
- **verb** **1** [I] to shine brightly with little flashes of light, like a diamond **SYN** SPARKLE: *The ceiling of the cathedral glittered with gold.* ◆ *The water glittered in the sunlight.* ➔ thesaurus box at SHINE **2** [I] **~ (with sth)** (of the eyes) to shine brightly with a particular emotion, usually a strong one: *His eyes glittered with greed.*
  IDM all that glitters is not gold (*saying*) not everything that seems good, attractive, etc. is actually good, etc.
- **noun** **1** [U] bright light consisting of many little flashes: *the glitter of diamonds* **2** [sing.] a bright expression in someone's eyes showing a particular emotion **SYN** GLINT: *There was a triumphant glitter in her eyes.* **3** [U] the attractive, exciting qualities that someone or something, especially a rich and famous person or place, seems to have **SYN** GLAMOUR: *the superficial glitter of show business* **4** [U] very small, shiny pieces of thin metal or paper that are stuck to things as a decoration: *gold/silver glitter*

glit·te·ra·ti /ˌɡlɪtəˈrɑti/ *noun* [pl.] (used in the media) fashionable, rich, and famous people

glit·ter·ing /ˈɡlɪtərɪŋ/ *adj.* [usually before noun] **1** very impressive and successful: *He has a glittering career ahead of him.* **2** very impressive and involving rich and successful people: *a glittering occasion/ceremony* ◆ *a glittering array of stars* **3** shining brightly with many small flashes of light **SYN** SPARKLING: *glittering jewels*

| t tea | ṭ butter | d did | k cat | ɡ got | tʃ chin | dʒ June | f fall |

glit·ter·y /ˈglɪṭəri/ adj. shining brightly with many little flashes of light: a glittery handbag

glitz /glɪts/ noun [U] (sometimes disapproving) the quality of appearing very attractive, exciting, and impressive, in a way that is not always genuine: the glitz and glamour of the music scene ▶ **glitz·y** adj.: a glitzy, Hollywood-style occasion

the gloam·ing /ˈgloʊmɪŋ/ noun [sing.] (literary) the faint light after the sun sets **SYN** DUSK, TWILIGHT

gloat /gloʊt/ verb [I] **~ (about/at/over sth)** to show that you are happy about your own success or someone else's failure, in an unpleasant way **SYN** CROW: She was still gloating over her rival's disappointment. ▶ **gloat·ing** adj.: a gloating look

glob /glɑb/ noun (informal) a small amount of a liquid or substance in a round shape: thick globs of paint on the floor

glob·al 🔑 **AWL** /ˈgloʊbl/ adj. [usually before noun]
1 covering or affecting the whole world: global issues ◆ The commission is calling for a global ban on whaling. ◆ the company's domestic and global markets ⊃ collocations at GLOBE, INTERNATIONAL **2** considering or including all parts of something: We need to take a more global approach to the problem. ◆ global searches on the database ◆ They sent a global e-mail to all staff. ▶ **glob·al·ly** **AWL** /-bəli/ adv.: We need to start thinking globally. ⊃ collocations at GLOBE

glob·al·i·za·tion **AWL** /ˌgloʊbələˈzeɪʃn/ noun [U] the fact that different cultures and economic systems around the world are becoming connected and similar to each other because of the influence of large MULTINATIONAL companies and of improved communication ⊃ collocations at INTERNATIONAL

glob·al·ize /ˈgloʊbəˌlaɪz/ verb [I, T] **~ (sth)** (economics) if something, for example a business company, **globalizes** or **is globalized**, it operates all around the world

global ˈvillage noun [sing.] the whole world, looked at as a single community that is connected by electronic communication systems

global ˈwarming noun [U] the increase in temperature of the earth's atmosphere, that is caused by the increase of particular gases, especially CARBON DIOXIDE ⊃ collocations at ENVIRONMENT ⊃ compare CLIMATE CHANGE ⊃ see also GREENHOUSE EFFECT

globe **AWL** /gloʊb/ noun **1** [C] an object shaped like a ball with a map of the world on its surface, usually on a stand so that it can be turned **2 the globe** [sing.] the world (used especially to emphasize its size): tourists from every corner of the globe **3** [C] a thing shaped like a ball

AWL COLLOCATIONS

globe
the globe noun
■ around, across, throughout, all over
In this study, archaeological accounts from around the globe provide rich and varied examples on which to draw.

global adj.
■ economy, market, marketplace | climate | capitalism | scale, reach
An emerging global economy heralded social and cultural changes.

globally adj.
■ reverberate | compete | expand | circulate | source something
The United States remains an attractive place for manufacturing companies to operate, and a base from which they can compete globally.
■ competitive | dispersed, distributed | recognized | oriented
The algae are globally distributed, with greatest densities occurring in the Caribbean Sea.

globalization noun
■ engender sth | entail sth
Globalization has entailed the closer economic integration of the countries of the world.
■ economic, free-market, market | corporate | cultural | political
In this article, I focus specifically on economic globalization.

ˌglobe ˈartichoke noun = ARTICHOKE

globe·trot·ting /ˈgloʊbˌtrɑtɪŋ/ adj. (informal) traveling in many countries all over the world: a globetrotting journalist ▶ **globe·trot·ter** noun **globetrotting** noun [U]

glob·u·lar /ˈglɑbyələr/ adj. shaped like a ball, GLOBE, or globule; consisting of globules

glob·ule /ˈglɑbyul/ noun a very small drop or ball of a liquid or of a solid that has been melted: a globule of fat

glo·cal·i·za·tion /ˌgloʊkələˈzeɪʃn/ noun [U] the fact of adapting products or services that are available all over the world to make them suitable for local needs

glock·en·spiel /ˈglɑkənˌʃpil; -ˌspil/ noun a musical instrument made of a row of metal bars of different lengths, that you hit with two small HAMMERS ⊃ picture at INSTRUMENT ⊃ compare XYLOPHONE

glom /glɑm/ verb (-mm-) **~ sth** (informal) to steal **PHR V** ˌglom ˈonto sth **1** to develop a strong interest in something: Kids soon glom onto the latest trend. **2** to become attached or stuck to something: A wad of chewing gum had glommed onto my foot.

gloom /glum/ noun **1** [U, sing.] a feeling of being sad and without hope **SYN** DEPRESSION: The gloom deepened as the election results came in. **2** [U] (literary) almost total DARKNESS: We watched the boats come back in the gathering gloom. **IDM** see DOOM

gloom·y /ˈglumi/ adj. (gloom·i·er, gloom·i·est) **1** nearly dark, or badly lit in a way that makes you feel sad **SYN** DEPRESSING: a gloomy room/atmosphere ◆ It was a wet and gloomy day. **2** sad and without hope **SYN** GLUM: a gloomy expression ◆ We sat in gloomy silence. **3** without much hope of success or happiness in the future **SYN** DEPRESSING: a gloomy picture of the country's economic future ◆ Suddenly, the future didn't look so gloomy after all. ▶ **gloom·i·ly** /-məli/ adv.: He stared gloomily at the phone. **gloom·i·ness** /-minəs/ noun [U]

glop /glɑp/ noun [U] (informal) a thick wet substance that looks, tastes, or feels unpleasant ▶ **glop·py** adj.

glo·ri·fied /ˈglɔrəˌfaɪd/ adj. [only before noun] making someone or something seem more important or better than they are: The restaurant was no more than a glorified fast-food joint.

glo·ri·fy /ˈglɔrəˌfaɪ/ verb (glo·ri·fies, glo·ri·fy·ing, glo·ri·fied, glo·ri·fied) **1 ~ sth** (often disapproving) to make something seem better or more important than it really is: He denies that the movie glorifies violence. **2 ~ sb** (formal) to praise and worship God ▶ **glo·ri·fi·ca·tion** /ˌglɔrəfəˈkeɪʃn/ noun [U]: the glorification of war

glo·ri·ous /ˈglɔriəs/ adj. **1** (formal) deserving or bringing great fame and success: a glorious victory ◆ a glorious chapter in our country's history ⊃ compare INGLORIOUS **2** (formal) very beautiful and impressive: a glorious sunset **3** extremely enjoyable **SYN** WONDERFUL: a glorious trip to the Caribbean **4** (of weather) hot, with the sun shining: They had three weeks of glorious sunshine. ▶ **glo·ri·ous·ly** adv.

glo·ry /ˈglɔri/ noun, verb
● noun **1** [U] fame, praise, or honor that is given to someone because they have achieved something important: Olympic glory in the 100 meters ◆ I do all the work and he gets all the glory. ◆ She wanted to enjoy her moment of glory. ◆ He came home a rich man, **covered in glory**. **2** [U] praise and worship of God: "Glory to God in the highest!" **3** [U] great beauty: The city was spread out beneath us **in all its glory**. ◆ The house has

*now been restored to its **former glory**.* **4** [C] a special cause for pride, respect, or pleasure: *The temple is one of the glories of ancient Greece.* ♦ *Her long black hair is her **crowning glory*** (= most impressive feature). ➲ **see also** REFLECTED GLORY

● ***verb*** (**glo·ries, glo·ry·ing, glo·ried, glo·ried**)

PHR V **ˈglory in sth** to get great pleasure or enjoyment from something **SYN** REVEL: *She gloried in her new-found independence.*

ˈglory ˌdays *noun* [pl.] a time in the past which people look back on as being better than the present

gloss /glɔs; glɑs/ *noun, verb*

● ***noun*** **1** [U, sing.] a shine on a smooth surface: *paper with a high gloss on one side* ♦ *The gel gives your hair a gloss.* ♦ *You can have the photos with either a gloss or a matte finish.* **2** [U] (often in compounds) a substance designed to make something shiny: *lip gloss* **3** [U, sing.] an attractive appearance that is only on the surface and hides what is not so attractive: *Beneath the gloss of success was a tragic private life.* ♦ *This scandal took the gloss off the occasion.* **4** [C] **~ (on sth)** a way of explaining something to make it seem more attractive or acceptable: *The director puts a Hollywood gloss on the civil war.* **5** [C] **~ (on sth)** a note or comment added to a piece of writing to explain a difficult word or phrase

● ***verb*** **~ sth (as sth)** to add a note or comment to a piece of writing to explain a difficult word or idea

PHR V **ˌgloss ˈover sth** to avoid talking about something unpleasant or embarrassing by not dealing with it in detail: *to gloss over a problem* ♦ *He glossed over any splits in the party.*

glos·sa·ry /ˈglɑsəri; ˈglɔ-/ *noun* (*pl.* **glos·sa·ries**) a list of technical or special words, especially those in a particular text, explaining their meanings

gloss·y /ˈglɔsi; ˈglɑ-/ *adj., noun*

● ***adj.*** (**gloss·i·er, gloss·i·est**) **1** smooth and shiny: *glossy hair* ♦ *a **glossy brochure/magazine*** (= printed on shiny paper) **2** giving an appearance of being important and expensive: *the glossy world of fashion*

● ***noun*** (*pl.*) a photograph printed on glossy paper

glot·tal /ˈglɑtl/ *noun* (*phonetics*) a speech sound produced by the glottis ▶ **glottal** *adj.*

ˌglottal ˈstop *noun* (*phonetics*) a speech sound made by closing and opening the glottis, which in English sometimes takes the place of a /t/, for example in *butter*

glot·tis /ˈglɑtəs/ *noun* (*anatomy*) the part of the throat that contains the VOCAL CORDS and the narrow opening between them

gloves

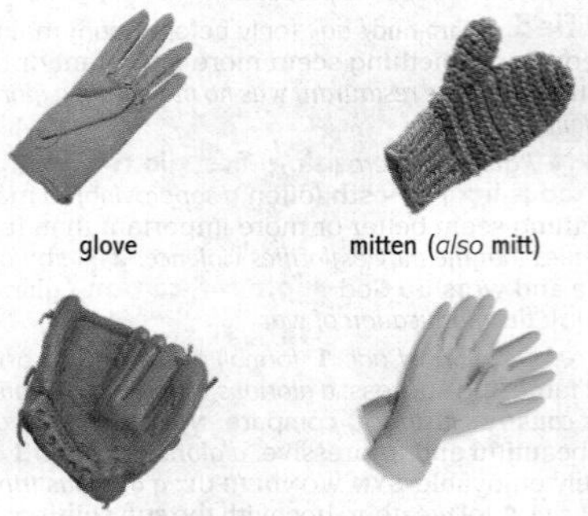

glove — mitten (*also* mitt) — baseball mitt — rubber gloves

glove 🔑 /glʌv/ *noun*

a covering for the hand, made of wool, leather, etc. with separate parts for each finger and the thumb: *a pair of gloves* ♦ ***rubber gloves*** ♦ *gardening gloves* ➲ **compare** MITTEN ➲ **see also** BOXING

IDM **the gloves are off** used to say that someone is ready for a fight or an argument ➲ **more at** FIT, HAND, KID

ˈglove comˌpartment (also **ˈglove box**) *noun* a small space or shelf facing the front seats of a car, used for keeping small things in ➲ **picture at** CAR

gloved /glʌvd/ *adj.* [usually before noun] (of a hand) wearing a glove

glow /gloʊ/ *verb, noun*

● ***verb*** **1** [I] (especially of something hot or warm) to produce a dull, steady light: *The embers still glowed in the hearth.* ♦ *The strap has a fluorescent coating that **glows in the dark**.* ♦ **+ adj.** *A cigarette end glowed red in the darkness.* ➲ **thesaurus box at** SHINE **2** [I] (of a person's body or face) to look or feel warm or pink, especially after exercise or because of excitement, embarrassment, etc.: *Her cheeks were glowing.* ♦ **~ with sth** *His face glowed with embarrassment.* **3** [I] **~ (with sth)** to look very pleased or satisfied: *She was positively glowing with pride.* ♦ *He gave her a warm glowing smile.* **4** [I] to appear a strong, warm color: **~ (with sth)** *The countryside glowed with fall colors.* ♦ **+ adj.** *The brick walls glowed red in the late afternoon sun.*

● ***noun*** [sing.] **1** a dull steady light, especially from a fire that has stopped producing flames: *The city was just a red glow on the horizon.* ♦ *There was no light except for the occasional glow of a cigarette.* **2** the pink color in your face when you have been doing exercise or feel happy and excited: *The fresh air had brought a healthy glow to her cheeks.* **3** a gold or red color: *the glow of autumn leaves* **4** a feeling of pleasure and satisfaction: *When she looked at her children, she felt a glow of pride.*

glow·er /ˈglaʊər/ *verb* [I] **~ (at sb/sth)** to look in an angry, aggressive way **SYN** GLARE ▶ **glow·er** *noun*

glow·ing /ˈgloʊɪŋ/ *adj.* giving enthusiastic praise: ***a glowing account/report/review*** ♦ *He spoke of her performance in the movie **in glowing terms*** (= praising her highly). ▶ **glow·ing·ly** *adv.*

glow·stick /ˈgloʊstɪk/ (also **ˈlight stick**) *noun* a plastic tube filled with chemicals that shines like a lamp when you bend it

glow·worm /ˈgloʊwərm/ *noun* a type of insect. The female has no wings and produces a green light at the end of the tail.

glu·cose /ˈglukoʊs/ *noun* [U] a simple type of sugar that is an important energy source in living things and which is a part of many CARBOHYDRATES

glue 🔑 /glu/ *noun, verb*

● ***noun*** [U, C] a sticky substance that is used for joining things together: *a tube of glue* ♦ *He sticks to her like glue* (= never leaves her). ➲ **picture at** STATIONERY

● ***verb*** to join two things together using glue **SYN** STICK: **~ A (to/onto B)** *She glued the label onto the box.* ♦ **~ A and B (together)** *Glue the two pieces of cardboard together.* ♦ *Make sure the edges are glued down.*

IDM **be glued to sth** (*informal*) to give all your attention to something; to stay very close to something: *He spends every evening glued to the TV.* ♦ *Her eyes were glued to the screen* (= she did not stop watching it). **glued to the spot** not able to move, for example because you are frightened or surprised

ˈglue ˌsniffing *noun* [U] the habit of breathing in the gases from some kinds of glue in order to produce a state of excitement; a type of SOLVENT ABUSE

glue·y /ˈglui/ *adj.* sticky like glue; covered with glue

glug /glʌg/ *verb, noun* (*informal*)

● ***verb*** (**-gg-**) **1** [I] **+ adv./prep.** (of liquid) to pour out quickly and noisily, especially from a bottle **2** [T] **~ sth (down)** to drink something quickly: *She glugged down a glass of water*

● ***noun*** a small amount of a drink or liquid poured out

glum /glʌm/ *adj.* sad, quiet, and unhappy **SYN** GLOOMY: *The players sat there with glum looks on their faces.* ▶ **glum·ly** *adv.*: *The three of us sat glumly looking out at the ocean.*

glut /glʌt/ *noun*, *verb*
- **noun** [usually sing.] ~ **(of sth)** a situation in which there is more of something than is needed or can be used **SYN** SURFEIT: *a glut of cheap DVDs on the market* **ANT** SHORTAGE
- **verb** (-tt-) [usually passive] ~ **sth (with sth)** to supply or provide something with too much of something: *The market is glutted with foreign cars.*

glu·ten /'glutn/ *noun* [U] a sticky substance that is a mixture of two PROTEINS and is left when STARCH is removed from flour, especially WHEAT flour: *We sell a range of gluten-free products* (= not containing gluten).

glutes /gluts/ *noun* [pl.] (*informal*) the muscles in the BUTTOCKS that move the top of the leg

glu·te·us /'glutiəs/ (also ˌgluteus ˈmuscle) *noun* (*anatomy*) any of the three muscles in each BUTTOCK

glu·ti·nous /'glutn·əs/ *adj.* sticky: *glutinous rice*

glut·ton /'glʌtn/ *noun* **1** (*disapproving*) a person who eats too much **2** ~ **for punishment/work** a person who enjoys doing difficult or unpleasant tasks ▶ **glut·ton·ous** /'glʌtn·əs/ *adj.* **SYN** GREEDY

glut·ton·y /'glʌtn·i/ *noun* [U] the habit of eating and drinking too much **SYN** GREED

gly·ce·mic index /glaɪˌsimɪk 'ɪndɛks/ *noun* = GI

glyc·er·in (also **glyc·er·ine**) /'glɪsərən/ *noun* [U] a thick, sweet, clear liquid made from fats and oils and used in medicines, beauty products, and EXPLOSIVES

glyph /glɪf/ *noun* a symbol CARVED out of stone, especially one from an ancient writing system

gm ♫ (also **gm.**) *abbr.* (*pl.* **gm** or **gms**) gram(s)

GMAT™ /'dʒimæt/ *abbr.* Graduate Management Admissions Test (a test taken by graduate students in the U.S. who want to study for a degree in Business)

GMO *noun* (*pl.* **GMOs**) the abbreviation for "genetically modified organism" (a plant, etc. that has had its genetic structure changed artificially, so that it will produce more fruit or not be affected by disease)

GMT /ˌdʒi ɛm 'ti/ *noun* [U] the abbreviation for "Greenwich Mean Time" (the time at Greenwich in England on the line of 0° LONGITUDE, used for calculating time everywhere in the world; also called Universal Time)

gnarled /narld/ (also **gnarl·y**) *adj.* **1** (of trees) twisted and rough; covered with hard lumps: *a gnarled oak/branch/trunk* **2** (of a person or part of the body) bent and twisted because of age or illness: *gnarled hands*

gnarl·y /'narli/ *adj.* **1** = GNARLED **2** (*slang*) difficult or dangerous **3** (*slang*) very good; excellent: *Wow, man! That's totally gnarly!*

gnash /næʃ/ *verb*
IDM **gnash your teeth** to feel very angry and upset about something, especially because you cannot get what you want: *He'll be gnashing his teeth when he hears that we lost the contract.*

gnat /næt/ *noun* a small fly with two wings, that bites

gnaw /nɔ/ *verb* [T, I] to keep biting something or chewing it hard, so that it gradually disappears: ~ **sth** *The dog was gnawing a bone.* ◆ ~ **through sth** *Rats had gnawed through the cable* ◆ ~ **at/on sth** *She gnawed at her fingernails.* ◆ ~ **away at/on sth** (*figurative*) *Self-doubt began to gnaw away at her confidence.*
PHR V **ˈgnaw at sb** to make someone feel anxious, frightened, or uncomfortable over a long period of time: *The problem had been gnawing at him for months.*

gnaw·ing /'nɔɪŋ/ *adj.* [only before noun] making you feel worried over a period of time: *gnawing doubts*

gneiss /naɪs/ *noun* [U] (*geology*) a type of METAMORPHIC rock formed at high pressure and temperature deep in the ground

gnoc·chi /'nyouki; 'nou-/ *noun* [pl.] an Italian dish consisting of small balls of potato mixed with flour and boiled, usually eaten with a sauce

gnome /noum/ *noun* **1** (in stories) a creature like a small man with a pointed hat, who lives under the ground and guards gold and TREASURE **2** a plastic or stone figure of a gnome, used as decoration

gno·mic /'noumɪk/ *adj.* (*formal*) (of a person or a remark) intelligent and wise but sometimes difficult to understand

GNP /ˌdʒi ɛn 'pi/ *noun* the abbreviation for "gross national product" (the total value of all the goods and services produced by a country in one year, including the total income from foreign countries) ⊃ compare GDP

gnu /nu/ *noun* (*pl.* **gnu** or **gnus**) = WILDEBEEST

go ♫ /gou/ *verb*, *noun*
- **verb** (**goes** /gouz/, **went** /wɛnt/, **gone** /gɔn; gɑn/)
  HELP Been is used as the past participle of **go** when someone has gone somewhere and come back.
  ▷ MOVE/TRAVEL **1** [I] to move or travel from one place to another: + *adv./prep.* *She went into her room and shut the door behind her.* ◆ *He goes to work by bus.* ◆ *I have to go to Omaha on business.* ◆ *She has gone to China* (= is now in China or is on her way there). ◆ *She has been to China* (= she went to China and has now returned). ◆ *I think you should go to the doctor.* ◆ *Are you going home for Christmas?* ◆ ~ **to do sth** *She went to see her sister this weekend.* **HELP** In spoken English **go** is used with **and** plus another verb to show purpose or to tell someone what to do: *I'll go and answer the door.* ◆ *Go and get me a drink!* The and is sometimes left out: *Go ask your mom!* **2** [I] ~ **(to sth) (with sb)** to move or travel, especially with someone else, to a particular place or in order to be present at an event: *Are you going to Dave's party?* ◆ *Who else is going?* ◆ *His dog goes everywhere with him.* **3** [I] to move or travel in a particular way or cover a particular distance: + *adv./prep.* *He's going too fast.* ◆ + *noun* *We had gone about fifty miles when the car broke down.* **4** [I] ~ **flying, singing, etc. (+ adv./prep.)** to move in a particular way or while doing something else: *The car went skidding off the road into a ditch.* ◆ *She went sobbing up the stairs.* ◆ *She crashed into a waiter and his tray of drinks went flying.*
  ▷ LEAVE **5** [I] to leave one place in order to reach another **SYN** DEPART: *I must be going now.* ◆ *It's time to go.* ◆ *Has she gone yet?* ◆ *He's been gone an hour* (= he left an hour ago). ◆ *When does the train go?* **6** [I] ~ **on sth** to leave a place and do something different: *to go on a tour/a trip/a cruise* ◆ *Richard has gone on vacation and won't be back for two weeks.*
  ▷ VISIT/ATTEND **7** [I] ~ **to sth** to visit or attend a place for a particular purpose: *I have to go to the hospital for an operation.* ◆ *to go to prison* (= to be sent there as punishment for a crime) ◆ *Do you go to church* (= regularly attend church services)?
  ▷ SWIMMING/FISHING/JOGGING, ETC. **8** [I] ~ **for sth** to leave a place or travel to a place in order to take part in an activity or a sport: *to go for a walk/drive/swim/run* ◆ *Let's go for a drink* (= at a bar) *after work.* ◆ *I have to go shopping this afternoon.* ◆ *We're going sailing on Saturday.*
  ▷ BE SENT **9** [I] (+ *adv./prep.*) to be sent or passed somewhere: *I want this memo to go to all managers.*
  ▷ LEAD **10** [I] ~ **(from...) to...** to lead or extend from one place to another: *a rope that will go from the top of the roof to the ground.* ◆ *Where does this road go?*
  ▷ PLACE/SPACE **11** [I] + *adv./prep.* to have as a usual or correct position; to be placed: *This dictionary goes on the top shelf.* ◆ *Where do you want the piano to go* (= be put)? **12** [I] **will/would not ~ (in/into sth)** used to say that something does/did not fit into a particular place or space: *My clothes won't all go in that one suitcase.* ◆ *He tried to push his hand through the gap but it wouldn't go.*
  ▷ NUMBERS **13** [I] if a number will **go into** another number, it is contained in that number an exact number of times: (+ *adj.*) *How many times will 3 go into 12? 4 times.* ◆ ~ **into sth** *7 won't go into 15.*
  ▷ PROGRESS **14** [I] + *adv./prep.* used to talk about how well or badly something makes progress or succeeds: *"How did your interview go?" "It went very well, thank you."* ◆ *Did*

---

everything go smoothly? ♦ How's it going (= is your life enjoyable, successful, etc. at the moment)? ♦ The way things are going the company will be bankrupt by the end of the year.
> STATE/CONDITION **15** [I] used in many expressions to show that someone or something has reached a particular state/is no longer in a particular state: ~ **to/into sth** She went to sleep. ♦ The boy went into a coma. ♦ ~ **out of sth** That color has gone out of fashion. **16** linking verb + adj. to become different in a particular way, especially a bad way: to go **bald/blind/crazy/bankrupt, etc.** ♦ Her hair is going gray. ♦ The milk had gone sour. ♦ The children went wild with excitement. ⊃ note at BECOME **17** [I] + adj. to live or move around in a particular state: to go naked/barefoot ♦ She cannot bear the thought of children going hungry. **18** [I] ~ **unnoticed, unre-ported, etc.** to not be noticed, reported, etc.: Police are worried that many crimes go unreported.
> SONG/STORY **19** [I, T] used to talk about what tune or words a song or poem has or what happens in a story: + **adv./prep.** How does that song go? ♦ I forget how the next line goes. ♦ ~ **that...** The story goes that she's been married five times.
> SOUND/MOVEMENT **20** [I] to make a particular sound or movement: + **noun** The gun went "bang." ♦ + **adv./prep.** She went like this with her hand.
> SAY **21** [T] + **speech** (informal) (used when telling a story) to say: I asked "How much?" and he goes, "Fifty" and I go, "Fifty? You must be joking!"
> START **22** [I] to start an activity: I'll say "One, two, three, go!" as a signal for you to start. ♦ As soon as he gets here we're ready to go.
> MACHINE **23** [I] if a machine goes, it works: This fan doesn't go.
> DISAPPEAR **24** [I] to stop existing; to be lost or stolen SYN DISAPPEAR: Has your headache gone yet?
> BE THROWN OUT **25** [I] sb/sth must/has to/can ~ used to talk about wanting to get rid of someone or something: The old sofa will have to go. ♦ He's useless—he'll have to go.
> NOT WORK **26** [I] to get worse; to become damaged or stop working correctly: Her sight is beginning to go. ♦ His mind is going (= he is losing his mental powers). ♦ I was driving home when my brakes went.
> DIE **27** [I] to die. People say "go" to avoid saying "die.": You can't take your money with you when you go.
> MONEY **28** [I] when money goes, it is spent or used for something: I don't know where the money goes! ♦ ~ **on sth** Most of her allowance goes on clothes. ♦ ~ **to do sth** The money will go to finance a new community center. **29** [I] ~ **(to sb) (for sth)** to be sold: We won't let the house go for less than $200,000. ♦ There was usually some bread going cheap (= being sold cheaply) at the end of the day. **30** [I] + **adv./prep.** to be willing to pay a particular amount of money for something: He offered $5,000 for the car and I don't think he'll go any higher. ♦ I'll go to $1,000 but that's my limit.
> HELP **31** [I] ~ **to do sth** to help; to play a part in doing something: This all goes to prove my theory. ♦ It (= what has just happened) just goes to show you can't always tell how people are going to react.
> BE AVAILABLE **32** be going [I] (informal) to be available: There just aren't any jobs going in this area.
> TIME **33** [I] + **adv./prep.** used to talk about how quickly or slowly time seems to pass: Hasn't the time gone quickly? ♦ Half an hour went past while we were sitting there.
> USE TOILET **34** [I] (informal) to use a toilet: Do you need to go, Billy?
IDM Most idioms containing **go** are at the entries for the nouns and adjectives in the idioms. For example, **go it alone** is at alone. **anything goes** (informal) anything that someone says or does is accepted or allowed, however shocking or unusual it may be: Almost anything goes these days. **as people, things, etc. go** in comparison with the average person, thing, etc.: As teachers go, he's not bad. **be going to do sth 1** used to show what someone intends to do in the future: We're going to buy a house after we save enough money. **2** used to show that something is likely to happen very soon or in the future: I think I'm going to faint. ♦ If the drought continues there's going to be a famine. **don't go doing sth** (informal) used to tell or warn someone not to do

something: Don't go getting yourself into trouble. **go all out for sth | go all out to do sth** to make a very great effort to get something or do something **go and do sth** used to show that you are angry or annoyed that someone has done something stupid: Trust him to go and mess things up! ♦ Why did you have to go and upset your mother like that? ♦ You've really gone and done it (= done something very stupid) now! **going on...** approaching a particular age or amount: My nephew is three going on four so he has a lot of energy. ♦ I was going on sixteen when we met in school. **go on** (old-fashioned) used to express the fact that you do not believe something, or that you disapprove of something **(have) a lot, nothing, etc. going for you** (to have) many/not many advantages: You're young, intelligent, attractive—you have a lot going for you! **a no go** (informal) not possible or allowed: If the bank won't lend us the money it's a no go, I'm afraid. **not (even) go there** (informal) used to say that you do not want to talk about something in any more detail because you do not even want to think about it: Don't ask me to choose. I don't want to go there. ♦ "There was a problem with his parents, wasn't there?" "Don't even go there!" **to go 1** remaining; still left: I only have one final exam to go. **2** (informal) if you buy cooked food **to go** in a restaurant or store, you buy it to take away and eat somewhere else: Two pizzas to go. **what goes around comes around** (saying) the way someone behaves toward other people will affect the way those people behave toward them in the future **where does sb go from here?** used to ask what action someone should take, especially in order to improve the difficult situation that they are in **who goes there?** used by a soldier who is guarding a place to order someone to say who they are: Halt, who goes there?
PHR V **'go about sth** to continue to do something; to keep busy with something: Despite the threat of war, people went about their business as usual. **,go a'bout sth** to start working on something SYN TACKLE: You're not going about the job in the right way. ♦ ~ **doing sth** How should I go about finding a job?
,go 'after sb to chase or follow someone: He went after the burglars. ♦ She left the room in tears so I went after her. **,go 'after sb/sth** to try to get someone or something: We're both going after the same job.
,go a'gainst sb to not be in someone's favor or not to their advantage: The jury's verdict went against him. **,go a'gainst sb/sth** to resist or oppose someone or something: He would not go against his parents' wishes. **,go a'gainst sth** to be opposed to something; to not fit or agree with something: Paying for a private room in the hospital goes against her principles. ♦ His thinking goes against all logic.
,go a'head 1 to travel in front of other people in your group and arrive before them: I'll go ahead and tell them you're on the way. **2** to happen; to be done SYN PROCEED: The building of the new bridge will go ahead as planned. ⊃ related noun GO-AHEAD **,go a'head (with sth)** to begin to do something, especially when someone has given per-mission or has expressed doubts or opposition: "May I start now?" "Yes, go ahead." ♦ The government intends to go ahead with major tax cuts. ⊃ related noun GO-AHEAD
,go a'long 1 to continue with an activity: He made up the story as he went along. **2** to make progress; to develop: Things are going along nicely. **,go a'long with sb/sth** to agree with someone or something: I don't go along with her views on health insurance. ⊃ thesaurus box at AGREE
,go a'round 1 to spin or turn: to go around in a circle **2** to be enough for everyone to have one or some: There aren't enough chairs to go around. **3** to often be in a particular state or behave in a particular way: She often goes around barefoot. ♦ ~ **doing sth** It's unprofessional to go around criticizing your colleagues. **4** to spread from person to person: There's a rumor going around that they're having an affair. **,go a'round (to...)** to visit someone or a place that is near: I went around to the post office. ♦ I'm going around to my sister's (= her house) later.
'go at sb to attack someone: They went at each other furiously. **'go at sth** to make great efforts to do something;

to work hard at something: *They went at the job as if their lives depended on it.*

,go a'way **1** to leave a person or place: *Just go away!* ♦ *Go away and think about it, then let me know.* **2** to leave home for a period of time, especially for a vacation: *They went away for a few days.* ♦ *I'm going away on business.* **3** to disappear: *The smell still hasn't gone away.*

,go 'back if two people **go back** a period of time (usually a long time), they have known each other for that time: *Dave and I go back twenty years.* ,go 'back (to…) to return to a place: *She doesn't want to go back to her husband* (= to live with him again). ♦ *This toaster will have to go back* (= be taken back to the store where it was bought) —*it's faulty.* ♦ *Of course we want to go back someday—it's our country, our real home.* ⊃ thesaurus box at RETURN ,go 'back (to sth) **1** to consider something that happened or was said at an earlier time: *Can I go back to what you said at the beginning of the meeting?* ♦ *Once you have made this decision, there will be **no going back*** (= you will not be able to change your mind). **2** to have existed since a particular time or for a particular period: *Their family goes back to the time of the Pilgrim Fathers.* ,go 'back on sth to fail to keep a promise; to change your mind about something: *He never **goes back on his word*** (= never fails to do what he has said he will do). ,go 'back to sth to start doing something again that you had stopped doing: *The kids go back to school next week.* ♦ [+ -ing] *She's decided to go back to teaching.*

,go be'fore to exist or happen in an earlier time: *The present crisis is worse than any that have gone before.* 'go before sb/sth to be presented to someone or something for discussion, decision, or judgment: *My application goes before the planning committee next week.*

,go be'yond sth to be more than something SYN EXCEED: *This year's sales figures go beyond all our expectations* (= are much better than we thought they would be).

,go 'by (of time) to pass: *Things will get easier **as time goes by.*** ♦ *The weeks went slowly by.* 'go by sth to be guided by something; to form an opinion from something: *That's a good rule to go by.* ♦ *If past experience **is anything to go by**, they'll be late.*

,go 'down **1** to fall to the ground: *She tripped and went down with a thump.* **2** if a ship, etc. **goes down**, it disappears below the water SYN SINK **3** when the sun or moon **goes down**, it disappears below the HORIZON SYN SET **4** if food or drink will/will not **go down**, it is easy/difficult to swallow: *She tried to swallow the medicine but it wouldn't go down.* **5** if the price of something, the temperature, etc. **goes down**, it becomes lower SYN FALL: *The price of oil is going down.* ♦ *Oil is going down in price.* ANT GO UP **6** (*informal*) to get worse in quality: *The neighborhood has gone down a lot recently.* **7** (*computing*) to stop working temporarily: *The system is going down in ten minutes.* **8** (*informal*) to happen: *You really don't know what's going down?* ,go 'down (in sth) to be written in something; to be recorded or remembered in something: *It all goes down* (= she writes it all) *in her notebook.* ♦ *He will **go down in history** as a great statesman.* ,go 'down (to sb) to be defeated by someone, especially in a game or competition: *Italy went down to Brazil by three goals to one.* ,go 'down (to…) to go from one place to another, especially somewhere nearby or further south: *She went down to Florida to see her parents.* ANT GO UP ,go 'down (with sb) to be received in a particular way by someone: *The suggestion didn't go down very well with her boss.*

'go for sb to attack someone: *She went for him with a knife.* 'go for sb/sth **1** to apply to someone or something: *What I said about Peter goes for you, too.* ♦ *They have a high level of unemployment—but **the same goes for** many other countries.* **2** to go to a place and bring someone or something back: *She's gone for some milk.* **3** to be attracted by someone or something; to like or prefer someone or something: *She goes for tall slim men.* ♦ *I don't really go for modern art.* 'go for sth **1** to choose something: *I think I'll go for the fruit salad.* ⊃ thesaurus box at CHOOSE **2** to put a lot of effort into something, so that you get or achieve something: *Go for it,*

John! You know you can beat him.* ♦ *It sounds like a great idea. **Go for it!***

,go 'in **1** to enter a room, house, etc.: *Let's go in, it's getting cold.* **2** if the sun or moon **goes in**, it disappears behind a cloud ,go 'in for sth to have something as an interest or a hobby: *She doesn't go in for team sports.* ,go 'in with sb to join someone in starting a business: *My brothers are opening a garage and they want me to go in with them.* ,go in on sth (with sb) (for sb) to share the cost of sth: *Do you want to go in on a wedding present for Doug and Cheryl with us?*

,go 'into sth **1** (of a vehicle) to hit something violently: *The car skidded and went into a tree.* **2** (of a vehicle or driver) to start moving in a particular way: *The plane went into a nosedive.* **3** to join an organization, especially in order to have a career in it: *to go into the Army/the priesthood* ♦ *to go into teaching/medicine/politics* **4** to begin to do something or behave in a particular way: *He went into a long explanation of the affair.* **5** to examine something carefully: *We need to go into the question of costs.* **6** (of money, time, effort, etc.) to be spent on something or used to do something: *More government money needs to go into the project.* ♦ [+ **-ing**] *Years of work went into researching the book.*

,go 'off **1** to leave a place, especially in order to do something: *She went off to get a drink.* **2** to be fired; to explode: *The gun went off by accident.* ♦ *The bomb went off in a crowded street.* ⊃ thesaurus box at EXPLODE **3** if an alarm, etc. **goes off**, it makes a sudden loud noise **4** if a light, the electricity, etc. **goes off**, it stops working: *Suddenly the lights went off.* ♦ *The heat goes off at night.* ANT GO ON **5** to happen in a particular way: *The meeting **went off well**.* ,go 'off (on sb) (*informal*) to suddenly become angry with someone ,go 'off with sb to leave your husband, wife, partner, etc. in order to have a relationship with someone else: *He went off with his best friend's wife.* ,go 'off with sth to take away from a place something that does not belong to you: *He went off with $10,000 of the company's money.*

,go 'on **1** when a performer **goes on**, they begin their performance: *She doesn't go on until Act 2.* **2** (in sports) to join a team as a SUBSTITUTE during a game: *Miller went on for Rose just before halftime.* **3** when a light, the electricity, etc. **goes on**, it starts to work: *Suddenly all the lights went on.* ANT GO OFF **4** (of time) to pass: *She became more and more talkative as the evening went on.* **5** usually **be going on** to happen: *What's going on here?* **6** if a situation **goes on**, it continues without changing: *This cannot be allowed to go on.* ♦ *How much longer will this hot weather go on for?* ♦ *We can't go on like this —we seem to be always arguing.* **7** to continue speaking, after a short pause: *She hesitated for a moment and then went on.* ♦ **+ speech** *"You know," he went on, "I think my brother could help you."* **8** used to encourage someone to do something: *Go on! Have another piece of cake!* ♦ *Go on—jump!* ,go on (ahead) to travel in front of someone else: *You go on ahead—I'll catch up with you in a few minutes.* 'go on sth (used in negative sentences and questions) to base an opinion or a judgment on something: *The police don't have much to go on.* ,go 'on (about sb/sth) (*informal*) to talk about someone or something for a long time, especially in a boring or complaining way: *He went on and on about how poor he was.* ♦ *She does go on sometimes!* ,go 'on (with sth) to continue an activity, especially after a pause or break: *That's enough for now—let's go on with it tomorrow.* ,go 'on doing sth to continue an activity without stopping: *He said nothing but just went on working.* ,go 'on to sth to pass from one item to the next: *Let's go on to the next item on the agenda.* ,go 'on to do sth to do something after completing something else: *The book goes on to describe his experiences in the army.*

,go 'out **1** to leave your house to go to a social event: *She goes out a lot.* ♦ *~ doing sth He goes out partying most weekends.* **2** when the TIDE **goes out**, it moves away from the land SYN EBB ANT COME IN **3** to be sent: *Have the invitations gone out yet?* **4** when news or information **goes out**, it is announced or published: *~ that... Word went out that the director had resigned* **5** if a fire or light **goes out**, it stops burning or shining ,go 'out (of sth) to be no longer fashionable or generally used: *Those skirts went out years* ago. ,go 'out of sb/sth (of a quality or a feeling) to be no longer present in someone or something; to disappear from someone or something: *All the fight seemed to go out of him.* ,go 'out to sb if your thoughts, etc. go out to someone, you think about them in a kind way and hope that the difficult situation that they are in will get better: go 'out (with sb) (especially of young people) to spend time with someone and have a romantic or sexual relationship with them: *Tom has been going out with Lucy for six weeks.* ◆ *How long have Tom and Lucy been going out?*

,go 'over sth 1 to examine or check something carefully: *Go over your work before you hand it in.* ➔ thesaurus box at CHECK 2 to study something carefully, especially by repeating it: *He went over the events of the day in his mind* (= thought about them carefully). ,go 'over (to…) to move from one place to another, especially when this means crossing something such as a room, town, or city: *He went over and shook hands with his guests.* ◆ *Many Irish people went over to America during the famine.* ,go 'over to sb/sth (in broadcasting) to change to a different person or place for the next part of a broadcast: *We are now going over to the news desk for an important announcement.* ,go 'over to sth to change from one side, opinion, habit, etc. to another: *Two Republicans have gone over to the Democrats.* ,go 'over (with sb) to be received in a particular way by someone: *The news of her promotion went over well with her colleagues.*

,go 'through if a law, contract, etc. goes through, it is officially accepted or completed: *The deal did not go through.* go through sth 1 to look at or examine something carefully, especially in order to find something: *I always start the day by going through my e-mail.* ◆ *She went through the company's accounts, looking for evidence of fraud.* 2 to study or consider something in detail, especially by repeating it: *Let's go through the arguments again.* ◆ *Could we go through* (= practice) *Act 2 once more?* 3 to perform a series of actions; to follow a method or procedure: *Certain formalities have to be gone through before you can emigrate.* 4 to experience or suffer something: *She's been going through a bad time recently.* ◆ *He's amazingly cheerful considering all he's had to go through.* 5 to use up or finish something completely: *The boys went through two whole loaves of bread.* ,go 'through with sth to do what is necessary to complete a course of action, especially one that is difficult or unpleasant: *She decided not to go through with* (= not to have) *the operation.*

'go to sb/sth to be given to someone or something: *Proceeds from the concert will go to charity.* ◆ *All her property went to her eldest son* (= when she died).

,go to'gether = GO WITH STH

'go toward sth to be used as part of the payment for something: *The money will go toward a new car.* ◆ ~ doing sth *Part of my paycheck went toward buying new speakers.*

,go 'under 1 (of something that floats) to sink below the surface 2 (*informal*) to become BANKRUPT (= be unable to pay what you owe): *The company will go under unless business improves.*

,go 'up 1 to be built: *New office buildings are going up everywhere.* 2 when the curtain across the stage in a theater goes up, it is raised or opened 3 to be destroyed by fire or an explosion: *The whole building went up in flames.* 4 if the price of something, the temperature, etc. goes up, it becomes higher SYN RISE: *The price of cigarettes is going up.* ◆ *Cigarettes are going up in price.* ANT GO DOWN ,go 'up (to…) to go from one place to another, especially further north: *When are you next going up to Seattle?* ◆ *We went up to Montreal last weekend.* ANT GO DOWN

'go with sb (*old-fashioned, informal*) to have a romantic relationship with someone 'go with sth 1 to be included with or as part of something: *A car goes with the job.* 2 to agree to accept something, for example a plan or an offer: *You're offering $500? I think we can go with that.* 3 (also go (together)) to combine well with something SYN MATCH: *Does this jacket go with this skirt?* ◆ *Those colors don't really go together.* 4 (also ,go to'gether) to exist at the same time or in the same place as something; to be found together: *Disease often goes with poverty.* ◆ *Disease and poverty often go together.*

,go wi'thout (sth) to manage without something that you usually have or need: *There wasn't time for breakfast, so I had to go without.* ◆ *How long can a human being go* (= survive) *without sleep?* ◆ ~ doing sth *She went without eating for three days.*

● **noun** (*pl.* **goes** /goʊz/) (also **try**) an attempt at doing something: *It took three goes to get it right.* ◆ *I doubt if he'll listen to advice from me, but I'll give it a go* (= I'll try but I don't think I will succeed).

IDM be a go (*informal*) to be planned and possible or allowed: *I'm not sure if Friday's trip is a go.* be on the go (also be on the move) (*informal*) to be very active and busy: *I've been on the go all day.* ◆ *Having four children keeps her on the go.* have a go (at sth/at doing sth) to make an attempt to do something: *"I can't start the engine." "Let me have a go."* ◆ *I'll have a go at fixing it tonight.* in one go (*informal*) all together on one occasion: *I'd rather do the trip in one go, and not stop on the way.* ◆ *They ate the whole bag of potato chips all in one go.* make a go of sth (*informal*) to be successful in something: *We've had a few problems in our marriage, but we're both determined to make a go of it.* ➔ more at LET

goad /goʊd/ *verb, noun*
● **verb** to keep irritating or annoying someone or something until they react: ~ sb/sth *Goaded beyond endurance, she finally lost her temper.* ◆ ~ sb/sth into sth/into doing sth *He finally goaded her into answering his question.*
PHR V ,goad sb↔'on to drive or encourage someone to do something: *The boxers were goaded on by the shrieking crowd.*
● **noun** 1 a pointed stick used for making cows, etc. move forward 2 something that makes someone do something, usually by annoying them

go-a,head *noun, adj.*
● **noun** the go-ahead [sing.] permission for someone to start doing something: *Management has given the go-ahead to start building.*
● **adj.** [usually before noun] willing to try new ideas, methods, etc. and therefore likely to succeed: *a go-ahead company*

goal 🖉 **AWL** /goʊl/ *noun*
1 something that you hope to achieve SYN AIM: *to work toward a goal* ◆ *to achieve/attain a goal* ◆ *You need to set yourself some long-term goals.* ◆ *Our ultimate goal must be the preservation of the environment.* ➔ thesaurus box at TARGET 2 (in sports) a frame with a net into which players must kick or hit the ball in order to score a point: *He headed the ball into an open goal* (= one that had no one defending it). ◆ *Who is in goal* (= is the goalkeeper) *for the Penguins?* ➔ picture at SPORT 3 the act of kicking or hitting the ball into the goal; a point that is scored for this: *The winning goal was scored by Pearce.* ◆ *The Rangers won by three goals to one.* ◆ *The Galaxy gave up two goals in the first half.* ◆ *a penalty goal*

goal·keep·er /'goʊlˌkipər/ (also *informal* **goal·ie** /'goʊli/, **goal·tend·er**, **keep·er**) *noun* (in SOCCER, HOCKEY, etc.) a player whose job is to stop the ball from going into his or her own team's goal ➔ picture at SPORT ▶ **goal·keep·ing** *noun* [U]: *goalkeeping techniques*

goal kick *noun* (in SOCCER) a kick taken by one team after the ball has been kicked over their GOAL LINE by the other team without a goal being scored

goal line *noun* (in football, HOCKEY, etc.) the line at either end of a sports field on which the goal stands or which the ball must cross to score a goal or TOUCHDOWN

goal·mouth /'goʊlmaʊθ/ *noun* the area directly in front of a goal

goal·post /'goʊlpoʊst/ (also **post**) *noun* one of the two vertical posts that form part of a goal ➔ picture at FOOTBALL
IDM move, etc. the goalposts (*informal, disapproving*) to change the rules for something, or conditions under which it is done, so that the situation becomes more difficult for someone

goal·scor·er /'goʊlˌskɔrər/ *noun* a player in a sports game who scores a goal

goal·tend·er /'goʊlˌtɛndər/ *noun* = GOALKEEPER

t tea   ţ butter   d did   k cat   g got   tʃ chin   dʒ June   f fall

go-a·round (also **go-round**) noun **1** (technical) a path taken by a plane after an unsuccessful attempt at landing, in order to get into a suitable position to try to land again **2** (informal) a disagreement or argument

goat /goʊt/ noun **1** an animal with horns and a coat of hair, that lives wild in mountain areas or is kept on farms for its milk or meat: *a mountain goat* ➲ picture at ANIMAL: *goat milk/cheese* ➲ see also BILLY GOAT, KID, NANNY GOAT **2** old **~** (informal) an unpleasant old man who is annoying in a sexual way
IDM **get sb's goat** (informal) to annoy someone very much

goat cheese noun [U] cheese made from the milk of a GOAT

goat·ee /goʊˈti/ noun a small pointed beard (= hair growing on a man's face) that is grown only on the chin ➲ picture at HAIR

goat·herd /ˈgoʊthɜrd/ noun a person whose job is to take care of a group of goats

goat·skin /ˈgoʊtskɪn/ noun [U] leather made from the skin of a goat

gob /gɑb/ noun (slang) **1** a small amount of a thick wet substance: *Gobs of paint ran down the sides of the can.* **2** [usually pl.] a large amount of something: *gobs of cash*

gob·bet /ˈgɑbət/ noun (old-fashioned) **~ (of sth)** a small amount of something: *gobbets of food*

gob·ble /ˈgɑbl/ verb **1** [T, I] to eat something very fast, in a way that people consider rude or GREEDY **SYN** WOLF: **~ (sth)** *Don't gobble your food like that!* ♦ **~ sth up/down** *They gobbled up all the sandwiches.* **2** [I] when a TURKEY gobbles, it makes a noise in its throat
PHR V **gobble sth↔up** (informal) **1** to use something very quickly: *Hotel costs gobbled up most of their vacation budget.* **2** if a business, company, etc. **gobbles up** a smaller one, it takes control of it

gob·ble·dy·gook (also **gob·ble·de·gook**) /ˈgɑbəldiɡʊk; -ˌguk/ noun [U] (informal) complicated language that is difficult to understand, especially when used in official documents: *It's all gobbledygook to me.*

gob·bler /ˈgɑblər/ noun (informal) a male TURKEY

go-be·tween noun a person who takes messages between one person or group and another: *to act as a go-between*

gob·let /ˈgɑblət/ noun a cup for wine, usually made of glass or metal, with a STEM and base but no handle

gob·lin /ˈgɑblən/ noun (in stories) a small ugly creature that likes to trick people or cause trouble

gob·stop·per /ˈgɑbˌstɑpər/ noun = JAWBREAKER

go·by /ˈgoʊbi/ noun (pl. **go·by** or **go·bies**) a small sea fish with a SUCKER underneath

go-cart = GO-KART

god 🔑 /gɑd/ noun
1 God [sing.] (not used with *the*) (in Christianity, Islam, and Judaism) the BEING or spirit that is worshiped and is believed to have created the universe: *Do you believe in God?* ♦ *Good luck and God bless you.* ♦ *the Son of God* (= Christ) ➲ collocations at RELIGION **2** [C] (in some religions) a BEING or spirit who is believed to have power over a particular part of nature or who is believed to represent a particular quality: *Mars was the Roman god of war.* ♦ *the rain god* ♦ *Greek gods* ➲ see also GODDESS **3** [C] a person who is loved or admired very much by other people: *To her fans she's a god.* ➲ see also GODDESS **4** [C] something to which too much importance or attention is given: *Money is his god.*
IDM **God| God almighty| God in heaven| good God| my God| oh God** (informal) used to emphasize what you are saying when you are surprised, shocked, or annoyed: *God, what a stupid thing to do!* **HELP** Some people find this use offensive. **God bless** used when you are leaving someone, to say that you hope they will be safe, etc.: *Goodnight, God bless.* **God rest his/her soul| God rest him/her** (old-fashioned, informal) used to show respect when you are talking about someone who is dead **God's gift (to**

sb/sth) (ironic) a person who thinks that they are particularly good at something or who thinks that someone will find them particularly attractive: *He seems to think he's God's gift to women.* **God willing** (informal) used to say that you hope that things will happen as you have planned and that there will be no problems: *I'll be back next week, God willing.* **play God** to behave as if you control events or other people's lives: *It is unfair to ask doctors to play God and end someone's life.* **to God/goodness/Heaven** used after a verb to emphasize a particular hope, wish, etc.: *I wish to God you'd learn to pay attention!* **HELP** Some people find this use offensive. ➲ more at ACT, FEAR, FORBID, GRACE, HELP, HONEST, KNOW, LOVE, MAN, NAME *n.*, PLEASE, THANK

god·aw·ful (also **god-awful**) /ˈgɑdˌɔfl/ adj. [usually before noun] (informal) extremely bad: *He made a god-awful mess of it!* **HELP** Some people find this use offensive.

god·child /ˈgɑdtʃaɪld/ noun (pl. **god·child·ren** /-ˌtʃɪldrən/) a child that a GODPARENT at a Christian BAPTISM ceremony promises to be responsible for and to teach about the Christian religion

god·daugh·ter /ˈgɑdˌdɔtər/ noun a female GODCHILD

god·dess /ˈgɑdəs/ noun **1** a female god: *Diana, the goddess of hunting* **2** a woman who is loved or admired very much by other people: *a screen goddess* (= a female movie star)

god·fa·ther /ˈgɑdˌfɑðər/ noun **1** a male GODPARENT **2** often Godfather a very powerful man in a criminal organization, especially the Mafia **3** **~ of sth** a person who began or developed something: *He's the godfather of punk.*

God-fearing adj. [usually before noun] living a moral life based on religious principles

god·for·sak·en /ˈgɑdfərˌseɪkən/ adj. [only before noun] (of places) boring, depressing, and ugly: *I can't stand living in this godforsaken place.*

God-given adj. [usually before noun] given or created by God: *a God-given talent* ♦ *What gives you a God-given right to know all my business?*

god·head /ˈgɑdhɛd/ noun the Godhead [sing.] (formal) used in the Christian religion to mean God, including the Father, Son, and HOLY SPIRIT

god·less /ˈgɑdləs/ adj. [usually before noun] not believing in or respecting God: *a godless generation/world* ▸ **god·less·ness** [U]

god·like /ˈgɑdlaɪk/ adj. like God or a god in some quality: *his godlike beauty*

god·ly /ˈgɑdli/ adj. [usually before noun] (old-fashioned) living a moral life based on religious principles: *a godly man* ▸ **god·li·ness** noun [U]

god·moth·er /ˈgɑdˌmʌðər/ noun a female GODPARENT ➲ see also FAIRY GODMOTHER

god·par·ent /ˈgɑdˌpɛrənt/ noun a person who promises at a Christian BAPTISM ceremony to be responsible for a child (= his or her GODCHILD) and to teach them about the Christian religion

God's country noun a beautiful and peaceful area that people love. The expression is often used to mean the U.S., especially the western states.

god·send /ˈgɑdsɛnd/ noun [sing.] **~ (for sb/sth)** | **~ (to sb/ sth)** something good that happens unexpectedly and helps someone or something when they need help: *This new benefit is a godsend for low-income families.*

god·son /ˈgɑdsʌn/ noun a male GODCHILD

God·speed /ˌgɑdˈspid; ˈgɑdspid/ exclamation (old-fashioned or literary) used to express good wishes to a person starting on a journey

the God squad noun [sing.] (informal, disapproving) Christians, especially ones who try to make people share their beliefs

-go·er /ˈgoʊər/ noun (in compounds) a person who regularly goes to the place or event mentioned: *a theater-goer* ♦ *a moviegoer*

go·fer (also **go·pher**) /ˈɡoʊfər/ noun (informal) a person whose job is to do small boring tasks for other people in a company

go-get·ter /ˌɡoʊ ˈɡɛtər; ˈɡoʊ ˌɡɛtər/ noun (informal) a person who is determined to succeed, especially in business

gog·gle /ˈɡɑɡl/ verb [I] ~ **(at sb/sth)** (old-fashioned, informal) to look at someone or something with your eyes wide open, especially because you are surprised or shocked

goggle-eyed adj. with your eyes wide open, staring at something, especially because you are surprised

gog·gles /ˈɡɑɡlz/ noun [pl.] a pair of glasses that fit closely to the face to protect the eyes from wind, dust, water, etc.: *a pair of swimming/ski/safety goggles* ⊃ picture at SPORT

go-go adj. **1** connected with a style of dancing to pop music in which women dance wearing very few clothes: *a go-go dancer* **2** (informal) of a period of time when businesses are growing and people are making money fast: *the go-go years of the 1990s*

go·ing /ˈɡoʊɪŋ/ noun, adj.

• noun **1** [U] (used with an adjective) the speed with which someone does something; how difficult it is to do something: *Walking four miles in an hour is pretty good going for me.* ♦ *She had her own company by 25—not bad going!* ♦ *It was hard going getting up at five every morning.* **2** [sing.] (formal) an act of leaving a place SYN DEPARTURE: *We were all sad at her going.* **3** [U] the condition of the ground, especially in horse racing: *The going is good to firm.* ⊃ see also OUTGOINGS IDM **when the going gets tough (the tough get going)** (saying) when conditions or progress become difficult (strong and determined people work even harder to succeed) **while the going/getting is good** before a situation changes and it is no longer possible to do something: *Don't you think we should quit while the going is good?* ⊃ more at COMING, HEAVY

• adj. **-going** (in compounds) going regularly to the place or event mentioned: *the theater-going public* ⊃ see also OCEANGOING, ONGOING, OUTGOING IDM **the best, fastest, etc. sth going** (informal) the best, fastest, etc. thing of its kind currently available: *It's a little expensive, but this computer is the best thing going right now.* **a going concern** a business or an activity that is making a profit and is expected to continue to do well: *He sold the café as a going concern.* **the going rate (for sth)** the usual amount of money paid for goods or services at a particular time: *They pay slightly more than the going rate.*

going-over noun [sing.] (informal) **1** a thorough examination of someone or something: *The garage gave the car a thorough going-over.* **2** a serious physical attack on someone: *The gang gave him a real going-over.*

goings-on noun [pl.] (informal) activities or events that are strange, surprising, or dishonest: *There were some strange goings-on next door last night.*

goi·ter (CanE usually **goi·tre**) /ˈɡɔɪtər/ noun [U, C] a swelling of the throat caused by a disease of the THYROID gland

go-kart (also **go-cart**) /ˈɡoʊ kɑrt/ noun a vehicle like a small low car with no roof or doors, used for racing

gold /ɡoʊld/ noun, adj.

• noun **1** [U] (symb. **Au**) a chemical element. Gold is a yellow PRECIOUS METAL used for making coins, jewelry, decorative objects, etc.: *a gold bracelet/ring/watch, etc.* ♦ *18-karat gold* ♦ *the country's gold reserves* ♦ *made of solid/pure gold* ⊃ see also FOOL'S GOLD **2** [U] money, jewelry, etc. that is made of gold: *His wife was dripping with* (= wearing a lot of) *gold.* **3** [U, C] the color of gold: *I love the reds and golds of the fall.* **4** [U, C] = GOLD MEDAL: *The team look set to win Olympic gold.* ♦ *He won three golds and a bronze.* IDM **a crock/pot of gold** a large prize or reward that someone hopes for but is unlikely to get **(as) good as gold** (informal) behaving in a way that other people approve of: *The kids have been as good as gold all day.* ⊃ more at GLITTER v., HEART, STREET n., STRIKE v., WORTH adj.

• adj. [only before noun] bright yellow in color, like gold: *The company name was spelled out in gold letters.*

gold brick noun (informal) a person who is lazy and tries to avoid work by pretending to be sick

gold·brick /ˈɡoʊldbrɪk/ verb [I] (informal) to be lazy and try to avoid work by pretending to be sick

gold card noun a type of credit card that enables a person to buy more goods and services than a normal card does

gold digger noun (informal, disapproving) a woman who uses the fact that she is attractive to get money from men

gold dust noun [U] gold in the form of powder

gold·en /ˈɡoʊldən/ adj. **1** (especially literary) made of gold: *a golden crown* **2** bright yellow in color like gold: *golden hair* ♦ *miles of golden beaches* **3** special; wonderful: *golden memories* ♦ *Businesses have a golden opportunity to expand into new markets.* ♦ *Hollywood's golden boy* IDM **be golden** (informal) be in a situation where you are successful or do not have any problems: *He thinks once he gets the money he'll be golden.* **the golden mean** (approving) a course of action that is not extreme ⊃ more at KILL, SILENCE

golden age noun [usually sing.] ~ **(of sth)** a period during which something is very successful, especially in the past: *the golden age of theater*

gold·en ag·er /ˌɡoʊldən ˈeɪdʒər/ noun (informal) an old person

golden anni·versary noun the 50th anniversary of a wedding or other important event ⊃ compare DIAMOND ANNIVERSARY, SILVER ANNIVERSARY

golden eagle noun a large BIRD OF PREY (= a bird that kills other creatures for food) of the EAGLE family, with light brown feathers, that lives in northern parts of the world

golden goose noun something that provides someone with a lot of money, that they must be very careful with in order not to lose it: *An increase in crime could kill the golden goose of tourism.*

golden handcuffs noun [pl.] a large sum of money and other financial benefits that are given to someone to persuade them to continue working for a company rather than leaving to work for another company

golden handshake noun a large sum of money that is given to someone when they leave their job, or to persuade them to leave their job

golden oldie noun (informal) **1** a song or movie that is fairly old but still well known and popular **2** a person who is no longer young but still successful in their particular career, sport, etc.

golden parachute noun (informal) part of a work contract in which a business person is promised a large amount of money if they have to leave their job

golden raisin noun a small, dried, white GRAPE without seeds

golden re·triever noun a large dog with thick yellow hair

gold·en·rod /ˈɡoʊldənˌrɑd/ noun a plant that has small, bright yellow flowers

golden rule noun [usually sing.] **1** an important principle that should be followed when doing something in order to be successful: *The golden rule in tennis is to keep your eye on the ball.* **2** often **Golden Rule** a principle that states that you should treat others in the same way that you want them to treat you

golden section noun (technical) the proportion that is considered to be the most attractive to look at when a line is divided into two

gold·field /ˈɡoʊldfild/ noun an area where gold is found in the ground

gold·finch /ˈɡoʊldfɪntʃ/ noun a small brightly colored bird of the FINCH family, with yellow feathers on its wings

gold·fish /ˈɡoʊldfɪʃ/ noun (pl. **gold·fish**) a small orange or red fish. Goldfish are kept as pets in bowls or PONDS.

| h **hat** | m **man** | n **no** | ŋ **sing** | l **leg** | r **red** | y **yes** | w **wet** |

'goldfish ¦bowl (also **fish·bowl**) *noun* **1** a glass bowl for keeping fish in as pets **2** a situation in which people can see everything that happens and nothing is private: *Living in this goldfish bowl of publicity would crack the strongest marriage.*

¦gold 'leaf *noun* [U] gold that has been made into a very thin sheet and is used for decoration

¦gold 'medal *noun* (also **gold**) a MEDAL made of gold that is given to the winner of a race or competition: *an Olympic gold medal winner* ➔ compare BRONZE MEDAL, SILVER MEDAL ▶ **¦gold 'medalist** *noun: an Olympic gold medalist*

'gold mine *noun* **1** a place where gold is dug out of the ground **2** a business or an activity that makes a large profit: *This restaurant is a potential gold mine.*

¦gold 'plate *noun* [U] **1** dishes, etc. made of gold **2** a thin layer of gold used to cover another metal; objects made in this way

¦gold-'plated *adj.* covered with a thin layer of gold: *gold-plated earrings*

¦gold 'record *noun* a gold record that is given to a singer or group that sells a particularly high number of records

'gold re¦serve *noun* [usually pl.] an amount of gold kept by a country's bank in order to support the supply of money

'gold rush *noun* a situation in which a lot of people suddenly go to a place where gold has recently been discovered

gold·smith /'ɡoʊldsmɪθ/ *noun* a person who makes, repairs, or sells articles made of gold

'gold ¦standard *noun* **1** usually **the gold standard** [sing.] an economic system in which the value of money is based on the value of gold **2** [usually sing.] a high level of quality that others try to copy: *Articles like his are the gold standard of news reporting.*

go·lem /'ɡoʊləm/ *noun* **1** (in Jewish stories) a figure made of CLAY that comes to life **2** a machine that behaves like a human

golf /ɡɑlf; ɡɔlf/ *noun* [U] a game played over a large area of ground using specially shaped sticks to hit a small hard ball (a **golf ball**) into a series of 9 or 18 holes, using as few strokes as possible: *He enjoyed a **round of golf** on Sunday morning.* ➔ picture at SPORT ➔ see also MINIATURE GOLF

'golf cart *noun* a small car, often without a roof or doors, used to drive people around a golf course

'golf club *noun* **1** (also **club**) a long metal stick with a piece of metal or wood at one end, used for hitting the ball in golf: *a set of golf clubs* ➔ picture at SPORT **2** an organization whose members play golf; the place where these people meet and play golf: *Pine Ridge Golf Club* ◆ *We're going to lunch at the golf club.*

'golf course (also **course**) *noun* a large area of land that is designed for playing golf on ➔ picture at SPORT

golf·er /'ɡɑlfər; 'ɡɔl-/ *noun* a person who plays golf ➔ picture at SPORT

golf·ing /'ɡɑlfɪŋ; 'ɡɔl-/ *adj.* [only before noun] playing golf; connected with golf: *a golfing vacation* ▶ **golfing** *noun* [U]: *a week spent golfing with friends*

'golf links (also **links**) *noun* (*pl.* **golf links**) a golf course, especially one by the ocean

Go·li·ath /ɡə'laɪəθ/ *noun* a person or thing that is very large or powerful: *a Goliath of a man* ◆ *a Goliath of the computer industry* ORIGIN From Goliath, a giant in the Bible who is killed by the boy David with a stone.

gol·ly /'ɡɑli/ *exclamation* (*old-fashioned, informal*) used to express surprise: *Golly, you're early!*

go·nad /'ɡoʊnæd/ *noun* (*anatomy*) a male sex organ that produces SPERM; a female sex organ that produces eggs

gon·do·la /'ɡɑndələ; ɡɑn'doʊlə/ *noun* **1** a long boat with a flat bottom and high parts at each end, used on CANALS in Venice **2** the part on a CABLE CAR or SKI LIFT where the passengers sit **3** the part of a hot air BALLOON or AIRSHIP where the passengers sit

gon·do·lier /ˌɡɑndə'lɪr/ *noun* a person whose job is to move and steer a gondola in Venice

Gond·wa·na /ɡɑn'dwɑnə/ (also **Gond·wa·na·land** /ɡɑn'dwɑnəˌlænd/) *noun* [sing.] (*geology*) a very large area of land that existed in the southern HEMISPHERE millions of years ago. It was made up of the present Arabia, S. America, Antarctica, Australia, and India.

gone /ɡɔn; ɡɑn/ *adj.* [not before noun] **1** (of a thing) used up: *"Where's the coffee?" "It's all gone."* **2** (of a person) having left a place; away from a place: *"Is Tom here?" "No, he was gone before I arrived."* **3** (*formal*) used to say that a particular situation no longer exists: *The days are gone when you could leave your door unlocked at night.* ➔ see also GO v.
IDM **going, going, gone** (also **going once, going twice, sold**) said by an AUCTIONEER to show that an item has been sold ➔ more at DEAD

gon·er /'ɡɔnər; 'ɡɑ-/ *noun* (*informal*) a person who is going to die soon or who cannot be saved from a dangerous situation

gong /ɡɑŋ; ɡɔŋ/ *noun* a round piece of metal that hangs in a frame and makes a loud, deep sound when it is hit with a stick. Gongs are used as musical instruments or to give signals, for example that a meal is ready.

gon·na /ɡənə; 'ɡɔnə/ (*informal, non-standard*) a way of saying or writing "going to" in informal speech, when it refers to the future: *What's she gonna do now?* **HELP** You should not write this form unless you are copying somebody's speech.

gon·or·rhe·a /ˌɡɑnə'riə/ *noun* [U] a disease of the sexual organs, caught by having sex with an infected person ➔ see also SEXUALLY TRANSMITTED DISEASE

gon·zo jour·nal·ism /ˌɡɑnzoʊ 'dʒərnəˌlɪzəm/ *noun* [U] (*informal*) reporting in newspapers that tries to shock or excite readers rather than to give true information

goo /ɡu/ *noun* [U] (*informal*) any unpleasant, sticky, wet substance ➔ see also GOOEY

goo·ber /'ɡubər/ *noun* (*informal*) **1** (also **'goober ¦pea**) a PEANUT **2** (*offensive*) a stupid person

good /ɡʊd/ *adj., noun, adv.*
● *adj.* (**bet·ter** /'bɛtər/, **best** /bɛst/)
▶ HIGH QUALITY **1** of high quality or an acceptable standard: *a good book* ◆ *good food* ◆ *The piano was in good condition.* ◆ *Your work is just not good enough.* ◆ *The results were pretty good.* ◆ *Sorry, my English is not very good.* ◆ *This is **as good a place as any** to spend the night.* ◆ *You'll never marry her—she's much too good for you.*
▶ PLEASANT **2** pleasant; that you enjoy or want: *Did you have a **good time** in London?* ◆ *It's good to see you again.* ◆ *This is very **good news.*** ◆ *Let's hope we have good weather tomorrow.* ◆ *We are still friends, though, which is good.* ◆ *It's a **good thing** (= it's lucky) you came early.* ➔ thesaurus box at FUN
▶ SENSIBLE/STRONG **3** sensible, logical, or strongly supporting what is being discussed: *Thank you, **good question.*** ◆ *Yes, that's a **good point.*** ◆ *I have **good reason** to be suspicious.* ◆ *What a **good idea!***
▶ FAVORABLE **4** showing or getting approval or respect: *The play had good reviews.* ◆ *The hotel has a good reputation.* ◆ *He comes from a good family.*
▶ SKILLFUL **5** able to do something well: *to be a good actor/cook* ◆ ~ **at sth** *to be good at languages/your job* ◆ ~ **at doing sth** *Nick has always been good at finding cheap flights.* **6** ~ **with sth/sb** able to use something or deal with people well: *She's good with her hands (= able to make things, etc.).* ◆ *He's very good with children.*
▶ MORALLY RIGHT **7** morally right; behaving in a way that is morally right: *She has tried to lead a **good life.*** ◆ *a **good deed*** ◆ *Giving her that money was a good thing to do.* ◆ *He is a very good man.*
▶ FOLLOWING RULES **8** following strictly a set of rules or principles: *It is **good practice** to supply a written report to the buyer.* ◆ *She was a good Catholic girl.*

> **KIND 9** willing to help; showing kindness to other people: ~ **(to sb)** *He was very good to me when I was sick.* ◆ ~ **(of sb) (to do sth)** *It was very good of you to come.* ◆ ~ **(about sth)** *I had to take a week off work but my colleagues were very good about it.*

> **CHILD 10** behaving well or politely: *You can stay up late if you're good.* ◆ *Get dressed now, that's a good girl.*

> **HEALTHY 11** healthy or strong: *Can you speak into my good ear?* ◆ *I don't feel too good today.* ◆ *"How are you?" "I'm good."* (= used as a general reply to a greeting) ⊃ **thesaurus box at WELL**

> **USEFUL/HELPFUL 12** ~ **(for sb/sth)** having a useful or helpful effect on someone or something: *Too much sun isn't good for you.* ◆ *It's probably good for you to get some criticism now and then.* ◆ (*informal*) *Shut your mouth, if you know what's good for you* (= used as a threat). **13 no** ~ **doing sth | no** ~ **to sb** not having a useful or helpful effect: *It's no good complaining—they never listen.* ◆ *This book is no good to me: I need the new edition.*

> **SUITABLE 14** suitable or appropriate: *Now is a good time to buy a house.* ◆ ~ **for sth/to do sth** *She would be good for the job.* ◆ ~ **for sb** *Can we change our meeting? Monday isn't good* (= convenient) *for me.*

> **SHOWING APPROVAL 15** (*informal*) used to show that you approve of or are pleased about something that has been said or done, or to show that you want to move on to a new topic of conversation: *"Dinner's ready." "Good—I'm starving."* ◆ *"I got the job." "Oh, good."* ◆ *Good, I think we've come to a decision.* **16** [only before noun] (*informal*) used as a form of praise: *Good old Jack!* ◆ *"I ordered some drinks." "Good man!"*

> **IN EXCLAMATIONS 17** (*informal*) used in exclamations: *Good heavens!* ◆ *Good God!* **HELP** Some people find this use offensive.

> **LARGE 18** [only before noun] great in number, amount, or degree: *a good many people* ◆ *The kitchen is a good size.* ◆ *We spent a good while* (= quite a long time) *looking for the house.* ◆ *He devoted a good deal of* (= a lot of) *attention to the problem.* ◆ *There's a good chance* (= it is likely) *that I won't be here next year.*

> **AT LEAST 19** not less than; rather more than: *We waited for a good hour.* ◆ *It's a good three miles to the station.*

> **THOROUGH 20** [only before noun] thorough; complete: *We had a good laugh about it afterward.* ◆ *You'll feel better after a good sleep.*

> **AMUSING 21** [usually before noun] amusing: *a good story/ joke* ◆ (*informal*) *That's a good one!*

> **FOR PARTICULAR TIME/DISTANCE 22** ~ **for sth** having enough energy, health, strength, etc. to last for a particular length of time or distance: *You're good for* (= you will live) *a few years yet.* **23** ~ **for sth** valid for something: *The ticket is good for three months.*

> **LIKELY TO PROVIDE 24** ~ **for sth** likely to provide something: *He's always good for a laugh.* ◆ *Bobby should be good for a few drinks.*

IDM Most idioms containing **good** are at the entries for the nouns and verbs in the idioms. For example, **(as) good as gold** is at **gold**. **as good as** very nearly: *The matter is as good as settled.* ◆ *He as good as called me a coward* (= suggested that I was a coward without actually using the word "coward"). **as good as it gets** used when you are saying that a situation is not going to get any better **good and…** (*informal*) completely: *I won't go until I'm good and ready.* **good for you, sb, them, etc.** (*informal*) used to praise someone for doing something well: *"I passed first time." "Good for you!"* **a good many** a lot of: *There are still a good many empty seats.*

● **noun** ⊃ see also **GOODS**

> **MORALLY RIGHT 1** [U] behavior that is morally right or acceptable: *the difference between good and evil* ◆ *Is religion always a force for good?* **2 the good** [pl.] people who live a moral life; people who are admired for the work they do to help other people: *a gathering of the great and the good*

> **SOMETHING HELPFUL 2** [U] something that helps someone or something: *Cuts have been made for the good of the company.* ◆ *I'm only telling you this for your own good.* ◆ *What's the good*

of (= how does it help you) *earning all that money if you don't have time to enjoy it?* ◆ *What good is it redecorating if you're thinking of moving?* ⊃ see also **DO-GOODER**

IDM **all to the good** used to say that if something happens, it will be good, even if it is not exactly what you were expecting: *If these measures also reduce unemployment, that is all to the good.* **be no good | not be any/much good 1** to not be useful; to have no useful effect: *This gadget isn't much good.* ◆ *It's no good trying to talk me out of leaving.* ◆ *Was his advice ever any good?* **2** to not be interesting or enjoyable: *His latest movie isn't much good.* **do good | do sb good** to have a useful effect; to help someone: *Do you think these latest changes will do any good?* ◆ *Don't you think talking to her would do some good?* ◆ *The fresh air will do you good* (= improve your health). **for good** permanently: *This time she's leaving for good* (= she will never return). **to the good** used to say that someone now has a particular amount of money that they did not have before: *We are $500 to the good.* **up to no good** (*informal*) doing something wrong or dishonest: *Those kids are always up to no good.* ⊃ more at **ILL, WORLD**

● **adv.** (*informal*) well: *"How's it going?" "Pretty good."* ◆ (*non-standard*) *Now, you listen to me good!*

WHICH WORD?

good / goodness

■ The noun **good** means actions and behavior that are morally right. You can talk about a person doing **good**: *The charity does a lot of good.* ◆ *the difference between good and evil.*

■ **Goodness** is the quality of being good. You can talk about a person's **goodness**: *Her goodness shone through.*

VOCABULARY BUILDING

good and very good

Instead of saying that something is **good** or **very good**, try to use more precise and interesting adjectives to describe things:

■ **delicious/tasty** food
■ an **exciting/entertaining/absorbing** movie
■ an **absorbing/a fascinating/an informative** book
■ a **pleasant/an enjoyable** trip
■ a **skillful/skilled/talented** player
■ **impressive/high-quality/superb** acting
■ **useful/helpful** advice

In conversation, you can use words like **great**, **super**, **wonderful**, and **excellent**.

⊃ note at **NICE**

good ˌafterˈnoon *exclamation* used to say hello formally when people first see each other in the afternoon

goodˈbye 🔊 /ˌɡʊdˈbaɪ; ɡəˈbaɪ/ *exclamation, noun* used when you are leaving someone or when someone else is leaving: *Goodbye! It was great to meet you.* ◆ *She didn't even say goodbye to her mother.* ◆ *We waved them goodbye.* ◆ *We've already said our goodbyes.* ◆ *Kiss me goodbye!* ◆ (*figurative*) *Buy our service contract and say goodbye to costly repair bills.* ⊃ compare **BYE** **IDM** see **KISS** *v.*

ˌgood ˈday *exclamation* (*old-fashioned*) used to say hello or goodbye politely when people first see each other or leave each other during the day: *Good day to you.*

ˌgood ˈevening *exclamation* used to say hello formally when people first see each other in the evening

ˌgood ˈfaith *noun* [U] the intention to be honest and helpful: *a gesture of good faith* ◆ *He acted in good faith.*

ˌgood-for-ˈnothing *noun* (*informal*) a person who is lazy and has no skills: *an idle good-for-nothing* ▶ **ˌgood-for-ˈnothing** *adj.* [usually before noun]: *Where's that good-for-nothing son of yours?*

Good ˈFriday *noun* [U, C] the Friday before Easter, the day when Christians remember the Crucifixion of Christ

good-ˈhearted *adj.* kind; willing to help other people

good ˈhumor (*CanE usually* **good ˈhumour**) *noun* [U, sing.] a cheerful mood: *Everyone admired her patience and unfailing good humor.* **ANT ILL HUMOR ▶ good-ˈhumored** (*CanE usually* **good-ˈhumoured**) *adj.*: *a good-humored atmosphere* **good-ˈhumoredly** (*CanE usually* **good-ˈhumouredly**) *adv.*

good·ie = GOODY

good·ish /ˈgʊdɪʃ/ *adj.* [only before noun] (*informal*) **1** fairly good rather than very good: *"Is the salary good?" "Goodish."* **2** quite large in size or amount: *It'll be a goodish while yet before I'm done.*

good-ˈlooking *adj.* (especially of people) physically attractive ➜ thesaurus box at BEAUTIFUL: *a good-looking man/couple* ♦ *She's strikingly good-looking.* **ANT UGLY**

good ˈlooks *noun* [pl.] the physical beauty of a person: *an actor famous for his rugged good looks*

good·ly /ˈgʊdli/ *adj.* [only before noun] **1** (*old-fashioned, formal*) quite large in size or amount: *a goodly number* **2** (*old use*) physically attractive; of good quality

good ˈmorning *exclamation* used to say hello politely when people first see each other in the morning; sometimes also used formally when people leave each other in the morning; in informal use people often just say *Morning.*

good ˈname *noun* [sing.] the good opinion that people have of someone or something **SYN REPUTATION**: *He told the police he didn't know her, to protect her good name.* ♦ *My election chances are not as important as the good name of the party.*

good ˈnature *noun* [U] the quality of being kind, friendly, and patient when dealing with people

good-ˈnatured *adj.* kind, friendly, and patient when dealing with people: *a good-natured person/discussion* **▶ good-ˈnaturedly** *adv.*: *to smile good-naturedly*

good·ness /ˈgʊdnəs/ *noun* [U] **1** the quality of being good: *the essential goodness of human nature* ♦ *evidence of God's goodness* ➜ note at GOOD **2** the part of something that has a useful effect on someone or something, especially someone's health: *These vegetables have had all the goodness boiled out of them.*
IDM **Goodness!** | **Goodness me!** | **My goodness!** | **Goodness gracious!** (*informal*) used to express surprise: *Goodness, what a big balloon!* ♦ *My goodness, you have been busy!* ♦ *Goodness me, no!* **out of the goodness of your heart** from feelings of kindness, without thinking about what advantage there will be for you: *You're not telling me he offered to lend you the money out of the goodness of his heart?* ➜ more at GOD, HONEST, KNOW, THANK

good ˈnight *exclamation* used when you are saying goodbye to someone late in the evening, or when they or you are going to bed; in informal use people often just say *Night.*

good old ˌboy *noun* (*informal*) a man who is considered typical of white men in the southern states of the U.S.

goods 🔑 /gʊdz/ *noun* [pl.]
1 things that are produced to be sold: *cheap/expensive goods* ♦ *leather/cotton/paper goods* ♦ *electrical/sports goods* ♦ *perishable/durable goods* ♦ *increased tax on goods and services* ➜ see also CONSUMER GOODS ➜ thesaurus box at PRODUCT **2** possessions that can be moved: *stolen goods* ♦ *The plastic bag contained all his worldly goods* (= everything he owned). ➜ thesaurus box at THING
IDM **deliver the goods** | **come up with the goods** (*informal*) to do what you have promised to do or what people expect or want you to do: *We expected great things from the new government, but so far they have failed to deliver the goods.*

good ˈsense *noun* [U] **~ (to do sth)** the ability to make the right decision about something; good judgment: *a man of*

honor and good sense ♦ *Eating a low-fat diet makes very good sense* (= is a sensible thing to do).

good-ˈtempered *adj.* cheerful and not easily made angry

good-time *adj.* [only before noun] only interested in pleasure, and not in anything serious or important: *I was too much of a good-time guy to do any serious studying.*

good·will /ˌgʊdˈwɪl/ *noun* [U] **1** friendly or helpful feelings toward other people or countries: *a spirit of goodwill in international relations* ♦ *a goodwill gesture/a gesture of goodwill* **2** the good relationship between a business and its customers that is calculated as part of its value when it is sold

goodwill amˈbassador *noun* a famous person who represents an organization by educating the public or promoting a good relationship with the public: *The singer is a goodwill ambassador for the American Heart Association.*

good·y /ˈgʊdi/ *noun, exclamation*
● *noun* (also **good·ie**) [usually pl.] (*pl.* **good·ies**) (*informal*) **1** a thing that is very nice to eat: *a basket of goodies for the children* **2** anything that is attractive and that people want to have: *We're giving away lots of free goodies—T-shirts, hats, and DVDs!*
● *exclamation* (becoming *old-fashioned*) a word children use when they are excited or pleased about something

goody ˌbag (also **ˈgoodie bag**) *noun* **1** a bag containing examples of a company's products, given away in order to advertise them **2** a bag containing candy and small presents, given to children to take home at the end of a party

goody-ˈgoody *noun* (*pl.* **goody-goodies**) (*informal, disapproving*) (used especially by and about children) a person who behaves very well to please people in authority such as parents or teachers

goody-ˈtwo-shoes *noun* (*pl.* **goody-two-shoes**) (*informal, disapproving*) a person who always behaves well, and often has a disapproving attitude to people who do not

goo·ey /ˈgui/ *adj.* (*informal*) soft and sticky: *a gooey mess* ♦ *gooey cakes*

goof /guf/ *verb, noun*
● *verb* [I] (*informal*) to make a stupid mistake: *Sorry, guys. I goofed.*
PHR V **goof aˈround** (*informal*) to spend your time doing silly or stupid things **SYN MESS AROUND** **goof ˈoff** (*informal*) to spend your time doing nothing, especially when you should be working
● *noun* (*informal*) **1** a stupid mistake **2** a silly or stupid person

goof·ball /ˈgufbɔl/ *noun* (*informal*) a stupid person **▶ goof·ball** *adj.* [only before noun]: *This is just another of his goofball ideas.*

goof-off *noun* (*slang*) a person who avoids work or responsibility

goof·y /ˈgufi/ *adj.* (*informal*) silly; stupid: *a goofy grin*

goo·gle /ˈgugl/ *verb* [T, I] **~ (sb/sth)** (*computing*) to type words into the SEARCH ENGINE Google® in order to find information about someone or something: *You can google someone to see what information is available about them on the Internet.* ♦ *I tried googling but couldn't find anything relevant.*

goog·ly eyes /ˌgugli ˈaɪz/ *noun* [pl.] (*informal*) eyes that stick out or are open very wide **▶ googly-eyed** /ˌgugli ˈaɪd/ *adj.* (*informal*): *They were staring, googly-eyed, at the strange scene in front of them.*

goo·gol /ˈgugɔl/ *noun* (*mathematics*) the number 10^{100}, or 1 followed by 100 zeros

goon /gun/ *noun* (*informal*) **1** a criminal who is paid to frighten or injure people **2** (*old-fashioned*) a stupid or silly person

goop /gup/ *noun* [U] (*informal*) a thick, soft, sticky substance that looks, tastes, or feels unpleasant

goose /gus/ *noun, verb*
● *noun* (*pl.* **geese** /gis/) **1** [C] a bird like a large DUCK with a

long neck. Geese either live wild or are kept on farms. **2** [U] meat from a goose: *roast goose* **3** [C] a female goose ⊃ compare GANDER **4** [C] (*old-fashioned*, *informal*) a silly person ⊃ see also WILD GOOSE CHASE **IDM** see COOK v., KILL v., SAUCE

● *verb* (*informal*) **1** ~ **sb** to touch or squeeze someone's bottom **2** ~ **sth (along/up)** to make something move or work faster

goose·ber·ry /ˈɡusˌbɛri/ *noun* (*pl.* goose·ber·ries) a small green fruit that grows on a bush with THORNS. Gooseberries taste sour and are usually cooked to make PIES, etc.: *a gooseberry bush*

goose·bumps /ˈɡusbʌmps/ *noun* [pl.] (*also less frequent* **goose·flesh** [U]) a condition in which there are raised spots on your skin because you feel cold, frightened, or excited: *It gave me goosebumps just to think about it.*

'goose egg *noun* (*informal*) a score of zero in a game

goose·flesh / ˈɡusflɛʃ/ *noun* [U] = GOOSEBUMPS

goose·neck /ˈɡusnɛk/ *noun* something such as a support or pipe that is curved and shaped like the neck of a GOOSE

'goose step *noun* [sing.] (*often disapproving*) a way of marching, used by soldiers in some countries, in which the legs are raised high and straight ▶ **'goose-step** *verb* (-pp-) [I]

GOP /ˌdʒi oʊ ˈpi/ *abbr.* Grand Old Party (the Republican political party in the U.S.)

go·pher /ˈɡoʊfər/ *noun* **1** (*also* **'ground ˌsquirrel**) a N. American animal like a RAT, that lives in holes in the ground ⊃ picture at RODENT **2** = GOFER

Gor·di·an knot /ˌɡɔrdiən ˈnɑt/ *noun* a very difficult or impossible task or problem: *to cut/untie the Gordian knot* (= to solve a problem by taking action) **ORIGIN** From the story in which King Gordius tied a very complicated knot and said that whoever undid it would become the ruler of Asia. Alexander the Great cut through the knot with his SWORD.

gore /ɡɔr/ *verb*, *noun*

● *verb* ~ **sb/sth** (of an animal) to wound a person or another animal with a horn or TUSK: *He was gored by a bull.*

● *noun* [U] thick blood that has flowed from a wound, especially in a violent situation: *The movie is not just blood and gore* (= scenes of violence); *it has a thrilling story.* ⊃ see also GORY

Gore-tex™ /ˈɡɔrtɛks/ *noun* [U] a light material that does not let water through but that allows air and water VAPOR through, used for making outdoor and sports clothes

gorge /ɡɔrdʒ/ *noun*, *verb*

● *noun* [C] a deep, narrow valley with steep sides: *the Columbia Gorge near Portland* **SYN** CANYON

IDM sb's gorge rises (*formal*) someone feels so angry about something that they feel physically sick

● *verb* [T, I] ~ **(yourself) (on sth)** (*sometimes disapproving*) to eat a lot of something, until you are too full to eat any more **SYN** STUFF YOURSELF

gor·geous /ˈɡɔrdʒəs/ *adj.* **1** (*informal*) very beautiful and attractive; giving pleasure and enjoyment **SYN** LOVELY: *a gorgeous girl/man* ◆ *a gorgeous view* ◆ *gorgeous weather* (= warm and with a lot of sun) ◆ *You look gorgeous!* ◆ *It was absolutely gorgeous.* ⊃ thesaurus box at BEAUTIFUL **2** [usually before noun] (of colors, clothes, etc.) with very deep colors; impressive: *exotic birds with feathers of gorgeous colors* ▶ **gor·geous·ly** *adv.*

Gor·gon /ˈɡɔrɡən/ *noun* **1** (in ancient Greek stories) one of three sisters with snakes on their heads instead of hair, who can change anyone that looks at them into stone **2** an ugly woman who behaves in an aggressive and frightening way

Gor·gon·zo·la /ˌɡɔrɡənˈzoʊlə/ *noun* [U] a type of Italian cheese with blue marks and a strong flavor

go·ril·la /ɡəˈrɪlə/ *noun* **1** a very large, powerful African APE (= an animal like a large MONKEY without a tail) covered

with black or brown hair **2** (*informal*) a large aggressive man

'go-round *noun* = GO-AROUND

gorp /ɡɔrp/ *noun* [U] a mixture of nuts, dried fruit, etc. eaten between meals to provide extra energy, especially by people on camping trips, etc.

gorilla

gorse /ɡɔrs/ *noun* [U] a bush with thin leaves with sharp points and small yellow flowers. Gorse often grows on land that is not used or cared for.

gor·y /ˈɡɔri/ *adj.* (gor·i·er, gor·i·est) **1** (*informal*) involving a lot of blood or violence; showing or describing blood and violence: *a gory accident* ◆ *the gory task of the pathologist* ◆ *a gory movie* ◆ (*humorous*) *He insisted on telling us all the gory details about their divorce* (= the unpleasant facts). **2** (*literary*) covered with blood **SYN** BLOODSTAINED: *a gory figure*

gosh /ɡɑʃ/ *exclamation* (*informal*) people say "**Gosh!**" when they are surprised or shocked: *Gosh, is that the time?*

gos·hawk /ˈɡɑshɔk/ *noun* a large HAWK with short wings

gos·ling /ˈɡɑzlɪŋ/ *noun* a young GOOSE (= a bird like a large DUCK)

gos·pel /ˈɡɑspl/ *noun* **1** [C] *also* **Gospel** one of the four books in the Bible about the life and teaching of Jesus: *the Gospel according to St. John* ◆ *St. Mark's Gospel* **2** [sing.] *also* **the Gospel** the life and teaching of Jesus as explained in the Bible: *preaching/spreading the gospel* ⊃ collocations at RELIGION **3** (*also* **'gospel ˌmusic**) [U] a style of religious singing developed by African Americans: *a gospel choir* **4** [C, usually sing.] a set of ideas that someone believes in and tries to persuade others to accept: *He preached a gospel of military strength.* **5** (*also* **'gospel ˈtruth**) [U] (*informal*) the complete truth: *Is that gospel?* ◆ *Don't take his word as gospel.*

gos·sa·mer /ˈɡɑsəmər/ *noun* [U] **1** the very fine thread made by spiders **2** (*literary*) any very light, delicate material: *a gown of gossamer silk* ◆ *the gossamer wings of a dragonfly*

gos·sip /ˈɡɑsəp/ *noun*, *verb*

● *noun* **1** [U] (*disapproving*) informal talk or stories about other people's private lives, that may be unkind or not true: *Don't believe all the gossip you hear.* ◆ *Tell me all the latest gossip!* ◆ *The gossip was that he had lost a fortune on the stock exchange.* ◆ *It was common gossip* (= everyone said so) *that they were having an affair.* ◆ *She's a great one for idle gossip* (= she enjoys spreading stories about other people that are probably not true). **2** [C, usually sing.] a conversation about other people and their private lives: *I love a good gossip.* ⊃ thesaurus box at DISCUSSION **3** [C] (*disapproving*) a person who enjoys talking about other people's private lives ⊃ thesaurus box at SPEAKER ▶ **gos·sip·y** /ˈɡɑsəpi/ *adj.*: *gossipy letter/neighbor*

● *verb* [I] to talk about other people's private lives, often in an unkind way: *I can't stand here gossiping all day.* ◆ ~ **about sb/sth** *She's been gossiping about you.*

'gossip ˌcolumn *noun* a piece of writing in a newspaper about social events and the private and personal lives of famous people ▶ **'gossip ˌcolumnist** *noun*

got *pt, pp of* GET

got·cha /ˈɡɑtʃə/ *exclamation* (*non-standard*) the written form of the way some people pronounce "I've got you," which is not considered to be correct: *"Gotcha!" I yelled as I grabbed him by the arm.* (= used when you have caught someone, or have beaten them at something) ◆ *"Don't let go." "Yeah, gotcha."* (= Yes, I understand.) **HELP** You should not write this form unless you are copying somebody's speech.

goth /ɡɑθ/ *noun* **1** [U] a style of rock music, popular in the 1980s, that developed from PUNK music. The words often expressed ideas about the end of the world, death, or the

DEVIL. **2** [C] a member of a group of people who listen to goth music, and wear black clothes and black and white MAKEUP ▶ **goth** (also **goth·ic**) adj.

Go·tham /'gɑθəm/ noun (informal) New York City

Goth·ic /'gɑθɪk/ adj., noun
● adj. **1** connected with the Goths (= a Germanic people who fought against the Roman Empire) **2** (architecture) built in the style that was popular in western Europe from the 12th to the 16th centuries, and which has pointed ARCHES and windows and tall thin PILLARS: a Gothic church **3** (of a novel, etc.) written in the style popular in the 18th and 19th centuries, which described romantic adventures in mysterious or frightening surroundings **4** (of type and printing) having pointed letters with thick lines and sharp angles. German books used to be printed in this style. **5** connected with goths
● noun [U] **1** the Gothic style of ARCHITECTURE **2** Gothic printing type or printed letters

go-to adj. [only before noun] used to refer to the person or place that someone goes to for help, advice, or information: He's the president's go-to guy on Asian politics.

got·ta /'gɑtə/ (informal, non-standard) the written form of the word some people use to mean "have got to" or "have got a," which is not considered to be correct: He's gotta go.
HELP You should not write this form unless you are copying somebody's speech.

got·ten pp of GET

gou·ache /gwɑʃ/ noun **1** [U] a method of painting using colors that are mixed with water and made thick with a type of glue; the paints used in this method **2** [C] a picture painted using this method

Gou·da /'gudə/ noun [U] a type of Dutch cheese that is covered with yellow WAX

gouge /gaʊdʒ/ verb, noun
● verb **1** ~ sth (in sth) to make a hole or cut in something with a sharp object in a rough or violent way: The lion's claws had gouged a wound in the horse's side. ◆ He accidentally gouged the wall with his screwdriver. **2** ~ sb/sth to force someone to pay an unfairly high price for something; to raise prices unfairly: Price gouging is widespread.
PHR V gouge sth↔'out (of sth) to remove or force something by digging into a surface: The man's eyes had been gouged out. ◆ Glaciers gouged out valleys from the hills.
● noun **1** a sharp tool for making hollow areas in wood **2** a deep, narrow hole or cut in a surface

gou·lash /'gulɑʃ/ noun [C, U] a hot, spicy Hungarian dish of meat that is cooked slowly in liquid with PAPRIKA

gourd /gɔrd; gʊrd/ /gʊrd/ noun a type of large fruit with hard skin and soft flesh. Gourds are often dried and used as containers. ⊃ see also CALABASH

gour·mand /gʊr'mɑnd; 'gʊrmɑnd/ noun (often disapproving) a person who enjoys eating and eats large amounts of food

gour·met /gʊr'meɪ; 'gʊrmeɪ/ noun a person who knows a lot about good food and wines and who enjoys choosing, eating, and drinking them ▶ **gourmet** adj. [only before noun]: gourmet food (= of high quality and often expensive)

gout /gaʊt/ noun [U] a disease that causes painful swelling in the joints, especially of the toes, knees, and fingers

gov·ern /'gʌvərn/ verb
1 [T, I] ~ (sth) to legally control a country or its people and be responsible for introducing new laws, organizing public services, etc.: The country is governed by elected representatives of the people. ◆ He accused the other candidate of being unfit to govern. **2** [T, often passive] ~ sth to control or influence someone or something or how something happens, functions, etc.: Prices are governed by market demand. ◆ All his decisions have been entirely governed by self-interest. ◆ We need changes in the law governing school attendance. **3** [T] ~ sth (grammar) if a word **governs** another word or phrase, it affects how that word or phrase is formed or used

gov·ern·ance /'gʌvərnəns/ noun [U] (technical) the activity of governing a country or controlling a company or an organization; the way in which a country is governed or a company or institution is controlled

gov·ern·ess /'gʌvərnəs/ noun (especially in the past) a woman employed to teach the children of a rich family in their home and to live with them

gov·ern·ing /'gʌvərnɪŋ/ adj. [only before noun] having the right and the authority to control something such as a country or an institution: The Republicans were then the **governing party**. ◆ The school's **governing body** (= the group of people who control the organization of the school) took responsibility for the decision.

gov·ern·ment /'gʌvərmənt; 'gʌvərnmənt/ noun
1 [C] (abbr. **govt.**) the group of people who are responsible for controlling a country or a state: to lead/form a government ◆ the last Democratic government ◆ the government of the day ◆ Foreign governments have been consulted about this decision. ◆ She has resigned from the Government. ◆ The Government has been considering further tax cuts. ◆ government policies/officials/ministers ◆ a government department/agency/grant ◆ government expenditure/intervention/subsidies ⊃ collocations at POLITICS **2** [U] a particular system or method of controlling a country: coalition/communist/democratic/totalitarian, etc. government ◆ Democratic government has now replaced military rule. ◆ central/federal government **3** [U] the activity or the manner of controlling a country: strong government ◆ The Democrats are now in government in the U.S. ⊃ see also BIG GOVERNMENT, STUDENT GOVERNMENT

gov·ern·men·tal /ˌgʌvər'mɛntl; ˌgʌvərn-/ adj. connected with government; of a government: governmental agencies ◆ governmental actions ⊃ compare NONGOVERNMENTAL

ˌgovernment and 'binding ˌtheory (also 'binding ˌtheory) noun [U] (linguistics) a theory of grammar based on the idea that a series of conditions relate the parts of a sentence together

gov·er·nor /'gʌvənər; 'gʌvərnər/ noun
1 also **Governor** a person who is chosen to be in charge of the government of a state in the U.S.: the governor of Arizona ◆ the Arizona governor ◆ Governor Arnold Schwarzenegger **2** also **Governor** a person who is the official head of a country or region that is governed by another country: the former governor of the colony ◆ a provincial governor

ˌGovernor 'General noun (pl. **Governors General**) the official representative of the British King or Queen in Canada or another COMMONWEALTH country

govt. (also **govt**) abbr. (in writing) government

gown /gaʊn/ noun **1** a woman's dress, especially a long one for special occasions: an evening/ball/wedding gown **2** a long, loose piece of clothing that is worn over other clothes by judges and by students or professors (at special ceremonies): a graduation gown **3** a loose piece of clothing worn by patients in a hospital, or worn by medical staff over other clothes to protect them: a hospital gown ⊃ see also NIGHTGOWN, TOWN AND GOWN

gowned /gaʊnd/ adj. wearing a gown

goy /gɔɪ/ noun (pl. **goy·im** /'gɔɪɪm/ or **goys**) (informal, often offensive) a word used by Jewish people for a person who is not Jewish

GP /ˌdʒi 'pi/ noun the abbreviation for "general practitioner" (a doctor who is trained in general medicine and who works in the local community, not in a hospital): Go and see your GP as soon as possible. ◆ There are four GPs in our local practice.

GPA /ˌdʒi pi 'eɪ/ abbr. GRADE POINT AVERAGE: He graduated with a GPA of 3.8.

GPRS /ˌdʒi pi ɑr 'ɛs/ abbr. general packet radio services (a way of sending electronic data as radio signals, used especially between cell phones and the Internet

GPS /ˌdʒi pi 'ɛs/ abbr. global positioning system (a system by which signals are sent from SATELLITES to a special device, used to show the position of a person or thing on the surface of the earth very accurately): *The drivers all have GPS in their trucks.*

grab /græb/ *verb, noun*

● *verb* (**-bb-**) **1** [T, I] to take or hold someone or something with your hand suddenly, firmly, or roughly **SYN** SEIZE: ~ **(sth)** *She grabbed the child's hand and ran.* ◆ *He grabbed hold of me and wouldn't let go.* ◆ *Don't grab—there's plenty for everyone.* ◆ ~ **sth from sb/sth** *Jim grabbed a cookie from the plate.* **2** [I] to try to take hold of something: ~ **at sth** *She grabbed at the branch, missed, and fell.* ◆ ~ **for sth** *Kate grabbed for the robber's gun.* **3** [T, I] to take advantage of an opportunity to do or have something **SYN** SEIZE: ~ **sth** *This was my big chance and I grabbed it with both hands.* ◆ ~ **at sth** *He'll grab at any excuse to avoid doing the dishes.* **4** [T] ~ **sth** to have or take something quickly, especially because you are in a hurry: *Let's grab a sandwich before we go.* ◆ *I managed to grab a couple of hours of sleep on the plane.* ◆ *Grab a seat, I'll only keep you a moment.* **5** [T] ~ **sth** to take something for yourself without thinking about other people: *By the time we arrived, someone had grabbed all the good seats.* **6** [T] ~ **sb/sth** to get someone's attention: *I'll see if I can grab the waitress and get the bill.* ◆ *The mayor's campaign scandal has grabbed the headlines tonight* (= been published as an important story in the newspapers).
IDM **how does…grab you?** (*informal*) used to ask someone whether they are interested in something or in doing something: *How does the idea of a trip to Rome grab you?*

● *noun* **1** [usually sing.] ~ **(at/for sb/sth)** a sudden attempt to take or hold someone or something: *He made a grab for her bag.* **2** ~ **(for sth)** an act of taking something quickly, unfairly, and usually by force: *The company made a land grab for the waterfront property.* **3** (*computing*) a picture taken from a television or video film, stored as an image on a computer: *a screen grab from Wednesday's program* **4** a piece of equipment that lifts and holds goods, for example the equipment that hangs from a CRANE
IDM **up for grabs** (*informal*) available for anyone who is interested: *There are $25,000 worth of prizes up for grabs in our competition!*

grab bag *noun* **1** a game in which people choose a present from a container of presents without being able to see what it is going to be **2** (*informal*) a mixed collection of things: *He offered a grab bag of reasons for his decision.*

grab·by /ˈgræbi/ *adj.* (*informal, disapproving*) having or showing a desire for something that is not yours or that you already have enough of: *a grabby child who always took all the toys*

grace /greɪs/ *noun, verb*

● *noun*

▷ OF MOVEMENT **1** [U] an attractive quality of movement that is smooth, elegant, and controlled: *She moves with the natural grace of a ballerina.*

▷ BEHAVIOR **2** [U] a quality of behavior that is polite and pleasant and deserves respect: *He conducted himself with grace and dignity throughout the trial.* **3** **graces** [pl.] ways of behaving that people think are polite and acceptable: *He was not particularly well versed in the social graces.*

▷ EXTRA TIME **4** [U] extra time that is given to someone to enable them to pay a bill, finish a piece of work, etc.: *They gave me a two-week grace period to get the money.*

▷ OF GOD **5** [U] the kindness that God shows toward the human race: *It was only by the grace of God that they survived.* ⟳ collocations at RELIGION

▷ PRAYER **6** [U, C] a short prayer that is usually said before a meal to thank God for the food: *Let's say grace.*

▷ TITLE **7** **His/Her/Your Grace** [C] used as a title of respect when talking to or about an ARCHBISHOP, a DUKE, or a DUCHESS: *Their Graces the Duke and Duchess of Kent.* ⟳ see also COUP DE GRÂCE, SAVING GRACE
IDM **be in sb's good graces** (*formal*) to have someone's approval and be liked by them **fall from grace** to lose the trust or respect that people have for you, especially by doing something wrong or immoral **sb's fall from grace** a situation in which someone loses the trust or respect that people have for them, especially because of something wrong or immoral that they have done **have the (good) grace to do sth** to be polite enough to do something, especially when you have done something wrong: *He didn't even have the good grace to look embarrassed.* **there but for the grace of God (go I)** (*saying*) used to say that you could easily have been in the same difficult or unpleasant situation that someone else is in **with bad grace** in an unwilling and/or rude way: *He handed over the money with typical bad grace.* **with good grace** in a willing and pleasant way: *You must learn to accept defeat with good grace.* ⟳ more at AIR, STATE, YEAR

● *verb* (*formal*) **1** ~ **sth** to make something more attractive; to decorate something: *The table had once graced a governor's dining room.* **2** (usually *ironic*) to bring honor to someone or something; to be kind enough to attend or take part in something: ~ **sb/sth** *She is one of the finest players ever to have graced the game.* ◆ ~ **sb/sth with sth** *Will you be gracing us with your presence tonight?*

grace·ful /ˈgreɪsfl/ *adj.* **1** moving in a controlled, attractive way or having a smooth, attractive form: *The dancers were all tall and graceful.* ◆ *He gave a graceful bow to the audience.* ◆ *the graceful curves of the hills* **2** polite and kind in your behavior, especially in a difficult situation: *His father had always taught him to be graceful in defeat.* ▶ **grace·ful·ly** /-fəli/ *adv.*: *The cathedral's white towers climb gracefully into the sky.* ◆ *I think we should just give in gracefully.* **grace·ful·ness** *noun* [U]

grace·less /ˈgreɪsləs/ *adj.* **1** not knowing how to be polite and pleasant to other people: *a graceless, angry young man* **2** not pleasing or attractive to look at: *the graceless architecture of the 1960s* **3** moving in an awkward way: *She swam with a graceless stroke.* **ANT** GRACEFUL ▶ **grace·less·ly** *adv.*

grace note *noun* (*music*) an extra note that is not a necessary part of a tune, but that is played before one of the notes of the tune as decoration

gra·cious /ˈgreɪʃəs/ *adj.* **1** (of people or behavior) kind, polite, and generous, especially to someone of a lower social position: *a gracious lady* ◆ *a gracious smile* ◆ *He has not yet learned how to be gracious in defeat.* **2** [usually before noun] showing the comfort and easy way of life that wealth can bring: *gracious living* **3** ~ **(to sb)** (of God) showing kindness and MERCY: *a gracious act of God* **4** (becoming *old-fashioned*) used for expressing surprise: *Goodness gracious!* ◆ *"I hope you didn't mind my calling you." "Good gracious, no, of course not."* ▶ **gra·cious·ly** *adv.*: *She graciously accepted our invitation.* **gra·cious·ness** *noun* [U]

grack·le /ˈgrækl/ *noun* an American bird with shiny black feathers

grad /græd/ *noun* (*informal*) **1** = GRADUATE **2** (*CanE*) a dinner and dance for all students who are finishing high school

grad·a·ble /ˈgreɪdəbl/ *adj.* (*grammar*) (of an adjective) that can be used in the comparative and superlative forms or be used with words like "very" and "less" **ANT** NONGRADABLE ▶ **grad·a·bil·i·ty** /ˌgreɪdəˈbɪləti/ *noun* [U]

gra·da·tion /greɪˈdeɪʃn; grə-/ *noun* **1** [C, U] (*formal*) any of the small changes or levels which something is divided into; the process or result of something changing gradually: *gradations of color* ◆ *gradation in size* **2** (also **grad·u·a·tion**) [C] a mark showing a division on a scale: *the gradations on a thermometer*

grade /greɪd/ **AWL** *noun, verb*

● *noun* **1** a letter or number given on an exam or for a piece of school work: *She got good grades on her exams.* ◆ *70% of students got a grade of C or above.* **2** one of the levels in a school with children of similar age: *Sam is in (the) second grade.* **3** the quality of a particular product or material: *All the materials used were of the highest grade.* **4** = GRADIENT **5** a level of ability or rank that someone has in an organization: *salary grades* (= levels of pay) **6** (*technical*) how serious an illness is: *low/high grade fever*

IDM **make the grade** (*informal*) to reach the necessary standard; to succeed: *About 10% of trainees fail to make the grade.*

- **verb 1** [often passive] to arrange people or things in groups according to their ability, quality, size, etc.: *~ sth/sb (by/according to sth) The containers are graded according to size.* ◆ *~ sth/sb from... to... Eggs are graded from small to extra large.* ◆ *Responses were graded from 1 (very satisfied) to 5 (not at all satisfied).* ◆ *~ sth (as) sth Ten beaches were graded as acceptable.* **2** to give a grade to a student or to a piece of their written work: *~ sb/sth I spent all weekend grading papers.* ◆ *~ sb/sth + noun The best students are graded A.* ➔ compare MARK

grad·ed **AWL** /ˈɡreɪdəd/ *adj.* arranged in order or in groups according to difficulty, size, etc.: *graded tests for language students* ◆ *graded doses of a drug*

grade point average *noun* [usually sing.] (*abbr.* **GPA**) the average of a student's grades over a period of time

grad·er /ˈɡreɪdər/ *noun* **1 first, second, etc. ~** a student who is in the grade mentioned: *The play is open to all seventh and eighth graders.* **2** a person who grades students' work or exams

grade school *noun* (*informal*) = ELEMENTARY SCHOOL

gra·di·ent /ˈɡreɪdiənt/ *noun* **1** (also **grade**) the degree to which the ground slopes, especially on a road or railroad: *a steep gradient* ◆ *a hill with a gradient of 1 in 4 (or 25%)* **2** (*technical*) the rate at which temperature, pressure, etc. changes, or increases and decreases, between one region and another

grad·ing **AWL** /ˈɡreɪdɪŋ/ *noun* [U] the activity of checking and correcting the written work or exams of students

gra·di·om·e·ter /ˌɡreɪdiˈɑmətər/ *noun* **1** (*technical*) an instrument for measuring the angle of a slope **2** (*physics*) an instrument for measuring the changes in an energy field

grad school *noun* (*informal*) = GRADUATE SCHOOL

grad·u·al 🔑 /ˈɡrædʒuəl/ *adj.*
1 happening slowly over a long period; not sudden: *a gradual change in the climate* ◆ *Recovery from the disease is very gradual.* **ANT** SUDDEN **2** (of a slope) not steep

grad·u·al·ism /ˈɡrædʒuəˌlɪzəm/ *noun* [U] a policy of gradual change in society rather than sudden change or revolution ▸ **grad·u·al·ist** /-lɪst/ *noun*

grad·u·al·ly 🔑 /ˈɡrædʒuəli; -dʒəli/ *adv.*
slowly, or over a long period of time: *The weather gradually improved.* ◆ *Gradually, the children began to understand.*

grad·u·ate 🔑 *noun, verb*
- **noun** /ˈɡrædʒuət/ (also *informal* **grad**) **1** a person who has a college or university degree: *a graduate of Yale/a Yale graduate* ◆ *a graduate student/course* (= for students doing further study after their first degree) **2** a person who has completed their studies at a school: *a high school graduate* ➔ note at STUDENT
- **verb** /ˈɡrædʒuˌeɪt/ **1** [I, T] to get a degree, especially your first degree, from a college or university: *~ (from...) She graduated from Harvard this year.* ◆ *He graduated from Amherst with a degree in psychology.* ◆ *~ sth She graduated college last year.* **2** [I, T] to complete a course in education, especially at high school: *~ (from...) Martha graduated from high school two years ago.* ◆ *~ sth Martha graduated high school two years ago.* **3** [T] *~ sb (from sth)* to give a degree, DIPLOMA, etc. to someone: *The college graduated 50 students last year.* **4** [I] *~ (from sth)* to start doing something more difficult or important than what you were doing before: *She recently graduated from being a dancer to having a small role in a movie.* ➔ collocations at EDUCATION

grad·u·a·ted /ˈɡrædʒuˌeɪtəd/ *adj.* **1** divided into groups or levels on a scale: *graduated lessons/taxes* **2** (of a container or measure) marked with lines to show measurements

SYN CALIBRATED: *a graduated measuring cup* ➔ picture at LABORATORY

Graduate Management Admissions Test ➔ GMAT™

grad·u·ate school /ˈɡrædʒuət ˌskul/ (also *informal* **grad school**) *noun* a part of a university where you can study for a degree or Ph.D.

grad·u·a·tion /ˌɡrædʒuˈeɪʃn/ *noun* **1** [U] the act of successfully completing a college or university degree, or getting a high school DIPLOMA: *It was my first job after graduation.* **2** [U, C] a ceremony at which degrees, etc. are officially given out: *graduation day* ◆ *My whole family came to my graduation.* **3** [C] = GRADATION (2): *The graduations are marked on the side of the flask.*

Graeco- (*CanE*) = GRECO-

graf·fi·ti /ɡrəˈfiti/ *noun* [U, pl.] drawings or writing done on a wall, etc. in a public place without permission: *The subway was covered in graffiti.*

graft /ɡræft/ *noun, verb*
- **noun 1** [C] a piece cut from a living plant and fixed in a cut made in another plant, so that it grows there; the process or result of doing this **2** [C] a piece of skin, bone, etc. removed from a living body and placed in another part of the body that has been damaged; the process or result of doing this: *a skin graft* **3** [U] the use of illegal or unfair methods, especially BRIBERY, to gain advantage in business, politics, etc.; money obtained in this way
- **verb 1** *~ sth (onto/to/into sth)* | *~ sth (on) (from sth)* to take a piece of skin, bone, etc. from one part of the body and attach it to a damaged part: *newly grafted tissue* ◆ *New skin had to be grafted on from his back.* **2** *~ sth (onto sth)* to cut a piece from a living plant and attach it to another plant **3** *~ sth (onto sth)* to make one idea, system, etc. become part of another one: *Old values are being grafted onto a new social class.*

graham cracker /ˈɡreɪəm ˌkrækər; ˈɡræm-/ *noun* a slightly sweet cookie made with WHOLE-WHEAT flour

grail /ɡreɪl/ (also **the Holy Grail**) *noun* **1** [sing.] the cup or bowl believed to have been used by Jesus Christ before he died, that became a holy thing that people wanted to find **2** [C] a thing that you try very hard to find or achieve, but never will

grain 🔑 /ɡreɪn/ *noun*
1 [U, C] the small hard seeds of food plants such as WHEAT, rice, etc.; a single seed of such a plant: *America's grain exports* ◆ *a few grains of rice* ➔ see also WHOLE-GRAIN ➔ picture at CEREAL **2** [C] a small hard piece of particular substances: *a grain of salt/sand/sugar* **3** [C] (used especially in negative sentences) a very small amount **SYN** IOTA: *There isn't a grain of truth in those rumors.* **4** [C] a small unit of weight, equal to 0.00143 of a pound or 0.0648 of a gram, used for example for weighing medicines **5** [U] the natural direction of lines in wood, cloth, etc. or of layers of rock; the pattern of lines that you can see: *to cut a piece of wood along/across the grain* **6** [U, C] how rough or smooth a surface feels: *wood of coarse/fine grain*

IDM **be/go against the grain** to be or do something different from what is normal or natural: *It really goes against the grain to have to work on a Sunday.* ➔ more at SALT *n.*

grained /ɡreɪnd/ *adj.* (of wood, stone, etc.) **1** having noticeable lines or a pattern on the surface **2** **-grained** having a TEXTURE of the type mentioned: *fine-grained stone*

grain·y /ˈɡreɪni/ *adj.* **1** (especially of photographs) not having completely clear images because they look as if they are made of a lot of small dots and marks: *The film is shot in grainy black and white.* **2** having a rough surface or containing small bits, seeds, etc.: *a grainy texture*

gram 🔑 /ɡræm/ *noun*
1 (*abbr.* **g, gm**) a unit for measuring weight. There are

1,000 grams in one kilogram. **2** **-gram** a thing that is written or drawn: *telegram* ♦ *hologram*

gram·mar 🔑 /ˈɡræmər/ *noun*
1 [U] the rules in a language for changing the form of words and joining them into sentences: *the basic rules of grammar* ♦ *English grammar* ⸰ see also GENERATIVE GRAMMAR **2** [U] a person's knowledge and use of a language: *His grammar is awful.* ♦ *bad grammar* **3** [C] a book containing a description of the rules of a language: *a French grammar*

gram·mar·i·an /ɡrəˈmɛriən/ *noun* a person who is an expert in the study of grammar

ˈgrammar ˌschool *noun* (*old-fashioned*) = ELEMENTARY SCHOOL

the ˌgrammar transˈlation ˌmethod *noun* [sing.] (*linguistics*) a traditional way of teaching a foreign language, in which the study of grammar is very important and very little teaching is in the foreign language

gram·mat·i·cal /ɡrəˈmætɪkl/ *adj.* **1** connected with the rules of grammar: *a grammatical error* **2** correctly following the rules of grammar: *That sentence is not grammatical.* ▸ **gram·mat·i·cally** /-kli/ *adv.*: *a grammatically correct sentence*

Gram·my /ˈɡræmi/ *noun* (*pl.* **Gram·mys** or **Gram·mies**) one of many prizes given each year to the best song, singer, recording, etc. in the music industry

gram·o·phone /ˈɡræməˌfoʊn/ *noun* (*old-fashioned*) = RECORD PLAYER

gramp /ɡræmp/ (also **gramps** /ɡræmps/, **gramp·y** /ˈɡræmpi/) *noun* [sing.] (*informal*) grandfather

gra·na·ry /ˈɡreɪnəri; ˈɡræ-/ *noun* (*pl.* **gra·na·ries**) **1** a building where grain is stored **2** a region that produces a lot of grain: *Iowa is the leading corn granary in the U.S.*

grand 🔑 /ɡrænd/ *adj., noun*
● *adj.* (**grand·er, grand·est**) **1** impressive and large or important: *It's not a very grand house.* ♦ *The wedding was a very grand occasion.* **2** **Grand** [only before noun] used in the names of impressive or very large buildings, etc.: *the Grand Canyon* ♦ *We left from Grand Central Station.* **3** needing a lot of effort, money, or time to succeed but intended to achieve impressive results: *a grand design/plan/strategy* ♦ *New Yorkers built their city* **on a grand scale**. **4** (of people) behaving in a proud way because they are rich or from a high social class **5** **Grand** used in the titles of people of very high social rank: *the Grand Duchess Elena* ⸰ see also GRANDEUR ▸ **grand·ly** *adv.*: *He described himself grandly as a "landscape architect."* **grand·ness** *noun* [U]
IDM **a/the grand old age** a great age: *She finally learned to drive at the grand old age of 70.* **a/the grand old man (of sth)** a man who is respected in a particular profession that he has been involved in for a long time: *James Lovelock, the grand old man of environmental science*
● *noun* (*pl.* **grand**) (*informal*) $1,000: *It'll cost you five grand!* **2** = GRAND PIANO ⸰ see also CONCERT GRAND

ˌGrand ˌCentral ˈStation *noun* used to describe a place that is very busy or crowded: *My hospital room was like Grand Central Station with everyone coming and going.* **ORIGIN** From the name of a very busy train station in New York City.

grand·child 🔑 /ˈɡræntʃaɪld/ *noun* (*pl.* **grand·child·ren** /-ˌtʃɪldrən/)
a child of your son or daughter

grand·dad /ˈɡrændæd/ *noun* (*informal*) grandfather

grand·dad·dy /ˈɡrænˌdædi/ *noun* (*informal*) **1** = GRAND-FATHER **2 the granddaddy** the first or greatest example of something

grand·daugh·ter 🔑 /ˈɡrænˌdɔtər/ *noun*
a daughter of your son or daughter ⸰ compare GRANDSON

grande dame /ˌɡrɑn ˈdɑm/ *noun* (*pl.* **grande dames** or **grandes dames** /ˌɡrɑn ˈdɑmz; -ˈdæm/) an older woman with a lot of experience and influence in a particular area: *the grande dame of literary criticism*

gran·dee /ɡrænˈdi/ *noun* **1** (in the past) a Spanish or Portuguese NOBLEMAN of high rank **2** a person of high social rank and importance

gran·deur /ˈɡrændʒər; -dʒʊr/ *noun* [U] **1** the quality of being great and impressive in appearance **SYN** SPLENDOR: *the grandeur and simplicity of Roman architecture* ♦ *The hotel had an air of faded grandeur.* **2** the importance or social status someone has or thinks they have: *He has a sense of grandeur about him.* ♦ *She is clearly suffering from* **delusions of grandeur** (= thinks she is more important than she really is). ⸰ see also GRAND

grand·fa·ther 🔑 /ˈɡrænˌfɑðər/ *noun, verb*
● *noun* the father of your father or mother ⸰ see also GRANDDAD, GRANDDADDY, GRANDPA ⸰ compare GRAND-MOTHER
● *verb* to give or be given official permission not to obey a new law or regulation that one would normally be required to obey: *~ sb/sth Workers who were here before the cut in benefits went into effect will be automatically grandfathered.* ♦ *~ sb/sth in Older cars have been grandfathered in and don't have to have air bags.*

ˈgrandfather ˌclause *noun* part of a new rule or law that excludes a particular group of people and allows them to continue following the old rule or law

ˈgrandfather ˌclock *noun* an old-fashioned type of clock in a tall wooden case that stands on the floor ⸰ picture at CLOCK

gran·dil·o·quent /ɡrænˈdɪləkwənt/ *adj.* (*formal, disapproving*) using long or complicated words in order to impress people **SYN** POMPOUS ▸ **gran·dil·o·quence** /-kwəns/ *noun* [U]

gran·di·ose /ˈɡrændiˌoʊs; ˌɡrændiˈoʊs/ *adj.* (*disapproving*) seeming very impressive but too large, complicated, expensive, etc. to be practical or possible: *The grandiose plan for a journey across the desert came to nothing.* ♦ *a grandiose opera house*

grand ˈjury *noun* (*law*) a jury that has to decide whether there is enough evidence against an accused person for a trial in court

grand·kid /ˈɡrænkɪd/ *noun* (*informal*) a grandchild

ˌgrand ˈlarceny *noun* [U] the crime of stealing something that is worth a lot of money ⸰ compare PETTY LARCENY

grand·ma /ˈɡrænmɑ; ˈɡræmɑ/ *noun* (*informal*) grandmother

grand mal /ˌɡrɑn ˈmɑl; ˌɡræn-/ *noun* [U] (from *French, medical*) a serious form of EPILEPSY in which someone becomes unconscious for fairly long periods ⸰ compare PETIT MAL

ˌgrand ˈmaster *noun* a CHESS player of the highest standard

grand·moth·er 🔑 /ˈɡrænˌmʌðər/ *noun*
the mother of your father or mother ⸰ see also GRANDMA, GRANNY ⸰ compare GRANDFATHER

ˈgrandmother ˌclock *noun* a clock similar to a GRAND-FATHER CLOCK but smaller

ˌgrand ˈopera *noun* [U, C] OPERA in which everything is sung and there are no spoken parts

grand·pa /ˈɡrænpɑ; ˈɡræmpɑ/ *noun* (*informal*) grandfather ⸰ see also GRANDDAD

grand·par·ent 🔑 /ˈɡrænˌpɛrənt/ *noun* [usually pl.]
the father or mother of your father or mother: *The children are staying with their grandparents.*

ˌgrand ˈpiano (also **grand**) *noun* a large piano in which the strings are horizontal ⸰ compare UPRIGHT PIANO

Grand Prix /ˌɡrɑn ˈpri; ˌɡrænd-/ *noun* (*pl.* **Grands Prix** /ˌɡrɑn ˈpri; ˌɡrænd-/) one of a series of important international races for racing cars or motorcycles

grand 'slam noun **1** also **Grand Slam** a very important sports event, contest, etc.: *a Grand Slam tournament/cup/title* **2** the winning of every part of a sports contest or all the main contests in a year for a particular sport: *Will Serena Williams win the grand slam this year?* (= in TENNIS) **3** (also **grand ,slam home 'run**) (in baseball) a HOME RUN that is worth four points **4** (in card games, especially BRIDGE) the winning of all the TRICKS in a single game

grand·son /ˈɡrænsʌn/ noun
a son of your son or daughter ⊃ compare GRANDDAUGHTER

grand·stand /ˈɡrænstænd; ˈɡrænd-/ noun a large covered structure with rows of seats for people to watch sports events: *The game was played to a packed grandstand.* ♦ *From her house, we had a **grandstand view** (= very good view) of the celebrations.*

grand·stand·ing /ˈɡrænˌstændɪŋ; ˈɡrænd-/ noun [U] (especially in business, politics, etc.) the fact of behaving or speaking in a way that is intended to make people impressed in order to gain some advantage for yourself

grand 'total noun the final total when a number of other totals have been added together

grand 'tour noun **1** (often *humorous*) a visit around a building or house in order to show it to someone: *Steve took us on a grand tour of the house and gardens.* **2** also **Grand Tour** a visit to the main cities of Europe made by rich young British or American people as part of their education in the past

grand 'unified ,theory noun (*physics*) a single theory that tries to explain all the behavior of SUBATOMIC PARTICLES

grange /ɡreɪndʒ/ noun a country house with farm buildings

gran·ite /ˈɡrænət/ noun [U] a type of hard gray stone, often used in building

gran·ny (also *less frequent* **gran·nie**) /ˈɡræni/ noun (*pl.* **gran·nies**) (*informal*) grandmother ⊃ see also GRANDMA
▶ **gran·ny** (also *less frequent* **gran·nie**) *adj.*: *a pair of granny glasses*

granny ,knot noun a SQUARE KNOT that is not tied correctly

gra·no·la /ɡrəˈnoʊlə/ noun, adj.
● *noun* [U] a type of breakfast CEREAL made of grains, nuts, etc. that have been TOASTED
● *adj.* [only before noun] (*informal*) (of a person) eating healthy food, supporting the protection of the environment, and having LIBERAL views

grant 〔AWL〕 /ɡrænt/ verb, noun
● *verb* **1** [often passive] to agree to give someone what they ask for, especially formal or legal permission to do something: *~ sth My request was granted.* ♦ *~ sb sth I was granted permission to visit the palace.* ♦ *She was granted a divorce.* ♦ *The bank finally granted me a $500 loan.* ♦ *~ sth to sb/sth The bank finally granted a $500 loan to me.* **2** to admit that something is true, although you may not like or agree with it: *~ sb She's a smart woman, I grant you, but she's no genius.* ♦ *~ (sb) (that)… I grant you (that) it looks good, but it's not exactly practical.*
IDM **take it for granted (that…)** to believe something is true without first making sure that it is: *I just took it for granted that he'd always be around.* **take sb/sth for granted** to be so used to someone or something that you do not recognize their true value anymore and do not show that you are grateful: *Her husband was always there and she just took him for granted.* ♦ *We take having an endless supply of clean water for granted.*
● *noun* ~ **(to do sth)** a sum of money that is given by the government or by another organization to be used for a particular purpose: *student grants* (= to pay for their education) ♦ *He has been awarded a research grant.*

grant·ed 〔AWL〕 /ˈɡræntəd/ adv., conj.
● *adv.* used to show that you accept that something is true, often before you make another statement about it: *"You could have done more to help." "Granted."* ♦ *Granted, it's not the most pleasant of jobs but it has to be done.*

● *conj.* ~ **(that…)** because of the fact that: *Granted that it is a simple test to perform, it should be easy to get results quickly.*

grant-in-'aid noun (*pl.* **grants-in-'aid**) a sum of money given to a local government or an institution, or to a particular person to allow them to study something

gran·u·lar /ˈɡrænyələr/ adj. consisting of small GRANULES; looking or feeling like a collection of GRANULES

granulated sugar /ˌɡrænyəleɪtəd ˈʃʊɡər/ noun [U] white sugar in the form of small grains

gran·ule /ˈɡrænyul/ noun [usually pl.] a small hard piece of something; a small grain: *instant coffee granules*

grape /ɡreɪp/ noun a small green or purple fruit that grows in bunches on a climbing plant (called a VINE). Wine is made from grapes: *a bunch of grapes* ♦ *black/white grapes* (= grapes that are actually purple/green in color) ⊃ picture at FRUIT **IDM** see SOUR

grape·fruit /ˈɡreɪpfrut/ noun (*pl.* **grape·fruit** or **grape-fruits**) [C, U] a large, round, yellow CITRUS fruit with a lot of slightly sour juice ⊃ picture at FRUIT

grape·shot /ˈɡreɪpʃɑt/ noun [U] a number of small iron balls that are fired together from a CANNON

grape·vine /ˈɡreɪpvaɪn/ noun
IDM **through the grapevine** by talking in an informal way to other people: *I heard through the grapevine that you're leaving.*

graphs and charts

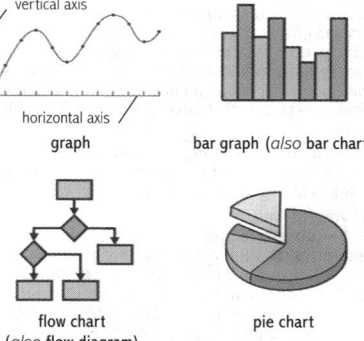

graph

bar graph (*also* bar chart)

flow chart
(*also* flow diagram)

pie chart

graph /ɡræf/ noun a planned drawing, consisting of a line or lines, showing how two or more sets of numbers are related to each other: *Plot a graph of height against age.* ♦ *The graph shows how house prices have risen since the 1980s.*

graph·eme /ˈɡræfim/ noun (*linguistics*) the smallest unit that has meaning in a writing system ⊃ compare PHONEME

graph·ic /ˈɡræfɪk/ adj., noun
● *adj.* **1** [only before noun] connected with drawings and design, especially in the production of books, magazines, etc.: *graphic design* ♦ *a graphic designer* **2** (of descriptions, etc.) very clear and full of details, especially about something unpleasant **SYN** VIVID: *a graphic account/description of a battle* ♦ *He kept telling us about his operation, in the most graphic detail.*
● *noun* a diagram or picture, especially one that appears on a computer screen or in a newspaper or book ⊃ compare GRAPHICS

graph·i·cal /ˈɡræfɪkl/ adj. **1** [only before noun] connected with art or computer graphics: *The system uses an impressive graphical interface.* **2** in the form of a diagram or graph: *a graphical presentation of results*

graph·i·cal·ly /ˈɡræfɪkli/ adv. **1** in the form of drawings or diagrams: *This data is shown graphically on the opposite page.* **2** very clearly and in great detail **SYN** VIVIDLY: *The murders are graphically described in the article.*

---

graphic 'arts *noun* [U] art based on the use of lines and shades of color ▶ **graphic 'artist** *noun*

graphic e'qualizer *noun* (*technical*) an electronic device or computer program that allows you to control the strength and quality of particular sound frequencies (FREQUENCY) separately

graphic 'novel *noun* a novel in the form of a COMIC STRIP

graph·ics /'græfɪks/ *noun* [pl.] designs, drawings, or pictures that are used especially in the production of books, magazines, etc.: *computer graphics* ◆ *Text and graphics are prepared separately and then combined.*

'graphics ,card *noun* (*computing*) = VIDEO CARD

graph·ite /'græfaɪt/ *noun* [U] a soft black mineral that is a form of CARBON. Graphite is used to make pencils, to LUBRICATE machinery, and in nuclear REACTORS.

graph·ol·o·gy /græ'fɒlədʒi/ *noun* [U] the study of HAND-WRITING, for example as a way of learning more about someone's character

'graph ,paper *noun* paper with small squares of equal size printed on it, used for drawing GRAPHS and other diagrams

-graphy /grəfi/ *combining form* (in nouns) **1** a type of art or science: *choreography* ◆ *geography* **2** a method of producing images: *radiography* **3** a form of writing or drawing: *calligraphy* ◆ *biography*

grap·pa /'grɑpə/ *noun* [U, C] a strong alcoholic drink from Italy, made from GRAPES

grap·ple /'græpl/ *verb* **1** [I, T] to take a firm hold of someone or something and struggle with them: ~ **(with sb/sth)** *Bystanders grappled with the man after the attack.* ◆ ~ **sb/sth (+ adv./prep.)** *They managed to grapple him to the ground.* **2** [I] to try hard to find a solution to a problem: ~ **with sth** *The new government has yet to grapple with the problem of air pollution.* ◆ ~ **to do sth** *I was grappling to find an answer to his question.*

grappling ,hook (also **'grappling ,iron**) *noun* a tool with several hooks attached to a long rope, used for dragging something along or holding a boat still

grasp /græsp/ *verb, noun*
● *verb* **1** ~ **sb/sth** to take a firm hold of someone or something SYN GRIP: *He grasped my hand and shook it warmly.* ◆ *Kay grasped him by the wrist.* ⊃ thesaurus box at HOLD **2** to understand something completely: ~ **sth** *They failed to grasp the importance of his words.* ◆ ~ **how, why, etc....** *She was unable to grasp how to do it.* ◆ ~ **that...** *It took him some time to grasp that he was now a public figure.* ⊃ thesaurus box at UNDERSTAND **3** ~ **a chance/an opportunity** to take an opportunity without hesitating and use it: *I grasped the opportunity to work in Europe.*
IDM see STRAW
PHR V **'grasp at sth 1** to try to take hold of something in your hands: *She grasped at his coat as he rushed past her.* **2** to try to take an opportunity
● *noun* [usually sing.] **1** a firm hold of someone or something or control over someone or something SYN GRIP: *I grabbed him, but he slipped from my grasp.* ◆ *She felt a firm grasp on her arm.* ◆ *Don't let the situation escape from your grasp.* **2** a person's understanding of a subject or of difficult facts: *He has a good grasp of German grammar.* ◆ *These complex formulae are beyond the grasp of the average student.* **3** the ability to get or achieve something: *Success was within her grasp.*

grasp·ing /'græspɪŋ/ *adj.* (*disapproving*) always trying to get money, possessions, power, etc. for yourself SYN GREEDY: *a grasping landlord*

grass 🔊 /græs/ *noun, verb*
● *noun* **1** [U] a very common plant with long, narrow, green leaves, that grows wild and in parks and yards, and is eaten by cows, horses, sheep, etc.: *a blade of grass* ◆ *The dry grass caught fire.* **2** [C] any type of grass: *ornamental grasses* **3** [sing., U] usually **the grass** an area of ground covered

with grass: *to cut/mow the grass* ◆ *Don't walk on the grass.* ◆ *Keep off the grass.* (= on a sign) **4** [U] (*slang*) MARIJUANA
IDM **the grass is (always) greener on the other side (of the fence)** (*saying*) said about people who never seem happy with what they have and always think that other people have a better situation than they have **not let the grass grow under your feet** to not delay in getting things done **put sb out to grass/pasture** (*informal*) to force someone to stop doing their job, especially because they are old ⊃ more at SNAKE *n.*
● *verb*
PHR V **grass sth↔'over** to cover an area with grass

grass 'court *noun* a TENNIS COURT with a grass surface

grassed /græst/ *adj.* covered with grass

grass·hop·per /'græs,hɒpər/ *noun* an insect with long back legs, that can jump very high and that makes a sound with its legs ⊃ picture at ANIMAL **IDM** see KNEE-HIGH

grass·land /'græslænd/ *noun* [U] also **grasslands** [pl.] a large area of open land covered with wild grass

grass 'roots *noun* [pl.] often **the grass roots** ordinary people in society or in an organization, rather than the leaders or people who make decisions: *the grass roots of the party* ▶ **grass-roots** *adj.* [only before noun]: *We need support at the grass-roots level.*

grass 'skirt *noun* a skirt made of long grass, worn by dancers in the Pacific islands

'grass snake *noun* a small harmless snake

grass 'widow *noun* a woman whose husband is away from home for long periods of time

grass·y /'græsi/ *adj.* (**grass·i·er, grass·i·est**) covered with grass

grate /greɪt/ *verb, noun*
● *verb* **1** [T] ~ **sth** to rub food against a GRATER in order to cut it into small pieces: *grated apple/carrots/cheese, etc.* ⊃ picture at COOKING ⊃ collocations at COOKING **2** [I] ~ **(on sb/sth)** to irritate or annoy someone: *Her voice really grates on me.* **3** [I, T] when two hard surfaces grate as they rub together, they make a sharp unpleasant sound; someone can also make one thing grate against another: *The rusty hinges grated as the gate swung shut.* ◆ ~ **sth (+ adv./prep.)** *He grated his knife across the plate.*
● *noun* **1** a metal frame for holding the wood or coal in a FIREPLACE **2** a frame of metal bars over the opening to a hole in the ground or a window SYN GRATING ⊃ see also SEWER GRATE

grate·ful 🔊 /'greɪtfl/ *adj.*
1 feeling or showing thanks because someone has done something kind for you or has done as you asked: ~ **(to sb) (for sth)** *I am extremely grateful to all the teachers for their help.*

WORD FAMILY
grateful *adj.* (≠ ungrateful)
gratefully *adv.*
gratitude *noun* (≠ ingratitude)

◆ *We would be grateful for any information you can give us.* ◆ ~ **(to do sth)** *She seems to think I should be grateful to have a job at all.* ◆ ~ **(that...)** *He was grateful that she didn't tell his parents about the incident.* ◆ *Kate gave him a grateful smile.*
2 used to make a request, especially in a letter or in a formal situation: *I would be grateful if you could send the completed form back as soon as possible.* ▶ **grate·ful·ly** /-fəli/ *adv.*: *He nodded gratefully.* ◆ *All donations will be gratefully received.* **IDM** see SMALL

grat·er /'greɪtər/ *noun* a kitchen UTENSIL (= a tool) with a rough surface, used for GRATING food into very small pieces: *a cheese/nutmeg grater* ⊃ picture at COOKING, KITCHEN

grat·i·fi·ca·tion /,grætəfə'keɪʃn/ *noun* [U, C] (*formal*) the state of feeling pleasure when something goes well for you or when your desires are satisfied; something that gives you pleasure SYN SATISFACTION: *sexual gratification* ◆ *Feeding will usually provide instant gratification to a crying baby.*

grat·i·fy /ˈɡrætəˌfaɪ/ verb (grat·i·fies, grat·i·fy·ing, grat·i-fied, grat·i·fied) **1** (formal) to please or satisfy someone: **it gratifies sb to do sth** It gratified him to think that it was all his work. ♦ ~ **sb** I was gratified by their invitation. **2** ~ **sth** (formal) to satisfy a wish, need, etc.: He only gave his consent in order to gratify her wishes. ▶ **grat·i·fied** adj. [not usually before noun] ~ **(at sth)** | ~ **(to find, hear, see, etc.)**: She was gratified to find that they had followed her advice.

grat·i·fy·ing /ˈɡrætəˌfaɪɪŋ/ adj. (formal) pleasing and giving satisfaction: It is gratifying to see such good results. ⊃ thesaurus box at SATISFYING ▶ **gra·ti·fy·ing·ly** adv.

grat·in /ˈɡrætn; ˈɡrætn; ɡraˈtæ/ noun [U] (from French) a cooked dish that is covered with a crisp layer of cheese or BREADCRUMBS ⊃ see also AU GRATIN

grat·ing /ˈɡreɪtɪŋ/ noun, adj.
• noun a flat frame with metal bars across it, used to cover a window, a hole in the ground, etc. **SYN** GRATE
• adj. (of a sound or someone's voice) unpleasant to listen to

grat·is /ˈɡrætəs/ adv. done or given without having to be paid for **SYN** FREE adv.: I knew his help wouldn't be given gratis. ▶ **grat·is** adj.: a gratis copy of a book

grat·i·tude /ˈɡrætəˌtud/ noun [U] the feeling of being grateful and wanting to express your thanks: He smiled at them **with gratitude**. ♦ ~ **(to sb) (for sth)** I would like to express my gratitude to everyone for their hard work. ♦ She was presented with the gift **in gratitude for** her long service. ♦ a deep sense of gratitude ♦ I owe you a great **debt of gratitude** (= feel extremely grateful). **ANT** INGRATITUDE

gra·tu·i·tous /ɡrəˈtuatəs/ adj. (disapproving) done without any good reason or purpose and often having harmful effects **SYN** UNNECESSARY: gratuitous violence on television ▶ **gra·tu·i·tous·ly** adv.

gra·tu·i·ty /ɡrəˈtuati/ noun (pl. gra·tu·i·ties) (formal) money that you give to someone who has provided a service for you **SYN** TIP

grave¹ 🔊 /ɡreɪv/ noun, adj. ⊃ see also GRAVE²
• noun **1** a place in the ground where a dead person is buried: We visited Grandma's grave. ♦ There were flowers on the grave. **2** [sing.] often **the grave** (usually literary) death; a person's death: Is there life beyond the grave (= life after death)? ♦ He followed her to the grave (= died soon after her). ♦ She smoked herself into an early grave (= died young as a result of smoking).
IDM **turn/roll (over) in his/her grave** (of a person who is dead) likely to be very shocked or angry: My father would turn over in his grave if he knew. ⊃ more at CRADLE n., DIG v., FOOT n.
• adj. (grav·er, grav·est) (formal) **1** (of situations, feelings, etc.) very serious and important; giving you a reason to feel worried: The police have expressed grave concern about the missing child's safety. ♦ The consequences will be very grave if nothing is done. ♦ We were in grave danger. **2** (of people) serious in manner, as if something sad, important, or worrying has just happened: She looked very grave as she entered the room. ⊃ see also GRAVITY ⊃ thesaurus box at SERIOUS ▶ **grave·ly** adv.: She is gravely ill. ♦ Local people are gravely concerned. ♦ He nodded gravely as I poured out my troubles.

grave² /ɡreɪv; ɡrɑv/ (also ˌgrave ˈaccent) noun a mark placed over a vowel in some languages to show how it should be pronounced, as over the e in the French word père ⊃ compare ACUTE ACCENT, CIRCUMFLEX, TILDE, UMLAUT ⊃ see also GRAVE¹

grave·dig·ger /ˈɡreɪvˌdɪɡər/ noun a person whose job is to dig graves

grav·el /ˈɡrævl/ noun [U] small stones, often used to make the surface of paths and roads: a gravel path ♦ a gravel pit (= a place where gravel is taken from the ground)

grav·eled /ˈɡrævld/ adj. (of a road, etc.) covered with gravel

gra·vel·ly /ˈɡrævəli/ adj. **1** full of or containing many small stones: a dry gravelly soil **2** (of a voice) deep and with a rough sound

grav·en im·age /ˌɡreɪvn ˈɪmɪdʒ/ noun (disapproving) a statue or image that people worship as a god or as if it were a god

ˈgrave ˌrobber noun a person who digs up graves to steal bodies or the valuable things buried with the bodies, especially from ancient graves

grave·side /ˈɡreɪvsaɪd/ noun the area around the edge of a grave: a graveside service

grave·stone /ˈɡreɪvstoʊn/ noun a stone that is put on a grave in a vertical position, showing the name, etc. of the person buried there **SYN** HEADSTONE ⊃ compare TOMB-STONE

grave·yard /ˈɡreɪvyard/ noun **1** an area of land, often near a church, where people are buried ⊃ compare CEMETERY, CHURCHYARD **2** a place where things or people that are not wanted are sent or left

ˈgraveyard ˌshift noun a period of time working at night or in the very early morning

grav·id /ˈɡrævəd/ adj. (technical) pregnant

grav·i·tas /ˈɡrævəˌtɑs/ noun [U] (formal) the quality of being serious **SYN** SERIOUSNESS: a book of extraordinary gravitas

grav·i·tate /ˈɡrævəˌteɪt/ verb (formal)
PHR V **ˈgravitate to/toward(s) sb/sth** to move toward someone or something that you are attracted to: College graduates tend to gravitate to the cities in search of work.

grav·i·ta·tion /ˌɡrævəˈteɪʃn/ noun [U] (physics) a force of attraction that causes objects to move toward each other

grav·i·ta·tion·al /ˌɡrævəˈteɪʃənl/ adj. connected with or caused by the force of gravity: a gravitational field ♦ the gravitational pull of the moon

grav·i·ty /ˈɡrævəti/ noun [U] **1** (abbr. g) the force that attracts objects in space toward each other, and that on the earth pulls them toward the center of the planet, so that things fall to the ground when they are dropped: Newton's law of gravity ⊃ see also CENTER OF GRAVITY **2** (formal) extreme importance and a cause for worry **SYN** SERIOUSNESS: I don't think you realize the gravity of the situation. ♦ Punishment varies according to the gravity of the offense. **3** (formal) serious behavior, speech, or appearance: They were asked to behave with the gravity that was appropriate in a court of law. ⊃ see also GRAVE¹

gra·vy /ˈɡreɪvi/ noun [U] **1** a brown sauce made by adding flour to the juices that come out of meat while it is cooking **2** (informal) something, especially money, that is obtained when you do not expect it

ˈgravy ˌboat noun a long low bowl used for serving and pouring gravy at a meal

ˈgravy ˌtrain noun (informal) a situation where people seem to be making a lot of money without much effort

gray (especially CanE **grey**) /ɡreɪ/ adj., noun, verb
• adj. **1** having the color of smoke or ASH: gray eyes/hair ♦ wisps of gray smoke ♦ a gray suit **2** [not usually before noun] having gray hair: He's gotten very gray. **3** (of a person's skin color) pale and dull, because they are sick, tired, or sad **4** (of the sky or weather) dull; full of clouds: gray skies ♦ I hate these gray days. **5** without interest or variety; making you feel sad: Life seems gray and pointless without him. **6** (disapproving) not interesting or attractive: The company was full of faceless gray men who all looked the same. **7** [only before noun] connected with old people: the gray vote ♦ gray power ▶ **gray·ness** noun [U, sing.]
• noun **1** [U, C] the color of smoke or ASH: the dull gray of the sky ♦ dressed in gray **2** [C] a gray or white horse: She's riding the gray.
• verb [I] (of hair) to become gray: His hair was graying at the sides. ♦ a tall woman with graying hair

ˈgray ˌarea noun an area of a subject or situation that is not clear or does not fit into a particular group and is therefore difficult to define or deal with: Exactly what can be called an offensive weapon is still a gray area.

gray·beard (*CanE usually* **grey·beard**) /ˈgreɪbɪrd/ *noun* (*informal*) an old man: *the graybeards of the art world*

gray-ˈhaired *adj.* with gray hair

gray·ish (*CanE usually* **grey·ish**) /ˈgreɪʃ/ *adj.* fairly gray in color: *grayish hair*

gray ˈmarket *noun* [usually sing.] **1** a system in which products are imported into a country and sold without the permission of the company that produced them **2** old people, when they are thought of as customers for goods

gray ˌmatter *noun* [U] (*informal*) a person's intelligence

gray·scale (*CanE usually* **grey·scale**) /ˈgreɪskeɪl/ *adj.* (*technical*) **1** (of an image) produced using only shades of gray, not color: *I printed out the pictures in grayscale.* **2** (of a printer or SCANNER) producing images using only shades of gray, not color

graze /greɪz/ *verb, noun*
• *verb* **1** [I, T] (of cows, sheep, etc.) to eat grass that is growing in a field: *There were cows grazing beside the river.* ◆ ~ **on sth** *The horses were grazing on the lush grass.* ◆ ~ **sth** *The field had been grazed by sheep.* **2** [T] ~ **sth** to put cows, sheep, etc. in a field so that they can eat the grass there: *The land is used by local people to graze their animals.* ⊃ collocations at FARMING **3** [I] ~ **(on sth)** (*informal*) to eat small amounts of food many times during the day, often while doing other things, instead of eating three meals: *I have this really bad habit of grazing on junk food.* **4** [T] ~ **sth (on sth)** to break the surface of your skin by rubbing it against something rough: *I fell and grazed my knee.* ⊃ collocations at INJURY **5** [T] ~ **sth** to touch something lightly while passing it: *The bullet grazed his cheek.*
• *noun* a small injury where the surface of the skin has been slightly broken by rubbing against something: *Adam walked away from the crash with just cuts and grazes.*

graz·ing /ˈgreɪzɪŋ/ *noun* [U] land with grass that cows, sheep, etc. can eat

GRE /ˌdʒi ɑr ˈi/ *abbr.* Graduate Record Examination (an examination taken by students who want to study for a further degree)

grease /gris/ *noun, verb*
• *noun* [U] **1** any thick OILY substance, especially one that is used to make machines run smoothly: *Grease marks can be removed with liquid detergent.* ◆ *Her hands were covered with oil and grease.* ◆ *the grease in his hair* ⊃ see also ELBOW GREASE **2** animal fat that has been made softer by cooking or heating: *plates covered with grease*
• *verb* ~ **sth** to rub grease or fat on something: *to grease a cake pan*
IDM **grease sb's palm** (*old-fashioned, informal*) to give someone money in order to persuade them to do something dishonest **SYN** BRIBE **grease the wheels** to help something to happen easily and without problems, especially in business or politics ⊃ more at LIGHTNING *n.*

ˈgrease gun *noun* a tool for applying grease to moving parts of a machine, etc.

ˈgrease ˌmonkey *noun* (*informal*) an offensive or humorous word for a person whose job is repairing cars **SYN** MECHANIC

grease·paint /ˈgrispeɪnt/ *noun* [U] a thick substance used by actors as makeup

greas·y /ˈgrisi; -zi/ *adj.* (**greas·i·er, greas·i·est**) **1** covered in a lot of GREASE or oil: *greasy fingers/marks/coveralls* **2** (*disapproving*) (of food) cooked with too much oil: *greasy french fries* **3** (*disapproving*) (of hair or skin) producing too much natural oil: *long greasy hair* **4** (*informal, disapproving*) (of people or their behavior) friendly in a way that does not seem sincere **SYN** OILY
IDM **the greasy pole** (*informal*) used to refer to the difficult way to the top of a profession

ˌgreasy ˈspoon *noun* (*informal, often disapproving*) a small cheap restaurant, usually one that is not very clean or attractive

great 🔑 /greɪt/ *adj., noun, adv.*
• *adj.* (**great·er, great·est**)
▸ LARGE **1** much more than average in degree or quantity: *a matter of great importance* ◆ *The concert had been a great success.* ◆ *Her death was a great shock to us all.* ◆ *It gives me great pleasure to welcome you here today.* ◆ *Take great care of it.* ◆ *You've been a great help.* ◆ *We are all* **to a great extent** *the products of our culture.* **2** [usually before noun] very large; much bigger than average in size or quantity: *A great crowd had gathered.* ◆ *People were arriving in great numbers.* ◆ *The* **great majority of** (= most) *people seem to agree with this view.* ◆ *He must have fallen from a great height.* ◆ *A great many people died in the attack.* **3** [only before noun] (*informal*) used to emphasize an adjective of size or quality: *There was a* **great** *big pile of books on the table.* ⊃ note at BIG
▸ ADMIRED **4** extremely good in ability or quality and therefore admired by many people: *He has been described as the world's greatest violinist.* ◆ *Sherlock Holmes, the great detective* ◆ *Great art has the power to change lives.*
▸ GOOD **5** (*informal*) very good or pleasant: *He's a great guy.* ◆ *It's great to see you again.* ◆ *What a great goal!* ◆ *We had a great time in Miami.* ◆ *"I'll pick you up at seven." "That would be great, thanks."* ◆ *"Tom's coming too." "Great!"* ◆ (*ironic*) *Oh great, they left without us.* ⊃ thesaurus box at FUN
▸ SKILLED **6** [not usually before noun] ~ **at (doing) sth** (*informal*) able to do something well: *She's great at chess.*
▸ USEFUL **7** ~ **for (doing) sth** (*informal*) very suitable or useful for something: *This gadget is great for opening jars.* ◆ *Try this cream—it's great for dry skin.*
▸ IMPORTANT/IMPRESSIVE **8** [only before noun] important and impressive: *The wedding was a great occasion.* ◆ *As the great day approached, she grew more and more nervous.* ◆ *One great advantage of this metal is that it doesn't rust.*
▸ WITH INFLUENCE **9** having high status or a lot of influence: *the great powers* (= important and powerful countries) ◆ *We can make this country great again.* ◆ *Alexander the Great*
▸ IN GOOD HEALTH **10** in a very good state of physical or mental health: *She seemed to be in great spirits* (= very cheerful). ◆ *I feel great today.* ◆ *Everyone's in great form.*
▸ FOR EMPHASIS **11** [only before noun] used when you are emphasizing a particular description of someone/something: *We are great friends.* ◆ *I've never been a great reader* (= I do not read much). ◆ *She's a great talker, isn't she?*
▸ FAMILY **12** **great-** added to words for family members to show a further stage in relationship: *my great-aunt* (= my father's or mother's aunt) ◆ *her great-grandson* (= the grandson of her son or daughter) ◆ *my great-great-grandfather* (= the grandfather of my grandfather)
▸ LARGER ANIMALS/PLANTS **13** [only before noun] used in the names of animals or plants which are larger than similar kinds: *a Great Dane*
▸ CITY NAME **14** **Greater** used with the name of a city to describe an area that includes the center of the city and a large area all around it: *Greater Chicago*

▸ **great·ness** **IDM** *see* OAK *noun* [U]
IDM **be going great guns** (*informal*) to be doing something quickly and successfully: *Work is going great guns now.* **be a great one for (doing) sth** to do something a lot; to enjoy something: *I've never been a great one for writing letters.* **be no great shakes** (*informal*) to be not very good, efficient, suitable, etc. **great and small** of all sizes or types: *all creatures great and small* **great minds think alike** (*informal, humorous*) used to say that you and another person must both be very smart because you have had the same idea or agree about something **the great ...in the sky** (*humorous*) used to refer to where a particular person or thing is imagined to go when they die or are no longer working, similar to the place they were connected with on earth: *Their pet rabbit had gone to the great rabbit hutch in the sky.* ⊃ more at PAINS, SUM
• *noun* [usually pl.] (*informal*) a very well-known and successful person or thing: *He was one of boxing's all-time greats.*
• *adv.* (*informal, non-standard*) very well: *You did great.*

great

cool ◆ fantastic ◆ fabulous ◆ terrific ◆ awesome

These are all informal words that describe someone or something that is very good, pleasant, enjoyable, etc.

great (*informal*) very good; giving a lot of pleasure: *We had a great time in Madrid.*

cool (*informal*) used to show that you admire or approve of something, often because it is fashionable, attractive, or different: *I think their new song's really cool.*

fantastic (*informal*) extremely good; giving a lot of pleasure: *I had a fantastic vacation in Mexico.*

fabulous (*informal*) extremely good: *Jane's a fabulous cook.* (**Fabulous** is slightly more old-fashioned than the other words in this set.)

terrific (*informal*) extremely good; wonderful: *She's doing a terrific job.*

awesome (*informal*) very good, impressive, or enjoyable: *The show was just awesome.*

PATTERNS

- to have a(n) great/fantastic/fabulous/terrific/ awesome time
- to look/sound great/cool/fantastic/fabulous/ terrific/awesome
- really great/cool/fantastic/fabulous/terrific/ awesome
- absolutely great/fantastic/fabulous/terrific/ awesome

ˌgreat ˈape *noun* [usually pl.] one of the large animals that are most similar to humans (CHIMPANZEES, GORILLAS, and ORANGUTANS)

ˌgreat ˈauk *noun* a large bird similar to a PENGUIN, that no longer exists

the ˌGreat ˈBear *noun* [sing.] (*astronomy*) = URSA MAJOR

ˌGreat ˈBritain *noun* [U] England, Scotland, and Wales, when considered as a unit. HELP Sometimes "Great Britain" (or "Britain") is wrongly used to refer to the political state, officially called the "United Kingdom of Great Britain and Northern Ireland" or the "U.K."

ˈgreat·coat /ˈgreɪtkoʊt/ *noun* a long heavy coat, especially one worn by soldiers

ˌGreat ˈDane /ˌgreɪt ˈdeɪn/ *noun* a very large dog with short hair

the ˌGreat Diˈvide *noun* [sing.] **1** = CONTINENTAL DIVIDE **2** ~ (**between A and B**) (sometimes *humorous*) a great difference between two groups of people that separates them from each other: *the Great Divide between liberals and conservatives*

ˈgreat·ly /ˈgreɪtli/ *adv.* (*formal*) (usually before a verb or participle) very much: *People's reaction to the film has varied greatly.* ◆ *a greatly increased risk* ◆ *Your help would be greatly appreciated.*

the ˌGreat ˈWar *noun* [sing.] (*old-fashioned*) = WORLD WAR I

ˌgreat white ˈshark *noun* a large aggressive SHARK with a brown or gray back, found in warm seas

the ˌGreat White ˈWay *noun* (*informal*) a name for Broadway in New York City that refers to the many bright lights of its theaters

grebe /grib/ *noun* a bird like a DUCK, that can also swim underwater: *a great crested grebe*

Gre·cian /ˈgriʃn/ *adj.* from ancient Greece or like the styles of ancient Greece: *Grecian architecture*

ˌGrecian ˈnose *noun* a straight nose that continues the line of the FOREHEAD

Greco- /ˈgrekoʊ/ *combining form* (in adjectives) Greek

greed /grid/ *noun* [U] (*disapproving*) **1** a strong desire for more wealth, possessions, power, etc. than a person needs: *His actions were motivated by greed.* ◆ ~ **for sth** *Nothing would satisfy her greed for power.* **2** a strong desire for more food or drinks when you are no longer hungry or thirsty: *I had another helping of ice cream out of pure greed.*

greed·y /ˈgridi/ *adj.* (greed·i·er, greed·i·est) wanting more money, power, food, etc. than you really need: *You greedy pig! You've already had two helpings!* ◆ *He stared at the diamonds with greedy eyes.* ◆ ~ **for sth** *The shareholders are greedy for profit.* ▶ greed·i·ly /ˈgridli/ *adv.*: *She ate noisily and greedily.*

Greek /grik/ *noun* **1** [C] a person from modern or ancient Greece **2** [U] the language of modern or ancient Greece **3** [C] a member of a FRATERNITY or a SORORITY at a college or university
IDM **it's all Greek to me** (*informal, saying*) I cannot understand it: *She tried to explain how the system works, but it's all Greek to me.*

ˌGreek ˈcross *noun* a cross with all arms of the same length

ˌGreek ˈsalad *noun* [C, U] a salad that is made with tomatoes, OLIVES, and FETA CHEESE

green ♪ /grin/ *adj., noun, verb*
● *adj.* (green·er, green·est)
> COLOR **1** having the color of grass or the leaves of most plants and trees: *green beans* ◆ *Wait for the light to turn green* (= on traffic lights).
> COVERED WITH GRASS **2** covered with grass or other plants: *green fields/hills* ◆ *After the rains, the land was green with new growth.*
> FRUIT **3** not yet ready to eat: *green tomatoes*
> PERSON **4** (*informal*) (of a person) young and lacking experience: *The new trainees are still very green.* **5** (of a person or their skin) being a pale color, as if the person is going to VOMIT: *It was a rough crossing and most of the passengers looked distinctly green.*
> POLITICS **6** concerned with the protection of the environment; supporting the protection of the environment as a political principle: *green politics* ◆ *Try to adopt a greener lifestyle.*
▶ green·ness *noun* [U]: *the greenness of the countryside* ◆ *Supermarkets have started proclaiming the greenness of their products.*
IDM **green with envy** very jealous ⊃ more at GRASS *n.*
● *noun*
> COLOR **1** [U, C] the color of grass and the leaves of most plants and trees: *the green of the countryside in spring* ◆ *The room was decorated in a combination of greens and blues.* ◆ *She was dressed all in green.*
> VEGETABLES **2** greens [pl.] vegetables with dark green leaves: *Eat up your greens.*
> AREA OF GRASS **3** [C] (in GOLF) an area of grass cut short around a hole in a GOLF COURSE: *the 18th green* ◆ *Did the ball land on the green?* ⊃ picture at SPORT ⊃ see also BOWLING GREEN, PUTTING GREEN
> POLITICS **4** Green [C] a person who supports a group or political party whose main aim is the protection of the environment
● *verb*
> CREATE PARKS **1** ~ sth to create parks and other areas with trees and plants in a city: *projects for greening the cities*
> POLITICS **2** ~ sb/sth to make someone more aware of issues connected with the environment; to make something less harmful to the environment: *an attempt to green industry bosses*
▶ green·ing *noun* [U]: *the greening of auto manufacturing*

ˌgreen ˈaudit *noun* an official examination of the effect of a company's business on the environment

green·back /ˈgrinbæk/ *noun* (*informal*) an American dollar note

ˈgreen bean (also ˈstring bean) *noun* a type of BEAN which

is a long, thin, green POD, cooked and eaten whole as a vegetable ⊃ picture at FRUIT

'green belt *noun* [U, C, usually sing.] an area of open land around a city where building is strictly controlled: *New roads are cutting into the green belt.*

,Green Be'ret *noun* a member of the U.S. Army Special Forces

'green bin *noun* (*CanE*) a green plastic container in which you can put garbage that will break down into the soil, such as fruit, vegetables, etc., for city workers to take away

'green card *noun* a document that legally allows someone from another country to live and work in the U.S.

green·er·y /'grinəri/ *noun* [U] attractive green leaves and plants: *The room was decorated with flowers and greenery.*

the ,green-eyed 'monster *noun* (*informal*) used as a way of talking about JEALOUSY

green·field /'grinfild/ *adj.* [only before noun] used to describe an area of land that has not yet had buildings on it, but for which building development may be planned: *a greenfield site*

green·gage /'gringeidʒ/ *noun* a small, soft, green fruit that is a type of PLUM: *a greengage tree*

green·gro·cer /'grin,grousər/ *noun* **1** a person who owns, manages, or works in a store selling fruit and vegetables **2** a store that sells fruit and vegetables

green·horn /'grinhɔrn/ *noun* (*informal*) a person who has little experience and can be easily tricked **SYN** TENDERFOOT

green·house /'grinhaus/ *noun* a building with glass sides and a glass roof for growing plants in ⊃ picture at BUILDING

the 'greenhouse ef,fect *noun* [sing.] the problem of the gradual rise in temperature of the earth's atmosphere, caused by an increase of gases such as CARBON DIOXIDE in the air surrounding the earth, which trap the heat of the sun ⊃ collocations at ENVIRONMENT ⊃ see also GLOBAL WARMING

'greenhouse 'gas *noun* any of the gases that are thought to cause the greenhouse effect, especially CARBON DIOXIDE ⊃ collocations at ENVIRONMENT

green·ing /'grinɪŋ/ *noun* [U] ⊃ GREEN

green·ish /'grinɪʃ/ *adj.* fairly green in color

green·keep·er /'grin,kipər/ *noun* = GREENSKEEPER

'green 'light *noun* [sing.] permission for a project, etc. to start or continue **SYN** GO-AHEAD: *The government has decided to give the green light to the plan.*

,green ma'nure *noun* [U, C] plants that are dug into the soil in order to improve its quality

,green 'onion *noun* = SCALLION ⊃ picture at FRUIT

,green 'pepper *noun* a hollow green fruit that is eaten, raw or cooked, as a vegetable

'green roof (also ,living 'roof) *noun* a type of roof that has plants growing on it that help to keep the building cool in summer and warm in winter

'green room *noun* a room in a theater, television studio, etc. where the performers can relax when they are not performing

,green 'salad *noun* [C, U] a salad that is made with raw green vegetables, especially LETTUCE **SYN** TOSSED SALAD: *Serve with a green salad.*

greens·keep·er /'grinz,kipər/ (also green·keep·er) *noun* a person whose job is to take care of a GOLF COURSE

green·sward /'grinswɔrd/ *noun* [U] (*literary*) a piece of ground covered with grass

,green 'tea *noun* [U] a pale tea made from leaves that have been dried but not FERMENTED

,green 'thumb *noun* [sing.] if you have a **green thumb**, you are good at making plants grow

,green 'vegetable *noun* [C, usually pl.] (also greens [pl.]) a

vegetable with dark green leaves, for example CABBAGE or SPINACH

green·wash /'grinwɑʃ; -wɔʃ/ *noun* [U] (*disapproving*) activities by a company or an organization that are intended to make people think that it is concerned about the environment, even if its real business actually harms the environment

Green·wich Mean Time /,grɛnɪtʃ 'min taɪm/ ⊃ GMT

greet /grit/ *verb* **1** to say hello to someone or to welcome them: **~ sb** *He greeted all the guests warmly as they arrived.* ♦ **~ sb with sth** *She greeted us with a smile.* **2** [usually passive] to react to someone or something in a particular way: **~ sb/ sth** *Loud cheers greeted the news.* ♦ **~ sb/sth with sth** *The changes were greeted with suspicion.* ♦ **~ sb/sth as sth** *The team's win was greeted as a major triumph.* **3** [usually passive] **~ sb** (of sights, sounds, or smells) to be the first thing that you see, hear, or smell at a particular time: *When she opened the door, she was greeted by a scene of utter confusion.*

greet·er /'gritər/ *noun* a person whose job is to meet and welcome people in a public place such as a restaurant or store

greet·ing /'gritɪŋ/ *noun* **1** [C, U] something that you say or do to greet someone: *She waved a friendly greeting.* ♦ *They exchanged greetings and sat down to lunch.* ♦ *He raised his hand in greeting.* **2 greetings** [pl.] a message of good wishes for someone's health, happiness, etc.: *Christmas/ birthday, etc. greetings* ♦ *My mother sends her greetings to you all.* **IDM** see SEASON

'greeting ,card *noun* a card with a picture on the front and a message inside that you send to someone on a particular occasion such as their birthday

gre·gar·i·ous /grɪ'gɛriəs/ *adj.* **1** liking to be with other people **SYN** SOCIABLE **2** (*biology*) (of animals or birds) living in groups ▶ **gre·gar·i·ous·ly** *adv.* **gre·gar·i·ous·ness** *noun* [U]

Gre·go·ri·an cal·en·dar /grɪ,gɔriən 'kæləndər/ *noun* [sing.] the system used since 1582 in Western countries of arranging the months in the year and the days in the months and of counting the years from the birth of Christ ⊃ compare JULIAN CALENDAR

Gre,gorian 'chant *noun* [U, C] a type of church music for voices alone, used since the Middle Ages

grem·lin /'grɛmlən/ *noun* an imaginary creature that people blame when a machine suddenly stops working

gre·nade /grə'neɪd/ *noun* a small bomb that can be thrown by hand or fired from a gun ⊃ see also HAND GRENADE

gren·a·dier /,grɛnə'dɪr/ *noun* a soldier who is trained to use GRENADES

gren·a·dine /'grɛnə,din; ,grɛnə'din/ *noun* [U] a sweet red liquid that is made from POMEGRANATES (= a TROPICAL fruit with many seeds). It is drunk mixed with water or alcoholic drinks.

grew pt of GROW

grey (*especially CanE*) = GRAY

grey·hound /'greɪhaund/ *noun* a large, thin dog with smooth hair and long, thin legs, that can run very fast and is used in the sport of **greyhound racing**

grid /grɪd/ *noun* **1** a pattern of straight lines, usually crossing each other to form squares: *New York's grid of streets* **2** a frame of metal or wooden bars that are parallel or cross each other ⊃ see also CATTLE GUARD **3** a pattern of squares on a map that are marked with letters or numbers to help you find the exact position of a place: *The grid reference is C8.* **4** a system of electric wires or pipes carrying gas, for sending power over a large area **5** (in motor racing) a pattern of lines marking the starting positions for the racing cars **6** often **the Grid** [sing.] (*computing*) a number of computers that are linked together using the Internet so that they can share power, data, etc. in order to work on difficult problems

IDM off the grid not using the public supplies of elec-

ʌ **cup**   ə **about**   eɪ **say**   aɪ **five**   ɔɪ **boy**   aʊ **now**   oʊ **go**   ər **bird**

tricity, gas, water, etc.: *The mountain cabin is entirely off the grid.* ➔ see also OFF-THE-GRID

grid·dle /ˈɡrɪdl/ *noun* a flat iron plate that is heated and used for cooking

grid·i·ron /ˈɡrɪdˌaɪərn/ *noun* **1** a field used for football, marked with a pattern of parallel lines **2** a frame made of metal bars that is used for cooking meat or fish on, over an open fire

grid·lock /ˈɡrɪdlɑk/ *noun* [U] **1** a situation in which there are so many cars in the streets of a town that the traffic cannot move at all **2** (usually in politics) a situation in which people with different opinions are not able to agree with each other and so no action can be taken: *Congress is in gridlock.* ▶ **grid·locked** *adj.*

grief /ɡrif/ *noun* [U] **1** ~ **(over/at sth)** a feeling of great sadness, especially when someone dies: *She was overcome with grief when her husband died.* ◆ *They were able to share their common joy and grief.* **2** (*informal*) problems and worry: *He caused his parents a lot of grief.*

IDM come to grief (*informal*) **1** to end in total failure **2** to be harmed in an accident: *Several pedestrians came to grief on the icy pavement.* **give sb grief (about/over sth)** (*informal*) to be annoyed with someone and criticize their behavior **good grief!** (*informal*) used to express surprise or shock: *Good grief! What a mess!*

grief–stricken *adj.* feeling extremely sad because of something that has happened, especially the death of someone

griev·ance /ˈɡrivəns/ *noun* ~ **(against sb)** something that you think is unfair and that you complain or protest about: *Parents were invited to **air their grievances** (= express them) at the meeting.* ◆ *He had been **nursing a grievance** against his boss for months.* ◆ *Does the company have a formal **grievance procedure** (= a way of telling someone your complaints at work)?*

grieve /ɡriv/ *verb* **1** [I, T] to feel very sad, especially because someone has died: ~ **(for/over sb/sth)** *They are still grieving for their son.* ◆ *grieving relatives* ◆ ~ **sb/sth** *She grieved the death of her husband.* **2** [T] (*formal*) to make you feel very sad **SYN PAIN: it grieves sb that…** *It grieved him that he could do nothing to help her.* ◆ ~ **sb** *Their lack of interest grieved her.* ◆ **it grieves sb to do sth** *It grieved her to leave.*

griev·ous /ˈɡrivəs/ *adj.* (*formal*) very serious and often causing great pain or suffering: *He had been the victim of a grievous injustice.* ▶ **griev·ous·ly** *adv.*: *grievously hurt/ wounded*

grif·fin (also **grif·fon**, **gryph·on**) /ˈɡrɪfən/ *noun* (in stories) a creature with a LION's body and an EAGLE's wings and head

grift·er /ˈɡrɪftər/ *noun* a person who tricks people into giving them money, etc.

grill /ɡrɪl/ *noun, verb*
● *noun* **1** a flat metal frame that you put food on to cook over a fire ➔ see also BARBECUE **2** a dish of grilled food, especially meat **3** (especially in names) a restaurant serving grilled food: *Harry's Bar and Grill* **4** = GRILLE
● *verb* **1** ~ **sth** to cook food over a fire, especially outdoors: *grilled meat and shrimp* **2** ~ **sb (about sth)** to ask someone a lot of questions about their ideas, actions, etc., often in an unpleasant way: *They grilled her about where she had been all night.* ➔ see also GRILLING

grille (also **grill**) /ɡrɪl/ *noun* a screen made of metal bars or wire that is placed in front of a window, door, or piece of machinery in order to protect it: *a radiator grille* (= at the front of a car)

grilling /ˈɡrɪlɪŋ/ *noun* [usually sing.] a period of being questioned closely about your ideas, actions, etc.: *The president faced a tough grilling at today's press conference.*

grilse /ɡrɪls/ *noun* a SALMON (= a type of fish) that has returned to a river or lake after spending one winter in the ocean

grim /ɡrɪm/ *adj.* (**grim·mer**, **grim·mest**) **1** looking or sounding very serious: *a grim face/look/smile* ◆ *She looked grim.* ◆ *with a look of grim determination on his face* ◆ *grim-faced policemen* **2** unpleasant and depressing: *grim news* ◆ *We face the grim prospect of still higher unemployment.* ◆ *The outlook is pretty grim.* ◆ *Things are looking grim for workers in the building industry.* **3** (of a place or building) not attractive; depressing: *The house looked grim and dreary in the rain.* ◆ *the grim walls of the prison* ▶ **grim·ly** *adv.*: *"It won't be easy,"* he said grimly. ◆ *grimly determined* **grim·ness** *noun* [U]

grim·ace /ˈɡrɪməs; ɡrɪˈmeɪs/ *verb, noun*
● *verb* [I] ~ **(at sb/sth)** to make an ugly expression with your face to show pain, disgust, etc.: *He grimaced at the bitter taste.* ◆ *She grimaced as the needle went in.*
● *noun* an ugly expression made by twisting your face, used to show pain, disgust, etc. or to make someone laugh: *to make a grimace of pain* ◆ *"What's that?"* she asked with a grimace.

grime /ɡraɪm/ *noun* [U] dirt that forms a layer on the surface of something **SYN DIRT**: *a face covered with grime and sweat*

the Grim Reaper *noun* an imaginary figure who represents death. It looks like a SKELETON, wears a long CLOAK, and carries a SCYTHE.

grim·y /ˈɡraɪmi/ *adj.* (**grim·i·er**, **grim·i·est**) covered with dirt **SYN DIRTY**: *grimy hands/windows*

grin /ɡrɪn/ *verb, noun*
● *verb* (-nn-) [I, T] to smile widely: *They grinned with delight when they heard our news.* ◆ *He was **grinning from ear to ear**.* ◆ ~ **at sb** *She grinned amiably at us.* ◆ ~ **sth** *He grinned a welcome.*

IDM grin and bear it (only used as an infinitive and in orders) to accept pain, disappointment, or a difficult situation without complaining: *There's nothing we can do about it. We'll just have to grin and bear it.*
● *noun* a wide smile: *She broke into a broad grin.* ◆ *a wry/ sheepish grin* ◆ *"No,"* he said *with a grin.* ◆ *Take that grin off your face!*

grind /ɡraɪnd/ *verb, noun*
● *verb* (**ground, ground** /ɡraʊnd/)
▷ FOOD/FLOUR/COFFEE **1** [T] ~ **sth (up)** | ~ **sth (to/into sth)** to break or crush something into very small pieces between two hard surfaces or using a special machine: *to grind coffee/corn* ➔ see also GROUND (4) **2** [T] ~ **sth** to produce something such as flour by crushing: *The flour is ground using traditional methods.* **3** [T] ~ **sth** to cut food, especially meat, into very small pieces using a special machine (called a meat GRINDER): *ground beef* ➔ compare MINCE ➔ see also HAMBURGER
▷ MAKE SHARP/SMOOTH **4** [T] ~ **sth** to make something sharp or smooth by rubbing it against a hard surface: *a special stone for grinding knives*
▷ PRESS INTO SURFACE **5** [T] to press or rub something into a surface: ~ **sth into sth** *He ground his cigarette into the ashtray.* ◆ ~ **sth in** *The dirt on her hands was ground in.*
▷ RUB TOGETHER **6** [I, T] to rub together, or to make hard objects rub together, often producing an unpleasant noise: ~ **(together)** *Parts of the machine were grinding together noisily.* ◆ ~ **sth (together)** *She grinds her teeth while she's sleeping.* ◆ *He ground the gears on the car.*
▷ MACHINE **7** [T] ~ **sth** to turn the handle of a machine that grinds something: *to grind a pepper mill*

IDM bring sth to a grinding halt to make something gradually go slower until it stops completely **grind to a halt| come to a grinding halt** to go slower gradually and then stop completely: *Production ground to a halt during the strike.* ➔ more at AX
PHR V grind sb↔down to treat someone in a cruel, unpleasant way over a long period of time, so that they become very unhappy: *Don't let them grind you down.* ◆ *Years of oppression had ground the people down.* **grind on** to continue for a long time, when this is unpleasant: *The argument ground on for almost two years.* **grind sth↔out** to produce something in large quantities, often something that is not good or interesting **SYN CHURN OUT**: *She grinds out romance novels at the rate of five a year.*

● *noun*

> BORING ACTIVITY **1** [sing.] (*informal*) an activity that is tiring or boring and takes a lot of time: *the **daily grind** of a long commute to work* ◆ *It's a long grind to the top of that particular profession.*

> OF MACHINES **2** [sing.] the unpleasant noise made by machines

> OF PERSON **3** [C] (*informal*) a person who spends too much time working or studying

grind·er /'graɪndər/ *noun* **1** a machine or tool for grinding a solid substance into a powder: *a coffee grinder* **2** a person whose job is to make knives sharper; a machine that does this ➔ see also ORGAN GRINDER **3** = SUBMARINE SANDWICH

grind·ing /'graɪndɪŋ/ *adj.* [only before noun] (of a difficult situation) that never ends or improves: *grinding poverty*

grind·stone /'graɪndstoʊn/ *noun* a round stone that is turned like a wheel and is used to make knives and other tools sharp **IDM** see NOSE

grin·go /'grɪŋgoʊ/ *noun* (*pl.* grin·gos) (*informal, disapproving*) used in Latin American countries to refer to a person from the U.S.

gri·ot /'griou/ *noun* (in W. Africa, especially in the past) a person who sings or tells stories about the history and traditions of their people and community

grip /grɪp/ *verb, noun*
● *verb* (-pp-)
> HOLD TIGHTLY **1** [T, I] to hold something tightly **SYN** GRASP: *~ sth* "*Please don't go,*" *he said, gripping her arm.* ◆ *~ on to sth She gripped onto the railing with both hands.* ➔ thesaurus box at HOLD

> INTEREST/EXCITE **2** [T] *~ sb* to interest or excite someone; to hold someone's attention: *The book grips you from start to finish.* ◆ *I was totally gripped by the story.* ➔ see also GRIPPING

> HAVE POWERFUL EFFECT **3** [T] *~ sb/sth* (of an emotion or a situation) to have a powerful effect on someone or something: *I was gripped by a feeling of panic.* ◆ *Terrorism has gripped the country for the past two years.*

> MOVE/HOLD WITHOUT SLIPPING **4** [T, I] *~ (sth)* to hold onto or to move over a surface without slipping: *tires that grip the road*

● *noun*
> HOLDING TIGHTLY **1** [C, usually sing.] *~ (on sb/sth)* an act of holding someone or something tightly; a particular way of doing this **SYN** GRASP: *Keep a tight grip on the rope.* ◆ *to loosen/release/relax your grip* ◆ *She tried to get a grip on the icy rock.* ◆ *The climber slipped and lost her grip.* ◆ *She struggled from his grip.* ◆ *Try adjusting your grip on the racket.*

> CONTROL/POWER **2** [sing.] *~ (on sb/sth)* control or power over someone or something: *The home team took a firm grip on the game.* ◆ *We need to tighten the grip we have on the market.*

> UNDERSTANDING **3** [sing.] *~ (on sth)* an understanding of something **SYN** GRASP: *I couldn't get a grip on what was going on.* ◆ *You need to keep a good grip on reality in this job.*

> MOVING WITHOUT SLIPPING **4** [C, U] the ability of something to move over a surface without slipping: *These tires give the bus a better grip in slippery conditions.*

> PART OF OBJECT **5** [C] a part of something that has a special surface so that it can be held without the hands slipping: *the grip on a golf club*

> JOB IN THE MOVIES **6** [C] a person who prepares and moves the cameras, and sometimes the lighting equipment, when a movie is being made

> BAG **7** [C] (*old-fashioned*) a large soft bag, used when traveling

IDM come to grips with sth to begin to understand and deal with something difficult: *I'm slowly coming to grips with the language.* get a grip (on yourself) to improve your behavior or control your emotions after being afraid, upset, or angry: *I have to get a grip on myself, he told himself firmly.* ◆ (*informal*) *Get a grip!* (= make an effort to control your emotions) in the grip of sth experiencing something unpleasant that cannot be stopped: *a country in the grip of recession* lose your grip (on sth) to become unable to

understand or control a situation: *Sometimes I feel like I'm losing my grip on reality.*

gripe /graɪp/ *noun, verb*
● *noun* (*informal*) a complaint about something: *My only gripe about the hotel was the food.*

● *verb* [I] *~ (about sb/sth)* (*informal*) to complain about someone or something in an annoying way: *He's always griping about the people at work.*

grip·ping /'grɪpɪŋ/ *adj.* exciting or interesting in a way that keeps your attention ➔ thesaurus box at INTERESTING

gris·ly /'grɪzli/ *adj.* [usually before noun] (gris·li·er, gris·li·est) extremely unpleasant and frightening and usually connected with death and violence: *a grisly crime*

gris·tle /'grɪsl/ *noun* [U] a hard substance in meat that is unpleasant to eat: *a lump of gristle*

Grit /grɪt/ *noun* [C] (*CanE*) a member or supporter of the Liberal Party in Canada

grit /grɪt/ *noun, verb*
● *noun* [U] **1** very small pieces of stone or sand: *I had a piece of grit in my eye.* ◆ *She asked the children to take off their boots so they wouldn't bring grit into the house.* **2** the courage and determination that makes it possible for someone to continue doing something difficult or unpleasant

● *verb* (-tt-)
IDM grit your teeth **1** to bite your teeth tightly together: *She gritted her teeth against the pain.* ◆ "*Stop it!*" *he said through gritted teeth.* **2** to be determined to continue to do something in a difficult or unpleasant situation: *It started to rain harder, but we gritted our teeth and kept going.*

grits /grɪts/ *noun* [pl.] CORN that is partly crushed before cooking, often eaten for breakfast or as part of a meal in the southern U.S.

grit·ty /'grɪti/ *adj.* **1** containing or like GRIT: *a layer of gritty dust* **2** showing the courage and determination to continue doing something difficult or unpleasant: *gritty determination* ◆ *a gritty performance from the halfback* **3** showing something unpleasant as it really is: *a gritty description of urban violence* ◆ *gritty realism* ➔ see also NITTY-GRITTY ▸ **grit·ti·ly** /-ṭəli/ *adv.* **grit·ti·ness** /-ṭinəs/ *noun* [U]

griz·zled /'grɪzld/ *adj.* (*literary*) having hair that is gray or partly gray

griz·zly bear /'grɪzli ˌbɛr/ (also **griz·zly**) *noun* a large aggressive brown BEAR that lives in N. America and parts of Russia

groan /groʊn/ *verb, noun*
● *verb* **1** [I, T] to make a long deep sound because you are annoyed, upset, or in pain, or with pleasure **SYN** MOAN: *He lay on the floor groaning.* ◆ *~ with sth to groan with pain/pleasure* ◆ *~ at sth We all groaned at his terrible jokes.* ◆ *~ about sth They were all moaning and groaning* (= complaining) *about the amount of work they had to do.* ◆ + *speech* "*It's a complete mess!*" *she groaned.* **2** [I] to make a sound like a person groaning **SYN** MOAN: *The trees creaked and groaned in the wind.*
IDM groan under the weight of sth (*formal*) used to say that there is too much of something
PHR V 'groan with sth (*formal*) to be full of something: *tables groaning with food*

● *noun* a long deep sound made when someone or something groans **SYN** MOAN: *She let out a groan of dismay.* ◆ *He fell to the floor with a groan.* ◆ *The house was filled with the cello's dismal squeaks and groans.*

gro·cer /'groʊsər/ *noun* (*old-fashioned*) a person who owns, manages, or works in a store selling food and other things used in the home

gro·cer·y 🔑 /'groʊsəri; 'groʊsri/ *noun* (*pl.* gro·cer·ies) **1** [C] = GROCERY STORE **2** gro·ceries [pl.] food and other goods sold in a grocery store or at a supermarket ➔ collocations at SHOPPING ▸ **gro·cer·y** *adj.* [only before noun]: *the grocery bill*

'grocery ˌstore (also gro·cer·y) *noun* a store that sells food

t **t**ea   ț **b**utter   d **d**id   k **c**at   g **g**ot   tʃ **ch**in   dʒ **J**une   f **f**all

and other things used in the home. "Grocery store" is often used to mean "supermarket." ⊃ compare SUPERMARKET

grog /grɑg/ *noun* [U] a strong alcoholic drink, originally RUM, mixed with water

grog·gy /'grɑgi/ *adj.* **(grog-gi-er, grog-gi-est)** [not usually before noun] (*informal*) weak and unable to think or move well because you are sick or very tired

groin /grɔɪn/ *noun* **1** the part of the body where the legs join at the top, including the area around the GENITALS (= sex organs): *She kicked her attacker in the groin.* ♦ *He's been out all season with a groin injury.* ⊃ picture at BODY **2** a low wall built out into the ocean to prevent it from washing away sand and stones from the beach

grok /grɑk/ (-kk-) *verb* ~ **sth** (*slang*) to understand something completely using your feelings rather than considering the facts: *Children grok this show immediately but their parents take longer to get it.*

grom·met /'grɑmət/ *noun* a small metal ring placed around a hole in cloth or leather, to make it stronger

groom /grum/ *verb, noun*
• *verb* **1** ~ **sth** to clean or brush an animal: *to groom a horse/dog/cat* ♦ *The horses are all well fed and groomed.* **2** ~ **sth** (of an animal) to clean the fur or skin of another animal or itself: *a female ape grooming her mate* **3** to prepare or train someone for an important job or position: ~ **sb (for/as sth)** *Our junior employees are being groomed for more senior roles.* ♦ ~ **sb to do sth** *The eldest son is being groomed to take over when his father dies.* **4** ~ **sb** (of a person who is sexually attracted to children) to prepare a child for a meeting, especially using an Internet CHAT ROOM, with the intention of performing an illegal sexual act
• *noun* **1** a person whose job is to feed and take care of horses, especially by brushing and cleaning them **2** = BRIDEGROOM

groomed /grumd/ *adj.* (usually following an adverb) used to describe the way in which a person cares for their clothes and hair: *She is always perfectly groomed.* ⊃ see also WELL GROOMED

groom·ing /'grumɪŋ/ *noun* [U] the things that you do to keep your clothes and hair clean and neat, or to keep an animal's fur or hair clean: *You should always pay attention to personal grooming.*

grooms·man /'grumzmən/ *noun* (*pl.* **grooms·men** /-mən/) a friend or relation of the BRIDEGROOM at a wedding, who has special duties

groove /gruv/ *noun* **1** a long narrow cut in the surface of something hard **2** (*informal*) a particular type of musical rhythm: *a jazz groove*

grooved /gruvd/ *adj.* having a groove or grooves

groov·y /'gruvi/ *adj.* (*old-fashioned, informal*) fashionable, attractive, and interesting

grope /group/ *verb*
• *verb* **1** [I] ~ **(around) (for sth)** to try and find something that you cannot see, by feeling with your hands: *He groped around in the dark for his other sock.* ♦ (*figurative*) *"It's so…, so…," I was groping for the right word to describe it.* **2** [T, I] to try to reach a place by feeling with your hands because you cannot see clearly ~ **your way + adv./prep.**: *He groped his way up the stairs in the dark.* ♦ + **adv./prep.** *She groped through the darkness toward the doors.* **3** [T] ~ **sb** (*informal*) to touch someone sexually, especially when they do not want you to
• *noun* (*informal*) an act of groping someone (= touching them sexually)

gross /grous/ *adj., adv., verb, noun*
• *adj.* **(gros·ser, gros·sest HELP** Senses 1 and 2 have no comparative or superlative.) **1** [only before noun] being the total amount of something before anything is taken away: *gross weight* (= including the container or wrapping) ♦ *gross income/salary* (= before taxes, etc. are taken away) ♦ *Investments showed a gross profit of 26%.* ⊃ compare NET **2** [only before noun] (*formal* or *law*) (of a crime, etc.) very obvious

and unacceptable: *gross indecency/negligence/misconduct* ♦ *a gross violation of human rights* **3** (*informal*) very unpleasant SYN DISGUSTING: *"He ate it with mustard." "Oh, gross!"* ⊃ thesaurus box at DISGUSTING **4** offensive SYN CRUDE: *gross behavior* **5** very fat and ugly: *She's not just fat, she's positively gross!* ▶ **gross·ness** *noun* [U]
• *adv.* in total, before anything is taken away: *She earns $50,000 a year gross.* ⊃ compare NET
• *verb* ~ **sth** to earn a particular amount of money before taxes are taken out: *It is one of the biggest grossing movies of all time.*
  PHR V ˌgross sb 'out (*informal*) to be very unpleasant and make someone feel disgusted SYN DISGUST: *His bad breath really grossed me out.*
• *noun* **1** (*pl.* **gross**) a group of 144 things: *two gross of apples* ♦ *to sell something by the gross* **2** (*pl.* **grosses**) a total amount of money earned by something, especially a movie, before any costs are taken away

gross do·mestic 'product *noun* [sing., U] = GDP

gross·ly /'grousli/ *adv.* (*disapproving*) (used to describe unpleasant qualities) extremely: *grossly overweight/unfair/inadequate* ♦ *Press reports have been grossly exaggerated.*

gross ˌnational 'product *noun* [sing., U] = GNP

gross-out *noun* (*informal*) something disgusting: *They eat flies? What a gross-out!* ▶ **gross-out** *adj.* [only before noun]: *gross-out movie scenes*

gro·tesque /grou'tɛsk/ *adj., noun*
• *adj.* **1** strange in a way that is unpleasant or offensive: *a grotesque distortion of the truth* ♦ *It's grotesque to expect a person of her experience to work for so little money.* **2** extremely ugly in a strange way that is often frightening or amusing: *a grotesque figure* ♦ *tribal dancers wearing grotesque masks* ▶ **gro·tesque·ly** *adv.*
• *noun* **1** [C] a person who is extremely ugly in a strange way, especially in a book or painting **2** the **grotesque** [sing.] a style of art using grotesque figures and designs

grot·to /'grɑtou/ *noun* (*pl.* **grot·toes** or **grot·tos**) a small CAVE, especially one that has been made artificially

grouch /grautʃ/ *noun* (*informal*) **1** a person who complains a lot **2** a complaint about something unimportant ▶ **grouch** *verb* [I]

grouch·y /'grautʃi/ *adj.* (*informal*) bad-tempered and often complaining SYN CRANKY

ground 🔊 /graund/ *noun, verb, adj.* ⊃ see also GRIND
• *noun*
  ⟩ SURFACE OF EARTH **1** often **the ground** [U] the solid surface of the earth: *I found her lying on the ground.* ♦ *He lost his balance and fell to the ground.* ♦ *6 feet above/below ground* ♦ *Most of the monkeys' food is found at ground level.* ♦ *ground forces* (= soldiers that fight on land, not in the air or at sea) ♦ *Houses and a luxury tourist hotel burned to the ground* (= were completely destroyed, so that there was nothing left). ⊃ thesaurus box at FLOOR
  ⟩ SOIL **2** [U] soil on the surface of the earth: *fertile ground for planting crops* ⊃ thesaurus box at SOIL
  ⟩ AREA OF LAND **3** [U] an area of open land: *The kids were playing on some open ground behind the school.* **4** [C] (often in compounds) an area of land that is used for a particular purpose or activity: *ancient burial grounds* ⊃ see also BREEDING GROUND, DUMPING GROUND, PARADE GROUND, STOMPING GROUND, TESTING GROUND ⊃ thesaurus box at LAND **5** **grounds** [pl.] a large area of land or ocean that is used for a particular purpose: *fishing grounds* ♦ *feeding grounds for birds*
  ⟩ GARDENS **6** **grounds** [pl.] the land or lawn around a large building: *the hospital grounds*
  ⟩ AREA OF KNOWLEDGE/IDEAS **7** [U] an area of interest, knowledge, or ideas: *He managed to cover a lot of ground in a short talk.* ♦ *We had to go over the same ground* (= talk about the same things again) *in class the next day.* ♦ *You're on dangerous ground* (= talking about ideas that are likely to offend someone or make people angry) *if you criticize his family.* ♦ *I thought I*

was **on safe ground** (= talking about a suitable subject) *discussing music with her.* ♦ *He was back on familiar ground, dealing with the customers.* ♦ *They are fighting the Republicans on their own ground.* ⊃ see also COMMON GROUND, MIDDLE GROUND

▷ **GOOD REASON 8** [C, usually pl.] **~ for sth/for doing sth** a good or true reason for saying, doing, or believing something: *You have no grounds for your accusation.* ♦ *What were his grounds for wanting a divorce?* ♦ *The case was dismissed on the grounds that there was not enough evidence.* ♦ *He left the job but feels he deserves compensation from his employer on medical grounds.* ♦ *Employers cannot discriminate on the grounds of age.* ⊃ thesaurus box at REASON

▷ **IN LIQUID 9 grounds** [pl.] the small pieces of solid MATTER (= a substance) in a liquid that have fallen to the bottom: *coffee grounds*

▷ **ELECTRICAL WIRE 10** [C, usually sing.] a wire that connects an electric CIRCUIT with the ground and makes it safe

▷ **BACKGROUND 11** [C] a background that a design is painted or printed on: *pink roses on a white ground*

IDM gain/make up ground (on sb/sth) to gradually get closer to someone or something that is moving or making progress in an activity: *The police car was gaining ground on the suspects.* ♦ *They needed to make up ground on their competitors.* **get (sth) off the ground** to start happening successfully; to make something start happening successfully: *Without more money, the production is unlikely to get off the ground.* ♦ *to get a new company off the ground* **give/lose ground (to sb/sth)** to allow someone to have an advantage; to lose an advantage for yourself: *They are not prepared to give ground on tax cuts.* ♦ *The Democrats lost a lot of ground to the Republicans in several state elections.* **hold/stand your ground 1** to continue with your opinions or intentions when someone is opposing you and wants you to change: *Don't let him persuade you—stand your ground.* **2** to face a situation and refuse to run away: *It is not easy to hold your ground in front of someone with a gun.* **on the ground** in the place where something is happening and among the people who are in the situation, especially a war: *On the ground, there are hopes that the fighting will soon stop.* ♦ *There's a lot of support for the policy on the ground.* **run/drive/work yourself into the ground** to work so hard that you become extremely tired **run sb/sth into the ground** to use something so much that it is broken; to make someone work so hard that they are no longer able to work ⊃ **more at** EAR, FIRM *adj.*, FOOT *n.*, GAIN *v.*, HIT *v.*, MORAL *adj.*, NEUTRAL *adj.*, NEW, PREPARE, RIVET *v.*, SHIFT *v.*, STONY

• **verb**

▷ **BOAT 1** [T, I] **~ (sth)** when a boat **grounds** or something **grounds** it, it touches the bottom of the ocean and is unable to move: *The fishing boat was grounded on the rocks off the coast of Maine.*

▷ **AIRCRAFT 2** [T, often passive] **~ sth** to prevent an aircraft from taking off: *The balloon was grounded by strong winds.* ♦ *All planes out of San Francisco are grounded because of fog.*

▷ **CHILD 3** [T, usually passive] **~ sb** to punish a child by not allowing them to go out with their friends for a period of time: *You're grounded for a week!*

▷ **ELECTRICITY 4** [T, usually passive] **~ sth** to make electrical equipment safe by connecting it to the ground with a wire ⊃ see also GROUNDED, GROUNDING

• **adj.** [only before noun] (of food) cut, chopped, or crushed into very small pieces or powder: *ground coffee* ♦ *ground beef* ⊃ see also HAMBURGER

ˌground ˈball (also ground·er) *noun* (in baseball) a ball that runs along the ground after it has been hit

ˌground ˈbeef *noun* [U] = HAMBURGER

ground·break·ing /ˈɡraʊndˌbreɪkɪŋ/ *adj.* [only before noun] making new discoveries; using new methods: *a groundbreaking piece of research*

ˈground cloth *noun* a large piece of material that is placed on the ground inside a tent and does not let water through

ˈground conˌtrol *noun* [U] the people and equipment on the ground that make sure that planes or SPACECRAFT take off and land safely

ˈground ˌcover *noun* [U] plants that cover the soil over a wide area

ˈground crew *noun* the people at an airport whose job is to take care of aircraft while they are on the ground

ground·ed /ˈɡraʊndəd/ *adj.* having a sensible and realistic attitude to life: *Away from Hollywood, he relies on his family and friends to keep him grounded.*

IDM (be) grounded in/on sth (to be) based on something: *His views are grounded on the assumption that all people are equal.*

ground·er /ˈɡraʊndər/ *noun* = GROUND BALL

ˌground ˈfloor *noun* the floor of a building that is at the same level as the ground outside (used especially about public buildings) **SYN** FIRST FLOOR: *a ground-floor window* ♦ *I live on the ground floor.* ⊃ note at FLOOR

IDM be/get in on the ground floor to become involved in a plan, project, etc. at the beginning

ground·hog /ˈɡraʊndhɔɡ; -hɑɡ/ *noun* = WOODCHUCK

ˈGroundhog ˌDay *noun* **1** (in the U.S.) February 2, when it is said that the groundhog comes out of its hole at the end of winter. If the sun shines and the groundhog sees its shadow, it is said that there will be another six weeks of winter. **2** an event that is repeated without changing: *The Government lost the vote then and it can expect a Groundhog Day next time.* **ORIGIN** From the movie *Groundhog Day* about a man who lives the same day many times.

ground·ing /ˈɡraʊndɪŋ/ *noun* **1** [sing.] **~ (in sth)** the teaching of the basic parts of a subject: *a good grounding in grammar* **2** [U, C] the act of keeping a plane on the ground or a ship in a port, especially because it is not in a good enough condition to travel

ground·less /ˈɡraʊndləs/ *adj.* not based on reason or evidence **SYN** UNFOUNDED: *groundless allegations* ♦ *Our fears proved groundless.* ▶ ground·less·ly *adv.*

ground·out /ˈɡraʊndaʊt/ *noun* (in baseball) a situation in which a player hits the ball along the ground but a FIELDER touches first BASE with it before the player reaches the BASE

ˈground plan *noun* **1** a plan of a floor of a building, drawn as if seen from above ⊃ compare ELEVATION (4), PLAN **2** a plan for future action

ˈground rules *noun* [pl.] the basic rules on which something is based: *The new code of conduct lays down the ground rules for management-union relations.*

ground·sel /ˈɡraʊnsl/ *noun* [U] a wild plant with yellow flowers, sometimes used as food for animals and birds

grounds·keep·er *noun* a person whose job is to take care of a sports field or a park

ˈground speed *noun* the speed of an aircraft relative to the ground ⊃ compare AIRSPEED

ˈground ˌsquirrel *noun* = GOPHER

ground·stroke /ˈɡraʊndstroʊk/ *noun* (in TENNIS) a hit that is made after the ball has BOUNCED

ground·swell /ˈɡraʊndswɛl/ *noun* [sing.] **~ (of sth)** (*formal*) the sudden increase of a particular feeling among a group of people: *a groundswell of support* ♦ *There was a groundswell of opinion that he should resign.*

ground·wa·ter /ˈɡraʊndˌwɔtər; -ˌwatər/ *noun* [U] water that is found under the ground in soil, rocks, etc.

ground·work /ˈɡraʊndwərk/ *noun* [U] **~ (for sth)** work that is done as preparation for other work that will be done later: *Officials are laying the groundwork for a summit conference of world leaders.* ⊃ thesaurus box at BASIS

ˌground ˈzero *noun* [U] **1** the point on the earth's surface where a nuclear bomb explodes **2 Ground Zero** the site of the World Trade Center in New York City, destroyed on September 11, 2001 **3** the beginning; a starting point for an activity

h **hat**　　m **man**　　n **no**　　ŋ **sing**　　l **leg**　　r **red**　　y **yes**　　w **wet**

group 🔑 /grup/ *noun, verb*

● **noun 1** a number of people or things that are together in the same place or that are connected in some way: *a group of girls/trees/houses* ◆ *A group of us are going to the theater this evening.* ◆ *Students stood around **in groups** waiting for the doors to open.* ◆ *The residents formed a community action group.* ◆ *English is a member of the Germanic group of languages* ◆ *The proportion of single parent families varies between different income groups.* ◆ *a minority group* ◆ *ethnic groups* ◆ *a **group activity** (= done by a number of people working together)* ◆ *She asked her students to **get into groups** of four.* ◆ *to work **in groups*** ⊃ see also SUBGROUP **HELP** There are many other compounds ending in **group**. You will find them at their place in the alphabet. **2** (*business*) a number of companies that are owned by the same person or organization: *a newspaper group* ◆ *the Burton group* ◆ *the group sales director* **3** a number of musicians who perform together, especially to play pop music: *She sings in a rock group.*

● **verb 1** [T, I] to gather into a group; to make someone or something form a group: *~ sb/sth/yourself (around sb/sth) The children grouped themselves around their teacher.* ◆ *~ around sb/sth We all grouped around the tree for a photograph.* ◆ *~ (sb/sth) together The colleges grouped together to offer a wider range of courses.* **2** [T] *~ sb/sth (together)* to divide people or things into groups of people or things that are similar in some way: *The books are grouped together by subject.* ◆ *Contestants were grouped according to age and ability.*

group·ie /'grupi/ *noun* a person, especially a young woman, who follows popular musicians or other famous people around and tries to meet them

group·ing /'grupɪŋ/ *noun* **1** [C] a number of people or organizations that have the same interests, aims, or characteristics and that are often part of a larger group: *These small nations constitute an important grouping within the UN.* **2** [U] the act of forming something into a group

group 'practice *noun* a group of several doctors or other medical workers who work together in the community and use the same building to see patients

group 'therapy *noun* [U] a type of PSYCHIATRIC treatment in which people with similar personal problems meet together to discuss them

group·ware /'grupwɛr/ *noun* [U] (*computing*) software that is designed to help a group of people on different computers to work together

grouse /graʊs/ *noun, verb*
● **noun 1** [C, U] (*pl.* **grouse**) a bird with a fat body and feathers on its legs, which people shoot for sport and food; the meat of this bird **2** [C] (*informal*) a complaint
● **verb** [I, T] *~ (about sb/sth)* | (+ *speech*) (*informal*) to complain about someone or something in a way that other people find annoying **SYN** GRUMBLE

grout /graʊt/ (also **grout·ing**) *noun* [U] a substance that is used between the TILES on the walls of kitchens, bathrooms, etc. ▶ **grout** *verb ~ sth*

grove /groʊv/ *noun* **1** (*literary*) a small group of trees: *a grove of birch trees* **2** a small area of land with fruit trees of particular types on it: *an olive grove* **3** used in the names of streets: *Elm Grove*

grov·el /'grævl; 'grʌvl/ *verb* **1** [I] *~ (to sb) (for sth)* (*disapproving*) to behave in a very HUMBLE way toward someone who is more important than you or who can give you something you want **2** [I] + *adv./prep.* to move along the ground on your hands and knees, especially because you are looking for something ▶ **grov·el·ing** *adj.* [only before noun]: *a groveling letter of apology*

grow 🔑 /groʊ/ *verb* (**grew** /gru/, **grown** /groʊn/)
▷ INCREASE **1** [I] to increase in size, number, strength, or quality: *The company profits grew by 5% last year.* ◆ *A growing number of people are becoming vegetarians.* ◆ *Fears are growing for the safety of a teenager who disappeared a week ago.* ◆ *~ in sth The family has grown in size recently.* ◆ *She is growing in*

confidence all the time. ◆ *+ adj. The company is growing bigger all the time.*
▷ OF PERSON/ANIMAL **2** [I] to become bigger or taller and develop into an adult: *You've grown since the last time I saw you!* ◆ *Larry grew almost an inch in the last month.* ◆ *+ adj. to grow bigger/taller*
▷ OF PLANT **3** [I, T] to exist and develop in a particular place; to make plants grow: *The region is too dry for plants to grow.* ◆ *Tomatoes grow best in direct sunlight.* ◆ *~ sth I didn't know they grew rice in France.* ⊃ see also HOMEGROWN
▷ OF HAIR/NAILS **4** [I, T] to become longer; to allow something to become longer by not cutting it: *I've decided to let my hair grow.* ◆ *~ sth I didn't recognize him—he's grown a beard.*
▷ BECOME/BEGIN **5** *linking verb + adj.* to begin to have a particular quality or feeling over a period of time: *to grow old/bored/calm* ◆ *As time went on he grew more and more impatient.* ◆ *The skies grew dark and it began to rain.* **6** [I] *~ to do sth* to gradually begin to do something: *I'm sure you'll grow to like her in time.*
▷ DEVELOP SKILLS **7** [I] *~ (as sth)* (of a person) to develop and improve particular qualities or skills: *She continues to grow as an artist.*
▷ BUSINESS **8** [T] *~ sth* to increase the size, quality, or number of something: *We are trying to grow the business.*
IDM **money doesn't grow on trees** (*saying*) used to tell someone not to use something or spend money carelessly because you do not have a lot of it ⊃ more at ABSENCE, GRASS n., OAK
PHR V **grow a'part (from sb)** to stop having a close relationship with someone over a period of time **grow 'back** to begin growing again after being cut off or damaged **grow 'into sth** [no passive] **1** to gradually develop into a particular type of person over a period of time **2** (of a child) to grow big enough to fit into a piece of clothing that used to be too big: *The dress is too long for her now but she'll grow into it.* **3** to become more confident in a new job, etc. and learn to do it better: *She's still growing into her new role as a mother.* **grow on sb** [no passive] if someone or something **grows on** you, you start to like them or it more and more **grow 'out** (of a HAIRSTYLE, etc.) to disappear as your hair grows: *I had a perm a year ago and it still hasn't grown out.* **grow sth↔'out** to allow your hair to grow in order to change the style: *I've decided to grow my layers out.* **grow 'out of sth** [no passive] **1** (of a child) to become too big to fit into a piece of clothing **SYN** OUTGROW: *He's already grown out of his baseball uniform.* **2** to stop doing something as you become older **SYN** OUTGROW: *Most children suck their thumbs but they grow out of it.* **3** to develop from something: *The idea for the book grew out of a visit to India.* **grow 'up 1** (of a person) to develop into an adult: *She grew up in Boston (= lived there as a child).* ◆ *Their children have all grown up and left home now.* ◆ *~ to do sth He grew up to become a famous pianist.* ⊃ related noun GROWN-UP **2** used to tell someone to stop behaving in a silly way: *Why don't you grow up!* ◆ *It's time you grew up.* **3** to develop gradually: *A closeness grew up between the two girls.*

grow·er /'groʊər/ *noun* **1** a person or company that grows plants, fruit, or vegetables to sell: *a tomato grower* ◆ *All our vegetables are supplied by local growers.* **2** a plant that grows in the way mentioned: *a fast/slow grower*

grow·ing /'groʊɪŋ/ *adj.* [only before noun] increasing in size, amount, or degree: *A growing number of people are returning to school full-time.* ◆ *one of the country's fastest growing industries* ◆ *There is growing concern over the safety of the missing teenager.*

growing ,pains *noun* [pl.] **1** pains that some children feel in their arms and legs when they are growing **2** emotional anxieties felt by young people as they grow up **3** problems that are experienced by a company when it begins operating but that are not likely to last

growing ,season *noun* [usually sing.] the period of the year during which the weather conditions are right for plants to grow

growl /graʊl/ verb, noun
- **verb 1** [I] ~ **(at sb/sth)** (of animals, especially dogs) to make a low sound in the throat, usually as a sign of anger **2** [T] to say something in a low angry voice: **+ speech (at sb)** "Who are you?" he growled at the stranger. ♦ ~ **sth (at sb)** She growled a sarcastic reply.
- **noun** a deep angry sound made when someone or something growls

grown /groʊn/ adj. [only before noun] (of a person) mentally and physically an adult: It's pathetic that grown men have to resort to violence like this. ⊃ see also FULL-GROWN, HOME-GROWN, GROW

grown-up¹ adj. **1** (of a person) mentally and physically an adult **SYN** ADULT: What do you want to be when you're grown-up? ♦ She has a grown-up son. **2** suitable for or typical of an adult: The child was clearly puzzled at being addressed in such a grown-up way.

grown-up² noun (used especially by and to children) an adult person **SYN** ADULT: If you're good you can eat with the grown-ups.

growth 🔑 /groʊθ/ noun
1 [U] (of people, animals, or plants) the process of growing physically, mentally, or emotionally: Lack of water will stunt the plant's growth. ♦ Remove dead leaves to encourage new growth. ♦ a concern with personal (= mental and emotional) growth and development ♦ growth hormones (= designed to make someone or something grow faster) **2** [U] ~ **(in/of sth)** an increase in the size, amount, or degree of something: population growth ♦ the rapid growth in violent crime **3** [U] an increase in economic activity: a disappointing year of little growth in America and Britain ♦ policies aimed at sustaining economic growth ♦ an annual growth rate of 10% ♦ a **growth area/industry** **4** [C] a lump caused by a disease that forms on or inside a person, an animal, or a plant: a **malignant/cancerous growth** **5** [U, C] something that has grown: The forest's dense growth provides nesting places for a wide variety of birds. ♦ several days' growth of beard

growth ring noun a layer of wood, shell, or bone developed in one year, or in another regular period of growth, that an expert can look at to find out how old something is

grub /grʌb/ noun, verb
- **noun 1** [C] the young form of an insect, that looks like a small fat WORM **2** [U] (informal) food: I'm hungry. Let's go get some grub.
- **verb** (-bb-) [I] ~ **(around/about) (for sth)** to look for something, especially by digging or by looking through or under other things: birds grubbing for worms

grub·by /ˈgrʌbi/ adj. (grub·bi·er, grub·bi·est) **1** fairly dirty, usually because it has not been washed or cleaned: grubby hands/clothes ⊃ thesaurus box at DIRTY **2** unpleasant because it involves activities that are dishonest or immoral **SYN** SORDID: a grubby scandal ▶ **grub·bi·ness** noun [U]

grudge /grʌdʒ/ noun, verb
- **noun** ~ **(against sb)** a feeling of anger or dislike toward someone because of something bad they have done to you in the past: I bear him **no grudge**. ♦ He has a grudge against the world. ♦ I don't **hold any grudges** now. ♦ He's a man with a grudge. ♦ They beat us in a **grudge match** (= a match where there is strong dislike between the teams).
- **verb 1** to do or give something unwillingly **SYN** BEGRUDGE: ~ **doing sth** I don't grudge paying a little extra for good service. ♦ ~ **sth** He grudges the time he spends traveling to work. **2** ~ **sb sth** to think that someone does not deserve to have something **SYN** BEGRUDGE: You surely don't grudge her her success?

grudg·ing /ˈgrʌdʒɪŋ/ adj. [usually before noun] given or done unwillingly **SYN** RELUCTANT: He couldn't help feeling a grudging admiration for the old lady. ▶ **grudg·ing·ly** (also less frequent be·grudg·ing·ly) adv.: She grudgingly admitted that I was right.

gru·el /ˈgruəl/ noun [U] a simple dish made by boiling OATS in milk or water, eaten especially in the past by poor people

gru·el·ing /ˈgruəlɪŋ/ adj. very difficult and tiring, needing great effort for a long time **SYN** PUNISHING: a grueling trip/schedule ♦ I've had a grueling day.

grue·some /ˈgrusəm/ adj. very unpleasant and filling you with horror, usually because it is connected with death or injury: a gruesome murder ♦ gruesome pictures of dead bodies ♦ (humorous) We spent a week in a gruesome apartment in Miami. ▶ **grue·some·ly** adv.

gruff /grʌf/ adj. **1** (of a voice) deep and rough, and often sounding unfriendly **2** (of a person's behavior) unfriendly and impatient: Beneath his gruff exterior, he's really a nice guy. ▶ **gruff·ly** adv.

grum·ble /ˈgrʌmbl/ verb, noun
- **verb 1** [I, T] to complain about someone or something in a bad-tempered way: ~ **(at/to sb) (about/at sb/sth)** She's always grumbling to me about how badly they treat her at work. ♦ **+ speech** "I'll just have to do it myself," he grumbled. ♦ ~ **that…** They kept grumbling that they were cold. ⊃ thesaurus box at COMPLAIN **2** [I] to make a deep continuous sound **SYN** RUMBLE: Thunder grumbled in the distance. ▶ **grum·bler** /-blər/ noun
- **noun 1** ~ **(about sth)** | ~ **(that…)** something that you complain about because you are not satisfied: My main grumble is about the lack of privacy. **2** a long low sound **SYN** RUMBLE: a distant grumble of thunder

grum·bling /ˈgrʌmblɪŋ/ noun **1** [U] the act of complaining about something: We didn't hear any grumbling about the food. **2** grum·blings [pl.] protests about something that come from a number of people but that are not expressed very clearly

grump /grʌmp/ noun (informal) a bad-tempered person

grump·y /ˈgrʌmpi/ adj. (grum·pi·er, grum·pi·est) (informal) bad-tempered ▶ **grump·i·ly** /-pəli/ adv.

grunge /grʌndʒ/ noun [U] **1** (informal) dirt of any kind **SYN** GRIME **2** (also **grunge rock**) a type of loud rock music that was popular in the early 1990s **3** a style of fashion worn by people who like grunge music, usually involving clothes that look messy

grun·gy /ˈgrʌndʒi/ adj. (informal) dirty in an unpleasant way

grunt /grʌnt/ verb, noun
- **verb 1** [I] (of animals, especially pigs) to make a short low sound in the throat **2** [I, T] (of people) to make a short low sound in your throat, especially to show that you are in pain, annoyed, or not interested; to say something using this sound: He pulled harder on the rope, grunting with the effort. ♦ When I told her what happened, she just grunted and turned back to her book. ♦ ~ **sth** He grunted something about being late and rushed out. ♦ **+ speech** "Thanks," he grunted.
- **noun 1** a short low sound made by a person or an animal (especially a pig): to give a **grunt of effort/pain** **2** (informal) a worker who does boring tasks for low pay **3** (informal) a soldier of low rank

grunt work noun [U] (informal) hard boring work: She has assistants to do the grunt work like research and proofreading.

Gru·yère /gruˈyɛr; grɪ-/ noun [U] a type of Swiss cheese with a strong flavor

gryph·on noun = GRIFFIN

GSM /ˌdʒi ɛs ˈɛm/ abbr. Global System/Standard for Mobile Communication(s) (an international system for digital communication by cell phone)

GSOH abbr. good sense of humor (used in personal advertisements)

GST /ˌdʒi ɛs ˈti/ noun [U] (CanE) goods and services tax (a tax that is added to the price of goods and services)

G-string noun a type of underwear that covers the sexual organs and is held up by a string around the waist

Gt. (also **Gt**) abbr. (in names of places) Great: Gt. Britain

gua·ca·mo·le /ˌgwɑkəˈmoʊli/ noun [U] (from Spanish) a

Mexican dish of crushed AVOCADO mixed with onion, tomatoes, CHILIES, etc.

gua·no /'gwɑnoʊ/ *noun* [U] the waste substance passed from the bodies of birds that live near the ocean, used to make plants and crops grow well

guar·an·tee 🔧 **AWL** /ˌgærən'ti/ *noun, verb*

● **noun 1** a written promise given by a company that something you buy will be replaced or repaired without payment if it goes wrong within a particular period **SYN** WARRANTY: *We provide a 5-year guarantee against rust.* ◆ *The watch is still* **under guarantee.** ◆ *The television comes with a year's guarantee.* ◆ *a money-back guarantee* **2** a firm promise that you will do something or that something will happen **SYN** ASSURANCE: *to give a guarantee of good behavior* ◆ *He gave me a guarantee that it would never happen again.* ◆ *They are demanding certain guarantees before they sign the treaty.* **3** something that makes something else certain to happen: **~ (of sth)** *Career success is no guarantee of happiness.* ◆ **~ (that...)** *There's no guarantee that she'll come* (= she may not come). **4** money or something valuable that you give or promise to a bank, for example, to make sure that you will do what you have promised: *We had to offer our house as a guarantee when we got the loan.* **5** a written promise to pay back money that someone else owes, or do something that someone else promised to do, if they cannot do it themselves: *A close relative, usually a parent, can provide a guarantee for the loan.*

● **verb 1** to promise to do something; to promise something will happen: **~ sth** *Basic human rights, including freedom of speech, are now guaranteed.* ◆ **~ (that)...** *We cannot guarantee (that) our flights will never be delayed.* ◆ **~ sb sth** *The ticket will guarantee you free entry.* ◆ **~ to do sth** *We guarantee to deliver your order within a week.* **2 ~ sth (against sth)** to give a written promise to replace or repair a product free if it goes wrong: *This iron is guaranteed for a year against faulty workmanship.* **3** to make something certain to happen: **~ sth** *Tonight's victory guarantees the team's place in the final.* ◆ **~ sb sth** *These days getting a degree doesn't guarantee you a job.* **4 ~ (that)...** to be certain that something will happen: *You can guarantee (that) the kids will start misbehaving as soon as they have to go to bed.* **5** to agree to be legally responsible for something or for doing something, especially for paying back money that someone else owes, if they cannot pay it back themselves: **~ sth** *to guarantee a bank loan* ◆ **~ to do sth** *to guarantee to pay someone's debts* ◆ **~ that...** *I guarantee that he will appear in court.*
IDM **be guaranteed to do sth** to be certain to have a particular result: *If we try to keep it a secret, she's guaranteed to find out.* ◆ *That kind of behavior is guaranteed to make him angry.* ⊃ thesaurus box at CERTAIN

guaranteed in'vestment cer'tificate *noun* (*CanE*) = GIC

guar·an·tor /ˌgærən'tɔr; 'gærən,tɔr/ *noun* (*formal or law*) a person who agrees to be responsible for someone or for making sure that something happens or is done: *The United Nations will act as guarantor of the peace settlement.*

guard 🔧 /gɑrd/ *noun, verb*

● **noun**
> **PEOPLE WHO PROTECT 1** [C] a person, such as a soldier, a police officer, or a prison officer, who protects a place or people, or prevents prisoners from escaping: *a security guard* ◆ *border guards* ◆ *The prisoner slipped past the guards at the gate and escaped.* ◆ *A guard was posted outside the building.* ⊃ see also BODYGUARD, COASTGUARD, LIFEGUARD **2** [C, usually sing.] a group of people, such as soldiers or police officers, who protect someone or something: *the captain of the guard* ◆ *the changing of the guard* (= when one group replaces another) ◆ *The guard is being inspected today.* ◆ *Fellow airmen provided a guard of honor at his wedding.* ◆ *The president always travels with an armed guard.* ⊃ see also NATIONAL GUARD, OLD GUARD, REARGUARD **3** [U] the act or duty of protecting property, places, or people from attack or danger; the act or duty of preventing prisoners from

escaping: *a sentry on guard* (= at his or her post, on duty) ◆ *to do guard duty* ◆ *The escaped prisoner was brought back under armed guard.* ◆ *The terrorist was kept under police guard.* ◆ *One of the men kept guard, while the other broke into the house.*
> AGAINST INJURY **4** [C] (often in compounds) something that covers a part of a person's body or a dangerous part of a machine to prevent injury: *Ensure the guard is in place before operating the machine.* ⊃ see also FIREGUARD, MUDGUARD, SAFEGUARD, SHIN GUARD
> IN BASKETBALL **5** [C] one of the two players on a basketball team who are mainly responsible for staying close to opposing players to stop them from scoring
> IN FOOTBALL **6** [C] one of the two players on a football team who play either side of the CENTER
> IN BOXING /FENCING **7** [U] a position you take to defend yourself, especially in a sport such as BOXING or FENCING: *to drop/keep up your guard* ◆ (*figurative*) *In spite of the awkward questions, the minister never let his guard down for a moment.*
IDM **be on your guard** to be very careful and prepared for something difficult or dangerous **stand/keep guard (over sb/sth)** to watch or protect someone or something: *Four soldiers stood guard over the coffin.* **off guard** not careful or prepared for something difficult or dangerous: *The lawyer's apparently innocent question was designed to catch the witness off guard.*

● **verb 1 ~ sb/sth** to protect property, places, or people from attack or danger: *The dog was guarding the house.* ◆ *political leaders guarded by the police* ◆ *You can't get in; the whole place is guarded.* ◆ (*figurative*) *a closely guarded secret* **2 ~ sb** to prevent prisoners from escaping: *The prisoners were guarded by soldiers.*
PHRV **'guard against sth** to take care to prevent something or to protect yourself from something: *to guard against accidents/disease*

'guard dog *noun* a dog that is kept to guard a building

guard·ed /'gɑrdəd/ *adj.* (of a person or a remark they make) careful; not showing feelings or giving much information **SYN** CAUTIOUS: *a guarded reply* ◆ *You should be more guarded in what you say to reporters.* ◆ *They gave the news a guarded welcome* (= did not show great enthusiasm about it). **ANT** UNGUARDED ▶ **guard·ed·ly** *adv.*

guard·house /'gɑrdhaʊs/ *noun* a building for soldiers who are guarding the entrance to a military camp or for keeping military prisoners in

guard·i·an /'gɑrdiən/ *noun* **1** a person who protects something **SYN** CUSTODIAN: *Farmers should be guardians of the countryside.* ◆ *The police are guardians of law and order.* **2** a person who is legally responsible for the care of another person, especially a child whose parents have died

guardian 'angel *noun* a spirit that some people believe protects and guides them, especially when they are in danger: *Quickly, he became their guardian angel, clearing away the obstacles in their path.*

guard·i·an·ship /'gɑrdiən,ʃɪp/ *noun* [U] (*formal or law*) the state or position of being responsible for someone or something

'guard rail *noun* **1** a rail placed on the edge of a path, a CLIFF, or a boat to protect people and prevent them falling over the edge **2** a strong low fence or wall at the side of a road or between the two halves of a major road such as a HIGHWAY or INTERSTATE

guard·room /'gɑrdrum; -rʊm/ *noun* a room for soldiers who are guarding the entrance to a building or for keeping military prisoners in

guards·man /'gɑrdzmən/ *noun* (*pl.* **guards·men** /-mən/) a soldier in the U.S. National Guard

gua·va /'gwɑvə/ *noun* the fruit of a tropical American tree, with yellow skin and pink flesh

gu·ber·na·to·ri·al /ˌgubərnə'tɔriəl/ *adj.* (*formal*) connected with the job of state governor: *a gubernatorial candidate* ◆ *gubernatorial duties*

Guern·sey /'gərnzi/ *noun* **1** a type of cow kept for its rich milk **2 guernsey** a thick sweater made with dark blue wool that has been specially treated so that it does not let water through, worn originally by fishermen (**FISHERMAN**)

guer·ril·la (also **guer·il·la**) /gəˈrɪlə/ *noun, adj.*
• *noun* a member of a small group of soldiers who are not part of an official army and who fight against official soldiers, usually to try to change the government: *urban guerrillas* (= those who fight in towns) ♦ *guerrilla war/warfare* (= fought by guerrillas on one or both sides) ♦ *a guerrilla movement* ➔ compare FREEDOM FIGHTER
• *adj.* [only before noun] organized in an informal way and without official permission or approval: *Guerrilla actors took to the streets in army fatigues to protest against the war.*
♦ *guerrilla marketing* (= marketing that uses unusual methods in order to achieve the greatest effect for the smallest amount of money)

guess 🔑 /gɛs/ *verb, noun*
• *verb* **1** [I, T] to try and give an answer or make a judgment about something without being sure of all the facts: *I don't really know. I'm just guessing.* ♦ **~ at sth** *We can only guess at her reasons for leaving.* ♦ **+ adj.** *He guessed right/wrong.* ♦ **~ (that)…** *I'd guess that she's about 30.* ♦ **~ where, who, etc.** *… Can you guess where I've been?* ♦ **~ sth** *Can you guess his age?* **2** [T] to find the right answer to a question or the truth without knowing all the facts: **~ sth** *She guessed the answer right away.* ♦ **~ what, where, etc.…** *You'll never guess what she told me.* ♦ **~ (that)…** *You would never guess (that) she had problems. She's always so cheerful.* ➔ see also SECOND-GUESS **3 I guess** [T, I] **~ (that)…** (*informal*) to suppose that something is true or likely: *I guess (that) you'll be looking for a new job now.* ♦ *"He didn't see me, I guess."* ♦ *"Are you ready to go?" "Yeah, I guess so."* ♦ *"They aren't coming, then?"* ♦ *" I guess not."* **4 guess…!** [T] used to show that you are going to say something surprising or exciting: **~ sth** *Guess what! He asked me out!* ♦ **~ who, where, etc.…** *Guess who I just saw!*
IDM **keep sb guessing** (*informal*) to not tell someone about your plans or what is going to happen next: *It's the kind of book that keeps you guessing right to the end.*
• *noun* an attempt to give an answer or an opinion when you cannot be certain if you are right: **~ (at sth)** *to take/make a guess* ♦ *Go on! Take a guess!* ♦ **~ (about sth)** *The article is based on guesses about what might happen in the future.* ♦ *They might be here by 3—but that's just a rough guess* (= not exact). ♦ **~ (that…)** *My guess is that we won't hear from him again.* ♦ *If I might hazard a guess, I'd say she was about thirty.* ♦ *Who do you think I saw yesterday? I'll give you three guesses.*
IDM **anybody's/anyone's guess** (*informal*) something that no one can be certain about: *What will happen next is anybody's guess.* **your guess is as good as mine** (*informal*) used to tell someone that you do not know any more about a subject than the person that you are talking to does: *"Who's going to win?" "Your guess is as good as mine."* ➔ more at EDUCATED, MISS v.

guessing game *noun* **1** a game in which you have to guess the answers to questions **2** a situation in which you do not know what is going to happen or what someone is going to do

guess·ti·mate (also **gues·ti·mate**) /ˈgɛstəmət/ *noun* (*informal*) an attempt to calculate something that is based more on guessing than on information

guess·work /ˈgɛswərk/ *noun* [U] the process of trying to find an answer by guessing when you do not have enough information to be sure: *It was pure guesswork on our part.*

guest 🔑 /gɛst/ *noun, verb*
• *noun* **1** a person that you have invited to your house or to a particular event that you are paying for: *We have guests staying this weekend.* ♦ *more than 100 wedding guests* ♦ *I went to the theater as Helen's guest.* ♦ *He was the guest of honor* (= the most important person invited to an event). ♦ *Liz was not on the guest list.* **2** a person who is staying at a hotel, etc.: *We have room for 500 guests.* ♦ *Guests should vacate their rooms by 10:30 a.m.* **3** a famous guest or performer who takes part in a television show or concert: *a guest artist/star/singer* ♦ *Our*

special guest tonight is…* ♦ *He made a guest appearance on the show.* **4** a person who is invited to a particular place or organization, or to speak at a meeting: *The scientists are here as guests of our government.* ♦ *a guest speaker*
IDM **be my guest** (*informal*) used to give someone permission to do something that they have asked you to do: *"Do you mind if I use the phone?" "Be my guest."*
• *verb* [I] **~ (on sth)** to take part in a television or radio show, a concert, a game, etc. as a visiting or temporary performer or player: *She guested on several talk shows while visiting New York.*

guest book (also **guest·book**) *noun* **1** a book in which visitors to a place or special event can write their names, addresses, and short remarks: *The wedding guests left their comments in the large guest book.* **2** usually **guestbook** a Web page where visitors to a site can leave their names and comments

guest house *noun* a small house built near a large house, for guests to stay in

gues·ti·mate = GUESSTIMATE

guest room *noun* a bedroom that is kept for guests to use

guest worker *noun* a person, usually from a poor country, who comes to another richer country in order to work there

guff /gʌf/ *noun* [U] (*informal*) ideas or talk that you think are stupid SYN NONSENSE

guf·faw /gəˈfɔ/ *verb* [I, T] (**+ speech**) to laugh noisily: *They all guffawed at his jokes.* ▶ **guf·faw** *noun*: *She let out a loud guffaw.*

GUI /ˈgui; ˌdʒi yu ˈaɪ/ *abbr.* (*computing*) graphical user interface (a way of giving instructions to a computer using things that can be seen on the screen such as symbols and menus)

guid·ance /ˈgaɪdns/ *noun* [U] **1 ~ (on sth)** help or advice that is given to someone, especially by someone older or with more experience: *guidance for teachers on how to use video in the classroom* ♦ *Activities all take place under the guidance of a responsible adult.* **2** the process of controlling the direction of a ROCKET, etc., using electronic equipment: *a missile guidance system*

guidance counselor (CanE usually **guidance coun·sellor**) *noun* a person who works in a school and is responsible for giving students advice about classes and helping them with personal problems

guide 🔑 /gaɪd/ *noun, verb*
• *noun*
> PERSON **1** a person who shows other people the way to a place, especially someone employed to show tourists around interesting places: *a tour guide* ♦ *We hired a local guide to get us across the mountains.* **2** a person who advises you on how to live and behave: *a spiritual guide*
> BOOK/MAGAZINE **3 ~ (to sth)** a book, magazine, etc. that gives you information, help, or instructions about something: *a Guide to Family Health* ♦ *Let's take a look at the TV guide and see what's on.* **4** (also **guide·book**) **~ (to sth)** a book that gives information about a place for travelers or tourists: *a guide to Italy* ♦ *travel guides*
> SOMETHING THAT HELPS YOU DECIDE **5** something that gives you enough information to be able to make a decision about something or form an opinion: *As a rough guide, allow half a cup of rice per person.* ♦ *I let my feelings be my guide.*
• *verb*
> SHOW THE WAY **1 ~ sb (to/through/around sth)** to show someone the way to a place, often by going with them; to show someone a place that you know well: *She guided us through the busy streets to the cathedral.* ♦ *We were guided around the museums.* ➔ thesaurus box at TAKE
> INFLUENCE BEHAVIOR **2 ~ sb** to direct or influence someone's behavior: *He was always guided by his religious beliefs.*
> EXPLAIN **3 ~ sb (through sth)** to explain to someone how to do something, especially something complicated or

difficult: *The health and safety officer will guide you through the safety procedures.*
▷ **HELP SOMEONE MOVE** **4** ~ **sb/sth** (+ *adv./prep.*) to help someone to move in a particular direction; to move something in a particular direction: *She took her arm and guided her across the busy road.* ♦ *He guided her hand to his face.* ⊃ see also GUIDING

guide·book /ˈɡaɪdbʊk/ *noun* = GUIDE

guid·ed /ˈɡaɪdəd/ *adj.* [usually before noun] that is led by someone who works as a guide: *a guided tour/walk*

ˌguided ˈmissile *noun* a MISSILE that can be controlled while in the air by electronic equipment

ˈguide dog (also ˌSeeing ˈEye dog™) *noun* a dog trained to guide a blind person

guide·line AWL /ˈɡaɪdlaɪn/ *noun* **1** guide·lines [pl.] rules or instructions that are given by an official organization telling you how to do something, especially something difficult: *The government has issued guidelines for controlling infection.* **2** [C] something that can be used to help you make a decision or form an opinion: *The figures are a useful guideline when buying a house.*

guide·post /ˈɡaɪdpoʊst/ *noun* **1** a sign or other indication that helps you make a decision: *The stock market is an important guidepost for the overall economy.* **2** a sign beside a road that tells you where to go **SYN** SIGNPOST

guid·ing /ˈɡaɪdɪŋ/ *adj.* [only before noun] giving advice and help; having a strong influence on people: *She was inexperienced and needed a guiding hand.* ♦ *a guiding force*

guild /ɡɪld/ *noun* **1** an organization of people who do the same job or who have the same interests or aims: *the Screen Actors' Guild* **2** an association of skilled workers in the Middle Ages

guild·er /ˈɡɪldər/ *noun* the former unit of money in the Netherlands (replaced in 2002 by the euro)

guild·hall /ˈɡɪldhɔl/ *noun* a building in which the members of a GUILD used to meet

guile /ɡaɪl/ *noun* [U] (*formal*) the use of skillful but dishonest behavior in order to trick people **SYN** DECEIT

guile·less /ˈɡaɪlləs/ *adj.* (*formal*) behaving in a very honest way; not knowing how to trick people ▶ **guile·less·ly** *adv.*

guil·le·mot /ˈɡɪləˌmɑt/ *noun* a black and white bird with a long narrow beak that lives near the ocean

guil·lo·tine /ˈɡɪləˌtin; ˈɡiə-; ˌɡiəˈtin/ *noun, verb*
● *noun* [sing.] a machine, originally from France, for cutting people's heads off. It has a heavy blade that slides down a wooden frame.
● *verb* ~ **sb** to kill someone by cutting off their head with a guillotine

guilt /ɡɪlt/ *noun, verb*
● *noun* [U] **1** ~ (**about sth**) the unhappy feelings caused by knowing or thinking that you have done something wrong: *She had feelings of guilt about leaving her children and going to work.* ♦ *Many survivors were left with a sense of guilt.* ♦ *a guilt complex* (= an exaggerated sense of guilt) **2** the fact that someone has done something illegal: *His guilt was proved beyond all doubt by the prosecution.* ♦ *an admission of guilt* **ANT** INNOCENCE **3** blame or responsibility for doing something wrong or for something bad that has happened: *The investigation will try to find out where the guilt for the disaster really lies.* ▶ **guilt·less** /ˈɡɪltləs/ *adj.*
IDM **a guilt trip** (*informal*) things you say to someone in order to make them feel guilty about something: *Don't lay a guilt trip on your child about schoolwork.*
● *verb*
PHR V ˈguilt sb into sth/into doing sth (*informal*) to make someone do something by persuading them that it is wrong not to do it: *I only went because she guilted me into it.*

guilt·y /ˈɡɪlti/ *adj.* (guilt·i·er, guilt·i·est)
HELP more guilty and most guilty are more common
1 ~ (**about sth**) feeling ashamed because you have done

something that you know is wrong or have not done something that you should have done: *I felt guilty about not visiting my parents more often.* ♦ *John had a guilty look on his face.* ♦ *I had a guilty conscience and could not sleep.* **2** ~ (**of sth**) having done something illegal; being responsible for something bad that has happened: *The jury found the defendant not guilty of the offense.* ♦ *He pleaded guilty to murder.* ♦ *the guilty party* (= the person responsible for something bad happening) ♦ *We've all been guilty of selfishness at some time in our lives.* **ANT** INNOCENT ⊃ collocations at JUSTICE ▶ **guilt·i·ly** /-təli/ *adv.*
IDM **a guilty secret** a secret that someone feels ashamed about ⊃ more at SIN *n.*

guin·ea fowl /ˈɡɪni ˌfaʊl/ *noun* [C, U] (*pl.* guin·ea fowl) a bird of the PHEASANT family, that has dark gray feathers with white dots, and is often used for food; the meat of this bird: *roast guinea fowl*

ˈguinea ˌpig *noun* **1** a small animal with short ears and no tail, often kept as a pet **2** a person used in medical or other experiments: *Students in fifty schools will be acting as guinea pigs for these new teaching methods.*

Guin·ness™ /ˈɡɪnəs/ *noun* [U, C] a type of very dark brown beer, with a white HEAD (= top) on it

guise /ɡaɪz/ *noun* a way in which someone or something appears, often in a way that is different from usual or that hides the truth about them or it: *His speech presented racist ideas under the guise of nationalism.* ♦ *The story appears in different guises in different cultures.*

gui·tar /ɡɪˈtar/ *noun*
a musical instrument that usually has six strings, that you play with your fingers or with a PICK: *an acoustic/an electric/a classical, etc. guitar* ♦ *a guitar player* ♦ *Do you play the guitar?* ♦ *She plays guitar in a band.* ♦ *As he sang, he strummed his guitar.* ⊃ see also AIR GUITAR, BASS¹

gui·tar·ist /ɡɪˈtarɪst/ *noun* a person who plays the guitar

Gu·lag /ˈɡulæɡ/ *noun* **1** a system of prison labor camps in the Soviet Union from 1930 to 1955, where many people died **2** gulag any political labor camp

gulch /ɡʌltʃ/ *noun* a narrow valley with steep sides, that was formed by a fast stream flowing through it

gulf /ɡʌlf/ *noun* **1** [C] a large area of ocean that is partly surrounded by land: *the Gulf of Mexico* **2** the Gulf [sing.] the area of ocean between the Arabian PENINSULA and Iran **3** [C, usually sing.] ~ (**between A and B**) a large difference between two people or groups in the way that they think, live, or feel: *The gulf between rich and poor is enormous.* **4** [C] a wide, deep crack in the ground
IDM see BRIDGE

ˈGulf States *noun* [pl.] **1** the countries around the Persian Gulf (Iran, Iraq, Kuwait, Saudi Arabia, Bahrain, Qatar, the United Arab Emirates, and Oman) **2** the U.S. states around the Gulf of Mexico (Florida, Alabama, Mississippi, Louisiana, and Texas)

the ˈGulf Stream *noun* [sing.] a warm current of water flowing across the Atlantic Ocean from the Gulf of Mexico toward Europe

gull /ɡʌl/ (also ˈsea·gull) *noun* a bird with long wings and usually white and gray or black feathers that lives near the ocean. There are several types of gulls. ⊃ picture at ANIMAL ⊃ see also HERRING GULL

Gul·lah /ˈɡʌlə/ *noun* [U] a language spoken by black people living on the coast of South Carolina, that is a combination of English and various W. African languages

gul·let /ˈɡʌlət/ *noun* the tube through which food passes from the mouth to the stomach **SYN** ESOPHAGUS ⊃ picture at BODY

gul·ley *noun* = GULLY

gul·li·ble /ˈɡʌləbl/ *adj.* too willing to believe or accept what other people tell you and therefore easily tricked **SYN** NAIVE ▶ **gul·li·bil·i·ty** /ˌɡʌləˈbɪləti/ *noun* [U]

gul·ly (also **gul·ley**) /ˈɡʌli/ *noun* (*pl.* gul·lies, gul·leys) **1** a small, narrow channel, usually formed by a stream or by rain **2** a deep DITCH

gulp /gʌlp/ *verb, noun*
● *verb* **1** [T, I] ~ (sth) | ~ sth **down** to swallow large amounts of food or drink quickly: *He gulped down the rest of his coffee and went out.* **2** [I, T] **(+ speech)** to swallow, but without eating or drinking anything, especially because of a strong emotion such as fear or surprise: *She gulped nervously before trying to answer.* **3** [I, T] to breathe quickly and deeply, because you need more air: ~ **(for sth)** *She came up gulping for air.* ♦ ~ sth **(in)** *He leaned against the car, gulping in the cold air.*
PHR V ,gulp sth↔'back to stop yourself from showing your emotions by swallowing hard: *She gulped back her tears and forced a smile.*
● *noun* **1** ~ **(of sth)** an amount of something that you swallow or drink quickly: *He took a gulp of water.* **2** an act of breathing in or of swallowing something: *He drank the glass of whiskey in one gulp.*

gum /gʌm/ *noun, verb*
● *noun* **1** (also 'chewing ,gum) [U] a candy that you chew but do not swallow: *Please do not chew gum in class.* ➷ see also BUBBLEGUM **2** [C, usually pl.] either of the firm areas of flesh in the mouth to which the teeth are attached: *gum disease* ➷ picture at BODY **3** [U] a sticky substance produced by some types of trees **4** [U] a type of glue used for sticking light things together, such as paper
IDM by gum! (*old-fashioned, informal*) used to show surprise
● *verb* (-mm-) **1** ~ **A to B** | ~ sth **(down)** (somewhat *old-fashioned*) to spread glue on the surface of something; to stick two things together with glue: *A large address label was gummed to the package.* ♦ *gummed labels* (= with glue on one side) **2** ~ sth chew something without teeth, like a baby: *The baby gummed the toy all morning.*
PHR V ,gum sth↔'up [usually passive] (*informal*) to cover or fill something with a sticky substance so that it stops moving or working as it should

gum·ball /'gʌmbɔl/ *noun* a small ball of GUM that looks like a piece of candy

gum·bo /'gʌmbou/ *noun* [U] a thick chicken or fish soup, usually made with the vegetable OKRA

gum·drop /'gʌmdrɑp/ *noun* a small piece of jelly candy that has sugar on the outside

gummed /gʌmd/ *adj.* [usually before noun] (of stamps, paper, etc.) covered with a type of glue that will become sticky when water is put on it

gum·my /'gʌmi/ *adj.* (*informal*) **1** sticky or covered in gum **2** a gummy smile shows your teeth and gums

gump·tion /'gʌmpʃn/ *noun* [U] (*old-fashioned, informal*) **1** courage and determination **2** the intelligence needed to know what to do in a particular situation

gum·shoe /'gʌmʃu/ *noun* (*old-fashioned; informal*) = DETECTIVE

'gum tree *noun* a EUCALYPTUS tree

gun ⚲ /gʌn/ *noun, verb*
● *noun* **1** [C] a weapon that is used for firing bullets or SHELLS: *to fire a gun at someone* ♦ *a toy gun* ♦ *antiaircraft guns* ♦ *Look out, he's got a gun!* ♦ *He pointed/aimed the gun at her head.* ♦ *The police officers drew their guns* (= took them out so they were ready to use). ♦ *She pulled a gun on me* (= took out a gun and aimed it at me). ♦ *The gun went off by accident.* ♦ *a gun battle between rival gangs* ➷ see also AIR GUN, HANDGUN, MACHINE GUN, SHOTGUN, STUN GUN, SUBMACHINE GUN, TOMMY GUN **2** [C] a tool that uses pressure to send out a substance or an object: *a staple gun* ➷ see also SPRAY GUN **3** the gun [sing.] the signal to begin a race, that is made by firing a special gun, called a STARTING PISTOL, into the air **4** [C] (*informal*) a person who is paid to shoot someone: *a hired gun* ➷ see also FLASHGUN, SON OF A GUN
IDM hold/put a gun to sb's head to force someone to do something that they do not want to do, by making threats **under the gun** (*informal*) experiencing a lot of pressure: *I'm*

really under the gun today. **(with) all/both guns blazing** (*informal*) with a lot of energy and determination: *The champions came out (with) all guns blazing.* ➷ more at GREAT *adj.*, JUMP *v.*, STICK *v.*
● *verb* (-nn-) **1** [I] (of an engine) to run very quickly: *a line of motorcycles with their engines gunning* **2** [T] ~ sth + adv./prep. to start driving a vehicle very fast: *He gunned the cab through the red light.*
PHR V be 'gunning for sb (*informal*) to be looking for an opportunity to blame or attack someone be 'gunning for sth to be competing for or trying hard to get something: *She's gunning for the top job.* ,gun sb↔'down [usually passive] to shoot someone, especially killing or seriously injuring them

gun·boat /'gʌnbout/ *noun* a small ship that has large guns on it

,gunboat di'plomacy *noun* [U] a way of making another country accept your demands by using the threat of force

'gun ,carriage *noun* a support on wheels for a large heavy gun

'gun con,trol *noun* [U] laws that restrict the sale and use of guns

'gun dog *noun* a dog trained to help in the sport of shooting, for example by finding birds that have been shot

gun·fight /'gʌnfaɪt/ *noun* a fight between people using guns ▸ gun·fight·er /-,faɪtər/ *noun*

gun·fire /'gʌn,faɪər/ *noun* [U] the repeated firing of guns; the sound of guns firing: *an exchange of gunfire with the police* ♦ *I could hear gunfire.*

gung-ho /,gʌŋ 'hou/ *adj.* (*informal, disapproving*) too enthusiastic about something, without thinking seriously about it, especially about fighting and war

gunk /gʌŋk/ *noun, verb*
● *noun* [U] (*informal*) any unpleasant, sticky, or dirty substance ▸ gun·ky *adj.*
● *verb*
PHR V ,gunk sth↔'up (*informal*) to make something dirty with a sticky substance; to ruin or break something with a sticky substance

gun·man /'gʌnmən/ *noun* (pl. gun·men /-mən/) a man who uses a gun to steal from or kill people

gun·met·al /'gʌn,mɛtl/ *noun* [U] **1** a metal that is a mixture of COPPER, tin, and ZINC **2** a dull, blue-gray color

gun·nel = GUNWALE

gun·ner /'gʌnər/ *noun* a member of the armed forces who is trained to use large guns

gun·ner·y /'gʌnəri/ *noun* [U] (*technical*) the operation of large military guns

gun·ny /'gʌni/ *noun* [U] a type of rough cloth used for making SACKS

gun·ny·sack /'gʌni,sæk/ *noun* a large bag made from rough material and used to store flour, potatoes, etc.

gun·point /'gʌnpɔɪnt/ *noun*
IDM at gunpoint while threatening someone or being threatened with a gun: *The driver was robbed at gunpoint.*

gun·pow·der /'gʌn,paʊdər/ (also pow·der) *noun* [U] EXPLOSIVE powder used especially in bombs or FIREWORKS

gun·run·ner /'gʌn,rʌnər/ *noun* a person who secretly and illegally brings guns into a country ▸ gun·run·ning *noun* [U]

gun·ship /'gʌnʃɪp/ *noun* an armed military HELICOPTER or other aircraft

gun·shot /'gʌnʃɑt/ *noun* **1** [U] the bullets that are fired from a gun: *gunshot wounds* **2** [C] the firing of a gun; the sound of it being fired: *I heard the sound of gunshots out in the street.* **3** [U] the distance that a bullet from a gun can travel: *He was out of/within gunshot.*

'gun-shy *adj.* **1** very careful or anxious about doing something, because of a previous bad experience: *Since last*

summer, Horace has been gun-shy about swimming in the lake.
2 (especially of a dog) nervous and scared at the sound of a gunshot

gun·sight /'gʌnsaɪt/ *noun* a part of a gun that you look through in order to aim it accurately

gun·sling·er /'gʌn,slɪŋər/ *noun* a person who is paid to kill people, especially in movies about the Wild West

gun·smith /'gʌnsmɪθ/ *noun* a person who makes and repairs guns

gun·wale (also **gun·nel**) /'gʌnl/ *noun* the upper edge of the side of a boat or small ship

gup·py /'gʌpi/ *noun* (*pl.* **gup·pies**) a small FRESHWATER fish, commonly kept in AQUARIUMS

gur·dwa·ra /gʊr'dwɑrə; gər-/ *noun* a building in which Sikhs worship

gur·gle /'gərgl/ *verb, noun*
• *verb* **1** [I] to make a sound like water flowing quickly through a narrow space: *Water gurgled through the pipes.* ◆ *a gurgling stream* **2** [I] if a baby **gurgles**, it makes a noise in its throat when it is happy
• *noun* **1** a sound like water flowing quickly through a narrow space **2** the sound that babies make in the throat, especially when they are happy

gur·ney /'gərni/ *noun* a type of CART which is used for moving patients in a hospital

gu·ru /'guru; 'gʊru/ *noun* **1** a Hindu or Sikh religious teacher or leader **2** (*informal*) a person who is an expert on a particular subject or who is very good at doing something: *a management/health/fashion, etc. guru*

gush /gʌʃ/ *verb, noun*
• *verb* **1** [I] ~ **out of/from/into sth** | ~ **out/in** to flow or pour suddenly and quickly out of a hole in large amounts: *blood gushing from a wound* ◆ *Water gushed out of the pipe.* **2** [T] ~ **sth** (of a container, vehicle, etc.) to suddenly let out large amounts of a liquid: *The tanker was gushing oil.* ◆ (*figurative*) *She absolutely gushed enthusiasm.* **3** [T, I] (**+ speech**) (*disapproving*) to express so much praise or emotion about someone or something that it does not seem sincere: *"You are just gorgeous," she gushed.* ◆ *The critics gushed with admiration for the novel.*
• *noun* [usually sing.] **1** ~ **(of sth)** a large amount of liquid suddenly and quickly flowing or pouring out of something: *a gush of blood* **2** ~ **(of sth)** a sudden strong expression of feeling: *a gush of emotion*

gush·er /'gʌʃər/ *noun* **1** an OIL WELL where the oil comes out quickly and in large quantities **2** a person who gushes

gush·ing /'gʌʃɪŋ/ *adj.* (*disapproving*) expressing so much enthusiasm, praise, or emotion that it does not seem sincere ▶ **gush·ing·ly** *adv.*

gus·set /'gʌsət/ *noun* an extra piece of cloth sewn into a piece of clothing to make it wider, stronger, or more comfortable

gus·sy /'gʌsi/ *verb* (**gus·sies, gus·sy·ing, gus·sied, gus·sied**)
PHRV gussy 'up (*informal*) to dress yourself in an attractive way **SYN DRESS UP**: *I had to get all gussied up for our night out.*

gust /gʌst/ *noun, verb*
• *noun* **1** a sudden strong increase in the amount and speed of wind that is blowing: *A gust of wind blew his hat off.* ◆ *The wind was blowing in gusts.* **2** a sudden strong expression of emotion: *a gust of laughter*
• *verb* [I] (of the wind) to suddenly blow very hard: *winds gusting up to 60 mph*

gus·ta·to·ry /'gʌstə,tɔri/ *adj.* (*formal*) connected with tasting or the sense of taste: *gustatory delights*

gus·to /'gʌstoʊ/ *noun* [U] enthusiasm and energy in doing something: *They sang with gusto.*

gust·y /'gʌsti/ *adj.* [usually before noun] with the wind blowing in GUSTS: *a gusty morning* ◆ *gusty winds*

gut /gʌt/ *noun, verb, adj.*
• *noun* **1** [C] the tube in the body through which food passes when it leaves the stomach **SYN INTESTINE 2 guts** [pl.] the organs in and around the stomach, especially in an animal: *I'll only cook fish if the guts have been removed.* **3** [C] (*informal*) a person's stomach, especially when it is large **SYN BELLY**: *Have you seen the gut on him!* ◆ *a beer gut* (= caused by drinking beer) **4 guts** [pl.] (*informal*) the courage and determination that it takes to do something difficult or unpleasant: *He doesn't have the guts to walk away from a high-paying job.* **5** [C] the place where your natural feelings that make you react in a particular way are thought to be: *I had a feeling in my gut that something was wrong.* **6 guts** [pl.] the most important part of something: *the guts of the problem* ⊃ see also CATGUT
  IDM run/sweat/work, etc. your guts out (*informal*) to work very hard to achieve something: *I ran my guts out and only finished fourth.* ⊃ more at BUST, HATE, SPILL
• *verb* (-tt-) **1** [usually passive] ~ **sth** to destroy the inside or contents of a building or room: *a factory gutted by fire* ◆ *The house was completely gutted.* **2** ~ **sth** to remove the organs from inside a fish or an animal to prepare it for cooking
• *adj.* [only before noun] based on feelings and emotions rather than thought or reason: *a gut feeling/reaction* ◆ *You have to work on gut instinct.*

gut·less /'gʌtləs/ *adj.* lacking courage or determination

guts·y /'gʌtsi/ *adj.* (*informal*) **1** showing courage and determination: *a gutsy fighter/win* **2** having strong and unusual qualities: *a gutsy red wine* ◆ *a gutsy song*

gut·ter /'gʌtər/ *noun, verb*
• *noun* **1** [C] a long curved channel made of metal or plastic that is attached under the edge of a roof to carry away the water when it rains: *a clogged/leaky gutter* ⊃ picture at HOUSE **2** [C] a channel at the edge of a road where water collects and is carried away to DRAINS **3 the gutter** [sing.] the bad social conditions or low moral standards sometimes connected with the lowest level of society: *She rose from the gutter to become a great star.* ◆ *gutter mouth* (= using offensive words)
• *verb* [I] (*literary*) (of a flame or CANDLE) to burn in an unsteady way

gut·ter·snipe /'gʌtər,snaɪp/ *noun* (*informal, old-fashioned, disapproving*) a poor and dirty child

gut·tur·al /'gʌtərəl/ *adj.* (of a sound) made or seeming to be made at the back of the throat: *guttural consonants* ◆ *a low guttural growl*

gut-,wrenching *adj.* (*informal*) very unpleasant; making you feel very upset

guy /gaɪ/ *noun*
1 [C] (*informal*) a man: *a big/nice/tough guy* ◆ *an Italian guy* ◆ *At the end of the movie, the bad guy gets shot.* ⊃ see also FALL GUY, WISE GUY **2 guys** [pl.] (*informal*) a group of people of either sex: *Come on, you guys, let's get going!* **3** (also **guy rope**) [C] a rope used to keep a pole or tent in a vertical position **IDM see** MR.

guz·zle /'gʌzl/ *verb* [T, I] ~ **(sth)** (*informal, usually disapproving*) to drink something quickly and in large amounts: *The kids seem to be guzzling soft drinks all day.* ◆ (*figurative*) *My car guzzles fuel.*

guz·zler /'gʌzlər/ *noun* (*informal*) = GAS GUZZLER

gym /dʒɪm/ *noun* (*informal*) **1** (also formal **gym·na·si·um** /dʒɪm'neɪziəm/) [C] a room or hall with equipment for doing physical exercise, for example in a school: *to play basketball in the gym* ◆ *The school recently built a new gym.* **2** [U] physical exercises done in a gym, especially at school: *I don't like gym.* ◆ *I have gym at 2:30.* ◆ *gym class* **3** [C] = HEALTH CLUB: *I just joined a gym.* ◆ *I work out at the gym almost every day.* ⊃ collocations at DIET

gym·na·si·um /dʒɪm'neɪziəm/ *noun* (*pl.* **gym·na·si·ums** or **gym·na·si·a** /-ziə/) (*formal*) = GYM

gym·nast /'dʒɪmnəst; -næst/ *noun* a person who performs gymnastics, especially in a competition

gym·nas·tics /dʒɪm'næstɪks/ *noun* [U] physical exercises that develop and show the body's strength and ability to move and bend easily, often done as a sport in competitions: *a gymnastics competition* ◆ (*figurative*) **mental/verbal gymnastics** (= quick or intelligent thinking or use of words) ⊃ **picture at SPORT** ▶ **gym·nas·tic** *adj.* [only before noun]

'gym shoe *noun* a light, simple, sports shoe made of CANVAS (= strong cotton cloth) or leather with a rubber SOLE

gy·ne·col·o·gist /ˌɡaɪnə'kɑlədʒɪst/ *noun* a doctor who studies and treats the medical conditions and diseases of women

gy·ne·col·o·gy /ˌɡaɪnə'kɑlədʒi/ *noun* [U] the scientific study and treatment of the medical conditions and diseases of women, especially those connected with sexual REPRODUCTION ▶ **gyn·e·co·log·i·cal** /ˌɡaɪnəkə'lɑdʒɪkl/ *adj.*: *a gynecological examination*

gyp /dʒɪp/ *noun, verb*
● *noun* [sing.] (*informal*) an act of charging too much money for something: *That meal was a real gyp.*
● *verb* (-pp-) ~ **sb** to cheat or trick someone, especially by taking their money

gyp·sum /'dʒɪpsəm/ *noun* [U] a soft white mineral like CHALK that is found naturally and is used in making PLASTER OF PARIS

gyp·sy (also **gip·sy**) /'dʒɪpsi/ *noun* (*pl.* **gyp·sies**) (sometimes *offensive*) a member of a group of people, originally from Asia, who traditionally travel from place to place instead of living in one place. Many people prefer to use the name Romani. ⊃ **see also ROMANI**

'gypsy moth *noun* a type of MOTH, the CATERPILLAR of which eats leaves and causes serious damage to trees and plants

gy·rate /'dʒaɪreɪt/ *verb* [I, T] to move around in circles; to make something, especially a part of your body, move around: *They began gyrating to the music.* ◆ ~ **sth** *As the lead singer gyrated his hips, the crowd screamed wildly.* ▶ **gy·ra·tion** /dʒaɪ'reɪʃn/ *noun* [C, usually pl., U]

gy·ro /'yɪrou; 'dʒaɪrou/ *noun* (*pl.* **gy·ros**) a type of Greek sandwich made with sliced meat and vegetables in PITA bread

gy·ro·scope /'dʒaɪrəˌskoup/ (also *informal* **gy·ro** /'dʒaɪrou/) *noun* a device consisting of a wheel that spins rapidly inside a frame and does not change position when the frame is moved. Gyroscopes are often used to keep ships and aircraft steady. ▶ **gy·ro·scop·ic** /ˌdʒaɪrə'skɑpɪk/ *adj.*

ʌ **cup**   ə **about**   eɪ **say**   aɪ **five**   ɔɪ **boy**   aʊ **now**   oʊ **go**   ɜr **bird**

Hh

H also **h** /eɪtʃ/ *noun* [C, U] (*pl.* Hs, H's, h's /'eɪtʃəz/) the 8th letter of the English alphabet: *"Hat" begins with (an) H/"H."* ⊃ compare AITCH ⊃ see also H-BOMB

ha¹ /hɑ/ *exclamation* **1** (also **hah**) the sound that people make when they are surprised or pleased or when they have discovered something: *Ha! It serves you right!* ◆ *Ha! I knew he was hiding something.* **2** (also **ha! ha!**) the word for the sound that people make when they laugh **3** (also **ha! ha!**) (*informal, ironic*) used to show that you do not think that something is funny: *Ha! Ha! Very funny! Now give me back my shoes.*

ha² *abbr.* (in writing) HECTARE

ha·be·as cor·pus /ˌheɪbiəs ˈkɔrpəs/ *noun* [U] (from *Latin, law*) a law that states that a person who has been arrested should not be kept in prison longer than a particular period of time unless a judge in court has decided that it is right

hab·er·dash·er /'hæbərˌdæʃər/ *noun* **1** (*pl.* **Hab·er·dash·ers**) (*old-fashioned*) a store selling small articles for sewing, for example, needles, pins, cotton, and buttons **Haber-dasher's 2** a person who owns, manages, or works in a store that makes and sells men's clothes

hab·er·dash·er·y /'hæbərˌdæʃəri/ *noun* (*pl.* **hab·er·dash-er·ies**) **1** [U] (*old-fashioned*) men's clothes **2** [C] (*old-fashioned*) a store or part of a store where haberdashery is sold

hab·it 🔑 /'hæbət/ *noun*
1 [C] a thing that you do often and almost without thinking, especially something that is hard to stop doing: *You need to change your eating habits.* ◆ *good/bad habits* ◆ *He has the irritating habit of biting his nails.* ◆ *It's all right to borrow money occasionally, but don't* **let it become a habit.** ◆ *I'd prefer you not to* **make a habit** *of it.* ◆ *I'm not in the habit of letting strangers into my apartment.* ◆ *I've* **gotten into the habit** *of turning on the TV as soon as I get home.* ◆ *I'm trying to* **break the habit** *of staying up too late.* **2** [U] usual behavior: *I only do it* **out of habit.** ◆ *I'm a* **creature of habit** (= I have a fixed and regular way of doing things). **3** [C] (*informal*) a strong need to keep using drugs, alcohol, or cigarettes regularly: *He began to finance his habit through burglary.* ◆ *She's tried to give up smoking but just can't* **kick the habit.** ◆ *a 50-a-day habit* **4** [C] a long piece of clothing worn by a MONK or NUN **IDM** see FORCE *n.*

hab·it·a·ble /'hæbətəbl/ *adj.* suitable for people to live in: *The house should be habitable by the new year.*
ANT UNINHABITABLE

hab·i·tat /'hæbəˌtæt/ *noun* [C, U] the place where a particular type of animal or plant is normally found: *The panda's natural habitat is the bamboo forest.* ◆ *the destruction of wildlife habitat* ⊃ collocations at ENVIRONMENT

hab·i·ta·tion /ˌhæbəˈteɪʃn/ *noun* **1** [U] the act of living in a place: *They looked around for any signs of habitation.* ◆ *The houses were unfit for human habitation* (= not clean or safe enough for people to live in). **2** [C] (*formal*) a place where people live: *The road serves the scattered habitations along the coast.*

habit-forming *adj.* a habit-forming activity or drug is one that makes you want to continue doing it or taking it

ha·bit·u·al /hə'bɪtʃuəl/ *adj.* **1** [only before noun] usual or typical of someone or something: *They waited for his habitual response.* **2** (of an action) done, often in a way that is annoying or difficult to stop: *habitual complaining* ◆ *the habitual use of heroin* **3** [only before noun] (of a person) doing something that has become a habit and is therefore difficult to stop: *a habitual criminal/drinker/liar, etc.* ▶ **ha·bit·u-al·ly** *adv.*: *the dark glasses he habitually wore*

ha·bit·u·at·ed /hə'bɪtʃuˌeɪtəd/ *adj.* ~ (to sth) (*formal*) familiar with something because you have done it or experienced it often **SYN** ACCUSTOMED

ha·bit·u·a·tion /həˌbɪtʃuˈeɪʃn/ *noun* [U] (*formal*) the action or condition of becoming used to something: *the habituation of animals to a new environment*

ha·bit·u·é /həˈbɪtʃuˌeɪ; həˌbɪtʃuˈeɪ/ *noun* (from *French, formal*) a person who goes regularly to a particular place or event: *a(n) habitué of upscale clubs* **SYN** REGULAR

ha·ci·en·da /ˌhasiˈɛndə; ˌɑsi-/ *noun* a large farm in a Spanish-speaking country

hack /hæk/ *verb, noun*
● *verb* **1** [T, I] to cut someone or something with rough, heavy blows: ~ **sb/sth + adv./prep.** *I hacked the dead branches off.* ◆ *They were hacked to death as they tried to escape.* ◆ *We had to* **hack our way** *through the jungle.* ◆ **+ adv./prep.** *We hacked away at the bushes.* **2** [I, T] (*computing*) to secretly find a way of looking at and/or changing information on someone else's computer system without permission: ~ **into sth** *He hacked into the bank's computer.* ◆ ~ **sth** *They had hacked secret data.* **3** [T] **can/can't hack it** (*informal*) to be able/not able to manage in a particular situation: *Lots of people leave this job because they can't hack it.*
● *noun* **1** (*disapproving*) a writer, especially of newspaper articles, who does a lot of low quality work and does not get paid much **2** (*disapproving*) a person who does the hard and often boring work for an organization, especially a politician: *a party hack* **3** an act of hitting something, especially with a cutting tool

hack·er /'hækər/ *noun* a person who secretly finds a way of looking at and/or changing information on someone else's computer system without permission

hacking cough *noun* [sing.] a dry painful cough that is repeated often

hack·les /'hæklz/ *noun* [pl.] the hairs on the back of the neck of a dog, cat, etc. that rise when the animal is afraid or angry
IDM **raise sb's hackles** to make someone angry **sb's hackles rise** to become angry: *Ben felt his hackles rise as the speaker continued.*

hack·neyed /'hæknid/ *adj.* used too often and therefore boring **SYN** CLICHÉ: *a hackneyed phrase/subject*

hack·saw /'hæksɔ/ *noun* a tool with a narrow blade in a frame, used for cutting metal ⊃ picture at TOOL

had /həd; əd; d; hæd/ ⊃ HAVE

had·dock /'hædək/ *noun* (*pl.* **had·dock**) [C, U] a sea fish like a COD but smaller, with white flesh that is used for food: *smoked haddock*

Ha·des /'heɪdiz/ *noun* [U] (in ancient Greek stories) the land of the dead **SYN** HELL

Ha·dith /hɑ'diθ/ *noun* (*pl.* **Ha·dith** or **Ha·diths**) (in Islam) **1** [sing.] a text containing things said by Muhammad and descriptions of his daily life, used by Muslims as a spiritual guide **2** [C] one of the things said by Muhammad, recorded in this text

had·n't /'hædnt/ *short form* had not

haf·ni·um /'hæfniəm/ *noun* [U] (*symb.* **Hf**) a RADIOACTIVE chemical element. Hafnium is a hard silver-gray metal.

haft /hæft/ *noun* the handle of a knife or weapon

hag /hæg/ *noun* (*offensive*) an ugly and/or unpleasant old woman

hag·gard /'hægərd/ *adj.* looking very tired because of illness, worry, or a lack of sleep **SYN** DRAWN

hag·gle /'hægl/ *verb* [I] ~ (with sb) (over sth) to argue with someone in order to reach an agreement, especially about the price of something: *I left him in the market haggling over the price of a shirt.*

hag·i·og·ra·pher /ˌhægiˈɑgrəfər; ˌheɪgi-; ˌheɪdʒi-/ *noun* (*formal*) **1** a person who writes the life story of a SAINT **2** a person who writes about another person's life in a way that praises them too much, and does not criticize them

---

hag·i·og·ra·phy /ˌhægiˈɑɡrəfi; ˌheɪɡi-; ˌheɪdʒi-/ *noun* (pl. **hag·i·og·ra·phies**) [C, U] (*formal*) a book about the life of a person that praises them too much; this style of writing

hah = HA¹

hai·ku /ˈhaɪkuː; haɪˈkuː/ *noun* (pl. **hai·ku** or **hai·kus**) (from *Japanese*) a poem with three lines and usually 17 syllables, written in a style that is traditional in Japan

hail /heɪl/ *verb, noun*
• *verb* **1** [T, usually passive] to describe someone or something as being very good or special, especially in newspapers, etc.: **~ sb/sth as sth** *The conference was hailed as a great success.* ♦ **~ sb/sth + noun** *Teenager Matt Brown is being hailed a hero for saving a young child from drowning.* **2** [T] **~ sth** to signal to a taxi or a bus, in order to get the driver to stop: *to hail a taxi/cab* **3** [T] **~ sb** (*literary*) to call to someone in order to say hello to them or attract their attention: *A voice hailed us from the other side of the street.* **4** [I] when **it hails**, small balls of ice fall like rain from the sky: *It's hailing!*
PHR V **'hail from...** (*formal*) to come from or have been born in a particular place: *His father hailed from Italy.*
• *noun* **1** [U] small balls of ice that fall like rain: *We drove through hail and snow.* **2** [sing.] **a ~ of sth** a large number or amount of something that is aimed at someone in order to harm them: *a hail of arrows/bullets* ♦ *a hail of abuse*

Hail Mar·y /ˌheɪl ˈmeri/ *noun* (pl. **Hail Ma·rys**) a Roman Catholic prayer to Mary, the mother of Jesus

hail·stone /ˈheɪlstoʊn/ *noun* [usually pl.] a small ball of ice that falls like rain

hail·storm /ˈheɪlstɔrm/ *noun* a storm during which hail falls from the sky

hair /her/ *noun*
1 [U, C] the substance that looks like a mass of fine threads growing especially on the head; one of these threads growing on the body of people and some animals: *fair/dark hair* ♦ *straight/curly/wavy hair* ♦ *to comb/brush your hair* ♦ (*informal*) *I'll be down in a minute. I'm doing* (= brushing, arranging, etc.) *my hair.* ♦ *I'm having my hair cut this afternoon.* ♦ *body/facial/pubic hair* ♦ *There's a hair in my soup.* ♦ *The rug was covered with cat hairs.* ➷ **picture at** BODY ➷ **collocations at** FASHION, PHYSICAL ➷ **see also** CAMEL HAIR, HORSEHAIR **2 -haired** (in adjectives) having the type of hair mentioned: *dark-haired* ♦ *long-haired* **3** [C] a thing that looks like a fine thread growing on the leaves and STEM of some plants
IDM **get in sb's hair** (*informal*) to annoy someone by always being near them, asking them questions, etc. **the hair of the dog (that bit you)** (*informal*) alcohol that you drink in order to make you feel better when you have drunk too much alcohol the night before **let your hair down** (*informal*) to relax and enjoy yourself, especially in a lively way **make sb's hair stand on end** to shock or frighten someone: *a chilling tale that will make your hair stand on end* **not harm/touch a hair on sb's head** to not hurt someone physically in any way **not have a hair out of place** (of a person) to look extremely clean and neat **not turn a hair** to show no emotion when something surprising, shocking, etc. happens ➷ **more at** HANG *v.*, HIDE *n.*, SPLIT *v.*, TEAR¹ *v.*

hair·band /ˈherbænd/ *noun* a strip of cloth or curved plastic worn by women in their hair, that fits closely over the top of the head and behind the ears

hair·brush /ˈherbrʌʃ/ *noun* a brush for making the hair neat or smooth ➷ **picture at** COMB

hair·cut /ˈherkʌt/ *noun* **1** the act of someone cutting your hair: *You need a haircut.* ♦ *I see you've had a haircut.* **2** the style in which someone's hair is cut: *What do you think of my new haircut?* ♦ *a trendy haircut* ➷ **collocations at** FASHION

hair·do /ˈherduː/ *noun* (pl. **hairdos**) (*old-fashioned, informal*) the style in which a woman's hair is arranged
SYN HAIRSTYLE

hair·dress·er /ˈherˌdresər/ *noun*
1 a person whose job is to cut, wash, and shape hair **2** a place where you can get your hair cut, washed, and shaped ➷ **compare** BARBER ▶ **hair·dress·ing** *noun* [U]

'hair dryer (also **'hair drier**) *noun* a small machine used for drying your hair by blowing hot air over it

hair·less /ˈherləs/ *adj.* without hair

hair·line /ˈherlaɪn/ *noun* **1** the edge of a person's hair, especially at the front: *a receding hairline* **2** (often used as an adjective) a very thin crack or line: *a hairline crack/fracture*

hair·net /ˈhernet/ *noun* a net worn over the hair to keep it in place

hair·piece /ˈherpiːs/ *noun* a piece of false hair worn to make your own hair look longer or thicker

hair·pin /ˈherpɪn/ *noun* **1** a small thin piece of wire that is folded in the middle, used by women for holding their hair in place ➷ **compare** BOBBY PIN **2** = HAIRPIN TURN

hairpin 'turn (also **hair·pin**) *noun* a very sharp bend in a road, especially a mountain road

'hair-ˌraising *adj.* extremely frightening but often exciting: *a hair-raising adventure/story*

'hair's breadth *noun* [sing.] a very small amount or distance: *We won by a hair's breadth.* ♦ *They were within a hair's breadth of being killed.*

'hair shirt *noun* a shirt made of rough cloth containing hair, worn in the past by people who wished to punish themselves for religious reasons

'hair-ˌsplitting *noun* [U] (*disapproving*) the act of giving too much importance to small and unimportant differences in an argument **SYN** QUIBBLE **IDM** **see** SPLIT

hair·spray /ˈherspreɪ/ *noun* [U, C] a substance sprayed onto the hair to hold it in a particular style

hair·style /ˈherstaɪl/ *noun* the style in which someone's hair is cut or arranged ➷ **collocations at** FASHION

hair·styl·ist /ˈherˌstaɪlɪst/ *noun* a person whose job is to cut, wash, and shape hair

hair·y /ˈheri/ *adj.* (**hairier**, **hairiest**) **1** covered with a lot of hair: *a hairy chest/monster* ♦ *plants with hairy stems* **2** (*informal*) dangerous or frightening but often exciting: *Driving on icy roads can be pretty hairy.* ♦ *a hairy experience* ▶ **hair·i·ness** *noun* [U]

hajj (also **haj**) /hædʒ; hɑdʒ/ *noun* usually **the Hajj** [sing.] the religious journey to Mecca that all Muslims try to make at least once in their lives

hake /heɪk/ *noun* [C, U] (pl. **hake**) a large sea fish that is used for food

Hak·ka /ˈhɑkə/ *noun* [U] a form of Chinese spoken by a group of people in south-eastern China

ha·lal /həˈlɑl/ *adj.* [only before noun] (of meat) from an animal that has been killed according to Muslim law: *halal meat* ♦ *a halal butcher* (= one who sells halal meat)

hal·berd /ˈhælbərd; ˈhɔl-/ *noun* a weapon used in the past that is a combination of a SPEAR and an AX

hal·cy·on /ˈhælsiən/ *adj.* [usually before noun] (*literary*) peaceful and happy: *the halcyon days of her youth*

hale /heɪl/ *adj.*
IDM **hale and hearty** (especially of an old person) strong and healthy

half /hæf/ *noun, det., pron., adv.*
• *noun* (pl. **halves** /hævz/) **1** either of two equal parts into which something is or can be divided: *two and a half pounds* (2½ lbs) ♦ *One and a half hours are allowed for the exam.* ♦ *An hour and a half is allowed for the exam.* ♦ *The second half of the book is more exciting.* ♦ *I've divided the money in half.* ♦ *We'll need to reduce the weight by half.* ➷ **note on page 678** ➷ **see also** HALVE **2** either of two periods of time into which a sports game, concert, etc. is divided: *No goals were scored in the first half.* **3** = HALFBACK ➷ **see also** CENTER HALF

t **tea**	t̬ **butter**	d **did**	k **cat**	g **got**	tʃ **chin**	dʒ **June**	f **fall**

hair

clean-shaven — mustache — stubble — beard — sideburn — goatee

crew cut · shaved head · bald head · receding hairline · long hair

straight hair — layered hair

flattop · spiky · dreadlocks (*also* dreads) · cornrows · bob · shoulder-length

widow's peak — ringlet

chignon · bun · French twist · long, wavy · curly · perm

bangs — part

braid · French braid · braids · pigtails · ponytail

IDM **and a half** (*informal*) bigger, better, more important, etc. than usual: *That was a game and a half!* **not do things/ anything by halves** to do whatever you do completely and thoroughly: *You're expecting twins? Well, you never did do things by halves.* **go halves (with sb)** to share the cost of something equally with someone: *We go halves on all the bills.* **the half of it** used in negative sentences to say that a situation is worse or more complicated than someone thinks: *"It sounds very difficult." " You don't know the half of it."* **how the other half lives** the way of life of a different social group, especially one much richer than you ⊃ more at MIND *n.*, SIX, TIME *n.*

• *det.*, *pron.* **1** an amount equal to half of something or someone: *half an hour* ◆ *Half (of) the fruit was bad.* ◆ *Half of the money was mine.* ◆ *He has a half share in the company.* ◆ *Out of 36 candidates, half passed.* ⊃ language bank at PROPORTION **2** ~ **the time, fun, trouble, etc.** the largest part of something: *Half the fun of gardening is never knowing exactly*

what's going to come up. ◆ *Half the time you don't even listen to what I say.*

IDM **half a loaf is better than none** (*saying*) you should be grateful for something, even if it is not as good, much, etc. as you really wanted; something is better than nothing **half a minute, second, etc.** (*informal*) a short time: *Hang on. I'll be ready in half a minute.* **half past one, two, etc.** 30 minutes after any hour on the clock

• *adv.* **1** to the extent of half: *The glass was half full.* **2** partly: *The chicken was only half cooked.* ◆ *half-closed eyes* ◆ *I'm half inclined to agree.*

IDM **half again as much** an increase of 50% of the existing number or amount: *Spending on health is half again as much as it was in 2009.* **not half** not nearly: *He's not half as rich as they say he is.* **not half bad** (*informal*) (used to show surprise) not bad at all; good: *It really isn't half bad, is it?*

half • whole • quarter

- **Quarter**, **half**, and **whole** can all be nouns: *Cut the apple into quarters.* ♦ *Two halves make a whole.*
- **Whole** is also an adjective: *I've been waiting here for a whole hour.*
- **Half** is also a determiner: *Half (of) the work is already finished.* ♦ *They spent half the time looking for a parking space.* ♦ *Her house is half a mile down the road.* Note that you do not put *a* or *the* in front of **half** when it is used in this way: *I waited for half an hour* ♦ ~~I waited for a half an hour.~~
- **Half** can also be used as an adverb: *This meal is only half cooked.*

,**half-and-'half** *noun* [U] a mixture of milk and cream that is used in coffee

half·back /ˈhæfbæk/ (also **half**) *noun* **1** [C] one of the defending players in HOCKEY or RUGBY whose position is between those who play at the front of a team and those who play at the back **2** (also **tail·back**) [C] one of the two offensive players in football whose position is behind the QUARTERBACK and beside the FULLBACK **3** (also **tail·back**) [U] the position a halfback plays at

,**half-'baked** *adj.* [usually before noun] (*informal*) not well planned or considered: *a half-baked idea*

'**half-,bath** *noun* a small room in a house, containing a SINK and a toilet but not a bathtub or shower **SYN** POWDER ROOM

'**half-,brother** *noun* a person's **half-brother** is a boy or man with either the same mother or the same father as they have ⊃ compare STEPBROTHER

,**half-'cocked** *adj.*
IDM **go off half-cocked** (*informal*) to start before preparations are complete, so that the effect or result is not as it should be

'**half day** *noun* a day on which people work or go to school only in the morning or in the afternoon: *Tuesday is her half day.*

,**half 'dollar** *noun* a U.S. coin worth 50 cents ⊃ picture at MONEY

,**half-'hearted** *adj.* done without enthusiasm or effort: *He made a half-hearted attempt to justify himself.* ▶ ,**half-'heartedly** *adv.*

,**half-'hour** (also ,**half an 'hour**) *noun* a period of 30 minutes: *He should arrive within the next half-hour.* ♦ *a half-hour drive*

,**half-'hourly** *adj.* happening every 30 minutes: *a half-hourly bus service* ▶ ,**half-'hourly** *adv.*: *The buses run half-hourly.*

'**half-life** *noun* [C] **1** (*physics*) the time taken for the radioactivity (RADIOACTIVE) of a substance to fall to half its original value **2** (*chemistry*) the time taken for the concentration of a REACTANT to fall to half of its original value in a chemical reaction

'**half-light** *noun* [sing., U] a dull light in which it is difficult to see things: *in the gray half-light of dawn*

'**half-,mast** *noun*
IDM **at half-mast** (of a flag) flown at the middle of the MAST as a sign of respect for an important person who has just died: *Flags were flown at half-mast on the day of his funeral.*

'**half ,measures** *noun* [pl.] a policy or plan of action that is weak and does not do enough: *There are no half measures with this company.*

,**half-'moon** *noun* **1** the moon when only half of it can be seen from the earth; the time when this happens ⊃ compare FULL MOON, HARVEST MOON, NEW MOON **2** a thing that is shaped like a half-moon

'**half note** *noun* (*music*) a note that lasts twice as long as a QUARTER NOTE ⊃ picture at MUSIC

'**half-pipe** *noun* a U-shaped structure, or U-shaped channel

cut into snow, used for performing complicated movements in skateboarding (SKATEBOARD), Rollerblading (ROLLERBLADE™), and SNOWBOARDING

,**half-'price** *adj.* costing half the usual price: *a half-price ticket* ▶ ,**half-'price** *adv.*: *Children aged under four go half-price.* ,**half 'price** *noun* [U]: *Many items are at half price.*

'**half-,sister** *noun* a person's **half-sister** is a girl or woman who has either the same mother or the same father as them ⊃ compare STEPSISTER

'**half step** (also '**half-tone**) *noun* (*music*) half a TONE on a musical SCALE, for example the INTERVAL between C and C♯ or between E and F ⊃ compare STEP

,**half-'timbered** *adj.* [usually before noun] (of a building) having walls that are made from a wooden frame filled with brick, stone, etc. so that the FRAMEWORK can still be seen

'**half-time** *noun* [U] a short period between the two halves of a sports game during which the players rest: *The score at half-time was two all.* ♦ *the half-time score* ⊃ compare FULL TIME

'**half-tone** *noun* **1** (*technical*) a print of a black and white photograph in which the different shades of gray are produced from small and large black dots **2** (*music*) = HALF STEP

'**half-truth** *noun* a statement that gives only part of the truth, especially when it is intended to cheat someone: *The newspaper reports are a mixture of gossip, lies, and half-truths.*

'**half-,volley** *noun* (in TENNIS and SOCCER) a stroke or kick immediately after the ball has BOUNCED

'**half·way** /ˌhæfˈweɪ/ *adv.* **1** at an equal distance between two points; in the middle of a period of time: *It's about halfway between Boston and Providence.* ♦ *He left halfway through the ceremony.* ♦ *I'm afraid we're not even halfway there yet.* **2** ~ **toward sth** | ~ **toward doing sth** part of the way toward doing or achieving something: *This only goes halfway toward explaining what really happened.* **3** ~ **decent** (*informal*) fairly, but not very, good: *Any halfway decent map will give you that information.* ▶ '**half·way** *adj.*: *the halfway point/stage* **IDM** see MEET v.

'**halfway ,house** *noun* a place where prisoners, mental patients, etc. can stay for a short time after leaving a prison or hospital, before they start to live on their own again

'**halfway ,line** *noun* a line across a sports field at an equal distance between the ends

'**half·wit** /ˈhæfwɪt/ *noun* (*informal*) a stupid person **SYN** IDIOT ▶ ,**half-'witted** *adj.*

'**hal·i·but** /ˈhæləbət/ *noun* (*pl.* **hal·i·but**) [C, U] a large, flat, ocean fish that is used for food

'**hal·i·to·sis** /ˌhæləˈtoʊsəs/ *noun* [U] (*medical*) a condition in which the breath smells unpleasant **SYN** BAD BREATH

hall 🔊 /hɔl/ *noun*
1 (also **hall·way**) a passage in a building with rooms down either side **SYN** CORRIDOR: *I headed for Scott's office down the hall.* **2** (also **hall·way**, **en·try**) a space or passage inside the entrance or front door of a building: *She ran into the hall and up the stairs.* **3** a building or large room for public meetings, meals, concerts, etc.: *a concert/banquet/exhibition, etc. hall* ♦ *There are three dining halls on campus.* ♦ *Carnegie Hall* ⊃ see also CITY HALL, DANCE HALL, GUILDHALL, MUSIC HALL, TOWN HALL **4** (also '**residence ,hall**) = DORMITORY (1): *She's living in Thayer Hall.*

hal·le·lu·jah /ˌhæləˈluyə/ (also **al·le·lu·ia**) *noun* a song or shout of praise to God ▶ **hal·le·lu·jah** *exclamation*

hall·mark /ˈhɔlmɑrk/ *noun, verb*
● *noun* **1** a feature or quality that is typical of someone or something: *Police said the explosion bore all the hallmarks of a terrorist attack.* **2** a mark put on gold, silver, and PLATINUM objects that shows the quality of the metal and gives information about when and where the object was made
● *verb* ~ **sth** to put a hallmark on metal goods

'**Hall of 'Fame** *noun* (*pl.* ,**Halls of 'Fame**) **1** a place for people to visit, like a museum, with things connected with famous people from a particular sport or activity: *the Country Music Hall of Fame* **2** [sing.] the group of people who have done a particular activity or sport particularly well

hal·loo /həˈluː; hæ-/ *exclamation* **1** used to attract someone's attention **2** used in hunting to tell the dogs to start chasing an animal ▶ **halloo** *verb* [T, I] **~ (sb)**

hal·lowed /ˈhæloʊd/ *adj.* [only before noun] **1** (especially of old things) respected and important **SYN** SACRED: *one of the theater's most hallowed traditions* **2** that has been made holy: *to be buried in hallowed ground* **SYN** SACRED

Hal·low·een (also **Hallowe'en**) /ˌhæləˈwin; ˌhɑ-/ *noun* [C, U] the night of October 31st when it was believed in the past that dead people appeared from their graves, and that is now celebrated by children who dress and visit people's houses to get candy ⊃ see also TRICK OR TREAT

hal·lu·ci·nate /həˈluːsəˌneɪt/ *verb* [I] to see or hear things that are not really there because of illness or drugs

hal·lu·ci·na·tion /həˌluːsəˈneɪʃn/ *noun* **1** [C, U] the fact of seeming to see or hear someone or something that is not really there, especially because of illness or drugs: *to have hallucinations* ◆ *High temperatures can cause hallucination.* **2** [C] something that is seen or heard when it is not really there: *Was the figure real or just a hallucination?*

hal·lu·ci·na·to·ry /həˈluːsənəˌtɔri/ *adj.* [only before noun] connected with or causing hallucinations: *a hallucinatory experience* ◆ *hallucinatory drugs*

hal·lu·ci·no·gen /hæˈluːsənədʒən/ *noun* a drug, such as LSD, that affects people's minds and makes them see and hear things that are not really there ▶ **hal·lu·ci·no·gen·ic** /həˌluːsənəˈdʒɛnɪk/ *adj.*: *hallucinogenic drugs/effects*

hall·way /ˈhɔlweɪ/ *noun* **1** = HALL (1) **2** = HALL (2)

ha·lo /ˈheɪloʊ/ *noun* (*pl.* **ha·loes** or **ha·los**) **1** (in paintings, etc.) a circle of light shown around or above the head of a holy person: *She played the part of an angel, complete with wings and a halo.* ◆ (*figurative*) *a halo of white frizzy hair* **2** (*informal*) = CORONA

hal·o·gen /ˈhælədʒən/ *noun* (*chemistry*) any of a set of five chemical elements, including FLUORINE, CHLORINE, and IODINE, that react with HYDROGEN to form acids from which simple salts can be made. Halogens, in the form of gas, are used in lamps and stoves.

hal·on /ˈheɪlɑn/ *noun* (*chemistry*) a gas that is made up of CARBON and one or more halogen, used especially to stop fires

halt /hɔlt/ *verb, noun*
● *verb* [I, T] to stop; to make someone or something stop: *She walked toward him and then halted.* ◆ *"Halt!" the Major ordered* (= used as a command to soldiers). ◆ *~ sb/sth The police were halting traffic on the parade route.* ◆ *The trial was halted after the first week.* **IDM** see TRACK *n.*
● *noun* [sing.] an act of stopping the movement or progress of someone or something: *Work came to a halt when the machine broke down.* ◆ *The thought brought her to an abrupt halt.* ◆ *The car skidded to a halt.* ◆ *Strikes have led to a halt in production.* ◆ *They decided it was time to call a halt to the project* (= stop it officially). **IDM** see GRIND *v.*

hal·ter /ˈhɔltər/ *noun* **1** a rope or narrow piece of leather put around the head of a horse for leading it with **2** (usually used as an adjective) a narrow piece of cloth around the neck that holds a woman's dress or shirt in position, with the back and shoulders not covered: *She was dressed in a halter top and shorts.*

halt·ing /ˈhɔltɪŋ/ *adj.* [usually before noun] (especially of speech or movement) stopping and starting often, especially because you are not certain or are not very confident **SYN** HESITANT: *a halting conversation* ◆ *a toddler's first few halting steps* ▶ **halt·ing·ly** *adv.*: *"Well…" she began haltingly.*

halve /hæv/ *verb* **1** [I, T] to reduce by a half; to make something reduce by a half: *The shares have halved in value.* ◆ *~ sth The company is halving its prices.* **2** [T] **~ sth** to divide something into two equal parts

halves pl. of HALF

hal·yard /ˈhælyərd/ *noun* (*technical*) a rope used for raising or taking down a sail or flag

ham /hæm/ *noun, verb*
● *noun* **1** [C, U] the top part of a pig's leg that has been CURED (= preserved using salt or smoke) and is eaten as food; the meat from this: *The hams were cooked whole.* ◆ *a slice of ham* ◆ *a ham sandwich* ⊃ compare BACON, PORK **2** [C] a person who sends and receives radio messages as a hobby rather than as a job: *a radio ham* **3** [C] (*informal*) (often used as an adjective) an actor who performs badly, especially by exaggerating emotions: *a ham actor* **4** [C, usually pl.] (*informal*) the back part of a person's leg above the knee ⊃ see also HAMSTRING
● *verb* (-mm-)
IDM **ham it up** (*informal*) (especially of actors) when people **ham it up**, they deliberately exaggerate their emotions or movements

ham·burg·er /ˈhæmˌbərgər/ (also **burg·er**) *noun* **1** finely ground (GRIND) beef made into a flat round shape that is then grilled, often served in a roll **2** (also ˈ**ham·burg·er meat**, ˌ**ground ˈbeef**) beef that has been finely ground (GRIND) in a special machine

ˈ**ham-ˌfisted** (also ˈ**ham-ˌhanded**) *adj.* (*informal*) lacking skill when using your hands or when dealing with people **SYN** CLUMSY: *his ham-fisted efforts to assist her*

ham·let /ˈhæmlət/ *noun* a very small VILLAGE

ham·mer 🔨 /ˈhæmər/ *noun, verb*
● *noun*
> TOOL **1** [C] a tool with a handle and a heavy metal head, used for breaking things or hitting nails: (*figurative*) *The decision is a hammer blow for the steel industry.* ⊃ picture at TOOL ⊃ see also SLEDGEHAMMER **2** [C] a tool with a handle and a wooden head, used by a person in charge of an AUCTION (= a sale at which things are sold to the person who offers the most money) to get people's attention when something is just being sold: *to come/go under the hammer* (= to be sold at AUCTION)
> IN PIANO **3** [C] a small wooden part inside a piano, that hits the strings to produce a sound
> IN GUN **4** [C] a part inside a gun that makes the gun fire
> SPORTS **5** [C] a metal ball attached to a wire, thrown as a sport ⊃ picture at SPORT **6** the hammer [sing.] the event or sport of throwing the hammer
IDM **hammer and tongs** if two people are **at it hammer and tongs** or **go at it hammer and tongs**, they argue or fight with a lot of energy and noise
● *verb*
> HIT WITH TOOL **1** [I, T] to hit something with a hammer: *I could hear someone hammering next door.* ◆ *~ sth (in/into/onto sth) She hammered the nail into the wall.* ◆ *~ sth + adj. He was hammering the sheet of copper flat.*
> HIT MANY TIMES **2** [I, T] to hit something hard many times, especially so that it makes a loud noise **SYN** POUND: *Someone was hammering at the door.* ◆ *Hail was hammering down onto the roof.* ◆ (*figurative*) *I was so scared my heart was hammering* (= beating very fast) *in my chest.* ◆ *~ sth He hammered the door with his fists.* ⊃ thesaurus box at BEAT
> KICK/HIT BALL **3** [T] **~ sth (+ adv./prep.)** (*informal*) to kick or hit a ball very hard: *He hammered the ball into the net.*
> DEFEAT EASILY **4** [T] **~ sb** (*informal*) to defeat someone very easily: *Our team was hammered 5–1.*
PHR V ˌ**hammer aˈway at sth** to work hard in order to finish or achieve something; to keep repeating something in order to get the result that you want ˌ**hammer sth↔ˈhome 1** to emphasize a point, an idea, etc. so that people fully understand it **2** to kick a ball hard and score a goal ˌ**hammer sth ˈinto sb** to make someone learn or remember something by repeating it many times ˌ**hammer ˈout sth 1** to discuss a plan, an idea, etc. until everyone agrees or a decision is made: *to hammer out a compromise* **2** to play a tune, especially on a piano, loudly and not very well

ham·mer and 'sick·le *noun* [sing.] tools representing the people who work in industry and farming, used on the flag of the former Soviet Union and as a symbol of Communism

hammered /ˈhæmərd/ *adj.* [not before noun] (*slang*) very drunk

ham·mer·head /ˈhæmərˌhed/ (also **hammerhead 'shark**) *noun* a SHARK with flat parts sticking out from either side of its head with eyes at the ends

ham·mer·ing /ˈhæmərɪŋ/ *noun* **1** [U, sing.] the sound of someone hitting something with a hammer or with their FISTS: *the sound of hammering from the next room* **2** [C, usually sing.] (*informal*) an act of defeating or criticizing someone severely: *Our team took a real hammering in the first half.*

'hammer ˌprice *noun* the last and highest amount offered for something at an AUCTION and that is the price for which it is sold

ham·mock /ˈhæmək/ *noun* a type of bed made from a net or from a piece of strong material, with ropes at each end that are used to hang it between two trees, posts, etc. ➔ picture at BED

ham·my /ˈhæmi/ *adj.* (**ham·mi·er**, **ham·mi·est**) (*informal*) (of a style of acting) artificial or exaggerated

ham·per /ˈhæmpər/ *verb, noun*
- *verb* [often passive] ~ **sb/sth** to prevent someone from easily doing or achieving something **SYN** HINDER
- *noun* **1** a large container that you keep your dirty clothes in until they are washed ➔ picture at BASKET **2** a large BASKET with a lid, especially one used to carry food in: *a picnic hamper*

ham·ster /ˈhæmstər/ *noun* an animal like a large mouse, with large cheeks for storing food. Hamsters are often kept as pets.

ham·string /ˈhæmstrɪŋ/ *noun, verb*
- *noun* **1** one of the five TENDONS behind the knee that connect the muscles of the upper leg to the bones of the lower leg: *a hamstring injury* • *She pulled a hamstring.* **2** a TENDON behind the middle joint (= HOCK) of the back leg of a horse and some other animals
- *verb* (**ham·strung**, **ham·strung** /-strʌŋ/) [often passive] ~ **sb/sth** to prevent someone or something from working or taking action in the way that is needed

hand ✎ /hænd/ *noun, verb*
- *noun*
> PART OF BODY **1** [C] the part of the body at the end of the arm, including the fingers and thumb: *I placed a hand on her shoulder.* • *Put your hand up if you know the answer.* • *Keep both hands on the steering wheel at all times.* • *She was on (her) hands and knees* (= CRAWLING on the floor) *looking for an earring.* • *Couples strolled past holding hands.* • *Give me your hand* (= hold my hand) *while we cross the road.* • *The crowd threw up their hands* (= lifted them into the air) *in dismay.* • *He killed the snake with his bare hands* (= using only his hands). • *a hand towel* (= a small towel for drying your hands on) • *a hand drill* (= one that is used by turning a handle rather than powered by electricity) ➔ picture at BODY ➔ collocations at PHYSICAL ➔ see also LEFT-HAND, RIGHT-HAND
> -HANDED **2** (in adjectives) using the hand or number of hands mentioned: *a one-handed catch* • *left-handed scissors* (= intended to be held in your left hand)
> HELP **3 a hand** [sing.] (*informal*) help in doing something: *Let me give you a hand with those bags* (= help you to carry them). • *Do you need a hand with those invoices?* • *The neighbors are always willing to lend a hand.*
> ROLE IN SITUATION **4** [sing.] ~ **in sth** the part or role that someone or something plays in a particular situation; someone's influence in a situation: *Early reports suggest the hand of rebel forces in the bombings.* • *Several of his colleagues had a hand in his downfall.* • *This appointment was an attempt to strengthen her hand in policy discussions.*
> ON CLOCK/WATCH **5** [C] (usually in compounds) a part of a clock or watch that points to the numbers ➔ see also HOUR HAND, MINUTE HAND, SECOND HAND

> WORKER **6** [C] a person who does physical work on a farm or in a factory ➔ see also FARMHAND, HIRED HAND, STAGE-HAND
> SAILOR **7** [C] a sailor on a ship: *All hands on deck!* ➔ see also DECKHAND
> HAND- **8** (in compounds) by a person rather than a machine: *hand-painted pottery* • *hand-knitted* • *This item should be hand washed.* ➔ see also HANDMADE
> IN CARD GAMES **9** [C] a set of PLAYING CARDS given to one player in a game: *to be dealt a good/bad hand* **10** [C] one stage of a game of cards: *I'll have to leave after this hand.*
> WRITING **11** [sing.] (*old use*) a particular style of writing ➔ see also FREEHAND
> MEASUREMENT FOR HORSE **12** [C] a unit for measuring the height of a horse, equal to 4 inches or 10.16 centimeters ➔ see also OLD HAND, SECONDHAND, UNDERHAND

IDM **all hands on deck** (*saying, humorous*) everyone helps or must help, especially in a difficult situation: *There are 30 people coming to dinner tonight, so it's all hands on deck.* **(close/near) at hand** close to you in time or distance: *Help was at hand.* • *The property is ideally located with all local amenities close at hand.* **at the hands of sb | at sb's hands** (*formal*) if you experience something **at the hands of someone**, they are the cause of it **be good with your hands** to be skillful at making or doing things with your hands **bind/tie sb hand and foot 1** to tie someone's hands and feet together so that they cannot move or escape **2** to prevent someone from doing what they want by creating rules, restrictions, etc. **by hand 1** by a person rather than a machine: *The fabric was painted by hand.* **2** if a letter is delivered **by hand**, it is delivered by the person who wrote it, or someone who is sent by them, rather than by mail **fall into sb's hands/the hands of sb** (*formal*) to become controlled by someone: *The town fell into enemy hands.* • *We don't want this document falling into the wrong hands.* **(at) first hand** by experiencing, seeing, etc. something yourself rather than being told about it by someone else: *The President visited the area to see the devastation at first hand.* **get your hands dirty** (also **dirty your hands**) to do physical or difficult work: *He's not frightened of getting his hands dirty.* **go cap/hat in hand (to sb)** to ask someone for something, especially money, in a very polite way that makes you seem less important: *There's no way he'll go cap in hand to his brother.* **sb's hand (in marriage)** (*old-fashioned*) permission to marry someone, especially a woman: *He asked the general for his daughter's hand in marriage.* **hand in glove (with sb)** working closely with someone, especially in a secret and/or illegal way **hand in hand 1** if two people are **hand in hand**, they are holding each other's hand **2** if two things **go hand in hand**, they are closely connected and one thing causes the other: *Poverty and poor health often go hand in hand.* **hands down** (*informal*) easily and without any doubt: *They won hands down.* • *It is hands down the best movie this year.* ➔ see also HANDS-DOWN *adj.* **(get/take) your hands off (sth/sb)** (*informal*) used to tell someone not to touch something or someone: *Get your hands off her!* • *Hey, hands off! That's my drink!* **hands up! 1** (*informal*) used to tell a group of people to raise one hand in the air if they know the answer to a question, etc.: *Hands up all those who want to go swimming.* **2** used by someone who is threatening people with a gun to tell them to raise both hands in the air **have your hands full** to be very busy or too busy to do something else: *She certainly has her hands full with four kids in the house.* **have your hands tied** to be unable to do what you want to do because of rules, promises, etc.: *I really wish I could help but my hands are tied.* **hold sb's hand** to give someone support in a difficult situation: *Do you want me to come along and hold your hand?* **in sb's capable, safe, etc. hands** being taken care of or dealt with by someone that you think you can rely on: *Can I leave these queries in your capable hands?* **in hand 1** if you have money **in hand**, it is left and available to be used **2** if you have a particular situation **in hand**, you are in control of it **3** the job, question, etc. **in hand** is the one that you are dealing with **in the hands of sb | in sb's hands** being taken care of or controlled by someone: *The matter is*

ʌ **cup**   ə **about**   eɪ **say**   aɪ **five**   ɔɪ **boy**   aʊ **now**   oʊ **go**   ər **bird**

now in the hands of my lawyer. ◆ At that time, the castle was in enemy hands. **keep your hand in** to occasionally do something that you used to do a lot so that you do not lose your skill at it: She retired last year but still teaches the odd class to keep her hand in. **lay/get your hands on sb** to catch someone that you are annoyed with: Wait till I get my hands on him! **lay/get your hands on sth** to find or get something: I know their address is here somewhere, but I can't lay my hands on it right now. **many hands make light work** (saying) used to say that a job is made easier if a lot of people help **off your hands** no longer your responsibility **on either/every hand** (literary) on both/all sides; in both/all directions **on hand** available, especially to help: The emergency services were on hand with medical advice. **on your hands** if you have someone or something **on your hands**, you are responsible for them or it: Let me take care of the invitations—you've enough on your hands with the caterers. **on the one hand… on the other (hand)…** used to introduce different points of view, ideas, etc., especially when they are opposites: On the one hand they'd love to have kids, but on the other, they don't want to give up their freedom. ⊃ language bank at CONTRAST **out of hand 1** difficult or impossible to control: Unemployment is getting out of hand. **2** if you reject, etc. something **out of hand**, you do so immediately without thinking about it fully or listening to other people's arguments: All our suggestions were dismissed out of hand. **out of your hands** no longer your responsibility: I'm afraid the matter is now out of my hands. **play into sb's hands** to do exactly what an enemy, opponent, etc. wants so that they gain the advantage in a particular situation: If we get the police involved, we'll be playing right into the protesters' hands. **(at) second, third, etc. hand** by being told about something by someone else who has seen it or heard about it, not by experiencing, seeing, etc. it yourself: I'm tired of hearing about these decisions third hand! **take sb in hand** to deal with someone in a strict way in order to improve their behavior **take sth into your own hands** to deal with a particular situation yourself because you are not happy with the way that others are dealing with it **throw your hand in** (informal) to stop doing something or taking part in something, especially because you are not successful **to hand** that you can reach or get easily: I'm afraid I don't have the latest figures to hand. **turn your hand to sth** to start doing something or be able to do something, especially when you do it well: Jim can turn his hand to most jobs around the house. ⊃ more at BIG adj., BIRD n., BITE v., BLOOD, CHANGE v., CLOSE² adv., DEAD adj., DEVIL, EAT, FIRM adj., FOLD v., FORCE v., FREE adj., HEAVY adj., HELP v., IRON adj., JOIN v., KNOW v., LAW, LIFE, LIVE¹, MONEY, OFFER v., OVERPLAY, PAIR n., PALM n., PUTTY, RAISE v., SAFE adj., SHOW v., SLEIGHT, STAY v., TIME n., TRY v., UPPER adj., WAIT v., WASH v., WHIP n., WIN v., WRING

● **verb** to pass or give something to someone: ~ **sth to sb** She handed the letter to me. ◆ ~ **sb sth** She handed me the letter. **IDM** **hand sth to sb on a plate** (informal) to give something to someone without the person concerned making any effort: Nobody's going to hand you success on a plate. **have to hand it to sb** (informal) used to say that someone deserves praise for something: You have to hand it to her— she's a great cook.

PHR V ,hand sth↔a'round to offer or pass something, especially food or drinks, to all the people in a group ,hand sth 'back (to sb) to give or return something to the person who owns it or to where it belongs ,hand sth↔'down (to sb) **1** [usually passive] to give or leave something to someone who is younger than you **SYN** PASS DOWN: These skills used to be handed down from father to son. ⊃ related noun HAND-ME-DOWN **2** to officially give a decision, statement, etc. **SYN** ANNOUNCE: The judge has handed down his verdict. ,hand sth↔'in (to sb) to give something to a person in authority, especially a piece of work or something that is lost: You must all hand in your projects by the end of next week. ◆ I handed the watch in to the police. ◆ to **hand in your notice/resignation** (= formally tell your employer that you want to stop working for them) ,hand sth↔'on (to sb) to give or leave something for another person to use or deal

with **SYN** PASS ON ,hand sth↔'out (to sb) **1** to give a number of things to the members of a group **SYN** DISTRIBUTE: Could you hand these books out, please? ⊃ related noun HANDOUT **2** to give advice, a punishment, etc.: He's always handing out advice to people. ,hand 'over (to sb) | ,hand sth↔'over (to sb) to give someone else your position of power or the responsibility for something: She resigned and handed over to one of her younger colleagues. ◆ He finally handed over his responsibility for the company last year. ⊃ related noun HANDOVER ,hand sb 'over to sb to let someone listen or speak to another person, especially on the telephone or in a news broadcast: I'll hand you over to my boss. ,hand sb/sth↔'over (to sb) to give something or someone officially or formally to another person: He handed over a check for $200,000. ◆ They handed the weapons over to the police. ⊃ related noun HANDOVER

VOCABULARY BUILDING

using your hands
touch

These verbs describe different ways of touching things:
- **brush** She brushed the silk with her fingertips.
- **feel** I felt the bag to see what was in it.
- **handle** Handle the fruit with care.
- **pat** He patted my arm and told me not to worry.
- **pet** The dog loves being petted.
- **rub** She rubbed her eyes wearily.
- **squeeze** I took his hand and squeezed it.
- **stroke** He stroked her hair lovingly.
- **tap** Someone was tapping lightly at the door.

hold

You can use these verbs to describe taking something quickly:
- **grab** I grabbed his arm to keep myself from falling.
- **snatch** She snatched the letter out of my hand.

These verbs describe holding things tightly:
- **clasp** Her hands were clasped behind her head.
- **clutch** The child was clutching a doll in her hand.
- **grasp** Grasp the rope with both hands and pull.
- **grip** He gripped the bag tightly and wouldn't let go.

---

hand·bag /'hændbæg/ noun = PURSE n. (1)

hand·ball /'hændbɔl/ noun **1** [U] a game in which players hit a small ball against a wall with their hand **2** [U] (also 'team ,handball) a team game for two teams of seven players, usually played indoors, in which players try to score goals by throwing a ball with their hand **3** [C, U] (in SOCCER) the offense of touching the ball with your hands

hand·bas·ket /'hænd,bæskət/ noun **IDM** see HELL

hand·bell /'hændbɛl/ noun a small bell with a handle, especially one of a set used by a group of people to play tunes

hand·bill /'hændbɪl/ noun a small printed advertisement that is given to people by hand

hand·book /'hændbʊk/ noun a book giving instructions on how to use something or information about a particular subject ⊃ compare MANUAL

hand·brake /'hændbreɪk/ noun = EMERGENCY BRAKE

hand·cart /'hændkɑrt/ noun = CART

hand·craft·ed /,hænd'kræftəd/ adj. skillfully made by hand, not by machine: a handcrafted chair

hand cream noun [U] cream that you put on your hands to prevent dry skin

hand·cuff /'hændkʌf/ verb [usually passive] ~ **sb** to put handcuffs on someone or to fasten someone to something or someone with handcuffs

hand·cuffs /'hændkʌfs/ (also informal cuffs) noun [pl.] a pair of metal rings joined by a chain, used for holding the wrists of a prisoner together: a pair of handcuffs ◆ She was led away in handcuffs. ⊃ see also GOLDEN HANDCUFFS

---

hand·ful /ˈhændfʊl/ *noun* **1** [C] ~ (of sth) the amount of something that can be held in one hand: *a handful of rice* **2** [sing.] ~ (of sb/sth) a small number of people or things: *Only a handful of people came.* **3** a ~ [sing.] (*informal*) a person or an animal that is difficult to control: *Her kids can be a real handful.*

ˈhand greˌnade *noun* a small bomb that is thrown by hand

hand·grip /ˈhændɡrɪp/ *noun* a handle for holding something

hand·gun /ˈhændɡʌn/ *noun* a small gun that you can hold and fire with one hand

ˈhand-held (also **hand·held** /ˈhændhɛld/) *adj.* [usually before noun] small enough to be held in the hand while being used ▶ **ˈhand-held** (also **hand·held**) *noun*

hand·hold /ˈhændhoʊld/ *noun* something on the surface of a steep slope, wall, etc. that a person can hold when climbing up it

hand·i·cap /ˈhændiˌkæp/ *noun, verb*
- **noun 1** [C, U] (becoming *old-fashioned*, sometimes *offensive*) a permanent physical or mental condition that makes it difficult or impossible to use a particular part of your body or mind **SYN** DISABILITY: *Despite her handicap, Jane is able to hold down a full-time job.* ♦ *mental/physical/visual handicap* ⊃ note at DISABLED **2** [C] something that makes it difficult for someone to do something **SYN** OBSTACLE: *Not speaking the language proved to be a bigger handicap than I'd imagined.* **3** [C] (*sports*) a race or competition in which the most skillful must run further, carry extra weight, etc. in order to give all those taking part an equal chance of winning; the disadvantage that is given to someone you are competing against in such a race or competition **4** [C] (in GOLF) an advantage given to a weaker player so that competition is more equal when they play against a stronger player. It is expressed as a number related to the number of times a player hits the ball and gets lower as he/she improves.
- **verb** (-pp-) [usually passive] ~ sb/sth to make something more difficult for someone to do: *The runners were handicapped by the strong wind.*

hand·i·capped /ˈhændiˌkæpt/ *adj.* (becoming *old-fashioned*, sometimes *offensive*) **1** suffering from a mental or physical handicap **SYN** DISABLED: *a visually handicapped child* ♦ *The accident left him physically handicapped.* ⊃ see also MENTALLY HANDICAPPED **2** **the handicapped** *noun* [pl.] people who are handicapped: *a school for the physically handicapped* ⊃ note at DISABLED

hand·i·craft /ˈhændiˌkræft/ *noun* [C, usually pl., U] **1** activities such as sewing and making cloth that use skill with your hands and artistic ability to make things: *to teach handicrafts* **2** things made in this way: *traditional handicrafts bought by tourists*

hand·i·ly /ˈhændəli/ *adv.* easily: *He handily defeated his challengers.*

hand·i·work /ˈhændiˌwɚk/ *noun* [U] **1** work that you do, or something that you have made, especially using your artistic skill: *We admired her exquisite handiwork.* **2** a thing done by a particular person or group, especially something bad: *This looks like the handiwork of an arsonist.*

hand·ker·chief /ˈhæŋkɚtʃɪf; -ˌtʃif/ *noun* (also *informal* **han·ky, han·kie**) a small piece of material that you use for blowing your nose, etc.

han·dle 🔑 /ˈhændl/ *verb, noun*
- **verb**
- ⟩DEAL WITH **1** [T] to deal with a situation, a person, an area of work, or a strong emotion: ~ sth *A new man was appointed to handle the crisis.* ♦ *She's very good at handling her patients.* ♦ *The sale was handled by Adams Commercial.* ♦ *We can handle up to 500 calls an hour at our new offices.* ♦ *We all have to learn to handle stress.* ♦ *This matter has been handled very badly.* ♦ (*informal*) *"Any problems?" "Nothing I can't handle."* ♦ (*informal*) *I have to go. I can't handle it anymore* (= deal with a difficult situation). ♦ ~ yourself (*informal*) *You have to know*

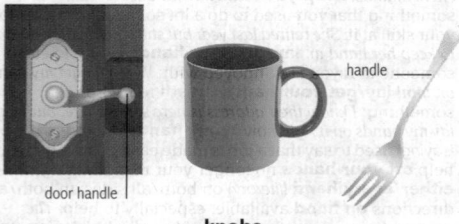
handles

door handle / handle

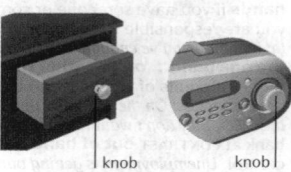
knobs

doorknob / knob / knob

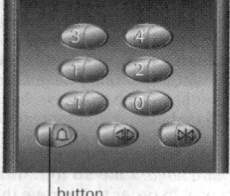
buttons

button / buttons

how to handle yourself in this business (= know the right way to behave).
- ⟩TOUCH WITH HANDS **2** [T] ~ sth to touch, hold, or move something with your hands: *Our cat hates being handled.* ♦ *The label on the box said: "Fragile. Handle with care."*
- ⟩CONTROL **3** [T] ~ sth to control a vehicle, an animal, a tool, etc.: *I wasn't sure if I could handle such a powerful car.* ♦ *She's a difficult horse to handle.* **4** [I] ~ well/badly to be easy/difficult to drive or control: *The car handles well in any weather.*
- ⟩BUY/SELL **5** [T] ~ sth to buy or sell something **SYN** DEAL IN: *They were arrested for handling stolen goods.*
- **noun**
- ⟩OF DOOR/DRAWER/WINDOW **1** the part of a door, drawer, window, etc. that you use to open it: *She turned the handle and opened the door.*
- ⟩OF CUP/BAG/TOOL **2** the part of an object, such as a cup, a bag, or a tool that you use to hold it, or carry it: *the handle of a knife* ♦ *a broom handle* ⊃ picture at CUP, KITCHEN ⊃ see also LOVE HANDLES
- ⟩-HANDLED **3** (in adjectives) having the number or type of handle mentioned: *a long-handled spoon*
- **IDM** **get/have a handle on sb/sth** (*informal*) to understand or know about someone or something, especially so that you can deal with it or them later: *I can't get a handle on these sales figures.* **give sb a handle (on sth)** (*informal*) to give someone enough facts or knowledge for them to be able to deal with something ⊃ more at FLY *v.*

han·dle·bar /ˈhændlˌbɑr/ *noun* [C] (also **han·dle·bars** [pl.]) a metal bar, with a handle at each end, that you use for steering a bicycle or motorcycle: *to hold onto the handlebars* ⊃ picture at BICYCLE

ˈhandlebar ˈmustache *noun* a MUSTACHE that is curved upward at each end

han·dler /ˈhændlɚ/ *noun* (especially in compounds) **1** a person who trains and controls animals, especially dogs **2** a person who carries or touches something as part of their job: *airport baggage handlers* ♦ *food handlers* **3** a person

t **tea**   ţ **butter**   d **did**   k **cat**   g **got**   tʃ **chin**   dʒ **June**   f **fall**

who organizes something or advises someone: *the President's campaign handlers*

hand·ling /ˈhændlɪŋ/ *noun* [U] **1** the way that someone deals with or treats a situation, a person, an animal, etc.: *I was impressed by his handling of the affair.* ♦ *This horse needs firm handling.* **2** the action of organizing or controlling something: *data handling on computers* **3** the action of touching, feeling, or holding something with your hands: *toys that can stand up to rough handling* **4** the cost of dealing with an order, delivering goods, booking tickets, etc.: *$12.95 for postage and handling* **5** the way in which a vehicle can be controlled by the driver: *a car designed for easy handling* **6** the act or cost of transporting goods from one place to another

ˈhand ˌluggage (also **ˈcarry-on ˌluggage**) *noun* [U] small bags that you can keep with you on an aircraft

hand·made /ˌhændˈmeɪd/ *adj.* made by a person using their hands rather than by machines ⊃ **compare** MACHINE-MADE

hand·maid·en /ˈhænd meɪdn/ (also **hand·maid** /ˈhændmeɪd/) *noun* **1** (*old-fashioned*) a female servant **2** (*formal*) something that supports and helps something else: *Mathematics was once dubbed the handmaiden of the sciences.*

ˈhand-me-ˌdown *noun* [usually pl.] a piece of clothing that used to belong to someone else: *She mostly wore her sister's hand-me-downs.* ⊃ **compare** CASTOFF ▶ **ˈhand-me-down** *adj.*

hand·off /ˈhændɔf; -ɑf/ *noun* **1** (in football) an act of giving the ball to another player on your team **2** (especially in RUGBY) an act of preventing an opponent from tackling (TACKLE) you by blocking them with your hand while keeping your arm straight

hand·out /ˈhændaʊt/ *noun* **1** (sometimes *disapproving*) food, money, or clothes that are given to a person who is poor **2** (often *disapproving*) money that is given to a person or an organization by the government, etc., for example to encourage commercial activity **3** a free document that gives information about an event or a matter of public interest, or that states the views of a political party, etc. ⊃ **see also** PRESS RELEASE **4** a document that is given to students in class and that contains a summary of the lesson, a set of exercises, etc.

hand·o·ver /ˈhænd oʊvər/ *noun* [C, U] **1** the act of moving power or responsibility from one person or group to another; the period during which this is done: *the smooth handover of power from a military to a civilian government* **2** the act of giving a person or thing to someone in authority: *the handover of the hostages*

hand·picked /ˌhændˈpɪkt/ *adj.* carefully chosen for a special purpose

hand·print /ˈhændprɪnt/ *noun* a mark left by the flat part of someone's hand on a surface

ˈhand ˌpuppet *noun* a type of PUPPET that you put over your hand and move using your fingers ⊃ **picture at** TOY

hand·rail /ˈhændreɪl/ *noun* a long narrow bar that you can hold onto for support, for example when you are going up or down stairs

hand·saw /ˈhændsɔ/ *noun* a SAW (= a tool with a long blade with sharp teeth along one edge) that is used with one hand only ⊃ **picture at** TOOL

ˌhands-ˈdown *adj.* [only before noun] ~ **winner/favorite/choice** (*informal*) easily the winner of a contest; definitely the one that people prefer: *These kits were hands-down favorites with our testers.* **IDM** **see** HAND *n.*

hand·set /ˈhændsɛt/ *noun* the part of a telephone that you hold close to your mouth and ear to speak into and listen ⊃ **compare** RECEIVER

ˈhands-free *adj.* (of a telephone, etc.) able to be used without needing to be held in the hand

hand·shake /ˈhændʃeɪk/ *noun* an act of shaking someone's hand with your own, used especially to say hello or goodbye or when you have made an agreement ⊃ **see also** GOLDEN HANDSHAKE

ˌhands-ˈoff *adj.* [usually before noun] dealing with people or a situation by not becoming involved and by allowing people to do what they want to: *a hands-off approach to staff management* ⊃ **compare** HANDS-ON

hand·some /ˈhænsəm/ *adj.* (**hand·som·er, hand·som·est**) **HELP** **more handsome** and **most handsome** are more common **1** (of men) attractive **SYN** GOOD-LOOKING: *a handsome face* ♦ *He's the most handsome man I've ever met.* ♦ *He was aptly described as "tall, dark, and handsome."* ⊃ note at BEAUTIFUL **2** (of women) attractive, with large strong features rather than small delicate ones: *a tall, handsome woman* ⊃ **thesaurus box at** BEAUTIFUL **3** beautiful to look at: *a handsome horse/house/city* ♦ *The two of them made a handsome couple.* **4** large in amount or quantity: *a handsome profit* ♦ *He was elected by a handsome majority* (= a lot of people voted for him). **5** generous: *She paid him a handsome compliment.* ▶ **hand·some·ly** *adv.*: *a handsomely dressed man* ♦ *a handsomely produced book* ♦ *to be paid/rewarded handsomely* **hand·some·ness** *noun* [U]

ˌhands-ˈon *adj.* [usually before noun] doing something rather than just talking about it: *hands-on computer training* ♦ *to gain hands-on experience in the industry* ♦ *a hands-on style of management* ⊃ **compare** HANDS-OFF

hand·spring /ˈhændsprɪŋ/ *noun* a movement in GYMNASTICS in which you jump through the air landing on your hands, then again landing on your feet

hand·stand /ˈhændstænd/ *noun* a movement in which you balance on your hands and put your legs straight up in the air

ˌhand-to-ˈhand *adj.* **hand-to-hand** fighting involves physical contact with your opponent

ˌhand-to-ˈmouth *adj.* [usually before noun] if you have a **hand-to-mouth** existence, you spend all the money you earn on basic needs such as food and do not have anything left **IDM** **see** LIVE¹

hand·wring·ing /ˈhænd rɪŋɪŋ/ *noun* [U] the behavior that comes from being nervous or worried: *The candidate and her supporters went through a lot of handwringing as they waited to see the results.*

hand·writ·ing /ˈhænd raɪtɪŋ/ *noun* [U] **1** writing that is done with a pen or pencil, not printed or typed **2** a person's particular style of writing in this way: *I can't read his handwriting.* **IDM** **see** WALL *n.*

hand·writ·ten /ˈhænd rɪtn/ *adj.* written by hand, not printed or typed: *a handwritten note*

hand·y /ˈhændi/ *adj.* (**han·di·er, han·di·est**) (*informal*) **1** easy to use or to do **SYN** USEFUL: *a handy little tool* ♦ *handy hints/tips for removing stains* **2** [not before noun] located near to someone or something; located or stored in a convenient place: *Always keep a first-aid kit handy.* ♦ *Do you have a pen handy?* **3** [not before noun] skillful in using your hands or tools to make or repair things: *to be handy around the house* ▶ **hand·i·ness** *noun* [U] **IDM** **come in handy** (*informal*) to be useful: *The extra money came in very handy.* ♦ *Don't throw that away—it might come in handy.*

ˌhandy-ˈdandy *adj.* (*informal, humorous*) very simple and easy to use: *a cell phone with a handy-dandy camera*

hand·y·man /ˈhændi mæn/ *noun* (*pl.* **hand·y·men** /- mɛn/) a man who is good at doing practical jobs inside and outside the house, either as a hobby or as a job

hang /hæŋ/ *verb, noun*
● *verb* (**hung, hung** /hʌŋ/, **HELP** In sense 4, **hanged** is used for the past tense and past participle.)
▷ **ATTACH FROM TOP** **1** [T, I] to attach something, or to be attached, at the top so that the lower part is free or loose: ~ **sth** + *adv./prep.* Hang your coat on the hook. ♦ ~ **sth up** *Should I hang your coat up?* ♦ ~ **sth (out)** *Have you hung the laundry out?* ♦ ~ *adv./prep.* There were several expensive suits hanging in his closet.

> **FALL LOOSELY** **2** [I] **~ adv./prep.** when something **hangs** in a particular way, it falls in that way: *Her hair hung down to her waist.* ◆ *He had lost weight and the suit hung loosely on him.*

> **BEND DOWNWARD** **3** [I, T] to bend or let something bend downward: **~ adv./prep.** *The dog's tongue was hanging out.* ◆ *Children hung* (= were leaning) *over the gate.* ◆ *A cigarette hung from her lips.* ◆ **~ sth** *She hung her head in shame.*

> **KILL SOMEONE** **4** (**hanged, hanged**) [T, I] **~ (sb/yourself)** to kill someone, usually as a punishment, by tying a rope around their neck and allowing them to drop; to be killed in this way: *He was the last man to be hanged for murder in this country.* ◆ *She had committed suicide by hanging herself from a beam.* ◆ *At that time you could hang for stealing.*

> **PICTURES** **5** [T, I] **~ (sth)** to attach something, especially a picture, to a hook on a wall; to be attached in this way: *We hung her portrait above the fireplace.* ◆ *Several of his paintings hang in the Guggenheim Museum.* **6** [T, usually passive] **~ sth with sth** to decorate a place by placing paintings, etc. on a wall: *The rooms were hung with tapestries.*

> **WALLPAPER** **7** [T] **~ sth** to stick WALLPAPER to a wall

> **DOOR/GATE** **8** [T] **~ sth** to attach a door or gate to a post so that it moves freely

> **STAY IN THE AIR** **9** [I] **+ adv./prep.** to stay in the air: *Smoke hung in the air above the city.*

> **SPEND TIIME** **10** [I] (*informal*) to spend a lot of time in a particular place, not doing very much: *We usually hang at Sue's house.*

IDM **hang a left/right** to take a left/right turn **hang by a hair/thread** (of a person's life) to be in great danger **hang in there** (*informal*) to remain determined to succeed even when a situation is difficult **hang on sb's words/on sb's every word** to listen with great attention to someone you admire **hang out your (own) shingle** to start a business as a doctor, lawyer, or other professional **hang tough** to be determined and refuse to change your attitude or ideas **let it all hang out** to express your feelings freely ⊃ more at BALANCE, FIRE, GRIM, HEAVY, LOOSE, PEG

PHR V **hang a'round (…)** (*informal*) to wait or stay near a place, not doing very much: *You hang around here in case he comes, and I'll go on ahead.* **hang a'round with sb** (*informal*) to spend a lot of time with someone **hang 'back** to remain in a place after all the other people have left **hang 'back (from sth)** to hesitate because you are nervous about doing or saying something: *I was sure she knew the answer but for some reason she hung back.* **hang 'on 1** to hold something tightly: *Hang on tight—we're off!* ⊃ thesaurus box at HOLD **2** (*informal*) used to ask someone to wait for a short time or to stop what they are doing: *Hang on—I'm not quite ready.* ◆ *Now hang on a minute—you can't really believe what you just said!* **3** to wait for something to happen: *I haven't heard about the new job yet—they've kept me hanging on for days.* **4** (*informal*) used on the telephone to ask someone who is calling to wait until they can talk to the person they want: *Hang on—I'll just see if he's here.* **5** to continue doing something in difficult circumstances: *The team hung on for victory.* **hang on sth** to depend on something: *A lot hangs on this decision.* **hang 'onto sth 1** to hold something tightly: *Hang onto that rope and don't let go.* **2** (*informal*) to keep something, not sell it or give it away: *Let's hang onto those old photos—they may be valuable.* **hang 'out** (*informal*) to spend a lot of time in a place: *The local kids hang out at the mall.* ⊃ related noun HANGOUT **hang 'out with sb** (*informal*) to spend a lot of time with someone **hang sth↔'out** to attach things that you have washed to a piece of thin rope or wire, etc. outside so that they can dry; to hang something such as a flag outside a window or in the street **hang 'over sb** if something bad or unpleasant is **hanging over** you, you think about it and worry about it a lot because it is happening or might happen: *The possibility of a court case is still hanging over her.* **hang to'gether 1** to fit together well; to be the same as or consistent with each other: *Their accounts of what happened don't hang together.* **2** (of people) to support or help one another **hang 'up** to end a telephone conversation by putting the telephone RECEIVER down or turning the telephone off: *After I hung up*

I remembered what I'd wanted to say. **hang sth↔'up** (*informal*) to finish using something for the last time: *Ruth has hung up her dancing shoes.* **hang 'up on sb** (*informal*) to end a telephone call by suddenly and unexpectedly putting the telephone receiver down or turning the telephone off: *Don't hang up on me—we need to talk!* ⊃ see also HUNG UP **'hang with sb** (*informal*) to spend a lot of time with someone

● **noun** [sing.] the way in which a dress, piece of cloth, etc. falls or moves

IDM **get the hang of sth** (*informal*) to learn how to do or to use something; to understand something: *It's not difficult once you get the hang of it.*

hang·ar /ˈhæŋər; ˈhæŋgər/ *noun* a large building in which aircraft are kept

hang·dog /ˈhæŋdɒg; -dɑg/ *adj.* [only before noun] if a person has a **hangdog** look, they look sad or ashamed

hang·er /ˈhæŋər/ (also **'coat ,hanger, 'clothes ,hanger**) *noun* a curved piece of wood, plastic, or wire, with a hook at the top, that you use to hang clothes up on ⊃ picture at CLOTHES

,hanger-'on *noun* (*pl.* ,hangers-'on) (*often disapproving*) a person who tries to be friendly with a famous person or who goes to important events, in order to get some advantage

'hang-,glider *noun* **1** the frame used in hang-gliding **2** a person who goes hang-gliding

'hang-,gliding *noun* [U] a sport in which you fly while hanging from a frame like a large KITE that you control with your body movements: *to go hang-gliding* ⊃ picture at SPORT

hang·ing /ˈhæŋɪŋ/ *noun* **1** [U, C] the practice of killing someone as a punishment by putting a rope around their neck and hanging them from a high place; an occasion when this happens: *to sentence someone to death by hanging* ◆ *public hangings* **2** [C, usually pl.] a large piece of material that is hung on a wall for decoration: *wall hangings*

,hanging 'valley *noun* (*technical*) a valley which joins a deeper valley, often with a WATERFALL where the two valleys join

hang·man /ˈhæŋmən/ *noun* (*pl.* **hang·men** /-mən/) **1** [U] a game for two people in which one player has to guess the letters of a word that the other person has chosen **2** (*old-fashioned*) a man whose job is to hang criminals

hang·nail /ˈhæŋneɪl/ *noun* a piece of skin near the bottom or at the side of your nail that is loose and sore

hang·out /ˈhæŋaʊt/ *noun* (*informal*) a place where someone lives or likes to go often **SYN** HAUNT

hang·o·ver /ˈhæŋˌoʊvər/ *noun* **1** the headache and sick feeling that you have the day after drinking too much alcohol: *She woke up with a terrible hangover.* **2** [usually sing.] **~ (from sth)** a feeling, custom, idea, etc. that remains from the past, although it is no longer practical or suitable: *the insecure feeling that was a hangover from her childhood* ◆ *hangover laws from the previous administration* ⊃ see also HOLDOVER

the Hang Seng Index /ˌhæŋ ˈsen ˌɪndeks/ *noun* a figure that shows the relative price of shares on the Hong Kong Stock Exchange

'hang-up *noun* (*informal*) **1 ~ (about sth)** an emotional problem about something that makes you embarrassed or worried: *He's got a real hang-up about his height.* **2** a problem that delays something being agreed or achieved

hank /hæŋk/ *noun* a long piece of wool, thread, rope, etc. that is wound into a large loose ball

hank·er /ˈhæŋkər/ *verb* [I] to have a strong desire for something: **~ after/for sth** *He had hankered after fame all his life.* ◆ **~ to do sth** *She hankered to go back to Australia.*

hank·er·ing /ˈhæŋkərɪŋ/ *noun* [usually sing.] **~ (for/after sth)** | **~ (to do sth)** a strong desire: *a hankering for a wealthy lifestyle*

| h hat | m man | n no | ŋ sing | l leg | r red | y yes | w wet |

han·ky (also **han·kie**) /ˈhæŋki/ noun (pl. **han·kies**) (informal)
= HANDKERCHIEF

han·ky-pan·ky /ˌhæŋki ˈpæŋki/ noun [U] (old-fashioned, informal) **1** sexual activity that is not considered acceptable **2** dishonest behavior

han·som /ˈhænsəm/ (also ˌhansom ˈcab) noun a CARRIAGE with two wheels, pulled by one horse, used in the past to carry two passengers

Ha·nuk·kah (also **Cha·nu·kah**) /ˈhɑnəkə; ˈxɑ-/ noun an eight-day Jewish festival and holiday in November or December when Jews remember the occasion when the TEMPLE in Jerusalem was DEDICATED again in 165 B.C.

hap·haz·ard /hæpˈhæzərd/ adj. (disapproving) with no particular order or plan; not organized well: *The books had been piled on the shelves in a haphazard fashion.* ◆ *The government's approach to the problem was haphazard.* ▶ **hap·haz·ard·ly** adv.

hap·less /ˈhæpləs/ adj. [only before noun] (formal) not lucky; unfortunate: *the hapless victims of exploitation*

hap·loid /ˈhæplɔɪd/ adj. (biology) (of a cell) containing the set of CHROMOSOMES from one parent only ⊃ compare DIPLOID

hap·pen 🔑 /ˈhæpən/ verb
1 [I] to take place, especially without being planned: *You'll never guess what's happened!* ◆ *Accidents like this happen all the time.* ◆ *Let's see what happens next week.* ◆ *I'll be there whatever happens.* ◆ *I don't know how this happened.* **2** [I] to take place as the result of something: *She pressed the button but nothing happened.* ◆ *What happens if no one comes to the party?* ◆ *Just plug it in and see what happens.* **3** [T] to do or be something by chance: **~ to be/do sth** *She happened to be out when we called.* ◆ *You don't happen to know his name, do you?* ◆ **it happens that...** *It happened that she was out when we called.* **4** [T] **~ to be sth** used to tell someone something, especially when you are disagreeing with them or annoyed by what they have said: *That happens to be my mother you're talking about!*
IDM **anything can/might happen** used to say that it is not possible to know what the result of something will be **as it happens/happened** used when you say something that is surprising, or something connected with what someone else has just said: *I agree with you, as it happens.* ◆ *As it happens, I have a spare set of keys in my office.* **it (just) so happens that...** by chance: *It just so happened they'd been invited too.* **these things happen** used to tell someone not to worry about something they have done: *"Sorry—I've spilled some wine." "Never mind. These things happen."* ⊃ more at ACCIDENT, EVENT, WAIT
PHR V ˈhappen on sth (old-fashioned) to find something by chance ˈhappen to sb/sth to have an effect on someone or something: *I hope nothing (= nothing unpleasant) has happened to them.* ◆ *It's the best thing that has ever happened to me.* ◆ *What's happened to your car?* ◆ *Do you know what happened to Jill (= do you have any news about her)?*

hap·pen·ing /ˈhæpənɪŋ; ˈhæpnɪŋ/ noun, adj.
● **noun 1** [usually pl.] an event; something that happens, often something unusual: *There have been strange happenings here lately.* **2** an artistic performance or event that is not planned
● **adj.** [only before noun] (informal) where there is a lot of exciting activity; fashionable: *a happening place*

hap·pen·stance /ˈhæpənˌstæns/ noun [U, C] (literary) chance, especially when it results in something good

hap·pi·ly 🔑 /ˈhæpəli/ adv.
1 in a cheerful way; with feelings of pleasure or satisfaction: *children playing happily on the beach* ◆ *to be happily married* ◆ *I think we can manage quite happily on our own.* ◆ *And they all lived happily ever after* (= used as the end of a FAIRY TALE). **2** by good luck **SYN** FORTUNATELY: *Happily, the damage was only slight.* **3** willingly: *I'll happily help, if I can.* **4** (formal) in a way that is suitable or appropriate: *This suggestion did not fit very happily with our existing plans.*

THESAURUS

happy
satisfied ◆ content ◆ contented ◆ joyful ◆ blissful
These words all describe feeling, showing, or giving pleasure or satisfaction.

happy feeling, showing, or giving pleasure; satisfied with something or not worried about it: *a happy marriage/memory/childhood* ◆ *I said I'd go, just to make him happy.*

satisfied pleased because you have achieved something or because something has happened as you wanted it to; showing this satisfaction: *She's never satisfied with what she has.* ◆ *a satisfied smile*

content [not before noun] happy and satisfied with what you have: *I'm perfectly content just to lie in the sun.*

contented happy and comfortable with what you have; showing this: *a contented baby* ◆ *a long, contented sigh*

CONTENT OR CONTENTED?
Being **contented** depends more on having a comfortable life; being **content** can depend more on your attitude to your life: you can *have to be content* or *learn to be content*. People or animals can be **contented** but only people can be **content**.

joyful (somewhat formal) very happy; making people very happy: *They had a joyful reunion in Phoenix.*

blissful (somewhat formal) making people very happy; showing this happiness: *three blissful weeks in Maui*

JOYFUL OR BLISSFUL?
Joy is a livelier feeling; **bliss** is more peaceful.

PATTERNS
- happy/satisfied/content **with** sth
- a happy/satisfied/contented/blissful **smile**
- a happy/joyful **occasion/celebration**
- to **be/feel** happy/satisfied/content/contented/joyful
- **very/perfectly/quite** happy/satisfied/content/contented

hap·py 🔑 /ˈhæpi/ adj.
(hap·pi·er, hap·pi·est)
▸FEELING/GIVING PLEASURE

WORD FAMILY
happy adj. (≠ unhappy)
happily adv. (≠ unhappily)
happiness noun
(≠ unhappiness)

1 feeling or showing pleasure; pleased: *a happy smile/face* ◆ *You don't look very happy today.* ◆ **~ to do sth** *We are happy to announce the engagement of our daughter.* ◆ **~ for sb** *I'm very happy for you.* ◆ **~ (that)...** *I'm happy (that) you could come.* ⊃ thesaurus box at GLAD
2 giving or causing pleasure: *a happy marriage/memory/childhood* ◆ *The story has a happy ending.* ◆ *Those were the happiest days of my life.*
▸AT CELEBRATION **3** if you wish someone a **Happy Birthday**, **Happy New Year**, etc. you mean that you hope they have a pleasant celebration
▸SATISFIED **4** satisfied that something is good or right; not anxious: **~ (with sb/sth)** *Are you happy with that arrangement?* ◆ *I'm not happy with his work this term.* ◆ *She was happy enough with her performance.* ◆ **~ (about sb/sth)** *If there's anything you're not happy about, come and ask.* ◆ *I'm not too happy about her living alone.* ◆ *I said I'd go just to keep him happy.*
▸WILLING **5** **~ to do sth** (formal) willing or pleased to do something: *I'm happy to leave it till tomorrow.* ◆ *He will be more than happy to come with us.*
▸LUCKY **6** lucky; successful **SYN** FORTUNATE: *By a happy coincidence, we arrived at exactly the same time.* ◆ *He is in the happy position of never having to worry about money.*
▸SUITABLE **7** (formal) (of words, ideas, or behavior) suitable and appropriate for a particular situation: *That wasn't the happiest choice of words.*

▶ **hap·pi·ness** *noun* [U]: *to find true happiness* ◆ *Her eyes shine with happiness.* ➔ thesaurus box at SATISFACTION **IDM (as) happy as a clam** (*informal*) very happy: *Thomas was as happy as a clam when the test was canceled.* **a happy camper** (*informal*) (especially after a negative) pleased about a situation: *She wasn't a happy camper at all.* **the happy event** (*old-fashioned*) the birth of a baby **a/the happy medium** something that is in the middle between two choices or two ways of doing something **many happy returns (of the day)** used to wish someone a happy and pleasant birthday

happy-go-'lucky *adj.* not caring or worrying about the future: *a happy-go-lucky attitude* ◆ *a happy-go-lucky sort of person*

'happy ,hour *noun* [usually sing.] (*informal*) a time, usually in the early evening, when a bar sells alcoholic drinks at lower prices than usual

hap·tic /'hæptɪk/ *adj.* (*technical*) relating to or involving the sense of touch: *Players use a haptic device such as a joystick to control the game.*

ha·ra-ki·ri /,hæ; rə 'kɪri; ,hɑrə-/ *noun* [U] (from *Japanese*) an act of killing yourself by cutting open your stomach with a SWORD, performed especially by the SAMURAI in Japan in the past, to avoid losing honor

ha·rangue /hə'ræŋ/ *verb, noun*
● *verb* ~ **sb** to speak loudly and angrily in a way that criticizes someone or something or tries to persuade people to do something
● *noun* a long, loud, angry speech that criticizes someone or something or tries to persuade people to do something

ha·rass /hə'ræs; 'hærəs/ *verb* **1** [often passive] ~ **sb** to annoy or worry someone by putting pressure on them or saying or doing unpleasant things to them: *He has complained of being harassed by the police.* ◆ *She claims she has been sexually harassed at work.* **2** ~ **sb/sth** to make repeated attacks on an enemy **SYN** HARRY ▶ **ha·rass·ment** *noun* [U]: *racial/ sexual harassment*

ha·rassed /hə'ræst; 'hærəst/ *adj.* tired and anxious because you have too much to do: *a harassed-looking waiter* ◆ *harassed mothers with their children*

har·bin·ger /'hɑrbəndʒər/ *noun* ~ **(of sth)** (*formal* or *literary*) a sign that shows that something is going to happen soon, often something bad

har·bor (*CanE usually* **har·bour**) /'hɑrbər/ *noun, verb*
● *noun* [C, U] an area of water on the coast, protected from the open ocean by strong walls, where ships can shelter: *Several boats lay at anchor in the harbor.* ◆ *to enter/leave harbor*
● *verb* **1** ~ **sb** to hide and protect someone who is hiding from the police: *Police believe someone must be harboring the killer.* **2** ~ **sth** to keep feelings or thoughts, especially negative ones, in your mind for a long time: *The arsonist may harbor a grudge against the company.* ◆ *She began to harbor doubts about the decision.* **3** ~ **sth** to contain something and allow it to develop: *Your dishcloth can harbor many germs.*

hard 🔊 /hɑrd/ *adj., adv.*
● *adj.* (**hard·er, hard·est**)
> SOLID/STIFF **1** solid, firm, or stiff and difficult to bend or break: *Wait for the concrete to go hard.* ◆ *a hard mattress* ◆ *Diamonds are the hardest known mineral.* **ANT** SOFT
> DIFFICULT **2** difficult to do, understand, or answer: *a hard choice/question* ◆ ~ **to do sth** *It is hard to believe that she's only nine.* ◆ *It's hard to see how they can lose.* ◆ *"When will the job be finished?" "It's hard to say."* (= it is difficult to be certain) ◆ *I find his attitude very hard to take* (= difficult to accept). ◆ *We're finding reliable staff hard to come by* (= difficult to get). ◆ ~ **for sb (to do sth)** *It's hard for old people to change their ways.* ◆ *It must be hard for her, bringing up four children on her own.* **ANT** EASY **3** full of difficulty and problems, especially because of a lack of money **SYN** TOUGH: *Times were hard at the end of the war.* ◆ *She's had a hard life.* **ANT** EASY
> NEEDING/USING EFFORT **4** needing or using a lot of physical strength or mental effort: *It's hard work shoveling snow.* ◆ *I've*

had a long hard day. ➔ thesaurus box at DIFFICULT **5** (of people) putting a lot of effort or energy into an activity: *She's a very hard worker.* ◆ *He's hard at work on a new novel.* ◆ *When I left they were all still hard at it* (= working hard). ➔ note at DIFFICULT **6** done with a lot of strength or force: *He gave the door a good hard kick.* ◆ *a hard punch*
> WITHOUT SYMPATHY **7** showing no sympathy or affection: *My father was a hard man.* ◆ *She gave me a hard stare.*
> FACTS/EVIDENCE **8** [only before noun] definitely true and based on information that can be proved: *Is there any hard evidence either way?* ◆ *The newspaper story is based on hard facts.*
> WEATHER **9** very cold and severe: *It had been a hard winter.* ◆ *There was a hard frost that night.* ➔ compare MILD
> DRINK **10** [only before noun] strongly alcoholic: *hard liquor* ◆ (*informal*) *a drop of the hard stuff* (= a strong alcoholic drink) ➔ compare SOFT DRINK
> WATER **11** containing CALCIUM and other mineral salts that make mixing with soap difficult: *a hard water area* ◆ *Our water is very hard.* **ANT** SOFT
> CONSONANTS **12** (*phonetics*) used to describe a letter *c* or *g* when pronounced as in "cat" or "go," rather than as in "city" or "giant" **ANT** SOFT

▶ **hard·ness** *noun* [U]: *water hardness* ◆ *hardness of heart* **IDM be hard on sb/sth 1** to treat or criticize someone in a very severe or strict way: *Don't be too hard on him—he's very young.* **2** to be difficult for or unfair to someone or something: *It's hard on people who don't have a car.* **3** to be likely to hurt or damage something: *Looking at a computer screen all day can be very hard on the eyes.* **fall on hard times** to find yourself in a bad situation in which you have many problems, usually about money: *After he lost his job, Mark had fallen on hard times.* **drive/strike a hard bargain** to argue in an aggressive way and force someone to agree on the best possible price or arrangement **give sb a hard time** to deliberately make a situation difficult and unpleasant for someone: *They really gave me a hard time at the interview.* **hard and fast** (especially after a negative) that cannot be changed in any circumstances: *There are no hard and fast rules about this.* **(as) hard as nails** showing no sympathy, kindness, or fear **hard going** difficult to understand or needing a lot of effort: *I'm finding his latest novel very hard going.* **the hard way** by having an unpleasant experience or by making mistakes: *She won't listen to my advice so she'll just have to learn the hard way.* **make hard work of sth** to use more time or energy on a task than is necessary **no hard feelings** used to tell someone you have been arguing with or have beaten in a contest that you would still like to be friendly with them: *It looks like I'm the winner again. No hard feelings, Dave, right?* **play hard to get** (*informal*) to make yourself seem more attractive or interesting by not immediately accepting an invitation to do something ➔ more at ACT *n.*, NUT, ROCK *n.*
● *adv.* (**hard·er, hard·est**)
> WITH EFFORT **1** with great effort; with difficulty: *to work hard* ◆ *You must try harder.* ◆ *She tried her hardest not to show how disappointed she was.* ◆ *Don't hit it so hard!* ◆ *He was still breathing hard after his run.* ◆ *Our victory was hard won* (= won with great difficulty).
> WITH FORCE **2** with great force: (*figurative*) *Small businesses have been hit hard / hard hit by the recession.*
> CAREFULLY **3** very carefully and thoroughly: *to think hard* ◆ *We thought long and hard before deciding to move into a new house.*
> A LOT **4** heavily; a lot or for a long time: *It was raining hard when we set off.*
> LEFT/RIGHT **5** at a sharp angle to the left/right: *Make a hard right at the next intersection.*
IDM be hard pressed/pushed/put to do sth to find it very difficult to do something: *He was hard put to explain her disappearance.* **be hard up for sth** to have too few or too little of something: *We're hard up for ideas.* ➔ see also HARD UP **hard on sth** very soon after: *His death followed hard on hers.* **take sth hard** to be very upset by something: *He took his wife's death very hard.* ➔ more at DIE *v.*, HEEL *n.*

ʌ cup   ə about   eɪ say   aɪ five   ɔɪ boy   aʊ now   oʊ go   ər bird

hard ◆ hardly

- The adverb from the adjective **hard** is hard: *I have to work hard today.* ◆ *She has thought very hard about her future plans.* ◆ *It was raining hard outside.*
- **Hardly** is an adverb meaning "almost not": *I hardly ever go to concerts.* ◆ *I can hardly wait for my birthday.* It cannot be used instead of **hard**: *I've been working hardly today.* ◆ *She has thought very hardly about her future plans.* ◆ *It was raining hardly outside.*
- ⊃ note at HARDLY

hard·back /'hɑrdbæk/ *noun* = HARDCOVER

hard·ball /'hɑrdbɔl/ *noun* **1** the game of baseball (when contrasted with SOFTBALL) **2** used to refer to a way of behaving, especially in politics, that shows that a person is determined to get what they want: *I want us to play hardball on this issue.* ◆ *hardball politics*

hard·bit·ten /ˌhɑrd'bɪtn/ *adj.* not easily shocked and not showing emotion, because you have experienced many unpleasant things

hard·board /'hɑrdbɔrd/ *noun* [U] a type of stiff board made by crushing very small pieces of wood together into thin sheets

hard-'boiled *adj.* **1** (of an egg) boiled until the inside is hard ⊃ compare SOFT-BOILED **2** (of people) not showing much emotion

hard·bound /'hɑrdbaʊnd/ *adj.* (of a book) having a hard cover, usually of stiff paper or cloth

hard 'by *prep.* (*old-fashioned*) very near something ▸ **hard 'by** *adv.*

hard 'candy *noun* [U] a firm candy made from boiled sugar, often with fruit flavors

hard 'cash *noun* = COLD CASH

hard-'charging *adj.* [only before noun] working or performing with a lot of energy and skill: *He changed from a goofy kid to a hard-charging soldier.*

hard 'cider *noun* [U, C] an alcoholic drink made from the juice of apples

hard-'code *verb* [T] ~ sth (*computing*) to write data so that it cannot easily be changed

hard 'copy *noun* [U, C] (*computing*) information from a computer that has been printed on paper

hard-'core *adj.* [only before noun] **1** having a belief or a way of behaving that will not change: *hard-core party members* **2** showing or describing sexual activity in a detailed or violent way: *They sell hard-core pornography.* ⊃ compare SOFT-CORE

hard court *noun* an area with a hard surface for playing TENNIS on, not grass

hard·cov·er /'hɑrdˌkʌvər/ (also hard·back) *noun* [C, U] a book that has a stiff cover: *What's the price of the hardcover?* ◆ *It was published in hardcover last year.* ◆ *hardcover books/ editions* ⊃ compare PAPERBACK

hard 'currency *noun* [U, C] money that is easy to exchange for money from another country, because it is not likely to lose its value

hard 'disk *noun* a disk inside a computer that stores data and programs ⊃ compare FLOPPY DISK

hard disk re'corder *noun* a digital recording system that records sound or video directly to a hard disk, without using tape

hard-'drinking *adj.* drinking a lot of alcohol

hard 'drive *noun* (*computing*) a part of a computer that reads data on a HARD DISK

hard 'drug *noun* [usually pl.] a powerful illegal drug, such as HEROIN, that some people take for pleasure and can become ADDICTED to ⊃ compare SOFT DRUG

hard-'earned *adj.* that you get only after a lot of work and effort: *hard-earned cash* ◆ *We finally pulled off a hard-earned victory.*

hard-'edged *adj.* powerful, true to life, and not affected by emotion: *the movie's hard-edged realism*

hard·en /'hɑrdn/ *verb* **1** [I, T] to become or make something become firm, stiff, or solid: *The varnish takes a few hours to harden.* ◆ ~ sth *a method for hardening and preserving wood* **2** [I, T] if your voice, face, etc. **hardens**, or you **harden** it, it becomes more serious or severe: *Her face hardened into an expression of hatred.* ◆ ~ sth *He hardened his voice when he saw she wasn't listening.* **3** [I, T] if someone's feelings or attitudes **harden** or someone or something **hardens** them, they become more fixed and determined: *Public attitudes to the strike have hardened.* ◆ *Their suspicions hardened into certainty.* ◆ ~ sth *The incident hardened her resolve to leave the company.* **4** [T, usually passive] ~ sb/sth/yourself to make someone less kind or less affected by extreme situations: *Joe sounded different, hardened by the war.* ◆ *They were hardened criminals* (= they showed no regret for their crimes). ◆ *In this job you have to harden your heart to pain and suffering.* ▸ **hardening** *noun* [U, sing.]: *hardening of the arteries* ◆ *a hardening of attitudes toward one-parent families*

hard-'fought *adj.* that involves fighting very hard: *a hard-fought battle/win/victory*

hard hat *noun* a hat worn by building workers, etc. to protect their heads ⊃ picture at HAT

hard·head·ed /ˌhɑrd'hɛdəd/ *adj.* determined and not allowing your emotions to affect your decisions

hard-'hearted *adj.* giving no importance to the feelings or problems of other people ⊃ compare SOFT-HEARTED

hard-'hitting *adj.* not afraid to talk about or criticize someone or something in an honest and very direct way: *a hard-hitting speech*

hard 'labor *noun* [U] punishment in prison that involves a lot of very hard physical work

hard 'line *noun* [sing.] a strict policy or attitude: *the judge's hard line against drug dealers* ◆ *The government took a hard line on the strike.*

hard-'line *adj.* [usually before noun] **1** (of a person) having very fixed beliefs and being unlikely or unwilling to change them: *a hard-line conservative* **2** (of ideas) very fixed and unlikely to change: *a hard-line attitude* ▸ **hard-'liner** *noun*: *a Republican hard-liner*

hard-'luck ˌstory *noun* a story about yourself that you tell someone in order to get their sympathy or help

hardly ◆ scarcely ◆ barely ◆ no sooner

- **Hardly**, **scarcely**, and **barely** can all be used to say that something is almost untrue or almost impossible. They are used with words like *any* and *anyone*, with adjectives and verbs, and are often placed between *can*, *could*, *have*, *be*, etc. and the main verb: *They have sold hardly any copies of the book.* ◆ *We had scarcely any time between dinner and the show.* ◆ *I barely recognized her.* ◆ *His words were barely audible.* ◆ *I can hardly believe it.* ◆ *I hardly can believe it.*
- **Hardly**, **scarcely**, and **barely** are negative words and should not be used with *not* or other negatives: *I can't hardly believe it.*
- You can also use **hardly**, **scarcely**, and **barely** to say that one thing happens immediately after another: *We had hardly/scarcely/barely sat down at the table, when the phone rang.* In formal, written English, especially in a literary style, these words can be placed at the beginning of the sentence and then the subject and verb are turned around: *Hardly/Scarcely had we sat down at the table, when the phone rang.* Note that you usually use *when* in these sentences, not *than*. You can also use *before*: *I scarcely had time to ring the bell before*

the door opened. **No sooner** can be used in the same way, but is always used with *than*: *No sooner had we sat down at the table than the phone rang.*

■ **Hardly** and **scarcely** can be used to mean "almost never," but **barely** is not used in this way: *She hardly (ever) sees her parents these days.* ◆ ~~She barely sees her parents these days.~~

hard·ly 🔊 /ˈhɑrdli/ *adv.*

1 almost no; almost none: *There's* **hardly** *any coffee left.* ◆ **Hardly** *anyone has bothered to reply.* ◆ *She* **hardly** *ever calls me* (= almost never). ◆ *We* **hardly** *know each other.* ◆ **Hardly** *a day goes by when I don't think about her* (= I think of her almost every day). **2** used especially after "can" or "could" and before the main verb, to emphasize that it is difficult to do something: *I can* **hardly** *keep my eyes open* (= I'm almost falling asleep). ◆ *I could* **hardly** *believe it when I read the letter.* **3** used to say that something has just begun, happened, etc.: *We can't stop for coffee now, we've* **hardly** *started.* ◆ *We had* **hardly** *sat down to supper when the phone rang.* ◆ *(formal)* **Hardly** *had she spoken than she regretted it bitterly.* **4** used to suggest that something is unlikely or unreasonable or that someone is silly for saying or doing something: *He is* **hardly** *likely to admit he was wrong.* ◆ *It's* **hardly** *surprising she was fired; she never did any work.* ◆ *It's* **hardly** *the time to discuss it now.* ◆ *You* **can hardly** *expect her to do it for free.* ◆ *"Couldn't you have just said no?" "Well,* **hardly** (= of course not), *she's my wife's sister."* ⊃ note at HARD

hard news *noun* [U] serious or important news stories: *Julia became a journalist so she could travel to war zones and report hard news.*

hard-nosed *adj.* not affected by feelings when trying to get what you want: *a hard-nosed journalist*

hard of hearing *adj.* [not before noun] **1** unable to hear very well **2 the hard of hearing** *noun* [pl.] people who are unable to hear very well: *subtitles for the deaf and the hard of hearing*

hard-pressed *adj.* **1** having a lot of problems, especially too much work, and too little time or money **2** ~ **to do sth** finding something very difficult to do: *You would be hard-pressed to find a better accountant.*

hard rock *noun* [U] a type of loud rock music with a very strong beat, played on electric GUITAR

hard science *noun* **1** [U] science that is based on the objective measurement and observation of physical facts or events **2** [C] a science that involves the objective measurement and observation of physical facts or events, such as physics and chemistry

hard·scrab·ble /ˈhɑrdˌskræbl/ *adj.* not having enough of the basic things you need to live: *a hardscrabble life/upbringing*

hard sell *noun* [sing.] a method of selling that puts a lot of pressure on the customer to buy ⊃ compare SOFT SELL

hard·ship /ˈhɑrdʃɪp/ *noun* [U, C] a situation that is difficult and unpleasant because you do not have enough money, food, clothes, etc.: *economic/financial, etc. hardship* ◆ *People suffered many hardships during that long winter.* ◆ *It was* **no hardship** *to walk home on such a beautiful night.*

hard·top /ˈhɑrdtɑp/ *noun* a car with a metal roof ⊃ see also SOFT TOP

hard up *adj.* *(informal)* **1** having very little money, especially for a short period of time ⊃ thesaurus box at POOR **2** ~ **(for sth)** lacking in something interesting to do, talk about, etc.: *"You could always go out with Steve." "I'm not that hard up!"*

hard·ware /ˈhɑrdwɛr/ *noun* [U] **1** *(computing)* the machinery and electronic parts of a computer system ⊃ compare SOFTWARE **2** tools and equipment that are used in the house and yard: *a hardware store* **3** the equipment, machinery, and vehicles used to do something: *tanks and other military hardware*

hardware store *noun* a store that sells tools and equipment for the house and yard

hard-wired *adj.* **1** *(technical)* (of computer functions) built into the permanent system and not provided by software **2** (of a skill, quality, or type of behavior) present when you are born and not changing during your life: *Many aspects of morality appear to be hard-wired in the brain.*

hard-won *adj.* [usually before noun] that you only get after fighting or working hard for it: *She was not going to give up her hard-won freedom so easily.*

hard·wood /ˈhɑrdwʊd/ *noun* [U, C] hard, heavy wood from a BROADLEAVED tree ⊃ compare SOFTWOOD

hard-working (also **hard·work·ing**) /ˌhɑrdˈwɜrkɪŋ/ *adj.* putting a lot of effort into a job and doing it well: *hard-working nurses*

har·dy /ˈhɑrdi/ *adj.* (**har·di·er**, **har·di·est**) **1** strong and able to survive difficult conditions and bad weather: *a hardy breed of sheep* **2** (of a plant) that can live outside through the winter ▶ **har·di·ness** *noun* [U]

hare /hɛr/ *noun* an animal like a large RABBIT with very strong back legs, that can run very fast ⊃ picture at RABBIT
IDM see MAD

hare·brained /ˈhɛrbreɪnd/ *adj.* *(informal)* crazy and unlikely to succeed: *a harebrained scheme/idea/theory*

Ha·re Krish·na /ˌhɑri ˈkrɪʃnə; ˌhæri-/ *noun* **1** [U] a religious group whose members wear orange ROBES and use the name of the Hindu god Krishna in their worship **2** [C] a member of this religious group

hare·lip /ˈhɛrlɪp/ *noun* an old-fashioned and now offensive word for CLEFT LIP

har·em /ˈhɛrəm/ *noun* **1** the women or wives belonging to a rich man, especially in some Muslim societies in the past **2** the separate part of a traditional Muslim house where the women live **3** *(technical)* a group of female animals that share the same male for reproducing

hark /hɑrk/ *verb* [I] *(old use)* used only as an order to tell someone to listen
PHRV **hark back (to sth)** **1** to remember or talk about something that happened in the past: *She's always harking back to how things used to be.* **2** to remind you of, or to be like, something in the past: *The newest styles hark back to the clothes of the Seventies.*

hark·en = HEARKEN

Har·le·quin /ˈhɑrləkwən; -kən/ *noun* an amusing character in some traditional plays, who wears special brightly colored clothes with a diamond pattern

har·lot /ˈhɑrlət/ *noun* *(old use, disapproving)* a PROSTITUTE, or a woman who looks and behaves like one

harm 🔊 /hɑrm/ *noun, verb*

• *noun* [U] damage or injury that is caused by a person or an event: *He would never frighten anyone or* **cause** *them* **any harm.** ◆ *He may look fierce, but he* **means no harm.** ◆ *The court case will* **do serious harm** *to my business.* ◆ *The accident could have been much worse; luckily* **no harm was done.** ◆ *Don't worry, we'll see that the children* **come to no harm.** ◆ *I can't say I like Mark very much, but I don't* **wish him any harm.** ◆ *Hard work* **never did anyone any harm.** ◆ *Look, we're just going out for a few drinks,* **where's the harm in that?** ◆ *The treatment they gave him did him* **more harm than good.**
IDM **it wouldn't do sb any harm (to do sth)** used to suggest that it would be a good idea for someone to do something: *It wouldn't do you any harm to clean yourself up.* **no harm done** *(informal)* used to tell someone not to worry because they have caused no serious damage or injury **out of harm's way** in a safe place where someone or something cannot be hurt or injured or do any damage to someone or something **there is no harm in (sb's) doing sth | it does no harm (for sb) to do sth** used to tell someone that something is a good idea and will not cause any problems: *He may say no, but there's no harm in asking.* ◆ *It does no harm to ask.*

| t **tea** | ţ **butter** | d **did** | k **cat** | g **got** | tʃ **chin** | dʒ **June** | f **fall**

- **verb** ~ **sb/sth** to hurt or injure someone or to damage something: *He would never harm anyone.* ◆ *Pollution can harm marine life.* ◆ *These revelations will harm her chances of winning the election.* **IDM** see HAIR ⟳ thesaurus box at DAMAGE

harm·ful 🔊 /ˈhɑːmfl/ *adj.*
causing damage or injury to someone or something, especially to a person's health or to the environment: *the harmful effects of alcohol* ◆ *the sun's harmful ultraviolet rays* ◆ *Many household products are potentially harmful.* ◆ ~ **to sb/ sth** *Fruit juices can be harmful to children's teeth.* ▶ **harm·ful·ly** /-fəli/ *adv.* **harm·ful·ness** *noun* [U]

harm·less 🔊 /ˈhɑːmləs/ *adj.*
1 ~ **(to sb/sth)** unable or unlikely to cause damage or harm: *The bacteria is harmless to humans.* **2** unlikely to upset or offend anyone **SYN** INNOCUOUS: *It's just a little harmless fun.* ▶ **harm·less·ly** *adv.*: *The missile fell harmlessly into the ocean.* **harm·less·ness** *noun* [U]

har·mon·ic /hɑːˈmɑnɪk/ *adj., noun*
- *adj.* [usually before noun] (*music*) relating to the way notes are played or sung together to make a pleasing sound
- *noun* [usually pl.] (*music*) **1** a note that sounds together with the main note being played and is higher and quieter than that note **2** a high, quiet note that can be played on some instruments like the VIOLIN by touching the string very lightly

har·mon·i·ca /hɑːˈmɑnɪkə/ (also *old-fashioned* ˈmouth ˌorgan) *noun* a small musical instrument that you hold near your mouth and play by blowing or sucking air through it ⟳ picture at INSTRUMENT

har·mo·ni·ous /hɑːˈmoʊniəs/ *adj.* **1** (of relationships, etc.) friendly, peaceful, and without any disagreement **ANT** INHARMONIOUS **2** arranged together in a pleasing way so that each part goes well with the others **SYN** PLEASING: *a harmonious combination of colors* **ANT** INHARMONIOUS **3** (of sounds) very pleasant when played or sung together ▶ **har·mo·ni·ous·ly** *adv.*: *They worked very harmoniously together.*

har·mo·ni·um /hɑːˈmoʊniəm/ *noun* a musical instrument like a small organ. Air is forced through metal pipes to produce the sound and the different notes are played on the keyboard.

har·mo·nize /ˈhɑːmənaɪz/ *verb* **1** [I] ~ **(with sth)** if two or more things **harmonize** with each other or one thing **harmonizes** with the other, the things go well together and produce an attractive result: *The new building does not harmonize with its surroundings.* **2** [T] ~ **sth** to make systems or rules similar in different countries or organizations: *the need to harmonize international accounting standards* **3** [I] ~ **(with sb/sth)** to play or sing music that combines with the main tune to make a pleasing sound ▶ **har·mo·ni·za·tion** /ˌhɑːmənəˈzeɪʃn/ *noun* [U, C]

Harmonized ˈSales Tax *noun* (*CanE*) = HST

har·mo·ny /ˈhɑːməni/ *noun* (*pl.* **har·mo·nies**) **1** [U] a state of peaceful existence and agreement: *the need to be in harmony with our environment* ◆ *to live together in perfect harmony* ◆ *social/racial harmony* ⟳ compare DISCORD **2** [U, C] (*music*) the way in which different notes that are played or sung together combine to make a pleasing sound: *to sing in harmony* ◆ *to study four-part harmony* ◆ *passionate lyrics and stunning vocal harmonies* ⟳ compare DISCORD **3** [C, U] a pleasing combination of related things: *the harmony of color in nature*

har·ness /ˈhɑːnəs/ *noun, verb*
- *noun* **1** a set of strips of leather and metal pieces that is put around a horse's head and body so that the horse can be controlled and fastened to a CARRIAGE, etc. **2** a set of strips of leather, etc. for fastening something to a person's body or to keep them from moving off or falling: *a safety harness*
- *verb* **1** to put a harness on a horse or other animal; to attach a horse or other animal to something with a harness: ~ **sth** *to harness a horse* ◆ ~ **sth to sth** *We harnessed two ponies to the cart.* ◆ (*figurative*) *In some areas, the poor feel*

harnessed to their jobs. **2** ~ **sth** to control and use the force or strength of something to produce power or to achieve something: *attempts to harness the sun's rays as a source of energy* ◆ *We must harness the skill and creativity of our workforce.*

harp /hɑːp/ *noun, verb*
- *noun* a large musical instrument with strings stretched on a vertical frame, played with the fingers ⟳ picture at INSTRUMENT ⟳ see also JEW'S HARP
- *verb*
  PHR V ˌharp ˈon (about sth) | ˈharp on sth to keep talking about something in a boring or annoying way

harp·ist /ˈhɑːpɪst/ *noun* a person who plays the harp

har·poon /hɑːˈpuːn/ *noun, verb*
- *noun* a weapon like a SPEAR that you can throw or fire from a gun and is used for catching large fish, WHALES, etc.
- *verb* ~ **sth** to hit something with a harpoon

harp·si·chord /ˈhɑːpsɪˌkɔːd/ *noun* an early type of musical instrument similar to a piano, but with strings that are PLUCKED (=pulled), not hit

harp·si·chord·ist /ˈhɑːpsɪˌkɔːdɪst/ *noun* a person who plays the harpsichord

har·py /ˈhɑːpi/ *noun* (*pl.* **har·pies**) **1** (in ancient Greek and Roman stories) a cruel creature with a woman's head and body and a bird's wings and feet **2** a cruel woman

har·ri·dan /ˈhærədən/ *noun* (*old-fashioned* or *literary*) a bad-tempered, unpleasant woman

har·ri·er /ˈhæriər/ *noun* a BIRD OF PREY (= a bird that kills other creatures for food) of the HAWK family

har·row /ˈhæroʊ/ *noun* a piece of farming equipment that is pulled over land that has been PLOWED to break up the earth before planting ▶ **harrow** *verb* ~ **sth**

har·row·ing /ˈhæroʊɪŋ/ *adj.* very shocking or frightening and making you feel very upset

har·rumph /həˈrʌmf/ *verb* [I] (*informal*) to express disagreement or disapproval, especially by making a sound in your throat like a cough ▶ **harrumph** *noun* [sing.]

har·ry /ˈhæri/ *verb* (**har·ries, har·ry·ing, har·ried, har·ried**) **1** ~ **sb** to annoy or upset someone by continuously asking them questions or for something **SYN** HARASS: *She has been harried by the press all week.* **2** ~ **sb/sth** to make repeated attacks on an enemy **SYN** HARASS

harsh /hɑːʃ/ *adj.* (**harsh·er, harsh·est**) **1** cruel, severe, and unkind: *The punishment was harsh and unfair.* ◆ *The minister received some harsh criticism.* ◆ *the harsh treatment of slaves* ◆ *He regretted his harsh words.* ◆ *We had to face up to the harsh realities of life sooner or later.* **2** (of weather or living conditions) very difficult and unpleasant to live in: *a harsh winter/wind/climate* ◆ *the harsh conditions of poverty which existed for most people at that time* **3** too strong and bright; ugly or unpleasant to look at: *harsh colors* ◆ *She was caught in the harsh glare of the headlights.* ◆ *the harsh lines of concrete buildings* **ANT** SOFT **4** unpleasant to listen to: *a harsh voice* **5** too strong and rough and likely to damage something: *harsh detergents* ▶ **harsh·ly** *adv.*: *She was treated very harshly.* ◆ *Alec laughed harshly.* **harsh·ness** *noun* [U]

hart /hɑːt/ *noun* a male DEER, especially a RED DEER; a STAG ⟳ compare BUCK, HIND

har·um-scar·um /ˌhærəm ˈskɛrəm/ *adj.* (*old-fashioned*) behaving in a wild and sometimes careless way

har·vest /ˈhɑːvəst/ *noun, verb*
- *noun* **1** [C, U] the time of year when the crops are gathered in on a farm, etc.; the act of cutting and gathering crops: *harvest time* ◆ *Farmers are extremely busy during the harvest.* **2** [C] the crops, or the amount of crops, cut and gathered: *the grain harvest* ◆ *a good/bad harvest* (= a lot of crops or few crops) ◆ (*figurative*) *The appeal produced a rich harvest of blankets, medicines, and clothing.* **IDM** see REAP
- *verb* **1** [I, T] ~ **(sth)** to cut and gather a crop; to catch a number of animals or fish to eat ⟳ collocations at FARMING **2** [T] ~ **sth** (*medical*) to collect cells or TISSUE from

someone's body for use in medical experiments or operations: *She had her eggs harvested and frozen for her own future use.*

har·vest·er /ˈhɑrvəstər/ *noun* **1** a machine that cuts and gathers grain ⊃ **see also** COMBINE HARVESTER **2** (*old-fashioned*) a person who helps to gather in the crops

'harvest ˌfestival *noun* a service held in Christian churches when people thank God for the crops that have been gathered ⊃ **compare** THANKSGIVING

ˌharvest 'moon *noun* [sing.] a full moon in the fall nearest the time when day and night are of equal length ⊃ compare FULL MOON, HALF-MOON

has /həz; əz; z; hæz/ ⊃ HAVE

has-been /ˈhæz bɪn/ *noun* (*informal, disapproving*) a person who is no longer as famous, successful, or important as they used to be

hash /hæʃ/ *noun, verb*
● *noun* **1** [U, C] a hot dish of cooked meat and potatoes that are cut into small pieces and mixed together **2** [U] (*informal*) = HASHISH
   IDM **make a hash of sth** (*informal*) to do something badly: *I made a real hash of the interview.*
● *verb*
   PHR V **hash sth↔'out** (*informal*) to discuss something thoroughly in order to reach an agreement or decide something

ˌhash 'browns *noun* [pl.] a dish of chopped potatoes and onions, fried until they are brown

hash·ish /hæˈʃiʃ; ˈhæʃiʃ/ (also *informal* hash) *noun* [U] a drug made from the RESIN of the HEMP plant, which gives a feeling of being relaxed when it is smoked or chewed. Use of the drug is illegal in many countries. **SYN** CANNABIS

Has·i·dism (also **Has·si·dism**) /ˈhɑsɪˌdɪzəm; ˈxɑ-/ *noun* [U] a form of the Jewish religion which has very strict beliefs
   ▶ **Ha·sid** (also **Has·sid**) /ˈhɑsɪd; ˈxɑ-/ *noun* **Ha·sid·ic** (also **Has·sid·ic**) /həˈsɪdɪk; xɑ-/ *adj.*

has·n't /ˈhæznt/ *short form* has not

hasp /hæsp/ *noun* a flat piece of metal with a long narrow hole in it, used with a PADLOCK to fasten doors, boxes, etc.

Has·si·dism = HASIDISM

has·si·um /ˈhæsiəm/ *noun* [U] (*symb.* Hs) a chemical element. Hassium is produced when atoms COLLIDE (= crash into each other).

has·sle /ˈhæsl/ *noun, verb*
● *noun* [C, U] (*informal*) **1** a situation that is annoying because it involves doing something difficult or complicated that needs a lot of effort: *Send them an e-mail—it's a lot less hassle than calling.* ◆ *legal hassles* **2** a situation in which people disagree, argue, or annoy you: *Do as you're told and don't give me any hassle!*
● *verb* ~ **sb (for sth/to do sth)** (*informal*) to annoy someone or cause them trouble, especially by asking them to do something many times **SYN** BOTHER: *Don't keep hassling me! I'll do it later.*

has·sock /ˈhæsək/ *noun* **1** a large thick CUSHION used as a seat or for resting your feet on **2** a thick firm CUSHION on which you rest your knees when saying prayers in a church

hast /hæst/ **thou hast** (*old use*) a way of saying "you have"

haste /heɪst/ *noun* [U] (*formal*) speed in doing something, especially because you do not have enough time **SYN** HURRY: *In her haste to complete the work on time, she made a number of mistakes.* ◆ *The letter had clearly been written in haste.* ◆ *After his first wife died, he married again with almost indecent haste.* ◆ (*old-fashioned*) *She made haste to open the door.* **IDM** see MARRY

has·ten /ˈheɪsn/ *verb* **1** [I] ~ **to do sth** to say or do something without delay: *She saw his frown and hastened to explain.* ◆ *He has been described as a "charmless bore"—not by me, I hasten to add.* **2** [T] ~ **sth** (*formal*) to make something happen sooner or more quickly: *The treatment she received*

may, in fact, have hastened her death. ◆ *News of the scandal certainly hastened his departure from office.* **3** [I] + **adv./prep.** (*literary*) to go or move somewhere quickly **SYN** HURRY

hast·y /ˈheɪsti/ *adj.* (**hasti·er, hasti·est**) **1** said, made, or done very quickly, especially when this has bad results **SYN** HURRIED: *a hasty departure/meal/farewell* ◆ *Let's not make any hasty decisions.* **2** ~ **in doing sth** (of a person) acting or deciding too quickly, without enough thought: *Perhaps I was too hasty in rejecting his offer.* **IDM** see BEAT *v.*
   ▶ **hast·i·ly** /-stəli/ *adv.*: *Perhaps I spoke too hastily.* ◆ *She hastily changed the subject.*

hat 🪢 /hæt/ *noun*

1 a covering made to fit the head, often with a BRIM (= a flat edge that sticks out) and worn out of doors: *a straw/woolen, etc. hat* ◆ *to put on/take off a hat* ⊃ picture on page 691 **2** (*informal*) a position or role, especially an official or professional role, when you have more than one such role: *I'm wearing two hats tonight—parent and teacher.* ◆ *I'm telling you this with my lawyer's hat on, you understand.* ⊃ see also OLD HAT
   IDM **hats off to sb** | **I take my hat off to sb** | **I tip my hat to sb** (*informal*) used to say that you admire someone very much for something they have done **keep sth under your hat** (*informal*) to keep something secret and not tell anyone else **my hat** (*old-fashioned*) used to express surprise **out of a/the hat** if something such as a name is picked **out of a/ the hat**, it is picked at RANDOM from a container into which all the names are put, so that each name has an equal chance of being picked, in a competition, etc. **throw your hat into the ring** to announce officially that you are going to compete in an election, a competition, etc. ⊃ **more at** DROP *n.*, EAT, HAND *n.*, PASS *v.*, PULL *v.*

hat·band /ˈhætbænd/ *noun* a band of cloth placed around a hat as decoration

hat·box /ˈhætbɑks/ *noun* a round box used for keeping a hat in, to stop it from being crushed or damaged

hatch /hætʃ/ *verb, noun*
● *verb* **1** [I] ~ **(out)** (of a young bird, fish, insect, etc.) to come out of an egg: *Ten chicks hatched (out) this morning.* **2** [I] ~ **(out)** (of an egg) to break open so that a young bird, fish, insect, etc. can come out: *The eggs are about to hatch.* ⊃ collocations at LIFE **3** [T] ~ **sth** to make a young bird, fish, insect, etc. come out of an egg: *The female must find a warm place to hatch her eggs.* **4** [T] ~ **sth (up)** to create a plan or idea, especially in secret: *Have you been hatching up a deal with her?* **IDM** see COUNT *v.*
● *noun* **1** (also **hatch·way**) an opening or a door in the DECK of a ship or the bottom of an aircraft, through which goods to be carried are passed **2** a door in an aircraft or a SPACECRAFT: *an escape hatch* **3** an opening or a door in a floor or ceiling: *a hatch to the attic*
   IDM **down the hatch** (*informal, saying*) used before drinking something, especially to express good wishes before drinking alcohol ⊃ **more at** BATTEN

hatch·back /ˈhætʃbæk/ *noun* a car with a sloping door at the back that opens upward ⊃ picture at CAR

hatch·er·y /ˈhætʃəri/ *noun* (*pl.* **hatch·er·ies**) a place for HATCHING eggs as part of a business: *a trout hatchery*

hatch·et /ˈhætʃət/ *noun* a small AX (= a tool with a heavy blade for chopping things) with a short handle **IDM** see BURY

'hatchet-ˌfaced *adj.* (*disapproving*) (of a person) having a long, thin face and sharp features

'hatchet ˌjob *noun* [usually sing.] ~ **(on sb/sth)** (*informal*) strong criticism that is often unfair and is intended to harm someone or something: *The press did a very effective hatchet job on her last movie.*

'hatchet ˌman *noun* (*informal*) a person employed by an organization to make changes that are not popular with the other people who work there

hatch·ling /ˈhætʃlɪŋ/ *noun* a baby bird or animal which has just come out of its shell

hatch·way /ˈhætʃweɪ/ *noun* = HATCH *n.* (1)

hats

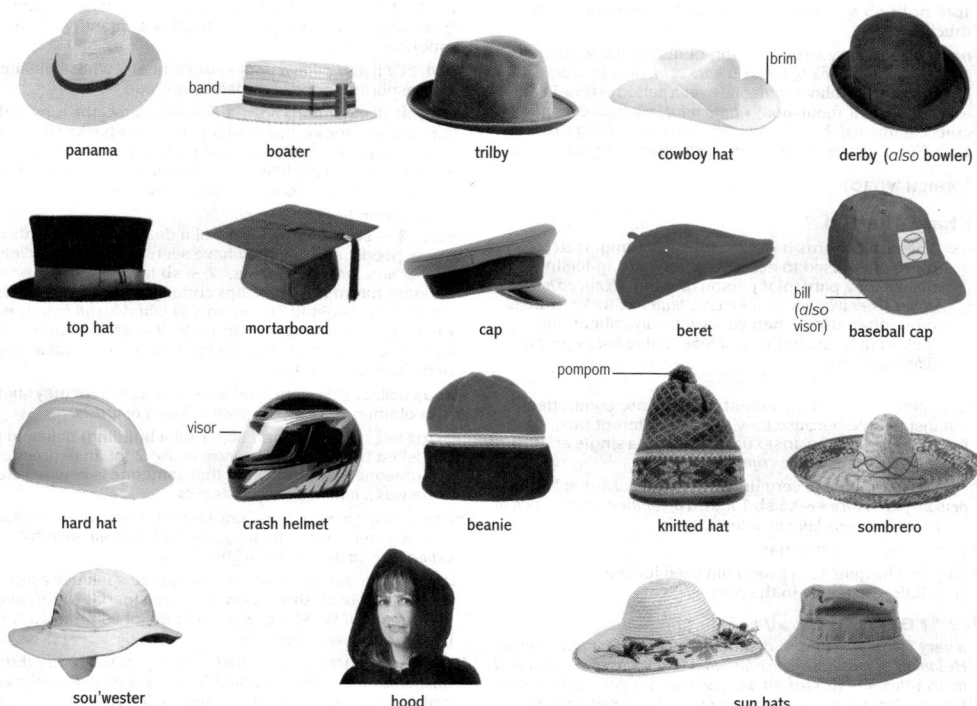

panama

boater (band)

trilby

cowboy hat (brim)

derby (*also* bowler)

top hat

mortarboard

cap

beret

baseball cap (bill *(also* visor))

hard hat

crash helmet (visor)

beanie

knitted hat (pompom)

sombrero

sou'wester

hood

sun hats

THESAURUS

hate

dislike ◆ can't stand ◆ despise ◆ can't bear ◆ loathe ◆ detest

These words all mean to have a strong feeling of dislike for someone or something.

hate to have a strong feeling of dislike for someone or something **NOTE** Although **hate** is generally a very strong verb, it is also commonly used in spoken or informal English to talk about people or things that you dislike in a less important way, for example a particular type of food: *He hates violence in any form.* ◆ *I've always hated cabbage.*

dislike (*somewhat formal*) to not like someone or something **NOTE** Dislike is a somewhat formal word; it is less formal, and more usual, to say that you *don't like* someone or something, especially in spoken English: *I don't like it when you call me so late at night.*

can't stand (*somewhat informal*) used to emphasize that you really do not like someone or something: *I can't stand his brother.* ◆ *She couldn't stand to be kept waiting.*

despise to dislike and have no respect for someone or something: *He despised himself for being so cowardly.*

can't bear used to say that you dislike something so much that you cannot accept or deal with it: *I can't bear the thought of being without you.*

CAN'T STAND OR CAN'T BEAR?

In many cases you can use either expression, but **can't bear** is stronger and more formal than **can't stand**.

loathe (*formal*) to hate someone or something very much: *They loathe each other.* **NOTE** Loathe is generally an even stronger verb than **hate**, but it can also be used more informally to say that you "really don't like" something: *I loathe country music.*

detest (*somewhat formal*) to hate someone or something very much: *They absolutely detest each other.*

PATTERNS

- I hate/dislike/can't stand/can't bear/loathe/detest **doing sth**
- I hate/can't stand **to do sth**
- I hate/dislike/can't stand/can't bear **it when…**
- I **really** hate/dislike/can't stand/despise/can't bear/detest sb/sth
- I **absolutely** hate/can't stand/loathe/detest sb/sth

---

hate 🔑 /heɪt/ *verb, noun*

● **verb** (not used in the progressive tenses) **1** to dislike something very much: **~ sth** *I hate spinach.* ◆ *I hate Monday mornings.* ◆ *I hate it when people cry.* ◆ *He hated it in France* (= did not like the life there). ◆ *I hate the way she always criticizes me.* ◆ **~ doing sth** *She hates making mistakes.* ◆ **~ to do sth** *He hated to be away from his family.* ◆ *She's a person who hates to make mistakes.* ◆ *I hate to think what would have happened if you hadn't been there.* ◆ **~ sb/sth doing sth** *He hates anyone parking in his space.* ◆ **~ sb/sth to do sth** *She would have hated him to see how her hands shook.* ◆ (*informal*) **~ for sb/sth to do sth** *I'd hate for anything to happen to him.* **2** to dislike someone very much: **~ sb/yourself** *The two boys hated each other.* ◆ *He was her most hated enemy.* ◆ **~ sb/ yourself for sth/for doing sth** *I hated myself for feeling jealous.* **3** [no passive] **~ to do sth** used when saying something that you would prefer not to have to say, or when politely asking to do something: *I hate to say it, but I don't think their marriage will last.* ◆ *I hate to trouble you, but*

---

could I use your phone? ▶ **hat·er** *noun*: *I'm not a woman hater, I just don't like Joan.*

IDM **hate sb's guts** (*informal*) to dislike someone very much

● **noun 1** [U] a very strong feeling of dislike for someone **SYN** HATRED: *a look of hate* ◆ *a hate campaign* (= cruel comments made about someone over a period of time in order to damage their reputation) ◆ *hate mail* (= letters containing cruel comments) **2** [C] (*informal*) a person or thing that you hate: *Plastic flowers have always been a particular hate of mine.*

> **WHICH WORD?**
>
> **hate ◦ hatred**
>
> ■ These two words have a similar meaning. **Hatred** is more often used to describe a very strong feeling of dislike for a particular person or thing: *Her deep hatred of her sister was obvious.* ◆ *a cat's hatred of water.* **Hate** is more often used when you are talking about this feeling in a general way: *a look of pure hate* ◆ *people filled with hate.*

hate crime *noun* **1** [U] violent acts that are committed against people because they are of a different race, because they are HOMOSEXUAL, etc. **2** [C] a single act of this type: *the victim of a hate crime*

hate·ful /ˈheɪtfl/ *adj.* very unkind or unpleasant: *a hateful person/place/face* ◆ *~ to sb The idea of fighting against men of their own race was hateful to them.*

hath /hæθ/ (*old use*) = HAS

hat·pin /ˈhætpɪn/ *noun* a long pin used for fastening a hat to your hair, especially in the past

ha·tred 🔑 /ˈheɪtrəd/ *noun* [U, C]
a very strong feeling of dislike for someone or something: *He looked at me with intense hatred.* ◆ *There was fear and hatred in his voice.* ◆ *~ (for/of sb/sth) She felt nothing but hatred for her attacker.* ◆ *a profound hatred of war* ◆ *~ (toward sb) feelings of hatred toward the bombers* ◆ *racial hatred* (= between people from different races) ◆ *The debate simply revived old hatreds.* ⊃ note at HATE

hat·stand /ˈhætstænd/ *noun* a vertical pole with large hooks around the top, for hanging hats and coats on

hat·ter /ˈhætər/ *noun* (*old-fashioned*) a person who makes and sells hats **IDM** see MAD

hat trick *noun* (especially in ICE HOCKEY or SOCCER) three points, goals, etc. scored by the same player in a particular match or game; three successes achieved by one person: *to score a hat trick*

haugh·ty /ˈhɔti/ *adj.* (**haught·ier, haught·iest**) behaving in an unfriendly way toward other people because you think that you are better than them **SYN** ARROGANT: *a haughty face/look/manner* ◆ *He replied with haughty disdain.*
▶ **haugh·ti·ly** /ˈhɔtləi/ *adv.* **haugh·ti·ness** /ˈhɔtinəs/ *noun* [U]

haul /hɔl/ *verb, noun*
● **verb 1** to pull something or someone with a lot of effort: *~ sth/sb The wagons were hauled by horses.* ◆ *~ sth/sb + adv./prep.* He reached down and hauled Liz up onto the wall. ⊃ thesaurus box at PULL **2 ~ yourself up/out of, etc.** to move yourself somewhere slowly and with a lot of effort: *She hauled herself out of bed.* **3 ~ sb + adv./prep.** to force someone to go somewhere they do not want to go: *A number of suspects have been hauled in for questioning.* **4** [usually passive] **~ sb (up) before sb/sth** to make someone appear in court in order to be judged: *He was hauled up before the local authorities for dangerous driving.*
● **noun 1** a large amount of something that has been stolen or that is illegal: *a haul of weapons* ◆ *a drug haul* **2** (especially in sports) a large number of points, goals, etc.: *His haul of 40 goals in a season is a record.* **3** [usually sing.] the distance

covered in a particular journey: *They began the long slow haul to the summit.* ◆ *Our camp is only a short haul from here.* ◆ *Take the highway—it'll be less of a haul* (= an easier trip). ⊃ see also LONG HAUL, SHORT-HAUL **4** a quantity of fish caught at one time

haul·er /ˈhɔlər/ *noun* a person or company whose business is transporting goods by road or railroad

haunch /hɔntʃ; hɑntʃ/ *noun* **1 haunches** [pl.] the tops of the legs and BUTTOCKS; the similar parts at the back of the body of an animal that has four legs: *to crouch/squat on your haunches* **2** [C] a back leg and LOIN of an animal that has four legs, eaten as food: *a haunch of venison*

haunt /hɔnt; hɑnt/ *verb, noun*
● **verb 1 ~ sth/sb** if the GHOST of a dead person **haunts** a place, people say that they have seen it there: *A headless rider haunts the country lanes.* **2 ~ sb** if something unpleasant **haunts** you, it keeps coming to your mind so that you cannot forget it: *The memory of that day still haunts me.* ◆ *For years she was haunted by guilt.* **3 ~ sb** to continue to cause problems for someone for a long time: *That decision came back to haunt him.*
● **noun** a place that someone visits often or where they spend a lot of time: *The café is a favorite haunt of artists.*

haunt·ed /ˈhɔntəd; ˈhɑn-/ *adj.* **1** (of a building) believed to be visited by GHOSTS: *a haunted house* **2** (of an expression on someone's face) showing that someone is very worried: *There was a haunted look in his eyes.*

haunt·ing /ˈhɔntɪŋ; ˈhɑn-/ *adj.* beautiful, sad, or frightening in a way that cannot be forgotten: *a haunting melody/experience/image* ▶ **haunt·ing·ly** *adv.*

Hau·sa /ˈhaʊsə; -zə/ *noun* [U] a language spoken by the Hausa people of Africa, now used in Nigeria, Niger, and other parts of W. Africa as a language of communication between different peoples

haute cou·ture /ˌoʊt kuˈtʊr/ *noun* [U] (from *French*) the business of making fashionable and expensive clothes for women; the clothes made in this business

haute cui·sine /ˌoʊt kwɪˈzin/ *noun* [U] (from *French*) cooking of a very high standard

hau·teur /hɔˈtər; hoʊ-; oʊ-/ *noun* [U] (*formal*) an unfriendly way of behaving toward other people suggesting that you think that you are better than they are

have 🔑 /həv; əv; v; hæv/ *verb, auxiliary verb*
⊃ IRREGULAR VERBS on page R5
● **verb** (In some senses **have got** is also used, although it is not as common as **have.**)
> OWN/HOLD **1** (also **have got**) **~ sth** (not used in the progressive tenses) to own, hold, or possess something: *He had a new car and a boat.* ◆ *I don't have that much money on me.* ◆ *She's got a B.A. in English.*
> CONSIST OF **2** (also **have got**) **~ sth** (not used in the progressive tenses) be made up of: *In 2008 the party had 10,000 members.*
> QUALITY/FEATURE **3** (also **have got**) (not used in the progressive tenses) to show a quality or feature: **~ sth** *The ham had a smoky flavor.* ◆ *The house has central heating.* ◆ *They have a lot of courage.* ◆ *~ sth + adj.* He has a front tooth missing. **4** (also **have got**) **~ sth to do sth** (not used in the progressive tenses) to show a particular quality by your actions: *Surely she didn't have the nerve to say that to him?*
> RELATIONSHIP **5** (also **have got**) **~ sb/sth** (not used in the progressive tenses) used to show a particular relationship: *He has three children.* ◆ *Do you have a client named Peters?*
> SOMETHING AVAILABLE **6** (also **have got**) **~ sth** (not used in the progressive tenses) to be able to make use of something because it is available: *Do you have time to call him?* ◆ *We have no choice in the matter.*
> SHOULD/MUST **7** (also **have got**) **~ sth** (not used in the progressive tenses) to be in a position where you ought to do something: *We have a duty to care for the refugees.* ⊃ note

at MUST **8** (also **have got**) (not used in the progressive tenses) to be in a position of needing to do something: ~ **sth** *I have a lot of homework tonight.* ♦ ~ **sth to do** *I should go—I have a bus to catch.*

> **HOLD 9** (also **have got**) (not used in the progressive tenses) ~ **sb/sth + adv./prep.** to hold someone or something in the way mentioned: *She had him by the collar.* ♦ *He had his head in his hands.*

> **PUT/KEEP IN A POSITION 10** (also **have got**) ~ **sth + adv./prep.** (not used in the progressive tenses) to place or keep something in a particular position: *Mary had her back to me.* ♦ *I soon had the fish in a net.*

> **FEELING/THOUGHT 11** (also **have got**) (not used in the progressive tenses) ~ **sth** to let a feeling or thought come into your mind: *He had the strong impression that someone was watching him.* ♦ *We have a few ideas for the title.* ♦ (*informal*) *I've got it! We'll call it "Word Magic."*

> **ILLNESS 12** (also **have got**) ~ **sth** (not used in the progressive tenses) to suffer from an illness or a disease: *I have a headache.*

> **EXPERIENCE 13** ~ **sth** to experience something: *I went to a few parties and had a good time.* ♦ *I was having difficulty in staying awake.* ♦ *She'll have an accident one day.*

> **EVENT 14** ~ **sth** to organize or hold an event: *Let's have a party.*

> **EAT/DRINK/SMOKE 15** ~ **sth** to eat, drink, or smoke something: *to have breakfast/lunch/dinner* ♦ *I'll have the salmon* (= for example, in a restaurant). ♦ *I had a cigarette while I was waiting.*

> **DO SOMETHING 16** ~ **sth** to perform a particular action: *I had a swim to cool down.*

> **GIVE BIRTH 17** ~ **sb/sth** to give birth to someone or something: *She's going to have a baby.*

> **EFFECT 18** ~ **sth** to produce a particular effect: *His paintings had a strong influence on me as a student.* ♦ *The color green has a restful effect.*

> **RECEIVE 19** ~ **sth** (not usually used in the progressive tenses) to receive something from someone: *Can I have the check, please?* **20** ~ **sth** to be given something; to have something done to you: *I'm having physical therapy for my back problem.* ♦ *How many driving lessons have you had so far?* **21** (also **have got**) (not used in the progressive tenses) ~ **sth doing sth** to experience the effects of someone's actions: *We have orders coming in from all over the world.*

> **HAVE SOMETHING DONE 22** (used with a past participle) ~ **sth done** to suffer the effects of what someone else does to you: *She had her purse stolen.* **23** (used with a past participle) ~ **sth done** to cause something to be done for you by someone else: *You've had your hair cut!* ♦ *We're having our car repaired.* **24** to tell or arrange for someone to do something for you: ~ **sb do sth** *He had the bouncers throw them out of the club.* ♦ (*informal*) *I'll have you know* (= I'm telling you) *I'm a black belt in judo.* ♦ ~ **sb + adv./prep.** *She's always having the handyman here to do something or other.*

> **ALLOW 25** (also **have got**) (used in negative sentences, especially after *will not, cannot*, etc.) to allow something; to accept something without complaining: ~ **sth** *I'm sick of your rudeness—I won't have it any longer!* ♦ ~ **sb/sth doing sth** *We can't have people arriving late all the time.*

> **PUT SOMEONE OR SOMETHING IN A CONDITION 26** to cause someone or something to be in a particular state; to make someone react in a particular way: ~ **sb/sth + adj.** *I want to have everything ready in good time.* ♦ ~ **sb/sth doing sth** *He had his audience listening attentively.*

> **IN ARGUMENT 27** (also **have got**) ~ **sb** (*informal*) (not used in the progressive tenses) to put someone at a disadvantage in an argument: *You've got me there. I hadn't thought of that.*

> **TRICK 28** [usually passive] ~ **sb** (*informal*) to trick or cheat someone: *I'm afraid you've been had.*

> **GUESTS 29** [no passive] ~ **sb/sth** to take care of someone or something in your home, especially for a limited period: *We're having the kids for the weekend.* **30** [no passive] ~ **sb + adv./prep.** to entertain someone in your home: *We had some friends to dinner last night.*

> **BE WITH 31** (also **have got**) ~ **sb with you** (not used in the progressive tenses) to be with someone: *She had some friends with her.*

> **FOR A JOB 32** [no passive] ~ **sb as sth** to take or accept someone for a particular role: *Who can we have as treasurer?*

IDM Most idioms containing **have** are at the entries for the nouns and adjectives in the idioms. For example, **have your eye on someone** is at **eye** *n.* **have had it** (*informal*) **1** to be in a very bad condition; to be unable to be repaired: *The car had had it.* **2** to be extremely tired: *I've had it! I'm going to bed.* **3** to have lost all chance of surviving something: *When the truck smashed into me, I thought I'd had it.* **4** to be going to experience something unpleasant: *Dad saw you scratch the car—you've had it now!* **5** to be unable to accept a situation any longer: *I've had it (up to here) with him—he's done it once too often.* **have it (that…)** to claim that it is a fact that…: *Rumor has it that we'll have a new manager soon.* **have (got) it/that coming (to you)** to be likely to suffer the unpleasant effects of your actions and to deserve to do so: *It was no surprise when she left him—everyone knew he had it coming to him.* **have it in for sb** (*informal*) to not like someone and be unpleasant to them **have it in you (to do sth)** (*informal*) to be capable of doing something: *Everyone thinks he has it in him to produce a literary classic.* ♦ *You were great. I didn't know you had it in you.* **have (got) nothing on sb/sth** (*informal*) to be not nearly as good as someone or something ⊃ see also HAVE (GOT) STH ON SB **not having any of it** (*informal*) not willing to listen to or believe something: *I tried to persuade her to wait but she wasn't having any of it.* **what have you** (*informal*) other things, people, etc. of the same kind: *There's room in the basement to store old furniture and what have you.*

PHR V **have (got) sth a'gainst sb/sth** (not used in the progressive tenses) to dislike someone or something for a particular reason: *What do you have against Ruth? She's always been good to you.* **have sb↔'back** to allow a husband, wife, or partner that you are separated from to return **have sth 'back** to receive something that someone has borrowed or taken from you: *You can have your files back after we've checked them.* **have (got) sth 'on** (not used in the progressive tenses) **1** to be wearing something: *She had a red jacket on.* ♦ *He had nothing* (= no clothes) *on.* **2** to leave a piece of equipment working: *She has her TV on all day.* **have (got) sth 'on sb** [no passive] (*informal*) (not used in the progressive tenses) to know something bad about someone, especially something that connects them with a crime: *I'm not worried—they have nothing on me.* **have sth 'out** to cause something, especially a part of your body, to be removed: *I had to have my appendix out.* **have sth 'out (with sb)** to try to settle a disagreement by discussing or arguing about it openly: *I need to have it out with her once and for all.*

● *auxiliary verb* used with the past participle to form perfect tenses: *I've finished my work.* ♦ *He's gone home, hasn't he?* ♦ *"Have you seen it?" "Yes, I have/No, I haven't."* ♦ *She'll have had the results by now.* ♦ *Had they left before you got there?* ♦ *If I hadn't seen it with my own eyes I wouldn't have believed it.* ♦ (*formal*) *Had I known that* (= if I had known that) *I would never have come.*

ha·ven /ˈheɪvn/ *noun* a place that is safe and peaceful where people or animals are protected: *The hotel is a haven of peace and tranquility.* ♦ *The river banks are a haven for wildlife.* ⊃ see also SAFE HAVEN, TAX HAVEN

the ˌhave-'nots *noun* [pl.] people who do not have money and possessions ⊃ compare THE HAVES

have·n't /ˈhævnt/ *short form* have not

hav·er·sack /ˈhævərˌsæk/ *noun* (*old-fashioned*) a bag that is carried on the back or over the shoulder, especially when walking in the country

the ˈhaves /hævz/ *noun* [pl.] people who have enough money and possessions: *the division between the haves and the have-nots* ⊃ compare THE HAVE-NOTS

have to /'hæf tə; -tu/ *modal verb* (**has to** /'hæs tə; -tu/, **had to, had to** /'hæd tə; -tu/)

1 (also **have got to**) used to show that you must do something: *Sorry, I've got to go.* ♦ *Did she have to pay a fine?* ♦ *You don't have to knock—just walk in.* ♦ *I've got to leave by seven.* ♦ *First, you have to think logically about your fears.* ♦ *I have to admit, the idea of marriage scares me.* ♦ *Do you have to go?* **2** (also **have got to**) used to give advice or recommend something: *You simply have to get a new job.* ♦ *You've got to try this recipe—it's delicious.* **3** (also **have got to**) used to say that something must be true or must happen: *There has to be a reason for his strange behavior.* ♦ *This war has got to end soon.* **4** used to suggest that an annoying event happens in order to annoy you, or that someone does something in order to annoy you: *Of course, it had to start raining as soon as we got to the beach.* ♦ *Do you have to hum so loudly?* (= it is annoying) ⊃ note at MODAL, MUST

hav·oc /'hævək/ *noun* [U] a situation in which there is a lot of damage, destruction, or confusion: *The floods caused havoc throughout the area.* ♦ *Continuing strikes are beginning to play havoc with the national economy.* ♦ *These insects can wreak havoc on crops.*

haw /hɔ/ *verb* **IDM** see HEM v.

Ha·wai·ian shirt /hə,waɪən 'ʃərt/ (also **a'loha ,shirt**) *noun* a loose cotton shirt with a brightly colored pattern and short sleeves

hawk /hɔk/ *noun, verb*
● *noun* **1** a strong fast BIRD OF PREY (= a bird that kills other creatures for food): *He waited, watching her like a hawk* (= watching her very closely). **2** a person, especially a politician, who supports the use of military force to solve problems **ANT** DOVE¹ **IDM** see EYE
● *verb* **1** [T] ~ **sth** to try to sell things by going from place to place asking people to buy them **SYN** PEDDLE **2** [I, T] ~ **(sth)** to get PHLEGM in your mouth when you cough

hawk·er /'hɔkər/ *noun* a person who makes money by hawking goods

hawk-eyed *adj.* (of a person) watching closely and carefully and noticing small details **SYN** EAGLE-EYED

hawk·ish /'hɔkɪʃ/ *adj.* preferring to use military action rather than peaceful discussion in order to solve a political problem **ANT** DOVISH

haw·ser /'hɔzər/ *noun* (*technical*) a thick rope or steel cable used on a ship

haw·thorn /'hɔθɔrn/ *noun* [U, C] a bush or small tree with THORNS, white or pink flowers, and small dark red berries (BERRY)

hay /heɪ/ *noun* [U] **1** grass that has been cut and dried and is used as food for animals: *a bale of hay* ⊃ compare STRAW **2** (*informal*) a small amount of money
IDM **make hay while the sun shines** (*saying*) to make good use of opportunities, good conditions, etc. while they last ⊃ more at HIT v., ROLL n.

hay ,fever *noun* [U] an illness that affects the nose, eyes, and throat and is caused by POLLEN from plants that is breathed in from the air

hay·loft /'heɪlɔft/ *noun* a place at the top of a farm building used for storing hay

hay·mak·ing /'heɪ,meɪkɪŋ/ *noun* [U] the process of cutting and drying grass to make hay

hay·ride /'heɪraɪd/ *noun* a ride for pleasure on a CART filled with hay, pulled by a horse or TRACTOR

hay·seed /'heɪsid/ *noun* (*informal, offensive*) a person who comes from the country and does not have much experience of the world or knowledge of culture: *a bunch of hayseed tourists*

hay·stack /'heɪstæk/ *noun* a large pile of hay, used as a way of storing it until it is needed **IDM** see NEEDLE n.

hay·wire /'heɪ,waɪər/ *adj.*
IDM **go haywire** (*informal*) to stop working correctly or become out of control: *After that, things started to go haywire.*

haz·ard /'hæzərd/ *noun, verb*
● *noun* a thing that can be dangerous or cause damage: *a fire/safety hazard* ♦ ~ **(to sb/sth)** *Growing levels of pollution represent a serious health hazard to the local population.* ♦ ~ **(of sth/of doing sth)** *Everybody is aware of the hazards of smoking.*
● *verb* **1** to make a suggestion or guess which you know may be wrong: ~ **sth** *Would you like to hazard a guess?* ♦ + speech *"Is it Tom you're going with?" she hazarded.* ♦ ~ **that…** *I would hazard that she is the sole reason we are here.* **2** ~ **sth** (*formal*) to risk something or put it in danger **SYN** ENDANGER: *Careless drivers hazard other people's lives as well as their own.*

hazard ,lights (also **haz·ards**) *noun* [pl.] lights on a car or other vehicle that flash and warn other drivers of a dangerous situation

haz·ard·ous /'hæzərdəs/ *adj.* involving risk or danger, especially to someone's health or safety: *hazardous waste/chemicals* ♦ *a hazardous journey* ♦ *It would be hazardous to invest so much.* ♦ *a list of products that are potentially hazardous to health*

hazard ,pay (also **'danger ,pay**) *noun* [U] extra pay for doing work that is dangerous

haze /heɪz/ *noun, verb*
● *noun* **1** [C, U] air that is difficult to see through because it contains very small drops of water, especially caused by hot weather: *a heat haze* **2** [sing.] air containing something that makes it difficult to see through it: *a haze of smoke/dust/steam* **3** [sing.] a mental state in which your thoughts, feelings, etc. are not clear: *an alcoholic haze*
● *verb* **1** [I, T] ~ **(sth)** to become covered or to cover something in a haze **2** ~ **sb** to play tricks on someone, especially a new student, or to give them very unpleasant things to do, sometimes as a condition for entering a FRATERNITY or SORORITY

ha·zel /'heɪzl/ *noun, adj.*
● *noun* [C, U] a small tree that produces small nuts (called hazelnuts) that can be eaten
● *adj.* (of eyes) greenish-brown or reddish-brown in color

ha·zel·nut /'heɪzl,nʌt/ (also fil·bert) *noun* the small brown nut of the hazel tree ⊃ picture at NUT

ha·zy /'heɪzi/ *adj.* (hazi·er, hazi·est) **1** not clear because of haze: *a hazy afternoon/sky* ♦ *hazy light/sunshine* ♦ *The mountains were hazy in the distance.* **2** not clear because of a lack of memory, understanding, or detail **SYN** VAGUE: *a hazy memory/idea* ♦ *What happened next is all very hazy.* **3** (of a person) uncertain or confused about something: *I'm a little hazy about what to do next.* ▶ **ha·zi·ly** /-zəli/ *adv.*: *"Why now?" she wondered hazily.*

'H-bomb *noun* = HYDROGEN BOMB

HCF /,eɪtʃ si 'ɛf/ *abbr.* (*mathematics*) HIGHEST COMMON FACTOR

HCFC /,eɪtʃ si ɛf 'si/ *noun* (*chemistry*) a type of gas used especially in AEROSOLS (= types of containers that release liquid in the form of a spray) instead of CFC, as it is less harmful to the layer of the gas OZONE in the earth's atmosphere (the abbreviation for "hydrochlorofluorocarbon")

HD /,eɪtʃ 'di/ *abbr.* high-definition (used of television, film, or video images that are extremely high quality, with very clear, sharp outlines and details): *The program was shot in HD.*

HDTV /,eɪtʃ di ti 'vi/ *noun* [U] (*technical*) the abbreviation for "high definition television" (technology that produces extremely clear images on a television screen)

he /hi; i; *strong form* hi/ *pron., noun*
● *pron.* (used as the subject of a verb) **1** a male person or animal that has already been mentioned or is easily identified: *Everyone liked my father—he was the perfect gentleman.* ♦ *He* (= the man we are watching) *went through that door.* **2** (becoming *old-fashioned*) a person, male or female, whose sex is not stated or known, especially when

referring to someone mentioned earlier or to a group in general: *Every child needs to know that he is loved.* ◆ (*saying*) *He who* (= anyone who) *hesitates is lost.* ⊃ note at GENDER **3** He used when referring to God ⊃ compare HIM

● **noun** /hi/ **1** [sing.] (*informal*) a male: *What a nice dog—is it a he or a she?* **2** he- (in compound nouns) a male animal: *a he-goat*

head ✎ /hed/ *noun, verb*

● **noun**

> **PART OF BODY 1** [C] the part of the body on top of the neck containing the eyes, nose, mouth, and brain: *She nodded her head in agreement.* ◆ *He shook his head in disbelief.* ◆ *The boys hung their heads in shame.* ◆ *The driver suffered head injuries.* ◆ *She always has her head in a book* (= is always reading). ◆ *He still has a good head of hair* (= a lot of hair). ⊃ picture at BODY ⊃ collocations at PHYSICAL ⊃ see also DEATH'S HEAD

> **MIND 2** [C] the mind or brain: *I sometimes wonder what goes on in that head of yours.* ◆ *I wish you'd use your head* (= think carefully before doing or saying something). ◆ *The thought never entered my head.* ◆ *I can't work it out in my head—I need a calculator.* ◆ *I can't get that tune out of my head.* ◆ *When will you get it into your head* (= understand) *that I don't want to discuss this anymore!* ◆ *For some reason, she's got it into her head* (= believes) *that the others don't like her.* ◆ *Who's been putting such weird ideas into your head* (= making you believe that)*?* ◆ *Try to put the exams out of your head* (= stop thinking about them) *for tonight.* ⊃ see also HOTHEAD

> **MEASUREMENT 3** a head [sing.] the size of a person's or animal's head, used as a measurement of distance or height: *She's a good head taller than her sister.* ◆ *The favorite won by a short head* (= a distance slightly less than the length of a horse's head).

> **PAIN 4** [C, usually sing.] (*informal*) a continuous pain in your head SYN HEADACHE: *I woke up with a really bad head this morning.*

> **OF GROUP/ORGANIZATION 5** [C, U] the person in charge of a group of people or an organization: *the heads of government/state* ◆ *the crowned heads* (= the kings and queens) *of Europe* ◆ *the head gardener/waiter, etc.*

> **SIDE OF COIN 6** heads [U] the side of a coin that has a picture of the head of a person on it, used as one choice when a coin is TOSSED to decide something ⊃ compare TAIL *n.*(7)

> **END OF OBJECT 7** [C, usually sing.] ~ (of sth) the end of a long narrow object that is larger or wider than the rest of it: *the head of a nail*

> **TOP 8** [sing.] ~ of sth the top or highest part of something: *at the head of the page* ◆ *They finished the season at the head of their league.*

> **OF RIVER 9** [sing.] the ~ of the river the place where a river begins SYN SOURCE

> **OF TABLE 10** [sing.] the ~ of the table the most important seat at a table: *The President sat at the head of the table.*

> **OF LINE OF PEOPLE 11** [sing.] the ~ of sth the position at the front of a line of people: *The prince rode at the head of his regiment.*

> **OF PLANT 12** [C] ~ (of sth) the mass of leaves or flowers at the end of a STEM: *Remove the dead heads to encourage new growth.*

> **ON BEER 13** [sing.] the mass of small bubbles on the top of a glass of beer

> **OF PIMPLE 14** [C] the part of a spot on your skin that contains a thick yellow liquid (= PUS) ⊃ see also BLACKHEAD

> **IN TAPE/VIDEO RECORDER 15** [C] the part of a TAPE RECORDER or VIDEO CASSETTE RECORDER that touches the tape and changes the electrical signals into sounds and/or pictures

> **NUMBER OF ANIMALS 16** ~ of sth [pl.] used to say how many animals of a particular type are on a farm, in a HERD, etc.: *200 head of sheep*

> **OF STEAM 17** a ~ of steam [sing.] the pressure produced by steam in a limited space

> **LINGUISTICS 18** [C] the central part of a phrase, which has the same GRAMMATICAL function as the whole phrase. In the phrase "the tall man in a suit," *man* is the head.

IDM a/per head for each person: *The meal worked out at $20 a head.* bang/knock your/their heads together (*informal*) to force people to stop arguing and behave in a sensible way be banging, etc. your head against a (brick) wall (*informal*) to keep trying to do something that will never be successful: *Trying to reason with them was like banging my head against a (brick) wall.* be/stand head and shoulders above sb/sth to be much better than other people or things bite/snap sb's head off (*informal*) to shout at someone in an angry way, especially without reason bring sth to a head | come to a head if you bring a situation to a head or if a situation comes to a head, you are forced to deal with it quickly because it suddenly becomes very bad bury/stick your head in the sand to refuse to admit that a problem exists or refuse to deal with it can't make heads or/nor tails of sth to be unable to understand something: *I couldn't make heads or tails of what he was saying.* do sth standing on your head (*informal*) to be able to do something very easily and without having to think too much from head to foot/toe covering your whole body: *We were covered from head to foot in mud.* go head to head (with sb) to deal with someone in a very direct and determined way go to sb's head **1** (of alcohol) to make you feel drunk: *That glass of wine has gone straight to my head.* **2** (of success, praise, etc.) to make you feel too proud of yourself in a way that other people find annoying have a good head on your shoulders to be a sensible person have a head for sth to be good at something: *to have a head for figures/business* have your head in the clouds **1** to be thinking about something that is not connected with what you are doing **2** to have ideas, plans, etc. that are not realistic have your head screwed on (straight/right) | get/have/keep your head on straight/right (*informal*) to be a sensible person: *I kept my head on straight and did what I had to.* get/have/keep your head straight (*informal*) to be a sensible person head first **1** moving forward or downward with your head in front of the rest of your body: *He fell head first down the stairs.* **2** without thinking carefully about something before acting: *She got divorced and rushed head first into another marriage.* head over heels in love loving someone very much: *He's fallen head over heels in love with his boss.* heads or tails? used to ask someone which side of a coin they think will be facing upward when it is TOSSED in order to decide something by chance heads will roll (for sth) (*informal*, usually *humorous*) used to say that some people will be punished because of something that has happened hold your head high | hold up your head to be proud of or not feel ashamed about something that you have done: *She managed to hold her head high and ignore what people were saying.* in over your head involved in something that is too difficult for you to deal with: *After a week in the new job, I soon realized that I was in over my head.* keep/get your head down to avoid attracting attention to yourself keep your head | keep a clear/cool head to remain calm in a difficult situation keep your head above water to deal with a difficult situation, especially one in which you have financial problems, and just manage to survive laugh, scream, etc. your head off (*informal*) to laugh, etc. a lot and very loudly lose your head to become unable to act in a calm or sensible way over sb's head **1** too difficult or complicated for someone to understand: *A lot of the jokes went* (= were) *right over my head.* **2** to a higher position of authority than someone: *I couldn't help feeling jealous when she was promoted over my head.* put our/your/their heads together to think about or discuss something as a group stand/turn sth on its head to make people think about something in a completely different way take it into your head to do sth to suddenly decide to do something, especially something that other people think is stupid turn sb's head (of success, praise, etc.) to make a person feel too proud in a way that other people find annoying two heads are better than one (*saying*) used to say that two people can achieve more than one person working alone ⊃ more at BLOCK *n.*, DRUM *v.*, EYE *n.*, GUN *n.*, HAIR, HEART,

HIT v., IDEA, LAUGH v., NEED v., PRICE n., REAR v., ROOF n., SCRATCH v., THICK adj., TOP n.

● **verb**

▷ **MOVE TOWARD 1** [I] (also **be headed**) + **adv./prep.** to move in a particular direction: *Where are we heading?* ◆ *Where are you two headed?* ◆ *Let's head back home.* ◆ *She headed for the door.* ◆ *(figurative) Can you forecast where the economy is heading?*

▷ **GROUP/ORGANIZATION 2** [T] **~ sth** (also ˌhead sth↔'up) to lead or be in charge of something: *She has been appointed to head the research team.*

▷ **LIST/LINE OF PEOPLE 3** [T] **~ sth** to be at the top of a list of names or at the front of a line of people: *Her name heads the list of nominees.* ◆ *to head a march/procession*

▷ **BE AT TOP 4** [T, usually passive] **~ sth** to put a word or words at the top of a page or section of a book as a title: *The chapter was headed "My Early Life."*

▷ **SOCCER 5** [T] **~ sth** to hit a soccer ball with your head: *Walsh headed the ball into an empty goal.*

PHR V be 'heading for sth (also be 'headed for sth) to be likely to experience something bad: *They look as though they're heading for divorce.* ˌhead sb↔'off to get in front of someone in order to make them turn back or change direction **SYN** INTERCEPT: *We'll head them off at the bridge!* ˌhead sth↔'off to take action in order to prevent something from happening: *He headed off efforts to replace him as leader.* ˌhead sth↔'up to lead or be in charge of a department, part of an organization, etc. ⊃ **see also** HEAD v. (2)

-head /hɛd/ *suffix* (*informal*) (in nouns) a person who is very enthusiastic about a particular thing or is addicted to a particular drug: *a gearhead* (= a person who is very enthusiastic about cars)

head·ache 🔑 /ˈhɛdeɪk/ *noun*
1 a continuous pain in the head: *to suffer from headaches* ◆ *Red wine gives me a headache.* ◆ *I have a splitting headache* (= a very bad one). **2** a person or thing that causes worry or trouble: *The real headache will be getting the bank to lend you the money.*

head·band /ˈhɛdbænd/ *noun* a strip of cloth worn around the head, especially to keep hair or sweat out of your eyes when playing sports

head·bang·er /ˈhɛdˌbæŋər/ *noun* (*informal*) a person who likes or performs HEAVY METAL music and shakes their head violently up and down while listening to it ▶ **head·bang·ing** *noun* [U]

head·board /ˈhɛdbɔrd/ *noun* the vertical board at the end of a bed where you put your head ⊃ **picture at** BED

head·cheese /ˈhɛdtʃiz/ *noun* [U] meat made from the head of a pig or CALF that has been boiled and pressed into a container, served cold in thin slices

head·count /ˈhɛdkaʊnt/ *noun* an act of counting the number of people who are at an event, employed by an organization, etc.; the number of people that have been counted in this way: *to do a headcount* ◆ *What's the latest headcount?*

head·dress /ˈhɛddrɛs/ *noun* a covering worn on the head on special occasions

head·ed /ˈhɛdəd/ *adj.* **1** (of writing paper) having the name and address of a person, an organization, etc. printed at the top: *headed notepaper* **2** -headed (in adjectives) having the type of head or number of heads mentioned: *a bald-headed man* ◆ *a three-headed monster* ⊃ **see also** BIG-HEADED, CLEAR-HEADED, COOL-HEADED, EMPTY-HEADED, HARDHEADED, LEVEL-HEADED, LIGHTHEADED, PIGHEADED, WRONG-HEADED

head·er /ˈhɛdər/ *noun* **1** (in SOCCER) an act of hitting the ball with your head **2** a line or block of text that is automatically added to the top of every page that is printed from a computer ⊃ **compare** FOOTER

head·gear /ˈhɛdgɪr/ *noun* [U] anything worn on the head, for example a hat: *protective headgear*

head·hunt /ˈhɛdhʌnt/ *verb* **~ sb** to find someone who is

suitable for a senior job and persuade them to leave their present job: *I was headhunted by a marketing agency.* ▶ **head·hunt·ing** *noun* [U]

head·hunt·er /ˈhɛdˌhʌntər/ *noun* **1** a person whose job is to find people with the necessary skills to work for a particular company and to persuade them to join this company **2** a member of a people that collects the heads of the people they kill

head·ing /ˈhɛdɪŋ/ *noun* **1** a title printed at the top of a page or at the beginning of a section of a book: *chapter headings* **2** the subject of each section of a speech or piece of writing: *The company's aims can be grouped under three main headings.*

head·lamp /ˈhɛdlæmp/ *noun* = HEADLIGHT

head·land /ˈhɛdlənd; -lænd/ *noun* a narrow piece of high land that sticks out from the coast into the ocean **SYN** PROMONTORY

head·less /ˈhɛdləs/ *adj.* [usually before noun] without a head: *a headless body/corpse*

head·light /ˈhɛdlaɪt/ *noun* (also **head·lamp**) a large light, usually one of two, at the front of a vehicle; the BEAM from this light ⊃ **picture at** CAR

head·line /ˈhɛdlaɪn/ *noun, verb*
● **noun 1** [C] the title of a newspaper article printed in large letters, especially at the top of the front page: *They ran the story under the headline "Home at last!"* ◆ *The scandal was in the headlines for several days.* ◆ *headline news* ⊃ **see also** BANNER HEADLINE **2 the headlines** [pl.] a short summary of the most important items of news, read at the beginning of a news program on the radio or television
IDM grab/hit/make the headlines to be an important item of news in newspapers or on the radio or television
● **verb 1** [T, usually passive] **~ sth + noun** to give a story or article a particular headline: *The story was headlined "Back to the future."* **2** [T, I] **~ (sth)** to be the main performer in a concert or show: *The concert was headlined by Elton John.*

head·lin·er /ˈhɛdˌlaɪnər/ *noun* the main performer or act in a show

head·lock /ˈhɛdlɑk/ *noun* (in WRESTLING) a way of holding an opponent's head so that they cannot move: *He had him in a headlock.*

head·long /ˈhɛdlɔŋ/ *adv.* **1** with the head first and the rest of the body following **SYN** HEAD FIRST: *She fell headlong into the icy pool.* **2** without thinking carefully before doing something: *The government is taking care not to rush headlong into another controversy.* **3** quickly and without looking where you are going: *He ran headlong into a police car.* ▶ **headlong** *adj.* [only before noun]: *a headlong dive/rush*

head·man /ˈhɛdmæn; -mən/ *noun* (*pl.* **head·men** /-mɛn; -mən/) the leader of a community **SYN** CHIEF: *the village headman*

head·mas·ter /ˈhɛdˌmæstər/, **head·mis·tress** /ˈhɛdˌmɪstrəs/ *noun* (*old-fashioned*) the person who is in charge of a private school; the principal

ˌhead 'office *noun* the main office of a company; the managers who work there: *Their head office is in New York.* ◆ *I don't know what head office will think about this proposal.*

ˌhead of 'state *noun* (*pl.* **heads of state**) the official leader of a country who is sometimes also the leader of the government

ˌhead-'on *adj.* [only before noun] **1** in which the front part of one vehicle hits the front part of another vehicle: *a head-on crash/collision* **2** in which people express strong views and deal with something in a direct way: *There was a head-on confrontation between management and unions.* ▶ ˌhead-'on *adv.*: *The cars crashed head-on.* ◆ *We hit the tree head-on.* ◆ *to tackle a problem head-on* (= without trying to avoid it)

head·phones /ˈhɛdfoʊnz/ (also **ear·phones**) *noun* [pl.] a piece of equipment worn over or in the ears that makes it possible to listen to music, the radio, etc. without other people hearing it: *a pair/set of headphones*

head·quar·tered /ˈhɛdˌkwɔrtərd; -ˌkwɔtərd/ *adj.* [not

before noun] having headquarters in a particular place: *CNN is headquartered in Atlanta.*

head·quar·ters /ˈhɛdˌkwɔrtərz; -ˌkwɑtərz/ *noun* [U, pl.] (*pl.* **head·quar·ters**) (*abbr.* **HQ**) a place from which an organization or a military operation is controlled; the people who work there: *The firm's headquarters are/is in New York.* ◆ *Several companies have their headquarters in the area.* ◆ *I'm now based at headquarters.* ◆ *police headquarters* ◆ *Headquarters in Boston has/have agreed.*

head·rest /ˈhɛdrɛst/ *noun* the part of a seat or chair that supports a person's head, especially on the front seat of a car ⊃ picture at CAR

head·room /ˈhɛdrum; -rʊm/ *noun* [U] the amount of space between the top of your head and the roof of a vehicle: *There's a lot of headroom for such a small car.*

head·scarf /ˈhɛdskɑrf/ *noun* (*pl.* **head·scarves**) a square piece of cloth tied around the head by women or girls

head·set /ˈhɛdsɛt/ *noun* a pair of HEADPHONES, especially one with a MICROPHONE attached to it, often used to talk on the phone ⊃ picture at COMPUTER

head·ship /ˈhɛdʃɪp/ *noun* ~ **(of sth)** the position of being in charge of an organization: *the headship of the department*

head·stand /ˈhɛdstænd/ *noun* a position in which a person has their head on the ground and their feet straight up in the air

ˌhead ˈstart *noun* [sing.] ~ **(on/over sb)** an advantage that someone already has before they start doing something: *Being able to speak French gave her a head start over the other candidates.*

head·stone /ˈhɛdstoʊn/ *noun* a piece of stone placed at one end of a grave, showing the name, etc. of the person buried there **SYN** GRAVESTONE ⊃ compare TOMBSTONE

head·strong /ˈhɛdstrɔŋ/ *adj.* (*disapproving*) a **headstrong** person is determined to do things their own way and refuses to listen to advice

ˌheads-ˈup *noun* (*pl.* **heads-up** or **heads-ups**) ~ **(about sth)** a piece of information given in advance of something or as advice: *Send everyone a heads-up about the changes well in advance.*

ˌhead ˈtable *noun* the table at which the most important guests sit at a formal dinner

ˌhead-to-ˈhead *adj.* [only before noun] in which two people or groups face each other directly in order to decide the result of a disagreement or competition: *a head-to-head battle/clash/contest* ▶ ˌhead-to-ˈhead *adv.*: *They are set to meet head-to-head in next week's final.*

head·waters /ˈhɛdˌwɔtərz; -ˌwɑtərz/ *noun* [pl.] streams forming the source of a river

head·way /ˈhɛdweɪ/ *noun* [U]
IDM **make headway** to make progress, especially when this is slow or difficult: *We are making little headway with the negotiations.* ◆ *The boat was unable to make much headway against the tide.*

head·wind /ˈhɛdwɪnd/ *noun* a wind that is blowing toward a person or vehicle, so that it is blowing from the direction in which the person or vehicle is moving ⊃ compare TAILWIND

head·word /ˈhɛdwərd/ *noun* (*technical*) a word that forms a HEADING in a dictionary, under which its meaning is explained

head·y /ˈhɛdi/ *adj.* (**head·i·er**, **head·i·est**) **1** [usually before noun] having a strong effect on your senses; making you feel excited and confident **SYN** INTOXICATING: *the heady days of youth* ◆ *the heady scent of hot spices* ◆ *a heady mixture of desire and fear* **2** [not before noun] (of a person) excited in a way that makes you do things without worrying about the possible results: *She felt heady with success.*

heal 🔑 /hil/ *verb*
1 [I, T] to become healthy again; to make something healthy again: *It took a long time for the wounds to heal.* ◆ ~ **up**

The cut healed up without leaving a scar. ◆ ~ **sth** *This will help to heal your cuts and scratches.* ◆ (*figurative*) *It was a chance to heal the wounds in the party* (= to repair the damage that had been done). **2** [T] ~ **sb (of sth)** (*old use* or *formal*) to cure someone who is sick; to make someone feel happy again: *the story of Jesus healing ten lepers of their disease* ◆ *I felt healed by his love.* **3** [T, I] ~ **(sth)** to put an end to something or make something easier to bear; to end or become easier to bear: *She was never able to heal the rift between herself and her father.* ◆ *The breach between them never really healed.*

heal·er /ˈhilər/ *noun* **1** a person who cures people of illnesses and disease using natural powers rather than medicine: *a faith/spiritual healer* **2** something that makes a bad situation easier to deal with: *Time is a great healer.*

heal·ing /ˈhilɪŋ/ *noun* [U] the process of becoming or making someone or something healthy again; the process of getting better after an emotional shock: *the healing process* ◆ *emotional healing* ⊃ see also FAITH HEALING

health 🔑 /hɛlθ/ *noun* [U]
1 the condition of a person's body or mind: *Exhaust fumes are bad for your health.* ◆ *to be in poor/good/excellent/the best of health* ◆ *Smoking can seriously damage your health.* ◆ *mental health* ⊃ see also ILL HEALTH ⊃ thesaurus box at ILLNESS **2** the state of being physically and mentally healthy: *He was nursed back to health by his wife.* ◆ *She was glowing with health and clearly enjoying life.* ◆ *As long as you have your health, nothing else matters.* **3** the work of providing medical services: *All parties are promising to increase spending on health.* ◆ *the Department of Health* ◆ *health insurance* ◆ *health and safety regulations* (= laws that protect the health of people at work) **4** how successful something is: *the health of your marriage/finances* **IDM** see CLEAN *adj.*, DRINK *v.*

ˈhealth card *noun* (*CanE*) a card that shows that a person has the right to receive free medical treatment

health·care (also **health care**) /ˈhɛlθkɛr/ *noun* [U] the service of providing medical care: *the costs of healthcare for the elderly* ◆ *healthcare workers/professionals*

ˈhealth ˌcenter (*CanE usually* ˈhealth ˌcentre) *noun* a building where a group of doctors see their patients and where some local medical services have their offices

ˈhealth club *noun* (also **gym**) a private club where people go to do physical exercise in order to stay or become healthy and fit

ˈhealth food *noun* [U, C, usually pl.] food that does not contain any artificial substances and is therefore thought to be good for your health

health·ful /ˈhɛlθfl/ *adj.* [usually before noun] good for your health ▶ **health·ful·ly** /-fəli/ *adv.*

ˈhealth ˌservice *noun* a public service providing medical care

ˈhealth spa *noun* = SPA (2)

health·y 🔑 /ˈhɛlθi/ *adj.* (**health·ier**, **health·iest**)
1 having good health and not likely to become sick: *a healthy child/animal/tree* ◆ *Stay healthy by eating well and exercising regularly.* **ANT** UNHEALTHY ⊃ thesaurus box at WELL **2** [usually before noun] good for your health: *a healthy diet/climate/lifestyle* **ANT** UNHEALTHY **3** [usually before noun] showing that you are in good health: *to have a healthy appetite* ◆ *a shampoo that keeps hair looking healthy* **4** normal and sensible: *The child showed a healthy curiosity.* ◆ *She has a healthy respect for her rival's talents.* ◆ *It's not healthy the way she clings to the past.* **ANT** UNHEALTHY **5** successful and working well: *a healthy economy* ◆ *Your car doesn't sound very healthy.* **6** [usually before noun] large and showing success: *a healthy bank balance* ◆ *a healthy profit* ▶ **health·i·ly** /-θəli/ *adv.*: *to eat healthily* **health·i·ness** /-θinəs/ *noun* [U]

heap /hip/ *noun, verb*
● *noun* **1** ~ **(of sth)** a messy pile of something: *The building was reduced to a heap of rubble.* ◆ *His clothes lay in a heap on the floor.* ◆ *Worn-out car tires were stacked in heaps.* ⊃ see also COMPOST HEAP, SCRAP HEAP, SLAG HEAP

2 [usually pl.] (*informal*) a lot of something: *There's heaps of time before the plane leaves.* ◆ *I've got heaps to tell you.*
3 (*informal, humorous*) a car that is old and in bad condition
IDM **at the top/bottom of the heap** high up/low down in the structure of an organization or a society: *These workers are at the bottom of the economic heap.* **collapse, fall, etc. in a heap** to fall down heavily and not move
● *verb* **1** ~ sth (up) to put things in an messy pile: *Rocks were heaped up on the side of the road.* **2** to put a lot of something in a pile on something: ~ A on B *She heaped food on my plate.* ◆ ~ B with A *She heaped my plate with food.* **3** to give a lot of something such as praise or criticism to someone: ~ A on B *He heaped praise on his team.* ◆ ~ B with A *He heaped his team with praise.* **IDM** see SCORN n.

heap·ing /ˈhipɪŋ/ *adj.* used to describe a spoon, etc. that has as much in it or on it as it can hold: *a heaping teaspoon of sugar* ◆ *heaping plates of scrambled eggs* ⊃ compare LEVEL

hear 🔊 /hɪr/ *verb* (heard, heard /hɜrd/)
1 [I, T] (not used in the progressive tenses) to be aware of sounds with your ears: *I can't hear very well.* ◆ ~ sth/sb *She heard footsteps behind her.* ◆ ~ sb/sth doing sth *He could hear a dog barking.* ◆ ~ sb/sth do sth *Did you hear him go out?* ◆ ~ what… *Didn't you hear what I said?* ◆ sb/sth is heard to do sth *She has been heard to make threats to her former lover.*
2 [T] (not used in the progressive tenses) to listen or pay attention to someone or something: ~ sth *Did you hear that interview on the radio last night?* ◆ ~ sb/sth/yourself do sth *Be quiet— I can't hear myself think!* (= it is so noisy that I can't think clearly) ◆ ~ what… *We'd better hear what they have to say.* ◆ *I hear what you're saying* (= I have listened to your opinion), *but you're wrong.* **3** [I, T] (not usually used in the progressive tenses) to be told about something: *Haven't you heard? She resigned.* ◆ *"I'm getting married." "So I've heard."* ◆ *Things are going well from what I hear.* ◆ ~ about sb/sth *I was sorry to hear about your accident.* ◆ *I've heard about people like you.* ◆ ~ sth *We had heard nothing for weeks.* ◆ ~ (that)… *I was surprised to hear (that) he was married.* ◆ *I hear you've been away this weekend.* ◆ ~ it said (that)… *I've heard it said (that) they met in Italy.* ◆ ~ what, how, etc.… *Did you hear what happened?* **4** [T] ~ sth to listen to and judge a case in court: *The appeal was heard in private.* ◆ *Today the jury began to hear the evidence.*
IDM **have you heard the one about…?** used to ask someone if they have heard a particular joke before **hear! hear!** used to show that you agree with or approve of what someone has just said, especially during a speech **hear tell (of sth)** (*old-fashioned*) to hear people talking about something: *I've often heard tell of such things.* **I've heard it all before** (*informal*) used to say that you do not really believe someone's promises or excuses because they are the same ones you have heard before **let's hear it for…** (*informal*) used to say that someone or something deserves praise: *Let's hear it for the teachers, for a change.* **not/never hear the end of it** to keep being reminded of something because someone is always talking to you about it: *If we don't get her a dog we'll never hear the end of it.* **you could hear a pin drop** it was extremely quiet: *The audience was so quiet you could have heard a pin drop.* **(do) you hear me?** (*informal*) used to tell someone in an angry way to pay attention and obey you: *You can't go—do you hear me?* ⊃ more at LAST¹ n., THING, VOICE n.
PHR V **'hear from sb** | **'hear sth from sb** to receive a letter, e-mail, phone call, etc. from someone: *I look forward to hearing from you.* ◆ *I haven't heard anything from her for months.* **'hear of sb/sth** | **'hear sth of sb/sth** to know about someone or something because you have been told about them: *I've never heard of the place.* ◆ *She disappeared and was never heard of again.* ◆ *The last I heard of him he was living in St. Louis.* ◆ *This is the first I've heard of it!* **not 'hear of sth** to refuse to let someone do something, especially because you want to help them: *She wanted to walk home but I wouldn't hear of it.* ◆ ~ sb doing sth *He wouldn't hear of my walking home alone.* ⊃ see also UNHEARD-OF, **,hear sb 'out**

to listen until someone has finished saying what they want to say

hear·er /ˈhɪrər/ *noun* a person who hears something or who is listening to someone

hear·ing 🔊 /ˈhɪrɪŋ/ *noun*
1 [U] the ability to hear: *Her hearing is poor.* ◆ *He's hearing-impaired* (= not able to hear well). ⊃ see also HARD OF HEARING **2** [C] an official meeting at which the facts about a crime, complaint, etc. are presented to the person or group of people who will have to decide what action to take: *a court/disciplinary hearing* ⊃ collocations at JUSTICE **3** [sing.] an opportunity to explain your actions, ideas, or opinions: *to get/give someone a fair hearing* ◆ *His views may be extreme but he deserves a hearing.*
IDM **in/within (sb's) hearing** near enough to someone so that they can hear what is said **SYN** WITHIN EARSHOT: *She shouldn't have said such things in your hearing.* ◆ *I had no reason to believe there was anyone within hearing.* **out of hearing** too far away to hear someone or something or to be heard: *She had moved out of hearing.* **IDM** see FAIR *adj.*

'hearing ,aid *noun* a small device that fits inside the ear and makes sounds louder, used by people who cannot hear well: *to have/wear a hearing aid*

'hearing ,dog *noun* a dog trained to make a deaf person (= person who cannot hear well) aware of sounds such as the ringing of a telephone or a DOORBELL

heark·en (also **hark·en**) /ˈhɑrkən/ *verb* [I] ~ (to sb/sth) (*old use*) to listen to someone or something

hear·say /ˈhɪrseɪ/ *noun* [U] things that you have heard from another person but do not (definitely) know to be true: *We can't make a decision based on hearsay and guesswork.* ◆ *hearsay evidence*

hearse /hɜrs/ *noun* a long vehicle used for carrying the COFFIN (= the box for the dead body) at a funeral

heart 🔊 /hɑrt/ *noun*
> **PART OF BODY 1** [C] the organ in the chest that sends blood around the body, usually on the left in humans: *The patient's heart stopped beating for a few seconds.* ◆ *heart trouble/failure/disease* ◆ *to have a weak heart* ◆ *I could feel my heart pounding in my chest* (= because of excitement etc.). ⊃ picture at BODY ⊃ see also OPEN-HEART SURGERY **2** [C] (*literary*) the outside part of the chest where the heart is: *She clasped the photo to her heart.*
> **FEELINGS/EMOTIONS 3** [C] the place in a person where the feelings and emotions are thought to be, especially those connected with love: *She has a kind heart.* ◆ *Have you no heart?* ◆ *He returned with a heavy heart* (= sad). ◆ *Her novels tend to deal with affairs of the heart.* ◆ *The story captured the hearts and minds of a generation.* ⊃ see also BROKEN HEART
> **-HEARTED 4** (in adjectives) having the type of character or personality mentioned: *cold-hearted* ◆ *kind-hearted*
> **IMPORTANT PART 5** [sing.] ~ (of sth) the most important part of something **SYN** CRUX: *the heart of the matter/problem* ◆ *The committee's report went to the heart of the government's dilemma.* ◆ *The distinction between right and wrong lies at the heart of all questions of morality.*
> **CENTER 6** [C, usually sing.] ~ (of sth) the part that is in the center of something: *a quiet hotel in the very heart of the city*
> **OF CABBAGE 7** [C] the smaller leaves in the middle of a CABBAGE, LETTUCE, etc.
> **SHAPE 8** [C] a thing shaped like a heart, often red and used as a symbol of love; a symbol shaped like a heart used to mean the verb "love": *The words "I love you" were written inside a big red heart.* ◆ (*informal*) *I ♡ New York.*
> **IN CARD GAMES 9 hearts** [pl.] one of the four sets of cards (called SUITS) in a DECK of cards, with red heart symbols on them: *the queen of hearts* ◆ *Hearts are trumps.* ⊃ picture at PLAYING CARD **10** [C] one card from the set of hearts: *Who played that heart?*
> **IDM** **at heart** used to say what someone is really like even though they may seem to be something different: *He's still a socialist at heart.* **break sb's heart** to make someone feel very unhappy: *She broke his heart when she called off the*

engagement. ♦ *It breaks my heart to see you like this.* **by heart** using only your memory: *I've dialed the number so many times I know it by heart.* **close/dear/near to sb's heart** having a lot of importance and interest for someone **from the (bottom of your) heart** in a way that is sincere: *I beg you, from the bottom of my heart, to spare his life.* ♦ *It was clearly an offer that came from the heart.* **give sb heart** to make someone feel positive, especially when they thought that they had no chance of achieving something **give your heart to sb** to give your love to one person **have a heart!** (*informal*) used to ask someone to be kind and/or reasonable **have a heart of gold** to be a very kind person **have a heart of stone** to be a person who does not show others sympathy **heart and soul** with a lot of energy and enthusiasm: *They threw themselves heart and soul into the project.* **your heart goes out to sb** used to say that you feel a lot of sympathy for someone: *Our hearts go out to the families of the victims.* **sb's heart is in their mouth** someone feels nervous or frightened about something **sb's heart is in the right place** used to say that someone's intentions are kind and sincere even though they sometimes do the wrong thing **your heart is not in sth** used to say that you are not very interested in or enthusiastic about something **sb's heart leaps** used to say that someone has a sudden feeling of happiness or excitement **sb's heart sinks** used to say that someone suddenly feels sad or depressed about something: *My heart sank when I saw how much work there was left.* ♦ *She watched him go with a sinking heart.* **sb's heart skips a beat** used to say that someone has a sudden feeling of fear, excitement, etc. **in your heart (of hearts)** if you know something **in your heart**, you have a strong feeling that it is true: *She knew in her heart of hearts that she was making the wrong decision.* **it does sb's heart good (to do sth)** it makes someone feel happy when they see or hear something: *It does my heart good to see the old place being taken care of so well.* **let your heart rule your head** to act according to what you feel rather than to what you think is sensible **lose heart** to stop hoping for something or trying to do something because you no longer feel confident **lose your heart (to sb/sth)** (*formal*) to fall in love with someone or something **a man/woman after your own heart** a man/woman who likes the same things or has the same opinions as you **my heart bleeds (for sb)** (*ironic*) used to say that you do not feel sympathy for someone: *"I have to go to Brazil on business." "My heart bleeds for you!"* **not have the heart (to do sth)** to be unable to do something because you know that it will make someone sad or upset **pour out/open your heart to sb** to tell someone all your problems, feelings, etc. **set your heart on sth | have your heart set on sth** to want something very much **take heart (from sth)** to feel more positive about something, especially when you thought that you had no chance of achieving something: *The government can take heart from the latest opinion polls.* **take sth to heart** to be very upset by something that someone says or does **tear/rip the heart out of sth** to destroy the most important part or aspect of something **to your heart's content** as much as you want: *a supervised play area where children can run around to their heart's content* **with all your heart/your whole heart** completely: *I hope with all my heart that things work out for you.* ⊃ more at ABSENCE, CHANGE *n.*, CROSS *v.*, EAT, ETCH, FIND *v.*, GOODNESS, HOME *n.*, INTEREST *n.*, SICK *adj.*, SOB *v.*, STEAL *v.*, STRIKE *v.*, TEAR[1] *v.*, WAY *n.*, WEAR *v.*, WIN *v.*, YOUNG *adj.*

heart·ache /'hɑrteɪk/ *noun* [U, C] a strong feeling of sadness or worry: *The relationship caused her a great deal of heartache.* ♦ *the heartaches of being a parent*

'heart at·tack *noun* a sudden serious medical condition in which the heart stops working normally, sometimes causing death ⊃ compare CORONARY THROMBOSIS

heart·beat /'hɑrtbit/ *noun* **1** [C, U] the movement or sound of the heart as it sends blood around the body: *a rapid/regular heartbeat* **2** [sing.] **the ~ of sth** an important feature of something, that is responsible for making it what it is:

The candidate said that he understood the heartbeat of the Hispanic community in California.
IDM **a heartbeat away (from sth)** very close to something **in a heartbeat** very quickly, without thinking about it: *If I was offered another job, I'd leave in a heartbeat.*

heart·break /'hɑrtbreɪk/ *noun* [U, C] a strong feeling of sadness: *They suffered the heartbreak of losing a child through cancer.* ▶ **'heart·break·ing** *adj.*: *a heartbreaking story* ♦ *It's heartbreaking to see him wasting his life like this.*

heart·bro·ken /'hɑrt,broʊkən/ *adj.* extremely sad because of something that has happened **SYN** BROKEN-HEARTED

heart·burn /'hɑrtbɜrn/ *noun* [U] a pain that feels like something burning in your chest caused by INDIGESTION

heart·en /'hɑrtn/ *verb* [usually passive] **~ sb** to give someone encouragement or hope **ANT** DISHEARTEN ▶ **heart·en·ing** *adj.*: *It is heartening to see the determination of these young people.*

'heart ˌfailure *noun* [U] a serious medical condition in which the heart does not work correctly

heart·felt /'hɑrtfelt/ *adj.* [usually before noun] showing strong feelings that are sincere **SYN** SINCERE: *a heartfelt apology/plea/sigh* ♦ *heartfelt sympathy/thanks*

hearth /hɑrθ/ *noun* **1** the floor at the bottom of a FIREPLACE (= the space for a fire in the wall of a room); the area in front of this: *A log fire roared in the open hearth.* ♦ *The cat dozed in its favorite spot on the hearth.* **2** (*literary*) home and family life: *a longing for hearth and home*

heart·i·ly /'hɑrtl·i/ *adv.* **1** with obvious enjoyment and enthusiasm: *to laugh/sing/eat heartily* **2** in a way that shows that you feel strongly about something: *I heartily agree with her on this.* **3** extremely: *heartily glad/relieved*

heart·land /'hɑrtlænd/ *noun* also **heartlands** [pl.] **1** the central part of a country or an area: *the great Russian heartlands* **2** an area that is important for a particular activity or political party: *the industrial heartland of Germany* ♦ *the traditional Democratic heartland in Pennsylvania*

heart·less /'hɑrtləs/ *adj.* feeling no sympathy for other people **SYN** CRUEL: *What a heartless thing to say!* ▶ **heart·less·ly** *adv.* **heart·less·ness** *noun* [U]

ˌheart-'lung maˌchine *noun* a machine that replaces the functions of the heart and lungs, for example during a medical operation on the heart

'heart-ˌrending *adj.* [usually before noun] causing feelings of great sadness **SYN** HEARTBREAKING: *a heart-rending story*

'heart-ˌsearching *noun* [U] the process of examining carefully your feelings or reasons for doing something

heart·sick /'hɑrtsɪk/ *adj.* [not usually before noun] (*literary*) extremely unhappy or disappointed

'heart-ˌstopping *adj.* [usually before noun] causing feelings of great excitement or worry: *For one heart-stopping moment she thought they were too late.*

heart·strings /'hɑrtstrɪŋz/ *noun* [pl.] strong feelings of love or sympathy: *to tug/pull at someone's heartstrings* (= to cause such feelings in someone)

heart·throb /'hɑrtθrɑb/ *noun* (used especially in newspapers) a famous man, usually an actor or a singer, that a lot of women find attractive

ˌheart-to-'heart *noun* [usually sing.] a conversation in which two people talk honestly about their feelings and personal problems: *to have a heart-to-heart with someone* ▶ **ˌheart-to-'heart** *adj.*: *a heart-to-heart talk*

heart·warm·ing /'hɑrt,wɔrmɪŋ/ *adj.* causing feelings of happiness and pleasure

heart·wood /'hɑrtwʊd/ *noun* [U] the hard, older, inner layers of the wood of a tree ⊃ compare SAPWOOD

heart·worm /'hɑrtwɜrm/ *noun* [C, U] a type of WORM that lives in a dog's heart and causes disease; the disease caused by these worms

heart·y /'hɑrti/ *adj.* (heart·i·er, heart·i·est) **1** [usually before noun] showing friendly feelings for someone: *a*

hearty welcome **2** (sometimes *disapproving*) loud, cheerful, and full of energy: *a hearty and boisterous fellow* ♦ *a hearty voice* **3** [only before noun] (of a meal or someone's APPETITE) large; making you feel full: *a hearty breakfast* ♦ *to have a hearty appetite* **4** [usually before noun] showing that you feel strongly about something: *He nodded his head in hearty agreement.* ♦ *Hearty congratulations to everyone involved.* ♦ *a hearty dislike of something* **IDM** see HALE
▶ **heart·i·ness** *noun* [U]

heat 🔑 /hiːt/ *noun, verb*

● **noun**
▷ BEING HOT/TEMPERATURE **1** [U] the quality of being hot: *He could feel the heat of the sun on his back.* ♦ *Heat rises.* ♦ *The fire gave off intense heat.* ⊃ see also WHITE HEAT **2** [U, C, usually sing.] the level of temperature: *to increase/reduce the heat* ♦ *Test the heat of the water before putting the baby in the bathtub.* ♦ *Set the oven to a low/high/moderate heat.* ⊃ see also BLOOD HEAT **3** [U] hot weather; the hot conditions in a building/vehicle, etc.: *You should not go out in the heat of the day* (= at the hottest time). ♦ *to suffer from the heat* ♦ *the afternoon/midday heat* ♦ *The heat in the factory was unbearable.* ⊃ see also PRICKLY HEAT
▷ FOR COOKING **4** [sing.] a source of heat, especially one that you cook food on: *Return the pan to the heat and stir.*
▷ IN BUILDING/ROOM **5** [U, sing.] the process of supplying heat to a room or building; a system used to do this: *The heat wasn't on and the house was freezing.* **SYN** HEATING
▷ STRONG FEELINGS **6** [U] strong feelings, especially of anger or excitement: *"No, I won't,"* he said with heat in his voice. ♦ *The chairman tried to take the heat out of the situation* (= to make people calmer). ♦ *In the heat of the moment she forgot what she wanted to say* (= because she was so angry or excited). ♦ *In the heat of the argument he said a lot of things he regretted later.*
▷ PRESSURE **7** [U] pressure on someone to do or achieve something: *The heat is on now that the election is only a week away.* ♦ *The Mavericks turned up the heat on their opponents with a second basket.* ♦ *Can she take the heat of this level of competition?*
▷ RACE **8** [C] one of a series of races or competitions, the winners of which then compete against each other in the next part of the competition: *a qualifying heat* ♦ *She won her heat.* ♦ *He did well in the heats; hopefully he'll do as well in the final.* ⊃ see also DEAD HEAT
▷ PHYSICS **9** [U] heat seen as a form of energy that can be transferred by CONDUCTION, CONVECTION, or RADIATION
IDM if you can't stand/take the heat (get out of the kitchen) (*informal*) used to tell someone to stop trying to do something if they find it too difficult, especially in order to suggest that they are less able than other people

● **verb** [T, I] ~ (sth) to make something hot or warm; to become hot or warm: *Heat the oil and add the onions.* ♦ *The system produced enough energy to heat several thousand homes.* ⊃ collocations at COOKING
PHR V heat 'up **1** to become hot or warm **SYN** WARM UP: *The oven takes a while to heat up.* **2** to become more exciting or to show an increase in activity: *The election contest is heating up.* heat sth↔'up to make something hot or warm **SYN** WARM UP: *Just heat up the food in the microwave.*

'heat capacity *noun* [U] (*chemistry*) the amount of heat needed to raise the temperature of something by one degree

heat·ed /'hiːtɪd/ *adj.* **1** (of a room, building, etc.) made warmer using a heater: *a heated swimming pool* **ANT** UNHEATED **2** (of a person or discussion) full of anger and excitement: *a heated argument/debate* ♦ *She became very heated.* ▶ **heat·ed·ly** *adv.*: *"You had no right!"* she said heatedly.

heat·er /'hiːtər/ *noun* a machine used for making air or water warmer: *a gas heater* ♦ *a water heater*

'heat ex,changer *noun* (*technical*) a device for making heat pass from one liquid to another without allowing the liquids to mix

'heat ex,haustion (also 'heat pros,tration) *noun* [U] an illness that happens when you are very active in hot conditions and that makes you feel very weak and sick

heath /hiːθ/ *noun* a large area of open land that is not used for farming and is covered with rough grass and other small wild plants

heath·en /'hiːðn/ *noun, adj.*
● **noun** (*old-fashioned, offensive*) **1** used by people who have a strong religious belief as a way of referring to a person who has no religion or who believes in a religion that is not one of the world's main religions **2** used to refer to a person who shows lack of education
● **adj.** (*old-fashioned, offensive*) connected with heathens: *heathen gods* ♦ *He set out to convert the heathen* (= people who are heathens).

heath·er /'hɛðər/ *noun* [U] a low wild plant with small purple, pink, or white flowers, that grows on hills and areas of wild open land (= MOORLAND)

heath·land /'hiːθlænd/ *noun* [U] (also heath·lands [pl.]) a large area of heath

'heat ,index *noun* [sing.] a measure of temperature and the effects of HUMIDITY combined. When the level of humidity is high, the air feels hotter and more uncomfortable.

heat·ing 🔑 /'hiːtɪŋ/ *noun* [U]
the process of supplying heat to a room or building; a system used to do this: *What type of heating do you have?* ♦ *a gas heating system* ♦ *heating bills* **SYN** HEAT ⊃ see also CENTRAL HEATING

'heat ,lightning *noun* [U] flashes of LIGHTNING without THUNDER, seen in the sky on hot nights

heat·proof /'hiːtpruːf/ *adj.* that cannot be damaged by heat: *a heatproof dish*

'heat pros,tration *noun* [U] = HEAT EXHAUSTION

'heat pump *noun* a machine or part of a machine that can move heat from one area to another

'heat-re,sistant *adj.* not easily damaged by heat

'heat-,seeking *adj.* [only before noun] (of a weapon) that moves toward the heat coming from the aircraft, etc. that it is intended to hit and destroy: *heat-seeking missiles*

heat·stroke /'hiːtstroʊk/ *noun* [U] an illness with fever and often loss of CONSCIOUSNESS, caused by being in too great a heat for too long

heat·wave /'hiːtweɪv/ *noun* a period of unusually hot weather

heave /hiːv/ *verb, noun*
● **verb** **1** [T, I] to lift, pull, or throw someone or something very heavy with one great effort: ~ sth/sb/yourself + adv./prep. *I managed to heave the suitcase into the trunk of the car.* ♦ *They heaved the body overboard.* ♦ + adv./prep. *We all heaved on the rope.* **2** [I] to rise up and down with strong, regular movements: *The boat heaved beneath them.* ♦ ~ with sth *Her shoulders heaved with suppressed laughter.* **3** [T] ~ a sigh, etc. to make a sound slowly and often with effort: *We all heaved a sigh of relief.* **4** [I] to experience the tight feeling in your stomach that you get before you VOMIT: *The thought of it makes me heave.*
IDM heave into sight/view (*formal*) (especially of ships) to appear, especially when moving gradually closer from a long way off: *A ship hove into sight.* **HELP** Hove is usually used for the past tense and past participle in this idiom.
PHR V ,heave 'to (*technical*) if a ship or its CREW (= the people sailing it) heave to, the ship stops moving **HELP** Hove is usually used for the past tense and past participle in this phrasal verb.
● **noun** **1** [C] an act of lifting, pulling, or throwing: *With a mighty heave he lifted the sack onto the truck.* **2** [U] (especially *literary*) a rising and falling movement: *the steady heave of the sea*

heave-ho /ˌhiːv 'hoʊ/ *noun* [sing.]
IDM give sb the (old) heave-ho (*informal*) to dismiss

someone from their job; to end a relationship with someone

heav·en 🔊 /'hɛvn/ noun
1 also **Heaven** [U] (used without *the*) (in some religions) the place believed to be the home of God where good people go when they die: *the kingdom of heaven* ◆ *I feel like I've died and gone to heaven.* **2** [U, C] (*informal*) a place or situation in which you are very happy: *This isn't exactly my idea of heaven!* ◆ *It was heaven being away from the office for a week.* ◆ *The island is truly a heaven on earth.* **3 the heavens** [pl.] (*literary*) the sky: *Four tall trees stretched up to the heavens.* **IDM Heaven forbid/forfend (that)…** (*humorous* or *old use*) used to say that you are frightened of the idea of something happening: *Heaven forbid that students are encouraged to think!* | **(Good) Heavens!** | **Heavens above!** (*informal*) used to show that you are surprised or annoyed: *Good heavens, what are you doing?* **the heavens opened** it began to rain heavily **made in heaven** (especially of a marriage or other relationship) seeming to be perfect ➲ more at GOD, HELP v., HIGH adj., KNOW v., MOVE v., NAME n., SEVENTH, THANK

heav·en·ly /'hɛvnli/ adj. **1** [only before noun] connected with heaven: *our heavenly Father* (= God) ◆ *the heavenly kingdom* **2** [only before noun] connected with the sky: *heavenly bodies* (= the sun, moon, stars, and planets) **3** (*informal*) very pleasant **SYN WONDERFUL**: *a heavenly morning/feeling* ◆ *This place is heavenly.*

heaven-'sent adj. [usually before noun] happening unexpectedly and at exactly the right time

heav·en·ward /'hɛvnwərd/ (also **heavenwards**) adv. (*literary*) toward heaven or the sky: *to cast/raise your eyes heavenward* (= to show you are annoyed or impatient)

heav·i·ly 🔊 /'hɛvəli/ adv.
1 to a great degree; in large amounts: *It was raining heavily.* ◆ *to drink/smoke heavily.* ◆ *heavily armed police* (= carrying a lot of weapons) ◆ *a heavily pregnant woman* (= one whose baby is nearly ready to be born) ◆ *They are both heavily involved in politics.* ◆ *He relies heavily on his parents.* ◆ *She has been heavily criticized in the press.* **2** with a lot of force or effort: *She fell heavily to the ground.* **3 ~ built** (of a person) with a large, solid, and strong body **4** slowly and loudly: *She was now breathing heavily.* ◆ *He was snoring heavily.* **5** in a slow way that sounds as though you are worried or sad: *He sighed heavily.* **6** in a way that makes you feel uncomfortable or anxious: *Silence hung heavily in the room.* ◆ *The burden of guilt weighed heavily on his mind.* **7 ~ loaded/laden** full of or loaded with heavy things: *a heavily loaded van*

heav·y 🔊 /'hɛvi/ adj., noun, adv.
● **adj.** (**heav·ier, heav·iest**)
▷ **WEIGHING A LOT 1** weighing a lot; difficult to lift or move: *She was struggling with a heavy suitcase.* ◆ *My brother is much heavier than me.* ◆ *He tried to push the heavy door open.* ◆ *How heavy is it* (= how much does it weigh)? ◆ *My sister has gotten a little heavy* (= fat). ◆ (*figurative*) *Her father carried a heavy burden of responsibility.* **ANT LIGHT**
▷ **WORSE THAN USUAL 2** more or worse than usual in amount, degree, etc.: *the noise of heavy traffic* ◆ *heavy frost/rain/snow* ◆ *the effects of heavy drinking* ◆ *There was heavy fighting in the capital last night.* ◆ *The penalty for speeding can be a heavy fine.* ◆ *She spoke with heavy irony.* **ANT LIGHT**
▷ **NOT DELICATE 3** (of someone/something's appearance or structure) large and solid; not delicate: *big, dark rooms full of heavy furniture* ◆ *He was tall and strong, with heavy features.*
▷ **MATERIAL 4** (of the material or substance that something is made of) thick: *heavy curtains* ◆ *a heavy coat* **ANT LIGHT**
▷ **FULL OF SOMETHING 5 ~ with sth** (*literary*) full of or loaded with something: *trees heavy with apples* ◆ *The air was heavy with the scent of flowers.* ◆ *His voice was heavy with sarcasm.*
▷ **MACHINES 6** [usually before noun] (of machines, vehicles, or weapons) large and powerful: *a wide range of engines and heavy machinery* ◆ *heavy trucks*
▷ **BUSY 7** [usually before noun] involving a lot of work or activity; very busy: *a heavy schedule* ◆ *She'd had a heavy day.*

▷ **WORK 8** hard, especially because it requires a lot of physical strength: *heavy digging/lifting*
▷ **FALL/HIT 9** falling or hitting something with a lot of force: *a heavy fall/blow*
▷ **MEAL/FOOD 10** large in amount or very solid: *a heavy lunch/dinner* ◆ *a heavy cake* **ANT LIGHT**
▷ **USING A LOT 11 ~ on sth** (*informal*) using a lot of something: *Older cars are heavy on gas.* ◆ *Don't go so heavy on the garlic.*
▷ **DRINKER/SMOKER/SLEEPER 12** [only before noun] (of a person) doing the thing mentioned more, or more deeply, than usual: *a heavy drinker/smoker* ◆ *a heavy sleeper*
▷ **SOUND 13** (of a sound that someone makes) loud and deep: *heavy breathing/snoring* ◆ *a heavy groan/sigh*
▷ **SERIOUS/DIFFICULT 14** (usually *disapproving*) (of a book, program, style, etc.) serious; difficult to understand or enjoy: *We found the play very heavy.* ◆ *The discussion got a little heavy.*
▷ **SEA/OCEAN 15** dangerous because of big waves, etc.: *strong winds and heavy seas*
▷ **AIR/WEATHER 16** hot and lacking fresh air, in a way that is unpleasant: *It feels very heavy—I think there's going to be a storm.*
▷ **SOIL 17** wet, sticky, and difficult to dig or to move over
▷ **ACCENT 18** (of someone's accent) very noticeable: *She has a heavy British accent.*
▶ **heav·i·ness** noun [U]
IDM get heavy (*informal*) to become very serious, because strong feelings are involved: *They started shouting at me. It got very heavy.* **heavy going** used to describe something that is difficult to deal with or understand: *I found the course to be heavy going.* **heavy hand** a way of doing something or of treating people that is much stronger and less sensitive than it needs to be: *the heavy hand of management* **a heavy heart** a feeling of great sadness: *She left her children behind with a heavy heart.* **a heavy silence/atmosphere** a situation when people do not say anything, but feel embarrassed or uncomfortable **make heavy weather of sth** to seem to find something more difficult or complicated than it needs to be ➲ more at TOLL n.

● **noun** (pl. **heav·ies**) (*informal*) a large strong man whose job is to protect a person or place, often using violence

● **adv.**
IDM hang/lie heavy 1 ~ (on/in sth) (of a feeling or something in the air) to be very noticeable in a particular place in a way that is unpleasant: *Smoke lay heavy on the far side of the water.* ◆ *Despair hangs heavy in the stifling air.* **2 ~ on sb/sth** to cause someone or something to feel uncomfortable or anxious: *The crime lay heavy on her conscience.*

heavy-'duty adj. [only before noun] **1** not easily damaged and therefore suitable for hard physical work or to be used all the time: *a heavy-duty carpet* **2** (*informal*) very serious or great in quantity: *I think you need some heavy-duty advice.*

heavy-'handed adj. **1** not showing a sympathetic understanding of the feelings of other people: *a heavy-handed approach* **2** using unnecessary force: *heavy-handed police methods* **3** (of a person) using too much of something in a way that can cause damage: *Don't be too heavy-handed with the salt.*

heavy 'hitter noun (*informal*) a person with a lot of power, especially in business or politics

heavy 'industry noun [U, C] industry that uses large machinery to produce metal, coal, vehicles, etc. ➲ compare **LIGHT INDUSTRY**

heavy 'metal noun **1** [U] a type of ROCK music with a very strong beat played very loud on electric GUITARS **2** [C] (*technical*) a metal that has a very high DENSITY (= the relation of its weight to its volume), such as gold or LEAD[2]

heavy-'set adj. having a broad heavy body **SYN THICKSET**

heavy 'water noun [U] (*chemistry*) water in which HYDROGEN is replaced by DEUTERIUM, used in nuclear reactions

heav·y·weight /'hɛviˌweɪt/ noun **1** a BOXER of the heaviest class in normal use, weighing 175 pounds or more: *a heavyweight champion* **2** a person or thing that weighs more than is usual **3** a very important person, organization, or thing that influences others: *a political heavyweight* ◆ *a heavyweight journal*

He·bra·ic /hɪˈbreɪɪk/ *adj.* of or connected with the Hebrew language or people: *Hebraic poetry*

He·brew /ˈhibru/ *noun* **1** a member of an ancient race of people living in what is now Israel and Palestine. Their writings and traditions form the basis of the Jewish religion. **2** the language traditionally used by the Hebrew people **3** a modern form of the Hebrew language which is the official language of modern Israel ⊃ compare YIDDISH ▸ **Hebrew** *adj.*

heck /hɛk/ *exclamation, noun* (*informal*) used to show that you are slightly annoyed or surprised: *Oh heck, I'm going to be late!* ◆ *We had to wait a heck of a long time!* ◆ *Who the heck are you?*
IDM **for the heck of it** (*informal*) just for pleasure rather than for a reason **what the heck!** (*informal*) used to say that you are going to do something that you know you should not do: *It means I'll be late for work but what the heck!*

heck·le /ˈhɛkl/ *verb* [T, I] ~ **(sb)** to interrupt a speaker at a public meeting by shouting out questions or rude remarks: *He was booed and heckled throughout his speech.* ▸ **heck·ler** /ˈhɛklər/ *noun* **heck·ling** *noun* [U]

hec·tare /ˈhɛktɛr/ *noun* (*abbr.* ha) a unit for measuring an area of land; 10,000 square meters or about 2.5 ACRES

hec·tic /ˈhɛktɪk/ *adj.* very busy; full of activity: *to lead a hectic life* ◆ *a hectic schedule*

hec·to·li·ter (*CanE* usually **hec·to·li·tre**) /ˈhɛktəˌlitər/ *noun* (*abbr.* hl) a unit for measuring volume; 100 liters

hec·tor /ˈhɛktər/ *verb* ~ **sb** | + speech (*formal*) to try to make someone do something by talking or behaving in an aggressive way **SYN** BULLY ▸ **hec·tor·ing** *adj.*: *a hectoring tone of voice*

he'd /hid; id; *strong form* hid/ *short form* **1** he had **2** he would

hedge /hɛdʒ/ *noun, verb*
● *noun* **1** a row of bushes or small trees planted close together, usually along the edge of a field, yard, or road: *a privet hedge* **2** ~ **against sth** a way of protecting yourself against the loss of something, especially money: *to buy gold as a hedge against inflation*
● *verb* **1** [I] to avoid giving a direct answer to a question or promising to support a particular idea, etc.: *Just answer "yes" or "no"—and stop hedging.* **2** [T] ~ **sth** to put a hedge around a field, etc. **3** [T, usually passive] (*formal*) to surround or limit someone or something: *His religious belief was always hedged with doubt.*
IDM **hedge your bets** to reduce the risk of losing or making a mistake by supporting more than one side in a competition, an argument, etc., or by having several choices available to you
PHR V **'hedge against sth** to do something to protect yourself against problems, especially against losing money: *a way of hedging against currency risks* **hedge sb/sth↔'in** to surround someone or something with something **SYN** HEM SB/STH IN: *The cathedral is now hedged in by other buildings.* ◆ (*figurative*) *Married life made him feel hedged in and restless.*

'hedge fund *noun* a group of people who take high risks to invest money and try to make a lot of money

hedge·hog /ˈhɛdʒhɔg; -hag/ *noun* a small, brown, European animal with stiff parts like needles (called SPINES) covering its back. Hedgehogs are NOCTURNAL (= active mostly at night) and can roll into a ball to defend themselves when they are attacked.

hedge·row /ˈhɛdʒroʊ/ *noun* (*literary*) a line of bushes planted along the edge of a field or road

he·don·ism /ˈhidnˌɪzəm/ *noun* [U] the belief that pleasure is the most important thing in life ▸ **he·don·is·tic** /ˌhidnˈɪstɪk/ *adj.*

he·don·ist /ˈhidnɪst/ *noun* a person who believes that pleasure is the most important thing in life

the hee·bie-jee·bies /ˌhibi ˈdʒibiz/ *noun* [pl.] (*old-fashioned, informal*) a feeling of nervous fear or worry

heed /hid/ *verb, noun*
● *verb* ~ **sb/sth** (*formal*) to pay careful attention to someone's advice or warning **SYN** TAKE NOTICE OF
● *noun* [U]
IDM **give/pay heed (to sb/sth)| take heed (of sb/sth)** (*formal*) to pay careful attention to someone or something

heed·ful /ˈhidfl/ *adj.* ~ **(of sb/sth)** (*formal*) paying careful attention to someone or something

heed·less /ˈhidləs/ *adj.* [not usually before noun] ~ **(of sb/sth)** (*formal*) not paying careful attention to someone or something ▸ **heed·less·ly** *adv.*

hee-haw /ˈhi hɔ/ *noun* the way of writing the sound made by a DONKEY

heel /hil/ *noun, verb*
● *noun*
▷ **PART OF FOOT 1** [C] the back part of the foot below the ankle ⊃ picture at BODY
▷ **PART OF SOCK/SHOE 2** [C] the part of a sock, etc. that covers the heel **3** [C] the raised part on the bottom of a shoe, boot, etc. that makes the shoe, etc. higher at the back: *shoes with a low/high heel* ◆ *a stiletto heel* ◆ *The sergeant clicked his heels and walked out.* ⊃ compare SOLE
▷ **-HEELED 4** (in adjectives) having the type of heel mentioned: *high-heeled shoes* ⊃ see also WELL HEELED
▷ **SHOES 5** **heels** [pl.] a pair of women's shoes that have high heels: *She doesn't often wear heels.* ⊃ picture at SHOE ⊃ see also KITTEN HEELS
▷ **PART OF HAND 6** [C] ~ **of your hand/palm** the raised part of the inside of the hand where it joins the wrist
▷ **UNPLEASANT MAN 7** [C] (*old-fashioned, informal*) a man who is unpleasant to other people and cannot be trusted ⊃ see also ACHILLES HEEL, DOWN AT HEEL
IDM **at/on sb's heels** following closely behind someone: *He ran from the stadium with the police at his heels.* **bring sb/sth to heel 1** to force someone to obey you and accept discipline **2** to make a dog come close to you **come to heel 1** (of a person) to agree to obey someone and accept their orders **2** (of a dog) to come close to the person who has called it **(close/hard/hot) on sb's/sth's heels** very close behind someone or something; very soon after something: *News of rising unemployment followed hard on the heels of falling export figures.* **take to your heels** (*old-fashioned* or *formal*) to run away from someone or something **turn/spin on your heel** to turn around suddenly so that you are facing in the opposite direction **under the heel of sb** (*literary*) completely controlled by someone ⊃ more at COOL *v.*, DIG *v.*, DRAG *v.*, HEAD *n.*, KICK *v.*
● *verb*
▷ **REPAIR SHOE 1** [T] ~ **sth** to repair the heel of a shoe, etc.
▷ **OF BOAT 2** [I] ~ **(over)** to lean over to one side: *The boat heeled over in the strong wind.*

Heelys™ /ˈhiliz/ *noun* [pl.] sports shoes that have one or more wheels underneath

heft /hɛft/ *verb, noun*
● *verb* **1** ~ **sth** (+ adv./prep.) to lift or carry something heavy from one position to another: *The two men hefted the box into the car.* **2** ~ **sth** to lift or hold something in order to estimate its weight: *Anna took the old sword and hefted it in her hands.*
● *noun* [U] the weight of someone or something: *She was surprised by the sheer heft of the package.*

heft·y /ˈhɛfti/ *adj.* (**hefti·er, hefti·est**) **1** (of a person or an object) big and heavy: *Her brothers were both hefty men in their forties.* **2** (of an amount of money) large; larger than usual or expected: *They sold it easily and made a hefty profit.* **3** using a lot of force: *He gave the door a hefty kick.* ▸ **heft·i·ly** /-təli/ *adv.*

he·gem·o·ny /hɪˈdʒɛməni; ˈhɛdʒəˌmoʊni/ *noun* [U, C] (*pl.*

h hat   m man   n no   ŋ sing   l leg   r red   y yes   w wet

he·gem·o·nies (*formal*) control by one country, organization, etc. over other countries, etc. within a particular group ▶ **heg·e·mon·ic** /ˌhedʒəˈmɑnɪk/ *adj.*: *hegemonic control*

He·gi·ra (also **He·ji·ra**) /hɪˈdʒaɪrə; ˈhedʒɪrə/ (also **Hi·jra**) *noun* [*sing.*] **1** usually **the Hegira** the occasion when Muhammad left Mecca to go to Medina in A.D.622 **2** the period which began at this time; the Muslim ERA

heif·er /ˈhefər/ *noun* a young female cow, especially one that has not yet had a CALF

height 🔊 /haɪt/ *noun*
> MEASUREMENT **1** [U, C] the measurement of how tall a person or thing is: *Height: 8.5 inches. Width: 2.25 inches. Length: 6.75 inches.* ♦ *Please state your height and weight.* ♦ *It is almost 6 feet in height.* ♦ *She is the same height as her sister.* ♦ *to be of medium/average height* ♦ *You can adjust the height of the chair.* ♦ *The table is available in several different heights.* ⊃ **picture at DIMENSION**
> BEING TALL **2** [U] the quality of being tall or high: *She worries about her height* (= that she is too tall). ♦ *The height of the mountain did not discourage them.*
> DISTANCE ABOVE GROUND **3** [C, U] a particular distance above the ground: *The plane flew at a height of 9,000 feet.* ♦ *The stone was dropped from a great height.* ♦ *The aircraft was gaining height.* ♦ *to be at shoulder/chest/waist height*
> HIGH PLACE **4** [C, usually pl.] (often used in names) a high place or position: *Brooklyn Heights* ♦ *a fear of heights* ♦ *We looked out over the city from the heights of the Space Needle.* ♦ *The pattern of the ancient fields is clearly visible from a height.*
> STRONGEST POINT/LEVEL **5** [*sing.*] the point when something is at its best or strongest: *He is at the height of his career.* ♦ *She is still at the height of her powers.* ♦ *I wouldn't go there at the height of summer.* ♦ *The fire reached its height around 2 a.m.* ♦ *The crisis was at its height in May.* **6 heights** [pl.] a better or greater level of something; a situation where something is very good: *Their success had reached new heights.* ♦ *She dreamed of reaching the dizzy heights of stardom.*
> EXTREME EXAMPLE **7** [*sing.*] **~ of sth** an extreme example of a particular quality: *She was dressed in the height of fashion.* ♦ *It would be the height of folly* (= very stupid) *to change course now.*

IDM **draw yourself up/rise to your full height** to stand straight and tall in order to show your determination or high status ⊃ **more at DIZZY**

height·en /ˈhaɪtn/ *verb* [I, T] if a feeling or an effect **heightens**, or something **heightens** it, it becomes stronger or increases **SYN** **INTENSIFY**: *Tension has heightened after the recent bomb attack.* ♦ **~ sth** *The campaign is intended to heighten public awareness of the disease.*

Heim·lich ma·neu·ver /ˈhaɪmlɪk məˌnuvər/ *noun* [C, usually *sing.*] a method to stop someone from choking (CHOKE) on food, in which you quickly and suddenly apply pressure to the top of their stomach to force the food up and out of their throat

hei·nous /ˈheɪnəs/ *adj.* [usually before noun] (*formal*) morally very bad: *a heinous crime* ▶ **hei·nous·ly** *adv.* **hei·nous·ness** *noun* [U]

heir /ɛr/ *noun* **~ (to sth)** | **~ (of sb) 1** a person who has the legal right to receive someone's property, money, or title when that person dies: *to be heir to a large fortune* ♦ *the heir to the throne* (= the person who will be the next king or queen) **2** a person who is thought to continue the work or a tradition started by someone else: *the president's political heirs* **HELP** Use **an**, not **a**, before **heir**.

heir ap·parent *noun* (*pl.* **heirs apparent**) **~ (to sth) 1** an HEIR whose legal right to receive someone's property, money, or title cannot be taken away because it is impossible for someone with a stronger claim to be born **2** a person who is expected to take the job of someone when that person leaves

heir·ess /ˈɛrəs/ *noun* **~ (to sth)** a female heir, especially one who has received or will receive a large amount of money **HELP** Use **an**, not **a**, before **heiress**.

heir·loom /ˈɛrlum/ *noun, adj.*
● *noun* a valuable object that has belonged to the same family for many years: *a family heirloom* **HELP** Use **an**, not **a**, before **heirloom**.
● *adj.* [only before noun] **heirloom** plants are varieties which were commonly grown in the past but are no longer grown as commercial crops

heir pre·sumptive *noun* (*pl.* **heirs presumptive**) an HEIR who may lose his or her legal right to receive someone's property, money, or title if someone with a stronger claim is born

heist /haɪst/ *noun, verb*
● *noun* (*informal*) an act of stealing something valuable from a store or bank **SYN** **ROBBERY**: *a bank heist*
● *verb* **~ sth** (*informal*) to steal something valuable from a store or bank

He·ji·ra = **HEGIRA**

held pt, pp of **HOLD**

hel·i·cal /ˈhelɪkl/ *adj.* (*technical*) like a HELIX

hel·i·cop·ter /ˈheləˌkɑptər/ (also *informal* **cop·ter**, **chop·per**) *noun* an aircraft without wings that has large blades on top that go around. It can fly straight up from the ground and can also stay in one position in the air: *He was rushed to the hospital by helicopter.* ♦ *a police helicopter* ♦ *a helicopter pilot* ⊃ **picture at PLANE**

helicopter pad *noun* = **HELIPAD**

helicopter view (*business*) a broad, general view or description of a problem **SYN** **10,000-FOOT VIEW**

he·li·o·cen·tric /ˌhiliəˈsentrɪk/ *adj.* (*astronomy*) with the sun as the center: *the heliocentric model of the solar system*

he·li·o·graph /ˈhiliəˌgræf/ *noun* **1** a device that gives signals by reflecting flashes of light from the sun **2** (also **he·li·o·gram** /ˈhiliəˌgræm/) a message that is sent using signals from a heliograph **3** a special camera that takes photographs of the sun

he·li·o·trope /ˈhiliəˌtroup/ *noun* **1** [C, U] a garden plant with pale purple flowers with a sweet smell **2** [U] a pale purple color

hel·i·pad /ˈheləˌpæd/ (also **helicopter pad**) *noun* a small area where HELICOPTERS can take off and land

hel·i·port /ˈheləˌpɔrt/ *noun* a place where HELICOPTERS take off and land

hel·i·ski·ing /ˈheləˌskiɪŋ/ *noun* [U] the sport of flying in a HELICOPTER to a place where there is a lot of snow on a mountain in order to SKI there

he·li·um /ˈhiliəm/ *noun* [U] (*symb.* **He**) a chemical element. Helium is a very light gas that does not burn, often used to fill BALLOONS and to freeze food.

he·lix /ˈhilɪks/ *noun* (*pl.* **hel·i·ces** /ˈheləsiz; ˈhi-/) a shape like a SPIRAL or a line curved around a CYLINDER or CONE ⊃ **see also DOUBLE HELIX**

helix

hell 🔊 /hel/ *noun*
1 [*sing.*] usually **Hell** (used without *a* or *the*) in some religions, the place believed to be the home of the DEVIL and where bad people go after death **2** [U, *sing.*] a very unpleasant experience or situation in which people suffer very much: *The last three months have been hell.* ♦ *He went through hell during the trial.* ♦ *Her parents made her life hell.* ♦ *Being totally alone is my idea of hell on earth.* **3** [U] a swear word that some people use when they are annoyed or surprised or to emphasize something. Its use is offensive to some people: *Oh hell, I've burned the pan.* ♦ *What the hell do you think you are doing?* ♦ *Go to hell!* ♦ *I can't really afford it, but, what the hell* (= it doesn't matter), *I'll get it anyway.* ♦ *He's as guilty as hell.* ♦ *"Do you understand?" "Hell, no. I don't."*

IDM **all hell broke loose** (*informal*) suddenly there was a lot of noise, arguing, fighting, or confusion: *There was a loud bang and then all hell broke loose.* **beat/kick (the) hell out of sb/sth | knock hell out of sb/sth** (*informal*) to hit someone or something very hard: *He was a dirty player and loved to kick hell out of the opposition.* **(just) for the hell of it** (*informal*) just for fun; for no real reason: *They stole the car just for the hell of it.* **from hell** (*informal*) used to describe a very unpleasant person or thing; the worst that you can imagine: *They are the neighbors from hell.* **get the hell out (of…)** (*informal*) to leave a place very quickly: *Let's get the hell out of here.* **give sb hell** (*informal*) **1** to make life unpleasant for someone: *He used to give his mother hell when he was a teenager.* ◆ *My new shoes are giving me hell* (= are hurting me). **2** to shout at or speak angrily to someone: *Dad will give us hell when he sees that mess.* **go to hell in a handbasket** (*informal*) to get into a very bad state **hell hath no fury (like a woman scorned)** used to refer to someone, usually a woman, who has reacted very angrily to something, especially the fact that her husband or lover has been UNFAITHFUL **(come) hell or high water** despite any difficulties: *I was determined to go, come hell or high water.* **like hell 1** (*informal*) used for emphasis: *She worked like hell to prepare for her exams.* ◆ *My broken finger hurt like hell.* **2** (*informal*) used when you are refusing permission or saying that something is not true: *"I'm coming with you." "Like hell you are."* (= you certainly are not) **a/one hell of a… | a/one helluva…** /'hɛləvə/ (*slang*) used to give emphasis to what a person is saying: *The firm was in a hell of a mess when he took over.* ◆ *It must have been one hell of a party.* ◆ *That's one helluva big house you've got.* **scare, annoy, etc. the hell out of sb** (*informal*) to scare, annoy, etc. someone very much **to hell and back** (*informal*) used to say that someone has been through a difficult situation: *We'd been to hell and back together and we were still good friends.* **to hell with sb/sth** (*informal*) used to express anger or dislike and to say that you no longer care about someone or something and will take no notice of them: *"To hell with him," she thought, "I'm leaving."* ⊃ more at BAT *n.*, CATCH *v.*, HOPE *n.*, PAY *v.*, RAISE *v.*, ROAD, SNOWBALL *n.*

he'll /hil; hɪl; *weak form* il; ɪl/ *short form* he will

hell·a·cious /hɛ'leɪʃəs/ *adj.* (*informal*) extremely difficult or bad: *hellacious traffic* ◆ *a hellacious storm*

hell-'bent *adj.* ~ **on sth/on doing sth** determined to do something even though the results may be bad: *He seems hell-bent on drinking himself to death.*

hel·le·bore /'hɛlə,bɔr/ *noun* a poisonous plant with divided leaves and large green, white, or purple flowers

Hel·lene /'hɛlin/ *noun* a person from Greece, especially ancient Greece

Hel·len·ic /hə'lɛnɪk/ *adj.* of or connected with ancient or modern Greece

Hel·len·is·tic /,hɛlə'nɪstɪk/ *adj.* of or connected with the Greek history, language, and culture of the 4th–1st centuries B.C.

hell·fire /'hɛl,faɪər/ *noun* [U] the fires that are believed by some religious people to burn in hell, where bad people go to be punished after they die

hell·hole /'hɛlhoʊl/ *noun* (*informal*) a very unpleasant place

hel·lion /'hɛlyən/ *noun* a badly behaved child who annoys other people

hell·ish /'hɛlɪʃ/ *adj.* (*informal*) extremely unpleasant

hel·lo 🔊 /hə'loʊ; hɛ-; 'hɛloʊ/ *exclamation, noun* (*pl.* hel·los)

1 used as a GREETING when you meet someone, when you answer the telephone, or when you want to attract someone's attention: *Hello John, how are you?* ◆ *Hello, is there anybody there?* ◆ *Say hello to Liz for me.* ◆ *They exchanged hellos* (= said hello to each other) *and forced smiles.* **2** (*informal*) used to show that you think someone has said something stupid or is not paying attention: *Hello? You didn't really mean that, did you?* ◆ *I'm like, "Hello! Did you even listen?"*

hell·rais·er /'hɛl,raɪzər/ *noun* a person who causes trouble by behaving loudly and often violently, especially when they have drunk too much alcohol

Hell's 'Angel *noun* a member of a group of people, usually men, who ride powerful motorcycles, wear leather clothes, and used to be known for their wild and violent behavior

hell·uv·a ⊃ HELL

helm /hɛlm/ *noun* a handle or wheel used for steering a boat or ship ⊃ compare TILLER
IDM **at the helm 1** in charge of an organization, project, etc. **2** steering a boat or ship **take the helm 1** to take charge of an organization, project, etc. **2** to begin steering a boat or ship

hel·met /'hɛlmət/ *noun* a type of hard hat that protects the head, worn, for example, by a police officer, a soldier, or a person playing some sports ⊃ picture at BICYCLE ⊃ see also CRASH HELMET ⊃ picture at FOOTBALL, SPORT

hel·met·ed /'hɛlmətəd/ *adj.* [only before noun] wearing a helmet

helms·man /'hɛlmzmən/ *noun* (*pl.* helms·men /-mən/) a person who steers a boat or ship

help 🔊 /hɛlp/ *verb, noun*
● **verb**
▷ **MAKE EASIER/BETTER 1** [I, T] to make it easier or possible for someone to do something by doing something for them or by giving them something that they need: *Help, I'm stuck!* ◆ ~ **with sth** *He always helps with the housework.* ◆ ~ **sb** *We must try and to help each other.* ◆ ~ **sb with sth** *Jo will help us with some of the organization.* ◆ ~ **(sb) in doing sth** *I need contacts that could help me in finding a job.* ◆ ~ **sb (to) do sth** *The college's goal is to help students (to) achieve their aspirations.* ◆ *This charity works to help people (to) help themselves.* ◆ *Come and help me lift this box.* ◆ ~ **(to) do sth** *She helped (to) organize the party.* **HELP** In verb patterns with a to infinitive, the "to" is often left out, especially in informal or spoken English. **2** [I, T] to improve a situation; to make it easier for something to happen: *It helped being able to talk about it.* ◆ ~ **sth** *It doesn't really help matters knowing that everyone is talking about us.* ◆ ~ **(to) do sth** *This should help (to) reduce the pain.*
▷ **SOMEONE TO MOVE 3** [T] ~ **sb + adv./prep.** to help someone move by letting them lean on you, guiding them,

ʌ cup   ə about   eɪ say   aɪ five   ɔɪ boy   aʊ now   oʊ go   ər bird

etc.: *She helped him to his feet.* ◆ *We were helped ashore by local people.*
> GIVE FOOD/DRINK **4** [T] to give yourself/someone food, drinks, etc.: **~ yourself** *If you want another drink, just help yourself.* ◆ **~ yourself/sb to sth** *Can I help you to some more salad?*
> STEAL **5** [T] **~ yourself to sth** (*informal, disapproving*) to take something without permission **SYN** STEAL: *He'd been helping himself to the money in the cash register.*
IDM **sb can (not) help (doing) sth | sb can not help but do sth** used to say that it is impossible to prevent or avoid something: *I can't help thinking he knows more than he has told us.* ◆ *She couldn't help but wonder what he was thinking.* ◆ *I always end up having an argument with her, I don't know why, I just **can't help it**.* ◆ *I couldn't **help it** if the bus was late* (= it wasn't my fault). ◆ *She burst out laughing—she **couldn't help herself*** (= couldn't stop herself). **it can't be helped** used to say that there is no way of avoiding a bad situation: *It couldn't be helped* (= there was no way of avoiding it and we must accept it). **give/lend a helping hand** to help someone **God/Heaven help sb** (*informal*) used to say that you are afraid someone will be in danger or that something bad will happen to them: *God help us if this doesn't work.* **HELP** Some people find this use offensive. **so help me (God)** used to swear that what you are saying is true, especially in a court of law
PHR V **help sb 'off/'on with sth** to help someone put on/ take off a piece of clothing: *Let me help you off with your coat.* **help 'out | help sb⟷'out** to help someone, especially in a difficult situation: *He's always willing to help out.* ◆ *When I bought the house, my sister helped me out with a loan.*

● *noun*
> MAKING EASIER/BETTER **1** [U] the act of helping someone to do something: *Thank you for all your help.* ◆ **~ (with sth)** *Do you need any help with that?* ◆ *Can I be of any help to you?* ◆ *None of this would have been possible without their help.* ◆ *She stopped smoking with the help of her family and friends.*
> BEING USEFUL **2** [U] the fact of being useful: *The map wasn't much help.* ◆ *With the help of a ladder, neighbors were able to rescue the children from the blaze.* ◆ *Just shouting at him isn't going to be a lot of help.*
> ADVICE/MONEY **3** [U] advice, money, etc. that is given to someone in order to solve their problems: *to seek financial/ legal/medical, etc. help* ◆ **~ in doing sth** *The organization offers practical help in dealing with paperwork.* ◆ **~ with sth** *You should qualify for help with your tuition and fees.* ◆ *a help key/screen* (= a function on a computer that provides information on how to use the computer)
> FOR SOMEONE IN DANGER **4** [U] the act of helping someone who is in danger: *Quick, get help!* ◆ *She screamed for help.*
> PERSON/THING **5** [sing.] **a ~ (to sb)** a person or thing that helps someone: *She was more of a hindrance than a help.* ◆ *Your advice was a big help.*
> IN HOUSE **6** **the help** [U] (*old-fashioned*) the person or people who are employed by someone to clean their house, etc.

help desk *noun* a service, usually in a business company, that gives people information and help, especially if they are having problems with a computer

help·er /'hɛlpər/ *noun* a person who helps someone to do something: *a willing helper*

help·ful 🎓 /'hɛlpfl/ *adj.*
1 able to improve a particular situation **SYN** USEFUL: *helpful advice/information/suggestions* ◆ *Sorry I can't be more helpful.* ◆ **~ (for sb) (to do sth)** *It would be helpful for me to see the damage for myself.* ◆ **~ in doing sth** *Role-play is helpful in developing communication skills.* ◆ **~ to sb** *The booklet should be very helpful to parents of disabled children.* **2** (of a person) willing to help someone: *I called the police but they weren't very helpful.* ◆ *The staff couldn't have been more helpful.* **ANT** UNHELPFUL ► **help·ful·ly** /-fəli/ *adv.*: *She helpfully suggested that I try the local library.* **help·ful·ness** *noun* [U]

help·ing /'hɛlpɪŋ/ *noun* **~ (of sth)** an amount of food given to someone at a meal **SYN** SERVING: *a small/generous helping* ◆ *We all had a second helping of pie.*

help·less /'hɛlpləs/ *adj.* **1** unable to take care of yourself or do things without the help of other people: *the helpless victims of war* ◆ *a helpless gesture/look* ◆ *He lay helpless on the floor.* ◆ *It's natural to feel helpless against so much abuse.* ◆ *The worst part is being helpless to change anything.* **2** unable to control a strong feeling: *helpless panic/rage* ◆ **~ with sth** *The audience was helpless with laughter.* ► **help·less·ly** *adv.*: *They watched helplessly as their home went up in flames.* **help·less·ness** *noun* [U]: *a feeling/sense of helplessness*

help·line /'hɛlplaɪn/ *noun* a telephone service that provides advice and information about particular problems

help·mate /'hɛlpmeɪt/ (also **help·meet** /'hɛlpmiːt/) *noun* (*formal* or *literary*) a helpful partner, especially a wife

hel·ter-skel·ter /ˌhɛltər 'skɛltər/ *adj.* [only before noun] done in a hurry and in a way that lacks organization: *a helter-skelter dash to meet the deadline* ► **hel·ter-skel·ter** *adv.*

hem /hɛm/ *noun, verb*
● *noun* the edge of a piece of cloth that has been folded over and sewn, especially on a piece of clothing: *to take up the hem of a dress* (= to make the dress shorter)
● *verb* (-mm-) **~ sth** to make a hem on something: *to hem a skirt*
IDM **hem and haw** to take a long time to make a decision or before you say something: *We hemmed and hawed for weeks before deciding to buy the house.*
PHR V **hem sb/sth⟷'in** to surround someone or something so that they cannot move or grow easily **SYN** HEDGE SB/STH IN: *The village is hemmed in on all sides by mountains.* ◆ (*figurative*) *She felt hemmed in by all their petty rules and regulations.*

'he-man *noun* (*pl.* **he-men**) (*often humorous*) a strong man with big muscles, especially one who likes to show other people how strong he is

he·ma·tite /'himəˌtaɪt/ *noun* [U] (*geology*) a dark red rock from which iron is obtained

he·ma·tol·o·gy /ˌhiməˈtɑlədʒi/ *noun* [U] the scientific study of the blood and its diseases ► **he·ma·to·log·i·cal** /ˌhimə-tlˈɑdʒɪkl/ *adj.* **he·ma·tol·o·gist** /ˌhiməˈtɑlədʒɪst/ *noun*

he·ma·to·ma /ˌhiməˈtoumə/ *noun* (*medical*) a swollen area on the body consisting of blood that has become thick

hem·i·sphere /'hɛmɪˌsfɪr/ *noun* **1** one half of the earth, especially the half above or below the EQUATOR: *the northern/southern hemisphere* ⟳ picture at EARTH **2** either half of the brain: *the left/right cerebral hemisphere* **3** one half of a SPHERE (= a round solid object)

hem·i·spher·i·cal /ˌhɛməˈsfɪrɪkl; -ˈsfɛr-/ *adj.* shaped like a hemisphere

hem·line /'hɛmlaɪn/ *noun* the bottom edge of a dress or skirt; the length of a dress or skirt: *Shorter hemlines are back in this season.*

hem·lock /'hɛmlɑk/ *noun* **1** [U, C] a poisonous plant with a mass of small white flowers growing at the end of a STEM that is covered in spots **2** [U] poison made from hemlock

hemo- /'himou; -mə/ *combining form* (in nouns and adjectives) connected with blood: *hemophilia*

he·mo·glo·bin /'himəˌgloubən/ *noun* [U] a red substance in the blood that carries OXYGEN and contains iron

he·mo·phil·i·a /ˌhiməˈfiliə; -ˈfilyə/ *noun* [U] a medical condition that causes severe loss of blood from even a slight injury because the blood fails to CLOT normally. It usually affects only men although it can be passed on by women.

he·mo·phil·i·ac /ˌhiməˈfiliæk; -ˈfi-/ *noun* a person who suffers from hemophilia

hem·or·rhage /'hɛmrɪdʒ; 'hɛmərɪdʒ/ *noun, verb*
● *noun* **1** [C, U] a medical condition in which there is severe loss of blood from inside a person's body: *a massive brain/ cerebral hemorrhage* ◆ *He was checked for any signs of hemorrhage.* **2** [C, usually sing.] **~ (of sb/sth)** a serious loss of people, money, etc. from a country, a group, or an

organization: *Poor working conditions have led to a steady hemorrhage of qualified teachers from our schools.*
- *verb* **1** [I] to lose blood heavily, especially from the inside of the body; to have a hemorrhage **2** [T] ~ **sb/sth** to lose money or people in large amounts at a fast rate

hem·or·rhag·ic /ˌhɛməˈrædʒɪk/ *adj.* (*medical*) happening with or caused by hemorrhage: *a hemorrhagic fever*

hem·or·rhoids /ˈhɛmrɔɪdz; ˈhɛməˌrɔɪdz/ *noun* [pl.] (*medical*) painful swollen VEINS at or near the ANUS

hemp /hɛmp/ *noun* [U] a plant which is used for making rope and cloth, and also to make the drug CANNABIS

hen /hɛn/ *noun* **1** a female chicken, often kept for its eggs or meat: *a small flock of laying hens* ◆ *battery hens* **2** (especially in compounds) any female bird: *a hen pheasant* ⊃ compare COCK ⊃ see also MOORHEN

hence AWL /hɛns/ *adv.* (*formal*)
for this reason: *We suspect they are trying to hide something, hence the need for an independent investigation.* ⊃ language bank at THEREFORE
IDM **... days, weeks, etc. hence** (*formal*) a number of days, etc. from now: *The true consequences will only be known several years hence.*

hence·forth /ˈhɛnsfɔrθ; ˌhɛnsˈfɔrθ/ (also **hence·for·ward** /ˌhɛnsˈfɔrwərd/) *adv.* (*formal*) starting from a particular time and at all times in the future: *Tuesday, October 29, 1929 was henceforth known as "Black Tuesday."*

hench·man /ˈhɛntʃmən/ *noun* (*pl.* **hench·men** /-mən/) a faithful supporter of a powerful person, for example a political leader or criminal, who is prepared to use violence or become involved in illegal activities to help that person

hen·dec·a·syl·la·ble /ˈhɛndɛkəˈsɪləbl; hɛnˈdɛkəˌsɪləbl/ *noun* (*technical*) a line of poetry with eleven syllables ▶ **hen·dec·a·syl·lab·ic** /ˌhɛnˌdɛkəsəˈlæbɪk/ *adj.*

hen·di·a·dys /hɛnˈdaɪədəs/ *noun* [U] (*grammar*) the use of two words joined with "and" to express a single idea, for example "nice and warm"

henge /hɛndʒ/ *noun* a circle of large, vertical, wooden or stone objects built in PREHISTORIC times

hen·na /ˈhɛnə/ *noun* [U] a reddish-brown DYE (= a substance used to change the color of something), used especially on the hair and skin

hen·pecked /ˈhɛnpɛkt/ *adj.* (*informal*) a man who people say is **henpecked** has a wife who is always telling him what to do, and is too weak to disagree with her

hen·ry /ˈhɛnri/ *noun* (*pl.* **hen·ries** or **hen·rys**) (*abbr.* H) a unit for measuring the INDUCTANCE in an electric CIRCUIT

he·pat·ic /hɪˈpætɪk/ *adj.* (*biology*) connected with the LIVER

hep·a·ti·tis /ˌhɛpəˈtaɪtəs/ *noun* [U] a serious disease of the LIVER. There are three main forms: **hepatitis A** (the least serious, caused by infected food), **hepatitis B**, and **hepatitis C** (both very serious and caused by infected blood).

hep·ta·gon /ˈhɛptəˌɡɑn/ *noun* (*geometry*) a flat shape with seven straight sides and seven angles ▶ **hep·tag·o·nal** /hɛpˈtæɡənl/ *adj.*

hep·tath·lon /hɛpˈtæθlən; -lɑn/ *noun* a sports event, especially one for women, in which people compete in seven different sports ⊃ compare BIATHLON, DECATHLON, PENTATHLON, TETRATHLON, TRIATHLON

her 🔑 /hər; ər; *strong form* hɑr/ *pron., det.*
- *pron.* used as the object of a verb, after the verb *be*, or after a preposition, to refer to a woman or girl who has already been mentioned or is easily identified: *We're going to name her Sophie.* ◆ *Please give her my regards.* ◆ *The manager will be available soon—you can wait for her here.* ◆ *That must be her now.* ⊃ compare SHE
- *det.* (the possessive form of *she*) of or belonging to a woman or girl who has already been mentioned or is easily identified: *Meg loves her job.* ◆ *She broke her leg skiing.* ⊃ see also HERS

her·ald /ˈhɛrəld/ *verb, noun*
- *verb* (*formal*) **1** ~ **sth** to be a sign that something is going to happen: *These talks could herald a new era of peace* **2** ~ **sb/sth (as sth)** [often passive] to say in public that someone or something is good or important: *The report is being heralded as a blueprint for the future of transportation.*
- *noun* **1** something that shows that something else is going to happen soon: *The government claims that the fall in unemployment is the herald of economic recovery.* **2** (in the past) a person who carried messages from a ruler

her·ald·ry /ˈhɛrəldri/ *noun* [U] the study of the COATS OF ARMS and the history of old families ▶ **he·ral·dic** /həˈrældɪk/ *adj.*

herb /ərb/ *noun* **1** a plant whose leaves, flowers, or seeds are used to flavor food, in medicines, or for their pleasant smell. PARSLEY, MINT, and OREGANO are all herbs: *an herb garden* ⊃ picture on page 707 **2** (*technical*) a plant with a soft STEM that dies down after flowering

her·ba·ceous /hərˈbeɪʃəs; ər-/ *adj.* (*technical*) connected with plants that have soft STEMS: *a herbaceous plant*

herb·al /ˈərbl; ˈhərbl/ *adj., noun*
- *adj.* connected with or made from HERBS: *herbal medicine/remedies*
- *noun* a book about HERBS, especially those used in medicines

her·bal·ism /ˈərbəˌlɪzəm; ˈhər-/ *noun* [U] the medical use of plants, especially as a form of ALTERNATIVE MEDICINE

herb·al·ist /ˈərbəlɪst; ˈhər-/ *noun* a person who grows, sells, or uses HERBS for medical purposes

herbal 'tea *noun* [U, C] a drink made from dried HERBS and hot water

herb·i·cide /ˈhərbəˌsaɪd; ˈər-/ *noun* [C, U] a chemical that is poisonous to plants, used to kill plants that are growing where they are not wanted ⊃ see also INSECTICIDE, PESTICIDE

her·biv·ore /ˈhərbəˌvɔr; ˈər-/ *noun* any animal that eats only plants ⊃ compare CARNIVORE, INSECTIVORE, OMNIVORE, VEGETARIAN ▶ **her·biv·o·rous** /hərˈbɪvərəs; ər-/ *adj.*: *herbivorous dinosaurs*

Her·cu·le·an /ˌhərkyəˈliən; hərˈkyuliən/ *adj.* [usually before noun] needing a lot of strength, determination, or effort: *a Herculean task* ORIGIN From the Greek myth in which Hercules proved his courage and strength by completing twelve very difficult tasks (called the Labors of Hercules).

herd /hərd/ *noun, verb*
- *noun* **1** a group of animals of the same type that live and feed together: *a herd of cows/deer/elephants* ◆ *a beef/dairy herd* ⊃ compare FLOCK **2** (usually *disapproving*) a large group of people of the same type: *She pushed her way through a herd of lunchtime drinkers.* ◆ *the common herd* (= ordinary people) ◆ *Why follow the herd* (= do and think the same as everyone else)? IDM see RIDE *v.*
- *verb* **1** [I, T] to move or make someone or something move in a particular direction: + *adv./prep.* *We all herded on to the bus.* ◆ ~ **sb/sth** + *adv./prep.* *They were herded together into trucks and driven away.* **2** [T] ~ **sth** to make animals move together as a group: *a shepherd herding his flock*

herd·er /ˈhərdər/ *noun* a person whose job is to take care of a group of animals such as sheep and cows in the countryside

'herd instinct *noun* [sing.] the natural tendency in people or animals to behave or think like other people or animals

herds·man /ˈhərdzmən/ *noun* (*pl.* **herds·men** /-mən/) a man whose job is to take care of a group of animals such as sheep and cows in the countryside

here 🔑 /hɪr/ *adv., exclamation*
- *adv.* **1** used after a verb or preposition to mean "in, at, or to this position or place": *I live here.* ◆ *Put the box here.* ◆ *Let's get out of here.* ◆ *Come over here.* **2** now; at this point: *The countdown to Christmas starts here.* ◆ *Here the speaker paused*

t tea   ṱ butter   d did   k cat   ɡ got   tʃ chin   dʒ June   f fall

herbs and spices

herbs

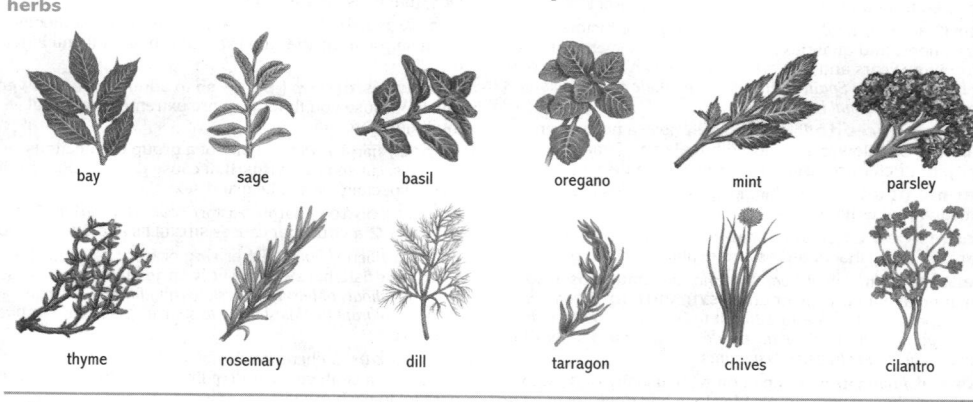

bay   sage   basil   oregano   mint   parsley

thyme   rosemary   dill   tarragon   chives   cilantro

spices

cloves   black peppercorns   star anise   cinnamon   cardamom   nutmeg

pod   mace   seeds

ginger   saffron   turmeric   paprika   cumin seeds   coriander seeds

to have a drink. **3** used when you are giving or showing something to someone: *Here's the money I promised you.* ◆ *Here's a dish that is simple and quick to make.* ◆ *Here is your opportunity.* ◆ *Here comes the bus.* ◆ *I can't find my keys. Oh, here they are.* ◆ *Here we are* (= we've arrived). **4 ~ to do sth** used to show your role in a situation: *I'm here to help you.* **5** (used after a noun, for emphasis): *My friend here saw it happen.*

IDM **here and there** in various places: *Papers were scattered here and there on the floor.* **here goes** (*informal*) used when you are telling people that you are just going to do something exciting, dangerous, etc. **here's to sb/sth** used to wish someone health or success, as you lift a glass and drink a TOAST: *Here's to your future happiness!* **here, there, and everywhere** in many different places; all around **here we go** (*informal*) said when something is starting to happen: *"Here we go," thought Fred, "she's sure to say something."* **here we go again** (*informal*) said when something is starting to happen again, especially something bad **here you are** (*informal*) used when you are giving something to someone: *Here you are. This is what you were asking for.* **here you go** (*informal*) used when you are giving something to someone: *Here you go. Four copies, right?* **neither here nor there** not important **SYN** IRRELEVANT: *What might have happened is neither here nor there.* ⊃ more at OUT

● *exclamation* used when offering something to someone: *Here, let me carry that for you.*

here·a·bouts /ˌhɪrəˈbaʊts/ (also **here·a·bout**) *adv.* near this place: *There aren't many houses hereabouts.*

here·af·ter /ˌhɪrˈæftər/ *adv., noun*
● *adv.* **1** (*formal*) from this time; in the future ⊃ compare THEREAFTER **2** (also **here·in·af·ter**) (*law*) (in legal documents, etc.) in the rest of this document **3** (*formal*) after death: *Do you believe in a life hereafter?*
● *noun* **the hereafter** [sing.] a life believed to begin after death

here·by /ˌhɪrˈbaɪ; ˈhɪrbaɪ/ *adv.* (in legal documents, etc.) as a result of this statement, and in a way that makes something legal

he·red·i·tar·y /həˈredəˌteri/ *adj.* **1** (especially of illnesses) given to a child by its parents before it is born: *a hereditary illness/disease/condition/problem* ◆ *Epilepsy is hereditary in her family.* **2** that is legally given to someone's child, when that person dies: *a hereditary title/monarchy* **3** holding a rank or title that is hereditary: *hereditary peers/rulers*

he·red·i·ty /həˈredəti/ *noun* [U] the process by which mental and physical characteristics are passed by parents to their children; these characteristics in a particular person: *the debate over the effects of heredity and environment*

here·in /ˌhɪrˈɪn/ *adv.* (*formal* or *law*) in this place, document, statement, or fact: *Neither party is willing to compromise and herein lies the problem.*

here·in·af·ter /ˌhɪrɪnˈæftər/ *adv.* (*law*) = HEREAFTER

here·of /ˌhɪrˈʌv/ *adv.* (*law*) of this: *a period of 12 months from the date hereof* (= the date of this document)

her·e·sy /ˈhɛrəsi/ *noun* (*pl.* **her·e·sies**) [U, C] **1** a belief or an opinion that is against the principles of a particular religion; the fact of holding such beliefs: *He was burned at the stake for heresy.* ◆ *the heresies of the early Protestants* ⊃ collocations at RELIGION **2** a belief or an opinion that disagrees strongly with what most people believe: *The idea is heresy to most employees of the company.*

her·e·tic /ˈhɛrəˌtɪk/ *noun* a person who is guilty of heresy ▶ **he·ret·i·cal** /həˈretɪkl/ *adj.*: *heretical beliefs*

here·to /ˌhɪrˈtu/ *adv.* (*law*) to this

here·to·fore /ˌhɪrtəˈfɔr; ˈhɪrtəˌfɔr/ *adv.* (*formal*) before this time

here·up·on /ˌhɪrəˈpɑn; -ˈpɔn/ *adv.* (*literary*) after this; as a direct result of this situation

here·with /ˌhɪrˈwɪθ; -ˈwɪð/ *adv.* (*formal*) with this letter, book, or document: *I enclose herewith a copy of the policy.*

her·it·a·ble /ˈherətəbl/ adj. (law) (of property) that can be passed from one member of a family to another

her·it·age /ˈherətɪdʒ/ noun [usually sing.] the history, traditions, and qualities that a country or society has had for many years and that are considered an important part of its character: *Spain's rich cultural heritage* ♦ *The building is part of our national heritage.*

her·maph·ro·dite /hərˈmæfrəˌdaɪt/ noun a person, an animal, or a flower that has both male and female sexual organs or characteristics ▶ **her·maph·ro·dite** adj.

her·me·neu·tic /ˌhərməˈnutɪk/ adj. (technical) relating to the meaning of written texts

her·me·neu·tics /ˌhərməˈnutɪks/ noun [pl.] (technical) the area of study that analyzes and explains written texts

her·met·ic /hərˈmetɪk/ adj. **1** (technical) tightly closed so that no air can escape or enter SYN AIRTIGHT **2** (formal, disapproving) closed and difficult to become a part of: *the strange, hermetic world of the theater* ▶ **her·met·i·cally** /-kli/ adv.: *a hermetically sealed container*

her·mit /ˈhərmət/ noun a person who, usually for religious reasons, lives a very simple life alone and does not meet or talk to other people.

her·mit·age /ˈhərmətɪdʒ/ noun a place where a hermit lives or lived

'hermit ˌcrab noun a CRAB (= a sea creature with eight legs and, usually, a hard shell) that has no shell of its own and has to use the empty shells of other sea creatures

her·ni·a /ˈhərniə/ noun [C, U] a medical condition in which part of an organ is pushed through a weak part of the body wall

her·ni·at·ed disc /ˌhərnieɪtəd ˈdɪsk/ noun (medical) = SLIPPED DISC

he·ro 🔑 /ˈhɪroʊ; ˈhiroʊ/ noun (pl. he·roes)
1 a person, especially a man, who is admired by many people for doing something brave or good: *a war hero* (= someone who was very brave during a war) ♦ *The Olympic skaters were given **a hero's welcome** on their return home.* ♦ *one of the country's **national heroes*** **2** the main male character in a story, novel, movie, etc.: *The hero of the novel is a ten-year old boy.* **3** a person, especially a man, that you admire because of a particular quality or skill that they have: *my childhood hero* ⊃ see also HEROINE **4** = SUBMARINE SANDWICH

he·ro·ic /həˈroʊɪk/ adj. **1** showing extreme courage and admired by many people SYN COURAGEOUS: *a heroic figure* ♦ *Rescuers made **heroic efforts** to save the crew.* **2** showing great determination to succeed or to achieve something, especially something difficult: *We watched our team's heroic struggle to win back the trophy.* **3** that is about or involves a hero: *a heroic story/poem* ♦ *heroic deeds/myths* **4** very large or great: *This was foolishness on a heroic scale.* ▶ **he·ro·i·cally** /-kli/ adv.

he·ˌroic 'couplet noun (technical) two lines of poetry one after the other that RHYME and usually contain ten syllables and five stresses

he·ro·ics /həˈroʊɪks/ noun [pl.] **1** (disapproving) talk or behavior that is too brave or dramatic for a particular situation: *Remember, no heroics, we just go in there and do our job.* **2** actions that are brave and determined: *Thanks to Bateman's heroics in the second half, the team won 2–0.*

her·o·in /ˈheroʊən/ noun [U] a powerful illegal drug made from MORPHINE, that some people take for pleasure and can become ADDICTED to: *a heroin addict*

her·o·ine /ˈheroʊən/ noun **1** a girl or woman who is admired by many people for doing something brave or good: *the heroines of the revolution* **2** the main female character in a story, novel, movie, etc.: *The heroine is played by Katie Holmes.* **3** a woman that you admire because of a particular quality or skill that she has: *Madonna was her teenage heroine.* ⊃ compare HERO

her·o·ism /ˈheroʊˌɪzəm/ noun [U] very great courage

her·on /ˈhɛrən/ noun a large bird with a long neck and long legs, that lives near water

'hero ˌworship noun [U] great admiration for someone because you think they are extremely beautiful, intelligent, etc.

'hero-ˌworship verb (-pp-) ~ sb to admire someone very much because you think they are extremely beautiful, intelligent, etc.

her·pes /ˈhərpiz/ noun [U] one of a group of infectious diseases, caused by a virus, that cause painful spots on the skin, especially on the face and sexual organs

her·pes zos·ter /ˌhərpiz ˈzastər/ noun [U] (medical) **1** = SHINGLES **2** a virus that causes SHINGLES and CHICKEN POX

her·ring /ˈhɛrɪŋ/ noun (pl. her·ring or her·rings) [U, C] a N. Atlantic fish that swims in very large groups and is used for food: *shoals of herring* ♦ *fresh herring fillets* ♦ *The mature herrings migrate to Akkeshi Bay to spawn.* ⊃ see also RED HERRING

her·ring·bone /ˈhɛrɪŋˌboʊn/ noun [U] a pattern used, for example, in cloth consisting of lines of V-shapes that are parallel to each other

'herring ˌgull noun a large N. Atlantic bird of the GULL family, with black tips to its wings

hers 🔑 /hərz/ pron.
of or belonging to her: *His eyes met hers.* ♦ *The choice was hers.* ♦ *a friend of hers*

her·self 🔑 /hərˈself; weak form ərˈself/ pron.
1 (the reflexive form of she) used when the woman or girl who performs an action is also affected by it: *She hurt herself.* ♦ *She must be very proud of herself.* **2** used to emphasize the female subject or object of a sentence: *She told me the news herself.* ♦ *Jane herself was at the meeting.*
IDM **be, seem, etc. herself** (of a woman or girl) to be in a normal state of health or happiness; not influenced by other people: *She didn't seem quite herself this morning.* ♦ *She needed space to be herself.* **(all) by herself 1** alone; without anyone else: *She lives by herself.* **2** without help: *She runs the business by herself.* **(all) to herself** for only her to have or use: *She wants a room all to herself.*

hertz /hərts/ noun (pl. hertz) (abbr. Hz) a unit for measuring the FREQUENCY of sound waves

he's /hiz; iz; strong form hiz/ short form **1** he is **2** he has

hes·i·tan·cy /ˈhezətənsi/ noun [U] the state or quality of being slow or uncertain in doing or saying something: *I noticed a certain hesitancy in his voice.*

hes·i·tant /ˈhezətənt/ adj. slow to speak or act because you feel uncertain, embarrassed, or unwilling: *a hesitant smile* ♦ *the baby's first few hesitant steps* ♦ ~ **about sth** *She's hesitant about signing the contract.* ♦ ~ **to do sth** *Doctors are hesitant to comment on the new treatment.* ▶ **hes·i·tant·ly** adv.

hes·i·tate 🔑 /ˈhezəˌteɪt/ verb
1 [I, T] to be slow to speak or act because you feel uncertain or nervous: *She hesitated before replying.* ♦ ~ **about/over sth** *I didn't hesitate for a moment about taking the job.* ♦ **+ speech** *"I'm not sure," she hesitated.* **2** [I] ~ **to do sth** to be worried about doing something, especially because you are not sure that it is right or appropriate: *Please do not hesitate to contact me if you have any queries.* ▶ **hes·i·ta·tion** /ˌhezə-ˈteɪʃn/ noun [U, C]: *She agreed without the slightest hesitation.* ♦ *I have no hesitation in recommending her for the job.* ♦ *He spoke fluently and without unnecessary hesitations.*
IDM **he who hesitates (is lost)** (saying) if you delay in doing something you may lose a good opportunity

hetero- /ˈhetəroʊ; -rə/ combining form (in nouns, adjectives, and adverbs) other; different: *heterogeneous* ♦ *heterosexual* ⊃ compare HOMO-

het·er·o·dox /ˈhetərəˌdaks/ adj. (formal) not following the usual or accepted beliefs and opinions ⊃ compare ORTHODOX, UNORTHODOX ▶ **het·er·o·dox·y** noun [U, C] (pl. het·er·o·dox·ies)

het·er·o·ge·ne·ous /ˌhɛtərəˈdʒiniəs; -ˈdʒinyəs/ adj. (formal) consisting of many different kinds of people or things: *the heterogeneous population of the United States* **ANT** HOMOGENEOUS ▸ **het·er·o·ge·ne·i·ty** /ˌhɛtəroudʒəˈniəti/ noun [U]

het·er·o·nym /ˈhɛtərənɪm/ noun (linguistics) **1** one of two or more words that have the same spelling but different meanings and pronunciation, for example "tear" meaning "rip" and "tear" meaning "liquid from the eye" **2** one of two or more words that refer to the same thing, for example "fall" and "autumn"

het·er·o·sex·u·al /ˌhɛtərəˈsɛkʃuəl/ noun a person who is sexually attracted to people of the opposite sex ⊃ compare BISEXUAL, HOMOSEXUAL ▸ **het·er·o·sex·u·al** adj.: *a heterosexual relationship* **het·er·o·sex·u·al·i·ty** /ˌhɛtərəˌsɛkʃuˈæləti/ noun [U]

het·er·o·zy·gote /ˌhɛtərəˈzaɪgout/ noun (biology) a living thing that has two varying forms of a particular gene, and whose young may therefore vary in a particular characteristic ▸ **het·er·o·zy·gous** /-gəs/ adj.

het up /ˌhɛt ˈʌp/ adj. [not before noun] ~ **(about/over sth)** (informal, becoming old-fashioned) anxious, excited, or slightly angry: *What are you getting so het up about?*

heu·ris·tic /hyuˈrɪstɪk/ adj. (formal) **heuristic** teaching or education encourages you to learn by discovering things for yourself

heuristics /hyuˈrɪstɪks/ noun [U] (formal) a method of solving problems by finding practical ways of dealing with them, learning from past experience

hew /hyu/ verb (hewed, hewed or hewn /hyun/) **1** ~ **sth** (old-fashioned) to cut something large with a tool: *to hew wood* **2** ~ **sth (out of sth)** (formal) to make or shape something large by cutting: *roughly hewn timber frames* ◆ *The statues were hewn out of solid rock.*

hex /hɛks/ verb ~ **sb** to use magic powers in order to harm someone ▸ **hex** noun: *to put a hex on someone* ⊃ compare CURSE

hexa- /ˈhɛksə/ (also **hex-**) combining form (in nouns, adjectives, and adverbs) six; having six

hex·a·dec·i·mal /ˌhɛksəˈdɛsəml/ (also **hex** /hɛks/) adj. (computing) a system for representing pieces of data using the numbers 0-9 and the letters A-F: *The number 107 is represented in hexadecimal as 6B.*

hex·a·gon /ˈhɛksəˌgan/ noun (geometry) a flat shape with six straight sides and six angles ⊃ picture at SHAPE ▸ **hex·ag·o·nal** /hɛkˈsægənl/ adj.

hex·a·gram /ˈhɛksəˌgræm/ noun (geometry) a shape made by six straight lines, especially a star made from two triangles with equal sides

hex·am·e·ter /hɛkˈsæmətər/ noun (technical) a line of poetry with six stressed syllables

hey /heɪ/ exclamation (informal) **1** used to attract someone's attention or to express interest, surprise, or anger: *Hey, can I just ask you something?* ◆ *Hey, leave my things alone!* **2** (informal) used to say hello: *Hey, Tony, how's it going?* **3** used to show that you do not really care about something or that you think it is not important: *That's the third time I've been late this week — but hey! — who's counting?* **IDM** **what the hey!** (informal) used to say that something does not matter or that you do not care about it: *This is probably a bad idea, but what the hey!*

hey·day /ˈheɪdeɪ/ noun [usually sing.] the time when someone or something had most power or success, or was most popular **SYN** PRIME: *In its heyday, the company ran trains every fifteen minutes.* ◆ *a fine example from the heyday of Italian cinema* ◆ *a picture of Marilyn Monroe in her heyday*

HFC /ˌeɪtʃ ɛf ˈsi/ noun [C, U] a type of gas used especially in AEROSOLS (= types of containers that release liquid in the form of a spray). HFCs are not harmful to the layer of the gas OZONE in the earth's atmosphere. (the abbreviation for "hydrofluorocarbon")

hg abbr. HECTOGRAM(S)

HHS /ˌeɪtʃ eɪtʃ ˈɛs/ abbr. Department of Health and Human Services (the federal government department responsible for national health programs and the SOCIAL SERVICES ADMINISTRATION)

HI abbr. (in writing) Hawaii

hi 🔑 /haɪ/ exclamation (informal) used to say hello: *Hi guys!* ◆ *Hi, there! How're you doing?*

hi·a·tus /haɪˈeɪtəs/ noun [sing.] (formal) **1** a pause in activity when nothing happens **2** a space, especially in a piece of writing or in a speech, where something is missing

hi·ba·chi /hɪˈbɑtʃi/ noun a small device used to cook food outdoors over CHARCOAL

hi·ber·nate /ˈhaɪbərˌneɪt/ verb [I] (of animals) to spend the winter in a state like deep sleep ⊃ collocations at LIFE ▸ **hi·ber·na·tion** /ˌhaɪbərˈneɪʃn/ noun [U]

hi·bis·cus /haɪˈbɪskəs; hɪ-/ noun [U, C] (pl. **hi·bis·cus**) a tropical plant or bush with large brightly colored flowers

hic·cup (also **hiccough**) /ˈhɪkʌp/ noun, verb
● noun **1** [C] a sharp, usually repeated, sound made in the throat, that is caused by a sudden movement of the DIAPHRAGM and that you cannot control: *She gave a loud hiccup.* **2** **(the) hiccups** [pl.] a series of hiccups: *I ate too quickly and got the hiccups.* ◆ *He had the hiccups.* **3** [C] (informal) a small problem or temporary delay: *There was a slight hiccup in the schedule.*
● verb [I] to have the hiccups or a single hiccup

hick /hɪk/ noun (informal) a person from the country who is considered to be stupid and to have little experience of life: *I was just a hick from Texas then.* ▸ **hick** adj.: *a hick town*

hick·ey /ˈhɪki/ noun a red mark on the skin that is caused by someone biting or sucking their partner's skin when they are kissing

hick·o·ry /ˈhɪkəri/ noun [U] the hard wood of the N. American **hickory tree**

hidden a·gen·da noun (disapproving) the secret intention behind what someone says or does: *There are fears of a hidden agenda behind this new proposal.*

hide 🔑 /haɪd/ verb, noun
● verb (hid /hɪd/, hid·den /ˈhɪdn/) **1** [T] to put or keep someone or something in a place where they/it cannot be seen or found **SYN** CONCEAL: *~ sb/sth He hid the letter in a drawer.* ◆ *I keep my private papers hidden.* ◆ *~ sb/sth from sth They hid me from the police in their attic.* ⊃ thesaurus box on page 710 **2** [I, T] to go somewhere where you hope you will not be seen or found: *Quick, hide!* ◆ *+ adv./prep. I hid under the bed.* ◆ *(figurative) He hid behind a false identity.* ◆ *~ yourself (+ adv./prep.) She hides herself away in her office all day.* **3** [T] to cover something so that it cannot be seen **SYN** CONCEAL: *~ sth + adv./prep. He hid his face in his hands.* ◆ *~ sth The house was hidden by trees.* ◆ *No amount of makeup could hide her age.* **4** [T] *~ sth* to keep something secret, especially your feelings **SYN** CONCEAL: *She struggled to hide her disappointment.* ◆ *I have never tried to hide the truth about my past.* ◆ *They claim that they* **have nothing to hide** (= there was nothing wrong or illegal about what they did). ◆ *She felt sure the letter had some* **hidden meaning**. **IDM** **hide your light under a bushel** to not let people know that you are good at something ⊃ more at MULTITUDE
● noun **1** [C, U] an animal's skin, especially when it is bought or sold or used for leather: *boots made from buffalo hide* **2** [sing.] (informal) used to refer to someone's life or safety when they are in a difficult situation: *All he's worried about is his own hide* (= himself). ◆ *She'd do anything to* **save her own hide.** **IDM** **have/tan sb's hide** (old-fashioned, informal, or humorous) to punish someone severely **not see hide nor hair of sb/sth** (informal) not to see someone or something for some time: *I haven't seen hide nor hair of her for a month.*

hide

conceal ♦ **cover** ♦ **disguise** ♦ **mask** ♦ **camouflage**

These words all mean to put or keep someone or something in a place where they/it cannot be seen or found, or to keep the truth or your feelings secret.

hide to put or keep someone or something in a place where they/it cannot be seen or found; to keep something secret, especially your feelings: *He hid the letter in a drawer.* ♦ *She hid her disappointment from her brother.*

conceal (*formal*) to hide someone or something; to keep something secret: *The paintings were concealed beneath a thick layer of plaster.* ♦ *Tim could barely conceal his disappointment.* **NOTE** When it is being used to talk about emotions, **conceal** is often used in negative statements.

cover to place something over or in front of something in order to hide it: *She covered her face with her hands.*

disguise to hide or change the nature of something, so that it cannot be recognized: *He tried to disguise his accent.*

mask to hide a feeling, smell, fact, etc. so that it cannot be easily seen or noticed: *She masked her anger with a smile.*

camouflage to hide someone or something by making them/it look like the things around, or like something else: *The soldiers camouflaged themselves with leaves and twigs.*

PATTERNS
- to hide/conceal/mask sth **behind** sth
- to hide/conceal sth **under** sth
- to hide/conceal sth **from** sb
- to hide/conceal/disguise/mask **the truth/the fact that...**
- to hide/conceal/disguise/mask **your feelings**

hide-and-seek /ˌhaɪd n ˈsik/ (also ˌhide-and-go-ˈseek) *noun* [U] a children's game in which one player covers his or her eyes while the other players hide, and then tries to find them

hide·a·way /ˈhaɪdəˌweɪ/ *noun* a place where you can go to hide or to be alone

hide·bound /ˈhaɪdbaʊnd/ *adj.* (*disapproving*) having old-fashioned ideas, rather than accepting new ways of thinking **SYN** NARROW-MINDED

ˌhi-ˈdef /ˌhaɪ ˈdef/ *adj.* [only before noun] (*informal*) = HIGH-DEFINITION

hid·e·ous /ˈhɪdiəs/ *adj.* very ugly or unpleasant **SYN** REVOLTING: *a hideous face/building/dress* ♦ *Their new color scheme is hideous!* ♦ *a hideous crime* ♦ *The whole experience had been like some hideous nightmare.*
▶ **hid·e·ous·ly** *adv.*: *His face was hideously deformed.*

hide·out /ˈhaɪdaʊt/ *noun* a place where someone goes when they do not want anyone to find them

hid·ey-hole (also **hidy-hole**) /ˈhaɪdi ˌhoʊl/ *noun* (*informal*) a place where someone hides, especially in order to avoid being with other people

hid·ing /ˈhaɪdɪŋ/ *noun* [U] the state of being hidden: *After the trial, she had to go into hiding for several weeks.* ♦ *He only came out of hiding ten years after the war was over.* ♦ *We spent months in hiding.*

ˈhiding ˌplace *noun* a place where someone or something can be hidden

hie /haɪ/ *verb* (hies, hy·ing, hied) [I] + **adv./prep.** (*old use*) to go quickly

hi·er·ar·chi·cal **AWL** /ˌhaɪəˈrɑrkɪkl/ *adj.* arranged in a

hierarchy: *a hierarchical society/structure/organization*
▶ **hi·er·ar·chi·cally** /-kli/ *adv.*

hi·er·ar·chy **AWL** /ˈhaɪəˌrɑrki/ *noun* (*pl.* **hierarchies**) **1** [C, U] a system, especially in a society or an organization, in which people are organized into different levels of importance from highest to lowest: *the social/political hierarchy* ♦ *She's quite high up in the management hierarchy.* **2** [C] the group of people in control of a large organization or institution **3** [C] (*formal*) a system that ideas or beliefs can be arranged into: *a hierarchy of needs*

hi·er·o·glyph /ˈhaɪərəˌglɪf; ˈhaɪrə-/ *noun* a picture or symbol of an object, representing a word, syllable, or sound, especially as used in ancient Egyptian and other writing systems ▶ **hi·er·o·glyph·ic** /ˌhaɪərəˈglɪfɪk; ˌhaɪrə-/ *adj.*

hi·er·o·glyph·ics /ˌhaɪərəˈglɪfɪks; ˌhaɪrə-/ *noun* [pl.] writing that uses hiero-glyphs

hieroglyphics

hi-fi /ˈhaɪ faɪ/ *noun* [C, U] (*old-fashioned*) equipment for playing recorded music that produces high-quality STEREO sound ▶ **hi-fi** *adj.* [usually before noun]: *a hi-fi system*

hig·gle·dy-pig·gle·dy /ˌhɪgəldi ˈpɪgəldi/ *adv.* (*informal*) in a messy way that lacks any order: *Files were strewn higgledy-piggledy over the floor.*
▶ **hig·gle·dy-pig·gle·dy** *adj.*: *a higgledy-piggledy collection of houses*

WHICH WORD?

high ♦ tall

- **High** is used to talk about the measurement from the bottom to the top of something: *The fence is over five feet high.* ♦ *He has climbed some of the world's highest mountains.* You also use **high** to describe the distance of something from the ground: *How high (up) was the plane when the engine failed?*

- **Tall** is used instead of **high** to talk about people: *My brother's much taller than me.* **Tall** is also used for things that are high and narrow, such as trees: *She ordered cold beer in a tall glass.* ♦ *tall factory chimneys.* Buildings can be **high** but they are much more frequently **tall**.

high 🔑 /haɪ/ *adj., noun, adv.*
● *adj.* (**high·er, high·est**)
▷ **FROM BOTTOM TO TOP 1** measuring a long distance from the bottom to the top: *What's the highest mountain in the U.S.?*

WORD FAMILY
high *adj., noun, adv.*
highly *adv.*
height *noun*
heighten *verb*

♦ *The house has a high wall all the way around it.* ♦ *shoes with high heels* ♦ *He has a round face with a high forehead.*
ANT LOW **2** used to talk about the distance that something measures from the bottom to the top: *How high is Everest?* ♦ *It's only a low wall—about a yard high.* ♦ *The grass was waist-high.*
▷ **FAR ABOVE GROUND 3** at a level that is a long way above the ground or above the level of the ocean: *a high branch/shelf/window* ♦ *The rooms had high ceilings.* ♦ *They were flying at high altitude.* ♦ *the grasslands of the high prairies* **ANT** LOW
▷ **GREATER THAN NORMAL 4** greater or better than normal in quantity or quality, size, or degree: *a high temperature/speed/price* ♦ *a high rate of inflation* ♦ *Demand is high at this time of year.* ♦ *a high level of pollution* ♦ *a high standard of craftsmanship* ♦ *high-quality goods* ♦ *A high degree of accuracy is needed.* ♦ *The tree blew over in the high winds.* ♦ *We had high hopes for the business* (= we believed it would be successful). ♦ *The cost in terms of human life was high.* ◗ compare LOW

> **CONTAINING A LOT 5** ~ **(in sth)** containing a lot of a particular substance **ANT** LOW: *foods which are high in fat* ♦ *a high potassium content* ♦ *a high-fat diet*

> **RANK/STATUS 6** (usually before noun) near the top in rank or status: *She has held high office under three presidents.* ♦ *He has friends in high places* (= among people of power and influence). **ANT** LOW

> **VALUABLE 7** of great value: *to play for high stakes* ♦ *My highest card is ten.*

> **IDEALS/PRINCIPLES 8** (usually before noun) morally good: *a man of high ideals/principles*

> **APPROVING 9** (usually before noun) showing a lot of approval or respect for someone: *She is held in very high regard by her colleagues.* ♦ *You seem to have a high opinion of yourself!* **ANT** LOW

> **SOUND 10** at the upper end of the range of sounds that humans can hear; not deep or low: *She has a high voice.* ♦ *That note is definitely too high for me.* **ANT** LOW

> **OF PERIOD OF TIME 11** [only before noun] used to describe the middle or the most attractive part of a period of time: *high noon* ♦ *high summer*

> **ON ALCOHOL/DRUGS 12** [not before noun] ~ **(on sth)** (*informal*) behaving in an excited way because of the effects of alcohol or drugs

> **PHONETICS 13** (*phonetics*) = CLOSE² *adj.* (14)
  IDM **be/get on your high horse** (*informal*) to behave in a way that shows you think you are better than other people **get off your high horse** (*informal*) to stop behaving in a way that shows you think you are better than other people **have a high old time** (*old-fashioned, informal*) to enjoy yourself very much **high and dry 1** (of a boat, etc.) in a position out of the water: *Their yacht was left high and dry on a sandbank.* **2** in a difficult situation, without help or money **high and mighty** (*informal*) behaving as though you think you are more important than other people **high as a kite** (*informal*) behaving in a very excited way because of being strongly affected by alcohol or drugs **in high dudgeon** (*old-fashioned, formal*) in an angry or offended mood, and showing other people that you are angry: *He stomped out of the room in high dudgeon.* **smell, stink, etc. to high heaven** (*informal*) **1** to have a strong unpleasant smell **2** to seem to be very dishonest or morally unacceptable ⊃ more at HELL, MORAL *adj.*, ORDER *n.*, PROFILE *n.*, TIME *n.*

● **noun**
> **LEVEL/NUMBER 1** the highest level or number: *Profits reached an all-time high last year.*

> **WEATHER 2** an area of high air pressure; an ANTICYCLONE: *A high over southern California is bringing fine, sunny weather to all parts.* **3** the highest temperature reached during a particular day, week, etc.: *Highs today will be in the region of 75°F.*

> **FROM DRUGS 4** (*informal*) the feeling of extreme pleasure and excitement that someone gets after taking some types of drugs: *The high lasted all night.*

> **FROM SUCCESS/ENJOYMENT 5** (*informal*) the feeling of extreme pleasure and excitement that someone gets from doing something enjoyable or being successful at something: *He was on a real high after winning the competition.* ♦ *the highs and lows of her acting career*

> **SCHOOL 6** used in the name of a high school: *He graduated from Little Rock High in 1982.*
  IDM **on high 1** (*formal*) in a high place: *We gazed down into the valley from on high.* **2** (*humorous*) the people in senior positions in an organization: *An order came down from on high that lunchbreaks were to be half an hour and no longer.* **3** in heaven: *The disaster was seen as a judgment from on high.*

● **adv.** (**high·er, high·est**)
> **FAR FROM GROUND/BOTTOM 1** at or to a position or level that is a long way up from the ground or from the bottom: *An eagle circled high overhead.* ♦ *I can't jump any higher.* ♦ *She never got very high in the company.* ♦ *His desk was piled high with papers.* ♦ *She's aiming high* (= hoping to be very successful) *in her exam.*

> **VALUE/AMOUNT 2** at or to a large cost, value, or amount: *Prices are expected to rise even higher this year.*

> **SOUND 3** at a high PITCH: *I can't sing that high.* **ANT** LOW
  IDM **high and low** everywhere: *I've searched high and low for my purse.* **run high** (especially of feelings) to be strong and angry or excited: *Feelings ran high as the election approached.* ⊃ more at FLY *v.*, HEAD *n.*, RIDE *v.*

high and 'tight *noun* a military HAIRSTYLE in which the sides of the head are shaved and the top is cut very short

high·ball /'haɪbɔl/ *noun, verb*
● *noun* a strong alcoholic drink, such as WHISKEY or GIN, mixed with water with bubbles in it, or with GINGER ALE, etc. and served with ice
● *verb* ~ **sth** (*informal*) to deliberately make an estimate of the cost, value, etc. of something that is too high: *He thought she was highballing her salary requirements.* **ANT** LOWBALL

'high beams *noun* [pl.] the lights on a car when they are pointing a long way ahead, not down at the road ⊃ compare LOW BEAMS
  IDM **on high beam** (of the lights on a car) pointing a long way ahead, not down at the road

high-born *adj.* (*old-fashioned* or *formal*) having parents who are members of the highest social class **SYN** ARISTOCRATIC **ANT** LOW-BORN

high·boy /'haɪbɔɪ/ *noun* a tall piece of furniture with drawers

high·brow /'haɪbraʊ/ *adj., noun*
● *adj.* (sometimes *disapproving*) concerned with or interested in serious artistic or cultural ideas **SYN** INTELLECTUAL: *highbrow newspapers* ♦ *highbrow readers* **ANT** LOWBROW ⊃ compare MIDDLEBROW
● *noun* (sometimes *disapproving*) a person who is interested in serious artistic or cultural ideas

'high chair *noun* a special chair with long legs and a little seat and table, for a small child to sit in when eating ⊃ picture at CHAIR

high-'class *adj.* **1** excellent; of good quality: *a high-class restaurant* ♦ *to stay in high-class accommodations* **2** connected with a high social class: *to come from a high-class background* **ANT** LOW-CLASS

high com'mand *noun* [usually sing.] the senior leaders of the armed forces of a country

high com'mission *noun* a group of people who are working for a government or an international organization on an important project: *the United Nations High Commission for Refugees*

High Com'missioner *noun* a person who is head of an important international project: *the United Nations High Commissioner for Refugees*

high 'court *noun* a name for the SUPREME COURT in some countries

high-defi'nition (also informal **hi-'def**, **high-'def**) *adj.* [only before noun] (*abbr.* HD *technical*) using or produced by a system that gives very clear, detailed images: *high-definition television* ♦ *high-definition displays*

high-'end *adj.* [only before noun] expensive and of high quality: *high-end restaurants*

higher /'haɪər/ *adj.* [only before noun] at a more advanced level; greater in rank or importance than others: *The case was referred to a higher court.* ♦ *higher mathematics* ♦ *My mind was on higher things.*

higher 'animals, **higher 'plants** *noun* [pl.] (*technical*) animals and plants that have reached an advanced stage of development

higher edu'cation *noun* [U] education at a college or a university, especially to a degree level

higher-'up *noun* (*informal*) a person who has a higher rank or who is more senior than you

highest common 'factor *noun* (*abbr.* HCF) (*mathematics*) the highest number that can be divided exactly into two or more numbers

high ex'plosive *noun* [C, U] a very powerful substance that is used in bombs and can damage a very large area

high·fa·lu·tin /ˌhaɪfəˈlutn/ *adj.* (*informal*) trying to be serious or important, but in a way that often appears silly and unnecessary **SYN** PRETENTIOUS

high fi'delity *noun* [U] (*old-fashioned*) = HI-FI

high 'five *noun* an action to celebrate victory or to express happiness in which two people raise one arm each and hit their open hands together: *Way to go! High five!*

high-'flown *adj.* (usually *disapproving*) (of language and ideas) very grand and complicated **SYN** BOMBASTIC: *His high-flown style just sounds absurd today.*

high-'flyer (also **high-'flier**) *noun* a person who has the desire and the ability to be very successful in their job or their studies: *academic high-flyers*

high-'flying *adj.* [only before noun] **1** very successful: *a high-flying career woman* **2** that flies very high in the air

high 'gear *noun* [U] the highest gear in a vehicle that is used when you are driving fast **IDM in/into high gear** in a state of intense activity: *Her career is back in high gear.* **kick/move/swing into high gear** to become more intense: *The campaign season for this year's elections doesn't really kick into high gear until June.*

high-'grade *adj.* [usually before noun] of very good quality: *high-grade steel*

high ground *noun* usually **the high ground** [sing.] the advantage in a discussion or an argument, etc.: *The government is claiming the high ground in the education debate.* **IDM** see MORAL *adj.*

high-'handed *adj.* (of people or their behavior) using authority in an unreasonable way, without considering the opinions of other people **SYN** OVERBEARING

'high-hat *noun* = HI-HAT ⊃ picture at INSTRUMENT

high 'heels *noun* [pl.] shoes that have very high heels, usually worn by women ► **high-'heeled** *adj.* [only before noun]: *high-heeled shoes/boots*

high jinks (also **hi-jinks**) /ˈhaɪ dʒɪŋks/ *noun* [pl.] (*old-fashioned, informal*) lively and excited behavior **SYN** FUN

the 'high jump *noun* [sing.] a sporting event in which people try to jump over a high bar that is gradually raised higher and higher: *She won a silver medal in the high jump.* ⊃ picture at SPORT

high·land /ˈhaɪlənd/ *adj., noun*
• *adj.* [only before noun] **1** connected with an area of land that has hills or mountains: *highland regions* **2** **Highland** connected with the Highlands of Scotland ⊃ compare LOWLAND
• *noun* **1** [C, usually pl.] an area of land with hills or mountains: *the Peruvian highlands* **2** **the Highlands** [pl.] the high mountain region of Scotland

high·land·er /ˈhaɪləndər/ *noun* **1** a person who comes from an area where there are a lot of mountains **2** **Highlander** a person who comes from the Scottish Highlands ⊃ compare LOWLANDER

high-'level *adj.* [usually before noun] **1** involving senior people: *high-level talks/negotiations* ◆ *high-level staff* **2** in a high position or place: *a high-level walk in the hills* **3** advanced: *a high-level course* **4** (*computing*) (of a computer language) similar to an existing language such as English, making it fairly simple to use **ANT** LOW-LEVEL

'high life *noun* also **the high life** [sing., U] (also **high 'living** [U]) (sometimes *disapproving*) a way of life that involves going to parties and spending a lot of money on food, clothes, etc.

high·light 🔑 **AWL** /ˈhaɪlaɪt/ *verb, noun*
• *verb* **1** ~ sth to emphasize something, especially so that people give it more attention: *The report highlights the major problems facing society today.* ⊃ language bank at EMPHASIS **2** ~ sth to mark part of a text with a special colored pen, or to mark an area on a computer screen, to emphasize it or

make it easier to see: *I've highlighted the important passages in yellow.* **3** ~ sth to make some parts of your hair a lighter color than the rest by using a chemical substance on them
• *noun* **1** the best, most interesting, or most exciting part of something: *One of the highlights of the trip was seeing the Taj Mahal.* ◆ *The highlights of the game will be shown later this evening.* **2** **highlights** [pl.] areas of hair that are lighter than the rest, usually because a chemical substance has been put on them ⊃ compare LOWLIGHTS **3** **highlights** [pl.] (*technical*) the light or bright part of a picture or photograph

high·light·er /ˈhaɪˌlaɪtər/ *noun* **1** (also **'highlighter ˌpen**) a special pen used for marking words in a text in bright colors ⊃ picture at STATIONERY **2** a colored substance that you put above your eyes or on your cheeks to make yourself more attractive

high·ly 🔑 /ˈhaɪli/ *adv.*
1 very: *highly successful/skilled/intelligent* ◆ *highly competitive/critical/sensitive* ◆ *It is highly unlikely that she'll be late.* **2** at or to a high standard, level, or amount: *highly trained/educated* ◆ *a highly paid job* **3** with admiration or praise: *His teachers think very highly of him* (= have a very good opinion of him). ◆ *She speaks highly of you.* ◆ *Her novels are very highly regarded.*

high-'maintenance *adj.* needing a lot of attention or effort: *a high-maintenance girlfriend* **ANT** LOW-MAINTENANCE

high-'minded *adj.* (of people or ideas) having strong moral principles ► **high-'mindedness** *noun* [U]

High·ness /ˈhaɪnəs/ *noun* **His/Her/Your Highness** a title of respect used when talking to or about a member of the royal family ⊃ see also ROYAL HIGHNESS

high 'noon *noun* **1** exactly twelve o'clock in the middle of the day **2** (*formal*) the most important stage of something, when something that will decide the future happens

high-'octane *adj.* [only before noun] **1** (of fuel used in engines) of very good quality and very efficient **2** (*informal*) full of energy; powerful: *a high-octane athlete*

high-per'formance *adj.* [only before noun] that can go very fast or do complicated things: *a high-performance car/computer, etc.*

high-'pitched *adj.* (of sounds) very high: *a high-pitched voice/whistle* **ANT** LOW-PITCHED

'high point *noun* the most interesting, enjoyable, or best part of something: *It was the high point of the evening.* **ANT** LOW POINT

high-'powered *adj.* **1** (of people) having a lot of power and influence; full of energy: *high-powered executives* **2** (of activities) important; with a lot of responsibility: *a high-powered job* **3** (also **high-'power**) (of machines) very powerful: *a high-powered car/computer, etc.*

high 'pressure *noun* [U] **1** the condition of air, gas, or liquid that is kept in a small space by force: *Water is forced through the pipes at high pressure.* **2** a condition of the air which affects the weather, when the pressure is higher than average ⊃ compare LOW PRESSURE

high-'pressure *adj.* [only before noun] **1** that involves a lot of worry and anxiety **SYN** STRESSFUL: *a high-pressure job* **2** that involves aggressive ways of persuading someone to do something or to buy something: *high-pressure sales techniques* **3** using or containing a great force of a gas or a liquid: *a high-pressure water-jet*

high-'priced *adj.* [usually before noun] expensive: *high-priced housing/cars* **ANT** LOW-PRICED

high 'priest *noun* **1** the most important priest in the Jewish religion in the past **2** (*feminine* **high 'priestess**) an important priest in some other non-Christian religions **3** (*feminine* **high 'priestess**) the most important person in a particular area of music, art, etc.: *Janis Joplin was known as the High Priestess of Rock.*

high-'profile *adj.* [usually before noun] receiving or involving a lot of attention and discussion on television, in

t **tea**   ʈ **butter**   d **did**   k **cat**   g **got**   tʃ **chin**   dʒ **June**   f **fall**

newspapers, etc.: *a high-profile campaign* ⟳ see also PROFILE

high-'ranking *adj.* senior; important: *a high-ranking officer/official* ◆ *a high-ranking position* **ANT** LOW-RANKING

high-reso'lution (also hi-res, high-res /ˌhaɪ ˈrɛz/) *adj.* (of a photograph or an image on a computer or television screen) showing a lot of clear sharp detail: *a high-resolution scan* **ANT** LOW-RESOLUTION

'high-rise *adj.* [only before noun] (of a building) very tall and having a lot of floors: *high-rise housing* ▶ **'high-rise** *noun*: *to live in a high-rise* ⟳ compare LOW-RISE

high-'risk *adj.* [usually before noun] involving a lot of danger and the risk of injury, death, damage, etc.: *a high-risk sport* ◆ *high-risk patients* (= who are very likely to get a particular illness) ⟳ compare LOW-RISK

'high road *noun* **1** (*old-fashioned*) a main or important road **2** ~ **(to sth)** the most direct way: *This is the high road to democracy.*
IDM **take the high road (in sth)** to take the most positive course of action: *He took the high road in his campaign.*

high 'roller *noun* (*informal*) a person who spends a lot of money, especially on gambling

'high school ✎ *noun* [C, U]
a school for young people between the ages of 14 and 18 ⟳ collocations at EDUCATION ⟳ see also JUNIOR HIGH SCHOOL, SENIOR HIGH SCHOOL

the ˌhigh 'seas *noun* [pl.] (*formal* or *literary*) the areas of ocean that are not under the legal control of any one country

high 'season *noun* [U, sing.] the time of year when a hotel or tourist area receives most visitors ⟳ compare OFF-SEASON

high-se'curity *adj.* [only before noun] **1** (of buildings and places) very carefully locked and guarded: *a high-security prison* **2** (of prisoners) kept in a prison that is very carefully locked and guarded

high-'sounding *adj.* (often *disapproving*) (of language or ideas) complicated and intended to sound important **SYN** PRETENTIOUS

high-'speed *adj.* [only before noun] that travels, works, or happens very fast: *a high-speed train* ◆ *a high-speed car chase* ◆ *high-speed Internet access*

high-'spirited *adj.* **1** (of people) very lively and active: *a high-spirited child* ◆ *high-spirited behavior* **2** (of animals, especially horses) lively and difficult to control **ANT** PLACID ⟳ see also SPIRIT

high-'strung *adj.* (of a person or an animal) nervous and easily upset ⟳ note at NERVOUS

high-tail /ˈhaɪteɪl/ *verb*
IDM **hightail it** (*informal*) to leave somewhere very quickly

high-'tech (also ˌhi-'tech) *adj.* (*informal*) **1** using the most modern methods and machines, especially electronic ones: *high-tech industries* **2** (of designs, objects, etc.) very modern in appearance; using modern materials: *a high-tech table made of glass and steel* ⟳ compare LOW-TECH

high tech'nology *noun* [U] the most modern methods and machines, especially electronic ones; the use of these in industry, etc.

high-'tension *adj.* [only before noun] carrying a very powerful electric current: *high-tension wires/lines*

high 'tide *noun* [U, C] the time when the ocean has risen to its highest level; the ocean at this time: *You can't walk along this beach at high tide.* ⟳ compare FLOOD TIDE, HIGH WATER **ANT** LOW TIDE

'high-tops *noun* [pl.] sports shoes that cover the ankle, worn especially for playing basketball ⟳ picture at SHOE ▶ **'high-top** *adj.* [usually before noun]: *high-top sneakers*

high 'treason *noun* [U] = TREASON

high 'water *noun* [U] the time when the ocean or the water

in a river has risen to its highest level: *Fishing is good at high water.* ⟳ compare HIGH TIDE **IDM** see HELL

high-'water ˌmark *noun* a line or mark showing the highest point that the ocean or FLOODWATER has reached: (*figurative*) *the high-water mark of Parisian fashion* (= the most successful time) ⟳ compare LOW-WATER MARK

high·way ✎ /ˈhaɪweɪ/
noun a main road for traveling long distances, especially one connecting and going through cities and towns: *an interstate highway* ◆ *Highway patrol officers closed the road.*
IDM **highway robbery** (*informal*) the fact of someone charging too much money for something: *You wouldn't believe some of the prices they charge; it's highway robbery.* ⟳ more at WAY

high·way·man /ˈhaɪweɪmən/ *noun* (*pl.* high·way·men /-mən/) a man, usually on a horse and carrying a gun, who stole from travelers on public roads in the past

'high wire *noun* [usually sing.] a rope or wire that is stretched high above the ground, and used by CIRCUS performers **SYN** TIGHTROPE

'hi-hat (also 'high-hat) /ˈhaɪ hæt/ *noun* a pair of CYMBALS on a set of drums, operated by the foot ⟳ picture at INSTRUMENT

hi·jab /hɪˈdʒɑb/ *noun* **1** [C] a head covering worn in public by some Muslim women **2** [U] the religious system which controls the wearing of such clothing ⟳ see also VEIL

hi·jack /ˈhaɪdʒæk/ *verb* **1** ~ sth to use violence or threats to take control of a vehicle, especially a plane, in order to force it to travel to a different place or to demand something from a government: *The plane was hijacked by two armed men on a flight from Miami to San Juan.* ⟳ collocations at CRIME **2** ~ sth (*disapproving*) to use or take control of something, especially a meeting, in order to advertise your own aims and interests ▶ **hi·jack·ing** (also hijack) *noun* [C, U]: *There has been a series of hijackings recently.* ◆ *an unsuccessful hijack* ⟳ compare CARJACKING

hi·jack·er /ˈhaɪˌdʒækər/ *noun* a person who hijacks a plane or other vehicle

hi·jinks = HIGH JINKS

Hij·ra /ˈhɪdʒrə/ *noun* = HEGIRA

hike /haɪk/ *noun, verb*
● *noun* **1** a long walk in the country: *They went on a ten-mile hike through the forest.* ◆ *We could go into town but it's a real hike* (= a long way) *from here.* **2** (*informal*) a large or sudden increase in prices, costs, etc.: *a tax/price hike* ◆ ~ **in sth** *the latest hike in interest rates*
IDM **take a hike** (*informal*) a rude way of telling someone to go away
● *verb* **1** [I, T] to go for a long walk in the country, especially for pleasure: *sturdy boots for hiking over rough terrain* ◆ ~ **sth** *to hike the Rockies* **2** [I] **go hiking** to spend time hiking for pleasure: *If the weather's good, we'll go hiking this weekend.* **3** [T] ~ **sth (up)** to increase prices, taxes, etc. suddenly by large amounts: *The state hiked up the price of gas by over 40%.* **PHR V** **ˌhike sth↔'up** (*informal*) to pull or lift something up, especially your clothing **SYN** HITCH UP: *She hiked up her skirt and waded into the river.*

hik·er /ˈhaɪkər/ *noun* a person who goes for long walks in the country for pleasure ⟳ see also HITCHHIKE

hik·ing /ˈhaɪkɪŋ/ *noun* [U] the activity of going for long walks in the country for pleasure: *to go hiking* ◆ *hiking boots*

hi·lar·i·ous /hɪˈlɛriəs/ *adj.* extremely funny: *a hilarious joke/story* ◆ *Lynn found the whole situation hilarious.* ◆ *Do you know Pete? He's hilarious.* ⟳ thesaurus box at FUNNY ▶ **hi·lar·i·ous·ly** *adv.*: *hilariously funny*

hi·lar·i·ty /hɪˈlærəti/ *noun* [U] a state of great AMUSEMENT which makes people laugh

hill ✎ /hɪl/ *noun*
1 [C] an area of land that is higher than the land around it, but not as high as a mountain: *a region of gently rolling hills* ◆ *a hill farm/town/fort* ◆ *the hill country* of North Mississippi

◆ *The house is built **on the side of a hill** overlooking the river.* ◆ *I love walking **in the hills*** (= in the area where there are hills). ➔ see also ANTHILL, FOOTHILL, MOLEHILL **2** [C] a slope on a road: *Always take care when driving down **steep hills**.* ◆ *a hill start* (= the act of starting a vehicle on a slope) ➔ see also DOWNHILL, UPHILL **3 the Hill** [sing.] (*informal*) = CAPITOL HILL

IDM **a hill of beans** (*old-fashioned, informal*) something that is not worth much **over the hill** (*informal*) (of a person) old and therefore no longer useful or attractive ➔ more at OLD

hill·bil·ly /ˈhɪlˌbɪli/ *noun* (*pl.* **hill·bil·lies**) **1** [C] (*disapproving*) a person who lives in the mountains and is thought to be stupid by people who live in the towns **2** [U] a type of COUNTRY MUSIC that began in the mountains of the southern states of the U.S.

hill·ock /ˈhɪlək/ *noun* a small hill

hill·side /ˈhɪlsaɪd/ *noun* the side of a hill: *The crops will not grow on exposed hillsides.* ◆ *Our hotel was on the hillside overlooking the lake.*

hill·top /ˈhɪltɑp/ *noun* the top of a hill: *the hilltop town of Urbino*

hill·y /ˈhɪli/ *adj.* (**hill·ier**, **hill·iest**) having a lot of hills: *a hilly area/region*

hilt /hɪlt/ *noun* the handle of a SWORD, knife, etc. ➔ picture at SWORD

IDM **(up) to the hilt** as much as possible: *We're mortgaged up to the hilt.* ◆ *They have promised to back us to the hilt.*

him 🔑 /ɪm; strong form hɪm/ *pron.*
1 used as the object of a verb, after the verb *be*, or after a preposition, to refer to a male person or animal that has already been mentioned or is easily identified: *When did you see him?* ◆ *I'm taller than him.* ◆ *It's him.* ➔ compare HE **2 Him** used when referring to God

him·self 🔑 /hɪmˈsɛlf; weak form ɪmˈsɛlf/ *pron.*
1 (the reflexive form of *he*) used when the man or boy who performs an action is also affected by it: *He introduced himself.* ◆ *Peter ought to be ashamed of himself.* **2** used to emphasize the male subject or object of a sentence: *The doctor said so himself.* ◆ *Did you see the manager himself?* **IDM** **be, seem, etc. himself** (of a man or boy) to be in a normal state of health or happiness; not influenced by other people: *He didn't seem quite himself this morning.* ◆ *He needed space to be himself.* **(all) by himself 1** alone; without anyone else: *He lives all by himself.* **2** without help: *He managed to repair the car by himself.* **(all) to himself** for only him to have or use: *He has the house to himself during the week.*

hind /haɪnd/ *adj., noun*
● *adj.* [only before noun] the **hind** legs or feet of an animal with four legs are those at the back: *The horse reared up on its hind legs.* **ANT** FORE, FRONT
● *noun* a female DEER, especially a RED DEER; a DOE ➔ compare HART

hind·brain /ˈhaɪndbreɪn/ *noun* (*anatomy*) the part of the brain near the base of the head

hind·er /ˈhɪndər/ *verb* to make it difficult for someone to do something or something to happen **SYN** HAMPER: ~ **sb/sth** *a political situation that hinders economic growth* ◆ *Some teachers felt hindered by a lack of resources.* ◆ ~ **sb/sth from sth/from doing sth** *An injury was hindering him from playing his best.* ➔ see also HINDRANCE

Hin·di /ˈhɪndi/ *noun* [U] one of the official languages of India, spoken especially in northern India ▶ **Hindi** *adj.*

hind·limb /ˈhaɪndlɪm/ *noun* one of the legs at the back of an animal's body

hind·quar·ters /ˈhaɪndˌkwɔrtərz; -ˌkwɔtərz/ *noun* [pl.] the back part of an animal that has four legs, including its two back legs

hin·drance /ˈhɪndrəns/ *noun* **1** [C, usually sing.] a person or thing that makes it more difficult for someone to do something or for something to happen: *To be honest, she was more of a hindrance than a help.* ◆ ~ **to sth/sb** *The high price is a major hindrance to potential buyers.* **2** [U] (*formal*) the act of making it more difficult for someone to do something or for something to happen: *They were able to complete their journey without further hindrance.* ➔ see also HINDER

hind·sight /ˈhaɪndsaɪt/ *noun* [U] the understanding that you have of a situation only after it has happened and that means you would have done things in a different way: *With hindsight it is easy to say they should not have released him.* ◆ *What looks obvious in hindsight was not at all obvious at the time.* ◆ *It's easy to criticize with the benefit of hindsight.* ➔ compare FORESIGHT

Hin·du /ˈhɪndu/ *noun* a person whose religion is Hinduism ▶ **Hindu** *adj.*: *a Hindu temple*

Hin·du·ism /ˈhɪnduˌɪzəm/ *noun* [U] the main religion of India and Nepal, which includes the worship of one or more gods and belief in REINCARNATION

hinge /hɪndʒ/ *noun, verb*

hinge

● *noun* a piece of metal, plastic, etc. on which a door, lid, or gate moves freely as it opens or closes: *The door had been pulled off its hinges.*
● *verb* [usually passive] ~ **sth** to attach something with a hinge ▶ **hinged** *adj.*: *a hinged door/lid*
PHR V **'hinge on/upon sth** (of an action, a result, etc.) to depend on something completely: *Everything hinges on the outcome of these talks.* ◆ ~ **how, what, etc....** *His success hinges on how well he does at the interview.*

hint /hɪnt/ *noun, verb*
● *noun* **1** something that you say or do in an indirect way in order to show someone what you are thinking: *He gave a **broad hint*** (= one that was obvious) *that he was thinking of retiring.* ◆ *Should I **drop a hint*** (= give a hint) *to Matt?* **2** something that suggests what will happen in the future **SYN** SIGN: *At the first hint of trouble, they left.* **3** [usually sing.] ~ **(of sth)** a small amount of something **SYN** SUGGESTION, TRACE: *a hint of a smile* ◆ *There was more than a hint of sadness in his voice.* ◆ *The walls were painted white with a hint of peach.* **4** [usually pl.] ~ **(on sth)** a small piece of practical information or advice **SYN** TIP: *handy hints on saving money* **IDM** **take a/the hint** to understand what someone wants you to do even though they tell you in an indirect way: *I thought they'd never go—some people just can't take a hint.* ◆ *Sarah hoped he'd take the hint and leave her alone.*
● *verb* [I, T] to suggest something in an indirect way: ~ **at sth** *What are you hinting at?* ◆ ~ **(that)...** *They hinted (that) there might be more job losses.* ◆ + **speech** *"I might know something about it,"* he hinted.

hin·ter·land /ˈhɪntərˌlænd/ (also **hin·ter·lands**) *noun* the areas of a country that are away from the coast, from the banks of a large river, or from the main cities: *the rural/remote hinterlands*

hip 🔑 /hɪp/ *noun, adj., exclamation*
● *noun* **1** the area at either side of the body between the top of the leg and the waist; the joint at the top of the leg: *She stood with her hands on her hips.* ◆ *These jeans are too tight around the hips.* ◆ *a hip replacement operation* ◆ *the hip bone* ◆ *She broke her hip in the fall.* ➔ picture at BODY ➔ collocations at PHYSICAL **2 -hipped** (in adjectives) having hips of the size or shape mentioned: *large-hipped* ◆ *slim-hipped* **3** (also **'rose hip**) the red fruit that grows on some types of wild ROSE bushes **IDM** SEE SHOOT
● *adj.* (**hip·per**, **hip·pest**) (*informal*) following or knowing what is fashionable in clothes, music, etc. **ANT** UNHIP
● *exclamation*
IDM **hip, hip, hooray!** (also *less frequent* **hip, hip, hurrah!**)

used by a group of people to show their approval of someone. One person in the group says "hip, hip" and the others then shout "hooray": *Three cheers for the bride and groom: "Hip, hip…" "Hooray!"*

'**hip bath** *noun* a small BATHTUB that you sit in rather than lie down in

'**hip flask** *noun* = FLASK (2)

'**hip-hop** *noun* [U] **1** a type of popular dance music with spoken words and a steady beat played on electronic instruments, originally played by young African Americans **2** the culture of the young African Americans and others who enjoy this type of music, including special styles of art, dancing, dress, etc.

hip-hug·gers /'hɪp ˌhʌgərz/ *noun* [pl.] pants that cover the hips but not the waist: *a pair of hip-huggers* ▶ '**hip-ˌhugger** *adj.* [only before noun]: *hip-hugger jeans*

'**hip joint** *noun* the joint that connects the leg to the body, at the top of the THIGH bone

hip·pie (also **hip·py**) /'hɪpi/ *noun* (*pl.* **hip·pies**) a person who rejected the way that most people live in Western society, often having long hair, wearing brightly colored clothes, and taking illegal drugs. The hippie movement was most popular in the 1960s.

hip·po /'hɪpoʊ/ *noun* (*pl.* **hip·pos**) (*informal*) = HIPPOPOTAMUS

hip·po·cam·pus /ˌhɪpə'kæmpəs/ *noun* (*pl.* **hip·po·cam·pi** /-paɪ; -pi/) (*anatomy*) either of the two areas of the brain thought to be the center of emotion and memory

ˌ**hip 'pocket** *noun* a pocket at the back or the side of a pair of pants or a skirt

the Hip·po·crat·ic oath /ˌhɪpə'krætɪk 'oʊθ/ *noun* [sing.] the promise that doctors make to keep to the principles of the medical profession

hip·po·drome /'hɪpəˌdroʊm/ *noun* **1** an ARENA, especially one used for horse shows **2** a track in ancient Greece or Rome on which horse races or CHARIOT races took place

hip·po·pot·a·mus /ˌhɪpə'pɑtəməs/ *noun* (*pl.* **hip·po·pot·a·mus·es** /-məsəz/ or **hip·po·pot·a·mi** /-maɪ/) (also *informal* **hip·po**) a large, heavy, African animal with thick dark skin and short legs, that lives in rivers and lakes

hippopotamus

hip·py = HIPPIE

hip·ster /'hɪpstər/ *noun* (*informal*) a person who follows what is fashionable in clothes, music, etc. ▶ **hip·ster** *adj.* [only before noun]: *a hipster bar*

hi·ra·ga·na /ˌhɪrə'gɑnə/ *noun* [U] (from *Japanese*) a set of symbols used in Japanese writing ➔ compare KATAKANA

hire 🔑 /'haɪər/ *verb, noun*

● *verb* **1** [T, I] ~ (**sb**) to give someone a job: *She was hired three years ago.* ◆ *He does the **hiring and firing** in our company.* ➔ collocations at JOB **2** [T] ~ **sb/sth** to employ someone to do a particular job: *to hire a lawyer* ◆ *They hired a firm of consultants to design the new system.* **PHR V** ˌ**hire yourself 'out (to sb)** to arrange to work for someone: *He hired himself out to whoever needed his services.*

● *noun* a person who has recently been given a job by a company

ˌ**hired 'hand** *noun* a person who is paid to work on a farm

hire·ling /'haɪərlɪŋ/ *noun* (*disapproving*) a person who is willing to do anything or work for anyone as long as they are paid

hi-res (also **high-res**) /ˌhaɪ 'rez/ *adj.* (*informal*) = HIGH-RESOLUTION

hir·sute /'hərsut; 'hɪr-; hər'sut; hɪr-/ *adj.* (*literary* or *humorous*) having a lot of hair on the face or body SYN HAIRY

his 🔑 /hɪz; ɪz; *strong form* hɪz/ *det., pron.*

● *det.* (the possessive form of *he*) **1** of or belonging to a man or boy who has already been mentioned or is easily identified: *James has sold his car.* ◆ *He broke his leg skiing.* **2** His of or belonging to God

● *pron.* of or belonging to him: *He took my hand in his.* ◆ *The choice was his.* ◆ *a friend of his* ➔ note at GENDER

His·pan·ic /hɪ'spænɪk/ *adj., noun*

● *adj.* of or connected with Spain or Spanish-speaking countries, especially those of Latin America

● *noun* a person whose first language is Spanish, especially one from a Latin American country living in the U.S. or Canada

Hispano- /hɪ'spænoʊ/ *combining form* (in nouns and adjectives) Spanish: *the Hispano-French border* ◆ *Hispanophile*

hiss /hɪs/ *verb, noun*

● *verb* **1** [I] ~ (**at sb/sth**) to make a sound like a long "s": *The steam escaped with a loud hissing noise.* ◆ *The snake lifted its head and hissed.* **2** [T, I] ~ (**sb/sth**) | ~ (**sb/sth + adv./prep.**) to make a sound like a long "s" to show disapproval of someone or something, especially an actor or a speaker: *He was booed and hissed off the stage.* **3** [I, T] to say something in a quiet angry voice: ~ **at sb** *He hissed at them to be quiet.* ◆ + *speech "Leave me alone!" she hissed.*

● *noun* a sound like a long "s"; this sound used to show disapproval of someone: *the hiss of the air brakes* ◆ *the snake's hiss* ◆ *The performance was met with boos and hisses.*

hissy fit /'hɪsi ˌfɪt/ *noun* [C, usually sing.] (*informal*) a state of being bad-tempered and unreasonable SYN TANTRUM: *She threw a hissy fit because her dressing room wasn't painted blue.*

his·ta·mine /'hɪstəˌmin; -mən/ *noun* [U] (*medical*) a chemical substance that is given out in the body in response to an injury or an ALLERGY ➔ see also ANTIHISTAMINE

his·to·gram /'hɪstəˌgræm/ *noun* (*technical*) a diagram which uses RECTANGLES (= bars) of different heights (and sometimes different widths) to show different amounts, so that they can be compared ➔ compare BAR GRAPH

his·tol·o·gy /hɪ'stɑlədʒi/ *noun* [U] the scientific study of the extremely small structures that form living TISSUE ▶ **his·tol·o·gist** /-dʒɪst/ *noun*

his·to·pa·thol·o·gy /ˌhɪstoʊpə'θɑlədʒi/ *noun* [U] the study of changes in cells where disease is present

his·to·ri·an /hɪ'stɔriən/ *noun* a person who studies or writes about history; an expert in history

his·tor·ic /hɪ'stɔrɪk; -'stɑr-/ *adj.* [usually before noun] **1** important in history; likely to be thought of as important at some time in the future: *a historic building/monument* ◆ *The area is of special historic interest.* ◆ *a historic occasion/decision/day/visit/victory* **2** of a period during which history was recorded: *in historic times* ➔ compare PREHISTORIC

WHICH WORD?

historic ◆ historical

■ **Historic** is usually used to describe something that is so important that it is likely to be remembered: *Today is a historic occasion for our country.* **Historical** usually describes something that is connected with the past or with the study of history, or something that really happened in the past: *I have been doing some historical research.* ◆ *Was Robin Hood a historical figure?*

his·tor·i·cal 🔑 /hɪ'stɔrɪkl; -'stɑr-/ *adj.* [usually before noun]

1 connected with the past: *the historical background to the war* ◆ *You must place these events in their **historical context**.* ➔ note at HISTORIC **2** connected with the study of history: *historical documents/records/research* ◆ *The building is of historical importance.* **3** (of a book, movie, etc.) about people and events in the past: *a historical novel*

▶ his·tor·i·cal·ly /-kli/ *adv.*: *The book is historically inaccurate.* ♦ *Historically, there has always been a great deal of rivalry between the two families.*

his·tor·i·cism /hɪˈstɔːrəˌsɪzəm; -ˈstɑːr-/ *noun* [U] the theory that cultural and social events and situations can be explained by history

the his·toric 'present *noun* [sing.] (*grammar*) the simple present tense used to describe events in the past in order to make the description more powerful

his·to·ri·og·ra·phy /hɪˌstɔːriˈɑːɡrəfi/ *noun* [U] the study of writing about history ▶ his·to·ri·o·graph·i·cal /hɪˌstɔːriəˈɡræfɪkl/ *adj.*

his·to·ry 🔑 /ˈhɪstəri; ˈhɪstri/ *noun* (*pl.* his·to·ries)

1 [U] all the events that happened in the past: *a turning point in human history* ♦ *one of the worst disasters in recent history* ♦ *a people with no sense of history* ♦ *Many people throughout history have dreamt of a world without war.* ♦ *The area was inhabited long before the dawn of recorded history* (= before people wrote about events). ♦ *These events changed the course of history.* ⊃ see also ANCIENT HISTORY **2** [sing., U] the past events concerned in the development of a particular place, subject, etc.: *the history of Texas/democracy/popular music* ♦ *The local history of the area is fascinating.* ♦ *The school traces its history back to 1865.* **3** [U] the study of past events as a subject in school or college: *a history teacher* ♦ *a degree in History* ♦ *social/economic/political history* ♦ *ancient/ medieval/modern history* ♦ *She's studying art history.* ⊃ see also NATURAL HISTORY **4** [C] a written or spoken account of past events: *She's writing a new history of New York.* ♦ *She went on to catalog a long history of disasters.* **5** [sing.] ~ (of sth) a record of something happening frequently in the past life of a person, family, or place; the set of facts that are known about someone's past life: *He has a history of violent crime.* ♦ *There is a history of heart disease in my family.* ♦ *a patient's medical history* ♦ *Do you have a good credit history?* (= a good record of paying back money that you borrow) ⊃ see also CASE HISTORY, LIFE HISTORY
IDM be history (*informal*) to be dead or no longer important: *Another mistake like that and you're history.* ♦ *We won't talk about that—that's history.* ♦ *That's past history now.* the history books the record of great achievements in history: *She has earned her place in the history books.* history repeats itself used to say that things often happen later in the same way as before make history | go down in history to be or do something so important that it will be recorded in history: *a discovery that made medical history* ⊃ more at REST *n.*

his·tri·on·ic /ˌhɪstriˈɑnɪk/ *adj.* [usually before noun] (*formal, disapproving*) histrionic behavior is very emotional and is intended to attract attention in a way that does not seem sincere ▶ his·tri·on·i·cally /-kli/ *adv.* his·tri·on·ics *noun* [pl.]: *She was used to her mother's histrionics.*

hit 🔑 /hɪt/ *verb, noun*

● **verb** (hit·ting, hit, hit)

▷ TOUCH SOMEONE OR SOMETHING WITH FORCE **1** [T] to bring your hand, or an object you are holding, against someone or something quickly and with force: ~ sb/sth *My parents never used to hit me.* ♦ ~ sb/sth with sth *He hit the nail squarely on the head with the hammer.* ♦ *She hit him on the head with her umbrella.* **IDM** see PANIC BUTTON **2** [T] ~ sth/sb to come against something or someone with force, especially causing damage or injury: *The bus hit the bridge.* ♦ *I was hit by a falling stone.* **3** [T] ~ sth (on/against sth) to knock a part of your body against something: *He hit his head on the low ceiling.* **4** [T, often passive] ~ sb/sth (of a bullet, bomb, etc. or a person using them) to reach and touch a person or thing suddenly and with force: *The town was hit by bombs again last night.* ♦ *He was hit by a sniper.*

▷ BALL **5** [T] ~ sth (+ adv./prep.) to bring a BAT, etc. against a ball and push it away with force: *She hit the ball too hard and it went out of the court.* ♦ *We've hit our ball over the fence!* **6** [T] ~ sth (*sports*) to score points by hitting a ball: *to hit a home run*

▷ HAVE BAD EFFECT **7** [T, I] ~ (sb/sth) to have a bad effect on someone or something: *The tax increases will certainly hit the poor.* ♦ *His death didn't really hit me at first.* ♦ *Rural areas have been worst hit by the strike.* ♦ *Spain was one of the hardest hit countries.* ♦ *A tornado hit on Tuesday night.*

▷ ATTACK **8** [T, I] ~ (sb/sth) to attack someone or something: *We hit the enemy when they least expected it.*

▷ REACH **9** [T] ~ sth to reach a place: *Follow this footpath and you'll eventually hit the road.* ♦ *The President hits town tomorrow.* **10** [T] ~ sth to reach a particular level: *Temperatures hit 100° yesterday.* ♦ *The dollar hit a record low in trading today.*

▷ PROBLEM/DIFFICULTY **11** [T] ~ sth (*informal*) to experience something difficult or unpleasant: *We seem to have hit a problem.* ♦ *Everything was going well but then we hit trouble.*

▷ SUDDENLY REALIZE **12** [T] ~ sb (*informal*) to come suddenly into your mind: *I couldn't remember where I'd seen him before, and then it suddenly hit me.*

▷ PRESS BUTTON **13** [T] ~ sth (*informal*) to press something such as a button to operate a machine, etc.: *Hit the brakes!*
IDM hit (it) big (*informal*) to be very successful: *The band has hit big in the U.S.* hit the ceiling/roof (*informal*) to suddenly become very angry hit the deck/dirt/ground (*informal*) to fall to the ground hit the ground running (*informal*) to start doing something and continue very quickly and successfully hit the hay/sack (*informal*) to go to bed hit a/the wall to reach a point when you cannot continue or make any more progress: *We hit a wall and we weren't scoring.* hit it (*informal*) used to tell someone to start doing something, such as playing music: *Hit it, Louis!* hit it off (with sb) (*informal*) to have a good, friendly relationship with someone: *We hit it off right away.* hit the jackpot **1** to make or win a lot of money quickly and unexpectedly **2** to have great or unexpected success hit the nail on the head to say something that is exactly right hit the road/trail (*informal*) to start a trip hit the spot (*informal*) if food or drink hits the spot, it is very satisfying and enjoyable hit the skids (*informal*) to suddenly stop being successful: *Sales of vehicles hit the skids in January.* hit the street(s) **1** to appear or become available to buy: *These new summer styles should be hitting the streets soon.* ♦ *In spite of increased efforts by the narcotics bureau, new drugs hit the street every day.* **2** to go out into the streets of a city, doing something or looking for something: *Thousands of demonstrators are getting ready to hit the streets in Washington, D.C.* hit sb when they're down to continue to hurt someone when they are already defeated hit sb where it hurts to affect someone where they will feel it most ⊃ more at HEADLINE, HOME *adv.*, KNOW *v.*, NERVE *n.*, NOTE *n.*, PAY DIRT, ROOF *n.*, STRIDE *n.*
PHR V hit 'back (at sb/sth) to reply to attacks or criticism: *In a TV interview she hit back at her critics.* **SYN** RETALIATE 'hit on sb (*slang*) to start talking to someone to show them that you are sexually attracted to them 'hit on/upon sth [no passive] to think of a good idea suddenly or by chance: *She hit upon the perfect title for her new novel.* ˌhit 'out (at sb/sth) to attack someone or something violently by fighting them or criticizing them: *I just hit out blindly in all directions.* ♦ *In a rousing speech the general hit out at racism in the armed forces.* ˌhit sb 'up for sth | 'hit sb for sth (*informal*) to ask someone for money: *Does he always hit you up for cash when he wants new clothes?* 'hit sb with sth (*informal*) to tell someone something, especially something that surprises or shocks them: *How much is it going to cost? Come on, hit me with it!*

● **noun**

▷ ACT OF HITTING **1** an act of hitting someone or something with your hand or with an object held in your hand: *Give it a good hit.* ♦ *He made the winning hit.* **2** an occasion when something that has been thrown, fired, etc. at an object reaches that object: *The bomber scored a direct hit on the bridge.* ♦ *We finished the first round with a score of two hits and six misses.*

▷ SOMETHING POPULAR **3** a person or thing that is very popular: *The duo was a real hit in last year's show.* ♦ *a hit musical* ♦ *Her new series is a smash hit.*

▷ POP MUSIC **4** a successful pop song or record: *They are about*

ʌ cup   ə about   eɪ say   aɪ five   ɔɪ boy   aʊ now   oʊ go   ər bird

to release an album of their greatest hits. ◆ She played all her old hits. ◆ *a hit record/single*
> COMPUTING **5** a result of a search on a computer, for example on the Internet
> OF DRUG **6** (*slang*) an amount of an illegal drug that is taken at one time
> MURDER **7** (*slang*) a violent crime or murder ⊃ see also HIT MAN
IDM **be/make a hit (with sb)** to be liked very much by someone when they first meet you **take a hit** to be damaged or badly affected by something: *The airline industry took a hit last year.*

THESAURUS

hit
knock ◆ bang ◆ strike ◆ bump ◆ bash
These words all mean to come against something with a lot of force.
hit to come against something with force, especially causing damage or injury: *The boy was hit by a speeding car.*
knock to hit something so that it moves or breaks; to put someone or something into a particular state or position by hitting them/it: *Someone had knocked a hole in the wall.*
bang to hit something in a way that makes a loud noise: *The baby was banging the table with his spoon.*
strike (*formal*) to hit someone or something hard: *The ship struck a rock.*
bump to hit someone or something accidentally: *In the darkness I bumped into a chair.*
bash (*informal*) to hit against something very hard: *I braked too late and bashed into the car in front of me.*

PATTERNS
▪ to knock/bang/bump/bash **into** sb/sth
▪ to knock/bang/bump/bash **on** sth
▪ to hit/knock/bang/strike/bump/bash sth **with** sth
▪ to hit/strike the **ground/floor/wall**

ˌhit-and-ˈmiss (also ˌhit-or-ˈmiss) *adj.* not done in a careful or planned way and therefore not likely to be successful
ˌhit-and-ˈrun *adj.* [only before noun] **1** (of a road accident) caused by a driver who does not stop to help: *a hit-and-run accident/death* ◆ *a hit-and-run driver* (= one who causes an accident but drives away without helping) **2** (of a military attack) happening suddenly and unexpectedly so that the people attacking can leave quickly without being hurt: *hit-and-run raids* ▶ ˌhit-and-ˈrun *noun*: *He was killed in a hit-and-run.*
hitch /hɪtʃ/ *verb, noun*
● *verb* **1** [T, I] to get a free ride in a person's car; to travel around in this way, by standing at the side of the road and trying to get passing cars to stop: ~ **sth** *They hitched a ride in a truck.* ◆ **(+ adv./prep.)** *We spent the summer hitching around New England.* ⊃ see also HITCHHIKE **2** [T] ~ **sth (up)** to pull up a piece of your clothing **SYN** HIKE UP: *She hitched up her skirt and waded into the river.* **3** [T] ~ **sth (to sth)** to attach something to something else with a rope, a hook, etc.: *We hitched the trailer to the pickup.* **4** [T] ~ **yourself (up, etc.)** to lift yourself into a higher position, or the position mentioned: *She hitched herself up.* ◆ *He hitched himself onto the bar stool.*
IDM **get hitched** (*informal*) to get married
● *noun* **1** a problem or difficulty that causes a short delay: *The ceremony went off **without a hitch**.* ◆ *a technical hitch* **2** a type of knot: *a clove hitch* **3** a device for attaching one thing, usually a vehicle, to another: *a trailer hitch* **4** (*informal*) a period of time spent in the armed forces: *a four-year hitch in the Army*
hitch·hike /ˈhɪtʃhaɪk/ *verb* [I] to travel by asking for free

rides in other people's cars, by standing at the side of the road and trying to get passing cars to stop: *They hitchhiked around the Midwest.* ⊃ see also HITCH ▶ hitch·hik·er (also hitch·er /ˈhɪtʃər/) *noun*: *He picked up two hitchhikers on the road to Cheyenne.*
hi-tech = HIGH-TECH
hith·er /ˈhɪðər/ *adv.* (*old use*) to this place
IDM **hither and thither | hither and yon** (especially *literary*) in many different directions
hith·er·to /ˌhɪðərˈtu; ˌhɪðərˈtu/ *adv.* (*formal*) until now; until the particular time you are talking about: *a hitherto unknown species of moth*
ˈhit list *noun* (*informal*) a list of people, organizations, etc. against whom some unpleasant action is being planned: *Which social services are on the government's hit list?* ◆ *She was at the top of the terrorists' hit list for over two years.*
ˈhit man *noun* (*informal*) a criminal who is paid to kill someone
ˌhit-or-ˈmiss *adj.* = HIT-AND-MISS
the ˈhit paˌrade *noun* (*old-fashioned*) a list published every week that shows which pop records have sold the most copies
ˈhit squad *noun* a group of criminals who are paid to kill a person
hit·ter /ˈhɪtər/ *noun* (often in compounds) **1** (in sports) a person who hits the ball in the way mentioned: *a big/long/hard hitter* **2** (in politics or business) a person who is powerful: *the heavy hitters of Japanese industry*
HIV /ˌeɪtʃ aɪ ˈvi/ *noun* [U] the abbreviation for "human immunodeficiency virus" (the virus that can cause AIDS): *to be infected with HIV* ◆ *to be HIV-positive/HIV-negative* (= to have had a medical test which shows that you are/are not infected with HIV)
hive /haɪv/ *noun* **1** (also bee·hive) [C] a structure made for BEES to live in **2** [C] the BEES living in a hive **3** hives (also ur·ti·car·i·a) [U] (*medical*) red spots on the skin that ITCH (= make you want to scratch), caused by an ALLERGIC reaction, for example to particular foods **IDM** see ACTIVITY
hi·ya /ˈhaɪyə/ *exclamation* used to say hello to someone in an informal way
hl *abbr.* HECTOLITER(S)
HM (also H.M.) *abbr.* Her/His Majesty('s): *HM the Queen* ◆ *HM Navy*
hm *abbr.* HECTOMETER(S)
hmm (also hm, h'm) /hm; m/ *exclamation* used in writing to show the sound that you make to express doubt or when you are hesitating
HMO /ˌeɪtʃ ɛm ˈoʊ/ *abbr.* health maintenance organization (an organization whose members pay regularly in order to receive medical treatment from its own doctors and hospitals when they need it) ⊃ compare PPO
HMS /ˌeɪtʃ ɛm ˈɛs/ *abbr.* Her/His Majesty's Ship (used before the name of a ship in the British navy): *HMS Apollo*
hoa·gie (also hoa·gy) /ˈhoʊgi/ *noun* = SUBMARINE SANDWICH
hoard /hɔrd/ *noun, verb*
● *noun* ~ **(of sth)** a collection of money, food, valuable objects, etc., especially one that someone keeps in a secret place so that other people will not find or steal it
● *verb* [I, T] ~ **(sth)** to collect and keep large amounts of food, money, etc., especially secretly ▶ hoard·er *noun*
hoard·ing /ˈhɔrdɪŋ/ *noun* [U] the act of hoarding things
hoar·frost /ˈhɔrfrɔst/ *noun* [U] a layer of small pieces of ice that look like white needles and that form on surfaces outside when temperatures are very low
hoarse /hɔrs/ *adj.* (of a person or voice) sounding rough and unpleasant, especially because of a sore throat: *He shouted himself hoarse.* ◆ *a hoarse cough/cry/scream* ▶ hoarse·ly *adv.* hoarse·ness *noun* [U]

---

hoar·y /ˈhɔri/ *adj.* [usually before noun] **1** (*old-fashioned*) very old and well known and therefore no longer interesting: *a hoary old joke* **2** (*literary*) (especially of hair) gray or white because a person is old

hoax /hoʊks/ *noun, verb*
- *noun* an act intended to make someone believe something that is not true, especially something unpleasant: *a bomb hoax* ◆ *hoax calls*
- *verb* ~ **sb** to trick someone by making them believe something that is not true, especially something unpleasant ▶ **hoax·er** *noun*

hob·ble /ˈhɑbl/ *verb* **1** [I] (+ *adv./prep.*) to walk with difficulty, especially because your feet or legs hurt **SYN** LIMP: *The old man hobbled across the road.* **2** [T] ~ **sth** to tie together two legs of a horse or other animal in order to stop it from running away **3** [T] ~ **sth** to make it more difficult for someone to do something or for something to happen

hob·by /ˈhɑbi/ *noun* (*pl.* **hob·bies**)
an activity that you do for pleasure when you are not working: *Her hobbies include swimming and gardening.* ◆ *I only play jazz as a hobby.* ⊃ picture on page 719 ⊃ thesaurus box at INTEREST

hob·by·horse /ˈhɑbiˌhɔrs/ *noun* **1** (sometimes *disapproving*) a subject that someone feels strongly about and likes to talk about: *to get on your hobbyhorse* (= talk about your favorite subject) **2** a toy made from a long stick that has a horse's head at one end. Children pretend to ride on it.

hob·by·ist /ˈhɑbiɪst/ *noun* (*formal*) a person who is very interested in a particular hobby

hob·gob·lin /ˈhɑbˌgɑblən/ *noun* (in stories) a small ugly creature that likes to trick people or cause laughter

hob·nail boot /ˌhɑbneɪl ˈbut/ (also **hob·nailed boot** /-ˌneɪld-/) *noun* [usually pl.] a heavy shoe whose SOLE is attached to the upper part with short heavy nails

hob·nob /ˈhɑbnɑb/ *verb* (-bb-) [I] ~ (**with sb**) (*informal*) to spend a lot of time with someone, especially someone who is rich and/or famous

ho·bo /ˈhoʊboʊ/ *noun* (*pl.* **ho·bos**) (*old-fashioned*) **1** a person who travels from place to place looking for work, especially on farms **2** = TRAMP

Hob·son's choice /ˌhɑbsnz ˈtʃɔɪs/ *noun* [U] a situation in which someone has no choice because if they do not accept what is offered, they will get nothing **ORIGIN** From Tobias Hobson, a man who hired out horses in the 17th century. He gave his customers the choice of the horse nearest the stable door or none at all.

hock /hɑk/ *noun, verb*
- *noun* **1** [U] (*informal*) if something that you own is in **hock**, you have exchanged it for money but hope to buy it back later: *He had to fight to get himself out of hock* (= to buy back the thing he had exchanged for money). **2** [C] the middle joint of an animal's back leg ⊃ picture at HORSE **3** [U, C] = KNUCKLE
  IDM **be in hock (to sb)** to owe someone something: *I'm in hock to the bank for $6,000.* **get/go into hock** to get into debt
- *verb* ~ **sth** (*informal*) to leave a valuable object with someone in exchange for money that you borrow **SYN** PAWN

hock·ey /ˈhɑki/ *noun* [U] **1** (also **ice hockey**) a game played on ice, in which players use long sticks to hit a hard rubber disk (called a PUCK) into the other team's goal ⊃ picture at SPORT ⊃ see also STREET HOCKEY **2** = FIELD HOCKEY

ho·cus-po·cus /ˌhoʊkəs ˈpoʊkəs/ *noun* [U] **1** language or behavior that is nonsense and is intended to hide the truth from people **2** a form of words used by someone performing a magic trick

hod /hɑd/ *noun* an open box attached to a pole, used by building workers for carrying bricks on the shoulder

hodge·podge /ˈhɑdʒpɑdʒ/ *noun* [sing.] a number of things mixed together without any particular order or reason

Hodg·kin's dis·ease /ˈhɑdʒkɪnz dɪˌziz/ *noun* [U] a serious disease of the LYMPH NODE, LIVER, and SPLEEN

hoe /hoʊ/ *noun, verb*
- *noun* a garden tool with a long handle and a blade, used for breaking up soil and removing WEEDS (= plants growing where they are not wanted) ⊃ picture at TOOL
- *verb* (hoe·ing, hoed, hoed) [T, I] ~ (**sth**) to break up soil, remove plants, etc. with a hoe: *to hoe the flower beds*

hoe·down /ˈhoʊdaʊn/ *noun* **1** a social occasion when lively dances are performed **2** a lively dance

hog /hɔg; hɑg/ *noun, verb*
- *noun* **1** a pig, especially one that is kept and made fat for eating **2** (*informal*) a person who wants to keep or use all of something rather than sharing or waiting their turn **SYN** PIG: *Stop being such a hog and let the rest of us have some.* ⊃ see also ROAD HOG, WARTHOG
  IDM **go hog wild** (*informal*) to do something in an extreme and uncontrolled way **go the whole hog** (*informal*) to do something thoroughly or completely
- *verb* (-gg-) ~ **sth** to use or keep most of something yourself and stop others from using or having it: *to hog the road* (= to drive so that other vehicles cannot pass) ◆ *to hog the bathroom* (= to spend a long time in it so that others cannot use it)

hog·nose snake /ˌhɑgnoʊz ˈsneɪk; ˌhag-/ (also **hog-nosed snake**) *noun* a harmless snake with a nose which is turned up

hog·wash /ˈhɔgwɑʃ; ˈhag-; -wɔʃ/ *noun* [U] (*informal*) an idea, argument, etc. that you think is stupid

ho ho /ˌhoʊ ˈhoʊ/ *exclamation* used to show the sound of a deep laugh

ho–hum /ˌhoʊ ˈhʌm/ *exclamation, adj.*
- *exclamation* used to show that you are bored
- *adj.* boring: *a ho-hum game*

hoick /hɔɪk/ *verb* ~ **sth** (+ *adv./prep.*) (*informal*) to lift or pull something in a particular direction, especially with a quick sudden movement **SYN** JERK

the hoi pol·loi /ˌhɔɪ pəˈlɔɪ/ *noun* [pl.] (*disapproving* or *humorous*) an insulting word for ordinary people

hoist /hɔɪst/ *verb, noun*
- *verb* ~ **sth** (+ *adv./prep.*) to raise or pull something up to a higher position, often using ropes or special equipment: *He hoisted himself onto a high stool.* ◆ *to hoist a flag/sail* ◆ *The cargo was hoisted aboard by crane.*
  IDM **be hoist/hoisted by/with your own petard** to be hurt or to have problems as a result of your own plans to hurt or trick others
- *noun* a piece of equipment used for lifting heavy things, or for lifting people who cannot stand or walk

hoi·ty-toi·ty /ˌhɔɪti ˈtɔɪti/ *adj.* (*old-fashioned, informal*) behaving in a way that suggests that you think you are more important than other people

hok·ey /ˈhoʊki/ *adj.* (*informal*) expressing emotions in a way that seems exaggerated or silly

ho·kum /ˈhoʊkəm/ *noun* [U] (*informal*) **1** a movie, play, etc. that is not realistic and has no artistic qualities **2** an idea, argument, etc. that you think is stupid: *What a bunch of hokum!*

hold /hoʊld/ *verb, noun*
- *verb* (held, held /hɛld/)
  > IN HAND/ARMS 1 [T] ~ **sb/sth** to carry something; to have someone or something in your hand, arms, etc.: *She was holding a large box.* ◆ *I held the mouse by its tail.* ◆ *The girl held her father's hand tightly.* ◆ *He was holding the baby in his arms.* ◆ *The winning captain held the trophy in the air.* ◆ *We were* ***holding hands*** (= holding each other's hands). ◆ *The lovers held each other close.* **2** [T] ~ **sth** to put your hand on part of your body, usually because it hurts: *She groaned and held her head.*

Hobbies

photography

painting

pottery

woodcarving

model making

stamp collecting

gardening

knitting

crochet

embroidery

sewing

skateboarding

bowling

Rollerblade™

pool

ice skating

darts

caving (*also* spelunking)

scuba diving

snorkeling

> **IN POSITION** **3** [T] to keep someone or something in a particular position: ~ **sth** (+ adv./prep.) *Hold your head up.* ♦ *Hold this position for a count of 10.* ♦ *The wood is held in position by a clamp.* ♦ *I had to hold my stomach in* (= pull the muscles flat) *to zip up my jeans.* ♦ ~ **sth** + **adj.** *I'll hold the door open for you.*

> **SUPPORT** **4** [T] ~ **sb/sth** to support the weight of someone or something: *I don't think that branch will hold your weight.*

> **CONTAIN** **5** [T] ~ **sb/sth** to have enough space for something or someone; to contain something or someone: *This barrel holds 25 gallons.* ♦ *The plane holds about 300 passengers.*

> **SOMEONE PRISONER** **6** [T] to keep someone and not allow them to leave: ~ **sb** *Police are holding two men in connection with last Thursday's bank robbery.* ♦ ~ **sb** + **noun** *He was held prisoner for two years.*

> **CONTROL** **7** [T] ~ **sth** to defend something against attack; to have control of something: *The rebels held the radio station.*

> **REMAIN** **8** [I] to remain strong and safe or in position: *They were afraid the dam wouldn't hold.* **9** [I] to remain the same: *How long will the good weather hold?* ♦ *If their luck holds, they could still win the championship.*

> **KEEP** **10** [T] ~ **sth** to keep someone's attention or interest: *There wasn't much in the museum to hold my attention.* **11** [T] ~ **sth (at sth)** to keep something at the same level, rate, speed, etc.: *Hold your speed at 50.* **12** [T] ~ **sth** to keep something so that it can be used later: *records held on computer* ♦ *Our attorney holds our wills.* ♦ *We can hold your reservation for three days.*

> **OWN** **13** [T] ~ **sth** to own or have something: *Employees hold 30% of the shares.*

> **JOB** **14** [T] ~ **sth** to have a particular job or position: *How long has he held office?*

> **RECORD/TITLE** **15** [T] ~ **sth** to have something you have gained or achieved: *Who holds the world record for the long jump?* ♦ *She held the title of world champion for three years.*

> **OPINION** **16** [T] to have a belief or an opinion about someone or something: ~ **sth** *He holds strange views on education.* ♦ ~ **sb/sth** + **adv./prep./adj.** *She is held in high regard by her students* (= they have a high opinion of her). ♦ *firmly-held beliefs* **17** [T] (*formal*) to consider that something is true: ~ **that…** *I still hold that the government's economic policies are mistaken.* ♦ ~ **sb/sth** + **adj.** *Parents will be held responsible for their children's behavior.* ♦ **be held to be sth** *These vases are held to be the finest examples of Greek art.*

> **MEETING** **18** [T, usually passive] ~ **sth** to have a meeting, competition, conversation, etc.: *The meeting will be held in the community center.* ♦ *It's impossible to hold a conversation with all this noise.*

> **ROAD/COURSE** **19** [T] ~ **the road** (of a vehicle) to be in close contact with the road and easy to control, especially when driven fast **20** [T] ~ **a course** (of a ship or an aircraft) to continue to move in a particular direction ⊃ picture at PLANE

> **IN MUSIC** **21** [T] ~ **sth** to make a note continue for a particular time

> **ON TELEPHONE** **22** [I, T] to wait until you can speak to the person you have telephoned: *That extension is busy right now. Can you hold?* ♦ ~ **the line** *She asked me to hold the line.*

> **STOP** **23** [T] ~ **sth** used to tell someone to stop doing something or not to do something: *Hold your fire!* (= don't shoot) ♦ *Hold the front page!* (= don't print it until a particular piece of news is available) ♦ (*informal*) *Give me a hot dog, but hold the* (= don't give me any) *mustard.*

IDM Most idioms containing **hold** are at the entries for the nouns and adjectives in the idioms. For example, **hold the fort** is at **fort**. **hold it** (*informal*) used to ask someone to wait, or not to move: *Hold it a second—I don't think everyone's arrived yet.* **there is no holding sb back** a person cannot be prevented from doing something: *Once she gets on to the subject of politics there's no holding her back.*

PHR V ,**hold sth a'gainst sb** to allow something that someone has done to make you have a lower opinion of them: *I admit I made a mistake—but don't hold it against me.* ,**hold sb**↔'**back** to prevent a school student from progressing to the next grade: *She was held back in first grade.*

,**hold sb/sth**↔'**back** **1** to prevent someone or something from moving forward or crossing something: *The police were unable to hold back the crowd.* **2** to prevent the progress or development of someone or something: *Do you think that mixed-ability classes hold back the better students?* ,**hold sth**↔'**back** **1** to not tell someone something they want or need to know: *to hold back information* **2** to stop yourself from expressing how you really feel: *She just managed to hold back her anger.* ♦ *He bravely held back his tears.* ,**hold 'back (from doing sth)** | ,**hold sb 'back (from doing sth)** to hesitate or to make someone hesitate to act or speak: *She held back, not knowing how to break the terrible news.* ♦ *I wanted to tell him the truth, but something held me back.* ,**hold sb**↔'**down** **1** to prevent someone from moving, using force: *It took three men to hold him down.* **2** to prevent someone from having their freedom or rights: *The people are held down by a repressive regime.* ,**hold sth**↔'**down** **1** to keep something at a low level: *The rate of inflation must be held down.* **2** [no passive] to keep a job for some time: *He was unable to hold down a job after his breakdown.* **3** [no passive] (*informal*) to limit something, especially a noise: *Hold it down, will you? I'm trying to sleep!* ,**hold 'forth** to speak for a long time about something in a way that other people might find boring ,**hold sth**↔'**in** to not express how you really feel: *to hold in your feelings/anger* **ANT** LET STH OUT ,**hold 'off** **1** (of rain or a storm) to not start: *The rain held off just long enough for us to have our picnic.* **2** to not do something immediately: *We could get a new computer now or hold off until prices are lower.* ♦ ~ **doing sth** *Could you hold off making your decision for a few days?* ,**hold sb/sth**↔'**off** to stop someone or something defeating you: *She held off all the last-minute challengers and won the race in a new record time.* ,**hold 'on** **1** (*informal*) used to tell someone to wait or stop **SYN** WAIT: *Hold on a minute while I get my breath back.* ♦ *Hold on! This isn't the right road.* **2** to survive in a difficult or dangerous situation: *They managed to hold on until help arrived.* **3** (*informal*) used on the telephone to ask someone to wait until they can talk to the person they want: *Can you hold on? I'll see if he's here.* ,**hold sth**↔'**on** to keep something in position: *These nuts and bolts hold the wheels on.* ♦ *The knob is only held on by duct tape.* ,**hold 'on (to sth/sb)** | ,**hold 'on to sth/sb** [no passive] to keep holding something or someone: *Hold on and don't let go until I say so.* ♦ *He held on to the back of the chair to stop himself from falling.* ⊃ note at HOLD ,**hold 'on to sth** | ,**hold 'on to sth** **1** to keep something that is an advantage for you; to not give or sell something to someone else: *You should hold on to your oil shares.* ♦ *She took an early lead in the race and held on to it for nine laps.* **2** to keep something for someone else or for longer than usual: *I'll hold on to your mail for you until you get back.* ,**hold 'out** **1** to last, especially in a difficult situation: *We can stay here for as long as our supplies hold out.* **2** to resist or survive in a dangerous or difficult situation: *The rebels held out in the mountains for several years.* ,**hold 'out sth** to offer a chance, hope, or possibility of something: *Doctors hold out little hope of her recovering.* ,**hold sth**↔'**out** to put your hand or arms, or something in your hand, toward someone, especially to give or offer something: *I held out my hand to steady her.* ♦ *He held out the keys and I took them.* ,**hold 'out for sth** [no passive] to cause a delay in reaching an agreement because you hope you will gain something: *The union negotiators are holding out for a more generous pay package.* ,**hold 'out on sb** (*informal*) to refuse to tell or give someone something ,**hold sth**↔'**over** [usually passive] **1** to not deal with something immediately; to leave something to be dealt with later **SYN** POSTPONE: *The matter was held over until the next meeting.* **2** to show a movie, play, etc. for longer than planned: *The movie proved so popular it was held over for another week.* ,**hold sth 'over sb** to use knowledge that you have about someone to threaten them or make them do what you want

'**hold sb to sth** **1** to make someone keep a promise **2** to

    h **hat**   m **man**   n **no**   ŋ **sing**   l **leg**   r **red**   y **yes**   w **wet**

stop an opposing team scoring more points, etc. than you: *Their opponents were held to a 0–0 draw.*

,hold to'gether | ,hold sth ↔ to'gether **1** to remain, or to keep something, united: *A political party should hold together.* ♦ *It's the mother who usually holds the family together.* **2** (of an argument, a theory, or a story) to be logical or consistent: *Their case doesn't hold together when you look at the evidence.* ⊃ compare HANG TOGETHER at HANG **3** if a machine or an object **holds together** or something **holds it together**, the different parts stay together so that it does not break

,hold 'up to remain strong and working effectively: *She's holding up well under the pressure.* ,hold sb/sth↔'up [often passive] **1** to support someone or something and stop them from falling **2** to delay or block the movement or progress of someone or something: *An accident is holding up traffic.* ⊃ related noun HOLDUP **3** to use or present someone or something as an example: *She's always holding up her children as models of good behavior.* ♦ *His ideas were held up to ridicule.* ,hold up 'sth to steal from a bank, store, etc. using a gun ⊃ related noun HOLDUP

'hold with sth [no passive] (used in negative sentences or in questions) to agree with something SYN APPROVE OF: *I don't hold with the use of force.* ♦ *~ doing sth They don't hold with letting children watch as much TV as they want.*

hold

hold on ♦ cling ♦ clutch ♦ grip ♦ grasp ♦ clasp ♦ hang on

These words all mean to have something or someone in your hands or arms.

hold to have something or someone in your hand or arms: *She was holding a large box.* ♦ *I held the baby gently in my arms.*

hold on (to sb/sth) to continue to hold something or someone; to put your hand on something or someone and not take your hand away: *Hold on and don't let go until I say so.*

cling to hold on to something or someone tightly, especially with your whole body: *Survivors clung to pieces of floating debris.*

clutch to hold something or someone tightly, especially in your hand; to take hold of something suddenly: *She stood there, the flowers still clutched in her hand.* ♦ *He felt himself slipping and clutched at a branch.*

grip to hold on to something very tightly with your hand: *Grip the rope as tightly as you can.*

grasp to take hold of something firmly: *He grasped my hand and shook it warmly.*

clasp (*formal*) to hold something or someone tightly in your hand or in your arms: *They clasped hands (= held each other's hands).* ♦ *She clasped the children to her breast.* **NOTE** The object of **clasp** is often your *hands*, someone else's *hand*, or another person.

hang on (to sth) to hold on to something very tightly, especially in order to support yourself or stop yourself from falling: *Hang on to the safety rope in case you slip and fall.*

PATTERNS
- to hold/clutch/grip/clasp sth **in your hand/hands**
- to hold/clasp sb/sth **in your arms**
- to hold/hang **on to sth**
- to hold/cling/hang **on**
- to hold/clutch/clasp sb/sth **to you**
- to hold/hold on to/cling to/clutch/grip/grasp/clasp/hang on to sb/sth **tightly**
- to hold/hold on to/cling to/clutch/grip/grasp/clasp sb/sth **firmly**
- to hold/hold on to/clutch/grip/clasp/hang on to sb/sth **tight**

● *noun*
> WITH HAND **1** [sing., U] the action of holding someone or something; the way you are holding someone or something SYN GRIP *n.*: *His hold on her arm tightened.* ♦ *She tried to keep hold of the child's hand.* ♦ *Make sure you've got a steady hold on the camera.*
> IN SPORTS **2** [C] a particular way of holding someone, especially in a sport such as WRESTLING or in a fight: *The wrestler put his opponent into a head hold.*
> POWER/CONTROL **3** [sing.] ~ (on/over sb/sth) influence, power, or control over someone or something: *What they knew about his past gave her a hold over him.* ♦ *He struggled to get a hold of his anger.* ⊃ see also STRANGLEHOLD
> IN CLIMBING **4** [C] a place where you can put your hands or feet when climbing ⊃ see also FOOTHOLD, HANDHOLD, TOEHOLD
> ON SHIP/PLANE **5** [C] the part of a ship or plane where the goods being carried are stored

IDM **catch, get, grab, take, etc. (a) hold of sb/sth** to have or take someone or something in your hands: *He caught hold of her wrists so she couldn't get away.* ♦ *Lee got hold of the dog by its collar.* ♦ *Quick, grab a hold of that rope.* ♦ *Gently, she took hold of the door handle and turned it.* **get hold of sb** to contact or find someone: *Where have you been? I've been trying to get hold of you all day.* **get hold of sth 1** to find something that you want or need: *I need to get hold of Tom's address.* ♦ *It's almost impossible to get hold of tickets for the final.* **2** to learn or understand something **no holds barred** with no rules or limits on what someone is allowed to do **on hold 1** delayed until a later time or date: *She put her career on hold to have a baby.* ♦ *The project is on hold until more money is available.* **2** if a person on the telephone is put **on hold**, they have to wait until the person that they want to talk to is free **take (a) hold** to begin to have complete control over someone or something; to become very strong: *Panic took hold of him and he couldn't move.* ♦ *They got out of the house just before the flames took hold.* ♦ *It is best to treat the disease early before it takes a hold.*

hold·er /'hoʊldər/ *noun* (often in compounds) **1** a person who has or owns the thing mentioned: *a license holder* ♦ *the current holder of the world record* ♦ *holders of high office* ♦ *the holder of a U.S. passport* ⊃ see also RECORD HOLDER, TITLE-HOLDER **2** a thing that holds the object mentioned: *a pen holder* ⊃ see also CIGARETTE HOLDER

hold·ing /'hoʊldɪŋ/ *noun* **1** ~ (in sth) a number of shares that someone has in a company: *She has a 40% holding in the company.* ⊃ see also FUNDHOLDING **2** an amount of property that is owned by a person, museum, library, etc.: *one of the most important private holdings of Indian art*

'holding ˌcompany *noun* a company that is formed to buy shares in other companies which it then controls

'holding ˌpattern *noun* **1** the route a plane travels in while it is flying above the landing place, waiting for permission to land **2** a situation of no progress or change when all you can do is wait

hold·o·ver /'hoʊldˌoʊvər/ *noun* **1** an idea, a fashion, etc. from an earlier time that still exists in the present **2** a person who keeps a position of power, for example someone who had a particular position in one ADMINISTRATION and who still has it in the next

hold·up /'hoʊldʌp/ *noun* **1** a situation in which something is prevented from happening for a short time SYN DELAY: *What's the holdup?* ♦ *We should finish by tonight, barring any holdups.* **2** (also 'stick-up) an act of stealing from a bank, etc. using a gun

hole 🔒 /hoʊl/ *noun, verb*
● *noun*
> HOLLOW SPACE **1** [C] a hollow space in something solid or in the surface of something: *He dug a deep hole in the garden.* ♦ *The bomb blew a huge hole in the ground.* ♦ *Water had collected in the holes in the road.*

> **OPENING** **2** [C] a space or opening that goes all the way through something: *to drill/bore/punch/kick a hole* in something ◆ *There were holes in the knees of his pants.* ◆ *The children climbed through a hole in the fence.* ◆ *a bullet hole* ◆ *the hole in the ozone layer* ⊃ see also OZONE HOLE

> **ANIMAL'S HOME** **3** [C] the home of a small animal: *a rabbit/mouse, etc. hole* ⊃ compare FOXHOLE, PIGEONHOLE

> **UNPLEASANT PLACE** **4** [C, usually sing.] (*informal, disapproving*) an unpleasant place to live or be in **SYN** DUMP: *I am not going to bring up my child in this hole.* ⊃ see also HELLHOLE

> **IN GOLF** **5** [C] a hollow in the ground that you must get the ball into; one of the sections of a GOLF COURSE with the TEE at the beginning and the hole at the end: *The ball rolled into the hole and she had won.* ◆ *an eighteen-hole golf course* ◆ *He liked to play a few holes after work.* ◆ *She won the first hole.* ⊃ picture at SPORT

> **FAULT/WEAKNESS** **6** [C, usually pl.] a fault or weakness in something such as a plan, law, or story: *He was found not guilty because of holes in the prosecution case.* ◆ *I don't believe what she says—her story is full of holes.* ⊃ see also LOOPHOLE

> **EMPTY PLACE/POSITION** **7** [sing.] a place or position that needs to be filled because someone or something is no longer there: *After his wife left, there was a gaping hole in his life.* ◆ *Buying the new equipment left a big hole in the company's finances.* **HELP** There are many other compounds ending in **hole**. You will find them at their place in the alphabet. **IDM** **in a hole** (*informal*) in a difficult situation: *He had gotten himself into a hole and it was going to be difficult to get out of it.* **in the hole** (*informal*) owing money **SYN** IN DEBT: *We start the current fiscal year $30 million in the hole.* **make a hole in sth** to use up a large amount of something that you have, especially money: *College tuition can make a big hole in your savings.* **pick/poke/punch holes in sth** to find the weak points in something such as a plan, suggestion, etc.: *It was easy to pick holes in his arguments.* ⊃ more at ACE *n.*, BURN *v.*, DIG *v.*, NEED *v.*

● *verb*
> **MAKE A HOLE** **1** [T, usually passive] **~ sth** to make a hole or holes in something, especially a boat or ship

> **IN GOLF** **2** [T, I] to hit a GOLF ball into the hole: **~ sth** *She holed a 25 foot putt.* ◆ **~ (out)** *He holed out from 25 feet.* **PHR V** **,hole 'up | be ,holed 'up** (*informal*) to hide in a place: *He'll hole up now and move again tomorrow, after dark.* ◆ *We believe the gang are holed up in the mountains.*

,hole in 'one *noun* (*pl.* **,holes in 'one**) an occasion in GOLF when a player hits the ball from the TEE into the hole using only one shot

,hole in the 'heart *noun* (*medical*) a condition in which a baby is born with a problem with the wall dividing the parts of its heart, so that it does not get enough OXYGEN in its blood

,hole in the 'wall *noun* (*informal*) a small dark store or restaurant ▶ **,hole-in-the-'wall** *adj.* [only before noun]: *hole-in-the-wall restaurants*

hol·ey /'houli/ *adj.* a **holey** piece of clothing or material has a lot of holes in it

hol·i·day ⚷ /'halə,deɪ/ *noun*
1 [C] a day when most people do not go to work or school, especially because of a religious or national celebration: *a national/state/religious holiday* ◆ *Today is a state holiday in Massachusetts.* ⊃ see also PUBLIC HOLIDAY **2 holidays** [pl.] the time in December and early January that includes Christmas, Hanukkah, and New Year: *Happy Holidays!*

ho·li·er-than-thou /ˌhouliər ðən 'ðaʊ/ *adj.* (*disapproving*) showing that you think that you are morally better than other people **SYN** SELF-RIGHTEOUS: *I can't stand his holier-than-thou attitude.*

ho·li·ness /'houlinəs/ *noun* **1** [U] the quality of being holy **2 His/Your Holiness** [C] a title of respect used when talking to or about the Pope and some other religious leaders: *His Holiness Pope Benedict XVI*

ho·lism /'houlɪzəm/ *noun* [U] **1** the idea that the whole of something must be considered in order to understand its

different parts ⊃ compare ATOMISM **2** the idea that the whole of a sick person, including their body, mind, and way of life, should be considered when treating them, and not just the SYMPTOMS (= effects) of the disease

ho·lis·tic /hou'lɪstɪk/ *adj.* **1** (*informal*) considering a whole thing or being to be more than a collection of parts: *a holistic approach to life* **2** (*medical*) treating the whole person rather than just the SYMPTOMS (= effects) of a disease: *holistic medicine* ▶ **ho·lis·ti·cally** /-kli/ *adv.*

hol·lan·daise sauce /'halənderz ,sɔs; ,halən'deɪz-/ *noun* [U] a sauce made with butter, egg YOLKS (= yellow parts), and VINEGAR

hol·ler /'halər/ *verb* [I, T] (*informal*) to shout loudly **SYN** YELL: **~ (at sb)** *Don't holler at me!* ◆ **+ speech** *"Look out!" I hollered.* ◆ **~ sth** *He hollered something I couldn't understand.*

hol·low ⚷ /'halou/ *adj., noun, verb*
● *adj.* **1** having a hole or empty space inside: *a hollow ball/center/tube* ◆ *The tree trunk was hollow inside.* ◆ *Her stomach felt hollow with fear.* **2** (of parts of the face) sinking deeply into the face: *hollow eyes/cheeks* ◆ *hollow-eyed from lack of sleep* **3** [usually before noun] (of sounds) making a low sound like that made by an empty object when it is hit: *a hollow groan* **4** [usually before noun] not sincere: *hollow promises/threats* ◆ *a hollow laugh* ◆ *Their appeals for an end to the violence had a hollow ring.* ◆ *His promise rang hollow* (= did not sound sincere). **5** [usually before noun] without real value: *to win a hollow victory* ▶ **hol·low·ly** *adv.*: *to laugh hollowly* **hol·low·ness** *noun* [U]: *the hollowness of the victory*

● *noun* **1** an area that is lower than the surface around it, especially on the ground: *muddy hollows* ◆ *The village lay secluded in a hollow of the hills* (= a small valley). ◆ *She noticed the slight hollows under his cheekbones.* **2** a hole or a small space in something: *The squirrel disappeared into a hollow at the base of the tree.*

● *verb* [usually passive] **~ sth** to make a flat surface curve in **PHR V** **,hollow sth↔'out 1** to make a hole in something by removing part of it: *Hollow out the cake and fill it with cream.* **2** to form something by making a hole in something else: *The cave has been hollowed out of the mountainside.*

hol·ly /'hali/ *noun* (*pl.* **hol·lies**) [U, C] a bush or small tree with hard shiny leaves with sharp points and bright red berries (BERRY) in winter, often used as a decoration at Christmas: *a sprig of holly*

hol·ly·hock /'hali,hak/ *noun* a tall garden plant with white, yellow, red, or purple flowers growing up its STEM

Hol·ly·wood /'hali,wʊd/ *noun* [U] the part of Los Angeles where the movie industry is based (used to refer to the U.S. movie industry and the way of life that is associated with it)

,Hollywood 'ending *noun* (usually *disapproving*) an ending in a movie, novel, etc., which happens in the way you expect, is full of exaggerated happiness, sadness, or love, and may not be very realistic: *The movie refuses to sell out and provide a Hollywood ending.*

hol·mi·um /'houlmiəm/ *noun* [U] (*symb.* **Ho**) a chemical element. Holmium is a soft silver-white metal.

hol·o·caust /'halə,kɔst; 'hou-/ *noun* **1** [C] a situation in which many things are destroyed and many people killed, especially because of a war or a fire: *a nuclear holocaust* **2 the Holocaust** [sing.] the killing of millions of Jews by the Nazis in the 1930s and 1940s

hol·o·gram /'halə,græm; 'hou-/ *noun* a special type of picture in which the objects seem to be THREE-DIMENSIONAL (= solid rather than flat)

hol·o·graph /'halə,græf; 'hou-/ *noun* (*technical*) a piece of writing that has been written by hand by its author

hol·o·graph·ic /ˌhalə'græfɪk; ˌhou-/ *adj.* [usually before noun] connected with holograms: *a holographic picture*

ho·loph·ra·sis /hə'lafrəsəs/ *noun* [U] (*linguistics*) the expression of a whole idea in a single word, for example a baby saying "up" for "I want you to pick me up" ▶ **hol·o·phras·tic** /ˌhalə'fræstɪk; ˌhou-/ *adj.*

ʌ **cup**   ə **about**   eɪ **say**   aɪ **five**   ɔɪ **boy**   aʊ **now**   oʊ **go**   ər **bird**

Hol·stein /'houlstaɪn; -staɪn/ *noun* a type of black and white cow that produces a lot of milk

hol·ster /'houlstər/ *noun, verb*
- *noun* a leather case worn on a belt or on a narrow piece of leather under the arm, used for carrying a small gun
- *verb* ~ sth to put a gun in a **holster**

ho·ly 🔑 /'houli/ *adj.* (ho·li·er, ho·li·est)
1 [usually before noun] connected with God or a particular religion: *the Holy Bible/Scriptures* ♦ *holy ground* ♦ *a holy war* (= one fought to defend the beliefs of a particular religion) ♦ *the holy city of Mecca* ♦ *Islam's holiest shrine* **ANT** UNHOLY ⊃ see also HOLY ORDERS **2** good in a moral and religious way: *a holy life/man* **ANT** UNHOLY **3** [only before noun] (*informal*) used to emphasize that you are surprised, afraid, etc.: *Holy cow! What was that?* ⊃ see also HOLIER-THAN-THOU, HOLINESS

Holy Com'munion *noun* [U] = COMMUNION

the Holy 'Father *noun* [sing.] the POPE

the Holy 'Ghost *noun* [sing.] = THE HOLY SPIRIT

the Holy 'Grail *noun* [sing.] = GRAIL

the holy of 'holies *noun* [sing.] **1** the most holy part of a religious building **2** (*humorous*) a special room or building that can only be visited by important people

holy 'orders *noun* [pl.] the official position of being a priest: *to take holy orders* (= to become a priest)

the Holy 'See *noun* [sing.] **1** the job or authority of the Pope **2** the Roman Catholic court at the Vatican in Rome

the Holy 'Spirit (also **the Holy 'Ghost**) *noun* [sing.] (in Christianity) God in the form of a spirit

holy water *noun* [U] water that has been BLESSED by a priest

Holy Week *noun* in the Christian Church, the week before Easter Sunday

Holy 'Writ *noun* [U] (*old-fashioned*) the Bible: (*figurative*) *You shouldn't take what he says as Holy Writ* (= accept that it is true without questioning it).

hom·age /'hɒmɪdʒ; 'ɑ-/ *noun* [U, C, usually sing.] ~ **(to sb/ sth)** (*formal*) something that is said or done to show respect for someone: *The kings of France paid homage to no one.* ♦ *He describes his book as "a homage to my father."* ♦ *They stood in silent homage around the grave.*

hom·bre /'ɑmbreɪ; 'oum-/ *noun* (*informal, from Spanish*) a man, especially one of a particular type: *Their quarterback is one tough hombre.*

hom·burg /'hɑmbɜrg/ *noun* a man's soft hat with a narrow, curled BRIM

home 🔑 /houm/ *noun, adj., adv., verb*
- *noun*
> **HOUSE, ETC. 1** [C, U] the house or apartment that you live in, especially with your family: *We are not far from my home now.* ♦ *Old people prefer to stay in their own homes.* ♦ *She leaves home at 7 every day.* ♦ *the family home* ♦ *While traveling she missed the comforts of home.* ♦ *He left home* (= left his parents and began an independent life) *at sixteen.* ♦ *Nowadays a lot of people work from home.* ♦ *I'll call you from home later.* ♦ (*figurative*) *We haven't found a home for all our books yet* (= a place where they can be kept). ♦ *stray dogs needing new homes* ⊃ see also STAY-AT-HOME **2** [C] a house or apartment, etc., when you think of it as property that can be bought and sold: *a summer home* ♦ *A lot of new homes are being built on the edge of town.* ♦ *Private home ownership is increasing faster than ever.* ♦ *They applied for a home improvement loan.* ⊃ picture at HOUSE ⊃ see also MOBILE HOME, SECOND HOME
> **TOWN/COUNTRY 3** [C, U] the town, district, country, etc. that you come from, or where you are living and that you feel you belong to: *I often think about my friends back home.* ♦ *Jane left Chicago and made Greece her home.* ♦ *Jamaica is home to over two million people.*
> **FAMILY 4** [C] used to refer to a family living together, and the way it behaves: *She came from a violent home.* ♦ *He had*

always wanted a real home with a wife and children. ⊃ see also BROKEN HOME
> **FOR OLD PEOPLE/CHILDREN 5** [C] a place where people who cannot care for themselves live and are cared for by others: *a children's home* ♦ *an old people's home* ♦ *a retirement home* ♦ *a home for the mentally ill* ♦ *She has lived in a home since she was six.* ⊃ see also NURSING HOME, REST HOME
> **OF PLANT/ANIMAL 6** [sing., U] the place where a plant or animal usually lives; the place where someone or something can be found: *This region is the home of many species of wild flower.* ♦ *The tiger's home is in the jungle.* ♦ *The Rockies are home to bears and mountain lions.*
> **WHERE SOMETHING FIRST DONE 7** [sing.] **the ~ of sth** the place where something was first discovered, made, or invented: *New Orleans, the home of jazz* ♦ *Greece, the home of democracy*
> **IN BASEBALL 8** [sing.] = HOME PLATE
IDM **at home 1** in a person's own house, apartment, etc.: *I phoned you last night, but you weren't at home.* ♦ *Oh no, I left my purse at home.* ♦ *He lived at home* (= with his parents) *until he was thirty.* **2** comfortable and relaxed: *Sit down and make yourself at home.* ♦ *Simon feels very at home on a horse.* **3** (*used especially in JOURNALISM*) in someone's own country, not in a foreign country: *The president is not as popular at home as he is abroad.* **4** if a sports team plays **at home**, it plays in the town, etc. that it comes from: *The Jets are playing at home this weekend.* ♦ *Is the game on Saturday at home or away?* **away from home 1** away from a person's own house, apartment, etc.: *He works away from home during the week.* ♦ *I don't want to be away from home for too long.* **2** if a sports team plays **away from home**, it plays in the town, etc. that its opponent comes from **a home away from home** a place where you feel relaxed and comfortable as if you were in your own home **home is where the heart is** (*saying*) a home is where the people you love are **home sweet home** (often *ironic*) used to say how pleasant your home is (especially when you really mean that it is not pleasant at all) ⊃ more at CHARITY, CLOSE² *adj.*, EAT, MAN *n.*, SPIRITUAL
- *adj.* [only before noun]
> **WHERE YOU LIVE 1** connected with the place where you live: *home life* (= with your family) ♦ *a person's home address/town* ♦ *We offer customers a free home delivery service.*
> **MADE/USED AT HOME 2** made or used at home: *home movies* ♦ *home cooking* ♦ *a home computer*
> **OWN COUNTRY 3** connected with your own country rather than foreign countries **SYN** DOMESTIC: *products for the home market* ♦ *home news/affairs* **ANT** FOREIGN, OVERSEAS
> **IN SPORTS 4** connected with a team's own sports ground: *a home game/win* ♦ *the home team* ♦ *The Rangers were playing in front of their home crowd.* ⊃ compare AWAY
- *adv.*
> **WHERE YOU LIVE 1** to or at the place where you live: *Come on, it's time to go home.* ♦ *What time did you get home last night?* ♦ *The trip has been exhausting and I'll be glad to be home.* ♦ *After a month, they went back home to the U.S.* ♦ *It was a beautiful day so I walked home.* ♦ *Anna will drive me home after work.* ♦ *Hopefully the doctors will allow her to go home tomorrow.* ♦ *I like to stay home in the evenings.*
> **INTO CORRECT POSITION 2** into the correct position: *She leaned on the door and pushed the bolt home.* ♦ *He drove the ball home* (= scored a goal) *from 50 feet.* ♦ *The torpedo struck home on the hull of the ship.*
IDM **be home free** to have done something successfully, especially when it was difficult: *I could see the finish line and thought I was home free.* **bring home the bacon** (*informal*) to be successful at something; to earn money for your family to live on **bring sth home to sb** to make someone realize how important, difficult, or serious something is: *The television pictures brought home to us the full horror of the attack.* **come home to sb** to become completely clear to someone, often in a way that is painful: *It suddenly came home to him that he was never going to see Julie again.* **sth comes home to roost** (also **the chickens come home to roost**) used to say that if someone says or does something

bad or wrong, it will affect them badly in the future **hit/ strike home** if a remark, etc. **hits/ strikes home**, it has a strong effect on someone, in a way that makes them realize what the true facts of a situation are: *Her face went pale as his words hit home.* ⊃ more at COW, DRIVE, PRESS, RAM, ROMP, WRITE

● *verb*

PHR V ˌhome ˈin on sth **1** to aim at something and move straight toward it: *The missile homed in on the target.* **2** to direct your thoughts or attention toward something: *I began to feel I was really homing in on the answer.*

ˌhome ˈbase *noun* [sing., U] **1** = HOME PLATE **2** the place where someone or something usually lives, works, or operates from

home·bod·y /ˈhoʊmˌbɑdi/ *noun* (*pl.* home·bod·ies) (*informal*) a person who enjoys spending time at home

home·boy /ˈhoʊmbɔɪ/ *noun* (*informal*) a male friend from the same town as you; a member of your GANG (= a group of young people who spend a lot of time together and often cause trouble or fight against other groups)

ˌhome ˈbrew *noun* [U] **1** beer that someone makes at home **2** something that someone makes at home rather than buying it: *The security software he uses is home brew.* ▸ ˌhome-ˈbrewed (also ˌhome-ˈbrew) *adj.*

home·buy·er /ˈhoʊmˌbaɪər/ *noun* a person who buys a house, an apartment, etc.

home·com·ing /ˈhoʊmˌkʌmɪŋ/ *noun* **1** [C, U] the act of returning to your home after being away for a long time **2** [C] a social event that takes place every year at a high school, college, or university for people who used to be students there

ˌhome conˈfinement *noun* [U] = HOUSE ARREST

ˌhome ecoˈnomics *noun* [U] cooking and other skills needed at home, taught as a subject in school

ˈhome fries (also ˌhome fried poˈtatoes) *noun* [pl.] potatoes that have been sliced and fried in a pan

ˈhome front *noun* [sing.] the people who do not go to fight in a war but who stay in a country to work
IDM **on the home front** happening at home, or in your own country

home·girl /ˈhoʊmgərl/ *noun* (*informal*) a female friend from the same town as you; a member of your GANG (= a group of young people who spend a lot of time together and often cause trouble or fight against other groups)

ˌhome ˈground *noun* [sing., U] a place where someone lives or works and where they feel confident, rather than a place that is not familiar to them: *I'd rather meet him here on my own home ground.*

home·grown /ˌhoʊmˈgroʊn/ *adj.* **1** (of plants, fruit, and vegetables) grown in a person's garden: *homegrown tomatoes* **2** made, trained, or educated in your own country, town, etc.: *The team has a wealth of homegrown talent.*

ˌhome imˈprovement *noun* [C, U] changes that are made to a house, that increase its value: *They've spent a lot of money on home improvements.* ◆ *home-improvement products* ⊃ collocations at DECORATE

home·land /ˈhoʊmlænd/ *noun* [usually sing.] the country where a person was born: *Many refugees have been forced to flee their homeland.*

ˌHomeland Seˈcurity *noun* [U] the activities and organizations whose aim is to prevent TERRORIST attacks: *the Department of Homeland Security*

home·less /ˈhoʊmləs/ *adj.* **1** having no home: *The program has been set up to help homeless people.* **2 the homeless** *noun* [pl.] people who have no home: *helping the homeless* ▸ home·less·ness *noun* [U]

ˌhome ˈloan *noun* (*informal*) = MORTGAGE

home·ly /ˈhoʊmli/ *adj.* (home·li·er, home·li·est) **1** (*disapproving*) (of a person's appearance) not attractive

SYN PLAIN: *a homely child* **2** (*approving*) simple and good: *homely cooking*

home·made /ˌhoʊmˈmeɪd/ *adj.* made at home, rather than produced in a factory and bought in a store

home·mak·er /ˈhoʊmˌmeɪkər/ *noun* a person who works at home and takes care of the house and family ▸ home·mak·ing *noun* [U]

ˌhome ˈoffice *noun* a room in someone's home that is used for work

ho·me·o·path /ˈhoʊmiəˌpæθ/ *noun* a person who treats illness using homeopathic methods

ho·me·op·a·thy /ˌhoʊmiˈɑpəθi/ *noun* [U] a system of treating diseases or conditions using very small amounts of the substance that causes the disease or condition ▸ ho·me·o·path·ic /ˌhoʊmiəˈpæθɪk/ *adj.*: *homeopathic medicines/remedies/treatments*

ho·me·o·sta·sis /ˌhoʊmioʊˈsteɪsəs/ *noun* [U] (*biology*) the process by which the body reacts to changes in order to keep conditions inside the body, for example temperature, the same

home·own·er /ˈhoʊmˌoʊnər/ *noun* a person who owns their house or apartment

ˈhome page *noun* (*computing*) **1** the main page created by a company, an organization, etc. on the Internet from which connections to other pages can be made **2** a page on the Internet that you choose to appear first on your screen whenever you make a connection to the Internet

ˌhome ˈplate (also ˌhome ˈbase, ˌhome ˈbase, plate) *noun* [sing.] (in baseball) the place where the person hitting the ball stands and where they must return to after running around all the bases ⊃ picture at BASEBALL

ho·mer /ˈhoʊmər/ *noun* (*informal*) = HOME RUN: *He hit a homer.*

home·room /ˈhoʊmrum; -rʊm/ *noun* [C, U] a room in a school where students go at the beginning of each school day, so that teachers can check who is in school; the time spent in this room

ˌhome ˈrule *noun* [U] the right of a country or region to govern itself, especially after another country or region has governed it

ˌhome ˈrun (also *informal* ho·mer) *noun* (in baseball) a hit that allows the person hitting the ball to run around all the bases without stopping SYN LONG BALL ⊃ note at BASEBALL

home·school·ing /ˈhoʊmˌskulɪŋ/ *noun* [U] the practice of educating children at home, not in schools ▸ home·school [T, I] ~ (sb)

ˌhome ˈshopping *noun* [U] the practice of ordering goods by phone or by e-mail and having them delivered to your home

home·sick /ˈhoʊmsɪk/ *adj.* sad because you are away from home and you miss your family and friends: *I felt homesick for Kansas.* ▸ home·sick·ness *noun* [U]

home·spun /ˈhoʊmspʌn/ *adj.* **1** (especially of ideas) simple and ordinary; not coming from an expert **2** (of cloth) made at home

home·stay /ˈhoʊmsteɪ/ *noun* [C, U] an arrangement that provides a place to stay for students or tourists in the home of a family in exchange for payment: *The trip includes a homestay in a traditional village.* ◆ *We are seeking homestay hosts for our Korean students.*

home·stead /ˈhoʊmstɛd/ *noun, verb*
● *noun* **1** a house with the land and buildings around it, especially a farm **2** (in the past) a piece of land given to someone by the government on condition that they lived on it and grew crops on it
● *verb* [I] (*old-fashioned*) to live and work on a homestead ▸ home·stead·er *noun*

home·stretch /ˌhoʊmˈstrɛtʃ/ (also ˌhome ˈstretch) *noun* [sing.] **1** the last part of a race **2** the last part of an activity, etc. when it is nearly completed

t tea   ţ butter   d did   k cat   g got   tʃ chin   dʒ June   f fall

home 'theater (CanE usually ˌhome 'theatre) noun [U] television and video equipment designed to give a similar experience to being in a movie theater, with high-quality pictures and sound and a large screen

home·town /ˌhoʊmˈtaʊn/ noun the place where you were born or lived as a child

home 'truth noun [usually pl.] a true but unpleasant fact about a person, usually told to them by someone else: *It's time you told him a few home truths.*

home·ward /ˈhoʊmwərd/ adj. going toward home: *the homeward journey* ▶ **home·ward** (also **home·wards**) adv.: *Commuters were heading homeward at the end of the day.* ♦ *We drove homeward in silence.* ♦ *We were homeward bound at last.*

home·work 🔑 /ˈhoʊmwərk/ noun [U]
1 work that is given by teachers for students to do at home: *I still haven't done my geography homework.* ♦ *How much homework do you get?* ♦ *I have to write up the notes for homework.* ⊃ compare CLASSWORK ⊃ collocations at EDUCATION **2** (informal) work that someone does to prepare for something: *You could tell that he had really done his homework* (= found out all he needed to know).

hom·ey /ˈhoʊmi/ /ˈhoʊmiəst/ adj., noun
● (also **hom·y**) adj. pleasant and comfortable, like home: *The hotel had a nice, homey atmosphere.*
● noun = HOMIE

hom·i·cid·al /ˌhɑməˈsaɪdl/ adj. likely to kill another person; making someone likely to kill another person: *a homicidal maniac* ♦ *He had clear homicidal tendencies.*

hom·i·cide /ˈhɑməˌsaɪd/ noun [C,U] (law) **1** the crime of killing someone deliberately **SYN** MURDER ⊃ compare CULPABLE HOMICIDE, MANSLAUGHTER **2** Homicide the police department that deals with cases of murder

hom·ie (also **hom·ey**) /ˈhoʊmi/ noun (informal) a HOMEBOY or HOMEGIRL

hom·i·ly /ˈhɑməli/ (pl. **hom·i·lies**) noun **1** a short speech given by a religious leader on a moral or religious subject **SYN** SERMON **2** (formal, often disapproving) a speech or piece of writing giving advice on the correct way to behave, etc.: *She delivered a homily on the virtues of family life.*

hom·ing /ˈhoʊmɪŋ/ adj. [only before noun] **1** (of a bird or an animal) trained, or having a natural ability, to find the way home from a long distance away: *Many birds have a remarkable homing instinct.* **2** (of a MISSILE, etc.) fitted with an electronic device that enables it to find and hit the place or object it is aimed at: *a homing device*

'homing ˌpigeon noun a PIGEON (= a type of bird) that has been trained to find its way home from a long distance away, and that people race against other pigeons for sport

hom·i·nid /ˈhɑmənɪd/ noun (technical) a human, or a creature that lived in the past that humans developed from

hom·i·noid /ˈhɑməˌnɔɪd/ noun (technical) a human, or a creature related to humans

hom·i·ny /ˈhɑməni/ noun [U] dried CORN, boiled in water or milk, eaten especially in the southern states

Ho·mo /ˈhoʊmoʊ/ noun (from Latin, technical) the GENUS (= group) of PRIMATES that includes early and modern humans

homo- /ˈhoʊmoʊ; ˈhɑ-; -mə/ combining form (in nouns, adjectives, and adverbs) the same ⊃ compare HETERO-

Ho·mo erec·tus /ˌhoʊmoʊ ɪˈrɛktəs/ noun [U] (from Latin, technical) an early form of human that was able to walk on two legs

ho·mo·e·rot·ic /ˌhoʊmoʊɪˈrɑtɪk/ adj. relating to HOMOSEXUAL sex and sexual desire

ho·mo·ge·ne·i·ty /ˌhoʊmədʒəˈniəti; -ˈneɪti/ noun [U] (formal) the quality of being homogeneous

ho·mo·ge·ne·ous /ˌhoʊməˈdʒiniəs; -ˈdʒinyəs/ adj. (formal) consisting of things or people that are all the same or all of the same type: *a homogeneous group/mixture/population* **ANT** HETEROGENEOUS

ho·mog·e·nized /həˈmɑdʒəˌnaɪzd/ adj. (of milk) treated so that the cream is mixed in with the rest

hom·o·graph /ˈhɑməˌgræf; ˈhoʊ-/ noun (grammar) a word that is spelled like another word but has a different meaning from it, and may have a different pronunciation, for example bow /baʊ/, bow /boʊ/

Ho·mo hab·ilis /ˌhoʊmoʊ ˈhæbələs/ noun [U] (from Latin, technical) an early form of human that was able to use tools

ho·mol·o·gous /həˈmɑləgəs/ adj. ~ (with sth) (technical) similar in position, structure, etc. to something else: *The seal's flipper is homologous with the human arm.*

hom·o·nym /ˈhɑmənɪm/ noun (grammar) a word that is spelled like another word (or pronounced like it) but which has a different meaning, for example can meaning "be able" and can meaning "put something in a container"

ho·mo·pho·bia /ˌhoʊməˈfoʊbiə/ noun [U] a strong dislike and fear of HOMOSEXUAL people ▶ **ho·mo·pho·bic** /-ˈfoʊbɪk/ adj.

ho·mo·phone /ˈhɑməˌfoʊn; ˈhoʊ-/ noun (grammar) a word that is pronounced like another word but has a different spelling or meaning, for example some, sum /sʌm/

ho·moph·o·nous /həˈmɑfənəs/ adj. (linguistics) (of a word) having the same pronunciation as another word but a different meaning or spelling: *"Bear" and "bare" are homophonous.*

Ho·mo sa·pi·ens /ˌhoʊmoʊ ˈseɪpiənz/ noun [U] (from Latin, technical) the kind or SPECIES of human that exists now

ho·mo·sex·u·al /ˌhoʊməˈsɛkʃuəl/ noun a person, usually a man, who is sexually attracted to people of the same sex: *a practicing homosexual* ⊃ compare BISEXUAL, GAY, HETEROSEXUAL, LESBIAN ▶ **homosexual** adj.: *a homosexual act/relationship* **ho·mo·sex·u·al·i·ty** /ˌhoʊməˌsɛkʃuˈæləti/ noun [U]

ho·mo·zy·gote /ˌhoʊməˈzaɪgoʊt/ noun (biology) a living thing that has only one form of a particular gene, and whose young are more likely to share a particular characteristic ▶ **ho·mo·zy·gous** /-gəs/ adj.

hom·y adj. = HOMEY adj.

Hon. abbr. **1** HONORABLE: *the Hon. Judge Wayne* **2** HONORARY (used in official titles of jobs): *Hon. Treasurer: D Shrimpton*

hon·cho /ˈhɑntʃoʊ/ noun (pl. **hon·chos**) (informal) the person who is in charge **SYN** BOSS: *Claude is the studio's head honcho.*

hone /hoʊn/ verb **1** to develop and improve something, especially a skill, over a period of time: *~ sth She honed her debating skills at college.* ♦ *It was a finely honed piece of writing.* ♦ *~ sth to sth His body was honed to perfection.* **2** *~ sth (to sth)* to make a blade sharp or sharper **SYN** SHARPEN

hon·est 🔑 /ˈɑnəst/ adj.
1 always telling the truth, and never stealing or cheating: *an honest man/woman* **ANT** DISHONEST **2** not hiding the truth about something: *an honest answer* ♦ *~ (about sth) Are you being completely honest about your feelings?* ♦ *~ (with sb) Thank you for being so honest with me.* ♦ *Give me your honest opinion.* ♦ *To be honest* (= what I really think is), *it was one of the worst books I've ever read.* ♦ *Let's be honest, she's only interested in Mike because of his money.* **3** showing an honest mind or attitude: *She's got an honest face.* **4** (of work or wages) earned or resulting from hard work: *He hasn't done an honest day's work in his life.* ♦ *It's quite a struggle to make an honest living.* **HELP** Use an, not a, before honest.
IDM **honest!** (informal) used to emphasize that you are not lying: *I didn't mean it, honest!* **honest to God/goodness** used to emphasize that what you are saying is true: *Honest to God, Mary, I'm not joking.* **HELP** Some people find this use offensive. **make an honest woman of sb** (old-fashioned, humorous) to marry a woman after having had a sexual relationship with her

---

v **voice**   θ **thin**   ð **then**   s **so**   z **zoo**   ʃ **she**   ʒ **vision**   x **Chanukah**

honest

direct ◆ open ◆ outspoken ◆ straight ◆ blunt ◆ frank

These words all describe people saying exactly what they mean without trying to hide feelings, opinions, or facts.

honest not hiding the truth about something: *Thank you for being so honest with me.*

direct saying exactly what you mean in a way that nobody can pretend not to understand: *You'll have to get used to his direct manner.* **NOTE** Being **direct** is sometimes considered positive but sometimes it is used as a "polite" way of saying that someone is rude.

open (*approving*) (of a person) not keeping thoughts and feelings hidden: *He was quite open about his reasons for leaving.*

outspoken saying exactly what you think, even if this shocks or offends people: *She was outspoken in her criticism of the plan.*

straight honest and direct: *I don't think you're being straight with me.*

blunt saying exactly what you think without trying to be polite: *She has a reputation for being blunt.*

frank (*somewhat formal*) honest in what you say, sometimes in a way that other people might not like: *To be frank with you, I think your son has little chance of passing the exam.*

WHICH WORD?

Honest and **frank** refer to *what* you say as much as *how* you say it: *a(n) honest/frank admission of guilt.* They are generally positive words, although it is possible to be *too* frank in a way that other people might not like. **Direct,** **outspoken,** and **blunt** all describe someone's manner of saying what they think. **Outspoken** suggests that you are willing to shock people by saying what you believe to be right. **Blunt** and **direct** often suggest that you think honesty is more important than being polite. **Open** is positive and describes someone's character: *I'm a very open person.*

PATTERNS

- honest/direct/open/outspoken/straight/frank **about** sth
- honest/direct/open/straight/blunt/frank **with** sb
- a(n) honest/direct/straight/blunt **answer**
- a direct/blunt/frank **manner**

honest broker *noun* a person or country that tries to get other people or countries to reach an agreement or to solve a problem, without getting involved with either side

hon·est·ly 🔑 /ˈɑnəstli/ *adv.*
1 in an honest way: *I can't believe he got that money honestly.* **ANT** DISHONEST **2** used to emphasize that what you are saying is true, however surprising it may seem: *I didn't tell anyone, honestly!* ◆ *I honestly can't remember a thing about last night.* ◆ *You can't honestly expect me to believe that!* **3** (*informal*) used to show that you disapprove of something and are irritated by it: *Honestly! What will they think of next?*

honest-to-goodness *adj.* [only before noun] (*approving*) simple and good: *honest-to-goodness country food*

hon·es·ty /ˈɑnəsti/ *noun* [U] the quality of being honest: *She answered all my questions with her usual honesty.* ◆ *His honesty is not in question.*
IDM **in all honesty** used to state a fact or an opinion that, though true, may seem disappointing: *The book isn't, in all honesty, as good as I expected.*

hon·ey /ˈhɑni/ *noun* **1** [U] a sweet sticky yellow substance made by BEES that is spread on bread, etc. like jam **2** [C] (*informal*) a way of addressing someone that you like or love:

Have you seen my keys, honey? **3** [C] (*informal*) a person that you like or love and think is very kind: *He can be a real honey when he wants to be.* **4** [sing.] (*informal*) an excellent example of something: *She has her own style and a honey of a voice.*
IDM see LAND *n.*

hon·ey·bee /ˈhɑniˌbi/ *noun* a BEE that makes honey

hon·ey·comb /ˈhɑniˌkoʊm/ (also **comb**) *noun* [C, U] a structure of cells with six sides, made by BEES for holding their honey and their eggs

hon·ey·combed /ˈhɑniˌkoʊmd/ *adj.* ~ **(with sth)** filled with holes, tunnels, etc.

hon·ey·dew mel·on /ˈhɑnidu ˌmɛlən/ *noun* a type of MELON with a pale skin and green flesh

hon·eyed /ˈhɑnid/ *adj.* (*literary*) **1** (of words) soft and intended to please, but often not sincere **2** tasting or smelling like honey, or having the color of honey

hon·ey·moon /ˈhɑniˌmun/ *noun, verb*
• *noun* [usually sing.] **1** a vacation taken by a couple who have just gotten married: *We went to Venice for our honeymoon.* ◆ *They're on their honeymoon.* **2** the period of time at the start of a new activity when nobody is criticized and people feel enthusiastic: *The honeymoon period for the new president is now over.*
• *verb* [I] + adv./prep. to spend your honeymoon somewhere ▶ **hon·ey·moon·er** *noun*

hon·ey·suck·le /ˈhɑniˌsʌkl/ *noun* [U, C] a climbing plant with white, yellow, or pink flowers with a sweet smell

honk /hɑŋk; hɔŋk/ *noun, verb*
• *noun* **1** the noise made by a GOOSE **2** the noise made by a car horn
• *verb* **1** [I, T] if a car horn **honks** or you **honk** or **honk the horn,** the horn makes a loud noise: *honking taxis* ◆ ~ **at sb/sth** *Why did he honk at me?* ◆ ~ **sth** *People honked their horns as they drove past.* **2** [I] when a GOOSE **honks,** it makes a loud noise

hon·ky-tonk /ˈhɑŋki ˌtɑŋk; ˈhɔŋki ˌtɔŋk/ *noun* **1** [C] a cheap, noisy bar or dance hall where COUNTRY MUSIC is played **2** [U] a type of lively JAZZ played on a piano **3** [U] a type of COUNTRY MUSIC

hon·or 🔑 (*CanE usually* **hon·our**) /ˈɑnər/ *noun, verb*
• *noun*
> **RESPECT 1** [U] great respect and admiration for someone: *the guest of honor* (= the most important one) ◆ *the seat/place of honor* (= given to the most important guest) ◆ *They stood in silence as a mark of honor to her.* ⊃ see also MAID OF HONOR, MATRON OF HONOR
> **PRIVILEGE 2** [sing.] (*formal*) something that you are very pleased or proud to do because people are showing you great respect: *It was a great honor to be invited here today.* **SYN** PRIVILEGE ⊃ thesaurus box at PLEASURE
> **MORAL BEHAVIOR 3** [U] the quality of knowing and doing what is morally right: *a man of honor* ◆ *Proving his innocence has become a matter of honor.*
> **REPUTATION 4** [U] a good reputation; respect from other people: *upholding the honor of your country* ◆ *The family honor is at stake.* ⊃ compare DISHONOR
> **SOMEONE OR SOMETHING CAUSING RESPECT 5** [sing.] ~ **to sth/sb** a person or thing that causes others to respect and admire something/someone: *She is an honor to the profession.*
> **AWARD 6** [C] an award, official title, etc. given to someone as a reward for something that they have done: *to win the highest honor* ◆ *He was buried with full military honors* (= with a special military service as a sign of respect).
> **IN EDUCATION 7 honors** [pl.] (often used as an adjective) a course that is at a higher level than a basic course: *an honors course* ◆ *I'm in honors English.* **8 honors** [pl.] if you pass an exam or graduate from a school **with honors,** you receive a special grade for having achieved a very high standard
> **JUDGE/MAYOR 9 His/Her/Your honor** [C] a title of respect used when talking to or about a judge or a MAYOR: *No more questions, Your honor.*

| h **hat** | m **man** | n **no** | ŋ **sing** | l **leg** | r **red** | y **yes** | w **wet**

IDM **do sb an honor| do sb the honor (of doing sth)** (*formal*) to do something to make someone feel very proud and pleased: *Would you do me the honor of dining with me?* **do the honors** to perform a social duty or ceremony, such as pouring drinks, making a speech, etc.: *Would you do the honors and draw the winning ticket?* **have the honor of sth/ of doing sth** (*formal*) to be given the opportunity to do something that makes you feel proud and happy: *May I have the honor of the next dance?* **(there is) honor among thieves** (*saying*) used to say that even criminals have standards of behavior that they respect **(feel) honor-bound to do sth** (*formal*) to feel that you must do something because of your sense of moral duty: *She felt honor-bound to attend as she had promised to.* ➔ compare DUTY-BOUND **in honor of sb/sth| in sb's/sth's honor** in order to show respect and admiration for someone or something: *a ceremony in honor of those killed in the explosion* ◆ *A banquet was held in her honor.* **on your honor** (*old-fashioned*) **1** used to promise very seriously that you will do something or that something is true: *I swear on my honor that I knew nothing about this.* **2** to be trusted to do something: *You're on your honor not to go into my room.* ➔ more at POINT *n.*

● *verb*
➢ SHOW RESPECT **1** ~ **sb (with sth)** to do something that shows great respect for someone or something: *The President honored us with a personal visit.* ◆ *our honored guests* ◆ (*ironic*) *I'm glad to see that you've decided to honor us with your presence!*
➢ GIVE AWARD **2** ~ **sb/sth (with sth) (for sth)** to give public praise, an award, or a title to someone for something they have done: *He has been honored with the Nobel Prize for his scientific work.*
➢ KEEP PROMISE **3** ~ **sth** to do what you have agreed or promised to do: *I have every intention of honoring our contract.* ◆ *to honor a check* (= to keep an agreement to pay it) **IDM** **be/feel honored (to do sth)** to feel proud and happy: *I was honored to have been mentioned in his speech.*

hon·or·a·ble (*CanE usually* **hon·our·a·ble**) /'ɑnərəbl/ *adj.* **1** deserving respect and admiration: *a long and honorable career in government* ◆ *They managed an honorable 2–2 tie.* ◆ *With a few honorable exceptions, the staff were found to be incompetent.* **2** showing high moral standards: *an honorable man* **3** allowing someone to keep their good name and the respect of others: *an honorable compromise* ◆ *They urged her to do the honorable thing and resign.* ◆ *He received an honorable discharge from the army.* **ANT** DISHONORABLE **4** (*abbr.* **Hon.**) a title of respect used by an official of high rank: *the Honorable Alan Simpson, U.S. senator* **HELP** Use **an**, not **a**, before **honorable**. ▶ **hon·or·a·bly** /-bli/ *adv.*:

,**honorable 'mention** (*CanE usually* ,**honourable 'mention**) *noun* special praise given in a competition for work that is of a very high standard but does not win a prize: *Three other entries received honorable mentions.*

hon·o·rar·i·um /,ɑnə'rɛriəm/ *noun* (*pl.* **hon·o·rar·i·a** /-'rɛriə/) (*formal*) a payment made for someone's professional services **HELP** Use **an**, not **a**, before **honorarium**.

hon·or·ar·y (*CanE also* **hon·our·ar·y**) /'ɑnə,rɛri/ *adj.* (*abbr.* **Hon.**) **1** (of a university degree, a rank, etc.) given as an honor, without the person having to have the usual qualifications: *an honorary doctorate/degree* **2** (of a position in an organization) not paid: *the honorary president* ◆ *The post of treasurer is a purely honorary position.* **3** treated like a member of a group without actually belonging to it: *She was treated as an honorary man.* **HELP** Use **an**, not **a**, before **honorary**.

'**honor code** (*CanE usually* '**honour code**) *noun* a system in which people are trusted to obey rules and not cheat: *Honor codes make cheating socially unacceptable.*

hon·o·ree (*CanE also* **hon·ou·ree**) /,ɑnə'ri/ *noun* a person or thing that wins an award: *The author is a Pulitzer Prize honoree.*

hon·or·if·ic /,ɑnə'rɪfɪk/ *adj.* (*formal*) showing respect for the person you are speaking to: *an honorific title* **HELP** Use **an**, not **a**, before **honorific**.

ho·no·ris cau·sa /ɑ,nɔrəs 'kaʊsə; -'kaʊzə/ *adv.* (from *Latin*) (especially of a degree) given to a person as a sign of honor and respect, without their having to take an exam: *She was awarded a degree honoris causa.*

'**honor ,roll** (*CanE usually* '**honour ,roll**) *noun* **1** [usually sing.] a list of people who are being praised officially for something they have done **2** a list of the best students in a college or high school ➔ compare DEAN'S LIST

'**honor so,ciety** *noun* an organization for students with the best grades at school or college

'**honor ,system** (*CanE usually* '**honour ,system**) *noun* [sing.] an agreement in which people are trusted to obey rules and act in an honest way, although no one checks to make sure this happens

hon·our (*CanE*) = HONOR

hon·our·a·ble (*CanE*) = HONORABLE

hooch /hutʃ/ *noun* [U] (*informal*) a strong alcoholic drink, especially something that has been made illegally

hood /hʊd/ *noun* **1** a part of a coat, etc. that you can pull up to cover the back and top of your head: *a jacket with a detachable hood* ➔ picture at CLOTHES, HAT **2** a piece of cloth put over someone's face and head so that they cannot be recognized or so that they cannot see **3** a piece of colored silk or fur worn over an academic GOWN to show the kind of degree held by the person wearing it **4** the metal part over the front of a vehicle, usually covering the engine ➔ picture at CAR ➔ collocations at DRIVING **5** a cover placed over a device or machine, for example, to protect it: *a lens hood* ◆ *an extractor hood* (= one that removes cooking smells from a kitchen) **6** (*slang*) = HOODLUM **7** also '**hood** (*slang*) a neighborhood, especially a person's own neighborhood

-hood /hʊd/ *suffix* (in nouns) **1** the state or quality of: *childhood* ◆ *falsehood* **2** a group of people of the type mentioned: *the priesthood*

hood·ed /'hʊdəd/ *adj.* **1** having or wearing a hood: *a hooded jacket* ◆ *A hooded figure waited in the doorway.* **2** (of eyes) having large EYELIDS that always look as if they are partly closed

hood·ie (also **hood·y**) /'hʊdi/ *noun* (*pl.* **hood·ies**) (*informal*) a jacket or a SWEATSHIRT with a hood ➔ picture at CLOTHES

hood·lum /'hʊdləm; 'hud-/ *noun* (*informal*) **1** (also *slang* **hood**) a violent criminal, especially one who is part of a GANG **2** a violent and noisy young man **SYN** HOOLIGAN

hoo·doo /'hudu/ *noun* (*pl.* **hoo·doos**) a person or thing that brings or causes bad luck

hood·wink /'hʊdwɪŋk/ *verb* ~ **sb (into doing sth)** to trick someone: *She was hoodwinked into buying a worthless necklace.*

hoo·ey /'hui/ *noun* [U] (*informal*) nonsense; stupid talk

hoof /hʊf; huf/ *noun, verb*
● *noun* (*pl.* **hoofs** or **hooves** /huvz; hʊvz/) the hard part of the foot of some animals, for example horses ➔ picture at ANIMAL, HORSE
IDM **on the hoof** meat that is sold, transported, etc. **on the hoof** is sold, etc. while the cow or sheep is still alive
● *verb*
IDM **hoof it** (*informal*) to go somewhere on foot; to walk somewhere: *We hoofed it all the way to 42nd Street.*

,**hoof-and-'mouth dis,ease** *noun* [U] = FOOT-AND-MOUTH DISEASE

hook 🎣 /hʊk/ *noun, verb*
● *noun* **1** a curved piece of metal, plastic, or wire for hanging things on, catching fish with, etc.: *a picture/ curtain/coat hook* ◆ *a fish hook* ◆ *Hang your towel on the hook.* ➔ see also BOATHOOK **2** (in boxing) a short hard blow that is made with the elbow bent: *a left hook to the jaw* **3** (in

hooks

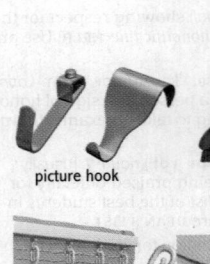
picture hook

coat hook

fish hook

curtain hook

hook and eye

left hook

GOLF) a way of hitting the ball so that it curves sideways instead of going straight ahead **4** a thing that is used to make people interested in something: *The images are used as a hook to get children interested in science.* **5** a part of a pop or rock song that makes it easy to remember: *There's an unforgettable hook in each and every song.*

IDM **by hook or by crook** using any method you can, even a dishonest one **hook, line, and sinker** completely: *What I said wasn't true, but he fell for it (= believed it) hook, line, and sinker.* **off the hook** (*informal*) **1** no longer in difficulty or trouble: *He apologized but she did not want to let him off the hook so easily.* ◆ *I don't think we're off the hook yet.* **2** if you leave or take the telephone **off the hook**, you take the RECEIVER (= the part that you pick up) off the place where it usually rests, so that no one can call you ⊃ more at RING¹, SLING

● *verb* **1** [T, I] to fasten or hang something on something else using a hook; to be fastened or hanging in this way: ~ **sth** + *adv./prep.* *She hooked the two pieces together.* ◆ + *adv./prep.* *a dress that hooks at the back* ⊃ picture at CLOTHES **2** [T, I] to put something, especially your leg, arm, or finger, around something else so that you can hold onto it or move it; to go around something else in this way: ~ **sth** + *adv./prep.* *He hooked his foot under the stool and dragged it over.* ◆ *Her thumbs were hooked into the pockets of her jeans.* ◆ + *adv./prep.* *Suddenly an arm hooked around my neck.* **3** [T] ~ **sth** to catch a fish with a hook: *It was the biggest trout I ever hooked.* ◆ (*figurative*) *She had managed to hook a wealthy husband.* **4** [T] ~ **sth** (especially in GOLF or SOCCER) to hit or kick a ball so that it goes to one side instead of straight ahead

PHR V ˌhook ˈup (to sth) | ˌhook sb/sth↔ˈup (to sth) to connect someone or something to a piece of electronic equipment, to a power supply, or to the Internet: *She was then hooked up to an IV drip.* ◆ *Check that the computer is hooked up to the printer.* ◆ *A large proportion of the nation's households are hooked up to the Internet.* ˌhook ˈup (with sb) (*informal*) **1** to meet someone and spend time with them **2** to start working with someone ˌhook sb ˈup with sb/sth (*informal*) to put someone in contact with someone who can help them; to get something for someone that they want: *Can you hook me up with someone with a car?*

hook·ah /ˈhukə; ˈhuː-/ *noun* a long pipe for smoking that passes smoke through a container of water to cool it

ˌhook and ˈeye *noun* (*pl.* hooks and eyes) a device for fastening clothes, consisting of a small metal ring and a hook that fits into it ⊃ picture at CLOTHES, HOOK

hooked /hukt/ *adj.* **1** curved; shaped like a hook: *a hooked nose/beak/finger* **2** [not before noun] ~ **(on sth)** (*informal*) enjoying something very much, so that you want to do it, see it, etc. as much as possible **3** [not before noun] ~ **(on sth)** (*informal*) needing something that is bad for you, especially a drug **4** having one or more hooks

hook·er /ˈhukər/ *noun* (*informal*) a PROSTITUTE

hook·ey = HOOKY

ˈhook shot *noun* (in basketball) a shot in which a player throws the ball toward the BASKET in a wide curve, by stretching their arm out to the side and throwing over their head

hook·up /ˈhukʌp/ *noun* a connection between two pieces of equipment, especially electronic equipment used in broadcasting, or computers: *a satellite hookup between the major European networks*

hook·worm /ˈhukwərm/ *noun* **1** [C] a WORM that lives in the INTESTINES of humans and animals **2** [U] a disease caused by hookworms

hook·y (also **hook·ey**) /ˈhuki/
IDM **play hooky** (*informal, old-fashioned*) to stay away from school without permission

hoo·li·gan /ˈhuligən/ *noun* a young person who behaves in an extremely noisy and violent way in public, usually in a group: *hooligans vandalizing the neighborhood* ▶ **hoo·li·gan·ism** /ˈhuligəˌnɪzəm/ *noun* [U]

hoop /hup/ *noun* **1** a large ring of plastic, wood, or iron: *a barrel bound with iron hoops* ◆ *hoop earrings* (= in the shape of a hoop) **2** the ring that the players throw the ball through in the game of basketball in order to score points: *Let's shoot some hoops.* ⊃ picture at SPORT **3** a large ring that was used as a children's toy in the past, or for animals or riders to jump through at a CIRCUS **4** = HULA HOOP **5** a small ARCH made of metal or plastic, put into the ground: *croquet hoops* ◆ *Grow lettuce under plastic stretched over wire hoops.* **IDM** see JUMP v.

hooped /hupt/ *adj.* shaped like a hoop: *hooped earrings*

hoop·la /ˈhuplə/ *noun* [U, sing.] (*informal*) excitement about something which gets a lot of public attention

hoo·ray (also **hur·ray**) /huˈreɪ; hə-/ *exclamation* (also **hur·rah**) used to show that you are happy or that you approve of something **IDM** see HIP *exclam.*.

hoot /hut/ *verb, noun*
● *verb* **1** [I] to make a loud noise: *He had the audience hooting with laughter.* ◆ *Some people hooted in disgust.* **2** [I] when an OWL hoots, it makes a long calling sound
● *noun* **1** [C] a short loud laugh or shout: *The suggestion was greeted with hoots of laughter.* **2** [sing.] (*informal*) a situation or a person that you find very funny: *You ought to meet her—she's a hoot!* **3** the cry of an OWL
IDM **not care/give a hoot** | **not care/give two hoots** (*informal*) not to care at all

hoot·en·an·ny /ˈhutnˌæni/ *noun* (*pl.* hoot·en·an·nies) an informal social event at which people play FOLK MUSIC, sing, and sometimes dance

hooves *pl.* of HOOF

hop /hap/ *verb, noun*
● *verb* (-pp-) **1** [I] (+ *adv./prep.*) (of a person) to move by jumping on one foot: *I couldn't put my weight on my ankle and had to hop everywhere.* ◆ *kids hopping over puddles* **2** [I] + *adv./prep.* (of an animal or a bird) to move by jumping with all or both feet together: *A robin was hopping around on the path.* **3** [I] + *adv./prep.* (*informal*) to go or move somewhere quickly and suddenly: *Hop in, I'll drive you home.* ◆ *to hop into/out of bed* ◆ *I hopped on the next train.* ◆ *We hopped over to Nantucket for the weekend.* **4** [T] ~ **a plane, bus, train, etc.** to get on a plane, bus, etc., especially when you make a quick decision to do so **5** [I] ~ **(from sth to sth)** to change from one activity or subject to another: *I like to hop from channel to channel when I watch TV.*
IDM **hop to it** (*informal*) = JUMP TO IT at JUMP *v.*
● *noun* **1** [C] a short jump by a person on one foot: *He crossed the hall with a hop, skip, and a jump.* **2** [C] a short jump by an animal or a bird with all or both feet together **3** [C] a short journey, especially by plane **4** [C] a tall climbing plant with green female flowers that are shaped like CONES **5** hops [pl.] the green female flowers of the hop plant that have been dried, used for making beer **6** [C] an occasion when a ball BOUNCES **7** [C] (*old-fashioned, informal*) a social event at which people dance in an informal way ⊃ see also HIP-HOP

ʌ cup   ə about   eɪ say   aɪ five   ɔɪ boy   aʊ now   oʊ go   ər bird

IDM **a hop, skip, and (a) jump** (*informal*) a short distance: *It's just a hop, skip, and jump from here.* ◗ **more at CATCH** *v.*

hope 🔑 /hoʊp/ *verb, noun*

● *verb* [I, T] to want something to happen and think that it is possible: ~ **(for sth)** *We are hoping for good weather on Sunday.* ◆ *All we can do now is wait and hope.* ◆ *"Do you think it will rain?" "I hope not."* ◆ *"Will you be back before dark?" "I hope so, yes."* ◆ **~ (that)...** *I hope (that) you're okay.* ◆ *Let's hope we can find a parking space.* ◆ **it is hoped (that)...** *It is hoped that over $10,000 will be raised.* ◆ **~ to do sth** *She is hoping to win the gold medal.* ◆ *We hope to arrive around two.*
HELP **Hope** can be used in the passive in the form **it is hoped that....** For must always be used with **hope** in other passive sentences: *The improvement that had been hoped for never came.* ◆ *The hoped-for improvement never came.*
IDM **hope against hope (that...)** to continue to hope for something although it is very unlikely to happen **hope for the best** to hope that something will happen successfully, especially where it seems likely that it will not **I should hope so/not| so I should hope** (*informal*) used to say that you feel very strongly that something should/should not happen: *"Nobody blames you." "I should hope not!"*

● *noun* **1** [U, C] a belief that something you want will happen: ~ **(of sth)** *There is now hope of a cure.* ◆ **~ (for sb/sth)** *Hopes for the missing men are fading.* ◆ **~ (that...)** *There is little hope that they will be found alive.* ◆ **~ (of doing sth)** *They have given up hope of finding any more survivors.* ◆ *She has high hopes of winning* (= is very confident about it). ◆ *The future is not without hope.* ◆ *Don't raise your hopes too high, or you may be disappointed.* ◆ *I'll do what I can, but don't get your hopes up.* ◆ *There is still a glimmer of hope.* ◆ *The situation is not good but we live in hope that it will improve.* **2** [C] **~ (of/for sth)** | **~ (for sb)** | **~ (that...)** | **~ (of doing sth)** something that you wish for: *She told me all her hopes, dreams, and fears.* ◆ *They have high hopes for their children.* **3** [C, usually sing.] **~ (of sth)** | **~ (for sb)** a person, a thing, or a situation that will help you get what you want: *He turned to her in despair and said, "You're my last hope."* ◆ *The operation was Kelly's only hope of survival.*
IDM **be beyond hope (of sth)** to be in a situation where no improvement is possible **hold out little, etc. hope (of sth/that...)| not hold out any, much hope (of sth/that...)** to offer little, etc. reason for believing that something will happen: *The doctors did not hold out much hope for her recovery.* **hope springs eternal** (*saying*) people never stop hoping **in the hope of sth| in the hope that...** (also **in hopes that...**) because you want something to happen: *I called early in the hope of catching her before she went to work.* ◆ *He asked her again in the vain hope that he could persuade her to come* (= it was impossible). **not have a hope (in hell) (of doing sth)** (*informal*) to have no chance at all: *She doesn't have a hope of winning.* ◗ **more at DASH, PIN** *v.*

hope chest *noun* items for the house collected by a woman, especially in the past, in preparation for her marriage (and often kept in a large **CHEST**)

hoped-for *adj.* [only before noun] wanted and thought possible: *The new policy did not bring the hoped-for economic recovery.*

hope·ful /ˈhoʊpfl/ *adj., noun*
● *adj.* **1** [not usually before noun] (of a person) believing that something you want will happen **SYN OPTIMISTIC**: **~ (that...)** *I feel hopeful that we'll find a larger house very soon.* ◆ **~ (about sth)** *He is not very hopeful about the outcome of the interview.* **ANT PESSIMISTIC 2** [only before noun] (of a person's behavior) showing hope: *a hopeful smile* **3** (of a thing) making you believe that something you want will happen; bringing hope **SYN PROMISING**: *The latest sales figures are a hopeful sign.* ◆ *The future did not seem very hopeful.* ▶ **hope·ful·ness** *noun* [U]
● *noun* a person who wants to succeed at something: *50 young hopefuls are trying out for a place in the show's chorus.*

hope·ful·ly 🔑 /ˈhoʊpfəli/ *adv.*
1 used to express what you hope will happen: *Hopefully,*

we'll arrive before dark. **2** showing hope: *"Are you free tonight?" she asked hopefully.*

hope·less /ˈhoʊpləs/ *adj.* **1** if something is **hopeless**, there is no hope that it will get better or succeed: *a hopeless situation* ◆ *It's hopeless trying to convince her.* ◆ *Most of the students are making good progress, but Michael is a hopeless case.* ◆ *He felt that his life was a hopeless mess.* **2** (of people) very bad; with no ability or skill **SYN TERRIBLE**: *a hopeless driver* ◆ *I can't help it. I'm a hopeless romantic* (= I will never change). ◆ **~ at sth** *I'm hopeless at science.* **3** feeling or showing no hope: *She felt lonely and hopeless.* ▶ **hope·less·ly** *adv.*: *hopelessly outnumbered* ◆ *They were hopelessly lost.* ◆ *to be hopelessly in love* ◆ *"I'll never manage it," he said hopelessly.* **hope·less·ness** *noun* [U]: *a sense/feeling of hopelessness*

Ho·pi /ˈhoʊpi/ *noun* (*pl.* **Ho·pi** or **Ho·pis**) a member of a Native American people, many of whom live in Arizona

hopped 'up *adj.* (*informal*) **~ (on sth)** (of a person) excited and energetic, especially because of having taken an illegal drug: *They were hopped up on cocaine.*

hop·per /ˈhɑpər/ *noun* **1** a container shaped like a V, that holds grain, coal, or food for animals, and lets it out through the bottom **2** often **the hopper** a box where proposed new laws are put before they are considered by Congress **3** (in baseball) a ball that hits the ground and **BOUNCES** up ◗ see also **CLODHOPPER**
IDM **in the hopper** waiting to be considered: *A lot of projects were in the hopper for next year.*

hop·ping /ˈhɑpɪŋ/ *adj., adv.*
● *adj.* (*informal*) very lively or busy: *The clubs in town are really hopping.*
● *adv.*
IDM **hopping mad** (*informal*) very angry

hop·scotch /ˈhɑpskɑtʃ/ *noun* [U] a children's game played on a pattern of squares marked on the ground. Each child throws a stone into a square then **HOPS** (= jumps on one leg) and jumps along the empty squares to pick up the stone again.

horde /hɔrd/ *noun* (sometimes *disapproving*) a large crowd of people: *There are always hordes of tourists here in the summer.* ◆ *Football fans turned up in hordes.*

ho·ri·zon /həˈraɪzn/ *noun* **1** **the horizon** [sing.] the furthest that you can see, where the sky seems to meet the land or the ocean: *The sun sank below the horizon.* ◆ *A ship appeared on the horizon.* **2** [C, usually pl.] the limit of your desires, knowledge, or interests: *She wanted to travel to broaden her horizons.* ◆ *The company needs new horizons now.*
IDM **on the horizon** likely to happen soon: *There's trouble looming on the horizon.*

hor·i·zon·tal 🔑 /ˌhɔrəˈzɑntl; ˌhɑr-/ *adj., noun*
● *adj.* flat and level; going across and parallel to the ground rather than going up and down: *horizontal lines* ◗ **picture at LINE** ◗ compare **VERTICAL** ▶ **hor·i·zon·tal·ly** /-təli/ *adv.*: *Cut the cake in half horizontally and spread frosting on one half.*
● *noun* **1** **the horizontal** [U] a horizontal position: *He shifted his position from the horizontal.* **2** [C] a horizontal line or surface

hor·mone /ˈhɔrmoʊn/ *noun* a chemical substance produced in the body or in a plant that encourages growth or influences how the cells and **TISSUES** function; an artificial substance that has similar effects: *growth hormones* ◆ *a hormone imbalance* ◆ *Estrogen is a female sex hormone.* ▶ **hor·mo·nal** /hɔrˈmoʊnl/ *adj.* [usually before noun]: *the hormonal changes occurring during pregnancy*

hormone re'placement ˌtherapy *noun* [U] = HRT

horn 🔑 /hɔrn/ *noun, verb*
● *noun* **1** [C] a hard pointed part that grows, usually in pairs, on the heads of some animals, such as sheep and cows. Horns are often curved. **2** [C] a horn on the head of a male **DEER SYN ANTLER** ◗ picture at **ANIMAL 3** [U] the hard substance of which animal horns are made **4** [C] a device

in a vehicle for making a loud sound as a warning or signal: *to honk your car horn* ⊃ picture at CAR ⊃ see also FOGHORN **5** [C] a simple musical instrument that consists of a curved metal tube that you blow into: *a hunting horn* **6** [C] = FRENCH HORN: *a horn concerto* ⊃ see also ENGLISH HORN **IDM** **be/get on the horn** (*informal*) to talk on the telephone **blow/toot your own horn** (*informal*) to praise your own abilities and achievements **SYN** BOAST **ORIGIN** This phrase refers to the custom of announcing important guests by blowing a horn. **draw/pull your horns in** to start being more careful in your behavior, especially by spending less money than before **on the horns of a dilemma** in a situation in which you have to make a choice between things that are equally unpleasant ⊃ more at BULL, LOCK *v.*

● *verb*
PHR V **horn 'in (on sb/sth)** (*informal*) to involve yourself in a situation that does not concern you: *I'm sure she doesn't want us horning in on her business.*

horn·beam /'hɔrnbim/ *noun* [C, U] a tree with smooth gray BARK and hard wood

horn·bill /'hɔrnbɪl/ *noun* a tropical bird with a very large curved beak

horned /hɔrnd/ *adj.* having horns or having something that looks like horns

hor·net /'hɔrnət/ *noun* a large WASP (= a black and yellow flying insect) that has a very powerful sting **IDM** **a hornets' nest** a difficult situation in which a lot of people get very angry: *His letter to the editor stirred up a real hornets' nest.*

horn of 'plenty *noun* = CORNUCOPIA

horn·pipe /'hɔrnpaɪp/ *noun* a fast dance for one person, traditionally performed by sailors; the music for the dance

horn-,rimmed *adj.* (of a pair of glasses) with frames made of material that looks like horn

horn·y /'hɔrni/ *adj.* **1** (*informal*) sexually excited: *to feel horny* **2** made of a hard substance like horn: *the bird's horny beak* **3** (of skin, etc.) hard and rough: *horny hands*

ho·rol·o·gy /hə'rɑlədʒi/ *noun* [U] **1** the study and measurement of time **2** the art of making clocks and watches

hor·o·scope /'hɔrə,skoʊp; 'hɑr-/ *noun* a description of what is going to happen to someone in the future, based on the position of the stars and the planets when the person was born

hor·ren·dous /hə'rɛndəs/ *adj.* **1** extremely shocking **SYN** HORRIFIC, HORRIFYING: *horrendous injuries* **2** extremely unpleasant and unacceptable **SYN** TERRIBLE: *horrendous traffic* ⊃ thesaurus box at TERRIBLE ▶ **hor·ren·dous·ly** *adv.*: *horrendously expensive*

hor·ri·ble /'hɔrəbl; 'hɑr-/ *adj.* **1** (*informal*) very bad or unpleasant; used to describe something that you do not like: *horrible weather/children/shoes* ◆ *The coffee tasted horrible.* ◆ *I have a horrible feeling she lied to us.* ⊃ thesaurus box at TERRIBLE **2** making you feel very shocked and frightened **SYN** TERRIBLE: *a horrible crime/nightmare* **3** (*informal*) (of people or their behavior) unfriendly, unpleasant, or unkind **SYN** NASTY, OBNOXIOUS: *a horrible man* ◆ *My sister was being horrible to me all day.* ◆ *What a horrible thing to say!* ▶ **hor·ri·bly** /-bli/ *adv.*: *It was horribly painful.* ◆ *The experiment went horribly wrong.*

hor·rid /'hɔrəd; 'hɑr-/ *adj.* **1** bad and shocking: *a horrid nightmare* **2** (*old-fashioned* or *informal*) very unpleasant or unkind **SYN** HORRIBLE: *a horrid child* ◆ *Don't be so horrid to your brother.*

hor·ri·fic /hə'rɪfɪk/ *adj.* **1** extremely bad and shocking or frightening **SYN** HORRIFYING: *a horrific murder/accident/attack, etc.* ◆ *Her injuries were horrific.* **2** (*informal*) very bad or unpleasant **SYN** HORRENDOUS: *We had a horrific trip.* ▶ **hor·rif·i·cally** /-kli/ *adv.*

hor·ri·fy /'hɔrə,faɪ; 'hɑr-/ *verb* (hor·ri·fies, hor·ri·fy·ing, hor·ri·fied, hor·ri·fied) to make someone feel extremely shocked, disgusted, or frightened **SYN** APPALL: ~ **sb** *The*

whole country was horrified by the kidnapping. ◆ **it horrifies sb to do sth** *It horrified her to think that he had killed someone.* ◆ **it horrifies sb that...** *It horrified her that he had actually killed someone.* ⊃ thesaurus box at SHOCK ▶ **hor·ri·fied** *adj.*: *He was horrified when he discovered the conditions in which they lived.* ◆ *She gazed at him in horrified disbelief.*

hor·ri·fy·ing /'hɔrə,faɪɪŋ; 'hɑr-/ *adj.* making you feel extremely shocked, disgusted, or frightened **SYN** HORRIFIC: *a horrifying sight/experience/story* ◆ *It's horrifying to see such poverty.* ▶ **hor·ri·fy·ing·ly** *adv.*

hor·ror /'hɔrər; 'hɑr-/ *noun*
1 [U] a feeling of great shock, fear, or disgust: *People watched in horror as the plane crashed to the ground.* ◆ *With a look of horror, he asked if the doctor thought he had cancer.* ◆ *The thought of being left alone filled her with horror.* ◆ *She recoiled in horror at the sight of an enormous spider.* ◆ **To his horror,** *he could feel himself starting to cry* (= it upset him very much). ◆ *Her eyes were wide with horror.* **2** [sing.] a great fear or hatred of something: ~ **of sth** *a horror of deep water* ◆ ~ **of doing sth** *Most people have a horror of speaking in public.* **3** [U] **the ~ of sth** the very unpleasant nature of something, especially when it is shocking or frightening: *The full horror of the accident was beginning to become clear.* ◆ *In his dreams he relives the horror of the attack.* **4** [C, usually pl.] a very unpleasant or frightening experience: *the horrors of war* **5** [U] a type of book, movie, etc. that is designed to frighten people: *In this section you'll find horror and science fiction.* ◆ *a horror movie* ⊃ see also HORROR STORY **IDM** **horror of horrors** (*humorous* or *ironic*) used to emphasize how bad a situation is: *I stood up to speak and—horror of horrors—realized I had left my notes behind.*

'horror ,story *noun* **1** a story about strange and frightening things that is designed to entertain people **2** (*informal*) a report that describes an experience of a situation as very unpleasant: *horror stories about visits to the dentist*

'horror-,stricken (also **'horror-,stricken**) *adj.* suddenly feeling very shocked, frightened, or disgusted

hors de com·bat /,ɔr də koʊm'ba/ *adj.* (*formal, from French*) unable to fight or to take part in an activity, especially because you are injured

hors d'oeuvre /ɔr 'dərv/ *noun* [C, U] (*pl.* hors d'oeuvres /ɔr 'dərvz/) (from *French*) a small amount of food, usually cold, served before the main part of a meal ⊃ compare APPETIZER

horse

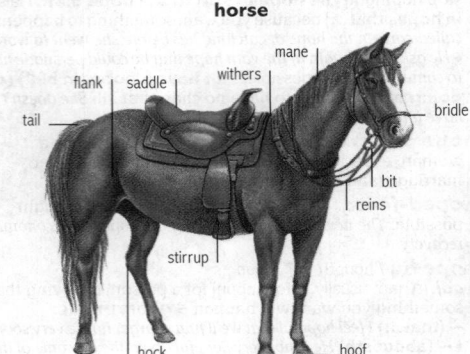

horse /hɔrs/ *noun, verb*
● *noun* **1** a large animal with four legs, a MANE (= long thick hair on its neck), and a tail. Horses are used for riding on, pulling CARRIAGES, etc.: *He mounted his horse and rode off.* ◆ *a horse and cart* ⊃ see also COLT, FILLY, FOAL, GELDING, MARE, STALLION **2 the horses** [pl.] (*informal*) horse racing: *He lost a lot of money on the horses* (= by gambling on races). **3** = VAULTING HORSE ⊃ see also CLOTHES HORSE, HOBBY-HORSE, QUARTER HORSE, ROCKING HORSE, SEA HORSE,

STALKING HORSE, TROJAN HORSE

IDM **a horse of a different color** (*informal*) a completely different situation or person from the one previously mentioned **change/switch horses in midstream** to change to a different or new activity while you are in the middle of doing something else; to change from supporting one person or thing to another **(straight) from the horse's mouth** (*informal*) (of information) given by someone who is directly involved and therefore likely to be accurate **hold your horses** (*informal*) used to tell someone that they should wait a moment and not be so excited that they take action without thinking about it first **a one, two, three, etc. horse race** a competition or an election in which there are only one, two, etc. teams or candidates with a chance of winning ⊃ more at BARN, CART *n.*, CHOKE *v.*, DARK *adj.*, DEAD, EAT, GIFT *n.*, HIGH *adj.*, LEAD¹ *v.*, WILD *adj.*, WISH *n.*

● *verb*
PHR V **horse a'round** (*informal*) to play in a way that is noisy and not very careful so that you could hurt someone or damage something

horse·back /'hɔrsbæk/ *noun, adj.*
● *noun*
IDM **on horseback** sitting on a horse; using horses: *a soldier on horseback*
● *adj.* [only before noun] sitting on a horse: *a horseback tour* ▶ **horseback** *adv.*: *to ride horseback*

horseback ,riding (also **rid·ing**) *noun* [U] the sport or activity of riding horses: *to go horseback riding*

horse ,chestnut *noun* **1** a large, tall tree with spreading branches, white, or pink flowers and nuts that grow inside cases which are covered with SPIKES ⊃ see also CHESTNUT **2** the smooth brown nut of the horse chestnut tree

horse–drawn *adj.* [only before noun] (of a vehicle) pulled by a horse or horses

horse·flesh /'hɔrsflɛʃ/ *noun* [U] horses, especially when being bought or sold

horse·fly /'hɔrsflaɪ/ *noun* (*pl.* **horse·flies**) a large fly that bites horses and cows

horse·hair /'hɔrshɛr/ *noun* [U] hair from the MANE or tail of a horse, used in the past for filling MATTRESSES, chairs, etc.

horse·man /'hɔrsmən/ *noun* (*pl.* **horse·men** /-mən/) a rider on a horse; a person who can ride horses: *a good horseman* ⊃ see also HORSEWOMAN

horse·man·ship /'hɔrsmənʃɪp/ *noun* [U] skill in riding horses

horse·play /'hɔrspleɪ/ *noun* [U] rough, noisy play in which people push or hit each other for fun

horse·pow·er /'hɔrsˌpaʊər/ *noun* [C, U] (*pl.* **horse·pow·er**) (*abbr.* **hp**) a unit for measuring the power of an engine: *a powerful car with a 170 horsepower engine*

horse race *noun* **1** a race between horses with riders **2** a very close contest, especially to gain political control or power

horse ,racing *noun* [U] a sport in which horses with riders race against each other ⊃ picture at SPORT

horse·rad·ish /'hɔrsˌrædɪʃ/ *noun* [U] **1** a hard white root vegetable that has a taste like pepper **2** (also ,horseradish 'sauce) a sauce made from horseradish, that is eaten with meat: *roast beef and horseradish*

horse·shoe /'hɔrʃʃu; 'hɔrsʃu/ *noun* (also **shoe**) **1** a piece of curved iron that is attached with nails to the bottom of a horse's foot. A horseshoe is often used as a symbol of good luck. **2** anything shaped like a horseshoe: *a horseshoe bend in the river* **3 horseshoes** [sing.] a game in which horse-shoes are thrown at a post in the ground

horse show *noun* a sports competition where people ride horses in different events

horse–,trading *noun* [U] the activity of discussing business with someone using skillful or secret methods in order to reach an agreement that suits you

horse ,trailer *noun* a vehicle for transporting horses in, pulled by another vehicle

horse·whip /'hɔrswɪp/ *noun, verb*
● *noun* a long stick with a long piece of leather attached to the end that is used to control or train horses
● *verb* (-pp-) ~ **sb** to beat someone with a horsewhip

horse·wom·an /'hɔrsˌwʊmən/ *noun* (*pl.* **horse·wom·en** /-ˌwɪmən/) a woman rider on a horse; a woman who can ride horses well: *a good horsewoman*

hors·ey (also **hors·y**) /'hɔrsi/ *adj.* **1** interested in and involved with horses or horse racing **2** connected with horses; like a horse: *She had a long, horsey face.*

hor·ti·cul·ture /'hɔrtəˌkʌltʃər/ *noun* [U] the study or practice of growing flowers, fruit, and vegetables: *a college of agriculture and horticulture* ⊃ compare GARDENING ▶ **hor·ti·cul·tur·al** /ˌhɔrtə'kʌltʃərəl/ *adj.*: *a horticultural show* **hor·ti·cul·tur·al·ist** /-'kʌltʃərəlɪst/**hor·ti·cul·tur·ist** /-'kʌltʃərɪst/ *noun*

ho·san·na (also **ho·san·nah**) /hoʊ'zænə/ *exclamation* used in worship to express praise, joy, and love for God, especially in the Christian and Jewish religions ▶ **hosanna** *noun*

hose /hoʊz/ *noun, verb*
● *noun* **1** (also **hose·pipe** /'hoʊzpaɪp/) [C, U] a long tube made of rubber, plastic, etc., that carries liquids and gases from one place to another. It is used especially for putting water onto fires, gardens, etc.: *a garden hose* ♦ *a length of hose* ⊃ picture at TOOL ⊃ see also FIRE HOSE **2** [pl.] = HOSIERY **3** [pl.] pants that fit tightly over the legs, worn by men in the past: *doublet and hose*
● *verb* **1** ~ **sth/sb** to wash or pour water on something or someone using a hose: *Firemen hosed the burning car.* **2** ~ **sb** usually **be/get hosed** (*slang*) to cheat someone **PHR V** **,hose sth/sb** ↔ **'down** to wash something or someone using a hose

ho·sier·y /'hoʊʒəri/ (also **hose**) *noun* [U] used especially in stores as a word for PANTYHOSE, STOCKINGS, and socks: *the hosiery department*

hos·pice /'hɑspəs/ *noun* a hospital for people who are dying: *an AIDS hospice*

hos·pi·ta·ble /hɑ'spɪtəbl; 'hɑspɪtəbl/ *adj.* **1** ~ **(to/toward sb)** (of a person) pleased to welcome guests; generous and friendly to visitors **SYN** WELCOMING: *The local people are very hospitable to strangers.* **2** having good conditions that allow things to grow; having a pleasant environment: *a hospitable climate* **ANT** INHOSPITABLE ▶ **hos·pi·ta·bly** /-bli/ *adv.*

hos·pi·tal 🔑 /'hɑspɪtl/ *noun* a large building where people who are sick or injured are given medical treatment and care: *He had to go to the hospital for treatment* ♦ *to be admitted to the hospital* ♦ *to be discharged from the hospital* ♦ *The injured were rushed to the hospital in an ambulance.* ♦ *He died in the hospital.* ♦ *I'm going to the hospital to visit my brother.* ♦ *a psychiatric/mental hospital* ♦ *hospital doctors/nurses/staff* ♦ *There is an urgent need for more hospital beds.*

hospital ,corners *noun* [pl.] a way of folding the sheets at the corners of a bed tightly and neatly, in a way that they are often folded in a hospital

hos·pit·a·list /'hɑspɪtlˌɪst/ *noun* a doctor who cares for patients in a hospital: *He was taken to the emergency room and examined by the hospitalist on duty.*

hos·pi·tal·i·ty /ˌhɑspə'tæləti/ *noun* [U] **1** friendly and generous behavior toward guests: *Thank you for your kind hospitality.* **2** food, drinks, or services that are provided by an organization for guests, customers, etc.: *We were entertained in the company's hospitality suite.* ♦ *the hospitality industry* (= hotels, restaurants, etc.)

hos·pi·tal·ize /'hɑspɪtlˌaɪz/ *verb* [usually passive] ~ **sb** to send someone to a hospital for treatment ▶ **hos·pi·tal·i·za·tion** /ˌhɑspɪtlˌæwːə'zeɪʃn/ *noun* [U]: *a long period of hospitalization*

host /hoʊst/ *noun, verb*

● *noun* **1** [C] a person who invites guests to a meal, a party, etc. or who has people staying at their house: *James, our host, introduced us to the other guests.* ➔ see also HOSTESS **2** [C] a country, a city, or an organization that holds and arranges a special event: *The college is playing host to a group of visiting Russian scientists.* **3** [C] a person who introduces a television or radio show, and talks to guests: *a TV game show host* ➔ see also ANNOUNCER **4** [C] (*technical*) an animal or a plant on which another animal or plant lives and feeds **5** [C] ~ **of sb/sth** a large number of people or things: *a host of possibilities* **6** [C] the main computer in a network that controls or supplies information to other computers that are connected to it: *transferring files from the host to your local computer* **7 the Host** [sing.] the bread that is used in the Christian service of COMMUNION, after it has been BLESSED

● *verb* **1** ~ **sth** to organize an event to which others are invited and make all the arrangements for them: *San Diego hosted the America's Cup regatta in 1995.* **2** ~ **sth** to introduce a television or radio program, a show, etc. **3** ~ **sth** to organize a party that you have invited guests to: *to host a dinner* **4** ~ **sth** to store a Web site on a computer connected to the Internet, usually in return for payment: *a company that builds and hosts e-commerce sites*

hos·tage /ˈhɑstɪdʒ/ *noun* a person who is captured and held prisoner by a person or group, and who may be injured or killed if people do not do what the person or group is asking: *Three children were taken hostage during the bank robbery.* ◆ *He was held hostage for almost a year.* ◆ *The government is negotiating the release of the hostages.* ◆ (*figurative*) *to be held hostage to the whims of dictators* **IDM a hostage to fortune** something that you have, or have promised to do, that could cause trouble or worry in the future

hostage-taker *noun* a person, often one of a group, who captures someone and holds them prisoner, and who may injure or kill them if people do not do what the person is asking ▶ **hostage-taking** *noun* [U]

hos·tel /ˈhɑstl/ *noun* a building that provides meals and a cheap place to stay to students, workers, or travelers ➔ see also YOUTH HOSTEL

hos·tel·ry /ˈhɑstəlri/ (*pl.* **hos·tel·ries**) *noun* (*old use* or *humorous*) a bar or hotel

host·ess /ˈhoʊstəs/ *noun* **1** a woman who invites guests to a meal, a party, etc.; a woman who has people staying at her home: *Mary was always the perfect hostess.* **2** a woman who introduces and talks to guests on a television or radio show **3** a woman who welcomes the customers in a restaurant ➔ see also HOST

hos·tile /ˈhɑstl; -taɪl/ *adj.* **1** very unfriendly or aggressive and ready to argue or fight: *The speaker got a hostile reception from the audience.* ◆ ~ **to/toward sb/sth** *She was openly hostile toward her parents.* **2** ~ (**to sth**) strongly rejecting something **SYN** OPPOSED TO: *hostile to the idea of change* **3** making it difficult for something to happen or to be achieved: *hostile conditions for plants to grow in* **4** belonging to a military enemy: *hostile territory* **5** (*business*) (of an offer to buy a company, etc.) not wanted by the company that is to be bought: *a hostile takeover bid*

hostile witness *noun* (*law*) a person who must answer questions in a court of law but might not want to tell the truth or might answer in a way that is bad for the people asking the questions

hos·til·i·ty /hɑˈstɪləti/ *noun* **1** [U] unfriendly or aggressive feelings or behavior: ~ (**to/toward sb/sth**) *feelings of hostility toward people from other backgrounds* ◆ ~ (**between A and B**) *There was open hostility between the two schools.* **2** [U] ~ (**to/toward sth**) strong and angry opposition toward an idea, a plan, or a situation: *public hostility to nuclear power* **3** *hostilities* [pl.] (*formal*) acts of fighting in a war: *the start/outbreak of hostilities between the two sides* ◆ *a cessation of hostilities* (= an end to fighting) ➔ collocations at WAR

hot /hɑt/ *adj.* (**hot·ter, hot·test**)

▷ TEMPERATURE **1** having a high temperature; producing heat: *Do you like this hot weather?* ◆ *It's hot today, isn't it?* ◆ *It was hot and getting hotter.* ◆ *It was the hottest July on record.* ◆ *a hot dry summer* ◆ *Be careful—the plates are hot.* ◆ *All rooms have hot and cold water.* ◆ *a hot bath* ◆ *a hot meal* (= one that has been cooked) ◆ *I couldn't live in a hot country* (= one which has high average temperatures). ◆ *Cook in a very hot oven.* ◆ *Eat it while it's hot.* ◆ *I touched his forehead. He felt hot and feverish.* ➔ see also BAKING HOT, PIPING HOT, RED-HOT, WHITE-HOT **2** (of a person) feeling heat in an unpleasant or uncomfortable way: *Is anyone too hot?* ◆ *I feel hot.* ◆ *Her cheeks were hot with embarrassment.* **3** making you feel hot: *San Antonio was hot and dusty.* ◆ *a long hot journey*

▷ FOOD WITH SPICES **4** containing pepper and spices and producing a burning feeling in your mouth: *hot spicy food* ◆ *You can make a curry hotter simply by adding chilies.* ◆ *hot mustard* **ANT** MILD

▷ CAUSING STRONG FEELINGS **5** involving a lot of activity, argument, or strong feelings: *Today we enter the hottest phase of the election campaign.* ◆ *The environment has become a very hot issue.* ◆ *Competition is getting hotter day by day.*

▷ DIFFICULT/DANGEROUS **6** difficult or dangerous to deal with and making you feel worried or uncomfortable: *When things got too hot most journalists left the area.* ◆ *They're making life hot for her.*

▷ POPULAR **7** (*informal*) new, exciting, and very popular: *This is one of the hottest clubs in town.* ◆ *They are one of this year's hot new bands.* ◆ *The couple is Hollywood's hottest property.*

▷ NEWS **8** fresh, very recent, and usually exciting: *I've got some hot gossip for you!* ◆ *a story that is hot off the press* (= has just appeared in the newspapers)

▷ TIP/FAVORITE **9** [only before noun] likely to be successful: *She seems to be the hot favorite for the job.* ◆ *Do you have any hot tips for today's race?*

▷ GOOD AT SOMETHING/KNOWING A LOT **10** [not before noun] ~ **at/on sth** (*informal*) very good at doing something; knowing a lot about something: *Don't ask me—I'm not too hot on Civil War history.*

▷ ANGER **11** if someone has a **hot temper** they become angry very easily

▷ SEXUAL EXCITEMENT **12** feeling or causing sexual attraction or excitement: ◆ *I've got a hot date tonight.* ◆ *He's hot for his new neighbor.*

▷ SHOCKING/CRITICAL **13** containing scenes, statements, etc. that are too shocking or too critical and are likely to cause anger or disapproval: *Some of the nude scenes were considered too hot for Broadway.* ◆ *The report was highly critical of certain managers and was considered too hot to publish.* ➔ see also HOT STUFF

▷ MUSIC **14** (of music, especially JAZZ) having a strong and exciting rhythm

▷ GOODS **15** stolen and difficult to get rid of because they can easily be recognized: *I'd never have touched those CDs if I'd known they were hot.*

▷ IN CHILDREN'S GAMES **16** [not before noun] used in children's games to say that the person playing is very close to finding a person or thing, or to guessing the correct answer: *You're getting hot!*

IDM be hot to trot (*informal*) **1** to be very enthusiastic about starting an activity **2** to be excited in a sexual way **be in/get into hot water** (*informal*) to be in or get into trouble **go hot and cold** to experience a sudden feeling of fear or anxiety: *When the phone rang I just went hot and cold.* **go/sell like hot cakes** to sell quickly or in great numbers **(all) hot and bothered** (*informal*) in a state of anxiety or confusion because you are under too much pressure, have a problem, are trying to hurry, etc. **hot on sb's/sth's heels** following someone or something very closely: *He turned and fled with Peter hot on his heels.* ◆ *Greater successes came hot on the heels of her first best-selling novel.* **hot on sb's/sth's tracks/trail** (*informal*) close to catching or finding the person or thing that you have been chasing or searching for **hot under the collar** (*informal*) angry or embarrassed: *He got very hot under the collar when I asked him where he'd been all day.* **in hot pursuit (of sb)** following someone closely and determined to catch them: *She sped away in her car with journalists in hot pursuit.* **not so/too hot 1** not very good in quality: *Her spelling isn't too hot.* **2** not feeling well: *"How are you today?" "Not so hot, I'm afraid."* ⟹ more at BLOW v., CAT, HEEL n., STRIKE v.

,hot 'air *noun* [U] (*informal*) claims, promises, or statements that sound impressive but have no real meaning or truth

,hot-'air bal,loon (also bal·loon) *noun* a large BALLOON made of strong material that is filled with hot air or gas to make it rise in the air, usually carrying a BASKET for passengers ⟹ picture at PLANE

hot·bed /'hɑtbɛd/ *noun* [usually sing.] **~ of sth** a place where a lot of a particular activity, especially something bad or violent, is happening: *The area was a hotbed of crime.*

,hot-'blooded *adj.* (of a person) having strong emotions and easily becoming very excited or angry **SYN** PASSIONATE ⟹ compare WARM-BLOODED

'hot ,button *noun* (*informal*) a subject or issue that people have strong feelings about and argue about a lot: *Race has always been a hot button in this country's history.* ◆ *the hot-button issue of nuclear waste disposal*

,hot 'chocolate *noun* [U, C] a drink made by mixing chocolate powder with hot water or milk; a cup of this drink: *Two cups of coffee and a hot chocolate, please.*

,hot cross 'bun *noun* a small sweet bread roll that contains CURRANTS or RAISINS and has a pattern of a cross on top, traditionally eaten around Easter

,hot-'desking *noun* [U] the practice in an office of giving desks to workers when they are required, rather than giving each worker their own desk

'hot dog *noun* **1** a SAUSAGE served warm in a long bread roll ⟹ see also CHILI DOG, CORN DOG **2** a person who performs skillful or dangerous tricks while SKIING, SNOWBOARDING, or SURFING: *He's a real hot dog.*

'hot-dog *verb* (-gg-) [I] (*informal*) to perform skillful or dangerous tricks while SKIING, SNOWBOARDING, or SURFING

ho·tel 🔊 /hou'tɛl/ *noun*
a building where people stay, usually for a short time, paying for their rooms and sometimes meals: *We stayed at/ in a hotel.* ◆ *hotel rooms/guests* ◆ *a two-star/five-star, etc. hotel* ◆ *a luxury hotel* ◆ *a friendly, family-run hotel* ⟹ collocations at TRAVEL

ho·te·lier /hou'tɛlyər; ,outɛl'yeɪ; ,hou-/ *noun* a person who owns or manages a hotel

hot·fix /'hɑtfɪks/ *noun* (*computing*) a file that is used to correct a fault in a computer program

'hot flash *noun* a sudden hot and uncomfortable feeling in the skin, especially experienced by women during the MENOPAUSE

hot·foot /'hɑtfʊt/ *verb*
IDM hotfoot it (*informal*) to walk or run somewhere quickly

hot·head /'hɑthɛd/ *noun* a person who often acts too quickly, without thinking of what might happen ▶ 'hot-,headed *adj.*

hot·house /'hɑthaʊs/ *noun* **1** a heated building, usually made of glass, used for growing delicate plants in: *hothouse flowers* **2** a place or situation that encourages the rapid development of someone or something, especially ideas and emotions

'hot key *noun* (*computing*) a key on a computer keyboard that you can press to perform a set of operations quickly, rather than having to press a number of different keys

hot·line /'hɑtlaɪn/ *noun* **1** a special telephone line that people can use in order to get information or to talk about something **2** a direct telephone line between the heads of government in different countries

'hot link *noun* = HYPERLINK

hot·list /'hɑtlɪst/ *noun* a list of popular, fashionable, or important people or things

hot·ly /'hɑtli/ *adv.* **1** done in an angry or excited way or with a lot of strong feeling: *a hotly debated topic* ◆ *Recent reports in the press have been hotly denied.* ◆ *"Nonsense!" he said hotly.* ◆ *The results were hotly disputed.* **2** done with a lot of energy and determination **SYN** CLOSELY: *hotly contested elections* ◆ *She ran out of the store, hotly pursued by the store detective.*

'hot pants *noun* [pl.] very short, tight women's SHORTS

,hot 'pink *noun* [U] a very bright pink color ▶ ,hot 'pink *adj.*

hot·plate /'hɑtpleɪt/ *noun* a flat heated metal surface that is used for cooking food or for keeping it hot

hot·pot /'hɑtpɑt/ *noun* a small electric pot that you can use to heat water or food

,hot po'tato *noun* [usually sing.] (*informal*) a problem, situation, etc. that is difficult and unpleasant to deal with

'hot rod *noun* a car that has been changed and improved to give it extra power and speed

hots /hɑts/ *noun* [pl.]
IDM get/have the hots for sb (*informal*) to be sexually attracted to someone

the 'hot seat *noun* [sing.] (*informal*) if someone is **in the hot seat**, they have to take responsibility for important or difficult decisions and actions

hot·shot /'hɑtʃɑt/ *noun* (*informal*) a person who is extremely successful in their career or at a particular sport ▶ hotshot *adj.* [only before noun]: *a hotshot lawyer*

'hot spot *noun* (*informal*) **1** a place where fighting is common, especially for political reasons **2** a place where there is a lot of activity or entertainment **3** a place that is very hot and dry, where a fire has been burning or is likely to start **4** (*computing*) an area on a computer screen that you can click on to start an operation such as loading a file **5** a place in a hotel, restaurant, airport, etc. that is fitted with a special device that enables you to connect a computer to the Internet without using wires

,hot 'stuff *noun* [U] (*informal*) **1** a person who is sexually attractive: *She's pretty hot stuff.* **2** a movie, book, etc. that is exciting in a sexual way **3 ~ (at sth)** a person who is very skillful at something: *She's really hot stuff at tennis.*

,hot-'tempered *adj.* tending to become very angry easily

hot·tie (also hot·ty) /'hɑti/ *noun* (*informal*) a person who is very sexually attractive

'hot tub *noun* a heated BATHTUB, often outside, that several people can sit in together to relax

,hot-'water ,bottle *noun* a rubber container that is filled with hot water and put in a bed to make it warm or as pain relief for sore muscles

'hot-wire *verb* **~ sth** (*informal*) to start the engine of a vehicle by using a piece of wire instead of a key

Hou·di·ni /hu'dini/ *noun* a person or animal that is very good at escaping **ORIGIN** From Harry Houdini, a famous performer in the U.S. who escaped from ropes, chains, boxes, etc.

hound /haʊnd/ *noun, verb*
• *noun* a dog that can run fast and has a good sense of smell, used for hunting ⟹ see also AFGHAN HOUND, BLOODHOUND, FOXHOUND, GREYHOUND, WOLFHOUND
• *verb* **~ sb** to keep following someone and not leave them alone, especially in order to get something from them or ask them questions **SYN** HARASS: *They were hounded day and night by the press.*
PHR V ,hound sb 'out (of sth) | 'hound sb from sth [usually passive] to force someone to leave a job or a place, especially by making their life difficult and unpleasant

'hound dog *noun* (especially in the southern states) a dog used in hunting

hounds·tooth /'haʊndztuθ/ *noun* [U] a type of large pattern with pointed shapes, often in black and white, used especially in cloth for jackets and suits

hour /'aʊər/ noun

HELP Use an, not a, before **hour**. **1** [C] (*abbr.* **hr., hr.**) 60 minutes; one of the 24 parts that a day is divided into: *It will take about an hour to get there.* ◆ *The interview lasted half an hour.* ◆ *It was a three-hour exam.* ◆ *I waited for an hour and then I left.* ◆ *He'll be back in an hour.* ◆ *We're paid by the hour.* ◆ *The minimum wage was set at $7.25 an hour.* ◆ *Top speed is 120 miles per hour.* ◆ *New York was within an hour's drive.* ◆ *Chicago is two hours away* (= it takes two hours to get there). ◆ *We're four hours ahead of Boston* (= referring to the time difference). ◆ *We hope to be there within the hour* (= in less than an hour). **2** [C, usually sing.] a period of about an hour, used for a particular purpose: *I use the Internet at work, during my lunch hour.* ➔ see also HAPPY HOUR, RUSH HOUR **3 hours** [pl.] a fixed period of time during which people work, an office is open, etc.: *Store hours are from 10 to 6 each day.* ◆ *Most people in this kind of job tend to work long hours.* ◆ *What are your office hours?* ◆ *a hospital's visiting hours* ◆ *This is the only place to get a drink after hours* (= after the normal closing time for bars). ◆ *Clients can now contact us by e-mail after hours* (= when the business is closed). ➔ see also AFTER-HOURS **4** [sing.] a particular point in time: *You can't turn him away at this hour of the night.* **5 hours** [pl.] a long time: *It took hours getting there.* ◆ *I've been waiting for hours.* ◆ *"How long did it last?" "Oh, hours and hours."* **6** [C, usually sing.] the time when something important happens: *This was often thought of as the country's finest hour.* ◆ *She thought her last hour had come.* ◆ *Don't desert me in my hour of need.* **7 the hour** [sing.] the time when it is exactly 1 o'clock, 2 o'clock, etc.: *There's a bus every hour on the hour.* ◆ *The clock struck the hour.* **8 hours** [pl.] used when giving the time according to the 24-hour clock, usually in military or other official language: *The first missile was launched at 23:00 hours* (= at 11 p.m.). **HELP** This is pronounced "23 hundred hours".

IDM **all hours** any time, especially a time that is not usual or suitable: *He's started staying out till all hours* (= until very late at night). ◆ *She thinks she can call me at all hours of the day and night.* **before/after the hour** used in giving the time to say the number of minutes before or after a particular hour: *It's twenty minutes before/after the hour* (= 11:40/12:20, 12:40/ 13:20, etc.). **keep… hours** if you keep regular, strange, etc. **hours**, the times at which you do things (especially getting up or going to bed) are regular, strange, etc. **of the hour** (of a person, an issue, etc.) very famous and talked about a lot now: *Jeff was the man of the hour today.* **the small/early hours** (also **the wee hours**) the period of time very early in the morning, soon after midnight: *We worked well into the small hours.* ◆ *The fighting began in the early hours of Saturday morning.* ➔ more at ELEVEN, KILL *v.*, UNEARTHLY, UNGODLY

hour·glass /'aʊər,glæs/ noun, adj.
● *noun* a glass container holding sand that takes exactly an hour to pass through a small opening between the top and bottom sections ➔ compare EGG TIMER
● *adj.* [only before noun] a woman who has an **hourglass** figure, shape, etc. has large breasts and hips and a small waist

'hour ,hand noun the small hand on a clock or watch that points to the hour ➔ picture at CLOCK

hour·ly /'aʊərli/ adj., adv. **HELP** Use an, not a, before hourly.
● *adj.* [only before noun] **1** done or happening every hour: *an hourly bus service* ◆ *Trains leave at hourly intervals.* **2** an **hourly wage, fee, rate, etc.** is the amount that you earn every hour or pay for a service every hour: *an hourly rate of $30 an hour*
● *adv.* every hour: *Reapply sunscreen hourly and after swimming.*

house /haʊs/ noun, verb
● *noun* /haʊs/ (*pl.* hous·es /'haʊzəz/)
➤ BUILDING **1** [C] a building for people to live in, usually for one family: *He went into the house.* ◆ *a two-bedroom house* ◆ *Let's have the party at my house.* ◆ *house prices* ◆ *What time do you leave the house in the morning?* (= to go to work)? ➔ picture on page 735 ➔ see also PENTHOUSE, SAFE HOUSE

➔ collocations at DECORATE **2** [sing.] all the people living in a house **SYN** HOUSEHOLD: *Be quiet or you'll wake the whole house!* **3** [C] (in compounds) a building used for a particular purpose, for example for holding meetings in or keeping animals or goods in: *an opera house* ◆ *a henhouse* ➔ see also DOGHOUSE, HALFWAY HOUSE, HOTHOUSE, LIGHTHOUSE, MADHOUSE, OUTHOUSE, STOREHOUSE, WAREHOUSE

TOPIC COLLOCATIONS

Houses and Apartments

renting
- **live in** a rental property
- **rent/share/move into** a furnished house/an apartment
- **rent** a studio/a studio apartment
- **find/get** a housemate/a roommate
- **sign/break/default on** a lease/rental agreement/ contract
- **extend/renew/terminate** the lease
- **afford/pay** the rent/the bills/the utilities
- **fall behind on** the rent
- **pay/lose/return** a security/key deposit
- **give/receive** a month's/two-weeks' notice to leave/ vacate the property

being a landlord
- **have an apartment/a room/a house** for rent
- **rent (out)/lease (out)/sublet** an apartment/a house/ a property
- **collect/increase/raise** the rent
- **evict** the existing tenants
- **attract/find** new/prospective tenants
- **invest in** rental property

buying
- **buy/acquire/purchase** a house/(a) property/(a piece of) prime real estate
- **call/contact/use** a real estate agent/broker
- **put in/make** an offer on a house
- **make/save for** a down payment on a house/home
- **apply for/be approved for/take out** a mortgage/ home loan
- **(struggle to) pay** the mortgage
- **make/meet/keep up/cover** the monthly mortgage payments
- **foreclose on** sb's home/house

selling
- **put your house/property** on the market/up for sale/ up for auction
- **increase/lower** your price/the asking price
- **have/hold/hand over** the deed to the house, land, etc.

➤ COMPANY/INSTITUTION **4** [C] (in compounds) a company involved in a particular kind of business; an institution of a particular kind: *a fashion/banking/publishing, etc. house* ◆ *a religious house* (= a CONVENT or a MONASTERY) ◆ *I work in house* (= in the offices of the company that I work for, not at home) ➔ see also CLEARING HOUSE, IN-HOUSE
➤ RESTAURANT **5** [C] (in compounds) a restaurant: *a steakhouse* ◆ *a coffee house* ◆ *a bottle of house wine* (= the cheapest wine available in a particular restaurant, sometimes not listed by name) ➔ see also ROADHOUSE
➤ PARLIAMENT **6** [C] often **House** a group of people who meet to discuss and make the laws of a country: *Legislation requires approval by both houses of Congress.* ➔ see also LOWER HOUSE, UPPER HOUSE **7 the House** [sing.] the House of Representatives
➤ IN THEATER **8** [C] the part of a theater where the audience sits; the audience at a particular performance: *playing to a full/packed/empty house* (= to a large/small audience) ◆ *The spotlight faded and the house lights came up.* ➔ see also FULL HOUSE

ʌ **cup**   ə **about**   eɪ **say**   aɪ **five**   ɔɪ **boy**   aʊ **now**   oʊ **go**   ər **bird**

House and Homes

house

①	chimney	⑥	gutter	⑪	windowsill	⑯	bay window	㉑	basement
②	antenna	⑦	downspout (*also* drainpipe)	⑫	porch	⑰	front door	㉒	step
③	roof	⑧	shutter	⑬	shingle	⑱	wall	㉓	driveway (*also* drive)
④	skylight	⑨	windowpane	⑭	door knocker	⑲	garage	㉔	lawn
⑤	doorbell	⑩	balcony	⑮	French door	⑳	window box	㉕	mailbox

homes

row house

apartment building

duplex

condominium

mobile home

townhouse

bungalow

> FAMILY **9** [C] usually the House of… an old and famous family: *the House of Windsor* (= the British royal family)

> MUSIC **10** [U] = HOUSE MUSIC ⊃ see also ACID HOUSE, ART-HOUSE, POWERHOUSE **HELP** There are many other compounds ending in **house**. You will find them at their place in the alphabet.

IDM **bring the house down** to make everyone laugh or CHEER, especially at a performance in the theater **get along like a house on fire** (*informal*) (of people) to become friends quickly and have a very friendly relationship **keep house** to cook, clean, and do all the other jobs around the house **on the house** drinks or meals that are **on the house** are provided free by the bar or restaurant and you do not have to pay **put/set your (own) house in order** to organize your own business or improve your own behavior before you try to criticize someone else **set up house** to make a place your home: *They set up house together in a small apartment in Brooklyn.* ⊃ more at CLEAN *v*., EAT, LADY, PEOPLE *n*.

● **verb** /haʊz/
> PROVIDE HOME **1** ~ sb to provide a place for someone to live: *The government is committed to housing the refugees.*
> KEEP SOMETHING **2** ~ sth to be the place where something is kept or where something operates from: *The gallery houses 2,000 works of modern art.* ◆ *The museum is housed in the Old Court House.*

house ar,rest (also ,home con'finement) *noun* [U] the state of being a prisoner in your own house rather than in a prison: *to be under house arrest* ◆ *She was placed under house arrest.*

house·boat /'haʊsboʊt/ *noun* a boat that people can live in, usually kept at a particular place on a river or CANAL or in a MARINA

house·bound /'haʊsbaʊnd/ *adj.* **1** unable to leave your house because you cannot walk very far as a result of being sick or old **2** **the housebound** *noun* [pl.] people who are housebound

house·boy /'haʊsbɔɪ/ *noun* a young male servant in a house

house·break·ing /'haʊs,breɪkɪŋ/ *noun* [U] the crime of entering a house illegally by using force, in order to steal things from it **SYN** BURGLARY ▶ **house·break·er** *noun*

house·brok·en /'haʊs,broʊkən/ *adj.* (of pet cats or dogs) trained to DEFECATE and URINATE outside the house or in a special box

house call *noun* a professional visit, especially by a doctor, to the home of a patient or client: *Doctors rarely make house calls these days.*

house·coat /'haʊskoʊt/ *noun* a long loose piece of clothing, worn in the house by women

house dust ,mite *noun* = DUST MITE

house·fly /'haʊsflaɪ/ *noun* (*pl.* **house·flies**) a common fly that lives in houses

house·ful /'haʊsfʊl/ *noun* [sing.] a large number of people in a house: *He grew up in a houseful of women.* ◆ *They had a houseful so we didn't stay.*

house guest *noun* a person who is staying in your house for a short time

house·hold 🔑 /'haʊshoʊld; 'haʊsoʊld/ *noun*
all the people living together in a house: *Most households now own at least one car.* ◆ *low-income/one-parent, etc. households* ◆ *the head of the household* ▶ **house·hold** *adj.* [only before noun]: *household bills/chores/goods* (= connected with looking after a house and the people living in it)

house·hold·er /'haʊs,hoʊldər; 'haʊ,soʊl-/ *noun* (*formal*) a person who owns or rents the house that they live in

household 'name (also *less frequent* ,household 'word) *noun* a name that has become very well known: *She became a household name in the 1960s.*

house-,hunting *noun* [U] the activity of looking for a house to buy ▶ **'house-,hunter** *noun*

house·hus·band /'haʊs,hʌzbənd/ *noun* a man who stays at home to cook, clean, take care of the children, etc. while his wife or partner goes out to work ⊃ compare HOUSEWIFE

house·keep·er /'haʊs,kipər/ *noun* **1** a person, usually a woman, whose job is to manage the shopping, cooking, cleaning, etc. in a house or an institution **2** a person whose job is to manage the cleaning of rooms in a hotel

house·keep·ing /'haʊs,kipɪŋ/ *noun* [U] **1** the work involved in taking care of a house, especially cleaning, shopping, and managing money **2** the department in a hotel, a hospital, an office building, etc. that is responsible for cleaning the rooms, etc.: *Call housekeeping and ask them to bring us some clean towels.* **3** jobs that are done to enable an organization or computer system to work well: *Most large companies now use computers for accounting and housekeeping operations.*

house·maid /'haʊsmeɪd/ *noun* (*old-fashioned*) a female servant in a large house who cleans the rooms, etc. and often lives there

house·man /'haʊsmən; -mæn/ *noun* (*pl.* **house·men** /-mən; -men/) a man employed to do general jobs in a house, hotel, etc.

house·mate /'haʊsmeɪt/ *noun* a person that you share a house with, but who is not one of your family

house·moth·er /'haʊs,mʌðər/ *noun* a woman who lives with and is in charge of a group of residents at a school or children's home

'house ,music (also house) *noun* [U] a type of electronic dance music with a fast beat

,house of 'cards *noun* [sing.] **1** a plan, an organization, etc. that is so badly arranged that it could easily fail **2** a structure built out of PLAYING CARDS

the ,House of 'Commons *noun* [sing.] **1** (in Canada and the U.K.) the part of Parliament whose members are elected by the people of the country **2** the building where the members of the House of Commons meet

,house of 'God *noun* (*pl.* **houses of God**) [usually sing.] (*literary*) a church or other religious building

the ,House of Repre'sentatives *noun* [sing.] the largest part of Congress, whose members are elected by the people of the country ⊃ compare SENATE

'house ,organ *noun* a magazine that is published by a company for its employees and customers, with articles about its products and services

'house ,party *noun* a party held at a large house in the country where guests stay for a few days; the guests at this party

house·plant /'haʊsplænt/ *noun* a plant that you grow in a pot and keep indoors

'house-sit *verb* (-tt-) [I] to live in someone's house while they are away in order to take care of it for them

,house 'style *noun* [U, C] the way a company such as a PUBLISHER prefers its written materials to be expressed and arranged

,house-to-'house *adj.* [only before noun] visiting every house in a particular area: *The police are making a house-to-house search.*

house·wares /'haʊswɛrz/ *noun* [pl.] (in stores) small items used in the house, especially kitchen equipment

house·warm·ing /'haʊs,wɔrmɪŋ/ *noun* a party given by someone who has just moved into a new house

house·wife /'haʊswaɪf/ *noun* (*pl.* **house·wives** /-waɪvz/) a woman who stays at home to cook, clean, take care of the children, etc. while her husband or partner goes out to work ⊃ compare HOUSEHUSBAND

house·work /'haʊswərk/ *noun* [U] the work involved in taking care of a home and family, for example cleaning and cooking: *to do the housework*

| t tea | ţ butter | d did | k cat | g got | tʃ chin | dʒ June | f fall |

hous·ing /ˈhaʊzɪŋ/ noun
1 [U] houses, apartments, etc. that people live in, especially when referring to their type, price, or condition: *public/ private housing* ♦ *poor housing conditions* ♦ *the housing shortage* ♦ *the housing market* (= the activity of buying and selling houses, etc.) **2** [U] the job of providing houses, apartments, etc. for people to live in: *the housing department* ♦ *the mayor's housing policy* **3** [C] a hard cover that protects part of a machine: *a car's rear axle housing*

housing de·velopment noun an area in which a large number of houses are planned and built together at the same time: *They live in a housing development.*

housing project (also pro·ject) noun a group of houses or apartments built for poor families, usually with government money

hove pt, pp of HEAVE

hov·el /ˈhʌvl; ˈhɑ-/ noun (*disapproving*) a house or room that is not fit to live in because it is dirty or in very bad condition

hov·er /ˈhʌvər/ verb **1** [I] (+ adv./prep.) (of birds, HELICOPTERS, etc.) to stay in the air in one place: *A hawk hovered over the hill.* **2** [I] (+ adv./prep.) (of a person) to wait somewhere, especially near someone, in a shy or uncertain manner: *He hovered nervously in the doorway.* **3** [I] + adv./ prep. to stay close to something, or to stay in an uncertain state: *Temperatures hovered around freezing.* ♦ *He hovered on the edge of consciousness.* ♦ *A smile hovered on her lips.* **4** [T] **~ sth over sth** (*computing*) to move a mouse or CURSOR over something on a computer screen: *Just hover your mouse over the folder and it will open.*

hov·er·craft /ˈhʌvərˌkræft/ noun a vehicle that travels just above the surface of water or land, held up by air being forced downward ⊃ picture at BOAT ⊃ compare HYDROFOIL

HOV lane /ˌeɪtʃ oʊ ˈvi leɪn/ noun high-occupancy vehicle lane (a part of the road that may only be used by vehicles that are carrying two or more people)

how /haʊ/ adv.
1 in what way or manner: *How does it work?* ♦ *He did not know how he ought to behave.* ♦ *I'll show you how to load the software.* ♦ *"Her behavior was very odd." "How so?" ♦ It's funny how* (= that) *people always remember him.* ♦ *Do you remember how* (= that) *the kids always loved going there?* ♦ *How ever did you get here so quickly?* ⊃ compare HOWEVER **2** used to ask about someone's health: *How are you?* ♦ *How are you feeling now?* **3** used to ask whether something is successful or enjoyable: *How was your trip?* ♦ *How did they play?* **4** used before an adjective or adverb to ask about the amount, degree, etc. of something, or about someone's age: *How often do you go swimming?* ♦ *I didn't know how much to bring.* ♦ *How much are those earrings?* (= What do they cost)? ♦ *How many people were there?* ♦ *How old is she?* **5** used to express surprise, pleasure, etc.: *How nice of you to help!* ♦ *How he wished he had been there!* **6** in any way in which **SYN** HOWEVER: *I'll dress how I like in my own house!* **IDM** **and how!** (*informal*) used to express strong agreement: *"Are you looking forward to it?" "And how!"* **how about…?** **1** used when asking for information about someone or something: *I'm not going. How about you?* **2** used to make a suggestion: *How about a break?* ♦ *How about going for a meal?* ♦ *How about we go for a meal?* **how can/could you!** (*informal*) used to show that you strongly disapprove of someone's behavior or are very surprised by it: *Ben! How could you? After all they've done for us!* ♦ *Ugh! How can you eat that stuff?* **how do you do** (becoming old-fashioned) used as a formal GREETING when you meet someone for the first time. The usual reply is also *How do you do?* **how's that?** (*informal*) **1** used to ask the reason for something: *"I left work early today." "How's that* (= Why)?" **2** used when you ask sb to repeat sth: *"How's that again? I think I missed something."* **3** used when asking someone's opinion of something: *I'll tuck your sheets in for you. How's that? Comfortable?* ♦ *Two o'clock on the dot! How's that for punctuality!* ⊃ more at COME v.

how·dy /ˈhaʊdi/ exclamation (*informal*, often *humorous*) used to say hello: *Howdy, partner.*

how·ev·er /haʊˈevər/ adv.
1 used with an adjective or adverb to mean "to whatever degree": *He wanted to take no risks, however small.* ♦ *She has the window open, however cold it is outside.* ♦ *However carefully I explained, she still didn't understand.* **HELP** When **ever** is used to emphasize **how**, meaning "In what way or manner?", it is usually written as a separate word: *How ever did you get here so quickly?* **2** in whatever way: *However you look at it, it's going to cost a lot.* **3** used to introduce a statement that contrasts with something that has just been said: *He was feeling bad. He went to work, however, and tried to concentrate.* ♦ *We thought the figures were correct. However, we have now discovered some errors.*

LANGUAGE BANK

however

ways of saying "but"

- Politicians have promised to improve road safety. So far, **however**, little has been achieved.
- **Despite/In spite of** clear evidence from road safety studies, no new measures have been introduced.
- Politicians have promised to improve road safety. **In spite of this/Despite this**, little has been achieved so far.
- **Although** politicians have promised to improve road safety, little has been achieved so far.
- Some politicians claim that the new transportation policy has been a success. **In fact**, it has been a total disaster.
- Government campaigns have had a measure of success, **but the fact remains that** large numbers of accidents are still caused by careless drivers.

⊃ Language Bank at NEVERTHELESS

---

how·itz·er /ˈhaʊətsər/ noun a heavy gun that fires SHELLS high into the air for a short distance

howl /haʊl/ verb, noun
● **verb 1** [I] (of a dog, WOLF, etc.) to make a long loud cry **2** [I] **~ (in/with sth)** to make a loud cry when you are in pain, angry, amused, etc.: *to howl in pain* ♦ *We howled with laughter.* ♦ *The baby was howling* (= crying loudly) *all the time I was there.* **3** [I] (of the wind) to blow hard and make a long loud noise: *The wind was howling around the house.* **4** [T] **~ sth | + speech** to say something loudly and angrily: *The crowd howled its displeasure.* **PHR V** **howl sb↔down** to prevent a speaker from being heard by shouting angrily **SYN** SHOUT SB DOWN
● **noun 1** a long loud cry made by a dog, WOLF, etc. **2** a loud cry showing that you are in pain, angry, amused, etc.: *to let out a howl of anguish* ♦ *The suggestion was greeted with howls of laughter.* **3** a long loud sound made when the wind is blowing strongly: *They listened to the howl of the wind through the trees.*

howl·er /ˈhaʊlər/ noun (*informal*) a stupid mistake, especially in what someone says or writes: *The report is full of howlers.*

howl·ing /ˈhaʊlɪŋ/ adj. [only before noun] **1** (of a storm, etc.) very violent, with strong winds: *a howling gale/storm/wind* **2** (*informal*) very great or extreme: *a howling success* ♦ *She flew into a howling rage.*

how-to adj. [only before noun] providing detailed instructions or advice on how to do something: *how-to books on computing* ▶ **how-to** noun (pl. **how-tos**): *Visit our downloads page for free how-tos and tutorials.*

hp /ˌeɪtʃ ˈpi/ abbr. HORSEPOWER

HQ /ˌeɪtʃ ˈkyu/ abbr. HEADQUARTERS: *See you back at HQ.* ♦ *police HQ*

HR /ˌeɪtʃ ˈɑr/ abbr. HUMAN RESOURCES

hr. abbr. (pl. **hrs.** or **hr.**) (in writing) hour: *Cover and chill for 1 hr.*

HRH /ˌeɪtʃ ɑr 'eɪtʃ/ abbr. His/Her Royal Highness: *HRH Prince Harry*

HRT /ˌeɪtʃ ɑr 'ti/ noun [U] the abbreviation for "hormone replacement therapy" (medical treatment for women going through MENOPAUSE in which HORMONES are added to the body)

Hsi·ang = XIANG

HST /ˌeɪtʃ ɛs 'ti/ abbr. (CanE) Harmonized Sales Tax (a tax that is added to the price of goods and services in parts of Canada)

HTML /ˌeɪtʃ ti ɛm 'ɛl/ abbr. (computing) Hypertext Mark-up Language (a system used to mark text for World Wide Web pages in order to obtain colors, style, pictures, etc.)

HTTP /ˌeɪtʃ ti ti 'pi/ abbr. (computing) Hypertext Transfer Protocol (the set of rules that control the way data is sent and received over the Internet)

hua·ra·che /wə'rɑtʃi/ noun a type of SANDAL (= open shoe) made of many narrow strips of leather twisted together

hub /hʌb/ noun **1** [usually sing.] ~ (of sth) the central and most important part of a particular place or activity: *the commercial hub of the city* ◆ *to be at the hub of things* (= where things happen and important decisions are made) ◆ *a hub airport* (= a large important one where people often change from one plane to another) **2** the central part of a wheel ⊃ picture at BICYCLE

hub·bub /'hʌbʌb/ noun [sing., U] **1** the loud sound made by a lot of people talking at the same time: *It was difficult to hear what he was saying over the hubbub.* **2** a situation in which there is a lot of noise, excitement, and activity: *the hubbub of city life*

hub·by /'hʌbi/ noun (pl. hub·bies) (informal) = HUSBAND

hub·cap /'hʌbkæp/ noun a round metal cover that fits over the HUB of a vehicle's wheel ⊃ picture at CAR

hu·bris /'hyubrəs/ noun [U] (literary) the fact of someone being too proud. In literature, a character with this pride ignores warnings and laws and this usually results in their DOWNFALL and death.

huck·le·ber·ry /'hʌkl̩ˌbɛri/ noun (pl. huck·le·ber·ries) a small, soft, round, purple North American fruit. The bush it grows on is also called a huckleberry.

huck·ster /'hʌkstər/ noun (old-fashioned) **1** (disapproving) a person who uses aggressive or annoying methods to sell something **2** a person who sells things in the street or by visiting people's houses

HUD /hʌd/ abbr. Department of Housing and Urban Development (the government department in charge of financial programs to build houses and to help people buy their own homes)

hud·dle /'hʌdl/ verb, noun
• verb **1** [I] ~ (up/together) (+ adv./prep.) (of people or animals) to gather closely together, usually because of cold or fear: *We huddled together for warmth.* ◆ *They all huddled around the fire.* **2** [I] ~ (up) (+ adv./prep.) to hold your arms and legs close to your body, usually because you are cold or frightened: *I huddled under a blanket on the floor.* **3** [I] (of football players) to gather around to hear the plan for the next part of the game ▶ hud·dled adj.: *People were huddled together around the fire.* ◆ *huddled figures in shop doorways* ◆ *We found him huddled on the floor.*
• noun **1** a small group of people, objects, or buildings that are close together, especially when they are not in any particular order: *People stood around in huddles.* ◆ *The track led them to a huddle of buildings.* **2** (in football) a time when the players gather around to hear the plan for the next part of the game
  IDM **get/go into a huddle (with sb)** to move close to someone so that you can talk about something without other people hearing

hue /hyu/ noun **1** (literary or technical) a color; a particular shade of a color: *His face took on an unhealthy whitish hue.* ◆ *Her paintings capture the subtle hues of the countryside in* the fall. ⊃ thesaurus box at COLOR **2** (formal) a type of belief or opinion: *supporters of every political hue*
  IDM **hue and cry** strong public protest about something

huff /hʌf/ verb, noun
• verb [T, I] (+ speech) to say something or make a noise in a way that shows you are offended or annoyed: *"Well, nobody asked you," she huffed irritably.*
  IDM **huff and puff** (informal) **1** to breathe in a noisy way because you are very tired: *Jack was huffing and puffing to keep up with her.* **2** to make it obvious that you are annoyed about something without doing anything to change the situation: *After much huffing and puffing, she finally agreed to help.*
• noun
  IDM **in a huff** (informal) in a bad mood, especially because someone has annoyed or upset you: *She went off in a huff.*

huff·y /'hʌfi/ adj. (informal) in a bad mood, especially because someone has annoyed or upset you ▶ huff·i·ly /'hʌfəli/ adv.

hug /hʌg/ verb, noun
• verb (-gg-) **1** [T, I] ~ (sb) to put your arms around someone and hold them tightly, especially to show that you like or love them SYN EMBRACE: *They hugged each other.* ◆ *She hugged him tightly.* ◆ *They put their arms around each other and hugged.* **2** [T] ~ sth to put your arms around something and hold it close to your body: *She sat in the chair, hugging her knees.* ◆ *He hugged the hot-water bottle to his chest.* **3** [T] ~ sth (of a path, vehicle, etc.) to keep close to something for a distance: *The track hugs the coast for a mile.* **4** [T] ~ sth to fit tightly around something, especially a person's body: *figure-hugging jeans*
• noun an act of putting your arms around someone and holding them tightly, especially to show that you like or love them: *She gave her mother a big hug.* ◆ *He stopped to receive hugs and kisses from the fans.* ⊃ see also BEAR HUG

huge 🔑 /hyudʒ/ adj.
1 extremely large in size or amount; great in degree SYN ENORMOUS, VAST: *a huge crowd* ◆ *He gazed up at her with huge brown eyes.* ◆ *huge debts* ◆ *a huge amount of data* ◆ *The sums of money involved are potentially huge.* ◆ *The party was a huge success.* ◆ *This is going to be a huge problem for us.* **2** (informal) very successful: *I think this band is going to be huge.*

huge·ly /'hyudʒli/ adv. **1** extremely: *hugely entertaining/ important/popular/successful* **2** very much: *They intended to invest hugely in new technology.* ◆ *He turned around, grinning hugely.*

huh /hʌ; hʌ̃/ exclamation **1** people use Huh? at the end of questions, suggestions, etc., especially when they want someone to agree with them: *So you won't be coming tonight, huh?* ◆ *Let's get out of here, huh?* **2** people say Huh? to show that they have not heard what someone has just said: *"Are you feeling OK?" "Huh?"* **3** people say Huh! to show anger, surprise, disagreement, etc. or to show that they are not impressed by something: *Huh! Is that all you've done?*

hu·la /'hulə/ noun a Hawaiian dance that is performed with gentle movements of the hips and hands

'hula ˌhoop (also 'Hula- ˌHoop™) noun a large plastic ring that you spin around your waist by moving your hips

hulk /hʌlk/ noun **1** the main part of an old vehicle, especially a ship, that is no longer used: *the hulk of a wrecked ship* **2** a very large person, especially one who moves in an awkward way: *a great hulk of a man* **3** a very large object, especially one that causes you to feel nervous or afraid

hulk·ing /'hʌlkɪŋ/ adj. [only before noun] very large or heavy, often in a way that causes you to feel nervous or afraid: *a hulking figure crouching in the darkness* ◆ *I don't want that hulking great computer in my office.*

hull /hʌl/ noun, verb
• noun the main, bottom part of a ship, that goes in the water: *a wooden/steel hull* ◆ *They climbed onto the upturned hull and waited to be rescued.*

h **h**at   m **m**an   n **n**o   ŋ si**ng**   l **l**eg   r **r**ed   y **y**es   w **w**et

• **verb** ~ **sth** to remove the outer covering of PEAS, BEANS, etc. or the ring of leaves attached to strawberries (STRAWBERRY)

hul·la·ba·loo /ˈhʌləbəˌlu; ˌhʌləbəˈlu/ *noun* [sing.] a lot of loud noise, especially made by people who are annoyed or excited about something **SYN** COMMOTION, UPROAR

hum /hʌm/ *verb, noun*
• **verb** (-mm-) **1** [I, T] to sing a tune with your lips closed: *She was humming softly to herself.* ◆ ~ **sth** *What's that tune you're humming?* ⊃ collocations at MUSIC **2** [I] to make a low continuous sound: *The computers were humming away.* **3** [I] to be full of activity: *The streets were beginning to hum with life.*
• **noun** [sing.] ~ **(of sth)** a low continuous sound: *the hum of bees/traffic/voices* ◆ *The room filled with the hum of conversation.*

hu·man 🔑 /ˈhyumən/ *adj., noun*
• **adj. 1** [only before noun] of or connected with people rather than animals, machines, or gods: *the human body/brain* ◆ *human anatomy/activity/behavior/experience* ◆ *a terrible loss of human life* ◆ *Contact with other people is a basic human need.* ◆ *This food is not fit for human consumption.* ◆ *human geography* (= the study of the way different people live around the world) ◆ *The hostages were used as a human shield* (= a person or group of people that is forced to stay in a particular place where they would be hurt or killed if their country attacked it). ◆ *Firefighters formed a human chain* (= a line of people) *to carry the children to safety.* ◆ *Human remains* (= the body of a dead person) *were found inside the house.* **2** showing the weaknesses that are typical of people, which means that other people should not criticize the person too much: *human weaknesses/failings* ◆ *We must allow for human error.* ◆ *It's only human to want the best for your children.* **3** having the same feelings and emotions as most ordinary people: *He's really very human when you get to know him.* ◆ *The public is always attracted to politicians who have the human touch* (= the ability to make ordinary people feel relaxed when they meet them). ⊃ compare INHUMAN, NONHUMAN
IDM **the human face of...** a person who is involved in a subject, issue, etc. and makes it easier for ordinary people to understand and have sympathy with it: *He is the human face of party politics.* **with a human face** that considers the needs of ordinary people: *This was science with a human face.* ⊃ more at MILK
• **noun** (also ˌhuman ˈbeing) a person rather than an animal or a machine: *Dogs can hear much better than humans.* ◆ *That is no way to treat another human being.*

ˌhuman ˈcapital *noun* [U] = HUMAN RESOURCES (1)

hu·mane /hyuˈmeɪn/ *adj.* showing kindness toward people and animals by making sure that they do not suffer more than is necessary: *a caring and humane society* ◆ *the humane treatment of refugees* ◆ *the humane killing of animals* **ANT** INHUMANE ▶ **hu·mane·ly** *adv.*: *to treat someone humanely* ◆ *meat that has been humanely produced* ◆ *The dog was humanely destroyed.*

ˌhuman ˈinterest *noun* [U] the part of a story in a newspaper, etc. that people find interesting because it describes the experiences, feelings, etc. of the people involved

hu·man·ism /ˈhyuməˌnɪzəm/ *noun* [U] a system of thought that considers that solving human problems with the help of reason is more important than religious beliefs. It emphasizes the fact that the basic nature of humans is good. ▶ **hu·man·is·tic** /ˌhyuməˈnɪstɪk/ *adj.*: *humanistic ideals*

hu·man·ist /ˈhyumənɪst/ *noun* a person who believes in humanism

hu·man·i·tar·i·an /hyuˌmænəˈtɛriən/ *adj.* [usually before noun] concerned with reducing suffering and improving the conditions that people live in: *to provide humanitarian aid to the war zone* ◆ *humanitarian issues* ◆ *a humanitarian organization* ◆ *They are calling for the release of the hostages on humanitarian grounds.* ◆ *The expulsion of thousands of people* represents a humanitarian catastrophe of enormous proportions. ▶ **hu·man·i·tar·i·an** *noun* **hu·man·i·tar·i·an·ism** /-əˌnɪzəm/ *noun* [U]

hu·man·i·ty /hyuˈmænəti/ *noun* **1** [U] people in general: *crimes against humanity* **2** [U] the state of being a person rather than a god, an animal, or a machine: *The story was used to emphasize the humanity of Jesus.* ◆ *united by a sense of common humanity* **3** [U] the quality of being kind to people and animals by making sure that they do not suffer more than is necessary; the quality of being HUMANE: *The judge was praised for his courage and humanity.* **ANT** INHUMANITY **4 (the) humanities** [pl.] the subjects of study that are concerned with the way people think and behave, for example literature, language, history, and philosophy ⊃ compare SCIENCE

hu·man·ize /ˈhyuməˌnaɪz/ *verb* ~ **sth** to make something more pleasant or suitable for people; to make something more HUMANE: *These measures are intended to humanize the prison system.*

hu·man·kind /ˈhyumənˌkaɪnd; ˌhyumənˈkaɪnd/ *noun* [U] people in general ⊃ see also MANKIND

hu·man·ly /ˈhyumənli/ *adv.* within human ability; in a way that is typical of human behavior, thoughts, and feelings: *The doctors did all that was humanly possible.* ◆ *He couldn't humanly refuse to help her.*

ˌhuman ˈnature *noun* [U] the ways of behaving, thinking, and feeling that are shared by most people and are considered to be normal: *Her kindness has restored my faith in human nature* (= the belief that people are good). ◆ *It's only human nature to be worried about change.*

hu·man·oid /ˈhyuməˌnɔɪd/ *noun* a machine or creature that looks and behaves like a human ▶ **humanoid** *adj.*

the ˌhuman ˈrace *noun* [sing.] all people, considered together as a group

ˌhuman ˈresources *noun* **1** [pl.] (also ˌhuman ˈcapital [U]) people's skills and abilities, seen as something a company, an organization, etc. can make use of **2** (*abbr.* HR) [U] the department in a company that deals with employing and training people **SYN** PERSONNEL: *the human resources director*

ˌhuman ˈright *noun* [usually pl.] one of the basic rights that everyone has to be treated fairly and not in a cruel way, especially by their government: *The country has a poor record on human rights.* ◆ *to campaign for human rights* ◆ *human rights abuses/violations*

hum·ble /ˈhʌmbl/ *adj., verb*
• **adj.** (hum·bler /-blər/, hum·blest /-bləst/) **1** showing you do not think that you are as important as other people **SYN** MODEST: *Be humble enough to learn from your mistakes.* ◆ *my humble tribute to this great man* ⊃ see also HUMILITY **2** (*ironic* or *humorous*) used to suggest that you are not as important as other people, but in a way that is not sincere or not very serious: *In my humble opinion, you were in the wrong.* ◆ *My humble apologies. I did not understand.* **3** having a low rank or social position: *a man of humble birth/origins* ◆ *a humble occupation* ◆ *the daughter of a humble shopkeeper* **4** (of a thing) not large or special in any way **SYN** MODEST: *a humble farmhouse* ◆ *The company has worked its way up from humble beginnings to become the market leader.* ▶ **hum·bly** /-bli/ *adv.*: *I would humbly suggest that there is something wrong here.* ◆ *"Sorry," she said humbly.* **IDM** see EAT
• **verb 1** ~ **sb** to make someone feel that they are not as good or important as they thought they were: *He was humbled by her generosity.* ◆ *a humbling experience* **2** [usually passive] ~ **sb** to easily defeat an opponent, especially a strong or powerful one: *The world champion was humbled last night in three rounds.* **3** ~ **yourself** to show that you are not too proud to ask for something, admit that you have been wrong, etc. ⊃ see also HUMILITY

hum·bug /ˈhʌmbʌg/ *noun* (*old-fashioned*) **1** [U] dishonest language or behavior that is intended to trick people: *political humbug* **2** [C] a person who is not sincere or honest

hum·ding·er /ˌhʌmˈdɪŋər/ noun [sing.] (informal) something that is very exciting or impressive: It turned into a real humdinger of a game.

hum·drum /ˈhʌmdrʌm/ adj. boring and always the same **SYN** DULL, TEDIOUS: a humdrum existence/job/life

hu·mec·tant /hyuˈmɛktənt/ noun (technical) **1** a substance added to foods to stop them from becoming dry **2** a substance added to skin cream to stop your skin from being dry

hu·mer·us /ˈhyumərəs/ noun (pl. hu·mer·i /-ˌraɪ/) (anatomy) the large bone in the top part of the arm between the shoulder and the elbow ⊃ picture at BODY

hu·mid /ˈhyuməd/ adj. (of the air or climate) warm and damp: These ferns will grow best in a humid atmosphere. ◆ The island is hot and humid in the summer.

hu·mid·ex /ˈhyuməˌdɛks/ noun [sing.] (CanE) a scale that measures how unpleasant hot and humid weather feels to people

hu·mid·i·fi·er /hyuˈmɪdəˌfaɪər/ noun a machine used for making the air in a room less dry ⊃ see also DEHUMIDIFIER

hu·mid·i·ty /hyuˈmɪdəti/ noun [U] **1** the amount of water in the air: high/low humidity ◆ 70% humidity **2** conditions in which the air is very warm and damp: These plants need heat and humidity to grow well. ◆ The humidity was becoming unbearable.

hu·mil·i·ate /hyuˈmɪliˌeɪt/ verb ~ sb/yourself/sth to make someone feel ashamed or stupid and lose the respect of other people: I didn't want to humiliate her in front of her colleagues. ◆ I've never felt so humiliated. ◆ The party was humiliated in the recent election. ▶ hu·mil·i·at·ing adj.: a humiliating defeat ▶ hu·mil·i·a·tion /hyuˌmɪliˈeɪʃn/ noun [U, C]: She suffered the humiliation of being criticized in public.

hu·mil·i·ty /hyuˈmɪləti/ noun [U] the quality of not thinking that you are better than other people; the quality of being humble: Her first defeat was an early lesson in humility. ◆ an act of genuine humility

Hu·mint /ˈhyumɪnt/ noun [U] the activity or job of collecting secret information about people or governments

hum·ming·bird /ˈhʌmɪŋˌbərd/ noun a small brightly colored bird that lives in warm countries and that can stay in one place in the air by beating its wings very fast, making a continuous low sound (= a HUMMING sound)

hum·mus /ˈhuməs; ˈhʌ-/ noun [U] a type of food, originally from the Middle East, that is a soft mixture of CHICKPEAS, oil, and GARLIC

hu·mon·gous (also hu·mun·gous) /hyuˈmʌŋɡəs/ adj. (informal) very big **SYN** ENORMOUS

hu·mor 🔑 /ˈhyumər/ (CanE usually hu·mour) noun, verb
• noun **1** [U] the quality in something that makes it funny or amusing; the ability to laugh at things that are amusing: a story full of gentle humor ◆ She ignored his feeble attempt at humor. ◆ They failed to see the humor of the situation. ◆ I can't stand people with no sense of humor. ◆ She smiled with a rare flash of humor. ◆ She has her very own brand of humor. ◆ The movie is only funny if you appreciate British humor (= things that cause British people to laugh). **2** [C, U] (formal) the state of your feelings or mind at a particular time: to be in the best of humors ◆ The meeting dissolved in ill humor. ◆ to be out of humor (= in a bad mood) ⊃ see also GOOD HUMOR, ILL HUMOR **3** [C] (old use) one of the four liquids that were thought in the past to be in a person's body and to influence health and character
• verb ~ sb to agree with someone's wishes, even if they seem unreasonable, in order to keep the person happy: She thought it best to humor him rather than get into an argument.

hu·mor·ist /ˈhyumərɪst/ noun a person who is famous for writing or telling amusing stories

hu·mor·less (CanE usually hu·mour·less) /ˈhyumərləs/ adj. not having or showing the ability to laugh at things that other people think are amusing ▶ hu·mor·less·ly (CanE usually hu·mour·less·ly) adv.

hu·mor·ous 🔑 /ˈhyumərəs/ adj. funny and entertaining; showing a sense of humor: He gave a humorous account of their trip to Spain. ◆ He had a wide mouth and humorous gray eyes. ⊃ thesaurus box at FUNNY ▶ hu·mor·ous·ly adv.: The poem humorously describes local characters and traditions.

hu·mour (CanE) = HUMOR

hu·mour·less (CanE) = HUMORLESS

hump /hʌmp/ noun **1** a large lump that sticks out above the surface of something, especially the ground: the dark hump of the mountain in the distance **2** a large lump on the back of some animals, especially CAMELS **3** a large lump on the back of a person, caused by an unusual curve in the SPINE (= the row of bones in the middle of the back) **IDM** be over the hump to have done the most difficult part of something

hump·back whale /ˌhʌmpbæk ˈweɪl/ (also hump·back) noun a large WHALE (= a very large sea animal) with a back shaped like a HUMP

humped /hʌmpt/ adj. having a HUMP or HUMPS; shaped like a HUMP: a humped back ◆ He was tall and broad with humped shoulders.

humph /hʌmf; hm/ exclamation the way of writing the sound /hʌmf/ that people use to show they do not believe something or do not approve of it

hu·mun·gous = HUMONGOUS

hu·mus /ˈhyuməs/ noun [U] a substance made from dead leaves and plants, added to soil to help plants grow

Hum·vee™ /ˌhʌmˈvi; ˈhʌmvi/ noun a modern military vehicle like a JEEP™

hunch /hʌntʃ/ verb, noun
• verb [I, T] to bend the top part of your body forward and raise your shoulders and back: (+ adv./prep.) She leaned forward, hunching over the desk. ◆ ~ sth He hunched his shoulders and thrust his hands deep into his pockets. ▶ hunched adj.: a hunched figure ◆ He sat hunched over his breakfast.
• noun a feeling that something is true even though you do not have any evidence to prove it: It seemed that the doctor's hunch had been right. ◆ I had a hunch (that) you'd be back.

hunch·back /ˈhʌntʃbæk/ noun (offensive) a person who has a HUMP on their back ▶ hunch·backed /-bækt/ adj.

hun·dred /ˈhʌndrəd/ number (plural verb) **1** 100: One hundred (of the children) have already been placed with foster families. ◆ There were just a hundred of them there. ◆ This vase is worth several hundred dollars. ◆ She must be over a hundred (= a hundred years old). ◆ Hundreds of thousands of people are at risk. ◆ a hundred-year lease **HELP** You say a, one, two, several, etc. hundred without a final "s" on "hundred." Hundreds (of…) can be used if there is no number or quantity before it. Always use a plural verb with hundred or hundreds, except when an amount of money is mentioned: Four hundred (people) are expected to attend. ◆ Two hundred (dollars) was withdrawn from the account. **2** a hundred or hundreds (of…) (usually informal) a large amount: hundreds of miles away ◆ for hundreds of years ◆ If I've said it once, I've said it a hundred times. ◆ I have a hundred and one things to do. ◆ (formal) Men died in the hundreds. **3** the hundreds [pl.] the numbers from 100 to 999: We're talking about a figure in the low hundreds. **4** the… hundreds [pl.] the years of a particular century: the early nineteen hundreds (= written "early 1900s") **5** one, two, three, etc. ~ hours used to express whole hours in the 24-hour system: twelve hundred hours (= 12:00, noon) **IDM** a/one hundred percent **1** in every way **SYN** COMPLETELY: I'm not a hundred percent sure. ◆ My family supports me one hundred percent. **2** completely fit and healthy: I still don't feel a hundred percent. **give a hundred (and ten) percent** to put as much effort into something as you can: Every player gave a hundred percent tonight. ⊃ more at NINETY

ʌ cup   ə about   eɪ say   aɪ five   ɔɪ boy   aʊ now   oʊ go   ər bird

hun·dredth /ˈhʌndrədθ; -drətθ/ *ordinal number, noun*
- **ordinal number** 100th: *her hundredth birthday*
- **noun** each of one hundred equal parts of something: *a/one hundredth of a second*

hun·dred·weight /ˈhʌndrədˌweɪt/ *noun* (*pl.* **hun·dred·weight**) (*abbr.* **cwt.**) a unit for measuring weight equal to 100 pounds. There are 20 hundredweight in a ton.

hung /hʌŋ/ *adj.* [only before noun] (of a jury) unable to agree about whether someone is guilty of a crime ⊃ see also HANG

hun·ger /ˈhʌŋɡər/ *noun, verb*
- **noun 1** [U] the feeling caused by a need to eat: *hunger pangs* ◆ *I felt faint with hunger.* **2** [U] the state of not having enough food to eat, especially when this causes illness or death SYN STARVATION: *Around fifty people die of hunger every day in the camp.* ◆ *The organization works to alleviate world hunger and disease.* **3** [sing.] ~ (**for sth**) (*formal*) a strong desire for something: *a hunger for knowledge* ◆ *Nothing seemed to satisfy their hunger for truth.*
- **verb**
  PHR V **ˈhunger for/after sth/sb** (*literary*) to have a strong desire or need for something or someone

ˈhunger ˌstrike *noun* [C, U] the act of refusing to eat for a long period of time in order to protest about something: *to be on/go on hunger strike* ▶ **ˈhunger ˌstriker** *noun*

hung·o·ver /ˌhʌŋˈoʊvər/ *adj.* [not usually before noun] a person who is **hungover** is feeling sick because they drank too much alcohol the night before ⊃ see also HANGOVER

hun·gry 🔑 /ˈhʌŋɡri/ *adj.* (**hun·gri·er**, **hun·gri·est**)
1 feeling that you want to eat something: *I'm really hungry.* ◆ *Is anyone getting hungry?* ◆ *All this talk of food is making me hungry.* ◆ *I have a hungry family to feed.* **2** not having enough food to eat: *Thousands are going hungry because of the failure of this year's harvest.* **3 the hungry** *noun* [pl.] people who do not have enough food to eat **4** [only before noun] causing you to feel that you want something: *All this gardening is hungry work.* **5** ~ (**for sth**) having or showing a strong desire for something: *Both parties are hungry for power.* ◆ *power-hungry* ◆ *The child is simply hungry for affection.* ◆ *His eyes had a wild hungry look in them.* ▶ **hun·gri·ly** /-ɡrəli/ *adv.*: *They gazed hungrily at the display of food.* ◆ *He kissed her hungrily.*

ˌhung ˈup *adj.* [not before noun] ~ (**on/about sth/sb**) (*informal, disapproving*) very worried about something or someone; thinking about something or someone too much: *You're not still hung up on that girl?* ◆ *He's too hung up about fitness.*

hunk /hʌŋk/ *noun* **1** a large piece of something, especially food, that has been cut or broken from a larger piece: *a hunk of bread/cheese/meat* **2** (*informal*) a man who is big, strong, and sexually attractive: *He's a real hunk.*

hunk·er /ˈhʌŋkər/ *verb*
PHR V **ˌhunker ˈdown 1** to sit on your heels with your knees bent up in front of you SYN SQUAT: *He hunkered down beside her.* **2** to prepare yourself to stay somewhere, keep an opinion, etc. for a long time **3** to refuse to change an opinion, way of behaving, etc.

hunk·y /ˈhʌŋki/ *adj.* (**hunk·i·er**, **hunk·i·est**) (of a man) big, strong, and sexually attractive

hunk·y-do·ry /ˌhʌŋki ˈdɔri/ *adj.* [not before noun] (*informal*) if you say that **everything is hunky-dory**, you mean that there are no problems and that everyone is happy

hunt 🔑 /hʌnt/ *verb, noun*
- **verb 1** [I, T] to chase wild animals or birds in order to catch or kill them for food or sport or to make money: *Lions sometimes hunt alone.* ◆ ~ **sth** *Whales are still being hunted and killed in the Arctic.* **2** [I] to look for something that is difficult to find SYN SEARCH: *I've hunted everywhere but I can't find it.* ◆ ~ **for sth** *She is still hunting for a new job.* **3** [T, I] to look for someone in order to catch them or harm them: ~ **sb** *Police are hunting an escaped criminal.* ◆ ~ **for sb** *Detectives are*

hunting for thieves who broke into a warehouse yesterday.
PHR V **ˌhunt sb↔ˈdown** to search for someone until you catch or find them, especially in order to punish or harm them **ˌhunt sth↔ˈout** to search for something until you find it
- **noun 1** [C, usually sing.] ~ (**for sb/sth**) an act of looking for someone or something that is difficult to find: *The hunt is on for a suitable candidate.* ◆ *Hundreds have joined a police hunt for the missing teenager.* ◆ *a murder hunt* (= to find the person who has killed someone) ⊃ see also TREASURE HUNT, WITCH-HUNT **2** [C] (often in compounds) an act of chasing wild animals to kill or capture them: *a tiger hunt*
  IDM **be in the hunt** to have a chance of winning: *The team is back in the hunt for the national title.*

ˌhunt-and-ˈpeck *adj.* (*informal*) using only one or two fingers when typing on a keyboard: *a hunt-and-peck typist*

hunt·ed /ˈhʌntəd/ *adj.* (of an expression on someone's face) showing that someone is very worried or frightened, as if they are being followed or chased: *His eyes had a hunted look.*

hunt·er /ˈhʌntər/ *noun* **1** a person who hunts wild animals for food or sport; an animal that hunts its food **2** (usually in compounds) a person who looks for and collects a particular kind of thing: *a bargain hunter* ⊃ see also HEADHUNTER **3** a dog used in hunting

ˌhunter-ˈgatherer *noun* a member of a group of people who do not live in one place but move around and live by hunting, fishing, and gathering plants

hunt·ing 🔑 /ˈhʌntɪŋ/ *noun* [U]
1 chasing and killing wild animals and birds as a sport or for food: *to go hunting* ⊃ see also FOX HUNTING **2** (in compounds) the process of looking for something: *We're going house-hunting at the weekend.* ◆ *How's the job-hunting going?*

ˈhunting ˌground *noun* **1** a place where people with a particular interest can easily find what they want: *Crowded markets are a happy hunting ground for pickpockets.* **2** a place where wild animals are hunted

hunt·ress /ˈhʌntrəs/ *noun* (*literary*) a woman who hunts wild animals

hunts·man /ˈhʌntsmən/ *noun* (*pl.* **hunts·men** /-mən/) a man who hunts wild animals

hur·dle /ˈhərdl/ *noun, verb*
- **noun 1** each of a series of vertical frames that a person or horse jumps over in a race: *His horse fell at the final hurdle.* ◆ *to clear a hurdle* (= jump over it successfully) ⊃ picture at SPORT **2 hurdles** [pl.] a race in which runners or horses have to jump over hurdles: *the 300-meter hurdles* **3** a problem or difficulty that must be solved or dealt with before you can achieve something SYN OBSTACLE: *The next hurdle will be getting her parents' agreement.*
- **verb 1** [T, I] to jump over something while you are running: ~ **sth** *He hurdled two barriers to avoid reporters.* ◆ ~ **over sth** *to hurdle over a fence* **2** [I] to run in a hurdle race

hur·dler /ˈhərdlər/ *noun* a person or horse that runs in races over hurdles

hur·dling /ˈhərdlɪŋ/ *noun* [U] the sport of racing over HURDLES ⊃ picture at SPORT

hur·dy-gur·dy /ˌhərdi ˈɡərdi/ *noun* (*pl.* **hur·dy-gur·dies**) a small musical instrument that is played by turning a handle

hurl /hərl/ *verb* **1** [T] ~ **sth/sb** + **adv./prep.** to throw something or someone violently in a particular direction: *He hurled a brick through the window.* ⊃ thesaurus box at THROW **2** [T] ~ **abuse, accusations, insults, etc. (at sb)** to shout insults, etc. at someone: *Rival fans hurled abuse at each other.* **3** [I] (*slang*) to VOMIT

hurl·y-burl·y /ˌhərli ˈbərli/ *noun* [U] a very noisy and busy activity or situation

hur·rah /həˈrɑ; -ˈrɔ/ (also **hur·ray** /həˈreɪ/) *exclamation* = HOORAY

---

hur·ri·cane /'hərəˌkeɪn/ *noun* a violent storm with very strong winds, especially in the western Atlantic Ocean: *hurricane-force winds* ◆ *Hurricane Betty is now approaching the coast of Florida.* ⊃ collocations at WEATHER ⊃ compare CYCLONE, TYPHOON

'hurricane ˌlamp *noun* a type of lamp with glass sides to protect the flame inside from the wind

hur·ried /'hərid/ *adj.* [usually before noun] done too quickly because you do not have enough time: *I ate a hurried breakfast and left.* **ANT** UNHURRIED ▶ **hur·ried·ly** /'hərədli; 'hərid-/ *adv.*: *I hurriedly got up and dressed.*

hur·ry 🔑 /'həri/ *verb, noun*
● *verb* (**hur·ries, hur·ry·ing, hur·ried, hur·ried**) **1** [I] to do something more quickly than usual because there is not much time **SYN** RUSH: *You'll have to hurry if you want to catch that train.* ◆ *The kids hurried to open their presents.* **HELP** In spoken English **hurry** can be used with **and** plus another verb, instead of with **to** and the infinitive, especially to tell someone to do something quickly: *Hurry and open your present—I want to see what it is!* **2** [I] + *adv./prep.* to move quickly in a particular direction **SYN** RUSH: *He picked up his bags and hurried across the courtyard.* ◆ *She hurried away without saying goodbye.* **3** [T] to make someone do something more quickly **SYN** RUSH: ~ *sb I don't want to hurry you, but we close in twenty minutes.* ◆ ~ *sb into doing sth She was hurried into making an unwise choice.* **4** [T] ~ *sth* + *adv./prep.* to deal with something quickly **SYN** RUSH: *Her application was hurried through.* **5** [T, usually passive] ~ *sth* to do something too quickly **SYN** RUSH: *A good meal should never be hurried.*
PHR V ˌhurry 'on to continue speaking without giving anyone else time to say anything ˌhurry 'up (with sth) to do something more quickly because there is not much time: *I wish the bus would hurry up and come.* ◆ *Hurry up! We're going to be late.* ◆ *Hurry up with the scissors. I need them.* ˌhurry sb/sth↔'up to make someone do something more quickly; to make something happen more quickly: *Can you do anything to hurry it up?*
● *noun* [U, sing.] the need or wish to get something done quickly: *Take your time—there's no hurry.* ◆ *In my hurry to leave, I forgot my passport.* ◆ *What's the hurry? The train doesn't leave for an hour.*
IDM in a hurry **1** very quickly or more quickly than usual: *He had to leave in a hurry.* **2** not having enough time to do something: *Sorry, I don't have time to do it now—I'm in a hurry.* in a hurry to do sth impatient to do something: *My daughter is in such a hurry to grow up.* ◆ *Why are you in such a hurry to sell?* in no hurry (to do sth) | not in a/any hurry (to do sth) **1** having plenty of time: *I don't mind waiting—I'm not in any particular hurry.* **2** not wanting or not willing to do something: *We were in no hurry to get back to work after the holiday.* sb will not do sth again in a hurry (*informal*) used to say that someone does not want to do something again because it was not so enjoyable: *I won't be going there again in a hurry—the food was terrible.*

hurt 🔑 /hərt/ *verb, adj., noun*
● *verb* (**hurt, hurt**) **1** [T, I] ~ *(sb/sth/yourself)* to cause physical pain to someone/yourself; to injure someone/yourself: *He hurt his back playing football.* ◆ *Did you hurt yourself?* ◆ *Stop it. You're hurting me.* ◆ *My back is really hurting me today.* ◆ *My shoes hurt—they're too tight.* ⊃ collocations at INJURY ⊃ thesaurus box at INJURE **2** [I] to feel painful: *My feet hurt.* ◆ *Ouch! That hurt!* ◆ *It hurts when I bend my knee.* **3** [I, T] to make someone unhappy or upset: *What really hurt was that he never answered my letter.* ◆ ~ *sb/sth I'm sorry, I didn't mean to hurt you.* ◆ *I didn't want to hurt his feelings.* ◆ it hurts (sb) to do sth *It hurt me to think that he would lie to me.* **4** [I] be hurting (*informal*) to feel unhappy or upset: *I know you're hurting and I want to help you.* **5** [T] ~ *sb/sth* to have a bad effect on someone or something: *Many people on low incomes will be hurt by the government's plans.* ⊃ thesaurus box at DAMAGE **6** [I] be hurting (for something) to be in a difficult situation because you need

something, especially money: *His campaign is already hurting for money.*
IDM it won't/wouldn't hurt (sb/sth) (to do sth) used to say that someone should do a particular thing: *It wouldn't hurt you to help with the housework occasionally.* not hurt a fly to be kind and gentle and unwilling to cause unhappiness ⊃ more at HIT
● *adj.* **1** injured physically: *None of the passengers was badly hurt.* **ANT** UNHURT **2** upset and offended by something that someone has said or done: *a hurt look/expression* ◆ *She was deeply hurt that she had not been invited.* ◆ *Martha's hurt pride showed in her eyes.*
● *noun* [U, sing.] a feeling of unhappiness because someone has been unkind or unfair to you: *There was hurt and real anger in her voice.* ◆ *It was a hurt that would take a long time to heal.*

THESAURUS

hurt

ache ◆ burn ◆ sting ◆ tingle ◆ itch ◆ throb

These are all words that can be used when part of your body feels painful.

hurt (of part of your body) to feel painful; (of an action) to cause pain: *My feet hurt.* ◆ *Stop it! That hurts!*
ache to feel a continuous dull pain: *I'm aching all over.*
burn (of part of your body) to feel very hot and painful: *Our eyes were burning from the chemicals in the air.*
sting to make someone feel a sharp burning pain or an uncomfortable feeling in part of their body; (of part of your body) to feel this pain: *My eyes were stinging from the smoke.*
tingle (of part of your body) to feel as if a lot of small sharp points are pushing into the skin there: *The cold air made her face tingle.*
itch to have an uncomfortable feeling on your skin that makes you want to scratch; to make your skin feel like this: *I itch all over.* ◆ *Does the rash itch?*
throb (of part of your body) to feel pain as a series of regular beats: *His head throbbed with pain.*

PATTERNS
■ your **eyes** hurt/ache/burn/sting/itch
■ your **skin** hurts/burns/stings/tingles/itches
■ your **flesh** hurts/burns/stings/tingles
■ your **head** hurts/aches/throbs
■ your **stomach** hurts/aches
■ to **really** hurt/ache/burn/sting/tingle/itch/throb
■ to hurt/ache/sting/itch badly/a lot
■ It hurts/stings/tingles/itches.

hurt·ful /'hərtfl/ *adj.* (of comments) making you feel upset and offended **SYN** UNKIND: *I cannot forget the hurtful things he said.* ◆ ~ to sb *The bad reviews of her new book were very hurtful to her.* ▶ **hurt·ful·ly** /-fəli/ *adv.*: *He said, rather hurtfully, that he had better things to do than come and see me.*

hur·tle /'hərtl/ *verb* [I] + *adv./prep.* to move very fast in a particular direction **SYN** CAREEN: *A runaway car came hurtling toward us.*

hus·band 🔑 /'hʌzbənd/ *noun, verb*
● *noun* (also *informal* hub·by) the man that a woman is married to; a married man: *This is my husband, Steve.* ⊃ collocations at MARRIAGE
IDM husband and wife a man and woman who are married to each other: *a husband-and-wife team*
● *verb* ~ *sth* (*formal*) to use something very carefully and make sure that you do not waste it

hus·band·ry /'hʌzbəndri/ *noun* **1** farming, especially when done carefully and well: *animal/crop husbandry* **2** (*old-fashioned*) the careful use of food, money, and supplies

---

| t tea | ṭ butter | d did | k cat | g got | tʃ chin | dʒ June | f fall |

hush /hʌʃ/ *verb, noun*

● *verb* **1** [I] (used especially in orders) to be quiet; to stop talking or crying: *Hush now and try to sleep.* **2** [T] ~ sb/sth to make someone or something become quieter; to make someone stop talking, crying, etc.

PHRV ˌhush sth↔ˈup to hide information about a situation because you do not want people to know about it: *He claimed that the whole affair had been hushed up by the government.*

● *noun* [sing., U] a period of silence, especially following a lot of noise, or when people are expecting something to happen: *There was **a deathly hush** in the theater.* ◆ *A hush descended over the waiting crowd.*

hushed /hʌʃt/ *adj.* **1** (of a place) quiet because nobody is talking; much quieter than usual: *A hushed courtroom listened as the boy gave evidence.* **2** [usually before noun] (of voices) speaking very quietly: *a hushed whisper*

ˌhush-ˈhush *adj.* (*informal*) secret and not known about by many people: *Their wedding was very hush-hush.*

ˈhush ˌmoney *noun* [U] money that is paid to someone to prevent them from giving other people information that could be embarrassing or damaging

ˈhush ˌpuppy *noun* a small fried cake made of CORNMEAL, eaten especially in the southern U.S.

husk /hʌsk/ *noun, verb*
● *noun* the dry outer covering of nuts, fruits, and seeds, especially of grain
● *verb* ~ sth to remove the husk from grain, seeds, nuts, etc.

husk·y /ˈhʌski/ *adj., noun*
● *adj.* (husk·i·er, husk·i·est) **1** (of a person or their voice) sounding deep, quiet, and rough, sometimes in an attractive way: *She spoke in a husky whisper.* **2** (of a man) big and strong ▶ **husk·i·ly** /-kəli/ *adv.* **husk·i·ness** /-kinəs/ *noun* [U]
● *noun* (also **hus·kie**) (*pl.* **husk·ies**) a large strong dog with thick hair, used for pulling SLEDS across snow

hus·sar /həˈzar/ *noun* (in the past) a CAVALRY soldier who carried light weapons

hus·sy /ˈhʌsi; -zi/ *noun* (*pl.* **hus·sies**) (*old-fashioned, disapproving*) a girl or woman who behaves in a way that is considered shocking or morally wrong

hust·ings /ˈhʌstɪŋz/ *noun* **the hustings** [pl.] the political meetings, speeches, etc. that take place in the period before an election: *Most candidates will be out **on the hustings** this week.*

hus·tle /ˈhʌsl/ *verb, noun*
● *verb* **1** [T] ~ sb + adv./prep. to make someone move quickly by pushing them in a rough and aggressive way: *He grabbed her arm and hustled her out of the room.* **2** [T] ~ sb (into sth) to force someone to make a decision before they are ready or sure **3** [T, I] ~ (sth) (*informal*) to sell or obtain something, often illegally: *to hustle dope* ◆ *They survive by hustling on the streets.* **4** [I] (*informal*) to act in an aggressive way or with a lot of energy **5** [I] to work as a PROSTITUTE
● *noun* **1** [U] busy noisy activity of a lot of people in one place: *We escaped from the **hustle and bustle** of the city for the weekend.* **2** [U] quick movement that uses a lot of energy and effort: *He forced a turnover with his hustle, diving after a loose ball.* **3** [C] (*informal*) a way of getting money that that is not honest: *He's tried every kind of hustle, from selling shoddy goods to dishonest gambling schemes.*

hus·tler /ˈhʌslər/ *noun* (*informal*) **1** a person who tries to trick someone into giving them money **2** a PROSTITUTE

hut /hʌt/ *noun* a small, simply built house or shelter: *a beach hut* ◆ *a wooden hut* ➷ picture at BUILDING

hutch /hʌtʃ/ *noun* **1** a wooden box with a front made of wire, used for keeping RABBITS or other small animals in **2** a large piece of wooden furniture with shelves in the top part and cupboards below, used for displaying and storing cups, plates, etc.

hy·a·cinth /ˈhaɪəsɪnθ/ *noun* a plant with a mass of small blue, white, or pink flowers with a sweet smell that grow closely together around a thick STEM

hy·brid /ˈhaɪbrɪd/ *noun* **1** an animal or plant that has parents of different SPECIES or varieties: *A mule is a hybrid of a male donkey and a female horse.* ➷ compare CROSS-BREED **2** ~ (between/of A and B) something that is the product of mixing two or more different things **SYN** MIXTURE: *The music was a hybrid of Western pop and traditional folk song.* **3** (also **hybrid car, hybrid vehicle**) a car that has both a gasoline engine and an electric motor and can run on either of these ▶ **hy·brid** *adj.*

hy·brid·ize /ˈhaɪbrəˌdaɪz/ *verb* [I, T] ~ (sth) (*technical*) if an animal or a plant **hybridizes** or **is hybridized** with an animal or a plant of another SPECIES, they join together to produce a hybrid ▶ **hy·brid·i·za·tion** /ˌhaɪbrədəˈzeɪʃn/ *noun* [U]

hy·dra /ˈhaɪdrə/ *noun* **1** Hydra (in ancient Greek stories) a snake with several heads. As one head was cut off, another one grew. In the end it was killed by Hercules. **2** (*formal*) a thing that is very difficult to deal with, because it continues for a long time or because it has many different aspects **3** (*biology*) an extremely small water creature with a body shaped like a tube and TENTACLES around its mouth

hy·dran·gea /haɪˈdreɪndʒə/ *noun* a bush with white, pink, or blue flowers that grow closely together in the shape of a large ball

hy·drant /ˈhaɪdrənt/ *noun* = FIRE HYDRANT

hy·drate /ˈhaɪdreɪt/ /haɪˈdreɪt/ *verb* ~ sth (*technical*) to make something absorb water ▶ **hy·dra·tion** /haɪˈdreɪʃn/ *noun* [U] ➷ compare DEHYDRATE

hy·drau·lic /haɪˈdrɔlɪk/ *adj.* [usually before noun] **1** (of water, oil, etc.) moved through pipes, etc. under pressure: *hydraulic fluid* **2** (of a piece of machinery) operated by liquid moving under pressure: *hydraulic brakes* **3** connected with hydraulic systems: *hydraulic engineering* ▶ **hy·drau·li·cally** /-kli/ *adv.*: *hydraulically operated doors*

hy·drau·lics /haɪˈdrɔlɪks/ *noun* **1** [pl.] machinery that works by the use of liquid moving under pressure **2** [U] the science of the use of liquids moving under pressure

hy·dro /ˈhaɪdroʊ/ *noun* [U] (*CanE*) electricity: *to pay your hydro bill*

hydro- /ˈhaɪdroʊ; -drə/ *combining form* (in nouns, adjectives, and adverbs) **1** connected with water **2** (*chemistry*) combined with HYDROGEN

hy·dro·car·bon /ˈhaɪdrəˌkɑrbən; ˌhaɪdrəˈkɑr-/ *noun* (*chemistry*) a chemical made up of HYDROGEN and CARBON only. There are many different hydrocarbons found in petroleum, coal, and natural gas.

hy·dro·chlo·ric ac·id /ˌhaɪdrəˌklɔrɪk ˈæsɪd/ *noun* [U] (*chemistry*) (*symb.* **HCl**) an acid containing HYDROGEN and CHLORINE

hy·dro·chlo·ro·fluor·o·car·bon /ˌhaɪdroʊˌklɔrouˈflɔrəˌkɑrbən; -ˈflʊrə-/ *noun* (*chemistry*) = HCFC

hy·dro·cor·ti·sone /ˌhaɪdrəˈkɔrtəˌsoʊn; -ˌzoʊn/ *noun* [U] a HORMONE produced in the body that is used in drugs to help with diseases of the skin and muscles

hy·dro·e·lec·tric /ˌhaɪdroʊɪˈlɛktrɪk/ *adj.* using the power of water to produce electricity; produced by the power of water: *a hydroelectric plant* ◆ *hydroelectric power* ▶ **hy·dro·e·lec·tric·i·ty** /-ɪˌlɛkˈtrɪsəti/ *noun* [U]

hy·dro·fluor·o·car·bon /ˌhaɪdroʊˈflɔrəˌkɑrbən; -ˈflʊrə-/ *noun* (*chemistry*) = HFC

hy·dro·foil /ˈhaɪdrəˌfɔɪl/ *noun* a boat which rises above the surface of the water when it is traveling fast ➷ picture at BOAT ➷ compare HOVERCRAFT

hy·dro·gen /ˈhaɪdrədʒən/ *noun* [U] (*symb.* **H**) a chemical element. Hydrogen is a gas that is the lightest of all the elements. It combines with OXYGEN to form water.

hy·dro·ge·nat·ed /haɪˈdrɑdʒəˌneɪtəd; ˈhaɪdrədʒə-/ *adj.* (*chemistry*) **hydrogenated** oils have had hydrogen added to them

hydrogen 'bomb (also **'H-bomb**) *noun* a very powerful nuclear bomb

hydrogen per'oxide *noun* [U] (*symb.* **H₂O₂**) (*chemistry*) = PEROXIDE

hy·drol·o·gy /haɪˈdrɑlədʒi/ *noun* [U] (*technical*) the scientific study of the earth's water, especially its movement in relation to land

hy·drol·y·sis /haɪˈdrɑləsəs/ *noun* [U] (*chemistry*) a reaction with water which causes a COMPOUND to separate into its parts

hy·dro·pho·bi·a /ˌhaɪdrəˈfoubiə/ *noun* [U] extreme fear of water, which happens with RABIES infection in humans ▶ **hy·dro·pho·bic** /-ˈfoubɪk/ *adj.*

hy·dro·plane /ˈhaɪdrəˌpleɪn/ *noun, verb*
• *noun* **1** a light boat with an engine and a flat bottom, designed to travel fast over the surface of water
2 = SEAPLANE
• *verb* (of a motor vehicle) to slide out of control on a wet road

hy·dro·plan·ing /ˈhaɪdrəˌpleɪnɪŋ/ *noun* [U] the fact of a vehicle sliding on a wet surface, so that it is out of control

hy·dro·pon·ics /ˌhaɪdrəˈpɑnɪks/ *noun* [U] the process of growing plants in water or sand, rather than in soil

hy·dro·ther·a·py /ˌhaɪdrəˈθɛrəpi/ *noun* [U] the treatment of disease or injury by doing physical exercises in water

hy·drox·ide /haɪˈdrɑksaɪd/ *noun* (*chemistry*) a chemical consisting of a metal and a combination of OXYGEN and HYDROGEN

hy·e·na /haɪˈinə/ *noun* a wild animal like a dog, that eats the meat of animals that are already dead and has a cry like a human laugh. Hyenas live in Africa and Asia.

hy·giene /ˈhaɪdʒin/ *noun* [U] the practice of keeping yourself and your living and working areas clean in order to prevent illness and disease: *food hygiene* ◆ *personal hygiene* ◆ *In the interests of hygiene, please wash your hands.*

hy·gien·ic /haɪˈdʒɛnɪk; -ˈdʒinɪk; ˌhaɪdʒiˈɛnɪk/ *adj.* clean and free of bacteria and therefore unlikely to spread disease: *Food must be prepared in hygienic conditions.*
ANT UNHYGIENIC ▶ **hy·gien·i·cally** /-kli/ *adv.*: *Medical supplies are disposed of hygienically.*

hy·gien·ist /haɪˈdʒɛnɪst; -ˈdʒinɪst; ˈhaɪdʒinɪst/ *noun* = DENTAL HYGIENIST

hy·men /ˈhaɪmən/ *noun* (*anatomy*) a piece of skin that partly covers the opening of the VAGINA in women who have never had sex

hymn /hɪm/ *noun* **1** a song of praise, especially one praising God and sung by Christians **2** [usually sing.] if a movie, book, etc. is a **hymn to something**, it praises it very strongly

'hymn book (also *old-fashioned* **hym·nal** /ˈhɪmnəl/) *noun* a book of hymns

hype /haɪp/ *noun, verb*
• *noun* [U] (*informal, disapproving*) advertisements and discussion on television, radio, etc. telling the public about a product and about how good or important it is: *marketing/media hype* ◆ *Don't believe all the hype—the book isn't that good.*
• *verb* (*informal, disapproving*) to advertise something a lot and exaggerate its good qualities, in order to get a lot of public attention for it: ~ **sth** *This week his much hyped new movie opens nationwide.* ◆ ~ **sth up** *The meeting was hyped up in the media as an important event.*

hyped 'up *adj.* (*informal*) (of a person) very worried or excited about something that is going to happen

hy·per /ˈhaɪpər/ *adj.* (*informal*) excited and nervous; having too much nervous energy

hyper- /ˈhaɪpər/ *prefix* (in adjectives and nouns) more than normal; too much: *hypercritical* ◆ *hypertension* ⊃ compare HYPO-

hy·per·ac·tive /ˌhaɪpərˈæktɪv/ *adj.* (especially of children and their behavior) too active and only able to keep quiet and still for short periods ▶ **hy·per·ac·tiv·i·ty** /-ækˈtɪvəti/ *noun* [U]

hy·per·bar·ic /ˌhaɪpərˈbɛrɪk; -ˈbær-/ *adj.* (*physics*) (of gas) at a higher pressure than normal

hy·per·bo·la /haɪˈpərbələ/ *noun* (*pl.* **hy·per·bo·las** or **hy·per·bo·lae** /-li/) a SYMMETRICAL open curve ⊃ picture at SHAPE

hy·per·bo·le /haɪˈpərbəli/ *noun* [U, C, usually sing.] a way of speaking or writing that makes something sound better, more exciting, dangerous, etc. than it really is
SYN EXAGGERATION

hy·per·bol·ic /ˌhaɪpərˈbɑlɪk/ *adj.* **1** (*mathematics*) of or related to a hyperbola **2** (of language) deliberately exaggerated; using hyperbole

hy·per·cor·rec·tion /ˌhaɪpərkəˈrɛkʃn/ *noun* [U, C] (*linguistics*) the use of a wrong form or pronunciation of a word by someone who is trying to show that they can use language correctly, for example, the use of *I* instead of *me* in the sentence "They invited my husband and I to dinner."

hy·per·gly·ce·mi·a /ˌhaɪpərglaɪˈsimiə/ *noun* [U] (*medical*) the condition of having too high a level of blood sugar

hy·per·in·fla·tion /ˌhaɪpərɪnˈfleɪʃn/ *noun* [U] a situation in which prices rise very fast, causing damage to a country's economy

hy·per·link /ˈhaɪpərˌlɪŋk/ (also **'hot link, link**) *noun* a place in an electronic document on a computer that is linked to another electronic document: *Click on the hyperlink.*

hy·per·me·di·a /ˈhaɪpərˌmidiə/ *noun* [U] (*computing*) a system that links text to files containing images, sound, or video

hy·per·nym /ˈhaɪpərnɪm/ *noun* (*linguistics*) = SUPERORDINATE ⊃ compare HYPONYM

hy·per·sen·si·tive /ˌhaɪpərˈsɛnsətɪv/ *adj.* ~ **(to sth) 1** very easily offended: *He's hypersensitive to any kind of criticism.* **2** extremely physically sensitive to particular substances, medicines, light, etc.: *Her skin is hypersensitive.* ▶ **hy·per·sen·si·tiv·i·ty** /-ˌsɛnsəˈtɪvəti/ *noun* [U]

hy·per·space /ˈhaɪpərˌspeɪs/ *noun* [U] **1** (*technical*) space which consists of more than three DIMENSIONS **2** (in stories) a situation in which it is possible to travel faster than light

hy·per·ten·sion /ˌhaɪpərˈtɛnʃn/ *noun* [U] (*medical*) blood pressure that is higher than is normal

hy·per·text /ˈhaɪpərˌtɛkst/ *noun* [U] text stored in a computer system that contains links that allow the user to move from one piece of text or document to another ⊃ see also HTML

hy·per·thy·roid·ism /ˌhaɪpərˈθaɪrɔɪˌdɪzəm/ *noun* [U] (*medical*) a condition in which the THYROID is too active, making the heart and other body systems function too quickly

hy·per·tro·phy /haɪˈpərtrəfi/ *noun* [U] (*biology*) an increase in the size of an organ or TISSUE because its cells grow in size

hy·per·ven·ti·late /ˌhaɪpərˈvɛntəˌleɪt/ *verb* [I] (*technical*) to breathe too quickly because you are very frightened or excited ▶ **hy·per·ven·ti·la·tion** /-ˌvɛntəˈleɪʃn/ *noun* [U]

hy·phen /ˈhaɪfn/ *noun* the mark (-) used to join two words together to make a new one, as in *knee-length*, or to show that a word has been divided between the end of one line and the beginning of the next ⊃ compare DASH

hy·phen·ate /ˈhaɪfəˌneɪt/ *verb* ~ **sth** to join two words together using a hyphen; to divide a word between two lines of text using a hyphen: *Is your name hyphenated?* ▶ **hy·phen·a·tion** /ˌhaɪfəˈneɪʃn/ *noun* [U]: *hyphenation rules*

hyp·no·sis /hɪpˈnoʊsəs/ *noun* [U] **1** an unconscious state in which someone can still see and hear and can be influenced to follow commands or answer questions: *She only remembered details of the accident* **under hypnosis**. **2** = HYPNOTISM: *He uses hypnosis as part of the treatment.* ◆ *Hypnosis helped me give up smoking.*

---

h **hat**   m **man**   n **no**   ŋ **sing**   1 **leg**   r **red**   y **yes**   w **wet**

hyp·no·ther·a·py /ˌhɪpnoʊˈθɛrəpi/ *noun* [U] a kind of treatment that uses hypnosis to help with physical or emotional problems

hyp·not·ic /hɪpˈnɑtɪk/ *adj.*, *noun*

● *adj.* **1** making you feel as if you are going to fall asleep, especially because of a regular, repeated noise or movement **SYN** SOPORIFIC: *hypnotic music* ◆ *His voice had an almost hypnotic effect.* **2** [only before noun] connected with or produced by hypnosis: *a hypnotic trance/state* **3** (of a drug) making you sleep

● *noun* (*technical*) a drug that makes you sleep; a SLEEPING PILL

hyp·no·tism /ˈhɪpnəˌtɪzəm/ (also **hyp·no·sis**) *noun* [U] the practice of hypnotizing a person (= putting them into an unconscious state)

hyp·no·tist /ˈhɪpnətɪst/ *noun* a person who hypnotizes people

hyp·no·tize /ˈhɪpnəˌtaɪz/ *verb* **1** ~ sb to produce a state of HYPNOSIS in someone **2** [usually passive] ~ sb (*formal*) to interest someone so much that they can think of nothing else **SYN** MESMERIZE

hypo- /ˈhaɪpoʊ; -pə/ (also **hyp-**) *prefix* (in adjectives and nouns) under; below normal: *hypodermic* ◆ *hypothermia* ⊃ compare HYPER-

hy·po·al·ler·gen·ic /ˌhaɪpoʊˌælərˈdʒɛnɪk/ *adj.* (*technical*) hypoallergenic substances and materials are unlikely to cause an ALLERGIC reaction in the person who uses them

hy·po·chon·dri·a /ˌhaɪpəˈkɑndriə/ *noun* [U] a state in which someone worries all the time about their health and believes that they are sick when there is nothing wrong with them

hy·po·chon·dri·ac /ˌhaɪpəˈkɑndriˌæk/ *noun* a person who suffers from hypochondria: *Don't be such a hypochondriac!—there's nothing wrong with you.* ▶ **hy·po·chon·dri·ac** (also **hy·po·chon·dri·a·cal** /ˌhaɪpəkənˈdraɪəkl/) *adj.*

hy·poc·ri·sy /hɪˈpɑkrəsi/ *noun* (*pl.* **hypocrisies**) [U, C] (*disapproving*) behavior in which someone pretends to have moral standards or opinions that they do not actually have: *He condemned the hypocrisy of those politicians who do one thing and say another.*

hyp·o·crite /ˈhɪpəˌkrɪt/ *noun* (*disapproving*) a person who pretends to have moral standards or opinions that they do not actually have ▶ **hyp·o·crit·i·cal** /ˌhɪpəˈkrɪtɪkl/ *adj.*: *It would be hypocritical of me to have a church wedding when I don't believe in God.* **hyp·o·crit·i·cal·ly** /-kli/ *adv.*

hy·po·der·mic /ˌhaɪpəˈdərmɪk/ (also ˌhypodermic 'needle, ˌhypodermic sy'ringe) *noun* a medical instrument with a long thin needle that is used to give someone an INJECTION under their skin ▶ **hypodermic** *adj.*: *a hypodermic injection* (= one under the skin)

hy·po·gly·ce·mi·a /ˌhaɪpoʊɡlaɪˈsimiə/ *noun* [U] (*medical*) the condition of having too low a level of blood sugar

hy·po·nym /ˈhaɪpənɪm/ *noun* (*linguistics*) a word with a particular meaning that is included in the meaning of a more general word, for example "dog" and "cat" are hyponyms of "animal" ⊃ compare HYPERNYM, SUPERORDINATE

hy·po·tax·is /ˌhaɪpoʊˈtæksəs/ *noun* [U] (*grammar*) the use of SUBORDINATE CLAUSE s ⊃ compare PARATAXIS

hy·pot·e·nuse /haɪˈpɑtnˌus/ *noun* (*geometry*) the side opposite the RIGHT ANGLE of a RIGHT-ANGLED triangle ⊃ picture at SHAPE

hy·po·thal·a·mus /ˌhaɪpəˈθæləməs/ *noun* (*anatomy*) an area in the central lower part of the brain that controls body temperature, HUNGER, and the release of HORMONES

hy·po·ther·mi·a /ˌhaɪpəˈθərmiə/ *noun* [U] a medical condition in which the body temperature is much lower than normal

hy·poth·e·sis **AWL** /haɪˈpɑθəsəs/ *noun* (*pl.* **hy·poth·e·ses** /-siz/) **1** [C] an idea or explanation of something that is based on a few known facts but that has not yet been proved to be true or correct **SYN** THEORY: *to formulate/confirm a hypothesis* ◆ *a hypothesis about the function of dreams* ⊃ collocations at SCIENTIFIC **2** [U] guesses and ideas that are not based on certain knowledge **SYN** SPECULATION: *It would be pointless to engage in hypothesis before we have the facts.*

hy·poth·e·size **AWL** /haɪˈpɑθəˌsaɪz/ *verb* [T, I] ~ (sth) | ~ that... (*formal*) to suggest a way of explaining something when you do not definitely know about it; to form a hypothesis

hy·po·thet·i·cal **AWL** /ˌhaɪpəˈθɛtɪkl/ *adj.* based on situations or ideas that are possible and imagined rather than real and true: *a hypothetical question/situation/example* ◆ *Let us take the hypothetical case of Sheila, a mother of two...* ◆ *I wasn't asking about anybody in particular—it was a purely hypothetical question.* ▶ **hy·po·thet·i·cally** **AWL** /-kli/ *adv.*

hy·po·thy·roid·ism /ˌhaɪpoʊˈθaɪrɔɪˌdɪzəm/ *noun* [U] (*medical*) a condition in which the THYROID is not active enough, making growth and mental development slower than normal

hy·pox·e·mi·a /ˌhaɪpɑkˈsimiə/ *noun* [U] (*medical*) a lower than normal amount of OXYGEN in the blood

hy·pox·i·a /haɪˈpɑksiə/ *noun* [U] (*medical*) a condition in which not enough OXYGEN reaches the body's TISSUES

hys·ter·ec·to·my /ˌhɪstəˈrɛktəmi/ *noun* (*pl.* **hys·ter·ec·to·mies**) [C, U] a medical operation to remove a woman's UTERUS

hys·te·ri·a /hɪˈstɛriə; -ˈstɪr-/ *noun* [U] **1** a state of extreme excitement, fear, or anger in which a person, or a group of people, loses control of their emotions and starts to cry, laugh, etc.: *There was mass hysteria when the band came on stage.* ◆ *A note of hysteria crept into her voice.* **2** (*disapproving*) an extremely excited and exaggerated way of behaving or reacting to an event: *the usual media hysteria that surrounds royal visits* ◆ *public hysteria about AIDS* **3** (*medical*) a condition in which someone experiences violent or extreme emotions that they cannot control, especially as a result of shock

hys·ter·i·cal /hɪˈstɛrɪkl/ *adj.* **1** in a state of extreme excitement, and crying, laughing, etc. in an uncontrolled way: *hysterical screams* ◆ *a hysterical giggle* ◆ *He became almost hysterical when I told him.* ◆ *Let's not get hysterical.* ◆ (*disapproving*) *He thought I was being a hysterical female.* **2** (*informal*) extremely funny **SYN** HILARIOUS: *She seemed to find my situation absolutely hysterical.* ▶ **hys·ter·i·cally** /-kli/ *adv.*: *to laugh/cry/scream/sob hysterically* ◆ *hysterically funny*

hys·ter·ics /hɪˈstɛrɪks/ *noun* [pl.] **1** an expression of extreme fear, excitement, or anger that makes someone lose control of their emotions and cry, laugh, etc.: *He went into hysterics when he heard the news.* **2** (*informal*) wild LAUGHTER: *She had the audience in hysterics.* **IDM** have hysterics (*informal*) to be extremely upset and angry: *My mom'll have hysterics when she sees the color of my hair.*

Hz *abbr.* (in writing) HERTZ

I i

I /aɪ/ *noun, pron., abbr., symbol*

- **noun** also **i** [C, U] (*pl.* **Is, I's, i's** /aɪz/) the 9th letter of the English alphabet: *"Island" begins with (an) I/"I."* **IDM** see DOT
- **pron.** used as the subject of a verb when the speaker or writer is referring to himself/herself: *I think I'd better go now.* ◆ *He and I are old friends.* ◆ *When they asked me if I wanted the job, I said yes.* ◆ *I'm not going to fall, am I?* ◆ *I'm taller than her, aren't I?* ⊃ see also ME
- **abbr.** (also **I.**) **1** (especially on maps) Island(s); ISLE(S) **2** INTERSTATE: *You can take I 95 all the way from Maine to Florida.*
- **symbol** also **i** the number 1 in ROMAN NUMERAL S

i- /aɪ/ *combining form* (in the names of products) (*computing*) INTERACTIVE (= allowing information to be passed continuously and in both directions between a computer and the person who uses it): *The i-Writer teaches you how to plan and write essays.*

I-9 form /ˌaɪ ˈnaɪn fɔrm/ *noun* an official document that an employer must have that shows that an employee has the right to work in the U.S.

IA *abbr.* (in writing) Iowa

-ial /iəl/ *suffix* (in adjectives) typical of: *dictatorial* ▸ **-ially** /iəli/ (in adverbs): *officially*

i·am·bic /aɪˈæmbɪk/ *adj.* (*technical*) (of rhythm in poetry) in which one weak or short syllable is followed by one strong or long syllable: *a poem written in iambic pentameters* (= in lines of ten syllables, five short and five long)

i·am·bus /aɪˈæmbəs/ *noun* (*pl.* **i·am·bi** /-baɪ/, **i·am·bus·es**) (also **i·amb** /ˈaɪæm; ˈaɪæmb/) (*technical*) a unit of sound in poetry consisting of one weak or short syllable followed by one strong or long syllable

-ian /iən/, **-an** *suffix* **1** (in nouns and adjectives) from; typical of: *Bostonian* ◆ *Brazilian* ◆ *Shakespearian* ◆ *Libran* **2** (in nouns) a specialist in: *mathematician*

-iana /iˈænə; iˈɑnə/, **-ana** *suffix* (in nouns) a collection of objects, facts, stories, etc. connected with the person, place, period, etc. mentioned: *Mozartiana* ◆ *Americana* ◆ *Victoriana*

IB /ˌaɪ ˈbi/ *abbr.* INTERNATIONAL BACCALAUREATE™: *to do the IB*

I·be·ri·an /aɪˈbɪriən/ *adj.* relating to Spain and Portugal: *the Iberian peninsula*

i·bex /ˈaɪbɛks/ *noun* (*pl.* **i·bex**) a mountain GOAT with long curved horns

ibid. /ˈɪbɪd/ (also **ib.**) *abbr.* in the same book or piece of writing as the one that has just been mentioned (from Latin "ibidem")

-ibility /əˈbɪləti/ ⊃ -ABLE

i·bis /ˈaɪbəs/ *noun* (*pl.* **i·bis·es**) a bird with a long neck, long legs, and a long beak that curves downward, that lives near water

-ible /əbl/, **-ibly** ⊃ -ABLE

I·bo /ˈiboʊ/ *noun* = IGBO

i·bu·pro·fen /ˌaɪbyuˈproʊfɛn; ˌaɪbyʊˈproʊfən/ *noun* [U] a drug used to reduce pain and INFLAMMATION

-ic /ɪk/ *suffix* **1** (in adjectives and nouns) connected with: *scenic* ◆ *economic* ◆ *Arabic* **2** (in adjectives) that performs the action mentioned: *horrific* ◆ *specific* ▸ **-ical** /ɪkl/ (in adjectives): *comical* **-ically** /ɪkli/ (in adverbs): *physically*

ice /aɪs/ *noun, verb*

- **noun 1** [U] water that has frozen and become solid: *There was ice on the windows.* ◆ *The lake was covered with a **sheet of ice**.* ◆ *My hands are as cold as ice.* ⊃ see also BLACK ICE, DRY ICE, ICY **2** [sing.] usually **the ice** a frozen surface that people SKATE on: *The dancers came out onto the ice.* ◆ *Both teams are on the ice, waiting for the whistle.* **3** [U] a piece of ice used to keep food and drinks cold: *I'll have lemonade please—no ice.* **4** [U] a type of sweet food that consists of ice that has been crushed and flavored
  IDM **break the ice** to say or do something that makes people feel more relaxed, especially at the beginning of a meeting, party, etc. ⊃ see also ICEBREAKER **cut no ice (with sb)** to have no influence or effect on someone: *His excuses cut no ice with me.* **on ice 1** (of wine, etc.) kept cold by being surrounded by ice **2** (of a plan, etc.) not being dealt with now; waiting to be dealt with at a later time: *We've had to **put** our plans **on ice** for the time being.* **3** (of entertainment, etc.) performed by SKATERS on an ICE RINK: *Cinderella on ice* ⊃ more at THIN
- **verb ~ sth** to cover a cake with ICING
  PHR V **ice 'over/'up** | **ice sth↔'over/'up** to cover something with ice; to become covered with ice

ice age often **the Ice Age** *noun* one of the long periods of time, thousands of years ago, when much of the earth's surface was covered in ice

ice ax *noun* a tool used by people climbing mountains for cutting steps into ice

ice bag *noun* = ICE PACK

ice·berg /ˈaɪsbərg/ *noun* an extremely large mass of ice floating in the ocean **IDM** see TIP *n.*

iceberg 'lettuce *noun* a type of LETTUCE (= a salad vegetable) with crisp, pale green leaves that form a tight ball

ice-'blue *adj.* (especially of eyes) very pale blue in color

ice·bound /ˈaɪsbaʊnd/ *adj.* surrounded by or covered in ice

ice·box /ˈaɪsbɑks/ *noun* **1** a cabinet with a place to put a block of ice, used in the past to keep food cold **2** (*old-fashioned*) a refrigerator

ice·break·er /ˈaɪsˌbreɪkər/ *noun* **1** a strong ship designed to break a way through ice, for example in the Arctic or Antarctic **2** a thing that you do or say, like a game or a joke, to make people feel less nervous when they first meet

ice bucket *noun* a container filled with ice and used for keeping bottles of wine, etc. cold

ice cap *noun* a layer of ice permanently covering parts of the earth, especially around the North and South Poles

ice chest *noun* a box with thick sides that you put ice in to keep things cold, especially food and drinks: *Put the soda cans in the ice chest.*

ice-'cold *adj.* **1** as cold as ice; very cold: *ice-cold beer* ◆ *My hands were ice-cold.* **2** not having or showing any emotion: *His eyes had grown ice-cold.*

ice 'cream *noun* [U, C]
a type of sweet frozen food made from milk fat, flavored with fruit, chocolate, etc. and often eaten as a DESSERT; a small amount of this food intended for one person, often served in a CONE: *Desserts are served with cream or ice cream.* ◆ *Who wants an ice cream?*

ice cube *noun* a small, usually square, piece of ice used for making drinks cold

iced /aɪst/ *adj.* **1** (of drinks) made very cold; containing ice: *iced coffee/tea* **2** (of a cake, etc.) covered with ICING: *an iced cake*

ice dancing (also **ice dance**) *noun* [U] the sport of dancing on ice ▸ **ice dancer** *noun*

ice field *noun* a large area of ice, especially one near the North or South Pole

ice floe (also **floe**) *noun* a large area of ice, floating in the ocean

---

ʌ **cup** ə **about** eɪ **say** aɪ **five** ɔɪ **boy** aʊ **now** oʊ **go** ər **bird**

ice hockey noun [U] = HOCKEY

ice house noun a building for storing ice in, especially in the past, usually underground or partly underground

ice pack (also **ice bag**) noun a plastic container filled with ice that is used to cool parts of the body that are injured, etc.

ice pick noun a tool with a very sharp point for breaking ice with

ice rink (also **skating rink, rink**) noun a specially prepared flat surface of ice, where you can ice-skate; a building where there is an ice rink ⟳ picture at HOBBY, SPORT

ice sheet noun (technical) a layer of ice that covers a large area of land for a long period of time

ice shelf noun (technical) a layer of ice that is attached to land and covers a large area of ocean

ice skate (also **skate**) noun a boot with a thin metal blade on the bottom, that is used for SKATING on ice

ice-skate verb [I] to SKATE on ice ▶ **ice skater** noun

ice skating noun [U] the sport or activity of SKATING on ice: to go ice skating ⟳ picture at HOBBY

ice water noun water with ice in it for drinking

i·ci·cle /ˈaɪsɪkl/ noun a pointed piece of ice that is formed when water freezes as it falls down from something such as a roof

i·ci·ly /ˈaɪsəli/ adv. said or done in a very unfriendly way: "I have nothing to say to you," she said icily.

ic·ing /ˈaɪsɪŋ/ noun [U] a sweet mixture of sugar and water, milk, or egg white that is used to cover and decorate cakes **SYN** FROSTING **IDM** see CAKE n.

icing sugar (CanE) noun [U] fine white powder made from sugar, that is mixed with water to make icing

ick·y /ˈɪki/ adj. (informal) unpleasant (used especially about something that is wet and sticky)

i·con /ˈaɪkɑn/ noun **1** (computing) a small symbol on a computer screen that represents a program or a file: Click on the printer icon with the mouse. **2** a famous person or thing that people admire and see as a symbol of a particular idea, way of life, etc.: Madonna and other pop icons of the 1980s ◆ a feminist/gay icon (= someone that feminists/gay people admire) **3** (also **i·kon**) (in the Orthodox Church) a painting or statue of a holy person that is also thought of as a holy object

i·con·ic /aɪˈkɑnɪk/ adj. acting as a sign or symbol of something

i·con·o·clast /aɪˈkɑnəˌklæst/ noun (formal) a person who criticizes popular beliefs or established customs and ideas

i·con·o·clas·tic /aɪˌkɑnəˈklæstɪk/ adj. (formal) criticizing popular beliefs or established customs and ideas ▶ **i·con·o·clasm** /aɪˈkɑnəˌklæzəm/ noun [U]: the iconoclasm of the early Christians

i·co·nog·ra·phy /ˌaɪkəˈnɑɡrəfi/ noun [U] the use or study of images or symbols in art

i·co·nol·o·gy /ˌaɪkəˈnɑlədʒi/ noun [U] the fact of a work of art being an image or symbol of something

–ics /ɪks/ suffix (in nouns) the science, art, or activity of: physics ◆ dramatics ◆ athletics

ICU /ˌaɪ si ˈyu/ abbr. intensive care unit (in a hospital)

i·cy /ˈaɪsi/ adj. (i·ci·er, i·ci·est) **1** very cold **SYN** FREEZING: icy winds/water ◆ My feet were icy cold. **2** covered with ice: icy roads **3** (of a person's voice, manner, etc.) not friendly or kind; showing feelings of dislike or anger: My eyes met his icy gaze. ⟳ see also ICILY ▶ **i·ci·ness** noun [U]

ID /ˌaɪ ˈdi/ noun, verb, abbr.
● **noun 1** [U, C] the abbreviation for "identification" or "identity" (an official way of showing who you are, for example a document with your name, date of birth, and often a photograph on it): You must carry ID at all times. ◆ The police checked IDs at the gate. ◆ an ID card **2** [C]IDENTIFICA-TION: The police need a witness to make a positive ID. ⟳ see also CALLER ID
● **verb** (ID's, ID'ing, ID'd, ID'd) (informal) = IDENTIFY

● **abbr.** (in writing) Idaho

Id = EID

id /ɪd/ noun (psychology) the part of the unconscious mind where many of a person's basic needs, feelings, and desires are supposed to exist ⟳ compare EGO, SUPEREGO

I'd /aɪd/ short form **1** I had **2** I would

I'D card noun the abbreviation for "identification card" or "identity card" (a card with a person's name, date of birth, photograph, etc. on it that proves who they are)

–ide /aɪd/ suffix (chemistry) (in nouns) a COMPOUND of: chloride

i·de·a 🔊 /aɪˈdiə/ noun
▷ PLAN/THOUGHT **1** [C] a plan, thought, or suggestion, especially about what to do in a particular situation: It would be a good idea to call before we leave. ◆ ~ (of sth/of doing sth) I like the idea of living on a boat. ◆ ~ (for sth) He already had an idea for his next novel. ◆ Her family expected her to go to college, but she had other ideas. ◆ The surprise party was Jane's idea. ◆ It might be an idea (= it would be sensible) to try again later. ◆ We've been toying with the idea of (= thinking about) getting a dog. ◆ It seemed like a good idea at the time, and then it all went horribly wrong. ◆ The latest big idea is to make women more interested in sports.
▷ IMPRESSION **2** [U, sing.] ~ (of sth) a picture or an impression in your mind of what someone or something is like: The brochure should give you a good idea of the hotel. ◆ I had some idea of what the job would be like. ◆ She doesn't seem to have any idea of what I'm talking about. ◆ I don't want anyone getting the wrong idea (= getting the wrong impression about something). ◆ A night at home watching TV is not my idea of a good time.
▷ OPINION **3** [C] ~ (about sth) an opinion or a belief about something: He has some very strange ideas about education.
▷ FEELING **4** [sing.] ~ (that…) a feeling that something is possible: What gave you the idea that he'd be here? ◆ I have a pretty good idea where I left it—I hope I'm right.
▷ AIM **5** the idea [sing.] ~ of sth/of doing sth the aim or purpose of something: You'll soon get the idea (= understand). ◆ What's the idea of the game? ⟳ thesaurus box at PURPOSE
IDM give sb ideas | put ideas into sb's head to give someone hopes about something that may not be possible or likely; to make someone act or think in an unreasonable way: Who's been putting ideas into his head? have no idea | not have the faintest, first, etc. idea (informal) used to emphasize that you do not know something: "What's she talking about?" "I have no idea." ◆ He hasn't the faintest idea how to manage people. have the right idea to have found a very good or successful way of living, doing something, etc.: He's certainly got the right idea—retiring at 55. that's an idea! (informal) used to reply in a positive way to a suggestion that someone has made: Hey, that's an idea! And we could get a band, as well. that's the idea! (informal) used to encourage people and to tell them that they are doing something right: That's the idea! You're doing great. you have no idea… (informal) used to show that something is hard for someone else to imagine: You have no idea how much traffic there was tonight.

i·de·al 🔊 /aɪˈdiəl/ adj., noun
● **adj. 1** ~ (for sth) perfect; most suitable: This beach is ideal for children. ◆ She's the ideal candidate for the job. ◆ The trip to Paris will be an ideal opportunity to practice my French. **2** [only before noun] existing only in your imagination or as an idea; not likely to be real: the search for ideal love ◆ In an ideal world there would be no poverty and disease. ▶ **i·de·al·ly** /aɪˈdiəli/ adv.: She's ideally suited for this job. ◆ Ideally, I'd like to live in New York, but that's not possible.
● **noun 1** [C] an idea or standard that seems perfect, and worth trying to achieve or obtain: political ideals ◆ She found it hard to live up to his high ideals. **2** [C, usually sing.] ~ (of sth) a person or thing that you think is perfect: It's my ideal of what a family home should be.

i·de·al·ism /aɪˈdiəˌlɪzəm/ noun [U] **1** the belief that a perfect life, situation, etc. can be achieved, even when this is not very likely: *He was full of youthful idealism.* **2** (*philosophy*) the belief that our ideas are the only things that are real and that we can know about ⭢ compare MATERIALISM, REALISM ▶ **i·de·al·ist** /-lɪst/ *noun: He's too much of an idealist for this government.*

i·de·al·is·tic /ˌaɪdiəˈlɪstɪk; aɪˌdiə-/ *adj.* having a strong belief in perfect standards and trying to achieve them, even when this is not realistic: *She's still young and idealistic.* ▶ **i·de·al·is·ti·cally** /-kli/ *adv.*

i·de·al·ize /aɪˈdiəˌlaɪz/ *verb* ~ sb/sth to consider or represent someone or something as being perfect or better than they really are: *It is tempting to idealize the past.* ◆ *an idealized view of married life* ▶ **i·de·al·i·za·tion** /aɪˌdiələˈzeɪʃn/ *noun* [U, C]

i·de·ate /ˈaɪdiˌeɪt/ *verb* (*formal*) **1** [T] ~ sth to form an idea of something; to imagine something **2** [I] to form ideas; to think ▶ **i·de·a·tion** /ˌaɪdiˈeɪʃn/ *noun* [U]

i·dée fixe /ˌideɪ ˈfiks/ *noun* (*pl.* **idées fixes** /ˌideɪ ˈfiks/) (from *French*) an idea or desire that is so strong you cannot think about anything else

i·dem /ˈɪdem; ˈaɪ-/ *adv.* (from *Latin*) from the same book, article, author, etc. as the one that has just been mentioned

i·den·ti·cal AWL /aɪˈdentɪkl/ *adj.* **1** similar in every detail: *a row of identical houses* ◆ *The two pictures are similar, although not identical.* ◆ ~ with sb/sth *Her dress is almost identical to mine.* ◆ ~ with sb/sth *The number on the card should be identical with the one on the checkbook.* ⭢ language bank at SIMILARLY **2** the identical [only before noun] the same: *This is the identical room we stayed in last year.* ▶ **i·den·ti·cally** AWL /-kli/ *adv.: The children were dressed identically.*

i·dentical 'twin (also *technical* **mon·o·zy·got·ic twin**) *noun* either of two children or animals born from the same mother at the same time who have developed from a single egg. Identical twins are of the same sex and look very similar. ⭢ compare DIZYGOTIC TWIN, FRATERNAL TWIN

i·den·ti·fi·a·ble AWL /aɪˌdentəˈfaɪəbl; aɪˈdentəˌfaɪ-/ *adj.* that can be recognized: *identifiable characteristics* ◆ *The house is easily identifiable by the large tree outside.* ANT UNIDENTIFIABLE ⭢ collocations at IDENTIFY

i·den·ti·fi·ca·tion AWL /aɪˌdentəfəˈkeɪʃn/ *noun* **1** [U, C] (*abbr.* ID) the process of showing, proving, or recognizing who or what someone or something is: *The identification of the crash victims was a long and difficult task.* ◆ *Each product has a number for easy identification.* ◆ *an identification number* ◆ *Only one witness could make a positive identification.* ⭢ collocations at IDENTIFY **2** [U] the process of recognizing that something exists, or is important: *The early identification of children with special educational needs is very important.* **3** (*abbr.* ID) [U] official papers or a document that can prove who you are: *Can I see some identification, please?* **4** [U, C] ~ (with sb/sth) a strong feeling of sympathy, understanding, or support for someone or something: *her emotional identification with the play's heroine* ◆ *their increasing identification with the struggle for independence* **5** [U, C] ~ (of sb) (with sb/sth) the process of making a close connection between one person or thing and another: *the voters' identification of the Democrats with high taxes*

identifi'cation ˌcard *noun* = ID CARD

i·den·ti·fi·er /aɪˈdentəˌfaɪər/ *noun* (*computing*) a series of characters used to refer to a program or set of data within a program

i·den·ti·fy 🔑 AWL /aɪˈdentəˌfaɪ/ *verb* (i·den·ti·fies, i·den·ti·fy·ing, i·den·ti·fied, i·den·ti·fied)

1 (also *informal* **ID**) to recognize someone or something and be able to say who or what they are: ~ sb/sth as sb/sth *The bodies were identified as those of two suspected drug dealers.* ◆ ~ sb/sth *He was able to identify his attacker.* ◆ *Passengers were asked to identify their own suitcases before they were put on the plane.* ◆ *Many of those arrested refused to identify themselves* (= would not say who they were). ◆ *First of all we must identify the problem areas.* **2** to find or discover someone or something: ~ sth *Scientists have identified a link*

between diet and cancer. ◆ *As yet they have not identified a buyer for the company.* ◆ ~ what, which, etc.... *They are trying to identify what is wrong with the present system.* **3** ~ sb/sth (as sb/sth) to make it possible to recognize who or what someone or something is: *In many cases, the clothes people wear identify them as belonging to a particular social class.* ▶ **i·den·ti·fied** AWL *adj.* **i·den·ti·fy·ing** AWL *adj.*

PHR V **i'dentify with sb** to feel that you can understand and share the feelings of someone else SYN SYMPATHIZE WITH: *I didn't enjoy the book because I couldn't identify with any of the main characters.* **i'dentify sb with sth** to consider someone to be something: *He was not the "tough guy" the public identified him with.* **i'dentify sth with sth** to consider something to be the same as something else SYN EQUATE: *You should not identify wealth with happiness.* **be i'dentified with sb/sth | i'dentify yourself with sth** to support someone or something; to be closely connected with someone or something: *The Church became increasingly identified with opposition to the regime.*

THESAURUS

identify

know ◆ recognize ◆ name ◆ make sb/sth out

These words all mean to be able to see or hear someone or something and especially to be able to say who or what they are.

identify to be able to say who or what someone or something is: *He was able to identify his attacker.*

know to be able to say who or what something is when you see or hear it because you have seen or heard it before **NOTE** *Know* is used especially to talk about sounds that seem familiar and when someone recognizes the quality or opportunity that someone or something represents: *I couldn't see who was speaking, but I knew the voice.* ◆ *She knows a bargain when she sees one.*

recognize to know who someone is or what something is when you see or hear them/it, because you have seen or heard them/it before: *I recognized him as soon as he came into the room.*

name to say the name of someone or something in order to show that you know who/what they are: *The victim has not yet been named in the newspapers.*

make sb/sth out to manage to see or hear someone or something that is not very clear: *I could just make out a figure in the darkness.*

PATTERNS

- to identify/know/recognize sb/sth **by** sth
- to identify/recognize/name sb/sth **as** sth
- to identify/know/recognize/make out **who/what/ how**...
- to **easily/barely/just** identify/recognize/make out sb/sth

---

AWL COLLOCATIONS

identify

identify *verb*

- **researcher, scholar, scientist, witness | analysis, report, research, study, survey**
  Prior research identified high school GPA as a predictor of students' academic performance.

- **target | pattern, trend | characteristic, element | variable | factor | cause | source**
  Chapter three identifies the patterns of growth over the past century.

- **previously | positively | accurately, correctly | easily, readily | clearly | incorrectly, mistakenly**
  The present research focuses on three behavioral outcomes previously identified.

---

t **t**ea   t̬ bu**tt**er   d **d**id   k **c**at   g **g**ot   tʃ **ch**in   dʒ **J**une   f **f**all

identifiable *adj.*
- easily, readily | individually | clearly
  The pineal gland is an easily identifiable point of reference in X-ray images of the brain.

identification *noun*
- allow, enable, facilitate, permit | preclude | verify
  This method facilitates the identification of a large number of herbs.
- accurate, correct, precise | positive | false, mistaken | eyewitness
  The more extensive analysis needed for precise identification is beyond the scope of this study.

identity *noun*
- cultural, ethnic, gender, national, racial, regional | collective | individual, personal | mistaken
  A weakening of national identity may well make regional ones stronger.
- a sense of ~
  Children often derive a sense of identity from their hometown.

identified *adj.*
- need | problem | factor | issue | cause | hazard, risk | gene
  This survey was designed to determine the level of importance of each of the identified issues.
- clearly, easily | newly | recently
  The newly identified chemical structures were recently named in a patent application.

identifying *adj.*
- characteristic, feature, mark
  The sawfish's most distinctive identifying feature is a broad snout with razor-sharp teeth.

i·den·ti·ty 🔑 **AWL** /aɪˈdɛntəti/ *noun* (*pl.* **i·den·ti·ties**)
1 [C, U] (*abbr.* ID) who or what someone or something is: *The police are trying to discover the identity of the killer.* ◆ *Their identities were kept secret.* ◆ *She is innocent; it was a **case of mistaken identity**.* ◆ *Do you have any proof of identity?* ◆ *The thief used a false identity.* ◆ *She went through an **identity crisis** in her teens (= was not sure of who she was or of her place in society).* **2** [C, U] the characteristics, feelings, or beliefs that distinguish people from others: *a sense of **national/cultural/personal/group identity*** ◆ *a plan to strengthen the corporate identity of the company* ⊃ collocations at IDENTIFY **3** [U] **~ (with sb/sth)** | **~ (between A and B)** the state or feeling of being very similar to and able to understand someone or something: *an identity of interests* ◆ *There's a close identity between fans and their team.*

iˈdentity ˌcard *noun* = ID CARD

iˈdentity ˌtheft *noun* [U] using someone else's name and personal information in order to obtain credit cards and other goods or to take money out of the person's bank accounts

id·e·o·gram /ˈɪdiəˌɡræm/ (also **id·e·o·graph** /ˈɪdiəˌɡræf/) *noun* **1** a symbol that is used in a writing system, for example Chinese, to represent the idea of a thing, rather than the sounds of a word **2** (*technical*) a sign or symbol for something

id·e·o·logue /ˈaɪdiəˌlɔɡ; -ˌlɑɡ; ˈɪdiə-/ (also **id·e·ol·o·gist** /ˌaɪdiˈɑlədʒɪst; ˌɪdi-/) *noun* (*formal, sometimes disapproving*) a person whose actions are influenced by belief in a set of principles (= an ideology)

id·e·ol·o·gy **AWL** /ˌaɪdiˈɑlədʒi; ˌɪdi-/ *noun* (*pl.* **id·e·ol·o·gies**) [C, U] (*sometimes disapproving*) **1** a set of ideas that an economic or political system is based on: *Marxist/capitalist ideology* **2** a set of beliefs, especially one held by a particular group, that influences the way people behave: *the ideology of gender roles* ◆ *alternative ideologies*

ideograms

Chinese character for earth

Roman numeral three

wheelchair access sign

biohazard sign

▶ **i·de·o·log·i·cal** **AWL** /ˌaɪdiəˈlɑdʒɪkl; ˌɪdiə-/ *adj.: ideological differences* **i·de·o·log·i·cally** **AWL** /-kli/ *adv.:*

ides /aɪdz/ *noun* [pl.] the middle day of the month in the ancient Roman system, from which other days were calculated: *the ides of March*

id·i·o·cy /ˈɪdiəsi/ *noun* (*pl.* **id·i·o·cies**) (*formal*) **1** [U] very stupid behavior; the state of being very stupid **SYN** STUPIDITY **2** [C] a very stupid act, remark, etc.: *the idiocies of bureaucracy*

id·i·o·lect /ˈɪdiəˌlɛkt/ *noun* [C, U] (*linguistics*) the way that a particular person uses language ⊃ compare DIALECT

id·i·om /ˈɪdiəm/ *noun* **1** [C] a group of words whose meaning is different from the meanings of the individual words: *"Let the cat out of the bag" is an idiom meaning to tell a secret by mistake.* ⊃ thesaurus box at WORD **2** [U, C] (*formal*) the kind of language and grammar used by particular people at a particular time or place **3** [U, C] (*formal*) the style of writing, music, art, etc. that is typical of a particular person, group, period, or place: *the classical/contemporary/popular idiom*

id·i·o·mat·ic /ˌɪdiəˈmætɪk/ *adj.* **1** containing expressions that are natural to a NATIVE SPEAKER of a language: *She speaks fluent and idiomatic English.* **2** containing an idiom: *an idiomatic expression* ▶ **id·i·o·mat·i·cally** /-kli/ *adv.*

id·i·o·syn·cra·sy /ˌɪdiəˈsɪŋkrəsi/ *noun* (*pl.* **id·i·o·syn·cra·sies**) [C, U] a person's particular way of behaving, thinking, etc., especially when it is unusual; an unusual feature **SYN** ECCENTRICITY: *The car has its little idiosyncrasies.* ▶ **id·i·o·syn·crat·ic** /ˌɪdioʊsɪŋˈkrætɪk/ *adj.: His teaching methods are idiosyncratic but successful.*

id·i·ot /ˈɪdiət/ *noun* **1** (*informal*) a very stupid person **SYN** FOOL: *When I lost my passport, I felt such an idiot.* ◆ *Not that switch, you idiot!* **2** (*old use, offensive*) a person with very low intelligence who cannot think or behave normally

id·i·ot·ic /ˌɪdiˈɑtɪk/ *adj.* very stupid **SYN** RIDICULOUS: *an idiotic question* ◆ *Don't be so idiotic!* ▶ **id·i·ot·i·cally** /-kli/ *adv.*

id·i·ot sa·vant /ˌɪdiət sæˈvɑnt; -sə-/ *noun* (*pl.* **id·i·ot sa·vants** or **id·i·ots sa·vants** /ˌɪdiət sæˈvɑnt; -sə-/) (*from French*) a person who has severe LEARNING DIFFICULTIES, but who has an unusually high level of ability in a particular skill, for example in art or music, or in remembering things

i·dle /ˈaɪdl/ *adj., verb*
● *adj.* **1** (of people) not working hard **SYN** LAZY: *an idle student* **2** (of machines, factories, etc.) not in use: *to lie/stand/remain idle* **3** (of people) without work **SYN** UNEMPLOYED: *Over ten percent of the workforce is now idle.* **4** [usually before noun] with no particular purpose or effect; useless: *idle chatter/curiosity* ◆ *It was just an idle threat* (= not serious). ◆ *It is idle to pretend that their marriage is a success.* **5** [usually before noun] (of time) not spent doing work or something particular: *In idle moments, he carved wooden figures.* **IDM** see DEVIL ▶ **i·dle·ness** *noun* [U]: *After a period of enforced idleness, she found a new job.*

• **verb 1** [T, I] to spend time doing nothing important: ~ **sth (+ adv./prep.)** *They idled the days away, talking and watching television.* ◆ **(+ adv./prep.)** *They idled along by the river* (= walked slowly and with no particular purpose). **2** [I] (of an engine) to run slowly while the vehicle is not moving: *She left the car idling at the curb.* **3** [T] ~ **sb/sth** to close a factory, etc. or stop providing work for the workers, especially temporarily: *The strikes have idled nearly 4000 workers.*

i·dler /'aɪdlər/ *noun* a person who is lazy and does not work **SYN** LOAFER

i·dly /'aɪdli/ *adv.* without any particular reason, purpose, or effort; doing nothing: *She sat in the sun, idly sipping a cool drink.* ◆ *He wondered idly what would happen.* ◆ *We can't* **stand idly by** (= do nothing) *and let people starve.*

i·dol /'aɪdl/ *noun* **1** a person or thing that is loved and admired very much: *a sports/teen, etc. idol* ◆ *the idol of countless teenagers* ◆ *a fallen idol* (= someone who is no longer popular) **2** a statue that is worshiped as a god

i·dol·a·try /aɪ'dɑlətri/ *noun* [U] **1** the practice of worshiping statues as gods **2** (*formal*) too much love or admiration for someone or something: *football fans whose support for their team borders on idolatry* ▶ **i·dol·a·trous** /-trəs/ *adj.*

i·dol·ize /'aɪdl̩ˌaɪz/ *verb* ~ **sb** to admire or love someone very much **SYN** WORSHIP: *a movie star idolized by millions of fans* ◆ *They idolize their kids.*

i·dyll /'aɪdl/ *noun* **1** (*literary*) a happy and peaceful place, event, or experience, especially one connected with the countryside **2** a short poem or other piece of writing that describes a peaceful and happy scene

i·dyl·lic /aɪ'dɪlɪk/ *adj.* peaceful and beautiful; perfect, without problems: *a house set in idyllic surroundings* ◆ *to lead an idyllic existence* ◆ *The cottage sounds idyllic.* ▶ **i·dyl·li·cally** /-kli/ *adv.*: *a house idyllically set in wooded grounds*

i.e. 🔑 /ˌaɪ 'i/ *abbr.*
used to explain exactly what the previous thing that you have mentioned means (from Latin "id est"): *the basic essentials of life (i.e., housing, food, and water)*

i.e.

explaining what you mean

- Some poems are mnemonics (**i.e.,** they are designed to help you remember something).
- Some poems are mnemonics; **that is to say,** they are designed to help you remember something.
- Mnemonic poems – **that is** – are poems designed to help you remember something – are an excellent way to learn lists.
- A limerick's rhyme scheme is A–A–B–B–A. **In other words,** the first, second, and fifth lines all rhyme with one another, while the third and fourth lines have their own rhyme.
- In this exercise, the reader is encouraged to work out the meaning, **or rather** the range of meanings, of the poem.
- This is a poem about death, **or, more precisely,** dying.
- He says his poems deal with "the big issues," **by which he means** love, loss, grief, and death.
⊃ Language Bank at ABOUT

-ie ⊃ -Y

IED /ˌaɪ i 'di/ *abbr.* improvised explosive device (a bomb made and used by people who are not members of the military forces of a country)

IELTS /'aɪɛlts/ *noun* [U] the abbreviation for "International English Language Testing System" (a British test, set by the University of Cambridge, that measures a person's ability to speak and write English at the level that is necessary to go to university in Britain, Canada, Australia, and New Zealand)

if ◆ whether

- Both **if** and **whether** are used in reporting questions which expect "yes" or "no" as the answer: *She asked if/whether I wanted a drink.*, although **whether** sounds more natural with particular verbs such as **discuss**, **consider**, and **decide**. When a choice is offered between alternatives, **if** or **whether** can be used: *We didn't know if/whether we should write or phone.* In this last type of sentence, **whether** is usually considered more formal and more suitable for written English.

if 🔑 /ɪf/ *conj., noun*
• *conj.* **1** used to say that one thing can, will, or might happen or be true, depending on another thing happening or being true: *If you see him, give him this note.* ◆ *I'll only stay if you offer me more money.* ◆ *If necessary I can come at once.* ◆ *You can stay for the weekend if you like.* ◆ *If anyone calls, tell them I'm not at home.* ◆ *If he improved his IT skills, he'd* (= he would) *easily get a job.* ◆ *You would know what was going on if you'd* (= you had) *listened.* ◆ *They would have been here by now if they'd caught the early train.* ◆ *If I were in charge, I'd do things differently.* ◆ **Even if** (= although) *you did see someone, you can't be sure it was him.* **2** when; whenever; every time: *If metal gets hot it expands.* ◆ *She glares at me if I go near her desk.* **3** (*formal*) used with *will* or *would* to ask someone politely to do something: *If you will sit down for a few moments, I'll tell the manager you're here.* ◆ *If you would care to leave your name, we'll contact you as soon as possible.* **4** used after *ask, know, find out, wonder*, etc. to introduce one of two or more possibilities **SYN** WHETHER: *Do you know if he's married?* ◆ *I wonder if I should wear a coat or not.* ◆ *He couldn't tell if she was laughing or crying.* ◆ *Listen to the tune and see if you can remember the words.* **5** used after verbs or adjectives expressing feelings: *I am sorry if I disturbed you.* ◆ *I'd be grateful if you would keep it a secret.* ◆ *Do you mind if I turn the TV off?* **6** used to admit that something is possible, but to say that it is not very important: *If she has any weakness, it is her Italian.* ◆ *So what if he was late. Who cares?* **7** used before an adjective to introduce a contrast: *He's a good driver, if a little overconfident.* ◆ *We'll only do it once— if at all.* **8** used to ask someone to listen to your opinion: *If you ask me, she's too scared to do it.* ◆ *If you think about it, those children must be at school by now.* ◆ *If you remember, Mary was always fond of animals.* **9** used before *could, may,* or *might* to suggest something or to interrupt someone politely: *If I may make a suggestion, perhaps we could begin a little earlier next week.* **IDM** **if and when** used to say something about an event that may or may not happen: *If and when we ever meet again I hope he remembers what I did for him.* **if anything** used to express an opinion about something, or after a negative statement to suggest that the opposite is true: *I'd say he was more like his father, if anything.* ◆ *She's not thin—if anything she's on the heavy side.* **if I were you** used to give someone advice: *If I were you I'd start looking for another job.* **if not 1** used to introduce a different suggestion, after a sentence with *if*: *I'll go if you're going. If not* (= if you are not) *I'd rather stay at home.* **2** used after a *yes/no* question to say what will or should happen if the answer is "no": *Are you ready? If not, I'm going without you.* ◆ *Do you want that cake? If not, I'll have it.* **3** used to suggest that something may be even larger, more important, etc. than was first stated: *They cost thousands if not millions of dollars to build.* **if only** used to say that you wish something was true or that something had happened: *If only I were rich.* ◆ *If only I knew her name.* ◆ *If only he'd remembered to send that letter.* ◆ *If only I had gone by taxi.* **it's not as if** used to say that something that is happening is surprising: *I'm surprised they've invited me to their wedding—it's not as if I know them well.* **only if** (*somewhat formal*) used to state the only situation in which something can happen: *Only if a teacher has given permission is a student allowed to leave the room.* ◆ *Only if the red light comes on is there any danger to employees.*

noun (*informal*) a situation that is not certain: *If he wins—and it's a big if—he'll be the first American to win for fifty years.* ◆ *There are still a lot of ifs and buts before everything's settled.*

iff /ɪf/ *conj.* (*mathematics*) an expression used in mathematics to mean "if and only if"

if·fy /ˈɪfi/ *adj.* (*informal*) not certain: *The weather looks slightly iffy.*

-ify /əfaɪ/, **-fy** *suffix* (in verbs) to make or become: *purify* ◆ *solidify*

Ig·bo /ˈɪgboʊ/ (also **I·bo**) *noun* [U] a language spoken in S.E. Nigeria

ig·loo /ˈɪglu/ *noun* (*pl.* **ig·loos**) a small round house or shelter built from blocks of hard snow by the Inuit people of northern N. America

ig·ne·ous /ˈɪgniəs/ *adj.* (*geology*) (of rocks) formed when MAGMA (= melted or liquid material lying below the earth's surface) becomes solid, especially after it has poured out of a VOLCANO

ig·nite /ɪgˈnaɪt/ *verb* (*formal*) **1** [I, T] to start to burn; to make something start to burn: *Gas ignites very easily.* ◆ ~ **sth** *Flames melted a lead pipe and ignited leaking gas.* **2** [T] ~ **sth** to cause a powerful emotion or reaction; to give force or energy to something: *His words ignited their anger.* ◆ *The book ignited a firestorm of debate.* ◆ *Legends often ignite the imagination of fiction writers.*

ig·ni·tion /ɪgˈnɪʃn/ *noun* **1** [C, usually sing.] the electrical system of a vehicle that makes the fuel begin to burn to start the engine; the place in a vehicle where you start this system: *to turn the ignition on/off* ◆ *to put the key in the ignition* ⊃ picture at CAR ⊃ collocations at DRIVING **2** [U] (*technical*) the action of starting to burn or of making something burn: *The flames spread to all parts of the house within minutes of ignition.*

ig·no·ble /ɪgˈnoʊbl/ *adj.* (*formal*) not good or honest; that should make you feel shame SYN BASE: *ignoble thoughts* ◆ *an ignoble person* ANT NOBLE

ig·no·min·i·ous /ˌɪgnəˈmɪniəs/ *adj.* (*formal*) that makes, or should make, you feel ashamed SYN DISGRACEFUL: *an ignominious defeat* ◆ *He made one mistake and his career came to an ignominious end.* ▶ **ig·no·min·i·ous·ly** *adv.*

ig·no·min·y /ˈɪgnəˌmɪni/ *noun* [U] (*formal*) public shame and loss of honor SYN DISGRACE: *They suffered the ignominy of defeat.*

ig·no·ra·mus /ˌɪgnəˈreɪməs; -ˈræ-/ *noun* (usually *humorous*) a person who does not have much knowledge: *When it comes to music, I'm a complete ignoramus.*

ig·no·rance AWL /ˈɪgnərəns/ *noun* [U] ~ **(of/about sth)** a lack of knowledge or information about something: *widespread ignorance of/about the disease* ◆ *They fought a long battle against prejudice and ignorance.* ◆ *She was kept in ignorance of her husband's activities.* ◆ *Children often behave badly out of/through ignorance.*
IDM **ignorance is bliss** (*saying*) if you do not know about something, you cannot worry about it: *Some doctors believe ignorance is bliss and don't give their patients all the facts.*

ig·no·rant AWL /ˈɪgnərənt/ *adj.* **1** lacking knowledge or information about something; not educated: *an ignorant person/question* ◆ *Never make your students feel ignorant.* ◆ ~ **about sth** *He's ignorant about modern technology.* ◆ ~ **of sth** *At that time I was ignorant of events going on elsewhere.* **2** (*informal*) with very bad manners SYN UNCOUTH: *a rude, ignorant person* ▶ **ig·no·rant·ly** *adv.*

ig·nore 🔑 AWL /ɪgˈnɔr/ *verb*
1 ~ **sth** to pay no attention to something SYN DISREGARD: *He ignored all the "No Smoking" signs and lit up a cigarette.* ◆ *I made a suggestion but they chose to ignore it.* ◆ *We cannot afford to ignore their advice.* **2** ~ **sb** to pretend that you have not seen someone or that someone is not there SYN TAKE NO NOTICE OF: *She ignored him and carried on with her work.*

i·gua·na /ɪˈgwanə/ *noun* a large tropical American LIZARD (= a type of REPTILE)

i·guan·o·don /ɪˈgwanəˌdɑn/ *noun* a large DINOSAUR

i·ke·ba·na /ˌikeɪˈbanə; ˌɪkɪ-/ *noun* [U] (from *Japanese*) Japanese flower arranging, that has strict formal rules

i·kon = ICON (3)

IL *abbr.* (in writing) Illinois

il- /ɪl/ *prefix* ⊃ IN-

il·e·um /ˈɪliəm/ *noun* (*pl.* **il·e·a** /ˈɪliə/) (*anatomy*) the third part of the small INTESTINE ⊃ compare DUODENUM, JEJUNUM ▶ **il·e·al** /ˈɪliəl/ *adj.*

ilk /ɪlk/ *noun* [usually sing.] (sometimes *disapproving*) type; kind: *the world of media people and their ilk* ◆ *I can't stand him, or any others of that ilk.*

ill 🔑 /ɪl/ *adj., adv., noun*
● *adj.* **1** [not usually before noun] suffering from an illness or disease; not feeling well SYN SICK: *Her father is seriously ill in St. Luke's hospital.* ◆ *She was taken ill suddenly.* ◆ *We both started to feel ill shortly after the meal.* ◆ *Uncle Harry is terminally ill with cancer* (= he will die from his illness). ◆ *the mentally ill* (= people with a mental illness) ◆ (*formal*) *He fell ill and died soon after.* **2** [usually before noun] bad or harmful: *He resigned because of ill health* (= he was often ill). ◆ *She suffered no ill effects from the experience.* ◆ *a woman of ill repute* (= considered to be immoral) **3** (*formal*) that brings, or is thought to bring, bad luck: *a bird of ill omen*
IDM **ill at ease** feeling uncomfortable and embarrassed: *I felt ill at ease in such formal clothes.* **it's an ill wind (that blows nobody any good)** (*saying*) no problem is so bad that it does not bring some advantage to someone ⊃ more at FEELING
● *adv.* **1** (especially in compounds) badly or in an unpleasant way: *The animals had been grossly ill-treated.* **2** (*formal*) badly; not in an acceptable way: *They live in an area ill served by public transport.* **3** (*formal*) only with difficulty: *We're wasting valuable time, time we can ill afford.*
IDM **speak/think ill of sb** (*formal*) to say or think bad things about someone: *Don't speak ill of the dead.*
● *noun* **1** [usually pl.] (*formal*) a problem or harmful thing; an illness: *social/economic ills* ◆ *the ills of the modern world* **2** [U] (*literary*) harm; bad luck: *I may not like him, but I wish him no ill.*

I'll /aɪl/ *short form* **1** I will **2** I shall

ill-ad·vised *adj.* not sensible; likely to cause difficulties in the future: *Her remarks were ill-advised, to say the least.* ◆ *You would be ill-advised to travel on your own.* ⊃ compare WELL-ADVISED ▶ **ill-ad·visedly** *adv.*

ill-as·sorted *adj.* (*old-fashioned*) (of a group of people or things) not seeming suited to each other: *It was an ill-assorted group.*

ill-bred *adj.* (*formal*) rude or badly behaved, especially because you have not been taught how to behave well ANT WELL-BRED

ill-con·cealed *adj.* (*formal*) (of feelings or expressions of feeling) not hidden well from other people

ill-con·ceived *adj.* badly planned or designed

ill-con·sidered *adj.* not carefully thought about or planned

ill-de·fined *adj.* **1** not clearly described: *an ill-defined role* **2** not clearly marked or easy to see: *an ill-defined path* ANT WELL DEFINED

ill-dis·posed *adj.* ~ **(toward sb)** (*formal*) not feeling friendly toward someone ANT WELL-DISPOSED

il·le·gal 🔑 AWL /ɪˈligl/ *adj., noun*
● *adj.* not allowed by the law: *illegal immigrants/aliens* ◆ *It's illegal to drive through a red light.* ANT LEGAL ▶ **il·le·gal·ly** AWL /-gəli/ *adv.*: *an illegally parked car* ◆ *He entered the country illegally.*
● *noun* a person who lives or works in a country illegally

il·le·gal·i·ty AWL /ˌɪliˈgæləti/ *noun* (*pl.* **il·le·gal·i·ties**) **1** [U] the state of being illegal: *No illegality is suspected.* **2** [C] an illegal act ⟁ compare LEGALITY

il·leg·i·ble /ɪˈlɛdʒəbl/ (also **un·read·a·ble**) *adj.* difficult or impossible to read: *an illegible signature* **ANT** LEGIBLE ▶ **il·leg·i·bly** *adv.* /-bli/

il·le·git·i·mate /ˌɪləˈdʒɪtəmət/ *adj.* **1** born to parents who are not married to each other **2** not allowed by a particular set of rules or by law **SYN** UNAUTHORIZED: *illegitimate use of company property* **ANT** LEGITIMATE ▶ **il·le·git·i·ma·cy** /-məsi/ *noun* [U] **il·le·git·i·mate·ly** *adv.*

ˌill-eˈquipped *adj.* ~ (for sth) | ~ (to do sth) not having the necessary equipment or skills

ˌill-ˈfated (also **fated**) *adj.* (*formal*) not lucky and ending sadly, especially in death or failure: *an ill-fated expedition*

ˌill-ˈfitting *adj.* not the right size or shape: *ill-fitting clothes*

ˌill-ˈfounded *adj.* (*formal*) not based on fact or truth: *All our fears proved ill-founded.* **ANT** WELL-FOUNDED

ˌill-ˈgotten *adj.* (*old-fashioned* or *humorous*) obtained dishonestly or unfairly: *ill-gotten gains* (= money that was not obtained fairly)

ˌill ˈhealth *noun* [U] (*formal*) the poor condition of a person's body or mind: *He retired early on grounds of ill health.*

ˌill ˈhumor (*CanE usually* **ˌill ˈhumour**) *noun* [U, C] (*literary*) a bad mood **ANT** GOOD HUMOR ▶ **ˌill-ˈhumored** (*CanE usually* **ˌill-ˈhumoured**) *adj.*

il·lib·er·al /ɪˈlɪbərəl; -brəl/ *adj.* (*formal*) not allowing much freedom of opinion or action **SYN** INTOLERANT: *illiberal policies*

il·lic·it /ɪˈlɪsət/ *adj.* **1** not allowed by the law **SYN** ILLEGAL: *illicit drugs* **2** not approved of by the normal rules of society: *an illicit love affair* ▶ **il·lic·it·ly** *adv.*

ˌill-inˈformed *adj.* having or showing little knowledge of something **ANT** WELL-INFORMED

il·lit·er·ate /ɪˈlɪtərət/ *adj., noun*
• *adj.* **1** (of a person) not knowing how to read or write **ANT** LITERATE **2** (of a document or letter) badly written, as if by someone without much education **3** (usually after a noun or adverb) not knowing very much about a particular subject area: *computer illiterate* ◆ *musically illiterate* ▶ **il·lit·er·a·cy** /ɪˈlɪtərəsi/ *noun* [U]
• *noun* a person who is illiterate

ˌill-ˈjudged *adj.* (*formal*) that has not been carefully thought about; not appropriate in a particular situation

ˌill-ˈmannered *adj.* (*formal*) not behaving well or politely in social situations **SYN** RUDE **ANT** WELL-MANNERED

ill·ness 🔑 /ˈɪlnəs/ *noun*
1 [U] the state of being physically or mentally ill: *mental illness* ◆ *I missed a lot of school through illness last year.* **2** [C] a type or period of illness: *minor/serious illnesses* ◆ *childhood illnesses* ◆ *He died after a long illness.* ⟁ thesaurus box at DISEASE

THESAURUS

illness

condition ◆ health problems/issues ◆ disability

These are all words for the state of someone's health, especially when they are physically or mentally ill.

illness the state of being physically or mentally ill

condition the state of someone's health or how fit they are, especially when they are ill: *She can't travel in her condition.* ◆ *My condition requires me to watch what I eat.*

health problems/issues any problems that someone has with their physical or mental health: *My parents have had a lot of health problems this year.* ◆ *Many of the patients at the clinic are dealing with serious mental health issues.* **NOTE** The term **health issues** is slightly more formal than **health problems**.

disability a physical or mental condition that means you

cannot use a part of your body completely or easily, or that you cannot learn easily: *His disability does not keep him from living a full and active life.*

PATTERNS

■ (a) **chronic** illness/condition/health problems/health issues/disability
■ to **suffer from** an illness/health problems/health issues
■ to **deal with/have** health problems/health issues/a disability

il·log·i·cal **AWL** /ɪˈlɑdʒɪkl/ *adj.* not sensible or thought out in a logical way: *illogical behavior/arguments* ◆ *She has an illogical fear of insects.* **ANT** LOGICAL ▶ **il·log·i·cal·i·ty** /ɪˌlɑdʒɪˈkæləti/ *noun* [U, C] **il·log·i·cally** **AWL** /ɪˈlɑdʒɪkli/ *adv.*

ˌill-ˈomened *adj.* (*formal*) (of an event or activity) seeming likely to be unlucky or unsuccessful because there are a lot of unlucky signs relating to it

ˌill-preˈpared *adj.* **1** ~ (for sth) not ready, especially because you were not expecting something to happen: *The team was ill-prepared for a disaster on that scale.* **2** badly planned or organized: *an ill-prepared speech*

ˌill-ˈstarred *adj.* (*formal*) not lucky and likely to bring unhappiness or to end in failure: *an ill-starred marriage*

ˌill-ˈsuited *adj.* [not before noun] ~ to/for sb/sth not appropriate or useful for a particular purpose or in a particular situation: *The small broom was ill-suited to the task of cleaning up such a big mess.* ⟁ compare SUITED (1)

ˌill-ˈtempered *adj.* (*formal*) angry and rude or irritated, especially when this seems unreasonable

ˌill-ˈtimed *adj.* done or happening at the wrong time: *an ill-timed visit* **ANT** WELL-TIMED

ˌill-ˈtreat *verb* ~ sb to treat someone in a cruel or unkind way **SYN** MISTREAT ▶ **ˌill-ˈtreatment** *noun* [U]: *the ill-treatment of prisoners*

il·lu·mi·nate /ɪˈluməˌneɪt/ (also *less frequent* **il·lu·mine**) *verb* **1** ~ sth to shine light on something: *Floodlights illuminated the stadium.* ◆ *The earth is illuminated by the sun.* **2** ~ sth (*formal*) to make something clearer or easier to understand **SYN** CLARIFY: *This text illuminates the philosopher's early thinking.* **3** ~ sth to decorate a street, building, etc. with bright lights for a special occasion **4** ~ sth (*literary*) to make a person's face, etc. seem bright and excited **SYN** LIGHT UP: *Her smile illuminated her entire being.*

il·lu·mi·nat·ed /ɪˈluməˌneɪtəd/ *adj.* [usually before noun] **1** lit with bright lights: *the illuminated city at night* **2** (of books, etc.) decorated with gold, silver, and bright colors in a way that was done in the past, by hand: *illuminated manuscripts*

il·lu·mi·nat·ing /ɪˈluməˌneɪtɪŋ/ *adj.* helping to make something clear or easier to understand: *We didn't find the examples he used particularly illuminating.*

il·lu·mi·na·tion /ɪˌluməˈneɪʃn/ *noun* **1** [U, C] light or a place that light comes from: *The only illumination in the room came from the fire.* **2** [C, usually pl.] a colored decoration, usually painted by hand, in an old book **3** [U] (*formal*) understanding or explanation of something: *spiritual illumination*

il·lu·mine /ɪˈlumən/ *verb* = ILLUMINATE

ˌill-ˈused *adj.* (*old-fashioned* or *formal*) badly treated

il·lu·sion /ɪˈluʒn/ *noun* **1** [C, U] a false idea or belief, especially about someone or about a situation: *She's under the illusion that* (= believes wrongly that) *she'll get the job.* ◆ *The new president has no illusions about the difficulties facing her country* (= she knows that the country has serious problems). ◆ *He could no longer distinguish between illusion and reality.* **2** [C] something that seems to exist but in fact does not, or seems to be something that it is not: *Mirrors in a room often give an illusion of space.* ◆ *The idea of absolute personal freedom is an illusion.*

il·lu·sion·ist /ɪˈluːʒənɪst/ *noun* an entertainer who performs tricks that seem strange or impossible to believe

il·lu·sive /ɪˈluːsɪv/ *adj.* (*literary, rare*) not real although seeming to be: *There is an illusive sense of depth.*
SYN ILLUSORY **HELP** *Illusive* is sometimes confused with *elusive* which has a different meaning.

il·lu·so·ry /ɪˈluːsəri; -zəri/ *adj.* (*formal*) not real, although seeming to be: *an illusory sense of freedom*

il·lus·trate 🖋 **AWL** /ˈɪləˌstreɪt/ *verb*
1 [usually passive]: to use pictures, photographs, diagrams, etc. in a book, etc.: **~ sth** *an illustrated textbook* ◆ **~ sth with sth** *His lecture was illustrated with slides taken during the expedition.* **2 ~ sth | ~ how, what, etc....** to make the meaning of something clearer by using examples, pictures, etc.: *To illustrate my point, let me tell you a little story.* ◆ *Last year's sales figures are illustrated in Figure 2.* ⟳ language bank at PROCESS[1] **3 ~ sth | ~ how, what, etc.... | ~ that...** to show that something is true or that a situation exists **SYN** DEMONSTRATE: *The incident illustrates the need for better security measures.*

LANGUAGE BANK

illustrate

referring to a chart, graph, or table

- This bar chart **illustrates** how many journeys people made on public transportation over a three-month period.
- This table **compares** bus, train, and taxi use between April and June.
- The results **are shown** in the chart below.
- In this pie chart, the survey results **are broken down** by age.
- This pie chart **breaks down** the survey results by age.
- **As can be seen from** these results, younger people use buses more than older people.
- **According to** these figures, bus travel accounts for 60% of public transportation use.
- **From** the data in the above graph, **it is apparent that** buses are the most widely used form of public transportation.
- ⟳ Language Banks at EVIDENCE, FALL, INCREASE, PROPORTION, SURPRISING

AWL COLLOCATIONS

illustrate

illustrate *verb*
to explain or make something clear using examples, pictures, or diagrams

- **amply | best**, **nicely | clearly**, **graphically**, **vividly**
  One of the stories in the collection best illustrates Jefferson's feelings about his mother.
  This model vividly illustrates the impact of one individual's behavior on the spread of disease.
- **importance | point**, **concept, principle, thesis | complexity, difficulty**
  These statistics illustrate two important points.
  A simple example will illustrate these concepts.
- **attempt to | serve to | suffice to**
  He attempts to illustrate his argument through detailed discussions.
  Two examples should suffice to illustrate the scale of the problem.
- **be intended to**
  The case studies are intended to illustrate a link between engineering and architecture.

illustration *noun*
an example that makes a point or an idea clear

- **striking, vivid | classic | graphical**
  The community development process in Chile offers vivid illustrations of a number of issues raised in this paper.
- **by way of ~**
  A number of examples of strikes in different parts of the country are provided by way of illustration.
- **for ~ purposes**
  The data are for illustration purposes only.

il·lus·tra·tion **AWL** /ˌɪləˈstreɪʃn/ *noun* **1** [C] a drawing or picture in a book, magazine, etc., especially one that explains something: *50 full-color illustrations* **2** [U] the process of illustrating something: *the art of book illustration* **3** [C, U] a story, an event, or an example that clearly shows the truth about something: *The statistics are a clear illustration of the point I am trying to make* ◆ *Let me, by way of illustration, quote from one of her poems.* ⟳ thesaurus box at EXAMPLE ⟳ collocations at ILLUSTRATE

il·lus·tra·tive **AWL** /ɪˈlʌstrətɪv; ˈɪləˌstreɪtɪv/ *adj.* (*formal*) helping to explain something or show it more clearly **SYN** EXPLANATORY: *an illustrative example*

il·lus·tra·tor /ˈɪləˌstreɪtər/ *noun* a person who draws or paints pictures for books, etc.

il·lus·tri·ous /ɪˈlʌstriəs/ *adj.* (*formal*) very famous and much admired, especially because of what you have achieved **SYN** DISTINGUISHED: *The composer was one of many illustrious visitors to the town.* ◆ *a long and illustrious career*

ill ˈwill *noun* [U] bad and unkind feelings toward someone: *I bear Sue no ill will.*

ILO /ˌaɪ ɛl ˈoʊ/ *abbr.* International Labor Organization (an organization within the United Nations concerned with work and working conditions)

I'm /aɪm/ *short form* I am

im- /ɪm/ ⟳ IN-

im·age 🖋 **AWL** /ˈɪmɪdʒ/ *noun*
1 [C, U] the impression that a person, an organization, or a product, etc. gives to the public: *His public image is very different from the real person.* ◆ *The advertisements are intended to improve the company's image.* ◆ *Image is very important in the music world.* ◆ *stereotyped images of women in children's books* **2** [C] a mental picture that you have of what someone or something is like or looks like: *images of the past* ◆ *I had a mental image of what she would look like.* **3** [C] (*formal*) a copy of someone or something in the form of a picture or statue: *Images of deer and hunters decorate the cave walls.* ◆ *a wooden image of the Hindu god Ganesh* **4** [C] a picture of someone or something seen in a mirror, through a camera, or on a television or computer: *He stared at his own image reflected in the water.* ◆ *Slowly, an image began to appear on the screen.* ⟳ see also MIRROR IMAGE **5** [C] a word or phrase used with a different meaning from its normal one, in order to describe something in a way that produces a strong picture in the mind: *poetic images of the countryside*
IDM **be the image of sb/sth** to look very like someone or something else: *He's the image of his father.* ⟳ see also SPITTING IMAGE

im·age·ry **AWL** /ˈɪmɪdʒri/ *noun* [U] **1** language that produces pictures in the minds of people reading or listening: *poetic imagery* ⟳ collocations at LITERATURE ⟳ see also METAPHOR **2** (*formal*) pictures, photographs, etc.: *satellite imagery* (= for example, photographs of the earth taken from space)

im·ag·i·na·ble /ɪˈmædʒənəbl/ *adj.* **1** used with superlatives, and with *all* and *every*, to emphasize that something is the best, worst, etc. that you can imagine, or includes every possible example: *The house has the most spectacular views imaginable.* ◆ *They stock every imaginable type of pasta.* **2** possible to imagine: *These technological developments were hardly imaginable 30 years ago.*

---

im·ag·i·nar·y 🔑 /ɪˈmædʒəˌnɛri/ adj.
existing only in your mind or imagination: imaginary fears ◆ The equator is an imaginary line around the middle of the earth.

imˌaginary ˈnumber noun (mathematics) a number expressed as the SQUARE ROOT of a negative number, especially the square root of -1 ⊃ compare COMPLEX NUMBER, REAL NUMBER

im·ag·i·na·tion 🔑 /ɪˌmædʒəˈneɪʃn/ noun
1 [U, C] the ability to create pictures in your mind; the part of your mind that does this: a vivid/fertile imagination ◆ He has no imagination. ◆ It doesn't take much imagination to guess what she meant. ◆ I won't tell you his reaction— I'll leave that to your imagination. ◆ Don't let your imagination run away with you (= don't use too much imagination). ◆ The new policies appear to have caught the imagination of the public (= they find them interesting and exciting). ◆ Nobody hates you—it's all in your imagination. ◆ (informal) Use your imagination! (= used to tell someone that they will have to guess the answer to the question they have asked you, usually because it is obvious or embarrassing) **2** [U] something that you have imagined rather than something that exists: She was no longer able to distinguish between imagination and reality. ◆ Is it my imagination or have you lost a lot of weight? **3** [U] the ability to have new and exciting ideas: His writing lacks imagination. ◆ With a little imagination, you could turn this place into a palace.
IDM **leave nothing/little to the imagination** (of clothes) to allow more of someone's body to be seen than usual: Her tight-fitting dress left nothing to the imagination. ⊃ more at FIGMENT, STRETCH n.

im·ag·i·na·tive /ɪˈmædʒənətɪv/ adj. having or showing new and exciting ideas **SYN** INVENTIVE: an imaginative approach/idea/child ◆ recipes that make imaginative use of seasonal vegetables **ANT** UNIMAGINATIVE ▶ **i·mag·i·na·tive·ly** adv.: The warehouse has been imaginatively converted into apartments.

THESAURUS

imagine

think ◆ see ◆ envision

These words all mean to form an idea in your mind of what someone or something might be like.

imagine to form an idea in your mind of what someone or something might be like: The house was just as she had imagined it.

think to imagine something that might happen: I can't think of a better place for a wedding. ◆ Just think —this time tomorrow we'll be lying on a beach.

see to consider something as a future possibility; to imagine someone as something: I can't see her changing her mind. ◆ His colleagues see him as a future director.

envision to imagine what a situation will be like in the future, especially a situation that you intend to work

toward: They envision an equal society, free from poverty and disease. ◆ In ten years, I envision myself running my own business. **NOTE** Envision is used especially in business and political contexts.

PATTERNS
- to imagine/see/envision sb/sth as sth
- to imagine/see/envision (sb) doing sth
- to be able to imagine/think/see/envision who/what/how...
- to imagine/think/envision that...

---

im·ag·ine 🔑 /ɪˈmædʒən/ verb
1 [T, I] to form a picture in your mind of what something might be like: ~ sth The house was just as she had imagined it. ◆ I can't imagine life without the kids now. ◆ ~ (that)... Close your eyes and imagine (that) you are in a forest. ◆ ~ what, how, etc.... Can you imagine what it must be like to lose your job after

20 years? ◆ ~ doing sth She imagined walking into the office and handing in her resignation. ◆ Imagine earning that much money! ◆ ~ sb/sth doing sth I can just imagine him saying that! ◆ ~ sb/sth to be/do sth I had imagined her to be older than that. ◆ ~ (sb + adj./noun) I can imagine him really angry. ◆ (informal) "He was furious." " I can imagine." **2** [T] to believe something that is not true: ~ (that)... He's always imagining (that) we're talking about him behind his back. ◆ ~ sth There's nobody there. You're imagining things. **3** [I, T] to think that something is probably true **SYN** ASSUME, SUPPOSE: "Can we still buy tickets for the concert?" "I imagine so." ◆ ~ (that)... I don't imagine (that) they'll refuse.

imaging /ˈɪmədʒɪŋ/ noun [U] (computing) the process of capturing, storing, and showing an image on a computer screen: imaging software

im·ag·in·ings /ɪˈmædʒənɪŋz/ noun [pl.] things that you imagine, that exist only in your mind

i·ma·go /ɪˈmeɪɡoʊ; ɪˈmɑ-/ noun **1** (psychology) a mental image of someone as being perfect that you do not realize you have and that influences your behavior **2** (pl. i·ma·gos or i·ma·gi·nes /ɪˈmeɪɡəniz; ɪˈmɑ-/) the final and fully developed adult stage of an insect, especially one with wings

i·mam /ɪˈmɑm/ noun (in Islam) **1** a religious man who leads the prayers in a MOSQUE **2** Imam the title of a religious leader

IMAX™ /ˈaɪmæks/ noun **1** [U] technology that allows movies to be shown on extremely large screens **2** [C] a movie theater or screen that uses IMAX

im·bal·ance /ɪmˈbæləns/ noun [C, U] a situation in which two or more things are not the same size or are not treated the same, in a way that is unfair or causes problems: ~ (in/of sth) a global imbalance in/of power ◆ ~ (between A and B) Attempts are being made to redress (= put right) the imbalance between our import and export figures.

im·be·cile /ˈɪmbəsl/ noun **1** a rude way to describe a person that you think is very stupid **SYN** IDIOT: They behaved like imbeciles. **2** (old-fashioned, offensive) a person who has a very low level of intelligence ▶ **im·be·cile** (also im·be·cil·ic /ˌɪmbəˈsɪlɪk/) adj. [usually before noun]: imbecile remarks **im·be·cil·i·ty** /ˌɪmbəˈsɪləti/ noun [U, C]

im·bed = EMBED

im·bibe /ɪmˈbaɪb/ verb **1** [I, T] ~ (sth) (formal or humorous) to drink something, especially alcohol **2** [T] ~ sth (formal) to absorb something, especially information

im·bro·glio /ɪmˈbroʊlyoʊ/ noun (pl. im·bro·glios) (formal) a complicated situation that causes confusion or embarrassment, especially one that is political

im·bue /ɪmˈbyu/ verb [often passive] ~ sb/sth (with sth) (formal) to fill someone or something with strong feelings, opinions, or values **SYN** INFUSE: Her voice was imbued with an unusual seriousness. ◆ He was imbued with a desire for social justice.

IMF /ˌaɪ ɛm ˈɛf/ abbr. International Monetary Fund (the organization within the United Nations which is concerned with trade and economic development)

im·i·tate /ˈɪməˌteɪt/ verb **1** ~ sb/sth to copy someone or something: Her style of painting has been imitated by other artists. ◆ Art imitates Nature. ◆ Teachers provide a model for children to imitate. ◆ No computer can imitate the complex functions of the human brain. **2** ~ sb to copy the way a person speaks or behaves, in order to amuse people **SYN** MIMIC: She knew that the girls used to imitate her and laugh at her behind her back.

im·i·ta·tion /ˌɪməˈteɪʃn/ noun **1** [C] a copy of something, especially something expensive: a poor/cheap imitation of the real thing ◆ This latest production is a pale imitation of the original (= it is not nearly as good). ◆ imitation leather/pearls ⊃ thesaurus box at ARTIFICIAL **2** [U] the act of copying someone or something: A child learns to talk by imitation. ◆ Many corporate methods have been adopted by American managers in imitation of Japanese practice. **3** [C] an act of copying the way someone talks and behaves, especially to

---

| t tea | ṭ butter | d did | k cat | g got | tʃ chin | dʒ June | f fall

make people laugh **SYN** IMPRESSION: *He does an imitation of Barack Obama.*

im·i·ta·tive /ˈɪməˌteɪtɪv/ *adj.* (*formal*, sometimes *disapproving*) that copies someone or something: *movies that encourage imitative crime* ♦ *His work has been criticized for being imitative and shallow.*

im·i·ta·tor /ˈɪməˌteɪtər/ *noun* a person or thing that copies someone or something else: *The band's success has inspired hundreds of would-be imitators.*

im·mac·u·late /ɪˈmækyələt/ *adj.* **1** extremely clean and neat **SYN** SPOTLESS: *She always looks immaculate.* ♦ *an immaculate uniform/room* **2** containing no mistakes **SYN** PERFECT: *an immaculate performance* ▶ **im·mac·u·late·ly** *adv.*: *immaculately dressed*

the Imˌmaculate Conˈception *noun* [sing.] (*religion*) the Catholic belief that the Virgin Mary's soul was free from ORIGINAL SIN from the moment of her CONCEPTION

im·ma·nent /ˈɪmənənt/ *adj.* (*formal*) present as a natural part of something; present everywhere

im·ma·te·ri·al /ˌɪməˈtɪriəl/ *adj.* **1** [not usually before noun] not important in a particular situation **SYN** IRRELEVANT: *The cost is immaterial.* ♦ ~ **to sb/sth** *It is immaterial to me whether he stays or goes.* **2** (*formal*) not having a physical form: *an immaterial God* **ANT** MATERIAL

im·ma·ture **AWL** /ˌɪməˈtʃʊr; -ˈtʊr/ *adj.* **1** behaving in a way that is not sensible and is typical of people who are much younger: *immature behavior* **2** not fully developed or grown: *immature plants* **ANT** MATURE ▶ **im·ma·tu·ri·ty** **AWL** /ˌɪməˈtʃʊrəti; -ˈtʊr-/ *noun* [U]

im·meas·ur·a·ble /ɪˈmeʒərəbl/ *adj.* (*formal*) too large, great, etc. to be measured: *to cause immeasurable harm* ▶ **im·meas·ur·a·bly** /-bli/ *adv.*: *Housing standards improved immeasurably after the war.* ♦ *Stress has an immeasurably more serious effect on our lives than we realize.*

im·me·di·a·cy /ɪˈmidiəsi/ *noun* [U] (*formal*) **1** the quality in something that makes it seem as if it is happening now and close to you and is therefore important, urgent, etc.: *the immediacy of threat* ♦ *E-mail lacks the immediacy of online chat.* **2** lack of delay; speed: *Our aim is immediacy of response to emergency calls.*

im·me·di·ate 🔑 /ɪˈmidiət/ *adj.*

1 happening or done without delay **SYN** INSTANT: *an immediate reaction/response* ♦ *to take immediate action* **2** [usually before noun] existing now and needing urgent attention: *Our immediate concern is to help the families of those who died.* ♦ *The effects of global warming, while not immediate, are potentially catastrophic.* ♦ *The hospital says she's out of immediate danger.* **3** [only before noun] next to or very close to a particular place or time: *in the immediate vicinity* ♦ *The prospects for the immediate future are good.* ♦ *The director is standing on her immediate right.* ♦ *my immediate predecessor in the job* (= the person who had the job just before me) **4** [only before noun] nearest in relationship or rank: *The funeral was attended by her immediate family* (= her parents, children, brothers, and sisters) *only.* ♦ *He is my immediate superior* (= the person directly above me) *in the company.* **5** [only before noun] having a direct effect: *The immediate cause of death is unknown.* **IDM** see EFFECT *n.*

im·me·di·ate·ly 🔑 /ɪˈmidiətli/ *adv.*, *conj.*

1 without delay **SYN** AT ONCE: *She answered almost immediately.* ♦ *The point of my question may not be immediately apparent.* **2** (usually with prepositions) next to or very close to a particular place or time: *Turn right immediately after the church.* ♦ *the years immediately before the war* **3** (usually with past participles) closely and directly: *Counseling is being given to those most immediately affected by the tragedy.*

im·me·mo·ri·al /ˌɪməˈmɔriəl/ *adj.* (*formal* or *literary*) that has existed for longer than people can remember: *an immemorial tradition* ♦ *My family has lived in this area from time immemorial* (= for hundreds of years).

im·mense /ɪˈmɛns/ *adj.* extremely large or great

SYN ENORMOUS: *There is still an immense amount of work to be done.* ♦ *The benefits are immense.* ♦ *a project of immense importance*

im·mense·ly /ɪˈmɛnsli/ *adv.* extremely; very much **SYN** ENORMOUSLY: *immensely popular/difficult/grateful* ♦ *We enjoyed ourselves immensely.*

im·men·si·ty /ɪˈmɛnsəti/ *noun* [U] the large size of something: *the immensity of the universe* ♦ *We were overwhelmed by the sheer immensity of the task.*

im·merse /ɪˈmərs/ *verb* **1** ~ **sb/sth (in sth)** to put someone or something into a liquid so that they or it are completely covered **2** ~ **yourself/sb in sth** to become or make someone completely involved in something: *She immersed herself in her work.* ♦ *Clare and Phil were immersed in conversation in the corner.*

im·mer·sion /ɪˈmərʒn; -ʃn/ *noun* [U] **1** ~ **(in sth)** the act of putting someone or something into a liquid so that they or it are completely covered; the state of being completely covered by a liquid: *Immersion in cold water resulted in rapid loss of heat.* ♦ *baptism by total immersion* (= putting the whole body underwater) **2** ~ **(in sth)** the state of being completely involved in something: *his long immersion in politics* ♦ *a two-week immersion course in French* (= in which the student will hear and use only French)

im·mer·sive /ɪˈmərsɪv/ *adj.* (*technical*) used to describe a computer system or image that seems to surround the user

im·mi·grant **AWL** /ˈɪməgrənt/ *noun* a person who has come to live permanently in a country that is not their own: *immigrant communities/families/workers* ♦ *illegal immigrants* ⊃ compare EMIGRANT, MIGRANT

im·mi·grate **AWL** /ˈɪməˌgreɪt/ *verb* ~ **(to…) (from…)** to come and live permanently in a country after leaving your own country ⊃ compare EMIGRATE

im·mi·gra·tion **AWL** /ˌɪməˈgreɪʃn/ *noun* [U] **1** the process of coming to live permanently in a country that is not your own; the number of people who do this: *laws restricting immigration into the U.S.* ♦ *a rise/fall in immigration* ♦ *immigration officers* **2** (also immiˈgration control) the place at a port, an airport, etc. where the passports and other documents of people coming into a country are checked: *to go through immigration*

im·mi·nent /ˈɪmənənt/ *adj.* (especially of something unpleasant) likely to happen very soon: *the imminent threat of invasion* ♦ *The system is in imminent danger of collapse.* ♦ *An announcement about his resignation is imminent.* ▶ **im·mi·nence** /-nəns/ *noun* [U]: *the imminence of death* **im·mi·nent·ly** *adv.*

im·mis·ci·ble /ɪˈmɪsəbl/ *adj.* (*technical*) (of liquids) that cannot be mixed together **ANT** MISCIBLE

im·mo·bile /ɪˈmoʊbl/ *adj.* **1** not moving **SYN** MOTIONLESS: *She stood immobile by the window.* **2** unable to move: *His illness has left him completely immobile.* **ANT** MOBILE ▶ **im·mo·bil·i·ty** /ˌɪmoʊˈbɪləti/ *noun* [U]

im·mo·bi·lize /ɪˈmoʊbəˌlaɪz/ *verb* ~ **sth** to prevent something from moving or from working normally: *a device to immobilize the car engine in case of theft* ♦ *Always immobilize a broken leg immediately.* ▶ **im·mo·bi·li·za·tion** /ɪˌmoʊbələˈzeɪʃn/ *noun* [U]

im·mo·bi·liz·er /ɪˈmoʊbəˌlaɪzər/ *noun* a device that is fitted to a car to stop it from moving if someone tries to steal it

im·mod·er·ate /ɪˈmɑdərət/ *adj.* [usually before noun] (*formal*, *disapproving*) extreme; not reasonable **SYN** EXCESSIVE: *immoderate drinking* **ANT** MODERATE ▶ **im·mod·er·ate·ly** *adv.*

im·mod·est /ɪˈmɑdəst/ *adj.* **1** (*disapproving*) having or showing a very high opinion of yourself and your abilities **SYN** CONCEITED **2** not considered to be socially acceptable by most people, especially concerning sexual behavior: *an immodest dress* **ANT** MODEST

im·mo·late /ˈɪməˌleɪt/ *verb* ~ **sb** (*formal*) to kill someone by burning them ▶ **im·mo·la·tion** /ˌɪməˈleɪʃn/ *noun* [U]

im·mor·al /ɪˈmɔrəl; ɪˈmɑr-/ *adj.*
1 (of people and their behavior) not considered to be good or honest by most people: *It's immoral to steal.* ♦ *There's nothing immoral about wanting to earn more money.* **2** not following accepted standards of sexual behavior: *an immoral act/life/person* ➔ compare AMORAL, MORAL
▶ **im·mo·ral·i·ty** /ˌɪməˈræləti/ *noun* (*pl.* **im·mo·ral·i·ties**) [U, C]: *the immorality of war* ♦ *a life of immorality* **im·mor·al·ly** /ɪˈmɔrəli; ɪˈmɑr-/ *adv.*

im·mor·tal /ɪˈmɔrtl/ *adj., noun*
● *adj.* **1** that lives or lasts forever: *The soul is immortal.* ANT MORTAL **2** famous and likely to be remembered forever: *the immortal Goethe* ♦ *In the immortal words of Henry Ford, "If it ain't broke, don't fix it."*
● *noun* **1** a person who is so famous that they will be remembered forever: *She is one of the Hollywood immortals.* **2** a god or other BEING who is believed to live forever

im·mor·tal·i·ty /ˌɪmɔrˈtæləti/ *noun* [U] the state of being immortal: *belief in the immortality of the soul* ♦ *He is well on his way to showbusiness immortality.*

im·mor·tal·ize /ɪˈmɔrtlˌaɪz/ *verb* ~ sb/sth (in sth) to prevent someone or something from being forgotten in the future, especially by mentioning them in literature, making movies about them, painting them, etc.: *The poet fell in love with her and immortalized her in his verse.*

im·mov·a·ble /ɪˈmuvəbl/ *adj.* **1** [usually before noun] that cannot be moved: *an immovable object* **2** (of a person or an opinion, etc.) impossible to change or persuade: *On this issue he is completely immovable.*

im·mune /ɪˈmyun/ *adj.* [not usually before noun] **1** ~ (to sth) that cannot catch or be affected by a particular disease or illness: *Adults are often immune to German measles.* **2** ~ (to sth) not affected by something: *You'll eventually become immune to criticism.* **3** ~ (from sth) protected from something and therefore able to avoid it SYN EXEMPT: *No one should be immune from prosecution.*

im·mune re·sponse *noun* (*biology*) the reaction of the body to the presence of an ANTIGEN (= a substance that can cause disease)

im·mune ·system *noun* the system in your body that produces substances to help it fight against infection and disease

im·mu·ni·ty /ɪˈmyunəti/ *noun* [U, C] (*pl.* **im·mu·ni·ties**) **1** the body's ability to avoid or not be affected by infection and disease: ~ (to sth) *immunity to infection* ♦ ~ (against sth) *The vaccine provides longer immunity against the flu.* **2** ~ (from sth) the state of being protected from something: *The spies were all granted immunity from prosecution.* ♦ *congressional immunity* (= protection against particular laws that is given to politicians) ♦ *Officials of all member states receive certain privileges and immunities.* ➔ see also DIPLOMATIC IMMUNITY

im·mu·nize /ˈɪmyəˌnaɪz/ *verb* ~ sb/sth (against sth) to protect a person or an animal from a disease, especially by giving them an INJECTION of a VACCINE ➔ compare INOCULATE, VACCINATE ▶ **im·mu·ni·za·tion** /ˌɪmyənəˈzeɪʃn/ *noun* [U, C]: *an immunization program to prevent epidemics*

im·mu·no·de·fi·cien·cy /ˌɪmyənoʊdɪˈfɪʃnsi; ɪˌmyunoʊ-/ (also **im·mune de·ficiency**) *noun* [U] a medical condition in which your body does not have the normal ability to resist infection: *human immunodeficiency virus or HIV*

im·mu·nol·o·gy /ˌɪmyəˈnɑlədʒi/ *noun* [U] the scientific study of protection against disease ▶ **im·mu·no·log·i·cal** /ˌɪmyənəˈlɑdʒɪkl/ *adj.*

im·mu·no·sup·pres·sion /ˌɪmyənoʊsəˈprɛʃn/ *noun* [U] (*medical*) the act of stopping the body from reacting against ANTIGENS, for example in order to prevent the body from rejecting a new organ ▶ **im·mu·no·sup·pres·sant** /-səˈprɛsənt/ *noun*

im·mure /ɪˈmyʊr/ *verb* ~ sb (*literary*) to shut someone in a place so that they cannot get out SYN IMPRISON

im·mu·ta·ble /ɪˈmyutəbl/ *adj.* (*formal*) that cannot be changed; that will never change SYN UNCHANGEABLE
▶ **im·mu·ta·bil·i·ty** /ˌɪmyutəˈbɪləti/ *noun* [U]

imp /ɪmp/ *noun* **1** (in stories) a small creature like a little man, that has magic powers and behaves badly **2** a child who behaves badly, but not in a serious way

im·pact 〔AWL〕 *noun, verb*
● *noun* /ˈɪmpækt/ [C, usually sing., U] **1** ~ (of sth) (on sb/sth) the powerful effect that something has on someone or something: *the environmental impact of tourism* ♦ *The report assesses the impact of AIDS on the gay community.* ♦ *Her speech made a profound impact on everyone.* ♦ *Businesses are beginning to feel the full impact of the recession.* **2** the act of one object hitting another; the force with which this happens: *craters made by meteorite impacts* ♦ *The impact of the blow knocked Jack off balance.* ♦ *The bomb explodes on impact* (= when it hits something). ♦ *The car is fitted with side impact bars* (= to protect it from a blow from the side).
● *verb* /ɪmˈpækt/ **1** [I, T] to have an effect on something SYN AFFECT: ~ on/upon sth *Her father's death impacted greatly on her childhood years.* ♦ ~ sth (*business*) *The company's performance was impacted by the high value of the dollar.* **2** [I, T] ~ (on/upon/with) sth (*formal*) to hit something with great force

im·pact·ed 〔AWL〕 /ɪmˈpæktəd/ *adj.* (of a tooth) that cannot grow correctly because it is under another tooth

im·pair /ɪmˈpɛr/ *verb* ~ sth (*formal*) to damage something or make something worse ➔ thesaurus box at DAMAGE

im·paired /ɪmˈpɛrd/ *adj.* **1** damaged or not functioning normally: *impaired vision/memory* **2** -impaired having the type of physical or mental problem mentioned: *hearing-impaired children* ♦ *Nowadays we say someone is "speech-impaired," not dumb.* ➔ note at DISABLED **3** (*CanE*) drunk when driving a vehicle

im·pair·ment /ɪmˈpɛrmənt/ *noun* [U, C] (*technical*) the state of having a physical or mental condition that means that part of your body or brain does not work correctly; a particular condition of this sort: *impairment of kidney function* ♦ *visual impairments*

im·pa·la /ɪmˈpælə; -ˈpɑlə/ *noun* (*pl.* **im·pal·a** or **im·pal·as**) an African ANTELOPE with curled horns

im·pale /ɪmˈpeɪl/ *verb* **1** ~ sth (on sth) to push a sharp pointed object through something SYN SPEAR: *She impaled a lump of meat on her fork.* **2** ~ sb/yourself on sth if you **impale** yourself on something, or **are impaled** on it, you have a sharp pointed object pushed into you and you may be caught somewhere by it: *He fell and was impaled on some iron railings.*

im·pal·pa·ble /ɪmˈpælpəbl/ *adj.* (*formal*) **1** that cannot be felt physically **2** very difficult to understand ANT PALPABLE

im·pan·el (also **em·pan·el**) /ɪmˈpænl/ *verb* (-l-) ~ sb/sth to choose the members of a jury in a court case; to choose someone as a member of a jury

im·part /ɪmˈpɑrt/ *verb* (*formal*) **1** ~ sth (to sb) to pass information, knowledge, etc. to other people SYN CONVEY **2** ~ sth (to sb) to give a particular quality to something SYN LEND: *The spice imparts an Eastern flavor to the dish.*

im·par·tial /ɪmˈpɑrʃl/ *adj.* not supporting one person or group more than another SYN NEUTRAL, UNBIASED: *an impartial inquiry/observer* ♦ *to give impartial advice* ♦ *As chairman, I must remain impartial.* ANT PARTIAL
▶ **im·par·ti·al·i·ty** /ˌɪmˌpɑrʃiˈæləti/ *noun* [U] **im·par·tial·ly** /ɪmˈpɑrʃəli/ *adv.*

im·pass·a·ble /ɪmˈpæsəbl/ *adj.* (of a road, an area, etc.) impossible to travel on or through, especially because it is in bad condition or it has been blocked by something ANT PASSABLE

im·passe /ˈɪmpæs/ *noun* [usually sing.] a difficult situation in which no progress can be made because the people involved cannot agree what to do **SYN** DEADLOCK: *to break/ end the impasse.* ◆ *Negotiations have reached an impasse.*

im·pas·sioned /ɪmˈpæʃnd/ *adj.* [usually before noun] (usually of speech) showing strong feelings about something **SYN** FERVENT: *an impassioned plea/speech/defense*

im·pas·sive /ɪmˈpæsɪv/ *adj.* not showing any feeling or emotion **SYN** EMOTIONLESS: *her impassive expression/face* ▶ **im·pas·sive·ly** *adv.*

im·pa·tiens /ɪmˈpeɪʃnz; -ʃns/ *noun* (*pl.* im·pa·tiens) a small plant with a lot of red, pink, or white flowers, often grown indoors or in gardens

im·pa·tient 🔑 /ɪmˈpeɪʃnt/ *adj.*
1 annoyed or irritated by someone or something, especially because you have to wait for a long time: *I'd been waiting for twenty minutes and I was getting impatient.* ◆ *~ (with sb/sth)* Try not to be too impatient with her.* ◆ *~ (at sth)* Sarah was becoming increasingly impatient at their lack of interest.* ◆ *He waved them away with an impatient gesture.* **2** wanting to do something soon; wanting something to happen soon: *~ to do sth She was clearly impatient to leave.* ◆ *~ for sth impatient for change* **3** *~ of sb/sth* (*formal*) unable or unwilling to accept something unpleasant: *impatient of criticism* ▶ **im·pa·tience** /ɪmˈpeɪʃns/ *noun* [U]: *She was bursting with impatience to tell me the news.* **im·pa·tient·ly** *adv.*: *We sat waiting impatiently for the movie to start.*

im·peach /ɪmˈpiːtʃ/ *verb* **1** *~ sb (for sth)* (of a court or other official body, especially in the U.S.) to charge an important public figure with a serious crime **2** *~ sth* (*formal*) to raise doubts about something **SYN** QUESTION: *to impeach someone's motives* ▶ **im·peach·ment** *noun* [U, C]

im·peach·a·ble /ɪmˈpiːtʃəbl/ *adj.* (of a crime) for which a politician or a person who works for the government can be impeached: *an impeachable offense*

im·pec·ca·ble /ɪmˈpɛkəbl/ *adj.* without mistakes or faults **SYN** PERFECT: *impeccable manners/taste* ◆ *Her written English is impeccable.* ◆ *He was dressed in a suit and an impeccable white shirt.* ▶ **im·pec·ca·bly** /-bli/ *adv.*: *to behave impeccably* ◆ *impeccably dressed*

im·pe·cu·ni·ous /ˌɪmpɪˈkyuːniəs/ *adj.* (*formal* or *humorous*) having little or no money **SYN** PENNILESS, POOR

im·ped·ance /ɪmˈpiːdns/ *noun* [U] (*physics*) a measurement of the total RESISTANCE of a piece of electrical equipment, etc. to the flow of an ALTERNATING CURRENT

im·pede /ɪmˈpiːd/ *verb* [often passive] *~ sth* (*formal*) to delay or stop the progress of something **SYN** HAMPER, HINDER: *Work on the building was impeded by severe weather.*

im·ped·i·ment /ɪmˈpɛdəmənt/ *noun* **1** *~ (to sth)* something that delays or stops the progress of something **SYN** OBSTACLE: *The level of inflation is a serious impediment to economic recovery.* **2** a physical problem that makes it difficult to speak normally: *a speech impediment*

im·ped·i·men·ta /ɪmˌpɛdəˈmɛntə/ *noun* [pl.] (*formal* or *humorous*) the bags and other equipment that you take with you, especially when traveling, and that are difficult to carry

im·pel /ɪmˈpɛl/ *verb* (-ll-) (*formal*) if an idea or feeling **impels** you to do something, you feel as if you are forced to do it: *~ sb to do sth He felt impelled to investigate further.* ◆ *~ sb (to sth)* There are various reasons that impel me to that conclusion.

im·pend·ing /ɪmˈpɛndɪŋ/ *adj.* [only before noun] (usually of an unpleasant event) that is going to happen very soon **SYN** IMMINENT: *his impending retirement* ◆ *warnings of impending danger/disaster*

im·pen·e·tra·ble /ɪmˈpɛnətrəbl/ *adj.* **1** that cannot be entered, passed through, or seen through: *an impenetrable jungle* ◆ *impenetrable darkness* **ANT** PENETRABLE **2** impossible to understand **SYN** INCOMPREHENSIBLE: *an impenetrable mystery* ◆ *~ to sb Their jargon is impenetrable to an outsider.* ▶ **im·pen·e·tra·bil·i·ty** /ɪmˌpɛnətrəˈbɪləti/ *noun* [U] **im·pen·e·tra·bly** /ɪmˈpɛnətrəbli/ *adv.*

im·pen·i·tent /ɪmˈpɛnətənt/ *adj.* (*formal*) not feeling ashamed or sorry about something bad you have done

im·per·a·tive /ɪmˈpɛrətɪv/ *adj., noun*
● *adj.* **1** [not usually before noun] (*formal*) very important and needing immediate attention or action **SYN** VITAL: *~ (that…) It is absolutely imperative that we finish by next week.* ◆ *~ (to do sth) It is imperative to continue the treatment for at least two months.* **2** (*formal*) expressing authority: *an imperative tone* **3** [only before noun] (*grammar*) expressing an order: *an imperative sentence*
● *noun* **1** (*formal*) a thing that is very important and needs immediate attention or action: *the economic imperative of quality education for all* **2** (*grammar*) the form of a verb that expresses an order; a verb in this form: *In "Go away!" the verb is in the imperative.* ◆ *"Go away!" is an imperative.*

im·per·cep·ti·ble /ˌɪmpərˈsɛptəbl/ *adj.* very small and therefore unable to be seen or felt: *imperceptible changes in temperature* **ANT** PERCEPTIBLE ▶ **im·per·cep·ti·bly** /-bli/ *adv.*

im·per·fect /ɪmˈpərfɪkt/ *adj., noun*
● *adj.* containing faults or mistakes; not complete or perfect **SYN** FLAWED: *an imperfect world* ◆ *an imperfect understanding of English* ◆ *All our sale items are slightly imperfect.* ▶ **im·per·fect·ly** *adv.*
● *noun* the imperfect (also the im·perfect 'tense) [sing.] (*grammar*) the verb tense that expresses action in the past that is not complete. It is often called the **past progressive** or **past continuous**: *In "while I was washing my hair," the verb is in the imperfect.*

im·per·fec·tion /ˌɪmpərˈfɛkʃn/ *noun* [C, U] a fault or weakness in someone or something: *They learned to live with each other's imperfections.*

im·pe·ri·al /ɪmˈpɪriəl/ *adj.* [only before noun] **1** connected with an empire: *the imperial family/palace/army* ◆ *imperial power/expansion* **2** connected with the system for measuring length, weight, and volume using pounds, inches, etc. ⟳ compare METRIC

im·pe·ri·al·ism /ɪmˈpɪriəˌlɪzəm/ *noun* [U] (usually *disapproving*) **1** a system in which one country controls other countries, often after defeating them in a war: *Roman imperialism* **2** the fact of a powerful country increasing its influence over other countries through business, culture, etc.: *cultural/economic imperialism* ▶ **im·pe·ri·al·ist** (also **im·pe·ri·al·is·tic** /ɪmˌpɪriəˈlɪstɪk/) *adj.*: *an imperialist power* ◆ *imperialist ambitions*

im·pe·ri·al·ist /ɪmˈpɪriəlɪst/ *noun* (usually *disapproving*) a person, such as a politician, who supports imperialism

im·per·il /ɪmˈpɛrəl/ *verb* (-l-) *~ sth/sb* (*formal*) to put something or someone in danger **SYN** ENDANGER

im·pe·ri·ous /ɪmˈpɪriəs/ *adj.* (*formal*) expecting people to obey you and treating them as if they are not as important as you: *an imperious gesture/voice/command* ▶ **im·pe·ri·ous·ly** *adv.*: *"Get it now," she demanded imperiously.*

im·per·ish·a·ble /ɪmˈpɛrɪʃəbl/ *adj.* (*formal* or *literary*) that will last for a long time or forever **SYN** ENDURING

im·per·ma·nent /ɪmˈpərmənənt/ *adj.* (*formal*) that will not last or stay the same forever **ANT** PERMANENT ▶ **im·per·ma·nence** /-nəns/ *noun* [U]

im·per·me·a·ble /ɪmˈpərmiəbl/ *adj.* *~ (to sth)* (*technical*) not allowing a liquid or gas to pass through **ANT** PERMEABLE

im·per·mis·si·ble /ˌɪmpərˈmɪsəbl/ *adj.* that cannot be allowed: *an impermissible invasion of privacy* **ANT** PERMISSIBLE

im·per·son·al /ɪmˈpərsənl/ *adj.* **1** (usually *disapproving*) lacking friendly human feelings or atmosphere; making you feel unimportant: *a vast impersonal organization* ◆ *an impersonal hotel room* ◆ *Business letters need not be formal and impersonal.* ◆ *a cold impersonal stare* **2** not referring to any particular person: *Let's keep the criticism general and impersonal.* **3** (*grammar*) an **impersonal** verb or sentence has "it" or "there" as the subject ▶ **im·per·son·al·i·ty** /ɪmˌpɜːrsə-ˈnæləti/ *noun* [U]: *the cold impersonality of some modern cities* **im·per·son·al·ly** /ɪmˈpɜːrsənəli/ *adv.*

impersonal

giving opinions using impersonal language

- **It is vital that** more is done to prevent the illegal trade in wild animals. ◆ (Compare: *We have to do more to stop people trading wild animals illegally.*)
- **It is clear that** more needs to be done to protect biodiversity. ◆ (Compare: *We clearly need to do more to protect biodiversity.*)
- **It is unfortunate that** the practice of keeping monkeys as pets still continues. ◆ (Compare: *It's absolutely terrible that people still keep monkeys as pets.*)
- **It is difficult** for many people **to** understand the reasons why certain individuals choose to hunt animals for sport. ◆ (Compare: *I can't understand why anyone would want to kill animals for fun.*)
- Unfortunately, **it would seem that** not enough is being done to support tiger conservation. ◆ (Compare: *Governments aren't doing enough to help tiger conservation.*)
- **There is no doubt that** the greatest threat to polar bears comes from global warming. ◆ (Compare: *I believe that the greatest threat…*)

➲ Language Banks at OPINION, PERHAPS, VITAL

im·personal ˈpronoun *noun* (*grammar*) a pronoun (in English, the pronoun "it") that does not refer to a person or thing or to any other part of the sentence, for example in "it was raining"

im·per·son·ate /ɪmˈpɜːrsəˌneɪt/ *verb* ~ **sb** to pretend to be someone in order to trick people or to entertain them: *He was caught trying to impersonate a security guard.* ◆ *They do a pretty good job of impersonating Laurel and Hardy.* ▶ **im·per·son·a·tion** /ɪmˌpɜːrsəˈneɪʃn/ *noun* [C, U] **SYN** IMPRESSION: *He did a very convincing impersonation of the singer.*

im·per·son·a·tor /ɪmˈpɜːrsəˌneɪtər/ *noun* a person who copies the way another person talks or behaves in order to entertain people: *The show included a **female impersonator*** (= a man dressed as a woman).

im·per·ti·nent /ɪmˈpɜːrtn·ənt/ *adj.* (*formal*) rude and not showing respect for someone who is older or more important **SYN** IMPOLITE: *an impertinent question/child* ◆ *Would it be impertinent to ask why you're leaving?* ➲ thesaurus box at RUDE ▶ **im·per·ti·nence** /-əns/ *noun* [U, C, usually sing.]: *She had the impertinence to ask my age!* **im·per·ti·nent·ly** *adv.*

im·per·turb·a·ble /ˌɪmpərˈtɜːrbəbl/ *adj.* (*formal*) not easily upset or worried by a difficult situation; calm ▶ **im·per·turb·a·bil·i·ty** /ˌɪmpərˌtɜːrbəˈbɪləti/ *noun* [U] **im·per·turb·a·bly** /ˌɪmpərˈtɜːrbəbli/ *adv.*

im·per·vi·ous /ɪmˈpɜːrviəs/ *adj.* **1** ~ **to sth** not affected or influenced by something: *impervious to criticism/pain* **2** (*technical*) not allowing a liquid or gas to pass through: *an impervious rock/layer* ◆ ~ **to sth** *impervious to moisture*

im·pe·ti·go /ˌɪmpəˈtaɪɡoʊ/ *noun* [U] an infectious disease that causes sore areas on the skin

im·pet·u·ous /ɪmˈpɛtʃuəs/ *adj.* acting or done quickly and without thinking carefully about the results **SYN** IMPULSIVE, RASH: *an impetuous young woman* ◆ *an impetuous decision* ▶ **im·pet·u·os·i·ty** /ɪmˌpɛtʃuˈɑsəti/ *noun* [U] **im·pet·u·ous·ly** /ɪmˈpɛtʃuəsli/ *adv.*

im·pe·tus /ˈɪmpətəs/ *noun* **1** [U, sing.] something that encourages a process or activity to develop more quickly **SYN** STIMULUS: *The debate seems to have lost much of its initial impetus.* ◆ ~ **to sth/to do sth** *to give (a) new/fresh impetus to something* ◆ ~ **for sth** *His articles provided the main impetus for change.* **2** [U] (*technical*) the force or energy with which something moves

im·pinge /ɪmˈpɪndʒ/ *verb* [I] ~ **(on/upon sth/sb)** (*formal*) to have a noticeable effect on something or someone, especially a bad one **SYN** ENCROACH: *He never allowed his work to impinge on his private life.*

im·pi·ous /ˈɪmpaɪəs; ˈɪmpiəs/ *adj.* (*formal*) showing a lack of respect for God and religion **ANT** PIOUS ▶ **im·pi·e·ty** /ɪmˈpaɪəti/ *noun* [U]

imp·ish /ˈɪmpɪʃ/ *adj.* showing a lack of respect for someone or something in a way that is amusing rather than serious **SYN** MISCHIEVOUS: *an impish grin/look* ➲ see also IMP ▶ **imp·ish·ly** *adv.*

im·plac·a·ble /ɪmˈplækəbl/ *adj.* **1** (of strong negative opinions or feelings) that cannot be changed: *implacable hatred* **2** (of a person) unwilling to stop opposing someone or something: *an implacable enemy* ▶ **im·plac·a·bly** /-bli/ *adv.*: *to be implacably opposed to the plan*

im·plant *verb, noun*
- *verb* /ɪmˈplænt/ **1** [T] ~ **sth (in/into sth)** to fix an idea, attitude, etc. firmly in someone's mind: *Prejudices can easily become implanted in the mind.* **2** [T] ~ **sth (in/into sth)** to put something (usually something artificial) into a part of the body for medical purposes, usually by means of an operation: *an electrode implanted into the brain* ➲ compare TRANSPLANT **3** [I] ~ **(in/into sth)** (of an egg or an EMBRYO) to become fixed inside the body of a person or an animal so that it can start to develop ▶ **im·plan·ta·tion** /ˌɪmplænˈteɪʃn/ *noun* [U]
- *noun* /ˈɪmplænt/ something that is put into a person's body in a medical operation: *silicone breast implants* ➲ compare TRANSPLANT

im·plau·si·ble /ɪmˈplɔːzəbl/ *adj.* not seeming reasonable or likely to be true: *an implausible claim/idea/theory* ◆ *It was all highly implausible.* **ANT** PLAUSIBLE ▶ **im·plau·si·bly** /-bli/ *adv.*

im·ple·ment AWL *verb, noun*
- *verb* /ˈɪmpləˌmɛnt/ ~ **sth** to make something that has been officially decided start to happen or be used **SYN** CARRY OUT: *to implement changes/decisions/policies/reforms* ▶ **im·ple·men·ta·tion** AWL /ˌɪmpləmənˈteɪʃn/ *noun* [U]: *the implementation of the new system*
- *noun* /ˈɪmpləmənt/ a tool or an instrument, often one that is quite simple and that is used outdoors: *agricultural implements*

im·pli·cate AWL /ˈɪmpləˌkeɪt/ *verb* **1** ~ **sb (in sth)** to show or suggest that someone is involved in something bad or criminal **SYN** INCRIMINATE: *He tried to avoid saying anything that would implicate him further.* **2** ~ **sth (in/as sth)** to show or suggest that something is the cause of something bad: *The results implicate poor hygiene as one cause of the outbreak.* **IDM** **be implicated in sth** to be involved in a crime; to be responsible for something bad: *Senior officials were implicated in the scandal.*

im·pli·ca·tion 🔑 AWL /ˌɪmpləˈkeɪʃn/ *noun* **1** [C, usually pl.] ~ **(of sth) (for sth)** a possible effect or result of an action or a decision: *They failed to consider the wider implications of their actions.* ◆ *The development of the site will have implications for the surrounding countryside.* **2** [C, U] something that is suggested or indirectly stated (= something that is implied): *The implication in his article is that being a housewife is greatly inferior to every other occupation.* ◆ *He criticized the Director and, by implication, the whole of the organization.* **3** [U] ~ **(of sb) (in sth)** the fact of being involved, or of involving someone, in something, especially a crime **SYN** INVOLVEMENT: *He resigned after his implication in a sex scandal.*

im·pli·ca·ture /ˈɪmplɪkətʃər/ *noun* (*technical*) **1** [U] the act of suggesting that you feel or think something is true, without saying so directly **2** [C] something that you can understand from what is said, but which is not stated directly: *An implicature of "Some of my friends came" is "Some of my friends did not come."*

im·plic·it AWL /ɪmˈplɪsət/ *adj.* **1** ~ **(in sth)** suggested

ʌ **cup**　　ə **about**　　eɪ **say**　　aɪ **five**　　ɔɪ **boy**　　aʊ **now**　　oʊ **go**　　ər **bird**

without being directly expressed: *Implicit in his speech was the assumption that they were guilty.* ◆ *implicit criticism* **2 ~ (in sth)** forming part of something (although perhaps not directly expressed): *The ability to listen is implicit in the teacher's role.* **3** complete and not doubted **SYN** ABSOLUTE: *She had the implicit trust of her staff.* ◒ compare EXPLICIT ▸ **im·plic·it·ly** **AWL** *adv.*: *It reinforces, implicitly or explicitly, the idea that money is all-important.* ◆ *I trust John implicitly.*

im·plode /ɪmˈploʊd/ *verb* **1** [I] to burst or explode and collapse into the center **2** [I] (of an organization, a system, etc.) to fail suddenly and completely ▸ **im·plo·sion** /ɪmˈploʊʒn/ *noun* [C, U]

im·plore /ɪmˈplɔːr/ *verb* (*formal* or *literary*) to ask someone to do something in an anxious way because you want or need it very much **SYN** BEG, BESEECH: ~ **sb to do sth** *She implored him to stay.* ◆ ~ **(sb) + speech** *"Help me," he implored.* ◆ ~ **sb** *Tell me it's true. I implore you.* ▸ **im·plor·ing** *adj.*: *She gave him an imploring look.*

im·ply 🔑 **AWL** /ɪmˈplaɪ/ *verb* (im·plies, im·ply·ing, im·plied, im·plied)
1 to suggest that something is true or that you feel or think something, without saying so directly: ~ **(that)…** *Are you implying (that) I am wrong?* ◆ ~ **sth** *I disliked the implied criticism in his voice.* ◆ **it is implied that…** *It was implied that we were at fault.* ◒ note at INFER **2** to make it seem likely that something is true or exists **SYN** SUGGEST: ~ **(that)…** *The survey implies (that) more people are moving away than was thought.* ◆ **it is implied that…** *It was implied in the survey that…* ◆ ~ **sth** *The fact that she was here implies a degree of interest.* **3** ~ **sth** (of an idea, action, etc.) to make something necessary in order to be successful **SYN** MEAN: *The project implies an enormous investment in training.* ◒ see also IM-PLICATION

im·po·lite /ˌɪmpəˈlaɪt/ *adj.* not polite **SYN** RUDE: *Some people think it is impolite to ask someone's age.* ◒ thesaurus box at RUDE ▸ **im·po·lite·ly** *adv.* **im·po·lite·ness** *noun* [U]

im·pol·i·tic /ɪmˈpɑləˌtɪk/ *adj.* (*formal*) not wise **SYN** UNWISE: *It would have been impolitic to refuse his offer.*

im·pon·der·a·ble /ɪmˈpɑndərəbl/ *noun* [usually pl.] (*formal*) something that is difficult to measure or estimate: *We can't predict the outcome. There are too many imponderables.* ▸ **im·pon·der·a·ble** *adj.*

im·port 🔑 *noun, verb*
● *noun* /ˈɪmpɔrt/ **1** [C, usually pl.] a product or service that is brought into one country from another: *food imports from abroad* **ANT** EXPORT ◒ collocations at ECONOMY **2** [U, pl.] the act of bringing a product or service into one country from another: *The report calls for a ban on the import of hazardous waste.* ◆ *import controls* ◆ *an import license* ◆ *imports of oil* **ANT** EXPORT **3** [U] (*formal*) importance: *matters of great import* **4** **the ~ (of sth)** [sing.] (*formal*) the meaning of something, especially when it is not immediately clear: *It is difficult to understand the full import of this statement.*
● *verb* /ɪmˈpɔrt; ˈɪmpɔrt/ **1** to bring a product, a service, an idea, etc. into one country from another: ~ **sth** *The country has to import most of its raw materials.* ◆ ~ **sth (from…) (into…)** *goods imported from Japan into the U.S.* ◆ *customs imported from the West* **2** ~ **sth (from…) (into…)** (*computing*) to get data from another program, changing its form so that the program you are using can read it **ANT** EXPORT ▸ **im·por·ta·tion** /ˌɪmpɔrˈteɪʃn/ *noun* [U, C] **SYN** IMPORT: *a ban on the importation of ivory*

im·por·tance 🔑 /ɪmˈpɔrtns/ *noun* [U]
the quality of being important: *She stressed the importance of careful preparation.* ◆ *It's a matter of the greatest importance to me.* ◆ *They attach great importance to the project* ◆ *the relative importance of the two ideas* ◆ *State your reasons in order of importance.* ◆ *He was very aware of his own importance.*

im·por·tant 🔑 /ɪmˈpɔrtnt/ *adj.*
1 having a great effect on people or things; of great value: *an important decision/factor* ◆ *I have an important announce-*

---

ment to make. ◆ *Money played an important role in his life.* ◆ *Listening is an important part of the job.* ◆ *one of the most important collections of American art* ◆ *It is important to follow the manufacturer's instructions.* ◆ *It is important that he attend every day.* ◆ *It is important for him to attend every day.* ◆ ~ **(to sb)** *It's very important to me that you should be there.* ◆ *The important thing is to keep trying.* ◒ language bank at EMPHASIS **2** (of a person) having great influence or authority: *an important member of the team* ◆ *He likes to feel important.* ▸ **im·por·tant·ly** *adv.*: *More importantly, can he be trusted?* ◆ *She was sitting importantly behind a big desk.*

im·port·er /ɪmˈpɔrtər; ˈɪmpɔrtər/ *noun* a person, company, etc. that buys goods from another country to sell them in their own country: *a New York-based importer of Italian goods* ◒ compare EXPORTER

im·por·tu·nate /ɪmˈpɔrtʃənət/ *adj.* (*formal*) asking for things many times in a way that is annoying

im·por·tune /ˌɪmpɔrˈtun/ *verb* ~ **sb (for sth)** | ~ **sb to do sth** (*formal*) to ask someone for something many times and in a way that is annoying **SYN** PESTER

im·pose 🔑 **AWL** /ɪmˈpoʊz/ *verb*
1 [T] ~ **sth (on/upon sth/sb)** to introduce a new law, rule, tax, etc.; to order that a rule, punishment, etc. be used: *A new tax was imposed on fuel.* **2** [T] ~ **sth (on/upon sb/sth)** to force someone or something to have to deal with something that is difficult or unpleasant: *to impose limitations/restrictions/constraints on something* ◆ *This system imposes additional financial burdens on many people.* **3** [T] ~ **sth (on/upon sb)** to make someone accept the same opinions, wishes etc. as your own: *She didn't want to impose her values on her family.* ◆ *It was noticeable how a few people managed to impose their will on the others.* **4** [I] to expect someone to do something for you or to spend time with you, when it may not be convenient for them: *"You must stay for lunch." "Well, thanks, but I don't want to impose…"* ◆ ~ **on/upon sb/sth** *Everyone imposes on Dave's good nature.* **5** [T] ~ **yourself (on/upon sb/sth)** to make someone or something accept or be aware of your presence or ideas: *European civilization was the first to impose itself across the whole world.*

im·pos·ing **AWL** /ɪmˈpoʊzɪŋ/ *adj.* impressive to look at; making a strong impression: *a grand and imposing building* ◆ *a tall imposing woman*

im·po·si·tion **AWL** /ˌɪmpəˈzɪʃn/ *noun* **1** [U] the act of introducing something such as a new law or rule, or a new tax: *the imposition of martial law* ◆ *the imposition of tax on domestic fuel* **2** [C] an unfair or unreasonable thing that someone expects or asks you to do: *I'd like to stay if it's not too much of an imposition.*

im·pos·si·ble 🔑 /ɪmˈpɑsəbl/ *adj.*
1 that cannot exist or be done; not possible: *almost/virtually impossible* ◆ *It's impossible for me to be there before eight.* ◆ *It's impossible to prove.* ◆ *I find it impossible to lie to her.* ◆ *an impossible dream/goal* **ANT** POSSIBLE **2** very difficult to deal with: *I've been placed in an impossible position.* ◆ *Honestly, you're impossible at times!* **3** **the impossible** *noun* [sing.] a thing that is or seems impossible: *to attempt the impossible* ▸ **im·pos·si·bil·i·ty** /ɪmˌpɑsəˈbɪləti/ *noun* (pl. im·pos·si·bil·i·ties) [U, C, usually sing.]: *the sheer impossibility of providing enough food for everyone* ◆ *a virtual impossibility* **im·pos·si·bly** /ɪmˈpɑsəbli/ *adv.*: *an impossibly difficult problem* (= impossible to solve) ◆ *He was impossibly handsome* (= it was difficult to believe that he could be so HANDSOME).

im·pos·tor (also **im·pos·ter**) /ɪmˈpɑstər/ *noun* a person who pretends to be someone else in order to trick people

im·pos·ture /ɪmˈpɑstʃər/ *noun* [U, C] (*formal*) an act of tricking people deliberately by pretending to be someone else

im·po·tent /ˈɪmpətənt/ *adj.* **1** having no power to change things or to influence a situation **SYN** POWERLESS: *Without the chairman's support, the committee is impotent.* ◆ *She blazed with impotent rage.* **2** (of a man) unable to achieve an ERECTION and therefore unable to have full sex

---

▶ **im·po·tence** /ˈɪmpətəns/ noun [U]: *a feeling of impotence in the face of an apparently insoluble problem* ♦ *male impotence*
im·po·tent·ly adv.

im·pound /ɪmˈpaʊnd/ verb (*law*) **1** ~ **sth** (of the police, courts of law, etc.) to take something away from someone, so that they cannot use it **SYN** CONFISCATE: *The car was impounded by the police after the accident.* **2** ~ **sth** to shut up dogs, cats, etc. found on the streets in a POUND, until their owners collect them

im·pov·er·ish /ɪmˈpɑvərɪʃ/ verb **1** ~ **sb** to make someone poor: *These changes are likely to impoverish single-parent families even further.* **2** ~ **sth** to make something worse in quality: *Intensive cultivation has impoverished the soil.*
▶ **im·pov·er·ish·ment** noun [U]

im·pov·er·ished /ɪmˈpɑvərɪʃt/ adj. **1** very poor; without money: *impoverished peasants* ♦ *the impoverished areas of the city* ⊃ thesaurus box at POOR **2** poor in quality, because something is missing

im·prac·ti·ca·ble /ɪmˈpræktɪkəbl/ adj. impossible or very difficult to do; not practical in a particular situation: *It would be impracticable for each member to be consulted on every occasion.* ⊃ compare IMPRACTICAL **ANT** PRACTICABLE
▶ **im·prac·ti·ca·bil·i·ty** /ɪmˌpræktɪkəˈbɪləti/ noun [U]

im·prac·ti·cal /ɪmˈpræktɪkl/ adj. **1** not sensible or realistic: *It was totally impractical to think that we could finish the job in two months.* **2** (of people) not good at doing things that involve using the hands; not good at planning or organizing things **ANT** PRACTICAL ⊃ compare IMPRACTICABLE
▶ **im·prac·ti·cal·i·ty** /ɪmˌpræktɪˈkæləti/ noun [U]

im·pre·ca·tion /ˌɪmprɪˈkeɪʃn/ noun (*formal*) a CURSE (= an offensive word that is used to express extreme anger)

im·pre·cise **AWL** /ˌɪmprɪˈsaɪs/ adj. not giving exact details or making something clear **SYN** INACCURATE: *an imprecise definition* ♦ *imprecise information* ♦ *The witness's descriptions were too imprecise to be of any real value.* **ANT** PRECISE
▶ **im·pre·cise·ly** adv.: *These terms are often used imprecisely and interchangeably.* **im·pre·ci·sion** /ˌɪmprɪˈsɪʒn/ noun [U]: *There is considerable imprecision in the terminology used.*

im·preg·na·ble /ɪmˈprɛgnəbl/ adj. **1** an **impregnable** building is so strongly built that it cannot be entered by force: *an impregnable fortress* **2** strong and impossible to defeat or change **SYN** INVINCIBLE: *The team built up an impregnable 5–1 lead.*

im·preg·nate /ɪmˈprɛgneɪt/ verb **1** [usually passive] ~ **sth (with sth)** to make a substance spread through an area so that the area is full of the substance: *The pad is impregnated with insecticide.* **2** ~ **sb/sth** (*formal*) to make a woman or female animal pregnant ▶ **im·preg·na·tion** /ˌɪmprɛgˈneɪʃn/ noun [U]

im·pre·sa·ri·o /ˌɪmprəˈsɑrioʊ; -ˈsɛr-/ noun (pl. **im·pre·sa·ri·os**) a person who arranges plays in the theater, etc., especially a person who manages a theater, OPERA, or BALLET company

im·press 🔑 /ɪmˈprɛs/ verb

1 [T, I] if a person or thing **impresses** you, you feel admiration for them or it: ~ **(sb)** *We interviewed a number of candidates but none of them impressed us.* ♦ *The Grand Canyon never fails to impress.* ♦ *His sincerity impressed her.* ♦ ~ **sb with sth/sb** *He impressed her with his sincerity.* ♦ **it impresses sb that…** *It impressed me that she remembered my name.* ♦ **sb is impressed that…** *I was impressed that she remembered my name.* ⊃ see also IMPRESSED, IMPRESSIVE **2** [T] ~ **sth on/ upon sb** (*formal*) to make someone understand how important, serious etc. something is by emphasizing it: *He impressed on us the need for immediate action.* **3** [T] ~ **sth/ itself on/upon sth** (*formal*) to have a great effect on something, especially someone's mind, imagination, etc.: *Her words impressed themselves on my memory.*

im·pressed 🔑 /ɪmˈprɛst/ adj.
feeling admiration for someone or something because you think they are particularly good, interesting, etc.: *I must*

admit I am impressed. ♦ ~ **by/with sb/sth** *We were all impressed by her enthusiasm.* ♦ *She was **suitably impressed** (= as impressed as someone had hoped) with the painting.* ⊃ see also UNIMPRESSED

im·pres·sion 🔑 /ɪmˈprɛʃn/ noun

> **IDEA/OPINION 1** an idea, a feeling, or an opinion that you get about someone or something, or that someone or something gives you: *a general/an overall impression* ♦ *an initial/a lasting impression* ♦ ~ **(of sb/sth)** *to get a good/bad impression of someone or something* ♦ *My first impression of him was favorable.* ♦ *She gives the impression of being very busy.* ♦ ~ **(that…)** *I did not get the impression that they were unhappy about the situation.* ♦ *My impression is that there are still a lot of problems.* ♦ *Try and smile. You don't want to **give people the wrong impression** (= that you are not friendly).*
> **EFFECT 2** the effect that an experience or a person has on someone or something: *a big impression* ♦ ~ **(on sb)** *His trip to India made a strong impression on him.* ♦ *My words made no impression on her.* ♦ *You'll have to play better than that if you really want to **make an impression** (= to make people admire you).*
> **DRAWING 3** a drawing showing what a person looks like or what a place or a building will look like in the future: *This is an artist's impression of the new stadium.*
> **AMUSING COPY OF SOMEONE 4** ~ **(of sb)** an amusing copy of the way a person acts or speaks: *He did his impression of Homer Simpson.*
> **FALSE APPEARANCE 5** an appearance that may be false: *Clever lighting creates an impression of space in a room.*
> **MARK 6** a mark that is left when an object is pressed hard into a surface
> **BOOK 7** all the copies of a book that are printed at one time, with few or no changes to the contents since the last time the book was printed ⊃ compare EDITION
> **IDM (be) under the impression that…** believing, usually wrongly, that something is true or is happening: *I was under the impression that the work had already been completed.* ⊃ thesaurus box at THINK

im·pres·sion·a·ble /ɪmˈprɛʃənəbl/ adj. (of a person, especially a young one) easily influenced or affected by someone or something: *children at an impressionable age*

Im·pres·sion·ism /ɪmˈprɛʃəˌnɪzəm/ noun [U] a style in painting developed in France in the late 19th century that uses color to show the effects of light on things and to suggest atmosphere rather than showing exact details
▶ **Im·pres·sion·ist** adj. [usually before noun]: *Impressionist landscapes*

im·pres·sion·ist /ɪmˈprɛʃənɪst/ noun **1** usually **Impressionist** an artist who paints in the style of Impressionism: *Impressionists such as Monet and Pissarro* **2** a person who entertains people by copying the way a famous person speaks or behaves

im·pres·sion·is·tic /ɪmˌprɛʃəˈnɪstɪk/ adj. giving a general idea rather than particular facts or details

im·pres·sive 🔑 /ɪmˈprɛsɪv/ adj.
(of things or people) making you feel admiration, because they are very large, good, skillful, etc.: *an impressive building with a huge tower* ♦ *an impressive performance* ♦ *one of the most impressive novels of recent years* ♦ *She was very impressive in the interview.* **ANT** UNIMPRESSIVE ▶ **im·pres·sive·ly** adv.: *impressively high* ♦ *an impressively detailed article*

im·pri·ma·tur /ˌɪmprəˈmɑtər/ noun [sing.] (*formal*) official approval of something, given by a person in a position of authority

im·print verb, noun
● **verb** /ɪmˈprɪnt/ **1** ~ **A in/on B** | ~ **B with A** to have a great effect on something so that it cannot be forgotten, changed, etc.: *The terrible scenes were indelibly imprinted on his mind.* **2** ~ **A in/on B** | ~ **B with A** to print or press a mark or design onto a surface: *clothes imprinted with the logos of sports teams*
● **noun** /ˈɪmprɪnt/ **1** ~ **(of sth) (in/on sth)** a mark made by

pressing or stamping something onto a surface: *the imprint of a foot in the sand* **2** [usually sing.] **~ (of sth) (on sb/sth)** (*formal*) the lasting effect that a person or an experience has on a place or a situation **3** (*technical*) the name of the PUBLISHER of a book, usually printed below the title on the first page

im·pris·on /ɪmˈprɪzn/ *verb* [often passive] **~ sb** to put someone in a prison or another place from which they cannot escape **SYN** JAIL: *They were imprisoned for possession of drugs.* ◆ (*figurative*) *Some young mothers feel imprisoned in their own homes.* ⊃ collocations at JUSTICE ▶ **im·pris·on·ment** *noun* [U]: *to be sentenced to* **life imprisonment** *for murder*

im·prob·a·ble /ɪmˈprɑbəbl/ *adj.* **1** not likely to be true or to happen **SYN** UNLIKELY: *an improbable story* ◆ *It all sounded* **highly improbable.** ◆ **~ that…** *It seems improbable that the current situation will continue.* **ANT** PROBABLE **2** seeming strange because it is not what you would expect **SYN** UNEXPECTED: *Her hair was an improbable shade of yellow.* ▶ **im·prob·a·bil·i·ty** /ɪmˌprɑbəˈbɪləti/ *noun* [U, C]: *the improbability of finding them alive* ◆ *statistical improbability* **im·prob·a·bly** /ɪmˈprɑbəbli/ *adv.*: *He claimed, improbably, that he had never been there.* ◆ *an improbably happy end*

im·promp·tu /ɪmˈprɑmptu/ *adj.* done without preparation or planning: *an impromptu speech*

im·prop·er /ɪmˈprɑpər/ *adj.* **1** dishonest or morally wrong: *improper business practices* ◆ *improper conduct* ◆ *There was nothing improper about our relationship.* **ANT** PROPER **2** (*formal*) not suited or appropriate to the situation **SYN** INAPPROPRIATE: *It would be improper to comment at this stage.* **ANT** PROPER **3** wrong; not correct: *improper use of the drug* ▶ **im·prop·er·ly** *adv.*: *to behave improperly* ◆ *He was improperly dressed for the occasion.* ◆ *improperly cooked meat*

im·prop·er ˈfraction *noun* (*mathematics*) a FRACTION in which the top number is greater than the bottom number, for example $\frac{7}{6}$

im·pro·pri·e·ty /ˌɪmprəˈpraɪəti/ *noun* [U, C] (*pl.* **im·pro·pri·e·ties**) (*formal*) behavior or actions that are dishonest, morally wrong, or not appropriate for a person in a position of responsibility **ANT** PROPRIETY

im·prov /ˈɪmprɑv/ *noun* [U] (*informal*) a type of performance, often involving comedy, that has not been REHEARSED (= practiced)

im·prove 🔑 /ɪmˈpruv/ *verb* [I, T]
to become better than before; to make something or someone better than before: *His quality of life has improved dramatically since the operation.* ◆ *The doctor says she should continue to improve* (= after an illness). ◆ **~ sth** *to improve standards* ◆ *The company needs to improve performance in all these areas.* ◆ *I need to improve my French.*
PHR V **im'prove on/upon sth** to achieve or produce something that is of a better quality than something else: *We've certainly improved on last year's figures.*

im·prove·ment 🔑 /ɪmˈpruvmənt/ *noun*
1 [U] the act of making something better; the process of something becoming better: *Sales figures continue to show signs of improvement.* ◆ *We expect to see* **further improvement** *over the coming year.* ◆ **~ in/on/to sth** *There is still room for* **improvement** *in your work.* **2** [C] a change in something that makes it better; something that is better than it was before: *a significant/substantial/dramatic improvement* ◆ *a slight/steady improvement* ◆ **~ in/on/to sth** *an improvement in Russo-American relations* ◆ *This is a great improvement on your previous work.* ◆ *improvements to the bus service*

im·prov·i·dent /ɪmˈprɑvədənt/ *adj.* (*formal*) not thinking about or planning for the future; spending money in a careless way **ANT** PROVIDENT ▶ **im·prov·i·dence** /-dəns/ *noun* [U]

im·pro·vise /ˈɪmprəˌvaɪz/ *verb* **1** [I, T] to make or do something using whatever is available, usually because you do not have what you really need: *There isn't much equipment. We're going to have to improvise.* ◆ **~ sth** *We improvised some shelves out of a few boards and bricks.* **2** [I, T] to invent music,

the words in a play, a statement, etc. while you are playing or speaking, instead of planning it in advance: *"It'll be ready some time next week, I imagine," she said, improvising.* ◆ **~ on sth** *He improvised on the melody.* ◆ **~ sth** *I had to improvise an introductory speech.* ▶ **im·prov·i·sa·tion** /ɪmˌprɑvəˈzeɪʃn/ *noun* [U, C] **im·pro·vised** *adj.*: *an improvised shelter/speech*

im·pru·dent /ɪmˈprudnt/ *adj.* (*formal*) not wise or sensible **SYN** UNWISE: *It would be imprudent to invest all your money in one company.* **ANT** PRUDENT ▶ **im·pru·dence** /ɪmˈprudns/ *noun* [U] **im·pru·dent·ly** *adv.*

im·pu·dent /ˈɪmpyədənt/ *adj.* (*formal*) rude; not showing respect for other people **SYN** IMPERTINENT: *an impudent young man* ◆ *an impudent remark* ▶ **im·pu·dence** /-dəns/ *noun* [U]

im·pugn /ɪmˈpyun/ *verb* **~ sth** (*formal*) to express doubts about whether something is right, honest, etc. **SYN** CHALLENGE

im·pulse /ˈɪmpʌls/ *noun* **1** [C, usually sing., U] **~ (to do sth)** a sudden strong wish or need to do something, without stopping to think about the results: *He had a sudden impulse to stand up and sing.* ◆ *I resisted the impulse to laugh.* ◆ *Her first impulse was to run away.* ◆ *The door was open and on (an)* **impulse** *she went inside.* ◆ *He tends to act* **on impulse.** **2** [C] (*technical*) a force or movement of energy that causes something else to react: *nerve/electrical impulses* **3** [C, usually sing., U] (*formal*) something that causes someone or something to do something or to develop and make progress: *to give an impulse to the struggling car industry*

ˈimpulse ˌbuying *noun* [U] buying goods without planning to do so in advance, and without thinking about it carefully ▶ **ˈimpulse ˌbuy** *noun*: *It was an impulse buy.*

im·pul·sion /ɪmˈpʌlʃn/ *noun* (*formal*) **1** [C] a strong desire to do something **2** [U] a reason for doing something: *Lack of food and water provided much of the impulsion for their speed.*

im·pul·sive /ɪmˈpʌlsɪv/ *adj.* (of people or their behavior) acting suddenly without thinking carefully about what might happen because of what you are doing **SYN** IMPETUOUS, RASH: *an impulsive decision/gesture* ◆ *You're so impulsive!* ◆ *He has an impulsive nature.* ▶ **im·pul·sive·ly** *adv.*: *Impulsively he reached out and took her hand.* **im·pul·sive·ness** *noun* [U]

im·pu·ni·ty /ɪmˈpyunəti/ *noun* [U] (*formal, disapproving*) if a person does something bad **with impunity,** they do not get punished for what they have done

im·pure /ɪmˈpyur/ *adj.* **1** not pure or clean; not consisting of only one substance but mixed with one or more substances, often of poorer quality: *impure gold* **2** (*old-fashioned* or *formal*) (of thoughts or feelings) morally bad, especially because they are connected with sex **ANT** PURE

im·pu·ri·ty /ɪmˈpyurəti/ *noun* (*pl.* **im·pu·ri·ties**) **1** [C] a substance that is present in small amounts in another substance, making it dirty or of poor quality: *A filter will remove most impurities found in water.* **2** [U] the state of being dirty or not pure **ANT** PURITY

im·pute /ɪmˈpyut/
PHR V **im'pute sth to sb/sth** (*formal*) to say, often unfairly, that someone is responsible for something or has a particular quality **SYN** ATTRIBUTE ▶ **im·pu·ta·tion** /ˌɪmpyəˈteɪʃn/ *noun* [U, C]

IN *abbr.* (in writing) Indiana

in 🔑 /ɪn/ *prep., adv., adj., noun*
● **prep. HELP** For the special uses of **in** in phrasal verbs, look at the entries for the verbs. For example, **deal in sth** is in the phrasal verb section at **deal.** **1** at a point within an area or a space: *a country in Africa* ◆ *The kids were playing in the street.* ◆ *It's in that drawer.* ◆ *I read about it in the paper.* **2** within the shape of something; surrounded by something: *She was lying in bed.* ◆ *sitting in an armchair* ◆ *Leave the key in the lock.* ◆ *Soak it in cold water.* **3** into something: *He dipped his brush in the paint.* ◆ *She got in her car and drove off.* **4** forming the whole or part of something or someone; contained within

---

something or someone: *There are 31 days in May.* ♦ *all the paintings in the collection* ♦ *I recognize his father in him* (= his character is similar to his father's). **5** during a period of time: *in 2012* ♦ *in the 18th century* ♦ *in spring/summer/winter* ♦ *in the fall* ♦ *in March* ♦ *in the morning/afternoon/evening* ♦ *I'm getting forgetful in my old age.* **6** after a particular length of time: *to return in a few minutes/hours/days/months.* ♦ *It will be ready in a week* (= one week from now). ♦ *She learned to drive in three weeks* (= after three weeks she could drive). **7** (used in negative sentences or after *first, last,* etc.) for a particular period of time: *I haven't seen him in years.* ♦ *It's the first rain we've had in ten days.* **8** wearing something: *dressed in their best clothes* ♦ *the man in the hat* ♦ *to be in uniform* ♦ *She was all in black.* **9** used to describe physical surroundings: *We went out in the rain.* ♦ *He was sitting alone in the darkness.* **10** used to show a state or condition: *I'm in love!* ♦ *The house is in good repair.* ♦ *I must put my affairs in order.* ♦ *a man in his thirties* ♦ *The daffodils were in full bloom.* **11** involved in something; taking part in something: *to act in a play* **12** used to show someone's job or profession: *He is in the army.* ♦ *She's in computers.* ♦ *in business* **13** used to show the form, shape, arrangement, or quantity of something: *a novel in three parts* ♦ *Roll it up in a ball.* ♦ *They sat in rows.* ♦ *People flocked in the thousands to see her.* **14** used to show the language, material, etc. used: *Say it in English.* ♦ *She wrote in pencil.* ♦ *Put it in writing.* ♦ *I paid in cash.* ♦ *He spoke in a loud voice.* **15** concerning something: *She was not lacking in courage.* ♦ *a country rich in minerals* ♦ *three yards in length* **16** while doing something; while something is happening: *In attempting to save the child from drowning, she nearly lost her own life.* ♦ *In all the commotion, I forgot to tell him the news.* **17** used to introduce the name of a person who has a particular quality: *We're losing a first-rate editor in Jen.* **18** used to show a rate or relative amount: *a gradient of one in five* ♦ *a dropout rate of one in ten*

IDM **in that** /ɪn ðæt/ (*formal*) for the reason that; because: *She was fortunate in that she had friends to help her.*

● **adv.** **HELP** For the special uses of **in** in phrasal verbs, look at the entries for the verbs. For example, **fill in (for sb)** is in the phrasal verb section at **fill**. **1** contained within an object, an area, or a substance: *We were locked in.* **2** into an object, an area, or a substance: *She opened the door and went in.* ♦ *The kids were playing by the river and one of them fell in.* **3** (of people) at home or at a place of work: *Nobody was in when we called.* **ANT** OUT **4** (of trains, buses, etc.) at the place where people can get on or off, for example the station: *The bus is due in* (= it should arrive) *at six.* **5** (of letters, etc.) received: *Applications must be in by April 30.* **6** (of the TIDE) at or toward its highest point on land: *Is the tide coming in or going out?* **7** elected: *Several new council members got in during the last election.* **8** (in TENNIS, etc.) if the ball is in, it has landed inside the line: *Her serve was barely in.*

IDM **be in at sth** to be present when something happens: *They were in at the beginning.* **be in for sth** (*informal*) to be going to experience something soon, especially something unpleasant: *He's in for a shock!* ♦ *I'm afraid we're in for a storm.* **be/get in on sth** (*informal*) to be/become involved in something; to share or know about something: *I'd like to be in on the plan.* ♦ *Is she in on the secret?* **be in with sb** (*informal*) to be (very) friendly with someone, and likely to get an advantage from the friendship **in and out (of sth)** going regularly to a place: *He was in and out of jail for most of his life.*

● **adj.** [usually before noun] (*informal*) popular and fashionable: *Purple is the in color this spring.* ♦ *Exotic pets are the in thing right now.* ♦ *Short skirts are in again.* ➔ see also IN-JOKE

● **noun**
IDM **an in to sth** = A WAY INTO STH at WAY *n.* **have an in with sb** to have influence with someone **the ins and outs (of sth)** all the details, especially the complicated or difficult ones: *the ins and outs of the problem* ♦ *He quickly learned the ins and outs of the job.*

in. *abbr.* (*pl.* **in.** or **ins.**) INCH: *Height: 6ft. 2in.*

in- *prefix* /ɪn/ **1** (also **il-, im-, ir-**) (in adjectives, adverbs, and

nouns) not; the opposite of: *infinite* ♦ *illogical* ♦ *immorally* ♦ *irrelevance* **2** (also **im-**) (in verbs) to put into the condition mentioned: *inflame* ♦ *imperil*

-in /ɪn/ *combining form* (in nouns) an activity in which many people take part: *a sit-in* ♦ *a teach-in*

in·a·bil·i·ty 🔑 /ˌɪnəˈbɪləti/ *noun* [U, sing.] ~ **(to do sth)** the fact of not being able to do something: *the government's inability to provide basic services* ♦ *Some families go without medical treatment because of their inability to pay.* **ANT** ABILITY

in ab·sen·tia /ˌɪn æbˈsɛnʃə; -ʃiə/ *adv.* (from *Latin*) while not present at the event being referred to: *Two foreign suspects will be tried in absentia.*

in·ac·ces·si·ble **AWL** /ˌɪnəkˈsɛsəbl/ *adj.* difficult or impossible to reach or to get: *They live in a remote area, inaccessible except by car.* ♦ ~ **to sb/sth** *The temple is now inaccessible to the public.* ♦ (*figurative*) *The language of teenagers is often completely inaccessible to* (= not understood by) *adults.* **ANT** ACCESSIBLE ▶ **in·ac·ces·si·bil·i·ty** /ˌɪnəkˌsɛsəˈbɪləti/ *noun* [U]

in·ac·cu·rate **AWL** /ɪnˈækyərət/ *adj.* not exact or accurate; with mistakes: *an inaccurate statement* ♦ *inaccurate information* ♦ *All the maps we had were wildly inaccurate.* **ANT** ACCURATE ➔ thesaurus box at WRONG ➔ collocations at ACCURATE ▶ **in·ac·cu·ra·cy** **AWL** /-rəsi/ *noun* [C, U] (*pl.* **in·ac·cu·ra·cies**): *The article is full of inaccuracies.* ♦ *The writer is guilty of bias and inaccuracy.* ➔ thesaurus box at MISTAKE **in·ac·cu·rate·ly** *adv.*

in·ac·tion /ɪnˈækʃn/ *noun* [U] (usually *disapproving*) lack of action; the state of doing nothing about a situation or a problem

in·ac·ti·vate /ɪnˈæktəˌveɪt/ *verb* ~ **sth** (*technical*) to make something stop doing something; to make something no longer active

in·ac·tive /ɪnˈæktɪv/ *adj.* **1** not doing anything; not active: *Some animals are inactive during the daytime.* ♦ *politically inactive* ♦ *The volcano has been inactive for 50 years.* **2** not in use; not working: *an inactive oil well* **3** having no effect: *an inactive drug/disease* **ANT** ACTIVE ▶ **in·ac·tiv·i·ty** /ˌɪnæk ˈtɪvəti/ *noun* [U]: *periods of enforced inactivity and boredom* ♦ *The inactivity of the local government was deplorable.*

in·ad·e·qua·cy **AWL** /ɪnˈædəkwəsi/ *noun* (*pl.* **in·ad·e·qua·cies**) **1** [U] ~ **(of sth)** the state of not being enough or good enough: *the inadequacy of our resources* **2** [U] a state of not being able or confident to deal with a situation: *a feeling/sense of inadequacy* **3** [C, usually pl.] ~ **(of/in sth)** a weakness; a lack of something: *gross inadequacies in the data* ♦ *He had to face up to his own inadequacies as a father.*

in·ad·e·quate **AWL** /ɪnˈædəkwət/ *adj.* **1** not enough; not good enough: *inadequate supplies* ♦ ~ **for sth** *The system is inadequate for the tasks it has to perform.* ♦ ~ **to do sth** *The food supplies are inadequate to meet the needs of the hungry.* **ANT** ADEQUATE **2** (of people) not able, or not confident enough, to deal with a situation **SYN** INCOMPETENT: *I felt totally inadequate as a parent.* ▶ **in·ad·e·quate·ly** **AWL** *adv.*: *to be inadequately prepared/insured/funded*

in·ad·mis·si·ble /ˌɪnədˈmɪsəbl/ *adj.* (*formal*) that cannot be allowed or accepted, especially in court: *inadmissible evidence* **ANT** ADMISSIBLE

in·ad·vert·ent·ly /ˌɪnədˈvərtntli/ *adv.* by accident; without intending to: *We inadvertently left without paying the bill.* ▶ **in·ad·vert·ent** *adj.*: *an inadvertent omission* **in·ad·vert·ence** /-ˈvərtns/ *noun* [U]

in·ad·vis·a·ble /ˌɪnədˈvaɪzəbl/ *adj.* [not usually before noun] ~ **(for sb) (to do sth)** (*formal*) not sensible or wise; that you would advise against: *It is inadvisable to bring children on this trip.* **ANT** ADVISABLE

in·al·ien·a·ble /ɪnˈeɪliənəbl/; -ˈeɪljə-/ (also *less frequent* **un·al·ien·a·ble**) *adj.* [usually before noun] (*formal*) that cannot be taken away from you: *the inalienable right to decide your own future*

in·am·o·ra·ta /ɪˌnæməˈrɑtə/ noun (from Italian, formal or humorous) a person's female lover

in·ane /ɪˈneɪn/ adj. stupid or silly; with no meaning: an inane remark ▶ **in·ane·ly** adv.: to grin inanely **in·an·i·ty** /ɪˈnænəti/ noun [U, C, usually pl.] (pl. **in·an·i·ties**)

in·an·i·mate /ɪnˈænəmət/ adj. **1** not alive in the way that people and animals are: A rock is an inanimate object. **ANT** ANIMATE **2** dead or appearing to be dead: A man was lying inanimate on the floor.

in·ap·pli·ca·ble /ɪnˈæplɪkəbl; ˌɪnəˈplɪkəbl/ adj. [not before noun] **~ (to sb/sth)** that cannot be used, or that does not apply, in a particular situation: These regulations are inapplicable to international students. **ANT** APPLICABLE

in·ap·pro·pri·ate AWL /ˌɪnəˈproupriət/ adj. not suitable or appropriate in a particular situation: inappropriate behavior/language ♦ **~ (for sb/sth) (to do sth)** It would be inappropriate for me to comment. ♦ **~ to/for sth** clothes inappropriate for the occasion **ANT** APPROPRIATE ▶ **in·ap·pro·pri·acy** AWL /ˌɪnəˈproupriəsi/ noun [U] **in·ap·pro·pri·ate·ly** adv.: She was inappropriately dressed for a funeral. **in·ap·pro·pri·ate·ness** noun [U]

in·ar·tic·u·late /ˌɪnɑrˈtɪkyələt/ adj. **1** (of people) not able to express ideas or feelings clearly or easily **2** (of speech) not using clear words; not expressed clearly: an inarticulate reply **ANT** ARTICULATE ▶ **in·ar·tic·u·late·ly** adv.

in·as·much as /ˌɪnəzˈmʌtʃ əz/ conj. (formal) used to add a comment on something that you have just said and to say in what way it is true: He was a very unusual musician inasmuch as he was totally deaf.

in·at·ten·tion /ˌɪnəˈtɛnʃn/ noun [U] (usually disapproving) lack of attention: The accident was the result of a moment's inattention.

in·at·ten·tive /ˌɪnəˈtɛntɪv/ adj. (disapproving) not paying attention to something or someone: an inattentive pupil ♦ **~ to sth/sb** inattentive to the needs of others **ANT** ATTENTIVE ▶ **in·at·ten·tive·ly** adv.

in·au·di·ble /ɪnˈɔdəbl/ adj. **~ (to sb)** that you cannot hear: The whistle was inaudible to the human ear. **ANT** AUDIBLE ▶ **in·au·di·bil·i·ty** /ɪnˌɔdəˈbɪləti/ noun [U] **in·au·di·bly** /ɪnˈɔdəbli/ adv.

in·au·gu·ral /ɪˈnɔgyərəl/ adj. [only before noun] (of an official speech, meeting, etc.) first, and marking the beginning of something important, for example the time when a new leader starts work, when a new organization is formed, or when something is used for the first time: the President's inaugural address ♦ the inaugural meeting of the geographical society ♦ the inaugural flight of the space shuttle ▶ **in·au·gu·ral** noun [C, usually sing.]: the presidential inaugural in January

in·au·gu·rate /ɪˈnɔgyəˌreɪt/ verb **1 ~ sb (as sth)** | **~ sb + noun** to introduce a new public official or leader at a special ceremony: He will be inaugurated (as) President in January. **2 ~ sth** to officially open a building or start an organization with a special ceremony: The new subway system was inaugurated by the mayor. **3 ~ sth** (formal) to introduce a new development or an important change: The moon landing inaugurated a new era in space exploration. ▶ **in·au·gu·ra·tion** /ɪˌnɔgyəˈreɪʃn/ noun [U, C]: the President's inauguration ♦ an inauguration speech

Inaugu'ration ,Day noun January 20, officially the first day of a new U.S. President's period of office

in·aus·pi·cious /ˌɪnɔˈspɪʃəs/ adj. (formal) showing signs that the future will not be good or successful: an inauspicious start **ANT** AUSPICIOUS ▶ **in·aus·pi·cious·ly** adv.

in·au·then·tic /ˌɪnɔˈθɛntɪk/ adj. not genuine; that you cannot believe or rely on **ANT** AUTHENTIC ▶ **in·au·then·tic·i·ty** /ˌɪnɔθɛnˈtɪsəti; -ʒθɛn-/ noun [U]

in·board /ˈɪnbɔrd/ adj. (technical) located on the inside of a boat, plane, or car: an inboard motor **ANT** OUTBOARD ▶ **in·board** adv.

in·born /ˌɪnˈbɔrn/ (also less frequent **in·bred**) adj. an **inborn** quality is one that you are born with **SYN** INNATE

in·bound /ˈɪnbaʊnd/ adj. (formal) traveling toward a place rather than leaving it: inbound flights/passengers **ANT** OUTBOUND

in·bounds /ˈɪnbaʊndz/ adj. (in basketball) relating to a throw that puts the ball into play again after it has gone out of play: an inbounds pass

in-box noun **1** (in an office) a container on your desk for letters that are waiting to be read or answered **2** the place on a computer where new e-mail messages are shown: I have hundreds of e-mails in my in-box. ➔ compare OUT-BOX

in·bred /ˌɪnˈbrɛd/ adj. **1** produced by breeding among closely related members of a group of animals, people, or plants: an inbred racehorse **2** = INBORN

in·breed·ing /ˈɪnˌbridɪŋ/ noun [U] breeding between closely related people or animals

Inc. /ɪŋk/ abbr. also **inc** Incorporated (used after the name of a company in the U.S.): Texaco, Inc.

in·cal·cu·la·ble /ɪnˈkælkyələbl/ adj. (formal) very large or very great; too great to calculate: The oil spill has caused incalculable damage to the environment. ➔ compare CALCULABLE ▶ **in·cal·cu·la·bly** /-bli/ adv.

in·can·des·cent /ˌɪnkænˈdɛsnt/ adj. **1** (technical) giving out light when heated: incandescent light bulbs **2** (formal) very bright: incandescent white **3** (formal) full of strong emotion: an incandescent musical performance ♦ She was incandescent with rage. ▶ **in·can·des·cence** /-ˈdɛsns/ noun [U]

in·can·ta·tion /ˌɪnkænˈteɪʃn/ noun [C, U] special words that are spoken or sung to have a magic effect; the act of speaking or singing these words

in·ca·pa·ble AWL /ɪnˈkeɪpəbl/ adj. **1** not able to do something: **~ of sth** incapable of speech ♦ **~ of doing sth** The children seem to be totally incapable of working by themselves. **2** not able to control yourself or your affairs; not able to do anything well: The manager was completely incapable and had to be let go. ♦ If people keep telling you that you're incapable, you begin to lose confidence in yourself. **ANT** CAPABLE

in·ca·pac·i·tate AWL /ˌɪnkəˈpæsəˌteɪt/ verb [usually passive] **~ sb/sth** (formal) to make someone or something unable to live or work normally

in·ca·pac·i·ty /ˌɪnkəˈpæsəti/ noun [U] (formal) **1 ~ (of sb/sth) (to do sth)** lack of ability or skill **SYN** INABILITY: their incapacity to govern effectively **2** the state of being too sick to do your work or take care of yourself: She returned to work after a long period of incapacity.

in-car adj. [only before noun] relating to something that you have or use inside a car, for example a radio or CD player: in-car entertainment

in·car·cer·ate /ɪnˈkɑrsəˌreɪt/ verb [usually passive] **~ sb (in sth)** (formal) to put someone in prison or in another place from which they cannot escape **SYN** IMPRISON ▶ **in·car·cer·a·tion** /ɪnˌkɑrsəˈreɪʃn/ noun [U]

in·car·nate adj., verb
● **adj.** /ɪnˈkɑrnət; -neɪt/ (usually after nouns) (formal) in human form: The leader seemed like the devil incarnate.
● **verb** /ɪnˈkɑrneɪt/ **~ sth** (formal) to give a definite or human form to a particular idea or quality **SYN** EMBODY

in·car·na·tion /ˌɪnkɑrˈneɪʃn/ noun **1** [C] a period of life in a particular form: one of the incarnations of the Hindu god Vishnu ♦ He believed he had been a prince in a previous incarnation. ♦ (figurative) I worked for her in her earlier incarnation (= her previous job) as a lawyer. **2** [C] a person who represents a particular quality, for example, in human form **SYN** EMBODIMENT: the incarnation of evil **3** [sing., U] also **the Incarnation** (in Christianity) the act of God coming to earth in human form as Jesus

in·cau·tious /ɪnˈkɔʃəs/ adj. (formal) done without thinking carefully about the results; not thinking about what might happen ▶ **in·cau·tious·ly** adv.

in·cen·di·ar·y /ɪnˈsɛndiˌɛri/ adj., noun
● **adj.** [only before noun] **1** designed to cause fires: an incendiary device/bomb/attack **2** (formal) causing strong

feelings or violence **SYN** INFLAMMATORY: *incendiary remarks*

● *noun* (pl. in·cen·di·a·ries) a bomb that is designed to make a fire start burning when it explodes **SYN** FIREBOMB

in·cense *noun, verb*
● *noun* /ˈɪnsɛns/ [U] a substance that produces a pleasant smell when you burn it, used particularly in religious ceremonies
● *verb* /ɪnˈsɛns/ ~ sb to make someone very angry: *The decision incensed the workforce.*

in·censed /ɪnˈsɛnst/ *adj.* very angry: *They were incensed at the decision.*

in·cen·tive **AWL** /ɪnˈsɛntɪv/ *noun* [C, U] ~ (for/to sb/sth) (to do sth) something that encourages you to do something: *tax incentives to encourage savings* ◆ *There is no incentive for people to save fuel.* **ANT** DISINCENTIVE

in·cen·tiv·ize /ɪnˈsɛntəˌvaɪz/ *verb* to encourage someone to behave in a particular way by offering them a reward: ~ sth *ways to incentivize innovation* ◆ ~ sb to do sth *You need to incentivize your existing customers to stay with you.*

in·cep·tion /ɪnˈsɛpʃn/ *noun* [sing.] (*formal*) the start of an institution, an organization, etc.: *Interest in the girls' basketball team has grown rapidly since its inception in 2009.*

in·ces·sant /ɪnˈsɛsnt/ *adj.* (*usually disapproving*) never stopping **SYN** CONSTANT: *incessant noise/rain/chatter* ◆ *incessant meetings* ▶ **in·ces·sant·ly** *adv.*: *to talk incessantly*

in·cest /ˈɪnsɛst/ *noun* [U] sexual activity between two people who are very closely related in a family

in·ces·tu·ous /ɪnˈsɛstʃuəs/ *adj.* **1** involving sex between two people in a family who are very closely related: *an incestuous relationship* **2** (*disapproving*) involving a group of people who have a close relationship and do not want to include anyone outside the group: *The music industry is an incestuous business.* ▶ **in·ces·tu·ous·ly** *adv.*

inch 🔑 /ɪntʃ/ *noun, verb*
● *noun* **1** (*abbr.* in.) a unit for measuring length, equal to 2.54 centimeters. There are 12 inches in a foot: *1.14 inches of rain fell last night.* ◆ *She's a few inches taller than me.* **2** a small amount or distance: *He escaped death by an inch.* ◆ *The car missed us by inches.* ◆ *He was just inches away from scoring.* **IDM** every inch **1** the whole of something: *The doctor examined every inch of his body.* ◆ (*figurative*) *If they try to fire me, I'll fight them every inch of the way.* **2** completely: *In his first game, the young player already looked every inch a winner.* give sb an inch (and they'll take a mile) (*saying*) used to say that if you allow some people a small amount of freedom or power they will see you as weak and try to take a lot more inch by inch very slowly and with great care or difficulty: *She crawled forward inch by inch.* not budge/give/move an inch to refuse to change your position, decision, etc. even a little: *We tried to negotiate a lower price but they wouldn't budge an inch.* within an inch of sth/of doing sth very close to something/doing something: *She was within an inch of being killed.* ◆ *They beat him (to) within an inch of his life* (= very severely). ⊃ more at TRUST *v.*
● *verb* [I, T] to move or make something move slowly and carefully in a particular direction: + adv./prep. *She moved forward, inching toward the rope.* ◆ ~ sth + adv./prep. *I inched the car forward.* ◆ *He inched his way through the narrow passage.*

in·cho·ate /ɪnˈkoʊət/ *adj.* (*formal*) just beginning to form and therefore not clear or developed: *inchoate ideas*

in·cho·a·tive /ɪnˈkoʊətɪv/ *adj.* (*grammar*) (of verbs) expressing a change of state that happens on its own. "Opened" in "the door opened" is an example of an inchoative verb. ⊃ compare CAUSATIVE, ERGATIVE

in·ci·dence **AWL** /ˈɪnsədəns/ *noun* **1** [C, usually sing.] ~ of sth (*formal*) the extent to which something happens or has an effect: *an area with a high incidence of crime* **2** [U] (*physics*) the way in which light meets a surface: *the angle of incidence*

in·ci·dent 🔑 **AWL** /ˈɪnsədənt/ *noun*
1 [C] something that happens, especially something unusual or unpleasant: *His bad behavior was just an isolated incident.* ◆ *One particular incident sticks in my mind.* **2** [C, U] a serious or violent event, such as a crime, an accident, or an attack: *There was a shooting incident near here last night.* ◆ *The demonstration went off without incident.* **3** [C] a disagreement between two countries, often involving military forces: *a border/diplomatic incident*

in·ci·den·tal /ˌɪnsəˈdɛntl/ *adj., noun*
● *adj.* **1** ~ (to sth) happening in connection with something else, but not as important as it, or not intended: *The discovery was incidental to their main research.* ◆ *incidental music* (= music used with a play or a movie to give atmosphere) ◆ *You may be able to get help with incidental expenses* (= small costs that you get in connection with something). **2** ~ to sth (*technical*) happening as a natural result of something: *These risks are incidental to the work of a firefighter.*
● *noun* [usually pl.] something that happens in connection with something else, but is less important: *You'll need money for incidentals such as tips and taxis.*

in·ci·den·tal·ly **AWL** /ˌɪnsəˈdɛntli; -ˈdɛntl·i/ *adv.* **1** used to introduce a new topic, or some extra information, or a question that you have just thought of **SYN** BY THE WAY: *Incidentally, have you heard the news about Sue?* **2** in a way that was not planned but that is connected with something else: *The information was only discovered incidentally.*

in·cin·er·ate /ɪnˈsɪnəˌreɪt/ *verb* [often passive] ~ sth to burn something until it is completely destroyed ▶ **in·cin·er·a·tion** /ɪnˌsɪnəˈreɪʃn/ *noun* [U]: *high-temperature incineration plants*

in·cin·er·a·tor /ɪnˈsɪnəˌreɪtər/ *noun* a container that is closed on all sides for burning waste at high temperatures

in·cip·i·ent /ɪnˈsɪpiənt/ *adj.* [usually before noun] (*formal*) just beginning: *signs of incipient unrest*

in·cise /ɪnˈsaɪz/ *verb* ~ sth (in/on/onto sth) (*formal*) to cut words, designs, etc. into a surface ⊃ compare ENGRAVE

in·ci·sion /ɪnˈsɪʒn/ *noun* [C, U] a sharp cut made in something, particularly during a medical operation; the act of making a cut in something: *Make a small incision below the ribs.*

in·ci·sive /ɪnˈsaɪsɪv/ *adj.* (*approving*) **1** showing clear thought and good understanding of what is important, and the ability to express this: *incisive comments/criticism/analysis* ◆ *an incisive mind* **2** showing someone's ability to make decisions and act with force: *an incisive performance* ▶ **in·ci·sive·ly** *adv.* **in·ci·sive·ness** *noun* [U]

in·ci·sor /ɪnˈsaɪzər/ *noun* one of the eight sharp teeth at the front of the mouth that are used for biting ⊃ compare CANINE, MOLAR

in·cite /ɪnˈsaɪt/ *verb* to encourage someone to do something violent, illegal, or unpleasant, especially by making them angry or excited: ~ sth *to incite crime/racial hatred/violence* ◆ ~ sb (to sth) *They were accused of inciting the crowd to violence.* ◆ ~ sb to do sth *He incited the workforce to go on strike.*

in·cite·ment /ɪnˈsaɪtmənt/ *noun* [U, C] ~ (to sth) the act of encouraging someone to do something violent, illegal, or unpleasant: *incitement to racial hatred*

in·ci·vil·i·ty /ˌɪnsəˈvɪləti/ *noun* (pl. in·ci·vil·i·ties) [U, C] (*formal*) rude behavior; rude remarks ⊃ see also UNCIVIL

incl. *abbr.* (in advertisements) including; included: *transportation not incl.* ◆ *$29.53 incl. tax*

in·clem·ent /ɪnˈklɛmənt/ *adj.* (*formal*) (of the weather) not pleasant; cold, wet, etc. **ANT** CLEMENT ▶ **in·clem·en·cy** /-mənsi/ *noun* [U]

in·cli·na·tion **AWL** /ˌɪnkləˈneɪʃn/ *noun* **1** [U, C] a feeling that makes you want to do something: ~ (to do sth) *He did not show the slightest inclination to leave.* ◆ *My natural inclination is to find a compromise.* ◆ *She had neither the time nor the* inclination to help them. ♦ **~ (toward/for sth)** She lacked any inclination for housework. ♦ He was a loner by nature and **by inclination**. ♦ You must follow your own inclinations when choosing a career. **2** [C] **~ to do sth** a tendency to do something: There is an inclination to treat geography as a less important subject. **3** [C, usually sing., U] (technical) a degree of sloping: an inclination of 45° ♦ the angle of inclination **4** [C] a small downward movement, usually of the head

in·cline AWL verb, noun
● **verb** /ɪnˈklaɪn/ **1** [I, T] (formal) to tend to think or behave in a particular way; to make someone do this: **~ to/toward sth** I incline to the view that we should take no action at this stage. ♦ **~ to do sth** Government is often more effective than we incline to think. ♦ **~ sb to/toward sth** Lack of money inclines many young people toward crime. ♦ **~ sb to do sth** His obvious sincerity inclined me to trust him. **2** [T] **~ your head** to bend your head forward, especially as a sign of agreement, welcome, etc. **3** [I, T] **~ (sth) (to/toward sth)** to lean or slope in a particular direction; to make something lean or slope: The land inclined gently toward the shore.
● **noun** /ˈɪnklaɪn/ a slope: a steep/slight incline

in·clined AWL /ɪnˈklaɪnd/ adj. **1** [not before noun] **~ (to do sth)** wanting to do something: She was inclined to trust him. ♦ He writes only when he feels inclined to. ♦ There'll be time for a swim if you **feel so inclined**. **2** **~ to do sth** tending to do something; likely to do something: He's inclined to be lazy. ♦ They'll be more inclined to listen if you don't shout. **3** **~ to agree, believe, think, etc.** used when you are expressing an opinion but do not want to express it very strongly: I'm inclined to agree with you. **4** (used with particular adverbs) having a natural ability for something; preferring to do something: **musically/academically inclined** children **5** sloping; at an angle

in·clude 🔑 /ɪnˈklud/ verb
1 (not used in the progressive tenses) if one thing **includes** another, it has the second thing as one of its parts: **~ sth** The tour included a visit to the Science Museum. ♦ Does the price include tax? ♦ **~ doing sth** Your responsibilities include opening mail and answering the phone. **2** to make someone or something part of something: **~ sb/sth (as/in/on sth)** You should include some examples in your essay. ♦ We all went, **myself included**. ♦ **~ sb/sth as sth** Representatives from the country were included as observers at the conference. ANT EXCLUDE

in·clud·ing 🔑 /ɪnˈkludɪŋ/ prep. (abbr. incl.)
having something as part of a group or set: We get three days off, including New Year's Day. ♦ Six people were killed in the riot, including a policeman. ♦ It's $10.95, **not including** tax. ANT EXCLUDING ⊃ language bank at E.G.

in·clu·sion /ɪnˈkluʒn/ noun **1** [U] the fact of including someone or something; the fact of being included: His inclusion on the team is in doubt. **2** [C] a person or thing that is included: There were some surprising inclusions on the list. ANT EXCLUSION

in·clu·sive /ɪnˈklusɪv/ adj. **1** having the total cost, or the cost of something that is mentioned, contained in the price: The **fully inclusive** fare for the cruise is $2,500. ♦ **~ of sth** The rent is inclusive of heat and electricity. ANT EXCLUSIVE **2** including a wide range of people, things, ideas, etc.: The party must adopt more inclusive strategies and a broader vision. ANT EXCLUSIVE ▶ **in·clu·sive·ly** adv.: The word "men" can be understood inclusively (= including men and women). **in·clu·sive·ness** noun [U]

in·cog·ni·to /ˌɪnkɑgˈnitoʊ/ adv. in a way that prevents other people from finding out who you are: Movie stars often prefer to travel incognito. ▶ **in·cog·ni·to** adj.: an incognito visit

in·co·her·ent AWL /ˌɪnkoʊˈhɪrənt; -ˈhɛr-/ adj. **1** (of people) unable to express yourself clearly, often because of emotion: She broke off, incoherent with anger. ANT COHERENT **2** (of sounds) not clear and hard to understand SYN UNINTELLIGIBLE: Rachel whispered something incoherent. **3** not logical or well organized: an incoherent

policy ANT COHERENT ▶ **in·co·her·ence** /-əns/ noun [U] **in·co·her·ent·ly** AWL adv.

in·come 🔑 AWL /ˈɪnkʌm; ˈɪŋ-/ noun [C, U]
the money that a person, a region, a country, etc. earns from work, from investing money, from business, etc.: **people with high/low incomes** ♦ a weekly **disposable income** (= the money that you have left to spend after tax, food, housing, etc.) of $800 ♦ a rise in **national income** ♦ They receive a proportion of their income from the sale of goods and services. ♦ Tourism is a major **source of income** for the area. ♦ **higher/middle/lower income** groups ⊃ compare EXPENDITURE ⊃ thesaurus box at POOR

THESAURUS

income

pay ♦ salary ♦ wage/wages ♦ overtime ♦ earnings

These are all words for money that a person earns or receives for their work.

income money that a person receives for their work, or from investments or business: people on low incomes

pay (often used in compounds) money that employees earn for doing their jobs: We all took **pay cuts** when sales figures fell. ♦ A large percentage of my **paycheck** goes towards health insurance for my family. ♦ The job offers good pay and benefits.

salary a fixed amount of money that employees earn (usually per year) for doing their jobs: She was offered a starting salary of $33,000 per year. NOTE A person's salary does not change, no matter how many hours per week the person works.

wage/wages (somewhat formal) money that a person receives for doing their job, usually calculated by the hour or by dividing an annual salary into a semi-monthly or monthly figure: By law, the **minimum wage** is $7.25 per hour. ♦ I earned $1,700 in wages last month.

PAY, SALARY, OR WAGE?

Pay is the most general of these three words. The term **wages** is used in accounting to describe the amount of money someone earns before any taxes or other payments are taken away. Employees who work in offices or professional people, such as teachers or doctors, usually receive a **salary** that is paid once or twice a month, but is usually expressed as an annual figure.

overtime money that a person earns for working more hours than they had originally agreed to work: She earned $500 in overtime by working the entire holiday weekend.

earnings (business) money that a person earns for their work: The industry has seen a rise in average earnings over the past two years.

PATTERNS

- (a) **high/low/basic** income/pay/salary/wage/earnings
- to **earn** an income/your pay/a salary/a wage/overtime
- to **earn $... in** income/pay/salary/wages/overtime
- to **live on/support a family on** a(n) income/salary/hourly wage of…

ˈincome ˌtax noun [U, C] the amount of money that you pay to the government according to how much you earn: Her income tax bracket is 15%.

in·com·ing /ˈɪnˌkʌmɪŋ/ adj. [only before noun] **1** recently elected or chosen: the incoming mayor/president/administration ANT OUTGOING **2** arriving somewhere or being received: incoming flights ♦ the incoming tide ♦ incoming calls/mail ANT OUTGOING

in·com·men·su·ra·ble /ˌɪnkəˈmɛnsərəbl; -ʃərəbl/ adj. **~ (with sth)** (formal) if two things are **incommensurable**, they are so completely different from each other that they cannot be compared

in·com·men·su·rate /ˌɪnkəˈmensərət; -ˈʃərət/ *adj.* **~ (with sth)** (*formal*) not matching something in size, importance, quality, etc. **ANT** COMMENSURATE

in·com·mode /ˌɪnkəˈmoʊd/ *verb* **~ sb** (*formal*) to cause someone difficulties or problems: *We are very sorry to have incommoded you.*

in·com·mu·ni·ca·do /ˌɪnkəˌmyunəˈkɑdoʊ/ *adj.* without communicating with other people, because you are not allowed to or because you do not want to: *The prisoner has been **held incommunicado** for more than a week.*

in·com·pa·ra·ble /ɪnˈkɑmpərəbl/ *adj.* so good or impressive that nothing can be compared to it **SYN** MATCHLESS: *the incomparable beauty of the Rocky Mountains* ▶ **in·com·pa·ra·bil·i·ty** /ɪnˌkɑmpərəˈbɪləti/ *noun* [U] **in·com·pa·ra·bly** /ɪnˈkɑmpərəbli/ *adv.*

in·com·pat·i·ble AWL /ˌɪnkəmˈpætəbl/ *adj.* **1 ~ (with sth)** two actions, ideas, etc. that are **incompatible** are not acceptable or possible together because of basic differences: *The hours of the job are incompatible with family life.* ♦ *These two objectives are **mutually incompatible**.* **2** two people who are **incompatible** are very different from each other and so are not able to live or work happily together **3 ~ (with sth)** two things that are **incompatible** are of different types so that they cannot be used or mixed together: *New computer software is often incompatible with older computers.* ♦ *Those two blood groups are incompatible.* **ANT** COMPATIBLE ▶ **in·com·pat·i·bil·i·ty** AWL /ˌɪnkəmˌpætəˈbɪləti/ *noun* (*pl.* **in·com·pat·i·bil·i·ties**) [U, C]

in·com·pe·tence /ɪnˈkɑmpətəns/ *noun* [U] the lack of skill or ability to do your job or a task as it should be done: *professional incompetence* ♦ *police incompetence* ♦ *He was dismissed for incompetence.*

in·com·pe·tent /ɪnˈkɑmpətənt/ *adj., noun*
● *adj.* not having the skill or ability to do your job or a task as it should be done: *an incompetent teacher* ♦ *his incompetent handling of the crisis* ♦ *The governor was accused of being incompetent to lead.* **ANT** COMPETENT ▶ **in·com·pe·tent·ly** *adv.*
● *noun* a person who does not have the skill or ability to do their job or a task as it should be done

in·com·plete /ˌɪnkəmˈplit/ *adj., noun*
● *adj.* not having everything that it should have; not finished or complete: *an incomplete set of figures* ♦ *Spoken language contains many incomplete sentences.* **ANT** COMPLETE ▶ **in·com·plete·ly** *adv.*: *The causes of the phenomenon are still incompletely understood.* **in·com·plete·ness** *noun* [U]
● *noun* the grade that a student gets for a course of study when they have not completed all the work for that course

in·com·pre·hen·si·ble /ˌɪnkɑmprɪˈhensəbl/ *adj.* **~ (to sb)** impossible to understand **SYN** UNINTELLIGIBLE: *Some application forms can be incomprehensible to ordinary people.* ♦ *He found his son's actions totally incomprehensible.* **ANT** COMPREHENSIBLE ▶ **in·com·pre·hen·si·bil·i·ty** /ˌɪnkɑmprɪˌhensəˈbɪləti/ *noun* [U] **in·com·pre·hen·si·bly** /ˌɪnkɑmprɪˈhensəbli/ *adv.*

in·com·pre·hen·sion /ˌɪnkɑmprɪˈhenʃn/ *noun* [U] the state of not being able to understand someone or something: *Anna read the letter with incomprehension.*

in·con·ceiv·a·ble AWL /ˌɪnkənˈsivəbl/ *adj.* impossible to imagine or believe **SYN** UNTHINKABLE: *It is inconceivable that the manager was not aware of the problem.* **ANT** CONCEIVABLE ▶ **in·con·ceiv·a·bly** AWL /ˌɪnkənˈsivəbli/ *adv.*

in·con·clu·sive AWL /ˌɪnkənˈklusɪv/ *adj.* not leading to a definite decision or result: *inconclusive evidence/results/tests* ♦ *inconclusive discussions* **ANT** CONCLUSIVE ⊃ collocations at CONCLUDE ▶ **in·con·clu·sive·ly** AWL *adv.*: *The last meeting ended inconclusively.*

in·con·gru·ous /ɪnˈkɑŋgruəs/ *adj.* strange, and not suitable in a particular situation **SYN** INAPPROPRIATE: *Such traditional methods seem incongruous in our technical age.*

▶ **in·con·gru·i·ty** /ˌɪnkənˈgruəti/ *noun* (*pl.* **in·con·gru·i·ties**) [U, C]: *She was struck by the incongruity of the situation.* **in·con·gru·ous·ly** *adv.*: *incongruously dressed*

in·con·se·quen·tial /ˌɪnkɑnsəˈkwenʃl/ *adj.* not important or worth considering **SYN** TRIVIAL: *inconsequential details* ♦ *inconsequential chatter* **ANT** CONSEQUENTIAL ▶ **in·con·se·quen·tial·ly** /-ˈʃəli/ *adv.*

in·con·sid·er·a·ble /ˌɪnkənˈsɪdərəbl/ *adj.*
IDM **not inconsiderable** (*formal*) large; large enough to be considered important: *We have spent a not inconsiderable amount of money on the project already.*

in·con·sid·er·ate /ˌɪnkənˈsɪdərət/ *adj.* (*disapproving*) not giving enough thought to other people's feelings or needs **SYN** THOUGHTLESS: *inconsiderate behavior* ♦ *It was inconsiderate of you not to call.* **ANT** CONSIDERATE ▶ **in·con·sid·er·ate·ly** *adv.*

in·con·sist·ent AWL /ˌɪnkənˈsɪstənt/ *adj.* **1** [not usually before noun] **~ (with sth)** if two statements, etc. are **inconsistent**, or one is **inconsistent with** the other, they cannot both be true because they give the facts in a different way: *The report is inconsistent with the financial statements.* ♦ *The witnesses' statements were inconsistent.* **2 ~ with sth** not matching a set of standards, ideas, etc.: *Her behavior was clearly inconsistent with her beliefs.* **3** (*disapproving*) tending to change too often; not staying the same: *inconsistent results* ♦ *Children find it confusing if a parent is inconsistent.* **ANT** CONSISTENT ▶ **in·con·sist·en·cy** AWL /-tənsi/ *noun* (*pl.* **in·con·sist·en·cies**) [U, C]: *There is some inconsistency between the witnesses' evidence and their earlier statements.* ♦ *I noticed a few minor inconsistencies in her argument.* **in·con·sist·ent·ly** *adv.*

in·con·sol·a·ble /ˌɪnkənˈsoʊləbl/ (also **un·con·sol·a·ble**) *adj.* very sad and unable to accept help or comfort: *They were inconsolable when their only child died.* ▶ **in·con·sol·a·bly** /-bli/ (also **un·con·sol·a·bly**) *adv.*: *to weep inconsolably*

in·con·spic·u·ous /ˌɪnkənˈspɪkyuəs/ *adj.* not attracting attention; not easy to notice **ANT** CONSPICUOUS ▶ **in·con·spic·u·ous·ly** *adv.*

in·con·stant /ɪnˈkɑnstənt/ *adj.* (*formal*) **1** not faithful in love or friendship **SYN** FICKLE **2** that frequently changes **ANT** CONSTANT ▶ **in·con·stan·cy** AWL /-stənsi/ *noun* [U]

in·con·test·a·ble /ˌɪnkənˈtestəbl/ *adj.* (*formal*) that is true and cannot be disagreed with or denied **SYN** INDISPUTABLE: *an incontestable right/fact* ▶ **in·con·test·a·bly** /-bli/ *adv.*

in·con·ti·nence /ɪnˈkɑntənəns; -ˈkɑntn·əns/ *noun* [U] the lack of ability to control the BLADDER and BOWELS **ANT** CONTINENCE ▶ **in·con·ti·nent** /ɪnˈkɑntənənt; -ˈkɑntn·ənt/ *adj.*: *Many of our patients are incontinent.*

in·con·tro·vert·i·ble /ˌɪnkɑntrəˈvərtəbl/ *adj.* (*formal*) that is true and cannot be disagreed with or denied **SYN** INDISPUTABLE: *incontrovertible evidence/proof* ▶ **in·con·tro·vert·i·bly** /-bli/ *adv.*

in·con·ven·ience /ˌɪnkənˈvinyəns/ *noun, verb*
● *noun* **1** [U] trouble or problems, especially concerning what you need or would like yourself: *We apologize for the delay and regret any inconvenience it may have caused.* ♦ *I have already been put to considerable inconvenience.* **2** [C] a person or thing that causes problems or difficulties **SYN** NUISANCE: *I can put up with minor inconveniences.*
● *verb* **~ sb** to cause trouble or difficulty for someone: *I hope that we didn't inconvenience you.*

in·con·ven·ient /ˌɪnkənˈvinyənt/ *adj.* causing trouble or problems, especially concerning what you need or would like yourself: *an inconvenient time/place* **ANT** CONVENIENT ▶ **in·con·ven·ient·ly** *adv.*

in·cor·po·rate AWL /ɪnˈkɔrpəˌreɪt/ *verb* **1** to include something so that it forms a part of something: **~ sth** *The new car design incorporates all the latest safety features.* ♦ **~ sth in/into/within sth** *We've incorporated all the latest safety features into the design.* ♦ *Many of your suggestions have been incorporated in the plan.* **2** [often passive] **~ sth** (*business*) to

t **t**ea   t̬ bu**tt**er   d **d**id   k **c**at   g **g**ot   tʃ **ch**in   dʒ **J**une   f **f**all

create a legally recognized company: *The company was incorporated in 2008.* ▶ **in·cor·po·ra·tion** [AWL] /ɪnˌkɔrpə-ˈreɪʃn/ *noun* [U]: *the incorporation of foreign words into the language* ♦ *the articles of incorporation of the company*

in·cor·por·at·ed [AWL] /ɪnˈkɔrpəˌreɪtəd/ *adj.* (*abbr.* **Inc.**) (*business*) formed into a business company with legal status

in·cor·po·re·al /ˌɪnkɔrˈpɔriəl/ *adj.* (*formal*) without a body or form

in·cor·rect /ˌɪnkəˈrɛkt/ *adj.* **1** not accurate or true: *incorrect information/spelling* ♦ *His version of what happened is incorrect.* ⊃ thesaurus box at WRONG **2** speaking or behaving in a way that does not follow the accepted standards or rules ⊃ see also POLITICALLY CORRECT **ANT** CORRECT ▶ **in·cor·rect·ly** *adv.*: *an incorrectly addressed letter* **in·cor·rect·ness** *noun* [U]

in·cor·ri·gi·ble /ɪnˈkɔrədʒəbl; -ˈkɑr-/ *adj.* (*disapproving* or *humorous*) having bad habits that cannot be changed or improved **SYN** INCURABLE: *Her husband is an incorrigible flirt.* ♦ *You're incorrigible!* ▶ **in·cor·ri·gi·bly** /-bli/ *adv.*

in·cor·rupt·i·ble /ˌɪnkəˈrʌptəbl/ *adj.* **1** (of people) not able to be persuaded to do something wrong or dishonest, even if someone offers them money **2** that cannot decay or be destroyed **ANT** CORRUPTIBLE ▶ **in·cor·rupt·i·bil·i·ty** /ˌɪnkəˌrʌptəˈbɪləti/ *noun* [U]

in·crease ✏ *verb, noun*

● *verb* /ɪnˈkris; ˈɪnkris/ [I, T] to become or to make something greater in amount, number, value, etc.: **~ (from A) (to B)** *The population has increased from 1.2 million to 1.8 million.* ♦ *increasing levels of carbon dioxide in the earth's atmosphere* ♦ *The price of oil increased.* ♦ **~ in sth** *Oil increased in price.* ♦ **~ by sth** *The rate of inflation increased by 2%.* ♦ **~ with sth** *Disability increases with age* (= the older someone is, the more likely they are to be disabled). ♦ **~ sth (from A) (to B)** *We need to increase productivity.* ♦ **~ sth (by sth)** *They increased the price by 50%.* **ANT** DECREASE ▶ **in·creased** *adj.* [only before noun]: *increased demand*

● *noun* /ˈɪnkris/ [C, U] **~ (in sth)** a rise in the amount, number, or value of something: *an increase in spending* ♦ *an increase in property taxes* ♦ *an increase of nearly 20%* ♦ *a* **significant/ substantial increase** *in sales* ♦ *price/tax/wage increases* ♦ *Homelessness is* **on the increase** (= increasing). **ANT** DECREASE

LANGUAGE BANK

increase

describing an increase

■ The number of foreign students in the U.S. **increased from** 622,000 in 2009 **to** just over 672,000 in 2010.

■ First-time student enrollments **shot up/increased dramatically** in 2010.

■ 2010 saw a significant **rise** in student numbers.

■ The number of foreign students **increased by** almost 8% compared with the previous year.

■ The 2010 figure was 672,000, **an increase of** 8% from the previous year.

■ The 2010 figure was 672,000, **up** 8% **from** the previous year.

■ As the chart shows, this can partly be explained by a **dramatic increase** in students from China.

■ The number of Chinese undergraduate students **rose sharply** from 81,000 in 2009 to 98,000 in 2010.

⊃ Language Banks at EXPECT, FALL, ILLUSTRATE, PROPORTION

in·creas·ing·ly ✏ /ɪnˈkrisɪŋli/ *adv.* more and more all the time: *increasingly difficult/important/ popular* ♦ *It is becoming increasingly clear that this problem will not be easily solved.* ♦ *Increasingly, training is taking place in the office rather than outside it.*

in·cred·i·ble /ɪnˈkrɛdəbl/ *adj.* **1** impossible or very difficult to believe **SYN** UNBELIEVABLE: *an incredible story* ♦ *It seemed incredible that she had been there a week already.* **2** (*informal*) extremely good or extremely large **SYN** UNBELIEVABLE: *The hotel was incredible.* ♦ *an incredible amount of work*

in·cred·i·bly /ɪnˈkrɛdəbli/ *adv.* **1** extremely: *incredibly lucky/stupid/difficult/beautiful* **2** in a way that is very difficult to believe: *Incredibly, she had no idea what was going on.*

in·cred·u·lous /ɪnˈkrɛdʒələs/ *adj.* not willing or not able to believe something; showing an inability to believe something: *"Here?" said Kate, incredulous.* ♦ *an incredulous look* ⊃ compare CREDULOUS ▶ **in·cre·du·li·ty** /ˌɪnkrəˈduləti; -ˈdʒu-/ *noun* [U] **SYN** DISBELIEF: *a look of surprise and incredulity* **in·cred·u·lous·ly** *adv.*: *He laughed incredulously.*

in·cre·ment /ˈɪŋkrəmənt/ *noun* a gradual increase in a number or an amount: *Your savings will grow in increments over a period of months.* ▶ **in·cre·men·tal** /ˌɪŋkrəˈmɛntl/ *adj.*: *incremental costs* **in·cre·men·tal·ly** /-ˈmɛntəli/ *adv.*: *The changes were introduced incrementally to avoid confusion.*

in·crim·i·nate /ɪnˈkrɪməˌneɪt/ *verb* **~ sb** to make it seem as if someone has done something wrong or illegal: *They were afraid of answering the questions and incriminating themselves.* ▶ **in·crim·i·nat·ing** *adj.* [usually before noun]: *incriminating evidence* **in·crim·i·na·tion** /ɪnˌkrɪməˈneɪʃn/ *noun* [U]

ˈin-crowd *noun* [sing.] a small group of people within a larger group who seem to be the most popular or fashionable

in·crus·ta·tion /ˌɪnkrʌˈsteɪʃn/ (also **en·crus·ta·tion**) *noun* [U, C] the process of forming a hard outer covering or layer; the covering or layer that is formed

in·cu·bate /ˈɪŋkyəˌbeɪt/ *verb* **1** [T] **~ sth** (of a bird) to sit on its eggs in order to keep them warm until they HATCH **2** [T] **~ sth** (*biology*) to keep cells, bacteria, etc. at a suitable temperature so that they develop **3** [T] **be incubating something** (*medical*) to have an infectious disease developing inside you before SYMPTOMS (= signs of illness) appear **4** [I] (*medical*) (of a disease) to develop slowly without showing any signs

in·cu·ba·tion /ˌɪŋkyəˈbeɪʃn/ *noun* **1** [U] the HATCHING of eggs **2** [C] (also **incuˈbation ˌperiod**) (*medical* or *biology*) the time between someone being infected with a disease and the appearance of the first SYMPTOMS (= signs) **3** [U] (*biology*) the development and growth of bacteria, etc.

in·cu·ba·tor /ˈɪŋkyəˌbeɪtər/ *noun* **1** a piece of equipment in a hospital that new babies are placed in when they are weak or born too early, in order to help them survive **2** a machine like a box where eggs are kept warm until the young birds are born

in·cu·bus /ˈɪŋkyəbəs/ *noun* (*pl.* **in·cu·bi** /-ˌbaɪ/) **1** a male evil spirit, supposed in the past to have sex with a sleeping woman ⊃ compare SUCCUBUS **2** (*literary*) a problem that makes you worry a lot

in·cul·cate /ɪnˈkʌlkeɪt; ˈɪnkʌlˌkeɪt/ *verb* (*formal*) to cause someone to learn and remember ideas, moral principles, etc., especially by repeating them often: **~ sth (in/into sb)** *to inculcate a sense of responsibility in someone* ♦ **~ sb with sth** *to inculcate someone with a sense of responsibility* ▶ **in·cul·ca·tion** /ˌɪnkʌlˈkeɪʃn/ *noun* [U]

in·cum·ben·cy /ɪnˈkʌmbənsi/ *noun* (*pl.* **in·cum·ben·cies**) (*formal*) an official position or the time during which someone holds it

in·cum·bent /ɪnˈkʌmbənt/ *noun, adj.*

● *noun* a person who has an official position: *the* **present incumbent** *of the White House*

● *adj.* **1** [only before noun] having an official position: *the incumbent president* **2** **~ upon/on sb** (*formal*) necessary as part of someone's duties: *It was incumbent on them to attend.*

in·cur /ɪnˈkər/ *verb* (-rr-) (*formal*) **1** **~ sth** if you incur something unpleasant, you are in a situation in which you have to deal with it: *She had incurred the wrath of her father by marrying without his consent* **2** **~ sth** if you incur costs, you have to pay them: *You risk incurring bank charges if you exceed your overdraft limit.*

| v **v**oice | θ **th**in | ð **th**en | s **s**o | z **z**oo | ʃ **sh**e | ʒ vi**s**ion | x **Ch**anukah | 767 |

in·cur·a·ble /ɪnˈkjʊərəbl/ *adj.* **1** that cannot be cured: *an incurable disease/illness* **ANT** CURABLE **2** that cannot be changed **SYN** INCORRIGIBLE: *She's an incurable optimist.* ▶ **in·cur·a·bly** /-bli/ *adv.*: *incurably ill/romantic*

in·cu·ri·ous /ɪnˈkjʊəriəs/ *adj.* (*formal*) having no interest in knowing or discovering things ▶ **in·cu·ri·ous·ly** *adv.*

in·cur·sion /ɪnˈkɜrʒn/ *noun* ~ **(into sth)** (*formal*) **1** a sudden attack on a place by foreign armies, etc. **2** the sudden appearance of something in a particular area of activity that is either not expected or not wanted

in·debt·ed /ɪnˈdɛtəd/ *adj.* **1** ~ **(to sb) (for sth)** (*formal*) grateful to someone for helping you: *I am deeply indebted to my family for all their help.* **2** (of countries, governments, organizations, etc.) owing money to other countries or organizations: *a list of the fifteen most heavily indebted nations* ▶ **in·debt·ed·ness** *noun* [U]

in·de·cen·cy /ɪnˈdisnsi/ *noun* (*pl.* **in·de·cen·cies**) **1** [U] behavior that is thought to be morally or sexually offensive: *an act of gross indecency* (= a sexual act that is a criminal offense) **2** [C] an indecent act, expression, etc.

in·de·cent /ɪnˈdisnt/ *adj.* **1** (of behavior, talk, etc.) thought to be morally offensive, especially because it involves sex or being naked: *indecent conduct/photos* ⊃ compare DECENT **2** (of clothes) showing parts of the body that are usually covered: *That skirt of hers is positively indecent.* **3** not done in the appropriate or usual amount of time: *They left the funeral with almost indecent haste* (= too quickly). ▶ **in·de·cent·ly** *adv.*: *He was charged with indecently assaulting five women.*

in·decent as·sault *noun* [C, U] (*law*) a sexual attack on someone, but one that does not include RAPE

in·decent ex·posure *noun* [U] (*law*) the crime of showing your sexual organs to other people in a public place

in·de·cipher·a·ble /ˌɪndɪˈsaɪfərəbl/ *adj.* (of writing or speech) impossible to read or understand

in·de·ci·sion /ˌɪndɪˈsɪʒn/ (also *less frequent* **in·de·ci·sive·ness**) *noun* [U] the state of being unable to decide: *After a moment's indecision, he said yes.* ⊃ compare DECISION

in·de·ci·sive /ˌɪndɪˈsaɪsɪv/ *adj.* **1** (of a person) unable to make decisions: *a weak and indecisive man* **2** not providing a clear and definite answer or result: *an indecisive battle* **ANT** DECISIVE ▶ **in·de·ci·sive·ly** *adv.* **in·de·ci·sive·ness** *noun* [U] = INDECISION

in·dec·o·rous /ɪnˈdɛkərəs/ *adj.* (*formal*) (of behavior) embarrassing or not socially acceptable

in·deed 🔑 /ɪnˈdid/ *adv.*
1 used to emphasize a positive statement or answer: *"Was he very angry?" "Indeed he was."* ◆ *"Do you agree?" "Yes, indeed/Indeed I do." ◆ "You said you'd help?" "I did indeed—yes." ◆ It is indeed a remarkable achievement.* **2** used after *very* and an adjective or adverb to emphasize a statement, description, etc.: *Thank you very much indeed! ◆ I was very sad indeed to hear of your father's death.* **3** (*formal*) used to add information to a statement: *I don't mind at all. Indeed, I would be delighted to help.* **4** (*informal*) used to show that you are surprised at something or that you find something ridiculous: *A ghost indeed! I've never heard anything so silly.* **5** (*informal*) used when you are repeating a question that someone has just asked and showing that you do not know the answer: *"Why did he do it?" "Why indeed?"* **IDM** see FRIEND

in·de·fat·i·ga·ble /ˌɪndɪˈfætɪgəbl/ *adj.* (*formal, approving*) never giving up or getting tired of doing something: *an indefatigable defender of human rights* ▶ **in·de·fat·i·ga·bly** /-bli/ *adv.*

in·de·fen·si·ble /ˌɪndɪˈfɛnsəbl/ *adj.* **1** that cannot be defended or excused because it is morally unacceptable: *indefensible behavior* ◆ *The assemblyman was accused of defending the indefensible.* **2** (of a place or building) impossible to defend from military attack

in·de·fin·a·ble /ˌɪndɪˈfaɪnəbl/ *adj.* difficult or impossible to define or explain: *She has that indefinable something that makes an actress a star.* ▶ **in·de·fin·a·bly** /-bli/ *adv.*

in·def·i·nite **AWL** /ɪnˈdɛfənət/ *adj.* **1** lasting for a period of time that has no fixed end: *She will be away for the indefinite future.* **2** not clearly defined **SYN** IMPRECISE: *an indefinite science*

in,definite ˈarticle *noun* (*grammar*) the word *a* or *an* in English, or a similar word in another language ⊃ compare DEFINITE ARTICLE

in·def·i·nite·ly **AWL** /ɪnˈdɛfənətli/ *adv.* for a period of time with no fixed limit: *The trial was postponed indefinitely.*

in,definite ˈpronoun *noun* (*grammar*) a pronoun that does not refer to any person or thing in particular, for example "anything" and "everyone"

in·del·i·ble /ɪnˈdɛləbl/ *adj.* **1** impossible to forget or remove **SYN** PERMANENT: *The experience made an indelible impression on me.* ◆ *Her unhappy childhood left an indelible mark.* **2** (of ink, pens, etc.) leaving a mark that cannot be removed **SYN** PERMANENT: *an indelible marker* ▶ **in·del·i·bly** /-bli/ *adv.*: *That day is stamped indelibly on my memory.*

in·del·i·cate /ɪnˈdɛlɪkət/ *adj.* (*formal*) likely to be thought rude or embarrassing: *an indelicate question* ▶ **in·del·i·ca·cy** /-kəsi/ *noun* [U]

in·dem·ni·fy /ɪnˈdɛmnəˌfaɪ/ *verb* (**in·dem·ni·fies**, **in·dem·ni·fy·ing**, **in·dem·ni·fied**, **in·dem·ni·fied**) (*law*) **1** ~ **sb (against sth)** to promise to pay someone an amount of money if they suffer any damage or loss **2** ~ **sb (for sth)** to pay someone an amount of money because of the damage or loss that they have suffered ▶ **in·dem·ni·fi·ca·tion** /ˌɪndɛmnəfəˈkeɪʃn/ *noun* [U]

in·dem·ni·ty /ɪnˈdɛmnəti/ *noun* (*pl.* **in·dem·ni·ties**) (*formal or law*) **1** [U] ~ **(against sth)** protection against damage or loss, especially in the form of a promise to pay for any that happens: *an indemnity clause/fund/policy* ◆ *indemnity insurance* **2** [C] a sum of money that is given as payment for damage or loss

in·dent *verb*, *noun*
● *verb* /ɪnˈdɛnt/ ~ **sth** to start a line of print or writing farther away from the edge of the page than the other lines: *The first line of each paragraph should be indented.*
● *noun* /ˈɪndɛnt; ɪnˈdɛnt/ = INDENTATION

in·den·ta·tion /ˌɪndɛnˈteɪʃn/ *noun* **1** [C] a cut or mark on the edge or surface of something: *The horse's hooves left deep indentations in the mud.* **2** (also **in·dent**) [C] a space left at the beginning of a line of print or writing **3** [U] the action of indenting something or the process of being indented

in·dent·ed /ɪnˈdɛntəd/ *adj.* (of an edge or a surface) an indented edge is not even, because parts of it are missing or have been cut away: *an indented coastline*

in·den·ture /ɪnˈdɛntʃər/ *noun* a type of contract in the past that forced a servant or APPRENTICE to work for their employer for a particular period of time ▶ **in·den·tured** *adj.*: *indentured servants/laborers*

in·de·pend·ence 🔑 /ˌɪndɪˈpɛndəns/ *noun* [U]
1 ~ **(from sb/sth)** (of a country) freedom from political control by other countries: *Cuba gained independence from Spain in 1898.* **2** the time when a country gains freedom from political control by another country: *independence celebrations* ◆ *the first elections since independence* **3** the freedom to organize your own life, make your own decisions, etc. without needing help from other people: *He values his independence.* ◆ *a woman's financial independence* **ANT** DEPENDENCE

Inde,pendence ˌDay *noun* July 4, celebrated in the U.S. as the anniversary of the day in 1776 when the Americans declared themselves independent of Britain ⊃ see also THE FOURTH OF JULY

in·de·pend·ent 🔑 /ˌɪndɪˈpɛndənt/ *adj., noun*

● *adj.*
> COUNTRY **1** ~ **(from/of sth)** (of countries) having their own government: *Mozambique became independent in 1975.*
> SEPARATE **2** done or given by someone who is not involved in a situation and so is able to judge it fairly: *an independent investigation/witness* ◆ *She went to a lawyer for some independent advice.* **3** ~ **(of sb/sth)** not connected with or influenced by something; not connected with each other: *The police force should be independent of direct government control.* ◆ *Two independent research bodies reached the same conclusions.*
> ORGANIZATION **4** not supported by public money or a large organization: *an independent bookstore/movie*
> PERSON **5** ~ **(of sb/sth)** confident and free to do things without needing help from other people: *Going away to college has made me much more independent.* ◆ *She's a very independent-minded young woman.* ◆ *Students should aim to become more independent of their teachers.* **ANT** DEPENDENT **6** ~ **(of sb/sth)** having or earning enough money so that you do not have to rely on someone else for help: *It was important to me to be financially independent of my parents.* ◆ *a man of independent means* (= with an income that he does not earn by working) **ANT** DEPENDENT
> POLITICIAN **7** not representing or belonging to a particular political party: *an independent candidate*
   ▶ **in·de·pend·ent·ly** *adv.*: ~ **(of sb/sth)** *The two departments work independently of each other.* ◆ *It was the first time that she had lived independently.* ◆ *Students should be able to work independently.*
● *noun* a member of parliament, candidate, etc. who does not belong to a particular political party

independent 'clause *noun* (*grammar*) = MAIN CLAUSE

independent 'school *noun* = PRIVATE SCHOOL

independent 'variable *noun* (*mathematics*) a VARIABLE whose value does not depend on another variable

in-'depth *adj.* [usually before noun] very thorough and detailed: *an in-depth discussion/study* ⊃ see also DEPTH

in·de·scrib·a·ble /ˌɪndɪˈskraɪbəbl/ *adj.* so extreme or unusual it is almost impossible to describe: *The pain was indescribable.* ▶ **in·de·scrib·a·bly** /-bli/ *adv.*: *indescribably beautiful/boring*

in·de·struct·i·ble /ˌɪndɪˈstrʌktəbl/ *adj.* that is very strong and cannot easily be destroyed: *plastic containers that are virtually indestructible* ◆ *an indestructible bond of friendship*

in·de·ter·mi·nate /ˌɪndɪˈtɜːmənət/ *adj.* that cannot be identified easily or exactly: *She was a tall woman of indeterminate age.* ▶ **in·de·ter·mi·na·cy** /-nəsi/ *noun* [U]

in·dex 🔑 /ˈɪndɛks/ *noun, verb*

● *noun* (*pl.* **in·dex·es** or **in·di·ces** /ˈɪndəsiz/) **HELP** In sense 4, **indices** is the only plural form. **1** a list of names or topics that are referred to in a book, etc., usually arranged at the end of a book in alphabetical order or listed in a separate file or book: *Look it up in the index.* ◆ *Author and subject indexes are available on a library database.* **2** a system that shows the level of prices and pay, etc. so that they can be compared with those of a previous date: *the cost-of-living index* ◆ *The Dow Jones index fell 15 points this morning.* ◆ *stock-market indices* ◆ *housing cost indexes* ⊃ see also STOCK INDEX **3** a sign or measure that something else can be judged by: *The number of new houses being built is a good index of a country's prosperity.* **4** (*mathematics*) the small number written above a larger number to show how many times that number must be multiplied by itself. In the EQUATION $4^2=16$, the number 2 is an index.
● *verb* **1** ~ **sth** to make an index of documents, the contents of a book, etc.; to add something to a list of this type: *All publications are indexed by subject and title.* **2** [usually passive] ~ **sth (to sth)** to link pay, etc. to the level of prices of food, clothing, etc. so that they both increase at the same rate

in·dex·a·tion /ˌɪndɛkˈseɪʃn/ *noun* [U] the linking of increases in pay, etc. to increases in prices

'index ˌcard *noun* a small card that you can write information on and keep with other cards in a box or file ⊃ picture at STATIONERY

'index ˌfinger (also ˌfirst 'finger) *noun* the finger next to the thumb ⊃ picture at BODY **SYN** FOREFINGER ⊃ compare POINTER FINGER

In·di·a ink /ˈɪndiə ˌɪŋk/ *noun* [U] a very black ink used in drawing and technical drawing

In·di·an /ˈɪndiən/ *noun* **1** a person from India **2** (somewhat *old-fashioned*, often *offensive*) = NATIVE AMERICAN **3** (somewhat *old-fashioned*, often *offensive*, *CanE*) a Native Canadian who is not Inuit or Métis ⊃ note at NATIVE AMERICAN ▶ **In·di·an** *adj.*

ˌIndian 'corn *noun* [U] a type of CORN with large brown and yellow grains, not usually eaten but sometimes used to make decorations, for example at Thanksgiving

ˌIndian 'summer *noun* **1** a period of dry warm weather in the fall **2** a pleasant period of success or improvement, especially later in someone's life

ˌIndia 'rubber *noun* [U] (*old-fashioned*) natural rubber

in·di·cate 🔑 **AWL** /ˈɪndəˌkeɪt/ *verb*
> SHOW **1** [T, I] to show that something is true or exists: ~ **sth** *Record profits in the retail market indicate a boom in the economy.* ◆ ~ **(that…)** *Research indicates that eating habits are changing fast.* ◆ *Croton-on-Hudson, as the name indicates, is situated on the banks of the Hudson River.* ◆ ~ **how, what, etc.…** *Our results indicate how misleading it could be to rely on this method.*
> SUGGEST **2** [T] to be a sign of something; to show that something is possible or likely: ~ **sth** *A red sky at night often indicates good weather the next day.* ◆ ~ **that…** *Early results indicate that the mayor will get a second term.*
> MENTION **3** [T] to mention something, especially in an indirect way: ~ **(to sb) (that)…** *In his letter, he indicated to us (that) he was willing to cooperate.* ◆ ~ **sth (to sb)** *He indicated his willingness to cooperate.* ◆ ~ **whether, when, etc.…** *Has she indicated yet whether she would like to be involved?* ⊃ thesaurus box at DECLARE
> POINT TO **4** [T] to make someone notice someone or something, especially by pointing or moving your head: ~ **sb/sth (to sb)** *She took out a map and indicated the quickest route to us.* ◆ ~ **where, which, etc.…** *He indicated where the furniture was to go.* ◆ ~ **that…** *She indicated that I was to sit down.*
> GIVE INFORMATION **5** [T] ~ **sth** to represent information without using words: *The results are indicated in Table 2.* **6** [T] to give information in writing: ~ **sth** *You are allowed 2 pieces of luggage unless your ticket indicates otherwise.* ◆ ~ **which, where, etc.…** *Please indicate clearly which color you require.*
> SHOW MEASUREMENT **7** [T] ~ **sth** | ~ **how much, how many, etc.…** (of an instrument for measuring things) to show a particular measurement: *When the temperature gauge indicates 90°F or more, turn off the engine.*
> BE RECOMMENDED **8** [T, usually passive] ~ **sth** (*formal*) to be necessary or recommended: *A course of chemotherapy was indicated.*

AWL COLLOCATIONS

indicate

indicate *verb*
■ data, evidence | finding, result | study | analysis, research
  The data indicate that UVA radiation exerts harmful effects on these organisms.
■ correlation | difference
  Comparison of color intensity with lead concentration indicated no correlation.

- presence | willingness | preference | extent | importance

Field studies indicate the importance of feathers in nest linings.

- clearly | strongly | reliably | (not) necessarily

These two examples clearly indicate that the potential incomes from market gardening are considerable.

- otherwise

Unless otherwise indicated, information presented in the article is based on interviews.

indication *noun*

- clear | strong | reliable | slight | early, preliminary | outward

There are strong indications that the situation is changing.

- give, offer, provide, yield | reveal, show | find | see

Red markings at the top of the gauge give an easy indication that water levels are too high.

- point to | suggest

All indications point to the fact that we have to address the issue as quickly as possible.

indicative *adj.*

- strongly | (not) necessarily

Heavy snoring and periods of stopped breathing are strongly indicative of sleep apnea.

indicator *noun*

a sign that shows you what something is like or how a situation is changing

- accurate, reliable | unreliable | key

Brand awareness is a key indicator of a brand's strength.

- economic, macroeconomic | socioeconomic | behavioral | performance

Living standards, defined by economic indicators such as wages, increased steadily.

- point to, signal, suggest

According to the report, there are currently no indicators suggesting this trend will change in the short-term.

in·di·ca·tion 🔑 **AWL** /ˌɪndəˈkeɪʃn/ *noun* [C, U]
a remark or sign that shows that something is happening or what someone is thinking or feeling: **~ (of sth)** *They gave no indication of how the work should be done.* ◆ **~ (of doing sth)** *He shows every indication (= clear signs) of wanting to accept the job.* ◆ **~ (that…)** *There are clear indications that the economy is improving.* ◆ *All the indications are that the deal will go ahead as planned.* ⊃ thesaurus box at SIGN ⊃ collocations at INDICATE

in·dic·a·tive **AWL** /ɪnˈdɪkətɪv/ *adj., noun*
- *adj.* **1** [not usually before noun] **~ (of sth)** (*formal*) showing or suggesting something: *Their failure to act is indicative of their lack of interest.* ⊃ collocations at INDICATE **2** [only before noun] (*grammar*) stating a fact
- *noun* the indicative [sing.] (*grammar*) the form of a verb that states a fact: *In "Ben likes school," the verb "like" is in the indicative.*

in·di·ca·tor **AWL** /ˈɪndəˌkeɪtər/ *noun* **1** a sign that shows you what something is like or how a situation is changing: *The economic indicators are better than expected.* ⊃ thesaurus box at SIGN ⊃ collocations at INDICATE **2** a device on a machine that shows speed, pressure, etc.: *a depth indicator*

in·di·ces pl. of INDEX

in·dict /ɪnˈdaɪt/ *verb* [usually passive] **~ sb (for sth)** | **~ sb (on charges/on a charge of sth)** (*law*) to officially charge someone with a crime: *She was indicted for murder.* ◆ *The senator was indicted on charges of corruption.* ⊃ collocations at JUSTICE

in·dict·a·ble /ɪnˈdaɪtəbl/ *adj.* (*law*) **1** (of a crime) for which you can be indicted: *an indictable offense* **2** (of a person) able to be indicted

in·dict·ment /ɪnˈdaɪtmənt/ *noun* **1** [C, usually sing.] **~ (of/on sb/sth)** a sign that a system, society, etc. is very bad or very wrong: *The poverty in our cities is a damning indictment of modern society.* **2** [C] a written statement accusing someone of a crime **3** [U] the act of officially accusing someone of a crime: *This led to his indictment on allegations of conspiracy.*

in·die /ˈɪndi/ *adj., noun*
- *adj.* (of a company, person, or product) not belonging to, working for, or produced by a large organization; independent: *an indie publisher/newspaper* ◆ *indie music* ◆ *an indie band/record label*
- *noun* a small independent company, or something produced by such a company

in·dif·fer·ence /ɪnˈdɪfrəns/ *noun* [U, sing.] **~ (to sb/sth)** a lack of interest, feeling, or reaction toward someone or something: *his total indifference to what people thought of him* ◆ *What she said is **a matter of complete indifference** to me.* ◆ *Their father treated them with indifference.* ◆ *an indifference to the needs of others*

in·dif·fer·ent /ɪnˈdɪfrənt/ *adj.* **1** [not usually before noun] **~ (to sb/sth)** having or showing no interest in someone or something: *The administration cannot afford to be indifferent to public opinion.* **2** not very good **SYN** MEDIOCRE: *an indifferent meal* ◆ *The festival has the usual mixture of movies— good, bad, and indifferent.* ▶ **in·dif·fer·ent·ly** *adv.*: *He shrugged indifferently.*

in·dig·e·nous /ɪnˈdɪdʒənəs/ *adj.* (*formal*) belonging to a particular place rather than coming to it from somewhere else **SYN** NATIVE: *the indigenous peoples/languages of the area* ◆ **~ to…** *The kangaroo is indigenous to Australia.*

in·di·gent /ˈɪndɪdʒənt/ *adj.* [usually before noun] (*formal*) very poor

in·di·gest·i·ble /ˌɪndɪˈdʒestəbl; ˌɪndaɪ-/ *adj.* **1** (of food) that cannot easily be DIGESTED in the stomach: *an indigestible meal* **2** (of facts, information, etc.) difficult to understand, and presented in a complicated way **ANT** DIGESTIBLE

in·di·ges·tion /ˌɪndɪˈdʒestʃən; ˌɪndaɪ-/ *noun* [U] pain caused by difficulty in DIGEST food **SYN** DYSPEPSIA

in·dig·nant /ɪnˈdɪɡnənt/ *adj.* feeling or showing anger and surprise because you think that you have been treated unfairly: *an indignant letter/look* ◆ **~ at/about sth** *She was very indignant at the way she had been treated.* ◆ **~ that…** *They were indignant that they hadn't been invited.* ⊃ thesaurus box at ANGRY ▶ **in·dig·nant·ly** *adv.*: *"I'm certainly not asking him!" she retorted indignantly.*

in·dig·na·tion /ˌɪndɪɡˈneɪʃn/ *noun* [U] **~ (at/about sth)** | **~ (that…)** a feeling of anger and surprise caused by something that you think is unfair or unreasonable: *The increase in plane fares has aroused public indignation.* ◆ *Joe quivered **with indignation** that Paul would speak to him like that.* ◆ *Some benefits apply only to men, much **to the indignation** of working women.* ◆ *to be full of **righteous indignation** (= the belief that you are right to be angry even though other people do not agree)*

in·dig·ni·ty /ɪnˈdɪɡnəti/ *noun* [U, C] (*pl.* **in·dig·ni·ties**) **~ (of sth/of doing sth)** a situation that makes you feel embarrassed or ashamed because you are not treated with respect; an act that causes these feelings: *The chairman **suffered the indignity of** being refused admission to the meeting.* ◆ *the daily indignities of imprisonment*

in·di·go /ˈɪndɪɡoʊ/ *adj.* very dark blue in color: *an indigo sky* ▶ **in·di·go** *noun* [U]

in·di·rect 🔑 /ˌɪndəˈrekt; ˌɪndaɪ-/ *adj.* [usually before noun]
1 happening not as the main aim, cause, or result of a particular action, but in addition to it: *the indirect effects of the war* ◆ *to find something out by indirect methods* ◆ *The building collapsed as an indirect result of the heavy rain.* ◆ *There would be some benefit, however indirect, to the state.* ◆ *indirect costs (= costs that are not directly connected with making a product, for example training, heat, rent, etc.)* **2** avoiding saying something in a clear and obvious way: *an indirect*

ʌ cup   ə about   eɪ say   aɪ five   ɔɪ boy   aʊ now   oʊ go   ər bird

attack **3** not going in a straight line: *an indirect route* **ANT** DIRECT ▸ in·di·rect·ly *adv.*: *The new law will affect us all, directly or indirectly.* in·di·rect·ness *noun* [U]

indirect ˈobject *noun* (*grammar*) a noun, noun phrase, or pronoun in a sentence, used after some verbs, that refers to the person or thing that an action is done to or for: *In "Give him the money," "him" is the indirect object and "money" is the direct object.*

indirect ˈquestion (also re·ported ˈquestion) *noun* (*grammar*) a question in REPORTED SPEECH, for example *She asked where I was going.* **HELP** Do not put a question mark after an indirect question.

indirect ˈspeech *noun* [U] (*grammar*) = REPORTED SPEECH ⊃ compare DIRECT SPEECH

indirect ˈtax *noun* [C, U] a tax that is added to the price of goods and services, instead of being collected directly from the person who pays it ⊃ compare DIRECT TAX ▸ indirect tax·ation *noun* [U]

in·dis·cern·i·ble /ˌɪndɪˈsɜrnəbl/ *adj.* that cannot be seen, heard, or understood

in·dis·ci·pline /ɪnˈdɪsəplən/ *noun* [U] (*formal*) a lack of control in the behavior of a group of people

in·dis·creet /ˌɪndɪˈskrit/ *adj.* not careful about what you say or do, especially when this embarrasses or offends someone **ANT** DISCREET ▸ in·dis·creet·ly *adv.*

in·dis·cre·tion /ˌɪndɪˈskrɛʃn/ *noun* **1** [C] an act or remark that is indiscreet, especially one that is not morally acceptable: *youthful indiscretions* **2** [U] the act of saying or doing something without thinking about the effect it may have, especially when this embarrasses or offends someone: *He talked to the press in a moment of indiscretion.* ⊃ compare DISCRETION

in·dis·crim·i·nate /ˌɪndɪˈskrɪmənət/ *adj.* **1** an indiscriminate action is done without thought about what the result may be, especially when it causes people to be harmed: *indiscriminate attacks on passersby by rival gangs* ◆ *Doctors have been criticized for their indiscriminate use of antibiotics.* **2** acting without careful judgment: *She's always been indiscriminate in her choice of friends.* ▸ in·dis·crim·i·nate·ly *adv.*: *The soldiers fired indiscriminately into the crowd.*

in·dis·pen·sa·ble /ˌɪndɪˈspɛnsəbl/ *adj.* too important to be without **SYN** ESSENTIAL: *Cars have become an indispensable part of our lives.* ◆ *~ to sb/sth She made herself indispensable to the department.* ◆ *~ for sth/for doing sth A good dictionary is indispensable for learning a foreign language.* **ANT** DISPENSABLE ⊃ thesaurus box at ESSENTIAL ⊃ language bank at VITAL

in·dis·posed /ˌɪndɪˈspoʊzd/ *adj.* (*formal*) **1** [not usually before noun] unable to do something because you are sick, or for a reason you do not want to give **2** [not before noun] *~ to do sth* not willing to do something

in·dis·po·si·tion /ˌɪndɪspəˈzɪʃn/ *noun* [C, U] (*formal*) a slight illness that makes you unable to do something

in·dis·put·a·ble /ˌɪndɪˈspyutəbl/ *adj.* that is true and cannot be disagreed with or denied **SYN** UNDENIABLE: *indisputable evidence* ◆ *an indisputable fact* ◆ *It is indisputable that the crime rate has been rising.* ⊃ compare DISPUTABLE ▸ in·dis·put·a·bly /-bli/ *adv.*: *This painting is indisputably one of his finest works.*

in·dis·sol·u·ble /ˌɪndɪˈsɑlyəbl/ *adj.* (*formal*) (of a relationship) that cannot be ended: *an indissoluble friendship* ▸ in·dis·sol·u·bly /-bli/ *adv.*: *indissolubly linked*

in·dis·tinct **AWL** /ˌɪndɪˈstɪŋkt/ *adj.* that cannot be seen, heard, or remembered clearly **SYN** HAZY, VAGUE ▸ in·dis·tinct·ly *adv.*

in·dis·tin·guish·a·ble /ˌɪndɪˈstɪŋgwɪʃəbl/ *adj.* **1** *~ (from sth)* if two things are indistinguishable, or one is indistinguishable from the other, it is impossible to see any differences between them: *The male of the species is almost indistinguishable from the female.* **2** not clear; not able to be clearly identified: *His words were indistinguishable.*

in·di·um /ˈɪndiəm/ *noun* [U] (*symb.* **In**) a chemical element. Indium is a soft silver-white metal.

in·di·vid·u·al ✍ **AWL** /ˌɪndəˈvɪdʒuəl/ *adj.*, *noun*

● *adj.* **1** [only before noun] (often used after *each*) considered separately rather than as part of a group: *We interviewed each individual member of the community.* ◆ *The prosecutor refused to comment on individual cases.* **2** [only before noun] connected with one person; designed for one person: *respect for individual freedom* ◆ *an individual pizza* **3** (usually *approving*) typical of one particular person or thing in a way that is different from others **SYN** DISTINCTIVE: *a highly individual style of dress*

● *noun* **1** a person considered separately rather than as part of a group: *The competition is open to both teams and individuals.* ◆ *Treatment depends on the individual involved.* ◆ *donations from private individuals* (= ordinary people rather than companies, etc.) **2** a person who is original and very different from others: *She's grown into quite an individual.* **3** (*informal*, usually *disapproving*) a person of a particular type, especially a strange one: *an odd-looking individual* ◆ *This is the same individual who's been hanging out on the corner lately.*

in·di·vid·u·al·ism **AWL** /ˌɪndəˈvɪdʒuəˌlɪzəm/ *noun* [U] **1** the quality of being different from other people and doing things in your own way **2** the belief that individual people in society should have the right to make their own decisions, etc., rather than be controlled by the government or public opinion: *Capitalism stresses innovation, competition, and individualism.* ▸ in·di·vid·u·al·ist **AWL** /-əlɪst/ *noun*: *She's a complete individualist in her art.* in·di·vid·u·al·is·tic **AWL** /ˌɪndəˌvɪdʒuəˈlɪstɪk/ (also in·di·vid·u·al·ist) *adj.*: *an individualistic culture* ◆ *His music is highly individualistic and may not appeal to everyone.*

in·di·vid·u·al·i·ty **AWL** /ˌɪndəˌvɪdʒuˈæləti/ *noun* [U] the qualities that make someone or something different from other people or things: *She expresses her individuality through her clothes.*

in·di·vid·u·al·ize /ˌɪndəˈvɪdʒuəˌlaɪz/ *verb* *~ sth* to make something different to suit the needs of a particular person, place, etc.: *to individualize children's learning*

in·di·vid·u·al·ized /ˌɪndəˈvɪdʒuəˌlaɪzd/ *adj.* designed for a particular person or thing; connected with a particular person or thing: *individualized instruction* ◆ *a highly individualized approach to management*

in·di·vid·u·al·ly **AWL** /ˌɪndəˈvɪdʒuəli/ *adv.* separately, rather than as a group: *individually wrapped chocolates* ◆ *The manager spoke to them all individually.* ◆ *The hotel has 100 individually designed rooms.*

in·di·vid·u·ate /ˌɪndəˈvɪdʒuˌeɪt/ *verb* *~ sb/sth* (*formal*) to make someone or something clearly different from other people or things of the same type

in·di·vis·i·ble /ˌɪndəˈvɪzəbl/ *adj.* that cannot be divided into separate parts **ANT** DIVISIBLE ▸ in·di·vis·i·bil·i·ty /ˌɪndəˌvɪzəˈbɪləti/ *noun* [U] in·di·vis·i·bly /ˌɪndəˈvɪzəbli/ *adv.*

Indo- /ˈɪndoʊ/ *combining form* (in nouns and adjectives) Indian: *the Indo-Pakistan border*

Indo-Caˈnadian *noun* a Canadian who was born in S. Asia, especially India, or whose family originally came from S. Asia

in·doc·tri·nate /ɪnˈdɑktrəˌneɪt/ *verb* *~ sb (with sth)* | *~ sb (to do sth)* (*disapproving*) to force someone to accept a particular belief or set of beliefs and not allow them to consider any others: *They had been indoctrinated from an early age with their parents' beliefs.* ▸ in·doc·tri·na·tion /ɪnˌdɑktrəˈneɪʃn/ *noun* [U]: *political/religious indoctrination*

Indo-Euroˈpean *adj.* of or connected with the family of languages spoken in most of Europe and parts of western Asia (including English, French, Latin, Greek, Swedish, Russian, and Hindi)

in·do·lent /ˈɪndələnt/ *adj.* (*formal*) not wanting to work **SYN** LAZY ▸ in·do·lence /-ləns/ *noun* [U]

in·dom·i·ta·ble /ɪnˈdɑmətəbl/ *adj.* (*formal*, *approving*) not willing to accept defeat, even in a difficult situation; very brave and determined

in·door 🔊 /'ɪndɔr/ *adj.* [only before noun]
located, done, or used inside a building: *an indoor swimming pool* ♦ *indoor games* ♦ *the world indoor 200 meters champion* **ANT** OUTDOOR

in·doors 🔊 /ˌɪnˈdɔrz/ *adv.*
inside or into a building: *to go/stay indoors* ♦ *Many herbs can be grown indoors.* **ANT** OUTDOORS

in·du·bi·ta·bly /ɪnˈdubəṭəbli/ *adv.* (*formal*) in a way that cannot be doubted; without question: *He was, indubitably, the most suitable candidate.* ▶ **in·du·bi·ta·ble** *adj.*: *indubitable proof*

in·duce **AWL** /ɪnˈdus/ *verb* **1** ~ **sb to do sth** (*formal*) to persuade or influence someone to do something: *Nothing would induce me to take the job.* **2** ~ **sth** (*formal*) to cause something: *drugs that induce sleep* ♦ *a drug-induced coma* **3** ~ **sb/sth** (*medical*) to make a woman start giving birth to her baby by giving her special drugs: *induced labor* ♦ *We'll have to induce her.*

in·duce·ment /ɪnˈdusmənt/ *noun* [C, U] ~ **(to/for sb) (to do sth)** something that is given to someone to persuade them to do something **SYN** INCENTIVE: *There is little inducement for them to work harder.* ♦ *Car dealers are offering generous financial inducements to encourage the sale of new vehicles.* ♦ *Government officials have been accused of accepting inducements* (= BRIBES) *from local businessmen.*

in·duct /ɪnˈdʌkt/ *verb* [often passive] ~ **sb (into sth) (as sth)** (*formal*) **1** to formally give someone a job or position of authority, especially as part of a ceremony **2** to officially introduce someone into a group or an organization: *This quarterback, inducted into the Hall of Fame over the summer, was second to none.* **3** to take someone into military service **4** to introduce someone to a particular area of knowledge: *They were inducted into the skills of magic.*

in·duc·tee /ˌɪndʌkˈti/ *noun* a person who is being, or who has just been, introduced into a special group of people, especially someone who has just joined the army

in·duc·tion **AWL** /ɪnˈdʌkʃn/ *noun* **1** [U, C] ~ **(into sth)** the process of introducing someone to a new job, skill, organization, etc.; a ceremony at which this takes place **2** [U, C] the act of making a pregnant woman start to give birth, using artificial means such as a special drug **3** [U] (*technical*) a method of discovering general rules and principles from particular facts and examples ⊃ compare DEDUCTION **4** [U] (*physics*) the process by which electricity or MAGNETISM passes from one object to another without them touching

in·duc·tive /ɪnˈdʌktɪv/ *adj.* **1** (*technical*) using particular facts and examples to form general rules and principles: *an inductive argument* ♦ *inductive reasoning* ⊃ compare DEDUCTIVE **2** (*physics*) connected with the INDUCTION of electricity ▶ **in·duc·tive·ly** *adv.*: *a theory derived inductively from the data*

in·dulge /ɪnˈdʌldʒ/ *verb* **1** [I, T] to allow yourself to have or do something that you like, especially something that is considered bad for you: ~ **in sth** *They went into town to indulge in some serious shopping.* ♦ ~ **yourself (with sth)** *I indulged myself with a long hot bath.* **2** [T] ~ **sth** to satisfy a particular desire, interest, etc.: *The inheritance enabled him to indulge his passion for art.* **3** [T] to be too generous in allowing someone to have or do whatever they like: ~ **sb (with sth)** *She did not believe in indulging the children with presents.* ♦ ~ **sth** *Her father had always indulged her every whim.* **4** [I] ~ **in sth** to take part in an activity, especially one that is illegal

in·dul·gence /ɪnˈdʌldʒəns/ *noun* **1** [U] (usually *disapproving*) the state or act of having or doing whatever you want; the state of allowing someone to have or do whatever they want: *to lead a life of indulgence* ♦ *Avoid excessive indulgence in sweets and sugary drinks.* ♦ *There is no limit to the indulgence he shows to his grandchildren.* **2** [C] something that you allow

yourself to have even though it is not essential: *The cruise was an extravagant indulgence.* **3** [U] (*formal*) willingness to ignore the weaknesses in someone or something **SYN** PATIENCE: *They begged the audience's indulgence.*

in·dul·gent /ɪnˈdʌldʒənt/ *adj.* **1** (usually *disapproving*) tending to allow someone to have or do whatever they want: *indulgent parents* ♦ *an indulgent smile* ⊃ see also SELF-INDULGENT **2** willing or too willing to ignore the weaknesses in someone or something **SYN** PATIENT: *to take an indulgent view of something* ▶ **in·dul·gent·ly** *adv.*: *to laugh indulgently*

in·dus·tri·al 🔊 /ɪnˈdʌstriəl/ *adj.* [usually before noun]
1 connected with industry: *industrial competition* ♦ *industrial output* ♦ *an industrial accident* ♦ *They had made industrial quantities of food* (= a lot). **2** used by industries: *industrial chemicals* **3** having many industries: *an industrial town* ♦ *an industrial society* ♦ *the world's leading industrial nations* ▶ **in·dus·tri·al·ly** *adv.*: *industrially advanced countries*

in,dustrial archae'ology *noun* [U] the study of machines, factories, bridges, etc. used in the past in industry

in,dustrial 'arts (also **shop**, **'shop class**) *noun* [U] a school subject in which students learn to make things from wood and metal using tools and machines

in·dus·tri·al·ism /ɪnˈdʌstriəˌlɪzəm/ *noun* [U] (*technical*) an economic and social system based on industry

in·dus·tri·al·ist /ɪnˈdʌstriəlɪst/ *noun* a person who owns or runs a large factory or industrial company

in·dus·tri·al·ize /ɪnˈdʌstriəˌlaɪz/ *verb* [T, I] ~ **(sth)** if a country or an area **is industrialized** or if it **industrializes**, industries are developed there: *The southern part of the country was slow to industrialize.* ▶ **in·dus·tri·al·i·za·tion** /ɪnˌdʌstriələˈzeɪʃn/ *noun* [U]: *the rapid industrialization of Japan* **in·dus·tri·al·ized** *adj.*: *an industrialized country*

in,dustrial 'park *noun* an area especially for office buildings or factories, on the edge of a town

in,dustrial re'lations *noun* [pl.] relations between employers and employees

the In,dustrial Revo'lution *noun* [sing.] the period in the 18th and 19th centuries in Europe and the U.S. when machines began to be used to do work and industry grew rapidly

in'dustrial-,strength *adj.* (often *humorous*) very strong or powerful: *industrial-strength cleaning agents* ♦ *industrial-strength coffee*

in·dus·tri·ous /ɪnˈdʌstriəs/ *adj.* (*approving*) working hard; busy **SYN** HARD-WORKING: *an industrious student* ▶ **in·dus·tri·ous·ly** *adv.*

in·dus·try 🔊 /'ɪndəstri/ *noun* (*pl.* **in·dus·tries**)
1 [U] the production of goods from raw materials, especially in factories: *heavy/light industry* ♦ *the needs of American industry* ♦ *This chemical is mostly used in industry.* ⊃ collocations at ECONOMY **2** [C] the people and activities involved in producing a particular thing, or in providing a particular service: *the steel industry* ♦ *the automotive/tourist, etc. industry* ♦ *We need to develop local industries.* ⊃ see also CAPTAIN OF INDUSTRY, COTTAGE INDUSTRY, HEAVY INDUSTRY, SMOKESTACK INDUSTRY **3** [U] (*formal*) the quality of working hard: *We were impressed by their industry.*

In·dy /'ɪndi/ (also **'Indy ,racing**, **'Indy ,car**, **'Indy car ,racing**) *noun* [U] motor racing around a track that is raised on both sides

'Indy ,car *noun* a car used in Indy racing

in·e·bri·at·ed /ɪˈnibriˌeɪṭɪd/ *adj.* (*formal* or *humorous*) drunk ▶ **in·e·bri·a·tion** /ɪˌnibriˈeɪʃn/ *noun* [U]

in·ed·i·ble /ɪnˈɛdəbl/ *adj.* that you cannot eat because it is of poor quality, or poisonous **ANT** EDIBLE

in·ef·fa·ble /ɪnˈɛfəbl/ *adj.* (*formal*) too great or beautiful to describe in words: *ineffable joy*

| t tea | ṭ butter | d did | k cat | g got | tʃ chin | dʒ June | f fall |

in·ef·fec·tive /ˌɪnɪˈfɛktɪv/ adj. not achieving what you want to achieve; not having any effect: *The new drug was ineffective.* ◆ *ineffective management* ◆ **~ in doing sth** *The law proved ineffective in dealing with the problem.* **ANT** EFFECTIVE ▸ **in·ef·fec·tive·ly** adv. **in·ef·fec·tive·ness** noun [U]

in·ef·fec·tu·al /ˌɪnɪˈfɛktʃuəl/ adj. (formal) without the ability to achieve much; not achieving what you want to do: *an ineffectual teacher* ◆ *an ineffectual attempt to reform the law* ▸ **in·ef·fec·tu·al·ly** adv.

in·ef·fi·cient /ˌɪnɪˈfɪʃnt/ adj. not doing a job well and not making the best use of time, money, energy, etc.: *an inefficient heating system* ◆ *inefficient management* ◆ *an extremely inefficient secretary* ◆ *inefficient use of time and energy* **ANT** EFFICIENT ▸ **in·ef·fi·cien·cy** /-ˈʃɑnsi/ noun [U, C] (pl. in·ef·fi·cien·cies): *waste and inefficiency in government* ◆ *inefficiencies in the system* **in·ef·fi·cient·ly** adv.

in·el·e·gant /ɪnˈɛləɡənt/ adj. not attractive or elegant **ANT** ELEGANT ▸ **in·el·e·gant·ly** adv.

in·el·i·gi·ble /ɪnˈɛlədʒəbl/ adj. not having the necessary qualifications to have or to do something: **~ (for sth)** *ineligible for financial aid* ◆ **~ (to do sth)** *ineligible to vote* **ANT** ELIGIBLE ▸ **in·el·i·gi·bil·i·ty** /ɪnˌɛlədʒəˈbɪləti/ noun [U]

in·e·luc·ta·ble /ˌɪnɪˈlʌktəbl/ adj. (formal) that you cannot avoid **SYN** UNAVOIDABLE ▸ **in·e·luc·ta·bly** /-ˈbli/ adv.

in·ept /ɪˈnɛpt/ adj. acting or done with no skill: *She was left feeling inept and inadequate.* ◆ *an inept remark* ▸ **in·ept·ly** adv.

in·ept·i·tude /ɪˈnɛptəˌtud/ noun [U] lack of skill: *the ineptitude of the police in handling the situation*

in·e·qual·i·ty /ˌɪnɪˈkwɑləti/ noun (pl. in·e·qual·i·ties) [U, C] the unfair difference between groups of people in society, when some have more wealth, status, or opportunities than others: *inequality of opportunity* ◆ *economic inequalities between different areas* ◆ *racial/gender inequality* ⊃ collocations at RACE **ANT** EQUALITY

in·eq·ui·ta·ble /ɪnˈɛkwətəbl/ adj. (formal) not fair; not the same for everyone **SYN** UNFAIR: *inequitable distribution of wealth* **ANT** EQUITABLE

in·eq·ui·ty /ɪnˈɛkwəti/ noun (pl. in·eq·ui·ties) [C, U] (formal) something that is unfair; the state of being unfair **SYN** INJUSTICE

in·e·rad·i·ca·ble /ˌɪnɪˈrædɪkəbl/ adj. (formal) (of a quality or situation) that cannot be removed or changed

in·ert /ɪˈnərt/ adj. **1** (formal) without power to move or act: *He lay inert with half-closed eyes.* **2** (chemistry) without active chemical or other properties (= characteristics)

in·ert ˈgas noun (chemistry) = NOBLE GAS

in·er·tia /ɪˈnərʃə/ noun [U] **1** (usually disapproving) lack of energy; lack of desire or ability to move or change: *I can't seem to get rid of this feeling of inertia.* ◆ *the forces of institutional inertia in the school system* **2** (physics) a property (= characteristic) of MATTER (= a substance) by which it stays still or, if moving, continues moving in a straight line unless it is acted on by a force outside itself

in·er·tial /ɪˈnərʃl/ adj. (technical) connected with or caused by inertia

in·es·cap·a·ble /ˌɪnɪˈskeɪpəbl/ adj. (of a fact or situation) that you cannot avoid or ignore **SYN** UNAVOIDABLE: *an inescapable fact* ◆ *This leads to the inescapable conclusion that the two things are connected.* ▸ **in·es·cap·a·bly** /-ˈbli/ adv.

in·es·sen·tial /ˌɪnɪˈsɛnʃl/ adj. not necessary: *inessential luxuries* ▸ **in·es·sen·tial** noun: *Few people had spare cash for inessentials.* ⊃ compare ESSENTIAL, NONESSENTIAL

in·es·ti·ma·ble /ɪnˈɛstəməbl/ adj. (formal) too great to calculate: *The information he provided was of inestimable value.*

in·ev·i·ta·ble 🔑 **AWL** /ɪnˈɛvətəbl/ adj.
1 that you cannot avoid or prevent **SYN** UNAVOIDABLE: *It was an inevitable consequence of the decision.* ◆ *It was inevitable that there would be job losses.* ◆ *It seems inevitable*

that interest rates will rise. **2** [only before noun] (often humorous) so frequent that you always expect it: *toddlers and their inevitable tantrums* **3** **the inevitable** noun [sing.] something that is certain to happen: *You have to accept the inevitable.* ◆ *The inevitable happened—I forgot my passport.* ▸ **in·ev·i·ta·bil·i·ty** **AWL** /ɪnˌɛvətəˈbɪləti/ noun [U, sing.]: *the inevitability of death* ◆ *There was an inevitability about their defeat.*

in·ev·i·ta·bly 🔑 **AWL** /ɪnˈɛvətəbli/ adv.
1 as is certain to happen: *Inevitably, the press exaggerated the story.* **2** (often humorous) as you would expect: *Inevitably, it rained on the day of the wedding.*

in·ex·act /ˌɪnɪɡˈzækt/ adj. not accurate or exact: *an inexact description* ◆ *Economics is an inexact science.*

in·ex·ac·ti·tude /ˌɪnɪɡˈzæktəˌtud/ noun [U] (formal) the quality of being not accurate or exact

in·ex·cus·a·ble /ˌɪnɪkˈskyuzəbl/ adj. too bad to accept or forgive **SYN** UNJUSTIFIABLE: *inexcusable rudeness* **ANT** EXCUSABLE ▸ **in·ex·cus·a·bly** /-ˈbli/ adv.

in·ex·haust·i·ble /ˌɪnɪɡˈzɔstəbl/ adj. that cannot be finished; very great: *an inexhaustible supply of good jokes* ◆ *Her energy is inexhaustible.*

in·ex·o·ra·ble /ɪnˈɛksərəbl; -ˈɛɡzə-/ adj. (formal) (of a process) that cannot be stopped or changed **SYN** RELENTLESS: *the inexorable rise of crime* ▸ **in·ex·o·ra·bil·i·ty** /ɪnˌɛksərəˈbɪləti; -ˌɛɡzə-/ noun [U]: *the inexorability of progress* **in·ex·o·ra·bly** /ɪnˈɛksərəbli; -ˈɛɡzə-/ adv.: *events leading inexorably toward a crisis*

in·ex·pe·di·ent /ˌɪnɪkˈspidiənt/ adj. [not usually before noun] (formal) (of an action) not fair or right: *It would be inexpedient to raise taxes further.* **ANT** EXPEDIENT

in·ex·pen·sive /ˌɪnɪkˈspɛnsɪv/ adj. not costing a lot of money: *a relatively inexpensive hotel* **ANT** EXPENSIVE ⊃ thesaurus box at CHEAP ▸ **in·ex·pen·sive·ly** adv.

in·ex·pe·ri·ence /ˌɪnɪkˈspɪriəns/ noun [U] lack of knowledge and experience: *His mistake was due to youth and inexperience.*

in·ex·pe·ri·enced /ˌɪnɪkˈspɪriənst/ adj. having little knowledge or experience of something: *inexperienced drivers/staff* ◆ *inexperienced in modern methods* ◆ *a child too young and inexperienced to recognize danger* **ANT** EXPERIENCED

in·ex·pert /ɪnˈɛkspərt/ adj. without much skill ⊃ compare EXPERT ▸ **in·ex·pert·ly** adv.

in·ex·pli·ca·ble /ˌɪnɪkˈsplɪkəbl/ adj. that cannot be understood or explained **SYN** INCOMPREHENSIBLE: *inexplicable behavior* ◆ *For some inexplicable reason, he gave up a fantastic job.* **ANT** EXPLICABLE ▸ **in·ex·pli·ca·bly** /-ˈbli/ adv.: *inexplicably delayed/absent* ◆ *She inexplicably withdrew the offer.*

in·ex·press·i·ble /ˌɪnɪkˈsprɛsəbl/ adj. (of feelings) too strong to be put into words: *inexpressible joy*

in ex·tre·mis /ˌɪn ɪkˈstrimɪs/ adv. (from Latin, formal) **1** in a very difficult situation when very strong action is needed **2** at the moment of death

in·ex·tri·ca·ble /ˌɪnɪkˈstrɪkəbl; ɪnˈɛkstrɪkəbl/ adj. (formal) too closely linked to be separated: *an inextricable connection between the past and the present*

in·ex·tri·ca·bly /ˌɪnɪkˈstrɪkəbli; ɪnˈɛkstrɪkəbli/ adv. if two things are **inextricably linked**, etc., it is impossible to separate them: *Europe's foreign policy is inextricably linked with that of the U.S.* ◆ *She had become inextricably involved in the campaign.*

in·fal·li·ble /ɪnˈfæləbl/ adj. **1** never wrong; never making mistakes: *infallible advice* ◆ *Doctors are not infallible.* **ANT** FALLIBLE **2** that never fails; always doing what it is supposed to do: *an infallible method of memorizing things* ▸ **in·fal·li·bil·i·ty** /ɪnˌfæləˈbɪləti/ noun [U]: *papal infallibility* **in·fal·li·bly** /ɪnˈfæləbli/ adv.

in·fa·mous /ˈɪnfəməs/ adj. (formal) well known for being bad or evil **SYN** NOTORIOUS: *a general who was infamous for his*

---

brutality ♦ *the most infamous concentration camp* ♦ (*humorous*) *Uncle Harry's infamous fruitcake* ⊃ compare FAMOUS

in·fa·my /ˈɪnfəmi/ *noun* (*pl.* **in·fa·mies**) (*formal*) **1** [U] the state of being well known for something bad or evil: *a day that will live in infamy* **2** [U, C] evil behavior; an evil act: *scenes of horror and infamy*

in·fan·cy /ˈɪnfənsi/ *noun* [U] **1** the time when a child is a baby: *to die in infancy* **2** the early development of something: *a time when the movie business was still in its infancy*

in·fant /ˈɪnfənt/ *noun, adj.*
● *noun* (*formal or law*) a baby, especially a very young one: *a day care center for infants* ♦ *their infant son* ♦ *She was seriously ill as an infant.* ♦ *the infant mortality rate*
● *adj.* [only before noun] **1** designed to be used by infants: *infant formula* (= milk for babies) **2** new and not yet developed: *infant industries*

in·fan·ti·cide /ɪnˈfæntəˌsaɪd/ *noun* (*formal*) **1** [U, C] the crime of killing a baby; a person who is guilty of this crime **2** [U] (in some cultures) the practice of killing babies that are not wanted, for example because they are girls and not boys

in·fan·tile /ˈɪnfənˌtaɪl/ *adj.* **1** (*disapproving*) typical of a small child (and therefore not suitable for adults or older children) SYN CHILDISH **2** [only before noun] (*formal*) connected with babies or very young children

in·fan·til·ism /ɪnˈfæntəˌlɪzəm/ *noun* [U] (*psychology*) the fact of adults continuing to behave like children, in a way that is not normal

in·fan·til·ize /ɪnˈfæntəˌlaɪz/ *verb* ~ **sb** (*formal*) to treat someone as though they are a child

in·fan·try /ˈɪnfəntri/ *noun* [U] soldiers who fight on foot: *infantry units* ♦ *The infantry was guarding the bridge.*

in·fan·try·man /ˈɪnfəntrimən/ *noun* (*pl.* **in·fan·try·men** /-mən/) a soldier who fights on foot

in·farc·tion /ɪnˈfɑrkʃn/ *noun* (*medical*) a condition in which the blood supply to an area of TISSUE is blocked and the TISSUE dies

in·fat·u·at·ed /ɪnˈfætʃuˌeɪtəd/ *adj.* ~ (**with sb/sth**) having a very strong feeling of love or attraction for someone or something so that you cannot think clearly and in a sensible way SYN BESOTTED: *She was completely infatuated with him.*

in·fat·u·a·tion /ɪnˌfætʃuˈeɪʃn/ *noun* [C, U] ~ (**with/for sb/sth**) very strong feelings of love or attraction for someone or something, especially when these are unreasonable and do not last long: *It isn't love, it's just a passing infatuation.*

in·fect 🔑 /ɪnˈfɛkt/ *verb*
1 to make a disease or an illness spread to a person, an animal, or a plant: ~ **sb/sth** *It is not possible to infect another person through kissing.* ♦ ~ **sb/sth with sth** *people infected with HIV* **2** ~ **sth** (**with sth**) [usually passive] to make a substance contain harmful bacteria that can spread disease SYN CONTAMINATE: *eggs infected with salmonella* **3** ~ **sth** (**with sth**) to make a computer virus spread to another computer or program **4** ~ **sb** (**with sth**) to make someone share a particular feeling: *She infected the children with her enthusiasm for music.*

in·fect·ed 🔑 /ɪnˈfɛktəd/ *adj.*
containing harmful bacteria: *The wound from the dog bite became infected.* ♦ *an infected water supply* ⊃ thesaurus box at PAINFUL

in·fec·tion 🔑 /ɪnˈfɛkʃn/ *noun*
1 [U] the act or process of causing or getting a disease: *to be exposed to infection* ♦ *to increase the risk of infection* **2** [C] an illness that is caused by bacteria or a virus: *an ear/sinus infection* ♦ *to spread an infection* ⊃ thesaurus box at DISEASE ⊃ compare CONTAGION

in·fec·tious 🔑 /ɪnˈfɛkʃəs/ *adj.*
1 an **infectious** disease can be passed easily from one person to another, especially through the air they breathe:

The flu is highly infectious. ♦ (*figurative*) *infectious laughter* **2** [not usually before noun] if a person or an animal is **infectious**, they have a disease that can be spread to others: *I'm still infectious.* ⊃ compare CONTAGIOUS ▶ **in·fec·tious·ly** *adv.*: *to laugh infectiously* **in·fec·tious·ness** *noun* [U]

in·fec·tive /ɪnˈfɛktɪv/ *adj.* (*medical*) able to cause infection

in·fer AWL /ɪnˈfər/ *verb* (-rr-) **1** to reach an opinion or decide that something is true on the basis of information that is available SYN DEDUCE: ~ **sth** (**from sth**) *Much of the meaning must be inferred from the context.* ♦ ~ **that...** *It is reasonable to infer that the government knew about these deals.* **2** ~ (**that**)... | ~ **sth** (*non-standard*) to suggest indirectly that something is true: *Are you inferring (that) I'm not capable of doing the job?*

> **WHICH WORD?**
>
> **infer ♦ imply**
>
> ■ **Infer** and **imply** have opposite meanings. The two words can describe the same event, but from different points of view. If a speaker or writer **implies** something, they suggest it without saying it directly: *The article implied that the pilot was responsible for the accident.* If you **infer** something from what a speaker or writer says, you come to the conclusion that this is what he or she means: *I inferred from the article that the pilot was responsible for the accident.*
>
> ■ **Infer** is now often used with the same meaning as **imply**. However, many people consider that a sentence such as *Are you inferring that I'm a liar?* is incorrect, although it is fairly common in speech.

in·fer·ence AWL /ˈɪnfərəns; -frəns/ *noun* **1** [C] something that you can find out indirectly from what you already know SYN DEDUCTION: *to draw/make inferences from the data* ♦ *The clear inference is that the universe is expanding.* ⊃ collocations at SCIENTIFIC **2** [U] the act or process of forming an opinion, based on what you already know: *If he is guilty, then by inference, so is his wife* (= it is logical to think so, from the same evidence).

in·fe·ri·or /ɪnˈfɪriər/ *adj., noun*
● *adj.* **1** not good or not as good as someone or something else: *of inferior quality* ♦ *inferior goods* ♦ *to make someone feel inferior* ♦ ~ **to sb/sth** *Modern music is often considered inferior to that of the past.* **2** [usually before noun] (*formal*) of lower rank; lower: *an inferior officer* ANT SUPERIOR
● *noun* a person who is not as good as someone else; a person who is lower in rank or status

in·fe·ri·or·i·ty /ɪnˌfɪriˈɔrəti; -ˈɑr-/ *noun* [U] the state of not being as good as someone or something else: *a sense of inferiority* ♦ *the inferiority of poorly made clothing* ANT SUPERIORITY

infe·ri·or·i·ty ˌcomplex *noun* a feeling that you are not as good, as important, or as intelligent as other people

in·fer·nal /ɪnˈfərnl/ *adj.* **1** [only before noun] (*old-fashioned*) extremely annoying: *Stop that infernal noise!* **2** (*literary*) connected with hell ▶ **in·fer·nal·ly** /-nəli/ *adv.*

in·fer·no /ɪnˈfərnoʊ/ *noun* (*pl.* **in·fer·nos**) [usually sing.] a very large, dangerous fire that is out of control: *a blazing/raging inferno*

in·fer·tile /ɪnˈfərtl/ *adj.* **1** (of people, animals, and plants) not able to have babies or produce young: *an infertile couple* **2** (of land) not able to produce good crops ANT FERTILE ▶ **in·fer·til·i·ty** /ˌɪnfərˈtɪləti/ *noun* [U]: *an infertility clinic* ♦ *infertility treatment for couples*

in·fest /ɪnˈfɛst/ *verb* [usually passive] ~ **sth** (especially of insects or animals such as RATS) to exist in large numbers in a particular place, often causing damage or disease: *shark-infested waters* ♦ *The kitchen was infested with ants.* ▶ **in·fes·ta·tion** /ˌɪnfɛˈsteɪʃn/ *noun* [C, U]: *an infestation of lice*

in·fi·del /ˈɪnfədəl; -ˌdɛl/ *noun* (*old use*) an offensive way of

| h **h**at | m **m**an | n **n**o | ŋ si**ng** | 1 **l**eg | r **r**ed | y **y**es | w **w**et |

referring to someone who does not believe in what the speaker considers to be the true religion

in·fi·del·i·ty /ˌɪnfəˈdɛləti/ *noun* (*pl.* **in·fi·del·i·ties**) [U, C] the act of not being faithful to your wife, husband, or partner, by having sex with someone else: *marital infidelity* ◆ *She could not forgive his infidelities.* **ANT** FIDELITY

in·field /ˈɪnfild/ *noun* **1** [sing.] the inner part of the field in baseball and some other sports ➔ compare OUTFIELD **2** the group of players who play in the infield: *The third baseman leads a strong infield.* **3** the area that is within a running track ▸ **in·field·er** *noun*: *four infielders and three outfielders*

in·fight·ing /ˈɪnˌfaɪtɪŋ/ *noun* [U] arguments and disagreements between people in the same group who are competing for power: *political infighting within the party*

in·fill /ˈɪnfɪl/ *noun* [U] **1** the filling in of a space with something, especially the building of new houses in spaces between existing ones: *infill development* **2** the material used to fill in a space or a hole: *gravel infill* ▸ **in·fill** *verb* [I, T] **~ (sth)**

in·fil·trate /ˈɪnfɪlˌtreɪt; ɪnˈfɪltreɪt/ *verb* **1** [T, I] to enter or make someone enter a place or an organization secretly, especially in order to get information that can be used against it: **~ sth** *The headquarters had been infiltrated by enemy spies.* ◆ **~ sb into sth** *Rebel forces were infiltrated into the country.* ◆ **~ into sth** *The CIA agents successfully infiltrated into the terrorist organizations.* **2** [I, T] **~ (into) sth** (*technical*) (especially of liquids or gases) to pass slowly into something: *Only a small amount of the rainwater actually infiltrates into the soil.* ▸ **in·fil·tra·tion** /ˌɪnfɪlˈtreɪʃn/ *noun* [U]: *the infiltration of terrorists from across the border* ◆ *the infiltration of rain into the soil*

in·fil·tra·tor /ˈɪnfɪlˌtreɪtər/ *noun* a person who secretly becomes a member of a group or goes to a place, to get information, or to influence the group

in·fi·nite **AWL** /ˈɪnfənət/ *adj., noun*
● *adj.* **1** very great; impossible to measure **SYN** BOUNDLESS: *an infinite variety of plants* ◆ *a teacher with infinite patience* ◆ (*ironic*) *The company, in its infinite wisdom, decided to close the employee cafeteria* (= they thought it was a good thing to do, but nobody else agreed). **2** without limit; without end: *an infinite universe* **ANT** FINITE
● *noun* [sing.] **1 the infinite** something that has no end **2 the Infinite** God

in·fi·nite·ly **AWL** /ˈɪnfənətli/ *adv.* **1** (used especially in comparisons) very much: *Your English is infinitely better than my German.* **2** extremely; with no limit: *Human beings are infinitely adaptable.*

in·fin·i·tes·i·mal /ˌɪnfɪnɪˈtɛsəml/ *adj.* (*formal*) extremely small **SYN** TINY: *infinitesimal traces of poison* ◆ *an infinitesimal risk* ▸ **in·fin·i·tes·i·mal·ly** /-məli/ *adv.*

in·fin·i·tive /ɪnˈfɪnətɪv/ *noun* (*grammar*) the basic form of a verb, such as *be* or *run*. In English, an infinitive is used by itself, for example *swim* in *She can swim* (this use is sometimes called the **bare infinitive**), or with *to* (the **to-infinitive**) as in *She likes to swim.* **IDM** see SPLIT *v.*

in·fin·i·ty /ɪnˈfɪnəti/ *noun* (*pl.* **in·fin·i·ties**) **1** [U] (also **in·fin·i·ties** [pl.]) the state of having no end or limit: *the infinity/infinities of space* **2** [U] a point far away that can never be reached: *The landscape seemed to stretch into infinity.* **3** (*symb.* ∞) [U, C] (*mathematics*) a number larger than any other **4** [sing.] a large amount that is impossible to count: *an infinity of stars*

in·fin·i·ty ˌpool *noun* a swimming pool that is specially designed so that, when you are in it, the pool seems to stretch to the HORIZON (= where the sky seems to meet the land or ocean)

in·firm /ɪnˈfərm/ *adj.* **1** weak and sick, especially over a long period or as a result of being old **2 the infirm** *noun* [pl.] people who are weak and sick for a long period: *care for the elderly and infirm*

in·fir·ma·ry /ɪnˈfərməri/ *noun* (*pl.* **in·fir·ma·ries**) **1** a special room in a school, prison, etc. for people who are sick

2 (often used in names) a hospital, especially a military hospital

in·fir·mi·ty /ɪnˈfərməti/ *noun* (*pl.* **in·fir·mi·ties**) [U, C] weakness or illness over a long period: *We all fear disability or infirmity.* ◆ *the infirmities of old age*

in·fix /ˈɪnfɪks/ *noun* (*grammar*) a letter or group of letters added to the middle of a word to change its meaning

in fla·gran·te /ˌɪn fləˈɡrɑnti/ (also **fla·gran·te de·lic·to** /ˌɪn fləˌɡrɑnti dəˈlɪktoʊ/) *adv.* (from *Latin, literary or humorous*) if someone is found or caught **in flagrante**, they are discovered doing something that they should not be doing, especially having sex

in·flame /ɪnˈfleɪm/ *verb* (*formal*) **1 ~ sb/sth** to cause very strong feelings, especially anger or excitement, in a person or in a group of people: *His comments have inflamed teachers all over the country.* **2 ~ sth** to make a situation worse or more difficult to deal with: *The situation was further inflamed by the arrival of the security forces.*

in·flamed /ɪnˈfleɪmd/ *adj.* **1** (of a part of the body) painful, swollen, and hot because of infection or injury ➔ thesaurus box at PAINFUL **2** (of people, feelings, etc.) very angry or excited

in·flam·ma·ble /ɪnˈflæməbl/ *adj.* **1** = FLAMMABLE: *inflammable material* **2** full of strong emotions or violence

in·flam·ma·tion /ˌɪnfləˈmeɪʃn/ *noun* [U, C] a condition in which a part of the body becomes red, sore, and swollen because of infection or injury

in·flam·ma·to·ry /ɪnˈflæməˌtɔri/ *adj.* **1** (*disapproving*) intended to cause very strong feelings of anger: *inflammatory remarks* **2** (*medical*) causing or involving inflammation

in·flat·a·ble /ɪnˈfleɪtəbl/ *adj., noun*
● *adj.* needing to be filled with air or gas before you use it: *an inflatable mattress*
● *noun* **1** an inflatable boat **2** a large object made of plastic or rubber and filled with air or gas, used for children to play on, or as an advertisement for something

in·flate /ɪnˈfleɪt/ *verb* **1** [T, I] **~ (sth)** to fill something or become filled with gas or air: *Inflate your life jacket by pulling sharply on the cord.* ◆ *The life jacket failed to inflate.* **2** [T] **~ sth** to make something appear to be more important or impressive than it really is **3** [T, I] **~ (sth)** to increase in price; to increase the price of something: *The principal effect of the demand for new houses was to inflate prices.* ◆ *Food prices are no longer inflating at the same rate as last year.* ➔ compare DEFLATE, REFLATE

in·flat·ed /ɪnˈfleɪtəd/ *adj.* **1** (especially of prices) higher than is acceptable or reasonable: *inflated prices/salaries* **2** (of ideas, claims, etc.) believing or claiming that someone or something is more important or impressive than they really are: *He has an inflated sense of his own importance.*

in·fla·tion /ɪnˈfleɪʃn/ *noun* [U] **1** a general increase in the prices of services and goods in a particular country, resulting in a fall in the value of money; the rate at which this happens: *the fight against rising inflation* ◆ *to control/curb inflation* ◆ *to reduce/bring down inflation* ◆ *a high/low rate of inflation* ◆ *an inflation rate of 3%* ◆ *Salary increases must be in line with inflation.* ◆ *Inflation is currently running at 3%.* ➔ collocations at ECONOMY **2** the act of filling something with air or gas: *life jackets with an automatic inflation device* **ANT** DEFLATION

in·fla·tion·ar·y /ɪnˈfleɪʃəˌneri/ *adj.* [usually before noun] causing or connected with a general increase in the prices of services and goods: *the inflationary effects of an increase in prices* ◆ *Our economy is in an **inflationary spiral** of salary and price increases* (= a continuing situation in which an increase in one causes an increase in the other).

in·flect /ɪnˈflɛkt/ *verb* [I] (*grammar*) if a word **inflects**, its ending or spelling changes according to its GRAMMATICAL function in a sentence; if a language **inflects**, it has words that do this ▸ **in·flect·ed** *adj.* [usually before noun]: *an inflected language/form/verb*

---

in·flec·tion /ɪnˈflɛkʃn/ *noun* [C, U] **1** a change in the form of a word, especially the ending, according to its GRAMMATICAL function in a sentence **2** a change in how high or low your voice is as you are speaking ▶ **in·flec·tion·al** *adj.*

in·flex·i·ble AWL /ɪnˈflɛksəbl/ *adj.* **1** (*disapproving*) that cannot be changed or made more suitable for a particular situation SYN RIGID: *an inflexible attitude/routine/system* **2** (*disapproving*) (of people or organizations) unwilling to change their opinions, decisions, etc., or the way they do things: *He's completely inflexible on the subject.* **3** (of a material) difficult or impossible to bend SYN STIFF ANT FLEXIBLE ▶ **in·flex·i·bil·i·ty** AWL /ɪnˌflɛksəˈbɪləti/ *noun* [U] **in·flex·i·bly** /ɪnˈflɛksəbli/ *adv.*

in·flict /ɪnˈflɪkt/ *verb* to make someone or something suffer something unpleasant: ~ **sth on/upon sb/sth** *They inflicted a humiliating defeat on the home team.* ♦ *Heavy casualties were inflicted on the enemy.* ♦ (*humorous*) *Do you have to inflict that music on us?* ♦ ~ **sth** *They surveyed the damage inflicted by the storm.* ▶ **in·flic·tion** /ɪnˈflɪkʃn/ *noun* [U]: *the infliction of pain*

'in-flight *adj.* [only before noun] provided or happening during a trip on a plane: *an in-flight magazine/movie* ♦ *in-flight refueling*

in·flow /ˈɪnfloʊ/ *noun* **1** [C, U] the movement of a lot of money, people, or things into a place from somewhere else SYN INFLUX **2** [sing., U] the movement of a liquid or of air into a place from somewhere else: *an inflow pipe* ANT OUTFLOW

in·flu·ence /ˈɪnfluəns/ *noun, verb*
- *noun* **1** [U, C] ~ **(on/upon sb/sth)** the effect that someone or something has on the way a person thinks or behaves or on the way that something works or develops: *to have/exert a strong influence on someone* ♦ *the influence of the climate on agricultural production* ♦ *What exactly is the influence of television on children?* **2** [U] the power that someone or something has to make someone or something behave in a particular way: ~ **(over sb/sth)** *Her parents no longer have any real influence over her.* ♦ ~ **(with sb)** *She could probably exert her influence with the manager and get you a job.* ♦ *He committed the crime under the influence of drugs.* **3** [C] a person or thing that affects the way a person behaves and thinks: *cultural influences* ♦ ~ **(on sb/sth)** *Those friends are a bad influence on her.* ♦ *His first music teacher was a major influence in his life.* IDM **under the influence** having had too much alcohol to drink: *She was charged with driving under the influence.* ⊃ see also DUI
- *verb* **1** to have an effect on the way that someone behaves or thinks, especially by giving them an example to follow: ~ **sb/sth** *His writings have influenced the lives of millions.* ♦ *to be strongly influenced by something* ♦ *Don't let me influence you either way.* ♦ ~ **how, whether, etc....** *The wording of questions can influence how people answer.* ♦ ~ **sb to do sth** *She was influenced to start doing volunteer work by her teacher.* **2** ~ **sth** | ~ **how, where, etc....** to have an effect on a particular situation and the way that it develops: *A number of social factors influence life expectancy.*

'influence ˌpeddling *noun* [U] the illegal activity of a politician doing something for someone in return for payment SYN CORRUPTION

in·flu·en·tial /ˌɪnfluˈɛnʃl/ *adj.* having a lot of influence on someone or something: *a highly influential book* ♦ ~ **in sth** *She is one of the most influential figures in local politics.* ♦ ~ **in doing sth** *The committee was influential in formulating government policy on employment.*

in·flu·en·za /ˌɪnfluˈɛnzə/ *noun* [U] (*formal*) = FLU

in·flux /ˈɪnflʌks/ *noun* [usually sing.] ~ **(of sb/sth) (into...)** the fact of a lot of people, money, or things arriving somewhere: *a massive/sudden influx of visitors* ♦ *the influx of wealth into the region*

in·fo /ˈɪnfoʊ/ *noun* **1** [U] (*informal*) information: *Did you get any more info about the job yet?* **2** info- (in nouns) connected with information: *an infosheet* ♦ *We send all potential clients an infopack.*

in·fo·mer·cial /ˈɪnfoʊˌmərʃl/ *noun* a long advertisement on television that tries to give a lot of information about a subject, so that it does not appear to be an advertisement

in·form /ɪnˈfɔrm/ *verb*
1 to tell someone about something, especially in an official way: ~ **sb (of/about sth)** *Please inform us of any changes of address.* ♦ ~ **sb that...** *I have been reliably informed* (= someone I trust has told me) *that the couple will marry next year.* ♦ ~ **sb + speech** *"He already left," she informed us.* ♦ ~ **sb when, where, etc....** *I have not been informed when the ceremony will take place.* **2** ~ **yourself (of/about sth)** to find out information about something: *We need time to inform ourselves thoroughly about the problem.* **3** ~ **sth** (*formal*) to have an influence on something: *Religion informs every aspect of their lives.*
PHRV **inˈform on sb** to give information to the police or someone in authority about the illegal activities of someone: *He informed on his own brother.*

in·for·mal /ɪnˈfɔrml/ *adj.*
1 relaxed and friendly; not following strict rules of how to behave or do something: *an informal atmosphere* ♦ *an informal arrangement/meeting/visit* ♦ *Discussions are held on an informal basis within the department.* **2** (of clothes) suitable for wearing at home or when relaxing rather than for a special or an official occasion SYN CASUAL ANT FORMAL **3** (of language) suitable for normal conversation and writing to friends rather than for serious speech and letters: *an informal expression* ⊃ compare FORMAL, SLANG ▶ **in·for·mal·i·ty** /ˌɪnfɔrˈmæləti/ *noun* [U] **in·for·mal·ly** /ɪnˈfɔrməli/ *adv.*: *They told me informally* (= not officially) *that I got the job.* ♦ *to dress informally*

in·form·ant /ɪnˈfɔrmənt/ *noun* **1** a person who gives secret information about someone or something to the police or a newspaper SYN INFORMER **2** (*technical*) a person who gives someone information about something, for example to help them with their research: *His informants were middle-class professional women.*

in·for·mat·ics /ˌɪnfərˈmætɪks/ *noun* [U] = INFORMATION SCIENCE

in·for·ma·tion /ˌɪnfərˈmeɪʃn/ (also *informal* **in·fo**) *noun* [U]
1 ~ **(on/about sb/sth)** facts or details about someone or something: *a piece of information* ♦ *a source of information* ♦ *to collect/gather/obtain/receive information* ♦ *to provide/give/pass on information* ♦ *For further information on the diet, write to us at this address.* ♦ *Our information is that the police will soon make an arrest.* ♦ *This leaflet is produced for the information of* (= to inform) *our customers.* ♦ *an information desk* ♦ *He refused to comment before he had seen all the relevant information.* **2** (*informal*) = DIRECTORY ASSISTANCE ▶ **in·for·ma·tion·al** /-ʃənl/ *adj.* [only before noun]: *the informational content of a book* ♦ *the informational role of the media* IDM **for your information 1** (*abbr.* FYI) (also **for information only**) written on documents that are sent to someone who needs to know the information in them but does not need to deal with them **2** (*informal*) used to tell someone that they are wrong about something: *For your information, I don't even have a car.* ⊃ more at MINE

inforˈmation 'science (also **in·for·mat·ics**) *noun* [U] (*computing*) the study of processes for storing and obtaining information

inforˌmation superˈhighway /ɪnfərˌmeɪʃn supərˈhaɪweɪ; ˈsupərhaɪweɪ/ *noun* (*old-fashioned, computing*) a large electronic network such as the Internet, used for sending information such as sound, pictures, and video quickly in digital form

inforˌmation techˈnology *noun* [U] (*abbr.* IT) the development, study, or use of electronic equipment, especially computers, for storing and analyzing information

ʌ cup   ə about   eɪ say   aɪ five   ɔɪ boy   aʊ now   oʊ go   ər bird

infor'mation ,theory *noun* [U] (*mathematics*) a theory that is used to calculate the most efficient way to send information over distances in the form of signals or symbols

in·for·ma·tive /ɪnˈfɔrmətɪv/ *adj.* giving useful information: *The talk was both informative and entertaining.* **ANT** UNINFORMATIVE

in·formed /ɪnˈfɔrmd/ *adj.* having or showing a lot of knowledge about a particular subject or situation: *an informed critic* ◆ *an informed choice/decision/guess/opinion* ◆ *They are not fully informed about the changes.* ◆ *Keep me informed of any developments.* **ANT** UNINFORMED ➔ see also ILL-INFORMED, WELL-INFORMED

in·form·er /ɪnˈfɔrmər/ *noun* a person who gives information to the police or other authority

in·fo·tain·ment /ˌɪnfoʊˈteɪnmənt/ *noun* [U] television programs, etc. that present news and serious subjects in an entertaining way

infra- /ˈɪnfrə/ *prefix* (in adjectives) below or beyond a particular limit: *infrared* ➔ compare ULTRA-

in·frac·tion /ɪnˈfrækʃn/ *noun* [C, U] (*formal*) an act of breaking a rule or law **SYN** INFRINGEMENT: *minor infractions of the club's regulations*

in·fra dig /ˌɪnfrə ˈdɪg/ *adj.* [not before noun] (*old-fashioned, informal*) considered to be below the standard of behavior appropriate in a particular situation or to someone's social position

in·fra·red /ˌɪnfrəˈred/ *adj.* (*physics*) having or using ELECTROMAGNETIC waves that are longer than those of red light in the SPECTRUM, and that cannot be seen: *infrared radiation* ◆ *an infrared lamp* ➔ compare ULTRAVIOLET

in·fra·struc·ture **AWL** /ˈɪnfrəˌstrʌktʃər/ *noun* [C, U] the basic systems and services that are necessary for a country or an organization to run smoothly, for example buildings, transportation, and water and power supplies ▸ **in·fra·struc·tur·al** /ˌɪnfrəˈstrʌktʃərəl/ *adj.* [usually before noun]: *infrastructural development*

in·fre·quent /ɪnˈfrikwənt/ *adj.* not happening often **SYN** RARE: *her infrequent visits home* ◆ *Muggings are relatively infrequent in this area.* **ANT** FREQUENT ▸ **in·fre·quent·ly** *adv.*: *This happens not infrequently* (= often).

in·fringe /ɪnˈfrɪndʒ/ *verb* **1** [T] ~ sth (of an action, a plan, etc.) to break a law or rule: *The material can be copied without infringing copyright.* **2** [T, I] to limit someone's legal rights: ~ sth *They said that compulsory identification cards would infringe civil liberties.* ◆ ~ on/upon sth *She refused to answer questions that infringed on her private affairs.* ▸ **in·fringe·ment** *noun* [U, C]: *copyright infringement* ◆ *an infringement of liberty*

in·fu·ri·ate /ɪnˈfyʊriˌeɪt/ *verb* to make someone extremely angry **SYN** ENRAGE: ~ sb *Her silence infuriated him even more.* ◆ *it infuriates sb that…/to do sth It infuriates me that she was not found guilty.*

in·fu·ri·at·ing /ɪnˈfyʊriˌeɪtɪŋ/ *adj.* making you extremely angry: *an infuriating child/delay* ◆ *It is infuriating to talk to someone who just looks out of the window.* ▸ **in·fu·ri·at·ing·ly** *adv.*: *to smile infuriatingly* ◆ *Infuriatingly, the store had just closed.*

in·fuse /ɪnˈfyuz/ *verb* **1** [T] ~ A into B | ~ B with A (*formal*) to make someone or something have a particular quality: *Her novels are infused with sadness.* **2** [T] ~ sth to have an effect on all parts of something: *Politics infuses all aspects of our lives.* **3** [I, T] ~ (sth) if you infuse HERBS, etc. or they infuse, you put them in hot water until the flavor has passed into the water **4** [T] ~ sth (into sb) (*medical*) to slowly put a drug or other substance into a person's VEIN

in·fu·sion /ɪnˈfyuʒn/ *noun* **1** [C, U] ~ of sth (into sth) (*formal*) the act of adding something to something else in order to make it stronger or more successful: *a cash infusion into the business* ◆ *an infusion of new talent into science education* ◆ *The company needs an infusion of new blood* (= new employees with new ideas). **2** [C] a drink or medicine made by leaving HERBS, etc. in hot water **3** [C, U] (*medical*) an act of slowly putting a drug or other substance into a person's VEIN; the drug that is used in this way

-ing /ɪŋ/ *suffix* used to make the present participle of regular verbs: *hating* ◆ *walking* ◆ *loving*

in·gen·ious /ɪnˈdʒinyəs/ *adj.* **1** (of an object, a plan, an idea, etc.) very suitable for a particular purpose and resulting from intelligent new ideas: *an ingenious device* ◆ *ingenious ways of saving energy* **2** (of a person) having a lot of intelligent new ideas and good at inventing things: *an ingenious cook* ◆ *She's very ingenious when it comes to finding excuses.* ▸ **in·gen·ious·ly** *adv.*: *ingeniously designed*

in·gé·nue /ˈænʒəˌnu; ˈɑn-/ *noun* (from *French*) an innocent young woman, especially in a movie or play

in·ge·nu·i·ty /ˌɪndʒəˈnuəti/ *noun* [U] the ability to invent things or solve problems in intelligent new ways **SYN** INVENTIVENESS

in·gen·u·ous /ɪnˈdʒenyuəs/ *adj.* (*formal*, sometimes *disapproving*) honest, innocent, and willing to trust people **SYN** NAIVE: *You're too ingenuous.* ◆ *An ingenuous smile* ◆ *It is ingenuous to suppose that money did not play a part in his decision.* ➔ compare DISINGENUOUS ▸ **in·gen·u·ous·ly** *adv.*

in·gest /ɪnˈdʒest/ *verb* ~ sth (*technical*) to take food, drugs, etc. into your body, usually by swallowing ▸ **in·ges·tion** /ɪnˈdʒestʃən/ *noun* [U]

in·gle·nook /ˈɪŋglˌnʊk/ *noun* a space at either side of a large FIREPLACE where you can sit

in·glo·ri·ous /ɪnˈglɔriəs/ *adj.* [usually before noun] (*literary*) causing feelings of shame **SYN** SHAMEFUL: *an inglorious chapter in the nation's history* ➔ compare GLORIOUS ▸ **in·glo·ri·ous·ly** *adv.*

in·got /ˈɪŋgət/ *noun* a solid piece of metal, especially gold or silver, usually shaped like a brick

in·grained /ˈɪngreɪnd; ɪnˈgreɪnd/ *adj.* **1** ~ (in sb/sth) (of a habit, an attitude, etc.) that has existed for a long time and is therefore difficult to change **SYN** DEEP-ROOTED: *ingrained prejudices* **2** (of dirt) under the surface of something and therefore difficult to get rid of

in·gra·ti·ate /ɪnˈgreɪʃiˌeɪt/ *verb* [no passive] ~ yourself (with sb) (*disapproving*) to do things in order to make someone like you, especially someone who will be useful to you: *The first part of his plan was to ingratiate himself with the members of the committee.*

in·gra·ti·at·ing /ɪnˈgreɪʃiˌeɪtɪŋ/ *adj.* (*disapproving*) trying too hard to please someone: *an ingratiating smile* ▸ **in·gra·ti·at·ing·ly** *adv.*

in·grat·i·tude /ɪnˈgrætəˌtud/ *noun* [U] the state of not feeling or showing that you are grateful for something **ANT** GRATITUDE

in·gre·di·ent 🔑 /ɪnˈgridiənt/ *noun* ~ (of/in/for sth) **1** one of the things from which something is made, especially one of the foods that are used together to make a particular dish: *Coconut is a basic ingredient for many curries.* ◆ *Our moisturizer contains only natural ingredients.* **2** one of the things or qualities that are necessary to make something successful: *the essential ingredients for success* ◆ *It has all the ingredients of a good mystery story.*

in·gress /ˈɪngres/ *noun* [U] (*formal*) the act of entering a place; the right to enter a place ➔ compare EGRESS

in-group *noun* (usually *disapproving*) a small group of people in an organization or a society whose members share the same interests, language, etc. and try to keep other people out **SYN** CLIQUE

in·grown /ˈɪngroʊn/ *adj.* [only before noun] (of the nail of a toe) growing into the skin

in·hab·it /ɪnˈhæbət/ *verb* ~ sth to live in a particular place: *some of the rare species that inhabit the area*

WORD FAMILY
inhabit *verb*
habitable *adj.* (≠ uninhabitable)
uninhabited *adj.*
inhabitant *noun*
habitation *noun*

in·hab·it·ant /ɪnˈhæbətənt/ *noun* a person or an animal that lives in a particular place: *the oldest inhabitant of the village* ◆ *a town of 11,000 inhabitants*

inhabited /ɪnˈhæbətəd/ *adj.* with people or animals living there: *The island is no longer inhabited.* ◆ *The building is now inhabited by birds.* **ANT UNINHABITED**

in·hal·ant /ɪnˈheɪlənt/ *noun* a drug or medicine that you breathe in

in·hale /ɪnˈheɪl; ˈɪnheɪl/ *verb* [I, T] to take air, smoke, gas, etc. into your lungs as you breathe **SYN** : *She closed her eyes and inhaled deeply.* ◆ *He inhaled deeply on another cigarette.* ◆ *~ sth Local residents needed hospital treatment after inhaling fumes from the fire.* **ANT EXHALE** ▶ **in·ha·la·tion** /ˌɪnhəˈleɪʃn/ *noun* [U]: *Hundreds of children were treated for smoke inhalation.*

in·hal·er /ɪnˈheɪlər/ *noun* a small device containing medicine that you breathe in through your mouth, used by people who have problems with breathing

in·har·mo·ni·ous /ˌɪnhɑrˈmoʊniəs/ *adj.* (*formal*) not combining well together or with something else **ANT HARMONIOUS**

in·here /ɪnˈhɪr/ *verb*
PHR V in·here in sth (*formal*) to be a natural part of something: *the meaning that inheres in words*

in·her·ent **AWL** /ɪnˈhɪrənt; -ˈher-/ *adj.* ~ **(in sb/sth)** that is a basic or permanent part of someone or something and that cannot be removed **SYN INTRINSIC**: *the difficulties inherent in a study of this type* ◆ *Violence is inherent in our society.* ◆ *an inherent weakness in the design of the machine* ▶ **in·her·ent·ly** **AWL** *adv.*: *an inherently unworkable system*

in·her·it /ɪnˈherət/ *verb* **1** [T, I] ~ **(sth) (from sb)** to receive money, property, etc. from someone when they die: *She inherited a fortune from her father.* ↪ compare **DISINHERIT** **2** [T] ~ **sth (from sb)** to have qualities, physical features, etc. that are similar to those of your parents, grandparents, etc.: *He has inherited his mother's patience.* ◆ *an inherited disease* **3** [T] ~ **sth (from sb)** if you **inherit** a particular situation from someone, you are now responsible for dealing with it, especially because you have replaced that person in their job: *policies inherited from the previous administration*

in·her·it·a·ble /ɪnˈherɪtəbl/ *adj.* (*biology*) (of a feature or disease) capable of being passed from a parent to a child in the **GENES**: *inheritable characteristics*

in·her·it·ance /ɪnˈherɪtəns/ *noun* **1** [C, usually sing., U] the money, property, etc. that you receive from someone when they die; the fact of receiving something when someone dies: *She spent all her inheritance in a year.* ◆ *The title passes by inheritance to the eldest son.* **2** [U, C] something from the past or from your family that affects the way you behave, look, etc.: *our cultural inheritance* ◆ *Physical characteristics are determined by genetic inheritance.*

in'heritance ˌtax *noun* [U] tax that you must pay on the money or property that you receive from someone when they die ↪ compare **ESTATE TAX**

in·her·i·tor /ɪnˈherətər/ *noun* **1** [usually pl.] ~ **of sth** a person who is affected by the work, ideas, etc. of people who lived before them **SYN HEIR**: *We are the inheritors of a great cultural tradition.* **2** a person who receives money, property, etc. from someone when they die **SYN HEIR**

in·hib·it **AWL** /ɪnˈhɪbɪt/ *verb* **1** ~ **sth** to prevent something from happening or make it happen more slowly or less frequently than normal: *A lack of oxygen may inhibit brain development in the unborn child.* **2** ~ **sb (from sth/from doing sth)** to make someone nervous or embarrassed so that they are unable to do something: *The managing director's presence inhibited them from airing their problems.*

in·hib·it·ed **AWL** /ɪnˈhɪbətəd/ *adj.* unable to relax or express your feelings in a natural way: *Boys are often more inhibited than girls about discussing their problems.* **ANT UNINHIBITED**

in·hi·bi·tion **AWL** /ˌɪnhəˈbɪʃn; ˌɪnə-/ *noun* **1** [C, U] a shy or nervous feeling that stops you from expressing your real thoughts or feelings: *The children were shy at first, but soon lost their inhibitions.* ◆ *She had no inhibitions about making her opinions known.* **2** [U] (*formal*) the act of restricting or preventing a process or an action: *the inhibition of growth*

in·hib·i·tor /ɪnˈhɪbɪtər/ *noun* **1** (*chemistry*) a substance that delays or prevents a chemical reaction **2** (*biology*) a gene that prevents another gene from being effective

in·hos·pi·ta·ble /ˌɪnhɑˈspɪtəbl/ *adj.* **1** (of a place) difficult to stay or live in, especially because there is no shelter from the weather **SYN UNWELCOMING**: *inhospitable terrain* ◆ *an inhospitable climate* **2** (of people) not giving a friendly or polite welcome to guests **ANT HOSPITABLE**

ˌin-'house *adj.* [only before noun] existing or happening within a company or an organization: *an in-house magazine* ◆ *in-house language training*

in·hu·man /ɪnˈhyumən/ *adj.* **1** lacking the qualities of kindness and sympathy; very cruel: *inhuman and degrading treatment* **2** not human; not seeming to be produced by a human and therefore frightening: *There was a strange inhuman sound.* ↪ compare **HUMAN, NONHUMAN, SUBHUMAN**

in·hu·mane /ˌɪnhyuˈmeɪn/ *adj.* not caring about the suffering of other people; very cruel **SYN CALLOUS**: *inhumane treatment of animals/prisoners* **ANT HUMANE** ▶ **in·hu·mane·ly** *adv.*

in·hu·man·i·ty /ˌɪnhyuˈmænəti/ *noun* [U] cruel behavior or treatment; the fact of not having the usual human qualities of kindness and sympathy: *man's inhumanity to man* ◆ *the inhumanity of the system* **ANT HUMANITY**

in·hu·ma·tion /ˌɪnhyuˈmeɪʃn/ *noun* [U] (*technical*) the act of burying dead people, used especially in relation to ancient times

in·im·i·cal /ɪˈnɪmɪkl/ *adj.* (*formal*) **1** ~ **to sth** harmful to something; not helping something: *These policies are inimical to the interests of society.* **2** unfriendly: *an inimical stare*

in·im·i·ta·ble /ɪˈnɪmətəbl/ *adj.* too good or individual for anyone else to copy with the same effect: *John related in his own inimitable way the story of his trip to Tibet.*

in·iq·ui·tous /ɪˈnɪkwətəs/ *adj.* (*formal*) very unfair or wrong **SYN WICKED**: *an iniquitous system/practice*

in·iq·ui·ty /ɪˈnɪkwəti/ *noun* (*pl.* **in·iq·ui·ties**) [U, C] (*formal*) the fact of being very unfair or wrong; something that is very unfair or wrong: *the iniquity of racial prejudice* ◆ *the iniquities of the criminal justice system*

in·i·tial 🔑 **AWL** /ɪˈnɪʃl/ *adj., noun, verb*
● *adj.* [only before noun] happening at the beginning; first: *an initial payment of $60 and ten installments of $25* ◆ *in the **initial stages** (= at the beginning) of the campaign* ◆ *My **initial reaction** was to decline the offer.*
● *noun* **1** [C] the first letter of a person's first name: *"What initial is it, Mrs. Owen?" "It's J, J for Jane."* **2 initials** [pl.] the first letters of all of a person's names: *John Fitzgerald Kennedy was often known by his initials JFK.* ◆ *Just write your initials.*
● *verb* (**-l-**, *CanE* **-ll-**) ~ **sth** to mark or sign something with your initials: *Please initial each page and sign in the space provided.*

in·i·tial·ize /ɪˈnɪʃəˌlaɪz/ *verb* ~ **sth** (*computing*) to make a computer program or system ready for use or **FORMAT** a disk ▶ **in·i·tial·i·za·tion** /ɪˌnɪʃələˈzeɪʃn/ *noun* [U]

in·i·tial·ly 🔑 **AWL** /ɪˈnɪʃəli/ *adv.*
at the beginning: *Initially, the system worked well.* ◆ *The death toll was initially reported at around 250, but was later revised to 300.*

in·i·ti·ate **AWL** *verb, noun*
● *verb* /ɪˈnɪʃiˌeɪt/ **1** ~ **sth** (*formal*) to make something begin **SYN SET IN MOTION**: *to initiate legal proceedings against someone* ◆ *The government has initiated a program of economic reform.* **2** ~ **sb (into sth)** to explain something to someone and/or make them experience it for the first time: *His uncle*

initiated him into the pleasures of sailing. **3 ~ sb (into sth)** to make someone a member of a particular group, especially as part of a secret ceremony: *Hundreds are initiated into the sect each year.*

• **noun** /ɪˈnɪʃiət/ a person who has been allowed to join a particular group, organization, or religion and is learning its rules and secrets

in·i·ti·a·tion **AWL** /ɪˌnɪʃiˈeɪʃn/ *noun* [U] **1** the act of someone becoming a member of a group, often with a special ceremony; the act of introducing someone to an activity or skill: *an initiation ceremony* • **~ into sth** *her initiation into the world of marketing* **2** (*formal*) the act of starting something: *the initiation of criminal proceedings*

in·i·ti·a·tive 🔑 **AWL** /ɪˈnɪʃətɪv/ *noun*
1 [C] a new plan for dealing with a particular problem or for achieving a particular purpose: *a United Nations peace initiative* • *a government initiative to combat unemployment* **2** [U] the ability to decide and act on your own without waiting for someone to tell you what to do: *You won't get much help. You'll have to* **use your initiative.** • *She did it* **on her own initiative** (= without anyone telling her to do it). **3 the initiative** [sing.] the power or opportunity to act and gain an advantage before other people do: *to seize/lose the initiative* • *It was up to the U.S. to* **take the initiative** *in repairing relations.* **4** [C] (*law*) (in some states of the U.S.) a process by which ordinary people can suggest a new law by signing a PETITION

in·i·ti·a·tor **AWL** /ɪˈnɪʃieɪtər/ *noun* (*formal*) the person who starts something

in·ject /ɪnˈdʒɛkt/ *verb* **1** to put a drug or other substance into a person's or an animal's body using a SYRINGE: **~ sth (into yourself/sb/sth)** *Adrenaline was injected into the muscle.* • **~ yourself/sb/sth (with sth)** *She has been injecting herself with insulin since the age of 16.* **2** to put a liquid into something using a SYRINGE or similar instrument: **~ A (with B)** *The fruit is injected with chemicals to reduce decay.* • **~ B (into A)** *Chemicals are injected into the fruit to reduce decay.* **3 ~ sth (into sth)** to add a particular quality to something: *His comments injected a note of humor into the proceedings.* **4 ~ sth (into sth)** to give money to an organization, a project, etc. so that it can function: *They are refusing to inject any more capital into the industry.*

in·jec·tion /ɪnˈdʒɛkʃn/ *noun* **1** [C, U] an act of injecting someone with a drug or other substance: *to give someone an injection* • *He was treated with penicillin injections.* • *An anesthetic was administered by injection.* • *daily injections of insulin* **2** [C] a large sum of money that is spent to help improve a situation, business, etc.: *The theater faces closure unless it gets an urgent cash injection.* **3** [U, C] an act of forcing liquid into something: *a fuel injection system*

in'jection ˌmolding *noun* [U] (*technical*) a way of shaping plastic or rubber by heating it and pouring it into a MOLD ▶ **in'jection- molded** *adj.*

'in-joke *noun* a joke that is only understood by a particular group of people

in·ju·di·cious /ˌɪndʒuˈdɪʃəs/ *adj.* (*formal*) not sensible or wise; not appropriate in a particular situation **SYN** UNWISE: *an injudicious remark* **ANT** JUDICIOUS ▶ **in·ju·di·cious·ly** *adv.*

in·junc·tion /ɪnˈdʒʌŋkʃn/ *noun* **1** an official order given by a court that demands that something must or must not be done: *to seek/obtain an injunction* • **~ against sb** *The court granted an injunction against the defendants.* ⊃ compare RESTRAINING ORDER **2** (*formal*) a warning or an order from someone in authority

in·jure 🔑 **AWL** /ˈɪndʒər/ *verb*
1 ~ sb/sth/yourself to harm yourself or someone else physically, especially in an accident: *He injured his knee playing hockey.* • *Three people were killed and five injured in the crash.* ⊃ collocations at INJURY **2 ~ sth** to damage someone's reputation, pride, etc.: *This could seriously injure the company's reputation.*

THESAURUS

injure

wound • hurt • bruise • sprain • pull • strain

These words all mean to harm yourself or someone else physically, especially in an accident.

injure to harm yourself or someone else physically, especially in an accident: *He injured his knee playing hockey.* • *Three people were injured in the crash.*

wound [often passive] (*somewhat formal*) to injure part of the body, especially by making a hole in the skin using a weapon: *Two people were killed and dozens more wounded in the attack.* **NOTE** Wound is often used to talk about people being hurt in war or in other attacks which affect a lot of people.

hurt (*somewhat informal*) to cause physical pain to someone or yourself; to injure someone or yourself: *Did you hurt yourself?*

INJURE OR HURT?

You can **hurt** or **injure** a part of the body in an accident. **Hurt** emphasizes the physical pain caused; **injure** emphasizes that the part of the body has been damaged in some way.

bruise to make a blue, brown, or purple mark (= a bruise) appear on the skin after someone has fallen or been hit; to develop a bruise

sprain to injure part of your body, especially your ankle, wrist, or knee, by suddenly bending it in an awkward way, causing pain and swelling

pull to damage a muscle, etc., by using too much force

strain to injure yourself or part of your body by making it work too hard: *Don't strain your eyes by reading in poor light.*

PATTERNS

- to injure/hurt/strain **yourself**
- to injure/hurt/pull/strain a **muscle**
- to injure/hurt/sprain your **ankle/knee/wrist**
- to injure/hurt/strain your **back/shoulder/eyes**
- to injure/hurt your **spine/neck**
- to be **badly/severely/slightly** injured/wounded/hurt/bruised/sprained

in·jured 🔑 **AWL** /ˈɪndʒərd/ *adj.*
1 physically hurt; having an injury: *an injured leg* • *Luckily, she isn't injured.* • *Carter is playing in place of the injured O'Reilly.* **ANT** UNINJURED **2 the injured** *noun* [pl.] the people injured in an accident, a battle, etc.: *Ambulances took the injured to a nearby hospital.* **3** (of a person or their feelings) upset or offended because something unfair has been done: *an injured look/tone* • *injured pride*

the ˌinjured 'party *noun* [sing.] (*law*) the person who has been treated unfairly, or the person who claims in court to have been treated unfairly

in·ju·ri·ous /ɪnˈdʒʊriəs/ *adj.* **~ (to sb/sth)** (*formal*) causing or likely to cause harm or damage **SYN** DAMAGING

in·ju·ry 🔑 **AWL** /ˈɪndʒəri/ *noun* (*pl.* in·ju·ries)
1 [C, U] harm done to a person's or an animal's body, for example in an accident: *serious injury/injuries* • *minor injuries* • *to sustain injuries/an injury* • **~ (to sb/sth)** *injury to the head* • *a head injury* • *Two players are out of the team* **because of injury.** • *There were* **no injuries** *in the crash* (= no people injured). ⊃ collocations on page 780 **2** [U] (*law*) damage to a person's feelings: *Damages may be awarded for emotional injury.* **IDM** see ADD

in·jus·tice /ɪnˈdʒʌstəs/ noun [U, C] the fact of a situation being unfair and of people not being treated equally; an unfair act or an example of unfair treatment: *fighting against poverty and injustice* ◆ *a burning sense of injustice* ◆ *social injustice* ◆ *She was enraged at the injustice of the remark.* ◆ *The report exposes the injustices of the system.* **ANT** JUSTICE **IDM** **do yourself/sb an injustice** to judge yourself/someone unfairly: *We may have been doing him an injustice. This work is good.*

ink 🔑 /ɪŋk/ noun, verb

- *noun* [U, C] colored liquid for writing, drawing, and printing: *written in ink* ◆ *a pen and ink drawing* ◆ *different colored inks* ➔ see also INKY
- *verb* **1** ~ sth to cover something with ink so that it can be used for printing **2** ~ sth (*informal*) to sign a document, especially a contract: *The group has just inked a $10 million deal.*
  PHR V ,ink sth↔'in to write or draw in ink over something that has already been written or drawn in pencil: (*figurative*) *The date for the presentation should have been inked in* (= made definite) *by now.*

ink-blot ,test noun (*psychology*) = RORSCHACH TEST

ink-jet ,printer noun a printer that uses very small JETS to blow ink onto paper in order to form letters, numbers, etc.

ink·ling /ˈɪŋklɪŋ/ noun [usually sing.] a slight knowledge of something that is happening or about to happen **SYN** SUSPICION: ~ (of sth) *He had no inkling of what was going on.* ◆ ~ (that…) *The first inkling I had that something was wrong was when I found the front door wide open.*

ink pad noun a thick piece of soft material full of ink, used with a rubber stamp ➔ picture at STATIONERY

ink·well /ˈɪŋkwɛl/ noun a pot for holding ink that fits into a hole in a desk (used in the past)

ink·y /ˈɪŋki/ adj. **1** black like ink: *the inky blackness of the cellar* **2** made dirty with ink: *inky fingers*

in·laid /ˈɪnleɪd; ˌɪnˈleɪd/ adj. (of furniture, floors, etc.) decorated with designs of wood, metal, etc. that are set into the surface: *an inlaid wooden box* ◆ ~ **with sth** *a box inlaid with gold*

in·land adv., adj.
- *adv.* /ˈɪnlænd; -lənd/ in a direction toward the middle of a country; away from the coast: *The town lies a few miles inland.* ◆ *We traveled further inland the next day.*
- *adj.* /ˈɪnlənd/ [usually before noun] located in or near the middle of a country, not near the edge or on the coast: *inland areas* ◆ *inland lakes* ➔ compare COASTAL

'in-law a,partment (also **'mother-in-law a,partment**) noun (*informal*) a set of rooms for an old person, especially in a relative's house

'in-laws noun [pl.] (*informal*) your relatives by marriage, especially the parents of your husband or wife: *We're visiting my in-laws on Sunday.*

in·lay verb, noun
- *verb* /ˈɪnleɪ; ˌɪnˈleɪ/ (in·lay·ing, in·laid, in·laid /ˈɪnleɪd; ˌɪnˈleɪd/) [often passive] ~ **A (with B)** | ~ **B (in/into A)** to decorate the surface of something by putting pieces of wood or metal into it in such a way that the surface remains smooth: *The lid of the box had been inlaid with silver.*
- *noun* /ˈɪnleɪ/ [C, U] a design or pattern on a surface made by setting wood or metal into it; the material that this design is made of: *The table was decorated with gold inlay.*

in·let /ˈɪnlɛt; -lət/ noun **1** a narrow strip of water that stretches into the land from the ocean or a lake, or between islands **2** (*technical*) an opening through which liquid, air, or gas can enter a machine: *a fuel inlet* **ANT** OUTLET

in·line /ˈɪnlaɪn/ adj. [only before noun] (of a reference) placed inside running text: *inline citations*

,in-line 'skate noun = ROLLERBLADE™ ▶ ,in-line 'skating noun [U]

in lo·co pa·ren·tis /ɪn ˌloʊkoʊ pəˈrɛntəs/ adv. (from Latin, formal) having the same responsibility for a child as a parent has: *The staff have a position of trust; they stand in loco parentis to all the children for whom they are responsible.*

in·mate /ˈɪnmeɪt/ noun one of the people living in an institution such as a prison or a mental hospital

in me·di·as res /ɪn ˌmeɪdiəs ˈreɪs/ adv. (from Latin, formal) straight into the main part of a story or account without giving any introduction: *He began his story in medias res.*

in me·mo·ri·am /ˌɪn məˈmɔriəm/ prep. (from Latin) used to mean "in memory of," for example on the stone over a grave

in·most /ˈɪnmoʊst/ adj. [only before noun] = INNERMOST

inn /ɪn/ noun **1** a small hotel, usually in the country **2** **Inn** used in the names of some hotels and restaurants: *Holiday Inn*

in·nards /ˈɪnərdz/ noun [pl.] (*informal*) **1** the organs inside the body of a person or an animal, especially the stomach **SYN** ENTRAILS, GUTS **2** the parts inside a machine

in·nate /ɪˈneɪt/ adj. (of a quality, feeling, etc.) that you have when you are born **SYN** INBORN: *the innate ability to learn* ▶ **in·nate·ly** adv.: *He believes that humans are innately violent.*

in·ner 🔑 /ˈɪnər/ adj. [only before noun]
1 inside; toward or close to the center of a place: *an inner courtyard* ◆ *the inner ear* **ANT** OUTER **2** (of feelings, etc.) private and secret; not expressed or shown to other people: *She doesn't reveal much of her inner self.*

,inner 'circle noun the small group of people who have a lot of power in an organization and who are close to its leader

,inner 'city noun the part near the center of a large city, which often has social problems: *There are huge problems in our inner cities.* ◆ *an inner-city area/school*

,inner 'ear noun (*anatomy*) the parts of the ear which form the organs of balance and hearing, including the COCHLEA

in·ner·most /ˈɪnərˌmoʊst/ adj. [only before noun] **1** (also *less* frequent in·most) most private, personal, and secret: *I could not express my innermost feelings to anyone.* **2** nearest to the center or inside of something: *the innermost shrine of the temple* **ANT** OUTERMOST

'inner ˌtube *noun* a rubber tube filled with air inside a tire

in·ning /'ɪnɪŋ/ *noun* (in baseball) one of the nine periods of a game in which each team has a turn at BAT

inn·keep·er /'ɪnˌkipər/ *noun* (*old-fashioned*) a person who owns or manages an INN

in·no·cence /'ɪnəsns/ *noun* [U] **1** the fact of not being guilty of a crime, etc.: *She protested her innocence* (= said repeatedly that she was innocent). ♦ *This new evidence will prove their innocence.* ♦ *I asked if she was married in all innocence* (= without knowing it was likely to offend or upset her). **ANT** GUILT **2** lack of knowledge and experience of the world, especially of evil or unpleasant things: *Children lose their innocence as they grow older.*

in·no·cent 🔑 /'ɪnəsnt/ *adj., noun*

• *adj.* **1** not guilty of a crime, etc.; not having done something wrong: *They have imprisoned an innocent man.* ♦ ~ (**of sth**) *She was found innocent of any crime.* ♦ *He was the innocent party* (= person) *in the breakdown of the marriage.* **ANT** GUILTY **2** [only before noun] suffering harm or being killed because of a crime, war, etc. although not directly involved in it: *an innocent bystander* ♦ *innocent victims of a bomb blast* **3** not intended to cause harm or upset someone **SYN** HARMLESS: *It was all innocent fun.* ♦ *It was a perfectly innocent remark.* **4** having little experience of the world, especially of sexual matters, or of evil or unpleasant things **SYN** NAIVE: *an innocent young child* ▶ in·no·cent·ly *adv.*: *"Oh, Sue went too, did she?" I asked innocently* (= pretending I did not know that this was important).

• *noun* an innocent person, especially a young child

in·noc·u·ous /ɪˈnɑkyuəs/ *adj.* (*formal*) **1** not intended to offend or upset anyone **SYN** HARMLESS: *It seemed a perfectly innocuous remark.* **2** not harmful or dangerous: *an innocuous substance* **SYN** HARMLESS

in·no·vate **AWL** /'ɪnəˌveɪt/ *verb* [I, T] to introduce new things, ideas, or ways of doing something: *We must constantly adapt and innovate to ensure success in a growing market.* ♦ ~ **sth** *to innovate new products* ▶ in·no·va·tor **AWL** /'ɪnəˌveɪtər/ *noun*

in·no·va·tion **AWL** /ˌɪnəˈveɪʃn/ *noun* **1** [U] ~ (**in sth**) the introduction of new things, ideas, or ways of doing something: *an age of technological innovation* **2** [C] ~ (**in sth**) a new idea, way of doing something, etc. that has been introduced or discovered: *recent innovations in steel-making technology*

in·no·va·tive **AWL** /'ɪnəˌveɪtɪv/ (also *less frequent* in·no·va·to·ry /'ɪnəvəˌtɔri; ˌɪnəˈveɪtəri/) *adj.* (*approving*) introducing or using new ideas, ways of doing something, etc.: *There will be a prize for the most innovative design.*

in·nu·en·do /ˌɪnyuˈɛndoʊ/ *noun* [C, U] (*pl.* in·nu·en·does or in·nu·en·dos) (*disapproving*) an indirect remark about someone or something, usually suggesting something bad or offensive; the use of remarks like this: *innuendoes about her private life* ♦ *The song is full of sexual innuendo.*

in·nu·mer·a·ble /ɪˈnumərəbl/ *adj.* too many to be counted; very many **SYN** COUNTLESS: *Innumerable books have been written on the subject.*

in·nu·mer·ate /ɪˈnumərət/ *adj.* unable to count or do simple mathematics **ANT** NUMERATE

in·oc·u·late /ɪˈnɑkyəˌleɪt/ *verb* ~ **sb** (**against sth**) to protect a person or an animal from catching a particular disease by INJECTING them with a mild form of the disease ⊃ compare IMMUNIZE, VACCINATE ▶ in·oc·u·la·tion /ɪˌnɑkyəˈleɪʃn/ *noun* [C, U]

in·of·fen·sive /ˌɪnəˈfɛnsɪv/ *adj.* not likely to offend or upset anyone: *a shy, inoffensive young man* **ANT** OFFENSIVE

in·op·er·a·ble /ɪnˈɑpərəbl; -'ɑprəbl/ *adj.* **1** (of an illness, especially cancer) not able to be cured by a medical operation: *an inoperable brain tumor* **2** (*formal*) that cannot be used or made to work; not practical: *The policy was thought to be inoperable.* **ANT** OPERABLE

in·op·er·a·tive /ɪnˈɑpərətɪv; -'ɑprətɪv/ *adj.* (*formal*) **1** (of a rule, system, etc.) not valid or able to be used **2** (of a machine) not working; not functioning correctly **ANT** OPERATIVE

in·op·por·tune /ɪnˌɑpərˈtun/ *adj.* (*formal*) happening at a bad time **SYN** INAPPROPRIATE, INCONVENIENT: *They arrived at an inopportune moment.* **ANT** OPPORTUNE

in·or·di·nate /ɪnˈɔrdnət/ *adj.* (*formal*) far more than is usual or expected **SYN** EXCESSIVE ▶ in·or·di·nate·ly *adv.*: *inordinately high prices*

in·or·gan·ic /ˌɪnɔrˈɡænɪk/ *adj.* not consisting of or coming from any living substances: *inorganic fertilizers* **ANT** ORGANIC

ˌinorganic 'chemistry *noun* [U] the branch of chemistry that deals with substances that do not contain CARBON ⊃ compare ORGANIC CHEMISTRY

in·pa·tient /'ɪnˌpeɪʃnt/ *noun* a person who stays in a hospital while receiving treatment ⊃ compare OUTPATIENT

in·put **AWL** /'ɪnpʊt/ *noun, verb*

• *noun* **1** [C, U] time, knowledge, ideas, etc. that you put into work, a project, etc. in order to make it succeed; the act of putting something in: ~ (**into/to sth**) *Her specialist input to the discussions has been very useful.* ♦ *I'd appreciate your input on this.* ♦ ~ (**of sth**) *There has been a big input of resources into the project from industry.* **2** [U] (*computing*) the act of putting information into a computer; the information that you put in: *data input* ♦ *This program accepts input from most word processors.* **3** [C] (*technical*) a place or means for electricity, data, etc. to enter a machine or system ⊃ compare OUTPUT

• *verb* (in·put·ting, in·put, in·put or in·put·ting, in·put·ted, in·put·ted) ~ **sth** to put information into a computer: *to input text/data/figures* ⊃ compare OUTPUT

in·quest /'ɪŋkwɛst/ *noun* **1** an official investigation to find out the cause of someone's death, especially when it has not happened naturally: *An inquest was held to discover the cause of death.* ♦ ~ (**on/into sth**) *a coroner's inquest into his death* **2** ~ (**on/into sth**) a discussion about something that has failed: *An inquest was held on the team's poor performance.*

in·quire (also en·quire) /ɪnˈkwaɪər/ *verb* [I, T] (*somewhat formal*) to ask someone for some information: ~ (**about sb/sth**) *I called the school to inquire about the application process.* ♦ ~ (**as to sth**) *She inquired as to your whereabouts.* ♦ ~ **why, where, etc....** *He inquired why you were so late.* ♦ ~ **sth** *He inquired her name.* ♦ + *speech* *"What is your name?" he inquired.* ⊃ thesaurus box at ASK

PHR V in'quire after sb (*formal*) to ask for information about someone, especially about their health or about what they are doing in'quire into sth to find out more information about something **SYN** INVESTIGATE: *A committee was appointed to inquire into the allegations.* in'quire sth of sb (*formal*) to ask someone something: (+ **speech**) *"Will you be staying for lunch?" she inquired of Charles.*

in·quir·er (also en·quir·er) /ɪnˈkwaɪərər/ *noun* (*formal*) a person who asks for information

in·quir·ing (also en·quir·ing) /ɪnˈkwaɪrɪŋ/ *adj.* [usually before noun] **1** showing an interest in learning new things: *a child with an inquiring mind* **2** asking for information: *an inquiring look* ▶ in·quir·ing·ly (also en·quir·ing·ly) /ɪnˈkwaɪrɪŋli/ *adv.*

in·quir·y 🔑 (also en·quir·y) /'ɪŋkwəri; ɪnˈkwaɪəri/ *noun*

(*pl.* in·quir·ies) **1** [C] an official process to find out the cause of something or to find out information about something: *a murder inquiry* ♦ ~ **into sth** *a public inquiry into the environmental effects of the proposed new road* ♦ *to hold/order an inquiry into the affair* **2** [C] a request for information about someone or something; a question about someone or something: *a telephone inquiry* ♦ ~ (**from sb**) (**about sb/sth**) *We received over 300 inquiries about the job.* ♦ *inquiries from prospective students* ♦ *I'll have to make a few inquiries* (=

try to find out about it) *and get back to you.* **3** [U] the act of asking questions or collecting information about someone or something: *scientific inquiry* ◆ *The police are following several lines of inquiry.*

in·qui·si·tion /ˌɪnkwəˈzɪʃn/ *noun* **1 the Inquisition** [sing.] the organization set up by the Roman Catholic Church to punish people who opposed its beliefs, especially from the 15th to the 17th century **2** [C] (*formal* or *humorous*) a series of questions that someone asks you, especially when they ask them in an unpleasant way ➲ **see also** SPANISH INQUISITION

in·quis·i·tive /ɪnˈkwɪzətɪv/ *adj.* **1** (*disapproving*) asking too many questions and trying to find out about what other people are doing, etc. **SYN** CURIOUS: *Don't be so inquisitive. It's none of your business!* **2** very interested in learning about many different things **SYN** INQUIRING: *an inquisitive mind* ▶ **in·quis·i·tive·ly** *adv.* **in·quis·i·tive·ness** *noun* [U]

in·quis·i·tor /ɪnˈkwɪzətər/ *noun* **1** a person who asks a lot of difficult questions, especially in a way that makes you feel threatened **2** an officer of the inquisition of the Roman Catholic Church ▶ **in·quis·i·to·ri·al** /ɪnˌkwɪzəˈtɔriəl/ *adj.*: *He questioned her in a cold inquisitorial voice.* **in·quis·i·to·ri·al·ly** *adv.*

in·road /ˈɪnroʊd/ *noun* **~ (into sth)** something that is achieved, especially by reducing the power or success of something else: *This deal is their first major inroad into the American market.*
IDM **make inroads into/on sth** if one thing **makes inroads into** another, it has a noticeable effect on the second thing, especially by reducing it or influencing it: *Tax rises have made some inroads into the country's national debt.*

in·rush /ˈɪnrʌʃ/ *noun* [usually sing.] a sudden flow toward the inside: *an inrush of air/water*

in·sa·lu·bri·ous /ˌɪnsəˈlubriəs/ *adj.* (*formal*) (of a place) dirty and with many things that need to be repaired, cleaned, or replaced

in·sane /ɪnˈseɪn/ *adj.* **1** seriously mentally ill and unable to live in normal society: *Doctors certified him as insane.* ◆ *The prisoners were slowly going insane.* **ANT** SANE ➲ **thesaurus box at** MENTALLY ILL **2 the insane** *noun* [pl.] people who are insane: *a hospital for the insane* **3** (*informal*) having a mind that does not work normally: *If I'll have to stay any longer, I'll go insane.* ➲ **thesaurus box at** CRAZY **4** (*informal*) very stupid, crazy, or dangerous: *I must have been insane to agree to the idea.* ◆ *This job is driving me insane* (= making me feel very angry). ➲ **see also** INSANITY ▶ **in·sane·ly** *adv.*: *He is insanely jealous.*

in·san·i·tar·y /ɪnˈsænəˌteri/ *adj.* = UNSANITARY

in·san·i·ty /ɪnˈsænəti/ *noun* [U] **1** the state of being INSANE: *He was found not guilty, by reason of insanity.* **ANT** SANITY **2** actions that are very stupid and possibly dangerous **SYN** MADNESS, LUNACY: *It would be sheer insanity to attempt the trip in such bad weather.*

in·sa·tia·ble /ɪnˈseɪʃəbl/ *adj.* always wanting more of something; not able to be satisfied: *an insatiable appetite/curiosity/thirst* ◆ *There seems to be an insatiable demand for more powerful computers.* ▶ **in·sa·tia·bly** /-bli/ *adv.*

in·scribe /ɪnˈskraɪb/ *verb* to write or cut words, your name, etc. onto something: **~ A (on/in B)** *His name was inscribed on the trophy.* ◆ *She signed the book and inscribed the words "with grateful thanks" on it.* ◆ **~ B (with A)** *The trophy was inscribed with his name.*

in·scrip·tion /ɪnˈskrɪpʃn/ *noun* words written in the front of a book or cut in stone or metal

in·scru·ta·ble /ɪnˈskrutəbl/ *adj.* if a person or their expression is **inscrutable**, it is hard to know what they are thinking or feeling, because they do not show any emotion ▶ **in·scru·ta·bil·i·ty** /ɪnˌskrutəˈbɪləti/ *noun* [U] **in·scru·ta·bly** /ɪnˈskrutəbli/ *adv.*

in·seam /ˈɪnsim/ *noun* [sing.] a measurement of the length of the inside of someone's leg, used for making or choosing pants of the correct size

in·sect 🔎 /ˈɪnsɛkt/ *noun* any small creature with six legs and a body divided into three parts. Insects usually also have wings. ANTS, BEES, and flies are all insects.: *insect species* ◆ *insect repellent* (= a chemical that keeps insects away) ◆ *an insect bite* ➲ **collocations at** LIFE ➲ **see also** STICK INSECT **HELP** Insect is often used to refer to other small creatures, for example spiders, although this is not correct scientific language.

in·sec·ti·cide /ɪnˈsɛktəsaɪd/ *noun* [C, U] a chemical used for killing insects ➲ **see also** HERBICIDE, PESTICIDE ▶ **in·sec·ti·cid·al** /ɪnˌsɛktəˈsaɪdl/ *adj.*

in·sec·ti·vore /ɪnˈsɛktəˌvɔr/ *noun* any animal that eats insects ➲ **compare** CARNIVORE, HERBIVORE, OMNIVORE ▶ **in·sec·tiv·o·rous** /ˌɪnsɛkˈtɪvərəs/ *adj.*

in·se·cure **AWL** /ˌɪnsɪˈkyʊr/ *adj.* **1** not confident about yourself or your relationships with other people: *He's very insecure about his appearance.* ◆ *She felt nervous and insecure.* **2** not safe or protected: *Jobs nowadays are much more insecure than they were ten years ago.* ◆ *As an artist, he was always financially insecure.* ◆ *Insecure doors and windows* (= for example, without good locks) *make life easy for burglars.* **ANT** SECURE ▶ **in·se·cure·ly** *adv.* **in·se·cu·ri·ty** **AWL** /ˌɪnsɪˈkyʊrəti/ *noun* (*pl.* **in·se·cu·ri·ties**) [U, C]: *feelings of insecurity* ◆ *job insecurity* ◆ *We all have our fears and insecurities.*

in·sem·i·nate /ɪnˈsɛməˌneɪt/ *verb* **~ sb/sth** (*technical*) to put SPERM into a woman or female animal in order to make her pregnant: *The cows are artificially inseminated.* ▶ **in·sem·i·na·tion** /ɪnˌsɛməˈneɪʃn/ *noun* [U] ➲ **see also** ARTIFICIAL INSEMINATION

in·sen·si·bil·i·ty /ɪnˌsɛnsəˈbɪləti/ *noun* [U] **1** (*formal*) the state of being unconscious **2** the fact of not being able to react to a particular thing: *insensibility to pain*

in·sen·si·ble /ɪnˈsɛnsəbl/ *adj.* (*formal*) **1** [not before noun] **~ (to sth)** unable to feel something or react to it: *insensible to pain/cold* **2** [not before noun] **~ (of sth)** not aware of a situation or of something that might happen **SYN** UNAWARE: *They were not insensible of the risks.* **ANT** SENSIBLE **3** unconscious as the result of injury, illness, etc.: *The blow knocked him insensible.* ▶ **in·sen·si·bly** /-bli/ *adv.*

in·sen·si·tive /ɪnˈsɛnsətɪv/ *adj.* **1** not realizing or caring how other people feel, and therefore likely to hurt or offend them **SYN** UNSYMPATHETIC: *an insensitive remark* ◆ **~ to sth** *She's completely insensitive to my feelings.* **2** **~ (to sth)** not aware of changing situations, and therefore of the need to react to them: *The government seems totally insensitive to the mood of the country.* **3** **~ (to sth)** not able to feel or react to something: *insensitive to pain/cold* ◆ *He seems completely insensitive to criticism.* **ANT** SENSITIVE ▶ **in·sen·si·tive·ly** *adv.* **in·sen·si·tiv·i·ty** /ɪnˌsɛnsəˈtɪvəti/ *noun* [U]

in·sep·a·ra·ble /ɪnˈsɛpərəbl; -ˈsɛprəbl/ *adj.* **1** **~ (from sth)** not able to be separated: *The welfare of birds is inseparable from that of the ecosystem to which they belong.* **2** if people are **inseparable**, they spend most of their time together and are very good friends ▶ **in·sep·a·ra·bil·i·ty** /ɪnˌsɛpərəˈbɪləti; -ˌsɛprə-/ *noun* [U] **in·sep·a·ra·bly** /ɪnˈsɛpərəbli; -ˈsɛprə-/ *adv.*: *Our lives were inseparably linked.*

in·sert **AWL** *verb, noun*
● *verb* /ɪnˈsərt/ **1** **~ sth (in/into/between sth)** to put something into something else or between two things: *Insert coins into the slot and press for a ticket.* ◆ *They inserted a tube in his mouth to help him breathe.* **2** to add something to a piece of writing: **~ sth** *Position the cursor where you want to insert a word.* ◆ **~ sth into sth** *Later, he inserted another paragraph into his will.*
● *noun* /ˈɪnsərt/ **~ (in sth)** **1** an extra section added to a book, newspaper, or magazine, especially to advertise something: *an 8-page insert on the new car models* **2** something

ʌ cup   ə about   eɪ say   aɪ five   ɔɪ boy   aʊ now   oʊ go   ər bird

that is put inside something else, or added to something else: *These inserts fit inside any style of shoe.*

in·ser·tion `AWL` /ɪnˈsɜrʃn/ *noun* **1** [U, C] ~ **(in/into sth)** the act of putting something inside something else; a thing that is put inside something else: *the insertion of a feeding tube* **2** [C, U] a thing that is added to a book, piece of writing, etc.; the act of adding something: *the insertion of an extra paragraph*

in-'service *adj.* [only before noun] (of training, courses of study, etc.) done while someone is working in a job, in order to learn new skills: *in-service training*

in·set /ˈɪnsɛt/ *noun, verb*
● *noun* **1** a small picture, map, etc. inside a larger one: *For downtown Providence, see inset.* **2** something that is added on to something else, or put inside something else: *The windows have beautiful stained glass insets.*
● *verb* (in·set·ting, in·set, in·set) **1** [usually passive] to fix something into the surface of something else, especially as a decoration: ~ **A (with B)** *The tables were inset with ceramic tiles.* ◆ ~ **B (into A)** *Ceramic tiles were inset into the tables.* **2** ~ **sth (into sth)** to put a small picture, map, etc. inside the borders of a bigger one

in·shore /ˈɪnʃɔr/ *adj.* [usually before noun] in the ocean but close to the SHORE: *an inshore breeze* ◆ *an inshore lifeboat* (= that stays close to the land) ▶ **in·shore** *adv.*: *The boat came inshore* (= toward the land). ⊃ compare OFFSHORE

in·side 🔑 *prep., adv., noun, adj.*
● *prep.* /ˌɪnˈsaɪd; ˈɪnsaɪd/ (also **inside of**) **1** on or to the inner part of something or someone; within something or someone: *Go inside the house.* ◆ *Inside the box was a gold watch.* ◆ *For years we had little knowledge of what life was like inside China.* ◆ *You'll feel better with a good meal inside you.* ◆ (*figurative*) *Inside most of us is a small child screaming for attention.* **ANT** OUTSIDE **2** in less than the amount of time mentioned: *The job is unlikely to be finished inside (of) a year*
● *adv.* /ˌɪnˈsaɪd/ **1** on or to the inside: *She shook it to make sure there was nothing inside.* ◆ *We had to move inside* (= indoors) *when it started to rain.* ◆ (*figurative*) *I pretended not to care but I was screaming inside.* **ANT** OUTSIDE **2** (*informal*) in prison: *He was sentenced to three years inside.*
● *noun* /ˌɪnˈsaɪd; ˈɪnsaɪd/ **1** [C, usually sing.] usually **the inside** the inner part, side, or surface of something: *The inside of the box was blue.* ◆ *The door was locked from the inside.* ◆ *The shell is smooth on the inside.* ◆ *the insides of the windows* **ANT** THE OUTSIDE **2** **the inside** [sing.] the part of a curved road or track nearest to the middle or shortest side of the curve: *The French runner is coming up fast on the inside.* **ANT** THE OUTSIDE **3** **insides** [pl.] (*informal*) a person's stomach and BOWELS: *She was so nervous, her insides were like jelly.*
IDM **inside out** with the part that is usually inside facing out: *You've got your sweater on inside out.* ◆ *Turn the bag inside out and let it dry.* **ANT** RIGHT SIDE OUT **on the inside** belonging to a group or an organization and therefore able to get information that is not available to other people: *The thieves must have had someone on the inside helping them.* **turn sth inside out 1** to make a place very messy when you are searching for something: *The burglars turned the house inside out.* **2** to cause large changes: *The new manager turned the old systems inside out.* ⊃ more at KNOW *v.*
● *adj.* /ˈɪnsaɪd/ [only before noun] **1** forming the inner part of something; not on the outside: *the inside pages of a newspaper* ◆ *an inside pocket* **2** known or done by someone in a group or an organization: *inside information* ◆ *Any newspaper would pay big money to get* **the inside story** *on her marriage.* ◆ *The robbery appeared to have been an* **inside job.**

in·sid·er /ˌɪnˈsaɪdər; ˈɪnˌsaɪdər/ *noun* a person who knows a lot about a group or an organization, because they are part of it: *The situation was described by one insider as "absolute chaos."* ⊃ compare OUTSIDER

insider 'trading *noun* [U] the crime of buying or selling shares in a company with the help of information known only by those connected with the business, before this information is available to everyone

inside 'track *noun* [sing.] a position in which you have an advantage over someone else

in·sid·i·ous /ɪnˈsɪdiəs/ *adj.* (*formal, disapproving*) spreading gradually or without being noticed, but causing serious harm: *the insidious effects of polluted water supplies* ▶ **in·sid·i·ous·ly** *adv.*

in·sight `AWL` /ˈɪnsaɪt/ *noun* **1** [U] (*approving*) the ability to see and understand the truth about people or situations: *a writer of great insight* ◆ *With a flash of insight, I realized what the dream meant.* **2** [C, U] ~ **(into sth)** an understanding of what something is like: *The book gives us fascinating insights into life in Mexico.*

in·sight·ful `AWL` /ɪnˈsaɪtfl; ˈɪnsaɪtfl/ *adj.* (*approving*) showing a clear understanding of a person or situation
SYN PERCEPTIVE

in·sig·ni·a /ɪnˈsɪgniə/ *noun* [U] the symbol, BADGE, or sign that shows someone's rank or that they are a member of a group or an organization: *the royal insignia* ◆ *His uniform bore the insignia of a captain.*

in·sig·nif·i·cant `AWL` /ˌɪnsɪgˈnɪfɪkənt/ *adj.* not big or valuable enough to be considered important: *an insignificant difference* ◆ *The levels of chemicals in the river are not insignificant.* ◆ *He made her feel insignificant and stupid.* **ANT** SIGNIFICANT ⊃ collocations at SIGNIFICANT ▶ **in·sig·nif·i·cance** /-kəns/ *noun* [U] **in·sig·nif·i·cant·ly** `AWL` *adv.*

in·sin·cere /ˌɪnsɪnˈsɪr/ *adj.* (*disapproving*) saying or doing something that you do not really mean or believe: *an insincere smile* **ANT** SINCERE ▶ **in·sin·cere·ly** *adv.* **in·sin·cer·i·ty** /ˌɪnsɪnˈsɛrəti/ *noun* [U]: *She accused him of insincerity.*

in·sin·u·ate /ɪnˈsɪnyueɪt/ *verb* **1** to suggest indirectly that something unpleasant is true **SYN** IMPLY: ~ **that...** *The article insinuated that he was having an affair with his friend's wife.* ◆ ~ **sth** *What are you trying to insinuate?* ◆ *an insinuating smile* **2** ~ **yourself into sth** (*formal, disapproving*) to succeed in gaining someone's respect, affection, etc. so that you can use the situation to your own advantage: *In the first act, the villain insinuates himself into the household of the man he intends to kill.* **3** ~ **yourself/sth + adv./prep.** (*formal*) to slowly move yourself or a part of your body into a particular position or place: *She insinuated her right hand under his arm.*

in·sin·u·a·tion /ɪnˌsɪnyuˈeɪʃn/ *noun* **1** [C] something that someone insinuates: *She resented the insinuation that she was too old for the job.* **2** [U] the act of insinuating something

in·sip·id /ɪnˈsɪpəd/ *adj.* (*disapproving*) **1** having almost no taste or flavor **SYN** FLAVORLESS: *a cup of insipid coffee* **2** not interesting or exciting **SYN** DULL: *After an hour of insipid conversation, I left.*

in·sist 🔑 /ɪnˈsɪst/ *verb*
1 [I, T] to demand that something happens or that someone agrees to do something: *I didn't really want to go but he insisted.* ◆ *"Please come with us." "OK, if you insist."* ◆ ~ **on sth/sb doing sth** (*formal*) *She insisted on his/him wearing a suit.* ◆ ~ **that...** *He insists that she come.* ⊃ thesaurus box at DEMAND **2** [I, T] to say firmly that something is true, especially when other people do not believe you: ~ **on sth** *He insisted on his innocence.* ◆ ~ **(that)...** *He insisted (that) he was innocent.* ◆ **+ speech** *"It's true," she insisted.*
PHRV **in'sist on/upon sth** to demand something and refuse to be persuaded to accept anything else: *We insisted on a refund of the full amount.* ◆ ~ **doing sth** *They insisted upon being given every detail of the case.* **in'sist on doing sth** to continue doing something even though other people think it is annoying: *They insist on playing their music late at night.*

in·sist·ence /ɪnˈsɪstəns/ *noun* [U] ~ **(on sth/on doing sth)** | ~ **(that...)** an act of demanding or saying something firmly and refusing to accept any opposition or excuses: *their insistence on strict standards of behavior* ◆ *At her insistence, the matter was dropped.*

in·sist·ent /ɪnˈsɪstənt/ *adj.* **1** demanding something firmly and refusing to accept any opposition or excuses: ~ **(on**

sth/on doing sth) *They were insistent on having a contract for the work.* ◆ **~ (that…)** *Why are you so insistent that we leave tonight?* ◆ *She didn't want to go but her brother was insistent.* **2** continuing for a long period of time in a way that cannot be ignored: *insistent demands* ◆ *the insistent ringing of the telephone* ▶ **in·sis·tent·ly** *adv.*

in si·tu /ˌɪn ˈsaɪtu; -ˈsɪtu/ *adv.* (from *Latin*) in the original or correct place

in·so·bri·e·ty /ˌɪnsəˈbraɪəti/ *noun* [U] (*formal*) the state of being drunk; wild and noisy behavior that is typical of this state

in·so·far as /ˌɪnsəˈfɑr əz/ = IN SO FAR AS at FAR

in·sole /ˈɪnsoʊl/ *noun* a piece of material shaped like your foot that is placed inside a shoe to make it more comfortable

in·so·lent /ˈɪnsələnt/ *adj.* extremely rude and showing a lack of respect: *an insolent child/smile* ⊃ thesaurus box at RUDE ▶ **in·so·lence** /-ləns/ *noun* [U]: *Her insolence cost her her job.* **in·so·lent·ly** *adv.*

in·sol·u·ble /ɪnˈsɑlyəbl/ *adj.* **1** (of a problem, mystery, etc.) that cannot be solved or explained **2** **(in sth)** (of a substance) that does not dissolve in a liquid ANT SOLUBLE

in·sol·vent /ɪnˈsɑlvənt/ *adj.* not having enough money to pay what you owe SYN BANKRUPT: *The company has been declared insolvent.* ANT SOLVENT ▶ **in·sol·ven·cy** /-vənsi/ *noun* [U, C] (*pl.* **in·sol·ven·cies**)

in·som·ni·a /ɪnˈsɑmniə/ *noun* [U] the condition of being unable to sleep: *to suffer from insomnia* ⊃ see also SLEEPLESS

in·som·ni·ac /ɪnˈsɑmniˌæk/ *noun* a person who finds it difficult to sleep

in·sou·ci·ance /ɪnˈsusiəns/ *noun* [U] (*formal*) the state of not being worried about anything: *She hid her worries behind an air of insouciance.* ▶ **in·sou·ci·ant** /-siənt/ *adj.* SYN NONCHALANT

in·spect AWL /ɪnˈspɛkt/ *verb* **1** to look closely at something or someone, especially to check that everything is as it should be SYN EXAMINE: **~ sth/sb** *The teacher walked around inspecting their work.* ◆ *Make sure you inspect the goods before signing for them.* ◆ **~ sth/sb for sth** *The plants are regularly inspected for disease.* ⊃ thesaurus box at CHECK **2 ~ sth** to officially visit a school, factory, etc. in order to check that rules are being obeyed and that standards are acceptable: *Public health officials were called in to inspect the premises.*

in·spec·tion AWL /ɪnˈspɛkʃn/ *noun* [U, C] **1** an official visit to a school, factory, etc. in order to check that rules are being obeyed and that standards are acceptable: *Regular inspections are carried out at the prison.* ◆ *The principal went on a tour of inspection of all the classrooms.* **2** the act of looking closely at something or someone, especially to check that everything is as it should be SYN EXAMINATION: *The documents are available for inspection.* ◆ *On closer inspection, the notes proved to be forgeries.* ◆ *Engineers carried out a thorough inspection of the track.*

in·spec·tor AWL /ɪnˈspɛktər/ *noun* **1** a person whose job is to visit schools, factories, etc. to check that rules are being obeyed and that standards are acceptable: *a school/building/health/safety inspector* **2** a high-ranking officer in a POLICE FORCE: *Inspector Maggie Forbes*

in·spi·ra·tion /ˌɪnspəˈreɪʃn/ *noun* **1** [U] **~ (to do sth)** | **~ (for sth)** the process that takes place when someone sees or hears something that causes them to have exciting new ideas or makes them want to create something, especially in art, music, or literature: *Dreams can be a rich source of inspiration for an artist.* ◆ *Both poets drew their inspiration from the countryside.* ◆ *Looking for inspiration for a new dessert? Try this recipe.* **2** [C, usually sing.] **~ (for sth)** a person or thing that is the reason why someone creates or does something: *He says my sister was the inspiration for his heroine.* ◆ *Clark was the inspiration behind Saturday's victory.* **3** [C, usually sing.] **~ (to/for sb)** a person or thing that makes you want to be better, more successful, etc.: *Her charity work is an inspiration to us all.* **4** [C, usually sing., U] a sudden good idea: *He had an inspiration: he'd give her a dog for her birthday.* ◆ *It came to me in a flash of inspiration.*

in·spi·ra·tion·al /ˌɪnspəˈreɪʃənl/ *adj.* providing inspiration: *an inspirational leader*

in·spire /ɪnˈspaɪər/ *verb* **1** to give someone the desire, confidence, or enthusiasm to do something well: **~ sb (with sth)** *The actors inspired the kids with their enthusiasm.* ◆ *The actors' enthusiasm inspired the kids.* ◆ **~ sb to sth** *His performance inspired the team to a thrilling win.* ◆ **~ sb to do sth** *By visiting schools, the actors hope to inspire children to put on their own productions.* **2** [usually passive] **~ sth** to give someone the idea for something, especially something artistic or that shows imagination: *The choice of decor was inspired by a trip to India.* **3** to make someone have a particular feeling or emotion: **~ sb (with sth)** *Her work didn't exactly inspire me with confidence.* ◆ **~ sth (in sb)** *As a general, he inspired great loyalty in his troops.*

in·spired /ɪnˈspaɪərd/ *adj.* **1** having excellent qualities or abilities; produced with the help of INSPIRATION: *an inspired performance* ◆ *an inspired choice/guess* (= one that is right but based on feelings rather than knowledge) ANT UNINSPIRED **2** -inspired used with nouns, adjectives and adverbs to form adjectives that show how something has been influenced: *politically-inspired killings*

in·spir·ing /ɪnˈspaɪərɪŋ/ *adj.* exciting and encouraging you to do or feel something: *an inspiring teacher* ◆ (*informal*) *The book is less than inspiring.* ANT UNINSPIRING ⊃ see also AWE-INSPIRING

in·sta·bil·i·ty AWL /ˌɪnstəˈbɪləti/ *noun* [U, C, usually pl.] (*pl.* **in·sta·bil·i·ties**) **1** the quality of a situation in which things are likely to change or fail suddenly: *political and economic instability* **2** a mental condition in which someone's behavior is likely to change suddenly: *mental/emotional instability* ANT STABILITY ⊃ see also UNSTABLE

in·stall 🔧 /ɪnˈstɔl/ *verb* **1 ~ sth** to put equipment or furniture in position so that it can be used: *He's getting a phone installed tomorrow.* ◆ *The hotel chain has recently installed a new booking system.* **2 ~ sth** (*computing*) to put a new program into a computer: *I'll need some help installing the software.* ANT UNINSTALL **3 ~ sb (as sth)** to put someone in a new position of authority, often with an official ceremony: *He was installed as president last May.* **4 ~ sb/yourself (+ adv./prep.)** to make someone/yourself comfortable in a particular place or position: *We installed ourselves in the front row.*

in·stal·la·tion /ˌɪnstəˈleɪʃn/ *noun* **1** [U, C] the act of putting equipment or furniture in position so that it can be used: *installation costs* ◆ *Installation of the new system will take several days.* **2** [C] a piece of equipment or machinery that has been put in position so that it can be used: *a heating installation* **3** [C] a place where specialist equipment is kept and used: *a military installation* **4** [U] the act of placing someone in a new position of authority, often with a ceremony: *the installation of the new vice chancellor* **5** [C] (*art*) a piece of modern SCULPTURE that is made using sound, light, etc. as well as objects

in·stall·ment /ɪnˈstɔlmənt/ *noun* **1** one of a number of payments that are made regularly over a period of time until something has been paid for: *We paid for the car by/in installments.* ◆ *The final installment on the loan is due next week.* ◆ *They were unable to keep up* (= continue to pay regularly) *the installments.* ⊃ thesaurus box at PAYMENT **2** one of the parts of a story that appears regularly over a period of time in a newspaper, on television, etc. SYN EPISODE

in'stallment ˌplan *noun* [U, C] a method of buying an article by making regular payments for it over several months or years. The article only belongs to the person who is buying it when all the payments have been made. ⊃ compare CREDIT

---

t tea   ṭ butter   d did   k cat   g got   tʃ chin   dʒ June   f fall

in·stance 🔑 **AWL** /ˈɪnstəns/ noun, verb

- *noun* a particular example or case of something: *The report highlights a number of instances of injustice.* ◆ *In most instances, there will be no need for further treatment.* ◆ *I would normally suggest taking time off work, but in this instance I'm not sure that would do any good.* ⊃ thesaurus box at EXAMPLE
IDM **for instance** for example: *What would you do, for instance, if you found a member of staff stealing?* ⊃ language bank at E.G. **in the first instance** (*formal*) as the first part of a series of actions: *In the first instance, notify the police and then contact your insurance company.*
- *verb* ~ sth (*formal*) to give something as an example

in·stant /ˈɪnstənt/ adj., noun

- *adj.* **1** [usually before noun] happening immediately **SYN** IMMEDIATE: *She took an instant dislike to me.* ◆ *This account gives you instant access to your money.* ◆ *The show was an instant success.* **2** [only before noun] (of food) that can be made quickly and easily, usually by adding hot water: *instant coffee*
- *noun* [usually sing.] **1** a very short period of time **SYN** MOMENT: *I'll be back in an instant.* ◆ *Just for an instant I thought he was going to refuse.* **2** a particular point in time: *At that (very) instant, the door opened.* ◆ *I recognized her the instant (that)* (= as soon as) *I saw her.* ◆ *Come here this instant!* (= immediately)

in·stan·ta·ne·ous /ˌɪnstənˈteɪniəs/ adj. happening immediately: *an instantaneous response* ◆ *Death was almost instantaneous.* ▶ **in·stan·ta·ne·ous·ly** adv.

in·stant·ly /ˈɪnstəntli/ adv. immediately: *Her voice is instantly recognizable.* ◆ *The driver was killed instantly.*

ˌinstant ˈmessaging noun [U] a system on the Internet that allows people to exchange written messages with each other very quickly

ˌinstant ˈreplay noun part of something, for example a sports game on television, that is immediately repeated, often more slowly, so that you can see a goal or another exciting or important moment again

in·stead 🔑 /ɪnˈstɛd/ adv.
in the place of someone or something: *Lee was sick so I went instead.* ◆ *He didn't reply. Instead, he turned on his heel and left the room.* ◆ *She said nothing, preferring instead to save her comments till later.*

in·stead of 🔑 prep.
in the place of someone or something: *We just had soup instead of a full meal.* ◆ *Now I can walk to work instead of driving.*

in·step /ˈɪnstɛp/ noun **1** the top part of the foot between the ankle and toes ⊃ picture at BODY **2** the part of a shoe that covers the instep

in·sti·gate /ˈɪnstəˌɡeɪt/ verb **1** ~ sth to cause something bad to happen: *They were accused of instigating racial violence.* **2** ~ sth to make something start or happen, usually something official: *The government has instigated a program of economic reform.*

in·sti·ga·tion /ˌɪnstəˈɡeɪʃn/ noun [U] the act of causing something to begin or happen: *An appeal fund was launched at the instigation of the President.* ◆ *It was done at his instigation.*

in·sti·ga·tor /ˈɪnstəˌɡeɪt̬ər/ noun ~ (of sth) a person who causes something to happen, especially something bad: *the instigators of the riots*

in·still /ɪnˈstɪl/ verb ~ sth (in/into sb) to gradually make someone feel, think, or behave in a particular way over a period of time: *to instill confidence/discipline/fear into someone*

in·stinct /ˈɪnstɪŋkt/ noun [U, C] **1** ~ (for sth/for doing sth) | ~ (to do sth) a natural tendency for people and animals to behave in a particular way, using the knowledge and abilities that they were born with rather than thought or training: *maternal instincts* ◆ *Children do not know by instinct the difference between right and wrong.* ◆ *His first instinct was to*

run away. ◆ *Horses have a well-developed instinct for fear.* ◆ *Even at school, he showed he had an instinct for* (= was naturally good at) *business.* **2** ~ (that...) a feeling that makes you do something or believe that something is true, even though it is not based on facts or reason **SYN** INTUITION: *Her instincts had been right.*

in·stinc·tive /ɪnˈstɪŋktɪv/ adj. based on instinct, not thought or training: *instinctive knowledge* ◆ *She's an instinctive player.* ◆ *My instinctive reaction was to deny everything.* ▶ **in·stinc·tive·ly** adv.: *He knew instinctively that something was wrong.*

in·stinc·tu·al /ɪnˈstɪŋktʃuəl/ adj. (*psychology*) based on natural instinct; not learned

in·sti·tute 🔑 **AWL** /ˈɪnstəˌtut/ noun, verb

- *noun* an organization that has a particular purpose, especially one that is connected with education or a particular profession; the building used by this organization: *a research institute* ◆ *institutes of higher education*
- *verb* ~ sth (*formal*) to introduce a system, policy, etc. or start a process: *to institute criminal proceedings against someone* ◆ *The new management intends to institute a number of changes.*

in·sti·tu·tion 🔑 **AWL** /ˌɪnstəˈtuʃn/ noun
1 [C] a large important organization that has a particular purpose, for example, a university or bank: *an educational/financial, etc. institution* ◆ *the Smithsonian Institution* **2** [C] (*usually disapproving*) a building where people with special needs are taken care of, for example because they are old or mentally ill: *a mental institution* ◆ *We want this to be like a home, not an institution.* **3** [C] a custom or system that has existed for a long time among a particular group of people: *the institution of marriage* **4** [U] the act of starting or introducing something such as a system or a law: *the institution of new safety procedures* **5** [C] (*informal, humorous*) a person who is well known because they have been in a particular place or job for a long time: *You must know him—he's an institution around here!*

in·sti·tu·tion·al **AWL** /ˌɪnstəˈtuʃənl/ adj. [usually before noun] connected with an institution: *institutional investors* ◆ *institutional care* ▶ **in·sti·tu·tion·al·ly** **AWL** /-ʃənəli/ adv.

in·sti·tu·tion·al·ize **AWL** /ˌɪnstəˈtuʃənəˌlaɪz/ verb **1** ~ sb to send someone who is not capable of living independently to live in a special building (= an institution) especially when it is for a long period of time **2** ~ sth to make something become part of an organized system, society, or culture, so that it is considered normal ▶ **in·sti·tu·tion·al·i·za·tion** /ˌɪnstəˌtuʃənələˈzeɪʃn/ noun [U]

in·sti·tu·tion·al·ized **AWL** /ˌɪnstəˈtuʃənəˌlaɪzd/ adj.
1 (*usually disapproving*) that has happened or been done for so long that it is considered normal: *institutionalized racism* **2** (of people) lacking the ability to live and think independently because they have spent so long in an institution: *institutionalized patients*

ˈin-store adj. [only before noun] within a large store: *an in-store bakery*

in·struct **AWL** /ɪnˈstrʌkt/ verb **1** (*formal*) to tell someone to do something, especially in a formal or official way **SYN** DIRECT, ORDER: ~ sb to do sth *The letter instructed him to report to headquarters immediately.* ◆ ~ sb where, what, etc.... *You will be instructed where to go as soon as the plane is ready.* ◆ ~ sb *She arrived at 10 o'clock as instructed.* ◆ ~ that... *He instructed that a wall be built around the city.* ◆ ~ (sb) + speech *"Put it there," she instructed (them).* ⊃ thesaurus box at ORDER **2** ~ sb (in sth) (*formal*) to teach someone something, especially a practical skill: *All our staff have been instructed in sign language.* **3** [usually passive] ~ sb that... (*formal*) to give someone information about something: *We have been instructed that a decision will not be made before the end of the week.* **4** ~ sb (to do sth) (*law*) to employ someone to represent you in a legal situation, especially as a lawyer

in·struc·tion 🔑 **AWL** /ɪnˈstrʌkʃn/ noun, adj.
- *noun* **1** instructions [pl.] detailed information on how to

do or use something **SYN** DIRECTIONS: *Follow the instructions on the packet carefully.* ◆ *Always read the instructions before you start.* ◆ **~ on how to do sth** *The plant comes with full instructions on how to care for it.* **2** [C, usually pl.] **~ (to do sth)** | **~ (that…)** something that someone tells you to do **SYN** ORDER: *to ignore/carry out someone's instructions* ◆ *I'm under instructions to keep my speech short.* **3** [C] a piece of information that tells a computer to perform a particular operation. **4** [U] **~ (in sth)** (*formal*) the act of teaching something to someone: *religious instruction*

● **adj.** [only before noun] giving detailed information on how to do or use something (= giving instructions): *an instruction book/manual*

in·struc·tion·al /ɪnˈstrʌkʃənl/ *adj.* [usually before noun] (*formal*) that teaches people something: *instructional materials*

in·struc·tive **AWL** /ɪnˈstrʌktɪv/ *adj.* giving a lot of useful information: *a most instructive experience* ◆ *It is instructive to see how other countries are tackling the problem.* ▶ **in·struc·tive·ly** *adv.*

in·struc·tor **AWL** /ɪnˈstrʌktər/ *noun* **1** a person whose job is to teach someone a practical skill or sport: *a driving instructor* **2** a teacher below the rank of ASSISTANT PROFESSOR at a college or university

in·stru·ment 🔑 /ˈɪnstrəmənt/ *noun*

1 a tool or device used for a particular task, especially for delicate or scientific work: *surgical/optical/precision, etc. instruments* ◆ *instruments of torture* **2** = MUSICAL INSTRUMENT: *Is he learning an instrument?* ◆ *brass/stringed, etc. instruments* ⊃ picture on page 787 **3** a device used for measuring speed, distance, temperature, etc. in a vehicle or on a piece of machinery: *the flight instruments* ◆ *the instrument panel* **4** (*formal*) something that is used by someone in order to achieve something; a person or thing that makes something happen: **~ for sth/for doing sth** *The law is not the best instrument for dealing with family matters.* ◆ **~ of sth** *an instrument of change* **5** **~ of sb/sth** (*formal*) a person who is used and controlled by someone or something that is more powerful: *an instrument of fate* **6** (*law*) a formal legal document

in·stru·men·tal /ˌɪnstrəˈmentl/ *adj., noun*

● **adj.** **1** **~ (in sth/in doing sth)** important in making something happen: *He was instrumental in bringing about an end to the conflict.* **2** made by or for musical instruments: *instrumental music* ▶ **in·stru·men·tal·ly** /-ˈmentl-i/ *adv.*

● **noun** **1** a piece of music (usually popular music) in which only musical instruments are used, with no singing **2** (*grammar*) (in some languages) the form of a noun, pronoun, or adjective when it refers to a thing that is used to do something

in·stru·men·tal·ist /ˌɪnstrəˈmentl-ɪst/ *noun* a person who plays a musical instrument ⊃ compare VOCALIST

in·stru·men·ta·tion /ˌɪnstrəmənˈteɪʃn; -men-/ *noun* [U] **1** a set of instruments used in operating a vehicle or a piece of machinery **2** the way in which a piece of music is written for a particular group of instruments

in·sub·or·di·na·tion /ˌɪnsəˌbɔrdnˈeɪʃn/ *noun* [U] (*formal*) the refusal to obey orders or show respect for someone who has a higher rank **SYN** DISOBEDIENCE ▶ **in·sub·or·di·nate** /ˌɪnsəˈbɔrdn-ət/ *adj.*

in·sub·stan·tial /ˌɪnsəbˈstænʃl/ *adj.* **1** not very large, strong, or important: *an insubstantial construction of wood and glue* ◆ *an insubstantial argument* **2** (*literary*) not real or solid: *as insubstantial as a shadow*

in·suf·fer·a·ble /ɪnˈsʌfərəbl; -ˈsʌfrəbl/ *adj.* extremely annoying, unpleasant, and difficult to bear **SYN** UNBEARABLE ▶ **in·suf·fer·a·bly** /-bli/ *adv.*: *insufferably hot*

in·suf·fi·cient **AWL** /ˌɪnsəˈfɪʃnt/ *adj.* **~ (to do sth)** | **~ (for sth)** not large, strong, or important enough for a particular purpose **SYN** INADEQUATE: *insufficient time* ◆ *His salary is insufficient to meet his needs.* **ANT** SUFFICIENT ▶ **in·suf·fi-**

cient·ly **AWL** *adv.* **in·suf·fi·cien·cy** /-ˈfənsi/ *noun* [U, sing.] (*technical*): *cardiac insufficiency*

in·su·lar /ˈɪnsələr/ *adj.* **1** (*disapproving*) only interested in your own country, ideas, etc. and not in those from outside: *The British are often accused of being insular.* **2** (*technical*) connected with an island or islands: *the coastal and insular areas* ▶ **in·su·lar·i·ty** /ˌɪnsəˈlærəti/ *noun* [U]

in·su·late /ˈɪnsəˌleɪt/ *verb* **1** **~ sth (from/against sth)** to protect something with a material that prevents heat, sound, electricity, etc. from passing through: *Homeowners are being encouraged to insulate their homes to save energy.* ⊃ collocations at DECORATE **2** **~ sb/sth from/against sth** to protect someone or something from unpleasant experiences or influences **SYN** SHIELD

in·su·lat·ed /ˈɪnsəˌleɪtəd/ *adj.* protected with a material that prevents heat, sound, electricity, etc. from passing through: *insulated wires* ◆ *a well-insulated house*

in·su·lat·ing /ˈɪnsəˌleɪtɪŋ/ *adj.* [only before noun] preventing heat, sound, electricity, etc. from passing through: *insulating materials*

insulating tape (also **friction tape**) *noun* [U] a strip of sticky material used for covering the ends of electrical wires to prevent the possibility of an electric shock

in·su·la·tion /ˌɪnsəˈleɪʃn/ *noun* [U] the act of protecting something with a material that prevents heat, sound, electricity, etc. from passing through; the materials used for this: *Better insulation of your home will help to reduce heating bills.* ◆ *foam insulation* ⊃ collocations at DECORATE

in·su·la·tor /ˈɪnsəˌleɪtər/ *noun* a material or device used to prevent heat, electricity, or sound from escaping from something

in·su·lin /ˈɪnsələn/ *noun* [U] a chemical substance produced in the body that controls the amount of sugar in the blood (by influencing the rate at which it is removed); a similar artificial substance given to people whose bodies do not produce enough naturally: *insulin-dependent diabetes*

in·sult 🔑 *verb, noun*

● **verb** /ɪnˈsʌlt/ **~ sb/sth** to say or do something that offends someone: *I have never been so insulted in my life!* ◆ *She felt insulted by the low offer.*

● **noun** /ˈɪnsʌlt/ a remark or an action that is said or done in order to offend someone: *The crowd was shouting insults at the police.* ◆ **~ to sb/sth** *His comments were seen as an insult to the president.* ◆ *The questions were an insult to our intelligence* (= too easy). **IDM** see ADD

in·sult·ing 🔑 /ɪnˈsʌltɪŋ/ *adj.*

causing or intending to cause someone to feel offended: *insulting remarks* ◆ **~ to sb/sth** *She was really insulting to me.*

in·su·per·a·ble /ɪnˈsupərəbl/ *adj.* (*formal*) (of difficulties, problems, etc.) that cannot be dealt with successfully **SYN** INSURMOUNTABLE

in·sup·port·a·ble /ˌɪnsəˈpɔrtəbl/ *adj.* so bad or difficult that you cannot accept it or deal with it **SYN** INTOLERABLE

in·sur·ance 🔑 /ɪnˈʃʊrəns/ *noun*

1 [U, C] an arrangement with a company in which you pay them regular amounts of money and they agree to pay the costs, for example, if you die or are sick, or if you lose or damage something: *health/life/car/travel, etc. insurance* ◆ *to have adequate insurance coverage* ◆ **~ (against sth)** *to take out insurance against fire and theft* ◆ *insurance premiums* (= the regular payments made for insurance) ◆ *Can you claim for the loss on your insurance?* **2** [U] the business of providing people with insurance: *an insurance broker/company* ◆ *He works in insurance.* **3** [U] money paid by or to an insurance company: *to pay insurance on your house* ◆ *When her husband died, she received $50,000 in insurance.* **4** [U, C] **~ (against sth)** something you do to protect yourself against something bad happening in the future: *At that time people had large families as an insurance against some children dying.*

Musical Instruments

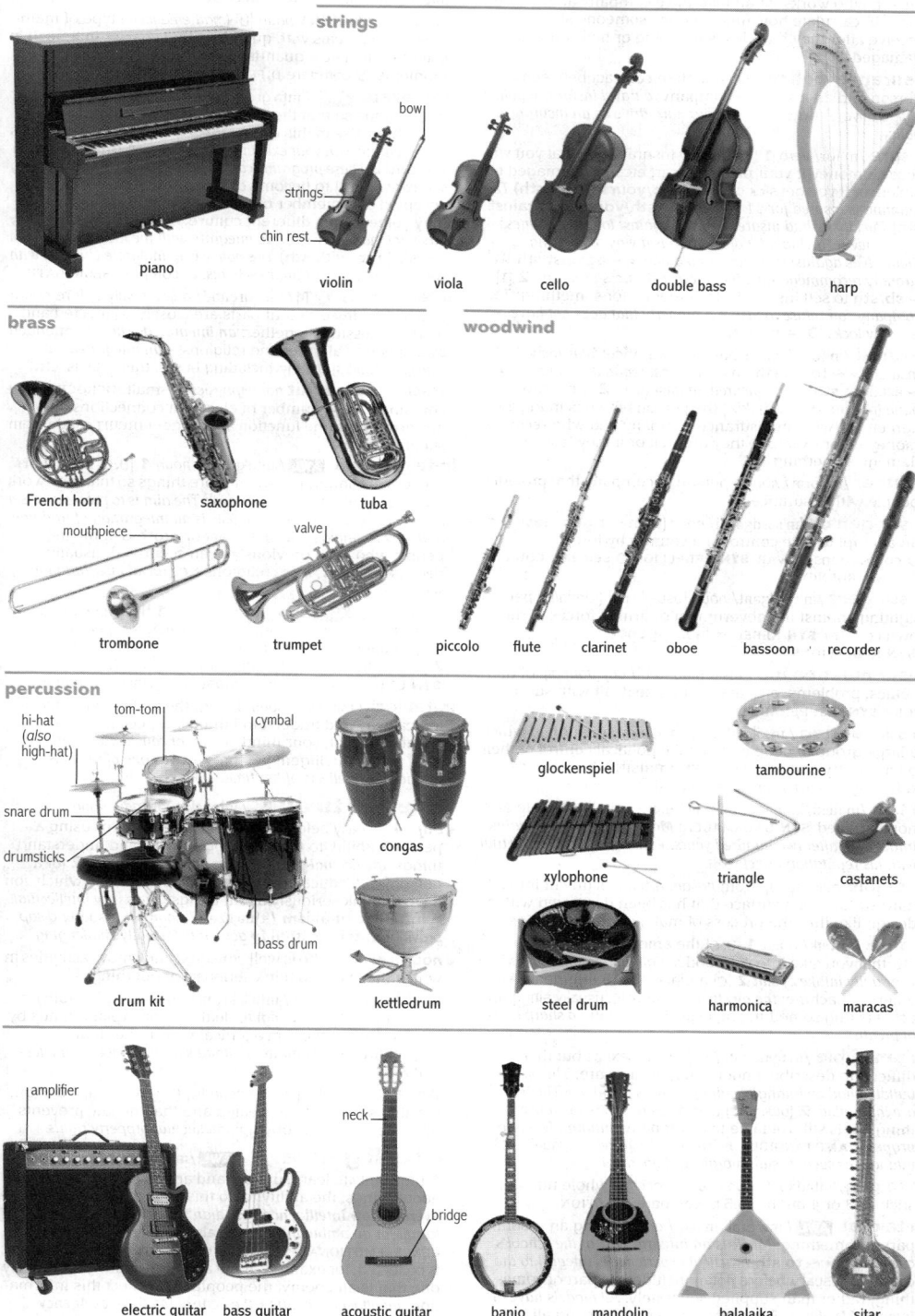

strings

bow

strings

chin rest

piano

violin

viola

cello

double bass

harp

brass

French horn

saxophone

tuba

mouthpiece

valve

trombone

trumpet

woodwind

piccolo

flute

clarinet

oboe

bassoon

recorder

percussion

hi-hat
(*also*
high-hat)

tom-tom

cymbal

snare drum

drumsticks

bass drum

drum kit

congas

kettledrum

glockenspiel

xylophone

steel drum

tambourine

triangle

castanets

harmonica

maracas

amplifier

neck

bridge

electric guitar

bass guitar

acoustic guitar

banjo

mandolin

balalaika

sitar

in·surance ad·juster (also **claims ad·juster**) *noun* person who works for an insurance company and whose job is to calculate how much money someone should receive after they have lost something or had something damaged

in·surance ,policy *noun* a written contract between a person and an insurance company: *a travel insurance policy* ◆ (*figurative*) *Always back up your hard drive as an insurance policy.*

in·sure /ɪnˈʃʊr/ *verb* **1** [T, I] to buy insurance so that you will receive money if your property, car, etc. gets damaged or stolen, or if you get sick or die: **~ sth/yourself (for sth)** *The painting is insured for $1 million.* ◆ **~ sth/yourself (against sth)** *Luckily he had insured himself against long-term illness.* ◆ (*figurative*) *Having a lot of children is a way of insuring themselves against loneliness in old age.* ◆ **~ against sth** *We strongly recommend insuring against sickness or injury.* **2** [T] **~ sb/sth** to sell insurance to someone for something: *The company can refuse to insure a property that does not have window locks.* **3** = ENSURE

in·sured /ɪnˈʃʊrd/ *adj.* **1** having insurance: *Was the vehicle insured?* ◆ **~ to do sth** *You're not insured to drive our car.* ◆ **~ against sth** *It isn't insured against theft.* **2 the insured** *noun* (*pl.* **the insured**) (*law*) the person who has made an agreement with an insurance company and who receives money if, for example, they are sick or if they lose or damage something

in·sur·er /ɪnˈʃʊrər/ *noun* a person or company that provides people with insurance

in·sur·gen·cy /ɪnˈsɜːrdʒənsi/ *noun* (*pl.* **in·sur·gen·cies**) [U, C] an attempt to take control of a country by force ⊃ collocations at WAR **SYN** REBELLION ⊃ see also COUN-TERINSURGENCY

in·sur·gent /ɪnˈsɜːrdʒənt/ *noun* [usually pl.] (*formal*) a person fighting against the government or armed forces of their own country **SYN** REBEL ▶ **in·sur·gent** *adj.* **SYN** REBELLIOUS

in·sur·mount·a·ble /ˌɪnsərˈmaʊntəbl/ *adj.* (*formal*) (of difficulties, problems, etc.) that cannot be dealt with success-fully **SYN** INSUPERABLE

in·sur·rec·tion /ˌɪnsəˈrekʃn/ *noun* [C, U] a situation in which a large group of people try to take political control of their own country with violence **SYN** UPRISING ▶ **in·sur·rec-tion·ar·y** /-ʃəˌneri/ *adj.* **in·sur·rec·tion·ist** *noun*

in·tact /ɪnˈtækt/ *adj.* [not usually before noun] complete and not damaged **SYN** UNDAMAGED: *Most of the house remains intact even after two hundred years.* ◆ *He emerged from the trial with his reputation intact.*

in·ta·glio *noun* [C, U] (from *Italian*, *art*) a design cut into a hard surface, or a surface that has been decorated with a design like this; the process of making intaglio designs

in·take /ˈɪnteɪk/ *noun* **1** [U, C] the amount of food, liquids, etc. that you take into your body: *high fluid intake* ◆ *to reduce your daily intake of salt* **2** [C] a place where liquid, air, etc. enters a machine: *the air/fuel intake* **3** [C, usually sing.] an act of taking something in, especially breath: *a sharp intake of breath*

in·tan·gi·ble /ɪnˈtændʒəbl/ *adj.* **1** that exists but that is difficult to describe, understand, or measure: *The old building had an intangible air of sadness about it.* ◆ *The benefits are intangible.* **2** (*business*) that does not exist as a physical thing but is still valuable to a company: *intangible assets/property* **ANT** TANGIBLE ▶ **in·tan·gi·ble** *noun* [usually pl.]: *intangibles such as staff morale and goodwill*

in·te·ger /ˈɪntədʒər/ *noun* (*mathematics*) a whole number, such as 3 or 4 but not 3.5 ⊃ compare FRACTION

in·te·gral **AWL** /ˈɪntɪɡrəl; ɪnˈteɡ-/ *adj.* **1** being an essential part of something: *Music is an integral part of the school's curriculum.* ◆ **~ to sth** *Practical experience is integral to the course.* **2** [usually before noun] included as part of something, rather than supplied separately: *All models have an integral CD player.* **3** [usually before noun] having all the parts that are necessary for something to be complete: *an integral system* ▶ **in·te·gral·ly** *adv.*

,integral 'calculus *noun* [U] (*mathematics*) a type of math-ematics that deals with quantities that change in time. It is used to calculate a quantity between two particular moments. ⊃ compare DIFFERENTIAL CALCULUS

in·te·grate **AWL** /ˈɪntəˌɡreɪt/ *verb* **1** [I, T] to combine two or more things so that they work together; to combine with something else in this way: **~ into/with sth** *These programs will integrate with your existing software.* ◆ **~ A (into/with B)** | **~ A and B** *These programs can be integrated with your existing software.* **2** [I, T] to become or make someone become accepted as a member of a social group, especially when they come from a different culture: **~ (into/with sth)** *They have not made any effort to integrate with the local community.* ◆ **~ sb (into/with sth)** *The policy is to integrate children with special needs into ordinary schools.* ⊃ compare SEGREGATE

in·te·grat·ed **AWL** /ˈɪntəˌɡreɪtəd/ *adj.* [usually before noun] in which many different parts are closely connected and work successfully together: *an integrated school* (= attended by students of all races and religions) ◆ *an integrated transportation system* (= including buses, trains, taxis, etc.)

,integrated 'circuit *noun* (*physics*) a small MICROCHIP that contains a large number of electrical connections and performs the same function as a larger CIRCUIT made from separate parts

in·te·gra·tion **AWL** /ˌɪntəˈɡreɪʃn/ *noun* **1** [U, C] the act or process of combining two or more things so that they work together (= of integrating them): *The aim is to promote closer economic integration.* ◆ *His music is an integration of tradition and new technology.* **2** [U] the act or process of mixing people who have previously been separated, usually because of color, race, religion, etc.: *racial integration in schools*

in·teg·ri·ty **AWL** /ɪnˈteɡrəti/ *noun* [U] **1** the quality of being honest and having strong moral principles: *personal/professional/artistic integrity* ◆ *to behave with integrity* **2** (*formal*) the state of being whole and not divided **SYN** UNITY: *to respect the territorial integrity of the nation*

in·tel·lect /ˈɪntəˌlekt/ *noun* **1** [U, C] the ability to think in a logical way and understand things, especially at an advanced level; your mind: *a man of considerable intellect* **2** [C] a very intelligent person: *She was one of the most formidable intellects of her time.*

in·tel·lec·tu·al ✎ /ˌɪntəˈlektʃuəl/ *adj.*, *noun*
● *adj.* **1** [usually before noun] connected with or using a person's ability to think in a logical way and understand things: *intellectual curiosity* ◆ *an intellectual novel* **2** (of a person) well educated and enjoying activities in which you have to think seriously about things: *She's very intellectual.* ▶ **in·tel·lec·tu·al·ism** /-tʃuəˌlɪzəm/ *noun* [U] (usually *disap-proving*) **in·tel·lec·tu·al·ly** *adv.*: *intellectually challenging*
● *noun* a person who is well educated and enjoys activities in which they have to think seriously about things

in·tel·lec·tu·al·ize /ˌɪntəˈlektʃuəˌlaɪz/ *verb* [T, I] **~ (sth)** (sometimes *disapproving*) to deal with or explain things by thinking about them in a logical way, rather than responding emotionally: *Religious faith cannot be intellec-tualized.*

,intellectual 'property *noun* [U] (*law*) an idea, a design, etc. that someone has created and that the law prevents other people from copying: *intellectual property rights*

in·tel·li·gence ✎ **AWL** /ɪnˈtelədʒəns/ *noun* [U] **1** the ability to learn, understand and think in a logical way about things; the ability to do this well: *a person of high/average/low intelligence* ◆ *He didn't even have the intelligence to call for an ambulance.* ⊃ see also ARTIFICIAL INTELLI-GENCE, EMOTIONAL INTELLIGENCE **2** secret information that is collected, for example about a foreign country, especially one that is an enemy; the people that collect this informa-tion: *intelligence reports* ◆ *the Central Intelligence Agency*

ʌ cup   ə about   eɪ say   aɪ five   ɔɪ boy   aʊ now   oʊ go   ər bird

in·tel·li·gence ˌquotient noun = IQ

in·tel·li·gence ˌtest noun a test to measure how well a person is able to understand and think in a logical way about things

in·tel·li·gent 🔑 **AWL** /ɪnˈtɛlədʒənt/ adj.
1 good at learning, understanding, and thinking in a logical way about things; showing this ability: *a highly intelligent child* • *to ask an intelligent question* **ANT** UNINTELLIGENT **2** (of an animal, a being, etc.) able to understand and learn things: *a search for intelligent life on other planets* **3** (*computing*) (of a computer, program, etc.) able to store information and use it in new situations: *intelligent software/systems* ▶ **in·tel·li·gent·ly** **AWL** adv.

THESAURUS

intelligent

smart ◆ brilliant ◆ bright ◆ sharp

These words all describe people who are good at learning, understanding, and thinking about things, and the actions that show this ability.

intelligent good at learning, understanding, and thinking in a logical way about things; showing this ability: *He's a* **highly intelligent** *man.* ◆ *She asked a lot of intelligent questions.*

smart quick at learning and understanding things; showing the ability to make good business or personal decisions: *She's smarter than her brother.* ◆ *That was a smart career move.*

brilliant extremely intelligent or skillful: *She's a brilliant young scientist.*

bright intelligent; quick to learn: *He's probably the brightest student in the class.* **NOTE** Bright is used especially to talk about young people. Common collocations of **bright** include *girl, boy, kid,* and *student.*

sharp bright: *You're a pretty sharp kid.*

PATTERNS

- a(n) intelligent/smart/brilliant/bright/sharp **child/kid/boy/girl**
- a(n) intelligent/smart/brilliant **man/woman**
- a(n) intelligent/smart/brilliant **thing to do**

---

inˌtelligent deˈsign noun [U] the belief that the universe and living things were created by an intelligent being: *the legal battle about the teaching of intelligent design as science* ⊃ compare CREATIONISM

in·tel·li·gent·si·a /ɪnˌtɛləˈdʒɛntsiə/ usually **the intelligentsia** noun [sing.] the people in a country or society who are well educated and are interested in culture, politics, literature, etc.

in·tel·li·gi·ble /ɪnˈtɛlədʒəbl/ adj. ~ **(to sb)** that can be easily understood **SYN** UNDERSTANDABLE: *His lecture was readily intelligible to all the students.* **ANT** UNINTELLIGIBLE ▶ **in·tel·li·gi·bil·i·ty** /ɪnˌtɛlədʒəˈbɪləti/ noun [U] **in·tel·li·gi·bly** /ɪnˈtɛlədʒəbli/ adv.

in·tem·per·ate /ɪnˈtɛmpərət/ adj. (*formal*) **1** showing a lack of control over yourself: *intemperate language* **ANT** TEMPERATE **2** regularly drinking too much alcohol ▶ **in·tem·per·ance** /-pərəns/ noun [U]

in·tend 🔑 /ɪnˈtɛnd/ verb
1 [I, T] to have a plan, result, or purpose in your mind when you do something: *We finished later than we had intended.* ◆ **~ to do sth** *I fully intended* (= definitely intended) *to pay for the damage.* ◆ **~ sb/sth to do sth** *The writer clearly intends his readers to identify with the main character.* ◆ **~ sth** *The company intends a slow-down in expansion.* ◆ **~ sb sth** *He intended her no harm* (= it was not his plan to harm her).

WORD FAMILY
intend verb
intended adj. (≠ unintended)
intention noun
intentional adj. (≠ unintentional)
intentionally adv. (≠ unintentionally)

◆ **it is intended that…** *It is intended that production will start next month.* ◆ **~ that…** *We intend that production will start next month.* **2** [T] to plan that something should have a particular meaning **SYN** MEAN: **~ sth (by sth)** *What exactly did you intend by that remark?* ◆ **~ sth (as sth)** *He intended it as a joke.*

in·tend·ed 🔑 /ɪnˈtɛndəd/ adj. [only before noun]
1 that you are trying to achieve or reach: *the intended purpose* ◆ *the intended audience* ◆ *The bullet missed its intended target.* **2** planned or designed for someone or something: **~ for sb/sth** *The book is intended for children.* ◆ **~ as sth** *The notes are intended as an introduction to the course.* ◆ **~ to be/do sth** *This list is not intended to be a complete catalog.* ⊃ see also UNINTENDED

in·tense 🔑 **AWL** /ɪnˈtɛns/ adj.
1 very great; very strong **SYN** EXTREME: *intense heat/cold/pain* ◆ *The President is under intense pressure to resign.* ◆ *the intense blue of her eyes* ◆ *intense interest/pleasure/desire/anger* **2** serious and often involving a lot of action in a short period of time: *intense competition* ◆ *It was a period of intense activity.* **3** (of a person) having or showing very strong feelings, opinions, or thoughts about someone or something: *an intense look* ◆ *He's very intense about everything.* ⊃ compare INTENSIVE ▶ **in·tense·ly** **AWL** adv.: *She disliked him intensely.*

in·ten·si·fi·er /ɪnˈtɛnsəˌfaɪər/ noun (*grammar*) a word, especially an adjective or an adverb, for example *so* or *very*, that makes the meaning of another word stronger

in·ten·si·fy **AWL** /ɪnˈtɛnsəˌfaɪ/ verb (in·ten·si·fies, in·ten·si·fy·ing, in·ten·si·fied, in·ten·si·fied) [I, T] to increase in degree or strength; to make something increase in degree or strength **SYN** HEIGHTEN: *Violence intensified during the night.* ◆ **~ sth** *The opposition leader has intensified his attacks on the government.* ▶ **in·ten·si·fi·ca·tion** **AWL** /ɪnˌtɛnsəfəˈkeɪʃn/ noun [U, sing.]

in·ten·si·ty **AWL** /ɪnˈtɛnsəti/ noun (pl. in·ten·si·ties)
1 [U, sing.] the state or quality of being intense: *intensity of light/sound/color* ◆ *intensity of feeling/concentration/relief* ◆ *He was watching her with an intensity that was unnerving.* ◆ *The storm resumed with even greater intensity.* **2** [U, C] (*technical*) the strength of something, for example light, that can be measured: *varying intensities of natural light*

in·ten·sive **AWL** /ɪnˈtɛnsɪv/ adj. **1** involving a lot of work or activity done in a short time: *an intensive language course* ◆ *two weeks of intensive training* ◆ *intensive diplomatic negotiations* **2** extremely thorough; done with a lot of care: *His disappearance has been the subject of intensive investigation.* **3** (of methods of farming) aimed at producing as much food as possible using as little land or as little money as possible: *Traditionally reared animals grow more slowly than those reared under intensive farming conditions.* ◆ *intensive agriculture* ⊃ see also CAPITAL-INTENSIVE, LABOR-INTENSIVE ▶ **in·ten·sive·ly** **AWL** adv.: *This case has been intensively studied.* ◆ *intensively farmed land*

inˌtensive ˈcare noun [U] **1** continuous care and attention, often using special equipment, for people in a hospital who are very seriously ill or injured: *She needed intensive care for several days.* ◆ *intensive care patients/beds* **2** (also inˌtensive ˈcare ˌunit [C]) (*abbr.* ICU) the part of a hospital that provides intensive care: *The baby was* **in intensive care** *for 48 hours.*

in·tent /ɪnˈtɛnt/ adj., noun
● *adj.* **1** showing strong interest and attention: *an intent gaze/look* ◆ *His eyes were suddenly intent.* **2** (*formal*) determined to do something, especially something that will harm other people: **~ on/upon sth** *They were intent on murder.* ◆ **~ on/upon doing sth** *Are you intent upon destroying my reputation?* **3** **~ on/upon sth** giving all your attention to something: *I was so intent on my work that I didn't notice the time.* ▶ **in·tent·ly** adv.: *She looked at him intently.*
● *noun* [U] **~ (to do sth)** (*formal* or *law*) what you intend to do **SYN** INTENTION: *She denies possessing the drug with intent to sell.* ◆ *a* **letter/statement of intent** ◆ *His intent is clearly not to placate his critics.*

IDM **for all intents and purposes** in the effects that something has, if not in reality; almost completely: *By 1981 the docks had, for all intents and purposes, closed.* ◆ *The two items are, for all intents and purposes, identical.*

in·ten·tion 🔑 /ɪnˈtɛnʃn/ *noun* [C, U]
what you intend or plan to do; your aim: ~ **(of doing sth)** *I have no intention of going to the wedding.* ◆ *He left the U.S. with the intention of traveling in Africa.* ◆ *I have every intention of paying her back what I owe her.* ◆ ~ **(to do sth)** *He has announced his intention to retire.* ◆ ~ **(that…)** *It was not my intention that she should suffer.* ◆ *The original intention was to devote three months to the project.* ◆ *She's full of good intentions but things rarely work out for her.* ◆ *I did it with the best (of) intentions* (= meaning to help)*, but I only succeeded in annoying them.* ➔ see also WELL INTENTIONED ➔ thesaurus box at PURPOSE **IDM** see ROAD

in·ten·tion·al /ɪnˈtɛnʃənl/ *adj.* done deliberately **SYN** DELIBERATE, INTENDED: *I'm sorry I left you off the list—it wasn't intentional.* **ANT** UNINTENTIONAL ▶ **in·ten·tion·al·ly** /-ʃənəli/ *adv.*: *She would never intentionally hurt anyone.* ◆ *I kept my statement intentionally vague.*

in·ter /ɪnˈtər/ *verb* (-rr-) [usually passive] ~ **sb** *(formal)* to bury a dead person **ANT** DISINTER ➔ see also INTERMENT

inter- /ˈɪntər/ *prefix* (in verbs, nouns, adjectives, and adverbs) between; from one to another: *interface* ◆ *interaction* ◆ *international* ➔ compare INTRA-

In·ter·ac /ˈɪntəræk/ *noun* (*CanE*) a system of payment in which you use a DEBIT CARD (= a plastic card that takes money directly from your bank account) to buy things

in·ter·act **AWL** /ˌɪntərˈækt/ *verb* **1** [I] ~ **(with sb)** to communicate with someone, especially while you work, play or spend time with them: *Teachers have a limited amount of time to interact with each child.* **2** [I] ~ **(with sth)** if one thing **interacts** with another, or if two things **interact**, the two things have an effect on each other: *Perfume interacts with the skin's natural chemicals.* ▶ **in·ter·ac·tion** **AWL** /-ˈækʃn/ *noun* [U, C]: ~ **(between sb/sth)** *the interaction between performers and their audience* ◆ ~ **(with sb/sth)** *the interaction of bacteria with the body's natural chemistry*

in·ter·ac·tive **AWL** /ˌɪntərˈæktɪv/ *adj.* **1** that involves people working together and having an influence on each other: *The school believes in interactive teaching methods.* **2** (*computing*) that allows information to be passed continuously and in both directions between a computer and the person who uses it: *interactive systems/video* ▶ **in·ter·ac·tive·ly** **AWL** *adv.* ▶ **in·ter·ac·tiv·i·ty** /ˌɪntəræk'tɪvəti/ *noun* [U]

in·ter a·li·a /ˌɪntər ˈeɪliə; -ˈeɪliə/ *adv.* (from *Latin*, *formal*) among other things

in·ter·breed /ˌɪntərˈbrid/ *verb* [I, T] ~ **(sth) (with sth)** if animals from different SPECIES **interbreed**, or someone **interbreeds** them, they produce young together

in·ter·cede /ˌɪntərˈsid/ *verb* [I] ~ **(with sb) (for/on behalf of sb)** *(formal)* to speak to someone in order to persuade them to be kind to someone else or to help settle an argument **SYN** INTERVENE: *They interceded with the authorities on behalf of the detainees.* ▶ **in·ter·ces·sion** /ˌɪntərˈsɛʃn/ *noun* [U]: *the intercession of a priest*

in·ter·cept /ˌɪntərˈsɛpt/ *verb, noun*
• *verb* **1** ~ **sb/sth** to stop someone or something that is going from one place to another from arriving: *Reporters intercepted him as he tried to leave the hotel.* ◆ *The letter was intercepted.* **2** ~ **sth** (especially in football) to catch a ball that is thrown to a player on the opposing team: *He intercepted two passes by Kramer.* ▶ **in·ter·cep·tion** /-ˈsɛpʃn/ *noun* [U, C]: *the interception of enemy radio signals* ◆ *He had two interceptions late in the game.*
• *noun* /ˈɪntərˌsɛpt/ /ˈɪntərˌsɛpt/ (*mathematics*) the point at which a line or curve crosses an AXIS

in·ter·cep·tor /ˌɪntərˈsɛptər/ *noun* a fast military plane that attacks enemy planes that are carrying bombs

in·ter·change *noun, verb*
• *noun* /ˈɪntərˌtʃeɪndʒ/ **1** [C, U] the act of sharing or exchan-

ging something, especially ideas or information: *a continuous interchange of ideas* ◆ *electronic data interchange* **2** [C] a place where a road joins a major road such as a highway, designed so that vehicles leaving or joining the road do not have to cross other lines of traffic
• *verb* /ˌɪntərˈtʃeɪndʒ/ **1** [T] ~ **sth** to share or exchange ideas, information, etc. **2** [T, I] to put each of two things or people in the other's place; to move or be moved from one place to another in this way: ~ **A and B** *to interchange the front and rear tires of a car* ◆ ~ **(A) (with B)** *to interchange the front tires with the rear ones* ◆ *The front and rear tires interchange* (= can be exchanged).

in·ter·change·a·ble /ˌɪntərˈtʃeɪndʒəbl/ *adj.* that can be exchanged, especially without affecting the way in which something works: *The two words are virtually interchangeable* (= have almost the same meaning). ◆ ~ **with sth** *The V8 engines are all interchangeable with each other.* ▶ **in·ter·change·a·bil·i·ty** /ˌɪntərˌtʃeɪndʒəˈbɪləti/ *noun* [U] **in·ter·change·a·bly** /ˌɪntərˈtʃeɪndʒəbli/ *adv.*: *These terms are used interchangeably.*

in·ter·cit·y /ˌɪntərˈsɪti/ *adj.* [usually before noun] (of transportation) traveling between cities, usually with not many stops on the way: *an intercity bus service* ◆ *intercity travel*

in·ter·col·le·giate /ˌɪntərkəˈlidʒət/ *adj.* involving competition between colleges: *intercollegiate football*

in·ter·com /ˈɪntərˌkɑm/ *noun* a system of communication by telephone or radio inside an office, plane, etc.; the device you press or turn on to start using this system: *to announce something over the intercom* ◆ *They called him on the intercom.*

in·ter·com·mu·ni·ca·tion /ˌɪntərkəˌmyunəˈkeɪʃn/ *noun* [U] the process of communicating between people or groups

in·ter·con·nect /ˌɪntərkəˈnɛkt/ *verb* [T, I] to connect similar things; to be connected to or with similar things: ~ **A with B** *Bad housing is interconnected with debt and poverty.* ◆ ~ **A and B** *Bad housing, debt, and poverty are interconnected.* ◆ ~ **(with sth)** *separate bedrooms that interconnect* ▶ **in·ter·con·nec·tion** /-kəˈnɛkʃn/ *noun* [C, U]: *interconnections between different parts of the brain*

in·ter·con·ti·nen·tal /ˌɪntərˌkɑntəˈnɛntl; -ˌkɑntnˈɛntl/ *adj.* [usually before noun] between continents: *intercontinental flights/missiles/travel/trade*

in·ter·course /ˈɪntərˌkɔrs/ *noun* [U] **1** = SEXUAL INTERCOURSE **2** (*old-fashioned*) communication between people, countries, etc.: *the importance of social intercourse between different age groups*

in·ter·cul·tur·al /ˌɪntərˈkʌltʃərəl/ *adj.* existing or happening between different cultures

in·ter·cut /ˌɪntərˈkʌt/ *verb* (in·ter·cut·ting, in·ter·cut, in·ter·cut) ~ **sth (with sth)** *(technical)* to put a movie scene between two parts of a different scene: *Scenes of city life were intercut with interviews with local people.*

in·ter·de·nom·i·na·tion·al /ˌɪntərdɪˌnɑməˈneɪʃənl/ *adj.* shared by different religious groups (= different DENOMINATIONS)

in·ter·de·part·men·tal /ˌɪntərˌdipɑrtˈmɛntl/ *adj.* between departments; involving more than one department

in·ter·de·pend·ent /ˌɪntərdɪˈpɛndənt/ *adj.* that depend on each other; consisting of parts that depend on each other: *interdependent economies/organizations/relationships* ◆ *The world is becoming increasingly interdependent.* ▶ **in·ter·de·pend·ence** /-dəns/ (also *less frequent* in·ter·de·pend·en·cy *pl.* in·ter·de·pend·en·cies) *noun* [U, C]

in·ter·dict /ˈɪntərˌdɪkt/ *noun* **1** (*law*) an official order from a court that orders you not to do something **2** (*technical*) (in the Roman Catholic Church) an order banning someone from taking part in church services, etc.

in·ter·dic·tion /ˌɪntərˈdɪkʃn/ *noun* [U] *(formal)* the act of stopping something that is being transported from one place from reaching another place, especially by using force: *the agency's drug interdiction programs*

in·ter·dis·ci·pli·nar·y /ˌɪntərˈdɪsəpləˌnɛri/ *adj.* involving

t **t**ea   ţ bu**tt**er   d **d**id   k **c**at   g **g**ot   tʃ **ch**in   dʒ **J**une   f **f**all

different areas of knowledge or study: *interdisciplinary research* ♦ *an interdisciplinary approach*

in·ter·est 🔑 /'ɪntrəst; -trest/ *noun, verb*

● *noun*

> **WANTING TO KNOW MORE 1** [sing., U] ~ **(in sb/sth)** the feeling that you have when you want to know or learn more about someone or something: *to feel/have/show/express (an) interest in something* ♦ *Do your parents take an interest in your friends?* ♦ *By that time I had lost (all) interest in the idea.* ♦ *I watched with interest.* ♦ *As a matter of interest,* (= I'd like to know) *what time did the party finish?* ♦ *Just out of interest, how much did it cost?* ➔ compare DISINTEREST

> **ATTRACTION 2** [U] the quality that something has when it attracts someone's attention or makes them want to know more about it: *There are many places of interest near the city.* ♦ *The subject is of no interest to me at all.* ♦ *These plants will add interest to your garden in winter.* ♦ *These documents are of great historical interest.* ♦ *be of cultural/scientific interest* ➔ see also HUMAN INTEREST, LOVE INTEREST

> **HOBBY 3** [C] an activity or a subject that you enjoy and that you spend your free time doing or studying: *Her main interests are music and tennis.* ♦ *He was a man of wide interests outside his work.* ➔ compare HOBBY

> **MONEY 4** [U] ~ **(on sth)** (*finance*) the extra money that you pay back when you borrow money or that you receive when you invest money: *to pay interest on a loan* ♦ *The money was repaid with interest.* ♦ *interest charges/payments* ♦ *Interest rates have risen by 1%.* ♦ *high rates of interest* ➔ see also COMPOUND INTEREST, SIMPLE INTEREST

> **ADVANTAGE 5** [C, usually pl., U] a good result or an advantage for someone or something: *to promote/protect/safeguard someone's interests* ♦ *She was acting entirely in her own interests.* ♦ *These reforms were in the best interests of local government.* ♦ *It is in the public interest that these facts are made known.* ➔ see also SELF-INTEREST

> **SHARE IN BUSINESS 6** [C, usually pl.] ~ **(in sth)** a share in a business or company and its profits: *She has business interests in France.* ♦ *American interests in Europe* (= money invested in European countries) ➔ see also CONTROLLING INTEREST

> **CONNECTION 7** [C, U] ~ **(in sth)** a connection with something that affects your attitude to it, especially because you may benefit from it in some way: *I should, at this point, declare my interest.* ♦ *Organizations have an interest in ensuring that employee motivation is high.* ➔ compare DISINTEREST ➔ see also VESTED INTEREST

> **GROUP OF PEOPLE 8** [C, usually pl.] a group of people who are in the same business or who share the same aims, which they want to protect: *powerful farming interests* ♦ *relationships between local government and business interests*

IDM **have sb's interests at heart** to want someone to be happy and successful even though your actions may not show this **in the interest(s) of sth** in order to help or achieve something: *In the interest(s) of safety, smoking is forbidden.* ➔ more at CONFLICT *n.*, PAY *v.*

● *verb* to attract your attention and make you feel interested; to make yourself give your attention to something: ~ **sb** *Politics doesn't interest me.* ♦ ~ **sb/yourself in sth** *She has always interested herself in charity work.* ♦ *it interests sb to do sth* *It may interest you to know that I didn't accept the job.*
PHR V **'interest sb in sth** to persuade someone to buy, do, or eat something: *Could I interest you in this model, Sir?*

THESAURUS

interest
hobby ♦ pastime

These are all words for activities that you do for pleasure in your spare time.

interest an activity or a subject that you do or study for pleasure in your spare time: *Her main interests are music and gardening.*

hobby an activity that you do for pleasure in your spare time: *His hobbies include swimming and cooking.*

pastime an activity that people do for pleasure in their spare time: *Eating out is the national pastime in France.*

INTEREST, HOBBY, OR PASTIME?

A **hobby** is often more active than an **interest**: *His main hobby is football* (= he plays football). ♦ *His main interest is football* (= he watches and reads about football, and may or may not play it). **Pastime** is used when talking about people in general; when you are talking about yourself or an individual person it is more usual to use **interest** or **hobby**: *Eating out is the national interest/hobby in France.* ♦ *Do you have any pastimes?*

in·ter·est·ed 🔑 /'ɪntrəstəd; 'ɪntəres-; 'ɪntres-/ *adj.*
1 giving your attention to something because you enjoy finding out about it or doing it; showing interest in something and finding it exciting: ~ **(in sth/sb)** *I'm very interested in history.* ♦ ~ **(in doing sth)** *Anyone interested in joining the club should contact us at the address below.* ♦ ~ **(to do sth)** *We would be interested to hear your views on this subject.* ♦ *an interested audience* ♦ *There's a talk on Italian art—are you interested* (= would you like to go)? ♦ *He sounded genuinely interested.* **2** in a position to gain from a situation or be affected by it: *As an interested party, I was not allowed to vote.* ♦ *Interested groups will be given three months to give their views on the new development.*

WHICH WORD?

interested ♦ **interesting** ♦ **uninterested** ♦ **disinterested** ♦ **uninteresting**

■ The opposite of **interested** is **uninterested** or **not interested**: *He is completely uninterested in politics.* ♦ *I am not really interested in politics.*

■ **Disinterested** means that you can be fair in judging a situation because you do not feel personally involved in it: *A lawyer can give you disinterested advice.* However, in speech it is sometimes used instead of **uninterested**, although this is thought to be incorrect.

■ The opposite of **interesting** can be **uninteresting**: *The food was bland and uninteresting.* It is more common to use a different word such as **dull** or **boring**.

interest-'free *adj.* with no interest charged on money borrowed: *an interest-free loan* ♦ *interest-free credit*

'interest group *noun* a group of people who work together to achieve something that they are particularly interested in, especially by putting pressure on the government, etc.: *a special interest group of U.S. lumber producers* ➔ compare ADVOCACY GROUP, PRESSURE GROUP

in·ter·est·ing 🔑 /'ɪntrəstɪŋ; 'ɪntəres-; 'ɪntres-/ *adj.*
attracting your attention because it is special, exciting, or unusual: *an interesting question/point/example* ♦ *interesting people/places/work* ♦ ~ **(to do sth)** *It would be interesting to know what he really believed.* ♦ ~ **(that...)** *I find it interesting that she claims not to know him.* ♦ *Can't we do something more interesting?* ♦ *Her account makes interesting reading.* ♦ *It is particularly interesting to compare the two versions.* ➔ note at INTERESTED ▶ **in·ter·est·ing·ly** *adv.*: *Interestingly, there are very few recorded cases of such attacks.* ➔ language bank at SURPRISING

THESAURUS

interesting
fascinating ♦ compelling ♦ stimulating ♦ gripping ♦ absorbing

These words all describe someone or something that attracts or holds your attention because they are/it is exciting, unusual, or full of good ideas.

interesting attracting your attention because it is exciting, unusual, or full of good ideas: *That's an interesting question, Daniel.*

fascinating extremely interesting or attractive: *The exhibition tells the fascinating story of the steam age.*

compelling (*somewhat formal*) so interesting or exciting that it holds your attention: *Her latest book makes for compelling reading.*

stimulating full of interesting or exciting ideas; making people feel enthusiastic: *We had a stimulating conversation over lunch.*

gripping so exciting or interesting that it holds your attention completely: *His books are always so gripping.*

absorbing so interesting or enjoyable that it holds your attention: *Chess can be a completely absorbing game.*

PATTERNS

- interesting/fascinating/stimulating **for** sb
- interesting/fascinating **to** sb
- interesting/fascinating **that…**
- interesting/fascinating **to see/hear/find/learn/know…**
- a(n) interesting/fascinating/compelling/stimulating/gripping **read/book**
- a(n) interesting/fascinating/compelling/gripping **story**
- a(n) interesting/fascinating/stimulating **experience/discussion/idea**
- to **find sth** interesting/fascinating/compelling/stimulating/gripping/absorbing

in·ter·face /ˈɪntərˌfeɪs/ *noun, verb*
- *noun* **1** (*computing*) the way a computer program presents information to a user or receives information from a user, in particular the LAYOUT of the screen and the menus: *the user interface* **2** (*computing*) an electrical CIRCUIT, connection, or program that joins one device or system to another: *the interface between computer and printer* **3** ~ **(between A and B)** the point where two subjects, systems, etc. meet and affect each other: *the interface between manufacturing and sales*
- *verb* [I, T] ~ **(sth) (with sth)** | ~ **A and B** (*computing*) to be connected with something using an interface; to connect something in this way: *The new system interfaces with existing telephone equipment.*

in·ter·faith /ˈɪntərˌfeɪθ/ *adj.* [only before noun] between or connected with people of different religions: *an interfaith marriage* ◆ *an interfaith memorial service*

in·ter·fere /ˌɪntərˈfɪr/ *verb* [I] to get involved in and try to influence a situation that does not concern you, in a way that annoys other people: *I wish my mother would stop interfering and let me make my own decisions.* ◆ ~ **in sth** *The police are very unwilling to interfere in family problems.*
PHR V **inter'fere with sb** to illegally try to influence someone who is going to give evidence in court, for example by threatening them or offering them money **inter'fere with sth 1** to prevent something from succeeding or from being done or happening as planned: *She never allows her personal feelings to interfere with her work.* **2** to touch, use, or change something, especially a piece of equipment, so that it is damaged or no longer works correctly: *I'd get fired if he found out I'd been interfering with his records.*

in·ter·fer·ence /ˌɪntərˈfɪrəns/ *noun* [U] **1** ~ **(in sth)** the act of interfering: *They resent foreign interference in the internal affairs of their country.* **2** interruption of a radio signal by another signal on a similar WAVELENGTH, causing extra noise that is not wanted **3** (in HOCKEY and other sports) the act, which is against the rules, of getting in the way of an opposing player's ability to run, hit, etc.: *rules on goalie interference*
IDM **run interference 1** (in football) to clear the way for

the player with the ball by blocking players from the opposing team **2** (*informal*) to help someone by dealing with problems for them so that they do not need to deal with them

in·ter·fer·ing /ˌɪntərˈfɪrɪŋ/ *adj.* [usually before noun] (*disapproving*) involving yourself in an annoying way in other people's private lives: *She's an interfering busybody!*

in·ter·fer·on /ˌɪntərˈfɪrɑn/ *noun* [U] (*biology*) a substance produced by the body to prevent harmful viruses from causing disease

in·ter·ga·lac·tic /ˌɪntərgəˈlæktɪk/ *adj.* [only before noun] existing or happening between galaxies (GALAXY) of stars: *intergalactic space/travel*

in·ter·gen·e·ra·tio·nal /ˌɪntərˌdʒɛnəˈreɪʃənl/ *adj.* including or involving people of different generations or age groups: *intergenerational conflict* ◆ *The school has started an intergenerational program in which seniors spend time helping the children.*

in·ter·gov·ern·men·tal /ˌɪntərˌgʌvərˈmɛntl; -ˌgʌvərn-/ *adj.* [only before noun] concerning the governments of two or more countries: *an intergovernmental conference*

in·ter·im /ˈɪntərəm/ *adj., noun*
- *adj.* [only before noun] **1** intended to last for only a short time until someone or something more permanent is found: *an interim government/measure/report* ◆ *The vice president took power in the interim period before the election.* **2** (*finance*) calculated before the final results of something are known **SYN** PROVISIONAL: *interim figures/profits/results*
- *noun*
IDM **in the interim** during the period of time between two events; until a particular event happens: *Despite everything that had happened in the interim, they remained good friends.* ◆ *Her new job does not start until May and she will continue in the old job in the interim.*

in·te·ri·or 🔑 /ɪnˈtɪriər/ *noun, adj.*
- *noun* **1** [C, usually sing.] the inside part of something: *the interior of a building/a car* **ANT** EXTERIOR **2 the interior** [sing.] the central part of a country or continent that is a long way from the coast: *an expedition into the interior of Australia* **3 the Interior** [sing.] a country's own affairs rather than those that involve other countries: *the Department/Secretary of the Interior*
- *adj.* [only before noun] connected with the inside part of something: *interior walls* **ANT** EXTERIOR

in,terior 'decorator *noun* a person whose job is to design and/or decorate a room or the inside of a house, etc. with paint, paper, carpets, etc. ▶ **in,terior deco'ration** *noun* [U]: *an interior decoration project*

in,terior de'sign *noun* [U] the art or job of choosing the paint, carpets, furniture, etc. to decorate the inside of a house ▶ **in,terior de'signer** *noun*

in,terior 'monologue *noun* (in literature) a piece of writing that expresses a character's inner thoughts and feelings

in·ter·ject /ˌɪntərˈdʒɛkt/ *verb* [T, I] + **speech** | ~ **(sth)** (*formal*) to interrupt what someone is saying with your opinion or a remark: *"You're wrong," interjected Susan.*

in·ter·jec·tion /ˌɪntərˈdʒɛkʃn/ *noun* (*grammar*) a short sound, word, or phrase spoken suddenly to express an emotion. *Oh!*, *Look out!*, and *Ow!* are interjections. **SYN** EXCLAMATION

in·ter·lace /ˌɪntərˈleɪs; ˈɪntərˌleɪs/ *verb* [T, I] ~ **(sth) (with sth)** (*formal*) to twist things together over and under each other; to be twisted together in this way: *Her hair was interlaced with ribbons and flowers.* ◆ *interlacing branches*

in·ter·lan·guage /ˈɪntərˌlæŋgwɪdʒ/ *noun* [U, C] (*linguistics*) a language system produced by someone who is learning a language, which has features of the language which they are learning and also of their first language

in·ter·leave /ˌɪntərˈliv/ *verb* ~ **sth (with sth)** to put something, especially thin layers of something, between things

in·ter·lin·e·ar /ˌɪntərˈlɪniər/ adj. (technical) written or printed between the lines of a text

in·ter·lin·gual /ˌɪntərˈlɪŋgwəl/ adj. (linguistics) **1** using, between, or relating to two different languages: interlingual communication **2** relating to an INTERLANGUAGE

in·ter·link /ˌɪntərˈlɪŋk/ verb [T, usually passive, I] ~ (sth) (with sth) to connect things; to be connected with other things: The two processes are interlinked. ◆ a series of short interlinking stories

in·ter·lock /ˌɪntərˈlɑk/ verb [I, T] ~ (sth) (with sth) to fit or be fastened firmly together: interlocking shapes/systems/pieces

in·ter·loc·u·tor /ˌɪntərˈlɑkyətər/ noun (formal) **1** a person taking part in a conversation with you **2** a person or an organization that talks to another person or organization on behalf of someone else

in·ter·lop·er /ˈɪntərˌloupər/ noun a person who is present in a place or a situation where they do not belong **SYN** INTRUDER

in·ter·lude /ˈɪntərˌlud/ noun **1** a period of time between two events during which something different happens: a romantic interlude (= a short romantic relationship) ◆ Apart from a brief interlude of peace, the war lasted nine years. **2** a short piece of music between the parts of a longer piece of music or between the parts of a play: a musical interlude

in·ter·mar·ry /ˌɪntərˈmæri/ verb (in·ter·mar·ries, in·ter·mar·ry·ing, in·ter·mar·ried, in·ter·mar·ried) **1** [I] to marry someone of a different race or from a different country or a different religious group: Blacks and whites often intermarried (= married each other). ◆ ~ with sb They were not forbidden to intermarry with the local people. **2** [I] to marry someone within your own family or group: cousins who intermarry ▶ **in·ter·mar·riage** /-ˈmærɪdʒ/ noun [U, C]: intermarriage between blacks and whites

in·ter·me·di·ary /ˌɪntərˈmidiˌɛri/ noun (pl. in·ter·me·di·ar·ies) ~ (between A and B) a person or an organization that helps other people or organizations to make an agreement by being a means of communication between them **SYN** GO-BETWEEN, MEDIATOR: Financial institutions act as intermediaries between lenders and borrowers. ◆ All talks have so far been conducted through an intermediary. ▶ **in·ter·me·di·ary** adj. [only before noun]: to play an intermediary role in the dispute

in·ter·me·di·ate **AWL** /ˌɪntərˈmidiət/ adj., noun
● adj. **1** [usually before noun] located between two places, things, states, etc.: an intermediate stage/step in a process ◆ ~ between A and B Liquid crystals are considered to be intermediate between liquid and solid. **2** having more than a basic knowledge of something but not yet advanced; suitable for someone who is at this level: an intermediate skier/student, etc. ◆ an intermediate textbook ◆ pre-/upper-intermediate classes
● noun a person who is learning something and who has more than a basic knowledge of it but is not yet advanced

inter·mediate tech·nology noun [U] technology that is suitable for use in developing countries as it is cheap and simple and can use local materials

in·ter·ment /ɪnˈtɜrmənt/ noun [C, U] (formal) the act of burying a dead person **SYN** BURIAL ➔ see also INTER

in·ter·mesh /ˌɪntərˈmɛʃ/ verb [I] (of two objects or parts) to fit closely together: intermeshing cogs

in·ter·mez·zo /ˌɪntərˈmɛtsoʊ; -ˈmɛdzoʊ/ noun (pl. in·ter·mez·zi /-ˈmɛtsi; -ˈmɛdzi/ or in·ter·mez·zos) (from Italian, music) a short piece of music for the ORCHESTRA that is played between two parts in an OPERA or other musical performance

in·ter·mi·na·ble /ɪnˈtɜrmənəbl/ adj. lasting a very long time and therefore boring or annoying **SYN** ENDLESS: an interminable speech/wait/discussion ◆ The drive seemed interminable. ▶ **in·ter·mi·na·bly** /-bli/ adv.: The meeting dragged on interminably.

in·ter·min·gle /ˌɪntərˈmɪŋgl/ verb [T, I] (formal) to mix people, ideas, colors, etc. together; to be mixed in this way: ~ A with B The book intermingles fact with fiction. ◆ ~ A and B The book intermingles fact and fiction. ◆ ~ (with sb/sth) tourists and local people intermingling in the market square

in·ter·mis·sion /ˌɪntərˈmɪʃn/ noun [C, U] **1** a short period of time between the parts of a play, movie, etc.: Coffee was served during the intermission. ◆ After intermission, the second band played. **2** a period of time during which something stops before continuing again: This state of affairs lasted without intermission for a hundred years.

in·ter·mit·tent /ˌɪntərˈmɪtnt/ adj. stopping and starting often over a period of time, but not regularly **SYN** SPORADIC: intermittent bursts of applause ◆ intermittent showers ▶ **in·ter·mit·tent·ly** adv.: Protests continued intermittently throughout November.

in·ter·mix /ˌɪntərˈmɪks/ verb [T, I] ~ (sth) (with sth) to mix things together; to be mixed together: Grass fields were intermixed with areas of woodland.

in·tern noun, verb
● noun /ˈɪntɜrn/ **1** an advanced student of medicine, whose training is nearly finished and who is working in a hospital to get further practical experience **2** a student or new graduate who is getting practical experience in a job, for example during the summer vacation: a summer intern at a law firm ➔ see also INTERNSHIP
● verb /ɪnˈtɜrn/ **1** [I] to work as an intern: She interned at the State House between her sophomore and junior year at college. **2** [T, often passive] ~ sb (in sth) to put someone in prison during a war or for political reasons, although they have not been charged with a crime ➔ see also INTERNEE ▶ **in·tern·ment** /ɪnˈtɜrnmənt/ noun [U]: the internment of suspected terrorists ◆ internment camps

in·ter·nal **AWL** /ɪnˈtɜrnl/ adj.
1 [only before noun] connected with the inside of something: the internal structure of a building ◆ internal doors **ANT** EXTERNAL **2** [only before noun] connected with the inside of your body: internal organs/injuries ◆ The medicine is not for internal use. **ANT** EXTERNAL **3** [usually before noun] involving or concerning only the people who are part of a particular organization rather than people from outside it: an internal investigation ◆ the internal workings of government ◆ internal divisions within the company **ANT** EXTERNAL **4** [only before noun] connected with a country's own affairs rather than those that involve other countries **SYN** DOMESTIC: internal affairs/trade/markets ◆ an internal flight (= within a country) **ANT** EXTERNAL **5** coming from within a thing itself rather than from outside it: a theory which lacks internal consistency (= whose parts are not in agreement with each other) ◆ Some photos contain internal evidence (= fashions, transportation, etc.) that may help to date them. **6** happening or existing in your mind **SYN** INNER: internal rage ▶ **in·ter·nal·ly** **AWL** /-nəli/ adv.: internally connected rooms ◆ The new positions were only advertised internally.

in,ternal–com'bustion ,engine noun a type of engine used in most cars that produces power by burning gas inside

in·ter·nal·ize **AWL** /ɪnˈtɜrnəˌlaɪz/ verb ~ sth (technical) to make a feeling, an attitude, or a belief part of the way you think and behave ➔ compare EXTERNALIZE ▶ **in·ter·nal·i·za·tion** /ɪˌtɜrnələˈzeɪʃn/ noun [U]

in,ternal 'medicine noun [U] the branch of medicine concerned with the treatment of diseases without doing medical operations: He trained in internal medicine at Mt. Sinai Hospital.

the In,ternal 'Revenue ,Service noun [sing.] (abbr. IRS) (in the U.S.) the government department that is responsible for collecting most national taxes, for example income tax

in·ter·na·tion·al /ˌɪntərˈnæʃənl/ adj., noun
● adj. [usually before noun] connected with or involving two or more countries: international trade/law/sports ◆ an international airport/school/company ◆ international relations ◆ a

pianist with an international reputation ▶ **in·ter·na·tion·al·ly** /-ʃənəli/ *adv.*: *internationally famous*

● *noun* a person from a foreign country: *an English course for internationals*

International Relations

trade

- facilitate/regulate trade (with other countries)
- form/join a trading bloc
- live in/compete in a global/the world economy
- support/promote free trade

- adopt/call for/oppose protectionist measures
- erect/impose/reduce/remove trade barriers
- impose/lift/raise/eliminate import tariffs (on sth)
- have/run a huge/large/growing trade surplus/deficit
- embrace/resist/drive globalization

politics and law

- handle/talk about/discuss foreign policy
- pursue an aggressive/a hawkish foreign policy
- require/use/conduct diplomacy
- establish/break off/sever/restore diplomatic relations/ties
- foster/promote/strengthen regional cooperation
- facilitate/achieve economic/political integration
- exercise/defend/protect/transfer/restore/regain national/state/full/limited sovereignty
- consolidate/extend/lose/retain your power (in the region)
- hold/maintain/change/alter/shift the balance of power (in the region)
- cause/create/open/expose/heal/repair a deep/growing/major/serious rift between X and Y

meetings and agreements

- have/hold/host/attend an international conference/an economic forum/a G20 summit
- lead/launch a new round of global/multilateral/world trade negotiations
- send/head/lead/meet a high-level/an official/a trade delegation
- facilitate/begin/start/continue/resume peace talks
- be committed to/be opposed to/disrupt/undermine/derail/sabotage the peace process
- negotiate/achieve a lasting political settlement
- broker/sign a peace deal/agreement/treaty

conflict

- be/constitute/pose a threat to global security
- compromise/endanger/protect national security
- justify/be in favor of/support/be against/oppose military intervention
- threaten/authorize/launch/take/support/oppose unilateral/preemptive military action
- impose/enforce/lift/end economic sanctions/an arms embargo/a naval blockade
- close/protect/secure/patrol the border
- lead/be involved in a peacekeeping operation

aid

- negotiate/announce a $15 billion aid package/an economic stimulus package
- send/provide/request/cut off military aid
- bring/provide emergency/humanitarian relief
- deliver/distribute medical supplies/food supplies
- fund/run a foreign/a local/an international NGO
- reduce/eradicate/combat/fight child/global/world poverty

the ˌInternational ˈDate Line (also ˈDate Line) *noun* [sing.] the imaginary line that goes from north to south through the Pacific Ocean. The date on the west side is different by one day from that on the east side. ⊃ picture at EARTH

the In·ter·na·tio·nale /ˌɪntərnæʃəˈnɑl/ *noun* [sing.] an international SOCIALIST song written in France that was the official ANTHEM of the USSR until 1944

in·ter·na·tion·al·ism /ˌɪntərˈnæʃənəˌlɪzəm/ *noun* [U] the belief that countries should work together in a friendly way

in·ter·na·tion·al·ist /ˌɪntərˈnæʃənəlɪst/ *noun* a person who believes that countries should work together in a friendly way ▶ **in·ter·na·tion·al·ist** *adj.*

in·ter·na·tion·al·ize /ˌɪntərˈnæʃənəˌlaɪz/ *verb* ~ **sth** to bring something under the control or protection of many nations; to make something international ▶ **in·ter·na·tion·al·i·za·tion** /ˌɪntərˌnæʃənələˈzeɪʃn/ *noun* [U]

the Interˌnational Phoˌnetic ˈAlphabet *noun* [sing.] (*abbr.* IPA) an alphabet that is used to show the pronunciation of words in any language

in·ter·ne·cine /ˌɪntərˈnesin; -ˈnisn/ *adj.* [only before noun] (*formal*) happening between members of the same group, country, or organization: *internecine struggles/warfare/feuds*

in·tern·ee /ˌɪntərˈni/ *noun* a person who is put in prison for political reasons, usually without a trial (= who is INTERNED)

In·ter·net 🔑 (also **in·ter·net**) /ˈɪntərˌnɛt/ *noun* usually **the Internet** (also *informal* **the Net**) [sing.] an international computer network connecting other networks and computers from companies, universities, etc.: *I looked it up on the Internet.* ◆ *You can buy our goods over the Internet.* ◆ *All the rooms have access to the Internet/Internet access.* ◆ *an Internet service provider* (= a company that provides you with an Internet connection and services such as e-mail, etc.) ⊃ collocations at E-MAIL ⊃ see also INTRANET, WWW

in·tern·ist /ˈɪnˌtərnɪst; ɪnˈtər-/ *noun* a doctor who is a specialist in internal medicine and who does not usually do medical operations

in·tern·ment ⊃ INTERN

in·tern·ship /ˈɪntərnˌʃɪp/ *noun* **1** a period of time during which a student or new graduate gets practical experience in a job, for example during the summer vacation: *an internship at a television station* **2** a job that an advanced student of medicine, whose training is nearly finished, does in a hospital to get further practical experience

in·ter·of·fice /ˌɪntərˈɔfəs; -ˈɑfəs/ *adj.* [only before noun] connected with or between two offices or departments in the same company: *We received an interoffice memo about health insurance.*

in·ter·op·er·a·ble /ˌɪntərˈɑpərəbl; -ˈɑprəbl/ *adj.* (*technical*) (of computer systems or programs) able to exchange information

in·ter·pen·e·trate /ˌɪntərˈpɛnəˌtreɪt/ *verb* [I, T] ~ **(sth)** (*formal*) to spread completely through something or from one thing to another in each direction ▶ **in·ter·pen·e·tra·tion** /-ˌpɛnəˈtreɪʃn/ *noun* [U, C]

in·ter·per·son·al /ˌɪntərˈpərsənl/ *adj.* [only before noun] connected with relationships between people: *interpersonal skills*

in·ter·plan·e·tar·y /ˌɪntərˈplænəˌtɛri/ *adj.* [only before noun] between planets: *interplanetary travel*

in·ter·play /ˈɪntərˌpleɪ/ *noun* [U, sing.] ~ **(of/between A and B)** (*formal*) the way in which two or more things or people affect each other: *the interplay between politics and the environment* ◆ *the subtle interplay of colors*

In·ter·pol /ˈɪntərˌpoʊl/ *noun* [sing.] an international organization that enables the police forces of different countries to help each other to solve crimes

in·ter·po·late /ɪnˈtərpəˌleɪt/ *verb* (*formal*) **1** + **speech** | ~ **sth** to make a remark that interrupts a conversation SYN INTERJECT: *"But why?" he interpolated.* **2** ~ **sth (into**

ʌ **cup** ə **about** eɪ **say** aɪ **five** ɔɪ **boy** aʊ **now** oʊ **go** ər **bird**

sth) to add something to a piece of writing **SYN** INSERT: *The lines were interpolated into the manuscript at a later date.* **3 ~ sth** (*mathematics*) to add a value into a series by calculating it from surrounding known values ▶ **in·ter·po·la·tion** /ɪnˌtɜːrpəˈleɪʃn/ *noun* [U, C]

in·ter·pose /ˌɪntərˈpoʊz/ *verb* (*formal*) **1 + speech** | **~ sth** to add a question or remark into a conversation: *"Just a minute," Charles interposed. "How do you know?"* **2 ~ sb/sth (between A and B)** to place something between two people or things: *He quickly interposed himself between Mel and the doorway.*

in·ter·pret ⚷ **AWL** /ɪnˈtɜːrprət/ *verb*
1 [T] **~ sth** to explain the meaning of something: *The students were asked to interpret the poem.* **2** [T] to decide that something has a particular meaning and to understand it in this way: **~ sth as sth** *I didn't know whether to interpret her silence as acceptance or refusal.* ◆ **~ sth** *The data can be interpreted in many different ways.* ➔ compare MISINTERPRET **3** [I] **~ (for sb)** to translate one language into another as you hear it: *She couldn't speak much English so her children had to interpret for her.* **4** [T] **~ sth** to perform a piece of music, a role in a play, etc. in a way that shows your feelings about its meaning: *He interpreted the role with a lot of humor.* ▶ **in·ter·pret·a·ble** /ɪnˈtɜːrprətəbl/ *adj.*: *interpretable data*

AWL COLLOCATIONS

interpret

interpret *verb*
▪ **be difficult to**
  The results of the three studies are inconsistent and difficult to interpret.
▪ **~ with caution**
  The results of this study, however, should be interpreted with caution because of several methodological flaws.
▪ **~ within a/the framework** | **~ within a/the context**
  The results should be interpreted within the context of a number of underlying assumptions.
▪ **be interpreted as**
  Typographical errors may be reasonably interpreted as resulting from carelessness.
▪ **broadly** | **narrowly, strictly** | **cautiously** | **accurately, correctly** | **erroneously, incorrectly** | **variously**
  Historians have variously interpreted the treaty's significance.
  The findings should be interpreted cautiously because of the small sample size.
▪ **data, finding, result** | **pattern** | **information** | **study** | **meaning** | **behavior** | **theory** | **text**
  To interpret the results, it is important to understand how the study was organized.

interpretation *noun*
▪ **broad** | **literal, narrow, strict** | **subjective** | **plausible** | **correct** | **erroneous**
  Alexander Hamilton advocated a broad interpretation of the Constitution, which President George Washington endorsed.
▪ **be open to, be subject to**
  Many ethical issues are complex and subject to multiple interpretations.
▪ **defy, preclude** | **complicate** | **confound, contradict** | **challenge, refute** | **favor, support**
  The small sample size precludes further interpretation of this finding.

misinterpret *verb*
▪ **easily** | **completely** | **willfully**
  Every clinician is at risk of making an error when confusing or easily misinterpreted abbreviations or symbols are used.

misinterpretation *noun*
▪ **common** | **gross, serious** | **deliberate** | **possible, potential**
  These small misinterpretations would often lead to gross misinterpretations of the text as a whole.
▪ **be open to, be subject to** | **lead to, result in** | **prone to** | **be based on, rest on** | **avoid, prevent**
  Unfortunately, his conclusions rested on a misinterpretation of the data.

in·ter·pre·ta·tion ⚷ **AWL** /ɪnˌtɜːrprəˈteɪʃn/ *noun* [C, U]
1 the particular way in which something is understood or explained: *Her evidence suggests a different interpretation of the events.* ◆ *It is not possible for everyone to put their own interpretation on the law.* ◆ *Dreams are* **open to interpretation** (= they can be explained in different ways). ➔ collocations at INTERPRET **2** the particular way in which someone chooses to perform a piece of music, a role in a play, etc.: *a modern interpretation of "King Lear"*

in·ter·pret·er /ɪnˈtɜːrprətər/ *noun* **1** a person whose job is to translate what someone is saying into another language: *Speaking* **through an interpreter**, *the President said that the talks were going well.* ◆ *a sign language interpreter* (= a person who translates what someone is saying into sign language for deaf people) ➔ compare TRANSLATOR **2** a person who performs a piece of music or a role in a play in a way that clearly shows their ideas about its meaning: *She is one of the finest interpreters of Debussy's music.* **3** (*computing*) a computer program that changes the instructions of another program into a form that the computer can understand and use

in·ter·pre·tive **AWL** /ɪnˈtɜːrprətɪv/ (also **in·ter·pre·ta·tive** /ɪnˈtɜːrprəˌteɪtɪv/) *adj.* [usually before noun] connected with the particular way in which something is understood, explained, or performed; providing an interpretation: *an interpretive problem* ◆ *an interpretive exhibition*

in·ter·ra·cial /ˌɪntərˈreɪʃl/ *adj.* [only before noun] involving people of different races: *interracial marriage*

in·ter·reg·num /ˌɪntərˈreɡnəm/ *noun* [usually sing.] (*formal*) a period of time during which a country, an organization, etc. does not have a leader and is waiting for a new one

in·ter·re·late /ˌɪntərɪˈleɪt/ *verb* [I, T, usually passive] if two or more things **interrelate**, or if they are **interrelated**, they are closely connected and they affect each other: *a discussion of how the mind and body interrelate* ◆ **~ with sth** *a discussion of how the mind interrelates with the body* ◆ **be interrelated** *a discussion of how the mind and body are interrelated* ▶ **in·ter·re·lat·ed** *adj.*: *a number of interrelated problems*

in·ter·re·la·tion·ship /ˌɪntərɪˈleɪʃnˌʃɪp/ (also **in·ter·re·la·tion** /ˌɪntərɪˈleɪʃn/) *noun* [C, U] **~ (of/between A and B)** the way in which two or more things or people are connected and affect each other

in·ter·ro·gate /ɪnˈterəˌɡeɪt/ *verb* **1 ~ sb** to ask someone a lot of questions over a long period of time, especially in an aggressive way: *He was interrogated by the police for over 12 hours.* **2 ~ sth** (*technical*) to obtain information from a computer or other machine ▶ **in·ter·ro·ga·tion** /ɪnˌterəˈɡeɪʃn/ *noun* [U, C]: *He confessed after four days* **under interrogation.** ◆ *She hated her parents' endless interrogations about where she'd been.* ➔ thesaurus box at INTERVIEW **in·ter·ro·ga·tor** /ɪnˈterəˌɡeɪtər/ *noun*

in·ter·rog·a·tive /ˌɪntəˈrɑːɡətɪv/ *adj., noun*
• *adj.* **1** (*formal*) asking a question; in the form of a question: *an interrogative gesture/remark/sentence* **2** (*grammar*) used in questions: *interrogative pronouns/determiners/adverbs* (= for example, *who, which*, and *why*) ▶ **in·ter·rog·a·tive·ly** *adv.*
• *noun* (*grammar*) a question word, especially a pronoun or a determiner such as *who* or *which*

ɪr **near**   er **hair**   ɑr **car**   ɔr **north**   ʊr **tour**   ɑ̃ **denouement**   p **pen**   b **bad**

in·ter·rog·a·to·ry /ˌɪntəˈrɑgəˌtɔri/ *adj., noun*
- *adj.* seeming to be asking a question or demanding an answer to something: *an interrogatory stare*
- *noun* (*pl.* in·ter·rog·a·to·ries) (*law*) a written question, asked by one party in a legal case, which must be answered by the other party

in·ter·rupt 🔑 /ˌɪntəˈrʌpt/ *verb*
1 [I, T] to say or do something that makes someone stop what they are saying or doing: *Sorry to interrupt, but there's someone to see you.* ♦ **~ with sth** *Would you mind not interrupting with questions all the time?* ♦ **~ sb/sth (with sth)** *I hope I'm not interrupting you.* ♦ *They were interrupted by a knock at the door.* ♦ **~ (sb) + speech** *"I have a question," she interrupted.* **2** [T] **~ sth** to stop something for a short time: *The game was interrupted several times by rain.* ♦ *We interrupt this program to bring you an important news bulletin.* **3** [T] **~ sth** to stop a line, surface, view, etc. from being even or continuous

in·ter·rup·tion 🔑 /ˌɪntəˈrʌpʃn/ *noun* [C, U]
1 something that temporarily stops an activity or a situation; a time when an activity is stopped: *an interruption in the power supply* ♦ *I managed to work for two hours without interruption.* **2** the act of interrupting someone or something and of stopping them from speaking: *He ignored her interruptions.* **2** *She spoke for 20 minutes without interruption.*

in·ter·scho·las·tic /ˌɪntərskəˈlæstɪk/ *adj.* [only before noun] (of a sports competition) involving or held between different schools: *an interscholastic athletic program*

in·ter·sect /ˌɪntərˈsɛkt/ *verb* **1** [I, T] (of lines, roads, etc.) to meet or cross each other: **~ (sth)** *a pattern of intersecting streets* ♦ *The lines intersect at right angles.* ♦ **~ with sth** *The path intersected with a busy road.* **2** [T, usually passive] **~ sth (with sth)** to divide an area by crossing it: *The landscape is intersected with spectacular gorges.*

in·ter·sec·tion /ˈɪntərˌsɛkʃn; ˌɪntərˈsɛkʃn/ *noun* **1** [C] a place where two or more roads, lines, etc. meet or cross each other: *Traffic lights have been placed at all major intersections.* **2** [U] the act of intersecting something

in·ter·sex /ˈɪntərˌsɛks/ *noun* [U] (*medical*) the physical condition of being partly male and partly female

in·ter·sperse /ˌɪntərˈspɜrs/ *verb* **be interspersed with/in sth** if things are **interspersed with/in** other things, the other things are put among or between them: *Lectures will be interspersed with practical demonstrations.*

in·ter·state /ˈɪntərˌsteɪt/ *adj., noun*
- *adj.* [only before noun] between states: *interstate commerce*
- *noun* (also ˌinterstate ˈhighway) a wide road, with at least two lanes in each direction, where traffic can travel fast for long distances across many states. You can only enter and leave interstates on special RAMPS.

in·ter·stel·lar /ˌɪntərˈstɛlər/ *adj.* [only before noun] between the stars in the sky ➔ compare STELLAR

in·ter·stice /ɪnˈtɜrstəs/ *noun* [usually pl.] (*formal*) a small crack or space in something

in·ter·sti·tial /ˌɪntərˈstɪʃl/ *adj.* (*medical*) in or related to small spaces between the parts of an organ or between groups of cells or TISSUES: *interstitial cells*

in·ter·tex·tu·al·i·ty /ˌɪntərˌtɛkstʃuˈæləti/ *noun* [U] (*technical*) the relationship between texts, especially literature

in·ter·twine /ˌɪntərˈtwaɪn/ *verb* **1** [I, T, usually passive] if two or more things **intertwine** or are **intertwined**, they are twisted together so that they are very difficult to separate: *intertwining branches* ♦ **~ sth (with sth)** *a necklace of rubies intertwined with pearls* **2** [T, usually passive, I] **~ (sth)** to be or become very closely connected with something or someone else: *Their political careers had become closely intertwined.*

in·ter·val 🔑 **AWL** /ˈɪntərvl/ *noun*
1 a period of time between two events: *The interval between major earthquakes might be 200 years.* **2** [usually pl.] a short period during which something different happens from what is happening the rest of the time: *She's delirious, but has lucid intervals.* **3** (*music*) a difference in PITCH (= how high or low a note sounds) between two notes: *an interval of one octave*
IDM **at (…) intervals 1** with time between: *Buses to the city leave at regular intervals.* ♦ *The runners started at 5-minute intervals.* **2** with spaces between: *Traffic cones were positioned at intervals along the road.*

ˈinterval ˌtraining *noun* [U] sports training consisting of different activities which require different speeds or amounts of effort

in·ter·vene **AWL** /ˌɪntərˈvin/ *verb* **1** [I] to become involved in a situation in order to improve or help it: *She might have been killed if the neighbors hadn't intervened.* ♦ **~ in sth** *The President intervened personally in the crisis.* **2** [T, I] (**+ speech**) to interrupt someone when they are speaking in order to say something: *"But," she intervened, "what about the others?"* **3** [I] to happen in a way that delays something or prevents it from happening: *They were planning to get married and then the war intervened.* **4** [I] (*formal*) to exist between two events or places: *I saw nothing of her during the years that intervened.* ▸ **in·ter·ven·tion** **AWL** /ˌɪntərˈvɛnʃn/ *noun* [U, C]: **~ (in sth)** *calls for government intervention to save the steel industry* ♦ *armed/military intervention*

in·ter·ven·ing **AWL** /ˌɪntərˈvinɪŋ/ *adj.* [only before noun] coming or existing between two events, dates, objects, etc.: *Little had changed in the intervening years.*

in·ter·ven·tion·ism /ˌɪntərˈvɛnʃəˌnɪzəm/ *noun* [U] the policy or practice of a government influencing the economy of its own country, or of becoming involved in the affairs of other countries ▸ **in·ter·ven·tion·ist** /-ʃənɪst/ *adj., noun*: *interventionist policies*

THESAURUS

interview

interrogation ♦ audience ♦ consultation

These are all words for a meeting or occasion when someone is asked for information, opinions, or advice.

interview a formal meeting at which someone is asked questions, for example, to see if they are suitable for a particular job or course of study, or in order to find out their opinions about something: *a job interview*

interrogation the process of asking someone a lot of questions, especially in an aggressive way, in order to get information; an occasion on which this is done: *He confessed after four days of interrogation.*

audience a formal meeting with an important person: *The Pope granted her a private audience.*

consultation a meeting with an expert, such as a lawyer or doctor, to get advice or treatment: *A 30-minute consultation will cost $50.*

PATTERNS
- an **in-depth** interview/consultation
- a **police** interview/interrogation
- to **have/request** a(n) interview/audience/consultation **with** sb
- to **give/grant** sb a(n) interview/audience/consultation
- to **carry out/conduct** an interview/interrogation

---

in·ter·view 🔑 /ˈɪntərˌvyu/ *noun, verb*
- *noun* **1** a formal meeting at which someone is asked questions to see if they are suitable for a particular job, or for a course of study at a college, university, etc.: *a job interview* ♦ *to be called for interview* ♦ **~ for a job, etc.** *He has an interview next week for the manager's job.* ➔ collocations at JOB **2** a meeting (often a public one) at which a journalist

asks someone questions in order to find out their opinions: *a television/radio/newspaper interview* ◆ *~* **(with sb)** *an interview with the new governor* ◆ *to give an interview* (= to agree to answer questions) ◆ *Yesterday, in a televised* **interview**, *the senator denied the reports.* ◆ *to conduct an* **interview** (= to ask someone questions in public) ◆ *The interview was published in all the papers.* **3 ~ (with sb)** a private meeting between people when questions are asked and answered: *an interview with the careers adviser*

● **verb 1** [T, I] **~ (someone) (for a job, etc.)** to talk to someone and ask them questions at a formal meeting to find out if they are suitable for a job, course of study, etc.: *Which position are you being interviewed for?* ◆ *We interviewed ten people for the job.* **2** [I] **~ (for a job, etc.)** to talk to someone and answer questions at a formal meeting to get a job, a place in a course of study, etc.: *The Web site gives you tips on interviewing for colleges.* ◆ *If you don't interview well you are unlikely to get the job.* **3** [T] to ask someone questions about their life, opinions, etc., especially on the radio or television or for a newspaper or magazine: **~ sb about sth** *Next week, I will be interviewing Spielberg about his latest movie.* ◆ *~* **sb** *The senator declined to be interviewed.* **4** [T] **~ sb (about sth)** to ask someone questions at a private meeting: *The police are waiting to interview the injured man.* ▶ **in·ter·view·ing** *noun* [U]: *The research involves in-depth interviewing.* ◆ *interviewing techniques* **in·ter·view·ee** /ˌɪntərvyuˈi/ *noun* the person who answers the questions in an interview

in·ter·view·er /ˈɪntərˌvyuər/ *noun* the person who asks the questions in an interview

in·ter·war /ˌɪntərˈwɔr/ *adj.* [only before noun] happening or existing between the First and the Second World Wars: *the interwar years/period*

in·ter·weave /ˌɪntərˈwiv/ *verb* (**in·ter·wove** /-ˈwoʊv/, **in·ter·wo·ven** /-ˈwoʊvn/) [T, usually passive, I] **~ (sth) (with sth)** to twist together two or more pieces of thread, wool, etc.: *The blue fabric was interwoven with red and gold thread.* ◆ (*figurative*) *The problems are inextricably interwoven* (= very closely connected).

in·tes·tate /ɪnˈtɛsteɪt/ *adj.* (*law*) not having made a WILL (= a legal document that says what is to happen to a person's property when they die) ▶ **in·tes·ta·cy** /ɪnˈtɛstəsi/ *noun* [U]

in·tes·tin·al **for·ti·tude** *noun* (*formal* or *humorous*) the courage and determination necessary to do something difficult or unpleasant (used when you want to avoid using the word GUTS): *He did not have the intestinal fortitude to implement the changes.*

in·tes·tine /ɪnˈtɛstən/ *noun* [usually pl.] a long tube in the body between the stomach and the ANUS. Food passes from the stomach to the **small intestine** and from there to the **large intestine**. ➔ picture at BODY ▶ **in·tes·ti·nal** /ɪn ˈtɛstənl/ *adj.* [usually before noun]

in·ti·ma·cy /ˈɪntəməsi/ *noun* (pl. **in·ti·ma·cies**) **1** [U] the state of having a close personal relationship with someone **2** [C, usually pl.] a thing that a person says or does to someone that they know very well **3** [U] (*formal* or *law*) sexual activity, especially an act of SEXUAL INTERCOURSE

in·ti·mate *adj.*, *verb*, *noun*

● **adj.** /ˈɪntəmət/ **1** (of people) having a close and friendly relationship: *intimate friends* ◆ *We're not* **on intimate terms with** *our neighbors.* **2** private and personal, often in a sexual way: *The article revealed intimate details about his family life.* ◆ *the most intimate parts of her body* **3** (of a place or situation) encouraging close, friendly relationships, sometimes of a sexual nature: *an intimate restaurant* ◆ *He knew an intimate little bar where they would not be disturbed.* **4** (of knowledge) very detailed and thorough: *an intimate knowledge of the countryside* **5** (of a link between things) very close: *an intimate connection between class and educational success* **6 ~ (with sb)** (*formal* or *law*) having a sexual relationship with someone ▶ **in·ti·mate·ly** *adv.*: *intimately connected/linked/related* ◆ *an area of the country that he knew intimately* ◆ *She was intimately involved in the project.*

● **verb** /ˈɪntəˌmeɪt/ (*formal*) to let someone know what you think or mean in an indirect way **SYN** MAKE KNOWN: **~ sth (to sb)** *He has already intimated to us his intention to retire.* ◆ **~ (that)…** *He has already intimated (that) he intends to retire.*

● **noun** /ˈɪntəmət/ (*formal*) a close personal friend

in·ti·ma·tion /ˌɪntəˈmeɪʃn/ *noun* [C, U] (*formal*) the act of stating something or of making it known, especially in an indirect way: *There was no intimation from his doctor that his condition was serious.*

in·tim·i·date /ɪnˈtɪməˌdeɪt/ *verb* **~ sb (into sth/into doing sth)** to frighten or threaten someone so that they will do what you want: *They were accused of intimidating people into voting for them.* ◆ *She refused to be intimidated by their threats.* ▶ **in·tim·i·da·tion** /ɪnˌtɪməˈdeɪʃn/ *noun* [U]: *the intimidation of witnesses*

in·tim·i·dat·ed /ɪnˈtɪməˌdeɪtəd/ *adj.* [not usually before noun] feeling frightened and not confident in a particular situation: *We try to make sure students don't feel intimidated on their first day at school.*

in·tim·i·dat·ing /ɪnˈtɪməˌdeɪtɪŋ/ *adj.* frightening in a way that makes a person feel less confident: *an intimidating manner* ◆ *~* **for/to sb** *This kind of questioning can be very intimidating to children.*

in·to 🔑 /ˈɪntə; strong form and before vowels ˈɪntu/ *prep.* **HELP** For the special uses of **into** in phrasal verbs, look at the entries for the verbs. For example, **lay into sb/sth** is in the phrasal verb section at **lay**. **1** to a position in or inside something: *Come into the house.* ◆ *She dove into the water.* ◆ *He threw the letter into the fire.* ◆ (*figurative*) *She turned and walked off into the night.* **2** in the direction of something: *Speak clearly into the microphone.* ◆ *Driving into the sun, we had to shade our eyes.* **3** to a point at which you hit someone or something: *The truck crashed into a parked car.* **4** to a point during a period of time: *She worked late into the night.* ◆ *He didn't get married until he was well into his forties.* **5** used to show a change in state: *The fruit can be made into jam.* ◆ *Can you translate this passage into German?* ◆ *They came into power in 2008.* ◆ *She was sliding into depression.* **6** used to show the result of an action: *He was shocked into a confession of guilt.* **7** about or concerning something: *an inquiry into safety procedures* **8** used when you are dividing numbers: *3 into 24 is 8.*

IDM **be into sb for sth** (*informal*) to owe someone money or be owed money by someone: *By the time he'd fixed the leak, I was into him for $500.* ◆ *The bank was into her for $100,000.* **be into sth** (*informal*) to be interested in something in an active way: *He's into surfing in a big way.*

in·tol·er·able /ɪnˈtɑlərəbl/ *adj.* so bad or difficult that you cannot TOLERATE it; completely unacceptable **SYN** UNBEARABLE: *an intolerable burden/situation* ◆ *The heat was intolerable.* ▶ **in·tol·er·ably** /-bli/ *adv.*: *intolerably hot*

in·tol·er·ant /ɪnˈtɑlərənt/ *adj.* **1 ~ (of sb/sth)** (*disapproving*) not willing to accept ideas or ways of behaving that are different from your own **ANT** TOLERANT **2** (*technical*) not able to eat particular foods, use particular medicines, etc.: *recipes for people who are gluten intolerant* ▶ **in·tol·er·ance** /-rəns/ *noun* [U, C]: *religious intolerance* ◆ *an intolerance to dairy products* ◆ *lactose intolerance*

in·to·na·tion /ˌɪntəˈneɪʃn; ˌɪntoʊ-/ *noun* **1** [U, C] (*phonetics*) the rise and fall of the voice in speaking, especially as this affects the meaning of what is being said: *intonation patterns* ◆ *In English, some questions have a rising intonation.* ➔ compare STRESS **2** [U] (*music*) the quality of playing or singing exactly in tune

in·tone /ɪnˈtoʊn/ *verb* **~ sth** | **+ speech** (*formal*) to say something in a slow and serious voice without much expression: *The priest intoned the final prayer.*

in to·to /ˌɪn ˈtoʊtoʊ/ *adv.* (from *Latin*, *formal*) completely; including all parts

in·tox·i·cant /ɪnˈtɑksəkənt/ *noun* (*technical*) a substance such as alcohol that produces false feelings of pleasure and a lack of control

in·tox·i·cat·ed /ɪnˈtɑksəˌkeɪtəd/ adj. (formal) **1** under the influence of alcohol or drugs: *He was arrested for DWI* (= driving while intoxicated). **2** ~ (by/with sb/sth) very excited by something, so that you cannot think clearly: *intoxicated with success* ▶ **in·tox·i·cate** verb ~ **sb**

in·tox·i·cat·ing /ɪnˈtɑksəˌkeɪtɪŋ/ adj. (formal) **1** (of drinks) containing alcohol **2** making you feel excited so that you cannot think clearly: *Power can be intoxicating.* ▶ **in·tox·i·ca·tion** /ɪnˌtɑksəˈkeɪʃn/ noun [U]

intra- /ˈɪntrə/ prefix (in adjectives and adverbs) inside; within: *intravenous* ◆ *intradepartmental* (= within a department) ⊃ compare INTER-

in·trac·ta·ble /ɪnˈtræktəbl/ adj. (formal) (of a problem or a person) very difficult to deal with ANT TRACTABLE ▶ **in·trac·ta·bil·i·ty** /ɪnˌtræktəˈbɪləti/ noun [U]

in·tra·mu·ral /ˌɪntrəˈmyʊrəl/ adj. taking place within a single institution, especially a school or college: *Jeff played intramural basketball in high school.*

in·tra·mus·cu·lar /ˌɪntrəˈmʌskyələr/ adj. (medical) happening inside a muscle or put into a muscle: *intramuscular pain* ◆ *an intramuscular injection*

in·tra·net /ˈɪntrəˌnɛt/ noun (computing) a computer network that is private to a company, university, etc. but is connected to and uses the same software as the Internet

in·tran·si·gent /ɪnˈtrænsədʒənt; -ˈtrænzə-/ adj. (formal, disapproving) (of people) unwilling to change their opinions or behavior in a way that would be helpful to others SYN STUBBORN ▶ **in·tran·si·gence** /-dʒəns/ noun [U]

in·tran·si·tive /ɪnˈtrænsətɪv; -ˈtrænzə-/ adj. (grammar) (of verbs) used without a DIRECT OBJECT: *The verb "die" as in "He died suddenly," is intransitive.* ANT TRANSITIVE ▶ **in·tran·si·tive·ly** adv.: *The verb is being used intransitively.*

in·tra·state /ˈɪntrəˌsteɪt/ adj. [only before noun] within a state: *Local calls are charged at the same rate as intrastate calls.*

in·tra·u·ter·ine /ˌɪntrəˈyutərən; -ˌraɪn/ adj. (medical) within the UTERUS

ˌintrauterine deˈvice noun = IUD

in·tra·ve·nous /ˌɪntrəˈvinəs/ adj. (abbr. IV) (medical) (of drugs or food) going into a VEIN: *intravenous fluids* ◆ *an intravenous injection* ◆ *an intravenous drug user* ▶ **in·tra·ve·nous·ly** adv.

in·trep·id /ɪnˈtrɛpəd/ adj. (formal, often humorous) very brave; not afraid of danger or difficulties SYN FEARLESS: *an intrepid explorer*

in·tri·ca·cy /ˈɪntrɪkəsi/ noun **1** in·tri·ca·cies [pl.] the ~ of sth the complicated parts or details of something: *the intricacies of economic policy* **2** [U] the fact of having complicated parts, details, or patterns: *the intricacy of the design*

in·tri·cate /ˈɪntrɪkət/ adj. having a lot of different parts and small details that fit together: *intricate patterns* ◆ *an intricate network of loyalties and relationships* ▶ **in·tri·cate·ly** adv.: *intricately carved*

in·trigue verb, noun
• **verb** /ɪnˈtrig/ **1** [T, often passive] ~ **sb** | it intrigues sb that... to make someone very interested so that they want to know more about something: *You've really intrigued me—tell me more!* **2** [I] ~ (with sb) (against sb) (formal) to secretly plan with other people to harm someone
• **noun** /ˈɪntrig; ɪnˈtrig/ **1** [U] the activity of making secret plans in order to achieve an aim, often by tricking people: *political intrigue* ◆ *The young heroine steps into a web of intrigue in the academic world.* **2** [C] a secret plan or relationship, especially one which involves someone else being tricked: *I soon learned about all the intrigues and scandals that went on in the little town.* **3** [U] the atmosphere of interest and excitement that surrounds something secret or important

in·trigued /ɪnˈtrigd/ adj. [not usually before noun] very interested in something or someone and wanting to know more about it/them: *He was intrigued by her story.* ◆ ~ to do sth *I'm intrigued to know what you thought of the movie.*

in·tri·guing /ɪnˈtrigɪŋ/ adj. very interesting because of being unusual or not having an obvious answer: *These discoveries raise intriguing questions.* ◆ *an intriguing possibility* ◆ *He found her intriguing.* ▶ **in·tri·guing·ly** adv.

in·trin·sic AWL /ɪnˈtrɪnzɪk; -sɪk/ adj. belonging to or part of the real nature of something or someone: *the intrinsic value of education* ◆ *These tasks were repetitive, lengthy, and lacking any intrinsic interest.* ◆ ~ to sth *Small local shops are intrinsic to the town's character.* ⊃ compare EXTRINSIC ▶ **in·trin·si·cally** AWL /-kli/ adv.: *There is nothing intrinsically wrong with the idea* (= it is good in itself but there may be outside circumstances that mean it is not suitable).

in·tro /ˈɪntroʊ/ noun (pl. in·tros) (informal) an introduction to something, especially to a piece of music or writing

in·tro·duce 🔑 /ˌɪntrəˈdus/ verb
▸ PEOPLE **1** to tell two or more people who have not met before what each other's names are; to tell someone what your name is: ~ **sb** *Can I introduce my wife?* ◆ ~ A to B (as sth) *He introduced me to a Greek girl at the party.* ◆ ~ A and B *We've already been introduced.* ◆ ~ **yourself (to sb)** *Can I introduce myself? I'm Helen Robins.* ◆ *"Kay, this is Steve." "Yes, I know—we've already introduced ourselves."*
▸ TV/RADIO SHOW **2** ~ **sb/sth** to be the main speaker in a television or radio show, who gives details about the show and who presents the people who are in it; to tell the audience the name of the person who is going to speak or perform: *The next program will be introduced by Mary David.* ◆ *I'd like to introduce my first guest on the show tonight...*
▸ NEW EXPERIENCE **3** to make someone learn about something or do something for the first time: ~ **sb to sth** *The first lecture introduces students to the main topics of the course.* ◆ ~ **sth (to sb)** *It was she who first introduced the pleasures of sailing to me.*
▸ NEW PRODUCT/LAW **4** to make something available for use, discussion, etc. for the first time SYN BRING IN: ~ **sth** *The company is introducing a new range of products this year.* ◆ *The new law was introduced in 2007.* ◆ ~ **sth into/to sth** *We want to introduce the latest technology into schools.*
▸ PLANT/ANIMAL/DISEASE **5** ~ **sth (to/into sth)** to bring a plant, an animal, or a disease to a place for the first time: *Vegetation patterns changed when goats were introduced to the island.*
▸ START **6** ~ **sth** to be the start of something new: *Bands from London introduced the craze for this kind of music.* ◆ *A slow theme introduces the first movement.*
▸ IN CONGRESS **7** ~ **sth** to formally present a proposed new law so that it can be discussed: *to introduce a bill (before Congress)*
▸ ADD **8** ~ **sth (into sth)** (formal) to put something into something: *Particles of glass had been introduced into the baby food.*

in·tro·duc·tion /ˌɪntrəˈdʌkʃn/ noun
▸ BRINGING INTO USE/TO A PLACE **1** [U] the act of bringing something into use or existence for the first time, or of bringing something to a place for the first time: *the introduction of new manufacturing methods* ◆ *the introduction of compulsory military service* ◆ *the 1,000th anniversary of the introduction of Christianity to Russia* **2** [C] a thing that is brought into use or introduced to a place for the first time: *The book lists plants suitable for your flower garden, among them many new introductions.*
▸ OF PEOPLE **3** [C] ~ **(to sb)** the act of making one person formally known to another, in which you tell each the other's name: *Introductions were made and the conversation started to flow.* ◆ *Our speaker today needs no introduction* (= is already well known). ◆ *a letter of introduction* (= a letter that tells someone who you are, written by someone who knows both you and the person reading the letter)
▸ FIRST EXPERIENCE **4** [sing.] ~ **(to sth)** a person's first experience of something: *This album was my first introduction to modern jazz.*
▸ OF BOOK/SPEECH **5** [C, U] ~ **(to sth)** the first part of a book or speech that gives a general idea of what is to follow: *a brief introduction* ◆ *a book with an excellent introduction and notes* ◆

| h **hat** | m **man** | n **no** | ŋ **sing** | l **leg** | r **red** | y **yes** | w **wet**

By way of introduction, let me give you the background to the story. ⊃ compare PREFACE

▸ TO SUBJECT **6** [C] ~ **(to sth)** a book or course for people beginning to study a subject: *An Introduction to Astronomy* ◆ *It's a useful introduction to an extremely complex subject.*

▸ IN MUSIC **7** [C] (*music*) a short section at the beginning of a piece of music: *an eight-bar introduction*

in·tro·duc·to·ry /ˌɪntrəˈdʌktəri/ *adj.* **1** written or said at the beginning of something as an introduction to what follows SYN OPENING: *introductory chapters/paragraphs/remarks* **2** intended as an introduction to a subject or an activity for people who have never done it before: *introductory courses/lectures* **3** offered for a short time only, when a product is first on sale: *a special introductory price of just $10* ◆ *This introductory offer is for three days only.*

in·tro·spec·tion /ˌɪntrəˈspɛkʃn/ *noun* [U], the careful examination of your own thoughts, feelings, and reasons for behaving in a particular way

in·tro·spec·tive /ˌɪntrəˈspɛktɪv/ *adj.* tending to think a lot about your own thoughts, feelings, etc.

in·tro·vert /ˈɪntrəˌvərt/ *noun* a quiet person who is more interested in their own thoughts and feelings than in spending time with other people ANT EXTROVERT ▸ **in·tro·ver·sion** /ˌɪntrəˈvərʒn/ *noun* [U]

in·tro·vert·ed /ˈɪntrəˌvərtəd/ (also **in·tro·vert**) *adj.* more interested in your own thoughts and feelings than in spending time with other people ANT EXTROVERT

in·trude /ɪnˈtrud/ *verb* **1** [I] to go or be somewhere where you are not wanted or are not supposed to be: *I'm sorry to intrude, but I need to talk to someone.* ◆ ~ **into/on/upon sb/sth** *legislation to stop newspapers from intruding on people's private lives* **2** [I] ~ **(on/into/upon sth)** to disturb something or have an unpleasant effect on it: *The sound of the telephone intruded into his dreams.*

in·trud·er /ɪnˈtrudər/ *noun* **1** a person who enters a building or an area illegally **2** a person who is somewhere where they are not wanted: *The people in the room seemed to regard her as an unwelcome intruder.*

in·tru·sion /ɪnˈtruʒn/ *noun* [U, C] **1** something that affects a situation or people's lives in a way that they do not want: ~ **(on/upon sth)** *They claim the noise from the new airport is an intrusion on their lives.* ◆ ~ **(into sth)** *This was another example of press intrusion into the affairs of celebrities.* **2** ~ **(into/on/upon sth)** the act of entering a place which is private or where you may not be wanted: *She apologized for the intrusion but said she had an urgent message.*

in·tru·sive /ɪnˈtrusɪv/ *adj.* too noticeable, direct, etc. in a way that is disturbing or annoying: *intrusive questions* ◆ *The constant presence of the media was very intrusive.*

in·tu·bate /ˈɪntuˌbeɪt/ *verb* [T, I] ~ **(sb/sth)** to put a tube into a hollow space in the body, for example to allow a person to breathe: *They managed to intubate the victim inside the wrecked car.* ◆ *to intubate the trachea* ◆ *We made the decision not to intubate.*

in·tu·it /ɪnˈtuət/ *verb* ~ **that...** | ~ **sth** | ~ **what, why, etc....** (*formal*) to know that something is true based on your feelings rather than on facts, what someone tells you, etc.: *She intuited that something was badly wrong.*

in·tu·i·tion /ˌɪntuˈɪʃn/ *noun* **1** [U] the ability to know something by using your feelings rather than considering the facts **2** [C] ~ **(that...)** an idea or a strong feeling that something is true although you cannot explain why: *I had an intuition that something awful was about to happen.*

in·tu·i·tive /ɪnˈtuətɪv/ *adj.* **1** (of ideas) obtained by using your feelings rather than by considering the facts: *He had an intuitive sense of what the reader wanted.* **2** (of people) able to understand something by using feelings rather than by considering the facts **3** (of computer software, etc.) easy to understand and to use ▸ **in·tu·i·tive·ly** *adv.*: *Intuitively, she knew that he was lying.*

In·u·it /ˈɪnyuət; ˈɪnuət/ *noun* [pl.] (*sing.* **I·nuk** /ɪˈnuk; ˈɪnʊk/) a race of people from northern Canada and parts of Green-

land and Alaska. The name is sometimes also wrongly used to refer to people from Siberia and S. and W. Alaska. ⊃ compare ESKIMO

I·nuk·ti·tut /ɪˈnʊktəˌtʊt; ɪˈnʊktəˌtut/ *noun* [U] the language of the Inuit people

in·un·date /ˈɪnʌnˌdeɪt/ *verb* [usually passive] **1** ~ **sb (with sth)** to give or send someone so many things that they cannot deal with them all SYN OVERWHELM, SWAMP: *We have been inundated with offers of help.* **2** ~ **sth** (*formal*) to cover an area of land with a large amount of water SYN FLOOD ▸ **in·un·da·tion** /ˌɪnʌnˈdeɪʃn/ *noun* [U, C]

in·ure /ɪˈnʊr; ɪˈnyʊr/ *verb*
PHR V **i·nure sb/yourself to sth** (*formal*) to make someone/yourself get used to something unpleasant so that they/you are no longer strongly affected by it

in·vade /ɪnˈveɪd/ *verb* **1** [I, T] to enter a country, town, etc. using military force in order to take control of it: *Troops invaded on August 9th that year.* ◆ ~ **sth** *When did the Romans invade Britain?* **2** [T] ~ **sth** to enter a place in large numbers, especially in a way that causes damage or confusion: *Demonstrators invaded the government buildings.* ◆ *As the final whistle blew, fans began invading the field.* ◆ *The cancer cells may invade other parts of the body.* **3** [T] ~ **sth** to affect something in an unpleasant or annoying way: *Does the press have the right to invade her privacy in this way?* ⊃ see also INVASION, INVASIVE

in·vad·er /ɪnˈveɪdər/ *noun* an army or a country that enters another country by force in order to take control of it; a soldier fighting in such an army: *a foreign invader* ◆ *They prepared to repel the invaders.* ◆ (*figurative*) *The white blood cells attack cells infected with an invader.*

in·val·id¹ /ɪnˈvæləd/ *adj.* **1** not legally or officially acceptable: *The treaty was declared invalid because it had not been ratified.* ◆ *People with invalid papers are deported to another country.* **2** not based on all the facts, and therefore not correct: *an invalid argument* **3** (*computing*) of a type that the computer cannot recognize: *An error code will be displayed if any invalid information has been entered.* ◆ *invalid characters* ANT VALID

in·va·lid² /ˈɪnvələd/ *noun* a person who needs other people to take care of them, because of illness that they have had for a long time: *She had been a delicate child and her parents had treated her as an invalid.* ◆ *his invalid wife*

in·val·i·date AWL /ɪnˈvæləˌdeɪt/ *verb* **1** ~ **sth** to prove that an idea, a story, an argument, etc. is wrong: *This new piece of evidence invalidates his version of events.* **2** ~ **sth** if you **invalidate** a document, contract, election, etc., you make it no longer valid or officially valid or acceptable ANT VALIDATE ▸ **in·val·i·da·tion** /ɪnˌvæləˈdeɪʃn/ *noun* [U]

in·va·lid·i·ty AWL /ˌɪnvəˈlɪdəti/ *noun* [U] (*formal*) the state of not being legally or officially acceptable ⊃ compare VALIDITY

in·val·u·a·ble /ɪnˈvælyəbl; -yuəbl/ *adj.* extremely useful: *invaluable information* ◆ ~ **to/for sb/sth** *The book will be invaluable for students in higher education.* ◆ ~ **in sth** *The research should prove invaluable in the study of children's language.* ⊃ compare VALUABLE HELP Invaluable means "very valuable or useful." The opposite of **valuable** is **valueless** or **worthless**.

in·var·i·a·ble AWL /ɪnˈvɛriəbl/ *adj.* always the same; never changing SYN UNCHANGING: *Her routine was invariable.* ◆ *his invariable courtesy and charm* ◆ *an invariable principle* ⊃ compare VARIABLE

in·var·i·a·bly AWL /ɪnˈvɛriəbli/ *adv.* always SYN WITHOUT FAIL: *This acute infection of the brain is almost invariably fatal.* ◆ *This is not invariably the case.* ◆ *Invariably the reply came back, "Not now!"*

in·var·i·ant /ɪnˈvɛriənt/ *adj.* (*technical*) always the same; never changing SYN INVARIABLE

in·va·sion /ɪnˈveɪʒn/ *noun* [C, U] **1** the act of an army entering another country by force in order to take control of it: *the German invasion of Poland in 1939* ◆ *the threat of invasion* ◆ *an invasion force/fleet* ⊃ collocations at WAR

2 the fact of a large number of people or things arriving somewhere, especially people or things that are disturbing or unpleasant: *the annual tourist invasion ◆ Farmers are struggling to cope with an invasion of slugs.* **3** an act or a process that affects someone or something in a way that is not welcome: *The actress described the photographs of her as an invasion of privacy.* ⟳ see also INVADE

in·va·sive /ɪnˈveɪsɪv/ *adj.* (*formal*) **1** (especially of diseases within the body) spreading very quickly and difficult to stop: *invasive cancer* **2** (of medical treatment) involving cutting into the body: *invasive surgery* **ANT** NONINVASIVE ⟳ see also INVADE

in·vec·tive /ɪnˈvektɪv/ *noun* [U] (*formal*) rude language and unpleasant remarks that someone shouts when they are very angry

in·veigh /ɪnˈveɪ/ *verb*
PHRV in'veigh against sb/sth (*formal*) to criticize someone or something strongly

in·vei·gle /ɪnˈveɪɡl/ *verb* ~ sb/yourself (into sth/into doing sth) (*formal*) to achieve control over someone or something in a dishonest but skillful way, especially so that they will do what you want: *He inveigled himself into her affections* (= dishonestly made her love him).

in·vent /ɪnˈvent/ *verb*
1 ~ sth to produce or design something that has not existed before: *Who invented the steam engine?* **2** ~ sth to say or describe something that is not true, especially in order to trick people: *What excuse did he invent this time?* ◆ *Many children invent an imaginary friend.*

in·ven·tion /ɪnˈvenʃn/ *noun*
1 [C] a thing or an idea that has been invented: *Fax machines were a wonderful invention at the time.* **2** [U] the act of inventing something: *Such changes have not been seen since the invention of the printing press.* **3** [C, U] the act of inventing a story or an idea and pretending that it is true; a story invented in this way: *This story is apparently a complete invention.* **4** [U] the ability to have new and interesting ideas: *John was full of invention—always making up new dance steps and sequences.* **IDM** see NECESSITY

in·ven·tive /ɪnˈventɪv/ *adj.* **1** (especially of people) able to think of new and interesting ideas **SYN** IMAGINATIVE: *She has a highly inventive mind.* **2** (of ideas) new and interesting ▶ **in·ven·tive·ly** *adv.* **in·ven·tive·ness** *noun* [U]

in·ven·tor /ɪnˈventər/ *noun* a person who has invented something or whose job is inventing things

in·ven·to·ry /ˈɪnvənˌtɔri/ *noun, verb*
● *noun* (pl. **in·ven·to·ries**) **1** [C] a written list of all the objects, furniture, etc. in a particular building: *an inventory of the museum's contents* **2** [U] all the goods in a store **SYN** STOCK: *The inventory will be disposed of over the next twelve weeks.* ◆ *inventory control*
● *verb* (**in·ven·to·ries**, **in·ven·to·ry·ing**, **in·ven·to·ried**, **in·ven·to·ried**) ~ sth (*formal*) to make a complete list of something: *I've inventoried my father's collection of prints.*

in·verse /ˌɪnˈvɜrs; ˈɪnvɜrs/ *adj.* **1** [only before noun] opposite in amount or position to something else: *A person's wealth is often in inverse proportion to their happiness* (= the more money they have, the less happy they are). ◆ *There is often an inverse relationship between the power of the tool and how easy it is to use.* **2** the ˈinverse *noun* [sing.] (*technical*) the exact opposite of something ▶ **in·verse·ly** *adv.*: *We regard health as inversely related to social class.*

in·ver·sion /ɪnˈvɜrʒn/ *noun* [U, C] (*technical*) the act of changing the position or order of something to its opposite, or of turning something upside down: *the inversion of normal word order* ◆ *an inversion of the truth*

in·vert /ɪnˈvɜrt/ *verb* ~ sth (*formal*) to change the normal position of something, especially by turning it upside down or by arranging it in the opposite order: *Place a plate over the cake pan and invert it.*

in·ver·te·brate /ɪnˈvɜrtəbrət; -ˌbreɪt/ *noun* (*technical*) any animal with no BACKBONE, for example a WORM ⟳ compare VERTEBRATE

in·vest /ɪnˈvest/ *verb* **AWL**
1 [I, T] to buy property, shares in a company, etc. in the hope of making a profit: ~ (in sth) *Now is a good time to invest in the property market.* ◆ ~ sth (in sth) *He invested his life savings in his daughter's business.* **2** [I, T] (of an organization or government, etc.) to spend money on something in order to make it better or more successful: ~ (in/on sth) *The government has invested heavily in public transportation.* ◆ ~ sth (in/on sth) *The college is to invest $2 million in a new theater.* ◆ *In his time managing the team he has invested millions on new players.* **3** [T] ~ sth (in sth) | ~ sth (in) doing sth to spend time, energy, effort, etc. on something that you think is good or useful: *She had invested all her adult life in the relationship.* **4** [T] (*formal*) to give someone power or authority, especially as part of their job: ~ sb (with sth) *The new position invested her with a good deal of responsibility.* ◆ ~ sb (as sth) *The interview was broadcast on the same day he was invested as president.* ⟳ see also INVESTITURE
PHRV in'vest in sth (*informal*, often *humorous*) to buy something that is expensive but useful: *Don't you think it's about time you invested in a new coat?* in'vest sb/sth with sth (*formal*) to make someone or something seem to have a particular quality: *Being a model invests her with a certain glamour.*

in·ves·ti·gate /ɪnˈvestəˌɡeɪt/ *verb* **AWL**
1 [I, T] to carefully examine the facts of a situation, an event, a crime, etc. to find out the truth about it or how it happened: *The FBI has been called in to investigate.* ◆ (*informal*) *"What was that noise?" "I'll go and investigate."* ◆ ~ sth *Police are investigating possible links between the murders.* ◆ ~ what, how, etc.... *Police are investigating what happened.* ⟳ collocations at CRIME **2** [T] ~ sb (for sth) to try to find out information about someone's character, activities, etc.: *This is not the first time he has been investigated by the police for fraud.* **3** [T, I] to find out information and facts about a subject or problem by study or research: ~ (sth) *Scientists are investigating the effects of diet on fighting cancer.* ◆ ~ how, what, etc.... *The research investigates how foreign speakers gain fluency.*

AWL COLLOCATIONS

investigate

investigate *verb*

■ **empirically**, **experimentally** | **theoretically** | **rigorously**, **systematically**, **thoroughly** | **extensively**, **further**
This theory has been investigated experimentally by heating volcanic rock.
This speculation needs to be investigated further.

■ **influence**, **interaction**, **relationship**, **role** | **effect**, **efficacy** | **hypothesis**
Our study aims to investigate the role of optimism in preventing illness.
To investigate our hypothesis, we will present two analyses.

investigation *noun*

■ **empirical**, **scientific** | **thorough** | **further**, **ongoing**
Proposals for scientific investigations will probably increase as new discoveries are made.
A thorough investigation of the evidence confirms this conclusion.

■ **conduct**, **undertake**
We conducted a follow-up investigation to determine whether or not the students enrolled in French the following year.

■ **demonstrate**, **reveal**, **show**, **uncover**, **yield**
Investigations showed no chemical contamination of the air or water.
Recent investigations have yielded new insight into sleep's role in memory and learning.

ʌ **cup**   ə **about**   eɪ **say**   aɪ **five**   ɔɪ **boy**   aʊ **now**   oʊ **go**   ər **bird**

in·ves·ti·ga·tion 🔑 **AWL** /ɪnˌvestəˈɡeɪʃn/ *noun*
[C, U]

1 an official examination of the facts about a situation, crime, etc.: *a criminal/murder/police investigation* ◆ *She is still under investigation.* ◆ *~ into sth The police have completed their investigations into the accident.* ⊃ collocations at CRIME **2** ~ **(into sth)** a scientific or academic examination of the facts of a subject or problem SYN INQUIRY ⊃ collocations at INVESTIGATE: *an investigation into the spending habits of teenagers*

in·ves·ti·ga·tive **AWL** /ɪnˈvestəɡeɪtɪv/ (also *less frequent* **in·ves·ti·ga·to·ry** /ɪnˈvestəɡəˌtɔri/) *adj.* [usually before noun] involving examining an event or a situation to find out the truth: *The article was an excellent piece of investigative journalism.* ◆ *The police have full investigatory powers.*

in·ves·ti·ga·tor **AWL** /ɪnˈvestəˌɡeɪtər/ *noun* a person who examines a situation such as an accident or a crime to find out the truth: *air safety investigators* ◆ *a private investigator* (= a DETECTIVE)

in·ves·ti·ture /ɪnˈvestətʃər; -ˌtʃʊr/ *noun* [U, C] a ceremony at which someone formally receives an official title or special powers

in·vest·ment 🔑 **AWL** /ɪnˈvestmənt/ *noun*
1 [U] the act of investing money in something: *to encourage foreign investment* ◆ *investment income* ◆ *~ in sth This country needs investment in education.* ⊃ collocations at ECONOMY **2** [C] the money that you invest, or the thing that you invest in: *a minimum investment of $10,000* ◆ *a high return on my investments* ◆ *Our investments are not doing well.* ◆ *We bought the house as an investment* (= to make money). ⊃ collocations at BUSINESS **3** [C] a thing that is worth buying because it will be useful or helpful: *A microwave is a good investment.* **4** [U, C] the act of giving time or effort to a particular task in order to make it successful: *The project has demanded considerable investment of time and effort.*

inˈvestment ˌbank *noun* a bank that deals with large businesses, and that buys and sells securities (SECURITY) such as SHARES ▶ **inˈvestment ˌbanker** *noun* **inˈvestment ˌbanking** *noun* [U]

in·ves·tor **AWL** /ɪnˈvestər/ *noun* a person or an organization that invests money in something: *small investors* (= private people) ◆ *institutional investors*

in·vet·er·ate /ɪnˈvetərət/ *adj.* [usually before noun] (*formal*, often *disapproving*) **1** (of a person) always doing something or enjoying something, and unlikely to stop: *an inveterate liar* **2** (of a bad feeling or habit) done or felt for a long time and unlikely to change: *inveterate hostility*

in·vid·i·ous /ɪnˈvɪdiəs/ *adj.* (*formal*) unpleasant and unfair; likely to offend someone or make them jealous: *We were in the invidious position of having to choose whether to break the law or risk lives.* ◆ *It would be invidious to single out any one person to thank.*

in·vig·or·ate /ɪnˈvɪɡəˌreɪt/ *verb* **1** [often passive] ~ **sb** to make someone feel healthy and full of energy: *The cold water invigorated him.* ◆ *They felt refreshed and invigorated after the walk.* **2** ~ **sth** to make a situation, an organization, etc. efficient and successful: *They are looking into ways of invigorating the department.* ▶ **in·vig·or·at·ing** *adj.*: *an invigorating walk/shower*

in·vin·ci·ble /ɪnˈvɪnsəbl/ *adj.* too strong to be defeated or changed SYN UNCONQUERABLE: *The team seemed invincible.* ◆ *an invincible belief in his own ability* ▶ **in·vin·ci·bil·i·ty** /ɪnˌvɪnsəˈbɪləti/ *noun* [U]

in·vi·o·la·ble /ɪnˈvaɪələbl/ *adj.* (*formal*) that must be respected and not attacked or destroyed: *the inviolable right to life* ◆ *inviolable territory* ◆ *an inviolable rule* ▶ **in·vi·o·la·bil·i·ty** /ɪnˌvaɪələˈbɪləti/ *noun* [U]

in·vi·o·late /ɪnˈvaɪələt/ *adj.* (*formal*) that has been, or must be, respected and cannot be attacked or destroyed

in·vis·i·ble **AWL** /ɪnˈvɪzəbl/ *adj.* that cannot be seen: *a wizard who could make himself invisible* ◆ *She felt invisible in the crowd.* ◆ *~ to sb/sth stars invisible to the naked eye*

ANT VISIBLE ▶ **in·vis·i·bil·i·ty** **AWL** /ɪnˌvɪzəˈbɪləti/ *noun* [U]: *The ink had faded to invisibility.* **in·vis·i·bly** /ɪnˈvɪzəbli/ *adv.*: *He looked at me and nodded, almost invisibly.*

in·vi·ta·tion 🔑 /ˌɪnvəˈteɪʃn/ *noun*
1 [C] a spoken or written request to someone to do something or to go somewhere: *to issue/extend an invitation* ◆ *to accept/turn down/decline an invitation* ◆ *~ to sth an invitation to the party* ◆ *~ to do sth I have an open invitation* (= not restricted to a particular date) *to visit my friend in Japan.* **2** [U] the act of inviting someone or of being invited: *A concert was held at the invitation of the mayor.* ◆ *Admission is by invitation only.* **3** [C] a card or piece of paper that you use to invite someone to something: *Have you ordered the wedding invitations yet?* **4** [sing.] ~ **to sb (to do sth)** | ~ **to sth** something that encourages someone to do something, usually something bad: *Leaving the doors unlocked is an open invitation to burglars.*

in·vi·ta·tion·al /ˌɪnvəˈteɪʃənl/ *noun* (often used in names) a sports event that you can take part in only if you are invited ▶ **in·vi·ta·tion·al** *adj.*

in·vite 🔑 *verb, noun*
● *verb* /ɪnˈvaɪt/ **1** to ask someone to come to a social event: ~ **sb to sth** *Have you been invited to their party?* ◆ ~ **sb** *I would have liked to go, but I wasn't invited.* ◆ ~ **sb to do sth** *They have invited me to go to Paris with them.* **2** (*formal*) to ask someone formally to go somewhere or do something: ~ **sb (to/for sth)** *Successful candidates will be invited for an interview next week.* ◆ ~ **sth (from sb)** *He invited questions from the audience.* ◆ ~ **sb to do sth** *Readers are invited to write in with their comments.* **3** ~ **sth** | ~ **sb/sth to do sth** to make something, especially something bad or unpleasant, likely to happen SYN ASK FOR: *Such comments are just inviting trouble.* ⊃ see also UNINVITED
PHR V **inˌvite sb aˈlong** to ask someone to go somewhere with you and other people: *Shall we invite your sister along?* **inˌvite sb ˈback 1** to ask someone to come to your home after you have been somewhere together: *After the movie, she invited me back for a drink.* **2** to ask someone to come to your home a second time, or to ask someone to come to your house after you have been to theirs **inˌvite sb ˈin/ˈup** to ask someone to come into your home, especially after you have been somewhere together **inˌvite sb ˈout** to ask someone to go to a social event with you: *My neighbor invited me out to a movie.* **inˌvite sb ˈover** to ask someone to come to your home

● *noun* /ˈɪnvaɪt/ (*informal*) an invitation: *Thanks for your invite.*

in·vit·ing /ɪnˈvaɪtɪŋ/ *adj.* making you want to do, try, taste, etc. something SYN ATTRACTIVE: *an inviting smell* ◆ *The water looks really inviting.* ▶ **in·vit·ing·ly** *adv.*

in vi·tro /ɪn ˈvitroʊ/ *adj.* (from Latin, *biology*) (of processes) taking place outside a living body, in scientific APPARATUS: *in vitro experiments* ◆ *the development of in vitro fertilization* ⊃ see also IVF ▶ **in vi·tro** *adv.*: *an egg fertilized in vitro*

in vi·vo /ɪn ˈvivoʊ/ *adj.* (from Latin, *biology*) (of processes) taking place in a living body ▶ **in vi·vo** *adv.*

in·vo·ca·tion /ˌɪnvəˈkeɪʃn/ *noun* [U, C] **1** (*formal*) the act of asking for help, from a god or from a person in authority; the act of referring to something or of calling for something to appear **2** (*computing*) the act of making a particular function start

in·voice /ˈɪnvɔɪs/ *noun, verb*
● *noun* a list of goods that have been sold, work that has been done, etc., showing what you must pay SYN BILL: *to send/issue/settle an invoice for the goods* ◆ *an invoice for $250*
● *verb* (*business*) to write or send someone a bill for work you have done or goods you have provided: ~ **sb (for sth)** *You will be invoiced for these items at the end of the month.* ◆ ~ **sth (to sb/sth)** *Invoice the goods to my account.* ⊃ thesaurus box at BILL

in·voke **AWL** /ɪnˈvoʊk/ *verb* **1** ~ **sth (against sb)** to mention or use a law, rule, etc. as a reason for doing something: *It is unlikely that libel laws will be invoked.* **2** ~ **sb/sth** to mention a person, a theory, an example, etc. to support your opinions or ideas, or as a reason for something: *She invoked several eminent scholars to back up her argument.* **3 ~ sth** to mention someone's name to make people feel a particular thing or act in a particular way: *His name was invoked as a symbol of the revolution.* **4 ~ sb** to make a request (for help) to someone, especially a god **5 ~ sth** to make someone have a particular feeling or imagine a particular scene **SYN** EVOKE: *The opening paragraph invokes a vision of England in the early Middle Ages.* **HELP** Some people think this use is not correct. **6 ~ sth** (*computing*) to begin to run a program, etc.: *This command will invoke the HELP system.* **7 ~ sb/sth** to make evil appear by using magic

in·vol·un·tar·y /ɪnˈvɑlənˌtɛri/ *adj.* **1** an **involuntary** movement, etc. is made suddenly, without you intending it or being able to control it: *an involuntary cry of pain* **ANT** VOLUNTARY **2** happening without the person concerned wanting it to: *the involuntary repatriation of immigrants* ◆ *involuntary childlessness* ▶ **in·vol·un·tar·i·ly** /ɪnˌvɑlənˈtɛrəli/ *adv.*

in·volve 🔑 **AWL** /ɪnˈvɑlv/ *verb*
1 if a situation, an event, or an activity **involves** something, that thing is an important or necessary part or result of it **SYN** ENTAIL: *~ sth Any investment involves an element of risk.* ◆ *Many of the crimes involved drugs.* ◆ *~ doing sth The test will involve answering questions about a photograph.* ◆ *~ sb/sth doing sth The job involves me traveling all over the country.* ◆ (*formal*) *The job involves my traveling all over the country.* **2 ~ sb/sth** if a situation, an event, or an activity **involves** someone or something, they take part in it or are affected by it: *There was a serious incident involving a group of youths.* ◆ *How many vehicles were involved in the crash?* **3** to make someone take part in something: *~ sb (in sth/in doing sth) We want to involve as many people as possible in the celebrations.* ◆ *~ yourself (in sth) Parents should involve themselves in their child's education.* **4 ~ sb (in sth)** to say or do something to show that someone took part in something, especially a crime **SYN** IMPLICATE: *His confession involved a number of other politicians in the scandal.* **PHRV in·volve sb in sth** to make someone experience something, especially something unpleasant: *Don't involve me in your family arguments!*

AWL COLLOCATIONS

involve

involve *verb*
▪ **actively, directly | typically, usually | necessarily**
The plots usually involve a virtuous hero who triumphs over evil.
In the context of climate change, many potential risks necessarily involve intervention by the state.

involved *adj.*
▪ **actively, directly | deeply, heavily**
Numerous researchers are actively involved in water table management research.
Already heavily involved in the church, Baptist women heightened that involvement for the duration of the war.
▪ **~ in**
The step-by-step activities involved in the process are detailed in this article.

involvement *noun*
the act of taking part in something
▪ **active, direct**
The matter of a national bank system drew some direct involvement from President Lincoln.
▪ **~ in | ~ with**
In the study, two questions inquired about adolescents' involvement in competitive sports.
The survey showed that producers in North Carolina had the lowest involvement with livestock.

in·volved 🔑 **AWL** /ɪnˈvɑlvd/ *adj.*
1 [not before noun] **~ (in sth)** taking part in something; being part of something or connected with something: *to be/become/get involved in politics* ◆ *We need to examine all the costs involved in the project first.* ◆ *We'll make our decision and contact the people involved.* ◆ *Some people tried to stop the fight but I didn't want to get involved.* **HELP** In this meaning, **involved** is often used after a noun. **ANT** UNINVOLVED ⊃ collocations at INVOLVE **2** [not usually before noun] giving a lot of time or attention to someone or something: **~ (with sth/sb)** *She was deeply involved with the local hospital.* ◆ *~ (in sth/sb) I was so involved in my book I didn't hear you knock.* ◆ *He's a very involved father* (= he spends a lot of time with his children). **ANT** UNINVOLVED **3** [not usually before noun] having a close personal relationship with someone: *They're not romantically involved.* ◆ *~ with sb She is involved with an older man.* **ANT** UNINVOLVED **4** complicated and difficult to understand **SYN** COMPLEX: *an involved plot*

in·volve·ment 🔑 **AWL** /ɪnˈvɑlvmənt/ *noun*
1 [U] **~ (in/with sth)** the act of taking part in something **SYN** PARTICIPATION ⊃ collocations at INVOLVE: *U.S. involvement in European wars* **2** [U, C] **~ (in/with sth)** the act of giving a lot of time and attention to something you care about: *her growing involvement with contemporary music* **3** [C, U] **~ (with sb)** a romantic or sexual relationship with someone that you are not married to: *He spoke openly about his involvement with the actress.*

in·vul·ner·a·ble /ɪnˈvʌlnərəbl/ *adj.* that cannot be harmed or defeated; safe: *to be in an invulnerable position* ◆ *~ to sth The submarine is invulnerable to attack while at sea.* **ANT** VULNERABLE ▶ **in·vul·ner·a·bil·i·ty** /ɪnˌvʌlnərəˈbɪləti/ *noun* [U]

in·ward /ˈɪnwərd/ *adj., adv.*
● *adj.* **1** [only before noun] inside your mind and not shown to other people: *an inward smile* ◆ *Her calm expression hid her inward panic.* **2** toward the inside or center of something: *an inward flow* ◆ *an inward curve* **ANT** OUTWARD
● *adv.* (also **in·wards**) **1** toward the inside or center: *The door opens inward.* **2** toward yourself and your interests: *Her thoughts turned inward.* ◆ (*disapproving*) *an inward-looking person* (= one who is not interested in other people) **ANT** OUTWARD

in·ward·ly /ˈɪnwərdli/ *adv.* in your mind; secretly: *She groaned inwardly.* ◆ *I was inwardly furious.* **ANT** OUTWARDLY

in·ward·ness /ˈɪnwərdnəs/ *noun* [U] (*formal* or *literary*) interest in feelings and emotions rather than in the world around you

in-your-'face *adj.* (*informal*) used to describe an attitude, a performance, etc. that is aggressive in style and deliberately designed to make people react strongly for or against it: *in-your-face action thrillers*

i·o·dide /ˈaɪəˌdaɪd/ *noun* (*chemistry*) a chemical that contains iodine

i·o·dine /ˈaɪəˌdaɪn; -ˌdin/ *noun* [U] (*symb.* **I**) a chemical element. Iodine is a substance found in ocean water. A liquid containing iodine is sometimes used as an ANTISEPTIC (= a substance used on wounds to prevent infection).

i·on /ˈaɪən; ˈaɪɑn/ *noun* (*physics* or *chemistry*) an atom or a MOLECULE with a positive or negative electric charge caused by its losing or gaining one or more ELECTRONS

-ion /ən; yən/ (also **-ation, -ition, -sion, -tion**) *suffix* (in nouns) the action or state of: *hesitation* ◆ *competition* ◆ *confession*

I·on·ic /aɪˈɑnɪk/ *adj.* (*architecture*) used to describe a style of ARCHITECTURE in ancient Greece that uses a curved decoration in the shape of a SCROLL

i·on·ic /aɪˈɑnɪk/ *adj.* (*chemistry*) **1** of or related to ions **2** (of a chemical BOND) using the electrical pull between positive and negative ions ⊃ compare COVALENT

i·on·ize /ˈaɪəˌnaɪz/ *verb* [T, I] **~ (sth)** (*technical*) to change something or be changed into IONS ▶ **i·on·i·za·tion** /ˌaɪənəˈzeɪʃn/ noun [U]

i·on·iz·er /ˈaɪəˌnaɪzər/ noun a device that is used to make air in a room fresh and healthy by producing negative IONS

i·on·o·sphere /aɪˈɑnəˌsfɪr/ noun **the ionosphere** [sing.] a layer of the earth's atmosphere between about 50 and 600 miles above the surface of the earth, that reflects radio waves around the earth つ compare STRATOSPHERE

i·o·ta /aɪˈoʊtə/ noun **1** [sing.] (usually used in negative sentences) an extremely small amount: *There is not one iota of truth* (= no truth at all) *to the story.* ◆ *I don't think that would help one iota.* **2** the 9th letter of the Greek alphabet (I, ι)

IOU /ˌaɪ oʊ ˈyu/ noun (informal) a written promise that you will pay someone the money you owe them (a way of writing "I owe you"): *an IOU for $20*

IPA /ˌaɪ pi ˈeɪ/ abbr. International Phonetic Alphabet (an alphabet that is used to show the pronunciation of words in any language)

IP ad·dress /ˌaɪ ˈpi əˌdrɛs/ noun (computing) a series of numbers separated by dots that identifies a particular computer connected to the Internet

IPM /ˌaɪ pi ˈɛm/ abbr. integrated pest management (a method of controlling insects that harm plants or crops, without using strong chemicals)

IPO /ˌaɪ pi ˈoʊ/ abbr. (business) initial public offering (the act of selling shares in a company for the first time)

iPod™ /ˈaɪpɑd/ noun a small piece of equipment that can store information taken from the Internet and that you carry with you, usually so that you can listen to music

ip·so fac·to /ˌɪpsoʊ ˈfæktoʊ/ adv. (from Latin, formal) because of the fact that has been mentioned: *You cannot assume that a speaker of English is ipso facto qualified to teach English.*

IP te·leph·ony noun = VoIP

IQ /ˌaɪ ˈkyu/ noun the abbreviation for "intelligence quotient" (a measurement of a person's intelligence that is calculated from the results of special tests): *an IQ of 120* ◆ *to have a high/low IQ* ◆ *IQ tests*

ir- /ɪr/ つ IN-

i·ras·ci·ble /ɪˈræsəbl/ adj. (formal) becoming angry very easily SYN IRRITABLE ▶ **i·ras·ci·bil·i·ty** /ɪˌræsəˈbɪləṭi/ noun [U]

i·rate /aɪˈreɪt/ adj. very angry: *irate customers* ◆ *an irate phone call* つ thesaurus box at ANGRY

IRC /ˌaɪ ɑr ˈsi/ abbr. Internet Relay Chat (an area of the Internet where users can communicate directly with each other)

ire /ˈaɪər/ noun [U] (formal or literary) anger SYN WRATH: *to arouse/raise/provoke the ire* of local residents ◆ *to draw the ire of local residents*

ir·i·des·cent /ˌɪrəˈdɛsnt/ adj. (formal) showing many bright colors that seem to change in different lights: *a bird with iridescent blue feathers* ▶ **ir·i·des·cence** /-ˈdɛsns/ noun [U]

i·rid·i·um /ɪˈrɪdiəm/ noun [U] (symb. Ir) a chemical element. Iridium is a very hard yellow-white metal, used especially in making ALLOYS.

i·ris /ˈaɪrəs/ noun **1** the round colored part that surrounds the PUPIL of your eye つ picture at BODY **2** a tall plant with long pointed leaves and large purple or yellow flowers つ picture at PLANT

I·rish /ˈaɪrɪʃ/ noun, adj.
● noun **1** (also Irish Gaelic, Gael·ic) [U] the Celtic language of Ireland **2** the Irish [pl.] the people of Ireland
● adj. of or connected with Ireland, its people, or its language

Irish coffee noun **1** [U] hot coffee mixed with WHISKEY and sugar, with thick cream on top **2** [C] a cup or glass of Irish coffee

irk /ərk/ verb ~ sb (to do sth) | it irks sb that... (formal or literary) to annoy or irritate someone: *Her flippant tone irked him.*

irk·some /ˈərksəm/ adj. (formal) annoying or irritating SYN TIRESOME: *I found the restrictions irksome.*

IRL /ˌaɪ ɑr ˈɛl/ abbr. (informal) in real life, not on the Internet (used in informal situations on the Internet): *If he did that IRL he'd have a bullet in his head.*

i·ron /ˈaɪərn/ noun, verb, adj.
● noun
▷ METAL **1** [U] (symb. Fe) a chemical element. Iron is a hard strong metal that is used to make steel and is also found in small quantities in blood and food: *cast/wrought iron* ◆ *iron gates/bars/railings* ◆ *an iron and steel works* ◆ *iron ore* (= rock containing iron) ◆ *patients with an iron deficiency* (= not enough iron in their blood) ◆ *iron pills* (= containing iron prepared as a medicine) ◆ (figurative) *She had a will of iron* (= it was very strong).
▷ TOOL **2** [C] a tool with a flat metal base that can be heated and used to make clothes smooth: *a steam iron* つ picture at CLEANING **3** [C] (usually in compounds) a tool made of iron or another metal つ see also BRANDING IRON, SOLDERING IRON, TIRE IRON
▷ FOR PRISONERS **4 irons** [pl.] chains or other heavy objects made of iron, attached to the arms and legs of prisoners, especially in the past
▷ IN GOLF **5** [C] one of the set of CLUBS (= sticks for hitting the ball with) that have a metal head つ compare WOOD
IDM **have several, etc. irons in the fire** to be involved in several activities or areas of business at the same time, hoping that at least one will be successful つ more at PUMP v., STRIKE v.
● verb [T, I] ~ (sth) to make clothes, etc. smooth by using an iron: *I'll need to iron that dress before I can wear it.* ◆ *He was ironing when I arrived.* つ see also IRONING
PHR V **iron sth↔out 1** to remove the CREASES (= folds that you do not want) from clothes, etc. by using an iron **2** to get rid of any problems or difficulties that are affecting something: *There are still a few details that need ironing out.*
● adj. [only before noun] very strong and determined: *She was known as the "Iron Lady."* ◆ *a man of iron will*
IDM **an iron fist/hand** if you use the words an iron fist/hand when describing the way that someone behaves, you mean that they treat people severely

the Iron Age noun [sing.] the historical period about 3,000 years ago when people first used iron tools

i·ron·clad /ˈaɪərnˌklæd/ adj. so strong that it cannot be challenged or changed: *an ironclad alibi/contract/excuse/guarantee* ◆ *His memo is ironclad proof he was involved.* つ compare CAST-IRON (2)

the Iron Curtain noun [sing.] the name that people used for the border that used to exist between Western Europe and the COMMUNIST countries of Central and Eastern Europe

iron-gray adj. dark gray in color: *iron-gray hair*

i·ron·ic /aɪˈrɑnɪk/ (also less frequent i·ron·i·cal /aɪˈrɑnɪkl/) adj. **1** showing that you really mean the opposite of what you are saying; expressing IRONY: *an ironic comment* **2** (of a situation) strange or amusing because it is very different from what you expect: *It's ironic that she became a teacher—she used to hate school.* つ see also IRONY ▶ **i·ron·i·cal·ly** /-kli/ adv.: *Ironically, the book she felt was her worst sold more copies than any of her others.* ◆ *He smiled ironically.*

i·ron·ing /ˈaɪərnɪŋ/ noun [U] **1** the task of pressing clothes, etc. with an iron to make them smooth: *to do the ironing* **2** the clothes, etc. that you have just ironed or that need to be done: *a pile of ironing*

ironing board noun a long narrow board covered with cloth, and usually with folding legs, that you iron clothes on つ picture at CLEANING

i·ron·stone /ˈaɪərnˌstoʊn/ noun [U] a type of rock that contains iron

i·ron·work /ˈaɪərnˌwɜrk/ noun [U] things made of iron, such as gates, parts of buildings, etc.

i·ron·works /ˈaɪərnˌwɜrks/ noun (pl. **i·ron·works**) a factory where iron is obtained from ORE (= rock containing metal), or where heavy iron goods are made

i·ro·ny /ˈaɪrəni; ˈaɪərni/ noun (pl. **i·ro·nies**) **1** [U, C] the amusing or strange aspect of a situation that is very different from what you expect; a situation like this: *The irony is that when he finally got the job, he discovered he didn't like it.* ◆ *It was one of life's little ironies.* **2** [U] the use of words that say the opposite of what you really mean, often as a joke and with a tone of voice that shows this: *"England is famous for its food," she said with heavy irony.* ◆ *There was a note of irony in his voice.* ◆ *She said it without a hint/trace of irony.*

ir·ra·di·ance /ɪˈreɪdiəns/ noun [U] (*physics*) a measurement of the amount of light that comes from something

ir·ra·di·ate /ɪˈreɪdiˌeɪt/ verb **1** ~ sth (*technical*) to treat food with GAMMA RADIATION in order to preserve it **2** ~ sth (with sth) (*literary*) to make something look brighter and happier: *faces irradiated with joy* ▶ **ir·ra·di·a·tion** /ɪˌreɪdiˈeɪʃn/ noun [U]

ir·ra·tion·al /ɪˈræʃənl/ adj. not based on, or not using, clear logical thought **SYN** UNREASONABLE: *an irrational fear* ◆ *You're being irrational.* **ANT** RATIONAL ▶ **ir·ra·tion·al·i·ty** /ɪˌræʃəˈnæləti/ noun [U, C, usually sing.] **ir·ra·tion·al·ly** /ɪˈræʃənli/ adv.: *to behave irrationally*

ir·ˌrational ˈnumber (also **surd**) noun (*mathematics*) a number, for example π or the SQUARE ROOT of 2, that cannot be expressed as the RATIO of two whole numbers

ir·rec·on·cil·a·ble /ɪˌrɛkənˈsaɪləbl/ adj. **1** if differences or disagreements are **irreconcilable**, they are so great that it is not possible to settle them **2** if an idea or opinion is **irreconcilable** with another, it is impossible for someone to have both of them together: *This view is irreconcilable with common sense.* **3** people who are **irreconcilable** cannot be made to agree: *irreconcilable enemies*

ir·re·cov·er·a·ble /ɪˌrɪˈkʌvərəbl/ adj. (*formal*) that you cannot get back; lost: *irrecoverable costs* ◆ *irrecoverable loss of sight* **ANT** RECOVERABLE ▶ **ir·re·cov·er·a·bly** /-bli/ adv.

ir·re·deem·a·ble /ɪˌrɪˈdiməbl/ adj. (*formal*) too bad to be corrected, improved, or saved **SYN** HOPELESS ▶ **ir·re·deem·a·bly** /-bli/ adv.: *irredeemably spoiled*

ir·re·duc·i·ble /ɪˌrɪˈdusəbl/ adj. (*formal*) that cannot be made smaller or simpler: *to cut staff to an irreducible minimum* ◆ *an irreducible fact* ▶ **ir·re·duc·i·bly** /-bli/ adv.

ir·ref·u·ta·ble /ɪˌrɪˈfyutəbl; ɪˈrɛfyətəbl/ adj. (*formal*) that cannot be proved wrong and that must therefore be accepted: *irrefutable evidence* ▶ **ir·ref·u·ta·bly** /-bli/ adv.

ir·reg·u·lar /ɪˈrɛgyələr/ adj., noun
● adj. **1** not arranged in an even way; not having an even, smooth pattern or shape **SYN** UNEVEN: *irregular teeth* ◆ *an irregular outline* **2** not happening at times that are at an equal distance from each other; not happening regularly: *irregular meals* ◆ *an irregular heartbeat* ◆ *irregular attendance at school* ◆ *He visited his parents at irregular intervals.* **3** not normal; not according to the usual rules **SYN** ABNORMAL: *an irregular practice* ◆ *His behavior is highly irregular.* **4** (*grammar*) not formed in the normal way: *an irregular verb* **5** (of a soldier etc.) not part of a country's official army **ANT** REGULAR ▶ **ir·reg·u·lar·ly** adv.
● noun a soldier who is not a member of a country's official army

ir·reg·u·lar·i·ty /ɪˌrɛgyəˈlærəti/ noun (pl. **ir·reg·u·lar·i·ties**) **1** [C, U] an activity or a practice which is not according to the usual rules, or not normal: *alleged irregularities in the election campaign* ◆ *suspicion of financial irregularity* **2** [C, U] something that does not happen at regular intervals: *a slight irregularity in his heartbeat* **3** [U, C] something that is not smooth or regular in shape or arrangement: *The paint will cover any irregularity in the surface of the walls.* ⟳ compare REGULARITY

ir·rel·e·vance **AWL** /ɪˈrɛləvəns/ (also *less frequent* **ir·rel·e·van·cy** /ɪˈrɛləvənsi/ *pl.* **ir·rel·e·van·cies**) noun **1** [U] lack of importance to or connection with a situation: *the irrelevance of the curriculum to children's daily life* **ANT** RELEVANCE **2** [C, usually sing.] something that is not important to or connected with a situation: *His idea was rejected as an irrelevance.*

ir·rel·e·vant **AWL** /ɪˈrɛləvənt/ adj. not important to or connected with a situation: *totally/completely/largely irrelevant* ◆ *irrelevant remarks* ◆ *Whether I believe you or not is irrelevant now.* ◆ ~ to sth/sb *That evidence is irrelevant to the case.* ◆ *Many people consider politics irrelevant to their lives.* **ANT** RELEVANT ⟳ collocations at RELEVANT ▶ **ir·rel·e·vant·ly** adv.

ir·re·li·gious /ɪˌrɪˈlɪdʒəs/ adj. (*formal*) without any religious belief; showing no respect for religion

ir·re·me·di·a·ble /ɪˌrɪˈmidiəbl/ adj. (*formal*) too bad to be corrected or cured: *an irremediable situation* **ANT** REMEDIABLE ▶ **ir·re·me·di·a·bly** /-bli/ adv.

ir·rep·a·ra·ble /ɪˈrɛpərəbl/ adj. (of a loss, injury, etc.) too bad or too serious to repair or put right: *to cause irreparable damage/harm to your health* ◆ *Her death is an irreparable loss.* **ANT** REPAIRABLE, REPARABLE ▶ **ir·rep·a·ra·bly** /-bli/ adv.: *irreparably damaged*

ir·re·place·a·ble /ɪˌrɪˈpleɪsəbl/ adj. too valuable or special to be replaced **ANT** REPLACEABLE ⟳ thesaurus box at VALUABLE

ir·re·press·i·ble /ɪˌrɪˈprɛsəbl/ adj. **1** (of a person) lively, happy, and full of energy **SYN** EBULLIENT **2** (of feelings, etc.) very strong; impossible to control or stop: *irrepressible confidence* ▶ **ir·re·press·i·bly** /-bli/ adv.

ir·re·proach·a·ble /ɪˌrɪˈproʊtʃəbl/ adj. (of a person or their behavior) free from fault and impossible to criticize **SYN** BLAMELESS

ir·re·sist·i·ble /ɪˌrɪˈzɪstəbl/ adj. **1** so strong that it cannot be stopped or resisted: *I felt an irresistible urge to laugh.* ◆ *His arguments were irresistible.* **ANT** RESISTIBLE **2** so attractive that you feel you must have it: *an irresistible bargain* ◆ *On such a hot day, the water was irresistible* (= it made you want to swim in it). ◆ ~ to sb *The bright colors were irresistible to the baby.* ▶ **ir·re·sist·i·bly** /-bli/ adv.: *They were irresistibly drawn to each other.*

ir·res·o·lute /ɪˈrɛzəˌlut; ɪˌrɛzəˈlut/ adj. (*formal*) not able to decide what to do **ANT** RESOLUTE ▶ **ir·res·o·lute·ly** adv. **ir·res·o·lu·tion** /ɪˌrɛzəˈluʃn/ noun [U]

ir·re·spec·tive of /ɪrɪˈspɛktɪv əv/ prep. without considering something or being influenced by it **SYN** REGARDLESS OF: *Everyone is treated equally, irrespective of race.* ◆ *The weekly rent is the same irrespective of whether there are three or four occupants.*

ir·re·spon·si·ble /ɪˌrɪˈspɑnsəbl/ adj. (*disapproving*) (of a person) not thinking enough about the effects of what they do; not showing a feeling of responsibility: *an irresponsible teenager* ◆ *an irresponsible attitude* ◆ *It would be irresponsible to ignore the situation.* **ANT** RESPONSIBLE ▶ **ir·re·spon·si·bil·i·ty** /ɪˌrɪˌspɑnsəˈbɪləti/ noun [U] **ir·re·spon·si·bly** /ɪˌrɪˈspɑnsəbli/ adv.

ir·re·triev·a·ble /ɪˌrɪˈtrivəbl/ adj. (*formal*) that you can never make right or get back: *an irretrievable situation* ◆ *the irretrievable breakdown of the marriage* ◆ *The money already paid is irretrievable.* ▶ **ir·re·triev·a·bly** /-bli/ adv.: *Some of our old traditions are irretrievably lost.*

ir·rev·er·ent /ɪˈrɛvərənt; ɪˈrɛvrənt/ adj. (usually *approving*) not showing respect to someone or something that other people usually respect: *irreverent wit* ◆ *an irreverent attitude to tradition* ▶ **ir·rev·er·ence** /-rəns/ noun [U] **ir·rev·er·ent·ly** adv.

ir·re·vers·i·ble **AWL** /ɪˌrɪˈvɜrsəbl/ adj. that cannot be changed back to what it was before: *an irreversible change/decline/decision* ◆ *irreversible brain damage* (= that will not improve) **ANT** REVERSIBLE ▶ **ir·re·vers·i·bly** /-bli/ adv.

ir·rev·o·ca·ble /ɪˈrɛvəkəbl/ adj. (*formal*) that cannot be changed **SYN** FINAL: *an irrevocable decision/step* ▶ **ir·rev·o·ca·bly** /-bli/ *adv.*: *irrevocably committed*

ir·ri·gate /ˈɪrəˌgeɪt/ *verb* **1** ~ **sth** to supply water to an area of land through pipes or channels so that crops will grow: *irrigated land/crops* **2** ~ **sth** (*medical*) to wash out a wound or part of the body with a flow of water or liquid ▶ **ir·ri·ga·tion** /ˌɪrəˈgeɪʃn/ *noun* [U]: *irrigation channels*

ir·ri·ta·ble /ˈɪrətəbl/ *adj.* getting annoyed easily; showing your anger **SYN** BAD-TEMPERED: *to be tired and irritable* ♦ *an irritable gesture* ▶ **ir·ri·ta·bil·i·ty** /ˌɪrətəˈbɪləti/ *noun* [U] **ir·ri·ta·bly** /ˈɪrətəbli/ *adv.*

ˌirritable ˈbowel ˌsyndrome *noun* [U] a condition of the BOWEL that causes pain and DIARRHEA or CONSTIPATION, often caused by stress or anxiety

ir·ri·tant /ˈɪrətənt/ *noun* **1** (*technical*) a substance that makes part of your body sore **2** something that makes you annoyed or causes trouble ▶ **ir·ri·tant** *adj.* [usually before noun]: *irritant substances*

ir·ri·tate 🔑 /ˈɪrəˌteɪt/ *verb*
1 ~ **sb** to annoy someone, especially by something you continuously do or by something that continuously happens: *The way she puts on that accent really irritates me.* **2** ~ **sth** to make your skin or a part of your body sore or painful: *Some drugs can irritate the lining of the stomach.* ▶ **ir·ri·tat·ing** *adj.*: *I found her extremely irritating* ♦ *an irritating habit* ♦ *an irritating cough/rash* **ir·ri·tat·ing·ly** *adv.* **ir·ri·ta·tion** /ˌɪrəˈteɪʃn/ *noun* [U, C]: *He noted, with some irritation, that the letter had not been sent.* ♦ *a skin irritation*

ir·ri·tat·ed 🔑 /ˈɪrəˌteɪtəd/ *adj.*
~ **(at/by/with sth)**
annoyed or angry: *She was getting more and more irritated at his comments.*

ir·rupt /ɪˈrʌpt/ *verb* [I] + **adv./prep.** (*formal*) to enter or appear somewhere suddenly and with a lot of force: *Violence once again irrupted into their peaceful lives.* ▶ **ir·rup·tion** /ɪˈrʌpʃn/ *noun* [U, C]

IRS /ˌaɪ ɑr ˈɛs/ *abbr.* Internal Revenue Service (the U. S. government department that is responsible for collecting most national taxes, for example income tax)

is /ɪz/ ⟳ BE

ISA /ˌaɪ ɛs ˈeɪ/ *abbr.* Industry Standard Architecture (the usual international system used for connecting computers and other devices)

ISBN /ˌaɪ ɛs bi ˈɛn/ *noun* the abbreviation for International Standard Book Number (a number that identifies an individual book and its PUBLISHER)

is·che·mi·a /ɪˈskimiə/ *noun* [U] (*medical*) the situation when the supply of blood to an organ or part of the body, especially the heart muscles, is less than is needed

ISDN /ˌaɪ ɛs di ˈɛn/ *abbr.* integrated services digital network (a system for carrying sound signals, images, etc. along wires at high speed): *an ISDN Internet connection*

-ish 🔑 /ɪʃ/ *suffix*
(in adjectives) **1** from the country mentioned: *Turkish* ♦ *Irish* **2** (sometimes *disapproving*) having the nature of; like: *childish* **3** fairly; approximately: *reddish* ♦ *thirtyish* ▶ **-ishly** (in adverbs): *foolishly*

Is·lam /ɪsˈlɑm; ɪz-; ˈɪslɑm; ˈɪz-/ *noun* [U] **1** the Muslim religion, based on belief in one God and REVEALED through Muhammad as the Prophet of Allah **2** all Muslims and Muslim countries in the world ▶ **Is·lam·ic** /ɪsˈlɑmɪk; ɪz-/ *adj.*: *Islamic law*

Is·la·mist /ˈɪslɑmɪst; ɪz-; ˈɪslɑmɪst; ˈɪz-/ *noun* a person who believes strongly in the teachings of Islam ▶ **Is·la·mism** /ˈɪslɑmɪzəm; ɪz-; ˈɪsləˌmɪzəm; ˈɪz-/ *noun* [U] **Is·la·mist** *adj.*

is·land 🔑 /ˈaɪlənd/ *noun*
(*abbr.* I, I.) a piece of land that is completely surrounded by water: *We spent a week on the Greek island of Kos.* ♦ *a remote island off the coast of Maine* ⊃ **see also** DESERT ISLAND, TRAFFIC ISLAND

ˈisland·er /ˈaɪləndər/ *noun* a person who lives on an island, especially a small one

ˈisland-ˌhopping *noun* [U] the activity of traveling from one island to another in an area that has lots of islands, especially as a tourist

isle /aɪl/ *noun* (*abbr.* I, I.) used especially in poetry and names to mean "island": *the Isle of Skye* ♦ *the British Isles*

is·let /ˈaɪlət/ *noun* a very small island

ism /ˈɪzəm/ *noun* (usually *disapproving*) used to refer to a set of ideas or system of beliefs or behavior: *You're always talking in isms—sexism, ageism, racism.*

-ism /ɪzəm/ *suffix* (in nouns) **1** the action or result of: *criticism* **2** the state or quality of: *heroism* **3** the teaching, system, or movement of: *Buddhism* **4** unfair treatment or hatred for the reason mentioned: *racism* **5** a feature of language of the type mentioned: *Americanism* ♦ *colloquialism* **6** a medical condition or disease: *alcoholism*

is·n't /ˈɪznt/ *short form* is not

ISO /ˌaɪ ɛs ˈoʊ/ *abbr.* International Organization for Standardization (an organization established in 1946 to make the measurements used in science, industry, and business standard throughout the world)

iso- /ˈaɪsoʊ; -sə/ *combining form* (in nouns, adjectives, and adverbs) equal: *isotope* ♦ *isometric*

i·so·bar /ˈaɪsəˌbɑr/ *noun* (*technical*) a line on a weather map that joins places that have the same air pressure at a particular time

i·so·late **AWL** /ˈaɪsəˌleɪt/ *verb* **1** to separate someone or something physically or socially from other people or things: ~ **sb/yourself/sth** *Patients with the disease should be isolated.* ♦ ~ **sb/yourself/sth from sb/sth** *He was immediately isolated from the other prisoners.* ♦ *This decision will isolate the country from the rest of Europe.* **2** ~ **sth (from sth)** to separate a part of a situation, problem, idea, etc. so that you can see what it is and deal with it separately: *It is possible to isolate a number of factors that contributed to her downfall.* **3** ~ **sth (from sth)** (*technical*) to separate a single substance, cell, etc. from others so that you can study it: *Researchers are still trying to isolate the gene that causes this abnormality.*

i·so·lat·ed **AWL** /ˈaɪsəˌleɪtəd/ *adj.* **1** (of buildings and places) far away from any others **SYN** REMOTE: *isolated rural areas* **2** without much contact with other people or other countries: *I felt very isolated in my new job.* ♦ *Elderly people easily become socially isolated.* ♦ *The decision left the country isolated from its allies.* **3** single; happening once: *The police said the attack was an isolated incident.*

i·so·lat·ing **AWL** /ˈaɪsəˌleɪtɪŋ/ *adj.* (*linguistics*) = ANALYTIC

i·so·la·tion **AWL** /ˌaɪsəˈleɪʃn/ *noun* [U] **1** the act of separating someone or something; the state of being separate: *geographical isolation* ♦ *an isolation hospital/ward* (= for people with infectious diseases) ♦ ~ **(from sb/sth)** *The country has been threatened with complete isolation from the international community unless the atrocities stop.* **2** ~ **(from sb/sth)** the state of being alone or lonely: *Many unemployed people experience feelings of isolation and depression.* **IDM** **in isolation (from sb/sth)** separately; alone: *To make sense, these figures should not be looked at in isolation.*

i·so·la·tion·ism **AWL** /ˌaɪsəˈleɪʃəˌnɪzəm/ *noun* [U] the policy of not becoming involved in the affairs of other countries or groups ▶ **i·so·la·tion·ist** /-ʃənɪst/ *adj., noun*: *an isolationist foreign policy*

i·so·mer /ˈaɪsəmər/ *noun* **1** (*chemistry*) one of two or more COMPOUNDS that have the same atoms, but in different arrangements **2** (*physics*) one of two or more nuclei (NUCLEUS) that have the same ATOMIC NUMBER, but different energy states ▶ **i·so·mer·ic** /ˌaɪsəˈmɛrɪk/ *adj.* **i·som·er·ism** /aɪˈsɑməˌrɪzəm/ *noun* [U]

i·so·met·ric /ˌaɪsəˈmɛtrɪk/ *adj.* **1** (*technical*) connected with a type of physical exercise in which muscles are made to work without the whole body moving **2** (*geometry*) connected with a style of drawing in three DIMENSIONS without PERSPECTIVE

i·so·met·rics /ˌaɪsəˈmetrɪks/ *noun* [pl.] physical exercises in which the muscles work against each other or against a fixed object

i·so·prene /ˈaɪsəˌprin/ *noun* [U] a liquid HYDROCARBON obtained from PETROLEUM that is used to make artificial rubber. Isoprene is also found in natural rubber.

i·sos·ce·les triangle /aɪˌsɑsəliz ˈtraɪæŋgl/ *noun* (*geometry*) a triangle with two of its three sides the same length ⟳ picture at SHAPE

i·so·therm /ˈaɪsəˌθərm/ *noun* (*technical*) a line on a weather map that joins places that have the same temperature at a particular time

i·so·ton·ic /ˌaɪsəˈtɑnɪk/ *adj.* (of a drink) with added minerals and salts, intended to replace those lost during exercise

i·so·tope /ˈaɪsəˌtoʊp/ *noun* (*physics, chemistry*) one of two or more forms of a chemical element that have the same number of PROTONS but a different number of NEUTRONS in their atoms. They have different physical properties (PROPERTY) (= characteristics) but the same chemical ones: *radioactive isotopes* ♦ *the many isotopes of carbon*

ISP /ˌaɪ ɛs ˈpi/ *abbr.* Internet Service Provider (a company that provides you with an Internet connection and services such as e-mail, etc.)

I-spy /ˌaɪ ˈspaɪ/ *noun* [U] a children's game in which one player gives the first letter of a thing that they can see and the others have to guess what it is

Is·ra·el·ite /ˈɪzriəˌlaɪt; ˈɪzreɪˌlaɪt/ *noun* a member of the ancient Hebrew nation described in the Bible

is·sue 🔑 AWL /ˈɪʃu/ *noun, verb*

● **noun**
❯ **TOPIC OF DISCUSSION 1** [C] an important topic that people are discussing or arguing about: *a key/sensitive/controversial issue* ♦ *This is a big issue; we need more time to think about it.* ♦ *She usually writes about environmental issues.* ♦ *The union plans to raise the issue of overtime.* ♦ *The party was divided on this issue.* ♦ *You're just avoiding the issue.* ♦ *Don't confuse the issue.*
❯ **PROBLEM/WORRY 2** [C] a problem or worry that someone has with something: *Money is not an issue.* ♦ *I don't think my private life is the issue here.* ♦ *I'm not bothered about the cost—you're the one who's making an issue of it.* ♦ *Because I grew up in a dysfunctional family, anger is a big issue for me.* ♦ *She's always on a diet—she has issues about food.* ♦ *He still has some issues with women* (= has problems dealing with them). ♦ *If you have any issues, please call this number.*
❯ **MAGAZINE/NEWSPAPER 3** [C] one of a regular series of magazines or newspapers: *the July issue of a popular food magazine* ♦ *The article appeared in issue 25.*
❯ **OF STAMPS/COINS/SHARES 4** [C] a number or set of things that are supplied and made available at the same time: *The company is planning a new share issue.* ♦ *a special issue of stamps*
❯ **MAKING AVAILABLE/KNOWN 5** [U] the act of supplying or making available things for people to buy or use: *I bought a set of the new stamps on the date of issue.* ♦ *the issue of blankets to the refugees* ♦ *the issue of a joint statement by the French and German foreign ministers*
❯ **CHILDREN 6** [U] (*law*) children of your own: *He died without issue.*
IDM **be at issue** to be the most important part of the subject that is being discussed: *What is at issue is whether she was responsible for her actions.* **take issue with sb (about/on/over sth)** (*formal*) to start disagreeing or arguing with someone about something: *I must take issue with you on that point.* ⟳ more at FORCE

● **verb**
❯ **MAKE KNOWN 1** ~ sth (to sb) to make something known formally: *They issued a joint statement denying the charges.* ♦ *The police have issued an appeal for witnesses.*
❯ **GIVE 2** [often passive] to give something to someone, especially officially: ~ sth *to issue passports/visas/tickets* ♦ ~ sb with sth *New members will be issued with a temporary identification card.* ♦ ~ sth to sb *Work permits were issued to only 5% of those who applied for them.*
❯ **LAW 3** ~ sth to start a legal process against someone, especially by means of an official document: *to issue a writ against someone* ♦ *A warrant has been issued for his arrest.*
❯ **MAGAZINE 4** ~ sth to produce something such as a magazine, article, etc.: *We issue a monthly newsletter.*
❯ **STAMPS/COINS/SHARES 5** ~ sth to produce new stamps, coins, shares, etc. for sale to the public: *They issued a special set of stamps to mark the occasion.*
PHR V **ˈissue from sth** (*formal*) to come out of something: *A weak trembling sound issued from his lips.* ▶ **is·su·er** *noun*: *credit-card issuers*

-ist /ɪst/ *suffix* (in nouns and some related adjectives) **1** a person who believes or practices something: *atheist* **2** a member of a profession or business activity: *dentist* **3** a person who uses a thing: *violinist* **4** a person who does something: *plagiarist*

-ista /ˈɪstə/ *suffix* (in nouns) a person who is very enthusiastic about something: *fashionistas who are slaves to the latest trends*

isth·mus /ˈɪsməs/ *noun* a narrow strip of land, with water on each side, that joins two larger pieces of land

IT /ˌaɪ ˈti/ *noun* [U] the abbreviation for "information technology" (the study and use of electronic processes and equipment to store and send information of all kinds, including words, pictures, and numbers)

it 🔑 /ɪt/ *pron.*
(used as the subject or object of a verb or after a preposition) **1** used to refer to an animal or a thing that has already been mentioned or that is being talked about now: *"Where's your car?" "It's in the garage."* ♦ *Did you see it?* ♦ *Start a new file and put this letter in it.* ♦ *Look! It's going up that tree.* ♦ *We have $500. Will it be enough for a deposit?* **2** used to refer to a baby, especially one whose sex is not known: *Her baby's due next month. She hopes it will be a boy.* **3** used to refer to a fact or situation that is already known or happening: *When the factory closes, it will mean 500 people losing their jobs.* ♦ *Yes, I was at home on Sunday. What about it?* (= Why do you ask?) ♦ *Stop it, you're hurting me!* **4** used to identify a person: *It's your mother on the phone.* ♦ *Hello, Peter, it's Mike here.* ♦ *Hi, it's me!* ♦ *Was it you who put these books on my desk?* **5** used in the position of the subject or object of a verb when the real subject or object is at the end of the sentence: *Does it matter what color it is?* ♦ *It's impossible to get there in time.* ♦ *It's no use shouting.* ♦ *She finds it boring at home.* ♦ *It appears that the two leaders are holding secret talks.* ♦ *I find it strange that she doesn't want to go.* **6** used in the position of the subject of a verb when you are talking about time, the date, distance, the weather, etc.: *It's ten after twelve.* ♦ *It's our anniversary.* ♦ *It's two miles to the beach.* ♦ *It's a long time since they left.* ♦ *It was raining this morning.* ♦ *It's quite warm at the moment.* **7** used when you are talking about a situation: *If it's convenient I can come tomorrow.* ♦ *It's good to talk.* ♦ *I like it here.* **8** used to emphasize any part of a sentence: *It's Jim who's the smart one.* ♦ *It's Spain that they're going to, not Portugal.* ♦ *It was three weeks later that he heard the news.* **9** exactly what is needed: *In this business, either you've got it or you don't.* ⟳ see also ITS
IDM **that is it 1** this/that is the important point, reason, etc.: *That's just it—I can't work when you're making so much noise.* **2** this/that is the end: *I'm afraid that's it—we've lost.* **this is it 1** the expected event is just going to happen: *Well, this is it! Wish me luck.* **2** this is the main point: *"You're doing too much." "Well, this is it. I can't cope with any more work."*

I·tal·ian·ate /ɪˈtælyəˌneɪt/ *adj.* in an Italian style

I·tal·ic /ɪˈtælɪk; aɪ-/ *adj.* [only before noun] of or connected with the branch of Indo-European languages that includes Latin and some other ancient languages of Italy, and the Romance languages

i·tal·ic /ɪˈtælɪk; aɪ-/ *adj.* (of printed or written letters) leaning

ʌ **cup**   ə **about**   eɪ **say**   aɪ **five**   ɔɪ **boy**   aʊ **now**   oʊ **go**   ər **bird**

to the right: *The example sentences in this dictionary are printed in italic type.* ◆ *Use an italic font.* ⊃ compare ROMAN

i·tal·i·cize /ɪˈtæləˌsaɪz; aɪ-/ *verb* [often passive] ~ sth to write or print something in italics

i·tal·ics /ɪˈtælɪks; aɪ-/ *noun* [pl.] (also **i·tal·ic** [sing.]) printed letters that lean to the right: *Examples in this dictionary are in italics.* ◆ *Use italics for the names of books or plays.* ⊃ compare ROMAN

Italo- /ɪˈtæloʊ/ *combining form* (with nouns and adjectives) Italian; Italian and something else: *Italo-Americans* ◆ *Italophiles*

itch /ɪtʃ/ *verb, noun*
● *verb* **1** [I] to have an uncomfortable feeling on your skin that makes you want to scratch; to make your skin feel like this: *I itch all over.* ◆ *Does the rash itch?* ◆ *This sweater really itches.* ⊃ thesaurus box at HURT **2** [I] (*informal*) (often used in the progressive tenses) to want to do something very much: ~ for sth *The crowd was itching for a fight.* ◆ ~ to do sth *He's itching to get back to work.*
● *noun* **1** [C, usually sing.] an uncomfortable feeling on your skin that makes you want to scratch yourself: *to get/have an itch* **2** [sing.] ~ (to do sth) (*informal*) a strong desire to do something: *She has an itch to travel.* ◆ *the creative itch* **IDM** see SEVEN

itch·y /ˈɪtʃi/ *adj.* having or producing an itch on the skin: *an itchy nose/rash* ◆ *I feel itchy all over.* ⊃ thesaurus box at PAINFUL ▶ **itch·i·ness** *noun* [U]
IDM (get/have) itchy feet (*informal*) to want to travel or move to a different place; to want to do something different

it'd /ˈɪtəd/ *short form* **1** it had **2** it would

-ite /aɪt/ *suffix* (in nouns) (often *disapproving*) a person who follows or supports someone or something: *Trotskyite*

i·tem ⚹ **AWL** /ˈaɪtəm/ *noun*
1 one thing on a list of things to buy, do, talk about, etc.: *What's the next item on the agenda?* **2** a single article or object: *Can I pay for each item separately?* ◆ *The computer was my largest single item of expenditure.* ◆ *This clock is a collector's item* (= because it is rare and valuable). **3** a single piece of news in a newspaper, on television, etc.: *an item of news/a news item*
IDM be an item (*informal*) to be involved in a romantic or sexual relationship: *Are they an item?*

i·tem·ize **AWL** /ˈaɪtəˌmaɪz/ *verb* ~ sth to produce a detailed list of things: *The report itemizes 23 different faults.* ◆ *an itemized phone bill* (= each call is shown separately)

it·er·ate /ˈɪtəˌreɪt/ *verb* [I] (*technical*) to repeat a mathematical (MATHEMATICS) or COMPUTING process, or set of instructions again and again, each time applying it to the result of the previous stage

it·er·a·tion /ˌɪtəˈreɪʃn/ *noun* **1** [U, C] the process of repeating a mathematical (MATHEMATICS) or COMPUTING process, or set of instructions again and again, each time applying it to the result of the previous stage **2** [C] a new version of a piece of computer software

i·tin·er·ant /aɪˈtɪnərənt/ *adj.* [usually before noun] (*formal*) traveling from place to place, especially to find work: *itinerant workers/musicians* ◆ *to lead an itinerant life* ▶ **i·tin·er·ant** *noun*: *homeless itinerants*

i·tin·er·ary /aɪˈtɪnəˌreri/ *noun* (*pl.* **i·tin·er·ar·ies**) a plan of a trip, including the route and the places that you visit ⊃ collocations at TRAVEL

-ition /ˈɪʃn/ ⊃ -ION

-itis /ˈaɪtəs/ *suffix* (in nouns) **1** (*medical*) a disease of: *tonsillitis* **2** (*informal*, especially *humorous*) too much of; too much interest in: *Super Bowl-itis*

it'll /ˈɪtl/ *short form* it will

its ⚹ /ɪts/ *det.*
belonging to or connected with a thing, an animal, or a baby: *Turn the box on its side.* ◆ *Have you any idea of its value?* ◆ *The dog had hurt its paw.* ◆ *The baby threw its food on the floor.*

it's /ɪts/ *short form* **1** it is **2** it has

it·self ⚹ /ɪtˈsɛlf/ *pron.*
1 (the reflexive form of *it*) used when the animal or thing that does an action is also affected by it: *The cat was washing itself.* ◆ *Does the machine turn itself off?* ◆ *The company has got itself into difficulties.* ◆ *There's no need for the team to feel proud of itself.* **2** (used to emphasize an animal, a thing, etc.): *The town itself is pretty, but the surrounding countryside is very dull.* **IDM** be patience, honesty, simplicity, etc. itself to be an example of complete patience, etc.: *The manager of the hotel was courtesy itself.* (all) by itself **1** automatically; without anyone doing anything: *The machine will start by itself in a few seconds.* **2** alone: *The house stands by itself in an acre of land.* in itself considered separately from other things; in its true nature: *In itself, it's not a difficult problem to solve.* to itself not shared with others: *It doesn't have the market to itself.*

it·ty-bit·ty /ˌɪti ˈbɪti/ (also **it·sy-bit·sy** /ˌɪtsi ˈbɪtsi/) *adj.* [only before noun] (*informal*) very small

-ity /əti/ *suffix* (in nouns) the quality or state of: *purity* ◆ *oddity*

IUD /ˌaɪ yu ˈdi/ (also **coil**) *noun* the abbreviation for "intra-uterine device" (a small plastic or metal object placed inside a woman's UTERUS (= where a baby grows before it is born) to stop her from becoming pregnant)

IV /ˌaɪ ˈvi/ *abbr., noun*
● *abbr.* INTRAVENOUS
● *noun* (also **drip**) a piece of equipment that passes liquid food, medicine, or blood very slowly through a tube into a patient's VEIN

I've /aɪv/ *short form* I have

-ive /ɪv/ *suffix* (in nouns and adjectives) tending to; having the nature of: *explosive* ◆ *descriptive*

IVF /ˌaɪ vi ˈɛf/ *noun* [U] (*technical*) the abbreviation for "in vitro fertilization" (a process that FERTILIZES an egg from a woman outside her body. The egg is then put inside her UTERUS to develop.) ⊃ see also TEST-TUBE BABY

i·vo·ry /ˈaɪvri; ˈaɪvəri/ *noun* (*pl.* **i·vo·ries**) **1** [U] a hard yellow-white substance like bone that forms the TUSKS (= long teeth) of ELEPHANTS and some other animals: *a ban on the ivory trade* ◆ *an ivory chess set* **2** [C] an object made of ivory **3** [U] a yellow-white color

ivory 'tower *noun* (*disapproving*) a place or situation where you are separated from the problems and practical aspects of normal life and therefore do not have to worry about or understand them: *academics living in ivory towers*

i·vy /ˈaɪvi/ *noun* (*pl.* **i·vies**) [U, C] a climbing plant, especially one with dark green shiny leaves with five points: *stone walls covered in ivy* ⊃ see also POISON IVY ⊃ picture at PLANT

the ˌIvy 'League *noun* [sing.] a group of eight traditional colleges and universities in the eastern U.S. with high academic standards and a high social status ▶ **ˌIvy 'League** *adj.*: *Ivy League colleges*

-ize /aɪz/ *suffix* (in verbs) **1** to become, make, or make like: *privatize* ◆ *fossilize* ◆ *Americanize* **2** to speak, think, act, treat, etc. in the way mentioned: *criticize* ◆ *theorize* ◆ *deputize* ◆ *pasteurize* **3** to place in: *hospitalize* ▶ **-ization** /əˈzeɪʃn/ (in nouns): *immunization* **-izationally** /əˈzeɪʃənəli/ (in adverbs): *organizationally*

Jj

J also j /dʒeɪ/ noun (pl. Js, J's, j's /dʒeɪz/) [C, U] the 10th letter of the English alphabet: *"Jelly" begins with (a) J/"J."*

jab /dʒæb/ verb, noun
- *verb* (-bb-) [T, I] to push a pointed object into someone or something, or in the direction of someone or something, with a sudden strong movement SYN PROD: ~ **sb/sth (in sth) (with sth)** *She jabbed him in the ribs with her finger.* ◆ ~ **sth in sth** *She jabbed her finger in his ribs.* ◆ ~ **(at sb/sth) (with sth)** *He jabbed at the picture with his finger.* ◆ *The boxer jabbed at his opponent.*
- *noun* a sudden strong hit with something pointed or with a FIST (= a tightly closed hand): *She gave him a jab in the stomach with her elbow.* ◆ *a boxer's left jab*

jab·ber /ˈdʒæbər/ verb [I, T] ~ **(about sth)** | + speech (*disapproving*) to talk quickly and in an excited way so that it is difficult to understand what you are saying: *What is he jabbering about now?* ▶ **jab·ber** noun [U]

jac·a·ran·da /ˌdʒækəˈrændə/ noun [C, U] a tropical tree with blue flowers and pleasant-smelling wood; the wood of this tree

jack /dʒæk/ noun, verb
- *noun* **1** [C] a device for raising heavy objects off the ground, especially vehicles, so that a wheel can be changed **2** [C] an electronic connection between two pieces of electrical equipment **3** [C] (in a DECK of cards) a card with a picture of a young man on it, worth more than a ten and less than a queen: *the jack of clubs* ➔ picture at PLAYING CARD **4 jacks** [pl.] a children's game in which players BOUNCE a small ball and pick up small metal objects, also called jacks, before catching the ball ➔ see also BLACKJACK, FLAPJACK, UNION JACK
  IDM **a jack of all trades** a person who can do many different types of work, but who perhaps does not do them very well ➔ more at WORK
- *verb*
  PHR V **jack sb aˈround** (*informal*) to treat someone in a way that is deliberately not helpful to them or wastes their time: *Let's go. We're being jacked around here.* **jack ˈin/ˈinto sth** (*informal*) to connect to a computer system: *I'm jacking into the Internet now.* **jack sth↔ˈup 1** to lift something, especially a vehicle, off the ground using a jack **2** (*informal*) to increase something, especially prices, by a large amount

jack·al /ˈdʒækl/ noun a wild animal like a dog, which eats the meat of animals that are already dead and lives in Africa and Asia

jack·a·napes /ˈdʒækəˌneɪps/ noun (*old use*) a person who is rude in an annoying way

jack·ass /ˈdʒækæs/ noun **1** (*informal*) a stupid person SYN ASS: *Careful, you jackass!* **2** a male DONKEY

jack·boot /ˈdʒækbut/ noun **1** [C] a tall boot that reaches up to the knee, worn by soldiers, especially in the past **2 the jackboot** [sing.] used to refer to cruel military rule: *to be under the jackboot of a dictatorial regime*

Jack cheese noun [U] = MONTEREY JACK

jack·daw /ˈdʒækdɔ/ noun a black and gray bird of the CROW family

jack·et 🔊 /ˈdʒækət/ noun
1 a piece of clothing worn on the top half of the body over a shirt, etc. that has sleeves and fastens down the front; a short, light coat: *a denim/wool jacket* ◆ *I have to wear a jacket and tie to work.* ➔ picture at CLOTHES ➔ see also BOMBER JACKET, DINNER JACKET, FLAK JACKET, LIFE JACKET, SMOKING JACKET, SPORTS JACKET, STRAITJACKET **2** (also ˈdust jacket) a loose paper cover for a book, usually with a

design or picture on it **3** an outer cover around a hot water pipe, etc., for example to reduce loss of heat **4** (also sleeve) a stiff paper envelope for a record: *a colorful jacket design*

Jack ˈFrost noun [sing.] FROST, considered as a person: *Jack Frost was threatening to kill the new plants.*

jack·fruit /ˈdʒækfrut/ noun **1** [C, U] a large tropical fruit **2** [C] the tree that jackfruits grow on

jack·ham·mer /ˈdʒækˌhæmər/ (also pneuˌmatic ˈdrill) noun a large powerful tool, worked by air pressure, used especially for breaking up road surfaces

ˈjack-in-the-ˌbox noun a toy in the shape of a box with a figure inside on a spring that jumps up when you open the lid

jack·knife /ˈdʒæknaɪf/ noun, verb
- *noun* (pl. jack·knives /-naɪvz/) a large knife with a folding blade
- *verb* [I] to form a V-shape. For example, if a truck that is in two parts **jackknifes**, the driver loses control and the back part moves toward the front part.

jack-o'-lan·tern /ˈdʒæk ə ˌlæntərn/ noun a PUMPKIN (= a large orange vegetable) with a face cut into it and a CANDLE put inside to shine through the holes

jack·pot /ˈdʒækpɑt/ noun a large amount of money that is the most valuable prize in a game of chance: *to win the jackpot* ◆ *jackpot winners* ◆ (*figurative*) *Their team hit the jackpot* (= was successful) *with a 5-0 win.*

jack·rab·bit /ˈdʒækˌræbət/ noun a large N. American HARE (= an animal like a large RABBIT) with very long ears

Jack Rus·sell /ˌdʒæk ˈrʌsl/ (also Jack ˌRussell ˈterrier) noun a small active dog with short legs

jack·straws /ˈdʒækstrɔz/ noun [U] a game in which you remove a small stick from a pile, without moving any of the other sticks

Jac·o·be·an /ˌdʒækəˈbiən/ adj. connected with the time when James I (1603–25) was King of England: *Jacobean drama*

Ja·cuz·zi™ /dʒəˈkuzi/ (also spa) noun a large BATHTUB with a PUMP that moves the water around, giving a pleasant feeling to your body

jade /dʒeɪd/ noun [U] **1** a hard stone that is usually green and is used in making jewelry and decorative objects: *a jade necklace* **2** objects made of jade: *a collection of Chinese jade* **3** (also jade ˈgreen) a bright green color

jad·ed /ˈdʒeɪdəd/ adj. tired and bored, usually because you have had too much of something: *I felt terribly jaded after working all weekend.* ◆ *It was a meal to tempt even the most jaded palate.*

jag /dʒæg/ noun (*informal*) a short period of doing something or of behaving in a particular way, especially in a way that you cannot control: *a crying jag*

jag·ged /ˈdʒægəd/ adj. with rough, pointed, often sharp edges: *jagged rocks/peaks/edges*

jag·uar /ˈdʒægwɑr/ noun a large animal of the cat family, that has yellow-brown fur with black rings and spots. Jaguars live in parts of Central and S. America.

jai a·lai /ˈhaɪ laɪ; ˈhaɪ əˌlaɪ/ noun [U] a game played on a court with large curved baskets that are used to catch and throw a small hard ball against a wall

jail 🔊 /dʒeɪl/ noun, verb
- *noun* [U, C] a prison, especially a small local prison: *She spent a month in jail.* ◆ *He was released from the county jail six days later.* ➔ collocations at JUSTICE ➔ note at SCHOOL
- *verb* [usually passive] ~ **sb (for sth)** to put someone in prison SYN IMPRISON: *He was jailed for life for murder.*

jail·bait /ˈdʒeɪlbeɪt/ noun [U] (*informal*) a girl or boy who is too young to have sex with legally

jail·bird /ˈdʒeɪlbərd/ noun (*old-fashioned, informal*) a person who has spent a lot of time in prison

jail·break /'dʒeɪlbreɪk/ *noun* an escape from prison, usually by several people

jail·er /'dʒeɪlər/ *noun* (*old-fashioned*) a person in charge of a prison and the prisoners in it

jail·house /'dʒeɪlhaʊs/ *noun* a jail

Jain /dʒaɪn; dʒeɪn/ *noun* a member of an Indian religion whose principles include not harming any living creature and a belief in REINCARNATION ▶ **Jain** *adj.* **Jain·ism** /'dʒaɪ-ˌnɪzəm; 'dʒeɪ-/ *noun* [U]

ja·la·pe·ño /ˌhɑləˈpeɪnyoʊ; ˌhæ-/ (*also* ˌjalapeño ˈpepper) *noun* (from *Spanish*) the small green fruit of a type of pepper plant, that has a very hot taste and is used in Mexican cooking

ja·lop·y /dʒəˈlɑpi/ *noun* (*pl.* **ja·lop·ies**) (*old-fashioned, informal*) an old car that is in bad condition

jam /dʒæm/ *noun, verb*
● *noun*
▷ SWEET FOOD **1** [U, C] a thick sweet food made by boiling fruit with sugar, often sold in JARS and spread on bread: *strawberry jam* ◆ *recipes for jams and preserves* ⊃ compare JELLY, MARMALADE
▷ MANY PEOPLE/VEHICLES **2** [C] a situation in which it is difficult or impossible to move because there are so many people or vehicles in one particular place: *The bus was delayed in a five-mile jam.* ◆ *As fans rushed to leave, jams formed at all the exits.* ⊃ see also TRAFFIC JAM
▷ MACHINE **3** [C] a situation in which a machine does not work because something is stuck in one position: *There's a paper jam in the photocopier.*
IDM **be in a jam** (*informal*) to be in a difficult situation
● *verb* (-mm-)
▷ PUSH WITH FORCE **1** [T] ~ **sth + adv./prep.** to push something somewhere with a lot of force: *He jammed his fingers in his ears.* ◆ *A stool had been jammed against the door.*
▷ STOP MOVING/WORKING **2** [I, T] to become unable to move or work; to make something do this: ~ **(up)** *The photocopier keeps jamming up.* ◆ ~ **sth (up)** *There's a loose part that keeps jamming the mechanism.* ◆ + **adj.** *The valve has jammed shut.* ◆ ~ **sth + adj.** *He jammed the door open with a piece of wood.*
▷ PUT INTO SMALL SPACE **3** [T, I] to put someone or something into a small space where there is very little room to move **SYN** SQUASH, SQUEEZE: ~ **sb/sth + adv./prep.** *Six of us were jammed into one small car.* ◆ *We were jammed together like sardines in a can.* ◆ *The cabinets were jammed full of old newspapers.* ◆ + **adv./prep.** *Nearly 1,000 students jammed into the hall.* ⊃ see also JAM-PACKED
▷ FILL WITH PEOPLE/THINGS **4** [T] ~ **sth (up) (with sb/sth)** to fill something with a large number of people or things so that it is unable to function as it should **SYN** BLOCK: *Viewers jammed the switchboard with complaints.*
▷ RADIO BROADCAST **5** [T] ~ **sth** (*technical*) to send out radio signals to prevent another radio broadcast from being heard
▷ PLAY MUSIC **6** [I, T] ~ **(sth)** to play music with other musicians in an informal way without preparing or practicing first
IDM **jam on the brake(s)| jam the brake(s) on** to operate the BRAKE or brakes on a vehicle suddenly and with force: *The car skidded as he jammed on the brakes.*

jamb /dʒæm/ *noun* a vertical post at the side of a door or window

jam·ba·lay·a /ˌdʒʌmbəˈlaɪə/ *noun* [U] a spicy dish of rice, SEAFOOD, chicken, etc. from the southern U.S.

jam·bo·ree /ˌdʒæmbəˈri/ *noun* **1** a large party or celebration: *the movie industry's annual jamboree at the festival in Cannes* **2** a large meeting of BOY SCOUTS and GIRL SCOUTS

jammed /dʒæmd/ *adj.* **1** [not before noun] not able to move **SYN** STUCK: *I can't get the door open—it's completely jammed.* **2** very full; crowded **SYN** JAM-PACKED: *Hundreds more people were waiting outside the jammed stadium.*

jam·mies /'dʒæmiz/ *noun* [pl.] (*informal*) a child's word for PAJAMAS

jam-ˈpacked *adj.* [not usually before noun] ~ **(with sb/sth)** (*informal*) very full or crowded: *The train was jam-packed with commuters.*

ˈjam ˌsession *noun* an occasion when musicians perform in an informal way without practicing first

Jane Doe /ˌdʒeɪn ˈdoʊ/ *noun* [sing.] **1** used to refer to a woman whose name is not known or is kept secret, especially in a court of law **2** an average woman ⊃ compare JOHN DOE

jan·gle /'dʒæŋgl/ *verb, noun*
● *verb* **1** [I, T] to make an unpleasant sound, like two pieces of metal hitting each other; to make something do this: *The bell jangled loudly.* ◆ ~ **sth** *He jangled the keys in his pocket.* **2** [I, T] ~ **(sth)** if your nerves **jangle**, or if someone or something **jangles** them, you feel anxious or upset: *She was suddenly wide awake, her nerves jangling.*
● *noun* [usually sing.] a hard noise like that of metal hitting metal

jan·i·tor /'dʒænətər/ *noun* a person whose job is to take care of a building such as a school or an apartment building **SYN** CUSTODIAN ⊃ see also CARETAKER

Jan·u·ar·y ⚘ /'dʒænyuˌeri/ *noun* [U, C] (*abbr.* **Jan.**) the 1st month of the year, between December and February. **HELP** To see how **January** is used, look at the examples at **April**.

jar /dʒɑr/ *noun, verb*
● *noun* **1** [C] a round glass container, with a lid, used for storing food: *a storage jar* ⊃ picture at PACKAGING **2** [C] a jar and what it contains: *a jar of coffee* **3** [C] a tall container with a wide mouth, with or without handles, used in the past for carrying water, etc.: *a water jar* ⊃ see also BELL JAR **4** [sing.] an unpleasant shock, especially from two things being suddenly shaken or hit: *The fall gave him a nasty jar.*
● *verb* (-rr-) **1** [T, I] to give or receive a sudden, sharp, painful knock: ~ **sth** *The jolt seemed to jar every bone in her body.* ◆ ~ **(sth) (on sth)** *The spade jarred on something metal.* **2** [I, T] ~ **(on sth)** | ~ **(sth)** to have an unpleasant or annoying effect **SYN** GRATE: *His constant complaining was beginning to jar on her nerves.* ◆ *There was a jarring note of triumph in his voice.* **3** [I] ~ **(with sth)** to be different from something in a strange or unpleasant way **SYN** CLASH: *Her brown shoes jarred with the rest of the outfit.*

jar·gon /'dʒɑrgən/ *noun* [U] (often *disapproving*) words or expressions that are used by a particular profession or group of people, and are difficult for others to understand: *medical/legal/computer, etc. jargon* ◆ *Try to avoid using too much technical jargon.*

jar·head /'dʒɑrhɛd/ *noun* (*informal*) a member of the U.S. Marine Corps (= American soldiers trained to serve on land or at sea)

jas·mine /'dʒæzmən/ *noun* [U, C] a plant with white or yellow flowers with a sweet smell, sometimes used to make PERFUME and to flavor tea

jaun·dice /'dʒɔndəs/ *noun* [U] a medical condition in which the skin and the white parts of the eyes become yellow

jaun·diced /'dʒɔndəst/ *adj.* **1** not expecting someone or something to be good or useful, especially because of experiences that you have had in the past: *He had a jaundiced view of life.* ◆ *She looked on politicians with a jaundiced eye.* **2** suffering from jaundice: *a jaundiced patient/liver*

jaunt /dʒɔnt/ *noun* (*old-fashioned* or *humorous*) a short trip that you make for pleasure **SYN** EXCURSION

jaun·ty /'dʒɔnti/ *adj.* (**jaun·ti·er**, **jaun·ti·est**) **1** showing that you are feeling confident and pleased with yourself **SYN** CHEERFUL: *a jaunty smile* **2** lively: *a jaunty tune* ▶ **jaun·ti·ly** /-təli/ *adv.*: *He set off jauntily, whistling to himself.* **jaun·ti·ness** /-tinəs/ *noun* [U]

java /'dʒɑvə; 'dʒævə/ *noun* [U] (*informal*) coffee

javelin /'dʒævəlɪn; 'dʒævə-/ *noun* **1** [C] a light SPEAR (= a long stick with a pointed end) that is thrown in a sports event ⊃ picture at SPORT **2 the javelin** [sing.] the event or sport of throwing a javelin as far as possible

jaw /dʒɔ/ *noun, verb*
- *noun* **1** [C] either of the two bones at the bottom of the face that contain the teeth and move when you talk or eat: *the top/upper jaw* ◆ *the bottom/lower jaw* ⊃ picture at BODY **2** [sing.] the lower part of the face; the lower jaw: *He has a strong square jaw.* ◆ *The punch broke my jaw.* **3 jaws** [pl.] the mouth and teeth of a person or an animal: *The alligator's jaws snapped shut.* **4 jaws** [pl.] the parts of a tool or machine that are used to hold things tightly: *the jaws of a vice*
  IDM **sb's jaw dropped/fell/sagged** used to say that someone suddenly looked surprised, shocked, or disappointed **the jaws of death, defeat, etc.** (*literary*) used to describe an unpleasant situation that almost happens: *The team snatched victory from the jaws of defeat.* **the jaws of a tunnel, etc.** the narrow entrance to a tunnel, etc., especially one that looks dangerous
- *verb* [I] (*informal*, often *disapproving*) to talk, especially to talk a lot or for a long time

jaw·bone /ˈdʒɔboʊn/ *noun* the bone that forms the lower jaw ⊃ picture at BODY SYN MANDIBLE

jaw·break·er /ˈdʒɔˌbreɪkər/ *noun* a very large, hard, round candy

ˈjaw-ˌdropping *adj.* (*informal*) so large or good that it amazes you: *a jaw-dropping 5 million dollars* ◆ *The production is absolutely jaw-dropping.* ▶ **ˈjaw-ˌdroppingly** *adv.*: *jaw-droppingly beautiful*

jaw·line /ˈdʒɔlaɪn/ *noun* the outline of the lower jaw

jay /dʒeɪ/ *noun* a bird of the CROW family, with bright feathers and a noisy call ⊃ see also BLUEJAY

Jay·cee /ˌdʒeɪˈsi/ *noun* (*informal*) a member of the United States Junior Chamber, an organization for people between the ages of 18 and 41 that provides help in local communities in the U.S. and other countries

jay·walk /ˈdʒeɪwɔk/ *verb* [I] to walk along or across a street illegally or without paying attention to the traffic ▶ **jay·walk·er** *noun* **jay·walk·ing** *noun* [U]

jazz /dʒæz/ *noun, verb*
- *noun* [U] a type of music with strong rhythms, in which the players often IMPROVISE (= make up the music as they are playing), originally created by African American musicians: *a jazz band/club* ◆ *traditional/modern jazz* ◆ *jazz musicians* ⊃ collocations at MUSIC ⊃ see also ACID JAZZ
  IDM **and all that jazz** (*informal*) and things like that: *How's it going? You know—love, life, and all that jazz.*
- *verb*
  PHRV **jazz sth↔ˈup** (*informal*) **1** to make something more interesting, exciting, or attractive **2** to make a piece of music sound more modern, or more like popular music or jazz: *It's a jazzed up version of an old tune.*

jazzed /dʒæzd/ *adj.* [not before noun] (*informal*) excited: *I was jazzed to meet someone so famous.*

jazz·y /ˈdʒæzi/ *adj.* (*informal*) **1** in the style of jazz: *a jazzy melody/tune* **2** (sometimes *disapproving*) brightly colored and likely to attract attention SYN SNAZZY: *That's a jazzy tie you're wearing.*

JCL /ˌdʒeɪ si ˈɛl/ *abbr.* job control language (a computer language that lets the user state what tasks they want the OPERATING SYSTEM to do)

J.D. (also **JD**) /ˌdʒeɪ ˈdi/ *noun* a degree from a law school (the abbreviation for "Juris Doctor"): *She has a J.D. from Georgetown University.*

jeal·ous 🔑 /ˈdʒɛləs/ *adj.*
1 feeling angry or unhappy because someone you like or love is showing interest in someone else: *a jealous wife/husband* ◆ *He's only talking to her to make you jealous.* **2 ~ (of sb/sth)** feeling angry or unhappy because you wish you had something that someone else has SYN ENVIOUS: *She's jealous of my success.* ◆ *Children often feel jealous when a new baby arrives.* **3 ~ (of sth)** wanting to keep or protect

something that you have because it makes you feel proud: *They are very jealous of their good reputation* (= they do not want to lose it). ▶ **jeal·ous·ly** *adv.*: *She eyed Natalia jealously.* ◆ *a jealously guarded secret*

jeal·ous·y /ˈdʒɛləsi/ *noun* (*pl.* **jeal·ous·ies**) **1** [U] a feeling of being jealous: *I felt sick with jealousy.* ◆ *sexual jealousy* **2** [C] an action or a remark that shows that a person is jealous: *I'm tired of her petty jealousies.*

jeans 🔑 /dʒinz/ *noun* [pl.]
pants made of strong cotton, especially DENIM: *a faded pair of blue jeans* ⊃ picture at CLOTHES ⊃ see also DENIM ORIGIN From **Janne**, the Old French name for Genoa, where the heavy cotton now used for jeans was first made.

Jeep™ /dʒip/ *noun* a small strong vehicle used for driving over rough ground ⊃ picture at CAR

jee·pers /ˈdʒipərz/ (also **jeepers ˈcreepers**) *exclamation* (*old-fashioned, informal*) used to express surprise or shock: *Jeepers! That car nearly hit us!*

jeer /dʒɪr/ *verb, noun*
- *verb* [I, T] to laugh at someone or shout rude remarks at them to show that you do not respect them SYN TAUNT: *a jeering crowd* ◆ **~ at sb** *The police were jeered at by the waiting crowd.* ◆ **~ sb** *The players were jeered by disappointed fans.* ◆ **+ speech** *"Coward!" he jeered.*
- *noun* [usually pl.] a rude remark that someone shouts at someone else to show that they do not respect or like them SYN TAUNT: *He walked on to the stage to be greeted with jeers and whistles.*

jeez /dʒiz/ *exclamation* (*informal*) used to express anger, surprise, etc.

Je·ho·vah /dʒɪˈhoʊvə/ (also **Yah·weh**) *noun* [U] the name of God that is used in the Old Testament of the Bible

Je·hovah's ˈWitness *noun* a member of a religious organization based on Christianity, that believes that the end of the world is near and that only its members will be saved from being DAMNED

je·june /dʒɪˈdʒun/ *adj.* (*formal*) **1** too simple SYN NAIVE **2** (of a speech, etc.) not interesting

je·ju·num /dʒɪˈdʒunəm/ *noun* (*anatomy*) the second part of the small INTESTINE ⊃ compare DUODENUM, ILEUM ▶ **je·ju·nal** /-ˈdʒunl/ *adj.*

Jek·yll and Hyde /ˌdʒɛkl ən ˈhaɪd/ *noun* [sing.] a person who is sometimes very pleasant (*Jekyll*) and sometimes very unpleasant (*Hyde*) or who leads two very separate lives ORIGIN From the story by Robert Louis Stevenson, *Dr. Jekyll and Mr. Hyde*, in which Dr. Jekyll takes a drug which separates the good and bad sides of his personality into two characters. All the negative aspects go into the character of Mr. Hyde.

jell (also **gel**) /dʒɛl/ *verb* **1** [I] (of two or more people) to work well together; to form a successful group: *We just didn't jell as a group.* **2** [I] (of an idea, a thought, a plan, etc.) to become clearer and more definite; to work well: *Ideas were beginning to jell in my mind.* ◆ *That day, everything jelled.* **3** [I] (*technical*) (of a liquid) to become thicker and more solid; to form a GEL

jel·lied /ˈdʒɛlid/ *adj.* [only before noun] prepared or cooked in jelly: *jellied cranberry sauce*

Jell-O™ /ˈdʒɛloʊ/ *noun* [U] a cold, sweet, transparent food made from GELATIN, sugar, and fruit juice, that shakes when it is moved: *Jell-O and ice cream*

jel·ly 🔑 /ˈdʒɛli/
(*pl.* **jel·lies**) *noun* **1** [U, C] a thick sweet food made by boiling fruit juice with sugar, but without any pieces of fruit in it, often sold in jars and spread on bread: *blackcurrant jelly* ⊃ compare JAM **2** [U] any thick, sticky substance, especially a type of cream used on the skin ⊃ see also PETROLEUM JELLY, ROYAL JELLY **3** [U] a thick, sticky substance made from GELATIN and meat juices, served around meat, fish, etc. SYN ASPIC: *chicken in jelly* **4** (also **ˈjelly ˌshoe**) [C] a light

plastic shoe designed for wearing on the beach and in the ocean

IDM **be/feel like jelly| turn to jelly** (of legs or knees) to feel weak because you are nervous

'jelly ,bean *noun* a small candy shaped like a BEAN, with a hard outside and a softer center

jel·ly·fish /'dʒelifɪʃ/ *noun* (*pl.* **jel·ly·fish**) a sea creature with a body like jelly and long thin parts called TEN-TACLES that can give a sharp sting

jellyfish

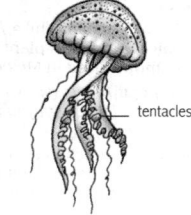

tentacles

'jelly ,roll *noun* a thin flat cake that is spread with jelly, etc. and rolled up

je ne sais quoi /,ʒə nə seɪ 'kwɑ/ *noun* [U] (from *French*, often *humorous*) a good quality that is difficult to describe: *He has that je ne sais quoi that distinguishes a professional from an amateur.*

jen·ny /'dʒeni/ *noun* (*pl.* **jen·nies**) a female DONKEY or ASS

jeop·ard·ize /'dʒepərˌdaɪz/ *verb* **~ sth/sb** (*formal*) to risk harming or destroying something or someone **SYN** ENDANGER: *He would never do anything to jeopardize his career.*

jeop·ard·y /'dʒepərdi/ *noun*
IDM **in jeopardy** in a dangerous position or situation and likely to be lost or harmed ⊃ see also DOUBLE JEOPARDY

jer·e·mi·ad /,dʒerə'maɪəd; -æd/ *noun* (*formal*) a very long sad complaint or list of complaints

jerk /dʒərk/ *verb, noun*
• *verb* [T, I] to move or to make something move with a sudden, short, sharp movement: **~ sth** (**+ adv./prep.**) *He jerked the phone away from her.* ♦ *She jerked her head up.* ♦ **+ adv./prep.** *The bus jerked to a halt.* ♦ *He grabbed a handful of hair and jerked at it.*
PHR V **jerk sb a'round** (*informal*) to make things difficult for someone, especially by not being honest with them: *Consumers are often jerked around by big companies.*
• *noun* **1** [C] a sudden, quick, sharp movement **SYN** JOLT: *She sat up* **with a jerk. 2** [C] (*informal*) a stupid or unpleasant person **3** [U] meat that is MARINATED (= left in a mixture of oil and spices before being cooked) to give it a strong flavor and then cooked over a wood fire: *jerk chicken*

jer·kin /'dʒərkən/ *noun* a short jacket without sleeves, especially one worn by men in the past

jerk·y /'dʒərki/ *adj., noun*
• *adj.* making sudden starts and stops and not moving smoothly ▶ **jerk·i·ly** /-kəli/ *adv.*: *The car moved off jerkily.*
• *noun* [U] meat that has been cut into long strips and smoked or dried: *beef jerky*

jer·o·bo·am /,dʒerə'bouəm/ *noun* a wine bottle which holds four or six times as much wine as an ordinary bottle ⊃ compare METHUSELAH, NEBUCHADNEZZAR

jer·ry–built /'dʒeri ,bɪlt/ *noun* (*old-fashioned, disapproving*) built quickly and cheaply without caring about quality or safety

jer·ry·can /'dʒeri ,kæn/ *noun* a large metal or plastic container with flat sides, used for carrying gas or water

Jer·sey /'dʒərzi/ *noun* a type of light brown cow that produces high quality milk

jer·sey /'dʒərzi/ *noun* **1** [C] a shirt worn by someone playing a sports game ⊃ picture at FOOTBALL **2** [U] a type of soft fine cloth that stretches easily, used for making clothes: *made from 100% cotton jersey* **3** [C] a tight-fitting piece of clothing made of wool or cotton for the upper part of the body, with long sleeves and no buttons; a type of sweater

Jerusalem 'artichoke /dʒə,rusələm 'ɑrtətʃouk/ *noun* a light brown vegetable that looks like a potato ⊃ compare ARTICHOKE

jest /dʒest/ *noun, verb*
• *noun* (*old-fashioned* or *formal*) something said or done to amuse people **SYN** JOKE
IDM **in jest** as a joke: *The remark was made half in jest.*
♦ *"Many a true word is spoken in jest,"* thought Rosie. (= people often say things as a joke that are actually true)
• *verb* [I, T] **~ (about sth)** | **+ speech** (*formal* or *humorous*) to say things that are not serious or true, especially in order to make someone laugh **SYN** JOKE: *Would I jest about such a thing?*

jest·er /'dʒestər/ *noun* a man employed in the past at the COURT of a king or queen to amuse people by telling jokes and funny stories: *the court jester*

Jes·u·it /'dʒeʒuət; -ʒuət/ *noun* a member of the Society of Jesus, a Roman Catholic religious group: *a Jesuit priest*

Je·sus /'dʒizəs; -zəz/ (also **Jesus 'Christ**) *noun* = CHRIST

jet /dʒet/ *noun, verb*
• *noun* **1** [C] a plane driven by JET ENGINES: *a jet aircraft/ fighter/airliner* ♦ *The accident happened as the jet was about to take off.* ⊃ see also JUMBO (JET), JUMP JET **2** [C] a strong narrow stream of gas, liquid, steam, or flame that comes very quickly out of a small opening. The opening is also called a jet: *The pipe burst and jets of water shot across the room.* ♦ *to clean the gas jets on the stove* **3** [U] a hard black mineral that can be polished and is used in jewelry
• *verb* (**-tt-**) [I] **+ adv./prep.** (*informal*) to fly somewhere in a plane

jet 'black *adj.* deep shiny black in color

jet 'engine *noun* an engine that drives an aircraft forward by pushing out a stream of gases behind it ⊃ picture at PLANE

jet·foil /'dʒetfɔɪl/ *noun* a passenger boat that rises above the surface of the water when it is traveling fast and has JET ENGINES

'jet lag *noun* [U] the feeling of being tired and slightly confused after a long plane trip, especially when there is a big difference in the time at the place you leave and that at the place you arrive in ⊃ collocations at TRAVEL ▶ **'jet-lagged** *adj.*

jet·lin·er /'dʒetˌlaɪnər/ *noun* a large plane with a jet engine, that carries passengers

jet-pro'pelled *adj.* driven by JET ENGINES

jet pro'pulsion *noun* [U] the use of JET ENGINES for power

jet·sam /'dʒetsəm/ *noun* things that are thrown away, especially from a ship at sea and that float toward land ⊃ compare FLOTSAM

the 'jet set *noun* [sing.] rich and fashionable people who travel a lot

'jet-,setter *noun* a rich fashionable person who travels a lot ▶ **'jet-,setting** *adj.* [usually before noun]: *her jet-setting millionaire boyfriend*

'Jet Ski™ *noun* a vehicle with an engine, like a motorcycle, for riding across water ▶ **'jet-,skiing** *noun* [U] ⊃ picture at SPORT

'jet stream *noun* **1** usually **the jet stream** [sing.] a strong wind that blows high above the earth and that has an effect on the weather **2** [C] the flow of gases from a plane's engine

jet·ti·son /'dʒetəsn; -zn/ *verb* **1 ~ sth** to throw something out of a moving plane or ship to make it lighter: *to jettison fuel* **2 ~ sth/sb** to get rid of something or someone that you no longer need or want **SYN** DISCARD: *He was jettisoned as team coach after the defeat.* **3 ~ sth** to reject an idea, belief, plan, etc. that you no longer think is useful or likely to be successful **SYN** ABANDON

jet·ty /'dʒeti/ *noun* (*pl.* **jet·ties**) (also **dock**) a wall or platform built out into the ocean, a river, etc., where boats can be tied and where people can get on and off boats

jet·way /'dʒetweɪ/ *noun* a bridge that can be moved and put against the door of an aircraft, so people can get on and off

Jew /dʒu/ *noun* a member of the people and cultural community whose traditional religion is Judaism and who come from the ancient Hebrew people of Israel; a person who believes in and practices Judaism

jew·el /'dʒuəl/ *noun* **1** a PRECIOUS STONE such as a diamond, RUBY, etc. **SYN GEM 2** [usually pl.] pieces of jewelry or decorative objects that contain PRECIOUS STONES: *The family jewels are locked away in a safe.* ➔ see also CROWN JEWELS **3** a small PRECIOUS STONE or piece of special glass that is used in the machinery of a watch **4** (*informal*) a person or thing that is very important or valuable ➔ compare GEM
  IDM the jewel in the crown the most attractive or valuable part of something

'jewel ˌcase *noun* a plastic box for holding a CD or DVD

jew·eled /'dʒuəld/ *adj.* decorated with jewels

jew·el·er /'dʒuələr/ *noun* **1** a person who makes, repairs, or sells jewelry and watches **2 jeweler's** (*pl.* **jewelers**) a store that sells jewelry and watches: *I bought it at the jeweler's near my office.*

jewelry

clasp
chain
pendant
medallion
locket
earrings
pin
pearl necklace
hoop earring
charm
bangle
bracelet
charm bracelet
cuff links
engagement ring
wedding ring
signet ring

jew·el·ry (CanE usually **jew·el·lery**) /'dʒuəlri/ *noun* [U]
objects such as rings and NECKLACES that people wear as decoration: *silver/gold jewelry* ◆ *She has some lovely pieces of jewelry.* ➔ collocations at FASHION ➔ see also COSTUME JEWELRY

Jew·ess /'dʒuəs/ *noun* (often *offensive*) an old-fashioned word for a Jewish woman

Jew·ish /'dʒuɪʃ/ *adj.* connected with Jews or Judaism; believing in and practicing Judaism: *We're Jewish.* ◆ *the local Jewish community* ▶ **Jew·ish·ness** *noun* [U]

Jew·ry /'dʒuri/ *noun* [U] (*formal*) Jewish people as a group: *North American Jewry*

'Jew's harp *noun* a small musical instrument which is held between the teeth and played with a finger

Je·ze·bel /'dʒɛzə,bɛl/ *noun* (*old-fashioned*) a woman who is thought to be sexually immoral **ORIGIN** From the name of the wife of a king of Israel in the Bible, who wore makeup and was criticized by Elijah for worshiping the god Baal.

jib /dʒɪb/ *noun* **1** a small sail in front of the large sail on a boat ➔ picture at BOAT **2** the arm of a CRANE that lifts things

jibe /dʒaɪb/ *noun, verb* [I]
● *verb* **1** ~ (**with sth**) (*informal*) to be the same as something or to match it: *Your statement doesn't jibe with the facts.* **2** = GIBE *v.* **3** to change direction when sailing with the wind behind you, by swinging the sail from one side of the boat to the other
● *noun* = GIBE *n.*

ji·ca·ma /'hikəmə; 'hɪkə-/ *noun* [U, C] the large root of a tropical American plant that has white flesh and is commonly used in Mexican cooking or eaten raw in salads

jif·fy /'dʒɪfi/ *noun* (*pl.* **jif·fies**) [usually sing.] (*informal*) a moment: *I'll be with you in a jiffy* (= very soon).

jig /dʒɪg/ *noun, verb*
● *noun* **1** a quick lively dance; the music for this dance: *an Irish jig* **2** a device that holds something in position and guides the tools that are working on it: *a carpenter's jig*
  IDM the game/jig is up (*informal*) said when someone who has done something wrong is caught and the crime or trick is discovered: *When they heard the police siren, they knew the jig was up.*
● *verb* (**-gg-**) [I, T] ~ (**sb/sth**) (+ *adv./prep.*) to move or to make someone or something move up and down with short quick movements: *He jigged up and down with excitement.*

jig·ger /'dʒɪgər/ *noun* **1** a very small glass for measuring alcohol; the amount a jigger can hold, about 1.5 OUNCES **2** = CHIGGER

jig·gle /'dʒɪgl/ *verb* [I, T] (*informal*) to move or make something move up and down or from side to side with short quick movements: (+ *adv./prep.*) *Stop jiggling around!* ◆ *She jiggled with the lock.* ◆ ~ **sth** (+ *adv./prep.*) *He stood jiggling his car keys in his hand.*

jig·saw /'dʒɪgsɔ/ *noun* **1** = JIGSAW PUZZLE **2** a mysterious situation in which it is not easy to understand all the causes of what is happening; a complicated problem **3** a SAW (= a type of tool) with a fine blade for cutting designs in thin pieces of wood or metal

'jigsaw ˌpuzzle (also **jig·saw, puz·zle**) *noun* a picture printed on heavy paper or wood, that has been cut up into a lot of small pieces of different shapes that you have to fit together again: *to do a jigsaw puzzle* ➔ picture at PUZZLE

ji·had /dʒɪ'had/ *noun* **1** (in Islam) a spiritual struggle within yourself to stop yourself from breaking religious or moral laws **2** a holy war fought by Muslims to defend Islam

jil·bab /dʒɪl'bab/ *noun* a full-length piece of clothing worn over other clothes by Muslim women

jilt /dʒɪlt/ *verb* [often passive] ~ **sb** to end a romantic relationship with someone in a sudden and unkind way: *He was jilted by his fiancée.* ◆ *a jilted bride/lover*

Jim Crow /,dʒɪm 'kroʊ/ *noun* [U] the former practice in the U.S. of using laws that allowed black people to be treated unfairly and kept separate from white people, for example in schools **ORIGIN** From the name of a black character in a song that was sung on the cotton plantations.

jim·my /'dʒɪmi/ *noun, verb*
● *noun* (*pl.* **jim·mies**) a short, heavy, metal bar used by thieves to force open doors and windows
● *verb* (**jim·my·ing, jim·mies, jim·mied**) ~ **sth** to force open a window or door with a jimmy

jin·gle /'dʒɪŋgl/ *noun, verb*
● *noun* **1** [sing.] a sound like small bells ringing that is made when metal objects are shaken together: *the jingle of coins in his pocket* **2** [C] a short song or tune that is easy to remember and is used in advertising on radio or television
● *verb* [I, T] ~ (**sth**) to make a pleasant gentle sound like small bells ringing; to make something do this: *The chimes jingled in the breeze.* ◆ *She jingled the coins in her pocket.*

jin·go·ism /'dʒɪŋgoʊ,ɪzəm/ *noun* [U] (*disapproving*) a strong belief that your own country is best, especially when this is expressed in support of war with another country ▸ jin·go·is·tic /ˌdʒɪŋɡoʊˈɪstɪk/ adj.

jinks /dʒɪŋks/ noun ⊃ HIGH JINKS

jinx /dʒɪŋks/ noun [sing.] ~ (on sb/sth) bad luck; someone or something that is thought to bring bad luck in a mysterious way: I'm convinced there's a jinx on this car. ▸ **jinx** verb ~ sb/sth

jinxed /dʒɪŋkst/ adj. (informal) having or bringing more bad luck than is normal: The whole family seemed to be jinxed.

JIT /ˌdʒeɪ aɪ ˈti/ abbr. JUST-IN-TIME

jit·ter·bug /ˈdʒɪtərˌbʌɡ/ noun a fast dance that was popular in the 1940s

jit·ters /ˈdʒɪtərz/ often **the jitters** noun [pl.] (informal) feelings of being anxious and nervous, especially before an important event or before having to do something difficult: I always **get the jitters** before exams.

jit·ter·y /ˈdʒɪtəri/ adj. (informal) anxious and nervous ⊃ thesaurus box at NERVOUS

jiu-jitsu = JU-JITSU

jive /dʒaɪv/ noun, verb
● noun 1 [U, sing.] a fast dance to music with a strong beat, especially popular in the 1950s 2 [U] (old-fashioned, informal) nonsense: to talk jive
● verb 1 [I] to dance to JAZZ or ROCK AND ROLL music 2 [I, T] ~ (sb) (old-fashioned, informal) to try to make someone believe something that is not true SYN KID

Job /dʒoʊb/ noun
IDM **the patience of Job** the fact of being extremely patient and not complaining: You need the patience of Job to deal with some of our customers. **ORIGIN** From **Job**, a man in the Bible who experienced much suffering, including losing his family, his home, and his possessions, but continued to believe in and trust God.

THESAURUS

job

position • post • vacancy • appointment

These are all words for a position doing work for which you receive regular payment.

job a position doing work for which you receive regular payment: He's trying to get a job at a bank.

position (formal) a job: I would like to apply for a position in sales.

JOB OR POSITION?

Position usually refers to a particular job within an organization, and is not usually used about about jobs generally. It is also often used in job applications, descriptions, and advertisements.

post (formal) an important job, especially one in government: She was offered a key post in the new government.

vacancy a job that is available for someone to do: We have several vacancies for nurses.

appointment (somewhat formal) a job or position of responsibility: After two years, you will become eligible for a permanent appointment.

PATTERNS
- a **permanent/temporary** job/position/post/vacancy/appointment
- a **full-time/part-time** job/position/post/vacancy/appointment
- to **have/have got** a(n) job/position/post/vacancy/appointment
- to **apply for/fill** a job/position/post/vacancy
- to **resign from/leave/quit** a job/position/post

---

job /dʒɑb/ noun
> **PAID WORK** **1** work for which you receive regular payment: He's trying to **get a job**. ◆ She **took a job** as a waitress. ◆ His brother's just **lost his job**. ◆ a temporary/permanent job ◆ I'm thinking of **applying for** a new job. ◆ The takeover of the company is bound to mean more job losses. ◆ Many women are in **part-time jobs**. ◆ Did they **offer you the job?** ◆ He certainly **knows his job** (= is very good at his job). ◆ I'm **only doing my job** (= I'm doing what I am paid to do). ◆ He's been **out of a job** (= unemployed) for six months now. ◆ She's never had a **steady job** (= a job that is not going to end suddenly). ⊃ collocations at UNEMPLOYMENT
> **TASK** **2** a particular task or piece of work that you have to do: I've got various jobs around the house. ◆ Sorting these papers out is going to be a long job. ◆ The builder has a couple of jobs going at the moment. ⊃ see also NOSE JOB ⊃ thesaurus box at TASK
> **DUTY** **3** [usually sing.] a responsibility or duty: It's not my job to lock up!
> **CRIME** **4** (informal) a crime, especially stealing: a bank job ◆ an inside job (= done by someone in the organization where the crime happens)
> **OBJECT** **5** (informal) a particular kind of thing: It's real wood—not one of those plastic jobs.
> **COMPUTING** **6** an item of work that is done by a computer as a single unit
IDM **do a good, bad, etc. job (on sth)** to do something well, badly, etc.: They did a very professional job. ◆ You've certainly done an excellent job on the kitchen (= for example, painting it). **do the job** (informal) to be effective or successful in doing what you want: This extra strong glue should do the job. **do a job on sb/sth** (informal) to harm or defeat someone, or to damage something: The hurricane really did a job on the city. **fall down on the job** to fail to do something that people expected you to do, or to do it badly: The government fell down on the job of monitoring this company. **good job!** (informal) used to tell someone that they have done well at something **on the job** while doing a particular job: No sleeping on the job! ◆ on-the-job training ⊃ more at WALK

TOPIC COLLOCATIONS

Jobs

getting a job
- **look for** work
- **look for/apply for/go for** a job
- **get/pick up/complete/fill out** an application (form)
- **send/e-mail** your résumé/CV/application/application form/cover letter
- **be called for/have/attend** an interview
- **offer sb** a job/work/employment/a promotion
- **find/get/land** a job
- **employ/hire/recruit** staff/workers/trainees
- **recruit/appoint** a manager

doing a job
- **arrive at/get to/leave** work/the office/the factory
- **start/finish** work/your shift
- **do/put in/work** overtime
- **have/gain/get/lack/need** experience/qualifications
- **do/get/have/receive** training
- **learn/pick up/improve/develop** (your) skills
- **cope with/manage/share/spread/delegate** the workload
- **improve your/achieve** a better work-life balance
- **have (no)** job satisfaction/job security

building a career
- **have** a job/work/a career/a vocation
- **find/follow/pursue** your vocation
- **enter/go into/join** a profession
- **choose/embark on/start/begin/pursue** a career
- **change** jobs/professions/careers
- **be/go/work** freelance

'job ,action *noun* action that workers take, such as a STRIKE (= stopping work), to protest something such as low pay

job·ber /'dʒɑbər/ *noun* (*finance*) a business that buys large amounts of particular goods and sells them to other businesses

job·bie /'dʒabi/ *noun* (*informal*) used to refer to an object of a particular kind: *Her bikini was one of those expensive designer jobbies.*

'job cre,ation *noun* [U] the process of providing opportunities for paid work, especially for people who are unemployed

'job de,scription *noun* a written description of the exact work and responsibilities of a job

'job-hunt *verb* [I] (usually used in the progressive tenses) to try to find a job: *At that time I had been job-hunting for six months.*

job·less /'dʒɑbləs/ *adj.* **1** without a job SYN UNEMPLOYED: *The closure left 500 people jobless.* **2 the jobless** *noun* [pl.] people who are unemployed ▸ **job·less·ness** *noun* [U]

'job lot *noun* (*informal*) a collection of different things, especially of poor quality, that are sold together

,job satis'faction *noun* [U] the good feeling that you get when you have a job that you enjoy

'job-,sharing *noun* [U] an arrangement for two people to share the hours of work and the pay of one job ▸ **'job-share** *noun*: *The company encourages job-shares and part-time work.* **'job-share** *verb* [I] ~ **(with sb)**

jock /dʒɑk/ *noun* **1** a person, especially a student, who plays a lot of sports **2** a person who likes a particular activity: *a computer jock* **3** = DISC JOCKEY ⊃ compare SHOCK JOCK

jock·ey /'dʒɑki/ *noun, verb*
• *noun* a person who rides horses in races, especially as a job ⊃ picture at SPORT
• *verb* [I] ~ **(with sb) (for sth)** | ~ **(with sb) (to do sth)** to try all possible ways of gaining an advantage over other people: *The runners jockeyed for position at the start.* ◆ *The bands are constantly jockeying with each other for the number one spot.*

'jock itch *noun* (*informal*) an infectious skin disease that affects the GROIN

jock·strap /'dʒɑkstræp/ (also ath'letic sup,porter) *noun* a piece of men's underwear worn to support or protect the sexual organs while playing sports

jo·cose /dʒə'koʊs/ *adj.* (*formal*) humorous

joc·u·lar /'dʒɑkyələr/ *adj.* (*formal*) **1** humorous: *a jocular comment* **2** (of a person) enjoying making people laugh SYN JOLLY ⊃ see also JOKE ▸ **joc·u·lar·i·ty** /,dʒɑkyə'lærəti/ *noun* [U] **joc·u·lar·ly** /'dʒɑkyələrli/ *adv.*

joc·und /'dʒɑkənd; 'dʒoʊ-/ *adj.* (*formal*) cheerful

jodh·purs /'dʒɑdpərz/ *noun* [pl.] pants that are loose above the knee and tight from the knee to the ankle, worn when riding a horse: *a pair of jodhpurs*

joe (also **Joe**) /dʒoʊ/ *noun* [usually sing.] (*informal*) an ordinary working man: *a fitness program for the average joe* IDM see CUP *n.*

,Joe 'Blow *noun* [sing.] (*informal*) a way of referring to a typical ordinary person

,Joe Six·pack /,dʒoʊ 'sɪkspæk/ *noun* (*informal*) a man who is considered typical of a person who does MANUAL work: *Joe Sixpack doesn't care about that.*

jo·ey /'dʒoʊi/ *noun* a young KANGAROO, WALLABY, or OPOSSUM ⊃ picture at ANIMAL

jog /dʒɑg/ *verb, noun*
• *verb* (-gg-) **1** also **go jogging** [I] to run slowly and steadily for a long time, especially for exercise: *I go jogging every morning.* **2** [T] ~ **sth/sb** to hit something lightly and by accident SYN NUDGE: *Someone jogged her elbow, making her spill her coffee.*
IDM **jog sb's memory** to say or do something that makes someone remember something
• *noun* [sing.] **1** a slow run, especially one done for physical exercise: *I like to go for a jog after work.* **2** a light push or knock SYN NUDGE

jog·ger /'dʒɑgər/ *noun* a person who jogs regularly for exercise

jog·ging /'dʒɑgɪn/ *noun* [U] the activity of running slowly and steadily as a form of exercise: *to go jogging* ⊃ picture at EXERCISE ⊃ collocations at DIET

'jogging ,suit *noun* = TRACKSUIT

jog·gle /'dʒɑgl/ *verb* [I, T] ~ **(sb/sth)** (*informal*) to move or to make someone or something move quickly up and down or from one side to another

john /dʒɑn/ *noun* (*informal*) a toilet

the John 'Birch So,ciety *noun* [sing.] a political organization of the far right that was started to fight Communism in the U.S.

John Doe /,dʒɑn 'doʊ/ *noun* [usually sing.] **1** a name used for a person whose name is not known or is kept secret, especially in a court of law **2** an average man ⊃ compare JANE DOE

John Hancock /,dʒɑn 'hæŋkɑk/ *noun* (*informal*) a person's signature

Johnny-come-lately /,dʒɑni kʌm 'leɪtli/ *noun* [sing.] (*disapproving* or *humorous*) a person who has only recently arrived in a place or started an activity, especially someone who is more confident than they should be

Johnny Reb /,dʒɑni 'rɛb/ *noun* (*informal*) a name for a soldier who fought for the Confederate States in the American Civil War

,John ,Q. 'Public *noun* [U] (*informal*) people in general; the public

joie de vi·vre /,ʒwɑ də 'vivrə; -'viv/ *noun* [U] (from *French*) a feeling of great happiness and enjoyment of life

join /dʒɔɪn/ *verb, noun*
• *verb*
▸ CONNECT **1** [T, I] to attach or connect two or more things together: ~ **A to B** *Join one section of pipe to the next.* ◆ *The island is joined to the mainland by a bridge.* ◆ ~ **(A and B) (together/up)** *Join the two sections of pipe together.* ◆ *Draw a line joining (up) all the dots.* ◆ *How do these two pieces join?*
▸ BECOME ONE **2** [I, T] if two things or groups **join**, or if one thing or group **joins** another, they come together to form one thing or group: *the place where the two paths join* ◆ ~ **sth** *The path joins the road near the trees.*
▸ CLUB/COMPANY **3** [T, I] ~ **(sth)** to become a member of an organization, a company, a club, etc.: *I've joined an aerobics class.* ◆ *She joined the company three months ago.* ◆ (*figurative*) *to join the ranks of the unemployed* ◆ *It costs $20 to join.*
▸ DO SOMETHING WITH SOMEONE ELSE **4** [T] to take part in something that someone else is doing or to go somewhere with them: ~ **sb (for sth)** *Will you join us for lunch?* ◆ *Do you mind if I join you?* ◆ ~ **sth** *Over 200 members of the staff joined the strike.* ◆ *Members of the public searched for the missing boy.* ◆ ~ **sb in doing sth** *I'm sure you'll all join me in wishing Ted and Laura a very happy marriage.*
IDM **join battle (with sb)** (*formal*) to begin fighting someone: (*figurative*) *Residents have joined battle with the local government over the lack of parking facilities.* **join the club** (*informal*) used when something bad that has happened to

someone else has also happened to you: *So you didn't get a job either? Join the club!* **join hands (with sb) 1** if two people **join hands**, they hold each other's hands **2** to work together in doing something: *Education has been reluctant to join hands with business.* ⊃ more at BEAT *v.*, FORCE *n.*
PHR V **join 'in (with/doing sth)** | **join 'in (with sb/sth)** to take part in an activity with other people: *She listens but she never joins in.* ♦ *I wish he would join in with the other kids.* **join 'up** to become a member of the armed forces **SYN** ENLIST **join 'up (with sb)** to combine with someone else to do something: *We'll join up with the other groups later.*

● **noun**
> CONNECTION a place where two things are fixed together: *The two pieces were stuck together so well that you could hardly see the join.*

join·er /'dʒɔɪnər/ *noun* **1** a person whose job is to make the wooden parts of a building, especially window frames, doors, etc. ⊃ compare CARPENTER **2** a person who joins an organization, club, etc.: *She's such a joiner that she belongs to eight or ten clubs.*

join·er·y /'dʒɔɪnəri/ *noun* [U] the work of a joiner or things made by a joiner

joint /dʒɔɪnt/ *adj., noun*
● **adj.** [only before noun] involving two or more people together: *a joint account* (= a bank account in the name of more than one person, for example a husband and wife) ♦ *The report was a joint effort* (= we worked on it together). ♦ *They finished in joint first place.* ♦ *They were joint owners of the house* (= they owned it together). ▸ **joint·ly** *adv.*: *The event was organized jointly by students and staff.*
● **noun 1** [C] a place where two bones are joined together in the body in a way that enables them to bend and move: *inflammation of the knee joint* ⊃ see also BALL-AND-SOCKET JOINT **2** [C] a place where two or more parts of an object are joined together, especially to form a corner **3** [C] (*informal*) a place where people meet to eat, drink, dance, etc., especially one that is cheap: *a fast-food joint* **4** the joint [sing.] (*informal*) prison; jail: *thirty years in the joint* **5** [C] (*informal*) a cigarette containing MARIJUANA (= an illegal drug)
IDM **out of joint 1** (of a bone) pushed out of its correct position **2** not working or behaving in the normal way ⊃ more at CASE, NOSE

Joint ,Chiefs of 'Staff *noun* [pl.] the leaders of the ARMED FORCES who advise the President on military matters

joint·ed /'dʒɔɪntɪd/ *adj.* [usually before noun] having parts that fit together and can move: *a doll with jointed arms/legs*

,joint reso'lution *noun* a decision that has been approved by the Senate and the House of Representatives

,joint-'stock ,company *noun* (*business*) a company that is owned by all the people who have shares in it

,joint 'venture *noun* (*business*) a business project or activity that is begun by two or more companies, etc., which remain separate organizations

joist /dʒɔɪst/ *noun* a long thick piece of wood or metal that is used to support a floor or ceiling in a building

jo·jo·ba /hou'houbə/ *noun* **1** [U] oil from the seeds of an American plant, often used in COSMETICS **2** [U, C] the plant that produces these seeds

joke /dʒouk/ *noun, verb*
● **noun 1** something that you say or do to make people laugh, for example a funny story that you tell: *I can't tell jokes.* ♦ *She's always cracking jokes.* ♦ *They often make jokes at each other's expense.* ♦ *I didn't get the joke* (= understand it). ♦ *I wish he wouldn't tell dirty jokes* (= about sex). ♦ *I only did it as a joke* (= it was not meant seriously). ⊃ see also IN-JOKE, PRACTICAL JOKE **2** [sing.] (*informal*) a person, thing, or situation that is ridiculous or annoying and cannot be taken seriously: *This latest pay offer is a joke.* ⊃ see also JOCULAR **IDM** **be no joke** to be difficult or unpleasant: *It's no joke trying to find a job these days.* **the joke's on sb** (*informal*) used

to say that someone who tried to make another person look ridiculous now looks ridiculous instead **make a joke of sth** to laugh about something that is serious or should be taken seriously **take a joke** to be able to laugh at a joke against yourself: *The trouble with her is she can't take a joke.*
● **verb ~ (with sb) (about sth) 1** [I, T] to say something to make people laugh; to tell a funny story: *She was laughing and joking with the children.* ♦ **~ about sth** *They often joked about all the things that could go wrong.* ♦ **+ speech** *"I cooked it myself, so be careful!" he joked.* **2** [I, T] to say something that is not true because you think it is funny: *I didn't mean that—I was only joking.* ♦ **~ that...** *She joked that she only loved him for his money.*
IDM **joking aside** used to show that you are now being serious after you have said something funny **you're joking| you must be joking** (*informal*) used to show that you are very surprised at what someone has just said: *No way am I doing that. You must be joking!* ♦ *She's going out with Dan? You're joking!*

jok·er /'dʒoukər/ *noun* **1** a person who likes making jokes or doing silly things to make people laugh **2** (*informal*) a person that you think is stupid because they annoy you **3** an extra PLAYING CARD that is used in some card games, usually as a WILD CARD ⊃ picture at PLAYING CARD

jok·ey (also **joky**) /'dʒouki/ *adj.* (*informal*) amusing; making people laugh

jok·ing·ly /'dʒoukɪŋli/ *adv.* in a way that is intended to be amusing and not serious

jol·ly /'dʒali/ *adj., verb, noun*
● **adj.** (jol·lier, jol·liest) **1** happy and cheerful: *a jolly crowd/face/mood* **2** (*old-fashioned*) enjoyable: *a jolly evening/party/time* ▸ **jol·li·ty** /'dʒalət̬i/ *noun* [U] (*old-fashioned*): *scenes of high-spirits and jollity*
● **verb** (jol·lies, jol·ly·ing, jol·lied, jol·lied)
PHR V **jolly sb a'long** to encourage someone in a cheerful way **jolly sb 'into sth/'doing sth** to persuade or encourage someone to do something by making them feel happy about it **jolly sb/sth 'up** to make someone or something more cheerful
● **noun**
IDM **get your jollies** (*informal*) to get pleasure or have fun: *He's one of those sad guys who gets his jollies from lurking in chat rooms.*

the ,Jolly 'Roger *noun* [sing.] a black flag with a white SKULL AND CROSSBONES on it, used in the past by PIRATES

jolt /dʒoult/ *verb, noun*
● **verb 1** [I, T] to move or to make someone or something move suddenly and roughly **SYN** JERK: (+ adv./prep.) *The truck jolted and rattled over the rough ground.* ♦ *The bus jolted to a halt.* ♦ (*figurative*) *Her heart jolted when she saw him.* ♦ **~ sb/sth (+ adv./prep.)** *He was jolted forward as the bus pulled out.* **2** [T] to give someone a sudden shock, especially so that they start to take action or deal with a situation: **~ sb/sth (into sth)** *His remark jolted her into action.* ♦ **~ sb/sth (out of sth)** *a method of jolting the economy out of recession* ♦ **~ sb/sth + adj.** *I was suddenly jolted awake.*
● **noun** [usually sing.] **1** a sudden rough movement **SYN** JERK: *The plane landed with a jolt.* **2** a sudden strong feeling, especially of shock or surprise: *a jolt of dismay*

Jones·es /'dʒounzəz/ *noun* [pl.]
IDM **keep up with the Joneses** (*informal*, often *disapproving*) to try to have all the possessions and social achievements that your friends and neighbors have

josh /dʒaʃ/ *verb* [I, T] **~ (sb)** | **+ speech** (*informal*) to gently make fun of someone or talk to them in a joking way **SYN** TEASE

joss stick /'dʒas stɪk/ *noun* a thin wooden stick covered with a substance that burns slowly and produces a sweet smell

jos·tle /'dʒasl/ *verb* [T, I] **~ (sb)** to push roughly against someone in a crowd: *The visiting president was jostled by*

angry demonstrators. ◆ *People were jostling, arguing, and complaining.*
PHR V **'jostle for sth** to compete strongly and with force with other people for something: *People in the crowd were jostling for the best positions.*

jot /dʒɑt/ *verb, noun*
● *verb* (-tt-)
PHR V **jot sth⟷'down** to write something quickly: *I'll just jot down the address for you.*
● *noun*
IDM **not a/one jot** (*old-fashioned*) used to mean "not even a small amount" when you are emphasizing a negative statement: *There's not a jot of truth in what he says* (= none at all).

jot·tings /'dʒɑtɪŋz/ *noun* [pl.] short notes that are written down quickly

joule /dʒul/ *noun* (*abbr.* J) (*physics*) a unit of energy or work

jour·nal **AWL** /'dʒɜrnl/ *noun* **1** a newspaper or magazine that deals with a particular subject or profession: *a scientific/trade journal* ◆ *the American Bar Association Journal* **2** used in the title of some newspapers: *the Wall Street Journal* **3** a written record of the things you do, see, etc. every day: *He kept a journal of his travels across Asia.* ⊃ compare DIARY

jour·nal·ese /ˌdʒɜrnə'liz/ *noun* [U] (usually *disapproving*) a style of language that is thought to be typical of that used in newspapers

jour·nal·ism /'dʒɜrnəˌlɪzəm/ *noun* [U] the work of collecting and writing news stories for newspapers, magazines, radio, or television

jour·nal·ist 🔧 /'dʒɜrnəlɪst/ *noun*
a person whose job is to collect and write news stories for newspapers, magazines, radio, or television ⊃ compare REPORTER

jour·nal·is·tic /ˌdʒɜrnə'lɪstɪk/ *adj.* [usually before noun] connected with the work of a journalist: *journalistic skills* ◆ *his journalistic background*

jour·ney 🔧 /'dʒɜrni/ *noun, verb*
● *noun* an act of traveling from one place to another, especially when they are far apart: *They went on a long train journey across Canada.* ◆ *Did you have a good journey?* ◆ *on the outbound/return journey* ◆ *We broke our journey* (= stopped for a short time) *in St. Louis.* ◆ *It's a day's journey by car.* ◆ (*informal*) *Bye! Safe journey!* (= used when someone is beginning a journey) ◆ (*figurative*) *The book describes a spiritual journey from despair to happiness.* ⊃ thesaurus box at TRIP
● *verb* [I] (**+ adv./prep.**) (*formal or literary*) to travel, especially a long distance: *They journeyed for seven long months.*

jour·ney·man /'dʒɜrnimən/ *noun* (*pl.* **jour·ney·men** /-mən/) **1** (in the past) a person who was trained to do a particular job and who then worked for someone else **2** a person who has training and experience in a job but who is only average at it

joust /dʒaʊst/ *verb* [I] **1** to fight on horses using a long stick (= a LANCE) to try to knock the other person off their horse, especially as part of a formal contest in the past **2** (*formal*) to argue with someone, especially as part of a formal or public debate ▶ **joust** *noun*

Jove /dʒoʊv/ *noun*
IDM **by Jove** (*old-fashioned, informal*) used to express surprise or to emphasize a statement

jo·vi·al /'dʒoʊviəl/ *adj.* very cheerful and friendly ▶ **jo·vi·al·i·ty** /ˌdʒoʊvi'æləti/ *noun* [U] **jo·vi·al·ly** /'dʒoʊviəli/ *adv.*

jowl /dʒaʊl/ *noun* [usually pl.] the lower part of someone's cheek when it is fat and hangs down below their chin: *a man with heavy jowls* **IDM** see CHEEK

joy 🔧 /dʒɔɪ/ *noun*
1 [U] a feeling of great happiness **SYN** DELIGHT: *the sheer joy of being with her again* ◆ *to dance for/with joy* ◆ *I didn't expect them to jump for joy at the news* (= to be very pleased). ◆ *To his*

great joy, she accepted. ⊃ thesaurus box at PLEASURE **2** [C] a person or thing that causes you to feel very happy: *the joys of fatherhood* ◆ *The game was a joy to watch.* **IDM** see PRIDE

joy·ful /'dʒɔɪfl/ *adj.* very happy; causing people to be happy ⊃ thesaurus box at HAPPY ▶ **joy·ful·ly** /-fəli/ *adv.* **joy·ful·ness** *noun* [U]

joy·less /'dʒɔɪləs/ *adj.* (*formal*) bringing no happiness; without joy: *a joyless childhood*

joy·ous /'dʒɔɪəs/ *adj.* (*literary*) very happy; causing people to be happy **SYN** JOYFUL: *joyous laughter* ▶ **joy·ous·ly** *adv.*

joy·pad /'dʒɔɪpæd/ *noun* a device used with some computer games, with buttons that you use to move images on the screen

joy·rid·ing /'dʒɔɪˌraɪdɪŋ/ *noun* [U] the crime of stealing a car and driving it for pleasure, usually in a fast and dangerous way ▶ **joy·ride** *noun* **joy·rid·er** *noun*

joy·stick /'dʒɔɪstɪk/ *noun* **1** a stick with a handle used with some computer games to move images on the screen **2** (*informal*) a stick with a handle in an aircraft that is used to control direction or height

JP /ˌdʒeɪ 'pi/ *abbr.* JUSTICE OF THE PEACE: *Helen Alvey JP*

JPEG (also **JPG**) /'dʒeɪpeg/ *noun* (*computing*) **1** [U] the abbreviation for "Joint Photographic Experts Group" (technology which reduces the size of files that contain images): *JPEG files* **2** [C] an image created using this technology: *You can download the pictures as JPEGs.*

Jr. *abbr.* JUNIOR ⊃ compare SR.

ju·bi·lant /'dʒubələnt/ *adj.* feeling or showing great happiness because of a success ▶ **ju·bi·lant·ly** *adv.*

ju·bi·la·tion /ˌdʒubə'leɪʃn/ *noun* [U] a feeling of great happiness because of a success

ju·bi·lee /ˌdʒubə'li; 'dʒubəli/ *noun* a special anniversary of an event, especially one that took place 25 or 50 years ago; the celebrations connected with it

Ju·da·ism /'dʒudiˌɪzəm; -deɪ-; -də-/ *noun* [U] the religion of the Jewish people, based mainly on the Bible (= the Christian Old Testament) and the Talmud ▶ **Ju·da·ic** /dʒu'deɪɪk/ *adj.* [only before noun]: *Judaic tradition*

Ju·das /'dʒudəs/ *noun* a person who treats a friend badly by not being loyal **SYN** TRAITOR **ORIGIN** From **Judas** in the Bible, the follower of Jesus who told the authorities where to find him and arrest him in return for payment.

judge 🔧 /dʒʌdʒ/ *noun, verb*
● *noun*
▸ IN COURT **1** a person in a court who has the authority to decide how criminals should be punished or to make legal decisions: *a Supreme Court judge* ◆ *a federal judge* ◆ *The case comes before Judge Cooper next week.* ◆ *The judge sentenced him to five years in prison.* ⊃ compare JUSTICE OF THE PEACE, MAGISTRATE
▸ IN COMPETITION **2** a person who decides who has won a competition: *the panel of judges at the flower show* ◆ *The judges' decision is final.*
▸ SOMEONE WHO GIVES OPINION **3** [usually sing.] a person who has the necessary knowledge or skills to give their opinion about the value or quality of someone or something: *She's a good judge of character.* ◆ *"I'm not sure that's a good way to do it." "Let me be the judge of that."*
● *verb*
▸ FORM OPINION **1** [I, T] to form an opinion about someone or something, based on the information you have: *As far as I can judge, all of them are to blame.* ◆ *Judging by her last letter, they are having a wonderful time.* ◆ *To judge from what he said, he was very disappointed.* ◆ *Each painting must be judged on its own merits.* ◆ ~ *sb/sth (on sth) Schools should not be judged only on exam results.* ◆ ~ *sb/sth + noun The tour was judged a great success.* ◆ ~ *sb/sth to be/do sth The tour was judged to have been a great success.* ◆ ~ *sb/sth + adj. They judged it wise to say nothing.* ◆ ~ *that... He judged that the risk was too great.* ◆ *it is judged that... It was judged that the risk*

h **hat**   m **man**   n **no**   ŋ **sing**   l **leg**   r **red**   y **yes**   w **wet**

was too great. ♦ **~ how, what, etc.…** *It was hard to judge how great the risk was.*
> ESTIMATE **2** [T] to guess the size, amount, etc. of something: **~ how, what, etc.…** *It's difficult to judge how long the journey will take.* ♦ **~ sb/sth to be/do sth** *I judged him to be about 50.*
> IN COMPETITION **3** [T, I] **~ (sth)** to decide the result of a competition; to be the judge in a competition: *She was asked to judge the essay competition.*
> GIVE OPINION **4** [T, I] **~ (sb)** to give your opinion about someone, especially when you disapprove of them: *What gives you the right to judge other people?*
> IN COURT **5** [T] to decide whether someone is guilty or innocent in a court: **~ sth** *to judge a case* ♦ **~ sb + adj.** *to judge someone guilty/not guilty*
IDM **don't judge a book by its cover** (*saying*) used to say that you should not form an opinion about someone or something from their appearance only

judg·ment 🔊 (also **judge·ment**) /ˈdʒʌdʒmənt/ *noun*
1 [U] the ability to make sensible decisions after carefully considering the best thing to do: *good/poor/sound judgment* ♦ *She showed a lack of judgment when she gave Mark the job.* ♦ *It's not something I can give you rules for; you'll have to use your judgment.* ♦ *He achieved his aim **more by luck than judgment.*** ♦ *The accident was caused by an **error of judgment** on the part of the pilot.* **2** [C, U] **~ (of/about/on sth)** an opinion that you form about something after thinking about it carefully; the act of making this opinion known to others: *He refused to **make a judgment** about the situation.* ♦ *Who am I to **pass judgment** on her behavior?* (= to criticize it) ♦ *I'd like to **reserve judgment** until I see the report.* ♦ *It was, **in her judgment**, the wrong thing to do.* ♦ *I did it **against my better judgment** (= although I thought it was perhaps the wrong thing to do).* **3** usually **judgment** [C, U] the decision of a court or a judge: *a judgment from the Court of Appeals* ♦ *The judgment will be given tomorrow.* ♦ *The court has yet to **pass judgment** (= say what its decision is) in this case.* **4** [C, usually sing.] **~ (on sth)** (*formal*) something bad that happens to someone that is thought to be a punishment from God
IDM see SIT

judg·men·tal (also **judge·men·tal**) /dʒʌdʒˈmɛntl/ *adj.*
1 (*disapproving*) judging people and criticizing them too quickly **ANT** NONJUDGMENTAL **2** (*formal*) connected with the process of judging things: *the judgmental process*

ˈjudgment ˌcall *noun* (*informal*) a decision you have to make where there is no clear rule about what the right thing to do is, so that you have to use your own judgment

ˈJudgment ˌDay (also the ˌDay of ˈJudgment, the ˌLast ˈJudgment) *noun* the day at the end of the world when, according to some religions, God will judge everyone who has ever lived

ju·di·ca·ture /ˈdʒudɪkətʃər/ *noun* (*law*) **1** [U] the system by which courts, judges, etc. are organized in a country **2** the judicature [sing.] judges when they are considered as a group

ju·di·cial /dʒuˈdɪʃl/ *adj.* [usually before noun] connected with a court, a judge, or a legal judgment: *judicial powers* ♦ *the judicial process/system* ▸ **ju·di·cial·ly** /-ʃəli/ *adv.*

ju‚dicial ˈactivism *noun* [U] (*law*) the idea that it is not necessary to follow the exact words of the Constitution when new laws are made

the ju‚dicial ˌbranch *noun* [sing.] the part of the U.S. government consisting of judges and courts that interpret the laws ⊃ compare EXECUTIVE BRANCH, LEGISLATIVE BRANCH

ju‚dicial reˈstraint *noun* [U] (*law*) the idea that judges of the Supreme Court or other courts should not try to change a law that is allowed by the Constitution

ju‚dicial reˈview *noun* [U] (*law*) the power of the Supreme Court to decide if something is allowed by the Constitution

ju·di·ci·ar·y /dʒuˈdɪʃiˌɛri; -ˈdɪʃəri/ *noun* usually **the judiciary** (*pl.* **ju·di·ci·ar·ies**) the judges of a country or a state, when

they are considered as a group: *an independent judiciary* ⊃ compare EXECUTIVE, LEGISLATURE

ju·di·cious /dʒuˈdɪʃəs/ *adj.* (*formal, approving*) careful and sensible; showing good judgment **ANT** INJUDICIOUS ▸ **ju·di·cious·ly** *adv.*: *a judiciously worded letter*

ju·do /ˈdʒudoʊ/ *noun* [U] (from *Japanese*) a sport in which two people fight and try to throw each other to the ground: *He does judo.* ♦ *She has a **black belt** in judo.*

jug /dʒʌg/ *noun* **1** a large deep container with a small opening and a handle, for holding liquids: *a one-gallon jug of milk* ⊃ picture at PITCHER **2** the amount of liquid contained in a jug: *She spilled a jug of water.*

jug·ful /ˈdʒʌgfʊl/ *noun* the amount of liquid contained in a jug

jug·ger·naut /ˈdʒʌgərˌnɔt; -ˌnɑt/ *noun* (*formal*) a large and powerful force or institution that cannot be controlled: *a bureaucratic juggernaut*

jug·gle /ˈdʒʌgl/ *verb* **1** [I, T] to throw a set of three or more objects such as balls into the air and catch and throw them again quickly, one at a time: *My uncle taught me to juggle.* ♦ **~ with sth** *to juggle with balls* ♦ **~ sth** (*figurative*) *I was juggling books, shopping bags, and the baby* (= I was trying to hold them all without dropping them). **2** [T, I] **~ (sth) (with sth)** to try to deal with two or more important jobs or activities at the same time so that you can fit all of them into your life: *Working mothers are used to juggling their jobs, their children's needs, and their housework.* **3** [T] **~ sth** to organize information, figures, the money you spend, etc. in the most useful or effective way

jug·gler /ˈdʒʌglər/ *noun* a person who juggles, especially an entertainer

jug·u·lar /ˈdʒʌgyələr/ (also ˈjugular ˌvein) *noun* any of the three large VEINS in the neck that carry blood from the head toward the heart
IDM **go for the jugular** (*informal*) to attack someone's weakest point during a discussion, in an aggressive way

juice 🔊 /dʒus/ *noun, verb*
● *noun* **1** [U, C] the liquid that comes from fruit or vegetables; a drink made from this: *Add the juice of two lemons.* ♦ *a carton of apple juice* ♦ *Two orange juices, please.* **2** [C, usually pl., U] the liquid that comes out of a piece of meat when it is cooked **3** [C, usually pl.] the liquid in the stomach that helps you to DIGEST food: *digestive/gastric juices* **4** [U] (*informal*) gas **5** [U] (*informal*) electricity **IDM** SEE STEW *v.*
● *verb* **~ sth** to get the juice out of fruit or vegetables: *Juice two oranges.*
PHRV ˌjuice sth↔ˈup (*informal*) to make something more exciting or interesting

ˈjuice ˌbar *noun* a café serving drinks made from freshly squeezed fruit

ˈjuice ˌbox *noun* a small box of juice for one person that usually has a STRAW attached to it ⊃ picture at PACKAGING

juiced /dʒust/ *adj.* (*informal*) drunk

juic·er /ˈdʒusər/ *noun* **1** a piece of electrical equipment for getting the juice out of fruit or vegetables ⊃ picture at KITCHEN **2** a kitchen UTENSIL (= a tool) for squeezing juice out of a fruit: *a lemon juicer*

juic·y /ˈdʒusi/ *adj.* (**juic·i·er**, **juic·i·est**) **1** (*approving*) containing a lot of juice and good to eat: *soft, juicy pears* ♦ *The meat was tender and juicy.* **2** (*informal*) interesting because you find it shocking or exciting: *juicy gossip* **3** (*informal*) attractive because it will bring you a lot of money or satisfaction: *a juicy prize*

ju·jit·su (also **jiu·jit·su**) /dʒu ˈdʒɪtsu/ *noun* [U] a Japanese system of fighting from which the sport of JUDO was developed

ju·ju /ˈdʒudʒu/ *noun* **1** [C] an object used in W. African magic **2** [U] a type of magic in W. Africa **3** [U] a type of Nigerian music that uses GUITARS and drums

juke /dʒuk/ *verb* [T, I] (*informal*) (in sports) to move or pretend to move in a way that tricks or confuses your opponent: ~ **(sb)** *to juke a defender* ◆ **+ adv./prep.** *The quarterback juked to the left side of the field.* ⊃ compare DUMMY *v.*

juke·box /'dʒukbɑks/ *noun* a machine in a bar, etc. that plays music when you put coins into it

'juke joint *noun* (*informal*) a bar where people can dance to music from a jukebox

ju·lep /'dʒuləp/ *noun* [U, C] **1** a sweet drink which may contain alcohol or medicine **2** = MINT JULEP

Jul·ian cal·en·dar /ˌdʒulyən 'kæləndər/ *noun* [sing.] the system of arranging days and months in the year introduced by Julius Caesar, and used in Western countries until the GREGORIAN CALENDAR replaced it

ju·li·enne /ˌdʒuli'ɛn/ (also **ju·li·enned** /ˌdʒuli'ɛnd/) *adj.* [only before noun] (of food, especially vegetables) cut into short, thin strips: *julienne carrots*

Ju·ly 🔊 /dʒʊ'laɪ/ *noun* [U, C] (*abbr.* **Jul.**) the 7th month of the year, between June and August
HELP To see how **July** is used, look at the examples at **April.**

jum·ble /'dʒʌmbl/ *verb, noun*
- *verb* [usually passive] ~ **sth (together/up)** to mix things together in a confused or messy way: *Books, shoes, and clothes were **jumbled together** on the floor.* ▸ **jum·bled** *adj.*: *a jumbled collection of objects* ◆ *jumbled thoughts*
- *noun* [sing.] ~ **(of sth)** a messy or confused mixture of things: *a jumble of books and paper* ◆ *The essay was a meaningless jumble of ideas.*

jum·bo /'dʒʌmboʊ/ *adj., noun*
- *adj.* [only before noun] (*informal*) very large; larger than usual: *a jumbo pack of cornflakes*
- *noun* (*pl.* **jum·bos**) (also **jumbo 'jet**) a large plane that can carry several hundred passengers, especially a Boeing 747

jump 🔊 /dʒʌmp/ *verb, noun*
- *verb*
> **MOVE OFF/TO GROUND 1** [I] to move quickly off the ground or away from a surface by pushing yourself with your legs and feet: *"Quick, jump!" he shouted.* ◆ **+ adv./prep.** *to jump into the air/over a wall/into the water* ◆ *The children were jumping up and down with excitement.* ◆ *She jumped down from the chair.* ◆ *The pilot jumped from the burning plane* (= with a PARACHUTE). ◆ **+ noun** *She has jumped 7.5 feet.*
> **PASS OVER SOMETHING 2** [T] to pass over something by jumping **SYN** LEAP: ~ **sth** *Can you jump that gate?* ◆ *His horse fell as it jumped the last hurdle.* ◆ ~ **sth + adv./prep.** *I jumped my horse over all the fences.*
> **MOVE QUICKLY 3** [I] **+ adv./prep.** to move quickly and suddenly: *He jumped to his feet when they called his name.* ◆ *She jumped up and ran out of the room.* ◆ *Do you want a ride? Jump in.* **4** [I] to make a sudden movement because of surprise, fear, or excitement: *A loud bang made me jump.* ◆ *Her heart jumped when she heard the news.* **5** [I] to take quick action; to do something immediately: *When the boss gives an order, you better jump!* ◆ **+ adv./prep.** *When someone criticized my work, Gordon jumped to my defense* (= was quick to defend me).
> **INCREASE 6** [I] to rise suddenly by a large amount **SYN** LEAP: **by...** *Prices jumped by 60% last year.* ◆ ~ **(from...) (to...)** *Sales jumped from $2.7 billion to $3.5 billion.*
> **CHANGE SUDDENLY 7** [I] ~ **(around) (from sth to sth)** to change suddenly from one subject to another: *I couldn't follow the talk because he kept jumping around from one topic to another.* ◆ *The story then jumps from her childhood in New York to her first visit to London.*
> **LEAVE OUT 8** [T] ~ **sth** to leave out something and pass to a further point or stage: *You seem to have jumped several steps in the argument.*
> **OF MACHINE/DEVICE 9** [I] (**+ adv./prep.**) to move suddenly and unexpectedly, especially out of the correct position: *The needle jumped across the dial.* ◆ *The film jumped during projection.*

> **ATTACK 10** [T, I] ~ **(on) sb** (*informal*) to attack someone suddenly: *The thieves jumped him in a dark alleyway.*
> **VEHICLE 11** [T] ~ **sth** to get on a vehicle very quickly: *to jump a bus* **12** = JUMP-START
> **BE LIVELY 13** be jumping [I] (*informal*) to be very lively: *The bar's jumping tonight.*
IDM be jumping up and down (*informal*) to be very angry or excited about something **jump down sb's throat** (*informal*) to react very angrily to someone **(go) jump in the lake** (*informal*) a rude way of telling someone to go away: *When he asked me for more money, I told him to jump in the lake.* **jump in with both feet** to get deeply involved with something that you are enthusiastic about: *When he saw the opportunities for volunteer work, he jumped in with both feet.* **jump the gun** to do something too soon, before the right time **jump out of your skin** (*informal*) to move violently because of a sudden shock **jump ship 1** to leave the ship on which you are serving, without permission **2** to leave an organization that you belong to, suddenly and unexpectedly **jump through hoops** to do something difficult or complicated in order to achieve something **jump to it** (also **hop to it**) (*informal*) used to tell someone to hurry and do something quickly **jump the tracks** (of a train) to leave the tracks suddenly ⊃ more at BAIL, BANDWAGON, CONCLUSION, DEEP, ROPE *n.*
PHR V '**jump at sth** to accept an opportunity, offer, etc. with enthusiasm **SYN** LEAP AT STH **jump 'in 1** to interrupt a conversation: *Before she could reply, Peter jumped in with an objection.* **2** to start to do something very quickly without spending a long time thinking first '**jump on sb** (also '**jump at sb**) (*informal*) to criticize someone **jump 'out at sb** to be very obvious and easily noticed **SYN** LEAP OUT AT: *The mistake in the figures jumped out at me.*

- *noun*
> **MOVEMENT 1** an act of jumping: *a jump of over six meters* ◆ *The story takes a jump back in time.* ◆ *Somehow he survived the jump from the third floor of the building.* ◆ *to do a parachute jump* ◆ *a ski jump champion* ◆ *I sat up with a jump* (= quickly and suddenly). ◆ *The negotiations took a jump forward yesterday* (= they made progress). ⊃ see also HIGH JUMP, LONG JUMP, SKI JUMP, TRIPLE JUMP
> **BARRIER 2** a barrier like a narrow fence that a horse or a runner has to jump over in a race or competition: *The horse fell at the last jump.*
> **INCREASE 3** ~ **(in sth)** a sudden increase in amount, price, or value: *a 20 percent jump in pre-tax profits* ◆ *unusually large price jumps*
IDM to keep, etc. one jump ahead (of sb) to keep your advantage over someone, especially your COMPETITORS, by taking action before they do or by making sure you know more than they do ⊃ more at HOP *n.*, RUNNING

'**jump ball** *noun* (in basketball) a ball that the REFEREE throws up between two opposing players to begin play

jump·cut /'dʒʌmpkʌt/ *noun* (*technical*) (in movies) a sudden change from one scene to another

jump·er /'dʒʌmpər/ *noun* **1** a loose dress with no sleeves, usually worn over a BLOUSE or sweater **2** a person, an animal, or an insect that jumps: *He's a good jumper.* **3** = JUMP SHOT

'**jumper ˌcable** *noun* [usually pl.] one of two cables that are used to start a car when it has no power in its battery. The jumper cables connect the battery to the battery of another car.

'**jumping ˌjack** *noun* [usually pl.] an exercise in which you stand with your legs together and your arms at your sides and jump to a position with your legs apart and your arms spread out

'**jumping-'off point** (also **jumping-'off place**) *noun* a place from which to start a trip or new activity

'**jump jet** *noun* an aircraft that can take off and land by going straight up or down, without needing a RUNWAY

'**jump rope** *noun* **1** [C] a piece of rope, usually with a handle at each end, that you hold, turn over your head and then jump over, for fun or for exercise ⊃ picture at TOY **2** [U] the activity of jumping over a rope, for fun or for exercise: *The kids played jump rope during recess.* **IDM** see ROPE *n.*

jump shot (also **jump·er**) *noun* (in basketball) a shot made while jumping

jump-start (also **jump**) *verb* **1** ~ sth to start the engine of a car by connecting the battery to the battery of another car with JUMPER CABLES **2** ~ sth to put a lot of energy into starting a process or an activity or into making it start more quickly

jump·suit /'dʒʌmpsut/ *noun* a piece of clothing that consists of pants and a jacket or shirt sewn together in one piece, worn especially by women

jump·y /'dʒʌmpi/ *adj.* (jump·i·er, jump·i·est) (*informal*) nervous and anxious, especially because you think that something bad is going to happen

junc·tion /'dʒʌŋkʃn/ *noun* **1** (also in·ter·sec·tion) the place where two or more roads or railroad lines meet: *It was near the junction of City Road and Old Street.* ♦ *Cheyenne was one of the most important railroad junctions in the West.* **2** a place where two or more cables, rivers, or other things meet or are joined: *a telephone junction box*

junc·ture /'dʒʌŋktʃər/ *noun* (*formal*) **1** a particular point or stage in an activity or a series of events: *The battle had reached a crucial juncture.* ♦ *At this juncture, I would like to make an important announcement.* **2** a place or point where two things are joined **SYN** JUNCTION: *At that time the city's position at the juncture of two major railroad lines made it attractive to businesses.*

June 🔑 /dʒun/ *noun* [U, C] (*abbr.* Jun.)
the 6th month of the year, between May and July **HELP** To see how **June** is used, look at the examples at **April.**

jun·gle /'dʒʌŋgl/ *noun* **1** [U, C] an area of tropical forest where trees and plants grow very thickly: *The area was covered in dense jungle.* ♦ *the jungles of southeast Asia* ♦ *jungle warfare* **2** [sing.] ~ (of sth) a confusing, complicated, or messy mixture of things **SYN** TANGLE: *a jungle of weeds.* ♦ *a jungle of wires* **3** [sing.] an unfriendly or dangerous place or situation, especially one where it is very difficult to be successful or to trust anyone: *It's a jungle out there—you've got to be strong to succeed.* ⊃ **see also** CONCRETE JUNGLE **IDM** see LAW

jungle 'gym *noun* a structure made of metal bars joined together for children to climb and play on ⊃ picture at TOY

jun·ior 🔑 /'dʒunyər/ *adj., noun*
● **adj.**
▷ SCHOOL/COLLEGE **1** [only before noun] connected with the year before the last year in a high school or college: *I spent my junior year in France.*
▷ SON **2 Junior** (*abbr.* Jr.) used after the name of a man who has the same name as his father, to avoid confusion ⊃ compare THE YOUNGER *at* YOUNG *adj.* (6)
▷ OF LOW RANK **3** [usually before noun] having a low rank in an organization or a profession: *junior employees* ♦ ~ to sb *She is junior to me.*
▷ IN SPORTS **4** [only before noun] connected with young people below a particular age, rather than with adults, especially in sports: *the world junior tennis championships* ⊃ compare SENIOR
● **noun**
▷ IN SCHOOL/COLLEGE **1** [C] a student in the year before the last year of high school or college ⊃ compare FRESHMAN, SENIOR *n.*, SOPHOMORE
▷ LOW LEVEL JOB **2** [C] a person who has a job at a low level within an organization: *office juniors*
▷ SON **3** [sing.] (*informal*) a person's young son: *I leave junior with Mom when I'm at work.*
IDM be…years sb's junior| be sb's junior (by…) to be younger than someone, by the number of years mentioned: *She's four years his junior.* ♦ *She's his junior by four years.*

junior 'college *noun* a college that offers programs that are two years long. Some students go to a college offering four-year programs after they have finished studying at a junior college.

junior 'high school (also **junior 'high**) *noun* [C, U] a school for young people between the ages of 12 and 14 ⊃ compare SENIOR HIGH SCHOOL

junior 'varsity *noun* a school or college sports team for players who are younger than or not as good as the main team

ju·ni·per /'dʒunəpər/ *noun* [U, C] a bush with purple berries (BERRY) that are used in medicine and to flavor GIN

junk /dʒʌŋk/ *noun, verb*
● **noun 1** [U] things that are considered useless or of little value **SYN** GARBAGE: *I've cleared out all that old junk in the attic.* ♦ *There's nothing but junk on TV.* ⊃ thesaurus box at THING **2** [U] = JUNK FOOD **3** [C] a Chinese boat with a square sail and a flat bottom **4** [U] (*slang*) a powerful illegal drug, especially HEROIN
● **verb** ~ sth (*informal*) to get rid of something because it is no longer valuable or useful

junk bond *noun* (*business*) a type of BOND that pays a high rate of interest because there is a lot of risk involved, often used to raise money quickly in order to buy the shares of another company

junk·er /'dʒʌŋkər/ *noun* (*informal*) an old car that is in bad condition

jun·ket /'dʒʌŋkət/ *noun* (*informal, disapproving*) a trip that is made for pleasure by someone who works for the government, etc. and that is paid for using public money

junk food (also **junk**) *noun* [U] also **junk foods** [pl.] (*informal, disapproving*) food that is quick and easy to prepare and eat but that is thought to be bad for your health

junk·ie (also **junk·y**) /'dʒʌŋki/ (*pl.* junkies) *noun* (*informal*) a drug ADDICT (= a person who is unable to stop taking dangerous drugs)

junk mail *noun* [U] (*disapproving*) advertising material that is sent to people who have not asked for it ⊃ compare SPAM

junk 'science *noun* [U] (*disapproving*) used to refer to ideas and theories that seem to be well researched and scientific but in fact have little evidence to support them

junk shop *noun* a shop that buys and sells old furniture and other objects, at cheap prices

junk·y /'dʒʌŋki/ *adj.* (*informal*) of poor quality or of little value

junk·yard /'dʒʌŋkyɑrd/ (also **scrap·yard**) *noun* a place where old cars, machines, etc. are collected, so that parts of them, or the metal they are made of, can be sold to be used again

jun·ta /'hʊntə/ *noun* a military government that has taken power by force

Ju·pi·ter /'dʒupətər/ *noun* the largest planet of the SOLAR SYSTEM, fifth in order of distance from the sun ⊃ picture at EARTH

Ju·ras·sic /dʒʊ'ræsɪk/ *adj.* (*geology*) of the PERIOD between around 208 to 146 million years ago, when the largest known dinosaurs lived; of the rocks formed during this time ▶ the Jurassic *noun* [sing.]

ju·rid·i·cal /dʒʊ'rɪdɪkl/ *adj.* [usually before noun] (*formal*) connected with the law, judges, or legal matters

ju·ris·dic·tion /ˌdʒʊrəs'dɪkʃn/ *noun* (*formal*) **1** [U, C] ~ (over sb/sth) | ~ (of sb/sth) (to do sth) the authority that an official organization has to make legal decisions about someone or something **2** [C] an area or a country in which a particular system of laws has authority ▶ ju·ris·dic·tion·al /-ʃənl/ *adj.*

ju·ris·pru·dence /ˌdʒʊrəs'prudns/ *noun* [U] (*technical*) the scientific study of law: *a professor of jurisprudence*

ju·rist /'dʒʊrɪst/ *noun* (*formal*) a person who is an expert in law

ju·ror /'dʒʊrər/ *noun* a member of a jury

ju·ry /'dʒʊri/ noun

(pl. jur·ies) **1** (also **pan·el**, **'jury ˌpanel**) a group of members of the public who listen to the facts of a case in a court and decide whether or not someone is guilty of a crime: *members of the jury* ◆ *to be/sit/serve on a jury* ◆ *The jury has returned a verdict of guilty.* ◆ *the right to trial by jury* ⊃ collocations at JUSTICE ⊃ see also GRAND JURY **2** a group of people who decide who is the winner of a competition **IDM** **the jury is (still) out on sth** used when you are saying that something is still not certain

'jury ˌduty noun [U] a period of time spent as a member of a jury in court, or attending jury selection where you may or may not be chosen to serve on a jury

'jury-ˌrig verb (-gg-) ~ **sth** to make or build something with whatever materials are available, especially for temporary use: *In the shed they jury-rigged a cooking stove to get some heat.*

jus noun ⊃ AU JUS

just /dʒʌst/ adv., adj.

• *adv.* **1** exactly: *This jacket is just my size.* ◆ *This gadget is just the thing for getting those nails out.* ◆ *Just my luck* (= the sort of bad luck I usually have). *The phone's not working.* ◆ *You're just in time.* ◆ ~ **like…** *She looks just like her mother.* ◆ ~ **what…** *It's just what I wanted!* ◆ ~ **as…** *It's just as I thought.* **2** ~ **as…** at the same moment as: *The clock struck six just as I arrived.* **3** ~ **as good, nice, easily, etc.** no less than; equally: *She's just as smart as her sister.* ◆ *You can get there just as cheaply by plane.* **4** (only) ~ | ~ **after, before, under, etc. sth** by a small amount: *I got here just after nine.* ◆ *I only just caught the train.* ◆ *Inflation fell to just over 4 percent.* **5** used to say that you/someone did something very recently: *I've just heard the news.* ◆ *When you arrived he had only just left.* ◆ *She has just been telling us about her trip to Rome.* ◆ *I just saw him a moment ago.* ◆ *I was just beginning to enjoy myself when we had to leave.* **6** at this/that moment; now: *I'm just finishing my book.* ◆ *I was just beginning to enjoy myself when we had to leave.* **7** ~ **about/going to do sth** going to do something only a few moments from now or then: *The water's just about to boil.* ◆ *I was just going to tell you when you interrupted.* **8** simply: *It was just an ordinary day.* ◆ *I can't just drop all my commitments.* ◆ *This essay is just not good enough.* ◆ *I didn't mean to upset you. It's just that I had to tell somebody.* ◆ *This is not just another disaster movie—it's a masterpiece.* ◆ *Just because you're older than me doesn't mean you know everything.* **9** (informal) really; completely: *The food was just wonderful!* ◆ *I can just imagine his reaction.* **10** only: ~ **(for sth)** *I decided to learn Japanese just for fun.* ◆ ~ **(to do sth)** *I waited an hour just to see you.* ◆ *There is just one method that might work.* ◆ *"Can I help you?" "No thanks, I'm just looking."* (= in a store) **11** used in orders to get someone's attention, give permission, etc.: *Just listen to what I'm saying!* ◆ *Just help yourselves!* **12** used to make a polite request, excuse, etc.: *Could you just help me with this box, please?* ◆ *I've just got a few things to do first.* **13** **could/might/may** ~ used to show a slight possibility that something is true or will happen: *Try his home number—he might just be there.* **14** used to agree with someone: *"He's very pompous." "Isn't he just?"*

IDM **could/might just as well…** used to say that you/someone would have been in the same position if you had done something else, because you got little benefit or enjoyment from what you did do: *The weather was so bad we might just as well have stayed at home.* **it is just as well (that…)** it is a good thing: *It is just as well that we didn't leave any later or we'd have missed him.* **just about** (informal) **1** almost; very nearly: *I've met just about everyone.* ◆ *"Did you reach your sales target?" "Just about."* **2** approximately: *She should be arriving just about now.* **just a minute/moment/second** (informal) used to ask someone to wait for a short time: *"Is Mr. Burns available?" "Just a second, please, I'll check."* **just like that** suddenly, without warning or explanation **just now 1** at this moment: *Come and see me later—I'm busy just now.* **2** during this present period: *Business is good just now.* **3** only a short time ago: *I saw her just now.* **just so** done or arranged very accurately or carefully: *He liked polishing the furniture and making everything just so.* **just**

then at that moment: *Just then, someone knocked at the front door.* **not just yet** not now but probably quite soon: *I can't give you the money just yet.* **I, etc. would just as soon do sth** used to say that you would equally well like to do something as do something else that has been suggested: *I'd just as soon stay at home as go out tonight.* ⊃ more at CASE

• *adj.* [usually before noun] **1** that most people consider to be morally fair and reasonable **SYN** FAIR: *a just decision/law/society* **2** **the just** *noun* [pl.] people who are just **3** appropriate in a particular situation: *a just reward/punishment* ◆ *I think she got her just deserts* (= what she deserved). **ANT** UNJUST ▶ **just·ly** *adv.*: *to be treated justly* ◆ *to be justly proud of something*

jus·tice /'dʒʌstəs/ noun

1 [U] the fair treatment of people: *laws based on the principles of justice* ◆ *They are demanding equal rights and justice.* **ANT** INJUSTICE ⊃ see also POETIC JUSTICE, ROUGH JUSTICE **2** [U] the quality of being fair or reasonable: *Who can deny the justice of their cause?* **ANT** INJUSTICE **3** [U] the legal system used to punish people who have committed crimes: *the criminal justice system* ◆ *The U.S. Department of Justice* ◆ *They were accused of attempting to obstruct justice.* ⊃ see also MISCARRIAGE OF JUSTICE **4** also **Justice** [C] a judge in a court (also used before the name of a judge) ⊃ see also CHIEF JUSTICE

IDM **bring sb to justice** to arrest someone for a crime and put them on trial in court **do justice to sb/sth; do sb/sth justice 1** to treat or represent someone or something fairly, especially in a way that shows how good, attractive, etc. they are: *That photo doesn't do you justice.* **2** to deal with someone or something correctly and completely: *You cannot do justice to such a complex situation in just a few pages.* **do yourself justice** to do something as well as you can in order to show other people how good you are: *She didn't do herself justice in the exam.* ⊃ more at OBSTRUCT

TOPIC COLLOCATIONS

Criminal Justice

breaking the law

- break/violate/obey/uphold the law
- be investigated/arrested/tried for a crime/a robbery/fraud
- be arrested/indicted/convicted on felony charges/on charges of rape/fraud
- be arrested on suspicion of arson/robbery/shoplifting
- be accused of/be charged with murder/homicide/four counts of fraud
- face two charges of assault and battery
- admit your guilt/liability/responsibility (for sth)
- deny the allegations/claims/charges
- confess to a crime
- be granted/be refused/be released on/skip/jump bail

the legal process

- stand/await/bring sb to/come to/be on trial
- take sb to/come to/settle sth out of court
- face/avoid/escape prosecution
- seek/retain/have the right to/be denied access to legal counsel
- hold/conduct/attend/adjourn a hearing/trial
- sit on/influence/persuade/convince/advise a jury
- stand/appear/be brought before a judge
- plead guilty/not guilty to a crime
- be called to/take/put sb on the stand/the witness stand
- call/subpoena/question/cross-examine a witness
- give/hear the evidence against/on behalf of sb
- raise/withdraw/overrule an objection
- reach a unanimous/majority verdict
- return/deliver/record a verdict of guilty/not guilty

---

t tea	ţ butter	d did	k cat	g got	tʃ chin	dʒ June	f fall

- **convict/acquit** the defendant of the crime
- **secure** a conviction/your acquittal
- **lodge/file** an appeal
- **appeal (against)/challenge/uphold/overturn** a conviction/verdict

sentencing and punishment

- **sentence sb to** 5 years in prison/2 years' probation
- **carry/face/serve** a seven-year/life sentence
- **receive/be given** the death penalty
- **be sentenced to** ten years (in prison/jail)
- **carry/impose/pay** a fine (of $3,000)/a penalty (of 14 years' imprisonment)
- **be imprisoned/jailed for** drug possession/fraud/murder
- **do/serve** time/ten years
- **be sent to/put sb in/be released from** jail/prison
- **be/put sb/spend** 13 years on death row
- **be granted/be denied/violate (your)** parole
- ⭯ more collocations at CRIME

Justice of the 'Peace noun (pl. Justices of the Peace) (abbr. JP) an official who acts as a judge in the lowest courts of law and can perform marriages **SYN** MAGISTRATE

jus·ti·fi·a·ble **AWL** /ˌdʒʌstəˈfaɪəbl; ˈdʒʌstəˌfaɪ-/ adj. existing or done for a good reason, and therefore acceptable **SYN** LEGITIMATE: justifiable pride ▶ **jus·ti·fi·a·bly** **AWL** /-bli/ adv.: The university can be justifiably proud of its record.

justifiable 'homicide noun [U] (law) in some countries, a killing which is not a criminal act, for example because you were trying to defend yourself ⭯ compare CULPABLE HOMICIDE

jus·ti·fi·ca·tion **AWL** /ˌdʒʌstəfəˈkeɪʃn/ noun [U, C] ~ (for sth/doing sth) a good reason why something exists or is done: I can see no possible justification for any further tax increases. ◆ He was getting angry—and with some justification. ⭯ thesaurus box at REASON
  IDM in justification (of sb/sth) as an explanation of why something exists or why someone has done something: All I can say in justification of her actions is that she was under a lot of pressure at work.

jus·ti·fied 🔑 **AWL** /ˈdʒʌstəˌfaɪd/ adj.
  1 ~ (in doing sth) having a good reason for doing something: She felt fully justified in asking for her money back. **2** existing or done for a good reason: His fears proved justified. **ANT** UNJUSTIFIED

jus·ti·fy 🔑 **AWL** /ˈdʒʌstəˌfaɪ/ verb (jus·ti·fies, jus·ti·fy·ing, jus·ti·fied, jus·ti·fied)
  1 to show that someone or something is right or reasonable: ~ (sb/sth) doing sth How can they justify paying such huge salaries? ◆ ~ sth Her success had justified the faith her teachers had put in her. **2** ~ sth/yourself (to sb) | ~ (sb/sth) doing sth to give an explanation or excuse for something or for doing something **SYN** DEFEND: The Secretary of Education has been asked to justify the decision to Congress. ◆ You don't need to justify yourself to me. **3** ~ sth (technical) to arrange lines of printed text so that one or both edges are straight **IDM** see END n.

just-in-'time adj. (abbr. JIT) (business) used to describe a system in which parts or materials are only delivered to a factory just before they are needed

jut /dʒʌt/ verb (-tt-) [I, T] to stick out further than the surrounding surface, objects, etc.; to make something stick out **SYN** PROTRUDE: ~ (out) (from, into, over sth) A row of small windows jutted out from the roof. ◆ A rocky headland jutted into the sea. ◆ a jutting chin ◆ ~ sth (out) She jutted her chin out stubbornly.

jute /dʒuːt/ noun [U] FIBER (= thin threads) from a plant, also called jute, used for making rope and rough cloth

ju·ve·nile /ˈdʒuːvəˌnaɪl; -nl/ adj., noun
  ● adj. **1** [only before noun] (formal or law) connected with young people who are not yet adults: juvenile crime/employment ◆ juvenile offenders **2** (disapproving) silly and more typical of a child than an adult **SYN** CHILDISH: juvenile behavior ◆ Don't be so juvenile!
  ● noun (formal or law) a young person who is not yet an adult

juvenile 'court noun a court that deals with young people who are not yet adults

juvenile de'linquent noun a young person who is not yet an adult and who is guilty of committing a crime ▶ **juvenile de'linquency** noun [U]

ju·ve·nil·i·a /ˌdʒuːvəˈnɪliə/ noun [pl.] (formal) writing, poetry, works of art, etc. produced by a writer or an artist when he/she was still young

jux·ta·pose /ˈdʒʌkstəˌpoʊz; ˌdʒʌkstəˈpoʊz/ verb [usually passive] ~ A and/with B (formal) to put people or things together, especially in order to show a contrast or a new relationship between them: In the exhibition, abstract paintings are juxtaposed with shocking photographs. ▶ **jux·ta·po·si·tion** /ˌdʒʌkstəpəˈzɪʃn/ noun [U, C]: the juxtaposition of realistic and surreal situations in the novel

K k

K /keɪ/ *noun, abbr., symbol*

• *noun* also **k** (*pl.* **Ks, K's, k's** /keɪz/) [C, U] the 11th letter of the English alphabet: *"King" begins with (a) K/"K."*

• *abbr.* (*pl.* **K**) **1** (*informal*) one thousand: *She earns 40K ($40,000) a year.* **2** kilometer(s): *a 10K race* **3** KELVIN(S) **4** KILOBYTE(S)

• *symbol* the symbol for the chemical element POTASSIUM

K-12 /ˌkeɪ 'twɛlv/ *adj.* relating to education from KINDERGARTEN (= the class that prepares children for school) to 12th GRADE

Kab·ba·lah (also **Ca·ba·la, Qa·ba·lah**) /kəˈbɑlə; ˌkɑbəˈlɑ/ *noun* (in Judaism) the ancient tradition of explaining holy texts through MYSTICAL means

ka·bu·ki /kəˈbuki/ *noun* [U] (from *Japanese*) traditional Japanese theater, in which songs, dance, and MIME are performed by men

ka-ching /kə ˈtʃɪŋ/ (also **cha-ching** /tʃə ˈtʃɪŋ/) *exclamation* (*informal*) used to say that someone is getting a lot of money: *The money was rolling in, ka-ching, ka-ching! ♦ Ka-ching! I just got my first check.* **ORIGIN** A way of representing the noise made by a CASH REGISTER.

kaf·fee·klatsch /ˈkɔfiˌklɑtʃ; ˈkɑfi-; -ˌklætʃ/ *noun* (from *German*) a social event at which people drink coffee

kaf·fi·yeh = KEFFIYEH

Kaf·ka·esque /ˌkɑfkəˈɛsk/ *adj.* used to describe a situation that is confusing and frightening, especially one involving complicated official rules and systems that do not seem to make any sense: *My attempt to get a new passport turned into a Kafkaesque nightmare.* **ORIGIN** From the name of the Czech writer Franz Kafka, whose novels often describe situations like this.

kaf·tan (also **caf·tan**) /ˈkæftæn/ *noun* **1** a long, loose piece of clothing, usually with a belt at the waist, worn by men in Arab countries **2** a woman's long, loose dress with long, wide sleeves

ka·hu·na /kəˈhunə/ *noun* (*informal*) an important person; the person in charge

kai·ser /ˈkaɪzər/ *noun* (from *German*) **1** Kaiser (in the past) a ruler of Germany, of Austria, or of the Holy Roman Empire: *Kaiser Wilhelm* **2** (also **'kaiser ˌroll**) a crisp bread roll

kai·zen /ˌkaɪˈzɛn/ *noun* [U] (*business*) the practice of continuously improving the way in which a company operates **ORIGIN** From the Japanese for **improvement**.

Ka·lash·ni·kov /kəˈlɑʃnəˌkɔf; -ˌkɑf/ *noun* a type of RIFLE (= a long gun) that can fire bullets very quickly

kale /keɪl/ *noun* [U] a dark green vegetable like a CABBAGE

ka·lei·do·scope /kəˈlaɪdəˌskoup/ *noun* **1** [C] a toy consisting of a tube that you look through with loose pieces of colored glass and mirrors at the end. When the tube is turned, the pieces of glass move and form different patterns **2** [sing.] a situation, pattern, etc. containing a lot of different parts that are always changing ▶ **ka·lei·do·scop·ic** /kəˌlaɪdəˈskɑpɪk/ *adj.*

ka·meez /kəˈmiz/ *noun* (*pl.* **ka·meez** or **ka·meez·es**) a piece of clothing like a long shirt worn by many people from S. Asia

ka·mi·ka·ze /ˌkɑmɪˈkɑzi/ *adj.* [only before noun] (from *Japanese*) used to describe the way soldiers attack the enemy, knowing that they too will be killed **SYN** SUICIDAL: *a kamikaze pilot/attack ♦* (*figurative*) *He made a kamikaze run across three lanes of traffic.*

kan·ga·roo /ˌkæŋgəˈru/ *noun* (*pl.* **kan·ga·roos**) a large Australian animal with a strong tail and back legs, that moves by jumping. The female carries its young in a pocket of skin (called a POUCH) on the front of its body. ➲ **picture at** ANIMAL

ˌkangaroo 'court *noun* (*disapproving*) an illegal court that punishes people unfairly

kan·ji /ˈkɑndʒi/ *noun* (*pl.* **kan·ji**) [U, C] (from *Japanese*) a Japanese system of writing based on Chinese symbols, called CHARACTERS; a symbol in this system

ka·o·lin /ˈkeɪələn/ (also ˌchina 'clay) *noun* [U] a type of fine white CLAY used in some medicines and in making PORCELAIN for cups, plates, etc.

ka·pok /ˈkeɪpɑk/ *noun* [U] a soft white material used for filling CUSHIONS, soft toys, etc.

kap·pa /ˈkæpə/ *noun* the 10th letter of the Greek alphabet (K, κ)

ka·put /kəˈpʊt/ *adj.* [not before noun] (*informal*) not working correctly; broken: *The truck's kaput.*

kar·a·bi·ner /ˌkærəˈbinər/ *noun* a metal ring that can open to allow a rope to pass through, used by rock CLIMBERS to attach themselves safely to things

kar·a·o·ke /ˌkæriˈouki/ *noun* [U] (from *Japanese*) a type of entertainment in which a machine plays only the music of popular songs so that people can sing the words themselves: *a karaoke machine/night/bar*

kar·at /ˈkærət/ *noun* a unit for measuring how pure gold is. The purest gold is 24 karats: *an 18-karat gold ring*

ka·ra·te /kəˈrɑti/ *noun* [U] a Japanese system of fighting in which you use your hands and feet as weapons: *a karate chop* (= a blow with the side of the hand)

kar·ma /ˈkɑrmə/ *noun* [U] **1** (in Buddhism and Hinduism) the sum of someone's good and bad actions in one of their lives, believed to decide what will happen to them in the next life **2 good/bad ~** (*informal*) the good/bad effect of doing a particular thing, being in a particular place, etc.: *Some vegetarians believe that eating meat is bad karma.*

kart /kɑrt/ *noun* a small motor vehicle used for racing

kart·ing /ˈkɑrtɪŋ/ *noun* [U] the sport of racing in karts

kas·bah = CASBAH

ka·ta·ka·na /ˌkɑtəˈkɑnə/ *noun* [U] (from *Japanese*) a set of symbols used in Japanese writing, used especially to write foreign words or to represent noises ➲ **compare** HIRAGANA

ka·ty·did /ˈkeɪtiˌdɪd/ *noun* a large, green, N. American insect, the male of which makes a noise that sounds like "katydid" when it rubs its wings together

kay·ak /ˈkaɪæk/ *noun, verb*

• *noun* a light CANOE in which the part where you sit is covered over ➲ **picture at** BOAT

• *verb* often **go kayaking** to travel in or use a kayak ▶ **kay·ak·er** /ˈkaɪækər/ *noun*: *three kayakers* **kay·ak·ing** *noun* [U]

kay·o /ˌkeɪˈou/ *noun* (*pl.* **kay·os**) = KO

ka·zoo /kəˈzu/ *noun* (*pl.* **ka·zoos**) a small simple musical instrument consisting of a hollow pipe with a hole in it, that makes a BUZZING sound when you sing into it

KB *abbr.* (in writing) KILOBYTE(S)

Kbps *abbr.* (in writing) kilobits per second (a unit for measuring the speed of a MODEM)

ke·bab /kəˈbɑb/ (also ˈshish keˌbab) *noun* small pieces of meat and vegetables cooked on a wooden or metal stick

keel /kil/ *noun, verb*

• *noun* the long piece of wood or steel along the bottom of a ship, on which the frame is built, and which sometimes sticks out below the bottom and helps to keep it in a vertical position in the water **IDM** see EVEN *adj.*

• *verb* [I, T] **~ (sth) (over)** (of a ship or boat) to fall over sideways; to make something fall over sideways **SYN** CAPSIZE **PHR V** ˌkeel 'over to fall over unexpectedly, especially because you feel sick: *Several of them keeled over in the heat.*

| h hat | m man | n no | ŋ sing | l leg | r red | y yes | w wet |

keel·haul /'kiːlhɔl/ verb **1** ~ sb (old use) to punish a sailor by pulling him under a ship, from one side to the other or from one end to the other **2** ~ sb (humorous) to punish someone very severely or speak very angrily to someone

keen 🔎 /kin/ adj., verb

● **adj.** (keen·er, keen·est)

> EAGER/ENTHUSIASTIC **1** wanting to do something or wanting something to happen very much **SYN** EAGER: ~ (to do sth) John was very keen to help. ♦ ~ (on doing sth) I wasn't too keen on going to the party. **2** [usually before noun] enthusiastic about or interested in an activity or idea, etc.: a keen fisherman ♦ one of the keenest supporters of the team
> INTELLIGENCE **3** [only before noun] quick to understand **SYN** ACUTE, SHARP: a keen mind/intellect
> IDEAS/FEELINGS **4** [usually before noun] strong or deep: a keen sense of tradition ♦ He took a keen interest in his grandson's education.
> SENSES **5** [only before noun] highly developed **SYN** SHARP: Dogs have a keen sense of smell. ♦ My friend has a keen eye for (= is good at noticing) a bargain.
> COMPETITION **6** involving people competing very hard with each other for something: There is keen competition to be admitted to the university.
> WIND **7** (literary) extremely cold
> KNIFE **8** [usually before noun] (literary) having a sharp edge or point

▶ **keen·ly** adv.: a keenly fought contest ♦ We were keenly aware of the danger. **keen·ness** noun [U]

● **verb** [I] (usually used in the progressive tenses) (old-fashioned) to make a loud, high, sad sound, when someone has died

keep 🔎 /kip/ verb, noun

● **verb** (kept, kept /kɛpt/)

> STAY **1** [I, T] to stay in a particular condition or position; to make someone or something do this: + adj. We huddled together to keep warm. ♦ + adv./prep. The sign said "Keep off (= Do not walk on) the grass". ♦ Keep left along the wall. ♦ ~ sb/ sth + adj. She kept the children amused for hours. ♦ ~ sb/sth (+ adv./prep.) He kept his coat on. ♦ Don't keep us in suspense —what happened next? ♦ She had trouble keeping her balance. ♦ ~ sb/sth doing sth I'm very sorry to keep you waiting.
> CONTINUE **2** [I] to continue doing something; to do something repeatedly: ~ doing sth Keep smiling! ♦ ~ on doing sth Don't keep on interrupting me!
> DELAY **3** [T] ~ sb to delay someone **SYN** HOLD SB UP: You're an hour late—what kept you?
> NOT GIVE BACK **4** [T] ~ sth to continue to have something and not give it back or throw it away: Here's a five dollar bill— please keep the change. ♦ I keep all her letters.
> PUT/STORE **5** [T] ~ sth + adv./prep. to put or store something in a particular place: Keep your passport in a safe place.
> ANIMALS **6** [T] ~ sth to own and care for animals: to keep bees/goats/hens
> ABOUT HEALTH **7** [I] + adv./prep. (old-fashioned, informal) used to ask or talk about someone's health: How is your mother keeping? ♦ We're all keeping well.
> OF FOOD **8** [I] to remain in good condition: Finish off the pie— it won't keep. ♦ (informal, figurative) "I'd love to hear about it, but I'm late already." "That's OK— it'll keep (= I can tell you about it later)."
> SECRET **9** [T] ~ a secret | ~ something secret (from someone) to know something and not tell it to anyone: Can you keep a secret? ♦ She kept her past secret from us all.
> PROMISE/APPOINTMENT **10** [T] ~ your promise/word | ~ an appointment to do what you have promised to do; to go where you have agreed to go: She kept her promise to visit them. ♦ He failed to keep his appointment at the clinic.
> DIARY/RECORD **11** [T] ~ a diary, an account, a record, etc. to write down something as a record: She kept a diary for over twenty years. ♦ Keep a note about where each item can be found.
> SUPPORT SOMEONE **12** [T] ~ sb/yourself to provide what is necessary for someone to live; to support someone by paying for food, etc.: He scarcely earns enough to keep himself and his family.

> PROTECT **13** [T] (formal) to protect someone from something: ~ sb May the Lord bless you and keep you (= used in prayers in the Christian Church). ♦ ~ sb from sth His only thought was to keep the boy from harm.
> IN SPORTS **14** [T] ~ goal (in SOCCER, HOCKEY, etc.) to guard or protect the goal ⊃ see also GOALKEEPER

IDM Most idioms containing **keep** are at the entries for the nouns and adjectives in the idioms. For example, **keep house** is at **house**. **keep going 1** to make an effort to live normally when you are in a difficult situation or when you have experienced great suffering: You just have to keep yourself busy and keep going. **2** (informal) used to encourage someone to continue doing something: Keep going, Sarah, you're nearly there. **keep sb going** (informal) to be enough for someone until they get what they are waiting for: Have an apple to keep you going till dinner time.

PHR V keep 'after sb to try to get someone to do something by constantly reminding them: If I didn't keep after the kids, they'd never clean their rooms. keep sb 'after to make a student stay at school after normal hours as a punishment
keep 'at sth to continue working at something: Come on, keep at it, you're nearly finished! keep sb 'at sth to make someone continue working at something: He kept us at it all day.
keep a'way (from sb/sth) to avoid going near someone or something: Keep away from the edge of the cliff. keep sb/ sth a'way (from sb/sth) to prevent someone or something from going somewhere: Her illness kept her away from work for several weeks.
keep 'back (from sb/sth) to stay at a distance from someone or something: Keep far back from the road. keep sb↔'back to make a student repeat a year at school because of poor grades keep sb↔'back (from sb/sth) to make someone stay at a distance from someone or something: Barricades were erected to keep back the crowds. keep sth↔'back to prevent a feeling, etc. from being expressed **SYN** RESTRAIN: She was unable to keep back her tears. keep sth↔'back (from sb) to refuse to tell someone something: I'm sure she's keeping something back from us.
keep 'down to hide yourself by not standing up straight: Keep down! You mustn't let anyone see you. keep sb↔'down to prevent a person, group, etc. from expressing themselves freely **SYN** OPPRESS: The people have been kept down for years by a brutal regime. keep sth↔'down **1** to make something stay at a low level; to avoid increasing something: to keep down salaries/prices/the cost of living ♦ Keep your voice down—I don't want anyone else to hear. ♦ Keep the noise down (= be quiet). **2** to not bring something back through the mouth from the stomach; to not VOMIT: She's had some water but she can't keep any food down.
'keep from sth | 'keep yourself from sth to prevent yourself from doing something: ~ doing sth She could hardly keep from laughing. ♦ I just managed to keep myself from falling. 'keep sb from sth to prevent someone from doing something: I hope I'm not keeping you from your work. ♦ ~ doing sth The church bells keep me from sleeping. 'keep sth from sb to avoid telling someone something: I think we ought to keep the truth from him until he's better. 'keep sth from sth to make something stay out of something: She could not keep the dismay from her voice.
keep sth↔'in to avoid expressing an emotion **SYN** RESTRAIN: He could barely keep in his indignation. keep sb 'in to make someone stay indoors or in a particular place 'keep sb/yourself in sth to provide someone/yourself with a regular supply of something
keep 'off sth to avoid mentioning a particular subject: It's best to keep off politics when my father's around. keep sb/ sth↔'off | keep sb/sth 'off sb/sth to prevent someone or something from coming near, touching, etc. someone or something: They lit a fire to keep off wild animals. ♦ Keep your hands off (= do not touch) me!
keep 'on to continue: Keep on until you get to the church. keep sb↔'on to continue to employ someone
keep 'out (of sth) to not enter a place; to stay outside: The sign said "Private Property—Keep Out!" keep sb/sth↔'out

(of sth) to prevent someone or something from entering a place: *Keep that dog out of my study!* **keep 'out of sth** | **keep sb 'out of sth** to avoid something; to prevent someone from being involved in something or affected by something: *That child can't keep out of mischief.* ◆ *Keep the baby out of the sun.*

'keep to sth 1 to avoid leaving a path, road, etc. **SYN** **STICK TO STH:** *Keep to the trail—the land is very boggy around here.* **2** to talk or write only about the subject that you are supposed to talk or write about: *Nothing is more irritating than people who do not keep to the point.* **3** to do what you have promised or agreed to do: *to keep to an agreement/an undertaking/a plan* **4** to stay in and not leave a particular place or position: *She's nearly 90 and mostly keeps to her room.* **keep (yourself) to your'self** to avoid meeting people socially or becoming involved in their affairs: *Nobody knows much about him; he keeps very much to himself.* **keep sth to your'self** to not tell other people about something: *I'd be grateful if you kept this information to yourself.*

keep 'up if particular weather **keeps up**, it continues without stopping: *The rain kept up all afternoon.* **keep 'up (with sb/sth)** to move, make progress, or increase at the same rate as someone or something: *Slow down—I can't keep up!* ◆ *I can't keep up with all the changes.* ◆ *Salaries are not keeping up with inflation.* **keep 'up with sb** to continue to be in contact with someone: *How many of your old school friends do you keep up with?* **keep 'up with sth 1** to learn about or be aware of the news, current events, etc.: *She likes to keep up with the latest fashions.* **2** to continue to pay or do something regularly: *If you do not keep up with the payments you could lose your home.* **keep sb 'up** to prevent someone from going to bed: *I hope we're not keeping you up.* **keep sth↔'up 1** to make something stay at a high level: *The high cost of raw materials is keeping prices up.* **2** to continue something at the same, usually high, level: *The enemy kept up the bombardment day and night.* ◆ *We're having difficulty keeping up our mortgage payments.* ◆ *Well done! Keep up the good work/Keep it up!* **3** to make something remain at a high level: *They sang songs to keep their spirits up.* **4** to continue to use or practice something: *to keep up old traditions* ◆ *Do you still keep up your Spanish?* **5** to take care of a house, yard, etc. so that it stays in good condition **SYN** MAINTAIN ◆ related noun UPKEEP

● **noun 1** [U] food, clothes, and all the other things that a person needs to live; the cost of these things: *It's about time you got a job to earn your keep.* **2** [C] a large strong tower, built as part of an old castle

IDM **for keeps** (*informal*) forever: *Is it yours for keeps or does he want it back?* ⊃ more at EARN

keep·er /'kipər/ *noun* **1** (especially in compounds) a person whose job is to take care of a building, its contents, or something valuable: *the keeper of geology at the museum* ⊃ see also STOREKEEPER **2** a person whose job is to take care of animals, especially in a ZOO ⊃ see also GAMEKEEPER, ZOOKEEPER **3** (*informal*) = GOALKEEPER **4** (*informal*) something worth keeping: *They were deciding which drawings to get rid of and which were keepers.*

IDM **keeper of the flame** someone who feels it is their responsibility to support an idea, philosophy, etc., even if it is not popular: *She was the keeper of the flame for her dead husband's vision of a utopian society.* **be sb's keeper** to be regarded as being in charge of someone else: *I'm his wife, not his keeper.* ⊃ more at FINDER

keep·ing /'kipɪŋ/ *noun*

IDM **in sb's keeping** being taken care of by someone ⊃ see also SAFEKEEPING **in keeping (with sth)** appropriate or expected in a particular situation; in agreement with something: *The latest results are in keeping with our earlier findings.* **out of keeping (with sth)** not appropriate or expected in a particular situation; not in agreement with something: *The painting is out of keeping with the rest of the room.*

keep·sake /'kipseɪk/ *noun* a small object that someone gives you so that you will remember them **SYN** MEMENTO

kef·fi·yeh (also **kaf·fi·yeh**) /kə'fiə/ *noun* a square of cloth worn on the head by Arab men and fastened by a band

keg /kɛg/ *noun* a round wooden or metal container with a flat top and bottom, used especially for storing beer, like a BARREL but smaller

keg·ger /'kɛgər/ (also **'keg ,party**) *noun* (*informal*) a party at which beer is served from kegs

keis·ter /'kistər/ *noun* (*informal*) the part of the body that you sit on **SYN** BACKSIDE

kelp /kɛlp/ *noun* [U] a type of brown SEAWEED, sometimes used as a FERTILIZER to help plants grow

kel·vin /'kɛlvən/ *noun* (*abbr.* K) (*pl.* **kel·vin** or **kel·vins**) a unit for measuring temperature. One kelvin is equal to one degree Celsius, but the **Kelvin scale** starts at ABSOLUTE ZERO and water freezes at 273.15 kelvin

the 'Kelvin ,scale *noun* [sing.] a scale of temperature in which water freezes at 273.15 degrees

ken /kɛn/ *noun*

● *noun*

IDM **beyond your ken** (*old-fashioned*) if something is **beyond your ken**, you do not know enough about it to be able to understand it

ken·do /'kɛndoʊ/ *noun* [U] (from *Japanese*) a Japanese form of the sport of FENCING, using light wooden weapons

ken·nel /'kɛnl/ *noun* **1** (also **'boarding ,kennel**) a place where people can leave their dogs to be taken care of when they go on vacation; a place where dogs are bred: *We left the dog at a kennel for a week.* **2** a small shelter for a dog or cat to sleep in **SYN** DOGHOUSE

kept *pt, pp of* KEEP

kept 'woman *noun* (*old-fashioned*, usually *humorous*) a woman who is given money and a home by a man who visits her regularly to have sex

ker·a·tin /'kɛrətən/ *noun* [U] (*biology*) a PROTEIN that forms hair, feathers, horns, HOOFS, etc.

ker·chief /'kɑrtʃəf/ *noun* (*old-fashioned*) a square piece of cloth worn on the head or around the neck

ker·nel /'kɑrnl/ *noun* **1** the inner part of a nut or seed **2** the central, most important part of an idea or a subject

ker·o·sene (also **ker·o·sine**) /'kɛrəsin; ,kɛrə'sin/ *noun* [U] a type of fuel oil that is made from PETROLEUM and that is used in the engines of planes and for heat and light: *a kerosene lamp*

kes·trel /'kɛstrəl/ *noun* a small BIRD OF PREY (= a bird that kills other creatures for food) of the FALCON family

ke·ta·mine /'kɛtə,min; 'ki-/ *noun* [U] a substance that is used as an ANESTHETIC, and also as a drug that is taken illegally for pleasure

ketch /kɛtʃ/ *noun* a SAILBOAT with two MASTS (= posts to support the sails)

ketch·up (also **cat·sup**) /'kɛtʃəp; 'kæ-/ *noun* [U] a thick cold sauce made from tomatoes, usually sold in bottles

ket·tle /'kɛtl/ *noun* a container with a lid, handle, and a SPOUT, used for boiling water: *an electric kettle* **IDM** see DIFFERENT, POT

ket·tle·drum /'kɛtl,drʌm/ *noun* a large metal drum with a round bottom and a thin plastic top that can be made looser or tighter to produce different musical notes. A set of kettledrums is usually called TIMPANI. ⊃ picture at INSTRUMENT

Kev·lar™ /'kɛvlɑr/ *noun* [U] an artificial substance used to give strength to tires and other rubber products, often used in clothing that protects people from bullets

key /ki/ *noun, verb, adj.*

● *noun*

> TOOL FOR LOCK **1** a specially shaped piece of metal used for locking a door, starting a car, etc.: *to insert/turn the key in the lock* ◆ *the car keys* ◆ *a bunch of keys* ◆ *the spare key to the front*

ʌ cup   ə about   eɪ say   aɪ five   ɔɪ boy   aʊ now   oʊ go   ər bird

keys

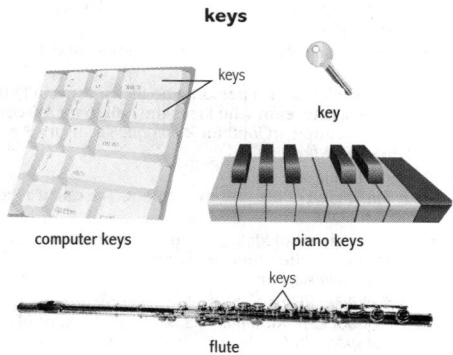

keys

key

computer keys   piano keys

keys

flute

door ♦ *We'll have a duplicate key cut* (= made). ➔ picture at PADLOCK
> MOST IMPORTANT THING **2** [usually sing.] a thing that makes you able to understand or achieve something **SYN** SECRET: *~ (to sth) The key to success is preparation.* ♦ *~ (to doing sth) The driver of the car probably holds the key to solving the crime.* ♦ *The key is, how long can the federal government control the inflation rate?*
> ON COMPUTER **3** any of the buttons that you press to operate a computer or TYPEWRITER: *Press the return key to enter the information.* ➔ picture at COMPUTER
> ON MUSICAL INSTRUMENT **4** any of the wooden or metal parts that you press to play a piano and some other musical instruments
> MUSIC **5** a set of related notes, based on a particular note. Pieces of music are usually written mainly using a particular key: *a sonata in the key of E flat major* ➔ compare SCALE ➔ see also OFF-KEY
> ANSWERS **6** a set of answers to exercises or problems: *Check your answers in the key at the back of the book.*
> ON MAP **7** an explanation of the symbols used on a map or plan ➔ see also LOW-KEY **IDM** see LOCK
• *verb* **1** ~ sth (in) | ~ sth (into sth) to put information into a computer using a keyboard **SYN** ENTER: *Key (in) your password.* **2** to deliberately damage a car by scratching it with a key
PHR V 'key sb/sth to sth [usually passive] to make someone or something suitable or appropriate for a particular purpose **SYN** GEAR: *The classes are keyed to the needs of advanced students.*
• *adj.* [usually before noun] most important; essential **SYN** CRITICAL, VITAL: *the key issue/factor/point* ♦ *He was a key figure in the campaign.* ♦ *She played a key role in the dispute.* ♦ *"Caution" is the key word in this situation.* ♦ *Good communication is key to our success.* ♦ *His contribution could be key.* ➔ thesaurus box at MAIN

key·board 🔑 /'kibɔrd/ *noun, verb*
• *noun* **1** the set of keys for operating a computer or TYPE-WRITER ➔ picture at COMPUTER **2** the set of black and white keys on a piano or other musical instrument **3** an electronic musical instrument that has keys like a piano and can be made to play in different styles or to sound like different instruments ➔ compare SYNTHESIZER
• *verb* [T, I] ~ (sth) to type information into a computer ▶ key·board·ing *noun* [U]
key·board·er /'ki,bɔrdər/ *noun* a person whose job is to type data into a computer
key·board·ist /'ki,bɔrdɪst/ *noun* a person who plays an electronic musical instrument with a keyboard
'**key card** (also '**card key**) *noun* a small plastic card that can be used in an electronic lock to open a door or gate ➔ compare SWIPE CARD

'**key chain** *noun* a small chain, often attached to a metal ring and a decoration, that you use to hold keys together
,**keyed** '**up** *adj.* [not before noun] nervous and excited, especially before an important event
key·hole /'kihoul/ *noun* the hole in a lock that you put a key in
key·log·ger /'ki,lɔgər; -,lɑ-/ *noun* (*computing*) a computer program that records all the keys that a user hits so that it is possible to discover secret information such as code words
key·note /'kinout/ *noun* **1** [usually sing.] the central idea of a book, a speech, etc.: *Choice is the keynote of the new education policy.* ♦ *a keynote address/speech/speaker* (= a very important one, introducing a meeting or its subject) **2** (*music*) the note on which the KEY is based ▶ **key·not·er** *noun*: *For the first time, a woman will be the keynoter at the convention this year.*
key·pad /'kipæd/ *noun* a small set of buttons with numbers on used to operate a telephone, television, etc.; the buttons on the right of a computer keyboard
'**key ring** *noun* a small ring that you put keys on to keep them together ➔ picture at RING[1]
'**key** ,**signature** *noun* (*music*) the set of marks at the beginning of a printed piece of music to show what KEY the piece is in ➔ picture at MUSIC
key·stone /'kistoun/ *noun* **1** (*architecture*) the central stone at the top of an ARCH that keeps all the other stones in position **2** [usually sing.] the most important part of a plan or argument that the other parts depend on
key·stroke /'kistrouk/ *noun* a single action of pressing a key on a computer or TYPEWRITER keyboard
key·word /'kiwərd/ *noun* **1** a word that tells you about the main idea or subject of something: *When you're studying a language, the keyword is patience.* **2** a word or phrase that you type on a computer keyboard to give an instruction or to search for information about something: *Enter the keyword "restaurants" and click on Search.*
kg *abbr.* (*pl.* **kg** or **kgs**) (in writing) kilogram(s): *10 kg*
the KGB /,keɪ dʒi 'bi/ *noun* [sing.] the state security police of the former USSR
khak·i /'kæki/ *noun* **1** [U] a strong greenish or yellowish brown cloth, used especially for making military uniforms **2** [U] a dull greenish or yellowish brown color **3 khakis** [pl.] pants made from khaki cloth: *He wore a pair of baggy khakis.* ▶ **khak·i** *adj.*: *khaki uniforms*
khan /kɑn/ *noun* a title given to rulers in some Muslim countries
khan·ate /'kɑneɪt/ *noun* **1** the area which is ruled by a khan **2** the position of a khan
kHz *abbr.* (in writing) KILOHERTZ
kib·ble /'kɪbl/ *noun* [U] grain and other ingredients, crushed to produce a powder and then shaped into small hard balls and used for pet food: *Our dog eats kibble and canned dog food.*
kib·butz /kɪ'buts/ *noun* (*pl.* **kib·but·zim** /,kɪbut'sɪm/) (in Israel) a type of farm or factory where a group of people live together and share all the work, decisions, and income
kib·itz /'kɪbəts/ *verb* (*informal*) **1** [I, T] (usually *disapproving*) to watch other people doing something and make comments or give advice about it, often in an annoying way: *It is rude to kibitz during a serious game.* ♦ *~ sth I paused to kibitz a poker game.* **2** [I] to talk in a friendly, informal way: *We sat around and kibitzed until about eleven.* ▶ **kib·itz·er** *noun*: *The kibitzers were second-guessing each move.*
kib·lah = QIBLA
ki·bosh /'kaɪbɑʃ; kɪ'bɑʃ/ *noun*
IDM put the kibosh on sth (*informal*) to stop something from happening; to spoil someone's plans

kick /kɪk/ verb, noun

• **verb** **1** [T, I] to hit someone or something with your foot: ~ **(sb/sth)** *She was punched and kicked by her attackers.* ◆ *Stop kicking—it hurts!* ◆ ~ **sb/sth + adv./prep./adj.** *The boys were kicking a ball around in the yard.* ◆ *Vandals had kicked the door down.* **2** [T, I] ~ **(sth)** to move your legs as if you were kicking something: *The dancers kicked their legs in the air.* ◆ *The child was dragged away,* **kicking and screaming.** **3** [T] ~ **yourself** (*informal*) to be annoyed with yourself because you have done something stupid, missed an opportunity, etc.: *He'll kick himself when he finds out he could have had the job.* **4** [T] ~ **sth** (in some sports) to score points by kicking the ball: *to kick a penalty/goal/fieldgoal*

IDM **kick ass/butt** (*slang*) (*impolite*) to succeed or win in an impressive way: *Let's show them that we're ready to kick some ass!* **kick sb's ass/butt** (*slang*) (*impolite*) to punish or defeat someone **kick the bucket** (*informal* or *humorous*) to die **kick the habit, drug, booze, etc.** to stop doing something harmful that you have done for a long time **kick sb in the teeth/stomach** to disappoint someone greatly or fail to give them help when they need it **kick up a fuss, stink, etc.** (*informal*) to complain loudly about something **kick up your heels** (*informal*) to be relaxed and enjoy yourself **kick sb upstairs** (*informal*) to move someone to a job that seems to be more important but which actually has less power or influence **kick sb when they're down** to continue to hurt someone when they are already defeated, etc. ➔ more at ALIVE, HELL, HIGH GEAR

PHRV **kick a'round** (*informal*) **1** (usually used in the progressive tenses) to be lying somewhere not being used: *There's a pen kicking around on my desk somewhere.* **2** to go from one place to another with no particular purpose: *They spent the summer kicking around Europe.* **kick sb a'round** (*informal*) to treat someone in a rough or unfair way **kick sth a'round** (*informal*) to discuss an idea, a plan, etc. in an informal way **kick against sth** to protest about or resist something: *Young people often kick against the rules.* **kick 'back** to relax: *Kick back and enjoy the summer.* **kick 'in** (*informal*) **1** to begin to take effect: *Reforms will kick in later this year.* **2** (also **kick 'in sth**) to give your share of money or help **kick 'off** when a football or SOCCER game or a team, etc. **kicks off,** the game starts ➔ related noun KICKOFF **kick 'off (with sth)** (*informal*) to start: *What time shall we kick off?* ◆ *Tom will kick off with a few comments.* ➔ related noun KICKOFF ➔ thesaurus box at START **kick sth↔'off** to remove something by kicking: *to kick off your shoes* **kick 'off sth** to start a discussion, a meeting, an event, etc. **SYN** OPEN **kick sb 'out (of sth)** (*informal*) to make someone leave or go away (from somewhere) **kick 'up** (of wind or a storm) to become stronger **kick sth↔'up 1** to make something, especially dust, rise from the ground **2** (*informal*) to increase the speed or amount of something: *We've got to kick up production if we're going to stay ahead of our competitors.*

• **noun** **1** a movement with the foot or the leg, usually to hit something with the foot: *the first kick of the game* ◆ *She gave him a kick on the shin.* ◆ *He aimed a kick at the dog.* ◆ *If the door won't open, give it a kick.* ◆ (*slang*) *She needs a kick in the pants* (= she needs to be strongly encouraged to do something or to behave better). ➔ see also FREE KICK, PENALTY KICK **2** (*informal*) a strong feeling of excitement and pleasure **SYN** THRILL: *I get a kick out of driving fast cars.* ◆ *He gets his kicks from hurting other people.* ◆ *What do you do for kicks?* **3** [usually sing.] (*informal*) the strong effect that a drug, an alcoholic drink, or spicy food has: *This drink has quite a kick.* **IDM** **a kick in the teeth** (*informal*) a great disappointment; something that hurts someone or something emotionally **be on a health, cultural, etc. kick** to have a particular temporary interest or enthusiasm: *She's been on a jogging kick for the past few weeks.*

kick·back /'kɪkbæk/ noun (*informal*) money paid illegally to someone in return for work or help **SYN** BRIBE

kick·ball /'kɪkbɔl/ noun [U] a game that is based on baseball in which players kick the ball instead of hitting it with a BAT

kick-‚boxing noun [U] a form of BOXING in which the

people fighting each other can kick as well as punch (= hit with their hands)

'kick drum noun (*informal*) a large drum played using a PEDAL

kick·er /'kɪkər/ noun **1** a person who kicks, especially the player in a sports team who kicks the ball to try to score points, for example in football **2** (*informal*) a surprising end to a series of events

kick·ing /'kɪkɪŋ/ adj., noun

• **adj.** (*informal*) full of life and excitement: *The club was really kicking last night.*

• **noun** [sing.] an act of kicking someone hard and repeatedly, especially when they are lying on the ground: *They gave him a good kicking.*

kick·off /'kɪkɔf; -ɑf/ noun **1** [C, U] the start of a game of football or SOCCER: *Kickoff is at 3.* **2** [sing.] the start of an activity: *A speech by the chancellor was the kickoff to our college reunion.*

kick·stand /'kɪkstænd/ noun a long straight piece of metal attached to a bicycle or a motorcycle, that is kept horizontal while the bicycle is being ridden but that can be moved to a vertical position when you need to stand the bicycle somewhere ➔ picture at BICYCLE

'kick-start verb, noun

• **verb 1** ~ **sth** to start a motorcycle by pushing down a LEVER with your foot **2** ~ **sth** to do something to help a process or project start more quickly: *The government's attempt to kick-start the economy has failed.*

• **noun 1** (also **'kick start,** **'kick ‚starter**) the part of a motorcycle that you push down with your foot in order to start it **2** a quick start that you give to something by taking some action

'kick turn noun **1** (in SKIING) a turn made by lifting and turning each SKI separately so that you face the opposite direction **2** a turn made with the front wheels of a SKATE-BOARD off the ground

kid /kɪd/ noun, verb, adj.

• **noun 1** [C] (*informal*) a child or young person: *A bunch of kids were hanging around outside.* ◆ *a 15-year-old kid* ◆ *She's a bright kid.* ◆ *How are the kids* (= your children)? ◆ *Do you have any kids?* **HELP** Kid is much more common than child in informal and spoken English. ➔ collocations at CHILD **2** [C] a young GOAT **3** [U] soft leather made from the skin of a young GOAT

IDM **handle/treat, etc. sb with kid gloves** to deal with someone in a very careful way so that you do not offend or upset them **kid stuff** (also **kids' stuff**) something that is so easy to do or understand that it is thought to be not very serious or only suitable for children ➔ more at NEW

• **verb** (**-dd-**) (*informal*) **1** [I, T] (usually used in the progressive tenses) to tell someone something that is not true, especially as a joke **SYN** JOKE: *I thought he was kidding when he said he was going out with a rock star.* ◆ *I didn't mean it. I was only kidding.* ◆ ~ **sb** *I'm not kidding you. It does work.* **2** [T] to allow someone/yourself to believe something that is not true **SYN** DECEIVE: ~ **sb/yourself** *They're kidding themselves if they think it's going to be easy.* ◆ ~ **sb/yourself (that)…** *I tried to kid myself (that) everything was normal.*

IDM **I kid you not** (*humorous*) used to stress the fact that you are telling the truth: *I kid you not – he ate 27 hot dogs!* **no kidding** (*informal*) **1** used to emphasize that something is true or that you agree with something that someone has just said: *"It's cold!" "No kidding!"* **2** used to show that you mean what you are saying: *I want the money back tomorrow. No kidding. Who is sb trying to kid?* (*informal*) used to show that people do not believe what someone says: *She says her father's a millionaire, but who is she trying to kid?* **you're kidding | you must be kidding** (*informal*) used to show that you are very surprised at something that someone has just said

PHRV **kid a'round** to behave in a silly way

| t tea | ţ butter | d did | k cat | g got | tʃ chin | dʒ June | f fall |

- *adj.* ~ **sister/brother** (*informal*) a person's younger sister/brother

kid·die (also **kid·dy**) /ˈkɪdi/ (*pl.* **kid·dies**) *noun* (*informal*) a young child: *a kiddies' party*

kid·do /ˈkɪdoʊ/ *noun* (*pl.* **kid·dos**) (*informal*) used when speaking to a friend or a child: *Cheer up, kiddo – you'll be OK in a few days.*

kid·nap /ˈkɪdnæp/ *verb* (-p-, *CanE usually* -pp-) ~ **sb** to take someone away illegally and keep them as a prisoner, especially in order to get money or something else for returning them **SYN** ABDUCT, SEIZE: *Two businessmen have been kidnapped by terrorists.* ▶ **kid·nap·per** *noun*: *The kidnappers are demanding a ransom of $1 million.* **kid·nap·ping** (also **kidnap**) *noun* [U, C]: *He pled guilty to the charge of kidnapping.* ◆ *the kidnap of 12 U.S. citizens*

kid·ney /ˈkɪdni/ *noun* **1** [C] either of the two organs in the body that remove waste products from the blood and produce URINE: *a kidney infection* ⊃ picture at BODY **2** [U, C] the kidneys of some animals that are cooked and eaten

kidney bean *noun* a type of reddish-brown BEAN shaped like a kidney that is usually dried before it is sold and then left in water before cooking ⊃ picture at FRUIT

kidney machine *noun* a machine that does the work of a KIDNEY for someone whose kidneys are damaged or have been removed

kid·ult /ˈkɪdʌlt/ *noun* (*informal*) an adult who likes doing or buying things that are usually thought more suitable for children

kiel·ba·sa /kɪlˈbɑsə; kil-/ *noun* [U, C] a type of spicy Polish SAUSAGE that is eaten hot

kill 🔎 /kɪl/ *verb, noun*

- *verb* **1** [T, I] ~ **(sb/sth/yourself)** to make someone or something die: *Cancer kills thousands of people every year.* ◆ *Three people were killed in the crash.* ◆ *He tried to kill himself with sleeping pills.* ◆ *I bought a spray to kill the weeds.* ◆ (*informal*) *My mother will kill me* (= be very angry with me) *when she finds out.* ◆ *Don't kill yourself trying to get the work done by tomorrow. It can wait.* ◆ *Drunk driving can kill.* **2** [T] ~ **sth** to destroy or spoil something or make it stop: *to kill a rumor* ◆ *Do you agree that television kills conversation?* ◆ *The defeat last night killed the team's chances of qualifying.* **3** [T] ~ **sb** | **it kills sb to do sth** (*informal*) (usually used in the progressive tenses and not used in the passive) to cause someone pain or suffering: *My feet are killing me.* **4** [T] ~ **sb** to make someone laugh a lot: *Stop it! You're killing me!* **IDM** **kill the goose that lays the golden egg/eggs** (*saying*) to destroy something that would make you rich, successful, etc. **kill time | kill an hour, a couple of hours, etc.** to spend time doing something that is not important while you are waiting for something else to happen: *We killed time playing cards.* **kill two birds with one stone** to achieve two things at the same time with one action **kill sb/sth with kindness** to be so kind to someone or something that you in fact harm them ⊃ more at CLOCK, CURIOSITY, DRESSED, LOOK, TIME **PHR V** **kill sb/sth↔off 1** to make a lot of plants, animals, etc. die: *Some drugs kill off useful bacteria in the user's body.* **2** to stop or get rid of something: *He has effectively killed off any political opposition.*
- *noun* [usually sing.] **1** an act of killing, especially when an animal is hunted or killed: *A cat often plays with a mouse before the kill.* ◆ *The plane prepared to move in for the kill.* ◆ (*figurative*) *I was in at the kill when she finally lost her job* (= present at the end of an unpleasant process). **2** an animal that has been hunted and killed: *lions feeding on their kill*

kill·er /ˈkɪlər/ *noun, adj.*

- *noun* **1** a person, an animal, or a thing that kills: *Police are hunting his killer.* ◆ *Heart disease is the biggest killer in the U.S.* ◆ *an electric insect killer* ◆ *The players lacked the killer instinct.* ⊃ see also LADYKILLER, SERIAL KILLER **2** (*informal*) something that is very difficult, very exciting, or very skillful: *The exam was a real killer.* ◆ *The new movie is a killer.*

- *adj.* (*informal*) **1** likely to cause great harm: *a killer tornado* **2** very attractive or impressive: *She was wearing a killer outfit.* **3** very difficult: *a killer math test*

killer application (also *informal* **killer app**) *noun* (*computing*) a computer program that is so popular that it encourages people to buy or use the OPERATING SYSTEM, etc. that it runs on

killer bee *noun* a type of BEE that is very aggressive

killer cell *noun* (*biology*) a white blood cell which destroys infected cells or cancer cells

killer whale (also or·ca) *noun* a black and white WHALE that kills and eats other animals

kill·ing 🔎 /ˈkɪlɪŋ/ *noun*

- *noun* an act of killing someone deliberately **SYN** MURDER: *brutal killings* ⊃ see also MERCY KILLING ⊃ collocations at CRIME **IDM** **make a killing** (*informal*) to make a lot of money quickly

killing fields *noun* [pl.] a place where very many people were killed, for example during a war

kill·joy /ˈkɪldʒɔɪ/ *noun* (*disapproving*) a person who likes to spoil other people's enjoyment

kiln /kɪln; kɪl/ *noun* a large oven for baking CLAY and bricks, drying wood and grain, etc.

ki·lo /ˈkiloʊ/ *noun* (*pl.* **ki·los**) = KILOGRAM

kilo- /ˈkɪloʊ; -lə/ *combining form* (in nouns; often used in units of measurement) one thousand: *kilojoule*

kil·o·bit /ˈkɪləˌbɪt/ *noun* a unit for measuring computer memory or information equal to 1,024 BITS ⊃ see also KBPS

kil·o·byte /ˈkɪləˌbaɪt/ *noun* (*abbr.* K, KB) a unit of computer memory equal to 1,024 BYTES

kil·o·gram 🔎 /ˈkɪləˌgræm/ (also **ki·lo**) *noun* (*abbr.* kg) a unit for measuring weight; 1,000 grams: *A kilogram is equivalent to around 2.2 pounds.*

kil·o·hertz /ˈkɪləˌhərts/ *noun* (*abbr.* kHz) (*pl.* **kil·o·hertz**) a unit for measuring radio waves

kil·o·joule /ˈkɪləˌdʒul/ *noun* (*abbr.* kJ) a measurement of the energy that you get from food; 1,000 JOULES

kil·o·me·ter 🔎 (*CanE usually* **kil·o·me·tre**) /kɪˈlɑmətər; ˈkɪləˌmitər/ *noun* (*abbr.* k, km) a unit for measuring distance; 1,000 meters

kil·o·watt /ˈkɪləˌwat/ *noun* (*abbr.* kW, kw) a unit for measuring electrical power; 1,000 WATTS

kilowatt-hour *noun* (*abbr.* kWh) a unit for measuring electrical energy equal to the power provided by one kilowatt in one hour

kilt /kɪlt/ *noun* a skirt made of TARTAN cloth that reaches to the knees and is traditionally worn by Scottish men; a similar skirt worn by women

kilt·ed /ˈkɪltəd/ *adj.* wearing a kilt

kil·ter /ˈkɪltər/ *noun* **IDM** **out of kilter 1** not agreeing with or the same as something else: *His views are out of kilter with world opinion.* **2** no longer continuing or working in the normal way: *Long flights throw my sleeping pattern out of kilter for days.*

kim·chi (also **kim·chee**) /ˈkɪmtʃi/ *noun* [U] a spicy Korean dish made with PICKLED CABBAGE, onions, peppers, etc.

ki·mo·no /kəˈmoʊnoʊ; -nə/ *noun* (*pl.* **ki·mo·nos**) (from *Japanese*) a traditional Japanese piece of clothing like a long loose dress with wide sleeves, worn on formal occasions; a ROBE in this style

kin /kɪn/ *noun* [pl.] (*old-fashioned* or *formal*) your family or your relatives ⊃ compare KINDRED ⊃ see also NEXT OF KIN **IDM** see KITH

kind /kaɪnd/ *noun, adj.*

● *noun* [C, U] a group of people or things that are the same in some way; a particular variety or type: *three kinds of cake* ◆ *music of all/various/different kinds* ◆ *Exercises of this kind are very popular.* ◆ *What kind of house do you live in?* ◆ *They sell all kinds of things.* ◆ *The school is the first of its kind in the city.* ◆ *She isn't that kind of girl.* ◆ *The regions differ in size, but not in kind.* ◆ *I need to buy paper and pencils, that kind of thing.* ◆ *I'll never have that kind of money* (= as much money as that). ◆ *(formal) Would you like a drink of some kind?* **IDM** **in kind 1** (of a payment) consisting of goods or services, not money **2** *(formal)* with the same thing: *She insulted him and he responded in kind.* **a kind of** *(informal)* used to show that something you are saying is not exact: *I had a kind of feeling this might happen.* **kind of** *(informal)* (also **kinda**) slightly; in some ways: *That made me feel kind of stupid.* ◆ *I like him, kind of.* **nothing of the kind/sort** used to emphasize that the situation is very different from what has been said: *"I was terrible!" "You were nothing of the kind."* **of a kind 1** *(disapproving)* not as good as it could be: *You're making progress of a kind.* **2** very similar: *They're two of a kind —both workaholics!* **one of a kind** the only one like this **SYN** UNIQUE: *My father was one of a kind—I'll never be like him.* **something of the/that kind** something like what has been said: *"He's resigning." "I'd suspected something of the kind."*

GRAMMAR

kind ◆ type ◆ sort

- Use the singular (**kind/type/sort**) or plural (**kinds/types/sorts**) depending on the word you use before them: *each/one/every kind of animal* ◆ *all/many/other types of animals*
- **Kind/type/sort of** is followed by a singular or uncountable noun: *This type of question often appears on the test.* ◆ *That sort of behavior is not acceptable.*
- **Kinds/types/sorts of** is followed by a plural or uncountable noun: *These types of questions often appear on the test.* ◆ *These sorts of behavior are not acceptable.*
- Other variations are possible in spoken English, but are less common, and are considered incorrect in formal written English: *These types of question often appear on the test.* ◆ *These kind of things don't happen in real life.*
- Note also that these examples are possible, especially in spoken English: *The shelf was full of the sort of books I like to read.* ◆ *He faced the same kind of problems as his predecessor.* ◆ *There are many different types of animal on the island.* ◆ *What kind of camera is this?* ◆ *What kind/kinds of cameras do you sell?* ◆ *There were three kinds of cakes/cake on the plate.*

● *adj.* (**kind·er**, **kind·est**) **1** caring about others; gentle, friendly, and generous: *a very kind and helpful person* ◆ *a kind heart/face* ◆ *a kind action/gesture/comment* ◆ *You've been very kind.* ◆ **~ (to sb/sth)** kind to animals ◆ *(figurative) The weather was very kind to us.* ◆ **~ (of sb) (to do sth)** *It was really kind of you to help me.* ◆ *(formal) Thank you for your kind invitation.* ◆ *(formal) "Please have another." "That's very kind of you* (= thank you)." **ANT** UNKIND **2** *(formal)* used to make a polite request or give an order: *Would you be kind enough to close the window.* ⤷ see also KINDLY, KINDNESS

kin·der·gar·ten /ˈkɪndərˌgɑrdn; -ˌgɑrtn/ *noun* [C, U] (from German) a school or class that prepares children aged five for first grade

kin·der·gar·ten·er (also **kin·der·gart·ner**) /ˈkɪndərˌgɑrdnər; -ˌgɑrt-/ *noun* a child who is in KINDERGARTEN

ˌkind-ˈhearted *adj.* kind and generous

kin·dle /ˈkɪndl/ *verb* **1** [I, T] to start burning; to make a fire start burning: *We watched as the fire slowly kindled.* ◆ **~ sth** *to kindle a fire/flame* **2** [T, I] **~ (sth)** to make something such as an interest, emotion, etc. start to grow in someone; to

start to be felt by someone: *It was her teacher who kindled her interest in music.* ◆ *Suspicion kindled within her.*

kin·dling /ˈkɪndlɪŋ/ *noun* [U] small dry pieces of wood, etc. used to start a fire

kind·ly /ˈkaɪndli/ *adv., adj.*

● *adv.* **1** in a kind way: *She spoke kindly to them.* ◆ *He has kindly agreed to help.* **2** *(old-fashioned, formal)* used to ask or tell someone to do something, especially when you are annoyed: *Kindly leave me alone!* ◆ *Visitors are kindly requested to sign the book.* **IDM** **look kindly on/upon sth/sb** *(formal)* to approve of something or someone: *He hoped they would look kindly on his request.* **not take kindly to sth/sb** to not like something or someone: *She doesn't take kindly to sudden change.*

● *adj.* [only before noun] *(old-fashioned* or *literary)* kind and caring ▶ **kind·li·ness** *noun* [U]

kind·ness /ˈkaɪndnəs/ *noun*

1 [U] the quality of being kind: *to treat someone with kindness and consideration* **2** [C] a kind act: *I can never repay your many kindnesses to me.* **IDM** see KILL v., MILK n.

kin·dred /ˈkɪndrəd/ *noun, adj.*

● *noun (old-fashioned* or *formal)* **1** [pl.] your family and relatives ⤷ compare KIN **2** [U] the fact of being related to another person: *ties of kindred*

● *adj.* [only before noun] *(formal)* very similar; related: *food and kindred products* ◆ *I knew I'd found a kindred spirit* (= a person with similar ideas, opinions, etc.)

ki·ne·sis /kɪˈnisəs/ *noun* [U] *(technical)* movement

ki·net·ic /kɪˈnɛtɪk/ *adj.* [usually before noun] *(technical)* of or produced by movement: *kinetic energy*

kiˌnetic ˈart *noun* [U] *(art)* art, especially SCULPTURE, with parts that move

kin·folk /ˈkɪnfoʊk/ *noun* [pl.] *(formal* or *old-fashioned)* a person's relatives

king /kɪŋ/ *noun*

1 the male ruler of an independent state that has a royal family: *the kings and queens of England* ◆ *to be crowned king* ◆ *King George V* **2** **~ (of sth)** a person, an animal, or a thing that is thought to be the best or most important of a particular type: *the king of comedy* ◆ *The lion is the king of the jungle.* **3** used in new words formed from two or more words, with the names of animals or plants to describe a very large type of the thing mentioned: *a king penguin* **4** the most important piece used in the game of CHESS, that can move one square in any direction ⤷ picture at TOY **5** a PLAYING CARD with the picture of a king on it ⤷ picture at PLAYING CARD **IDM** **a king's ransom** *(literary)* a very large amount of money **SYN** FORTUNE **IDM** see UNCROWNED

king·dom /ˈkɪŋdəm/ *noun* **1** a country ruled by a king or queen: *the United Kingdom* ◆ *the kingdom of God* (= heaven) **2** an area controlled by a particular person or where a particular thing or idea is important **3** one of the three traditional divisions of the natural world: *the animal, vegetable, and mineral kingdoms* **4** *(biology)* one of the five major groups into which all living things are organized **IDM** **blow sb/sth to kingdom come** *(informal)* to completely destroy someone or something with an explosion **till/until kingdom come** *(old-fashioned)* forever

king·fish /ˈkɪŋfɪʃ/ *noun* a long FRESHWATER fish with two parts that function as lungs and make it able to breathe air

king·fish·er /ˈkɪŋˌfɪʃər/ *noun* a brightly-colored bird with a blue-gray body and a long beak, that catches fish in rivers

king·ly /ˈkɪŋli/ *adj.* *(literary)* like a king; connected with or good enough for a king **SYN** REGAL

king·mak·er /ˈkɪŋˌmeɪkər/ *noun* a person who has a very strong political influence and is able to bring someone else to power as a leader

king·pin /ˈkɪŋpɪn/ *noun* the most important person in an organization or activity

king·ship /ˈkɪŋʃɪp/ noun [U] the state of being a king; the official position of a king

ˈking-size (also **ˈking-sized**) adj. [usually before noun] very large; larger than normal when compared with a range of sizes: a king-size bed

kink /kɪŋk/ noun, verb
- noun **1** a bend or twist in something that is usually straight: a dog with a kink in its tail ◆ (figurative) We need to iron out the kinks in the new system. **2** (informal, disapproving) an unusual feature in a person's character or mind, especially one that does not seem normal **3** = CRICK
- verb [I, T] ~ (sth) to develop or make something develop a bend or twist

kink·y /ˈkɪŋki/ adj. **1** (informal, usually disapproving) used to describe sexual behavior that most people would consider strange or unusual **2** tightly curled or twisted: kinky hair

kin·ship /ˈkɪnʃɪp/ noun (formal) **1** [U] the fact of being related in a family: the ties of kinship **2** [U, sing.] a feeling of being close to someone because you have similar origins or attitudes **SYN** AFFINITY

kins·man /ˈkɪnzmən/, **kins·wom·an** /ˈkɪnzˌwʊmən/ nouns (pl. **kins·men** /-mən/, **kins·wom·en** /-ˌwɪmən/) (old-fashioned or literary) a relative

ki·osk /ˈkiɑsk/ noun a small store, open at the front, where newspapers, drinks, etc. are sold. **SYN** STAND

kip·pa (also **kip·pah**) /kiˈpɑ/ noun = YARMULKE

kip·per /ˈkɪpər/ noun a HERRING (= a type of fish) that has been preserved using salt, then smoked

kis·met /ˈkɪzmɛt; -mət/ noun [U] (literary) the idea that everything that happens to you in your life is already decided and that you cannot do anything to change or control it **SYN** DESTINY, FATE

kiss /kɪs/ verb, noun
- verb **1** [I, T] to touch someone with your lips as a sign of love, affection, sexual desire, etc., or when saying hello or goodbye: They stood in a doorway kissing (= kissing each other). ◆ Do people in the U.S. kiss when they meet? ◆ ~ **sb** Go and kiss your mother goodnight. ◆ She kissed him on both cheeks. ◆ He lifted the trophy up and kissed it. ⊃ see also AIR KISS **2** [T] ~ **sth** (literary) to gently move or touch something: The sunlight kissed the warm stones.
  IDM **kiss and make up** to become friends again after having an argument or disagreement: After a bitter political campaign, the two candidates kissed and made up. **kiss and tell** a way of referring to someone talking publicly, usually for money, about a past sexual relationship with someone famous **kiss sth better** (informal) to take away the pain of an injury by kissing it: Come here and let me kiss it better. **kiss sth goodbye** (informal) to accept that you will lose something or be unable to do something: Well, you can kiss your chances of promotion goodbye.
  PHRV **kiss sth↔aˈway** to stop someone feeling sad or angry by kissing them: He kissed away her tears. ˌkiss sb/sth↔ˈoff (informal) to reject someone or something in a way that shows very little care or thought: They say she kissed him off after having spent a great deal of his money. ˌkiss sth↔ˈoff (informal) to accept a loss or failure: I guess we can kiss off any hopes of winning the game now. ˌkiss ˈup to sb (informal, usually disapproving) to behave in a way that pleases someone because you want them to do something for you: I refuse to kiss up to the boss in order to get promoted.
- noun the act of kissing someone or something: Come here and give me a kiss! ◆ a kiss on the cheek ◆ We were greeted with hugs and kisses.
  IDM **the kiss of death** (informal, especially humorous) an event that seems good, but is certain to make something else fail ⊃ more at STEAL v.

kiss·er /ˈkɪsər/ noun **1 good, bad, etc.** ~ a person who is very good, bad, etc. at kissing **2** (informal) a person's mouth

ˌkissing ˈcousin noun (old-fashioned) **1** a distant relative who you know well enough to kiss when you meet them **2** (figurative) something that is a lot like something else

ˈkiss-off noun [usually sing.] (informal) an occasion when someone is suddenly told they are no longer wanted, especially by a lover or by a company: She gave her husband the kiss-off. ◆ He got the kiss-off from his job.

the ˈKISS ˌprinciple noun the idea that products and advertising should be as simple as possible **ORIGIN** Formed from the first letters of the expression "Keep it simple, stupid."

Ki·swa·hi·li /ˌkiswɑˈhili/ noun [U] = SWAHILI

kit /kɪt/ noun **1** [C] a set of parts ready to be made into something: a kit for a model plane **2** [C, U] a set of tools or equipment that you use for a particular purpose: a first-aid kit ◆ a drum kit ⊃ see also TOOLKIT ⊃ thesaurus box at EQUIPMENT **IDM** SEE CABOODLE

kitch·en /ˈkɪtʃən/ noun
a room in which meals are cooked or prepared: She's in the kitchen. ◆ We ate at the kitchen table. ⊃ see also SOUP KITCHEN ⊃ picture on page 830
IDM **everything but the kitchen sink** (informal, humorous) a very large number of things, probably more than is necessary ⊃ more at COOK, HEAT

kitch·en·ette /ˌkɪtʃəˈnet/ noun a small room or part of a room used as a kitchen, for example in an apartment

ˌkitchen-ˈsink adj. [only before noun] (of plays, movies, novels, etc.) dealing with ordinary life and ordinary people, especially when this involves describing the boring or difficult side of their lives: a kitchen-sink drama

kitch·en·ware /ˈkɪtʃənˌwɛr/ noun [U] used in stores to describe objects that you use in a kitchen, such as pans, bowls, etc.

kite /kaɪt/ noun, verb
- noun **1** a toy made of a light frame covered with paper, cloth, etc., that you fly in the air at the end of one or more long strings: to fly a kite ⊃ picture at TOY **2** a BIRD OF PREY (= a bird that eats other creatures) of the HAWK family **3** (mathematics) a shape that has four sides of two different lengths. The sides of the same length are next to each other and opposite sides are of different lengths, so that none of the sides are PARALLEL. **IDM** see FLY v., HIGH adj.
- verb ~ **sth** (informal) to use an illegal check to obtain money or to dishonestly change the amount written on a check: to kite checks ◆ check kiting

kite·surf·ing /ˈkaɪtˌsərfɪŋ/ (also **kite·board·ing** /ˈkaɪtˌbɔrdɪŋ/) noun [U] the sport of riding on water while standing on a short wide board and being pulled along by wind power, using a large kite

kith /kɪθ/ noun
IDM **kith and kin** (old-fashioned) friends and relatives

kitsch /kɪtʃ/ noun [U] (disapproving) works of art or objects that are popular but that are considered to have no real artistic value and to be lacking in good taste, for example because they are SENTIMENTAL ▶ **kitsch** (also **kitsch·y**) adj.

kit·ten /ˈkɪtn/ noun a young cat

ˈkitten ˌheels noun [pl.] small, thin, curved heels on women's shoes ⊃ picture at SHOE

kit·ten·ish /ˈkɪtnæwˌɪʃ/ adj. (old-fashioned) (of a woman) lively, and trying to attract men's attention

kit·ti·wake /ˈkɪtiˌweɪk/ noun a bird that lives in groups on ocean CLIFFS

kit·ty /ˈkɪti/ noun (pl. **kit·ties**) **1** (informal) if money is put in a kitty, a group of people all give an amount and the money is spent on something they all agree on: We each put $20 in the kitty to cover the bills. **2** (in card games, etc.) the sum of money that all the players bet, which is given to the winner **3** (informal) a way of referring to a cat

ˈkitty-ˌcorner(ed) (also ˈcatty-ˌcorner(ed)) adj., adv. (informal) opposite and at a DIAGONAL angle from something or someone: a restaurant kitty-corner from the theater ◆ Bikers cut kitty-cornered across his yard.

Kitchen Utensils

cutting

bread knife | serrated blade

carving knife | point | edge

cleaver | handle

chopping block (*also* cutting board)

peeler

paring knife

kitchen scissors

opening

corkscrew

can opener

bottle opener

crushing, grating, squeezing

potato masher | grater | zester | nutcracker | garlic press | pepper mill | juicer | pestle and mortar

measuring

measuring spoons

dry measuring cups

liquid measuring cup

timer

appliances

electric whisk

blender

food processor

hand blender

pestle | mortar

other utensils

colander

sieve (*also* sifter)

ramekin

tongs

ice-cream scoop

cake server

ladle | wooden spoon | whisk | pastry brush | spatulas

rolling pin

ki·wi /'kiwi/ *noun* **1** = KIWI FRUIT ⊃ picture at FRUIT **2** Kiwi (*informal*) a person from New Zealand **3** a New Zealand bird with a long beak, short wings, and no tail, that cannot fly

'kiwi ,fruit *noun* (*pl.* kiwi fruit) (also kiwi) a small fruit with thin brown skin covered with small hairs, soft green flesh, and black seeds

kJ *abbr.* KILOJOULE(S)

KKK /,keɪ keɪ 'keɪ/ *abbr.* Ku Klux Klan

klatch, klatsch ⊃ COFFEE KLATCH

Klax·on™ /'klæksn/ *noun* a horn, originally on a vehicle, that makes a loud sound as a warning

Kleen·ex™ /'kliːnɛks/ *noun* [U, C] (*pl.* Kleen·ex) a paper HANDKERCHIEF; a TISSUE: *a box of Kleenex* ◆ *Here, have a Kleenex to dry your eyes.*

klep·to·ma·ni·a /,klɛptə'meɪniə/ *noun* [U] a mental illness in which someone has a strong desire, that they cannot control, to steal things ▶ **klep·to·ma·ni·ac** /-'meɪni,æk/ *noun*: *She's a kleptomaniac.*

klez·mer /'klɛzmər/ (also 'klezmer ,music) *noun* [U] traditional Eastern European Jewish music: *a klezmer band*

klick (also **click**) /klɪk/ *noun* (*informal*) a kilometer: *We're twenty klicks south of your position.*

kludge /kludʒ/ *noun* (*computing*) a solution to a computer problem that has been quickly and badly put together ▶ **kludge** *verb* [I, T] ~ (sth)

klutz /klʌts/ *noun* (*informal*) a person who often drops things, is not good at sports, etc. ▶ **klutz·y** *adj.*

km *abbr.* (*pl.* km or kms) (in writing) kilometer(s)

knack /næk/ *noun* [sing.] **1** a special skill or ability that you have naturally or can learn: *It's easy, once you've got the knack.* ◆ ~ of/for (doing) sth *He's got a real knack for making money.* **2** ~ of doing sth a habit of doing something: *She has the unfortunate knack of always saying the wrong thing.*

knap·sack /'næpsæk/ *noun* a small BACKPACK

knave /neɪv/ *noun* **1** (*old-fashioned*) = JACK: *the knave of clubs* **2** (*old use*) a dishonest man or boy

knead /nid/ *verb* **1** ~ sth to press and stretch DOUGH, wet CLAY, etc. with your hands to make it ready to use ⊃ picture at COOKING **2** ~ sth to rub and squeeze muscles, etc. especially to relax them or to make them less painful

knee /ni/ *noun, verb*

• *noun* **1** the joint between the top and bottom parts of the leg where it bends in the middle: *a knee injury* ◆ *I grazed my knee when I fell.* ◆ *He went down on one knee and asked her to marry him.* ◆ *She was on her knees scrubbing the kitchen floor.* ⊃ picture at BODY **2** the part of a piece of clothing that covers the knee: *These jeans are torn at the knee.* ◆ *a knee patch* **3** the top surface of the upper part of the legs when you are sitting down SYN LAP: *Come and sit on Daddy's knee.* IDM **bring sb to their knees** to defeat someone, especially in a war **bring sth to its knees** to badly affect an organization, etc. so that it can no longer function: *The strikes brought the industry to its knees.* **put sb over your knee** to punish someone by making them lie on top of your knee and hitting their BUTTOCKS ⊃ more at BEE, BEND, MOTHER, WEAK

• *verb* (kneed, kneed) ~ sb/sth to hit or push someone or something with your knee: *He kneed his attacker in the stomach.*

knee·cap /'niːkæp/ *noun, verb*

• *noun* the small bone that covers the front of the knee ⊃ picture at BODY SYN PATELLA

• *verb* (-pp-) ~ sb to shoot or break someone's kneecaps as a form of punishment that is not official and is illegal ▶ **knee·cap·ping** *noun* [C, U]

,knee-'deep *adj.* up to your knees: *The snow was knee-deep*

in places. ◆ (*figurative*) *I was knee-deep in work.* ▶ ,knee-'deep *adv.*: *I waded in knee-deep.*

,knee-'high *adj.* high enough to reach your knees IDM **knee-high to a grasshopper** (*informal, humorous*) very small; very young

'knee-jerk *adj.* [only before noun] (*disapproving*) produced automatically, without any serious thought: *It was a knee-jerk reaction on her part.*

kneel /nil/ *verb* (knelt /nɛlt/ or kneeled) [I] to be in or move into a position where your body is supported on your knee or knees: *a kneeling figure* ◆ ~ (down) *We knelt (down) on the ground to examine the tracks.*

'knee-length *adj.* long enough to reach your knees: *knee-length shorts/socks*

knell /nɛl/ *noun* [sing.] = DEATH KNELL

knelt *pt, pp of* KNEEL

knew *pt of* KNOW

knick·ers /'nɪkərz/ *noun* [pl.] short, loose pants that fit tightly just below the knee, worn especially in the past

knick-knack /'nɪk næk/ *noun* [usually pl.] (sometimes *disapproving*) a small decorative object in a house SYN ORNAMENT

knife /naɪf/ *noun, verb*

• *noun* (*pl.* knives /naɪvz/) a sharp blade with a handle, used for cutting or as a weapon: *knives and forks* ◆ *a sharp knife* ◆ *a bread knife* (= one for cutting bread) ⊃ see also JACKKNIFE, PALETTE KNIFE, PENKNIFE IDM **the knives are out (for sb)** the situation has become so bad that people are preparing to make one person take the blame, for example by taking away their job **like a knife through butter** (*informal*) easily; without meeting any difficulty **put/stick the knife in | put/stick the knife into sb** (*informal*) to be very unfriendly to someone and try to harm them **turn/twist the knife (in the wound)** to say or do something unkind deliberately; to make someone who is unhappy feel even more unhappy **under the knife** (*informal*) having a medical operation

• *verb* ~ sb to injure or kill someone with a knife SYN STAB

'knife edge *noun* [usually sing.] the sharp edge of a knife IDM **on a knife edge 1** (of a situation, etc.) finely balanced between success and failure: *The economy is balanced on a knife edge.* **2** (of a person) very worried or anxious about the result of something

knife·point /'naɪfpɔɪnt/ *noun* IDM **at knifepoint** while being threatened, or threatening someone, with a knife: *He was mugged at knifepoint.*

knight /naɪt/ *noun, verb*

• *noun* **1** (in the Middle Ages) a man of high social rank who had a duty to fight for his king. Knights are often shown in pictures riding horses and wearing ARMOR. ⊃ see also BLACK KNIGHT, WHITE KNIGHT **2** (in Britain) a man who has been given a special honor by the king or queen and has the title *Sir* before his name ⊃ compare BARONET **3** a piece used in the game of CHESS that is shaped like a horse's head ⊃ picture at TOY IDM **a knight in shining armor** (usually *humorous*) a man who saves someone, especially a woman, from a dangerous situation

• *verb* [usually passive] ~ sb to give someone the rank and title of a knight: *He was knighted by Queen Elizabeth II for his services to industry.*

,knight 'errant *noun* (*pl.* ,knights 'errant) (in the Middle Ages) a KNIGHT who traveled around, looking for adventure

knight·hood /'naɪthʊd/ *noun* the rank or title of a KNIGHT

knight·ly /'naɪtli/ *adj.* [usually before noun] (*literary*) consisting of knights; typical of a knight SYN CHIVALROUS

knit /nɪt/ *verb, noun*

• *verb* (knit·ted, knit·ted) HELP In senses 3 and 4 knit is usually used for the past tense and past participle.

1 [T, I] to make clothes, etc. from wool or cotton thread using two long, thin, knitting needles or a machine: ~ **(sth)** *I knitted this sweater myself.* ◆ *Lucy was sitting on the sofa, knitting.* ◆ **~ sb sth** *She's knitting the baby a blanket.* **2** [T, I] **~ (sth)** to use a basic STITCH in knitting: *Knit one row, purl one row.* **3** [T, I] **~ (sb/sth) (together)** to join people or things closely together or to be joined closely together: *a closely/tightly knit community* (= one in which relationships are very close) ◆ *Society is knit together by certain commonly held beliefs.* **4** [I, T] **~ (sth)** (of broken bones) to grow together again to form one piece; to make broken bones grow together again **SYN** MEND: *The bone failed to knit correctly.*

IDM **knit your brow(s)** to move your EYEBROWS together, to show that you are thinking hard, feeling angry, etc. **SYN** FROWN

● **noun** [usually pl.] a piece of clothing that has been knitted: *winter knits* ⊃ picture at HAT

knit·ted /ˈnɪtəd/ (also **knit**) *adj.* made by knitting wool or thread: *knitted gloves* ◆ *a white knit dress* ◆ *a hand-knitted sweater* ◆ *a cotton-knit shirt*

knit·ter /ˈnɪtər/ *noun* a person who knits

knit·ting /ˈnɪtɪŋ/ *noun* [U] **1** an item that is being knitted: *Where's my knitting?* **2** the activity of knitting ⊃ picture at HOBBY

ˈ**knitting** ˌ**needle** *noun* a long thin stick with a round end that you use for knitting by hand ⊃ picture at HOBBY

knit·wear /ˈnɪtwɛr/ *noun* [U] items of clothing that have been knitted

knives pl. of KNIFE

knob /nɑb/ *noun* **1** a round switch on a machine such as a television that you use to turn it on and off, etc.: *the volume control knob* **2** a round handle on a door or a drawer ⊃ picture at HANDLE **3** a round lump on the surface or end of something

knob·by /ˈnɑbi/ (also **knob·bly** /ˈnɑbli/) *adj.* having small hard lumps: *knobby knees*

knock 🔑 /nɑk/ *verb, noun*
● **verb**
> **AT DOOR/WINDOW 1** [I] to hit a door, etc. firmly in order to attract attention **SYN** RAP: *He knocked three times and waited.* ◆ **~ at/on sth** *Somebody was knocking on the window.*
> **HIT 2** [T, I] to hit something, often by accident, with a short, hard blow: **~ sth (against/on sth)** *Be careful you don't knock your head on this low beam.* ◆ **~ against/on sth** *Her hand knocked against the glass.* **3** [T] to put someone or something into a particular state by hitting them/it: **~ sb/sth + adj.** *The blow knocked me flat.* ◆ *He was knocked unconscious by the blow.* ◆ **~ sb/sth doing sth** *She knocked my drink flying.* ⊃ thesaurus box at HIT **4** [T] to hit something so that it moves or breaks: **~ sth + adv./prep.** *He'd knocked over a glass of water.* ◆ *I knocked the nail into the wall.* ◆ *They had to knock the door down to get in.* ◆ **~ sth** *(figurative)* *The criticism had knocked* (= damaged) *her self-esteem.* ⊃ note at HIT **5** [T] **~ sth + adv./prep.** to make a hole in something by hitting it hard: *They managed to knock a hole in the wall.*
> **OF HEART/KNEES 6** [I] if your heart knocks, it beats hard; if your knees **knock**, they shake, for example from fear: *My heart was knocking wildly.*
> **OF ENGINE/PIPES 7** [I] to make a regular sound of metal hitting metal, especially because there is something wrong
> **CRITICIZE 8** [T] **~ sb/sth** *(informal)* to criticize someone or something, especially when it is being treated unfairly: *The newspapers are always knocking the Raiders.* ◆ *"Plastics?" " Don't knock it —there's a great future in plastics."*

IDM **I'll knock your block/head off!** *(informal)* used to threaten someone that you will hit them **knock sb dead** *(informal)* to impress someone very much: *You look fabulous —you'll knock 'em dead tonight.* **knock it off!** *(informal)* used to tell someone to stop making a noise, annoying you, etc. **knock sb off their pedestal/perch** to make someone lose their position as someone or something successful or admired **knock on wood** *(saying)* used when you have just

mentioned some way in which you have been lucky in the past, to avoid bringing bad luck **knock the stuffing out of sb** *(informal)* to make someone lose their confidence and enthusiasm **you could have knocked me down with a feather** *(informal)* used to express surprise ⊃ more at DAYLIGHTS, HEAD, HELL, SENSE, SHAPE, SOCK

PHR V ˌ**knock a'round...** *(informal)* **1** to travel and live in various places: *He spent a few years knocking around Europe.* **2** used to say that something is in a place but you do not know exactly where: *It must be knocking around here somewhere.* ˌ**knock a'round with sb/together** *(informal)* to spend a lot of time with sb/together ˌ**knock sb/sth a'round** *(informal)* to hit someone or something repeatedly; to treat someone or something roughly
ˌ**knock sth↔'back** *(informal)* to drink something quickly, especially an alcoholic drink
ˌ**knock sb 'down (from sth) (to sth)** *(informal)* to persuade someone to reduce the price of something: *I managed to knock him down to $400.* ˌ**knock sb↔'down/'over** to hit someone and make them fall to the ground: *She was knocked down by a bus.* ◆ *He knocked his opponent down three times in the first round.* ˌ**knock sth↔'down** to destroy a building by breaking its walls **SYN** DEMOLISH: *These old houses are going to be knocked down.* ˌ**knock sth↔'down (from sth) (to sth)** *(informal)* to reduce the price of something: *He knocked down the price from $80 to $50.* ⊃ see also KNOCK-DOWN
ˌ**knock 'off | ˌknock 'off sth** *(informal)* to stop doing something, especially work: *Do you want to knock off early today?* ◆ *What time do you knock off work?* ˌ**knock sb↔'off** *(slang)* to murder someone ˌ**knock sth↔'off** *(informal)* to complete something quickly and without much effort: *He knocks off three novels a year.* ˌ**knock sth↔'off | ˌknock sth↔'off sth** to reduce the price or value of something: *They knocked off $60 because of a scratch.* ◆ *The news knocked 13% off the company's shares.*
ˌ**knock sb↔'out 1** to make someone fall asleep or become unconscious: *The blow knocked her out.* **2** (in boxing) to hit an opponent so that they cannot get up within a limited time and therefore lose the fight ⊃ related noun KNOCKOUT **3** *(informal)* to surprise and impress someone very much: *The movie just knocked me out.* ⊃ related noun KNOCKOUT ˌ**knock sb/yourself 'out** to make someone/yourself very tired **SYN** WEAR OUT ˌ**knock sb↔'out (of sth)** to defeat someone so that they cannot continue competing **SYN** ELIMINATE: *The White Sox had been knocked out of the World Series.* ⊃ see also KNOCKOUT ˌ**knock sth↔'out** *(informal)* to produce something, especially quickly and easily: *He knocks out five books a year.*
ˌ**knock sb/sth↔'over 1** = KNOCK SB DOWN **2** *(informal)* to rob a place: *The two men knocked over a jewelry store last night.* ˌ**knock sth↔to'gether** *(informal)* to make or complete something quickly and often not very well: *I knocked some bookshelves together from old planks.*
ˌ**knock 'up** (in TENNIS, etc.) to practice for a short time before the start of a game ˌ**knock sb↔'up** *(informal)* to make a woman pregnant

● **noun**
> **AT DOOR/WINDOW 1** the sound of someone hitting a door, window, etc. with their hand or with something hard to attract attention: *There was a **knock** on/at the door.*
> **HIT 2** a sharp blow from something hard **SYN** BANG: *He had a nasty knock on the head.*

IDM **take a (hard, nasty, etc.) knock** to have an experience that makes someone or something less confident or successful; to be damaged

ˈ**knock-down** *adj., noun*
● **adj.** [only before noun] *(informal)* **1** (of prices, etc.) much lower than usual **SYN** ROCK-BOTTOM **2** using a lot of force: *a knock-down punch*
● **noun** (in boxing) an act of falling to the ground after being hit

ˌ**knock-down-'drag-out** *adj.* [only before noun] *(informal)* (of a fight or an argument) very aggressive and unpleasant

| t tea | ţ butter | d did | k cat | g got | tʃ chin | dʒ June | f fall |

knock·er /'nɑkər/ (also 'door ˌknocker) noun a metal object attached to the outside of the door of a house, etc. which you hit against the door to attract attention

'**knock-kneed** adj. having legs that turn toward each other at the knees

'**knock knees** noun [pl.] legs that turn toward each other at the knees

knock·off /'nɑkɔf; -ɑf/ noun (informal) a cheap copy of something expensive: She was selling knockoffs of designer jeans on the street.

knock·out /'nɑkaʊt/ noun, adj.
• noun **1** (abbr. KO) (in boxing) a blow that makes an opponent fall to the ground and be unable to get up, so that he or she loses the fight **2** (informal) a person or thing that is very attractive or impressive
• adj. [only before noun] **1** a **knockout** competition is one in which the winning player/team at each stage competes in the next stage and the losing one no longer takes part in the competition: the knockout stages of the tournament **2** a **knockout** blow is one that hits someone so hard that they can no longer get up

knoll /noʊl/ noun a small round hill SYN MOUND

knots

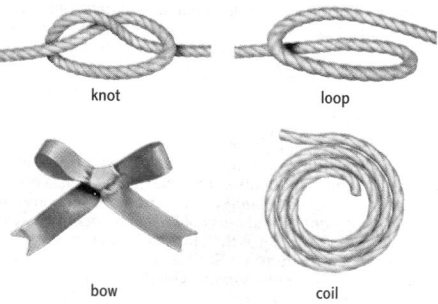

knot   loop

bow   coil

knot /nɑt/ noun, verb
• noun
▷ IN STRING/ROPE **1** a join made by tying together two pieces or ends of string, rope, etc.: to tie a knot ◆ Tie the two ropes together with a knot. ◆ (figurative) hair full of knots and tangles (= twisted in a way that is difficult to COMB)
▷ OF HAIR **2** a way of twisting hair into a small round shape at the back of the head: She had her hair in a knot.
▷ IN WOOD **3** a hard round spot in a piece of wood where there was once a branch
▷ GROUP OF PEOPLE **4** a small group of people standing close together
▷ OF MUSCLES **5** a tight, hard feeling in the stomach, throat, etc. caused by nerves, anger, etc.: My stomach was in knots. ◆ I could feel a knot of fear in my throat.
▷ SPEED OF BOAT/PLANE **6** a unit for measuring the speed of boats and aircraft; one NAUTICAL MILE per hour IDM see TIE v.
• verb (-tt-)
▷ TIE WITH KNOT **1** [T] ~ sth to fasten something with a knot or knots: He carefully knotted his tie.
▷ TWIST **2** [I] to become twisted into a knot SYN TANGLE **3** [T] ~ sth to twist hair into a particular shape: She wore her hair loosely knotted on top of her head.
▷ MUSCLES **4** [I, T] ~ (sth) if muscles, etc. knot or something knots them, they become hard and painful because of fear, excitement, etc.: She felt her stomach knot with fear.

knot·ty /'nɑti/ adj. (knot·ti·er, knot·ti·est) **1** complicated and difficult to solve SYN THORNY: a knotty problem **2** having parts that are hard and twisted together: the knotty roots of the old oak tree

know /noʊ/ verb, noun
• verb (knew /nu/, known /noʊn/) (not used in the progressive tenses)
▷ HAVE INFORMATION **1** [T, I] to have information in your mind as a result of experience or because you have learned or been told it: ~ sth Do you know his address? ◆ The cause of the fire is not yet known. ◆ All I know is that she used to work in a bank (= I have no other information about her). ◆ ~ (that)... I know (that) people's handwriting changes as they get older. ◆ it is known that... It is widely known that CFCs can damage the ozone layer. ◆ ~ where, what, etc.... I knew where he was hiding. ◆ I didn't know what he was talking about. ◆ ~ (of/about sth) "You've got a flat tire." "I know." ◆ "What's the answer?" "I don't know." ◆ "There's no one home." "How do you know?" ◆ You know about Amanda's baby, don't you? ◆ I don't know about you, but I'm ready for something to eat. ◆ I know of at least two people who did the same thing. ◆ "Is anyone else coming?" " Not that I know of. " ◆ "Isn't that his car?" "I wouldn't know./How should I know? " (= I don't know and I am not the person you should ask). ◆ (informal) "What are you two whispering about?" "You don't want to know" (= because you would be shocked or wouldn't approve). ◆ ~ to do sth Does he know to come here (= that he should come here) first? ◆ ~ sb/sth to be/do sth We know her to be honest. ◆ Two women are known to have died. ⊃ see also NEED-TO-KNOW
▷ REALIZE **2** [T, I] to realize, understand, or be aware of something: ~ (that)... As soon as I walked in the room I knew (that) something was wrong. ◆ She knew she was dying. ◆ ~ what, how, etc.... I knew perfectly well what she meant. ◆ I know exactly how you feel. ◆ ~ (sth) This case is hopeless and he knows it (= although he will not admit it). ◆ "Martin was lying the whole time." " I should have known."
▷ FEEL CERTAIN **3** [T, I] to feel certain about something: ~ (that)... He knew (that) he could trust her. ◆ I know it's here somewhere! ◆ I don't know that I can finish it by next week. ◆ ~ (sth) "You were right—someone's been spreading rumors about you." "I knew it!" ◆ "She's the worst player in the team." "Oh, I don't know (= I am not sure that I agree) —she played well yesterday."
▷ BE FAMILIAR **4** [T] ~ sb/sth to be familiar with a person, place, thing, etc.: I've known David for 20 years. ◆ Do you two know each other (= have you met before)? ◆ She's very nice when you get to know her. ◆ Knowing Ben, we could be waiting a long time (= it is typical of him to be late). ◆ This man is known to the police (= as a criminal). ◆ I know Savannah well. ◆ Do you know the play (= have you seen or read it before)? ◆ The new rules could mean the end of football as we know it (= in the form that we are familiar with).
▷ REPUTATION **5** [T, usually passive] to think that someone or something is a particular type of person or thing or has particular characteristics: ~ sb/sth as sth It's known as the most dangerous part of the city. ◆ ~ sb/sth for sth She is best known for her work on the human brain. ◆ ~ sb/sth to be/do sth He's known to be an outstanding physicist.
▷ GIVE NAME **6** [T] ~ sb/sth as sth [usually passive] to give someone or something a particular name or title: Ascorbic acid is more commonly known as Vitamin C. ◆ Peter Wilson, also known as "the Tiger."
▷ RECOGNIZE **7** [T] ~ sb/sth to be able to recognize someone or something: I couldn't see who was speaking, but I knew the voice. ◆ She knows a bargain when she sees one. ⊃ thesaurus box at IDENTIFY
▷ DISTINGUISH **8** [T] ~ sb/sth from sb/sth to be able to distinguish one person or thing from another SYN DIFFERENTIATE: I hope we have taught our children to know right from wrong.
▷ SKILL/LANGUAGE **9** [T] to have learned a skill or language and be able to use it: ~ sth Do you know any Japanese? ◆ ~ how, what, etc.... Do you know how to use spreadsheets?
▷ EXPERIENCE **10** [T] (only used in the perfect tenses) to have seen, heard, or experienced something: ~ sb/sth (to) do sth I've never known it (to) snow in July before. ◆ be known to do sth He has been known to spend all morning in the bathroom. **11** [T] ~ sth to have personal experience of something: He has known both poverty and wealth. ◆ She may be successful now, but she has known what it is like to be poor.

IDM **before you know where you are** very quickly or suddenly: *We were whisked off in a taxi before we knew where we were.* **for all you, I, they, etc. know** (*informal*) used to emphasize that you do not know something and that it is not important to you: *She could be dead for all I know.* **God/goodness/Heaven knows** (*informal*) **1** used to emphasize that you do not know something: *God knows what else they might find.* ◆ *"Where are they?" "Goodness knows."*

HELP Some people may find the use of **God knows** offensive. **2** used to emphasize the truth of what you are saying: *She ought to pass the exam—goodness knows she's been working hard enough.* **I don't know how, why, etc....** (*informal*) used to criticize someone's behavior: *I don't know how you can say things like that.* **I know** (*informal*) **1** used to agree with someone or to show sympathy: *"What a ridiculous situation!" "I know."* **2** used to introduce a new idea or suggestion: *I know, let's see what's playing at the theater.* **know sth as well as I do** used to criticize someone by saying that they should realize or understand something: *You know as well as I do that you're being unreasonable.* **know sb/sth backward and forward** (*informal*) to know someone or something extremely well: *She must know the play backward and forward by now.* **know best** to know what should be done, etc. better than other people: *The doctor told you to stay in bed, and she knows best.* **know better (than that/than to do sth)** to be sensible enough not to do something: *He knows better than to judge by appearances.* **know sb by sight** to recognize someone without knowing them well **know different/differently/otherwise** (*informal*) to have information or evidence that the opposite is true: *He says he doesn't care about what the critics write, but I know different.* **know full well** to be very aware of a fact and unable to deny or ignore it: *He knew full well what she thought of it.* **know sb/sth inside out | know sb/sth like the back of your hand** (*informal*) to be very familiar with something: *This is where I grew up. I know this area like the back of my hand.* **know your own mind** to have very firm ideas about what you want to do **know your stuff** (*informal*) to know a lot about a particular subject or job **know your way around** to be familiar with a place, subject, etc. **know what you're talking about** (*informal*) to have knowledge about something from your own experience **know which side your bread is buttered (on)** (*informal*) to know where you can get an advantage for yourself **let it be known/make it known that...** (*formal*) to make sure that people are informed about something, especially by getting someone else to tell them: *The President has let it be known that he does not intend to run for re-election.* **let sb know** to tell someone about something: *Let me know how I can help.* **make yourself known to sb** to introduce yourself to someone: *I made myself known to the hotel manager.* **not know any better** to behave badly, usually because you have not been taught the correct way to behave **not know beans about sth** (*informal*) to know nothing about a subject **not know the first thing about sb/sth** to know nothing at all about someone or something **not know sb from Adam** (*informal*) to not know at all who someone is **not know what hit you** (*informal*) to be so surprised by something that you do not know how to react **not know where to look** (*informal*) to feel great embarrassment and not know how to react **not know whether you're coming or going** (*informal*) to be so excited or confused that you cannot behave or think in a sensible way **there's no knowing** used to say that it is impossible to say what might happen: *There's no knowing how he'll react.* **what does... know?** used to say that someone knows nothing about the subject you are talking about: *What does he know about football, anyway?* **what do you know?** (*informal*) used to express surprise: *Well, what do you know?* **Look who's here!** **you know** (*informal*) **1** used when you are thinking of what to say next: *Well, you know, it's difficult to explain.* **2** used to show that what you are referring to is known or understood by the person you are speaking to: *Guess who I've just seen? Maggie! You know— Jim's wife.* ◆ *You know that restaurant around the corner? It's closing down.* **3** used to emphasize something that you are saying: *I'm not stupid, you know.* **you know something/**

what? (*informal*) used to introduce an interesting or surprising opinion, piece of news, etc.: *You know something? I've never really enjoyed Christmas.* **you know who/what** (*informal*) used to refer to someone or something without mentioning a name **you never know** (*informal*) used to say that you can never be certain about what will happen in the future, especially when you are suggesting that something good might happen ➔ more at ANSWER, COST, DAY, DEVIL, FAR, LORD, OLD, PAT, ROPE, THING, TRUTH

● *noun*
IDM **in the know** (*informal*) having more information about something than most people: *Somebody in the know told me he's going to resign.*

Know·bot™ /ˈnoʊbɑt/ *noun* (*computing*) a program that is designed to search for data in a large number of DATABASES when a user of a network has asked for information

'know-how *noun* [U] (*informal*) knowledge of how to do something and experience in doing it: *We need skilled workers and technical know-how.*

know·ing /ˈnoʊɪŋ/ *adj.* [usually before noun] showing that you know or understand about something that is supposed to be secret: *a knowing smile* ➔ compare UNKNOWING

know·ing·ly /ˈnoʊɪŋli/ *adv.* **1** while knowing the truth or likely result of what you are doing **SYN** DELIBERATELY: *She was accused of knowingly making a false statement to the police.* **2** in a way that shows that you know or understand about something that is supposed to be secret: *He glanced at her knowingly.*

'know-it-ˌall *noun* (*informal*, *disapproving*) a person who behaves as if they know everything

knowl·edge 🔑 /ˈnɑlɪdʒ/ *noun*
1 [U, sing.] the information, understanding, and skills that you gain through education or experience: *practical/medical/scientific knowledge* ◆ *~ of/about sth He has a wide knowledge of painting and music.* ◆ *There is a lack of knowledge about the tax system.* **2** [U] the state of knowing about a particular fact or situation: *She sent the letter without my knowledge.* ◆ *The film was made with the Governor's full knowledge and approval.* ◆ *She was impatient in the knowledge that time was limited.* ◆ *I went to sleep secure in the knowledge that I was not alone in the house.* ◆ *They could relax safe in the knowledge that they had the funding for the project.* ◆ *He denied all knowledge of the affair.* **3** ~ economy/industry/worker working with information rather than producing goods **IDM** **be common/public knowledge** to be something that everyone knows, especially in a particular community or group **come to sb's knowledge** (*formal*) to become known by someone: *It has come to our knowledge that you have been taking time off without permission.* **to your knowledge** from the information you have, although you may not know everything: *"Are they divorced?" "Not to my knowledge."*

knowl·edge·a·ble /ˈnɑlɪdʒəbl/ *adj.* ~ (about sth) knowing a lot **SYN** WELL-INFORMED: *She is very knowledgeable about plants.* ► **know·ledge·a·bly** /-bli/ *adv.*

known /noʊn/ *adj.* [only before noun] known about, especially by a lot of people: *He's a known thief.* ◆ *The disease has no known cure.* ➔ see also KNOW

knuck·le /ˈnʌkl/ *noun, verb*
● *noun* **1** [C] any of the joints in the fingers, especially those connecting the fingers to the rest of the hand ➔ picture at BODY **2** (also hock) [U, C] a piece of meat from the lower part of an animal's leg, especially a pig **IDM** see RAP *n.*, *v.*
● *verb*
PHRV **knuckle 'down (to sth)** (*informal*) to begin to work hard at something **SYN** GET DOWN TO: *I'm going to have to knuckle down to some serious study.* **knuckle 'under (to sb/sth)** (*informal*) to accept someone else's authority

knuckle-dragger /ˈnʌkl ˌdrægər/ *noun* (*informal*) a stupid man who thinks and behaves in simple, basic ways

knuck·le·dust·er /ˈnʌklˌdʌstər/ *noun* = BRASS KNUCKLES

knuck·le·head /ˈnʌklˌhɛd/ *noun* (*informal*) a person who behaves in a stupid way

ˌknuckle ˈsandwich *noun* (*slang*) a punch in the mouth

KO (also **kay·o**) /ˌkeɪ ˈoʊ/ *abbr.* KNOCKOUT

ko·a·la /kouˈɑlə/ (also koˈala ˌbear) *noun* an Australian animal with thick gray fur, large ears, and no tail. Koalas live in trees and eat leaves. ➲ picture at ANIMAL

kohl /koʊl/ *noun* [U] a black powder that is used especially in Eastern countries. It is put around the eyes to make them more attractive.

kohl·ra·bi /ˌkoʊlˈrɑbi/ *noun* [U] a vegetable of the CABBAGE family whose thick, round, white STEM is eaten

koi /kɔɪ/ *noun* (*pl.* **koi**) a large fish originally from Japan, often kept in fish PONDS

ˈkola ˌnut *noun* = COLA NUT

Ko·mo·do drag·on /kəˌmoudou ˈdrægən/ *noun* a very large LIZARD from Indonesia

kook /kuk/ *noun* (*informal*) a person who acts in a strange or crazy way ▶ **kook·y** *adj.*

kook·a·bur·ra /ˈkʊkəˌbərə/ *noun* an Australian bird that makes a strange laughing cry

Ko·ran (also **Qur'an**) /kəˈrɑn; -ˈræn/ *noun* **the Koran** [sing.] the holy book of the Islamic religion, written in Arabic, containing the word of Allah as REVEALED to the Prophet Muhammad ▶ **Ko·ran·ic** /kəˈrænɪk; -ˈrɑ-/ *adj.*

ko·sher /ˈkoʊʃər/ *adj.* **1** (of food) prepared according to the rules of Jewish law: *They attend synagogue and keep kosher* (= obey the Jewish food laws). **2** (*informal*) honest or legal: *Their business deals are not always completely kosher.*

kow·tow /ˈkaʊtaʊ/ *verb* [I] **~ (to sb/sth)** (*informal, disapproving*) to show someone in authority too much respect and be too willing to obey them

KP /ˌkeɪ ˈpi/ *noun* [U] work in the kitchen done by soldiers or children at camp: *The sergeant assigned him to KP.* **ORIGIN** From "kitchen police," a name for the soldiers.

kph /ˌkeɪ pi ˈeɪtʃ/ *abbr.* kilometers per hour

the Krem·lin /ˈkrɛmlən/ *noun* [sing.] **1** the buildings in Moscow where the offices of the Russian government are located **2** a way of referring to the government of Russia or the former Soviet Union: *relations between the White House and the Kremlin*

krill /krɪl/ *noun* [pl.] very small SHELLFISH that live in the ocean around the Antarctic and are eaten by WHALES

Kris Krin·gle /ˌkrɪs ˈkrɪŋgl/ *noun* = SANTA CLAUS **ORIGIN** From *Christkindl*, the German for "Christ child."

kro·na /ˈkroʊnə/ *noun* (*pl.* **kro·nor** /-ˈnɔr; -nər/) the unit of money in Sweden and Iceland

kro·ne /ˈkroʊnə/ *noun* (*pl.* **kro·ner** /-nər/) the unit of money in Denmark and Norway

kryp·ton /ˈkrɪptɑn/ *noun* [U] (*symb.* **Kr**) a chemical element. Krypton is a gas that does not react with anything, used in FLUORESCENT lights and LASERS.

kryp·ton·ite /ˈkrɪptəˌnaɪt/ *noun* [U] a chemical element that exists only in stories, especially in stories about Superman, a character with special powers which he loses when he is near to kryptonite

KS *abbr.* (in writing) Kansas

ku·dos /ˈkudous; -douz; -dɑs/ *noun* [U] the admiration and respect that goes with a particular achievement or position **SYN** PRESTIGE: *the kudos of playing for such a famous team*

kud·zu /ˈkʊdzu; ˈkʌd-/ *noun* [U] a climbing plant with purple flowers that grows very fast and is used as a food and in medicines. It is common in the southern states.

Ku Klux Klan /ˌku klʌks ˈklæn/ *noun* [sing.] (*abbr.* KKK) a secret organization of white men in the southern states who use violence to oppose social change and equal rights for black people

kum·quat /ˈkʌmkwɑt/ *noun* a fruit like a very small orange with sweet skin that is eaten, and sour flesh

kung fu /ˌkʌŋ ˈfu/ *noun* [U] (from *Chinese*) a Chinese system of fighting without weapons, similar to KARATE

kvetch /kvɛtʃ; kfɛtʃ/ *verb* [I] (*informal*) to complain about something all the time **SYN** WHINE

kW *abbr.* (in writing) KILOWATT(S): *a 2kW electric heater*

Kwan·zaa /ˈkwɑnzə/ *noun* [U] a cultural festival that is celebrated by some African Americans from December 26 to January 1 **ORIGIN** From a phrase in Swahili that means "first fruits."

kwash·i·or·kor /ˌkwɑʃiˈɔrkər/ *noun* [U] a dangerous form of MALNUTRITION that is caused by not eating enough PROTEIN

kWh *abbr.* (*pl.* **kWh**) (in writing) KILOWATT-HOUR(S)

KY *abbr.* (in writing) Kentucky

L l

L /ɛl/ *noun, abbr., symbol*
- *noun* also **l** [C, U] (*pl.* **Ls, L's, l's** /ɛlz/) the 12th letter of the English alphabet: *"Lion" begins with (an) L/"L."* ➲ see also **L-PLATE**
- *abbr.* **1** **L.** (especially on maps) Lake: *L. Erie* **2** (especially for sizes of clothes) large: *S, M, and L* (= small, medium, and large)
- *symbol* also **l** the number 50 in ROMAN NUMERALS

l 🖉 *abbr.*
1 (*pl.* **l**) (in writing) liter(s) **2** (also **l.**) (*pl.* **ll**) (in writing) line (on a page in a book)

LA /ɛl ˈeɪ/ *abbr.* **1** (also **L.A.**) the city of Los Angeles **2** (in writing) Louisiana

la /lɑ/ *noun* (*music*) the 6th note of a MAJOR SCALE ➲ see also A, LA

Lab /læb/ *noun* (*informal*) = LABRADOR

lab /læb/ *noun* (*informal*) = LABORATORY: *science labs* ◆ *a lab technician* ◆ *a lab coat* (= a white coat worn by scientists, etc. working in a laboratory)

label   price tag   ticket

la·bel 🖉 **AWL** /ˈleɪbl/ *noun, verb*
- *noun* **1** a piece of paper, etc. that is attached to something and that gives information about it **SYN** TAG, TICKET: *The washing instructions are on the label.* ◆ *price/address labels* ◆ *He'll only wear designer labels* (= clothes with designer labels). ➲ picture at PACKAGING **2** (*disapproving*) a word or phrase that is used to describe someone or something in a way that seems too general, unfair, or not correct: *I hated the label "housewife."* **3** a company that produces and sells recorded music: *the Virgin record label* ◆ *It's his first release for a major label.* ➲ see also OFF-LABEL
- *verb* (**-l-**, *CanE usually* **-ll-**) [often passive] **1** ~ sth to attach a label on something or write information on something: *We carefully labeled each item with the contents and the date.* ◆ *The file was labeled "Private."* **2** to describe someone or something in a particular way, especially unfairly: ~ sb/sth (as) sth | ~ sb/sth + noun/adj. *It is unfair to label a small baby as naughty.* ◆ *He was labeled (as) a traitor by his former colleagues.*

THESAURUS

label
tag ◆ sticker
These are all words for a piece of paper, fabric, or plastic that is attached to something and gives information about it.
label a small piece of paper, fabric, or plastic that is attached to something in order to show what it is or give information about it: *The washing instructions are on the label.* ◆ *address labels* ◆ *He'll only wear clothes with a designer label.*
tag (often used in compounds) a small piece of paper, fabric, or plastic that is attached to something, or that someone wears, in order to give information about it/

them: *Everyone at the conference had to wear a name tag.*

LABEL OR TAG?
Labels in clothes are often made of fabric and sewn in. **Tags** on clothes are usually made of cardboard and cut off before you wear the clothes. A *name tag* can be stuck or tied onto someone to show who they are: *All babies in the hospital have name tags wrapped around their ankles.* *Price tag* is much more frequent than *price label* and is used for both literal and figurative meanings: *What does the price tag say?* ◆ *There is a $20 million price tag on the team's star player.* A **label** can also be a **sticker** that you put on an envelope.
sticker a sticky label with a picture or message on it, that you stick on to something.

PATTERNS
- a price tag/sticker
- to have a label/tag/sticker
- to attach/put on/stick on a label/tag/sticker
- The label/tag/sticker says…

---

la·bi·a /ˈleɪbiə/ *noun* [pl.] the four folds of skin at the entrance to a woman's VAGINA

la·bi·al /ˈleɪbiəl/ *noun* (*phonetics*) a speech sound made with the lips, for example /m/, /p/, and /v/ in *me, pen,* and *very* ▶ **labial** *adj.*

la·bi·o·den·tal /ˌleɪbioʊˈdɛntl/ *noun* (*phonetics*) a speech sound made by placing the top teeth against the bottom lip, for example /f/ and /v/ in *fan* and *van* ▶ **labiodental** *adj.*

la·bi·o·ve·lar /ˌleɪbioʊˈvilər/ *noun* (*phonetics*) a speech sound made using the lips and soft PALATE, for example /w/ in *we* ▶ **la·bi·o·ve·lar** *adj.*

la·bor 🖉 **AWL** (*CanE usually* **la·bour**) /ˈleɪbər/ *noun, verb*
- *noun*
> **WORK 1** [U] work, especially physical work: *manual labor* (= work using your hands) ◆ *The price will include the labor and materials.* ◆ *The company wants to keep down labor costs.* ◆ *He was sentenced to two years in a labor camp* (= a type of prison where people have to do hard physical work). ➲ see also DAY LABOR **2** [C, usually pl.] (*formal*) a task or period of work: *He was so exhausted from the day's labors that he went straight to bed.*
> **PEOPLE WHO WORK 3** [U] the people who work or are available for work in a country or company: *a shortage of labor* ◆ *Employers are using immigrants as cheap labor.* ◆ *Repairs involve skilled labor, which can be expensive.* ◆ *good labor relations* (= the relationship between workers and employers)
> **HAVING BABY 4** [U, C, usually sing.] the period of time or the process of giving birth to a baby: *Jane was in labor for ten hours.* ◆ *She went into labor early.* ◆ *labor pains*
> **IDM** **a labor of love** a hard task that you do because you want to, not because it is necessary
- *verb*
> **STRUGGLE 1** [I] to try very hard to do something difficult: ~ (away) *He was in his study laboring away over some old papers.* ◆ ~ to do sth *They labored for years to clear their son's name.*
> **WORK HARD 2** [I] to do hard physical work: *We labored all day in the fields.* ◆ (*old-fashioned*) *the laboring classes* (= the working class)
> **MOVE WITH DIFFICULTY 3** [I] (+ adv./prep.) to move with difficulty and effort **SYN** STRUGGLE: *The horses labored up the steep slope.*
> **IDM** **labor the point** to continue to repeat or explain something that has already been said and understood
> **PHR V** **'labor under sth** (*formal*) to believe something that is not true: *to labor under a misapprehension/delusion, etc.* ◆ *He's still laboring under the impression that he's written a great book.*

---

laboratory equipment

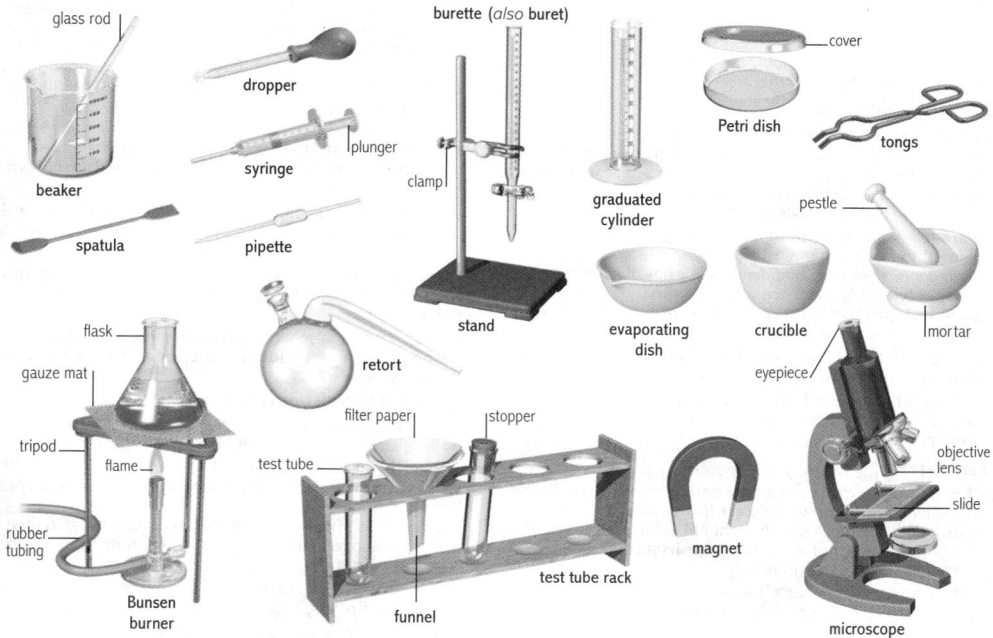

glass rod

dropper

burette (*also* buret)

cover

Petri dish

tongs

plunger

syringe

beaker

clamp

graduated
cylinder

pestle

spatula

pipette

flask

gauze mat

retort

evaporating
dish

crucible

mortar

eyepiece

tripod

filter paper

stopper

stand

flame

test tube

objective
lens

rubber
tubing

slide

magnet

Bunsen
burner

funnel

test tube rack

microscope

lab·o·ra·to·ry /ˈlæbrəˌtɔri/ *noun* (*pl.* lab·o·ra·to-ries) (*also informal* lab)
a room or building used for scientific research, experiments, testing, etc.: *a research laboratory* ♦ *laboratory experiments/tests* ➔ see also LANGUAGE LABORATORY

Labor Day (*CanE usually* **Labour Day**) *noun* a public holiday on the first Monday of September, in honor of working people ➔ compare MAY DAY

la·bored AWL (*CanE usually* **la·boured**) /ˈleɪbərd/ *adj.* **1** (of breathing) slow and taking a lot of effort **2** (of writing, speaking, etc.) not natural and seeming to take a lot of effort

la·bor·er (*CanE usually* **la·bour·er**) /ˈleɪbərər/ *noun* a person whose job involves hard physical work that is not skilled, especially work that is done outdoors

labor force (*CanE usually* **labour force**) *noun* all the people who work for a company or in a country **SYN** WORKFORCE: *a skilled/an unskilled labor force*

la·bor·ing AWL (*CanE usually* **la·bour·ing**) /ˈleɪbərɪŋ/ *noun* [U] hard physical work that is not skilled: *a laboring job*

labor-in·ten·sive (*CanE usually* **labour-in·ten·sive**) *adj.* (of work) needing a lot of people to do it, or taking a lot of time or effort: *labor-intensive methods* ♦ *This recipe is labor-intensive, but it's worth it.* ➔ compare CAPITAL-INTENSIVE

la·bo·ri·ous /ləˈbɔriəs/ *adj.* taking a lot of time and effort **SYN** ONEROUS, TAXING: *a laborious task/process* ♦ *Checking all the information will be slow and laborious.* ▶ **la·bo·ri·ous·ly** *adv.*

labor market (*CanE usually* **labour market**) *noun* the number of people who are available for work in relation to the number of jobs available: *young people about to enter the labor market*

labor-saving (*CanE usually* **labour-saving**) *adj.* [usually before noun] designed to reduce the amount of work or effort needed to do something: *modern labor-saving devices such as washing machines and dishwashers*

labor union (*CanE usually* **labour union**) *noun* an organization of workers, usually in a particular industry, that exists to protect their interests, improve conditions of work, etc.

la·bour (*CanE*) = LABOR

Lab·ra·dor /ˈlæbrəˌdɔr/ (*also* **Labrador re·triev·er**, *informal* **Lab**) *noun* a large dog that can be yellow, black, or brown in color, often used by blind people as a guide: *a yellow/black/chocolate Labrador*

la·bur·num /ləˈbɜrnəm/ *noun* [C, U] a small tree with hanging bunches of yellow flowers

lab·y·rinth /ˈlæbərɪnθ/ *noun* (*formal*) a complicated series of paths, which it is difficult to find your way through: *We lost our way in the labyrinth of streets.* ♦ (*figurative*) *a labyrinth of rules and regulations* ➔ compare MAZE ▶ **lab·y·rin·thine** /ˌlæbəˈrɪnθən; -θin/ *adj.* (*formal*): *labyrinthine corridors* ♦ *labyrinthine legislation*

lace /leɪs/ *noun, verb*
• *noun* **1** [U] a delicate material made from threads of cotton, silk, etc. that are twisted into a pattern of holes: *a lace handkerchief* ♦ *a tablecloth edged with lace* ♦ *lace curtains* ➔ see also LACY **2** [C] = SHOELACE: *Your laces are undone.* ➔ picture at CLOTHES
• *verb* **1** [I, T] to be fastened with lace; to fasten something with lace: ~ **(up)** *She was wearing a dress that laced up at the side.* ♦ ~ **(up)** *He was sitting on the bed lacing up his shoes.* ➔ see also LACE-UP **2** [T] ~ **sth** to put a lace through the holes in a shoe, a boot, etc. ➔ related noun LACE-UP **3** [T] ~ **sth (with sth)** to add a small amount of alcohol, a drug, poison, etc. to a drink **SYN** SPIKE: *He had laced her milk with rum.* **4** [T] ~ **sth (with sth)** to add a particular quality to a book, speech, etc.: *Her conversation was laced with witty asides.* **5** [T] ~ **sth** to twist something together with another thing: *They sat with their fingers laced.*

lac·er·ate /ˈlæsəˌreɪt/ *verb* (*formal*) **1** ~ **sth** to cut skin or flesh with something sharp: *His hand had been badly lacerated.* **2** ~ **sb** to criticize someone very severely ▶ **lac·er·a·tion** /ˌlæsəˈreɪʃn/ *noun* [C, U]: *She suffered multiple lacerations to the face.*

lace-up *noun* [usually pl.] a shoe that is fastened with laces: *a pair of lace-ups* ◆ *lace-up boots*

lace·wing /'leɪswɪŋ/ *noun* an insect that has large transparent wings with lines on them

lach·ry·mose /'lækrəmoʊs/ *adj.* (*formal*) having a tendency to cry easily **SYN** TEARFUL

lack 🔑 /læk/ *noun, verb*
● *noun* [U, sing.] **~ (of sth)** the state of not having something or not having enough of something **SYN** DEARTH, SHORTAGE: *a lack of food/money/skills* ◆ *The trip was canceled due to lack of* (= because there was not enough) *interest.* ◆ *There was no lack of volunteers.* **IDM** see TRY *v.*
● *verb* [no passive] **~ sth** to have none or not enough of something: *Some houses still lack basic amenities such as bathrooms.* ◆ *He lacks confidence.* ◆ *She has the determination that her brother lacks.* ⊃ see also LACKING **IDM** **lack (for) nothing** (*formal*) to have everything that you need ⊃ more at COURAGE

lack·a·dai·si·cal /ˌlækə'deɪzɪkl/ *adj.* not showing enough care or enthusiasm

lack·ey /'læki/ *noun* **1** (*old-fashioned*) a servant **2** (*disapproving*) a person who is treated like a servant or who behaves like one

lack·ing 🔑 /'lækɪŋ/ *adj.* [not before noun]
1 ~ (in sth) having none or not enough of something: *She's not usually lacking in confidence.* ◆ *He was hired as a teacher but was found lacking* (= was thought not to be good enough). **2** not present or not available **SYN** MISSING: *I feel there is something lacking in my life.*

lack·lus·ter (*CanE usually* **lack·lus·tre**) /'lækˌlʌstər/ *adj.* not interesting or exciting; dull: *a lackluster performance* ◆ *lackluster hair*

la·con·ic /lə'kɑnɪk/ *adj.* using only a few words to say something ▸ **la·con·i·cal·ly** /-kli/ *adv.*

lac·quer /'lækər/ *noun, verb*
● *noun* [U] a liquid that is used on wood or metal to give it a hard shiny surface
● *verb* **~ sth** to cover wood or metal with lacquer

la·crosse /lə'krɔs/ *noun* [U] a game played on a field by two teams of ten players who use sticks with curved nets on them to catch, carry, and throw the ball

lac·tate /'lækteɪt/ *verb* [I] (*technical*) (of a woman or female animal) to produce milk from the breasts to feed a baby or young animal ▸ **lac·ta·tion** /læk'teɪʃn/ *noun* [U]: *the period of lactation*

lac·tic ac·id /ˌlæktɪk 'æsɪd/ *noun* [U] an acid that forms in sour milk and is also produced in the muscles during hard exercise

lac·to·ba·cil·lus /ˌlæktoʊbə'sɪləs/ *noun* (*biology*) a type of bacteria that produces lactic acid

lac·tose /'læktoʊs/ *noun* [U] (*chemistry*) a type of sugar found in milk and used in some baby foods

la·cu·na /lə'kunə; -'kyu-/ *noun* (*pl.* **la·cu·nae** /-ni/ *or* **la·cu·nas**) (*formal*) a place where something is missing in a piece of writing or in an idea, a theory, etc. **SYN** GAP

lac·y /'leɪsi/ *adj.* made of or looking like LACE: *lacy underwear*

lad /læd/ *noun* (*informal*) a boy or young man: *Things have changed since I was a lad.* ⊃ compare LASS

lad·der /'lædər/ *noun* **1** a piece of equipment for climbing up and down a wall, the side of a building, etc., consisting of two lengths of wood or metal that are joined together by steps or RUNGS: *to climb up/fall off a ladder* ⊃ picture at TOOL ⊃ see also STEPLADDER **2** [usually sing.] a series of stages by which you can make progress in a career or an organization: *to move up or down the social ladder* ◆ *the career ladder* **3** (*also* **ladder tournament**) a competition in a particular sport or game in which teams or players are arranged in a list and they can move up the list by defeating one of the teams or players above

lad·en /'leɪdn/ *adj.* **1 ~ (with sth)** heavily loaded with something: *passengers laden with luggage* ◆ *The trees were laden with apples.* ◆ *a heavily/fully laden truck* ⊃ compare UNLADEN **2 ~ (with sth)** (*literary*) full of something, especially something unpleasant: *His voice was soft, yet laden with threat.* **3 -laden** used to form adjectives showing that something is full of, or loaded with, the thing mentioned: *calorie-laden cheesecake*

la-di-da (*also* **lah-di-dah**) /ˌlɑ di 'dɑ/ *adj., exclamation*
● *adj.* (*informal*) used to describe a way of speaking or behaving that is typical of upper-class people but that is not natural or sincere **SYN** AFFECTED
● *exclamation* used when someone is irritating you, because they seem to think they are more important then they really are

ladies' man (*also* **lady's man**) *noun* a man who enjoys spending time with women and thinks he is attractive to them

ladies' room (*also* **women's room**) *noun* a bathroom for women in a public building or place: *Could you tell me where the ladies' room is?*

lad·ing *noun* ⊃ BILL OF LADING

la·dle /'leɪdl/ *noun, verb*
● *noun* a large, deep spoon with a long handle, used especially for serving soup ⊃ picture at COOKING, KITCHEN
● *verb* **~ sth** to place food on a plate with a large spoon or in large quantities **PHR V** **ladle sth↔'out** (sometimes *disapproving*) to give someone a lot of something, especially money or advice **SYN** DOLE STH OUT

la dol·ce vi·ta /lɑ ˌdoʊltʃeɪ 'vitə/ *noun* [sing.] (from *Italian*) a life of pleasure and expensive things, without any worries

la·dy 🔑 /'leɪdi/ *noun* (*pl.* **la·dies**)
1 [C] a word used to mean "woman" that some people, especially older people, consider is more polite: *There's a lady waiting to see you.* ◆ *He was with an attractive young lady.* ◆ *the ladies' golf championship* ◆ *a cleaning lady* (= a woman who cleans an office or a private home) ◆ (*approving*) *She's a tough lady.* ◆ *a lady doctor/golfer* **HELP** Some women object to the way **lady** is used in some of these examples and prefer it to be avoided if possible: *a doctor/a woman doctor* ◆ *There's someone waiting to see you.* ⊃ see also BAG LADY, CLEANING LADY, FIRST LADY, LEADING LADY, OLD LADY **2** [C] a woman who is polite and well educated, has excellent manners, and always behaves well: *His wife was a real lady.* ⊃ compare GENTLEMAN **3** [C, usually pl.] (*formal*) used when speaking to or about a girl or woman, especially someone you do not know: *Can I take your coats, ladies?* ◆ *Could I have your attention, ladies and gentlemen?* **HELP** Some women do not like **ladies** used on its own, as in the first example, and prefer it to be left out. **4** [sing.] an informal way to talk to a woman, showing a lack of respect: *Listen, lady, don't shout at me.* **5** (*also* **lady friend**) [C] (*old-fashioned*) a girlfriend: *Max and his lady went dancing last night.* **6** [C] (*old-fashioned*) a woman belonging to a high social class: *the lords and ladies of the court* ◆ *a lady's maid* **7 Lady** [C] a title used by a woman who is a member of the British NOBILITY, or by someone who has been given the title "lady" as an honor. The wives and daughters of some members of the NOBILITY and the wives of KNIGHTS are also called "Lady": *Lady Howe* ◆ *Lady Jane Gray* ⊃ compare LORD, SIR **8 Our Lady** [sing.] a title used to refer to Mary, the mother of Christ, especially in the Roman Catholic Church: *Our Lady of Lourdes* **IDM** **lady of the house** (*old-fashioned*) a woman who is in charge of a household: *The salesman asked if the lady of the house was at home.* ⊃ more at FAT, LEISURE

la·dy·bug /'leɪdiˌbʌg/ *noun* a small flying insect, usually red with black spots ⊃ picture at ANIMAL

la·dy·fin·ger /'leɪdiˌfɪŋgər/ *noun* a small, long, thin cake made with eggs, sugar, and flour

t tea   ţ butter   d did   k cat   g got   tʃ chin   dʒ June   f fall

lady-in-ˈwaiting *noun* (*pl.* **ladies-in-waiting**) a woman who goes to places with, and helps, a queen or princess

la·dy·kill·er /ˈleɪdiˌkɪlər/ *noun* (*old-fashioned* or *informal*) a man who is sexually attractive and successful with women, but who does not stay in a relationship with anyone for long

la·dy·like /ˈleɪdiˌlaɪk/ *adj.* (*old-fashioned*) polite and quiet; typical of what is supposed to be socially acceptable for a woman **SYN REFINED**: *ladylike behavior* ◆ *Her language was not very ladylike.*

la·dy·ship /ˈleɪdiˌʃɪp/ *noun* **Her/Your Ladyship** a title used when talking to or about a woman who is a member of the British **NOBILITY**: *Does Your Ladyship require anything?* ⊃ compare **LORDSHIP**

lady's ˌman = LADIES' MAN

lag /læg/ *verb, noun*
● *verb* (-gg-) [I] **~ (behind sb/sth)** | **~ (behind)** to move or develop slowly or more slowly than other people, organizations, etc. **SYN TRAIL**: *The little boy lagged behind his parents.* ◆ *We still lag far behind many of our competitors in using modern technology.*
● *noun* = TIME LAG ⊃ see also JET LAG

la·ger /ˈlɑgər/ *noun* **1** [U, C] a type of light pale beer that usually has a lot of bubbles: *German lagers* **2** [C] a glass, can, or bottle of this

lag·gard /ˈlægərd/ *noun* (*old-fashioned*) a slow and lazy person, organization, etc.

la·goon /ləˈgun/ *noun* **1** a lake of salt water that is separated from the ocean by a REEF or an area of rock or sand **2** a small area of fresh water near a lake or river **3** (*technical*) an artificial area built to hold waste water before it is treated at a SEWAGE TREATMENT PLANT

lah-di-dah = LA-DI-DA

laid *pt, pp of* LAY

ˌlaid-ˈback /ˌleɪd ˈbæk/ *adj.* (*informal*) calm and relaxed; seeming not to worry about anything **SYN EASYGOING**: *a laid-back attitude to life*

lain *pt of* LIE¹

lair /lɛr/ *noun* [usually sing.] **1** a place where a wild animal sleeps or hides **2** a place where someone goes to hide or to be alone **SYN DEN, HIDEOUT**

lais·sez-faire /ˌlɛseɪ ˈfɛr; ˌlezeɪ-/ *noun* [U] (from *French*) the policy of allowing private businesses to develop without government control ▶ **lais·sez-faire** *adj.*: *a laissez-faire economy* ◆ *They have a laissez-faire approach to bringing up their children* (= they give them a lot of freedom).

la·i·ty /ˈleɪəti/ *noun* **the laity** [sing.] all the members of a Church who are not CLERGY ⊃ see also LAYMAN

lake 🔑 /leɪk/ *noun* (*abbr.* **L.**)
a large area of water that is surrounded by land: *We swam in the lake.* ◆ *Lake Ontario* **IDM** see JUMP *v.*

lake·front /ˈleɪkfrʌnt/ *noun* [sing.] the land along the edge of a lake: *They have a beautiful home on the lakefront.* ◆ *a lakefront cottage*

lake·side /ˈleɪksaɪd/ *noun* [sing.] the area around the edge of a lake: *We went for a walk by the lakeside.* ◆ *a lakeside hotel*

la-la land /ˈlɑ lɑ ˌlænd/ *noun* [U] (*informal, disapproving*) if you say that someone is living **in la-la land**, you mean that they do not understand what a situation is really like, but think it is much better than it is

lam /læm/ *noun*
IDM on the lam (*informal*) escaping from someone, especially from the police

la·ma /ˈlɑmə/ *noun* **1** a title given to a spiritual leader in Tibetan Buddhism **2** a Buddhist MONK from Tibet or Mongolia

La·ma·ism /ˈlɑməˌɪzəm/ *noun* [U] Tibetan Buddhism

lamb /læm/ *noun, verb*
● *noun* **1** [C] a young sheep **2** [U] meat from a young sheep: *a leg of lamb* ◆ *lamb chops* ⊃ compare MUTTON **3** [C] (*informal*) used to describe or address someone with affection or sadness: *You poor lamb!*
IDM (like) a lamb/lambs to the slaughter used to describe people who are going to do something dangerous without realizing it
● *verb* [I] (of a sheep) to give birth to a lamb

lam·ba·da /læmˈbɑdə/ *noun* a fast Brazilian dance performed by couples who hold each other closely

lam·baste (also **lam·bast**) /læmˈbeɪst; -ˈbæst/ *verb* **~ sb/sth** (*formal*) to attack or criticize someone or something very severely, especially in public **SYN LAY INTO**

lamb·da /ˈlæmdə/ *noun* the 11th letter of the Greek alphabet (Λ, λ)

lamb·skin /ˈlæmskɪn/ *noun* [U] prepared skin from a lamb, either with the wool on or as leather: *a lambskin jacket*

lambs·wool /ˈlæmzwʊl/ *noun* [U] soft fine wool from lambs, used for knitting clothes: *a lambswool sweater*

lame /leɪm/ *adj.* **1** (of people or animals) unable to walk well because of an injury to the leg or foot **2** (of an excuse, explanation, etc.) weak and difficult to believe **SYN FEEBLE, UNCONVINCING 3** (*informal*) not interesting, exciting, or fashionable: *What a lame party!* ▶ **lame·ness** *noun* [U]: *The disease has left her with permanent lameness.*

la·mé /læˈmeɪ; lɑ-/ *noun* [U] a type of cloth into which gold or silver thread has been twisted

lame·brain /ˈleɪmbreɪn/ *noun* (*informal*) a stupid person ▶ **lame·brain** (also **lame·brained**) *adj.*: *They invented some lamebrain scheme to get rich quick.*

ˌlame ˈduck *noun* (*informal*) a politician or government whose period of office will soon end and that will not be elected again: *a lame-duck president/administration*

lame·ly /ˈleɪmli/ *adv.* in a way that does not sound very confident, or that does not persuade other people **SYN FEEBLE**: *"I must have made a mistake," she said lamely.*

la·ment /ləˈment/ *verb, noun*
● *verb* **~ sth** | **~ that…** | **+ speech** (*formal*) to feel or express great sadness or disappointment about someone or something **SYN BEMOAN, BEWAIL**: *In the poem he laments the destruction of the countryside.*
● *noun* (*formal*) a song, poem, or other expression of great sadness for someone who has died or for something that has ended

lam·en·ta·ble /ləˈmentəbl/ *adj.* (*formal*) very disappointing **SYN DEPLORABLE, REGRETTABLE**: *She shows a lamentable lack of understanding.* ▶ **la·men·ta·bly** /-bli/ *adv.*

lam·en·ta·tion /ˌlæmənˈteɪʃn/ *noun* [C, U] (*formal*) an expression of great sadness or disappointment

la·ment·ed /ləˈmentəd/ *adj.* (*formal* or *humorous*) (of someone or something that has died or disappeared) missed very much: *her late lamented husband* ◆ *the last edition of the much lamented newspaper*

lam·i·nate /ˈlæmənət/ *noun* [U, C] a material that is laminated

lam·i·nat·ed /ˈlæməˌneɪtəd/ *adj.* **1** (of wood, plastic, etc.) made by sticking several thin layers together **2** covered with thin transparent plastic for protection: *laminated membership cards*

lamp 🔑 /læmp/ *noun*
1 a device that uses electricity, oil, or gas to produce light: *a table/desk/bicycle, etc. lamp* ◆ *to switch on/turn off a lamp* ◆ *a streetlamp* ⊃ see also FLOOR LAMP, HURRICANE LAMP, LAVA LAMP **2** an electrical device that produces RAYS of heat and that is used for medical or scientific purposes: *an infra-red/ultraviolet lamp* ⊃ see also SUNLAMP

lamp·light /ˈlæmplaɪt/ *noun* [U] light from a lamp

lamp·lit /ˈlæmplɪt/ *adj.* [usually before noun] given light by lamps; seen by the light from lamps: *a lamplit room* ◆ *a lamplit figure in the chair*

lam·poon /læm'puːn/ *verb, noun*

- *verb* ~ sb/sth to criticize someone or something publicly in an amusing way that makes them or it look ridiculous **SYN** SATIRIZE: *His cartoons mercilessly lampooned the politicians of his time.*
- *noun* a piece of writing that criticizes someone or something and makes them or it look ridiculous

lamp·post /'læmppoʊst/ *noun* a tall post in the street with a lamp at the top: *The car skidded and hit a lamppost.*
⊃ compare STREETLIGHT

lam·prey /'læmpri/ *noun* a fish with a round mouth that attaches itself to other fish and sucks their blood

lamp·shade /'læmpʃeɪd/ *noun* a decorative cover for a lamp that is used to make the light softer or to direct it
⊃ picture at LIGHT

LAN /læn/ *noun* (*computing*) the abbreviation for "local area network" (a system for communicating by computer within a large building or group of buildings) ⊃ compare WAN

lance /læns/ *noun, verb*

- *noun* a weapon with a long wooden handle and a pointed metal end that was used by people fighting on horses in the past
- *verb* **1** [T] ~ sth to cut open an infected place on someone's body with a sharp knife in order to let out the PUS (= a yellow substance produced by infection): *to lance an abscess* **2** [I] + adv./prep. (of a pain) to move suddenly and quickly and be very sharp: *Pain lanced through his body.*

lance corporal *noun* a member of one of the lower ranks in the Marine Corps: *Lance Corporal Alan Smith*

lanc·er /'lænsər/ *noun* in the past, a member of a REGIMENT that used LANCES

lan·cet /'lænsət/ *noun* a knife with a sharp point and two sharp edges, used by doctors for cutting skin and flesh

land 🔑 /lænd/ *noun, verb*

- *noun*
- ⟩ SURFACE OF EARTH **1** [U] the surface of the earth that is not ocean: *It was good to be back on land.* ♦ *We made the trip by land, though flying would have been cheaper.* ♦ *In the distance the crew sighted land.* ♦ *The elephant is the largest living land animal.* ⊃ see also DRY LAND ⊃ thesaurus box at FLOOR
- ⟩ AREA OF GROUND **2** [U] also **lands** [pl.] an area of ground, especially of a particular type or used for a particular purpose **SYN** TERRAIN: *fertile/arid/stony, etc. land* ♦ *flat/undulating/hilly, etc. land* ♦ *agricultural/arable/industrial, etc. land* ♦ *The land was very dry and hard after the long hot summer.* ♦ *The land rose in the east.* ♦ *a piece of waste/derelict land* ♦ *Some of the country's richest grazing lands are in these valleys.* ⊃ thesaurus box at SOIL **3** [U] (also *formal* **lands** [pl.]) the area of ground that someone owns, especially when you think of it as property that can be bought or sold: *The price of land is rising rapidly.* ♦ *During the war their lands were occupied by the enemy.* ⊃ see also NO-MAN'S-LAND
- ⟩ COUNTRYSIDE **4** the land [U] an area for farming: *At the beginning of the 20th century almost a third of the population lived off the land* (= grew or produced their own food). ♦ *Many people leave the land to find work in towns and cities.* ⊃ thesaurus box at COUNTRY
- ⟩ COUNTRY/REGION **5** [C] (*literary*) used to refer to a country or region in a way which appeals to the emotions or the imagination: *She longed to return to her native land.* ♦ *They dreamed of traveling to foreign lands.* ♦ *America is the land of freedom and opportunity.* ⊃ see also CLUBLAND, DOCKLAND, DREAMLAND, FAIRYLAND, LA-LA LAND, NEVER-NEVER LAND, THE PROMISED LAND, WONDERLAND **HELP** There are many other compounds ending in **land**. You will find them at their place in the alphabet.
  IDM in the land of the living (often *humorous*) awake or alive or no longer sick the land of milk and honey a place where life is pleasant and easy and people are very happy in the land of Nod (*old-fashioned, humorous*) asleep: *Pete and Jo were still in the land of Nod, so I went out for a walk in the morning sunshine.* ⊃ more at LIVE¹

- *verb*
- ⟩ OF BIRD/PLANE/INSECT **1** [I] to come down through the air onto the ground or another surface: *The plane landed safely.* ♦ *A fly landed on his nose.* **ANT** TAKE OFF
- ⟩ OF PILOT **2** [T] ~ sth to bring a plane down to the ground in a controlled way: *The pilot landed the plane safely.*
- ⟩ ARRIVE IN PLANE/BOAT **3** [I] to arrive somewhere in a plane or a boat: *We will be landing shortly. Please fasten your seatbelts.* ♦ *The troops landed at dawn.* ♦ *They were the first men to land on the moon.* ♦ *The ferry is due to land at 3 o'clock.* **4** [T] ~ sb/sth to put someone or something on land from an aircraft, a boat, etc.: *The troops were landed by helicopter.*
- ⟩ FALL TO GROUND **5** [I] to come down to the ground after jumping, falling, or being thrown: *I fell and landed heavily at the bottom of the stairs.* ♦ *A large stone landed right beside him.*
- ⟩ DIFFICULTIES **6** [I] + adv./prep. to arrive somewhere and cause difficulties that have to be dealt with: *Why do complaints always land on my desk* (= why do I always have to deal with them)?
- ⟩ JOB **7** [T] (*informal*) to succeed in getting a job, etc., especially one that a lot of other people want: ~ sth *He's just landed a starring role in Spielberg's next movie.* ♦ ~ sb/ yourself sth *She's just landed herself a company directorship.*
- ⟩ FISH **8** [T] ~ sth to catch a fish and bring it out of the water on to the land
  IDM land a blow, punch, etc. to succeed in hitting someone or something: *She landed a punch on his chin.* land on your feet to be lucky in finding yourself in a good situation, or in getting out of a difficult situation
  PHR V 'land in sth | 'land sb/yourself in sth (*informal*) to get someone/yourself into a difficult situation: *She was arrested and landed in court.* ♦ *His hot temper has landed him in trouble before.* 'land sb/yourself with sth/sb (*informal*) to give someone/yourself something unpleasant to do, especially because nobody else wants to do it: *As usual, I got landed with all the boring jobs.*

THESAURUS

land

lot · ground · space · plot

These words all mean an area of land that is used for a particular purpose.

land an area of ground, especially one that is used for a particular purpose: *agricultural land*

lot a piece of land that is used or intended for a particular purpose: *building lots* ♦ *a parking lot*

ground (often used in compounds) an area of land that is used for a particular purpose: *The kids were playing on a playground near the school.* ♦ *the site of an ancient burial ground*

LAND, LOT, OR GROUND?

Land is used for large areas of open land in the country, especially when it is used for farming. A **lot** is often a smaller piece of land in a town or city, especially one intended for building or parking on. **Ground** is any area of open land; a **ground** is an area of land designed or used for a particular purpose or activity.

space a large area of land that has no buildings on it: *The city has plenty of open space.* ♦ *the wide open spaces of the Canadian prairies*

plot a small piece of land used or intended for a particular purpose: *She bought a small plot of land to build a house.* ♦ *a vegetable plot*

LOT OR PLOT?

Either a **lot** or a **plot** can be used for building on. Only a **plot** can also be used for growing vegetables or burying people.

PATTERNS
- (an) open land/ground/space
- (a/an) empty/vacant land/lot/ground/plot

| h hat | m man | n no | ŋ sing | l leg | r red | y yes | w wet |

lan·dau /'lændɔ; -də/ *noun* a CARRIAGE with four wheels and a roof that folds down in two sections, that is pulled by horses

land-based *adj.* [usually before noun] located on or living on the land: *land-based missiles ♦ land-based animals*

land bridge *noun* a strip of land between two large land masses, especially one that existed a long time ago and that humans and animals could cross, but was later covered by the sea: *The Bering Straits were once a land bridge between Asia and North America.*

land·ed /'lændəd/ *adj.* [only before noun] **1** owning a lot of land: *the landed gentry* **2** including a large amount of land: *landed estates*

landed immigrant *noun* (CanE) a person from another country who has permission to live permanently in Canada

land·fall /'lændfɔl/ *noun* [U, C] (*literary*) the land that you see or arrive at first after a journey by ocean or by air: *After three weeks they made landfall on the coast of South Carolina.*

land·fill /'lændfɪl/ *noun* **1** [C, U] an area of land where large amounts of waste material are buried under the earth: *The map shows the position of the new landfills. ♦ a landfill site* **2** [U] the process of burying large amounts of waste material: *the choice of landfill or incineration* **3** [U] waste material that will be buried

land·form /'lændfɔrm/ *noun* (*geology*) a natural feature of the earth's surface

land·hold·ing /'lænd,hoʊldɪŋ/ *noun* [C, U] (*technical*) a piece of land that someone owns or rents; the fact of owning or renting land ▸ **land·hold·er** *noun*: *farmers and landholders*

land·ing /'lændɪŋ/ *noun* **1** [C] the area at the top of a set of stairs where you arrive before you go into an upstairs room or move onto another set of stairs **2** [C, U] an act of bringing an aircraft or a SPACECRAFT down to the ground: *a perfect/smooth/safe landing ♦ the first Apollo moon landing ♦ The pilot was forced to make an emergency landing. ♦ a landing site* **ANT** TAKEOFF **3** [C] an act of bringing soldiers to land in an area that is controlled by the enemy **4** [C] a flat wooden platform on the water where boats let people get on and off, and load and unload goods **SYN** JETTY

landing craft *noun* (*pl.* **landing craft**) a boat with a flat bottom, carried on a ship. Landing craft open at one end so soldiers and equipment can be brought to land.

landing gear *noun* [U] = UNDERCARRIAGE ➾ picture at PLANE

landing lights *noun* [pl.] **1** bright lamps on a plane that are switched on before it lands **2** lights that are arranged along the sides of a RUNWAY to guide a pilot when he or she is landing a plane

landing page *noun* (*computing*) the part of a Web site that you reach first when you click on a link on the Internet: *Have a different landing page for each advertising campaign.*

landing strip *noun* = AIRSTRIP

land·la·dy /'lænd,leɪdi/ *noun* (*pl.* **land·la·dies**) a woman from whom you rent a room, a house, etc.

land·less /'lændləs/ *adj.* [usually before noun] not owning land for farming; not allowed to own land

land·line /'lændlaɪn/ *noun* a telephone connection that uses wires carried on poles or under the ground, in contrast to a cell phone: *I'll call you later on the landline.* ➾ collocations at PHONE

land·locked /'lændlɑkt/ *adj.* almost or completely surrounded by land: *Switzerland is completely landlocked.*

land·lord /'lændlɔrd/ *noun* a person or company from whom you rent a room, a house, an office, etc.

land·lub·ber /'lænd,lʌbər/ *noun* (*informal*) a person with not much knowledge or experience of the ocean or sailing

land·mark /'lændmɑrk/ *noun* **1** something, such as a large building, a mountain, etc., that you can see clearly from a distance and that will help you to know where you are: *The Empire State Building is a familiar landmark on the New York* skyline. **2** ~ (in sth) an event, a discovery, an invention, etc. that marks an important stage in something **SYN** MILESTONE: *The ceasefire was seen as a major landmark in the fight against terrorism. ♦ a landmark decision/ruling in the courts* **3** a building or a place that is very important because of its history, and that should be preserved **SYN** MONUMENT

land·mass /'lændmæs/ *noun* (*technical*) a large area of land, for example a continent

land mine *noun* a bomb placed on or under the ground, that explodes when vehicles or people move over it

land office *noun* a government office that keeps a record of areas of land and who owns them **IDM** **do a land-office business** to do a lot of business and make a lot of money, usually in a short time: *Sellers of Yankees baseball paraphernalia did a land-office business when the team won the World Series.*

land·own·er /'lænd,oʊnər/ *noun* a person who owns land, especially a large area of land ▸ **land·own·er·ship** /'lændoʊnər,ʃɪp/ (also **land·own·ing**) *noun* [U]: *private land-ownership* **land·own·ing** *adj.* [only before noun]: *the great landowning families*

land reform *noun* [U, C] the principle of dividing land for farming into smaller pieces so that more people can own some

land·scape 🔑 /'lændskeɪp/ *noun, verb*
● *noun* **1** [C, usually sing.] everything you can see when you look across a large area of land, especially in the country: *the bleak/rugged/dramatic, etc. landscape of the area ♦ the mountains and deserts that are typical features of the Western landscape ♦ an urban/industrial landscape ♦ (figurative) We can expect changes in the political landscape.* ➾ thesaurus box at COUNTRY **2** [C, U] a painting of a view of the countryside; this style of painting: *an artist famous for his landscapes* ➾ collocations at ART **3** [U] (*technical*) the way of printing a document in which the top of the page is one of the longer sides: *Select the landscape option when printing the file.* ➾ compare PORTRAIT **IDM** see BLOT
● *verb* ~ sth to improve the appearance of an area of land by changing the design and planting trees, flowers, etc.

landscape architect *noun* a person whose job is planning and designing the environment, especially so that roads, buildings, etc. combine with the landscape in an attractive way ▸ **landscape architecture** *noun* [U]

landscape gardener *noun* a person whose job is designing and creating attractive parks and gardens ▸ **landscape gardening** *noun* [U]

land·slide /'lændslaɪd/ *noun* **1** a mass of earth, rock, etc. that falls down the slope of a mountain or a CLIFF ➾ see also LANDSLIP **2** an election in which one person or party gets very many more votes than the other people or parties: *She was expected to win by a landslide. ♦ a landslide victory* ➾ collocations at VOTE

land·slip /'lændslɪp/ *noun* a mass of rock and earth that falls down a slope, usually smaller than a landslide

land·ward /'lændwərd/ *adj.* [only before noun] facing the land; away from the water ▸ **land·ward** (also **land·wards**) *adv.*: *After an hour, the ship turned landward.*

land yacht *noun* **1** a small vehicle with a sail and no engine, that is used on land **2** (*informal*) a large car

lane 🔑 /leɪn/ *noun*
1 a narrow road in the country: *winding country lanes ♦ We drove along a muddy lane to reach the farmhouse.* ➾ see also MEMORY LANE **2** (especially in place names) a street in a town: *Rosemary Lane* **3** a section of a wide road, that is marked by painted white lines, to keep lines of traffic separate: *the northbound/southbound lane ♦ to change lanes ♦ She signaled and pulled over into the right lane. ♦ a four-lane highway* ➾ see also BIKE LANE, BUS LANE, EXPRESS LANE, FAST LANE, HOV LANE, PASSING LANE, SLOW LANE **4** a narrow marked section of a track or a swimming pool that

is used by one person taking part in a race: *The Ohio State freshman in lane four is coming up fast from behind.* ⊃ **picture** at SPORT, HOBBY **5** a route used by ships or aircraft on regular journeys: *one of the world's busiest **shipping/sea lanes*** **IDM** see FAST LANE

lan·gous·tine /ˈlɒŋɡəˌstin; ˌlɒŋɡəˈstin/ *noun* a type of SHELLFISH like a small LOBSTER

lan·guage 🔑 /ˈlæŋɡwɪdʒ/ *noun*
> OF A COUNTRY **1** [C] the system of communication in speech and writing that is used by people of a particular country or area: *the Japanese language* ♦ *It takes a long time to learn to **speak a language** well.* ♦ *Italian is my **first language**.* ♦ *All the students are required to learn a **foreign language**.* ♦ *She has a **good command of** the Spanish language.* ♦ *English is her **second language**.* ♦ *They fell in love in spite of **the language barrier*** (= the difficulty of communicating when people speak different languages). ♦ *Why study Latin? It's a **dead language*** (= no longer spoken by anyone). ♦ *Is English an **official language** in your country?* ⊃ see also MODERN LANGUAGE
> COMMUNICATION **2** [U] the use by humans of a system of sounds and words to communicate: *theories about the origins of language* ♦ *a study of **language acquisition** in two-year-olds*
> STYLE OF SPEAKING/WRITING **3** [U] a particular style of speaking or writing: ***bad/foul/strong language*** (= words that people may consider offensive) ♦ *literary/poetic language* ♦ *the language of the legal profession* ♦ *Give your instructions in everyday language.* ⊃ see also BAD LANGUAGE
> MOVEMENTS/SYMBOLS/SOUND **4** [C, U] a way of expressing ideas and feelings using movements, symbols, and sound: *the language of mime* ♦ *the **language of dolphins/bees*** ⊃ see also BODY LANGUAGE, SIGN LANGUAGE
> COMPUTING **5** [C, U] a system of symbols and rules that is used to operate a computer: *a programming language*
IDM **speak/talk the same language** to be able to communicate easily with another person because you share similar opinions and experience ⊃ more at WATCH *v.*

language

vocabulary ♦ terms ♦ wording ♦ terminology

These are all terms for the words and expressions people use when they speak or write, or for a particular style of speaking or writing.

language a particular style of speaking or writing: *Give your instructions in everyday language.* ♦ *the language of the legal profession*

vocabulary all the words that a person knows or uses, or all the words in a particular language; the words that people use when they are talking about a particular subject: *to have a large/wide/limited vocabulary* ♦ *The word has become part of everyday vocabulary.*

terms a way of expressing yourself or of saying something: *I'll try to explain in simple terms.*

wording [usually sing.] the words that are used in a piece of writing or a speech, especially when they have been carefully chosen: *It was the standard form of wording for a wedding invitation.*

terminology (*somewhat formal*) the set of technical words or expressions used in a particular subject; words used with particular meanings: *medical terminology* ♦ *Scientists are constantly developing new terminologies.*
NOTE *Literary/poetic terminology* is used for talking about literature or poetry. *Literary/poetic language* is used for writing in a literary or poetic style.

PATTERNS
- **formal/informal/simple/everyday** language/vocabulary/terms
- **business/scientific/technical/specialized** language/vocabulary/terminology
- A word **enters** the language/the vocabulary.

language engi·neering *noun* [U] (*computing*) the use of computers to process languages for industrial purposes

language labora·tory (also **language lab**) *noun* a room in a school or college that contains special equipment to help students learn foreign languages by listening to tapes or CDs, watching videos, recording themselves, etc.

language transfer *noun* [U] (*linguistics*) the process of using your knowledge of your first language or another language that you know when speaking or writing a language that you are learning

langue /lɒŋ/ *noun* (*linguistics*) (from *French*) a language considered as a communication system of a particular community, rather than the way individual people speak ⊃ compare PAROLE

lan·guid /ˈlæŋɡwəd/ *adj.* moving slowly in an elegant manner, not needing energy or effort: *a languid wave of the hand* ♦ *a languid afternoon in the sun* ▶ **lan·guid·ly** *adv.*: *He moved languidly across the room.*

lan·guish /ˈlæŋɡwɪʃ/ *verb* (*formal*) **1** [I] ~ **(in sth)** to be forced to stay somewhere or suffer something unpleasant for a long time: *She continues to languish in a foreign prison.* **2** [I] to become weaker or fail to make progress: *Share prices languished at the closing bell.*

lan·guor /ˈlæŋɡər/ *noun* [U, sing.] (*literary*) the pleasant state of feeling lazy and without energy: *A delicious languor was stealing over him.* ▶ **lan·guor·ous** /ˈlæŋɡərəs/ *adj.*: *a languorous pace of life* ▶ **lan·guor·ous·ly** *adv.*

La Ni·ña /lɑ ˈninyə/ *noun* [U] the cooling of the water in the central and eastern Pacific Ocean that happens every few years and that affects the weather in many parts of the world ⊃ compare EL NIÑO

lank /læŋk/ *adj.* (of hair) straight, dull, and not attractive

lank·y /ˈlæŋki/ *adj.* (lank·i·er, lank·i·est) (of a person) having long, thin arms and legs and moving in an awkward way **SYN** GANGLING: *a tall, lanky teenager*

lan·o·lin /ˈlænələn/ *noun* [U] an oil that comes from sheep's wool and is used to make skin creams

lan·tern /ˈlæntərn/ *noun* a light in a transparent case, often a metal case with glass sides, that has a handle, so that you can carry it outside ⊃ see also CHINESE LANTERN

lantern jaw *noun* a long thin JAW with a large chin ▶ **lantern–jawed** *adj.*

lan·tha·num /ˈlænθənəm/ *noun* [U] (*symb.* **La**) a chemical element. Lanthanum is a silver-white metal.

lan·yard /ˈlænyərd/ *noun* **1** a string that you wear around your neck or wrist for holding something: *A lanyard is useful for carrying your ID card.* ♦ *a whistle lanyard* **2** a piece of equipment that you wear around your neck to hold the wire of an IPOD™: *lanyard headphones for use with your iPod* **3** a rope used to fasten something, for example the sail of a ship

lap /læp/ *noun, verb*
● *noun* **1** [usually sing.] the top part of your legs that forms a flat surface when you are sitting down: *There's only one seat so you'll have to sit **on my lap**.* ♦ *She sat with her hands **in her lap**.* **2** one trip from the beginning to the end of a track used for running, a lane used for swimming, etc.: *the fastest lap on record* ♦ *She has completed six laps.* ♦ *Two people passed him on the final lap.* ♦ *to do a **victory lap*** (= go around the track again to celebrate winning) **3** a section of a trip, or of a piece of work, etc.: *They're off on the first lap of their round-the-world tour.* ♦ *We're almost finished with this proposal. We're **on the last lap** now.*
IDM **drop/dump sth in sb's lap** (*informal*) to make something the responsibility of another person: *They dropped the problem back in my lap.* **sth drops/falls into sb's lap** somebody has the opportunity to do something pleasant without having to make any effort: *My dream job just fell into my lap.* **in the lap of luxury** in easy, comfortable conditions, and enjoying the advantages of being rich
● *verb* (-pp-) **1** [I] (of water) to touch something gently and regularly, often making a soft sound: *The waves lapped*

around our feet. ◆ *the sound of water lapping against the boat*
2 [T] **~ sth** (of animals) to drink something with quick
movements of the tongue **3** [T] **~ sb** (in a race) to pass
another runner on a track who is one or more laps behind
you **4** [T] **~ sth (over sth)** to fold something partly over
itself or something else to form layers: *Lap the two pieces of
fabric over each other to form a pocket.*
PHRV **lap sth↔'up 1** (*informal*) to accept or receive
something with great enjoyment, without thinking about
whether it is good, true, or sincere: *It's a terrible movie but
audiences everywhere are lapping it up.* ◆ *She simply lapped up
all the compliments.* **2** to drink all of something with great
enjoyment: *The calf lapped up the bucket of milk.*

lap·a·ros·co·py /ˌlæpəˈrɑskəpi/ *noun* (pl. **lap·a·ros·co·pies**)
(*medical*) an examination of the inside of the body using a
tube-shaped instrument that can be put through the wall of
the ABDOMEN ▶ **lap·a·ro·scop·ic** /ˌlæpərəˈskɑpɪk/ *adj.*:
laparoscopic surgery

lap·a·rot·o·my /ˌlæpəˈrɑtəmi/ *noun* (pl. **lap·a·rot·o·mies**)
(*medical*) a cut in the ABDOMEN in order to perform an
operation or an examination

'lap belt *noun* a type of SEAT BELT that goes across your
waist

lap·dog (also **'lap dog**) /'læpdɔg/ *noun* **1** a pet dog that is
small enough to be carried **2** (*disapproving*) a person who is
under the control of another person or group

la·pel /ləˈpɛl/ *noun* one of the two front parts of the top of a
coat or jacket that are joined to the COLLAR and are folded
back ⟳ picture at CLOTHES

lap·i·dar·y /'læpəˌdɛri/ *adj.* **1** (*formal*) (especially of written
language) elegant and exact **SYN** CONCISE: *in lapidary style*
2 (*technical*) connected with stones and the work of cutting
and polishing them

lap·is laz·u·li /ˌlæpəs ˈlæzəli; -ˈlæʒəli/ *noun* [U] a bright blue
stone, used in making jewelry

lap·sang sou·chong /ˌlɑpsaŋ ˈsutʃaŋ; ˌlæpsæn-; -ˈsuʃaŋ/
noun [U] a type of tea that has a taste like smoke

lapse /læps/ *noun, verb*
● *noun* **1** a small mistake, especially one that is caused by
forgetting something or by being careless: *a lapse of
concentration/memory* ◆ *A momentary lapse in the final set cost
her the match.* **2** a period of time between two things that
happen **SYN** INTERVAL: *After a lapse of six months we met
again.* **3** an example or period of bad behavior from
someone who normally behaves well
● *verb* **1** [I] (of a contract, an agreement, etc.) to be no longer
valid because the period of time that it lasts has come to an
end: *She allowed her membership to lapse.* **2** [I] to gradually
become weaker or come to an end **SYN** EXPIRE: *His
concentration lapsed after a few minutes.* **3** [I] **~ (from sth)** to
stop believing in or practicing your religion: *He lapsed from
Judaism when he was a student.* ▶ **lapsed** *adj.* [only before
noun]: *a lapsed subscription* ◆ *lapsed faith* ◆ *a lapsed Catholic*
PHRV **'lapse into sth 1** to gradually pass into a worse or
less active state or condition: *to lapse into unconsciousness/a
coma* ◆ *She lapsed into silence again.* **2** to start speaking or
behaving in a different way, often one that is less acceptable: *He soon lapsed back into his old ways.*

lap·top /'læptɑp/ (also **'laptop com'puter**) *noun* a small
computer that can work with a battery and be easily carried
⟳ picture at COMPUTER **SYN** NOTEBOOK ⟳ compare
DESKTOP COMPUTER, NETBOOK, SUBNOTEBOOK

lar·ce·ny /'lɑrsəni/ *noun* [U, C] (pl. **lar·ce·nies**) (*law*) the crime
of stealing something from someone; an occasion when
this takes place **SYN** THEFT: *The couple were charged with
larceny.* ⟳ see also GRAND LARCENY, PETTY LARCENY

larch /lɑrtʃ/ *noun* [C, U] a tree with sharp pointed leaves that
fall in winter and hard dry fruit called CONES

lard /lɑrd/ *noun, verb*
● *noun* [U] a firm white substance made from the melted fat
of pigs that is used in cooking

● *verb* **~ sth** to put small pieces of fat on or into something
before cooking it
PHRV **'lard sth with sth** [usually passive] (often *disapproving*) to include a lot of a particular kind of word or
expressions in a speech or in a piece of writing: *His
conversation was larded with Russian proverbs.*

lard·er /'lɑrdər/ *noun* a closet or small room in a house,
used for storing food, especially in the past **SYN** PANTRY

large 🔑 /lɑrdʒ/ *adj.* (**larg·er, larg·est**)
1 big in size or quantity: *a large area/family/house/car/
appetite* ◆ *a large number of people* ◆ *very large sums of money*
◆ *He's a very large child for his age.* ◆ *A large proportion of elderly
people live alone.* ◆ *Women usually do the larger share of the
housework.* ◆ *Brazil is the world's largest producer of coffee.*
◆ *Who's the rather large (= fat) lady in the hat?* **2** (*abbr.* L) used
to describe one size in a range of sizes of clothes, food,
products used in the house, etc.: *small, medium, large*
3 wide in range and involving many things: *a large and
complex issue* ◆ *Some drugs are being used on a much larger
scale than previously.* ◆ *If we look at the larger picture of the
situation, the differences seem slight.* ⟳ note at BIG ▶ **large-
ness** *noun* [U]
IDM **at large 1** (used after a noun) as a whole; in general:
the opinion of the public at large **2** (of a dangerous person or
animal) not captured; free: *Her killer is still at large.* **by and
large** used when you are saying something that is
generally, but not completely, true: *By and large, I enjoyed
my high school years.* ⟳ language bank at GENERALLY **in
large part** | **in large measure** (*formal*) to a great extent:
Their success is due in large part to their determination. **(as)
large as life** (*humorous*) used to show surprise at seeing
someone or something: *I turned around and there was my
favorite movie actor standing right next to me, (as) large as life.*
larger than life looking or behaving in a way that is more
interesting or exciting than other people, and so is likely to
attract attention: *He's a larger-than-life character.*
SYN FLAMBOYANT **IDM** see LOOM *v.*, WRIT

large·ly 🔑 /'lɑrdʒli/ *adv.*
to a great extent; mostly or mainly: *the manager, who is
largely responsible for the team's victory* ◆ *It was largely a
matter of trial and error.* ◆ *He resigned largely because of the
stories in the media.*

'large-scale *adj.* [usually before noun] **1** involving many
people or things, especially over a wide area: *large-scale
development* ◆ *the large-scale employment of women* **2** (of a
map, model, etc.) drawn or made to a scale that shows a
small area of land or a building in great detail **ANT** SMALL-
SCALE

lar·gesse (also **lar·gess**) /lɑrˈdʒɛs; -ˈʒɛs/ *noun* [U] (*formal or
humorous*) the act or quality of being generous with money;
money that you give to people who have less than you: *She
is not noted for her largesse* (= she is not generous). ◆ *to dispense
largesse to the poor*

larg·ish /'lɑrdʒɪʃ/ *adj.* (*informal*) fairly large

lar·go /'lɑrgoʊ/ *adv., adj., noun* (from *Italian, music*)
● *adv., adj.* (used as an instruction) in a slow, serious way
● *noun* (pl. **lar·gos**) a piece of music to be performed in a
slow, serious way

lar·i·at /'læriət/ *noun* a LASSO

lark /lɑrk/ *noun* **1** a small brown bird with a pleasant song
⟳ see also SKYLARK **2** [usually sing.] (*informal*) a thing that
you do for fun or as a joke: *The boys didn't mean any harm—
they just did it as a lark.*

lark·spur /'lɑrkspər/ *noun* [C, U] a tall garden plant with
blue, pink, or white flowers growing up its STEM

lar·va /'lɑrvə/ *noun* (pl. **lar·vae** /-vi/) an insect at the stage
when it has just come out of an egg and looks like a short fat
WORM ⟳ picture at ANIMAL ▶ **lar·val** /'lɑrvl/ *adj.* [only
before noun]: *an insect in its larval stage*

la·ryn·ge·al /ləˈrɪndʒəl; -dʒiəl/ *adj.* (*anatomy, phonetics*)
related to or produced by the larynx

lar·yn·gi·tis /ˌlærənˈdʒaɪtəs/ *noun* [U] an infection of the larynx that makes speaking painful or difficult

lar·ynx /ˈlærɪŋks/ *noun* (*pl.* **la·ryn·ges** /ləˈrɪndʒiːz/ or **la·rynx·es**) (*anatomy*) the area at the top of the throat that contains the VOCAL CORDS **SYN** VOICE BOX

la·sa·gna (also **lasagne**) /ləˈzænyə/ *noun* **1** [U] large flat pieces of PASTA **2** [U, C] an Italian dish made from layers of lasagna, finely chopped meat and/or vegetables, and tomato sauce

las·civ·i·ous /ləˈsɪviəs/ *adj.* (*formal, disapproving*) feeling or showing strong sexual desire: *a lascivious person* ◆ *lascivious thoughts* ▶ **las·civ·i·ous·ly** *adv.* **las·civ·i·ous·ness** *noun* [U]

la·ser /ˈleɪzər/ *noun* a device that gives out light in which all the waves OSCILLATE (= change direction and strength) together, typically producing a very strong line of light that can be used for cutting metal, in medical operations, etc.: *a laser beam* ◆ *a laser navigation device* ◆ *The bar codes on the products are read by lasers.* ◆ *a laser show* (= laser used as entertainment) ◆ *She had laser surgery on her eye.*

la·ser·disc (also **laser disc**) /ˈleɪzərˌdɪsk/ *noun* a plastic disk like a large CD on which large amounts of information, such as video or music, can be stored, and which can be read by a laser BEAM

ˈlaser ˌgun *noun* a piece of equipment that uses a laser BEAM to read a BAR CODE or to find out how fast a vehicle or other object is moving

ˈlaser ˌprinter *noun* a printer that produces good quality printed material by means of a laser BEAM

lash /læʃ/ *verb, noun*
• *verb* **1** [I, T] to hit someone or something with great force **SYN** POUND: + *adv./prep.* *The rain lashed at the windows.* ◆ *~ sth Huge waves lashed the shore.* ⊃ thesaurus box at BEAT **2** [T] *~ sb/sth* to hit a person or an animal with a WHIP, rope, stick, etc. **SYN** BEAT **3** [T] *~ sb/sth* to criticize someone or something in a very angry way **SYN** ATTACK **4** [T] *~ sth + adv./prep.* to fasten something tightly to something else with ropes: *Several logs were lashed together to make a raft.* ◆ *During the storm everything on deck had to be lashed down.* **5** [I, T] *~ (sth)* to move or to move something quickly and violently from side to side: *The crocodile's tail was lashing furiously from side to side.*
PHR V ˌlash ˈout (at sb/sth) **1** to suddenly try to hit someone: *She suddenly lashed out at the boy.* **2** to criticize someone in an angry way: *In a bitter article he lashed out at his critics.*
• *noun* **1** = EYELASH: *her long dark lashes* **2** a hit with a WHIP, given as a form of punishment: *They each received 20 lashes for stealing.* ◆ (*figurative*) *to feel the lash of someone's tongue* (= to be spoken to in an angry and critical way) **3** the thin leather part at the end of a WHIP

lash·ing /ˈlæʃɪŋ/ *noun* **1** an act of hitting someone with a WHIP as a punishment: (*figurative*) *He was given a severe tongue-lashing* (= angry criticism). **2** [usually pl.] a rope used to fasten something tightly to something else

Las·sa fe·ver /ˌlæsə ˈfivər; ˌlɑsə-/ *noun* [U] a serious disease, usually caught from RATS and found especially in W. Africa

las·si /ˈlæsi; ˈlʌsi/ *noun* [U] a drink made from YOGURT and water

las·si·tude /ˈlæsəˌtud/ *noun* [U] (*formal*) a state of feeling very tired in mind or body; lack of energy

las·so *noun, verb*
• *noun* /ˈlæsoʊ/ (*pl.* **las·sos** or **-oes, las·soes**) a long rope with one end tied into a LOOP that is used for catching horses, cows, etc.
• *verb* *~ sth* to catch an animal using a lasso

last¹ /læst/ *det., adv., noun, verb* ⊃ see also LAST²
• *det.* **1** happening or coming after all other similar things or people: *We caught the last bus home.* ◆ *It's the last house on the left.* ◆ *She was last to arrive.* **2** [only before noun] most recent: *last night/Tuesday/month/summer/year* ◆ *her last book* ◆ *This last point is crucial.* ◆ *The last time I saw him was in*

May. **3** [only before noun] only remaining **SYN** FINAL: *This is our last bottle of water.* ◆ *He knew this was his last hope of winning.* **4** used to emphasize that someone or something is the least likely or suitable: *The last thing she needed was more work.* ◆ *He's the last person I'd trust with a secret.*
IDM **be on your/its last legs** to be going to die or stop functioning very soon; to be very weak or in bad condition **the Monday, week, month, etc. before last** the Monday, week, etc. just before the most recent one; two days, weeks, etc. ago: *I haven't seen him since the summer before last.* **every last…** every person or thing in a group; all of something: *I remember absolutely every last detail.* **every/sb's last penny** the only remaining money: *They spent their last penny on that house, and it turned out to be a good investment.* **have the last laugh** to be successful when you were not expected to be, making your opponents look stupid or silly **your/the last gasp** the point at which you/something can no longer continue living, fighting, existing, etc. ⊃ see also LAST-GASP **the last minute/moment** the latest possible time before an important event: *They changed their plans at the last minute.* ◆ *Don't leave your decision to the last moment.* **a/your last resort** the person or thing you rely on when everything else has failed: *I've tried everyone else and now you're my last resort.* **the last word (in sth)** the most recent, fashionable, advanced, etc. thing: *These apartments are the last word in luxury.* ⊃ more at ANALYSIS, BREATH, FAMOUS, LONG, MAN, STRAW, THING, WEEK, WORD
• *adv.* **1** after anyone or anything else; at the end: *He came in last in the race.* ◆ *They arrived last of all.* **2** most recently: *When did you see him last?* ◆ *I saw him last/I last saw him in New York two years ago.* ◆ *They last won the cup in 2006.*
IDM **last but not least** used when mentioning the last person or thing of a group, in order to say that they are not less important than the others: *Last but not least, I'd like to thank all the catering staff.* ⊃ more at FIRST, LAUGH
• *noun* **the last** (*pl.* **the last**) **1** the person or thing that comes or happens after all other similar people or things: *Sorry I'm late—am I the last?* ◆ *They were the last to arrive.* **2** *~ of sth* the only remaining part or items of something: *These are the last of our apples.*
IDM **at (long) last** after much delay, effort, etc.; in the end **SYN** FINALLY: *At last we're home!* ◆ *At long last the check arrived.* ⊃ note at LASTLY **hear/see the last of sb/sth** to hear/see someone or something for the last time: *That was the last I ever saw of her.* ◆ *Unfortunately, I don't think we've heard the last of this affair.* **the last I heard** used to give the most recent news you have about someone or something: *The last I heard he was still working at the garage.* **next/second to last** the one before the last one: *She finished second to last.* **to/till the last** until the last possible moment, especially until death: *He died protesting his innocence to the last.* ⊃ more at BREATHE, FIRST
• *verb* **1** [I] (not used in the progressive tenses) to continue for a particular period of time: *The meeting only lasted (for) a few minutes.* ◆ *Each game lasts about an hour.* ◆ *How long does the play last?* **2** [I, T] to continue to exist or to function well: *This weather won't last.* ◆ *He's making a big effort now, and I hope it lasts.* ◆ *~ sb These shoes should last you till next year.* **3** [I, T] to survive something or manage to stay in the same situation, despite difficulties: *She won't last long in that job.* ◆ *~ sth Doctors say that she probably won't last the night* (= she will probably die before the morning). ◆ *He was injured early on and didn't last the inning.* **4** [I, T] to be enough for someone to use, especially for a particular period of time: *Will the coffee last till next week?* ◆ *~ sb (sth) We've got enough food to last us (for) three days.*

| t tea | ţ butter | d did | k cat | g got | tʃ chin | dʒ June | f fall |

last? ♦ *The movie lasted over two hours.* **Last** does not always need an expression of time: *His annoyance won't last.* **Last** is also used to say that you have enough of something: *We have enough money to last until the end of the month.*

■ **Take** is used to talk about the amount of time you need in order to go somewhere or do something. It must be used with an expression of time: *It takes (me) at least an hour to get home from work.* ♦ *How long will the flight take?* ♦ *The water took forever to boil.*

last² /læst/ *noun* a block of wood or metal shaped like a foot, used in making and repairing shoes ⊃ see also LAST¹

ˌlast ˈcall *noun* the last opportunity for people to buy drinks in a bar before it closes

ˌlast-ˈditch *adj.* [only before noun] used to describe a final attempt to achieve something, when there is not much hope of succeeding: *a heart transplant was a last-ditch attempt to save her.*

ˌlast-ˈgasp *adj.* [only before noun] done at the last possible moment

last·ing /ˈlæstɪŋ/ *adj.* [usually before noun] continuing to exist or to have an effect for a long time: *Her words left a lasting impression on me.* ♦ *I formed several lasting friendships at college.* ♦ *The training was of no lasting value.* ⊃ see also LONG-LASTING ▶ **last·ing·ly** *adv.*

the ˌLast ˈJudgment *noun* [sing.] = JUDGMENT DAY

last·ly /ˈlæstli/ *adv.* **1** used to introduce the final point that you want to make **SYN** FINALLY: *Lastly, I'd like to ask you about your plans.* ⊃ language bank at FIRST **2** at the end; after all the other things that you have mentioned: *Lastly, add the lemon juice.*

WHICH WORD?

lastly ♦ at last

■ **Lastly** is used to introduce the last in a list of things or the final point you are making: *Lastly, I would like to thank my parents for all their support.*

■ **At last** is used when something happens after a long time, especially when there has been some difficulty or delay: *At last, after twenty hours on the boat, they arrived at their destination.* You can also use **finally**, **eventually**, or **in the end** with this meaning, but not **lastly**.

ˌlast-ˈminute *adj.* [usually before noun] done, decided, or organized just before something happens or before it is too late: *a last-minute vacation*

ˈlast name (also sur·name) *noun* your family name (written last in English names) ⊃ compare FAMILY NAME

the ˌlast ˈrites *noun* [pl.] a Christian religious ceremony that a priest performs for, and in the presence of, a dying person: *to administer the last rites to someone* ♦ *to receive the last rites*

lat. *abbr.* (in writing) LATITUDE

latch /lætʃ/ *noun, verb*
● *noun* a small metal bar that is used to fasten a door or a gate. You raise it to open the door, and drop it into a metal hook to fasten it: *He lifted the latch and opened the door.*
● *verb* ~ sth to fasten something with a latch
PHR V ˌlatch ˈon (to sth) | ˌlatch ˈonto sth (*informal*) to understand an idea or what someone is saying: *It was a difficult concept to grasp, but I soon latched on.* ˌlatch ˈon (to sb/sth) | ˌlatch ˈonto sb/sth (*informal*) **1** to become attached to someone or something: *antibodies that latch onto germs* **2** to join someone and stay in their company, especially when they would prefer that you not be with them **3** to develop a strong interest in something: *She always latches on to the latest craze.*

latch·key /ˈlætʃki/ *noun* a key for the front or the outer door of a house, etc.

ˈlatchkey ˌchild (also ˈlatchkey ˌkid) *noun* (usually *disapproving*) a child who is at home alone after school because both parents are at work

late /leɪt/ *adj., adv.*
● *adj.* (lat·er, lat·est) **1** [only before noun] near the end of a period of time, a person's life, etc.: *in the late afternoon* ♦ *in late summer* ♦ *She married in her late twenties* (= when she was 28 or 29). ♦ *In later life he started playing golf.* ♦ *The school was built in the late 1970s.* **ANT** EARLY **2** [not usually before noun] arriving, happening, or done after the expected, arranged, or usual time: *I'm sorry I'm late.* ♦ *She's late for work every day.* ♦ *My flight was an hour late.* ♦ *We apologize for the late arrival of this train.* ♦ *Because of the cold weather the crops are later this year.* ♦ *Interest will be charged for late payment.* ♦ *Here is a late news flash.* **ANT** EARLY **3** near the end of the day: *Let's go home—it's getting late.* ♦ *Look at the time—it's much later than I thought.* ♦ *What are you doing up at this late hour?* ♦ *What is the latest appointment you can give me?* ♦ *I've had too many late nights recently* (= when I've gone to bed very late). **ANT** EARLY **4** [only before noun] (of a person) no longer alive: *her late husband* ♦ *the late Paul Newman* ▶ **late·ness** *noun* [U]: *Despite the lateness of the hour, the children were not in bed.* ⊃ see also LATER, LATEST
IDM be too late happening after the time when it is possible to do something: *It's too late to save her now.* ♦ *Buy now before it's too late.*
● *adv.* (comparative lat·er, no superlative) **1** after the expected, arranged, or usual time: *I got up late.* ♦ *Can I stay up late tonight?* ♦ *She has to work late tomorrow.* ♦ *Most stores are open later on Thursdays.* ♦ *She married late.* ♦ *The birthday card arrived three days late.* **2** near the end of a period of time, a person's life, etc.: *late in March/the afternoon* ♦ *It happened late last year.* ♦ *As late as* (= as recently as) *the 1950s, tuberculosis was still a fatal illness.* ♦ *He became an author late in life.* **3** near the end of the day: *There's a good movie on late.* ♦ *Late that night, there was a knock at the door.* ♦ *Share prices fell early on but rose again late in the day.* **ANT** EARLY ⊃ see also LATER
IDM better late than never (*saying*) used especially when you, or someone else, arrive/arrives late, or when something such as success happens late, to say that this is better than not coming or happening at all late in the game/day (*disapproving*) after the time when an action could be successful: *He finally came up with some great ideas, but it was much too late in the game to be of any use.* late of... (*formal*) until recently working or living in the place mentioned: *Professor Jones, late of Stanford University* of late (*formal*) recently: *I haven't seen him of late.* too late after the time when it is possible to do something successfully: *She arrived too late to get a ticket.* ♦ *I realized the truth too late.* ⊃ more at SOON

GRAMMAR

late ♦ lately

■ **Late** and **lately** are both adverbs, but **late** is used with similar meanings to the adjective **late**, whereas **lately** can only mean "recently": *We arrived two hours late.* ♦ *I haven't heard from him lately.* **Lately** is usually used with a perfect tense of the verb.
■ Look also at the idioms **be too late** (at the adjective) and **too late** (at the adverb).

late·com·er /ˈleɪtkʌmər/ *noun* a person who arrives late

late·ly /ˈleɪtli/ *adv.*
recently; in the recent past: *Have you seen her lately?* ♦ *It's only lately that she's been well enough to go out.* ♦ *I haven't been sleeping well lately.* ⊃ note at LATE

ˌlate-ˈnight *adj.* [only before noun] happening late at night; available after other things finish: *a late-night movie* ♦ *late-night shopping*

la·tent /ˈleɪtnt/ *adj.* [usually before noun] existing, but not yet very noticeable, active, or well developed: *latent disease* ◆ *These children have a huge reserve of latent talent.* ▶ **la‑ten‑cy** /ˈleɪtnsi/ *noun* [U]

lat·er 🔊 /ˈleɪtər/ *adv.*, *adj.*
● *adv.* **1** at a time in the future; after the time you are talking about: *See you later.* ◆ *I met her again three years later.* ◆ *His father died later that year.* ◆ *We're planning a road trip for later in the year.* ◆ *She later became a doctor.* **2 Later!** (*informal*) a way of saying goodbye, used by young people: *Later, guys!* **IDM later on** (*informal*) at a time in the future; after the time you are talking about: *I'm going out later on.* ◆ *Much later on, she realized what he had meant.* **not/no later than...** by a particular time and not after it: *Please arrive no later than 8 o'clock.*
● *adj.* [only before noun] **1** coming after something else or at a time in the future: *This is discussed in more detail in a later chapter.* ◆ *The game has been postponed to a later date.* **2** near the end of a period of time, life, etc.: *the later part of the seventeenth century* ◆ *She found happiness in her later years.* **IDM see SOON**

lat·er·al /ˈlætərəl/ *adj.*, *noun*
● *adj.* [usually before noun] (*technical*) connected with the side of something or with movement to the side: *the lateral branches of a tree* ◆ *lateral eye movements* ▶ **lat·er·al·ly** *adv.*
● *noun* (also ˌlateral ˈconsonant) (*phonetics*) a consonant sound that is produced by placing a part of the tongue against the PALATE so that air flows around it on both sides, for example /l/ in *lie*

latest 🔊 /ˈleɪtəst/ *adj.*, *noun*
● *adj.* [only before noun] the most recent or newest: *the latest unemployment figures* ◆ *the latest craze/fashion/trend* ◆ *her latest novel* ◆ *Have you heard the latest news?*
● *noun* [U] **the latest** (*informal*) the most recent or the newest thing or piece of news: *This is the latest in robot technology.* ◆ *Have you heard the latest?* **IDM at the latest** no later than the time or the date mentioned: *Applications should be in by next Monday at the latest.*

la·tex /ˈleɪtɛks/ *noun* [U] **1** a thick white liquid that is produced by some plants and trees, especially rubber trees. Latex becomes solid when exposed to air, and is used to make medical products: *latex gloves* **2** an artificial substance similar to this that is used to make paints, glues, etc.

lath /læθ/ *noun* (*pl.* **laths** /læðz; læθs/) a thin narrow strip of wood that is used to support PLASTER (= material used for covering walls) on the inside walls and the ceilings of buildings

lathe /leɪð/ *noun* a machine that shapes pieces of wood or metal by holding and turning them against a fixed cutting tool

lath·er /ˈlæðər/ *noun*, *verb*
● *noun* [U, sing.] a white mass of small bubbles that is produced by mixing soap with water **IDM get into a lather | work yourself into a lather** (*informal*) to get anxious or angry about something, especially when it is not necessary
● *verb* **1** [T] ~ **sth** to cover something with lather: *I lathered my face and started to shave.* **2** [I] to produce lather: *Soap does not lather well in hard water.*

Lat·in /ˈlætn/ *noun*, *adj.*
● *noun* **1** [U] the language of ancient Rome and the official language of its empire **2** [C] a person from countries where languages that have developed from Latin, such as Spanish, Portuguese, Italian, or French, are spoken **3** [U] music of a kind that came originally from Latin America, typically with strong dance rhythms
● *adj.* **1** of or in the Latin language: *Latin poetry* **2** connected with or typical of the countries or peoples using languages developed from Latin, such as Spanish, Portuguese, Italian, or French: *a Latin temperament*

La·ti·na /ləˈtinə/ *noun* a woman or girl, especially one who

is living in the U.S., who comes from Latin America, or whose family came from there ⟳ compare **LATINO** ▶ **Latina** *adj.* [usually before noun]

ˌLatin Aˈmerica *noun* [U] the parts of the Americas in which Spanish or Portuguese is the main language ⟳ note at **AMERICAN** ⟳ compare **SOUTH AMERICA**

Lat·in·ate /ˈlætnˌeɪt/ *adj.* (of words or language) from Latin, or relating to Latin: *formal Latinate terms*

La·ti·no /ləˈtinoʊ/ *noun* (*pl.* **La·ti·nos**) a person, especially one who is living in the U.S., who comes from Latin America, or whose family came from there ⟳ compare **CHICANO** ▶ **Latino** *adj.* [usually before noun]

lat·i·tude /ˈlætəˌtud/ *noun* **1** (*abbr.* **lat.**) [U] the distance of a place north or south of the EQUATOR (= the line around the world dividing north and south), measured in degrees ⟳ picture at **EARTH** ⟳ compare **LONGITUDE** **2 latitudes** [pl.] a region of the world that is a particular distance from the EQUATOR: *the northern latitudes* **3** [U] (*formal*) freedom to choose what you do or the way that you do it **SYN LIBERTY**

la·trine /ləˈtrin/ *noun* a toilet in a camp, etc., especially one made by digging a hole in the ground

lat·te /ˈlɑteɪ/ (also **caffè latte**) *noun* (from *Italian*) a drink made by adding a small amount of strong coffee to a glass or cup of FROTHY steamed milk

lat·ter 🔊 /ˈlætər/ *adj.*
1 the latter... used to refer to the second of two things, people, or groups that have just been mentioned, or the last in a list: *The latter point is the most important.* ⟳ compare **FORMER 2** *pron.* the second of two things, people, or groups that have just been mentioned, or the last in a list: *He presented two solutions. The latter seems much better.* ◆ *The town has a concert hall and two theaters. The latter were both built in the 1950s.* ⟳ compare **FORMER 3** nearer to the end of a period of time than the beginning: *the latter half of the year*

ˈlatter-ˌday *adj.* [only before noun] being a modern version of a person or thing in the past: *a latter-day Robin Hood*

lat·ter·ly /ˈlætərli/ *adv.* (*formal*) **1** most recently: *Latterly his painting has shown a new freedom of expression.* **2** toward the end of a period of time: *Her health declined rapidly and latterly she never left the house.*

lat·tice /ˈlætəs/ *noun* [U, C] (also **lat·tice·work** [U]) a structure that is made of strips of wood or metal that cross over each other with spaces shaped like a diamond between them, used, for example, as a fence; any structure or pattern like this: *a low wall of stone latticework* ◆ *a lattice of branches* ▶ **lat·ticed** /ˈlætəst/ *adj.*

ˌlattice ˈwindow (also ˌlatticed ˈwindow) *noun* a window with small pieces of glass shaped like diamonds in a FRAMEWORK of metal strips

laud /lɔd/ *verb* ~ **sb/sth** (*formal*) to praise someone or something

laud·a·ble /ˈlɔdəbl/ *adj.* (*formal*) deserving to be praised or admired, even if not really successful **SYN COMMENDABLE**: *a laudable aim/attempt* ▶ **laud·a·bly** /-bli/ *adv.*

lau·da·num /ˈlɔdn·əm/ *noun* [U] a drug made from OPIUM. In the past, people used to take laudanum to reduce pain and anxiety, and to help them sleep.

laud·a·to·ry /ˈlɔdəˌtɔri/ *adj.* (*formal*) expressing praise or admiration

laugh 🔊 /læf/ *verb*, *noun*
● *verb* [I, T] to make the sounds and movements of your face that show you are happy or think something is funny: *to laugh loudly/aloud/out loud* ◆ ~ **(at/about sth)** *You never laugh at my jokes!* ◆ *The show was hilarious—I couldn't stop laughing.* ◆ *She always makes me laugh.* ◆ *He burst out laughing* (= suddenly started laughing). ◆ *She laughed to cover her nervousness.* ◆ *I told him I was worried but he laughed scornfully.* ◆ **+ speech** *"You're crazy!" she laughed.* **IDM don't make me laugh** (*informal*) used to show that you think what someone has just said is impossible or

stupid: *"Will your dad lend you the money?" "Don't make me laugh!"* **he who laughs last laughs best/longest** (*saying*) used to tell someone not to be too proud of their present success; in the end another person may be more successful **laugh all the way to the bank** (*informal*) to make a lot of money easily and feel very pleased about it **laugh in sb's face** to show in a very obvious way that you have no respect for someone **laugh sb/sth out of town** (*informal*) to completely reject an idea, a story, etc. that you think is not worth taking seriously at all **laugh until you cry** to laugh so long and hard that there are tears in your eyes **laugh up your sleeve (at sb/sth)** (*informal*) to be secretly amused about something **laugh your head off** to laugh very loudly and for a long time **not know whether to laugh or cry** (*informal*) to be unable to decide how to react to a bad or unfortunate situation **you have/you've got to laugh** (*informal*) used to say that you think there is a funny side to a situation: *Well, I'm sorry you lost your shoes, but you have to laugh, don't you?*

PHR V **'laugh at sb/sth** to make someone or something seem stupid or not serious by making jokes about them/it **SYN** RIDICULE: *Everybody laughs at my accent.* ◆ *She is not afraid to laugh at herself* (= not be too serious about herself). **laugh sth↔'off** (*informal*) to try to make people think that something is not serious or important, especially by making a joke about it: *He laughed off suggestions that he was going to resign.*

VOCABULARY BUILDING

different ways of laughing

- **cackle** to laugh in a loud unpleasant way, especially in a high voice
- **chuckle** to laugh quietly, especially because you are thinking about something funny
- **giggle** to laugh in a silly way because you are amused, embarrassed, or nervous
- **guffaw** to laugh noisily
- **roar** to laugh very loudly
- **snicker/snigger** to laugh in a quiet unpleasant way, especially at something rude or at someone's problems or mistakes
- **titter** to laugh quietly, in a nervous or embarrassed way

You can also be **convulsed with laughter** or **dissolve into laughter** when you find something very funny. People might also **shriek with laughter** or **howl with laughter**.

● *noun* **1** [C] the sound you make when you are amused or happy: *to give a laugh* ◆ *a short/nervous/hearty laugh* ◆ *His first joke got the biggest laugh of the night.* ⊃ see also BELLY LAUGH **2 a laugh** [sing.] (*informal*) an enjoyable and amusing occasion or thing that happens: *And he didn't realize it was you? What a laugh!*

IDM **do sth for a laugh/for laughs** to do something for fun as a joke: *I just did it for a laugh, but it got out of hand.* **have a (good) laugh (about sth)** to find something amusing: *I was angry at the time but we had a good laugh about it afterward.* ⊃ more at BARREL, LAST[1]

laugh·a·ble /'læfəbl/ *adj.* silly or ridiculous, and not worth taking seriously **SYN** ABSURD ▶ **laugh·a·bly** /-bli/ *adv.*

laugh·ing /'læfɪŋ/ *adj.* showing AMUSEMENT or happiness: *his laughing blue eyes* ◆ *laughing faces*
IDM **be no laughing matter** to be something serious that you should not joke about ⊃ more at DIE *v.*

'laughing ˌgas *noun* [U] (*informal*) = NITROUS OXIDE

laugh·ing·ly /'læfɪŋli/ *adv.* **1** in an amused way: *He laughingly agreed.* **2** used to show that you think a particular word is not at all a suitable way of describing something and therefore seems ridiculous: *I finally reached what we laughingly call civilization.*

'laughing ˌstock *noun* [usually sing.] a person that everyone laughs at because they have done something stupid: *I can't wear that! I'd be the laughing stock of my school.*

ˌlaugh-out-'loud *adj.* (*abbr.* LOL) [only before noun] (*informal*) extremely funny: *a laugh-out-loud moment* ◆ *The best scenes in the movie are laugh-out-loud funny.* **HELP** The abbreviation **LOL** is also used in text messages, e-mails, or Internet chat, to show that you think something is funny or do not mean it seriously.

laugh·ter /'læftər/ *noun* [U] the act or sound of laughing: *to roar with laughter* ◆ *tears/gales/howls/shrieks of laughter* ◆ *to burst/dissolve into laughter* ◆ *a house full of laughter* (= with a happy atmosphere)

'laugh track *noun* a recording of laughter played during a television show to make it sound as though the audience is laughing

launch 🔈 /lɔntʃ/ *verb, noun*

● *verb* **1** ~ sth to start an activity, especially an organized one: *to launch an appeal/an investigation/a campaign* ◆ *to launch an attack/invasion* **2** ~ sth to make a product available to the public for the first time: *a party to launch his latest novel* ◆ *The new model will be launched in July.* **3** ~ sth to put a ship or boat into the water, especially one that has just been built: *The Navy is to launch a new warship today.* ◆ *The lifeboat was launched immediately.* **4** ~ sth to send something such as a SPACECRAFT, weapon, etc. into space, into the sky, or through water: *to launch a communications satellite* ◆ *to launch a missile/rocket/torpedo* **5** ~ yourself at, from, etc. sth | ~ yourself forward, etc. to jump forward with a lot of force: *Without warning he launched himself at me.* **6** ~ sth (*computing*) to start a computer program: *You can launch programs and documents from your keyboard.*

PHR V **'launch into sth** | **'launch yourself into sth** to begin something in an enthusiastic way, especially something that will take a long time: *He launched into a lengthy account of his career.* **ˌlaunch 'out** to do something new in your career, especially something more exciting: *It's time for me to launch out on my own.*

● *noun* **1** [usually sing.] the action of launching something; an event at which something is launched: *the successful launch of the spacecraft* ◆ *a product launch* ◆ *The official launch date is in May.* **2** a large boat with a motor

launch·er /'lɔntʃər/ *noun* (often in compounds) a device that is used to send a ROCKET, a MISSILE, etc. into the sky: *a rocket launcher*

'launch pad (also **'launching ˌpad**) *noun* a platform from which a SPACECRAFT, etc. is sent into the sky: (*figurative*) *She regards the job as a launch pad for her career in the media.*

laun·der /'lɔndər/ *verb* **1** ~ sth (*formal*) to wash, dry, and iron clothes, etc.: *freshly laundered sheets* **2** ~ sth to move money that has been obtained illegally into foreign bank accounts or legal businesses so that it is difficult for people to know where the money came from

Laun·dro·mat™ /'lɔndrəˌmæt/ *noun* a place where you can wash and dry your clothes in machines that you operate by putting in coins

laun·dry 🔈 /'lɔndri/ *noun* (*pl.* **laun·dries**)
1 [U] clothes, sheets, etc. that need washing, that are being washed, or that have been washed recently: *a pile of clean/dirty laundry* ◆ *a laundry basket/room* **2** [U, sing.] the process or the job of washing clothes, sheets, etc.: *to do the laundry* ◆ *The hotel has a laundry service.* **3** [C] a business or place where you send sheets, clothes, etc. to be washed **IDM** see AIR *v.*

'laundry ˌlist *noun* (*informal*) a long list of things: *a laundry list of problems*

Laur·a·sia /lɔ'reɪʒə/ *noun* [sing.] (*geology*) a very large area of land that existed in the northern HEMISPHERE millions of years ago. It was made up of the present N. America, Greenland, Europe, and most of Asia.

lau·re·ate /ˈlɔriət/ *noun* **1** a person who has been given an official honor or prize for something important they have achieved: *a Nobel laureate* **2** = POET LAUREATE

lau·rel /ˈlɔrəl/ *noun* **1** [U, C] a bush with dark, smooth, shiny leaves that remain on the bush and stay green through the year **2 laurels** [pl.] honor and praise given to someone because of something that they have achieved
IDM rest/sit on your laurels (usually *disapproving*) to feel so satisfied with what you have already achieved that you do not try to do any more

laurel wreath *noun* a ring of laurel leaves that were worn on the head in the past as a sign of victory

la·va /ˈlɑvə/ *noun* [U] **1** hot liquid rock that comes out of a VOLCANO ⊃ picture at VOLCANO: *molten lava* **2** this type of rock when it has cooled and become hard

la·vage /ləˈvɑʒ/ *noun* (*medical*) the process of washing a space inside the body such as the stomach or COLON

lava lamp *noun* an electric lamp that contains a liquid in which a colored substance like oil moves up and down in shapes that keep changing ⊃ picture at LIGHT

lav·a·to·ry /ˈlævəˌtɔri/ *noun* (*pl.* lav·a·to·ries) a room with a toilet and a sink, especially on a plane

lav·en·der /ˈlævəndər/ *noun* [U] **1** a garden plant or bush with bunches of purple flowers with a sweet smell **2** the flowers of the lavender plant that have been dried, used for making sheets, clothes, etc. smell nice: *lavender oil* **3** a pale purple color

lav·ish /ˈlævɪʃ/ *adj., verb*
● *adj.* **1** large in amount, or impressive, and usually costing a lot of money SYN EXTRAVAGANT: *lavish gifts/costumes/celebrations* ◆ *They lived a very lavish lifestyle.* ◆ *They rebuilt the house on an even more lavish scale than before.* **2** ~ (with/in sth) giving or doing something generously: *He was lavish in his praise for her paintings.* ▶ **lav·ish·ly** *adv.: lavishly illustrated*
● *verb*
PHR V **lavish sth on/upon sb/sth** to give a lot of something, often too much, to someone or something: *She lavishes most of her attention on her youngest son.*

law 🔑 /lɔ/ *noun*

▷ SYSTEM OF RULES **1** also **the law** [U] the whole system of rules that everyone in a country or society must obey: *If they entered the building they would be breaking the law.* ◆ *In this city, it is against the law to sleep in an abandoned building.* ◆ *Defense attorneys can use any means within the law to get their client off.* ◆ *Anyone who operates a motor vehicle is required by law to have a driver's license.* ◆ *The reforms recently became law.* ◆ *Do not think you are above the law* (= think that you cannot be punished by the law). ◆ *the need for better law enforcement* ◆ (*humorous*) *Kate's word was law in the Brown household.* ⊃ collocations at JUSTICE **2** [U] a particular branch of the law: *corporate/international/tax, etc. law* ⊃ see also CANON LAW, CASE LAW, CIVIL LAW, COMMON LAW, CRIMINAL LAW, STATUTE LAW
▷ ONE RULE **3** [C] a rule that deals with a particular crime, agreement, etc.: ~ (against sth) *a law against the hiring of illegal immigrants* ◆ ~ (on sth) *The government has introduced some tough new laws on food hygiene.* ◆ *strict gun laws* ◆ *a federal/state law* ◆ *to pass a law* (= officially make it part of the system of laws) ◆ (*informal*) *There ought to be a law against it!* ⊃ see also BYLAW, LEMON LAW
▷ SUBJECT/PROFESSION **4** [U] the study of the law as a subject at a university, etc.; the profession of being a lawyer: *Jane is studying law.* ◆ *He's in law school.* ◆ *What made you go into law?* ◆ *a law firm*
▷ POLICE **5** **the law** [sing.] used to refer to the police and the legal system: *Jim is always getting into trouble with the law.*
▷ OF ORGANIZATION/ACTIVITY **6** [C] one of the rules that control an organization or activity: *the laws of the Roman Catholic Church* ◆ *The first law of kung fu is to defend yourself.* ◆ *the laws of tennis*
▷ OF GOOD BEHAVIOR **7** [C] a rule for good behavior or how you should behave in a particular place or situation: *moral laws* ◆ *the unspoken law of the street*
▷ IN BUSINESS/NATURE/SCIENCE **8** [C] the fact that something always happens in the same way in an activity or in nature SYN PRINCIPLE: *the law of supply and demand* ◆ *the law of gravity* **9** [C] a scientific rule that someone has stated to explain a natural process: *the first law of thermodynamics* ⊃ see also LEGAL, LEGALIZE, LEGISLATE, MURPHY'S LAW, PARKINSON'S LAW
IDM **be a law unto yourself** to behave in an independent way and ignore rules or what other people want you to do **law and order** a situation in which people obey the law and behave in a peaceful way: *The government struggled to maintain law and order.* ◆ *After the riots, the military was brought in to restore law and order.* ◆ *They claim to be the party of law and order.* **the law of averages** the principle that one thing will happen as often as another if you try enough times: *Keep looking, and by the law of averages you'll find a job sooner or later.* **the law of the jungle** a situation in which people are prepared to harm other people in order to succeed **lay down the law** to tell someone with force what they should or should not do **take the law into your own hands** to do something illegal in order to punish someone for doing something wrong, instead of letting the police deal with them **there's no law against sth | sth is not against the law** (*informal*) used to tell someone who is criticizing you that you are not doing anything wrong: *I'll sing if I want to—there's no law against it.* ⊃ more at LETTER *n.*, POSSESSION, RULE *n.*, WRONG *adj.*

law-a·bid·ing *adj.* obeying and respecting the law: *law-abiding citizens*

law·break·er /ˈlɔˌbreɪkər/ *noun* a person who does not obey the law ▶ **law·break·ing** *noun* [U]

law court *noun* = COURT OF LAW

law·ful /ˈlɔfl/ *adj.* (*formal*) allowed or recognized by law; legal: *his lawful heir* ANT UNLAWFUL ▶ **law·ful·ly** /-fəli/ *adv.: a lawfully elected governor* **law·ful·ness** *noun* [U]

law·less /ˈlɔləs/ *adj.* **1** (of a country or an area) where laws do not exist or are not obeyed: *lawless streets* ◆ *the lawless days of the Wild West* **2** (of people or their actions) without respect for the law SYN WILD: *lawless gangs* ▶ **law·less·ness** *noun* [U]

law·mak·er /ˈlɔˌmeɪkər/ *noun* a person in government who makes the laws of a country SYN LEGISLATOR

law·man /ˈlɔmən; -mæn/ *noun* (*pl.* law·men /-mən; -mɛn/) an officer responsible for keeping law and order, especially a SHERIFF

lawn /lɔn/ *noun* **1** [C] an area of ground covered in short grass in a yard or park: *In summer we have to mow the lawn twice a week.* ⊃ picture at HOUSE **2** [U] a type of fine cotton or LINEN cloth used for making clothes

lawn bowling (also **bowls**) *noun* [U] a game played on an area of very smooth grass, in which players take turns to roll BOWLS as near as possible to a small ball

lawn chair *noun* a chair that can be folded and that people use when sitting outside

lawn mower (also **mow·er**) *noun* a machine for cutting the grass on a LAWN ⊃ picture at TOOL

lawn sign *noun* a board that people put outside their house in order to advertise something or to show that they support a particular politician or political party

law·ren·ci·um /lɔˈrɛnsiəm/ *noun* [U] (*symb.* **Lr**) a chemical element. Lawrencium is a RADIOACTIVE metal.

law·suit /ˈlɔsut/ (also **suit**) *noun* a claim or complaint against someone that a person or an organization can make in court: *He filed a lawsuit against his record company.*

law·yer 🔑 /ˈlɔɪər; ˈlɔyər/ *noun*

a person who is trained and qualified to advise people about the law and to represent them in court, and to write legal documents

MORE ABOUT

lawyers

- **Lawyer** is a general term for a person who is qualified to advise people about the law, to prepare legal documents for them, and/or to represent them in a court of law.
- **Attorney** is a more formal word used for a **lawyer** and is used especially in job titles: *district attorney*
- **Counsel** is the formal legal word used for a lawyer who is representing someone in court: *counsel for the prosecution*
- After a lawyer passes the exam allowing him or her to represent someone in court in a particular state, you say that he or she has **passed the bar** or is a **member of the bar** in that state.

lax /læks/ *adj.* **1** (*disapproving*) not strict, severe, or careful enough about work, rules, or standards of behavior **SYN** SLACK, CARELESS: *lax security/discipline* ♦ *a lax attitude to health and safety regulations* **2** (*phonetics*) (of a speech sound) produced with the muscles of the speech organs relaxed **ANT** TENSE ▶ **lax·i·ty** /ˈlæksəti/ *noun* [U]

lax·a·tive /ˈlæksətɪv/ *noun* a medicine, food, or drink that makes someone empty their BOWELS easily ▶ **laxative** *adj.*

lay /leɪ/ *verb, adj., noun* ⊃ see also LIE[1]
• *verb* (laid, laid /leɪd/)
▷ PUT DOWN/SPREAD **1** [T] to put someone or something in a particular position, especially when it is done gently or carefully: *~ sb/sth (+ adv./prep.)* *She laid the baby down gently on the bed.* ♦ *He laid a hand on my arm.* ♦ *The horse laid back its ears.* ♦ *Relatives laid wreaths on the grave.* ♦ *~ sb/sth + adj.* *The cloth should be laid flat.* **HELP** Some speakers confuse this sense of **lay** with **lie**, especially in the present and progressive tenses. However, **lay** has an object and **lie** does not: *She was lying on the beach.* ♦ *She was laying on the beach.* ♦ *Why don't you lie on the bed?* ♦ *Why don't you lay on the bed?* In the past tenses **laid** (from *lay*) is often wrongly used for **lay** or **lain** (from *lie*): *She had lain there all night.* ♦ *She had laid there all night.* **2** [T] *~ sth (down)* to put something down, especially on the floor, ready to be used: *to lay a carpet/cable/pipe* ♦ *The foundations of the house are being laid today.* ♦ (*figurative*) *They had laid the groundwork for future development.* **3** [T] to spread something on something; to cover something with a layer of something: *~ A (on/over B)* *Before they started they laid newspaper on the floor.* ♦ *The grapes were laid to dry on racks.* ♦ *~ B with A* *The floor was laid with newspaper.*
▷ EGGS **4** [T, I] *~ (sth)* if a bird, an insect, a fish, etc. lays eggs, it produces them from its body: *The cuckoo lays its eggs in other birds' nests.* ♦ *newly laid eggs* ♦ *The hens are not laying well* (= not producing many eggs).
▷ PRESENT PROPOSAL **5** [T] *~ sth + adv./prep.* to present a proposal, some information, etc. to someone for them to think about and decide on: *They laid their case before the judge.*
▷ DIFFICULT SITUATION **6** [T] *~ sth/sb + adv./prep.* (*formal*) to put someone or something in a particular position or state, especially a difficult or unpleasant one **SYN** PLACE: *to lay a responsibility/burden on someone* ♦ *to lay someone under an obligation to do something*
▷ WITH NOUNS **7** [T] *~ sth + adv./prep.* used with a noun to form a phrase that has the same meaning as the verb related to the noun: *to lay the blame on someone* (= to blame someone) ♦ *Our teacher lays great stress on good spelling* (= stresses it strongly).
▷ PLAN/TRAP **8** [T] *~ sth* to prepare something in detail: *to lay a trap for someone* ♦ *She began to lay her plans for her escape.* ♦ *Bad weather can upset even the best-laid plans.*
▷ FIRE **9** [T] *~ sth* to prepare a fire by arranging wood, sticks, or coal
▷ BET **10** [T] *~ sth* to bet money on something; to place a bet: *~ sth to lay a bet* ♦ *~ sth on sth* *She laid $100 on the favorite.*

IDM Idioms containing **lay** are at the entries for the nouns and adjectives in the idioms. For example, **lay something bare** is at **bare**.
PHR V ˌlay sthↄˈaˈside** (*formal*) **1** to put something on one side and not use it or think about it **SYN** SET ASIDE: *He laid aside his book and stood up.* ♦ (*figurative*) *Doctors have to lay their personal feelings aside.* **2** to keep something to use, or deal with later **SYN** PUT ASIDE: *They had laid money aside for their old age.* ˌlay sthↄˈdown to put something down or stop using it: *She laid the book down on the table.* ♦ *Both sides were urged to lay down their arms* (= stop fighting). ♦ *They laid down their tools and walked out.* ˌlay sthↄˈin/ˈup to collect and store something to use in the future: *to lay in food supplies* ˌlay ˈinto sb/sth (*informal*) to attack someone violently with blows or words: *His parents really laid into him for wasting so much money.* ˌlay ˈoff | ˌlay ˈoff sb/sth (*informal*) used to tell someone to stop doing something: *Lay off me will you—it's got nothing to do with me.* ♦ *~ doing sth Lay off bullying Jack.* ˌlay sbↄˈoff to stop employing someone because there is not enough work for them to do ⊃ related noun LAYOFF ˌlay ˈoff sth (*informal*) to stop using something: *I think you'd better lay off fatty foods for a while.* ˌlay sth ˈon sb (*informal*) to make someone have to deal with something unpleasant or difficult: *Stop laying a guilt trip on me* (= making me feel guilty). ˌlay sbↄˈout **1** to knock someone unconscious **2** to prepare a dead body to be buried ˌlay sthↄˈout **1** to spread something out so that it can be seen easily or is ready to use: *He laid the map out on the table.* ♦ *+ adj. Lay the material out flat.* **2** [often passive] to plan how something should look and arrange it in this way: *The gardens were laid out with lawns and flower beds.* ♦ *a well laid out magazine* ⊃ related noun LAYOUT **3** to present a plan, an argument, etc. clearly and carefully **SYN** SET OUT: *All the terms and conditions are laid out in the contract.* **4** (*informal*) to spend money **SYN** FORK OUT: *I had to lay out a fortune on a new car.* ⊃ related noun OUTLAY ˌlay ˈover (at/in…) to stay somewhere for a short time during a long journey ⊃ related noun LAYOVER ⊃ see also STOP OVER ˌlay sb ˈup [usually passive] if someone is **laid up**, they are unable to work, etc. because of an illness or injury: *She's laid up with a broken leg.* ˌlay sth↔ˈup **1** = LAY STH IN **2** to stop using a ship or other vehicle while it is being repaired
• *adj.* [only before noun] **1** not having expert knowledge or professional qualifications in a particular subject: *His book explains the theory for the lay public.* **2** not in an official position in a church: *a lay preacher* ⊃ see also LAYMAN, LAYPERSON, LAYWOMAN
• *noun* (*old use*) a poem that was written to be sung, usually telling a story
IDM the lay of the land **1** the way the land in an area is formed and what physical characteristics it has **2** the way a situation is now and how it is likely to develop

lay·a·way /ˈleɪəˌweɪ/ *noun* [U] a system of buying goods in a store, where the customer pays a small amount of the price for an article and the store keeps the goods until the full price has been paid

lay·er /ˈleɪər/ **AWL** *noun, verb*
• *noun* **1** a quantity or thickness of something that lies over a surface or between surfaces: *A thin layer of dust covered everything.* ♦ *How many layers of clothing are you wearing?* **2** a level or part within a system or set of ideas: *There were too many layers of management in the company.* ♦ *the layers of meaning in the poem*
• *verb* [often passive] *~ sth* to arrange something in layers: *Layer the potatoes and onions in a dish.*

lay·ette /leɪˈɛt/ *noun* a set of clothes and other things for a new baby

lay·man /ˈleɪmən/ *noun* (*pl.* lay·men /-mən/) (also **lay·per·son**) **1** a person who does not have expert knowledge of a particular subject: *a book written for professionals and laymen alike* ♦ *to explain something in layman's terms* (= in simple language) **2** a person who is a member of a church but is not a priest or member of the CLERGY ⊃ see also LAYWOMAN

lay·off /ˈleɪɔf/ noun **1** an act of making people unemployed because there is no more work left for them to do **2** a period of time when someone is not working or not doing something that they normally do regularly: *an eight-week layoff with a broken leg*

lay·out /ˈleɪaʊt/ noun [usually sing.] the way in which the parts of something such as the page of a book, a garden, or a building are arranged: *the layout of streets* ◆ *the magazine's attractive new page layout*

lay·o·ver /ˈleɪˌoʊvər/ noun a short stay somewhere between two parts of a trip **SYN** STOPOVER: *We had a three-hour layover in Houston.*

lay·per·son /ˈleɪˌpərsn/ noun (pl. **lay·peo·ple**) a LAYMAN or LAYWOMAN: *The layperson cannot really understand mental illness.*

ˈlay-up noun (in GOLF) a shot made from a difficult position to a position that will allow an easier next shot

lay·up /ˈleɪʌp/ noun (in basketball) a shot made with one hand from under or beside the BASKET

lay·wom·an /ˈleɪˌwʊmən/ noun (pl. **lay·wom·en** /-ˌwɪmən/) a woman who is a member of a church but is not a priest or a member of the CLERGY **⊃** see also LAYMAN, LAYPERSON

Laz·a·rus /ˈlæzərəs/ noun used to refer to someone who improves or starts to be successful again after a period of failure **ORIGIN** From the story of **Lazarus** in the Bible. He was a man who died but was then brought back to life by Jesus Christ.

laze /leɪz/ verb [I] to relax and do very little: *We lazed by the pool all day.* ◆ *~ around I spent the afternoon just lazing around.* **SYN** LOUNGE
  PHR V **ˈlaze sth↔away** to spend time relaxing and doing very little: *They lazed away the long summer days.*

la·zy 🔖 /ˈleɪzi/ adj. (la·zi·er, la·zi·est)
1 (*disapproving*) unwilling to work or be active; doing as little as possible **SYN** IDLE: *He was not stupid, just lazy.* ◆ *I was feeling too lazy to go out.* **2** not involving much energy or activity; slow and relaxed: *We spent a lazy day on the beach.* **3** (*disapproving*) showing a lack of effort or care: *a lazy piece of work* **4** (*literary*) moving slowly **SYN** TORPID: *the lazy river*
  ▶ **la·zi·ly** /-zəli/ adv.: *She woke up and stretched lazily.*
  la·zi·ness /-zinəs/ noun [U]

la·zy·bones /ˈleɪziˌboʊnz/ noun [sing.] (*old-fashioned, informal*) used to refer to a lazy person

ˌlazy ˈeye noun an eye that does not see well because it is not used enough

la·zy Su·san /ˌleɪzi ˈsuzn/ noun a round plate or TRAY on a base, which can be spun around so that the objects on it can be easily reached

lb. abbr. (pl. **lbs.** or **lb.**) a pound in weight, equal to about 454 grams (from Latin "libra"). The are 16 ounces in a pound.

l.c. /ˌɛl ˈsi/ abbr. **1** in the piece of text that has been quoted (from Latin "loco citato") **2** (in writing) LETTER OF CREDIT **3** (in writing) LOWERCASE

LCD /ˌɛl si ˈdi/ abbr. **1** liquid crystal display (a way of showing information in electronic equipment. An electric current is passed through a special liquid and numbers and letters can be seen on a small screen.): *a pocket calculator with LCD* ◆ *an LCD screen* **2** LEAST/LOWEST COMMON DENOMINATOR

lea /li/ noun (*literary*) an open area of land covered in grass

leach /litʃ/ verb (*technical*) **1** [I] *~ (from sth) (into sth)* | *~ out/away* (of chemicals, minerals, etc.) to be removed from soil, etc. by water passing through it: *Nitrates leach from the soil into rivers.* **2** [T] *~ sth (from sth) (into sth)* | *~ sth out/away* (of a liquid) to remove chemicals, minerals, etc. from soil: *The nutrient is quickly leached away.*

lead¹ 🔖 /lid/ verb, noun **⊃** see also LEAD²
● **verb** (led, led /lɛd/)
▷ **SHOW THE WAY** **1** [I, T] to go with or in front of a person or an animal to show the way or to make them go in the right direction: *If you lead, I'll follow.* ◆ *~ sb/sth + adv./prep. He led us out onto the grounds.* ◆ *The receptionist led the way to the boardroom.* ◆ *She led the horse back into the stable.* ◆ (*figurative*) *I tried to lead the discussion back to the main issue.* **⊃** thesaurus box at TAKE
▷ **CONNECT TWO THINGS** **2** [I] *~ from/to sth (to/from sth)* to connect one object or place to another: *the pipe leading from the top of the water tank* ◆ *The wire led to a speaker.*
▷ **OF ROAD/PATH/DOOR** **3** [I, T] to go in a particular direction or to a particular place: *+ adv./prep. A path led up the hill.* ◆ *Which door leads to the yard?* ◆ *~ sb + adv./prep. The trail led us through the woods.*
▷ **CAUSE** **4** [I] *~ to sth* to have something as a result **SYN** RESULT IN: *Eating too much sugar can lead to health problems.* **⊃** language bank at CAUSE **5** [T] to be the reason why someone does or thinks something: *~ sb (to sth) What led you to this conclusion?* ◆ *He's too easily led* (= easily persuaded to do or think something). ◆ *~ sb to do sth This has led scientists to speculate on the existence of other galaxies.* ◆ *The situation is far worse than we had been led to believe.*
▷ **LIFE** **6** [T] *~ sth* to have a particular type of life: *to lead a quiet life/a life of luxury/a miserable existence*
▷ **BE BEST/FIRST** **7** [T, I] to be the best at something; to be in first place: *~ (sb/sth) (in sth) The department led the world in cancer research.* ◆ *We lead the way in space technology.* ◆ *~ (sb/sth) by sth The champion is leading (her nearest rival) by 18 seconds.*
▷ **BE IN CONTROL** **8** [T, I] *~ (sth)* to be in control of something; to be the leader of something: *to lead an expedition* ◆ *to lead a discussion* ◆ *Who will lead the list of candidates in the next election?*
▷ **IN CARD GAMES** **9** [I, T] to play first; to play something as your first card: *It's your turn to lead.* ◆ *~ (with) sth to lead the ten of clubs/to lead with a club*
  IDM **lead sb by the nose** to make someone do everything you want; to control someone completely **lead sb down the garden path** to make someone believe something that is not true **SYN** MISLEAD **lead from the front** to take an active part in what you are telling or persuading others to do **lead (sb) nowhere** to have no successful result for someone: *This discussion is leading us nowhere.* **you can lead a horse to water, but you can't make it drink** (*saying*) you can give someone the opportunity to do something, but you cannot force them to do it if they do not want to **⊃** more at BLIND adj., LIFE, THING
  PHR V **lead ˈoff (from) sth** to start at a place and go away from it: *narrow streets leading off from the main square* **lead ˈoff** | **lead sth↔ˈoff** to start something: *Who would like to lead off the debate?* **lead sb ˈon** (*informal*) to make someone believe something that is not true, especially that you love them or find them attractive **lead ˈup to sth** to be an introduction to or the cause of something: *the weeks leading up to the final exam* ◆ *the events leading up to the strike* **lead with sth** **1** (of a newspaper) to have something as the main item of news **2** (in boxing) to use a particular hand to begin an attack: *to lead with your right/left*

● **noun**
▷ **FIRST PLACE** **1** **the lead** [sing.] the position ahead of everyone else in a race or competition: *She took the lead in the second lap.* ◆ *He has gone into the lead.* ◆ *The Democrats now appear to be in the lead.* ◆ *to hold/lose the lead* ◆ *The lead car is now three minutes ahead of the rest of the field.* **2** [sing.] *~ (over sb/sth)* the amount or distance that someone or something is in front of someone or something else **SYN** ADVANTAGE: *He managed to hold a lead of two seconds over his closest rival.* ◆ *The polls have given the incumbent a five-point lead.* ◆ *a commanding/comfortable lead* ◆ *to increase/widen your lead* ◆ *Miami lost their early two-point lead.*
▷ **EXAMPLE** **3** [sing.] an example or action for people to copy: *If one bank raises interest rates, all the others will follow their lead.* ◆ *If we take the lead in this* (= start to act), *others may follow.* ◆ *You go first. I'll take my lead from you.*
▷ **INFORMATION** **4** [C] a piece of information that may help to find out the truth or facts about a situation, especially a crime **SYN** CLUE: *The police will follow up all possible leads.*
▷ **ACTOR/MUSICIAN** **5** [C] the main part in a play, movie, etc.;

---

t tea   **ṭ** butter   **d** did   **k** cat   **g** got   **tʃ** chin   **dʒ** June   **f** fall the person who plays this part: *Who is playing the lead?* ♦ *the male/female lead* ♦ *a lead role* ♦ *the lead singer in a band*

lead² /lɛd/ *noun* ⊃ see also LEAD¹ **1** [U] (*symb.* **Pb**) a chemical element. Lead is a heavy, soft, gray metal, used especially in the past for water pipes or to cover roofs. **2** [C, U] the thin black part of a pencil that marks paper **IDM go over like a lead balloon** (*informal*) to be very unsuccessful; to not be accepted by people

lead·ed /'lɛdəd/ *adj.* [usually before noun] (of gasoline, metal, etc.) with lead² added to it **ANT UNLEADED**

lead·en /'lɛdn/ *adj.* (*literary*) **1** dull gray in color, like LEAD²: *leaden skies* **2** dull, heavy, or slow: *a leaden heart* (= because you are sad)

lead·er 🖉 /'lidər/ *noun*
1 a person who leads a group of people, especially the head of a country, an organization, etc.: *a political/spiritual, etc. leader* ♦ *the leader of the movement* ♦ *union leaders* ♦ *He was not a natural leader.* ♦ *She's a born leader.* **2** a person or thing that is the best, or in first place in a race, business, etc.: *She was among the leaders of the race from the start.* ♦ *The company is a world leader in electrical goods.* ⊃ see also MARKET LEADER

'leader ,board *noun* a sign showing the names and scores of the top players, especially in a GOLF competition

lead·er·less /'lidərləs/ *adj.* without a leader: *Her sudden death left the organization leaderless.*

lead·er·ship /'lidərˌʃɪp/ *noun* **1** [U] the state or position of being a leader: *a leadership contest* ♦ *The company thrived under his leadership.* **2** [U] the ability to be a leader or the qualities a good leader should have: *leadership qualities/ skills* ♦ *The organization is in need of strong leadership.* **3** [C] a group of leaders of a particular organization, etc.: *The party leadership is divided.*

lead-free /ˌlɛd 'fri/ *adj.* (of gasoline, paint, etc.) without any of the metal LEAD² added to it

lead guitar /ˌlid gɪˈtɑr/ *noun* [U] a GUITAR style that consists mainly of SOLOS and tunes rather than only CHORDS ⊃ compare RHYTHM GUITAR

lead-in /'lid ɪn/ *noun* an introduction to a subject, story, show, etc.

lead·ing¹ 🖉 /'lidɪŋ/ *adj.* [only before noun]
1 most important or most successful: *leading experts* ♦ *She was offered the leading role in the new TV series.* ♦ *He played a leading part in the negotiations.* **2** ahead of others in a race or contest: *She started the last lap just behind the leading group.* ♦ *These are the leading first-round scores.*

lead·ing² /'lɛdɪŋ/ *noun* [U] (*technical*) the amount of white space between lines of printed text

lead·ing edge /ˌlidɪŋ 'ɛdʒ/ *noun* **1** [sing.] the most important and advanced position in an area of activity, especially technology: *at the leading edge of scientific research* **2** [C] (*technical*) the front or forward edge of something, especially an aircraft ⊃ picture at PLANE
▶ ˌleading-ˈedge *adj.* [only before noun] **SYN CUTTING EDGE**: *leading-edge technology*

leading lady /ˌlidɪŋ 'leɪdi/, **leading man** /ˌlidɪŋ 'mæn/ *noun* the actor with the main female or male part in a play or movie

leading light /ˌlidɪŋ 'laɪt/ *noun* an important, active, or respected person in a particular area of activity: *She's one of the leading lights in the opera world.*

leading question /ˌlidɪŋ 'kwɛstʃən/ *noun* a question that you ask in a particular way in order to get the answer you want

lead-off /'lid ɔf/ *adj.* being the first of a series: *the lead-off track on the album*

lead shot /ˌlɛd 'ʃɑt/ *noun* = SHOT *n.* (3)

lead story /ˌlid 'stɔri/ *noun* the main or first item of news in a newspaper, magazine, or news broadcast

lead time /'lid taɪm/ *noun* the time between starting and completing a production process

leaf 🖉 /lif/ *noun, verb*
• *noun* (*pl.* **leaves** /livz/) **1** [C] a flat green part of a plant, growing from a STEM or branch or from the root: *lettuce/ cabbage/oak leaves* ♦ *The trees are just coming into leaf.* ♦ *the dead leaves of autumn* ⊃ collocations at LIFE ⊃ picture at TREE ⊃ see also BAY LEAF, FIG LEAF **2 -leaf, -leafed, -leaved** (in adjectives) having leaves of the type or number mentioned: *a four-leaf clover* ♦ *a broad-leaved plant* **3** [C] a sheet of paper, especially a page in a book ⊃ see also FLYLEAF, LOOSE-LEAF, OVERLEAF **4** [U] metal, especially gold or silver, in the form of very thin sheets: *gold leaf* **5** [C] a part of a table that can be lifted up or pulled into position in order to make the table bigger **IDM** see BOOK *n.*, NEW
• *verb*
PHR V 'leaf through sth to quickly turn over the pages of a book, etc. without reading them or looking at them carefully

leaf·less /'lifləs/ *adj.* having no leaves **SYN BARE**

leaf·let /'liflət/ *noun, verb*
• *noun* a printed sheet of paper or a few printed pages that are given free to advertise or give information about something **SYN BOOKLET, PAMPHLET**: *a leaflet on local places of interest*
• *verb* [I, T] ~ (sb/sth) to give out leaflets to people: *We did a lot of leafleting in the area.*

'leaf mold *noun* [U] soil consisting mostly of dead, decayed leaves

leaf·y /'lifi/ *adj.* (**leaf·i·er, leaf·i·est**) **1** having a lot of leaves: *Eat plenty of leafy green vegetables.* **2** (*approving*) (of a place) having a lot of trees and plants: *leafy suburbs* **3** made by a lot of leaves or trees: *We sat in the leafy shade of an oak tree.*

league 🖉 /lig/ *noun*
1 a group of sports teams who all play each other to find out which team is best: *major-league baseball* ♦ *The Dodgers were the league champions last season.* ⊃ see also MINOR-LEAGUE **2** (*informal*) a level of quality, ability, etc.: *As a painter, he is in a league of his own* (= much better than others). ♦ *They're in a different league from us.* ♦ *When it comes to cooking, I'm not in her league* (= she is much better than me). ♦ *A house like that is out of our league* (= too expensive for us). **3** a group of people or nations who have combined for a particular purpose **SYN ALLIANCE**: *the League of Nations* ♦ *a meeting of the League of Women Voters* ⊃ see also IVY LEAGUE **4** (*old use*) a unit for measuring distance, equal to about 3 miles or 4,000 meters
IDM in league (with sb) making secret plans with someone

leak /lik/ *verb, noun*
• *verb* **1** [I, T] to allow liquid or gas to get in or out through a small hole or crack: *a leaking pipe* ♦ *The roof was leaking.* ♦ ~ sth *The tank had leaked a small amount of water.* **2** [I] (of a liquid or gas) to get in or out through a small hole or crack in something: *Water had started to leak into the cellar.* **3** [T] ~ sth (to sb) to give secret information to the public, for example by telling a newspaper **SYN DISCLOSE**: *The contents of the report were leaked to the press.* ♦ *a leaked document*
PHR V ,leak 'out (of secret information) to become known to the public: *Details of the plan soon leaked out.*
• *noun* **1** a small hole or crack that lets liquid or gas flow in or out of something by accident: *a leak in the roof* ♦ *a leak in the gas line* **2** liquid or gas that escapes through a hole in something: *a gas leak* ♦ *oil leaks* ⊃ collocations at DECORATE **3** a deliberate act of giving secret information to the newspapers, etc.: *a leak to the press about government plans on tax reform* **4** (*slang*) an act of passing URINE from the body: *to have/take a leak* **IDM** see SPRING *v.*

leak·age /'likɪdʒ/ *noun* [C, U] an amount of liquid or gas escaping through a hole in something; an occasion when there is a leak: *a leakage of toxic waste into the ocean* ♦ *Check bottles for leakage before use.*

leak·y /'liki/ *adj.* (**leak·i·er, leak·i·est**) having holes or cracks that allow liquid or gas to escape: *a leaky roof*

lean 🔑 /lin/ *verb, adj., noun*
● **verb 1** [I] (+ *adv./prep.*) to bend or move from a vertical position: *I leaned back in my chair.* ♦ *The tower is leaning dangerously.* ♦ *A man was leaning out of the window.* **2** [I] to rest on or against something for support: ~ **against sth** *A shovel was leaning against the wall.* ♦ ~ **on sth** *She walked slowly, leaning on her son's arm.* **3** [T] ~ **sth against/on sth** to make something rest against something in a sloping position: *Can I lean my bike against the wall?* **IDM** see BACKWARD
PHR V 'lean on sb/sth 1 to depend on someone or something for help and support **SYN** RELY ON: *He leans heavily on his family.* **2** to try to influence someone by threatening them: *Lobbyists have been leaning on several members of Congress not to endorse the plan.* **'lean to/toward sth** to have a tendency to prefer something, especially a particular opinion or interest: *The U.K. leaned toward the U.S. proposal.*
● **adj.** (**lean·er, lean·est**) **1** (usually *approving*) (of people, especially men, or animals) without much flesh; thin and fit: *a lean, muscular body* ♦ *He was tall, lean, and handsome.* **2** (of meat) containing little or no fat **3** [usually before noun] (of a period of time) difficult and not producing much money, food, etc.: *a lean period* ♦ *The company recovered well after going through several lean years.* **4** (of organizations, etc.) strong and efficient because the number of employees has been reduced: *The changes made the company leaner and more competitive.*
IDM lean and mean efficient and using resources well with little waste: *a lean and mean organization* ▶ **lean·ness** /'linnəs/ *noun* [U]
● **noun** [U] the part of meat that has little or no fat

lean·ing /'linɪŋ/ *noun* [usually pl.] ~ (**toward(s) sth**) a tendency to prefer something or to believe in particular ideas, opinions, etc. **SYN** INCLINATION, TENDENCY: *a leaning toward comedy rather than tragedy* ♦ *a person with socialist leanings*

'lean-to *noun* (*pl.* **'lean-tos** /-tuz/) a small building with its roof leaning against the side of a large building, wall, or fence: *a lean-to garage*

leap /lip/ *verb, noun*
● **verb** (**leaped, leaped** or **leapt, leapt** /lɛpt/) **1** [I, I] to jump high or a long way: + **adv./prep.** *A dolphin leaped out of the water.* ♦ *We leaped over the stream.* ♦ ~ **sth** *The horse leaped a five-foot wall.* **2** [I] + **adv./prep.** to move or do something suddenly and quickly: *She leaped out of bed.* ♦ *He leaped across the room to answer the door.* ♦ *I leaped to my feet* (= stood up quickly). ♦ *They leaped into action* immediately. ♦ (*figurative*) *She was quick to leap to my defense* (= speak in support of me). ♦ *The photo seemed to leap off the page* (= it got your attention immediately). ♦ *His name leaped out at me* (= I saw it immediately). **3** [I] ~ (**in sth**) (**from…**) (**to…**) to increase suddenly and by a large amount **SYN** SHOOT UP: *Shares leaped in value yesterday.*
IDM look before you leap (*saying*) used to advise someone to think about the possible results or dangers of something before doing it ⊃ more at CONCLUSION, HEART
PHR V 'leap at sth to accept a chance or an opportunity quickly and with enthusiasm **SYN** JUMP AT: *I leaped at the chance to go to the Virgin Islands.*
● **noun 1** a long or high jump: *a leap of six meters* ♦ *She took a flying leap and landed on the other side of the stream.* ♦ (*figurative*) *His heart gave a sudden leap when he saw her.* ♦ (*figurative*) *Few people successfully make the leap from television to the movies.* **2** ~ (**in sth**) a sudden large change or increase in something: *a leap in profits* ⊃ see also QUANTUM LEAP
IDM by/in leaps and bounds very quickly; in large amounts: *Her health has improved by leaps and bounds.* **a leap**

in the dark an action or a risk that you take without knowing anything about the activity or what the result will be

leap·frog /'lipfrɔg; -frag/ *noun, verb*
● **noun** [U] a children's game in which players take turns to jump over the backs of other players who are bending down
● **verb** (**-gg-**) [T, I] ~ (**sb/sth**) to get to a higher position or rank by going past someone else or by missing some stages: ~ **over sb** *She leapfrogged over several of her colleagues to become vice president of the company after only a year.*

'leap year *noun* one year in every four years when February has 29 days instead of 28

learn 🔑 /lərn/ *verb*
1 [T, I] to gain knowledge or skill by studying, from experience, from being taught, etc.: ~ **sth** *to learn a language/a musical instrument/a skill* ♦ ~ **sth from sb/sth** *I learned a lot from my father.* ♦ ~ **sth from doing sth** *I learned a lot about basketball just from watching him play.* ♦ ~ (**about sth**) *She's very eager to learn about Japanese culture.* ♦ *The book is about how children learn.* ♦ ~ **to do sth** *He's learning to dance.* ♦ ~ **how, what, etc.…** *Today we learned how to use the new software.* **2** [I, T] to become aware of something by hearing about it from someone else **SYN** DISCOVER: ~ **of/about sth** *I learned of her arrival from a close friend.* ♦ ~ (**that**) … *We were very surprised to learn (that) she got married again.* ♦ ~ **who, what, etc.…** *We only learned who the new teacher was a few days ago.* ♦ ~ **sth** *How did they react when they learned the news?* ♦ **it is learned that…** *It has been learned that 500 jobs will be lost at the factory.* **3** [T] ~ **sth** to study and repeat something in order to be able to remember it **SYN** MEMORIZE: *We have to learn one of Hamlet's speeches for school tomorrow.* **4** [I, T] to gradually change your attitudes about something so that you behave in a different way: ~ (**from sth**) *I'm sure she'll learn from her mistakes.* ♦ ~ (**that**) … *He'll just have to learn (that) he can't always have his own way.* ♦ ~ **to do sth** *I soon learned not to ask too many questions.*
IDM learn (sth) the hard way to find out how to behave by learning from your mistakes or from unpleasant experiences, rather than from being told **learn your lesson** to learn what to do or not to do in the future because you have had a bad experience in the past ⊃ more at COST, LIVE[1], ROPE

different ways of learning
- **learn** *He's learning Spanish/to swim.*
- **study** *She studied chemistry for three years.* ♦ *I have to study for my test tomorrow.*
- **review** *In this class we'll review what we did last week.*
- **practice** *If you practice speaking English, you'll soon get better and better.*
- **rehearse** *We had only two weeks to rehearse the play.*

learn·ed *adj.* [usually before noun] **1** /'lərnəd/ (*formal*) having a lot of knowledge because you have studied and read a lot: *a learned professor* **2** /'lərnəd/ (*formal*) connected with or for learned people; showing and expressing deep knowledge **SYN** SCHOLARLY: *a learned journal* **3** /lərnd/ developed by training or experience; not existing at birth: *a learned skill*

learn·er /'lərnər/ *noun* **1** a person who is finding out about a subject or how to do something: *a slow/fast learner* ♦ *a dictionary for learners of English* ♦ *learner-centered teaching methods* **2** a person who is learning to drive a car

'learner's permit *noun* an official document that you must have when you start to learn to drive

learn·ing /'lərnɪŋ/ *noun* [U] **1** the process of learning something: *computer-assisted learning* ♦ *Last season was a learning experience for me.* ⊃ see also DISTANCE LEARNING

2 knowledge that you get from reading and studying: *a woman of great learning*

'learning ˌcurve *noun* the rate at which you learn a new subject or a new skill; the process of learning from the mistakes you make

'learning disaˌbility *noun* [usually pl.] a mental problem that people may have from birth, or that may be caused by illness or injury, that affects their ability to learn things

lease /liːs/ *noun, verb*
- **noun** a legal agreement that allows you to use a car, a building, a piece of equipment, or some land for a period of time, usually in return for a regular payment: *to sign a lease on an apartment* ◆ *The lease expires/runs out next year.* ◆ *Under the terms of the lease, you have to pay maintenance charges.* **IDM** **a (new) lease on life** the chance to live or last longer, or with a better quality of life: *Since her hip operation she has a new lease on life.*
- **verb** to use or let someone use something, especially property or equipment, in exchange for rent or a regular payment **SYN** RENT: *~ sth We lease all our computer equipment.* ◆ *~ sth from sb They lease the land from a local farmer.* ◆ *~ sb sth A local farmer leased them the land.* ◆ *~ sth (out) (to sb) Parts of the building are leased out to tenants.*

lease·back /ˈliːsbæk/ *noun* [U] (*law*) the process of allowing the former owner of a property to continue to use it if they pay rent to the new owner; a legal agreement where this happens

leash /liːʃ/ *noun, verb*
- **noun** a long piece of leather, chain, or rope used for holding and controlling a dog: *All dogs must be kept on a leash in public places.* **IDM** **see STRAIN**
- **verb** *~ sth* to control an animal, especially a dog, with a LEASH

least 🔑 /liːst/ *det., pron., adv.*
- **det., pron.** usually **the least** smallest in size, amount, degree, etc.: *He's the best teacher, even though he has the least experience.* ◆ *She never had the least idea what to do about it.* ◆ *He gave (the) least of all toward the wedding present.* ◆ *How others see me is the least of my worries* (= I have more important things to worry about). ◆ *It's the least I can do to help* (= I feel I should do more). **IDM** **at the (very) least** used after amounts to show that the amount is the lowest possible: *It'll take a year, at the very least.* **not in the least** not at all: *Really, I'm not in the least tired.* ◆ *"Do you mind if I put the television on?" "No, not in the least."* ➡ **more at SAY**
- **adv.** to the smallest degree: *He always turns up just when you least expect him.* ◆ *She chose the least expensive of the hotels.* ◆ *I never hid the truth, least of all from you.* **IDM** **at least 1** not less than: *It'll cost at least 500 dollars.* ◆ *She must be at least 40.* ◆ *Cut the grass at least once a week in summer.* ◆ *I've known her at least as long as you have.* **2** used to add a positive comment about a negative situation: *She may be slow but at least she's reliable.* **3** even if nothing else is true or you do nothing else: *You could at least listen to what he says.* ◆ *Well, at least they weren't bored.* **4** used to limit or make what you have just said less definite **SYN** ANYWAY: *They seldom complained—officially at least.* ◆ *It works, at least I think it does.* **not least** especially: *The documentary caused a lot of bad feeling, not least among the workers whose lives it described.* ➡ **more at LAST¹**

ˌleast ˌcommon deˈnominator (also ˌlowest ˌcommon deˈnominator) *noun* **1** (*mathematics*) the smallest number that the bottom numbers of a group of FRACTIONS can be divided into exactly **2** (*disapproving*) something that is simple enough to seem interesting to, or to be understood by, the highest number of people in a particular group; the sort of people who are least intelligent or accept something that is of low quality: *The school syllabus seems aimed at the least common denominator.*

ˌleast ˌcommon ˈmultiple (also ˌlowest ˌcommon ˈmultiple) *noun* (*mathematics*) the smallest number that a group of numbers can be divided into exactly

least·ways /ˈliːstweɪz/ (also **least·wise** /ˈliːstwaɪz/) *adv.* (*informal*) at least: *It isn't cheap to get there, leastways not at this time of year.*

leath·er 🔑 /ˈleðər/ *noun*
[U, C] material made by removing the hair or fur from animal skins and preserving the skins using special processes: *a leather jacket* ◆ *The soles are made of leather.* ◆ *a leather-bound book* ➡ **see also CHAMOIS LEATHER, PATENT LEATHER**

leath·er·back /ˈleðərbæk/ (also ˌleatherback ˈturtle) *noun* a very large sea TURTLE with a shell that looks like leather

leath·er·ette /ˌleðəˈret/ *noun* [U] an artificial material that looks and feels like leather

leath·er·y /ˈleðəri/ *adj.* that looks or feels hard and tough like leather: *leathery skin*

leave 🔑 /liːv/ *verb, noun*
- **verb** (left, left /left/)
- ▸ PLACE/PERSON **1** [I, T] to go away from a person or a place: *Come on, it's time we left.* ◆ *~ for... The plane leaves for Dallas at 12:35.* ◆ *~ sth I hate leaving home.* ◆ *The plane leaves LAX at 12:35.*
- ▸ HOME/JOB/SCHOOL **2** [I, T] to stop living at a place, belonging to a group, working for an employer, etc.: *My assistant threatened to leave if I didn't pay her more.* ◆ *~ sth He left college after his freshman year.*
- ▸ WIFE/HUSBAND **3** [T] *~ sb (for sb)* to leave your wife, husband, or partner permanently: *She's leaving him for another man.*
- ▸ SOMETHING TO DO LATER **4** [T] to not do something or deal with something immediately: *~ sth Leave the dishes—I'll do them later.* ◆ *~ sth until... Why do you always leave everything until the last minute?*
- ▸ SOMEONE OR SOMETHING IN CONDITION/PLACE **5** [T] to make or allow someone or something to remain in a particular condition, place, etc.: *~ sb/sth (+ adj.) Leave the door open, please.* ◆ *The bomb blast left 25 people dead.* ◆ *~ sb/sth doing sth Don't leave her waiting outside in the rain.* ◆ *~ sb/sth to do sth Leave the rice to cook for 20 minutes.* **6** [T] to make something happen or remain as a result: *~ sth Red wine leaves a stain.* ◆ *~ sb with sth She left me with the impression that she was unhappy with her job.* ◆ *~ sb sth I'm afraid you leave me no choice.* **7** *be left* [T] to remain to be used, sold, etc.: *Is there any coffee left?* ◆ *How many tickets do you have left?* ◆ *~ of sth* (*figurative*) *They are fighting to save what is left of their business.* ◆ *~ to sb The only course of action left to me was to notify her employer.* **8** [T] to go away from a place without taking something or someone with you: *~ sth/sb (+ adv./prep.) I left my bag on the bus.* ◆ *~ sth/sb behind Don't leave any of your belongings behind.* ◆ *He wasn't feeling well, so we had to leave him behind.*
- ▸ MATHEMATICS **9** [T] *~ sth* to have a particular amount remaining: *Seven from ten leaves three.*
- ▸ AFTER DEATH **10** [T] to give something to someone when you die **SYN** BEQUEATH: *~ sth (to sb) She left $1 million to her daughter.* ◆ *~ sb sth She left her daughter $1 million.* **11** [T] *~ sb* to have family remaining after your death: *He leaves a wife and two children.*
- ▸ RESPONSIBILITY TO SOMEONE **12** [T] to allow someone to take care of something: *~ sb/sth + adv./prep. You can leave the cooking to me.* ◆ *She left her assistant in charge.* ◆ *Leave it with me—I'm sure I can figure it out.* ◆ *"Where should we eat?" "I'll leave it entirely (up) to you (= you can decide)."* ◆ *After making a big mess, they left me with the cleanup.* ◆ *~ sb/ sth to do sth I was left to cope on my own.*
- ▸ DELIVER **13** [T] to deliver something and then go away: *~ sth (for sb) Someone left this note for you.* ◆ *~ sb sth Someone left you this note.*
- **IDM** Most idioms containing **leave** are at the entries for the nouns and adjectives in the idioms. For example, **leave someone in the lurch** is at **lurch**.

| i see | ɪ sit | ɛ ten | æ cat | ɑ hot | ɔ saw | ʊ put | u too | 853 |

leave it at that (*informal*) to say or do nothing more about something: *We'll never agree, so let's just leave it at that.* ➔ more at TAKE

PHR V ,leave sth↔a'side to not consider something: *Leaving the expense aside, do we actually need a second car?* ,leave sb/sth be'hind **1** [usually passive] to make much better progress than someone: *Our manufacturers are being left behind in the race for new markets.* **2** to leave a person, place, or state permanently: *She knew that she had left childhood behind.* ➔ see also LEAVE(8) ,leave 'off (*informal*) to stop doing something: *Start reading from where you left off last time.* ♦ ~ doing sth *He left off playing the piano to answer the door.* ,leave sb/sth↔'off (sth) to not include someone or something on a list, etc.: *You left off a zero.* ♦ *We left him off the list.* ,leave sb/sth 'out (of sth) to not include or mention someone or something in something: *Leave me out of this argument, please.* ♦ *He wasn't invited to the party and was feeling very left out.* ♦ *She left out an "m" in "accommodation."* be ,left 'over (from sth) to remain when all that is needed has been used: *There was lots of food left over.* ➔ related noun LEFTOVER

● **noun** [U] **1** a period of time when you are allowed to be away from work for a vacation or for a special reason: *to take a month's paid/unpaid leave* ♦ *soldiers home on leave* ♦ *to be on maternity leave* ♦ *How much annual leave do you get?* ➔ see also COMPASSIONATE LEAVE, SICK LEAVE **2** (*formal*) official permission to do something: *to be absent without leave* ♦ ~ to do sth *The court granted him leave to appeal against the sentence.* ♦ *She asked for a leave of absence* (= permission to be away from work) *to attend a funeral.*
IDM by/with your leave (*formal*) with your permission take leave of your senses (*old-fashioned*) to start behaving as if you are crazy take (your) leave (of sb) (*formal*) to say goodbye: *With a nod and a smile, she took leave of her friends.* without a by your leave; without so much as a by your leave (*old-fashioned*) without asking permission; rudely ➔ more at BEG

-leaved /livd/ ➔ LEAF

leav·en /'lɛvn/ *noun*, *verb*
● (also **leav·en·ing**) *noun* [U] a substance, especially YEAST, that is added to bread before it is cooked to make it rise: (*figurative*) *A few jokes add leavening to a boring speech.*
● *verb* [often passive] ~ sth (with sth) (*formal*) to make something more interesting or cheerful by adding something to it: *Her speech was leavened with a touch of humor.*

leaves pl. of LEAF

'leave-,taking *noun* [U, C, usually sing.] (*formal*) the act of saying goodbye **SYN** FAREWELL

leav·ings /'livɪŋz/ *noun* [pl.] (*old-fashioned*) something that you leave because you do not want it, especially food

lech·er /'lɛtʃər/ *noun* (*disapproving*) a man who is always thinking about sex and looking for sexual pleasure ▶ **lech·er·y** /'lɛtʃəri/ *noun* [U]

lec·i·thin /'lɛsəθən/ *noun* [U] a natural substance found in animals, plants, and in egg YOLKS. Lecithin is used as an ingredient in some foods.

lec·tern /'lɛktərn/ (also **po·di·um**) *noun* a stand for holding a book, notes, etc. when you are reading in church, giving a talk, etc.

lec·ture 🔑 **AWL** /'lɛktʃər/ *noun*, *verb*
● *noun* ~ (to sb) (on/about sth) **1** a talk that is given to a group of people to teach them about a particular subject, often as part of a course of study: *to deliver/give a lecture to first-year students* ♦ *to attend a series of lectures on Jane Austen* ♦ *a lecture hall/room* ➔ thesaurus box at SPEECH ➔ collocations at EDUCATION **2** a long angry talk that someone gives to one person or a group of people because they have done something wrong: *I know I should stop smoking—don't give me a lecture about it.*
● *verb* **1** [I] ~ (on/in sth) to give a talk or a series of talks to a group of people on a subject, especially as a way of teaching in a university or college: *She lectures on Russian*

literature. **2** [T] ~ sb (about/on sth) | ~ sb (about doing sth) to criticize someone or tell them how you think they should behave, especially when it is done in an annoying way: *He's always lecturing me about the way I dress.*

'lecture ,hall *noun* a large room with rows of seats on a slope, where lectures are given

lec·tur·er **AWL** /'lɛktʃərər/ *noun* **1** a person who gives a lecture: *She's an excellent lecturer.* **2** a person who teaches at a university or college on a temporary basis: *He's a lecturer in French at Princeton.*

LED /,ɛl i 'di/ *abbr.* light emitting diode (a device that produces a light on electrical and electronic equipment): *A single red LED shows that the power is switched on.*

led /lɛd/ **1** pt, pp of LEAD¹ **2** **-led** (in adjectives) influenced or organized by: *a consumer-led society* ♦ *student-led activities*

ledge /lɛdʒ/ *noun* **1** a narrow, flat piece of rock that sticks out from a CLIFF: *seabirds nesting on rocky ledges* **2** a narrow, flat shelf attached to a wall, especially one below a window: *She put the vase of flowers on the window ledge.* ➔ see also SILL

ledg·er /'lɛdʒər/ *noun* a book in which a bank, a business, etc. records the money it has paid and received: *to enter figures in the purchase/sales ledger*

lee /li/ *noun* **1** [sing.] the side or part of something that provides shelter from the wind ➔ compare LEEWARD, WINDWARD **2** lees [pl.] the substance that is left at the bottom of a bottle of wine, a container of beer, etc. **SYN** DREGS

leech /litʃ/ *noun* **1** a small WORM that usually lives in water and that attaches itself to other creatures and sucks their blood. Leeches were used in the past by doctors to remove blood from sick people. **2** (*disapproving*) a person who depends on someone else for money, or takes the profit from someone else's work

leek /lik/ *noun* a vegetable like a long onion with many layers of wide, flat leaves that are white at the bottom and green at the top. Leeks are eaten cooked. ➔ picture at FRUIT

leer /lɪr/ *verb*, *noun*
● *verb* [I] ~ (at sb) to look or smile at someone in an unpleasant way that shows an evil or sexual interest in them
● *noun* an unpleasant look or smile that shows someone is interested in a person in an evil or sexual way: *He looked at her with an evil leer.*

leer·y /'lɪri/ *adj.* (*informal*) ~ (of sth/sb) | ~ (of doing sth) suspicious or careful about something or someone, and trying to avoid doing it or dealing with them **SYN** WARY: *The governor is leery of changing the current law.*

lee·ward /'liwərd/ *or, in nautical use* /'luərd/ *adj.*, *noun*
● *adj.* on the side of something that is sheltered from the wind: *a harbor on the leeward side of the island* ▶ **lee·ward** *adv.* ➔ compare WINDWARD
● *noun* [U] the side or direction that is sheltered from the wind ➔ compare WINDWARD

lee·way /'liweɪ/ *noun* [U] the amount of freedom that you have to change something or to do something in the way you want to **SYN** LATITUDE: *How much leeway should parents give their children?*

left 🔑 /lɛft/ *adj.*, *adv.*, *noun* ➔ see also LEAVE
● *adj.* [only before noun] on the side of your body that is toward the west when you are facing north: *Fewer people write with their left hand than with their right.* ♦ *Take a left turn at the intersection.* ♦ *I broke my left leg.* ♦ *the left side of the field* ♦ *The university is on the left bank of the river.* ♦ (*sports*) *a left back/wing* ♦ *a left hook* **ANT** RIGHT
IDM have two left feet (*informal*) to be very awkward in your movements, especially when you are dancing or playing a sport
● *adv.* on or to the left side: *Turn left at the intersection.* ♦ *Look left and right before you cross the road.*
IDM left and right (*informal*) everywhere: *He's giving away money left and right.*

ʌ cup   ə about   eɪ say   aɪ five   ɔɪ boy   aʊ now   oʊ go   ər bird

● ***noun* 1** **the/someone's left** [sing.] the left side or direction: *She was sitting **on my left**.* ◆ *Twist your body to the left, then to the right.* ◆ *Take the next road **on the left**.* ◆ *To the left of the library is the bank.* **2** [sing.] **the first, second, etc. left** the first, second, etc. street on the left side: *Take the first left.* **3** a **left** [sing.] a turn to the left: *to **hang/make a left*** **4** **the left, the Left** [sing.] political groups who support the ideas and beliefs of SOCIALISM: *The Left only has a small chance of winning power.* ◆ *a left-leaning newspaper* **5** **the left** [sing.] the part of a political party whose members are most in favor of social change: *She is on the far left of the party.* **6** [C] (in boxing) a blow that is made with your left hand: *He hit him with two sharp lefts.* **ANT** RIGHT

ˌleft ˈbrain *noun* [U, sing.] the left side of the human brain, that is thought to be used for analyzing and for processing language ➔ compare RIGHT BRAIN

ˌleft ˈfield *noun* [U] **1** (in baseball) the left part of the field from where the player who is hitting the ball (the BATTER) is standing; the position played by the person who is there **2** (*informal*) an opinion or a position that is strange or unusual and a long way from the normal position: *The governor is **way out in left field** on this issue.*

ˈleft-field *adj.* (*informal*) not following what is usually done; different, surprising, and interesting: *left-field ideas*

ˈleft-hand *adj.* [only before noun] **1** on the left side of something: *the left-hand side of the street* ◆ *the top left-hand corner of the page* **2** connected with a person's left hand: *a tennis player with a left-hand grip* ◆ *a left-hand glove* **ANT** RIGHT-HAND

ˌleft-ˈhanded *adj.* **1** (of a person) finding it easier to use the left hand to write, hit a ball, etc. than the right: *a left-handed golfer* ◆ *I'm left-handed.* **2** (of tools, etc.) designed to be used by someone who finds it easier to use their left hand: *left-handed scissors* **3** (of actions, etc.) done with your left hand: *a left-handed serve* **ANT** RIGHT-HANDED ▶ ˌleft-ˈhanded *adv.*: *She writes left-handed.* ˌleft-ˈhandedness *noun* [U] **IDM** see COMPLIMENT *n.*

ˌleft-ˈhander /ˌleft ˈhændər/ *noun* a person who finds it easier to use their left hand to write, etc. with than their right **ANT** RIGHT-HANDER

ˈleft·ist /ˈleftɪst/ *noun* a person who supports LEFT-WING political parties and their ideas **ANT** RIGHTIST ▶ ˈleft·ism /ˈleftɪzəm/ *noun* [U] **leftist** *adj.*: *leftist groups*

ˈleft·most /ˈleftmoʊst/ *adj.* [only before noun] farthest to the left

ˌleft-of-ˈcenter *adj.* = CENTER-LEFT

ˈleft·o·ver /ˈleftˌoʊvər/ *noun* **1** [usually pl.] food that has not been eaten at the end of a meal **2** an object, a custom, or a way of behaving that remains from an earlier time **SYN** RELIC: *He's a leftover from the hippies in the 1960s.* ▶ **leftover** *adj.* [only before noun] **SYN** SURPLUS: *Use any leftover turkey to make soup.*

ˈleft·ward /ˈleftwərd/ *adj.* [only before noun] toward the left: *a leftward swing in public opinion* ◆ *to move your eyes in a leftward direction* ▶ ˈleft·ward *adv.*

ˌleft ˈwing *noun* **1** [sing.] the part of a political party whose members are most in favor of social change: *on the left wing of the party* **2** [C, U] an attacking player or position on the left side of the field in a sports game

ˌleft-ˈwing *adj.* strongly supporting the ideas of SOCIALISM: *left-wing groups*

ˌleft-ˈwinger *noun* **1** a person on the LEFT WING of a political party: *a democratic left-winger* **2** a person who plays on the left side of the field in a sports game **ANT** RIGHT-WINGER

ˈleft·y /ˈlefti/ *noun* (*pl.* **left·ies**) (*informal*) **1** a person who uses their left hand to write, hit a ball, etc. **2** (*disapproving*) a person who has SOCIALIST views ▶ **left·y** *adj.*: *a lefty pitcher*

leg 🖉 /lɛg/ *noun*
> PART OF BODY **1** [C] one of the long parts that connect the feet to the rest of the body: *I broke my leg playing football.*

◆ *How many legs does a centipede have?* ◆ **front/back legs** ◆ **foreleg/hind legs** ◆ *a wooden leg* ➔ picture at BODY ➔ collocations at PHYSICAL ➔ see also BOW LEGS, DADDY LONGLEGS, INSIDE LEG, LEGGY, LEGROOM, PEG LEG, SEA LEGS
> MEAT **2** [C, U] the leg of an animal, especially the top part, cooked and eaten: *Would you like a leg or a breast?* ◆ *chicken legs* ◆ **~ of sth** *roast leg of lamb*
> OF PANTS **3** [C] the part of a pair of pants that covers the leg: *a pant leg* ◆ *These jeans are too long **in the leg**.*
> OF TABLE/CHAIR **4** [C] one of the long, thin parts on the bottom of a table, chair, etc. that support it: *a chair leg*
> -LEGGED **5** /ˈlɛgd; lɛgd/ (in adjectives) having the number or type of legs mentioned: *a three-legged stool* ◆ *a long-legged insect* **HELP** When **-legged** is used with numbers, it is nearly always pronounced /ˈlɛgəd/; in other adjectives it can be pronounced /ˈlɛgəd/ or /lɛgd/ (but /ˈlɛgəd/ is more common). ➔ see also CROSS-LEGGED
> OF TRIP/RACE **6** [C] **~ (of sth)** one part of a trip or race **SYN** SECTION, STAGE **IDM** **break a leg!** (*informal*) used to wish someone good luck **give sb a leg up** (*informal*) **1** to help someone to get on a horse, over a wall, etc. by allowing them to put their foot in your hands and lifting them up **2** to help someone to improve their situation **have legs** (*informal*) if you say that a news story, etc. **has legs**, you mean that people will continue to be interested in it for a long time **not have a leg to stand on** (*informal*) to be in a position where you are unable to prove something or explain why something is reasonable: *Without written evidence, we don't have a leg to stand on.* **IDM** see ARM *n.*, FAST *adv.*, LAST¹ *adj.*, PULL *v.*, , SHAKE *v.*, STRETCH *v.*, TAIL *n.*

leg·a·cy /ˈlɛgəsi/ *noun, adj.*
● *noun* (*pl.* **legacies**) **1** money or property that is given to you by someone when they die **SYN** INHERITANCE: *They each received a legacy of $5,000.* **2** a situation that exists now because of events, actions, etc. that took place in the past: *Future generations will be left with a legacy of pollution and destruction.*
● *adj.* [only before noun] used to describe a computer system or product that is no longer available to buy but is still used because it would be too difficult or expensive to replace it: *How can we integrate new technology with our legacy systems?* ◆ *legacy hardware/software*

le·gal 🖉 **AWL** /ˈligl/ *adj.*
1 [only before noun] connected with the law: *the legal profession/system* ◆ *to get/seek **legal advice*** ◆ *a legal adviser* ◆ *legal costs* **2** allowed or required by law: *The driver was more than three times over the **legal limit** (= the amount of alcohol you are allowed to have in your body when you are driving).* ◆ *Should euthanasia be made legal?* **ANT** ILLEGAL ▶ **le·gal·ly** **AWL** /-gəli/ *adv.*: *a **legally binding** agreement* ◆ *to be legally responsible for someone or something*

ˌlegal ˈaction *noun* [U] (also ˌlegal proˈceedings) the act of using the legal system to settle a disagreement, etc.: *to take/begin legal action against someone* ◆ *They have threatened us with legal action.*

ˌlegal ˈage *noun* [sing., U] the age when someone has the legal rights and responsibilities of an adult: *~ to do sth/ ~ for sth What's the legal age to vote in England?* ◆ *Both witnesses must be of legal age.*

ˌlegal ˈaid *noun* [U] money that is given by a special organization to someone who needs help to pay for legal advice or a lawyer

ˌlegal ˈeagle (also ˌlegal ˈbeagle) *noun* (*humorous*) a lawyer, especially one who is very smart

le·gal·ese /ˌligəˈliz; -ˈlis/ *noun* [U] (*informal*) the sort of language used in legal documents that is difficult to understand

ˌlegal ˈholiday *noun* a public holiday that is established by law

le·gal·is·tic /ˌligəˈlɪstɪk/ *adj.* (*disapproving*) obeying the law too strictly: *a legalistic approach to family disputes*

le·gal·i·ty AWL /liˈgæləti/ *noun* (*pl.* **le·gal·i·ties**) **1** [U] the fact of being legal: *They intended to challenge the legality of his claim in the courts.* ◆ *The arrangement is of doubtful legality.* **2** [C, usually pl.] the legal aspect of an action or a situation: *You need a lawyer to explain all the legalities of the contracts.* ⟳ compare ILLEGALITY

le·gal·ize /ˈliɡəˌlaɪz/ *verb* ~ **sth** to make something legal ► **le·gal·i·za·tion** /ˌliɡələˈzeɪʃn/ *noun* [U]

ˈlegal ˌpad *noun* a number of sheets of paper with lines on them, fastened together at one end. A legal pad is longer than regular paper and usually yellow.

ˌlegal proˈceedings *noun* [pl.] = LEGAL ACTION

ˈlegal-ˌsize (also **le-gal**) *adj.* (of paper) 8½ inches wide and 14 inches long ⟳ see also LETTER-SIZE

ˌlegal ˈtender *noun* [U] money that can be legally used to pay for things in a particular country

leg·ate /ˈlɛɡət/ *noun* the official representative of the Pope in a foreign country: *a papal legate*

leg·a·tee /ˌlɛɡəˈti/ *noun* (*law*) a person who receives money or property (= a LEGACY) when someone dies

le·ga·tion /lɪˈɡeɪʃn/ *noun* **1** a group of DIPLOMATS representing their government in a foreign country in an office that is below the rank of an EMBASSY **2** the building where these people work

le·ga·to /lɪˈɡɑtoʊ/ *adj.* (from *Italian*, *music*) to be played or sung in a smooth, even manner ► **legato** *adv.* **ANT** STACCATO

leg·end /ˈlɛdʒənd/ *noun* **1** [C, U] a story from ancient times about people and events, that may or may not be true; this type of story **SYN** MYTH: *the legend of Robin Hood* ◆ *the heroes of Greek legend* ◆ **Legend has it** *that the lake was formed by the tears of a god.* ⟳ see also URBAN LEGEND **2** [C] a very famous person, especially in a particular field, who is admired by other people: *a jazz/tennis, etc. legend* ◆ *She was a legend in her own lifetime.* ◆ *Many of golf's living legends were playing.* **3** [C] (*technical*) the explanation of a map or diagram in a book **SYN** KEY **4** [C] (*formal*) a piece of writing on a sign, a label, a coin, etc.

leg·end·ar·y /ˈlɛdʒənˌdɛri/ *adj.* **1** very famous and talked about a lot by people, especially in a way that shows admiration: *a legendary figure* ◆ *the legendary Orson Welles* ◆ *Her patience and tact are legendary.* **2** [only before noun] mentioned in stories from ancient times: *legendary heroes* ⟳ compare FABLED

leg·er·de·main /ˌlɛdʒərdəˈmeɪn/ *noun* [U] (*formal*, from *French*) = SLEIGHT OF HAND

leg·gings /ˈlɛɡɪnz/ *noun* [pl.] **1** pants for women that fit tightly over the legs, made of cloth that stretches easily: *a pair of leggings* **2** outer coverings for the legs, worn as protection

leg·gy /ˈlɛɡi/ *adj.* (*informal*) (especially of girls and women) having long legs: *a tall, leggy model*

leg·i·ble /ˈlɛdʒəbl/ *adj.* (of written or printed words) clear enough to read: *legible handwriting* ◆ *The signature was still legible.* **ANT** ILLEGIBLE ► **leg·i·bil·i·ty** /ˌlɛdʒəˈbɪləti/ *noun* [U] **leg·i·bly** /ˈlɛdʒəbli/ *adv.*

le·gion /ˈlidʒən/ *noun, adj.*
● *noun* **1** a large group of soldiers that forms part of an army, especially the one that existed in ancient Rome: *the French Foreign Legion* ◆ *Caesar's legions* **2** (*formal*) a large number of people of one particular type: *legions of photographers*
● *adj.* [not before noun] (*formal*) very many **SYN** NUMEROUS: *The medical uses of herbs are legion.*

le·gion·ar·y /ˈlidʒəˌnɛri/ *noun* (*pl.* **le·gion·ar·ies**) a soldier who is part of a legion ► **le·gion·ar·y** *adj.* [only before noun]

le·gion·naire /ˌlidʒəˈnɛr/ *noun* a member of a LEGION, especially the French Foreign Legion

legionˈnaires' disˌease *noun* [U] a serious lung disease caused by bacteria, especially spread by AIR CONDITIONING and similar systems

leg·is·late AWL /ˈlɛdʒəsˌleɪt/ *verb* [I] ~ **(for/against/on sth)** (*formal*) to make a law affecting something: *The government will legislate against discrimination in the workplace.* ◆ (*figurative*) *You can't legislate against bad luck!* ◆ *They promised to legislate to protect people's right to privacy.*

leg·is·la·tion AWL /ˌlɛdʒəsˈleɪʃn/ *noun* [U] **1** a law or a set of laws passed by a government body: *an important piece of legislation* ◆ *New legislation on the sale of drugs will be introduced next year.* ⟳ collocations at POLITICS **2** the process of making and passing laws: *Legislation will be difficult and will take time.*

leg·is·la·tive AWL /ˈlɛdʒəsˌleɪtɪv/ *adj.* [only before noun] connected with the act of making and passing laws: *a legislative assembly/body/council* ◆ *legislative powers*

the ˈlegislative ˌbranch *noun* [sing.] the part of the U.S. government, consisting of the House of Representatives and the Senate, that has the power to make laws ⟳ compare EXECUTIVE BRANCH, JUDICIAL BRANCH

leg·is·la·tor AWL /ˈlɛdʒəsˌleɪtər/ *noun* a member of a group of people that has the power to make laws

leg·is·la·ture AWL /ˈlɛdʒəsˌleɪtʃər/ *noun* **1** a group of people who have the power to make and change laws: *a democratically elected legislature* ◆ *the national/state legislature* ⟳ compare EXECUTIVE, JUDICIARY **2** (*CanE*) the legislative building

le·git /lɪˈdʒɪt/ *adj.* (*informal*) legal, or acting according to the law or the rules: *The business seems legit.*

le·git·i·mate /lɪˈdʒɪtəmət/ *adj.* **1** for which there is a fair and acceptable reason **SYN** JUSTIFIABLE, VALID: *a legitimate grievance* ◆ *It seemed like a perfectly legitimate question.* ◆ *Politicians are legitimate targets for satire.* **2** allowed and acceptable according to the law **SYN** LEGAL: *the legitimate government of the country* ◆ *Is his business strictly legitimate?* **ANT** ILLEGITIMATE **3** (of a child) born when its parents are legally married to each other **ANT** ILLEGITIMATE ► **le·git·i·ma·cy** /lɪˈdʒɪtəməsi/ *noun* [U]: *the dubious legitimacy of her argument* ◆ *I intend to challenge the legitimacy of his claim.* **le·git·i·mate·ly** *adv.*: *She can now legitimately claim to be the best in the world.*

le·git·i·mize /lɪˈdʒɪtəˌmaɪz/ *verb* (*formal*) **1** ~ **sth** to make something that is wrong or unfair seem acceptable: *The movie has been criticized for apparently legitimizing violence.* **2** ~ **sth** to make something legal **SYN** LEGALIZE **3** ~ **sb** to give a child whose parents are not married to each other the same rights as those whose parents are

leg·less /ˈlɛɡləs/ *adj.* without legs

Le·go™ /ˈlɛɡoʊ/ *noun* [U] a children's toy that consists of small colored bricks that fit together

leg·room /ˈlɛɡrum; -rʊm/ *noun* [U] the amount of space available for your legs when you are sitting in a car, plane, theater, etc.

leg·ume /ˈlɛɡyum; lɪˈɡyum/ *noun* (*technical*) any plant that has seeds in long PODS. PEAS and BEANS are legumes.

le·gu·mi·nous /lɪˈɡyumənəs/ *adj.* [usually before noun] (*technical*) relating to plants of the legume family

ˈleg ˌwarmer *noun* [usually pl.] a kind of sock without a foot that covers the leg from the ankle to the knee, often worn when doing exercise

leg·work /ˈlɛɡwərk/ *noun* [U] (*informal*) difficult or boring work that takes a lot of time and effort, but that is thought to be less important

lei /leɪ/ *noun* a WREATH (= circle) of flowers that is placed around the necks of visitors to Hawaii

lei·sure /ˈliʒər; ˈlɛ-/ *noun* [U] time that is spent doing what you enjoy when you are not working or studying: *These days we have more money and more leisure to enjoy it.* ◆ *leisure activities/interests/pursuits*
IDM **at leisure 1** with no particular activities; free: *After a tour of the university, we were at leisure for the rest of the*

t **tea**   ţ **butter**   d **did**   k **cat**   g **got**   tʃ **chin**   dʒ **June**   f **fall**

afternoon. **2** without hurrying: *Let's have lunch so we can talk at leisure.* **at your leisure** when you have the time to do something without hurrying: *I suggest you take the forms away and read them at your leisure.* **a gentleman/lady/man/woman of leisure** (*humorous*) a man/woman who does not have to work

lei·sured /ˈliʒərd; ˈlɛ-/ *adj.* **1** [only before noun] not having to work and therefore having a lot of time to do what you enjoy: *the leisured class* **2** = LEISURELY

lei·sure·ly /ˈliʒərli; ˈlɛ-/ (also **lei·sured**) *adj.* [usually before noun] done without hurrying: *a leisurely meal* ◆ *They set off at a leisurely pace.* ▶ **leisurely** *adv.*: *Couples strolled leisurely along the beach.*

leisure ˌsuit *noun* an informal suit consisting of a shirt and pants made of the same cloth, popular in the 1970s

lei·sure·wear /ˈliʒərˌwɛr; ˈlɛ-/ *noun* [U] (used especially by stores and clothing companies) informal clothes worn for relaxing or playing sports in

leit·mo·tif (also **leit·mo·tiv**) /ˈlaɪtmoʊˌtif/ *noun* (from German) **1** (*music*) a short tune in a piece of music that is often repeated and is connected with a particular person, thing, or idea **2** an idea or a phrase that is repeated often in a book or work of art, or is typical of a particular person or group

lem·ma /ˈlɛmə/ *noun* (*pl.* **lem·mas** or **lem·ma·ta** /-ˈmətə/) **1** (*technical*) a statement that is assumed to be true in order to test the truth of another statement **2** (*linguistics*) the basic form of a word, for example the singular form of a noun or the infinitive form of a verb, as it is shown at the beginning of a dictionary entry

lem·ming /ˈlɛmɪŋ/ *noun* a small animal like a mouse, that lives in cold northern countries. Sometimes large groups of lemmings MIGRATE (= move from one place to another) in search of food. Many of them die on these journeys and there is a popular belief that lemmings kill themselves by jumping off CLIFFS: *Lemming-like we rushed into certain disaster.*

lem·on 🔊 /ˈlɛmən/ *noun, adj.*
● *noun* **1** [C, U] a yellow CITRUS fruit with a lot of sour juice. Slices of lemon and lemon juice are used in cooking and drinks: *lemon tea* ◆ *You need a lot of lemons to make lemonade.* ◆ *Squeeze the juice of half a lemon over the fish.* ◆ *a lemon tree* ⊃ picture at FRUIT **2** [U] lemon juice or a drink made from lemon **3** (also ˌlemon ˈyellow) [U] a pale yellow color **4** [C] (*informal*) a thing, especially a car, that is useless because it does not work as it should **SYN** DUD
● *adj.* (also ˌlemon ˈyellow) pale yellow in color

lem·on·ade /ˌlɛməˈneɪd; ˈlɛməˌneɪd/ *noun* **1** [U] a drink made from lemon juice, sugar, and water **2** [C] a glass, can, or bottle of lemonade ⊃ compare ORANGEADE

lemon ˌbalm *noun* [U] an HERB with leaves that taste of lemon

lemon ˌcurd *noun* [U] a thick, sweet, yellow substance made from lemon, sugar, eggs, and butter

lem·on·grass /ˈlɛmənˌgræs/ *noun* [U] a type of grass with a lemon flavor that grows in hot countries and is used especially in S.E. Asian cooking

lemon ˌlaw *noun* a law that states that you can return a motor vehicle to get it repaired or your money back if the vehicle is no good

lem·on·y /ˈlɛməni/ *adj.* tasting or smelling of lemon: *a lemony flavor*

lemon ˈyellow *noun* [U] = LEMON *n.* (3)

le·mur /ˈlimər/ *noun* an animal like a MONKEY, with thick fur and a long tail, that lives in trees in Madagascar

lend 🔊 /lɛnd/ *verb*
(lent, lent /lɛnt/) **1** [T] to give something to someone or allow them to use something that belongs to you, which they have to return to you later **SYN** LOAN: ~ **(out) sth (to sb)** *I lent the car to a friend.* ◆ ~ **sb sth** *Can you lend me your car*

tonight? ◆ *Has he returned that book you lent him?* ⊃ note at BORROW **2** [T, I] (of a bank or financial institution) to give money to someone on condition that they pay it back over a period of time and pay interest on it **SYN** LOAN: ~ **(sth) (to sb)** *The bank refused to lend the money to us.* ◆ ~ **sb sth** *They refused to lend us the money.* ⊃ compare BORROW **3** [T] (*formal*) to give a particular quality to a person or a situation: ~ **sth (to sb/sth)** *The setting sun lent an air of melancholy to the scene.* ◆ ~ **sb/sth sth** *Her presence lent the occasion a certain dignity.* **4** [T] to give or provide help, support, etc.: ~ **sth (to sb/sth)** *I was more than happy to lend my support to such a good cause.* ◆ ~ **sb/sth sth** *He came along to lend me moral support.*
IDM **lend an ear (to sb/sth)** to listen in a patient and sympathetic way to someone **lend (sb) a (helping) hand (with sth)** (*informal*) to help someone with something: *I went over to see if I could lend a hand.* **lend your name to sth** (*formal*) **1** to let it be known in public that you support or agree with something: *I am more than happy to lend my name to this campaign.* **2** to have a place named after you **lend support, weight, credence, etc. to sth** to make something seem more likely to be true or genuine: *This latest evidence lends support to her theory.* ⊃ more at HELP
PHR V **ˈlend itself to sth** to be suitable for something: *Her voice doesn't really lend itself well to blues singing.*

lend·er /ˈlɛndər/ *noun* (*finance*) a person or an organization that lends money ⊃ compare BORROWER ⊃ see also MONEYLENDER

lend·ing /ˈlɛndɪŋ/ *noun* [U] (*finance*) the act of lending money: *Lending by banks rose to $10 billion last year.* ⊃ see also PREDATORY LENDING

ˈlending ˌlibrary *noun* a public library from which you can borrow books and take them away to read at home ⊃ compare REFERENCE LIBRARY

ˈlending ˌrate *noun* (*finance*) the rate of interest that you must pay when you borrow money from a bank or another financial organization

length 🔊 /lɛŋkθ; lɛŋθ/ *noun*
▷ **SIZE/MEASUREMENT 1** [U, C] the size or measurement of something from one end to the other: *This room is twice the length of the kitchen.* ◆ *The river is 300 miles in length.* ◆ *The snake usually reaches a length of 6 ft.* ◆ *He ran the entire length of the beach* (= from one end to the other). ◆ *Did you see the length of his hair?* ⊃ picture at DIMENSION ⊃ compare BREADTH, WIDTH
▷ **TIME 2** [U, C] the amount of time that something lasts: *We discussed shortening the length of the course.* ◆ *He was disgusted at the length of time he had to wait.* ◆ *She got a headache if she had to read for any length of time* (= for a long time). ◆ *The size of the pension depends partly on the individual's length of service with the company.* ◆ *Each class is 45 minutes in length.*
▷ **OF BOOK/MOVIE 3** [U, C] the amount of writing in a book, or a document, etc.; the amount of time that a movie lasts: *Her novels vary in length.*
▷ **-LENGTH 4** (in adjectives) having the length mentioned: *shoulder-length hair* ⊃ see also FULL-LENGTH, KNEE-LENGTH
▷ **OF SWIMMING POOL 5** [C] the distance from one end of a swimming pool to the other: *He swims 50 lengths a day.* ⊃ compare WIDTH
▷ **IN RACE 6** [C] the size of a horse or boat from one end to the other, when it is used to measure the distance between two horses or boats taking part in a race: *The horse won by two lengths.*
▷ **LONG THIN PIECE 7** [C] a long, thin piece of something: *a length of rope/string/wire* ⊃ see also LONG
IDM **at length** | **at... length 1** for a long time and in detail: *He quoted at length from the report.* ◆ *We have already discussed this matter at great length.* **2** (*literary*) after a long time: *"I'm still not sure," he said at length.* **go to any, some, great, etc. lengths (to do sth)** to put a lot of effort into doing something, especially when this seems extreme: *She goes to extraordinary lengths to keep her private life private.* **the length and breadth of...** in or to all parts of a place: *They*

have traveled the length and breadth of North America giving concerts. ⊃ more at ARM

length·en /'lɛŋθən; 'lɛŋθən/ *verb* [I, T] to become longer; to make something longer: *The afternoon shadows lengthened.* ◆ ~ *sth I need to lengthen this skirt.* **ANT** SHORTEN

length·wise /'lɛŋkθwaɪz; 'lɛŋθ-/ *adv.* (also **length·ways** /'lɛŋkweɪz; 'lɛŋθ-/) in the same direction as the longest side of something: *Cut the banana in half lengthwise.* ⊃ compare WIDTHWISE ▶ **length·wise** *adj.: a lengthwise cut*

length·y /'lɛŋkθi; 'lɛŋθi/ *adj.* (**length·i·er, length·i·est**) very long, and often too long, in time or size: *lengthy delays* ◆ *the lengthy process of obtaining a visa* ◆ *a lengthy explanation*

le·ni·ent /'linyənt/ *adj.* not as strict as expected when punishing someone or when making sure that rules are obeyed: *a lenient sentence/fine* ◆ *The judge was far too lenient with him.* ▶ **le·ni·ency** /-yənsi/ (also *less frequent* **le·ni·ence** /-yəns/) *noun* [U]: *She appealed to the judge for leniency.* **le·ni·ent·ly** *adv.: to treat someone leniently*

Le·nin·ism /'lɛnə,nɪzəm/ *noun* [U] the political and economic policies of Lenin, the first leader of the Soviet Union, which were based on Marxism ▶ **Le·nin·ist** /-nɪst/ *noun*

lens /lɛnz/ *noun* **1** a curved piece of glass or plastic that makes things look larger, smaller, or clearer when you look through it: *a pair of glasses with tinted lenses* ◆ *a camera with an adjustable lens* ◆ *a lens cap/cover* ⊃ picture at FRAME, LABORATORY ⊃ see also FISHEYE LENS, TELEPHOTO LENS, WIDE-ANGLE LENS, ZOOM LENS **2** (*informal*) = CONTACT LENS: *Have you got your lenses in?* **3** (*anatomy*) the transparent part of the eye, behind the PUPIL, that focuses light so that you can see clearly ⊃ picture at BODY

lens·man /'lɛnzmən/ *noun* (*pl.* **lens·men** /-mən/) a professional photographer or CAMERAMAN

Lent /lɛnt/ *noun* [U] in the Christian Church, the period of 40 days from Ash Wednesday to the day before Easter, during which some Christians give up some type of food or activity that they enjoy in memory of Christ's suffering

lent pt, pp of LEND

len·ti·go /lɛn'taɪgoʊ/ *noun* [U] (*medical*) a condition in which small brown areas appear on the skin, usually in old people ⊃ see also LIVER SPOT

len·til /'lɛntəl/ *noun* a small green, orange, or brown seed that is usually dried and used in cooking, for example in soup or STEW

Le·o /'lioʊ/ *noun* **1** [U] the fifth sign of the ZODIAC, the Lion [C] (*pl.* **Leos**) a person born under the influence of this sign, that is between July 23 and August 22, approximately

le·o·nine /'liə,naɪn/ *adj.* (*literary*) like a LION

leop·ard /'lɛpərd/ *noun* a large animal of the cat family, that has yellowish-brown fur with black spots. Leopards live in Africa and southern Asia. ⊃ compare LEOPARDESS

leopard

IDM a leopard cannot change its spots (*saying*) people cannot change their character, especially if they have a bad character

leop·ard·ess /'lɛpərdəs/ *noun* a female leopard

le·o·tard /'liə,tard/ *noun* a piece of clothing that fits tightly over the body from the neck down to the tops of the legs, worn by dancers, women doing physical exercises, etc.

LEP /,ɛl i 'pi/ *abbr.* [only before noun] (*technical*) Limited English Proficient (used to describe students who cannot speak English very well): *schools with large numbers of LEP children*

lep·er /'lɛpər/ *noun* **1** a person suffering from LEPROSY **2** a

person that other people avoid because they have done something that these people do not approve of

lep·re·chaun /'lɛprə,kɑn; -,kɔn/ *noun* (in Irish stories) a creature like a little man, with magic powers

lep·ro·sy /'lɛprəsi/ *noun* [U] an infectious disease that causes painful white areas on the skin and can destroy nerves and flesh ⊃ see also LEPER

lep·rous /'lɛprəs/ *adj.* affected by LEPROSY

les·bi·an /'lɛzbiən/ *noun* a woman who is sexually attracted to other women: *lesbians and gays* ⊃ compare GAY, HOMOSEXUAL ▶ **lesbian** *adj.: the lesbian and gay community* ◆ *a lesbian relationship* **les·bi·an·ism** /'lɛzbiə,nɪzəm/ *noun* [U]

lese-maj·es·ty /,liz 'mædʒəsti; ,leɪz-/ *noun* [U] (from *French, formal*) the act or crime of insulting the king, queen, or other ruler

le·sion /'liʒn/ *noun* (*medical*) damage to the skin or part of the body caused by injury or by illness: *skin/brain lesions*

less /lɛs/ *det., pron., adv., prep.*

● **det., pron.** used with noncountable nouns to mean "a smaller amount of": *less butter/time/importance* ◆ *He was advised to smoke fewer cigarettes and drink less beer.* ◆ *We have less to worry about now.* ◆ *It is less of a problem than I expected.* ◆ *The victory was nothing less than a miracle.* **HELP** People often use **less** with countable nouns: *There were less cars on the road then.* This is not considered correct by some people, and **fewer** should be used instead.
IDM less and less smaller and smaller amounts: *As time passed, she saw less and less of all her old friends at home.* **less is more** (*saying*) include only what is essential in order to create an effective product or result: *His simple, elegant paintings reflect his principle that less is more.* **no less** (often *ironic*) used to suggest that something is surprising or impressive: *She's having lunch with the director, no less.* **no less than...** used to emphasize a large amount: *The guide contains details of no less than 115 hiking routes.*

● **adv.** to a smaller degree; not so much: *less expensive/likely/intelligent* ◆ *less often/enthusiastically* ◆ *I read much less now than I used to.* ◆ *The receptionist was less than* (= not at all) *helpful.* ◆ *She wasn't any the less happy* (= she was perfectly happy) *being on her own.* ◆ *That this is a positive stereotype makes it no less a stereotype, and therefore unacceptable.* **IDM less and less** continuing to become smaller in amount: *She found the job less and less interesting.* **much less** and certainly not: *No explanation was offered, much less an apology.* **the less, more, etc...., the less, more, etc....,** used to show that two things change to the same degree: *The less said about the whole thing, the happier I'll be.* ⊃ see also MORE

● **prep.** used before a particular amount that must be taken away from the amount just mentioned **SYN** MINUS: *a weekly salary of $500 less taxes*

-less /ləs/ *suffix* (in adjectives) **1** without: *treeless* ◆ *meaningless* **2** not doing; not affected by: *tireless* ◆ *selfless* ▶ **-less·ly** (in adverbs): *hopelessly* **-less·ness** (in nouns): *helplessness*

les·see /lɛ'si/ *noun* (*law*) a person who has use of a building, an area of land, etc. on a LEASE ⊃ compare LESSOR

less·en /'lɛsn/ *verb* [I, T] to become or make something become smaller, weaker, less important, etc. **SYN** DIMINISH: *The noise began to lessen.* ◆ ~ *sth to lessen the risk/impact/effect of something* ▶ **less·en·ing** *noun* [sing., U]: *a lessening of tension*

less·er /'lɛsər/ *adj.* [only before noun] **1** not as great in size, amount, or importance as something or someone else: *people of lesser importance* ◆ *They were all involved to a greater or lesser degree* (= some were more involved than others). ◆ *The law was designed to protect wives, and, to a lesser extent, children.* ◆ *He was encouraged to plead guilty to the lesser offense.* **2** used in the names of some types of animals, birds, and plants that are smaller than similar kinds

| h hat | m man | n no | ŋ sing | l leg | r red | y yes | w wet |

ANT GREAT ▶ **lesser** *adv.*: *one of the lesser-known Caribbean islands*
IDM **the lesser of two evils| the lesser evil** the less unpleasant of two unpleasant choices

les·son /'lɛsn/ *noun* **1** a period of time in which someone is taught something: *She gives piano lessons.* ◆ *All new students are given lessons in/on how to use the library.* ◆ *I'm taking driving lessons.* ⊃ compare CLASS ⊃ collocations at EDUCA-TION **2** something that is intended to be learned: *The textbook is divided into 30 lessons.* ◆ *Other countries can teach us a lesson or two on industrial policy.* **3** an experience, especially an unpleasant one, that someone can learn from so that it does not happen again in the future: *a salutary lesson* ◆ *The accident taught me a lesson I'll never forget.* ◆ *~ to sb Let that be a lesson to you* (= so that you do not make the same mistake again). ⊃ see also OBJECT LESSON **4** a passage from the Bible that is read to people during a church service **IDM** see LEARN

les·sor /'lɛsɔr; lɛ'sɔr/ *noun* (*law*) a person who gives someone the use of a building, an area of land, etc. on a LEASE ⊃ compare LESSEE

lest /lɛst/ *conj.* (*formal* or *literary*) **1** in order to prevent something from happening: *He gripped his brother's arm lest he be trampled by the mob.* **2** used to introduce the reason for the particular emotion mentioned **SYN** IN CASE: *She was afraid lest she had revealed too much.*

let 🔑 /lɛt/ *verb, noun*
● *verb* (**let·ting, let, let**)
> ALLOW **1** [no passive] to allow someone to do something or something to happen without trying to stop it: *~ sb/sth do sth Let them splash around in the pool for a while.* ◆ *Don't let her upset you.* ◆ *Let your body relax.* ◆ *~ sb/sth He'd eat chocolate all day long if I let him.* **2** to give someone permission to do something: *~ sb/sth do sth They won't let him leave the country.* ◆ *~ sb/sth She wanted to lend me some money but I wouldn't let her.* **3** *~ sb/sth + adv./prep.* to allow someone or something to go somewhere: *to let someone into the house* ◆ *I'll give you a key so that you can let yourself in.* ◆ *Please let me past.* ◆ *The cat wants to be let out.*
> MAKING SUGGESTIONS **4** **let's** [no passive] *~ (do sth)* used for making suggestions: *Let's go to the beach.* ◆ *Let's not tell her what we did.* ◆ *I don't think we'll make it, but let's try anyway.* ◆ *"Shall we check it again?" "Yes, let's."*
> OFFERING HELP **5** [no passive] *~ sb/sth do sth* used for offering help to someone: *Here, let me do it.* ◆ *Let us get those boxes down for you.*
> MAKING REQUESTS **6** [no passive] *~ sb/sth do sth* used for making requests or giving instructions: *Let me have your report by Friday.*
> CHALLENGING **7** [no passive] *~ sb/sth do sth* used to show that you are not afraid or worried about someone doing something: *If he thinks he can cheat me, just let him try!*
> WISHING **8** [no passive] *~ sb/sth do sth* (*literary*) used to express a strong wish for something to happen: *Let her come home safely!*
> INTRODUCING SOMETHING **9** [no passive] *~ sb/sth do sth* used to introduce what you are going to say or do: *Let me give you an example.* ◆ *Let me just finish this and then I'll come.*
> IN CALCULATING **10** [no passive] *~ sb/sth do sth* (*technical*) used to say that you are supposing something to be true when you calculate something: *Let line AB be equal to line CD.*
IDM Most idioms containing **let** are at the entries for the nouns and adjectives in the idioms. For example, **let alone** is at **alone**. **let sb go 1** to allow someone to be free **SYN** FREE: *Will they let the hostages go?* **2** to make someone have to leave their job: *They had to let 100 employees go because of falling profits.* **let sb/sth go| let go (of sb/sth) 1** to stop holding someone or something: *Don't let the rope go.* ◆ *Don't let go of the rope.* ◆ *Let go! You're hurting me!* **2** to give up an idea or an attitude, or control of something: *It's time to let the past go.* ◆ *It's time to let go of the past.* **let sth go** to stop taking care of a house, garden, etc.: *I'm afraid I've let the garden go this year.* **let yourself go 1** to behave in a

relaxed way without worrying about what people think of your behavior: *Come on, enjoy yourself, let yourself go!* **2** to stop being careful about how you look and dress, etc.: *He has let himself go since he lost his job.* **let sb have it** (*informal*) to attack someone physically or with words **let it go (at that)** to say or do no more about something: *I don't entirely agree, but I'll let it go at that.* ◆ *I thought she was hinting at something, but I let it go.* **let me see/think** used when you are thinking or trying to remember something: *Now let me see—where did he say he lived?* **let us say** used when making a suggestion or giving an example: *I can let you have it for, well let's say $100.*
PHR V **let sb↔down** to fail to help or support someone as they had hoped or expected: *I'm afraid she let us down badly.* ◆ *This machine won't let you down.* ◆ *He trudged home feeling lonely and let down.* ⊃ related noun LETDOWN **let sth↔'down 1** to let or make something go down: *We let the bucket down by a rope.* **2** to make a dress, skirt, coat, etc. longer, by reducing the amount of material that is folded over at the bottom **let sb/yourself 'in for sth** (*informal*) to involve someone/yourself in something that is likely to be unpleasant or difficult: *I volunteered to help, and then I thought "Oh no, what have I let myself in for!"* **let sb 'in on sth** (*informal*) to allow someone to share a secret: *Are you going to let them in on your plans?* **let sb 'off (with sth)** to not punish someone for something they have done wrong, or to give them only a light punishment: *They let us off lightly.* ◆ *She was let off with a warning.* **let sth 'off** to fire a gun or make a bomb, etc. explode: *The boys were letting off fireworks.* **let 'on (to sb)** (*informal*) to tell a secret: *I'm getting married next week, but please don't let on to anyone.* ◆ *~ that... She let on that she was leaving.* **let 'out** (of school classes, movies, meetings, etc.) to come to an end, so that it is time for people to leave: *The movie has just let out.* **let sth 'out 1** to give a cry, etc.: *to let out a scream of terror* ◆ *to let out a gasp of delight* **ANT** HOLD IN **2** to make a shirt, coat, etc. looser or larger **ANT** TAKE IN **let 'up** (*informal*) **1** to become less strong: *The pain finally let up.* **2** to make less effort: *We mustn't let up now.* ⊃ related noun LETUP
● *noun* (in TENNIS) a SERVE that lands in the correct part of the COURT but must be taken again because it touched the top of the net

-let /lət/ *suffix* (in nouns) small; not very important: *booklet* ◆ *piglet* ◆ *starlet*

let·down /'lɛtdaʊn/ *noun* [C, usually sing., U] something that is disappointing because it is not as good as you expected it to be **SYN** DISAPPOINTMENT, ANTICLIMAX

le·thal /'liːθl/ *adj.* **1** causing or able to cause death **SYN** DEADLY, FATAL: *a lethal dose of poison* ◆ *a lethal weapon* ◆ (*figurative*) *The closure of the factory dealt a lethal blow to the town.* **2** (*informal*) causing or able to cause a lot of harm or damage: *You and that car—it's a lethal combination!* ▶ **le·thal·ly** /-θəli/ *adv.*

leth·ar·gy /'lɛθərdʒi/ *noun* [U] the state of not having any energy or enthusiasm for doing things **SYN** INERTIA ▶ **le·thar·gic** /lə'θɑrdʒɪk/ *adj.*: *The weather made her lethargic.*

Le·the /'liːθi/ *noun* [U] (in ancient Greek stories) an imaginary river whose water, when drunk, was thought to make the dead forget their life on Earth

let's /lɛts/ short form of LET US: *Let's break for lunch.*

let·ter 🔑 /'lɛtər/ *noun, verb*
● *noun* **1** a message that is written down or printed on paper and usually put in an envelope and sent to someone: *a business/thank-you, etc. letter* ◆ *a letter of complaint* ◆ *to mail a letter* ◆ *There's a letter for you from your mother. You will be notified by letter.* **HELP** You will find compounds ending in **letter** at their place in the alphabet. **2** a written or printed sign representing a sound used in speech: *"B" is the second letter of the alphabet.* ◆ *Write your name in capital letters.* **3** a sign in the shape of a letter that is sewn onto clothes and that is given to a person in a school or college sports team who plays very well

IDM **the letter of the law** (often *disapproving*) the exact words of a law or rule rather than its general meaning: *They insist on sticking to the letter of the law.* **to the letter** doing/following exactly what someone or something says, paying attention to every detail: *I followed your instructions to the letter.*

• *verb* **1** [T, usually passive] **~ sth (+ noun)** to give a letter to something as part of a series or list: *the stars lettered Alpha and Beta* **2** [T, usually passive] **~ sth (in sth)** to print, paint, sew, etc. letters onto something: *a black banner lettered in white* **3** [I] to receive a letter made of cloth that you sew onto your clothes for playing very well in a school or college sports team

'**letter ˌbomb** (also '**mail bomb**) *noun* a small bomb that is sent to someone hidden in a letter that explodes when the envelope is opened

let·ter·box /'lɛtərˌbaks/ *noun, verb*
• *noun* [U] = WIDESCREEN
• *verb* **~ sth** to present a movie on television with the width a lot greater than the height, and with a black band at the top and bottom: *a letterboxed edition*

'**letter ˌcarrier** *noun* = MAILMAN

let·ter·head /'lɛtərˌhɛd/ *noun* the name and address of a person, a company, or an organization printed at the top of their writing paper

let·ter·ing /'lɛtərɪŋ/ *noun* [U] **1** letters or words that are written or printed in a particular style: *Gothic lettering* **2** the process of writing, drawing, or printing letters or words

ˌ**letter of 'credit** *noun* (*pl.* '**letters of ˌcredit**) (*finance*) a letter from a bank that allows you to get a particular amount of money from another bank

'**letter ˌopener** *noun* a knife or something with a sharp edge that is used for opening envelopes

ˌ**letter-'perfect** *adj.* **1** correct in all details **2** able to remember and repeat something exactly without making any mistakes

'**letter-ˌsize** (also '**letter**) *adj.* (of paper) 8½ inches wide and 11 inches long ⊃ see also LEGAL-SIZE

let·tuce /'lɛtəs/ *noun* [U, C] a plant with large green leaves that are eaten raw, especially in salad. There are many types of lettuce: *a bacon, lettuce, and tomato sandwich* ◆ *Buy a lettuce and some tomatoes.* ⊃ picture at FRUIT

let·up /'lɛtʌp/ *noun* [U, sing.] **~ (in sth)** a period of time during which something stops or becomes less strong, difficult, etc.; a reduction in the strength of something **SYN** LULL: *There is no sign of a letup in the recession.*

leu·ke·m·ia /lu'kimiə/ *noun* [U] a serious disease in which too many white blood cells are produced, causing weakness and sometimes death

leu·ko·cyte /'lukəˌsaɪt/ *noun* (*biology*) = WHITE BLOOD CELL

lev·ee /'lɛvi/ *noun* **1** a low wall built at the side of a river to prevent it from flooding **2** a place on a river where boats can let passengers on or off

lev·el 🔑 /'lɛvl/ *noun, adj., verb*
• *noun*
> **AMOUNT 1** [C] the amount of something that exists in a particular situation at a particular time: *a test that checks the level of alcohol in the blood* ◆ *a relatively low/high level of crime* ◆ *low/high pollution levels* ◆ *Profits were at the same level as the year before.*
> **STANDARD 2** [C, U] a particular standard or quality: *a high level of achievement* ◆ *a game with 15 levels* ◆ *What is the level of this course?* ◆ *I refuse to sink to their level* (= behave as badly as them). ⊃ see also ENTRY-LEVEL
> **RANK IN SCALE 3** [U, C] a position or rank in a scale of size or importance: *a decision made at board level* ◆ *Discussions are currently being held at national level.*
> **POINT OF VIEW 4** [C] a particular way of looking at, reacting to, or understanding sth: *On a more personal level, I would like to thank Jean for all the help she has given me.* ◆ *Fables can be understood on various levels.*

> **HEIGHT 5** [C, U] the height of something in relation to the ground or to what it used to be: *the level of water in the bottle* ◆ *The cables are buried one yard below ground level.* ◆ *The floodwater nearly reached roof level.* ⊃ see also EYE LEVEL, SEA LEVEL
> **FLOOR/LAYER 6** [C] a floor of a building; a layer of ground: *The library is all on one level.* ◆ *Archaeologists found pottery in the lowest level of the site.* ◆ *a multilevel parking lot* ⊃ see also SPLIT-LEVEL
> **TOOL 7** [C] = SPIRIT LEVEL
> **IDM** **on the level** (also **on the up and up**) (*informal*) honest; legal **SYN** ABOVEBOARD: *I'm not convinced he's on the level.* ◆ *Are you sure this deal is on the level?*

• *adj.*
> **FLAT 1** having a flat surface that does not slope: *Pitch the tent on level ground.* ◆ *Add a level tablespoon of flour* (= enough to fill the spoon but not so much that it goes above the level of the top edge of the spoon). ⊃ compare HEAPING
> **EQUAL 2** having the same height, position, value, etc. as something: *Are these pictures level?* ◆ **~ with sth** *This latest raise is intended to keep salaries level with inflation.* ◆ *She drew level with* (= came beside) *the police car.*
> **VOICE/LOOK 3** not showing any emotion; steady **SYN** EVEN: *a level gaze* ⊃ see also LEVELLY
> **IDM** **do/try your level best (to do sth)** to do as much as you can to try to achieve something **a level playing field** a situation in which everyone has the same opportunities

• *verb* (-l-)
> **MAKE FLAT 1** [T] **~ sth (off/out)** to make something flat or smooth: *If you're laying tiles, the floor will need to be leveled first.*
> **DESTROY 2** [T] **~ sth** to destroy a building or a group of trees completely by knocking it down **SYN** RAZE: *The blast leveled several buildings in the area.*
> **MAKE EQUAL 3** [T] **~ sth** to make something equal or similar: *Davies leveled the score at 2 all.*
> **POINT 4** [T] **~ sth (at sb)** to point something, especially a gun, at someone: *I had a gun leveled at my head.*
> **IDM** **level the playing field** to create a situation where everyone has the same opportunities
> **PHR V** **level sth against/at sb** to say publicly that someone is to blame for something, especially a crime or a mistake: *The speech was intended to answer the charges leveled against him by his opponents.* ˌ**level 'off/'out 1** to stop rising or falling and remain horizontal: *The plane leveled off at 1,500 feet.* ◆ *After the long hill, the road leveled out.* **2** to stay at a steady level of development or progress after a period of sharp rises or falls: *Sales have leveled off after a period of rapid growth.* '**level with sb** (*informal*) to tell someone the truth and not hide any unpleasant facts from them

lev·el·er /'lɛvələr/ *noun* [usually sing.] an event or a situation that makes everyone equal whatever their age, importance, etc.: *death, the great leveler*

ˌ**level-'headed** *adj.* calm and sensible; able to make good decisions even in difficult situations

lev·el·ly /'lɛvəli/ *adv.* in a calm and steady way: *She looked at him levelly.*

lev·er /'lɛvər; 'li-/ *noun, verb*
• *noun* **1** a handle used to operate a vehicle or piece of machinery: *Pull the lever toward you to adjust the speed.* ⊃ see also GEAR LEVER **2** a long piece of wood, metal, etc. used for lifting or opening something by someone placing one end of it under an object and pushing down on the other end **3 ~ (for/against sth)** an action that is used to put pressure on someone to do something they do not want to do: *The threat of sanctions is our most powerful lever for peace.*
• *verb* to move something with a lever **SYN** PRIZE: **~ sth + adv./prep.** *I levered the lid off the can of paint with a knife.* ◆ **~ sth + adj.** *They managed to lever the door open.*

lev·er·age /'lɛvərɪdʒ; 'lɛvrɪdʒ/ *noun, verb*
• *noun* [U] **1** (*formal*) the ability to influence what people do: *diplomatic leverage* **2** (*technical*) the act of using a lever to open or lift something; the force used to do this **3** (*finance*) the relationship between the amount of money that a

ʌ **cup**   ə **about**   eɪ **say**   aɪ **five**   ɔɪ **boy**   aʊ **now**   oʊ **go**   ər **bird**

company owes and the value of its shares

- **verb** ~ **sth** (*business*) to get as much advantage or profit as possible from something that you have: *The company needs to leverage its resources.*

leveraged buyout *noun* (*business*) the act of a small company buying a larger company using money that is borrowed based on the value of this larger company

le·vi·a·than /ləˈvaɪəθən/ *noun* **1** (in the Bible) a very large sea MONSTER **2** (*literary*) a very large and powerful thing: *the leviathan of government bureaucracy*

lev·i·tate /ˈlɛvəˌteɪt/ *verb* [I, T] ~ (**sth**) to rise and float in the air with no physical support, especially by means of magic or by using special mental powers; to make something rise in this way ▶ **lev·i·ta·tion** /ˌlɛvəˈteɪʃn/ *noun* [U]

lev·i·ty /ˈlɛvəti/ *noun* [U] (*formal*) behavior that shows a lack of respect for something serious and that treats it in an amusing way **SYN** FRIVOLITY

le·vy **AWL** /ˈlɛvi/ *noun, verb*
- **noun** (*pl.* **le·vies**) ~ (**on sth**) an extra amount of money that has to be paid, especially as a tax to the government: *to put/impose a levy on oil imports*
- **verb** (**le·vies, le·vy·ing, le·vied, le·vied**) ~ **sth** (**on sb/sth**) to use official authority to demand and collect a payment, tax, etc.: *a tax levied by the government on excess company profits*

lewd /lud/ *adj.* referring to sex in an offensive way **SYN** OBSCENE: *lewd behavior/jokes/suggestions* ▶ **lewd·ly** *adv.* **lewd·ness** *noun* [U]

lex·eme /ˈlɛksim/ (also **lexical unit**) *noun* (*linguistics*) a word or several words that have a meaning that is not expressed by any of its separate parts

lex·i·cal /ˈlɛksɪkl/ *adj.* [usually before noun] (*linguistics*) connected with the words of a language: *lexical items* (= words and phrases) ▶ **lex·i·cally** /-kli/ *adv.*

lexical meaning *noun* [U, C] the meaning of a word, without paying attention to the way that it is used or to the words that occur with it

lexical unit *noun* = LEXEME

lex·i·cog·ra·pher /ˌlɛksəˈkɑgrəfər/ *noun* a person who writes and EDITS dictionaries

lex·i·cog·ra·phy /ˌlɛksəˈkɑgrəfi/ *noun* [U] the theory and practice of writing dictionaries

lex·i·col·o·gy /ˌlɛksəˈkɑlədʒi/ *noun* [U] the study of the form, meaning, and behavior of words

lex·i·con /ˈlɛksəˌkɑn/ *noun* **1** also **the lexicon** [sing.] (*linguistics*) all the words and phrases used in a particular language or subject; all the words and phrases used and known by a particular person or group of people: *the lexicon of finance and economics* **2** [C] a list of words on a particular subject or in a language in alphabetical order: *a lexicon of technical scientific terms* **3** [C] a dictionary, especially one of an ancient language, such as Greek or Hebrew

lex·is /ˈlɛksəs/ *noun* [U] (*linguistics*) all the words and phrases of a particular language **SYN** VOCABULARY

ley /leɪ/ *noun* **1** (also **ley line**) an imaginary line that is believed to follow the route of an ancient track and to have special powers **2** (*technical*) an area of land where grass is grown temporarily instead of crops

l.h. *abbr.* (in writing) LEFT HAND

li·a·bil·i·ty /ˌlaɪəˈbɪləti/ *noun* (*pl.* **li·a·bil·i·ties**) **1** [U] ~ (**for sth**) | ~ (**to do sth**) the state of being legally responsible for something: *The company cannot accept liability for any damage caused by natural disasters.* **2** [C, usually sing.] (*informal*) a person or thing that causes you a lot of problems: *Since his injury, Jones has become more of a liability than an asset to the team.* **3** [C, usually pl.] the amount of money that a person or company owes: *The company is reported to have liabilities of nearly $90,000.* ⊃ compare ASSET

li·a·ble /ˈlaɪəbl/ *adj.* [not before noun] **1** ~ (**for sth**) legally responsible for paying the cost of something: *You will be*

liable for any damage caused. ◆ *The court ruled he could not be held personally liable for his wife's debts.* **2** /also ˈlaɪbl/ ~ **to do sth** likely to do something: *We're all liable to make mistakes when we're tired.* ◆ *The bridge is liable to collapse at any moment.* **3** /also ˈlaɪbl/ ~ **to sth** likely to be affected by something **SYN** PRONE: *You are more liable to injury if you exercise infrequently.* **4** ~ **to sth** likely to be punished by law for something: *Offenders are liable to fines of up to $500.* **5** ~ **for/to sth** | ~ **to do sth** having to do something by law: *People who earn under a certain amount are not liable to pay tax.*

li·aise /liˈeɪz/ *verb* **1** [I] ~ (**with sb**) to work closely with someone and exchange information with them: *He had to liaise directly with the police while writing the report.* **2** [I] ~ (**between A and B**) to act as a link between two or more people or groups: *Her job is to liaise between students and teachers.*

li·ai·son /liˈeɪzɑn; ˈliəˌzɑn/ *noun* **1** [U, sing.] ~ (**between A and B**) a relationship between two organizations or different departments in an organization, involving the exchange of information or ideas: *Our role is to ensure liaison between schools and parents.* ◆ *We work in close liaison with the police.* **2** [C] ~ (**to/with sb/sth**) a person whose job is to make sure there is a good relationship between two groups or organizations: *the White House liaison to organized labor* **3** [C] ~ (**with sb**) a secret sexual relationship, especially if one or both partners are married **SYN** AFFAIR

liaison officer *noun* a person whose job is to make sure that there is a good relationship between two groups of people, organizations, etc. ⊃ see also LIAISON

li·ar /ˈlaɪər/ *noun* a person who tells lies

lib /lɪb/ *noun* (*informal*) the abbreviation for "liberation" (used in the names of organizations demanding greater freedom, equal rights, etc.): *women's lib*

li·ba·tion /laɪˈbeɪʃn/ *noun* **1** (*formal*) (in the past) a gift of wine to a god **2** (*humorous*) an alcoholic drink

li·bel /ˈlaɪbl/ *noun, verb*
- **noun** [U, C] the act of printing a statement about someone that is not true and that gives people a bad opinion of them: *He sued the newspaper for libel.* ◆ *a libel action* (= a case in a court of law) ⊃ compare SLANDER
- **verb** (-l-, *CanE usually* -ll-) ~ **sb** to publish a written statement about someone that is not true: *He claimed he had been libeled in an article the magazine had published.* ⊃ compare SLANDER

li·bel·ous (*CanE usually* **li·bel·lous**) /ˈlaɪbələs/ *adj.* containing a LIBEL about someone: *a libelous statement*

lib·er·al 🔑 **AWL** /ˈlɪbərəl; ˈlɪbrəl/ *adj., noun*
- **adj.**
> RESPECTING OTHER OPINIONS **1** willing to understand and respect other people's behavior, opinions, etc., especially when they are different from your own; believing people should be able to choose how they behave: *liberal attitudes/views/opinions*
> POLITICS **2** wanting or allowing a lot of political and economic freedom and supporting gradual social, political, or religious change: *Some politicians want more liberal trade relations with Europe.* ◆ *liberal democracy* ◆ *liberal theories* ◆ *a liberal politician* **3** Liberal connected with the Liberal Party, a political party in Canada
> GENEROUS **4** ~ (**with sth**) generous; given in large amounts **SYN** LAVISH: *She is very liberal with her money.* ◆ *I think Sam is too liberal with his criticism* (= he criticizes people too much).
> EDUCATION **5** concerned with increasing someone's general knowledge and experience rather than particular skills: *a liberal education*
> NOT EXACT **6** not completely accurate or exact **SYN** FREE: *a liberal translation of the text* ◆ *a liberal interpretation of the law*

  ▶ **lib·er·al·ly** **AWL** *adv.*: *Apply the cream liberally.* ◆ *The word "original" is liberally interpreted in copyright law.*

• **noun**

> SOMEONE WHO RESPECTS OTHERS **1** a person who understands and respects other people's opinions and behavior, especially when they are different from their own

> POLITICS **2** a person who supports political, social, and religious change: *Reform is popular with middle-class liberals.* **3 Liberal** (*politics*) a member of the Liberal Party, a political party in Canada

liberal ˈarts *noun* [pl.] subjects of study that develop students' general knowledge and ability to think, rather than their technical skills

lib·er·al·ism **AWL** /ˈlɪbərəˌlɪzəm; ˈlɪbrə-/ *noun* [U] liberal opinions and beliefs, especially in politics

lib·er·al·i·ty /ˌlɪbəˈræləti/ *noun* [U] (*formal*) **1** respect for political, religious, or moral views, even if you do not agree with them **2** the quality of being generous

lib·er·al·ize **AWL** /ˈlɪbərəˌlaɪz; ˈlɪbrə-/ *verb* ~ sth to make something such as a law or a political or religious system less strict ▶ **lib·er·al·i·za·tion** **AWL** /ˌlɪbərələˈzeɪʃn; ˌlɪbrə-/ *noun* [U]

the ˈLiberal ˈParty *noun* [sing.] (*CanE*) one of the three main political parties in Canada, in favor of some political and social change, but not extreme

lib·er·ate **AWL** /ˈlɪbəˌreɪt/ *verb* **1** ~ sb/sth (from sb/sth) to free a country or a person from the control of someone else: *The city was liberated by the advancing army.* **2** ~ sb (from sth) to free someone from something that restricts their enjoyment of life: *Writing poetry liberated her from the routine of everyday life.* ▶ **lib·er·a·tion** **AWL** /ˌlɪbəˈreɪʃn/ *noun* [U, sing.]: *a war of liberation* ◆ *liberation from poverty* ◆ *women's liberation* **lib·er·a·tor** **AWL** /ˈlɪbəˌreɪtər/ *noun*

lib·er·at·ed **AWL** /ˈlɪbəˌreɪtəd/ *adj.* free from the restrictions of traditional ideas about social and sexual behavior

liberˌation theˈology *noun* [U] a Christian movement, developed mainly by Latin American Catholics, which deals with social justice and the problems of people who are poor, as well as with spiritual matters

lib·er·tar·i·an /ˌlɪbərˈtɛriən/ *noun* a person who strongly believes that people should have the freedom to do and think as they like

lib·er·tine /ˈlɪbərˌtin/ *noun* (*formal, disapproving*) a person, usually a man, who leads an immoral life and is interested in pleasure, especially sexual pleasure

lib·er·ty /ˈlɪbərti/ *noun* (*pl.* **lib·er·ties**) **1** [U] freedom to live as you choose without too many restrictions from government or authority: *the fight for justice and liberty* **2** [U] the state of not being a prisoner or a SLAVE: *the salves struggle for liberty* **3** [C] the legal right and freedom to do something: *The right to vote should be a liberty enjoyed by all.* ◆ *People fear that security cameras could infringe personal liberties.* ➔ see also CIVIL LIBERTY **4** [sing.] an act or a statement that may offend or annoy someone, especially because it is done without permission or does not show respect: *He took the liberty of reading my files while I was away.*
IDM at liberty (*formal*) (of a prisoner or an animal) no longer in prison or in a CAGE **SYN** FREE at liberty to do sth (*formal*) having the right or freedom to do something **SYN** FREE: *You are at liberty to say what you like.* take liberties with sb/sth **1** to make important and unreasonable changes to something, especially a book: *The movie takes considerable liberties with the novel that it is based on.* **2** (*old-fashioned*) to be too friendly with someone, especially in a sexual way

li·bid·i·nous /lɪˈbɪdn·əs/ *adj.* (*formal*) having or expressing strong sexual feelings

li·bi·do /lɪˈbidoʊ/ *noun* (*pl.* **li·bi·dos**) [U, C, usually sing.] (*technical*) sexual desire: *loss of libido*

Li·bra /ˈlibrə/ *noun* **1** [U] the 7th sign of the ZODIAC, the SCALES **2** [C] a person born under the influence of this sign, that is between September 23 and October 22, approximately ▶ **Li·bran** /-brən/ *noun, adj.*

li·brar·i·an /laɪˈbrɛriən/ *noun* a person who is in charge of or works in a library ▶ **li·brar·i·an·ship** /-ənˌʃɪp/ *noun* [U]: *a degree in librarianship*

li·brar·y 🔑 /ˈlaɪˌbreri/ *noun* (*pl.* **li·brar·ies**)
1 a building in which collections of books, CDs, newspapers, etc. are kept for people to read, study, or borrow: *a public/reference/university, etc. library* ◆ *a library book* **2** a room in a large house where most of the books are kept **3** (*formal*) a personal collection of books, music, etc.: *a new edition to add to your library* **4** a series of books, recordings, etc. produced by the same company and similar in appearance: *a library of children's classics*

the ˌLibrary of ˈCongress *noun* [sing.] the U.S. national library

li·bret·tist /lɪˈbrɛtɪst/ *noun* a person who writes the words for an OPERA or a musical play

li·bret·to /lɪˈbrɛtoʊ/ *noun* (*pl.* **li·bret·tos** or **li·bret·ti** /-ˈbrɛti/) (*music*) the words that are sung or spoken in an OPERA or a musical play

lice *pl.* of LOUSE

li·cence (*CanE*) = LICENSE *n.*

li·cense 🔑 **AWL** /ˈlaɪsns/ *noun, verb*
• **noun** (*CanE also* **li·cence**) **1** [C] an official document that shows that permission has been given to do, own, or use something: *a driver's license* ◆ ~ (for sth) *a license for the software* ◆ *Is there a license fee?* ◆ *James lost his license for six months* (= had his license taken away by the police as a punishment). ◆ ~ (to do sth) *You need a license to fish in this river.* ◆ *a license holder* (= a person who has been given a license) **2** [U, sing.] ~ (to do sth) (*formal*) freedom to do or say whatever you want, often something bad or unacceptable: *Lack of punishment seems to give youngsters license to break the law.* **3** [U] (*formal*) freedom to behave in a way that is considered sexually immoral
IDM artistic/poetic license the freedom of artists or writers to change facts in order to make a story, painting, etc. more interesting or beautiful a license to print money (*disapproving*) used to describe a business which makes a lot of money with little effort under license (of a product) made with the permission of a company or an organization
• **verb** to give someone official permission to do, own, or use something: ~ sth *The new drug has not yet been licensed in the U.S.* ◆ ~ sb/sth to do sth *They licensed the company to produce the drug.*

li·censed **AWL** /ˈlaɪsnst/ *adj.* **1** that you have official permission to own: *Is that gun licensed?* **2** having official permission to do something: *She is licensed to fly solo.*

ˌlicensed ˌpractical ˈnurse *noun* (*abbr.* LPN) a nurse who has passed an exam to be allowed to work under the direction of a REGISTERED NURSE or a doctor

li·cen·see /ˌlaɪsənˈsi/ *noun* a person or company that has a license to make something or to use something

ˈlicense ˌnumber *noun* the series of letters and numbers that are shown on the LICENSE PLATE of a vehicle to identify it

ˈlicense ˌplate *noun* a metal or plastic plate on a vehicle that shows its LICENSE NUMBER

li·cen·ti·ate /laɪˈsɛnʃiət/ *noun* (*technical*) a person with official permission to work in a particular profession

li·cen·tious /laɪˈsɛnʃəs/ *adj.* (*formal, disapproving*) behaving in a way that is considered sexually immoral ▶ **li·cen·tious·ness** *noun* [U]

li·chee = LYCHEE

li·chen /ˈlaɪkən/ *noun* [U, C] a very small gray or yellow plant that spreads over the surface of rocks, walls, and trees and does not have any flowers ➔ compare MOSS ➔ picture at PLANT

lich·gate ➔ LYCHGATE

lic·it /ˈlɪsət/ *adj.* (*formal*) allowed or legal **ANT** ILLICIT ▶ **lic·it·ly** *adv.*

lick /lɪk/ *verb, noun*

● *verb* **1** [T] to move your tongue over the surface of something in order to eat it, make it wet, or clean it: **~ sth** *He licked his fingers.* ♦ *I'm tired of licking envelopes.* ♦ *The cat sat licking its paws.* ♦ **~ sth + adj.** *She licked the spoon clean.* **2** [T] **~ sth + adv./prep.** to eat or drink something by licking it: *The cat licked up the milk.* ♦ *She licked the honey off the spoon.* **3** [T, I] (of flames) to touch something lightly: **~ sth** *Flames were soon licking the curtains.* ♦ **~ at sth** *The flames were now licking at their feet.* **4** [T] **~ sb/sth** (*informal*) to easily defeat someone or deal with something: *We thought we **had them licked**.* ♦ *It was a tricky problem but I think we've licked it.*

IDM **lick sb's boots** (*disapproving*) to show too much respect for someone in authority because you want to please them **lick your wounds** to spend time trying to get your strength or confidence back after a defeat or disappointment ➪ more at LIP, SHAPE

● *noun* **1** [C] an act of licking something with the tongue: *Can I have a lick of your ice cream?* **2** [sing.] **a ~ of paint** (*informal*) a small amount of paint, used to make a place look better: *What this room needs is a lick of paint.* **3** [C] (*informal*) a short piece of music which is part of a song and is played on a GUITAR: *a guitar/blues lick* **4** [C] (*informal*) a hard hit: *Hockey players have to take a lot of licks.* ♦ (*figurative*) *The store didn't hire him, but he got in a few licks himself when he started his own successful business across the street.*

IDM **a lick and a promise** (*informal*) the act of performing a task quickly and carelessly, especially of washing or cleaning something quickly **at a (good) lick** (*informal*) fast; at a high speed

lick·e·ty-split /ˌlɪkəti ˈsplɪt/ *adv.* (*old-fashioned, informal*) very quickly; immediately

lick·ing /ˈlɪkɪŋ/ *noun* [sing.] (*informal*) a severe defeat in a battle, game, etc. **SYN** THRASHING

lick·spit·tle /ˈlɪkˌspɪtl/ *noun* (*disapproving, old-fashioned*) a person who tries to gain the approval of an important person

lic·o·rice /ˈlɪkərɪʃ/ *noun* [U] a firm black substance with a strong flavor, obtained from the root of a plant, used in medicine and to make candy; a candy made from this substance

lid /lɪd/ *noun*

1 a cover over a container that can be removed or opened by turning it or lifting it: *a trash can lid* ♦ *I can't get the lid off this jar.* ➪ picture at COOKING, PACKAGING **2** = EYELID
IDM **keep a/the lid on sth 1** to keep something secret or hidden **2** to keep something under control: *The government is keeping the lid on inflation.* **lift the lid on sth | take/blow the lid off sth** to tell people unpleasant or shocking facts about something: *Her article lifts the lid on child prostitution.* **put a lid on sth** (*informal*) **1** to stop a bad situation from getting worse: *We've got to put a lid on these rumors that the mayor is taking kickbacks.* **2** to stop someone from saying something: *If everyone would put a lid on their gossiping, we could get something done at this meeting.* ➪ more at FLIP

THESAURUS

lid

top ♦ cork ♦ cap ♦ plug

These are all words for a cover for a container.

lid a cover over a container that can be removed or opened by twisting or lifting it off: *a jar with a tight-fitting lid*

top a thing that you put over the end of something such as a pen or bottle in order to close it

cork a small round object made of cork or plastic that is used for closing bottles, especially wine bottles

cap (often in compounds) a top for something such as a bottle, or a protective cover for something such as the lens of a camera

---

plug a round piece of material that you put into a hole in order to block it; a flat round rubber or plastic thing that you put into the hole of a sink in order to stop the water from flowing out: *a drain plug*

PATTERNS
- a **tight-fitting** lid/top/cap
- a **screw** top/cap
- a **pen** lid/top
- to **put on/screw on/take off/unscrew** the lid/top/cap
- to **pull out** the cork/plug

lid·ded /ˈlɪdəd/ *adj.* [usually before noun] **1** (of containers) having a lid **2** (*literary*) used to describe a person's expression when their EYELIDS appear large or their eyes are almost closed: *heavy-lidded eyes* ♦ *his lidded gaze*

li·do·caine /ˈlaɪdəˌkeɪn/ *noun* [U] a substance used as a LOCAL ANESTHETIC, for example to stop people from feeling pain when teeth are removed

lie[1] /laɪ/ *verb* (lies, ly·ing, lay /leɪ/, lain /leɪn/) ➪ see also LIE[2]

1 [I] (of a person or an animal) to be or put yourself in a flat or horizontal position so that you are not standing or sitting: **+ adv./prep.** *Lie on your back/side/front* ♦ **+ adj.** *The cat was lying fast asleep by the fire.* **2** [I] (of a thing) to be or remain in a flat position on a surface: **+ adv./prep.** *Clothes were lying all over the floor.* ♦ **+ adj.** *The book lay open on his desk.* **3** [I] to be, remain, or be kept in a particular state: **+ adj.** *Snow was lying thick on the ground.* ♦ *These machines have lain idle since the factory closed.* ♦ **+ adv./prep.** *a ship lying at anchor* ♦ *I'd rather use my money than leave it lying in the bank.* **4** [I] **+ adv./prep.** (of a town, natural feature, etc.) to be located in a particular place: *The town lies on the coast.* **5** [I] **+ adv./prep.** to be spread out in a particular place: *The valley lay below us.* **6** [I] **~ (in sth)** (of ideas, qualities, problems, etc.) to exist or be found: *The problem lies in deciding when to intervene.* ➪ compare LAY
IDM **lie ahead/in store** to be going to happen to someone in the future: *You are young and your whole life lies ahead of you.* **lie in state** (of the dead body of an important person) to be placed on view in a public place before being buried **lie in wait (for sb)** to hide, waiting to surprise, attack, or catch someone: *He was surrounded by reporters who had been lying in wait for him.* **lie low** (*informal*) to try not to attract attention to yourself **take sth lying down** to accept an insult or offensive act without protesting or reacting ➪ more at BED, HEAVY, SLEEP
PHR V **lie a·round 1** to be left somewhere in a messy or careless way, not put away in the correct place: *Don't leave toys lying around—someone might trip over them.* **2** (of a person) to spend time doing nothing and being lazy **lie back** to do nothing except relax: *You don't have to do anything—just lie back and enjoy the ride.* **lie be·hind sth** to be the real reason for something, often hidden: *What lay behind this strange outburst?* **lie down** to be or get into a flat position, especially in bed, in order to sleep or rest: *Go and lie down for a while.* ♦ *He lay down on the sofa and soon fell asleep.* **lie with sb (to do sth)** (*formal*) to be someone's duty or responsibility: *It lies with you to accept or reject the proposals.*

lie[2] /laɪ/ *verb, noun* ➪ see also LIE[1]

● *verb* (lies, ly·ing, lied, lied) [I] to say or write something that you know is not true: *You could see from his face that he was lying.* ♦ **~ (to sb) (about sth)** *Don't lie to me!* ♦ *She lies about her age.* ♦ *The camera cannot lie* (= give a false impression). ➪ see also LIAR ➪ thesaurus box at CHEAT
IDM **lie through your teeth** (*informal*) to say something that is not true at all: *The witness was clearly lying through his teeth.* **lie your way into/out of sth** to get yourself into or out of a situation by lying

● *noun* a statement made by someone knowing that it is not true: *to tell a lie* ♦ *The whole story is nothing but a pack of lies.*

♦ *a barefaced lie* (= a lie that is deliberate and shocking) ⊃ see also WHITE LIE

IDM **give the lie to sth** (*formal*) to show that something is not true ⊃ more at LIVE¹, TISSUE

Lieb·frau·milch /ˈliːbfraʊˌmɪlk; -ˌmɪlʃ; -ˌmɪlx/ *noun* [U, C] a type of German white wine

lied /liːd/ *noun* (*pl.* **lie·der** /ˈliːdər/) a German song for one singer and piano

'lie de,tector (also *formal* or *technical* **pol·y·graph**) *noun* a piece of equipment that is used, for example by the police, to find out if someone is telling the truth

lief /liːf/ *adv.* (*old use*) willingly; happily: *I would as lief kill myself as betray my master.*

liege /liːdʒ/ (also *,liege 'lord*) *noun* (*old use*) a king or lord

lien /liːn/ *noun* ~ **(in/over sth)** (*law*) the right to keep someone's property until a debt is paid

lieu /luː/ *noun* (*formal*)

IDM **in lieu (of sth)** instead of: *They took cash in lieu of the prize they had won.* ♦ *We work on Saturdays and have a day off in lieu during the week.*

Lieut. (also **Lt.**) *abbr.* (in writing) LIEUTENANT

lieu·ten·ant /luːˈtɛnənt/ *noun* (*abbr.* **Lieut., Lt.**) **1** an officer of middle rank in the army, navy, or AIR FORCE: *Lieutenant Paul Fisher* ⊃ see also SECOND LIEUTENANT **2** (in compounds) an officer just below the rank mentioned: *a lieutenant colonel* **3** a police officer or FIREFIGHTER of fairly high rank **4** a person who helps someone who is above them in rank or who performs their duties when that person is unable to

lieu,tenant 'colonel *noun* an officer of middle rank in the army and AIR FORCE

lieu,tenant com'mander *noun* an officer of middle rank in the navy

lieu,tenant 'general *noun* an officer of very high rank in the army

lieu,tenant 'governor *noun* (in Canada) the representative of the CROWN in a PROVINCE

life 🔊 /laɪf/ *noun* (*pl.* **lives** /laɪvz/)

▷ STATE OF LIVING **1** [U] the ability to breathe, grow, reproduce, etc. that people, animals, and plants have before they die and that objects do not have: *life and death* ♦ *The body was cold and showed no signs of life.* ♦ *My father died last year—I wish I could bring him back to life.* ♦ *In spring the countryside bursts into life.* **2** [U, C] the state of being alive as a human; an individual person's existence: *The floods caused a massive loss of life* (= many people were killed). ♦ *He risked his life to save his daughter from the fire.* ♦ *Hundreds of lives were threatened when the building collapsed.* ♦ *The operation saved her life.* ♦ *My grandfather lost his life* (= was killed) *in the war.* ♦ *Several attempts have been made on the President's life* (= several people have tried to kill him).

▷ LIVING THINGS **3** [U] living things: *plant/animal life* ♦ *marine/pond life* ♦ *Is there intelligent life on other planets?*

▷ PERIOD OF TIME **4** [C, U] the period between someone's birth and their death; a part of this period: *He's lived here all his life.* ♦ *I've lived in Iowa for most of my life.* ♦ *to have a long/short life* ♦ *He became very weak toward the end of his life.* ♦ *Brenda took up tennis late in life.* ♦ *He will spend the rest of his life* (= until he dies) *in a wheelchair.* ♦ *There's no such thing as a job for life any longer.* ♦ *She is a life member of the club.* ♦ *in early/adult life* ⊃ see also CHANGE OF LIFE **5** [C] (used with an adjective) a period of someone's life when they are in a particular situation or job: *She has been an accountant all her working life.* ♦ *He met a lot of interesting people during his life as a student.* ♦ *They were very happy throughout their married life.* **6** [C] the period of time when something exists or functions: *That building started life as a drugstore.* ♦ *They could see that the company had a limited life* (= it was going to close). ♦ *In Italy the average life of a government is eleven months.* ⊃ see also SHELF LIFE

▷ PUNISHMENT **7** [U] the punishment of being sent to prison

for life; life IMPRISONMENT: *The judge gave him life.*

▷ EXPERIENCE/ACTIVITIES **8** [U] the experience and activities that are typical of all people's existences: *the worries of everyday life* ♦ *He is young and has little experience of life.* ♦ *Commuting is a part of daily life for many people.* ♦ *Jill wants to travel and see life for herself.* ♦ *We bought a dishwasher to make life easier.* ♦ *In Africa life can be hard.* ♦ *In real life* (= when she met him) *he wasn't how she had imagined him at all.* ♦ *Life isn't like in the movies, you know.* **9** [U, C] the activities and experiences that are typical of a particular way of living: *country/city life* ♦ *She enjoyed political life.* ♦ *family/married life* ♦ *How do you find life in Japan?* **10** [C] a person's experiences during their life; the activities that form a particular part of a person's life: *He has had a good life.* ♦ *a hard/an easy life* ♦ *My day-to-day life is not very exciting.* ♦ *a life of luxury* ♦ *Her daily life involved meeting lots of people.* ♦ *Many of these children have led very sheltered lives* (= they have not had many different experiences). ♦ *They emigrated to start a new life in Canada.* ♦ *He doesn't like to talk about his private life.* ♦ *She has a full social life.* ♦ *articles about the love lives of the stars* ⊃ see also SEX LIFE

▷ ENERGY/EXCITEMENT **11** [U] the quality of being active and exciting **SYN** VITALITY: *This is a great vacation resort that is full of life.*

▷ IN ART **12** [U] a living model or a real object or scene that people draw or paint: *She had lessons in drawing from life.* ♦ *a life class* (= one in which art students draw a naked man or woman) ⊃ see also STILL LIFE

▷ STORY OF LIFE **13** [C] a story of someone's life **SYN** BIOGRAPHY: *She wrote a life of Mozart.*

▷ IN CHILDREN'S GAMES **14** [C] one of a set number of chances before a player is out of a game: *He's lost two lives, so he's only got one left.*

IDM **be sb's life** be the most important person or thing to someone: *My children are my life.* ♦ *Writing is his life.* **bring sb/sth to life** to make someone or something more interesting or exciting: *The new teacher really brought French to life for us.* ♦ *Flowers can bring a dull room back to life.* **come to life 1** to become more interesting, exciting, or full of activity: *The game finally came to life in the final quarter.* **2** to start to act or move as if alive: *In my dream all my toys came to life.* **for dear life| for your life** as hard or as fast as possible: *She was holding on to the rope for dear life.* ♦ *Run for your life!* **for the life of you** (*informal*) however hard you try: *I cannot for the life of me imagine why they want to leave.* **full of life** having a lot of energy **get a life** (*informal*) used to tell someone to stop being boring and to do something more interesting **lay down your life (for sb/sth)** (*literary*) to die in order to save someone or something **SYN** SACRIFICE YOURSELF **lead/live the life of Riley** (*old-fashioned, often disapproving*) to live an enjoyable and comfortable life with no problems or responsibilities **life after death** the possibility or belief that people continue to exist in some form after they die **the life of the party** the most amusing and interesting person at a party, etc. **life is cheap** (*disapproving*) used to say that there is a situation in which it is not thought to be important if people somewhere die or are treated badly **(have) a life of its own** (of an object) seeming to move or function by itself without a person touching or working it **life's too short** (*informal*) used to say that it is not worth wasting time doing something that you dislike or that is not important **make life difficult (for sb)** to cause problems for someone **the man/woman in your life** (*informal*) the man or woman that you are having a sexual or romantic relationship with **not on your life** (*informal*) used to refuse very firmly to do something **scare/frighten the life out of sb** to frighten someone very much **take sb's life** to kill someone **take your (own) life** to kill yourself **take your life in your hands** to risk being killed: *You take your life in your hands just crossing the street here.* **that's life** (*informal*) used when you are disappointed about something but know that you must accept it **where there's life (, there's hope)** (*saying*) in a bad situation you must not give up hope because there is always a chance that it will improve ⊃ more at BET *v.*, BREATH, BREATHE, DEPART,

DOG n., END v., FACT, FEAR n., FIGHT v., LARGE, LEASE n., LIGHT n., MATTER n., MISERY, NINE, RISK v., SAVE v., SLICE n., SPRING v., STAFF n., STORY, TIME n., TRUE, VARIETY, WALK n., WAY n.

TOPIC COLLOCATIONS

The Living World

animals

- animals **mate/breed/reproduce/feed (on sth)**
- fish/amphibians **swim/spawn** (= lay eggs)
- birds **fly/migrate/nest/sing**
- insects **crawl/fly/bite/sting**
- insects/bees/locusts **swarm**
- bees **collect/gather** nectar/pollen
- spiders **spin/weave** a web
- snakes/lizards **shed their skins**
- bears/hedgehogs/frogs **hibernate**
- insect larvae **grow/develop/pupate**
- an egg/a chick/a larva **hatches**
- **attract/find/choose** a mate
- **produce/release** eggs/sperm
- **lay/fertilize/incubate/hatch** eggs
- **inhabit** a forest/a reef/the coast
- **mark/enter/defend** (a) territory
- **stalk/hunt/capture/catch/kill** prey

plants and fungi

- trees/plants **grow/bloom/blossom/flower**
- a seed **germinates/sprouts**
- leaves/buds/roots/shoots **appear/develop/form**
- flower buds **swell/open**
- a fungus **grows/spreads/colonizes sth**
- **pollinate/fertilize** a flower/plant
- **produce/release/spread/disperse** pollen/seeds/spores
- **produce/bear** fruit
- **develop/grow/form** roots/shoots/leaves
- **provide/supply/absorb/extract/release** nutrients
- **perform/increase/reduce** photosynthesis

bacteria and viruses

- bacteria/microbes/viruses **grow/spread/multiply**
- bacteria/microbes **live/thrive in/on sth**
- bacteria/microbes/viruses **evolve/colonize sth/cause disease**
- bacteria **break sth down/convert sth (into sth)**
- a virus **enters/invades** sth/the body
- a virus **mutates/evolves/replicates (itself)**
- be **infected with/contaminated with/exposed to** a new strain of a virus/drug-resistant bacteria
- **contain/carry/harbor** bacteria/a virus
- **kill/destroy/eliminate** harmful/deadly bacteria

ˌlife-and-ˈdeath (also ˌlife-or-ˈdeath) adj. [only before noun] extremely serious, especially when there is a situation in which people might die: a life-and-death decision/struggle

life·belt /ˈlaɪfbɛlt/ noun a special belt worn to help someone float in water ⊃ see also LIFE JACKET, LIFE PRESERVER

life·blood /ˈlaɪfblʌd/ noun [U] 1 ~ (of sth) the thing that keeps something strong and healthy and is necessary for successful development: Tourism is the lifeblood of the city. 2 (literary) a person's blood, when it is thought of as the thing that is necessary for life

life·boat /ˈlaɪfboʊt/ noun 1 a small boat carried on a ship in order to save the people on board if the ship sinks 2 a special boat that is sent out to rescue people who are in danger at sea: a lifeboat crew/station

life·bu·oy /ˈlaɪfˌbui; -ˌbɔɪ/ noun a piece of material that floats well, used to rescue someone who has fallen into water, by keeping them above water

ˈlife coach noun a person who is employed by someone to give them advice about how to achieve the things they want in their life and work ▶ ˈlife ˌcoaching noun [U]

ˈlife ˌcycle noun 1 (biology) the series of forms into which a living thing changes as it develops: the life cycle of the butterfly 2 the period of time during which something, for example a product, is developed and used

ˈlife-enˌhancing adj. making you feel happier and making life more enjoyable

ˈlife exˌpectancy (also expecˌtation of ˈlife) noun [U, C] the number of years that a person is likely to live; the length of time that something is likely to exist or continue for

ˈlife force noun [U] 1 the force that gives someone or something their strength or energy: He looked very weak—his life force seemed to have drained away. 2 the force that keeps all life in existence: In Hindu philosophy, the life force is known as prana.

ˈlife form noun (technical) a living thing such as a plant or an animal

ˈlife-ˌgiving adj. [usually before noun] (literary) that gives life or keeps something alive

ˈlife·guard /ˈlaɪfɡɑrd/ noun a person who is employed at a beach or a swimming pool to rescue people who are in danger in the water

ˈlife ˈhistory noun all the events that happen in the life of a person, animal, or plant

ˈlife inˌsurance noun [U] a type of insurance in which you make regular payments so that you receive a sum of money when you are a particular age, or so that your family will receive a sum of money when you die: a life insurance policy

ˈlife ˌjacket (also ˈlife vest) noun a jacket without sleeves designed to help you float if you fall in water ⊃ picture at BOAT

life·less /ˈlaɪfləs/ adj. 1 (formal) dead or appearing to be dead SYN INANIMATE 2 not living; not having living things growing on or in it: lifeless machines ◆ a lifeless planet 3 dull; lacking the qualities that make something or someone interesting and full of life SYN LACKLUSTER: his lifeless performance on stage

life·like /ˈlaɪflaɪk/ adj. exactly like a real person or thing SYN REALISTIC: a lifelike statue/drawing/toy

life·line /ˈlaɪflaɪn/ noun 1 a line or rope thrown to rescue someone who is in difficulty in the water 2 a line attached to someone who goes deep under the ocean 3 something that is very important for someone and that they depend on: The support group is a lifeline for many single mothers.

life·long /ˈlaɪflɔŋ/ adj. [only before noun] lasting or existing all through your life

ˌlife-or-ˈdeath adj. = LIFE-AND-DEATH

ˈlife preˌserver noun a piece of material that floats well, or a jacket made of such material, used to rescue a person who has fallen into water, by keeping them above water

lif·er /ˈlaɪfər/ noun (informal) 1 a person who has been sent to prison for their whole life 2 a person who has been in the same job, club, etc. for their whole life: Joe's a lifer here.

ˈlife raft noun an open rubber boat filled with air, used for rescuing people from sinking ships or planes

life·sav·er /ˈlaɪfˌseɪvər/ noun a thing that helps someone in a difficult situation; something that saves someone's life: The new drug is a potential lifesaver.

ˈlife-ˌsaving (also life-sav·ing) /ˈlaɪfˌseɪvɪŋ/ adj. [usually before noun] that is going to save someone's life: a life-saving heart operation

life·sav·ing /ˈlaɪfˌseɪvɪŋ/ noun [U] the skills needed to save someone who is in water and is DROWNING: lifesaving certification

ˈlife ˌsciences noun [pl.] the sciences concerned with studying humans, animals, or plants ⊃ compare EARTH SCIENCE, NATURAL SCIENCE, PHYSICAL SCIENCE

ˌlife ˈsentence noun the punishment in which someone spends the rest of their life in prison

ˈlife-size (also ˈlife-sized) adj. the same size as a person or thing really is: a life-size statue

---

life·span /'laɪfspæn/ *noun* the length of time that something is likely to live, continue, or function: *Worms have a lifespan of a few months.*

life 'story *noun* the story that someone tells you about their whole life

life·style /'laɪfstaɪl/ *noun* [C, U] the way in which a person or a group of people lives and works: *a comfortable/healthy/lavish, etc. lifestyle* ◆ *It was a big change in lifestyle when we moved to the country.* ◆ *the lifestyle section of the newspaper* (= the part that deals with clothes, furniture, hobbies, etc.)

life sup·port *noun* [U] the medical equipment or treatment used to keep someone alive when they are extremely sick: *Families want the right to refuse life support.* ◆ *She's critically ill, on life support.*

life-·threatening *adj.* that is likely to kill someone: *His heart condition is not life-threatening.*

life·time /'laɪftaɪm/ *noun* the length of time that someone lives or that something lasts: *His diary was not published during his lifetime.* ◆ *a lifetime of experience* ◆ *in the lifetime of the present government*
  IDM **the chance, etc. of a lifetime** a wonderful opportunity, etc. that you are not likely to get again **once in a lifetime** used to describe something special that is not likely to happen to you again: *An opportunity like this comes once in a lifetime.* ◆ *a once-in-a-lifetime experience*

life vest *noun* = LIFE JACKET ⊃ picture at BOAT

life·work /ˌlaɪf'wərk/ *noun* [sing.] the main purpose or activity in a person's life, or their greatest achievement

lift /lɪft/ *verb, noun*
● *verb*
> RAISE **1** [T, I] to raise someone or something or be raised to a higher position or level: *~ sb/sth (up) (+ adv./prep.)* *He stood there with his arms lifted above his head.* ◆ *I lifted the lid of the box and peered in.* ◆ *(figurative) John lifted his eyes* (= looked up) *from his book.* ◆ *~ (up) Her eyebrows lifted. "Apologize? Why?"*
> MOVE SOMEONE OR SOMETHING **2** [T] *~ sb/sth (+ adv./prep.)* to take hold of someone or something and move them/it to a different position: *I lifted the baby out of the crib.* ◆ *He lifted the suitcase down from the rack.* **3** [T] *~ sb/sth (+ adv./prep.)* to transport people or things by air: *The survivors were lifted to safety by helicopter.* ⊃ see also AIRLIFT
> REMOVE LAW/RULE **4** [T] *~ sth* to remove or end restrictions: *to lift a ban/curfew/blockade* ◆ *Martial law has now been lifted.*
> HEART/SPIRITS **5** [I, T] to become or make someone more cheerful: *His heart lifted at the sight of her.* ◆ *~ sth The news lifted our spirits.*
> OF MIST/CLOUDS **6** [I] to rise and disappear **SYN** DISPERSE: *The fog began to lift.* ◆ *(figurative) Gradually my depression started to lift.*
> STEAL **7** [T] *~ sth (from sb/sth)* *(informal)* to steal something: *He had been lifting electrical goods from the store where he worked.* ⊃ see also SHOPLIFTING
> COPY IDEAS/WORDS **8** [T] *~ sth (from sth)* to use someone's ideas or words without asking permission or without saying where they come from **SYN** PLAGIARIZE: *She lifted most of the ideas from a book she had been reading.*
> INCREASE **9** [T, I] *~ (sth)* to make the amount or level of something greater; to become greater in amount or level: *Interest rates were lifted yesterday.*
  IDM **not lift a finger (to do sth)** *(informal)* to do nothing to help someone: *The kids never lift a finger to help around the house.*
  PHR V **lift 'off** (of a ROCKET, a SPACECRAFT, or, less frequently, an aircraft) to leave the ground and rise into the air ⊃ related noun LIFT-OFF
● *noun*
> FREE RIDE **1** [C] a free ride in a car, etc. to a place you want to get to: *I'll give you a lift to the train station.*
> HAPPIER FEELING **2** [sing.] a feeling of being happier or more confident than before **SYN** BOOST: *Passing the exam gave him a real lift.*

> RISING MOVEMENT **3** [sing.] a movement in which something rises or is lifted up: *the puzzled lift of his eyebrows*
> ON AIRCRAFT **4** [U] the upward pressure of air on an aircraft when flying ⊃ compare DRAG

lift-off *noun* [C, U] the act of a SPACECRAFT leaving the ground and rising into the air **SYN** BLASTOFF: *Ten minutes to lift-off.*

lig·a·ment /'lɪgəmənt/ *noun* a strong band of TISSUE in the body that connects bones and supports organs and keeps them in position: *I tore a ligament.* ⊃ collocations at INJURY

li·gate /'laɪgeɪt/ *verb* *~ sth* *(medical)* to tie up an ARTERY or other BLOOD VESSEL or tube in the body, with a LIGATURE ▶ **li·ga·tion** /laɪ'geɪʃn/ *noun* [U]

li·ga·ture /'lɪgətʃər; -tʃʊr/ *noun* *(technical)* something that is used for tying something very tightly, for example to stop the loss of blood from a wound

lights

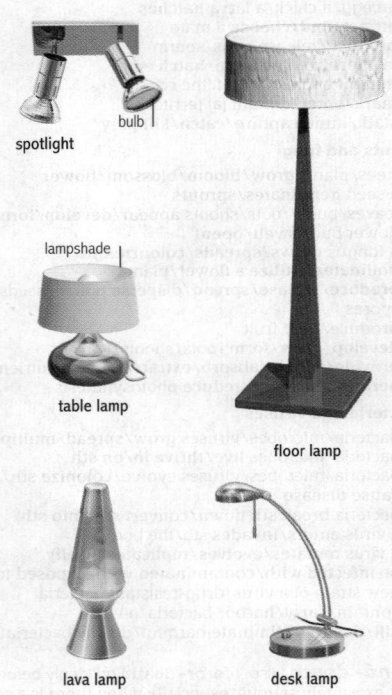

spotlight
bulb
lampshade
table lamp
floor lamp
lava lamp
desk lamp

light /laɪt/ *noun, adj., verb, adv.*
● *noun*
> FROM SUN/LAMPS **1** [U] the energy from the sun, a lamp, etc. that makes it possible to see things: *bright/dim light* ◆ *a room with good natural light* ◆ *in the fading light of a summer's evening* ◆ *The light was beginning to fail* (= it was beginning to get dark). ◆ *She could just see by the light of the candle.* ◆ *Bring it into the light so I can see it.* ◆ *a beam/ray of light* ◆ *The knife gleamed as it caught the light* (= as the light shone on it). ⊃ see also FIRST LIGHT **2** [C] a particular type of light with its own color and qualities: *A cold gray light crept under the curtains.* ⊃ see also THE NORTHERN LIGHTS
> LAMP **3** [C] a thing that produces light, especially an electric light: *to turn/switch the lights on/off* ◆ *to turn out the light(s)* ◆ *Suddenly all the lights went out.* ◆ *It was an hour before the lights came on again.* ◆ *to turn down/dim the lights* ◆ *A light was still burning in the bedroom.* ◆ *ceiling/wall lights* ◆ *Keep going—the light* (= traffic light) *is green.* ◆ *Check your car before you drive to make sure that your lights are working.* ⊃ see also

BRAKE LIGHT, FOG LIGHT, GREEN LIGHT, HEADLIGHT, LEADING LIGHT, RED LIGHT ⊃ picture at BICYCLE
> FOR CIGARETTE **4** [sing.] a match or device with which you can light a cigarette: *Do you have a light?*
> EXPRESSION IN EYES **5** [sing.] an expression in someone's eyes which shows what they are thinking or feeling: *There was a soft light in her eyes as she looked at him.*
> IN PICTURE **6** [U] light colors in a picture, which contrast with darker ones: *the artist's use of light and shade*
> WINDOW **7** [C] (*architecture*) a window or an opening to allow light in ⊃ see also SKYLIGHT
IDM be/go out like a light (*informal*) to go to sleep very quickly be in sb's light to be between someone and a source of light: *Could you move—you're in my light.* bring sth to light to make new information known to people: *These facts have only just been brought to light.* cast/shed/throw light on sth to make a problem, etc. easier to understand: *Recent research has thrown new light on the causes of the disease.* come to light to become known to people: *New evidence has recently come to light.* in a good, bad, favorable, etc. light if you see something or put something in a good, bad, etc. light, it seems good, bad, etc.: *You must not view what happened in a negative light.* ◆ *They want to present their policies in the best possible light.* in light of sth after considering something: *He rewrote the book in light of further research.* light at the end of the tunnel something that shows you are nearly at the end of a long and difficult time or situation (the) light dawned (on sb) someone suddenly understood or began to understand something: *I puzzled over the problem for ages before the light suddenly dawned.* the light of sb's life the person someone loves more than any other run a (red) light| run the light(s) (*informal*) to fail to stop at a red traffic light see the light **1** to finally understand or accept something, especially something obvious **2** to begin to believe in a religion see the light of day to begin to exist or to become publicly known: *He's written a lot of good material that has never seen the light of day.* ⊃ more at BRIGHT, COLD, SWEETNESS

● *adj.* (light·er, light·est)
> WITH NATURAL LIGHT **1** full of light; having the natural light of day: *We'll leave in the morning as soon as it's light.* ◆ *It gets light at about 6 o'clock.* ◆ *It was a light, spacious apartment at the top of the building.* **ANT** DARK
> COLORS **2** pale in color: *light blue eyes* ◆ *Lighter shades suit you best.* ◆ *People with pale complexions should avoid wearing light colors.* **ANT** DARK
> WEIGHT **3** easy to lift or move; not weighing very much: *Modern video cameras are light and easy to carry.* ◆ *Carry this bag—it's the lightest.* ◆ *He's lost a lot of weight—he's thirty pounds lighter than he was.* ◆ *The little girl was **as light as a feather**.* ◆ *The aluminum body is 12% lighter than the steel one.* **ANT** HEAVY **4** [usually before noun] of less than average or usual weight: *light summer clothes* ◆ *Only light vehicles are allowed over the old bridge.* **ANT** HEAVY **5** used with a unit of weight to say that something weighs less than it should: *The delivery of potatoes was several pounds light.*
> GENTLE **6** [usually before noun] gentle or delicate; not using much force: *She felt a light tap on her shoulder.* ◆ *the sound of quick light footsteps* ◆ *You only need to apply light pressure.* ◆ *As a boxer, he was always light on his feet* (= quick and elegant in the way he moved). **ANT** HEAVY
> WORK/EXERCISE **7** [usually before noun] easy to do; not making you tired: *After his accident he was moved to lighter work.* ◆ *some light housework* ◆ *You are probably well enough to get a little light exercise.*
> NOT GREAT **8** not great in amount, degree, etc.: *light traffic* ◆ *The forecast is for light showers.* ◆ *light winds* ◆ *Trading on the stock exchange was light today.* **ANT** HEAVY
> NOT SEVERE/SERIOUS **9** not severe: *He was convicted of assaulting a police officer but he got off with a **light sentence**.* **10** entertaining rather than serious and not needing much mental effort: *light reading for the beach* ◆ *a concert of light classical music* **11** not serious: *She kept her tone light.* ◆ *This program looks at the **lighter side** of politics.* ◆ *On a **lighter note**, we end the news today with a story about a duck called Quackers.*
> CHEERFUL **12** [usually before noun] free from worry; cheerful: *I left the island with a light heart.*
> FOOD **13** (of a meal) small in quantity: *a light supper/snack* ◆ *I just want something light for lunch.* **ANT** HEAVY **14** not containing much fat or not having a strong flavor and therefore easy for the stomach to DIGEST: *Stick to a light diet.* ⊃ see also LITE **15** containing a lot of air: *This batter is so light.*
> DRINK **16** low in alcohol: *a light beer*
> SLEEP **17** [only before noun] a person in a light sleep is easy to wake: *She drifted into a light sleep.* ◆ *I've always been a light sleeper.* **ANT** DEEP

▶ light·ness *noun* [U] ⊃ see also LIGHTLY
IDM a light touch the ability to deal with something in a delicate and relaxed way: *She handles this difficult subject with a light touch.* make light of sth to treat something as not being important and not serious make light work of sth to do something quickly and with little effort ⊃ more at HAND

● *verb* (lit, lit /lɪt/ **HELP** Lighted is also used for the past tense and past participle, especially in front of nouns.)
> START TO BURN **1** [T] ~ sth to make something start to burn: *She lit a candle.* ◆ *The candles were lit.* ◆ *I put a lighted match to the letter and watched it burn.* **2** [I] to start to burn: *The fire wouldn't light.*
> GIVE LIGHT **3** [T, usually passive] ~ sth to give light to something or to a place: *The stage was lit by bright spotlights.* ◆ *well/badly lit streets* **4** [T] ~ sth (*literary*) to guide someone with a light: *Our way was lit by a full moon.*
PHR V 'light on/upon sth (*literary*) to see or find something by accident: *His eye lit upon a small boat on the horizon.* ,light 'up | ,light sth↔'up **1** (*informal*) to begin to smoke a cigarette: *They all lit up as soon as he left the room.* ◆ *He sat back and lit up a cigarette.* **2** to become or to make something become bright with light or color: *There was an explosion and the whole sky lit up.* **3** if someone's eyes or face light up, or something lights them up, they show happiness or excitement: *His eyes lit up when she walked into the room.* ◆ *A smile lit up her face.*
● *adv.* **IDM** see TRAVEL *v.*

,light 'aircraft *noun* (*pl.* light aircraft) a small plane with seats for no more than about six passengers ⊃ picture at PLANE

'light bulb *noun* = BULB ⊃ picture at LIGHT

,light-'colored (*CanE usually* ,light-'coloured) *adj.* pale in color; not dark

light·ed /'laɪtəd/ *adj.* **1** a lighted CANDLE, cigarette, match, etc. is burning **2** a **lighted** window is bright because there are lights on inside the room **ANT** UNLIT

light·en /'laɪtn/ *verb* **1** [T] ~ sth to reduce the amount of work, debt, worry, etc. that someone has **SYN** LESSEN: *equipment to **lighten the load** of domestic work* ◆ *The measures will lighten the tax burden on small businesses.* **2** [I, T] to become or make something become brighter or lighter in color: *The sky began to lighten in the east.* ◆ *~ sth Use bleach to lighten the wood.* **3** [I, T] to feel or make someone feel less sad, worried, or serious **SYN** CHEER: *~ (up) My mood gradually lightened.* ◆ *~ sth (up) She told a joke to lighten the atmosphere.* **4** [T] ~ sth to make something lighter in weight
PHR V ,lighten 'up (*informal*) used to tell someone to

become less serious or worried about something: *Come on, John. Lighten up!*

light·er /ˈlaɪtər/ *noun* **1** (also **ciga'rette ˌlighter**) a small device that produces a flame for lighting cigarettes, etc. **2** a boat with a flat bottom used for carrying goods to and from ships in a HARBOR

ˈlight-ˌfingered *adj.* (*informal*) likely to steal things

ˈlight-ˌfooted *adj.* moving quickly and easily, in an elegant way

light·head·ed /ˈlaɪtˌhɛdəd/ *adj.* not completely in control of your thoughts or movements; slightly faint: *After four glasses of wine he began to feel lightheaded.*

light·heart·ed /ˈlaɪtˌhɑrtəd/ *adj.* **1** intended to be amusing or easily enjoyable rather than too serious: *a lighthearted speech* **2** cheerful and without problems: *She felt light-hearted and optimistic.* ▶ **light·heart·ed·ly** *adv.*

light·house /ˈlaɪthaʊs/ *noun* a tower or other building that contains a strong light to warn and guide ships near the coast ⊃ **picture at** BUILDING

ˌlight 'industry *noun* [U, C] industry that produces small or light objects such as things used in the house ⊃ **compare** HEAVY INDUSTRY

light·ing /ˈlaɪtɪŋ/ *noun* [U] **1** the arrangement or type of light in a place: *electric/natural lighting* ◆ *good/poor lighting* ◆ *The play had excellent sound and lighting effects.* ⊃ **see also** TRACK LIGHTING **2** the use of electric lights in a place: *the cost of heating and lighting* ◆ *street lighting* ⊃ **note at** LIGHT

ˈlighting engiˌneer *noun* a person who works in television, the theater, etc. and whose job is to control and take care of the lights

light·ly 🔑 /ˈlaɪtli/ *adv.*
1 gently; with very little force or effort: *He kissed her lightly on the cheek.* **2** to a small degree; not much: *It began to snow lightly.* ◆ *She tends to sleep lightly nowadays* (= it is easy to wake her). ◆ *I try to eat lightly* (= not to eat heavy or GREASY food). **3** in a way that sounds as though you are not particularly worried or interested **SYN** : *"I'll be all right," he said lightly.* **4** without being seriously considered: *This is not a problem we should take lightly.*
IDM **get off/be let off lightly** (*informal*) to be punished or treated in a way that is less severe than you deserve or may have expected

ˈlight ˌmeter *noun* a device used to measure how bright the light is before taking a photograph

light·ning /ˈlaɪtnɪŋ/ *noun, adj.*
● *noun* [U] a flash, or several flashes, of very bright light in the sky caused by electricity: *a flash of lightning* ◆ *a violent storm with thunder and lightning* ◆ *He was struck by lightning and killed.* ◆ *Lightning strikes caused scores of fires across the state.* ⊃ **collocations at** WEATHER
IDM **lightning never strikes (in the same place) twice** (*saying*) an unusual or unpleasant event is not likely to happen in the same place or to the same people twice **like (greased) lightning** very fast
● *adj.* [only before noun] very fast or sudden

ˈlightning ˌbug *noun* = FIREFLY

ˈlightning ˌrod *noun* **1** a long straight piece of metal or wire leading from the highest part of a building to the ground, put there to prevent lightning from damaging the building **2** a person or thing that attracts criticism, especially if the criticism is then not directed at someone or something else

ˈlightning ˌstrike *noun* an incident in which LIGHTNING hits someone or something

ˈlight pen *noun* **1** a piece of equipment, shaped like a pen, that is sensitive to light and that can be used to pass information to a computer when it touches the screen **2** a similar piece of equipment that is used for reading BAR CODES

ˈlight polˌlution *noun* [U] the existence of too much

artificial light in the environment, for example from street lights, which makes it difficult to see the stars

light·ship /ˈlaɪtʃɪp/ *noun* a small ship that stays at a particular place at sea and that has a powerful light on it to warn and guide other ships

ˈlight show *noun* a display of changing colored lights, for example at a concert

ˈlight stick *noun* = GLOWSTICK

ˈlight ˌwater *noun* [U] **1** (*chemistry*) water that contains the normal amount of DEUTERIUM ⊃ **compare** HEAVY WATER **2** (*technical*) a type of FOAM (= mass of bubbles) used to put out fires

light·weight /ˈlaɪtweɪt/ *adj., noun*
● *adj.* **1** made of thinner material and less heavy than usual: *a lightweight jacket* **2** (*disapproving*) not very serious or impressive: *a lightweight book* ◆ *He was considered too lightweight for the job.*
● *noun* **1** a BOXER weighing between 126 and 135 pounds (57–61 kg), heavier than a FEATHERWEIGHT: *a lightweight champion* **2** a person or thing that weighs less than is usual **3** (*informal, disapproving*) a person or thing of little importance or influence: *a political lightweight* ◆ *He's an intellectual lightweight* (= he does not think very deeply or seriously).

ˈlight year *noun* **1** (*astronomy*) the distance that light travels in one year, about $5.88×10^{12}$ miles ($9.4607 ×10^{12}$ kilometers): *The nearest star to earth is about 4 light years away.* **2** **light years** [pl.] a very long time: *Full employment still seems light years away.*

lig·nite /ˈlɪgnaɪt/ *noun* [U] a soft brown type of coal

lik·a·ble (also **like·a·ble**) /ˈlaɪkəbl/ *adj.* pleasant and easy to like: *a very likable man*

like 🔑 /laɪk/ *prep., verb, conj., noun, adj., adv.*
● *prep.* **1** similar to someone or something: *She's wearing a dress like mine.* ◆ *He's very much like his father.* ◆ *She looks nothing like* (= not at all like) *her mother.* ◆ *That sounds like* (= I think I can hear) *him coming now.* **2** used to ask someone's opinion of someone or something: *What's it like studying in Spain?* ◆ *This new girlfriend of his—what's she like?* **3** used to show what is usual or typical for someone: *It's just like her to tell everyone about it.* **4** in the same way as someone or something: *Students were angry at being treated like children.* ◆ *He ran like the wind* (= very fast). ◆ *You do it like this.* ◆ *I, like everyone else, had read these stories in the press.* ◆ *Don't look at me like that.* ◆ (*informal*) *The candles are arranged like so* (= in this way). ⊃ **language bank at** SIMILARLY **5** for example: *antiutopian novels like "Animal Farm" and "1984"* ⊃ **note at** AS
IDM **more like...** used to give a number or an amount that is more accurate than one previously mentioned: *He believes the figure should be more like $10 million.* **more like (it)** (*informal*) **1** better; more acceptable: *This is more like it! Real food—not that canned junk.* **2** used to give what you think is a better description of something: *Just talking? Arguing is more like it.*
● *verb* (not usually used in the progressive tenses) **1** [T] to find someone or something pleasant, attractive, or of a good enough standard; to enjoy something: ~ *sb/sth She's nice. I like her.* ◆ *Do you like their new house?* ◆ *Which tie do you like best?* ◆ *How did you like Japan* (= did you find it pleasant)? ◆ *I don't like the way he's looking at me.* ◆ *You have to go to school, whether you like it or not.* ◆ ~ *doing sth She's never liked swimming.* ◆ ~ *sb/sth doing sth I didn't like him taking all the credit.* ◆ (*formal*) *I didn't like his taking all the credit.* ◆ ~ *to do sth I like to see them enjoying themselves.* ◆ ~ *it when... I like it when you do that.* **2** [T, no passive] to prefer to do something; to prefer something to be made or to happen in a particular way: ~ *to do sth On weekends I like to sleep late.* ◆ ~ *sth + adj. I like my coffee strong.* **3** (*informal*) **what/ whatever sb** ~ to want: *Do what you like—I don't care.* ◆ *You can dye your hair whatever color you like.* **4** [T] used in negative sentences to mean "to be unwilling to do sth": ~ *to do sth I didn't like to disturb you.* ◆ ~ *doing sth He*

doesn't like asking his parents for help. **5** [T, I] used with *would* or *should* as a polite way to say what you want or to ask what someone wants: **~ sth** *Would you like a drink?* ♦ **~ to do sth** *I'd like to think it over.* ♦ *Would you like to come with us?* ♦ (*formal*) *We would like to apologize for the delay.* ♦ *How can they afford it? That's what I'd like to know.* ♦ **~ sb/sth to do sth** *We'd like you to come and visit us.* ♦ (*informal*) **~ for sb to do sth** *I'd like for us to work together.* ⊃ note at WANT

IDM **how would you like it?** used to emphasize that something bad has happened to you and you want some sympathy: *How would you like it if someone called you a liar?* **if you like 1** used to politely agree to something or to suggest something: *"Shall we stop now?" "If you like." ♦ If you like, we could go out this evening.* **2** (*formal*) used when you express something in a new way or when you are not confident about something: *It was, if you like, the dawn of a new era.* **I like that!** (*old-fashioned, informal*) used to protest that something that has been said is not true or fair: *"She called you a cheat." "Well, I like that!"* **I/I'd like to think** used to say that you hope or believe that something is true: *I like to think I'm broad-minded.* **what's not to like?** (*informal, humorous*) used to say that something is very good or enjoyable: *You get paid to eat chocolate. So what's not to like!*

● **conj.** (*informal*) **1** in the same way as: *No one sings the blues like she did.* ♦ *It didn't turn out like I intended.* ♦ *Like I said* (= as I said before), *you're always welcome to stay.* **2** as if: *She acts like she owns the place.* **HELP** You will find more information about this use of **like** at the entries for the verbs **act**, **behave**, **feel**, **look**, and **sound** and in the note at **as**.

● **noun 1 likes** [pl.] the things that you like: *We all have different likes and dislikes.* **2** [sing.] a person or thing that is similar to another: *jazz, rock,* **and the like** (= similar types of music) ♦ *a man whose like we shall not see again* ♦ *You're not comparing like with like.* **3 the likes of sb/sth** (*informal*) used to refer to someone or something that is considered as a type, especially one that is considered as good as someone or something else: *She didn't want to associate with the likes of me.*

● **adj.** [only before noun] (*formal*) having similar qualities to another person or thing: *a chance to meet people of like mind* (= with similar interests and opinions) ♦ *She responded in like manner.*

● **adv. 1** used in very informal speech, for example when you are thinking what to say next, explaining something, or giving an example of something: *It was, like, weird.* ♦ *It was kind of scary, like.* ♦ *It's really hard. Like I have no time for my own work.* **2** used in very informal speech to show that what you are saying may not be exactly right but is nearly so: *I'm leaving in like twenty minutes.* ♦ *It's going to cost like a hundred dollars.* **3 I'm, he's, she's, etc. ~** used in very informal speech, to mean "I say", "he/she says", etc.: *And then I'm like "No way!"* **4** used in informal speech instead of *as* to say that something happens in the same way: *There was silence, but not like before.* ⊃ note at AS

IDM **(as) like as not| like enough| most/very like** (*old-fashioned*) quite probably: *She would be in bed by now, as like as not.*

THESAURUS

like

love ♦ **be fond of sth** ♦ **be crazy about sth** ♦ **adore**

These words all mean to find something pleasant, attractive, or satisfactory, or to enjoy something.

like to find something pleasant, attractive, or satisfactory; to enjoy something: *Do you like their new house?* ♦ *I like to see them enjoying themselves.*

love to like or enjoy something very much: *He loved the way she smiled.*

be fond of sth (*somewhat formal*) to like or enjoy something, especially something you have liked or enjoyed for a long time: *We were fond of the house and didn't want to leave.*

be crazy about sth (*informal*) to be very enthusiastic or excited about something: *Rick is crazy about football.* ♦ *She's not crazy about being told what to do.*

adore (*informal*) to like or enjoy something very much: *He adores working with children.*

LOVE OR ADORE?

Adore is more informal than **love**, and is used to express a stronger feeling.

PATTERNS

- to like/love/be fond of/be crazy about/adore **doing sth**
- to like/love **to do sth**
- to like/love sth **very much**
- I like/love/adore **it** here/there/when…
- to like/love/adore **the way** sb does sth
- to **really** like/love/adore sb/sth
- to be **really** fond of/crazy about sth

-like /laɪk/ *combining form* (in adjectives) similar to; typical of: *childlike* ♦ *shell-like*

like·a·ble = LIKABLE

like·li·hood /ˈlaɪkliˌhʊd/ *noun* [U, sing.] the chance of something happening; how likely something is to happen **SYN** PROBABILITY: *There is very little likelihood of that happening.* ♦ **In all likelihood** (= very probably) *the meeting will be canceled.* ♦ **The likelihood is that** (= it is likely that) *unemployment figures will continue to fall.*

like·ly 🔑 /ˈlaɪkli/ *adj., adv.*

● **adj.** (**like·li·er, like·li·est**) **HELP** more **likely** and most **likely** are the usual forms **1** probably true or probably going to happen; expected: *the most likely outcome* ♦ **~ (to do sth)** *Tickets are likely to be expensive.* ♦ **~ (that…)** *It's more than likely that the thieves don't know how much it is worth.* ♦ *They might refuse to let us do it, but it's* **hardly likely**. ⊃ language bank at EXPECT **2** seeming suitable for a purpose **SYN** PROMISING: *She seems the most likely candidate for the job.*

IDM **a likely story** (*informal, ironic*) used to show that you do not believe what someone has said

● **adv.**

IDM **as likely as not| most/very likely** very probably: *As likely as not she's forgotten all about it.* **not likely!** (*informal*) used to disagree strongly with a statement or suggestion: *Me? Join the army? Not likely!*

GRAMMAR

likely

- The adverb **likely** is often used with a word such as *most*, *more*, or *very*: *We will most likely see him later.* In informal English, **likely** is sometimes used on its own: *We will likely see him later.* ♦ *He said that he would likely run for President.*

---

like-'minded *adj.* having similar ideas and interests

lik·en /ˈlaɪkən/ *verb*

PHR V **'liken sth/sb to sth/sb** (*formal*) to compare one thing or person to another and say they are similar: *Life is often likened to a journey.*

like·ness /ˈlaɪknəs/ *noun* **1** [C, U] the fact of being similar to another person or thing, especially in appearance; an example of this **SYN** RESEMBLANCE: *Joanna bears a strong likeness to her father.* ♦ *Do you notice any family likeness between them?* **2** [C, usually sing.] a painting, drawing, etc. of a person, especially one that looks very like them: *The drawing is said to be* **a good likeness** *of the girl's attacker.*

likes *noun* ⊃ LIKE *n.* (1)

like·wise **AWL** /ˈlaɪkwaɪz/ *adv.* **1** (*formal*) the same; in a similar way: *He voted for the change and he expected his* colleagues to **do likewise**. **2** (*formal*) also: *Her second marriage was likewise unhappy.* **3** (*informal*) used to show that you feel the same toward someone or about something: *"Let me know if you ever need any help." "Likewise."*

lik·ing /ˈlaɪkɪŋ/ *noun* [sing.] **~ (for sb/sth)** the feeling that you like someone or something; the enjoyment of something: *He had a liking for fast cars.* ◆ *She had taken a liking to him on their first meeting.*
IDM for your liking if you say, for example, that something is too hot **for your liking**, you mean that you would prefer it to be less hot: *The town was too crowded for my liking.* **to sb's liking** (*formal*) suitable, and how someone likes something: *The coffee was just to his liking.*

li·lac /ˈlaɪlæk; -lɑk; -lək/ *noun* **1** [U, C] a bush or small tree with purple or white flowers with a sweet smell, that grow closely together in the shape of a CONE **2** [U] a pale purple color ▶ **li·lac** *adj.*: *a lilac dress*

Lil·li·pu·tian /ˌlɪləˈpyuʃn/ *adj.* (*formal*) extremely small **SYN** DIMINUTIVE, TINY **ORIGIN** From the land of **Lilliput**, in Jonathan Swift's *Gulliver's Travels*, where the people are only 6 inches high.

lilt /lɪlt/ *noun* [sing.] **1** the pleasant way in which a person's voice rises and falls: *Her voice had a soft Caribbean lilt to it.* **2** a regular rising and falling pattern in music, with a strong rhythm ▶ **lilt·ing** *adj.*

lil·y /ˈlɪli/ *noun* (*pl.* **lil·ies**) a large white or brightly colored flower with PETALS that curl back from the center. There are many types of lilies. ⊃ **picture at PLANT** ⊃ **see also** DAYLILY, WATER LILY **IDM see** GILD

lil·y-liv·ered /ˈlɪli ˌlɪvərd/ *adj.* (*old-fashioned*) lacking courage **SYN**

lily of the ˈvalley *noun* (*pl.* **lilies of the valley**) [C, U] a plant with small white flowers shaped like bells

ˈlily ˌpad *noun* a round floating leaf of a WATER LILY

ˌlily-ˈwhite *adj.* **1** almost pure white in color: *lily-white skin* **2** morally perfect: *They want me to conform, to be lily-white.*

li·ma bean /ˈlaɪmə ˌbin/ *noun* a type of round, pale green BEAN. Several lima beans grow together inside a flat POD.

limb /lɪm/ *noun* **1** an arm or a leg; a similar part of an animal, such as a wing: *For a while, she lost the use of her limbs.* **2** **-limbed** (in adjectives) having the type of limbs mentioned: *long-limbed* ◆ *loose-limbed* **3** a large branch of a tree ⊃ **picture at TREE**
IDM out on a limb (*informal*) not supported by other people: *Are you prepared to go out on a limb* (= risk doing something that other people are not prepared to do) *and make your suspicions public?* **tear/rip sb limb from limb** (often *humorous*) to attack someone very violently ⊃ **more at** RISK

lim·ber /ˈlɪmbər/ *verb, adj.*
● *verb*
PHR V **ˌlimber ˈup** to do physical exercises in order to stretch and prepare your muscles before taking part in a race, sports game, etc. **SYN** WARM UP
● *adj.* (of a person or their body) able to move and bend easily **SYN** SUPPLE: *He still looks pretty limber for a 47-year-old.*

lim·bic sys·tem /ˈlɪmbɪk ˌsɪstəm/ *noun* (*biology*) a system of nerves in the brain involving several different areas, concerned with basic emotions such as fear and anger and basic needs such as the need to eat and to have sex

lim·bo /ˈlɪmboʊ/ *noun* **1** [U, sing.] a situation in which you are not certain what to do next, cannot take action, etc., especially because you are waiting for someone else to make a decision: *the limbo of the stateless person* ◆ *His life seemed stuck in limbo; he could not go forward and he could not go back.* **2** [C] a Caribbean dance in which you lean backward and go under a bar that is made lower each time you go under it

lime /laɪm/ *noun, verb*
● *noun* **1** [C, U] a green fruit, like a lemon, with a lot of sour juice, used in cooking and in drinks; the juice of this fruit: *lime juice* ◆ *slices of lime* ⊃ **picture at** FRUIT **2** (also **ˈlime tree**) [C] a tree on which limes grow **3** (also

quick·lime) [U] a white substance obtained by heating LIMESTONE, used in building materials and to help plants grow **4** (also **ˈlime tree**) [C] = LINDEN **5** [U] = LIME GREEN
● *verb* **~ sth** to add the substance lime to soil, especially in order to control the acid in it

lime·ade /laɪmˈeɪd; ˈlaɪmeɪd/ *noun* [U, C] a drink made from lime juice, sugar, and water

ˌlime ˈgreen *adj.* (also **lime**) bright yellowish green in color ▶ **ˌlime ˈgreen** (also **lime**) *noun* [U]

lime·light /ˈlaɪmlaɪt/ *usually* **the limelight** *noun* [U] the center of public attention: *to be in the limelight* ◆ *to stay out of the limelight* ◆ *to steal/hog the limelight* (= take attention away from other people)

lim·er·ick /ˈlɪmərɪk/ *noun* a humorous short poem, with two long lines that RHYME with each other, followed by two short lines that rhyme with each other, and ending with a long line that rhymes with the first two

lime·stone /ˈlaɪmstoʊn/ *noun* [U] a type of white stone that contains CALCIUM, used in building and in making CEMENT

ˈlime ˌwater *noun* [U] (*chemistry*) a liquid containing CALCIUM HYDROXIDE that shows the presence of CARBON DIOXIDE by turning white

Lim·ey /ˈlaɪmi/ *noun* (*old-fashioned*) a slightly insulting word for a British person

lim·it 🔑 /ˈlɪmət/ *noun, verb*
● *noun* **1 ~ (to sth)** a point at which something stops being possible or existing: *There is a limit to the amount of pain we can bear.* ◆ *The team performed to the limit of its capabilities.* ◆ *She knew the limits of her power.* ◆ *to push/stretch/test someone or something to the limit* ◆ *His arrogance knew* (= had) *no limits.* **2 ~ (on sth)** the greatest or smallest amount of something that is allowed **SYN** RESTRICTION: *a time/speed/age limit* ◆ *The agency has set strict limits on levels of pollution.* ◆ *They were traveling at a speed that was double the legal limit.* ◆ *You can't drive—you're over the limit* (= you have drunk more alcohol than is legal when driving). **3** the furthest edge of an area or a place: *We were reaching the limits of civilization.* ◆ *the city limits* (= the imaginary line which officially divides the city from the area outside) ⊃ **see also** OFF-LIMITS
IDM be the limit (*old-fashioned, informal*) to be extremely annoying **within limits** to some extent; with some restrictions: *I'm willing to help, within limits.* ⊃ **more at** SKY
● *verb* **1 ~ sth (to sth)** to stop something from increasing beyond a particular amount or level **SYN** RESTRICT: *measures to limit carbon dioxide emissions from cars* ◆ *The amount of money you have to spend will limit your choice.* **2 ~ yourself/sb (to sth)** to restrict or reduce the amount of something that you or someone can have or use: *Families are limited to four free tickets each.* ◆ *I've limited myself to 1,000 calories a day to try and lose weight.*
PHR V **ˈlimit sth to sb/sth** [usually passive] to make something exist or happen only in a particular place or within a particular group: *Violent crime is not limited to big cities.* ◆ *The teaching of history should not be limited to dates and figures.*

THESAURUS

limit

restriction ◆ control ◆ constraint ◆ restraint ◆ limitation

These are all words for something that limits what you can do or what can happen.

limit the greatest or smallest amount of something that is allowed: *The government has set strict limits on spending.* ◆ *the speed limit*

restriction (*somewhat formal*) a rule or law that limits what you can do: *There are no restrictions on the amount of money you can withdraw.*

control (often in compounds) the act of limiting or

| h hat | m man | n no | ŋ sing | l leg | r red | y yes | w wet |

managing something; a method of doing this: *crowd control*

constraint (*somewhat formal*) a fact or decision that limits what you can do: *The agency is operating under severe budget constraints.*

restraint (*somewhat formal*) a decision, a rule, an idea, etc. that limits what you can do; the act of limiting something because it is necessary or sensible to do so: *The new law has imposed restraints on exports to Russia.*

limitation the act or process of limiting something; a rule, fact, or condition that limits something: *They would resist any limitation of their powers.*

RESTRICTION, CONSTRAINT, RESTRAINT, OR LIMITATION?

These are all things that limit what you can do. A **restriction** is a rule or law that is made by someone in authority. A **constraint** is something that exists rather than something that is made, although it may exist as a result of someone's decision. A **restraint** is also something that exists: it can exist outside yourself, as the result of someone else's decision; but it can also exist inside you, as a fear of what other people may think or as your own feeling about what is acceptable: *moral/social/cultural restraints.* A **limitation** is more general and can be a rule that someone makes or a fact or condition that exists.

PATTERNS

- limits/restrictions/controls/constraints/restraints/limitations **on** sth
- limits/limitations **to** sth
- **severe** limits/restrictions/controls/constraints/restraints/limitations
- **tight** limits/restrictions/controls/constraints
- to **impose/remove** limits/restrictions/controls/constraints/restraints/limitations
- to **ease/lift** restrictions/controls/constraints/restraints

lim·i·ta·tion /ˌlɪməˈteɪʃn/ *noun* **1** [U] the act or process of limiting or controlling someone or something **SYN** RESTRICTION: *They would resist any limitation of their powers.* ⊃ see also DAMAGE LIMITATION ⊃ thesaurus box at LIMIT **2** [C] ~ **(on sth)** a rule, fact, or condition that limits something **SYN** CURB, RESTRAINT: *to impose limitations on imports* ◆ *Disability is a physical limitation on your life.* ⊃ see also STATUTE OF LIMITATIONS **3** [C, usually pl.] a limit on what someone or something can do or how good they or it can be: *This technique is useful, but it has its limitations.*

lim·it·ed 🔑 /ˈlɪmətəd/ *adj.*
1 not very great in amount or extent: *We are doing our best with the limited resources available.* **2** ~ **(to sth)** restricted to a particular limit of time, numbers, etc.: *This offer is for a limited period only.*

limited eˈdition *noun* a fixed, usually small, number of copies of a book, picture, etc. produced at one time

limited liaˈbility *noun* [U] (*law*) the legal position of having to pay only a limited amount of your or your company's debts

lim·it·ing /ˈlɪmətɪŋ/ *adj.* putting limits on what is possible: *Lack of cash is a limiting factor.*

lim·it·less /ˈlɪmətləs/ *adj.* without a limit; very great **SYN** INFINITE: *the limitless variety of consumer products* ◆ *The possibilities were almost limitless.*

lim·o /ˈlɪmoʊ/ *noun* (*pl.* lim·os) (*informal*) = LIMOUSINE

lim·ou·sine /ˈlɪməˌzin; ˌlɪməˈzin/ (also *informal* lim·o) *noun*
1 a large, expensive, comfortable car: *a long black chauffeur-driven limousine* ⊃ see also STRETCH LIMO **2** a van or small bus that takes people to and from an airport

limp /lɪmp/ *adj.*, *verb*, *noun*
● *adj.* **1** lacking strength or energy: *His hand went limp and*

the knife clattered to the ground. ◆ *She felt limp and exhausted.* **2** not stiff or firm: *The hat had become limp and shapeless.*
▶ **limp·ly** *adv.*: *Her hair hung limply over her forehead.*
● *verb* **1** [I] to walk slowly or with difficulty because one leg is injured: *She had twisted her ankle and was limping.* ◆ + *adv./prep.* Matt limped painfully off the field. **2** [I] + *adv./prep.* to move slowly or with difficulty after being damaged: *The plane limped back to the airport.* ◆ (*figurative*) *The government was limping along after the scandal.*
● *noun* [usually sing.] a way of walking in which one leg is used less than normal because it is injured or stiff: *to walk with a slight/pronounced limp*

lim·pet /ˈlɪmpət/ *noun* a small SHELLFISH that sticks very tightly to rocks: *He clung to his job like a limpet, despite calls for him to resign.*

lim·pid /ˈlɪmpɪd/ *adj.* (*literary*) (of liquids, etc.) clear **SYN** TRANSPARENT: *limpid eyes/water*

LINC /lɪŋk/ *abbr.* Language Instruction for Newcomers to Canada (free language classes provided by the government to people from other countries who come to live in Canada)

linch·pin (also **lynch·pin**) /ˈlɪntʃpɪn/ *noun* a person or thing that is the most important part of an organization, a plan, etc., because everything else depends on them or it

Lin·coln's Birth·day /ˌlɪŋkənz ˈbɜrθdeɪ/ *noun* [U] (in some U.S. states) a legal holiday on February 12 in memory of the birthday of Abraham Lincoln

lin·den /ˈlɪndən/ (also **ˈlime tree, ˈlinden ˌtree**) *noun* [C] a large tree with light green heart-shaped leaves and yellow flowers

lines

straight   curved

wavy

zigzag   dotted

vertical   parallel lines   diagonal

horizontal

line 🔑 /laɪn/ *noun*, *verb*
● *noun*
> LONG THIN MARK **1** [C] a long thin mark on a surface: *a straight/wavy/dotted/diagonal line* ◆ *a vertical/horizontal line* ◆ *parallel lines* ◆ *Draw a thick black line across the page.*
2 [C] a long thin mark on the ground to show the limit or border of something, especially of a playing area in some sports: *The ball went over the line.* ◆ *Be careful not to cross the line* (= the broken line painted down the middle of the road). ◆ *Your feet must be behind the line when you serve* (= in TENNIS). ◆ *They were all waiting on the starting line.* ⊃ see also FINISH LINE, GOAL LINE, SIDELINE, TOUCHLINE **3** [C] a mark like a line on someone's skin that people usually get as they get older **SYN** WRINKLE: *He has fine lines around his eyes.*
> DIVISION **4** [C] an imaginary limit or border between one place or thing and another: *He was convicted of illegally importing weapons across state lines.* ◆ *a district/county line* ◆ *lines of longitude and latitude* ⊃ see also COASTLINE, DATE LINE, DIVIDING LINE, PICKET LINE, TREELINE, WATERLINE **5** [C] the division between one area of thought or behavior and another: *We want to cut across lines of race, sex, and religion.* ◆ *There is a fine line between showing interest in what someone is doing and interfering in it.* ⊃ see also RED LINE

> **SHAPE 6** [C] the edge, outline, or shape of someone or something: *He traced the line of her jaw with his finger.* ◆ *a beautiful sports car with sleek lines* ⊃ see also BIKINI LINE

> **ROW OF PEOPLE/THINGS 7** [C] a row of people or things next to each other or behind each other: *to stand/wait in line for something* ◆ *A line formed at each ticket window.* ◆ *There's no need to cut in line* (= push in front of people standing in a line), *as there are plenty of seats for everyone.* ◆ *The children all stood in a line.* ◆ *a long line of trees* ◆ *They were stuck in a line of traffic.*

> **IN FACTORY 8** [C] a system of making something, in which the product moves from one worker to the next until it is finished ⊃ see also ASSEMBLY LINE, PRODUCTION LINE

> **SERIES 9** [C, usually sing.] a series of people, things, or events that follow one another in time: *She came from a long line of doctors.* ◆ *to pass something down through the male/female line* ◆ *This novel is the latest of a long line of thrillers that he has written.* **10** [C, usually sing.] a series of people in order of importance: *Orders came down the line from the very top.* ◆ *a line of command* ◆ *He is second in line to the chairman.* ◆ *to be next in line* to the throne ⊃ see also LINE MANAGEMENT

> **WORDS 11** [C] (*abbr.* l) a row of words on a page or the empty space where they can be written; the words of a song or poem: *Look at line 5 of the text.* ◆ *Write the title of your essay on the top line.* ◆ *I can only remember the first two lines of that song.* ⊃ see also BOTTOM LINE **12** [C] the words spoken by an actor in a play or movie: *to learn your lines* ◆ *a line from the movie "Casablanca"* **13** [C] (*informal*) a remark, especially when someone says it to achieve a particular purpose: *Don't give me that line about having to work late again.*

> **ROPE/WIRE/PIPE 14** [C] a long piece of rope, thread, etc., especially when it is used for a particular purpose: *a fishing line* ◆ *He hung the towels out on the line* (= clothesline). ◆ *They dropped the sails and threw a line to a man on the dock.* ⊃ see also LIFELINE **15** [C] a pipe or thick wire that carries water, gas, or electricity from one place to another ⊃ see also POWER LINE

> **TELEPHONE 16** [C] a telephone connection; a particular telephone number: *Your bill includes line rental.* ◆ *The company's lines have been jammed* (= busy) *all day with people making complaints.* ◆ *I was talking to John when the line suddenly went dead.* ⊃ see also HELPLINE, HOTLINE, LANDLINE, OFFLINE, ONLINE

> **RAILROAD 17** [C] a railroad track; a section of a railroad system: *The train was delayed because a tree had fallen across the line.* ◆ *a branch line* ◆ *the northeastern line* ⊃ see also MAIN LINE

> **ROUTE/DIRECTION 18** [C, usually sing.] the direction that someone or something is moving or located in: *Just keep going in a straight line; you can't miss it.* ◆ *The town is in a direct line between here and the coast.* ◆ *Please move; you're right in my line of vision* (= the direction I am looking in). ◆ *They followed the line of the river for three miles.* ◆ *Be careful to stay out of the line of fire* (= the direction someone is shooting in). **19** [C] a route from one place to another especially when it is used for a particular purpose: *Their aim was to block guerrilla supply lines.*

> **ATTITUDE/ARGUMENT 20** [C, usually sing.] an attitude or a belief, especially one that someone states publicly: *The government is taking a firm line on terrorism.* ◆ *He supported the official line on education.* ⊃ see also HARD LINE, PARTY LINE[1] **21** [C] a method or way of doing or thinking about something: *I don't follow your line of reasoning.* ◆ *She decided to try a different line of argument* (= way of persuading someone of something). ◆ *someone's first line of attack/defense* ◆ *The police are pursuing a new line of questioning* (= way of finding out information).

> **ACTIVITY 22** [sing.] a type or area of business, activity, or interest: *My line of work pays pretty well.* ◆ *What line of business are you in?* ⊃ see also SIDELINE

> **PRODUCT 23** [C] a type of product: *We are starting a new line in casual clothes.* ◆ *Some lines sell better than others.* ⊃ see also TOP OF THE LINE

> **TRANSPORTATION 24** [C] (often used in names) a company that provides transporation for people or goods: *a shipping/bus line* ⊃ see also AIRLINE

> **SOLDIERS 25** [C] a row or series of military defenses where the soldiers are fighting during a war: *The regiment was sent to fight in the front line* (= the position nearest the enemy). ◆ *They were trapped behind enemy lines* (= in the area controlled by the enemy).

IDM **along/down the line** (*informal*) at some point during an activity or a process: *Somewhere along the line a large amount of money was stolen.* ◆ *We'll make a decision on that further down the line.* **along/on (the)... lines 1** (*informal*) in the way that is mentioned: *The new system will operate along the same lines as the old one.* ◆ *They voted along class lines.* **2** (*informal*) similar to the way or thing that is mentioned: *Those aren't his exact words, but he said something along those lines.* **bring sb/sth, come, get, fall, etc. into line (with sb/sth)** to behave or make someone or something behave in the same way as other people or how they should behave: *Other politicians fell into line behind the president in support of the war.* **hold the line (against/on sth)** to keep something at a particular level and not allow any more increases or changes: *Foreign auto makers will try to hold the line on prices to maintain U.S. market share.* **in (a) line (with sth)** in a position that forms a straight line with something: *An eclipse happens when the earth and moon are in line with the sun.* **in line for sth** likely to get something: *She is in line for promotion.* **in the line of duty** while doing a job: *A policeman was injured in the line of duty yesterday.* **in line with sth** similar to something or so that one thing is closely connected with another: *Annual pay increases will be in line with inflation.* **lay it on the line** (*informal*) to tell someone clearly what you think, especially when they will not like what you say: *The manager laid it on the line—some people would have to lose their jobs.* **(choose, follow, take, etc.) the line of least resistance** (to choose, etc.) the easiest way of doing something **on line** = ONLINE *adv.* **(put sth) on the line** (*informal*) at risk: *If we don't make a profit, my job is on the line.* **out of line (with sb/sth) 1** not forming a straight line **2** different from something: *The prices here are way out of line with the rest of the country.* **3** (*informal*) behaving in a way that is not acceptable or right **walk/tread a fine/thin line** to be in a difficult or dangerous situation where you could easily make a mistake: *He was walking a fine line between being funny and being rude.* ⊃ more at BATTLE *n.*, END *n.*, FIRING LINE, FRONT LINE, HOOK *n.*, OVERSTEP, PITCH *v.*, READ, RESISTANCE, SIGN *v.*, STEP *v.*, TOE *v.*

● *verb*

> **COVER INSIDE 1** [often passive] **~ sth (with sth)** to cover the inside of something with a layer of another material to keep it clean, make it stronger, etc.: *Line the pan with aluminum foil.* **2 ~ sth** to form a layer on the inside of something: *the membranes that line the nose*

> **FORM ROWS 3** [often passive] to form lines or rows along something: **~ sth** *Crowds of people lined the streets to watch the race.* ◆ **~ sth with sth** *The walls were lined with books.* ⊃ see also LINED

IDM **line your (own)/sb's pockets** to get richer or make someone richer, especially by taking unfair advantage of a situation or by being dishonest

PHR V **line 'up** to stand in a line or row; to form a line: *Line up, children!* ◆ *Cars lined up waiting to board the ship.* **line sb/sth↔'up 1** to arrange people or things in a straight line or row: *The suspects were lined up against the wall.* ◆ *He lined the bottles up along the shelf.* **2** to arrange for an event or activity to happen, or arrange for sb to be available to do something: *Mark had a job lined up when he left college.* ◆ *I have a lot lined up this week* (= I'm very busy). ◆ *She's lined up a live band for the party.* **line sth↔'up (with sth)** to move one thing into a correct position in relation to another thing

lin·e·age /ˈlɪniɪdʒ/ *noun* [U, C] (*formal*) the series of families that someone comes from originally **SYN** ANCESTRY

lin·e·al /ˈlɪniəl/ *adj.* [only before noun] (*formal*) coming directly from a later generation of the same family as someone: *a lineal descendant of the company's founder*

lineaments /ˈlɪniəmənts/ *noun* [pl.] (*formal*) the typical features of something

lin·e·ar /ˈlɪniər/ *adj.* **1** of or in lines: *In his art he broke the laws of scientific linear perspective.* **2** going from one thing to another in a single series of stages: *Students do not always progress in a linear fashion.* **ANT** NONLINEAR **3** of length: *linear measurement* (= for example feet, inches, etc.) **4** (*mathematics*) able to be represented by a straight line on a GRAPH: *linear equations* ▶ **lin·e·ar·i·ty** /ˌlɪniˈærəti/ *noun* [U]: *She abandoned the linearity of the conventional novel.* **lin·e·ar·ly** /ˈlɪniərli/ *adv.*

Linear B *noun* [U] the later of two early forms of writing found on stones in Crete

line·back·er /ˈlaɪnˌbækər/ *noun* (in football) a DEFENSIVE player who tries to TACKLE members of the other team

line-caught *adj.* (of fish) caught with a hook, not in a net: *We sell only line-caught wild fish.*

lined /laɪnd/ *adj.* **1** (of skin, especially on the face) having folds or lines because of age, worry, etc. **SYN** WRINKLED: *a deeply lined face* **2** (of paper) having lines printed or drawn across it: *Lined paper helps keep handwriting neat.* **3** (of clothes) having a LINING inside them: *a lined skirt* **4** -lined having the object mentioned along an edge or edges, or as a LINING: *a tree-lined road*

line dance *noun* a dance in which people stand next to or in front of each other in a line and do the same steps together, especially to COUNTRY MUSIC ➔ compare SQUARE DANCE ▶ **'line dance** *verb* [I]: *Do you like to line dance?* **'line dancing** *noun* [U]

'line ˌdrawing *noun* a drawing that consists only of lines

ˌline 'drive *noun* (in BASEBALL) a powerful hit in a straight line near to the ground

ˌline-item 'veto *noun* [sing.] (*politics*) the power of a president or governor to reject one or more parts of a bill that has been approved by a LEGISLATURE without rejecting the whole bill

line·man /ˈlaɪnmən/ *noun* (*pl.* line·men /-mən/) **1** a player in the front line of a football team **2** a person whose job is to repair telephone or electricity power lines

lin·en /ˈlɪnən/ *noun* [U] **1** a type of cloth made from FLAX, used to make high quality clothes, sheets, etc.: *a linen tablecloth* **2** sheets, TABLECLOTHS, PILLOWCASES, etc.: *a linen closet* ➔ see also BED LINEN **IDM** see AIR

ˌline of 'scrimmage *noun* (in football) the imaginary line separating two football teams, where the football is placed at the beginning of each play

ˌline of 'sight (also ˌline of 'vision, 'sight line) *noun* an imaginary line that goes from someone's eye to something that they are looking at: *There was a column directly in my line of sight, so I could only see half the stage.*

'line ˌprinter *noun* a machine that prints very quickly, producing a complete line of print at a time

lin·er /ˈlaɪnər/ *noun* **1** a large ship that carries passengers: *an ocean liner* ◆ *a luxury cruise liner* ➔ picture at BOAT **2** (especially in compounds) a piece of material used to cover the inside surface of something **3** = EYELINER ➔ picture at MAKEUP

'liner ˌnote *noun* [usually pl.] information about the music or the performers that comes with a CD or is printed on the cover of a record

lines·man /ˈlaɪnzmən/ *noun* (*pl.* lines·men /-mən/) an official who helps the REFEREE in some games that are played on a field or court, especially in deciding whether or where a ball crosses one of the lines.

line-up /ˈlaɪnʌp/ *noun* [usually sing.] **1** the people who are going to take part in a particular event: *an impressive lineup of speakers* ◆ *the starting lineup* (= the players who will begin the game) **2** a set of items, events, etc. arranged to follow one another **SYN** PROGRAM: *A horror movie completes this evening's TV lineup.* **3** a row of people, including one person who is suspected of a crime, who are shown to a witness to see if he or she can recognize the criminal

-ling /lɪŋ/ *suffix* (in nouns) (sometimes *disapproving*) small; not important: *duckling* ◆ *princeling*

lin·ger /ˈlɪŋgər/ *verb* **1** [I] to continue to exist for longer than expected: *The faint smell of her perfume lingered in the room.* ◆ ~ **on** *The civil war lingered on well into the 1930s.* **2** [I] (+ adv./prep.) to stay somewhere for longer because you do not want to leave; to spend a long time doing something: *She lingered for a few minutes to talk to Nick.* ◆ *We lingered over breakfast on the terrace.* **3** [I] ~ **(on sb/sth)** to continue to look at someone or something or think about something for longer than usual: *His eyes lingered on the diamond ring on her finger.* **4** [I] ~ **(on)** to stay alive but become weaker: *He lingered on for several months after the heart attack.*

lin·ge·rie /ˌlɑːnʒəˈreɪ; ˌlændʒə-/ *noun* [U] (used especially by stores) women's underwear

lin·ger·ing /ˈlɪŋgərɪŋ/ *adj.* slow to end or disappear: *a painful and lingering death* ◆ *a last lingering look* ◆ *lingering doubts* ◆ *a lingering smell of machine oil* ▶ **lin·ger·ing·ly** *adv.*

lin·go /ˈlɪŋgoʊ/ *noun* [sing.] (*informal*) **1** expressions used by a particular group of people **SYN** JARGON: *baseball lingo* **2** (often *humorous*) a language, especially a foreign language: *He doesn't speak the lingo.*

lin·gua fran·ca /ˌlɪŋgwə ˈfræŋkə/ *noun* [usually sing.] (*linguistics*) a shared language of communication used between people whose main languages are different: *English has become a lingua franca in many parts of the world.*

lin·gual /ˈlɪŋgwəl/ *adj.* **1** (*anatomy*) related to the tongue **2** related to speech or language **3** (*phonetics*) (of a speech sound) produced using the tongue ▶ **lin·gual·ly** *adv.*

lin·gui·ne (also **lin·gui·ni**) /lɪŋˈgwini/ *noun* [U, pl.] PASTA in the shape of long, narrow, flat pieces

lin·guist /ˈlɪŋgwɪst/ *noun* **1** a person who knows several foreign languages well: *She's an excellent linguist.* ◆ *I'm afraid I'm no linguist* (= I find foreign languages difficult). **2** a person who studies languages or LINGUISTICS

lin·guis·tic /lɪŋˈgwɪstɪk/ *adj.* connected with language or the scientific study of language: *linguistic and cultural barriers* ◆ *a child's innate linguistic ability* ◆ *new developments in linguistic theory* ▶ **lin·guis·ti·cally** /-kli/ *adv.*

lin·guis·tics /lɪŋˈgwɪstɪks/ *noun* [U] the scientific study of language or of particular languages: *a course in applied linguistics*

lin·i·ment /ˈlɪnəmənt/ *noun* [C, U] a liquid, especially one made with oil, that you rub on a painful part of your body to reduce the pain

lin·ing /ˈlaɪnɪŋ/ *noun* **1** [C, U] a layer of material used to cover the inside surface of something: *a pair of leather gloves with cashmere lining* ➔ picture at CLOTHES **2** [U] the covering of the inner surface of a part of the body: *the stomach lining* **IDM** see CLOUD

link /lɪŋk/ **AWL** *noun, verb*
● *noun* **1** ~ **(between A and B)** a connection between two or more people or things: *Police suspect there may be a link between the two murders.* ◆ *evidence for a strong causal link between exposure to sun and skin cancer* ➔ see also MISSING LINK **2** a relationship between two or more people, countries, or organizations: ~ *to establish trade links with Asia* ◆ ~ **(between A and B)** *Social customs provide a vital link between generations.* **3** a means of traveling or communicating between two places: *a high-speed rail link* ◆ *a video link* ◆ *The speech was broadcast via a satellite link.* **4** (*computing*) a place in an electronic document that is connected to another electronic document or to another part of the same document **SYN** HYPERLINK: *To visit similar Web sites to this one, click on the links at the bottom of the page.* **5** each ring of a chain ➔ picture at ROPE ➔ see also CUFF LINK **6** (also **link sausage, sausage link**) a chain of long thin SAUSAGES; an individual long thin SAUSAGE: *They sell breakfast sausages in links or patties.*

IDM **a link in the chain** one of the stages in a process or a line of argument ⊃ more at WEAK

• *verb* [often passive] **1** to make a physical or electronic connection between one object, machine, place, etc. and another **SYN** CONNECT: *~ A to B The video cameras are linked to a powerful computer.* ♦ *~ A with B An underground tunnel links the library's basement with the Faculty of Law.* ♦ *~ A and B* **(together)** *When computers are networked, they are linked together so that information can be transferred between them.* **2** if something **links** two things, facts, or situations, or they **are linked**, they are connected in some way: *~ A to/with B Exposure to ultraviolet light is closely linked to skin cancer.* ♦ *~ A and B The two factors are directly linked.* ♦ *The personal and social development of the child are inextricably linked* (= they depend on each other). **3** *~ A and B/with B* | *~ A and B* to state that there is a connection or relationship between two things or people **SYN** ASSOCIATE: *Detectives have linked the break-in to a similar crime in the area last year.* ♦ *Newspapers have linked his name with the singer.* **4** *~ A and B* to join two things by putting one through the other: *The two girls linked arms as they strolled down the street.*
PHR V **,link 'up (with sb/sth)** to join or become joined with someone or something: *The two spacecraft will link up in orbit.* ♦ *The bands have linked up for a charity concert.* ⊃ related noun LINKUP

link·age **AWL** /'lɪŋkɪdʒ/ *noun* **1** [U, C] *~* **(between A and B)** the act of linking things; a link or system of links **SYN** CONNECTION: *This chapter explores the linkage between economic development and the environment.* **2** [C] a device that links two or more things

'linking ,verb (also **cop·u·la**) *noun* (*grammar*) a verb such as *be* or *become* that connects a subject with the adjective or noun (called the COMPLEMENT) that describes it: *In "She became angry," the verb "became" is a linking verb.*

links /lɪŋks/ *noun* = GOLF LINKS

'link ,sausage *noun* = LINK n. (6)

link·up /'lɪŋkʌp/ *noun* a connection formed between two things, for example two companies or two broadcasting systems: *a live satellite linkup with the conference*

Lin·nae·an (also **Lin·ne·an**) /lɪ'niən; -'neɪən/ *adj.* (*biology*) relating to the system of naming and arranging living things into scientific groups, invented by Carolus Linnaeus (Carl von Linné)

li·no·cut /'laɪnoʊˌkʌt/ *noun* a design or shape cut in a piece of LINOLEUM, used to make a print; a print made in this way

li·no·le·um /lɪ'noʊliəm/ *noun* [U] a type of strong material with a hard shiny surface, used for covering floors

Lin·o·type™ /'laɪnəˌtaɪp/ *noun* a machine used in the past for printing newspapers, that produces a line of words as one strip of metal

lin·seed oil /'lɪnsid ˌɔɪl/ (also **'flaxseed ,oil**) *noun* [U] an oil made from FLAX seeds, used in paint or to protect wood, etc.

lint /lɪnt/ *noun* [U] **1** small soft pieces of wool, cotton, etc. that stick on the surface of cloth **2** (*technical*) short fine FIBERS that come off the surface of cloth when it is being made

lin·tel /'lɪntl/ *noun* (*architecture*) a piece of wood or stone over a door or window, that forms part of the frame

Lin·ux™ /'lɪnəks/ *noun* [U] (*computing*) an OPERATING SYSTEM based on UNIX™ that is available free in the basic version

li·on /'laɪən/ *noun* a large powerful animal of the cat family, that hunts in groups and lives in parts of Africa and southern Asia. Lions have yellowish-brown fur and the male has a MANE (= long thick hair around its neck).
⊃ picture at ANIMAL ⊃ see also MOUNTAIN LION ⊃ compare LIONESS
IDM **the lion's den** a difficult situation in which you have to face a person or people who are unfriendly or aggressive toward you **the lion's share (of sth)** the largest or best part of something when it is divided

li·on·ess /'laɪənəs/ *noun* a female lion

li·on·ize /'laɪəˌnaɪz/ *verb* *~* **sb** (*formal*) to treat someone as a famous or important person

lip 🔊 /lɪp/ *noun*
1 [C] either of the two soft edges at the opening to the mouth: *The assistant pursed her lips.* ♦ *your* **upper/lower/top/ bottom lip** ♦ *She kissed him* **on the lips.** ♦ *Not a drop of alcohol* **passed my lips** (= I didn't drink any). ⊃ picture at BODY ⊃ collocations at PHYSICAL **2** **-lipped** (in adjectives) having the type of lips mentioned: *thin-lipped* ♦ *thick-lipped* ⊃ see also TIGHT-LIPPED **3** [C] *~* **(of sth)** the edge of a container or a hollow place in the ground **SYN** RIM: *He ran his finger around the lip of the cup.* ♦ *Lava bubbled a few feet below the lip of the crater.* **4** [U] (*informal*) words spoken to someone that are rude and show a lack of respect for that person: *Don't let him give you any lip!*
IDM **lick/smack your lips 1** to move your tongue over your lips, especially before eating something good **2** (*informal*) to show that you are excited about something and want it to happen soon: *They were licking their lips at the thought of clinching the deal.* **my lips are sealed** used to say that you will not repeat someone's secret to other people **on everyone's lips** if something is **on everyone's lips**, they are all talking about it ⊃ more at BITE, PASS, READ, SLIP, STIFF

li·pase /'laɪpeɪs; 'lɪ-/ *noun* [U] (*chemistry*) an ENZYME (= a chemical substance in the body) that makes fats change into acids and alcohol

'lip balm *noun* [U] a substance in the form of a stick, like a LIPSTICK, that you put on your lips to stop them from becoming sore

lip·gloss (also **'lip gloss**) /'lɪpglɔs; -glɑs/ *noun* [U, C] a substance that is put on the lips to make them look shiny ⊃ picture at MAKEUP

lip·id /'lɪpəd/ *noun* (*chemistry*) any of a group of natural substances which do not dissolve in water, including plant oils and STEROIDS

'lip ,liner *noun* [U] a substance that is put on the outline of the lips, to prevent LIPSTICK from spreading ⊃ picture at MAKEUP

lip·o·pro·tein /'lɪpoʊˌproʊtin; 'laɪ-/ *noun* (*biology*) a PROTEIN that combines with a lipid and carries it to another part of the body in the blood

lip·o·some /'lɪpəˌsoʊm; 'laɪ-/ *noun* a very small bag formed of lipid MOLECULES, used to carry a drug to a particular part of the body

lip·o·suc·tion /'lɪpəˌsʌkʃn; 'laɪ-/ *noun* [U] a way of removing fat from someone's body by using SUCTION

lip-read /'lɪp rid/ *verb* [I, T] *~* **(sb)** to understand what someone is saying by watching the way their lips move ▶ **'lip-,reading** *noun* [U]

'lip ,service *noun* [U] if someone pays **lip service** to something, they say that they approve of it or support it, without proving their support by what they actually do: *All the parties pay lip service to environmental issues.*

lip·stick /'lɪpstɪk/ *noun* [U, C] a substance made into a small stick, used for coloring the lips; a small stick of this substance: *She was wearing bright red lipstick.* ⊃ picture at MAKEUP

lip-sync (also **lip-synch**) /'lɪp sɪŋk/ *verb* [I, T] to move your mouth, without speaking or singing, so that its movements match the sound on a recorded song, etc.: *~* **(to sth)** *She lip-synced to a Beatles song.* ♦ *~ sth He lip-synced "Return to Sender."*

liq·ue·fy /'lɪkwəˌfaɪ/ *verb* (liq·ue·fies, liq·ue·fy·ing, liq·ue·fied, liq·ue·fied) [I, T] *~* **(sth)** (*formal*) to become liquid; to make something liquid

li·queur /lɪ'kər; -'kur; -'kyur/ (also **cor·dial**) *noun* **1** [U, C] a strong, sweet, alcoholic drink, sometimes flavored with fruit. It is usually drunk in very small glasses after a meal. **2** [C] a glass of liqueur

| t tea | ţ butter | d did | k cat | g got | tʃ chin | dʒ June | f fall |

liq·uid /ˈlɪkwəd/ *noun, adj.*

● *noun* [U, C] a substance that flows freely and is not a solid or a gas, for example water or oil: *She poured the dark brown liquid down the sink.* ◆ *the transition from liquid to vapor*

● *adj.* **1** in the form of a liquid; not a solid or a gas: *liquid soap* ◆ **liquid nitrogen** ◆ *The detergent comes in powder or* **liquid form.** ◆ *a bar selling snacks and* **liquid refreshment** (= drinks) **2** (*finance*) that can easily be changed into cash: *liquid assets* **3** (*literary*) clear, like water **SYN** LIMPID: *liquid blue eyes* **4** (*literary*) (of sounds) clear, pure, and flowing: *the liquid song of a blackbird*

liq·ui·date /ˈlɪkwəˌdeɪt/ *verb* **1** [I, T] ~ (sth) to close a business and sell everything it owns in order to pay debts **2** [T] ~ sth (*finance*) to sell something in order to get money: *to liquidate assets* **3** [T] ~ sth (*finance*) to pay a debt **4** [T] ~ sb/sth to destroy or remove someone or something that causes problems **SYN** ANNIHILATE: *The government tried to liquidate the rebel movement and failed.*

liq·ui·da·tion /ˌlɪkwəˈdeɪʃn/ *noun* [U] the action of liquidating someone or something: *The company has* **gone into liquidation.** ➔ collocations at BUSINESS

liq·ui·da·tor /ˈlɪkwəˌdeɪtər/ *noun* a person responsible for closing down a business and using any profits from the sale to pay its debts

liquid ˈcrystal disˌplay *noun* = LCD

liq·uid·i·ty /lɪˈkwɪdəti/ *noun* [U] (*finance*) the state of owning things of value that can easily be exchanged for cash

liq·uor /ˈlɪkər/ *noun* [U] strong alcoholic drink: *hard liquor* ◆ *She drinks wine and beer but no liquor.* ➔ see also MALT LIQUOR

ˈliquor ˌstore *noun* a store that sells alcoholic drinks in bottles and cans to take home

li·ra /ˈlɪrə/ *noun* (*pl.* lire /ˈlɪreɪ/) (*abbr.* l.) the unit of money in Turkey, and formerly in Italy (replaced there in 2002 by the EURO)

lisle /laɪl/ *noun* [U] a fine, smooth, cotton thread used in the past especially for making PANTYHOSE and STOCKINGS

lisp /lɪsp/ *noun, verb*

● *noun* [usually sing.] a speech fault in which the sound "s" is pronounced "th": *She spoke with a slight lisp.*

● *verb* [I, T] (+ speech) to speak with a lisp

lis·some /ˈlɪsəm/ *adj.* (*literary*) (of someone's body) thin and attractive **SYN** LITHE

list /lɪst/ *noun, verb*

● *noun* **1** [C] a series of names, items, figures, etc., especially when they are written or printed: *a shopping/wine/price list* ◆ *to* **make a list** *of things to do* ◆ (*formal*) *to* **draw up a list** ◆ *Is your name* **on the list?** ◆ *Having to wait hours came* **high on the list** *of complaints.* ➔ see also A-LIST, HIT LIST, LAUNDRY LIST, MAILING LIST, SHORT LIST, WAITING LIST, WAIT LIST **2** [sing.] the fact of a ship leaning to one side

● *verb* **1** [T] ~ sth to write a list of things in a particular order: *We were asked to list our ten favorite songs.* ◆ *Towns in the guide are listed alphabetically.* **2** [T] ~ sb/sth to mention or include someone or something in a list: *The koala is listed among Australia's endangered animals.* ◆ *soldiers listed as missing* **3** [I, T] ~ (at/for sth) | ~ sth to be put or put something in a list of things for sale: *This DVD player lists at $200.* **4** [I] (of a ship) to lean to one side

lis·ten /ˈlɪsn/ *verb*

1 [I] to pay attention to someone or something that you can hear: *Listen! What's that noise? Can you hear it?* ◆ *Sorry, I wasn't really listening.* ◆ ~ **to sb/sth** *to listen to music* ◆ *I listened carefully to her story.* **HELP** You cannot "listen sth" (without "to"): *I'm fond of listening to classical music.* ◆ *I'm fond of listening classical music.* **2** [I] ~ (to sb/sth) to take notice of what someone says to you so that you follow their advice or believe them: *None of this would have happened if you'd listened to me.* ◆ *Why won't you* **listen to reason?** **3** [I] (*informal*)

used to tell someone to take notice of what you are going to say: *Listen, there's something I have to tell you.*

PHR V ˈlisten for sth | ˌlisten ˈout for sth to be prepared to hear a particular sound: *Can you listen out for the doorbell?* ˌlisten ˈin (on/to sth) **1** to listen to a conversation that you are not supposed to hear: *You shouldn't listen in on other people's conversations.* **2** to listen to a radio broadcast ˌlisten ˈup (*informal*) used to tell people to listen carefully because you are going to say something important

lis·ten·a·ble /ˈlɪsənəbl/ *adj.* (*informal*) pleasant to listen to

lis·ten·er /ˈlɪsənər/ *noun* **1** a person who listens: *a good listener* (= someone who you can rely on to listen with attention or sympathy) **2** a person listening to a radio program

ˈlistening ˌpost *noun* a place where people who are part of an army listen to enemy communications to try to get information that will give them an advantage

lis·te·ri·a /lɪˈstɪriə/ *noun* [U] a type of bacteria that makes people sick if they eat infected food

list·ing /ˈlɪstɪŋ/ *noun* **1** [C] a list, especially an official or published list of people or things, often arranged in alphabetical order: *a comprehensive listing of all airlines* **2 listings** [pl.] information in a newspaper or magazine, or on the internet about what movies, plays, etc. are being shown in a particular city or town: *Check the listings to see what time the movie starts.* **3** [C] a position or an item on a list: (*business*) *The company is seeking a stock exchange listing* (= for trading shares).

list·less /ˈlɪstləs; ˈlɪsləs/ *adj.* having no energy or enthusiasm *The illness left her feeling listless and depressed.* ▸ **list·less·ly** *adv.* **list·less·ness** *noun* [U]

ˈlist price *noun* [usually sing.] (*business*) the price at which goods are advertised for sale, for example in a CATALOG

lit pt, pp of LIGHT

lit·a·ny /ˈlɪtnæwi/ *noun* (*pl.* lit·a·nies) **1** a series of prayers to God for use in church services, spoken by a priest, etc., with set responses by the people **2** ~ (of sth) (*formal*) a long boring account of a series of events, reasons, etc.: *a litany of complaints*

li·tchi = LYCHEE

lite /laɪt/ *adj.* (*informal*) **1** (of food or drinks) containing fewer CALORIES than other types of food, and therefore less likely to make you fat (a way of spelling "light"): *lite ice cream* **2** (used after a noun) (*disapproving*) used to say that a thing is similar to something else but lacks many of its serious or important qualities: *I would describe this movie as "Hitchcock lite."*

li·ter (*CanE usually* li·tre) /ˈlitər/ *noun* (*abbr.* l) a unit for measuring volume, equal to 1.057 liquid QUARTS: *3 liters of water* ◆ *a liter bottle of wine* ◆ *a car with a 3.5 liter engine*

lit·er·a·cy /ˈlɪtərəsi/ *noun* [U] the ability to read and write: *a campaign to promote adult literacy* ◆ *basic literacy skills* **ANT** ILLITERACY ➔ compare NUMERACY

lit·er·al /ˈlɪtərəl/ *adj.* **1** [usually before noun] being the basic or usual meaning of a word or phrase: *I am not referring to "small" people in the literal sense of the word.* ◆ *The literal meaning of "petrify" is "turn to stone."* ➔ compare FIGURATIVE, METAPHORICAL **2** [usually before noun] that follows the original words exactly: *a literal translation* ➔ compare FREE **3** (*disapproving*) lacking imagination: *Her interpretation of the music was too literal.* ▸ **lit·er·al·ness** *noun* [U]

lit·er·al·ly /ˈlɪtərəli/ *adv.* **1** in a literal way **SYN** EXACTLY: *The word "planet" literally means "wandering body."* ◆ *When I told you to "get lost" I didn't expect to* **be taken literally.** **2** used to emphasize the truth of something that may seem surprising: *There are literally hundreds of prizes to win.* **3** (*informal*) used to emphasize a word or phrase, even if it is not literally true: *I literally jumped out of my skin.* **HELP** Although this is a common use of **literally**, some people think it is not correct.

---

lit·er·ar·y /ˈlɪtəˌreri/ adj. **1** connected with literature: *literary criticism/theory* **2** (of a language or style of writing) suitable for or typical of a work of literature: *It was Chaucer who really turned English into a literary language.* **3** liking literature very much; studying or writing literature: *a literary man*

'literary ˌagent noun a person whose job is to represent authors and persuade companies to publish their work

lit·er·ate /ˈlɪtərət/ adj. able to read and write
ANT ILLITERATE ⊃ see also NUMERACY, COMPUTER-LITERATE

lit·e·ra·ti /ˌlɪtəˈrɑti/ **the literati** noun [pl.] (*formal*) educated and intelligent people who enjoy literature

lit·er·a·ture 🔊 /ˈlɪtərətʃər; -ˌtʃʊr/ noun [U]
1 pieces of writing that are valued as works of art, especially novels, plays, and poems (in contrast to technical books and newspapers, magazines, etc.): *French literature* ◆ *great works of literature* ⊃ see also COMPARATIVE LITERATURE **2** ~ **(on sth)** pieces of writing or printed information on a particular subject: *I've read all the available literature on keeping rabbits.* ◆ *sales literature*

TOPIC COLLOCATIONS

Literature

being a writer

- **write/publish** literature/poetry/fiction/a book/a story/a poem/a novel/a review/an autobiography
- **become** a writer/novelist/playwright
- **find/have** a publisher/an agent
- **have** a new book out
- **edit/revise/proofread** a book/text/manuscript
- **dedicate** a book/poem to…

plot, character, and atmosphere

- **construct/create/weave/weave sth into** a complex narrative
- **advance/drive** the plot
- **introduce/present** the protagonist/a character
- **describe/depict/portray** a character (as…)/(sb as) a hero/villain
- **create** an exciting/a tense atmosphere
- **build/heighten** the suspense/tension
- **evoke/capture** the pathos of the situation
- **convey** emotion/an idea/an impression/a sense of…
- **engage** the reader
- **seize/capture/grip** the (reader's) imagination
- **arouse/elicit** emotion/sympathy (in the reader)
- **lack** imagination/emotion/structure/rhythm

language, style, and imagery

- **use/employ** language/imagery/humor/an image/a symbol/a metaphor/a device
- **use/adopt/develop** a style/technique
- **be rich in/be full of** symbolism
- **evoke** images of…/a sense of…/a feeling of…
- **create/achieve** an effect
- **maintain/lighten** the tone
- **introduce/develop** an idea/a theme
- **inspire** a novel/a poet/sb's work/sb's imagination

reading and criticism

- **read** an author/sb's work/fiction/poetry/a text/an article/a poem/a novel/a chapter/a passage
- **review** an article/a book/a novel/sb's work
- **give sth/get/have/receive** a good/bad review
- **be hailed (as)/be recognized as** a masterpiece
- **quote** a phrase/a line/a stanza/a passage/an author
- **provoke/spark** discussion/criticism
- **study/interpret/understand** a text/passage
- **translate** sb's work/a text/a passage/a novel/a poem

lithe /laɪð/ adj. (of a person or their body) moving or bending easily, in a way that is elegant ▶ **lithe·ly** adv.

lith·i·um /ˈlɪθiəm/ noun [U] (*symb.* **Li**) a chemical element. Lithium is a soft, very light, silver-white metal used in batteries and ALLOYS.

lith·o·graph /ˈlɪθəˌgræf/ noun a picture printed by lithography

li·thog·ra·phy /lɪˈθɑgrəfi/ noun (also *informal* **li·tho** /ˈlɪθoʊ/) [U] the process of printing from a smooth surface, for example a metal plate, that has been specially prepared so that ink only sticks to the design to be printed ▶ **lith·o·graph·ic** /ˌlɪθəˈgræfɪk/ adj.

li·thol·o·gy /lɪˈθɑlədʒi/ noun [U] the study of the general physical characteristics of rocks

lith·o·sphere /ˈlɪθəˌsfɪr/ noun [sing.] (*geology*) the layer of rock that forms the outer part of the earth

lit·i·gant /ˈlɪtəgənt/ noun (*law*) a person who is making or defending a claim in court

lit·i·gate /ˈlɪtəˌgeɪt/ verb [I, T] ~ **(sth)** (*law*) to take a claim or disagreement to court ▶ **lit·i·ga·tor** /-ˌgeɪtər/ noun

lit·i·ga·tion /ˌlɪtəˈgeɪʃn/ noun [U] (*law*) the process of making or defending a claim in court: *The company has been in litigation with its previous auditors for a full year.*

li·ti·gious /lɪˈtɪdʒəs/ adj. (*formal, disapproving*) too ready to take disagreements to court ▶ **li·ti·gious·ness** noun [U]

lit·mus /ˈlɪtməs/ noun [U] a substance that turns red when it touches an acid and blue when it touches an ALKALI: *litmus paper*

'litmus ˌtest noun **1** = ACID TEST: *The outcome will be seen as a litmus test of government concern for conservation issues.* **2** a test using litmus

li·to·tes /laɪˈtoʊtiz; ˈlaɪtəˌtiz/ noun [U] (*technical*) the use of a negative or weak statement to emphasize a positive meaning, for example *he wasn't slow to accept the offer* (= he was quick to accept the offer) ⊃ compare UNDERSTATEMENT

lit·ter /ˈlɪtər/ noun, verb
● **noun 1** [U] small pieces of garbage such as paper, cans, and bottles, that people have left lying in a public place: *There will be fines for people who **drop litter**.* **2** [sing.] ~ **of sth** a number of things that are lying in a messy way: *The floor was covered with a litter of newspapers, clothes, and empty cups.* **3** [U] a dry substance that is put in a shallow open box for pets, especially cats, to use as a toilet when they are indoors: *cat litter* ◆ *a litter box* **4** [C] a number of baby animals that one mother gives birth to at the same time: *a litter of puppies* ◆ *the runt* (= the smallest and weakest baby) *of the litter* **5** [U] the substance, especially STRAW, that is used for farm animals to sleep on **6** [C] a kind of chair or bed that was used in the past for carrying important people
● **verb 1** [T] ~ **sth** to be spread around a place, making it look messy: *Piles of books and newspapers littered the floor.* ◆ *Broken glass littered the streets.* **2** [T, usually passive, I] ~ **(sth) (with sth)** to leave things in a place, making it look messy: *The floor was littered with papers.* ◆ *He was arrested for littering.* **3** [T] **be littered with sth** to contain or involve a lot of a particular type of thing, usually something bad: *Your essay is littered with spelling mistakes.*

lit·ter·bug /ˈlɪtərˌbʌg/ noun (*informal, disapproving*) a person who leaves litter in public places

lit·tle 🔊 /ˈlɪtl/ adj., det., pron., adv.
● **adj.** [usually before noun] **HELP** The forms **lit·tler** /ˈlɪtlər/ and **lit·tlest** /ˈlɪtləst/ are rare. It is more common to use **small·er** and **small·est**. **1** not big; small; smaller than others: *a little house* ◆ *a little old lady* ◆ *the classic little black dress* ◆ *"Which do you want?" "I'll take the little one."* ◆ *She gave a little laugh.* ◆ *Here's a little something* (= a small present) *for your birthday.* **2** used after an adjective to show affection or dislike, especially in a PATRONIZING way (= one that suggests that you think you are better than someone): *The poor little thing! It's lost its mother.* ◆ *What a nasty little man!* ◆ *She's a good little worker.* ◆ *He'd become quite the little gentleman.* **3** young: *a little boy/girl* ◆ *my little brother/sister* (= younger brother/sister) ◆ *I lived in an apartment when I was*

little. **4** (of distance or time) short: *A **little** while later the phone rang.* ◆ *Let's walk a **little** way.* **5** not important; not serious: *I can't remember every **little** detail.* ◆ *You soon get used to the **little** difficulties.* ▶ **lit·tle·ness** *noun* [U]

IDM **a little bird/birdie told me** (*informal*) used to say that someone told you something but you do not want to say who it was ⊃ more at OAK, WONDER *n.*

• **det., pron. 1** used with uncountable nouns to mean "not much": *There was **little** doubt in my mind.* ◆ *Students have **little** or no choice in the matter.* ◆ *I understood **little** of what he said.* ◆ *She said **little or nothing** about her experience.* ◆ *Tell him **as little as possible**.* **2 a little** used with uncountable nouns to mean "a small amount," "some": *a little milk/sugar/tea* ◆ *If you have any spare milk, could you give me a little?* ◆ *I've only read a little of the book so far.* ◆ (*formal*) *It caused **not a little/no little** (= a lot of) confusion.* ◆ *After a little (= a short time) he got up and left.*

IDM **little by little** slowly; gradually: *Little by little the snow disappeared.* ◆ *His English is improving little by little.*

• **adv.** (less, least) **1** not much; only slightly: *He is **little** known as an artist.* ◆ *I slept very **little** last night.* ◆ *Little did I know that this spelled the end of my career.* **2 a little (bit)** to a small degree: *She seemed **a little** afraid of going inside.* ◆ *These shoes are **a little (bit)** too big for me.* ◆ (*formal*) *She felt tired and **more than a little** worried.*

the ˌLittle ˈBear *noun* = URSA MINOR

ˌlittle ˈfinger *noun* the smallest finger of the hand ⊃ picture at BODY **SYN** PINKIE

IDM **twist/wrap/wind sb around your little finger** (*informal*) to persuade someone to do anything that you want

ˈLittle ˌLeague *noun* [sing., U] a baseball league for children

ˈlittle ˌpeople *noun* [pl.] **1** all the people in a country who have no power **2** extremely small people, who will never grow to a normal size because of a physical problem **3 the little people** small imaginary people with magic powers **SYN** FAIRY

lit·to·ral /ˈlɪtərəl; lɪˈtɔrəl/ *noun* (*technical*) the part of a country that is near the coast ▶ **lit·to·ral** *adj.* [only before noun]: *littoral states*

lit·ur·gy /ˈlɪtərdʒi/ *noun* (*pl.* **lit·ur·gies**) a fixed form of public worship used in churches ▶ **li·tur·gi·cal** /lɪˈtərdʒɪkl/ *adj.* **li·tur·gi·cal·ly** /-kli/ *adv.*

liv·able (also **live·a·ble**) /ˈlɪvəbl/ *adj.* **1** (of a house, etc.) fit to live in **SYN** HABITABLE: *safer and more livable residential areas* **2** (of life) worth living **3** [only before noun] (of a wage, etc.) enough to live on: *a livable salary*

live¹ 🔊 /lɪv/ *verb* ⊃ see also LIVE²

▷ **IN A PLACE 1** [I] + **adv./prep.** to have your home in a particular place: *to live in a house* ◆ *Where do you live?* ◆ *She needs to find **somewhere to live**.* ◆ *We used to live in Chicago.* ◆ *Both her children still live at home.* ◆ (*informal*) *Where do these plates live (= where are they usually kept)?*

▷ **BE ALIVE 2** [I] to remain alive: *The doctors said he only had six months to live.* ◆ *Spiders can live for several days without food.* ◆ **~ to do sth** *She lived to see her first grandchild.* **3** [I] to be alive, especially at a particular time: *When did Handel live?* ◆ *He's the greatest player who ever lived.*

▷ **TYPE OF LIFE 4** [I, T] to spend your life in a particular way: *He lived in poverty most of his life.* ◆ **~ sth** *She lived a very peaceful life.* ◆ **+ noun** *She lived and died a single woman.*

▷ **BE REMEMBERED 5** [I] to continue to exist or be remembered **SYN** REMAIN: *This moment will live in our memory for many years to come.* ◆ *Her words have lived with me all my life.*

▷ **HAVE EXCITEMENT 6** [I] to have a full and exciting life: *I don't want to be stuck in an office all my life—I want to live!*

IDM **live and breathe sth** to be very enthusiastic about something: *He just lives and breathes football.* **(you) live and learn** used to express surprise at something new or unexpected you have been told **live and let live** (*saying*) used to say that you should accept other people's opinions

and behavior even though they are different from your own **live by your wits** to earn money by being able to think quickly or sometimes by dishonest means **live (from) hand to mouth** to spend all the money you earn on basic needs such as food without being able to save any money **live in the past** to behave as though society, etc. has not changed, when in fact it has **live in sin** (*old-fashioned* or *humorous*) to live together and have a sexual relationship without being married **live it up** (*informal*) to enjoy yourself in an exciting way, usually spending a lot of money **live a lie** to keep something important about yourself a secret from other people, so that they do not know what you really think, what you are really like, etc. **live off the fat of the land** to have enough money to be able to afford expensive things, food, drink, etc. **live off the land** to eat whatever food you can grow, kill, or find yourself **live to fight/see another day** (*saying*) used to say that although you have failed or had a bad experience, you will continue **you haven't lived** used to tell someone that if they have not had a particular experience their life is not complete: *You've never been to New York? You haven't lived!* ⊃ more at BORROW, CLOVER, HALF *n.*, LAND *n.*, LIFE, LONG *adv.*, PEOPLE

PHR V **ˈlive by sth** to follow a particular belief or set of principles: *That's a philosophy I could live by.* **ˈlive by doing sth** to earn money or to get the things you need by doing a particular thing: *a community that lives by fishing* **ˌlive sth↔ˈdown** to be able to make people forget about something embarrassing you have done: *She felt so stupid. She'd never be able to live it down.* **ˈlive for sb/sth** to think that someone or something is the main purpose of or the most important thing in your life: *She lives for her work.* ◆ *After his wife died, he had nothing to live for.* **ˌlive ˈin** to live at the place where you work or study: *They have an au pair living in.* ⊃ see also LIVE-IN **ˈlive off sb/sth** (often *disapproving*) to receive the money you need to live from someone or something because you do not have any yourself: *She's still living off her parents.* ◆ *to live off welfare* **ˈlive off sth** to have one particular type of food as the main thing you eat in order to live: *He seems to live off junk food.* **ˌlive ˈon** to continue to live or exist: *She died ten years ago but her memory lives on.* **ˈlive on sth 1** to eat a particular type of food to live: *Small birds live mainly on insects.* **2** (often *disapproving*) to eat only or a lot of a particular type of food: *She lives on burgers.* **3** to have enough money for the basic things you need to live: *You can't live on ninety dollars a week.* **ˌlive ˈout sth 1** to actually do what you have only thought about doing before: *to live out your fantasies* **2** to spend the rest of your life in a particular way: *He lived out his days alone.* **ˌlive ˈthrough sth** to experience a disaster or other unpleasant situation and survive it: *He has lived through two world wars.* **ˈlive together** (also **ˈlive with sb**) **1** to live in the same house **2** to share a home and have a sexual relationship without being married **SYN** COHABIT **ˌlive ˈup to sth** to do as well as or be as good as other people expect you to: *He failed to live up to his parents' expectations.* ◆ *The team called "The No-Hopers" certainly lived up to its name.* **ˈlive with sb** = LIVE¹ **ˈlive with sth** to accept something unpleasant: *I just had to learn to live with the pain.*

live² 🔊 /laɪv/ *adj., adv.* ⊃ see also LIVE¹

• **adj.** [usually before noun]

▷ **NOT DEAD 1** living; not dead: *live animals* ◆ *the number of live births (= babies born alive)* ◆ *We saw a **real live** rattlesnake!*

▷ **NOT RECORDED 2** (of a broadcast) sent out while the event is actually happening, not recorded first and broadcast later: *live coverage of the World Cup* **3** (of a performance) given or made when people are watching, not recorded: *The club has live music most nights.* ◆ *a live recording made at Carnegie Hall* ◆ *the band's new live album* ◆ *It was the first interview I'd done in front of a **live audience** (= with people watching).*

▷ **ELECTRICITY 4** (of a wire or device) connected to a source of electrical power: *That terminal is live.*

▷ **BULLETS/MATCHES 5** still able to explode or light; ready for use: *live ammunition*

▷ **COALS 6** **live** coals are burning or are still hot and red

> QUESTION/SUBJECT **7** of interest or importance at the present time: *Pollution is still very much a live issue.*
> INTERNET **8** (of an electronic link) functioning correctly, so that it is connected to another document or page on the Internet: *Here are some live links to other aviation-related web pages.*
> IN SPORTS **9** used to describe the ball at a time when play is continuing, not stopped because the ball is out of BOUNDS **ANT** DEAD
> **IDM** **a live wire** a person who is lively and full of energy
> • **adv.** broadcast at the time of an actual event; played or recorded at an actual performance: *The show is going out live.*
> **IDM** **go live** (*computing*) (of a computer system) to become OPERATIONAL (= ready to be used)

live·a·ble = LIVABLE

live ac·tion /ˌlaɪv ˈækʃn/ *noun* [U] part of a movie that is made using real people or animals, rather than using drawings, models, or computers ▶ **live-'action** *adj.* [only before noun]: *a live-action movie*

'lived-in *adj.* (of a place) that has been used so continuously for so long that it does not look new: (*approving*) *The room had a comfortable, lived-in feel about it.*

live-in /ˈlɪv ɪn/ *adj.* **1** (of an employee) living in the house where they work: *a live-in nanny* **2 ~ lover, boyfriend, girlfriend, etc.** a person who lives with their sexual partner but is not married to them

live·li·hood /ˈlaɪvliˌhʊd/ *noun* [C, usually sing., U] a means of earning money in order to live **SYN** LIVING: *Communities on the island depended on whaling for their livelihood.* ♦ *a means/ source of livelihood*

live·long /ˈlɪvlɔŋ/ *adj.*
> **IDM** **the livelong day** (*literary*) the whole length of the day

live·ly /ˈlaɪvli/ *adj.*
(live·li·er, live·li·est) **1** full of life and energy; active and enthusiastic **SYN** ANIMATED, VIVACIOUS: *an intelligent and lively young woman* ♦ *a lively and inquiring mind* ♦ *He showed a lively interest in politics.* **2** (of a place, an event, etc.) full of interest or excitement **SYN** BUSTLING: *a lively bar* ♦ *a lively debate* **3** (of colors) strong and definite: *a lively shade of pink* **4** busy and active: *They do a lively trade in souvenirs and gifts.* ▶ **live·li·ness** *noun* [U]

liv·en /ˈlaɪvn/ *verb*
> **PHRV** **liven 'up** | **liven sb/sth 'up** to become or to make someone or something more interesting or exciting: *The game didn't liven up till the second half.* ♦ *Let's put some music on to liven things up.*

liv·er /ˈlɪvər/ *noun* **1** [C] a large organ in the body that cleans the blood and produces BILE ➔ picture at BODY **2** [U, C] the liver of some animals that is cooked and eaten: *liver and onions* ♦ *chicken livers*

'liver ˌfluke *noun* a small WORM that, in an adult form, lives in the liver of people or animals, often causing disease

liv·er·ied /ˈlɪvərid/ *adj.* wearing LIVERY: *liveried servants*

'liver ˌspot *noun* a small brown spot on the skin, especially found in older people

liv·er·wurst /ˈlɪvərˌwərst/ *noun* [U] a type of soft SAUSAGE made from finely chopped liver, usually spread cold on bread

liv·er·y /ˈlɪvəri/ *noun* [U, C] (*pl.* liv·er·ies) a special uniform worn by servants or officials, especially in the past

'livery ˌstable *noun* a place where people can pay to keep their horses or can rent a horse

lives *pl.* of LIFE

live·stock /ˈlaɪvstɑk/ *noun* [U, pl.] the animals kept on a farm, for example cows or sheep

live·ware /ˈlaɪvwer/ *noun* [U] (*informal*) people who work with computers, rather than the programs or computers with which they work

liv·id /ˈlɪvəd/ *adj.* **1** extremely angry **SYN** FURIOUS **2** dark blue-gray in color: *a livid bruise*

liv·ing /ˈlɪvɪŋ/ *adj., noun*
• **adj.** **1** alive now: *all living things* ♦ *living organisms* ♦ *the finest living pianist* **2** [only before noun] used or practiced now: *living languages* (= those still spoken) ♦ *a living faith*
> **IDM** **be living proof of sth/that...** to show by your actions or qualities that a particular fact is true: *He is living proof that not all engineers are boring.* **within/in living memory** at a time, or during the time, that is remembered by people still alive: *the coldest winter in living memory* ➔ more at DAYLIGHTS
• **noun** **1** [C, usually sing.] money to buy the things that you need in life: *She earns her living as a freelance journalist.* ♦ *to make a good/decent/meager living* ♦ *What do you do for a living?* **2** [U] a way or style of life: *everyday living* ♦ *communal living* ♦ *plain living* ♦ *Their standard of living is very low.* ♦ *The cost of living has risen sharply.* ♦ *poor living conditions/ standards* **3** **the living** [pl.] people who are alive now: *the living and the dead* **IDM** see LAND *n.*

ˌliving 'death *noun* [sing.] a life that is worse than being dead

ˌliving 'hell *noun* [sing.] a very unpleasant situation that causes a lot of suffering and lasts a long time

ˌliving 'roof *noun* = GREEN ROOF

ˌliving ˌroom *noun* a room in a house where people sit together, watch television, etc.

ˌliving 'wage *noun* [sing.] a wage that is high enough for someone to buy the things they need in order to live

ˌliving 'will *noun* a document stating your wishes concerning medical treatment in the case that you become so sick that you can no longer make decisions about it, in particular asking doctors to stop treating you and let you die

liz·ard /ˈlɪzərd/ *noun* a small REPTILE with a rough skin, four short legs, and a long tail

lizard

ll *abbr.* (in writing) lines (the plural form of "l")

lla·ma /ˈlɑmə/ *noun* a S. American animal kept for its soft wool or for carrying loads

LL.B. /ˌɛl ɛl ˈbi/ *noun* a first university degree in law (the abbreviation for "Bachelor of Laws")

LL.D. /ˌɛl ɛl ˈdi/ *noun* the highest university degree in law (the abbreviation for "Doctor of Laws")

LL.M. /ˌɛl ɛl ˈɛm/ *noun* a second university degree in law (the abbreviation for "Master of Laws")

lm *abbr.* LUMEN

LMS /ˌɛl ɛm ˈɛs/ *noun* a software system for managing training and education using the Internet (the abbreviation for "learning management system")

lo /loʊ/ *exclamation* (*old use* or *humorous*) used for calling attention to a surprising thing
> **IDM** **lo and behold** (*humorous*) used for calling attention to a surprising or annoying thing

load /loʊd/ *noun, verb*
• **noun**
> SOMETHING CARRIED **1** [C] something that is being carried (usually in large amounts) by a person, vehicle, etc. **SYN** CARGO: *The trucks waited at the warehouse to pick up their loads.* ♦ *The women came down the hill with their loads of firewood.* ♦ *These backpacks are designed to carry a heavy load.* **2** [C] (often in compounds) the total amount of something that something can carry or contain: *a busload of tourists* ♦ *They ordered three truckloads of sand.* ♦ *He put half a load of laundry in the machine.* ♦ *The plane took off with a full load.*

ʌ cup   ə about   eɪ say   aɪ five   ɔɪ boy   aʊ now   oʊ go   ər bird

> **WEIGHT 3** [C, usually sing.] the amount of weight that is pressing down on something: *a load-bearing wall* ◆ *Modern backpacks spread the load over a wider area.*

> **LARGE AMOUNT 4** [sing.] **a load** (also **loads** [pl.]) **~ (of sth)** (*informal*) a large number or amount of someone or something; plenty: *Uncle Jim brought a whole load of presents for the kids.* ◆ *She has loads of friends.* ◆ *There's loads to do today.* ◆ *He wrote loads and loads of letters to people.*

> **WRONG OR STUPID THING 5** [sing.] **~ of garbage, trash, etc.** (*informal*) used to emphasize that something is wrong, stupid, bad, etc.

> **WORK 6** [C] an amount of work that a person or machine has to do: *Teaching loads have increased in all types of schools.* ⊃ see also CASELOAD, WORKLOAD

> **RESPONSIBILITY/WORRY 7** [C, usually sing.] a feeling of responsibility or worry that is difficult to deal with **SYN** BURDEN: *She thought she would not be able to bear the load of bringing up her family alone.* ◆ *Knowing that they had arrived safely took a load off my mind.*

> **ELECTRICAL POWER 8** [C] the amount of electrical power that is being supplied at a particular time

IDM **get a load of sb/sth** (*informal*) used to tell someone to look at or listen to someone or something: *Get a load of that dress!*

• *verb*

> **GIVE/RECEIVE LOAD 1** [T, I] to put a large quantity of things or people onto or into something: **~ sth** *We loaded the car in ten minutes.* ◆ *Can you help me load the dishwasher?* ◆ **~ sth (up) (with sth)** *Men were loading up a truck with timber.* ◆ **~ sth/sb (into/onto sth)** *Sacks were being loaded onto the truck.* ◆ **~ (up)** | **~ (up with sth)** *We finished loading and set off.* [I] **ANT** UNLOAD **2** [I] to receive a load: *The ship was still loading.* **ANT** UNLOAD **3** [T] **~ sb with sth** to give someone a lot of things, especially things they have to carry: *They loaded her with gifts.*

> **GUN/CAMERA 4** [T, I] to put something into a weapon, camera, or other piece of equipment so that it can be used: **~ sth (into sth)** *She loaded film into the camera.* ◆ **~ sth (with sth)** *She loaded the camera with film.* ◆ **~ (sth)** *Is the gun loaded?* **ANT** UNLOAD

> **COMPUTING 5** [T, I] **~ (sth)** to put data or a program into the memory of a computer: *Have you loaded the software?* ◆ *Wait for the game to load.* ⊃ compare DOWNLOAD

IDM **load the dice (against sb)** [usually passive] to put someone at a disadvantage: *He has always felt that the dice were loaded against him in life.*

PHR V **,load sb/sth 'down (with sth)** [usually passive] to give someone or something a lot of heavy things to carry **SYN** WEIGH DOWN: *She was loaded down with bags of groceries.*

load·ed /'loʊdəd/ *adj.*

> **FULL 1** carrying a load; full and heavy **SYN** LADEN: *a fully loaded truck* ◆ **~ (with sth)** *a truck loaded with supplies* ◆ *She came into the room carrying a loaded tray.* **2 ~ with sth** (*informal*) full of a particular thing, quality, or meaning: *desserts loaded with calories*

> **RICH 3** [not before noun] (*informal*) very rich: *Let her pay— she's loaded.*

> **ADVANTAGE/DISADVANTAGE 4 ~ in favor of sb/sth** | **~ against sb/sth** acting either as an advantage or a disadvantage to someone or something in a way that is unfair: *a system that is loaded in favor of the young* (= gives them an advantage)

> **WORD/STATEMENT 5** having more meaning than you realize at first and intended to make you think in a particular way: *It was a loaded question and I preferred not to comment.*

> **GUN/CAMERA 6** containing bullets, film, etc.: *a loaded shotgun*

> **DRUNK 7** (*informal*) very drunk

'**load line** *noun* = PLIMSOLL LINE

loaf /loʊf/ *noun, verb*

• *noun* (*pl.* **loaves** /loʊvz/) an amount of bread that has been shaped and baked in one piece: *a loaf of bread* ◆ *Two white loaves, please.* ◆ *a sliced loaf* ⊃ see also MEATLOAF **IDM** see HALF

• *verb* [I] **~ (around)** (*informal*) to spend your time not doing anything, especially when you should be working **SYN** HANG AROUND: *A group of kids were loafing around outside.*

loaf·er /'loʊfər/ *noun* **1** a person who wastes their time rather than working **2** **Loafer**™ a flat leather shoe that you can put on your foot without fastening it ⊃ picture at SHOE

loam /loʊm/ *noun* [U] (*technical*) good quality soil containing sand, CLAY, and decayed vegetable matter ▶ **loam·y** *adj.*

loan 🔑 /loʊn/ *noun, verb*

• *noun* **1** [C] money that an organization such as a bank lends and someone borrows: *to take out/repay a loan* (= to borrow money/pay it back) ◆ *bank loans with low interest rates* ◆ *It took three years to repay my student loan* (= money lent to a student). ◆ *a car loan* (= a loan to buy a car) **2** [sing., U] **~ (of sth)** the act of lending something; the state of being lent: *I appreciate the loan of your car yesterday.* ◆ *an exhibition of paintings on loan* (= borrowed) *from private collections*

• *verb* **1** to lend something to someone, especially money: **~ sth (to sb)** *The bank is happy to loan money to small businesses.* ◆ **~ sb sth** *A friend loaned me $1,000.* **2** to lend a valuable object to a museum, etc.: **~ sth (out) (to sb/sth)** *This exhibit was kindly loaned by the artist's family.* ◆ **~ sb sth** *He loaned the museum his entire collection.* ⊃ compare BORROW

loan·er /'loʊnər/ *noun* something lent to someone by a repair shop while their car or other item is being repaired: *My car's at the garage being repaired, so I'm driving a loaner today.*

'**loan shark** *noun* (*disapproving*) a person who lends money at very high rates of interest

'**loan trans·lation** *noun* (*linguistics*) = CALQUE

loan·word /'loʊnwərd/ *noun* (*linguistics*) a word from another language used in its original form: *"Latte" is a loanword from Italian.*

loath (also *less frequent* **loth**) /loʊθ; loʊð/ *adj.* **~ to do sth** (*formal*) not willing to do something: *He was loath to admit his mistake.*

loathe /loʊð/ *verb* (not used in the progressive tenses) **~ sb/sth** | **~ doing sth** (*formal*) to dislike someone or something very much **SYN** DETEST: *I loathe modern art.* ◆ *They loathe each other.* ⊃ thesaurus box at HATE

loath·ing /'loʊðɪŋ/ *noun* [sing., U] **~ (for/of sb/sth)** (*formal*) a strong feeling of hatred: *She looked at her attacker with fear and loathing.* ◆ *Many soldiers returned with a deep loathing of war.*

loath·some /'loʊðsəm; 'loʊθ-/ *adj.* (*formal*) extremely unpleasant; disgusting **SYN** REPULSIVE

loaves pl. of LOAF

lob /lɑb/ *verb* (-bb-) **1 ~ sth + adv./prep.** (*informal*) to throw something so that it goes quite high through the air: *She lobbed a snowball at her brother.* ⊃ thesaurus box at THROW **2 ~ sth (+ adv./prep.)** (*sports*) to hit or kick a ball in a high curve through the air, especially so that it lands behind the person you are playing against: *He lobbed the ball over the defender's head.* ▶ **lob** *noun*: *to hit a lob in tennis*

lob·by /'lɑbi/ *noun, verb*

• *noun* (*pl.* **lob·bies**) **1** a large area inside the entrance of a public building where people can meet and wait **SYN** FOYER: *a hotel lobby* **2** a group of people who try to influence politicians on a particular issue: *The gun lobby is against any change in the law.*

• *verb* (**lob·bies, lob·by·ing, lob·bied, lob·bied**) [T, I] **~ (sb) (for/against sth)** to try to influence a politician or the government and, for example, persuade them to support or oppose a change in the law: *Farmers will lobby Congress for higher subsidies.* ◆ *Women's groups are lobbying to get more public money for children.*

lob·by·ist /'lɑbiɪst/ *noun* a person whose job involves trying to influence politicians or the government on a particular issue or change in the law: *She is a paid lobbyist for a drug company.*

lobe /loʊb/ *noun* **1** = EARLOBE **2** a part of an organ in the body, especially the lungs or brain

lo·bel·ia /loʊˈbilyə/ *noun* [C, U] a small garden plant with small blue, red, or white flowers

lo·bot·o·mize /ləˈbɑtəˌmaɪz/ *verb* **1** ~ sb to perform a LOBOTOMY on someone **2** ~ sb to make someone less intelligent or less mentally active

lo·bot·o·my /ləˈbɑtəmi/ *noun* (*pl.* **lo·bot·o·mies**) a rare medical operation that cuts into part of a person's brain in order to treat mental illness

lob·ster /ˈlɑbstər/ *noun* **1** [C] a sea creature with a hard shell, a long body divided into sections, eight legs, and two large CLAWS (= curved and pointed arms for catching and holding things). Its shell is black but turns bright red when it is boiled. ➔ picture at SHELLFISH **2** [U] meat from a lobster, used for food

ˈlobster ˌpot *noun* a trap for lobsters that is shaped like a BASKET

lo·cal ♪ /ˈloʊkl/ *adj., noun*

• *adj.* [usually before noun] **1** belonging to or connected with the particular place or area that you are talking about or with the place where you live: *a local farmer* ♦ *A local man was accused of the murder.* ♦ *Our children go to the local school.* ♦ *a local newspaper* (= one that gives local news) ♦ *local radio* (= a radio station that broadcasts to one area only) ♦ *decisions made at local rather than national level* ♦ *It was difficult to understand the local dialect.* **2** affecting only one part of the body: *Her tooth was extracted under local anesthetic.* ➔ compare GENERAL *adj.* (6) ▸ **lo·cal·ly** /-kəli/ *adv.*: *to work locally* ♦ *Do you* **live locally** (= in this area)? ♦ *locally grown fruit*
• *noun* **1** [usually pl.] a person who lives in a particular place or district: *The locals are very friendly.* **2** a branch of a LABOR UNION **3** a bus or train that stops at all places on the route

lo-cal /ˌloʊ ˈkæl/ *adj.* (*informal*) = LOW-CAL

ˌlocal ˌarea ˈnetwork *noun* = LAN

ˈlocal ˌcall *noun* a telephone call to a place that is near

ˈlocal ˈcolor (*CanE usually* **ˌlocal ˈcolour**) *noun* [U] the typical things, customs, etc. in a place that make it interesting, and that are used in a picture, story, or movie to make it seem real

lo·cale /loʊˈkæl/ *noun* (*formal or technical*) a place where something happens

ˌlocal ˈgovernment *noun* [C] the organization that is responsible for the government of a local area and for providing services, etc.: *state and local governments*

lo·cal·i·ty /loʊˈkæləti/ *noun* (*pl.* **lo·cal·i·ties**) (*formal*) **1** the place where someone or something exists: *We talk of the brain as the locality of thought.* ♦ *The birds are found in over 70 different localities.* **2** a small geographical area including a city, town, etc.: *The state school board works closely with locality officials.*

lo·cal·ize /ˈloʊkəˌlaɪz/ *verb* **1** ~ sth to limit something or its effects to a particular area SYN CONFINE **2** ~ sth (*formal*) to find out where something is: *animals' ability to localize sounds* ▸ **lo·cal·i·za·tion** /ˌloʊkələˈzeɪʃn/ *noun* [U]

lo·cal·ized /ˈloʊkəˌlaɪzd/ *adj.* (*formal*) happening within one small area: *a localized infection* (= in one part of the body) ♦ *localized fighting*

ˈlocal ˌtime *noun* [U] the time of day in the particular part of the world that you are talking about: *We reach Delhi at 2 o'clock local time.*

lo·cate ♪ AWL /ˈloʊkeɪt/ *verb*

1 [T] ~ sb/sth to find the exact position of someone or something: *The mechanic located the fault immediately.* ♦ *Rescue planes are trying to locate the missing sailors.* **2** [T] ~ sth + adv./prep. to put or build something in a particular place SYN SITE: *They located their headquarters in Boston.* ➔ compare RELOCATE **3** [I] + adv./prep. to start a

business in a particular place: *There are tax breaks for businesses that locate in rural areas.*

lo·cat·ed AWL /ˈloʊkeɪtəd/ *adj.* [not before noun] if something is **located** in a particular place, it exists there or has been put there SYN SITUATED: *a small town located 30 miles south of Chicago* ♦ *The offices are conveniently located just a few minutes from the main station.*

lo·ca·tion ♪ AWL /loʊˈkeɪʃn/ *noun* **1** [C] a place where something happens or exists; the position of something: *a honeymoon in a secret location* ♦ *What is the exact location of the ship?* ➔ thesaurus box at PLACE **2** [C, U] a place outside a movie studio where scenes of a movie are made: *A mountain in the Rockies became the location for a movie about Everest.* ♦ *The movie was shot entirely* **on location** *in Italy.* **3** [U] the act of finding the position of someone or something

loc·a·tive /ˈlɑkətɪv/ *adj.* (*grammar*) (in some languages) the form of a noun, pronoun or adjective when it expresses the idea of place ➔ see also ABLATIVE, ACCUSATIVE, DATIVE, GENITIVE, NOMINATIVE, VOCATIVE

lo·ca·tor /ˈloʊkeɪtər/ *noun* a device or system for finding something: *The company lists 5,000 stores on the store locator part of its Web site.*

loc. cit. /ˌlɑk ˈsɪt/ *abbr.* in the piece of text quoted (from Latin "loco citato")

loch /lɑk; lɑx/ *noun* (in Scotland) a lake or a narrow strip of ocean almost surrounded by land

lo·ci *pl.* of LOCUS

lock ♪ /lɑk/ *verb, noun*

• *verb* **1** [T, I] ~ (sth) to fasten something with a lock; to be fastened with a lock: *Did you lock the door?* ♦ *This suitcase doesn't lock.* **2** [T] ~ sth + adv./prep. to put something in a safe place and lock it: *She locked her passport and money in the safe.* **3** [I, T] ~ (sth) (in/into/around, etc. sth) | ~ (sth) **(together)** to become or make something become fixed in one position and unable to move: *The brakes locked and the car skidded.* ♦ *He locked his helmet into position with a click.* **4** [T] **be locked in/into something** to be involved in a difficult situation, an argument, a disagreement, etc.: *The two sides are locked into a bitter dispute.* ♦ *She felt locked in a loveless marriage.* **5** [T] **be locked together/in something** to be held very tightly by someone: *They were locked in a passionate embrace.* **6** [T] ~ sth (*computing*) to prevent computer data from being changed or looked at by someone without permission: *These files are locked to protect confidentiality.*
IDM **lock horns (with sb) (over sth)** to get involved in an argument or a disagreement with someone: *The company has locked horns with the unions over proposed pay cuts.*
PHRV **ˌlock sb/sth aˈway** = LOCK SB/STH UP **ˌlock sb/ yourself ˈin (…)** to prevent someone from leaving a place by locking the door: *At 9 p.m. the prisoners are locked in for the night.* **ˌlock ˈonto sth** (of a MISSILE, etc.) to find the thing that is being attacked and follow it **ˌlock sb/yourself ˈout (of sth)** to prevent someone from entering a place by locking the door: *I'd locked myself out of the house and had to break a window to get in.* **ˌlock sb ˈout** (of an employer) to refuse to allow workers into their place of work until they agree to particular conditions ➔ related noun LOCKOUT **ˌlock ˈup | ˌlock sth↔ˈup** to make a building safe by locking the doors and windows: *Don't forget to lock up at night.* ♦ *He locked up the shop and went home.* **ˌlock sb↔ˈup/aˈway** (*informal*) to put someone in prison ➔ related noun LOCKUP **ˌlock sth↔ˈup/aˈway** **1** to put something in a safe place that can be locked **2** to put money into an investment that you cannot easily turn into cash: *Their capital is all locked up in property.*
• *noun* **1** [C] a device that keeps a door, window, lid, etc. shut, usually needing a key to open it: *She turned the key in the lock.* ➔ see also COMBINATION LOCK **2** [C] a device with a key that prevents a vehicle or machine from being used: *a bicycle lock* ♦ *a steering lock* **3** [U] a state in which the parts of a machine, etc. do not move **4** [C] a section of CANAL or

t tea   t̮ butter   d did   k cat   g got   tʃ chin   dʒ June   f fall

river with a gate at either end, in which the water level can be changed so that boats can move from one level of the canal or river to another **5** [C] a few hairs that hang or lie together on your head: *John brushed a lock of hair from his eyes.* **6 locks** [pl.] (*literary*) a person's hair: *She shook her long, flowing locks.* **7** [sing.] **a ~ (on sth)** total control of something: *One company had a virtual lock on all orange juice sales in the state.* ⊃ see also ARMLOCK, HEADLOCK **IDM** **lock, stock, and barrel** including everything: *He sold the business lock, stock, and barrel.* **(keep sth/put sth/be) under lock and key** locked up safely somewhere; in prison: *We keep our valuables under lock and key.* ♦ *I will not rest until the murderer is under lock and key.* ⊃ more at PICK *v.*

lock·a·ble /ˈlɑkəbl/ *adj.* that you can lock with a key

lock·box /ˈlɑkbɑks/ *noun* a box that locks, usually for storing money or other valuable things

lock·down /ˈlɑkdaʊn/ *noun* [C, U] an official order to control the movement of people or vehicles because of a dangerous situation: *a three-day lockdown of American airspace* ♦ *Prisoners have been placed on lockdown to prevent further violence at the jail.*

lock·er /ˈlɑkər/ *noun* a small cabinet that can be locked, where you can leave your clothes, bags, etc. while you play a sport or go somewhere

ˈlocker ˌroom *noun* a room with lockers in it, at a school, GYM, etc., where people can change their clothes ⊃ compare CHANGING ROOM

lock·et /ˈlɑkət/ *noun* a piece of jewelry in the form of a small case that you wear on a chain around your neck and in which you can put a picture, piece of hair, etc. ⊃ picture at JEWELRY

lock·jaw /ˈlɑkdʒɔ/ *noun* [U] (*old-fashioned, informal*) a form of the disease TETANUS in which the JAWS become stiff and closed

ˈlock-ˌkeeper *noun* a person who is in charge of a LOCK on a CANAL or river, and opens and closes the gates

lock·out /ˈlɑkaʊt/ *noun* a situation when an employer refuses to allow workers into their place of work until they agree to various conditions

lock·smith /ˈlɑksmɪθ/ *noun* a person whose job is making, fitting, and repairing locks

lock·step /ˈlɑkstɛp/ *noun* [U] **1** a way of walking together where people move their feet at the same time: *The coffin was carried by six soldiers walking in lockstep.* ♦ (*figurative*) *Politicians and the media are marching in lockstep on this issue* (= they agree). **2** a situation where things happen at the same time or change at the same rate: *a lockstep approach to teaching* ♦ *Cases of breathing difficulties increase in lockstep with air pollution.*

lock·up /ˈlɑkʌp/ *noun* a small prison where prisoners are kept for a short time

lo·co /ˈloʊkoʊ/ *adj.* [not before noun] (*slang*) crazy

lo·co·mo·tion /ˌloʊkəˈmoʊʃn/ *noun* [U] (*formal*) movement or the ability to move

lo·co·mo·tive /ˌloʊkəˈmoʊtɪv/ *noun, adj.*
• *noun* a railroad engine that pulls a train: *steam/diesel/electric locomotives* ⊃ picture at TRAIN
• *adj.* (*formal*) connected with movement

lo·cus /ˈloʊkəs/ *noun* (*pl.* lo·ci /ˈloʊsaɪ; -kaɪ; -ki/) (*formal or technical*) the exact place where something happens or that is thought to be the center of something

lo·cust /ˈloʊkəst/ *noun* a large insect that lives in hot countries and flies in large groups, destroying all the plants and crops of an area: *a swarm of locusts*

lo·cu·tion /loʊˈkyuʃn/ *noun* (*technical*) **1** [U] a style of speaking **2** [C] a particular phrase, especially one used by a particular group of people

lode /loʊd/ *noun* a line of ORE (= metal in the ground or in rocks)

lode·star /ˈloʊdstɑr/ *noun* **1** the POLE STAR (= a star that is used by sailors to guide a ship) **2** (*formal*) a principle that guides someone's behavior or actions

lode·stone /ˈloʊdstoʊn/ *noun* a piece of iron that acts as a MAGNET

lodge /lɑdʒ/ *noun, verb*
• *noun* **1** a building or hotel in the country where people stay when they want to take part in some types of outdoor sports: *a ski lodge* ♦ *a hunting lodge* **2** the members of a branch of a society such as the Freemasons; the building where they meet: *a Masonic lodge* **3** the home of a BEAVER or an OTTER **4** a Native American's tent or home built of LOGS **5** a small house at the gates of a park or on the land belonging to a large house
• *verb* **1** [T] **~ sth (with sb) (against sb/sth)** to make a formal statement about something to a public organization or authority **SYN** SUBMIT: *They lodged a compensation claim against the factory.* ♦ *Portugal has lodged a complaint with the International Court of Justice.* **2** [I, T] to become fixed or stuck somewhere; to make something become fixed or stuck somewhere: **~ in sth** *One of the bullets lodged in his chest.* ♦ **~ sth in sth** *She lodged the number firmly in her mind.* **3** [T] **~ sth with sb/in sth** to leave money or something valuable in a safe place **SYN** DEPOSIT: *Your will should be lodged with your lawyer.* **4** [T] **~ sb (+ adv./prep.)** to provide someone with a place to sleep or live **SYN** ACCOMMODATE: *The refugees are being lodged at an old army base.* **5** [I] **+ adv./prep.** (*old-fashioned*) to pay to live in a room in someone's house **SYN** BOARD: *He lodged with Mrs. Brown when he arrived in the city.*

lodg·er /ˈlɑdʒər/ *noun* a person who pays rent to live in someone's house

lodg·ing /ˈlɑdʒɪŋ/ *noun* a place to live or stay for a short period of time: *budget lodging in New York City*

loft /lɔft/ *noun, verb*
• *noun* **1** an upper level in a church, or a farm or factory building: *the organ loft* **2** an apartment in a former factory, etc., that has been made suitable for living in: *They lived in a SoHo loft.* **3** a part of a room that is on a higher level than the rest: *The children slept in a loft in the upstairs bedroom.*
• *verb* **~ sth** (*sports*) to hit, kick, or throw a ball very high into the air

loft·y /ˈlɔfti/ *adj.* (loft·i·er, loft·i·est) (*formal*) **1** (of buildings, mountains, etc.) very high and impressive: *lofty ceilings/rooms/towers* **2** [usually before noun] (of a thought, an aim, etc.) deserving praise because of its high moral quality: *lofty ambitions/ideals/principles* **3** (*disapproving*) showing a belief that you are worth more than other people **SYN** HAUGHTY: *her lofty disdain for other people* ▶ **loft·i·ly** /-təli/ *adv.* **loft·i·ness** /-tinəs/ *noun* [U]

log /lɔg; lɑg/ *noun, verb*
• *noun* **1** a thick piece of wood that is cut from or has fallen from a tree: *logs for the fire* ⊃ picture at TREE **2** (also **log·book**) an official record of events during a particular period of time, especially a journey on a ship or plane: *The captain keeps a log.* **3** (*informal*) = LOGARITHM **IDM** see EASY, SLEEP
• *verb* (-gg-) **1 ~ sth** to put information in an official record or write a record of events **SYN** RECORD: *The police log all phone calls.* **2 ~ sth** to travel a particular distance or for a particular length of time **SYN** CLOCK UP: *The pilot has logged 1,000 hours in the air.* **3 ~ sth** to cut down trees in a forest for their wood **PHR V** **ˌlog ˈin/ˈon** (*computing*) to perform the actions that allow you to begin using a computer system: *You need a password to log on.* **ˌlog sb** ↔ **ˈin/ˈon** (*computing*) to allow someone to begin using a computer system: *The system is unable to log you on.* **ˌlog ˈoff/ˈout** (*computing*) to perform the actions that allow you to finish using a computer system **ˌlog sb** ↔ **ˈoff/ˈout** (*computing*) to cause someone to finish using a computer system

-log /lɔg; lɑg/ *combining form* (in nouns) talk or speech: *a catalog*

lo·gan·ber·ry /ˈloʊɡənˌbɛri/ *noun* (*pl.* lo·gan·ber·ries) a soft, dark red fruit, like a large RASPBERRY, that grows on a bush

log·a·rithm /ˈlɔɡəˌrɪðəm; ˈlɑ-/ (also *informal* log) *noun* (*mathematics*) any of a series of numbers set out in lists which make it possible to work out problems by adding and SUBTRACTING instead of multiplying and dividing ▶ **log·a·rith·mic** /ˌlɔɡəˈrɪðmɪk; ˌlɑ-/ *adj.*

log·book /ˈlɔɡbʊk; ˈlɑɡ-/ *noun* = LOG

log ˈcabin *noun* a small house built of logs ⟳ picture at BUILDING

log·ger /ˈlɔɡər; ˈlɑ-/ *noun* = LUMBERJACK

log·ger·heads /ˈlɔɡərˌhɛdz; ˈlɑ-/ *noun*
IDM **at loggerheads (with sb) (over sth)** in strong disagreement: *The two governments are still at loggerheads over the island.*

log·gia /ˈloʊdʒiə; -dʒə/ *noun* a room or passage with one or more open sides, especially one that forms part of a house and has one side open to the garden

log·ging /ˈlɔɡɪŋ; ˈlɑ-/ *noun* [U] the work of cutting down trees for their wood

log·ic 🖋 **AWL** /ˈladʒɪk/ *noun*
1 [U] a way of thinking or explaining something: *I fail to see the logic behind his argument.* ◆ *The two parts of the plan were governed by the same logic.* **2** [U, sing.] sensible reasons for doing something: *Linking the proposals in a single package did have a certain logic.* ◆ *a strategy based on sound commercial logic* ◆ *There is **no logic to/in** any of their claims.* **3** [U] (*philosophy*) the science of thinking about or explaining the reason for something using formal methods: *the rules of logic* **4** [U] (*computing*) a system or set of principles used in preparing a computer to perform a particular task

log·i·cal 🖋 **AWL** /ˈladʒɪkl/ *adj.*
1 (of an action, event, etc.) seeming natural, reasonable. or sensible: *a logical thing to do in the circumstances* ◆ *It was a logical conclusion from the child's point of view.* **2** following or able to follow the rules of logic in which ideas or facts are based on other true ideas or facts: *a logical argument* ◆ *Computer programming needs someone with a logical mind.* **ANT** ILLOGICAL ▶ **log·i·cally** **AWL** /-kli/ *adv.*: *to argue logically*

-logical, -logic ⟳ -OLOGY

ˌlogical ˈpositivism *noun* [U] (*philosophy*) the belief that the only problems which have meaning are those that can be solved using logical thinking

ˈlogic ˌcircuit *noun* (*computing*) a series of logic gates that performs operations on data that is put into a computer

ˈlogic ˌgate (also **gate**) *noun* (*computing*) an electronic switch that reacts in one of two ways to data that is put into it. A computer performs operations by passing data through a very large number of logic gates.

lo·gi·cian **AWL** /ləˈdʒɪʃn; loʊ-/ *noun* a person who studies or is skilled in logic

log·in /ˈlɔɡɪn; ˈlɑɡ-/ (also **log-on**) *noun* **1** [U] the act of starting to use a computer system, usually by typing a name or word that you choose to use: *If you've forgotten your login ID, click this link.* **2** [C] the name that you use to enter a computer system: *Enter your login and password and press "go."*

-logist ⟳ -OLOGY

lo·gis·tics /ləˈdʒɪstɪks/ *noun* **1** [U, pl.] **~ (of sth)** the practical organization that is needed to make a complicated plan successful when a lot of people and equipment are involved: *the logistics of moving the company to a new building* **2** [U] (*business*) the business of transporting and delivering goods **3** [U] the activity of moving equipment, supplies, and people for military operations: *a revolution in military logistics* ▶ **lo·gis·tic** (also **lo·gis·tic·al** /ləˈdʒɪstɪkl/) *adj.*: *logistic support* ◆ *Organizing famine relief presents huge logistical problems.* **lo·gis·ti·cally** /-kli/ *adv.*

log·jam /ˈlɔɡdʒæm; ˈlɑɡ-/ *noun* **1** a mass of LOGS floating on a river, that are blocking it **2** a difficult situation in which you cannot make progress easily because there are too many things to do **SYN** BOTTLENECK

lo·go /ˈloʊɡoʊ/ *noun* (*pl.* lo·gos) a printed design or symbol that a company or an organization uses as its special sign

log·off /ˈlɔɡɔf; ˈlɑɡ-; -ɑf/ (also **log·out**) *noun* [U] the act of finishing using a computer system

log·o·gram /ˈlɔɡəˌɡræm; ˈlɑ-/ (also **log·o·graph** /ˈlɔɡəˌɡræf; ˈlɑ-/) *noun* (*technical*) a symbol that represents a word or phrase, for example those used in ancient writing systems

log·on /ˈlɔɡɑn; ˈlɑɡ-; -ɔn/ *noun* = LOGIN

log·out /ˈlɔɡaʊt; ˈlɑɡ-/ *noun* = LOGOFF

log·roll·ing /ˈlɔɡˌroʊlɪŋ; ˈlɑɡ-/ *noun* [U] **1** (*politics*) the practice of agreeing with someone that you will vote to pass a law that they support so that they will later vote to pass a law that you support **2** a sport in which two people stand on a LOG floating on water and try to knock each other off by moving the log with their feet

-logue /lɔɡ; lɑɡ/ *combining form* (in nouns) talk or speech: *a monologue*

-logy ⟳ -OLOGY

loin /lɔɪn/ *noun* **1** [U, C] a piece of meat from the back or sides of an animal, near the tail: *loin of pork* **2** **loins** [pl.] (*old-fashioned*) the part of the body around the hips between the waist and the tops of the legs **3** **loins** [pl.] (*literary*) a person's sex organs **IDM** see GIRD

loin·cloth /ˈlɔɪnklɔθ/ *noun* a piece of cloth worn around the body at the hips by men in some hot countries, sometimes as the only piece of clothing worn

loi·ter /ˈlɔɪtər/ *verb* [I] to stand or wait somewhere especially with no obvious reason **SYN** HANG AROUND: *Teenagers were loitering in the street.*

LOL /ˌɛl oʊ ˈɛl/ *abbr.* LAUGH-OUT-LOUD

loll /lɑl/ *verb* **1** [I] + **adv./prep.** to lie, sit, or stand in a lazy, relaxed way: *He lolled back in his chair by the fire.* **2** [I] + **adv./prep.** (of your head, tongue, etc.) to move or hang in a relaxed way: *My head lolled against his shoulder.*

lol·li·pop /ˈlɑliˌpɑp/ (also *informal* **sucker**) *noun* a hard round or flat candy made of boiled sugar on a small stick

lone /loʊn/ *adj.* [only before noun] without any other people or things **SYN** SOLITARY ⟳ note at ALONE: *a lone sailor crossing the Atlantic*
IDM **a lone wolf** a person who prefers to be alone

lone·ly 🖋 /ˈloʊnli/ *adj.*
(lone·li·er, lone·li·est) **1** unhappy because you have no friends or people to talk to: *She lives alone and often feels lonely.* **2** (of a situation or period of time) sad and spent alone: *all those lonely nights at home watching TV* **3** [only before noun] (of places) where only a few people ever come or visit **SYN** ISOLATED: *a lonely beach* ⟳ note at ALONE ▶ **lone·li·ness** *noun* [U]: *a period of loneliness in his life*

ˌlonely ˈhearts *adj.* [only before noun] a **lonely hearts column** in a newspaper is where people can advertise for a new lover or friend: *He placed a lonely hearts ad in a magazine.*

lon·er /ˈloʊnər/ *noun* a person who is often alone or who prefers to be alone, rather than with other people

lone·some /ˈloʊnsəm/ *adj., noun*
● *adj.* **1** unhappy because you are alone and do not want to be or because you have no friends: *I felt so lonesome after he left.* **2** (of a place) where not many people go; a long way from where people live: *a lonesome road* ⟳ note at ALONE
● *noun*
IDM **(all) by/on your lonesome** (*informal*) alone: *Are you here all by your lonesome?*

long

long /lɔŋ/ *adj., adv., verb*

- **adj.** (**long·er** /'lɔŋɡər/, **long·est** /'lɔŋɡəst/)

WORD FAMILY
long *adj., adv.*
length *noun*
lengthy *adj.*
lengthen *verb*

> **DISTANCE 1** measuring or covering a great length or distance, or a greater length or distance than usual: *She had long dark hair.* ◆ *He walked down the long corridor.* ◆ *It was the world's longest bridge.* ◆ *a long journey/walk/drive/flight* ◆ *We're a long way from anywhere here.* ◆ *It's a long way away.* **ANT** SHORT ⊃ picture at HAIR **2** used for asking or talking about particular lengths or distances: *How long is the River Nile?* ◆ *The table is six feet long.* ◆ *The report is only three pages long.*

> **TIME 3** lasting or taking a great amount of time or more time than usual: *He's been sick (for) a long time.* ◆ *There was a long silence before she spoke.* ◆ *I like it now that the days are getting longer* (= it stays light for more time each day). ◆ *a long book/movie/list* (= taking a lot of time to read/watch/deal with) ◆ *Nurses have to work long hours* (= for more hours in the day than is usual). ◆ *He stared at them for the longest time* (= for a very long time) *before answering.* **ANT** SHORT **4** used for asking or talking about particular periods of time: *How long is the course?* ◆ *I think it's only three weeks long.* ◆ *How long a stay did you have in mind?* **5** seeming to last or take more time than it really does because, for example, you are very busy or not happy: *I'm tired. It's been a long day.* ◆ *We were married for ten long years.* **ANT** SHORT

> **CLOTHES 6** covering all or most of your legs or arms: *She usually wears long skirts.* ◆ *a long-sleeved shirt*

> **VOWEL SOUNDS 7** (*phonetics*) taking more time to make than a short vowel sound in the same position **ANT** SHORT
IDM **as long as your arm** (*informal*) very long: *There's a list of repairs as long as your arm.* **at long last** after a long time **SYN** FINALLY: *At long last his prayers had been answered.* **at the longest** not longer than the particular time given: *It will take an hour at the longest.* **by a long way** by a great amount **go back a long way** (of two or more people) to have known each other for a long time: *We go back a long way, he and I.* **go a long way** (of money, food, etc.) to last a long time: *She seems to make her money go a long way.* ◆ *A small amount of this paint goes a long way* (= covers a large area). ◆ (*ironic*) *I find that a little of Jerry's company can go a long way* (= I quickly get tired of being with him). ◆ see also WAY *n.* **have come a long way** to have made a lot of progress: *We've come a long way since the early days of the project.* **have a long way to go** to need to make a lot of progress before you can achieve something: *She still has a long way to go before she's fully recovered.* **in the long run** concerning a longer period in the future: *This measure inevitably means higher taxes in the long run.* **it's a long story** (*informal*) used to say that the reasons for something are complicated and you would prefer not to give all the details **the long arm of sth** the power and/or authority of something: *There is no escape from the long arm of the law.* **the long and (the) short of it** used when you are telling someone the essential facts about something or what effect it will have, without explaining all the details **(pull, wear, etc.) a long face** (to have) an unhappy or disappointed expression **long in the tooth** (*humorous*) old or too old **ORIGIN** This originally referred to the fact that a horse's teeth appear to be longer as it grows older, because its gums shrink. **long on sth** (*informal*) having a lot of a particular quality: *The government is long on ideas but short on performance.* **a long shot** an attempt or a guess that is not likely to be successful but is worth trying: *It's a long shot, but it just might work.* **long time no see** (*informal*) used to say hello to someone you have not seen for a long time **not by a long shot** not nearly; not at all: *It's not over yet—not by a long shot.* **take a long (cool/hard) look at sth** to consider a problem or possibility very carefully and without hurrying: *We need to take a long hard look at all the options.* **take the long view (of sth)** to consider what is likely to happen or be important over a long period of time rather than only considering the present situation **to make a long story short** (*informal*) used when you are saying that

you will get to the point of what you are saying quickly, without including all the details ⊃ more at TERM *n.*, WAY *n.*

- **adv.** (**long·er** /'lɔŋɡər/, **long·est** /'lɔŋɡəst/) **1** for a long time: *Have you been here long?* ◆ *Stay as long as you like.* ◆ *The party went on long into the night.* ◆ *This may take longer than we thought.* ◆ *I won't be long* (= I'll return, be ready, etc. soon). ◆ *How long have you been waiting?* ◆ *These reforms are long overdue.* **2** a long time before or after a particular time or event: *He retired long before the war.* ◆ *It wasn't long before she had persuaded him* (= it only took a short time). ◆ *We'll be home before long* (= soon). ◆ *The house was pulled down long ago.* ◆ *They had long since* (= a long time before the present time) *moved away.* **3** used after a noun to emphasize that something happens for the whole of a particular period of time: *We had to wait all day long.* ◆ *The baby was crying all night long.* ◆ *They stayed up the whole night long.*
IDM **as/so long as 1** only if: *We'll go as long as the weather is good.* **2** since; to the extent that: *So long as there is a demand for these drugs, the financial incentive for drug dealers will be there.* **for (so) long** for (such) a long time: *Will you be away for long?* ◆ *I'm sorry I haven't written to you for so long.* **how long do you have?** (*informal*) used to say that something is going to take a long time to explain: *What do I think about it? How long do you have?* **long live sb/sth** used to say that you hope someone or something will live or last for a long time **no/any longer** used to say that something which was possible or true before, is not now: *I can't wait any longer.* ◆ *He no longer lives here.* **so long** (*informal*) goodbye

---

WHICH WORD?

(for) long ◆ (for) a long time

- Both **(for) long** and **(for) a long time** are used as expressions of time. In positive sentences **(for) a long time** is used: *We've been friends (for) a long time.* **(For) long** is not used in positive sentences unless it is used with *too, enough, as, so, seldom,* etc: *I stayed out in the sun for too long.* ◆ *You've been waiting for long enough.* Both **(for) long** and **(for) a long time** can be used in questions, but **(for) long** is usually preferred: *Have you been waiting long?*

- In negative sentences, **(for) a long time** sometimes has a different meaning from **(for) long.** Compare: *I haven't been here for a long time* (= It is a long time since the last time I was here) and *I haven't been here long* (= I arrived here only a short time ago).

- **verb** [I] to want something very much especially if it does not seem likely to happen soon **SYN** YEARN: **~ for sb/sth** *Lucy had always longed for a brother.* ◆ **~ for sb to do sth** *He longed for Pat to call.* ◆ **~ to do sth** *I'm longing to see you again.* ⊃ see also LONGED-FOR

long. *abbr.* (in writing) LONGITUDE

long-a·wait·ed *adj.* that people have been waiting for for a long time: *her long-awaited new novel*

long ball *noun* (in baseball) a HOME RUN

long·board /'lɔŋbɔrd/ *noun* **1** a long board used in SURFING **2** a long SKATEBOARD

long·boat /'lɔŋboʊt/ *noun* a large ROWBOAT, used especially for traveling on the ocean

long·bow /'lɔŋboʊ/ *noun* a large BOW[2] made of a long thin curved piece of wood that was used in the past for shooting arrows

long-'distance *adj.* [only before noun] **1** traveling or involving travel between places that are far apart: *a long-distance commuter* ◆ *long-distance flights* **2** operating between people and places that are far apart: *a long-distance phone call* ▶ **long 'distance** *adv.*: *It's a comfortable car to drive long distance.* ◆ *to call long distance*

long di'vision *noun* [U] (*mathematics*) a method of dividing

---

one number by another in which all the stages involved are written down

long-drawn-'out (also ˌdrawn-'out) *adj.* lasting a very long time, often too long **SYN** PROTRACTED: *long-drawn-out negotiations*

'longed-for *adj.* [only before noun] that someone has been wanting or hoping for very much: *the birth of a longed-for baby*

lon·gev·i·ty /lɑnˈdʒɛvəti; lɔn-/ *noun* [U] (*formal*) long life; the fact of lasting a long time: *We wish you both health and longevity.* ◆ *He prides himself on the longevity of the company.*

long·hair /ˈlɔŋhɛr/ *noun* a breed of cat with long hair ⊃ picture at HAIR ⊃ compare SHORTHAIR

long·hand /ˈlɔŋhænd/ *noun* [U] ordinary writing, not typed or written in SHORTHAND

ˌlong 'haul *noun* [usually sing.] a difficult task that takes a long time and a lot of effort to complete: *She knows that becoming world champion is going to be a long haul.*
  IDM **be in sth for the long haul** to be willing to continue doing a task until it is finished: *I promise I am in this for the long haul.* **over the long haul** over a long period of time

'long-haul *adj.* [only before noun] involving the transport of goods or passengers over long distances: *long-haul flights/routes* **ANT** SHORT-HAUL

long·horn /ˈlɔŋhɔrn/ *noun* a cow with long horns

long·house /ˈlɔŋhaʊs/ *noun* a traditional house used by some Native Americans

long·ing /ˈlɔŋɪŋ/ *noun, adj.*
  ● *noun* [C, U] a strong feeling of wanting something or someone: **~ (for sb/sth)** *a longing for home* ◆ **~ (to do sth)** *She was filled with longing to hear his voice again.* ◆ *romantic longings*
  ● *adj.* [only before noun] feeling or showing that you want something very much: *He gave a longing look at the ice cream.* ▶ **long·ing·ly** *adv.*: *We looked longingly toward the hills.*

long·ish /ˈlɔŋɪʃ/ *adj.* [only before noun] fairly long: *longish hair* ◆ *There was a longish pause.*

lon·gi·tude /ˈlɑndʒəˌtud/ *noun* [U] (*abbr.* **long.**) the distance of a place east or west of the Greenwich MERIDIAN, measured in degrees: *the longitude of the island* ⊃ picture at EARTH ⊃ compare LATITUDE

lon·gi·tu·di·nal /ˌlɑndʒəˈtudnæwˌəl/ *adj.* (*technical*) **1** going downward rather than across: *The plant's stem is marked with thin green longitudinal stripes.* **2** concerning the development of something over a period of time: *a longitudinal study of aging* **3** connected with longitude: *the town's longitudinal position* ▶ **lon·gi·tu·di·nal·ly** *adv.*

longi·tudinal 'wave *noun* (*physics*) a wave that VIBRATES in the direction that it is moving ⊃ compare TRANSVERSE WAVE

'long johns *noun* [pl.] (*informal*) warm underwear with long legs down to the ankles: *a pair of long johns*

the ˈlong jump (also the ˈbroad jump) *noun* [sing.] a sporting event in which people try to jump as far forward as possible after running up to a line

ˌlong-'lasting *adj.* that can or does last for a long time **SYN** DURABLE: *long-lasting effects* ◆ *a long-lasting agreement*

ˌlong-'life *adj.* made to last longer than the ordinary type: *long-life batteries*

long-lived /ˌlɔŋ ˈlɪvd; -ˈlaɪvd/ *adj.* having a long life; lasting for a long time ⊃ thesaurus box at OLD

'long-lost *adj.* [only before noun] that you have not seen or received any news of for a long time: *a long-lost friend*

'long-range *adj.* [only before noun] **1** traveling a long distance: *long-range missiles* **2** made for a period of time that will last a long way into the future: *a long-range weather forecast* ◆ *long-range plans* ⊃ compare SHORT-RANGE

ˌlong-'running *adj.* [only before noun] that has been continuing for a long time: *a long-running dispute* ◆ *a long-running TV series*

ˌlong-'serving *adj.* [only before noun] having had the job or position mentioned for a long time: *long-serving employees*

long·ship /ˈlɔŋʃɪp/ *noun* a long narrow ship used by the Vikings

long·shore drift /ˌlɔŋʃɔr ˈdrɪft/ *noun* [U] (*technical*) the movement of sand, etc. along a beach caused by waves hitting the beach at an angle

long·shore·man /ˌlɔŋˈʃɔrmən; ˈlɔŋˌʃɔr-/ *noun* (*pl.* **long·shore·men** /-mən/) a man whose job is moving goods on and off ships

ˌlong-'standing *adj.* [usually before noun] that has existed or lasted for a long time: *a long-standing relationship*

ˌlong-'suffering *adj.* bearing problems or another person's unpleasant behavior with patience: *his long-suffering wife*

ˌlong-'term *adj.* [usually before noun] **1** that will last or have an effect over a long period of time: *a long-term strategy* ◆ *the long-term effects of fertilizers* ◆ *a long-term investment* **2** that is not likely to change or be solved quickly: *long-term unemployment* ⊃ compare SHORT-TERM

long·time /ˈlɔŋtaɪm/ *adj.* [only before noun] having been the particular thing mentioned for a long time: *his longtime colleague*

longueurs /lɔŋˈgərz/ *noun* [pl.] (from *French, literary*) very boring parts or aspects of something

'long wave *noun* [U, C] (*abbr.* **LW**) a radio wave with a length of more than 1,000 meters: *to broadcast on long wave* ⊃ compare SHORTWAVE

ˌlong 'weekend *noun* a vacation of three or four days from Friday or Saturday to Sunday or Monday

long-wind·ed /ˌlɔŋ ˈwɪndəd/ *adj.* (*disapproving*) (especially of talking or writing) continuing for too long and therefore boring **SYN** TEDIOUS

long·wise /ˈlɔŋwaɪz/ (also **long·ways** /ˈlɔŋweɪz/) *adv.* in the same direction as the longest side of something **SYN** LENGTHWISE

loo·fah (also **loo·fa**) /ˈlufə/ *noun* a long bath SPONGE made from the dried fruit of a tropical plant

look 🔑 /lʊk/ *verb, noun, exclamation*
  ● *verb*
  ▷ USE EYES **1** [I] to turn your eyes in a particular direction: *If you look carefully you can just see our house from here.* ◆ **~ (at sb/sth)** *She looked at me and smiled.* ◆ *"Has the mail come yet?" "I'll look and see."* ◆ *Look! I'm sure that's Brad Pitt!* ◆ *Don't look now, but there's someone staring at you!* ⊃ see also FORWARD-LOOKING
  ▷ SEARCH **2** [I] to try to find someone or something: *I can't find my book—I've looked everywhere.* ◆ **~ for sb/sth** *Where have you been? We've been looking for you.* ◆ *Are you still looking for a job?*
  ▷ PAY ATTENTION **3** [I, T] to pay attention to something: **~ (at sth)** *Look at the time! We're going to be late.* ◆ **~ where, what, etc....** *Can't you look where you're going?*
  ▷ APPEAR/SEEM **4** *linking verb* to seem; to appear: **+ adj.** *to look pale/happy/tired* ◆ *That book looks interesting.* ◆ **~ (to sb) like sb/sth** *That looks like an interesting book.* ⊃ see also GOOD-LOOKING **5** [I] (not usually used in the progressive tenses) to have a similar appearance to someone or something; to have an appearance that suggests that something is true or will happen: **~ (to sb) like sb/sth** *That photograph doesn't look like her at all.* ◆ *It looks like rain* (= it looks as if it's going to rain). ◆ **~ (to sb) as if.../as though...** *You look as though you slept badly.* **HELP** In spoken English people often use **like** instead of **as if** or **as though** in this meaning: *You look like you slept badly.* **6** [I] to seem most likely: **~ (to sb) as if.../as though...** *It doesn't look as if we'll be moving after all.* ◆ **~ (to sb) like...** (*informal*) *It doesn't look like we'll be moving after all.*

ʌ cup   ə **about**   eɪ **say**   aɪ **five**   ɔɪ **boy**   aʊ **now**   oʊ **go**   ər **bird**

▸FACE **7** [I] + **adv./prep.** to face a particular direction: *The house looks east.* ♦ *The hotel looks out over the harbor.*

IDM Most idioms containing **look** are at the entries for the nouns and adjectives in the idioms. For example, **look for trouble** is at **trouble**. be just looking used in a store to say that you are not ready to buy something: *"Can I help you?" "I'm just looking, thank you."* be looking to do sth to try to find ways of doing something: *The government is looking to reduce inflation.* look bad | not look good to be considered bad behavior or bad manners: *It looks bad not to go to your own brother's wedding.* look bad (for sb) to show that something bad might happen: *He's had another heart attack; things are looking bad for him, I'm afraid.* look good to show success or that something good might happen: *This year's sales figures are looking good.* look here (*old-fashioned*) used to protest about something: *Now look here, it wasn't my fault.* look how/what/who... used to give an example that proves what you are saying or makes it clearer: *Look how lazy we've become.* ♦ *Be careful climbing that ladder. Look what happened last time.* look sb up and down to look at someone in a careful or critical way (not) look yourself to not have your normal healthy appearance: *You're not looking yourself today* (= you look tired or sick). never/not look back (*informal*) to become more and more successful: *Her first novel was published in 2009 and since then she hasn't looked back.* not much to look at (*informal*) not attractive to look at sb/sth judging by the appearance of someone or something: *To look at him you'd never think he was nearly fifty.*
PHR V look after yourself/sb/sth **1** to be responsible for or to take care of someone or something: *Who's going to look after the children while you're away?* ♦ *Don't worry about me—I can look after myself* (= I don't need any help). **2** to make sure that things happen to someone's advantage: *He's good at looking after his own interests.*
look a'head (to sth) to think about what is going to happen in the future
look a'round to turn your head so that you can see something: *People came out of their houses and looked around.*
look a'round (sth) to visit a place or building, walking around it to see what is there: *Let's look around the town this afternoon.* look a'round for sth to search for something in a number of different places: *We're looking around for a house in this area.*
look at sth **1** to examine something closely: *Your ankle's swollen; I think the doctor ought to look at it.* ♦ *I haven't had time to look at* (= read) *the paper yet.* **2** to think about, consider, or study something: *The implications of the new law will need to be looked at.* ⟳ thesaurus box at EXAMINE **3** to view or consider something in a particular way: *Looking at it from that point of view, his decision is easier to understand.*
look 'back (on sth) to think about something in your past **SYN** REFLECT ON: *to look back on your childhood*
look 'down on sb/sth to think that you are better than someone or something: *She looks down on people who haven't gone to college.*
look for sth to hope for something; to expect something: *We will be looking for an improvement in your work this semester.*
look 'forward to sth to be thinking with pleasure about something that is going to happen (because you expect to enjoy it): *I'm looking forward to the weekend.* ♦ ~ doing sth *We're really looking forward to seeing you again.*
look 'in (on sb) to make a short visit to a place, especially someone's house when they are sick or need help: *She looks in on her elderly neighbor every evening.*
look 'into sth to examine something: *A committee has been set up to look into the problem.*
look 'on to watch something without becoming involved in it yourself: *Passers-by simply looked on as he was attacked.* ⟳ related noun ONLOOKER look on sb/sth as sb/sth to consider someone or something to be someone or something: *She's looked on as the leading authority on the subject.*
look on sb/sth with sth to consider someone or something in a particular way **SYN** REGARD: *They looked on his behavior with contempt.*
look 'out used to warn someone to be careful, especially when there is danger **SYN** WATCH OUT: *Look out! There's a car coming.* look 'out for sb to take care of someone and make sure nothing bad happens to them look 'out for sb/ sth **1** to try to avoid something bad happening or doing something bad **SYN** WATCH OUT: *You should look out for pickpockets.* ♦ *Look out for spelling mistakes in your work.* **2** to keep trying to find something or meet someone: *I'll look out for you at the conference.* ⟳ related noun LOOKOUT look 'out for sb/yourself to think only of someone's/your own advantage, without worrying about other people: *You should look out for yourself from now on.*
look sth↔'over to examine something to see how good, big, etc. it is: *We looked over the house again before we decided we would rent it.*
look 'through sb [no passive] to ignore someone by pretending not to see them: *She just looked straight through me.* look through sth [no passive] to examine or read something quickly: *She looked through her notes before the exam.*
look to sb for sth | look to sb to do sth to rely on or expect someone to provide something or do something: *We are looking to you for help.* look to sth (*formal*) to consider something and think about how to make it better: *We need to look to ways of improving our marketing.*
look 'up (*informal*) (of business, someone's situation, etc.) to become better **SYN** IMPROVE: *At last things were beginning to look up.* look 'up (from sth) to raise your eyes when you are looking down at something: *She looked up from her book as I entered the room.* look sb↔'up [no passive] (*informal*) to visit or make contact with someone, especially when you have not seen them for a long time: *Look me up the next time you're in San Francisco.* look sth↔'up to look for information in a dictionary or REFERENCE BOOK, or by using a computer: *Can you look up the address on the Web site?* ♦ *I looked it up in the dictionary.* look 'up to sb to admire or respect someone

---

THESAURUS

look

watch ♦ see ♦ view ♦ observe

These words all mean to turn your eyes in a particular direction.

look to turn your eyes in a particular direction: *If you look carefully, you can just see our house from here.* ♦ *She looked at me and smiled.*

watch to look at someone or something for a time, paying attention to what happens: *to watch television* ♦ *Watch what I do, then you try.*

see to watch a game, television program, performance, etc: *In the evening we went to see a movie.*

view (*formal*) to look at something, especially when you look carefully; to watch television, a movie, etc: *People came from all over the world to view her artwork.*

WATCH, SEE, OR VIEW?

You can *see/view a movie/program/show* but you cannot: *see/view television*. View is more formal than see and is used especially in business contexts.

observe (*formal*) to watch someone or something carefully, especially to learn more about them or it: *The patients were observed over a period of several months.*

PATTERNS
- to look/watch **for** sb/sth
- to watch/observe **what/who/how...**
- to look (at)/watch/view/observe (sb/sth) **with** amazement/surprise/disapproval, etc.
- to watch/see/view a **movie/show/program**
- to watch/see a **game/fight/match**
- to look (at sb/sth)/watch (sb/sth)/observe sb/sth **carefully/closely**

- **noun**
> USING EYES **1** [C, usually sing.] ~ **(at sb/sth)** an act of looking at someone or something: *Take a look at these figures!* ◆ *Make sure you get a good look at their faces.* ◆ *One look at his face and Jenny stopped laughing.* ◆ *A look passed between them* (= they looked at each other). ◆ *It's an interesting place. Do you want to take a look around?* ◆ *We'll be taking a close look at these proposals* (= examining them carefully).
> SEARCH **2** [C, usually sing.] ~ **(for sth/sb)** an act of trying to find something or someone: *We'll begin our look for a new apartment next week.*
> EXPRESSION **3** [C] an expression in your eyes or on your face: *a look of surprise* ◆ *He didn't like the look in her eyes.* ◆ *She had a worried look on her face.*
> APPEARANCE **4** [C, usually sing.] the way someone or something looks; the appearance of someone or something: *It's going to rain today by the look of it* (= judging by appearances). ◆ *Looks can be deceptive.* ◆ *I don't like the look of that guy* (= I don't trust him, judging by his appearance). **5** looks [pl.] a person's appearance, especially when the person is attractive: *She has her father's good looks.* ◆ *He lost his looks* (= became less attractive) *in later life.* ⊃ see also GOOD-LOOKING
> FASHION **6** [sing.] a fashion; a style: *The punk look is back in fashion.* ◆ *They've given the place a completely new look.*
  IDM if looks could kill... used to describe the very angry or unpleasant way someone is/was looking at you: *I don't know what I've done to upset him, but if looks could kill...* ⊃ more at DIRTY, LONG
- **exclamation** used to make someone pay attention to what you are going to say, often when you are annoyed: *Look, I think we should go now.* ◆ *Look, that's not fair.*

THESAURUS

look

glance ◆ gaze ◆ stare ◆ glimpse ◆ glare

These are all words for an act of looking, when you turn your eyes in a particular direction.

look an act of looking at someone or something: *Here, take a look at this.*

glance a quick look: *She stole a glance at her watch.*

gaze a long steady look at someone or something: *He felt embarrassed under her steady gaze.*

stare a long look at someone or something, especially in a way that is unfriendly or that shows surprise: *She gave the officer a blank stare and shrugged her shoulders.*

glimpse a look at someone or something for a very short time, when you do not see the person or thing completely: *He caught a glimpse of her in the crowd.*

glare a long angry look at someone or something: *She gave her questioner a hostile glare.*

PATTERNS
- a look/glance **at** sb/sth
- a **penetrating/piercing** look/glance/gaze/stare
- a **long** look/glance/stare
- a **brief** look/glance/glimpse
- to **have/get/take** a look/glance/glimpse
- to **avoid** sb's glance/gaze/stare

look-a,like *noun* (often used after a person's name) a person who looks very similar to the person mentioned: *an Elvis look-alike*

look·er /'lʊkər/ *noun* (*informal*) a way of describing an attractive person, usually a woman: *She's a real looker!*

looking ,glass *noun* (*old-fashioned*) a mirror

look·out /'lʊkaʊt/ *noun* **1** a place for watching from, especially for danger or an enemy coming toward you: *a lookout point/tower* **2** a person who has the responsibility of watching for something, especially danger, etc.: *One of the men stood at the door to act as a lookout.*

IDM be on the lookout (for sb/sth)| keep a lookout (for sb/sth) (*informal*) to watch carefully for someone or something in order to avoid danger, etc. or in order to find something you want: *The public should be on the lookout for symptoms of the disease.*

look-'see *noun* [sing.] (*informal*) a quick look at something: *Come and have a look-see.*

loom /lum/ *verb, noun*
- **verb 1** [I] (+ **adv./prep.**) to appear as a large shape that is not clear, especially in a frightening or threatening way: *A dark shape loomed up ahead of us.* **2** [I] to appear important or threatening and likely to happen soon: *There was a crisis looming.*
  IDM loom large to be worrying or frightening and seem hard to avoid: *The prospect of war loomed large.*
- **noun** a machine for making cloth by twisting threads between other threads that go in a different direction

loon /lun/ *noun* **1** a large N. American bird that eats fish and has a cry like a laugh **2** = LOONY

loon·ie /'luni/ *noun* (CanE) the Canadian dollar or a Canadian one-dollar coin

loon·y /'luni/ *adj., noun*
- **adj.** (*informal*) crazy or strange
- **noun** (*pl.* loon·ies) (also loon) (*informal*) a person who has strange ideas or who behaves in a strange way

loony ,bin *noun* (*old-fashioned*, *slang*) a humorous and sometimes offensive way of referring to a hospital for people who are mentally ill

loop /lup/ *noun, verb*
- **noun 1** a shape like a curve or circle made by a line curving all the way around and crossing itself: *The road went in a huge loop around the lake.* **2** a piece of rope, wire, etc. in the shape of a curve or circle: *He tied a loop of rope around his arm.* ◆ *Make a loop in the string.* ◆ *a belt loop* (= on pants, etc. for holding a belt in place) ◆ picture at KNOT **3** a strip of film or tape on which the pictures and sound are repeated continuously: *The film is on a loop.* ◆ (*figurative*) *His mind kept turning in an endless loop.* **4** (*computing*) a set of instructions that is repeated again and again until a particular condition is satisfied **5** a complete CIRCUIT for electrical current **6** the Loop (*informal*) the business center of the city of Chicago
  IDM in the loop| out of the loop (*informal*) part of a group of people that is dealing with something important; not part of this group knock/throw sb for a loop (*informal*) to shock or surprise someone
- **verb 1** [T] ~ **sth + adv./prep.** to form or bend something into a loop : *He looped the strap over his shoulder.* **2** [I] + **adv./prep.** to move in a way that makes the shape of a loop : *The river loops around the valley.* ◆ *The ball looped high up in the air.*
  IDM loop the loop to fly or make a plane fly in a circle going up and down

loop·hole /'luphoʊl/ *noun* ~ **(in sth)** a mistake in the way a law, contract, etc. has been written that enables people to legally avoid doing something that the law, contract, etc. had intended them to do: *a legal loophole* ◆ *to close existing loopholes*

loop·y /'lupi/ *adj.* (*informal*) not sensible; strange **SYN** CRAZY

loose 🔑 /lus/ *adj., verb, noun*
- **adj.** (loos·er, loos·est)
> NOT FIXED/TIED **1** not firmly fixed where it should be; able to become separated from something: *a loose button/tooth* ◆ *Check that the plug has not come loose.* **2** not tied together; not held in position by anything or contained in anything: *She usually wears her hair loose.* ◆ *The potatoes were sold loose, not in bags.* **3** [not usually before noun] free to move around without control; not tied up or shut in somewhere: *The sheep had got out and were loose on the road.* ◆ *The horse had broken loose* (= escaped) *from its tether.* ◆ *During the night, someone had cut the boat loose from its moorings.*
> CLOTHES **4** not fitting closely: *a loose shirt* **ANT** TIGHT

---

t **t**ea   ţ bu**tt**er   d **d**id   k **c**at   g **g**ot   tʃ **ch**in   dʒ **J**une   f **f**all

> NOT SOLID/HARD **5** not tightly packed together; not solid or hard: *loose soil* ♦ *a fabric with a loose weave*
> NOT STRICT/EXACT **6** not strictly organized or controlled: *a loose alliance/coalition/federation* **7** not exact; not very careful: *a loose translation* ♦ *loose thinking*
> IMMORAL **8** [usually before noun] (*old-fashioned*) having or involving an attitude to sexual relationships that people consider to be immoral: *a young man of loose morals*
> BALL **9** (*sports*) not in any player's control: *He pounced on a loose ball*.
> BODY WASTE **10** having too much liquid in it: *a baby with loose bowel movements*
> ▶ **loose·ness** *noun* [U]

IDM break/cut/tear (sb/sth) loose from sb/sth to separate yourself or someone or something from a group of people or their influence, etc.: *The organization broke loose from its sponsors.* ♦ *He cut himself loose from his family.* cut loose (*informal*) to do something or to happen in a way that is not controlled: *Teenagers need a place to cut loose.* hang/ stay loose (*informal*) to remain calm; to not worry: *It's OK— hang loose and stay cool.* have a loose tongue to talk too much, especially about things that are private let loose sth to make a noise or remark, especially in a loud or sudden way: *She let loose a stream of abuse.* let sb/sth loose **1** to free someone or something from whatever holds them/it in place: *She let her hair loose and it fell around her shoulders.* ♦ *Who's let the dog loose?* **2** to give someone complete freedom to do what they want in a place or situation: *He was at last let loose in the kitchen.* ♦ *A team of professionals were let loose on the project.* ⊃ more at FAST *adv.*, HELL, SCREW *n.*

● **verb** (*formal*)
> RELEASE **1** ~ sth (on/upon sb/sth) to release something or let it happen or be expressed in an uncontrolled way: *His speech loosed a tide of nationalist sentiment.*
> MAKE SOMETHING LOOSE **2** ~ sth to make something loose, especially something that is tied or held tightly **SYN** LOOSEN: *He loosed the straps that bound her arms.*
> FIRE BULLETS **3** ~ sth (off) (at sb/sth) to fire bullets, arrows, etc. **HELP** Do not confuse this verb with to lose = "to be unable to find something."

● **noun**
IDM on the loose (of a person or an animal) having escaped from somewhere; free **SYN** AT LARGE: *Three prisoners are still on the loose.*

,loose 'cannon *noun* a person, usually a public figure, who often behaves in a way that no one can predict

,loose 'change *noun* [U] coins that you have in a pocket or a bag

,loose 'end *noun* [usually pl.] a part of something, such as a story, that has not been completely finished or explained: *The play has too many loose ends.* ♦ *There are still a few loose ends to tie up* (= a few things to finish).
IDM at loose ends/at a loose end having nothing to do and not knowing what you want to do: *Come and see us, if you're at loose ends.*

,loose-'fitting *adj.* (of clothes) not fitting the body tightly

'loose-leaf *adj.* [usually before noun] (of a book, notebook, etc.) having pages that can be taken out and put in separately: *a loose-leaf binder*

,loose-'limbed *adj.* (*literary*) (of a person) moving in an easy, not stiff, way

loose·ly 🔑 /'lusli/ *adv.*
1 in a way that is not firm or tight: *She fastened the belt loosely around her waist.* **2** in a way that is not exact: *to use a term loosely* ♦ *The play is loosely based on his childhood in Russia.*

loos·en /'lusn/ *verb* **1** [T, I] ~ (sth) to make something less tight or firmly fixed; to become less tight or firmly fixed **SYN** SLACKEN: *First loosen the nuts, then take off the wheel.* ♦ *The rope holding the boat loosened.* **2** [T] ~ sth to make a piece of clothing, hair, etc. loose, when it has been tied or fastened **3** [T] ~ your hands, hold, etc. to hold someone or something less tightly: *He loosened his grip and let her go.* ♦ (*figurative*) *The military regime has not loosened its hold on*

power. **4** [T] ~ sth to make something weaker or less controlled than before **SYN** RELAX: *The party has loosened its links with big business.* **ANT** TIGHTEN
IDM loosen sb's tongue to make someone talk more freely than usual: *A bottle of wine had loosened Harry's tongue.* **PHR V** ,loosen 'up to relax and stop worrying: *Come on, Jo. Loosen up.* ,loosen 'up | ,loosen sb/sth↔'up to relax your muscles or parts of the body or to make them relax, before exercising, etc.

loosey-goosey /,lusi 'gusi/ *adj.* (*informal*) **1** relaxed and without tension; comfortable: *Some guys can goof around, be all loosey-goosey before a game.* **2** not precise or careful enough: *She sometimes took a loosey-goosey approach to her studies.*

loot /lut/ *verb, noun*
● **verb** [T, I] ~ (sth) to steal things from stores or buildings after a RIOT, fire, etc.: *More than 20 stores were looted.*
▶ **loot·er** *noun* **loot·ing** *noun* [U]
● **noun** [U] **1** money and valuable objects taken by soldiers from the enemy after winning a battle **SYN** BOOTY **2** (*informal*) money and valuable objects that have been stolen by thieves **3** (*informal*) money

lop /lɑp/ *verb* (-pp-) ~ sth to cut down a tree, or cut some large branches off it
PHR V lop sth↔'off (sth) **1** to remove part of something by cutting it, especially to remove branches from a tree **SYN** CHOP **2** to make something smaller or less by a particular amount: *They lopped $20 off the price.*

lope /loʊp/ *verb* [I] + *adv./prep.* to run taking long relaxed steps: *The dog loped along beside her.* ♦ *He set off with a loping stride.* ▶ **lope** *noun* [usually sing.]

'lop-ears *noun* [pl.] ears that hang down at the side of an animal's head ▶ 'lop-eared *adj.*: *a lop-eared rabbit*

lop·sid·ed /'lɑp,saɪdəd/ *adj.* having one side lower, smaller, etc. than the other: *a lopsided grin/mouth* ♦ (*figurative*) *The article presents a somewhat lopsided view of events.* ▶ **lop-sid·ed·ly** *adv.*

lo·qua·cious /loʊ'kweɪʃəs/ *adj.* (*formal*) talking a lot **SYN** TALKATIVE ▶ **lo·quac·i·ty** /loʊ'kwæsəti/ *noun* [U]

lo·quat /'loʊkwɑt/ *noun* a round, pale orange fruit that grows on bushes in China, Japan, and the Middle East

lord 🔑 /lɔrd/ *noun, verb*
● **noun 1** [C] a powerful man, especially in MEDIEVAL Europe, who owned a lot of land and property: *a feudal lord* ♦ *the lord of the manor* ⊃ see also OVERLORD, WARLORD **2** usually the Lord [sing.] a title used to refer to God or Christ: *Love the Lord with all your heart.* **3** Our Lord [sing.] a title used to refer to Christ **4** [C] (in compounds) a powerful criminal of a particular type: *gang lords* ⊃ see also DRUG LORD **5** [C] (in Britain) a man of high rank in the NOBILITY (= people of high social class), or someone who has been given the title "lord" as an honor ⊃ compare LADY **6** Lord (in Britain) the title used by a lord: *Lord Beaverbrook*
IDM (good) Lord! | oh Lord! used to show that you are surprised, annoyed, or worried about something: *Good Lord, what have you done to your hair!* Lord knows... used to emphasize what you are saying: *Lord knows, I tried to teach her.* Lord (only) knows (what, where, why, etc.)... (*informal*) used to say that you do not know the answer to something: *"Why did she say that?" "Lord knows!"* **HELP** Some people may find the use of **Lord** in these expressions offensive. **IDM** see NAME *n.*, YEAR
● **verb**
IDM lord it over sb (*disapproving*) to act as if you are better or more important than someone

lord·ly /'lɔrdli/ *adj.* **1** behaving in a way that suggests that you think you are better than other people **SYN** HAUGHTY **2** large and impressive; suitable for a lord **SYN** IMPOSING: *a lordly mansion*

lord·ship /'lɔrdʃɪp/ *noun* **1** His/Your Lordship a title of respect used when speaking to or about a NOBLEMAN: *His Lordship is away on business.* ⊃ compare LADYSHIP **2** [U] the power or position of a lord

the ¡Lord's 'Prayer *noun* [sing.] the prayer that Jesus Christ taught the people who followed him, that begins "Our Father…"

lore /lɔr/ *noun* [U] knowledge and information related to a particular subject, especially when this is not written down; the stories and traditions of a particular group of people: *basketball lore* ◆ *traditional Hawaiian lore* ⊃ see also FOLKLORE

lo-res /ˌloʊ 'rɛz/ *adj.* = LOW-RESOLUTION

lor·gnette /lɔrˈnyɛt/ *noun* an old-fashioned pair of glasses that you hold to your eyes on a long handle

lose /luz/ *verb* (lost, lost /lɔst/)

> **NOT FIND 1** [T] ~ **sth/sb** to be unable to find something or someone **SYN** MISPLACE: *I've lost my keys.* ◆ *The tickets seem to have gotten lost.* ◆ *She lost her husband in the crowd.*
> **HAVE SOMETHING OR SOMEONE TAKEN AWAY 2** [T] ~ **sth/sb** to have something or someone taken away from you as a result of an accident, getting old, dying, etc.: *She lost a leg in a car crash.* ◆ *to lose your hair/teeth* (= as a result of getting old) ◆ *He's lost his job.* ◆ *Some families lost everything* (= all they owned) *in the flood.* ◆ *They lost both their sons* (= they were killed) *in the war.* ◆ *The ship was lost at sea* (= it sank). ◆ *Many people lost their lives* (= were killed). **3** [T] ~ **sth (to sb/sth)** to have something taken away by someone or something: *The company has lost a lot of business to its competitors.* **4** [T] ~ **sth** to have to give up something; to fail to keep something: *You will lose your deposit if you cancel the order.* ◆ *Sit down or you'll lose your seat.*
> **HAVE LESS 5** [T] ~ **sth** to have less and less of something, especially until you no longer have any of it: *He lost his nerve at the last minute.* ◆ *She seemed to have lost interest in food.* ◆ *At that moment he lost his balance and fell.* ◆ *I've lost ten pounds since I started this diet.* ◆ *The train was losing speed.*
> **NOT UNDERSTAND/HEAR 6** [T] ~ **sth** to fail to get, hear, or understand something: *His words were lost* (= could not be heard) *in the applause.* **7** [T] ~ **sb** (*informal*) to be no longer understood by someone: *I'm afraid you've lost me there.*
> **ESCAPE 8** [T] ~ **sb/sth** to escape from someone or something **SYN** EVADE, SHAKE OFF: *We managed to lose our pursuers in the darkness.*
> **NOT WIN 9** [T, I] to be defeated; to fail to win a competition, a court case, an argument, etc.: ~ **sth (to sb)** *to lose a game/a race/an election/a battle/a war* ◆ ~ **to sb** *We lost to a stronger team.* ◆ ~ **(sth) (by sth)** *He lost by less than 100 votes.*
> **NOT KEEP 10** [T, I] to fail to keep something you want or need, especially money; to cause someone to fail to keep something: ~ **sth** *The business is losing money.* ◆ *Poetry always loses something in translation.* ◆ ~ **sth (on sth/by doing sth)** *You have nothing to lose by telling the truth.* ◆ ~ **on sth/by doing sth** *We lost on that deal.* ◆ ~ **sb sth** *His carelessness lost him the job.*
> **TIME 11** [T] ~ **sth** to waste time or an opportunity: *We lost twenty minutes changing a tire.* ◆ *Hurry— there's no time to lose!* ◆ *He lost no time in setting out for his uncle's house.* **12** [T, I] ~ **(sth)** if a watch or clock **loses** or **loses time**, it goes too slowly or becomes a particular amount of time behind the correct time: *This clock loses two minutes a day.*

ANT GAIN

IDM Most idioms containing **lose** are at the entries for the nouns and adjectives in the idioms. For example, **lose your bearings** is at **bearing**. **lose it** (*informal*) to be unable to stop yourself from crying, laughing, etc.; to become crazy: *Then she just lost it and started screaming.*

PHR V **'lose yourself in sth** to become so interested in something that it takes all your attention ˌlose 'out (on sth) (*informal*) to not get something you wanted or feel you should have: *While the stores make big profits, it's the customer who loses out.* ˌlose 'out to sb/sth (*informal*) to not get business, etc. that you expected or used to get because someone or something else has taken it: *Small businesses are losing out to the large chains.*

los·er /'luzər/ *noun* **1** a person who is defeated in a competition: *winners and losers* ◆ *He's a good/bad loser* (= he accepts defeat well/badly). **2** a person who is regularly unsuccessful, especially when you have a low opinion of them: *She's one of life's losers.* ◆ *He's a born loser.* **3** a person who suffers because of a particular action, decision, etc.: *The real losers in all of this are the students.*

loss /lɔs/ *noun*
1 [U, C, usually sing.] the state of no longer having something or as much of something; the process that leads to this: *I want to report the loss of a package.* ◆ *loss of blood* ◆ *weight loss* ◆ *The closure of the factory will lead to a number of job losses.* ◆ *When she died I was filled with a sense of loss.* ◆ *loss of earnings* (= the money you do not earn because you are prevented from working) **2** [C] money that has been lost by a business or an organization: *The company has announced net losses of $1.5 million.* ◆ *We took a loss on* (= lost money on) *the deal.* ◆ *We are now operating at a loss.* **ANT** PROFIT ⊃ see also CAPITAL LOSS **3** [C, U] the death of a person: *The loss of his wife was a great blow to him.* ◆ *Enemy troops suffered heavy losses.* ◆ *The drought has led to widespread loss of life.* **4** [sing.] the disadvantage that is caused when someone leaves or when a useful or valuable object is taken away; a person who causes a disadvantage by leaving: *Her departure is a big loss to the school.* ◆ *She will be a great loss to the school.* ◆ *If he isn't prepared to accept this money, then that's his loss.* **5** [C] a failure to win a contest: *Brazil's 2–1 loss to Argentina*
IDM **at a loss** not knowing what to say or do: *His comments left me at a loss for words.* ◆ *I'm at a loss what to do next.* **cut your losses** to stop doing something that is not successful before the situation becomes even worse

'loss-ˌleader *noun* an item that a store sells at a very low price to attract customers

loss·less /'lɔsləs/ *adj.* (*technical*) involving no loss of data or electrical energy **ANT** LOSSY

loss·y /'lɔsi/ *adj.* (*technical*) involving the loss of data or electrical energy **ANT** LOSSLESS

lost /lɔst/ *adj.*
1 unable to find your way; not knowing where you are: *We always get lost in this city.* ◆ *We're completely lost.* **2** that cannot be found or brought back: *I'm still looking for that lost file.* ◆ *Your check must have gotten lost in the mail.* **3** [usually before noun] that cannot be obtained; that cannot be found or created again: *The strike cost them thousands of dollars in lost business.* ◆ *She's trying to recapture her lost youth.* ◆ *He regretted the lost* (= wasted) *opportunity to apologize to her.* **4** [not usually before noun] unable to deal successfully with a particular situation: *We would be lost without your help.* ◆ *I felt so lost after my mother died.* ◆ *He's a lost soul* (= a person who does not seem to know what to do, and seems unhappy). **5** [not before noun] unable to understand something because it is too complicated: *They spoke so quickly I just got lost.* ◆ *Hang on a minute—I'm lost.* ⊃ see also LOSE
IDM **all is not lost** there is still some hope of making a bad situation better **be lost for words** to be so surprised, confused, etc. that you do not know what to say **be lost in sth** to be giving all your attention to something so that you do not notice what is happening around you: *to be lost in thought* **be lost on sb** to be not understood or noticed by someone: *His jokes were completely lost on most of the students.* **be lost to the world** to be giving all your attention to something so that you do not notice what is happening around you **get lost** (*informal*) a rude way of telling someone to go away, or of refusing something **give sb up for lost** (*formal*) to stop expecting to find someone alive **make up for lost time** to do something quickly or very often because you wish you had started doing it sooner ⊃ more at LOVE *n.*

ˌlost-and-'found *noun* [U] the place where items that have been found are kept until they are collected

ˌlost 'cause *noun* something that has failed or that cannot succeed

lot /lɑt/ *pron., det., adv., noun*
● *pron.* **a lot** (also *informal* **lots**) ~ **(to do)** a large number or amount: *"How many do you need?" "A lot."* ◆ *Have some more*

cake. There's lots left. ◆ *She still has **an awful lot*** (= a very large amount) *to learn.* ◆ *He has invited nearly a hundred people but a lot aren't able to come.* ➔ note at MANY, MUCH

● **det. a lot of** (also *informal* **lots of**) a large number or amount of someone or something: *What a lot of presents!* ◆ *A lot of people are coming to the meeting.* ◆ *black coffee with lots of sugar* ◆ *I saw a lot of her* (= I saw her often) *last summer.* ➔ note at MANY, MUCH

● **adv.** (*informal*) **1 a lot** (also *informal* **lots**) used with adjectives and adverbs to mean "much": *I'm feeling a lot better today.* ◆ *I eat lots less than I used to.* **2 a lot** used with verbs to mean "a great amount": *I care a lot about you.* ◆ *Thanks a lot for your help.* ◆ *I play tennis quite a lot* (= often) *in the summer.* ➔ note at MUCH

● **noun**
  ▷ AREA OF LAND **1** [C] an area of land used for a particular purpose: *a parking lot* ◆ *a vacant lot* (= one available to be built on or used for sth) ◆ *We're going to build a house on this lot.* ➔ thesaurus box at LAND
  ▷ LUCK/SITUATION **2** [sing.] a person's luck or situation in life SYN DESTINY: *She was feeling dissatisfied with her lot.*
  ▷ WHOLE AMOUNT/NUMBER **3 the lot, the whole lot** [sing.] (*informal*) the whole number or amount of people or things: *He's bought a new PC, color printer, scanner—the lot.* ◆ *This series is the best of the lot.*
  ▷ GROUP/SET **4** [C] a group or set of people or things: *The first lot of visitors have arrived.*
  ▷ ITEMS TO BE SOLD **5** [C] an item or a number of items to be sold, especially at an AUCTION: *Lot 46: six chairs*
  IDM **all over the lot** = ALL OVER THE PLACE at PLACE *n.* **by lot** using a method of choosing someone to do something in which each person takes a piece of paper, etc. from a container and the one whose paper has a special mark is chosen **draw/cast lots (for sth/to do sth)** to choose someone or something by lot: *They drew lots for the right to go first.* **throw in your lot with sb** to decide to join someone and share their successes and problems

lo-tech = LOW-TECH

loth = LOATH

lo·tion /ˈloʊʃn/ *noun* [C, U] a liquid used for cleaning, protecting, or treating the skin: *(a) body/hand lotion*

lot·ta /ˈlɑtə/ (also **lots·a** /ˈlɑtsə/) (*informal, non-standard*) a written form of "lot of" or "lots of" that shows how it sounds in informal speech: *We're gonna have a lotta fun.* **HELP** You should not write this form unless you are copying someone's speech.

lot·ter·y /ˈlɑtəri/ *noun* (*pl.* **lot·ter·ies**) **1** [C] a way of raising money for a government, charity, etc. by selling tickets that have different numbers on them that people have chosen. Numbers are then chosen by chance and the people who have those numbers on their tickets win prizes: *the state lottery* ◆ *a lottery ticket* ➔ compare DRAWING (4), RAFFLE **2** [C, U] a way of choosing who will get something, for example tickets for an event, in which people's names are chosen by chance: *Students were selected by lottery, since demand for the program was high.* **3** [sing.] (often *disapproving*) a situation whose success or result is based on luck rather than on effort or careful organization SYN GAMBLE: *Some people think that marriage is a lottery.*

lot·to /ˈlɑtoʊ/ *noun* (*pl.* **lot·tos**) **1** [U] a game of chance similar to BINGO but with the numbers drawn from a container by the players instead of being called out **2** [C] a lottery

lo·tus /ˈloʊtəs/ *noun* **1** a tropical plant with white or pink flowers that grows on the surface of lakes in Africa and Asia: *a lotus flower* ➔ picture at PLANT **2** a picture in the shape of the lotus plant, used in art and ARCHITECTURE, especially in ancient Egypt **3** (in ancient Greek stories) a fruit that is supposed to make you feel happy and relaxed when you have eaten it, as if in a dream

lotus po·sition *noun* [sing.] a way of sitting with your legs crossed, used especially when people do YOGA

louche /luʃ/ *adj.* (*formal*) not socially acceptable, but often still attractive despite this

loud 🔊 /laʊd/ *adj., adv.*

● **adj.** (**loud·er, loud·est**) **1** making a lot of noise: *loud laughter* ◆ *a deafeningly loud bang* ◆ *She spoke in a very loud voice.* ◆ *That music's too loud—please turn it down.* **2** (of a person or their behavior) talking very loudly, too much, and in a way that is annoying **3** (of colors, patterns, etc.) too bright and lacking good taste SYN GARISH, GAUDY ▶ **loud·ly** *adv.*: *She screamed as loudly as she could.* **loud·ness** /ˈlaʊdnəs/ *noun* [U]

● **adv.** (**loud·er, loud·est**) (*informal*) in a way that makes a lot of noise or can be easily heard SYN LOUDLY: *Do you have to play that music so loud?* ◆ *You'll have to speak louder—I can't hear you.*

IDM **loud and clear** in a way that is very easy to understand: *The message is coming through loud and clear.* **out loud** in a voice that can be heard by other people: *I laughed out loud.* ◆ *Please read the letter out loud.* ➔ compare ALOUD ➔ more at ACTION, CRY *v.*, THINK *v.*

WHICH WORD?

loud ◆ loudly ◆ aloud

■ **Loudly** is the usual adverb from the adjective **loud**: *The audience laughed loudly at the joke.*

■ **Loud** is very common as an adverb in informal language. It is nearly always used in phrases such as **loud enough, as loud as**, or with *too, very, so*, etc.: *Don't play your music too loud.* ◆ *I shouted as loud as I could.*

■ **Louder** is also used in informal styles to mean "more loudly": *Can you play any louder?*

■ **Out loud** is a common adverb meaning "so that people can hear": *Can you read the letter out loud?* ◆ *He laughed out loud at his own joke.* **Aloud** has the same meaning but is fairly formal. It can also mean "in a loud voice."

---

loud·mouth /ˈlaʊdmaʊθ/ *noun* (*informal*) a person who is annoying because they talk too loudly or too much in an offensive or stupid way ▶ **loud-mouthed** /-maʊðd; -maʊθt/ *adj.*

loud·speak·er /ˈlaʊdˌspikər/ *noun* **1** a piece of equipment that changes electrical signals into sound, used in public places for announcing things, playing music, etc.: *Their names were called over the loudspeaker.* ➔ see also PUBLIC ADDRESS SYSTEM **2** (*old-fashioned*) the part of a radio or piece of musical equipment that the sound comes out of SYN SPEAKER

lounge /laʊndʒ/ *noun, verb*
● **noun 1** a room for waiting in at an airport, etc.: *the departure lounge* **2** a public room in a hotel, club, etc. for waiting or relaxing in: *the television lounge*
● **verb** [I] (+ *adv./prep.*) to stand, sit, or lie in a lazy way SYN LAZE AROUND: *Several students were lounging around, reading newspapers.*

lounge chair *noun* = CHAISE LONGUE (2)

lounge lizard *noun* (*old-fashioned, informal*) a person who does no work and who likes to be with rich fashionable people

loung·er /ˈlaʊndʒər/ *noun* = CHAISE LONGUE (2)

lour *verb* = LOWER[2]

louse /laʊs/ *noun, verb*
● **noun 1** (*pl.* **lice** /laɪs/) a small insect that lives on the bodies of humans and animals: *head lice* ➔ see also WOOD LOUSE **2** (*pl.* **lous·es**) (*informal, disapproving*) a very unpleasant person
● **verb**
  PHR V **louse sth↔up** (*informal*) to spoil something or do it very badly

---

lous·y /ˈlaʊzi/ adj. (informal) (lous·i·er, lous·i·est) **1** very bad **SYN** AWFUL, TERRIBLE: *What lousy weather!* ♦ *She felt lousy* (= sick). **2** [only before noun] used to show that you feel annoyed or insulted because you do not think that something is worth very much: *All she bought me was this lousy T-shirt.* **3** ~ **with sth/sb** having too much of something or too many people: *This place is lousy with tourists in August.*

lout /laʊt/ noun a man or boy who behaves in a rude and aggressive way ▶ **lout·ish** adj.: *loutish behavior*

lou·ver /ˈluvər/ noun one of a set of narrow strips of wood, plastic, etc. in a door or a window that are designed to let air and some light in, but to keep out strong light or rain; a door or a window that has these strips across it ▶ **lou·vered** adj.

lov·a·ble (also **love·able**) /ˈlʌvəbl/ adj. having qualities that people find attractive and easy to love, often despite any faults **SYN** ENDEARING: *a lovable child* ♦ *a lovable rogue*

love 🔑 /lʌv/ noun, verb

● **noun**

> AFFECTION **1** [U] a strong feeling of deep affection for someone or something, especially a member of your family or a friend: *a mother's love for her children* ♦ *love of your country* ♦ *He seems incapable of love.*

> ROMANTIC **2** [U] a strong feeling of affection for someone that you are sexually attracted to: *a love song/story* ♦ *We're in love!* ♦ *She was in love with him.* ♦ *They fell in love with each other.* ♦ *It was love at first sight* (= they were attracted to each other the first time they met). ♦ *They're madly in love.* ♦ *Their love grew with the years.* ⊃ collocations at MARRIAGE

> ENJOYMENT **3** [U, sing.] the strong feeling of enjoyment that something gives you: *a love of learning* ♦ *He's in love with his work.* ♦ *I fell in love with the house.*

> SOMEONE OR SOMETHING YOU LIKE **4** [C] a person, a thing, or an activity that you like very much: *Take care, my love.* ♦ *He was the love of my life* (= the person I loved most). ♦ *I like most sports but tennis is my first love.*

> IN TENNIS **5** [U] a score of zero (points or games): *40–love!* ♦ *She won the first set six–love/six games to love.*

IDM **(just) for love** | **(just) for the love of sth** without receiving payment or any other reward: *They're all volunteers, working for the love of it.* **for the love of God** (old-fashioned, informal) used when you are expressing anger and the fact that you are impatient: *For the love of God, tell me what he said!* **give/send my love to sb** (informal) used to send good wishes to someone: *Give my love to Mary when you see her.* ♦ *Bob sends his love.* **love (from)** | **lots of love (from)** (informal) used at the end of a letter to a friend or to someone you love, followed by your name: *Lots of love, Jenny* **love is blind** (saying) when you love someone, you cannot see their faults **make love (to sb)** to have sex **not for love or/nor money** if you say you cannot do something **for love nor money**, you mean it is completely impossible to do it **there's little/no love lost between A and B** they do not like each other: *There's no love lost between her and her in-laws.* ⊃ more at FAIR adj., HEAD, LABOR

● **verb**

> FEEL AFFECTION **1** ~ **sb/sth** (not used in the progressive tenses) to have very strong feelings of affection for someone: *I love you.* ♦ *If you love each other, why not get married?* ♦ *Her much-loved brother lay dying of cancer.* ♦ *He had become a well-loved member of our club.* ♦ *Relatives need time to grieve over loved ones they have lost.* ♦ *to love your country*

> LIKE/ENJOY **2** to like or enjoy something very much **SYN** ADORE: ~ **sth** *I really love summer evenings.* ♦ *I just love it when you bring me presents!* ♦ *He loved the way she smiled.* ♦ *I love it in Spain* (= I like the life there). ♦ *It was one of his best-loved songs.* ♦ (ironic) *You're going to love this. They've changed their minds again.* ♦ ~ **doing sth** *My dad loves going to baseball games.* ♦ ~ **to do sth** *I love to go out dancing.* ♦ ~ **sb/sth to do sth** *He loved her to sing to him.* ⊃ thesaurus box at LIKE

3 **would love** used to say that you would very much like something: ~ **to do sth** *Come on Rory, the kids would love to hear you sing.* ♦ *I haven't been to Brazil, but I'd love to go.* ♦ ~ **for**

sb/sth to do sth *I'd love for her to come and live with us.* ♦ ~ **sth** *"Cigarette?" "I'd love one, but I've just quit."*

love af·fair noun **1** a romantic and/or sexual relationship between two people who are in love and not married to each other **2** great enthusiasm for something **SYN** PASSION: *her love affair with gardening*

love·bird /ˈlʌvbərd/ noun **1** [C] a small African PARROT (= a bird with brightly colored feathers) **2** lovebirds [pl.] (humorous) two people who love each other very much and show this in their behavior

love child noun (used especially in newspapers, etc.) a child born to parents who are not married to each other

love handles noun [pl.] (informal, humorous) extra fat on a person's waist

love-hate relationship noun [usually sing.] a relationship in which your feelings for someone or something are a mixture of love and hatred

love-in noun (informal) **1** (old-fashioned) a party at which people freely show their affection and sexual attraction for each other, associated with HIPPIES in the 1960s **2** (disapproving) an occasion when people are being especially pleasant to each other, in a way that you believe is not sincere

love interest noun [C, usually sing.] a character in a movie or story who has a romantic role, often as the main character's lover

love·less /ˈlʌvləs/ adj. without love: *a loveless marriage*

love letter noun a letter that you write to someone telling them that you love them

love life noun the part of your life that involves your romantic and sexual relationships

love·li·ness /ˈlʌvlinəs/ noun [U] (formal) the state of being very attractive **SYN** BEAUTY

love·lorn /ˈlʌvlɔrn/ adj. (literary) unhappy because the person you love does not love you

love·ly /ˈlʌvli/ adj., noun

● **adj.** (love·li·er, love·li·est) **HELP** You can also use **more lovely** and **most lovely**. **1** beautiful; attractive: *lovely countryside/eyes/flowers* ♦ *She looked particularly lovely that night.* ⊃ thesaurus box at BEAUTIFUL **2** (informal) very enjoyable and pleasant; wonderful: *"Can I get you anything?" "A cup of coffee would be lovely."* ♦ *What a lovely surprise!* ♦ *How lovely to see you!* ♦ (ironic) *You've got yourself into a lovely mess, haven't you?* **3** (informal) (of a person) very kind, generous, and friendly **HELP** **Very lovely** is not very common and is only used about the physical appearance of a person or thing.

● **noun** (pl. love·lies) (old-fashioned) a beautiful woman

love·mak·ing /ˈlʌvˌmeɪkɪŋ/ noun [U] sexual activity between two lovers, especially the act of having sex

love match noun a marriage of two people who are in love with each other

love nest noun [usually sing.] (informal) a house or an apartment where two people who are not married but are having a sexual relationship can meet

lov·er 🔑 /ˈlʌvər/ noun

1 a partner in a sexual relationship outside marriage: *He denied that he was her lover.* ♦ *They were lovers for several years.* ♦ *The park was full of young lovers holding hands.* **2** (often in compounds) a person who likes or enjoys a particular thing: *a lover of music* ♦ *an art-lover* ♦ *a nature-lover*

love seat noun a comfortable seat with a back and arms, for two people to sit on

love·sick /ˈlʌvsɪk/ adj. unable to think clearly or behave in a sensible way because you are in love with someone, especially someone who is not in love with you

love triangle noun [usually sing.] a situation that involves three people, each of whom loves at least one of the others

ʌ **cup**   ə **about**   eɪ **say**   aɪ **five**   ɔɪ **boy**   aʊ **now**   oʊ **go**   ər **bird**

love·y-dove·y /ˌlʌvi ˈdʌvi/ adj. (informal) expressing romantic love in a way that is slightly silly

lov·ing /ˈlʌvɪŋ/ adj. **1** feeling or showing love and affection for someone or something **SYN** AFFECTIONATE, TENDER: *a warm and loving family* ◆ *She chose the present with loving care.* **2** -**loving** (in adjectives) enjoying the object or activity mentioned: *fun-loving young people* ▶ **lov·ing·ly** adv.: *He gazed lovingly at his children.* ◆ *The house has been lovingly restored.*

'loving ˌcup noun (old use) a large cup with two handles, which guests pass around and drink from

low /loʊ/ adj., adv., noun, verb

● **adj.** (low·er, low·est)
▷ NOT HIGH/TALL **1** not high or tall; not far above the ground: *a low wall/building/table* ◆ *a low range of hills* ◆ *low clouds* ◆ *flying at low altitude* ◆ *The sun was low in the sky.* **ANT** HIGH
▷ NEAR BOTTOM **2** at or near the bottom of something: *lower back pain* ◆ *the lower slopes of the mountain* ◆ *temperatures in the low 60s* (= no higher than 61–63°) **ANT** HIGH
▷ CLOTHING **3** not high at the neck: *a dress with a low neckline* ⊃ see also LOW-CUT
▷ LEVEL/VALUE **4** also low- (often in compounds) below the usual or average amount, level, or value: *low prices* ◆ *low-income families* ◆ *a low-cost airline* ◆ *the lowest temperature ever recorded* ◆ *a low level of unemployment* ◆ *Yogurt is usually very low in fat.* ◆ *low-fat yogurt* ◆ *low-tar cigarettes* **ANT** HIGH **5** having a reduced amount or not enough of something: *The reservoir was low after the long drought.* ◆ *Our supplies are running low* (= we only have a little left). ◆ *They were low on fuel.*
▷ SOUND **6** not high; not loud: *The cello is lower than the violin.* ◆ *They were speaking in low voices.* **ANT** HIGH
▷ STANDARD **7** below the usual or expected standard: *students with low grades on their exams* ◆ *a low standard of living* **ANT** HIGH
▷ STATUS **8** below other people or things in importance or status: *low forms of life* (= creatures with a very simple structure) ◆ *jobs with low status* ◆ *Training was given a very low priority.* ◆ *the lower classes of society* **ANT** HIGH
▷ DEPRESSED **9** weak or depressed; with very little energy **SYN** DOWN: *I'm feeling really low.* ◆ *They were in low spirits.*
▷ OPINION **10** [usually before noun] not very good **SYN** POOR: *She has a very low opinion of her own abilities.* **ANT** HIGH
▷ NOT HONEST **11** (of a person) not honest **SYN** DISREPUTABLE: *He mixes with some pretty low types.*
▷ LIGHT **12** not bright **SYN** DIM: *The lights were low and romance was in the air.*
▷ IN VEHICLE **13** if a vehicle is in **low gear**, it travels at a slower speed in relation to the speed of the engine
▷ PHONETICS **14** (phonetics) = OPEN
IDM **at a low ebb** in a poor state; worse than usual: *Morale among teachers is at a low ebb.* **be brought low** (old-fashioned) to lose your wealth or your high position in society **lay sb low** if someone is laid low by/with an injury or illness, they feel very weak and are unable to do much **the lowest of the low** people who are not respected at all because they are dishonest, immoral, or not at all important ⊃ more at PROFILE *n.*

● **adv.** (low·er, low·est)
▷ NOT HIGH **1** in or into a low position, not far above the ground: *to crouch/bend low* ◆ *a plane flying low over the town* ◆ *low-flying aircraft* ◆ *The sun sank lower toward the horizon.*
▷ NEAR BOTTOM **2** in or into a position near the bottom of something: *a window set low in the wall* ◆ *The candles were burning low.*
▷ LEVEL **3** (especially in compounds) at a level below what is usual or expected: *low-priced goods* ◆ *a low-powered PC* ◆ *a very low-scoring game*
▷ SOUND **4** not high; not loudly: *He's singing an octave lower than the rest of us.* ◆ *Can you turn the music lower—you'll wake the baby.* **IDM** see HIGH adv., LIE¹, SINK v., STOOP v.

● **noun**
▷ LEVEL/VALUE **1** a low level or point; a low figure: *The yen has fallen to an all-time low against the dollar.* ◆ *The temperature*

reached a record low last night. ◆ *The government's popularity has hit a new low.*
▷ DIFFICULT TIME **2** a very difficult time in someone's life or career: *The breakup of her marriage marked an all-time low in her life.*
▷ WEATHER **3** an area of low pressure in the atmosphere: *Another low is moving in from the Atlantic.* **ANT** HIGH

● **verb** [I] (literary) when a cow **lows**, it makes a deep sound **SYN** MOO

low·ball /ˈloʊbɔl/ verb ~ sth (informal) to deliberately make an estimate of the cost, value, etc. of something that is too low: *He lowballed the cost of the project in order to obtain federal funding.* **ANT** HIGHBALL

'low beams noun [pl.] the lights on a car when they are pointing down at the road, not a long way ahead: *Use your low beams for city driving.* ⊃ compare HIGH BEAMS
IDM **on low beam** (of the lights on a car) pointing down at the road, not a long way ahead: *Always have your lights on low beam when another car is coming toward you.*

'low-born adj. (old-fashioned or formal) having parents who are members of a low social class **ANT** HIGH-BORN

low·brow /ˈloʊbraʊ/ adj., noun
● **adj.** (usually disapproving) having no connection with or interest in serious artistic or cultural ideas **ANT** HIGHBROW ⊃ compare MIDDLEBROW
● **noun** (usually disapproving) a person who has no interest in serious artistic or cultural ideas

low-cal (also **lo-cal**) /ˌloʊ ˈkæl/ adj. (informal) (of food and drinks) containing very few CALORIES

ˌlow-'carb adj. [usually before noun] relating to food or a diet that is low in CARBOHYDRATES: *She's on a low-carb diet, so she doesn't eat much bread, pasta, or potatoes.*

ˌlow-'class adj. **1** of poor quality or a low standard **2** connected with a low social class **ANT** HIGH-CLASS

the ˌLow ˌCountries noun [pl.] the region of Europe which consists of the Netherlands, Belgium, and Luxembourg (used especially in the past)

ˌlow-'cut adj. (of dresses etc.) with the top very low so that you can see the neck and the top of the chest

low·down /ˈloʊdaʊn/ adj., noun
● **adj.** [only before noun] (informal) not fair or honest **SYN** MEAN: *What a dirty, lowdown trick!*
● **noun the lowdown** [sing.] ~ **on (sb/sth)** (informal) the true facts about someone or something, especially those considered most important to know: *Jane gave me the lowdown on the other guests at the party.*

'low-end adj. [usually before noun] at the cheaper end of a range of similar products

low·er¹ /ˈloʊər/ adj., verb ⊃ see also LOWER²
● **adj.** [only before noun] **1** located below something else, especially something of the same type, or the other of a pair: *the lower deck of a ship* ◆ *His lower lip trembled.* **2** at or near the bottom of something: *the mountain's lower slopes* **3** (of a place) located toward the coast, on low ground, or toward the south of an area: *the lower reaches of the Nile* **ANT** UPPER
● **verb 1** [T] to let or make something or someone go down: ~ **sth** *He had to lower his head to get through the door.* ◆ *She lowered her newspaper and looked around.* ◆ ~ **sth/sb + adv./prep.** *They lowered him down the cliff on a rope.* **ANT** RAISE **2** [T, I] ~ **(sth)** to reduce something or to become less in value, quality, etc.: *He lowered his voice to a whisper.* ◆ *This drug is used to lower blood pressure.* ◆ *Her voice lowered as she spoke.* **ANT** RAISE
IDM **lower the bar** to set a new lower standard of quality or performance: *In the current economic climate we may need to lower the bar on quotas.* **lower yourself (by doing sth)** (usually used in negative sentences) to behave in a way that makes other people respect you less **SYN** DEMEAN: *I wouldn't lower myself by working for him.* ⊃ more at SIGHT *n.*, TEMPERATURE

---

low·er² (also **lour**) /ˈlaʊər/ verb [I] (*literary*) (of the sky or clouds) to be dark and threatening ⊃ see also LOWER¹

low·er·case (also ˌlower ˈcase) /ˌloʊərˈkeɪs/ noun [U] (in printing and writing) small letters: *The text is all in lowercase.* ⊃ compare CAPITAL, UPPERCASE ▶ **low·er·case** *adj.*: *lowercase letters*

ˌlower ˈchamber noun = LOWER HOUSE

the ˌlower ˈclass noun the group of people who are considered to have the lowest social status and who have less money and/or power than other people in society ▶ **ˌlower-ˈclass** *adj.*: *They considered their daughter's new boyfriend too lower class for her.* ♦ *a lower-class accent* ♦ compare UPPER CLASS

ˌlower ˈhouse (also ˌlower ˈchamber) noun [sing.] the larger group of people who make laws in a country, usually consisting of elected representatives, such as the House of Representatives ⊃ compare UPPER HOUSE

ˌlowest ˌcommon deˈnominator noun ⊃ see also LEAST COMMON DENOMINATOR

ˌlowest ˌcommon ˈmultiple noun = LEAST COMMON MULTIPLE

ˌlow-ˈfat *adj.* [usually before noun] containing only a very small amount of fat

ˌlow-ˈgrade *adj.* [usually before noun] **1** of low quality **2** (*medical*) of a less serious type: *a low-grade infection*

ˌlow-ˈimpact *adj.* [usually before noun] **1** involving movements that do not put a lot of stress on the body: *low-impact aerobics* **2** not causing very many problems or changes, especially in the environment: *low-impact tourism*

ˌlow-ˈkey *adj.* not intended to attract a lot of attention: *Their wedding was very low-key.*

low·land /ˈloʊlənd; -lænd/ *adj., noun*
- *adj.* [only before noun] connected with an area of land that is fairly flat and not very high above sea level ⊃ compare HIGHLAND
- *noun* [pl., U] an area of land that is fairly flat and not very high above sea level: *the lowlands of Peru* ♦ *Much of the region is lowland.* ⊃ compare HIGHLAND

low·land·er /ˈloʊləndər; -lændər/ noun a person who comes from an area that is flat and low ⊃ compare HIGH-LANDER

ˌlow-ˈlevel *adj.* [usually before noun] **1** close to the ground: *low-level bombing attacks* **2** of low rank; involving people of junior rank: *a low-level job* ♦ *low-level negotiations* **3** not containing much of a particular substance, especially a RADIOACTIVE substance: *low-level radioactive waste* **4** (*computing*) (of a computer language) similar to MACHINE CODE in form ANT HIGH-LEVEL

low·life /ˈloʊlaɪf/ noun **1** [C] (*informal, disapproving*) someone who is unacceptable to most people because they are a criminal, of poor moral character, lazy, etc.: *Why do you want to hang out with all those lowlifes?* **2** [U] the life and behavior of people who are outside normal society, especially criminals ▶ **low·life** *adj.* [only before noun] (*informal*): *a lowlife bar* ♦ *a bunch of lowlife characters*

low·lights /ˈloʊlaɪts/ noun [pl.] areas of hair that have been made darker than the rest, with the use of a chemical substance ⊃ compare HIGHLIGHT

low·ly /ˈloʊli/ *adj.* (low·li·er, low·li·est) (often *humorous*) low in status or importance SYN HUMBLE, OBSCURE

ˌlow-ˈlying *adj.* (of land) not high, and usually fairly flat

ˌlow-ˈmaintenance *adj.* not needing much attention or effort: *a low-maintenance garden* ANT HIGH-MAINTENANCE

ˌlow-ˈpaid *adj.* earning or providing very little money: *low-paid workers* ♦ *It is one of the lowest-paid jobs.*

ˌlow-ˈpitched *adj.* (of sounds) deep; low: *a low-pitched voice* ANT HIGH-PITCHED

ˈlow point noun the least interesting, least enjoyable, or worst part of something ANT HIGH POINT

ˌlow ˈpressure noun [U] **1** the condition of air, gas, or liquid that is kept in a container with little force: *Water supplies to the house are at low pressure.* **2** a condition of the air that affects the weather when the pressure is lower than average ⊃ compare HIGH PRESSURE

ˌlow-ˈprofile *adj.* [only before noun] receiving or involving very little attention: *a low-profile campaign* ⊃ see also PROFILE

ˌlow-ˈranking *adj.* junior; not very important: *a low-ranking officer/official* ANT HIGH-RANKING

ˌlow-ˈrent *adj.* of poor quality or low social status: *her low-rent boyfriend*

ˌlow-resoˈlution (also **lo-res, low-res** /ˌloʊ ˈrez/) *adj.* (of a photograph or an image on a computer or television screen) not showing a lot of clear detail: *a low-resolution scan* ANT HIGH-RESOLUTION

ˈlow-rise *adj.* [only before noun] **1** (of a building) low, with only a few floors: *low-rise housing* **2** (of a pair of jeans, etc.) cut so that the top is much lower than the waist ▶ **ˈlow-rise** noun ⊃ compare HIGH-RISE

ˌlow-ˈrisk *adj.* [usually before noun] involving only a small amount of danger and little risk of injury, death, damage, etc. SYN SAFE: *a low-risk investment* ♦ *low-risk patients* (= who are very unlikely to get a particular illness) ANT HIGH-RISK

ˌlow ˈslung *adj.* very low and close to the ground

ˌlow-ˈtech (also **ˌlo-ˈtech**) *adj.* (*informal*) not involving the most modern technology or methods ANT HIGH-TECH

ˌlow ˈtide (also ˌlow ˈwater) noun [U, C] the time when the ocean is at its lowest level; the ocean at this time: *The island can only be reached at low tide.* ANT HIGH TIDE

ˌlow-ˈwater ˌmark noun a line or mark showing the lowest point that the ocean reaches at low tide ANT HIGH-WATER MARK

lox /lɑks/ noun [U] smoked SALMON (= a type of fish)

loy·al 🔑 /ˈlɔɪəl/ *adj.* ~ (to sb/sth) remaining faithful to someone or something and supporting them or it SYN TRUE: *a loyal friend/supporter* ♦ *She has always remained loyal to her political principles.* ANT DISLOYAL ▶ **loy·al·ly** *adv.*

loy·al·ist /ˈlɔɪəlɪst/ noun **1** a person who is loyal to the ruler or government, or to a political party, especially during a time of change **2 Loyalist** an American who supported the British during the AMERICAN REVOLUTION: *Many Loyalists eventually moved to Canada or the Bahamas.*

loy·al·ty /ˈlɔɪəlti/ noun (pl. loy·al·ties) **1** [U] ~ (to/toward sb/sth) the quality of being faithful in your support of someone or something: *They swore their loyalty to the king.* ♦ *Can I count on your loyalty?* **2** [C, usually pl.] a strong feeling that you want to be loyal to someone or something: *a case of divided loyalties* (= with strong feelings of support for two different causes, people, etc.)

loz·enge /ˈlɑzəndʒ/ noun **1** (*geometry*) a figure with four sides in the shape of a diamond that has two opposite angles more than 90° and the other two less than 90° **2** a small candy, often in a lozenge shape, especially one that contains medicine and that you dissolve in your mouth: *throat/cough lozenges*

LP /ˌɛl ˈpi/ noun the abbreviation for "long-playing record" (a record that plays for about 25 minutes each side and turns 33 times per minute)

LPG /ˌɛl pi ˈdʒi/ noun [U] the abbreviation for "liquefied petroleum gas" (a fuel which is a mixture of gases kept in a liquid form by the pressure in a container)

LPN /ˌɛl pi ˈɛn/ abbr. LICENSED PRACTICAL NURSE

LSAT /ˈɛlsæt; ˌɛl ɛs eɪ ˈti/ abbr. Law School Admission Test (a test taken by students who want to study law)

LSD /ˌɛl ɛs ˈdi/ (also slang **ac·id**) noun [U] a powerful illegal drug that affects people's minds and makes them see and hear things that are not really there

Lt. abbr. (in writing) LIEUTENANT: *Lt. (Helen) Brown*

---

t **t**ea   t̮ bu**tt**er   d **d**id   k **c**at   g **g**ot   tʃ **ch**in   dʒ **J**une   f **f**all

lu·au /ˈluaʊ/ *noun* a Hawaiian party with traditional foods and entertainment

lu·bri·cant /ˈlubrəkənt/ (also *informal* **lube** /lub/) *noun* [U, C] a substance, for example oil, that you put on surfaces or parts of a machine so that they move easily and smoothly

lu·bri·cate /ˈlubrəˌkeɪt/ *verb* ~ **sth** to put a lubricant on something such as the parts of a machine, to help them move smoothly **SYN** GREASE, OIL ▶ **lu·bri·ca·tion** /ˌlubrəˈkeɪʃn/ *noun* [U]

lu·bri·cious /luˈbrɪʃəs/ *adj.* (*formal*) showing a great interest in sex in a way that is considered unpleasant or unacceptable **SYN** LEWD

lu·cid /ˈlusɪd/ *adj.* **1** clearly expressed; easy to understand **SYN** CLEAR: *a lucid style/explanation* **2** able to think clearly, especially during or after a period of illness or confusion: *In a rare lucid moment, she looked at me and smiled.* ▶ **lu·cid·i·ty** /luˈsɪdəti/ *noun* [U] **lu·cid·ly** *adv.*

Lu·ci·fer /ˈlusəfər/ *noun* [sing.] the DEVIL **SYN** Satan

luck 🔔 /lʌk/ *noun, verb*

● *noun* [U] **1** good things that happen to you by chance, not because of your own efforts or abilities: *With (any) luck, we'll be home before dark.* ◆ *So far I have had no luck with finding a job.* ◆ *I could hardly believe my luck when he said yes.* ◆ *It was a* **stroke of luck** *that we found you.* ◆ *By sheer luck no one was hurt in the explosion.* ◆ *We* **wish her luck** *in her new career.* ◆ *You're* **in luck** (= lucky)—*there's one ticket left.* —*You're* **out of luck.** *She's not here.* ◆ *What a* **piece of luck!** ⊃ see also BEGINNER'S LUCK **2** chance; the force that causes good or bad things to happen to people **SYN** FORTUNE: *to have good/bad luck* ⊃ see also HARD-LUCK STORY, POTLUCK

IDM **any luck?** (*informal*) used to ask someone if they have been successful with something: *"Any luck?" "No, they're all too busy to help."* **as luck would have it** in the way that chance decides what will happen: *As luck would have it, the train was late.* **bad, hard, etc. luck (on sb)** used to express sympathy for someone: *Bad luck, Helen, you played very well.* ◆ *It's hard luck on him that he wasn't chosen.* **be down on your luck** (*informal*) to have no money because of a period of bad luck **(the) best of luck (with sth) | good luck (with sth)** (*informal*) used to wish someone success with something: *Best of luck with your exams.* ◆ *I wish you the best of luck.* ◆ *Good luck! I hope it goes well.* **better luck next time** (*informal*) used to encourage someone who has not been successful at something **for luck** because you believe it will bring you good luck, or because this is a traditional belief: *Take something blue. It's for luck.* **good luck to sb** (*informal*) used to say that you do not mind what someone does as it does not affect you, but you hope they will be successful: *It's not something I would care to try myself but if she wants to, good luck to her.* **just my/sb's luck** (*informal*) used to show you are not surprised something bad has happened to you, because you are not often lucky: *Just my luck to arrive after they had left.* **your/sb's luck is in** used to say that someone has been lucky or successful **the luck of the draw** the fact that chance decides something, in a way that you cannot control **no such luck** used to show disappointment that something you were hoping for did not happen ⊃ more at PUSH *v.*, TOUGH *adj.*, TRY *v.*

● *verb*
PHR V **luck 'out** (*informal*) to be lucky: *I guess I really lucked out when I met her.*

THESAURUS

luck

chance • coincidence • accident • fate • destiny

These are all words for things that happen or the force that causes them to happen.

luck the force that causes good or bad things to happen to people: *This ring has always brought me good luck.*

chance the way that some things happen without any cause that you can see or understand: *The results could simply be due to chance.*

coincidence the fact of two things happening at the same time by chance, in a surprising way: *They met through a series of strange coincidences.*

accident something that happens unexpectedly and is not planned in advance: *I discovered the book by accident while shopping for a birthday present.*

fate the power that is believed to control everything that happens and that cannot be stopped or changed: *Fate decreed that she would not get married that day.*

destiny the power that is believed to control events: *I believe there's some force guiding us—call it God, destiny, or fate.*

FATE OR DESTINY?

Fate can be kind, but this is an unexpected gift; just as often, **fate** is cruel and makes people feel helpless. **Destiny** is more likely to give people a sense of power: people who have *a strong sense of destiny* usually believe that they are meant to be great or do great things.

PATTERNS

- **by** ...luck/chance/coincidence/accident
- **It's no** coincidence/accident that...
- **pure/sheer** luck/chance/coincidence/accident
- to **believe in** luck/coincidences/fate/destiny

luck·less /ˈlʌkləs/ *adj.* having bad luck **SYN** UNLUCKY: *the luckless victim of the attack*

luck·y 🔔 /ˈlʌki/ *adj.* (luck·i·er, luck·i·est)

1 having good luck **SYN** FORTUNATE: ~ **(to do sth)** *His friend was killed and he knows he is lucky to be alive.* ◆ *She was lucky enough to be chosen for the team.* ◆ ~ **(that...)** *You were lucky (that) you spotted the danger in time.* ◆ *You can* **think yourself lucky** *you didn't get mugged.* ◆ *She* **counted herself lucky** *that she still had a job.* ◆ *Mark is* **one of the lucky ones**—*he at least has somewhere to sleep.* ◆ *the lucky winners* **2** ~ **(for sb) (that...)** being the result of good luck: *It was lucky for us that we were able to go.* ◆ *That was the luckiest escape of my life.* ◆ *a lucky guess* **3** bringing good luck: *a lucky charm* ▶ **luck·i·ly** /ˈlʌkəli/ *adv.*: ~ **(for sb)** *Luckily for us, the train was late.* ◆ *Luckily, I am a good swimmer.*

IDM **lucky you, me, etc.** (*informal*) used to show that you think someone is lucky to have something, be able to do something, etc.: *"I'm off to Paris." "Lucky you!"* **you, etc. should be so lucky** (*informal*) used to tell someone that they will probably not get what they are hoping for, and may not deserve it ⊃ more at STRIKE *v.*, THANK

lu·cra·tive /ˈlukrətɪv/ *adj.* producing a large amount of money; making a large profit: *a lucrative business/contract/market* ⊃ thesaurus box at SUCCESSFUL ▶ **lu·cra·tive·ly** *adv.*

lu·cre /ˈlukər/ *noun* [U] (*disapproving*) money, especially when it has been obtained in a way that is dishonest or immoral: *the lure of* **filthy lucre**

Lud·dite /ˈlʌdaɪt/ *noun* (*disapproving*) a person who is opposed to new technology or working methods **ORIGIN** Named after Ned Lud, one of the workers who destroyed machinery in factories in the early 19th century, because they believed it would take away their jobs.

lu·dic /ˈludɪk/ *adj.* (*formal*) showing a tendency to play and have fun, make jokes, etc., especially when there is no particular reason for doing this

lu·di·crous /ˈludəkrəs/ *adj.* unreasonable; that you cannot take seriously **SYN** ABSURD, RIDICULOUS: *a ludicrous suggestion* ◆ *It was ludicrous to think that the plan could succeed.* ▶ **lu·di·crous·ly** *adv.*: *ludicrously expensive* **lu·di·crous·ness** *noun* [U]

lug /lʌg/ *verb, noun*
● *verb* (-gg-) ~ **sth + adv./prep.** (*informal*) to carry or drag something heavy with a lot of effort: *I had to lug my bags up to the fourth floor.*

• **noun 1** (*technical*) a part of something that sticks out, used as a handle or support **2** (*informal*) a man who is large, awkward, or not very intelligent: *He's a big lug, but very sweet.*

luge /luʒ/ *noun* **1** [C] a type of SLED (= a vehicle for sliding over ice) for racing, used by one person lying on their back with their feet pointing forward ⊃ **picture at SPORT 2 the luge** [sing.] the event or sport of racing down a track of ice on a luge

Lu·ger™ /'luɡər/ *noun* a type of small gun which was made in Germany

lug·gage /'lʌɡɪdʒ/ *noun* [U] bags, cases, etc. that someone carries when they are traveling: *There's room for one more piece of luggage.* ◆ *You stay there with the luggage while I find a cab.* ◆ *I need to buy some new luggage for my vacation next month.* ⊃ **see also HAND LUGGAGE** ⊃ **note at BAGGAGE** ⊃ **collocations at TRAVEL**

'luggage ,rack *noun* **1** a shelf for luggage above the seats in a train, bus, etc. ⊃ **picture at RACK 2** = **ROOF RACK**

'lug nut *noun* a small piece of metal with a hole through it that screws on to the BOLTS that attach a wheel to a vehicle

lu·gu·bri·ous /lə'ɡubriəs/ *adj.* (*formal*) sad and serious **SYN** DOLEFUL: *a lugubrious expression* ▶ **lu·gu·bri·ous·ly** *adv.*

lug·worm /'lʌɡwərm/ *noun* a large WORM that lives in the sand by the ocean. Lugworms are often used as BAIT on a hook to catch fish.

luke·warm /,luk'wɔrm/ *adj.* (often *disapproving*) **1** slightly warm **SYN** TEPID: *Our food was only lukewarm.* ⊃ **thesaurus box at COLD 2** not interested or enthusiastic: *a lukewarm response* ◆ **~ about sb/sth** *She was lukewarm about the plan.*

lull /lʌl/ *noun, verb*
• *noun* [usually sing.] **~ (in sth)** a quiet period between times of activity: *a lull in the conversation/fighting* ◆ *Just before an attack everything would go quiet but we knew it was just the lull before the storm* (= before a time of noise or trouble).
• *verb* **1** [T] **~ sb** to make someone relaxed and calm **SYN** SOOTHE: *The vibration of the engine lulled the children to sleep.* **2** [T, I] **~ (sth)** to make something, or to become, less strong: *His father's arrival lulled the boy's anxiety.* **PHR V** ,lull sb 'into sth to make someone feel confident and relaxed, especially so that they do not expect it when someone does something bad or dishonest: *His friendly manner lulled her into a false sense of security* (= made her feel safe with him when she wasn't really safe).

lull·a·by /'lʌləˌbaɪ/ *noun* (*pl.* **lull·a·bies**) a soft gentle song sung to make a child go to sleep

lum·ba·go /lʌm'beɪɡoʊ/ *noun* [U] pain in the muscles and joints of the lower back

lum·bar /'lʌmbər/ *adj.* [only before noun] (*medical*) relating to the lower part of the back

,lumbar 'puncture (also **'spinal tap**) *noun* (*medical*) the removal of liquid from the lower part of the SPINE with a hollow needle

lum·ber /'lʌmbər/ *noun, verb*
• *noun* [U] (also **tim·ber**) wood that is prepared for use in building, etc.
• *verb* [I] **+ adv./prep.** to move in a slow, heavy, and awkward way: *A family of elephants lumbered by.*

lum·ber·ing /'lʌmbərɪŋ/ *adj.* moving in a slow, heavy, and awkward way: *a lumbering dinosaur*

lum·ber·jack /'lʌmbərˌdʒæk/ (also **log·ger**) *noun* a person whose job is cutting down trees or cutting or transporting wood

lum·ber·yard /'lʌmbərˌyard/ *noun* a place where wood for building, etc. is stored and sold

lu·men /'lumən/ *noun* (*abbr.* lm) (*physics*) a unit for measuring the rate of flow of light

lu·mi·nance /'lumənəns/ *noun* [U] (*physics*) the amount of light given out in a particular direction from a particular area

lu·mi·nar·y /'luməˌnɛri/ *noun* (*pl.* **lu·mi·nar·ies**) a person who is an expert or a great influence in a special area or activity

lu·mi·nes·cence /,lumə'nɛsns/ *noun* [U] (*technical* or *literary*) a quality in something that produces light ▶ **lu·mi·nes·cent** *adj.*

lu·mi·nous /'lumənəs/ *adj.* **1** shining in the dark; giving out light: *luminous paint* ◆ *luminous hands on a clock* ◆ *staring with huge luminous eyes* ◆ (*figurative*) *the luminous quality of the music* **2** very bright in color: *They painted the door a luminous green.* ⊃ **note at BRIGHT** ▶ **lu·mi·nous·ly** *adv.* **lu·mi·nos·i·ty** /,lumə'nasəti/ *noun* [sing., U]

lump ✏ /lʌmp/ *noun, verb*
• *noun* **1** a piece of something hard or solid, usually without a particular shape: *a lump of coal/cheese/wood* ◆ *This sauce has lumps in it.* **2** = SUGAR CUBE **3** a swelling under the skin, sometimes a sign of serious illness: *He was unhurt apart from a lump on his head.* ◆ *Check your breasts for lumps every month.* **4** (*informal*) a heavy, lazy, or stupid person **IDM have, etc. a lump in your throat** to feel pressure in the throat because you are very sad or emotional **take your lumps** (*informal*) to accept bad things that happen to you without complaining
• *verb* **~ A and B together** | **~ A (in) with B** to put or consider different things together in the same group: *You can't lump all Asian languages together.* **IDM lump it** (*informal*) to accept something unpleasant because there is no other choice: *I'm sorry you're not happy about it but you'll just have to lump it.* ◆ *That's the situation—like it or lump it!*

lump·ec·to·my /,lʌm'pɛktəmi/ *noun* (*pl.* **lump·ec·to·mies**) an operation to remove a TUMOR from someone's body, especially from a woman's breast

lump·ish /'lʌmpɪʃ/ *adj.* heavy and awkward; stupid **SYN** CLUMSY

,lump 'sum (also **,lump ,sum 'payment**) *noun* an amount of money that is paid at one time and not on separate occasions

lump·y /'lʌmpi/ *adj.* full of lumps; covered in lumps: *lumpy sauce* ◆ *a lumpy mattress*

lu·na·cy /'lunəsi/ *noun* [U] **1** behavior that is stupid or crazy **SYN** MADNESS: *It's sheer lunacy to drive in this weather.* **2** (*old-fashioned*) mental illness **SYN** MADNESS

lu·nar /'lunər/ *adj.* [usually before noun] connected with the moon: *a lunar eclipse/landscape*

,lunar 'cycle *noun* (*astronomy*) a period of 19 years, after which the new moon and full moon return to the same day of the year

,lunar 'month *noun* the average time between one new moon and the next (about 29½ days) ⊃ **compare CALENDAR MONTH**

,lunar 'year *noun* a period of twelve lunar months (about 354 days)

lu·na·tic /'lunəˌtɪk/ *noun, adj.*
• *noun* **1** a person who does crazy things that are often dangerous **SYN** MANIAC: *This lunatic in a white van pulled out right in front of me!* **2** (*old-fashioned*) a person who is severely mentally ill (the use of this word is now offensive) **ORIGIN** Originally from the Latin *lunaticus* (*luna* = moon), because people believed that the changes in the moon made people go mad temporarily.
• *adj.* crazy, ridiculous, or extremely stupid: *lunatic ideas* ◆ *a lunatic smile* **IDM the lunatic fringe** (*disapproving*) those members of a political or other group whose views are considered to be very extreme and crazy

'lunatic a,sylum *noun* (*old-fashioned*) an institution where mentally ill people live (the use of this expression is now offensive)

| h hat | m man | n no | ŋ sing | l leg | r red | y yes | w wet |

lunch /lʌntʃ/ noun, verb
- **noun** [U, C] a meal eaten in the middle of the day: *She went to lunch.* ◆ *I'm ready for some lunch.* ◆ *What should we have for lunch?* ◆ *We serve hot and cold lunches.* ◆ *a one-hour lunch break* ◆ *Let's do lunch together.* ⊃ see also BAG LUNCH, BOX LUNCH ⊃ collocations at RESTAURANT **IDM out to lunch** (*informal*) behaving in a strange or confused way ⊃ more at FREE *adj.*
- **verb** [I] (*formal*) to have lunch, especially at a restaurant: *He lunched with a client at an expensive French restaurant.*

lunch·box /'lʌntʃbɑks/ noun **1** a container to hold a meal that you take from home to eat **2** a small computer that you can carry around

lunch·eon /'lʌntʃən/ noun [C, U] a formal lunch or a formal word for lunch: *a charity luncheon* ◆ *Luncheon will be served at one, Madam.*

lunch·eon·ette /ˌlʌntʃə'nɛt/ noun (*old-fashioned*) a small restaurant serving simple meals

lunch hour noun the time around the middle of the day when you stop work or school to eat lunch: *I usually go to the gym during my lunch hour.*

lunch lady noun a woman whose job is to serve meals to children in schools

lunch·meat /'lʌntʃmit/ (also **luncheon meat**) noun [U] cooked meat that is sold in slices

lunch·room /'lʌntʃrum; -rʊm/ noun a large room in a school or office where people eat lunch

lunch·time /'lʌntʃtaɪm/ noun [U, C] the time around the middle of the day when people usually eat lunch: *The package still hadn't arrived by lunchtime.* ◆ *a lunchtime concert* ◆ *The sandwich bar is generally packed at lunchtimes.*

lung /lʌŋ/ noun
either of the two organs in the chest that you use for breathing: *lung cancer* ⊃ picture at BODY **IDM** see TOP *n.*

lunge /lʌndʒ/ verb, noun
- **verb** [I] ~ **(at/toward/for sb/sth)** | ~ **(forward)** to make a sudden, powerful, forward movement, especially in order to attack someone or take hold of something
- **noun** [usually sing.] **1** ~ **(at sb)** | ~ **(for sb/sth)** a sudden, powerful, forward movement of the body and arm that a person makes toward another person or thing, especially when attacking or trying to take hold of them: *He made a lunge for the phone.* **2** (in the sport of FENCING) a THRUST made by putting one foot forward and making the back leg straight

lung·fish /'lʌŋfɪʃ/ noun (*pl.* **lung·fish**) a long fish that can breathe air and survive for a period of time out of water

lung·ful /'lʌŋfʊl/ noun the amount of something such as air or smoke that is breathed in at one time

lunk·head /'lʌŋkhɛd/ noun (*informal*) a stupid person

lu·pine¹ /'lupɪn/ noun a tall garden plant with many small flowers growing up its thick STEM

lu·pine² /'lupaɪn/ adj. (*formal*) like a WOLF; connected with a wolf or wolves

lu·pus /'lupəs/ noun [U] a disease that affects the skin or sometimes the joints

lurch /lɑrtʃ/ verb, noun
- **verb** **1** [I] (+ adv./prep.) to make a sudden unsteady movement forward or sideways **SYN** STAGGER, SWAY: *Suddenly the horse lurched to one side and the child fell off.* ◆ *The man lurched drunkenly out of the bar.* ◆ (*figurative*) *Their relationship seems to lurch from one crisis to the next.* **2** [I] if your heart or stomach **lurches**, you have a sudden feeling of fear or excitement
- **noun** [usually sing.] a sudden strong movement that moves you forward or sideways and rarely makes you lose your balance: *The train stopped with a lurch.* **IDM leave sb in the lurch** (*informal*) to fail to help someone when they are relying on you to do so

lure /lʊr/ verb, noun
- **verb** ~ **sb** (+ adv./prep.) (*disapproving*) to persuade or trick someone to go somewhere or to do something by promising them a reward **SYN** ENTICE: *The child was lured into a car but managed to escape.* ◆ *Young people are lured to the city by the prospect of a job and money.*
- **noun** **1** [usually sing.] the attractive qualities of something: *Few can resist the lure of adventure.* **2** a thing that is used to attract fish or animals, so that they can be caught

Lur·ex™ /'lʊrɛks/ noun [U] a type of thin metal thread; a cloth containing this thread, used for making clothes

lu·rid /'lʊrəd/ adj. (*disapproving*) **1** too bright in color, in a way that is not attractive **2** (especially of a story or piece of writing) shocking and violent in a way that is deliberate: *lurid headlines* ◆ *The paper gave all the lurid details of the murder.* ▶ **lu·rid·ly** adv.

lurk /lɑrk/
- **verb** **1** [I] (+ adv./prep.) to wait somewhere secretly, especially because you are going to do something bad or illegal **SYN** SKULK: *Why are you lurking around outside my house?* ◆ *A crocodile was lurking just below the surface.* **2** [I] (+ adv./prep.) when something unpleasant or dangerous lurks, it is present but not in an obvious way: *At night, danger lurks in these streets.* **3** [I] (*computing*) to read a discussion in a CHAT ROOM, etc. on the Internet, without taking part in it yourself

lus·cious /'lʌʃəs/ adj. **1** having a strong pleasant taste **SYN** DELICIOUS: *luscious fruit* **2** (of cloth, colors, or music) soft and deep or heavy in a way that is pleasing to feel, look at, or hear **SYN** RICH: *luscious silks and velvets* **3** (especially of a woman) sexually attractive

lush /lʌʃ/ adj., noun
- **adj.** **1** (of plants, gardens, etc.) growing thickly and strongly in a way that is attractive; covered in healthy grass and plants **SYN** LUXURIANT: *lush vegetation* ◆ *the lush green countryside* **2** beautiful and making you feel pleasure; seeming expensive: *a lush apartment*
- **noun** (*informal*) = ALCOHOLIC

lu·so·phone /'lusəˌfoʊn/ adj. (*technical*) speaking Portuguese as the main language

lust /lʌst/ noun, verb
- **noun** (often *disapproving*) [U, C] **1** ~ **(for sb)** very strong sexual desire, especially when love is not involved: *Their affair was driven by pure lust.* **2** ~ **(for sth)** very strong desire for something or enjoyment of something: *to satisfy his lust for power* ◆ *She has a real lust for life* (= she really enjoys life). ⊃ see also BLOODLUST
- **verb** **PHR V lust after/for sb/sth** (often *disapproving*) to feel an extremely strong, especially sexual, desire for someone or something

lus·ter (*CanE usually* **lus·tre**) /'lʌstər/ noun [U] **1** the shining quality of a surface **SYN** SHEEN: *Her hair had lost its luster.* **2** the quality of being special in a way that is exciting: *The presence of the prince added luster to the occasion.* ⊃ compare LACKLUSTER

lust·ful /'lʌstfl/ adj. (often *disapproving*) feeling or showing strong sexual desire **SYN** LASCIVIOUS

lus·trous /'lʌstrəs/ adj. (*formal*) soft and shining **SYN** GLOSSY: *thick lustrous hair*

lust·y /'lʌsti/ adj. healthy and strong **SYN** VIGOROUS: *a lusty young man* ◆ *lusty singing* ▶ **lust·i·ly** /-təli/ adv.: *singing lustily*

lute /lut/ noun an early type of musical instrument with strings, played like a GUITAR

lu·te·nist (also **lu·ta·nist**) /'lutn·ɪst/ noun a person who plays the lute

lu·te·ti·um /lu'tiʃiəm/ noun [U] (*symb.* **Lu**) a chemical element. Lutetium is a rare silver-white metal used in the nuclear industry.

Lu·ther·an /'luθərən/ noun a member of a Christian

Protestant Church that follows the teaching of the 16th century German religious leader Martin Luther ▸ **Lu·ther·an** *adj.*

lux·u·ri·ant /lʌgˈʒʊriənt/ *adj.* **1** (of plants or hair) growing thickly and strongly in a way that is attractive: *luxuriant vegetation* ◆ *thick, luxuriant hair* **2** (especially of art or the atmosphere of a place) rich in something that is pleasant or beautiful: *the poet's luxuriant imagery* ▸ **lux·u·ri·ance** /-əns/ *noun* [U]: *the luxuriance of the tropical forest*

lux·u·ri·ant·ly /lʌgˈʒʊriəntli/ *adv.* **1** in a way that is thick and attractive: *a tall, luxuriantly bearded man* **2** (especially of a way of moving your body) in a way that is comfortable and enjoyable: *She turned luxuriantly on her side, yawning.*

lux·u·ri·ate /lʌgˈʒʊriˌeɪt/ *verb*
PHR V **luˈxuriate in sth** to relax while enjoying something very pleasant: *She luxuriated in all the attention she received.*

lux·u·ri·ous /lʌgˈʒʊriəs/ *adj.* very comfortable; containing expensive and enjoyable things **SYN** SUMPTUOUS: *a luxurious hotel* ◆ *luxurious surroundings* **ANT** SPARTAN ▸ **lux·u·ri·ous·ly** *adv.*: *luxuriously comfortable* ◆ *a luxuriously furnished apartment* ◆ *She stretched luxuriously on the bed.*

lux·u·ry /ˈlʌkʃəri; ˈlʌgʒə-/ *noun* (*pl.* **lux·u·ries**) **1** [U] the enjoyment of special and expensive things, particularly food and drinks, clothes, and surroundings: *Now we'll be able to live in luxury for the rest of our lives.* ◆ *to lead a life of luxury* ◆ *a luxury hotel* ◆ *luxury goods* **2** [C] a thing that is expensive and enjoyable but not essential **SYN** EXTRAVAGANCE: *small luxuries like chocolate and flowers* ◆ *I love having a long, hot bath—it's one of life's little luxuries.* ◆ *It was a luxury if you had a washing machine in those days.* **3** [U, sing.] a pleasure or an advantage that you do not often have **SYN** INDULGENCE: *We had the luxury of being able to choose from four good candidates for the job.* **IDM** see LAP *n.*

LW *abbr.* LONG WAVE: *1500 m. LW*

-ly /li/ *suffix* **1** (in adverbs) in the way mentioned: *happily* ◆ *stupidly* **2** (in adjectives) having the qualities of: *cowardly* ◆ *scholarly* **3** (in adjectives and adverbs) at intervals of: *hourly* ◆ *daily*

ly·chee (also **li·chee, li·tchi**) /ˈliːtʃi/ *noun* a small Chinese fruit with thick, rough, pink-red skin, white flesh, and a large seed inside ᕲ picture at FRUIT

lych·gate (also **lich·gate**) /ˈlɪtʃɡeɪt/ *noun* a gate with a roof at the entrance to a CHURCHYARD

Ly·cra™ /ˈlaɪkrə/ *noun* [U] an artificial material that stretches, used for making clothes that fit close to the body

lye /laɪ/ *noun* [U] a chemical used in various industrial processes, including washing

ly·ing pres part of LIE¹

lying-ˈin *noun* [sing.] (*old-fashioned*) the period of time during which a woman in the past stayed in bed before and after giving birth to a child

lying-inˈstate *noun* [U] the period when the dead body of a ruler is displayed to the public before being buried; the display of the body in this way

Lyme disˈease /ˈlaɪm dɪˌziz/ *noun* [U] a serious disease that causes fever and pain in the joints of the body, caused by bacteria carried by TICKS (= small insects)

lymph /lɪmf/ *noun* [U] a clear liquid containing white blood cells that helps to clean the TISSUES of the body and helps to prevent infections from spreading ▸ **lym·phat·ic** /lɪmˈfætɪk/ *adj.* [only before noun]: *the lymphatic system*

ˈlymph node (also **ˈlymph gland**) *noun* one of the small round parts of the lymphatic system that stores lymphocytes and helps fight infection

lym·pho·cyte /ˈlɪmfəˌsaɪt/ *noun* (*biology*) a type of small white blood cell with one round NUCLEUS, found especially in the lymphatic system

lym·pho·ma /lɪmˈfoʊmə/ *noun* [U] cancer of the LYMPH NODES

lynch /lɪntʃ/ *verb* ~ **sb** if a crowd of people **lynches** someone whom they consider guilty of a crime, they capture them, do not allow them to have a trial in court, and kill them illegally, usually by hanging ▸ **lynch·ing** *noun* [C, U]

ˈlynch mob *noun* a crowd of people who gather to lynch someone

lynch·pin = LINCHPIN

lynx /lɪŋks/ *noun* (*pl.* **lynx** or **lynx·es**) a wild animal of the cat family, with spots on its fur and a very short tail

lyre /ˈlaɪər/ *noun* an ancient musical instrument with strings fastened in a frame shaped like a U. It was played with the fingers.

lyre·bird /ˈlaɪərˌbərd/ *noun* a large Australian bird

lyr·ic /ˈlɪrɪk/ *adj., noun*
● *adj.* **1** (of poetry) expressing a person's personal feelings and thoughts ᕲ compare EPIC **2** connected with, or written for, singing
● *noun* **1** [C] a lyric poem ᕲ compare EPIC **2 lyrics** [pl.] the words of a song: *music and lyrics by Rodgers and Hart*

lyr·i·cal /ˈlɪrɪkl/ *adj.* expressing strong emotion in a way that is beautiful and shows imagination **SYN** EXPRESSIVE: *a lyrical melody* ◆ *He began to **wax lyrical** (= talk in an enthusiastic way) about his new car.*

lyr·i·cal·ly /ˈlɪrɪkli/ *adv.* **1** in a way that expresses strong emotion **2** connected with the words of a song: *Both musically and lyrically it is very effective.*

lyr·i·cism /ˈlɪrəˌsɪzəm/ *noun* [U] the expression of strong emotion in poetry, art, music, etc.

lyr·i·cist /ˈlɪrəsɪst/ *noun* a person who writes the words of songs

ʌ **cup**   ə **about**   eɪ **say**   aɪ **five**   ɔɪ **boy**   aʊ **now**   oʊ **go**   ər **bird**

Mm

M /ɛm/ noun, abbr., symbol
- **noun** also **m** [C, U] (pl. **Ms, M's, m's** /ɛmz/) the 13th letter of the English alphabet: *"Milk" begins with (an) M/"M."*
- **abbr.** (also **med.**) (especially for sizes of clothes) medium: *S, M, and L* (= small, medium, and large)
- **symbol** also **m** the number 1,000 in ROMAN NUMERALS

m. (also **m**) abbr. **1** male **2** married **3** meter(s): *the 100m sprint* **4** million(s): *population: 10 m.*

MA abbr. (in writing) Massachusetts

M.A. (also **MA**) /ˌɛm ˈeɪ/ noun a second university degree in an ARTS subject (the abbreviation for "Master of Arts"): *to have/get an M.A.*

ma /mɑ/ noun (informal) mother: *I'm going now, ma.* ◆ *"I want my ma," sobbed the little girl.*

ma'am /mæm/ noun [sing.] used as a polite way of addressing a woman: *"Can I help you, ma'am?"* ➔ compare SIR

Mac /mæk/ noun [sing.] (informal) used to address a man whose name you do not know

ma·ca·bre /məˈkɑbrə; -ˈkɑb/ adj. unpleasant and strange because connected with death and frightening things **SYN** GRISLY: *a macabre tale/joke/ritual*

mac·ad·am /məˈkædəm/ noun [U] a road surface made of layers of broken stones, mixed with TAR

mac·a·da·mi·a /ˌmækəˈdeɪmiə/ (also **maca'damia ˌnut**) noun the round nut of an Australian tree ➔ picture at NUT

ma·caque /məˈkæk; -ˈkɑk/ noun a type of MONKEY that lives in Africa and Asia

mac·a·ro·ni /ˌmækəˈrouni/ noun [U] PASTA in the shape of hollow tubes

ˌmacaroni and ˈcheese noun [U] a hot dish of macaroni in a cheese sauce

mac·a·roon /ˌmækəˈrun/ noun a soft, round, sweet cookie made with ALMONDS or COCONUT

ma·caw /məˈkɔ/ noun a large Central and S. American tropical bird of the PARROT family, with bright feathers and a long tail

Mace™ /meɪs/ noun [U] a chemical that makes your eyes and skin sting, that some people, including police officers, carry in spray cans so that they can defend themselves against people attacking them

mace /meɪs/ noun **1** [C] a decorative stick, carried by an official as a sign of authority ➔ compare SCEPTER¹ **2** [C] a large heavy stick that has a head with metal points on it, used in the past as a weapon **3** [U] the dried outer covering of NUTMEG (= the hard nut of a tropical tree), used in cooking as a spice ➔ picture at HERB

mac·er·ate /ˈmæsəˌreɪt/ verb [T, I] ~ (**sth**) (technical) to make something (especially food) soft by leaving it in a liquid; to become soft in this way

Mach /mɑk/ noun [U] (often followed by a number) a measurement of speed, used especially for aircraft. Mach 1 is the speed of sound.: *a fighter plane with a top speed of Mach 3* (= 3 times the speed of sound)

ma·chet·e /məˈʃɛti/ noun a broad heavy knife used as a cutting tool and as a weapon

Mach·i·a·vel·li·an /ˌmækiəˈvɛliən/ adj. (formal, disapproving) using intelligent or skillful plans to achieve what you want, without people realizing what you are doing **SYN** CUNNING, UNSCRUPULOUS **ORIGIN** From the name of Niccolò Machiavelli, an Italian politician (1469-1527), who explained in his book, *The Prince*, that it was often necessary for rulers to use immoral methods in order to achieve power and success.

mach·i·na·tion /ˌmækəˈneɪʃn; ˌmæʃə-/ noun [usually pl.] (disapproving) a secret and complicated plan **SYN** INTRIGUE, PLOT

ma·chine /məˈʃin/ noun, verb
- **noun 1** (often in compounds) a piece of equipment with moving parts that is designed to do a particular job. The power used to work a machine may be electricity, steam, gas, etc. or human power.: *Machines have replaced human labor in many industries.* ◆ *to operate/run a machine* ◆ *How does this machine work?* ◆ *a washing/sewing machine* ◆ *a machine for making plastic toys* ◆ *I left a message on her answering machine.* ◆ *The potatoes are planted by machine.* ➔ see also VOTING MACHINE **2** (informal) a particular machine, for example in the home, when you do not refer to it by its full name: *Just put those clothes in the machine* (= the washing machine). ◆ *The new machines* (= computers) *will be shipped next month.* **3** a group of people that control an organization or part of an organization: *the president's propaganda machine* **4** (often disapproving) a person who acts automatically, without allowing their feelings to show or to affect their work ➔ see also MECHANICAL, SLOT MACHINE, TIME MACHINE **HELP** You will find other compounds ending in **machine** at their place in the alphabet. **IDM** see COG
- **verb** [T, I] ~ (**sth**) (technical) to make or shape something with a machine: *This material can be cut and machined easily.*

ma'chine code (also **ma'chine ˌlanguage**) noun [C, U] (computing) a code in which instructions are written in the form of numbers so that a computer can understand and act on them

ma'chine gun noun a gun that automatically fires many bullets one after the other very quickly: *a burst/hail of machine-gun fire*

ma'chine-gun verb (-nn-) ~ **sb/sth** to shoot at someone or something with a machine gun

ma'chine-made adj. made by a machine ➔ compare HANDMADE

ma,chine-ˈreadable adj. (of data) in a form that a computer can understand

ma·chin·er·y /məˈʃinəri/ noun
1 [U] machines as a group, especially large ones: *agricultural/industrial machinery* ◆ *a piece of machinery* **2** [U] the parts of a machine that make it work **3** [U, sing.] the organization or structure of something; the system for doing something: ~ (**of sth**) *the machinery of government* ◆ ~ (**for doing sth**) *There is no machinery for resolving disputes.*

ma'chine tool noun a tool for cutting or shaping metal, wood, etc., driven by a machine

ma,chine transˈlation noun [U] the process of translating language by computer

ma·chin·ist /məˈʃinɪst/ noun **1** a person whose job is operating a machine, especially machines used in industry for cutting and shaping things, or a sewing machine **2** a person whose job is to make or repair machines

ma·chis·mo /mɑˈtʃizmou; məˈtʃɪz-/ noun [U] (from Spanish, usually disapproving) aggressive male behavior that emphasizes the importance of being strong rather than being intelligent and sensitive

ma·cho /ˈmɑtʃou/ adj. (usually disapproving) male in an aggressive way: *He's too macho to ever admit he was wrong.* ◆ *macho pride/posturing*

mack·er·el /ˈmækərəl; ˈmækrəl/ noun (pl. **mack·er·el**) [C, U] an ocean fish with green-blue bands on its body, that is used for food: *smoked mackerel*

mac·ra·mé /ˈmækrəˌmeɪ/ noun [U] the art of tying knots in string in a decorative way, to make things

mac·ro /ˈmækrou/ noun (pl. **mac·ros**) (computing) a single instruction in a computer program that automatically causes a complete series of instructions to be put into effect, in order to perform a particular task

macro- /'mækrou/ *combining form* (in nouns, adjectives, and adverbs) large; on a large scale: *macroeconomics* **ANT** MICRO-

mac·ro·bi·ot·ic /ˌmækroubaɪˈɑtɪk/ *adj.* consisting of whole grains and vegetables grown without chemical treatment: *a macrobiotic diet*

mac·ro·cosm /'mækrəˌkɑzəm/ *noun* any large complete structure that contains smaller structures, for example the universe ➔ compare MICROCOSM

mac·ro·ec·o·nom·ics /ˌmækrouˌɛkəˈnɑmɪks; -ˌikə-/ *noun* [U] the study of large economic systems, such as those of whole countries or areas of the world ▶ **mac·ro·ec·o·nom·ic** *adj.*: *macroeconomic policy*

ma·cron /'meɪkrɑn/ *noun* (*linguistics*) the mark (¯) that is placed over a vowel in some languages and in the International Phonetic Alphabet to show that the vowel is stressed or long

mac·ro·phage /'mækrəˌfeɪdʒ/ *noun* (*biology*) a large cell that is able to remove harmful substances from the body, and is found in blood and TISSUE

mad 🖉 /mæd/ *adj.* (**mad·der**, **mad·dest**)
1 [not before noun] ~ (**at sb**) | ~ (**about sth**) (*informal*) very angry: *He got mad and walked out.* ◆ *She's mad at me for being late.* ➔ thesaurus box at ANGRY **2** done without thought or control; wild and excited: *The crowd made a mad rush for the exit.* ◆ *Only a mad dash got them to the meeting on time.*
3 having a mind that does not work normally; mentally ill: *They realized that he had gone mad.* ◆ *Inventors are not mad scientists.* ◆ *I'll go mad if I have to wait much longer.* ◆ *She seemed to have gone stark raving mad.* **4** [not usually before noun] ~ (**about sth/sb**) (*informal*) liking something or someone very much; very interested in something: *to be mad about tennis* ◆ *He's always been mad about kids.* ◆ *She's completely power-mad.* **5** (*informal*) very stupid; not at all sensible: *You must be mad to risk it.* ◆ *It was a mad idea.* ➔ compare CRAZY
IDM **like crazy/mad** (*informal*) very fast, hard, much, etc.: *I had to run like mad to catch the bus.* **(as) mad as a hatter/a March hare** (*informal*) (of a person) mentally ill; very silly **ORIGIN** From the Mad Hatter, a character in Lewis Carroll's *Alice's Adventures in Wonderland*. Because of the chemicals used in hat-making, workers often suffered from mercury poisoning, which can cause loss of memory and damage to the nervous system. A **March hare** was called mad because of the strange behavior of hares during the mating season. ➔ more at HOPPING

mad·am /'mædəm/ *noun* **1** [sing.] (*formal*) used when speaking or writing to a woman in a formal or business situation: *Can I help you, madam?* ◆ *Dear Madam* (= used like *Dear Sir* in a letter) **2** used before an official title to address or refer to a woman holding that rank or position : *Madam President* ◆ *Madam Ambassador* **3** [C] a woman who is in charge of the PROSTITUTES in a BROTHEL

mad·cap /'mædkæp/ *adj.* [usually before noun] (*informal*) (of people, plans etc.) crazy and not caring about danger; not sensible **SYN** RECKLESS: *madcap schemes/escapades*

mad 'cow dis·ease *noun* [U] (*informal*) = BSE

mad·den /'mædn/ *verb* [usually passive] ~ **sb/sth** to make a person or an animal very angry or crazy **SYN** INFURIATE ▶ **mad·den·ing** /'mædn·ɪŋ; 'mædnɪŋ/ *adj.*: *maddening delays* **mad·den·ing·ly** *adv.*: *Progress is maddeningly slow.*

mad·ding /'mædɪŋ/ *adj.* (*literary*) behaving in a crazy way; making you feel angry or crazy
IDM **far from the madding crowd** in a quiet and private place

made /meɪd/ **1** pt, pp of MAKE **2** **-made** (in adjectives) made in the way, place, etc. mentioned: *well-made* ◆ *homemade* ➔ see also SELF-MADE
IDM **have (got) it made** (*informal*) to be sure of success; to

have everything that you want **(be) made for sb/each other** to be completely suited to someone/each other: *Peter and Judy seem made for each other, don't they?* **what sb is made of** (*informal*) how someone reacts in a difficult situation

Ma·dei·ra /məˈdɪrə; -ˈdɛrə/ (also **Ma·deira 'wine**) *noun* **1** [U, C] a strong, sweet, white wine from the island of Madeira **2** [C] a glass of Madeira

mad·e·leine /'mædl·ən; ˌmædlˈeɪn; -ˈɛn/ *noun* a type of small cake

made to 'measure *adj.* (of clothes, curtains, etc.) made specially to fit a particular person, window, etc.

made to 'order *adj.* (of clothes, furniture, etc.) made specially for a particular customer

made-'up *adj.* **1** wearing makeup: *a heavily made-up face/woman* **2** not true or real; invented: *a made-up story/word/name*

mad·house /'mædhaʊs/ *noun* **1** [usually sing.] (*informal*) a place where there is confusion and noise: *Don't work in that department; it's a madhouse.* **2** (*old use*) a hospital for people who are mentally ill

Mad·i·son Av·e·nue /ˌmædəsn ˈævənu/ *noun* [U] the U.S. advertising industry **ORIGIN** From the name of the street in New York where many advertising companies have their offices.

mad·ly /'mædli/ *adv.* **1** (only used *after* a verb) in a way that shows a lack of control: *She was rushing around madly trying to put out the fire.* ◆ *His heart thudded madly against his ribs.* **2** (*informal*) very; extremely: *madly excited/jealous* ◆ *She's madly in love with him.*

mad·man /'mædmæn; -mən/ *noun* (*pl.* **mad·men** /-mɛn; -mən/) a man who has a serious mental illness or acts in a wild or uncontrolled way: *The killing was the act of a madman.* ◆ *He drove like a madman.* ◆ *Some madman* (= stupid person) *deleted all the files.* ➔ see also MADWOMAN

mad·ness /'mædnəs/ *noun* [U] **1** (*old-fashioned*) the state of having a serious mental illness **SYN** INSANITY: *There may be a link between madness and creativity.* **2** crazy or stupid behavior that could be dangerous: *It would be sheer madness to trust a man like that.* ◆ *In a moment of madness she had agreed to go out with him.* ➔ see also MARCH MADNESS
IDM see METHOD

ma·don·na /məˈdɑnə/ *noun* **1** the Madonna [sing.] the Virgin Mary, mother of Jesus Christ **2** [C] a statue or picture of the Virgin Mary

ma·dra·sa (also **ma·dra·sah** /məˈdrɑsə; -ˈdræsə/) *noun* a college where the Islamic faith is taught

mad·ri·gal /'mædrɪɡl/ *noun* a song for several singers, usually without musical instruments, popular in the 16th century

mad·wom·an /'mædˌwʊmən/ *noun* (*pl.* **mad·wom·en** /-ˌwɪmən/) a woman who has a serious mental illness or acts in a wild or uncontrolled way ➔ see also MADMAN

mael·strom /'meɪlstrɑm; -strəm/ *noun* [usually sing.] **1** (*literary*) a situation full of strong emotions or confusing events, that is hard to control and makes you feel frightened **2** a very strong current of water that moves in circles **SYN** WHIRLPOOL

maes·tro /'maɪstrou/ *noun* (*pl.* **maes·tros**) (often used as a way of addressing someone, showing respect) a great performer, especially a musician: *Maestro Giulini* ◆ *The winning goal was scored by the maestro himself.*

Ma·fi·a /'mɑfiə/ *noun* **1** the Mafia [sing.] a secret organization of criminals, that is active especially in Sicily, Italy, and the U.S. **2** mafia [C] a group of people within an organization or a community who use their power to get advantages for themselves: *a member of the local mafia* ◆ *Politics is still dominated by the middle-class mafia.*

Ma·fi·o·so /ˌmɑfiˈousou/ *noun* (*pl.* **Ma·fi·o·si** /-si/) a member of the Mafia

mag·a·zine 🔑 /ˈmægəˌziːn; ˌmægəˈziːn/ noun
1 (also informal **mag** /mæg/) a type of large thin book with a paper cover that you can buy every week or month, containing articles, photographs, etc., often on a particular topic: *a weekly/monthly magazine* ♦ *a magazine article/interview* ♦ *Her designer clothes were from the pages of a glossy fashion magazine.* **2** a radio or television program that is about a particular topic: *a regional news magazine on TV* ♦ *a magazine program* **3** the part of a gun that holds the bullets before they are fired **4** a room or building where weapons, EXPLOSIVES, and bullets are stored

ma·gen·ta /məˈdʒentə/ adj. red-purple in color
▶ **ma·gen·ta** noun [U]

mag·got /ˈmægət/ noun a creature like a small short WORM, that is the young form of a fly and is found in decaying meat and other food. Maggots are often used as BAIT on a hook to catch fish.

Ma·gi /ˈmeɪdʒaɪ/ **the Magi** noun [pl.] (in the Bible) the three wise men from the East who are said to have brought presents to the baby Jesus ⊃ see also MAGUS

mag·ic 🔑 /ˈmædʒɪk/ noun, adj., verb
● **noun** [U] **1** the secret power of appearing to make impossible things happen by saying special words or doing special things: *Do you believe in magic?* ♦ *He suddenly appeared as if by magic.* ♦ *A passage was cleared through the crowd like magic.* ⊃ see also BLACK MAGIC **2** the art of doing tricks that seem impossible in order to entertain people **SYN** CONJURING **3** a special quality or ability that someone or something has, that seems too wonderful to be real **SYN** ENCHANTMENT: *dance and music which capture the magic of India* ♦ *Like all truly charismatic people, he can work his magic on both men and women.* ♦ *Our year in Italy was pure/sheer magic.* **IDM** see WEAVE v.
● **adj. 1** having or using special powers to make impossible things happen or seem to happen: *a magic spell/charm/potion/trick* ♦ *There is no magic formula for passing exams—only hard work.* **2** (informal) having a special quality that makes something seem wonderful: *It was a magic moment when the two sisters were reunited after 30 years.* ♦ *She has a magic touch with the children and they do everything she asks.* ♦ *Trust is the magic ingredient in our relationship.*
● **verb** (-ck-) ~ sb/sth + adv./prep. to make someone or something appear somewhere, disappear, or turn into something, by magic, or as if by magic

mag·i·cal /ˈmædʒɪkl/ adj. **1** containing magic; used in magic: *magical powers* ♦ *Her words had a magical effect on us.* **2** (informal) wonderful; very enjoyable **SYN** ENCHANTING: *a truly magical feeling* ♦ *We spent a magical week in Paris.*
▶ **mag·i·cally** /-kli/ adv.

ˌ**magical 'realism** noun [U] = MAGIC REALISM

ˌ**magic 'bullet** noun **1** (medical) a medical treatment that works very quickly and effectively against a particular illness **2** a fast and effective solution to a serious problem **SYN** SILVER BULLET

ˌ**magic 'carpet** noun (in stories) a carpet that can fly and carry people

ma·gi·cian /məˈdʒɪʃn/ noun **1** a person who can do magic tricks **SYN** CONJUROR **2** (in stories) a person who has magic powers **SYN** SORCERER

ˌ**magic 'lantern** noun a piece of equipment used in the past to make pictures appear on a white wall or screen

ˌ**Magic 'Marker™** noun a type of pen with a thick point that writes in permanent ink

ˌ**magic 'mushroom** (also **shroom**) noun (informal) a type of MUSHROOM that has an effect like some drugs and that may make people who eat it HALLUCINATE (= see things that are not there)

ˌ**magic 'realism** (also ˌ**magical 'realism**) noun [U] a style of writing that mixes realistic events with FANTASY

ˌ**magic 'wand** noun = WAND: *I wish I could wave a magic wand and make everything all right again.*

mag·is·te·ri·al /ˌmædʒəˈstɪriəl/ adj. (formal) **1** (especially of a person or their behavior) having or showing power or authority: *He talked with the magisterial authority of the head of the family.* **2** (of a book or piece of writing) showing great knowledge or understanding **SYN** AUTHORITATIVE: *his magisterial work "The Roman Wall in Scotland"* **3** [only before noun] connected with a magistrate ▶ **mag·is·te·ri·al·ly** adv.

the mag·is·tra·cy /ˈmædʒəstrəsi/ noun [sing.] magistrates as a group

mag·is·trate /ˈmædʒəˌstreɪt/ noun an official who acts as a judge in the lowest courts of law **SYN** JUSTICE OF THE PEACE: *a magistrates' court* ♦ *to come up before the magistrates*

mag·ma /ˈmægmə/ noun [U] (technical) very hot liquid rock found below the earth's surface ⊃ picture at VOLCANO

Mag·na Car·ta /ˌmægnə ˈkɑrtə/ noun a document officially stating the political and legal rights of the English people, that King John was forced to sign in 1215 (often referred to as the basis for modern English law)

mag·na cum lau·de /ˌmægnə kʊm ˈlaʊdə; -kʌm ˈlɔːdə; -di/ adv., adj. (from Latin) at the second of the three highest levels of achievement that students can reach when they finish their studies at college: *She graduated magna cum laude from UCLA.* ⊃ compare CUM LAUDE, SUMMA CUM LAUDE

mag·nan·i·mous /mægˈnænəməs/ adj. (formal) kind, generous, and forgiving, especially toward an enemy or a rival: *a magnanimous gesture* ♦ *He was magnanimous in defeat and praised his opponent's skill.* ▶ **mag·na·nim·i·ty** /ˌmægnəˈnɪməti/ noun [U]: *She accepted the criticism with magnanimity.* **mag·nan·i·mous·ly** adv.

mag·nate /ˈmægneɪt; -nət/ noun a person who is rich, powerful, and successful, especially in business: *a media/property/shipping magnate*

mag·ne·sia /mægˈniʒə/ noun [U] a white substance containing magnesium, used to help with INDIGESTION

mag·ne·si·um /mægˈniziəm/ noun [U] (symb. **Mg**) a chemical element. Magnesium is a light, silver-white metal that burns with a bright white flame.

mag·net /ˈmægnət/ noun **1** a piece of iron that attracts objects made of iron toward it, either naturally or because of an electric current that is passed through it ⊃ picture at LABORATORY **2** [usually sing.] ~ (for sb/sth) a person, place, or thing that someone or something is attracted to: *In the 1990s the area became a magnet for new investment.* **3** an object with a magnetic surface that you can stick onto a metal surface: *refrigerator magnets*

mag·net·ic /mægˈnetɪk/ adj. [usually before noun]
1 behaving like a magnet: *magnetic materials* ♦ *The block becomes magnetic when the current is switched on.*
2 connected with or produced by magnetism: *magnetic properties/forces* ♦ *a magnetic disk* (= one containing magnetic tape that stores information to be used by a computer) **3** that people find very powerful and attractive: *a magnetic personality* ▶ **mag·net·i·cally** /-kli/ adv.

mag·netic 'compass noun = COMPASS

mag·netic 'field noun an area around a MAGNET or MAGNETIC object, where there is a force that will attract some metals toward it

mag·netic 'media noun [pl., U] the different methods, for example MAGNETIC TAPE, that are used to store information for computers

mag·netic 'north noun [U] the direction that is approximately north as it is shown on a COMPASS ⊃ compare TRUE NORTH

mag·netic 'pole noun **1** one of the two points on the earth, near the North and South Poles, toward which a COMPASS needle points **2** either of the two ends of a MAGNET

mag·netic 'storm noun a situation in which the magnetic field of the earth or of another planet, star, etc. is disturbed

mag,netic 'strip noun a line of magnetic material on a plastic card, containing information

mag,netic 'tape noun [U] a type of plastic tape that is used for recording sound, pictures, or computer information

mag·net·ism /ˈmægnəˌtɪzəm/ noun [U] **1** a physical property (= characteristic) of some metals such as iron, produced by electric currents, that causes forces between objects, either pulling them toward each other or pushing them apart **2** the qualities of something, especially a person's character, that people find powerful and attractive: *She exudes sexual magnetism.*

mag·net·ize /ˈmægnəˌtaɪz/ verb **1** [usually passive] ~ sth (*technical*) to make something metal behave like a MAGNET **2** ~ sb to strongly attract someone: *Cities have a powerful magnetizing effect on young people.*

mag·ne·to /mægˈniɾoʊ/ noun (pl. **mag·ne·tos**) a small piece of equipment that uses MAGNETS to produce the electricity that lights the fuel in the engine of a car, etc.

magnet ,school noun a school in a large city that offers extra courses in some subjects in order to attract students from other areas of the city

mag·ni·fi·ca·tion /ˌmægnəfəˈkeɪʃn/ noun **1** [U] the act of making something look larger: *The insects were examined under magnification.* **2** [C, U] the degree to which something is made to look larger; the degree to which something is able to make things look larger: *a magnification of 10 times the actual size* ◆ *high/low magnification* ◆ *The telescope has a magnification of 50.*

mag·nif·i·cent /mægˈnɪfəsnt/ adj. extremely attractive and impressive; deserving praise **SYN** SPLENDID: *The Taj Mahal is a magnificent building.* ◆ *She looked magnificent in her wedding dress.* ◆ *You've all done a magnificent job.*
▶ **mag·nif·i·cence** /-sns/ noun [U]: *the magnificence of the scenery* **mag·nif·i·cent·ly** adv.: *The public has responded magnificently to our appeal.*

mag·ni·fi·er /ˈmægnəˌfaɪər/ noun a piece of equipment that is used to make things look larger

mag·ni·fy /ˈmægnəˌfaɪ/ verb (**mag·ni·fies, mag·ni·fy·ing, mag·ni·fied, mag·ni·fied**) **1** ~ sth (to/by sth) to make something look bigger than it really is, for example by using a LENS or MICROSCOPE **SYN** ENLARGE: *bacteria magnified to 1,000 times their actual size* ◆ *an image magnified by a factor of 4* **2** ~ sth to make something bigger, louder, or stronger: *The sound was magnified by the high roof.* ◆ *The dry summer has magnified the problem of water shortages.* **3** ~ sth to make something seem more important or serious than it really is **SYN** EXAGGERATE

magnifying ,glass noun a piece of glass, usually with a handle, that you look through and that makes things look bigger than they really are ⊃ picture at HOBBY

mag·ni·tude /ˈmægnəˌtud/ noun ~ (of sth) **1** [U] (*formal*) the great size or importance of something; the degree to which something is large or important: *We did not realize the magnitude of the problem.* ◆ *a discovery of the first magnitude* **2** [C, U] (*astronomy*) the degree to which a star is bright: *The star varies in brightness by about three magnitudes.* **3** [C, U] (*geology*) the size of an EARTHQUAKE

mag·no·lia /mægˈnoʊlyə/ noun a tree with large white, pink, or purple flowers that smell sweet

mag·num /ˈmægnəm/ noun a bottle containing 1.5 liters of wine, etc.

magnum 'opus noun [sing.] (from *Latin*) a work of art, music, or literature that people think is the best that the artist, etc. has ever produced

mag·pie /ˈmægpaɪ/ noun a black and white bird with a long tail and a noisy cry. There is a popular belief that magpies like to steal small bright objects.

ma·gus /ˈmeɪgəs/ noun (pl. **ma·gi** /ˈmeɪdʒaɪ/) **1** a member of the group to which priests in ancient Persia belonged **2** a man with magic powers ⊃ see also MAGI

ma·ha·ra·ja (also **ma·ha·ra·jah**) /ˌmɑhəˈrɑdʒə; -ˈrɑʒə/ noun an Indian prince, especially one who ruled over one of the states of India in the past

ma·ha·ra·ni (also **ma·ha·ra·nee**) /ˌmɑhəˈrɑni/ noun the wife of a maharaja

Ma·ha·ri·shi /ˌmɑhəˈrɪʃi/ noun a Hindu spiritual leader or wise man

ma·hat·ma /məˈhɑtmə/ noun **1** a holy person in S. Asia who is respected by many people **2 the Mahatma** Mahatma Gandhi, the Indian spiritual leader who opposed British rule in India

Ma·ha·ya·na /ˌmɑhəˈyɑnə/ (also **,Maha,yana 'Buddhism**) noun [U] one of the two major forms of Buddhism ⊃ compare THERAVADA

Ma·hi·can /məˈhikən/ (also **Mo·hi·can**) noun a member of a Native American people originally from the northeastern states, around the Hudson River valley

mah·jong (also **mah·jongg**) /ˈmɑʒɑŋ; -ʒɔŋ; -dʒɑŋ; -dʒɔŋ/ noun [U] (from *Chinese*) a Chinese game played with small pieces of wood with symbols on them

ma·hog·a·ny /məˈhɑgəni/ noun [U] **1** the hard red-brown wood of a tropical tree, used for making furniture: *a mahogany table* **2** a red-brown color: *skin tanned to a deep mahogany*

ma·hout /məˈhaʊt/ noun a person who works with, rides, and cares for an ELEPHANT

maid /meɪd/ noun **1** (often in compounds) a female servant in a house or hotel: *There is a maid to do the housework.* ⊃ see also CHAMBERMAID, DAIRYMAID, HOUSEMAID, MILKMAID, NURSEMAID **2** (*old use*) a young woman who is not married ⊃ see also OLD MAID

maid·en /ˈmeɪdn/ noun, adj.
• **noun 1** (*literary*) a young girl or woman who is not married: *stories of knights and fair maidens*
• **adj.** [only before noun] being the first of its kind: *a maiden flight/voyage* (= the first journey made by a plane/ship)

,maiden 'aunt noun (*old-fashioned*) an aunt who has not married

maid·en·hair /ˈmeɪdnˌhɛr/ (also **,maidenhair 'fern**) noun [U, C] a type of FERN with long thin STEMS and delicate pale green leaves that are shaped like fans

maidenhair ,tree noun = GINKGO

maid·en·head /ˈmeɪdnˌhɛd/ noun (*old use*) **1** the state of being a VIRGIN **2** = HYMEN

,maiden 'name noun a woman's family name before marriage: *Kate kept her maiden name when she got married* (= did not change her surname to that of her husband).

,maid of 'honor noun (pl. **maids of honor**) a young woman or girl who is not married and who is the main BRIDESMAID at a wedding ⊃ compare MATRON OF HONOR

maid·serv·ant /ˈmeɪdˌsərvənt/ noun (*old-fashioned*) a female servant in a house

mail /meɪl/ noun, verb
• **noun** [U] **1** the official system used for sending and delivering letters, packages, etc.: *a mail service/train/truck* ◆ *Your check is in the mail.* ◆ *We do our business by mail.* ⊃ see also AIRMAIL, SNAIL MAIL, VOICE MAIL **2** letters, packages, etc. that are sent and delivered: *There isn't much mail today.* ◆ *I sat down to open the mail.* ◆ *Is there a letter from them in the mail?* ◆ *hate mail* (= letters containing insults and threats) ⊃ see also JUNK MAIL, RETURN MAIL, SURFACE MAIL **3** messages that are sent or received on a computer: *Check regularly for new mail.* ⊃ see also ELECTRONIC MAIL, E-MAIL **4** = CHAIN MAIL: *a coat of mail*
• **verb 1** to send something to someone using the POSTAL system: ~ sth (to sb/sth) *Don't forget to mail that letter to your mother.* ◆ ~ sb sth *Don't forget to mail your mother that letter.* **2** to send a message to someone by e-mail: ~ sb *Please mail us at the following e-mail address.* ◆ ~ sth (to sb/sth) *The virus mails itself forward to everyone in your address*

book. ♦ **~ sb sth** *Can you mail me that document you mentioned?*

PHR V ˌmail sth↔ˈout to send out a large number of letters, etc. at the same time: *The brochures were mailed out last week.*

mail·bag /ˈmeɪlbæg/ *noun* **1** a large strong bag that is used for carrying letters and packages **2** [usually sing.] all the letters, e-mails, etc. received by a newspaper, a TV station, a Web site, or an important person at a particular time or about a particular subject

ˈmail bomb *noun, verb*
- *noun* **1** = LETTER BOMB **2** an extremely large number of e-mail messages that are sent to someone
- *verb* ˈmail-bomb **~ sb/sth** to send someone an extremely large number of e-mail messages: *The newspaper was mail-bombed by angry readers after the article was published.*

mail·box /ˈmeɪlbɑks/ *noun*
1 a small box near the main door of a building or by the road, which mail is delivered to ⊃ picture at HOUSE **2** a public box, for example in the street, that you put letters into when you send them **3** the area of a computer's memory where e-mail messages are stored

mailboxes

ˈmail ˌcarrier (also ˈletter ˌcarrier) *noun* ⊃ MAILMAN

ˈmail drop *noun* **1** an address where someone's mail is delivered, which is not where they live or work **2** a box in a building where someone's mail is kept for them to collect

mail·er /ˈmeɪlər/ *noun* **1** an envelope, box, etc. for sending small things by mail **2** = MAILING

mail·ing /ˈmeɪlɪŋ/ *noun* **1** [U] the act of sending items by mail: *The strike has delayed the mailing of tax reminders.* ♦ *a mailing address* **2** (also mail·er) [C] a letter or package that is sent by mail, especially one that is sent to a large number of people: *An order form is included in the mailing.*

ˈmailing ˌlist *noun* **1** a list of the names and addresses of people who are regularly sent information, advertising material, etc. by an organization: *I am already on your mailing list.* **2** a list of names and e-mail addresses kept on a computer so that you can send a message to a number of people at the same time

mail·man /ˈmeɪlmæn/ *noun* (*pl.* mail·men /-mɛn/) (also ˈmail ˌcarrier, ˈletter ˌcarrier) a person whose job is to collect and deliver letters, etc.

Mail·merge™ /ˈmeɪlmərdʒ/ *noun* [U] a computer program that allows names and addresses to be automatically added to letters and envelopes, so that letters with the same contents can be sent to many different people

ˈmail ˌorder *noun* [U] a system of buying and selling goods through the mail: *All our products are available by mail order.* ♦ *a mail-order company* ♦ *a mail-order catalog*

ˈmail slot *noun* a narrow opening in a door or wall through which mail is delivered

maim /meɪm/ *verb* **~ sb** to injure someone seriously, causing permanent damage to their body
SYN INCAPACITATE: *Hundreds of people are killed or maimed in car accidents every week.*

main 🔑 /meɪn/ *adj., noun*
- *adj.* [only before noun] being the largest or most important of its kind: *Be careful crossing the main road.* ♦ *the main course* (= of a meal) ♦ *Reception is in the main building.* ♦ *Poor housing and unemployment are the main problems.* ♦ *The main thing is to stay calm.*
- *noun* **1** [C] a large pipe that carries water or gas to a building; a large cable that carries electricity to a building: *a leaking gas main* ⊃ see also WATER MAIN **2** a large pipe that carries waste water and SEWAGE (= human waste, etc.) away from a building

IDM in the main used to say that a statement is true in most cases: *The service here is, in the main, reliable.*

main

major ◆ key ◆ central ◆ principal ◆ chief ◆ prime

These words all describe something that is the largest or most important of its kind.

main [only before noun] largest or most important: *Turn left onto the main road.* ♦ *The main thing is to remain calm.*

major [usually before noun] very large or important: *He played a major role in setting up the system.* **NOTE** Major is most often used after *a* with a singular noun, or no article with a plural noun. When it is used with *the* or *my/your/his/her/our/their*, it means "the largest or most important": *Our major concern here is combatting poverty.* In this meaning it is only used to talk about ideas or worries that people have, not physical things, and it is also more formal than **main**: ~~*Turn left onto the major road.*~~ ♦ ~~*The major thing is to remain calm.*~~

key [usually before noun] most important; essential: *He was a key figure in the campaign.* **NOTE** Key is used most frequently in business and political contexts. It can be used to talk about ideas, or the part that someone plays in a situation, but not physical things. It is slightly more informal than **major**, especially when used after a noun and linking verb: *Speed is key at this point.*

central (*somewhat formal*) most important: *The central issue is that of widespread racism.* **NOTE** Central is used in a similar way to **key**, but is more formal. It is most frequently used in the phrase *sth is central to sth else*.

principal [only before noun] (*somewhat formal*) most important: *The principal reason for this omission is a lack of time.* **NOTE** Principal is mostly used for statements of fact about which there can be no argument. To state an opinion, or to try to persuade someone of the facts as you see them, it is more usual to use **key** or **central**: *The key/central issue here is...*

chief [only before noun] (*somewhat formal*) most important: *Malnutrition is the chief cause of preventable blindness.*

prime [only before noun] (*somewhat formal*) most important; to be considered first: *My prime concern is to protect my property.*

PATTERNS
- a/the main/major/key/central/principal/chief/ prime **aim/concern**
- a/the main/major/principal **road/town/city**
- the main/key **thing** is to...
- to be **of** major/key/central/prime **importance**

ˌmain ˈclause (also ˌindependent ˈclause) *noun* (*grammar*) a group of words that includes a subject and a verb and can form a sentence ⊃ compare SUBORDINATE CLAUSE

ˌmain ˈcourse (also ˌmain ˈdish) *noun* (in a restaurant or at a formal meal) the main or largest part of the meal: *I had salmon, rice, and mixed vegetables as a main course.*

the ˌmain ˈdrag *noun* [sing.] (*informal*) the most important or the busiest street in a town

main·frame /ˈmeɪnfreɪm/ (also ˌmainframe comˈputer) *noun* a large powerful computer, usually the center of a network and shared by many users ⊃ compare MICRO-COMPUTER, MINICOMPUTER, PERSONAL COMPUTER

the ˈmain·land /ˈmeɪnlænd; -lənd/ *noun* [sing.] the main area of land of a country, not including any islands near to it: *a boat to/from the mainland* ♦ *The hurricane is now threatening the U.S. mainland.* ▶ **mainland** *adj.* [only before noun]: *mainland Greece*

ˌmain ˈline *noun* an important railroad line between two cities ▶ ˌmain-ˈline *adj.*: *a main-line station*

main·line /'meɪnlaɪn/ adj., verb
• **adj.** belonging to the system, or connected with the ideas that most people accept or believe in **SYN** MAINSTREAM: *mainline churches/faiths*
• **verb** [T, I] ~ (sth) (*slang*) to take an illegal drug by INJECTING it into a VEIN: *At 18 he was mainlining heroin.*

main·ly 🔑 /'meɪnli/ adv.
1 more than anything else; also used to talk about the most important reason for something **SYN** CHIEFLY, PRIMARILY: *They eat mainly fruit and nuts.* ♦ *"Where do you export to?" "France, mainly."* ♦ *The population almost doubles in summer, mainly because of the jazz festival.* **2** used to talk about the largest part of a group of people or things: *The people in the hotel were mainly foreign tourists.* ⟳ **language bank** at GENERALLY

main 'man noun [sing.] (*informal*) a man who is important to you because he is a trusted friend or employee: *'Course I trust you—you're my main man!*

main·sail /'meɪnseɪl; 'meɪnsl/ noun the largest and most important sail on a boat or ship ⟳ **picture at** BOAT

main·spring /'meɪnsprɪŋ/ noun **1** [usually sing.] ~ (of sth) (*formal*) the most important part of something; the most important influence on something **2** the most important spring in a watch, clock, etc.

main·stay /'meɪnsteɪ/ noun [usually sing.] ~ (of sth) a person or thing that is the most important part of something and enables it to exist or be successful: *Cocoa is the country's economic mainstay.*

main·stream /'meɪnstriːm/ noun, adj., verb
• **noun** the mainstream [sing.] the ideas and opinions that are thought to be normal because they are shared by most people; the people whose ideas and opinions are most accepted: *His radical views place him outside the mainstream of American politics.* ▶ **main·stream** adj. [usually before noun]: *mainstream education*
• **verb 1** ~ sth to make a particular idea or opinion accepted by most people: *Vegetarianism has been mainstreamed.* **2** ~ sb to include children with mental or physical problems in ordinary school classes

'main street noun **1** [C] (especially in names) the main street of a town, where most stores, banks, etc. are **2** Main Street [U] typical middle-class Americans: *Main Street won't be happy with this new program.*

main·tain 🔑 **AWL** /meɪn'teɪn/ verb
1 ~ sth to make something continue at the same level, standard, etc. **SYN** PRESERVE: *to maintain law and order/ standards/a balance* ♦ *The two countries have always maintained close relations.* ♦ (*formal*) *She maintained a dignified silence.* ♦ *to maintain prices* (= prevent them falling or rising) **2** ~ sth to keep a building, a machine, etc. in good condition by checking or repairing it regularly: *The house is large and difficult to maintain.* **3** to keep stating that something is true, even though other people do not agree or do not believe it **SYN** INSIST: ~ (that)… *The men maintained (that) they were out of the country when the crime was committed.* ♦ ~ sth *She has always maintained her innocence.* ♦ + speech *"But I'm innocent!" she maintained.* ⟳ **language bank** at ARGUE **4** ~ sb/sth to support someone or something over a long period of time by giving money, paying for food, etc. **SYN** KEEP: *Her income was barely enough to maintain one child, let alone three.*

main·te·nance **AWL** /'meɪntn·əns/ noun [U] **1** ~ (of sth) the act of keeping something in good condition by checking or repairing it regularly: *The school pays for heating and the maintenance of the buildings.* ♦ *car maintenance* **2** ~ (of sth) the act of making a state or situation continue: *the maintenance of international peace*

'main verb noun [usually sing.] (*grammar*) the verb in a MAIN CLAUSE

maî·tre d' /ˌmeɪtrə 'di; ˌmeɪtər-/ noun (pl. maître d's /-'diz/) (also *formal* maître d'hôtel /ˌmeɪtrə doʊ'tɛl/ pl. maîtres

d'hôtel /ˌmeɪtrə doʊ'tɛl/) (from *French*, *informal*) a head waiter

Maj. abbr. (in writing) MAJOR: *Maj. (Tony) Davies* ♦ *Maj. Gen.* (= Major General)

ma·jes·tic /mə'dʒɛstɪk/ adj. impressive because of size or beauty **SYN** AWE-INSPIRING, SPLENDID: *a majestic castle/ river/view* ▶ **ma·jes·ti·cally** /-kli/ adv.

maj·es·ty /'mædʒəsti/ noun (pl. maj·es·ties) **1** [U] the impressive and attractive quality that something has: *the sheer majesty of St. Peter's in Rome* ♦ *the majesty of the music* **2** [C] His/Her/Your Majesty a title of respect used when speaking about or to a king or queen **3** [U] royal power

ma·jor 🔑 **AWL** /'meɪdʒər/ adj., noun, verb
• **adj. 1** [usually before noun] very large or important: *a major road* ♦ *major international companies* ♦ *to play a major role in something* ♦ *We have encountered major problems.* ♦ *There were calls for major changes to the welfare system.* **ANT** MINOR ⟳ **see also** MAJOR-LEAGUE ⟳ **thesaurus box** at MAIN **2** [not before noun] serious: *Never mind—it's nothing major.* **3** (*music*) based on a SCALE (= a series of eight notes) in which the third note is two whole TONES/STEPS higher than the first note: *the key of D major* ⟳ **compare** MINOR **4** related to someone's main subject of study in college
• **noun 1** [C] (*abbr.* Maj.) an officer of fairly high rank in the army or the AIR FORCE: *Major Smith* ♦ *He's a major in the U.S. army.* ⟳ **see also** DRUM MAJOR, SERGEANT MAJOR **2** [C] the main subject or course of a student at college or university: *Her major is French.* ⟳ **compare** MINOR **3** [C] a student studying a particular subject as the main part of their course: *She's a French major.* **4** the majors [pl.] (*sports*) the MAJOR LEAGUES
• **verb**
PHR V 'major in sth to study something as your main subject at a university or college: *She majored in history at Stanford.*

ma·jor-do·mo /ˌmeɪdʒər 'doʊmoʊ/ noun (pl. ma·jor-do·mos) a senior servant who manages a large house

ma·jor·ette /ˌmeɪdʒə'rɛt/ (also 'drum major·ette) noun a girl in special brightly colored clothes who walks in front of a marching band spinning, throwing, and catching a long stick (called a BATON)

ˌmajor 'general noun an officer of very high rank in the army or the AIR FORCE: *Major General William Hunt*

ma·jor·i·ty 🔑 **AWL** /mə'dʒɔːrəti; -'dʒɑr-/ noun (pl. ma·jor·i·ties) **1** [sing.] ~ (of sb/sth) the largest part of a group of people or things: *The majority of people interviewed prefer TV to radio.* ♦ *The majority was in favor of banning smoking .* ♦ *This treatment is not available in the vast majority of hospitals.* ♦ *a majority decision* (= one that is decided by what most people want) ♦ *In the nursing profession, women are in a/ the majority.* **ANT** MINORITY ⟳ **see also** MORAL MAJORITY, THE SILENT MAJORITY **2** [C] the number of votes by which one political party wins an election; the number of votes by which one side in a discussion, etc. wins: *She was elected by/ with a majority of the electoral votes.* ♦ *a clear* (= large) *majority* ♦ ~ (over sb) *They had a large majority over their nearest rivals.* ♦ *The Republicans do not have an overall majority* (= more members than all the other parties added together). ♦ *The resolution was carried by a huge majority.* ⟳ **collocations** at VOTE ⟳ **see also** ABSOLUTE MAJORITY **3** [C] the difference between the number of votes given to the candidate who wins the election and the total number of votes of all the other candidates ⟳ **see also** PLURALITY **4** [U] (*law*) the age at which you are legally considered to be an adult

ma'jority ˌleader noun the leader of the political party that has the majority in either the House of Representatives or the Senate

ma'jority 'rule noun [U] a system in which power is held by the group that has the largest number of members

ma'jority 'verdict noun (*law*) a decision made by a jury in a court case that most members, but not all, agree with

ʌ **cup**   ə **about**   eɪ **say**   aɪ **five**   ɔɪ **boy**   aʊ **now**   oʊ **go**   ər **bird**

ma·jority 'whip noun (*politics*) a member of the political party in Congress with the most representatives, who influences other party members to vote a particular way

major-'league adj. [only before noun] **1** (*sports*) connected with teams that play in the major leagues, especially in baseball: *a major-league team* **2** very important and having a lot of influence: *a major-league business*

Major 'Leagues (also the ma·jors) noun [pl.] (*informal*) the two highest leagues of professional baseball teams in the U.S. ⊃ compare MINOR LEAGUE ▶ **major 'leaguer** noun

ma·jor·ly /'meɪdʒərli/ adv. (used before an adjective) (*informal*) very; extremely: *majorly disappointed*

make 🔑 /meɪk/ verb, noun

● **verb** (made, made /meɪd/)

> **CREATE 1** to create or prepare something by combining materials or putting parts together: *~ sth to make a table/ dress/cake* ◆ *to make bread/cement/paper* ◆ *She makes her own clothes.* ◆ *made in China* (= on a label) ◆ *~ sth (out) of sth What's your shirt made of?* ◆ *~ sth from sth Wine is made from grapes.* ◆ *~ sth into sth The grapes are made into wine.* ◆ *~ sth for sb She made coffee for us all.* ◆ *~ sb sth She made us all coffee.* ⊃ note at DO¹ **2** *~ sth* to write, create, or prepare something: *These regulations were made to protect children.* ◆ *My lawyer has been urging me to make a will.* ◆ *She has made* (= directed or acted in) *several movies.*

> **A BED 3** *~ a bed* to arrange a bed so that it is neat and ready for use

> **CAUSE TO APPEAR/HAPPEN/BECOME/DO 4** *~ sth (+ adv./ prep.)* to cause something to appear as a result of breaking, tearing, hitting, or removing material: *The stone made a dent in the roof of the car.* ◆ *The holes in the cloth were made by moths.* **5** *~ sth* to cause something to exist, happen, or be done: *to make a noise/mess/fuss* ◆ *She tried to make a good impression on the interviewer.* ◆ *I keep making the same mistakes.* **6** *~ sb/sth/yourself + adj.* to cause someone or something to be or become something: *The news made him very happy.* ◆ *She made her objections clear.* ◆ *He made it clear that he objected.* ◆ *The full story was never made public.* ◆ *Can you make yourself understood in Russian?* ◆ *She couldn't make herself heard above the noise of the traffic.* ◆ *The terrorists made it known that tourists would be targeted.* **7** *~ sb/sth do sth* to cause someone or something to do something: *She always makes me laugh.* ◆ *This dress makes me look fat.* ◆ *What makes you say that* (= why do you think so?)*?* ◆ *Nothing will make me change my mind.* **8** to cause someone or something to be or become something: *~ sth of sb/sth This isn't very important —I don't want to make an issue of it.* ◆ *Don't make a habit of it.* ◆ *You've made a terrible mess of this job.* ◆ *It's important to try and make something of* (= achieve something in) *your life.* ◆ *We'll make a tennis player of you yet.* ◆ *~ sth + noun I made painting the house my project for the summer.* ◆ *She made it her business to find out who was responsible.*

> **A DECISION/GUESS/COMMENT, ETC. 9** *~ a decision, guess, comment, etc.* to decide, guess, etc. something: *Come on! It's time we made a start.* **HELP** Make can be used in this way with a number of different nouns. These expressions are included at the entry for each noun.

> **FORCE 10** to force someone to do something: *~ sb do sth They made me repeat the whole story.* ◆ *be made to do sth She must be made to comply with the rules.* ◆ *~ sb He never cleans his room and his mother never tries to make him.*

> **REPRESENT 11** to represent someone or something as being or doing something: *~ sb/sth + adj. You've made my nose too big* (= for example in a drawing)*.* ◆ *~ sb/sth + noun He makes King Lear a truly tragic figure.*

> **APPOINT 12** *~ sb + noun* to elect or choose someone as something: *She made him her assistant.*

> **BE SUITABLE 13** *linking verb ~ sb/sth + noun* to become or develop into something; to be suitable for something: *She would have made an excellent teacher.* ◆ *This room would make a nice office.*

> **EQUAL 14** *linking verb + noun* to add up to or equal something: *5 and 7 make 12.* ◆ *A hundred cents make one dollar.* **15** *linking verb + noun* to be a total of something:

That makes the third time he's failed his driving test!

> **MONEY 16** *~ sth* to earn or gain money: *She makes $100,000 a year.* ◆ *to make a profit/loss* ◆ *We need to think of ways to make money.* ◆ *He made a fortune on the stock market.* ◆ *He makes a living as a stand-up comic.*

> **CALCULATE 17** [no passive] *~ sth + noun* to think or calculate something to be something: *What time do you make it?* ◆ *I make that exactly $50.*

> **REACH 18** [no passive] *~ sth* to manage to reach or go to a place or position: *Do you think we'll make Denver by 12?* ◆ *I'm sorry I couldn't make your party last night.* ◆ *He'll never make* (= get a place in) *the team.* ◆ *The story made* (= appeared on) *the front page of the newspaper.* ◆ *We just managed to make the deadline* (= to finish something in time).

> **SOMETHING SUCCESSFUL 19** *~ sth* to cause something to be a success: *Good wine can make a meal.* ◆ *The news really made my day.*

IDM Most idioms containing **make** are at the entries for the nouns and adjectives in the idioms. For example, **make merry** is at **merry**. **make as if to do sth** to make a movement that makes it seem as if you are just going to do something: *He made as if to speak.* **make do (with sth)** to manage with something that is not really good enough: *We were in a hurry so we had to make do with a quick snack.* **make good** to become rich and successful **make sth good 1** to pay for, replace, or repair something that has been lost or damaged: *She promised to make good the damage.* **2** to do something that you have promised, threatened, etc. to do **SYN** FULFILL **make it 1** to be successful in your career: *He never really made it as an actor.* **2** to succeed in reaching a place in time, especially when this is difficult: *The flight leaves in twenty minutes—we'll never make it.* **3** to be able to be present at a place: *I'm sorry I won't be able to make it* (= for example, to a party) *on Saturday.* **4** to survive after a serious illness or accident; to deal successfully with a difficult experience: *The doctors think he's going to make it.* ◆ *I don't know how I made it through the week.* **make it with sb** (*slang*) to have sex with someone **make like…** (*informal*) to pretend to be, know, or have something in order to impress people: *He makes like he's the greatest actor of all time.* **make the most of sth/sb/yourself** to gain as much advantage, enjoyment, etc. as you can from someone or something: *It's my first trip abroad so I'm going to make the most of it.* ◆ *She doesn't know how to make the most of herself* (= make herself appear in the best possible way). **make much of sth/sb** to treat something or someone as very important: *He always makes much of his humble origins.* **make or break sth** to be the thing that makes someone or something either a success or a failure: *This movie will make or break him as a director.* ◆ *It's make-or-break time for the company.* **make something of yourself** to be successful in your life

PHRV **make for sth 1** to move toward something **SYN** HEAD FOR **2** to help to make something possible: *Constant arguing doesn't make for a happy marriage.* ⊃ see also BE MADE FOR SB/EACH OTHER at MADE

make sb/sth into sb/sth to change someone or something into someone or something **SYN** TURN INTO: *We're making our attic into an extra bedroom.*

make sth of sb/sth to understand the meaning or character of someone or something: *What do you make of it all?* ◆ *I can't make anything of this note.* ◆ *I don't know what to make of* (= think of) *the new manager.*

make 'off to hurry away, especially in order to escape **make 'off with sth** to steal something and hurry away with it

make 'out 1 (*informal*) used to ask if someone managed well or was successful in a particular situation: *How did he make out while his wife was away?* **2** ~ (with sb) (*informal*) to kiss and touch someone in a sexual way **make sb 'out** to understand someone's character **make sb/sth↔'out 1** to manage to see someone or something either a course and or hear something **SYN** DISTINGUISH: *I could just make out a figure in the darkness.* ◆ *~ what, who, etc…. I could hear voices but I couldn't make out what they were saying.* ⊃ thesaurus box at IDENTIFY **2** to say that something is true when it may not be

SYN CLAIM: *She's not as rich as people make out.* ◆ ~ **that...** *He made out that he had been robbed.* ◆ ~ **to be/do sth** *She makes herself out to be smarter than she really is.* ˌmake sth↔'out **1** to write out or complete a form or document: *He made out a check for $100.* ◆ *The doctor made out a prescription for me.* **2** (used in negative sentences and questions) to understand something; to see the reasons for something: *How do you make that out?* (= what are your reasons for thinking that)? ◆ ~ **what, why, etc.... ** *I can't make out what she wants.*

ˌmake sb/sth↔'over to change something in order to make it look different or use it for a different purpose; to give someone a different appearance by changing their clothes, hair, etc. **SYN** TRANSFORM ➔ related noun MAKE-OVER ˌmake sth↔'over (to sb/sth) to legally give something to someone: *He made over the property to his eldest son.* 'make toward sth to start moving toward something: *He made toward the door.*

ˌmake 'up | ˌmake yourself/sb↔'up to put powder, LIPSTICK, etc. on your/someone's face to make it more attractive or to prepare for an appearance in the theater, on television, etc. ➔ related noun MAKEUP ˌmake sth↔'up **1** to form something **SYN** CONSTITUTE: *Women make up 56% of the student population.* ➔ related noun MAKEUP ➔ thesaurus box at CONSIST OF ➔ language bank at PROPORTION **2** to put something together from several different things ➔ related noun MAKEUP **3** to invent a story, etc., especially in order to trick or entertain someone: *He made up some excuse about his daughter being sick.* ◆ *I told the kids a story, making it up as I went along.* ◆ *You made that up!* **4** to complete a number or an amount required: *We need one more person to make up a team.* **5** to replace something that has been lost; to COMPENSATE for something: *Can I leave early this afternoon and make up the time tomorrow?* **6** to prepare a medicine by mixing different things together **7** to prepare a bed for use; to create a temporary bed: *We made up the bed in the guest room.* ◆ *They made up a bed for me on the sofa.* **8** to clean a hotel room and make the bed: *The maid asked if she could make up the room.* ˌmake 'up for sth to do something that corrects a bad situation **SYN** COMPENSATE: *Nothing can make up for the loss of a child.* ◆ *After all the delays, we were anxious to make up for lost time.* ◆ *Her enthusiasm makes up for her lack of experience.* ˌmake 'up (to sb) for sth to do something for someone or give them something because you have caused them trouble, suffering, or disappointment and wish to show that you are sorry **SYN** COMPENSATE: *How can I make up for the way I've treated you?* ◆ (*informal*) *I'll make it up to you, I promise.* ˌmake 'up (with sb) to end a disagreement with someone and become friends again: *Why don't you two kiss and make up?* ◆ *Has he made up with her yet?* ◆ *Have they made up yet?*

● **noun ~ (of sth)** the name or type of a machine, piece of equipment, etc. that is made by a particular company: *What make of car does he drive?* ◆ *There are so many different makes to choose from.* ◆ *a Swiss make of watch*
IDM **on the make** (*informal, disapproving*) trying to get money or an advantage for yourself

---

THESAURUS

make

do ◆ create ◆ develop ◆ produce ◆ generate ◆ form

These words all mean to make something from parts or materials, or to cause something to exist or happen.

make to create or prepare something by combining materials or putting parts together; to cause something to exist or happen: *She makes her own clothes.*
◆ *She made a good impression on the interviewer.*

do (*somewhat informal*) to make or prepare something, especially something artistic or being to eat: *He did a beautiful drawing of a house.* ◆ *Who's doing the food for the party?*

create to make something exist or happen, especially something new that did not exist before: *Scientists*

---

disagree about how the universe was created.

MAKE OR CREATE?

Make is a more general word and is more often used for physical things: you would usually *make a table/dress/cake* but *create jobs/wealth*. You can use **create** for something physical in order to emphasize how original or unusual the object is: *Try this new dish, created by our head chef.*

develop (used especially in business contexts) to think of and produce a new product: *to develop new software*

produce to make things to be sold; to create something using skill: *a factory that produces microchips*

generate to produce or create something, especially power, money, or ideas: *to generate electricity* ◆ *Brainstorming is a good way of generating ideas.*

form [often passive] to make something from something else; to make something into something else: *Rearrange the letters to form a new word.* ◆ *The chain is formed from 136 links.*

PATTERNS

- to make/create/develop/produce/generate/form sth **from/out of** sth
- to make/form sth **into** sth
- to make/produce **wine/cheese**
- to create/develop a **new product**
- to create/produce/generate **income/profits/wealth**
- to produce/generate **electricity/heat/power**

'make-beˌlieve *noun* [U] **1** (*disapproving*) imagining or pretending things to be different or more exciting than they really are **SYN** FANTASY: *They live in a world of make-believe.* **2** imagining that something is real, or that you are someone else, for example in a child's game: *"Let's play make-believe," said Sam.*

make·o·ver /'meɪkˌoʊvər/ *noun* [C, U] the process of improving the appearance of a person or a place, or of changing the impression that something gives

mak·er /'meɪkər/ *noun* **1** [C] ~ **(of sth)** (often in compounds) a person, company, or piece of equipment that makes or produces something: *a decision/law/policy maker* ◆ *program makers* ◆ *a new movie from the makers of "Terminator"* ◆ *an electric coffee maker* ◆ *one of the best winemakers in France* ➔ see also PEACEMAKER, TROUBLEMAKER **2 the, his, your, etc. Maker** [sing.] God **IDM** see MEET *v.*

make·shift /'meɪkʃɪft/ *adj.* [usually before noun] used temporarily for a particular purpose because the real thing is not available **SYN** IMPROVISED, PROVISIONAL: *A few cushions formed a makeshift bed.*

make·up 🔑 (also 'make-up) /'meɪkʌp/ *noun* **1** [U] substances used especially by women to make their faces look more attractive, or used by actors to change their appearance: *eye makeup* ◆ *to put on your makeup* ◆ *She never wears makeup.* ◆ *a makeup artist* (= a person whose job is to put makeup on the faces of actors and models) ➔ collocations at FASHION **2** [sing.] the different qualities that combine to form someone's character or being: *Jealousy is not part of his makeup.* ◆ *a person's genetic makeup* **3** [sing.] ~ **(of sth)** the different things, people, etc. that combine to form something; the way in which they combine: *the makeup of a TV audience* ◆ (*technical*) *the page makeup of a text* (= the way in which the words and pictures are arranged on a page) **4** [C] a special exam taken by students who missed or failed an earlier one

make·weight /'meɪkweɪt/ *noun* an unimportant person or thing that is only added or included in something in order to make it the correct number, quantity, size, etc.

'make-work *noun* [U] work that has little value but is given to people to keep them busy: *In some departments there is too*

---

t **tea**   t̬ **butter**   d **did**   k **cat**   g **got**   tʃ **chin**   dʒ **June**   f **fall**

makeup

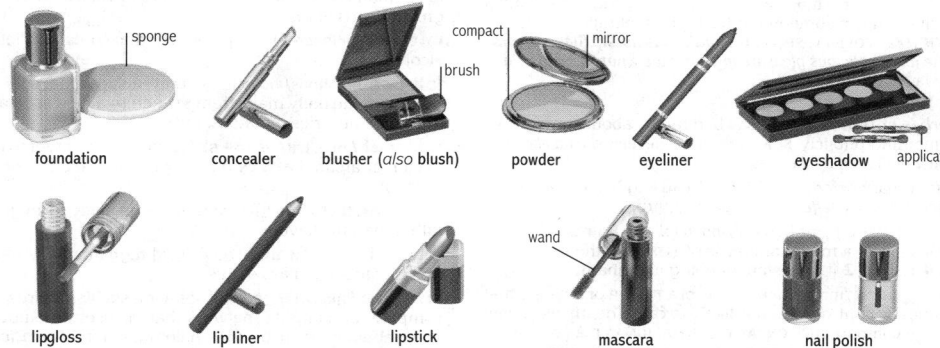

foundation   concealer   blusher (*also* blush)   powder   eyeliner   eyeshadow   applicator

sponge   compact   mirror   brush

lipgloss   lip liner   lipstick   mascara   nail polish   wand

much **make-work**. ◆ *These are simply make-work schemes for accountants.*

mak·ing /ˈmeɪkɪŋ/ *noun* [U] **~ (of sth)** (often in compounds) the act or process of making or producing something: *strategic decision making* ◆ *filmmaking* ◆ *dressmaking* ◆ *tea and coffee making facilities* ◆ *the making of social policy* ➔ see also HAYMAKING
IDM **be the making of sb** to make someone become a better or more successful person: *College was the making of Joe.* **have the makings of sth** to have the qualities that are necessary to become something: *Her first novel has all the makings of a classic.* **in the making** in the process of becoming something or of being made: *This model was two years in the making.* ◆ *These events are* **history in the making.** **of your own making** (of a problem, difficulty, etc.) created by you rather than by someone or something else

mal- /mæl/ *combining form* (in nouns, verbs, and adjectives) bad or badly; not correct or correctly: *malpractice* ◆ *malodorous* ◆ *malfunction*

mal·a·chite /ˈmæləkaɪt/ *noun* [U] a green mineral that can be polished, used to make decorative objects

mal·ad·just·ed /ˌmæləˈdʒʌstəd/ *adj.* (especially of children) having mental and emotional problems that lead to unacceptable behavior ➔ compare WELL ADJUSTED
▶ **mal·ad·just·ment** /ˌmæləˈdʒʌstmənt/ *noun* [U]

mal·ad·min·is·tra·tion /ˌmælədˌmɪnəˈstreɪʃn/ *noun* [U] (*formal*) the fact of managing a business or an organization in a bad or dishonest way

mal·a·droit /ˌmæləˈdrɔɪt/ *adj.* (*formal*) done without skill, especially in a way that annoys or offends people
SYN CLUMSY

mal·a·dy /ˈmælədi/ *noun* (*pl.* **mal·a·dies**) **1** (*formal*) a serious problem **SYN** ILL: *Violent crime is only one of the maladies afflicting modern society.* **2** (*old use*) an illness

ma·laise /məˈleɪz; mæ-/ *noun* [U, sing.] (*formal*) **1** the problems affecting a particular situation or group of people that are difficult to explain or identify: *economic/financial/social malaise* **2** a general feeling of being sick, unhappy, or not satisfied, without signs of any particular problem **SYN** UNEASE: *a serious malaise among the employees*

mal·a·prop·ism /ˈmæləprɑˌpɪzəm/ *noun* an amusing mistake someone makes when they use a word that sounds similar to the word they wanted to use, but means something different **ORIGIN** From Mrs. Malaprop, a character in Richard Brinsley Sheridan's play *The Rivals*, who confuses words like this all the time.

ma·lar·i·a /məˈleriə/ *noun* [U] a disease that causes fever and SHIVERING (= shaking of the body) caused by the bite of some types of MOSQUITOES ▶ **ma·lar·i·al** /-iəl/ *adj.*: *malarial insects/patients/regions*

ma·lar·key /məˈlɑrki/ *noun* [U] (*informal, disapproving*)

behavior or an idea that you think is nonsense or has no meaning

mal·con·tent /ˌmælkənˈtɛnt/ *noun* [usually pl.] (*formal, disapproving*) a person who is not satisfied with a situation and who complains about it, or causes trouble in order to change it

male 🔑 /meɪl/ *adj., noun*
● *adj.* **1** (*abbr.* **m.**) belonging to the sex that does not give birth to babies; connected with this sex: *a male cat* ◆ *All the attackers were male, aged between 25 and 30.* ◆ *a male nurse/model/colleague* ◆ *male attitudes to women* ◆ **male bonding** (= the act of forming close friendships between men) ➔ compare MASCULINE ➔ see also ALPHA MALE **2** (*biology*) (of most plants) producing POLLEN: *a male flower* **3** (*technical*) (of electrical PLUGS, parts of tools, etc.) having a part that sticks out which is designed to fit into a hole, OUTLET, etc. ➔ compare FEMALE ▶ **male·ness** *noun* [U]: *the chromosome that determines maleness*
● *noun* a male person, animal, or plant: *The body is that of a white male aged around 40.* ◆ *The male of the species has a white tail.* ◆ *a male-dominated profession* ➔ compare FEMALE

male ˈchauvinism (also **chau·vin·ism**) *noun* [U] (*disapproving*) the belief held by some men that men are more important, intelligent, etc. than women

male ˈchauvinist (also **chau·vin·ist**) *noun* (*disapproving*) a man who believes men are more important, intelligent, etc. than women: *I hate working for that* **male chauvinist pig** *Steve.*

mal·e·fac·tor /ˈmæləˌfæktər/ *noun* (*rare, formal*) a person who does wrong, illegal, or immoral things

ma·lev·o·lent /məˈlɛvələnt/ *adj.* [usually before noun] having or showing a desire to harm other people **SYN** MALICIOUS, WICKED **ANT** BENEVOLENT ▶ **ma·lev·o·lence** /-ləns/ *noun* [U]: *an act of pure malevolence* **ma·lev·o·lent·ly** *adv.*

malfeasance /mælˈfizns/ *noun* [U] (*law*) illegal actions, especially those of a government official or large business company

mal·for·ma·tion /ˌmælfɔrˈmeɪʃn; -fər-/ *noun* **1** [C] a part of the body that is not formed correctly: *Some fetal malformations cannot be diagnosed until late in pregnancy.* **2** [U] the state of not being correctly formed

mal·formed /ˌmælˈfɔrmd/ *adj.* (*technical*) badly formed or shaped

mal·func·tion /ˌmælˈfʌŋkʃn/ *verb* [I] (of a machine, etc.) to fail to work correctly ▶ **mal·func·tion** *noun* [C, U]

mal·ice /ˈmæləs/ *noun* [U] a feeling of hatred for someone that causes a desire to harm them: *He sent the letter out of malice.* ◆ *She is entirely without malice.* ◆ *He certainly bears you no malice* (= does not want to harm you).

IDM **with malice aforethought** (*law*) with the deliberate intention of committing a crime or harming someone

ma·li·cious /məˈlɪʃəs/ *adj.* having or showing hatred and a desire to harm someone or hurt their feelings **SYN** MALEVOLENT, SPITEFUL: *malicious gossip/lies/rumors* ◆ *He took malicious pleasure in telling me what she had said.* ▶ **ma·li·cious·ly** *adv.*

ma·lign /məˈlaɪn/ *verb, adj.*
● *verb* ~ **sb/sth** (*formal*) to say bad things about someone or something publicly **SYN** SLANDER: *She feels she has been much maligned by the press.*
● *adj.* [usually before noun] (*formal*) causing harm: *a malign force/influence/effect* ⊃ compare BENIGN

ma·lig·nan·cy /məˈlɪɡnənsi/ *noun* (*pl.* **ma·lig·nan·cies**) (*formal*) **1** [C] a malignant mass of TISSUE in the body **SYN** TUMOR **2** [U] the state of being malignant

ma·lig·nant /məˈlɪɡnənt/ *adj.* **1** (of a TUMOR or disease) that cannot be controlled and is likely to cause death: *malignant cells* ⊃ compare BENIGN **ANT** NONMALIGNANT **2** (*formal*) having or showing a strong desire to harm someone **SYN** MALEVOLENT

ma·lin·ger /məˈlɪŋɡər/ *verb* usually **be malingering** [I] (*disapproving*) to pretend to be sick, especially in order to avoid work ▶ **ma·lin·ger·er** *noun*

mall 🔑 /mɔl/ *noun*
= SHOPPING MALL: *Let's go to the mall.* ◆ *Some teenagers were hanging out at the mall.* ⊃ collocations at SHOPPING

mal·lard /ˈmælərd/ *noun* (*pl.* **mal·lards** or **mal·lard**) a common wild DUCK

mal·le·a·ble /ˈmæliəbl/ *adj.* **1** (*technical*) (of metal, etc.) that can be hit or pressed into different shapes easily without breaking or cracking **2** (of people, ideas, etc.) easily influenced or changed ▶ **mal·le·a·bil·i·ty** /ˌmæliəˈbɪləti/ *noun* [U]

mal·let /ˈmælət/ *noun* **1** a hammer with a large wooden head ⊃ picture at TOOL **2** a hammer with a long handle and a wooden head, used for hitting the ball in the games of CROQUET and POLO

mal·low /ˈmæloʊ/ *noun* [C, U] a plant with STEMS covered with small hairs and pink, purple, or white flowers

mall·rat /ˈmɔlræt/ *noun* (*informal*) a young person who spends a lot of time in SHOPPING MALLS, often in a large group of friends

mal·nour·ished /ˌmælˈnərɪʃt/ *adj.* in bad health because of a lack of food or a lack of the right type of food

mal·nu·tri·tion /ˌmælnuˈtrɪʃn/ *noun* [U] a poor condition of health caused by a lack of food or a lack of the right type of food ⊃ compare NUTRITION

mal·o·dor·ous /ˌmælˈoʊdərəs/ *adj.* (*formal or literary*) having an unpleasant smell

mal·prac·tice /ˌmælˈpræktəs/ *noun* [U, C] (*law*) careless, wrong, or illegal behavior while in a professional job: *medical malpractice* ◆ *a malpractice suit* ◆ *He is currently standing trial for alleged malpractices.*

malt /mɔlt/ *noun* **1** [U] grain, usually BARLEY, that has been left in water for a period of time and then dried, used for making beer, WHISKEY, etc. **2** [U, C] = MALT WHISKY **3** [U, C] = MALTED MILK

malt·ed /ˈmɔltəd/ *adj.* [only before noun] **1** having been made into malt: *malted barley* **2** having had malt added to it

malted ˈmilk (also **malt**) *noun* [U, C] a hot or cold drink made from MALT and dried milk mixed with water or milk and usually sugar, sometimes with ice cream and/or chocolate added

Mal·tese /mɔlˈtiz; -ˈtis/ *adj., noun* (*pl.* **Mal·tese**)
● *adj.* from or connected with Malta
● *noun* **1** [C] a person from Malta **2** [U] the language of Malta

Maltese ˈcross *noun* a cross whose arms are equal in length and have wide ends with V-shapes cut out of them

Mal·thu·sian /mælˈθuʒən/ *adj.* related to the theory of Thomas Malthus that, since populations naturally grow faster than the supply of food, failure to control their growth leads to disaster

malt ˈliquor *noun* [U] a type of beer that contains a lot of alcohol

malt·ose /ˈmɔltoʊs/ *noun* [U] (*biology*) a sugar that substances in the body make from STARCH (= a food substance found in flour, rice, potatoes, etc.)

mal·treat /ˌmælˈtrit/ *verb* ~ **sb/sth** to be very cruel to a person or an animal **SYN** ILL-TREAT ▶ **mal·treat·ment** *noun* [U]

malt ˈvinegar *noun* [U] VINEGAR that is made from grain rather than from wine

malt ˈwhisky (also **malt**) *noun* [U, C] high quality WHISKEY from Scotland; a glass of this

mal·ware /ˈmælwɛr/ *noun* [U] software such as a virus on a computer or computer network that the user does not know about or want **ORIGIN** A combination of *malicious* and *software*.

ma·ma /ˈmɑmə/ *noun* **1** (also **mam·ma, mom·ma**) mother ⊃ see also MOMMY **2** in some places in Africa, a mother or older woman (often used as a title that shows respect): *Leave this work to us, mama.* ◆ *Miriam Makeba became known as Mama Africa.* ◆ *Mama Ngina Kenyatta*

mama's ˌboy *noun* (*disapproving*) a boy or man who depends too much on his mother

mam·ba /ˈmɑmbə/ *noun* a black or green poisonous African snake

mam·bo /ˈmɑmboʊ/ *noun* (*pl.* **mam·bos**) **1** a lively Latin American dance **2** a female VOODOO priest

mam·mal /ˈmæml/ *noun* any animal that gives birth to live babies, not eggs, and feeds its young on milk. Cows, humans, and WHALES are all mammals. ▶ **mam·ma·li·an** /məˈmeɪliən/ *adj.*

mam·ma·ry /ˈmæməri/ *adj.* [only before noun] (*biology*) connected with the breasts: *mammary glands* (= parts of the breast that produce milk)

mam·mo·gram /ˈmæməˌɡræm/ *noun* an examination of a breast using X-RAYS to check for cancer

mam·mog·ra·phy /mæˈmɑɡrəfi/ *noun* [U] the use of X-RAYS to check for cancer in a breast

Mam·mon /ˈmæmən/ *noun* [U] (*formal, disapproving*) a way of talking about money and wealth when it has become the most important thing in someone's life and as important as a god

mam·moth /ˈmæməθ/ *noun, adj.*
● *noun* an animal like a large ELEPHANT covered with hair, that lived thousands of years ago and is now EXTINCT
● *adj.* [usually before noun] extremely large **SYN** HUGE: *a mammoth task* ◆ *a financial crisis of mammoth proportions*

mam·my /ˈmæmi/ *noun* (*pl.* **mam·mies**) **1** (*informal*) mother **2** an offensive word used in the past in the southern states for a black woman who cared for a white family's children

man 🔑 /mæn/ *noun, verb, exclamation*
● *noun* (*pl.* **men** /mɛn/)
▷ MALE PERSON **1** [C] an adult male human: *a good-looking young man* ◆ *the relationships between men and women* ⊃ see also DIRTY OLD MAN, LADIES' MAN, MEN'S ROOM
▷ HUMANS **2** [U] humans as a group or from a particular period of history: *the damage caused by man to the environment* ◆ *early/modern/Prehistoric man* ⊃ note at GENDER **3** [C] (*literary or old-fashioned*) a person, either male or female: *All men must die.*
▷ PARTICULAR TYPE OF MAN **4** /mæn; mən/ [C] (in compounds) a man who comes from the place mentioned or whose job or interest is connected with the thing mentioned: *a Frenchman* ◆ *a businessman* ◆ *a medical man* ◆ *a sportsman* ⊃ note at GENDER **5** [C] a man who likes or who does the thing mentioned: *a betting/drinking/fighting man* ⊃ see

also FAMILY MAN **6** [C] a man who works for or supports a particular organization, comes from a particular town, etc.: *CNN's man in Moscow* (= the man who reports on news from Moscow) ◆ *a loyal Republican Party man* ⊃ see also RIGHT-HAND MAN, YES-MAN
> SOLDIER/WORKER **7** [C, usually pl.] a soldier or a male worker who obeys the instructions of a person of higher rank: *The officer refused to let his men take part in the operation.* **8** [C] a man who comes to your house to do a job: *the gas man* ◆ *The cable man's coming to fix the TV today.*
> FORM OF ADDRESS **9** [sing.] (*informal*) used for addressing a male person: *Nice shirt, man!* ◆ *Hey man. Back off!* **10** [sing.] (*old-fashioned*) used for addressing a male person in an angry or impatient way: *Don't just stand there, man—get a doctor!*
> HUSBAND/BOYFRIEND **11** [C] (sometimes *disapproving*) a husband or sexual partner: *What's her new man like?* ◆ *I now pronounce you man and wife* (= you are now officially married). ⊃ see also OLD MAN
> STRONG/BRAVE PERSON **12** [C] a person who is strong and brave or has other qualities that some people think are particularly male: *Come on, now—be a man.* ◆ *She's more of a man than he is.* ⊃ see also HE-MAN, MUSCLEMAN, SUPERMAN
> SERVANT **13** [sing.] (*old-fashioned, formal*) a male servant: *My man will drive you home.*
> IN CHESS **14** [C] one of the figures or objects that you play with in a game such as CHESS ⊃ see also CHESSMAN
 IDM **as one man** with everyone doing or thinking the same thing at the same time; in agreement **be sb's man** to be the best or most suitable person to do a particular job, etc.: *For a fabulous haircut, David's your man.* **be man enough (to do sth/for sth)** to be strong or brave enough: *He was not man enough to face up to his responsibility.* **every man for himself** (*saying*) people must take care of themselves and not give or expect any help: *In business, it's every man for himself.* **make a man (out) of sb** to make a young man develop and become more adult **a/the man about town** a man who frequently goes to fashionable parties, clubs, theaters, etc. **the man (and/or woman) on the street** an average or ordinary person, either male or female: *Politicians often don't understand the views of the man on the street.* **a man of God/the cloth** (*old-fashioned, formal*) a religious man, especially a priest or a minister **a man of the people** (especially of a politician) a man who understands and is sympathetic to ordinary people **man's best friend** a way of describing a dog **a man's home is his castle** (*saying*) a person's home is a place where they can be private and safe and do as they like **a man's man** a man who is more popular with men than with women **be your own man/woman** to act or think independently, not following others or being ordered **man to man** between two men who are honest and treat each other honestly and equally: *I'm telling you all this man to man.* ◆ *a man-to-man talk* **one man's meat is another man's poison** (*saying*) used to say that different people like different things; what one person likes very much, another person does not like at all **to a man | to the last man** used to emphasize that something is true of all the people being described: *They answered "Yes," to a man.* ◆ *They were all destroyed, to the last man.* **you can't keep a good man down** (*saying*) a person who is determined or wants something very much will succeed ⊃ more at GRAND *adj.*, HEART, LEISURE, MARKED, NEXT *adj.*, ODD, PART *n.*, POOR, POSSESSED, SEPARATE *v.*, SUBSTANCE, THING, WORD *n.*, WORLD
● **verb** (-nn-) ~ **sth** to work at a place or be in charge of a place or a machine; to supply people to work somewhere **SYN** CREW, STAFF: *Soldiers manned barricades around the city.* ◆ *The telephones are manned 24 hours a day by volunteers.*
● **exclamation** (*informal*) used to express surprise, anger, etc.: *Man, that was great!*

man·a·cle /ˈmænəkl/ *noun, verb*
● **noun** [usually pl.] one of two metal bands joined by a chain, used for fastening a prisoner's ankles or wrists together
● **verb** [usually passive] ~ **sb/sth** to put manacles on

someone's wrists or ankles, to stop them from escaping

man·age 🔎 /ˈmænɪdʒ/ *verb*
> DO SOMETHING DIFFICULT **1** [T, I] to succeed in doing something, especially something difficult: ~ **sth** *In spite of his disappointment, he managed a weak smile.* ◆ *I don't know exactly how we'll manage it, but we will, somehow.* ◆ ~ **(to do sth)** *We managed to get to the airport in time.* ◆ *How did you manage to persuade him?* ◆ *We couldn't have managed without you.* ◆ *"Need any help?" "No, thanks. I can manage."* ⊃ note at CAN¹
> BUSINESS/TEAM **2** [T, I] ~ **(sth)** to control or be in charge of a business, a team, an organization, etc.: *to manage a factory/ bank/hotel/baseball team* ◆ *to manage a department/project* ◆ *We need people who are good at managing.*
> MONEY/TIME/INFORMATION **3** [I] ~ **(on sth)** to be able to live without having much money: *He has to manage on less than $150 a week.* **4** [T] ~ **sth** to use money, time, information, etc. in a sensible way: *Don't tell me how to manage my business.* ◆ *a computer program that helps you manage data efficiently* **5** [T] ~ **sth** to be able to do something at a particular time: *Let's meet again—can you manage one day next week for lunch?*
> DEAL WITH PROBLEMS **6** [I] to be able to solve your problems, deal with a difficult situation, etc. **SYN** COPE: *She's 82 and can't manage on her own any more.* ◆ ~ **with/without sb/sth** *How do you manage without a car?*
> CONTROL **7** [T] ~ **sb/sth** to keep someone or something under control; to be able to deal with someone or something: *It's like trying to manage a difficult child.* ◆ *Can you manage that suitcase?*

man·age·a·ble /ˈmænɪdʒəbl/ *adj.* possible to deal with or control: *Use conditioner regularly to make your hair soft and manageable.* ◆ *The debt has been reduced to a more manageable level.* **ANT** UNMANAGEABLE ▶ **man·age·a·bil·i·ty** /ˌmænɪdʒəˈbɪləti/ *noun* [U]

man·aged /ˈmænɪdʒd/ *adj.* [only before noun] carefully taken care of and controlled: *The money will be invested in managed funds.* ◆ *Only wood from managed forests is used in our furniture.*

managed 'care *noun* [U] a healthcare system that controls medical costs by requiring patients to visit only certain doctors and hospitals

man·age·ment 🔎 /ˈmænɪdʒmənt/ *noun*
1 [U] the act of running and controlling a business or similar organization: *a career in management* ◆ *hotel/project management* ◆ *a management training course* ◆ *The report cites bad management as the primary cause of the problem.* **2** [C, U] the people who run and control a business or similar organization: *(The) management is considering closing the factory.* ◆ *The store is now under new management.* ◆ *junior/ middle/senior management* ◆ *a management decision/job* ◆ *My role is to act as a mediator between employees and management.* ◆ *The managements of most manufacturers are eager to avoid strikes.* **3** [U] the act or skill of dealing with people or situations in a successful way: *classroom management* ◆ *time management* (= the way in which you organize how you spend your time) ◆ *management of staff* ◆ *Diet plays an important role in the management of heart disease.*

man·ag·er 🔎 /ˈmænɪdʒər/ *noun*
1 a person who is in charge of running a business, a store, or a similar organization or part of one: *a bank/hotel manager* ◆ *the sales/marketing/personnel manager* ◆ *a meeting of area managers* **2** a person who deals with the business affairs of an actor, a musician, etc. **3** a person who trains and organizes a sports team: *the new manager of the Yankees*

man·a·ge·ri·al /ˌmænəˈdʒɪriəl/ *adj.* [usually before noun] connected with the work of a manager: *Does she have any managerial experience?*

managing di'rector *noun* the person who is in charge of a large business or organization

managing '**editor** *noun* a person who manages the work of preparing books, magazines, or newspapers to be published

ma·ña·na /mənˈyɑnə; mɑn-/ *adv.* (from *Spanish*) at some time in the future (used when a person cannot or will not say exactly when)

man·a·tee /ˈmænəˌti/ *noun* a large water animal with front legs and a strong tail but no back legs, that lives in America and Africa

man·da·la /ˈmændələ; ˈmʌn-/ *noun* a round picture that represents the universe in some Eastern religions

man·da·rin /ˈmændərən/ *noun* **1 Mandarin** [U] the standard form of Chinese, which is the official language of China **2** (also ˌmandarin ˈorange) [C] a type of small orange with loose skin that comes off easily **3** [C] a government official of high rank in China in the past **4** [C] a powerful official of high rank, especially in the CIVIL SERVICE **SYN** BUREAUCRAT

ˌmandarin ˈcollar *noun* a small COLLAR that stands up and fits closely around the neck

man·date /ˈmændeɪt/ *noun, verb*
● *noun* **1** the authority to do something, given to a government or other organization by the people who vote for it in an election: ~ **(to do sth)** *The election victory gave the mayor a clear mandate to continue her program of reform.* ◆ ~ **(for sth)** *a mandate for an end to the civil war* **2** the period of time for which a government is given power: *The presidential mandate is limited to two terms of four years each.* **3** ~ **(to do sth)** (*formal*) an official order given to someone to perform a particular task: *The bank had no mandate to honor the check.* **4** the power given to a country to govern another country or region, especially in the past
● *verb* [often passive] (*formal*) **1** ~ **that...** | ~ **sb (to do sth)** to order someone to behave, do something, or vote in a particular way: *The law mandates that imported goods be identified as such.* **2** ~ **sb/sth to do sth** to give someone, especially a government or a committee, the authority to do something: *The assembly was mandated to draft a constitution.*

man·dat·ed /ˈmændeɪtəd/ *adj.* [only before noun] (*formal*) **1** required by law: *a mandated curriculum* **2** (of a country or state) placed under the rule of another country: *mandated territories* **3** having a mandate to do something: *a mandated government*

man·da·to·ry /ˈmændəˌtɔri/ *adj.* (*formal*) required by law **SYN** COMPULSORY: *The offense carries a mandatory life sentence.* ◆ ~ **(for sb) (to do sth)** *It is mandatory for blood banks to test all donated blood for the virus.*

man·di·ble /ˈmændəbl/ *noun* (*anatomy*) **1** the JAWBONE Ɔ picture at BODY **2** the upper or lower part of a bird's beak **3** either of the two parts that are at the front and on either side of an insect's mouth, used especially for biting and crushing food

man·do·lin /ˌmændəˈlɪn; ˈmændələn/ *noun* a musical instrument with metal strings (usually eight) arranged in pairs, and a curved back, played with a PLECTRUM Ɔ picture at INSTRUMENT

man·drake /ˈmændreɪk/ *noun* [C, U] a poisonous plant used to make drugs, especially ones to make people sleep, thought in the past to have magic powers

mane /meɪn/ *noun* **1** the long hair on the neck of a horse or a LION Ɔ picture at ANIMAL, HORSE **2** (*informal* or *literary*) a person's long or thick hair

man·eat·er /ˈmænˌitər/ *noun* **1** a wild animal that attacks and eats humans **2** (*humorous*) a woman who has many sexual partners ▶ ˈman-ˌeating *adj.* [only before noun]: *a man-eating tiger*

ma·neu·ver /məˈnuvər/ *noun, verb*
● *noun* **1** [C] a movement performed with care and skill: *a complicated/skillful maneuver* ◆ *You will be asked to perform some standard maneuvers during your driving test.* **2** [C, U] a skillful plan, action, or movement that is used to give someone an advantage **SYN** MOVE: *diplomatic maneuvers* ◆ *a complex maneuver in a game of chess* **3 maneuvers** [pl.] military exercises involving a large number of soldiers, ships, etc.: *The army is on maneuvers in the desert.*
● *verb* **1** [I, T] to move or turn skillfully or carefully; to move or turn something skillfully or carefully: ~ **(for sth)** *The yachts maneuvered for position.* ◆ *There was very little room to maneuver.* ◆ ~ **sth (+ adv./prep.)** *She maneuvered the car carefully into the garage.* **2** [I, T] to control or influence a situation in a skillful but sometimes dishonest way: *The new laws leave us little room to maneuver* (= not much opportunity to change or influence a situation). ◆ ~ **sth + adv./prep.** *She maneuvered her way to the top of the company.*

ma·neu·ver·a·ble /məˈnuvərəbl/ *adj.* that can easily be moved into different positions: *a highly maneuverable vehicle* ▶ **ma·neu·ver·a·bil·i·ty** /məˌnuvərəˈbɪləti/ *noun* [U]

ma·neu·ver·ing /məˈnuvərɪŋ/ *noun* [U, C] skillful and often dishonest ways of achieving your aims

man 'Friday *noun* a male assistant who does many different kinds of work Ɔ compare GIRL FRIDAY **ORIGIN** From a character in Daniel Defoe's novel *Robinson Crusoe* who is rescued by Crusoe and works for him.

man·ful·ly /ˈmænfəli/ *adv.* using a lot of effort in a brave and determined way ▶ **man·ful** *adj.* [only before noun]

man·ga /ˈmɑŋɡə/ *noun* [C, U] (from *Japanese*) a Japanese form of COMIC STRIP, often one with violent or sexual contents

man·ga·nese /ˈmæŋɡəˌniz; -ˌnis/ *noun* [U] (*symb.* **Mn**) a chemical element. Manganese is a gray-white metal that breaks easily, used in making glass and steel.

mange /meɪndʒ/ *noun* [U] a skin disease that affects MAMMALS, caused by a PARASITE Ɔ see also MANGY

man·ger /ˈmeɪndʒər/ *noun* a long open box that horses and cows can eat from **IDM** see DOG *n.*

man·gle /ˈmæŋɡl/ *verb, noun*
● *verb* [usually passive] **1** ~ **sth** to crush or twist something so that it is badly damaged: *His hand was mangled in the machine.* **2** ~ **sth** to spoil something, for example a poem or a piece of music, by saying it wrongly or playing it badly **SYN** RUIN ▶ **man·gled** *adj.*: *mangled bodies/remains*
● *noun* (also **wringer**) a machine with two ROLLERS used especially in the past for squeezing the water out of clothes that had been washed

man·go /ˈmæŋɡoʊ/ *noun* [C, U] (*pl.* **man·goes** or **man·gos**) a tropical fruit with smooth yellow or red skin, soft orange flesh, and a large seed inside Ɔ picture at FRUIT

man·go·steen /ˈmæŋɡəˌstin/ *noun* a tropical fruit with a thick red-brown skin and sweet white flesh with a lot of juice

man·grove /ˈmæŋɡroʊv/ *noun* a tropical tree that grows in mud or at the edge of rivers and has roots that are above ground: *mangrove swamps*

man·gy /ˈmeɪndʒi/ *adj.* [usually before noun] **1** (of an animal) suffering from MANGE: *a mangy dog* **2** (*informal*) dirty and in bad condition **SYN** MOTH-EATEN: *a mangy old coat*

man·han·dle /ˈmænˌhændl/ *verb* **1** ~ **sb** to push, pull, or handle someone roughly: *Bystanders claim they were manhandled by security guards.* **2** ~ **sb + adv./prep.** to move or lift a heavy object using a lot of effort **SYN** HAUL: *They were trying to manhandle an old sofa across the road.*

man·hat·tan /mænˈhætn; mən-/ *noun* an alcoholic drink made by mixing WHISKEY or another strong alcoholic drink with VERMOUTH

man·hole /ˈmænhoʊl/ *noun* a hole in the street that is covered with a lid, used when someone needs to go down to examine the pipes or SEWERS below the street

man·hood /ˈmænhʊd/ *noun* **1** [U] the state or time of being an adult man rather than a boy **2** [U] the qualities that a man is supposed to have, for example courage, strength, and sexual power: *Her newfound power was a threat to his manhood.* **3** [sing.] (*literary* or *humorous*) a man's PENIS.

ʌ cup ə about eɪ say aɪ five ɔɪ boy aʊ now oʊ go ər bird

People use "manhood" to avoid saying "penis." **4** [U] (*literary*) all the men of a country: *The nation's manhood died on the battlefields of World War I.* ◌ compare WOMANHOOD

man-hour *noun* [usually pl.] the amount of work done by one person in one hour

man·hunt /'mænhʌnt/ *noun* an organized search by a lot of people for a criminal or a prisoner who has escaped

ma·ni·a /'meɪniə/ *noun* **1** [C, usually sing., U] ~ **(for sth/for doing sth)** an extremely strong desire or enthusiasm for something, often shared by a lot of people at the same time **SYN** CRAZE: *The Super Bowl was approaching and football mania was sweeping the country.* **2** [U] (*psychology*) a mental illness in which someone has an OBSESSION about something that makes them extremely anxious, violent, or confused

-mania /'meɪniə/ *combining form* (in nouns) mental illness of a particular type: *kleptomania* ▸ **-maniac** /'meɪniˌæk/ (in nouns): *a pyromaniac*

ma·ni·ac /'meɪniˌæk/ *noun* **1** (*informal*) a person who behaves in an extremely dangerous, wild, or stupid way **SYN** MADMAN: *He was driving like a maniac.* **2** a person who has an extremely strong desire or enthusiasm for something, to an extent that other people think is not normal **SYN** FANATIC **3** (*psychology*) a person suffering from mania: *a homicidal maniac* ▸ **ma·ni·ac** *adj.* [only before noun]: *a maniac driver/fan/killer*

ma·ni·a·cal /məˈnaɪəkl/ *adj.* wild or violent: *maniacal laughter* ▸ **ma·ni·a·cally** /-kli/ *adv.*

man·ic /'mænɪk/ *adj.* **1** (*informal*) full of activity, excitement, and anxiety; behaving in a busy, excited, anxious way **SYN** HECTIC: *Things are manic at the office right now.* ◆ *The performers had manic energy and enthusiasm.* **2** (*psychology*) connected with MANIA: *manic mood swings* ▸ **man·i·cally** /-kli/ *adv.*: *I rushed around manically, trying to finish the housework.*

manic de·pression *noun* [U] = BIPOLAR DISORDER

manic-de·pressive *adj., noun* = BIPOLAR

Man·i·chae·an (also **Man·i·che·an**) /ˌmænəˈkiən/ *adj.* (*religion, philosophy*) based on the belief that there are two opposites in everything, for example good and evil or light and dark

man·i·cure /'mænəˌkyʊr/ *noun, verb*
● *noun* [C, U] the care and treatment of a person's hands and nails: *to have a manicure* ◌ compare PEDICURE
● *verb* ~ **sth** to care for and treat your hands and nails

man·i·cured /'mænəˌkyʊrd/ *adj.* **1** (of hands or fingers) with nails that are neatly cut and polished **2** (of gardens, a LAWN, etc.) very neat and well cared for

man·i·cur·ist /'mænəˌkyʊrɪst/ *noun* a person whose job is the care and treatment of the hands and nails

man·i·fest /'mænəˌfɛst/ *verb, adj., noun*
● *verb* (*formal*) **1** ~ **sth (in sth)** to show something clearly, especially a feeling, an attitude, or a quality **SYN** DEMONSTRATE: *Social tensions were manifested in the recent political crisis.* **2** ~ **itself (in sth)** to appear or become noticeable **SYN** APPEAR: *The symptoms of the disease manifested themselves ten days later.*
● *adj.* ~ **(to sb) (in sth)** (*formal*) easy to see or understand **SYN** CLEAR: *His nervousness was manifest to all those present.* ◆ *The anger he felt is manifest in his paintings.* ▸ **man·i·fest·ly** *adv.*: *manifestly unfair* ◆ *The current administration has manifestly failed to achieve its goals.*
● *noun* (*technical*) a list of goods or passengers on a ship or an aircraft

man·i·fes·ta·tion /ˌmænəfəˈsteɪʃn/ *noun* (*formal*) **1** [C, U] ~ **(of sth)** an event, action, or thing that is a sign that something exists or is happening; the act of appearing as a sign that something exists or is happening: *The riots are a clear manifestation of the people's discontent.* ◆ *Some manifestation of your concern would have been appreciated.* **2** [C] an

appearance of a GHOST or spirit: *The church is the site of a number of supernatural manifestations.*

man·i·fes·to /ˌmænəˈfɛstoʊ/ *noun* (pl. **man·i·fes·tos**) a written statement in which a group of people, especially a political party, explain their beliefs and say what they will do if they win an election: *an election manifesto* ◆ *the party manifesto*

man·i·fold /'mænəˌfoʊld/ *adj., noun*
● *adj.* (*formal*) many; of many different types: *The possibilities were manifold.*
● *noun* (*technical*) a pipe or chamber with several openings for taking gases in and out of a car engine: *the exhaust manifold*

man·i·kin (also **man·ni·kin**) /'mænəkən/ *noun* **1** a model of the human body that is used for teaching art or medicine **2** (*old-fashioned*) a very small man **SYN** DWARF

Ma·nil·a (also **Ma·nil·la**) /məˈnɪlə/ *noun* [U] strong brown paper, used especially for making envelopes

man·i·oc /'mæniˌɑk/ *noun* [U] = CASSAVA

ma·nip·u·late **AWL** /məˈnɪpyəˌleɪt/ *verb* **1** (*disapproving*) to control or influence someone or something, often in a dishonest way so that they do not realize it: *She uses her charm to manipulate people.* ◆ *As a politician, he knows how to manipulate public opinion.* ◆ ~ **sb into sth/into doing sth** *They managed to manipulate us into agreeing to help.* **2** ~ **sth** to control or use something in a skillful way: *to manipulate the gears and levers of a machine* ◆ *Computers are very efficient at manipulating information.* **3** ~ **sth** (*technical*) to move a person's bones or joints into the correct position ▸ **ma·nip·u·la·tion** **AWL** /məˌnɪpyəˈleɪʃn/ *noun* [U, C]: *the manipulation of children through advertising* ◆ *data manipulation* ◆ *manipulation of the bones of the back*

ma·nip·u·la·tive **AWL** /məˈnɪpyələtɪv; -ˌleɪtɪv/ *adj.* **1** (*disapproving*) skillful at influencing someone or forcing someone to do what you want, often in an unfair way **2** (*formal*) connected with the ability to handle objects skillfully: *manipulative skills such as typing and knitting*

ma·nip·u·la·tor /məˈnɪpyəˌleɪtər/ *noun* (often *disapproving*) a person who is skillful at influencing people or situations in order to get what they want

man·kind /ˌmænˈkaɪnd/ *noun* [U] all humans, thought about as one large group; the human race: *the history of mankind* ◆ *an invention for the good of all mankind* ◌ see also HUMANKIND ◌ compare WOMANKIND

man·ly /'mænli/ *adj.* (often *approving*) (**man·li·er, man·li·est**) having the qualities or physical features that are admired or expected in a man ▸ **man·li·ness** *noun* [U]

man-made *adj.* made by people; not natural **SYN** ARTIFICIAL: *a man-made lake* ◆ *man-made fibers such as nylon and polyester* ◌ thesaurus box at ARTIFICIAL

man·na /'mænə/ *noun* [U] (in the Bible) the food that God provided for the people of Israel during their 40 years in the desert: (*figurative*) *To the refugees, the food shipments were manna from heaven* (= an unexpected and very welcome gift).

manned /mænd/ *adj.* if a machine, a vehicle, a place, or an activity is **manned**, it has or needs a person to control or operate it **ANT** UNMANNED: *manned space flight*

man·ne·quin /'mænəkən/ *noun* **1** a model of a human body, used for displaying clothes in stores **2** (*old-fashioned*) a person whose job is to wear and display new styles of clothes **SYN** MODEL

man·ner /'mænər/ *noun*
1 [sing.] (*formal*) the way that something is done or happens: *She answered in a businesslike manner.* ◆ *The manner in which the decision was announced was extremely regrettable.* **2** [sing.] the way that someone behaves and speaks toward other people: *to have an aggressive/a friendly/a relaxed manner* ◆ *His manner was polite but cool.* ◌ see also BEDSIDE MANNER **3** **manners** [pl.] behavior that is considered to be polite in a particular society or culture: *to have good/bad manners* ◆ *It is bad manners to talk with your*

---

mouth full. ◆ *He has no manners* (= behaves very badly). ⮕ see also TABLE MANNERS **4** manners [pl.] (*formal*) the habits and customs of a particular group of people: *the social morals and manners of the seventeenth century*

IDM all manner of sb/sth many different types of people or things: *The problem can be solved in all manner of ways.* in a manner of speaking if you think about it in a particular way; true in some but not all ways: *All these points of view are related, in a manner of speaking.* in the manner of sb/sth (*formal*) in a style that is typical of someone or something: *a painting in the manner of Raphael* (as/as if) to the manner born (*formal*) as if something is natural for you and you have done it many times in the past what manner of... (*formal* or *literary*) what kind of...: *What manner of man could do such a terrible thing?*

man·nered /ˈmænərd/ *adj.* **1** (*disapproving*) (of behavior, art, writing, etc.) trying to impress people by being formal and not natural **SYN** AFFECTED **2** -mannered (in compounds) having the type of manners mentioned: *a bad-mannered child* ⮕ see also ILL-MANNERED, MILD-MANNERED, WELL MANNERED

man·ner·ism /ˈmænəˌrɪzəm/ *noun* **1** [C] a particular habit or way of speaking or behaving that someone has but is not aware of: *nervous/odd/irritating mannerisms* **2** [U] too much use of a particular style in painting or writing **3** Mannerism [U] a style in 16th-century Italian art that did not show things in a natural way but made them look strange or out of their usual shape

man·ner·ist /ˈmænərɪst/ usually **Mannerist** *adj.* (of painting or writing) in the style of mannerism

man·ni·kin = MANIKIN

man·nish /ˈmænɪʃ/ *adj.* (usually *disapproving*) (of a woman or of something belonging to a woman) having qualities that are thought of as typical of or suitable for a man

ma·no-a-ma·no /ˌmɑnoʊ ɑ ˈmɑnoʊ/ *adv.*, *noun* (*informal*, from *Spanish*)
- *adv.* with two people facing each other directly in order to decide an argument or a competition: *It's time to settle this mano-a-mano.*
- *noun* (*pl.* ma·no-a-ma·nos) a fight or contest, especially one between two people

man of ˈletters *noun* a man who is a writer, or who writes about literature

man-of-ˈwar (also **man-o'-ˈwar**) /ˌmæn ə ˈwɔr/ *noun* (*pl.* ˌmen-of-ˈwar, ˌmen-o'-ˈwar) a sailing ship used in the past for fighting

man·or /ˈmænər/ *noun* **1** (also ˈmanor ˌhouse) a large country house surrounded by land that belongs to it **2** an area of land with a manor house on it

ma·no·ri·al /məˈnɔriəl/ *adj.* typical of or connected with a manor, especially in the past

man·pow·er /ˈmænˌpaʊər/ *noun* [U] the number of workers needed or available to do a particular job: *a need for trained/skilled manpower* ◆ *a manpower shortage*

man·qué /mɑŋˈkeɪ/ *adj.* (following nouns) (from *French*, *formal* or *humorous*) used to describe a person who hoped to follow a particular career but who failed in it or never tried it: *He's really an artist manqué.*

man·sard /ˈmænsɑrd; -sərd/ (also ˌmansard ˈroof) *noun* (*technical*) a roof with a double slope in which the upper part is less steep than the lower part

manse /mæns/ *noun* the house of a minister, especially a Presbyterian one

man·serv·ant /ˈmænˌsɜrvənt/ *noun* (*pl.* men·serv·ants /ˈmɛnˌsɜrvənts/) (*old-fashioned*) a male servant, especially a man's personal servant

man·sion /ˈmænʃn/ *noun* a large impressive house: *the governor's mansion* ⮕ picture at BUILDING

man-sized *adj.* [only before noun] suitable or large enough for a man: *a man-sized breakfast*

man·slaugh·ter /ˈmænˌslɔtər/ *noun* [U] (*law*) the crime of killing someone illegally but not deliberately ⮕ compare CULPABLE HOMICIDE, HOMICIDE, MURDER

man·ta /ˈmæntə/ (also ˈmanta ˌray) *noun* a large fish that lives in tropical seas and swims by moving two parts like large flat wings

man·tel (also man·tle) /ˈmæntl/ (also man·tel·piece, man·tle·piece /ˈmæntlˌpis/) *noun* a shelf above a FIREPLACE

man·tis /ˈmæntəs/ *noun* (*pl.* man·tis·es or man·tis) = PRAYING MANTIS

man·tle /ˈmæntl/ *noun*, *verb*
- *noun* **1** [sing.] the ~ of sb/sth (*literary*) the role and responsibilities of an important person or job, especially when they are passed on from one person to another: *The vice president must now take on the mantle of power.* **2** [C] (*literary*) a layer of something that covers a surface: *hills with a mantle of snow* **SYN** COVERING **3** [C] a loose piece of clothing without sleeves, worn over other clothes, especially in the past **SYN** CLOAK **4** (also ˈgas ˌmantle) [C] a cover around the flame of a gas lamp that becomes very bright when it is heated **5** [sing.] (*geology*) the part of the earth below the CRUST and surrounding the core
- *verb* ~ sth (*literary*) to cover the surface of something

man·tra /ˈmɑntrə/ *noun* a word, phrase, or sound that is repeated again and again, especially during prayer or MEDITATION: *a Buddhist mantra*

man·trap /ˈmæntræp/ *noun* a trap used in the past for catching people, especially people who tried to steal things from someone's land

man·u·al **AWL** /ˈmænyuəl/ *adj.*, *noun*
- *adj.* **1** (of work, etc.) involving using the hands or physical strength: *manual labor/jobs/skills* ◆ *manual and non-manual workers* **2** operated or controlled by hand rather than automatically or using electricity, etc.: *The car has a manual shift.* ◆ *My camera has manual and automatic functions.* **3** connected with using the hands: *manual dexterity* ▶ man·u·al·ly **AWL** *adv.*: *manually operated*
- *noun* a book that tells you how to do or operate something, especially one that comes with a machine, etc. when you buy it: *a computer/car/instruction manual* ⮕ compare HANDBOOK
  IDM on manual not being operated automatically: *Leave the controls on manual.*

man·u·fac·ture 🔑 /ˌmænyəˈfæktʃər/ *verb*, *noun*
- *verb* **1** ~ sth to make goods in large quantities, using machinery **SYN** MASS-PRODUCE: *manufactured goods* **2** ~ sth to invent a story, an excuse, etc.: *a news story manufactured by an unscrupulous reporter* **3** ~ sth (*technical*) to produce a substance: *Vitamins cannot be manufactured by our bodies.*
- *noun* **1** [U] the process of producing goods in large quantities: *the manufacture of cars* **2** manufactures [pl.] (*technical*) manufactured goods: *a major importer of cotton manufactures*

man·u·fac·tur·er 🔑 /ˌmænyəˈfæktʃərər/ *noun* a person or company that produces goods in large quantities **SYN** MAKER: *a car/computer manufacturer* ◆ *Always follow the manufacturer's instructions.* ◆ *Faulty goods should be returned to the manufacturer.*

man·u·fac·tur·ing 🔑 /ˌmænyəˈfæktʃərɪŋ/ *noun* [U] the business or industry of producing goods in large quantities in factories, etc.: *Many jobs in manufacturing were lost during the recession.*

man·u·mis·sion /ˌmænyəˈmɪʃn/ *noun* [U] the act of releasing a person from SLAVERY: *manumission in ancient Greece* ▶ man·u·mit /ˌmænyəˈmɪt/ *verb*: ~ sb *Many slaves were manumitted by their masters.*

ma·nure /məˈnʊr/ *noun*, *verb*
- *noun* [U] the waste matter from animals that is spread over or mixed with the soil to help plants and crops grow **SYN** DUNG

• *verb* ~ **sth** to put manure on or in soil to help plants grow

man·u·script /ˈmænyəˌskrɪpt/ *noun* (*abbr.* MS, ms) **1** a copy of a book, piece of music, etc. before it has been printed: *an unpublished/original manuscript* ♦ *I read her poems in manuscript.* **2** a very old book or document that was written by hand before printing was invented: *medieval illuminated manuscripts*

Manx /mæŋks/ *adj.* of or connected with the Isle of Man, its people, or the language once spoken there

Manx ˈcat *noun* a breed of cat with no tail

man·y /ˈmɛni/ *det., pron.*

1 used with plural nouns and verbs, especially in negative sentences or in more formal English, to mean "a large number of." Also used in questions to ask about the size of a number, and with "as," "so," and "too.": *We don't have very many copies left.* ♦ *You can't each have one. We haven't got many.* ♦ *Many people feel that the law should be changed.* ♦ *Many of those present disagreed.* ♦ *How many children do you have?* ♦ *There are too many mistakes in this essay.* ♦ *He made ten mistakes in as many* (= in ten) *lines.* ♦ *New drivers have twice as many accidents as experienced drivers.* ♦ *Don't take so many.* ♦ *I've known her for a great many* (= very many) *years.* ♦ *Even if one person is hurt that is one too many.* ♦ *It was one of my many mistakes.* ♦ *a many-headed monster* ♦ **the many** used with a plural verb to mean "most people": *a government that improves conditions for the many* **3 many a** (*formal*) used with a singular noun and verb to mean "a large number of": *Many a good man has been destroyed by drinking.*

IDM **as many as…** used to show surprise that the number of people or things involved is so large: *There were as many as 200 people at the lecture.* **have had one too many** (*informal*) to be slightly drunk **many's the…** (*formal*) used to show that something happens often: *Many's the time I heard her use those words.*

Mao·ism /ˈmaʊˌɪzəm/ *noun* [U] the ideas of the 20th century Chinese COMMUNIST leader Mao Zedong ▶ **Mao·ist** /ˈmaʊɪst/ *noun, adj.*

Ma·o·ri /ˈmaʊri/ *noun* **1** [C] a member of a race of people who were the original people living in New Zealand **2** [U] the language of the Maori people ▶ **Ma·o·ri** *adj.*

map /mæp/ *noun, verb*

• *noun* a drawing or plan of the earth's surface or part of it, showing countries, towns, rivers, etc.: *a map of California* ♦ *a street map of Miami* ♦ *to read a/the map* (= understand the information on a map) ♦ *large-scale maps* ♦ *Can you find the Black Hills on the map?* ♦ *I'll draw you a map of how to get to my house.* ⊃ see also ROAD MAP

IDM **put sb/sth on the map** to make someone or something famous or important: *The exhibition helped put the city on the map.* ⊃ more at WIPE

• *verb* (-pp-) **1** ~ **sth** to make a map of an area **SYN** CHART: *an unexplored region that has not yet been mapped* **2** ~ **sth** to discover or give information about something, especially the way it is arranged or organized: *It is now possible to map the different functions of the brain.* ▶ **map·ping** *noun* [U]: *the mapping of the Indian subcontinent* ♦ *gene mapping*

PHR V **ˈmap sth on/onto sth** to link a group of qualities, items, etc. with their source, cause, position on a scale, etc.: *Grammar information enables students to map the structure of a foreign language onto their own.* **ˌmap sth↔ˈout** to plan or arrange something in a careful or detailed way: *He has his career path clearly mapped out.*

ma·ple /ˈmeɪpl/ *noun* **1** [C, U] (also **ˈmaple ˌtree**) a tall tree with leaves that have five points and turn bright red or yellow in the fall. Maples grow in northern countries. ⊃ see also SUGAR MAPLE ⊃ picture at TREE **2** [U] the wood of the maple tree

ˈmaple ˌleaf *noun* **1** [C] the leaf of the maple tree, used as a symbol of Canada **2 the Maple Leaf** [sing.] the flag of Canada

ˌmaple ˈsugar *noun* [U] a type of sugar obtained by boiling liquid (called SAP) obtained from some types of maple trees

ˌmaple ˈsyrup *noun* [U] a sweet sticky sauce made with liquid obtained from some types of maple trees, often eaten with PANCAKES

mar /mɑr/ *verb* (-rr-) ~ **sth** to damage or spoil something good **SYN** BLIGHT, RUIN: *His face was marred by an old knife wound.* ♦ *The elections were marred by violence.*

ma·rac·as /məˈrɑkəz/ *noun* [pl.] a pair of simple musical instruments consisting of hollow balls containing BEADS or BEANS that are shaken to produce a sound ⊃ picture at INSTRUMENT

mar·a·schi·no /ˌmærəˈskinoʊ; -ˈʃinoʊ/ *noun* (*pl.* **mar·a·schi·nos**) **1** (also **ˌmaraschino ˈcherry**) [C] a preserved CHERRY used to decorate alcoholic drinks and DESSERTS **2** [U, C] a strong, sweet, alcoholic drink made from black cherries

mar·a·thon /ˈmærəˌθɑn/ *noun* **1** a long running race of about 26 miles or 42 kilometers: *the Chicago marathon* ♦ *to run a marathon* **2** an activity or a piece of work that lasts a long time and requires a lot of effort and patience: *The interview was a real marathon.* **ORIGIN** From the story that in ancient Greece a messenger ran from Marathon to Athens (22 miles) with the news of a victory over the Persians. ▶ **marathon** *adj.* [only before noun]: *a marathon car trip lasting 56 hours* ♦ *a marathon legal battle*

mar·a·thon·er /ˈmærəˌθɑnər/ *noun* a person who runs in a marathon

ma·raud·ing /məˈrɔdɪŋ/ *adj.* [only before noun] (of people or animals) going around a place in search of things to steal or people to attack: *marauding wolves* ▶ **ma·raud·er** *noun*

mar·ble /ˈmɑrbl/ *noun* **1** [U] a type of hard stone that is usually white and often has colored lines in it. It can be polished and is used in building and for making statues, etc.: *a slab/block of marble* ♦ *a marble floor/sculpture* **2** [C] a small ball of colored glass that children roll along the ground in a game **3 marbles** [U] a game played with marbles: *Three boys were playing marbles.* **4 marbles** [pl.] (*informal*) a way of referring to someone's intelligence or mental ability: *He's losing his marbles* (= he's not behaving in a sensible way).

mar·bled /ˈmɑrbld/ *adj.* having the colors and/or patterns of marble: *marbled wallpaper*

mar·bling /ˈmɑrblɪŋ/ *noun* [U] the method of decorating something with a pattern that looks like MARBLE

marc /mɑrk/ *noun* **1** [U, sing.] the substance left after GRAPES have been pressed to make wine **2** [U, C] a strong alcoholic drink made from this substance

---

March 🔑 /mɑrtʃ/ *noun* [U, C] (*abbr.* **Mar.**)
the 3rd month of the year, between February and April
HELP To see how **March** is used, look at the examples at
April. **IDM** see MAD

march 🔑 /mɑrtʃ/ *verb, noun*

• *verb* **1** [I] to walk with stiff regular steps like a soldier:
(+ **adv./prep.**) *Soldiers were marching up and down outside
the government buildings.* ♦ + **noun** *They marched 20 miles to
reach the capital.* **2** [I] + **adv./prep.** to walk somewhere
quickly in a determined way: *She marched over to me and
demanded an apology.* **3** [T] ~ **sb** + **adv./prep.** to force
someone to walk somewhere with you: *The guards marched
the prisoner away.* **4** [I] to walk through the streets in a large
group in order to protest about or support something
SYN DEMONSTRATE
IDM **get your marching orders** (*informal*) to be ordered to
leave a place, a job, etc. **give sb their marching orders**
(*informal*) to order someone to leave a place, their job, etc.
march to (the beat of) a different drummer/drum to
behave in a different way from other people; to have
different attitudes or ideas: *She was a gifted and original artist
who marched to a different drummer.*
PHR V **march 'on** to move on or pass quickly: *Time marches
on and we still have not made a decision.* **'march on...** to
march to a place to protest about something or to attack it:
Several thousand people marched on City Hall.

• *noun* **1** [C] an organized walk by many people from one
place to another, in order to protest about something, or to
express their opinions: *protest marches* ⊃ compare DEMON-
STRATION **2** [C] an act of marching; a journey made by
marching: *The army began their long march to the coast.*
3 [sing.] **the ~ of sth** the steady development or forward
movement of something: *the march of progress/technology/
time* **4** [C] a piece of music written for marching to: *a funeral
march*
IDM **on the march** marching somewhere: *The enemy is on
the march.*

march·er /ˈmɑrtʃər/ *noun* a person who is taking part in a
march as a protest **SYN** DEMONSTRATOR

'marching ˌband *noun* a group of musicians who play
while they are marching

mar·chion·ess /ˈmɑrʃənəs; ˌmɑrʃəˈnɛs/ *noun* **1** a woman
who has the rank of a MARQUESS **2** the wife of a MARQUESS
⊃ compare MARQUISE

ˌMarch 'Madness *noun* [U] a period during the month of
March when the annual NCAA (National Collegiate Athletic
Association) basketball TOURNAMENT takes place

Mar·di Gras /ˈmɑrdi ˌgrɑ; -ˌgrɔ/ *noun* [U] (from *French*) the
day before the beginning of Lent, celebrated as a holiday in
some countries, with music and dancing in the streets
⊃ compare SHROVE TUESDAY

mare /mɛr/ *noun* a female horse or DONKEY ⊃ compare
BROOD MARE, FILLY, STALLION
IDM **a mare's nest 1** a discovery that seems interesting
but is found to have no value **2** a very complicated
situation

mar·ga·rine /ˈmɑrdʒərən/ *noun* [U] a yellow substance like
butter made from animal or vegetable fats, used in cooking
or spread on bread, etc.

mar·ga·ri·ta /ˌmɑrgəˈritə/ *noun* an alcoholic drink made by
mixing fruit juice with TEQUILA

mar·gin **AWL** /ˈmɑrdʒən/ *noun* [C] **1** the empty space at the
side of a written or printed page: *the left-hand/right-hand
margin* ♦ *a narrow/wide margin* ♦ *notes scribbled in the
margin* **2** [usually sing.] the amount of time, or number of
votes, etc. by which someone wins something: *He won by a
narrow margin.* ♦ *She beat the other runners by a margin of ten
seconds.* **3** (*business*) = PROFIT MARGIN: *What are your
average operating margins?* ♦ *a gross margin of 45%* **4** [usually
sing.] an extra amount of something such as time, space,
money, etc. that you include in order to make sure that

something is successful: *a safety margin* ♦ *The narrow
passageway left me little margin for error as I reversed the car.*
⊃ see also MARGIN OF ERROR **5** (*formal*) the extreme edge or
limit of a place: *the eastern margin of the Indian Ocean*
6 [usually pl.] the part that is not included in the main part of
a group or situation **SYN** FRINGE: *people living on the
margins of society*

mar·gin·al **AWL** /ˈmɑrdʒənl/ *adj.* **1** small and not important **SYN** SLIGHT: *a marginal improvement in weather conditions* ♦ *The story will only be of marginal interest to our readers.*
2 not part of a main or important group or situation:
marginal groups in society **3** [only before noun] written in the
margin of a page: *marginal notes/comments* **4** (of land) that
cannot produce enough good crops to make a profit

mar·gi·na·li·a /ˌmɑrdʒəˈneɪliə/ *noun* [pl.] **1** notes written in
the MARGINS of a book, etc. **2** facts or details that are not
very important

mar·gin·al·ize /ˈmɑrdʒənəˌlaɪz/ *verb* ~ **sb** to make
someone feel as if they are not important and cannot
influence decisions or events; to put someone in a position
in which they have no power ▶ **mar·gin·al·i·za·tion**
/ˌmɑrdʒənələˈzeɪʃn/ *noun* [U]: *the marginalization of the elderly*

mar·gin·al·ly **AWL** /ˈmɑrdʒənəli/ *adv.* very slightly; not
very much: *They now cost marginally more than they did last
year.*

ˌmargin of 'error *noun* [usually sing.] an amount that you
allow when you calculate something, for the possibility that
a number is not completely accurate: *The survey has a
margin of error of 2.5%.*

mar·gue·rite /ˌmɑrgəˈrit/ *noun* a small, white, garden
flower with a yellow center

ma·ri·a·chi /ˌmɑriˈɑtʃi; ˌmær-/ *noun* [C, U] a musician who
plays traditional Mexican music, usually as part of a small
group that travels from place to place; the type of music
played by these musicians: *a mariachi band*

Mar·i·an /ˈmɛriən/ *adj.* (*religion*) relating to the Virgin Mary
in the Christian church

mar·i·cul·ture /ˈmærəˌkʌltʃər/ *noun* [U] (*technical*) a type of
farming in which fish or other sea animals and plants are
bred or grown for food

mar·i·gold /ˈmærəˌgoʊld/ *noun* an orange or yellow garden
flower. There are several types of marigolds.

ma·ri·jua·na (also **ma·ri·hua·na** /ˌmærəˈwɑnə/) (also
informal **pot**) *noun* [U] a drug (illegal in many countries)
made from the dried leaves and flowers of the HEMP plant,
which gives the person smoking it a feeling of being
relaxed **SYN** CANNABIS

ma·rim·ba /məˈrɪmbə/ *noun* a musical instrument like a
XYLOPHONE

ma·ri·na /məˈrinə/ *noun* a specially designed HARBOR for
sail- and motor boats

mar·i·nade /ˈmærəˌneɪd; ˌmærəˈneɪd/ *noun* [C, U] a mixture of
oil, wine, spices, etc., in which meat or fish is left before it is
cooked in order to make it softer or to give it a particular
flavor

ma·ri·na·ra /ˌmærəˈnærə/ *noun* [U] (from *Italian*) **marinara**
sauce is made from tomatoes and onions and served
especially with PASTA

mar·i·nate /ˈmærəˌneɪt/ (also **mar·i·nade**) *verb* [T, I] ~ **(sth)** if
you **marinate** food or it **marinates**, you leave it in a
marinade before cooking it

ma·rine /məˈrin/ *adj., noun*

• *adj.* [only before noun] **1** connected with the ocean and the
creatures and plants that live there: *marine life* ♦ *a marine
biologist* (= a scientist who studies life in the ocean)
2 connected with ships or trade at sea

• *noun* **1** a soldier who is trained to serve on land or at sea
2 Marine a member of the U.S. Marine Corps

mar·i·ner /ˈmærənər/ *noun* (*old-fashioned* or *literary*) a sailor

h **hat**	m **man**	n **no**	ŋ **sing**	l **leg**	r **red**	y **yes**	w **wet**

mar·i·on·ette /ˌmæriəˈnɛt/ *noun* a PUPPET whose arms, legs, and head are moved by strings

mar·i·tal /ˈmærətl/ *adj.* [only before noun] connected with marriage or with the relationship between a husband and wife: *marital difficulties/breakdown*

ˌmarital ˈstatus *noun* [U] (*formal*) (used especially on official forms) the fact of whether you are single, married, etc.: *questions about age, sex, and marital status*

mar·i·time /ˈmærəˌtaɪm/ *adj.* **1** connected with the ocean or ships: *a maritime museum* **2** (*formal*) near the ocean: *maritime Antarctica*

the Mar·i·times /ˈmærəˌtaɪmz/ *noun* [pl.] the Canadian PROVINCES (= government divisions) of New Brunswick, Nova Scotia, and Prince Edward Island ⟳ compare ATLANTIC CANADA

mar·jo·ram /ˈmɑrdʒərəm/ *noun* [U] a plant with leaves that smell sweet and are used in cooking as an HERB, often when dried

mark ✎ /mɑrk/ *verb, noun*

• *verb*

> **WRITE/DRAW 1** [T] to write or draw a symbol, line, etc. on something in order to give information about it: **~ A (with B)** *Items marked with an asterisk can be omitted.* ◆ **~ B on A** *Prices are marked on the goods.* ◆ **~ sb/sth + adj.** *The teacher marked her absent* (= made a mark by her name to show that she was absent). ◆ *Why did you mark this wrong?* ◆ *Do not open any mail marked "Confidential."*

> **SPOIL/DAMAGE 2** [T, I] **~ (sth)** to make a mark on something in a way that spoils or damages it; to become spoiled or damaged in this way: *A large purple scar marked his cheek.* ◆ *The surfaces are made from a material that doesn't mark.*

> **SHOW POSITION 3** [T] **~ sth** to show the position of something **SYN** INDICATE: *The cross marks the spot where the body was found.* ◆ *The route is marked in red.*

> **CELEBRATE 4** [T] **~ sth** to celebrate or officially remember an event that you consider to be important: *a ceremony to mark the 50th anniversary of the end of the war*

> **SHOW CHANGE 5** [T] **~ sth** to be a sign that something new is going to happen: *This speech may mark a change in the country's monetary policy.* ◆ *The agreement marks a new phase in international relations.*

> **GIVE MARK/GRADE 6** [T] **~ (sth)** to give marks to students' work: *I hate marking papers.* ⟳ compare GRADE

> **GIVE PARTICULAR QUALITY 7** [T, usually passive] (*formal*) to give someone or something a particular quality or character **SYN** CHARACTERIZE: **~ sb/sth** *a life marked by suffering* ◆ **~ sb/sth as sth** *He was marked as an enemy of the poor.*

> **PAY ATTENTION 8** [T] (*old-fashioned*) used to tell someone to pay careful attention to something: **~ sth** *There'll be trouble over this, mark my words.*

IDM **mark time 1** to pass the time while you wait for something more interesting: *I'm just marking time in this job —I'm hoping to get into journalism.* **2** (of soldiers) to make marching movements without moving forward

PHR V ˌmark sth↔ˈdown to reduce the price of something: *All goods have been marked down by 15%.* **ANT** MARK UP ⟳ related noun MARKDOWN ˌmark sth↔ˈoff to separate something by marking a line between it and something else: *The playing area was marked off with a white line.* ˌmark sth↔ˈout to draw lines to show the edges of something: *They marked out a basketball court on the driveway.* ˌmark sth↔ˈup **1** to increase the price of something: *All the prices are marked up during the tourist season.* **ANT** MARK DOWN ⟳ related noun MARKUP **2** (*technical*) to mark or correct a text, etc., for example for printing: *to mark up a manuscript*

• *noun*

> **SPOT/DIRT 1** a small area of dirt, a spot, or a cut on a surface that spoils its appearance: *The kids left dirty marks all over the kitchen floor.* ◆ *a burn/scratch mark* ◆ *Detectives found no marks on the body.* **2** a noticeable spot or area of color on the body of a person or an animal that helps you to recognize them: *a horse with a white mark on its head* ◆ *He was about six feet tall,* with no *distinguishing marks.* ⟳ see also BIRTHMARK, MARKING ⟳ thesaurus box at PATCH

> **SYMBOL 3** a written or printed symbol that is used as a sign of something, for example the quality of something or who made or owns it: *punctuation/proofreading marks* ◆ *Any piece of silver bearing his mark is extremely valuable.* ◆ *I put a mark in the margin to remind me to check the figure.* ⟳ see also QUESTION MARK, QUOTATION MARKS, TRADEMARK

> **SIGN 4** a sign that a quality or feeling exists: *On the day of the funeral businesses remained closed as a mark of respect.* ◆ *Such coolness under pressure is the mark of a champion.*

> **STANDARD/GRADE 5** a number or letter that is given to show the standard of someone's work or performance: *to get a good/low mark in English* ◆ *to give someone a high/low mark* ◆ *The administration's handling of the crisis deserves top marks.* ⟳ see also BLACK MARK, GRADE

> **LEVEL 6** a level or point that something reaches that is thought to be important: *Unemployment has passed the four million mark.* ◆ *She was leading at the halfway mark.*

> **MACHINE/VEHICLE 7** Mark (followed by a number) a particular type or model of a machine or vehicle: *the Mark II engine*

> **SIGNATURE 8** a cross made on a document instead of a signature by someone who is not able to write their name

> **TARGET 9** (*formal*) *Of the blows delivered, barely half found their mark.* ◆ *to hit/miss the mark*

> **GERMAN MONEY 10** = DEUTSCHMARK

IDM be close to/near the mark to be fairly accurate in a guess, statement, etc. be off the mark not to be accurate in a guess, statement, etc.: *No, you're way off the mark.* be on the mark to be accurate or correct: *That estimate was right on the mark.* hit/miss the mark to succeed/fail in achieving or guessing something: *He blushed furiously and Robyn knew she had hit the mark.* leave your/a mark (on sth/sb) to have an effect on something or someone, especially a bad one, that lasts for a long time: *Such a traumatic experience was bound to leave its mark on the children.* make your/a mark (on sth) to become famous and successful in a particular area on your mark, get set, go! used to tell runners in a race to get ready and then to start quick/slow off the mark fast/slow in reacting to a situation ⟳ more at OVERSTEP, TOE *v.*, WIDE *adj.*

THESAURUS

mark

stain ◆ **fingerprint** ◆ **streak** ◆ **speck** ◆ **blot** ◆ **smear** ◆ **spot**

These are all words for a small area of dirt or another substance on a surface.

mark a small area of dirt or other substance on the surface of something, especially one that spoils its appearance: *The kids left dirty marks all over the kitchen floor.*

stain a dirty mark on something that is difficult to remove, especially one made by a liquid: *blood stains*

fingerprint a mark on a surface made by the pattern of lines on the end of a person's finger, often used by the police to identify criminals: *Her fingerprints were all over the gun.*

streak a long thin mark or line that is a different color from the surface it is on: *She had streaks of gray in her hair.*

speck a very small mark, spot, or piece of a substance on something: *There isn't a speck of dust anywhere in the house.*

blot a spot or dirty mark left on something by a substance such as ink being dropped on a surface: *an ink blot*

smear a mark made by something such as oil or paint being spread or rubbed on a surface: *She had smears of paint on her dress.*

spot a small dirty mark on something: *He found grease spots all over the walls.*

---

mark·down /'mɑrkdaʊn/ noun [usually sing.] a reduction in price

marked /mɑrkt/ adj. **1** easy to see **SYN** DISTINCT, NOTICE-ABLE: *a marked difference/improvement* ◆ *a marked increase in profits* ◆ *She is quiet and studious, in marked contrast to her sister.* **2** (linguistics) (of a word or form of a word) showing a particular feature or style, such as being formal or informal **ANT** UNMARKED ▶ **mark·ed·ly** /'mɑrkədli/ adv.: *Her background is markedly different from her husband's.* ◆ *This year's sales have risen markedly.*
IDM **a marked man/woman** a person who is in danger because their enemies want to harm them

mark·er /'mɑrkər/ noun **1** [C] an object or a sign that shows the position of something: *a boundary marker* ◆ *He placed a marker where the ball landed.* **2** [sing.] **a ~ (of/for sth)** a sign that something exists or that shows what it is like: *Price is not always an accurate marker of quality.* **3** a pen with a thick FELT tip ⊃ picture at STATIONERY

mar·ket 🔑 /'mɑrkət/ noun, verb
- **noun** **1** [C] an occasion when people buy and sell goods; the open area or building where they meet to do this: *a fruit/flower/livestock* ◆ *a street/an open-air/a covered market* ◆ *market stalls/traders* ◆ *Thursday is market day.* ⊃ see also FARMERS' MARKET **2** [C] a store that sells food or one kind of goods: *There is a nice fish market down the street.* ◆ *I stopped at the fruit and vegetable market on my way home from work.* ⊃ see also SUPERMARKET **3** [sing.] business or trade, or the amount of trade in a particular type of goods: *the world market in coffee* ◆ *They have increased their share of the market by 10%.* ◆ *the housing/job market* (= the number and type of houses, jobs, etc. that are available) ◆ *They've cornered the market in sportswear* (= sell the most). ⊃ collocations at BUSINESS **4** [C] a particular area, country, or section of the population that might buy goods: *the Japanese market* ◆ *the global/domestic market* ◆ *These movies are obviously made for the youth market.* **5** [sing.] **~ (for sth)** the number of people who want to buy something **SYN** DEMAND: *a growing/declining market for used cars* **6** often **the market** [sing.] people who buy and sell goods in competition with each other: *The market will decide if the TV station has any future.* ◆ *a market-based/market-driven/market-led economy* ⊃ see also BLACK MARKET, MARKET FORCES **7** [C] = STOCK MARKET: *the futures market* ◆ *a market crash* **HELP** There are many other compounds ending in **market**. You will find them at their place in the alphabet.
  IDM **in the market for sth** interested in buying something: *I'm not in the market for a new car right now.* **on the market** available for people to buy: *to put your house on the market* ◆ *The house came on the market last year.* ◆ *There are hundreds of different brands on the market.* **on the open market** available to buy without any restrictions **play the market** to buy and sell STOCKS and shares in order to make a profit ⊃ more at BUYER, PRICE v., SELLER
- **verb** **~ sth (to sb) (as sth)** to advertise and offer a product for sale; to present something in a particular way and make people want to buy it **SYN** PROMOTE: *It is marketed as a low-alcohol wine.* ◆ *School meals need to be marketed to children in the same way as other food.* ⊃ see also MARKETING

mar·ket·a·ble /'mɑrkətəbl/ adj. easy to sell; attractive to customers or employers: *marketable products/skills/quali-fications* ▶ **mar·ket·a·bil·i·ty** /ˌmɑrkətə'bɪləti/ noun [U]

mar·ket·eer /ˌmɑrkə'tɪr/ noun (usually in compounds) a person who is in favor of a particular system of buying and selling: *a free marketeer* (= a person who believes in a FREE MARKET system of trade) ⊃ see also BLACK MARKETEER

market 'forces noun [pl.] a free system of trade in which prices and wages rise and fall without being controlled by the government

mar·ket·ing 🔑 /'mɑrkətɪŋ/ noun [U] the activity of presenting, advertising, and selling a company's products in the best possible way: *a marketing campaign* ◆ *She works in sales and marketing.* ⊃ see also DIRECT MARKETING ⊃ collocations at BUSINESS ▶ **mar·ket·er** /'mɑrkɪtər/ noun: *a company that is a developer and marketer of software*

'marketing ˌmix noun (business) the combination of the features of a product, its price, the way it is advertised and where it is sold, each of which a company can adjust to persuade people to buy the product

'market 'leader noun **1** the company that sells the largest quantity of a particular kind of product **2** a product that is the most successful of its kind

mar·ket·place /'mɑrkətˌpleɪs/ noun **1** **the marketplace** [sing.] the activity of competing with other companies to buy and sell goods, services, etc.: *Companies must be able to survive in the marketplace.* ◆ *the education marketplace* **2** [C] an open area in a town where a market is held

'market ˌprice noun the price that people are willing to pay for something at a particular time

'market re'search (also ˌmarket 'research) noun [U] the work of collecting information about what people buy and why

'market ˌshare noun [U, sing.] (business) the amount that a company sells of its products or services compared with other companies selling the same things: *They claim to have a 40% worldwide market share.* ⊃ collocations at BUSINESS

'market ˌvalue noun [U, sing.] what something would be worth if it were sold

mark·ing /'mɑrkɪŋ/ noun **1** [C, usually pl.] a pattern of colors or marks on animals, birds, or wood **2** [C, usually pl.] lines, colors, or shapes painted on roads, vehicles, etc.: *Road markings indicate where you can stop.* **3** [U] = GRADING
IDM **have (all) the markings of sth** to have all the unique features of something: *It has all the markings of a hit musical.*

marks·man /'mɑrksmən/, **marks·wom·an** /'mɑrksˌwʊmən/ noun (pl. marks·men /-mən/, marks·wom·en /-ˌwɪmən/) a person who is skilled in accurate shooting

marks·man·ship /'mɑrksmənˌʃɪp/ noun [U] skill in shooting

mark·up /'mɑrkʌp/ noun **1** [usually sing.] an increase in the price of something based on the difference between the cost of producing it and the price it is sold for: *an average markup of 50%* **2** [U] (computing) the symbols used in computer documents which give information about the structure of the document and tell the computer how it is to appear on the computer screen, or how it is to appear when printed: *a markup language*

marl /mɑrl/ noun [U, C] soil consisting of CLAY and LIME

mar·lin /'mɑrlən/ noun (pl. mar·lin) a large ocean fish with a long sharp nose, that people catch for sport

mar·ma·lade /'mɑrməˌleɪd/ noun [U] a soft sweet food made from oranges, lemons, etc., often spread on bread for breakfast ⊃ compare JAM

mar·mo·re·al /mɑr'mɔriəl/ adj. (literary) made of or similar to MARBLE

mar·mo·set /'mɑrməˌset; -ˌzet/ noun a small MONKEY with a long thick tail, that lives in Central and S. America

mar·mot /'mɑrmət/ noun a small American or European animal that lives in holes in the ground

ma·roon /mə'run/ adj., noun, verb
- **adj.** dark brown-red in color
- **noun** [U] a dark brown-red color

● *verb* [usually passive] ~ **sb** to leave someone in a place that they cannot escape from, for example an island **SYN** STRAND: *"Lord of the Flies" is a novel about English schoolboys marooned on a desert island.*

marque /mɑrk/ *noun* (*formal*) a well-known make of a product, especially a car, that is expensive and fashionable: *the Porsche marque*

mar·quee /mɑrˈki/ *noun, adj.*
● *noun* **1** a large tent used at social events **2** a covered entrance to a theater, hotel, etc. often with a sign on or above it
● *adj.* [only before noun] (especially in sports) most important or most popular: *He is one of the marquee names in men's tennis.*

mar·quess /ˈmɑrkwəs/ (also **mar·quis**) *noun* (in Britain) a NOBLEMAN of high rank between an EARL and a DUKE: *the Marquess of Bath* ⊃ compare MARCHIONESS

mar·que·try /ˈmɑrkətri/ *noun* [U] patterns or pictures made of pieces of wood on the surface of furniture, etc.; the art of making these patterns

mar·quis /mɑrˈki; ˈmɑrkwəs/ *noun* **1** (in some European countries but not Britain) a NOBLEMAN of high rank between a COUNT and a DUKE **2** = MARQUESS

mar·quise /mɑrˈkiz/ *noun* **1** the wife of a marquis **2** a woman who has the rank of a marquis ⊃ compare MARCHIONESS

mar·ram grass /ˈmærəm ˌgræs/ (also **mar·ram**) *noun* [U] a type of grass that grows in sand, often planted to prevent sand DUNES from being destroyed by the wind, rain, etc.

mar·riage 🗝 /ˈmærɪdʒ/ *noun*
1 [C] the legal relationship between a husband and wife: *a happy/unhappy marriage* ◆ *All of her children's marriages ended in divorce.* ◆ *an arranged marriage* (= one in which the parents choose a husband or wife for their child) ◆ *She has two children by a previous marriage.* ⊃ see also MIXED **2** [U] the state of being married: *They don't believe in marriage.* ◆ *My parents are celebrating 30 years of marriage.* **3** [C] the ceremony in which two people become husband and wife: *Their marriage took place in a local church.* **HELP** Wedding is more common in this meaning.
IDM **by marriage** when you are related to someone **by marriage**, they are married to someone in your family, or you are married to someone in their family ⊃ more at HAND *n.*

TOPIC COLLOCATIONS

Marriage and Divorce
romance
- fall/be (madly/deeply/hopelessly) in love (with sb)
- be/believe in/fall in love at first sight
- be/find true love/the love of your life
- suffer (from) (the pains/pangs of) unrequited love
- have/feel/show/express great/deep/genuine affection for sb/sth
- meet/marry your husband/wife/partner/fiancé/fiancée/boyfriend/girlfriend
- have/go on a (blind) date
- be going out with/dating a guy/girl/boy/man/woman
- move in with/live with your boyfriend/girlfriend

weddings
- get/be engaged/married/divorced
- arrange/plan a wedding
- have a big wedding/a honeymoon/a happy marriage
- have/enter into an arranged marriage
- call off/cancel/postpone your wedding
- invite sb to/go to/attend a wedding/a wedding ceremony/a wedding reception
- conduct/perform a wedding ceremony
- exchange rings/wedding vows/marriage vows

- congratulate/toast/raise a glass to the happy couple
- be/go on your honeymoon (with your wife/husband)
- celebrate your first (wedding) anniversary

separation and divorce
- be unfaithful to/ (*informal*) cheat on your husband/wife/partner/fiancé/fiancée/boyfriend/girlfriend
- have an affair (with sb)
- break off/end an engagement/a relationship
- break up with/ (*informal*) dump your boyfriend/girlfriend
- separate from/be separated from/leave/divorce your husband/wife
- annul/dissolve a marriage
- file for/ask for/go through/get a divorce
- get/gain/be awarded/have/lose custody of the children
- pay alimony/child support (to your ex-wife/husband)

mar·riage·a·ble /ˈmærɪdʒəbl/ *adj.* (*old-fashioned*) suitable for marriage: *She had reached marriageable age.*

marriage broker *noun* a person who is paid to arrange for two people to meet and marry

marriage certificate *noun* a legal document that proves two people are married

marriage counseling (CanE usually **marriage counselling**) *noun* [U] advice that is given by specially trained people to couples with problems in their marriage
▶ **marriage counselor** (CanE usually **marriage counsellor**) *noun*

marriage license (CanE **marriage licence**) *noun* a legal document that allows two people to get married

marriage of convenience *noun* a marriage that is made for practical, financial, or political reasons and not because the two people love each other

mar·ried 🗝 /ˈmærid/ *adj.*
1 having a husband or wife: *a married man/woman* ◆ *Is he married?* ◆ *a happily married couple* ◆ *She's married to John.* ◆ *Rachel and David are getting married on Saturday.* ◆ *How long have you been married?* **ANT** UNMARRIED ⊃ collocations at MARRIAGE **2** [only before noun] connected with marriage: *Are you enjoying married life?* ◆ *Her married name* (= the family name of her husband) *is Jones.* **3** ~ **to sth** very involved in something so that you have no time for other activities or interests: *My brother is married to his job.*

mar·row /ˈmæroʊ/ *noun* [U] = BONE MARROW

mar·row·bone /ˈmæroʊˌboʊn/ *noun* a bone that still contains the MARROW (= the substance inside) and is used in making food

mar·ry 🗝 /ˈmæri/ *verb*
(mar·ries, mar·ry·ing, mar·ried, mar·ried) **1** [T, I] to become the husband or wife of someone; to get married to someone: ~ **(sb)** *She married a Canadian.* ◆ *He never married.* ◆ *I guess I'm not the marrying kind* (= the kind of person who wants to get married). ◆ + *adj.* *They married young.* **HELP** It is more common to say: *They're getting married next month.* than: *They're marrying next month.* ⊃ collocations at MARRIAGE **2** [T] ~ **sb** to perform a ceremony in which a man and woman become husband and wife: *They were married by a Baptist minister.* **3** [T] ~ **sb (to sb)** to find a husband or wife for someone, especially your daughter or son **4** [T] ~ **sth and/to/with sth** (*formal*) to combine two different things, ideas, etc. successfully **SYN** UNITE: *The music business marries art and commerce.*
IDM **marry in haste (, repent at leisure)** (*saying*) people who marry quickly, without really getting to know each other, may discover later that they have made a mistake **marry money** to marry a rich person
PHRV **marry into sth** to become part of a family or group because you have married someone who belongs to it: *She*

WORD FAMILY
marry *verb*
marriage *noun*
married *adj.* (≠ unmarried)

married into a wealthy family. ˌmarry sb↔ˈoff (to sb) (disapproving) to find a husband or wife for someone, especially your daughter or son

Mars /marz/ noun the planet in the SOLAR SYSTEM that is fourth in order of distance from the sun, between the Earth and Jupiter ➪ picture at EARTH

Mar·sa·la /marˈsalə/ noun [U] a dark, strong, sweet wine from Sicily. It is usually drunk with the sweet course of a meal.

marsh /marʃ/ noun [C, U] an area of low land that is always soft and wet because there is nowhere for the water to flow away to: They went duck hunting in the marshes. ▶ **marsh·y** adj.: marshy ground/land

mar·shal /ˈmarʃl/ noun, verb
• noun **1** a person responsible for making sure that public events, especially sports events and PARADES, take place without any problems, and for controlling crowds **2** an officer whose job is to put court orders into effect: a federal marshal **3** (in some cities) an officer of high rank in a police or fire department ➪ see also AIR MARSHAL, FIELD MARSHAL
• verb (formal) **1** ~ sth to gather together and organize the people, things, ideas, etc. that you need for a particular purpose SYN MUSTER: They have begun **marshaling forces** to send relief to the hurricane victims. ◆ to **marshal your arguments/thoughts/facts 2** ~ sb to control or organize a large group of people: Police were brought in to marshal the crowd.

ˈmarsh gas noun [U] a gas that is produced in a marsh when plants decay

marsh·land /ˈmarʃlænd/ noun [U, C] an area of soft wet land

marsh·mal·low /ˈmarʃˌmɛloʊ/ noun [C, U] a white candy that feels soft and ELASTIC when you chew it

mar·su·pi·al /marˈsupiəl/ noun any animal that carries its young in a pocket of skin (called a POUCH) on the mother's stomach. KANGAROOS, KOALAS, and OPOSSUMS are marsupials. ▶ **mar·su·pi·al** adj.

mart /mart/ noun a place where things are bought and sold: a used car mart

mar·ten /ˈmartn/ noun a small wild animal with a long body, short legs, and sharp teeth. Martens live in forests and eat smaller animals: a pine marten

mar·tial /ˈmarʃl/ adj. (formal) [only before noun] connected with fighting or war

ˌmartial ˈart noun [usually pl.] any of the fighting sports that include JUDO and KARATE

ˌmartial ˈlaw noun [U] a situation where the army of a country controls an area instead of the police during a time of trouble: to declare/impose/lift martial law ◆ The city remains firmly under martial law.

Mar·tian /ˈmarʃn/ adj., noun
• adj. (astronomy) related to or coming from the planet Mars
• noun an imaginary creature from the planet Mars

mar·ti·net /ˌmartnˈɛt/ noun (formal) a very strict person who demands that other people obey orders or rules completely

mar·ti·ni /marˈtini/ noun **1** [U] an alcoholic drink made by mixing GIN or VODKA with VERMOUTH **2** [C] a glass of martini: a dry martini

Martin Luther King Jr. Day /ˌmartn ˌluθər ˌkɪŋ ˈdʒunyər ˌdeɪ/ (also **Martin Luther King Day** /ˌmartn ˌluθər ˈkɪŋ deɪ/) noun a national holiday in the U.S. on the third Monday in January to celebrate the birthday of Martin Luther King, Jr., who was active in the struggle to win more rights for Black Americans

mar·tyr /ˈmartər/ noun, verb
• noun **1** a person who suffers very much or is killed because of their religious or political beliefs: the early Christian martyrs ◆ a martyr to the cause of freedom **2** (usually disapproving) a person who tries to get sympathy from other people by telling them how much he or she is suffering **3** ~ to sth (informal) a person who suffers very much

because of an illness, problem, or situation: She's a martyr to her allergies.
• verb [usually passive] ~ sb to kill someone because of their religious or political beliefs

mar·tyr·dom /ˈmartərdəm/ noun [U] the suffering or death of a martyr

mar·tyred /ˈmartərd/ adj. [usually before noun] (disapproving) showing pain or suffering so that people will be kind and sympathetic toward you: She wore a perpetually martyred expression.

mar·vel /ˈmarvl/ noun, verb
• noun **1** a wonderful and surprising person or thing SYN WONDER: the marvels of nature/technology **2** marvels [pl.] wonderful results or things that have been achieved SYN WONDERS: The doctors have done marvels for her.
• verb (-l-, CanE usually -ll-) [I, T] ~ (at sth) | ~ that... | + speech to be very surprised or impressed by something: Everyone marveled at his courage.

mar·vel·ous (CanE usually **mar·vel·lous**) /ˈmarvələs/ adj. extremely good; wonderful SYN FANTASTIC, SPLENDID: This will be a marvelous opportunity for her. ◆ The weather was marvelous. ◆ It's marvelous what modern technology can do. ▶ **mar·vel·ous·ly** adv.

Marx·ism /ˈmarksɪzəm/ noun [U] the political and economic theories of Karl Marx (1818-83), which explain the changes and developments in society as the result of opposition between the social classes ▶ **Marx·ist** /ˈmarksɪst/ noun **Marx·ist** adj.: Marxist theory/doctrine/ideology

mar·zi·pan /ˈmarzəˌpæn/ noun [U] a sweet firm substance, sometimes with yellow color added, made from ALMONDS, sugar, and eggs and used to make candy

mas·car·a /mæˈskærə/ noun [U] a substance that is put on EYELASHES to make them look dark and thick ➪ picture at MAKEUP

mas·cot /ˈmæskat/ noun an animal, a toy, etc. that people believe will bring them good luck, or that represents an organization, etc.: The team's mascot is a giant bear. ◆ the official mascot of the U.S. Marine Corps

mas·cu·line /ˈmæskyələn/ adj., noun
• adj. **1** having the qualities or appearance considered to be typical of men; connected with or like men: He was handsome and strong, and very masculine. ◆ That suit makes her look very masculine. ➪ compare FEMININE, MALE **2** (grammar) belonging to a class of words that refer to male people or animals and often have a special form: "He" and "him" are masculine pronouns. **3** (grammar) (in some languages) belonging to a class of nouns, pronouns, or adjectives that have masculine GENDER, not FEMININE or NEUTER: The French word for "sun" is masculine.
• noun **1** the masculine [sing.] the masculine GENDER (= form of nouns, adjectives, and pronouns) **2** [C] a masculine word or word form ➪ compare FEMININE, NEUTER

mas·cu·lin·i·ty /ˌmæskyəˈlɪnəti/ noun [U] the quality of being masculine: He felt it was a threat to his masculinity.

mas·cu·lin·ize /ˈmæskyələˌnaɪz/ verb ~ sth/sb (formal) to make something or someone more like a man

mash /mæʃ/ verb, noun
• verb ~ sth (up) to crush food into a soft mass: Mash the fruit up with a fork. ➪ picture at COOKING ➪ collocations at COOKING ▶ **mashed** adj.: mashed banana
• noun [U] **1** a mixture of MALT grains and hot water, used for making beer, etc. **2** grain cooked in water until soft, used to feed farm animals ➪ see also MISHMASH

ˌmashed poˈtatoes noun [pl.] potatoes that have been boiled and crushed into a soft mass, often with butter and milk

mash·up /ˈmæʃʌp/ noun a combination of elements from different sources used to create a new song, video, computer file, program, etc.: a video mashup

mask /mæsk/ noun, verb
• noun **1** a covering for part or all of the face, worn to hide or protect it: a gas/surgical mask ◆ The robbers were wearing

| t tea | ţ butter | d did | k cat | g got | tʃ chin | dʒ June | f fall

stocking masks. ◆ He was carrying a baseball bat, gloves, and a catcher's mask. ⊃ picture at HOBBY ⊃ see also OXYGEN MASK **2** something that covers your face and has another face painted on it: *The kids were all wearing Halloween masks.* ⊃ see also DEATH MASK **3** a thick cream made of various substances that you

masks

surgical mask   Halloween mask

put on your face and neck in order to improve the quality of your skin: *a facial mask* **4** [usually sing.] a manner or an expression that hides your true character or feelings: *He longed to throw off the mask of respectability.* ◆ *Her face was a cold blank mask.*

● **verb** ~ **sth** to hide a feeling, smell, fact, etc. so that it cannot be easily seen or noticed **SYN** DISGUISE, VEIL: *She masked her anger with a smile.* ⊃ thesaurus box at HIDE

masked /mæskt/ *adj.* wearing a MASK: *a masked gunman*

ˌmasked ˈball *noun* a formal party at which guests wear masks

ˈmasking ˌtape *noun* [U] sticky tape that you use to keep an area clean or protected when you are painting around or near it

mas·och·ism /ˈmæsəˌkɪzəm/ *noun* [U] **1** the practice of getting sexual pleasure from being physically hurt ⊃ compare SADISM **2** (*informal*) the enjoyment of something that most people would find unpleasant or painful: *You spent the whole weekend in a tent in the rain? That's masochism!* ▶ **mas·och·ist** /-kɪst/ *noun* **mas·och·is·tic** /ˌmæsə-ˈkɪstɪk/ *adj.*: *masochistic behavior/tendencies*

ma·son /ˈmeɪsn/ *noun* **1** a person who builds using stone, or works with stone **2 Mason** = FREEMASON

the Ma·son-Dix·on Line /ˌmeɪsn ˈdɪksn laɪn/ *noun* [sing.] the border between the U.S. states of Maryland and Pennsylvania that is thought of as the dividing line between the south of the U.S. and the north. In the past it formed the northern border of the states where SLAVES were owned.

Ma·son·ic /məˈsɑnɪk/ *adj.* connected with FREEMASONS

Ma·son·ite™ /ˈmeɪsəˌnaɪt/ *noun* [U] a make of board that is used in building, made of small pieces of wood that are pressed together and stuck with glue

ma·son·ry /ˈmeɪsənri/ *noun* [U] the parts of a building that are made of stone: *She was injured by falling masonry.* ◆ *He acquired a knowledge of carpentry and masonry* (= building with stone).

masque /mæsk/ *noun* a play written in VERSE, often with music and dancing, popular in England in the 16th and 17th centuries

mas·quer·ade /ˌmæskəˈreɪd/ *noun, verb*
● **noun 1** a type of party where people wear special COSTUMES and MASKS over their faces, to hide their identities **2** (*formal*) a way of behaving that hides the truth or a person's true feelings
● **verb** [I] ~ **as sth** to pretend to be something that you are not: *commercial advertisers masquerading as private individuals*

Mass /mæs/ *noun* **1** sometimes **mass** [U, C] (especially in the Roman Catholic Church) a ceremony held in memory of the last meal that Christ had with his DISCIPLES: *to go to Mass* ◆ *a priest celebrating/saying Mass* ⊃ see also COMMUNION, EUCHARIST **2** [C] a piece of music that is written for the prayers, etc. of this ceremony: *Bach's Mass in B minor*

mass /mæs/ *noun, adj., verb*
● **noun 1** [C] ~ **(of sth)** a large amount of a substance that does not have a definite shape or form: *a mass of snow and rocks falling down the mountain* ◆ *The hill appeared as a black mass in the distance.* ◆ *The sky was full of dark masses of*

clouds. **2** [C, usually sing.] ~ **of sth** a large amount or quantity of something: *a mass of blonde hair* ◆ *I began sifting through the mass of evidence.* **3** [sing.] ~ **of sth** a large number of people or things grouped together, often in a confused way: *I struggled through the mass of people to the exit.* ◆ *The page was covered with a mass of figures.* **4 masses** [pl.] ~ **of sth** (*informal*) a large number or amount of something **SYN** LOTS: *The trees were filled with masses of white blossoms.* **5 the masses** [pl.] the ordinary people in society who are not leaders or who are considered to be not very well educated: *government attempts to suppress dissatisfaction among the masses* ◆ *a TV program that brings science to the masses* **6 the mass of sth** [sing.] the most; the majority: *The reforms are unpopular with the mass of teachers and parents.* **7** [U] (*technical*) the quantity of material that something contains: *calculating the mass of a planet* **HELP** Weight is used in nontechnical language for this meaning. ⊃ see also BIOMASS, CENTER OF MASS, CRITICAL MASS, LANDMASS
IDM **be a mass of** to be full of or covered with something: *The rose bushes are a mass of flowers in June.* ◆ *Her arm was a mass of bruises.*

● **adj.** [only before noun] affecting or involving a large number of people or things: *mass unemployment/hysteria* ◆ *weapons of mass destruction* ◆ *Their latest product is aimed at the mass market.* ⊃ see also MASS-MARKET

● **verb** [I, T] to come together in large numbers; to gather people or things together in large numbers: **(+ adv./prep.)** *Demonstrators had massed outside the embassy.* ◆ *Dark clouds massed on the horizon.* ◆ ~ **sb/sth** *The general massed his troops for a final attack.* ▶ **massed** *adj.*: *the massed ranks of his political opponents*

mas·sa·cre /ˈmæsəkər/ *noun, verb*
● **noun** [C, U] **1** the killing of a large number of people especially in a cruel way: *the bloody massacre of innocent civilians* ◆ *Nobody survived the massacre.* **2** (*informal*) a very big defeat in a game or competition: *The game was a 10–0 massacre for our team.*
● **verb 1** ~ **sb** to kill a large number of people, especially in a cruel way **2** ~ **sb** (*informal*) to defeat someone in a game or competition by a high score

mas·sage /məˈsɑʒ, -ˈsɑdʒ/ *noun, verb*
● **noun** [U, C] the action of rubbing and pressing a person's body with the hands to reduce pain in the muscles and joints: *Massage will help the pain.* ◆ *a back massage* ◆ *to give someone a massage* ◆ *massage oils*
● **verb 1** ~ **sth** to rub and press a person's body with the hands to reduce pain in the muscles and joints: *He massaged the aching muscles in her feet.* ◆ (*figurative*) *to massage someone's ego* (= to make someone feel better, more confident, attractive, etc.) **2** ~ **sth into sth** to rub a substance into the skin, hair, etc.: *Massage the cream into your skin.* **3** ~ **sth** (*disapproving*) to change facts, figures, etc. in order to make them seem better than they really are: *The government was accused of massaging the unemployment figures.*

masˈsage ˌparlor (*CanE usually* **masˈsage ˌparlour**) *noun* **1** a place where you can pay to have a massage **2** a place that is supposed to offer the service of massage, but is also where men go to pay for sex with PROSTITUTES

masse ⊃ EN MASSE

mas·seur /mæˈsər; mə-; -ˈsʊr/ *noun* a person whose job is giving people massages

mas·seuse /mæˈsus; mə-; -ˈsuz/ *noun* a woman whose job is giving people massages

mas·sif /mæˈsif/ *noun* (*technical*) a group of mountains that form a large mass

mas·sive /ˈmæsɪv/ *adj.*
1 very large, heavy, and solid: *a massive rock* ◆ *the massive walls of the castle* **2** extremely large or serious: *The explosion made a massive hole in the ground.* ◆ *a massive increase in*

spending ♦ *He had a massive heart attack.* ▶ **mas·sive·ly** *adv.*

ˌmass-ˈmarket *adj.* [only before noun] (of goods etc.) produced for very large numbers of people: *mass-market paperbacks*

the ˌmass ˈmedia *noun* [pl.] sources of information and news such as newspapers, magazines, radio, and television, that reach and influence large numbers of people

ˈmass noun *noun* (*grammar*) **1** an uncountable noun **2** a noun that is usually uncountable but can be made plural or used with *a* or *an* when you are talking about different types of something. For example, *bread* is used as a mass noun in *the store sells several different breads.*

ˈmass ˌnumber *noun* (*chemistry*) the total number of PROTONS and NEUTRONS in an atom

ˌmass-proˈduce *verb* ~ sth to produce goods in large quantities, using machinery ▶ **mass-proˈduced** *adj.*: *mass-produced goods* ˌmass proˈduction *noun* [U]: *the mass production of consumer goods*

ˌmass ˈtransit (also ˌpublic ˈtransit) *noun* [U] the system of public transportation in cities, including the SUBWAY, buses, etc. ⊃ **compare** RAPID TRANSIT

mast /mæst/ *noun* **1** a tall pole on a boat or ship that supports the sails ⊃ **picture at** BOAT **2** a tall pole that is used for holding a flag **3** a tall metal tower with an AERIAL that sends and receives radio or television signals ⊃ **see also** HALF-MAST

mas·tec·to·my /mæˈstɛktəmi/ *noun* (*pl.* mas·tec·to·mies) a medical operation to remove a person's breast

mas·ter 🔑 /ˈmæstər/ *noun, verb, adj.*

• *noun*
> OF SERVANTS **1** (*old-fashioned*) a man who has people working for him, often as servants in his home: *They lived in fear of their master.*
> PERSON IN CONTROL **2** ~ of sth a person who is able to control something: *She was no longer master of her own future.*
> SKILLED PERSON **3** ~ (of sth) a person who is skilled at something: *a master of disguise* ♦ *a master of the serve-and-volley game* ⊃ **see also** PAST MASTER
> DOG OWNER **4** the owner of a dog: *The dog saved its master's life.*
> UNIVERSITY DEGREE **5** master's (also ˈmaster's ˌdegree) a second university degree, such as an M.A. or an M.S.: *He has a Master's in Business Administration.* ⊃ **see also** M.A., M.B. A., M.S. **6** usually Master a person who has a master's degree: *a Master of Arts/Science*
> CAPTAIN OF SHIP **7** the captain of a ship that transports goods
> FAMOUS PAINTER **8** a famous painter who lived in the past: *an exhibition of work by the French master Monet* ⊃ **see also** OLD MASTER
> ORIGINAL CD/MOVIE **9** (often used as an adjective) a version of a CD, movie, etc. from which copies are made: *the master copy*
> TITLE **10** Master (*old-fashioned*) a title used when speaking to or about a boy who is too young to be called *Mr.* (also used in front of the name on an envelope, etc.) **11** Master a title used for speaking to or about some religious teachers or leaders **HELP** There are many other compounds ending in master. You will find them at their place in the alphabet.
IDM be your own master to be free to make your own decisions rather than being told what to do by someone else ⊃ **more at** SERVE *v.*

• *verb*
> LEARN/UNDERSTAND **1** ~ sth to learn or understand something completely: *to master new skills/techniques* ♦ *French was a language he had never mastered.*
> CONTROL **2** ~ sth to manage to control an emotion: *She struggled hard to master her temper.* **3** ~ sth/sb to gain control of an animal or a person

• *adj.* [only before noun]
> SKILLED **1** ~ chef/electrician/mason, etc. used to describe a person who is very skilled at the job mentioned

> MOST IMPORTANT **2** the largest and/or most important: *the master bedroom* ♦ *a master file/switch*

ˈmaster class (also ˌmas·ter·ˈclass) *noun* a lesson, especially in music, given by a famous expert to very skilled students

mas·ter·ful /ˈmæstərfl/ *adj.* **1** (of a person, especially a man) able to control people or situations in a way that shows confidence as a leader **2** = MASTERLY: *a masterful performance* ▶ **mas·ter·ful·ly** /-fəli/ *adv.*: *He took her arm masterfully and led her away.*

ˈmaster ˌkey *noun* = PASS KEY

mas·ter·ly /ˈmæstərli/ (also ˌmas·ter·ˈful) *adj.* showing great skill or understanding: *a masterly performance* ♦ *Her handling of the situation was masterly.* ⊃ **see also** MASTERFUL (2)

mas·ter·mind /ˈmæstərmaɪnd/ *noun, verb*
• *noun* [usually sing.] an intelligent person who plans and directs a complicated project or activity (often one that involves a crime)
• *verb* ~ sth to plan and direct a complicated project or activity

ˌmaster of ˈceremonies *noun* (*abbr.* MC) a person who introduces guests or entertainers at a formal occasion

mas·ter·piece /ˈmæstərˌpis/ (also ˌmas·ter·ˈwork) *noun* a work of art such as a painting, movie, book, etc. that is an excellent, or the best, example of the artist's work: *The museum houses several of his Cubist masterpieces.* ♦ *Her work is a masterpiece of* (= an excellent example of) *simplicity.*

ˈmaster ˌplan *noun* [sing.] a detailed plan that will make a complicated project successful

ˈmaster's ˌdegree (also master's) *noun* a further university degree that you study for after a first degree

the ˈMaster's ˌTournament (also the Master's) *noun* a GOLF competition held in the U.S., in which skilled players are invited to compete

mas·ter·stroke /ˈmæstərˌstroʊk/ *noun* [usually sing.] something smart that you do that gives a successful result

mas·ter·work /ˈmæstərˌwərk/ *noun* = MASTERPIECE

mas·ter·y /ˈmæstəri/ *noun* **1** [U, sing.] ~ (of sth) great knowledge about or understanding of a particular thing **SYN** COMMAND: *She has a mastery of several languages.* **2** [U] ~ (of/over sb/sth) control or power: *human mastery of the natural world*

mast·head /ˈmæsthɛd/ *noun* **1** the top of a MAST on a ship **2** the name of a newspaper at the top of the front page **3** the part of a newspaper or a news Web site that gives details of the people who work on it and other information about it

mas·tic /ˈmæstɪk/ *noun* [U] **1** a substance that comes from the BARK of a tree and is used in making VARNISH **2** a substance that is used in building to fill holes and keep out water

mas·ti·cate /ˈmæstəˌkeɪt/ *verb* [I] (*technical*) to chew food ▶ **mas·ti·ca·tion** /ˌmæstəˈkeɪʃn/ *noun* [U]

mas·tiff /ˈmæstɪf/ *noun* a large strong dog with short hair, often used to guard buildings

mas·ti·tis /mæˈstaɪtəs/ *noun* [U] (*medical*) painful swelling of the breast or UDDER, usually because of infection

mas·tur·bate /ˈmæstərˌbeɪt/ *verb* **1** [I, T] ~ (yourself) to give yourself sexual pleasure by rubbing your sexual organs **2** [T] ~ sb to give someone sexual pleasure by rubbing their sexual organs ▶ **mas·tur·ba·tion** /ˌmæstərˈbeɪʃn/ *noun* [U] **mas·tur·ba·to·ry** /ˈmæstərbəˌtɔri/ *adj.*

mat /mæt/ *noun, adj.*
• *noun* **1** a small piece of thick carpet or strong material that is used to cover part of a floor: *Wipe your feet on the mat before you come in, please.* ⊃ **see also** BATH MAT, DOORMAT **2** a piece of thick material such as rubber or plastic used especially in some sports for people to lie on or fall onto: *a judo/an exercise mat* **3** a small piece of plastic, wood, or cloth used on a table to protect the surface from heat or

damage ⊃ see also PLACE MAT **4** a thick mass of something that is stuck together: *a mat of hair* ⊃ see also MATTED
IDM go to the mat (with sb) (for sb/sth) (*informal*) to support or defend someone or something in an argument with someone **take sb/sth to the mat** (*informal*) to get involved in an argument with someone or something ⊃ see also WELCOME MAT

• *adj.* = MATTE

mat·a·dor /ˈmætəˌdɔr/ *noun* (from *Spanish*) a person who fights and kills the BULL in a BULLFIGHT

Ma·ta Ha·ri /ˌmɑtə ˈhɑri/ *noun* an attractive female SPY
ORIGIN From the name of a Dutch dancer who worked as a spy for the German government during World War I.

match 🔑 /mætʃ/ *noun, verb*
• *noun*
▶ FOR LIGHTING FIRES **1** [C] a small stick made of wood or thick paper that is used for lighting a fire, cigarette, etc.: *a box of matches* ◆ *to strike/light a match* (= to make it burn)
▶ IN SPORTS **2** [C] a sports event in which people compete against each other: *a tennis/golf match* ◆ *to win/lose a match* ⊃ see also SHOOTING MATCH, SHOUTING MATCH
▶ AN EQUAL **3** [sing.] **a ~ for sb | sb's match** a person who is equal to someone else in strength, skill, intelligence, etc.: *I was no match for him at tennis.* ◆ *I was his match at tennis.*
▶ SOMEONE OR SOMETHING THAT COMBINES WELL **4** [sing.] a person or thing that combines well with someone or something else: *The curtains and rug are a good match.* ◆ *Christy and John are a perfect match for each other.*
▶ SOMETHING THE SAME **5** [C] a thing that looks exactly the same as or very similar to something else: *I've found a vase that is an exact match of the one I broke.*
▶ MARRIAGE **6** [C] (*old-fashioned*) a marriage or a marriage partner ⊃ see also LOVE MATCH
IDM find/meet your match (in sb) to meet someone who is equal to, or even better than you in strength, skill, or intelligence

• *verb*
▶ COMBINE WELL **1** [T, I] **~ (sth)** if two things **match**, or if one thing **matches** another, they have the same color, pattern, or style and therefore look attractive together: *The doors were painted blue to match the walls.* ◆ *a scarf with gloves to match* ◆ *None of these glasses match* (= they are all different). ⊃ see also MATCHING
▶ BE THE SAME **2** [T, I] **~ (sth)** if two things **match** or if one thing **matches** another, they are the same or very similar: *Her fingerprints match those found at the scene of the crime.* ◆ *As a couple they are not very well matched* (= they are not very suitable for each other). ◆ *The two sets of figures don't match.*
▶ FIND SOMETHING SIMILAR/CONNECTED **3** [T] **~ sb/sth (to/ with sb/sth)** to find someone or something that goes together with or is connected with another person or thing: *The aim of the competition is to match the quote to the person who said it.*
▶ BE EQUAL/BETTER **4** [T] **~ sb/sth** to be as good, interesting, successful, etc. as someone or something else **SYN** EQUAL: *We have never matched the profits we made in the first year.* ◆ *The teams were evenly matched.* **5** [T] **~ sth** to make something the same or better than something else: *The company was unable to match his current salary.*
▶ PROVIDE SOMETHING SUITABLE **6** [T] **~ sth** to provide something that is suitable for or enough for a particular situation: *Investment in hospitals is needed now to match the future needs of the country.* **IDM see MIX** *v.*
PHR V match sth against/with sth to compare something with something else in order to find things that are the same or similar: *New information is matched against existing data in the computer.* **match sb/sth against/with sth** to arrange for someone to compete in a game or competition against someone else: *We were matched against last year's champions in the first round.* **match 'up to sb/sth** (usually used in negative sentences) to be as good, interesting, or successful as someone or something **SYN** MEASURE UP: *The trip failed to match up to her expectations.* **match 'up (with sth)** to

be the same or similar **SYN** AGREE, TALLY: *The suspects' stories just don't match up.* **match sth↔'up (with sth)** to find things that belong together or that look attractive together: *She spent the morning matching up orders with invoices.*

match·book /ˈmætʃbʊk/ *noun* a piece of folded card containing matches and a surface to light them on

match·box /ˈmætʃbɑks/ *noun* a small box for holding matches ⊃ picture at PACKAGING

match·ing 🔑 /ˈmætʃɪŋ/ *adj.* [only before noun] (of clothing, material, objects, etc.) having the same color, pattern, style, etc. and therefore looking attractive together: *a pine table with four matching chairs*

match·less /ˈmætʃləs/ *adj.* (*formal*) so good that nothing can be compared with it **SYN** INCOMPARABLE: *matchless beauty/ skill*

match·mak·er /ˈmætʃˌmeɪkər/ *noun* a person who tries to arrange marriages or relationships between others
▶ **match·mak·ing** *noun* [U]

'match play *noun* [U] a way of playing GOLF in which your score depends on the number of holes that you win rather than the number of times you hit the ball in the whole game ⊃ compare STROKE PLAY

match 'point *noun* [U, C] (especially in TENNIS) a point that, if won by a player, will also win them the match

match·stick /ˈmætʃstɪk/ *noun* a single wooden match: *starving children with legs like matchsticks*

mate 🔑 /meɪt/ *noun, verb*
• *noun*
▶ SOMEONE YOU SHARE WITH **1** [C] (in compounds) a person you share an activity or living space with: *teammates/ playmates/classmates* ◆ *my roommate* ⊃ see also RUNNING MATE, SOULMATE
▶ BIRD/ANIMAL **2** [C] either of a pair of birds or animals: *A male bird sings to attract a mate.*
▶ SEXUAL PARTNER **3** [C] (*informal*) a husband, wife, or other sexual partner
▶ ON SHIP **4** [C] an officer in a commercial ship below the rank of captain or MASTER ⊃ see also FIRST MATE
▶ IN CHESS **5** [U] = CHECKMATE

• *verb*
▶ ANIMALS/BIRDS **1** [I] **~ (with sth)** (of two animals or birds) to have sex in order to produce young: *Do foxes ever mate with dogs?* ⊃ see also MATING **2** [T] **~ sth (to/with sth)** to put animals or birds together so that they will have sex and produce young
▶ IN CHESS **3 ~ sb/sth** = CHECKMATE

ma·te·ri·al 🔑 /məˈtɪriəl/ *noun, adj.*
• *noun* **1** [U, C] cloth used for making clothes, curtains, etc. **SYN** FABRIC: *a piece of material* ◆ *"What material is this dress made out of?" "Cotton."* ⊃ thesaurus box at FABRIC **2** [C, U] a substance that things can be made from: *building materials* (= bricks, sand, glass, etc.) ⊃ see also RAW MATERIAL **3** [C, usually pl., U] things that are needed in order to do a particular activity: *teaching materials* ◆ *The company produces its own training material.* ◆ (*figurative*) *The teacher saw her as good college material* (= good enough to go to college). ⊃ thesaurus box at EQUIPMENT **4** [U] information or ideas used in books, etc.: *She's collecting material for her latest novel.* **5** [U] items used in a performance: *The band played all new material at the gig.*
• *adj.* **1** [only before noun] connected with money, possessions, etc. rather than with the needs of the mind or spirit: *material comforts* ◆ *changes in your material circumstances* **ANT** SPIRITUAL **2** [only before noun] connected with the physical world rather than with the mind or spirit: *the material world* **ANT** IMMATERIAL **3** (*formal* or *law*) important and needing to be considered: *material evidence* ◆ **~ to sth** *She omitted information that was material to the case.* ⊃ see also IMMATERIAL ▶ **ma·te·ri·al·ly** /-iəli/ *adv.*: *Materially they*

are no better off. ♦ *Their comments have not materially affected our plans* (= in a noticeable or important way).

ma·te·ri·al·ism /məˈtɪriəˌlɪzəm/ *noun* [U] **1** (usually *disapproving*) the belief that money, possessions, and physical comforts are more important than spiritual values **2** (*philosophy*) the belief that only material things exist ⊃ **compare** IDEALISM

ma·te·ri·al·ist /məˈtɪriəlɪst/ *noun* **1** a person who believes that money, possessions, and physical comforts are more important than spiritual values in life **2** a person who believes in the philosophy of materialism

ma·te·ri·al·is·tic /məˌtɪriəˈlɪstɪk/ *adj.* (*disapproving*) caring more about money and possessions than anything else

ma·te·ri·al·ize /məˈtɪriəˌlaɪz/ *verb* **1** [I] (usually used in negative sentences) to take place or start to exist as expected or planned: *The promotion he was promised failed to materialize.* **2** [I] to appear suddenly and/or in a way that cannot be explained: *A tall figure suddenly materialized at her side.* ♦ (*informal*) *The train failed to materialize* (= it did not come). ▶ **ma·te·ri·al·i·za·tion** /məˌtɪriələˈzeɪʃn/ *noun* [U]

ma·te·ri·el /məˌtɪriˈɛl/ *noun* [U] (*technical*) military weapons and equipment

ma·ter·nal /məˈtɜrnl/ *adj.* **1** having feelings that are typical of a caring mother toward a child: *maternal love* ♦ *I'm not very maternal.* ♦ *She didn't have any maternal instincts.* **2** connected with being a mother: *Maternal age affects the baby's survival rate.* **3** [only before noun] related through the mother's side of the family: *my maternal grandfather* (= my mother's father) ▶ **ma·ter·nal·ly** /-nəli/ *adv.*: *She behaved maternally toward her students.* ⊃ **compare** PATERNAL

ma·ter·ni·ty /məˈtɜrnəti/ *noun* [U] the state of being or becoming a mother: *maternity clothes* (= clothes for women who are pregnant) ♦ *a maternity ward/hospital* (= one where women go to give birth to their babies)

maˈternity ˌleave *noun* [U] a period of time when a woman temporarily leaves her job to have a baby: *She's on maternity leave until June.* ⊃ **collocations** at CHILD ⊃ **see also** PARENTAL LEAVE, PATERNITY LEAVE

math 🔑 /mæθ/ *noun* [U]
1 mathematics, especially as a subject in school: *a math teacher* **2** the process of calculating using numbers: *Is your math correct?* ♦ *If my math is right, the answer is 142.*
IDM **do the math** to think carefully about something before doing it so that you know all the relevant facts or figures: *If only someone had done the math!*

math·e·ma·ti·cian /ˌmæθəməˈtɪʃn/ *noun* a person who is an expert in mathematics

math·e·mat·ics 🔑 /ˌmæθəˈmætɪks/ (*formal*) (also **math**) *noun*
1 [U] the science of numbers and shapes. Branches of mathematics include ARITHMETIC, ALGEBRA, GEOMETRY, and TRIGONOMETRY: *the school mathematics curriculum* **2** [U] the process of calculating using numbers: *He worked out the very difficult mathematics in great detail.* ▶ **math·e·mat·i·cal** /ˌmæθəˈmætɪkl/ *adj.*: *mathematical calculations/problems/models* ♦ *to assess children's mathematical ability* **math·e·mat·i·cal·ly** /-kli/ *adv.*: *It's mathematically impossible.* ♦ *Some people are very mathematically inclined* (= interested in and good at mathematics).

mat·i·nee (also **mat·i·née**) /ˌmætnˈeɪ/ *noun* an afternoon performance of a play, etc.; an afternoon showing of a movie

matiˈnee ˌidol (also **matiˈnée ˌidol**) *noun* (*old-fashioned*) an actor who is popular with women

mat·ing /ˈmeɪtɪŋ/ *noun* [U, C] sex between animals: *the mating season*

mat·ins /ˈmætnz/ *noun* [U] the service of morning prayer, especially in the Anglican Church ⊃ **compare** EVENSONG, VESPERS

ma·tri·arch /ˈmeɪtriˌɑrk/ *noun* a woman who is the head of a family or social group ⊃ **compare** PATRIARCH

ma·tri·ar·chal /ˌmeɪtriˈɑrkl/ *adj.* (of a society or system) controlled by women rather than men; passing power, property, etc. from mother to daughter rather than from father to son: *The animals live in matriarchal groups.* ⊃ **compare** PATRIARCHAL

ma·tri·ar·chy /ˈmeɪtriˌɑrki/ *noun* (*pl.* **ma·tri·ar·chies**) a social system that gives power and authority to women rather than men ⊃ **compare** PATRIARCHY

ma·tri·ces *pl.* of MATRIX

mat·ri·cide /ˈmætrəˌsaɪd/ *noun* [U, C] (*formal*) the crime of killing your mother; a person who is guilty of this crime ⊃ **compare** FRATRICIDE, PARRICIDE, PATRICIDE

ma·tric·u·late /məˈtrɪkyəˌleɪt/ *verb* [I] (*formal*) to officially become a student at a university: *She matriculated in 1995.* ▶ **ma·tric·u·la·tion** /məˌtrɪkyəˈleɪʃn/ *noun* [U]

mat·ri·lin·e·al /ˌmætrəˈlɪniəl/ *adj.* (*technical*) used to describe the relationship between mother and children that continues in a family with each generation, or something that is based on this relationship: *She traced her family history by matrilineal descent* (= starting with her mother, her mother's mother, etc.). ⊃ **compare** PATRILINEAL

mat·ri·mo·ni·al /ˌmætrəˈmouniəl/ *adj.* [usually before noun] (*formal* or *technical*) connected with marriage or with being married: *matrimonial problems* ♦ *the matrimonial home*

mat·ri·mo·ny /ˈmætrəˌmouni/ *noun* [U] (*formal* or *technical*) marriage; the state of being married: *holy matrimony*

ma·trix /ˈmeɪtrɪks/ *noun* (*pl.* **ma·tri·ces** /ˈmeɪtrəˌsiz/ or **ma·trix·es**) **1** (*mathematics*) an arrangement of numbers, symbols, etc. in rows and columns, treated as a single quantity **2** (*formal*) the formal social, political, etc. situation from which a person or society grows and develops: *the North American cultural matrix* **3** (*formal* or *literary*) a system of lines, roads, etc. that cross each other, forming a series of squares or shapes in between **SYN** NETWORK: *a matrix of paths* **4** (*technical*) a MOLD in which something is shaped **5** (*computing*) a group of electronic CIRCUIT elements arranged in rows and columns like a GRID ⊃ **see also** DOT MATRIX PRINTER **6** (*geology*) a mass of rock in which minerals, PRECIOUS STONES, etc. are found in the ground

ma·tron /ˈmeɪtrən/ *noun* **1** (becoming *old-fashioned*) an older married woman **2** a woman who is in charge of women or children in a prison or school

ma·tron·ly /ˈmeɪtrənli/ *adj.* (of a woman) no longer young, and somewhat fat

ˌmatron of ˈhonor *noun* [sing.] a married woman who is the most important BRIDESMAID at a wedding ⊃ **compare** MAID OF HONOR

mat·ro·nym·ic /ˌmætrəˈnɪmɪk/ *noun* (*technical*) a name formed from the name of your mother or a female ANCESTOR, especially by adding something to the beginning or end of their name ⊃ **compare** PATRONYMIC

matte (also **mat**) /mæt/ *adj.* (of a color, surface, or photograph) not shiny: *a matte finish* ♦ *matte white paint* ♦ *Prints are available on matte or glossy paper.*

mat·ted /ˈmætəd/ *adj.* (of hair, etc.) forming a thick mass, especially because it is wet and dirty

mat·ter 🔑 /ˈmætər/ *noun*, *verb*
● *noun*
▷ SUBJECT/SITUATION **1** [C] a subject or situation that you must consider or deal with **SYN** AFFAIR: *It's a private matter.* ♦ *They had important matters to discuss.* ♦ *She may need your help with some business matters.* ♦ *I always consulted him on matters of policy.* ♦ *It's a matter for the police* (= for them to deal with). ♦ *That's a matter for you to take up with your boss.* ♦ *Let's deal with the matter at hand* (= what we need to deal with now). ♦ *I wasn't prepared to let the matter drop* (= stop discussing it). ♦ *It was no easy matter getting him to change his mind.* ♦ *It should have been a simple matter to check.* ♦ (*ironic*) *And then there's the little matter of the fifty dollars you owe me.* ♦ (*formal*) *It was a matter of some concern to most of those present*

ʌ **cup**   ə **about**   eɪ **say**   aɪ **five**   ɔɪ **boy**   aʊ **now**   oʊ **go**   ər **bird**

(= something they were worried about). ◆ *I did not feel that we ever got to **the heart of the matter*** (= the most important part). ◆ *And that is **the crux of the matter*** (= the most important thing about the situation). **2 matters** [pl.] the present situation, or the situation that you are talking about **SYN** THINGS: *Unfortunately, there is nothing we can do to improve matters.* ◆ *I'd forgotten the keys, which didn't **help matters**.* ◆ *And then, **to make matters worse**, his parents turned up.* ◆ *I decided to **take matters into my own hands*** (= deal with the situation myself). ◆ ***Matters came to a head*** (= the situation became very difficult) *with his resignation.*

> PROBLEM **3 the matter** [sing.] used (to ask) if someone is upset, unhappy, etc. or if there is a problem: *What's the matter?* ◆ *Is there something wrong?* ◆ *Is anything the matter?* ◆ **~ with sb/sth** *Is something the matter with Bob? He seems very down.* ◆ *There's something the matter with my eyes.* ◆ *"We bought a new TV." "What was the matter with the old one?"* ◆ *What's the matter with you today* (= why are you behaving like this)?

> A MATTER OF SOMETHING/OF DOING SOMETHING **4** [sing.] a situation that involves something or depends on something **SYN** QUESTION: *Learning to drive is all a matter of coordination.* ◆ *Planning a project is just a matter of working out the right order to do things in.* ◆ *That's not a problem. It's **simply a matter of** letting people know in time.* ◆ *Some people prefer the older version to the new one. It's **a matter of taste**.* ◆ *She resigned as **a matter of principle**.* ◆ *The health department has to deal with this as **a matter of urgency**.* ◆ *Just as **a matter of interest*** (= because it is interesting, not because it is important), *how much did you pay for it?* ◆ *"I think this is the best so far." "Well, that's **a matter of opinion***" (= other people may think differently).

> SUBSTANCE **5** [U] (*technical*) physical substance in general that everything in the world consists of; not mind or spirit: *to study the properties of matter* **6** [U] a substance or things of a particular sort: *Add plenty of organic matter to improve the soil.* ◆ *elimination of **waste matter** from the body* ◆ *She didn't approve of their choice of **reading matter**.* ➜ see also SUBJECT MATTER

IDM **as a matter of fact 1** used to add a comment on something that you have just said, usually adding something that you think the other person will be interested in: *It's a nice place. We've stayed there ourselves, as a matter of fact.* **2** used to disagree with something that someone has just said **SYN** ACTUALLY: *"I suppose you'll be leaving soon, then?" "No, as a matter of fact I'll be staying for another two years."* **be another/a different matter** to be very different: *I know which neighborhood they live in, but whether I can find their house is a different matter.* **for that matter** used to add a comment on something that you have just said: *I didn't like it much. Nor did the kids, for that matter.* **it's just/only a matter of time (before…)** used to say that something will definitely happen, although you are not sure when: *It's only a matter of time before they bring out their own version of the software.* **(as) a matter of course** (as) the usual and correct thing to do: *We always check people's addresses as a matter of course.* **a matter of hours, minutes, etc.| a matter of inches, feet, etc.** only a few hours, minutes, etc.: *It was all over in a matter of minutes.* ◆ *The bullet missed her by a matter of inches.* **a matter of life and death** used to describe a situation that is very important or serious **a matter of record** (*formal*) something that has been recorded as being true **no matter** used to say that something is not important **no matter who, what, where, etc.** used to say that something is always true, whatever the situation is, or that someone should certainly do something: *They don't last long no matter how careful you are.* ◆ *Call me when you get there, no matter what the time is.* ➜ more at FACT, LAUGHING

● **verb** [I, T] (not used in the progressive tenses) to be important or have an important effect on someone or something: **~ (to sb)** *The children matter more to her than anything else in the world.* ◆ *"What did you say?" "Oh, it doesn't matter"* (= it is not important enough to repeat)." ◆ *"I'm afraid I forgot that book again." "It doesn't matter* (= it is not important enough to worry about)." ◆ *What does it matter if I spent $100*

on it—it's my money!* ◆ *As long as you're happy, that's **all that matters**.* ◆ *After his death, nothing seemed to matter any more.* ◆ *He's been in prison, you know— **not that it matters*** (= that information does not affect my opinion of him). ◆ **~ (to sb) who, what, etc.…** *Does it really matter who did it?* ◆ *It doesn't matter to me what you do.* ◆ **~ (to sb) that…** *It didn't matter that the weather was bad.*

matter-of-'fact *adj.* said or done without showing any emotion, especially in a situation in which you would expect someone to express their feelings **SYN** UNEMOTIONAL: *She told us the news of his death in a very matter-of-fact way.* ▶ **matter-of-'factly** *adv.*

mat·ting /'mætɪŋ/ *noun* rough WOVEN material for making MATS: *coconut matting*

mat·tock /'mætək/ *noun* a heavy garden tool with a long handle and a metal head, used for breaking up soil, cutting roots, etc.

mat·tress /'mætrəs/ *noun* the soft part of a bed, that you lie on: *a soft/hard mattress* ➜ picture at BED

mat·u·ra·tion **AWL** /ˌmætʃə'reɪʃn/ *noun* [U] (*formal*) **1** the process of becoming or being made mature (= ready to eat or drink after being left for a period of time) **2** the process of becoming adult ▶ **mat·u·ra·tion·al** **AWL** *adj.*

ma·ture **AWL** /mə'tʃʊr; -'tʊr/ *adj., verb*

● *adj.* **HELP** maturer is occasionally used instead of **more mature**

> SENSIBLE **1** (of a child or young person) behaving in a sensible way, like an adult: *Jane is very mature for her age.* ◆ *a mature and sensible attitude* **ANT** IMMATURE

> FULLY GROWN **2** (of a person, a tree, a bird, or an animal) fully grown and developed: *sexually mature* ◆ *a mature oak/eagle/elephant* **ANT** IMMATURE ➜ thesaurus box at OLD

> WINE/CHEESE **3** developed over a period of time to produce a strong, rich flavor

> NO LONGER YOUNG **4** used as a polite or humorous way of saying that someone is no longer young: *clothes for the mature woman* ◆ *a man of mature years*

> WORK OF ART **5** created late in an artist's life and showing great understanding and skill

> INSURANCE POLICY **6** (*business*) ready to be paid

▶ **ma·ture·ly** *adv.*

IDM **on mature reflection/consideration** (*formal*) after thinking about something carefully and for a long time

● *verb*

> BECOME FULLY GROWN **1** [I] to become fully grown or developed: *This particular breed of cattle matures early.* ◆ *Technology in this field has matured considerably over the last decade.*

> BECOME SENSIBLE **2** [I] to develop emotionally and start to behave like a sensible adult: *He has matured a great deal over the past year.*

> DEVELOP SKILL **3** [I] **~ (into sth)** to fully develop a particular skill or quality: *She has matured into one of the country's finest actresses.*

> WINE/CHEESE **4** [I, T] **~ (sth)** if wine, cheese, etc. **matures** or **is matured**, it develops over a period of time to produce a strong, rich flavor

> INSURANCE POLICY **5** [I] (*business*) to reach the date when it must be paid

ma·tu·ri·ty **AWL** /mə'tʃʊrəti; -'tʊr-/ *noun* [U] **1** the quality of thinking and behaving in a sensible, adult manner: *He has maturity beyond his years.* ◆ *Her poems show great maturity.* **2** (of a person, an animal, or a plant) the state of being fully grown or developed: *The forest will take 100 years to **reach maturity**.* **3** (*business*) (of an insurance policy, etc.) the time when money you have invested is ready to be paid

mat·zo /'mɑtsə/ *noun* [U, C] (*pl.* **mat·zos**) (also **mat·zoh**) (also **mat·zah**) a type of large, flat, hard bread, traditionally eaten by Jews during Passover; a piece of this bread

maud·lin /'mɔdlən/ *adj.* **1** talking in a silly, emotional way, often feeling sorry for yourself, especially when drunk **SYN** SENTIMENTAL **2** (of a book, movie, or song) expressing or causing exaggerated emotions, especially in way that is not sincere **SYN** SENTIMENTAL

maul /mɔl/ *verb* **1** ~ **sb** (of an animal) to attack and injure someone by tearing their flesh **SYN** SAVAGE **2** ~ **sb/sth** to touch someone or something in an unpleasant and/or violent way **3** ~ **sth/sb** to criticize something or someone severely and publicly **SYN** SAVAGE **4** ~ **sb** (*informal*) to defeat someone easily

Maun·dy Thurs·day /ˌmɔndi ˈθɜrzdeɪ; -ˈθɜrzdi/ *noun* [U, C] (in the Christian Church) the Thursday before Easter

mau·so·le·um /ˌmɔsəˈliəm; ˌmɔzə-/ *noun* a special building made to hold the dead body of an important person or the dead bodies of a family: *the family's mausoleum*

mauve /moʊv; mɔv/ *adj.* pale purple in color ▶ **mauve** *noun* [U]

ma·ven /ˈmeɪvn/ *noun* (*informal*) an expert on something: *My uncle's a baseball maven.*

mav·er·ick /ˈmævrɪk; ˈmævərɪk/ *noun* a person who does not behave or think like everyone else, but who has independent, unusual opinions ▶ **mav·er·ick** *adj.* [only before noun]: *a maverick film director*

maw /mɔ/ *noun* **1** (*literary*) something that seems like a big mouth that swallows things up completely **2** (*old-fashioned*) an animal's stomach or throat

mawk·ish /ˈmɔkɪʃ/ *adj.* (*disapproving*) expressing or sharing emotion in a way that is exaggerated or embarrassing **SYN** SENTIMENTAL: *a mawkish poem* ▶ **mawk·ish·ness** *noun* [U]

max **AWL** /mæks/ *abbr.*, *verb*
• *abbr.* **1** (also **max.**) maximum: *max temperature 85°F* **ANT** MIN. **2** (*informal*) at the most: *It'll cost $50 max.* **IDM** **to the max** (*informal*) to the highest level or greatest amount possible: *She believes in living life to the max.*
• *verb*
PHR V ˌmax (sth) ˈout (*informal*) to reach, or make something reach, the limit at which nothing more is possible: *The car maxed out at 150 mph.*

max·i /ˈmæksi/ *noun* a long coat, dress, or skirt that reaches to the ankles

max·il·la /mækˈsɪlə/ *noun* (*pl.* **max·il·lae** /-li/) (*anatomy*) the JAW ▶ **max·il·lar·y** /ˈmæksəˌleri/ *adj.*: *a maxillary fracture*

max·im /ˈmæksəm/ *noun* a well-known phrase that expresses something that is usually true or that people think is a rule for sensible behavior

max·i·mal /ˈmæksəml/ *adj.* [usually before noun] (*technical*) as great or as large as possible ⊃ compare MINIMAL

max·i·mize **AWL** /ˈmæksəˌmaɪz/ *verb* **1** ~ **sth** to increase something as much as possible: *to maximize efficiency/ fitness/profits* ◆ (*computing*) *Maximize the window to full screen.* **2** ~ **sth** to make the best use of something: *to maximize opportunities/resources* **ANT** MINIMIZE ▶ **max·i·mi·za·tion** **AWL** /ˌmæksəməˈzeɪʃn/ *noun* [U]

max·i·mum /ˈmæksəməm/ **AWL** *adj.*, *noun*
• *adj.* [only before noun] (*abbr.* **max**) as large, fast, etc. as is possible, or the most that is possible or allowed: *the maximum speed/temperature/volume* ◆ *For maximum effect, do the exercises every day.* ◆ *a maximum security prison* ⊃ compare MINIMUM
• *noun* [usually sing.] (*pl.* **max·i·ma** /ˈmæksəmə/) (*abbr.* **max**) the greatest amount, size, speed, etc. that is possible, recorded, or allowed: *a maximum of 30 children in a class* ◆ *The job will require you to use all your skills to the maximum.* ◆ *The July maximum* (= the highest temperature recorded in July) *was 105°F.* ◆ *What is the absolute maximum you can afford to pay?* ⊃ compare MINIMUM

May /meɪ/ *noun* [U, C]
the fifth month of the year, between April and June **HELP** To see how **May** is used, look at the examples at **April.**

may /meɪ/ *modal verb* (*negative* **may not**, *rare short form*

may·n't /ˈmeɪənt/, *pt* **might** /maɪt/, *negative* **might not**, *rare short form* **might·n't** /ˈmaɪtnt/) **1** used to say that something is possible: *That may or may not be true.* ◆ *He may have* (= perhaps he has) *missed his plane.* ◆ *They may well win.* ◆ *There are numerous programs on the market that may be described as design aids.* **2** used when admitting that something is true before introducing another point, argument, etc.: *He may be a good father but he's a terrible husband.* **3** (*formal*) used to ask for or give permission: *May I come in?* ◆ *You may come in if you wish.* ⊃ note at CAN¹ **4** (*formal*) used as a polite way of making a comment, asking a question, etc.: *You look lovely, if I may say so.* ◆ *May I ask why you made that decision?* ◆ *If I may just add one thing…* **5** (*formal*) used to express wishes and hopes: *May she rest in peace.* ◆ *Business has been thriving in the past year. Long may it continue to do so.* **6** (*formal*) used to say what the purpose of something is: *There is a need for more resources so that all children may be entitled to a decent education.* ⊃ note at MODAL **IDM** **be that as it may** (*formal*) despite that **SYN** NEVERTHELESS: *I know that he tries hard; be that as it may, his work just isn't good enough.*

may·be /ˈmeɪbi/ *adv.*
1 used when you are not certain that something will happen or that something is true or is a correct number **SYN** PERHAPS: *Maybe he'll come, maybe he won't.* ◆ *"Are you going to sell your house?" "Maybe."* ◆ *It will cost two, maybe three hundred dollars.* ◆ *We go there maybe once or twice a month.* **2** used when making a suggestion **SYN** PERHAPS: *I thought maybe we could go together.* ◆ *Maybe you should tell her.* **3** used to agree with someone, and to add more information that should be thought about **SYN** PERHAPS: *"You should stop work when you have the baby." "Maybe, but I can't afford to."* **4** used when replying to a question or an idea, when you are not sure whether to agree or disagree **SYN** PERHAPS: *"I think he should resign." "Maybe."*

'May Day *noun* the first day of May, celebrated as a spring festival and, in some countries, as a holiday in honor of working people ⊃ compare LABOR DAY

May·day /ˈmeɪdeɪ/ *noun* [U] an international radio signal used by ships and aircraft needing help when they are in danger **ORIGIN** From the French *venez m'aider* "come and help me."

may·fly /ˈmeɪflaɪ/ *noun* (*pl.* **may·flies**) a small insect that lives near water and only lives for a very short time

may·hem /ˈmeɪhɛm/ *noun* [U] confusion and fear, usually caused by violent behavior or by some sudden shocking event: *There was absolute mayhem when everyone tried to get out at once.*

may·on·naise /ˈmeɪəˌneɪz; ˌmeɪəˈneɪz/ (also *informal* **mayo** /ˈmeɪoʊ/) *noun* [U] a thick, cold, white sauce made from eggs, oil, and VINEGAR, used to add flavor to SANDWICHES, salads, etc.

may·or /ˈmeɪər; ˈmɛr/ *noun*
the head of the government of a town or city, etc., elected by the public: *the Mayor of New York* ◆ *Mayor Bob Anderson* ▶ **may·or·al** /ˈmeɪərəl/ *adj.* [only before noun]: *mayoral responsibilities/duties*

may·or·al·ty /ˈmeɪərəlti/ *noun* (*pl.* **may·or·al·ties**) (*formal*) **1** the title or position of a mayor **2** the period of time during which a person is a mayor

may·pole /ˈmeɪpoʊl/ *noun* a decorated pole that people dance around in ceremonies on MAY DAY

maze /meɪz/ *noun* **1** a system of paths separated by walls or HEDGES built in a park or garden, that is designed so that it is difficult to find your way through: *We got lost in the maze.* ◆ (*figurative*) *The building is a maze of corridors.* ⊃ compare LABYRINTH **2** [usually sing.] a large number of complicated rules or details that are difficult to understand: *a maze of regulations* **3** a printed PUZZLE in which you have to draw a line that shows a way through a complicated pattern of lines

t tea   t̬ butter   d did   k cat   g got   tʃ chin   dʒ June   f fall

ma·zur·ka /məˈzərkə/ *noun* a fast Polish dance for four or eight couples, or a piece of music for this dance

MB *abbr.* MEGABYTE: *512MB of memory*

Mb *abbr.* MEGABIT

M.B.A. (also **MBA**) /ˌɛm biː ˈeɪ/ *noun* a second university degree in business (the abbreviation for "Master of Business Administration"): *to earn an M.B.A.*

MC /ˌɛm ˈsiː/ *noun* **1** the abbreviation for MASTER OF CEREMONIES **2 M.C.** the abbreviation for "Member of Congress" **3** a person who speaks the words of a RAP song

MCAT /ˈɛmkæt/ *abbr.* Medical College Admission Test (a test that students must pass in order to study medicine in the U.S.)

Mc·Car·thy·ism /məˈkɑrθiˌɪzəm/ *noun* [U] an aggressive investigation during the 1950s against people in the U.S. government and other institutions who were thought to be COMMUNIST, in which many people lost their jobs

Mc·Coy /məˈkɔɪ/ *noun*
IDM **the real Mc·Coy** (*informal*) something that is genuine and that has value, not a copy: *It's one of Elvis's suits, the real McCoy.*

M.D. (also **MD**) /ˌɛm ˈdiː/ *noun* the abbreviation for "Doctor of Medicine": *Paula Clark M.D.*

MD *abbr.* (in writing) Maryland

ME *abbr.* **1** MEDICAL EXAMINER **2** (in writing) Maine

me /miː/ *pron.*
the form of *I* that is used when the speaker or writer is the object of a verb or preposition, or after the verb *be*: *Don't hit me.* ◆ *Excuse me!* ◆ *Give it to me.* ◆ *You're taller than me.* ◆ *Hello, it's me.* ◆ *"Who's there?" "Only me."* **HELP** The use of **me** in the last three examples is correct in modern standard English. I in these sentences would be considered much too formal for almost all contexts.

me·a cul·pa /ˌmeɪə ˈkʊlpə/ *exclamation* (from *Latin*, often *humorous*) used when you are admitting that something is your fault

mead /miːd/ *noun* [U] a sweet alcoholic drink made from HONEY and water, drunk especially in the past

mead·ow /ˈmɛdoʊ/ *noun* a field covered in grass, used especially for HAY

mead·ow·lark /ˈmɛdoʊˌlɑrk/ *noun* a singing bird that lives on the ground

mea·ger (*CanE usually* **mea·gre**) /ˈmiːgər/ *adj.* small in quantity and poor in quality: *a meager diet of bread and water* ◆ *She supplements her meager income by cleaning offices at night.*

meal /miːl/ *noun*
1 [C] an occasion when people sit down to eat food, especially breakfast, lunch, or dinner: *Try not to eat between meals.* ◆ *Lunch is his main meal of the day.* ◆ *to go out for a meal* (= to go to a restaurant to have a meal) ◆ *What time would you like your evening meal?* ➔ collocations at RESTAURANT **2** [C] the food that is eaten at a meal: *Enjoy your meal.* ◆ *a three-course meal* **3** [U] (often in compounds) grain that has been crushed to produce a powder, used as food for animals and for making flour ➔ see also BONEMEAL, OATMEAL, WHOLEMEAL **IDM** see SQUARE *adj.*

meals on wheels *noun* [pl.] a service that takes meals to elderly or sick people in their homes

meal ticket *noun* **1** (*informal*) a person or thing that you see only as a source of money and food: *He suspected that he was just a meal ticket for her.* **2** a card or ticket that gives you the right to have a cheap or free meal, for example at school

meal·time /ˈmiːltaɪm/ *noun* a time in the day when you eat a meal

meal·worm /ˈmiːlwərm/ *noun* a LARVA that is used to feed pet birds

meal·y /ˈmiːli/ *adj.* (especially of vegetables or fruit) soft and dry when you eat them

meal·y-mouthed /ˈmiːli ˌmaʊðd; -ˌmaʊθt/ *adj.* (*disapproving*) not willing or honest enough to speak in a direct or open way about what you really think: *mealy-mouthed politicians*

mean /miːn/ *verb, adj., noun*
● ***verb*** (meant, meant /mɛnt/)
> **HAVE AS MEANING 1** (not used in the progressive tenses) to have something as a meaning: **~ sth** *What does this sentence mean?* ◆ *What is meant by "batch processing?"* ◆ **~ sth to sb** *Does the name "David Berwick" mean anything to you* (= do you know who he is)? ◆ **~ (that)…** *The flashing light means (that) you must stop.*
> **INTEND AS MEANING 2** (not used in the progressive tenses) to intend to say something on a particular occasion: **~ sth** *What did he mean by that remark?* ◆ *"Maybe we should try another approach." "What do you mean?"* (= I don't understand what you are suggesting.)" ◆ *What do you mean, you thought I wouldn't mind?* (= of course I mind and I am very angry.) ◆ *What she means is that there's no point in waiting here.* ◆ *I always found him a little strange, if you know what I mean* (= if you understand what I mean by "strange"). ◆ *I know what you mean* (= I understand and feel sympathy). *I hated learning to drive too.* ◆ (*informal*) *It was like—weird. Know what I mean?* ◆ *I see what you mean* (= I understand although I may not agree), *but I still think it's worth trying.* ◆ *See what I mean* (= I was right and this proves it, doesn't it)? *She never agrees to anything I suggest.* ◆ *"But Pete doesn't know we're here!" "That's what I mean!* (= that's what I have been trying to tell you.) " ◆ *Do you mean Ann Smith or Mary Smith?* ◆ **~ (that)…** *Did he mean (that) he was dissatisfied with our service?* ◆ *You mean* (= are you telling me) *we have to start all over again?* ➔ **language bank** at I.E.
> **HAVE AS PURPOSE 3** to have something as a purpose or intention **SYN** INTEND: **~ sth** *What did she mean by leaving so early* (= why did she do it)? ◆ *Don't laugh! I mean it* (= I am serious). ◆ **~ to be/do sth** *Do you mean it seriously?* ◆ **~ sth as sth** *Don't be upset—I'm sure she meant it as a compliment.* ◆ **~ what…** *He means what he says* (= is not joking, exaggerating, etc.). ◆ **~ sth for sb/sth** *The chair was clearly meant for a child.* ◆ *Don't be angry. I'm sure she meant it for the best* (= intended to be helpful). ◆ **~ to do sth** *She means to succeed.* ◆ *I'm sorry I hurt you. I didn't mean to.* ◆ *I'm feeling very guilty— I've been meaning to call my parents for days, but still haven't got around to it.* ◆ **~ sb/sth to do sth** *I didn't mean you to read the letter.* ◆ *You're meant to* (= you are supposed to) *pay before you go in.* ◆ **~ (that)…** (*formal*) *I never meant (that) you should come alone.*
> **INTEND SOMEONE TO BE/DO SOMETHING 4** [often passive] to intend someone to be or do something: **~ sb for sth/sb** *I was never meant for the army* (= did not have the qualities needed to become a soldier). ◆ *Philip and Kim were meant for each other* (= are very suitable as partners). ◆ **~ sb/sb to be sth** *His father meant him to be an engineer.* ◆ *She did everything to get the two of them together, but I guess it just wasn't meant to be.*
> **HAVE AS RESULT 5** to have something as a result or a likely result **SYN** ENTAIL: **~ sth** *Spending too much now will mean a shortage of cash next year.* ◆ **~ sth to sb** *Do you have any idea what it means to be poor?* ◆ **~ (that)…** *We'll have to be careful with money but that doesn't mean (that) we can't enjoy ourselves.* ◆ **~ doing sth** *This new order will mean working overtime.* ◆ **~ sb/sth doing sth** *The injury could mean him missing next week's game.*
> **BE IMPORTANT 6** [no passive] **~ sth to sb** to be of value or importance to someone: *Your friendship means a great deal to me.* ◆ *$50 means a lot* (= represents a lot of money) *when you live on $300 a week.* ◆ *Money means nothing to him.* ◆ *His children mean the world to him.*
IDM **I mean** (*informal*) used to explain or correct what you have just said: *It was so boring—I mean, nothing happened for the first hour!* ◆ *She's French—French-Canadian, I mean.* **mean business** (*informal*) to be serious in your intentions: *He has the look of a man who means business.* **mean (sb) no harm | not mean (sb) any harm** to not have any intention of hurting someone **mean to say** used to emphasize what you are saying or to ask someone if they really mean what

they say: *I mean to say, you should have known how he would react!* ♦ *Do you mean to say you lost it?* **mean well** (usually disapproving) to have good intentions, although their effect may not be good **this means war!** (*informal*) used to say that you are ready to argue or defend yourself

● **adj.** (**mean·er, mean·est**)
> UNKIND **1** ~ (**to sb**) (of people or their behavior) unkind, for example by not letting someone have or do something: *Don't be so mean to your little brother!*
> ANGRY/VIOLENT **2** likely to become angry or violent: *That's a mean-looking dog.*
> SKILLFUL **3** (*informal*) very good and skillful: *He's a mean tennis player.* ♦ *She plays a mean game of chess.*
> AVERAGE **4** [only before noun] (*technical*) average; between the highest and the lowest, etc.: *the mean temperature*
> POOR **5** (*literary*) poor and dirty in appearance: *mean houses/streets* **6** (*old-fashioned*) born into or coming from a low social class
   ▶ **mean·ly** *adj.* **mean·ness** /'minnəs/ *noun* [U]
   IDM **be no mean...** (*approving*) used to say that someone is very good at doing something: *His mother was a painter, and he's no mean artist himself.*

● **noun** ⟹ see also MEANS
> MIDDLE WAY **1** ~ (**between A and B**) a quality, condition, or way of doing something that is in the middle of two extremes and better than either of them: *He needed to find a mean between frankness and rudeness.*
> AVERAGE **2** (also **arithmetic 'mean**) (*mathematics*) the value found by adding together all the numbers in a group, and dividing the total by the number of numbers ⟹ see also GEOMETRIC MEAN, MEDIAN, MODE **IDM** SEE GOLDEN

me·an·der /mi'ændər/ *verb* **1** [I] (+ *adv./prep.*) (of a river, road, etc.) to curve a lot rather than being in a straight line: *The stream meanders slowly down to the river.* **2** [I] (+ *adv./prep.*) to walk slowly and change direction often, especially without a particular aim **SYN** WANDER **3** [I] (+ *adv./prep.*) (of a conversation, discussion, etc.) to develop slowly and change subject often, in a way that makes it boring or difficult to understand ▶ **me·an·der** *noun*: *the meanders of a river*

me·an·der·ings /mi'ændərɪŋz/ *noun* [pl.] **1** a course that does not follow a straight line: *the meanderings of a river/path* **2** walking or talking without any particular aim: *his philosophical meanderings*

mean·ie (also **mean·y**) /'mini/ *noun* (*pl.* **mean·ies**) (*informal*) used especially by children to describe an unkind person who will not give them what they want

mean·ing /'minɪŋ/ *noun, adj.*
● **noun**
> OF SOUND/WORD/SIGN **1** [U, C] ~ (**of sth**) the thing or idea that a sound, word, sign, etc. represents: *What's the meaning of this word?* ♦ *Words often have several meanings.* ♦ *"Honesty?" He doesn't know the meaning of the word!*
> OF WHAT SOMEONE SAYS/DOES **2** [U, C] the things or ideas that someone wishes to communicate to you by what they say or do: *I don't quite get your meaning* (= understand what you mean to say). ♦ *What's the meaning of this? I explicitly told you not to leave the room.*
> OF FEELING/EXPERIENCE **3** [U] the real importance of a feeling or experience: *With Anna he learned the meaning of love.*
> OF BOOK/PAINTING **4** [U, C] the ideas that a writer, artist, etc. wishes to communicate through a book, painting, etc.: *several layers of meaning* ♦ *There are, of course, deeper meanings in the poem.*
> SENSE OF PURPOSE **5** [U] the quality or sense of purpose that makes you feel that your life is valuable: *Her life seemed to have lost all meaning.* ♦ *Having a child gave new meaning to their lives.*
● **adj.** [usually before noun] = MEANINGFUL

mean·ing·ful /'minɪŋfl/ *adj.* **1** serious and important: *a meaningful relationship/discussion/experience* **2** (also *less frequent* **meaning**) intended to communicate or express

something to someone, without any words being spoken: *She gave me a meaningful look.* **3** having a meaning that is easy to understand: *These statistics are not very meaningful.*
   ▶ **mean·ing·ful·ly** /-fəli/ *adv.* **mean·ing·ful·ness** *noun* [U]

mean·ing·less /'minɪŋləs/ *adj.* **1** without any purpose or reason and therefore not worth doing or having
   SYN POINTLESS: *a meaningless existence* ♦ *We fill up our lives with meaningless tasks.* **2** not considered important
   SYN IRRELEVANT: *Fines are meaningless to a huge company like that.* **3** not having a meaning that is easy to understand: *To me that painting is completely meaningless.* ▶ **mean·ing·less·ly** *adv.* **mean·ing·less·ness** *noun* [U]

means /minz/ *noun*
(*pl.* **means**) **1** [C] ~ (**of sth/of doing sth**) an action, an object, or a system by which a result is achieved; a way of achieving or doing something: *Television is an effective means of communication.* ♦ *Is there any means of contacting him?* ♦ *Have you any means of identification?* ♦ *We needed to get to Madison but we had no means of transportation.* **2** [pl.] the money that a person has: *People should pay according to their means.* ♦ *He doesn't have the means to support a wife and child.* ♦ *Private schools are beyond the means of most people* (= more than they can afford). ♦ *Are the monthly payments within your means* (= can you afford them)? ♦ *Try to live within your means* (= not spend more money than you have). ♦ *a man of means* (= a rich man)
   IDM **by all means** used to say that you are very willing for someone to have something or do something: *"Do you mind if I have a look?" "By all means."* **by means of sth** (*formal*) with the help of something: *The load was lifted by means of a crane.* **by no means | not by any means** not at all: *She is by no means an inexperienced teacher.* ♦ *We haven't won yet, not by any means.* **a means to an end** a thing or action that is not interesting or important in itself but is a way of achieving something else: *He doesn't particularly like the work but he sees it as a means to an end.* ⟹ more at END, FAIR *adj.*, WAY

'means test *noun* an official check of someone's wealth or income in order to decide if they are poor enough to receive money from the government, etc. for a particular purpose ▶ **'means-test** *verb* ~ **sb**

'means-tested *adj.* paid to someone according to the results of a means test: *means-tested aid*

meant pt, pp OF MEAN

mean·time /'mintaɪm/ *noun, adv.*
● **noun**
   IDM **in the meantime 1** for a short period of time but not permanently: *I'm changing my e-mail address, but in the meantime you can use the old one.* **2** in the period of time between two times or two events **SYN** MEANWHILE: *My first novel was rejected by six publishers. In the meantime I wrote a play.*
● **adv.** (*informal*) = MEANWHILE: *I'll contact them soon. Meantime don't tell them I'm back.*

mean·while /'minwaɪl/ *adv.*
1 (also *informal* **mean·time**) while something else is happening: *Bob spent fifteen months alone on his yacht. Ann, meanwhile, took care of the children by herself.* **2** (also *informal* **mean·time**) in the period of time between two times or two events: *The doctor will see you again next week. Meanwhile, you must rest as much as possible.* **3** used to compare two aspects of a situation: *Stress can be extremely damaging to your health. Exercise, meanwhile, can reduce its effects.*

mean·y *noun* = MEANIE

mea·sles /'mizlz/ *noun* [U] an infectious disease, especially of children, that causes a fever and small red spots that cover the whole body ⟹ see also GERMAN MEASLES

mea·sly /'mizli/ *adj.* (*informal, disapproving*) very small in size or quantity; not enough: *I get a measly $8.50 an hour.*

meas·ur·a·ble /'mɛʒərəbl/ *adj.* **1** that can be measured **2** [usually before noun] large enough to be noticed or to have a clear and noticeable effect: *measurable improve-*

h hat   m man   n no   ŋ sing   l leg   r red   y yes   w wet

ments ▸ **meas·ur·a·bly** /-bli/ *adv.*: *Working conditions have changed measurably in the last ten years.*

meas·ure 🔑 /ˈmɛʒər/ *verb, noun*

● ***verb***

▷ SIZE/QUANTITY **1** to find the size, quantity, etc. of something in standard units: ~ **sth (in sth)** *A ship's speed is measured in knots.* ◆ *a device that measures the level of radiation in the atmosphere* ◆ *measuring equipment/instruments* ◆ ~ **sb/sth for sth** *He's being measured for a costume in the school play.* ◆ ~ **how much, how long, etc.…** *A dipstick is used to measure how much oil is left in an engine.* **2** *linking verb* (not used in the progressive tenses) + **noun** to be a particular size, length, amount, etc.: *The bedroom measures 12 ft. by 15 ft.* ◆ *The pond measures about 20 yards across.*

▷ JUDGE **3** ~ **sth** | ~ **how, what, etc.…** to judge the importance, value, or effect of something **SYN** ASSESS: *It is difficult to measure the success of the campaign at this stage.*

PHR V ˌmeasure **sb/sth against sb/sth** to compare someone or something with someone or something: *The figures are not very good when measured against those of our competitors.* ˌmeasure **sth↔ˈout** to take the amount of something that you need from a larger amount: *He measured out a cup of milk and added it to the mixture.* ˌmeasure ˈup to measure something: *We spent the morning measuring up and deciding where the furniture would go.* ˌmeasure ˈup (to sth/sb) (usually used in negative sentences and questions) to be as good, successful, etc. as expected or needed **SYN** MATCH UP: *Last year's team just didn't measure up.* ◆ *The job failed to measure up to her expectations.*

● ***noun***

▷ OFFICIAL ACTION **1** [C] an official action that is done in order to achieve a particular aim: *safety/security/austerity measures* ◆ *a temporary/an emergency measure* ◆ ~ **(to do sth)** *We must take preventive measures to reduce crime in the area.* ◆ *The police department is introducing tougher measures to combat crime.* ◆ *measures against racism* ◆ *Police in riot gear were in attendance as a precautionary measure.* ⊃ see also HALF MEASURES ⊃ thesaurus box at ACTION

▷ AMOUNT **2** [sing.] a particular amount of something, especially a fairly large amount **SYN** DEGREE: *A measure of technical knowledge is desirable in this job.* ◆ *She achieved some measure of success with her first book.*

▷ WAY OF SHOWING/JUDGING **3** [sing.] a sign of the size or the strength of something: *Sending flowers is a measure of how much you care.* **4** [C] a way of judging or measuring something: *an accurate measure of ability* ◆ *Is this test a good measure of reading comprehension?*

▷ UNIT OF SIZE/QUANTITY **5** [C, U] a unit used for stating the size, quantity, or degree of something; a system or a scale of these units: *weights and measures* ◆ *The Richter Scale is a measure of ground motion.* ◆ *liquid/dry measure* ◆ *Which measure of weight do pharmacists use?* **6** [C] (especially of alcohol) a standard quantity: *a generous measure of whiskey*

▷ INSTRUMENT FOR MEASURING **7** [C] an instrument such as a stick, a long tape, or a container that is marked with standard units and is used for measuring ⊃ see also TAPE MEASURE

▷ SUGGESTED NEW LAW **8** [C] a written suggestion, especially one for a new law: *a motion to refer the measure to another committee* ◆ *a ballot measure* (= a change in the law that voters decide on)

▷ IN MUSIC **9** [C] one of the short sections of equal length that a piece of music is divided into, and the notes that are in it ⊃ picture at MUSIC

IDM beyond ˈmeasure (*formal*) very great or very much: *Our gratitude to all of you who helped us is beyond measure.* for good ˈmeasure as an extra amount of something in addition to what has already been done or given: *Use a half cup of rice per person and an extra spoonful for good measure.* full ˈmeasure the whole of something: *We experienced the full measure of their hospitality.* in full ˈmeasure (*formal*) to the greatest possible degree get/take/have the ˈmeasure of sb| get/have/take sb's ˈmeasure (*formal*) to form an opinion about someone's character or abilities so that you

can deal with them: *After only one game, the chess champion had the measure of his young opponent.* in no small ˈmeasure| in some, equal, etc. ˈmeasure (*formal*) to a large extent or degree; in some, etc. extent or degree: *The introduction of a new sales tax accounted in no small measure for the downfall of the governor.* ◆ *Our thanks are due in equal measure to every member of the team.* ⊃ more at LARGE

meas·ured /ˈmɛʒərd/ *adj.* [only before noun] slow and careful; controlled: *She replied in a measured tone to his threat.* ◆ *He walked down the corridor with measured steps.*

meas·ure·less /ˈmɛʒərləs/ *adj.* (*literary*) very great or without limits: *the measureless oceans*

meas·ure·ment 🔑 /ˈmɛʒərmənt/ *noun* **1** [U] the act or the process of finding the size, quantity, or degree of something: *the metric system of measurement* ◆ *Accurate measurement is very important in science.* ⊃ collocations at SCIENTIFIC **2** [C, usually pl.] the size, length, or amount of something: *to take someone's chest/waist measurement* ◆ *Do you know your measurements* (= the size of parts of your body)? ◆ *The exact measurements of the room are 20 feet 6 inches by 15 feet 3 inches.*

ˈmeasuring ˌcup *noun* a metal, glass, or plastic container used for measuring quantities when cooking ⊃ picture at KITCHEN

ˈmeasuring ˌspoon *noun* a metal or plastic spoon used for measuring quantities when cooking ⊃ picture at KITCHEN

ˈmeasuring ˌtape *noun* = TAPE MEASURE

meat 🔑 /mit/ *noun* **1** [U, C] the flesh of an animal or a bird eaten as food; a particular type of this: *a piece/slice of meat* ◆ *horse meat* (= from a horse) ◆ *meat-eating animals* ◆ *There's not much meat on this chop.* ◆ (*figurative, humorous*) *There's not much meat on her* (= she is very thin). ⊃ see also LUNCHMEAT, MINCEMEAT, RED MEAT, SAUSAGE MEAT, WHITE MEAT **2** [U] ~ **(of sth)** the important or interesting part of something **SYN** SUBSTANCE: *This chapter contains the real meat of the writer's argument.* **IDM** see DEAD, MAN

ˌmeat and poˈtatoes *noun* [U] the most basic and important aspects or parts of something: *Issues like this are the newspaper's meat and potatoes.*

ˌmeat-and-poˈtatoes *adj.* [only before noun] **1** dealing with the most basic and important aspects of something: *a meat-and-potatoes argument* **2** liking plain, simple things: *He's a real meat-and-potatoes guy.*

meat·ball /ˈmitbɔl/ *noun* a small ball of finely chopped meat, usually eaten hot with a sauce: *spaghetti and meatballs*

ˈmeat ˌgrinder *noun* a machine for cutting food, especially meat, into very small pieces

meat·loaf /ˈmitloʊf/ *noun* [C, U] finely chopped meat, onions, etc. that are mixed together and shaped like a LOAF of bread and then baked

ˈmeat ˌmarket *noun* **1** a place where meat is sold **2** (*informal*) a meeting place for people seeking sexual partners: *It's a meat market and the drinks are cheap.*

meat·pack·ing /ˈmitˌpækɪŋ/ *noun* [U] the process of killing animals and preparing the meat for sale

meat·y /ˈmiti/ *adj.* (**meat·i·er**, **meat·i·est**) **1** containing a lot of meat **2** smelling or tasting like meat: *a meaty taste* **3** (*approving*) containing a lot of important or interesting ideas **SYN** SUBSTANTIAL: *a meaty discussion* **4** (*informal*) large and fat; with a lot of flesh **SYN** FLESHY: *a meaty hand* ◆ *big, meaty tomatoes*

Mec·ca /ˈmɛkə/ *noun* **1** a city in Saudi Arabia that is the holiest city of Islam, being the place where the Prophet Muhammad was born **2** usually **mecca** a place that many people like to visit, especially for a particular reason: *Miami Beach is a mecca for tourists.*

me·chan·ic /məˈkænɪk/ *noun* **1** a person whose job is repairing machines, especially the engines of vehicles: *a car mechanic* **2 mechanics** [U] the science of movement and force ⟳ see also QUANTUM MECHANICS **3 mechanics** [U] the practical study of machinery: *The school's shop classes are where students learn basic mechanics.* **4 the mechanics** [pl.] the way something works or is done: *The exact mechanics of how payments are to be made will be decided later.*

me·chan·i·cal /məˈkænɪkl/ *adj.* **1** operated by power from an engine: *a mechanical device/toy/clock* ◆ *mechanical parts* **2** connected with machines and engines: *mechanical problems/defects* ◆ *The breakdown was due to a mechanical failure.* **3** (*disapproving*) (of people's behavior and actions) done without thinking, like a machine **SYN** ROUTINE: *a mechanical gesture/response* **4** connected with the physical laws of movement and cause and effect (= with MECHANICS): *mechanical processes* **5** (of a person) good at understanding how machines work ▶ **me·chan·i·cal·ly** /-kli/ *adv.*: *a mechanically powered vehicle* ◆ *She spoke mechanically, as if thinking of something else.* ◆ *He's always been mechanically minded.*

meˌchanical engiˈneering *noun* [U] the study of how machines are designed, built, and repaired ▶ **meˌchanical engiˈneer** *noun*

meˌchanical ˈpencil *noun* a pencil with a LEAD¹ that can be moved down for writing by turning or pushing the top of the pencil

mech·an·ism [AWL] /ˈmekəˌnɪzəm/ *noun* **1** a set of moving parts in a machine that performs a task: *a delicate watch mechanism* **2** a method or a system for achieving something: *mechanisms for dealing with complaints from the general public* **3** a system of parts in a living thing that together perform a particular function: *the balance mechanism in the ears* ◆ *Pain acts as a natural defense mechanism.*

mech·a·nis·tic /ˌmekəˈnɪstɪk/ *adj.* (often *disapproving*) connected with the belief that all things in the universe can be explained as if they were machines: *the mechanistic philosophy that compares the brain to a computer* ▶ **mech·a·nis·ti·cally** /-kli/ *adv.*

mech·a·nize /ˈmekəˌnaɪz/ *verb* [usually passive] ~ **sth** to change a process, so that the work is done by machines rather than people **SYN** AUTOMATE: *The production process is now highly mechanized.* ▶ **mech·a·ni·za·tion** /ˌmekənəˈzeɪʃn/ *noun* [U]: *the increasing mechanization of farm work*

med /med/ *adj.* (*informal*) = MEDICAL: *a med student* ◆ *She's in med school.*

medals   shield

trophy   rosette   cup

med·al /ˈmedl/ *noun, verb*
● *noun* a flat piece of metal, usually shaped like a coin, that is given to the winner of a competition or to someone who has been brave, for example in war: *to win a gold medal in the Olympics* ◆ *to award a medal for bravery* **IDM** see DESERVE

● *verb* (-l-, *CanE usually* -ll-) [I] to win a medal in a competition: *She medaled in tennis last year.*

med·al·ist (*CanE usually* **med·al·list**) /ˈmedl-ɪst/ *noun* a person who has received a medal, usually for winning a competition in a sport: *an Olympic medalist* ◆ *a gold/silver/bronze medalist*

me·dal·lion /məˈdælyən/ *noun* a piece of jewelry in the shape of a large flat coin worn on a chain around the neck ⟳ picture at JEWELRY

ˌMedal of ˈFreedom *noun* the highest award that the U.S. gives to a CIVILIAN who has achieved something very important

ˌMedal of ˈHonor *noun* the highest award that the U.S. gives to a member of the armed forces who has shown very great courage in a war

ˈmedal ˌplay *noun* [U] = STROKE PLAY

med·dle /ˈmedl/ *verb* (*disapproving*) **1** [I] ~ **(in/with sth)** to become involved in something that does not concern you **SYN** INTERFERE: *He had no right to meddle in her affairs.* **2** [I] ~ **(with sth)** to touch something in a careless way, especially when it is not yours or when you do not know how to use it correctly: *Somebody was meddling with her computer.* ▶ **med·dling** *noun* [U]

med·dler /ˈmedlər/ *noun* (*disapproving*) a person who tries to get involved in something that does not concern them **SYN** BUSYBODY

med·dle·some /ˈmedlsəm/ *adj.* (*disapproving*) (of people) enjoying getting involved in situations that do not concern them **SYN** INTERFERING

med·e·vac (also **med·i·vac**) /ˈmedɪˌvæk/ *noun* **1** [U] the transportation of injured soldiers or other people to the hospital in a HELICOPTER or other aircraft **2** [C] a HELICOPTER or other aircraft used to take sick or injured people to the hospital ▶ **med·e·vac** (also **med·i·vac**) *verb* (-ck-): ~ **sb** *The injured crew members were medevacked out.*

me·di·a 🔑 [AWL] /ˈmidiə/ *noun* **1 the media** [U, pl.] the main ways that large numbers of people receive information and entertainment, that is television, radio, newspapers, and the Internet: *the news/broadcasting/national media* ◆ *The trial was fully reported in the media.* ◆ *The media was accused of influencing the final decision.* ◆ *Any event attended by the actor received widespread media coverage.* ⟳ see also MASS MEDIA, NEW MEDIA, SOCIAL MEDIA **2** *pl.* of MEDIUM

me·di·ae·val = MEDIEVAL

me·di·al /ˈmidiəl/ *adj.* (*technical*) located in the middle, especially of the body or of an organ

me·di·an /ˈmidiən/ *adj., noun*
● *adj.* [only before noun] (*technical*) **1** having a value in the middle of a series of values: *the median age/price* **2** located in or passing through the middle: *a median point/line*
● *noun* **1** (*mathematics*) the middle value of a series of numbers arranged in order of size **2** (*geometry*) a straight line passing from a point of a triangle to the center of the opposite side. **3** (also **ˈmedian ˌstrip**) a narrow strip of land that separates the two sides of a major highway such as an INTERSTATE

ˈmedia ˌstudies *noun* [U] the study of newspapers, television, radio, etc. as a subject at college, etc.

me·di·ate [AWL] /ˈmidiˌeɪt/ *verb* **1** [I, T] to try to end a disagreement between two or more people or groups by talking to them and trying to find things that everyone can agree on: ~ **(in sth)** *The mayor was asked to mediate in the dispute.* ◆ ~ **between A and B** *An independent body was brought in to mediate between staff and management.* ◆ ~ **sth** to *mediate differences/disputes/problems* **2** [T] ~ **sth** to succeed in finding a solution to a disagreement between people or groups **SYN** NEGOTIATE: *They mediated a settlement.* **3** [T, usually passive] ~ **sth** (*formal* or *technical*) to influence something and/or make it possible for it to happen: *Educational success is mediated by economic factors.* ▶ **me·di·a·tion** `AWL` /ˌmidiˈeɪʃn/ *noun* [U]

me·di·a·tor /ˈmidiˌeɪtər/ *noun* a person or an organization that tries to help reach an agreement or settlement

med·ic /ˈmɛdɪk/ *noun* a person who is trained to give medical treatment, especially someone in the armed forces

Med·i·caid /ˈmɛdɪˌkeɪd/ *noun* [U] the insurance system that provides medical care for poor people in the U.S.

med·i·cal 🔑 `AWL` /ˈmɛdɪkl/ *adj., noun*
- *adj.* [usually before noun] **1** connected with illness and injury and their treatment: *medical advances/care/research ◆ her medical condition/history/records ◆ the medical profession ◆ a medical student/school* ⊃ see also MED **2** connected with ways of treating illness that do not involve cutting the body: *medical or surgical treatment* ▶ **med·i·cally** `AWL` /-kli/ *adv.*
- *noun* (also ˌmedical examiˈnation) a thorough examination of your body that a doctor does, for example, before you start a particular job ⊃ see also EXAM

ˈmedical exˌaminer *noun* (*abbr.* ME) a doctor whose job is to examine a dead body in order to find out the cause of death ⊃ compare PATHOLOGIST

ˈmedical ˌschool (also ˈmed school, *informal*) *noun* a (part of a) university where students study to obtain a degree in medicine

Med·i·care /ˈmɛdɪˌkɛr/ *noun* [U] **1** (in the U.S.) the federal insurance system that provides medical care for people over 65 **2 medicare** (in Canada) the national medical care system for all people that is paid for by taxes

med·i·cate /ˈmɛdɪˌkeɪt/ *verb* ~ **sb** to give someone medicine, especially a drug that affects their behavior

medicated /ˈmɛdɪˌkeɪtəd/ *adj.* containing a substance for preventing or curing infections of your skin or hair: *medicated shampoo/soap*

med·i·ca·tion /ˌmɛdəˈkeɪʃn/ *noun* [U, C] a drug or another form of medicine that you take to prevent or to treat an illness: *to be on medication ◆ Are you currently taking any medication? ◆ Many flu medications are available without a prescription.*

me·dic·i·nal /məˈdɪsənl/ *adj.* helpful in the process of healing illness or infection: *medicinal herbs/plants ◆ medicinal properties/use ◆* (*humorous*) *He claims he keeps a bottle of brandy only for medicinal purposes.*

med·i·cine 🔑 /ˈmɛdəsn/ *noun*
1 [U] the study and treatment of diseases and injuries: *advances in modern medicine ◆ to study/practice medicine ◆ traditional/conventional/orthodox medicine ◆ alternative medicine* ⊃ see also AYURVEDIC MEDICINE, DEFENSIVE MEDICINE, FAMILY MEDICINE, INTERNAL MEDICINE, SPORTS MEDICINE **2** [U, C] a substance, especially a liquid that you drink or a PILL that you swallow, used to treat an illness: *Did you take your medicine? ◆ cough medicine ◆ Chinese herbal medicines*
IDM the best medicine the best way of improving a situation, especially of making you feel happier: *Laughter is the best medicine.* **a taste/dose of your own medicine** the same bad treatment that you have given to others: *Let the bully have a taste of his own medicine.* ⊃ more at STRONG

ˈmedicine ˌball *noun* a large heavy ball that is thrown and caught as a form of exercise

ˈmedicine ˌman *noun* a person who is believed to have special magic powers of healing, especially among Native Americans ⊃ compare WITCH DOCTOR

med·i·co /ˈmɛdɪkoʊ/ *noun* (*pl.* med·i·cos) (*informal*) a doctor

me·di·e·val (also me·di·ae·val) /ˌmidiˈivl; ˌmɛdi-; ˌmɪdˈivl/ *adj.* [usually before noun] connected with the Middle Ages (about AD 1000 to AD 1450): *medieval architecture/castles/manuscripts ◆ the literature of the late medieval period*

me·di·o·cre /ˌmidiˈoʊkər/ *adj.* (*disapproving*) not very good;

of only average standard: *a mediocre musician/talent/performance ◆ I thought the play was only mediocre.*

me·di·oc·ri·ty /ˌmidiˈɑkrəti/ *noun* (*pl.* me·di·oc·ri·ties) (*disapproving*) **1** [U] the quality of being average or not very good: *His acting career started brilliantly, then sank into mediocrity.* **2** [C] a person who is not very good at something: *an outstanding leader, surrounded by mediocrities*

med·i·tate /ˈmɛdəˌteɪt/ *verb* **1** [I] ~ **(on/upon sth)** to think deeply, usually in silence, especially for religious reasons or in order to make your mind calm **2** [T] ~ **sth** (*formal*) to plan something in your mind; to consider doing something **SYN** CONTEMPLATE: *They were meditating revenge.*

med·i·ta·tion /ˌmɛdəˈteɪʃn/ *noun* **1** [U] the practice of thinking deeply in silence, especially for religious reasons or in order to make your mind calm: *She found peace through yoga and meditation. ◆ He was deep in meditation and didn't see me come in.* **2** [C, usually pl.] ~ **(on sth)** (*formal*) serious thoughts on a particular subject that someone writes down or speaks: *his meditations on life and art*

med·i·ta·tive /ˈmɛdəˌteɪtɪv/ *adj.* (*formal*) thinking very deeply; involving deep thought **SYN** THOUGHTFUL: *She found him in a meditative mood. ◆ a meditative poem*

Med·i·ter·ra·ne·an /ˌmɛdətəˈreɪniən/ *adj.* [only before noun] connected with the Mediterranean Sea or the countries and regions that surround it; typical of this area: *a Mediterranean country/climate ◆ Mediterranean food*

me·di·um 🔑 `AWL` /ˈmidiəm/ *adj., noun*
- *adj.* [usually before noun] (*abbr.* M) in the middle between two sizes, amounts, lengths, temperatures, etc. **SYN** AVERAGE: *a medium-size car/business/town ◆ a man of medium height/build ◆ There are three sizes—small, medium and large. ◆ Cook over a medium heat for 15 minutes. ◆ a medium dry white wine ◆ Choose medium to large tomatoes.* **IDM** see TERM
- *noun* (*pl.* me·di·a /ˈmidiə/ or mediums) **1** a way of communicating information, etc. to people: *the medium of radio/television ◆ electronic/audio-visual media ◆ Television is the modern medium of communication. ◆ A T-shirt can be an excellent medium for getting your message across.* **HELP** The plural in this meaning is usually **media**. ⊃ see also MASS MEDIA, MEDIA **2** something that is used for a particular purpose: *English is the medium of instruction* (= the language used to teach other subjects). *◆ Video is a good medium for learning a foreign language.* **3** the material or the form that an artist, a writer, or a musician uses: *the medium of paint/poetry/drama ◆ Watercolor is his favorite medium.* **4** (*biology*) a substance that something exists or grows in or that it travels through: *The bacteria were growing in a sugar medium.* **5** (*pl.* med·i·ums) a person who claims to be able to communicate with the spirits of dead people **IDM** see HAPPY

ˈmedium-ˌsized *adj.* of average size: *a medium-sized frying pan*

ˈmedium-ˌterm *adj.* used to describe a period of time that is a few weeks or months into the future: *the Fed's medium-term financial strategy*

ˈmedium ˌwave (*abbr.* MW) *noun* [U] also **the medium wave** [sing.] a band of radio waves with a length of between 100 and 1,000 meters ⊃ compare SHORTWAVE

med·i·vac *noun* = MEDEVAC

med·ley /ˈmɛdli/ *noun* **1** a piece of music consisting of several songs or tunes played or sung one after the other: *a medley of Beatles hits* **2** a mixture of people or things of different kinds: *a medley of flavors/smells* **3** a swimming race in which each member of a team uses a different stroke: *the 4×100 meters medley*

ˈmed school *noun* (*informal*) = MEDICAL SCHOOL

meek /mik/ *adj.* (meek·er, meek·est) **1** quiet, gentle, and always ready to do what other people want without expressing your own opinion **SYN** COMPLIANT, SELF-EFFACING: *They called her Miss Mouse because she was so meek and mild.* **2 the meek** *noun* [pl.] people who are meek

▶ **meek·ly** adv.: *He meekly did whatever was asked of him.*
meek·ness noun [U]

meer·kat /ˈmɪrkæt/ noun a small southern African animal that has a long tail and often stands up on its back legs. Meerkats are a type of MONGOOSE.

meet 🔑 /mit/ verb, noun

● **verb** (met, met /mɛt/)

▷ **BY ARRANGEMENT 1** [I, T, no passive] to come together formally in order to discuss something: *The committee meets on Fridays.* ◆ **~ sb** *World leaders are meeting in Paris next month for talks.* ◆ **~ with sb** *The President met with senior White House aides.* **2** [I, T, no passive] to come together socially after you have arranged it: **~ (for sth)** *Let's meet for a drink after work.* ◆ **~ sb (for sth)** *We're meeting them outside the theater at 7.* **3** [T] **~ sb/sth** to go to a place and wait there for a particular person to arrive: *Will you meet me at the airport?* ◆ *The hotel bus meets all incoming flights.* ◆ *I met his plane at 6 o'clock, but he wasn't on it.*

▷ **FOR THE FIRST TIME 4** [T, no passive, I] **~ (sb)** to see and know someone for the first time; to be introduced to someone: *Where did you first meet your husband?* ◆ **Pleased to meet you.** ◆ *Nice meeting you.* ◆ *There's someone I want you to meet.* ◆ *I don't think we've met.*

▷ **BY CHANCE 5** [I, T, no passive] to be in the same place as someone by chance and talk to them: *Maybe we'll meet again some time.* ◆ **~ sb** *Did you meet anyone in town?*

▷ **IN CONTEST 6** [I, T, no passive] to play, fight, etc. together as opponents in a competition: *Smith and Jones met in last year's final.* ◆ **~ sb** *Smith met Jones in last year's final.*

▷ **EXPERIENCE SOMETHING 7** [T] **~ sth** to experience something, often something unpleasant: *Others will have met similar problems.* ◆ *How she met her death will probably never be known.* **SYN** COME ACROSS, ENCOUNTER

▷ **TOUCH/JOIN 8** [I, T] to touch something; to join: *The curtains don't meet in the middle.* ◆ **~ sth** *That's where the river meets the ocean.* ◆ *His hand met hers.*

▷ **SATISFY 9** [T] **~ sth** to do or satisfy what is needed or what someone asks for **SYN** FULFILL: *How can we best meet the needs of all the different groups?* ◆ *Until these conditions are met we cannot proceed with the sale.* ◆ *I can't possibly meet that deadline.*

▷ **PAY 10** [T] **~ sth** to pay something: *The cost will be met by the company.*

IDM **meet sb's eye(s) 1** [T, I] (also **meet sb's ˈgaze, ˈlook,** etc., **people's ˈeyes meet**) if you **meet someone's eye(s)**, you look directly at them as they look at you; if two people's **eyes meet**, they look directly at each other: *She was afraid to meet my eye.* ◆ *Their eyes met across the crowded room.* ◆ *She met his gaze without flinching.* **2** [T] **~ your eyes** if a sight **meets your eyes**, you see it: *A terrible sight met their eyes.* **meet sb halfway** to reach an agreement with someone by giving them part of what they want **meet your Maker** (especially *humorous*) to die **there is more to sb/sth than meets the eye** a person or thing is more complicated or interesting than you might think at first ⊃ **more at** END *n.*, MATCH *n.*, TWAIN

PHR V **ˌmeet ˈup (with sb)** to meet someone, especially by arrangement: *They met up again later for a drink.* **ˈmeet with sb** to meet someone, especially for discussions: *The President met with senior White House aides.* **ˈmeet with sth 1** to be received or treated by someone in a particular way: *Her proposal met with resistance from the Republicans.* ◆ *to meet with success/failure* **2** to experience something unpleasant: *She was worried that he might have met with an accident.* **ˈmeet sth with sth** to react to something in a particular way **SYN** RECEIVE: *His suggestion was met with howls of protest.*

● **noun** a sports competition: *a track/swim meet*

meet·ing 🔑 /ˈmitɪŋ/ noun

1 [C] an occasion when people come together to discuss or decide something: *to have/hold/call/attend a meeting* ◆ *a committee/staff meeting* ◆ *What time is the meeting?* ◆ *Helen will chair the meeting* (= be in charge of it). ◆ *I'll be in a meeting all morning—can you take my calls?* ◆ *a meeting of the United Nations Security Council* **2 the meeting** [sing.] the people at a meeting: *The meeting voted to accept the pay offer.* **3** [C] a situation in which two or more people meet together, because they have arranged it or by chance **SYN** ENCOUNTER: *At our first meeting I was nervous.* ◆ *It was a chance meeting that would change my life.* ◆ *He remembered their childhood meetings with nostalgia.*

IDM **a meeting of minds** a close understanding between people with similar ideas, especially when they meet to do something or meet for the first time

ˈmeeting ˌhouse noun a place where Quakers meet for worship

ˈmeeting ˌplace noun a place where people often meet: *The café is a popular meeting place for students.*

meg /mɛg/ noun (*informal*) = MEGABYTE: *more than 512 megs of memory* ◆ *24-meg broadband*

meg·a /ˈmɛgə/ adj. [usually before noun] (*informal*) very large or impressive **SYN** GREAT, HUGE: *The song was a mega hit last year.* ▶ **mega** adv.: *They're mega rich.*

mega- /ˈmɛgə/ combining form (in nouns) **1** very large or great: *a megastore* **2** (in units of measurement) one million: *a megawatt* **3** (*computing*) 1,048,576 (= 2^{20}): *megabyte*

meg·a·bit /ˈmɛgəˌbɪt/ noun (*abbr.* Mb) (*computing*) a unit of computer memory which is roughly equal to 1 million BITS

meg·a·bucks /ˈmɛgəˌbʌks/ noun [pl.] (*informal*) a very large amount of money: *He earns megabucks.*

meg·a·byte /ˈmɛgəˌbaɪt/ noun (*abbr.* MB) (*informal*) (*abbr.* meg) a unit of computer memory, equal to 2^{20} (or about 1 million) BYTES: *a 512-megabyte flash drive*

meg·a·hertz /ˈmɛgəˌhərts/ noun (*pl.* meg·a·hertz) (*abbr.* MHz) a unit for measuring radio waves and the speed at which a computer operates; 1,000,000 HERTZ

meg·a·lith /ˈmɛgəlɪθ/ noun a very large stone, especially one put in a place that was used for ceremonies in ancient times ▶ **meg·a·lith·ic** /ˌmɛgəˈlɪθɪk/ adj.

meg·a·lo·ma·ni·a /ˌmɛgəlouˈmeɪniə/ noun [U] **1** (*technical*) a mental illness or condition in which someone has an exaggerated belief in their own importance or power **2** a strong feeling that you want to have more and more power

meg·a·lo·ma·ni·ac /ˌmɛgəlouˈmeɪniæk/ noun a person suffering from or showing megalomania ▶ **meg·a·lo·ma·ni·ac** adj.

meg·a·lop·o·lis /ˌmɛgəˈlɑpələs/ noun (*formal*) a very large city or group of cities where a great number of people live

meg·a·phone /ˈmɛgəˌfoun/ noun a device for making your voice sound louder, that is wider at one end, like a CONE, and is often used at outdoor events ⊃ compare BULL-HORN

megaphone

meg·a·pix·el /ˈmɛgəˌpɪksl/ noun a million PIXELS (= very small individual areas on a computer screen), used to measure the quality of a DIGITAL screen or image: *a 12 megapixel digital camera*

meg·a·star /ˈmɛgəˌstɑr/ noun (*informal*) a very famous singer, actor, or entertainer

meg·a·store /ˈmɛgəˌstɔr/ noun a very large store, especially one that sells one type of product, for example computers or furniture

meg·a·ton /ˈmɛgəˌtʌn/ noun a unit for measuring the power of an EXPLOSIVE, equal to one million tons of TNT: *a one megaton nuclear bomb*

meg·a·watt /ˈmɛgəˌwɑt/ noun (*abbr.* MW) a unit for measuring electrical power; one million WATTS

meh /mɛ/ exclamation, adj. (*informal*) used to show that you are not at all interested in or impressed by something: *"So how was the movie?" "Meh. The action scenes aren't awful, but*

t tea   ţ butter   d did   k cat   g got   tʃ chin   dʒ June   f fall

there's nothing great about it." ♦ She does an OK job on a meh song.

mei·o·sis /maɪˈoʊsəs/ *noun* [U] (*biology*) the division of a cell in two stages that results in four cells, each with half the number of CHROMOSOMES of the original cell

-meister /ˈmaɪstər/ *combining form* (in nouns) (*informal*) a person thought of as skilled at a particular activity or important in a particular field: *a horror-meister*

meit·ner·i·um /maɪtˈnɛriəm; -ˈnɪr-/ *noun* [U] (*symb.* **Mt**) a RADIOACTIVE chemical element. Meitnerium is produced when atoms COLLIDE (= crash into each other).

mel·a·mine /ˈmɛləˌmin/ *noun* [U] a strong, hard, plastic material, used especially for covering surfaces such as the tops of tables, and for making cups, etc.

mel·an·cho·li·a /ˌmɛlənˈkoʊliə/ *noun* (*old-fashioned*) a mental illness in which the patient is depressed and worried by unnecessary fears

mel·an·chol·ic /ˌmɛlənˈkɑlɪk/ *adj.* (*old-fashioned* or *literary*) feeling or expressing sadness, especially when the sadness is like an illness

mel·an·chol·y /ˈmɛlənˌkɑli/ *noun, adj.*
• *noun* [U] (*formal*) a deep feeling of sadness that lasts for a long time and often cannot be explained: *A mood of melancholy descended on us.*
• *adj.* very sad or making you feel sadness **SYN** MOURNFUL, SOMBER: *melancholy thoughts/memories* ♦ *The melancholy song died away.*

me·lange /meɪˈlɑnʒ/ *noun* (from *French, formal*) a mixture or variety of different things: *a melange of different cultures*

mel·a·nin /ˈmɛlənɪn/ *noun* [U] (*technical*) a dark substance in the skin and hair that causes the skin to change color in the sun's light

mel·a·no·ma /ˌmɛləˈnoʊmə/ *noun* [C, U] (*medical*) a type of cancer that appears as a dark spot or TUMOR on the skin

mel·a·to·nin /ˌmɛləˈtoʊnən/ *noun* [U] (*biology*) a HORMONE that causes changes in skin color

meld /mɛld/ *verb* [I, T] ~ **(A) with B** | ~ **(A and B) (together)** (*formal*) to combine with something else; to make something combine with something else **SYN** BLEND: *The chocolate and coffee flavors meld beautifully in this dessert.*

me·lee /ˈmeɪleɪ; meɪˈleɪ/ *noun* [sing.] (from *French*) a situation in which a crowd of people are rushing or pushing each other in a confused way

mel·lif·lu·ous /məˈlɪfluəs/ *adj.* (*formal*) (of music or of someone's voice) sounding sweet and smooth; very pleasant to listen to

mel·low /ˈmɛloʊ/ *adj., verb*
• *adj.* (**mel·low·er**, **mel·low·est**) **1** (of color or sound) soft, rich, and pleasant: *mellow autumn colors* ♦ *Mellow music and lighting helped to create the right atmosphere.* **2** (of a taste or flavor) smooth and pleasant: *a mellow, fruity wine* **3** (of people) calm, gentle, and reasonable because of age or experience: *Dad's certainly grown mellower with age.* **4** (*informal*) (of people) relaxed, calm, and happy, especially after drinking alcohol: *After two glasses of wine, I was feeling mellow.*
• *verb* **1** [I, T] to become or make someone become less extreme in behavior, etc., especially as a result of growing older: *She had mellowed a great deal since their days at college.* ♦ ~ **sb** *A period spent working abroad had done nothing to mellow him.* **2** [I, T] ~ **(sth)** to become, or make a color become, less bright, especially over a period of time **3** [I, T] ~ **(sth)** to develop or make wine develop a pleasant and less bitter taste over a period of time
PHR V **mellow 'out** (*informal*) to enjoy yourself by relaxing and not doing much

me·lod·ic /məˈlɑdɪk/ *adj.* **1** [only before noun] connected with the main tune in a piece of music: *The melodic line is carried by the two clarinets.* **2** = MELODIOUS

me·lod·i·ca /məˈlɑdɪkə/ *noun* a musical instrument that has a keyboard and a part that you blow into

me·lo·di·ous /məˈloʊdiəs/ (also **me·lod·ic**) *adj.* pleasant to listen to, like music: *a rich melodious voice* ▶ **me·lo·di·ous·ly** *adv.*

mel·o·dist /ˈmɛlədɪst/ *noun* a person who sings or writes tunes; a person who is very good at singing or writing tunes

mel·o·dra·ma /ˈmɛləˌdrɑmə/ *noun* [U, C] **1** a story, play, or novel that is full of exciting events and in which the characters and emotions seem too exaggerated to be real: *a gripping Victorian melodrama* ♦ *Instead of tragedy, we got melodrama.* **2** events, behavior, etc. that are exaggerated or extreme: *Her love of melodrama meant that any small problem became a crisis.*

mel·o·dra·mat·ic /ˌmɛlədrəˈmætɪk/ *adj.* (often *disapproving*) full of exciting and extreme emotions or events; behaving or reacting to something in an exaggerated way: *a melodramatic plot full of deceit and murder* ▶ **mel·o·dra·mat·i·cal·ly** /-kli/ *adv.*

mel·o·dra·mat·ics /ˌmɛlədrəˈmætɪks/ *noun* [pl.] behavior or events that are melodramatic: *No more melodramatics, please.*

mel·o·dy /ˈmɛlədi/ *noun* (*pl.* **mel·o·dies**) **1** [C] a tune, especially the main tune in a piece of music written for several instruments or voices: *a haunting melody* ♦ *The melody is then taken up by the flutes.* ⊃ collocations at MUSIC **2** [C] a piece of music or a song with a clear or simple tune: *old Irish melodies* **3** [U] the arrangement of musical notes in a tune: *a few bars of melody drifted toward us*

mel·on /ˈmɛlən/ *noun* [C, U] a large fruit with hard green, yellow, or orange skin, sweet flesh and juice, and a lot of seeds: *a slice of melon* ⊃ see also HONEYDEW MELON, WATERMELON

melt 🔊 /mɛlt/ *verb*
1 [I, T] to become or make something become liquid as a result of heating: *The snow showed no sign of melting.* ♦ *melting ice* ♦ ~ **sth** *The sun had melted the snow.* ♦ *First, melt two ounces of butter.* ⊃ collocations at COOKING ⊃ compare DEFROST, DE-ICE **2** [I, T] to become or to make a feeling, an emotion, etc. become gentler and less strong: *The tension in the room began to melt.* ♦ ~ **sth** *Her trusting smile melted his heart.*
IDM **melt in your mouth** (of food) to be soft and very good to eat ⊃ more at BUTTER *n.*
PHR V ,melt a'way | ,melt sth↔a'way to disappear or make something disappear gradually: *At the first sign of trouble, the crowd melted away.* ,melt sth↔'down to heat a metal or WAX object until it is liquid, especially so that the metal or wax can be used to make something else ⊃ related noun MELTDOWN 'melt into sth to gradually become part of something and therefore become difficult to see

melt·down /ˈmɛltdaʊn/ *noun* **1** [U, C] a serious accident in which the central part of a nuclear REACTOR melts, causing harmful RADIATION to escape **2** [U, C] (*economics*) a situation where something fails or becomes weaker in a sudden or dramatic way: *The country is in economic meltdown.* ♦ *a meltdown on the New York Stock Exchange* **3** (*informal*) a loss of control over your emotions that happens very fast: *My little brother had a meltdown when he couldn't get a new toy.*

melt·ing /ˈmɛltɪŋ/ *adj.* [usually before noun] persuading you to feel love or sympathy: *his melting eyes* ▶ **melt·ing·ly** *adv.*

'melting ,point *noun* [U, C] the temperature at which a substance will melt

'melting ,pot *noun* [usually sing.] a place or situation in which large numbers of people, ideas, etc. are mixed together: *the vast melting pot of American society*

mem·ber 🔊 /ˈmɛmbər/ *noun*
1 ~ **(of sth)** a person, an animal, or a plant that belongs to a particular group: *a member of society/the family* ♦ *characteristics common to all members of the species* **2** a person, a country, or an organization that has joined a particular group, club, or team: ♦ *staff/party/union members* ♦ *a meeting of member countries/states* ♦ *How much*

---

does it cost to become a member? ◆ **~ of sth** an active member of the local church **3** (old use or literary) a part of the body, especially an arm or a leg **4** PENIS. People say "member" to avoid saying "penis."

Member of Parliament noun = MP

mem·ber·ship 🔑 /'mɛmbərˌʃɪp/ noun
1 [U] **~ (in sth)** the state of being a member of a group, a club, an organization, etc.: Who is eligible to apply for membership in the association? ◆ a **membership card/fee 2** [C] the members of, or the number of members in, a group, a club, an organization, etc.: The membership has not yet voted. ◆ The club has a membership of more than 500.

mem·brane /'mɛmbreɪn/ noun [C, U] **1** a thin layer of skin or TISSUE that connects or covers parts inside the body ⊃ see also MUCOUS MEMBRANE **2** a very thin layer found in the structure of cells in plants **3** a thin layer of material used to prevent air, liquid, etc. from entering a particular part of something: a waterproof membrane ▶ **mem·bra·nous** /'mɛmbrənəs/ adj.

meme /mim/ noun (biology) a type of behavior that is passed from one member of a group to another, not in the GENE but by another means such as people copying it

me·men·to /mə'mɛntoʊ/ noun (pl. me·men·tos or me·men·toes) a thing that you keep or give to someone to remind you or them of a person or place SYN SOUVENIR: a memento of our trip to Italy

me·men·to mo·ri /məˌmɛntoʊ 'mɔri/ noun (pl. me·men·to mo·ri) an object or symbol that reminds or warns you of death

mem·o /'mɛmoʊ/ noun (pl. memos) (also formal memoran-dum) **~ (to sb)** an official note from one person to another in the same organization: to write/send/circulate a memo

mem·oir /'mɛmwɑr/ noun **1** memoirs [pl.] an account written by someone, especially someone famous, about their life and experiences **2** [C] (formal) a written account of someone's life, a place, or an event, written by someone who knows it well

mem·o·ra·bil·i·a /ˌmɛmərə'bɪliə; -'biliə/ noun [pl.] things that people collect because they once belonged to a famous person, or because they are connected with a particular interesting place, event, or activity: baseball/Beatles memorabilia

mem·o·ra·ble /'mɛmərəbl/ adj. **~ (for sth)** special, good, or unusual and therefore worth remembering or easy to remember SYN UNFORGETTABLE: a truly memorable occasion ▶ **mem·o·ra·bly** /-bli/ adv.

mem·o·ran·dum /ˌmɛmə'rændəm/ noun (pl. mem·o·ran-da /-də/) **1** (formal) = MEMO: an internal memorandum **2** (law) a record of a legal agreement that has not yet been formally prepared and signed **3** a proposal or report on a particular subject for a person, an organization, a committee, etc.: a detailed memorandum to the commission on employment policy

me·mo·ri·al /mə'mɔriəl/ noun, adj.
● noun **1** [C] a statue, stone, etc. that is built in order to remind people of an important past event or of a famous person who has died: a war memorial (= in memory of soldiers who died in a war) ◆ **~ to sb/sth** a memorial to victims of the Holocaust **2** [sing.] **~ to sb/sth** a thing that will continue to remind people of someone or something: The painting will be a lasting memorial to a remarkable woman.
● adj. [only before noun] created or done in order to remember someone who has died: a **memorial statue/plaque/prize** ◆ The **memorial service** will be held at a local church. ◆ the John F. Kennedy Memorial Hospital

Me·mo·rial Day noun a holiday in the U.S., usually the last Monday in May, in honor of members of the armed forces who have died in war ⊃ see also VETERANS DAY

me·mo·ri·al·ize /mə'mɔriəˌlaɪz/ verb **~ sb/sth** (formal) to produce something that will continue to exist and remind people of someone who has died or something that has gone SYN COMMEMORATE

memoriam /mə'mɔriəm/ ⊃ IN MEMORIAM

mem·o·rize /'mɛməˌraɪz/ verb **~ sth** to learn something carefully so that you can remember it exactly: to memorize a poem

mem·o·ry 🔑 /'mɛməri; 'mɛmri/ noun (pl. mem·o·ries)
> ABILITY TO REMEMBER **1** [C, U] **~ (for sth)** your ability to remember things: I have a bad memory for names. ◆ People have **short memories** (= they soon forget). ◆ He had a **long memory** for people who had disappointed him. ◆ She can recite the whole poem **from memory**. ◆ He suffered loss of memory for weeks after the accident. ◆ Are you sure? Memory can play tricks on you. **2** [U] the period of time that someone is able to remember events: There hasn't been peace in the country **within my memory**. ◆ It was the worst storm in recent memory. ◆ This hasn't happened **in living memory** (= nobody alive now can remember it happening).
> SOMETHING YOU REMEMBER **3** [C] a thought of something that you remember from the past SYN RECOLLECTION: childhood memories ◆ I have vivid memories of my grand-parents. ◆ What is your earliest memory? ◆ The photos **bring back** lots of good **memories**. **4** [U] (formal) what is remem-bered about someone after they have died: Her memory lives on (= we still remember her).
> COMPUTING **5** [C, U] the part of a computer where informa-tion is stored; the amount of space in a computer for storing information ⊃ see also RAM
IDM if (my) memory serves me well, correctly, etc. if I remember correctly **in memory of sb | to the memory of sb** intended to show respect and remind people of someone who has died: He founded the charity in memory of his late wife. ⊃ more at ETCH, JOG v., SIEVE n.

memory bank noun the memory of a device such as a computer

memory card noun an electronic device that can be used to store data, used especially with DIGITAL cameras, cell phones, music players, etc. ⊃ compare SD CARD, SDHC CARD

memory lane noun
IDM a trip/walk down memory lane time that you spend thinking about and remembering the past or going to a place again in order to remind yourself of past experiences

memory stick noun = FLASH DRIVE

men pl. of MAN

men·ace /'mɛnəs/ noun, verb
● noun **1** [C, usually sing.] **~ (to sb/sth)** a person or thing that causes, or may cause, serious damage, harm, or danger SYN THREAT: a new initiative aimed at beating the menace of illegal drugs **2** [U] an atmosphere that makes you feel threatened or frightened: a sense/an air/a hint of **menace** in his voice **3** [C, usually sing.] (informal) a person or thing that is annoying or causes trouble SYN NUISANCE
● verb **~ sth/sb** (formal) to be a possible danger to something or someone SYN THREATEN: Many of our coastal wetlands are being menaced by major development projects.

men·ac·ing /'mɛnəsɪŋ/ adj. seeming likely to cause you harm or danger SYN THREATENING: a menacing face/tone ◆ At night, the dark streets become menacing. ▶ **men·ac·ing·ly** adv.: The thunder growled menacingly.

mé·nage /meɪ'nɑʒ/ noun [usually sing.] (from French, formal or humorous) all the people who live together in one house SYN HOUSEHOLD

me·nag·er·ie /mə'nædʒəri; -'næʒə-/ noun a collection of wild animals

mend /mɛnd/ verb, noun
● verb **1** [T] **~ sth** to repair a hole in a piece of clothing, etc.: He mended a rip in his pants. **2** [T] **~ sth** to find a solution to a problem or disagreement: They tried to mend their differ-ences. ⊃ see also FENCE-MENDING **3** [I] (old-fashioned) (of a person) to improve in health after being ill/sick SYN RECOVER: He's mending slowly after the operation. **4** [I] (of a broken bone) to heal

---

h **h**at   m **m**an   n **n**o   ŋ si**ng**   l **l**eg   r **r**ed   y **y**es   w **w**et

IDM mend (your) fences (with sb) to find a solution to a disagreement with someone mend your ways to stop behaving badly

● **noun**
IDM on the mend (*informal*) getting better after an illness or injury; improving after a difficult situation: *My leg is definitely on the mend now.* ◆ *Does he believe the economy's really on the mend?*

men·da·cious /mɛnˈdeɪʃəs/ *adj.* (*formal*) not telling the truth **SYN** LYING

men·dac·i·ty /mɛnˈdæsəti/ *noun* [U] (*formal*) the act of not telling the truth **SYN** LYING

men·de·le·vi·um /ˌmɛndəˈliviəm; -ˈleɪ-/ *noun* [U] (*symb.* **Md**) a chemical element. Mendelevium is a RADIOACTIVE element that does not exist naturally.

men·di·cant /ˈmɛndɪkənt/ *adj.* (*formal*) (especially of members of religious groups) living by asking people for money and food ▶ **men·di·cant** *noun*

men·folk /ˈmɛnfoʊk/ *noun* [pl.] (*old-fashioned*) men of a particular family or community: *a society sending its menfolk off to war* ⊃ compare WOMENFOLK

me·ni·al /ˈminiəl/ *adj., noun*
● *adj.* (usually *disapproving*) (of work) not skilled or important, and often boring or badly paid: *menial jobs/work* ◆ *menial tasks like cleaning the floor*
● *noun* (*old-fashioned*) a person with a menial job

me·nin·ges /məˈnɪndʒiz/ *noun* [pl.] (*anatomy*) the three MEMBRANES (= thin layers of material) that surround the brain and SPINAL CORD

men·in·gi·tis /ˌmɛnənˈdʒaɪtəs/ *noun* [U] a serious disease in which the TISSUES surrounding the brain and SPINAL CORD become infected and swollen, causing severe headache, fever, and sometimes death

me·nis·cus /məˈnɪskəs/ *noun* (*pl.* me·nis·ci /-saɪ; -skaɪ; -ski/ or meniscuses) **1** (*physics*) the curved surface of a liquid in a tube **2** (*anatomy*) a thin layer of CARTILAGE between the surfaces of some joints, for example the knee

Men·non·ite /ˈmɛnəˌnaɪt/ *noun* a member of a PROTESTANT religious group that lives in the U.S. and Canada. Mennonites live a simple life and do not work as public officials or soldiers.

men·o·pause /ˈmɛnəˌpɔz/ *noun* [U] (also *informal* the change of life, the change) [sing.] the time during which a woman gradually stops menstruating (MENSTRUATE), usually at around the age of 50: *to reach menopause* ▶ **men·o·pau·sal** /ˌmɛnəˈpɔzl/ *adj.*: *menopausal women/symptoms*

me·nor·ah /məˈnɔrə/ *noun* a traditional Jewish object to hold seven or nine CANDLES

Men·sa /ˈmɛnsə/ *noun* [U] an organization for people who have achieved a very high score in a test of intelligence

mensch /mɛnʃ; mɛntʃ/ *noun* (*informal*) a good person, especially someone who does something kind or helpful

men·ses /ˈmɛnsiz/ *noun* often the menses [pl.] (*technical*) the flow of blood each month from a woman's body

men's room *noun* a public bathroom for men

men·stru·al /ˈmɛnstruəl; -strəl/ *adj.* connected with the time when a woman menstruates each month: *The average length of a woman's menstrual cycle is 28 days.* ◆ *menstrual blood* ◆ (*formal*) *a menstrual period* ⊃ compare PREMEN-STRUAL

men·stru·ate /ˈmɛnstruˌeɪt/ *verb* [I] (*formal*) when a woman menstruates, there is a flow of blood from her womb, usually once a month

men·stru·a·tion /ˌmɛnstruˈeɪʃn/ *noun* [U] (*formal*) the process or time of menstruating menstruate ⊃ compare PERIOD

mens·wear /ˈmɛnzwɛr/ *noun* [U] used especially in stores to describe clothes for men: *the menswear department*

-ment /mənt/ *suffix* (in nouns) the action or result of:

bombardment ◆ development ▶ -mental /ˈmɛntl/ (in adjectives): *governmental* ◆ *judgmental*

men·tal ♪ **AWL** /ˈmɛntl/ *adj.*
1 [usually before noun] connected with or happening in the mind; involving the process of thinking: *the mental process of remembering* ◆ *Do you have a mental picture of what it will look like?* ◆ *I made a mental note to talk to her about it.* ◆ *He has a complete mental block* (= difficulty in understanding or remembering) *when it comes to physics.* **2** [usually before noun] connected with the state of health of the mind or with the treatment of illnesses of the mind **SYN** PSYCHOLOGICAL: *mental health* ◆ *a mental disorder/illness/hospital* ◆ *She was suffering from physical and mental exhaustion.* ⊃ compare PSYCHIATRIC

mental age *noun* [C, usually sing.] the level of someone's ability to think, understand, etc. that is judged by comparison with the average ability for children of a particular age: *She is sixteen but has a mental age of five.* ⊃ compare CHRONOLOGICAL

mental arithmetic *noun* [U] adding, multiplying, etc. numbers in your mind without writing anything down or using a CALCULATOR

men·tal·i·ty **AWL** /mɛnˈtæləti/ *noun* [usually sing.] (*pl.* men·tal·i·ties) the particular attitude or way of thinking of a person or group **SYN** MINDSET: *I cannot understand the mentality of video gamers.* ◆ *a criminal/ghetto mentality* ⊃ see also SIEGE MENTALITY

men·tal·ly ♪ **AWL** /ˈmɛntəli/ *adv.*
connected with or happening in the mind: *mentally ill* ◆ *The baby is very mentally alert.* ◆ *Mentally, I began making a list of things I had to do.*

THESAURUS

mentally ill
insane ● depressed ● neurotic ● psychotic ● disturbed ● unstable

These words all describe someone who is suffering from a mental illness.

mentally ill suffering from an illness of the mind, especially in a way that affects the way you think and behave

insane [not usually before noun] (*somewhat formal*) suffering from a serious mental illness and unable to live in normal society: *The question is, was the woman insane when she committed the crime?* **NOTE** In informal English, **insane** can describe someone who is not suffering from a mental illness but whose mind does not work normally, especially because they are under pressure. This meaning is used especially in the phrases *go insane* and *drive sb insane*.

depressed (*medical*) suffering from a medical condition in which a person feels very sad and anxious over a long period of time, and often has physical symptoms such as being unable to sleep: *He was diagnosed as clinically depressed.* **NOTE** In informal English, **depressed** is sometimes used to describe someone who is just feeling very sad, but in correct medical usage it only describes people who feel very sad for weeks at a time.

neurotic (*medical*) suffering from or connected with neurosis (= a mental illness in which a person suffers strong feelings of fear and worry): *the treatment of anxiety in neurotic patients* **NOTE** In informal English **neurotic** is also used to describe someone who is not suffering from a mental illness, but is not behaving in a calm way because they are worried about something: *He became neurotic about keeping the house clean.*

psychotic (*medical*) suffering from or connected with psychosis (a serious mental illness in which thought and emotions lose connection with external reality). **NOTE** In informal English, **psychotic** is sometimes

---

used to describe anyone suffering from a mental illness, but in correct medical usage it only describes people who have difficulty relating to external reality. It contrasts with **neurotic** which describes people who are less seriously mentally ill and are still able to distinguish what is real from what is not.

disturbed mentally ill, especially because of very unhappy or shocking experiences: *He works with emotionally disturbed children.*

unstable having emotions and behavior that are likely to change suddenly and unexpectedly

PATTERNS
- neurotic/psychotic/disturbed/unstable **behavior**
- neurotic/psychotic **illnesses/disorders/symptoms/patients**
- **seriously** mentally ill/depressed/neurotic/psychotic/disturbed
- **emotionally/mentally** disturbed/unstable

ˌmentally ˈhandicapped *adj.* (*old-fashioned*) (of a person) slow to learn or to understand things because of a problem with the brain **HELP** It is now more usual to say that people with this kind of problem **have learning disabilities**.

men·tee /ˌmɛnˈti/ *noun* a person who is advised and helped by a more experienced person over a period of time: *the mentor/mentee relationship* ⟳ compare MENTOR

men·thol /ˈmɛnθɒl; -θɔl/ *noun* [U] a substance that tastes and smells of MINT, that is used in some medicines for colds and to give a strong cool flavor to cigarettes, TOOTHPASTE, etc.

men·tho·lat·ed /ˈmɛnθəˌleɪtəd/ *adj.* containing menthol: *mentholated cough drops*

men·tion 🔑 /ˈmɛnʃn/ *verb, noun*
- *verb* to write or speak about something or someone, especially without giving much information: ~ **sth/sb (to sb)** *Nobody mentioned anything to me about it.* ◆ *Sorry, I won't mention it again.* ◆ *Now that you mention it, she did seem to be in a strange mood.* ◆ ~ **sth/sb as sth/sb** *His name has been mentioned as a future mayor.* ◆ ~ **where, why, etc....** *Did she mention where she was going?* ◆ ~ **that...** *You mentioned in your letter that you might be moving to Albuquerque.* ◆ ~ **doing sth** *Did I mention going to see Vicky on Sunday?* ⟳ see also ABOVE-MENTIONED, AFOREMENTIONED
  IDM don't ˈmention it (*informal*) used as a polite answer when someone has thanked you for something: *"Thanks for all your help." "Don't mention it."* **SYN** YOU'RE WELCOME **not to mention** used to introduce extra information and emphasize what you are saying: *He has a New York apartment and a large country house, not to mention his villa in France.*
- *noun* [U, C, usually sing.] an act of referring to someone or something in speech or writing: *He made no mention of her work.* ◆ *The concert didn't even get a mention in the newspapers.* ◆ *Richard deserves (a) special mention for all the help he gave us.* ⟳ see also HONORABLE MENTION

THESAURUS

mention

refer to sb/sth ◆ speak of/about sb/sth ◆ cite ◆ quote

These words all mean to write or speak about someone or something, often in order to give an example or prove something.

mention to write or speak about someone or something, especially without giving much information: *Nobody mentioned anything to me about the party.*

refer to sb/sth (*somewhat formal*) to mention or speak about someone or something: *I promised not to refer to the matter again.*

speak of/about sb/sth to mention or describe someone or something: *Witnesses spoke of a great ball of flame.*

cite (*formal*) to mention something as a reason or an example, or in order to support what you are saying: *She cited her heavy workload as the reason for her breakdown.*

quote to mention an example of something to support what you are saying: *Can you quote me an instance of this happening?*

CITE OR QUOTE?

You can **cite** reasons or examples, but you can only **quote** examples: *She quoted her heavy workload as the reason for her breakdown.* **Cite** is a more formal word than **quote** and is often used in more formal situations, for example in descriptions of legal cases.

PATTERNS
- to mention/refer to/speak of/cite/quote sb/sth **as** sb/sth
- to mention/refer to/cite/quote a(n) **example/instance/case** of sth
- **frequently/often** mentioned/referred to/spoken of/cited/quoted
- the example mentioned/referred to/cited/quoted **above/earlier/previously**

men·tor /ˈmɛntɔr; -tər/ *noun* an experienced person who advises and helps someone with less experience over a period of time ⟳ compare MENTEE ▶ **men·tor·ing** *noun* [U]: *a mentoring program*

men·u 🔑 /ˈmɛnyu/ *noun*
1 a list of the food that is available at a restaurant or to be served at a meal: *to ask for/look at the menu* ◆ *What's on the menu* (= for dinner) *tonight?* ⟳ collocations at RESTAURANT
2 (*computing*) a list of possible choices that are shown on a computer screen: *a pull-down menu* ⟳ see also DROP-DOWN MENU

ˈmenu ˌbar *noun* (*computing*) a horizontal bar at the top of a computer screen that contains PULL-DOWN menus such as "File," "Edit," and "Help"

me·ow /miˈaʊ/ /miˈaʊ/ *noun* the crying sound made by a cat **IDM** see CAT ⟳ see also MEW ▶ **me·ow** *verb* [I]

MEP /ˌɛm i ˈpi/ *noun* the abbreviation for "Member of the European Parliament"

Meph·is·to·phe·li·an /məˌfɪstəˈfiliən; ˌmɛfəstə-/ *adj.* (*formal*) very evil; like the DEVIL **ORIGIN** From Mephistopheles, an evil spirit to whom, according to the German legend, Faust sold his soul.

mer·can·tile /ˈmərkənˌtaɪl; -ˌtil/ *adj.* (*formal*) connected with trade and commercial affairs

mer·can·til·ism /ˈmərkəntəˌlɪzəm; -taɪ-; -ti-/ *noun* [U] the economic theory that trade increases wealth ▶ **mer·can·til·ist** /-lɪst/ *adj.* **mer·can·til·ist** *noun*

Mer·ca·tor pro·jec·tion /mərˈkeɪtər prəˌdʒɛkʃn/ *noun* [sing.] a traditional map of the world, on which the relative size of some countries is not accurate ⟳ compare PETERS PROJECTION

mer·ce·nar·y /ˈmərsəˌnɛri/ *noun, adj.*
- *noun* (pl. **mer·ce·nar·ies**) a soldier who will fight for any country or group that offers payment: *foreign mercenaries* ◆ *mercenary soldiers*
- *adj.* (*disapproving*) only interested in making or getting money: *a mercenary society/attitude* ◆ *She's interested in him for purely mercenary reasons.*

mer·chan·dise *noun, verb*
- *noun* /ˈmərtʃənˌdaɪz; -ˌdaɪs/ [U] **1** (*formal*) goods that are bought or sold; goods that are for sale in a store: *a wide selection of merchandise* ⟳ thesaurus box at PRODUCT
2 things you can buy that are connected with or that advertise a particular event or organization: *official NBA merchandise*

• **verb** /ˈmɑrtʃənˌdaɪz/ **~ sth** to sell something using advertising, etc.

mer·chan·dis·ing /ˈmɑrtʃənˌdaɪzɪŋ/ *noun* [U] **1** the activity of selling goods, or of trying to sell them, by advertising or displaying them **2** products connected with a popular movie, person, or event; the process of selling these goods: *The Batman movies always have strong earnings from merchandising.*

mer·chant /ˈmɑrtʃənt/ *noun, adj.*
• **noun 1** a person who buys and sells goods in large quantities, especially one who imports and exports goods: *a cotton/wine merchant* ◆ *Venice was once a city of rich merchants.* **2** (*old-fashioned*) a person who owns or manages a store **SYN** SHOPKEEPER **IDM** see DOOM *n.*
• **adj.** [only before noun] connected with the transportation of goods by ocean: *merchant seamen*

mer·chant·a·ble /ˈmɑrtʃəntəbl/ *adj.* (*law*) in a good enough condition to be sold

mer·chant·man /ˈmɑrtʃəntmən/ (*pl.* **merchantmen** /-mən/) (also **ˈmerchant ˌship**) *noun* a ship used for carrying goods for trade rather than a military ship

ˌmerchant maˈrine *noun* a country's commercial ships and the people who work on them

mer·ci·ful /ˈmərsɪfl/ *adj.* **1** ready to forgive people and show them kindness **SYN** HUMANE: *a merciful God* ◆ *They asked her to be merciful to the prisoners.* **2** (of an event) seeming to be lucky, especially because it brings an end to someone's problems or suffering: *Death came as a merciful release.* ⊃ see also MERCY

mer·ci·ful·ly /ˈmərsɪfli; -fəli/ *adv.* **1** used to show that you feel someone or something is lucky because a situation could have been much worse **SYN** THANKFULLY: *Deaths from the disease are mercifully rare.* ◆ *Mercifully, everyone arrived on time.* **2** in a kind way: *He was treated mercifully.*

mer·ci·less /ˈmərsɪləs/ *adj.* showing no kindness or sympathy **SYN** CRUEL: *a merciless killer/attack* ◆ *the merciless heat of the sun* ⊃ see also MERCY ▶ **mer·ci·less·ly** *adv.*

mer·cu·ri·al /mərˈkyʊriəl/ *adj.* **1** (*literary*) often changing or reacting in a way that is unexpected **SYN** VOLATILE: *Emily's mercurial temperament made her difficult to live with.* **2** (*literary*) lively and quick: *a brilliant, mercurial mind* **3** (*technical*) containing MERCURY

Mer·cu·ry /ˈmərkyəri/ *noun* the smallest planet in the SOLAR SYSTEM, nearest to the sun ⊃ picture at EARTH

mer·cu·ry /ˈmərkyəri/ *noun* [U] (*symb.* **Hg**) a chemical element. Mercury is a poisonous, silver, liquid, metal, used in THERMOMETERS.

mer·cy /ˈmərsi/ *noun* (*pl.* **mer·cies**) **1** [U] a kind or forgiving attitude toward someone that you have the power to harm or the right to punish **SYN** HUMANITY: *to ask/beg/plead for mercy* ◆ *They showed no mercy to their hostages.* ◆ *God have mercy on us.* ◆ *The troops are on a mercy mission* (= a journey to help people) *in the war zone.* **2** [C, usually sing.] (*informal*) an event or a situation to be grateful for, usually because it stops something unpleasant: *It's a mercy she wasn't seriously hurt.* ⊃ see also MERCIFUL, MERCILESS **IDM** **at the mercy of sb/sth** not able to stop someone or something harming you because they have power or control over you: *I'm not going to put myself at the mercy of the bank.* ◆ *We were at the mercy of the weather.* **leave sb/sth to the mercy/mercies of sb/sth** to leave someone or something in a situation that may cause them to suffer or to be treated badly **throw yourself on sb's mercy** (*formal*) to put yourself in a situation where you must rely on someone to be kind to you and not harm or punish you ⊃ more at SMALL *adj.*

ˈmercy ˌkilling *noun* [C, U] the act of killing someone out of sympathy or kindness, for example because they are in severe pain **SYN** EUTHANASIA

mere /mɪr/ *adj.* (*superlative* **mer·est**, no *comparative*) [only before noun] **1** used when you want to emphasize how small, unimportant, etc. someone or something is: *It took her a mere 20 minutes to win.* ◆ *A mere 2% of their budget was spent on publicity.* ◆ *He seemed so young, a mere boy.* ◆ *You've got the job. The interview will be a mere formality.* **2** used when you are saying that the fact that a particular thing is present in a situation is enough to have an influence on that situation: *His mere presence* (= just the fact that he was there) *made her feel afraid.* ◆ *The mere fact that they were prepared to talk was encouraging.* ◆ *The mere thought of eating made him feel sick.* ◆ *The merest* (= the slightest) *hint of smoke is enough to make her cough.*

mere·ly /ˈmɪrli/ *adv.* used meaning "only" or "simply" to emphasize a fact or something that you are saying: *It is not merely a job, but a way of life.* ◆ *He said nothing, merely smiled and watched her.* ◆ *They agreed to go merely because they were getting paid for it.* ◆ *I'm merely stating what everybody knows anyway.*

mer·e·tri·cious /ˌmɛrəˈtrɪʃəs/ *adj.* (*formal*) seeming attractive, but in fact having no real value

merge /mərdʒ/ *verb* **1** [I, T] to combine or make two or more things combine to form a single thing: *The banks are set to merge next year.* ◆ *The two groups have merged to form a new coalition.* ◆ **~ with sth** *His department will merge with mine.* ◆ **~ into sth** *The villages expanded and merged into one large town.* ◆ **~ (A and B) (together)** *Fact and fiction merge together in his latest thriller.* ◆ **~ A with B** *His department will be merged with mine.* ◆ **~ sth** *The company was formed by merging three smaller firms.* **2** [I] **~ (into sth)** if two things **merge**, or if one thing **merges into** another, the differences between them gradually disappear so that it is impossible to separate them: *The hills merged into the dark sky behind them.* **IDM** **merge into the background** (of a person) to behave quietly when you are with a group of people so that they do not notice you

merg·er /ˈmərdʒər/ *noun* [C] the act of joining two or more organizations or businesses into one: **~ (between/of A and B)** *a merger between the two banks* ◆ **~ (with sth)** *our proposed merger with the university* ⊃ collocations at BUSINESS

me·rid·i·an /məˈrɪdiən/ *noun* one of the lines that is drawn from the North Pole to the South Pole on a map of the world

me·ringue /məˈræŋ/ *noun* [U, C] a sweet white mixture made from egg whites and sugar, usually baked until crisp and used to make cakes and desserts, or placed under fruit or ice cream; a small cake made from this mixture: *a lemon meringue pie*

me·ri·no /məˈrinoʊ/ *noun* (*pl.* **me·ri·nos**) **1** [C] a breed of sheep with long fine wool **2** [U] the wool of the merino sheep or a type of cloth made from this wool, used for making clothes

mer·it /ˈmɛrət/ *noun, verb*
• **noun 1** [U] (*formal*) the quality of being good and of deserving praise, reward, or admiration **SYN** WORTH: *a work of outstanding artistic merit* ◆ *The plan is entirely without merit.* ◆ *I want to get the job on merit and not because I know the president of the company.* **2** [C, usually pl.] a good feature that deserves praise, reward, or admiration **SYN** STRENGTH: *We will consider each case on its (own) merits* (= without considering any other issues, feelings, etc.). ◆ *They weighed the relative merits of the four candidates.*
• **verb** (not used in the progressive tenses) **~ (doing) sth** (*formal*) to do something to deserve praise, attention, etc. **SYN** DESERVE: *He claims that their success was not merited.* ◆ *The case does not merit further investigation.*

mer·i·toc·ra·cy /ˌmɛrəˈtɑkrəsi/ *noun* (*pl.* **mer·i·toc·ra·cies**) **1** [C, U] a country or social system where people get power or money on the basis of their ability **2** **the meritocracy** [sing.] the group of people with power in this kind of social system ▶ **mer·i·to·crat·ic** /ˌmɛrətəˈkrætɪk/ *adj.*

---

mer·i·to·ri·ous /ˌmɛrəˈtɔriəs/ adj. (formal) deserving praise **SYN** PRAISEWORTHY

mer·lin /ˈmɜrlən/ noun a small BIRD OF PREY (= a bird that kills other creatures for food) of the FALCON family

mer·maid /ˈmɜrmeɪd/ noun (in stories) a creature with a woman's head and body, and a fish's tail instead of legs

mer·man /ˈmɜrmæn/ noun (pl. mer·men /-mɛn/) (in stories) a creature with a man's head and body, and a fish's tail instead of legs, like a male MERMAID

mer·ri·ly /ˈmɛrəli/ adv. **1** in a happy, cheerful way: *They chatted merrily.* **2** without thinking about the problems that your actions might cause: *She continued merrily, not realizing the offense she was causing.*

mer·ri·ment /ˈmɛrimənt/ noun [U] (formal) happy talk, enjoyment, and the sound of people laughing **SYN** JOLLITY, MIRTH

mer·ry /ˈmɛri/ adj. (mer·ri·er, mer·ri·est) **1** (old-fashioned) happy and cheerful **SYN** CHEERY: *a merry grin* **2** Merry Christmas used at Christmas to say that you hope that someone has an enjoyable holiday
IDM **make merry** (old-fashioned) to enjoy yourself by singing, laughing, drinking, etc. **the ˌmore the ˈmerrier** (saying) the more people or things there are, the better the situation will be or the more fun people will have: *"Can I bring a friend to your party?" "Sure—the more the merrier!"* ➔ more at EAT

ˈmerry-go-ˌround noun **1** (also car·ou·sel) a round platform with model horses, cars, etc. that turns around and around and that children ride on **2** a round platform for children to play on in a park, etc. that is pushed around while the children are sitting on it **3** continuous busy activity or a continuous series of changing events: *He was tired of the merry-go-round of romance and longed to settle down.*

mer·ry·mak·ing /ˈmɛriˌmeɪkɪŋ/ noun [U] (literary) fun and enjoyment with singing, laughing, drinking, etc. **SYN** REVELRY

me·sa /ˈmeɪsə/ noun (pl. me·sas) a hill with a flat top and steep sides that is common in the southwest of the U.S.

mes·cal /ˈmɛˈskæl/ noun = PEYOTE

mes·ca·line /ˈmɛskələn/ noun [U] a drug obtained from a type of CACTUS, that affects people's minds and makes them see and hear things that are not really there

mes·clun /ˈmɛsklən/ noun [U] salad made from young leaf vegetables such as LETTUCE, ARUGULA, MUSTARD GREENS, and RADICCHIO

mesh /mɛʃ/ noun, verb
• noun **1** [U, C] material made of threads of plastic rope or wire that are twisted together like a net: *wire mesh over the door of the cage* **2** [C, usually sing.] a complicated situation or system that it is difficult to escape from **SYN** SPIDERWEB
• verb (formal) **1** [I, T] to fit together or match closely, especially in a way that works well; to make things fit together successfully: *~ (sth) (with sth) This evidence meshes with earlier reports of an organized riot.* ◆ *~ (sth) (together) His theories mesh together various political and religious beliefs.* **2** [I] (technical) (of parts of a machine) to fit together as they move: *If the cogs don't mesh correctly, the gears will keep slipping.*

mes·mer·ic /mɛzˈmɛrɪk/ adj. [usually before noun] (formal) having such a strong effect on people that they cannot give their attention to anything else **SYN** HYPNOTIC

mes·mer·ize /ˈmɛzməˌraɪz/ verb [usually passive] *~ sb* to have such a strong effect on you that you cannot give your attention to anything else **SYN** FASCINATE ▶ **mes·mer·iz·ing** adj.: *Her performance was mesmerizing.*

mes·o·phyll /ˈmɛzəfɪl/ noun [U] (biology) the material that the inside of a leaf is made of

mes·o·sphere /ˈmɛzəˌsfɪr/ noun [usually sing.] the part of the earth's atmosphere that is between 30 and 50 miles from the ground, between the STRATOSPHERE and the THERMOSPHERE

mes·quite /mɛˈskit/ (also mesˈquite tree) noun a N. American tree, often used for making CHARCOAL for GRILLING food: *mesquite-grilled chicken*

mess /mɛs/ noun, verb
• noun
➤ DIRTY STATE **1** [C, usually sing.] a condition in which things are dirty or not neat: *The room was a mess.* ◆ *The kids made a mess in the bathroom.* ◆ *" What a mess!" she said, surveying the scene after the party.* ◆ *My hair's a real mess!*
➤ DIFFICULT SITUATION **2** [C, usually sing.] a situation that is full of problems, usually because of a lack of organization or because of mistakes that someone has made: *The economy is in a mess.* ◆ *I feel like I made a mess of things.* ◆ *The whole situation is a mess.* ◆ *Let's try to sort out this mess.* ◆ *The biggest question is how they got into this mess in the first place.*
➤ PERSON **3** [sing.] a person who is dirty or whose clothes and hair are not neat: *You're a mess!* **4** [sing.] (informal) a person who has serious problems and is in a bad mental condition
➤ ANIMAL WASTE **5** [U, C] (informal) the EXCREMENT (= solid waste matter) of an animal, usually a dog or cat
➤ A LOT **6** [sing.] **a ~ of sth** (informal) a lot of something: *There's a mess of fish down there, so get your lines in the water.*
➤ ARMED FORCES **7** [C] (also ˈmess hall) a building or room in which members of the armed forces have their meals: *the officers' mess*
• verb
➤ MAKE UNTIDY **1** [T] *~ sth* (informal) to make something dirty or not neat: *Careful—you're messing my hair.*
➤ OF AN ANIMAL **2** [I] to empty its BOWELS somewhere that it should not
IDM **not mess around** (informal) to do something quickly, efficiently, or in the right way: *When they decide to have a party they don't mess around.*
PHRV **ˌmess aˈround 1** to behave in a silly and annoying way, especially instead of doing something useful **SYN** FOOL AROUND: *Will you stop messing around and get some work done?* ◆ *Look - I'm not messing around. I've got to go now!* **2** to spend time doing something for pleasure in a relaxed way: *We spent the day messing around on the river.* **ˌmess aˈround with sb** to have a sexual relationship with someone, especially when you should not **ˌmess aˈround with sth 1** to touch or use something in a careless and/or annoying way: *Who's been messing around with my computer?* **2** to spend time playing with something, repairing something, etc. **ˌmess ˈup | ˌmess sth↔ˈup** to spoil something or do it badly: *I've really messed up this time.* ◆ *If you cancel now you'll mess up all my arrangements.* **ˌmess sb↔ˈup 1** (informal) to cause someone to have serious emotional or mental problems **2** (informal) to physically hurt someone, especially by hitting them: *He was messed up pretty bad by the other guy.* **ˌmess sth↔ˈup** to make something dirty or not neat: *I don't want you messing up my nice clean kitchen.* **ˈmess with sb/sth** (usually used in negative sentences) to get involved with someone or something that may be harmful: *I wouldn't mess with him if I were you.*

mes·sage /ˈmɛsɪdʒ/ noun, verb
• noun *~ (from sb) (to sb)* **1** a written or spoken piece of information, etc. that you send to someone or leave for someone when you cannot speak to them yourself: *There were no messages for me at the hotel.* ◆ *I left a message on your voice mail.* ◆ *Jenny's not here right now. Can I take a message?* ◆ *We got an urgent message saying that your father's not well.* ◆ *a televised message from the President to the American people* ◆ *Messages of support have been arriving from all over the country* ◆ *an e-mail message* ◆ *I've been trying to get you all day —don't you ever listen to your messages?* ➔ see also ERROR MESSAGE **2** a piece of information sent in electronic form, for example by e-mail or cell phone: *There were four messages in my in-box.* ◆ *He sent me a message.* **3** [usually sing.] an important moral, social, or political idea that a book, speech, etc. is trying to communicate: *a film with a*

strong religious message ♦ *The campaign is trying to get the message across to young people that drugs are dangerous.* **4** a piece of information that is sent from the brain to a part of the body, or from a part of the body to the brain: *The message arrives in your brain in a fraction of a second.* **IDM** **get the** ˈmessage (*informal*) to understand what someone is trying to tell you indirectly: *When he started looking at his watch, I got the message and left.* **on/off** ˈmessage (of a politician) stating/not stating the official view of their political party

• *verb* to send a message to someone using a computer or other electronic device: **~ sb** *Faith just messaged me.* ♦ **~ sb sth** *Brian messaged me the news.* **Ͽ** see also TEXT ▶ **mes·sag·ing** /ˈmɛsɪdʒɪŋ/ *noun* [U]: *a multimedia messaging service* ♦ *picture messaging*

ˈmessage ˌboard *noun* a place on a Web site where a user can write or read messages: *I posted a question on the message board.*

mes·sen·ger /ˈmɛsəndʒər/ *noun* a person who gives a message to someone or who delivers messages to people as a job: *He sent the order by messenger.* ♦ *a motorcycle messenger* **IDM** see SHOOT *v.*

Mes·si·ah /məˈsaɪə/ *noun* **1** the Messiah [sing.] (in Christianity) Jesus Christ who was sent by God into the world to save people from evil and SIN **2** the Messiah [sing.] (in Judaism) a king who will be sent by God to save the Jewish people **3** messiah a leader who people believe will solve the problems of a country or the world **SYN** SAVIOR: *He's seen by many as a political messiah.*

mes·si·an·ic /ˌmɛsiˈænɪk/ *adj.* (*formal*) **1** relating to a Messiah **2** attempting to make big changes in society or to a political system in an extremely determined and enthusiastic way: *The reforms were carried out with an almost messianic zeal.*

Messrs. /ˈmɛsərz/ *abbr.* (*formal, old-fashioned*) used as the plural of "Mr." before a list of names and before names of business companies: *Messrs. Smith, Brown, and Jones* ♦ *Messrs. T. Brown and Co.*

mess·y 🔑 /ˈmɛsi/ *adj.* (mes·si·er, mes·si·est) **1** dirty and/or not neat **SYN** CHAOTIC: *The house was always messy.* **2** making someone or something dirty and/or not neat: *It was a messy job.* **3** (of a situation) unpleasant, confused, or difficult to deal with: *The divorce was painful and messy.*

mes·ti·za /mɛˈstizə/ *noun* a female MESTIZO

mes·ti·zo /mɛˈstizoʊ/ *noun* (*pl.* mes·ti·zos) a Latin American who has both Spanish and Native American ANCESTORS

Met /mɛt/ *abbr.* (*informal*) **1 met.** METEOROLOGY: *the met. office weather forecast service* **2 the Met** the Metropolitan Opera House (in New York City) **3 the Met** the Metropolitan Museum (in New York City)

met pt, pp of MEET

meta- /ˈmɛtə/ *combining form* (in nouns, adjectives, and verbs) **1** connected with a change of position or state: *metamorphosis* ♦ *metabolism* **2** higher; beyond: *metaphysics* ♦ *metalanguage*

me·tab·o·lism /məˈtæbəˌlɪzəm/ *noun* [U, sing.] (*biology*) the chemical processes in living things that change food, etc. into energy and materials for growth: *The body's metabolism is slowed down by extreme cold.* ▶ **met·a·bol·ic** /ˌmɛtəˈbɑlɪk/ *adj.* [usually before noun]: *a metabolic process/disorder* ♦ *a high/low metabolic rate*

me·tab·o·lize /məˈtæbəˌlaɪz/ *verb* **~ sth** (*biology*) to turn food, minerals, etc. in the body into new cells, energy, and waste products by means of chemical processes

met·a·car·pal /ˌmɛtəˈkɑrpl/ *noun* (*anatomy*) any of the five bones in the hand between the wrist and the fingers

met·a·da·ta /ˈmɛtəˌdeɪtə; -ˌdætə/ *noun* [U] information that describes other information in order to help you understand or use it: *In the metadata she found the author and location of the file.*

met·a·fic·tion /ˈmɛtəˌfɪkʃn/ *noun* [U] a type of play, novel, etc. in which the author deliberately reminds the audience, reader, etc. that it is FICTION and not real life

met·al 🔑 /ˈmɛtl/ *noun* [C, U] a type of solid mineral substance that is usually hard and shiny and that heat and electricity can travel through, for example tin, iron, and gold: *a piece of metal* ♦ *a metal pipe/ bar/box* ♦ *The frame is made of metal.* **Ͽ** see also HEAVY METAL, PRECIOUS METAL

met·a·lan·guage /ˈmɛtəˌlæŋgwɪdʒ/ *noun* [C, U] (*linguistics*) the words and phrases that people use to talk about or describe language or a particular language

ˈmetal deˌtector *noun* **1** an electronic device that you use to look for metal objects that are buried under the ground **2** an electronic machine that is used, for example at an airport, to see if people are hiding metal objects such as weapons

ˈmetal faˌtigue *noun* [U] weakness in metal that is frequently put under pressure that makes it likely to break

met·a·lin·guis·tic /ˌmɛtəlɪŋˈgwɪstɪk/ *adj.* (*linguistics*) related to metalanguage ▶ **met·a·lin·guis·tics** /-tɪks/ *noun* [U]

me·tal·lic /məˈtælɪk/ *adj.* [usually before noun] **1** that looks, tastes, or sounds like metal: *metallic paint/colors/blue* ♦ *a metallic taste* ♦ *a metallic sound/click* ♦ *a metallic voice* (= that sounds unpleasant) **2** made of or containing metal: *a metallic object* ♦ *metallic compounds*

met·al·loid /ˈmɛtlˌɔɪd/ *noun* (*chemistry*) a chemical element that has properties both of metals and of other solid substances

met·al·lur·gist /ˈmɛtlˌərdʒɪst/ *noun* a scientist who studies metallurgy

met·al·lur·gy /ˈmɛtlˌərdʒi/ *noun* [U] the scientific study of metals and their uses ▶ **met·al·lur·gi·cal** /ˌmɛtlˈərdʒɪkl/ *adj.*

met·al·work /ˈmɛtlˌwərk/ *noun* [U] the activity of making objects out of metal; objects that are made out of metal ▶ **met·al·work·er** *noun*

met·a·mor·phic /ˌmɛtəˈmɔrfɪk/ *adj.* (*geology*) (of rocks) formed by the action of heat or pressure

met·a·mor·phose /ˌmɛtəˈmɔrfoʊz/ *verb* [I, T] **~ (sth/sb) (from sth) (into sth)** (*formal*) to change or make something or someone change into something completely different, especially over a period of time **SYN** TRANSFORM: *The caterpillar will eventually metamorphose into a butterfly.*

met·a·mor·pho·sis /ˌmɛtəˈmɔrfəsəs/ *noun* (*pl.* met·a·mor·pho·ses /-siz/) [C, U] (*formal*) a process in which someone or something changes completely into something different **SYN** TRANSFORMATION: *the metamorphosis of a caterpillar into a butterfly* ♦ *She had undergone an amazing metamorphosis from awkward schoolgirl to beautiful woman.*

met·a·phor /ˈmɛtəˌfɔr/ *noun* [C, U] a word or phrase used to describe someone or something else, in a way that is different from its normal use, in order to show that the two things have the same qualities and to make the description more powerful, for example *She has a heart of stone*; the use of such words and phrases: *a football game used as a metaphor for the competitive struggle of life* ♦ *the writer's striking use of metaphor* **Ͽ** collocations at LITERATURE **Ͽ** compare SIMILE

met·a·phor·i·cal /ˌmɛtəˈfɔrɪkl; -ˈfɑr-/ *adj.* connected with or containing metaphor: *metaphorical language* **Ͽ** compare FIGURATIVE, LITERAL ▶ **met·a·phor·i·cally** /-kli/ *adv.*: *I'll leave you in Robin's capable hands— metaphorically speaking, of course!*

ˌmetaˌphysical ˈpoets *noun* [pl.] a group of 17th century English POETS who explored the nature of the world and human life, and who used images that were surprising at that time

met·a·phys·ics /ˌmɛtəˈfɪzɪks/ *noun* [U] the branch of philosophy that deals with the nature of existence, truth, and knowledge ▶ **met·a·phys·i·cal** /ˌmɛtəˈfɪzɪkl/ *adj.*: *meta-physical problems/speculation*

me·tas·ta·sis /məˈtæstəsəs/ *noun* (*pl.* **me·tas·ta·ses** /-siz/) [U, C] (*medical*) the development of TUMORS in different parts of the body resulting from cancer that has started in another part of the body; a TUMOR of this type ▶ **met·a-stat·ic** /ˌmɛtəˈstætɪk/ *adj.*

met·a·tar·sal /ˌmɛtəˈtɑrsl/ *noun* (*anatomy*) any of the bones in the part of the foot between the ankle and the toes

mete /mit/ *verb*
PHR V ˌmete sth↔ˈout (to sb) (*formal*) to give someone a punishment; to make someone suffer bad treatment: *Severe penalties were meted out by the court.* ◆ *the violence meted out to the prisoners*

me·te·or /ˈmitiər/ *noun* a piece of rock from outer space that makes a bright line across the night sky as it burns up while falling through the earth's atmosphere: *a meteor shower* ⊃ see also SHOOTING STAR

me·te·or·ic /ˌmitiˈɔrɪk; -ˈɑr-/ *adj.* **1** achieving success very quickly: *a meteoric rise to fame* ◆ *a meteoric career* **2** connected with meteors: *meteoric craters*

me·te·or·ite /ˈmitiəˌraɪt/ *noun* a piece of rock from outer space that hits the earth's surface

me·te·or·ol·o·gist /ˌmitiəˈrɑlədʒɪst/ *noun* a scientist who studies meteorology

me·te·or·ol·o·gy /ˌmitiəˈrɑlədʒi/ *noun* [U] the scientific study of the earth's atmosphere and its changes, used especially in forecasting the weather (= saying what it will be like) ▶ **me·te·or·o·log·i·cal** /ˌmitiərəˈlɑdʒɪkl/ *adj.*

me·ter (*CanE usually* **me·tre**) /ˈmitər/ *noun, verb*
● *noun* **1** [C] (*abbr.* m.) a unit for measuring length; a hundred centimeters **2** [C, U] (*abbr.* m.) used in the name of races: *She came in second in the 200 meters.* ◆ *the 4×100 meter(s) relay* **3** (especially in compounds) a device that measures and records the amount of electricity, gas, water, etc. that you have used or the time and distance you have traveled, etc.: *A man came to read the gas meter.* ◆ *a water meter* ◆ *The cab driver left the meter running while he waited for us.* ⊃ see also LIGHT METER **4** = PARKING METER **5** [U, C] the arrangement of strong and weak stresses in lines of poetry that produces the rhythm; a particular example of this
● *verb* ~ sth to measure something (for example how much gas, electricity, etc. has been used) using a meter

meth /mɛθ/ (*also* ˌcrystal ˈmeth, crystal) *noun* [U] (*informal*) a powerful illegal drug, METHAMPHETAMINE, that looks like small pieces of glass: *the growing meth problem in our rural communities*

meth·a·done /ˈmɛθəˌdoʊn/ *noun* [U] a drug that is used to treat people who are trying to stop taking the illegal drug HEROIN

meth·am·phet·a·mine /ˌmɛθæmˈfɛtəˌmin; -mən/ (*also informal* meth, ˌcrystal ˈmeth) *noun* [U] a powerful illegal drug

meth·ane /ˈmɛθeɪn/ *noun* [U] (*symb.* **CH₄**) a gas without color or smell, that burns easily and is used as fuel. Natural gas consists mainly of methane.

meth·a·nol /ˈmɛθəˌnɔl; -ˌnɑl/ *noun* [U] (*symb.* **CH₃OH**) a poisonous form of alcohol formed when METHANE reacts with OXYGEN

meth·i·cil·lin /ˌmɛθəˈsɪlən/ *noun* [U] a drug that can be used against infections where PENICILLIN is not effective

me·thinks /mɪˈθɪŋks/ *verb* (*pt* me·thought) (not used in the perfect tenses) [I, T] ~ (that)... (*old use or humorous*) I think

meth·od ✐ **AWL** /ˈmɛθəd/ *noun*
1 [C] a particular way of doing something: ~ (of sth) *a reliable/effective/scientific method of data analysis* ◆ ~ (of doing sth) *a new method of solving the problem* ◆ *traditional/alternative methods* ◆ ~ (for sth/for doing sth) *the best method for arriving at an accurate prediction of the costs* ⊃ see

also DIRECT METHOD **2** [U] the quality of being well planned and organized
IDM there's (a) method in sb's madness there is a reason for someone's behavior and it is not as strange or as stupid as it seems

ˈmethod ˌacting *noun* [U] a method of preparing for a role in which an actor tries to experience the life and feelings of the character he or she will play ▶ ˈmethod ˌactor *noun*

me·thod·i·cal **AWL** /məˈθɑdɪkl/ *adj.* **1** done in a careful and logical way: *a methodical approach/study* **2** (of a person) doing things in a careful and logical way **SYN** DISCIPLINED, PRECISE: *to have a methodical mind* ▶ **me·thod·i·cally** /-kli/ *adv.*: *They sorted slowly and me-thodically through the papers.*

Meth·od·ist /ˈmɛθədɪst/ *noun* a member of a Christian Protestant Church that broke away from the Church of England in the 18th century, and that follows the teachings of John Wesley ▶ **Meth·od·ism** /ˈmɛθəˌdɪzəm/ *noun* [U] **Meth·od·ist** *adj.*: *a Methodist church/minister*

meth·od·ol·o·gy **AWL** /ˌmɛθəˈdɑlədʒi/ *noun* (*pl.* **meth·od·ol·o·gies**) [C, U] (*formal*) a set of methods and principles used to perform a particular activity: *recent changes in the methodology of language teaching* ▶ **meth·od·o·log·i·cal** **AWL** /ˌmɛθədəˈlɑdʒɪkl/ *adj.* [usually before noun]: *methodo-logical problems* **meth·od·o·log·i·cally** /-kli/ *adj.*

Me·thu·se·lah /məˈθuzələ/ *noun* used to describe a very old person: *I'm feeling older than Methuselah.* **ORIGIN** From Methuselah, a man in the Bible who is supposed to have lived for 969 years.

me·tic·u·lous /məˈtɪkyələs/ *adj.* paying careful attention to every detail **SYN** FASTIDIOUS, THOROUGH: *meticulous planning/records/research* ◆ ~ in sth/doing sth *He's always meticulous in keeping the records up to date.* ◆ ~ about sth *My father was meticulous about his appearance.* ▶ **me·tic·u·lous·ly** *adv.*: *a meticulously planned schedule* ◆ *meticulously clean* **me·tic·u·lous·ness** *noun* [U]

mé·tier /mɛˈtyeɪ; meɪ-/ *noun* [usually sing.] (from *French, formal*) a person's work, especially when they have a natural skill or ability for it

ˈme time (*also* ˈme-time) *noun* [U] (*informal*) time when a person who is normally very busy relaxes or does something they enjoy: *The spa is popular with women who want a little me time.*

Mé·tis /meɪˈti; -ˈtis/ *noun* (*pl.* **Mé·tis** /meɪˈti; -ˈtis; -ˈtiz/) (*CanE*) (especially in Canada) a person whose family comes from both Aboriginal and European backgrounds

me·ton·y·my /məˈtɑnəmi/ *noun* [U] (*technical*) the act of referring to something by the name of something else that is closely connected with it, for example using *the White House* for *the U.S. president*

ˌme-ˈtoo *adj.* [only before noun] (*informal*) done or produced because of something successful that someone else has done: *The magazine "People" gave rise to a number of me-too publications.*

met·ric /ˈmɛtrɪk/ *adj.* **1** based on the metric system: *metric units/measurements/sizes* **2** made or measured using the metric system: *This tape measure is metric.* ⊃ compare IMPERIAL **3** = METRICAL

met·ri·cal /ˈmɛtrɪkl/ (*also* met·ric) *adj.* connected with the rhythm of a poem, produced by the arrangement of stress on the syllables in each line

met·ri·ca·tion /ˌmɛtrɪˈkeɪʃn/ *noun* [U] the process of changing to using the metric system

the ˈmetric ˌsystem *noun* [sing.] the system of measure-ment that uses the meter, the kilogram, and the liter as basic units

ˌmetric ˈton (*also* tonne) *noun* a unit for measuring weight, equal to 1,000 kilograms ⊃ compare TON

met·ro /ˈmɛtroʊ/ *noun, adj.*
● *noun* (*pl.* metros) **1** *also* the **Met·ro** [sing.] an under-ground train system, for instance the ones in Paris and

Washington, D.C.: *to travel* **on the metro** ◆ *the Paris Metro* ◆ *a metro station*

● *adj.* (*informal*) = METROPOLITAN: *the New York metro area*

me·trol·o·gy /mə'trɑlədʒi/ *noun* [U] the scientific study of measurement ▶ **met·ro·log·i·cal** /ˌmɛtrə'lɑdʒɪkl/ *adj.*

met·ro·nome /'mɛtrəˌnoʊm/ *noun* a device that makes a regular sound like a clock and is used by musicians to help them keep the correct rhythm when playing a piece of music ▶ **met·ro·nom·ic** /ˌmɛtrə'nɑmɪk/ *adj.* (*figurative*): *His financial problems hit the headlines with almost metronomic regularity.*

metronome

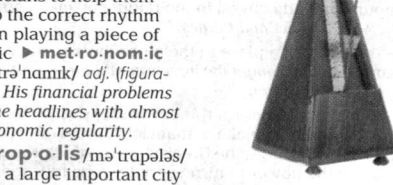

me·trop·o·lis /mə'trɑpələs/ *noun* a large important city (often the capital city of a country or region)

met·ro·pol·i·tan /ˌmɛtrə'pɑlətn/ *adj.* [only before noun] **1** (also *informal* **met·ro**) connected with a large or capital city: *the Dallas-Fort Worth metropolitan area* ◆ **metropolitan districts/regions 2** connected with a particular country rather than with the other regions of the world that the country controls: *metropolitan France/Spain*

met·ro·sex·ual /ˌmɛtrə'sɛkʃuəl/ *noun* (*informal*) a HETEROSEXUAL man who lives in a city and is interested in things like fashion and shopping ▶ **met·ro·sex·ual** *adj.*

met·tle /'mɛtl/ *noun* [U] the ability and determination to do something successfully despite difficult conditions: *The next game will be a real test of their mettle.*
IDM **on your 'mettle** prepared to use all your skills, knowledge, etc. because you are being tested

mew /myu/ *noun* the soft high noise that a cat makes ▶ **mew** *verb* [I]: *The kitten mewed pitifully.*

mewl /myul/ *verb* [I] to make a weak crying sound: *mewling babies* ▶ **mewl·ing** *noun* [U]

mews /myuz/ *noun* (*pl.* **mews**) a short narrow street with a row of stables (= buildings used to keep horses in) that have been made into small houses

Mex·i·can /'mɛksɪkən/ *adj., noun*
● *adj.* from or connected with Mexico
● *noun* a person from Mexico

Mexican 'jumping 'bean *noun* = JUMPING BEAN

me·zu·zah (also **me·zu·za**) /mə'zuzə/ *noun* (*pl.* **me·zu·zahs**, **me·zu·zas** or **me·zu·zot** /mə'zuzoʊt/) a small piece of paper with writing from the Bible on one side and a name for God on the other side, inside a case that is put on the side of an entrance door in many Jewish homes

mez·za·nine /'mɛzəˌnin; ˌmɛzə'nin/ *noun* **1** a floor that is built between two floors of a building and is smaller than the other floors: *an office on the mezzanine* ◆ *a mezzanine floor* **2** the first area of seats above the ground floor in a theater; the first few rows of these seats ➔ see also DRESS CIRCLE

mez·zo·so·pra·no /ˌmɛtsoʊ sə'prænoʊ; ˌmɛdzoʊ-/ (also **mez·zo**) *noun* (*pl.* **mezzo-sopranos, mezzos**) (from *Italian*) a singing voice with a range between SOPRANO and ALTO; a woman with a mezzo-soprano voice

mg 🔊 *abbr.*
(in writing) milligram(s)

mgr *abbr.* **1** (in writing) manager **2** **Mgr** (in writing) MONSIGNOR

MHA /ˌɛm eɪtʃ 'eɪ/ *abbr.* (*CanE*) Member of the House of Assembly (the parliament in Newfoundland and Labrador)

MHz *abbr.* (in writing) MEGAHERTZ

MI *abbr.* (in writing) Michigan

mi /mi/ *noun* (*music*) the third note in a MAJOR SCALE

MIA /ˌɛm aɪ 'eɪ/ *abbr.* (of a soldier) missing in action (missing after a battle)

mi·as·ma /maɪ'æzmə; mi-/ *noun* [C, usually sing., U] (*literary*) a mass of air that is dirty and smells unpleasant: *A miasma of stale alcohol and cigarettes hung around him.* ◆ (*figurative*) *the miasma of depression*

mic (also **mike**) /maɪk/ *noun* (*informal*) = MICROPHONE

mi·ca /'maɪkə/ *noun* [U] a clear mineral that splits easily into thin flat layers and is used to make electrical equipment

mice pl. of MOUSE

Mick·ey Finn /ˌmɪki 'fɪn/ (also **mick·ey**) *noun* a drink containing a drug or a lot of alcohol, given to someone who does not realize what is in it

Mickey 'Mouse *adj.* (*disapproving*) not of high quality; too easy: *They did a real Mickey Mouse job on the plumbing.* ◆ *He's taking some Mickey Mouse course at college.*

mi·cro /'maɪkroʊ/ *noun* (*pl.* **mi·cros**) = MICROCOMPUTER

micro- /'maɪkroʊ; -krə/ *combining form* **1** (in nouns, adjectives, and adverbs) small; on a small scale: *microchip* ◆ *microorganism* **ANT** MACRO- **2** (in nouns; used in units of measurement) one millionth: *a microlitre*

mi·crobe /'maɪkroʊb/ *noun* an extremely small living thing that you can only see under a MICROSCOPE and that may cause disease ➔ collocations at LIFE

mi·cro·bi·ol·o·gist /ˌmaɪkroʊbaɪ'ɑlədʒɪst/ *noun* a scientist who studies microbiology

mi·cro·bi·ol·o·gy /ˌmaɪkroʊbaɪ'ɑlədʒi/ *noun* [U] the scientific study of very small living things, such as bacteria ▶ **mi·cro·bi·o·log·i·cal** /ˌmaɪkroʊˌbaɪə'lɑdʒɪkl/ *adj.*

mi·cro·blog·ging /'maɪkroʊˌblɑgɪn; -ˌblɔgɪn/ *noun* [U] the activity of sending regular short messages, photos, or videos over the Internet, either to a selected group of people, or so that they can be viewed by anyone, as a means of keeping people informed about your activities and thoughts ➔ compare TWITTER ▶ **mi·cro·blog** *noun* **mi·cro·blog** *verb* (**-gg-**) [I]

mi·cro·brew /'maɪkroʊˌbru/ *noun* [C, U] a beer made in a microbrewery

mi·cro·brew·er·y /'maɪkroʊˌbruəri/ *noun* (*pl.* **mi·cro·brew·er·ies**) a small BREWERY that often sells its beer there or only locally: *a microbrewery with a capacity of about 12,000 barrels a year*

mi·cro·chip /'maɪkroʊˌtʃɪp/ *noun, verb*
● *noun* (also **chip**) a very small piece of a material that is a SEMICONDUCTOR, used to carry a complicated electronic CIRCUIT
● *verb* (**-pp-**) ~ **sth** to put a microchip under the skin of an animal as a way of identifying it

mi·cro·cli·mate /'maɪkroʊˌklaɪmət/ *noun* (*technical*) the weather in a particular small area, especially when this is different from the weather in the surrounding area

mi·cro·com·pu·ter /'maɪkroʊkəmˌpyutər/ (also **mi·cro**) *noun* a small computer that contains a MICROPROCESSOR ➔ compare MAINFRAME, MINICOMPUTER, PERSONAL COMPUTER

mi·cro·cosm /'maɪkrəˌkɑzəm/ *noun* a thing, place, or group that has all the features and qualities of something much larger: *The family is a microcosm of society.* ➔ compare MACROCOSM
IDM **in microcosm** on a small scale: *The developments in this town represent in microcosm what is happening in the country as a whole.*

mi·cro·dot /'maɪkroʊˌdɑt/ *noun* **1** a very small photograph about one millimeter in size, usually of a printed document **2** a very small round piece of a drug, especially the illegal drug LSD

mi·cro·e·lec·tron·ics /ˌmaɪkroʊɪˌlɛk'trɑnɪks/ *noun* [U] the design, production, and use of very small electronic CIRCUITS ▶ **mi·cro·e·lec·tron·ic** *adj.* [only before noun]

mi·cro·fi·ber /'maɪkroʊˌfaɪbər/ *noun* [U] a very light and warm artificial material that is used especially for making coats and jackets

mi·cro·fiche /ˈmaɪkrəˌfiːʃ/ *noun* [U, C] a piece of film with written information on it in print of very small size. Microfiches can only be read with a special machine: *The directory is available on microfiche.*

mi·cro·film /ˈmaɪkrəˌfɪlm/ *noun* [U, C] film used for storing written information on, using print of very small size

mi·cro·fi·nance /ˈmaɪkroʊˌfaɪnæns; -fəˌnæns/ *noun* [U] a system of providing services such as lending and saving money for people who are too poor to use banks

mi·cro·gram /ˈmaɪkrəˌɡræm/ *noun* (*symb.* **µg**) a unit for measuring weight; a millionth of a gram

mi·cro·man·age /ˌmaɪkroʊˈmænɪdʒ/ *verb* [T, I] **~ (sth)** (*disapproving*) to control every detail of a business, especially your employees' work: *The problem may be that you are micromanaging your team.* ♦ *bosses who micromanage* ▶ **mi·cro·man·age·ment** *noun* [U] **mi·cro·man·ag·er** *noun*

mi·cro·me·ter (*CanE usually* **mi·cro·me·tre**) /maɪˈkrɑmətər/ *noun* **1** (*symb.* **µm**) a unit for measuring length, equal to one millionth of a meter **2** a device used for measuring very small distances or spaces, using a screw with a very fine THREAD

mi·cron /ˈmaɪkrɑn/ *noun* (*old-fashioned*) = MICROMETER (1)

micro-organism *noun* (*technical*) a very small living thing that you can only see under a MICROSCOPE

mi·cro·phone /ˈmaɪkrəˌfoʊn/ (*also informal* mic, mike) *noun* a device that is used for recording sounds or for making your voice louder when you are speaking or singing to an audience: *to speak into the microphone* ♦ *Their remarks were picked up by the hidden microphones.* ⊃ **picture at** COMPUTER

mi·cro·por·tal /ˈmaɪkroʊˌpɔrtl/ *noun* (*computing*) a Web site that is used as a point of entry to the Internet where information has been collected that will be useful to a particular person or group

mi·cro·proc·es·sor /ˌmaɪkroʊˈprɑsesər/ *noun* (*computing*) a small unit of a computer that contains all the functions of the CENTRAL PROCESSING UNIT

mi·cro·scope /ˈmaɪkrəˌskoʊp/ *noun* an instrument used in scientific study for making very small things look larger so that you can examine them carefully: *a microscope slide* ♦ *The bacteria were then examined under a/the microscope.* ♦ (*figurative*) *In the play, love and marriage are put under the microscope.* ⊃ **picture at** LABORATORY ⊃ **see also** ELECTRON MICROSCOPE

mi·cro·scop·ic /ˌmaɪkrəˈskɑpɪk/ *adj.* **1** [usually before noun] extremely small and difficult or impossible to see without a microscope: *a microscopic creature/particle* ♦ (*humorous*) *The restaurant was very fancy, but the portions were microscopic!* **2** [only before noun] using a microscope: *a microscopic analysis/examination* ▶ **mi·cro·scop·i·cally** /-kli/ *adv.*: *microscopically small creatures* ♦ *All samples are examined microscopically.*

mi·cros·co·py /maɪˈkrɑskəpi/ *noun* [U] (*technical*) the use of MICROSCOPE to look at very small creatures, objects, etc.

mi·cro·sec·ond /ˈmaɪkroʊˌsɛkənd/ *noun* (*technical*) (*symb.* **µs**) one millionth of a second

mi·cro·sur·ger·y /ˈmaɪkroʊˌsərdʒəri/ *noun* [U] the use of extremely small instruments and MICROSCOPES in order to perform very detailed and complicated medical operations

mi·cro·wave /ˈmaɪkrəˌweɪv/ *noun, verb*
• *noun* **1** (*also formal* microwave oven) a type of oven that cooks or heats food very quickly using ELECTROMAGNETIC waves rather than heat: *Reheat the soup in the microwave.* ♦ *microwave cooking/meals* ⊃ **compare** OVEN **2** (*technical*) an ELECTROMAGNETIC wave that is shorter than a radio wave but longer than a light wave
• *verb* **~ sth** to cook or heat something in a microwave ⊃ **collocations at** COOKING ▶ **mi·cro·wav·a·ble** (*also* **mi·cro·wave·a·ble**) /ˈmaɪkrəˌweɪvəbl/ (*also*) *adj.*: *micro-wavable meals*

mic·tu·rate /ˈmɪktʃəˌreɪt/ *verb* [I] (*formal*) to URINATE ▶ **mic·tu·ri·tion** /ˌmɪktʃəˈrɪʃn/ *noun* [U]

MID /mɪd/ *noun* a small computer that you can hold in your hand, larger than a SMARTPHONE but smaller than a TABLET PC. MIDs offer Internet-based services mainly for personal rather than business use. (MID is the abbreviation for "mobile internet device") ⊃ **compare** MOBILE DEVICE

mid /mɪd/ *prep.* (*literary*) = AMID

mid- 🔑 /mɪd/ *combining form*
(in nouns and adjectives) in the middle of: *mid-morning coffee* ♦ *She's in her mid-thirties.*

mid-air *noun* [U] a place in the air or the sky, not on the ground: *The bird caught the insects in mid-air* ▶ **mid-air** *adj.*: *a mid-air collision*

Midas touch /ˈmaɪdəs ˌtʌtʃ/ *noun* usually **the Midas touch** [sing.] the ability to make a financial success of everything you do **ORIGIN** From the Greek story in which King Midas was given the power to turn everything he touched into gold.

mid-Atlantic *adj.* [only before noun] **1** connected with the area on the east coast of the U.S. that is near New York and immediately to the south of it: *the mid-Atlantic states/coast* **2** in the middle of the Atlantic ocean: (*figurative*) *a mid-Atlantic accent* (= a form of English that uses a mixture of British and American sounds)

mid·brain /ˈmɪdbreɪn/ *noun* (*anatomy*) a small central part of the brain

mid·day /ˌmɪdˈdeɪ; ˈmɪddeɪ/ *noun* [U] 12 o'clock in the middle of the day; the period around this time **SYN** NOON: *a midday meal* ♦ *the heat of the midday sun*

mid·den /ˈmɪdn/ *noun* (in the past) a pile of waste near a house

mid·dle 🔑 /ˈmɪdl/ *noun, adj.*
• *noun* **1** the middle [sing.] the part of something that is at an equal distance from all its edges or sides; a point or a period of time between the beginning and the end of something: *a lake with an island in the middle* ♦ *He was standing in the middle of the room.* ♦ *The phone rang in the middle of the night.* ♦ *This chicken isn't cooked in the middle.* ♦ *His picture was right* (= exactly) *in the middle of the front page.* ♦ *Take a sheet of paper and draw a line down the middle.* ♦ *I should be finished by the middle of the week.* **2** [C, usually sing.] (*informal*) a person's waist: *He grabbed her around the middle.* **IDM be in the middle of sth/of doing sth** to be busy doing something: *They were in the middle of dinner when I called.* ♦ *I'm in the middle of writing a difficult letter.* **the middle of nowhere** (*informal*) a place that is a long way from other buildings, towns, etc.: *She lives on a small farm in the middle of nowhere.* **split/divide sth down the middle** to divide something into two equal parts: *The town was split down the middle over the referendum* (= half supported it, half did not).
• *adj.* [only before noun] in a position in the middle of an object, group of objects, people, etc. between the beginning and the end of something: *Pens are kept in the middle drawer.* ♦ *She's the middle child of three.* ♦ *He was very successful in his middle forties.* ♦ *Thomas A. Edison's middle initial stood for "Alva."* ♦ *the middle-income groups in society* **IDM (steer, take, etc.) a middle course | (find, etc.) a/ the middle way** (to take/find) an acceptable course of action that avoids two extreme positions

middle age *noun* [U] the period of your life when you are neither young nor old, between the ages of about 45 and 60: *a pleasant woman in early/late middle age* ⊃ **collocations at** AGE

middle-aged *adj.* **1** (of a person) neither young nor old **2** the middle aged *noun* [pl.] people who are middle-aged **3** (*disapproving*) (of a person's attitudes or behavior) boring and old-fashioned

ʌ **cup**   ə **about**   eɪ **say**   aɪ **five**   ɔɪ **boy**   aʊ **now**   oʊ **go**   ər **bird**

the ˌMiddle ˈAges noun [pl.] in European history, the period from about AD1000 to AD1450

ˌmiddle-age ˈspread (also ˌmiddle-aged ˈspread) noun [U] (humorous) the fat around the stomach that some people develop in middle age

ˌMiddle Aˈmerica noun [U] the middle class in the U.S., especially those people who represent traditional social and political values, and who come from small towns and SUBURBS rather than cities

mid·dle·brow /ˈmɪdlˌbraʊ/ adj., noun
• adj. [usually before noun] (usually disapproving) (of books, music, art, etc.) of good quality but not needing a lot of thought to understand ⊃ compare HIGHBROW, LOWBROW
• noun (usually disapproving) a person who enjoys books, music, etc. that are not very serious or difficult to understand

ˌmiddle ˈC noun [U] the musical note C near the middle of the piano keyboard

the ˌmiddle ˈclass noun the social class whose members are neither very rich nor very poor and that includes professional and business people: the upper/lower middle class ◆ the growth of the middle class ⊃ compare UPPER CLASS, WORKING CLASS

ˌmiddle-ˈclass adj. 1 connected with the middle social class: a middle-class background/family/suburb 2 (disapproving) typical of people from the middle social class, for example having traditional views: middle-class views ◆ The magazine is very middle-class.

the ˌmiddle ˈdistance noun [sing.] the part of a painting or a view that is neither very close nor very far away: His eyes were fixed on a small house in the middle distance.

ˌmiddle-ˈdistance adj. [only before noun] (sports) connected with running a race over a distance that is neither very short nor very long: a middle-distance runner (= for example, somebody who runs 800 or 1500 meter races)

ˌmiddle ˈear noun [sing.] the part of the ear behind the EARDRUM, containing the little bones that transfer sound VIBRATIONS

the ˌMiddle ˈEast (also the Mid·east) (also less frequent the ˌNear ˈEast) noun [sing.] an area that covers S.W. Asia and N. E. Africa ⊃ compare THE FAR EAST ► ˌMiddle ˈEastern (also ˌMid·east·ern) (also less frequent ˌNear ˈEastern) adj.

ˌMiddle ˈEnglish noun [U] an old form of English that was used between about AD1150 and AD1500 ⊃ compare OLD ENGLISH

ˌMiddle-Euroˈpean adj. of or related to central Europe or its people

ˌmiddle ˈfinger noun the longest finger in the middle of each hand ⊃ picture at BODY

ˌmiddle ˈground noun [U] a set of opinions, decisions, etc. that two or more groups who oppose each other can agree on; a position that is not extreme: Negotiations have failed to establish any middle ground. ◆ The dance company now occupies the middle ground between classical ballet and modern dance.

mid·dle·man /ˈmɪdlˌmæn/ noun (pl. mid·dle·men /-ˌmɛn/)
1 a person or a company that buys goods from the company that makes them and sells them to someone else: Buy direct from the manufacturer and cut out the middleman.
2 a person who helps to arrange things between people who do not want to talk directly to each other SYN GO-BETWEEN, INTERMEDIARY

ˌmiddle ˈmanagement noun [U] the people who are in charge of small groups of people and departments within a business organization but who are not involved in making important decisions that will affect the whole organization ► ˌmiddle ˈmanager noun

ˌmiddle ˈname noun a name that comes between your first name and your family name
IDM be sb's middle ˈname (informal) used to say that someone has a lot of a particular quality: "Patience" is my middle name!

ˌmiddle-of-the-ˈroad adj. (of people, policies, etc.) not extreme; acceptable to most people SYN MODERATE: a middle-of-the-road newspaper ◆ Their music is very middle-of-the-road.

ˌmiddle-ˈranking adj. [only before noun] having a responsible job or position, but not one of the most important

ˈmiddle ˌschool noun a school for children between the ages of about 11 and 14 ⊃ compare ELEMENTARY SCHOOL, HIGH SCHOOL

mid·dle·ware /ˈmɪdlˌwɛr/ noun [U] (computing) software that allows different programs to work with each other

mid·dle·weight /ˈmɪdlˌweɪt/ noun a BOXER weighing between 147 and 160 pounds (67-72 kg), heavier than a WELTERWEIGHT: a middleweight champion

the ˌMiddle ˈWest noun [sing.] = MIDWEST

mid·dling /ˈmɪdlɪŋ/ adj. [usually before noun] of average size, quality, status, etc. SYN MODERATE, UNREMARKABLE: a golfer of middling talent IDM see FAIR adv.

the Mid·east noun = MIDDLE EAST

mid·field /ˈmɪdfild; ˌmɪdˈfild/ noun [U, C, sing.] the central part of a playing field in sports such as football and SOCCER; the group of players in this position: He plays (in) midfield. ◆ The team's midfield looks strong. ◆ a midfield player ► mid·field·er /ˈmɪdˌfildər; ˌmɪdˈfil-/ noun

midge /mɪdʒ/ noun a small flying insect that lives especially in damp places and that bites humans and animals

mid·get /ˈmɪdʒət/ noun, adj.
• noun 1 (offensive) an extremely small person, who will never grow to a normal size because of a physical problem; a person suffering from DWARFISM 2 (informal) a very small person or animal
• adj. [only before noun] very small

MIDI /ˈmɪdi/ noun [U] a connection or program that connects electronic musical instruments and computers

mid·life /ˌmɪdˈlaɪf/ noun [U] the middle part of your life when you are neither young nor old: It is not difficult to take up a new career in midlife ◆ midlife stresses

ˌmidlife ˈcrisis noun [usually sing.] the feelings of worry, disappointment, or lack of confidence that a person may feel in the middle part of their life ⊃ collocations at AGE

mid·night 🔑 /ˈmɪdnaɪt/ noun [U]
1 12 o'clock at night: They had to leave at midnight. ◆ at/on the stroke of midnight/shortly after midnight ◆ She heard the clock strike midnight. ◆ We have to catch the midnight train.
2 = MIDNIGHT BLUE IDM see BURN v.

ˌmidnight ˈblue noun [U] a very dark blue color ► ˌmidnight ˈblue adj.

the ˌmidnight ˈsun noun [sing.] the sun that you can see in the middle of the summer near the North and South Poles

mid·point /ˈmɪdpɔɪnt/ noun [usually sing.] the point that is at an equal distance between the beginning and the end of something; the point that is at an equal distance between two things: the midpoint of the decade ◆ At its midpoint, the race had no clear winner. ◆ the midpoint between the first number and the last

mid·range /ˈmɪdreɪndʒ/ adj. [only before noun] (especially of a product for sale) neither the best nor the worst that is available: a midrange computer

mid·riff /ˈmɪdrɪf/ noun the middle part of the body between the chest and the waist: a bare midriff

mid·ship·man /ˈmɪdˌʃɪpmən; ˌmɪdˈʃɪp-/ noun (pl. mid·ship·men /-mən/) a person training to be an officer in the navy: Midshipman Paul Brooks

mid·size /ˈmɪdsaɪz/ (also mid·sized) adj. of average size, neither large nor small

midst /mɪdst/ noun (formal) (used after a preposition) the

middle part of something **SYN** MIDDLE: *Such beauty was unexpected in the midst of the city.*
IDM **in the midst of sth/of doing sth** while something is happening or being done; while you are doing something: *a country in the midst of recession* ◆ *She discovered it in the midst of sorting out her father's things.* **in their/our/its/your midst** (*formal*) among or with them/us/it/you: *There is a traitor in our midst.*

mid·stream /ˌmɪdˈstriːm/ *noun* [U] the middle part of a river, stream, etc.: *We anchored in midstream.*
IDM **(in) midstream** in the middle of doing something; while something is still happening: *Their conversation was interrupted midstream by the baby crying.* ⊃ more at HORSE *n.*

mid·sum·mer /ˌmɪdˈsʌmər/ *noun* [U] the middle of summer, especially the period in June in northern parts of the world, in December in southern parts: *a midsummer evening*

mid·term /ˈmɪdtɜːrm/ *adj., noun*
● *adj.* [only before noun] **1** in the middle of the period that a government, a council, etc. is elected for: *midterm elections* **2** for or connected with a period of time that is neither long nor short; in the middle of a particular period: *a midterm solution* ◆ *midterm losses* ⊃ see also LONG-TERM, SHORT-TERM **3** in the middle of one of the main periods of the academic year: *a midterm examination/break*
● *noun* a test that students take in the middle of one of the main periods of the academic year: *I have two midterms tomorrow! I have to study!*

mid·town /ˈmɪdtaʊn/ *noun* [U] the part of a city that is between the central business area and the outer parts: *a house in midtown* ◆ *midtown Manhattan* ⊃ compare DOWNTOWN, UPTOWN

mid·way *adv., noun*
● *adv.* /ˌmɪdˈweɪ; ˈmɪdweɪ/ in the middle of a period of time; between two places **SYN** HALFWAY: *The touchdown was scored midway through the first half.* ▶ **mid·way** *adj.*: *to reach the midway point*
● *noun* /ˈmɪdweɪ/ the area at a FAIR where games, small shows, and food are located: *The kids headed straight for the midway.*

mid·week /ˌmɪdˈwiːk/ *noun* [U] the middle of the week: *By midweek he was too tired to go out.* ◆ *a midweek defeat for the team* ▶ **mid·week** *adv.*: *It's cheaper to travel midweek.*

the Mid·west /ˌmɪdˈwest/ (also the ˌMiddle ˈWest) *noun* [sing.] the northern central part of the U.S. ▶ **Mid·west·ern** /ˌmɪdˈwestərn/ *adj.*

mid·wife /ˈmɪdwaɪf/ *noun* (*pl.* **mid·wives** /-waɪvz/) a person, especially a woman, who is trained to help women give birth to babies ⊃ compare DOULA

mid·wife·ry /ˌmɪdˈwɪfəri; -ˈwaɪ-/ *noun* [U] the profession and work of a midwife

mid·win·ter /ˌmɪdˈwɪntər/ *noun* [U] the middle of winter, around December in northern parts of the world, June in southern parts: *midwinter weather*

mid·year *noun* **1** /ˌmɪdˈjɪr; ˈmɪdjɪr/ [U] the middle of the year: *Our annual reviews will take place at midyear.* **2** /ˈmɪdjɪr/ [C] an exam taken in the middle of the year at school or college ▶ **mid·year** /ˈmɪdjɪr/ *adj.*: *midyear elections*

mien /miːn/ *noun* [sing.] (*formal* or *literary*) a person's appearance or manner that shows how they are feeling

miffed /mɪft/ *adj.* [not before noun] (*informal*) slightly angry or upset **SYN** ANNOYED

might 🔑 /maɪt/ *modal verb, noun*
● *modal verb* (*negative* **might not**, *short form* **might·n't** /ˈmaɪtnt/) **1** used as the past tense of *may* when reporting what someone has said: *He said he might come tomorrow.* **2** used when showing that something is or was possible: *He might get there in time, but I can't be sure.* ◆ *I know Vicky doesn't like the job, but I might not find it too bad.* ◆ *The pills might have helped him, if only he'd taken them regularly.* ◆ *He might say that now (= it is true that he does), but he'll probably change his mind.* **3** used to make a polite suggestion: *You*

might try calling the help desk. ◆ *I thought we might go to the zoo on Saturday.* **4** (*formal*) used to ask for information: *How might we improve the plans?* ◆ *And who might she be?* **5** used to show that you are annoyed about something that someone could do or could have done: *I think you might at least offer to help!* ◆ *Honestly, you might have told me!* **6** used to say that you are not surprised by something: *I might have guessed it was you!* **7** used to emphasize that an important point has been made: *"And where is the money coming from?" "You might well ask!"* ⊃ note at MODAL **IDM** see WELL *adv.*
● *noun* [U] (*formal* or *literary*) great strength, energy, or power: *America's military might* ◆ *I pushed the rock with all my might.* **IDM** **might is/makes right** (*saying*) having the power to do something gives you the right to do it: *Their foreign policy is based on the principle that "might is right."*

might-have-been /ˈmaɪt əv ˌbɪn/ *noun* [usually pl.] (*informal*) an event or situation that could have happened or that you wish had happened, but that did not happen

might·i·ly /ˈmaɪtl·i/ *adv.* (*old-fashioned*) **1** very; very much: *mightily impressed/relieved* **2** (*formal*) with great strength or effort: *We have struggled mightily to win back lost trade.*

might·y /ˈmaɪti/ *adj., adv.*
● *adj.* (**might·i·er**, **might·i·est**) **1** (especially *literary*) very strong and powerful: *a mighty warrior* ◆ *He struck him with a mighty blow across his shoulder.* **2** large and impressive **SYN** GREAT: *the mighty Mississippi river* **IDM** see HIGH *adj.*, PEN
● *adv.* (*informal*) (with adjectives and adverbs) very **SYN** REALLY: *mighty difficult* ◆ *driving mighty fast*

mi·graine /ˈmaɪɡreɪn/ *noun* [C, U] a very severe type of headache that often makes a person feel sick and have difficulty in seeing: *severe migraine* ◆ *I'm getting a migraine.*

mi·grant **AWL** /ˈmaɪɡrənt/ *noun* **1** a person who moves from one place to another, especially in order to find work: *migrant workers* ⊃ see also ECONOMIC MIGRANT ⊃ compare EMIGRANT, IMMIGRANT **2** a bird or an animal that moves from one place to another according to the season

mi·grate **AWL** /ˈmaɪɡreɪt/ *verb* **1** [I] (of birds, animals, etc.) to move from one part of the world to another according to the season: *Swallows migrate south in winter.* **2** [I] (of a lot of people) to move from one town, country, etc. to go and live and/or work in another **SYN** EMIGRATE: *Thousands were forced to migrate from rural to urban areas in search of work.* **3** [I] (*technical*) to move from one place to another: *The infected cells then migrate to other areas of the body.* **4** [I, T] **~ (sb)** (*computing*) to change, or cause someone to change, from one computer system to another **5** [T] **~ sth** (*computing*) to move programs or HARDWARE from one computer system to another

mi·gra·tion **AWL** /maɪˈɡreɪʃn/ *noun* [U, C] **1** the movement of large numbers of people, birds, or animals from one place to another: *seasonal migration* ◆ *mass migrations* **2** the fact of changing from one computer system to another; the act of moving programs, etc. from one computer system to another

mi·gra·to·ry **AWL** /ˈmaɪɡrəˌtɔri/ *adj.* (*technical*) connected with, or having the habit of, regular migration: *migratory flights/birds*

mi·ka·do /mɪˈkɑdoʊ/ *noun* (*pl.* **mi·ka·dos**) (from *Japanese*) a title given in the past to the EMPEROR of Japan

mike (also **mic**) /maɪk/ *noun* (*informal*) = MICROPHONE ⊃ see also OPEN MIKE

mi·la·dy /mɪˈleɪdi/ *noun* (*pl.* **mi·la·dies**) (*old use* or *humorous*) used when talking to or about a woman who is a member of the British NOBILITY or of high class ⊃ compare MILORD

mil·age = MILEAGE

mild 🔑 /maɪld/ *adj.*
(**mild·er**, **mild·est**) **1** not severe or strong: *a mild form of the disease* ◆ *a mild punishment/criticism* ◆ *It's safe to take a mild sedative.* ◆ *Use a soap that is mild to the skin.* **2** (of weather) not very cold, and therefore pleasant: *the mildest winter since*

t **tea**   t̬ **butter**   d **did**   k **cat**   ɡ **got**   tʃ **chin**   dʒ **June**   f **fall**

records began ◆ *a mild climate* ⟹ compare HARD **3** (of feelings) not great or extreme SYN SLIGHT: *mild irritation/ amusement/disapproval* ◆ *She looked at him in mild surprise.* **4** (of people or their behavior) gentle and kind; not usually getting angry or violent SYN EQUABLE: *a mild woman, who never shouted* **5** (of a flavor) not strong, spicy, or bitter: *mild salsa* ◆ *mild cheese* ANT HOT ▶ **mild·ness** noun [U]: *the mildness of a sunny spring day* ◆ *her mildness of manner*

mil·dew /'mɪldu/ *noun* [U] a very small white FUNGUS that grows on walls, plants, food, etc. in warm wet conditions **mil·dewed** /'mɪldud/ *adj.* with MILDEW growing on it

mild·ly /'maɪldli/ *adv.* **1** slightly; not very much: *mildly surprised/irritated/interested* **2** in a gentle manner: *"I didn't mean to upset you," he said mildly.* **IDM** **to put it mildly** used to show that what you are talking about is much more extreme, etc. than your words suggest: *The result was unfortunate, to put it mildly* (= it was extremely unfortunate).

mild-'mannered *adj.* (of a person) gentle and not usually getting angry or violent

mild 'steel *noun* [U] a type of steel containing very little CARBON that is very strong but not easy to shape

mile ♪ /maɪl/ *noun*
1 [C] a unit for measuring distance equal to 1,760 yards or 1,609 meters: *a 20-mile drive to work* ◆ *an area of four square miles* ◆ *a mile-long procession* ◆ *The nearest bank is about half a mile down the street.* ◆ *We did about 30 miles a day on our cycling trip.* ◆ *The car must have been doing at least 100 miles an hour.* ◆ *My car gets 35 miles to the gallon.* ⟹ see also AIR MILES™, MPH, NAUTICAL MILE **2 miles** [pl.] a large area or a long distance: *miles and miles of desert* ◆ *There isn't a house for miles around here.* ◆ *I'm not walking—it's miles away.* **3** [C] (*informal*) very much; far: *The two sides in the dispute are still miles apart.* ◆ *She's taller than you by a mile.* **4 the mile** [sing.] a race over one mile: *He ran the mile in less than four minutes.* ◆ *a four-minute mile* **IDM** **be miles away** (*informal*) to be thinking deeply about something and not aware of what is happening around you **go the extra mile (for sb/sth)** to make a special effort to achieve something, help someone, etc. **miles from anywhere** (*informal*) in a place that is a long way from a town and surrounded only by a lot of open country, ocean, etc.: *We broke down miles from anywhere.* **see, spot, tell, smell, etc. sth a mile off** (*informal*) to see or realize something very easily and quickly: *He's wearing a wig—you can see it a mile off.* **stand/stick out a mile** to be very obvious or noticeable ⟹ more at INCH *n.*

mile·age (also **mil·age**) /'maɪlɪdʒ/ *noun* **1** [U, C, usually sing.] the distance that a vehicle has traveled, measured in miles: *My annual mileage is about 10,000.* ◆ *a used car with one owner and low mileage* ◆ *The car rental included unlimited mileage, but not fuel.* ◆ *I get a mileage allowance if I use my car for work* (= an amount of money paid for each mile I travel). **2** [U, C] the number of miles that a vehicle can travel using a particular amount of fuel: *If you drive carefully you can get better mileage from your car.* **3** [U] (*informal*) the amount of advantage or use that you can get from a particular event or situation: *I don't think the press can get any more mileage out of that story.*

mile·post /'maɪlpoʊst/ *noun* **1** a post by the side of the road that shows how far it is to the next town and to other places **2** = MILESTONE

mile·stone /'maɪlstoʊn/ *noun* **1** (also **mile·post**) a very important stage or event in the development of something SYN LANDMARK **2** a stone by the side of a road that shows how far it is to the next town and to other places

mi·lieu /mil'yu; mil-; -'yu/ *noun* [C, usually sing.] (*pl.* **mi·lieus** or **mi·lieux** /-'yuz; -'yuz/) (from *French, formal*) the social environment that you live or work in SYN BACKGROUND

mil·i·tant /'mɪlətənt/ *adj.* using, or willing to use, force or strong pressure to achieve your aims, especially to achieve social or political change: *militant groups/leaders* ▶ **mil·i·tan·cy** /-tənsi/ *noun* [U]: *a growing militancy among*

the unemployed **mil·i·tant** *noun*: *Student militants were fighting with the police.* **mil·i·tant·ly** *adv.*

mil·i·ta·rism /'mɪlətə,rɪzəm/ *noun* [U] (usually *disapproving*) the belief that a country should have great military strength in order to be powerful ▶ **mil·i·ta·rist** /-rɪst/ *noun*: *Militarists ran the country.* **mil·i·ta·ris·tic** /,mɪlətə'rɪstɪk/ *adj.*: *militaristic government*

mil·i·ta·rize /'mɪlətə,raɪz/ *verb* [usually passive] **1** ~ sth to send armed forces to an area: *a militarized zone* ANT DEMILITARIZE **2** ~ sth to make something similar to an army: *a militarized police force* ▶ **mil·i·ta·ri·za·tion** /,mɪlətərə'zeɪʃn/ *noun* [U]

mil·i·tar·y ♪ AWL /'mɪlə,teri/ *adj., noun*
• *adj.* [usually before noun] connected with soldiers or the armed forces: *military training/intelligence* ◆ *a military coup* ◆ *military uniforms* ◆ *We may have to take military action.* ⟹ collocations at WAR ⟹ compare CIVILIAN ▶ **mil·i·tar·i·ly** /,mɪlə'terəli/ *adv.*: *a militarily superior country* ◆ *We may have to intervene militarily in the area.*
• *noun* **the military** [sing.] soldiers; the armed forces: *The military was called in to deal with the riot.*

military ,band *noun* a large group of soldiers who play wind instruments and drums, sometimes while marching ⟹ compare CONCERT BAND

military po'lice *noun* (*abbr.* MP) often **the military police** [pl.] the police force that is responsible for the army, navy, etc.

military 'service *noun* [U] **1** a period during which young people train in the armed forces: *to be called up for military service* ◆ *She has to do her military service.* **2** the time someone spends in the armed forces: *He completed 30 years of active military service.*

mil·i·tate /'mɪlə,teɪt/ *verb* **PHR V** **'militate against sth** (*formal*) to prevent something; to make it difficult for something to happen or exist: *The supervisor's presence militated against a relaxed atmosphere.* SYN HINDER

mi·li·tia /mə'lɪʃə/ *noun* a group of people who are not professional soldiers but who have had military training and can act as an army

mi·li·tia·man /mə'lɪʃəmən/ *noun* (*pl.* **mi·li·tia·men** /-mən/) a member of a militia

milk ♪ /mɪlk/ *noun, verb*
• *noun* [U] **1** the white liquid produced by cows, GOATS, and some other animals as food for their babies and used as a drink by humans: *a pint/gallon of milk* ◆ *a bottle/carton of milk* ◆ *fresh/dried/powdered milk* ◆ *Do you take milk in your tea?* ◆ *milk products* (= butter, cheese, etc.) ⟹ see also BUTTERMILK, CONDENSED MILK, EVAPORATED MILK, MALTED MILK, SKIM MILK, WHOLE MILK **2** the white liquid that is produced by women and female MAMMALS for feeding their babies: *breast milk* **3** the white juice of some plants and trees, especially the COCONUT ⟹ see also SOY MILK **IDM** **the milk of human kindness** (*literary*) kind behavior, considered to be natural to humans ⟹ more at CRY, LAND
• *verb* **1** ~ sth to take milk from a cow, GOAT, etc. **2** (*disapproving*) to obtain as much money, advantage, etc. for yourself as you can from a particular situation, especially in a dishonest way: *~ A (from B) She's milked a small fortune from the company over the years.* ◆ *~ B (of A) She's milked the company of a small fortune.* ◆ *I know he's had a hard time lately, but he's certainly milking it for all it's worth* (= using it as an excuse to do things that people would normally object to). **IDM** see DRY *adj.*

milk 'chocolate *noun* [U] light brown chocolate made with milk ⟹ compare DARK CHOCOLATE, WHITE CHOCOLATE

milk·ing /'mɪlkɪŋ/ *noun* [U] the process of taking milk from a cow, etc.: *milking machines/sheds*

milk·maid /'mɪlkmeɪd/ *noun* (in the past) a woman whose job was to take milk from cows and make butter and cheese

milk·man /ˈmɪlkmæn/ noun (pl. **milk·men** /-mən/) a person whose job is to deliver milk to customers each morning

Milk of Mag·ne·sia™ noun [U] a white liquid that is used to help with INDIGESTION

milk·shake /ˈmɪlkʃeɪk/ (also **shake**) noun a drink made of milk and ice cream, with an added flavor of fruit or chocolate, which is mixed or shaken until it is full of bubbles: *a banana milkshake*

milk·sop /ˈmɪlksɑp/ noun (disapproving, old-fashioned) a man or boy who is not brave or strong

milk·weed /ˈmɪlkwid/ noun [C, U] a N. American plant that produces a white juice like milk

milk·y /ˈmɪlki/ adj. **1** made of milk; containing a lot of milk: *milky tea/coffee* **2** like milk: *milky* (= not clear) *blue eyes* ♦ *milky* (= white) *skin*

the Milky Way noun [sing.] = THE GALAXY

mill /mɪl/ noun, verb
• noun **1** a building fitted with machinery for GRINDING grain into flour ➔ see also WATERMILL, WINDMILL **2** (often in compounds) a factory that produces a particular type of material: *a cotton/cloth/steel/paper mill* ♦ *mill owners/workers* ➔ see also ROLLING MILL, SAWMILL ➔ thesaurus box at FACTORY **3** (often in compounds) a small machine for crushing or GRINDING a solid substance into powder: *a pepper mill* ➔ see also RUN-OF-THE-MILL, TREADMILL
  IDM go through the mill| put sb through the mill to have or make someone have a difficult time ➔ more at GRIST
• verb [often passive] **~ sth** to crush or GRIND something in a mill
  PHRV mill a·round/a·bout (especially of a large group of people) to move around an area without seeming to be going anywhere in particular: *Fans were milling around outside the hotel.* ➔ see also MILLING

mil·le·nar·i·an /ˌmɪləˈnɛriən/ noun a member of a religious group which believes in a future age of happiness and peace when Christ will return to Earth ▶ **mil·le·nar·i·an** adj. **mil·le·nar·i·an·ism** /-iəˌnɪzəm/ noun [U]

mil·len·ni·um /məˈlɛniəm/ noun (pl. **mil·len·ni·a** /-niə/ or **mil·len·ni·ums**) **1** a period of 1,000 years, especially as calculated before or after the birth of Christ: *the second millennium A.D.* **2** **the millenium** the time when one period of 1,000 years ends and another begins: *How did you celebrate the millennium?*

mill·er /ˈmɪlər/ noun a person who owns or works in a MILL for making flour

mil·let /ˈmɪlət/ noun [U] a type of plant that grows in hot countries and produces very small seeds. The seeds are used as food, mainly to make flour, and also to feed to birds and animals. ➔ picture at CEREAL

milli- /ˈmɪlə; -li/ combining form (in nouns; used in units of measurement) one thousandth: *milligram*

mil·li·bar /ˈmɪləˌbɑr/ noun a unit for measuring the pressure of the atmosphere. One thousand millibars are equal to one BAR.

mil·li·gram ⚲ /ˈmɪləˌɡræm/ noun (abbr. mg) a unit for measuring weight; a 1,000th of a gram

mil·li·li·ter (CanE usually **mil·li·li·tre**) /ˈmɪləˌlitər/ noun (abbr. ml) a unit for measuring the volume of liquids and gases; a 1,000th of a liter

mil·li·me·ter ⚲ (CanE usually **mil·li·me·tre**) /ˈmɪləˌmitər/ noun (abbr. mm) a unit for measuring length; a 1,000th of a meter

mil·li·ner /ˈmɪlənər/ noun a person whose job is making and/or selling women's hats

mil·li·ner·y /ˈmɪləˌnɛri/ noun [U] **1** the work of a milliner **2** hats sold in stores

mil·ling /ˈmɪlɪŋ/ adj. [only before noun] (of people) moving around in a large mass: *I had to fight my way through the milling crowd.*

mil·lion /ˈmɪlyən/ number (plural verb) **1** (abbr. m.) 1,000,000: *a population of half a million* ♦ *tens of millions of dollars* ♦ *It must be worth a million* (= dollars). **HELP** You say a, one, two, several, etc. million without a final "s" on "million." **Millions (of…)** can be used if there is no number or quantity before it. Always use a plural verb with million or millions, except when an amount of money is mentioned: *Four million (people) were affected.* ♦ *Two million (dollars) was withdrawn from the account.* **2** a million or millions (of…) (informal) a very large amount: *I still have a million things to do.* ♦ *There were millions of people there.* ♦ *He made his millions* (= all his money) *on currency deals.* **HELP** There are more examples of how to use numbers at the entry for **hundred**.
  IDM look/feel like a million dollars/bucks (informal) to look/feel extremely good **one in a million** a person or thing that is very unusual or special: *He's one in a million.*

mil·lion·aire /ˌmɪlyəˈnɛr; ˈmɪlyəˌnɛr/ noun a person who has a million dollars; a very rich person: *an oil millionaire* ♦ *She's a millionaire several times over.* ♦ *a millionaire businessman*

mil·lion·air·ess /ˌmɪlyəˈnɛrəs/ noun (old-fashioned) a woman who is a millionaire

mil·lionth /ˈmɪlyənθ/ ordinal number, noun
• ordinal number 1,000,000th
• noun each of one million equal parts of something: *a/one millionth of a second*

mil·li·pede /ˈmɪləˌpid/ noun a small creature like an insect, with a long thin body divided into many sections, each with two pairs of legs

mil·li·sec·ond /ˈmɪləˌsɛkənd/ noun (technical) a 1,000th of a second: *(figurative) I hesitated a millisecond too long.*

mil·li·volt /ˈmɪləˌvoʊlt/ noun (physics) a unit for measuring the force of an electric current; a 1,000th of a VOLT

mill·pond /ˈmɪlpɑnd/ noun a small area of water used especially in the past to make the wheel of a MILL turn: *The ocean was as calm as a millpond.*

mill·stone /ˈmɪlstoʊn/ noun one of two flat round stones used, especially in the past, to crush grain to make flour
  IDM a millstone around your neck a difficult problem or responsibility that it seems impossible to solve or get rid of: *My debts are a millstone around my neck.*

mill·stream /ˈmɪlstrim/ noun a stream whose water turns a wheel that provides power for machinery in a WATERMILL

mill wheel noun a large wheel that is turned by water and that makes the machinery of a MILL work

mime /maɪm/ noun, verb
• noun **1** [U, C] (especially in the theater) the use of movements of your hands or body and the expressions on your face to tell a story or to act something without speaking; a performance using this method of acting: *The performance consisted of dance, music, and mime.* ♦ *a mime artist* ♦ *She performed a brief mime.* **2** an actor who performs mime
• verb [T, I] to act, tell a story, etc. by moving your body and face but without speaking: **~ (sth)** *Each player has to mime the title of a movie, play, or book.* ♦ **~ doing sth** *He mimed climbing a mountain.*

mi·me·sis /mɪˈmisəs/ noun [U] **1** (technical) the way in which the real world and human behavior are represented in art or literature **2** (technical) the fact of a particular social group changing its behavior by copying the behavior of another social group **3** (biology) the fact of a plant or animal developing a similar appearance to another plant or animal. **4** (medical) the fact of a set of SYMPTOMS suggesting that someone has a particular disease, when in fact that person has a different disease or none

mi·met·ic /mɪˈmɛtɪk/ adj. (technical or formal) copying the behavior or appearance of someone or something else

mim·ic /ˈmɪmɪk/ verb, noun
• verb (-ck-) **1 ~ sb/sth | + speech** to copy the way

someone speaks, moves, behaves, etc., especially in order to make other people laugh: *She's always mimicking the teachers.* ♦ *He mimicked her southern accent.* **2 ~ sth** to look or behave like something else **SYN** IMITATE: *The robot was programmed to mimic a series of human movements.*
● *noun* a person or an animal that can copy the voice, movements, etc. of others

mim·ic·ry /ˈmɪmɪkri/ *noun* [U] the action or skill of being able to copy the voice, movements, etc. of others: *a talent for mimicry*

mi·mo·sa /mɪˈmoʊsə/ *noun* [C, U] **1** an alcoholic drink made by mixing SPARKLING white wine (= with bubbles) with orange juice **2** a tropical bush or tree with balls of yellow flowers and leaves that are sensitive to touch and light

Min /mɪn/ *noun* [U] a form of Chinese spoken mainly in southeast China

min. *abbr.* **1** (in writing) minute(s): *Cook for 8–10 min. until tender.* **2** (in writing) minimum: *min. charge $4.50* **ANT** MAX

min·a·ret /ˌmɪnəˈrɛt/ *noun* a tall thin tower, usually forming part of a MOSQUE, from which Muslims are called to prayer

min·a·to·ry /ˈmɪnəˌtɔri/ *adj.* (*formal*) threatening: *minatory words*

mince /mɪns/ *verb* **1** [T] **~ sth** to cut food into very small pieces: *minced garlic/onions/herbs* ➜ compare GRIND *v.* (3) **2** [I] **+ adv./prep.** (*disapproving*) to walk with quick short steps, in a way that is not natural: *He minced over to serve us.*
IDM **not mince (your) words** to say something in a direct way even though it might offend other people

mince·meat /ˈmɪnsmit/ *noun* [U] a mixture of dried fruit, spices, etc. used especially for making PIES
IDM **make mincemeat of sb** (*informal*) to defeat someone completely in a fight, an argument, or a competition

minc·ing /ˈmɪnsɪŋ/ *adj.* (*disapproving*) (of a way of walking or speaking) very delicate, and not natural: *short mincing steps*

mind 🔊 /maɪnd/ *noun, verb*
● *noun*
> ABILITY TO THINK **1** [C, U] the part of a person that makes them able to be aware of things, to think, and to feel: *the conscious/subconscious mind* ♦ *There were all kinds of thoughts running through my mind.* ♦ *There was no doubt in his mind that he'd get the job.* ♦ *"Drugs" are associated in most people's minds with drug abuse.* ♦ *She was in a disturbed state of mind.* ♦ *I could not have complete peace of mind before they returned.* ➜ see also FRAME OF MIND, PRESENCE OF MIND
2 [C] your ability to think and reason; your intelligence; the particular way that someone thinks **SYN** INTELLECT: *to have a brilliant/good mind* ♦ *a creative/evil/suspicious mind* ♦ *She had a lively and inquiring mind.* ♦ *His mind is as sharp as ever.* ♦ *I have no idea how her mind works!* ♦ *He had the body of a man and the mind of a child.* ♦ *insights into the criminal mind* ➜ see also ONE-TRACK MIND
> INTELLIGENT PERSON **3** [C] a person who is very intelligent: *She was one of the greatest minds of her generation.* **SYN** BRAIN ➜ see also MASTERMIND
> THOUGHTS **4** [C] your thoughts, interest, etc.: *Keep your mind on your work!* ♦ *Her mind is completely occupied by the new baby.* ♦ *The lecture dragged on and my mind wandered.* ♦ *He gave his mind to the arrangements for the next day.* ♦ *As for avoiding you, nothing could be further from my mind* (= I was not thinking of it at all).
> MEMORY **5** [C, usually sing.] your ability to remember things: *When I saw the exam questions my mind just went blank* (= I couldn't remember anything). ♦ *Sorry—your name has gone right out of my mind.*
IDM **be all in sb's/the mind** to be something that only exists in someone's imagination: *These problems are all in your mind, you know.* **bear/keep sb/sth in mind | bear/keep in mind that…** to remember someone or something; to remember or consider that… **be bored, frightened, stoned, etc. out of your mind** (*informal*) to be extremely bored, etc. **be/go out of your mind** (*informal*) to be unable to think or behave in a normal way; to become crazy: *You're*

lending them money? You must be out of your mind! ➜ thesaurus box at CRAZY **be of one/the same mind (about sb/sth)** to have the same opinion about someone or something **be out of your mind with worry, etc.** to be extremely worried, etc. **bring/call sb/sth to mind** (*formal*) **1** to remember someone or something **SYN** RECALL: *She couldn't call to mind where she had seen him before.* **2** to remind you of someone or something **SYN** RECALL: *The painting brings to mind some of Picasso's early works.* **come/spring to mind** if something **comes/springs to mind**, you suddenly remember or think of it: *When discussing influential modern artists, three names immediately come to mind.* **have a good mind to do sth | have half a mind to do sth 1** used to say that you think you will do something, although you are not sure: *I've half a mind to come with you tomorrow.* **2** used to say that you disapprove of what someone has done and should do something about it, although you probably will not: *I've a good mind to write and tell your parents about it.* **have sb/sth in mind (for sth)** to be thinking of someone or something, especially for a particular job, etc.: *Do you have anyone in mind for this job?* ♦ *Watching TV all evening wasn't exactly what I had in mind!* **have it in mind to do sth** (*formal*) to intend to do something **have a mind of your own** to have your own opinion and make your own decisions without being influenced by other people: *She has a mind of her own and isn't afraid to say what she thinks.* ♦ (*humorous*) *My computer seems to have a mind of its own!* **lose your mind** to become mentally ill **make up your mind | make your mind up** to decide something: *They're both beautiful—I can't make up my mind.* ♦ *Have you made up your minds where to go for your honeymoon?* ♦ *You'll never persuade him to stay—his mind's made up* (= he has definitely decided to go). ♦ *Come on—it's make your mind up time!* **mind over matter** the use of the power of your mind to deal with physical problems **your mind's eye** your imagination: *He pictured the scene in his mind's eye.* **on your mind** if someone or something is **on your mind**, you are thinking and worrying about them/it a lot: *You've been on my mind all day.* ♦ *Don't bother your father tonight—he's got a lot on his mind.* **put/get sth out of your mind** to stop thinking about someone or something; to deliberately forget someone or something: *I just can't get her out of my mind.* **put sb in mind of sb/sth** (*old-fashioned*) to make someone think of someone or something; to remind someone of someone or something **put/set sb's mind at ease/rest** to do or say something to make someone stop worrying about something **SYN** REASSURE **put/set/turn your mind to sth | set your mind on sth** to decide you want to achieve something and give this all your attention: *She could have been a brilliant pianist if she'd put her mind to it.* **take your mind off sth** to make you forget about something unpleasant for a short time **SYN** DISTRACT **to my mind** in my opinion: *It was a ridiculous thing to do, to my mind.* ➜ more at BACK *n.*, BEND *v.*, BLOW *v.*, BOGGLE, CAST *v.*, CHANGE *v.*, CHANGE *n.*, CLOSE[1] *v.*, CROSS *v.*, ETCH, GREAT *adj.*, KNOW *v.*, MEETING, OPEN *adj.*, OPEN *v.*, PIECE *n.*, PREY *v.*, PUSH *v.*, RIGHT *adj.*, SIEVE *n.*, SIGHT *n.*, SLIP *v.*, SPEAK, STICK *v.*, TURN *n.*, TWO, UNSOUND

● *verb*
> BE UPSET/ANNOYED **1** [T, I] (used especially in questions or with negatives; not used in the passive) to be upset, annoyed, or worried by something: **~ (sth)** *I don't mind the cold—it's the rain I don't like.* ♦ *I hope you don't mind the noise.* ♦ *He wouldn't have minded so much if she'd told him the truth.* ♦ **~ about sth** *Did she mind about not getting the job?* ♦ **~ doing sth** *Did she mind not getting the job?* ♦ **~ sb/sth doing sth** *Do your parents mind you leaving home?* ♦ (*formal*) *Do your parents mind your leaving home?* ♦ **~ how, what, etc.** *…She never minded how hot it was.* ♦ **~ that…** *He minded that he hadn't been asked.*
> ASKING PERMISSION **2** [I, T] used to ask for permission to do something, or to ask someone in a polite way to do something: *Do you mind if I open the window?* ♦ **~ sb doing sth** *Are you married, if you don't mind me asking?* ♦ (*formal*) *Are you married, if you don't mind my asking?* ♦ **~ doing sth** *Would*

you mind explaining that again, please? ◆ Do you mind driving? I'm feeling pretty tired.

> NOT CARE/WORRY **3** not mind [I, T, no passive] to not care or not be concerned about something: "Would you like tea or coffee?" "I don't mind—either's fine." ◆ ~ **sb** Don't mind her—she didn't mean what she said. ◆ Don't mind me (= don't let me disturb you) —I'll just sit here quietly.

> BE WILLING **4** not mind doing something [T] to be willing to do something: I don't mind helping if you can't find anyone else.

> OBEY **5** [T] ~ **sb** to pay attention to what someone says, and obey them: And the moral of the story is: always mind your mother!

> TAKE CARE OF **6** [T] ~ **sb/sth** to take care of someone or something SYN WATCH v. (2): Who's minding the children this evening? ◆ Could you mind my bags for a moment?

IDM **do you mind?** (ironic) used to show that you are annoyed about something that someone has just said or done: Do you mind? I was here before you. **I don't mind admitting, telling...,** etc. used to emphasize what you are saying, especially when you are talking about something that may be embarrassing for you: I was scared, I don't mind telling you! **I don't mind if I do** (informal) used to say politely that you would like something you have been offered: "Cup of tea, Brian?" "I don't mind if I do." **if you don't mind| if you wouldn't mind 1** used to check that someone does not object to something you want to do, or to ask someone politely to do something: I'd like to ask you a few questions, if you don't mind. ◆ Can you read that form carefully, if you wouldn't mind, and then sign it? **2** (often ironic) used to show that you object to something that someone has said or done: I give the orders around here, if you don't mind. **3** used to refuse an offer politely: "Will you come with us tonight?" "I won't, if you don't mind—I've got a lot of work to do." **if you don't mind me/my saying so...** used when you are going to criticize someone or say something that might upset them: That color doesn't really suit you, if you don't mind my saying so. **I wouldn't mind sth/doing sth** used to say politely that you would very much like sth/to do something: I wouldn't mind a cup of coffee, if it's no trouble. ◆ I wouldn't mind having his money! **mind your own business** (informal) to think about your own affairs and not ask questions about or try to get involved in other people's lives: "What are you reading?" "Mind your own business!" ◆ I was just sitting there, minding my own business, when a man started shouting at me. **mind the store** to be in charge of something for a short time while someone is away: Who's minding the store while the boss is abroad? **mind you** (informal) used to add something to what you have just said, especially something that makes it less strong: I've heard they're getting divorced. Mind you, I'm not surprised—they were always arguing. **mind your Ps and Qs** (informal) to behave in the most polite way you can **never mind 1** used to suggest that something is not important: This isn't where I intended to take you—but never mind, it's just as good. **2** used to tell someone not to worry or be upset: Have you broken it? Never mind, we can buy another one. **3** used to emphasize that what is true about the first thing you have said is even more true about the second SYN LET ALONE: I never thought she'd win once, never mind twice! **never mind (about) (doing) sth** used to tell someone they should not think about something or do something because it is not as important as something else, or because you will do it: Never mind your car—what about the damage to my fence? ◆ Never mind washing the dishes—I'll do them later. **never you mind** (informal) used to tell someone not to ask about something because you are not going to tell them: "Who told you about it?" "Never you mind!" ◆ Never you mind how I found out—it's true, isn't it?

mind-,bending adj. (informal) (especially of drugs) having a strong effect on your mind

mind-,blowing adj. (informal) very exciting, impressive, or surprising: Watching your baby being born is a mind-blowing experience.

mind-,boggling adj. (informal) very difficult to imagine or

to understand; extremely surprising: a problem of mind-boggling complexity ⊃ compare BOGGLE

mind·ed /'maɪndəd/ adj. **1** (used with adjectives to form compound adjectives) having the way of thinking, the attitude, or the type of character mentioned: a fair-minded employer ◆ high-minded principles ◆ I appeal to all like-minded people to support me. ⊃ see also ABSENTMINDED, BLOODY-MINDED, SINGLE-MINDED **2** (used with adverbs to form compound adjectives) having the type of mind that is interested in or able to understand the areas mentioned: I'm not very politically minded. **3** (used with nouns to form compound adjectives) interested in or enthusiastic about the thing mentioned: a reform-minded government

mind·ful /'maɪndfl/ adj. ~ **of sb/sth** | ~ **that...** (formal) remembering someone or something and considering them or it when you do something SYN CONSCIOUS: mindful of our responsibilities ◆ Mindful of the danger of tropical storms, I decided not to go out.

'mind game noun something that you do or say in order to make someone feel less confident, especially to gain an advantage for yourself

mind·less /'maɪndləs/ adj. **1** done or acting without thought and for no particular reason or purpose; SYN SENSELESS: mindless violence ◆ mindless vandals **2** not needing thought or intelligence SYN DULL: a mindless and repetitive task **3** ~ **of sb/sth** (formal) not remembering someone or something and not considering them or it when you do something: We explored the whole town, mindless of the cold and rain. ▶ **mind·less·ly** adv.

'mind-,numbing adj. very boring: mind-numbing conversation ▶ **'mind-,numbingly** adv.: The lecture was mind-numbingly tedious.

'mind reader noun (often humorous) a person who knows what someone else is thinking without being told

mind·set /'maɪndsɛt/ noun a set of attitudes or fixed ideas that someone has and that are often difficult to change SYN MENTALITY: a conservative mindset ◆ the mindset of the computer generation

mind·share /'maɪndʃɛr/ noun [U] (business) the extent of knowledge of a company or product among consumers, compared with their knowledge of others of the same type

mine 🔑 /maɪn/ pron., noun, verb

● **pron.** (the possessive form of I) of or belonging to the person writing or speaking: That's mine. ◆ He's a friend of mine (= one of my friends). ◆ She wanted one like mine (= like I have).

● **noun 1** a deep hole or holes under the ground where minerals such as coal, gold, etc. are dug: a **copper/diamond mine** ⊃ see also COAL MINE, GOLD MINE, MINING ⊃ compare QUARRY **2** a type of bomb that is hidden under the ground or in the ocean and that explodes when someone or something touches it ⊃ see also LAND MINE

IDM **a mine of information (about/on sb/sth)** a person, book, etc. that can give you a lot of information on a particular subject

● **verb 1** [T, I] to dig holes in the ground in order to find and obtain coal, diamonds, etc.: ~ **sth (for sth)** The area has been mined for slate for centuries. ◆ ~ **(for sth)** They were mining for gold. **2** [T] ~ **sth** to place MINES below the surface of an area of land or water; to destroy a vehicle with mines: The coastal route had been mined. ◆ The UN convoy was mined on its way to the border.

mine·field /'maɪnfild/ noun **1** an area of land or water where MINES (= bombs that explode when they are touched) have been hidden **2** a situation that contains hidden dangers or difficulties: a legal minefield ◆ Tax laws can be a minefield.

min·er /'maɪnər/ noun a person who works in a mine taking out coal, gold, diamonds, etc. ⊃ see also COAL MINER

min·er·al 🔑 /'mɪnərəl/ noun [C, U]
a substance that is naturally present in the earth and is not

formed from animal or vegetable matter, for example gold and salt. Some minerals are also present in food and drink and in the human body and are essential for good health: *mineral deposits/extraction* ♦ *the recommended intake of vitamins and minerals* ⊃ collocations at DIET

min·er·al·o·gist /ˌmɪnəˈrælədʒɪst; -ˈrælə-/ *noun* a scientist who studies mineralogy

min·er·al·o·gy /ˌmɪnəˈrælədʒi; -ˈrælə-/ *noun* [U] the scientific study of minerals ▶ **min·er·al·og·i·cal** /ˌmɪnərəˈlɑdʒɪkl/ *adj.*

ˌmineral ˈoil *noun* [U] a liquid with no color and no smell that comes from PETROLEUM and is used in medicines and COSMETICS

ˌmineral ˈwater *noun* **1** [U, C] water from a SPRING in the ground that contains mineral salts or gases: *A glass of mineral water, please.* **2** [C] a glass or bottle of mineral water

mine·shaft /ˈmaɪnʃæft/ *noun* a deep narrow hole that goes down to a mine

min·e·stro·ne /ˌmɪnəˈstrouni/ *noun* [U] an Italian soup containing small pieces of vegetables and PASTA

mine·sweep·er /ˈmaɪnˌswipər/ *noun* a ship used for finding and clearing away MINES (= bombs that explode when they are touched)

min·gle /ˈmɪŋɡl/ *verb* **1** [I, T] to combine or make one thing combine with another: *The sounds of laughter and singing mingled in the night air.* ♦ ~ **(A) (with B)** *Her tears mingled with the blood on her face.* ♦ *He felt a kind of happiness mingled with regret.* ♦ ~ **(A and B) (together)** *The flowers mingle together to form a blaze of color.* ⊃ thesaurus box at MIX **2** [I] to move among people and talk to them, especially at a social event **SYN** CIRCULATE: *The princess was not recognized and mingled freely with the crowds.* ♦ *If you'll excuse me, I must go and mingle* (= talk to other guests).

min·i /ˈmɪni/ *noun* = MINISKIRT

mini- /ˈmɪni/ *combining form* (in nouns) small: *a minibus* ♦ *minigolf*

min·i·a·ture /ˈmɪniətʃər; -ˌtʃʊr; ˈmɪnə-/ *adj., noun*
● *adj.* [only before noun] very small; much smaller than usual: *miniature roses* ♦ *a rare breed of miniature horses* ♦ *It looks like a miniature version of James Bond's car.*
● *noun* **1** a very small detailed painting, often of a person **2** a very small copy or model of something; a very small version of something: *She collects miniatures for her dollhouse.*
 IDM in miniature on a very small scale: *a doll's house with everything in miniature* ♦ *Through play, children act out in miniature the dramas of adult life.*

ˌminiature ˈgolf (also min·i·golf) *noun* [U] a type of GOLF in which people go around a small course, hitting a ball through or over little tunnels, hills, bridges, and other objects

min·i·a·tur·ist /ˈmɪniətʃərɪst; -ˌtʃʊrɪst; ˈmɪnə-/ *noun* a painter who paints small works of art

min·i·a·tur·ize /ˈmɪniətʃəˌraɪz; ˈmɪnə-/ *verb* ~ sth to make a much smaller version of something ▶ **min·i·a·tur·i·za·tion** /ˌmɪniətʃərəˈzeɪʃn; ˌmɪnə-/ *noun* [U] **min·i·a·tur·ized** *adj.* [only before noun]: *a miniaturized listening device*

min·i·bar /ˈmɪniˌbɑr/ *noun* a small refrigerator in a hotel room, with drinks in it for guests to use

min·i·bus /ˈmɪniˌbʌs/ *noun* a small vehicle with seats for about twelve people

min·i·cam /ˈmɪniˌkæm/ *noun* a video camera that is small enough to hold in one hand

min·i·com·pu·ter /ˈmɪnikəmˌpyutər/ *noun* a computer that is smaller and slower than a MAINFRAME but larger and faster than a MICROCOMPUTER

min·i·disc /ˈmɪniˌdɪsk/ *noun* a disk like a small CD that can record and play sound or data

min·i·dress /ˈmɪniˌdrɛs/ *noun* a very short dress

min·i·golf /ˈmɪniˌɡɑlf; -ˌɡɔlf/ *noun* [U] = MINIATURE GOLF

min·i·mal AWL /ˈmɪnəməl/ *adj.* very small in size or amount; as small as possible: *The work was carried out at minimal cost.* ♦ *There's only a minimal amount of risk involved.* ♦ *The damage to the car was minimal.* ⊃ compare MAXIMAL ▶ **min·i·mal·ly** AWL *adv.*: *minimally invasive surgery* ♦ *The episode was reported minimally in the press.*

min·i·mal·ist AWL /ˈmɪnəməlɪst/ *noun* an artist, a musician, etc. who uses very simple ideas or a very small number of simple things in their work ▶ **min·i·mal·ism** /-ˌlɪzəm/ *noun* [U] **min·i·mal·ist** *adj.*

ˌminimal ˈpair *noun* (*phonetics*) a pair of words, sounds, etc. that are distinguished from each other by only one feature, for example *pin* and *bin*

min·i·mart /ˈmɪniˌmɑrt/ *noun* a small store that sells food, newspapers, etc. and stays open very late

min·i·mize AWL /ˈmɪnəˌmaɪz/ *verb* **1** ~ sth to reduce something, especially something bad, to the lowest possible level: *Good hygiene helps to minimize the risk of infection.* **ANT** MAXIMIZE **2** ~ sth to try to make something seem less important than it really is **SYN** PLAY DOWN: *He always tried to minimize his own faults, while exaggerating those of others.* **3** ~ sth to make something small, especially on a computer screen: *Minimize any windows you have open.* **ANT** MAXIMIZE ▶ **min·i·mi·za·tion** /ˌmɪnəməˈzeɪʃn/ *noun* [U]

min·i·mum 🔑 AWL /ˈmɪnəməm/ *adj., noun*
● *adj.* [usually before noun] (*abbr.* **min.**) the smallest that is possible or allowed; extremely small: *a minimum charge/price* ♦ *the minimum age for retirement* ♦ *The work was done with the minimum amount of effort.* **ANT** MAXIMUM ▶ **min·i·mum** *adv.*: *You'll need $500 minimum for your vacation expenses.*
● *noun* (*pl.* **min·i·ma** /-mə/) [C, usually sing.] **1** (*abbr.* **min.**) the smallest or lowest amount that is possible, required, or recorded: *Costs should be kept to a minimum.* ♦ *The class needs a minimum of six students to continue.* ♦ *As an absolute minimum, you should spend two hours studying every night.* ♦ *Temperatures will fall to a minimum of 10 degrees.* **2** [sing.] an extremely small amount: *He did the bare minimum but still passed his exam.* **ANT** MAXIMUM

ˌminimum ˈwage *noun* [sing.] the lowest wage that an employer is allowed to pay by law

min·ing /ˈmaɪnɪŋ/ *noun* [U] the process of getting coal and other minerals from under the ground; the industry involved in this: *coal/diamond/gold/tin mining* ♦ *a mining company/community/engineer* ⊃ see also MINE, PLACER MINING

min·ion /ˈmɪnyən/ *noun* (*disapproving* or *humorous*) an unimportant person in an organization who has to obey orders; a servant

min·i·se·ries /ˈmɪniˌsɪriz/ *noun* (*pl.* **min·i·se·ries**) a television show that is divided into a number of parts and shown on different days

min·i·skirt /ˈmɪniˌskərt/ (also min·i) *noun* a very short skirt

min·is·ter 🔑 /ˈmɪnəstər/ *noun, verb*
● *noun* **1** (in some Protestant Christian churches) a trained religious leader: *a Methodist minister* ⊃ compare PASTOR, PRIEST, VICAR **2** often **Minister** (in some countries) a senior member of the government who is in charge of a government department or a branch of one: *cabinet ministers* ⊃ see also PRIME MINISTER **3** a person, lower in rank than an AMBASSADOR, whose job is to represent their government in a foreign country
● *verb*
 PHR V ˈminister to sb/sth (*formal*) to care for someone, especially someone who is sick or old, and make sure that they have everything they need **SYN** TEND

min·is·te·ri·al AWL /ˌmɪnəˈstɪriəl/ *adj.* connected with a government minister or ministers: *decisions taken at ministerial level* ♦ *to hold ministerial office* (= to have the job of a government minister)

min·is·ter·ing AWL /ˈmɪnəstərɪŋ/ *adj.* [only before noun] (*formal*) caring for people: *She could not see herself in the role of ministering angel.*

min·is·tra·tions /ˌmɪnəˈstreɪʃnz/ *noun* [pl.] (*formal or humorous*) the act of helping or caring for someone, especially when they are sick or in trouble

min·is·try 🔑 **AWL** /ˈmɪnəstri/ *noun*
(*pl.* **ministries**) **1 the Ministry** [sing.] ministers of religion, especially Protestant ministers, when they are mentioned as a group **2** [C, usually sing.] the work and duties of a minister in the church; the period of time spent working as a minister in the church **3** [C] (in some countries) a government department that has a particular area of responsibility: *the Ministry of Defense ◆ a ministry spokesperson*

min·i·van /ˈmɪniˌvæn/ *noun* a large car, like a van, designed to carry up to eight people ⊃ **picture at CAR**

mink /mɪŋk/ *noun* (*pl.* **mink** or **minks**) **1** [C] a small wild animal with thick shiny fur, a long body, and short legs. Mink are often kept on farms for their fur: *a mink farm* **2** [U] the skin and shiny brown fur of the mink, used for making expensive coats, etc.: *a mink jacket* **3** [C] a coat or jacket made of mink

min·ke /ˈmɪŋki; -kə/ (also **minke whale**) *noun* a small WHALE that is dark gray on top and white underneath

min·now /ˈmɪnoʊ/ *noun* **1** a very small FRESHWATER fish **2** a company or sports team that is small or unimportant

mi·nor 🔑 **AWL** /ˈmaɪnər/ *adj., noun, verb*
● *adj.* **1** [usually before noun] not very large, important, or serious: *a minor road ◆ minor injuries ◆ to undergo minor surgery ◆ youths imprisoned for minor offenses ◆ There may be some minor changes to the schedule. ◆ Women played a relatively minor role in the organization.* **ANT MAJOR 2** (*music*) based on a SCALE in which the third note is a HALF STEP higher than the second note: *the key of C minor* ⊃ compare MAJOR
● *noun* **1** (*law*) a person who is under the age at which you legally become an adult and are responsible for your actions: *It is an offense to serve alcohol to minors.* **2** a subject that some people study at college in addition to their MAJOR
● *verb*
PHR V 'minor in sth to study something at college, but not as your main subject ⊃ compare MAJOR

mi·nor·i·ty 🔑 **AWL** /məˈnɔrəti; maɪ-; -ˈnɑr-/ *noun*
(*pl.* **mi·nor·i·ties**) **1** [sing.] the smaller part of a group; less than half of the people or things in a large group: *Only a small minority of students is/are interested in politics these days. ◆ minority shareholders in the bank* **ANT MAJORITY 2** [C] a small group within a community or country that is different because of race, religion, language, etc.: *the rights of ethnic/racial minorities ◆ minority languages ◆ a large German-speaking minority in the east of the country ◆ The school is 95 percent minority* (= 95 percent of children are not white Americans but from different groups). *◆ minority neighborhoods* (= where no or few white people live) **3** [U] (*law*) the state of being under the age at which you are legally an adult
IDM be in a/the minority to form less than half of a large group **be a minority of one** (often *humorous*) to be the only person to have a particular opinion or to vote a particular way

mi'nority 'government *noun* [C, U] (in some countries) a government that has fewer seats in parliament than the total number held by all the other parties

mi'nority ,leader *noun* the leader of the political party that does not have a majority in either the House of Representatives or the Senate

,minor 'league (also **,Minor 'league**) *noun* a league of professional baseball teams that play at at a lower level than the Major Leagues ▶ **minor-'leaguer** *noun*

minor-'league *adj.* [only before noun] **1** (*sports*) connected with teams in the minor leagues in baseball: *a minor-league team* **2** not very important and having little influence: *a minor-league business*

Min·o·taur /ˈmɪnəˌtɔr; ˈmaɪ-/ *noun* (in ancient Greek stories) an imaginary creature who was half man and half BULL

min·strel /ˈmɪnstrəl/ *noun* a musician or singer in the Middle Ages

mint /mɪnt/ *noun, verb*
● *noun* **1** [U] a plant with dark green leaves that have a fresh smell and taste, used to flavor or decorate food and drinks: *roast lamb with mint sauce ◆ I decorated the fruit salad with a sprig of mint. ◆ mint-flavored toothpaste* ⊃ **picture at HERB** **2** [C] a candy flavored with a type of mint called PEPPERMINT: *after-dinner mints* **3** [C] a place where money is made: *the United States Mint* (= where American coins are made) **4 a mint** [sing.] (*informal*) a large amount of money: *to make/cost a mint*
IDM in mint condition new or as good as new; in perfect condition
● *verb* **~ sth** to make a coin from metal

mint·ed /ˈmɪntəd/ *adj.* **1 freshly/newly ~** recently produced, invented, etc.: *a newly minted expression* **2** (of food) flavored with mint

,mint 'julep (also **ju·lep**) *noun* [U, C] an alcoholic drink made by mixing BOURBON with crushed ice, sugar, and MINT

mint·y /ˈmɪnti/ *adj.* tasting or smelling of MINT: *a minty flavor/smell*

min·u·et /ˌmɪnjuˈɛt/ *noun* a slow elegant dance that was popular in the 17th and 18th centuries; a piece of music for this dance

mi·nus /ˈmaɪnəs/ *prep., noun, adj.*
● *prep.* **1** used when you SUBTRACT (= take away) one number or thing from another one: *Seven minus three equals four (7−3=4).* **2** used to express temperature below zero degrees: *It was minus ten. ◆ The temperature dropped to minus 15 degrees Fahrenheit (−15°F).* **3** (*informal*) without something that was there before: *We're going to be minus a car for a while. ◆ the former Soviet Union, minus the Baltic republics and Georgia* **ANT PLUS¹ IDM see PLUS¹**
● *noun* **1** (also **'minus ,sign**) The symbol (−), used in mathematics **2** (*informal*) a negative quality; a disadvantage: *Let's consider the pluses and minuses of changing the system.* **ANT PLUS¹**
● *adj.* **1** (*mathematics*) lower than zero: *a minus figure/number* **2** making something seem negative and less attractive or good: *What are the car's minus points* (= the disadvantages)? *◆ On the minus side, rented property is expensive and difficult to find.* **3** [not before noun] (used in a system of grades) slightly lower than the grade A, B, etc.: *I got a B minus (B−) on the test.* **ANT PLUS¹**

mi·nus·cule /ˈmɪnəˌskyul/ *adj.* extremely small

mi·nute¹ 🔑 /ˈmɪnət/ *noun, verb* ⊃ **see also MINUTE²**
● *noun*
▷ **PART OF HOUR 1** [C] (*abbr.* **min.**) each of the 60 parts of an hour, that are equal to 60 seconds: *It's four minutes to six. ◆ I'll be back in a few minutes. ◆ Boil the rice for 20 minutes. ◆ a ten-minute bus ride ◆ I enjoyed every minute of the party.*
▷ **VERY SHORT TIME 2** [sing.] (*informal*) a very short time: *It only takes a minute to make a salad. ◆ Hang on a minute—I'll just get my coat. ◆ I just have to finish this—I won't be a minute. ◆ Could I see you for a minute? ◆ I'll be with you in a minute, Jo. ◆ Typical Seattle weather—one minute it's raining and the next minute the sun is shining.*
▷ **EXACT MOMENT 3** [sing.] an exact moment in time: *At that very minute, Tom walked in.*
▷ **ANGLES 4** [C] each of the 60 equal parts of a degree, used in measuring angles: *37 degrees 30 minutes (37° 30′)*
▷ **RECORD OF MEETING 5 the minutes** [pl.] a summary or record of what is said or decided at a formal meeting: *We read through the minutes of the last meeting. ◆ Who is going to take the minutes* (= write them)?

   t **t**ea   t̬ bu**tt**er   d **d**id   k **c**at   g **g**ot   tʃ **ch**in   dʒ **J**une   f **f**all

> SHORT NOTE **6** [C] a short note on a subject, especially one that recommends a course of action

IDM **(at) any minute (now)** very soon: *Hurry up! He'll be back any minute now.* **the minute (that)…** as soon as…: *I want to see him the minute he arrives.* **not for a/one minute** certainly not; not at all: *I don't think for a minute that she'll accept but you can ask her.* **this minute** immediately; now: *Come down this minute!* ◆ *I don't know what I'm going to do yet —I've just this minute found out.* **to the minute** exactly: *The train arrived at 9:05 to the minute.* **up to the minute** (*informal*) **1** having the latest information: *The traffic reports are up to the minute.* ⊃ see also UP-TO-THE-MINUTE **2** fashionable and modern: *Her styles are always up to the minute.* ⊃ more at BORN, JUST, LAST¹, WAIT

● **verb** **~ sth** | **~ that…** to write down something that is said at a meeting in the official record (= the minutes): *I'd like that last remark to be minuted.*

mi·nute² /maɪˈnut/ *adj.* ⊃ see also MINUTE¹ (*superlative* **mi·nut·est**, no *comparative*) **1** extremely small **SYN** TINY: *minute amounts of chemicals in the water* ◆ *The kitchen on the boat is minute.* **2** very detailed, careful, and thorough: *a minute examination/inspection* ◆ *She remembered everything in minute detail/in the minutest detail(s).* ▶ **mi·nute·ly** *adv.*: *The agreement has been examined minutely.*

min·ute hand /ˈmɪnət ˌhænd/ *noun* [usually sing.] the hand on a watch or clock that points to the minutes ⊃ picture at CLOCK

min·ute·man /ˈmɪnətˌmæn/ *noun* (*pl.* **min·ute·men** /-ˌmɛn/) (during the American Revolution) a member of a group of men who were not soldiers but who were ready to fight immediately when they were needed

mi·nu·ti·ae /mɪˈnuʃiˌi; -ʃə/ *noun* [pl.] very small details: *the minutiae of the contract*

minx /mɪŋks/ *noun* [sing.] (*old-fashioned* or *humorous*) a confident girl or young woman who gets what she wants and does not show respect

MIPS /mɪps/ *abbr.* (*computing*) million instructions per second (a unit for measuring computer speed)

mir·a·cle /ˈmɪrəkl/ *noun* **1** [C] an act or event that does not follow the laws of nature and is believed to be caused by God **SYN** WONDER **2** [sing.] (*informal*) a lucky thing that happens that you did not expect or think was possible **SYN** WONDER: *an economic miracle* ◆ *It's a miracle (that) nobody was killed in the crash.* ◆ *It would take a miracle to make this business profitable.* ◆ *a miracle cure/drug* **3** [C] **~ of sth** a very good example or product of something **SYN** WONDER: *The car is a miracle of engineering.*
IDM **work/perform miracles** to achieve very good results: *Her exercise program has worked miracles for her.*

mi·rac·u·lous /məˈrækyələs/ *adj.* like a miracle; completely unexpected and very lucky **SYN** EXTRAORDINARY, PHE-NOMENAL: *miraculous powers of healing* ◆ *She's made a miraculous recovery.* ▶ **mi·rac·u·lous·ly** *adv.*: *They miraculously survived the plane crash.*

mi·rage /məˈrɑʒ/ *noun* **1** an effect caused by hot air in deserts or on roads, that makes you think you can see something, such as water, that is not there **2** a hope or wish that you cannot make happen because it is not realistic **SYN** ILLUSION: *His idea of love was a mirage.*

Mi·ran·da /məˈrændə/ *adj.* relating to the fact that the police must tell someone who has been arrested about their rights, including the right not to answer questions, and warn them that anything they say may be used as evidence against them: *The police read him his Miranda rights.* **ORIGIN** From the decision of the Supreme Court on the case of Miranda v. the State of Arizona in 1966.

mire /ˈmaɪər/ *noun* [U] an area of deep mud **SYN** BOG: *The wheels sank deeper into the mire.* ◆ (*figurative*) *My name had been dragged through the mire* (= my reputation was ruined). ◆ (*figurative*) *The government was sinking deeper and deeper into the mire* (= getting further into a difficult situation).

mired /ˈmaɪərd/ *adj.* [not before noun] **~ in sth** (*literary*) **1** in a difficult or unpleasant situation that you cannot escape from: *The country was mired in recession.* **2** stuck in deep mud

mir·ror 🔧 /ˈmɪrər/ *noun, verb*
● **noun** **1** [C] a piece of special flat glass that reflects images, so that you can see yourself when you look in it: *He looked at himself in the mirror.* ◆ *a rear-view mirror* (= in a car, so that the driver can see what is behind) ◆ *a side-view mirror* (= on the side of a car) ⊃ picture at MAKEUP, BICYCLE **2 a ~ of sth** [sing.] something that shows what something else is like: *The face is the mirror of the soul.*
● **verb** **1 ~ sth** to have features that are similar to something else and that show what it is like **SYN** REFLECT: *The music of the time mirrored the feeling of optimism in the country.* **2 ~ sb/sth** to show the image of someone or something on the surface of water, glass, etc. **SYN** REFLECT: *She saw herself mirrored in the window.*

mir·ror·ball /ˈmɪrərˌbɔl/ *noun* a decoration consisting of a large ball covered in small mirrors that hangs from the ceiling and turns to produce lighting effects

mir·rored /ˈmɪrərd/ *adj.* [only before noun] having a mirror or mirrors or behaving like a mirror: *mirrored doors/sunglasses*

mirror image *noun* an image of something that is like a REFLECTION of it, either because it is exactly the same or because the right side of the original object appears on the left and the left side appears on the right

mirror site (also **mir·ror**) *noun* (*computing*) a Web site that is a copy of another Web site but has a different address on the Internet

mirth /mərθ/ *noun* [U] (*formal*) happiness, fun, and the sound of people laughing **SYN** MERRIMENT: *The performance produced much mirth among the audience.*

mirth·less /ˈmərθləs/ *adj.* (*formal*) showing no real enjoyment or AMUSEMENT: *a mirthless laugh/smile* ▶ **mirth·less·ly** *adv.*

MIS /ˌɛm aɪ ˈɛs/ *abbr.* (*computing*) management information system (a system that stores information for use by business managers)

mis- /mɪs/ *prefix* (in verbs and nouns) bad or wrong; badly or wrongly: *misbehavior* ◆ *misinterpret*

mis·ad·ven·ture /ˌmɪsədˈvɛntʃər/ *noun* [C, U] (*formal*) bad luck or a small accident **SYN** MISHAP

mis·a·ligned /ˌmɪsəˈlaɪnd/ *adj.* not in the correct position in relation to something else: *a misaligned vertebra* ▶ **mis·a·lign·ment** /ˌmɪsəˈlaɪnmənt/ *noun* [U]: *The tests revealed a slight misalignment of the eyes.*

mis·an·thrope /ˈmɪsənˌθroʊp/ *noun* (*formal*) a person who hates and avoids other people

mis·an·throp·ic /ˌmɪsənˈθrɑpɪk/ *adj.* (*formal*) hating and avoiding other people ▶ **mis·an·thro·py** /mɪˈsænθrəpi/ *noun* [U]

mis·ap·pli·ca·tion /ˌmɪsæpləˈkeɪʃn/ *noun* [U, C] (*formal*) the use of something for the wrong purpose or in the wrong way

mis·ap·ply /ˌmɪsəˈplaɪ/ *verb* (**mis·ap·plies**, **mis·ap·ply·ing**, **mis·ap·plied**, **mis·ap·plied**) [usually passive] **~ sth** (*formal*) to use something for the wrong purpose or in the wrong way

mis·ap·pre·hen·sion /ˌmɪsæprɪˈhɛnʃn/ *noun* [U, C] (*formal*) a wrong idea about something, or something you believe to be true that is not true: *I was under the misapprehension that the course was for complete beginners.*

mis·ap·pro·pri·ate /ˌmɪsəˈproʊpriˌeɪt/ *verb* **~ sth** (*formal*) to take someone else's money or property for yourself, especially when they have trusted you to take care of it **SYN** EMBEZZLE ⊃ compare APPROPRIATE ▶ **mis·ap·pro·pri·a·tion** /ˌmɪsəˌproʊpriˈeɪʃn/ *noun* [U]

mis·be·got·ten /ˌmɪsbɪˈɡɑtn/ *adj.* [usually before noun] (*formal*) badly designed or planned

---

mis·be·have /ˌmɪsbɪˈheɪv/ verb [I, T] to behave badly: *Any child caught misbehaving had to stand at the front of the class.* ◆ **~ yourself** *I see the dog has been misbehaving itself again.* **ANT** BEHAVE ▶ **mis·be·hav·ior** /ˌmɪsbɪˈheɪvyər/ noun [U]

mis·cal·cu·late /ˌmɪsˈkælkyəˌleɪt/ verb **1** [T, I] to estimate an amount, a figure, a measurement, etc. wrongly: **~ (sth)** *They had seriously miscalculated the amount they would need.* ◆ **~ how long, how much, etc....** *He had miscalculated how long the trip would take.* **2** [T, I] **~ (sth)** | **~ how, what, etc....** to judge a situation wrongly **SYN** MISJUDGE: *She miscalculated the level of opposition to her proposals.* ▶ **mis·cal·cu·la·tion** /ˌmɪsˌkælkyəˈleɪʃn/ noun [C, U]: *to make a miscalculation*

mis·car·riage /ˈmɪsˌkærɪdʒ; ˌmɪsˈkærɪdʒ/ noun [C, U] the process of giving birth to a baby before it is fully developed and able to survive; an occasion when this happens: *to have a miscarriage* ◆ *The pregnancy ended in miscarriage at 11 weeks.* ➔ collocations at CHILD ➔ compare ABORTION

mis·carriage of ˈjustice noun [U, C] (*law*) a situation in which a court makes a wrong decision, especially when someone is punished when they are innocent

mis·car·ry /ˌmɪsˈkæri; ˈmɪsˌkæri/ verb (mis·car·ries, mis·car·ry·ing, mis·car·ried, mis·car·ried) **1** [I, T] **~ (sth)** to give birth to a baby before it is fully developed and able to live: *The shock caused her to miscarry.* **2** [I] (*formal*) (of a plan) to fail **SYN** COME TO NOTHING

mis·cast /ˌmɪsˈkæst/ verb (mis·cast, mis·cast) [usually passive] **~ sb (as sb/sth)** to choose an actor to play a role for which they are not suitable

mis·ceg·e·na·tion /mɪˌsedʒəˈneɪʃn; ˌmɪsɪdʒə-/ noun [U] (*formal*) the fact of children being produced by parents who are of different races, especially when one parent is white

mis·cel·la·ne·ous /ˌmɪsəˈleɪniəs/ adj. [usually before noun] consisting of many different kinds of things that are not connected and do not easily form a group **SYN** DIVERSE, VARIOUS: *a sale of miscellaneous household items* ◆ *She gave me some money to cover any miscellaneous expenses.*

mis·cel·la·ny /ˈmɪsəˌleɪni/ noun [sing.] (*formal*) a group or collection of different kinds of things **SYN** ASSORTMENT

mis·chance /ˌmɪsˈtʃæns/ noun [U, C] (*formal*) bad luck

mis·chief /ˈmɪstʃəf/ noun [U] **1** bad behavior (especially of children) that is annoying but does not cause any serious damage or harm: *Those children are always getting into mischief.* ◆ *I try to keep out of mischief.* ◆ *It's very quiet upstairs; they must be up to some mischief!* **2** the wish or tendency to behave or play in a way that causes trouble: *Her eyes were full of mischief.* **3** (*formal*) harm or injury that is done to someone or to their reputation: *The incident caused a great deal of political mischief.* **IDM** **make mischief** to do or say something deliberately to upset other people, or cause trouble between them

ˈmischief-ˌmaking noun [U] the act of deliberately causing trouble for people, such as harming their reputation

mis·chie·vous /ˈmɪstʃəvəs/ adj. **1** enjoying playing tricks and annoying people **SYN** NAUGHTY: *a mischievous boy* ◆ *a mischievous grin/smile/look* **2** (*formal*) (of an action or a statement) causing trouble, such as damaging someone's reputation: *mischievous lies/gossip* ▶ **mis·chie·vous·ly** adv.

mis·ci·ble /ˈmɪsəbl/ adj. (*technical*) (of liquids) that can be mixed together **ANT** IMMISCIBLE

mis·con·ceive /ˌmɪskənˈsiv/ verb **~ sth** (*formal*) to understand something in the wrong way **SYN** MISUNDERSTAND

mis·con·ceived /ˌmɪskənˈsivd/ adj. badly planned or judged; not carefully thought about: *a misconceived education policy* ◆ *their misconceived expectations of country life*

mis·con·cep·tion /ˌmɪskənˈsepʃn/ noun [C, U] **~ (about sth)** a belief or an idea that is not based on correct information, or that is not understood by people: *frequently held misconceptions about the disease* ◆ *a popular misconception* (= one that a lot of people have) ◆ *Let me deal with some common misconceptions.* ◆ *views based on misconception and prejudice* ➔ compare PRECONCEPTION

mis·con·duct /ˌmɪsˈkɑndʌkt/ noun [U] (*formal*) **1** unacceptable behavior, especially by a professional person: *a doctor accused of gross misconduct* (= very serious misconduct) ◆ *professional misconduct* **2** bad management of a company, etc.: *misconduct of the company's financial affairs*

mis·con·struc·tion /ˌmɪskənˈstrʌkʃn/ noun [U, C] (*formal*) a completely wrong understanding of something

mis·con·strue /ˌmɪskənˈstru/ verb **~ sth (as sth)** (*formal*) to understand someone's words or actions wrongly **SYN** MISINTERPRET: *It is easy to misconstrue confidence as arrogance.*

mis·count /ˌmɪsˈkaʊnt/ verb [T, I] **~ (sth)** to count something wrongly: *The votes had been miscounted.*

mis·cre·ant /ˈmɪskriənt/ noun (*literary*) a person who has done something wrong or illegal

mis·deed /ˌmɪsˈdid/ noun [usually pl.] (*formal*) a bad or evil act **SYN** WRONGDOING

mis·de·mean·or (CanE usually **mis·de·mean·our**) /ˌmɪsdɪˈminər/ noun **1** (*formal*) an action that is bad or unacceptable, but not very serious: *youthful misdemeanors* **2** (*law*) a crime that is not considered to be very serious ➔ compare FELONY

mis·di·ag·nose /ˌmɪsˈdaɪəgˌnoʊs; ˌmɪsdaɪəgˈnoʊs/ verb **~ sth (as sth)** to give an explanation of the nature of an illness or a problem that is not correct: *Her depression was misdiagnosed as stress.* ▶ **mis·di·ag·no·sis** /ˌmɪsdaɪəgˈnoʊsəs/ noun (pl. mis·di·ag·no·ses /-siz/)

mis·di·al /ˌmɪsˈdaɪəl; -ˈdaɪl/ verb [I, T] **~ (sth)** to call the wrong telephone number by mistake

mis·di·rect /ˌmɪsdəˈrɛkt; -daɪˈrɛkt/ verb **1** [usually passive] **~ sth** to use something in a way that is not appropriate to a particular situation: *Their efforts over the past years have been largely misdirected.* **2** **~ sb/sth** to send someone or something in the wrong direction or to the wrong place **3** **~ sb/sth** (*law*) (of a judge) to give a jury (= the group of people who decide if someone is guilty of a crime) wrong information about the law ▶ **mis·di·rec·tion** /ˌmɪsdəˈrɛkʃn; -daɪˈrɛk-/ noun [U]

mise en scène /ˌmiz ɑn ˈsɛn/ noun [sing.] (from French) **1** the arrangement of SCENERY, furniture, etc. used on the stage for a play in the theater **2** (*formal*) the place or scene where an event takes place: *Venice provided the mise-en-scène for the conference.*

mi·ser /ˈmaɪzər/ noun (*disapproving*) a person who loves money and hates spending it

mis·er·a·ble /ˈmɪzrəbl; ˈmɪzərə-/ adj. **1** very unhappy or uncomfortable: *We were cold, wet, and thoroughly miserable.* ◆ *Don't look so miserable!* **2** making you feel very unhappy or uncomfortable **SYN** DEPRESSING: *miserable housing conditions* ◆ *I spent a miserable weekend alone at home.* ◆ *What a miserable day* (= cold and wet)*!* ◆ *She knows how to make life miserable for her employees.* ◆ *The play was a miserable failure.* **3** [only before noun] (*disapproving*) (of a person) always unhappy, bad-tempered, and unfriendly **SYN** GRUMPY: *He was a miserable old man.* **4** too small in quantity **SYN** PALTRY: *How can anyone live on such a miserable wage?* ▶ **mis·er·a·bly** /-bli/ adv.: *They wandered around miserably.* ◆ *a miserably cold day* ◆ *He failed miserably as an actor.* **IDM** see SIN n.

mi·ser·ly /ˈmaɪzərli/ adj. (*disapproving*) **1** (of a person) hating to spend money **SYN** MEAN **2** (of a quantity or amount) too small **SYN** PALTRY

mis·er·y /ˈmɪzəri/ noun (pl. mis·er·ies) **1** [U] great suffering of the mind or body **SYN** DISTRESS: *Fame brought her nothing but misery.* **2** [U] very poor living conditions **SYN** POVERTY: *The vast majority of the population lives in utter misery.* **3** [C] something that causes great suffering of mind or body: *the miseries of unemployment* **IDM** **make sb's life a misery** to behave in a way that makes someone else feel very unhappy **put an animal, a**

bird, etc. out of its misery to kill a creature because it has an illness or injury that cannot be treated **put sb out of their misery** (*informal*) to stop someone from worrying by telling them something that they are anxious to know: *Put me out of my misery—did I pass or didn't I?*

mis·file /ˌmɪsˈfaɪl/ *verb* ~ **sth** to put away a document in the wrong place: *The missing letter had been misfiled.*

mis·fire /ˌmɪsˈfaɪər/ *verb* **1** [I] (of a plan or joke) to fail to have the effect that you had intended **SYN** GO WRONG: *The boys didn't know that their plot had misfired.* **2** (also **miss**) [I] (of an engine) to not work correctly because the gas does not burn at the right time: *The car sometimes misfires in cold weather.* **3** [I] (of a gun, etc.) to fail to send out a bullet, etc. when fired: *My rifle misfired twice.* ⊃ compare BACKFIRE ▸ **mis·fire** /ˈmɪsˌfaɪər/ *noun: How do you repair an engine misfire?* • *the misfire of a weapon*

mis·fit /ˈmɪsfɪt/ *noun* a person who is not accepted by a particular group of people, especially because their behavior or their ideas are very different: *a social misfit*

mis·for·tune /ˌmɪsˈfɔrtʃən/ *noun* **1** [U] bad luck: *He has known great misfortune in his life.* • *We had the misfortune to run into a violent storm.* **2** [C] an unfortunate accident, condition, or event **SYN** BLOW, DISASTER: *She bore her misfortunes bravely.*

mis·giv·ing /ˌmɪsˈɡɪvɪŋ/ *noun* [C, usually pl., U] ~ **about sth/about doing sth** feelings of doubt or anxiety about what might happen, or about whether or not something is the right thing to do: *I had grave misgivings about making the trip.* • *I read the letter with a sense of misgiving.*

mis·gov·ern /ˌmɪsˈɡʌvərn/ *verb* ~ **sth** to govern a country or state badly or unfairly ▸ **mis·gov·ern·ment** /ˌmɪsˈɡʌvərmənt; -ˈɡʌvərnmənt/ *noun* [U]

mis·guid·ed /ˌmɪsˈɡaɪdəd/ *adj.* wrong because you have understood or judged a situation badly **SYN** INAPPROPRIATE: *She only did it in a misguided attempt to help.* ⊃ thesaurus box at WRONG ▸ **mis·guid·ed·ly** *adv.*

mis·han·dle /ˌmɪsˈhændl/ *verb* **1** ~ **sth** to deal badly with a problem or situation **SYN** MISMANAGE: *The entire campaign had been badly mishandled.* **2** ~ **sb/sth** to touch or treat someone or something in a rough and careless way: *The equipment could be dangerous if mishandled.* ▸ **mis·hand·ling** *noun* [U]: *the government's mishandling of the economy*

mis·hap /ˈmɪshæp/ *noun* [C, U] a small accident or piece of bad luck that does not have serious results: *a slight mishap* • *a series of mishaps* • *I managed to get home without further mishap.*

mis·hear /ˌmɪsˈhɪr/ *verb* (mis·heard, mis·heard /-ˈhərd/) [T, I] ~ **(sb)** | ~ **what...** to fail to hear correctly what someone says, so that you think they said something else: *You may have misheard her—I'm sure she didn't mean that.* • *I thought he said he was coming today, but I must have misheard.*

mis·hit /ˌmɪsˈhɪt/ *verb* (mis·hit·ting, mis·hit, mis·hit) ~ **sth** (in a game) to hit the ball badly so that it does not go where you had intended ▸ **mis·hit** /ˈmɪshɪt/ *noun*

mish·mash /ˈmɪʃmæʃ; -maʃ/ *noun* [sing.] (*informal*, usually *disapproving*) a confused mixture of different kinds of things, styles, etc.

mis·in·form /ˌmɪsɪnˈfɔrm/ *verb* [often passive] ~ **sb** (about sth) to give someone wrong information about something: *They were deliberately misinformed about their rights.* • *a misinformed belief* (= based on wrong information) ▸ **mis·in·for·ma·tion** /ˌmɪsɪnfərˈmeɪʃn/ *noun* [U]: *a campaign of misinformation*

mis·in·ter·pret **AWL** /ˌmɪsɪnˈtərprət/ *verb* ~ **sth (as sth/doing sth)** to understand something or someone wrongly **SYN** MISCONSTRUE, MISREAD: *His comments were misinterpreted as a criticism of the project.* ⊃ compare INTERPRET ⊃ collocations at INTERPRET ▸ **mis·in·ter·pre·ta·tion** **AWL** /ˌmɪsɪnˌtərprəˈteɪʃn/ *noun* [U, C]: *A number of these statements could be open to misinterpretation* (= could be understood wrongly).

mis·judge /ˌmɪsˈdʒʌdʒ/ *verb* **1** ~ **sb/sth** | ~ **how, what,** etc.... to form a wrong opinion about a person or situation, especially in a way that makes you deal with them or it unfairly: *She now realizes that she misjudged him.* **2** ~ **sth** | ~ **how long, how far, etc....** to estimate something such as time or distance wrongly: *He misjudged the distance and his ball landed in the lake.* ▸ **mis·judg·ment** (also **mis·judge·ment**) *noun* [C, U]

mis·lay /ˌmɪsˈleɪ/ *verb* (mis·laid, mis·laid /-ˈleɪd/) ~ **sth** to put something somewhere and then be unable to find it again, especially for only a short time **SYN** LOSE: *I seem to have mislaid my keys.*

mis·lead /ˌmɪsˈlid/ *verb* (mis·led, mis·led /-ˈlɛd/) ~ **sb** (about sth) | ~ **sb** (into doing sth) to give someone the wrong idea or impression and make them believe something that is not true **SYN** DECEIVE: *He deliberately misled us about the nature of their relationship.*

mis·lead·ing /ˌmɪsˈlidɪŋ/ *adj.* giving the wrong idea or impression and making you believe something that is not true **SYN** DECEPTIVE: *misleading information/advertisements* ▸ **mis·lead·ing·ly** *adv.*: *These bats are sometimes misleadingly referred to as "flying foxes."*

mis·man·age /ˌmɪsˈmænɪdʒ/ *verb* ~ **sth** to deal with or manage something badly **SYN** MISHANDLE ▸ **mis·man·age·ment** *noun* [U]: *accusations of corruption and financial mismanagement*

mis·match /ˈmɪsmætʃ/ *noun* ~ **(between A and B)** a combination of things or people that do not go together well or are not suitable for each other: *a mismatch between people's real needs and the available facilities* ▸ **mis·match** /ˌmɪsˈmætʃ/ *verb* [often passive]: ~ **sb/sth** *They made a mismatched couple.*

mis·name /ˌmɪsˈneɪm/ *verb* [usually passive] ~ **sb/sth** to give someone or something a name that is wrong or not appropriate

mis·no·mer /ˌmɪsˈnoʊmər; ˈmɪsˌnoʊ-/ *noun* a name or a word that is not appropriate or accurate: *"Villa" was something of a misnomer; the place was no more than an old farmhouse.*

mi·so /ˈmisoʊ/ *noun* [U] a substance made from BEANS, used in Japanese cooking

mi·sog·y·nist /mɪˈsɑdʒənɪst/ *noun* (*formal*) a man who hates women ▸ **mi·sog·y·nis·tic** /mɪˌsɑdʒəˈnɪstɪk/ (also **mi·sog·y·nist**) *adj.*: *misogynistic attitudes* **mi·sog·y·ny** /mɪˈsɑdʒəni/ *noun* [U]

mis·place /ˌmɪsˈpleɪs/ *verb* ~ **sth** to put something somewhere and then be unable to find it again, especially for a short time **SYN** MISLAY

mis·placed /ˌmɪsˈpleɪst/ *adj.* **1** not appropriate or correct in the situation: *misplaced confidence/optimism/fear* **2** (of love, trust, etc.) given to a person who does not deserve or return those feelings: *misplaced loyalty*

mis·print /ˈmɪsprɪnt/ *noun* a mistake such as a spelling mistake that is made when a book, etc. is printed ⊃ thesaurus box at MISTAKE

mis·pro·nounce /ˌmɪsprəˈnaʊns/ *verb* ~ **sth** to pronounce a word wrongly ▸ **mis·pro·nun·ci·a·tion** /ˌmɪsprəˌnʌnsiˈeɪʃn/ *noun* [C, U]

mis·quote /ˌmɪsˈkwoʊt/ *verb* ~ **sb/sth** to repeat what someone has said or written in a way that is not correct: *The senator claims to have been misquoted in the article.* ▸ **mis·quo·ta·tion** /ˌmɪskwoʊˈteɪʃn/ *noun* [C, U]

mis·read /ˌmɪsˈrid/ *verb* (mis·read, mis·read /-ˈrɛd/) **1** to understand someone or something wrongly **SYN** MISINTERPRET: ~ **sth** *I'm afraid I completely misread the situation.* • ~ **sth as sth** *His confidence was misread as arrogance.* **2** ~ **sth (as sth)** to read something wrongly: *I misread the 1 as a 7.*

mis·re·port /ˌmɪsrɪˈpɔrt/ *verb* ~ **sth** | ~ **what, how, etc....** | **it is misreported that...** to give a report of an event, etc. that is not correct: *The newspapers misreported the facts of the case.*

mis·rep·re·sent /ˌmɪsreprɪˈzɛnt/ *verb* [often passive] to give information about someone or something that is not true or complete so that other people have the wrong impression about them/it: ~ **sb/sth** *He felt that the book misrepresented his opinions.* ◆ ~ **sb/sth as sth** *In the article she was misrepresented as an uncaring mother.* ◆ ~ **what, how, etc.…** *The report misrepresented what the group believes.* ▶ **mis·rep·re·sen·ta·tion** /ˌmɪsˌreprɪzen'teɪʃn; -zən-/ *noun* [C, U]: *a deliberate misrepresentation of the facts*

mis·rule /ˌmɪs'rul/ *noun* [U] (*formal*) bad government: *The regime finally collapsed after 25 years of misrule.*

miss 🔑 /mɪs/ *verb, noun*

● **verb**

> NOT HIT, CATCH, ETC. **1** [T, I] to fail to hit, reach, catch, etc. something: ~ **(sb/sth)** *How many goals has he missed this season?* ◆ *The bullet missed her by about six inches.* ◆ *She threw a plate at him and only **narrowly missed**.* ◆ ~ **doing sth** *She narrowly missed hitting him.*

> NOT HEAR/SEE **2** [T] ~ **sth** to fail to hear, see, or notice something: *The hotel is the only white building on the road—you can't miss it.* ◆ *Don't miss next week's issue!* ◆ *I missed her name.* ◆ *Your mother will know who's moved in—she **doesn't miss much**.*

> NOT UNDERSTAND **3** [T] ~ **sth** to fail to understand something: *He completely missed the joke.* ◆ *You're **missing the point** (= failing to understand the main part) of what I'm saying.*

> NOT BE/GO SOMEWHERE **4** [T] ~ **sth** to fail to be or go somewhere: *She hasn't missed a game all year.* ◆ *You missed a good party last night (= the party was good but you did not go).* ◆ *"Are you coming to the school play?" "**I wouldn't miss it for the world.**"*

> NOT DO SOMETHING **5** [T] ~ **sth** to fail to do something: *You can't afford to miss meals (= not eat meals) when you're in training.* ◆ *to miss a turn (= to not play when it is your turn in a game)* **6** [T] ~ **(doing) sth** to not take the opportunity to do something: *The sale prices were **too good to miss**.* ◆ *It was an **opportunity not to be missed**.*

> BE LATE **7** [T] ~ **sth/sb** | ~ **doing sth** to be or arrive too late for something: *If I don't leave now I'll miss my plane.* ◆ *Sorry I'm late—have I missed anything?* ◆ *"Is Ann there?" "You've just missed her (= she has just left)."*

> FEEL SAD **8** [T] to feel sad because you can no longer see someone or do something that you like: ~ **sb/sth** *She will be greatly missed when she leaves.* ◆ *What did you miss most when you were in France?* ◆ ~ **(sb/sth) doing sth** *I don't miss getting up at six every morning!*

> NOTICE SOMETHING NOT THERE **9** [T] ~ **sb/sth** to notice that someone or something is not where they/it should be: *When did you first miss the necklace?* ◆ *We seem to be missing some students this morning.*

> AVOID SOMETHING BAD **10** [T] to avoid something unpleasant **SYN** ESCAPE: ~ **sth** *If you go now you should miss the crowds.* ◆ ~ **doing sth** *He fell and just missed knocking the whole display over.*

> OF ENGINE **11** = MISFIRE

IDM **he, she, etc. doesn't miss a trick** (*informal*) used to say that someone notices every opportunity to gain an advantage **miss the boat** (*informal*) to be unable to take advantage of something because you are too late: *If you don't buy now, you may find that you've missed the boat.* **miss your guess** (*informal*) to make a mistake: *Unless I miss my guess, your computer needs a new hard drive.* **not miss a beat** | **without missing a beat** to do something or continue doing something without showing surprise or shock: *Despite the unexpected remark, she continued her speech without missing a beat.* ➔ more at MARK *n.*

PHRV **miss 'out (on sth)** to fail to benefit from something useful or enjoyable by not taking part in it: *Of course I'm coming—I don't want to miss out on all the fun!*

● **noun**

> TITLE/FORM OF ADDRESS **1 Miss** used before the family name, or the first and family name, of a woman who is not married, in order to speak or write to her politely: *That's all, thank you, Miss Lipman.* ➔ compare MRS., MS. **2 Miss** a title given to the winner of a beauty contest in a particular

country, town, etc.: *Miss California* ◆ *the Miss America contest* **3 Miss** (*informal*) used especially by men to address a young woman when they do not know her name: *Will that be all, Miss?* **4 Miss** used before a woman's first name, to speak to her politely, especially in the southern U.S.: *How are you, Miss Ellie?* **5 Miss** (*informal, humorous*) used before a description as a humorous name for a woman with that quality: *Carol is such a Miss Know-it-all—she has an answer for everything.* **6** (*old-fashioned*) a girl or young woman

> NOT HIT, CATCH, ETC. **7** a failure to hit, catch, or reach something: *He hit twelve in a row without a miss.* ➔ see also NEAR MISS

mis·sal /'mɪsl/ *noun* a book that contains the prayers, etc. that are used at MASS in the Roman Catholic Church

mis·shap·en /ˌmɪs'ʃeɪpən; ˌmɪʃ'ʃeɪ-/ *adj.* with a shape that is not normal or natural: *misshapen feet*

mis·sile /'mɪsl/ *noun* **1** a weapon that is sent through the air and that explodes when it hits the thing that it is aimed at: *nuclear missiles* ◆ *a missile base/site* ➔ collocations at WAR ➔ see also BALLISTIC MISSILE, CRUISE MISSILE, GUIDED MISSILE **2** an object that is thrown at someone to hurt them **SYN** PROJECTILE

miss·ing 🔑 /'mɪsɪŋ/ *adj.*

1 that cannot be found or that is not where they/it should be **SYN** LOST: *I never found the missing piece.* ◆ *My gloves have been missing for ages.* ◆ *Two files have gone missing.* ◆ *They still hoped to find their missing son.* **2** that has been removed, lost, or destroyed, and has not been replaced: *The book has two pages missing/two missing pages.* ◆ *He didn't notice there was anything missing from his room until later on.* **3** (of a person) not present after an accident, battle, etc. but not known to have been killed: *He was reported missing, presumed dead.* ◆ *Many soldiers were listed as missing in action.* **4** not included, often when it should have been: *Fill in the missing words in this text.* ◆ *There were several candidates missing from the list.*

,missing 'link *noun* **1** [C] something, such as a piece of information, that is necessary for someone to be able to understand a problem or in order to make something complete **2 the missing link** [sing.] an animal similar to humans that was once thought to exist at the time that APES were developing into humans

,missing 'person *noun* (*pl.* missing persons) a person who has disappeared from their home and whose family is trying to find them with the help of the police

mis·sion /'mɪʃn/ *noun*

> OFFICIAL JOB/GROUP **1** [C] an important official job that a person or group of people is given to do, especially when they are sent to another country: *a trade mission to China* ◆ *a fact-finding mission* ◆ *a mercy mission to aid homeless refugees* ➔ thesaurus box at TASK **2** [C] a group of people doing an important official job; the place where they work: *the head of the U.S. mission in Spain*

> TEACHING CHRISTIANITY **3** [C, U] the work of teaching people about Christianity, especially in a foreign country; a group of people doing such work: *a Catholic mission in Africa* **4** [C] a building or group of buildings used by a Christian mission

> YOUR DUTY **5** [C] particular work that you feel it is your duty to do: *Her mission in life was to work with the homeless.* **SYN** VOCATION

> SPACE FLIGHT **6** [C] a flight into space: *a U.S. space mission* ◆ *mission control (= the people on Earth who control and communicate with the people on the mission)*

IDM **mission accomplished** used when you have successfully completed what you had to do

mis·sion·ar·y /'mɪʃəˌneri/ *noun* (*pl.* mis·sion·ar·ies) a person who is sent to a foreign country to teach people about Christianity: *Baptist missionaries* ◆ *missionary work* ◆ (*figurative*) *She spoke about her new project with missionary zeal (= with great enthusiasm).*

the 'missionary po,sition *noun* [sing.] a position for having sex in which a man and a woman face each other, with the man lying on top of the woman

ʌ **cup**   ə **about**   eɪ **say**   aɪ **five**   ɔɪ **boy**   aʊ **now**   oʊ **go**   ɜr **bird**

mission-'critical *adj.* essential for an organization to function successfully: *mission-critical employees*

'mission ˌstatement *noun* an official statement of the aims of a company or an organization

mis·sive /'mɪsɪv/ *noun* (*formal* or *humorous*) a letter, especially a long or an official one

mis·spell /ˌmɪs'spɛl/ *verb* (**mis·spelled** or **mis·spelt** /ˌmɪs'spɛlt/) **~ sth** to spell a word wrongly ▶ **mis·spell·ing** *noun* [C, U]

mis·spend /ˌmɪs'spɛnd/ *verb* (**mis·spent, mis·spent** /-'spɛnt/) [usually passive] **~ sth** to spend time or money in a careless rather than a useful way **SYN** WASTE: *He joked that being good at cards was the sign of **a misspent youth** (= having wasted his time when he was young).*

mis·step /ˌmɪs'stɛp/ 'mɪsstɛp/ *noun* a mistake; a wrong action

mis·sus /'mɪsəz/ *noun* (*old-fashioned, informal*) (used after "the," "my," "your," "his") a man's wife: *How's the missus* (= your wife)?

miss·y /'mɪsi/ *noun* used when talking to a young girl, especially to express anger or affection: *Don't you speak to me like that, missy!*

mist /mɪst/ *noun, verb*
● *noun* **1** [U, C] a cloud of very small drops of water in the air just above the ground, that make it difficult to see: *The hills were shrouded in mist.* ◆ *Early morning mist patches will soon clear.* ◆ (*figurative*) *The origins of the story are lost in the mists of time* (= forgotten because it happened such a long time ago). ◆ (*figurative*) *She gazed at the scene through a mist of tears.* ⟳ collocations at WEATHER ⟳ compare FOG ⟳ see also MISTY **2** [sing.] a fine spray of liquid, for example, from an AEROSOL can
● *verb* **1** [T, I] **~ (sth) (up)** | **~ (over)** when something such as glass **mists** or is **misted**, it becomes covered with very small drops of water, so that it is impossible to see through it: *The windows were misted up with condensation.* ◆ *As he came in from the cold, his glasses misted up.* **2** [I, T] if your eyes **mist**, they fill with tears: **~ (over/up)** *Her eyes misted over as she listened to the speech.* ◆ **~ sth (up)** *Tears misted his eyes.* **3** [T] **~ sth** to spray the leaves of a plant with very small drops of water

mis·take 🔎 /mɪ'steɪk/ *noun, verb*
● *noun* **1** an action or an opinion that is not correct, or that produces a result that you did not want: *It's easy to make a mistake.* ◆ *This letter is addressed to someone else—there must be some mistake.* ◆ *It would be a mistake to ignore his opinion.* ◆ *Don't worry, we all make mistakes.* ◆ *You must try to learn from your mistakes.* ◆ *Leaving school so young was the biggest mistake of my life.* ◆ *I made the mistake of giving him my address.* ◆ *It was a big mistake on my part to have trusted her.* ◆ *a great/serious/terrible mistake* ◆ *It's a common mistake* (= one that a lot of people make). **2** a word, figure, etc. that is not said or written down correctly **SYN** ERROR: *It's a common mistake among learners of English.* ◆ *The waiter made a mistake (in) adding up the bill.* ◆ *Her essay is full of spelling mistakes.* **IDM by mistake** by accident; without intending to: *I took your bag instead of mine by mistake.* **make no mistake (about sth)** used to emphasize what you are saying, especially when you want to warn someone about something: *Make no mistake (about it), this is one crisis that won't just go away.*
● *verb* (**mis·took** /mɪ'stʊk/, **mis·tak·en** /mɪ'steɪkən/) to not understand or judge someone or something correctly **SYN** MISCONSTRUE: **~ sb/sth** *I admit that I mistook his intentions.* ◆ *There was no mistaking* (= it was impossible to mistake) *the bitterness in her voice.* ◆ **~ sb/sth as sb/sth** *I mistook her offer as a threat.* ◆ **~ what…** *Sorry—I mistook what you said.*
PHR V mi'stake sb/sth for sb/sth to think wrongly that someone or something is someone or something else **SYN** CONFUSE: *I think you must be mistaking me for someone else.*

THESAURUS

mistake

error ◆ inaccuracy ◆ slip ◆ misprint

These are all words for a word, figure, or fact that is not said, written down, or typed correctly.

mistake a word or figure that is not said or written down correctly: *It's a common mistake among learners of English.* ◆ *spelling mistakes*

error (*somewhat formal*) a word, figure, etc. that is not said or written down correctly: *There are too many errors in your work.* **NOTE** Error is a more formal way of saying **mistake**.

inaccuracy (*somewhat formal*) a piece of information that is not exactly correct: *The article is full of inaccuracies.*

slip a small mistake, usually made by being careless or not paying attention

misprint a small mistake in a printed text

PATTERNS
- a(n) mistake/error/inaccuracy/slip/misprint **in** sth
- to **make** a(n) mistake/error/slip
- to **contain/be full of/include** mistakes/errors/inaccuracies/misprints

mis·tak·en 🔎 /mɪ'steɪkən/ *adj.*
1 [not before noun] **~ (about sb/sth)** wrong in your opinion or judgment: *You are completely mistaken about Jane.* ◆ *Unless I'm very much mistaken, that's Paul's wife over there.* ⟳ thesaurus box at WRONG **2** based on a wrong opinion or bad judgment **SYN** MISGUIDED: *mistaken views/ideas* ◆ *I told her my secret in the mistaken belief that I could trust her.* ▶ **mis·tak·en·ly** *adv.*: *He mistakenly believed that his family would stand by him.*

misˌtaken iˈdentity *noun* [U] a situation in which you think wrongly that you recognize someone or have found the person you are looking for: *He was shot in what seems to have been a case of mistaken identity.*

mis·ter /'mɪstər/ *noun* **1 Mister** the full form, not often used in writing, of the abbreviation *Mr.* **2** (*informal*) used, especially by children, to address a man whose name they do not know: *Please, mister, can we have our ball back?*

mis·time /ˌmɪs'taɪm/ *verb* **~ sth** to do something at the wrong time, especially when this makes something bad or unpleasant happen: *The horse completely mistimed the jump and threw its rider.* ▶ **mis·tim·ing** *noun* [U]: *The failure of the talks was mainly due to insensitivity and mistiming.*

mis·tle·toe /'mɪslˌtoʊ/ *noun* [U] a plant with small, shiny, white berries (BERRY) that grows on other trees and is often used as a decoration at Christmas: *the tradition of kissing under the mistletoe*

mis·took pt of MISTAKE

mis·treat /ˌmɪs'trit/ *verb* **~ sb/sth** to treat a person or an animal in a cruel, unkind, or unfair way **SYN** ILL-TREAT, MALTREAT ▶ **mis·treat·ment** *noun* [U]

mis·tress /'mɪstrəs/ *noun* **1** a man's (usually a married man's) **mistress** is a woman that he is having a regular sexual relationship with and who is not his wife **2** (in the past) the female head of a house, especially one who employed servants: *the mistress of the house* **3** (*formal, old-fashioned*) the female owner of a dog or other animal **4** (**of sth**) (*formal*) a woman who is in a position of authority or control, or who is highly skilled in something: *She wants to be mistress of her own affairs* (= to organize her own life). ⟳ compare MASTER

mis·tri·al /'mɪsˌtraɪəl/ *noun* (*law*) **1** a trial that is not considered valid because of a mistake in the way it has been conducted **2** a trial in which the jury cannot reach a decision

mis·trust /ˌmɪsˈtrʌst/ *verb, noun*

- **verb ~ sb/sth** to have no confidence in someone or something because you think they may be harmful; to not trust someone or something **SYN** DISTRUST ⊃ note at DISTRUST

- **noun** [U, sing.] a feeling that you cannot trust someone or something **SYN** SUSPICION: *a climate of mistrust and fear* ♦ *She has a deep mistrust of strangers.* ▸ **mis·trust·ful** /ˌmɪsˈtrʌstfl/ *adj.*: **~ (of sb/sth)** *Some people are very mistrustful of computers.* **mis·trust·ful·ly** /-fəli/ *adv.*

mist·y /ˈmɪsti/ *adj.* **1** with a lot of MIST: *a misty morning* **2** not clear or bright **SYN** BLURRED: *misty memories* ♦ (*literary*) *His eyes grew misty* (= full of tears) *as he talked.*

ˈmisty-ˌeyed *adj.* feeling full of emotion, as if you are going to cry

mis·un·der·stand /ˌmɪsʌndərˈstænd/ *verb* (mis·un·der·stood, mis·un·der·stood /-ˈstʊd/) [T, I] **~ (sb/sth)** | **~ what, how, etc....** to fail to understand someone or something correctly: *I completely misunderstood her intentions.* ♦ *Don't misunderstand me—I am grateful for all you've done.* ♦ *I thought he was her husband—I must have misunderstood.*

mis·un·der·stand·ing /ˌmɪsʌndərˈstændɪŋ/ *noun* **1** [U, C] a situation in which a comment, an instruction, etc. is not understood correctly: *There must be some misunderstanding —I thought I ordered the smaller model.* ♦ **~ of/about sth** *There is still a fundamental misunderstanding about the real purpose of this work.* ♦ **~ between A and B** *All contracts are translated to avoid any misunderstanding between the companies.* **2** [C] a slight disagreement or argument: *We had a little misunderstanding over the bill.*

mis·un·der·stood /ˌmɪsʌndərˈstʊd/ *adj.* having qualities that people do not see or fully understand: *a much misunderstood illness* ♦ *She felt very alone and misunderstood.*

mis·use *noun, verb*

- **noun** /ˌmɪsˈyus/ [U, C, usually sing.] the act of using something in a dishonest way or for the wrong purpose **SYN** ABUSE: *alcohol/drug misuse* ♦ *the misuse of power/authority*

- **verb** /ˌmɪsˈyuz/ **1 ~ sth** to use something in the wrong way or for the wrong purpose **SYN** ABUSE, ILL-TREAT: *individuals who misuse power for their own ends* **2 ~ sb** to treat someone badly and/or unfairly

mite /maɪt/ *noun* **1** a very small creature like a spider that lives on plants, animals, carpets, etc. ⊃ see also DUST MITE **2** (*old-fashioned*) a small child or animal, especially one that you feel sorry for: *Poor little mite!* **3** (*old-fashioned*) a small amount of something: *The place looked a mite* (= a little) *expensive.*

mi·ter /ˈmaɪtər/ *noun, verb*

- **noun 1** a tall pointed hat worn by a BISHOP at special ceremonies as a symbol of their position and authority **2** (also ˈmiter joint) a corner joint, formed by two pieces of wood each cut at an angle, as in a picture frame ⊃ picture at DOVETAIL

- **verb ~ sth** (*technical*) to join two pieces of wood together with a miter joint

mit·i·gate /ˈmɪtəˌgeɪt/ *verb* **~ sth** (*formal*) to make something less harmful, serious, etc. **SYN** ALLEVIATE: *action to mitigate poverty* ♦ *Soil erosion was mitigated by the planting of trees.*

mit·i·gat·ing /ˈmɪtəˌgeɪtɪŋ/ *adj.* [only before noun] **~ circumstances/factors** (*formal* or *law*) circumstances or factors that make a crime or someone's actions easier to understand, so that the punishment may be less severe

mit·i·ga·tion /ˌmɪtəˈgeɪʃn/ *noun* [U] (*formal*) a reduction in how unpleasant, serious, etc. something is **IDM** **in mitigation** (*law*) with the aim of making a crime seem less serious or easier to forgive: *In mitigation, the defense lawyer said his client was seriously depressed at the time of the assault.*

mi·to·chon·dri·on /ˌmaɪtəˈkɑndriən/ *noun* (*pl.* mi·to·chon·dri·a /-driə/) (*biology*) a small part found in most cells,

in which the energy in food is released ▸ **mi·to·chon·dri·al** /-driəl/ *adj.*: *mitochondrial DNA*

mi·to·sis /maɪˈtoʊsəs/ *noun* [U] (*biology*) the process of cell division

mitt /mɪt/ *noun* **1** (in baseball) a large, thick, leather glove worn for catching the ball ⊃ picture at BASEBALL, GLOVE ⊃ see also OVEN MITT **2** [usually pl.] (*slang*) a hand: *I'd love to get my mitts on one of those.* **3** = MITTEN

mit·ten /ˈmɪtn/ (also mitt) *noun* a type of glove that covers the four fingers together and the thumb separately ⊃ picture at GLOVE

THESAURUS

mix

stir ♦ mingle ♦ blend

These words all refer to substances, qualities, ideas, or feelings combining or being combined.

mix to combine two or more substances, qualities, ideas, or feelings, usually in a way that means they cannot easily be separated; to be combined in this way: *Mix all the ingredients together in a bowl.* ♦ *Oil and water do not mix.*

stir to move a liquid or substance around, using a spoon or something similar, in order to mix it thoroughly: *She stirred her coffee.*

mingle to combine or be combined **NOTE** Mingle can be used to talk about sounds, colors, feelings, ideas, qualities, or substances. It is used in written English to talk about how a scene or event appears to someone or how they experience it: *The sounds of laughter and singing mingled in the evening air.* ♦ *He felt a kind of happiness mingled with regret.*

blend to mix two or more substances or flavors together; to be mixed together: *Blend the flour with the milk to make a smooth paste.*

MIX OR BLEND?

If you **blend** things when you are cooking, you usually combine them more completely than if you just **mix** them. Mix can be used to talk about colors, feelings, or qualities as well as food and substances. In this meaning, **blend** is mostly used in the context of cooking. It is also, used to talk about art, music, fashion, etc. with the meaning of "combine in an attractive way."

PATTERNS

- to mix/mingle/blend (sth) **with** sth
- to mix/stir/blend sth **into** sth
- to mix/stir/mingle/blend sth **together**
- to mix/stir/blend **ingredients**
- to mix/mingle/blend **flavors**
- to mix/blend **colors**
- to mix/stir/blend sth **thoroughly/well/gently**

---

mix /mɪks/ *verb, noun*

- **verb**

▷ **COMBINE 1** [I, T] if two or more substances **mix** or you **mix** them, they combine, usually in a way that means they cannot easily be separated: *Oil and water do not mix.* ♦ **~ with sth** *Oil does not mix with water.* ♦ **~ A and B (together)** *Mix all the ingredients together in a bowl.* ♦ *If you mix blue and yellow, you get green.* ♦ **~ A with B** *I don't like to mix business with pleasure* (= combine social events with doing business). **2** [T] to prepare something by combining two or more different substances: **~ sth** *With this line of paints, you can mix your own colors.* ♦ **~ sth for sb** *Why don't you mix a cocktail for our guests?* ♦ **~ sb sth** *Why don't you mix our guests a cocktail?* **3** [I] if two or more things, people, or activities **do not mix**, they are likely to cause problems or danger if they are combined: *Children and fireworks don't mix.*

▷ **MEET PEOPLE 4** [I] **~ (with sb)** to meet and talk to different

---

t **tea** ţ **butter** d **did** k **cat** g **got** tʃ **chin** dʒ **June** f **fall**

people, especially at social events **SYN** SOCIALIZE: *They don't mix much with the neighbors.*
> MUSIC/SOUNDS **5** [T] ~ sth (*technical*) to combine different recordings of voices and/or instruments to produce a single piece of music
IDM be/get mixed up in sth to be/become involved in something, especially something illegal or dishonest be/get mixed up with sb to be/become friendly with or involved with someone that other people do not approve of mix and match to combine things in different ways for different purposes: *You can mix and match courses to suit your requirements.* mix it up (with sb) (*informal*) to argue with someone or cause trouble
PHRV ,mix sth↔'in (with sth) to add one substance to others, especially in cooking: *Mix the remaining cream in with the sauce.* 'mix sth into sth to combine one substance with others, especially in cooking: *Mix the fruit into the rest of the batter.* 'mix sth into/to sth to produce something by combining two or more substances, especially in cooking **SYN** BLEND: *Add the milk and mix to a smooth dough.* ,mix sth↔'up to change the order or arrangement of a group of things, especially by mistake or in a way that you do not want: *Someone has mixed up all the application forms.* ⊃ related noun MIX-UP ,mix sb/sth 'up (with sb/sth) to think wrongly that someone or something is someone or something else **SYN** CONFUSE: *I think you must be mixing me up with someone else.* ⊃ see also MIXED-UP

• noun
> COMBINATION **1** [C, usually sing.] a combination of different people or things **SYN** BLEND: *a school with a good social mix of children* ♦ *The town offers a fascinating mix of old and new.* **2** [C, U] a combination of things that you need to make something, often sold as a powder to which you add water, etc.: *a cake mix* ♦ *cement mix*
> IN POPULAR MUSIC **3** [C] = REMIX **4** [sing.] the particular way that instruments and voices are arranged in a piece of music **5** [C] an arrangement of several songs or pieces of music into one continuous piece, especially for dancing

mixed 🔑 /mɪkst/ *adj.*
1 having both good and bad qualities or feelings: *The weather has been very mixed recently.* ♦ *I still have mixed feelings about going to Brazil* (= I am not sure what to think). ♦ *The play was given a mixed reception by the critics* (= some liked it, some did not). ♦ *U.S. athletes had mixed fortunes in yesterday's competition.* **2** [only before noun] consisting of different kinds of people, for example, people from different races and cultures: *a mixed community* ♦ *people of mixed race* ♦ *a mixed marriage* (= between two people of different races or religions) **3** [only before noun] consisting of different types of the same thing: *a mixed salad* **4** [usually before noun] of or for both males and females: *I'd rather not talk about it in mixed company.* **IDM** SEE BLESSING

,mixed-a'bility *adj.* [usually before noun] with or for students who have different levels of ability: *a mixed-ability class* ♦ *mixed-ability teaching*
,mixed 'bag *noun* [sing.] (*informal*) a collection of things or people of very different types
,mixed 'doubles *noun* [U] (in TENNIS, etc.) a game in which a man and a woman play together against another man and woman
,mixed e'conomy *noun* an economic system in a country in which some companies are owned by the state and some are private
,mixed 'farming *noun* [U] a system of farming in which farmers both grow crops and keep animals
,mixed 'metaphor *noun* a combination of two or more METAPHORS or IDIOMS that produces a ridiculous effect, for example, "He put his foot down with a firm hand."
,mixed 'number *noun* (*mathematics*) a number consisting of a whole number and a PROPER FRACTION, for example 3¼
,mixed-'up *adj.* (*informal*) confused because of mental, emotional, or social problems: *a mixed-up kid/teenager*

mix·er /ˈmɪksər/ *noun* **1** a machine or device used for mixing things: *a food mixer* ⊃ see also CEMENT MIXER **2** a drink such as fruit juice that is not alcoholic and that can be mixed with alcohol: *low-calorie mixers* **3** (*technical*) a device used for mixing together different sound or picture signals in order to produce a single sound or picture; a person whose job is to operate this device **4** (*old-fashioned*) a party where people can meet one another and make new friends
'mixing ,bowl *noun* a large bowl for mixing food in
'mixing ,desk *noun* a piece of electronic equipment for mixing sounds, used especially when recording music or to improve its sound after recording it

mix·ture 🔑 /ˈmɪkstʃər/ *noun*
1 [C, U] a substance made by mixing other substances together: *a soy sauce and garlic mixture* ♦ *Add the eggs to the mixture and beat well.* **2** [C, usually sing.] a combination of different things: *The city is a mixture of old and new buildings.* ♦ *We listened to the news with a mixture of surprise and horror.* **3** [C] (*technical*) a combination of two or more substances that mix together without any chemical reaction taking place ⊃ compare COMPOUND **4** [U] the act of mixing different substances together

'mix-up *noun* (*informal*) a situation that is full of confusion, especially because someone has made a mistake: *There has been a mix-up over the dates.*
miz·zen (also mizen) /ˈmɪzn/ *noun* (*technical*) **1** (also miz-zen-mast /ˈmɪzn,mæst/) the MAST of a ship that is behind the main mast **2** (also miz·zen·sail /ˈmɪzn,seɪl/) a sail on the mizzen of a ship
ml *abbr.* (*pl.* ml or mls) MILLILITER(S): *25ml water*
MLA /ˌɛm ɛl ˈeɪ/ *abbr.* (*CanE*) Member of the Legislative Assembly (the parliament of a PROVINCE)

mm 🔑 *abbr., exclamation*
• **abbr.** MILLIMETER(S): *rainfall 6mm* ♦ *a 35mm camera*
• **exclamation** (also mmm) /m; mm/ the way of writing the sound that people make to show that they are listening to someone or that they agree, they are thinking, they like something, they are not sure, etc.: *Mm, I know what you mean.* ♦ *Mm, what a delicious cake!* ♦ *Mmm, I'm not so sure that's a good idea.*
MMR /ˌɛm ɛm ˈɑr/ *abbr.* MEASLES, MUMPS, RUBELLA: *an MMR jab* (= a VACCINE shot to prevent these three diseases)
MMS /ˌɛm ɛm ˈɛs/ *noun* [U, C] the abbreviation for "Multimedia Messaging Service" (a system for sending color pictures and sounds as well as short written messages from one cell phone to another): *an MMS message* ♦ *He sent me an MMS.* ⊃ see also TEXT
MN *abbr.* (in writing) Minnesota
MNA /ˌɛm ɛn ˈeɪ/ *abbr.* (*CanE*) Member of the National Assembly (the parliament in Québec)
mne·mon·ic /nɪˈmɑnɪk/ *noun* a word, sentence, poem, etc. that helps you to remember something ▶ mne·mon·ic *adj.* [only before noun]: *a mnemonic device*
MO /ˌɛm ˈoʊ/ *abbr.* **1** (also M.O.) MODUS OPERANDI **2** (in writing) Missouri
moan /moʊn/ *verb, noun*
• **verb 1** [I, T] (of a person) to make a long deep sound, usually expressing unhappiness, suffering, or physical pleasure **SYN** GROAN: *The injured man was lying on the ground, moaning.* ♦ ~ in/with sth *to moan in/with pain* ♦ + speech *"I might never see you again," she moaned.* **2** [I] ~ (about sth) (*informal*) to complain about something in a way that other people find annoying: *They're always moaning and groaning about how much they have to do.* **3** [I] (*literary*) (especially of the wind) to make a long deep sound ▶ moan·er *noun*
• **noun 1** [C] a long deep sound, usually expressing unhappiness, suffering, or physical pleasure **SYN** GROAN: *a low moan of despair/anguish* **2** [sing.] (*literary*) a long deep sound, especially the sound that is made by the wind
moat /moʊt/ *noun* a deep wide channel that was dug around a castle, etc. and filled with water to make it more

difficult for enemies to attack ⊃ **picture at** BUILDING
▶ **moat·ed** /'moʊtəd/ adj. [usually before noun]: *a moated manor house*

mob /mɑb/ noun, verb
● **noun 1** [C] a large crowd of people, especially one that may become violent or cause trouble: *an angry/unruly mob* ◆ *The mob was preparing to storm the building.* ◆ *an excited mob of fans* ◆ **mob rule** (= a situation in which a mob has control, rather than people in authority) ⊃ **see also** LYNCH MOB **2 the Mob** [sing.] (*informal*) the people involved in organized crime; the MAFIA
● **verb** (-bb-) [usually passive] **1** ~ **sth** if a crowd of birds or animals **mobs** another bird or animal, they gather around it and attack it **2** ~ **sb** if a person is **mobbed** by a crowd of people, the crowd gathers around them in order to see them and get their attention SYN BESIEGE

mob cap noun a light cotton cap covering all the hair, worn by women in the 18th and 19th centuries

mo·bile 🔍 adj., noun
● **adj.** /'moʊbl/ **1** [usually before noun] that is not permanently in one place and can be moved easily and quickly: *mobile equipment* ◆ *a mobile classroom/clinic/library* (= one inside a vehicle) ⊃ **compare** STATIONARY **2** [not usually before noun] (of a person) able to move or travel around easily: *a kitchen especially designed for the elderly or people who are less mobile* ◆ *You really need to be mobile* (= have a car) *if you live in the country.* ANT IMMOBILE **3** (of people) able to change your social class, your job, or the place where you live easily: *a highly mobile workforce* (= people who can move easily from place to place) ⊃ **see also** UPWARDLY MOBILE **4** (of a face or its features) changing shape or expression easily and often
● **noun 1** /'moʊbil/ a decoration made from wire, etc. that is hung from the ceiling and that has small objects hanging from it that move when the air around them moves **2** /'moʊbl/ = CELL PHONE

mobile de·vice noun any small computing device that will fit into your pocket, such as a PDA or SMARTPHONE ⊃ **compare** MID

mobile home noun a small building for people to live in that is made in a factory and moved to a permanent place ⊃ **picture at** HOUSE ⊃ **compare** TRAILER

mobile phone noun = CELL PHONE

mo·bil·i·ty /moʊ'bɪləti/ noun [U] **1** the ability to move easily from one place, social class, or job to another: *social/geographical/career mobility* ◆ *Is a college education the ticket to upward mobility?* **2** the ability to move or travel around easily: *An electric wheelchair has given her greater mobility.*

mo·bi·lize /'moʊbəˌlaɪz/ verb **1** [T, I] ~ **(sb)** to work together in order to achieve a particular aim; to organize a group of people to do this SYN RALLY: *The unions mobilized thousands of workers in a protest against the cuts.* **2** [T] ~ **sth** to find and start to use something that is needed for a particular purpose SYN MARSHAL: *They were unable to mobilize the resources they needed.* **3** [T, I] ~ **(sb/sth)** if a country **mobilizes** its army, or if a country or army **mobilizes**, it makes itself ready to fight in a war: *The troops were ordered to mobilize.* ⊃ **compare** DEMOBILIZE ▶ **mo·bi·li·za·tion** /ˌmoʊbələ'zeɪʃn/ noun [U]

Mö·bi·us strip (also **Moe-bi·us strip**) /'moʊbiəs ˌstrɪp/ noun a surface with one continuous side, formed by joining the ends of a strip of material after twisting one end through 180 degrees

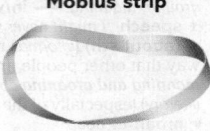
Möbius strip

mob·ster /'mɑbstər/ noun a member of a group of people who are involved in organized crime, especially the MAFIA

moc·ca·sin /'mɑkəsn/ noun a flat shoe that is made from soft leather and has large STITCHES around the front, of a type originally worn by Native Americans ⊃ **picture at** SHOE

mo·cha /'moʊkə/ noun **1** [U] a type of coffee of very good quality **2** [C, U] a drink made or flavored with this, often with chocolate added

mock /mɑk/ verb, adj.
● **verb 1** [T, I] ~ **(sb/sth)** | ~ **(sb)** + **speech** to laugh at someone or something in an unkind way, especially by copying what they say or do SYN MAKE FUN OF: *He's always mocking my French accent.* ◆ *The other children mocked her, laughing behind their hands.* ◆ *You can mock, but at least I'm willing to have a try!* **2** [T] ~ **sth** (*formal*) to show no respect for something: *The new exam mocked the needs of the majority of children.* ▶ **mock·er** noun
● **adj.** [only before noun] **1** not sincere SYN SHAM: *mock horror/surprise* **2** that is a copy of something; not real: *a mock election* ◆ *a mock interview/exam* (= used to practice for the real one)

mock·er·y /'mɑkəri/ noun **1** [U] comments or actions that are intended to make someone or something seem ridiculous SYN RIDICULE, SCORN: *She couldn't stand any more of their mockery.* **2** [sing.] (*disapproving*) an action, a decision, etc. that is a failure and that is not as it is supposed to be SYN TRAVESTY: *It was a mockery of a trial.*
IDM **make a mockery of sth** to make something seem ridiculous or useless: *The trial made a mockery of justice.*

mock·ing /'mɑkɪŋ/ adj. (of behavior, an expression, etc.) showing that you think someone or something is ridiculous SYN CONTEMPTUOUS: *a mocking smile* ◆ *Her voice was faintly mocking.* ▶ **mock·ing·ly** adv.

mock·ing·bird /'mɑkɪŋˌbərd/ noun a gray and white bird that can copy the songs of other birds

mock turtleneck noun a type of shirt or sweater that fits very closely around the lower neck

mock-up noun a model or a copy of something, often the same size as it, that is used for testing, or for showing people what the real thing will look like

mod verb ⊃ MODDING

mod·al /'moʊdl/ (also **modal verb**, **modal auxiliary**, **modal auxiliary verb**) noun (*grammar*) a verb such as *can*, *may*, or *will* that is used with another verb (not a modal) to express possibility, permission, intention, etc. ▶ **mod·al** adj. ⊃ **compare** AUXILIARY

modal verbs

- The **modal verbs** are **can**, **could**, **may**, **might**, **must**, **ought to**, **shall**, **should**, **will**, and **would**. Dare, need, have to, and used to also share some of the features of modal verbs.
- Modal verbs have only one form. They have no past or present participles and do not add -s to the 3rd person singular form: *He can speak three languages.* ◆ *She will try and visit tomorrow.*
- Modal verbs are followed by the infinitive of another verb without **to**. The exceptions are **ought to** and **used to**: *You must find a job.* ◆ *You ought to stop smoking.* ◆ *I used to smoke, but I quit two years ago.*
- Questions are formed without **do/does** in the present or **did** in the past: *Can I invite Mary?* ◆ *Should I have invited Mary?*
- Negative sentences are formed with **not** or the short form **-n't** and do not use **do/does** or **did**: *You shouldn't invite Mary.* ◆ *The error will not have affected our results.*
- You will find more help with how to use modal verbs at the dictionary entries for each verb.

mo·dal·i·ty /moʊ'dæləti/ noun (pl. **mo·dal·i·ties**) **1** [C] (*formal*) the particular way in which something exists, is experienced, or is done: *They are researching a different modality of treatment for the disease.* **2** [U] (*linguistics*) the ideas expressed by modals **3** [C] (*biology*) one of the kind of senses that the body uses to experience things: *the visual and auditory modalities*

mod·ding /'mɑdɪŋ/ *noun* [U] (*informal, computing*) the activity of changing a piece of computer equipment or a computer program so that it works in a way that was not intended by the producer: *There are stiff penalties for illegal modding.*
▶ **mod** *verb* (-dd-): ~ **sth** *a specially modded system*

mode **AWL** /moʊd/ *noun* **1** [C] a particular way of doing something; a particular type of something: *a mode of communication* ◆ *a mode of behavior* ◆ *environmentally-friendly modes of transport* **2** [C, U] the way in which a piece of equipment is set to perform a particular task: *Switch the camera into (the) automatic mode.* **3** [U] a particular way of feeling or behaving: *to be in holiday mode* **4** [C, usually sing.] a particular style or fashion in clothes, art, etc.: *a rock video made by a director who really understands the mode* ⮕ see also A LA MODE, MODISH **5** [sing.] (*technical*) a set of notes in music that form a SCALE: *the major/minor mode* **6** [sing.] (*mathematics*) the value that appears most frequently in a series of numbers

mod·el 🔑 /'mɑdl/ *noun, verb*
● *noun*
▸ SMALL COPY **1** a copy of something, usually smaller than the original object: *a **working model** (= one in which the parts move) of a fire engine* ◆ *a model airplane* ◆ *The architect had produced a **scale model** of the proposed shopping complex.*
▸ FASHION **2** a person whose job is to wear and show new styles of clothes and be photographed wearing them: *a fashion model* ◆ *a male model*
▸ DESIGN **3** a particular design or type of product: *The latest models will be on display at the motor show.*
▸ FOR ARTIST **4** a person who is employed to be painted, drawn, photographed, etc. by an artist or photographer
▸ EXAMPLE TO COPY **5** something such as a system that can be copied by other people: *The nation's constitution provided a model that other countries followed.* **6** (*approving*) a person or thing that is considered an excellent example of something: *It was a model of clarity.* ◆ *a model student* ◆ *a model farm* (= one that has been specially designed to work well) ⮕ see also ROLE MODEL
▸ DESCRIPTION OF SYSTEM **7** a simple description of a system, used for explaining how something works or for calculating what might happen, etc.: *a mathematical model for determining the safe level of pesticides in food* ⮕ collocations at SCIENTIFIC
● *verb* (-l-, *CanE usually* -ll-)
▸ WORK AS MODEL **1** [I] to work as a model for an artist or in the fashion industry
▸ CLOTHES **2** [T] ~ **sth** to wear clothes in order to show them to people who might want to buy them: *The wedding gown is being modeled for us by the designer's daughter.*
▸ CREATE COPY **3** [T] ~ **sth** to create a copy of an activity, a situation, etc. so that you can study it before dealing with the real thing SYN SIMULATE: *The program can model a typical home page for you.*
▸ CLAY, ETC. **4** [T] ~ **sth** to shape CLAY, etc. in order to make something: *a statue modeled in bronze*
PHR V **'model yourself on sb** to copy the behavior, style, etc. of someone you like and respect in order to be like them: *As a politician, he modeled himself on Kennedy.* **'model sth on/after sth** to make something so that it looks, works, etc. like something else: *The country's government is modeled on the U.S. system.*

mod·el·er /'mɑdl·ər/ *noun* **1** a person who makes models of objects **2** a person who makes a simple description of a system or a process that can be used to explain it, etc.

model 'home *noun* a house in a group of new houses that has been painted and filled with furniture, so that people can see what the houses will be like

mod·el·ing /'mɑdl·ɪŋ/ *noun* [U] **1** the work of a fashion model: *a career in modeling* ◆ *a modeling agency* **2** the activity of making models of objects: *clay modeling* **3** the work of making a simple description of a system or a process that can be used to explain it, etc.: *mathematical/statistical/computer modeling*

mo·dem /'moʊdəm/ *noun* a device that connects one computer system to another using a telephone line so that data can be sent

mod·er·ate *adj., verb, noun*
● *adj.* /'mɑdərət/ **1** that is neither very good, large, hot, etc. nor very bad, small, cold, etc.: *students of moderate ability* ◆ *Even moderate amounts of the drug can be fatal.* ◆ *The team enjoyed only moderate success last season.* ◆ *Cook over a moderate heat.* **2** having or showing opinions, especially about politics, that are not extreme: *moderate views/policies* ◆ *a moderate Republican* **3** staying within limits that are considered to be reasonable by most people: *a moderate drinker* ◆ *moderate salary demands* ANT IMMODERATE
● *verb* /'mɑdə,reɪt/ **1** [I, T] to become or make something become less extreme, severe, etc.: *By evening the wind had moderated slightly.* ◆ ~ **sth** *We agreed to moderate our original demands.* **2** [T, I] ~ **(sth)** to be in charge of a discussion or debate and make sure it is fair: *The television debate was moderated by a law professor.* ◆ *a moderated newsgroup*
● *noun* /'mɑdərət/ a person who has opinions, especially about politics, that are not extreme

mod·er·ate·ly /'mɑdərətli/ *adv.* **1** to an average extent; fairly but not very SYN REASONABLY: *a moderately successful career* ◆ *She only did moderately well on the exam.* ◆ *Cook in a moderately hot oven.* **2** within reasonable limits: *He only drinks (alcohol) moderately.*

mod·er·a·tion /,mɑdə'reɪʃn/ *noun* [U] the quality of being reasonable and not being extreme: *There was a call for moderation on the part of the trade unions.* ◆ *Alcohol should only ever be consumed in moderation* (= in small quantities).

mod·er·a·tor /'mɑdə,reɪtər/ *noun* **1** a person whose job is to help the two sides in a disagreement to reach an agreement ⮕ see also MEDIATOR **2** a person whose job is to make sure that a discussion or a debate is fair **3** (*computing*) a person who is responsible for preventing offensive material from being published on a Web site: *moderators of online discussion groups*

mod·ern 🔑 /'mɑdərn/ *adj.*
1 [only before noun] of the present time or recent times SYN CONTEMPORARY: *the modern industrial world* ◆ *Modern European history* ◆ *modern Greek* ◆ *Stress is a major problem of modern life.* **2** [only before noun] (of styles in art, music, fashion, etc.) new and intended to be different from traditional styles SYN CONTEMPORARY: *modern art/architecture/drama/jazz* **3** (*usually approving*) using the latest technology, designs, materials, etc. SYN UP-TO-DATE: *a modern computer system* ◆ *modern methods of farming* ◆ *the most modern, well-equipped hospital in Seattle* **4** (of ways of behaving, thinking, etc.) new and not always accepted by most members of society: *She has very modern ideas about educating her children.*

modern 'dance *noun* [U] a form of dance that was developed in the early 20th century by people who did not like the restrictions of traditional BALLET

modern-'day *adj.* [only before noun] **1** of the present time SYN CONTEMPORARY: *modern-day America* **2** used to describe a modern form of someone or something, usually someone or something bad or unpleasant, that existed in the past: *It has been called modern-day slavery.*

modern 'English *noun* [U] the English language in the form it has been in since about 1500

mod·ern·ism /'mɑdər,nɪzəm/ *noun* [U] **1** modern ideas or methods **2** a style and movement in art, ARCHITECTURE, and literature popular in the middle of the 20th century in which modern ideas, methods, and materials were used rather than traditional ones ⮕ compare POSTMODERNISM
▶ **mod·ern·ist** /-nɪst/ *adj.* [only before noun]: *modernist art* **mod·ern·ist** *noun*

mod·ern·is·tic /,mɑdər'nɪstɪk/ *adj.* (of a painting, building, piece of furniture, etc.) painted, designed, etc. in a very modern style

mo·der·ni·ty /məˈdɜrnəti; mɑ-/ noun [U] the condition of being new and modern

mod·ern·ize /ˈmɑdərˌnaɪz/ verb **1** [T] ~ sth to make a system, methods, etc. more modern and more suitable for use at the present time **SYN** UPDATE: *The company is investing $9 million to modernize its factories.* **2** [I] to start using modern equipment, ideas, etc.: *Unfortunately we lack the resources to modernize.* ► **mod·ern·i·za·tion** /ˌmɑdərnəˈzeɪʃn/ noun [U]

modern ˈlanguage noun a language that is spoken or written now, especially a European language, such as French or Spanish, that you study at school, college, or university: *the department of modern languages* ♦ *a degree in modern languages*

mod·est /ˈmɑdəst/ adj. **1** (approving) not talking much about your own abilities or possessions: *She's very modest about her success.* ♦ *You're too modest!* **ANT** IMMODEST **2** not very large, expensive, important, etc.: *modest improvements/reforms* ♦ *He charged a relatively modest fee.* ♦ *a modest little house* ♦ *The research was carried out on a modest scale.* **3** (of people, especially women, or their clothes) shy about showing much of the body; not intended to attract attention, especially in a sexual way **SYN** DEMURE: *a modest dress* **ANT** IMMODEST ► **mod·est·ly** adv.

mod·es·ty /ˈmɑdəsti/ noun [U] **1** the fact of not talking much about your abilities or possessions: *He accepted the award with characteristic modesty.* ♦ *I hate false* (= pretended) *modesty.* **2** the action of behaving or dressing so that you do not show your body or attract sexual attention **3** the state of being not very large, expensive, important, etc.: *They tried to disguise the modesty of their achievements.*

mod·i·cum /ˈmɑdɪkəm/ noun [sing.] (formal) a fairly small amount, especially of something good or pleasant: *They should win, given a modicum of luck.*

mod·i·fi·ca·tion [AWL] /ˌmɑdəfəˈkeɪʃn/ noun [U, C] ~ (of/to/ in sth) the act or process of changing something in order to improve it or make it more acceptable; a change that is made **SYN** ADAPTATION: *Considerable modification of the existing system is needed.* ♦ *It might be necessary to make a few slight modifications to the design.*

mod·i·fi·er /ˈmɑdəˌfaɪər/ noun (grammar) a word, such as an adjective or adverb, that describes another word or group of words, or restricts its/their meaning in some way: *In "speak quietly," the adverb "quietly" is a modifier.* ⊃ compare POSTMODIFIER, PREMODIFIER

mod·i·fy [AWL] /ˈmɑdəˌfaɪ/ verb (mod·i·fies, mod·i·fy·ing, mod·i·fied, mod·i·fied) **1** ~ sth to change something slightly, especially in order to make it more suitable for a particular purpose **SYN** ADAPT: *The software we use has been modified for us.* ♦ *Patients are taught how to modify their diet.* **2** ~ sth to make something less extreme **SYN** ADJUST: *to modify your behavior/language/views* **3** ~ sth (grammar) a word, such as an adjective or adverb, that **modifies** another word or group of words describes it or restricts its meaning in some way: *In "walk slowly," the adverb "slowly" modifies the verb "walk."*

mod·ish /ˈmoʊdɪʃ/ adj. (sometimes disapproving) fashionable

mod·u·lar /ˈmɑdʒələr/ adj. (of machines, buildings, etc.) consisting of separate parts or units that can be joined together

mod·u·late /ˈmɑdʒəˌleɪt/ verb **1** [T] ~ sth (formal) to change the quality of your voice in order to create a particular effect by making it louder, softer, lower, etc. **2** [I] ~ (from sth) (to/into sth) (music) to change from one musical KEY (= set of notes) to another **3** [T] ~ sth (technical) to affect something so that it becomes more regular, slower, etc.: *drugs that effectively modulate the disease process* **4** [T] ~ sth (technical) to change the rate at which a sound wave or radio signal VIBRATES (= the FREQUENCY) so that it is clearer ► **mod·u·la·tion** /ˌmɑdʒəˈleɪʃn/ noun [U, C]

mod·ule /ˈmɑdʒul/ noun **1** (computing) a unit of a computer system or program that has a particular function **2** one of a set of separate parts or units that can be joined together to make a machine, a piece of furniture, a building, etc. **3** a unit of a SPACECRAFT that can function independently of the main part: *the lunar module*

mo·dus op·e·ran·di /ˌmoʊdəs ˌɑpəˈrændi; -daɪ/ noun [sing.] (from Latin, formal) (abbr. MO) a particular method of working

mo·dus vi·ven·di /ˌmoʊdəs vɪˈvɛndi; -daɪ/ noun [sing.] (from Latin, formal) an arrangement that is made between people, institutions, or countries that have very different opinions or ideas, so that they can live or work together without arguing

Moe·bi·us strip = MÖBIUS STRIP

mo·gul /ˈmoʊgl/ noun **1** a very rich, important, and powerful person **SYN** MAGNATE: *a movie mogul* **2** Mogul (also **Mo·ghul, Mu·ghal** /ˈmugl/) a member of the Muslim race that ruled much of India from the 16th to the 19th century **3** a raised area of hard snow that you jump over when you are SKIING

mo·hair /ˈmoʊhɛr/ noun [U] soft wool or cloth made from the fine hair of the ANGORA GOAT, used for making clothes: *a mohair sweater*

Mo·ham·med = MUHAMMAD

Mo·hawk /ˈmoʊhɔk/ noun **1** (pl. Mo·hawk or Mo·hawks) a member of a Native American people, many of whom live in New York State and Ontario, Canada **2** a way of cutting the hair in which the head is shaved except for a strip of hair in the middle that is sometimes made to stick up

Mo·he·gan /moʊˈhigən/ noun a member of a Native American people originally from the northeastern states, especially Connecticut

Mo·hi·can /moʊˈhikən/ noun = MAHICAN

moi /mwɑ/ exclamation (humorous, from French) me: *"Did you eat all the cookies?" "Who? Moi?"*

moiety /ˈmɔɪəti/ noun (formal) a half of something

moi·re (also moiré) /mwɑˈreɪ; mɔ-/ noun [U] a type of silk cloth with a pattern on its surface like small waves

moist /mɔɪst/ adj. slightly wet: *warm moist air* ♦ *a rich moist cake* ♦ *Water the plants regularly to keep the soil moist.* ♦ *Her eyes were moist* (= with tears). ⊃ thesaurus box at WET ► **moist·ness** noun [U]

mois·ten /ˈmɔɪsn/ verb [T, I] ~ (sth) to become or make something slightly wet: *He moistened his lips before he spoke.*

mois·ture /ˈmɔɪstʃər/ noun [U] very small drops of water that are present in the air, on a surface, or in a substance: *the skin's natural moisture* ♦ *a material that is designed to absorb/ retain moisture*

mois·tur·ize /ˈmɔɪstʃəˌraɪz/ verb [T, I] ~ (sth) to put a special cream on your skin to make it less dry: *a moisturizing cream/lotion* ♦ *a product that soothes and moisturizes*

mois·tur·iz·er /ˈmɔɪstʃəˌraɪzər/ noun [C, U] a cream that is used to make the skin less dry

mo·jo /ˈmoʊdʒoʊ/ noun (pl. mo·jos) **1** [U] magic power **2** [C] a small object, or a collection of small objects in a bag, that is believed to have magic powers **3** [U] the power of someone's attractive personality

mo·lar /ˈmoʊlər/ noun any of the twelve large teeth at the back of the mouth used for crushing and chewing food ⊃ compare CANINE, INCISOR

mo·las·ses /məˈlæsəz/ noun [U] a thick, black, sweet, sticky liquid produced when sugar is REFINED (= made pure), used in cooking

mold /moʊld/ noun, verb
● **noun 1** [C] a container that you pour a liquid or soft substance into, which then becomes solid in the same shape as the container, for example when it is cooled or cooked: *A clay mold is used for casting bronze statues.* ♦ *Pour the chocolate into a heart-shaped mold.* ♦ *They broke the mold when they made you* (= there is nobody like you). **2** [C, usually sing.] a particular style showing the characteristics,

ʌ cup   ə about   eɪ say   aɪ five   ɔɪ boy   aʊ now   oʊ go   ər bird

attitudes, or behavior typical of someone or something: *a hero in the "Superman" mold* ◆ *He is cast in a different mold from his predecessor.* ◆ *She doesn't fit (into) the traditional mold of an academic.* **3** [U, C] a soft green, gray, or black substance like fur that grows on old food or on objects that are left in warm wet air: *There's mold on the cheese.* ◆ *molds and fungi* ◆ *mold growth* ⊃ see also LEAF MOLD
IDM **break the mold (of sth)** to change what people expect from a situation, especially by acting in a dramatic and original way
• *verb* **1** [T] to shape a soft substance into a particular form or object by pressing it or by putting it into a mold: *~ A (into B) First, mold the clay into the desired shape.* ◆ *~ B (from/out of/in A) The figure had been molded in clay.* **2** [T] to strongly influence the way someone's character, opinions, etc. develop: *~ sb/sth The experience had molded and colored her whole life.* ◆ *~ sb/sth into sb/sth He molded them into a winning team.* **3** [I, T] *~ (sth) to sth* to fit or make something fit tightly around the shape of something: *The fabric molds to the body.*

mold·er /'mouldər/ *verb* [I] to decay slowly and steadily: *The room smelled of disuse and moldering books.*

mold·ing /'mouldɪŋ/ *noun* a decorative strip of plastic, stone, wood, etc. around the top edge of a wall, on a door, etc.

mold·y /'mouldi/ *adj.* **1** covered with or containing MOLD: *moldy bread/cheese* ◆ *Strawberries go moldy very quickly.* **2** old and not in good condition

mole¹ /moul/ *noun* **1** a small dark brown mark on the skin, sometimes slightly higher than the skin around it ⊃ compare FRECKLE **2** a small animal with dark gray fur, that is almost blind and digs tunnels under the ground to live in ⊃ see also MOLEHILL **3** a person who works within an organization and secretly passes important information to another organization or country **4** (*chemistry*) a unit for measuring the chemical mass of a substance ⊃ see also MOLE²

mo·le² /'moulei/ *noun* [U] a spicy sauce used in Mexican cooking that is eaten with meat ⊃ see also MOLE¹

mol·e·cule /'malə,kyul/ *noun* (*chemistry*) the smallest unit, consisting of a group of atoms, into which a substance can be divided without a change in its chemical nature: *A molecule of water consists of two atoms of hydrogen and one atom of oxygen.* ⊃ picture at ATOM ▶ **mo·lec·u·lar** /mə'lɛkyələr/ *adj.* [only before noun]: *molecular structure/biology*

mole·hill /'moulhɪl/ *noun* a small pile of earth that a mole ¹ leaves on the surface of the ground when it digs underground **IDM** see MOUNTAIN

mole·skin /'moulskɪn/ *noun* [U] **1** a type of strong cotton cloth with a soft surface, used for making clothes **2** a type of soft thick bandage that is wrapped around your feet to prevent injuries caused by your feet rubbing against your shoes

mo·lest /mə'lɛst/ *verb* **1** *~ sb* to attack someone, especially a child, sexually **SYN** ABUSE **2** *~ sb* (*old-fashioned*) to attack someone physically ▶ **mo·les·ta·tion** /,moulɛ'steɪʃn; ,ma-/ *noun* [U] **mo·lest·er** /mə'lɛstər/ *noun*: *a child molester*

moll /mal/ *noun* (*old-fashioned, slang*) the female friend of a criminal

mol·li·fy /'malə,faɪ/ *verb* (**mol·li·fies**, **mol·li·fy·ing**, **mol·li·fied**, **mol·li·fied**) *~ sb* (*formal*) to make someone feel less angry or upset **SYN** PLACATE

mol·lusk (also **mol·lusc**) /'maləsk/ *noun* (*technical*) any creature with a soft body that is not divided into different sections, usually with a hard outer shell. SNAILS and SLUGS are mollusks. ⊃ compare BIVALVE, SHELLFISH

mol·ly·cod·dle /'mali,kadl/ *verb* *~ sb* (*disapproving, becoming old-fashioned*) to protect someone too much and make their life too comfortable and safe ⊃ compare CODDLE

Mo·lo·tov cock·tail /,malətɔf 'kakteɪl; ,mɔlə-/ *noun* a simple bomb that consists of a bottle filled with gasoline

and a piece of cloth in the end that is made to burn just before the bomb is thrown

molt /moult/ *verb* [I] (of a bird or an animal) to lose feathers or hair before new feathers or hair grow

mol·ten /'moultn/ *adj.* (of metal, rock, or glass) heated to a very high temperature so that it becomes liquid

mo·lyb·de·num /mə'lɪbdənəm/ *noun* [U] (*symb.* **Mo**) a chemical element. Molybdenum is a silver-grey metal that breaks easily and is used in some ALLOY steels.

mom 🔊 /mam/ *noun* (*informal*)
a mother: *Where's my mom?* ◆ *Mom and Dad* ◆ *Are you listening, Mom?* ⊃ see also SOCCER MOM

mom-and-'pop *adj.* [only before noun] (of a store or business) owned and run by a husband and wife, or by a family

mo·ment 🔊 /'moumənt/ *noun*
1 a very short period of time: *Could you wait a moment, please?* ◆ *One moment, please* (= Please wait a short time). ◆ *He thought for a moment before replying.* ◆ *I'll be back in a moment.* ◆ *We arrived not a moment too soon* (= almost too late). ◆ *Moments later* (= a very short time later), *I heard a terrible crash.* **2** [sing.] an exact point in time: *We're busy at the moment* (= now). ◆ *I agreed in a moment of weakness.* ◆ *At that very moment, the phone rang.* ◆ *From that moment on, she never felt really well again.* **3** [C] a particular occasion; a time for doing something: *I'm waiting for the right moment to tell him the bad news.* ◆ *That was one of the happiest moments of my life.* ◆ *Have I caught you at a bad moment?* ⊃ see also SENIOR MOMENT
IDM **(at) any moment (now)** very soon: *Hurry up! He'll be back any moment now.* **at this moment in time** (*informal*) now, at the present time: *At this moment in time, I don't know what my decision will be.* **for the moment/present** for now; for a short time: *This house is big enough for the moment, but we'll have to move if we have children.* **have its/your moments** to have short times that are better, more interesting, etc. than others: *The job isn't exciting all the time, but it has its moments.* **the moment of truth** a time when someone or something is tested, or when important decisions are made **the moment (that)…** as soon as…: *I want to see him the moment he arrives.* **not for a/one moment** certainly not; not at all: *I don't think for a moment that she'll accept, but you can ask her.* **of moment** (*formal*) very important: *matters of great moment* **of the moment** (of a person, a job, an issue, etc.) famous, important, and talked about a lot now: *She's the fashion designer of the moment.* ⊃ more at JUST, LAST¹, NOTICE, PSYCHOLOGICAL, SPUR, WAIT

mo·men·tar·i·ly /,moumən'tɛrəli/ *adv.* **1** for a very short time **SYN** BRIEFLY: *He paused momentarily.* **2** very soon; in a moment: *I'll be with you momentarily.*

mo·men·tar·y /'moumən,tɛri/ *adj.* lasting for a very short time **SYN** BRIEF: *a momentary lapse of concentration* ◆ *momentary confusion*

mo·men·tous /mou'mɛntəs; mə-/ *adj.* very important or serious, especially because there may be important results **SYN** HISTORIC: *a momentous decision/event/occasion*

mo·men·tum /mou'mɛntəm; mə-/ *noun* [U] **1** the ability to keep increasing or developing: *The fight for his release gathers momentum each day.* ◆ *They began to lose momentum in the second half of the game.* **2** a force that is gained by movement: *The vehicle gained momentum as the road dipped.* **3** (*technical*) the quantity of movement of a moving object, measured as its mass multiplied by its speed

mom·ma /'mamə/ *noun* (*informal*) = MAMA

mom·my (also **mom·mie**) /'mami/ *noun* (*pl.* **mom·mies**) (*informal*) a child's word for a mother

'mommy ,track *noun* [C, usually sing.] (*informal*) work arrangements for female employees who want to spend more time with their children, usually involving certain disadvantages: *She's **on the mommy track**, with flexible hours and lower pay.*

mon- /mɑn/ ➜ MONO-

mon·ad /'moʊnæd/ *noun* (*philosophy*) a single simple thing that cannot be divided, for example an atom or a person

mon·arch /'mɑnərk; -nɑrk/ *noun* a person who rules a country, for example a king or a queen

monarch 'butterfly *noun* a large butterfly (= a flying insect) with orange and black wings

mo·nar·chi·cal /məˈnɑrkɪkl/ *adj.* [usually before noun] (*formal*) connected with a ruler such as a king or a queen or with the system of government by a king or queen

mon·ar·chist /'mɑnərkɪst/ *noun* a person who believes that a country should be ruled by a king or queen ▶ **monarchist** *adj.*

mon·ar·chy /'mɑnərki/ *noun* (*pl.* **mon·ar·chies**) **1** the **monarchy** [sing.] a system of government by a king or a queen: *plans to abolish the monarchy* ➜ collocations at POLITICS **2** [C] a country that is ruled by a king or a queen: *There are several constitutional monarchies in Europe.* ➜ compare REPUBLIC **3** the **monarchy** [sing.] the king or queen of a country and their family

mon·as·ter·y /'mɑnəˌstɛri/ *noun* (*pl.* **mon·as·ter·ies**) a building in which MONKS (= members of a male religious community) live together ➜ collocations at RELIGION

mo·nas·tic /məˈnæstɪk/ *adj.* **1** connected with MONKS or monasteries **2** (of a way of life) simple and quiet and possibly CELIBATE **SYN** ASCETIC

mo·nas·ti·cism /məˈnæstəˌsɪzəm/ *noun* [U] the way of life of MONKS in monasteries

Mon·day 🔑 /'mʌndeɪ; -di/ *noun* [C, U] (*abbr.* **Mon.**) the day of the week after Sunday and before Tuesday; the first day of the working week: *It's Monday today, isn't it?* ✦ *She started work **last Monday**.* ✦ *Are you busy **next Monday**?* ✦ ***Monday morning/afternoon/night*** ✦ *We'll discuss this at **Monday's** meeting.* ✦ *Do we still have **Monday's** paper?* ✦ *I work Monday to Friday.* ✦ *I work Mondays to Fridays.* ✦ ***On Monday(s)*** (= Every Monday) *I do yoga.* ✦ *He was born on a Monday.* ✦ *I went to Charleston on Thursday, and came back the **following Monday**.* ✦ *We'll meet **on Monday**.* ✦ (*informal*) *We'll meet Monday.* **ORIGIN** From the Old English for "day of the moon," translated from Latin *lunae dies.*

Monday morning 'quarterback *noun* (*informal, disapproving*) a person who criticizes or comments on an event after it has happened **ORIGIN** The quarterback directs the play in a football game and games are usually played on the weekend.

mon·e·ta·rism /'mɑnətəˌrɪzəm/ *noun* [U] the policy of controlling the amount of money available in a country as a way of keeping the economy strong

mon·e·ta·rist /'mɑnətərɪst/ *noun* a person who supports monetarism ▶ **monetarist** *adj.*: *a monetarist economic policy*

mon·e·tar·y /'mɑnəˌtɛri/ *adj.* [only before noun] connected with money, especially all the money in a country: *monetary policy/growth* ✦ *an item of little monetary value* ✦ *closer North American political, monetary, and economic union* ➜ thesaurus box at ECONOMIC

mon·ey 🔑 /'mʌni/ *noun*
1 [U] what you earn by working or selling things, and use to buy things: *to borrow/save/spend/earn money* ✦ *How much money is there in my account?* ✦ *The money is much better in my new job.* ✦ *If the item is not satisfactory, you will get your money back.* ✦ *We'll need to raise more money* (= collect or borrow it) *next year.* ✦ *Can you lend me some money until tomorrow?* ✦ *Be careful with that —it cost a lot of money.* **2** [U] coins or paper notes: *I counted the money carefully.* ✦ *Where can I change my money into dollars?* ➜ see also FUNNY MONEY, PAPER MONEY, READY MONEY **3** [U] a person's wealth including their property: *He lost all his money.* ✦ *The family made their money in the 18th century.* **4** **moneys** or **monies** [pl.] (*old use* or *law*)

coins

penny

nickel

dime

quarter

half dollar

dollar

bill

credit card

sums of money: *a statement of all monies paid into your account* **HELP** You will find other compounds ending in **money** at their place in the alphabet.

IDM **be in the money** (*informal*) to have a lot of money to spend **for my money** (*informal*) in my opinion: *For my money, he's one of the greatest comedians of all time.* **get your money's worth** to get enough value or enjoyment out of something, considering the amount of money, time, etc. that you are spending on it **good money** a lot of money; money that you earn with hard work: *Thousands of people paid good money to watch the band perform.* ✦ *Don't waste good money on that!* **have money to burn** to have so much money that you do not have to be careful with it **made of money** (*informal*) very rich **make money** to earn a lot of money; to make a profit: *The movie should make money.* ✦ *There's money to be made from tourism.* **make/lose money hand over fist** to make/lose money very fast and in large quantities **money is no object** money is not something that needs to be considered, because there is plenty of it available: *She travels around the world as if money is no object.* **money talks** (*saying*) people who have a lot of money have more power and influence than others **on the money** correct; accurate: *His prediction was right on the money.* **put money into sth** to invest money in a business or a particular project: *We would welcome interest from anyone prepared to put money into the club.* **put your money on sb/sth 1** to bet that a particular horse, dog, etc. will win a race **2** to feel very sure that something is true or that someone will succeed: *He'll be there tonight. I'd put money on it.* **put your money where your mouth is** (*informal*) to support what you say by doing something practical; to show by your actions that you really mean something **throw your money around** (*informal*) to spend money in a careless and obvious way **throw good money after bad** (*disapproving*) to spend more money on something, when you have wasted a lot on it already **throw money at sth** (*disapproving*) to try to deal with a problem or improve a situation by spending money on it, when it would be better to deal with it in other ways: *It is inappropriate simply to throw money at these problems.* ➔ more at BEST, CAREFUL, COLOR *n.*, EASY *adj.*, FOOL *n.*, GROW, LICENSE *n.*, LOVE *n.*, MARRY, OBJECT *n.*, ROLL *v.*, RUN *n.*, TIME *n.*

THESAURUS

money

cash ◆ change ◆ bills

These are all words for money in the form of coins or paper notes.

money money in the form of coins or paper notes: *I counted the money carefully.* ◆ *Where can I change my money into dollars?* ◆ **paper money** (= money that is made of paper, not coins)

cash money in the form of coins or paper notes: *How much cash do you have on you?* ◆ *Payments can be made by credit card or in cash.*

MONEY OR CASH?

If it is important to contrast money in the form of coins and notes and money in other forms, use **cash**: *How much money/cash do you have on you?* ◆ *Payments can be made by credit card or in money.* ◆ *Customers are offered a discount if they pay money.*

change the money that you get back when you have paid for something giving more money than the amount it costs; coins rather than paper money: *The ticket machine doesn't give change.* ◆ *I don't have any* **small change** (= coins of low value).

bills paper money rather than coins: *The machine only accepts small bills* (= $20 or less).

PATTERNS

- to **get (out)/take out/withdraw** money/cash
- **ready** money/cash (= money that you have available to spend immediately)
- **small** change/bills

money-back guaran'tee *noun* an official promise by a store, etc. to return the money you have paid for something if it is not of an acceptable standard

mon·ey·bags /ˈmʌniˌbæɡz/ *noun* (*pl.* **mon·ey·bags**) (*informal, humorous*) a very rich person

mon·eyed (also **mon·ied**) /ˈmʌnid/ *adj.* [only before noun] (*formal*) having a lot of money **SYN** RICH: *the moneyed classes*

money-grubbing (also **money-grabbing**) *adj.* [only before noun] (*informal, disapproving*) trying to get a lot of money ▶ **money-grubber** (also **money-grabber**) *noun*

mon·ey·lend·er /ˈmʌniˌlɛndər/ *noun* (*old-fashioned*) a person whose business is lending money, usually at a very high rate of interest

mon·ey·mak·er /ˈmʌniˌmeɪkər/ *noun* a product, business, etc. that produces a large profit ▶ **mon·ey·mak·ing** *adj.*: *a moneymaking movie* **mon·ey·mak·ing** *noun* [U]

money market *noun* the banks and other institutions that lend or borrow money, and buy and sell foreign money

money order *noun* an official document that you can buy at a bank or a post office and send to someone so that they can exchange it for money

money-saving *adj.* [only before noun] that helps you spend less money: *money-saving offers/tips*

money supply *noun* [sing., U] (*economics*) the total amount of money that exists in the economy of a country at a particular time

money transfer *noun* = CASH TRANSFER

mon·goose /ˈmɑŋɡus/ *noun* (*pl.* **mon·goos·es** /-səz/) a small tropical animal with fur, that kills snakes, RATS, etc.

mon·grel /ˈmʌŋɡrəl; ˈmɑŋ-/ *noun* a dog that is a mixture of different breeds **SYN** MUTT

mon·ied = MONEYED

mon·i·ker /ˈmɑnɪkər/ *noun* (*humorous*) a name

mon·ism /ˈmoʊnɪzəm; ˈmɑ-/ *noun* (*religion*) the belief that there is only one God

mon·i·tor 🔑 AWL /ˈmɑnətər/ *noun, verb*

● *noun* **1** a television screen used to show particular kinds of information; a screen that shows information from a computer: *The arrival times of today's flights are displayed on the monitor.* ◆ *a PC with a 17-inch color monitor* ➔ picture at COMPUTER ➔ see also VDU **2** a piece of equipment used to check or record something: *a heart monitor* **3** a student in a school who performs special duties, such as helping the teacher **4** a person whose job is to check that something is done fairly and honestly, especially in a foreign country: *U.N. monitors declared the referendum fair.* **5** a large tropical LIZARD (= a type of REPTILE)

● *verb* **1** ~ sth | ~ what, how, etc.... to watch and check something over a period of time in order to see how it develops, so that you can make any necessary changes **SYN** TRACK: *Each student's progress is closely monitored.* **2** ~ sth to listen to telephone calls, foreign radio broadcasts, etc. in order to find out information that might be useful

monk /mʌŋk/ *noun* a member of a religious group of men who often live apart from other people in a MONASTERY and who do not marry or have personal possessions: *Benedictine/Buddhist monks* ➔ compare FRIAR, NUN ➔ see also MONKISH

mon·key /ˈmʌŋki/ *noun* **1** an animal with a long tail, that climbs trees and lives in hot countries. There are several types of monkeys and they are related to APES and humans. ➔ picture at ANIMAL **2** (*informal*) a child who is active and likes playing tricks on people: *Come here, you little monkey!*
IDM **make a monkey (out) of sb** to make someone seem stupid

monkey bars *noun* [pl.] = JUNGLE GYM

monkey business *noun* [U] (*informal*) dishonest or silly behavior

monkey puzzle (also **monkey puzzle tree**) *noun* a CONIFER tree with leaves like scales, that are thin, tough, and very sharp

monkey wrench *noun* a tool that can be adjusted to hold and turn things of different widths ➔ picture at TOOL
IDM **throw a monkey wrench in/into the works** (also **throw a wrench in/into the works**) (*informal*) to do something to spoil someone's plans

monk·ish /ˈmʌŋkɪʃ/ *adj.* like a MONK; connected with MONKS

mon·o /ˈmɑnoʊ/ *adj., noun*
● *adj.* (also **mon·o·phon·ic**) (*music*) recording or producing sound which comes from only one direction: *a mono recording* ➔ compare STEREO
● *noun* [U] **1** a system of recording or producing sound that comes from only one direction: *recorded in mono* ➔ compare STEREO **2** (*informal*) = MONONUCLEOSIS

mono- /ˈmɑnoʊ; -nə/ (also **mon-**) *combining form* (in nouns and adjectives) one; single: *monorail* ◆ *monogamy*

mon·o·chrome /ˈmɑnəˌkroʊm/ *adj.* **1** (of photographs, etc.) using only black, white, and shades of gray: *monochrome illustrations/images* ◆ (*figurative*) *a dull monochrome life* **2** using different shades of one color ▶ **mon·o·chro·mat·ic** /ˌmɑnəkroʊˈmætɪk; -krə-/ *adj.*: *a monochromatic color scheme* **monochrome** *noun* [U]: *an artist who works in monochrome*

mon·o·cle /ˈmɑnəkl/ *noun* a single glass LENS for one eye, held in place by the muscles around the eye and used by people in the past to help them see clearly

mon·o·cot·y·le·don /ˌmɑnoʊˌkɑtlˈidn/ (also **mon·o·cot** /ˈmɑnəˌkɑt/) *noun* (*biology*) a plant whose seeds form EMBRYOS that produce a single leaf ➔ compare DICOTYLEDON

mon·o·cul·ture /'manə,kʌltʃər/ noun **1** [U] the practice of growing only one type of crop on a certain area of land **2** [C, U] a society consisting of people who are all the same race, all share the same beliefs, etc.: *a global economic monoculture*

mon·o·cy·cle /'manə,saikl/ noun = UNICYCLE

mon·o·cyte /'manə,sait/ noun (*biology*) a type of large white blood cell with a simple round NUCLEUS that can remove harmful substances from the body

mo·nog·a·my /mə'nagəmi/ noun [U] **1** the fact or custom of being married to only one person at a particular time ➔ compare BIGAMY, POLYGAMY **2** the practice or custom of having a sexual relationship with only one partner at a particular time ▶ **mo·nog·a·mous** /mə'nagəməs/ adj.: *a monogamous marriage* ♦ *Most birds are monogamous.*

mon·o·glot /'manə,glat/ noun (*technical*) a person who speaks only one language ➔ compare POLYGLOT

mon·o·gram /'manə,græm/ noun two or more letters, usually the first letters of someone's names, that are combined in a design and marked on items of clothing, etc. that they own ▶ **mon·o·grammed** adj.: *a monogrammed handkerchief*

mon·o·graph /'manə,græf/ noun (*technical*) a detailed written study of a single subject, usually in the form of a short book

mon·o·lin·gual /,manə'lɪŋgwəl/ (especially CanE **u·ni·lin·gual**) adj. speaking or using only one language: *a monolingual dictionary* ➔ compare BILINGUAL, MULTILINGUAL

mon·o·lith /'manə,lɪθ/ noun **1** a large single vertical block of stone, especially one that was shaped into a column by people living in ancient times, and that may have had some religious meaning **2** (often *disapproving*) a single, very large organization, etc. that is very slow to change and not interested in individual people ▶ **mon·o·lith·ic** /,manə'lɪθɪk/ adj.: *a monolithic block* ♦ *the monolithic structure of the state*

mon·o·logue (also **mon·o·log**) /'manə,lɔg; -,lag/ noun **1** [C] a long speech by one person during a conversation that stops other people from speaking or expressing an opinion: *He went into a long monologue about life in Texas.* **2** [U, C] a long speech in a play, movie, etc. spoken by one actor, especially when alone **3** [C, U] a dramatic story, especially in VERSE, told or performed by one person: *a dramatic monologue* ➔ compare DIALOGUE, SOLILOQUY

mon·o·ma·ni·a /,manə'meɪniə/ noun [U] (*psychology*) too much interest in or enthusiasm for just one thing, so that it is not healthy

mon·o·nu·cle·o·sis /,manou,nukli'ousəs/ (also *informal* **mo·no**) noun [U] (*medical*) an infectious disease that causes swelling of the LYMPH NODES and makes the person feel very weak for a long time

mon·o·phon·ic /,manə'fanɪk/ adj. (*music*) = MONO

mon·o·plane /'manə,pleɪn/ noun an early type of plane with one set of wings ➔ compare BIPLANE

mo·nop·o·list /mə'napəlɪst/ noun (*technical*) a person or company that has a MONOPOLY

mo·nop·o·lis·tic /mə,napə'lɪstɪk/ adj. (*formal*) controlling or trying to get complete control over something, especially an industry or a company

mo·nop·o·lize /mə'napə,laɪz/ verb **1** ~ sth to have or take control of the largest part of something so that other people are prevented from sharing in it: *Men traditionally monopolized jobs in the printing industry.* ♦ *As usual, she completely monopolized the conversation.* **2** ~ sb to have or take a large part of someone's attention or time so that they are unable to speak to or deal with other people ▶ **mo·nop·o·li·za·tion** /mə,napələ'zeɪʃn/ noun [U]

mo·nop·o·ly /mə'napəli/ noun (pl. **mo·nop·o·lies**) **1** ~ (in/of/on sth) (*business*) the complete control of trade in particular goods or of the supply of a particular service; a type of goods or a service that is controlled in this way: *The software company had a monopoly on the market.* ♦ *Electricity, gas, and water were considered to be natural monopolies.* ➔ compare DUOPOLY **2** [usually sing.] ~ in/of/on sth the complete control, possession, or use of something; a thing that belongs only to one person or group and that other people cannot share: *Managers do not have a monopoly on stress.* ♦ *A good education should not be the monopoly of the rich.* **3** Monopoly™ a BOARD GAME in which players have to pretend to buy and sell land and houses, using pieces of paper that look like money

Mo'nopoly ,money noun [U] money that does not really exist or has no real value: *Inflation was so high that the notes were like Monopoly money.* **ORIGIN** From the toy money used in the board game *Monopoly.*

mon·o·rail /'manə,reɪl/ noun **1** [U] a railroad system in which trains travel along a track consisting of a single rail, usually one placed high above the ground **2** [C] a train used in a monorail system

mon·o·so·di·um glu·ta·mate /,manə,soudiəm 'glutə,meɪt/ noun [U] (*abbr.* MSG) a chemical that is sometimes added to food to improve its flavor

mon·o·syl·lab·ic /,manəsɪ'læbɪk/ adj. **1** having only one syllable: *a monosyllabic word* **2** (of a person or their way of speaking) saying very little, in a way that appears rude to other people

mon·o·syl·la·ble /'manə,sɪləbl/ noun a word with only one syllable, for example, "it" or "no"

mon·o·the·ism /'manəθi,ɪzəm/ noun [U] the belief that there is only one God ➔ compare POLYTHEISM ▶ **mon·o·the·ist** /'manə,θiɪst/ noun **mon·o·the·is·tic** /,manəθi'ɪstɪk/ adj.

mon·o·tone /'manə,toun/ noun, adj.
• noun [sing.] a dull sound or way of speaking in which the tone and volume remain the same and therefore seem boring: *He spoke in a flat monotone.*
• adj. [only before noun] without any changes or differences in sound or color: *He spoke in a monotone drawl.* ♦ *monotone engravings*

mo·not·o·nous /mə'natn-əs/ adj. never changing and therefore boring SYN DULL, REPETITIOUS: *a monotonous voice/diet/routine* ♦ *monotonous work* ♦ *New secretaries came and went with monotonous regularity.* ▶ **mo·not·o·nous·ly** adv.

mo·not·o·ny /mə'natnæː/ noun [U] boring lack of variety: *She watches TV to relieve the monotony of everyday life.*

mon·o·treme /'manə,trim/ noun (*technical*) a class of animals including the ECHIDNA and the PLATYPUS, that lay eggs, but also give milk to their babies

mon·o·un·sat·u·rat·ed fat /,manouʌn,sætʃəreɪtəd 'fæt/ noun [C, U] a type of fat found, for example, in OLIVES and nuts, which does not encourage the harmful development of CHOLESTEROL ➔ see also POLYUNSATURATED FAT, SATURATED FAT, TRANS-FATTY ACID, UNSATURATED FAT

mon·o·zy·got·ic twin /,manouzaɪ,gatɪk 'twɪn/ (also **mon·o·zy·gous twin** /,manou,zaɪgəs 'twɪn/) adj. (*technical*) = IDENTICAL TWIN ➔ compare DIZYGOTIC TWIN

the Mon·roe Doc·trine /mən,rou 'daktrən; ,manrou-/ noun a part of U.S. foreign policy that states that the U.S. will act to protect its own interests in N. and S. America **ORIGIN** From the name of U.S. President James Monroe, who first stated the policy in 1823.

Mon·si·gnor /man'sinyər/ noun (*abbr.* Mgr) used as a title when speaking to or about a priest of high rank in the Roman Catholic Church

mon·soon /,man'sun/ noun **1** a period of heavy rain in summer in S. Asia; the rain that falls during this period **2** a wind in S. Asia that blows from the southwest in summer, bringing rain, and the northeast in winter

mons pu·bis /,manz 'pyubəs/ (also **mons Ven·er·is** /,manz 'venərəs/) noun (*formal*) the curved area of fat over the joint of the PUBIC bones, especially in women

---

h **hat**   m **man**   n **no**   ŋ **sing**   l **leg**   r **red**   y **yes**   w **wet**

mon·ster /ˈmɑnstər/ *noun, adj.*
- *noun* **1** (in stories) an imaginary creature that is very large, ugly, and frightening: *a monster with three heads* ♦ *prehistoric monsters* **2** an animal or a thing that is very large or ugly: *Their dog's an absolute monster!* **3** a person who is very cruel and evil **4** (*humorous*) a child who behaves badly
- *adj.* [only before noun] (*informal*) unusually large **SYN** GIANT: *monster mushrooms*

ˌmonster ˈtruck *noun* an extremely large PICKUP TRUCK with very large wheels, often used for racing

mon·stros·i·ty /mɑnˈstrɑsəti/ *noun* (*pl.* mon·stros·i·ties) something that is very large and very ugly, especially a building **SYN** EYESORE: *a concrete monstrosity*

mon·strous /ˈmɑnstrəs/ *adj.* **1** considered to be shocking and unacceptable because it is morally wrong or unfair **SYN** OUTRAGEOUS: *a monstrous lie/injustice* **2** very large **SYN** GIGANTIC: *a monstrous wave* **3** very large, ugly, and frightening **SYN** HORRIFYING: *a monstrous figure/creature* ▸ **mon·strous·ly** *adv.*: *monstrously unfair* ♦ *a monstrously fat man*

mon·tage /mɑnˈtɑʒ; ˌmoʊn-/ *noun* **1** [C] a picture, movie, or piece of music or writing that consists of many separate items put together, especially in an interesting or unusual combination: *a photographic montage* **2** [U] the process of making a montage

mon·tane /mɑnˈteɪn; ˈmɑnteɪn/ *adj.* [only before noun] (*technical*) connected with mountains

Mon·te·rey Jack /ˌmɑntəreɪ ˈdʒæk/ (also ˈJack cheese) *noun* [U] a type of white cheese with a mild flavor

month /mʌnθ/ *noun*
1 [C] any of the twelve periods of time into which the year is divided, for example May or June: *the month of August* ♦ *We're moving next month.* ♦ *She earns $2,000 a month.* ♦ *The rent is $800 per month.* ♦ *Have you read this month's "Physics World?"* ♦ *Prices continue to rise month after month* (= over a period of several months). ♦ *Her anxiety mounted month by month* (= as each month passed). ⊃ see also CALENDAR MONTH **2** [C] a period of about 30 days, for example, June 3rd to July 3rd: *The baby is three months old.* ♦ *a three-month-old baby* ♦ *They lived in Toronto during their first few months of marriage.* ♦ *several months later* ♦ *a six-month contract* ♦ *a month-long strike* ♦ *He visits Portland once or twice a month.* ⊃ see also LUNAR MONTH **3** months [pl.] a long time, especially a period of several months: *He had to wait for months for the visas to come through.* ♦ *It will be months before we get the results.* **IDM** see FLAVOR *n.*

month·ly /ˈmʌnθli/ *adj., adv., noun*
- *adj.* **1** happening once a month or every month: *a monthly meeting/visit/magazine* **2** paid, valid, or calculated for one month: *a monthly salary of $2,000* ♦ *a monthly season ticket* ♦ *Summers are hot, with monthly averages above 80°F.*
- *adv.* every month or once a month: *She gets paid monthly.*
- *noun* (*pl.* month·lies) a magazine published once a month: *the fashion monthlies*

mon·u·ment /ˈmɑnyəmənt/ *noun* **1** ~ (to sb/sth) a building, column, statue, etc. built to remind people of a famous person or event: *A monument to him was erected in Washington, D.C.* **2** a building that has special historical importance: *an ancient monument* **3** ~ to sth a thing that remains as a good example of someone's qualities or of what they did: *These recordings are a monument to his talent as a pianist.*

mon·u·men·tal /ˌmɑnyəˈmɛntl/ *adj.* **1** [usually before noun] very important and having a great influence, especially as the result of years of work **SYN** HISTORIC: *Gibbon's monumental work "The Rise and Fall of the Roman Empire"* **2** [only before noun] very large, good, bad, stupid, etc. **SYN** MAJOR: *a book of monumental significance* ♦ *We have a monumental task ahead of us.* ♦ *It seems like an act of monumental folly.* **3** [only before noun] appearing in or serving as a

monument: *a monumental inscription/tomb* ♦ *a monumental mason* (= a person who makes monuments)

mon·u·men·tal·ly /ˌmɑnyəˈmɛntl·i/ *adv.* (used to describe negative qualities) extremely: *monumentally difficult/stupid*

moo /mu/ *noun* (*pl.* moos) the long deep sound made by a cow ▸ **moo** *verb* [I]

mooch /mutʃ/ *verb* (*informal*) [I, T] ~ (sth) (off sb) to get money, food, etc. from someone else instead of paying for it yourself **SYN** SPONGE: *He's always mooching off his friends.*

mood /mud/ *noun*
1 [C] the way you are feeling at a particular time: *She's in a good mood today* (= happy and friendly). ♦ *He's always in a bad mood* (= unhappy, or angry and impatient). ♦ *to be in a foul/filthy mood* ♦ *Some addicts suffer violent mood swings* (= changes of mood) *if deprived of the drug.* ♦ *I'm just not in the mood for a party tonight.* ♦ *I'm not really in the mood to go out tonight.* ♦ *He was in no mood for being polite to visitors.* **2** [C] a period of being angry or impatient: *I wonder why he's in such a mood today.* ♦ *She was in one of her moods* (= one of her regular periods of being angry or impatient). **3** [sing.] the way a group of people feel about something; the atmosphere in a place or among a group of people: *The mood of the meeting was distinctly pessimistic.* ♦ *The movie captures the mood of the interwar years perfectly.* **4** [C] (*grammar*) any of the sets of verb forms that show whether what is said or written is certain, possible, necessary, etc. **5** [C] (*grammar*) one of the categories of verb use that expresses facts, orders, questions, wishes, or conditions: *the indicative/imperative/subjunctive mood*

mood–altering *adj.* (of drugs) having an effect on your mood: *mood-altering substances*

mood music *noun* [U] music intended to create a particular atmosphere, especially a relaxed or romantic one

mood·y /ˈmudi/ *adj.* (mood·i·er, mood·i·est) **1** having moods that change regularly and often: *Moody people are very difficult to deal with.* **2** bad-tempered or upset, often for no particular reason **SYN** GRUMPY: *Why are you so moody today?* **3** (of a movie, piece of music, or place) suggesting particular emotions, especially sad ones ▸ **mood·i·ly** /ˈmudl·i/ *adv.*: *He stared moodily into the fire.* **mood·i·ness** /ˈmudinəs/ *noun* [U]

moon /mun/ *noun, verb*
- *noun* **1** usually the moon, also the Moon [sing.] the round object that moves around the earth once every 27½ days and shines at night by light reflected from the sun: *the surface of the moon* ♦ *a moon landing* **2** [sing.] the moon as it appears in the sky at a particular time: *a crescent moon* ♦ *There's no moon tonight* (= no moon can be seen). ♦ *By the light of the moon I could just make out shapes and outlines.* ⊃ see also FULL MOON, HALF-MOON, NEW MOON **3** [C] a natural SATELLITE that moves around a planet other than the earth: *How many moons does Jupiter have?*
  IDM ask, cry, etc. for the moon (*informal*) to ask for something that is difficult or impossible to get or achieve many moons ago (*literary*) a very long time ago ⊃ more at ONCE, PROMISE
- *verb* [I] (*informal*) to show your naked backside to people in a public place as a joke or an insult
  PHR V moon over sb (*informal*) to spend time thinking about someone that you love, especially when other people think this is silly or annoying **SYN** PINE FOR

moon·beam /ˈmunbim/ *noun* a stream of light from the moon

Moon Boot™ *noun* a thick warm boot made of cloth or plastic, worn in snow or cold weather

moon·less /ˈmunləs/ *adj.* without a moon that can be seen: *a moonless night/sky*

moon·light /ˈmunlaɪt/ *noun, verb*
- *noun* [U] the light of the moon: *to go for a walk by moonlight/in the moonlight*

verb (moon·light·ed, moon·light·ed) [I] (*informal*) to have a second job that you do secretly, usually without paying tax on the extra money that you earn

moon·lit /'munlɪt/ *adj.* lit by the moon: *a moonlit night/beach*

moon·scape /'munskeɪp/ *noun* **1** a view of the surface of the moon **2** an area of land that is empty, with no trees, water, etc., and looks like the surface of the moon

moon·shine /'munʃaɪn/ *noun* [U] **1** (*old-fashioned*) WHISKEY or other strong alcoholic drinks made and sold illegally **2** (*informal*) silly talk SYN NONSENSE

moon·stone /'munstoʊn/ *noun* [C, U] a smooth, white, shiny SEMI-PRECIOUS stone

moon·struck /'munstrʌk/ *adj.* slightly crazy, especially because you are in love

moon·walk /'munwɔk/ *verb* **1** [I] to walk on the moon **2** [I] to do a dance movement which consists of walking backward, sliding the feet smoothly over the floor ▶ **moonwalk** *noun*

Moor /mʊr/ *noun* a member of a race of Muslim people living in N.W. Africa who entered and took control of part of Spain in the 8th century ▶ **Moor·ish** /'mʊrɪʃ/ *adj.*: *the Moorish architecture of Cordoba*

moor /mʊr/ *noun, verb*
• **noun 1** [C, usually pl.] a high open area of land that is not used for farming, especially an area covered with rough grass and HEATHER: *to go for a walk on the moors* **2** [U] = MOORLAND: *moor and rough grassland*
• **verb** [I, T] to attach a boat, ship, etc. to a fixed object on the land with a rope, or to ANCHOR it SYN TIE UP: *We moored off the north coast of the island.* ◆ *~ sth (to sth)* A number of fishing boats were moored to the dock.

moor·hen /'mʊrhɛn/ *noun* a small black bird with a short reddish-yellow beak that lives on or near water

moor·ing /'mʊrɪŋ/ *noun* **1 moorings** [pl.] the ropes, chains, etc. by which a ship or boat is moored: *The boat slipped its moorings and drifted out to sea.* **2** [C] the place where a ship or boat is moored: *private moorings* ◆ *to find a mooring* ◆ *mooring ropes*

moor·land /'mʊrlənd/ (also **moor**) *noun* [U, C, usually pl.] land that consists of moors: *walking across open moorland*

moose /mus/ *noun* (*pl.* **moose**) a large DEER that lives in N. America, the north of Europe, and Asia

moose

moot /mut/ *adj., verb*
• **adj.** unlikely to happen and therefore not worth considering: *He argued that the issue had become moot since the board had changed its policy.*
  IDM a moot point/question a matter about which there may be disagreement or confusion
• **verb** [usually passive] *~ sth* (*formal*) to suggest an idea for people to discuss SYN PROPOSE, PUT FORWARD

moot 'court *noun* a MOCK court in which law students practice trials

mop /mɑp/ *noun, verb*
• **noun 1** a tool for washing floors that has a long handle with a bunch of thick strings or soft material at the end: *a mop and bucket* ⊃ picture at CLEANING **2** a mass of thick, often messy, hair: *a mop of curly red hair*
• **verb** (-pp-) **1** *~ sth* to clean something with a mop: *She wiped all the surfaces and mopped the floor.* **2** *~ sth (from sth)* to remove liquid from the surface of something using a cloth: *He took out a handkerchief to mop his brow* (= to remove the sweat). **IDM see FLOOR**
  PHR V ,mop sth↔'up 1 to remove the liquid from something using something that absorbs it: *Do you want some bread to mop up that sauce?* **2** to complete or end something

by dealing with the final parts: *There are a few things that need mopping up before I can leave.* ◆ *Troops combed the area to mop up any remaining resistance.* ◆ *A number of smaller companies were mopped up* (= taken over) *by the big multinational.* ◆ *New equipment mopped up* (= used up) *what was left of this year's budget.*

mope /moʊp/ *verb* [I] to spend your time doing nothing and feeling sorry for yourself SYN BROOD: *It won't do any good to mope!*
  PHR V ,mope a'round (…) (*disapproving*) to spend time walking around a place with no particular purpose, especially because you feel sorry for yourself: *Instead of moping around the house all day, you should be out there looking for a job.*

mo·ped /'moʊpɛd/ *noun* a motorcycle with a small engine and also PEDALS

mop·pet /'mɑpət/ *noun* (*informal*) an attractive small child, especially a girl

mo·quette /moʊ'kɛt/ *noun* [U] a type of thick cloth with a soft surface made of a mass of small threads, used for making carpets and covering furniture

mo·raine /mə'reɪn/ *noun* [U, C] (*technical*) a mass of earth, stones, etc., carried along by a GLACIER and left when it melts

mor·al 🔊 /'mɔrəl; 'mar-/ *adj., noun*
• **adj. 1** [only before noun] concerned with principles of right and wrong behavior: *a moral issue/dilemma/question* ◆ *traditional moral values* ◆ *a decline in moral standards* ◆ *moral philosophy* ◆ *a deeply religious man with a highly developed moral sense* ◆ *The newspapers were full of moral outrage at the weakness of other countries.* **2** [only before noun] based on your own sense of what is right and fair, not on legal rights or duties SYN ETHICAL: *moral responsibility/duty* ◆ *Governments have at least a moral obligation to answer these questions.* ◆ *The job was to call on all her diplomatic skills and moral courage* (= the courage to do what you think is right). **3** following the standards of behavior considered acceptable and right by most people SYN GOOD, HONORABLE: *He led a very moral life.* ◆ *a very moral person* ⊃ compare AMORAL, IMMORAL **4** [only before noun] able to understand the difference between right and wrong: *Children are not naturally moral beings.*
  IDM take, claim, seize, etc. the moral high ground to claim that your side of an argument is morally better than your opponent's side; to argue in a way that makes your side seem morally better
• **noun 1 morals** [pl.] standards or principles of good behavior, especially in matters of sexual relationships: *Young people these days have no morals.* ◆ *The play was considered an affront to public morals.* ◆ (*old-fashioned*) *a woman of loose morals* (= with a low standard of sexual behavior) **2** [C] a practical lesson that a story, an event, or an experience teaches you: *And the moral is that crime doesn't pay.*

mo·rale /mə'ræl/ *noun* [U] the amount of confidence and enthusiasm, etc. that a person or a group has at a particular time: *to boost/raise/improve morale* ◆ *Morale among the players is very high at the moment.* ◆ *The staff is suffering from low morale.*

moral 'fiber *noun* [U] the inner strength to do what you believe to be right in difficult situations

mor·al·ist /'mɔrəlɪst; 'mar-/ *noun* **1** (often *disapproving*) a person who has strong ideas about moral principles, especially one who tries to tell other people how they should behave **2** a person who teaches or writes about moral principles

mor·al·is·tic /,mɔrə'lɪstɪk; ,mar-/ *adj.* (usually *disapproving*) having or showing very fixed ideas about what is right and wrong, especially when this causes you to judge other people's behavior

mo·ral·i·ty /mə'ræləti/ *noun* (*pl.* **mo·ral·i·ties**) **1** [U] principles concerning right and wrong or good and bad

ʌ **cup**   ə **about**   eɪ **say**   aɪ **five**   ɔɪ **boy**   aʊ **now**   oʊ **go**   ər **bird**

behavior: *matters of **public/private morality*** ♦ *Standards of morality seem to be dropping.* **2** [U] the degree to which something is right or wrong, good or bad, etc. according to moral principles: *a debate on the morality of abortion* **3** [U, C] a system of moral principles followed by a particular group of people **SYN** ETHICS ⮑ compare IMMORALITY

mo·'rality ˌplay *noun* a type of play that was popular in the 15th and 16th centuries and was intended to teach a moral lesson, using characters to represent good and bad qualities

mor·al·ize /'mɔrə.laɪz; 'mɑr-/ *verb* [I] (usually *disapproving*) to tell other people what is right and wrong, especially in order to emphasize that your opinions are correct **SYN** PREACH

mor·al·ly 🔑 /'mɔrəli; 'mɑr-/ *adv.*
according to principles of good behavior and what is considered to be right or wrong: *to act morally* ♦ *morally right/wrong/justified/unacceptable* ♦ *He felt morally responsible for the accident.*

the ˌmoral ma'jority *noun* [sing.] the largest group of people in a society, considered as having very traditional ideas about moral matters, religion, sexual behavior, etc.

ˌmoral sup'port *noun* [U] the act of giving encouragement by showing your approval and interest, rather than by giving financial or practical support: *My sister came along just to give me some moral support.*

ˌmoral 'victory *noun* a situation in which your ideas or principles are proved to be right and fair, even though you may not have succeeded where practical results are concerned

mo·rass /mə'ræs/ *noun* [usually sing.] (*formal*) **1** an unpleasant and complicated situation that is difficult to escape from **SYN** QUAGMIRE **2** a dangerous area of low, soft, wet land **SYN** BOG, QUAGMIRE

mor·a·to·ri·um /ˌmɔrə'tɔriəm/ *noun* (*pl.* **mor·a·to·ri·ums** or **mor·a·to·ri·a** /-iə/) ~ **(on sth)** a temporary stopping of an activity, especially by official agreement: *The convention called for a two-year moratorium on commercial whaling.*

mo·ray /'mɔreɪ; mɔ'reɪ/ (also ˌmoray 'eel) *noun* a type of EEL that hides among rocks in tropical waters

mor·bid /'mɔrbəd/ *adj.* **1** having or expressing a strong interest in sad or unpleasant things, especially disease or death: *He had a morbid fascination with blood.* ♦ *"He might even die." "Don't be so morbid."* **2** (*medical*) connected with disease ▶ **mor·bid·i·ty** /mɔr'bɪdəti/ *noun* [U] **mor·bid·ly** *adv.*

mor·dant /'mɔrdnt/ *adj.* (*formal*) critical and unkind, but funny **SYN** CAUSTIC: *His mordant wit appealed to students.* ▶ **mor·dant·ly** *adv.*

more 🔑 /mɔr/ *det., pron., adv.*
● **det., pron.** (used as the comparative of "much," "a lot of," or "many") ~ **(sth/of sth) (than…)** a larger number or amount of: *more bread/cars* ♦ *Only two more days to go!* ♦ *people with more money than sense* ♦ *I can't stand much more of this.* ♦ *She earns a lot more than I do.* ♦ *There is room for no more than three cars.* ♦ *I hope we'll see more of you* (= see you again or more often).
IDM **more and more** continuing to become larger in number or amount: *More and more people are using the Internet.* ♦ *She spends more and more time alone in her room.*
● **adv.** ~ **(than…)** **1** used to form the comparative of adjectives and adverbs with two or more syllables: *She was far more intelligent than her sister.* ♦ *He read the letter more carefully the second time.* **2** to a greater degree than something else; to a greater degree than usual: *I like her more than her husband.* ♦ *a course for more advanced students* ♦ *It had more the appearance of a deliberate crime than of an accident.* ♦ *Could you repeat that once more* (= one more time)? ♦ *Signing the forms is little more than* (= only) *a formality.* ♦ *I'm more than happy* (= extremely happy) *to take you there in my car.* ♦ *She was more than a little shaken* (= extremely shaken) *by the*

experience. ♦ (*formal*) *I will torment you no more* (= no longer).
⮑ see also ANYMORE
IDM **more and more** continuing to become larger in number or amount **SYN** INCREASINGLY: *I was becoming more and more irritated by his behavior.* **more or less 1** almost: *I've more or less finished the book.* **2** approximately: *She could earn $200 a night, more or less.* **the more, less, etc.…, the more, less, etc.…** used to show that two things change to the same degree: *The more she thought about it, the more depressed she became.* ⮑ see also LESS **what is more** used to add a point that is even more important: *You're wrong, and what's more you know it!* ⮑ language bank at ADDITION

mo·rel /mə'rɛl/ (also moˌrel 'mushroom) *noun* a type of MUSHROOM that you can eat, with a top that is full of holes

more·o·ver 🔑 /mɔr'oʊvər/ *adv.* (*formal*)
used to introduce some new information that adds to or supports what you have said previously **SYN** IN ADDITION: *A talented artist, he was, moreover, a writer of some note.* ⮑ language bank at ADDITION

mo·res /'mɔreɪz/ *noun* [pl.] (*formal*) the customs and behavior that are considered typical of a particular social group or community **SYN** CONVENTIONS

morgue /mɔrg/ *noun* a building in which dead bodies are kept until they can be identified or until they are buried or CREMATED (= burned) ⮑ compare MORTUARY

mor·i·bund /'mɔrə.bʌnd; 'mɑr-/ *adj.* (*formal*) **1** (of an industry, an institution, a custom, etc.) no longer effective and about to come to an end completely **2** in a very bad condition; dying: *a moribund patient/tree*

Mor·mon /'mɔrmən/ *noun* a member of a religion formed by Joseph Smith in the U.S. in 1830, officially called "the Church of Jesus Christ of Latter-day Saints" ▶ **Mor·mon** *adj.*: *a Mormon church/chapel* **Mor·mon·ism** *noun* [U]

morn /mɔrn/ *noun* [usually sing.] (*literary*) morning

morn·ing 🔑 /'mɔrnɪŋ/ *noun*
1 the early part of the day, from the time when people wake up until noon, or before lunch: *They left for Mexico early this morning.* ♦ *See you tomorrow morning.* ♦ *I prefer coffee in the morning.* ♦ *She woke up every morning at the same time.* ♦ *Our group meets on Friday mornings.* ♦ *I walk to work most mornings.* ♦ *We got the news on the morning of the wedding.* ♦ *He's been in a meeting all morning.* ♦ *the morning papers* ⮑ see also GOOD MORNING **2** the part of the day from midnight to noon: *I didn't get home until two in the morning!* ♦ *He died in the early hours of Sunday morning.* **3** mornings *adv.* in the early part of the day, before lunch: *I only work mornings.*
IDM **in the morning 1** before midday of the next day; tomorrow morning: *I'll give you a call in the morning.* **2** between midnight and noon: *It must have happened at about five o'clock in the morning.* **morning, noon, and night** at all times of the day and night (used to emphasize that something happens very often or that it happens continuously): *She talks about him morning, noon, and night.* ♦ *The work continues morning, noon, and night.* ⮑ more at OTHER

ˌmorning-'after *adj.* [only before noun] **1** happening the next day, after an exciting or important event: *After his election victory, the president held a morning-after news conference.* **2** used to describe how someone feels the next morning, after an occasion when they have drunk too much alcohol: *a morning-after headache*

ˌmorning-'after ˌpill *noun* a drug that a woman can take some hours after having sex in order to avoid becoming pregnant

'morning ˌglory *noun* [C, U] a climbing plant with flowers shaped like TRUMPETS that open in the morning and close in late afternoon

'morning ˌroom *noun* (*old-fashioned*) (in some large houses, especially in the past) a room that you sit in in the morning

'morning ˌsickness *noun* [U] the need to VOMIT that some women feel, often only in the morning, when they are pregnant, especially in the first months

the ˌmorning ˈstar *noun* [sing.] the planet Venus, when it shines in the east before the sun rises

mo·roc·co /məˈrɑkoʊ/ *noun* [U] fine soft leather made from the skin of a GOAT, used especially for making shoes and covering books

mo·ron /ˈmɔrɑn/ *noun* (*informal*) an offensive way of referring to someone that you think is very stupid: *They're a bunch of morons.* ◆ *You moron—now look what you've done!* ▶ **mo·ron·ic** /məˈrɑnɪk; mɔ-/ *adj.*: *a moronic stare* ◆ *a moronic TV program*

mo·rose /məˈroʊs/ *adj.* unhappy, bad-tempered, and not talking very much **SYN** GLOOMY: *She just sat there looking morose.* ▶ **mo·rose·ly** *adv.*

morph /mɔrf/ *verb* **1** [I, T] ~ (sth) (into sth) to change smoothly from one image to another using computer ANIMATION; to make an image change in this way **2** [I, T] ~ (sb/sth) (into sb/sth) to change, or make someone or something change, into something different

mor·pheme /ˈmɔrfim/ *noun* (*grammar*) the smallest unit of meaning that a word can be divided into: *The word "like" contains one morpheme but "un·like·ly" contains three.*

mor·phine /ˈmɔrfin/ (also *old-fashioned* **mor·phi·a** /ˈmɔrfiə/) *noun* [U] a powerful drug that is made from OPIUM and used to reduce pain

mor·phol·o·gy /mɔrˈfɑlədʒi/ *noun* [U] **1** (*biology*) the form and structure of animals and plants, studied as a science **2** (*linguistics*) the forms of words, studied as a branch of linguistics ⊃ **compare** GRAMMAR, SYNTAX ▶ **mor·pho·log·i·cal** /ˌmɔrfəˈlɑdʒɪkl/ *adj.*

mor·row /ˈmɑroʊ; ˈmɔr-/ *noun* **the morrow** [sing.] (*old-fashioned, literary*) the next day; tomorrow: *We had to leave on the morrow.* ◆ *Who knows what the morrow* (= the future) *will bring?*

Morse code /ˌmɔrs ˈkoʊd/ *noun* [U] a system for sending messages, using combinations of long and short sounds or flashes of light to represent letters of the alphabet and numbers

mor·sel /ˈmɔrsl/ *noun* a small amount or a piece of something, especially food: *a tasty morsel of food* ◆ *He ate it all, down to the last morsel.*

mor·tal /ˈmɔrtl/ *adj., noun*
● *adj.* **1** that cannot live for ever and must die: *We are all mortal.* **ANT** IMMORTAL **2** (*literary*) causing death or likely to cause death; very serious: *a mortal blow/wound* ◆ *to be in mortal danger* ◆ (*figurative*) *Her reputation suffered a mortal blow as a result of the scandal.* ⊃ **compare** FATAL **3** [only before noun] (*formal*) lasting until death **SYN** DEADLY: *mortal enemies* ◆ *They were locked in mortal combat* (= a fight that will only end with the death of one of them). **4** [only before noun] (*formal*) (of fear, etc.) extreme: *We lived in mortal dread of him discovering our secret.*
● *noun* (often *humorous*) a human, especially an ordinary person with little power or influence **SYN** HUMAN BEING: *old stories about gods and mortals* ◆ (*humorous*) *Such things are not for mere mortals like ourselves.* ◆ (*humorous*) *She can deal with complicated numbers in her head, but we lesser mortals need calculators!*

mor·tal·i·ty /mɔrˈtæləti/ *noun* (*pl.* **mor·tal·i·ties**) **1** [U] the state of being human and not living for ever: *After her mother's death, she became acutely aware of her own mortality.* **2** [U] the number of deaths in a particular situation or period of time: *the infant mortality rate* (= the number of babies that die at or just after birth) ◆ *Mortality from lung cancer is still increasing.* **3** [C] (*technical*) a death: *hospital mortalities* (= deaths in hospital)

mor·tal·ly /ˈmɔrtl·i/ *adv.* (*literary*) **1** causing or resulting in death **SYN** FATALLY: *mortally wounded/ill* **2** extremely: *mortally afraid/offended*

ˌmortal ˈsin *noun* [C,U] (in the Roman Catholic Church) a very serious SIN for which you can be sent to HELL unless you CONFESS and are forgiven

mor·tar /ˈmɔrtər/ *noun, verb*
● *noun* **1** [U] a mixture of sand, water, LIME, and CEMENT used in building for holding bricks and stones together **2** [C] a heavy gun that fires bombs and SHELLS high into the air; the bombs that are fired by this gun: *to come under mortar fire/attack* **3** [C] a small hard bowl in which you can crush substances such as seeds and grains into powder with a special object (called a PESTLE) ⊃ **picture at** KITCHEN, LABORATORY **IDM** see BRICK
● *verb* [I, T] ~ (sb/sth) to attack someone or something using a mortar *n.* (2)

mor·tar·board /ˈmɔrtərˌbɔrd/ *noun* a black hat with a stiff square top, worn at special ceremonies at high school or college, especially when students graduate ⊃ **picture at** HAT ⊃ **compare** CAP

mort·gage /ˈmɔrgɪdʒ/ *noun, verb*
● *noun* (also *informal* ˌhome ˈloan) a legal agreement by which a bank or similar organization lends you money to buy a house, etc., and you pay the money back over a particular number of years; the sum of money that you borrow: *to apply for/take out/pay off a mortgage* ◆ *mortgage rates* (= of interest) ◆ *a mortgage on the house* ◆ *a mortgage of $260,000* ◆ *monthly mortgage repayments*
● *verb* ~ sth to give a bank, etc. the legal right to own your house, land, etc. if you do not pay the money back that you have borrowed from the bank to buy the house or land: *He had to mortgage his house to pay his legal costs.*

mort·ga·gee /ˌmɔrgɪˈdʒi/ *noun* (*technical*) a person or an organization that lends money to people to buy houses, etc.

mort·ga·gor /ˌmɔrgɪˈdʒɔr; ˈmɔrgɪdʒər/ *noun* (*technical*) a person who borrows money from a bank or a similar organization to buy a house, etc.

mor·ti·cian /mɔrˈtɪʃn/ *noun* = FUNERAL DIRECTOR

mor·ti·fy /ˈmɔrtəˌfaɪ/ *verb* (**mor·ti·fies, mor·ti·fy·ing, mor·ti·fied, mor·ti·fied**) [usually passive] ~ sb (to do sth) | it **mortifies sb that...** to make someone feel very ashamed or embarrassed **SYN** HUMILIATE: *She was mortified to realize he had heard every word she said.* ▶ **mor·ti·fi·ca·tion** /ˌmɔrtəfəˈkeɪʃn/ *noun* [U] **mor·ti·fy·ing** *adj.*: *How mortifying to have to apologize to him!*

mor·tise (also **mor·tice**) /ˈmɔrtɪs/ *noun* (*technical*) a hole cut in a piece of wood, etc. to receive the end of another piece of wood, so that the two are held together ⊃ **see also** TENON

ˈmortise ˌlock *noun* a lock that is fitted inside a hole cut into the edge of a door, not one that is screwed into the surface of one side

mor·tu·ar·y /ˈmɔrtʃuˌeri/ *noun* (*pl.* **mor·tu·ar·ies**) **1** a room or building, for example part of a hospital, in which dead bodies are kept before they are buried or CREMATED (= burned) **2** = FUNERAL PARLOR ⊃ **compare** MORGUE

mo·sa·ic /moʊˈzeɪɪk/ *noun* [C, U] a picture or pattern made by placing together small pieces of glass, stone, etc. of different colors: *a Roman mosaic* ◆ *a design in mosaic* ◆ *mosaic tiles* ◆ (*figurative*) *A mosaic of fields, rivers, and woods lay below us.*

Mo·selle /moʊˈzɛl/ (also **Mo·sel** /ˈmoʊzɛl/) *noun* [U, C] a type of German white wine

mo·sey /ˈmoʊzi/ *verb* [I] + adv./prep. (*informal*) to go in a particular direction slowly and with no definite purpose: *He moseyed on over to the bar.*

mosh /mɑʃ/ *verb* [I] to dance and jump up and down violently or without control at a concert where ROCK music is played

ˈmosh pit *noun* the place, just in front of the stage, where the audience at a concert of ROCK music moshes

Mos·lem /ˈmɑzləm/ *noun* = MUSLIM ▶ **Moslem** *adj.* = MUSLIM **HELP** The form **Moslem** is sometimes considered old-fashioned. Use **Muslim**.

mosque /mɑsk/ *noun* a building in which Muslims worship

| t **t**ea | ţ bu**tt**er | d **d**id | k **c**at | g **g**ot | tʃ **ch**in | dʒ **J**une | f **f**all |

mos·qui·to /məˈskitoʊ/ noun (pl. **mos·qui·toes** or **mos-qui·tos**) a flying insect that bites humans and animals and sucks their blood. One type of mosquito can spread the disease MALARIA: *a mosquito bite* ➔ picture at ANIMAL

mosˈquito ˌnet noun a net that you hang over a bed, etc. to keep mosquitoes away from you

moss /mɔs/ noun [U, C] a very small green or yellow plant without flowers that spreads over damp surfaces, rocks, etc.: *moss-covered walls* ➔ picture at PLANT ➔ compare LICHEN ➔ see also PEAT MOSS, SPANISH MOSS **IDM** see ROLL v.

moss·y /ˈmɔsi/ adj. covered with moss

most 🔑 /moʊst/ det., pron., adv.
• **det., pron.** (used as the superlative of "much," "a lot of," or "many") **1** the largest in number or amount: *Who do you think will get (the) most votes?* ◆ *She had the most money of all of them.* ◆ *I spent the most time on the first question.* ◆ *Who ate the most?* ◆ *The director has the most to lose.* **HELP** The can be left out in informal English. **2** more than half of someone or something; almost all of someone or something: *I like most vegetables.* ◆ *Most classical music puts me to sleep.* ◆ *As most of you know, I've decided to resign.* ◆ *Most of the people I had invited turned up.* ◆ *There are thousands of verbs in English and most (of them) are regular.* **HELP** The is not used with **most** in this meaning.
IDM at (the) most not more than: *As a news item it merits a short paragraph at most.* ◆ *There were 50 people there, at the very most.*
• **adv. 1** used to form the superlative of adjectives and adverbs of two or more syllables: *the most boring/beautiful part* ◆ *It was the people with the least money who gave most generously.* **HELP** When **most** is followed only by an adverb, the is not used: *This reason is mentioned most frequently,* but: *This is the most frequently mentioned reason.* **2** to the greatest degree: *What did you enjoy (the) most?* ◆ *It was what she wanted most of all.* **HELP** The is often left out in informal English. **3** (formal) very; extremely; completely: *It was most kind of you to meet me.* ◆ *We shall most probably never meet again.* ◆ *This technique looks easy, but it most certainly is not.* **4** (informal) almost: *I go to the store most every day.*

-most /moʊst/ suffix (in adjectives) the furthest: *inmost* (= the furthest in) ◆ *southernmost* ◆ *topmost* (= the furthest up/nearest to the top)

ˌmost favored ˈnation noun a country to which another country allows the most advantages in trade, because they have a good relationship

most·ly 🔑 /ˈmoʊstli/ adv.
mainly; generally: *The sauce is mostly cream.* ◆ *We're mostly out on Sundays.* ◆ *Mostly, I feel like sleeping.*

mote /moʊt/ noun (old-fashioned) a very small piece of dust **SYN** SPECK

mo·tel /moʊˈtɛl/ (also **ˈmotor ˌinn**, **ˈmotor ˌlodge**) noun a hotel for people who are traveling by car, with space for parking cars near the rooms

mo·tet /moʊˈtɛt/ noun a short piece of church music, usually for voices only ➔ compare CANTATA

moth /mɔθ/ noun a flying insect with a long thin body and four large wings, like a BUTTERFLY, but less brightly colored. Moths fly mainly at night and are attracted to bright lights. ➔ picture at ANIMAL ➔ see also GYPSY MOTH

moth·ball /ˈmɔθbɔl/ noun, verb
• **noun** a small white ball made of a chemical with a strong smell, used for keeping moths away from clothes
IDM in mothballs stored and not in use, often for a long time
• **verb** [usually passive] ~ sth to decide not to use or develop something for a period of time, especially a piece of equipment or a plan: *The original proposal had been mothballed years ago.* **SYN** SHELVE

ˈmoth-ˌeaten adj. **1** (of clothes, etc.) damaged or

destroyed by moths **2** (informal, disapproving) very old and in bad condition **SYN** SHABBY

moth·er 🔑 /ˈmʌðər/ noun, verb
• **noun 1** a female parent of a child or animal; a person who is acting as a mother to a child: *I want to buy a present for my mother and father.* ◆ *the relationship between mother and baby* ◆ *She's the mother of twins.* ◆ *a mother of three* (= with three children) ◆ *an expectant* (= pregnant) *mother* ◆ *She was a wonderful mother to both her natural and adopted children.* ◆ *the mother chimpanzee caring for her young* **2** the title of a woman who is head of a CONVENT (= a community of NUNS) ➔ see also MOTHER SUPERIOR
IDM at your mother's knee when you were very young: *I learned these songs at my mother's knee.* the mother of (all) sth (informal) used to emphasize that something is very large, unpleasant, important, etc.: *I got stuck in the mother of all traffic jams.* ➔ more at NECESSITY, OLD
• **verb** ~ sb/sth to care for someone or something because you are their mother, or as if you were their mother: *He was a disturbed child who needed to be mothered.* ◆ *Stop mothering me!*

moth·er·board /ˈmʌðərˌbɔrd/ noun (computing) the main board of a computer, containing all the CIRCUITS

ˈmother ˌcountry noun [sing.] **1** the country where you or your family were born and that you feel a strong emotional connection with ➔ compare MOTHERLAND **2** the country that controls or used to control the government of another country

ˈmother ˌfigure noun an older woman that you go to for advice, support, help, etc., as you would to a mother ➔ see also FATHER FIGURE

ˌmother ˈhen noun (usually disapproving) a woman who likes to care for and protect people and who worries about them a lot

moth·er·hood /ˈmʌðərˌhʊd/ noun [U] the state of being a mother: *Motherhood suits her.*

moth·er·ing /ˈmʌðərɪŋ/ noun [U] the act of caring for and protecting children or other people: *an example of good/poor mothering*

ˈmother-in-ˌlaw noun (pl. mothers-in-law) the mother of your husband or wife ➔ compare FATHER-IN-LAW

ˈmother-in-law aˌpartment noun = IN-LAW APARTMENT

moth·er·land /ˈmʌðərˌlænd/ noun (formal) the country that you were born in and that you feel a strong emotional connection with ➔ see also FATHERLAND

moth·er·less /ˈmʌðərləs/ adj. having no mother because she has died or does not live with you

ˈmother ˌlode noun [usually sing.] a very rich source of gold, silver, etc. in a mine: (figurative) *Her own experiences have provided her with a mother lode of material for her songs.*

moth·er·ly /ˈmʌðərli/ adj. having the qualities of a good mother; typical of a mother **SYN** MATERNAL: *motherly love* ◆ *She was a kind, motherly woman.*

ˌMother ˈNature noun [U] the natural world, when you consider it as a force that affects the world and humans

ˌmother-of-ˈpearl (also pearl) noun [U] the hard, smooth, shiny substance in various colors that forms a layer inside the shells of some types of SHELLFISH and is used in making buttons, decorative objects, etc.

ˈMother's ˌDay noun a day on which mothers traditionally receive cards and gifts from their children, celebrated on the 2nd Sunday in May

ˈmother ˌship noun a large ship or SPACECRAFT that smaller ones go out from

ˌmother's ˈmilk noun [U] a thing that a person really needs or enjoys: *Jazz is mother's milk to me.*

ˌMother Suˈperior noun a woman who is the head of a female religious community, especially a CONVENT (= a community of NUNS)

mother-to-'be *noun* (*pl.* mothers-to-be) a woman who is pregnant

mother 'tongue *noun* the language that you first learn to speak when you are a child **SYN** FIRST LANGUAGE

mo·tif /moʊˈtiːf/ *noun* **1** a design or a pattern used as a decoration: *wallpaper with a flower motif* **2** (also **mo·tive**) a subject, an idea, or a phrase that is repeated and developed in a work of literature or a piece of music **SYN** THEME ⊃ see also LEITMOTIF

mo·tion ♪ /ˈmoʊʃn/ *noun, verb*
• *noun* **1** [U, sing.] the act or process of moving or the way something moves: *Newton's laws of motion* ◆ *The swaying motion of the ship was making me feel seasick.* ◆ *(formal) Do not exit while the train is still in motion* (= moving). ◆ *Rub the cream in with a circular motion.* ⊃ see also SLOW MOTION **2** [C] a particular movement made usually with your hand or your head, especially to communicate something **SYN** GESTURE: *At a single motion of his hand, the room fell silent.* **3** [C] a formal proposal that is discussed and voted on at a meeting: *to table/make a motion* ◆ *to propose a motion* (= to be the main speaker in favor of a motion) ◆ *The motion was adopted/carried by six votes to one.*
IDM **go through the motions (of doing sth)** to do or say something because you have to, not because you really want to **set/put sth in motion** to start something moving: *They set the machinery in motion.* ◆ *(figurative) The wheels of change have been set in motion.*
• *verb* [I, T] to make a movement, usually with your hand or head, to show someone what you want them to do: **~ to sb (to do sth)** *I motioned to the waiter.* ◆ **~ (for) sb to do sth** *He motioned for us to follow him.* ◆ **~ sb + adv./prep.** *She motioned him into her office.*

mo·tion·less /ˈmoʊʃnləs/ *adj.* not moving; still: *She stood absolutely motionless.*

motion 'picture *noun* a movie

'motion ˌsickness *noun* [U] the unpleasant feeling that you are going to VOMIT, that some people have when they are moving, especially in a vehicle

mo·ti·vate **AWL** /ˈmoʊtəˌveɪt/ *verb* **1** [often passive] **~ sb** to be the reason why someone does something or behaves in a particular way: *He is motivated entirely by self-interest.* **2** to make someone want to do something, especially something that involves hard work and effort: **~ sb** *She's very good at motivating her students.* ◆ **~ sb to do sth** *The plan is designed to motivate employees to work more efficiently.*
▶ **mo·ti·va·ted** **AWL** *adj.*: *a racially motivated attack* ◆ *a highly motivated student* (= one who is very interested and works hard) **ANT** UNMOTIVATED **mo·ti·va·tion** **AWL** /ˌmoʊtəˈveɪʃn/ *noun* [C, U]: *What is the motivation behind this sudden change?* ◆ *Most people said that pay was their main motivation for working.* ◆ *He's intelligent enough but he lacks motivation.* **mo·ti·va·tion·al** /-ʃənl/ *adj.* (*formal*): *an important motivational factor* **mo·ti·va·tor** /ˈmoʊtəˌveɪtər/ *noun*: *Desire for status can be a powerful motivator.*

mo·tive **AWL** /ˈmoʊtɪv/ *noun, adj.*
• *noun* **1 ~ (for sth)** a reason for doing something: *There seemed to be no motive for the murder.* ◆ *I'm suspicious of his motives.* ◆ *the profit motive* (= the desire to make a profit) ◆ *I have an ulterior motive in offering to help you.* ⊃ thesaurus box at REASON **2** = MOTIF (2) ▶ **mo·tive·less** /-ləs/ *adj.*: *an apparently motiveless murder/attack*
• *adj.* [only before noun] (*technical*) causing movement or action: *motive power/force* (= for example, electricity, to operate machinery)

mot juste /ˌmoʊ ˈʒuːst/ *noun* (*pl.* mots justes /ˌmoʊ ˈʒuːst/) (from *French*) the exact word that is appropriate for the situation

mot·ley /ˈmɑtli/ *adj.* [only before noun] (*disapproving*) consisting of many different types of people or things that do not seem to belong together: *The room was filled with a motley collection of furniture and paintings.* ◆ *The audience was a motley crew of students and tourists.*

mo·to·cross /ˈmoʊtoʊˌkrɔs/ *noun* [U] the sport of racing motorcycles over rough ground

mo·to·neu·ron /ˌmoʊtəˈnʊrɑn/ *noun* = MOTOR NEURON

mo·tor ♪ /ˈmoʊtər/ *noun, adj.*
• *noun* a device that uses electricity, gas, etc. to produce movement and makes a machine, a vehicle, a boat, etc. work: *an electric motor* ◆ *He started the motor.* ⊃ see also OUTBOARD MOTOR
• *adj.* [only before noun] **1** having an engine; using the power of an engine: *motor vehicles* **2** connected with vehicles that have engines: *the motor industry* ◆ *motor oil* ◆ *motor sports* **3** (*technical*) connected with movement of the body that is produced by muscles; connected with the nerves that control movement: *uncoordinated motor activity* ◆ *motor skills* ◆ *Both motor and sensory functions are affected.*

mo·tor·bike /ˈmoʊtərˌbaɪk/ *noun* **1** a small motorcycle **2** a bicycle that has a small engine

mo·tor·boat /ˈmoʊtərˌboʊt/ *noun* a small fast boat driven by an engine

mo·tor·cade /ˈmoʊtərˌkeɪd/ *noun* a line of vehicles including one or more that famous or important people are traveling in: *The President's motorcade glided by.*

'motor ˌcar *noun* (*old-fashioned*) a car

mo·tor·cy·cle ♪ /ˈmoʊtərˌsaɪkl/ *noun* a road vehicle with two wheels, driven by an engine, with one seat for the driver and often a seat for a passenger behind the driver: *motorcycle racing* ◆ *a motorcycle accident* ⊃ picture at BICYCLE ⊃ collocations at DRIVING

mo·tor·cy·cling /ˈmoʊtərˌsaɪklɪŋ/ *noun* [U] the sport of riding motorcycles

mo·tor·cy·clist /ˈmoʊtərˌsaɪklɪst/ *noun* a person riding a motorcycle: *a police motorcyclist* ◆ *leather-clad motorcyclists*

'motor ˌhome *noun* a large vehicle with a kitchen, beds, etc. designed for people to live in when they are traveling ⊃ compare CAMPER, RV

mo·tor·ist /ˈmoʊtərɪst/ *noun* a person driving a car ⊃ compare PEDESTRIAN

mo·tor·ized /ˈmoʊtəˌraɪzd/ *adj.* [only before noun] **1** having an engine: *motorized vehicles* ◆ *a motorized wheelchair* **2** (of groups of soldiers, etc.) using vehicles with engines: *motorized forces/divisions*

'motor ˌlodge (also **'motor ˌinn**) *noun* = MOTEL

mo·tor·man /ˈmoʊætusɪpɑːrmən/ *noun* (*pl.* **mo·tor·men** /-mən/) a man who drives a SUBWAY train, a STREETCAR, a CABLE CAR, etc.

mo·tor·mouth /ˈmoʊtərˌmaʊθ/ *noun* (*pl.* **mo·tor·mouths** /-ˌmaʊðz/) (*informal*) a person who talks loudly and too much

'motor ˌneuron (also **mo·to·neu·ron**) *noun* (*biology*) a nerve cell that sends signals to a muscle or GLAND

'motor ˌneuron disˌease (also **ˌmoto'neuron disease**) *noun* [U] a disease in which the nerves and muscles become gradually weaker until the person dies

'motor ˌpool *noun* a group of cars owned by a company or an organization, that its staff can use

'motor ˌscooter *noun* = SCOOTER

mo·tor·sport /ˈmoʊtərˌspɔrt/ *noun* [U] (also **mo·tor·sports** [pl.]) the sport of racing fast cars or motorcycles on a special track

'motor ˌvehicle *noun* any road vehicle driven by an engine

Mo·town /ˈmoʊtaʊn/ *noun* [U] a style of music popular in the 1960s and 1970s, produced by a black music company based in Detroit **ORIGIN** From the informal name for the city of Detroit.

mot·tled /ˈmɑtld/ *adj.* marked with shapes of different colors without a regular pattern

mot·to /ˈmɑtoʊ/ *noun* (*pl.* **mot·toes** or **mot·tos**) a short sentence or phrase that expresses the aims and beliefs of a person, a group, an institution, etc. and is used as a rule of

h **hat**   m **man**   n **no**   ŋ **sing**   l **leg**   r **red**   y **yes**   w **wet**

behavior: *The school's motto is: "Duty, Honor, Country."* ◆ *"Live and let live." That's my motto.* ◆ *Our national motto is: "In God we trust."*

mound /maʊnd/ *noun* **1** a large pile of earth or stones; a small hill: *an ancient burial mound* ◆ *The fort was built on top of a natural grassy mound.* **2** a pile **SYN** HEAP: *a small mound of rice/sand* **3** ~ **of sth** (*informal*) a large amount of something **SYN** HEAP: *I have a mound of paperwork to do.* **4** (in baseball) the small hill where the player who throws the ball (called the PITCHER) stands ⊃ **picture at** BASEBALL

mount 🔑 /maʊnt/ *verb, noun*
● *verb*
⊳ GO UP SOMETHING **1** [T] ~ **sth** (*formal*) to go up something, or up on to something that is raised **SYN** ASCEND: *She slowly mounted the steps.* ◆ *He mounted the platform and addressed the crowd.*
⊳ INCREASE **2** [I] to increase gradually: *Pressure is mounting on the government to change the law.* ◆ *The death toll continues to mount.* ⊃ **see also** MOUNTING
⊳ PICTURE/JEWEL, ETC. **3** [T] ~ **sth (on/onto/in sth)** to put something into position on something, so that you can use it, look at it, or study it: *The specimens were mounted on slides.* ◆ *The diamond is mounted in gold.*
⊳ ORGANIZE **4** [T] ~ **sth** to organize and begin something **SYN** ARRANGE: *to mount a protest/campaign/an exhibition*
⊳ BICYCLE/HORSE **5** [T, I] ~ **(sth)** to get on a bicycle, horse, etc. in order to ride it: *He mounted his horse and rode away.* **ANT** DISMOUNT ⊃ **see also** MOUNTED
⊳ OF MALE ANIMAL **6** [T] ~ **sth** to get onto the back of a female animal in order to have sex
PHR V ˌmount ˈup to increase gradually in size and quantity: *Meanwhile, my debts were mounting up.* **SYN** BUILD UP
● *noun*
⊳ MOUNTAIN **1** Mount (*abbr.* Mt.) (used in modern English only in place names) a mountain or a hill: *Mt. Everest* ◆ *Mount Rainier*
⊳ HORSE **2** (*formal or literary*) a horse that you ride on
⊳ FOR DISPLAYING/SUPPORTING SOMETHING **3** something such as a piece of heavy paper or glass that you put something on or attach something to, to display it **4** = MOUNTING: *an engine/gun mount*

moun·tain 🔑 /ˈmaʊntn/ *noun*
1 a very high hill, often with rocks near the top: *a chain/range of mountains* ◆ *to climb a mountain* ◆ *We spent a week walking in the mountains.* ◆ *to enjoy the mountain air/scenery* ◆ *mountain roads/streams/villages* ◆ *a mountain rescue team* **2** ~ **of sth** (*informal*) a very large amount or number of something: *a mountain of work* ◆ *We made mountains of sandwiches.*
IDM **make a mountain out of a molehill** (*disapproving*) to make an unimportant matter seem important

ˈmountain ˌash *noun* a small tree that has red berries (BERRY) in the autumn

ˈmountain ˌbike *noun* a bicycle with a strong frame, wide tires, and many gears, designed for riding on rough ground ⊃ **picture at** BICYCLE ⊃ **compare** DIRT BIKE
▶ ˈmountain ˌbiking *noun* [U]

ˈmoun·tain·board /ˈmaʊntnˌbɔrd/ (also ˌall-terrain ˈboard) *noun* a short narrow board with wheels like a SKATEBOARD that can be used for going down mountains
▶ ˈmoun·tain·board·ing *noun* [U]

ˌmoun·tain·eer /ˌmaʊntnˈɪr/ *noun* a person who climbs mountains as a sport

ˌmoun·tain·eer·ing /ˌmaʊntnˈɪrɪŋ/ *noun* [U] the sport or activity of climbing mountains: *to go mountaineering* ◆ *a mountaineering expedition*

ˈmountain ˌlion *noun* = COUGAR

ˈmountain ˌman *noun* a man who lives alone in the mountains, especially one who catches and kills animals for their fur

moun·tain·ous /ˈmaʊntn·əs/ *adj.* **1** having many moun-

tains: *a mountainous region/terrain* **2** very large in size or amount; like a mountain **SYN** HUGE: *mountainous waves*

moun·tain·side /ˈmaʊntnˌsaɪd/ *noun* the side or slope of a mountain: *Tracks led up the mountainside.*

ˈMountain ˌtime *noun* [U] the standard time system that is used in the parts of the U.S. and Canada that are near the Rocky Mountains ⊃ **compare** ATLANTIC TIME, CENTRAL TIME, EASTERN TIME, PACIFIC TIME

moun·tain·top /ˈmaʊntnˌtɑp/ *noun* the top of a mountain
▶ **moun·tain·top** *adj.* [only before noun]: *a mountaintop ranch*

moun·te·bank /ˈmaʊntɪˌbæŋk/ *noun* (*old-fashioned*) a person who tries to trick people, especially in order to get their money

mount·ed /ˈmaʊntəd/ *adj.* [only before noun] **1** (of a person, especially a soldier or a police officer) riding a horse: *mounted policemen* **2** placed on something or attached to something for display or support: *a mounted photograph* **3** -mounted (in compounds) attached to the thing mentioned for support: *a ceiling-mounted fan* ⊃ **see also** WALL-MOUNTED

Moun·tie /ˈmaʊnti/ *noun* (*informal*) a member of the Royal Canadian Mounted Police

mount·ing /ˈmaʊntɪŋ/ *adj., noun*
● *adj.* [only before noun] increasing, often in a manner that causes or expresses anxiety **SYN** GROWING: *mounting excitement/concern/tension* ◆ *There is mounting evidence of serious effects on people's health.*
● *noun* (also **mount**) something that an object stands on or is attached to for support: *The engine came loose from its mountings.*

mourn /mɔrn/ *verb* [T, I] to feel and show sadness because someone has died; to feel sad because something no longer exists or is no longer the same **SYN** GRIEVE: ~ **sth** *He was still mourning his brother's death.* ◆ *They mourn the passing of a simpler way of life.* ◆ ~ **(for sb/sth)** *Today we mourn for all those who died in two world wars.* ◆ *She mourned for her lost childhood.*

mourn·er /ˈmɔrnər/ *noun* a person who attends a funeral, especially a friend or a relative of the dead person

mourn·ful /ˈmɔrnfl/ *adj.* very sad **SYN** MELANCHOLY: *mournful eyes* ◆ *mournful music* ◆ *I couldn't bear the mournful look on her face.* ▶ **mourn·ful·ly** /-fəli/ *adv.*: *The dog looked mournfully after its owner.*

mourn·ing /ˈmɔrnɪŋ/ *noun* [U] **1** sadness that you show and feel because someone has died **SYN** GRIEF: *The government announced a day of national mourning for the victims.* ◆ *She was still in mourning for her husband.* **2** clothes that people wear to show their sadness at someone's death

mouse 🔑 /maʊs/ *noun, verb*
● *noun* (pl. **mice** /maɪs/) **1** a small animal that is covered in fur and has a long thin tail. Mice live in fields, in people's houses, or where food is stored: *a house mouse* ◆ *The storerooms were overrun with rats and mice.* ◆ *She crept upstairs, quiet as a mouse.* ◆ (*figurative*) *He was a weak little mouse of a man.* ⊃ **see also** DORMOUSE, FIELD MOUSE ⊃ **picture at** RODENT **2** (pl. also **mous·es**) (*computing*) a small device that is moved by hand across a surface to control the movement of the CURSOR on a computer screen: *Click the left mouse button twice to start the program.* ◆ *Use the mouse to drag the icon to a new position.* ⊃ **picture at** COMPUTER **IDM** see CAT
● *verb*
PHR V ˈmouse over sth (*computing*) to use the mouse to move over something on a computer screen: *Mouse over the link in the original message.* ▶ **mouse·o·ver** /ˈmaʊsˌoʊvər/ *noun*: *the use of mouseovers in web design*

ˈmouse pad *noun* a small square of plastic that is the best kind of surface on which to use a computer mouse

ˈmouse po·ta·to *noun* (*disapproving, informal*) a person who spends too much time using a computer

mous·er /ˈmaʊsər/ *noun* a cat that catches mice

mouse·trap /ˈmaʊstræp/ *noun* a trap with a powerful spring that is used, for example in a house, for catching mice

mous·ey = MOUSY

mous·sa·ka /muˈsɑːkə; ˌmusəˈkɑː/ *noun* [U, C] a Greek dish made from layers of EGGPLANT and finely chopped meat with cheese on top

mousse /mus/ *noun* [C, U] **1** a cold DESSERT (= a sweet dish) made with cream and egg whites and flavored with fruit, chocolate, etc.; a similar dish flavored with fish, vegetables, etc.: *a chocolate/strawberry mousse* ◆ *salmon/mushroom mousse* **2** a substance that is sold in AEROSOLS, for example the light white substance that is used on hair to give it a particular style or to improve its condition

mous·y (also **mousey**) /ˈmaʊsi/ *adj.* **1** (of hair) of a dull brown color **2** (usually *disapproving*) (of people) shy and quiet; without a strong personality

mouth ℒ *noun, verb*

● *noun* /maʊθ/ (*pl.* **mouths** /maʊðz/)

> **PART OF FACE 1** the opening in the face used for speaking, eating, etc.; the area inside the head behind this opening: *She opened her mouth to say something.* ◆ *His mouth twisted into a wry smile.* ◆ *Their mouths fell open* (= they were surprised). ◆ *Don't talk with your mouth full* (= when eating). ◆ *The creature was foaming at the mouth.* ⊃ **picture at BODY** ⊃ **see also FOOT-AND-MOUTH DISEASE**

> **PERSON NEEDING FOOD 2** a person considered only as someone who needs to be provided with food: *Now there would be another mouth to feed.* ◆ *The world will not be able to support all these extra hungry mouths.*

> **ENTRANCE/OPENING 3** ~ (**of sth**) the entrance or opening of something: *the mouth of a cave/tunnel* ⊃ **see also GOAL-MOUTH**

> **OF RIVER 4** the place where a river joins the ocean

> **WAY OF SPEAKING 5** a particular way of speaking: *He has a foul mouth on him!* ◆ *Watch your mouth* (= stop saying things that are rude and/or offensive)! ⊃ **see also LOUDMOUTH**

> **-MOUTHED 6** /maʊðd; maʊθt/ (in adjectives) having the type or shape of mouth mentioned: *a wide-mouthed old woman* ◆ *a narrow-mouthed cave* ⊃ **see also OPEN-MOUTHED 7** (in adjectives) having a particular way of speaking: *a rather crude-mouthed individual* ⊃ **see also FOUL-MOUTHED, MEALY-MOUTHED**

IDM **be all mouth** (*informal*) if you say someone is **all mouth**, you mean that they talk a lot about doing something, but are, in fact, not brave enough to do it **down in the mouth** unhappy and depressed **keep your mouth shut** (*informal*) to not talk about something to someone because it is a secret or because it will upset or annoy them: *I've warned them to keep their mouths shut about this.* ◆ *Now she's upset—why couldn't you keep your mouth shut?* **out of/from the mouths of babes** (*saying*) used when a small child has just said something that seems very wise or intelligent **run off at the mouth** (*informal*) to talk too much, in a way that is not sensible ⊃ **more at BIG, BORN, BREAD, BUTTER, FOAM** *v.*, **FOOT** *n.*, **GIFT, HEART, HORSE, LIVE**[1], **MELT, MONEY, SHOOT** *v.*, **SHUT** *v.*, **TASTE** *n.*, **WATCH** *v.*, **WORD** *n.*

● *verb* /maʊð/ **1** ~ **sth** | + **speech** to move your lips as if you were saying something, but without making a sound: *He mouthed a few obscenities at us and then moved off.* **2** ~ **sth** | + **speech** (*disapproving*) to say something that you do not really feel, believe, or understand: *They're just mouthing empty slogans.*

PHRV **mouth 'off (at sb/about sth)** (*informal*) to talk or complain loudly about something

mouth·ful /ˈmaʊθfʊl/ *noun* **1** [C] an amount of food or drink that you put in your mouth at one time: *She took a mouthful of water.* **2** [sing.] (*informal*) a word or a phrase that is long and complicated or difficult to pronounce

IDM **say a mouthful** (*informal*) to say something important using only a few words

mouth·guard /ˈmaʊθɡɑrd/ *noun* a cover that a sports

player wears in his/her mouth to protect the teeth and GUMS

mouth ˌorgan *noun* (*old-fashioned*) = HARMONICA

mouth·piece /ˈmaʊθpis/ *noun* **1** the part of the telephone that is next to your mouth when you speak **2** the part of a musical instrument that you place between your lips ⊃ **picture at INSTRUMENT 3** (usually *disapproving*) ~ (**of/for sb**) a person, newspaper, etc. that speaks on behalf of another person or group of people: *The newspaper has become the official mouthpiece of the opposition party.* ◆ *The Press Secretary serves as the President's mouthpiece.*

mouth-to-ˌmouth resusciˈtation (also ˌmouth-to-ˈmouth) *noun* [U] the act of breathing into the mouth of an unconscious person in order to fill their lungs with air ⊃ **compare ARTIFICIAL RESPIRATION**

mouth·wash /ˈmaʊθwɑʃ; -wɔʃ/ *noun* [C, U] a liquid used to make the mouth fresh and healthy

mouth-ˌwatering *adj.* (*approving*) **mouth-watering** food looks or smells so good that you want to eat it immediately **SYN** TEMPTING: *a mouth-watering display of cakes* ◆ (*figurative*) *mouth-watering travel brochures*

mouth·y /ˈmaʊθi; -ði/ *adj.* (*informal, disapproving*) used to describe a person who talks a lot, sometimes expressing their opinions strongly and in a rude way

mov·a·ble (also **move·a·ble**) /ˈmuvəbl/ *adj., noun*

● *adj.* **1** that can be moved from one place or position to another: *movable partitions* ◆ *a doll with a movable head* **2** (*law*) (of property) able to be taken from one house, etc. to another

● *noun* [C, usually pl.] (*law*) a thing that can be moved from one house, etc. to another; a personal possession

ˌmovable ˈfeast *noun* a religious festival, such as Easter, whose date changes from year to year

move ℒ /muv/ *verb, noun*

● *verb*

> **CHANGE POSITION 1** [I, T] to change position or make someone or something change position in a way that can be seen, heard, or felt: *Don't move—stay perfectly still.* ◆ *The bus was already moving when I jumped onto it.* ◆ + **adv./prep.** *He could hear someone moving around in the room above.* ◆ *Phil moved toward the window.* ◆ *You can hardly move in this club on Saturdays* (= because it is so crowded). ◆ *You can't move for books in her room* (= her room is full of books). ◆ ~ **sth** *I can't move my fingers.* ◆ ~ **sth** + **adv./prep.** *We moved our chairs a little nearer.*

> **CHANGE HOUSE/JOB 2** [I] to change the place where you live, have your work, etc.: *We don't like it here so we've decided to move.* ◆ ~ (**from...**) (**to...**) *The company's moving to Indiana.* ◆ ~ **away** *She's been all on her own since her daughter moved away.* **3** [T] ~ **sb** (**from...**) (**to...**) to make someone change from one job, class, etc. to another **SYN** TRANSFER: *I'm being moved to the New York office.*

> **MAKE PROGRESS 4** [I] ~ (**on/ahead**) to make progress in the way or direction mentioned **SYN** PROGRESS: *Time is moving on.* ◆ *Share prices moved ahead today.* ◆ *Things are not moving as fast as we hoped.*

> **GO FAST 5** [I] (*informal*) to go very fast: *Japan's high-speed trains can really move!*

> **CAUSE STRONG FEELINGS 6** [T] to cause someone to have strong feelings, especially of sympathy or sadness: ~ **sb** *We were deeply moved by her plight.* ◆ ~ **sb to sth** *Grown men were moved to tears at the horrific scenes.* ⊃ **see also MOVING**

> **MAKE SOMEONE DO SOMETHING 7** [T] (*formal*) to cause someone to do something **SYN** PROMPT: ~ **sb to do sth** *She felt moved to address the crowd.* ◆ ~ **sb** *He works when the spirit moves him* (= when he wants to).

> **TAKE ACTION 8** [I] to take action; to do something **SYN** ACT: *The police moved quickly to dispel the rumors.* ⊃ **thesaurus box at ACTION**

> **CHANGE IDEAS/TIME 9** [I, T] to change; to change something **SYN** SHIFT: (+ **adv./prep.**) *The government has not moved on this issue.* ◆ ~ **sth** (+ **adv./prep.**) *Let's move the meeting to Wednesday.*

ʌ cup	ə about	eɪ say	aɪ five	ɔɪ boy	aʊ now	oʊ go	ər bird

> **IN BOARD GAMES 10** [I, T] (in CHESS and other board games) to change the position of a piece: *It's your turn to move.* ◆ **~ sth** *She moved her queen.*
> **SELL SOMETHING 11** [T] **~ sth** (*informal*) to sell something: *I need to move ten boxes of perfume by next week.*
> **SUGGEST FORMALLY 12** [T] (*formal*) to suggest something formally so that it can be discussed and decided **SYN** PUT FORWARD: **~ sth** *The Senator from Delaware moved an amendment to the Bill.* ◆ **~ that…** *I move that a vote be taken on this.*
> **IDM** get moving (*informal*) to begin, leave, etc. quickly: *It's late—we'd better get moving.* get sth moving (*informal*) to cause something to make progress: *The new director has really got things moving.* move heaven and earth to do everything you possibly can in order to achieve something move with the times to change the way you think and behave according to changes in society ⊃ more at FORWARD *adv.*, HIGH GEAR
> **PHRV** move a'long to go to a new position, especially in order to make room for other people: *The bus driver asked them to move along.* ,move 'in | ,move 'into sth to start to live in your new home: *Our new neighbors moved in yesterday.* **ANT** MOVE OUT 'move in sth to live, spend your time, etc. in a particular social group: *She only moves in the best circles.* ,move 'in (on sb/sth) to move toward someone or something from all directions, especially in a threatening way: *The police moved in on the terrorists.* ,move 'in with sb to start living with someone in the house or apartment where they already live ,move 'off (especially of a vehicle) to start moving; to leave ,move 'on (to sth) to start doing or discussing something new: *I've been in this job long enough —it's time I moved on.* ◆ *Can we move on to the next item on the agenda?* ,move sb 'on (of police, etc.) to order someone to move away from the scene of an accident, etc. ,move 'out to leave your old home **ANT** MOVE IN ,move 'over (also ,move 'up) to change your position in order to make room for someone: *There's room for another one if you move up a bit.*

● *noun*
> **ACTION 1 ~ (toward/to sth) | ~ (to do sth)** an action that you do or need to do to achieve something: *This latest move by the government has aroused fierce opposition.* ◆ *The management has made no move to settle the strike.* ◆ *Getting a job in marketing was a good career move.* ⊃ see also FALSE MOVE
> **CHANGE OF POSITION 2** [usually sing.] a change of place or position **SYN** MOVEMENT: *Don't make a move!* ◆ *Every move was painful.* ◆ *She felt he was watching her every move.*
> **CHANGE OF IDEAS/BEHAVIOR 3 ~ to/away from sth** a change in ideas, attitudes, or behavior **SYN** SHIFT, TREND: *There has been a move away from nuclear energy.*
> **CHANGE OF HOUSE/JOB 4** an act of changing the place where you live or work: *What's the date of your move?* ◆ *Their move from Italy to the U.S. has not been a success.* ◆ *Her new job is just a sideways move.*
> **IN BOARD GAMES 5** an act of changing the position of a piece in CHESS or other games that are played on a board: *The game was over in only six moves.* ◆ *It's your move.*
> **IDM** be on the move **1** to be traveling from place to place: *With this job, I'm constantly on the move.* **2** to be moving; to be going somewhere: *The car was already on the move.* ◆ *The company is on the move to larger offices.* **3** = BE ON THE GO get a move on (*informal*) you tell someone to **get a move on** when you want them to hurry make the first move to do something before someone else, for example in order to end an argument or to begin something: *If he wants to see me, he should make the first move.* make a move on sb (*informal*) **1** to try to start a sexual relationship with someone **2** (*sports*) to try to pass someone who is in front of you in a race make a, your, etc. move to do the action that you intend to do or need to do in order to achieve something: *The rebels waited until nightfall before they made their move.*

move·a·ble = MOVABLE

move·ment 🔊 /'muvmənt/ *noun*
> **CHANGING POSITION 1** [C, U] an act of moving the body or part of a body: *hand/eye movements* ◆ *She observed the gentle movement of his chest as he breathed.* ◆ *Loose clothing gives you greater freedom of movement.* ◆ *There was a sudden movement in the undergrowth.* **2** [C, U] an act of moving from one place to another or of moving something from one place to another: *enemy troop movements* ◆ *laws to allow free movement of goods and services*
> **GROUP OF PEOPLE 3** [C] a group of people who share the same ideas or aims: *the women's/peace movement* ◆ *the Romantic movement* (= for example in literature) ◆ *a mass movement for change* ⊃ collocations at POLITICS
> **PERSON'S ACTIVITIES 4** movements [pl.] a person's activities over a period of time, especially as watched by someone else: *The police are keeping a close watch on the suspect's movements.*
> **CHANGE OF IDEAS/BEHAVIOR 5** [sing.] **~ (away from/ towards sth)** a gradual change in what people in society do or think **SYN** TREND: *a movement toward greater sexual equality*
> **PROGRESS 6** [U] **~ (in sth)** progress, especially in a particular task: *It needs cooperation from all the countries to get any movement in arms control.*
> **CHANGE IN AMOUNT 7** [U, C] **~ (in sth)** a change in amount: *There has been no movement in oil prices.*
> **MUSIC 8** [C] any of the main parts that a long piece of music is divided into: *the slow movement of the First Concerto*
> **OF BOWELS 9** [C] (*technical*) = BOWEL MOVEMENT

mov·er /'muvər/ *noun* **1** a person or thing that moves in a particular way: *a great mover on the dance floor* ⊃ see also PRIME MOVER **2** a machine or a person that moves things from one place to another, especially someone who moves furniture from one house to another: *an earth mover* ◆ *professional furniture movers* ⊃ see also REMOVER
> **IDM** movers and shakers people with power in important organizations

mov·ie 🔊 /'muvi/ *noun*
1 [C] a series of moving pictures recorded with sound that tells a story, shown at the movie theater **SYN** FILM: *to make a horror movie* ◆ *Have you seen the latest Miyazaki movie?* ◆ *a famous movie director/star* ◆ *The movie was shot on location in Florida.* ⊃ see also ROAD MOVIE **2** the movies [pl.] when you go to the movies, you go to a movie theater to see a movie: *Let's go to the movies.* **3** the movies [pl.] movies as an art or an industry: *I've always wanted to work in the movies.*

TOPIC COLLOCATIONS

The Movies

watching
- go to/take sb to (see) a movie
- go to/sit in the (movie) theater
- rent a movie/DVD
- download a movie/a video
- burn/copy/rip a DVD
- see/watch/stream a movie/DVD/video/preview/trailer

showing
- show/screen a movie/a documentary
- promote/distribute/review a movie
- be out in theaters
- be released on/come out on/be out on DVD
- captivate/delight/grip/thrill the audience
- do well/badly at the box office
- get a lot of/live up to the hype/buzz

filmmaking
- write/co-write a movie/script/screenplay
- direct/produce/make/shoot/edit a movie/sequel/video
- make a romantic comedy/a thriller/an action movie
- do/work on a sequel/remake
- film/shoot the opening scene/an action sequence/footage (of sth)
- compose/create/do/write the soundtrack

- cut/edit (out) a scene/sequence

acting

- have/get/do an audition
- get/have/play a leading/starring/cameo role/part
- play a character/Indiana Jones/the bad guy
- act in/appear in/star in a movie/remake
- do/perform/attempt a stunt
- work in/make it big in Hollywood
- forge/carve/make/pursue a career in Hollywood

describing movies

- the camera pulls back/pans over sth/zooms in (on sth)
- the camera focuses on sth/lingers on sth
- shoot sb/show sb in extreme close-up
- use odd/unusual camera angles
- be filmed/shot on location/in a studio
- be set/take place in New York/in the '60s
- have a happy ending/plot twist

mov·ie·go·er /ˈmuviˌɡoʊər/ noun a person who goes to the movies, especially when they do it regularly

ˈmovie ˌstar noun a male or female actor who is famous for being in movies

ˈmovie ˌtheater 🔑 (CanE usually ˈmovie ˌtheatre) noun
= THEATER (2): The documentary opens tomorrow in movie theaters nationwide.

mov·ing 🔑 /ˈmuvɪŋ/ adj.
1 causing you to have deep feelings of sadness or sympathy: a deeply moving experience **2** [only before noun] (of things) changing from one place or position to another: the moving parts of a machine ◆ fast-moving water ◆ a moving target ▶ **mov·ing·ly** adv.: She described her experiences in Africa very movingly.

ˈmoving ˌvan noun a large van used for moving furniture from one house to another

mow /moʊ/ verb (mowed, mown /moʊn/ or mowed) [T, I]
~ (sth) to cut grass, etc. using a machine or tool with a special blade or blades: I mow the lawn every week in the summer. ◆ the smell of new-mown hay
PHR V ˌmow sb↔ˈdown to kill someone using a vehicle or a gun, especially when several people are all killed at the same time

mow·er /ˈmoʊər/ noun (especially in compounds) a machine that cuts grass: a lawn mower ◆ a motor/rotary mower

mox·ie /ˈmɑksi/ noun [U] (informal) courage, energy, and determination

moz·za·rel·la /ˌmɑtsəˈrɛlə/ noun [U] a type of soft, white, Italian cheese with a mild flavor

MP /ˌɛm ˈpi/ noun **1** a member of the MILITARY POLICE **2** (CanE) the abbreviation for "Member of Parliament" (a person who has been elected to represent the people of a particular area in a parliament): Scott Andrews MP

MP3 /ˌɛm pi ˈθri/ noun [C, U] a method of reducing the size of a computer file containing sound, or a file that is reduced in size in this way

MP3 ˌplayer noun a piece of computer equipment that can open and play MP3 files ⇒ picture at COMPUTER

MP4 /ˌɛm pi ˈfɔr/ noun [C, U] a method of reducing the size of a computer file containing sound and images; a file that is reduced in size in this way

MPEG /ˈɛmpɛɡ/ noun (computing) **1** [U] technology that reduces the size of files that contain video images or sounds: an MPEG file **2** [C] a file produced using this technology

mpg /ˌɛm pi ˈdʒi/ abbr. miles per gallon (used for saying how much gas a vehicle uses): It gets 40 mpg.

mph /ˌɛm pi ˈeɪtʃ/ abbr. miles per hour: a 60 mph speed limit

MPP /ˌɛm pi ˈpi/ abbr. (CanE) Member of the Provincial Parliament in Ontario, Canada

Mr. 🔑 /ˈmɪstər/ abbr.
1 a title that comes before a man's family name, or before his first and family names together: Mr. Brown ◆ Mr. John Brown ◆ Mr. and Mrs. Brown **2** a title used to address a man in some official positions: Thank you, Mr. Chairman. ◆ Mr. President **3** (informal, humorous) used before a description as a humorous name for a man with that quality: Jack is known as Mr. Sensitive because he cries a lot. ⇒ see also MISTER
IDM Mr. Big (informal) the most important man in a group, especially the leader of a group of criminals **Mr. Clean** (informal) a man, especially a politician, who is considered to be very honest and good: The scandal destroyed his image as Mr. Clean. **Mr. Nice Guy** (informal) a way of describing a man who is very honest and thinks about the wishes and feelings of other people: I was tired of helping other people. From now on it was no more Mr. Nice Guy (= I would stop being pleasant and kind). **Mr. Right** (informal) the man who would be the right husband for a particular woman: I'm not getting married in a hurry—I'm waiting for Mr. Right to come along.

MRE /ˌɛm ɑr ˈi/ abbr. meal ready to eat (an individual packaged meal used especially by soldiers)

Mr. Fixit /ˌmɪstər ˈfɪksɪt/ noun (informal) a person who organizes things and solves problems

MRI /ˌɛm ɑr ˈaɪ/ abbr. (medical) magnetic resonance imaging (a method of using a strong MAGNETIC FIELD to produce an image of the inside of a person's body): an MRI scan ⇒ compare CAT SCAN

Mrs. 🔑 /ˈmɪsəz/ abbr.
1 a title that comes before a married woman's family name or before her first and family names together: Mrs. Hill ◆ Mrs. Susan Hill ◆ Mr. and Mrs. Hill ⇒ compare MISS n., Ms. **2** (informal, humorous) used before a description as a humorous name for a married woman with that quality: Carol is such a Mrs. Know-it-all—she has an answer for everything.

MRSA /ˈmɑrsə; ˌɛm ɑr ɛs ˈeɪ/ noun [U] the abbreviation for "methicillin-resistant Staphylococcus aureus" (a type of bacteria that cannot be killed by standard ANTIBIOTICS): rising rates of MRSA infections in hospitals ⇒ see also SUPERBUG

MS /ˌɛm ˈɛs/ abbr. **1** MULTIPLE SCLEROSIS **2** MANUSCRIPT **3** = M.S. **4** (in writing) Mississippi

M.S. (also MS) /ˌɛm ˈɛs/ noun a second university degree in science (the abbreviation for "Master of Science"): to have/do an M.S. ◆ J Stevens M.S.

Ms. 🔑 /mɪz/ abbr.
1 a title that comes before a woman's family name or before her first and family names together, and that can be used when you do not want to state whether she is married or not: Ms. Murphy ◆ Ms. Jean Murphy ⇒ compare MISS n., MRS. **2** (informal, humorous) used before a description as a humorous name for a woman with that quality: Carol is such a Ms. Know-it-all—she has an answer for everything.

MSG /ˌɛm ɛs ˈdʒi/ abbr. MONOSODIUM GLUTAMATE

MSM /ˌɛm ɛs ˈɛm/ noun [U] (computing) the abbreviation for "mainstream media" (traditional media such as newspapers and broadcasting): The line is beginning to blur between influential blogs and MSM.

MT abbr. (in writing) Montana

Mt. abbr. (especially on maps) MOUNT: Mt. Kenya

MTV™ /ˌɛm ti ˈvi/ abbr. music television (a television channel that shows music videos and other light entertainment programs)

mu /mu; myu/ noun the 12th letter of the Greek alphabet (M, μ)

| t tea | t̮ butter | d did | k cat | ɡ got | tʃ chin | dʒ June | f fall |

much /mʌtʃ/ det., pron., adv.
- **det., pron.** used with uncountable nouns, especially in negative sentences to mean "a large amount of something," or after "how" to ask about the amount of something. It is also used with "as," "so," and "too.": *I don't have much money with me.* ◆ *"Got any money?" "Not much."* ◆ *How much water do you need?* ◆ *How much is it* (= What does it cost)? ◆ *Take as much time as you like.* ◆ *There was so much traffic that we were an hour late.* ◆ *I've got far too much to do.* ◆ (*formal*) *I lay awake for much of the night.* ◆ (*formal*) *There was much discussion about the reasons for the failure.* **IDM** **as much** the same: *Please help me get this job—you know I would do as much for you.* ◆ *"Roger stole the money." "I thought as much."* **as much as sb can do** used to say that something is difficult to do: *No dessert for me, thanks. It was as much as I could do to finish the main course.* **not much of a…** not a good…: *He's not much of a tennis player.* **this much** used to introduce something positive or definite: *I'll say this much for him—he never leaves a piece of work unfinished.*
- **adv.** (**more, most**) to a great degree: *Thank you very much for the flowers.* ◆ *I would very much like to see you again.* ◆ *He isn't in the office much* (= often). ◆ *You worry too much.* ◆ *My new job is much the same as the old one.* ◆ *Much to her surprise he came back the next day.* ◆ *She's much better today.* ◆ *The other one was much too expensive.* ◆ *Nikolai's English was much the worst.* ◆ *We are very much aware of the lack of food supplies.* ◆ *I'm not much good at tennis.* ◆ *He was much loved by all who knew him.* ◆ *an appeal to raise much-needed cash* **IDM** **much as** although: *Much as I would like to stay, I really must go home.* ⊃ more at **LESS** *adv.*

GRAMMAR

much ◆ a lot of ◆ lots of
- **Much** is used only with uncountable nouns. It is used mainly in questions and negative sentences: *Do you have much free time?* ◆ *How much experience do you have?* ◆ *I don't have much free time.*
- In statements **a lot of** or **lots of** (*informal*) is much more common: *She earns a lot of money.* You can also use **plenty (of)**. These phrases can also be used in questions and negative sentences.
- A lot of/lots of is still felt to be informal, especially in writing, so in formal writing it is better to use **much, a great deal of**, or **a large amount of**.
- Very much and a lot can be used as adverbs: *I miss my family very much.* ◆ ~~I miss very much my family.~~ ◆ *I miss my family a lot.* ◆ *Thanks a lot.* In negative sentences you can use **much**: *I didn't enjoy the movie (very) much.*
⊃ note at **MANY, VERY**

muck /mʌk/ noun, verb
- **noun** **1** waste matter from farm animals **SYN** MANURE: *to spread muck on the fields* **2** (*informal*) dirt or mud: *Can you wipe the muck off the windows?* **3** (*informal*) something very unpleasant: *I can't eat this muck!*
- **verb** **PHR V** **muck 'out** | **muck sth↔'out** to clean out the place where an animal lives **muck sth↔'up** (*informal*) **1** to do something badly so that you fail to achieve what you wanted or hoped to achieve **SYN** MESS STH UP: *He completely mucked up his English exam.* **2** to spoil a plan or an arrangement **SYN** MESS STH UP **3** to make something dirty: *I don't want you mucking up my nice clean floor.*

muck·rak·ing /'mʌkˌreɪkɪŋ/ noun [U] (*informal, disapproving*) the activity of looking for information about people's private lives that they do not wish to make public

muck·y /'mʌki/ adj. (*informal*) dirty: *mucky hands*

mucous 'membrane noun (*anatomy*) a thin layer of skin that covers the inside of the nose and mouth and the outside of other organs in the body, producing mucus to prevent these parts from becoming dry

mu·cus /'myukəs/ noun [U] a thick liquid that is produced in parts of the body, such as the nose, by a mucous membrane ▶ **mu·cous** /'myukəs/ adj.: *mucous glands*

MUD /mʌd/ noun [U] (*computing*) the abbreviation for "multi-user dungeon/dimension" (a computer game played over the Internet by several players at the same time)

mud /mʌd/ noun [U]
wet earth that is soft and sticky: *The car got stuck in the mud.* ◆ *Your boots are covered in mud.* ◆ *mud bricks/huts* (= made of dried mud) ⊃ **thesaurus box at** SOIL **IDM** **fling, sling, etc. mud (at sb)** to criticize someone or accuse someone of bad or shocking things in order to damage their reputation, especially in politics ⊃ **see also** MUDSLINGING ⊃ **more at** CLEAR *adj.*, DRAG *v.*, NAME *n.*

mud bath noun **1** a bath in hot mud that contains a lot of minerals, which is taken, for example, to help with RHEUMATISM **2** a place where there is a lot of mud: *Heavy rain turned the campsite into a mud bath.*

mud·dle /'mʌdl/ verb, noun
- **verb** **PHR V** **muddle a'long** to continue doing something without any clear plan or purpose: *We can't just keep muddling along like this.* **muddle 'through** to achieve your aims even though you do not know exactly what you are doing and do not have the correct equipment, knowledge, etc.: *We'll muddle through somehow.*
- **noun** [C, usually sing., U] a state of confusion in which things are messy **SYN** MESS: *The story is a hopeless muddle, with too many different strands.*

mud·dled /'mʌdld/ adj. confused: *muddled thinking*

muddle-headed adj. confused or with confused ideas: *muddle-headed thinkers*

mud·dy /'mʌdi/ adj., verb
- **adj.** (**mud·di·er, mud·di·est**) **1** full of or covered in mud: *a muddy field/track* ◆ *muddy boots/knees* ⊃ **thesaurus box at** DIRTY **2** (of a liquid) containing mud; not clear: *muddy water* ◆ *a muddy pond* **3** (of colors) not clear or bright: *muddy green/brown*
- **verb** (**mud·dies, mud·dy·ing, mud·died, mud·died**) **~ sth** to make something muddy **IDM** **muddy the waters, issue, etc.** (*disapproving*) to make a simple situation confused and more complicated than it really is

mud flap noun one of a set of pieces of FLEXIBLE material that are attached behind the wheels of a car, motorcycle, etc. to prevent them from throwing up mud, stones, or water

mud·flat /'mʌdflæt/ noun [usually pl.] an area of flat muddy land that is covered by the ocean when it comes in at HIGH TIDE

mud pack noun a substance containing CLAY that you put on your face and take off after a short period of time, used to improve the condition of your skin

mud pie noun **1** wet earth that is made into the shape of a PIE as part of a game played by children **2** a DESSERT (= a sweet dish) made with chocolate and ice cream

mud·room /'mʌdrum; -rʊm/ noun a small area where people can leave their dirty or wet clothing and shoes when they enter a house

mud·slide /'mʌdslaɪd/ noun a large amount of mud sliding down a mountain, often destroying buildings and injuring or killing people below

mud·sling·ing /'mʌdˌslɪŋɪŋ/ noun [U] (*disapproving*) the act of criticizing someone and accusing them of something in order to damage their reputation

Muen·ster /'mʌnstər; 'mʊn-/ (also Muenster 'cheese) noun [U] a light yellow cheese with a mild flavor

mues·li /'myusli; 'myuz-/ noun [U] a mixture of grains, nuts, dried fruit, etc. served with milk and eaten for breakfast

mu·ez·zin /muˈɛzn/ noun a man who calls Muslims to prayer, usually from the tower of a MOSQUE

muff /mʌf/ noun, verb
- **noun** a short tube of fur or other warm material that you put your hands into to keep them warm in cold weather ⊃ see also EARMUFFS
- **verb ~ sth** (informal, disapproving) to miss an opportunity to do something well: *He muffed his lines* (= he forgot them or said them wrongly). ◆ *It was a really simple shot, and I muffed it.*

muf·fin /ˈmʌfən/ noun a small cake in the shape of a cup, often containing small pieces of fruit, etc.: *a blueberry muffin* ⊃ compare ENGLISH MUFFIN

muf·fle /ˈmʌfl/ verb **1 ~ sth** to make a sound quieter or less clear: *He tried to muffle the alarm clock by putting it under his pillow.* **2 ~ sb/sth (up) in sth** to wrap or cover someone or something in order to keep them/it warm: *She muffled the child up in a blanket.*

muf·fled /ˈmʌfld/ adj. (of sounds) not heard clearly because something is in the way that stops the sound from traveling easily: *muffled voices from the next room*

muf·fler /ˈmʌflər/ noun **1** (old-fashioned) a thick piece of cloth worn around the neck for warmth SYN SCARF **2** a device that is fixed to the EXHAUST of a vehicle in order to reduce the amount of noise that the engine makes ⊃ picture at BICYCLE

muf·ti /ˈmʌfti/ noun **1** [C] also **Muf·ti** a Muslim who is an expert in legal matters connected with Islam **2** [U] (old-fashioned) ordinary clothes worn by people such as soldiers who wear uniforms in their job: *officers in mufti*

mug /mʌg/ noun, verb
- **noun 1** a tall cup for drinking from, usually with straight sides and a handle, used without a SAUCER: *a coffee mug* ◆ *a beer mug* (= a large glass with a handle) ⊃ picture at CUP **2** a mug and what it contains: *a mug of coffee* **3** (slang) a person's face: *I never want to see his ugly mug again.*
- **verb** (-gg-) **1** [T] **~ sb** to attack someone violently in order to steal their money, especially in a public place: *She had been mugged in the street in broad daylight.* **2** [I] **~ (for sb/sth)** (informal) to make silly expressions with your face or behave in a silly, exaggerated way, especially on the stage or before a camera: *to mug for the cameras*

mug·ger /ˈmʌgər/ noun a person who threatens or attacks someone in order to steal their money, especially in a public place

mug·ging /ˈmʌgɪŋ/ noun [U, C] the crime of attacking someone violently, or threatening to do so, in order to steal their money, especially in a public place: *Mugging is on the increase.* ◆ *There have been several muggings here recently.*

mug·gy /ˈmʌgi/ adj. (of weather) warm and damp in an unpleasant way SYN CLOSE² : *a muggy August day*

Mu·ghal /ˈmugl/ noun = MOGUL

mug·shot /ˈmʌgʃɑt/ noun (informal) a photograph of someone's face kept by the police in their records to identify criminals

mug·wump /ˈmʌgwʌmp/ noun (often disapproving) a person who cannot decide how to vote or who refuses to support a political party

Mu·ham·mad (also **Mo·ham·med**) /mʊˈhɑməd; -ˈhæməd; moʊ-/ noun the Arab PROPHET through whom the Koran was REVEALED and the religion of Islam established and completed

mu·ja·hi·deen (also **mu·ja·he·din, mu·ja·hi·din, mu·ja·hed·din**) /muˌdʒɑhəˈdin; ˌmudʒə-/ noun [pl.] (in some Muslim countries) soldiers fighting in support of their strong Muslim beliefs

mu·lat·to /məˈlɑtoʊ/ /məˈlætoʊ/ noun (pl. **mu·lat·tos** or **mu·lat·toes**) (offensive, old-fashioned) a person with one black parent and one white parent

mul·ber·ry /ˈmʌlˌbɛri/ noun (pl. **mul·ber·ries**) **1** (also **ˈmulberry tree**) [C] a tree with broad dark green leaves and berries (BERRY) that can be eaten. SILKWORMS (that make silk) eat the leaves of the white mulberry. **2** [C] the small purple or white BERRY of the mulberry tree **3** [U] a deep reddish-purple color

mulch /mʌltʃ/ noun, verb
- **noun** [C, U] material, for example, decaying leaves, that you put around a plant to protect its base and its roots, to improve the quality of the soil, or to stop WEEDS from growing
- **verb ~ sth** to cover the soil or the roots of a plant with a mulch

mule /myul/ noun **1** an animal that has a horse and a DONKEY as parents, used especially for carrying loads: *He's as stubborn as a mule.* **2** (slang) a person who is paid to take drugs illegally from one country to another **3** a SLIPPER (= a soft shoe for wearing indoors) that is open around the heel ⊃ picture at SHOE

mu·le·teer /ˌmyuləˈtɪr/ noun a person who controls MULES (= the animals) and makes them go in the right direction

mul·ish /ˈmyulɪʃ/ adj. (disapproving) unwilling to change your mind or attitude or to do what other people want you to do SYN STUBBORN

mull /mʌl/ verb
PHRV ˌmull sth↔ˈover to spend time thinking carefully about a plan or proposal SYN CONSIDER: *I need some time to mull it over before making a decision.*

mul·lah /ˈmʌlə; ˈmʊlə/ noun a Muslim teacher of religion and holy law

mulled /mʌld/ adj. [only before noun] **mulled** wine has been mixed with sugar and spices and heated

mul·let /ˈmʌlət/ noun **1** (pl. **mul·let**) [C, U] an ocean fish that is used for food. The two main types are **red mullet** and **gray mullet**. **2** [C] (informal) a HAIRSTYLE for men in which the hair is short at the front and sides and long at the back

mul·li·ga·taw·ny /ˌmʌlɪgəˈtɔni/ noun [U] a hot, spicy soup, originally from India ORIGIN From a Tamil word meaning "pepper water."

mul·lion /ˈmʌlyən/ noun (architecture) a solid vertical piece of stone, wood, or metal between two parts of a window ▶ **mul·lioned** /ˈmʌlyənd/ adj. [only before noun]: *mullioned windows*

multi– /ˈmʌlti; -taɪ; -ti/ combining form (in nouns and adjectives) more than one; many: *multicolored* ◆ *a multimillionaire* ◆ *a multimillion-dollar business* ◆ *multifamily housing*

multi–ˈaccess adj. (computing) allowing several people to use the same system at the same time

mul·ti·cast /ˈmʌltiˌkæst; ˈmʌltaɪ-/ verb **~ sth** (technical) to send data across a computer network to several users at the same time ▶ **mul·ti·cast** noun [U, C]

mul·ti·cel·lu·lar /ˌmʌltiˈsɛlyələr; ˌmʌltaɪ-/ adj. (biology) having many cells: *Plants and animals are multicellular organisms.*

mul·ti·chan·nel /ˈmʌltiˌtʃænl; ˈmʌltaɪ-/ adj. having or using many different television or communication channels

mul·ti·col·ored (CanE usually **mul·ti·col·oured**) /ˈmʌltiˌkʌlərd/ (also **mul·ti·col·or**, CanE usually **mul·ti·col·our**) adj. consisting of or decorated with many colors, especially bright ones: *a multicolored dress*

mul·ti·cul·tur·al /ˌmʌltiˈkʌltʃərəl; ˌmʌltaɪ-/ adj. for or including people of several different races, religions, languages, and traditions: *We live in a multicultural society.* ◆ *a multicultural approach to education*

mul·ti·cul·tur·al·ism /ˌmʌltiˈkʌltʃərəˌlɪzəm; ˌmʌltaɪ-/ noun [U] the practice of giving importance to all cultures in a society

mul·ti·di·men·sion·al /ˌmʌltidɪˈmɛnʃənl; ˌmʌltaɪ-/ adj. having several DIMENSIONS (= measurements in space) or aspects: *multidimensional space* ◆ *multidimensional problems*

mul·ti·dis·ci·plin·ar·y /ˌmʌltiˈdɪsəpləˌnɛri; ˌmʌltaɪ-/ adj. involving several different subjects of study: *a multidisciplinary course*

mul·ti·eth·nic /ˌmʌltiˈɛθnɪk; ˌmʌltaɪ-/ *adj.* consisting of people from many different races or cultures: *New York City is one of the country's most multiethnic cities.*

mul·ti·fac·et·ed /ˌmʌltiˈfæsətəd; ˌmʌltaɪ-/ *adj.* (*formal*) having many different aspects to be considered: *a complex and multifaceted problem*

mul·ti·far·i·ous /ˌmʌltəˈfɛriəs/ *adj.* (*formal*) of many different kinds; having great variety: *the multifarious life forms in the coral reef* ♦ *a vast and multifarious organization*

mul·ti·func·tion·al /ˌmʌltiˈfʌŋkʃənl; ˌmʌltaɪ-/ *adj.* having several different functions: *a multifunctional device*

mul·ti·grain /ˈmʌltiˌgreɪn/ *adj.* containing several different types of grain: *multigrain bread*

mul·ti·lat·er·al /ˌmʌltiˈlætərəl/ *adj.* **1** in which three or more groups, nations, etc. take part: *multilateral negotiations* **2** having many sides or parts ⊃ compare BILATERAL, TRILATERAL, UNILATERAL

mul·ti·lat·er·al·ism /ˌmʌltiˈlætərəlˌlɪzəm/ *noun* [U] (*politics*) the policy of trying to make multilateral agreements, especially in order to achieve nuclear DISARMAMENT

mul·ti·lin·gual /ˌmʌltiˈlɪŋwəl; ˌmʌltaɪ-/ *adj.* **1** speaking or using several different languages: ***multilingual translators/communities/societies*** ♦ *a multilingual classroom* **2** written or printed in several different languages: *a multilingual phrase book* ⊃ compare BILINGUAL, MONOLINGUAL

mul·ti·me·di·a /ˌmʌltiˈmidiə; ˌmʌltaɪ-/ *adj.* [only before noun] **1** (in computing) using sound, pictures, and film in addition to text on a screen: ***multimedia systems/products*** ♦ *the multimedia industry* (= producing CD-ROMS etc.) **2** (in teaching and art) using several different ways of giving information or several different materials: *a multimedia approach to learning* ▶ **mul·ti·me·di·a** *noun* [U]: *the use of multimedia in museums*

mul·ti·mil·lion·aire /ˌmʌltiˌmɪljəˈnɛr; ˌmʌltaɪ-; -ˈmɪljəˌnɛr/ *noun* a person who has money and possessions worth several million dollars

mul·ti·na·tion·al /ˌmʌltiˈnæʃənl; ˌmʌltaɪ-/ *adj.*, *noun*
● *adj.* existing in or involving many countries: ***multinational companies/corporations*** ♦ *A multinational force is being sent to the trouble spot.*
● *noun* a company that operates in several different countries, especially a large and powerful company

mul·ti·par·ty /ˈmʌltiˌpɑrti; ˈmʌltaɪ-/ *adj.* [only before noun] involving several different political parties

mul·ti·ple /ˈmʌltəpl/ *adj.*, *noun*
● *adj.* [only before noun] many in number; involving many different people or things: *multiple copies of documents* ♦ *a multiple entry visa* ♦ *to suffer multiple injuries* (= in many different places in the body) ♦ *a multiple birth* (= several babies born to a mother at one time) ♦ *a multiple pile-up* (= a crash involving many vehicles) ♦ *a house in **multiple ownership/occupancy*** (= owned/occupied by several different people or families)
● *noun* (*mathematics*) a quantity that contains another quantity an exact number of times: *14, 21, and 28 are all multiples of 7.* ♦ *18 is the lowest **common multiple** of 6 and 9.* ♦ *Traveler's checks are available in multiples of $10* (= to the value of $10, $20, $30, etc.).

multiple-ˈchoice *adj.* (of questions) showing several possible answers from which you must choose the correct one

multiple-personˈality disˌorder (also *less frequent* **ˌsplit-personˈality disˌorder**) *noun* (*psychology*) a rare condition in which a person seems to have one or more different personalities

ˌmultiple scleˈrosis *noun* [U] (*abbr.* MS) a disease of the nervous system that gets worse over a period of time, with loss of feeling and loss of control of movement and speech

mul·ti·plex /ˈmʌltɪˌplɛks/ *noun* a large movie theater with several separate rooms with screens

mul·ti·pli·ca·tion /ˌmʌltəpləˈkeɪʃn/ *noun* [U] the act or process of multiplying: *the multiplication sign* (×) ♦ *Multiplication of cells leads to rapid growth of the organism.* ⊃ compare DIVISION

multipliˈcation ˌtable (also **times table, ta·ble**) *noun* a list showing the results when a number is multiplied by a set of other numbers, especially 1 to 12, in turn

mul·ti·plic·i·ty /ˌmʌltəˈplɪsəti/ *noun* [sing., U] (*formal*) a great number and variety of something: *This situation can be influenced by a multiplicity of different factors.*

mul·ti·pli·er /ˈmʌltəˌplaɪər/ *noun* (*mathematics*) a number by which another number is multiplied

mul·ti·ply /ˈmʌltəˌplaɪ/ *verb* (**mul·ti·plies, mul·ti·ply·ing, mul·ti·plied, mul·ti·plied**)
1 [I, T] to add a number to itself a particular number of times: *The children are already learning to multiply and divide.* ♦ **~ A by B** *2 multiplied by 4 is/equals/makes 8* (2×4=8) ♦ **~ A and B (together)** *Multiply 2 and 6 together and you get 12.* **2** [I, T] to increase or make something increase very much in number or amount: *Our problems have multiplied since last year.* ♦ *Cigarette smoking multiplies the risk of cancer.* **3** [I, T] (*biology*) to reproduce in large numbers; to make something do this: *Rabbits multiply rapidly.* ♦ **~ sth** *It is possible to multiply these bacteria in the laboratory.*

mul·ti·proc·es·sor /ˌmʌltiˈprɑsesər; ˌmʌltaɪ-/ *noun* a computer with more than one CENTRAL PROCESSING UNIT

mul·ti·pur·pose /ˌmʌltiˈpɜrpəs/ *adj.* able to be used for several different purposes: *a **multipurpose tool/machine***

mul·ti·ra·cial /ˌmʌltiˈreɪʃl; ˌmʌltaɪ-/ *adj.* including or involving several different races of people: *a multiracial society*

mul·ti·skill·ing /ˈmʌltiˌskɪlɪŋ; ˈmʌltaɪ-/ *noun* [U] (*business*) the fact of a person being trained in several different jobs that require different skills

mul·ti·task /ˈmʌltiˌtæsk/ *verb* **1** [I] (of a computer) to operate several programs at the same time **2** [I] to do several things at the same time: *Women seem to be able to multitask better than men.*

mul·ti·task·ing /ˈmʌltiˌtæskɪŋ/ *noun* [U] **1** (*computing*) the ability of a computer to operate several programs at the same time **2** the ability to do several things at the same time

mul·ti·track /ˈmʌltiˌtræk/ *adj.* (*technical*) relating to the mixing of several different pieces of music

mul·ti·tude /ˈmʌltəˌtud/ *noun* (*formal*) **1** [C] **~ (of sth/sb)** an extremely large number of things or people: *a multitude of possibilities* ♦ *multitudes of birds* ♦ *These elements can be combined in a multitude of different ways.* ♦ *a multitude of outstanding actors* **2 the multitude** [sing.] also **the multitudes** [pl.] (sometimes *disapproving*) the mass of ordinary people: *It was an elite that believed its task was to enlighten the multitude.* ♦ *to feed the starving multitudes* **3** [C] (*literary*) a large crowd of people **SYN** THRONG: *He preached to the assembled multitude.*
IDM **cover/hide a multitude of sins** (often *humorous*) to hide the real situation or facts when these are not good or pleasant

mul·ti·tu·di·nous /ˌmʌltəˈtudn·əs/ *adj.* (*formal*) extremely large in number

mul·ti·us·er /ˌmʌltiˈyuzər; ˌmʌltaɪ-/ *adj.* (*computing*) able to be used by more than one person at the same time: *a multiuser software license*

mul·ti·vi·ta·min /ˈmʌltiˌvaɪtəmən; ˌmʌltiˈvaɪtəmən/ *noun* a pill or medicine containing several VITAMINS

mul·ti·word /ˈmʌltiˌwɜrd; ˈmʌltaɪ-/ *adj.* [only before noun] (*linguistics*) consisting of more than one word: *multiword units such as "fall in love"*

mum /mʌm/ *adj.* saying nothing; silent
IDM **keep mum** (*informal*) to say nothing about something; to stay quiet: *He kept mum about what he'd seen.* **mum's the word!** (*informal*) used to tell someone to say nothing about something and keep it secret

mum·ble /ˈmʌmbl/ *verb, noun*

● *verb* [I, T] to speak or say something in a quiet voice, in a way that is not clear **SYN** MUTTER: ~ **(to sb/yourself)** *I could hear him mumbling to himself.* ◆ ~ **sth (to sb/yourself)** *She mumbled an apology and left.* ◆ + **speech** *"Sorry," she mumbled.* ◆ ~ **that…** *She mumbled that she was sorry.*

● *noun* [usually sing.] (also **mum·bling** [C, usually pl., U]) speech or words that are spoken in a quiet voice, in a way that is not clear: *He spoke in a low mumble, as if to himself.* ◆ *They tried to make sense of her mumblings.*

mum·bo-jum·bo /ˌmʌmboʊ ˈdʒʌmboʊ/ *noun* [U] (*informal, disapproving*) language or a ceremony that seems complicated and important but is actually without real sense or meaning; nonsense

mum·mer /ˈmʌmər/ *noun* an actor in an old form of drama without words

mum·mi·fy /ˈmʌməˌfaɪ/ *verb* (**mum·mi·fies, mum·mi·fy·ing, mum·mi·fied, mum·mi·fied**) [usually passive] ~ **sth** to preserve a dead body by treating it with special oils and wrapping it in cloth **SYN** EMBALM

mum·my /ˈmʌmi/ *noun* (*pl.* **mum·mies**) a body of a human or of an animal that has been preserved by treating it with special oils and wrapping it in cloth: *an Egyptian mummy*

mumps /mʌmps/ *noun* [U] a disease, especially of children, that causes painful swellings in the neck

munch /mʌntʃ/ *verb* [I, T] to eat something steadily and often noisily, especially something crisp **SYN** CHOMP: ~ **on/at sth** *She munched on an apple.* ◆ ~ **sth** *He sat in a chair munching his toast.* ◆ *I munched my way through a huge bowl of cereal.*

Mun·chau·sen's syn·drome /ˈmʌntʃaʊzənz ˌsɪndroʊm; ˈmʊn-/ *noun* [U] a mental condition in which someone keeps pretending that they are sick in order to receive hospital treatment

munch·ies /ˈmʌntʃiz/ *noun* [pl.] (*informal*) small pieces of food for eating with drinks at a party
IDM have the munchies (*informal*) to feel hungry

munch·kin /ˈmʌntʃkɪn/ *noun* (*informal*) a very short person or a child

mun·dane /mʌnˈdeɪn/ *adj.* (often *disapproving*) not interesting or exciting **SYN** DULL, ORDINARY: *a mundane task/job* ◆ *I lead a pretty mundane existence.* ◆ *On a more mundane level, can we talk about the schedule for next week?*

mung /mʌŋ/ *noun* **1** (also **ˈmung bean**) a small, round, green BEAN **2** the tropical plant that produces these beans

mu·nic·i·pal /mjuˈnɪsəpl/ *adj.* [usually before noun] connected with or belonging to a town, city, or district that has its own local government: *municipal elections/councils* ◆ *municipal workers* ◆ *the Los Angeles Municipal Art Gallery*

mu·nic·i·pal·i·ty /mjuˌnɪsəˈpæləti/ *noun* (*pl.* **mu·nic·i·pal·i·ties**) a town, city, or district with its own local government; the group of officials who govern it

mu·nif·i·cent /mjuˈnɪfəsnt/ *adj.* (*formal*) extremely generous: *a munificent patron/gift/gesture* ▶ **mu·nif·i·cence** /-sns/ *noun* [U]

mu·ni·tions /mjuˈnɪʃnz/ *noun* [pl.] military weapons, AMMUNITION, and equipment: *a shortage of munitions* ◆ *a munitions factory* ▶ **mu·ni·tion** *adj.* [only before noun]: *a munition store*

munt·jac (also **munt·jak**) /ˈmʌntdʒæk/ *noun* a type of small DEER, originally from S.E. Asia

mu·ral /ˈmjʊrəl/ *noun* a painting, usually a large one, done on a wall, sometimes on an outside wall of a building ▶ **mural** *adj.*: *mural paintings*

mur·der 🔑 /ˈmərdər/ *noun, verb*

● *noun* **1** [U, C] the crime of killing someone deliberately **SYN** HOMICIDE: *He was found guilty of murder.* ◆ *She has been charged with the attempted murder of her husband.* ◆ *to commit (a) murder* ◆ *a murder case/investigation/trial* ◆ *The rebels were responsible for the mass murder of 400 civilians.* ◆ *What* was the **murder weapon**? ◆ *The play is a **murder mystery**.* ⟳ collocations at CRIME ⟳ compare MANSLAUGHTER **2** [U] (*informal*) used to describe something that is difficult or unpleasant: *It's murder trying to get to the airport at this time of day.* ◆ *It was murder* (= very busy and unpleasant) *in the office today.*
IDM get away with murder (*informal*, often *humorous*) to do whatever you want without being stopped or punished ⟳ more at SCREAM

● *verb* **1** ~ **sb** to kill someone deliberately and illegally: *He denies murdering his wife's lover.* ◆ *The murdered woman was well known in the area.* **2** ~ **sth** to spoil something because you do not do it very well **SYN** BUTCHER: *Critics accused him of murdering the English language* (= writing or speaking it very badly). **3** ~ **sb** (*informal*) to defeat someone completely, especially in a team sport **SYN** THRASH
IDM sb will murder you (*informal*) used to warn someone that another person will be very angry with them

mur·der·er /ˈmərdərər/ *noun* a person who has killed someone deliberately and illegally **SYN** KILLER: *a convicted murderer* ◆ *a mass murderer* (= who has killed a lot of people)

mur·der·ess /ˈmərdərəs/ *noun* (*old-fashioned*) a woman who has killed someone deliberately and illegally; a female murderer

mur·der·ous /ˈmərdərəs/ *adj.* intending or likely to murder **SYN** SAVAGE: *a murderous villain/tyrant* ◆ *a murderous attack* ◆ *She gave him a murderous look* (= a very angry one). ▶ **mur·der·ous·ly** *adv.*

murk /mərk/ *noun* usually **the murk** [U] DARKNESS caused by smoke, FOG, etc. **SYN** GLOOM

murk·y /ˈmərki/ *adj.* (**murk·i·er, murk·i·est**) **1** (of a liquid) not clear; dark or dirty with mud or another substance **SYN** CLOUDY: *She gazed into the murky depths of the water.* **2** (of air, light, etc.) dark and unpleasant because of smoke, FOG, etc.: *a murky night* **3** (*disapproving* or *humorous*) (of people's actions or character) not clearly known and suspected of not being honest: *He had a somewhat murky past.* ◆ *the murky world of arms dealing*

mur·mur /ˈmərmər/ *verb, noun*

● *verb* **1** [T, I] ~ **(sth)** | + **speech** | ~ **that…** to say something in a soft, quiet voice that is difficult to hear or understand: *She murmured her agreement.* ◆ *He murmured something in his sleep.* ◆ *She was murmuring in his ear.* **2** [I] to make a quiet continuous sound: *The wind murmured in the trees.* **3** [I] ~ **(against sb/sth)** (*literary*) to complain about someone or something, but not openly

● *noun* **1** [C] a quietly spoken word or words: *She answered in a faint murmur.* ◆ *Murmurs of "Praise God" went around the circle.* **2** [C] (also **mur·mur·ings** [pl.]) a quiet expression of feeling: *a murmur of agreement/approval/complaint* ◆ *He paid the extra cost without a murmur* (= without complaining at all). ◆ *polite murmurings of gratitude* **3** (also **mur·mur·ing**) [sing.] a low continuous sound in the background: *the distant murmur of traffic* **4** [C] (*medical*) a faint sound in the chest, usually a sign of damage or disease in the heart: *a heart murmur*

Mur·phy's Law /ˌmərfiz ˈlɔ/ *noun* [U] (*humorous*) a statement of the fact that, if anything can possibly go wrong, it will go wrong

Mus·ca·det /ˌmʌskəˈdeɪ; ˌmʊs-/ *noun* [U, C] a type of dry, white, French wine

mus·cat /ˈmʌskæt; -kət/ *noun* [U, C] **1** a type of GRAPE which can be eaten or used to make wine or RAISINS **2** (also **mus·ca·tel** /ˌmʌskəˈtɛl/) a type of wine made from muscat GRAPES, especially a strong, sweet, white wine

mus·cle 🔑 /ˈmʌsl/ *noun, verb*

● *noun* **1** [C, U] a piece of body TISSUE that you contract and relax in order to move a particular part of the body; the TISSUE that forms the muscles of the body: *a calf/neck/thigh muscle* ◆ *to pull/tear/strain a muscle* ◆ *This exercise will work the muscles of the lower back.* ◆ *He didn't move a muscle* (= stood completely still). ⟳ collocations at INJURY **2** [U] physical strength: *He's an intelligent player but lacks the muscle of older competitors.* **3** [U] the power and influence to make others do what you want: *to exercise political/industrial/financial muscle* ▸ **mus·cled** *adj.*: *heavily muscled shoulders* **IDM** see **FLEX**

● *verb*
PHR V **muscle 'in (on sb/sth)** (*informal, disapproving*) to involve yourself in a situation when you have no right to do so, in order to get something for yourself

muscle–bound *adj.* having large stiff muscles as a result of too much exercise

mus·cle·man /ˈmʌsl̩ˌmæn/ *noun* (*pl.* **mus·cle·men** /-ˌmɛn/) a big strong man, especially one employed to protect someone or something

mus·cu·lar /ˈmʌskyələr/ *adj.* **1** connected with the muscles: *muscular tension/power/tissue* **2** (also *informal* **mus·cly** /ˈmʌsli/) having large strong muscles: *a muscular body/build/chest* ◆ *He was tall, lean, and muscular.*

mus·cu·lar dys·tro·phy /ˌmʌskyələr ˈdɪstrəfi/ *noun* [U] a medical condition that some people are born with, in which the muscles gradually become weaker

mus·cu·la·ture /ˈmʌskyələtʃər; -ˌtʃʊr/ *noun* [U, sing.] (*biology*) the system of muscles in the body or in part of the body

muse /myuz/ *noun, verb*
● *noun* **1** a person or spirit that gives a writer, painter, etc. ideas and the desire to create things **SYN** **INSPIRATION**: *He felt that his muse had deserted him* (= that he could no longer write, paint, etc.). **2 Muse** (in ancient Greek and Roman stories) one of the nine **GODDESSES** who encouraged poetry, music, and other branches of art and literature
● *verb* (*formal*) **1** [I] ~ **(about/on/over/upon sth)** to think carefully about something for a time, ignoring what is happening around you **SYN** **PONDER**: *I sat quietly, musing on the events of the day.* ⊃ see also **MUSING 2** [T] + **speech** | ~ **that…** to say something to yourself in a way that shows you are thinking carefully about it: *"I wonder why?" she mused.*

mu·se·um 🔊 /myuˈziəm/ *noun*
a building in which objects of artistic, cultural, historical, or scientific interest are kept and shown to the public: *a museum of modern art* ◆ *a science museum*

mu'seum piece *noun* **1** an object that has enough historical or artistic value to be in a museum **2** (*humorous*) a thing or person that is old-fashioned, or old and no longer useful

mush /mʌʃ/ *noun, verb, exclamation*
● *noun* **1** also /mʊʃ/ [U, sing.] (*usually disapproving*) a soft thick mass or mixture: *The vegetables had turned to mush.* ◆ *His insides suddenly felt like mush.* **2** [U] a type of soft thick food made from **CORNMEAL** (= flour made from **CORN**) **3** also /mʊʃ/ [U] (*informal, disapproving*) words or events in a book, movie, etc. that are too emotional in a way that is embarrassing: *The movie was just romantic mush.*
● *verb* **1** also /mʊʃ/ [T] ~ **sth (up)** to crush a substance, especially food, into a soft thick mass: *He likes to mush up his peas.* **2** [I, T] to drive a **SLED** (= a vehicle that slides over snow) pulled by dogs, or to urge the dogs to pull the **SLED**: *By the end of winter he will have mushed over 700 miles.* ◆ ~ **sth** *I mushed my team 75 miles from my home.* ▸ **mushed** *adj.*: *mushed berries*
● *exclamation* used as a command to tell dogs to start pulling a **SLED** or to pull it faster

mush·er /ˈmʌʃər/ *noun* a person who drives a **DOGSLED**

mush·room /ˈmʌʃrum; -rəm/ *noun, verb*
● *noun* a **FUNGUS** with a round flat head and short **STEM**. Many mushrooms can be eaten: *fried mushrooms* ◆ *cream of mushroom soup* ⊃ picture at **FRUIT** ⊃ see also **BUTTON MUSHROOM, TOADSTOOL**
● *verb* **1** [I] to rapidly grow or increase in number: *We expect the market to mushroom in the next two years.* **2** usually **go mushrooming** [I] to gather mushrooms in a field or wood

mushroom cloud *noun* a large cloud, shaped like a mushroom, that forms in the air after a nuclear explosion

mush·y /ˈmʌʃi; ˈmʊʃi/ *adj.* (**mush·i·er, mush·i·est**) **1** soft and thick, like mush: *Cook until the fruit is soft but not mushy.* **2** (*informal, disapproving*) too emotional in a way that is embarrassing **SYN** **SENTIMENTAL**: *mushy romantic novels*

music

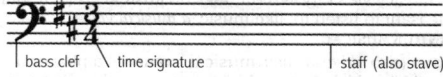

mu·sic 🔊 /ˈmyuzɪk/ *noun* [U]
1 sounds that are arranged in a way that is pleasant or exciting to listen to. People sing music or play it on instruments: *pop/dance/classical/church music* ◆ *to listen to music* ◆ *She could hear music playing somewhere.* ◆ *It was a charming piece of music.* ◆ *the popularity of Mozart's music* ◆ *He wrote the music but I don't know who wrote the words.* ◆ *The poem has been set to music.* ◆ *Every week they get together to make music* (= to play music or sing). ⊃ see also **CHAMBER MUSIC, COUNTRY MUSIC, ROCK MUSIC 2** the art of writing or playing music: *to study music* ◆ *a career in music* ◆ *music lessons* ◆ *the music business/industry* **3** the written or printed signs that represent the sounds to be played or sung in a piece of music: *Can you read music* (= understand the signs in order to play or sing a piece of music)? ◆ *I had to play it without the music.* ◆ *The music was still open on the piano* (= the paper or book with the musical notes on it). ⊃ see also **SHEET MUSIC**
IDM **music to your ears** news or information that you are very pleased to hear ⊃ more at **FACE** *v.*

TOPIC COLLOCATIONS

Music
listening
- **listen to/enjoy/love/**(*informal*) **be into** music/classical music/jazz/pop/hip-hop, etc.
- **listen to** the radio/an MP3 player/a CD
- **put on/play** a CD/a song/some music
- **turn down/up** the music/radio/volume/bass
- **go to** a concert/festival/gig/performance/recital
- **copy/burn/rip** music/a CD/a DVD
- **download** music/an album/a song/a demo/a video

playing

- **play** a musical instrument/the piano/percussion/a note/a riff/the melody/a concerto/a duet/by ear
- **sing** an anthem/a ballad/a solo/an aria/the blues/in a choir/soprano/alto/tenor/bass/out of tune
- **hum** a tune/a theme song/a lullaby
- **accompany** a singer/choir
- **strum** a chord/guitar

performing

- **form/start/join/quit/leave** a band
- (*informal*) **get/put** a band **together**
- **give** a performance/concert/recital
- **do** a concert/recital/gig
- **play** a concert/gig/festival/venue
- **perform** a concert/(live) in concert
- **appear** at a festival/live
- **go on/embark on** a (world) tour

recording

- **write/compose** music/a ballad/a melody/a tune/a song/a theme song/an opera/a symphony
- **land/get/sign** a record deal
- **be signed to/be dropped by** a record company
- **record/release/put out** an album/a single/a CD
- **be on top of/top** the charts
- **get to/go straight to/go straight in at/enter the charts** at number one

mu·si·cal 🔑 /'myuzɪkl/ *adj., noun*

● *adj.* **1** [only before noun] connected with music; containing music: *the musical director of the show* ♦ *musical talent/ability/skill* ♦ *musical styles/tastes* ♦ *a musical production/entertainment* **2** (of a person) with a natural skill or interest in music: *She's very musical.* **ANT** UNMUSICAL **3** (of a sound) pleasant to listen to, like music: *a musical voice* **ANT** UNMUSICAL

● *noun* (also *old-fashioned* ˌmusical ˈcomedy) a play or a movie in which part or all of the story is told using songs and often dancing

ˌmusical ˈchairs *noun* [U] **1** a children's game in which players run around a row of chairs while music is playing. Each time the music stops, players try to sit down on one of the chairs, but there are always more players than chairs. **2** (often *disapproving*) a situation in which people frequently exchange jobs or positions

ˌmusical diˈrector *noun* the person who is in charge of the music in a show in the theater

ˌmusical ˈinstrument (also in·stru·ment) *noun* an object used for producing musical sounds, for example a piano or a drum: *Most students learn (to play) a musical instrument.* ♦ *the instruments of the orchestra* ⊃ picture at INSTRUMENT

mu·si·cal·i·ty /ˌmyuzɪ'kæləti/ *noun* [U] (*formal*) skill and understanding in performing music

mu·si·cal·ly /'myuzɪkli/ *adv.* **1** in a way that is connected with music: *musically gifted* ♦ *Musically speaking, their latest album is nothing special.* **2** with musical skill: *He plays really musically.* **3** in a way that is pleasant to listen to, like music: *to laugh/speak musically*

ˈmusic ˌbox *noun* a box containing a device that plays a tune when the box is opened

ˈmusic ˌhall *noun* a theater used for popular entertainment in the late 19th and early 20th centuries

mu·si·cian 🔑 /myu'zɪʃn/ *noun*
a person who plays a musical instrument or writes music, especially as a job: *a jazz/rock musician*

mu·si·cian·ship /myu'zɪʃnˌʃɪp/ *noun* [U] skill in performing or writing music

mu·si·col·o·gy /ˌmyuzɪ'kɑlədʒi/ *noun* [U] the study of the history and theory of music ► mu·si·col·o·gist /-dʒɪst/ *noun*

ˈmusic ˌstand *noun* a frame, especially one that you can fold, that is used for holding sheets of music while you play a musical instrument

ˈmusic ˌvideo *noun* = VIDEO (4)

mus·ing /'myuzɪŋ/ *noun* [U, C, usually pl.] a period of thinking carefully about something or telling people your thoughts about it: *We had to sit and listen to his musings on life.*

musk /mʌsk/ *noun* [U] a substance with a strong smell that is used in making some PERFUMES. It is produced naturally by a type of male DEER. ► musk·y *adj.*: *a musky perfume* (= smelling of or like musk)

mus·ket /'mʌskət/ *noun* an early type of long gun that was used by soldiers in the past

mus·ket·eer /ˌmʌskə'tɪr/ *noun* a soldier who uses a musket

musk·ox /'mʌskɑks/ *noun* (pl. musk·ox·en /-ˌɑksn/) a large animal of the cow family that is covered with hair and has curved horns

musk·rat /'mʌskræt/ *noun* a water animal that has a strong smell and is hunted for its fur

Mus·lim /'mʌzləm; 'mʊz-; 'mʌs-/ *noun* a person whose religion is Islam ► Muslim *adj.* ⊃ see also MOSLEM

mus·lin /'mʌzlən/ *noun* [U] a type of fine cotton cloth that is almost transparent, used, especially in the past, for making clothes and curtains

muss /mʌs/ *verb* ~ **sth (up)** to make someone's clothes or hair messy: *Hey, don't muss up my hair!*

mus·sel /'mʌsl/ *noun* a small SHELLFISH that can be eaten, with a black shell in two parts ⊃ picture at SHELLFISH

must 🔑 *modal verb, noun*

● *modal verb* /məst; strong form mʌst/ (*negative* must not, short form must·n't /'mʌsnt/) **1** used to say that something is necessary or very important (sometimes involving a rule or a law): *All visitors must report to reception.* ♦ *Cars must not park in front of the entrance* (= it is not allowed). ♦ (*formal*) *I must ask you not to do that again.* ♦ *You mustn't say things like that.* ♦ *I must go to the bank and get some money.* ♦ *I must admit* (= I feel that I should admit) *I was surprised it cost so little.* ♦ *Must you always question everything I say?* (= it is annoying) ♦ *"Do we have to finish this today?" "Yes, you must."* **HELP** Note that the negative for the last example is: *"No, you don't have to."* **2** used to say that something is likely or logical: *You must be hungry after all that walking.* ♦ *He must have known* (= surely he knew) *what she wanted.* ♦ *I'm sorry, she's not here. She must have left already* (= that is the likely explanation). **3** used to recommend that someone do something because you think it is a good idea: *You simply must read this book.* ♦ *We must get together soon for lunch.* ⊃ note at MODAL
IDM **if you must (do sth)** used to say that someone may do something, but you do not really want them to: *"Can I smoke?" "If you must."* ♦ *It's from my boyfriend, if you must know.* **must-see/must-read/must-have, etc.** used to tell people that something is so good or interesting that they should see, read, get it, etc.: *Sydney is one of the world's must-see cities.* ♦ *The magazine is a must-read in the show business world.* ⊃ more at NEED

● *noun* /mʌst/ [usually sing.] (*informal*) something that you must do, see, buy, etc.: *His new novel is a must for all lovers of crime fiction.*

GRAMMAR

must ♦ have (got) to ♦ must not ♦ don't have to

necessity and obligation

- **Must** and **have (got) to** are used in the present to say that something is necessary or should be done.
- **Have to** is more common, especially in speech: *You have to be home by 11 o'clock.* ♦ *I have to wash the car tomorrow.* ♦ *I have to collect the children from school at 3 o'clock.*

t **t**ea	ţ bu**tt**er	d **d**id	k **c**at	g **g**ot	tʃ **ch**in	dʒ **J**une	f **f**all

- **Must** is stronger and more formal: ◆ *All nurses must wear uniform.* ◆ *Changes must be recorded in the log book.*
- There are no past or future forms of **must**. To talk about the past, you use **had to** and **has had to**: *I had to wait half an hour for a bus.* **Will have to** is used to talk about the future, or **have to** if an arrangement has already been made: *We'll have to borrow the money we need.* ◆ *I have to go to the dentist tomorrow.*
- Questions with **have to** are formed using **do**: *Do the children have to wear uniforms?* In negative sentences, both **must not** and **don't have to** are used, but with different meanings. **Must not** is used to tell someone not to do something: *Employees must not smoke in the building.* The short form **mustn't** is rare and very formal: *You mustn't leave the gate open.* **Don't have to** is used when it is not necessary to do something: *You don't have to pay for the tickets in advance.* ◆ *She doesn't have to work on weekends.*
- ⊃ note at NEED

certainty
- Both **must** and **have (got) to** are used to say that you are certain about something. **Have to** is the usual verb in this meaning: *He has (got) to be the worst actor on TV!* If you are talking about the past, use **must have**: *Your trip must have been fun!*

mus·tache /'mʌstæʃ; mə'stæʃ/ **1** a line of hair that a man allows to grow on his upper lip **2 mustaches** [pl.] a very long mustache ⊃ compare BEARD ⊃ picture at HAIR

mus·tached /'mʌstæʃt/ adj. [usually before noun] having a mustache ⊃ compare MUSTACHIOED

mus·ta·chioed /mə'stæʃi,oud/ adj. (literary) having a large mustache with curls at the ends

mus·tang /'mʌstæŋ/ noun a small wild horse

mus·tard /'mʌstərd/ noun [U] **1** a thick, cold, yellow or brown sauce that tastes hot and spicy and is usually eaten with meat: *a jar of mustard* ◆ *mustard powder* ◆ *French/English mustard* **2** a small plant with yellow flowers, grown for its seeds that are crushed to make mustard **3** a brown-yellow color ▶ **mus·tard** adj.: *a mustard sweater*
IDM (not) cut the mustard to (not) be as good as expected or required: *I didn't cut the mustard as a hockey player.*

ˈmustard ˌgas noun [U] a poisonous gas that burns the skin, used in chemical weapons, for example during the First World War

ˈmustard ˌgreens noun [pl.] the dark green leaves of a type of mustard plant that are cooked or eaten raw in salads, especially in the South

mus·ter /'mʌstər/ verb, noun
- **verb 1** [T] ~ sth (up) to find as much support, courage, etc. as you can **SYN** SUMMON: *We mustered what support we could for the plan.* ◆ *She left the room with all the dignity she could muster.* **2** [I, T] to come together; to bring people, especially soldiers, together, for example for military action **SYN** GATHER: *The troops mustered.* ◆ *~ sb/sth to muster an army*
- **noun** a group of people, especially soldiers, that have been brought together: *muster stations* (= parts of a building, a ship, etc. that people must go to if there is an emergency)
IDM see PASS

mus·ty /'mʌsti/ adj. (mus·ti·er, mus·ti·est) smelling damp and unpleasant because of a lack of fresh air **SYN** DANK: *a musty room*

mu·ta·ble /'myuṭəbl/ adj. (formal) that can change; likely to change ▶ **mu·ta·bil·i·ty** /,myuṭə'bɪləṭi/ noun [U]

mu·tant /'myutnt/ adj., noun
- **adj.** (biology) (of a living thing) different in some way from others of the same kind because of a change in its GENETIC structure: *a mutant gene*
- **noun 1** (biology) a living thing with qualities that are different from its parents' qualities because of a change in its GENETIC structure **2** (informal) (in stories about space, the

future, etc.) a living thing with an unusual and frightening appearance because of a change in its GENETIC structure

mu·tate /'myuteɪt/ verb **1** [I, T] to develop or make something develop a new form or structure, because of a GENETIC change: ~ (into sth) *the ability of the virus to mutate into new forms* ◆ ~ sth *mutated genes* **2** [I] ~ (into sth) to change into a new form: *Rhythm and blues mutated into rock and roll.* ⊃ see also MUTATION

mu·ta·tion /myu'teɪʃn/ noun **1** [U, C] (biology) a process in which the GENETIC material of a person, a plant, or an animal changes in structure when it is passed on to children, etc., causing different physical characteristics to develop; a change of this kind: *cells affected by mutation* ◆ *genetic mutations* **2** [U, C] a change in the form or structure of something: (linguistics) *vowel mutation*

mu·ta·tis mu·tan·dis /mu,taṭəs mu'tandəs; myu,taṭəs myu-/ adv. (from Latin, formal) (used when you are comparing two or more things or situations) making the small changes that are necessary for each individual case, without changing the main points: *The same contract, mutatis mutandis, will be given to each employee* (= the contract is basically the same for everyone, but the names, etc. are changed).

mute /myut/ adj., noun, verb
- **adj. 1** not speaking **SYN** SILENT: *The child sat mute in the corner of the room.* ◆ *a look of mute appeal* **2** (old-fashioned) (of a person) unable to speak **SYN** DUMB
- **noun 1** a device on a television, phone, or other piece of equipment that turns off the sound: *Use the remote to put the TV on mute.* **2** (music) a device made of metal, rubber, or plastic that you use to make the sound of a musical instrument softer **3** (old-fashioned) a person who is not able to speak
- **verb 1** ~ sth to make the sound of something quieter; to make something silent: *I always mute the TV during the commercials.* **2** ~ sth to make the sound of a musical instrument quieter or softer using a mute: *He muted the strings with his palm.* **3** ~ sth to make something weaker or less severe **SYN** TONE DOWN: *She thought it better to mute her criticism.*

ˈmute ˌbutton noun **1** a button on a telephone that you press in order to stop yourself from being heard by the person at the other end of the line (while you speak to someone else) **2** a button that you press in order to turn off a television's sound

mut·ed /'myuṭəd/ adj. **1** (of sounds) quiet; not as loud as usual: *They spoke in muted voices.* **2** (of emotions, opinions, etc.) not strongly expressed: *The proposals received only a muted response.* **3** (of colors, light, etc.) not bright: *a dress in muted shades of blue* **4** (of musical instruments) used with a mute: *muted trumpets*

mute·ly /'myutli/ adv. without speaking **SYN** SILENTLY

mu·ti·late /'myutl,eɪt/ verb **1** ~ sb/sth to damage someone's body very severely, especially by cutting or tearing off part of it: *The body had been badly mutilated.* **2** ~ sth to damage something very badly **SYN** VANDALIZE: *Intruders slashed and mutilated several paintings.* ▶ **mu·ti·la·tion** /,myutl'eɪʃn/ noun [U, C]: *Thousands suffered death or mutilation in the bomb blast.*

mu·ti·neer /,myutn'ɪr/ noun a person who takes part in a mutiny

mu·ti·nous /'myutn·əs/ adj. **1** refusing to obey the orders of someone in authority; wanting to do this **SYN** REBELLIOUS: *mutinous workers* ◆ *a mutinous expression* **2** taking part in a mutiny ▶ **mu·ti·nous·ly** adv.

mu·ti·ny /'myutn·i/ noun, verb
- **noun** (pl. mu·ti·nies) [U, C] the act of refusing to obey the orders of someone in authority, especially by soldiers or sailors: *Discontent among the ship's crew finally led to the outbreak of mutiny.* ◆ *the famous movie "Mutiny on the Bounty"* ◆ *We have a family mutiny on our hands!*
- **verb** (mu·ti·nies, mu·ti·ny·ing, mu·ti·nied, mu·ti·nied) [I]

(especially of soldiers or sailors) to refuse to obey the orders of someone in authority

mut·ism /ˈmyutɪzəm/ *noun* [U] (*medical*) a medical condition in which a person is unable to speak

mutt /mʌt/ *noun* (*informal*) a dog, especially one that is not of a particular breed **SYN** MONGREL

mut·ter /ˈmʌtər/ *verb*, *noun*

● *verb* **1** [T, I] to speak or say something in a quiet voice that is difficult to hear, especially because you are annoyed about something: **+ speech** *"How dare she," he muttered under his breath.* ◆ *~ (sth) (to sb/yourself) (about sth) She just sat there muttering to herself.* ◆ *I muttered something about needing to get back to work.* ◆ *~ that... He muttered that he was sorry.* **2** [I, T] *~ (about sth)* | *~ that...* to complain about something, without saying publicly what you think **SYN** GRUMBLE: *Workers continued to mutter about the management.*

● *noun* [usually sing.] a quiet sound or words that are difficult to hear: *the soft mutter of voices*

mut·ter·ing /ˈmʌtərɪŋ/ *noun* [U] **1** (also **mut·ter·ings** [pl.]) complaints that you express privately rather than openly: *There have been mutterings about his leadership.* **2** words that you speak very quietly to yourself

mut·ton /ˈmʌtn/ *noun* [U] meat from a fully grown sheep ◔ compare LAMB

mutton chops (also **mutton chop whiskers**) *noun* [pl.] hair at the sides of a man's face that is grown so that it is very wide and round in shape at the bottom

mu·tu·al **AWL** /ˈmyutʃuəl/ *adj.* **1** used to describe feelings that two or more people have for each other equally, or actions that affect two or more people equally: *mutual respect/understanding* ◆ *mutual support/aid* ◆ *I don't like her, and I think the feeling is mutual* (= she doesn't like me either). **2** [only before noun] shared by two or more people: *We met at the home of a mutual friend.* ◆ *They soon discovered a mutual interest in music.* ▶ **mu·tu·al·i·ty** /ˌmyutʃuˈæləti/ *noun* [U, C] (*formal*)

mutual fund *noun* a company that offers a service to people by investing their money in various businesses

mu·tu·al·ly **AWL** /ˈmyutʃuəli; -tʃəli/ *adv.* felt or done equally by two or more people: *a mutually beneficial/ supportive relationship* ◆ *Can we find a mutually convenient time to meet?* ◆ *The two views are not mutually exclusive* (= both can be true at the same time).

Mu·zak™ /ˈmyuzæk/ *noun* [U] (often *disapproving*) continuous recorded music that is played in stores, restaurants, airports, etc. ◔ compare PIPED MUSIC

muz·zle /ˈmʌzl/ *noun*, *verb*

● *noun* **1** the nose and mouth of an animal, especially a dog or a horse ◔ picture at ANIMAL ◔ compare SNOUT **2** a device made of leather or plastic that you put over the nose and mouth of an animal, especially a dog, to prevent it from biting people **3** the open end of a gun, where the bullets come out

● *verb* **1** [usually passive] *~ sth* to put a muzzle over a dog's nose and mouth to prevent it from biting people **2** *~ sb/ sth* to prevent someone from expressing their opinions in public as they want to **SYN** GAG: *They accused the government of muzzling the press.*

MVP /ˌɛm vi ˈpi/ *abbr.* most valuable player (the best player on a team): *He has just earned his fourth MVP award this season.*

MW *abbr.* (in writing) **1** MEDIUM WAVE **2** (*pl.* MW) MEGA-WATT(S)

mwah (also **mwa**) /mwɑ/ *exclamation* used to represent the sound that some people make when they kiss someone on the cheek

my /maɪ/ *det.* (the possessive form of *I*)
1 of or belonging to the speaker or writer: *Where's my passport?* ◆ *My feet are cold.* **2** used in exclamations to express surprise, etc.: *My goodness! Look at the time!* **3** used

when addressing someone, to show affection: *my dear/ darling/love* **4** used when addressing someone that you consider to have a lower status than you: *My dear girl, you're wrong.*

my·al·gi·a /maɪˈældʒə/ *noun* [U] (*medical*) pain in a muscle ▶ **my·al·gic** /-dʒɪk/ *adj.*

my·col·o·gy /maɪˈkɑlədʒi/ *noun* [U] the scientific study of FUNGUS ◔ see also FUNGUS ▶ **my·col·o·gist** *noun*

my·e·lin /ˈmaɪələn/ *noun* [U] (*biology*) a mixture of PROTEINS and fats that surrounds many nerve cells, increasing the speed at which they send signals

my·e·lo·ma /ˌmaɪəˈloumə/ (*pl.* my·e·lo·mas or my·e·lo·ma·ta /-mətə/) *noun* (*medical*) a type of cancer found as a TUMOR inside the bone

my·nah /ˈmaɪnə/ (also **mynah bird**) *noun* a S.E. Asian bird with dark feathers, that can copy human speech

my·o·pi·a /maɪˈoupiə/ *noun* [U] **1** (*technical*) the inability to see things clearly when they are far away **SYN** NEARSIGHTEDness **2** (*formal*, *disapproving*) the inability to see what the result of a particular action or decision will be; the inability to think about anything outside your own situation **SYN** SHORTSIGHTEDness ▶ **my·op·ic** /maɪˈɑpɪk/ *adj.* (*technical*): *a myopic child/eye* ◆ (*disapproving*) *a myopic strategy* ◆ *myopic voters* ◔ see also NEARSIGHTED, SHORT-SIGHTED **my·op·i·cally** /-kli/ *adv.*

myr·i·ad /ˈmɪriəd/ *noun* (*literary*) an extremely large number of something: *Designs are available in a myriad of colors.* ▶ **myriad** *adj.*: *the myriad problems of modern life*

myrrh /mər/ *noun* [U] a sticky substance with a sweet smell that comes from trees and is used to make PERFUME and INCENSE

myr·tle /ˈmərtl/ *noun* [U, C] a bush with shiny leaves, pink or white flowers, and bluish-black berries (BERRY)

my·self /maɪˈsɛlf/ *pron.*
1 (the reflexive form of *I*) used when the speaker or writer is also the person affected by an action: *I cut myself on a knife.* ◆ *I wrote a message to myself.* ◆ *I found myself unable to speak.* ◆ *I haven't been feeling myself recently* (= I have not felt well). ◆ *I needed space to be myself* (= not be influenced by other people). **2** used to emphasize the fact that the speaker is doing something: *I'll speak to her myself.* ◆ *I myself do not agree.*
IDM **(all) by myself 1** alone; without anyone else: *I live by myself.* **2** without help: *I painted the room all by myself.* **(all) to myself** for the speaker or writer alone; not shared: *I had a whole pizza to myself.*

mys·te·ri·ous /mɪˈstɪriəs/ *adj.*
1 difficult to understand or explain; strange: *He died in mysterious circumstances.* ◆ *A mysterious illness is affecting all the animals.* **2** (especially of people) strange and interesting because you do not know much about them **SYN** ENIGMATIC: *A mysterious young woman is living next door.* **3** (of people) not saying much about something, especially when other people want to know more: *He was being very mysterious about where he was going.* ▶ **mys·te·ri·ous·ly** *adv.*: *My watch had mysteriously disappeared.* ◆ *Mysteriously, the streets were deserted.* ◆ *She was silent, smiling mysteriously.* **mys·te·ri·ous·ness** *noun* [U]

mys·ter·y /ˈmɪstəri/ *noun* (*pl.* mys·ter·ies)
1 [C] something that is difficult to understand or to explain: *It is one of the great unsolved mysteries of this century.* ◆ *Their motives remain a mystery.* ◆ *It's a complete mystery to me why they chose him.* **2** [C] (often used as an adjective) a person or thing that is strange and interesting because you do not know much about them or it: *He's a bit of a mystery.* ◆ *There was a mystery guest on the program.* **3** [U] the quality of being difficult to understand or to explain, especially when this makes someone or something seem interesting and exciting: *Mystery surrounds her disappearance.* ◆ *His past is shrouded in mystery* (= not much is known about it). ◆ *The dark glasses give her an air of mystery.* **4** [C] a story, a movie, or a

h **hat**   m **man**   n **no**   ŋ **sing**   l **leg**   r **red**   y **yes**   w **wet**

play in which crimes and strange events are only explained at the end: *I enjoy murder mysteries.* **5 mysteries** [pl.] secret religious ceremonies; secret knowledge: *(figurative) the teacher who initiated me into the mysteries of mathematics* **6** [C] a religious belief that cannot be explained or proved in a scientific way: *the mystery of creation*

'mystery ,play *noun* a type of play that was popular between the 11th and 14th centuries and was based on events in the Bible or the lives of the Christian SAINTS

,mystery 'shopper *noun* a person whose job is to visit or telephone a store or other business pretending to be a customer, in order to get information on the quality of the service, the facilities, etc. ▶ **,mystery 'shopping** *noun* [U]

mys·tic /'mɪstɪk/ *noun, adj.*
• *noun* a person who tries to become united with God through prayer and MEDITATION and to understand important things that are beyond normal human understanding
• *adj.* = MYSTICAL

mys·ti·cal /'mɪstɪkl/ (also *less frequent* **mys·tic**) *adj.* **1** having spiritual powers or qualities that are difficult to understand or to explain: *mystical forces/powers* ◆ *mystic beauty* ◆ *Watching the sun rise over the mountain was an almost mystical experience.* **2** connected with mysticism: *the mystical life* ▶ **mys·ti·cally** /-kli/ *adv.*

mys·ti·cism /'mɪstə,sɪzəm/ *noun* [U] the belief that knowledge of God and of real truth can be found through prayer and MEDITATION rather than through reason and the senses: *Eastern mysticism*

mys·ti·fy /'mɪstə,faɪ/ *verb* (**mys·ti·fies, mys·ti·fy·ing, mys·ti·fied, mys·ti·fied**) ~ **sb** to make someone confused because they do not understand something **SYN** BAFFLE: *They were totally mystified by the girl's disappearance.* ▶ **mys·ti·fi·ca·tion** /,mɪstəfə'keɪʃn/ *noun* [U]: *He looked at her in mystification.* **mys·ti·fy·ing** *adj.*

mys·tique /mɪ'stik/ *noun* [U, sing.] the quality of being mysterious or secret that makes someone or something seem interesting or attractive: *The mystique surrounding the monarchy has gone forever.*

myth /mɪθ/ *noun* [C, U] **1** a story from ancient times, especially one that was told to explain natural events or to describe the early history of a people; this type of story **SYN** LEGEND: *ancient Greek myths* ◆ *a creation myth* (= that explains how the world began) ◆ *the heroes of myth and legend* **2** something that many people believe but that does not exist or is false **SYN** FALLACY: *It is time to dispel the myth of a classless society* (= to show that it does not exist). ◆ *Contrary to popular myth, women are not worse drivers than men.*

myth·ic /'mɪθɪk/ *adj.* **1** (also **myth·i·cal**) that has become very famous, like someone or something in a myth **SYN** LEGENDARY: *Scott of the Antarctic was a national hero of mythic proportions.* **2** = MYTHICAL (1), MYTHICAL (2)

myth·i·cal /'mɪθɪkl/ *adj.* [usually before noun] **1** (also *less frequent* **myth·ic**) existing only in ancient myths **SYN** LEGENDARY: *mythical beasts/heroes* **2** (also *less frequent* **myth·ic**) that does not exist or is not true **SYN** FICTITIOUS: *the mythical "rich uncle" that he boasts about* **3** = MYTHIC (1)

myth·o·log·i·cal /,mɪθə'lɑdʒɪkl/ *adj.* [usually before noun] connected with ancient myths: *mythological subjects/figures/stories*

my·thol·o·gy /mɪ'θɑlədʒi/ *noun* (*pl.* **my·thol·o·gies**) [U, C] **1** ancient myths in general; the ancient myths of a particular culture, society, etc.: *Greek mythology* ◆ *a study of the religions and mythologies of ancient Rome* **2** ideas that many people think are true but that do not exist or are false: *the popular mythology that life begins at forty*

myx·o·ma·to·sis /,mɪksəmə'toʊsəs/ *noun* [U] an infectious disease of RABBITS that usually causes death

---

Nn

N /ɛn/ *noun, abbr., symbol*

● **noun** also **n** (*pl.* **Ns, N's, n's** /ɛnz/) **1** [C, U] the 14th letter of the English alphabet: *"Night" begins with (an) N/"N."* **2 n** [U] (*mathematics*) used to represent a number whose value is not mentioned: *The equation is impossible for any value of n greater than 2.* ⊃ see also NTH

● **abbr.** (in writing) **1** usually **N.** (also **No.**) north; northern: *N. Ireland* **2** NEWTON(S)

● **symbol** the symbol for the chemical element NITROGEN

n. *abbr.* noun

n/a *abbr.* **1** not applicable (used on a form as an answer to a question that does not apply to you) **2** not available

NAACP /ˌɛn dʌbəl ˌeɪ si ˈpi/ *abbr.* National Association for the Advancement of Colored People (an organization that works for the rights of African Americans)

naan (also **nan**) /nɑn/ *noun* [U] a type of soft, flat, S. Asian bread

nab /næb/ *verb* (**-bb-**) (*informal*) **1 ~ sb** to catch or arrest someone who is doing something wrong **SYN** COLLAR: *He was nabbed by the police for speeding.* **2 ~ sth** to take or get something: *Who's nabbed my drink?*

na·bob /ˈneɪbɒb/ *noun* a rich or important person

na·chos /ˈnɑtʃoʊz/ *noun* [pl.] (from *Spanish*) a Mexican dish of crisp pieces of TORTILLA served with BEANS, cheese, spices, etc.

na·da /ˈnɑdə/ *noun* [U] (from *Spanish, informal*) nothing: *What is it worth? Zero, zilch, nada!*

na·dir /ˈneɪdər; -dɪr/ *noun* [sing.] (*formal*) the worst moment of a particular situation: *the nadir of his career* ◆ *Company losses reached their nadir in 2009.* **ANT** ZENITH

nag /næg/ *verb, noun*

● **verb** (**-gg-**) **~ (at sb) 1** [I, T] (*disapproving*) to keep complaining to someone about their behavior or keep asking them to do something **SYN** PESTER: *Stop nagging—I'll do it as soon as I can.* ◆ **~ sb (to do sth)** *She had been nagging him to paint the fence.* **2** [I, T] to worry or irritate you continuously: **~ at sb** *A feeling of unease nagged at her.* ◆ **~ sb** *Doubts nagged me all evening.*

● **noun** (*informal*) **1** (*disapproving*) a person who often complains to someone about their behavior or keeps asking them to do something: *Don't be a nag—you'll get an answer when I make a decision.* **2** (*old-fashioned*) a horse

nag·ging /ˈnæɡɪŋ/ *adj.* [only before noun] **1** continuing for a long time and difficult to cure or remove: *a nagging pain/doubt* **2** complaining: *a nagging voice*

nah /næ; nɑ/ *exclamation* (*slang*) = NO

nai·ad /ˈnaɪæd/ *noun* (*pl.* **nai·ads** or **nai·ad·es** /ˈnaɪədiz/) (in ancient stories) a water spirit

nail 🔨 /neɪl/ *noun, verb*

● **noun 1** a thin hard layer covering the outer tip of the fingers or toes: *Stop biting your nails!* ⊃ see also FINGERNAIL, TOENAIL **2** a small, thin, pointed piece of metal with a flat head, used for hanging things on a wall or for joining pieces of wood together: *She hammered the nail in.* ⊃ picture at TOOL ⊃ collocations at DECORATE ⊃ compare SCREW

IDM **a nail in sb's/sth's coffin** something that makes the end or failure of an organization, someone's plans, etc. more likely to happen ⊃ more at FIGHT, HARD, HIT, TOUGH

● **verb 1 ~ sth (+ adv./prep./adj.)** to fasten something to something with a nail or nails: *I nailed the sign to a tree.* **2 ~ sb** (*informal*) to catch someone and prove they are guilty of a crime or of doing something bad: *The police haven't been* able to nail the killer. **3 ~ sth** (*informal*) to tell the truth about something and prove that it is illegal, false, etc.: *We must nail this lie.* **4 ~ sth** (*informal*) to achieve something or do something right, especially in sports: *He nailed a victory in the semifinals.*

PHR V ˌnail sth↔ˈdown **1** to fasten something down with a nail or nails **2** to reach an agreement or a decision, usually after a lot of discussion: *All the parties seem anxious to nail down a ceasefire.* ˌnail sb↔ˈdown (to sth) to force someone to give you a definite promise or tell you exactly what they intend to do **SYN** PIN DOWN: *She says she'll come, but I can't nail her down to a specific time.* ˌnail sth↔ˈup **1** to fasten something to a wall, post, etc. with a nail or nails **2** to put nails into a door or window so that it cannot be opened

ˈnail-ˌbiter (also **ˈnail ˌbiter**) *noun* a situation that makes you feel excited or anxious because you do not know what is going to happen: *The final game of the competition was a real nail-biter.*

ˈnail-ˌbiting *adj.* [usually before noun] making you feel very excited or anxious because you do not know what is going to happen: *a nail-biting finish* ◆ *It's been a nail-biting couple of weeks waiting for my results.*

ˈnail brush *noun* a small stiff brush for cleaning your nails

ˈnail ˌclippers *noun* [pl.] a small tool for cutting the nails on your fingers and toes

ˈnail file *noun* a small metal tool with a rough surface for shaping your nails ⊃ see also EMERY BOARD

ˈnail ˌpolish *noun* [U] clear or colored liquid that you paint on your nails to make them look attractive: *nail polish remover* ⊃ picture at MAKEUP

ˈnail ˌscissors *noun* [pl.] small scissors that are usually curved, used for cutting the nails on your fingers and toes: *a pair of nail scissors*

na·ive (also **naïve**) /naɪˈiv/ *adj.* **1** (*disapproving*) lacking knowledge, experience of life, or good judgment, and willing to believe that people always tell you the truth: *to be politically naive* ◆ *I can't believe you were so naive as to trust him!* ◆ *a naive question* **2** (*approving*) (of people and their behavior) innocent and simple **SYN** ARTLESS: *Their approach to life is refreshingly naive.* ⊃ compare SOPHISTICATED **3** (*technical*) (of art) in a style which is deliberately very simple, often uses bright colors, and is similar to that produced by a child ▸ **na·ive·ly** (also **naïve·ly**) *adv.*: *I naively assumed that I would be paid for the work.* **na·ive·té** (also **na·ive·té**) /ˌnaɪivˈteɪ; naɪˈivteɪ/ *noun* [U]: *They laughed at the naiveté of his suggestion.* ◆ *She has lost none of her naiveté.*

WHICH WORD?

naked • bare

Both these words can be used to mean "not covered with clothes" and are frequently used with the following nouns:

naked ~	bare ~
body	feet
man/woman	arms
flame	walls
aggression	branches
fear	essentials

- **Naked** is more often used to describe a person or their body and **bare** usually describes a part of the body.
- **Bare** can also describe other things with nothing on them: *bare walls* ◆ *a bare hillside.* **Naked** can mean "without a protective covering": *a naked sword*
- **Bare** can also mean "just enough": *the bare minimum.*
- **Naked** can be used to talk about strong feelings that are not hidden: *naked fear.* Note also the idiom: *(visible) with/to the naked eye*

ʌ **cup**   ə **about**   eɪ **say**   ɪə **five**   ɔɪ **boy**   aʊ **now**   oʊ **go**   ər **bird**

na·ked 🔊 /ˈneɪkəd/ adj.

1 not wearing any clothes **SYN** BARE: *a naked body* ♦ *naked shoulders* ♦ *They often wandered around the house* **stark naked** (= completely naked). ♦ *They found him* **half naked** *and bleeding to death.* ♦ *The prisoners were* **stripped naked**. ⤷ see also BUCK NAKED **2** [usually before noun] without the usual covering **SYN** BARE: *a naked light* ♦ *a naked sword* ♦ *Mice are born naked* (= without fur). **3** [only before noun] (of emotions, attitudes, etc.) expressed strongly and not hidden: *naked aggression* ♦ *the naked truth* **4** [not usually before noun] unable to protect yourself from being harmed, criticized, etc. **SYN** HELPLESS: *He still felt naked and drained after his ordeal.* ▸ **na·ked·ly** adv.: *nakedly aggressive* **na·ked·ness** noun [U]

IDM **the naked eye** the normal power of your eyes without the help of an instrument: *The planet should be visible* **with/to the naked eye**.

nam·by-pam·by /ˌnæmbi ˈpæmbi/ adj. (informal, disapproving) weak and too emotional

name 🔊 /neɪm/ noun, verb

● **noun 1** a word or words that a particular person, animal, place, or thing is known by: *What's your name?* ♦ *What is/was the name, please?* (= a polite way of asking someone's name) ♦ *Please write your full name and address below.* ♦ *Do you know the name of this flower?* ♦ *Rubella is just another name for German measles.* ♦ *Are you changing your name when you get married?* ⤷ see also ASSUMED NAME, BRAND NAME, CODE NAME, FAMILY NAME, FILENAME, FIRST NAME, HOUSEHOLD NAME, LAST NAME, MAIDEN NAME, MIDDLE NAME, NICKNAME, PEN-NAME, PET NAME, PLACE NAME, SURNAME, TRADE NAME, USERNAME **2** [usually sing.] a reputation that someone or something has; the opinion that people have about someone or something: *She first* **made her name** *as a writer of children's books.* ♦ *He's* **made** *quite* **a name for himself** (= he has become famous). ♦ *The college has* **a good name** *for languages.* ♦ *This kind of behavior* **gives** *students* **a bad name**. **3** (in compound adjectives) having a name or a reputation of the kind mentioned, especially one that is known by a lot of people: *a big-name company* ♦ *brand-name goods* ⤷ see also HOUSEHOLD NAME **4** a famous person: *Some of the biggest names in the art world were at the party.*

IDM **by name** using the name of someone or something: *She asked for you by name.* ♦ *The principal knows all the students by name.* ♦ *I only know her by name* (= I have heard about her but I have not met her). **by the name of…** (formal) who is called: *a young actor by the name of Tom Rees* **give your name to sth** to invent something which then becomes known by your name **go by the name of…** to use a name that may not be your real one **have your/sb's name on it | with your/sb's name on it** (informal) if something **has your name on it**, or there is something **with your name on it**, it is intended for you: *He took my place and got killed. It should have been me — that bullet had my name on it.* ♦ *Are you coming for dinner tonight? I have a steak here with your name on it!* **in all but name** used to describe a situation which exists in reality but that is not officially recognized: *He runs the company in all but name.* **in God's/Heaven's name | in the name of God/Heaven** used especially in questions to show that you are angry, surprised, or shocked: *What in God's name was that noise?* ♦ *Where in the name of Heaven have you been?* **in the name of sb/sth | in sb's/sth's name 1** for someone; showing that something officially belongs to someone: *We reserved two tickets in the name of Brown.* ♦ *The car is registered in my name.* **2** using the authority of someone or something; as a representative of someone or something: *I arrest you in the name of the law.* **3** used to give a reason or an excuse for doing something, often when what you are doing is wrong: *crimes committed in the name of religion* **in name only** officially recognized but not existing in reality: *He's party leader in name only.* **sb's name is mud** (informal, usually humorous) used to say that someone is not liked or popular because of something they have done **the name of the game** (informal) the most important aspect of an activity; the most important quality needed for an activity: *Hard work is the name of the game if*

you want to succeed in business. **a name to reckon with** a person or thing that is well known and respected in a particular field: *Miyazaki is still a name to reckon with among anime fans.* **put a name to sb/sth** to know or remember what someone or something is called: *I recognize the tune but I can't put a name to it.* **take God's/the Lord's name in vain** (old-fashioned) to use the words "God," "Jesus," etc. in a way that shows a lack of respect **take sb's name in vain** to show a lack of respect when using someone's name: (humorous) *Have you been taking my name in vain again?* **(have sth) to your name** to have or own something: *an Olympic athlete with five gold medals to his name* ♦ *She doesn't have a penny/cent to her name* (= she is very poor). **under the name (of)…** using a name that may not be your real name ⤷ more at ANSWER v., BIG, CALL v., DROP v., LEND, MIDDLE NAME, ROSE n.

● **verb 1** to give a name to someone or something **SYN** CALL: **~ sb/sth (after/for sb)** *He was named after his father* (= given his father's first name). ♦ **~ sb/sth + noun** *They named their son John.* **2** to say the name of someone or something **SYN** IDENTIFY: **~ sb/sth** *The victim has not yet been named.* ♦ *Can you name all the American states?* ♦ **~ sb/sth as sb/sth** *The missing man has been named as James Kelly.* ⤷ thesaurus box at IDENTIFY **3 ~ sth** to state something exactly **SYN** SPECIFY: *Name your price.* ♦ *They're engaged, but they haven't yet* **named the day** (= chosen the date for their wedding). ◆ *Activities available include squash, archery, and swimming,* **to name (but) a few.** ◆ *Chairs, tables, cabinets— you name it, she makes it* (= she makes anything you can imagine). **4** to choose someone for a job or position **SYN** NOMINATE: ~ **sb (as) sth** *I had no hesitation in naming him (as) captain.* ◆ ~ **sb (to sth)** *When she resigned, he was named to the committee in her place.*

IDM **name names** to give the names of the people involved in something, especially something wrong or illegal

'name-,calling noun [U] the act of using rude or insulting words about someone

'name-check noun, verb
• **noun** an occasion when the name of a person or thing is mentioned or included in a list: *She started her speech by giving a name-check to all the people who had helped her.*
• **verb** ~ **sb/sth** to mention or include someone or something in a list: *The songs name-check other artists and bands.* ◆ *The book was name-checked in today's paper.*

'name day noun a day that is special for a Christian with a particular name, because it is the day that celebrates a SAINT with the same name

'name-,dropping noun [U] (*disapproving*) the act of mentioning the names of famous people you know or have met in order to impress other people ▶ **'name-drop** verb [I] ⊃ see also DROP NAMES

name·less /'neɪmləs/ adj. **1** [usually before noun] having no name; whose name you do not know: *a nameless grave* ◆ *thousands of nameless and faceless workers* **2** whose name is kept secret **SYN** ANONYMOUS: *a nameless source in the government* ◆ *a well-known public figure* **who shall remain nameless 3** [usually before noun] (*literary*) difficult or too unpleasant to describe: *nameless horrors* ◆ *a nameless longing*

name·ly /'neɪmli/ adv. used to introduce more exact and detailed information about something that you have just mentioned: *We need to concentrate on our target audience, namely women aged between 20 and 30.*

name·plate /'neɪmpleɪt/ noun **1** a sign on the door or the wall of a building showing the name of a company or the name of a person who is living or working there **2** a piece of metal or plastic on an object showing the name of the person who owns it, made it, or presented it

name·sake /'neɪmseɪk/ noun a person or thing that has the same name as someone or something else: *Unlike his more famous namesake, this Richard Nixon has little interest in politics.*

'name tag noun a small piece of plastic, paper, or metal that you wear, with your name on it

name·tape /'neɪmteɪp/ noun a small piece of cloth that is sewn or stuck onto a piece of clothing and that has the name of the owner on it

nan = NAAN

nan·a /'nænə/ noun (*informal*) (used by children, especially as a form of address) a grandmother

Na·naimo Bar /nə'naɪmou ˌbɑr/ noun (*CanE*) a sweet square with chocolate, nuts, and COCONUT on the bottom, white ICING, and chocolate on top

nan·ny /'næni/ noun (*pl.* **nan·nies**) a woman whose job is to take care of young children in the children's own home
IDM **the nanny state** a disapproving way of talking about the fact that government seems to get too much involved in people's lives and to protect them too much, in a way that limits their freedom

'nanny ˌgoat noun a female GOAT ⊃ compare BILLY GOAT

na·no- /'nænou; -nə/ combining form (*technical*) (in nouns and adjectives; used especially in units of measurement) one billionth: *nanosecond* ◆ *nanometer*

nan·o·me·ter (*CanE usually* **nan·o·me·tre**) /'nænəˌmitər/ noun (*abbr.* **nm**) one billionth of a meter

nan·o·par·ti·cle /'nænouˌpɑrtɪkl/ noun a piece of matter less than 100 NANOMETERS long

nan·o·scale /'nænəˌskeɪl/ adj. [usually before noun] of a size that can be measured in nanometers: *nanoscale particles/ devices/electronics*

nan·o·sec·ond /'nænəˌsɛkənd/ noun (*abbr.* **ns**) one billionth of a second

nan·o·tech·nol·o·gy /ˌnænoutɛk'nalədʒi/ noun [U] the branch of technology that deals with structures that are less than 100 nanometers long. Scientists often build these structures using individual MOLECULES of substances.
▶ **nan·o·tech·nol·o·gist** /-dʒɪst/ noun **nan·o·tech·no·log·i·cal** /-ˌtɛknə'ladʒɪkl/ adj.: *nanotechnological research*

nap /næp/ noun, verb
• **noun** **1** [C] a short sleep, especially during the day **SYN** SNOOZE: *to take a nap* ⊃ see also CATNAP, POWER NAP ⊃ compare SIESTA ⊃ thesaurus box at SLEEP **2** [sing.] the short fine threads on the surface of some types of cloth, usually lying in the same direction
• **verb** (-pp-) [I] to sleep for a short time, especially during the day **IDM** see CATCH v.

na·pa noun [U] = NAPPA

na·palm /'neɪpɑm/ noun [U] a substance like jelly, made from gas, that burns and is used in making bombs

nape /neɪp/ noun [sing.] ~ **(of someone's neck)** the back of the neck: *Her hair was cut short at the nape of her neck.* ⊃ picture at BODY

naph·tha /'næfθə; 'næpθə/ noun [U] a type of oil that starts burning very easily, used as fuel or in making chemicals

naph·tha·lene /'næfθəˌlin; 'næpθə-/ noun [U] (*chemistry*) a substance used in products that keep MOTHS away from clothes, and in industrial processes

nap·kin /'næpkən/ noun **1** (*CanE* **serviette**) a piece of cloth or paper used at meals for protecting your clothes and cleaning your lips and fingers **2** = SANITARY NAPKIN

nap·pa (also **na·pa**) /'næpə/ noun [U] a type of soft leather made from the skin of sheep or GOATS

nappe /næp/ noun [U] (*geology*) a thin layer of rock that lies on top of a different type of rock

nap·py /'næpi/ adj. (*informal*) (of hair) having short, tight curls

narc /nɑrk/ (also **nar·co** /'nɑrkou/) noun (*informal*) a police officer whose job is to stop people from selling or using drugs illegally

nar·cis·sism /'nɑrsəˌsɪzəm/ noun [U] (*formal, disapproving*) the habit of admiring yourself too much, especially your appearance ▶ **nar·cis·sist** noun **nar·cis·sis·tic** /ˌnɑrsə-'sɪstɪk/ adj. **ORIGIN** From the Greek myth in which **Narcissus**, a beautiful young man, fell in love with his own reflection in a pool. He died and was changed into the flower which bears his name.

nar·cis·sus /nɑr'sɪsəs/ noun (*pl.* **nar·cis·si** /-'sɪsaɪ; -'sɪsi/ or **narcissuses**) a plant with white or yellow flowers that appear in spring. There are many types of narcissi, including the DAFFODIL.

nar·co·lep·sy /'nɑrkəˌlɛpsi/ noun [U] (*medical*) a condition in which someone falls into a deep sleep whenever they are in relaxing surroundings

nar·co·sis /nɑr'kousəs/ noun [U] (*medical*) a state caused by drugs in which someone is unconscious or keeps falling asleep

nar·cot·ic /nɑr'katɪk/ noun, adj.
• **noun** **1** a powerful illegal drug that affects the mind in a harmful way. HEROIN and COCAINE are narcotics: *a narcotics agent* (= a police officer investigating the illegal trade in drugs) **2** (*medical*) a substance that relaxes you, reduces pain, or makes you sleep: *a mild narcotic*
• **adj.** **1** (of a drug) that affects your mind in a harmful way **2** (of a substance) making you sleep: *a mild narcotic effect*

nar·rate /'næreɪt/ verb **1** ~ sth (formal) to tell a story **SYN** RELATE: *She entertained them by narrating her adventures in Africa.* **2** ~ sth to speak the words that form the text of a DOCUMENTARY film or program: *The film was narrated by an unknown actor.*

nar·ra·tion /næ'reɪʃn/ noun (formal) **1** [U, C] the act or process of telling a story, especially in a novel, a movie, or a play **2** [C] a description of events that is spoken during a movie, a play, etc. or with music: *He has recorded the narration for the production.*

nar·ra·tive /'nærətɪv/ noun (formal) **1** [C] a description of events, especially in a novel **SYN** STORY: *a gripping narrative of their journey up the Amazon* ⟳ collocations at LITERATURE **2** [U] the act, process, or skill of telling a story: *The novel contains too much dialogue and not enough narrative.* ▶ **narrative** adj. [only before noun]: *narrative fiction*

nar·ra·tor /'næˌreɪtər; 'nærətər/ noun a person who tells a story, especially in a book, play, or movie; the person who speaks the words in a television program but who does not appear in it: *a first-person narrator*

nar·row 🔑 /'næroʊ/ adj., verb

• **adj.** (nar·row·er, nar·row·est) **1** measuring a short distance from one side to the other, especially in relation to length: *narrow streets* ◆ *a narrow bed/doorway/shelf* ◆ *narrow shoulders/hips* ◆ *There was only a narrow gap between the bed and the wall.* ◆ *(figurative) the narrow confines of prison life* **ANT** BROAD, WIDE **2** [usually before noun] only just achieved or avoided: *a narrow victory* ◆ *He lost the race by the narrowest of margins.* ◆ *She was elected by a narrow majority.* ◆ *He had a narrow escape when his car skidded on the ice.* **3** limited in a way that ignores important issues or the opinions of other people: *narrow interests* ◆ *She has a very narrow view of the world.* **ANT** BROAD **4** limited in variety or numbers **SYN** RESTRICTED: *The shop sells only a narrow range of goods.* ◆ *a narrow circle of friends* **ANT** WIDE **5** limited in meaning; exact: *I am using the word "education" in the narrower sense.* **ANT** BROAD ▶ **nar·row·ness** noun [U]: *The narrowness of the streets caused many traffic problems.* ◆ *We were surprised by the narrowness of our victory.* ◆ *His attitudes show a certain narrowness of mind.* **IDM** see STRAIGHT adj.

• **verb** [I, T] to become or make something narrower: *This is where the river narrows.* ◆ *The gap between the two teams has narrowed to three points.* ◆ *Her eyes narrowed (= almost closed) menacingly.* ◆ ~ sth *He narrowed his eyes at her.* ◆ *We're doing it to try to narrow the gap between rich and poor.* **PHRV** ,narrow sth↔'down (to sth) to reduce the number of possibilities or choices: *We have narrowed down the list to four candidates.*

WHICH WORD?

narrow • thin

These adjectives are frequently used with the following nouns:

narrow ~	thin ~
road	man
entrance	legs
bed	ice
stairs	line
majority	layer
victory	material
range	cream

- **Narrow** describes something that is a short distance from side to side. **Thin** describes people, or something that has a short distance through it from one side to the other.
- **Thin** is also used of things that are not as thick as you expect. **Narrow** can be used with the meanings "barely achieved" and "limited."

---

nar·row·band /'næroʊˌbænd/ noun [U] (technical) signals that use a narrow range of FREQUENCY ⟳ compare BROAD-BAND

nar·row·cast /'næroʊˌkæst/ verb [I] (technical) to send information by television or the Internet to a particular group of people ⟳ compare BROADCAST

,narrow 'gauge noun [U] a size of railroad track that is not as wide as the standard track that is used in the U.S. and many other countries: *a narrow-gauge railroad*

nar·row·ly /'næroʊli/ adv. **1** only by a small amount: *The car narrowly missed a girl crossing the street.* ◆ *She narrowly escaped injury.* ◆ *The team lost narrowly.* **2** (sometimes disapproving) in a way that is limited: *a narrowly defined task* ◆ *a narrowly specialized education* **3** closely; carefully: *She looked at him narrowly.*

,narrow-'minded adj. (disapproving) not willing to listen to new ideas or to the opinions of others **SYN** BIGOTED, INTOLERANT: *a narrow-minded attitude* ◆ *a narrow-minded nationalist* **ANT** BROAD-MINDED, OPEN-MINDED ▶ ,narrow-'mindedness noun [U]

nar·rows /'næroʊz/ noun [pl.] a narrow channel that connects two larger areas of water

nar·whal /'narwəl/ noun a small white WHALE from the Arctic region. The male narwhal has a long TUSK (= outer tooth).

nar·y /'nɛri/ adj. (old use or dialect) not a; no

NASA /'næsə/ abbr. National Aeronautics and Space Administration (a U.S. government organization that does research into space and organizes space travel)

na·sal /'neɪzl/ adj. **1** connected with the nose: *the nasal passages* ◆ *a nasal spray* **2** (of someone's voice) sounding as if it is produced partly through the nose: *a nasal accent* **3** (phonetics) (of a speech sound) produced by sending a stream of air through the nose. The nasal consonants in English are /m/, /n/, and /ŋ/, as in *sum, sun,* and *sung.*

na·sal·ize /'neɪzəˌlaɪz/ verb ~ sth (phonetics) to produce a speech sound, especially a vowel, with the air in the nose vibrating (VIBRATE) ▶ **na·sal·i·za·tion** /ˌneɪzələ'zeɪʃn/ noun [U]

NASCAR /'næskɑr/ abbr. National Association for Stock Car Auto Racing

nas·cent /'neɪsnt; 'næ-/ adj. (formal) beginning to exist; not yet fully developed

the NASDAQ /'næzdæk/ noun [sing.] National Association of Securities Dealers Automated Quotations (a computer system in the U.S. that supplies the current price of shares to the people who sell them)

nas·tur·tium /nə'stɔrʃəm/ noun a garden plant with round flat leaves and red, orange, or yellow flowers that are sometimes eaten in salads

nas·ty /'næsti/ adj. (nas·ti·er, nas·ti·est) **1** very bad or unpleasant: *a nasty accident* ◆ *The news gave me a nasty shock.* ◆ *I had a nasty feeling that he would follow me.* ◆ *This coffee has a nasty taste.* **2** unkind; unpleasant **SYN** MEAN: *to make nasty remarks about someone* ◆ *the nastier side of her character* ◆ *to have a nasty temper* ◆ *Don't be so nasty to your brother.* ◆ *That was a nasty little trick.* ◆ *Life has a nasty habit of repeating itself.* **3** dangerous or serious: *a nasty bend (= dangerous for cars going fast)* ◆ *a nasty injury* **4** offensive; in bad taste: *to have a nasty mind* ◆ *nasty jokes* ▶ **nas·ti·ly** /-təli/ adv.: *"I hate you," she said nastily.* **nas·ti·ness** /-tinəs/ noun [U] **IDM** get/turn nasty **1** to become threatening and violent: *You'd better do what he says or he'll turn nasty.* **2** to become bad or unpleasant: *It looks as though the weather is going to turn nasty again.* ⟳ more at TASTE n.

na·tal /'neɪtl/ adj. [only before noun] (formal) relating to the place where or the time when someone was born: *her natal home*

na·tal·i·ty /neɪ'tæləti/ noun [U] (technical) the number of births every year for every 1,000 people in the population **SYN** BIRTH RATE

natch /nætʃ/ adv. (informal) used to say that something is obvious or exactly as you would expect **SYN** NATURALLY: *He was wearing the latest T-shirt, natch.*

---

na·tion 🔊 /ˈneɪʃn/ noun
1 [C] a country considered as a group of people with the same language, culture, and history, who live in a particular area under one government: *an independent nation* ◆ *the African nations* **2** [sing.] all the people in a country **SYN** POPULATION: *The entire nation, it seemed, was watching TV.*

na·tion·al 🔊 /ˈnæʃnəl/ adj., noun
● *adj.* [usually before noun] **1** connected with a particular nation; shared by a whole nation: *national and local newspapers* ◆ *national and international news* ◆ *national and regional politics* ◆ *a national election* ◆ *These buildings are part of our national heritage.* ◆ *They are afraid of losing their national identity.* **2** owned, controlled, or paid for by the government: *a national airline/museum/theater*
● *noun* (*technical*) a citizen of a particular country: *Polish nationals living in Germany*

national 'anthem noun the official song of a nation that is sung on special occasions

national con'vention noun a meeting held by a political party to choose a candidate to take part in the election for President

national 'costume noun [C, U] (also **national 'dress** [U]) the clothes traditionally worn by people from a particular country, especially on special occasions or for formal ceremonies

national 'debt noun [usually sing.] the total amount of money that the government of a country owes

the National 'Guard noun [sing.] **1** the army in each state of the U.S. that can be used by the federal government if needed **2** a small army, often used to protect a political leader

na·tion·al·ism /ˈnæʃnəˌlɪzəm/ noun [U] **1** the desire by a group of people who share the same race, culture, language, etc. to form an independent country: *Scottish nationalism* **2** (sometimes *disapproving*) a feeling of love for and pride in your country; a feeling that your country is better than any other

na·tion·al·ist /ˈnæʃnəlɪst/ noun **1** a person who wants their country to become independent: *Scottish nationalists* **2** (sometimes *disapproving*) a person who has a great love for and pride in their country; a person who has a feeling that their country is better than any other ▶ **nationalist** *adj.*: *nationalist sentiments*

na·tion·al·is·tic /ˌnæʃnəˈlɪstɪk/ adj. (usually *disapproving*) having very strong feelings of love for and pride in your country, so that you think that it is better than any other

na·tion·al·i·ty /ˌnæʃəˈnæləti/ noun (pl. **na·tion·al·i·ties**)
1 [U, C] the legal right of belonging to a particular nation: *to have/hold French nationality* ◆ *All applicants will be considered regardless of age, sex, religion, or nationality.* ◆ *The college attracts students of all nationalities.* ◆ *She has dual nationality* (= is a citizen of two countries). **2** [C] a group of people with the same language, culture, and history who form part of a political nation: *Kazakhstan alone contains more than a hundred nationalities.*

na·tion·al·ize /ˈnæʃnəˌlaɪz/ verb **~ sth** to put an industry or a company under the control of the government, which becomes its owner: *nationalized industries*
ANT DENATIONALIZE, PRIVATIZE ▶ **na·tion·al·i·za·tion** /ˌnæʃnələˈzeɪʃn/ noun [U, C]

the National 'League noun (in the U.S.) one of the two organizations for professional baseball ⊃ see also AMERICAN LEAGUE

na·tion·al·ly /ˈnæʃnəli/ adv. relating to a country as a whole; relating to a particular country: *The program was broadcast nationally.* ◆ *Meetings were held locally and nationally.* ◆ *He's a talented athlete who competes nationally and internationally.*

national 'park noun an area of land that is protected by the government for people to visit because of its natural beauty and historical or scientific interest

National 'Socialism noun [U] (*politics*) the policies of the German Nazi party ▶ **National 'Socialist** noun, adj.

na·tion·hood /ˈneɪʃnˌhʊd/ noun [U] the state of being a nation: *Citizenship is about the sense of nationhood.*

'nation state noun a group of people with the same culture, language, etc. who have formed an independent country

na·tion·wide /ˌneɪʃnˈwaɪd/ adj. happening or existing in all parts of a particular country: *a nationwide campaign* ▶ **na·tion·wide** adv.: *The company has over 500 stores nationwide.*

na·tive 🔊 /ˈneɪtɪv/ adj., noun
● *adj.* **1** [only before noun] connected with the place where you were born and lived for the first years of your life: *your native land/country/city* ◆ *It is a long time since he has visited his native Chile.* ◆ *Her native language is Korean.* ⊃ see also NATIVE SPEAKER **2** [only before noun] connected with the place where you have always lived or have lived for a long time: *a native of New York* **3** [only before noun] connected with the people who originally lived in a country before other people, especially white people, came there: *native peoples* ◆ *native art* **4 ~ (to…)** (of animals and plants) existing naturally in a place **SYN** INDIGENOUS: *the native plants of America* ◆ *The tiger is native to India.* ◆ *native species* **5** [only before noun] that you have naturally, without having to learn it **SYN** INNATE: *native cunning*
IDM **go native** (often *humorous*) (of a person staying in another country) to try to live and behave like the local people
● *noun* **1** a person who was born in a particular country or area: *a native of New York* **2** a person who lives in a particular place, especially someone who has lived there a long time **SYN** LOCAL: *You can always tell the difference between the tourists and the natives.* ◆ *She speaks Italian like a native.* **3** (*old-fashioned, offensive*) a word used in the past by Europeans to describe a person who lived in a place originally, before white people arrived there: *disputes between early settlers and natives* **4** an animal or a plant that lives or grows naturally in a particular area: *The kangaroo is a native of Australia.*

Native A'merican (also A,merican 'Indian) noun a member of any of the races of people who were the original people living in America ▶ **Native A'merican** adj.: *Native American languages*

MORE ABOUT

Native American • First Nations

■ In the U.S., **Native American** is the term most widely used and generally accepted to describe a member of one of the races of people who lived in America before Europeans arrived in 1492. The term **American Indian** is also often used, although some people find it offensive. The word **Indian** by itself should only be used to describe a person from India. To refer to an individual person you can also say which Native American people they belong to: *He's an Apache/a Cherokee.*

■ In Canada, the term **Native American** is not used, and the most usual way to refer to the Aboriginal peoples of Canada, other than the Inuit and Métis, is **First Nations**. The term **Indian** is still used in some official contexts, but many people now consider it old-fashioned or offensive. To refer to an individual person, state which First Nation they belong to: *She's a Cree/Mohawk.*

| h hat | m man | n no | ŋ sing | l leg | r red | y yes | w wet |

Native Ca·nadian *noun* an Aboriginal Canadian; a Canadian Indian, Inuit, or Métis ⊃ note at NATIVE AMERICAN

native 'speaker *noun* a person who speaks a language as their first language and has not learned it as a foreign language

na·tiv·i·ty /nə'tɪvəti/ *noun* **1 the Nativity** [sing.] the birth of Jesus Christ, celebrated by Christians at Christmas **2** a picture or a model of the baby Jesus Christ and the place where he was born

na'tivity ˌplay *noun* a play about the birth of Jesus Christ, usually performed by children at Christmas

NATO also **Nato** /'neɪtoʊ/ *abbr.* North Atlantic Treaty Organization. NATO is an organization to which the U.S. and Canada and many European countries belong. They agree to give each other military help if necessary.

nat·ter /'næt̬ər/ *verb* [I] ~ **(away/on) (about sth)** (*old-fashioned, informal*) to talk for a long time, especially about unimportant things **SYN** CHAT

nat·ty /'næt̬i/ *adj.* (*old-fashioned, informal*) neat and fashionable: *a natty suit* ▶ **nat·ti·ly** /'næt̬l·i/ *adv.*

nat·u·ral /'næt̬ʃrəl; 'næt̬ʃərəl/ *adj., noun*

● *adj.*

> IN NATURE **1** [only before noun] existing in nature; not made or caused by humans: *natural disasters* ♦ *the natural world* (= of trees, rivers, animals, and birds) ♦ *a country's natural resources* (= its coal, oil, forests, etc.) ♦ *wildlife in its natural habitat* ♦ *My hair soon grew back to its natural color* (= after being DYED). ♦ *The clothes are available in warm natural colors.* ⊃ compare SUPERNATURAL

> EXPECTED **2** normal; as you would expect: *to die of natural causes* (= not by violence, but normally, of old age) ♦ *He thought social inequality was all part of the natural order of things.* ♦ *She was the natural choice for the job.* ⊃ compare UNNATURAL

> BEHAVIOR **3** used to describe behavior that is part of the character that a person or an animal was born with: *the natural agility of a cat* ♦ *the natural processes of language learning* ♦ *It's only natural to worry about your children.*

> ABILITY **4** [only before noun] having an ability that you were born with: *He's a natural leader.*

> RELAXED **5** relaxed and not pretending to be someone or something different: *It's difficult to look natural when you're feeling nervous.*

> PARENTS/CHILDREN **6** [only before noun] (of parents or their children) related by blood: *His natural mother was unable to care for him so he was raised by an aunt.* **7** [only before noun] (*old use* or *formal*) (of a son or daughter) born to parents who are not married **SYN** ILLEGITIMATE: *She was a natural daughter of King James II.*

> BASED ON HUMAN REASON **8** [only before noun] based on human reason alone: *natural justice/law*

> IN MUSIC **9** used after the name of a note to show that the note is neither SHARP nor FLAT. The written symbol is (♮): *B natural* ⊃ picture at MUSIC

● *noun*

> PERSON **1** ~ **(for sth)** a person who is very good at something without having to learn how to do it, or who is perfectly suited for a particular job: *She took to flying like a natural.* ♦ *He's a natural for the role.*

> IN MUSIC **2** a normal musical note, not its SHARP or FLAT form. The written symbol is (♮).

ˈnatural-ˌborn *adj.* [only before noun] having a natural ability or skill that you have not had to learn

ˌnatural 'childbirth *noun* [U] a method of giving birth to a baby in which a woman chooses not to take drugs and does special exercises to make her relaxed

ˌnatural dis'aster *noun* a sudden and violent event in nature (such as an EARTHQUAKE, HURRICANE, or flood) that kills a lot of people or causes a lot of damage

ˌnatural 'gas *noun* [U] gas that is found under the ground or the ocean and that is used as a fuel

ˌnatural 'history *noun* [U, C] the study of plants and animals; an account of the plant and animal life of a particular place: *the Natural History Museum* ♦ *He has written a natural history of California.*

nat·u·ral·ism /'næt̬ʃrəˌlɪzəm; 'næt̬ʃərə-/ *noun* [U] **1** a style of art or writing that shows people, things, and experiences as they really are **2** (*philosophy*) the theory that everything in the world and life is based on natural causes and laws, and not on spiritual or SUPERNATURAL ones

nat·u·ral·ist /'næt̬ʃrəlɪst; 'næt̬ʃərə-/ *noun* a person who studies animals, plants, birds, and other living things

nat·u·ral·is·tic /ˌnæt̬ʃrə'lɪstɪk; ˌnæt̬ʃərə-/ *adj.* **1** (of artists, writers, etc. or their work) showing things as they appear in the natural world **2** copying the way things are in the natural world: *to study behavior in laboratory and naturalistic settings*

nat·u·ral·ize /'næt̬ʃrəˌlaɪz; 'næt̬ʃərə-/ *verb* [usually passive] **1** [T] ~ **sb** to make someone who was not born in a particular country a citizen of that country **2** [T] ~ **sth** to introduce a plant or an animal to a country where it is not NATIVE **3** [I] (of a plant or an animal) to start growing or living naturally in a country where it is not NATIVE ▶ **nat·u·ral·i·za·tion** /ˌnæt̬ʃrələ'zeɪʃn; ˌnæt̬ʃərə-/ *noun* [U]

ˌnatural 'language *noun* [C, U] a language that has developed in a natural way and is not designed by humans

ˌnatural 'language ˌprocessing *noun* [U] (*abbr.* NLP) the use of computers to process natural languages, for example for translating

ˌnatural 'law *noun* [U] a set of moral principles on which human behavior is based

nat·u·ral·ly /'næt̬ʃrəli; 'næt̬ʃərə-/ *adv.*

1 in a way that you would expect **SYN** OF COURSE: *Naturally, I get upset when things go wrong.* ♦ *After a while, we naturally started talking about the children.* ♦ *"Did you complain about the noise?" "Naturally."* **2** without special help, treatment, or action by someone: *naturally occurring chemicals* ♦ *plants that grow naturally in poor soils* **3** as a normal, logical result of something: *This leads naturally to my next point.* **4** in a way that shows or uses abilities or qualities that a person or an animal is born with: *to be naturally artistic* ♦ *a naturally gifted athlete* **5** in a relaxed and normal way: *Just act naturally.* **IDM** **come naturally (to sb/sth)** if something **comes naturally** to you, you are able to do it very easily and very well: *Making money came naturally to her.*

nat·u·ral·ness /'næt̬ʃrəlnəs; 'næt̬ʃərəl-/ *noun* [U] **1** the state or quality of being like real life: *The naturalness of the dialogue made the book so true to life.* **2** the quality of behaving in a normal, relaxed, or innocent way: *Teenagers lose their childhood simplicity and naturalness.* **3** the style or quality of happening in a normal way that you would expect: *the naturalness of her reaction*

ˌnatural 'number *noun* (*mathematics*) a positive whole number such as 1, 2, or 3, and sometimes also zero

ˌnatural phi'losophy *noun* [U] (*old use*) the study of the physical world, which developed into the natural sciences

ˌnatural 'science *noun* [C, U] a science concerned with studying the physical world. Chemistry, biology, and physics are all natural sciences. ⊃ compare EARTH SCIENCE, LIFE SCIENCES

ˌnatural se'lection *noun* [U] the process by which the plants, animals, etc. that can adapt to their environment survive and reproduce, while the others disappear

na·ture /'neɪtʃər/ *noun*

> PLANTS, ANIMALS **1** often **Nature** [U] all the plants, animals, and things that exist in the universe that are not made by people: *the beauties of nature* ♦ *man-made substances not found in nature* ♦ *nature conservation* **HELP** You cannot use "the nature" in this meaning: ~~the beauties of the nature~~. It is often better to use another

WORD FAMILY
nature *noun*
natural *adj.* (≠ unnatural)
naturally *adv.* (≠ unnaturally)

appropriate word, for example **the countryside, the scenery**, or the **wildlife**: *We stopped to admire the scenery.* ◆ ~~We stopped to admire the nature.~~ **2** often **Nature** [U] the way that things happen in the physical world when it is not controlled by people: *the forces/laws of nature* ◆ *Just let nature take its course.* ◆ *Her illness was Nature's way of telling her to do less.* ⊃ see also MOTHER NATURE
‣ CHARACTER **3** [C, U] the usual way that a person or an animal behaves that is part of their character: *It's not in his nature to be unkind.* ◆ *She is very sensitive by nature.* ◆ *We appealed to his better nature* (= his kindness). ⊃ see also GOOD NATURE, HUMAN NATURE, SECOND NATURE
‣ BASIC QUALITIES **4** [sing., U] the basic qualities of a thing: *the changing nature of society* ◆ *It's difficult to define the exact nature of the problem.* ◆ *My work is very specialized in nature.*
‣ TYPE/KIND **5** [sing.] a type or kind of something: *books of a scientific nature* ◆ *Don't worry about things of that nature.*
‣ -NATURED **6** (in adjectives) having the type of character or quality mentioned: *a good-natured man*
IDM **against nature** not natural; not moral: *Murder is a crime against nature.* **(get, go, etc.) back to nature** to return to a simple kind of life in the country, away from cities **in the nature of sth** similar to something; a type of something; in the style of something: *His speech was in the nature of an apology.* **in the nature of things** in the way that things usually happen: *In the nature of things, young people often rebel against their parents.* ⊃ more at CALL, FORCE

'**nature re**,**serve** *noun* an area of land where the animals and plants are protected

'**nature** ,**trail** *noun* a path through countryside that you can follow in order to see the interesting plants and animals that are found there

na·tur·ism /ˈneɪtʃəˌrɪzəm/ *noun* [U] = NUDISM

na·tur·ist /ˈneɪtʃərɪst/ *noun* = NUDIST

na·tur·op·a·thy /ˌneɪtʃəˈrɑpəθi/ *noun* [U] a system for treating diseases or conditions using natural foods and HERBS and various other techniques, rather than artificial drugs ▶ **na·tur·o·path** /ˈneɪtʃərəˌpæθ/ *noun*: *A medical herbalist or naturopath will be able to advise on individual treatment plans.* **na·tur·o·path·ic** /ˌneɪtʃərəˈpæθɪk/ *adj.* [only before noun]: *naturopathic medicine* ◆ *a naturopathic physician*

naught *noun* = NOUGHT

naugh·ty /ˈnɔti/ *adj.* (**naugh·ti·er**, **naugh·ti·est**) **1** (especially of children) behaving badly; not willing to obey: *a naughty boy/girl* ◆ (*humorous*) *I'm being very naughty—I've ordered champagne!* **2** (*informal*, often *humorous*) slightly offensive and connected with sex **SYN** RISQUE: *a naughty joke/word* ▶ **naugh·ti·ly** /ˈnɔtəli/ *adv.* **naugh·ti·ness** /ˈnɔtinəs/ *noun* [U]

nau·se·a /ˈnɔziə; ˈnɔʒə; ˈnɔʃə/ *noun* [U] the feeling that you have when you want to VOMIT, for example because you are sick or are disgusted by something: *A wave of nausea swept over her.* ◆ *Nausea and vomiting are common symptoms.* ⊃ see also AD NAUSEAM

nau·se·ate /ˈnɔziˌeɪt; -ʒi-/ *verb* **1** ~ **sb** to make someone feel that they want to VOMIT **2** ~ **sb** to make someone feel disgusted **SYN** REVOLT, SICKEN: *I was nauseated by the violence in the movie.* ▶ **nau·se·at·ing** *adj.*: *a nauseating smell* ◆ *his nauseating behavior* **nau·se·at·ing·ly** *adv.*

nau·seous /ˈnɔʃəs/ *adj.* **1** feeling as if you want to VOMIT: *She felt dizzy and nauseous.* **2** making you feel as if you want to VOMIT: *a nauseous smell*

nau·ti·cal /ˈnɔtɪkl/ *adj.* connected with ships, sailors, and sailing: *nautical terms*

,**nautical** '**mile** (also '**sea mile**) *noun* a unit for measuring distance at sea; 1852 meters

nau·ti·lus /ˈnɔtləs/ *noun* (pl. **nau·ti·lus·es** or **nau·ti·li** /-tlˌaɪ/) a creature with a shell that lives in the ocean. It has TENTACLES around its mouth and its shell fills with gas to help it float.

Nav·a·jo (also **Nav·a·ho**) /ˈnævəˌhoʊ; ˈnɑ-/ *noun* (pl. **Nav·a·jo** or **Na·va·jos**) a member of the largest group of Native American people, most of whom live in the states of Arizona, New Mexico, and Utah

na·val /ˈneɪvl/ *adj.* connected with the navy of a country: *a naval base/officer/battle*

nave /neɪv/ *noun* the long central part of a church, where most of the seats are ⊃ compare TRANSEPT

na·vel /ˈneɪvl/ (also *informal* '**belly** ,**button**) *noun* the small hollow part or lump in the middle of the stomach where the UMBILICAL CORD was cut at birth ⊃ picture at BODY

'**navel-** ,**gazing** *noun* [U] (*disapproving*) the fact of thinking too much about a single issue and how it could affect you, without thinking about other things that could also affect the situation

'**navel** ,**orange** *noun* a large orange without seeds that has a part at the top that looks like a navel

nav·i·ga·ble /ˈnævɪgəbl/ *adj.* (of rivers, etc.) wide and deep enough for ships and boats to sail on ▶ **nav·i·ga·bil·i·ty** /ˌnævɪgəˈbɪləti/ *noun* [U]

nav·i·gate /ˈnævəˌgeɪt/ *verb* **1** [I, T] to find your position or the position of your ship, plane, car, etc. and the direction you need to go in, for example by using a map: *I'll drive, and you can navigate.* ◆ *to navigate by the stars* ◆ ~ **your way...** *How do you navigate your way through a forest?* **2** [T] ~ **sth** to sail along, over, or through an ocean, river, etc.: *The river became too narrow and shallow to navigate.* **3** [T] ~ **sth** to find the right way to deal with a difficult or complicated situation: *We next had to navigate a complex network of committees.* **4** [I, T] ~ **(sth)** (*computing*) to find your way around on the Internet or on a particular Web site

nav·i·ga·tion /ˌnævəˈgeɪʃn/ *noun* [U] **1** the skill or the process of planning a route for a ship or other vehicle and taking it there: *navigation systems* ◆ *an expert in navigation* **2** the movement of ships or aircraft: *the right of navigation through international waters* ▶ **nav·i·ga·tion·al** /-ʃənl/ *adj.*: *navigational aids*

nav·i·ga·tor /ˈnævəˌgeɪtər/ *noun* a person who navigates, for example on a ship or an aircraft

na·vy /ˈneɪvi/ *noun* (pl. **na·vies**) **1** [C] the part of a country's armed forces that fights at sea, and the ships that it uses: *the Canadian and American navies* ◆ *He's joined the navy/the Navy.* ◆ *an officer in the navy/the Navy* ◆ *The navy is considering buying six new warships.* ⊃ collocations at WAR ⊃ see also NAVAL **2** [U] = NAVY BLUE

'**navy** ,**bean** *noun* a type of small white BEAN that is usually dried before it is sold and then left in water before cooking

,**navy** '**blue** (also **na·vy**) *adj.* very dark blue in color: *a navy blue suit* ◆ ,**navy** '**blue** (also **na·vy**) *noun* [U]: *She was dressed in navy blue.*

nay /neɪ/ *adv., noun*
● *adv.* **1** (*old-fashioned*) used to emphasize something you have just said by introducing a stronger word or phrase: *Such a policy is difficult, nay impossible.* **2** (*old use* or *politics*) no: *Many senators voted nay on the bill.* **ANT** YEA
● *noun* a vote against something, such as a new plan or law; a person who votes against something: *On this vote, there are 65 yeas and 32 nays.* **ANT** YEA ⊃ compare AYE

nay·say·er /ˈneɪˌseɪər/ *noun* a person who opposes or expresses doubts about something: *There are always naysayers who claim the plan won't work.*

Na·zi /ˈnɑtsi/ *noun* **1** a member of the National Socialist party, which controlled Germany from 1933 to 1945 **2** (*disapproving*) a person who uses their power in a cruel way; a person with extreme and unreasonable views about race ▶ **Na·zi** *adj.* **Na·zism** /ˈnɑtsɪzəm/ *noun* [U]

N.B. (also **NB**) /ˌɛn ˈbi/ *abbr.* used in writing to make someone take notice of a particular piece of information that is important (from Latin "nota bene"): *N.B. The office will be closed from July 1.*

NBA /ˌɛn bi ˈeɪ/ *abbr.* National Basketball Association (the U.S. organization responsible for professional basketball)

ʌ cup   ə about   eɪ say   aɪ five   ɔɪ boy   aʊ now   oʊ go   ər bird

NBC /ˌɛn bi ˈsi/ abbr. National Broadcasting Company (a U.S. company that produces television and radio programs): NBC News

NC abbr. (in writing) North Carolina

NC-17 /ˌɛn si ˌsɛvənˈtin/ used to show that no one younger than 17 will be allowed to see a particular movie (the symbol for No Children under 17) ⊃ compare G, PG, PG-13, R, X

NCAA /ˌɛn si ˌdʌbl ˈeɪ; ˌɛn si eɪ ˈeɪ/ abbr. National Collegiate Athletic Association (an organization that organizes sports events for colleges in the U.S.)

NCO /ˌɛn si ˈoʊ/ abbr. noncommissioned officer (a soldier who has a rank such as CORPORAL or SERGEANT)

ND abbr. (in writing) North Dakota

NDP /ˌɛn di ˈpi/ noun (CanE) = NEW DEMOCRATIC PARTY

NE abbr. (in writing) 1 usually N.E. northeast; northeastern: N.E. New York 2 Nebraska

Ne·an·der·thal /niˈændərˌθɔl; -ˌtɔl; -ˌtal/ adj. also **nean-derthal** 1 used to describe a type of human being who used stone tools and lived in Europe during the early period of human history 2 (disapproving) very old-fashioned and not wanting any change: neanderthal attitudes 3 (disapproving) (of a man) unpleasant, rude, and not behaving in a socially acceptable way ▶ **Ne·an·der·thal** noun

neap tide /ˈnip taɪd/ (also **neap**) noun a TIDE in the ocean in which there is only a very small difference between the level of the water at HIGH TIDE and LOW TIDE

near 🔑 /nɪr/ adj., adv., prep., verb
● **adj.** (near·er, near·est) **HELP** In senses 1 to 4 **near** and **nearer** do not usually go before a noun; **nearest** can go either before or after a noun. 1 a short distance away **SYN** CLOSE[1]: His house is very near. ◆ Where's the nearest bank? ⊃ note at NEXT 2 a short time away in the future: The conflict is unlikely to be resolved **in the near future** (= very soon). 3 coming next after someone or something: She has a 12-point lead over her nearest rival. 4 usually **nearest** similar; most similar: He was **the nearest thing to** (= the person most like) a father she had ever had. 5 [only before noun] (no comparative or superlative) close to being someone or something: The election proved to be a near disaster for the party. ◆ a near impossibility 6 ~ **relative/relation** used to describe a close family connection: Only the nearest relatives were present at the funeral. ▶ **near·ness** noun [U]: the nearness of death
IDM **your nearest and dearest** (informal) your close family and friends **a near thing** a situation in which you are successful, but which could also have ended badly: Phew! That was a near thing! It could have been a disaster. ◆ We won in the end, but it was a near thing. **to the nearest…** followed by a number when counting or measuring approximately: We calculated the cost to the nearest 50 dollars.

WHICH WORD?

near ◆ close
■ The adjectives **near** and **close** are often the same in meaning, but in some phrases only one of them may be used: the near future ◆ a near neighbor ◆ a near miss ◆ a close contest ◆ a close encounter ◆ a close call.
■ **Close** is more often used to describe a relationship between people: a close friend ◆ close family ◆ close links. You do not usually use **near** in this way.

● **adv.** (near·er, near·est) 1 at a short distance away: A bomb exploded somewhere near. ◆ She took a step nearer. ◆ Visitors came from **near and far**. 2 a short time away in the future: The exams are **drawing near**. 3 (especially in compounds) almost: a near-perfect performance ◆ I'm as near certain as can be.

IDM **as near as** as accurately as: There were about 3,000 people there, as near as I could judge. **not anywhere near/nowhere near** far from; not at all: The job doesn't pay anywhere near enough for me. **so near and yet so far** used to comment on something that was almost successful, but in fact failed ⊃ more at PRETTY
● **prep.** (also **near to, near·er (to), near·est (to)**) **HELP** Near to is not usually used before the name of a place, person, festival, etc. 1 at a short distance away from someone or something: Do you live near here? ◆ Go and sit nearer (to) the fire. ⊃ note at NEXT 2 a short period of time from something: My birthday is very near Christmas. ◆ I'll think about it nearer (to) the time (= when it is just going to happen). 3 used before a number to mean "approximately," "just below," or "above": Share prices are near their record high of last year. ◆ Profits fell from $11 million to nearer $8 million. 4 similar to someone or something in quality, size, etc.: Nobody else comes near her in intellect. ◆ He's nearer 70 than 60. ◆ This color is nearest (to) the original. 5 ~ (doing) sth close to a particular state: a state near (to) death ◆ She was near to tears (= almost crying). ◆ We came near to being killed. **IDM** see HAND n., HEART
● **verb** [T, I] ~ (sth) (somewhat formal) to come close to something in time or space **SYN** APPROACH: The project is nearing completion. ◆ She was nearing the end of her life. ◆ We neared the top of the hill. ◆ As Christmas neared, the children became more and more excited.

near·by 🔑 adj., adv.
● **adj.** /ˈnɪrbaɪ; ˌnɪrˈbaɪ/ [usually before noun] near in position; not far away: Her mother lived in a nearby town. ◆ There were complaints from nearby residents.
● **adv.** /ˌnɪrˈbaɪ/ a short distance from someone or something; not far away: They live nearby. ◆ The car is parked nearby.

near-death ex'perience noun an occasion when you almost die, which is often remembered as leaving your body or going down a tunnel

the ˌNear ˈEast noun [sing.] = THE MIDDLE EAST

near·ly 🔑 /ˈnɪrli/ adv.
almost; not quite; not completely: The bottle's nearly empty. ◆ I've worked here for nearly two years. ◆ It's nearly time to leave. ◆ The audience were nearly all men. ◆ He's nearly as tall as you are. ◆ They're nearly always late. ⊃ note at ALMOST
IDM **not nearly** much less than; not at all: It's not nearly as hot as last year. ◆ There isn't nearly enough time to get there now. ⊃ more at PRETTY

ˌnear ˈmiss noun 1 a situation when a serious accident or a disaster nearly happens 2 a bomb or a shot that nearly hits what it is aimed at, but misses it: (figurative) He should have won the match—it was a near miss.

near·sight·ed /ˈnɪrˌsaɪtəd/ adj. able to see things clearly only if they are very close to you: She needs glasses because she's very nearsighted. **ANT** FARSIGHTED ▶ **near·sight·ed·ness** noun [U]

neat 🔑 /nit/ adj. (neat·er, neat·est)
1 clean and in order; carefully done or arranged: a neat desk ◆ neat handwriting ◆ neat rows of books ◆ She was wearing a neat black suit. ◆ They sat in her **neat and clean** kitchen. 2 (of people) liking to keep things clean and in order; having a clean appearance or doing things in an organized way: Try and be neater! 3 small, with a pleasing shape or appearance **SYN** TRIM: her neat figure 4 simple but effective: a neat explanation ◆ a neat solution to the problem 5 (informal) good; excellent: It's a really neat movie. ◆ We had a great time—it was pretty neat. ▶ **neat·ly** adv.: neatly folded clothes ◆ The box fitted neatly into the drawer. ◆ She summarized her plan very neatly. **neat·ness** /ˈnitnəs/ noun [U]

neat·en /ˈnitn/ verb ~ sth to make something neat

neb·ish /ˈnɛbɪʃ/ noun (informal) a man who behaves in an anxious and nervous way and without confidence

neb·u·la /ˈnɛbyələ/ noun (pl. **neb·u·lae** /-li/) (astronomy) a mass of dust or gas that can be seen in the night sky, often appearing very bright; a bright area in the night sky caused by a large cloud of stars that are far away

neb·u·liz·er /ˈnɛbyəˌlaɪzər/ *noun* a device for producing a fine spray of liquid, used especially for taking certain medicines

neb·u·lous /ˈnɛbyələs/ *adj.* (*formal*) not clear **SYN** VAGUE: *a nebulous concept*

nec·es·sar·ies /ˈnɛsəˌsɛriz/ *noun* [pl.] (*old-fashioned*) the things that you need, especially in order to live

nec·es·sar·i·ly 🔑 /ˌnɛsəˈsɛrəli/ *adv.*
used to say that something cannot be avoided: *The number of places available is necessarily limited.*
IDM **not necessarily** used to say that something is possibly true but not definitely or always true: *The more expensive articles are not necessarily better.* ◆ *Biggest doesn't necessarily mean best.* ◆ *"We're going to lose." "Not necessarily."*

nec·es·sar·y 🔑 /ˈnɛsəˌsɛri/ *adj.*
1 ~ (for sb/sth) (to do sth) that is needed for a purpose or a reason **SYN** ESSENTIAL: *It may be necessary to buy a new one.* ◆ *It doesn't seem necessary for us to meet.* ◆ *Only use your car when absolutely necessary.* ◆ *If necessary, you can contact me at home.* ◆ *I'll make the necessary arrangements.* **2** [only before noun] that must exist or happen and cannot be avoided **SYN** INEVITABLE: *This is a necessary consequence of progress.*
IDM **a necessary evil** a thing that is bad or that you do not like but which you must accept for a particular reason

ne·ces·si·tate /nəˈsɛsəˌteɪt/ *verb* (*formal*) to make something necessary: ~ **sth** *Recent financial scandals have necessitated changes in agency procedures.* ◆ ~ **doing sth** *Increased traffic necessitated widening the road.* ◆ ~ **sb/sth doing sth** *His new job necessitated him/his getting up at six.*

ne·ces·si·ty /nəˈsɛsəti/ *noun* **1** [U] the fact that something must happen or be done; the need for something: ~ **(for sth)** *We recognize the necessity for a written agreement.* ◆ ~ **(of sth/of doing sth)** *We were discussing the necessity of employing more staff.* ◆ ~ **(for sb) to do sth** *There had never been any necessity for her to go out to work.* ◆ *This is, of necessity, a brief and incomplete account.* **2** [C] a thing that you must have and cannot manage without: *Many people cannot even afford **basic necessities** such as food and clothing.* ◆ *Air-conditioning is an absolute necessity in this climate.* **3** [C, usually sing.] a situation that must happen and that cannot be avoided: *Living in a big city, he felt, was an unfortunate necessity.*
IDM **necessity is the mother of invention** (*saying*) a difficult new problem forces people to think of a solution to it ⊃ more at VIRTUE

neck — neck

V-neck sweater

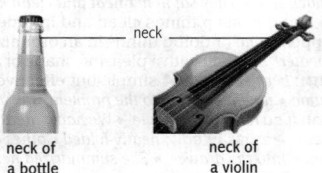

neck — neck of a bottle   neck of a violin

neck 🔑 /nɛk/ *noun, verb*
● *noun* **1** [C] the part of the body between the head and the shoulders: *He tied a scarf around his neck.* ◆ *Giraffes have very long necks.* ◆ *She craned (= stretched) her neck to get a better view.* ◆ *He broke his neck in the fall.* ◆ *Somebody's going to break*

their neck (= injure themselves) *on these steps.* ⊃ **picture at** BODY ⊃ **collocations at** PHYSICAL **2** [C] the part of a piece of clothing that fits around the neck: *What neck size do you take?* ⊃ **see also** CREW NECK, V-NECK **3** -necked (in adjectives) having the type of neck mentioned: *a round-necked sweater* ⊃ **see also** OPEN-NECKED, STIFF-NECKED **4** [C] ~ (of sth) a long, narrow part of something: *the neck of a bottle* ◆ *a neck of land* **5** [U] the neck of an animal, cooked and eaten: *lamb neck* ⊃ **see also** BOTTLENECK, REDNECK, ROUGHNECK
IDM **be up to your neck in sth** to have a lot of something to deal with: *We're up to our neck in debt.* ◆ *He's in it (= trouble) up to his neck.* **by a neck** if a person or an animal wins a race **by a neck**, they win it by a short distance **neck and neck (with sb/sth)** (also **nip and tuck (with sb)**) level with someone in a race or competition **neck of the woods** (*informal*) a particular place or area: *He's from your neck of the woods* (= the area where you live). ⊃ **more at** BLOCK, BREATHE, MILLSTONE, PAIN, RISK, SAVE, SCRUFF, STICK, WRING
● *verb* usually **be necking** [I] (*old-fashioned, informal*) when two people **are necking**, they are kissing each other in a sexual way

neck·er·chief /ˈnɛkərtʃɪf; -ˌtʃif/ *noun* a square of cloth that you wear around your neck

neck·lace /ˈnɛkləs/ *noun* a piece of jewelry consisting of a chain, string of BEADS, etc. worn around the neck: *a diamond necklace* ⊃ **picture at** JEWELRY

neck·line /ˈnɛklaɪn/ *noun* the edge of a piece of clothing, especially a woman's, which fits around or below the neck: *a dress with a low/round/plunging neckline*

neck·tie /ˈnɛktaɪ/ *noun* = TIE *n.* (1)

nec·ro·man·cer /ˈnɛkrəˌmænsər/ *noun* a person who claims to communicate by magic with people who are dead

nec·ro·man·cy /ˈnɛkrəˌmænsi/ *noun* [U] **1** the practice of claiming to communicate by magic with the dead, in order to learn about the future **2** the use of magic powers, especially evil ones

ne·crop·o·lis /nəˈkrɑpələs/ *noun* (*pl.* **ne·crop·o·lis·es** /-ləsəz/) a CEMETERY (= place where dead people are buried), especially a large one in an ancient city

nec·rop·sy /ˈnɛkrɑpsi/ *noun* (*pl.* **nec·rop·sies**) an official examination of a dead body (especially that of an animal) in order to discover the cause of death **SYN** AUTOPSY

ne·cro·sis /nəˈkroʊsəs/ *noun* [U] (*medical*) the death of most or all of the cells in an organ or TISSUE caused by injury, disease, or a loss of blood supply

nec·tar /ˈnɛktər/ *noun* [U] **1** a sweet liquid that is produced by flowers and collected by BEES for making HONEY: (*figurative*) *On such a hot day, even water was nectar* (= very good). **2** the thick juice of some fruits as a drink: *peach nectar*

nec·tar·ine /ˌnɛktəˈrin/ *noun* a round red and yellow fruit, like a PEACH with smooth skin

née /neɪ/ *adj.* (from *French*) a word used after a married woman's name to introduce the family name that she had when she was born: *Jane Smith, née Brown*

need 🔑 /nid/ *verb, modal verb, noun*
● *verb* **1** to require something or someone because they are essential or very important, not just because you would like to have them: ~ **sth/sb** *Do you need any help?* ◆ *It's here if you need it.* ◆ *Don't go—I might need you.* ◆ *They badly needed a change.* ◆ *Food aid is urgently needed.* ◆ *What do you need your own computer for? You can use ours.* ◆ *I don't need your comments, thank you.* ◆ ~ **to do sth** *I need to get some sleep.* ◆ *He needs to win this game to stay in the match.* ◆ *You don't need to leave yet, do you?* ◆ *This shirt needs to be washed.* ◆ ~ **doing sth** *This shirt needs washing.* ⊃ **note at** REASON **2** ~ **to do sth** used to show what you should or have to do: *All you need to do is complete this form.* ◆ *I didn't need to go to the bank after all—Mary lent me the money.*
IDM **need sth like a hole in the head** (*informal*) to have no

t tea   ṭ butter   d did   k cat   g got   tʃ chin   dʒ June   f fall

need or desire for something **need (to have) your head examined** (*informal*) to be crazy

● **modal verb** (*negative* **need not**, *short form* **need·n't** /'nidnt/) (*formal*) used to state that something is/was not necessary or that only very little is/was necessary; used to ask if something is/was necessary: **~ (not) do sth** *You needn't bother asking Rick—I know he's too busy.* ◆ *I need hardly tell you* (= you must already know) *that the work is dangerous.* ◆ *If she wants anything, she need only ask.* ◆ *All you need bring are sheets.* ◆ **~ (not) have done sth** *You needn't have worried* (= it was not necessary for you to worry, but you did) *—it all turned out fine.* ➔ note at MODAL

● **noun 1** [sing., U] a situation when something is necessary or must be done: *to satisfy/meet/identify a need* ◆ **~ (for sth)** *There is an urgent need for qualified teachers.* ◆ *We will contact you again if the need arises.* ◆ *The house is **in need of** a thorough cleaning.* ◆ **~ (for sb/sth) to do sth** *There is no need for you to get up early tomorrow.* ◆ *I had no need to open the letter—I knew what it would say.* ◆ *There's no need to cry* (= stop crying). **2** [C, U] a strong feeling that you want someone or something or must have something: *to fulfill an emotional need* ◆ *She felt the need to talk to someone.* ◆ *I'm **in need of** some fresh air.* ◆ *She had no more need of me.* **3** [C, usually pl.] the things that someone requires in order to live in a comfortable way or achieve what they want: *financial needs* ◆ *a program to **suit** your individual needs* ◆ *to **meet** children's special educational needs* **4** [U] the state of not having enough food, money, or support **SYN** HARDSHIP: *The charity aims to provide assistance to people **in need**.* ◆ *He helped me in my **hour of need**.* ➔ see also NEEDY

IDM **if need be** if necessary: *There's always food in the freezer if need be.* ➔ more at CRYING, FRIEND

GRAMMAR

need

■ There are two separate verbs **need**.
■ **Need** as a main verb has the question form **do you need?**, the negative **you don't need**, and the past forms **needed**, **did you need?**, and **didn't need**. It has two meanings: 1. to require something or to think that something is necessary: *Do you need any help?* ◆ *I needed to get some sleep.* 2. to have to or to be obliged to do something: *Will we need to show our passports?*
■ **Need** as a modal verb has **need** for all forms of the present tense, **need you?** as the question form, and **need not/needn't** as the negative. The past is **need have/needn't have**. It is used to say that something is or is not necessary: *Need I pay the whole amount now?* **Need** as a modal verb is used rarely and only in quite formal situations. In all ordinary situations use **have to**.
➔ note at MUST

---

need-blind *adj.* (of a university's or college's policy of choosing which people to admit to a course of study) depending only on someone's academic ability, without considering their ability to pay for it: *a need-blind admissions policy*

need·ful /'nidfl/ *adj.* (*old-fashioned*) necessary

nee·dle 🔑 /'nidl/ *noun, verb*

● **noun** [C]

▷ **FOR SEWING 1** a small thin piece of steel that you use for sewing, with a point at one end and a hole for the thread at the other: *a needle and thread* ◆ *the eye* (= hole) *of a needle* ➔ see also PINS AND NEEDLES ➔ picture at HOBBY

▷ **FOR KNITTING 2** a long thin piece of plastic or metal with a point at one end that you use for KNITTING. You usually use two together: *knitting needles*

▷ **FOR DRUGS 3** a very thin, pointed piece of steel used on the end of a SYRINGE for putting a drug into someone's body, or for taking blood out of it: *a hypodermic needle*

▷ **ON INSTRUMENT 4** a thin piece of metal on a scientific instrument that moves to point to the correct measurement or direction: *The compass needle was pointing north.*

▷ **ON PINE TREE 5** [usually pl.] the thin, hard, pointed leaf of a PINE tree ➔ picture at TREE

▷ **ON RECORD PLAYER 6** the very small pointed piece of metal that touches a record that is being played in order to produce the sound **SYN** STYLUS

IDM **a needle in a haystack** a thing that is almost impossible to find: *Searching for one man in this city is like looking for a needle in a haystack.*

● **verb ~ sb** (*informal*) to deliberately annoy someone, especially by criticizing them continuously **SYN** ANTAGONIZE: *Don't let her needle you.*

nee·dle·point /'nidl,pɔɪnt/ *noun* [U] a type of decorative sewing in which you use very small STITCHES to make a picture on strong cloth

need·less /'nidləs/ *adj.* **needless** death or suffering is not necessary because it could have been avoided **SYN** UNNECESSARY: *needless suffering* ◆ *Banning smoking would save needless deaths.* ▶ **need·less·ly** *adv.*: *Many soldiers died needlessly.* ◆ *The process was needlessly slow.* **IDM** **needless to say** used to emphasize that the information you are giving is obvious: *The problem, needless to say, is the cost involved.*

nee·dle·wom·an /'nidl,wʊmən/ *noun* (*pl.* **needlewomen** /-,wɪmən/) a woman who sews well

nee·dle·work /'nidl,wɜrk/ *noun* [U] things that are sewn by hand, especially for decoration; the activity of making things by sewing

need·n't short form of NEED NOT

needs /nidz/ *adv.* (*old use*) in a way that cannot be avoided: *We must needs depart.* **IDM** **needs must (when the Devil drives)** (*saying*) in certain situations it is necessary for you to do something that you do not like or enjoy

need-to-'know *adj.* **IDM** **on a need-to-know basis** with people being told only the things they need to know when they need to know them, and no more than that: *Information will be released strictly on a need-to-know basis.*

need·y /'nidi/ *adj.* (**need·i·er**, **need·i·est**) **1** (of people) not having enough money, food, clothes, etc. ➔ thesaurus box at POOR **2 the needy** *noun* [pl.] people who do not have enough money, food, etc. **3** (of people) not confident, and needing a lot of love and emotional support from other people

ne'er /nɛr/ *adv.* (*literary*) = NEVER

ne'er-do-,well *noun* (*old-fashioned*) a useless or lazy person

ne·far·i·ous /nɪ'fɛriəs/ *adj.* (*formal*) criminal; immoral: *nefarious activities*

neg. *abbr.* (in writing) NEGATIVE

ne·gate **AWL** /nɪ'geɪt/ *verb* (*formal*) **1 ~ sth** to stop something from having any effect **SYN** NULLIFY: *Alcohol negates the effects of the drug.* **2 ~ sth** to state that something does not exist

ne·ga·tion /nɪ'geɪʃn/ *noun* (*formal*) **1** [C, usually sing., U] the exact opposite of something; the act of causing something not to exist or to become its opposite: *This political system was the negation of democracy.* **2** [U] disagreement or refusal: *She shook her head in negation.*

neg·a·tive 🔑 **AWL** /'nɛgətɪv/ *adj., noun, verb*

● **adj.**

▷ **BAD 1** bad or harmful: *The crisis had a **negative effect on** trade.* ◆ *The whole experience was definitely more positive than negative.* **ANT** POSITIVE

▷ **NOT HOPEFUL 2** considering only the bad side of something or someone; lacking enthusiasm or hope: *Scientists have a fairly **negative attitude** toward the theory.* ◆ *"He probably won't show up." "Don't be so negative."* **ANT** POSITIVE

| v **v**oice | θ **thin** | ð **then** | s **so** | z **zoo** | ʃ **she** | ʒ **vision** | x **Chanukah** | 989 |

> NO **3** expressing the answer "no": *His response was negative.* ◆ *They received a negative reply.* **ANT** AFFIRMATIVE

> GRAMMAR **4** containing a word such as "no," "not," "never," etc.: *a negative form/sentence*

> SCIENTIFIC TEST **5** (*abbr.* **neg.**) not showing any evidence of a particular substance or medical condition: *Her pregnancy test was negative.* **ANT** POSITIVE

> ELECTRICITY **6** (*technical*) containing or producing the type of electricity that is carried by an ELECTRON: *a negative charge/current* ◆ *the negative terminal of a battery* **ANT** POSITIVE

> NUMBER/QUANTITY **7** less than zero: *a negative trade balance* **ANT** POSITIVE

▶ **neg·a·tive·ly** **AWL** *adv.*: *to react negatively to stress* ◆ *to respond negatively* ◆ *negatively charged electrons*

● *noun*

> NO **1** a word or statement that means "no"; a refusal or DENIAL: (*formal*) *She answered in the negative* (= said "no"). **ANT** AFFIRMATIVE

> IN PHOTOGRAPHY **2** a developed film showing the dark areas of an actual scene as light and the light areas as dark ⊃ compare POSITIVE

> IN SCIENTIFIC TEST **3** the result of a test or an experiment that shows that a substance or condition is not present: *The percentage of false negatives generated by the cancer test is of great concern.* **ANT** POSITIVE

● *verb* (*formal*) **1** ~ sth to refuse to agree to a proposal or a request **2** ~ sth to prove that something is not true

negative 'equity *noun* [U] the situation in which the value of someone's house is less than the amount of money that is still owed to a MORTGAGE company, such as a bank

neg·a·tiv·ity /ˌnɛɡəˈtɪvəti/ (also **neg·a·tiv·ism** /ˈnɛɡətɪˌvɪzəm/) *noun* [U] (*formal*) a tendency to consider only the bad side of something or someone; a lack of enthusiasm or hope

neg·lect /nɪˈɡlɛkt/ *verb, noun*
● *verb* **1** ~ sb/sth to fail to take care of someone or something: *She denies neglecting her baby.* ◆ *The buildings had been neglected for years.* **2** ~ sth to not give enough attention to something: *Dance has been neglected by television.* ◆ *She has neglected her studies.* **3** ~ to do sth (*formal*) to fail or forget to do something that you ought to do **SYN** OMIT: *You neglected to mention the name of your previous employer.* ⊃ see also NEGLIGENCE
● *noun* [U] ~ (of sth/sb) the fact of not giving enough care or attention to something or someone; the state of not receiving enough care or attention: *The law imposes penalties for the neglect of children.* ◆ *The buildings are crumbling from years of neglect.* ◆ *The place smelled of decay and neglect.*

ne·glect·ed /nɪˈɡlɛktəd/ *adj.* not receiving enough care or attention: *neglected children* ◆ *a neglected area of research*

ne·glect·ful /nɪˈɡlɛktfl/ *adj.* (*formal*) not giving enough care or attention to someone or something: *neglectful parents* ◆ ~ of sth/sb *She became neglectful of her appearance.*

neg·li·gee (also **neg·li·gée**) /ˌnɛɡləˈʒeɪ; ˈnɛɡləˌʒeɪ/ *noun* a loose, pretty coat of very light material, worn by women before going to bed

neg·li·gence /ˈnɛɡlədʒəns/ *noun* [U] (*formal* or *law*) the failure to give someone or something enough care or attention: *The accident was caused by negligence on the part of the driver.* ◆ *The doctor was sued for medical negligence.*

neg·li·gent /ˈnɛɡlədʒənt/ *adj.* **1** (*formal* or *law*) failing to give someone or something enough care or attention, especially when this has serious results: *The school had been negligent in not informing the child's parents about the incident.* ◆ *grossly negligent* **2** (*literary*) (of a person or their manner) relaxed; not formal or awkward **SYN** NONCHALANT: *He waved his hand in a negligent gesture.* ▶ **neg·li·gent·ly** *adv.*: *The defendant drove negligently and hit a street light.* ◆ *She was leaning negligently against the wall.*

neg·li·gi·ble /ˈnɛɡlɪdʒəbl/ *adj.* of very little importance or

size and not worth considering **SYN** INSIGNIFICANT: *The cost was negligible.* ◆ *a negligible amount*

ne·go·tia·ble /nɪˈɡoʊʃəbl/ *adj.* **1** that you can discuss or change before you make an agreement or a decision: *The terms of employment are negotiable.* ◆ *The price was not negotiable.* **2** (*business*) that you can exchange for money or give to another person in exchange for money **ANT** NONNEGOTIABLE

ne·go·ti·ate /nɪˈɡoʊʃiˌeɪt/ *verb* **1** [I] ~ (with sb) (for/about sth) to try to reach an agreement by formal discussion: *The government will not negotiate with terrorists.* ◆ *We have been negotiating for more pay.* ◆ *a strong negotiating position* ◆ *negotiating skills* **2** [T] ~ sth to arrange or agree to something by formal discussion: *to negotiate a deal/contract/treaty/settlement* ◆ *We successfully negotiated the release of the hostages.* **3** [T] ~ sth to successfully get over or past a difficult part on a path or route: *The climbers had to negotiate a steep rock face.*

the ne'gotiating ˌtable *noun* [sing.] (used mainly in newspapers) a formal discussion to try to reach an agreement: *We want to get all the parties back to the negotiating table.*

ne·go·ti·a·tion /nɪˌɡoʊʃiˈeɪʃn/ *noun* [C, usually pl., U] formal discussion between people who are trying to reach an agreement: *peace/trade/wage, etc. negotiations* ◆ *They begin another round of negotiations today.* ◆ *to enter into/open/conduct negotiations with someone* ◆ *The rent is a matter for negotiation between the landlord and the tenant.* ◆ *A contract is prepared in negotiation with our clients.* ◆ *The issue is still under negotiation.* ◆ *The price is generally open to negotiation.* ⊃ collocations at INTERNATIONAL

ne·go·ti·a·tor /nɪˈɡoʊʃiˌeɪtər/ *noun* a person who is involved in formal political or financial discussions, especially because it is their job

ne·gri·tude /ˈnɛɡrəˌtud; ˈni-/ *noun* [U] (*formal*) the quality or fact of being of black African origin

Ne·gro /ˈnɪɡroʊ/ *noun* (*pl.* **Ne·groes**) (*old-fashioned*, often *offensive*) a member of a race of people with dark skin who originally came from Africa

neigh /neɪ/ *verb* [I] when a horse **neighs**, it makes a long high sound ▶ **neigh** *noun*

neigh·bor 🔑 (*CanE* usually **neigh·bour**) /ˈneɪbər/ *noun*
1 a person who lives next to you or near you: *We've had a lot of support from all our friends and neighbors.* ◆ *Our next-door neighbors are very noisy.* **2** a country that is next to or near another country: *America's nearest neighbor is Canada.* **3** a person or thing that is standing or located next to another person or thing: *Stand quietly, children, and try not to talk to your neighbor.* ◆ *The tree fell slowly, its branches caught in those of its neighbors.* **4** (*literary*) any other human: *We should all love our neighbors.*

neigh·bor·hood 🔑 (*CanE* usually **neigh·bour·hood**) /ˈneɪbərˌhʊd/ *noun*
1 a district or an area of a town; the people who live there: *We grew up in the same neighborhood.* ◆ *a poor/quiet/residential neighborhood* ◆ *Manhattan is divided into distinct neighborhoods.* ◆ *the neighborhood police* ◆ *He shouted so loudly that the whole neighborhood could hear him.* **2** the area that you are in or the area near a particular place **SYN** VICINITY: *We searched the surrounding neighborhood for the missing boy.* ◆ *Houses in the neighborhood of Paris are extremely expensive.*
IDM **in the neighborhood of** (of a number or an amount) approximately; not exactly: *It cost in the neighborhood of $500.*

ˌneighborhood 'watch (*CanE* usually **ˌneighbourhood 'watch**) *noun* [U] an arrangement by which a group of people in an area watch each other's houses regularly as a way of preventing crime

neigh·bor·ing (*CanE* usually **neigh·bour·ing**) /ˈneɪbərɪŋ/ *adj.* [only before noun] located or living near or next to a place or person: *a neighboring house* ♦ *neighboring towns* ♦ *a neighboring farmer*

neigh·bor·ly (*CanE* usually **neigh·bour·ly**) /ˈneɪbərli/ *adj.* **1** involving people, countries, etc. that live or are located near each other: *the importance of good neighborly relations between the two states* ♦ *neighborly help* ♦ *a neighborly dispute* **2** friendly and helpful **SYN** KIND: *It was a neighborly gesture of theirs.* ▶ **neigh·bor·li·ness** (*CanE* usually **neighbour·li·ness**) *noun* [U]: *good neighborliness* ♦ *a sense of community and neighborliness*

neigh·bour (*CanE*) = NEIGHBOR

nei·ther 🔊 /ˈniðər; ˈnaɪ-/ *det., pron., adv.*
● *det., pron.* not one nor the other of two things or people: *Neither answer is correct.* ♦ *Neither of them has/have a car.* ♦ *They produced two reports, neither of which contained any useful suggestions.* ♦ *"Which do you like?" "Neither. I think they're both ugly."*
● *adv.* **1** used to show that a negative statement is also true of someone or something else: *He didn't remember and neither did I.* ♦ *I hadn't been to New York before and neither had Jane.* ♦ *"I can't understand a word of it." "Neither can I."* ♦ (*informal*) *"I don't know." "Me neither."* **2** **neither... nor...** used to show that a negative statement is true of two things: *I neither knew nor cared what had happened to him.* ♦ *Their house is neither big nor small.* ♦ *Neither the TV nor the DVD player actually works/work.*

GRAMMAR

neither ♦ either

- After **neither** and **either**, you use a singular verb: *Neither candidate was selected for the job.*
- **Neither of** and **either of** are followed by a plural noun or pronoun and a singular or plural verb. A singular verb should be used in formal writing. A plural verb is more informal: *Neither of my parents speaks/speak a foreign language.*
- When **neither... nor...** or **either... or...** is used with two singular nouns, the verb is singular. When one of the nouns is plural, the verb agrees with the noun closest to it: *Either she or her teachers are going to speak to the principal.*

---

nel·son /ˈnɛlsn/ *noun* a move in which a WRESTLER stands behind his/her opponent, puts one or both arms underneath the opponent's arm(s), and holds the back of the opponent's neck. When done with one arm it is called a **half nelson**, and with both arms a **full nelson**.

nem·a·tode /ˈnɛməˌtoʊd/ (also **nematode ˈworm**) *noun* a WORM with a thin, tube-shaped body that is not divided into sections

nem·e·sis /ˈnɛməsəs/ *noun* [U, sing.] (*formal*) punishment or defeat that is deserved and cannot be avoided

neo- /ˈnioʊ/ *combining form* (in adjectives and nouns) new; in a later form: *neo-Georgian* ♦ *neo-fascist*

ne·o·clas·si·cal /ˌnioʊˈklæsɪkl/ *adj.* [usually before noun] used to describe art and ARCHITECTURE that is based on the style of ancient Greece or Rome, or music, literature, etc. that uses traditional ideas or styles

ne·o·co·lo·ni·al·ism /ˌnioʊkəˈloʊniəˌlɪzəm/ *noun* [U] (*disapproving*) the use of economic or political pressure by powerful countries to control or influence other countries

ne·o·con·serv·a·tive /ˌnioʊkənˈsərvətɪv/ *adj.* (*politics*) relating to political, economic, religious, etc. beliefs that return to traditional conservative views in a slightly changed form ▶ **ne·o·con·serv·a·tive** (also **ne·o·con** /ˈnioʊˌkɑn/) *noun*

ne·o·cor·tex /ˌnioʊˈkɔrtɛks/ *noun* (*anatomy*) the part of the brain that controls sight and hearing

ne·o·dym·i·um /ˌnioʊˈdɪmiəm/ *noun* [U] (*symb.* **Nd**) a chemical element. Neodymium is a silver-white metal.

ne·o·lib·er·al /ˌnioʊˈlɪbərəl; -ˈlɪbrəl/ *adj.* [usually before noun] (*politics*) relating to a type of LIBERALISM that believes in a global free market, without government regulation, with businesses and industry controlled and run for profit by private owners

Ne·o·lith·ic /ˌniəˈlɪθɪk/ *adj.* of the later part of the STONE AGE: *Neolithic stone axes* ♦ *Neolithic settlements*

ne·ol·o·gism /niˈɑləˌdʒɪzəm/ *noun* (*formal*) a new word or expression, or a new meaning of a word

ne·on /ˈniɑn/ *noun* [U] (*symb.* **Ne**) a chemical element. Neon is a gas that does not react with anything and that shines with a bright light when electricity is passed through it: *neon lights/signs*

ne·o·na·tal /ˌniˈoʊˈneɪtl/ *adj.* (*technical*) connected with a child that has just been born: *the hospital's neonatal unit* ♦ *neonatal care*

ne·o·nate /ˈniəˌneɪt/ *noun* (*medical*) a baby that has recently been born, especially within the last four weeks

ne·o·phyte /ˈniəˌfaɪt/ *noun* (*formal*) **1** a person who has recently started an activity: *The site gives neophytes the chance to learn from experts.* **2** a person who has recently changed to a new religion **3** a person who has recently become a priest or recently entered a religious order

ne·o·prene /ˈniəˌprin/ *noun* [U] an artificial material that looks like rubber, used for making WETSUITS

neph·ew 🔊 /ˈnɛfyu/ *noun* the son of your brother or sister; the son of your husband's or wife's brother or sister ⊃ compare NIECE

ne plus ul·tra /ˌneɪ plʌs ˈʌltrə; ˌni-/ *noun* (from *Latin, formal*) the perfect example of something

nep·o·tism /ˈnɛpəˌtɪzəm/ *noun* [U] (*disapproving*) giving unfair advantages to your own family if you are in a position of power, especially by giving them jobs

Nep·tune /ˈnɛptun/ *noun* a planet in the SOLAR SYSTEM that is 8th in order of distance from the sun ⊃ picture at EARTH

nep·tu·ni·um /nɛpˈtuniəm/ *noun* [U] (*symb.* **Np**) a chemical element. Neptunium is a RADIOACTIVE metal.

nerd /nərd/ *noun* (*informal, disapproving*) **1** a person who is boring, uncomfortable in social situations, and not fashionable **2** a person who is very interested in computers **SYN** GEEK ▶ **nerd·y** *adj.*

nerve 🔊 /nərv/ *noun, verb*
● *noun* **1** [C] any of the long threads that carry messages between the brain and parts of the body, enabling you to move, feel pain, etc.: *the optic nerve* ♦ *nerve cells* ♦ *nerve endings* ♦ *Every nerve in her body was tense.* ⊃ picture at BODY **2 nerves** [pl.] feelings of worry or anxiety: *Even after years as a singer, he still suffers from nerves before a performance.* ♦ *I need something to calm/steady my nerves.* ♦ *Everyone's nerves were on edge* (= everyone felt TENSE). **3** [U] the courage to do something difficult or dangerous **SYN** GUTS: *It took a lot of nerve to take the company to court.* ♦ *I was going to try parachuting but lost my nerve at the last minute.* **4** [sing., U] (*informal*) a way of behaving that other people think is rude or not appropriate: *I don't know how you have the nerve to show your face after what you said!* ♦ *He has some nerve asking us for money!* ♦ *"Then she demanded to see the manager!" "What nerve!"*
IDM **be a bag/bundle of nerves** (*informal*) to be very nervous **get on sb's nerves** (*informal*) to annoy someone **have nerves of steel** to be able to remain calm in a difficult or dangerous situation **hit/touch a (raw/sensitive) nerve** to mention a subject that makes someone feel angry, upset, embarrassed, etc.: *You touched a raw nerve when you mentioned his first wife.* ⊃ more at STRAIN, WAR
● *verb* ~ **yourself for sth/to do sth** to give yourself the courage or strength to do something: *He nerved himself to ask her out.*

ˈnerve ˌcenter (*CanE* usually **ˈnerve ˌcentre**) *noun* the place from which an activity or organization is controlled and instructions are sent out

nerve gas *noun* a poisonous gas used in war that attacks your CENTRAL NERVOUS SYSTEM

nerve·less /'nɜrvləs/ *adj.* **1** having no strength or feeling: *The knife fell from her nerveless fingers.* **2** having no fear: *She is a nerveless rider.* **ANT** NERVOUS

nerve-ˌracking (also **'nerve- wracking**) *adj.* making you feel very nervous and worried

nerv·ous 🔑 /'nɜrvəs/ *adj.*
1 anxious about something or afraid of something: **~ (about sth)** *Consumers are very nervous about the future.* ◆ **~ (about doing sth)** *He had been nervous about inviting us.* ◆ *I felt really nervous before the interview.* ◆ *a **nervous glance/smile/voice** (= one that shows that you feel anxious)* ◆ *By the time the police arrived, I was a **nervous wreck**.* **ANT** CONFIDENT ⊃ thesaurus box at WORRIED **2** easily worried or frightened: *She was a thin, nervous girl.* ◆ *He's not the nervous type.* ◆ *She was **of a nervous disposition**.* **3** connected with the body's nerves and often affecting you mentally or emotionally: *a **nervous condition/disorder/disease*** ◆ *She was in a state of **nervous exhaustion**.* **IDM** see SHADOW ▶ **ner·vous·ly** *adv.*: *She smiled nervously.* **ner·vous·ness** *noun* [U]: *He tried to hide his nervousness.*

THESAURUS

nervous
neurotic ◆ **on edge** ◆ **jittery**

These words all describe people who are easily frightened or who are behaving in a frightened way.

nervous easily worried or frightened; anxious about something or afraid of something: *She has a nervous temperament.* ◆ *I felt really nervous about meeting him.* **NOTE** See also the entry for **worried**.

neurotic not able to behave in a reasonable, calm way, because you are always worried about something: *He became neurotic about keeping the house clean.*

on edge nervous or bad-tempered, especially because you are worried about what might happen: *She was always on edge before an interview.*

jittery (*informal*) anxious and nervous about what might happen: *All this talk of job losses was making him jittery.*

PATTERNS
- a nervous/neurotic **man/woman/lady/girl/boy**
- to **feel** nervous/on edge/jittery
- **a bit** nervous/on edge/jittery

ˌnervous 'breakdown (also **break·down**) *noun* a period of mental illness in which someone becomes very depressed, anxious, and tired, and cannot deal with normal life: *to have a nervous breakdown*

'nervous ˌsystem *noun* the system of all the nerves in the body ⊃ see also CENTRAL NERVOUS SYSTEM

nerv·y /'nɜrvi/ *adj.* (*informal*) brave and confident in a way that might offend other people, or show a lack of respect

-ness /nəs/ *suffix* (in nouns) the quality, state, or character of: *dryness* ◆ *blindness* ◆ *silliness*

nest 🔑 /nɛst/ *noun, verb*
- *noun* **1** [C] a hollow place or structure that a bird makes or chooses for laying its eggs in and sheltering its young ⊃ picture at ANIMAL **2** [C] a place where insects or other small creatures live and produce their young **3** [sing.] a secret place which is full of bad people and their activities: *a nest of thieves* **4** [sing.] the home, thought of as the safe place where parents bring up their children: *to **leave the nest** (= leave your parents' home)* ⊃ see also EMPTY NEST **5** [C, usually sing.] a group or set of similar things that are made to fit inside each other: *a nest of tables* **IDM** see FEATHER *v.*, FLY *v.*, HORNET, MARE
- *verb* **1** [I] to make and use a nest: *Thousands of seabirds are nesting on the cliffs.* **2** [T] **~ sth** (*technical*) to put types of

information together, or inside each other, so that they form a single unit

'nest box (also **'nesting ˌbox**) *noun* a box provided for a bird to make its nest in

'nest egg *noun* (*informal*) a sum of money that you save to use in the future

nes·tle /'nɛsl/ *verb* **1** [I] + **adv./prep.** to sit or lie down in a warm or soft place: *He hugged her and she nestled against his chest.* **2** [T] **~ sb/sth** + **adv./prep.** to put or hold someone or something in a comfortable position in a warm or soft place: *He nestled the baby in his arms.* **3** [I] + **adv./prep.** to be located in a position that is protected, sheltered, or partly hidden: *The little town nestles snugly at the foot of the hill.*

nest·ling /'nɛstlɪŋ; 'nɛslɪŋ/ *noun* a bird that is too young to leave the nest

net 🔑 /nɛt/ *noun, adj., adv., verb*
- *noun* **1** [U] a type of material that is made of string, thread, or wire twisted or tied together, with small spaces in between ⊃ see also FISHNET, NETTING **2** [C] (especially in compounds) a piece of net used for a particular purpose, such as catching fish or covering something: *fishing nets* ◆ *a mosquito net* (= used to protect you from MOSQUITOES) ⊃ see also HAIRNET, SAFETY NET **3 the net** [sing.] (in sports) the frame covered in net that forms the goal: *to kick the ball **into the back of the net*** **4 the net** [sing.] (in TENNIS, etc.) the piece of net between the two players that the ball goes over ⊃ picture at SPORT **5 the Net** (also **the net**) (*informal*) = THE INTERNET **IDM** see CAST *v.*, SLIP *v.*, SPREAD *v.*
- *adj.* **1** [usually before noun] a **net** amount of money is the amount that remains when nothing more is to be taken away: *a net profit of $500* ◆ *net income/earnings* (= after tax has been paid) ⊃ compare GROSS **2** [only before noun] the **net** weight of something is the weight without its container or the material it is wrapped in: *15 oz. net weight* ⊃ compare GROSS **3** [only before noun] final, after all the important facts have been included: *The net result is that small storeowners are being forced out of business.* ◆ *Canada is now a substantial net importer of medicines* (= it imports more than it exports). ◆ *a net gain* ▶ **net** *adv.*: *a salary of $50,000 net* ◆ *Interest on the investment will be paid net* (= tax will already have been taken out). ⊃ compare GROSS
- *verb* (**-tt-**) **1** **~ sth** to earn an amount of money as a profit after you have paid tax on it: *The sale of paintings netted $17,000.* **2** **~ sth** to catch something, especially fish, in a net **3** **~ sb/sth** to catch someone or obtain something in a skillful way: *A swoop by customs officers netted a large quantity of drugs.* **4** **~ sth** to kick or hit a ball into the goal **SYN** SCORE: *He has netted 21 goals so far this season.* **5** **~ sth** to cover something with a net or nets

net·book /'nɛtbʊk/ a small LAPTOP computer, designed especially for using the Internet and e-mail ⊃ compare NOTEBOOK

neth·er /'nɛðər/ *adj.* [only before noun] (*literary* or *humorous*) lower: *a person's nether regions* (= their GENITALS)

the neth·er·world /'nɛðər wɜrld/ *noun* [sing.] (*literary*) the world of the dead **SYN** HELL

net·i·quette /'nɛtəkət/ *noun* [U] (*informal*) the rules of correct or polite behavior among people using the Internet

net·i·zen /'nɛtəzn/ *noun* (*informal*) a person who uses the Internet a lot

net·ting /'nɛtɪŋ/ *noun* [U] material that is made of string, thread, or wire twisted or tied together, with spaces in between: *wire netting*

net·tle /'nɛtl/ *noun, verb*
- *noun* (also **'stinging ˌnettle**) a wild plant with leaves that have pointed edges, are covered in fine hairs, and sting if you touch them ⊃ picture at PLANT
- *verb* [usually passive] **~ sb** | **it nettles sb that...** (*informal*) to make someone slightly angry **SYN** ANNOY: *My remarks clearly nettled her.*

net·tle·some /'nɛtlsəm/ *adj.* causing trouble or difficulty

ʌ cup   ə about   eɪ say   aɪ five   ɔɪ boy   aʊ now   oʊ go   ər bird

net·work /ˈnɛtwərk/ noun, verb

● **noun** **1** a complicated system of roads, lines, tubes, nerves, etc. that cross each other and are connected to each other: *a rail/road/canal network* ♦ *a network of veins* **2** a closely connected group of people, companies, etc. that exchange information, etc.: *a communications/distribution network* ♦ *a network of friends* **3** (*computing*) a number of computers and other devices that are connected together so that equipment and information can be shared: *The office network allows users to share files and software, and to use a central printer.* ➋ **see also** LAN, WAN **4** a group of radio or television stations in different places that are connected and that broadcast the same programs at the same time **IDM see** OLD BOY

● **verb** **1** [T] ~ sth (*computing*) to connect a number of computers and other devices together so that equipment and information can be shared **2** [T] ~ sth to broadcast a television or radio program on stations in several different areas at the same time **3** [I] to try to meet and talk to people who may be useful to you in your work: *Conferences are a good place to network.*

net·work·ing AWL /ˈnɛtˌwərkɪŋ/ noun [U] a system of trying to meet and talk to other people who may be useful to you in your work

neu·ral /ˈnʊrəl/ adj. (*technical*) connected with a nerve or the NERVOUS SYSTEM: *neural processes*

neu·ral·gia /nʊˈrældʒə/ noun [U] (*medical*) a sharp pain felt along a nerve, especially in the head or face ► **neu·ral·gic** /-dʒɪk/ adj.

neural network (also **neural net**) noun (*computing*) a system with a structure that is similar to the human brain and nervous system

neur·as·the·ni·a /ˌnʊrəsˈθiniə/ noun [U] (*old-fashioned*) a condition in which someone feels tired and depressed over a long period of time

neuro- /ˈnʊroʊ/ combining form (in nouns, adjectives, and adverbs) connected with the nerves: *neuroscience* ♦ *a neurosurgeon*

neu·ro·lin·guis·tic pro·gram·ming /ˌnʊroʊlɪŋˌgwɪstɪk ˈproʊgræmɪŋ/ noun [U] (*abbr.* NLP) (*psychology*) a technique that people use to help themselves or others think in a more positive way, and that uses neurolinguistics as its basis

neu·ro·lin·guis·tics /ˌnʊroʊlɪŋˈgwɪstɪks/ noun [U] (*psychology*) the study of the way the human brain processes language

neu·rolog·i·cal /ˌnʊrəˈlɑdʒɪkl/ adj. relating to nerves or to the science of NEUROLOGY: *neurological damage*

neu·rol·o·gist /nʊˈrɑlədʒɪst/ noun a doctor who studies and treats diseases of the nerves

neu·rol·o·gy /nʊˈrɑlədʒi/ noun [U] the scientific study of nerves and their diseases

neu·ron /ˈnʊrɑn/ noun (*biology*) a cell that carries information within the brain and between the brain and other parts of the body; a nerve cell ➋ **see also** MOTOR NEURON DISEASE

neu·ro·phys·i·ol·o·gy /ˌnʊroʊˌfɪziˈɑlədʒi/ noun [U] the scientific study of the normal functions of the NERVOUS SYSTEM

neu·ro·sci·ence /ˈnʊroʊˌsaɪəns/ noun [U] the science that deals with the structure and function of the brain and the NERVOUS SYSTEM ► **neu·ro·sci·en·tist** /ˌnʊroʊˈsaɪəntɪst/ noun

neu·ro·sis /nʊˈroʊsəs/ noun (*pl.* **neu·ro·ses** /-siz/) [C, U] **1** (*medical*) a mental illness in which a person suffers strong feelings of fear and worry **2** a strong fear or worry **SYN** ANXIETY

neu·ro·sur·ger·y /ˈnʊroʊˌsərdʒəri/ noun [U] medical operations performed on the nervous system, especially the brain ► **neu·ro·sur·geon** /-ˌsərdʒən/ noun

neu·rot·ic /nʊˈrɑtɪk/ adj., noun

● **adj.** **1** caused by or suffering from neurosis: *neurotic obsessions* ➋ thesaurus box at MENTALLY ILL **2** not behav-

ing in a reasonable, calm way, because you are worried about something: *He became neurotic about keeping the house clean.* ♦ *a brilliant but neurotic actor* ➋ thesaurus box at NERVOUS ► **neu·rot·i·cally** /-kli/ adv.

● **noun** a neurotic person

neu·ro·tox·in /ˈnʊroʊˌtɑksən/ noun (*technical*) a poison that affects the NERVOUS SYSTEM

neu·ro·trans·mit·ter /ˌnʊroʊˈtrænsmɪtər; -ˈtrænz-/ noun (*biology*) a chemical that carries messages from nerve cells to other nerve cells or muscles

neu·ter /ˈnutər/ adj., verb

● **adj.** (*grammar*) (in some languages) belonging to a class of nouns, pronouns, adjectives, or verbs whose GENDER is not FEMININE or MASCULINE: *The Polish word for "window" is neuter.*

● **verb** **1** ~ sth to remove part of the sex organs of an animal so that it cannot produce young: *Has your cat been neutered?* **2** ~ sth (*disapproving*) to prevent something from having the effect that it ought to have

neu·tral AWL /ˈnutrəl/ adj., noun

● **adj.**

> IN DISAGREEMENT/CONTEST **1** not supporting or helping either side in a disagreement, competition, etc. **SYN** IMPARTIAL, UNBIASED: *Journalists are supposed to be politically neutral.* ♦ *I didn't take my father's or my mother's side; I tried to remain neutral.*

> IN WAR **2** not belonging to any of the countries that are involved in a war; not supporting any of the countries involved in a war: *neutral territory/waters* ♦ *Switzerland was neutral during the war.*

> WITHOUT STRONG FEELING **3** deliberately not expressing any strong feeling: *"So you told her?" he said in a neutral tone of voice.*

> COLOR **4** not very bright or strong, such as gray or light brown: *a neutral color scheme* ♦ *neutral tones*

> CHEMISTRY **5** neither acid nor ALKALINE

> ELECTRICAL **6** (*abbr.* N.) having neither a positive nor a negative electrical charge: *the neutral wire in a plug* ➋ see also GENDER-NEUTRAL ► **neu·tral·ly** adv.

IDM on neutral ground/territory in a place that has no connection with either of the people or sides who are meeting and so does not give an advantage to either of them: *We decided to meet on neutral ground.*

● **noun**

> IN VEHICLE **1** [U] the position of the gears of a vehicle in which no power is carried from the engine to the wheels: *to leave the car in neutral*

> IN DISAGREEMENT/WAR **2** [C] a person or country that does not support either side in a disagreement, competition, or war

> COLOR **3** [C] a color that is not bright or strong, such as gray or light brown: *The room was decorated in neutrals.*

neu·tral·ist /ˈnutrəlɪst/ noun a person who does not support either side in a war ► **neu·tral·ist** adj.: *a neutralist state*

neu·tral·i·ty AWL /nuˈtræləti/ noun [U] the state of not supporting either side in a disagreement, competition, or war

neu·tral·ize AWL /ˈnutrəˌlaɪz/ verb **1** ~ sth to stop something from having any effect: *The latest figures should neutralize the fears of inflation.* **2** ~ sth (*chemistry*) to make a substance NEUTRAL **3** ~ sb/sth to remove the threat of someone or something that might be dangerous, especially by killing them or destroying it. People say "neutralize" to avoid saying "kill" or "destroy": *The military carried out its operation to "neutralize and eliminate" the insurgents.* **4** ~ sth to make a country or an area NEUTRAL ► **neu·tral·i·za·tion** AWL /ˌnutrələˈzeɪʃn/ noun [U]

neutral zone noun **1** (in HOCKEY) an area that covers the central part of the ICE RINK, between two blue lines **2** (in football) an imaginary area between the teams where no player except the CENTER is allowed to step until play has started

neu·tri·no /nuˈtrinoʊ/ noun (*pl.* **neu·tri·nos**) (*physics*) an extremely small PARTICLE that has no electrical charge, and that rarely reacts with other matter

neu·tron /'nutrɑn/ *noun* (*physics*) a very small piece of matter (= a substance) that carries no electrical charge and that forms part of the NUCLEUS (= central part) of an atom ⊃ picture at ATOM ⊃ see also ELECTRON, PROTON

'neutron ˌbomb *noun* a bomb that can kill people by giving out neutrons, but does not cause a lot of damage to buildings

nev·er ℒ /'nɛvər/ *adv.*, *exclamation*
- **adv. 1** not at any time; not on any occasion: *You never help me.* ◆ *He has never been abroad.* ◆ *"Would you vote for him?" "Never."* ◆ *"I work for a company called Orion Technology." "Never heard of them."* ◆ *Never in all my life have I seen such a horrible thing.* ◆ *Never ever tell anyone your password.* **2** used to emphasize a negative statement instead of "not": *I never knew* (= didn't know until now) *you had a twin sister.* ◆ *Someone might find out, and that would never do* (= that is not acceptable). ◆ *He never so much as smiled* (= did not smile even once). ◆ (*old-fashioned* or *humorous*) *Never fear* (= Do not worry), *everything will be all right.*
  IDM Well, I never! (*old-fashioned*) used to express surprise or disapproval
- **exclamation** (*informal*) used to show that you are very surprised about something because you do not believe it is possible: *"I got the job." "Never!"*

ˌnever-'ending *adj.* seeming to last forever **SYN** ENDLESS, INTERMINABLE: *Housework is a never-ending task.*

nev·er·more /ˌnɛvər'mɔr/ *adv.* (*old use*) never again

ˌnever-'never ˌland *noun* [sing.] an imaginary place where everything is wonderful

nev·er·the·less ℒ **AWL** /ˌnɛvərðə'lɛs/ *adv.*
despite something that you have just mentioned **SYN** NONETHELESS: *There is little chance that we will succeed in changing the law. Nevertheless, it is important that we try.* ◆ *Our defeat was expected, but it is disappointing nevertheless.*

new ℒ /nu/ *adj.* (**new·er, new·est**)
▷ **NOT EXISTING BEFORE 1** not existing before; recently made, invented, introduced, etc.: *Have you read her new novel?* ◆ *new ways of doing things* ◆ *This idea isn't new.* ◆ *The latest model has over 100 new features.* **ANT** OLD ⊃ see also BRAND-NEW **2 the new** *noun* [U] something that is new: *It was a good mix of the old and the new.*

▷ **RECENTLY BOUGHT 3** recently bought: *Let me show you my new dress.*
▷ **NOT USED BEFORE 4** not used or owned by anyone before: *A used car costs a fraction of a new one.*
▷ **DIFFERENT 5** different from the previous one: *I like your new hairstyle.* ◆ *When do you start your new job?* ◆ *He's made a lot of new friends.* **ANT** OLD
▷ **NOT FAMILIAR 6** already existing but not seen, experienced, etc. before; not familiar: *This is a new experience for me.* ◆ *I'd like to learn a new language.* ◆ *the discovery of a new star* ◆ *~ to sb Our system is probably new to you.*
▷ **RECENTLY ARRIVED 7 ~ (to sth)** not yet familiar with something because you have only just started, arrived, etc.: *I should tell you, I'm completely new to this kind of work.* ◆ *I am new to the town.* ◆ *a new arrival/recruit* ◆ *You're new here, aren't you?*
▷ **NEW- 8** used in compounds to describe something that has recently happened: *He was enjoying his newfound freedom.* ◆ *the sweetness of new-mown hay*
▷ **MODERN 9** (usually with *the*) modern; of the latest type: *the new morality* ◆ *They called themselves the New Romantics.*
▷ **JUST BEGINNING 10** [usually before noun] just beginning or beginning again: *a new day* ◆ *It was a new era in the history of our country.* ◆ *She went to Australia to start a new life.*
▷ **WITH FRESH ENERGY 11** having fresh energy, courage, or health: *Since he changed jobs he's looked like a new man.*
▷ **RECENTLY PRODUCED 12** only recently produced or developed: *The new buds are appearing on the trees now.* ◆ *new potatoes* (= ones dug from the soil early in the season)

  ► **new·ness** *noun* [U] ⊃ see also NEWLY

IDM break new ground to make a new discovery or do something that has not been done before ⊃ see also GROUNDBREAKING **(as) good as new** **| like new** in very good condition, as it was when it was new: *I had your coat cleaned—it's as good as new now.* **... is the new ...** (*informal*) used to say that something has become very fashionable and can be thought of as replacing something else: *Brown is the new black.* ◆ *Comedy is the new rock and roll.* ◆ *Fifty is the new forty.* **a/the new kid on the block** (*informal*) a person who is new to a place, an organization, etc.: *Despite his six years in politics, he was still regarded by many as the new kid on the block.* **a new one on me** (*informal*) used to say that you have not heard a particular idea, piece of information, joke, etc. before: *"Have you come across this before?" "No, it's a new one on me."* **turn over a new leaf** to change your way of life, to become a better, more responsible person **what's new?** (*informal*) used as a friendly GREETING: *Hi! What's new?* ⊃ more at BLOOD, BRAVE *adj.*, BREATHE, COMPLEXION, SHINY, TEACH

ˌNew 'Age *adj.* connected with a way of life that rejects modern Western values and is based on spiritual ideas and beliefs, ASTROLOGY, etc.: *a New Age festival* ► **ˌNew 'Age** *noun* [U]

new·bie /'nubi/ *noun* (*informal*) a person who is new and has little experience in doing something, especially in using computers **SYN** NOVICE

new·born /'nubɔrn/ *adj.* [only before noun] recently born: *a newborn baby*

new·com·er /'nuˌkʌmər/ *noun* **~ (to sth)** a person who has only recently arrived in a place or started an activity

the ˌNew Demoˌcratic 'Party *noun* [sing.] (*CanE*) (*abbr.* NDP) one of the three main political parties in Canada, in favor of social reform

new·el post /'nuəl ˌpoust/ (also **new·el**) *noun* a post at the top or bottom of a set of stairs

ˌNew 'England *noun* an area in the NORTHEASTERN U.S. that includes the states of Maine, New Hampshire, Vermont, Massachusetts, Rhode Island, and Connecticut

new·fan·gled /'nuˌfæŋgld/ *adj.* [usually before noun] (*disapproving*) used to describe something that has recently been invented or introduced, but that you do not like because it is not what you are used to, or is too complicated

new·fie /'nufi/ *noun* (*CanE, informal*) a person from Newfoundland in Canada

new·found /'nufaʊnd/ *adj.* [only before noun] recently discovered or achieved: *How is she handling her newfound fame?* ◆ *his newfound freedom/confidence/enthusiasm*

New·found·land Time /'nufənlənd ˌtaɪm; -fənd-; -lænd-/ *noun* [U] (*CanE*) the standard time system that is used in an area that includes the island of Newfoundland

new·ly /'nuli/ *adv.*
(usually before a past participle) recently: *a newly qualified doctor* ◆ *a newly created job* ◆ *a newly independent republic*

new·ly·wed /'nuliˌwɛd/ *noun* [usually pl.] a person who has recently got married ▶ **new·ly·wed** *adj.*

ˌnew ˈmedia *noun* [pl.] new information and entertainment technologies, such as the Internet and DIGITAL TELEVISION

ˌnew ˈmoon *noun* **1** the moon when it looks like a thin curved shape (= a CRESCENT) **2** the time of the month when the moon has this shape ⊃ compare FULL MOON, HALF-MOON

the ˌNew ˈRight *noun* [sing.] politicians and political groups that support conservative social and political policies and religious ideas based on Christian FUNDAMENTALISM

news /nuz/ *noun* [U]
1 new information about something that has happened recently: *What's the latest news?* ◆ *Have you heard the news? Pat's leaving!* ◆ *That's great news.* ◆ *Tell me all your news.* ◆ *Any news on the deal?* ◆ *Messengers brought news that the battle had been lost.* ◆ *Do you want the good news or the bad news first?* ◆ *a piece of news* ◆ (*informal*) *It's news to me* (= I haven't heard it before). **2** reports of recent events that appear in newspapers or on television or radio: *national/international news* ◆ *a news story/item/report/article* ◆ *News of a serious traffic accident is just coming in.* ◆ *breaking news* (= news that is arriving about events that have just happened) ◆ *She is always in the news.* ◆ *The wedding was front-page news.* ⊃ see also HARD NEWS **3** the news a regular television or radio broadcast of the latest news: *to listen to/watch the news* ◆ *Can you put the news on?* ◆ *I saw it on the news.* ◆ *Cities covered the event for the evening news.* ⊃ see also SHIPPING NEWS **4** a person, thing, or event that is considered to be interesting enough to be reported as news: *Pop stars are always news.* ⊃ see also NEWSY
IDM **be bad news (for sb/sth)** to be likely to cause problems: *Central heating is bad news for indoor plants.* **break the news (to sb)** to be the first to tell someone some bad news **be good news (for sb/sth)** to be likely to be helpful or give an advantage: *The cut in interest rates is good news for homeowners.* **no news is good news** (*saying*) if there were bad news we would hear it, so since we have heard nothing, it is likely that nothing bad has happened

ˈnews ˌagency (also **ˈpress ˌagency**) *noun* an organization that collects news and supplies it to newspapers and television and radio companies

news·cast /'nuzkæst/ *noun* a news program on radio or television

news·cast·er /'nuzˌkæstər/ *noun* a person who reads the news on television or radio

ˈnews ˌconference *noun* = PRESS CONFERENCE

news·deal·er /'nuzˌdilər/ *noun* a person who owns or works in a store selling newspapers and magazines, and often candy and cigarettes

ˈnews desk *noun* the department of a newspaper office or a radio or television station where news is received and prepared for printing or broadcasting: *She works on the news desk.*

ˈnews flash (also **flash**) *noun* a short item of important news that is broadcast on radio or television, often interrupting a program

ˈnews-ˌgathering *noun* [U] the process of doing research

on news items, especially ones that will be broadcast on television or printed in a newspaper ▶ **ˈnews-ˌgatherer** *noun*

ˈnews·group /'nuzgrup/ *noun* a place in a computer network, especially the Internet, where people can discuss a particular subject and exchange information about it

news·let·ter /'nuzˌlɛtər/ *noun* a report containing news of the activities of a club or an organization that is sent regularly to all its members

news·man /'nuzmæn; -mən/, **news·wom·an** /'nuzˌwʊmən/ *noun* (*pl.* **news·men** /-mɛn; -mən/, **news·wom·en** /-ˌwɪmən/) a journalist who works for a newspaper or a television or radio station: *a crowd of reporters and TV newsmen*

news·pa·per /'nuzˌpeɪpər/ *noun*
1 [C] a set of large printed sheets of paper containing news, articles, advertisements, etc. and published every day or every week: *a daily/weekly newspaper* ◆ *a local/national newspaper* ◆ *an online newspaper* ◆ *a newspaper article* ◆ *I read about it in the newspaper.* ◆ *a newspaper clipping* ◆ *She works for the local newspaper* (= the company that produces it). ⊃ see also PAPER **2** [U] paper taken from old newspapers: *Wrap all your glasses in newspaper.*

news·pa·per·man /'nuzpeɪpərˌmæn/, **news·pa·per·wom·an** /'nuzpeɪpərˌwʊmən/ *noun* (*pl.* **news·pa·per·men** /-ˌmɛn/, **news·pa·per·wom·en** /-ˌwɪmən/) a journalist who works for a newspaper

new·speak /'nuspik/ *noun* [U] language that is not clear or honest, for example the language that is used in political PROPAGANDA **ORIGIN** From the novel *1984* by George Orwell.

news·print /'nuzprɪnt/ *noun* [U] the cheap paper that newspapers are printed on

news·reel /'nuzril/ *noun* a short film of news that was shown in the past in movie theaters

news·room /'nuzrum; -rʊm/ *noun* the room at a newspaper office or a radio or television station where news is received and prepared for printing or broadcasting

news·stand /'nuzstænd/ *noun* a place on the street, at a station, etc. where you can buy newspapers and magazines

ˈnews ˌticker (also **tick·er**) *noun* a line of text containing news which passes across the screen of a computer or television

news·wire /'nuzˌwaɪər/ *noun* a service that provides the latest news, for example using the Internet

news·wor·thy /'nuzˌwərði/ *adj.* interesting and important enough to be reported as news

news·y /'nuzi/ *adj.* (*informal*) full of interesting and entertaining news: *a newsy letter*

newt /nut/ *noun* a small animal with short legs, a long tail, and cold blood, that lives both in water and on land (= is an AMPHIBIAN)

the ˌNew ˈTestament *noun* [sing.] the second part of the Bible, that describes the life and teachings of Jesus Christ ⊃ compare THE OLD TESTAMENT

new·ton /'nutn/ *noun* (*abbr.* N.) (*physics*) a unit of force. One newton is equal to the force that would give a mass of one kilogram an ACCELERATION (= an increase in speed) of one meter per second per second.

ˈnew town *noun* a planned urban center with community services and facilities, created in a previously open or rural area

ˌnew ˌvariant ˈCJˈD *noun* [U] a disease similar to CREUTZFELDT-JAKOB DISEASE (= a brain disease in humans that causes death) that is thought to be connected with BSE

ˌnew ˈwave *noun* [U, sing.] **1** [C, usually sing.] a group of people who together introduce new styles and ideas in art, music, movies, etc.: *one of the most exciting directors of the Australian new wave* ◆ *new wave films* **2** [C, usually sing., U]

new styles and ideas introduced in music, art, movies, etc: *The current generation of musicians has created a new wave of American music.* **3** [U] a style of ROCK music popular in the 1970s and 1980s

the ˌNew ˈWorld *noun* [sing.] a way of referring to North, Central, and South America, used especially in the past ⊃ compare THE OLD WORLD

ˈnew year *noun* **1** ˈNew Year [U] January 1, or the first few days of the year: *Happy New Year!* ◆ *We're going to Germany for Christmas and New Year.* **2** ˌnew ˈyear [sing.] the year that is about to start or has just started: *I'll see you in the new year.* ⊃ see also RESOLUTION

ˌNew Year's ˈDay (also ˌNew Year's) *noun* [U] January 1

ˌNew Year's ˈEve (also ˌNew Year's) *noun* [U] December 31, especially the evening of that day

next 🔊 /nɛkst/ *adj., adv., noun*

● *adj.* [only before noun] **1** (usually with *the*) coming straight after someone or something in time, order, or space: *The next train to Baltimore is at ten.* ◆ *The next six months will be the hardest.* ◆ *the next chapter* ◆ *the woman in the next room* ◆ *I fainted, and the next thing I knew I was in the hospital.* ◆ (*informal*) *Around here, you leave school at sixteen and next thing you know, you're married with three kids.* **2** (used without *the*) ~ **Monday, week, summer, year, etc.** the Monday, week, etc. immediately following: *Next Thursday is April 12.* ◆ *Next time I'll bring a book.*
IDM the next man, woman, person, etc. the average person: *I can enjoy a joke as well as the next man, but this is going too far.* ⊃ more at DAY, LUCK *n.*

● *adv.* **1** after something else; then; afterward: *What happened next?* ◆ *Next, I heard the sound of voices.* ◆ *Who's next?* ⊃ language bank at FIRST, PROCESS¹ **2** ~ **best, biggest, most important, etc.... (after/to sb/sth)** following in the order mentioned: *Jo was the next oldest after Martin.* ◆ *The next best thing to flying is gliding.* **3** used in questions to express surprise or confusion: *You're going bungee jumping? What next?*

● *noun* usually **the next** [sing.] a person or thing that is next: *One moment he wasn't there, the next he was.* ◆ *the week after next*

WHICH WORD?

next ◆ nearest

■ (**The**) **next** means "after this/that one" in time or in a series of events, places, or people: *When is your next appointment?* ◆ *Take a left at the next traffic light.* ◆ *Who's next?* (**The**) **nearest** means "closest" in space: *Where's the nearest grocery store?*

■ Notice the difference between the prepositions **nearest to** and **next to**: *Janet's sitting nearest to the window* (= of all the people in the room). ◆ *Sarah's sitting next to the window* (= right beside it).

ˌnext ˈdoor *adv., adj.*

● *adv.* in the next room, house, or building: *The cat is from the house next door.* ◆ *The manager's office is just next door.* ◆ *We live next door to the bank.* ▶ **ˈnext-door** *adj.* [only before noun]: *our next-door neighbors*

ˌnext of ˈkin *noun* (*pl.* **next of kin**) [C, U] your closest living relative or relatives: *I'm her next of kin.* ◆ *Her next of kin have been informed.* ◆ *The form must be signed by next of kin.*

ˈnext to 🔊 *prep.*

1 in or into a position right beside someone or something: *We sat next to each other.* ⊃ note at NEXT **2** following in order or importance after someone or something: *Next to skiing my favorite sport is skating.* **3** almost: *Charles knew next to nothing about farming.* ◆ *The horse came next to last* (= the one before the last one) *in the race.* **4** in comparison with someone or something: *Next to her I felt like a fraud.*

nex·us /ˈnɛksəs/ *noun* [sing.] (*formal*) a complicated series of connections between different things

Nez Per·cé /ˌnɛz ˈpərs/ *noun* (*pl.* **Nez Per·cé** or **Nez Percés**) a member of a Native American people, many of whom now live in the state of Idaho **ORIGIN** From the French for "pierced nose."

the NFC /ˌɛn ɛf ˈsi/ *abbr.* the National Football Conference (one of the two groups of teams in the National Football League) ⊃ see also AFC

the NFL /ˌɛn ɛf ˈɛl/ *abbr.* the National Football League (the organization for professional football with two groups of teams, the National Football Conference and the American Football Conference)

NGO /ˌɛn dʒi ˈoʊ/ *noun* (*pl.* **NGOs**) a charity, association, etc. that is independent of government and business (the abbreviation for "nongovernmental organization")

NH *abbr.* (in writing) New Hampshire

ni·a·cin /ˈnaɪəsən/ (also ˌnic·o·tin·ic ˈac·id) *noun* [U] a VITAMIN of the B group that is found in foods such as milk and meat

nib /nɪb/ *noun* the metal point of a pen

nib·ble /ˈnɪbl/ *verb, noun*

● *verb* **1** [T, I] to take small bites of something, especially food: ~ **sth** *We sat drinking wine and nibbling olives.* ◆ *He nibbled her ear playfully.* ◆ ~ **(at/on sth)** *She took some cake from the tray and nibbled at it.* **2** [I] ~ **(at sth)** to show a slight interest in an offer, idea, etc.: *He nibbled at the idea, but would not make a definite decision.*
PHR V ˌnibble aˈway at sth to take away small amounts of something, so that the total amount is gradually reduced **SYN** ERODE: *Inflation is nibbling away at spending power.*

● *noun* **1** [C] a small bite of something **2** nib·bles [pl.] small things to eat with a drink before a meal or at a party

VOCABULARY BUILDING

nice and very nice

Instead of saying that something is **nice** or **very nice**, try to use more precise and interesting adjectives to describe things:

■ **pleasant/perfect/beautiful** weather
■ a **cozy**/a **comfortable**/an **attractive** room
■ a **pleasant**/an **interesting**/an **enjoyable** experience
■ **expensive/fashionable/stylish** clothes
■ a **kind**/a **charming**/an **interesting** man
■ The party was **fun**.
■ In conversation, you can also use **great**, **wonderful**, and **fantastic**: *The party was great.* ◆ *We had a fantastic weekend.*
⊃ note at GOOD

nice 🔊 /naɪs/ *adj.* (nic·er, nic·est)
> PLEASANT/ATTRACTIVE **1** pleasant, enjoyable, or attractive: *a nice day/smile/place* ◆ *nice weather* ◆ *Did you have a nice time?* ◆ *You look very nice.* ◆ "*Do you want to come, too?*" "*Yes, that would be nice.*" ◆ *The nicest thing about her is that she never criticizes us.* ◆ ~ **(to do sth)** *Nice to meet you!* (= a friendly GREETING when you meet someone for the first time) ◆ ~ **(doing sth)** *It's been nice meeting you.* ◆ ~ **(that...)** *It's nice that you can come with us.* ◆ *It would be nice if he moved to our neighborhood.* ◆ *We all had the flu last week—it wasn't very nice.* ◆ *It's nice to know that someone appreciates what I do.* **2** used before adjectives or adverbs to emphasize how pleasant something is: *a nice hot bath* ◆ *a nice long walk* ◆ *It was nice and warm yesterday.* ◆ *Everyone arrived nice and early.*
HELP Nice and with another adjective cannot be used before a noun: *a nice and quiet place.*
> KIND/FRIENDLY **3** kind; friendly: *Our new neighbors are very nice.* ◆ *He's a really nice guy.* ◆ ~ **to sb** *Be nice to me. I'm not feeling well.* ◆ ~ **of sb (to do sth)** *It was nice of them to invite us.* ◆ ~ **about sth** *I complained to the manager and he was very nice about it.* ◆ *I asked him in the nicest possible way to put his cigarette out.* **ANT** NASTY
> NOT NICE **4** (*ironic*) bad or unpleasant: *That's a nice thing to say!* ◆ *That's a nice way to speak to your mother!*

> SMALL DETAILS 5 (*formal*) involving a very small detail or difference **SYN** SUBTLE: *a nice point of law* (= one that is difficult to decide)

▶ **nice·ness** *noun* [U]: *In some professions, niceness does not get you very far.*

IDM **as nice as pie** (*informal*) very kind and friendly, especially when you are not expecting it **have a nice day!** (*informal*) a friendly way of saying goodbye, especially to customers **nice work if you can get it** (*informal*) used when you wish that you had someone's success or good luck and think they have achieved it with little effort ⊃ more at MR.

nice-'looking *adj.* attractive: *What a nice-looking young man!*

nice·ly /ˈnaɪsli/ *adv.*

1 in an attractive or acceptable way; well: *The room was nicely furnished.* ♦ *The plants are coming along nicely* (= growing well). **2** in a kind, friendly, or polite way: *If you ask her nicely she might say yes.* **3** (*formal*) carefully; exactly: *His novels nicely describe life in Britain between the wars.* **IDM** **do nicely 1** to be making good progress: *Her new business is doing very nicely.* **2** to be acceptable: *Tomorrow at ten will do nicely* (= will be a good time).

ni·ce·ty /ˈnaɪsəti/ *noun* (*pl.* **ni·ce·ties**) (*formal*) **1** [C, usually pl.] a small detail or point of difference, especially concerning the correct way of behaving or of doing things **2** [U] (*formal*) the quality of being very detailed or careful about something **SYN** PRECISION: *the nicety of his argument*

niche /nɪtʃ; niʃ/ *noun* **1** a comfortable or suitable role, job, way of life, etc.: *He eventually found his niche in sports journalism.* **2** (*business*) an opportunity to sell a particular product to a particular group of people: *They spotted a niche in the market, with no serious competition.* ♦ *a niche market* ♦ *the development of niche marketing* (= aiming products at particular groups) **3** a small hollow place, especially in a wall to contain a statue, etc., or in the side of a hill **SYN** NOOK **4** (*biology*) the conditions of its environment within which a particular type of living thing can live successfully

nick /nɪk/ *noun, verb*
● *noun* a small cut in the edge or surface of something **IDM** **in the nick of time** (*informal*) at the very last moment; just in time before something bad happens
● *verb* ~ **sth/yourself** to make a small cut in something: *He nicked himself while shaving.*

nick·el /ˈnɪkl/ *noun* **1** [U] (*symb.* **Ni**) a chemical element. Nickel is a hard silver-white metal used in making some types of steel and other ALLOYS. **2** [C] a coin of the U.S. and Canada worth 5 cents ⊃ picture at MONEY

nickel-and-'dime *adj., verb*
● *adj.* (*informal*) involving only a small amount of money; not important
● *verb* ~ **sth/sb** to spend or save very small amounts of money; to charge small amounts of money for lots of extra items: *Set the money aside so you don't nickel-and-dime it away.* ♦ *She's careful not to nickel-and-dime clients for extra charges.*

nick·name /ˈnɪkneɪm/ *noun, verb*
● *noun* an informal, often humorous, name for a person that is connected with their real name, their personality or appearance, or with something they have done ⊃ note at NAME
● *verb* [often passive] ~ **sb/sth + noun** to give a nickname to someone or something: *She was nicknamed "The Ice Queen."*

nic·o·tine /ˈnɪkəˌtin/ *noun* [U] a poisonous substance in TOBACCO that people become ADDICTED to, so that it is difficult to stop smoking

nic·o·tin·ic ac·id /ˌnɪkətɪnɪk ˈæsɪd; -tɪnɪk-/ *noun* [U] = NIACIN

niece /nis/ *noun*
the daughter of your brother or sister; the daughter of your husband's or wife's brother or sister ⊃ compare NEPHEW

nif·ty /ˈnɪfti/ *adj.* (*informal*) **1** skillful and accurate: *There's some nifty guitar work on his latest CD.* **2** practical; working well **SYN** HANDY: *a nifty little gadget for slicing cucumbers*

nig·gard·ly /ˈnɪɡərdli/ *adj.* (*formal, disapproving*) **1** unwilling to be generous with money, time, etc. **SYN** MEAN **2** (of a gift or an amount of money) not worth much and given unwillingly **SYN** MISERLY

nig·gle /ˈnɪɡl/ *verb* **1** [I, T] ~ **(at sb)** to irritate or annoy someone slightly; to make someone slightly worried **SYN** BOTHER: *A doubt niggled at her.* **2** [I] ~ **(about/over sth)** to argue about something unimportant; to criticize someone for something that is not important **SYN** QUIBBLE

nig·gling /ˈnɪɡlɪŋ/ *adj.* **1** used to describe a slight feeling of worry or pain that does not go away: *She had niggling doubts about their relationship.* **2** not important: *niggling details* **SYN** PETTY

nigh /naɪ/ *adv.* **1** ~ **on** (*old-fashioned*) almost; nearly: *They've lived in that house for nigh on 30 years.* ⊃ see also WELL-NIGH **2** (*old use* or *literary*) near: *Winter was drawing nigh.*

night /naɪt/ *noun* [U, C]
1 the time between one day and the next when it is dark, when people usually sleep: *These animals only come out at night.* ♦ *They sleep by day and hunt by night.* ♦ *The accident happened on Friday night.* ♦ *on the night of January 10* ♦ *Did you hear the storm last night?* ♦ *I lay awake all night.* ♦ *Where did you spend the night?* ♦ *You're welcome to stay the night here.* ♦ *What is he doing calling at this time of night?* ♦ *You'll feel better after you've had a good night's sleep.* ♦ *The trip was for ten nights.* ♦ *The hotel costs $65 per person per night.* ♦ *the night train/boat/flight* ♦ *Night fell* (= it became dark). **2** the evening until you go to bed: *Let's go out on Saturday night.* ♦ *Bill's parents came for dinner last night.* ♦ *She doesn't like to walk home late at night.* ♦ *I saw her in town the other night* (= a few nights ago). ♦ *I'm working late tomorrow night.* ⊃ see also GOOD NIGHT **3** an evening when a special event happens: *the first/opening night* (= of a play, movie, etc.) ♦ *a karaoke night* ♦ *an Irish/a Scandinavian, etc. night* (= with Irish/ Scandinavian music, entertainment, etc.) ▶ **nights** *adv.*: *He can't get used to working nights* (= at night).
IDM **have an early/a late night** to go to bed earlier or later than usual: *I've had a lot of late nights recently.* **have a good/bad night** to sleep well/badly during the night **like night and day** if two people or things are **like night and day**, they are completely different from each other **night and day | day and night** all the time; continuously: *The machines are kept running night and day.* **nighty/night night** used by children or to children, to mean "Good night": *"Nighty night, sleep tight!"* **a night out** an evening that you spend enjoying yourself away from home: *They enjoy a night out occasionally.* ⊃ more at ALL RIGHT, DANCE, DEAD, MORNING, SPEND, STILL, THING

night·cap /ˈnaɪtkæp/ *noun* **1** a drink, usually containing alcohol, taken before going to bed **2** (in the past) a soft cap worn in bed

night·clothes /ˈnaɪtkloʊz; -kloʊðz/ *noun* [pl.] clothes that you wear in bed

night·club /ˈnaɪtklʌb/ *noun* a place that is open late in the evening where people can go to dance, drink, etc.

night de'pository *noun* a SAFE in the outside wall of a bank where money, etc. can be left when the bank is closed

night ˌduty *noun* [U] work that people have to do at night, for example in a hospital: *to be on night duty*

night·fall /ˈnaɪtfɔl/ *noun* [U] (*formal* or *literary*) the time in the evening when it becomes dark **SYN** DUSK

night·gown /ˈnaɪtɡaʊn/ *noun* a long loose piece of clothing like a thin dress, worn by a woman or girl in bed: *I prefer pajamas to nightgowns.* ⊃ picture at CLOTHES

night·ie /ˈnaɪti/ *noun* (*informal*) = NIGHTGOWN

night·in·gale /ˈnaɪtnˌɡeɪl; ˈnaɪtɪŋ-/ *noun* a small brown bird, the male of which has a beautiful song

night·jar /ˈnaɪtdʒɑr/ noun a brown bird with a long tail and a rough, unpleasant cry, that is active mainly at night

night·life /ˈnaɪtlaɪf/ noun [U] entertainment that is available in the evening and at night ⊃ collocations at TOWN

night light noun a light or CANDLE that is left on at night

night-long adj. [only before noun] lasting all night

night·ly /ˈnaɪtli/ adj. happening every night: a nightly news bulletin ▶ **night·ly** adv.

night·mare /ˈnaɪtmɛr/ noun **1** a dream that is very frightening or unpleasant: He still has nightmares about the accident. **2** ~ (for sb) an experience that is very frightening and unpleasant, or very difficult to deal with: The trip turned into a nightmare when they both got sick. ◆ (informal) Nobody knows what's going on— it's a nightmare! ◆ (informal) Filling in all those forms was a nightmare. ◆ Losing a child is most people's worst nightmare. ◆ If it goes ahead, it will be the nightmare scenario (= the worst thing that could happen). ◆ a nightmare situation ▶ **night·mar·ish** /ˈnaɪtˌmɛrɪʃ/ adj.: nightmarish living conditions

night owl noun (informal) a person who enjoys staying up late at night

night school noun [U, C] classes for adults, held in the evening

night shift noun [C, usually sing.] **1** a period of time at night during which a group of workers regularly work: He works the night shift at a clothing factory. **2** the workers who work during this period of time: The night shift had already gone home.

night·shirt /ˈnaɪtʃɜrt/ noun a long loose shirt worn in bed

night·spot /ˈnaɪtspɑt/ noun (informal) a place people go to for entertainment at night **SYN** NIGHTCLUB

night·stand /ˈnaɪtstænd/ (also **night table**) noun a small table beside a bed

night·stick /ˈnaɪtstɪk/ noun a short thick stick that police officers carry as a weapon **SYN** BATON

night table noun = NIGHTSTAND

night·time /ˈnaɪttaɪm/ noun [U] the time when it is dark: This area can be very noisy at nighttime.

night watchman noun (pl. **night watchmen**) a man whose job is to guard a building such as a factory at night

night·wear /ˈnaɪtwɛr/ noun [U] a word used by stores for clothes that are worn in bed

ni·hil·ism /ˈnaɪəˌlɪzəm; ˈniə-/ noun [U] (philosophy) the belief that nothing has any value, especially that religious and moral principles have no value ▶ **ni·hil·is·tic** /ˌnaɪəˈlɪstɪk; ˌniə-/ adj.: Her latest play is a nihilistic vision of the world of the future.

ni·hil·ist /ˈnaɪəlɪst; ˈniə-/ noun a person who believes in nihilism

the Nik·kei in·dex /ˈnɪkeɪ ˌɪndɛks/ (also the **Nikkei average**) noun [sing.] a figure that shows the relative price of shares on the Tokyo Stock Exchange

nil /nɪl/ noun [U] nothing: The doctors rated her chances as nil (= there were no chances).

nim·ble /ˈnɪmbl/ adj. (**nim·bler** /-blər/, **nim·blest** /-bləst/) **1** able to move quickly and easily **SYN** AGILE: You need nimble fingers for that job. ◆ She was extremely nimble on her feet. **2** (of the mind) able to think and understand quickly ▶ **nim·bly** /-bli/ adv.

nim·bus /ˈnɪmbəs/ noun (technical) **1** [C, usually sing., U] a large, gray, rain cloud **2** [C, usually sing.] a circle of light

NIM·BY /ˈnɪmbi/ (also **Nim·by**) noun (pl. **NIMBYs**) (humorous, disapproving) a person who claims to be in favor of a new development or project, but objects if it is too near their home and will disturb them in some way **ORIGIN** Formed from the first letters of "not in my backyard."

nin·com·poop /ˈnɪŋkəmˌpup/ noun (old-fashioned, informal) a stupid person

nine /naɪn/ number
9 **HELP** There are examples of how to use numbers at the entry for **five**.
IDM have nine lives (especially of a cat) to be very lucky in dangerous situations **nine times out of ten** almost every time: I'm always emailing her, but nine times out of ten she doesn't reply. **nine to five** the normal working hours in an office: I work nine to five. ◆ a nine-to-five job **the whole nine yards** (informal) everything, or a situation that includes everything: When Dan cooks dinner he always goes the whole nine yards, with three courses and a choice of dessert. ⊃ more at DRESSED, POSSESSION

nine·teen /ˌnaɪnˈtin/ number
19 ▶ **nine·teenth** /ˌnaɪnˈtinθ/ ordinal number, noun
HELP There are examples of how to use ordinal numbers at the entry for **fifth**.

nine·ty /ˈnaɪnti/ **1** number 90 **2** noun **the nine·ties** [pl.] numbers, years, or temperatures from 90 to 99: The temperature must be in the nineties today. ▶ **nine·ti·eth** /ˈnaɪntiəθ/ ordinal number, noun **HELP** There are examples of how to use ordinal numbers at the entry for **fifth**.
IDM in your nineties between the ages of 90 and 99 **ninety-nine times out of a hundred** almost always

nin·ja /ˈnɪndʒə/ noun (pl. **nin·jas** or **nin·ja**) (from Japanese) a person trained in traditional Japanese skills of fighting and moving quietly

nin·ny /ˈnɪni/ noun (pl. **nin·nies**) (old-fashioned, informal) a stupid person

ninth /naɪnθ/ ordinal number, noun
● **ordinal number** 9th **HELP** There are examples of how to use ordinal numbers at the entry for **fifth**.
● **noun** each of nine equal parts of something

ni·o·bi·um /naɪˈoʊbiəm/ noun [U] (symb. **Nb**) a chemical element. Niobium is a silver-gray metal used in steel ALLOYS.

nip /nɪp/ verb, noun
● **verb** (-pp-) **1** [T, I] to give someone or something a quick painful bite or PINCH (= squeezing their skin between your finger and thumb): ~ sth He winced as the dog nipped his ankle. ◆ ~ (at sth) She nipped at my arm. **2** [I, T] (of cold, wind, etc.) to harm or damage something: ~ (at sth) The icy wind nipped at our faces. ◆ ~ sth growing shoots nipped by frost **IDM nip sth in the bud** to stop something when it has just begun because you can see that problems will come from it **PHR V nip sth↔off** to remove a part of something with your finger or with a tool
● **noun 1** the act of giving someone a small bite or PINCH (= squeezing their skin between your finger and thumb) **2** (informal) a feeling of cold: There was a real nip in the air. ⊃ see also NIPPY **3** (informal) a small drink of strong alcohol

nip and tuck adj., adv., noun
● **adj., adv.** = NECK AND NECK: The presidential contest is nip and tuck.
● **noun** (informal) a medical operation in which skin is removed or made tighter to make someone look younger or more attractive, especially a FACELIFT

nip·ple /ˈnɪpl/ noun **1** either of the two small, round, dark parts on a person's chest. Babies can suck milk from their mother's breasts through the nipples. ⊃ picture at BODY **2** the rubber part at the end of a baby's bottle that the baby sucks in order to get milk, etc. from the bottle **3** a small metal, plastic, or rubber object that is shaped like a nipple with a small hole in the end, especially one that is used as part of a machine to direct oil, etc. into a particular place: a grease nipple

nip·py /ˈnɪpi/ adj. (informal) (of the weather) cold

nir·va·na /nɪrˈvɑnə; nər-/ noun [U] (in Buddhism) the state of peace and happiness that a person achieves after giving up all personal desires

nit /nɪt/ noun the egg or young form of a LOUSE (= a small insect that lives in human hair)

ʌ cup ə about eɪ say aɪ five ɔɪ boy aʊ now oʊ go ər bird

'nit·pick·ing noun [U] (informal, disapproving) the habit of finding small mistakes in someone's work or paying too much attention to small details that are not important ▶ **'nit·pick·er** noun **'nit·pick·ing** adj.

ni·trate /'naɪtreɪt/ noun [U, C] (chemistry) a COMPOUND containing NITROGEN and OXYGEN. There are several different nitrates and they are used especially to make soil better for growing crops: *We need to cut nitrate levels in water.*

ni·tric ac·id /ˌnaɪtrɪk 'æsɪd/ noun [U] (chemistry) (symb. **HNO₃**) a powerful clear acid that can destroy most substances and is used to make EXPLOSIVES and other chemical products

ni·tri·fy /'naɪtrəˌfaɪ/ verb (ni·tri·fies, ni·tri·fy·ing, ni·tri·fied, ni·tri·fied) ~ sth (chemistry) to change a substance into a COMPOUND that contains NITROGEN ⊃ see also NITRATE

ni·trite /'naɪtraɪt/ noun [U, C] (chemistry) a COMPOUND containing nitrogen and OXYGEN. There are several different nitrites.

ni·tro·gen /'naɪtrədʒən/ noun [U] (symb. **N**) a chemical element. Nitrogen is a gas that is found in large quantities in the earth's atmosphere. ▶ **ni·trog·e·nous** /naɪ'trɑdʒ-ənəs/ adj.

'nitrogen ˌcycle noun [C, U] the processes by which nitrogen is passed from one part of the environment to another, for example when plants decay

ˌnitrogen diˈoxide noun [U] (chemistry) a brown poisonous gas. Nitrogen dioxide is formed when some metals are dissolved in NITRIC ACID.

ni·tro·gly·ce·rin (also ni·tro·gly·ce·rine) /ˌnaɪtroʊˈglɪ-sərən/ noun [U] a powerful liquid EXPLOSIVE

ni·trous ox·ide /ˌnaɪtrəs 'ɑksaɪd/ (also informal 'laughing ˌgas) noun [U] a gas used especially in the past by dentists to prevent you from feeling pain

the nit·ty-grit·ty /ˌnɪti 'grɪti/ noun [sing.] (informal) the basic or most important details of an issue or a situation: *Time ran out before we could get down to the real nitty-gritty.*

nit·wit /'nɪtwɪt/ noun (informal) a stupid person

nix /nɪks/ verb ~ sth (informal) to prevent something from happening by saying "no" to it

NJ abbr. (in writing) New Jersey

NLP /ˌɛn ɛl 'pi/ abbr. **1** NATURAL LANGUAGE PROCESSING **2** NEUROLINGUISTIC PROGRAMMING

NM abbr. (in writing) New Mexico

N.N.E. (also NNE) abbr. (in writing) NORTH-NORTHEAST

N.N.W. (also NNW) abbr. (in writing) NORTH-NORTHWEST

No noun [U] = NOH

No. abbr. **1** also **no.** (pl. **Nos.**, **nos.**) (in writing) number: *Room No. 145* **2** north; northern

no 🔑 /noʊ/ exclamation, det., adv., noun
● **exclamation 1** used to give a negative reply or statement: *Just say yes or no.* ◆ *"Are you ready?" "No, I'm not."* ◆ *Sorry, the answer's no.* ◆ *"Another drink?" "No, thanks."* ◆ *It's about 70—no, I'm wrong—80 miles from Rome.* ◆ *No! Don't touch it! It's hot.* ◆ *"It was Tony." "No, you're wrong. It was Ted."* ◆ *"It's not very good, is it?" "No, you're right, it isn't (= I agree)."* **2** used to express shock or surprise at what someone has said: *"She's had an accident." "Oh, no!"* ◆ *"I'm leaving!" "No!"*
IDM **not take no for an answer** to refuse to accept that someone does not want something, will not do something, etc.: *You're coming and I won't take no for an answer!* ⊃ more at YES
● **det. 1** not one; not any; not a: *No student is to leave the room.* ◆ *There were no letters this morning.* ◆ *There's no bread left.* ◆ *No two days are the same.* ⊃ see also NO ONE **2** used, for example on notices, to say that something is not allowed: *No smoking!* **3** there's ~ doing sth used to say that it is impossible to do something: *There's no telling what will happen next.* **4** used to express the opposite of what is mentioned: *She's no fool (= she's intelligent).* ◆ *It was no easy matter (= it was difficult).*

● **adv.** used before adjectives and adverbs to mean "not": *She's feeling no better this morning.* ◆ *Reply by no later than July 21.*

● **noun** (pl. **noes** /noʊz/) **1** an answer that shows you do not agree with an idea, a statement, etc.; a person who says "no": *Can't you give me a straight yes or no?* ◆ *When we took a vote there were nine yesses and 3 noes.* ◆ *I'll put you down as a no.* **2** the noes the total number of people saying "no" when voting

No·ah's ark /ˌnoʊəz 'ɑrk/ noun = ARK

no·bel·i·um /noʊ'beliəm/ noun [U] (symb. **No**) a chemical element. Nobelium is a RADIOACTIVE metal that does not exist naturally and is produced from CURIUM.

No·bel Prize /ˌnoʊbel 'praɪz; noʊˌbel-/ noun one of six international prizes given each year for excellent work in physics, chemistry, medicine, literature, economics, and work toward world peace

no·bil·i·ty /noʊ'bɪləti/ noun **1** the nobility [sing.] people of high social position who have titles such as that of DUKE or DUCHESS SYN THE ARISTOCRACY **2** [U] (formal) the quality of being noble in character

no·ble /'noʊbl/ adj., noun
● **adj.** (no·bler /-blər/, no·blest /-bləst/) **1** having fine personal qualities that people admire, such as courage, HONESTY, and care for others: *a noble leader* ◆ *noble ideals* ◆ *He died for a noble cause.* ⊃ compare IGNOBLE **2** very impressive in size or quality SYN SPLENDID: *a noble building* **3** belonging to the nobility (= families of high social rank) SYN ARISTOCRATIC: *a man of noble birth* ▶ **no·bly** /-bli/ adv.: *She bore the disappointment nobly.* ◆ *to be nobly born*
● **noun** a person who comes from a family of high social rank; a member of the nobility

ˌnoble 'gas (also iˌnert 'gas, ˌrare 'gas) noun (chemistry) any of a group of gases that do not react with other chemicals. ARGON, HELIUM, KRYPTON, and NEON are noble gases.

no·ble·man /'noʊblmən/, **no·ble·wom·an** /'noʊbl-ˌwʊmən/ nouns (pl. no·ble·men /-mən/, no·ble·wom·en /-ˌwɪmən/) a person from a family of high social rank; a member of the NOBILITY SYN ARISTOCRAT

ˌnoble 'savage noun a word used in the past to refer in a positive way to a person or people who did not live in an advanced human society: *The book contrasts modern civilization with the ideal of the noble savage who lived in harmony with nature.*

noblesse oblige /noʊˌblɛs ə'bliʒ/ noun [U] (from French) the idea that people who have special advantages of wealth, etc. should help other people who do not have these advantages

no·bod·y 🔑 /'noʊbədi; -ˌbɑdi; -ˌbʌdi/ pron., noun
● **pron.** = NO ONE: *Nobody knew what to say.* **HELP** Nobody is more common than **no one** in spoken English.
ANT SOMEBODY
● **noun** (pl. no·bod·ies) a person who has no importance or influence SYN NONENTITY: *She rose from being a nobody to become a superstar.* ⊃ compare SOMEONE

no-brain·er /ˌnoʊ 'breɪnər/ noun (informal) a decision or a problem that you do not need to think about much because it is obvious what you should do

noc·tur·nal /nɑk'tɜrnl/ adj. **1** (of animals) active at night **ANT** DIURNAL **2** (formal) happening during the night: *a nocturnal visit*

noc·turne /'nɑktɜrn/ noun a short piece of music in a romantic style, especially for the piano

Nod /nɑd/ noun [U] **IDM** see LAND n.

nod 🔑 /nɑd/ verb, noun
● **verb** (-dd-) **1** [I, T] if you **nod** or **nod** your head or if your head **nods**, you move your head up and down to show agreement, understanding, etc.: *I asked him if he would help me and he nodded.* ◆ *Her head nodded in agreement.* ◆ ~ sth *He*

nodded his head sympathetically. ◆ She nodded approval.
2 [I, T] to move your head down and up once to say hello to someone or to give them a sign to do something: **~ (to/at sb)** The president nodded to the crowd as he passed in the motorcade. ◆ **~ to/at sb to do sth** She nodded at him to begin speaking. ◆ **~ sth (to/at sb)** to nod a greeting **3** [I] + **adv./ prep.** to move your head in the direction of someone or something to show that you are talking about them/it: I asked where Steve was and she nodded in the direction of the kitchen. **4** [I] to let your head fall forward when you are sleeping in a chair: He sat nodding in front of the fire.
IDM have a nodding acquaintance with sb/sth to only know someone or something slightly
PHR V ,nod 'off (informal) to fall asleep for a short time while you are sitting in a chair

● **noun** a small quick movement of the head down and up again: to give a nod of approval/agreement/encouragement
IDM get the nod (informal) to be chosen for something; to be given permission or approval to do something: He got the nod from the team manager (= he was chosen for the team). give sb/sth the nod (informal) **1** to give permission for something; to agree to something: We've been given the nod to expand the business. ◆ I hope he'll give the nod to the plan. **2** to choose someone for something

node /noʊd/ noun **1** (technical, computing) a point at which two lines or systems meet or cross: a network node **2** (anatomy) a small hard mass of TISSUE, especially near a joint in the human body: a lymph node **3** (biology) a place on the STEM of a plant from which a branch or leaf grows **4** (biology) a small swelling on a root or branch ▶ nod·al /ˈnoʊdl/ adj.

nod·ule /ˈnɑdʒul/ noun a small round lump or swelling, especially on a plant

No·el /noʊˈɛl/ noun [C, U] a word for "Christmas" used especially in songs or on cards: Joyful Noel

noes pl. of NO

,no-'fault adj. [only before noun] (law) not involving a decision as to who is to blame for something: no-fault insurance (= in which the insurance company pays for damage, etc. without asking whose fault it was)

,no-'fly zone noun an area above a country where planes from other countries are not allowed to fly

,no-'frills adj. [only before noun] (especially of a service or product) including only the basic features, without anything that is unnecessary, especially things added to make something more attractive or comfortable: a no-frills airline

,no-'good adj. [only before noun] (slang) (of a person) bad or useless

Noh (also **No**) /noʊ/ noun [U] traditional Japanese theater in which songs, dance, and MIME are performed by people wearing MASKS

,no-'hitter noun a baseball game in which the PITCHER (= the player who throws the ball) does not allow the players on the opposing team to get any hits: Friday night he pitched a no-hitter.

noise 🔑 /nɔɪz/ noun
1 [C, U] a sound, especially when it is loud, unpleasant, or disturbing: a rattling noise ◆ What's that noise? ◆ Don't make a noise. ◆ They were making too much noise. ◆ I was woken by the noise of a car starting up. ◆ We had to shout above the noise of the traffic. ◆ to reduce noise levels **2** [U] (technical) extra electrical or electronic signals that are not part of the signal that is being broadcast or TRANSMITTED and that may damage it **3** [U] information that is not wanted and that can make it difficult for the important or useful information to be seen clearly: There is some noise in the data that needs to be reduced.
IDM make a noise (about sth) (informal) to complain loudly make noises (about sth) (informal) **1** to talk in an indirect way about something that you think you might do: The company has been making noises about closing several

factories. **2** to complain about something make soothing, encouraging, reassuring, etc. noises to make remarks of the kind mentioned, even when that is not what you really think: He made all the right noises at the meeting yesterday (= he said what people wanted to hear).

WHICH WORD?

noise ● sound

■ **Noise** is usually loud and unpleasant. It can be countable or uncountable: Try not to make so much noise. ◆ What a terrible noise!
■ **Sound** is a countable noun and means something that you hear: All she could hear was the sound of the waves. You do not use words like much or a lot of with **sound**.

noise·less /ˈnɔɪzləs/ adj. (formal) making little or no noise **SYN** SILENT: He moved with noiseless steps. ▶ noise·less·ly adv.

noi·some /ˈnɔɪsəm/ adj. (formal) extremely unpleasant or offensive: noisome smells

nois·y 🔑 /ˈnɔɪzi/ adj. (nois·i·er, nois·i·est)
1 making a lot of noise: noisy children/traffic/crowds ◆ a noisy protest (= when people shout) ◆ The engine is very noisy at high speed. **2** full of noise: a noisy classroom ▶ nois·i·ly /-zəli/ adv.: The children were playing noisily upstairs.

no·mad /ˈnoʊmæd/ noun a member of a community that moves with its animals from place to place ▶ no·mad·ic /noʊˈmædɪk/ adj.: nomadic tribes ◆ (figurative) the nomadic life of a foreign correspondent

'no-man's-,land noun [U, sing.] an area of land between the borders of two countries or between two armies, that is not controlled by either

nom de guerre /ˌnɑm də ˈɡɛr/ noun (pl. noms de guerre /ˌnɑm də ˈɡɛr/) (from French, formal) a false name that is used, for example, by someone who belongs to a military organization that is not official

nom de plume /ˌnɑm də ˈplum/ noun (pl. noms de plume /ˌnɑm də ˈplum/) (from French) a name used by a writer instead of their real name **SYN** PEN-NAME, PSEUDONYM

no·men·cla·ture /ˈnoʊmənˌkleɪtʃər/ noun [U, C] (formal) a system of naming things, especially in a branch of science

nom·i·nal /ˈnɑmənl/ adj. **1** being something in name only, and not in reality: the nominal leader of the party ◆ He remained in nominal control of the business for another ten years. **2** (of a sum of money) very small and much less than the normal cost or change **SYN** TOKEN: We only pay a nominal rent. **3** (grammar) connected with a noun or nouns ▶ nom·i·nal·ly /-nəli/ adv.: He was nominally in charge of the company.

nom·i·nal·ize /ˈnɑmənəˌlaɪz/ verb ~ sth (grammar) to form a noun from a verb or adjective, for example "truth" from "true" ▶ nom·i·nal·i·za·tion /ˌnɑmənələˈzeɪʃn/ noun [U, C]

nom·i·nate /ˈnɑməˌneɪt/ verb **1** to formally suggest that someone be chosen for an important role, prize, position, etc. **SYN** PROPOSE: ~ sb (for sth) She has been nominated for the presidency. ◆ ~ sb (as) sth | ~ sb + noun He was nominated (as) best actor. ◆ ~ sb to do sth I nominated Paul to take on the role of treasurer. **2** to choose someone to do a particular job **SYN** APPOINT: ~ sb (to/as sth) I have been nominated to the committee. ◆ ~ sb to do sth She was nominated to speak on our behalf. **3** ~ sth (as sth) to choose a time, date, or title for something **SYN** SELECT: December 1 has been nominated as the day of the election.

nom·i·na·tion /ˌnɑməˈneɪʃn/ noun [U, C] the act of suggesting or choosing someone as a candidate in an election, or for a job or an award; the fact of being suggested for this: Membership in the club is by nomination only. ◆ He won the nomination as Democratic candidate for the presidency. ◆ They opposed her nomination to the post of Deputy Director. ◆ He has had nine Oscar nominations.

nom·i·na·tive /ˈnɑmənətɪv/ (also **sub·jec·tive**) *noun* (*grammar*) (in some languages) the form of a noun, a pronoun, or an adjective when it is the subject of a verb ⊃ compare ABLATIVE, ACCUSATIVE, DATIVE, GENITIVE, VOCATIVE ▶ **nom·i·na·tive** *adj.*: *nominative pronouns*

nom·i·nee /ˌnɑməˈni/ *noun* **1** a person who has been formally suggested for a job, a prize, etc.: *a presidential nominee* ◆ *an Oscar nominee* **2** (*business*) a person in whose name money is invested in a company, etc.

non- /nɑn/ *prefix* (in nouns, adjectives, and adverbs) not: *nonsense* ◆ *nonfiction* ◆ *nonalcoholic* ◆ *nonprofit* ◆ *noncommittally*

non·a·ge·nar·i·an /ˌnɑnədʒəˈnɛriən; ˌnoʊnə-/ *noun* a person who is between 90 and 99 years old ▶ **non·a·ge·nar·i·an** *adj.*

non·ag·gres·sion /ˌnɑnəˈɡrɛʃn/ *noun* [U] (often used as an adjective) a relationship between two countries that have agreed not to attack each other: *a policy of nonaggression* ◆ *a nonaggression pact/treaty*

non·al·co·hol·ic /ˌnɑnælkəˈhɔlɪk; -ˈhɑlɪk/ *adj.* (of a drink) not containing any alcohol: *a nonalcoholic drink* ◆ *Can I have something nonalcoholic?*

non·a·ligned /ˌnɑnəˈlaɪnd/ *adj.* not providing support for or receiving support from any of the powerful countries in the world ▶ **non·a·lign·ment** /-əˈlaɪnmənt/ *noun* [U]: *a policy of nonalignment*

'no-name *adj.* **1** not famous: *a no-name comedian* **2** not having a BRAND NAME (= a name given to a product): *cheap, no-name soda*

non·ap·pear·ance /ˌnɑnəˈpɪrəns/ *noun* [U] (*formal*) failure to be in a place where people expect to see you

non·at·tend·ance /ˌnɑnəˈtɛndəns/ *noun* [U] failure to go somewhere where you are expected

non·be·liev·er /ˌnɑnbɪˈlivər/ *noun* a person who lacks religious faith or does not believe in a certain philosophy: *an effort to convert nonbelievers* ANT BELIEVER ⊃ compare UNBELIEVER

non·bind·ing /ˌnɑnˈbaɪndɪŋ/ *adj.* that not does not have to be obeyed because it is not ordered by law: *We have a nonbinding agreement to sell the business.* ANT BINDING

non·bi·o·de·grad·a·ble /ˌnɑnˌbaɪoʊdɪˈɡreɪdəbl/ *adj.* a substance or chemical that is **nonbiodegradable** cannot be changed to a harmless natural state by the action of bacteria, and may therefore damage the environment ANT BIODEGRADABLE

nonce /nɑns/ *adj.* a **nonce** word or expression is one that is invented for one particular occasion

non·cha·lant /ˌnɑnʃəˈlɑnt/ *adj.* behaving in a calm and relaxed way; giving the impression that you are not feeling any anxiety SYN CASUAL: *to appear/look/sound nonchalant* ◆ *"It'll be fine," she replied, with a nonchalant shrug.* ▶ **non·cha·lance** /-ˈlɑns/ *noun* [U] SYN INSOUCIANCE: *an air of nonchalance* **non·cha·lant·ly** *adv.*: *He was leaning nonchalantly against the wall.*

non·ci·ti·zen /ˌnɑnˈsɪtəzn/ *noun* = ALIEN

non·com·bat·ant /ˌnɑnkəmˈbætnt/ *noun* **1** a member of the armed forces who does not actually fight in a war, for example an army doctor **2** in a war, a person who is not a member of the armed forces SYN CIVILIAN ⊃ compare COMBATANT

noncommissioned officer /ˌnɑnkəˌmɪʃnd ˈɔfəsər; -ˈɑfə-/ *noun* (*abbr.* NCO) a soldier in the army, etc. who has a rank such as SERGEANT or CORPORAL, but not a high rank ⊃ compare COMMISSIONED OFFICER

non·com·mit·tal /ˌnɑnkəˈmɪtl/ *adj.* not giving an opinion; not showing which side of an argument you agree with: *a noncommittal reply/tone* ◆ *The doctor was noncommittal about when I could drive again.* ⊃ see also COMMIT ▶ **non·com·mit·tal·ly** *adv.*

non·com·pli·ance /ˌnɑnkəmˈplaɪəns/ *noun* [U] ~ **(with sth)** the fact of failing or refusing to obey a rule: *There are penalties for noncompliance with the fire regulations.* ANT COMPLIANCE

non com·pos men·tis /ˌnɑn ˌkɑmpəs ˈmɛntəs/ (also ˌnon ˈcompos) *adj.* (*formal*) not in a normal mental state ANT COMPOS MENTIS

non·con·form·ist AWL /ˌnɑnkənˈfɔrmɪst/ *noun* a person who does not follow normal ways of thinking or behaving ▶ **non·con·form·ist** *adj.*

non·con·form·i·ty AWL /ˌnɑnkənˈfɔrməti/ (also **non·con·form·ism** /-kənˈfɔrmɪzəm/) *noun* [U] the fact of not following normal ways of thinking and behaving

non·con·trib·u·to·ry /ˌnɑnkənˈtrɪbyəˌtɔri/ *adj.* (of an insurance or pension plan) paid for by the employer and not the employee ANT CONTRIBUTORY

non·con·tro·ver·sial /ˌnɑnkɑntrəˈvərʃl/ *adj.* not causing, or not likely to cause, any disagreement ANT CONTROVERSIAL HELP This is not as strong as **uncontroversial**, which is more common.

non·co·op·er·a·tion /ˌnɑnkoʊˌɑpəˈreɪʃn/ *noun* [U] refusal to help a person in authority by doing what they have asked you to do, especially as a form of protest: *A strike is unlikely, but some forms of noncooperation are being considered.*

non·count /ˌnɑnˈkaʊnt/ *adj.* (*grammar*) = UNCOUNTABLE

non·cus·to·di·al /ˌnɑnkʌˈstoʊdiəl/ *adj.* [only before noun] (*law*) (of a parent) not having CUSTODY of a child ANT CUSTODIAL

non·dair·y /ˌnɑnˈdɛri/ *adj.* [only before noun] not made with milk or cream: *a nondairy whipped topping*

non·de·fin·ing /ˌnɑndɪˈfaɪnɪŋ/ *adj.* = NONRESTRICTIVE

non·de·nom·i·na·tion·al /ˌnɑndɪˌnɑməˈneɪʃənl/ *adj.* open or acceptable to people of any religious group, especially any branch of the Christian Church: *a nondenominational memorial service* ANT DENOMINATIONAL

non·de·script /ˌnɑndɪˈskrɪpt/ *adj.* (*disapproving*) having no interesting or unusual features or qualities SYN DULL

none /nʌn/ *pron., adv.*

● **pron.** ~ **(of sb/sth)** not one of a group of people or things; not any: *None of these pens work.* ◆ *We have three sons but none of them live nearby.* ◆ *We saw several houses but none we really liked.* ◆ *Tickets for Friday? Sorry we've got none left.* ◆ *He told me all the news but none of it was very exciting.* ◆ *"Is there any more milk?" "No, none at all."* ◆ (*formal*) *Everybody liked him but none* (= no one) *more than I.* IDM **none but** (*literary*) only: *None but he knew the truth.* **none other than** used to emphasize who or what someone or something is, when this is surprising: *Her first customer was none other than Mrs. Obama.* **have/want none of sth** to refuse to accept something: *I offered to pay but he was having none of it.* **none the less** = NONETHELESS

● **adv. 1** used with *the* and a comparative to mean "not at all": *She told me what it meant at great length but I'm afraid I'm none the wiser.* ◆ *He seems none the worse for the experience.* **2** used with *too* and an adjective or adverb to mean "not at all" or "not very": *She was looking none too pleased.*

GRAMMAR

none of

- When you use **none of** with an uncountable noun, the verb is singular: *None of the work was done.*
- When you use **none of** with a plural noun, the verb is plural: *None of the trains are going to Boston.*
- When you use **none of** with a noun referring to a group of people or things, the verb is usually singular: *None of her family has been to college.*

non·en·ti·ty /nɑnˈɛntəti/ *noun* (*pl.* **non·en·ti·ties**) (*disapproving*) a person without any special qualities, who has not achieved anything important SYN NOBODY

non·es·sen·tial /ˌnɑnɪˈsɛnʃl/ *adj.* [usually before noun] not completely necessary ➔ compare ESSENTIAL **HELP** This is not as strong as **inessential** and is more common. **Inessential** can suggest disapproval. ▶ **non·es·sen·tial** *noun* [usually pl.]: *I have no money for nonessentials.*

no·net /nou'nɛt/ *noun* **1** a group of nine people or things, especially nine musicians **2** a piece of music for nine singers or musicians

none·the·less **AWL** /ˌnʌnðə'lɛs/ also ˌnone the 'less *adv.* (*formal*) despite this fact **SYN** NEVERTHELESS: *The book is too long but, nonetheless, informative and entertaining.* ◆ *The problems are not serious. Nonetheless, we shall need to tackle them soon.* ➔ language bank at NEVERTHELESS

non·e·vent /ˌnɑni'vɛnt/ *noun* (*informal*) an event that was expected to be interesting, exciting, and popular but is in fact very disappointing **SYN** ANTICLIMAX

non·ex·ist·ent /ˌnɑnɪg'zɪstənt/ *adj.* not existing; not real: *a nonexistent problem* ◆ "*How's your social life?*" "*Nonexistent, I'm afraid.*" ◆ *Hospital beds were scarce and medicines were practically nonexistent.* ➔ compare EXISTENT ▶ **non·ex·ist·ence** /-təns/ *noun* [U]

non·fat /ˌnɑn'fæt/ *adj.* [usually before noun] containing no fat: *nonfat yogurt* ➔ compare LOW-FAT

non·fic·tion /ˌnɑn'fɪkʃn/ *noun* [U] books, articles, or texts about real facts, people, and events: *I prefer reading nonfiction.* ◆ *the nonfiction section of the library* **ANT** FICTION

non·fi·nite /ˌnɑn'faɪnaɪt/ *adj.* (*grammar*) a **nonfinite** verb form or **clause** does not show a particular tense, PERSON, or NUMBER **ANT** FINITE

non·flam·ma·ble /ˌnɑn'flæməbl/ *adj.* not likely to burn easily: *nonflammable nightwear* **ANT** FLAMMABLE

non·gov·ern·men·tal /ˌnɑnˌgʌvər'mɛntl; -ˌgʌvərn-/ *adj.* [only before noun] (especially of an organization) not part of or associated with any government: *nongovernmental charities* ➔ compare NGO, GOVERNMENTAL

non·grad·a·ble /ˌnɑn'greɪdəbl/ *adj.* (*grammar*) (of an adjective) that cannot be used in the comparative and superlative forms, or be used with words like "very" and "less" **ANT** GRADABLE

non·hu·man /ˌnɑn'hyumən/ *adj.* not human: *similarities between human and nonhuman animals* ➔ compare HUMAN, INHUMAN

non·in·ter·ven·tion /ˌnɑnɪntər'vɛnʃn/ (also **non·in·ter·fer·ence** /ˌnɑnɪntər'fɪrəns/) *noun* [U] the policy or practice of not becoming involved in other people's disagreements, especially those of foreign countries ▶ **non·in·ter·ven·tion·ism** /-ʃə,nɪzəm/ *noun* [U] **non·in·ter·ven·tion·ist** /-ʃənɪst/ *adj.*

non·in·va·sive /ˌnɑnɪn'veɪsɪv/ *adj.* (of medical treatment) not involving cutting into the body

non·is·sue /ˌnɑn'ɪʃu/ *noun* a subject of little or no importance

non·judg·men·tal (also **non·judge·men·tal**) /ˌnɑndʒʌdʒ-'mɛntl/ *adj.* avoiding moral judgments; not quick to judge people and criticize them: *You need to be a more nonjudgmental listener.* **ANT** JUDGMENTAL

non·lin·e·ar /ˌnɑn'lɪniər/ *adj.* (*technical*) that does not develop from one thing to another in a single smooth series of stages **ANT** LINEAR

non·ma·lig·nant /ˌnɑnmə'lɪgnənt/ *adj.* (of a TUMOR) not caused by cancer and not likely to be dangerous **SYN** BENIGN **ANT** MALIGNANT

non·na·tive /ˌnɑn'neɪtɪv/ *adj.* **1** (of animals, plants, etc.) not existing naturally in a place but coming from somewhere else **2** a **nonnative** speaker of a language is one who has not spoken it from the time they first learned to talk **ANT** NATIVE

non·ne·go·tia·ble /ˌnɑnnɪ'gouʃəbl/ *adj.* **1** that cannot be discussed or changed **2** (of a check, etc.) that cannot be changed for money by anyone except the person whose name is on it **ANT** NEGOTIABLE

'**no-no** *noun* [sing.] (*informal*) a thing or a way of behaving that is not acceptable in a particular situation

non·ob·serv·ance /ˌnɑnəb'zərvəns/ *noun* [U] (*formal*) the failure to keep or to obey a rule, custom, etc. **ANT** OBSERVANCE

ˌno-'nonsense *adj.* [only before noun] simple and direct; only paying attention to important and necessary things

non·pa·reil /ˌnɑnpə'rɛl/ *noun* [sing.] (*formal*) a person or thing that is better than others in a particular area

non·par·ti·san /ˌnɑn'pɑrtəzn; -sn/ *adj.* [usually before noun] not supporting the ideas of one particular political party or group of people strongly **ANT** PARTISAN

non·pay·ment /ˌnɑn'peɪmənt/ *noun* [U] (*formal*) failure to pay a debt, a tax, rent, etc.

non·per·son /ˌnɑn'pərsn/ *noun* (*pl.* **non·per·sons**) a person who is thought not to be important, or who is ignored

non·plussed (also **non·plused**) /ˌnɑn'plʌst/ *adj.* so surprised and confused that you do not know what to do or say **SYN** DUMBFOUNDED

non·pre·scrip·tion /ˌnɑnprɪ'skrɪpʃn/ *adj.* (of drugs) that you can buy directly without a PRESCRIPTION (= a special form from a doctor)

non·pro·fes·sion·al /ˌnɑnprə'fɛʃənl/ *adj.* **1** having a job that does not need a high level of education or special training; connected with a job of this kind: *training for nonprofessional staff* **2** doing something as a hobby rather than as a paid job: *nonprofessional actors* ➔ compare PROFESSIONAL, UNPROFESSIONAL ➔ see also AMATEUR

non·prof·it /ˌnɑn'prɑfət/ (also ˌnot-for-'profit) *adj.* (of an organization) without the aim of making a profit: *an independent nonprofit organization* ◆ *The center is run on a nonprofit basis.* ◆ *The charity is nonprofit.* ▶ **non·prof·it** *noun*: *a coalition of businesses, nonprofits, and government agencies*

non·pro·lif·er·a·tion /ˌnɑnprə,lɪfə'reɪʃn/ *noun* [U] a limit to the increase in the number of nuclear and chemical weapons that are produced

non·pro·pri·e·tar·y /ˌnɑnprə'praɪə,tɛri/ *adj.* not made by or belonging to a particular company: *nonproprietary medicines* **ANT** PROPRIETARY

non·re·fund·a·ble /ˌnɑnrɪ'fʌndəbl/ (also **non·re·turn·able**) *adj.* (of a sum of money) that cannot be returned: *a nonrefundable deposit* ◆ *a nonrefundable ticket* (= you cannot return it and get your money back)

non·re·new·a·ble /ˌnɑnrɪ'nuəbl/ *adj.* **1** (of natural resources such as gas or oil) that cannot be replaced after use **2** that cannot be continued or repeated for a further period of time after it has ended: *a nonrenewable contract* **ANT** RENEWABLE

non·res·i·dent /ˌnɑn'rɛzədənt; -dɛnt/ *adj., noun*
● *adj.* (*formal*) **1** (of a person or company) not living or located permanently in a particular place or country **2** not living in the place where you work or in a house that you own **3** not staying at a particular hotel: *Nonresident guests are welcome to use the hotel swimming pool.*

● *noun* **1** a person who does not live permanently in a particular country **2** a person not staying at a particular hotel

non·res·i·den·tial /ˌnɑnrɛzə'dɛnʃl/ *adj.* **1** that is not used for people to live in **2** that does not require you to live in the place where you work or study: *a nonresidential course*

ˌnon·re·stric·tive /ˌnɑnrɪ'strɪktɪv/ *adj.* (also **non·de·fin·ing**) (*grammar*) (of RELATIVE CLAUSES) giving extra information about a noun phrase, inside commas in writing or in a particular INTONATION in speech. In "My brother, who lives in Austin, is coming to Florida with us," the part between the commas is a nonrestrictive relative clause. ➔ compare RESTRICTIVE

non·re·turn·a·ble /ˌnɑnrɪ'tərnəbl/ *adj.* **1** = NONREFUNDABLE **2** that you cannot give back, for example to a store, to be used again; that will not be given back to you:

| h **h**at | m **m**an | n **n**o | ŋ si**ng** | l **l**eg | r **r**ed | y **y**es | w **w**et |

nonreturnable bottles ◆ *a nonreturnable deposit* **ANT** RETURNABLE

non·sci·en·tif·ic /ˌnɑnsaɪən'tɪfɪk/ *adj.* not involving or connected with science or scientific methods ➔ **compare** SCIENTIFIC, UNSCIENTIFIC

non·sec·tar·i·an /ˌnɑnsɛk'tɛriən/ *adj.* not involving or connected with a specific religion or religious group: *a nonsectarian school* **ANT** SECTARIAN

non·sense 🔑 /'nɑnsɛns; -səns/ *noun* [U]
1 ideas, statements, or beliefs that you think are ridiculous or not true: *Reports that he has resigned are nonsense.* ◆ *You're talking nonsense!* ◆ *"I won't go." "Nonsense! You must go!"* ◆ *It's nonsense to say they don't care.* **2** silly or unacceptable behavior: *The new teacher won't stand for any nonsense.* ➔ **see also** NO-NONSENSE **3** spoken or written words that have no meaning or make no sense: *Most of the translation he did for me was complete nonsense.* ◆ *a book of children's nonsense poems*
IDM **make nonsense of sth** to reduce the value of something by a lot; to make something seem ridiculous: *If people can bribe police officers, it makes complete nonsense of the legal system.* ➔ **more at** STUFF *n.*

'nonsense ˌword *noun* a word with no meaning

non·sen·si·cal /nɑn'sɛnsɪkl/ *adj.* ridiculous; with no meaning **SYN** ABSURD

non se·qui·tur /ˌnɑn 'sɛkwətər/ *noun* (from *Latin, formal*) a statement that does not seem to follow what has just been said in any natural or logical way

non·slip /ˌnɑn'slɪp/ *adj.* that helps to prevent someone or something from slipping; that does not slip: *a nonslip bath mat*

non·smok·er /ˌnɑn'smoʊkər/ *noun* a person who does not smoke **ANT** SMOKER

non·smok·ing /ˌnɑn'smoʊkɪŋ/ *adj.* [usually before noun]
1 (of a place) where people are not allowed to smoke: *a nonsmoking area in a restaurant* **2** (of a person) who does not smoke: *She's a nonsmoking, nondrinking fitness fanatic.* ▶ **non·smok·ing** *noun* [U]: *Nonsmoking is now the norm in most workplaces.*

non·spe·cif·ic /ˌnɑnspə'sɪfɪk/ *adj.* [usually before noun]
1 not definite or clearly defined; general: *The candidate's speech was nonspecific.* **2** (*medical*) (of pain, a disease, etc.) with more than one possible cause

non·stand·ard /ˌnɑn'stændərd/ *adj.* **1** (of language) not considered correct by most educated people: *nonstandard dialects* ◆ *nonstandard English* ➔ **compare** STANDARD **2** not the usual size, type, etc.: *The paper was of nonstandard size.*

non·start·er /ˌnɑn'stɑrtər/ *noun* (*informal*) a thing or a person that has no chance of success: *As a business proposition, it's a nonstarter.*

non·stick /ˌnɑn'stɪk/ *adj.* [usually before noun] (of a pan or a surface) covered with a substance that prevents food from sticking to it

non·stop /ˌnɑn'stɑp/ *adj.* **1** (of a train, a trip, etc.) without any stops **SYN** DIRECT: *a nonstop flight to Tokyo* ◆ *a nonstop train/service* **2** without any pauses or stops **SYN** CONTINUOUS: *nonstop entertainment/work* ▶ **non·stop** *adv.*: *We flew nonstop from Paris to Chicago.* ◆ *It rained nonstop all week.*

non·threat·en·ing /ˌnɑn'θrɛtn·ɪŋ/ *adj.* not likely to frighten anyone; not threatening: *Use a nonthreatening tone of voice.* **ANT** THREATENING

non·tox·ic /ˌnɑn'tɑksɪk/ *adj.* not poisonous or not harmful to your health: *The insect bait is nontoxic to pets and humans.* ◆ *a nontoxic paint* **ANT** TOXIC

non·tra·di·tion·al /ˌnɑntrə'dɪʃənl/ *adj.* new and different from what was done or considered usual in the past: *students from nontraditional backgrounds* ◆ *nontraditional occupations for women* **ANT** TRADITIONAL

non·un·ion /ˌnɑn'yunyən/ (also *less frequent* ˌnon-'union-ized) *adj.* [usually before noun] **1** not belonging to a LABOR UNION: *nonunion labor/workers* **2** (of a business, company, etc.) not accepting LABOR UNIONS or employing LABOR UNION members

non·ver·bal /ˌnɑn'vərbl/ *adj.* [usually before noun] not involving words or speech: *nonverbal communication*

non·vi·o·lence /ˌnɑn'vaɪələns/ *noun* [U] the policy of using peaceful methods, not force, to bring about political or social change

non·vi·o·lent /ˌnɑn'vaɪələnt/ *adj.* **1** using peaceful methods, not force, to bring about political or social change: *nonviolent resistance* ◆ *a nonviolent protest* **2** not involving force, or injury to someone: *nonviolent crimes*

non·white /ˌnɑn'waɪt/ *noun* a person who is not a member of a race of people who have white skin ▶ **non·white** *adj.*

noo·dle /'nudl/ *noun* **1** [usually pl.] a long thin strip of PASTA, used especially in Chinese and Italian cooking: *chicken noodle soup* ◆ *Would you prefer rice or noodles?* **2** [C] (*old-fashioned, slang*) your head; your brain

nook /nʊk/ *noun* a small quiet place or corner that is sheltered or hidden from other people: *a shady nook in the garden* ◆ *dark woods full of secret nooks and crannies*
IDM **every nook and cranny** (*informal*) every part of a place; every aspect of a situation

noon /nun/ *noun* [U] 12 o'clock in the middle of the day **SYN** MIDDAY: *We should be there by noon.* ◆ *The conference opens at 12 noon on Saturday.* ◆ *the noon deadline for the end of hostilities* ◆ *I'm leaving on the noon train.* ◆ *the glaring light of high noon* **IDM** **see** MORNING

noon·day /'nundeɪ/ *adj.* [only before noun] (*old-fashioned* or *literary*) happening or appearing at noon: *the noonday sun*

'no one 🔑 (also **no·bod·y**) *pron.*
not anyone; no person: *No one was at home.* ◆ *There was no one else around.* ◆ *We were told to speak to no one.* **HELP** No one is much more common than **nobody** in written English.

noon·tide /'nuntaɪd/ *noun* [U] (*literary*) around 12 o'clock in the middle of the day

noose /nus/ *noun* a circle that is tied in a rope with a knot that allows the circle to get smaller as the rope is pulled: *a hangman's noose* ◆ (*figurative*) *His debts were a noose around his neck.*

nope /noʊp/ *exclamation* (*informal*) used to say "no": *"Have you seen my pen?" "Nope."*

'no place *adv.* (*informal*) = NOWHERE: *I have no place else to go.*

nor 🔑 /nɔr/ *conj.*
1 **neither… nor…** | **not… nor…** and not: *She seemed neither surprised nor worried.* ◆ *He wasn't there on Monday. Nor on Tuesday, for that matter.* ◆ (*formal*) *Not a building nor a tree was left standing.* **2** used before a positive verb to agree with something negative that has just been said: *She doesn't like them, nor does Jeff.* ◆ *"I'm not going." "Nor am I."*

Nor·dic /'nɔrdɪk/ *adj.* **1** of or connected with the countries of Scandinavia, Finland, and Iceland **2** typical of a member of a European race of people who are tall and have blue eyes and blond hair

ˌNordic 'walking *noun* [U] the sport of walking with special poles attached to your wrists

nor'easter /ˌnɔr'istər/ (also **northeaster** /ˌnɔrθ'istər/) *noun* a strong wind or storm that comes from the northeast, especially in New England

norm **AWL** /nɔrm/ *noun, verb*
● *noun* **1** often **the norm** [sing.] a situation or a pattern of behavior that is usual or expected **SYN** RULE: *a departure from the norm* ◆ *Older parents seem to be the norm rather than the exception nowadays.* **2** **norms** [pl.] standards of behavior that are typical of or accepted within a particular group or society: *social/cultural norms* **3** [C] a required or agreed standard, amount, etc.: *detailed education norms for children of particular ages*

• **verb** ~ **sth** to adjust something so that it is of the required standard; to establish a required or agreed standard for something: *You can use the information to norm the test.* ◆ *to norm the practice of trading on the Internet*

nor·mal 🔑 **AWL** /ˈnɔːml/ *adj., noun*
• *adj.* **1** typical, usual, or ordinary; what you would expect: *perfectly* (= completely) *normal* ◆ *Her temperature is normal.* ◆ *It's normal to feel tired after such a long trip.* ◆ *Divorce is complicated enough in normal circumstances, but this situation is even worse.* ◆ *Under normal circumstances, I would say "yes."* ◆ *He should be able to lead a perfectly normal life.* ◆ *In the normal course of events I wouldn't go to that part of town.* ◆ *We are open during normal office hours.* **2** not suffering from any mental DISORDER: *People who commit such crimes aren't normal.* **ANT** ABNORMAL **IDM** see PER
• *noun* [U] the usual or average state, level, or standard: *above/below normal* ◆ *Things soon returned to normal.*

normal distri·bution *noun* (*statistics*) the usual way in which a particular feature varies among a large number of things or people, represented on a GRAPH by a line that rises to a high SYMMETRICAL curve in the middle ⊃ compare BELL CURVE

nor·mal·i·ty **AWL** /nɔːˈmæləti/ (also **nor·mal·cy** /ˈnɔːmlsi/) *noun* [U] a situation where everything is normal or as you would expect it to be: *They are hoping for a return to normality now that the war is over.*

nor·mal·ize **AWL** /ˈnɔːrməˌlaɪz/ *verb* [T, I] ~ **(sth)** (*formal*) to fit or make something fit a normal pattern or condition: *a lotion to normalize oily skin* ◆ *The two countries agreed to normalize relations* (= return to a normal, friendly relationship, for example after a disagreement or war). ◆ *It took time until the political situation had normalized.* ▶ **nor·mal·i·za·tion** **AWL** /ˌnɔːrmələˈzeɪʃn/ *noun* [U]: *the normalization of relations*

nor·mal·ly 🔑 **AWL** /ˈnɔːrməli/ *adv.*
1 usually; in normal circumstances: *I'm not normally allowed to stay out late.* ◆ *It's normally much warmer than this in July.* ◆ *It normally takes 20 minutes to get there.* **2** in the usual or ordinary way: *Her heart is beating normally.* ◆ *Just try to behave normally.*

Nor·man /ˈnɔːrmən/ *adj.* **1** used to describe the style of ARCHITECTURE in Britain in the 11th and 12th centuries that developed from the ROMANESQUE style: *a Norman church/castle* **2** connected with the Normans (= the people from northern France who defeated the English in 1066 and then ruled the country): *the Norman Conquest*

nor·ma·tive /ˈnɔːrmətɪv/ *adj.* (*formal*) describing or setting standards or rules of behavior: *a normative approach*

Norse /nɔːrs/ *noun* [U] the Norwegian language, especially in an ancient form, or the Scandinavian language group

north 🔑 /nɔːrθ/ *noun, adj., adv.*
• *noun* [U, sing.] (*abbr.* N., N, No.) **1** (also **the north**) the direction that is on your left when you watch the sun rise; one of the four main points of the COMPASS: *Which way is north?* ◆ *cold winds coming from the north* ◆ *Mount Kenya is to the north of* (= further north than) *Nairobi.* ⊃ picture at COMPASS ⊃ compare EAST, SOUTH, WEST ⊃ see also MAGNETIC NORTH, TRUE NORTH **2 the north** the northern part of a country, a region, or the world: *birds migrating from the north* ◆ *The temperature is much warmer in the north* (= of the state) *than in the south.* **3 the North** the northeastern states of the U.S. that fought against the South in the American Civil War **4 the North** the richer and more developed countries of the world, especially in N. America and Europe
• *adj.* [only before noun] **1** (*abbr.* N., N) in or toward the north: *North Minneapolis* ◆ *the north bank of the river* **2** a **north wind** blows from the north ⊃ compare NORTHERLY
• *adv.* **1** toward the north: *The house faces north.* **2** ~ **of sth** nearer to the north than something: *They live ten miles north of Boston.* **3** ~ **of sth** (*informal* or *finance*) more or higher

than something: *The estimated value is north of $5.4 billion.* **ANT** SOUTH
IDM **up north** (*informal*) to or in the north of a country: *They've gone to live up north.*

North A·mer·i·ca *noun* [U] the continent consisting of Canada, the United States, Mexico, the countries of Central America, and Greenland

the North At·lan·tic 'Drift *noun* [sing.] (*technical*) a current of warm water in the Atlantic Ocean that has the effect of making the climate of N.W. Europe warmer

north·bound /ˈnɔːrθbaʊnd/ *adj.* traveling or leading toward the north: *northbound traffic* ◆ *the northbound lane of the highway*

north·east /ˌnɔːrθˈiːst/ *noun* usually **the northeast** [sing.] (*abbr.* N.E., NE) the direction or region at an equal distance between north and east ⊃ picture at COMPASS ▶ **north·east** *adv., adj.*

north·east·er·ly /ˌnɔːrθˈiːstərli/ *adj.* **1** [only before noun] in or toward the northeast: *traveling in a northeasterly direction* **2** [usually before noun] (of winds) blowing from the northeast

north·east·ern /ˌnɔːrθˈiːstərn/ *adj.* [only before noun] (*abbr.* N.E., NE) connected with the northeast

north·east·ward /ˌnɔːrθˈiːstwərd/ (also **north·east·wards**) *adv.* toward the northeast ▶ **north·east·ward** *adj.*

north·er·ly /ˈnɔːrðərli/ *adj., noun*
• *adj.* **1** [only before noun] in or toward the north: *traveling in a northerly direction* **2** [usually before noun] (of winds) blowing from the north: *a northerly breeze* ⊃ compare NORTH
• *noun* (*pl.* **north·er·lies**) a wind that blows from the north

north·ern 🔑 /ˈnɔːrðərn/ also **Northern** *adj.* [usually before noun] (*abbr.* N., N, No.)
located in the north or facing north; connected with or typical of the north part of the world or a region: *the northern slopes of the mountains* ◆ *northern New York State*

north·ern·er /ˈnɔːrðərnər/ *noun* a person who comes from or lives in the northern part of a country

the Northern 'Lights *noun* [pl.] (also **au·rora bore·alis**) bands of colored light, mainly green and red, that are sometimes seen in the sky at night in the most northern countries of the world

north·ern·most /ˈnɔːrðərnˌmoʊst/ *adj.* [usually before noun] farthest north: *the northernmost city in the world*

north-north'east *noun* [sing.] (*abbr.* N.N.E., NNE) the direction at an equal distance between north and northeast ▶ **north-north'east** *adv.*

north-north'west *noun* [sing.] (*abbr.* N.N.W., NNW) the direction at an equal distance between north and northwest ▶ **north-north'west** *adv.*

the North 'Pole *noun* [sing.] the point on the surface of the earth that is farthest north ⊃ picture at EARTH

north·ward /ˈnɔːrθwərd/ (also **north·wards**) *adv.* toward the north: *to go/look/turn northward* ▶ **north·ward** *adj.*: *in a northward direction*

north·west /ˌnɔːrθˈwɛst/ *noun* usually **the northwest** [sing.] (*abbr.* N.W., NW) the direction or region at an equal distance between north and west ⊃ picture at COMPASS ▶ **north·west** *adv., adj.*

north·west·er·ly /ˌnɔːrθˈwɛstərli/ *adj.* **1** [only before noun] in or toward the northwest **2** (of winds) blowing from the northwest

north·west·ern /ˌnɔːrθˈwɛstərn/ *adj.* [only before noun] (*abbr.* N.W., NW) connected with the northwest

north·west·ward /ˌnɔːrθˈwɛstwərd/ (also **north·west·wards**) *adv.* toward the northwest ▶ **north·west·ward** *adj.*

Nor·way rat /ˈnɔːrweɪ ˈræt/ *noun* = BROWN RAT

nose 🔑 /noʊz/ *noun, verb*
• *noun* **1** [C] the part of the face that sticks out above the

mouth, used for breathing and smelling things: *He broke his nose in the fight.* ♦ *She wrinkled her nose in disgust.* ♦ *He blew his nose* (= cleared it by blowing strongly into a HANDKERCHIEF). ♦ *a stuffed-up/runny nose* ♦ *Stop picking your nose!* (= removing dried MUCUS from it with your finger) ⊃ picture at BODY ⊃ collocations at PHYSICAL ⊃ see also NASAL, POPE'S NOSE, ROMAN NOSE **2** -nosed (in adjectives) having the type of nose mentioned: *red-nosed* ♦ *large-nosed* ⊃ see also HARD-NOSED **3** [C] the front part of a plane, SPACECRAFT, etc. ⊃ picture at PLANE **4** [sing.] **a ~ for sth** a special ability for finding or recognizing something **SYN** INSTINCT: *As a journalist, she has always had a nose for a good story.* **5** [sing.] a sense of smell: *a dog with a good nose* **6** [sing.] (of wine) a characteristic smell **SYN** BOUQUET
IDM **cut off your nose to spite your face** (*informal*) to do something when you are angry that is meant to harm someone else but that also harms you **have your nose in sth** (*informal*) to be reading something and giving it all your attention **keep your nose clean** (*informal*) to avoid doing anything wrong or illegal: *Since leaving prison, he's managed to keep his nose clean.* **keep your nose out of sth** to try not to become involved in things that do not concern you **keep your nose to the grindstone** (*informal*) to work hard for a long period of time without stopping **look down your nose at sb/sth** (*informal*) to behave in a way that suggests that you think that you are better than someone or that something is not good enough for you **SYN** LOOK DOWN ON **on the nose** (*informal*) exactly: *The budget should hit the $136 billion target on the nose.* **poke/stick your nose into sth** (*informal*) to try to become involved in something that does not concern you **put sb's nose out of joint** (*informal*) to upset or annoy someone, especially by not giving them enough attention **turn your nose up at sth** (*informal*) to refuse something, especially because you do not think that it is good enough for you **under sb's nose** (*informal*) **1** if something is **under someone's nose**, it is very close to them but they cannot see it: *I searched everywhere for the letter and it was under my nose all the time!* **2** if something happens **under someone's nose**, they do not notice it even though it is not being done secretly: *The police didn't know the drug ring was operating right under their noses.* **with your nose in the air** (*informal*) in a way that is unfriendly and suggests that you think that you are better than other people ⊃ more at FOLLOW, LEAD¹ *v.*, PAY *v.*, PLAIN *adj.*, POWDER *v.*, RUB *v.*, SKIN *n.*, THUMB *v.*
● *verb* **1** [I, T] to move forward slowly and carefully: + **adv./prep.** *The plane nosed down through the thick clouds.* ♦ **~ your way** + **adv./prep.** *The taxi nosed its way back into the traffic.* **2** [I] + **adv./prep.** (of an animal) to search for something or push something with its nose: *Dogs nosed around in piles of refuse.*
PHR V ,nose a'round (for sth) to look for something, especially information about someone **SYN** POKE ABOUT/AROUND: *We found a man nosing around in our backyard.* ,nose sth↔'out (*informal*) to discover information about someone or something by searching for it: *Reporters nosed out all the details of the affair.*
nose·band /'noʊzbænd/ *noun* a leather band that passes over a horse's nose and under its chin and is part of its BRIDLE
nose·bleed /'noʊzblid/ *noun* a flow of blood that comes from the nose
'nose cone *noun* the pointed front end of a ROCKET, an aircraft, etc.
nose·dive /'noʊzdaɪv/ *noun, verb*
● *noun* [sing.] **1** a sudden steep fall or drop; a situation where something suddenly becomes worse or begins to fail: *Oil prices took a nosedive in the crisis.* ♦ *These policies have sent the construction industry into an abrupt nosedive.* **2** a sudden sharp fall of an aircraft toward the ground with its front part pointing down
● *verb* **1** [I] (of prices, costs, etc.) to fall suddenly **SYN** PLUMMET: *Building costs have nosedived.* **2** [I] (of an

aircraft) to fall suddenly with the front part pointing toward the ground
'nose·gay /'noʊzɡeɪ/ *noun* (*old-fashioned*) a small bunch of flowers
'nose job *noun* (*informal*) a medical operation on the nose to improve its shape
'nose ring *noun* **1** a ring that is put in an animal's nose for leading it **2** a ring worn in the nose as a piece of jewelry
nos·ey = NOSY
nosh /nɑʃ/ *noun, verb*
● *noun* a small meal that you eat quickly between main meals
● *verb* [I, T] **~ (sth)** (*informal*) to eat a small meal
'no-show *noun* (*informal*) a person who is expected to be somewhere and does not come; a situation where this happens
nos·tal·gia /nə'stældʒə; nɑ-/ *noun* [U] a feeling of sadness mixed with pleasure and affection when you think of happy times in the past: *a sense/wave/pang of nostalgia* ♦ *She is filled with nostalgia for her own college days.* ▶ **nos·tal·gic** /nə'stældʒɪk; nɑ-/ *adj.*: *nostalgic memories* ♦ *I feel quite nostalgic for the place where I grew up.* **nos·tal·gi·cally** /-kli/ *adv.*: *to look back nostalgically to your childhood*
nos·tril /'nɑstrəl/ *noun* either of the two openings at the end of the nose that you breathe through ⊃ picture at BODY
nos·trum /'nɑstrəm/ *noun* **1** (*formal, disapproving*) an idea that is intended to solve a problem but that will probably not succeed **2** (*old-fashioned*) a medicine that is not made in a scientific way, and that is not effective
nos·y (also **nos·ey**) /'noʊzi/ *adj.* (*informal, disapproving*) too interested in things that do not concern you, especially other people's affairs **SYN** INQUISITIVE: *nosy neighbors* ♦ *Don't be so nosy—it's none of your business.* ▶ **nos·i·ly** /-zəli/ *adv.* **nos·i·ness** /-zinəs/ *noun* [U]

not 🔑 /nɑt/ *adv.*
1 used to form the negative of the verbs *be, do,* and *have* and modal verbs like *can* or *must* and often reduced to *n't*: *She did not/didn't see him.* ♦ *It's not/It isn't raining.* ♦ *I can't see from here.* ♦ *He must not go.* ♦ *Don't you eat meat?* ♦ *It's cold, isn't it?* **2** used to give the following word or phrase a negative meaning, or to reply in the negative: *He warned me not to be late.* ♦ *I was sorry not to have seen them.* ♦ *Not everybody agrees.* ♦ *"Who's next?" "Not me."* ♦ *"What did you do at school?" "Not a lot."* ♦ *It's not easy being a parent* (= it's difficult). **3** used after *hope, expect, believe,* etc. to give a negative reply: *"Will she be there?" "I hope not."* ♦ *"Is it ready?" "I'm afraid not."* ♦ *(formal) "Does he know?" "I believe not."* **4 or ~** used to show a negative possibility: *I don't know if he's telling the truth or not.* **5** used to say that you do not want something or will not allow something: *"Some more?" "Not for me, thanks."* ♦ *"Can I throw this out?" "Certainly not."*
IDM **not a...| not one...** used for emphasis to mean "no thing or person": *He didn't speak to me—not one word.* **not at all** used to politely accept thanks or to agree to something: *"Thanks a lot." "Not at all."* ♦ *"Will it bother you if I smoke?" "Not at all."* **not only... (but) also...** used to emphasize that something else is also true: *She not only wrote the text but also selected the illustrations.* **not that** used to state that you are not suggesting something: *She hasn't written—not that she said she would.*
no·ta·ble /'noʊtəbl/ *adj., noun*
● *adj.* deserving to be noticed or to receive attention; important **SYN** STRIKING: *a notable success/achievement/example* ♦ *His eyes are his most notable feature.* ♦ **~ (for sth)** *The town is notable for its ancient harbor.* ♦ *With a few notable exceptions, such as rayon, most synthetic fibers come from petrochemicals.*
● *noun* [usually pl.] (*formal*) a famous or important person: *All the usual local notables were there.*
no·ta·bly /'noʊtəbli/ *adv.* **1** used for giving a good or the most important example of something **SYN** ESPECIALLY:

The house had many drawbacks, most notably its price. **2** to a great degree: *This has not been a notably successful project.*

no·ta·rize /ˈnoʊtəˌraɪz/ *verb* **~ sth** (*law*) if a document is **notarized**, it is given legal status by a notary

no·ta·ry /ˈnoʊtəri/ *noun* (*pl.* **no·ta·ries**) (also ˌnotary ˈpublic *pl.* ˌnotaries ˈpublic) (*technical*) a person, especially a lawyer, with official authority to be a witness when someone signs a document and to make this document valid in law

no·ta·tion /noʊˈteɪʃn/ *noun* [U, C] a system of signs or symbols used to represent information, especially in mathematics, science, and music

notch /nɑtʃ/ *noun, verb*
- *noun* **1** a level on a scale, often marking quality or achievement: *The quality of the food here has dropped a notch recently.* ➔ see also TOP-NOTCH **2** a V-shape or a circle cut in an edge or a surface, sometimes used to keep a record of something: *For each day he spent on the island, he cut a new notch in his stick.* ◆ *She tightened her belt an extra notch.*
- *verb* **1 ~ sth (up)** (*informal*) to achieve something such as a win or a high score: *The team has notched up 20 goals already this season.* **2 ~ sth** to make a small V-shaped cut in an edge or a surface

note 🔑 /noʊt/ *noun, verb*
- *noun*
> TO REMIND YOU **1** [C] a short piece of writing to help you to remember something: *Please **make a note** of the dates.* ◆ *She **made a mental note** (= decided that she must remember) to ask Alan about it.*
> SHORT LETTER **2** [C] a short informal letter: *Just a quick note to say thank you for a wonderful evening.* ◆ *She left a note for Ben on the kitchen table.*
> IN BOOK **3** [C] a short comment on a word or passage in a book: *a new edition of "Hamlet," with explanatory notes* ◆ *See note 3, page 259.* ➔ see also FOOTNOTE
> INFORMATION **4 notes** [pl.] information that you write down when someone is speaking, or when you are reading a book, etc.: *He sat **taking notes** on everything that was said.* ◆ *Can I borrow your **lecture notes**?* **5** [C, usually pl.] information about a performance, an actor's career, a piece of music, etc. printed in a special book or on a CD case, DVD, etc.: *The liner notes include a short biography of the performers on this recording.*
> IN MUSIC **6** [C] a single sound of a particular length and PITCH (= how high or low the sound is), made by the voice or a musical instrument; the written or printed sign for a musical note: *He played the first few notes of the tune.* ◆ *high/ low notes* ➔ picture at MUSIC
> QUALITY **7** [sing.] **~ (of sth)** a particular quality in something, for example in someone's voice or the atmosphere at an event **SYN** AIR: *There was a note of amusement in his voice.* ◆ *On a more serious note* (= speaking more seriously), … ◆ *On a slightly different note* (= changing the subject slightly), *let's talk about…*
> OFFICIAL DOCUMENT **8** [C] an official document with a particular purpose: *a sick note from your doctor* ◆ *The buyer has to sign a delivery note as proof of receipt.* ➔ see also PROMISSORY NOTE **9** [C] (*technical*) an official letter from the representative of one government to another: *an exchange of diplomatic notes*
IDM of note of importance or of great interest: *a scientist of note* ◆ *The museum contains nothing of great note.* **hit/strike the right/wrong note** to do, say, or write something that is suitable/not suitable for a particular occasion **sound/ strike a note (of sth)** to express feelings or opinions of a particular kind: *She sounded a note of caution in her speech.* **take note (of sth)** to pay attention to something and be sure to remember it: *Take note of what he says.* ➔ more at COMPARE *v.*
- *verb* (somewhat *formal*) **1** to notice or pay careful attention to something: **~ sth** *Note the fine Baroque altar inside the chapel.* ◆ **~ (that)…** *Please note (that) the office will be closed on Monday.* ◆ **~ how, where, etc.…** *Note how these animals*

sometimes walk with their tails up in the air. ◆ **it is noted that…** *It should be noted that dissertations submitted late will not be accepted.* ➔ thesaurus box at NOTICE ➔ language bank at EMPHASIS **2 ~ sth** | **~ that…** | **~ how, where, etc.…** | **it is noted that…** to mention something because it is important or interesting: *It is worth noting that the most successful companies had the lowest prices.* ➔ thesaurus box at COMMENT ➔ language bank at ARGUE
PHR V ˌnote sth↔ˈdown to write down something important so that you will not forget it **SYN** JOT DOWN

note·book /ˈnoʊtbʊk/ *noun* **1** a small book of plain paper for writing notes in ➔ picture at STATIONERY **2** a small book for students to write their work in **3** (also ˌnotebook comˈputer) a small computer that can work with a battery and be easily carried **SYN** LAPTOP ➔ compare DESKTOP COMPUTER, NETBOOK

note·card /ˈnoʊtkɑrd/ *noun* **1** a small folded card, sometimes with a picture on the front, that you use for writing a short letter on **2** a card on which notes are written, for example by someone to use when making a speech

not·ed /ˈnoʊtəd/ *adj.* well known because of a special skill or feature **SYN** FAMOUS: *a noted dancer* ◆ **for sth** *He is not noted for his sense of humor* (= he has no sense of humor). ◆ **~ as sth** *The lake is noted as a home to many birds.*

note·pad /ˈnoʊtpæd/ *noun* sheets of paper that are held together at the top and used for writing notes on: *a notepad by the phone for messages* ➔ picture at STATIONERY

note·pa·per /ˈnoʊtˌpeɪpər/ (also ˈwriting ˌpaper) *noun* [U] paper for writing letters on

note·wor·thy /ˈnoʊtˌwɜrði/ *adj.* deserving to be noticed or to receive attention because it is unusual, important, or interesting **SYN** SIGNIFICANT

ˌnot-for-ˈprofit *adj.* = NONPROFIT

ˈnoth·er /ˈnʌðər/ *adj.* (*non-standard*) = ANOTHER: *Now that's a whole 'nother question.*

noth·ing 🔑 /ˈnʌθɪŋ/ *pron.*
1 not anything; no single thing: *There was nothing in her bag.* ◆ *There's nothing you can do to help.* ◆ *The doctor said there was nothing wrong with me.* ◆ *Nothing else matters to him apart from his job.* ◆ *It cost us nothing to go in.* **2** something that is not at all important or interesting: *"What's that in your pocket?" "Oh, nothing."* ◆ *We did nothing this weekend.* ➔ see also DO-NOTHING
IDM be nothing to sb to be a person for whom someone has no feelings: *I used to love her but she's nothing to me anymore.* **be/have nothing to do with sb/sth** to have no connection with someone or something: *Get out! It's nothing to do with you* (= you have no right to know about it). ◆ *That has nothing to do with what we're discussing.* **for nothing 1** without payment **SYN** FREE: *She's always trying to get something for nothing.* **2** with no reward or result: *All that preparation was for nothing because the visit was cancelled.* **have nothing on sb** (*informal*) **1** to have much less of a particular quality than someone or something: *I'm a fast worker, but I've got nothing on her!* **2** (of the police, etc.) to have no information that could show someone to be guilty of something **not for nothing** for a very good reason: *Not for nothing was he called the king of rock and roll.* **nothing but** only; no more/less than: *Nothing but a miracle can save her now.* ◆ *I want nothing but the best for my children.* **nothing if not** extremely; very: *The trip was nothing if not varied.* **nothing less than** used to emphasize how great or extreme something is: *It was nothing less than a disaster.* **nothing like** (*informal*) **1** not at all like: *It looks nothing like a horse.* **2** not nearly; not at all: *I had nothing like enough time to answer all the questions.* **nothing much** not a great amount of something; nothing of great value or importance: *There's nothing much in the refrigerator.* ◆ *I got up late and did nothing much all day.* **(there's) nothing to it** (it's) very easy: *You'll soon learn. There's nothing to it really.* **there is/was nothing in sth** something is/was not true: *There was a rumor she was going to resign, but there was nothing in it.* **there's nothing like sth** used to say that you enjoy something very much:

| t tea | ţ butter | d did | k cat | g got | tʃ chin | dʒ June | f fall

There's nothing like a brisk walk on a cold day! ⊃ more at ALL, STOP *v.*, SWEET *adj.*

noth·ing·ness /ˈnʌθɪŋnəs/ *noun* [U] a situation where nothing exists; the state of not existing

no·tice 🔑 /ˈnoʊṭəs/ *noun, verb*

● *noun*

▸ PAYING ATTENTION **1** [U] the fact of someone paying attention to someone or something or knowing about something: *Don't take any notice of what you read in the papers.* ◆ *Take no notice of what he says.* ◆ *These protests have really made the government sit up and take notice* (= realize the importance of the situation). ◆ *It was Susan who brought the problem to my notice* (= told me about it). ◆ *Normally, the letter would not have come to my notice* (= I would not have known about it). ◆ *(formal) It will not have escaped your notice that there have been some major changes in the company.*

▸ GIVING INFORMATION **2** [C] a sheet of paper giving written or printed information, usually put in a public place: *There was a notice on the board saying the class had been cancelled.* **3** [C] a board or sign giving information, an instruction, or a warning: *a notice saying "Keep off the Grass"*

▸ ANNOUNCING SOMETHING **4** [C] a small advertisement or ANNOUNCEMENT in a newspaper or magazine: *notices of births, marriages, and deaths* **5** [C] a short ANNOUNCEMENT made at the beginning or end of a meeting, a church service, etc.: *There are just two notices this week.*

▸ WARNING **6** [U] information or a warning given in advance of something that is going to happen: *She left without giving notice.* ◆ *Prices may be altered without notice.* ◆ *The bar is closed until further notice* (= until you are told that it is open again). ◆ *You are welcome to come and stay as long as you give us plenty of notice.*

▸ WHEN LEAVING JOB/HOUSE **7** [U] a formal letter or statement saying that you will or must leave your job or house at the end of a particular period of time: *He has handed in his notice.* ◆ *They gave her two weeks' notice.*

▸ REVIEW OF BOOK/PLAY **8** [C] a short article in a newspaper or magazine, giving an opinion about a book, play, etc.
IDM **on short notice| at a moment's notice** not long in advance; without warning or time for preparation: *This was the best room we could get on such short notice.* ◆ *You must be ready to leave at a moment's notice.*

● *verb* (not usually used in the progressive tenses)

▸ SEE/HEAR **1** [I, T] to see or hear someone or something; to become aware of someone or something: *People were making fun of him but he didn't seem to notice.* ◆ *~ sb/sth The first thing I noticed about the room was the smell.* ◆ *~ (that)... I couldn't help noticing (that) she was wearing a wig.* ◆ *~ how, what, etc.... Did you notice how Rachel kept looking at her watch?* ◆ *~ sb/sth do sth I noticed them come in.* ◆ *~ sb/sth doing sth I didn't notice him leaving.*

▸ PAY ATTENTION **2** [T] *~ sb/sth* to pay attention to someone or something: *She wears those strange clothes just to get herself noticed.*

◆ *The police observed a van leaving the parking lot.*
witness *(somewhat formal)* to see something happen: *Police have asked anyone who witnessed the robbery to contact them.*

PATTERNS
- to notice/note/detect/observe that/how/what/where/who...
- to notice/observe/witness sth happen/sb do sth

no·tice·a·ble 🔑 /ˈnoʊṭəsəbl/ *adj.*
easy to see or notice; clear or definite: *a noticeable improvement* ◆ *~ in sb/sth This effect is particularly noticeable in younger patients.* ◆ *~ that... It was noticeable that none of the family were present.* ▶ **no·tice·a·bly** /-bli/ *adv.: Her hand was shaking noticeably.* ◆ *Grades were noticeably higher for girls than for boys.*

no·ti·fi·a·ble /ˈnoʊṭəˌfaɪəbl; ˌnoʊṭəˈfaɪ-/ *adj.* [usually before noun] *(formal)* (of a disease or a crime) so dangerous or serious that it must by law be reported officially to the authorities

no·ti·fi·ca·tion /ˌnoʊṭəfəˈkeɪʃn/ *noun* [U, C] *(formal)* the act of giving or receiving official information about something: *advance/prior notification* (= telling someone in advance about something) ◆ *written notification* ◆ *You should receive (a) notification of our decision in the next week.*

no·ti·fy /ˈnoʊṭəˌfaɪ/ *verb* (no·ti·fies, no·ti·fy·ing, no·ti·fied, no·ti·fied) to formally or officially tell someone about something **SYN** INFORM: *~ sb Competition winners will be notified by mail.* ◆ *~ sb of sth The police must be notified of the date of the demonstration.* ◆ *~ sb that... Members have been notified that there will be a small increase in the fee.*

no·tion 🔑 **AWL** /ˈnoʊʃn/ *noun*
an idea, a belief, or an understanding of something: *~ (of sth) a political system based on the notions of equality and liberty* ◆ *She had only a vague notion of what might happen.* ◆ *~ (that...) I have to reject the notion that greed can be a good thing.*

no·tion·al /ˈnoʊʃənl/ *adj.* *(formal)* based on a guess, estimate, or theory; not existing in reality ▶ **no·tion·al·ly** /-ʃənəli/ *adv.*

no·to·ri·e·ty /ˌnoʊṭəˈraɪəti/ *noun* [U, sing.] fame for being bad in some way: *~ (for sth) She achieved notoriety for her affair with the senator.* ◆ *~ (as sth) He gained a certain notoriety as a gambler.*

no·to·ri·ous /noʊˈtɔriəs/ *adj.* well known for being bad: *a notorious criminal* ◆ *~ for sth/for doing sth The country is notorious for its appalling prison conditions.* ◆ *~ as sth The bar has become notorious as a meeting-place for drug dealers.* ▶ **no·to·ri·ous·ly** *adv.: Mountain weather is notoriously difficult to predict.*

not·with·stand·ing **AWL** /ˌnɑtwɪθˈstændɪŋ; -wɪð-/ *prep., adv.* *(formal)*

● *prep.* (also used following the noun it refers to) without being affected by something; despite something: *Notwithstanding some major financial problems, the school has had a successful year.* ◆ *The bad weather notwithstanding, the event was a great success.*

● *adv.* despite this **SYN** HOWEVER, NEVERTHELESS: *Notwithstanding, the problem is a significant one.*

nou·gat /ˈnugət/ *noun* [U] a hard candy that has to be chewed a lot, often containing nuts, cherries (CHERRY), etc. and pink or white in color

nought (also **naught**) /nɔt/ *noun* [U] *(literary)* used in particular phrases to mean "nothing": *All our efforts have come to nought* (= have not been successful).

noun /naʊn/ *noun* (*abbr.* n.) *(grammar)* a word that refers to a person (such as *Ann* or *doctor*), a place (such as *Paris* or *city*), or a thing, a quality, or an activity (such as *plant, happiness,* or *football*) ⊃ see also ABSTRACT NOUN, COMMON NOUN, PROPER NOUN

'noun phrase *noun* (*grammar*) a word or group of words in a sentence that behaves in the same way as a noun, that is, as a subject, an object, a COMPLEMENT, or as the object of a preposition: *In the sentence "I spoke to the driver of the car," "the driver of the car" is a noun phrase.*

nour·ish /'nɔrɪʃ/ *verb* **1 ~ sb/sth** to keep a person, an animal, or a plant alive and healthy with food, etc.: *All the children were well nourished and in good physical condition.* **2 ~ sth** (*formal*) to allow a feeling, an idea, etc. to develop or grow stronger: *By investing in education, we nourish the talents of our children.* ▶ **nour·ish·ing** *adj.*: *nourishing food*

nour·ish·ment /'nɔrɪʃmənt/ *noun* [U] (*formal or technical*) food that is needed to stay alive, grow, and stay healthy: *Can plants obtain adequate nourishment from such poor soil?* ♦ (*figurative*) *As a child, she was starved of intellectual nourishment.*

nou·veau riche /ˌnuvoʊ 'riʃ/ *noun* (*pl.* **nou·veaux riches** /ˌnuvoʊ 'riʃ/ *or the* **nouveau riche**) (*from French, disapproving*) a person who has recently become rich and likes to show how rich they are in a very obvious way ▶ **nou·veau riche** *adj.*

nou·velle cui·sine /nuˌvɛl kwi'zin/ *noun* [U] (*from French*) a style of cooking that avoids heavy foods and serves small amounts of different dishes arranged in an attractive way on the plate

no·va /'noʊvə/ *noun* (*pl.* **no·vae** /-vi/ *or* **no·vas**) (*astronomy*) a star that suddenly becomes much brighter for a short period ⊃ compare SUPERNOVA

nov·el /'nɑvl/ *noun, adj.*
• *noun* a story long enough to fill a complete book, in which the characters and events are usually imaginary: *to write/ publish/read a novel* ♦ *detective/historical/romantic novels* ♦ *the novels of Henry James* ⊃ collocations at LITERATURE
• *adj.* (*often approving*) different from anything known before; new, interesting, and often seeming slightly strange: *a novel feature*

nov·el·ette /ˌnɑvə'lɛt/ *noun* a short novel, especially a romantic novel that is considered to be badly written

nov·el·ist /'nɑvəlɪst/ *noun* a person who writes novels: *a romantic/historical novelist* ⊃ collocations at LITERATURE

nov·el·is·tic /ˌnɑvə'lɪstɪk/ *adj.* (*formal*) typical of or used in novels

no·vel·la /noʊ'vɛlə/ *noun* a short novel

nov·el·ty /'nɑvəlti/ *noun, adj.*
• *noun* (*pl.* **nov·el·ties**) **1** [U] the quality of being new, different, and interesting: *It was fun working there at first but the novelty soon wore off* (= it became boring). ♦ *There's a certain novelty value in this approach.* **2** [C] a thing, person, or situation that is interesting because it is new, unusual, or has not been known before: *Electric cars are still something of a novelty.* **3** [C] a small cheap object sold as a toy or a decorative object
• *adj.* [only before noun] different and unusual; intended to be amusing and to catch people's attention: *a novelty teapot*

No·vem·ber /noʊ'vɛmbər/ *noun* [U, C] (*abbr.* **Nov.**) the 11th month of the year, between October and December **HELP** To see how **November** is used, look at the examples at **April**.

nov·ice /'nɑvəs/ *noun* **1** a person who is new and has little experience in a skill, job, or situation: *I'm a complete novice at skiing.* ♦ *computer software for novices/the novice user* **2** a person who has joined a religious group and is preparing to become a MONK or a NUN **3** a horse that has not yet won an important race

no·vi·ti·ate (also **no·vi·ci·ate**) /noʊ'vɪʃiət; -ʃət/ *noun* (*formal*) a period of being a novice

no·vo·caine (also **No·vo·cain™**) /'noʊvəˌkeɪn/ *noun* [U] (*medical*) = PROCAINE

now /naʊ/ *adv., conj.*
• *adv.* **1** (at) the present time: *Where are you living now?* ♦ *It's been two weeks now since she called.* ♦ *It's too late now.* ♦ *From now on I'll be more careful.* ♦ *He'll be home by now.* ♦ *I've lived at home up till now.* ♦ *That's all for now.* **2** at or from this moment, but not before: *Start writing now.* ♦ *I am now ready to answer your questions.* **3** (*informal*) used to show that you are annoyed about something: *Now they want to tax food!* ♦ *What do you want now?* ♦ *It's broken. Now I'll have to get a new one.* **4** used to get someone's attention before changing the subject or asking them to do something: *Now, listen to what she's saying.* ♦ *Now, the next point is quite complex.* ♦ *Now come and sit down.* ♦ *Now let me think…*
IDM **(every) now and again/then** from time to time; occasionally: *Every now and again she checked to see if he was still asleep.* **now for sb/sth** used when turning to a fresh activity or subject: *And now for some travel news.* **now, now** (also **now then**) used to show in a mild way that you do not approve of something: *Now then, that's enough noise.* **now… now…** at one time… at another time…: *Her moods kept changing—now happy, now sad.* **(it's) now or never** this is the only opportunity someone will have to do something **now then 1** = NOW, NOW **2** used when making a suggestion or an offer: *Now then, who wants to come for a walk?* **now what?** (*informal*) **1** (also **what is it now?**) used when you are annoyed because someone is always asking questions or interrupting you: *"Yes, but Dad…" "Now what?"* **2** used to say that you do not know what to do next in a particular situation
• *conj.* **~ (that)…** because the thing mentioned is happening or has just happened: *Now that the kids have left home we have a lot of extra space.*

now·a·days /'naʊəˌdeɪz/ *adv.* at the present time, in contrast with the past: *Nowadays most kids prefer watching TV to reading.*

no·where /'noʊwɛr/ (also **'no place**) *adv.* not in or to any place: *This animal is found in Australia, and nowhere else.* ♦ *There was nowhere for me to sit.* ♦ *"Where are you going this weekend?" "Nowhere special."* ♦ *Nowhere is the effect of government policy more apparent than in agriculture.*
IDM **get/go nowhere | get sb nowhere** to make no progress or have no success; to allow someone to do this: *We discussed it all morning but got nowhere.* ♦ *Talking to him will get you nowhere.* **nowhere to be found/seen | nowhere in sight** impossible for anyone to find or see: *The children were nowhere to be seen.* ♦ *A peace settlement is nowhere in sight* (= is not likely in the near future). ⊃ more at LEAD[1] *v.*, MIDDLE *n.*, NEAR *adv.*

no-'win *adj.* [only before noun] (of a situation, policy, etc.) that will end badly whatever you decide to do: *We are considering the options available to us in this no-win situation.*

nox·ious /'nɑkʃəs/ *adj.* (*formal*) poisonous or harmful: *noxious fumes*

noz·zle /'nɑzl/ *noun* a narrow piece that is attached to the end of a pipe or tube to direct the stream of liquid, air, or gas passing through ⊃ picture at PACKAGING

NPR /ˌɛn pi 'ɑr/ *abbr.* National Public Radio (a national organization of radio stations that do not broadcast commercials)

NRA /ˌɛn ɑr 'eɪ/ *abbr.* National Rifle Association (an organization that supports the right of citizens to own a gun)

ns *abbr.* NANOSECOND(S)

nth /ɛnθ/ *adj.* (*informal*) [only before noun] used when you are stating that something is the last in a long series and emphasizing how often something has happened: *It's the nth time I've explained it to you.*
IDM **to the nth degree** extremely; to an extreme degree

nu /nu/ *noun* the 13th letter of the Greek alphabet (N, ν)

nu·ance /'nuɑns/ *noun* [C, U] a very slight difference in meaning, sound, color, or someone's feelings that is not usually very obvious: *He watched her face intently to catch every nuance of expression.*

h **hat**   m **man**   n **no**   ŋ **sing**   l **leg**   r **red**   y **yes**   w **wet**

nub /nʌb/ *noun* **1** [sing.] **the ~ (of sth)** the central or essential point of a situation, problem, etc.: *The nub of the matter is that business is declining.* **2** [C] a small, round piece of something: *a nub of gold*

nu·bile /ˈnuːbaɪl; ˈnubl/ *adj.* (of a girl or young woman) sexually attractive

nu·cle·ar 🔑 **AWL** /ˈnuːkliər/ *adj.* [usually before noun] **1** using, producing, or resulting from nuclear energy: *a nuclear power station* ◆ *the nuclear industry* **2** connected with weapons that use nuclear energy: *a nuclear weapon/bomb/missile* ◆ *nuclear-powered submarines* ◆ *a nuclear explosion/attack/war* ◆ *the country's nuclear capability* (= the fact that it has nuclear weapons) ◆ *nuclear capacity* (= the number of nuclear weapons a country has) **3** (*physics*) of the NUCLEUS (= central part) of an atom: *nuclear particles* ◆ *a nuclear reaction*

ˌnuclear ˈenergy (also ˌnuclear ˈpower) *noun* [U] a powerful form of energy produced by splitting the nuclei (= central parts) of atoms. It is used to produce electricity. **SYN** ATOMIC ENERGY

ˌnuclear ˈfamily *noun* (*technical*) a family that consists of parents and children, when it is thought of as a unit in society ⊃ compare EXTENDED FAMILY

ˌnuclear ˈfission *noun* [U] = FISSION

ˌnuclear-ˈfree *adj.* [usually before noun] (of a country or a region) not having or allowing nuclear energy, weapons, or materials: *a nuclear-free zone*

ˌnuclear ˈfuel *noun* a substance that can be used as a source of NUCLEAR ENERGY because it is capable of NUCLEAR FISSION

ˌnuclear ˈfusion *noun* [U] = FUSION

ˌnuclear ˈoption *noun* (*politics*) the most extreme possible response to a particular situation: *Currency controls would be the nuclear option.*

ˌnuclear ˈphysics *noun* [U] the area of physics that deals with the nuclei (NUCLEUS) of atoms and with nuclear energy ► ˌnuclear ˈphysicist *noun*

ˌnuclear ˈpower *noun* [U] = NUCLEAR ENERGY

ˌnuclear reˈactor *noun* = REACTOR

ˌnuclear ˈwaste *noun* [U] waste material that is RADIOACTIVE, especially used fuel from nuclear power stations

ˌnuclear ˈwinter *noun* a period without light, heat, or growth that scientists believe would follow a nuclear war

nu·cle·ic ac·id /nuˌkliːɪk ˈæsɪd; -ˌkleɪɪk-/ *noun* [U] (*chemistry*) either of two acids, DNA and RNA, that are present in all living cells

nu·cle·o·tide /ˈnuːkliəˌtaɪd/ *noun* (*chemistry*) one of the many small MOLECULES that combine to form DNA and RNA

nu·cle·us /ˈnuːkliəs/ *noun* (*pl.* nu·cle·i /-kliˌaɪ/) **1** (*physics*) the part of an atom that contains most of its mass and that carries a positive electric charge ⊃ picture at ATOM ⊃ see also NEUTRON, PROTON **2** (*biology*) the central part of some cells, containing the GENETIC material **3** the central part of something, around which other parts are located or collected: *These paintings will form the nucleus of a new collection.*

nude /nuːd/ *adj., noun*
● *adj.* **1** (especially of a human figure in art) not wearing any clothes **SYN** NAKED: *a nude model* ◆ *He asked me to pose nude for him.* **2** involving people who are naked: *a nude photograph* ◆ *Are there any nude scenes in the movie?* **3** (of PANTYHOSE, etc.) skin-colored
● *noun* a work of art consisting of a naked human figure; a naked human figure in art: *a bronze nude by Rodin* ◆ *a reclining nude*
IDM **in the nude** not wearing any clothes **SYN** NAKED: *She refuses to be photographed in the nude.*

nudge /nʌdʒ/ *verb, noun*
● *verb* **1** [T] **~ sb/sth** to push someone gently, especially with your elbow, in order to get their attention: *He nudged me and whispered, "Look who just came in."* **2** [T] **~ sb/sth + adv./prep.** to push someone or something gently or gradually in a particular direction: *He nudged the ball past the goalie and into the net.* ◆ *She nudged me out of the way.* ◆ (*figurative*) *He nudged the conversation toward the subject of money.* ◆ (*figurative*) *She tried to nudge him into changing his mind* (= persuade him to do it). **3** [T, I] **~ (sth) + adv./prep.** to move forward by pushing with your elbow: *He nudged his way through the crowd.* **4** [T] **~ sth (+ adv./prep.)** to reach or make something reach a particular level: *Inflation is nudging 20%.* ◆ *This afternoon's sunshine could nudge the temperature above freezing.*
● *noun* a slight push, usually with the elbow: *She gave me a gentle nudge in the ribs to tell me to shut up.* ◆ (*figurative*) *He can work hard but he needs a nudge now and then.*

nud·ie /ˈnuːdi/ *adj.* (*informal*) showing or including people wearing no clothes: *nudie photographs*

nud·ism /ˈnuːdɪzəm/ (also **na·tur·ism**) *noun* [U] the practice of not wearing any clothes because you believe this is more natural and healthy

nud·ist /ˈnuːdɪst/ (also **na·tur·ist**) *noun* a person who does not wear any clothes because they believe this is more natural and healthy: *a nudist beach/camp*

nu·di·ty /ˈnuːdəti/ *noun* [U] the state of being naked: *The committee claimed that there was too much nudity on television.*

'nuff /nʌf/ *adj., pron.* (*non-standard*) a way of writing the word "enough," representing informal speech: *Boston is the best team there is.* ***'Nuff said.***

nu·ga·to·ry /ˈnuːɡəˌtɔri/ *adj.* (*formal*) having no purpose or value **SYN** WORTHLESS

nug·get /ˈnʌɡət/ *noun* **1** a small lump of a valuable metal or mineral, especially gold, that is found in the earth **2** a small round piece of some types of food: *chicken nuggets* **3** a small thing, such as an idea or a fact, that people think of as valuable **SYN** SNIPPET: *a useful nugget of information*

nui·sance /ˈnuːsns/ *noun* **1** [C, usually sing.] a thing, person, or situation that is annoying or causes trouble or problems: *I don't want to be a nuisance, so tell me if you want to be alone.* ◆ *I hope you're not making a nuisance of yourself.* ◆ *It's a nuisance having to go back tomorrow.* ◆ *What a nuisance!* **2** [C, U] (*law*) behavior by someone that annoys other people and that a court can order the person to stop: *He was charged with causing a public nuisance.*

nuke /nuːk/ *verb, noun* (*informal*)
● *verb* **1** **~ sth** to attack a place with nuclear weapons **2** **~ sth** to cook something in a MICROWAVE oven
● *noun* a nuclear weapon

null /nʌl/ *adj.* (*technical*) having the value zero: *a null result* **IDM** **null and void** (*law*) (of an election, an agreement, etc.) having no legal force; not valid: *The contract was declared null and void.*

'null hyˌpothesis *noun* (*statistics*) the idea that an experiment that is done using two groups of people will show the same results for each group

nul·li·fy /ˈnʌləˌfaɪ/ *verb* (nul·li·fies, nul·li·fy·ing, nul·li·fied, nul·li·fied) (*formal*) **1** **~ sth** to make something such as an agreement or order lose its legal force **SYN** INVALIDATE: *Judges were unwilling to nullify government decisions.* **2** **~ sth** to make something lose its effect or power **SYN** NEGATE: *An unhealthy diet will nullify the effects of training.* ► **nul·li·fi·ca·tion** *noun* [U, C]

nul·li·ty /ˈnʌləti/ *noun* [sing.] (*formal or law*) the fact of something, for example a marriage, having no legal force or no longer being valid; something which is no longer valid

numb /nʌm/ *adj., verb*
● *adj.* **1** if a part of your body is **numb**, you cannot feel anything in it, for example because of cold: *to be/go numb* ◆ *numb with cold* ◆ *I just came back from the dentist and my face*

is still numb. **2** unable to feel, think, or react in the normal way: *He felt numb with shock.* ⊃ see also NUMBING
▶ **numb·ly** *adv.*: *Her life would never be the same again, she realized numbly.* **numb·ness** *noun* [U]: *pain and numbness in my fingers* ◆ *He was still in a state of numbness and shock from the accident.*
● *verb* **1** ~ sth to make a part of your body unable to feel anything, for example because of cold: *His fingers were numbed with the cold.* **2** ~ sb to make someone unable to feel, think, or react in a normal way, for example because of an emotional shock **SYN** STUN: *We sat there in silence, numbed by the shock of her death.*

num·ber 🔑 /ˈnʌmbər/ *noun, verb*
● *noun*
> WORD/SYMBOL **1** [C] a word or symbol that represents an amount or a quantity **SYN** FIGURE: *Think of a number and multiply it by two.* ◆ *a high/low number* ◆ *even numbers* (= 2, 4, 6, etc.) ◆ *odd numbers* (= 1, 3, 5, etc.) ◆ *You owe me 27 dollars? Make it 30, that's a nice round number.* ⊃ see also CARDINAL NUMBER, ORDINAL, PRIME NUMBER, WHOLE NUMBER
> POSITION IN SERIES **2** [C] (*abbr.* No.) (*symb.* #) used before a figure to show the position of something in a series: *They live at number 26.* ◆ *The song reached number 5 on the charts.*
> TELEPHONE, ETC. **3** [C] (often in compounds) a number used to identify something or communicate by telephone, FAX, etc.: *My phone number is 266-9982.* ◆ *I'm sorry, I think you have the wrong number* (= wrong telephone number). ◆ *What is your account number, please?* ⊃ see also BOX NUMBER, PIN, REGISTRATION NUMBER, SERIAL NUMBER
> QUANTITY **4** [C] ~ (of sb/sth) a quantity of people or things: *A large number of people have applied for the job.* ◆ *The number of homeless people has increased dramatically.* ◆ *Huge numbers of* (= very many) *animals have died.* ◆ *A number of* (= some) *problems have arisen.* ◆ *I could give you any number of* (= a lot of) *reasons for not going.* ◆ *We were eight in number* (= there were eight of us). ◆ *Nurses are leaving the profession in increasing numbers.* ◆ *Sheer weight of numbers* (= the large number of soldiers) *secured them victory in the battle.* ◆ *staff/student numbers* **HELP** A plural verb is needed after a/an **(large, small, etc.) number of…**
> INFORMATION **5** the numbers [pl.] information that is given in the form of numbers: *Tell Tommy to run the numbers for the annual report.*
> SONG/DANCE **6** [C] a song or dance, especially one of several in a performance: *They sang a slow romantic number.*
> THING ADMIRED **7** [sing.] (*informal*) (following one or more adjectives) a thing, such as a dress or a car, that is admired: *She was wearing a black velvet number.*
> GROUP OF PEOPLE **8** [sing.] (*formal*) a group or quantity of people: *one of our number* (= one of us) ◆ *The congressman's proposal is supported by his number.*
> GRAMMAR **9** [U] the form of a word, showing whether one or more than one person or thing is being talked about: *The word "men" is plural in number.* ◆ *The subject of a sentence and its verb must agree in number.*
IDM **by numbers** following a set of simple instructions identified by numbers: *painting by numbers* **by the numbers** following closely the accepted rules for doing something **do a number on sb/sth** (*informal*) to hurt someone or damage something, either emotionally or physically: *The divorce really did a number on her ability to trust people.* **have (got) sb's number** (*informal*) to know what someone is really like and what they plan to do: *He thinks he can fool me, but I've got his number.* **your number is up** (*informal*) the time has come when you will die or lose everything **numbers game** a way of considering an activity, etc. that is concerned only with the number of people doing something, things achieved, etc., not with who or what they are: *Candidates were playing the numbers game as the crucial vote drew closer.* ⊃ more at OPPOSITE *adj.*, SAFETY, WEIGHT *n.*
● *verb*
> MAKE A SERIES **1** [T] to give a number to something as part of a series or list: ~ sth *All the seats in the stadium are*

numbered. ◆ *I couldn't figure out the numbering system for the hotel rooms.* ◆ ~ sth from… to… *Number the car's features from 1 to 10 according to importance.* ◆ ~ sth + noun *The doors were numbered 2, 4, 6, and 8.*
> MAKE SOMETHING AS TOTAL **2** [I] + noun to make a particular number when added together: *The crowd numbered more than a thousand.* ◆ *We numbered 20* (= there were 20 of us in the group).
> INCLUDE **3** [T, I] (*formal*) to include someone or something in a particular group; to be included in a particular group: ~ sb/sth among sth *I number her among my closest friends.* ◆ ~ among sth *He numbers among the best classical American actors.* **IDM** see DAY

ˈnumber ˌcruncher (also ˈnumber-ˌcruncher) *noun* (*informal*) **1** a person whose job involves working with numbers, such as an ACCOUNTANT **2** a computer or computer program that works with numbers and calculates data

ˈnumber ˌcrunching *noun* [U] (*informal*) the process of calculating numbers, especially when a large amount of data is involved and the data is processed in a short space of time

num·bered /ˈnʌmbərd/ *adj.* having a number to show that it is part of a series or list: *The players all wear numbered shirts.* **IDM** see DAY

num·ber·less /ˈnʌmbərləs/ *adj.* (*literary*) too many to be counted **SYN** INNUMERABLE

ˌnumber ˈone *noun, adj.* (*informal*)
● *noun* **1** [U] the most important or best person or thing: *We're number one in the used car business.* **2** [U, C] the song or ALBUM (= collection of songs) that has sold the most copies in a particular week: *She's had three number ones.* ◆ *The new album went straight to number one.* **3** [U] yourself: *Looking out for number one is all she cares about.* **4** [sing.] an expression used especially by children or when speaking to talk about passing liquid waste from the body: *It's only a number one.* ⊃ compare NUMBER TWO
● *adj.* most important or best: *the world's number one athlete* ◆ *the number one priority*

ˌnumber ˈtwo *noun* [sing.] (*informal*) an expression used especially by children or when speaking to children to talk about passing solid waste from the body: *Mommy, I need to do a number two.* ⊃ compare NUMBER ONE

numb·ing /ˈnʌmɪŋ/ *adj.* (of an experience or a situation) making you unable to feel anything: *numbing cold/fear* ◆ *Watching television had a numbing effect on his mind.*

numb·skull (also **num·skull**) /ˈnʌmskʌl/ *noun* (*informal*) a stupid person

nu·mer·a·cy /ˈnuːmərəsi/ *noun* [U] a good basic knowledge of mathematics; the ability to understand and work with numbers: *standards of literacy and numeracy* ▶ **nu·mer·ate** /ˈnuːmərət/ *adj.*: *All students should be numerate and literate when they finish school.* **ANT** INNUMERATE

nu·mer·al /ˈnuːmərəl/ *noun* a sign or symbol that represents a number ⊃ see also ARABIC NUMERAL, ROMAN NUMERAL

nu·mer·a·tor /ˈnuːməˌreɪtər/ *noun* (*mathematics*) the number above the line in a FRACTION, for example 3 in the FRACTION ¾ ⊃ compare DENOMINATOR

nu·mer·i·cal /nuːˈmɛrɪkl/ (also *less frequent* **nu·mer·ic** /nuːˈmɛrɪk/) *adj.* relating to numbers; expressed in numbers: *numerical data* ◆ *The results are expressed in descending numerical order.* ▶ **nu·mer·i·cally** /-kli/ *adv.*: *to express the results numerically*

nu·mer·ol·o·gy /ˌnuːməˈrɑlədʒi/ *noun* [U] the use of numbers to try to tell someone what will happen in the future ▶ **nu·mer·o·log·i·cal** /ˌnuːmərəˈlɑdʒɪkl/ *adj.*

nu·mer·ous 🔑 /ˈnuːmərəs/ *adj.* (*formal*)
existing in large numbers **SYN** MANY: *He has been late on numerous occasions.* ◆ *The advantages of this system are too numerous to mention.*

nu·mi·nous /ˈnuːmənəs/ *adj.* (*formal*) having a strong religious and spiritual quality that makes you feel that God is present

nu·mis·mat·ics /ˌnuːmɪzˈmætɪks/ *noun* [U] the study of coins and MEDALS ▶ **nu·mis·mat·ic** *adj.*

nu·mis·ma·tist /nuˈmɪzmətɪst/ *noun* a person who collects or studies coins or MEDALS

num·skull = NUMBSKULL

nun /nʌn/ *noun* a member of a religious community of women who promise to serve God all their lives and often live together in a CONVENT ⊃ compare MONK

nun·ci·o /ˈnʌnsiou; ˈnun-/ *noun* (pl. **nun·ci·os**) a representative of the POPE (= the leader of the Roman Catholic Church) in a foreign country: *a papal nuncio*

nun·ner·y /ˈnʌnəri/ *noun* (pl. **nun·ner·ies**) (*old-fashioned* or *literary*) = CONVENT

nup·tial /ˈnʌpʃl/ *adj.* [only before noun] (*formal*) connected with marriage or a wedding: *nuptial bliss* ◆ *a nuptial mass*

nup·tials /ˈnʌpʃlz/ *noun* [pl.] (*old-fashioned*) a wedding

nurse 🔎 /nɜːrs/ *noun, verb*

• *noun* **1** a person whose job is to take care of sick or injured people, usually in a hospital: *a licensed/registered nurse* ◆ *student nurses* ◆ *a male nurse* ◆ *a nurse midwife* (= one who helps women with the birth of babies) ◆ *a psychiatric nurse* (= one who helps people with mental illnesses) ◆ *Nurse Bennett* ◆ *We need a nurse in here!* ⊃ see also PRACTICAL NURSE, REGISTERED NURSE, VISITING NURSE ⊃ note at GENDER **2** (also **nurse·maid**) (*old-fashioned*) (in the past) a woman or girl whose job was to take care of babies or small children in the children's own home ⊃ see also WET NURSE

• *verb* **1** [T] ~ **sb** to care for someone who is sick or injured: *He worked in a hospital for ten years, nursing cancer patients.* ◆ *She nursed her daughter **back to health**.* **2** [T] ~ **sth** to take care of an injury or illness: *Several weeks after the game, he was still nursing a shoulder injury.* ◆ *You'd better go to bed and nurse that cold.* ◆ (*figurative*) *She was nursing her hurt pride.* **3** [T] ~ **sth** (*formal*) to have a strong feeling or idea in your mind for a long time SYN HARBOR: *to nurse an ambition/a grievance/a grudge* ◆ *She had been nursing a secret desire to see him again.* **4** [T] ~ **sth** to give special care or attention to something: *to nurse tender young plants* **5** [T] ~ **sb/sth** to hold someone or something carefully in your arms or close to your body: *He sat nursing his cup of coffee.* **6** [I, T] (of a woman or female animal) to feed a baby with milk from the breast SYN SUCKLE: *a nursing mother* ◆ ~ **sb/sth** *The lioness is still nursing her cubs.* ⊃ compare BREASTFEED **7** [I] (of a baby) to suck milk from its mother's breast SYN SUCKLE

nurse·maid /ˈnɜːrsmeɪd/ *noun* (*old-fashioned*) = NURSE *n.* (2)

nurse prac·ti·tion·er *noun* a nurse who is trained to do many of the tasks usually done by a doctor

nurs·er·y /ˈnɜːrsəri/ *noun* (pl. **nurs·er·ies**) **1** = NURSERY SCHOOL **2** a place where young plants and trees are grown for sale or for planting somewhere else **3** (*old-fashioned*) a room in a house where a baby sleeps **4** (*old-fashioned*) a room in a house where young children can play

nurs·er·y·man /ˈnɜːrsərimən/ *noun* (pl. **nurs·er·y·men** /-mən/) a person who owns or works in a nursery

nursery rhyme *noun* a simple traditional poem or song for children

nursery school *noun* a school for children between the ages of about two and five ⊃ compare PLAY GROUP

nurs·ing /ˈnɜːrsɪŋ/ *noun* [U] the job or skill of caring for people who are sick or injured: *a career in nursing* ◆ *nursing care* ◆ *the nursing profession*

nursing home *noun* a small private hospital, especially one where old people live and are cared for

nur·ture /ˈnɜːrtʃər/ *verb, noun*

• *verb* (*formal*) **1** ~ **sb/sth** to care for and protect someone or something while they are growing and developing: *These delicate plants need careful nurturing.* ◆ *children nurtured by loving parents* **2** ~ **sth** to help someone or something to develop and be successful SYN FOSTER: *It's important to nurture a good working relationship.* **3** ~ **sth** to have a feeling, an idea, a plan, etc. for a long time and encourage it to develop: *She secretly nurtured a hope of becoming famous.*

• *noun* [U] (*formal*) care, encouragement, and support given to someone or something while they are growing

nuts

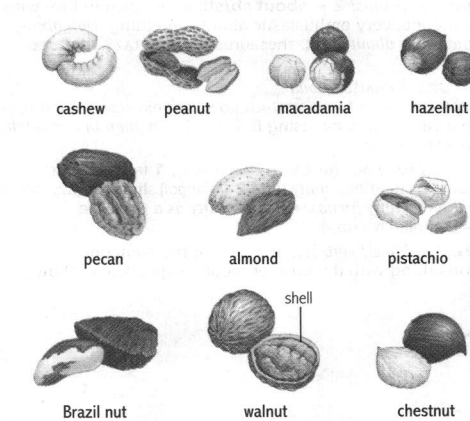

cashew   peanut   macadamia   hazelnut

pecan   almond   pistachio

shell

Brazil nut   walnut   chestnut

nut 🔎 /nʌt/ *noun*
1 (often in compounds) a small hard fruit with a very hard shell that grows on some trees: *to crack a nut* (= open it) ◆ *a Brazil nut* ◆ *a hazelnut* ◆ *nuts and raisins* **2** a small piece of metal with a hole through the center that is screwed onto a BOLT to hold pieces of wood, machinery, etc. together: *to tighten a nut* ◆ *a wing nut* ⊃ picture at TOOL **3** (*informal*) a strange or crazy person: *He's a complete nut, if you ask me.* ⊃ see also NUTS, NUTTY **4** (*informal*) (in compounds) a person who is extremely interested in a particular subject, activity, etc.: *a fitness/tennis/computer, etc. nut* **IDM** **a hard/tough nut** (*informal*) a person who is difficult to deal with or to influence **a hard/tough nut (to crack)** a difficult problem or situation to deal with **the nuts and bolts (of sth)** (*informal*) the basic practical details of a subject or an activity

nut-brown *adj.* dark brown in color: *nut-brown hair*

nut case *noun* (*informal*) a crazy person

nut·crack·er /ˈnʌtˌkrækər/ *noun* a tool for cracking open the shells of nuts ⊃ picture at KITCHEN

nut·house /ˈnʌthaʊs/ *noun* (*informal*) **1** (*offensive*) a hospital for people who are mentally ill **2** (*disapproving*) a place that is loud and confusing

nut·meg /ˈnʌtmeg/ *noun* [U, C] the hard seed of a tropical tree imported from southeast Asia, used in cooking as a spice, especially to give flavor to cakes and sauces: *freshly grated nutmeg* ⊃ picture at HERB

nu·tra·ceu·ti·cal /ˌnuːtrəˈsuːtɪkl/ *noun* food that has had substances that are good for your health specially added to it

nu·tri·ent /ˈnuːtriənt/ *noun* (*technical*) a substance that is needed to keep a living thing alive and to help it to grow: *a lack of essential nutrients* ◆ *Plants draw minerals and other nutrients from the soil.* ◆ *children suffering from a serious nutrient deficiency* ⊃ collocations at LIFE, DIET

nu·tri·tion /nuˈtrɪʃn/ *noun* [U] the process by which living things receive the food necessary for them to grow and be healthy: *advice on diet and nutrition* ◆ *to study food science and nutrition* ⊃ collocations at DIET ⊃ compare MALNUTRITION ▶ **nu·tri·tion·al** /-ʃənl/ (also *less frequent* **nu·tri·tive** /ˈnuːtrətɪv/) *adj.*: *the nutritional value of milk* **nu·tri·tion·al·ly** /-ʃənəli/ *adv.*: *a nutritionally balanced menu*

nu·tri·tion·ist /nuˈtrɪʃənɪst/ *noun* a person who is an expert

on the relationship between food and health ⊃ **see also**
DIETITIAN

nu·tri·tious /nuˈtrɪʃəs/ *adj.* (*approving*) (of food) very good
for you; containing many of the substances that help the
body to grow **SYN** NOURISHing: *tasty and nutritious meals*

nuts /nʌts/ *adj.* [not before noun] (*informal*) **1** crazy: *My friends
think I'm nuts for saying yes.* ♦ *That phone ringing all the time is
driving me nuts!* **2** ~ **about sb/sth** very much in love with
someone; very enthusiastic about something: *He's absolutely nuts about her.* ⊃ **thesaurus box at** CRAZY **IDM** see
SOUP *n.*

nut·shell /ˈnʌtʃel/ *noun*
IDM **(put sth) in a nutshell** (to say or express something)
in a very clear way, using few words: *To put it in a nutshell,
we're bankrupt.*

nut·ty /ˈnʌti/ *adj.* (nut·ti·er, nut·ti·est) **1** tasting of or
containing nuts: *a nutty taste* **2** (*informal*) slightly crazy: *She's
got some nutty friends.* ♦ *He's as nutty as a fruitcake*
(= completely crazy).

nuz·zle /ˈnʌzl/ *verb* [T, I] to touch or rub someone or
something with the nose or mouth, especially to show

affection: ~ **sb/sth** *She nuzzled his ear.* ♦ + **adv./prep.** *The
child nuzzled up against his mother.*

NV *abbr.* (in writing) Nevada

N.W. (also NW) *abbr.* (in writing) northwest; northwestern:
N.W. Australia

NY *abbr.* (in writing) New York

NYC *abbr.* (in writing) New York City

ny·lon /ˈnaɪlɒn/ *noun* **1** [U] a very strong artificial material,
used for making clothes, rope, brushes, etc.: *a nylon fishing
line* ♦ *This material is 45% nylon.* **2** nylons [pl.] (*old-fashioned*)
women's STOCKINGS or PANTYHOSE made of nylon

nymph /nɪmf/ *noun* **1** (in ancient Greek and Roman stories)
a spirit of nature in the form of a young woman, that lives in
rivers, woods, etc. **2** (*biology*) a young insect that has a body
form that compares with that of the adult: *a dragonfly nymph*

nym·pho·ma·ni·ac /ˌnɪmfəˈmeɪniˌæk/ *noun* (*disapproving*) a
woman who has, or wants to have, sex very often
▶ **nym·pho·ma·ni·a** /-ˈmeɪniə/ *noun* [U]

NYSE /ˌɛn waɪ ɛs ˈi/ *abbr.* New York Stock Exchange

NZ *abbr.* (in writing) New Zealand

Oo

O /oʊ/ noun, exclamation, symbol
- **noun** also **o** (pl. **Os, O's, o's** /oʊz/) **1** [C, U] the 15th letter of the English alphabet: *"Orange" begins with (an) O/"O."* **2** used to mean "zero" when saying telephone numbers, etc.: *My number is six o three three* (= 6033).
- **exclamation** (especially *literary*) = OH
- **symbol** the symbol for the chemical element OXYGEN

o' /ə/ prep. used in written English to represent an informal way of saying *of*: *a couple o' times*

oaf /oʊf/ noun a stupid, unpleasant, or awkward person, especially a man: *Watch that cup, you clumsy oaf!* ▶ **oaf·ish** /'oʊfɪʃ/ adj.

oak /oʊk/ noun **1** [C, U] (also **oak tree**) a large tree that produces small nuts called ACORNS. Oaks are common in northern countries and can live to be hundreds of years old: *a gnarled old oak tree* ◆ *forests of oak and pine* ⊃ see also POISON OAK ⊃ picture at TREE **2** [U] the hard wood of the oak tree: *oak beams* ◆ *This table is made of solid oak.*
IDM **great/tall oaks from little acorns grow** (*saying*) something large and successful often begins in a very small way

oak·en /'oʊkən/ adj. [only before noun] (*literary*) made of oak

oa·kum /'oʊkəm/ noun [U] a material obtained by pulling old rope to pieces, a job done in the past by prisoners

OAP /ˌoʊ eɪ 'pi/ abbr. (CanE) OLD-AGE PENSION

oar /ɔr/ noun a long pole with a flat blade at one end that is used for ROWING a boat: *He pulled as hard as he could on the oars.* ⊃ picture at BOAT ⊃ compare PADDLE

oar·lock /'ɔrlɑk/ noun a device attached to the side of a boat for holding an OAR

oars·man /'ɔrzmən/, **oars·wom·an** /'ɔrzˌwʊmən/ noun (pl. **oars·men** /-mən/, **oars·wom·en** /-ˌwɪmən/) a person who ROWS a boat, especially as a member of a CREW (= team)

OAS /ˌoʊ eɪ 'ɛs/ abbr. (CanE) OLD-AGE SECURITY

o·a·sis /oʊ'eɪsəs/ noun (pl. **o·a·ses** /-siz/) **1** an area in the desert where there is water and where plants grow **2** a pleasant place or period of time in the middle of something unpleasant or difficult **SYN** HAVEN: *an oasis of calm* ◆ *a green oasis in the heart of the city*

oat /oʊt/ adj. [only before noun] made from or containing OATS: *oat bran* ⊃ see also OATMEAL

oat·er /'oʊtər/ noun (*informal*) a movie about life in the western U.S. in the 19th century

oath /oʊθ/ noun (pl. **oaths** /oʊðz; oʊθs/) **1** a formal promise to do something or a formal statement that something is true: *to take/swear an oath* of allegiance ◆ *Before giving evidence, witnesses in court have to take the oath* (= promise to tell the truth). ⊃ collocations at VOTE **2** (*old-fashioned*) an offensive word or phrase used to express anger, surprise, etc.; a swear word: *She heard the sound of breaking glass, followed by a muttered oath.*
IDM **under oath** (*law*) having made a formal promise to tell the truth in court: *Is she prepared to give evidence under oath?* ◆ *The judge reminded the witness that he was still under oath.*

oat·meal /'oʊtmil/ noun [U] **1** flour made from crushed oats, used to make cookies, breakfast CEREAL, etc. **2** a type of soft, thick, pale brown food made by boiling OATS in milk or water, eaten hot, especially for breakfast **3** a pale brown color ▶ **oat·meal** adj.: *an oatmeal carpet*

oats /oʊts/ noun [pl.] grain grown in cool countries as food for animals and for making flour, OATMEAL, etc. ⊃ picture at CEREAL ⊃ see also OAT **IDM** see SOW¹

ob·li·ga·to (also **o·bli·ga·to**) /ˌɑblə'ɡɑtoʊ/ noun (pl. **ob·bli·ga·tos**) (*music*) (from *Italian*) an important part for an instrument in a piece of music that cannot be left out

ob·du·rate /'ɑbdərət/ adj. (*formal*, usually *disapproving*) refusing to change your mind or your actions in any way **SYN** STUBBORN ▶ **ob·du·ra·cy** /'ɑbdərəsi/ noun [U] **ob·du·rate·ly** adv.

o·be·di·ent /oʊ'bidiənt; ə'bi-/ adj. doing what you are told to do; willing to obey: *an obedient child* ◆ *~ to sb/sth He was always obedient to his father's wishes.* **ANT** DISOBEDIENT ▶ **o·be·di·ence** /-əns/ noun [U]: *blind/complete/unquestioning/total obedience* ◆ *~ to sb/sth He has acted in obedience to the law.* **o·be·di·ent·ly** adv.
IDM **your obedient servant** (*old use*) used to end a formal letter

o·bei·sance /oʊ'bisns; oʊ'beɪ-/ noun (*formal*) **1** [U] respect for someone or something or willingness to obey someone **2** [C] the act of bending your head or the upper part of your body in order to show respect for someone or something

ob·e·lisk /'ɑbəlɪsk/ noun a tall, pointed, stone column with four sides, put up in memory of a person or an event ⊃ picture at ARCHITECTURE

o·bese /oʊ'bis/ adj. (*formal* or *medical*) (of people) very fat, in a way that is not healthy ⊃ collocations at DIET ▶ **o·be·si·ty** /oʊ'bisəti/ noun [U]: *Obesity can increase the risk of heart disease.*

o·bey 🔑 /oʊ'beɪ; ə'beɪ/ verb [T, I] **~ (sb/sth)** to do what you are told or expected to do: *to obey a command/an order/rules/the law* ◆ *He had always obeyed his parents without question.* ◆ *"Sit down!" Meekly, she obeyed.* **ANT** DISOBEY

ob·fus·cate /'ɑbfəˌskeɪt/ verb [I, T] **~ (sth)** (*formal*) to make something less clear and more difficult to understand, usually deliberately **SYN** OBSCURE ▶ **ob·fus·ca·tion** /ˌɑbfə'skeɪʃn/ noun [U, C]

ob-gyn /ˌoʊ bi ˌdʒi waɪ 'ɛn/ noun (*informal*) **1** [U] the branches of medicine concerned with the birth of children (= OBSTETRICS) and the diseases of women (= GYNECOLOGY) **2** [C] a doctor who is trained in this type of medicine

o·bi /'oʊbi/ noun (from *Japanese*) a wide piece of cloth worn around the waist of a Japanese KIMONO

o·bit·u·ar·y /oʊ'bɪtʃuˌɛri/ noun (pl. **o·bit·u·ar·ies**) (also *informal* **o·bit** /'oʊbɪt/) an article about someone's life and achievements, printed in a newspaper soon after they have died

ob·ject 🔑 noun, verb
- **noun** /'ɑbdʒɛkt; -dʒɪkt/ **1** a thing that can be seen and touched, but is not alive: *everyday objects such as cups and saucers* ◆ *Glass and plastic objects lined the shelves.* ⊃ see also UFO **2 ~ of desire, study, attention, etc.** a person or thing that someone DESIRES, studies, pays attention to, etc. ⊃ see also SEX OBJECT **3** an aim or a purpose: *Her sole object in life is to become a travel writer.* ◆ *The object is to educate people about road safety.* ◆ *If you're late, you'll defeat the whole object of the exercise.* ⊃ thesaurus box at TARGET **4** (*grammar*) a noun, noun phrase, or pronoun that refers to a person or thing that is affected by the action of the verb (called the DIRECT OBJECT), or that the action is done to or for (called the INDIRECT OBJECT) ⊃ compare SUBJECT
IDM **money, price, etc. is no object** used to say that you are willing to spend a lot of money: *He always travels first class—money is no object.*

VOCABULARY BUILDING

objects you can use

It is useful to know some general words to help you describe objects, especially if you do not know the name of a particular object.

- A **device** is something that has been designed to do a

particular job: *Have you seen the new device for cars that warns drivers about traffic jams ahead?*

- A **gadget** is a small object that does something useful, but is not really necessary: *His kitchen is full of gadgets he never uses.*
- An **instrument** is used especially for delicate or scientific work: *A thermometer is an instrument that measures temperature.*
- A **tool** is something that you use for making and repairing things: *A tool for turning screws is called a screwdriver.*
- A **machine** has moving parts and is used for a particular job. It usually stands on its own: *A blender is an electric machine for mixing soft food or liquid.*
- An **appliance** is a large machine that you use in the house, such as a washing machine.
- **Equipment** means all the things you need for a particular activity: *rock climbing equipment.*
- **Apparatus** means all the tools, machines, or equipment that you need for something: *firefighters wearing breathing apparatus.*

● **verb** /əb'dʒɛkt/ **1** [I] to say that you disagree with, disapprove of, or oppose something: ~ **(to sb/sth)** *Many local people object to the building of the new airport.* ◆ *If no one objects, we'll postpone the meeting till next week.* ◆ ~ **to doing sth/to sb doing sth** *I really object to being charged for parking.* **2** [T] ~ **that...** | **+ speech** to give something as a reason for opposing something **SYN** PROTEST: *He objected that the police had arrested him without sufficient evidence.* ↪ thesaurus box at COMPLAIN

'**object** ˌ**code** (also '**object** ˌ**language**) *noun* [U] (*computing*) the language into which a program is translated using a COMPILER or an ASSEMBLER

ob·jec·ti·fi·ca·tion /əbˌdʒɛktəfə'keɪʃn/ *noun* [U] (*formal*) the act of treating people as if they are objects, without rights or feelings of their own

ob·jec·ti·fy /əb'dʒɛktəˌfaɪ/ *verb* (**ob·jec·ti·fies**, **ob·jec·ti·fy·ing**, **ob·jec·ti·fied**, **ob·jec·ti·fied**) ~ **sb/sth** (*formal*) to treat someone or something as an object

ob·jec·tion /əb'dʒɛkʃn/ *noun* ~ **(to sth/to doing sth)** | ~ **(that...)** a reason why you do not like or are opposed to something; a statement about this: *I have no objection to him coming to stay.* ◆ *I'd like to come too, if you have no objection.* ◆ *The main objection to the plan was that it would cost too much.* ◆ *to raise an objection to something* ◆ *No objections were raised at the time.* ◆ *The proposal will go ahead despite strong objections from the public.*

ob·jec·tion·a·ble /əb'dʒɛkʃənəbl/ *adj.* (*formal*) unpleasant or offensive: *objectionable people/odors* ◆ *Why are you being so objectionable today?*

ob·jec·tive 🔑 **AWL** /əb'dʒɛktɪv/ *noun, adj.*

● **noun 1** something that you are trying to achieve **SYN** GOAL: *the main/primary/principal objective* ◆ *to meet/achieve your objectives* ◆ *You must set realistic aims and objectives for yourself.* ◆ *The main objective of this meeting is to give more information on our plans.* ↪ thesaurus box at TARGET **2** (also **ob·jective** ˈ**lens**) (*technical*) the LENS in a TELESCOPE or MICROSCOPE that is nearest to the object being looked at ↪ picture at LABORATORY

● **adj. 1** not influenced by personal feelings or opinions; considering only facts **SYN** UNBIASED: *an objective analysis/assessment/report* ◆ *objective criteria* ◆ *I find it difficult to be objective where he's concerned.* **ANT** SUBJECTIVE **2** (*philosophy*) existing outside the mind; based on facts that can be proved: *objective reality* **ANT** SUBJECTIVE **3** [only before noun] (*grammar*) the **objective** case is the one which is used for the object of a sentence ▶ **ob·jec·tive·ly** **AWL** *adv.*: *Looked at objectively, the situation is not too bad.* ◆ *Can these effects be objectively measured?* **ob·jec·tiv·i·ty** **AWL** /ˌɑbdʒɛk'tɪvəti/ *noun* [U]: *There was a lack of objectivity in the way the candidates were judged.* ◆ *scientific objectivity*

'**object** ˌ**language** *noun* **1** [C] (*linguistics*) = TARGET LANGUAGE **2** [U] (*computing*) = OBJECT CODE

'**object** ˌ**lesson** *noun* [usually sing.] a practical example of what you should or should not do in a particular situation

ob·jec·tor /əb'dʒɛktər/ *noun* ~ **(to sth)** a person who objects to something: *There were no objectors to the plan.* ↪ see also CONSCIENTIOUS OBJECTOR

ob·jet d'art /ˌɔbʒeɪ 'dɑr/ *noun* (*pl.* **ob·jets d'art** /ˌɔbʒeɪ 'dɑr/) (from *French*) a small artistic object, used for decoration

ob·li·gat·ed /'ɑbləˌɡeɪtəd/ *adj.* ~ **(to do sth)** having a moral or legal duty to do something **SYN** OBLIGED: *He felt obligated to help.*

ob·li·ga·tion /ˌɑblə'ɡeɪʃn/ *noun* **1** [U] ~ **(to do sth)** the state of being forced to do something because it is your duty, or because of a law, etc.: *You are under no obligation to buy anything.* ◆ *She did not feel under any obligation to tell him the truth.* ◆ *I don't want people coming to see me out of a sense of obligation.* ◆ *We will send you an estimate for the work without obligation* (= you do not have to accept it). **2** [C] something that you must do because you have promised, because of a law, etc. **SYN** COMMITMENT: *to fulfill your legal/professional/financial obligations* ◆ *They reminded him of his contractual obligations.* ◆ ~ **to do sth** *We have a moral obligation to protect the environment.*

ob·li·ga·to = OBBLIGATO

o·blig·a·to·ry /ə'blɪɡəˌtɔri/ *adj.* **1** ~ **(for sb) (to do sth)** (*formal*) that you must do because of the law, rules, etc. **SYN** COMPULSORY: *It is obligatory for all employees to wear protective clothing.* **ANT** OPTIONAL **2** (often *humorous*) that you do because you always do it, or other people in the same situation always do it: *In the mid 60s he took the almost obligatory trip to India.*

o·blige /ə'blaɪdʒ/ *verb* **1** [T, usually passive] ~ **sb to do sth** to force someone to do something, because it is a duty, etc.: *Parents are obliged by law to send their children to school.* ◆ *I felt obliged to ask them to dinner.* ◆ *He suffered a serious injury that obliged him to give up work.* **2** [I, T] to help someone by doing what they ask or what you know they want: *Call me if you need any help—I'd be happy to oblige.* ◆ ~ **sb (with sth)** (*formal*) *Would you oblige me with some information?* ◆ ~ **sb (by doing sth)** *Oblige me by keeping your suspicions to yourself.*

o·bliged /ə'blaɪdʒd/ *adj.* [not before noun] ~ **(to sb) (for sth/for doing sth)** (*formal*) used when you are expressing thanks or asking politely for something, to show that you are grateful to someone: *I'm much obliged to you for helping us.* ◆ *I'd be obliged if you would keep this to yourself.*

o·blig·ing /ə'blaɪdʒɪŋ/ *adj.* very willing to help **SYN** HELPFUL: *They were very obliging and offered to wait for us.* ▶ **o·blig·ing·ly** *adv.*

o·blique /ə'blik; ou-/ *adj.* **1** not expressed or done in a direct way **SYN** INDIRECT: *an oblique reference/approach/comment* **2** (of a line) sloping at an angle ▶ **o·blique·ly** *adv.*: *He referred only obliquely to their recent problems.* ◆ *Always cut stems obliquely to enable flowers to absorb more water.*

o·blique ˈ**angle** *noun* an angle that is not an angle of 90° ↪ compare ACUTE ANGLE, OBTUSE ANGLE, REFLEX ANGLE, RIGHT ANGLE

ob·lit·er·ate /ə'blɪtəˌreɪt/ *verb* [often passive] ~ **sth** to remove all signs of something, either by destroying or covering it completely: *The building was completely obliterated by the bomb.* ◆ *The snow had obliterated their footprints.* ◆ (*figurative*) *Everything that happened that night was obliterated from his memory.* ▶ **ob·lit·er·a·tion** /əˌblɪtə'reɪʃn/ *noun* [U]

ob·liv·i·on /ə'blɪviən/ *noun* [U] **1** a state in which you are not aware of what is happening around you, usually because you are unconscious or asleep: *He often drinks himself into oblivion.* ◆ *Sam longed for the oblivion of sleep.* **2** the state in which someone or something has been forgotten and is no longer famous or important

SYN OBSCURITY: *An unexpected victory saved him from political oblivion.* ◆ *Most of his inventions have been consigned to oblivion.* **3** a state in which something has been completely destroyed: *Hundreds of homes were bombed into oblivion during the first weeks of the war.*

ob·liv·i·ous /ə'blɪviəs/ *adj.* [not usually before noun] not aware of something: **~ (of sth)** *He drove off, oblivious of the damage he had caused.* ◆ **~ (to sth)** *You eventually become oblivious to the noise.* ▶ **ob·liv·i·ous·ly** *adv.*

ob·long /'ɑblɔŋ/ *adj.* **1** an oblong shape has four straight sides, two of which are longer than the other two, and four angles of 90° **2** used to describe any shape that is longer than it is wide: *an oblong melon* ▶ **oblong** *noun: a tiny oblong of glass in the roof* ⟳ see also RECTANGLE

ob·lo·quy /'ɑbləkwi/ *noun* [U] (*formal*) **1** strong public criticism **2** loss of respect and honor

ob·nox·ious /əb'nɑkʃəs/ *adj.* extremely unpleasant, especially in a way that offends people **SYN** OFFENSIVE: *obnoxious behavior* ◆ *a thoroughly obnoxious little man* ◆ *obnoxious odors* ▶ **ob·nox·ious·ly** *adv.*

obo (also **o.b.o.**) *abbr.* or best offer (used in small advertisements to show that something may be sold at a lower price than the price that has been asked): *$800 obo*

o·boe /'oʊboʊ/ *noun* a musical instrument of the WOODWIND group. It is shaped like a pipe and has a double REED at the top that you blow into. ⟳ picture at INSTRUMENT

o·bo·ist /'oʊboʊɪst/ *noun* a person who plays the oboe

ob·scene /əb'sin/ *adj.* **1** connected with sex in a way that most people find offensive: *obscene gestures/language/books* ◆ *an obscene phone call* (= in which someone says obscene things) **2** extremely large in size or amount in a way that most people find unacceptable and offensive **SYN** OUTRAGEOUS: *He earns an obscene amount of money.* ◆ *It's obscene to spend so much on food when millions are starving.* ▶ **ob·scene·ly** *adv.: to behave obscenely* ◆ *obscenely rich*

ob·scen·i·ty /əb'sɛnəti/ *noun* (*pl.* **ob·scen·i·ties**) **1** [U] obscene language or behavior: *The editors are being prosecuted for obscenity.* ◆ *the laws on obscenity* **2** [C, usually pl.] an obscene word or act: *She screamed a string of obscenities at the judge.*

ob·scu·rant·ism /əb'skyʊrən,tɪzəm/ *noun* [U] (*formal*) the practice of deliberately preventing someone from understanding or discovering something ▶ **ob·scu·rant·ist** /-tɪst/ *adj.*

ob·scure /əb'skyʊr/ *adj., verb*
• *adj.* **1** not well known **SYN** UNKNOWN: *an obscure German poet* ◆ *He was born around 1650 but his origins remain obscure.* **2** difficult to understand: *I found her lecture very obscure.* ◆ *For some obscure reason, he failed to show up.* ▶ **ob·scure·ly** *adv.: They were making her feel obscurely worried* (= for reasons that were difficult to understand).
• *verb* **~ sth** to make it difficult to see, hear, or understand something: *The view was obscured by fog.* ◆ *We mustn't let these minor details obscure the main issue.*

ob·scu·ri·ty /əb'skyʊrəti/ *noun* (*pl.* **ob·scu·ri·ties**) **1** [U] the state in which someone or something is not well known or has been forgotten: *The actress was only 17 when she was plucked from obscurity and made a star.* ◆ *He spent most of his life working in obscurity.* **2** [U, C, usually pl.] the quality of being difficult to understand; something that is difficult to understand: *The course teaches students to avoid ambiguity and obscurity of expression.* ◆ *a speech full of obscurities* **3** [U] (*literary*) the state of being dark; DARKNESS

ob·se·quies /'ɑbsəkwiz/ *noun* [pl.] (*formal*) funeral ceremonies: *state obsequies*

ob·se·qui·ous /əb'sikwiəs/ *adj.* (*formal, disapproving*) trying too hard to please someone, especially someone who is important **SYN** SERVILE: *an obsequious manner* ▶ **ob·se·qui·ous·ly** *adv.: smiling obsequiously* **ob·se·qui·ous·ness** *noun* [U]

ob·serv·a·ble /əb'zərvəbl/ *adj.* that can be seen or noticed: *observable differences* ◆ *Similar trends are observable in mainland Europe.* ▶ **ob·serv·a·bly** /-bli/ *adv.*

ob·serv·ance /əb'zərvəns/ *noun* **1** [U, sing.] the practice of obeying a law, celebrating a festival, or behaving according to a particular custom: *observance of the law* ◆ *a strict observance of the Sabbath* **ANT** NONOBSERVANCE **2** [C, usually pl.] an act performed as part of a religious or traditional ceremony: *religious observances*

ob·serv·ant /əb'zərvənt/ *adj.* **1** good at noticing things around you **SYN** SHARP-EYED: *Observant walkers may see red deer along this stretch of the road.* ◆ *How very observant of you!* **2** (*formal*) careful to obey religious laws and customs

ob·ser·va·tion 🔊 /,ɑbzər'veɪʃn; -sər-/ *noun* **1** [U, C] the act of watching someone or something carefully for a period of time, especially to learn something: *Most information was collected by direct observation of the animals' behavior.* ◆ *results based on scientific observations* ◆ *We managed to escape observation* (= we were not seen). ◆ *The patient is being kept under observation* (= watched closely by the doctors). ◆ *She has outstanding powers of observation* (= the ability to notice things around her). ◆ *an observation post/tower* (= a place from where someone, especially an enemy, can be watched) ⟳ collocations at SCIENTIFIC **2** [C] **~ (about/on sth)** a comment, especially based on something you have seen, heard, or read **SYN** REMARK: *He began by making a few general observations about the report.* ◆ *She has some interesting observations on possible future developments.* ▶ **ob·ser·va·tion·al** /-ʃənl/ *adj.*

obser'vation car *noun* a car on a train with large windows, designed to give passengers a good view of the landscape

ob·serv·a·to·ry /əb'zərvə,tɔri/ *noun* (*pl.* **ob·serv·a·to·ries**) a special building from which scientists watch the stars, the weather, etc.

ob·serve 🔊 /əb'zərv/ *verb* (*formal*) **1** [T] (not used in the progressive tenses) to see or notice someone or something: **~ sb/sth** *Have you observed any changes lately?* ◆ *All the characters in the novel are closely observed* (= seem like people in real life). ◆ **~ sb/sth do sth** *The police observed a man enter the bank.* ◆ **~ sb/sth doing sth** *They observed him entering the bank.* ◆ **~ that…** *She observed that all the chairs were already occupied.* ◆ **be observed to do sth** *He was observed to follow her closely.* **HELP** This pattern is only used in the passive. ⟳ thesaurus box at COMMENT, NOTICE **2** [T, I] to watch someone or something carefully, especially to learn more about them **SYN** MONITOR: **~ (sb/sth)** *I felt he was observing everything I did.* ◆ *The patients were observed over a period of several months.* ◆ *He observes keenly, but says little.* ◆ **~ how, what, etc.…** *They observed how the parts of the machine fitted together.* ⟳ thesaurus box at LOOK **3** [T] **~ that…** | **+ speech** (*formal*) to make a remark **SYN** COMMENT: *She observed that it was getting late.* **4** [T] **~ sth** to obey rules, laws, etc.: *Will the rebels observe the ceasefire?* ◆ *The crowd observed a minute's silence* (= were silent for one minute) *in memory of those who had died.* **5** [T] **~ sth** (*formal*) to celebrate festivals, birthdays, etc.: *Do they observe Christmas?*

ob·serv·er /əb'zərvər/ *noun* **1** a person who watches someone or something: *According to observers, the plane exploded shortly after takeoff.* ◆ *To the casual observer* (= someone who does not pay much attention), *the system appears confusing.* ⟳ thesaurus box at WITNESS **2** a person who attends a meeting, lesson, etc. to listen and watch but not to take part: *A team of officials was sent as observers to the conference.* **3** a person who watches and studies particular events, situations, etc. and is therefore considered to be an expert on them: *a celebrity observer*

ob·sess /əb'sɛs/ *verb* **1** [T, often passive] **~ sb** to completely fill your mind so that you cannot think of anything else, in a way that is not normal: *He's obsessed by computers.* ◆ *She's completely obsessed with him.* ◆ *The need to produce the most exciting newspaper story obsesses most journalists.* **2** [I] **~ (about sth)** to be always talking or worrying about a particular thing, especially when this annoys other people: *I think you should try to stop obsessing about food.*

ob·ses·sion /əbˈsɛʃn/ *noun* **1** [U] the state in which a person's mind is completely filled with thoughts of one particular thing or person, in a way that is not normal: *Her fear of flying is bordering on obsession.* ◆ **~ with sb/sth** *The media's obsession with the young prince continues.* **2** [C] **~ (with sb)** a person or thing that someone thinks about too much: *Fitness has become an obsession with him.*

ob·ses·sion·al /əbˈsɛʃənl/ *adj.* thinking too much about one particular person or thing, in a way that is not normal: *She is obsessional about cleanliness.* ◆ *obsessional behavior* ▶ **ob·ses·sion·al·ly** /-ʃənəli/ *adv.*

ob·ses·sive /əbˈsɛsɪv/ *adj., noun*
● *adj.* thinking too much about one particular person or thing, in a way that is not normal: *He's becoming more and more obsessive about punctuality.* ◆ *an obsessive attention to detail* ▶ **ob·ses·sive·ly** *adv.*: *obsessively jealous* ◆ *He worries obsessively about his appearance.*
● *noun* (*psychology*) a person whose mind is filled with thoughts of one particular thing or person, so that they cannot think of anything else

ob·ses·sive com·pul·sive dis·order *noun* [U] (*abbr.* OCD) a mental DISORDER in which someone feels they have to repeat certain actions or activities to get rid of fears or unpleasant thoughts

ob·sid·i·an /əbˈsɪdiən/ *noun* [U] a type of dark rock that looks like glass and comes from VOLCANOES

ob·so·les·cence /ˌɑbsəˈlɛsns/ *noun* [U] (*formal*) the state of becoming old-fashioned and no longer useful (= becoming obsolete): *products with **built-in/planned obsolescence*** (= designed not to last long so that people will have to buy new ones) ▶ **ob·so·les·cent** /-ˈlɛsnt/ *adj.*

ob·so·lete /ˌɑbsəˈlit/ *adj.* no longer used because something new has been invented **SYN** OUT OF DATE: *obsolete technology* ◆ *With technological changes many traditional skills have become obsolete.*

ob·sta·cle /ˈɑbstɪkl/ *noun* **1 ~ (to sth/to doing sth)** a situation, an event, etc. that makes it difficult for you to do or achieve something **SYN** HINDRANCE: *A lack of qualifications can be a major obstacle to finding a job.* ◆ *So far, we have managed to overcome all the obstacles that have been placed in our path.* **2** an object that is in your way and that makes it difficult for you to move forward: *The area was full of streams and bogs and other natural obstacles.*

obstacle course *noun* **1** a series of objects that people taking part in a race have to climb over, under, through, etc. **2** an area of land with many objects that are difficult to climb, jump over, or go through, that is used by soldiers for improving physical skills and strength **3** a series of difficulties that people have to deal with in order to achieve a particular aim

obstacle race *noun* a race in which the people taking part have to climb over, under, through, etc. various objects

ob·ste·tri·cian /ˌɑbstəˈtrɪʃn/ *noun* a doctor who is trained in obstetrics

ob·stet·rics /əbˈstɛtrɪks/ *noun* [U] the branch of medicine concerned with the birth of children ▶ **ob·stet·ric** *adj.*: *obstetric medicine*

ob·sti·nate /ˈɑbstənət/ *adj.* **1** (often *disapproving*) refusing to change your opinions, way of behaving, etc. when other people try to persuade you to; showing this **SYN** STUBBORN: *He can be very obstinate when he wants to be!* ◆ *her obstinate refusal to comply with their request* **2** [usually before noun] difficult to get rid of or deal with **SYN** STUBBORN: *the obstinate problem of unemployment* ◆ *an obstinate stain* ▶ **ob·sti·na·cy** /ˈɑbstənəsi/ *noun* [U]: *an act of*

sheer obstinacy **ob·sti·nate·ly** *adv.*: *He obstinately refused to consider the future.*

ob·strep·er·ous /əbˈstrɛpərəs/ *adj.* (*formal* or *humorous*) noisy and difficult to control

ob·struct /əbˈstrʌkt/ *verb* **1 ~ sth** to block a road, an entrance, a passage, etc. so that someone or something cannot get through, see past, etc.: *You can't park here, you're obstructing my driveway.* ◆ *First check that the patient doesn't have an obstructed airway.* ◆ *The pillar obstructed our view of the stage.* **2 ~ sb/sth** to prevent someone or something from doing something or making progress, especially when this is done deliberately **SYN** HINDER: *They were charged with obstructing the police in the course of duty.* ◆ *terrorists attempting to obstruct the peace process*
IDM **obstruct justice** (*law*) to tell a lie or to do something in order to prevent the police, etc. from finding out the truth about a crime

ob·struc·tion /əbˈstrʌkʃn/ *noun* **1** [U, C] the fact of trying to prevent something or someone from making progress: *the obstruction of justice* ◆ *He was arrested for obstruction of a police officer in the execution of his duty.* **2** [U, C] the fact of blocking a road, an entrance, a passage, etc.: *obstruction of the factory gates* ◆ *The abandoned car was causing an obstruction.* **3** [C] something that blocks a road, an entrance, etc.: *It is my job to make sure that all pathways are clear of obstructions.* **4** [C, U] something that blocks a passage or tube in your body; a medical condition resulting from this **SYN** BLOCKAGE: *He had an operation to remove an obstruction in his throat.* ◆ *bowel/intestinal obstruction* **5** [U] (*sports*) the offense of unfairly preventing a player of the other team from moving to get the ball

ob·struc·tion·ism /əbˈstrʌkʃəˌnɪzəm/ *noun* [U] (*formal*) the practice of trying to prevent a political group or a committee from making progress, passing laws, etc. ▶ **ob·struc·tion·ist** /-nɪst/ *noun, adj.*

ob·struc·tive /əbˈstrʌktɪv/ *adj.* **1** trying to prevent someone or something from making progress: *Of course she can do it. She's just being deliberately obstructive.* ➔ compare CONSTRUCTIVE **2** [only before noun] (*medical*) connected with a passage, tube, etc. in your body that has become blocked: *obstructive lung disease*

ob·tain 🔑 **AWL** /əbˈteɪn/ *verb* (*formal*)
1 [T] **~ sth** to get something, especially by making an effort: *to obtain advice/information/permission* ◆ *I finally managed to obtain a copy of the report.* ◆ *To obtain the overall score, add up the totals in each column.* **2** [I] (not used in the progressive tenses) (of rules, systems, customs, etc.) to exist **SYN** APPLY: *These conditions no longer obtain.*

ob·tain·a·ble **AWL** /əbˈteɪnəbl/ *adj.* [not usually before noun] that can be obtained **SYN** AVAILABLE: *Full details are obtainable from any post office.*

ob·trude /əbˈtrud/ *verb* [I, T] **~ (sth/yourself) (on/upon sb)** (*formal*) to become or make something noticed, especially in a way that is not wanted: *Music from the next room obtruded upon his thoughts.*

ob·tru·sive /əbˈtrusɪv/ *adj.* noticeable in an unpleasant way: *The sofa would be less obtrusive in a paler color.* ◆ *They tried to ensure that their presence was not too obtrusive.* ▶ **ob·tru·sive·ly** *adv.*

ob·tuse /əbˈtus/ *adj.* (*formal, disapproving*) slow or unwilling to understand something: *Are you being deliberately obtuse?* ▶ **ob·tuse·ness** *noun* [U]

obtuse angle *noun* an angle between 90° and 180° ➔ picture at SHAPE ➔ compare ACUTE ANGLE, OBLIQUE ANGLE, REFLEX ANGLE, RIGHT ANGLE

ob·verse /ˈɑbvərs/ *noun* usually **the obverse** [sing.] **1** (*formal*) the opposite of something: *The obverse of love is hate.* **2** (*technical*) the side of a coin or MEDAL that has the head or main design on it

ob·vi·ate /ˈɑbviˌeɪt/ *verb* **~ sth** (*formal*) to remove a problem or the need for something **SYN** PRECLUDE: *This new evidence obviates the need for any further enquiries.*

ob·vi·ous 🔑 **AWL** /ˈɑbviəs/ *adj.*

1 ~ (to sb) (that…) easy to see or understand **SYN** CLEAR: *It was obvious to everyone that the child had been badly treated.* ◆ *It's obvious from what she said that something is wrong.* ◆ *I know you don't like her, but try not to make it so obvious.* ◆ *He agreed with obvious pleasure.* ◆ **For obvious reasons**, *I'd prefer not to give my name.* ◆ *The reasons for this decision were not immediately obvious.* ➔ **thesaurus box at CLEAR 2** that most people would think of or agree to: *She was the obvious choice for the job.* ◆ *There's no obvious solution to the problem.* ◆ *This seemed the most obvious thing to do.* **3** (*disapproving*) not interesting, new, or showing imagination; unnecessary because it is clear to everyone: *The ending was pretty obvious.* ◆ *I may be **stating the obvious**, but without more money the project cannot survive.* ▸ **ob·vi·ous·ness** *noun* [U]

ob·vi·ous·ly 🔑 **AWL** /ˈɑbviəsli/ *adv.*

1 used when giving information that you expect other people to know already or agree with **SYN** CLEARLY: *Obviously, we don't want to spend too much money.* ◆ *Diet and exercise are obviously important.* **2** used to say that a particular situation or fact is easy to see or understand: *He was obviously drunk.* ◆ *They're obviously not coming.* ◆ *"I didn't realize it was a formal occasion." "Obviously!"* (= I can see by the way you are dressed.)

oc·a·ri·na /ˌɑkəˈriːnə/ *noun* a small egg-shaped musical instrument that you blow into, with holes for the fingers

oc·ca·sion 🔑 /əˈkeɪʒn/ *noun, verb*

● *noun* **1** [C] a particular time when something happens: *on this/that occasion* ◆ *I've met him on several occasions.* ◆ *I can remember **occasions** when he had to cancel because of poor health.* ◆ *They have been seen together on two **separate** occasions.* ◆ *On one occasion, she called me in the middle of the night.* ◆ *He used the occasion to announce further tax cuts.* **2** [C] a special event, ceremony, or celebration: *a great/memorable/happy occasion* ◆ *Turn every meal into **a special occasion**.* ◆ *They **marked the occasion** (= celebrated it) with an open-air concert.* ◆ *Their wedding turned out to be quite an occasion.* ◆ *He was presented with the watch **on the occasion of** his retirement.* **3** [sing.] ~ (for sth/doing sth) a suitable time for something: *It should have been an occasion for rejoicing, but she could not feel any real joy.* ◆ *I'll speak to him about it **if the occasion arises** (= if I get a chance).* **4** [U, sing.] (*formal*) a reason or cause: ~ (to do sth) *I've had no occasion to visit him recently.* ◆ ~ (of/for sth) *Her death was the occasion of mass riots.* ◆ *I'm willing to go to court over this **if the occasion arises** (= if it becomes necessary).*
IDM on occasion sometimes, but not often: *He has been known on occasion to lose his temper.* ➔ more at SENSE *n.*

● *verb* (*formal*) to cause something: ~ sth *The flight delay was occasioned by the need for a further security check.* ◆ ~ sb sth *The decision occasioned us much anxiety.*

oc·ca·sion·al /əˈkeɪʒənl/ *adj.* [only before noun] happening or done sometimes, but not often: *He works for us on an occasional basis.* ◆ *I enjoy the occasional glass of wine.* ◆ *He spent five years in Paris, with occasional visits to Italy.* ◆ *an occasional smoker* (= a person who smokes, but not often)

oc·ca·sion·al·ly 🔑 /əˈkeɪʒənəli/ *adv.*
sometimes, but not often: *We occasionally meet for a drink after work.* ◆ *This type of allergy can very occasionally be fatal.*

oc'casional ˌtable *noun* a small, light table that is easy to move, used for different things at different times

the Oc·ci·dent /ˈɑksədənt; -ˌdɛnt/ *noun* [sing.] (*formal*) the western part of the world, especially Europe and America ➔ compare ORIENT ▸ **oc·ci·den·tal** /ˌɑksəˈdɛntl/ *adj.*

oc·clude /əˈklud/ *verb* ~ sth (*technical*) to cover or block something: *an occluded artery* ▸ **oc·clu·sion** /əˈkluːʒn/ *noun* [U]

oc·cult /əˈkʌlt/ *adj.* **1** [only before noun] connected with magic powers and things that cannot be explained by reason or science **SYN** SUPERNATURAL: *occult practices*

2 the occult *noun* [sing.] everything connected with occult practices, etc.: *He's interested in witchcraft and the occult.*

oc·cult·ist /əˈkʌltɪst/ *noun* a person who is involved in the occult

oc·cu·pan·cy **AWL** /ˈɑkyəpənsi/ *noun* [U] (*formal*) the act of living in or using a building, room, piece of land, etc.: *Prices are based on full occupancy of an apartment.* ◆ *to be in sole occupancy*

oc·cu·pant **AWL** /ˈɑkyəpənt/ *noun* **1** a person who lives or works in a particular house, room, building, etc.: *All outstanding bills will be paid by the previous occupants.* **2** a person who is in a vehicle, seat, etc. at a particular time: *The car was badly damaged but the occupants were unhurt.*

oc·cu·pa·tion **AWL** /ˌɑkyəˈpeɪʃn/ *noun* **1** [C] a job or profession: *Please state your name, age, and occupation below.* ➔ **thesaurus box at WORK 2** [C] the way in which you spend your time, especially when you are not working: *Her main occupation seems to be shopping.* **3** [U] the act of moving into a country, town, etc. and taking control of it using military force; the period of time during which a country, town, etc. is controlled in this way: *the Roman occupation of Britain* ◆ *The areas **under occupation** contained major industrial areas.* ◆ *occupation forces* **4** [U] (*formal*) the act of living in or using a building, room, piece of land, etc.: *The offices will be ready for occupation in June.* ◆ *The following applies only to tenants in occupation after January 1, 2010.* ◆ *The level of **owner occupation** (= people owning their homes) has increased rapidly in the last 30 years.*

oc·cu·pa·tion·al **AWL** /ˌɑkyəˈpeɪʃənl/ *adj.* [only before noun] connected with a person's job or profession: *occupational health* ◆ *an **occupational risk/hazard*** ▸ **oc·cu·pa·tion·al·ly** /-ʃənəli/ *adv.*: *occupationally induced disease* ➔ see also OSHA

occuˌpational 'therapist *noun* (*abbr.* OT) a person whose job is to help people get better after illness or injury by giving them special activities to do

occuˌpational 'therapy *noun* (*abbr.* OT) [U] the work of an occupational therapist

oc·cu·pied 🔑 **AWL** /ˈɑkyəˌpaɪd/ *adj.*
1 [not before noun] being used by someone: *Only half of the rooms are occupied at the moment.* ➔ see also OWNER-OCCUPIED **2** [not before noun] busy: ~ (doing sth/in doing sth/in sth) *He's fully occupied taking care of three small children.* ◆ ~ (with sth/with doing sth) *Only half her time is occupied with politics.* ◆ *The most important thing is to **keep yourself occupied**.* **3** (of a country, etc.) controlled by people from another country, etc., using military force: *He spent his childhood in occupied Europe.* **ANT** UNOCCUPIED

oc·cu·pi·er **AWL** /ˈɑkyəˌpaɪər/ *noun* **1** ~ (of sth) (*formal*) a person who lives in or uses a building, room, piece of land, etc. **SYN** OCCUPANT: *The letter was addressed to the occupier of the house.* ➔ see also OWNER-OCCUPIER **2** [usually pl.] a member of an army that is occupying a foreign country, etc.

oc·cu·py 🔑 **AWL** /ˈɑkyəˌpaɪ/ *verb* (oc·cu·pies, oc·cu·py·ing, oc·cu·pied, oc·cu·pied)
1 ~ sth to fill or use a space, an area, or an amount of time **SYN** TAKE UP: *The bed seemed to occupy most of the room.* ◆ *How much memory does the program occupy?* ◆ *Administrative work occupies half of my time.* **2** ~ sth (*formal*) to live or work in a room, house, or building: *He occupies an office on the 12th floor.* **3** ~ sth to enter a place in a large group and take control of it, especially by military force: *The capital has been occupied by the rebel army.* ◆ *Protesting students occupied the TV station.* **4** to fill your time or keep you busy doing something: ~ sb/sth/yourself *a game that will occupy the kids for hours* ◆ *Problems at work continued to occupy his mind for some time.* ◆ ~ sb/sth/yourself with sb/sth *She occupied herself with routine office tasks.* ◆ ~ sb/sth/yourself doing sth *She occupied herself doing routine office tasks.* **5** ~ sth to have an official job or position **SYN** HOLD: *The president occupies the position for four years.*

oc·cur /ə'kər/ *verb* (-rr-)

1 [I] (*formal*) to happen: *When exactly did the incident occur?* ◆ *Something unexpected occurred.* **2** [I] + *adv./prep.* to exist or be found somewhere: *Sugar occurs naturally in fruit.* **PHR V** **oc·cur to sb** (of an idea or a thought) to come into your mind: *The idea occurred to him in a dream.* ◆ *~ that... It didn't occur to him that his wife was having an affair.* ◆ *~ to do sth It didn't occur to her to ask for help.*

oc·cur·rence /ə'kərəns/ *noun* **1** [C] something that happens or exists: *a common/everyday/frequent/regular occurrence* ◆ *Vandalism used to be a rare occurrence here.* ◆ *The program counts the number of occurrences of any word within the text.* **2** [U] *~ (of sth)* the fact of something happening or existing: *a link between the occurrence of skin cancer and the use of tanning salons*

OCD /ˌoʊ si 'di/ *abbr.* OBSESSIVE COMPULSIVE DISORDER

o·cean /'oʊʃn/ *noun*

1 usually the ocean [sing.] the mass of salt water that covers most of the earth's surface: *the depths of the ocean* ◆ *People were swimming in the ocean despite the hurricane warning.* ◆ *The plane hit the ocean several miles offshore.* ◆ *Our beach house is just a couple of miles from the ocean.* ◆ *an ocean liner* ◆ *Ocean levels are rising.* **2** usually Ocean [C] one of the five large areas that the ocean is divided into: *the Antarctic/Arctic/Atlantic/Indian/Pacific Ocean* **IDM** **an ocean of sth** (also **oceans of sth**) (*informal*) a large amount of something

o·cea·nar·i·um /ˌoʊʃə'nɛriəm/ *noun* an extremely large container in which fish and other sea creatures are kept to be seen by the public or to be studied by scientists ⊃ see also AQUARIUM

o·cean·front /'oʊʃn̩frʌnt/ (also **sea·front**) *noun* [sing.] often **the oceanfront** the land that faces the ocean: *condos and apartments along the oceanfront* ◆ *an oceanfront hotel*

o·cean·go·ing /'oʊʃn̩ɡoʊɪŋ/ *adj.* [only before noun] (of ships) made for crossing the ocean, not for trips along the coast or up rivers

O·ce·an·i·a /ˌoʊʃi'æniə/ *noun* [U] a large region of the world consisting of the Pacific islands and the oceans around them

o·ce·an·ic /ˌoʊʃi'ænɪk/ *adj.* [usually before noun] (*technical*) connected with the ocean: *oceanic fish*

o·cea·nog·ra·phy /ˌoʊʃə'nɑɡrəfi/ *noun* [U] the scientific study of the ocean ▶ **o·cea·nog·ra·pher** /-fər/ *noun*

ocean 'trench *noun* = TRENCH (3)

oc·e·lot /'ɑsəˌlɑt/ *noun* a wild animal of the cat family that has yellow fur with black lines and spots, found in Central and South America

o·cher (also **o·chre**) /'oʊkər/ *noun* [U] **1** a type of red or yellow earth used in some paints and DYES **2** the red or yellow color of ocher

o'clock /ə'klɑk/ *adv.*

used with the numbers 1 to 12 when telling the time, to mean an exact hour: *He left between five and six o'clock.* ◆ *at/after/before eleven o'clock*

OCR /ˌoʊ si 'ɑr/ *abbr.* (*computing*) OPTICAL CHARACTER RECOGNITION

-ocrat /əkræt/ *combining form* (in nouns) a member or supporter of a particular type of government or system: *democrat* ▶ **-ocratic** /əkrætɪk/ (in adjectives): *aristocratic*

oc·ta·gon /'ɑktəˌɡɑn/ *noun* (*geometry*) a flat shape with eight straight sides and eight angles ⊃ picture at SHAPE ▶ **oc·tag·o·nal** /ɑk'tæɡənl/ *adj.*: *an octagonal coin*

oc·tane /'ɑkteɪn/ *noun* a chemical substance in gas, used as a way of measuring its quality: *high-octane fuel*

oc·tave /'ɑktɪv/ *noun* (*music*) the difference (called the INTERVAL) between the first and last notes in a series of eight notes on a SCALE: *to play an octave higher* ◆ *Orbison's vocal range spanned three octaves.*

oc·ta·vo /ɑk'teɪvoʊ; -'tɑ-/ *noun* (*pl.* **oc·ta·vos**) (*technical*) a size of a book page that is made by folding each sheet of paper into eight LEAVES (= 16 pages)

oc·tet /ɑk'tɛt/ *noun* **1** a group of eight singers or musicians **2** a piece of music for eight singers or musicians

octo- /'ɑktoʊ; -tə/ (also **oct-**) *combining form* (in nouns, adjectives, and adverbs) eight; having eight: *octagon*

Oc·to·ber /ɑk'toʊbər/ *noun* [U, C] (*abbr.* Oct.) the 10th month of the year, between September and November **HELP** To see how **October** is used, look at the examples at **April**.

oc·to·ge·nar·i·an /ˌɑktədʒə'nɛriən/ *noun* a person between 80 and 89 years old

oc·to·pus /'ɑktəpəs; -ˌpʊs/ *noun* [C, U] a sea creature with a soft round body and eight long arms, that is sometimes used for food ⊃ picture at ANIMAL

oc·to·syl·la·ble /'ɑktəˌsɪləbl/ *noun* (*technical*) a line of poetry consisting of eight syllables ▶ **oc·to·syl·la·bic** /ˌɑktoʊsɪ'læbɪk/ *adj.*

oc·u·lar /'ɑkyələr/ *adj.* [only before noun] **1** (*technical*) connected with the eyes: *ocular muscles* **2** (*formal*) that can be seen: *ocular proof*

oc·u·list /'ɑkyəlɪst/ *noun* (*old-fashioned*) a doctor who examines and treats people's eyes

OD /ˌoʊ 'di/ *verb* (OD's, OD'ing, OD'd, OD'd) [I] *~ (on sth)* (*informal*) = OVERDOSE

odd /ɑd/ *adj.* (**odd·er**, **odd·est**)

▷ STRANGE **1** strange or unusual: *They're very odd people.* ◆ *There's something odd about that man.* ◆ *Doesn't it strike you as odd that she hasn't written?* ◆ *The odd thing was that he didn't recognize me.* ◆ *She had the oddest feeling that he was avoiding her.* ⊃ compare PECULIAR

▷ ODD- **2** (in compounds) strange or unusual in the way mentioned: *an odd-looking house* ◆ *an odd-sounding name*

▷ NOT REGULAR/OFTEN **3** the odd [only before noun] (no comparative or superlative) happening or appearing occasionally; not very regular or frequent **SYN** OCCASIONAL: *He makes the odd mistake—nothing too serious.*

▷ VARIOUS **4** [only before noun] (no comparative or superlative) of no particular type or size; various: *decorations made of odd scraps of paper*

▷ NOT MATCHING **5** [usually before noun] (no comparative or superlative) not with the pair or set that it belongs to; not matching: *You're wearing odd socks!*

▷ NUMBERS **6** (no comparative or superlative) (of numbers) that cannot be divided exactly by the number two: *1, 3, 5, and 7 are odd numbers.* **ANT** EVEN

▷ APPROXIMATELY **7** (no comparative or superlative; usually placed immediately after a number) approximately, or a little more than the number mentioned: *How old is she—seventy odd?* ◆ *He's worked there for twenty-odd years.*

▶ **odd·ness** *noun* [U]: *the oddness of her appearance* ◆ *His oddness frightened her.*

IDM **the odd man/one out** a person or thing that is different from others or does not fit easily into a group or set: *At school he was always the odd man out.* ◆ *Dog, cat, horse, shoe—which is the odd one out?*

odd·ball /'ɑdbɔl/ *noun* (*informal*) a person who behaves in a strange or unusual way ▶ **odd·ball** *adj.*: *oddball characters*

odd·i·ty /'ɑdəti/ *noun* (*pl.* **odd·i·ties**) **1** [C] a person or thing that is strange or unusual: *The book deals with some of the oddities of grammar and spelling.* **2** [U] the quality of being strange or unusual: *She suddenly realized the oddity of her remark and blushed.*

odd 'jobs *noun* [pl.] small jobs of various types: *to do odd jobs around the house*

odd·ly /'ɑdli/ *adv.*

1 in a strange or unusual way **SYN** STRANGELY: *She's been behaving very oddly lately.* ◆ *oddly colored clothes* ◆ *He looked at her in a way she found oddly disturbing.* **2** used to show that

t **t**ea   ţ bu**tt**er   d **d**id   k **c**at   ɡ **g**ot   tʃ **ch**in   dʒ **J**une   f **f**all

something is surprising **SYN** SURPRISINGly: *She felt, oddly, that they had been happier when they had no money.* ◆ *Oddly enough, the most expensive tickets sold fastest.*

odd·ments /ˈɑdmənts/ *noun* [pl.] **1** small pieces of cloth, wood, etc. that are left after a larger piece has been used to make something **SYN** REMNANT **2** small items that are not valuable or are not part of a larger set **SYN** BITS AND PIECES

odds **AWL** /ɑdz/ *noun* [pl.] **1** usually **the odds** the degree to which something is likely to happen: *The odds are very much in our favor* (= we are likely to succeed). ◆ *The odds are heavily against him* (= he is not likely to succeed). ◆ *The odds are that* (= it is likely that) *she'll win.* ◆ *What are the odds* (= how likely is it) *he won't show up?* **2** something that makes it seem impossible to do or achieve something: *They secured a victory in the face of overwhelming odds.* ◆ *Against all (the) odds, he made a full recovery.* **3** (in betting) the connection between two numbers that shows how much money someone will receive if they win a bet: *odds of ten to one* (= ten times the amount of money that has been bet by someone will be paid to them if they win) ◆ *They are offering long/short odds* (= the prize money will be high/low because there is a high/low risk of losing) *on the defending champion.* ◆ (*figurative*) *I'll lay odds on him getting the job* (= I'm sure he will get it).
IDM **be at odds (with sth)** to be different from something, when the two things should be the same **SYN** CONFLICT: *These findings are at odds with what is going on in the rest of the country.* **be at odds (with sb) (over/on sth)** to disagree with someone about something: *He's always at odds with his father over politics.* ⟳ more at STACKED

ˌodds and ˈends *noun* [pl.] (*informal*) small items that are not valuable or are not part of a larger set: *She spent the day sorting through a box full of odds and ends.* ◆ *I've got a few odds and ends* (= small jobs) *to do before leaving.*

ˌodds-ˈon *adj.* very likely to happen, win, etc.: *the odds-on favorite* (= the person, horse, etc. that is most likely to succeed, to win a race, etc.) ◆ *It's odds-on that he'll be late.* ◆ *Arazi is odds-on to win the Kentucky Derby.*

ode /oʊd/ *noun* a poem that speaks to a person or thing or celebrates a special event: *Keats's "Ode to a Nightingale"*

o·di·ous /ˈoʊdiəs/ *adj.* (*formal*) extremely unpleasant **SYN** HORRIBLE: *What an odious man!*

o·di·um /ˈoʊdiəm/ *noun* [U] (*formal*) a feeling of hatred that a lot of people have toward someone, because of something they have done

o·dom·e·ter /oʊˈdɑmətər/ (also *informal* **the clock**) *noun* an instrument in a vehicle that measures the number of miles it has traveled ⟳ picture at CAR

o·don·tol·o·gy /ˌoʊdɑnˈtɑlədʒi/ *noun* [U] the scientific study of the diseases and structure of teeth ▸ **o·don·tol·o·gist** /-dʒɪst/ *noun*

o·dor (*CanE usually* **o·dour**) /ˈoʊdər/ *noun* [C, U] (*formal*) a smell, especially one that is unpleasant: *a foul/musty/pungent, etc. odor* ◆ *the stale odor of cigarette smoke* ◆ (*figurative*) *the odor of suspicion* ⟳ see also BODY ODOR
IDM **be in good/bad odor (with sb)** (*formal*) to have/not have someone's approval and support

o·dor·less (*CanE usually* **o·dour·less**) /ˈoʊdərləs/ *adj.* without a smell: *an odorless liquid*

o·dor·ous /ˈoʊdərəs/ *adj.* (*literary* or *technical*) having a smell: *odorous gases*

od·ys·sey /ˈɑdəsi/ *noun* [sing.] (*literary*) a long journey full of experiences **ORIGIN** From the **Odyssey**, a Greek poem that is said to have been written by Homer, about the adventures of **Odysseus**. After a battle in Troy, Odysseus had to spend ten years traveling before he could return home.

OECD /ˌoʊ i si ˈdi/ *abbr.* Organization for Economic Cooperation and Development (an organization of industrial countries that encourages trade and economic growth)

the OED /ˌoʊ i ˈdi/ *abbr.* the Oxford English Dictionary (the largest dictionary of the English language, which was first published in Britain in 1928)

Oed·i·pal /ˈɛdəpl/ *adj.* [usually before noun] connected with an Oedipus complex

Oed·i·pus com·plex /ˈɛdəpəs ˌkɑmplɛks/ *noun* [sing.] (*psychology*) (in FREUDIAN theory) a young boy's unconscious sexual attraction to his mother and the jealous feelings that this causes toward his father ⟳ compare ELECTRA COMPLEX **ORIGIN** From the Greek story of **Oedipus**, whose father Laius had been told by the oracle that his son would kill him. Laius left Oedipus on a mountain to die, but a shepherd rescued him. Oedipus returned home many years later but did not recognize his parents. He killed his father and married his mother, Jocasta.

o'er /ɔr/ *adv., prep.* (*old use*) over

oeu·vre /ˈʊvrə/ *noun* [sing.] (from *French, formal*) all the works of a writer, an artist, etc.: *Picasso's oeuvre*

of 🔑 /əv; *before consonants often* ə; *strong form* ʌv/ *prep.*
1 belonging to someone; relating to someone: *a friend of mine* ◆ *the love of a mother for her child* ◆ *the role of the teacher* ◆ *Can't you throw out that old bike of Tommy's?* ◆ *the paintings of Monet* **HELP** When you are talking about everything someone has painted, written, etc., use of. When you are referring to one or more examples of someone's work, use by: *a painting by Monet* **2** belonging to something; being part of something; relating to something: *the lid of the box* ◆ *the president of the company* ◆ *a member of the team* ◆ *the result of the debate* **3** coming from a particular background or living in a place: *a woman of Italian descent* ◆ *the people of Kansas* **4** concerning or showing someone or something: *a story of passion* ◆ *a photo of my dog* ◆ *a map of India* **5** used to say what someone or something is, consists of, or contains: *the city of Las Vegas* ◆ *the issue of housing* ◆ *a crowd of people* ◆ *a glass of milk* **6** used with measurements and expressions of time, age, etc.: *2 pounds of potatoes* ◆ *an increase of 2%* ◆ *a girl of 12* ◆ *the fourth of July* ◆ *the year of his birth* ◆ (*old-fashioned*) *We would often have a walk of an evening.* **7** used to show that someone or something belongs to a group, often after *some, a few,* etc.: *some of his friends* ◆ *a few of the problems* ◆ *the most famous of all the stars* **8** used to show the position of something or someone in space or time: *just north of Detroit* ◆ *at the time of the revolution* ◆ *at a quarter of eleven tonight* (= 10:45 p.m.) **9** used after nouns formed from verbs. The noun after "of" can be either the object or the subject of the action: *the arrival of the police* (= they arrive) ◆ *criticism of the police* (= they are criticized) ◆ *fear of the dark* ◆ *the howling of the wind* **10** used after some verbs before mentioning someone or something involved in the action: *to deprive someone of something* ◆ *He was cleared of all blame.* ◆ *Think of a number.* **11** used after some adjectives before mentioning someone or something that a feeling relates to: *to be proud of something* ◆ *fear of the dark* **12** used to give your opinion of someone's behavior: *It was kind of you to offer.* **13** used when one noun describes a second one: *Where's that idiot of a boy?* (= the boy that you think is stupid)
IDM **of all** used before a noun to say that something is very surprising: *I'm surprised that you of all people should say that.* **of all the…** used to express anger: *Of all the nerve!*

off 🔑 /ɔf; ɑf/ *adv., prep., adj., verb*
• *adv.* **HELP** For the special uses of **off** in phrasal verbs, look at the entries for the verbs. For example, **come off** is in the phrasal verb section at **come**. **1** away from a place; at a distance in space or time: *I called him but he ran off.* ◆ *Sarah is off in India somewhere.* ◆ *I need to be off soon* (= leave). ◆ *Off you go!* ◆ *Summer's not far off now.* ◆ *A solution is still some way off.* **2** used to say that something has been removed: *He's had his beard shaved off.* ◆ *Take your coat off.* ◆ *Don't leave the toothpaste with the top off.* **3** starting a race: *They're off* (= the race has begun). **4** no longer going to happen; canceled: *The wedding is off.* **5** not connected or functioning: *The water is off.* ◆ *Make sure the TV is off.* **6** away from work or duty: *She's off today.* ◆ *I've got three days off next week.* ◆ *How*

many days did you **take off**? ◆ *I need some time off.* **7** taken from the price: *shoes with $20 off* ◆ *All shirts have/are 10% off.* **8** behind or at the sides of the stage in a theater **SYN** OFFSTAGE

IDM be well/better/badly, etc. off used to say how much money someone has: *Families will be better off under the new law* (= will have more money). ◆ *They are both comfortably off* (= have enough money to be able to buy what they want without worrying too much about the cost). be better/worse off (doing sth) to be in a better or worse situation: *She's better off without him.* ◆ *The weather was so bad we'd have been better off staying at home.* ◆ *We can't be any worse off than we are already.* off and on/on and off from time to time; now and again: *It rained on and off all day.*

• *prep.* **HELP** For the special uses of **off** in phrasal verbs, look at the entries for the verbs. For example, **take something off something** is in the phrasal verb section at **take**. **1** down or away from a place or at a distance in space or time: *I fell off the ladder.* ◆ *Keep off the grass!* ◆ *an island off the coast of Maine* ◆ *They were still 100 meters off the summit.* ◆ *We're getting right of the subject.* **2** leading away from something, for example a road or room: *We live off Main Street.* ◆ *There's a bathroom off the main bedroom.* **3** used to say that something has been removed: *You need to take the top off the bottle first!* ◆ *I want about an inch off the back of my hair.* **4** away from work or duty: *He's had ten days off school.* **5** away from a price: *They knocked $500 off the car.* **6** off of (*informal*) off; from: *Scientists are still a long way off of finding a cure.* ◆ *I got it off of my brother.* **7** not wanting or liking something that you usually eat or use: *I'm off* (= not drinking) *alcohol for a week.* ◆ *He's finally off drugs* (= he no longer takes them).

• *adj.* used to describe someone performing or feeling worse than usual: *Her tennis game was really off last night.* ◆ *~ day/week I was having an off day and couldn't get anything done.*

• *verb* (*informal*) *~ sb* to kill someone

off- /ɔf; ɑf/ *prefix* (in nouns, adjectives, verbs, and adverbs) not on; away from: *offstage* ◆ *offload*

off-'air *adj.* (in radio and television) not being broadcast: *off-air recording* **ANT** ON-AIR ▶ **off-air** *adv.*: *to record off-air*

of·fal /'ɔfl; 'ɑfl/ *noun* [U] (also va'riety ˌmeats [pl.]) the inside parts of an animal, such as the heart and LIVER, cooked and eaten as food

off·beat /ˌɔf'bit; ˌɑf-/ *adj.* [usually before noun] (*informal*) different from what most people expect **SYN** UNCONVENTIONAL: *offbeat humor* ◆ *an offbeat approach to interviewing*

off-'Broadway *adj.* **1** (of a theater or play) not on Broadway, New York's main theater district **2** (of a play) unusual in some way and often by a new writer

off-'center (*CanE usually* **off-'centre**) *adv., adj.* not exactly in the center of something

'off chance *noun*
IDM do sth on the off chance to do something even though you think that there is only a small possibility of it being successful: *She scanned the crowd on the off chance of seeing someone she knew.* ◆ *I stopped by the office on the off chance that you would still be there.*

off-'color (*CanE usually* **off-'colour**) *adj.* [usually before noun] an **off-color** joke is one that people think is rude, usually because it is about sex

off-'duty *adj.* not at work: *an off-duty policeman*

of·fend ${\wp}$ /ə'fɛnd/ *verb*
1 [T, often passive, I] *~ (sb)* to make someone feel upset because of something you say or do that is rude or embarrassing: *They'll be offended if you don't go to their wedding.* ◆ *Neil did not mean to offend anyone with his joke.* ◆ *A TV interviewer must be careful not to offend.* **2** [T] *~ sb/sth* to seem unpleasant to someone: *The smell from the farm offended some people.* ◆ *an ugly building that offends the eye* **3** [I] (*formal*) to commit a crime or crimes: *He started offending at the age of 16.* **4** [I] *~ (against sb/sth)* (*formal*) to

be against what people believe is morally right: *comments that offend against people's religious beliefs* ▶ **of·fend·ed** *adj.*: *Alice looked kind of offended.*

of·fend·er /ə'fɛndər/ *noun* **1** a person who commits a crime: *a persistent/serious/violent, etc. offender* ◆ *a young offender institution* ⊃ see also FIRST OFFENDER, SEX OFFENDER **2** a person or thing that does something wrong: *When it comes to pollution, the chemical industry is a major offender.*

of·fend·ing /ə'fɛndɪŋ/ *adj.* [only before noun] **1** causing you to feel annoyed or upset; causing problems: *The offending paragraph was deleted.* ◆ *The traffic jam soon cleared once the offending vehicle had been removed.* **2** guilty of a crime: *The offending driver received a large fine.*

of·fense /ə'fɛns/ *noun* **1** [C] *~ (against sb/sth)* an illegal act **SYN** CRIME: *a criminal/serious/minor/sexual, etc. offense* ◆ *a first offense* (= the first time that someone has been found guilty of a crime) ◆ *a capital offense* (= one for which someone may be punished by death) ◆ *He was not aware that he had committed an offense.* ◆ *an offense against society/humanity/the state* ◆ *New legislation makes it an offense to carry guns.* **2** [U] the act of upsetting or insulting someone: *I'm sure he meant no offense when he said that.* ◆ *The photo may cause offense to some people.* ◆ *No one will take offense* (= feel upset or insulted) *if you leave early.* ◆ *Don't be so quick to take offense.* **3** /'ɔfɛns; 'ɑ-/ [sing., U] (*sports*) the members of a team whose main aim is to score points against the other team; a method of scoring points: *The Redskins' offense is stronger than their defense.* ◆ *He played offense for the Cowboys.* ⊃ compare DEFENSE
IDM no offense (*informal*) used to say that you do not mean to upset or insult someone by something you say or do: *No offense, but I'd really like to be by myself.*

of·fen·sive ${\wp}$ /ə'fɛnsɪv/ *adj., noun*
• *adj.* **1** rude in a way that causes you to feel upset, insulted, or annoyed: *offensive remarks* ◆ *The program contains language which some viewers may find offensive.* ◆ *~ to sb His comments were deeply offensive to a large number of single mothers.* **ANT** INOFFENSIVE **2** (*formal*) extremely unpleasant **SYN** OBNOXIOUS: *an offensive smell* ⊃ thesaurus box at DISGUSTING **3** [only before noun] connected with the act of attacking someone or something: *an offensive war* ◆ *offensive action* ◆ *He was charged with carrying an offensive weapon.* ⊃ compare DEFENSIVE **4** (*sports*) connected with the team that has control of the ball; connected with the act of scoring points: *offensive play* ⊃ compare DEFENSIVE ▶ **of·fen·sive·ly** *adv.* **of·fen·sive·ness** *noun* [U]

• *noun* **1** a military operation in which large numbers of soldiers, etc. attack another country **SYN** STRIKE: *an air offensive* ◆ *They launched the offensive on January 10.* **2** a series of actions aimed at achieving something in a way that attracts a lot of attention **SYN** CAMPAIGN: *The government has launched a new offensive against crime.* ◆ *a sales offensive* ◆ *The public seems unconvinced by their latest charm offensive* (= their attempt to make people like them).
IDM be on the offensive to be attacking someone or something rather than waiting for them to attack you go on (to) the offensive | take the offensive to start attacking someone or something before they start attacking you

of·fer ${\wp}$ /'ɔfər; 'ɑfər/ *verb, noun*
• *verb* **1** [T, I] to say that you are willing to do something for someone or give something to someone: *~ (sth) Josie had offered her services as a guide.* ◆ *He offered some useful advice.* ◆ *I don't think they need help, but I think I should offer anyway.* ◆ *~ sth (to sb) (for sth) He offered $4,000 for the car.* ◆ *They decided to offer the job to Jo.* ◆ *~ sb sth They decided to offer Jo the job.* ◆ *I gratefully took the cup of coffee she offered me.* ◆ *Taylor offered him 500 dollars to do the work.* ◆ *~ to do sth The kids offered to do the dishes.* ◆ *+ speech "I'll do it," she offered.* **2** [T] *~ sth* to make something available or to provide the opportunity for something: *The hotel offers excellent facilities for families.* ◆ *The job didn't offer any prospects for promotion.* ◆ *He did not offer any explanation for*

| h hat | m man | n no | ŋ sing | l leg | r red | y yes | w wet |

his behavior. **3** [T] ~ sth/sb (up) (to sb) (formal) to give something to God: *We offered up our prayers for the men's safe return.*

IDM **have sth to offer** to have something available that someone wants: *Orlando has a lot to offer visitors in the way of entertainment.* ♦ *a young man with a great deal to offer* (= who is intelligent, has many skills, etc.) **offer your hand** (formal) to hold out your hand for someone to shake

● **noun 1** an act of saying that you are willing to do something for someone or give something to someone: ~ (of sth) *Thank you for your kind offer of help.* ♦ *I took him up on his offer of a loan.* ♦ *You can't just turn down offers of work like that.* ♦ *an offer of marriage* ♦ *to accept/refuse/decline an offer* ♦ ~ *to do sth I accepted her offer to pay.* **2** ~ (for sth) an amount of money that someone is willing to pay for something: *I've had an offer of $2,500 for the car.* ♦ *They decided to accept our original offer.* ♦ *The offer has been withdrawn.* ♦ *They made me an offer I couldn't refuse.* ♦ *The original price was $3,000, but I'm open to offers* (= willing to consider offers that are less than that). ◯ *see also* OBO **3** a reduction in the normal price of something, usually for a short period of time: *This special offer is valid until the end of the month.* ♦ *See next week's issue for details of more free offers.* **IDM** **on offer** that can be bought, used, etc.: *The following is a list of courses currently on offer.* ♦ *Over 50 wines are on offer, many by the glass.*

of·fer·ing /'ɔfərɪŋ; 'af-/ *noun* **1** something that is produced for other people to use, watch, enjoy etc.: *the latest offering from the Canadian-born writer* **2** something that is given to a god as part of religious worship ◯ *see also* BURNT OFFERING, PEACE OFFERING

of·fer·to·ry /'ɔfər,tɔri; 'af-/ *noun* (pl. of·fer·to·ries) **1** the offering of bread and wine to God at a church service **2** an offering or a collection of money during a church service

off-'grid *adj.* = OFF-THE-GRID

off·hand /,ɔf'hænd; ,af-/ *adj., adv.*
● **adj. 1** said or done without much thought or preparation: *an offhand remark* **2** (disapproving) not showing much interest in someone or something: *an offhand manner* ♦ *He was very offhand with me.* ▶ **off·hand·ed·ly** /,ɔf'hændədli; ,af-/ *adv.: He spoke offhandedly, making it clear I had no say in the matter.*
● **adv.** without being able to check something or think about it: *I don't know offhand how much we made last year.*

of·fice 🔊 /'ɔfəs; 'afəs/ *noun*
▷ROOM/BUILDING **1** [C] a room, set of rooms, or building where people work, usually sitting at desks: *The company is moving to new offices on the other side of town.* ♦ *Are you going to the office today?* ♦ *an office job* ♦ *office workers* ◯ collocations at JOB ◯ *see also* BACK OFFICE, HEAD OFFICE **2** [C] a room in which a particular person works, usually at a desk: *Some people have to share an office.* ♦ *Come into my office.* **3** [C] a place where a doctor, dentist, or VETERINAR-IAN sees patients: *a doctor's/dentist's office* **4** [C] (often in compounds) a room or building used for a particular purpose, especially to provide information or a service: *the local tourist office* ♦ *a ticket office* ◯ *see also* BOX OFFICE, REGISTRY OFFICE
▷IMPORTANT POSITION **5** [U, C] an important position of authority, especially in government; the work and duties connected with this: *She held office as governor for eight years.* ♦ *How long has he been in office?* ♦ *The former senator has been out of office for many years.* ♦ *The present incumbent took office in 2009.* ♦ *to seek/run for office* ♦ *the office of treasurer* ◯ collocations at VOTE
▷GOVERNMENT DEPARTMENT **6** Office [sing.] used in the names of some government departments: *the Office of Management and Budget*
IDM **through sb's good offices** (formal) with someone's help

office ,boy, 'office ,girl *noun* (old-fashioned) a young person employed to do simple tasks in an office

'office ,building *noun* a large building that contains offices, usually belonging to more than one company

of·fice·hold·er /'ɔfəs,houldər; 'af-/ *noun* a person who is in a position of authority, especially in the government or a government organization

'office ,hours *noun* [pl.] **1** the time when people in offices are normally working: *Our telephone lines are open during normal office hours.* **2** the time during which a doctor or dentist is available to see patients **3** the time when a professor meets with students in his or her office: *Professor Chen's office hours are Tuesday and Thursday from 3 to 5 p.m.*

of·fi·cer 🔊 /'ɔfəsər; 'af-/ *noun*
1 a person who is in a position of authority in the armed forces: *army/air force/naval, etc. officers* ♦ *The matter was passed on to me, as your commanding officer.* ◯ *see also* PETTY OFFICER, PILOT OFFICER, WARRANT OFFICER **2** (often in compounds) a person who is in a position of authority in the government or a large organization: *a customs/prison/court officer* ♦ *officers of state* (= people in high positions in the government) ◯ *see also* CHIEF EXECUTIVE OFFICER, MEDICAL OFFICER, PRESS OFFICER, PROBATION OFFICER **3** (often used as a form of address) = POLICE OFFICER: *the officer in charge of the case* ♦ *the investigating officer* ♦ *Yes, officer, I saw what happened.* **4** a title for a police officer: *Officer Daley*

'office ,worker *noun* a person who works in the offices of a business or company

of·fi·cial 🔊 /ə'fɪʃl/ *adj., noun*
● **adj. 1** [only before noun] connected with the job of someone who is in a position of authority: *official responsibilities* ♦ *the governor's official residence* ♦ *He attended in his official capacity as mayor.* ♦ *This was her first official engagement.* ♦ *He made an official visit to Tokyo in March.* **2** [usually before noun] agreed to, said, done, etc. by someone who is in a position of authority: *an official announcement/decision/statement* ♦ *according to official statistics/figures* ♦ *An official inquiry has been launched into the cause of the accident.* ♦ *The country's official language is Spanish.* ♦ *I intend to lodge an official complaint* (= to complain to someone in authority). ♦ *The news is not yet official.* **3** [only before noun] that is told to the public but may not be true: *I only knew the official version of events.* ♦ *The official story has always been that they are just good friends.* **4** [only before noun] formal and attended by people in authority: *an official function/reception* ♦ *The official opening is planned for October.* **ANT** UNOFFICIAL
● **noun** (often in compounds) a person who is in a position of authority in a large organization: *a bank/company/court/government official* ♦ *a senior official in the State Department*

of·fi·cial·dom /ə'fɪʃldəm/ *noun* [U] (disapproving) people who are in positions of authority in large organizations when they seem to be more interested in following rules than in being helpful

of·fi·cial·ese /ə,fɪʃə'liz/ *noun* [U] (disapproving) language used in official documents that is thought by many people to be too complicated and difficult to understand

of·fi·cial·ly 🔊 /ə'fɪʃəli/ *adv.*
1 publicly and by someone who is in a position of authority: *The library will be officially opened by the mayor.* ♦ *We haven't yet been told officially about the closure.* ♦ *The institute is not an officially recognized English language school.* **2** according to a particular set of rules, laws, etc.: *Many of those living on the streets are not officially homeless.* ♦ *I'm not officially supposed to be here.* **3** according to information that has been told to the public but may not be true: *Officially, he resigned because of bad health.*

of·fi·ci·ate /ə'fɪʃi,eɪt/ *verb* **1** [I, T] ~ (at sth) | ~ sth to act as an official in charge of something, especially a sports event: *A new referee will officiate (at) the game.* **2** [I] ~ (at sth) (formal) to do the official duties at a public or religious ceremony

of·fi·cious /ə'fɪʃəs/ *adj.* (disapproving) too ready to tell people what to do or to use the power you have to give orders **SYN** SELF-IMPORTANT: *a nasty, officious, little man* ▶ **of·fi·cious·ly** *adv.*: *"You can't park here," he said officiously.* **of·fi·cious·ness** *noun* [U]

off·ing /ˈɔfɪŋ; ˈɑf-/ *noun*
  IDM **in the offing** (*informal*) likely to appear or happen soon: *I hear there are more staff changes in the offing.*

off-ˈkey *adj.* **1** (of a voice or a musical instrument) not in tune **2** not suitable or correct in a particular situation **SYN** INAPPROPRIATE: *Some of his remarks were very off-key.* ▶ **off-ˈkey** *adv.*: *to sing off-key*

off-ˈkilter *adj.* **1** not perfectly straight or balanced; not in line with something else: *a slightly off-kilter, hand-drawn circle* **2** slightly strange or unusual: *an off-kilter comedy*

off-ˈlabel *adj.* relating to the use of a drug for something other than what it was originally created for: *This drug has been found useful in several off-label treatments.* ▶ **off ˈlabel** *adv.*: *Many physicians prescribe the drug off label.*

off-ˈlimits *adj.* **1** ~ (to sb) (of a place) where people are not allowed to go: *The site is off-limits to the general public.* **2** not allowed to be discussed: *The subject was ruled off-limits.*

off·line (also **off-line**) /ˌɔfˈlaɪn; ˌɑf-/ *adj.* (*computing*) not directly controlled by or connected to a computer or to the Internet: *For offline orders, call this number.* ▶ **off·line** *adv.*: *How do I write an e-mail offline?* ⊃ **see also** ONLINE

off·load (also **off-load**) /ˈɔfloʊd; ˈɑf-; ˌɔfˈloʊd; ˌɑf-/ *verb* **1** to take a load of goods off a ship, train, or truck **SYN** UNLOAD (1): *~ sth The goods were offloaded at the dock.* ✦ *They will be offloading the truck tomorrow morning.* ✦ *~ sth from sth The cargo containers were offloaded from the ships.* **2** to get rid of something that you do not need or want by passing it to someone else: *~ sth They should stop offloading waste from oil tankers into the sea.* ✦ *~ sth on/onto sb The broker offloaded 5,000 shares on a client.*

off-ˈpeak *adj.* [only before noun] happening or used at a time that is less popular or busy, and therefore cheaper: *off-peak travel/rates* ▶ **off-ˈpeak** *adv.*: *The fare is much lower off-peak.* ⊃ **compare** PEAK

off-ˈpiste *adj.* away from the tracks of firm snow that have been prepared for SKIING on: *off-piste skiing* ▶ **off-ˈpiste** *adv.*: *We enjoy skiing off-piste.*

off·print /ˈɔfprɪnt; ˈɑf-/ *noun* a separate printed copy of an article that first appeared as part of a newspaper, magazine, etc.

off-ˈputting *adj.* not pleasant, in a way that prevents you from liking someone or something: *I find his manner very off-putting.*

off-ramp *noun* a road used for driving off a major road such as an INTERSTATE ⊃ **compare** ON-RAMP

off-ˈroad *adj.* [usually before noun] not on the public road: *an off-road vehicle* (= one for driving on rough ground)

off-ˈroader *noun* **1** a vehicle that is driven across rough ground as a sport **2** a person who drives a vehicle across rough ground as a sport ▶ **off-ˈroading** *noun* [U]

off-ˈscreen *adj.* [only before noun] in real life, not in a movie: *They were off-screen lovers.* ▶ **off-ˈscreen** *adv.*: *She looks totally different off-screen.* ⊃ **compare** ON-SCREEN

off-ˈseason *noun* [sing.] **1** the time of the year that is less busy in business and travel **SYN** LOW SEASON **2** (*sports*) the time during the year when teams do not play important games ▶ **off-ˈseason** *adj.* [only before noun]: *off-season prices* **off-ˈseason** *adv.*: *We prefer to travel off-season.*

off·set **AWL** /ˈɔfset; ˈɑf-/ *verb, adj.*
  • *verb* (off·set·ting, off·set, off·set) to use one cost, payment, or situation in order to cancel or reduce the effect of another: *~ sth Prices have risen in order to offset the increased cost of materials.* **~ sth against sth**
  • *adj.* [only before noun] used to describe a method of printing in which ink is put onto a metal plate, then onto a rubber surface and only then onto the paper

off·shoot /ˈɔfʃut; ˈɑf-/ *noun* **1** a thing that develops from

something, especially a small organization that develops from a larger one **2** (*technical*) a new STEM that grows on a plant

off·shore /ˈɔfˈʃɔr; ˌɑf-/ *adj.* [usually before noun] **1** happening or existing in the ocean, not far from the land: *offshore drilling* ✦ *an offshore island* **2** (of winds) blowing from the land toward the ocean: *offshore breezes* **3** (*business*) (of money, companies, etc.) kept or located in a country that has more generous tax laws than other places: *offshore investments* ▶ **offshore** *adv.*: *a ship anchored offshore* ✦ *profits earned offshore* ⊃ **compare** INSHORE, ONSHORE

off·shor·ing /ˈɔfˈʃɔrɪŋ; ˌɑf-; ˈɔfˌʃɔrɪŋ; ˈɑf-/ *noun* [U] the practice of a company in one country arranging for people in another country to do work for it: *the offshoring of call-center jobs to India* ▶ **off·shore** *verb* ~ **sth**

off·side /ˌɔfˈsaɪd; ˌɑf-/ (also **off·sides**) *adj.* (in some sports, for example football, SOCCER, and HOCKEY) a player is **offside** if he or she is in a position, usually ahead of the ball, that is not allowed: *He was offside when he scored.* ✦ *the offside rule* ⊃ **compare** ONSIDE ▶ **off·side** (also **off·sides**) *noun* [U]

off·spring /ˈɔfsprɪŋ; ˈɑf-/ *noun* (*pl.* **off·spring**) (*formal* or *humorous*) **1** a child of a particular person or couple: *the problems parents have with their teenage offspring* ✦ *to produce/raise offspring* **2** the young of an animal or a plant

off·stage /ˌɔfˈsteɪdʒ; ˌɑf-/ *adj.* **1** not on the stage in a theater; not where the audience can see: *offstage sound effects* **2** happening to an actor in real life, not on the stage: *The stars were having an offstage relationship.* ▶ **off·stage** *adv.*: *The hero dies offstage.* ⊃ **compare** ONSTAGE

off-street *adj.* [usually before noun] not on a public street: *an apartment with off-street parking* **ANT** ON-STREET

off-the-ˈcuff ⊃ CUFF **HELP** You will also find other compounds beginning **off-the-** at the entry for the last word in the compound.

off-the-ˈgrid (also **off-ˈgrid**) *adj.* not using the public supplies of electricity, gas, water, etc.: *an off-the-grid house, independent of traditional utility services* ⊃ **see also** GRID

off-the-ˈshelf *adj.* [only before noun] (of a product) that can be bought immediately and does not have to be specially designed or ordered: *off-the-shelf software packages* ⊃ **see also** SHELF

off-ˈwhite *adj.* very pale yellowish-white in color ▶ **off-ˈwhite** *noun* [U]

off year *noun* a year in which there are no important elections, especially no election for president ▶ **off-year** *adj.*: *off-year elections for U.S. Representatives*

oft /ɔft; ɑft/ *adv.* (*old use*) often

oft- /ɔft; ɑft/ *prefix* (in adjectives) often: *an oft-repeated claim*

of·ten 🔑 /ˈɔfn; ˈɑfn; ˈɔftən; ˈɑf-/ *adv.*
  1 many times **SYN** FREQUENTLY: *We often go there.* ✦ *I've often wondered what happened to him.* ✦ *How often do you go to the theater?* ✦ *I see her quite often.* ✦ *Try to exercise as often as possible.* ✦ *We should meet for lunch more often.* ✦ *It is not often that you get such an opportunity.* **2** in many cases **SYN** COMMONLY: *Old houses are often damp.* ✦ *People are often afraid of things they don't understand.* ✦ *All too often the animals die because of neglect.*
  IDM **as often as not | more often than not** usually; in a way that is typical of someone or something: *As often as not, he's late for work.* **every so often** occasionally; sometimes ⊃ **more at** ONCE *adv.*

of·ten·times /ˈɔfnˌtaɪmz; ˈɔftən-; ˈɑf-/ *adv.* often

o·gle /ˈoʊgl; ˈɑgl/ *verb* [T, I] ~ (sb) to look hard at someone in an offensive way, usually showing sexual interest: *He was not in the habit of ogling women.*

o·gre /ˈoʊgər/ *noun* **1** (in stories) a cruel and frightening giant who eats people **2** a very frightening person: *My boss is a real ogre.*

o·gress /ˈoʊgrəs/ *noun* a female ogre

OH *abbr.* (in writing) Ohio

oh 🔑 (also less frequent **O**) /oʊ/ exclamation
1 used when you are reacting to something that has been said, especially if you did not know it before: *"I saw Ben yesterday." "Oh yes, how is he?"* ♦ *"Erica has a new job." "Oh, she does?"* **2** used to express surprise, fear, joy, etc.: *Oh, how wonderful!* ♦ *Oh no, I've broken it!* **3** used to attract someone's attention: *Oh, Sue! Could you help me for a minute?* **4** used when you are thinking of what to say next: *I've been in this job for, oh, about six years.*

ohm /oʊm/ noun (physics) a unit for measuring electrical RESISTANCE

ohm·me·ter /'oʊm,miṭər/ noun (physics) a device for measuring electrical RESISTANCE

oh-oh exclamation = UH-OH

oh-so adv. (informal) extremely: *their oh-so ordinary lives*

-oid /ɔɪd/ suffix (in adjectives and nouns) similar to: *humanoid* ♦ *rhomboid*

oil 🔑 /ɔɪl/ noun, verb
● *noun* **1** [U] a thick liquid that is found in rock underground **SYN** PETROLEUM: *drilling for oil* **2** [U] a form of PETROLEUM that is used as fuel and to make parts of machines move smoothly: *engine oil* ♦ *an oil burner/lamp* ♦ *Put some oil in the car.* **3** [U, C] a smooth thick liquid that is made from plants or animals and is used in cooking: *olive oil* ♦ *vegetable oils* **4** [U, C] a smooth thick liquid that is made from plants, minerals, etc. and is used on the skin or hair: *lavender bath oil* ♦ *baby oil* ⊃ see also ESSENTIAL OIL **5** [U] also *oils* [pl.] colored paint containing oil used by artists: *a painting done in oils* ♦ *landscapes in oil* ⊃ see also OIL PAINT ⊃ collocations at ART **6** [C] = OIL PAINTING: *Among the more important Turner oils was "Venus and Adonis."* ⊃ see also CASTOR OIL, COD LIVER OIL, LINSEED OIL, OILY **IDM** see BURN v.
● *verb* ~ sth to put oil onto or into something, for example a machine, in order to protect it or make it work smoothly: *He oiled his bike and pumped up the tires.*

oil-bearing adj. [only before noun] producing or containing oil

oil·can /'ɔɪlkæn/ noun a metal container for oil, especially one with a long thin SPOUT, used for putting oil onto machine parts

oil·cloth /'ɔɪlklɔθ/ noun [U] a type of cotton cloth that is covered on one side with a layer of oil so that water cannot pass through it, used especially in the past for covering tables

oil color (CanE usually **oil colour**) noun [C, U] = OIL PAINT

oil field /' / noun an area where oil is found in the ground or under the ocean

oil·man /'ɔɪlmæn/ noun (pl. oil·men /-mɛn/) a man who owns an oil company or works in the oil industry

oil paint (also **oil color**) noun [C, U] a type of paint that contains oil

oil painting noun **1** (also oil) [C] a picture painted in OIL PAINT **2** [U] the art of painting in OIL PAINT

oil pan noun the place under an engine that holds the engine oil

oil rig (also **oil platform**) noun a large structure with equipment for getting oil from under the ground or under the ocean ⊃ picture at BUILDING

oil·skin /'ɔɪlskɪn/ noun **1** [U] a type of cotton cloth that has had oil put on it in a special process so that water cannot pass through it, used for making WATERPROOF clothing **2** [C] a coat or jacket made of oilskin **3** oilskins [pl.] a set of clothes made of oilskin, worn especially by sailors

oil slick (also **slick**) noun an area of oil that is floating on the surface of the ocean

oil tanker noun a large ship with containers for carrying oil

oil well (also **well**) noun a hole made in the ground to obtain oil

oil·y /'ɔɪli/ adj. (oil·i·er, oil·i·est) **1** containing or covered with oil: *oily fish* ♦ *an oily rag* **2** feeling, tasting, smelling, or looking like oil: *an oily substance* **3** (disapproving) (of a person or their behavior) trying to be too polite, in a way that is annoying **SYN** OBSEQUIOUS: *an oily smile* ▸ oil·i·ness noun [U]

oink /ɔɪŋk/ exclamation, noun used to represent the sound a pig makes

oint·ment /'ɔɪntmənt/ noun [U, C] a smooth substance that you rub on the skin to heal a wound or sore place **SYN** CREAM: *antiseptic ointment* **IDM** see FLY n.

OJ /'oʊ dʒeɪ/ noun [U] (informal) the abbreviation for "orange juice"

O·jib·wa /oʊ'dʒɪbweɪ/ noun (pl. O·jib·wa or O·jib·was) = ANISHINABE

OK 🔑 (also **okay**) /,oʊ'keɪ/ exclamation, adj., adv., noun, verb, abbr.
● *exclamation* (informal) **1** used to express agreement or give permission for something: *"Shall we go for a walk?" "OK."* ♦ (computing) *Click on OK to terminate the application.* **2** used to attract someone's attention or to introduce a comment: *Okay, let's go.* **3** used to make sure that someone agrees with you or understands you: *The meeting's at 2, OK?* ♦ *I'll do it my way, OK?* **4** used to stop people from arguing with you or criticizing you: *OK, so I was wrong. I'm sorry.*
● *adj., adv.* (informal) **1** safe and well; in a calm or happy state: *Are you OK?* ⊃ thesaurus box at WELL **2** ~ (for sb) (to do sth) all right; acceptable; in an acceptable way: *Is it OK if I leave now?* ♦ *Is it OK for me to come too?* ♦ *Does my hair look okay?* ♦ *I think I did OK on the exam.* ♦ *Whatever you decide, it's okay with/by me.* ♦ *an okay movie*
● *noun* [sing.] (informal) permission **SYN** GO AHEAD: *I'm still waiting for the boss to give me the OK.*
● *verb* (OK's, OK'ing, OK'd, OK'd) ~ sth (informal) to officially agree to something or allow it to happen **SYN** APPROVE: *She filled in an expenses claim and her manager OK'd it.*
● *abbr.* (in writing) Oklahoma

o·ka·pi /oʊ'kɑpi/ noun an African animal that belongs to the same family as the GIRAFFE, but is smaller, with a dark body and white lines across its legs

o·key-doke /,oʊki 'doʊk/ (also **okey-dokey** /,oʊki 'doʊki/) exclamation (informal) used to express agreement **SYN** OK

o·kra /'oʊkrə/ noun [U] the green seed cases of the okra plant, eaten as a vegetable ⊃ picture at FRUIT

old 🔑 /oʊld/ adj. (old·er, old·est)
▷ AGE **1** be… years, months, etc. ~ of a particular age: *The baby was only a few hours old.* ♦ *In those days most people left school when they were only fifteen years old.* ♦ *At thirty years old, he was already earning $100,000 a year.* ♦ *two fourteen-year-old boys* ♦ *a class for five-year-olds* (= children who are five) ♦ *I didn't think she was old enough for the responsibility.* ♦ *How old is this building?* ♦ *He's the oldest player on the team.* ♦ *She's much older than me.*
▷ NOT YOUNG **2** having lived for a long time; no longer young: *to get/grow old* ♦ *The old man lay propped up on cushions.* **ANT** YOUNG **3** the old noun [pl.] old people: *The old feel the cold more than the young.*
▷ NOT NEW **4** having existed or been used for a long time: *old habits* ♦ *He always gives the same old excuses.* ♦ *This couch is getting pretty old now.* **ANT** NEW **5** [only before noun] former; belonging to past times or a past time in your life: *Things were different in the old days.* ♦ *I went back to visit my old school.* ♦ *Old and Middle English* **6** [only before noun] used to refer to something that has been replaced by something else: *We had more room in our old house.* **ANT** NEW **7** [only before noun] known for a long time: *She's an old friend of mine* (= I have known her for a long time). ♦ *We're old rivals.* ⊃ compare RECENT
▷ GOOD OLD/POOR OLD **8** [only before noun] (informal) used to show affection or a lack of respect: *Good old Dad!* ♦ *Our poor*

old dog is deaf and lame, but we love him so! ◆ I hate him, the silly old fool!

IDM **any old how** (*informal*) in a careless or messy way: *The books were piled up all over the floor any old how.* **any old...** (*informal*) any item of the type mentioned (used when it is not important which particular item is chosen): *Any old room would have been okay.* **as old as the hills** very old; ancient **for old times' sake** if you do something **for old times' sake**, you do it because it is connected with something good that happened to you in the past **the good/bad old days** an earlier period of time in your life or in history that is seen as better/worse than the present: *That was in the bad old days of rampant inflation.* **of old** (*formal* or *literary*) in or since past times: *in days of old* **old enough to be sb's father/mother** (*disapproving*) very much older than someone (especially used to suggest that a romantic relationship between the two people is not appropriate) **old enough to know better** old enough to behave in a more sensible way than you actually did **the (same) old story** what usually happens: *It's the same old story of a badly managed project with inadequate funding.* **an old wives' tale** (*disapproving*) an old idea or belief that has been proved not to be scientific ⊃ **see also** OLD-SCHOOL **IDM** **see** CHIP n., FOOL n., GRAND adj., HEAVE-HO, HIGH adj., RIPE, SETTLE v., TEACH, TOUGH adj., TRICK n.

THESAURUS

old

elderly ◆ aged ◆ long-lived ◆ mature

These words all describe someone who or something that has lived for a long time or that usually lives for a long time.

old having lived for a long time; no longer young: *She's getting old—she'll be 75 next year.*

elderly (*somewhat formal*) used as a polite word for "old": *He is very busy caring for two elderly relatives.*

aged (*formal*) very old: *Having aged relatives visiting you can be quite stressful.*

long-lived having a long life; lasting for a long time: *Everyone in my family is exceptionally long-lived.*

mature used as a polite or humorous way of saying that someone is no longer young: *clothes for the mature woman*

PATTERNS

- a(n) old/elderly/aged/long-lived/mature **man/woman**
- a(n) old/elderly/aged/mature **gentleman/lady/couple**

WHICH WORD?

older ◆ elder

- The usual comparative and superlative forms of **old** are **older** and **oldest**: *My brother is older than me.* ◆ *The palace is the oldest building in the city.* In literary or formal writing, **elder** and **eldest** may be used when comparing the ages of people, especially members of the same family. As adjectives, they are only used before a noun and you cannot say "elder than": *my older/elder sister* ◆ *the older/elder of their two children* ◆ *I'm the oldest/eldest in the family.*

,old 'age *noun* [U] the time of your life when you are old: *Old age can bring many problems.* ◆ *He lived alone in his old age.* ⊃ **collocations at** AGE

,old-age 'pension *noun* (*CanE*) a regular income paid by the state to people over the age of 65

,old-age 'pensioner *noun* (*abbr.* OAP) (*CanE*) a person who receives an old-age pension ⊃ **see also** SENIOR CITIZEN

,old-age se'curity *noun* [U] (*abbr.* OAS) (*CanE*) a regular income paid by the government to people above the age of 65

,old 'boy *noun*
IDM **the old-boy network** (*informal*) the practice of men who went to the same school using their influence to help each other at work or socially ⊃ **see also** GOOD OLD BOY

the 'old ,country *noun* [sing.] the country where you were born, especially when you have left it to live somewhere else

olde /ould; 'ouldi/ *adj.* [only before noun] a way of spelling "old" that was used in the past and is now sometimes used in names and advertisements to give the impression that something is traditional: *a restaurant that tries to recreate the flavor of olde England*

old·en /'ouldən/ *adj.* [only before noun] existing a long time ago in the past: *What was life like in the olden days, Grandma?*

,Old 'English (also ,Anglo-'Saxon) *noun* [U] the English language before about 1150, very different from modern English

,Old ,English 'sheepdog *noun* a very large dog with very long gray and white hair

,old-es'tablished *adj.* [only before noun] that has existed for a long time

,old-'fashioned ♪ *adj.* (*sometimes disapproving*)
1 not modern; no longer fashionable **SYN** DATED: *old-fashioned clothes/styles/methods/equipment* ⊃ **compare** FASHIONABLE **2** (of a person) believing in old or traditional ways; having traditional ideas: *My parents are old-fashioned about relationships and marriage.*

,old 'flame *noun* a former boyfriend or girlfriend: *She met an old flame from high school at the party.*

,Old 'Glory *noun* a name for the U.S. flag

the ,old 'guard *noun* [sing.] the original members of a group or an organization, who are often against change

,old 'hand *noun* ~ (at sth/at doing sth) a person with a lot of experience and skill in a particular activity: *She's an old hand at dealing with the press.*

,old 'hat *noun* [U] something that is old-fashioned and no longer interesting: *Today's hits rapidly become old hat.*

old·ie /'ouldi/ *noun* (*informal*) an old thing ⊃ **see also** GOLDEN OLDIE

old·ish /'ouldıʃ/ *adj.* fairly old

,old 'lady *noun* (*informal*) a person's wife or mother

,old 'maid *noun* (*old-fashioned*, *disapproving*) a woman who has never married and is now no longer young

,old 'man *noun* (*informal*) a person's husband or father

,old 'master *noun* **1** a famous painter, especially of the 13th–17th centuries in Europe **2** a picture painted by an old master

,Old 'Nick *noun* (*old-fashioned*, *humorous*) the DEVIL

'old-school *adj.* old-fashioned or traditional

old·ster /'ouldstər/ *noun* (*informal*) an old person

'old-style *adj.* [only before noun] typical of past fashions or times: *an old-style dress shop* ◆ *old-style politics*

the ,Old 'Testament *noun* [sing.] the first part of the Bible, that tells the history of the Jews, their beliefs, and their relationship with God before the birth of Christ ⊃ **compare** THE NEW TESTAMENT

'old-time *adj.* [only before noun] typical of the past: *old-time music*

,old-'timer *noun* **1** a person who has been connected with a club or an organization, or who has lived in a place, for a long time **SYN** VETERAN **2** an old man

the ,Old 'World *noun* [sing.] Europe, Asia, and Africa ⊃ **compare** THE NEW WORLD

'old-world *adj.* [only before noun] (*approving*) belonging to

---

past times; not modern: *an old-world hotel with character and charm*

o·lé /oʊˈleɪ/ *exclamation* (*informal*, from *Spanish*) used for showing approval or happiness

ole /oʊl/ *adj.* used in written English to represent how some people say the word "old": *My ole man used to work there.*

o·le·ag·i·nous /ˌoʊliˈædʒənəs/ *adj.* (*formal*) covered in oil or GREASE, or containing a lot of oil or grease

o·le·an·der /ˈoʊliˌændər/ *noun* [C, U] a bush with white, pink, or red flowers and long, pointed, thick leaves

O·les·tra™ /oʊˈlɛstrə/ *noun* [U] a substance that is used instead of fat in some foods

ol·fac·to·ry /ɑlˈfæktəri; oʊl-/ *adj.* [only before noun] (*technical*) connected with the sense of smell: *olfactory cells/nerves/organs*

ol·i·garch /ˈɑləˌgɑrk/ *noun* **1** a member of an oligarchy **2** an extremely rich and powerful person, especially a Russian who became rich in business after the end of the former Soviet Union

ol·i·gar·chy /ˈɑləˌgɑrki/ *noun* (*pl.* **ol·i·gar·chies**) **1** [U] a form of government in which only a small group of people hold all the power **2** [C] the people who hold power in an oligarchy **3** [C] a country governed by an oligarchy

ol·ive /ˈɑlɪv/ *noun, adj.*
- **noun 1** [C] a small green or black fruit with a strong taste, used in cooking and for its oil **2** (also ˈolive ˌtree) [C] a tree on which olives grow: *olive groves* **3** (also ˌolive ˈgreen) [U] a yellowish-green color
- **adj. 1** (also ˌolive-ˈgreen) yellowish-green in color **2** (of skin) yellowish-brown in color: *an olive complexion*

ˈolive ˌbranch *noun* [usually sing.] a symbol of peace; something you say or do to show that you wish to make peace with someone: *Management is holding out an olive branch to the strikers.*

ˌolive ˈdrab *noun* [U] a dull green color, used in some military uniforms

ˈolive ˈoil *noun* [U] oil produced from olives, used in cooking and on salad ⊃ see also EXTRA VIRGIN

ol·lie /ˈɑli/ *noun* (in SKATEBOARDING) a jump that is done by pushing one foot down hard on the back of the board

ol·o·gy /ˈɑlədʒi/ *noun* (*pl.* **ol·o·gies**) (*informal, humorous*) a subject of study: *They come here with their ologies, knowing nothing about life.*

-ology /ˈɑlədʒi/, **-logy** *combining form* (in nouns) **1** a subject of study: *sociology ◆ genealogy* **2** a characteristic of speech or writing: *phraseology ◆ trilogy* ▶ **-ological** /əˈlɑdʒɪkl/ **-logical** (also **-ologic, -logic**) (in adjectives): *pathological* **-ologist** /ˈɑlədʒɪst/**-logist** (in nouns): *biologist*

O·lym·pi·ad /əˈlɪmpiˌæd/ *noun* **1** an occasion when the modern Olympic games are held: *The 26th Olympiad took place in Atlanta, Georgia.* **2** an international competition in a particular subject, especially a science: *the 14th International Physics Olympiad*

O·lym·pi·an /əˈlɪmpiən/ *noun, adj.*
- **noun** a person who competes in the Olympic Games
- **adj.** (*formal*) like a god; powerful and impressive

O·lym·pic /əˈlɪmpɪk/ *adj.* [only before noun] connected with the Olympic Games: *an Olympic athlete/medalist*

the O·lympic ˈGames (also **the Olympics**) *noun* [pl.] an international sports festival held every four years in a different country: *the Beijing Olympics, held in 2008*

om·buds·man /ˈɑmbədzmən; -ˌbʊdz-/ *noun* (*pl.* **om·buds·men** /-mən/) an official whose job is to examine and report on complaints made by ordinary people about companies, the government, or public authorities

o·me·ga /oʊˈmeɪgə/ *noun* the last letter of the Greek alphabet (Ω, ω)

O·me·ga-3 /oʊˌmeɪgə ˈθri/ (also **O·mega-ˈ3 ˌfatty ˈacid**)

noun any of a group of acids, found mainly in fish oils, that many people think are important for human health

ome·let (also **ome·lette**) /ˈɑmlət/ *noun* a hot dish of eggs mixed together and fried, often with cheese, meat, vegetables, etc. added: *a cheese and mushroom omelet* **IDM** **you can't make an omelet without breaking eggs** (*saying*) you cannot achieve something important without causing a few small problems

o·men /ˈoʊmən/ *noun* a sign of what is going to happen in the future **SYN** PORTENT: *a good/bad omen* ◆ *an omen of death/disaster* ◆ **~ for sth** *The omens for their future success are not good.*

om·i·cron /ˈɑmɪˌkrɑn; ˈoʊ-/ *noun* the 15th letter of the Greek alphabet (O, o)

om·i·nous /ˈɑmənəs/ *adj.* suggesting that something bad is going to happen in the future **SYN** FOREBODING: *There were ominous dark clouds gathering overhead.* ◆ *She picked up the phone but there was an ominous silence at the other end.* ▶ **om·i·nous·ly** *adv.*

o·mis·sion /oʊˈmɪʃn; ə-/ *noun* **1** [U] **~ (from sth)** the act of not including someone or something or not doing something; the fact of not being included/done: *Everyone was surprised at her omission from the team.* ◆ *The play was shortened by the omission of two scenes.* ◆ *sins of omission* (= not doing things that should be done) **2** [C] a thing that has not been included or done: *There were a number of errors and omissions in the article.*

o·mit /oʊˈmɪt; ə-/ *verb* (**-tt-**) (*formal*) **1** to not include something or someone, either deliberately or because you have forgotten it/them **SYN** LEAVE OUT: **~ sth/sb** *If you are a student, you can omit questions 16–18.* ◆ **~ sth/sb from sth** *People were surprised that Sam's name was omitted from the list of honorees.* **2** **~ to do sth** to not do or fail to do something: *She omitted to mention that they were staying the night.*

omni- /ˈɑmni/ *combining form* (in nouns, adjectives, and adverbs) of all things; in all ways or places: *omnivore* ◆ *omnipresent*

om·ni·bus /ˈɑmnɪbəs/ *noun, adj.*
- **noun 1** a large book that contains a number of books, for example novels by the same author **2** (*old-fashioned*) a bus
- **adj.** including many things or different types of things: *an omnibus law*

om·ni·di·rec·tion·al /ˌɑmnɪdəˈrɛkʃənl; -daɪ-/ *adj.* (*technical*) receiving or sending signals in all directions: *an omnidirectional microphone*

om·nip·o·tent /ɑmˈnɪpətənt/ *adj.* (*formal*) having total power; able to do anything: *an omnipotent God* ▶ **om·nip·o·tence** /-ətəns/ *noun* [U]: *the omnipotence of God*

om·ni·pres·ent /ˌɑmnɪˈprɛznt/ *adj.* (*formal*) present everywhere: *These days the media are omnipresent.* ▶ **om·ni·pres·ence** /-ˈprɛzns/ *noun* [U]

om·nis·cient /ɑmˈnɪʃnt/ *adj.* (*formal*) knowing everything: *The novel has an omniscient narrator.* ▶ **om·nis·cience** /-ʃns/ *noun* [U]

om·ni·vore /ˈɑmnəˌvɔr/ *noun* an animal or a person that eats all types of food, especially both plants and meat ⊃ compare CARNIVORE, HERBIVORE, INSECTIVORE

om·niv·o·rous /ɑmˈnɪvərəs/ *adj.* **1** (*technical*) eating all types of food, especially both plants and meat ⊃ compare CARNIVORE, HERBIVORE **2** (*formal*) having wide interests in a particular area or activity: *She has always been an omnivorous reader.*

on /ɑn; ɔn/ *prep., adv.*
- **prep.** **HELP** For the special uses of **on** in phrasal verbs, look at the entries for the verbs. For example, **turn on someone** is in the phrasal verb section at **turn**. **1** in or into a position covering, touching, or forming part of a surface: *a picture on a wall* ◆ *There's a spot on your skirt.* ◆ *the diagram on page 5* ◆ *Put it down on the table.* ◆ *He was hit on the head.* ◆ *She climbed on to the bed.* **HELP** This could also be written: *onto the bed* **2** supported by someone or something: *She*

was standing on one foot. ♦ Try lying on your back. ♦ Hang your coat on that hook. **3** used to show a means of transportation: He was on the plane from New York. ♦ to travel on the bus/subway/ferry ♦ I came on my bike. ♦ a woman on horseback **4** used to show a day or date: He came on Sunday. ♦ We meet on Tuesdays. ♦ on May the first/the first of May ♦ on the evening of May the first ♦ on one occasion ♦ on your birthday **5** immediately after something: On arriving home I discovered they had gone. ♦ Please report to reception on arrival. ♦ There was a letter waiting for him on his return. **6** about something or someone: a book on Southern cooking ♦ She tested us on irregular verbs. **7** being carried by someone; in the possession of someone: Have you got any money on you? **8** used to show that someone belongs to a group or an organization: to be on the committee/staff/jury/panel ♦ Whose side are you on (= which of two or more different views do you support)? **9** eating or drinking something; using a drug or a medicine regularly: He lived on a diet of junk food. ♦ The doctor put me on antibiotics. **10** used to show direction: on the left/right ♦ He turned his back on us. **11** at or near a place: a town on the coast ♦ a house on Lake Michigan ♦ We lived on the outskirts of town. **12** used to show the basis or reason for something: a story based on fact ♦ On their advice I applied for the job. **13** paid for by something: to live on Social Security/a student grant ♦ to be on a low wage ♦ You can't feed a family on $100 a week. ♦ Drinks are on me (= I am paying). **14** by means of something; using something: She played a tune on her guitar. ♦ The information is available on the Internet. ♦ We spoke on the phone. ♦ What's on TV? ♦ The movie is on PBS later tonight. **15** used with some nouns or adjectives to say who or what is affected by something: a ban on smoking ♦ He's hard on his kids. ♦ Go easy on the mayo! (= do not give me too much) **16** compared with someone or something: These sales figures are an improvement on last year's totals. **17** used to describe an activity or a state: to be away on business/vacation ♦ The book is currently on loan.

● **adv.** **HELP** For the special uses of on in phrasal verbs, look at the entries for the verbs. For example, get on is in the phrasal verb section at get. **1** used to show that something continues: He worked on without a break. ♦ If you like a good story, read on. **2** used to show that someone or something moves or is sent forward: She stopped for a moment, then walked on. ♦ He handed me a form to fill out and moved on to the next person. ♦ From then on he never trusted her again. ♦ Please send the letter on to my new address. **3** on someone's body; being worn: Put your coat on. ♦ I didn't have my glasses on. ♦ What did she have on (= what was she wearing)? **4** covering, touching, or forming part of something: Make sure the lid is on. **5** connected or operating; being used: The lights were all on. ♦ The TV is always on in their house. ♦ We were without electricity for three hours but it's on again now. **6** happening: There was a war on at the time. ♦ What's on at the movies? ♦ The band is on (= performing) in ten minutes. **7** planned to take place in the future: The game is still on (= it has not been canceled). ♦ I don't think we have anything on this weekend. ♦ I'm sorry we can't come—we have a lot on. **8** on duty; working: I'm on now till 8 tomorrow morning. **9** in or into a vehicle: The bus stopped and four people got on. ♦ They hurried on to the plane. ⊃ see also ONTO

IDM **on and on** without stopping; continuously: She went on and on about her trip. **on and off** = OFF adv. **what are you, etc. on?** (informal) used when you are very surprised at someone's behavior and are suggesting that they are acting in a similar way to someone using drugs **you're on** (informal) used when you are accepting a bet ⊃ more at OFF adv.

on-'air adj. (in radio and television) being broadcast: She explains how she deals with on-air technical problems. **ANT** OFF-AIR ⊃ see also AIR n.

on-'board adj. [only before noun] **1** on a ship, aircraft, or vehicle: an on-board motor **2** (computing) relating to, or controlled by, part of the main CIRCUIT BOARD: a PC with on-board sound

on-'call [only before noun] (of a doctor, police officer, etc.)

available for work if necessary, especially in an emergency: on-call doctors ⊃ see also CALL n.

once 🔑 /wʌns/ adv., conj.

● **adv.** **1** on one occasion only; one time: I've only been there once. ♦ He washes his car once a week. ♦ She only sees her parents once every six months. **2** at some time in the past: I once met your mother. ♦ He once lived in Alaska. ♦ This book was famous once, but nobody reads it today. **3** used in negative sentences and questions, and after if to mean "ever" or "at all": He never once offered to help. ♦ If she once decides to do something, you can't change her mind.

IDM **all at once 1** suddenly: All at once she lost her temper. **2** all together; at the same time: I can't do everything all at once—you'll have to be patient. **at once 1** immediately; without delay: Come here at once! **2** at the same time: Don't all speak at once! ♦ I can't do two things at once. **(just) for once| just this once** (informal) on this occasion (which is in contrast to what happens usually): For once he arrived on time. ♦ Can't you be nice to each other just this once? **going once, going twice, sold** = GONE **once again| once more** one more time; another time: Once again the plane was late. ♦ Let me hear it just once more. **once a…, always a…** used to say that someone cannot change: Once an actor, always an actor. **once and for all** now and for the last time; finally or completely: We need to settle this once and for all. **once bitten, twice shy** (saying) after an unpleasant experience you are careful to avoid something similar **once in a blue moon** (informal) very rarely **(every) once in a while** occasionally **once or twice** a few times: I don't know her well, I've only met her once or twice. **once too often** used to say that someone has done something wrong or stupid again, and this time they will suffer because of it: You've tried that trick once too often. **once upon a time** used, especially at the beginning of stories, to mean "a long time in the past": Once upon a time there was a beautiful princess.

● **conj.** as soon as; when: We didn't know how we would cope once the money was gone. ♦ The water is fine once you're in!

once-,over noun

IDM **give sb/sth a/the once-over** (informal) **1** to look at someone or something quickly to see what they or it are like **2** to clean something quickly: She gave the room a quick once-over before the guests arrived.

on·col·o·gy /aŋˈkɑlədʒi/ noun [U] the scientific study of and treatment of TUMORS in the body ▶ **on·col·o·gist** /-dʒɪst/ noun

on·com·ing /ˈɑnˌkʌmɪŋ; ˈɔn-/ adj. [only before noun] coming toward you **SYN** APPROACHing: Always walk facing the oncoming traffic.

on-de'mand adj. [only before noun] done or happening whenever someone asks: The new network promises lightning-fast access to on-demand video. ⊃ see also DEMAND n., PRINT ON DEMAND

one 🔑 /wʌn/ number, det., pron.

● **number, det.** **1** the number 1: Do you want one or two? ♦ There's only room for one person. ♦ One more, please! ♦ a one-bedroom apartment ♦ I'll see you at one (= one o'clock). **2** used in formal language or for emphasis before hundred, thousand, etc., or before a unit of measurement: It cost one hundred and fifty dollars. ♦ He lost by less than one second. **3** used for emphasis to mean "a single" or "just one": There's only one thing we can do. **4** a person or thing, especially when they are part of a group: One of my friends lives in Boston. ♦ One place I'd really like to visit is Bali. **5** used for emphasis to mean "the only one" or "the most important one": He's the one person I can trust. ♦ Her one concern was for the health of her baby. ♦ It's the one thing I can't stand about him. **6** used when you are talking about a time in the past or the future, without actually saying which one: I saw her one afternoon last week. ♦ One day (= at some time in the future) you'll understand. **7** the same: They all went off in one direction. **8** (informal) used for emphasis instead of a or an: That was one hell of a game! ♦ She's one snazzy dresser. **9** used with a person's name to show that the speaker does not

know the person **SYN** A CERTAIN: *He worked as an assistant to one Jonathan Jones.*
IDM **as one** (*formal*) in agreement; all together: *We spoke as one on this matter.* **(be) at one (with sb/sth)** (*formal*) to feel that you completely agree with someone or something, or that you are part of something: *a place where you can feel at one with nature* **for one** used to emphasize that a particular person does something and that you believe other people do too: *I, for one, would prefer to postpone the meeting.* **get one over (on) sb/sth** (*informal*) to get an advantage over someone or something: *I'm not going to let them get one over on me!* **go one better (than sb/sth)** to do something better than someone else or than you have done before **SYN** OUTDO: *She did well this year and next year she hopes to go one better.* **in one** used to say that someone or something has different roles, contains different things, or is used for different purposes: *She's a mother and successful career woman in one.* ♦ *It's a public relations office, a press office, and a private office all in one.* ⊃ see also ALL-IN-ONE **one after another/the other** first one person or thing, and then another, and then another, up to any number or amount: *The bills kept coming in, one after another.* **one and all** (*old-fashioned, informal*) everyone: *Happy New Year to one and all!* **one and only** used to emphasize that someone is famous: *Here he is, the one and only Van Morrison!* **one and the same** used for emphasis to mean "the same": *I never realized that Ruth Rendell and Barbara Vine were one and the same* (= the same person using two different names). **one by one** separately and in order: *I went through the items on the list one by one.* **one or two** a few: *We've had one or two problems—nothing serious.* **one up (on sb)** having an advantage over someone **once/when you've seen, heard, etc. one, you've seen, heard, etc. them all** (*saying*) used to say that all types of the things mentioned are very similar: *I don't like science fiction novels much. Once you've read one, you've read them all.* ⊃ more at ALL *pron.*, MINORITY, SQUARE *n.*
• *pron.* **1** used to avoid repeating a noun, when you are referring to someone or something that has already been mentioned, or that the person you are speaking to knows about: *I'd like an ice-cream cone. Are you having one, too?* ♦ *Our car's always breaking down. But we're getting a new one soon.* ♦ *She was wearing her new dress, the red one.* ♦ *My favorite band? Oh, that's a hard one* (= a hard question). ♦ *What made you choose the one rather than the other?* **2** used when you are identifying the person or thing you are talking about: *Our house is the one next to the school.* ♦ *The students who are most successful are usually the ones who come to all the classes.* **3 ~ of** a person or thing belonging to a particular group: *It's a present for one of my children.* ♦ *We think of you as one of the family.* **4** a person of the type mentioned: *10 o'clock is too late for the little ones* (= young children). ♦ *He ached to be home with his loved ones.* ♦ *~ to do sth She was never one to criticize.* **5** (*formal*) used to mean "people in general" or "I," when the speaker is referring to himself or herself: *One should never criticize if one is not sure of one's facts.* ♦ *One gets the impression that they disapprove.* This use of **one** is very formal and now sounds old-fashioned. It is much more usual to use **you** for "people in general" and I when you are talking about yourself. **6 the ~ about sth** the joke: *Have you heard the one about the pink elephant?*
IDM **be (a) one for (doing) sth** to be a person who enjoys something, or who does something often or well: *I've never been a great one for camping.*

GRAMMAR

one + ones

- **One/ones** is used to avoid repeating a countable noun, but there are some times when you should not use it, especially in formal speech or writing:
- After a possessive (*my, your, Mary's*, etc.), *some, any, both*, or a number, unless it is used with an adjective: *"Did you get any postcards?" "Yes, I bought four nice ones."* ♦ ~~I bought four ones.~~ ♦ *Yes, I bought four.*
- It can be left out after superlatives, *this, that, these,*

those, *either, neither, another, which*, etc.: *"Here are the designs. Which (one) do you prefer?" "I think that (one) looks the most original."*
- **These ones** and **those ones** are not used in formal English: *Do you prefer these designs or those?*
- It is never used to replace uncountable nouns and is unusual with abstract countable nouns: *The American legal system is not the same as the Canadian system,* is better than *…as the Canadian one.*

one an`other ⚲ *pron.*
one another is used when you are saying that each member of a group does something to or for the other people in the group: *We all try and help one another.* ♦ *I think we've learned a lot about one another in this session.*
one-armed `bandit *noun* = SLOT MACHINE
one-horse `town *noun* (*informal*) a small town with not many interesting things to do or places to go to
one-`liner *noun* (*informal*) a short joke or funny remark: *He came out with some good one-liners.*
one-man *adj.* [only before noun] done or controlled by one person only; suitable for one person: *a one-man show/business* ♦ *a one-man tent* ⊃ see also ONE-WOMAN
one-man `band *noun* a street musician who plays several instruments at the same time: (*figurative*) *He runs the business as a one-man band* (= one person does everything).
one·ness /ˈwʌnnəs/ *noun* [U] (*formal*) the state of being completely united with someone or something, or of being in complete agreement with someone: *a sense of oneness with the natural world*
one-on-`one** (also **one-to-`one) *adj.* [usually before noun] between two people only: *a one-on-one meeting* ▶ **one-on-`one** *adv.*: *He teaches one-on-one.*
one-parent `family *noun* a family in which the children live with one parent rather than two ⊃ see also SINGLE PARENT
one-piece *adj.* [only before noun] (especially of clothes) consisting of one piece, not separate parts: *a one-piece swimsuit*
on·er·ous /ˈɑnərəs; ˈoʊ-/ *adj.* (*formal*) needing great effort; causing trouble or worry **SYN** TAXING: *an onerous duty/task/responsibility*
one's /wʌnz/ *det.* the possessive form of *one*: *One tries one's best.*
one·self /wʌnˈsɛlf/ *pron.* (*formal*) **1** (the reflexive form of *one*) used as the object of a verb or preposition when "one" is the subject of the verb or is understood as the subject: *One has to ask oneself what the purpose of the exercise is.* ♦ *One cannot choose freedom for oneself without choosing it for others.* ♦ *It is difficult to make oneself concentrate for long periods.* **2** used to emphasize *one*: *One likes to do it oneself.* **HELP** **One** and **oneself** are very formal words and now sound old-fashioned. It is much more usual to use **you** and **yourself** for referring to people in general and **I** and **myself** when the speaker is referring to himself or herself.
IDM **be oneself** to be in a normal state of body and mind, not influenced by other people: *One needs space to be oneself.* **(all) by oneself 1** alone; without anyone else **2** without help **(all) to oneself** not shared with anyone
one-shot *adj.* [only before noun] made or happening only once and not regularly: *a one-shot bonus*
one-`sided *adj.* **1** (*disapproving*) (of an argument, opinion, etc.) showing only one side of the situation; not balanced **SYN** BIASED: *The media were accused of presenting a very one-sided picture of the issue.* **2** (of a competition or a relationship) involving people who have different abilities; involving one person more than another: *a totally one-sided match* ♦ *a one-sided conversation* (= in which one person talks most of the time)
one-size-fits-`all *adj.* [only before noun] designed to be

suitable for a wide range of situations or needs: *a one-size-fits-all monetary policy*

'one-star *adj.* [usually before noun] **1** having one star in a system that measures quality. The highest standard is usually represented by four or five stars: *a one-star hotel* **2** having the fifth-highest military rank, and wearing a uniform that has one star on it: *a one-star general*

'one-stop *adj.* [only before noun] in which you can buy or do everything you want in one place: *Come see us for one-stop shopping. You can get everything you need here.*

'one-time *adj.* [only before noun] **1** former: *her one-time best friend, Anna* **2** not to be repeated: *a one-time fee of $500*

,one-to-'one *adj.* [usually before noun] **1** = ONE-ON-ONE **2** matching something else in an exact way: *There is no one-to-one correspondence between sounds and letters.*
▶ **,one-to-'one** *adv.* = ONE-ON-ONE

,one-track 'mind *noun* if someone has a **one-track mind**, they can only think about one subject

,one-trick 'pony *noun* (becoming *old-fashioned, disapproving*) a performer who is only famous for one song, etc.; a person or business that is only good at doing one thing: *This comedian is no one-trick pony.*

one-up·man·ship /,wʌn ˈʌpmənʃɪp/ *noun* [U] (*disapproving*) the skill of getting an advantage over other people

,one-'way *adj.* [usually before noun] **1** moving or allowing movement in only one direction: *one-way traffic* ◆ *a one-way street* ◆ *a one-way valve* **2** (also) a **one-way** ticket, etc. can be used for traveling to a place but not back again ⊃ compare ROUND TRIP **3** operating in only one direction: *Theirs was a one-way relationship* (= one person made all the effort). ◆ *They observed the prisoners through a one-way mirror* (= a mirror that allows a person standing behind it to see through it).

'one-,woman *adj.* [only before noun] done or controlled by one woman only: *a one-woman show*

,on-'field *adj.* at or on a sports field: *on-field medical treatment*

on·go·ing AWL /ˈɑnˌgoʊɪŋ; ˈɔn-/ *adj.* [usually before noun] continuing to exist or develop: *an ongoing debate/discussion/process* ◆ *The police investigation is ongoing.*

on·ion 🔊 /ˈʌnyən/ *noun* [C, U]
a round vegetable with many layers inside each other and a brown, red, or white skin. Onions have a strong smell and flavor: *Chop the onions finely.* ◆ *French onion soup* ⊃ picture at FRUIT

'onion ,ring *noun* [usually pl.] a slice of onion that has been covered with BATTER (= a mixture of flour and egg) or BREADCRUMBS and fried

on·ion·skin paper /ˈʌnyənskɪn ˈpeɪpər/ (also **on·ion·skin**) *noun* [U] very thin, smooth writing paper

on·line 🔊 /ˌɑnˈlaɪn; ˌɔn-/ *adj., adv.*
● *adj.* controlled by or connected to a computer or to the Internet: *Online shopping is both cheap and convenient.* ◆ *an online database*
● *adv.* (also **on line**) **1** using or connected to a computer or the Internet: *The new working methods will come online in June.* ◆ *All the new homes are online.* **2** working or functioning: *The new working methods will come online in June.* ⊃ collocations at E-MAIL

,online 'dating (also **,Internet ,dating**) *noun* [U] using the Internet to arrange to meet someone and possibly begin a romantic relationship with them: *an online dating service/site*

on·look·er /ˈɑnˌlʊkər; ˈɔn-/ *noun* a person who watches something that is happening but is not involved in it SYN BYSTANDER: *A crowd of onlookers gathered at the scene of the accident.* ⊃ thesaurus box at WITNESS

on·ly 🔊 /ˈoʊnli/ *adj., adv., conj.*
● *adj.* [only before noun] **1** used to say that no other or others of the same group exist or are there: *She's their only*

daughter. ◆ *We were the only people there.* ◆ *His only answer was a grunt.* **2** used to say that someone or something is the best and you would not choose any other: *She's the only person for the job.*
IDM **the only thing is…** (*informal*) used before mentioning a worry or problem you have with something: *I'd love to come—the only thing is I might be late.* ⊃ more at NAME, ONE
● *adv.* **1** nobody or nothing except: *There are only a limited number of tickets available.* ◆ *The bar is for members only.* ◆ *You only have to look at her to see she doesn't eat enough.* ◆ *Only five people turned up.* **2** in no other situation, place, etc.: *I agreed, but only because I was frightened.* ◆ *Children are admitted only if accompanied by an adult.* HELP In formal written English **only**, or **only if** and its clause, can be placed first in the sentence. In the second part of the sentence, **be, do, have,** etc. come before the subject and the main part of the verb: *Only in the Southwest do you find scenery like this.* ◆ *Only if these conditions are fulfilled can the application proceed to the next stage.* **3** no more important, interesting, serious, etc. than: *It was only a suggestion.* ◆ *Don't blame me, I'm only the messenger!* ◆ *He was only teasing you.* **4** no more than; no longer than: *She's only 21 and she runs her own business.* ◆ *It only took a few seconds.* ◆ *It took only a few seconds.* **5** not until: *We only got here yesterday.* ◆ (*formal*) *Only then did she realize the stress he was under.* HELP When **only** begins a sentence **be, do, have,** etc. come before the subject and the main part of the verb. **6** used to say that someone can do no more than what is mentioned, although this is probably not enough: *We can only guess what happened.* ◆ *He could only watch helplessly as the car plunged into the ravine.* ◆ *I only hope that she never finds out.* **7** used to say that something will have a bad effect: *If you do that, it will only make matters worse.* ◆ *Trying to reason with him only enrages him even more.* **8 ~ to do sth** used to mention something that happens immediately afterward, especially something that causes surprise, disappointment, etc.: *She turned into the driveway, only to find her way blocked.*
IDM **not only… but (also)…** both… and…: *He not only read the book, but also remembered what he had read.* ◆ language bank at ACCORDING TO **only just 1** not long ago/before: *We've only just arrived.* **2** almost not: *He only just caught the train.* ◆ *I can afford it, but only just.* **only too…** very: *I was only too pleased to help.* ◆ *Children can be difficult, as we know only too well.* **you're only young once** (*saying*) young people should enjoy themselves as much as possible, because they will have to work and worry later in their lives ⊃ more at EYE *n.*, IF
● *conj.* (*informal*) except that; but: *I'd love to come, only I have to work.* ◆ *It tastes like chicken, only stronger.*

,only 'child *noun* a child who has no brothers or sisters: *I'm an only child.*

on-'off *adj.* [only before noun] **1** (of a switch) having the positions "on" and "off": *an on-off switch* **2** (of a relationship) interrupted by periods when the relationship is not continuing

on·o·mas·tics /ˌɑnəˈmæstɪks/ *noun* [U] the study of the history and origin of names, especially names of people

on·o·mat·o·poe·ia /ˌɑnəˌmætəˈpiə; -ˌmɑtə-/ *noun* [U] (*technical*) the fact of words containing sounds similar to the noises they describe, for example *hiss*; the use of words like this in a piece of writing ▶ **on·o·mat·o·poe·ic** /-ˈpiɪk/ *adj.*: *"Bang" and "pop" are onomatopoeic words.*

on-ramp *noun* a road used for driving onto a major road such as an INTERSTATE ⊃ compare OFF-RAMP

on·rush /ˈɑnrʌʃ; ˈɔn-/ *noun* [sing.] a strong movement forward; the sudden development of something

,on-'screen *adj.* [only before noun] **1** appearing or written on the screen of a computer, television, or movie theater: *on-screen courtroom dramas* ◆ *on-screen messages* **2** connected with the imaginary story of a movie and not with real life: *His on-screen father is also his father in real life.* ⊃ compare OFF-SCREEN ▶ **,on-'screen** *adv.*

on·set /ˈɑnsɛt; ˈɔn-/ *noun* [sing.] the beginning of something, especially something unpleasant: *the onset of disease/old age/winter*

on·shore /ˌɑnˈʃɔr; ˌɔn-/ *adj.* [usually before noun] **1** on the land rather than at sea: *an onshore oil field* **2** (of wind) blowing from the ocean toward the land ▶ **on·shore** *adv.* ➲ compare OFFSHORE

on·side /ˌɑnˈsaɪd; ˌɔn-/ *adj.* (in football, SOCCER, HOCKEY, etc.) in a position on the field where you are allowed to play the ball or PUCK ▶ **on·side** *adv.* ➲ compare OFFSIDE

on·slaught /ˈɑnslɔt; ˈɔn-/ *noun* a strong or violent attack: **~ (against/on sb/sth)** *the enemy onslaught on our military forces* ◆ **~ (of sth)** *The town survives the onslaught of tourists every summer.* ◆ *an onslaught of abuse*

on·stage /ˌɑnˈsteɪdʒ; ˌɔn-/ *adj.* on the stage in a theater; in front of an audience: *onstage fights* ▶ **on·stage** *adv.* ➲ compare OFFSTAGE

ˈon-street *adj.* [only before noun] (of parking facilities) located at the side of a public road rather than in a garage, a driveway, etc. **ANT** OFF-STREET

on·to /ˈɑntə; ˈɔn-; *before vowels* ˈɑntu; ˈɔn-/ also **on to** *prep.*
1 used with verbs to express movement on or to a particular place or position: *Move the books onto the second shelf.* ◆ *She stepped down from the train onto the platform.*
2 used to show that something faces in a particular direction: *The window looked out onto the terrace.*
PHR V be ˈonto sb 1 (*informal*) to know about what someone has done wrong: *She knew the police would be onto them.* **2** to be talking to someone, usually in order to ask or tell them something: *They've been onto me for ages to get a job.* **be ˈonto sth** to know about something or be in a situation that could lead to a good result for you: *Scientists believe they are onto something big.* ◆ *She's onto a good thing with that new job.*

on·tol·o·gy /ɑnˈtɑlədʒi/ *noun* **1** [U] a branch of philosophy that deals with the nature of existence **2** [C] (*computing*) a list of concepts and categories in a subject area that shows the relationships between them: *a guide to creating a marketing ontology* ▶ **on·to·log·i·cal** /ˌɑntəˈlɑdʒɪkl/ *adj.*

o·nus /ˈoʊnəs/ *noun* usually **the onus** [sing.] (*formal*) the responsibility for something: *The **onus is on** employers to follow health and safety laws.*

on·ward /ˈɑnwərd; ˈɔn-/ *adv., adj.*
• ***adv.*** (also **onwards**) **1 from... onward** continuing from a particular time: *They lived there from the 1980s onward.* ◆ *The pool is open from 7 a.m. onward.* **2** (*formal*) forward: *We drove onward toward the coast.*
• ***adj.*** [only before noun] (*formal*) continuing or moving forward: *Oil was pumped to a port for onward shipment.*

on·yx /ˈɑnɪks/ *noun* [U] a type of stone that has layers of different colors in it, usually used for decorative objects

oo·dles /ˈudlz/ *noun* [pl.] **~ (of sth)** (*old-fashioned, informal*) a large amount of something **SYN** LOADS

ooh /u/ *exclamation* used for expressing surprise, happiness, or pain

oom·pah /ˈʊmpɑ; ˈum-/ (also **ˈoompah-ˌpah**) *noun* (*informal*) used to refer to the sound produced by a group of BRASS instruments: *an oompah band*

oomph /ʊmf/ *noun* [U] (*informal*) energy; a special good quality: *a styling product to give your hair more oomph*

oops /ʊps; ups/ *exclamation* **1** used when someone has almost had an accident, broken something, etc.: *Oops! I almost spilled the wine.* **2** used when you have done something embarrassing, said something rude by accident, told a secret, etc.: *Oops, I shouldn't have said that.*

oops-a-daisy /ˈʊpsə ˌdeɪzi/ *exclamation* = UPSY-DAISY

ooze /uz/ *verb, noun*
• ***verb*** **1** [I, T] if a thick liquid **oozes** from a place, or if something **oozes** a thick liquid, the liquid flows from the place slowly: **~ from/out of/through sth** | **~ out** *Blood oozed out of the wound.* ◆ **~ with sth** *an ugly swelling oozing with pus* ◆ **~ sth** *The wound was oozing blood.* ◆ *a plate of toast oozing butter* **2** [T, I] if someone or something **oozes** a particular characteristic, quality, etc., they show it strongly **SYN** EXUDE: **~ sth** *She walked into the party oozing confidence.* ◆ **~ with sth** *His voice oozed with charm.*
• ***noun*** **1** [U] very soft mud, especially at the bottom of a lake or river **2** [sing.] the very slow flow of a thick liquid ▶ **ooz·y** *adj.*

Op. *abbr.* also **op.** OPUS: *Webern's Five Pieces, Op. 10*

o·pac·i·ty /oʊˈpæsət̬i/ *noun* [U] **1** (*technical*) the fact of being difficult to see through; the fact of being OPAQUE **2** (*formal*) the fact of being difficult to understand; the fact of being OPAQUE **ANT** TRANSPARENCY

o·pal /ˈoʊpl/ *noun* [C, U] a white or almost clear SEMI-PRECIOUS STONE in which changes of color are seen, used in jewelry: *an opal ring*

o·pal·es·cent /ˌoʊpəˈlɛsnt/ *adj.* (*formal* or *literary*) changing color like an opal

o·paque /oʊˈpeɪk/ *adj.* **1** (of glass, liquid, etc.) not clear enough to see through or allow light through: *opaque glass* ◆ *opaque stockings* **2** (of speech or writing) difficult to understand; not clear **SYN** IMPENETRABLE: *The jargon in his talk was opaque to me.* **ANT** TRANSPARENT

op art /ˈɑp ɑrt/ *noun* [U] a style of modern art that uses patterns and colors in a way that makes the images seem to move as you look at them

op. cit. *abbr.* used in formal writing to refer to a book or an article that has already been mentioned

op·code /ˈɑpkoʊd/ *noun* = OPERATION CODE

OPEC /ˈoʊpɛk/ *abbr.* Organization of Petroleum Exporting Countries (an organization of countries that produce and sell oil)

op-ed /ˌɑp ˈɛd/ (also **ˌop-ˈed page**) *noun* the page in a newspaper opposite the EDITORIAL page that contains comment on the news and articles on particular subjects

o·pen /ˈoʊpən/ *adj., verb, noun*
• ***adj.***
› **NOT CLOSED 1** allowing things or people to go through: *A wasp flew in the open window.* ◆ *She had left the door **wide open**.* **ANT** CLOSED **2** (of someone's eyes, mouth, etc.) with EYELIDS or lips apart: *She had difficulty keeping her eyes open* (= because she was very tired). ◆ *He was breathing through his open mouth.* **ANT** CLOSED **3** spread out; with the edges apart: *The flowers are all open now.* ◆ *The book lay open on the table.* **ANT** CLOSED **4** not blocked by anything: *The mountain pass is **kept open** year-round.* **ANT** CLOSED
› **NOT FASTENED 5** not fastened or covered, so that things can easily come out or be put in: *Leave the envelope open.* ◆ *The bag burst open and everything fell out.* **6** (of clothes) not fastened: *Her coat was open.*
› **NOT ENCLOSED 7** not surrounded by anything; not closed in: ***open country*** (= without forests, buildings, etc.) ◆ *a city with a lot of parks and **open spaces*** ◆ *driving along the **open road*** (= part of a road in the country, where you can drive fast)
› **NOT COVERED 8** with no cover or roof on: *an open drain* ◆ *people working in **the open air*** (= not in a building) ◆ *The building's interior courtyard was open to the sky.* ◆ *an open wound* (= with no skin covering it) ◆ *an open flame*
› **FOR CUSTOMERS/VISITORS 9** [not usually before noun] if a store, bank, business, etc. is **open**, it is ready for business and will admit customers or visitors: *Is the museum open on Sundays?* ◆ *The new store will be open in the spring.* ◆ *The house was **thrown open** to the public.* ◆ *I declare this festival open.* **ANT** CLOSED
› **OF COMPETITION/BUILDING 10** if a competition, etc. is **open**, anyone can enter it **SYN** PUBLIC: *an open debate/championship/scholarship* ◆ *She was tried in **open court*** (= the public could go and listen to the trial). ◆ *The debate was **thrown open** to the audience.* **11** [not before noun] **~ to sb** if a competition, building, etc. is **open** to particular people, those people can enter it: *The competition is open to young people*

under the age of 18. ♦ *The house is not open to the public.* **ANT** CLOSED

> AVAILABLE **12** [not before noun] ~ **(to sb)** to be available and ready to use: *What options are open to us?* ♦ *Is the offer still open?* ♦ *I want to keep my savings account open.* **ANT** CLOSED

> NOT PROTECTED **13** ~ **(to sth)** likely to suffer something such as criticism, injury, etc. **SYN** VULNERABLE: *The system is open to abuse.* ♦ *He laid himself wide open to political attack.*

> NOT HIDDEN **14** known to everyone; not kept hidden: *an open quarrel* ♦ *open government* ♦ *their open display of affection* ♦ *His eyes showed open admiration as he looked at her.*

> PERSON'S CHARACTER **15** honest; not keeping thoughts and feelings hidden **SYN** FRANK: *She was always open with her parents.* ♦ *He was quite open about his reasons for leaving.* ⊃ thesaurus box at HONEST **16** ~ **to sth** (of a person) willing to listen to and think about new ideas: *I'm open to suggestions for what you would like to do in our classes.*

> NOT YET DECIDED **17** ~ **(to sth)** not yet finally decided or settled: *The race is still wide open* (= anyone could win). ♦ *The price is not open to negotiation.* ♦ *Some phrases in the contract are open to interpretation.* ♦ *Which route is better remains an open question* (= it is not decided). ♦ *In an interview try to ask open questions* (= to which the answer is not just "yes" or "no").

> CLOTH **18** with wide spaces between the threads: *an open weave*

> PHONETICS **19** (also low) (of a vowel) produced by opening the mouth wide ⊃ compare CLOSE¹

IDM **have/keep an open mind (about/on sth)** to be willing to listen to or accept new ideas or suggestions **keep your ears/eyes open (for sth)** to be quick to notice or hear things **an open book** if you describe someone or their life as **an open book**, you mean that you can easily understand them and know everything about them **an open invitation (to sb)** **1** an invitation to someone to visit you at any time **2** if something is **an open invitation** to criminals, etc., it encourages them to commit a crime by making it easier: *Leaving your camera on the seat of the car is an open invitation to thieves.* **an open secret** if something is **an open secret**, many people know about it, although it is supposed to be a secret **with open arms** if you welcome someone **with open arms**, you are extremely happy and pleased to see them ⊃ more at BURST *v.*, DOOR, EYE *n.*, MARKET *n.*, OPTION

● **verb**

> DOOR/WINDOW/LID **1** [T] ~ **sth** to move a door, window, lid, etc. so that it is no longer closed: *Mr. Chen opened the car door for his wife.* **ANT** CLOSE¹ **2** [I] to move or be moved so that it is no longer closed: *The door opened and Alan walked in.* **ANT** CLOSE¹

> CONTAINER/PACKAGE **3** [T] ~ **sth** to remove the lid, undo the FASTENER, etc. of a container, etc. in order to see or get what is inside: *Should I open another bottle?* ♦ *He opened the letter and read it.*

> EYES **4** [T, I] ~ **(sth)** if you **open** your eyes or your eyes **open**, you move your EYELIDS upward so that you can see **ANT** CLOSE¹

> MOUTH **5** [T, I] ~ **(sth)** if you **open** your mouth or your mouth **opens**, you move your lips, for example in order to speak: *He hardly ever opens his mouth* (= speaks).

> BOOK **6** [T] ~ **sth** to turn the cover or the pages of a book so that it is no longer closed: *Open your books to page 25.* **ANT** CLOSE¹

> SPREAD OUT **7** [I, T] to spread out or UNFOLD; to spread something out or UNFOLD it: *What if the parachute doesn't open?* ♦ *The flowers are starting to open.* ♦ ~ **sth** *Open the map on the table.* ♦ *He opened his arms wide to embrace her.*

> BORDER/ROAD **8** [T] ~ **sth** to make it possible for people, cars, goods, etc. to pass through a place: *When did the country open its borders?* ♦ *The road will be opened again in a few hours after police clear it.* **ANT** CLOSE¹

> FOR CUSTOMERS/VISITORS **9** [I, T] (of a shop/store, business, etc.) to start business for the day; to start business for the first time: *What time does the bank open?* ♦ ~ **sth** *The company opened its doors for business a month ago.* **ANT** CLOSE¹ **10** [I] to be ready for people to go to: *The new hospital opens on July 1st.* ♦ *When does the play open?* **ANT** CLOSE¹

> START SOMETHING **11** [T] to start an activity or event: ~ **sth** *You need just one dollar to open a bank account with us.* ♦ *The police have opened an investigation into the death.* ♦ *Troops opened fire on* (= started shooting at) *the crowds.* ♦ ~ **sth with sth** *They will open the new season with a performance of "Carmen."* ⊃ thesaurus box at START **12** [I] ~ **(with sth)** (of a story, movie, etc.) to start in a particular way: *The story opens with a murder.*

> WITH CEREMONY **13** [T] ~ **sth** to perform a ceremony showing that a building can start being used: *The bridge was opened by the governor.*

> COMPUTING **14** [T, I] ~ **(sth)** to start a computer program or file so that you can use it on the screen

IDM **open doors for sb** to provide opportunities for someone to do something and be successful **open your/sb's eyes (to sth)** to realize or make someone realize the truth about something: *Traveling really opens your eyes to other cultures.* **open your/sb's mind to sth** to become or make someone aware of new ideas or experiences **open the way for sb/sth (to do sth)** to make it possible for someone to do something or for something to happen ⊃ more at HEART, HEAVEN

PHR V **open into/onto sth** to lead to another room, area or place **open 'out** to become bigger or wider: *The street opened out into a small square.* **open 'up 1** to talk about what you feel and think: *It helps to discuss your problems but I find it hard to open up.* **2** to begin shooting: *Anti-aircraft guns opened up.* **3** (often used in orders) to open a door, container, etc.: *Open up or we'll break the door down!* **open sth↔'up** | **open 'up 1** to become or make something possible, available, or able to be reached: *The transcontinental railroad opened up the American West.* ♦ *Exciting possibilities were opening up for her in the new job.* **2** to begin business for the day; to start a new business: *I open up the store for the day at 9.* **ANT** CLOSE UP **3** to start a new business: *There's a new Thai restaurant opening up in town.* **ANT** CLOSE DOWN **4** to develop or start to happen or exist; to develop or start something: *A division has opened up between the two senators over the issue.* ♦ *Scott opened up a 3-point lead in the first game.* **5** to appear and become wider; to make something wider when it is narrow or closed: *The wound opened up and started bleeding.* ♦ *The operation will open up the blocked passages around his heart.* **ANT** CLOSE UP **open sth↔'up** to make something open that is shut, locked, etc.: *She laid the book flat and opened it up.*

● **noun** the open [sing.]

> OUTDOORS **1** outdoors; the countryside: *Children need to play out in the open.*

> NOT HIDDEN **2** not hidden or secret: *Government officials do not want these comments in the open.* ♦ *They intend to bring their complaints out into the open.*

the ˌopen 'air *noun* [sing.] a place outside rather than in a building: *He likes to cook in the open air.*

ˌopen- 'air *adj.* [only before noun] happening or existing outside rather than inside a building: *an open-air performance space*

ˌopen-and-shut 'case *noun* a legal case or other matter that is easy to decide or solve: *The murder was an open-and-shut case.*

ˌopen 'bar *noun* [U, C] an occasion when all the drinks at a party or other event have been paid for by someone else or are included in the ticket price

ˌopen 'door *noun, adj.*

● *noun* [sing.] a situation that allows something to happen, or that allows people to go to a place or get information without restrictions: *The current government policy is an open door to disaster.* ♦ *An insecure computer system is an open door to criminals.*

● *adj.* ˌopen-'door [only before noun] **1** (of a policy, system, principle, etc.) allowing people or goods freedom to come into a country; allowing people to go to a place or get information without restrictions: *the country's open-door policy for refugees* **2** a policy within a company or other organization designed to allow people to freely commu-

t tea   t̬ butter   d did   k cat   g got   tʃ chin   dʒ June   f fall

nicate with the people in charge: *We operate an open-door policy here, and are always willing to listen to our students' suggestions.*

ˌopen-'ended *adj.* without any limits, aims, or dates fixed in advance: *an open-ended discussion* ♦ *The contract is open-ended.*

o·pen·er /'oʊpənər/ *noun* **1** (usually in compounds) a tool that is used to open things: *a can opener* ♦ *a bottle opener* ⊃ see also EYE-OPENER **2** the first in a series of things such as sports games; the first action in an event, a game, etc.: *They won the season opener 4–2.* ♦ *Jones scored the opener.* ♦ *a good conversation opener*
IDM for openers (*informal*) as a beginning or first part of a process

ˌopen-faced 'sandwich (also open-face 'sandwich) *noun* a slice of bread with meat, cheese, etc. on top but without a second slice of bread to cover this

o·pen·handed /ˌoʊpən'hændəd/ *adj.* **1** generous and giving willingly: *an openhanded host* **2** using the flat part of the hand: *an openhanded blow*

ˌopen-'hearted *adj.* kind and friendly

ˌopen-ˌheart 'surgery *noun* [U] a medical operation on the heart, during which the patient's blood is kept flowing by a machine

ˌopen 'house *noun* **1** [U, sing.] a place or a time at which visitors are welcome: *It's always open house at their place.* ♦ *We're having a New Year's Day open house from 2 to 6.* **2** [C] a day when people can visit a school, an organization, etc. and see the work that is done there **3** [C] a time when people who are interested in buying a particular house or apartment can look around it

o·pen·ing 🔊 /'oʊpənɪŋ/ *noun, adj.*
• *noun* **1** [C] a space or hole that someone or something can pass through: *We could see the stars through an opening in the roof.* **2** [C, usually sing.] the beginning or first part of something: *The movie has an exciting opening.* **ANT** ENDING **3** [C, usually sing.] a ceremony to celebrate the start of a public event or the first time a new building, road, etc. is used: *the opening of the Olympic Games* ♦ *the official opening of the new hospital* **4** [C, U] the act or process of making something open or of becoming open: *the opening of a flower* ♦ *the opening of the new play* ♦ *The new store will have its grand opening next week.* **ANT** CLOSING **5** [C] a job that is available **SYN** VACANCY: *There are several openings in the sales department.* **6** [C] a good opportunity for someone: *Winning the competition was the opening she needed for her career.* **7** [C] part of a piece of clothing that is made to open and close so that it can be put on easily: *The skirt has a side opening.*
• *adj.* [only before noun] first; beginning: *his opening remarks* ♦ *the opening chapter of the book* **ANT** CLOSING

'opening ˌhours *noun* [pl.] the time during which a store, bank, etc. is open for business

ˌopening 'night *noun* [usually sing.] the first night that, for example, a play is performed or a movie is shown to the public

ˌopening 'up *noun* [sing.] **1** the process of removing restrictions and making something such as land or jobs available to more people: *the opening up of new opportunities for women in business* **2** the process of making something ready for use: *the opening up of a new stretch of highway*

ˌopen 'letter *noun* a letter of complaint or protest to an important person or group that is printed in a newspaper so that the public can read it

o·pen·ly 🔊 /'oʊpənli/ *adv.*
without hiding any feelings, opinions, or information: *Can you talk openly about the problem with your parents?* ♦ *The men in prison would never cry openly* (= so that other people could see).

ˌopen 'market *noun* [sing.] a situation in which companies can trade without restrictions, and prices depend on the

amount of goods and the number of people buying them: *to buy/sell/trade on the open market*

ˌopen 'mike (also ˌopen 'mic) *noun* [U] an occasion in a club when anyone can sing, play music, or tell jokes: *open-mike night*

ˌopen-'minded *adj.* willing to listen to, think about, or accept different ideas **SYN** BROAD-MINDED **ANT** NARROW-MINDED ▶ ˌopen-'mindedness *noun* [U]

ˌopen-'mouthed *adj.* with your mouth open because you are surprised or shocked

ˌopen-'necked (also ˌopen-'neck) *adj.* (of a shirt) worn without a tie and with the top button undone

o·pen·ness /'oʊpənnəs/ *noun* [U] **1** the quality of being honest and not hiding information or feelings **2** the quality of being able to think about, accept, or listen to different ideas or people **3** the quality of not being closed in or covered

ˌopen-'pit *adj.* [usually before noun] in **open-pit** mines, coal is taken out of the ground near the surface ⊃ see also STRIP MINING

ˌopen-'plan *adj.* an **open-plan** building or area does not have inside walls dividing it up into rooms: *an open-plan office*

ˌopen 'sandwich *noun* a SANDWICH that is served on a plate with no top piece of bread

ˌopen 'season *noun* [sing.] **1** ~ (for sth) the time in the year when it is legal to hunt and kill particular animals or birds, or to catch fish, for sport **ANT** CLOSED SEASON **2** ~ for/on sb/sth a time when there are no restrictions on criticizing particular groups of people or treating them unfairly: *It seems to be open season on teachers now.*

ˌopen 'sesame *noun* [sing.] an easy way to gain or achieve something that is usually very difficult to get: *Academic success is not always an open sesame to a well-paid job.* **ORIGIN** From the fairy tale *Ali Baba and the Forty Thieves*, in which the magic words **open sesame** had to be said to open the cave where the thieves kept their treasure.

ˌopen-'source *adj.* (*computing*) used to describe software for which the original SOURCE CODE is made available to anyone

ˌopen 'syllable *noun* (*phonetics*) a syllable that does not end with a consonant, for example *so*

ˌopen-'toed *adj.* (of shoes) not covering the toes: *open-toed pumps*

o·pe·ra /'ɑprə; 'ɑpərə/ *noun* **1** [C, U] a dramatic work in which all or most of the words are sung to music; works of this type as an art form or entertainment: *Puccini's operas* ♦ *to go to the opera* ♦ *an opera singer* ♦ *light/grand opera* ⊃ see also SOAP OPERA **2** [C] a company that performs opera; a building in which operas are performed: *the Metropolitan Opera* ▶ op·er·at·ic /ˌɑpə'rætɪk/ *adj.*: *operatic arias/composers*

op·er·a·ble /'ɑpərəbl; 'ɑprə-/ *adj.* **1** that functions; that can be used: *When will the new system be operable?* **2** (of a medical condition) that can be treated by an operation **ANT** INOPERABLE

'opera ˌglasses *noun* [pl.] small BINOCULARS that people use in a theater to see the actors or singers on the stage

'opera ˌhouse *noun* a theater where operas are performed

op·er·and /'ɑpəˌrænd/ *noun* (*mathematics*) the number on which an operation is to be done

op·er·ate 🔊 /'ɑpəˌreɪt/ *verb*
▷ MACHINE **1** [I] + adv./prep. to work in a particular way **SYN** FUNCTION: *Most domestic freezers operate at below 0°F.* ♦ *Solar panels can only operate in sunlight.* ♦ (*figurative*) *Some people only operate well under pressure.* **2** [T] ~ sth to use or control a machine or make it work: *What skills are needed to operate this machinery?*
▷ SYSTEM/PROCESS/SERVICE **3** [I, T] to be used or working; to use something or make it work: *A new late-night service is*

now operating. ◆ *The regulation operates in favor of married couples.* ◆ **~ sth** *The airline operates flights to 25 countries.* ◆ *The government operates a system of subsidized loans to dairy farmers.*

▷ OF BUSINESS/ORGANIZATION **4** [I] **+ adv./prep.** to work in a particular way or from a particular place: *They plan to operate from a new office in St. Louis.* ◆ *Illegal drinking clubs continue to operate in the city.*

▷ MEDICAL **5** [I] to cut open someone's body in order to remove a part that has a disease or to repair a part that is damaged: *The doctors operated last night.* ◆ **~ (on sb) (for sth)** *We will have to operate on his eyes.*

▷ OF SOLDIERS **6** [I] **(+ adv./prep.)** to be involved in military activities in a place: *Troops are operating from bases in the north.*

'operating ˌroom *noun* a room in a hospital used for medical operations

'operating ˌsystem *noun* a set of programs that controls the way a computer works and runs other programs

'operating ˌtable *noun* a special table that you lie on to have a medical operation in a hospital: *The patient died on the operating table* (= during an operation).

op·er·a·tion 🔑 /ˌɑpəˈreɪʃn/ *noun*

▷ MEDICAL **1** [C] the process of cutting open a part of a person's body in order to remove or repair a damaged part: *Will I need to have an operation?* ◆ *He underwent a three-hour heart operation.* ◆ **~ (on sb/sth) (to do sth)** *an operation on her lung to remove a tumor* ◆ **~ (on sb/sth) (for sth)** *Doctors performed an emergency operation for appendicitis last night.*

▷ ORGANIZED ACTIVITY **2** [C] an organized activity that involves several people doing different things: *a security operation* ◆ *The police have launched a major operation against drug dealers.* ◆ *the UN peacekeeping operations*

▷ BUSINESS **3** [C] a business or company involving many parts: *a huge multinational operation* **4** [C] the activity or work done in an area of business or industry: *the firm's banking operations overseas*

▷ COMPUTER **5** [C, U] an act performed by a machine, especially a computer: *The whole operation is performed in less than three seconds.*

▷ MACHINE/SYSTEM **6** [U] the way that parts of a machine or a system work; the process of making something work: *Regular servicing guarantees the smooth operation of the engine.* ◆ *Operation of the device is extremely simple.*

▷ MILITARY ACTIVITY **7** [C, usually pl.] military activity: *He was the officer in charge of operations.*

▷ MATHEMATICS **8** [C] a process in which a number or quantity is changed by adding, multiplying, etc.
IDM **in operation** working, being used, or having an effect: *The system has been in operation for six months.* ◆ *Temporary traffic controls are in operation on Route 47.* **come into operation** to start working; to start having an effect **SYN** COME INTO FORCE: *The new rules will come into operation next week.* **put sth into operation** to make something start working; to start using something: *It's time to put our plan into operation.*

op·er·a·tion·al /ˌɑpəˈreɪʃənl/ *adj.* **1** [usually before noun] connected with the way in which a business, machine, system, etc. works: *operational activities/costs/difficulties* **2** [not usually before noun] ready to be used: *The new airport is now fully operational.* **3** [only before noun] connected with a military operation: *operational headquarters* ▶ **op·er·a·tion·al·ly** /-ʃənəli/ *adv.*

oper'ation ˌcode (also **op·code**) *noun* [U, C] (*computing*) an instruction written in MACHINE CODE that relates to a particular task

oper'ations ˌresearch (also **operational ˌresearch**) *noun* [U] (*technical*) the study of how businesses are organized, in order to make them more efficient

oper'ations ˌroom *noun* a room from which military or police activities are controlled

op·er·a·tive /ˈɑpərətɪv; ˈɑprə-/ *noun, adj.*
● *noun* **1** (*technical*) a worker, especially one who works with

their hands: *a factory operative* ◆ *skilled/unskilled operatives* **2** a person who does secret work, especially for a government organization: *an intelligence operative*
● *adj.* **1** [not usually before noun] ready to be used; in use **SYN** FUNCTIONAL: *This law becomes operative immediately.* ◆ *The station will be fully operative again in January.* **2** [only before noun] (*medical*) connected with a medical operation: *operative treatment* ⊃ see also POSTOPERATIVE
IDM **the operative word** used to emphasize that a particular word or phrase is the most important one in a sentence: *I was in love with her—"was" being the operative word.*

op·er·a·tor /ˈɑpəˌreɪtər/ *noun* **1** (often in compounds) a person who operates equipment or a machine: *a computer/ machine operator* **2** a person who works on the telephone SWITCHBOARD of a large company or organization, especially at a TELEPHONE EXCHANGE **3** (often in compounds) a person or company that runs a particular business: *a tour operator* ◆ *a bus operator* **4** (*informal*, especially *disapproving*) a person who is skillful at getting what they want, especially when this involves behaving in a dishonest way: *a smooth/slick/shrewd operator* **5** (*mathematics*) a symbol or function that represents an operation in mathematics

op·er·et·ta /ˌɑpəˈrɛtə/ *noun* a short OPERA, usually with a humorous subject

oph·thal·mic /ɑfˈθælmɪk; ɑp-/ *adj.* (*medical*) connected with the eye: *ophthalmic surgery*

oph·thal·mol·o·gist /ˌɑfθəˈmɑlədʒɪst; -θəl-; ˌɑp-/ *noun* a doctor who studies and treats the diseases of the eye

oph·thal·mol·o·gy /ˌɑfθəˈmɑlədʒi; -θəl-; ˌɑp-/ *noun* [U] the scientific study of the eye and its diseases

o·pi·ate /ˈoʊpiət/ *noun* (*formal*) a drug containing OPIUM

o·pine /oʊˈpaɪn/ *verb* **~ that…** (*formal*) to express a particular opinion: *She opined that San Francisco had the most beautiful views of any city in the United States.*

LANGUAGE BANK

opinion
giving your personal opinion

■ **In my opinion**, everyone should have some understanding of science.

■ Everyone should, **in my opinion**, have some understanding of science.

■ **It seems to me that** many people in this country have a flawed understanding of science.

■ This is, **in my view**, the result of a failure of the scientific community to get its message across.

■ Another reason why so many people have such a poor understanding of science is, **I believe**, the lack of adequate funding for science in schools.

■ Smith argues that science is separate from culture. **My own view is that** science belongs with literature, art, philosophy, and religion as an integral part of our culture.

■ **In this writer's opinion**, the more the public knows about science, the less they will fear and distrust it.

⊃ Thesaurus at THINK

⊃ Language Banks at ACCORDING TO, ARGUE, IMPERSONAL, NEVERTHELESS, PERHAPS

---

o·pin·ion 🔑 /əˈpɪnyən/ *noun*

1 [C] your feelings or thoughts about someone or something, rather than a fact **SYN** VIEW: **~ (about/of/on sb/sth)** *We were invited to give our opinions about how the work should be done.* ◆ *I've recently changed my opinion of her.* ◆ *Everyone had an opinion on the subject.* ◆ **~ (that…)** *The chairman expressed the opinion that job losses were inevitable.* ◆ *He has very strong political opinions.* ◆ **In my opinion**, *it's a very sound investment.* ◆ (*formal*) *It is our opinion that he should resign.* ◆ *If you want my opinion, I think you'd be crazy not to accept.* **2** [U] the beliefs or views of a group of people: *legal/medical/*

political opinion (= the beliefs of people working in the legal, etc. profession) ◆ *There is* ***a difference of opinion*** (= people disagree) *as to the merits of the plan.* ◆ *Opinion is divided* on the issue. ◆ *There is a wide body of opinion that supports this proposal.* ◆ *Which is the better choice is* ***a matter of opinion*** (= people have different opinions about it). see also PUBLIC OPINION **3** [C] advice from a professional person: *They called in a psychologist to give an independent opinion.* ◆ *I'd like* ***a second opinion*** (= advice from another person) *before I make a decision.*
IDM **be of the opinion that…** (*formal*) to believe or think that… **have a good, bad, high, low, etc. opinion of sb/ sth** to think that someone or something is good, bad, etc.: *The boss has a very high opinion of her.* more at CONSIDER

o·pin·ion·at·ed /ə'pɪnyəˌneɪtəd/ (also ˌself-o'pinionated) *adj.* (*disapproving*) having very strong opinions that you are not willing to change

o'pinion ˌpoll *noun* = POLL

o·pi·um /'oʊpiəm/ *noun* [U] a powerful drug made from the juice of a type of POPPY (= a kind of flower), used in the past in medicines to reduce pain and help people sleep. Some people take opium illegally for pleasure and can become ADDICTED to it.

o·pos·sum /ə'pasəm/ (also *informal* pos·sum) *noun* a small N. American or Australian animal that lives in trees and carries its young in a POUCH (= a pocket of skin on the front of the mother's body)

opossum

op·po·nent /ə'poʊnənt/ *noun*
1 a person that you are playing or fighting against in a game, competition, argument, etc. **SYN** ADVERSARY: *a political opponent* ◆ *a* ***dangerous/worthy/formidable opponent*** ◆ *The team's opponents are unbeaten so far this season.* **2 ~ (of sth)** a person who is against something and tries to change or stop it: *opponents of abortion* ◆ *opponents of the regime*

op·por·tune /ˌapər'tun/ *adj.* (*formal*) **1** (of a time) suitable for doing a particular thing, so that it is likely to be successful **SYN** FAVORABLE: *The offer could not have come at a more opportune moment.* **2** (of an action or event) done or happening at the right time to be successful: *an opportune remark* **ANT** INOPPORTUNE ▶ **op·por·tune·ly** *adv.*

op·por·tun·ism /ˌapər'tunɪzəm/ *noun* [U] (*disapproving*) the practice of using situations unfairly to gain advantage for yourself without thinking about how your actions will affect other people

op·por·tun·ist /ˌapər'tunɪst/ *noun, adj.*
● *noun* (often *disapproving*) a person who makes use of an opportunity, especially to get an advantage for himself or herself: *80% of burglaries are committed by casual opportunists.*
● *adj.* [usually before noun] = OPPORTUNISTIC (1)

op·por·tun·is·tic /ˌapərtu'nɪstɪk/ *adj.* **1** (also op·por·tun·ist) (*disapproving*) making use of an opportunity, especially to get an advantage for yourself; not done in a planned way: *an opportunistic crime* **2** [only before noun] (*medical*) harmful to people whose IMMUNE SYSTEM has been made weak by disease or drugs: *an opportunistic infection*

op·por·tu·ni·ty /ˌapər'tunəti/ *noun* [C, U] (*pl.* op·por·tu·ni·ties)
a time when a particular situation makes it possible to do or achieve something **SYN** CHANCE: **~ (to do sth)** *You'll have the opportunity to ask any questions at the end.* ◆ **~ (for sth/for doing sth)** *There was no opportunity for further discussion.* ◆ **~ (of doing sth)** *At least give him the opportunity of explaining what happened.* ◆ *Our company promotes* ***equal opportunities*** *for women* (= women are given the same jobs, pay, etc. as men). ◆ ***career/employment/job opportunities*** ◆ *I'd like to* ***take this opportunity*** *to thank my colleagues for their support.* ◆ *He is*

rude to me *at every opportunity* (= whenever possible). ◆ *They intend to close the school at the earliest opportunity* (= as soon as possible). ◆ *a* ***window of opportunity*** (= a period of time when the circumstances are right for doing something) see also PHOTO OPPORTUNITY

op·pos·a·ble /ə'poʊzəbl/ *adj.* (of a thumb) capable of touching the other fingers on the same hand in order to hold things: *the opposable thumb of humans and monkeys*

op·pose /ə'poʊz/ *verb*
1 to disagree strongly with someone's plan, policy, etc. and try to change it or prevent it from succeeding: **~ sb/sth** *This party would bitterly oppose the reintroduction of the death penalty.* ◆ *He threw all those who opposed him into prison.* ◆ **~ (sb/sth) doing sth** *I would oppose changing the law.* compare PROPOSE **2 ~ sb** to compete with someone in a contest: *She intends to oppose the incumbent in the next election.*

op·posed /ə'poʊzd/ *adj.* [not usually before noun] **~ (to sth)**
1 (of a person) disagreeing strongly with something and trying to stop it: *She remained bitterly opposed to the idea of moving to Tulsa.* ◆ *They are totally opposed to abortion.* **2** (of ideas, opinions, etc.) very different from something: *Our views are* ***diametrically opposed*** *on this issue.*
IDM **as opposed to** used to make a contrast between two things: *200 attended, as opposed to 300 the previous year.* ◆ *This exercise develops suppleness as opposed to* (= rather than) *strength.*

op·pos·ing /ə'poʊzɪŋ/ *adj.* [only before noun]
1 (of teams, armies, forces, etc.) playing, fighting, working, etc. against each other: *a player from the opposing team* ◆ *It is time for opposing factions to unite and work toward a common goal.* **2** (of attitudes, views etc.) very different from each other

op·po·site /'apəzət; -sət/ *adj., adv., noun, prep.*
● *adj.* **1** [only before noun] on the other side of a particular area from someone or something, and usually facing them: *Answers are given on the opposite page.* ◆ *We live farther down on the opposite side of the street.* ◆ *It's not easy having a relationship when you live on opposite ends of the country.* **2** (used after the noun) facing the speaker or someone or something that has been mentioned: *I could see smoke coming from the windows of the house directly opposite.* ◆ *He sat down in the chair opposite.* **3** [usually before noun] as different as possible from something: *I watched them leave and then drove off in the opposite direction.* ◆ *She tried calming him down but it seemed to be having the opposite effect.* ◆ *students at opposite ends of the ability range* ▶ **op·po·site** *adv.*: *A newly married couple lived opposite* (= on the other side of the street) *to them.* ◆ *See opposite* (= on the opposite page) *for further details.*
IDM **your opposite number** a person who does the same job as you in another organization: *The Secretary of State is currently having talks with her opposite number in the British Government.* **the opposite sex** the other sex: *He found it difficult to talk to members of the opposite sex.* more at PULL *v.*
● *noun* a person or thing that is as different as possible from someone or something else: *Hot and cold are opposites.* ◆ *What is the opposite of heavy?* ◆ *I thought she would be small and blonde but she's the complete opposite.* ◆ *Exactly the opposite is true.* ◆ *"Is it better now?" "Quite the opposite, I'm afraid."*
IDM **opposites attract** used to say that people who are very different are often attracted to each other
● *prep.* **1** on the other side of a particular area from someone or something, and usually facing them: *I sat opposite him during the meal* (= on the other side of the table). ◆ *The bank is opposite the supermarket* (= on the other side of the street). ◆ *Write your address opposite* (= next to) *your name.* **2** acting in a movie or play as the partner of someone: *She starred opposite Tom Hanks.*

op·po·si·tion 🔑 /ˌɑpəˈzɪʃn/ noun
1 [U] ~ **(to sb/sth)** the act of strongly disagreeing with someone or something, especially with the aim of preventing something from happening: *Delegates expressed* **strong opposition** *to the plans.* ◆ *The army* **met with fierce opposition** *in every town.* ◆ *He spent five years in prison for his opposition to the regime.* ◆ **opposition forces** (= people who are arguing, fighting, etc. with another group) **2** **the opposition** [sing.] the people you are competing against in business, a competition, a game, etc.: *He went to work for the opposition.* ◆ *The opposition, in the form of innovative new companies, is mounting a strong challenge to our business.* ◆ *The Cavaliers couldn't match the opposition in the final game and lost 106–93.* **3** **the opposition** (also **the Opposition**) [sing.] the main political party that is opposed to the party that is in power; the political parties that are in a parliament, but not part of the government: *the leader of the opposition* ◆ **opposition parties** ◆ *The opposition candidate stressed the need for more funds for education.* **4** [U, C] (*formal*) the state of being as different as possible; two things that are as different as possible: *the opposition between good and evil* ◆ *His poetry is full of oppositions and contrasts.* ▶ **op·po·si·tion·al** /-ʃənl/ *adj.* [usually before noun] (*formal*): *oppositional groups/tactics*
IDM **in opposition to sb/sth** **1** disagreeing strongly with someone or something, especially with the aim of preventing something from happening: *Protest marches were held in opposition to the proposed law.* **2** contrasting two people or things that are very different: *Leisure is often defined in opposition to work.*

op·press /əˈprɛs/ *verb* **1** ~ **sb** to treat someone in a cruel and unfair way, especially by not giving them the same freedom, rights, etc. as other people: *The regime is accused of oppressing religious minorities.* **2** ~ **sb** to make someone only able to think about sad or worrying things **SYN** WEIGH DOWN: *The gloomy atmosphere in the office oppressed her.* ▶ **op·pres·sion** /əˈprɛʃn/ *noun* [U]: *victims of oppression*

op·pressed /əˈprɛst/ *adj.* **1** treated in a cruel and unfair way and not given the same freedom, rights, etc. as other people: *oppressed minorities* **2** **the oppressed** *noun* [pl.] people who are oppressed

op·pres·sive /əˈprɛsɪv/ *adj.* **1** treating people in a cruel and unfair way and not giving them the same freedom, rights, etc. as other people: *oppressive laws* ◆ *an oppressive government* **2** (of the weather) extremely hot and unpleasant and lacking fresh air: *oppressive heat* **3** making you feel unhappy and anxious: *an oppressive relationship* ▶ **op·pres·sive·ly** *adv.*: *to behave oppressively* ◆ *oppressively hot* ◆ *He suffered from an oppressively dominant mother.*

op·pres·sor /əˈprɛsər/ *noun* a person or group of people that treats someone in a cruel and unfair way, especially by not giving them the same rights, etc. as other people

op·pro·bri·um /əˈproʊbriəm/ *noun* [U] (*formal*) severe criticism of a person, country, etc. by a large group of people ▶ **op·pro·bri·ous** /əˈproʊbriəs/ *adj.*: *an opprobrious remark*

opt /ɑpt/ *verb* [I, T] to choose to take or not to take a particular course of action: ~ **for/against sth** *After graduating she opted for a career in music.* ◆ ~ **to do sth** *Many workers opted to leave their jobs rather than take a pay cut.* ⊃ **thesaurus box at** CHOOSE
PHR V **opt ˈin (to sth)** to choose to be part of a system or an agreement **opt ˈout (of sth)** to choose not to take part in something: *Employees may opt out of the company's pension plan.* ⊃ **related noun** OPT-OUT

op·tic /ˈɑptɪk/ *adj.* [usually before noun] connected with the eye or the sense of sight: *the optic nerve* (= from the eye to the brain) ⊃ **picture at** BODY

op·ti·cal /ˈɑptɪkl/ *adj.* [usually before noun] **1** connected with the sense of sight or the relationship between light and sight: *optical effects* **2** used to help you see something more clearly: *optical aids* ◆ *optical instruments such as microscopes and telescopes* **3** (*computing*) using light for reading or storing information: *optical storage* ◆ *an optical disk* ▶ **op·ti·cal·ly** /-kli/ *adv.*

optical ˈcharacter recogˌnition *noun* [U] (*abbr.* OCR) (*computing*) the process of using light to record printed information onto disks for use in a computer system

optical ˈfiber (also) *noun* [C, U] a thin glass thread through which light can be TRANSMITTED (= sent)

optical ilˈlusion *noun* something that tricks your eyes and makes you think that you can see something that is not there, or makes you see something as different from what it really is

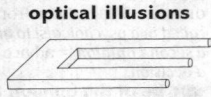

optical illusions

Are there two prongs or three?

op·ti·cian /ɑpˈtɪʃn/ *noun* **1** (also) a person whose job is to test people's eyes and to recommend and sell glasses ⊃ **see also** OPTOMETRIST **2** a person who makes LENSES, glasses, etc.

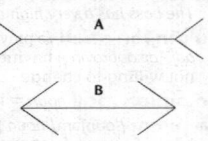

A

B

Horizontal line A and horizontal line B are of equal length, but horizontal line A appears to be longer.

op·tics /ˈɑptɪks/ *noun* [U] the scientific study of sight and light ⊃ **see also** FIBER OPTICS

op·ti·mal /ˈɑptəməl/ *adj.* = OPTIMUM ▶ **op·ti·mal·ly** *adv.*

op·ti·mism /ˈɑptəˌmɪzəm/ *noun* [U] ~ **(about/for sth)** a feeling that good things will happen and that something will be successful; the tendency to have this feeling: *optimism about/for the future* ◆ *We may now look forward with* **optimism.** ◆ *a mood of* **cautious optimism** ◆ *There are very real grounds for optimism.* **ANT** PESSIMISM

op·ti·mist /ˈɑptəmɪst/ *noun* a person who always expects good things to happen or things to be successful **ANT** PESSIMIST

op·ti·mis·tic /ˌɑptəˈmɪstɪk/ *adj.* expecting good things to happen or something to be successful; showing this feeling **SYN** POSITIVE: ~ **(about sth)** *She's not very optimistic about the outcome of the talks.* ◆ ~ **(that…)** *They are cautiously optimistic that the reforms will take place.* ◆ *We are now taking a more optimistic view.* ◆ *in an optimistic mood* ◆ *I think you're being overly optimistic.* **ANT** PESSIMISTIC ▶ **op·ti·mis·ti·cally** /-kli/ *adv.*

op·ti·mize /ˈɑptəˌmaɪz/ *verb* ~ **sth** to make something as good as it can be; to use something in the best possible way: *to optimize the use of resources*

op·ti·mum /ˈɑptəməm/ *adj.* [only before noun] **1** (also **optimal**) the best possible; producing the best possible results: *optimum growth* ◆ *the optimum use of resources* ◆ *the optimum conditions for effective learning* **2** **the optimum** *noun* [sing.] the best possible result, set of conditions, etc. **SYN** IDEAL

op·tion 🔑 **AWL** /ˈɑpʃn/ *noun, verb*
• *noun* **1** [C, U] something that you can choose to have or do; the freedom to choose what you do: *As I see it, we have two options…* ◆ *There are various options open to you.* ◆ *Going to college was not an option for me.* ◆ *I had* **no option but to** (= I had to) *ask him to leave.* ◆ ~ **(of doing sth)** *Students have the option of studying abroad in their second year.* ◆ ~ **(to do sth)** *A savings plan that gives you the option to vary your monthly payments.* ◆ *This particular model comes with a wide range of options* (= things you can choose to have when buying something but that you will have to pay extra for). **2** [C] the right to buy or sell something at some time in the future: ~ **(on sth)** *We have an option on the house.* ◆ *He has promised me first option on his car* (= the opportunity to buy it before anyone else). ◆ ~ **(to do sth)** *The property is for rent with an option to buy at any time.* ◆ **stock options** (= the right to buy stock in a company) **3** [C] (*computing*) one of the choices you can make when using a computer program: *Choose the "Cut" option from the Edit menu.*

IDM **keep/leave your options open** to avoid making a decision now so that you still have a choice in the future **the easy/soft option** (often *disapproving*) a choice that is thought to be easier because it involves less effort, difficulty, etc.: *They are anxious that the new course should not be seen as a soft option.* ◆ *He decided to **take the easy option** and give them what they wanted.*

THESAURUS

option

choice ◆ alternative ◆ possibility

These are all words for something that you choose to do in a particular situation.

option something that you can choose to have or do; the freedom to choose what you do: *We are currently studying all the options available.* ◆ *He was given one month's imprisonment without the option of a fine.* **NOTE** **Option** is also the word used in computing for one of the choices you can make when using a computer program: *Choose the "Cut" option from the Edit menu.*

choice the freedom to choose what you do; something that you can choose to have or do: *If I had the choice, I would stop working tomorrow.* ◆ *She has a number of choices available to her.*

alternative something that you can choose to have or do out of two or more possibilities: *You can be paid in cash weekly or by check monthly: Those are the two alternatives.*

OPTION, CHOICE, OR ALTERNATIVE?

Choice is slightly less formal than **option**, and **alternative** is slightly more formal. **Choice** is most often used for "the freedom to choose," although you can sometimes also use **option** (but not usually **alternative**): *If I had the choice/option, I would...* ◆ *If I had the alternative, I would...* ◆ *parental choice in education* ◆ *parental option/alternative in education.* Things that you can choose are **options**, **choices**, or **alternatives**. However, **alternative** is more frequently used to talk about choosing between two things rather than several.

possibility one of the different things that you can do in a particular situation: *We need to explore a wide range of possibilities.* ◆ *The possibilities are endless.* **NOTE** **Possibility** can be used in a similar way to **option**, **choice**, and **alternative**, but the emphasis here is less on the need to make a choice, and more on what is available.

PATTERNS

- with/without the option/choice/possibility of sth
- a(n) good/acceptable/reasonable/possible option/choice/alternative
- the only option/choice/alternative/possibility open to sb
- to have a/an the option/choice of doing sth
- to have no option/choice/alternative but to do sth
- a number/range of options/choices/alternatives/possibilities

---

● **verb** ~ **sth** to buy or sell the right to own or use something at some time in the future: *The novel was optioned for the screen by his production company.*

op·tion·al **AWL** /ˈɑpʃənl/ *adj.* that you can choose to do or have if you want to: *Certain courses are compulsory, others are optional.*

op·tom·e·trist /ɑpˈtɑmətrɪst/ *noun* a person whose job is to examine people's eyes for medical conditions and to find out if they need glasses ⊃ **see also** OPTICIAN

op·tom·e·try /ɑpˈtɑmətri/ *noun* [U] the job of examining people's eyes for medical conditions and checking how well they can see and whether they need glasses

'opt-out *noun* (often used as an adjective) the act of choosing not to be involved in something, such as an agreement: *an opt-out clause* ◆ *They hoped to reverse the union's opt-out from the contract.*

op·u·lent /ˈɑpyələnt/ *adj.* (*formal*) **1** made or decorated using expensive materials **SYN** LUXURIOUS **2** (of people) extremely rich **SYN** WEALTHY ▶ **op·u·lence** /-ləns/ *noun* [U] **op·u·lent·ly** *adv.*

o·pus /ˈoʊpəs/ *noun* (*pl.* o·pus·es or o·pe·ra /ˈoʊpərə/ ˈɑ-/) [usually sing.] **1** (*abbr.* **op.**) a piece of music written by a famous COMPOSER and usually followed by a number that shows when it was written: *Beethoven's Opus 18* **2** (*formal*) an important piece of literature, etc., especially one that is on a large scale **SYN** WORK ⊃ **see also** MAGNUM OPUS

OR *abbr.* (in writing) Oregon

or 🔊 /ər; *strong form* ɔr/ *conj.*
1 used to introduce another possibility: *Is your sister older or younger than you?* ◆ *Are you coming or not?* ◆ *Is it a boy or a girl?* ◆ *It can be black, white, or gray.* ⊃ **compare** EITHER... OR... **2** used in negative sentences when mentioning two or more things: *He can't read or write.* ◆ *There are people without homes, jobs, or family.* ⊃ **compare** NEITHER... NOR... **3** (also **or else**) used to warn or advise someone that something bad could happen; otherwise: *Turn the heat down or it'll burn.* **4** used between two numbers to show approximately how many: *There were six or seven of us there.* **5** used to introduce a word or phrase that explains or means the same as another: *geology, or the science of the earth's crust* ◆ *It weighs a kilo, or just over two pounds.* **6** used to say why something must be true: *He must like her, or he wouldn't keep calling her.* **7** used to introduce a contrasting idea: *He was lying—or was he?*
IDM **or so** about: *It'll cost $150 or so.* **or somebody/something/somewhere| somebody/something/somewhere or other** (*informal*) used when you are not exactly sure about a person, thing, or place: *He's a factory supervisor or something.* ◆ *"Who said so?" "Oh, somebody or other. I can't remember who it was."*

-or /ər/ *suffix* (in nouns) a person or thing that: *actor* ⊃ **compare** -AR, -EE, -ER

or·a·cle /ˈɔrəkl; ˈɑr-/ *noun* [C] **1** (in ancient Greece) a place where people could go to ask the gods for advice or information about the future; the priest or PRIESTESS through whom the gods were thought to give their message: *They consulted the oracle at Delphi.* **2** (in ancient Greece) the advice or information that the gods gave, which often had a hidden meaning **3** [usually sing.] a person or book that gives valuable advice or information: *My sister's the oracle on investment matters.*

o·rac·u·lar /əˈrækyələr/ *adj.* (*formal* or *humorous*) of or like an oracle; with a hidden meaning

o·ral /ˈɔrəl/ *adj., noun*
● *adj.* **1** [usually before noun] spoken rather than written: *a test of both oral and written French* ◆ *oral evidence* ⊃ **compare** VERBAL ⊃ **thesaurus box at** SPOKEN **2** [only before noun] connected with the mouth: *oral hygiene* **3** (*phonetics*) (of a speech sound) produced without the air in the nose vibrating (VIBRATE) ⊃ **compare** NASAL ▶ **o·ral·ly** *adv.*: *Answers can be written or presented orally on tape.* ◆ *not to be taken orally* (= a warning on some medicines to show that they must not be swallowed)
● *noun* a spoken exam

oral 'history *noun* [U] the collection and study of historical information using sound recordings of interviews with people who remember past events

o·ral·ism /ˈɔrəˌlɪzəm/ *noun* [U] the system of teaching deaf people to communicate using speech and LIP-READING ▶ **o·ral·ist** /-lɪst/ *adj.*

oral 'surgeon (also **'dental ,surgeon**) *noun* a dentist who performs surgery inside the mouth

---

or·ange /ˈɔrɪndʒ; ˈɑr-/ *noun, adj.*

• *noun* [C, U] **1** a round CITRUS fruit with thick reddish-yellow skin and a lot of sweet juice: *orange peel* ♦ *an orange tree* ♦ *freshly squeezed orange juice* ♦ *orange groves* (= groups of orange trees) ♦ *orange blossom* ⊃ **picture at FRUIT** ⊃ **see also BLOOD ORANGE 2** a bright color that is between red and yellow **IDM see APPLE**

• *adj.* of a bright color that is between red and yellow: *yellow and orange flames*

or·ange·ade /ˌɔrɪnˈdʒeɪd; ˌɑr-/ *noun* **1** [U] a sweet drink with an orange flavor, sometimes with bubbles **2** [C] a glass of orangeade ⊃ **compare LEMONADE**

or·ange·ry /ˈɔrɪndʒri; ˈɑr-/ *noun* (*pl.* **or·ange·ries**) a glass building where orange trees are grown

o·rang·u·tan /əˈræŋəˌtæn; -ˌtæn/ *noun* a large APE (= an animal like a large MONKEY with no tail) with long arms and reddish hair, that lives in Borneo and Sumatra **ORIGIN** From Malay *orang utan/hutan*, meaning "person of the forest."

o·ra·tion /ɔˈreɪʃn/ *noun* (*formal*) a formal speech made on a public occasion, especially as part of a ceremony

or·a·tor /ˈɔrətər; ˈɑr-/ *noun* (*formal*) a person who makes formal speeches in public or is good at public speaking: *a fine political orator*

or·a·tor·i·cal /ˌɔrəˈtɔrɪkl; ˌɑrəˈtɑr-/ *adj.* (*formal*, sometimes *disapproving*) connected with the art of public speaking: *oratorical skills*

or·a·to·ri·o /ˌɔrəˈtɔrioʊ; ˌɑr-/ *noun* (*pl.* **or·a·to·ri·os**) a long piece of music for singers and an ORCHESTRA, usually based on a story from the Bible ⊃ **compare CANTATA**

or·a·to·ry /ˈɔrəˌtɔri; ˈɑr-/ *noun* (*pl.* **or·a·to·ries**) **1** [U] the skill of making powerful and effective speeches in public **SYN RHETORIC 2** [C] a room or small building that is used for private prayer or worship

orb /ɔrb/ *noun* **1** (*literary*) an object shaped like a ball, especially the sun or moon **2** a gold ball with a cross on top, carried by a king or queen at formal ceremonies as a symbol of power ⊃ **compare SCEPTER**

or·bit /ˈɔrbət/ *noun, verb*

• *noun* **1** [C, U] a curved path followed by a planet or an object as it moves around another planet, star, moon, etc.: *the earth's orbit around the sun* ♦ *a space station in orbit around the moon* ♦ *A new satellite has been put into orbit around the earth.* ⊃ **picture at EARTH 2** [sing.] an area that a particular person, organization, etc. deals with or is able to influence: *to come/fall/be within someone's orbit*

• *verb* [T, I] ~ **(around)** sth to move in an orbit (= a curved path) around a much larger object, especially a planet, star, etc.: *The earth takes a year to orbit the sun.*

or·bit·al /ˈɔrbətl/ *adj.* [only before noun] connected with the orbit of a planet or an object in space

or·bit·er /ˈɔrbətər/ *noun* a SPACECRAFT designed to move around a planet or moon rather than to land on it

or·ca /ˈɔrkə/ *noun* = KILLER WHALE

or·chard /ˈɔrtʃərd/ *noun* a piece of land, normally separated from the surrounding area, in which fruit trees are grown

or·ches·tra /ˈɔrkəstrə/ *noun* **1** [C] a large group of people who play various musical instruments together, led by a CONDUCTOR: *She plays the flute in the school orchestra.* ♦ *the Philadelphia Symphony Orchestra* ⊃ **see also CHAMBER ORCHESTRA, SYMPHONY ORCHESTRA 2 the orchestra** [sing.] the seats that are nearest to the stage in a theater: *We have orchestra seats for the ballet.*

or·ches·tral /ɔrˈkɛstrəl/ *adj.* connected with an orchestra: *orchestral music*

ˈorchestra ˌpit (also **pit**) *noun* the place in a theater just in front of the stage where the orchestra sits and plays for an OPERA, a BALLET, etc.

or·ches·trate /ˈɔrkəˌstreɪt/ *verb* **1** ~ sth to arrange a piece of music in parts so that it can be played by an orchestra

2 ~ sth to organize a complicated plan or event very carefully or secretly **SYN STAGE-MANAGE:** *a carefully orchestrated publicity campaign* ▶ **or·ches·tra·tion** /ˌɔrkəˈstreɪʃn/ *noun* [C, U]

or·chid /ˈɔrkəd/ *noun* a plant with brightly colored flowers of unusual shapes. There are many different types of orchids and some of them are very rare. ⊃ **picture at PLANT**

or·dain /ɔrˈdeɪn/ *verb* **1** ~ sb (as sth) | ~ sb + noun to make someone a priest, minister, or RABBI: *He was ordained (as) a priest last year.* ⊃ **see also ORDINATION 2** ~ sth | ~ that... (*formal*) (of God, the law, or FATE) to order or command something; to decide something in advance: *Fate had ordained that they would never meet again.*

or·deal /ɔrˈdil/ *noun* [usually sing.] ~ **(of sth/of doing sth)** a difficult or unpleasant experience: *They are to be spared the ordeal of giving evidence in court.* ♦ *The hostages spoke openly about the terrible ordeal they had been through.* ♦ *The interview was less of an ordeal than she expected.*

or·der /ˈɔrdər/ *noun, verb*

• *noun*

> ARRANGEMENT **1** [U, C] the way in which people or things are placed or arranged in relation to each other: *The names are listed in alphabetical order.* ♦ *in chronological/numerical order* ♦ *arranged in order of priority/importance/size* ♦ *The results, ranked in descending/ascending order, are as follows:* ♦ *All the procedures must be done in the correct order.* ♦ *Let's take the problems in a different order.* **2** [U] the state of being carefully and neatly arranged: *It was time for her to get her life in order.* ♦ *The house had been kept in good order.* ♦ *Get your ideas into some sort of order before you begin to write.* ♦ *It is one of the functions of art to bring order out of chaos.* **ANT DISORDER**

> CONTROLLED STATE **3** [U] the state that exists when people obey laws, rules, or authority: *The army has been sent in to maintain order in the capital.* ♦ *Some teachers find it difficult to keep their classes in order.* ♦ *The police are trying to restore public order.* ♦ *The argument continued until the chairman called them both to order* (= ordered them to obey the formal rules of the meeting). ⊃ **compare DISORDER** ⊃ **see also POINT OF ORDER**

> INSTRUCTIONS **4** [C] something that someone is told to do by someone in authority: ~ **(for sb/sth to do sth)** *He gave orders for the work to be started.* ♦ ~ **(to do sth)** *The general gave the order to advance.* ♦ *I'm under orders not to let anyone in.* ♦ *She takes orders only from the president.* ♦ *Dogs can be trained to obey orders.* ♦ (*informal*) *No sugar for me—doctor's orders.* ♦ *Interest rates are controlled by order of the Fed.*

> GOODS **5** [C, U] ~ **(for sth)** a request to make or supply goods: *I would like to place an order for ten copies of this book.* ♦ *an order form* ♦ *The machine parts are still on order* (= they have been ordered but have not yet been received). ♦ *These items can be made to order* (= produced especially for a particular customer). ⊃ **see also BACK ORDER, MAIL ORDER 6** [C] goods supplied in response to a particular order that someone has placed: *The office supplies order is here.*

> FOOD/DRINKS **7** [C] a request for food or drinks in a restaurant, bar etc.; the food or drinks that you ask for: *May I take your order?* ♦ *two orders of fried shrimp to go* ♦ *a side order* (= for example, vegetables or salad that you eat with your main dish) ⊃ **collocations at RESTAURANT**

> LEGAL DOCUMENT **8** [C] a legal document from a court or judge stating that something must happen: *a judge's order forbidding the reporting of evidence* ♦ *a restraining order* ⊃ **see also COURT ORDER**

> SYSTEM **9** [C, usually sing.] (*formal*) the way that a society, the world, etc. is arranged, with its system of rules and customs: *a change in the political and social order* ♦ *the natural order of things* ♦ *He was seen as a threat to the established order.* ♦ *A new order seems to be emerging.*

> BIOLOGY **10** [C] a group into which animals, plants, etc. that have similar characteristics are divided, smaller than a CLASS and larger than a FAMILY: *the order of primates* ⊃ **compare GENUS**

> RELIGIOUS COMMUNITY **11** [C] a group of people living in a

t **tea**   ṭ **butter**   d **did**   k **cat**   g **got**   tʃ **chin**   dʒ **June**   f **fall**

religious community, especially MONKS or NUNS: *religious orders* ◆ *the Benedictine order*

> SPECIAL HONOR **12** [C] a group of people who have been given a special honor by a queen, king, president, etc.: *The Order of the Garter is an ancient order of chivalry.*

> ORGANIZATION OR SOCIETY **13** [C] a society whose members help each other and who meet for special ceremonies: *the Benevolent and Protective Order of Elks* ⟳ see also BANKER'S ORDER, MONEY ORDER, STANDING ORDER

IDM **be in/take (holy) orders** to be/become a priest **in order 1** (of an official document) that can be used because it is all correct and legal SYN VALID: *Is your work permit in order?* **2** (*formal*) as it should be: *Is everything in order, sir?* **3** if something is **in order**, it is a suitable thing to do or say on a particular occasion: *I think a drink would be in order.* **in order that...** (*formal*) so that something can happen: *Everyone concerned must work together in order that we can reach an agreement on this issue.* **in order to do sth** with the purpose or intention of doing or achieving something: *She arrived early in order to get a good seat.* ◆ *In order to get a complete picture, we will need further information.* ⟳ language bank at PROCESS¹ **in running/working order** (especially of machines) working well: *The engine is now in perfect working order.* **of a high order** | **of the highest/first order** of a high quality or degree; of the highest quality or greatest degree: *The job requires diplomatic skills of a high order.* ◆ *She was a snob of the first order.* **on the order of sth** (*formal*) about something; approximately something: *She earns something on the order of $100,000 a year.* **the order of the day** common, popular, or suitable at a particular time or for a particular occasion: *Pessimism seems to be the order of the day.* **Order! Order!** used to remind people to obey the rules of a formal meeting or debate **out of order 1** (of a machine, etc.) not working correctly: *The phone is out of order.* **2** not arranged correctly or neatly: *I checked the files, and some of the papers were out of order.* **3** (*formal*) not allowed by the rules of a formal meeting or debate: *His objection was ruled out of order.* ⟳ more at CALL v., HOUSE n., LAW, MARCH v., PECK v., SHORT adj., TALL

● *verb*

> GIVE INSTRUCTIONS **1** [T] to use your position of authority to tell someone to do something or say that sth must happen: *~ sb to do sth The company was ordered to pay compensation to its former employees.* ◆ *The officer ordered them to fire.* ◆ *~ sb + adv./prep. They were ordered out of the class for fighting.* ◆ *~ sth The federal government has ordered an investigation into the accident.* ◆ *~ that... They ordered that for every tree cut down two more be planted.* ◆ *~ (sb) + speech "Sit down and be quiet," she ordered.*

> GOODS/SERVICE **2** [T] to ask for goods to be made or supplied; to ask for a service to be provided: *~ sth (from sb) These boots can be ordered direct from the manufacturer.* ◆ *~ sb sth Should I order you a limo?* ◆ *~ sth for sb Should I order a limo for you?* ⟳ see also BACK ORDER

> FOOD/DRINK **3** [T, I] to ask for something to eat or drink in a restaurant, bar, etc.: *~ (sth) I ordered a beer and a sandwich.* ◆ *Have you ordered yet?* ◆ *~ sb/yourself sth He ordered himself a double whiskey.* ◆ *~ (sth) (for sb) Will you order for me while I make a phone call?*

> ORGANIZE/ARRANGE **4** [T] *~ sth* (*formal*) to organize or arrange something: *I need time to order my thoughts* ⟳ see also DISORDERED, ORDERED IDM see DOCTOR n.

PHR V **order sb a'round** (*disapproving*) to keep telling someone what to do in a way that is annoying or unpleasant

order

tell ◆ instruct ◆ direct ◆ command

These words all mean to use your position of authority to say to someone that they must do something.

order to use your position of authority to tell someone to do something: *The company was ordered to clean up the*

pollution in the river. ◆ *"Come here at once!" she ordered.*

tell to say to someone that they must or should do something: *He was told to sit down and wait.* ◆ *Don't tell me what to do!*

instruct (*somewhat formal*) to tell someone to do something, especially in a formal or official way: *The letter instructed him to report to headquarters immediately.*

direct (*formal*) to give an official order: *The police officer directed me to pull over and stop the car.*

command to use your position of authority to tell someone to do something: *He commanded his men to retreat.*

ORDER OR COMMAND?

Order is a more general word than **command** and can be used about anyone in a position of authority, such as a parent, teacher, or government, telling someone to do something. **Command** is slightly stronger than **order** and is the normal word to use about an army officer giving orders, or in any context where it is normal to give orders without any discussion about them. It is less likely to be used about a parent or teacher.

PATTERNS

■ to order/tell/instruct/direct/command sb **to do sth**
■ to order/instruct/direct/command **that...**
■ to **do** sth as ordered/told/instructed/directed/commanded

'order ,book noun a record kept by a business of the products it has agreed to supply to its customers, often used to show how well the business is doing: *We have a full order book for the coming year.*

or·dered /'ɔrdərd/ adj. [usually before noun] carefully arranged or organized SYN ORDERLY: *an ordered existence* ◆ *a well-ordered society* ANT DISORDERED

'order ,form noun a document filled in by customers when ordering goods

or·der·ing /'ɔrdərɪŋ/ noun [C, U] the way in which something is ordered or arranged; the act of putting something into an order SYN ARRANGEMENT: *Many possible orderings may exist.* ◆ *the successful ordering of complex data*

or·der·ly /'ɔrdərli/ adj., noun

● *adj.* **1** arranged or organized in a neat, careful, and logical way SYN TIDY: *a calm and orderly life* ◆ *vegetables planted in orderly rows* **2** behaving well; peaceful: *an orderly demonstration* ANT DISORDERLY ▶ or·der·li·ness noun [U]

● *noun* (pl. or·der·lies) **1** a person who works in a hospital, usually doing jobs that do not need any special training **2** a soldier who does jobs that do not need any special training

,order of 'magnitude noun (*mathematics*) a level in a system of ordering things by size or amount, where each level is higher by a FACTOR of ten: *The actual measurement is two orders of magnitude (= a hundred times) greater than we expected.* ◆ (*figurative*) *The problem is of the same order of magnitude for all concerned.*

or·di·nal /'ɔrdn·l; 'ɔrdnəl/ (also ,ordinal 'number) noun a number that refers to the position of something in a series, for example "first," "second," etc. ⟳ compare CARDINAL ▶ ordinal adj.

or·di·nance /'ɔrdn·əns/ noun [C, U] (*formal*) a law or rule made by a government or someone in a position of authority

or·di·nand /'ɔrdn,ænd/ noun a person who is preparing to become a priest, minister, or RABBI

or·di·nar·i·ly /,ɔrdn'erəli/ adv. **1** in a normal way SYN NORMALLY: *To the untrained eye, the children were behaving ordinarily.* **2** used to say what normally happens in a particular situation, especially because something different is happening this time SYN USUALLY: *Ordinarily,* *she wouldn't have bothered to argue with him.* ◆ *We do not ordinarily carry out this type of work.*

or·di·nar·y 🔑 /ˈɔrdnɛri; ˈɔrdnˌɛri/ *adj.*
1 [usually before noun] not unusual or different in any way: *an ordinary sort of day* ◆ *in the ordinary course of events* ◆ *ordinary people like you and me* ◆ *This was no ordinary meeting.* **2** (*disapproving*) having no unusual or interesting features: *The meal was very ordinary.* ⊃ compare EXTRAOR-
DINARY ▶ **or·di·nar·i·ness** *noun* [U]
IDM **out of the ordinary** unusual or different: *I'm looking for something a little more out of the ordinary.*

ˌordinary ˈshare *noun* a fixed unit of a company's capital. People who own ordinary shares have voting rights in the company.

or·di·nate /ˈɔrdnˌət/ *noun* (*mathematics*) the COORDINATE that gives the distance along the vertical AXIS ⊃ compare ABSCISSA

or·di·na·tion /ˌɔrdnˈeɪʃn/ *noun* [U, C] the act or ceremony of making someone a priest, minister, or RABBI ⊃ see also ORDAIN

ord·nance /ˈɔrdnəns/ *noun* [U] **1** large guns on wheels **SYN** ARTILLERY **2** military supplies and materials: *an ordnance depot*

or·dure /ˈɔrdʒər/ *noun* [U] (*formal*) solid waste from the body of a person or an animal **SYN** FECES

ore /ɔr/ *noun* [U, C] rock, earth, etc. from which metal can be obtained: *iron ore*

o·reg·a·no /əˈrɛgəˌnoʊ/ *noun* [U] a plant with leaves that have a sweet smell and are used in cooking as an HERB ⊃ picture at HERB

or·gan 🔑 /ˈɔrgən/ *noun*
1 a part of the body that has a particular purpose, such as the heart or the brain; part of a plant with a particular purpose: *the internal organs* ◆ *the sense organs* (= the eyes, ears, nose, etc.) ◆ *the sexual/reproductive organs* ◆ *an organ transplant/donor* ⊃ picture at BODY **2** (especially *humorous*) a PENIS: *the male organ* **3** (also ˈpipe ˈorgan) a large musical instrument with keys like a piano. Sounds are produced by air forced through pipes: *She plays the organ in church.* ◆ *organ music* ⊃ compare HARMONIUM **4** a musical instrument similar to a pipe organ, but without pipes: *an electric organ* ⊃ see also BARREL ORGAN, MOUTH ORGAN **5** (*formal*) an official organization that is part of a larger organization and has a special purpose: *the organs of government* **6** (*formal*) a newspaper or magazine that gives information about a particular group or organization; a means of communicating the views of a particular group: *The People's Daily is the official organ of the Chinese Communist Party.* ⊃ see also HOUSE ORGAN

or·gan·dy (also **or·gan·die**) /ˈɔrgəndi/ *noun* [U] a type of thin cotton cloth that is slightly stiff, used especially for making formal dresses

ˈorgan ˌgrinder *noun* a person who plays a BARREL ORGAN (= a large musical instrument played by turning a handle): (*humorous*) *He's only the organ grinder's monkey* (= an unimportant person who does what he is told to do).

or·gan·ic /ɔrˈgænɪk/ *adj.* [usually before noun] **1** (of food, farming methods, etc.) produced or practiced without using artificial chemicals: *organic cheese/vegetables/wine, etc.* ◆ *an organic farmer/gardener* ◆ *organic farming/horti-culture* **2** produced by or from living things: *Improve the soil by adding organic matter.* ◆ *organic compounds* **ANT** INORGANIC **3** (*technical*) connected with the organs of the body: *organic disease* **4** (*formal*) consisting of different parts that are all connected to each other: *the view of society as an organic whole* **5** (*formal*) happening in a slow and natural way, rather than suddenly: *the organic growth of foreign markets* ▶ **or·gan·i·cally** /-kli/ *adv.*: *organically grown fruit* ◆ *The cardboard disintegrates organically.* ◆ *Doctors could find nothing organically wrong with her.* ◆ *The organization should be allowed to develop organically.*

orˌganic ˈchemistry *noun* [U] the branch of chemistry that deals with substances that contain CARBON ⊃ compare INORGANIC CHEMISTRY

or·gan·ism /ˈɔrgəˌnɪzəm/ *noun* **1** a living thing, especially one that is extremely small ⊃ see also MICRO-ORGANISM **2** a system consisting of parts that depend on each other: *the social organism* (= society)

or·gan·ist /ˈɔrgənɪst/ *noun* a person who plays the organ

or·gan·i·za·tion 🔑 /ˌɔrgənəˈzeɪʃn/ *noun*
1 [C] a group of people who form a business, club, etc. together in order to achieve a particular aim: *to work for a business/political/voluntary organization* ◆ *the World Health Organization* ◆ *He's the president of a large international organization.* **2** [U] the act of making arrangements or preparations for something **SYN** PLANNING: *I leave most of the organization of these conferences to my assistant.* **3** [U] the way in which the different parts of something are arranged **SYN** STRUCTURE: *The report studies the organization of labor within the company.* **4** [U] the quality of being arranged in a neat, careful, and logical way: *She is highly intelligent but her work lacks organization.* ▶ **or·gan·i·za·tion·al** /-ʃənl/ *adj.*: *organizational skills* ◆ *organizational change* **or·gan·i·za·tion·al·ly** /-ʃənəli/ *adv.*

organiˈzation ˌchart *noun* a diagram showing the structure of an organization, especially a large business, showing the relationships between all the jobs in it

or·gan·ize 🔑 /ˈɔrgəˌnaɪz/ *verb*
1 [T] ~ sth to arrange for something to happen or to be provided: *to organize a meeting/party/trip* ◆ *I'll invite people if you can organize food and drinks.* **2** [T] ~ sth to arrange something or the parts of something into a particular order or structure: *Modern computers can organize large amounts of data very quickly.* ◆ *You should try and organize your time better.* ◆ *We do not fully understand how the brain is organized.* **3** [T] ~ yourself/sb to plan your/someone's work and activities in an efficient way: *I'm sure you don't need me to organize you.* **4** [T, I] ~ (sb/yourself) (into sth) to form a group of people with a shared aim, especially a union or political party: *the right of workers to organize themselves into unions* ⊃ see also DISORGANIZED ▶ **or·gan·iz·er** *noun*: *the organizers of the festival* ⊃ see also PERSONAL ORGANIZER

or·gan·ized 🔑 /ˈɔrgəˌnaɪzd/ *adj.*
1 [only before noun] involving large numbers of people who work together to do something in a way that has been carefully planned: *an organized body of workers* ◆ *organized religion* (= traditional religion followed by large numbers of people who obey a fixed set of rules) ◆ *organized crime* (= committed by professional criminals working in large groups) ⊃ compare UNORGANIZED **2** arranged or planned in the way mentioned: *a carefully organized campaign* ◆ *a well-organized office* ⊃ compare DISORGANIZED **3** (of a person) able to plan your work, life, etc. well and in an efficient way: *a very organized person* ◆ *Isn't it time you started to get organized?* ⊃ compare DISORGANIZED

ˈorgan ˌloft *noun* a place where there is an organ high above the ground in a church or concert hall

or·ga·no·phos·phate /ˌɔrˌgænoʊˈfɑsfeɪt/ *noun* a chemical containing CARBON and PHOSPHORUS

or·gan·za /ɔrˈgænzə/ *noun* [U] a type of thin, stiff, transparent cloth, used for making formal dresses

or·gasm /ˈɔrˌgæzəm/ *noun* [U, C] the moment during sexual activity when feelings of sexual pleasure are at their strongest: *to achieve/reach orgasm* ◆ *to have an orgasm*

or·gas·mic /ɔrˈgæzmɪk/ *adj.* [only before noun] connected with or like an orgasm

or·gi·as·tic /ˌɔrdʒiˈæstɪk/ *adj.* [usually before noun] (*formal*) typical of an orgy

or·gy /ˈɔrdʒi/ *noun* (*pl.* **or·gies**) **1** a party at which there is a lot of eating, drinking, and sexual activity: *a drunken orgy* **2** ~ (of sth) (*disapproving*) an extreme amount of a particular activity: *The rebels went on an orgy of killing.*

h **h**at	m **m**an	n **n**o	ŋ si**ng**	l **l**eg	r **r**ed	y **y**es	w **w**et

o·ri·el /'ɔriəl/ noun (architecture) a part of a building, like a small room with windows, that sticks out from a wall above the ground: an oriel window

O·ri·ent /'ɔriɛnt; -ˌɛnt/ **the Orient** noun [sing.] (literary) the eastern part of the world, especially China and Japan ⊃ compare OCCIDENT

o·ri·ent AWL /'ɔriˌɛnt/ (also **o·ri·en·tate**) verb **1** [usually passive] ~ sb/sth (to/toward sb/sth) to direct someone or something toward something; to make or adapt someone or something for a particular purpose: Our students are oriented toward science subjects. ♦ policies oriented to the needs of working mothers ♦ We run a commercially oriented operation. ♦ profit-orientated organizations ♦ Neither of them is politically oriented (= interested in politics). **2** ~ yourself to find your position in relation to your surroundings: The mountaineers found it hard to orient themselves in the fog. **3** ~ yourself to make yourself familiar with a new situation: It took him some time to orient himself in his new school. ⊃ compare DISORIENT

o·ri·en·tal /ˌɔri'ɛntl/ adj. connected with or typical of the eastern part of the world, especially China and Japan, and the people who live there: oriental languages

o·ri·en·tal·ist /ˌɔri'ɛntəlɪst/ noun a person who studies the languages, arts, etc. of Oriental countries

o·ri·en·tate AWL /'ɔriənˌteɪt/ verb = ORIENT

o·ri·en·ta·tion AWL /ˌɔriən'teɪʃn/ noun **1** [U, C] the type of aims or interests that a person or an organization has; the act of directing your aims toward a particular thing: The course is essentially theoretical in orientation. ♦ ~ to/toward sth Companies have been forced into a greater orientation to the market. **2** [U, C] a person's basic beliefs or feelings about a particular subject: religious/political orientation ♦ a person's sexual orientation (= whether they are attracted to men, women, or both) **3** [U] training or information that you are given before starting a new job, course, etc.: an orientation course **4** [C] (technical) the direction in which an object faces: The orientation of the planet's orbit is changing continuously.

o·ri·en·teer·ing /ˌɔriən'tɪrɪŋ/ noun [U] the sport of following a route across country on foot, as quickly as possible, using a map and COMPASS

or·i·fice /'ɔrəfəs; 'ar-/ noun (formal or humorous) a hole or opening, especially one in the body: the nasal orifice

o·ri·ga·mi /ˌɔrə'gami/ noun [U] the Japanese art of folding paper into attractive shapes

or·i·gin 🔑 /'ɔrədʒən; 'ar-/ noun [C, U] (also **or·i·gins** [pl.]) **1** the point from which something starts; the cause of something: the origins of life on earth ♦ Most coughs are viral in origin (= caused by a virus). ♦ The origin of the word remains obscure. ♦ This particular custom has its origins in the South. **2** a person's social and family background: She has risen from humble origins to immense wealth. ♦ children of various ethnic origins ♦ people of German origin ♦ a person's country of origin (= where they were born)

o·rig·i·nal 🔑 /ə'rɪdʒənl/ adj., noun
- adj. **1** [only before noun] existing at the beginning of a particular period, process, or activity: The room still has many of its original features. ♦ I think you should go back to your original plan. **2** new and interesting in a way that is different from anything that has existed before; able to produce new and interesting ideas: an original idea ♦ That's not a very original suggestion. ♦ an original thinker **3** [usually before noun] painted, written, etc. by the artist rather than copied: an original painting by a local artist ♦ The original manuscript has been lost. ♦ Only original documents (= not photocopies) will be accepted as proof of status.
- noun **1** a document, work of art, etc. produced for the first time, from which copies are later made: This painting is a copy; the original is in Madrid. ♦ Send out the photocopies and keep the original. **2** (formal) a person who thinks, behaves, dresses, etc. in an unusual way
  IDM **in the original** in the language in which a book, etc.

was first written, before being translated: I studied Italian so that I would be able to read Dante in the original.

o·rig·i·nal·i·ty /əˌrɪdʒə'næləti/ noun [U] the quality of being new and interesting in a way that is different from anything that has existed before: This latest collection lacks style and originality.

o·rig·i·nal·ly 🔑 /ə'rɪdʒənəli/ adv. used to describe the situation that existed at the beginning of a particular period or activity, especially before something was changed: The school was originally very small. ♦ She comes originally from New York. ♦ Originally, we had intended to go to Italy, but then we won the trip to Greece.

o·rig·i·nal 'sin noun [U] (in Christianity) the tendency to be evil that is believed to be present in everyone from birth

o·rig·i·nate /ə'rɪdʒəˌneɪt/ verb (formal) **1** [I] (+ adv./prep.) to happen or appear for the first time in a particular place or situation: The disease is thought to have originated in the tropics. **2** [T] ~ sth to create something new: Locke originated this theory in the 17th century. ▶ **o·rig·i·na·tor** /-ˌneɪt̮ər/ noun

o·ri·ole /'ɔriˌoʊl/ noun **1** a N. American bird: the male is black and orange and the female is yellow-green **2** a European bird, the male of which is bright yellow with black wings

or·mo·lu /'ɔrməˌlu/ noun [U] a gold metal made of a mixture of other metals, used to decorate furniture, make decorative objects, etc.

or·na·ment noun, verb
- noun /'ɔrnəmənt/ (formal) **1** [C] an object that is used as decoration in a room, garden, etc. rather than for a particular purpose: a china/glass ornament **2** [C] (formal) an object that is worn as jewelry **3** [U] (formal) the use of objects, designs, etc. as decoration: The clock is simply for ornament; it doesn't work anymore. **4** ~ to sth a person or thing whose good qualities improve something: The building is an ornament to the city. **5 ornaments** [pl.] (music) features that are added when playing individual notes to make them more beautiful or interesting
- verb /'ɔrnəˌmɛnt/ [usually passive] ~ sth (formal) to add decoration to something SYN DECORATE: a room richly ornamented with carving

or·na·men·tal /ˌɔrnə'mɛntl/ adj. used as decoration rather than for a practical purpose SYN DECORATIVE: an ornamental fountain ♦ The fireplace is purely ornamental.

or·na·men·ta·tion /ˌɔrnəmən'teɪʃn; -mɛn-/ noun [U] the use of objects, designs, etc. to decorate something

or·nate /ɔr'neɪt/ adj. covered with a lot of decoration, especially when this involves very small or complicated designs: a mirror in an ornate gold frame ▶ **or·nate·ly** adv.: ornately carved chairs

or·ner·y /'ɔrnəri/ adj. (informal) bad-tempered and difficult to deal with

or·ni·thol·o·gist /ˌɔrnə'θalədʒɪst/ noun a person who studies birds ⊃ compare BIRDWATCHER

or·ni·thol·o·gy /ˌɔrnə'θalədʒi/ noun [U] the scientific study of birds ▶ **or·ni·tho·log·i·cal** /ˌɔrnəθə'ladʒɪkl/ adj.

o·rog·e·ny /ɔ'radʒəni/ noun [U] (geology) a process in which the outer layer of the earth is folded to form mountains

or·o·graph·ic /ˌɔrə'græfɪk/ adj. (geology) connected with mountains, especially with their position and shape

o·ro·tund /'ɔrəˌtʌnd/ adj. (formal) (of the voice or the way something is said) using full and impressive sounds and language ▶ **o·ro·tun·di·ty** /ˌɔrə'tʌndət̮i/ noun [U]

or·phan /'ɔrfən/ noun, verb
- noun a child whose parents are dead: He was an orphan and lived with his uncle. ♦ orphan boys/girls
- verb [usually passive] ~ sb to make a child an orphan: She was orphaned in the war.

or·phan·age /'ɔrfənɪdʒ/ noun a home for children whose parents are dead

ortho- /'ɔrθoʊ; -θə/ *combining form* (in nouns, adjectives, and adverbs) correct; standard: *orthodox* ♦ *orthography*

or·tho·don·tics /ˌɔrθə'dɑntɪks/ *noun* [U] the treatment of problems concerning the position of the teeth and JAWS ▶ **or·tho·don·tic** *adj.*: *orthodontic treatment*

or·tho·don·tist /ˌɔrθə'dɑntɪst/ *noun* a dentist who treats problems concerning the position of the teeth and JAWS

or·tho·dox /'ɔrθəˌdɑks/ *adj.* **1** (especially of beliefs or behavior) generally accepted or approved of; following generally accepted beliefs **SYN** TRADITIONAL: *orthodox medicine* **ANT** UNORTHODOX ⊃ compare HETERODOX **2** following closely the traditional beliefs and practices of a religion: *an orthodox Jew* **3 Orthodox** belonging to or connected with the Orthodox Church

the ˌOrthodox ˈChurch (also **the ˌEastern ˌOrthodox ˈChurch**) *noun* [sing.] a branch of the Christian Church in eastern Europe and Greece: *the Greek/Russian Orthodox Church*

or·tho·dox·y /'ɔrθəˌdɑksi/ *noun* (*pl.* **or·tho·dox·ies**) **1** [C, U] (*formal*) an idea or view that is generally accepted: *an economist arguing against the current financial orthodoxy* **2** [U, C, usually pl.] the traditional beliefs or practices of a religion, etc. **3 Orthodoxy** [U] the Orthodox Church, its beliefs and practices

or·thog·ra·phy /ɔr'θɑgrəfi/ *noun* [U] (*formal*) the system of spelling in a language ▶ **or·tho·graph·ic** /ˌɔrθə'græfɪk/ *adj.*

or·tho·pe·dics /ˌɔrθə'pidɪks/ *noun* [U] the branch of medicine concerned with injuries and diseases of the bones or muscles ▶ **or·tho·pe·dic** *adj.*: *an orthopedic surgeon/hospital*

Or·well·i·an /ɔr'wɛliən/ *adj.* used to describe a political system in which a government tries to have complete control over people's behavior and thoughts **ORIGIN** From the name of the English writer George Orwell, whose novel *Nineteen Eighty-Four* describes a government that has total control over the people.

-ory /ɔri; əri/ *suffix* **1** (in adjectives) that does: *explanatory* **2** (in nouns) a place for: *observatory*

o·ryx /'ɔrɪks/ *noun* a large ANTELOPE with long straight horns

or·zo /'ɔrzoʊ/ *noun* [U] PASTA in the shape of rice grains

OS /ˌoʊ 'ɛs/ *abbr.* (*computing*) OPERATING SYSTEM

Os·car™ /'ɑskər/ *noun* = ACADEMY AWARD™: *The movie was nominated for an Oscar.* ♦ *an Oscar nomination/winner*

os·cil·late /'ɑsəˌleɪt/ *verb* **1** [I] ~ **(between A and B)** (*formal*) to keep changing from one extreme of feeling or behavior to another, and back again **SYN** SWING: *Her moods oscillated between depression and elation.* **2** [I] (*physics*) to keep moving from one position to another and back again: *Watch how the needle on the dial oscillates.* **3** [I] (*physics*) (of an electric current, radio waves, etc.) to change in strength or direction at regular intervals

os·cil·la·tion /ˌɑsə'leɪʃn/ *noun* (*formal*) **1** [U, sing.] a regular movement between one position and another or between one amount and another: *the oscillation of the compass needle* ♦ ~ **between A and B** *the economy's continual oscillation between growth and recession* **2** [C] ~ **(between A and B)** | ~ **(of sth) (against sth)** a single movement from one position to another of something that is oscillating: *the oscillations of the dollar against foreign currency* **3** [U, C] ~ **(between A and B)** a repeated change between different feelings, types of behavior, or ideas: *his oscillation, as a teenager, between science and art*

os·cil·la·tor /'ɑsəˌleɪtər/ *noun* (*physics*) a piece of equipment for producing oscillating electric currents

os·cil·lo·scope /ə'sɪləˌskoʊp/ *noun* (*physics*) a piece of equipment that shows changes in electrical current as waves in a line on a screen

OSHA /'oʊʃə/ *abbr.* Occupational Safety and Health Administration (the U.S. government department that is responsible for making sure that places where people work are safe)

o·sier /'oʊʒər/ *noun* a type of WILLOW tree, with thin branches that bend easily and are used for making BASKETS

os·mi·um /'ɑzmiəm/ *noun* [U] (*symb.* **Os**) a chemical element. Osmium is a hard silver-white metal.

os·mo·sis /ɑz'moʊsəs; ɑs-/ *noun* [U] **1** (*biology* or *chemistry*) the gradual passing of a liquid through a MEMBRANE (= a thin layer of material) as a result of there being different amounts of dissolved substances on either side of the membrane: *Water passes into the roots of a plant by osmosis.* **2** the gradual process of learning or being influenced by something, as a result of being in close contact with it ▶ **os·mot·ic** /ɑz'mɑtɪk; ɑs-/ *adj.*: *osmotic pressure*

os·prey /'ɑspreɪ; -pri/ *noun* a large BIRD OF PREY (= a bird that kills other creatures for food) that eats fish

os·se·ous /'ɑsiəs/ *adj.* (*technical*) made of or turned into bone

os·si·fy /'ɑsəˌfaɪ/ *verb* [usually passive] (**os·si·fies**, **os·si·fy·ing**, **os·si·fied**, **os·si·fied**) (*formal*, *disapproving*) **1** [I, T, usually passive] ~ **(sth)** to become or make something fixed and unable to change: *an ossified political system* **2** [I, T, usually passive] ~ **(sth)** (*technical*) to become or make something hard like bone ▶ **os·si·fi·ca·tion** /ˌɑsəfə'keɪʃn/ *noun* [U] (*formal*)

os·ten·si·ble /ɑ'stɛnsəbl/ *adj.* [only before noun] seeming or stated to be real or true, when this is perhaps not the case **SYN** APPARENT: *The ostensible reason for his absence was illness.* ▶ **os·ten·si·bly** /-bli/ *adv.*: *Troops were sent in, ostensibly to protect the civilian population.*

os·ten·ta·tion /ˌɑstɛn'teɪʃn/ *noun* [U] (*disapproving*) an exaggerated display of wealth, knowledge, or skill that is made in order to impress people

os·ten·ta·tious /ˌɑstɛn'teɪʃəs/ *adj.* **1** (*disapproving*) expensive or noticeable in a way that is intended to impress people **SYN** SHOWY **2** (*disapproving*) behaving in a way that is meant to impress people by showing how rich, important, etc. you are **3** (of an action) done in a very obvious way so that people will notice it: *He gave an ostentatious yawn.* ▶ **os·ten·ta·tious·ly** *adv.*: *ostentatiously dressed*

osteo- /'ɑstioʊ/ *combining form* (in nouns and adjectives) connected with bones: *osteopath*

os·te·o·ar·thri·tis /ˌɑstioʊɑr'θraɪtəs/ *noun* [U] (*medical*) a disease that causes painful swelling and permanent damage in the joints of the body, especially the hips, knees, and thumbs

os·te·o·path /'ɑstiəˌpæθ/ *noun* a person whose job involves treating some diseases and physical problems by pressing and moving the bones and muscles ⊃ compare CHIRO-PRACTOR

os·te·op·a·thy /ˌɑsti'ɑpəθi/ *noun* [U] the treatment of some diseases and physical problems by pressing and moving the bones and muscles ▶ **os·te·o·path·ic** /ˌɑstiə'pæθɪk/ *adj.*

os·te·o·po·ro·sis /ˌɑstioʊpə'roʊsəs/ (also **ˌbrittle ˈbone disˌease**) *noun* [U] (*medical*) a condition in which the bones become weak and are easily broken, usually when people get older or because they do not eat enough of certain substances

os·tra·cism /'ɑstrəˌsɪzəm/ *noun* [U] (*formal*) the act of deliberately not including someone in a group or activity; the state of not being included

os·tra·cize /'ɑstrəˌsaɪz/ *verb* ~ **sb** (*formal*) to refuse to let someone be a member of a social group; to refuse to meet or talk to someone **SYN** SHUN: *He was ostracized by his colleagues for refusing to support the strike.*

os·trich /'ɑstrɪtʃ/ *noun* **1** a very large African bird with a long neck and long legs, that cannot fly but can run very fast **2** (*informal*) a person who prefers to ignore problems rather than try and deal with them

ʌ **cup**   ə **about**   eɪ **say**   aɪ **five**   ɔɪ **boy**   aʊ **now**   oʊ **go**   ər **bird**

OT /ˌoʊ ˈti/ *abbr.* OCCUPATIONAL THERAPY or OCCUPATIONAL THERAPIST: *Can you recommend a good OT?*

OTC /ˌoʊ ti ˈsi/ *abbr.* = OVER-THE-COUNTER: *OTC medicines and food supplements* ◆ *OTC trading of securities*

oth·er 🔑 /ˈʌðər/ *adj., pron.*
1 used to refer to people or things that are additional to or different from people or things that have been mentioned or are known about: *Mr. Harris and Mrs. Bate and three other teachers were there.* ◆ *Are there any other questions?* ◆ *I can't see you now—some other time, maybe.* ◆ *Two buildings were destroyed and many others damaged in the blast.* ◆ *This option is preferable to any other.* ◆ *Some designs are better than others.* ⊃ compare ANOTHER **2 the, my, your, etc. ~** used to refer to the second of two people or things: *My other sister is a doctor.* ◆ *One son went to live in Australia and the other one was killed in a car crash.* ◆ *He raised one arm and then the other.* ◆ *You must ask one or other of your parents.* ◆ (*humorous*) *You'll have to ask my other half* (= husband, wife, or partner). **3 the, my, your, etc. ~** used to refer to the remaining people or things in a group: *I'll wear my other shoes—these are dirty.* ◆ *"I like this one." "What about the other ones?"* ◆ *I went swimming while the others played tennis.* **4 the other…** used to refer to a place, direction, etc. that is the opposite to where you are, are going, etc.: *I work on the other side of town.* ◆ *He crashed into a car coming the other way.* ◆ *He found me, not the other way around.*
IDM Most idioms containing **other** are at the entries for the nouns and verbs in the idioms. For example, **in other words** is at **word**. **the other day/morning/evening/week** recently: *I saw Jack the other day.* **other than** (usually used in negative sentences) **1** except: *I don't know any French people other than you.* ◆ *We're going away in June but other than that I'll be here all summer.* **2** (*formal*) different or in a different way from; not: *I have never known him to behave other than selfishly.*

oth·er·ness /ˈʌðərnəs/ *noun* [U] (*formal*) the quality of being different or strange: *the otherness of an alien culture*

oth·er·wise 🔑 /ˈʌðərˌwaɪz/ *adv.*
1 used to state what the result would be if something did not happen or if the situation were different: *My parents lent me the money. Otherwise, I couldn't have afforded the trip.* ◆ *Shut the window, otherwise it'll get too cold in here.* ◆ *We're committed to the project. We wouldn't be here otherwise.* **2** apart from that: *There was some music playing upstairs. Otherwise the house was silent.* ◆ *He was slightly bruised but otherwise unhurt.* **3** in a different way to the way mentioned; differently: *Bismarck, otherwise known as "the Iron Chancellor"* ◆ *It is not permitted to sell or otherwise distribute copies of past examination papers.* ◆ *You know what this is about. Why pretend otherwise* (= that you do not)? ◆ *I wanted to see him but he was otherwise engaged* (= doing something else).
IDM **or otherwise** used to refer to something that is different from or the opposite of what has just been mentioned: *It was necessary to discover the truth or otherwise of these statements.* ◆ *We insure against all damage, accidental or otherwise.* ⊃ more at KNOW *v.*

ˌother ˈwoman *noun* [usually sing.] a woman with whom a man is having a sexual relationship, although he already has a wife or partner

ˌother-ˈworldly *adj.* concerned with spiritual thoughts and ideas rather than with ordinary life ▶ **ˌother-ˈworldliness** *noun* [U]

o·ti·ose /ˈoʊʃiˌoʊs; ˈoʊti-/ *adj.* (*formal*) having no useful purpose **SYN** UNNECESSARY: *an otiose round of meetings*

o·ti·tis /oʊˈtaɪtəs/ *noun* [U] (*medical*) a painful swelling of the ear, caused by an infection

ot·ter /ˈɑtər/ *noun* a small animal that has four WEBBED feet (= with skin between the toes), a tail, and thick brown fur. Otters live in rivers and eat fish.

ot·to /ˈɑtoʊ/ *noun* = ATTAR

ot·to·man /ˈɑtəmən/ *noun* a piece of furniture like a large box with a soft top, used for storing things in and sitting on

ouch /aʊtʃ/ *exclamation* used to express sudden pain: *Ouch! That hurt!*

ought to 🔑 /ˈɔtə; *before vowels and finally* ˈɔt tu/ *modal verb* (*negative* **ought not to**, *short form* (*old-fashioned*) **oughtn't to**)
1 used to say what is the right thing to do: *They ought to apologize.* ◆ *"Should I to write to say thank you?" "Yes, I think you ought (to)."* ◆ *They ought to have apologized* (= but they didn't). ◆ *Such things ought not to be allowed.* ◆ *He oughtn't to have been driving so fast.* ⊃ note at SHOULD **2** used to say what you expect or would like to happen: *Children ought to be able to read by the age of 7.* ◆ *Nurses ought to earn more.* **3** used to say what you advise or recommend: *We ought to be leaving now.* ◆ *This is delicious. You ought to try some.* ◆ *You ought to have come to the meeting. It was interesting.* **4** used to say what has probably happened or is probably true: *If he started out at nine, he ought to be here by now.* ◆ *That ought to be enough food for the four of us.* ⊃ note at MODAL

Oui·ja board™ /ˈwidʒə ˌbɔrd; ˈwidʒi-/ *noun* a board marked with letters of the alphabet and other signs, used in SEANCES to receive messages said to come from people who are dead

ounce 🔑 /aʊns/ *noun*
1 [C] (*abbr.* **oz.**) a unit for measuring weight, 1/16 of a pound, equal to 28.35 grams ⊃ see also FLUID OUNCE **2** [sing.] **~ of sth** (*informal*) (used especially with negatives) a very small quantity of something: *There's not an ounce of truth in her story.*
IDM **an ounce of prevention is better than a pound of cure** (*saying*) it is better to stop something bad from happening rather than try to deal with the problems after it has happened

our 🔑 /ɑr; ˈaʊər/ *det.* (the possessive form of *we*)
1 belonging to us; connected with us: *our daughter/dog/house* ◆ *We showed them some of our photos.* ◆ *Our main export is rice.* ◆ *And now, over to our Rome correspondent…* **2** used to refer to or address God or a holy person: *Our Father* (= God) ◆ *Our Lady* (= the Virgin Mary)

ours 🔑 /ɑrz; ˈaʊərz/ *pron.*
the one or ones that belong to us: *Their house is very similar to ours, but ours is bigger.* ◆ *No, those are Ellie's kids. Ours are upstairs.* ◆ *He's a friend of ours.*

our·selves 🔑 /ɑrˈsɛlvz; aʊər-/ *pron.*
1 the reflexive form of *we*; used when you and another person or other people together cause and are affected by an action: *We shouldn't blame ourselves for what happened.* ◆ *Let's just relax and enjoy ourselves.* ◆ *We'd like to see it for ourselves.* **2** used to emphasize *we* or *us*; sometimes used instead of these words: *We've often thought of going there ourselves.* ◆ *The only people there were ourselves.*
IDM **(all) by ourselves 1** alone; without anyone else **2** without help **(all) to ourselves** for us alone; not shared with anyone: *We had the pool all to ourselves.*

-ous /əs/ *suffix* (in adjectives) having the nature or quality of: *poisonous* ◆ *mountainous* ▶ **-ously** (in adverbs): *gloriously* **-ousness** (in nouns): *spaciousness*

oust /aʊst/ *verb* to force someone out of a job or position of power, especially in order to take their place: **~ sb (as sth)** *He was ousted as chairman.* ◆ **~ sb (from sth)** *The rebels finally managed to oust the government from power.*

oust·er /ˈaʊstər/ *noun* the act of removing someone from a position of authority in order to put someone else in their place; the fact of being removed in this way: *the president's ouster by the military*

out 🔑 /aʊt/ *adv., prep., noun, adj., verb*
● *adv., prep.* **HELP** For the special uses of **out** in phrasal verbs, look at the entries for the verbs. For example, **burst out** is in the phrasal verb section at **burst**. **1 ~ (of sth)** away from the inside of a place or thing: *She ran out into the corridor.* ◆ *She shook the bag and some coins fell out.* ◆ *I got out*

of bed. ◆ *He opened the box and out jumped a frog.* ◆ **Out you go!** (= used to order someone to leave a room) ◆ *(informal) He ran out the door.* **2 ~ (of sth)** (of people) away from or not at home or their place of work: *I called Liz but she was out.* ◆ *Let's go out this evening* (= for example to a restaurant or club). ◆ *We haven't had a **night out** for weeks.* ◆ *Mr. Green is out of town this week.* **3 ~ (of sth)** away from the edge of a place: *The boy dashed out into the road.* ◆ *Don't lean out of the window.* **4 ~ (of sth)** a long or a particular distance away from a place or from land: *She's working out in Australia.* ◆ *He lives right out in the country.* ◆ *The boats are all out at sea.* ◆ *The ship sank ten miles out of Stockholm.* **5 ~ (of sth)** used to show that something or someone is removed from a place, job, etc.: *This detergent is good for getting stains out.* ◆ *We want this government out.* ◆ *He got thrown out of the restaurant.* **6 ~ of sth/sb** used to show that something comes from or is obtained from something or someone: *He drank his beer out of the bottle.* ◆ *a statue made out of bronze* ◆ *a romance straight out of a fairy tale* ◆ *I paid for the damage out of my savings.* ◆ *We'll get the truth out of her.* **7 ~ of sth** used to show that someone or something does not have any of something: *We're out of milk.* ◆ *He's been **out of work** for six months.* ◆ *You're **out of luck** —she left ten minutes ago.* **8 ~ of sth** used to show that someone or something is not or no longer in a particular state or condition: *Try and stay out of trouble.* ◆ *I watched the car until it was **out of sight**.* **9 ~ (of sth)** used to show that someone is no longer involved in something: *It was an awful job and I'm glad to be out of it.* ◆ *He gets out of the army in a few weeks.* ◆ *They'll be out* (= of prison) *on bail in no time.* ◆ *Brown goes on to the semifinals but Lee is out.* **10 ~ of sth** used to show the reason why something is done: *I asked out of curiosity.* ◆ *She did it out of spite.* **11 ~ of sth** from a particular number or set: *You scored six out of ten.* ◆ *Two out of three people think the President should resign.* **12** (of a book, etc.) not in the library; borrowed by someone else: *The book you wanted is out.* **13** (of the TIDE) at or toward its lowest point on land: *I like walking on the wet sand when the tide is out.* **14** if the sun, moon, or stars are or come out, they can be seen from the earth and are not hidden by clouds **15** (of flowers) fully open: *There should be some snowdrops out by now.* **16** available to everyone; known to everyone: *When does her new book come out?* ◆ *Word always gets out* (= people find out about things) *no matter how careful you are.* ◆ *Out with it!* (= say what you know) **17** clearly and loudly so that people can hear: *to call/cry/shout out* ◆ *Read it out loud.* ◆ *Nobody spoke out in his defense.* **18** *(informal)* having told other people that you are HOMOSEXUAL: *I had been out since I was 17.* **19** (in baseball) if a team or team member is out, it is no longer their turn with the BAT ⊃ note at BASEBALL **20** (in TENNIS, etc.) if the ball is out, it landed outside the line: *The umpire said the ball was out.* **21** not possible or not allowed: *Swimming is out until the weather gets warmer.* **22** not fashionable: *Black is out this year.* **23** (of fire, lights, or burning materials) not or no longer burning or lit: *Suddenly all the lights went out.* ◆ *The fire had burned itself out.* **24** at an end: *It was summer and school was out.* ◆ *She was to regret her words **before the day was out**.* **25** unconscious: *He was out for more than an hour and came around in the hospital.* ◆ *She was knocked **out cold**.* **26** to the end; completely: *Hear me out before you say anything.* ◆ *We left them to **fight it out*** (= settle a disagreement by fighting or arguing). ⊃ see also ALL-OUT **IDM** **be out for sth/to do sth** to be trying to get or do something: *I'm not out for revenge.* ◆ *She's **out for what she can get*** (= trying to get something for herself). ◆ *The company is out to capture the Canadian market.* **out and about 1** able to go outside again after an illness **2** traveling around a place: *We've been out and about talking to people all over the country.* **out of here** *(informal)* going or leaving: *As soon as I get my money I'm out of here!* **out of it** *(informal)* **1** sad because you are not included in something: *We've only just moved here so we feel a little out of it.* **2** not aware of what is happening, usually because of drinking too much alcohol or taking drugs

● **noun 1** [sing.] a way of avoiding having to do something: *She was desperately looking for an out.* **2** [C] (in baseball) an

act of putting a player out, so that is no longer their turn with the bat: *to make an out* **IDM** see IN n.

● **adj.** *(informal)* having told other people that you are HOMOSEXUAL: *an out gay man*

● **verb ~ sb** to say publicly that someone is HOMOSEXUAL, especially when they would prefer to keep the fact a secret: *He is the latest politician to be outed by gay activists.*

out- /aʊt/ *prefix* **1** (in verbs) greater, better, further, longer, etc.: *outnumber* ◆ *outwit* ◆ *outgrow* ◆ *outlive* **2** (in nouns and adjectives) outside; OUTWARD; away from: *outbuildings* ◆ *outpatient* ◆ *outlying* ◆ *outgoing*

out·age /ˈaʊtɪdʒ/ *noun* a period of time when the supply of electricity, etc. is not working

out-and-ˈout *adj.* [only before noun] in every way **SYN** COMPLETE: *What she said was an out-and-out lie.*

the out·back /ˈaʊtbæk/ *noun* [sing.] the area of Australia that is a long way from the coast and the towns, where few people live

out·bid /ˌaʊtˈbɪd/ *verb* (out·bid·ding, out·bid, out·bid) **~ sb (for sth)** to offer more money than someone else in order to buy something, for example at an AUCTION

out·board /ˈaʊtbɔrd/ *adj.* (technical) on, toward, or near the outside of a ship or an aircraft

outboard ˈmotor (also **outboard ˈengine**) *noun* an engine that you can attach to the back of a small boat

out·bound /ˈaʊtbaʊnd/ *adj.* (formal) traveling from a place rather than arriving in it: *outbound flights/passengers* **ANT** INBOUND

out-box *noun* (computing) **1** (in an office) a container on your desk for letters or documents that are waiting to be sent out or passed to someone else **2** the place on a computer where new e-mail messages that you write are stored before you send them ⊃ compare IN-BOX

out·break /ˈaʊtbreɪk/ *noun* the sudden start of something unpleasant, especially violence or a disease: *the outbreak of war* ◆ *an outbreak of typhoid* ◆ *Outbreaks of rain are expected in the afternoon.*

out·build·ing /ˈaʊtˌbɪldɪŋ/ *noun* [usually pl.] a building such as a SHED or STABLE that is built near to, but separate from, a main building

out·burst /ˈaʊtbɜrst/ *noun* **1** a sudden strong expression of an emotion: *an outburst of anger* ◆ *She was alarmed by his violent outburst.* **2** a sudden increase in a particular activity or attitude: *an outburst of racism*

out·cast /ˈaʊtkæst/ *noun* a person who is not accepted by other people and who sometimes has to leave their home and friends: *People with the disease were often treated as social outcasts.* ▸ **out·cast** *adj.*

out·class /ˌaʊtˈklæs/ *verb* [often passive] **~ sb/sth** to be much better than someone you are competing against: *Kennedy was outclassed 0–6 0–6 in the final.*

out·come **AWL** /ˈaʊtkʌm/ *noun* the final result of an action or event: *We are waiting to hear the outcome of the negotiations.* ◆ *These costs are payable whatever the outcome of the case.* ◆ *We are confident of a successful outcome.* ◆ *Four possible outcomes have been identified.* ⊃ thesaurus box at RESULT

out·crop /ˈaʊtkrɑp/ *noun* a large mass of rock that stands above the surface of the ground

out·cry /ˈaʊtkraɪ/ *noun* (pl. out·cries) [C, U] **~ (at/over/against sth)** a reaction of anger or strong protest shown by people in public: *an outcry over the proposed change* ◆ *The new tax provoked a public outcry.* ◆ *There was outcry at the judge's statement.*

out·dat·ed /ˌaʊtˈdeɪtəd/ *adj.* no longer useful because of being old-fashioned: *outdated equipment* ◆ *These figures are now outdated.* ⊃ compare OUT OF DATE

out·dis·tance /ˌaʊtˈdɪstəns/ *verb* **~ sb/sth** to leave someone or something behind by going faster, further,

t tea   ţ butter   d did   k cat   g got   tʃ chin   dʒ June   f fall

etc.; to be better than someone or something **SYN** OUTSTRIP

out·do /ˌaʊtˈdu/ verb (out·does /-ˈdʌz/, out·did /-ˈdɪd/, out·done /-ˈdʌn/) ~ **sb/sth** to do more or better than someone else **SYN** BEAT: *Sometimes small firms can outdo big business when it comes to customer care.* ◆ *Not to be outdone* (= not wanting to let someone else do better), *she tried again.*

out·door 🔑 /ˈaʊtdɔr/ adj. [only before noun] used, happening, or located outside rather than in a building: *outdoor clothing/activities* ◆ *an outdoor swimming pool* ◆ *I'm not really the outdoor type* (= I prefer indoor activities). **ANT** INDOOR

out·doors 🔑 /ˌaʊtˈdɔrz/ adv., noun
● *adv.* outside, rather than in a building: *The rain prevented them from eating outdoors.* **ANT** INDOORS
● *noun* the out·doors [sing.] the countryside, away from buildings and busy places: *They both have a love of the outdoors.* ◆ *Come to Canada and enjoy* ***the great outdoors.*** ⊃ collocations at TOWN

out·doors·man /ˌaʊtˈdɔrzmən/, **out·doors·wom·an** /ˌaʊtˈdɔrzˌwʊmən/ noun (pl. out·doors·men /-ˈdɔrzmən/, pl. out·doors·wom·en /-ˈdɔrzˌwɪmən/) a man or woman who spends a lot of time doing outdoor sports and activities, especially in the countryside

out·doors·y /ˌaʊtˈdɔrzi/ adj. (informal) enjoying outdoor sports and activities, especially in the countryside: *I'm not as outdoorsy as he is.*

out·er 🔑 /ˈaʊtər/ adj. [only before noun]
1 on the outside of something **SYN** EXTERNAL: *the outer layers of the skin* **2** furthest from the inside or center of something: *I walked along the outer edge of the track.* ◆ *the outer suburbs of the city* ◆ *Outer Mongolia* ◆ *(figurative) to explore the outer* (= most extreme) *limits of human experience* **ANT** INNER

out·er·most /ˈaʊtərˌmoʊst/ adj. [only before noun] furthest from the inside or center: *the outermost planet* ◆ *He fired and hit the outermost ring of the target.* **ANT** INNERMOST

outer ˈspace noun [U] = SPACE: *radio waves from outer space*

out·er·wear /ˈaʊtərˌwɛr/ noun [U] clothes such as coats, hats, etc. that you wear outside

out·face /ˌaʊtˈfeɪs/ verb ~ **sb** (formal) to defeat an enemy or opponent by being brave and remaining confident

out·fall /ˈaʊtfɔl/ noun (technical) the place where a river, pipe, etc. flows out into the ocean: *a sewage outfall*

out·field /ˈaʊtfild/ noun, adv.
● *noun* [sing.] the outer part of the field in baseball and some other sports ⊃ compare INFIELD
● *adv.* in or to the outfield

out·field·er /ˈaʊtˌfildər/ noun (in baseball) a player in the outfield

out·fit /ˈaʊtfɪt/ noun, verb
● *noun* **1** a set of clothes that you wear together, especially for a particular occasion or purpose: *She was wearing an expensive new outfit.* ◆ *a wedding outfit* ◆ *a cowboy/Superman outfit* (= one that you wear for fun in order to look like the type of person mentioned) **2** (informal) a group of people working together as an organization, business, team, etc.: *a market research outfit* ◆ *This was the fourth album by the top rock outfit.* **3** a set of equipment that you need for a particular purpose: *a bicycle repair outfit*
● *verb* (-tt-) [often passive] ~ **sth/sb (with sth)** to provide someone or something with equipment or clothes for a special purpose **SYN** EQUIP: *The ship was outfitted with a 12-bed hospital.*

out·fit·ter (also out·fit·ters) /ˈaʊtˌfɪtər/ noun a store that sells equipment for camping and other outdoor activities

out·flank /ˌaʊtˈflæŋk/ verb **1** ~ **sb/sth** to move around the side of an enemy or opponent, especially in order to attack them from behind **2** ~ **sb/sth** to gain an advantage over

someone, especially by doing something unexpected **SYN** OUTMANEUVER

out·flow /ˈaʊtfloʊ/ noun ~ **(of sth/sb) (from sth)** the movement of a large amount of money, liquid, people, etc. out of a place: *There was a capital outflow of $22 billion in 2008.* ◆ *a steady outflow of oil from the tank* ◆ *the outflow of refugees* **ANT** INFLOW

out·fox /ˌaʊtˈfɑks/ verb ~ **sb** to gain an advantage over someone by being smarter than they are **SYN** OUTWIT

out·go·ing /ˈaʊtˌgoʊɪŋ/ adj. **1** liking to meet other people, enjoying their company, and being friendly toward them **SYN** SOCIABLE: *an outgoing personality* **2** [only before noun] leaving the position of responsibility mentioned: *the outgoing president/government* **ANT** INCOMING **3** [only before noun] going away from a particular place rather than arriving in it: *This telephone should be used for outgoing calls.* ◆ *outgoing flights/passengers* ◆ *the outgoing tide* **ANT** INCOMING

ˈout-group noun the people who do not belong to a particular IN-GROUP in a society

out·grow /ˌaʊtˈgroʊ/ verb (out·grew /-ˈgru/, out·grown /-ˈgroʊn/) **1** ~ **sth** to grow too big to be able to wear or fit into something **SYN** GROW OUT OF: *She's outgrown most of her clothes.* ◆ *The company has outgrown its offices.* **2** ~ **sb** to grow taller, larger, or more quickly than another person: *He's already outgrown his older brother.* **3** ~ **sth** to stop doing something or lose interest in something as you become older **SYN** GROW OUT OF: *He's outgrown his passion for rock music.*

out·growth /ˈaʊtgroʊθ/ noun **1** (technical) a thing that grows out of something else: *The eye first appears as a cup-shaped outgrowth from the brain.* **2** (formal) a natural development or result of something: *The law was an outgrowth of the last presidential election.*

out·gun /ˌaʊtˈgʌn/ verb (-nn-) [often passive] ~ **sb/sth** to have greater military strength than someone: *(figurative) Our team was completely outgunned.*

out·house /ˈaʊthaʊs/ noun a toilet in a small building of its own

out·ing /ˈaʊtɪŋ/ noun **1** [C] ~ **(to…)** a trip that you go on for pleasure or education, usually with a group of people and lasting no more than one day **SYN** EXCURSION: *We went* ***on an outing*** *to the park.* ◆ *a family outing* ⊃ thesaurus box at TRIP **2** [C] (sports) (informal) an occasion when someone takes part in a competition **3** [U,C] the practice of naming people as HOMOSEXUAL in public, when they do not want anyone to know

out·land·ish /aʊtˈlændɪʃ/ adj. (usually disapproving) strange or extremely unusual **SYN** BIZARRE: *outlandish costumes/ideas* ▸ **out·land·ish·ly** adv.

out·last /ˌaʊtˈlæst/ verb ~ **sb/sth** to continue to exist or take part in an activity for a longer time than someone or something: *He can outlast anyone on the dance floor.*

out·law /ˈaʊtlɔ/ verb, noun
● *verb* **1** ~ **sth** to make something illegal **SYN** BAN: *plans to outlaw the carrying of knives* ◆ *the outlawed nationalist party* **2** ~ **sb** (in the past) to make someone an outlaw
● *noun* (used especially about people in the past) a person who has done something illegal and is hiding to avoid being caught; a person who is not protected by the law: *Robin Hood, the world's most famous outlaw*

out·lay /ˈaʊtleɪ/ noun [C, U] ~ **(on sth)** the money that you have to spend in order to start a new project: *The business quickly repaid the initial outlay on advertising.* ◆ *a massive financial/capital outlay* ⊃ thesaurus box at COST

out·let /ˈaʊtlɛt; -lət/ noun **1** ~ **(for sth)** a way of expressing or making good use of strong feelings, ideas, or energy: *She needed to find an outlet for her many talents and interests.* ◆ *Sports became the perfect outlet for his aggression.* **2** (business) a store or an organization that sells goods made by a particular company or of a particular type: *The business has 34 retail outlets in this state alone.* **3** a store that sells goods of a particular make at reduced prices: *the Nike outlet in the outlet mall* **4** a pipe or hole through which liquid or gas can flow out: *a sewage outlet* ◆ *an outlet pipe* ➔ picture at PLUG **ANT** INLET **5** (also re·cep·ta·cle, sock·et) a device in a wall that you put a plug into in order to connect electrical equipment to the power supply of a building

out·line 🔑 /'aʊtlaɪn/ *verb, noun*
- *verb* **1** ~ sth (to sb) | ~ what, how, etc.... to give a description of the main facts or points involved in something **SYN** SKETCH: *We outlined our proposals to the committee.* **2** [usually passive] ~ sth (against sth) to show or mark the outer edge of something: *They saw the huge building outlined against the sky.*
- *noun* [C, U] **1** a description of the main facts or points involved in something: *This is a brief outline of the events.* ◆ *You should draw up a plan or outline for the essay.* ◆ *The book describes* in outline *the main findings of the research.* ◆ *an outline agreement/proposal* **2** the line that goes around the edge of something, showing its main shape but not the details: *At last we could see the dim outline of an island.* ◆ *an outline map/sketch* ◆ *She drew the figures* in outline.

out·live /ˌaʊt'lɪv/ *verb* **1** ~ sb to live longer than someone: *He outlived his wife by three years.* **2** ~ sth to continue to exist after something else has ended or disappeared: *The machine had outlived its usefulness* (= was no longer useful).

out·look /'aʊtlʊk/ *noun* **1** [usually sing.] ~ (on sth) the attitude to life and the world of a particular person, group, or culture: *He had a practical outlook on life.* ◆ *Most Western societies are liberal* in outlook. **2** ~ (for sth) the expected future for someone or something; what is likely to happen **SYN** PROSPECT: *The outlook for jobs is bleak.* ◆ *The country's economic outlook* ◆ *The outlook* (= the expected weather) *for the weekend is dry and sunny.* **3** a view from a particular place: *The house has a pleasant outlook over the valley.*

out·ly·ing /'aʊtˌlaɪɪŋ/ *adj.* [only before noun] far away from the cities of a country or from the main part of a place: *outlying areas*

out·ma·neu·ver /ˌaʊtmə'nuvər/ *verb* ~ sb/sth to do better than an opponent by acting in a way that is smarter or more skillful: *The president has so far managed to outmaneuver his critics.*

out·mod·ed /ˌaʊt'moʊdəd/ *adj.* (*disapproving*) no longer fashionable or useful: *an outmoded attitude*

out·num·ber /ˌaʊt'nʌmbər/ *verb* ~ sb/sth to be greater in number than someone or something: *The demonstrators were heavily outnumbered by the police.* ◆ *In this profession, women outnumber men by two to one* (= there are twice as many women as men).

out-of-ˌbody exˈperience *noun* a feeling of being outside your own body, especially when you feel that you are watching yourself from a distance

out of ˈdate *adj.* **1** old-fashioned or without the most recent information and therefore no longer useful: *These figures are very out of date.* ◆ *Suddenly she felt old and out of date.* ◆ *an out-of-date map* ◆ *out-of-date technology* ➔ compare OUTDATED **2** no longer valid: *an out-of-date driver's license* ➔ see also UP TO DATE

out-of-ˈpocket *adj.* ~ expenses/costs/expenditure/spending small business expenses that you pay yourself, with your employer paying you back later: *On business trips she has some travel and other out-of-pocket expenses.*

out-of-ˈstate *adj.* [only before noun] coming from or happening in a different state: *out-of-state license plates*

out-of-the-ˈway *adj.* far from a town or city: *a little out-of-the-way place on the coast*

out-of-ˈtown *adj.* [only before noun] **1** coming from or happening in a different place: *an out-of-town guest* ◆ *an out-of-town performance* **2** located away from the center of a town or city: *out-of-town superstores*

out-of-ˈwork *adj.* [only before noun] unemployed: *an out-of-work actor*

out·pace /ˌaʊt'peɪs/ *verb* ~ sb/sth to go, rise, improve, etc. faster than someone or something **SYN** OUTSTRIP: *He easily outpaced the other runners.* ◆ *Demand is outpacing production.*

out·pa·tient /'aʊtˌpeɪʃnt/ *noun* a person who goes to a hospital for treatment but does not stay there: *an outpatient clinic* ➔ compare INPATIENT

out·per·form /ˌaʊtpər'fɔrm/ *verb* ~ sb/sth to achieve better results than someone or something ▶ out·per·for·mance /ˌaʊtpər'fɔrməns/ *noun* [U]

out·place·ment /'aʊtˌpleɪsmənt/ *noun* [U] (*business*) the process of helping people to find new jobs after they have become unemployed

out·play /ˌaʊt'pleɪ/ *verb* ~ sb to play much better than someone you are competing against: *We were totally outplayed and lost 106–74.*

out·point /ˌaʊt'pɔɪnt/ *verb* ~ sb (especially in boxing) to defeat someone by scoring more points

out·post /'aʊtpoʊst/ *noun* **1** a small military camp away from the main army, used for watching an enemy's movements, etc. **2** a small town or group of buildings in a lonely part of a country: *a remote outpost* ◆ *the last outpost of civilization*

out·pour·ing /'aʊtˌpɔrɪŋ/ *noun* **1** [usually pl.] a strong and sudden expression of feeling: *spontaneous outpourings of praise* **2** a large amount of something produced in a short time: *a remarkable outpouring of new ideas*

out·put 🔑 **AWL** /'aʊtpʊt/ *noun, verb*
- *noun* [U, sing.] **1** the amount of something that a person, a machine, or an organization produces: *Manufacturing output has increased by 8%.* **2** (*computing*) the information, results, etc. produced by a computer: *data output* ◆ *an output device* ➔ compare INPUT **3** the power, energy, etc. produced by a piece of equipment: *an output of 100 watts* **4** a place where energy, power, information, etc. leaves a system: *Connect a cable to the output.*
- *verb* (out·put·ting, out·put, out·put) ~ sth (*computing*) to supply or produce information, results, etc.: *Computers can now output data much more quickly.* ➔ compare INPUT

out·rage /'aʊtreɪdʒ/ *noun, verb*
- *noun* **1** [U] a strong feeling of shock and anger: *The judge's remarks caused public outrage.* ◆ *Environmentalists have expressed outrage at the ruling.* **2** [C] an act or event that is violent, cruel, or very wrong and that shocks people or makes them very angry **SYN** ATROCITY: *No one has yet claimed responsibility for this latest bomb outrage.*
- *verb* [often passive] ~ sb to make someone very shocked and angry: *He was outraged at the way he had been treated.*

out·ra·geous /aʊt'reɪdʒəs/ *adj.* **1** very shocking and unacceptable **SYN** SCANDALOUS: *outrageous behavior* ◆ *"That's outrageous!" he protested.* **2** very unusual and slightly shocking: *She says the most outrageous things sometimes.* ◆ *outrageous clothes* ▶ out·ra·geous·ly *adv.*: *an outrageously expensive meal* ◆ *They behaved outrageously.*

out·ran *pt of* OUTRUN

out·rank /ˌaʊt'ræŋk/ *verb* ~ sb to be of higher rank, quality, etc. than someone

ou·tré /u'treɪ/ *adj.* (from French, *formal*) very unusual and slightly shocking

out·reach /'aʊtritʃ/ *noun* [U] the activity of an organization that provides a service or advice to people in the community, especially those who cannot or are unlikely to come to an office, a hospital, etc. for help: *an outreach and education program* ◆ *outreach workers* ◆ *efforts to expand the outreach to black voters*

out·rid·er /'aʊtˌraɪdər/ *noun* a person who rides a motorcycle or a horse in front of or beside the vehicle of an important person in order to give protection

out·rig·ger /'aʊtˌrɪɡər/ *noun* a wooden structure that is fixed to the side of a boat or ship in order to keep it steady in the water; a boat fitted with such a structure

out·right adj., adv.
- **adj.** /ˈaʊtraɪt/ [only before noun] **1** complete and total: *an outright ban/rejection/victory* ◆ *She was the outright winner.* ◆ *No one party is expected to gain an outright majority.* **2** open and direct: *There was outright opposition to the plan.*
- **adv.** /ˌaʊtˈraɪt; ˈaʊtraɪt/ **1** in a direct way and without trying to hide anything: *Why don't you ask him outright if it's true?* ◆ *She couldn't help herself and she laughed outright.* **2** clearly and completely: *Neither candidate won outright.* ◆ *The group rejects outright any negotiations with the government.* **3** not gradually; immediately: *Most of the crash victims were* **killed outright.** ◆ *We had saved enough money to buy the house outright.*

out·run /ˌaʊtˈrʌn/ verb (out·run·ning, out·ran /-ˈræn/, out·run) **1 ~ sb/sth** to run faster or further than someone or something: *He couldn't outrun his pursuers.* **2 ~ sth** to develop faster than something **SYN** OUTSTRIP: *Demand for the new model is outrunning supply.*

out·sell /ˌaʊtˈsɛl/ verb (out·sold, out·sold /-ˈsoʊld/) **~ sb/ sth** to sell more or to be sold in larger quantities than someone or something: *We are now outselling all our competitors.* ◆ *This year the newspaper has outsold its main rival.*

out·set /ˈaʊtsɛt/ noun
  IDM **at/from the outset (of sth)** at/from the beginning of something: *I made it clear right from the outset that I disapproved.*

out·shine /ˌaʊtˈʃaɪn/ verb (out·shone, out·shone /-ˈʃoʊn/) **~ sb/sth** to be more impressive than someone or something; to be better than someone or something

out·side 🔑 noun, adj., prep., adv.
- **noun** /ˌaʊtˈsaɪd; ˈaʊtsaɪd/ **1** usually **the outside** [C, usually sing.] the outer side or surface of something **SYN** EXTERIOR: *The outside of the house needs painting.* ◆ *You can't open the door from the outside.* **2** [sing.] the area that is near or around a building, etc.: *I walked around the outside of the building.* ◆ *I didn't go into the temple—I only saw it from the outside.* **3** [sing.] the part of a road nearest to the middle: *Always overtake* **on the outside. 4** [sing.] the part of a curving road or track furthest from the inner or shorter side of the curve **ANT** THE INSIDE
  IDM **at the outside** at the most; as a maximum: *There was room for 20 people at the outside.* **on the outside 1** used to describe how someone appears or seems: *On the outside she seems calm, but I know she's worried.* **2** not in prison: *Life on the outside took some getting used to again.*
- **adj.** /ˈaʊtsaɪd/ [only before noun] **1** of, on, or facing the outer side **SYN** EXTERNAL: *The outside walls were damp.* **2** not located in the main building; going out of the main building **SYN** EXTERNAL: *an outside toilet* ◆ *You have to pay to make outside calls.* ◆ *I can't get an outside line.* **3** not included in or connected with your group, organization, country, etc.: *We plan to use an outside firm of consultants.* ◆ *She has a lot of* **outside interests** (= not connected with her work). ◆ *They felt cut off from the* **outside world** (= from other people and from other things that were happening). **4** used to say that something is very unlikely: *They have only an* **outside chance** *of winning.* ◆ *150 is an outside estimate* (= it is very likely to be less).
- **prep.** /ˌaʊtˈsaɪd; ˈaʊtsaɪd/ (also **outside of**) **1** on or to a place on the outside of something: *You can park your car outside our house.* **ANT** INSIDE **2** away from or not in a particular place: *It's the biggest theme park outside the United States.* ◆ *We live in a small town* **just outside** *St. Louis.* **3** not part of something: *The matter is outside my area of responsibility.* ◆ *You may do as you wish outside working hours.* **ANT** WITHIN **4 outside of** apart from: *There was nothing they could do, outside of hoping things would get better.* **IDM** **see** THINK v.
- **adv.** /ˌaʊtˈsaɪd/ **1** not in a room, building, or container but on or to the outside of it: *I'm seeing a patient—please wait outside.* ◆ *The house is painted green outside.* **2** not inside a building: *It's warm enough to eat outside.* ◆ *Go outside and see if it's raining.* **ANT** INSIDE

out·sid·er /ˌaʊtˈsaɪdər; ˈaʊtˌsaɪdər/ noun **1** a person who is not accepted as a member of a society, group, etc.: *Here she felt she would always be an outsider.* **2** a person who is not part of a particular organization or profession: *They have decided to hire outsiders for some of the key positions.* ◆ *To an outsider it may appear to be a glamorous job.* **3** a person or an animal taking part in a race or competition that is not expected to win: *The race was won by a 20–1 outsider.* ◆ *To everyone's surprise, the job went to* **a rank outsider** (= a complete outsider).

out·size /ˈaʊtsaɪz/ (also **out·sized** /ˈaʊtsaɪzd/) adj. [usually before noun] **1** larger than the usual size: *an outsize desk* **2** designed for large people: *outsize clothes*

out·skirts /ˈaʊtskərts/ noun [pl.] the parts of a town or city that are farthest from the center: *They live* **on the outskirts of** *Milan.*

out·smart /ˌaʊtˈsmart/ verb **~ sb** to gain an advantage over someone by tricking them or using your intelligence **SYN** OUTWIT: *She always managed to outsmart her political rivals.*

out·source /ˈaʊtsɔrs/ verb [T, I] **~ (sth)** (business) to arrange for someone outside a company to do work or provide goods for that company: *We outsource all our computing work.* ▶ **out·sourc·ing** noun [U]

out·spo·ken /ˌaʊtˈspoʊkən/ adj. saying exactly what you think, even if this shocks or offends people **SYN** BLUNT: *an outspoken opponent of the leader* ◆ *outspoken comments* ◆ **~ in sth** *She was outspoken in her criticism of the plan.* ⊃ thesaurus box at HONEST ▶ **out·spok·en·ly** adv. **out·spok·en·ness** noun [U]

out·spread /ˌaʊtˈsprɛd/ adj. (formal) spread out completely: *The bird soared high, with outspread wings.*

out·stand·ing 🔑 /aʊtˈstændɪŋ/ adj.
  1 extremely good; excellent: *an outstanding player/achievement/success* ◆ *an area of* **outstanding natural beauty** ⊃ thesaurus box at EXCELLENT **2** [usually before noun] very obvious or important **SYN** PROMINENT: *the outstanding features of the landscape* **3** (of payment, work, problems, etc.) not yet paid, done, solved, etc.: *She has outstanding debts of over $500.* ◆ *A lot of work is still outstanding.*

out·stand·ing·ly /aʊtˈstændɪŋli/ adv. **1** used to emphasize the good quality of something: *outstandingly successful* **2** extremely well: *He performed well but not outstandingly.*

out·stay /ˌaʊtˈsteɪ/ verb **IDM** **see** WELCOME n.

out·stretched /ˌaʊtˈstrɛtʃt/ adj. (of parts of the body) stretched or spread out as far as possible: *He ran toward her* **with arms outstretched/with outstretched arms.**

out·strip /ˌaʊtˈstrɪp/ verb (-pp-) **1 ~ sth** to become larger, more important, etc. than someone or something: *Demand is outstripping supply.* **2 ~ sth** to be faster, better, or more successful than someone you are competing against **SYN** SURPASS: *Their latest computer outstrips all its rivals.* **3 ~ sb** to run faster than someone in a race so that you pass them

out·ta (also **out·a**) /ˈaʊtə/ prep. used for writing the way "out of" is sometimes pronounced in informal speech: *I'm outta here!* (= I'm leaving now.)

out·take /ˈaʊtteɪk/ noun a piece of a movie that is removed before the movie is shown, for example because it contains a mistake

out-there adj. (informal) (of people) different, confident, having strong opinions, and attracting attention to yourself; (of ideas) different from what most people consider normal, but exciting: *Wow, this is such an out-there character. This role is definitely going to be cool.* ◆ *It may be totally out-there but I think it could work.*

out·vote /ˌaʊtˈvoʊt/ verb [usually passive] **~ sb/sth** to defeat someone or something by winning a larger number of votes **SYN** VOTE SB/STH DOWN: *His proposal was outvoted by 10 votes to 8.*

out·ward /ˈaʊtwərd/ *adj., adv.*

- *adj.* [only before noun] **1** connected with the way people or things seem to be rather than with what is actually true: *Mark showed no outward signs of distress.* ◆ *She simply observes the outward forms of religion.* ◆ *To all outward appearances* (= as far as it was possible to judge from the outside) *they were perfectly happy.* **ANT** INWARD **2** going away from a particular place, especially one that you are going to return to: *the outward voyage/journey* **3** away from the center or a particular point: *outward movement* ◆ *outward investment* (= in other countries) ◆ *Managers need to become more outward-looking* (= more open to new ideas). **ANT** INWARD

- *adv.* (also **outwards**) **~ (from sth)** toward the outside; away from the center or from a particular point: *The door opens outward.* ◆ *Factories were spreading outward from the old heart of the town.* ◆ *Lie on your stomach with your elbows pointing outward.* ◆ *The country is looking outward and is opening its economy to trade and investment.* **ANT** INWARD

Outward 'Bound™ *noun* [U] an international organization that provides training in outdoor activities including sports for young people

outward 'bound *adj.* going away from home or a particular place

out·ward·ly /ˈaʊtwərdli/ *adv.* on the surface; in appearance: *Though badly frightened, she remained outwardly composed.* ◆ *Outwardly, the couple seemed perfectly happy.* **ANT** INWARDLY

out·weigh /ˌaʊtˈweɪ/ *verb* **~ sth** to be greater or more important than something: *The advantages far outweigh the disadvantages.*

out·wit /ˌaʊtˈwɪt/ *verb* (-tt-) **~ sb/sth** to defeat someone or something or gain an advantage over them by doing something smart or by tricking them **SYN** OUTSMART: *Somehow he always manages to outwit his opponents.*

out·worn /ˈaʊtwɔrn/ *adj.* [usually before noun] old-fashioned and no longer useful **SYN** OBSOLETE: *outworn institutions* ➔ compare WORN OUT

ou·zo /ˈuzoʊ/ *noun* [U] a strong alcoholic drink from Greece, made from ANISEED and usually drunk with water

o·va pl. of OVUM

o·val /ˈoʊvl/ *adj., noun*

- *adj.* shaped like an egg: *an oval face*
- *noun* an oval shape

the ˌOval 'Office *noun* [sing.] **1** the office of the U.S. President in the White House **2** a way of referring to the U. S. President and the part of the government that is controlled by the President: *Congress is waiting to see how the Oval Office will react.*

o·va·ry /ˈoʊvəri/ *noun* (pl. **o·va·ries**) **1** either of the two organs in a woman's body that produce eggs; a similar organ in female animals, birds, and fish **2** the part of a plant that produces seeds ➔ picture at PLANT ▶ **o·var·i·an** /oʊˈveriən/ *adj.* [only before noun]: *ovarian cancer*

o·va·tion /oʊˈveɪʃn/ *noun* enthusiastic CLAPPING by an audience as a sign of their approval: *to give someone a huge/rapturous/rousing ovation* ◆ *The soloist got a ten-minute standing ovation* (= in which people stand up from their seats).

ov·en /ˈʌvn/ *noun*
the part of a stove shaped like a box with a door on the front, in which food is cooked or heated: *Take the cake out of the oven.* ◆ *a gas/an electric oven* ◆ *a cool/hot/moderate oven* ◆ *Open a window, it's like an oven in here!* ➔ see also CONVECTION OVEN ➔ compare MICROWAVE **IDM** see BUN

'oven ˌmitt (also **'oven ˌglove**) *noun* a glove made of thick material, used for holding hot dishes from an oven

ov·en·proof /ˈʌvnpruf/ *adj.* suitable for use in a hot oven: *an ovenproof dish*

ˌoven-'ready *adj.* [usually before noun] (of food) bought already prepared and ready for cooking

ov·en·ware /ˈʌvnˌwer/ *noun* [U] dishes that can be used for cooking food in an oven

o·ver /ˈoʊvər/ *adv., prep.*

- *adv.* **HELP** For the special uses of **over** in phrasal verbs, look at the entries for the verbs. For example, **take sth over** is in the phrasal verb section at **take**. **1** downward and away from a vertical position: *Try not to knock that vase over.* ◆ *The wind must have blown it over.* **2** from one side to another side: *She turned over onto her front.* ◆ *The car skidded off the road and rolled over and over.* **3** across a street, an open space, etc.: *I stopped and crossed over.* ◆ *He rowed us over to the other side of the lake.* ◆ *They have gone over to France.* ◆ *This is my aunt who's over from Ireland.* ◆ *I went over* (= across the room) *and asked her name.* ◆ *Let's ask some friends over* (= to our home). ◆ *Put it down over there.* **4** so as to cover someone or something completely: *The lake was frozen over.* ◆ *Cover her over with a blanket.* **5** above; more: *children of 14 and over* ◆ *You get an A grade for scores of 75 and over.* **6** remaining; not used or needed: *If there's any food left over, put it in the refrigerator.* **7** again: *He repeated it several times over until he could remember it.* ◆ *It's all wrong—you'll have to do it over.* **8** ended: *By the time we arrived the meeting was over.* ◆ *Thank goodness that's over!* ◆ *I was glad when it was over and done with.* **9** used to talk about someone or something changing position: *He's gone over to the enemy* (= joined them). ◆ *Please change the wheels over* (= for example, put the front wheels at the back). ◆ *Hand over the money!* **10** used when communicating by radio: *Message received. Over* (= it is your turn to speak). ◆ *Message understood. Over and out.* **IDM** **(all) over again** a second time from the beginning: *He did the work so badly that I had to do it all over again myself.* **over against sth** in contrast with something **over and over (again)** many times; repeatedly: *I've told you over and over again not to do that.* **over to you** used to say that it is someone's turn to do something

- *prep.* **HELP** For the special uses of **over** in phrasal verbs, look at the entries for the verbs. For example, **get over something** is in the phrasal verb section at **get**. **1** resting on the surface of someone or something and partly or completely covering them/it: *She put a blanket over the sleeping child.* ◆ *He wore an overcoat over his suit.* ◆ *She put her hand over her mouth to stop herself from screaming.* **2** in or to a position higher than but not touching someone or something; above someone or something: *They held a large umbrella over her.* ◆ *The balcony juts out over the street.* ◆ *There was a lamp hanging over the table.* **3** from one side of something to the other; across something: *a bridge over the river* ◆ *They ran over the grass.* ◆ *They had a wonderful view over the park.* **4** on the far or opposite side of something: *He lives over the road.* **5** so as to cross something and be on the other side: *She climbed over the wall.* **6** falling from or down from a place: *The car had toppled over the cliff.* ◆ *He didn't dare look over the edge.* **7** all **~** in or on all or most parts of something: *Snow is falling all over the country.* ◆ *They've traveled all over the world.* ◆ *There were papers lying around all over the place.* **8** more than a particular time, amount, cost, etc.: *over 3 million copies sold* ◆ *She stayed in Lagos for over a month.* ◆ *He's over sixty.* **9** used to show that someone has control or authority: *She has only the director over her.* ◆ *He ruled over a great empire.* ◆ *She has editorial control over what is included.* **10** during something: *We'll discuss it over lunch.* ◆ *Over the next few days they got to know the town well.* ◆ *She has not changed much over the years.* ◆ *He built up the business over a period of ten years.* ◆ *We're away over* (= until after) *the New Year.* **11** past a particular difficult stage or situation: *We're over the worst of the recession.* ◆ *It took her ages to get over her illness.* **12** because of or concerning something; about something: *an argument over money* ◆ *a disagreement over the best way to proceed* **13** using something; by means of something: *We heard it over the radio.* ◆ *She wouldn't tell me over the phone.* **14** louder than something: *I couldn't hear what he said over the noise of the traffic.* ➔ note at ABOVE **IDM** **over and above** in addition to something: *There are other factors over and above those we have discussed.*

over- /ˈoʊvər/ prefix (in nouns, verbs, adjectives, and adverbs) **1** more than usual; too much: *overproduction* ♦ *overload* ♦ *overoptimistic* ♦ *overconfident* ♦ *overanxious* **2** completely: *overjoyed* **3** upper; outer; extra: *overcoat* ♦ *overtime* **4** over; above: *overcast* ♦ *overhang*

o·ver·a·chieve /ˌoʊvərəˈtʃiv/ verb **1** [I] to do better than expected in your studies or work **2** [I] to try too hard to be successful in your work

o·ver·a·chiev·er /ˌoʊvərəˈtʃivər/ noun someone who does better than expected in school or work, or who places too much importance on being successful: *Both her parents are overachievers at the top of their professions and they expect the same from her.* **ANT** UNDERACHIEVER

o·ver·act /ˌoʊvərˈækt/ verb [I, T] ~ **(sth)** (disapproving) to behave in a way that is exaggerated and not natural, especially when you are acting a part in a play

o·ver·ac·tive /ˌoʊvərˈæktɪv/ adj. [usually before noun] **1** (of an organ or part of the body) causing harm by doing something too much: *an overactive thyroid* **2** (of someone's imagination) too active, especially so that they imagine things that are not true: *She suffers from an overactive imagination.*

o·ver·age /ˌoʊvərˈeɪdʒ/ adj. too old to be allowed to do a particular thing

o·ver·all 🔑 [AWL] *adj., adv., noun*

● **adj.** /ˈoʊvərˌɔl/ [only before noun] including all the things or people that are involved in a particular situation; general: *the person with overall responsibility for the project* ♦ *There will be winners in each of three age groups, and one overall winner.* ♦ *an overall improvement in standards of living* (= affecting everyone) ♦ *When she finished painting, she stepped back to admire the overall effect.*

● **adv.** /ˌoʊvərˈɔl/ **1** including everything or everyone; in total: *The company will invest $1.6 m. overall in new equipment.* **2** generally; when you consider everything: *Overall, this is a very useful book.* ⊃ **language bank at** CONCLUSION

● **noun** /ˈoʊvərˌɔl/ **overalls** (also ˌbib ˈoveralls) [pl.] a piece of clothing that consists of pants with an extra piece of cloth covering the chest, held up by strips of cloth over the shoulders

o·ver·am·bi·tious /ˌoʊvəræmˈbɪʃəs/ adj. **1** (of a person) too determined to be successful, rich, powerful, etc. **2** (of a plan, task, etc.) unsuccessful or likely to be unsuccessful because of needing too much effort, money, or time: *Her plans were overambitious.*

o·ver·arch·ing /ˌoʊvərˈɑrtʃɪŋ/ adj. [usually before noun] (formal) very important, because it includes or influences many things

o·ver·ate pt of OVEREAT

o·ver·awe /ˌoʊvərˈɔ/ verb [usually passive] ~ **sb** to impress someone so much that they feel nervous or frightened ▶ **o·ver·awed** adj.

o·ver·bear·ing /ˌoʊvərˈbɛrɪŋ/ adj. (disapproving) trying to control other people in an unpleasant way **SYN** DOMINEERING: *an overbearing manner*

o·ver·bite /ˈoʊvərˌbaɪt/ noun (technical) a condition in which a person's or animal's upper JAW is too far forward in relation to their lower JAW

o·ver·blown /ˌoʊvərˈbloʊn/ adj. **1** that is made to seem larger, more impressive, or more important than it really is **SYN** EXAGGERATED **2** (of flowers) past the best, most beautiful stage

o·ver·board /ˈoʊvərˌbɔrd/ adv. over the side of a boat or a ship into the water: *to fall/jump overboard* ♦ *Huge waves washed him overboard.* **IDM** **go overboard** (informal) to be too excited or enthusiastic about something or about doing something: *Don't go overboard on fitness.* **throw sb/sth overboard** to get rid of someone or something that you think is useless

o·ver·book /ˌoʊvərˈbʊk/ verb [T, I] ~ **(sth)** to sell more tickets on a plane or reserve more rooms in a hotel than there are places available: *The flight was heavily overbooked.* ⊃ compare DOUBLE-BOOK

o·ver·bur·den /ˌoʊvərˈbərdn/ verb [usually passive] ~ **sb/ sth (with sth)** to give someone or something more work, worry, etc. than they can deal with

o·ver·came pt of OVERCOME

o·ver·ca·pac·i·ty /ˌoʊvərkəˈpæsəti/ noun [U, sing.] (business) the situation in which an industry or a factory cannot sell as much as it is designed to produce

o·ver·cast /ˈoʊvərˌkæst/ adj. covered with clouds; dull: *an overcast sky/day* ♦ *Today it will be cool and overcast.*

o·ver·cau·tious /ˌoʊvərˈkɔʃəs/ adj. too careful

o·ver·charge /ˌoʊvərˈtʃɑrdʒ/ verb [T, I] ~ **(sb) (for sth)** to make someone pay too much for something: *Make sure they don't overcharge you for the drinks.* ♦ *We were overcharged by $5.* **ANT** UNDERCHARGE

o·ver·coat /ˈoʊvərˌkoʊt/ noun a long warm coat worn in cold weather ⊃ picture at CLOTHES

o·ver·come 🔑 /ˌoʊvərˈkʌm/ verb (o·ver·came /-ˈkeɪm/, o·ver·come)

1 ~ **sth** to succeed in dealing with or controlling a problem that has been preventing you from achieving something: *She overcame injury to win the Olympic gold medal.* ♦ *The two parties managed to overcome their differences on the issue.* **2** ~ **sb/sth** to defeat someone: *In the final game Sweden easily overcame France.* **3** [usually passive] ~ **sb** to be extremely strongly affected by something **SYN** OVERWHELM: *Her parents were overcome with grief at the funeral.* ♦ *The dead woman had been overcome by smoke.*

o·ver·com·pen·sate /ˌoʊvərˈkɑmpənˌseɪt/ verb [I] ~ **(for sth) (by doing sth)** to do too much when trying to correct a problem and so cause a different problem: *She overcompensated for her shyness by talking too much and laughing too loud.*

o·ver·con·fi·dent /ˌoʊvərˈkɑnfədənt/ adj. too confident

o·ver·cook /ˌoʊvərˈkʊk/ verb ~ **sth** to cook food for too long

o·ver·crit·i·cal /ˌoʊvərˈkrɪtɪkl/ adj. too critical

o·ver·crowd·ed /ˌoʊvərˈkraʊdəd/ adj. (of a place) with too many people or things in it: *overcrowded cities/prisons* ♦ *Too many poor people are living in overcrowded conditions.*

o·ver·crowd·ing /ˌoʊvərˈkraʊdɪŋ/ noun [U] the situation when there are too many people or things in one place

o·ver·de·vel·oped /ˌoʊvərdɪˈvɛləpt/ adj. that has grown too large: *overdeveloped muscles* ♦ *an overdeveloped sense of humor* ▶ **o·ver·de·vel·op** verb ~ **sth**

o·ver·do /ˌoʊvərˈdu/ verb (o·ver·does /-ˈdʌz/, o·ver·did /-ˈdɪd/, o·ver·done /-ˈdʌn/) **1** ~ **sth** to do something too much; to exaggerate something: *She really overdid the sympathy* (= and so did not seem sincere). **2** ~ **sth** to use too much of something: *Don't overdo the salt in the food.* ♦ *Use illustrations where appropriate but don't overdo it.* **3** [usually passive] ~ **sth** to cook something for too long: *The fish was overdone and very dry.* **IDM** **overdo it/things** to work, study, etc. too hard or for too long: *He's been overdoing things recently.* ♦ *I overdid it in the gym and hurt my back.*

o·ver·dog /ˈoʊvərˌdɔg/ noun (disapproving) a person, organization, or country that is successful or in a stronger position than others, especially when they seem to have an unfair advantage: *political leaders who support the interests of the overdog* **ANT** UNDERDOG

o·ver·dose /ˈoʊvərˌdoʊs/ noun, verb
● **noun** too much of a drug taken at one time: *a drug overdose* ♦ *She took a massive overdose of sleeping pills.*
● **verb** (also informal OD) [I] ~ **(on sth)** to take too much of a drug at one time, so that it is dangerous: *He had overdosed on heroin.* ♦ *(figurative) I had overdosed on sun.*

o·ver·draft /ˈoʊvərˌdræft/ noun the amount of money that you owe to a bank when you have spent more money than is in your bank account; an arrangement that allows you to do this: *to run up/pay off an overdraft*

o·ver·draw /ˌoʊvərˈdrɔ/ *verb* (o·ver·drew /-ˈdru/, o·ver-drawn /-ˈdrɔn/) [T, I] **~ (sth)** to take out more money from a bank account than it contains: *Customers who overdraw their accounts will be charged a fee.*

o·ver·drawn /ˌoʊvərˈdrɔn/ *adj.* **1** [not usually before noun] (of a person) having taken more money out of your bank account than you have in it: *I'm overdrawn by $100.* **2** (of a bank account) with more money taken out than was paid in or left in: *an overdrawn account* ◆ *Your account is $200 overdrawn.*

o·ver·dressed /ˌoʊvərˈdrɛst/ *adj.* (usually *disapproving*) wearing clothes that are too formal or too elegant for a particular occasion **ANT** UNDERDRESSED

o·ver·drive /ˈoʊvərˌdraɪv/ *noun* [U] an extra high gear in a vehicle, that you use when you are driving at high speeds: *to be in overdrive*
IDM **go into overdrive** to start being very active and working very hard: *As the wedding approached, the whole family went into overdrive.*

o·ver·dub /ˌoʊvərˈdʌb/ *verb* (-bb-) **~ sb** to record new sounds over the sounds on an original recording so that both can be heard

o·ver·due /ˌoʊvərˈdu/ *adj.* **1** not paid, done, returned, etc. by the required or expected time: *an overdue payment/ library book* ◆ *The rent is now overdue.* ◆ *Her baby is two weeks overdue.* **2** that should have happened or been done before now: *overdue reforms* ◆ *A book like this is **long overdue***.

,over ˈeasy *adj.* (of fried eggs) turned over when almost cooked and fried for a short time on the other side

o·ver·eat /ˌoʊvərˈit/ *verb* (o·ver·ate /-ˈeɪt/, o·ver·eat·en /-ˈitn/) [I] to eat more than you need or more than is healthy ▶ **o·ver·eat·ing** *noun* [U]: *She went through periods of compulsive overeating.*

o·ver·em·pha·sis /ˌoʊvərˈɛmfəsəs/ *noun* [U, sing.] **~ (on sth)** too much emphasis or importance: *an overemphasis on curing illness rather than preventing it* ▶ **o·ver·em·pha·size** /ˌoʊvərˈɛmfəˌsaɪz/ *verb*: **~ sth** *The importance of preparation cannot be overemphasized.*

o·ver·es·ti·mate **AWL** *verb, noun*
• *verb* /ˌoʊvərˈɛstəˌmeɪt/ **~ sth** to estimate something to be larger, better, more important, etc. than it really is: *They overestimated his ability when they promoted him.* ◆ *The importance of these findings cannot be overestimated* (= is very great). **ANT** UNDERESTIMATE ⊃ collocations at ESTIMATE ▶ **o·ver·es·ti·ma·tion** *noun* [U, C]
• *noun* /ˌoʊvərˈɛstəmət/ [usually sing.] an estimate about the size, cost, etc. of something that is too high **ANT** UNDERESTIMATE

o·ver·ex·cit·ed /ˌoʊvərɪkˈsaɪtəd/ *adj.* too excited and not behaving in a calm or sensible way: *Don't get the children overexcited just before bedtime.*

o·ver·ex·pose /ˌoʊvərɪkˈspoʊz/ *verb* [usually passive] **1 ~ sth** to affect the quality of a photograph or film by allowing too much light to enter the camera **ANT** UNDEREXPOSE **2 ~ sb/sth** to allow someone or something to be seen too much on television, in the newspapers, etc.: *The club is careful not to let the younger players be overexposed, and rarely allows them to be interviewed.* ▶ **o·ver·ex·po·sure** /-ɪkˈspoʊʒər/ *noun* [U]

o·ver·ex·tend·ed /ˌoʊvərɪkˈstɛndəd/ *adj.* [not usually before noun] involved in more work or activities, or spending more money, than you can manage without problems ▶ **o·ver·ex·tend** *verb*: **~ yourself** *They should not overextend themselves on the mortgage.*

o·ver·feed /ˌoʊvərˈfid/ *verb* (o·ver·fed, o·ver·fed /-ˈfɛd/) **~ sb/sth** to give someone or something too much food ▶ **o·ver·fed** *adj.* **ANT** UNDERFED

o·ver·fish·ing /ˌoʊvərˈfɪʃɪŋ/ *noun* [U] the process of taking so many fish from the ocean, a river, etc. that the number of fish in it becomes very low

o·ver·flow *verb, noun*
• *verb* /ˌoʊvərˈfloʊ/ **1** [I, T] to be so full that the contents go over the sides: *The bathtub is overflowing.* ◆ **~ with sth** *Plates overflowed with party food.* ◆ (*figurative*) *Her heart overflowed with love.* ◆ **~ sth** *The river overflowed its banks.* **2** [I] **~ (with sth)** (of a place) to have too many people in it: *The streets were overflowing with the crowds.* ◆ *The hospitals are filled to overflowing* (= with patients). **3** [I, T] **~ (into sth)** | **~ (sth)** to spread beyond the limits of a place or container that is too full: *The meeting overflowed into the street.*
• *noun* /ˈoʊvərˌfloʊ/ **1** [U, sing.] a number of people or things that do not fit into the space available: *A new office building was built to accommodate the overflow of staff.* ◆ *an overflow garage* **2** [U, sing.] the action of liquid flowing out of a container, etc. that is already full; the liquid that flows out: *an overflow of water from the lake* ◆ (*figurative*) *an overflow of powerful emotions* **3** (also ˈoverflow pipe) [C] a pipe that allows extra liquid to escape **4** [C, usually sing.] (*computing*) a fault that happens because a number or data item (for example, the result of a calculation) is too large for the computer to represent it exactly

o·ver·fly /ˌoʊvərˈflaɪ/ *verb* (o·ver·flies, o·ver·fly·ing, o·ver-flew /-ˈflu/, o·ver·flown /-ˈfloʊn/) [T, I] **~ (sth)** to fly over a place: *We overflew the war zone, taking photographs.* ◆ *the noise from overflying planes* ▶ **o·ver·flight** /ˈoʊvərˌflaɪt/ *noun*

o·ver·gar·ment /ˈoʊvərˌgarmənt/ *noun* (*formal*) an item of clothing that is worn over other clothes

o·ver·gen·er·al·ize /ˌoʊvərˈdʒɛnərəˌlaɪz; -ˈdʒɛnrə-/ *verb* [I] to make a statement that is not accurate because it is too general ▶ **o·ver·gen·er·al·i·za·tion** /ˌoʊvərˌdʒɛnərələ-ˈzeɪʃn; -ˌdʒɛnrə-/ *noun* [C, U]

o·ver·gen·er·ous /ˌoʊvərˈdʒɛnərəs/ *adj.* **~ (with sth)** giving too much of something: *She is not overgenerous with praise.*

o·ver·graze /ˌoʊvərˈgreɪz/ *verb* **~ sth** if land is **overgrazed**, it is damaged by having too many animals feeding on it

o·ver·grown /ˌoʊvərˈgroʊn/ *adj.* **1** (of gardens, etc.) covered with plants that have been allowed to grow wild and have not been controlled: *an overgrown path* ◆ **~ with sth** *The garden's completely overgrown with weeds.* **2** (often *disapproving*) that has grown too large: *an overgrown village* ◆ *They act like a pair of overgrown children* (= they are adults but they behave like children).

o·ver·growth /ˈoʊvərˌgroʊθ/ *noun* [U, sing.] (*technical*) too much growth of something, especially something that grows on or over something else

o·ver·hand /ˈoʊvərˌhænd/ *adv.* if you throw a ball **overhand**, you throw it with your arm swung backward and then lifted high above your shoulder ⊃ compare UNDERHAND ▶ **o·ver·hand** *adj.*

o·ver·hang *verb, noun*
• *verb* /ˌoʊvərˈhæŋ/ (o·ver·hung, o·ver·hung /-ˈhʌŋ/) [T, I] **~ (sth)** to stick out over and above something else: *His big fat belly overhung his belt.* ◆ *The path was cool and dark with overhanging trees.*
• *noun* /ˈoʊvərˌhæŋ/ **1** the part of something that sticks out over and above something else: *The roof has an overhang to protect the walls from the rain.* ⊃ picture at OVERLAP **2** the amount by which something hangs over and above something else **3** [usually sing.] (*business*) the state of being extra to what is required; the things that are extra: *attempts to reduce the overhang of unsold goods*

o·ver·hast·y /ˌoʊvərˈheɪsti/ *adj.* done too soon or doing something too soon, especially without enough thought: *an overhasty decision* ◆ *We were overhasty in making the choice.*

o·ver·haul *noun, verb*
• *noun* /ˈoʊvərˌhɔl/ an examination of a machine or system, including doing repairs on it or making changes to it: *a complete/major overhaul* ◆ *A radical overhaul of the tax system is necessary.*
• *verb* /ˌoʊvərˈhɔl; ˈoʊvərˌhɔl/ **1 ~ sth** to examine every part of a machine, system, etc. and make any necessary

t **tea**   ţ **butter**   d **did**   k **cat**   g **got**   tʃ **chin**   dʒ **June**   f **fall**

changes or repairs: *The engine has been completely over-hauled.* **2 ~ sb** to come from behind a person you are competing against in a race and go past them **SYN** OVERTAKE: *He managed to overhaul the leader on the final lap.*

o·ver·head *adv., adj., noun*
- *adv.* /ˌoʊvərˈhɛd/ above your head; in the sky: *Planes flew overhead constantly.* ◆ *Thunder boomed in the sky overhead.*
- *adj.* /ˈoʊvərˌhɛd/ **1** above your head; raised above the ground: *overhead power lines* **2** [only before noun] connected with the general costs of running a business or an organization, for example paying for rent or electricity: *overhead costs*
- *noun* /ˈoʊvərˌhɛd/ [U] regular costs that you have when you are running a business or an organization, such as rent, electricity, wages, etc. ⊃ **thesaurus box at** COST

overhead pro·jector *noun* a piece of equipment that projects an image onto a wall or screen so that many people can see it ⊃ **compare** DATA PROJECTOR, SLIDE PRO-JECTOR

o·ver·hear /ˌoʊvərˈhɪr/ *verb* (o·ver·heard, o·ver·heard /-ˈhɜrd/) to hear, especially by accident, a conversation in which you are not involved: **~ sb/sth** *We talked quietly so as not to be overheard.* ◆ *I overheard a conversation between two boys on the bus.* ◆ **~ sb doing sth** *We overheard them arguing.* ◆ **~ sb do sth** *I overheard him say he was going to France.* ⊃ **compare** EAVESDROP

o·ver·heat /ˌoʊvərˈhit/ *verb* **1** [I, T] to become or to make something become too hot: *The engine is overheating.* ◆ **~ sth** *It's vital not to overheat the liquid.* **2** [I] (of a country's economy) to be too active, with rising prices ▸ **o·ver·heat·ing** *noun* [U]

o·ver·heat·ed /ˌoʊvərˈhitəd/ *adj.* **1** too hot: *Don't sleep in an overheated room.* **2** too interested or excited: *the figment of an overheated imagination* **3** (of a country's economy) too active in a way that may cause problems

o·ver·hung pt of OVERHANG

o·ver·in·dulge /ˌoʊvərɪnˈdʌldʒ/ *verb* **1** [I] **~ (in sth)** to have too much of something nice, especially food or drink **2** [T] **~ sb** to give someone more than is good for them: *His mother overindulged him.*

o·ver·in·flat·ed /ˌoʊvərɪnˈfleɪtəd/ *adj.* **1** (of a price or value) too high: *overinflated house prices* **2** made to seem better, worse, more important, etc. than it really is **SYN** EXAGGERATED **3** filled with too much air: *Overinflated tires burst more easily.*

o·ver·joyed /ˌoʊvərˈdʒɔɪd/ *adj.* [not before noun] extremely happy or pleased **SYN** DELIGHTED: **~ (at sth)** *He was overjoyed at my success.* ◆ **~ (to do sth)** *We were overjoyed to hear their good news.* ◆ **~ (that…)** *She was overjoyed that her article had been published.*

o·ver·kill /ˈoʊvərˌkɪl/ *noun* [U] (*disapproving*) too much of something that reduces the effect it has: *There is a danger of overkill if you plan everything too carefully.*

o·ver·laid pt, pp of OVERLAY

o·ver·land /ˈoʊvərˌlænd/ *adj.* across the land; by land, not by ocean or by air: *an overland route* ▸ **o·ver·land** *adv.*: *to travel overland*

o·ver·lap AWL *verb, noun*
- *verb* /ˌoʊvərˈlæp/ (-pp-) **1** [T, I] **~ (sth)** if one thing **overlaps** another, or the two things **overlap**, part of one thing covers part of the other: *A fish's scales overlap each other.* ◆ *The floor was protected with overlapping sheets of newspaper.* **2** [T] **~ sth** to make two or more things overlap: *You will need to overlap the pieces of wood slightly.* **3** [I, T] **~ (sth)** if two events **overlap** or **overlap** each other, the second one starts before the first one has finished **4** [I, T] to cover part of the same area of interest, knowledge, responsibility, etc.: *Our jobs overlap slightly, which sometimes causes difficulties.* ◆ **~ (with) sth** *The language of science overlaps with that of everyday life.*
- *noun* /ˈoʊvərˌlæp/ **1** [C, U] **~ (between sth and sth)** a

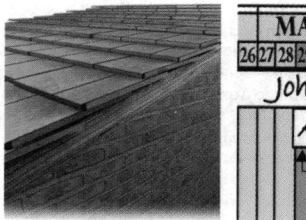

overlapping tiles   overlapping dates

overhanging branches

shared area of interest, knowledge, responsibility, etc.: *There is (a) considerable overlap between the two subjects.* **2** [C, U] the amount by which one thing covers another thing: *an overlap of 5 inches on each roof tile* **3** [sing.] a period of time in which two events or activities happen together: *There will be an overlap of a week while John teaches Anne the job.*

o·ver·lay *verb, noun*
- *verb* /ˌoʊvərˈleɪ/ (o·ver·laid, o·ver·laid /-ˈleɪd/) [usually passive] **1 ~ sth (with sth)** (*technical*) to put something on top of a surface so as to cover it completely; to lie on top of a surface: *wood overlaid with gold* **2 ~ sth (with sth)** (*literary*) to add something, especially a feeling or quality, to something else so that it seems to cover it: *The place was overlaid with memories of his childhood.*
- *noun* /ˈoʊvərˌleɪ/ **1** a transparent sheet with drawings, figures, etc. on it that can be placed on top of another sheet in order to change it: *An overlay showing population can be placed on top of the map.* **2** a thing that is laid on top of or covers something else: *an overlay of fiberglass insulation*

o·ver·leaf /ˈoʊvərˌlif/ *adv.* on the other side of the page of a book, etc.: *Complete the form overleaf.* ◆ *The changes are explained in detail overleaf.*

o·ver·lie /ˌoʊvərˈlaɪ/ *verb* (o·ver·ly·ing, o·ver·lay /-ˈleɪ/, o·ver·lain /-ˈleɪn/) [I, T] **~ (sth)** (*technical*) to lie over something: *overlying rock*

o·ver·load *verb, noun*
- *verb* /ˌoʊvərˈloʊd/ [often passive] **1 ~ sth** to put too great a load on something: *an overloaded truck* **2 ~ sb (with sth)** to give someone too much of something: *He's overloaded with responsibilities.* ◆ *Don't overload the students with information.* **3 ~ sth** to put too great a demand on a computer, an electrical system, etc. causing it to fail
- *noun* /ˈoʊvərˌloʊd/ [U, sing.] too much of something: *In these days of technological change we all suffer from information overload.*

o·ver·long /ˌoʊvərˈlɔŋ/ *adj.* too long: *an overlong agenda*

o·ver·look *verb, noun*
- *verb* /ˌoʊvərˈlʊk/ **1 ~ sth** to fail to see or notice something: *He seems to have overlooked one important fact.* **2 ~ sth** to see something wrong or bad but decide to ignore it **SYN** TURN A BLIND EYE TO: *We could not afford to overlook such a serious offense.* **3 ~ sth** if a building, etc. **overlooks** a place, you can see that place from the building: *a restaurant*

overlooking the lake ♦ *Our backyard is overlooked by several houses.* **4** ~ **sb (for sth)** to not consider someone for a job or position, even though they might be suitable **SYN PASS OVER**: *She's been overlooked for promotion several times.*

• **noun** /'oʊvər,lʊk/ a place from which you can look down at a view: *Be sure to stop at this scenic overlook.*

o·ver·lord /'oʊvər,lɔrd/ *noun* (especially in the past) a person who has power over many other people: *feudal overlords*

o·ver·ly /'oʊvərli/ *adv.* (before an adjective) too; very: *I'm not overly fond of pasta.* ♦ *We think you are being overly optimistic.*

o·ver·manned /,oʊvər'mænd/ *adj.* (of a company, office, etc.) having more workers than are needed **SYN OVERSTAFFED ANT UNDERMANNED ▶ o·ver·man·ning** /-'mænɪŋ/ *noun* [U]: *the problems of overmanning in industry*

o·ver·much /,oʊvər'mʌtʃ/ *adv.* (also **overly much**) (especially with a negative verb) too much; very much: *She didn't worry overmuch about it.*

o·ver·night *adv., adj.*

• **adv.** /,oʊvər'naɪt/ **1** during or for the night: *We stayed overnight in the city after the theater.* **2** suddenly or quickly: *Don't expect it to improve overnight.*

• **adj.** /'oʊvər,naɪt/ [only before noun] **1** happening during the night; for a night: *an overnight flight ♦ overnight accommodations ♦ She took only an overnight bag* (= containing the things needed for a night spent away from home). **2** happening suddenly or quickly: *The play was an overnight success.*

o·ver·op·ti·mis·tic /,oʊvər,ɑptə'mɪstɪk/ *adj.* **1** too confident that something will be successful: *I'm not overoptimistic about my chances of getting the job.* **2** showing more confidence that something will be successful than is justified by later events: *The sales forecasts turned out to be overoptimistic.*

o·ver·pass /'oʊvər,pæs/ *noun* a bridge that carries one road over another one ➔ compare UNDERPASS

o·ver·pay /,oʊvər'peɪ/ *verb* (o·ver·paid, o·ver·paid /-'peɪd/) [usually passive] ~ **sb** to pay someone too much; to pay someone more than their work is worth **ANT UNDERPAY ▶ o·ver·pay·ment** /-'peɪmənt/ *noun* [C, U]

o·ver·play /,oʊvər'pleɪ/ *verb* ~ **sth** to give too much importance to something **ANT UNDERPLAY**
IDM overplay your hand to spoil your chance of success by judging your position to be stronger than it really is

o·ver·pop·u·la·ted /,oʊvər'pɑpyə,leɪtəd/ *adj.* (of a country or city) with too many people living in it **▶ o·ver·pop·u·la·tion** /,oʊvər,pɑpyə'leɪʃn/ *noun* [U]: *the problems of overpopulation*

o·ver·pow·er /,oʊvər'paʊər/ *verb* **1** ~ **sb** to defeat or gain control over someone completely by using greater strength: *Police finally managed to overpower the gunman.* **2** ~ **sb/sth** to be so strong or great that it affects or disturbs someone or something seriously **SYN OVERWHELM**: *Her beauty overpowered him.* ♦ *The flavor of the garlic overpowered the meat.*

o·ver·pow·er·ing /,oʊvər'paʊərɪŋ/ *adj.* very strong or powerful: *an overpowering smell of fish ♦ an overpowering personality ♦ The heat was overpowering.* **▶ o·ver·pow·er·ing·ly** *adv.*

o·ver·priced /,oʊvər'praɪst/ *adj.* too expensive; costing more than it is worth ➔ thesaurus box at EXPENSIVE

o·ver·print /,oʊvər'prɪnt/ *verb* ~ **A (on B)** | ~ **B with A** to print something on a document, etc. that already has printing on it

o·ver·pro·duce /,oʊvərprə'dus/ *verb* [T, I] ~ **(sth)** to produce more of something than is wanted or needed **▶ o·ver·pro·duc·tion** /-prə'dʌkʃn/ *noun* [U]

o·ver·pro·tec·tive /,oʊvərprə'tɛktɪv/ *adj.* too anxious to protect someone from being hurt, in a way that restricts their freedom: *overprotective parents*

o·ver·qual·i·fied /,oʊvər'kwɑlə,faɪd/ *adj.* having more experience or training than is necessary for a particular job, so that people do not want to employ you

o·ver·ran pt of OVERRUN

o·ver·rate /,oʊvər'reɪt/ *verb* [usually passive] ~ **sb/sth** to have too high an opinion of someone or something; to put too high a value on someone or something: *In my opinion, that painting has been vastly overrated.* **ANT UNDERRATE**

o·ver·reach /,oʊvər'ritʃ/ *verb* [T, I] ~ **(yourself)** to fail by trying to achieve more than is possible: *In making these promises, the company had clearly overreached itself.*

o·ver·re·act /,oʊvərri'ækt/ *verb* [I] ~ **(to sth)** to react too strongly, especially to something unpleasant **▶ o·ver·re·ac·tion** /-ri'ækʃn/ *noun* [sing., U]

o·ver·ride *verb, noun*

• **verb** /,oʊvər'raɪd/ (o·ver·rode /-'roʊd/, o·ver·rid·den /-'rɪdn/) **1** ~ **sth** to use your authority to reject someone's decision, order, etc. **SYN OVERRULE**: *The chairman overrode the committee's objections and signed the agreement.* **2** ~ **sth** to be more important than something: *Considerations of safety override all other concerns.* **3** ~ **sth** to stop a process that happens automatically and control it yourself: *A special code is needed to override the time lock.*

• **noun** /'oʊvər,raɪd/ **1** an act of using your authority to reject someone's decisions, order, etc. **2** a system or piece of equipment that allows you to stop a process that happens automatically and control it yourself: *He used his override code to shut down security and enter the room.*

o·ver·rid·ing /,oʊvər'raɪdɪŋ/ *adj.* [only before noun] more important than anything else in a particular situation: *the overriding factor/consideration/concern ♦ Their overriding aim was to keep costs low.*

o·ver·ripe /,oʊvər'raɪp/ *adj.* too RIPE: *overripe fruit*

o·ver·rule /,oʊvər'rul/ *verb* [often passive] ~ **sb/sth** to change a decision or reject an idea from a position of greater power **SYN OVERRIDE**: *to overrule a decision/an objection ♦ The verdict was overruled by the Supreme Court.*

o·ver·run /,oʊvər'rʌn/ *verb* (o·ver·ran /-'ræn/, o·ver·run) **1** [T, often passive] ~ **sth** (especially of something bad or not wanted) to fill or spread over an area quickly, especially in large numbers: *The house was completely overrun with mice.* ♦ *Enemy soldiers had overrun the island.* **2** [I, T] to take more time or money than was intended: *Her lectures never overrun.* ♦ ~ **sth** *You've overrun your time by 10 minutes.* **▶ o·ver·run** /'oʊvər,rʌn/ *noun*: *a cost overrun*

o·ver·seas ♪ **AWL** /,oʊvər'siz/ *adj., adv.*

• **adj.** connected with foreign countries, especially those separated from your country by the ocean: *overseas development/markets/trade ♦ overseas students/visitors* ➔ compare HOME

• **adv.** to or in a foreign country, especially those separated from your country by the ocean **SYN ABROAD**: *to live/work/go overseas ♦ The product is sold both at home and overseas.*

o·ver·see /,oʊvər'si/ *verb* (o·ver·saw /-'sɔ/, o·ver·seen /-'sin/) ~ **sb/sth** to watch someone or something and make sure that a job or an activity is done correctly **SYN SUPERVISE**

o·ver·se·er /'oʊvər,siər; -,sɪr/ *noun* **1** (old-fashioned) a person whose job is to make sure that other workers do their work **2** a person or an organization that is responsible for making sure that a system is working as it should

o·ver·sell /,oʊvər'sɛl/ *verb* (o·ver·sold, o·ver·sold /-'soʊld/) [often passive] **1** ~ **sb/sth/yourself** to say that someone or something is better than they really are: *He has a tendency to oversell himself.* **2** ~ **sth** (business) to sell too much or more of something than is available: *The seats on the plane were oversold.*

o·ver·sen·si·tive /,oʊvər'sensətɪv/ *adj.* too easily upset or offended

o·ver·sexed /,oʊvər'sɛkst/ *adj.* having stronger sexual desire than is usual

o·ver·shad·ow /ˌouvərˈʃædou/ *verb* [often passive] **1** ~ sb/ sth to make someone or something seem less important or successful: *He had always been overshadowed by his elder sister.* **2** ~ sth to make an event less enjoyable than it should be **SYN** CLOUD: *News of the accident overshadowed the day's events.* **3** ~ sth to throw a shadow over something: *The garden is overshadowed by tall trees.*

o·ver·shoe /ˈouvərˌʃu/ *noun* a shoe worn over another shoe, especially in wet weather or to protect a floor

o·ver·shoot /ˌouvərˈʃut/ *verb* (o·ver·shot, o·ver·shot /-ˈʃɑt/) **1** [T, I] to go further than the place you intended to stop or turn: ~ sth *The aircraft overshot the runway.* ◆ ~ (sth) (by sth) *She had overshot by 20 yards.* **2** [T] ~ sth (by sth) to do more or to spend more money than you originally planned: *The department may overshoot its cash limit this year.*

o·ver·sight /ˈouvərˌsaɪt/ *noun* **1** [C, U] the fact of making a mistake because you forget to do something or you do not notice something **SYN** OMISSION: *I didn't mean to leave her name off the list; it was an oversight.* **2** [U] (*formal*) the state of being in charge of someone or something: *The committee has oversight of finance and general policy.*

o·ver·sim·pli·fy /ˌouvərˈsɪmpləˌfaɪ/ *verb* (o·ver·sim·pli·fies, o·ver·sim·pli·fy·ing, o·ver·sim·pli·fied, o·ver·sim·pli·fied) [T, I] ~ (sth) to describe a situation, a problem, etc. in a way that is too simple and ignores some of the facts: *It's easy to oversimplify the issues involved.* ◆ *an oversimplified view of human nature* ▶ **o·ver·sim·pli·fi·ca·tion** /ˌouvərˌsɪmpləfə- ˈkeɪʃn/ *noun* [C, usually sing., U]: *This is a gross oversimplification of the facts.* ⊃ compare SIMPLIFICATION

o·ver·sized /ˈouvərˌsaɪzd/ (also *less frequent* o·ver·size /ˈouvərˌsaɪz/) *adj.* bigger than the normal size; too big

o·ver·sleep /ˌouvərˈslip/ *verb* (o·ver·slept, o·ver·slept /-ˈslɛpt/) [I] to sleep longer than you intended: *I overslept and missed the bus.*

o·ver·spend /ˌouvərˈspɛnd/ *verb* (o·ver·spent, o·ver·spent /-ˈspɛnt/) [I, T] to spend too much money or more than you planned: ~ (on sth) *The company has overspent on marketing.* ◆ ~ sth *Many departments have overspent their budgets this year.* ▶ **o·ver·spent** /ˌouvərˈspɛnt/ *adj.*: *The organization is heavily overspent.*

o·ver·staffed /ˌouvərˈstæft/ *adj.* (of a company, office, etc.) having more workers than are needed **SYN** OVERMANNED **ANT** UNDERSTAFFED

o·ver·state /ˌouvərˈsteɪt/ *verb* ~ sth to say something in a way that makes it seem more important than it really is **SYN** EXAGGERATE: *He tends to overstate his case when talking politics.* ◆ *The seriousness of the crime cannot be overstated.* **ANT** UNDERSTATE ▶ **o·ver·state·ment** /ˈouvərˌsteɪtmənt/ *noun* [C, U]: *It is not an overstatement to say a crisis is imminent.*

o·ver·stay /ˌouvərˈsteɪ/ *verb* ~ sth to stay longer than the length of time you are expected or allowed to stay: *They overstayed their visa.* **IDM** see WELCOME

o·ver·step /ˌouvərˈstɛp/ *verb* (-pp-) ~ sth to go beyond what is normal or allowed: *to overstep your authority* ◆ *He tends to overstep the boundaries of good taste.* **IDM** overstep the mark/line to behave in a way that people think is not acceptable

o·ver·stock /ˌouvərˈstɑk/ *verb* **1** [T, I] ~ (sth) to buy or make more of something than you need or can sell **2** [T, I] ~ (sth) to put too many animals in a place where there is not enough room or food for them

o·ver·stretch /ˌouvərˈstrɛtʃ/ *verb* ~ sb/sth/yourself to do more than you are capable of; to make someone or something do more than they are capable of: *This will overstretch the prison service's resources.* ◆ *Credit cards can tempt you to overstretch yourself (= spend more money than you can afford).* ▶ **o·ver·stretched** *adj.*: *overstretched muscles* ◆ *overstretched services*

o·ver·sub·scribed /ˌouvərsəbˈskraɪbd/ *adj.* if an activity, service, etc. is oversubscribed, there are fewer places, tickets, etc. than the number of people who are asking for them

o·vert /ouˈvərt; ˈouvərt/ *adj.* [usually before noun] (*formal*) done in an open way and not secretly: *There was little overt support for the project.* ⊃ compare COVERT ▶ **o·vert·ly** *adv.*: *overtly political activities*

o·ver·take /ˌouvərˈteɪk/ *verb* (o·ver·took /-ˈtuk/, o·ver·tak·en /-ˈteɪkən/) **1** [T] ~ sb/sth to become greater in number, amount, or importance than something else **SYN** OUTSTRIP: *Nuclear energy may overtake oil as the main fuel.* ◆ *We must not let ourselves be overtaken by our competitors.* **2** [T, often passive] ~ sb/sth if something unpleasant overtakes a person, it unexpectedly starts to happen and to affect them: *The climbers were overtaken by bad weather.* ◆ *Sudden panic overtook her.* ◆ *Our original plan was overtaken by events (= the situation changed very rapidly) and we had to make a new one.* **3** [T, I] ~ (sb/sth) to go past a moving vehicle or person ahead of you because you are going faster than they are: *He pulled out to overtake a truck.* ◆ *It's dangerous to overtake on a curve.*

o·ver·tax /ˌouvərˈtæks/ *verb* **1** ~ sb/sth/yourself to do more than you are able or want to do; to make someone or something do more than they are able or want to do: *to overtax your strength* ◆ *Take it easy. Don't overtax yourself.* **2** ~ sb/sth to make a person or an organization pay too much tax

over-the-ˈcounter *adj.* [only before noun] (*abbr.* OTC) **1** (of drugs and medicines) that can be obtained without a PRESCRIPTION (= a written order from a doctor) **2** (*business*) (of stocks and shares) not appearing on an official STOCK EXCHANGE list

o·ver·throw *verb, noun*
- *verb* /ˌouvərˈθrou/ (o·ver·threw /-ˈθru/, o·ver·thrown /-ˈθroun/) ~ sb/sth to remove a leader or a government from a position of power by force: *The president was overthrown in a military coup.*
- *noun* /ˈouvərˌθrou/ [usually sing.] the act of taking power by force from a leader or government

o·ver·time /ˈouvərˌtaɪm/ *noun* [U] **1** time that you spend working at your job after you have worked the normal hours: *to do/work overtime* ◆ *overtime pay/earnings/hours* ◆ *The union announced a ban on overtime.* ⊃ collocations at JOB **2** the money someone earns for doing overtime: *They pay $150 a day plus overtime.* ⊃ thesaurus box at INCOME **3** (*sports*) a set period of time that is added to the end of a sports game, etc., if there is no winner at the end of the normal period
IDM be working overtime (*informal*) to be very active or too active: *There was nothing to worry about. It was just her imagination working overtime.*

o·ver·tired /ˌouvərˈtaɪərd/ *adj.* extremely tired, so that you become irritated easily

o·ver·tone /ˈouvərˌtoun/ *noun* [usually pl.] an attitude or an emotion that is suggested and is not expressed in a direct way: *There were political overtones to the point he was making.* ⊃ compare UNDERTONE

o·ver·took pt of OVERTAKE

o·ver·train /ˌouvərˈtreɪn/ *verb* [I] (of an ATHLETE) to train too hard or for too long

o·ver·ture /ˈouvərtʃər; -ˌtʃur/ *noun* **1** a piece of music written as an introduction to an OPERA or a BALLET: *Prokofiev's overture to "Romeo and Juliet"* **2** [usually pl.] ~ (to sb) a suggestion or an action by which someone tries to make friends, start a business relationship, have discussions, etc. with someone else: *He began making overtures to a number of investment banks.*

o·ver·turn /ˌouvərˈtərn/ *verb* **1** [I, T] if something overturns, or if someone overturns it, it turns upside down or on its side: *The car skidded and overturned.* ◆ ~ sth *He stood up quickly, overturning his chair.* **2** [T] ~ sth to officially decide that a legal decision etc. is not correct, and to make it no longer valid: *to overturn a decision/conviction/verdict* ◆ *His sentence was overturned by the appeals court.*

o·ver·use /ˌouvərˈyuz/ *verb* ~ sth to use something too much or too often: *"Nice" is a very overused word.* ▶ o·ver·use /ˌouvər'yus; 'ouvər,yus/ *noun* [U, sing.]

o·ver·val·ue /ˌouvər'vælyu/ *verb* [often passive] ~ sth to put too high a value on something: *Intelligence cannot be overvalued.* ◆ (*business*) *overvalued currencies/stocks*

o·ver·view /'ouvər,vyu/ *noun* a general description or an outline of something **SYN** SURVEY ⊃ **language bank at** ABOUT

o·ver·ween·ing /ˌouvər'winɪŋ/ *adj.* [only before noun] (*formal, disapproving*) showing too much confidence or pride **SYN** ARROGANT

o·ver·weight /ˌouvər'weɪt; 'ouvər,weɪt/ *adj.* **1** (of people) too heavy and fat: *She was only a few pounds overweight.* **ANT** UNDERWEIGHT ⊃ **collocations at** DIET **2** above an allowed weight: *overweight baggage*

o·ver·whelm /ˌouvər'wɛlm/ *verb* [often passive] **1** ~ sb to have such a strong emotional effect on someone that it is difficult for them to resist or know how to react **SYN** OVERCOME: *She was overwhelmed by feelings of guilt.* ◆ *The beauty of the landscape overwhelmed me.* **2** ~ sb to defeat someone completely **SYN** OVERPOWER: *The army was overwhelmed by the rebels.* **3** ~ sb to be so bad or so great that a person cannot deal with it; to give too much of a thing to a person: *We were overwhelmed by requests for information.* **4** ~ sb/sth (*literary*) (of water) to cover someone or something completely **SYN** FLOOD

o·ver·whelm·ing /ˌouvər'wɛlmɪŋ/ *adj.* very great or very strong; so powerful that you cannot resist it or decide how to react: *The evidence against him was overwhelming.* ◆ *The* **overwhelming majority** *of those present were in favor of the plan.* ◆ *an* **overwhelming sense of** *loss* ◆ *She had the almost overwhelming desire to tell him the truth.* ◆ *You may find it somewhat overwhelming at first.* ▶ o·ver·whelm·ing·ly *adv.*: *They voted overwhelmingly against the proposal.*

o·ver·win·ter /ˌouvər'wɪntər/ *verb* [I, T] ~ (sth) (of animals, birds, and plants) to spend the winter months in a place; to stay alive or to keep something alive during the winter ⊃ **compare** WINTER

o·ver·work *verb, noun*
• *verb* /ˌouvər'wɜrk/ [I, T] to work too hard; to make a person or an animal work too hard: *You look tired. Have you been overworking?* ◆ ~ sb/sth *She overworks her staff.*
• *noun* /'ouvər,wɜrk; ,ouvər'wɜrk/ [U] the fact of working too hard: *His illness was brought on by money worries and overwork.*

o·ver·worked /ˌouvər'wɜrkt/ *adj.* **1** made to work too hard or too much: *overworked nurses* **2** (of words or phrases) used too often so that the meaning or effect has become weaker

o·ver·write /ˌouvər'raɪt/ *verb* (o·ver·wrote /-'rout/, o·ver·writ·ten /-'rɪtn/) ~ sth (*computing*) to replace information on the screen or in a file by putting new information over it

o·ver·wrought /ˌouvər'rɔt/ *adj.* very worried and upset; excited in a nervous way **SYN** DISTRAUGHT

o·ver·zeal·ous /ˌouvər'zɛləs/ *adj.* showing too much energy or enthusiasm: *An overzealous fan ran onto the stage during the concert.*

o·vi·duct /'ouvə,dʌkt/ *noun* (*anatomy*) either of the tubes that carry eggs from the OVARY in women and female animals

o·vine /'ouvaɪn/ *adj.* (*technical*) relating to sheep

o·vip·a·rous /ou'vɪpərəs/ *adj.* (*biology*) (of an animal) producing eggs rather than live babies ⊃ **compare** OVOVI-VIPAROUS, VIVIPAROUS

o·void /'ouvɔɪd/ *adj.* (*formal*) shaped like an egg ▶ o·void *noun*

o·vo·vi·vip·a·rous /ˌouvouvaɪ'vɪpərəs/ *adj.* (*biology*) (of an animal) producing babies by means of eggs that are HATCHED inside the body of the parent, like some snakes ⊃ **compare** OVIPAROUS, VIVIPAROUS

ov·u·late /'avyə,leɪt/ *verb* [I] (of a woman or a female animal) to produce an egg (called an OVUM), from the OVARY

▶ ov·u·la·tion /ˌavyə'leɪʃn/ *noun* [U]: *methods of predicting ovulation*

ov·ule /'ouvyul; 'av-/ *noun* (*biology*) the part of the OVARY of a plant containing the female cell, which becomes the seed when it is FERTILIZED ⊃ **picture at** PLANT

o·vum /'ouvəm/ *noun* (pl. o·va /'ouvə/) (*biology*) a female cell of an animal or a plant that can develop into a young animal or plant when FERTILIZED

ow /au/ *exclamation* used to express sudden pain: *Ow! That hurt!*

owe 🔑 /ou/ *verb* (not used in the progressive tenses) **1** to have to pay someone for something that you have already received or return money that you have borrowed: ~ sb sth *She still owes her father $3,000.* ◆ (*figurative*) *I'm still owed three days' vacation.* ◆ ~ sb sth for sth *How much do I owe you for the groceries?* ◆ ~ sth (to sb) (for sth) *She still owes $3,000 to her father.* ◆ *The country owes billions of dollars to foreign creditors.* **2** to feel that you ought to do something for someone or give them something, especially because they have done something for you: ~ sth to sb *I owe a debt of gratitude to all my family.* ◆ *You* **owe it to** *your staff to be honest with them.* ◆ ~ sb sth *You owe me a favor!* ◆ *Thanks for sticking up for me—I* **owe you one** (= I owe you a favor). ◆ *I think you owe us an explanation.* ◆ *I think we're owed an apology.* **HELP** The passive is not used in this meaning except with a person as the subject: *An apology is owed to us.* **3** to exist or be successful because of the help or influence of someone or something: ~ sth to sb/sth *He owes his success to hard work.* ◆ *The play owes much to French tragedy.* ◆ *I owe everything to him.* ◆ ~ sb sth *I owe him everything.* ◆ *I knew that I owed the surgeon my life.* **4** ~ allegiance/loyalty/obedi-ence (to sb) (*formal*) to have to obey or be loyal to someone who is in a position of authority or power

ow·ing /'ouɪŋ/ *adj.* [not before noun] money that is owing has not been paid yet: *$100 is still owing on the loan.*

'owing to *prep.* because of: *The game was canceled owing to torrential rain.*

owl /aul/ *noun* a BIRD OF PREY (= a bird that kills other creatures for food) with large round eyes, that hunts at night. Owls are traditionally thought to be wise: *An owl hooted nearby.* ⊃ **picture at** ANIMAL ⊃ **see also** BARN OWL, NIGHT OWL

owl·et /'aulət/ *noun* a young owl

owl·ish /'aulɪʃ/ *adj.* looking like an owl, especially because you are wearing round glasses, and therefore seeming serious and intelligent ▶ owl·ish·ly *adv.*: *She blinked at them owlishly.*

own 🔑 /oun/ *adj., pron., verb*
• *adj., pron.* **1** used to emphasize that something belongs to or is connected with someone: *It was her own idea.* ◆ *I saw it with my own eyes* (= I didn't hear about it from someone else). ◆ *Is the car your own?* ◆ *Your day off is your own* (= you can spend it as you wish). ◆ *Our children are grown up and have children of their own.* ◆ *For reasons of his own* (= particular reasons that perhaps only he knew about), *he refused to join the club.* ◆ *The accident happened through no fault of her own.* ◆ *He wants to come into the business on his own terms.* ◆ *I need a room of my own.* ◆ *I have my very own room at last.* **HELP** Own cannot be used after an article: *I need my own room.* ◆ *I need an own room.* ◆ *It's good to have your own room.* ◆ *It's good to have the own room.* **2** done or produced by and for yourself: *She makes all her own clothes.* ◆ *He has to cook his own meals.*

IDM come into your/its own to have the opportunity to show how good or useful you are or something is: *When the traffic's this bad, a bicycle really comes into its own.* hold your own (against sb/sth) (in sth) to remain in a strong position when someone is attacking you, competing with you, etc.: *Business isn't good but we're managing to hold our own.* ◆ *She can hold her own against anybody in an argument.* ◆ *The patient is holding her own although she is still very sick.* (all) on your own **1** alone; without anyone else: *I'm all on* *my own today.* ◆ *She lives on her own.* **2** without help: *He did it on his own.* ⊃ more at DEVIL, MIND *n.*, SAKE[1], SOUND *n.*

● *verb* (not used in the progressive tenses) **1** [T] ~ **sth** to have something that belongs to you, especially because you have bought it: *Do you own your house or do you rent it?* ◆ *I don't own anything of any value.* ◆ *Most of the apartments are privately owned.* ◆ *an American-owned company* **2** [I, T] (*old-fashioned*) to admit that something is true: ~ **to sth/to doing sth** *He owned to a feeling of guilt.* ◆ ~ **(that)…** *She owned (that) she had been present.*
IDM behave/act as if you own the place| think you own the place (*disapproving*) to behave in a very confident way that annoys other people, for example by telling them what to do
PHRV own 'up (to sth/to doing sth) to admit that you are responsible for something bad or wrong **SYN** CONFESS: *I'm still waiting for someone to own up to the breakages.*

own·er 🔊 /'oʊnər/ *noun*
a person who owns something: *a dog/factory owner* ◆ *The painting has been returned to its rightful owner.* ◆ *He's now the proud owner of a new restaurant in Houston.* ⊃ see also HOMEOWNER, LANDOWNER

ˌowner-'occupied *adj.* (of a house, etc.) lived in by the owner rather than rented to someone else

ˌowner-'occupier *noun* a person who owns the house, apartment, etc. that they live in

own·er·ship /'oʊnərˌʃɪp/ *noun* [U] the fact of owning something: *a growth in home ownership* ◆ *Ownership of the land is currently being disputed.* ◆ *to be in joint/private/public ownership* ◆ *The restaurant is under new ownership.*

ˌown 'goal *noun* [usually sing.] (in SOCCER) a goal that is scored by mistake by a player against their own team

ox /ɑks/ *noun* (*pl.* ox·en /'ɑksn/) **1** a BULL (= a male cow) that has been CASTRATED (= had part of its sex organs removed), used, especially in the past, for pulling farm equipment, etc. ⊃ compare BULLOCK, STEER **2** (*old-fashioned*) any cow or BULL on a farm ⊃ see also CATTLE

oxbow

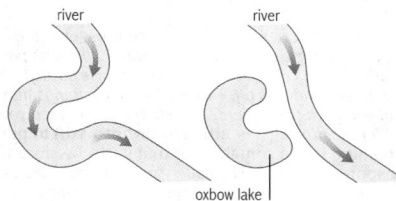

river   river

oxbow lake

ox·bow /'ɑksboʊ/ *noun* (*technical*) a bend in a river that almost forms a full circle; a lake that forms when this bend is separated from the river

ox·ford /'ɑksfərd/ *noun* **1** oxfords [pl.] leather shoes that fasten with LACES ⊃ picture at SHOE **2** [U] = OXFORD CLOTH: *an oxford shirt*

oxford ˌcloth (also **ox·ford**) *noun* [U] a type of heavy cotton cloth used mainly for making shirts

ox·i·dant /'ɑksədənt/ *noun* (*chemistry*) a substance that makes another substance combine with OXYGEN

ox·ide /'ɑksaɪd/ *noun* [U, C] (*chemistry*) a COMPOUND of OXYGEN and another chemical element: *iron oxide* ◆ *an oxide of tin*

ox·i·dize /'ɑksəˌdaɪz/ *verb* [T, I] ~ **(sth)** (*chemistry*) to remove one or more ELECTRON from a substance, or to combine or to make something combine with OXYGEN, especially when this causes metal to become covered with RUST ▶ **ox·i·da·tion** /ˌɑksə'deɪʃn/ *noun* [U] ⊃ compare REDUCE, REDUCTION

ox·tail /'ɑksteɪl/ *noun* [U, C] meat from the tail of a cow, used especially for making soup: *oxtail soup*

ox·y·a·cet·y·lene /ˌɑksiə'setlˌin; -ən/ *adj.* connected with a mixture of oxygen and ACETYLENE gas that produces a very hot flame, used especially for cutting or joining metal: *an oxyacetylene torch*

ox·y·gen /'ɑksɪdʒən/ *noun* [U] (*symb.* **O**) a chemical element. Oxygen is a gas that is present in air and water and is necessary for people, animals, and plants to live.

ox·y·gen·ate /'ɑksɪdʒəˌneɪt/ *verb* ~ **sth** (*technical*) to supply something with oxygen ▶ **ox·y·gen·a·tion** /ˌɑksɪdʒə'neɪʃn/ *noun* [U]

ox·y·gen·a·tor /'ɑksɪdʒəˌneɪtər/ *noun* **1** (*medical*) a device for putting oxygen into the blood **2** a water plant that puts oxygen into the water around it

'oxygen ˌbar *noun* a place where you can pay to breathe pure oxygen in order to improve your health and help you relax

'oxygen ˌmask *noun* a device placed over the nose and mouth through which a person can breathe OXYGEN, for example in an aircraft or a hospital

'oxygen ˌtent *noun* (*medical*) a structure like a tent that can be used to increase someone's supply of oxygen and help them to breathe

ox·y·mo·ron /ˌɑksɪ'mɔrɑn/ *noun* (*technical*) a phrase that combines two words that seem to be the opposite of each other, for example *a human robot*

oy /ɔɪ/ *exclamation* = OY VEY

o·yez (also **o·yes**) /'oʊyeɪ/ *exclamation* used by a TOWN CRIER or an officer in court to tell people to be quiet and pay attention

oys·ter /'ɔɪstər/ *noun* a large flat SHELLFISH. Some types of oysters can be eaten and others produce shiny white JEWELS called PEARLS.: *Oyster beds, on the mudflats, are a form of fish farming.* ⊃ picture at SHELLFISH **IDM** see WORLD

oys·ter·catch·er /'ɔɪstərˌkætʃər/ *noun* a black bird with long legs and a long red beak that lives near the coast and feeds on SHELLFISH

'oyster ˌmushroom *noun* a type of wide flat FUNGUS that grows on trees and that you can eat

oy vey /ˌɔɪ 'veɪ/ (also **oy**) *exclamation* used for showing disappointment or sadness (mainly by Yiddish speakers or Jewish people)

oz. *abbr.* .OUNCE(S): *4 oz. sugar*

o·zone /'oʊzoʊn/ *noun* [U] (*chemistry*) a poisonous gas with a strong smell that is a form of OXYGEN

ˌozone-'friendly *adj.* not containing substances that will damage the ozone layer

'ozone ˌhole *noun* an area in the ozone layer where the amount of ozone has been very much reduced so that harmful RADIATION from the sun can pass through it

'ozone ˌlayer *noun* [sing.] a layer of ozone high above the earth's surface that helps to protect the earth from harmful RADIATION from the sun ⊃ collocations at ENVIRONMENT

Pp

P also **p** /pi/ noun [C, U] (pl. **Ps**, **P's**, **p's** /piz/) the 16th letter of the English alphabet: *"Pizza" begins with (a) P/"P."* **IDM** see **MIND** v.

p *abbr.*
1 usually **p.** (pl. **pp.**) page: *See p. 34 and pp. 63-72.* **2** (*music*) quietly (from Italian "piano") ⟳ see also **P.&H.**

PA /ˌpi ˈeɪ/ *abbr.* **1** PUBLIC ADDRESS (SYSTEM): *Announcements were made over the PA.* **2** PHYSICIAN'S ASSISTANT **3** (in writing) Pennsylvania

Pa *abbr.* PASCAL

pa /pɑ/ *noun* (*old-fashioned, informal*) father: *I used to know your pa.*

p.a. *abbr.* per year (from Latin "per annum"): *an increase of 3% p.a.*

PAC /pæk/ *abbr.* POLITICAL ACTION COMMITTEE

pace¹ /peɪs/ *noun, verb* ⟳ see also **PACE²**
• *noun* **1** [sing., U] the speed at which someone or something walks, runs, or moves: *to set off at a steady/gentle/leisurely pace* ◆ *Congestion frequently reduces traffic to walking pace.* ◆ *The ball gathered pace as it rolled down the hill.* ◆ *The runners have noticeably quickened their pace.* **2** [sing., U] ~ **(of sth)** the speed at which something happens: *It is difficult to keep up with the rapid pace of change.* ◆ *We encourage all students to work at their own pace* (= at the speed which is best for them). ◆ *I prefer the relaxed pace of life in the country.* ◆ *rumors of corruption and scandal gathered pace* (= increased in number). **3** [C] an act of stepping once when walking or running; the distance traveled when doing this **SYN** STEP: *She took two paces forward.* **4** [U] the fact of something happening, changing, etc. quickly: *He gave up his job in advertising because he couldn't stand the pace.* ◆ *The novel lacks pace* (= it develops too slowly).
IDM **go through your paces| show your paces** to perform a particular activity in order to show other people what you are capable of doing **keep pace (with sb/sth)** to move, increase, change, etc. at the same speed as someone or something: *She found it hard to keep pace with him as he strode off.* ◆ *Until now, wage increases have always kept pace with inflation.* **off the pace** (in sports) behind the leader or the leading group in a race or a competition: *Mickelson is still three shots off the pace* (= in GOLF). **put sb/sth through their/its paces** to give someone or something a number of tasks to perform in order to see what they are capable of doing **set the pace 1** to do something at a particular speed or to a particular standard so that other people are then forced to copy it if they want to be successful: *The company is no longer setting the pace in the home computer market.* **2** (in a race) to run faster than the other people taking part, at a speed that they then try to copy ⟳ more at **FORCE** v., **SNAIL**
• *verb* **1** [I, T] to walk up and down in a small area many times, especially because you are feeling nervous or angry: + **adv./prep.** *She paced up and down outside the room.* ◆ ~ **sth** *Ted paced the floor restlessly.* **2** [T] ~ **sth** to set the speed at which something happens or develops: *He paced his game skillfully.* **3** [T] ~ **yourself** to find the right speed or rhythm for your work or an activity so that you have enough energy to do what you have to do: *He'll have to learn to pace himself in this job.*
PHR V **pace sth↔'off/'out** to measure the size of something by walking across it with regular steps

pa·ce² /'pɑtʃeɪ; 'pɑːkeɪ; 'peɪsi/ *prep.* (from Latin, *formal*) used before a person's name to express polite disagreement with what they have said: *The evidence suggests, pace Professor Jones, that…* (= Professor Jones has a different opinion). ⟳ see also **PACE¹**

pace·mak·er /'peɪsˌmeɪkər/ *noun* **1** an electronic device that is put inside a person's body to help their heart beat regularly **2** = PACESETTER (1) **3** = PACESETTER (2)

pace·set·ter /'peɪsˌsɛtər/ *noun* (also **pace·mak·er**) **1** a person or an animal that begins a race quickly so that the other people taking part will try to copy the speed and run a fast race: (*figurative*) *The big banks have been the pacesetters in developing the system.* **2** a person or team that is winning in a sports competition: *The local club is now only one point off the pacesetter.*

pa·chin·ko /pə'tʃɪŋkoʊ/ *noun* [U] (from *Japanese*) a Japanese form of PINBALL, in which you can win prizes

pach·y·derm /'pækɪˌdərm/ *noun* (*technical*) a type of animal with a very thick skin, for example, an ELEPHANT

pa·cif·ic /pə'sɪfɪk/ *adj.* [usually before noun] (*literary*) peaceful; loving peace

the Pa·cific 'Rim *noun* [sing.] the countries around the Pacific Ocean, especially the countries of eastern Asia, considered as an economic group

Pa'cific ˌtime *noun* [U] the standard time system that is used in the western part of the U.S. and Canada ⟳ compare ATLANTIC TIME, CENTRAL TIME, EASTERN TIME, MOUNTAIN TIME

pac·i·fi·er /'pæsəˌfaɪər/ *noun* a specially shaped rubber or plastic object for a baby to suck

pac·i·fism /'pæsəˌfɪzəm/ *noun* [U] the belief that war and violence are always wrong

pac·i·fist /'pæsəfɪst/ *noun* a person who believes in pacifism and who refuses to fight in a war ⟳ compare CONSCIENTIOUS OBJECTOR ▶ **pac·i·fist** *adj.* [usually before noun]: *pacifist beliefs*

pac·i·fy /'pæsəˌfaɪ/ *verb* (pac·i·fies, pac·i·fy·ing, pac·i·fied, pac·i·fied) **1** ~ **sb** to make someone who is angry or upset become calm and quiet **SYN** PLACATE: *The baby could not be pacified.* ◆ *The speech was designed to pacify the irate crowd.* **2** ~ **sth** to bring peace to an area where there is fighting or a war ▶ **pa·cif·i·ca·tion** /ˌpæsəfə'keɪʃn/ *noun* [U]

pack /pæk/ *verb, noun*
• *verb*
‣ **PUT INTO CONTAINER 1** [I, T] to put clothes, etc. into a bag in preparation for a trip away from home: *I haven't packed yet.* ◆ ~ **sth** *I haven't packed my suitcase yet.* ◆ *He packed a bag with a few things and was off.* ◆ *He packed a few things into a bag.* ◆ *Did you pack the camera?* ◆ ~ **sb sth** *I've packed you some food for the trip.* **2** [T] ~ **sth (up) (in/into sth)** to put something into a container so that it can be stored, transported, or sold: *The pottery was packed in boxes and shipped to the U.S.* ◆ *I carefully packed up the gifts.* **ANT** UNPACK
‣ **PROTECT 3** [T] ~ **sth (in/with sth)** to protect something that breaks easily by surrounding it with soft material: *The paintings were carefully packed in newspaper.*
‣ **PRESERVE FOOD 4** [T] ~ **sth (in sth)** to preserve food in a particular substance: *fish packed in ice*
‣ **FILL 5** [I, T] to fill something with a lot of people or things: + **adv./prep.** *We all packed together into one car.* ◆ ~ **sth (with sth)** *Fans packed the hall to see the band.* ⟳ see also PACKED
‣ **SNOW/SOIL 6** [T] ~ **sth (down)** to press something such as snow or soil to form a thick hard mass: *Pack the earth down around the plant.* ◆ *a patch of packed snow*
‣ **CARRY GUN 7** [T, I] ~ **(sth)** (*informal*) to carry a gun: *to pack a gun* ◆ *Is he packing?*
‣ **STORM 8** [T] ~ **sth** to have something: *A storm packing 75 mph winds swept across the area last night.*
IDM **pack a (powerful, real, etc.) punch** (*informal*) **1** (of a BOXER) to be capable of hitting someone very hard **2** to have a powerful effect on someone: *The advertising campaign packs quite a punch.* **pack your bags** (*informal*) to leave a person or place permanently, especially after a disagreement ⟳ more at SEND
PHR V **pack a'way** to be capable of being folded up small when it is not being used: *The tent packs away in a small bag.*

t **tea**   ţ **butter**   d **did**   k **cat**   g **got**   tʃ **chin**   dʒ **June**   f **fall**

,pack sth↔a'way to put something in a box, etc. when you have finished using it: *We packed away the summer clothes.* ,pack sb↔'in [no passive] (of plays, performers, etc.) to attract a lot of people to see it/them: *The show is still packing them in.* ,pack sth↔'in (*informal*) to stop doing something **SYN** GIVE UP: *She decided to pack in her job.* ,pack sb/sth 'in/ 'into sth 1 to do a lot of things in a limited period of time: *You seem to have packed a lot into your life!* 2 to put a lot of things or people into a limited space **SYN** CRAM IN: *They've managed to pack a lot of information into a very small book.* ,pack 'into sth to go somewhere in large numbers so that all available space is filled **SYN** CRAM: *Over 80,000 fans packed into the stadium to watch the final.* ➔ see also PACK (5) ,pack sb↔'off (to…) (*informal*) to send someone somewhere, especially because you do not want them with you: *My parents always packed me off to bed early.* ,pack 'up | ,pack sth↔'up to put your possessions into a bag, etc. before leaving a place: *Are you packing up already? It's only 4 o'clock.* ◆ *We arrived just as the musicians were packing up their instruments.*

● **noun**
> CONTAINER 1 a container, usually made of paper, that holds a number of the same things or an amount of something, ready to be sold: *a pack of cigarettes/gum* ◆ *You can buy the envelopes in packs of ten.* ➔ picture at PACKAGING ➔ compare PACKAGE, PACKET ➔ see also SIX-PACK
> SET 2 a set of different things that are supplied together for a particular purpose: *Send for your free information pack today.*
> THINGS TIED FOR CARRYING 3 a number of things that are wrapped or tied together, especially for carrying: *donkeys carrying packs of wool* ◆ (*figurative*) *Everything she told us is a pack of lies* (= a story that is completely false).
> LARGE BAG 4 a large bag that you carry on your back: *We passed a group of walkers, carrying huge packs.* ➔ see also BACKPACK
> OF ANIMALS 5 a group of animals that hunt together or are kept for hunting: *packs of savage dogs* ◆ *wolves hunting in packs* ◆ *a pack of hounds*
> OF PEOPLE 6 a group of similar people or things, especially one that you do not like or approve of: *We avoided a pack of journalists waiting outside.* ◆ *He's the leader of the pack.* 7 all the people who are behind the leaders in a race, competition, etc.: *measures aimed at keeping the company ahead of the pack*
> OF CARDS 8 = DECK n. (3)
> OF CUB SCOUTS/BROWNIES 9 an organized group of CUB SCOUTS or BROWNIES: *to join a Brownie pack*
> FOR WOUND 10 a hot or cold piece of soft material that absorbs liquid, used for treating a wound ➔ see also ICE PACK, MUD PACK

pack·age ✎ /'pækɪdʒ/ *noun, verb*
● **noun** 1 (*abbr.* pkg.) something that is wrapped in paper or put into a thick envelope so that it can be sent by mail, carried easily, or given as a present: *A large package has arrived for you.* ➔ compare PACK 2 a box, bag, etc. in which things are wrapped or packed; the contents of a box, etc.: *Check the list of ingredients on the side of the package.* ◆ *a package of hamburger buns* ➔ picture on page 1056 ➔ compare PACKET 3 (also 'package ,deal) a set of items or ideas that must be bought or accepted together: *a benefits package* ◆ *an aid package* ◆ *a package of measures to help small businesses* 4 (also 'software ,package) (*computing*) a set of related programs for a particular type of task, sold and used as a single unit: *The system came with a database software package.*
● **verb** (*often passive*) 1 to put something into a box, bag, etc. to be sold or transported: *~ sth We package our products in recyclable materials.* ◆ *~ sth up The orders were already packaged up, ready to be sent.* 2 *~ sb/sth (as sth)* to present someone or something in a particular way: *an attempt to package news as entertainment*

'package ,store *noun* (in some parts of the U.S.) a LIQUOR STORE

'package ,tour *noun* a vacation that is organized by a company at a fixed price and that includes the cost of travel, hotels, etc.

pack·ag·ing /'pækɪdʒɪŋ/ *noun* [U] 1 materials used to wrap or protect goods that are sold in stores: *Attractive packaging can help to sell products.* ➔ picture on page 1056 2 the process of wrapping goods: *His company offers a flexible packaging service for the food industry.*

'pack ,animal *noun* an animal used for carrying loads, for example a horse

packed /pækt/ *adj.* 1 extremely full of people **SYN** CROWDED: *The restaurant was packed.* ◆ *The show played to packed houses* (= large audiences). 2 containing a lot of a particular thing: *~ with sth The book is packed with information.* ◆ *-packed an information-packed book* 3 tightly *~* pressed closely together: *The birds' nests are lined with tightly packed leaves.* 4 [not before noun] (*informal*) having put everything you need into cases, boxes, etc. before you go somewhere: *I'm all packed and ready to go.*

pack·er /'pækər/ *noun* a person, machine, or company that puts food, goods, etc. into containers to be sold or sent to someone

pack·et /'pækət/ *noun* 1 a small paper container in which goods are packed for selling: *a packet of sugar/wildflower seed packets* ➔ picture at PACKAGING ➔ compare PACK n. (1), PACKAGE 2 a set of documents that are supplied together for a particular purpose: *a training packet* 3 (*computing*) a piece of information that forms part of a message sent through a computer network

'packet ,switching *noun* [U] (*computing*) a process in which data is separated into parts before being sent, and then joined together after it arrives

pack·horse /'pækhɔrs/ *noun* a horse that is used to carry heavy loads

'pack ice *noun* [U] a large mass of ice floating in the ocean, formed from smaller pieces that have frozen together

pack·ing /'pækɪŋ/ *noun* [U] 1 the act of putting your possessions, clothes, etc. into bags or boxes in order to take or send them somewhere: *Have you finished your packing?* 2 (also 'packing ma,terial) material used for wrapping around delicate objects in order to protect them, especially before sending them somewhere 3 the act or process of putting things such as food or commercial goods into containers so they can be sold: *a meat packing plant* ◆ *the handling, packing, and shipping of products*

'pack rat *noun* 1 a person who collects and stores things that they do not really need 2 a small N. American animal like a mouse that collects small sticks, etc. in its hole

pact /pækt/ *noun ~ (between A and B)* | *~ (with sb) (to do sth)* a formal agreement between two or more people, groups, or countries, especially one in which they agree to help each other: *a nonaggression pact* ◆ *They have made a pact with each other not to speak about their differences in public.* ◆ *a suicide pact* (= an agreement by two or more people to kill themselves at the same time)

pad /pæd/ *noun, verb*
● **verb** (-dd-)
> ADD SOFT MATERIAL 1 [T, often passive] *~ sth (with sth)* to put a layer of soft material in or on something in order to protect it, make it thicker, or change its shape: *All the sharp corners were padded with foam.* ◆ *a padded jacket* ◆ *a padded envelope* (= for sending delicate objects)
> WALK QUIETLY 2 [I] + adv./prep. to walk with quiet steps: *She padded across the room to the window.*
> BILLS 3 [T] *~ sth* to dishonestly add items to bills to obtain more money: *to pad bills/expense accounts*
PHR V ,pad sth↔'out 1 to put soft material into a piece of clothing in order to change its shape 2 to make something such as an article seem longer or more impressive by adding things that are unnecessary: *The report was padded out with extracts from previous documents.*

Packaging

packs

stick

a pack of gum

blister pack

packets

a packet of ketchup

tube

cap (also top)

Toothpaste

a tube of toothpaste

boxes

straw

Juice

a box of chocolates

juice box matchbox

Corn Flakes

rolls

a roll of toilet paper

tubs

spread

Ice Cream

a tub of ice cream

cartons

Soup

milk

Yogurt Cream

a carton of milk

bottles

cork

screw top

OLIVE OIL

BALSAMIC VINEGAR

KETCHUP

LEMONADE

a bottle of vinegar

jar

label

a jar of honey

tray

a tray of meat

stick

BUTTER

a stick of butter

cans

nozzle

lid

pull tab

BAKED BEANS

Sardines

TUNA

COLA

aerosol can a can of beans

tin

lid

a tin of cookies

package

a package of cookies

bags

Flour

a bag of potato chips

shopping bag

plastic bag

baskets

a basket of strawberries

shopping basket

shopping cart

h **h**at   m **m**an   n **n**o   ŋ si**ng**   l **l**eg   r **r**ed   y **y**es   w **w**et

● *noun*

> OF SOFT MATERIAL **1** a thick piece of soft material that is used, for example, for absorbing liquid, cleaning, or protecting something: *medicated cleansing pads for sensitive skin* ♦ *sanitary pads* (= that a woman uses during her PERIOD) ⊃ see also SHOULDER PAD

> OF PAPER **2** a number of pieces of paper for writing or drawing on, that are fastened together at one edge: *a sketch/writing pad* ⊃ see also NOTEPAD, SCRATCH PAD

> OF ANIMAL'S FOOT **3** the soft part under the foot of a cat, dog, etc.

> FOR CLEANING **4** a small piece of rough material used for cleaning pans, surfaces, etc.: *a scouring pad*

> FOR SPACECRAFT/HELICOPTER **5** a flat surface where a SPACECRAFT or a HELICOPTER takes off and lands ⊃ see also HELIPAD, LAUNCH PAD

> FOR PROTECTION **6** [usually pl.] a piece of thick material that you wear in some sports, for example football and HOCKEY, to protect your legs, elbows, etc.

> OF WATER PLANTS **7** the large flat leaf of some water plants, especially the WATER LILY: *floating lily pads*

> APARTMENT **8** [usually sing.] (*old-fashioned, informal*) the place where someone lives, especially an apartment ⊃ see also INK PAD, KEYPAD

ˌpadded ˈcell *noun* a room in a hospital for mentally ill people, with soft walls to prevent violent patients from injuring themselves

pad·ding /ˈpædɪŋ/ *noun* [U] **1** soft material that is placed inside something to make it more comfortable or to change its shape **2** words that are used to make a speech, piece of writing, etc. longer, but that do not contain any interesting information

pad·dle /ˈpædl/ *noun, verb*
● *noun* **1** [C] a short pole with a flat wide part at one or both ends, that you hold in both hands and use for moving a small boat, especially a CANOE, through water ⊃ picture at BOAT, SPORT ⊃ compare OAR **2** [C] a tool or part of a machine shaped like a paddle, especially one used for mixing food **3** [C] a BAT used for playing TABLE TENNIS **4** [C] a piece of wood with a handle, used for hitting children as a punishment ⊃ see also DOG-PADDLE **IDM** see CREEK
● *verb* **1** [I, T] to move a small boat through water using a paddle: (+ adv./prep.) *We paddled downstream for about a mile.* ♦ ~ *sth* (+ adv./prep.) *We paddled the canoe along the coast.* **2** [I] to swim with short movements of your hands or feet up and down **3** [T] ~ *sb/sth* to hit a child with a flat piece of wood as a punishment

pad·dle·boat /ˈpædlˌboʊt/ *noun* **1** a small pleasure boat that you move through the water by pushing PEDALS with your feet ⊃ picture at BOAT **2** = PADDLE WHEELER

ˈpaddle ˌwheel *noun* a large wheel on a boat that has boards around its outer edge and is driven by steam to move the boat through the water ⊃ picture at BOAT

ˈpaddle ˌwheeler (also pad·dle·boat) *noun* an old-fashioned type of boat driven by steam and moved forward by a large wheel or wheels at the side

pad·dock /ˈpædək/ *noun* **1** a small field in which horses are kept **2** (in horse racing or auto racing) an area where horses or cars are taken before a race and shown to the public

pad·dy /ˈpædi/ *noun* (*pl.* pad·dies) (also ˈpaddy ˌfield) a field in which rice is grown: *a rice paddy*

ˈpaddy ˌwagon *noun* (*informal*) = PATROL WAGON

pad·lock /ˈpædlɑk/ *noun, verb*
● *noun* a type of lock that is used to fasten two things together or to fasten one thing to another. Padlocks are used with chains on gates, etc.
● *verb* to lock something with

padlock

key

a padlock: ~ *sth to sth She always padlocked her bike to the railings.* ♦ ~ *sth The doors were padlocked.*

pa·dre /ˈpɑdreɪ/ *noun* (often used as a form of address) a priest, or other Christian minister, especially in the armed forces ⊃ compare CHAPLAIN

pae·an /ˈpiən/ *noun* (*literary*) a song of praise or victory

pa·el·la /pɑˈeɪjə; -ˈeɪlyə/ *noun* [U, C] a Spanish dish of rice, chicken, fish, and vegetables, cooked and served in a large shallow pan

pa·gan /ˈpeɪɡən/ *noun* (often *disapproving*) **1** a person who holds religious beliefs that are not part of any of the world's main religions **2** used in the past by Christians to describe a person who did not believe in Christianity ▶ pa·gan *adj.*: *a pagan festival* pa·gan·ism /ˈpeɪɡəˌnɪzəm/ *noun* [U]

page 🔑 /peɪdʒ/ *noun, verb*
● *noun* **1** (*abbr.* p.) one side or both sides of a sheet of paper in a book, magazine, etc.: *Turn to page 64.* ♦ *Someone has torn a page out of this book.* ♦ *a blank/new page* ♦ *the sports/financial pages of the newspaper* ♦ *on the opposite/facing page* ♦ *over the page* (= on the next page) ⊃ see also FRONT PAGE, FULL-PAGE, YELLOW PAGES **2** a section of data or information that can be shown on a computer screen at any one time ⊃ see also HOME PAGE **3** (*literary*) an important event or period of history: *a glorious page of Arab history* **4** = PAGEBOY **5** a student who works as an assistant to a member of the U.S. Congress **6** (in the Middle Ages) a boy or young man who worked for a KNIGHT while training to be a knight himself
IDM on the same page if two or more people or groups are **on the same page**, they agree about what they are trying to achieve **turn the page** to begin doing things in a different way and thinking in a more positive way after a period of difficulties ⊃ more at BOOK *n.*, PRINT *v.*
● *verb* **1** ~ *sb* to call someone's name over a PUBLIC ADDRESS SYSTEM in order to find them and give them a message: *Why don't you have him paged at the airport?* **2** ~ *sb* to contact someone by sending a message to their PAGER: *Page Dr. Green immediately.*
PHR V ˌpage ˈthrough sth to quickly turn the pages of a book, magazine, etc. and look at them without reading them carefully or in detail **SYN** FLICK THROUGH STH, LEAF THROUGH STH

pag·eant /ˈpædʒənt/ *noun* **1** a competition for young women in which their beauty, personal qualities, and skills are judged: *a beauty pageant* ⊃ compare BEAUTY CONTEST **2** a public entertainment in which people dress in historical COSTUME and give performances of scenes from history **3** ~ (of sth) (*literary*) something that is considered as a series of interesting and different events: *life's rich pageant*

pag·eant·ry /ˈpædʒəntri/ *noun* [U] impressive and exciting events and ceremonies involving a lot of people wearing special clothes: *the pageantry of royal occasions*

page·boy /ˈpeɪdʒbɔɪ/ *noun* **1** a HAIRSTYLE for women in which the hair reaches to the shoulders and is turned under at the ends **2** (also page) (*old-fashioned*) a boy or young man, usually in uniform, employed in a hotel to open doors, deliver messages for people, etc.

pag·er /ˈpeɪdʒər/ *noun* a small electronic device that you carry around with you and that shows a message or lets you know when someone is trying to contact you, for example by making a sound ⊃ see also BEEPER

ˈpage-ˌturner *noun* (*informal*) a book that is very exciting

ˈpage view *noun* [C, sing.] (*business*) one visit to a single page on a Web site: *a surge in page views*

pag·i·nate /ˈpædʒəˌneɪt/ *verb* ~ *sth* (*technical*) to give a number to each page of a book, piece of writing, etc.

pag·i·na·tion /ˌpædʒəˈneɪʃn/ *noun* [U] (*technical*) the process of giving a page number to each page of a book; the page numbers given

pa·go·da /pəˈɡoʊdə/ *noun* a TEMPLE (= religious building) in S. or E. Asia in the form of a tall tower with several levels, each of which has its own roof that extends beyond the walls ➲ picture at BUILDING

p.&h. /ˌpiː ən ˈeɪtʃ/ *abbr.* postage and handling

paid /peɪd/ *adj., verb*

● *adj.* [usually before noun] **1** (of work, etc.) for which people receive money: *Neither of them is currently in paid employment.* ◆ *a well-paid job* **2** (of a person) receiving money for doing work: *Men still outnumber women in the paid workforce.* ◆ *a poorly paid teacher* **ANT** UNPAID
  IDM **put paid to sth** (*informal*) to stop or destroy something, especially what someone plans or wants to do

● *verb* pt, pp of PAY

paid-up *adj.* [only before noun] having paid all the money necessary to be a member of a club or an organization: *a fully paid-up member*

pail /peɪl/ *noun* = BUCKET

pail·ful /ˈpeɪlfʊl/ *noun* = BUCKET (3)

pain 🖋 /peɪn/ *noun, verb*

● *noun* ➲ see also PAINS **1** [U, C] the feelings that you have in your body when you have been hurt or when you are sick: *a cry of pain* ◆ *She was clearly in a lot of pain.* ◆ *He felt a sharp pain in his knee.* ◆ *patients suffering from acute back pain* ◆ *stomach/chest pains* ◆ *You get more aches and pains as you get older.* ◆ *The booklet contains information on pain relief during labor.* ◆ *This cream should help to relieve the pain.* ➲ see also GROWING PAINS **2** [U, C] mental or emotional suffering: *the pain of separation* ◆ *I never meant to cause her pain.* ◆ *the pleasures and pains of growing old*
  IDM **no pain, no gain** (*saying*) used to say that you need to suffer if you want to achieve something **on/under pain of sth** (*formal*) with the threat of having something done to you as a punishment if you do not obey: *They were required to cut pollution levels, on pain of a $10,000 fine if they disobeyed.* **a pain in the butt/neck** (*informal*) a person or thing that is very annoying

● *verb* (not used in the progressive tenses) (*formal*) to cause someone pain or make them unhappy **SYN** HURT: *~ sb She was deeply pained by the accusation.* ◆ (*old use*) *The wound still pained him occasionally.* ◆ **it pains sb to do sth** *It pains me to see you like this.* ◆ **it pains sb that…** *It pained him that she would not acknowledge him.*

pain barrier *noun* [usually sing.] the moment at which someone doing hard physical activity feels the greatest pain, after which the pain becomes less: *He broke through the pain barrier at 15 miles and went on to win his first marathon.*

pained /peɪnd/ *adj.* showing that someone is feeling annoyed or upset: *a pained expression/voice*

pain·ful 🖋 /ˈpeɪnfl/ *adj.*
  1 causing you pain: *Is your back still painful?* ◆ *a painful death* ◆ *My ankle is still too painful to walk on.* **2** ~ (for sb) (to do sth) | ~ (doing sth) causing you to feel upset or embarrassed: *a painful experience/memory* ◆ *Their efforts were painful to watch.* **3** unpleasant or difficult to do **SYN** TRYING: *Applying for jobs can be a long and painful process.*

THESAURUS

painful

sore ◆ raw ◆ inflamed ◆ infected ◆ excruciating ◆ burning ◆ itchy

These words all describe something that causes you physical pain.

painful causing you physical pain **NOTE** Painful can describe a part of the body, an illness, an injury, a treatment, or a death: *Is your knee still painful?* ◆ *a series of painful injections* ◆ *a slow and painful death*

sore (of a part of the body) painful and often red, especially because of infection or being used too

---

much: *a sore throat* ◆ *Their feet were sore after hours of walking.*

raw (of a part of the body) red and painful, for example because of an infection or because the skin has been damaged: *The skin on her heels had been rubbed raw.*

inflamed (of a part of the body) painful, swollen, and hot because of an infection or injury: *If your tonsils become inflamed, you should see a doctor.*

infected containing harmful bacteria: *The wound became infected.*

excruciating extremely painful **NOTE** Excruciating can describe feelings, treatments, or death but not parts of the body: *an excruciating throat/back/knee.*

burning painful and giving a feeling of being very hot: *She felt a burning sensation in her throat.*

itchy giving an uncomfortable feeling on your skin that makes you want to scratch; having this feeling: *an itchy rash* ◆ *I feel itchy all over.*

PATTERNS
  ▪ sore/inflamed/itchy **eyes**
  ▪ raw/inflamed/itchy **skin**
  ▪ a painful/an excruciating **death**
  ▪ a painful/burning **sensation**
  ▪ excruciating/burning **pain**

---

pain·ful·ly /ˈpeɪnfəli/ *adv.* **1** extremely, and in a way that makes you feel annoyed, upset, etc.: *Their son was painfully shy.* ◆ *The dog was painfully thin.* ◆ *He was painfully aware of his lack of experience.* ◆ *Progress has been painfully slow.* **2** in a way that causes you physical or emotional pain: *He banged his knee painfully against the desk.* **3** with a lot of effort and difficulty: *painfully acquired experience*

pain·kil·ler /ˈpeɪnˌkɪlər/ *noun* a drug that reduces pain: *She's on (= taking) painkillers.* ▶ **pain·kill·ing** *adj.*: *painkilling drugs/injections*

pain·less /ˈpeɪnləs/ *adj.* **1** causing you no pain: *a painless death* ◆ *The treatment is painless.* **2** not unpleasant or difficult to do: *The interview was relatively painless.* ▶ **pain·less·ly** *adv.*

pains /peɪnz/ *noun* [pl.]
  IDM **be at pains to do sth** to put a lot of effort into doing something correctly: *She was at great pains to stress the advantages of the new system.* **take (great) pains (to do sth)** | **go to great pains (to do sth)** to put a lot of effort into doing something: *The couple went to great pains to keep their plans secret.* **take (great) pains with/over sth** to do something very carefully: *He always takes great pains with his lectures.*

pains·tak·ing /ˈpeɪnˌsteɪkɪŋ/ *adj.* [usually before noun] needing a lot of care, effort, and attention to detail **SYN** THOROUGH: *painstaking research* ◆ *The event had been planned with painstaking attention to detail.* ▶ **pains·tak·ing·ly** *adv.*

paint 🖋 /peɪnt/ *noun, verb*

● *noun* **1** [U] a liquid that is put on surfaces to give them a particular color; a layer of this liquid when it has dried on a surface: *white paint* ◆ *gloss/mat/acrylic paint* ◆ *The woodwork has recently been given a fresh coat of paint.* ◆ *Wet paint!* (= used as a sign) ◆ *The paint is starting to peel off.* ➲ see also GREASEPAINT, OIL PAINT, WARPAINT **2 paints** [pl.] tubes or blocks of paint used for painting pictures: *oil paints*

● *verb* **1** [T, I] ~ sth (with sth) to cover a surface or object with paint: *~ (sth) We've had the house painted.* ◆ *Paint the shed with weather-resistant paint.* ◆ *a brightly painted barge* ◆ *~ sth + adj./noun The walls were painted yellow.* ➲ collocations at DECORATE **2** [T, I] to make a picture or design using paints: *~ sth/sb to paint portraits* ◆ *A friend painted the children for me* (= painted a picture of the children). ◆ *~ sth on sth Slogans had been painted on the walls.* ◆ *~ (in sth) She paints in oils.* ◆ *My mother paints well.* ➲ collocations

---

at ART **3** [T] to give a particular impression of someone or something **SYN** PORTRAY: ~ sb/sth as sth *The article paints them as a bunch of petty criminals.* ◆ ~ sb/sth in… *The documentary painted her in a bad light.* **4** [T] ~ sth to put colored makeup on your nails, lips, etc.

IDM **paint a (grim, gloomy, rosy, etc.) picture of sb/sth** to describe something in a particular way; to give a particular impression of someone or something: *The report paints a vivid picture of life in the city.* ◆ *Journalists paint a grim picture of conditions in the camps.* **paint the town (red)** (*informal*) to go to a lot of different bars, clubs, etc. and enjoy yourself **paint sth with a broad brush** to describe something in a general way, ignoring the details ⊃ more at BLACK *adj.*

PHR V ,paint sth↔'out to cover part of a picture, sign, etc. with another layer of paint ,paint 'over sth to cover something with a layer of paint: *We painted over the dirty marks on the wall.*

paint·ball /ˈpeɪntbɔl/ *noun* [U] a game in which people shoot balls of paint at each other

paint·box /ˈpeɪntbɑks/ *noun* a box containing a set of paints

paint·brush /ˈpeɪntbrʌʃ/ *noun* a brush that is used for painting ⊃ picture at CLEANING

,**paint-by-'numbers** *adj.* [only before noun] **1** (of pictures) having sections with different numbers showing which colors should be used to fill them in **2** (*disapproving*) used to describe something that is produced without using the imagination: *He accused the government of relying on paint-by-numbers policies.*

,**paint chip** *noun* **1** a small piece of paint that has broken off something or the small area where the paint has come off **2** a strip of card with samples of paint in different colors, provided in stores to help customers decide which paint to buy

,**painted 'lady** *noun* a BUTTERFLY that has orange-brown wings with darker marks on them

paint·er ✿ /ˈpeɪntər/ *noun*
1 a person whose job is painting buildings, walls, etc.: *He works as a painter and decorator.* **2** an artist who paints pictures: *a famous painter* ◆ *a portrait/landscape painter* **3** a rope fastened to the front of a boat, used for tying it to a post, ship, etc.

paint·er·ly /ˈpeɪntərli/ *adj.* typical of artists or painting **SYN** ARTISTIC

paint·ing ✿ /ˈpeɪntɪŋ/ *noun*
1 [C] a picture that has been painted: *a collection of paintings by American artists* ◆ *cave paintings* ⊃ see also OIL PAINTING ⊃ thesaurus box at PICTURE ⊃ collocations at ART **2** [U] the act or art of using paint to produce pictures: *Her hobbies include music and painting.* ⊃ picture at HOBBY **3** [U] the act of putting paint onto the surface of objects, walls, etc.: *painting and decorating*

,**paint ,stripper** *noun* [U] a liquid used to remove old paint from surfaces

pair ✿ /pɛr/ *noun, verb*
● *noun*
▶ TWO THINGS THE SAME **1** two things of the same type, especially when they are used or worn together: *a pair of gloves/shoes/earrings, etc.* ◆ *a huge pair of eyes* ◆ *The vase is one of a matching pair.*
▶ TWO PARTS JOINED **2** an object consisting of two parts that are joined together: *a pair of pants/jeans, etc.* ◆ *a pair of glasses/binoculars/scissors, etc.* **HELP** A plural verb is sometimes used with **pair** in the singular in senses 1 and 2. In informal English some people use **pair** as a plural form: *three pair of shoes.* This is not considered correct in written English.
▶ TWO PEOPLE **3** two people who are doing something together or who have a particular relationship: *Get pairs of students to act out the dialogue in front of the class.* ◆ (*informal*) *I've had enough of the pair of you!* **HELP** A plural verb is

usually used: *A pair of children were kicking a ball around.* ◆ *The pair are planning a trip to India together.*
▶ TWO ANIMALS/BIRDS **4** two animals or birds of the same type that are breeding together: *a breeding pair* ◆ *a pair of swans* ⊃ see also AU PAIR
IDM **a pair of hands** (*informal*) a person who can do, or is doing, a job: *We need an extra pair of hands if we're going to finish on time.* ◆ *Colleagues regard him as a safe pair of hands* (= someone who can be relied on to do a job well). **in pairs** in groups of two objects or people: *Students worked in pairs on the project.* **I only have one pair of hands** (*informal*) used to say that you are too busy to do anything else
● *verb*
▶ MAKE GROUPS OF TWO **1** [T, usually passive] to put people or things into groups of two: ~ A with B *Each blind student was paired with a sighted student.* ◆ ~ A and B (together) *All the shoes on the floor were neatly paired.*
▶ OF ANIMALS/BIRDS **2** [I] (*technical*) to come together in order to breed: *Many of the species pair for life.*
PHR V ,pair 'off (with sb) | ,pair sb↔'off (with sb) to come together, especially in order to have a romantic relationship; to bring two people together for this purpose: *It seemed that all her friends were pairing off.* ◆ *He's always trying to pair me off with his cousin.* ,pair 'up (with sb) | ,pair sb↔'up (with sb) to come together or to bring two people together to work, play a game, etc.

pair·ing /ˈpɛrɪŋ/ *noun* [C] two people or things that work together or are placed together; the act of placing them together: *Tonight they take on a Chinese pairing in their bid to reach the final tomorrow.*

pais·ley /ˈpeɪzli/ *noun* [U] a detailed pattern of curved shapes that look like feathers, used especially on cloth: *a paisley tie*

Pai·ute /ˈpaɪut/ *noun* (*pl.* Pai·ute or Pai·utes) a member of a Native American people, many of whom live in the southwestern U.S.

pa·ja·mas /pəˈdʒɑməz; -ˈdʒæ-/ (also *informal* jam·mies) *noun* [pl.] a loose jacket and pants worn in bed: *a pair of pajamas* ⊃ picture at CLOTHES **IDM** see CAT ▶ **pa·ja·ma** *adj.* [only before noun]: *pajama bottoms*

pal /pæl/ *noun, verb*
● *noun* **1** (*informal*, becoming *old-fashioned*) a friend: *We've been pals for years.* ⊃ see also PEN PAL **2** (*informal*) used to address a man in an unfriendly way: *If I were you, pal, I'd stay away from her!* ▶ **pal·ly** /ˈpæli/ *adj.*: *I got very pally* (= friendly) *with him.*
● *verb* (-ll-)
PHR V ,pal a'round (with sb) (*informal*) to do things with someone as a friend: *I palled around with him and his sister at school.*

pal·ace ✿ /ˈpæləs/ *noun*
1 [C] the official home of a king, queen, president, etc.: *Buckingham Palace* ◆ *the royal/presidential palace* ⊃ picture at BUILDING **2** [C] any large impressive house: *The Old Town has a whole collection of churches, palaces, and mosques.* **3** [C] (*old-fashioned*) (sometimes used in the names of buildings) a large public building, such as a hotel or movie theater: *the Palace Hotel*

,**palace 'coup** (also ,palace revo'lution) *noun* a situation in which a ruler or leader has their power taken away from them by someone within the same party, etc.

pal·at·a·ble /ˈpælətəbl/ *adj.* **1** (of food or drink) having a pleasant or acceptable taste **2** ~ (to sb) pleasant or acceptable to someone: *Some of the dialogue has been changed to make it more palatable to an American audience.* **ANT** UNPALATABLE

pal·a·tal /ˈpælətl/ *noun* (*phonetics*) a speech sound made by placing the tongue against or near the hard palate of the mouth, for example /j/ at the beginning of *yes* ▶ **pal·a·tal** *adj.*

pal·a·tal·ize /ˈpælətlˌaɪz/ *verb* ~ sth (*phonetics*) to make a speech sound by putting your tongue against or near your hard palate ▶ **pal·a·tal·i·za·tion** /ˌpælətlˌəˈzeɪʃn/ *noun* [U]

pal·ate /ˈpælət/ *noun* **1** the top part of the inside of the mouth: *the **hard/soft palate** (= the hard/soft part at the front/back of the palate)* ➔ see also CLEFT PALATE **2** [usually sing.] the ability to recognize and/or enjoy good food and drink: *a menu to tempt even the most **jaded palate***

pa·la·tial /pəˈleɪʃl/ *adj.* [usually before noun] (of a room or building) very large and impressive, like a palace **SYN** SPLENDID

pa·lat·i·nate /pəˈlætnˌət/ *noun* **1** [C] the area ruled by a Count Palatine (= a ruler with the power of a king or queen) **2 the Palatinate** [sing.] the land of the German Empire that was ruled over by the Count Palatine of the Rhine

pal·a·tine /ˈpæləˌtaɪn/ *adj.* [only before noun] **1** (of an official, etc. in the past) having the power in a particular area that a king or queen usually has **2** (of an area of land) ruled over by someone who has the power of a king or queen

pa·lav·er /pəˈlævər, -ˈlɑ-/ *noun* (*informal*) [U] talk that does not have any meaning; nonsense: *He's talking palaver.*

pa·laz·zo pants /pəˈlɑtsoʊ ˌpænts/ *noun* [pl.] women's pants with wide loose legs

pale 🖉 /peɪl/ *adj., verb, noun*
- *adj.* (**pal·er, pal·est**) **1** (of a person, their face, etc.) having skin that is almost white; having skin that is whiter than usual because of illness, a strong emotion, etc.: *a pale complexion ♦ pale with fear ♦ to go/turn pale ♦ You look pale. Are you OK? ♦ The ordeal left her looking pale and drawn.* **2** light in color; containing a lot of white: *pale blue eyes ♦ a paler shade of green ♦ a pale sky* **ANT** DARK, DEEP **3** (of light) not strong or bright: *the cold pale light of dawn* ➔ see also PALLID, PALLOR ▶ **pale·ly** /ˈpeɪlli/ *adv.*: *Mark stared palely (= with a pale face) at his plate.* **pale·ness** *noun* [U]
- *verb* [I] **~ (at sth)** to become paler than usual: *She (= her face) paled visibly at the sight of the police car. ♦ The blue of the sky paled to a light gray.* **IDM** **pale beside/next to sth| pale in/by comparison (with/to sth)| pale into insignificance** to seem less important when compared with something else: *Last year's riots pale in comparison with this latest outburst of violence.*
- *noun* **IDM** **beyond the pale** considered by most people to be unacceptable or unreasonable: *His remarks were clearly beyond the pale.*

paleo- /ˈpeɪlioʊ/ *combining form* (in nouns, adjectives, and adverbs) connected with ancient times

pa·le·og·ra·phy /ˌpeɪliˈɑgrəfi/ *noun* [U] the study of ancient writing systems ▶ **pa·le·og·ra·pher** /-fər/ *noun*

Pa·le·o·lith·ic /ˌpeɪliəˈlɪθɪk/ *adj.* from or connected with the early part of the Stone Age

pa·le·on·tol·o·gist /ˌpeɪliənˈtɑlədʒɪst/ *noun* a person who studies FOSSILS

pa·le·on·tol·o·gy /ˌpeɪliənˈtɑlədʒi/ *noun* [U] the study of FOSSILS (= the remains of animals or plants in rocks) as a guide to the history of life on earth

pal·ette /ˈpælət/ *noun* **1** a thin board with a hole in it for the thumb to go through, used by an artist for mixing colors on when painting ➔ picture at HOBBY **2** [usually sing.] (*technical*) the colors used by a particular artist: *Greens and browns are typical of Ribera's palette.*

ˈpalette ˌknife *noun* a knife with a blade that bends easily and has a round end, used by artists

pal·i·mo·ny /ˈpæləˌmoʊni/ *noun* [U] (*informal*) money that a court orders someone to pay regularly to a former partner when they have lived together without being married ➔ compare ALIMONY

pal·imp·sest /ˈpæləmpˌsest/ *noun* **1** an ancient document from which some or all of the original text has been removed and replaced by a new text **2** (*formal*) something that has many different layers of meaning or detail

pal·in·drome /ˈpælənˌdroʊm/ *noun* a word or phrase that reads the same backward as forward, for example *madam* or *nurses run*

pal·ing /ˈpeɪlɪŋ/ *noun* [C, usually pl., U] a metal or wooden post that is pointed at the top; a fence made of these posts

pal·i·sade /ˌpæləˈseɪd/ *noun* **1** a fence made of strong wooden or metal posts that are pointed at the top, especially used to protect a building in the past **2 pal·i·sades** [pl.] a line of high steep CLIFFS, especially along a river or by the ocean

pall /pɔl/ *noun, verb*
- *noun* **1** [usually sing.] **~ of sth** a thick dark cloud of something: *a pall of smoke/dust ♦* (*figurative*) *News of her death cast a pall over the event.* **2** a cloth spread over a COFFIN (= a box used for burying a dead person in)
- *verb* [I] (not used in the progressive tenses) **~ (on sb)** to become less interesting to someone over a period of time because they have done or seen it too much: *Even the impressive scenery began to pall on me after a few hundred miles.*

pal·la·di·um /pəˈleɪdiəm/ *noun* [U] (*symb.* **Pd**) a chemical element. Palladium is a rare silver-white metal that looks like PLATINUM.

pall·bear·er /ˈpɔlˌberər/ *noun* a person who walks beside or helps to carry the COFFIN at a funeral

pal·let /ˈpælət/ *noun* **1** a heavy wooden or metal base that can be used for moving or storing goods **2** a cloth bag filled with STRAW, used for sleeping on

pal·li·ate /ˈpæliˌeɪt/ *verb* **~ sth** (*formal*) to make a disease or an illness less painful or unpleasant without curing it

pal·li·a·tive /ˈpæliətɪv/ *noun* **1** (*medical*) a medicine or medical treatment that reduces pain without curing its cause **2** (*formal*, usually *disapproving*) an action, a decision, etc. that is designed to make a difficult situation seem better without actually solving the cause of the problems ▶ **pal·li·a·tive** *adj.* [usually before noun]: *palliative treatment ♦ short-term palliative measures*

pal·lid /ˈpæləd/ *adj.* **1** (of a person, their face, etc.) pale, especially because of illness: *a pallid complexion* **2** (of colors or light) not strong or bright, and therefore not attractive: *a pallid sky*

pal·lor /ˈpælər/ *noun* [U] pale coloring of the face, especially because of illness or fear: *Her cheeks had an unhealthy pallor.*

pal·ly *adj.* ➔ PAL

palm /pɑm; pɑlm/ *noun, verb*
- *noun* **1** the inner surface of the hand between the wrist and the fingers: *He held the bird gently in **the palm of his hand**. ♦ sweaty palms ♦ to read someone's palm (= to say what you think will happen to someone by looking at the lines on their palm)* ➔ picture at BODY **2** (also **ˈpalm tree**) a straight tree with a mass of long leaves at the top, growing in tropical countries. There are several types of palm trees, some of which produce fruit: *a date palm ♦ a coconut palm ♦ palm leaves/fronds/groves* ➔ picture at TREE **IDM** **have sb in the palm of your hand** to have complete control or influence over someone ➔ more at CROSS, GREASE
- *verb* **~ sth** to hide a coin, card, etc. in your hand, especially when performing a trick **PHR V** **ˌpalm sb↔ˈoff (with sth)** (*informal*) to persuade someone to believe an excuse or an explanation that is not true, in order to stop them from asking questions or complaining **ˌpalm sth↔ˈoff (on/onto sb)** (*informal*) to persuade someone to accept something that has no value or that you do not want, especially by tricking them: *She's always palming the worst jobs off on her assistant.* **ˌpalm sth ˈoff as sth** (*informal*) to tell someone that something is better than it is, especially in order to sell it: *They were trying to palm the table off as a genuine antique.*

t **t**ea   ț **butt**er   d **d**id   k **c**at   g **g**ot   tʃ **ch**in   dʒ **J**une   f **f**all

pal·met·to /pæl'mɛtoʊ; pəl-; pə-/ noun (pl. pal·met·tos) a small palm tree that grows in the southeastern U.S.

palm·ist /'pɑmɪst; 'pɑl-/ noun a person who claims to be able to tell what a person is like and what will happen to them in the future, by looking at the lines on the palm of their hand

palm·is·try /'pɑməstri; 'pɑl-/ noun [U] the art of telling what a person is like and what will happen to them by looking at the lines on the PALM of their hand

'palm oil noun [U] oil obtained from the fruit of some types of PALM trees, used in cooking and in making soap, CANDLES, etc.

Palm 'Sunday noun [U, C] (in the Christian Church) the Sunday before Easter

palm·top /'pɑmtɑp; 'pɑlm-/ noun a small computer that can be held in the PALM of one hand

palm·y /'pɑmi; 'pɑl-/ adj. (palm·i·er, palm·i·est) used to describe a time in the past when life was good: That's a picture of me in my palmier days.

pal·o·mi·no /ˌpælə'minoʊ/ noun (pl. pal·o·mi·nos) a horse that is a cream or gold color with a white MANE and tail

pal·pa·ble /'pælpəbl/ adj. that is easily noticed by the mind or the senses: a **palpable sense** of relief ◆ The tension in the room was almost palpable. ▶ **pal·pa·bly** /-bli/ adv.: It was palpably clear what she really meant.

pal·pate /'pælpeɪt/ verb ~ sth (medical) to examine part of the body by touching it ▶ **pal·pa·tion** /pæl'peɪʃn/ noun [U]

pal·pi·tate /'pælpəteɪt/ verb [I] (of the heart) to beat rapidly and/or in an IRREGULAR way, especially because of fear or excitement

pal·pi·ta·tions /ˌpælpə'teɪʃnz/ noun [pl.] a physical condition in which your heart beats very quickly and in an IRREGULAR way: Just the thought of flying gives me palpitations (= makes me very nervous).

pal·sy /'pɔlzi/ noun [U] (old-fashioned) PARALYSIS (= loss of control or feeling in part or most of the body), especially when the arms and legs shake without control ⊃ see also CEREBRAL PALSY ▶ **pal·sied** /'pɔlzid/ adj.

pal·try /'pɔltri/ adj. [usually before noun] **1** (of an amount) too small to be considered as important or useful **SYN** MEAGER: This account offers a paltry 1% return on your investment. ◆ a paltry sum **2** having no value or useful qualities: a paltry gesture

pam·pas /'pæmpəs; 'pɑm-; -pəz/ noun usually **the pampas** [sing.] the large area of land in S. America that has few trees and is covered in grass

pam·pas grass /'pæmpəs ˌgræs/ noun [U] a type of tall grass from S. America that is often grown in yards for its long silver-white flowers that look like feathers

pam·per /'pæmpər/ verb ~ sb (sometimes disapproving) to take care of someone very well and make them feel as comfortable as possible: Pamper yourself with our new range of beauty treatments. ◆ a spoiled and pampered child

pam·phlet /'pæmflət/ noun a very thin book with a paper cover, containing information about a particular subject **SYN** LEAFLET

pam·phlet·eer /ˌpæmflə'tɪr/ noun a person who writes pamphlets on particular subjects

pan 🔑 /pæn/ noun, verb
● **noun 1** a container, usually made of metal, with a handle or handles, used for cooking food in: pots and pans ◆ a large stainless steel pan ⊃ see also FRYING PAN, SAUCEPAN **2** the amount contained in a pan: a pan of boiling water **3** a metal container used for BAKING food in: a cake pan ⊃ picture at COOKING **4** either of the dishes on a pair of SCALES that you put things into in order to weigh them ⊃ see also BEDPAN, DUSTPAN, SKIDPAN, WARMING PAN **IDM** see FLASH
● **verb** (-nn-) **1** [T, usually passive] ~ sth (informal) to severely criticize something such as a play or a movie **SYN** SLATE **2** [I, T] if a television or video camera **pans** somewhere, or a person **pans** or **pans a camera**, the camera moves in a particular direction, to follow an object or to film a wide

area: + adv./prep. The camera panned back to the audience. ◆ ~ sth + adv./prep. He panned the camera along the row of faces. **3** [I, T] ~ **(for) sth** to wash soil or small stones in a pan to find gold or other valuable minerals: panning for gold **PHR V** ˌpan **'out** (informal) (of events or a situation) to develop in a particular way: I'm happy with the way things have panned out.

pan- /pæn/ combining form (in adjectives and nouns) including all of something; connected with the whole of something: pan-African ◆ pandemic

pan·a·ce·a /ˌpænə'siə/ noun ~ **(for sth)** something that will solve all the problems of a particular situation

pa·nache /pə'næʃ; -'nɑʃ/ noun [U] the quality of being able to do things in a confident and elegant way that other people find attractive **SYN** FLAIR, STYLE

pan·a·ma /'pænəˌmɑ/ (also ˌpanama 'hat) noun a man's hat made from fine STRAW ⊃ picture at HAT

pan-A'merican (also ˌPan-A'merican) adj. connected with or involving all the countries of North, Central, and South America: The **Pan-American Games** are held every four years.

pan·cake /'pænkeɪk/ noun **1** [C] a thin, flat, round cake made from a mixture of flour, eggs, and milk that is fried on both sides, usually eaten hot for breakfast **2** [U] thick makeup for the face, used especially in the theater **IDM** see FLAT

pan·cre·as /'pæŋkriəs/ noun an organ near the stomach that produces INSULIN and a liquid that helps the body to DIGEST food ⊃ picture at BODY ▶ **pan·cre·at·ic** /ˌpæŋkri-'ætɪk/ adj. [only before noun]

pan·da /'pændə/ noun
1 (also ˌgiant 'panda) a large black and white animal like a BEAR, that lives in China and is very rare **2** (also ˌred 'panda) an Asian animal like a RACCOON, with red-brown fur and a long thick tail

panda

pan·dem·ic /pæn'dɛmɪk/ noun a disease that spreads over a whole country or the whole world ▶ **pan·dem·ic** adj.: a pandemic disease ⊃ compare ENDEMIC, EPIDEMIC

pan·de·mo·ni·um /ˌpændə'moʊniəm/ noun [U] a situation in which there is a lot of noise, activity, and confusion, especially because people are feeling angry or frightened **SYN** CHAOS: Pandemonium broke out when the news was announced.

pan·der /'pændər/ verb
PHR V 'pander to sth/sb (disapproving) to do what someone wants, or try to please them, especially when this is not acceptable or reasonable: to pander to someone's wishes ◆ The speech was pandering to racial prejudice.

Pan·do·ra's box /pænˌdɔrəz 'bɑks/ noun [sing., U] a process that, if started, will cause many problems that cannot be solved: This court case could **open a Pandora's box** of similar claims. **ORIGIN** From the Greek story in which **Pandora** was created by the god Zeus and sent to the earth with a box containing many evils. When she opened the box, the evils came out and infected the earth.

pan·dow·dy /pæn'daʊdi/ noun (pl. pan·dow·dies) [C, U] a sweet dish of apples and spices covered with a mixture of butter, milk, and eggs and baked

pane /peɪn/ noun a single sheet of glass in a window: a pane of glass ◆ a windowpane

pan·e·gyr·ic /ˌpænə'dʒɪrɪk; -'dʒaɪrɪk/ noun (formal) a speech or piece of writing praising someone or something

pan·el 🔑 **AWL** /'pænl/ noun, verb
● **noun 1** a square or rectangular (RECTANGLE) piece of wood, glass, or metal that forms part of a larger surface such as a door or wall: One of the glass panels in the front door

was cracked. ⊃ see also SOLAR PANEL **2** a piece of metal that forms part of the outer frame of a vehicle **3** a piece of cloth that forms part of a piece of clothing: *The pants have double thickness knee panels for extra protection.* **4** a group of specialists who give their advice or opinion about something; a group of people who discuss topics of interest on television or radio: *an advisory panel* ◆ *a panel of experts* ◆ *We have two politicians on tonight's panel.* ◆ *a panel discussion* **5** (also ˌjury ˈpanel) = JURY **6** a flat board in a vehicle or on a piece of machinery where the controls and instruments are fixed: *an instrument panel* ◆ *a control/display panel*

• **verb** [usually passive] ~ sth to cover or decorate a surface with flat strips of wood, glass, etc.: *The walls were paneled in oak.* ◆ *a glass-/wood-paneled door*

pan·el·ing (CanE usually pan·el·ling) /ˈpænl·ɪŋ/ noun [U] square or rectangular (RECTANGLE) pieces of wood used to cover and decorate walls, ceilings, etc.

pan·el·ist /ˈpænl·ɪst/ noun a person who is a member of a panel answering questions during a discussion, for example on radio or television

ˈpanel ˌtruck noun a small truck, especially one without windows at the sides or seats for passengers

pan-fry verb (pan-fries, pan-frying, pan-fried, pan-fried) ~ sth to fry food in a pan in a small amount of fat: *pan-fried chicken*

pang /pæŋ/ noun a sudden strong feeling of physical or emotional pain: *hunger pangs/pangs of hunger* ◆ *a sudden pang of jealousy*

Pan·gae·a /pænˈdʒiːə/ noun [sing.] (geology) an extremely large area of land that existed millions of years ago, made up of all the present continents

pan·go·lin /ˈpæŋɡələn/ (also ˌscaly ˈanteater) noun a small animal from Africa or Asia that eats insects, and has a long nose, tongue, and tail, and hard SCALES on its body

pan·han·dler /ˈpænˌhændlər/ noun (informal) a person who asks other people for money in the street ▶ **pan·han·dle** verb [I]

pan·ic /ˈpænɪk/ noun, verb
• **noun** [U, C, usually sing.] **1** a sudden feeling of great fear that cannot be controlled and prevents you from thinking clearly: *a moment of panic* ◆ *They were in a state of panic.* ◆ *Office workers fled in panic as the fire took hold.* ◆ *There's no point getting into a panic about the exams.* ◆ *a panic attack* (= a condition in which you suddenly feel very anxious, causing your heart to beat faster, etc.) ◆ *a panic decision* (= one that is made when you are in a state of panic) ⊃ thesaurus box at FEAR **2** a situation in which people are made to feel very anxious, causing them to act quickly and without thinking carefully: *News of the losses caused (a) panic among investors.* ◆ *Careful planning at this stage will help to avoid a last-minute panic.* ◆ *There's no panic* (= we do not need to rush), *we've got plenty of time.* ◆ *panic buying/selling* (= the act of buying/selling things quickly and without thinking carefully because you are afraid that a particular situation will become worse)
• **verb** (-ck-) [I, T] to suddenly feel frightened so that you cannot think clearly and you say or do something stupid, dangerous, etc.; to make someone do this: *I panicked when I saw smoke coming out of the engine.* ◆ ~ sb/sth *The gunfire panicked the horses.*
PHR V ˈpanic sb into doing sth [usually passive] to make someone act too quickly because they are afraid of something

ˈpanic ˌbutton noun a button that someone working in a bank, etc. can press to call for help if they are in danger
IDM hit/press/push the panic button to react in a sudden or extreme way to something unexpected that has frightened you

pan·ick·y /ˈpænɪki/ adj. (informal) anxious about something; feeling or showing panic **SYN** HYSTERICAL

ˈpanic ˌroom (also ˈsafe room) noun a room in a home or an office building where people can go to avoid a dangerous situation

ˈpanic-ˌstricken adj. extremely anxious about something, in a way that prevents you from thinking clearly **SYN** HYSTERICAL

pa·ni·ni /pəˈniːni/ (also pa·ni·no /pəˈniːnoʊ/) noun (pl. pa·ni·ni or pa·ni·nis) a sandwich made with Italian bread, usually toasted

pan·nier /ˈpænjər/ noun each of a pair of bags or boxes carried on either side of the back wheel of a bicycle or motorcycle; each of a pair of BASKETS carried on either side of its back by a horse or DONKEY

pan·o·ply /ˈpænəpli/ noun [sing., U] (formal) a large and impressive number or collection of something **SYN** ARRAY

pan·o·ram·a /ˌpænəˈræmə; -ˈrɑːmə/ noun **1** a view of a wide area of land **SYN** VISTA: *There is a superb panorama of the mountains from the hotel.* ⊃ thesaurus box at VIEW **2** a description, study, or set of pictures that presents all the different aspects or stages of a particular subject, event, etc. ▶ **pan·o·ram·ic** /ˌpænəˈræmɪk/ adj. [usually before noun]: *a panoramic view over the valley*

ˈpan pipes noun [pl.] (also pan-pipe [C]) a musical instrument made of a row of pipes of different lengths that you play by blowing across the open ends

pan·sy /ˈpænzi/ noun (pl. pan·sies) a small garden plant with brightly colored flowers

pant /pænt/ verb [I, T] (+ speech) to breathe quickly with short breaths, usually with your mouth open, because you have been doing some physical exercise, or because it is very hot: *She finished the race panting heavily.* ◆ *She could hear him panting up the stairs* (= running up and breathing quickly). ◆ *He found her panting for breath at the top of the hill.* ▶ **pant** noun [usually pl.]: *His breath came in short pants.* ⊃ see also PANTS **IDM** See PUFF
PHR V ˈpant for/after sb/sth to want something or someone very much: *The end of the novel leaves you panting for more.*

pan·ta·loons /ˌpæntəˈluːnz/ noun [pl.] (in the past) men's tight pants fastened at the foot

pan·the·ism /ˈpænθiˌɪzəm/ noun [U] **1** the belief that God is present in all natural things **2** belief in many or all gods ▶ **pan·the·ist** /-θiːɪst/ noun **pan·the·is·tic** /ˌpænθiˈɪstɪk/ adj.

pan·the·on /ˈpænθiˌɑn/ noun **1** (technical) all the gods of a nation or people: *the ancient Egyptian pantheon* **2** (formal) a group of people who are famous within a particular area of activity **3** a TEMPLE (= religious building) built in honor of all the gods of a nation; a building in which famous dead people of a nation are buried or HONORED

pan·ther /ˈpænθər/ noun
1 a black LEOPARD (= a large wild animal of the cat family) **2** = COUGAR

panther

pant·ies /ˈpæntiz/ noun [pl.] a piece of women's underwear that covers the body from the waist to the tops of the legs

pan·tile /ˈpæntaɪl/ noun a curved TILE used for roofs

pan·to·graph /ˈpæntəˌɡræf/ noun a device used for copying a drawing in a bigger or smaller size

pan·to·mime /ˈpæntəˌmaɪm/ noun [U, C, usually sing.] the use of movement and the expression of your face to communicate something or to tell a story **SYN** MIME

pan·try /ˈpæntri/ noun (pl. pan·tries) a closet or small room in a house, used for storing food **SYN** LARDER

pants 🔊 /pænts/ noun [pl.]
a piece of clothing that covers the body from the waist down and is divided into two parts to cover each leg separately: *a new pair of pants* ◆ *ski pants* ⊃ picture at CLOTHES ⊃ see also CARGO PANTS
IDM bore, scare, etc. the pants off sb (informal) to make

someone extremely bored, frightened, etc. ⊃ more at ANT, CATCH v., SEAT n., WEAR v., WET v.

pant·suit /ˈpæntsut/ *noun* a woman's suit of jacket and pants

pant·y·hose /ˈpæntiˌhoʊz/ *noun* [pl.] a piece of clothing made of very thin cloth that fits closely over a woman's hips, legs, and feet ⊃ compare STOCKING

pap /pæp/ *noun* [U] **1** (*disapproving*) books, magazines, television programs, etc. that have no real value **2** soft or almost liquid food eaten by babies or people who are sick

pa·pa /ˈpɑpə/ *noun* (*old-fashioned*) used to talk about or to address your father

pa·pa·cy /ˈpeɪpəsi/ *noun* **1** the **pa·pa·cy** [sing.] the position or the authority of the POPE **2** [C, usually sing.] the period of time when a particular POPE is in power

pa·pal /ˈpeɪpl/ *adj.* [only before noun] connected with the POPE: *papal authority* ◆ *a papal visit to Mexico*

pa·pa·raz·zo /ˌpɑpəˈrɑtsoʊ/ *noun* (*pl.* **pa·pa·raz·zi** /-ˈrɑtsi/) [usually pl.] a photographer who follows famous people around in order to get interesting photographs of them to sell to a newspaper

pa·pa·ya /pəˈpaɪə/ *noun* a tropical fruit with yellow and green skin, sweet orange or red flesh, and round black seeds

pa·per 🔑 /ˈpeɪpər/ *noun, verb*

● *noun*
> FOR WRITING/WRAPPING **1** [U] (often in compounds) the thin material that you write and draw on and that is also used for wrapping and packing things: *a piece/sheet of paper* ◆ *a package wrapped in brown paper* ◆ *recycled paper* ◆ *She wrote her name and address on a **slip** (= a small piece) **of paper**.* ◆ *Experience is more important for this job than **paper qualifications** (= that exist on paper, but may not have any real value).* ◆ ***paper losses/profits** (= that are shown in accounts but which may not exist in reality)* ◆ *This journal is available in paper and electronic form.* ⊃ see also NOTEPAPER, WRAPPING PAPER,
> NEWSPAPER **2** [C] a newspaper: *a local/national paper* ◆ *a daily/evening/Sunday paper* ◆ *I read about it **in the paper**.* ◆ *Have you seen today's paper?* ◆ ***The papers** (= newspapers in general) soon got hold of the story.*
> DOCUMENTS **3** **papers** [pl.] pieces of paper with writing on them, such as letters, pieces of work, or private documents: *His desk was covered with books and papers.* **4** **papers** [pl.] official documents that prove your identity, give you permission to do something, etc.: *divorce/identification papers* ⊃ see also WALKING PAPERS, WORKING PAPERS
> ARTICLE **5** [C] an academic article about a particular subject that is written by and for specialists: *a recent paper in the Journal of Medicine* ◆ *She was invited to **give a paper** (= a talk) on the results of her research.* ⊃ collocations at SCIENTIFIC ⊃ see also POSITION PAPER, WORKING PAPER (1) **6** [C] a piece of written work done by a student: *Your grade will be based on four papers and a final exam.* ⊃ see also TERM PAPER
> ON WALLS **7** [C, U] paper that you use to cover and decorate the walls of a room: **SYN** WALLPAPER *The room was damp and the paper was peeling off.* **HELP** There are many other compounds ending in **paper**. You will find them at their place in the alphabet.
> **IDM** **on paper 1** when you put something **on paper**, you write it down **2** judged from written information only, but not proved in practice: *The idea **looks good on paper**.* ⊃ more at PEN n., WORTH adj.

● *verb* ~ **sth** to decorate the walls of a room by covering them with WALLPAPER
PHRV **paper 'over sth 1** to cover a wall with WALLPAPER in order to hide something **SYN** WALLPAPER: *The previous owners had obviously papered over any damp patches.* **2** to try to hide a problem or disagreement in a way that is temporary and not likely to be successful: *We can't just paper over the problem.*

pa·per·back /ˈpeɪpərˌbæk/ *noun* [C, U] a book that has a thick paper cover: *a cheap paperback* ◆ *When is it coming out in paperback?* ◆ *a paperback book/edition* ⊃ compare HARDCOVER

pa·per·board /ˈpeɪpərˌbɔrd/ *noun* [U] a type of thick stiff paper or thin board made of many layers of paper stuck together: *The cover of the book was made of paperboard.*

'paper ˌboy, **'paper ˌgirl** *noun* a boy or girl who delivers newspapers to people's houses

'paper ˌchase *noun* (*informal*) the fact of producing too much work on paper

'paper ˌclip *noun* a piece of bent wire or plastic that is designed to hold loose sheets of paper together ⊃ picture at STATIONERY

'paper ˌcutter *noun* [C] a device with a long blade for cutting paper

ˌpaper 'doll *noun* a piece of thick paper cut into the shape of a human figure, often as part of a set for children to play with

pa·per·less /ˈpeɪpərləs/ *adj.* using computers, telephones, etc. rather than paper to exchange information: *the paperless office* ◆ *a system of paperless business transactions*

ˌpaper 'money *noun* [U] money that is made of paper, not coins

ˌpaper 'plate *noun* a cardboard plate that can be thrown away after it is used

'paper–ˌpusher *noun* (*disapproving*) a person who does unimportant office work as their job

'paper ˌroute *noun* the job of delivering newspapers to houses; the route taken when doing this

ˌpaper–'thin *adj.* (of objects) very thin and delicate: *paper-thin slices of meat* ⊃ compare WAFER-THIN

ˌpaper 'tiger *noun* a person, a country, or a situation that seems or claims to be powerful or dangerous but is not really

ˌpaper 'towel *noun* **1** [C] a thick sheet of paper that you use to dry your hands or to absorb water **2** [U] thick paper on a roll, used for cleaning up liquid, food, etc.

'paper ˌtrail *noun* (*informal*) a series of documents that provide evidence of what you have done or what has happened: *He was a shrewd lawyer with a talent for uncovering paper trails of fraud.*

pa·per·weight /ˈpeɪpərˌweɪt/ *noun* a small heavy object that you put on top of loose papers to keep them in place

pa·per·work /ˈpeɪpərˌwɑrk/ *noun* [U] **1** the written work that is part of a job, such as filling in forms or writing letters and reports: *We're trying to cut down on the amount of paperwork involved.* **2** all the documents that you need for something, such as a court case or buying a house: *How quickly can you prepare the paperwork?*

pa·per·y /ˈpeɪpəri/ *adj.* like paper; thin and dry

pa·pier mâ·ché /ˌpeɪpər məˈʃeɪ/ *noun* [U] (from *French*) paper mixed with glue or flour and water, that is used to make decorative objects

pap·il·lo·ma /ˌpæpəˈloʊmə/ *noun* (*medical*) a small lump like a WART that grows on the skin and is usually harmless

pa·poose /pæˈpus/ *noun* a type of bag that can be used for carrying a baby in, on your back or in front of you

pap·ri·ka /pæˈprikə; pə-/ *noun* [U] a red powder made from a type of PEPPER, used in cooking as a spice

Pap smear /ˈpæp smɪr/ *noun* a medical test in which a very small amount of TISSUE from a woman's CERVIX is removed and examined for cancer cells

pa·py·rus /pəˈpaɪrəs/ *noun* (*pl.* **pa·py·ri** /-raɪ; -ri/) **1** [U] a tall plant with thick STEM that grows in water **2** [U] paper made from the STEM of the papyrus plant, used in ancient Egypt for writing and drawing on **3** [C] a document or piece of paper made of papyrus

par /pɑr/ *noun* [U] **1** (in GOLF) the number of strokes a good player should need to complete a course or to hit the ball into a particular hole: *a par five hole* ♦ *Par for the course is 72.* **2** (also ˈpar ˌvalue) (*business*) the value that a share in a company had originally: *to be redeemed at par* **IDM below/under par** less well, good, etc. than is usual or expected: *Teaching in some subjects has been well below par.* **be par for the course** (*disapproving*) to be just what you would expect to happen or expect someone to do in a particular situation **SYN THE NORM**: *Starting early and working long hours is par for the course in this job.* **on a par with sb/sth** as good, bad, important, etc. as someone or something else **up to par** as good as usual or as good as it should be **SYN UP TO SCRATCH**

par. (also **para.**) *abbr.* (in writing) paragraph: *See par. 3.*

par·a /ˈpærə/ *noun* (*informal*) = **PARATROOPER**

para- /ˈpærə/ *prefix* (in nouns and adjectives) **1** beyond: *paranormal* **2** similar to but not official or not fully qualified: *paramilitary* ♦ *a paramedic*

par·a·ble /ˈpærəbl/ *noun* a short story that teaches a moral or spiritual lesson, especially one of those told by Jesus as recorded in the Bible

pa·rab·o·la /pəˈræbələ/ *noun* (*geometry*) a curve like the path of an object thrown into the air and falling back to earth ➔ picture at SHAPE ▶ **par·a·bol·ic** /ˌpærəˈbɒlɪk/ *adj.*: *parabolic curves*

par·a·chute /ˈpærəʃuːt/ *noun, verb*
● *noun* (also *informal* **chute**) a device that is attached to people or objects to make them fall slowly and safely when they are dropped from an aircraft. It consists of a large piece of thin cloth that opens out in the air to form an umbrella shape: *Planes dropped supplies by parachute.* ♦ *a parachute drop/jump* ♦ *a parachute regiment*
● *verb* **1** [I] (+ *adv./prep.*) to jump from an aircraft using a parachute: *The pilot was able to parachute to safety.* ♦ *She regularly goes parachuting.* **2** [T] ~ sb/sth + *adv./prep.* to drop someone or something from an aircraft by parachute

par·a·chut·ist /ˈpærəʃuːtɪst/ *noun* a person who jumps from a plane using a parachute

pa·rade /pəˈreɪd/ *noun, verb*
● *noun*
▷ **PUBLIC CELEBRATION 1** [C] a public celebration of a special day or event, usually with bands in the streets and decorated vehicles **SYN PROCESSION**: *the St. Patrick's Day parade in New York*
▷ **OF SOLDIERS 2** [C, U] a formal occasion when soldiers march or stand in lines so that they can be examined by their officers or other important people: *a military parade* ♦ *They stood as straight as soldiers on parade.* ♦ (*figurative*) *The latest software will be on parade at the exhibition.*
▷ **SERIES 3** [C] a series of things or people: *Each generation passes through a similar parade of events.*
▷ **WEALTH/KNOWLEDGE 4** [C, usually sing.] ~ of wealth, knowledge, etc. (often *disapproving*) an obvious display of something, particularly in order to impress other people **IDM** see RAIN *v.*
● *verb*
▷ **WALK TO CELEBRATE/PROTEST 1** [I] (+ *adv./prep.*) to walk somewhere in a formal group of people, in order to celebrate or protest about something: *The victorious team will parade through the city tomorrow morning.*
▷ **SHOW IN PUBLIC 2** [I] + *adv./prep.* to walk around in a way that makes other people notice you: *People were parading up and down showing off their finest clothes.* **3** [T] ~ sb/sth + *adv./prep.* to show someone or something in public so that people can see them/it: *The trophy was paraded around the stadium.* ♦ *The prisoners were paraded in front of the crowd.* ♦ (*figurative*) *He is not one to parade his achievements.*
▷ **OF SOLDIERS 4** [I, T] to come together, or to bring soldiers together, in order to march in front of other people: + *adv./prep. The crowds applauded as the guards paraded past.* ♦ ~ sb + *adv./prep. The colonel paraded his men before the Queen.*
▷ **PRETEND 5** [I, T] to pretend to be, or to make someone or something seem to be, good or important when they are

not: ~ **as sth** *myth parading as fact* ♦ ~ **sb/sth/yourself as sth** *He paraded himself as a loyal supporter of the party.*

paˈrade ˌground *noun* a place where soldiers gather to march or to be INSPECTED by an officer or an important visitor

par·a·digm **AWL** /ˈpærəˌdaɪm/ *noun* (*formal* or *technical*) **1** a typical example or pattern of something: *a paradigm for students to copy* ♦ *The war was a paradigm of the destructive side of human nature.* **2** (*grammar*) a set of all the different forms of a word: *verb paradigms* ▶ **par·a·dig·mat·ic** /ˌpærədɪɡˈmætɪk/ *adj.*

ˈparadigm ˌshift *noun* a great and important change in the way something is done or thought about

par·a·dise /ˈpærəˌdaɪs; -ˌdaɪz/ *noun* **1** often **Par·a·dise** [U] (in some religions) a perfect place where people are said to go when they die **SYN HEAVEN**: *The ancient Egyptians saw paradise as an idealized version of their own lives.* **2** [C] a place that is extremely beautiful and that seems perfect, like heaven: *a tropical paradise* **3** [C] a perfect place for a particular activity or kind of person: *The area is a bird-watcher's paradise.* **4** [U] a state of perfect happiness **SYN BLISS**: *Being alone is his idea of paradise.* **5** **Par·a·dise** [U] (in the Bible) the garden of Eden, where Adam and Eve lived

par·a·dox /ˈpærəˌdɒks/ *noun* **1** [C] a person, thing, or situation that has two opposite features and therefore seems strange: *He was a paradox—a loner who loved to chat to strangers.* ♦ *It is a curious paradox that professional comedians often have unhappy personal lives.* **2** [C, U] a statement containing two opposite ideas that make it seem impossible or unlikely, although it is probably true; the use of this in writing: *"More haste, less speed" is a well-known paradox.* ♦ *It's a work full of paradox and ambiguity.* ▶ **par·a·dox·i·cal** /ˌpærəˈdɒksɪkl/ *adj.*: *It is paradoxical that some of the poorest people live in some of the richest areas of the country.* ▶ **par·a·dox·i·cally** /-kli/ *adv.*: *Paradoxically, the less she ate, the fatter she got.*

par·af·fin /ˈpærəfən/ *noun* [U] a soft white substance that is made from PETROLEUM or coal, and is used especially for making CANDLES

par·a·glid·er /ˈpærəˌɡlaɪdər/ *noun* **1** a structure consisting of a big thin piece of cloth like a PARACHUTE, and a HARNESS that is attached to a person when they jump from a plane or a high place in the sport of paragliding **2** a person who goes paragliding

par·a·glid·ing /ˈpærəˌɡlaɪdɪŋ/ *noun* [U] a sport in which you wear a special structure like a PARACHUTE, jump from a plane or a high place, and are carried along by the wind before coming down to earth: *to go paragliding* ➔ picture at SPORT

par·a·gon /ˈpærəˌɡɒn/ *noun* a person who is perfect or who is a perfect example of a particular good quality: *I make no claim to be a paragon.* ♦ *He wasn't the paragon of virtue she had expected.*

par·a·graph **AWL** /ˈpærəˌɡræf/ *noun* (*abbr.* **par., para.**) a section of a piece of writing, usually consisting of several sentences dealing with a single subject. The first sentence of a paragraph starts on a new line: *an opening/introductory paragraph* ♦ *Write a paragraph on each of the topics given below.* ♦ *See paragraph 15 of the handbook.*

par·a·graph·ing /ˈpærəˌɡræfɪŋ/ *noun* [U] the way that a piece of writing is divided into paragraphs

par·a·keet /ˈpærəkiːt/ *noun* a small bird of the PARROT family, usually with a long tail

par·a·le·gal /ˌpærəˈliːɡl/ *noun* a person who is trained to help a lawyer ▶ **par·a·le·gal** *adj.*

par·a·lin·guis·tic /ˌpærəlɪŋˈɡwɪstɪk/ *adj.* (*linguistics*) relating to communication through ways other than words, for example tone of voice, expressions on your face, and actions

par·al·lax /ˈpærəˌlæks/ *noun* [U] (*technical*) the effect by which the position or direction of an object appears to change when the object is seen from different positions

par·al·lel 🔧 **AWL** /ˈpærəˌlel/ *adj., noun, verb*
● *adj.* **1** two or more lines that are **parallel** to each other are the same distance apart at every point: *parallel lines* ◆ *~ to/with sth The road and the canal are parallel to each other.* ➲ picture at LINE **2** very similar or taking place at the same time: *a parallel case* ◆ *parallel trends* **3** (*computing*) involving several computer operations at the same time: *parallel processing* ▶ **par·al·lel** *adv.: The road and the canal run parallel to each other.* ◆ *The plane flew parallel to the coast.*
● *noun* **1** [C, U] a person, a situation, an event, etc. that is very similar to another, especially one in a different place or time **SYN** EQUIVALENT: *These ideas have parallels in Freud's thought too.* ◆ *This is an achievement without parallel in modern times.* ◆ *This tradition has no parallel in our culture.* **2** [C, usually pl.] similar features: *There are interesting parallels between the 1960s and the late 1990s.* ◆ *It is possible to draw a parallel between* (= find similar features in) *their experience and ours.* **3** (also parallel of latitude) [C] an imaginary line around the earth that is always the same distance from the EQUATOR; this line on a map: *the 49th parallel*
IDM **in parallel (with sth/sb)** with and at the same time as something or someone else: *The new degree and the existing certificate courses would run in parallel.*
● *verb* **1** ~ sth to be similar to something; to happen at the same time as something: *Their legal system parallels our own.* ◆ *The rise in unemployment is paralleled by an increase in petty crime.* **2** ~ sth to be as good as something **SYN** EQUAL: *a level of achievement that has never been paralleled* ➲ compare UNPARALLELED

parallel 'bars *noun* [pl.] two bars on posts that are used for doing exercises

parallel 'imports *noun* [pl.] (*economics*) goods that are imported into a country without the permission of the company that produced them, and sold at a lower price than the company sells them at

par·al·lel·ism /ˈpærəleˌlɪzəm/ *noun* [U, C] (*formal*) the state of being similar; a similar feature: *I think he exaggerates the parallelism between the two cases.*

par·al·lel·o·gram /ˌpærəˈleləˌgræm/ *noun* (*geometry*) a flat shape with four straight sides, the opposite sides being parallel and equal to each other

parallel 'park *verb* [I, T] ~ (sth) to park a car or other vehicle parallel to the SIDEWALK: *I never learned how to parallel park.* ▶ **parallel 'parking** *noun* [U]

parallel 'port *noun* (*computing*) a point on a computer where you connect a device such as a printer that sends or receives more than one piece of data at a time

parallel 'processing *noun* [U] (*computing*) the division of a process into different parts, which are performed at the same time by different PROCESSORS in a computer

parallel 'ruler *noun* a device for drawing lines that are always the same distance apart, consisting of two connected rulers

the Par·a·lym·pics /ˌpærəˈlɪmpɪks/ *noun* [pl.] an international ATHLETICS competition for people who are DISABLED

pa·ral·y·sis /pəˈræləsəs/ *noun* (*pl.* **pa·ral·y·ses** /-siz/) **1** [U, C] a loss of control of, and sometimes feeling in, part or most of the body, caused by disease or an injury to the nerves: *paralysis of both legs* **2** [U] a total inability to move, act, function, etc.: *The strike caused total paralysis in the city.*

par·a·lyt·ic /ˌpærəˈlɪtɪk/ *adj.* [usually before noun] (*formal*) suffering from paralysis; making someone unable to move: *a paralytic illness* ◆ *paralytic fear*

par·a·lyze /ˈpærəˌlaɪz/ *verb* [often passive] **1** ~ sb to make someone unable to feel or move all or part of their body: *The accident left him paralyzed from the waist down.* ◆ (*figurative*) *paralyzing heat* ◆ (*figurative*) *She stood there, paralyzed with fear.* **2** ~ sth to prevent something from functioning normally: *The airport is still paralyzed by the strike.*

par·a·med·ic /ˌpærəˈmedɪk/ *noun* a person whose job is to help people who are sick or injured, but who is not a doctor or a nurse: *Paramedics treated the injured at the roadside.* ▶ **par·a·med·i·cal** /-ˈmedɪkl/ *adj.: paramedical staff*

pa·ram·e·ter **AWL** /pəˈræmɪtər/ *noun* [usually pl.] something that decides or limits the way in which something can be done: *to set/define the parameters* ◆ *We had to work within the parameters that had already been established.*

par·a·mil·i·tar·y /ˌpærəˈmɪləˌteri/ *adj., noun*
● *adj.* [usually before noun] **1** a **paramilitary** organization is an illegal group that is organized like an army: *a right-wing paramilitary group* **2** helping the official army of a country: *paramilitary police, such as the CRS in France*
● *noun* (*pl.* **par·a·mil·i·tar·ies**) [usually pl.] **1** a member of an illegal paramilitary group or organization **2** a member of an organization that helps the official army of a country

par·a·mount /ˈpærəˌmaʊnt/ *adj.* **1** more important than anything else: *This matter is of paramount importance.* ◆ *Safety is paramount.* ➲ language bank at VITAL **2** (*formal*) having the highest position or the greatest power: *China's paramount leader* ▶ **par·a·mount·cy** /-ˌmaʊntsi/ *noun* [U]

par·a·mour /ˈpærəˌmʊr/ *noun* (*old-fashioned* or *literary*) a person that someone is having a romantic or sexual relationship with **SYN** LOVER

par·a·noi·a /ˌpærəˈnɔɪə/ *noun* [U] **1** (*medical*) a mental illness in which a person may wrongly believe that other people are trying to harm them or that they are someone very important, etc. **2** (*informal*) fear or suspicion of other people when there is no evidence or reason for this

par·a·noid /ˈpærəˌnɔɪd/ *adj., noun*
● *adj.* (also less frequent **par·a·noi·ac** /ˌpærəˈnɔɪæk; -ˈnɔɪɪk/) **1** afraid or suspicious of other people and believing that they are trying to harm you, in a way that is not reasonable: *She's getting really paranoid about what other people say about her.* ➲ thesaurus box at AFRAID **2** suffering from a mental illness in which you wrongly believe that other people are trying to harm you or that you are very important: *paranoid delusions* ◆ *paranoid schizophrenia* ◆ *a paranoid killer*
● *noun* (also **par·a·noi·ac** /ˌpærəˈnɔɪæk; -ˈnɔɪɪk/) a person who suffers from paranoia

par·a·nor·mal /ˌpærəˈnɔrml/ *adj.* **1** that cannot be explained by science or reason and that seems to involve mysterious forces **SYN** SUPERNATURAL **2** the par·a·nor·mal *noun* [sing.] events or subjects that are paranormal **SYN** THE SUPERNATURAL

par·a·pet /ˈpærəpət; -ˌpet/ *noun* a low wall along the edge of a bridge, a roof, etc. to stop people from falling

par·a·pher·na·lia /ˌpærəfəˈneɪlyə; -fərˈneɪl-/ *noun* [U] a large number of objects or personal possessions, especially the equipment that you need for a particular activity: *skiing paraphernalia* ◆ *an electric kettle and all the paraphernalia for making tea and coffee*

par·a·phrase /ˈpærəˌfreɪz/ *verb, noun*
● *verb* [T, I] ~ (sth) to express what someone has said or written using different words, especially in order to make it easier to understand: *Try to paraphrase the question before you answer it.*
● *noun* a statement that expresses something that someone has written or said using different words, especially in order to make it easier to understand

par·a·ple·gi·a /ˌpærəˈplidʒə/ *noun* [U] PARALYSIS (= loss of control or feeling) in the legs and lower body

par·a·ple·gic /ˌpærəˈplidʒɪk/ *noun* a person who suffers from paraplegia ▶ **par·a·ple·gic** *adj.*

par·a·psy·chol·o·gy /ˌpærəsaɪˈkɑlədʒi/ *noun* [U] the study of mental powers that seem to exist but that cannot be explained by scientific knowledge

par·a·quat /ˈpærəˌkwɑt/ *noun* [U] an extremely poisonous liquid used to kill plants that are growing where they are not wanted

par·a·sail·ing /ˈpærəˌseɪlɪŋ/ *noun* [U] the sport of being pulled up into the air behind a boat while wearing a special PARACHUTE

par·a·site /ˈpærəˌsaɪt/ *noun* **1** a small animal or plant that lives on or inside another animal or plant and gets its food from it **2** (*disapproving*) a person who always relies on or benefits from other people and gives nothing back

par·a·sit·ic /ˌpærəˈsɪtɪk/ (also *less frequent* **par·a·sit·i·cal** /ˌpærəˈsɪtɪkl/) *adj.* **1** caused by a parasite: *a parasitic disease/infection* **2** living on another animal or plant and getting its food from it: *a parasitic mite* **3** (*disapproving*) (of a person) always relying on or benefiting from other people and giving nothing back ▸ **par·a·sit·i·cally** /-kli/ *adv.*

par·a·sol /ˈpærəˌsɒl; -ˌsɔl/ *noun* **1** a type of light umbrella that women in the past carried to protect themselves from the sun **2** a large umbrella that is used for example on beaches or outside restaurants to protect people from hot sun ⊃ compare SUNSHADE

par·a·stat·al /ˌpærəˈsteɪtl/ *adj.* (*technical*) (of an organization) having some political power and serving the state

par·a·tax·is /ˌpærəˈtæksəs/ *noun* [U] (*grammar*) the placing of clauses and phrases one after the other, without words to link them or show their relationship ⊃ compare HYPOTAXIS

par·a·troop·er /ˈpærəˌtruːpər/ (also *informal* **par·a**) *noun* a member of the paratroops

par·a·troops /ˈpærəˌtruːps/ *noun* [pl.] soldiers who are trained to jump from planes using a PARACHUTE ▸ **par·a·troop** *adj.* [only before noun]: *a paratroop regiment*

par·boil /ˈpɑːrbɔɪl/ *verb* ~ sth to boil food, especially vegetables, until it is partly cooked

par·cel /ˈpɑːrsl/ *noun, verb*
• *noun* **1** = PACKAGE **2** a piece of land: *50 five-acre parcels have already been sold.* **3** a small amount of food that is wrapped in something, usually PASTRY, before it is cooked: *filo pastry parcels* **IDM** see PART
• *verb*
  PHR V ˌparcel sth↔ˈoff to divide something into smaller parts, especially in order to sell them: *The developer bought a large tract of farmland and parceled it off into several lots.* ◆ *The corporation parceled off some of its less profitable divisions.* ˌparcel sth↔ˈout to divide something into parts or between several people: *The land was parceled out into small lots.*

ˌparcel ˈpost *noun* [U] a service that is used to mail packages and thick envelopes: *I sent the boxes (by) parcel post.*

parch /pɑːrtʃ/ *verb* ~ sth (especially of hot weather) to make an area of land very dry

parched /pɑːrtʃt/ *adj.* **1** very dry, especially because the weather is hot: *dry parched land* ◆ *soil parched by drought* ◆ *She licked her parched lips.* **2** (*informal*) very thirsty: *Let's get a drink—I'm parched.*

Par·chee·si™ /pɑːrˈtʃiːzi/ *noun* [U] a simple game played with DICE and COUNTERS on a special board

parch·ment /ˈpɑːrtʃmənt/ *noun* **1** [U] material made from the skin of a sheep or GOAT, used in the past for writing on: *parchment scrolls* **2** [U] a thick, pale, yellow type of paper **3** [C] a document written on a piece of parchment

pard·ner /ˈpɑːrdnər/ *noun* (*informal, non-standard*) a way of saying or writing "partner" in informal speech

par·don /ˈpɑːrdn/ *exclamation, noun, verb*
• *exclamation* **1** (also ˌpardon ˈme) used to ask someone to repeat something because you did not hear it or did not understand it: *"You're very quiet today." "Pardon me?" "I said you're very quiet today."* **2** (also ˌpardon ˈme) used by some people to say "sorry" when they have accidentally made a rude noise, or said or done something wrong
• *noun* **1** [C] an official decision not to punish someone for a crime, or to say that someone is not guilty of a crime: *to ask/grant/receive a pardon* ◆ *a presidential/royal pardon* **2** [U] (*formal*) ~ (for sth) the action of forgiving someone for

something **SYN** FORGIVENESS: *He asked her pardon for having deceived her.* **IDM** see BEG
• *verb* (not usually used in the progressive tenses) **1** ~ sb to officially allow someone who has been found guilty of a crime to leave prison and/or avoid punishment: *She was pardoned after serving ten years of a life sentence.* **2** to forgive someone for something they have said or done (used in many expressions when you want to be polite) **SYN** EXCUSE: *~ sth Pardon my ignorance, but what is a "duplex"?* ◆ *The place was, if you'll pardon the expression, a dump.* ◆ *~ sb (for sth/for doing sth) You could be pardoned for thinking* (= it is easy to understand why people think) *that education is not the government's priority.* ◆ *Pardon me for interrupting you.* ◆ *~ sb doing sth Pardon my asking, but is that your husband?*
  IDM ˌpardon me for doing sth used to show that you are upset or offended by the way that someone has spoken to you: *"Oh, just shut up!" "Well, pardon me for breathing!"* ⊃ more at FRENCH

par·don·a·ble /ˈpɑːrdn·əbl/ *adj.* that can be forgiven or excused **SYN** EXCUSABLE **ANT** UNPARDONABLE

pare /pɛr/ *verb* **1** to remove the thin outer layer of something, especially of fruit: *~ sth She pared the apple.* ◆ *~ sth from sth First, pare the rind from the lemon.* ◆ *~ sth off/away He pared away the excess glue with a razor blade.* **2** ~ sth (back/down) to gradually reduce the size or amount: *The training budget has been pared back to a minimum.* ◆ *The workforce has been pared to the bone* (= reduced to the lowest possible level). ⊃ see also PARINGS

par·ent 🔑 /ˈpɛrənt/ *noun*
1 [usually pl.] a person's father or mother: *He's still living with his parents.* ◆ *her adoptive parents* ◆ *Sue and Ben have recently become parents.* ⊃ see also ONE-PARENT FAMILY, SINGLE PARENT, STEPPARENT **2** an animal or a plant which produces other animals or plants: *the parent bird/tree* **3** (often used as an adjective) an organization that produces and owns or controls smaller organizations of the same type: *a parent bank and its subsidiaries* ◆ *the parent company*

par·ent·age /ˈpɛrəntɪdʒ/ *noun* [U] the origin of a person's parents and who they are: *a young American of German parentage* ◆ *Nothing is known about her parentage and background.*

pa·ren·tal /pəˈrɛntl/ *adj.* [usually before noun] connected with a parent or parents: *parental responsibility/rights* ◆ *parental choice in education* ◆ *the parental home*

pa·rental con·trols *noun* [pl.] (also pa·rental ˈlock [C]) a feature that is offered in some computer, cell phone, and DIGITAL television services that enables parents or other adults to control children's access to material that is not suitable for them ▸ **pa·rental con·trol** *adj.* [only before noun]: *parental control software*

pa·rental ˈleave *noun* [U] time when a parent is allowed to be away from work to care for a child: *paid/unpaid parental leave* ◆ *fathers who take parental leave* ⊃ see also MATERNITY LEAVE, PATERNITY LEAVE

pa·ren·the·sis /pəˈrɛnθəsəs/ *noun* (*pl.* **pa·ren·the·ses** /-siːz/) **1** [usually pl.] either of a pair of marks, (), placed around extra information in a piece of writing or part of a problem in mathematics: *Irregular forms are given in parentheses.* **2** a word, sentence, etc. that is added to a speech or piece of writing, especially in order to give extra information. In writing, it is separated from the rest of the text using parentheses, commas, or DASHES.

par·en·thet·i·cal /ˌpærənˈθɛtɪkl/ (also **par·en·thet·ic** /ˌpærənˈθɛtɪk/) *adj.* [usually before noun] (*formal*) given as extra information in a speech or piece of writing: *parenthetical remarks* ▸ **par·en·thet·i·cally** /-kli/ *adv.*

par·ent·hood /ˈpɛrəntˌhʊd/ *noun* [U] the state of being a parent: *the responsibilities/joys of parenthood*

par·ent·ing /ˈpɛrəntɪŋ/ *noun* [U] the process of caring for your child or children: *good/poor parenting* ♦ *parenting skills* ➔ collocations at CHILD

parentis ➔ IN LOCO PARENTIS

parents-in-law *noun* [pl.] the parents of your husband or wife ➔ see also IN-LAWS

parent-teacher association *noun* = PTA

par·ex·cel·lence /ˌpɑr ˌɛksəˈlɑns/ *adj.* (from *French*) (only used after the noun it describes) better than all the others of the same kind; a very good example of something: *She turned out to be an organizer par excellence.* ▶ **par ex·cel·lence** *adv.*: *Chemistry was par excellence the laboratory science of the early nineteenth century.*

pa·ri·ah /pəˈraɪə/ *noun* a person who is not acceptable to society and is avoided by everyone **SYN** OUTCAST

paring knife *noun* a small sharp knife, used especially for cutting and PEELING fruit ➔ picture at KITCHEN ➔ see also PARE

par·ings /ˈpɛrɪŋz/ *noun* [pl.] thin pieces that have been cut off something: *cheese parings* ➔ see also PARE

par·ish /ˈpærɪʃ/ *noun* **1** an area that has its own church and that a priest is responsible for: *a parish church/priest* ♦ *He is vicar of a large rural parish.* **2** the people living in a particular area, especially those who go to church **3** an area of Louisiana that has its own government, like a county in other states

par·ish·ion·er /pəˈrɪʃənər/ *noun* a person living in a parish, especially one who goes to church regularly

parish register *noun* a book that has a list of all the BAPTISMS, marriages, and funerals that have taken place at a particular parish church

par·i·ty /ˈpærəti/ *noun* (*pl.* **par·i·ties**) **1** [U] ~ **(with sb/sth)** | ~ **(between A and B)** (*formal*) the state of being equal, especially the state of having equal pay or status: *Prison officers are demanding pay parity with the police force.* **2** [U, C] (*finance*) the fact that the units of money of two different countries being equal: *to achieve parity with the dollar*

park 🔑 /pɑrk/ *noun, verb*
• *noun* **1** [C] an area of public land in a town or a city where people go to walk, play, and relax: *We went for a walk in the park.* ♦ *a park bench* **2** [C] **Park** (*abbr.* **Pk**) used in the names of places, especially in towns: *Prospect Park* **3** [C] (in compounds) an area of land used for a particular purpose: *a business/science park* ♦ *a wildlife park* ➔ see also AMUSEMENT PARK, INDUSTRIAL PARK, NATIONAL PARK, SAFARI PARK, THEME PARK **4** [C] a piece of land for playing sports, especially baseball ➔ see also BALLPARK **5** [U] (in a vehicle) the position in which the gears are locked, preventing the vehicle's movement: *He put the car in park.* ➔ compare DRIVE *n.* (3) **IDM** see WALK
• *verb* **1** [I, T] ~ **(sth)** to leave a vehicle that you are driving in a particular place for a period of time: *You can't park here.* ♦ *You can't park the car here.* ♦ *He's parked very badly.* ♦ *a badly parked truck* ♦ *A red van was parked in front of the house.* ♦ *a parked car* ♦ (*informal, figurative*) *Just park your bags in the hall until your room is ready.* ➔ see also DOUBLE-PARK, PARALLEL PARK **2** [T] ~ **yourself** + *adv./prep.* (*informal*) to sit or stand in a particular place for a period of time: *She parked herself on the edge of the bed.* **3** [T] ~ **sth** (*informal, business*) to decide to leave an idea or issue to be dealt with or considered at a later meeting: *Let's park that until our next meeting.*

par·ka /ˈpɑrkə/ *noun* a very warm jacket or coat with a HOOD that often has fur inside

par·kade /pɑrˈkeɪd/ *noun* (*CanE*) a parking garage for many cars

park and ride *noun* [U] a system designed to reduce traffic in cities, in which people park their cars on the edge of a city and then take a special bus or train to the center of the city; the area where people park their cars before taking the bus: *Use the park and ride.* ♦ *I've left my car in the park and ride.* ♦ *a park-and-ride service*

park·ing /ˈpɑrkɪŋ/ *noun* [U] **1** the act of stopping a vehicle at a place and leaving it there for a period of time: *There is no parking here between 9 a.m. and 6 p.m.* ♦ *I managed to find a parking space.* ♦ *a parking fine* (= for parking illegally) **2** a space or an area for leaving vehicles: *The hotel is centrally situated with ample free parking.*

parking brake *noun* = EMERGENCY BRAKE

parking garage *noun* a large building with several floors for parking cars in

parking lot *noun* an area where people can leave their cars

parking meter (also **me·ter**) *noun* a machine that you put money into when you park your car in the street

parking ticket (also **tick·et**) *noun* an official notice that is put on your car when you have parked illegally, ordering you to pay money

Par·kin·son's dis·ease /ˈpɑrkənsnz dɪˌziz/ (also **Par·kin·son·ism** /ˈpɑrkənsəˌnɪzəm/) *noun* [U] a disease of the nervous system that gets worse over a period of time and causes the muscles to become weak and the arms and legs to shake

Parkinson's law *noun* [U] (*humorous*) the idea that work will always take as long as the time available for it

park·land /ˈpɑrklænd/ *noun* [U] open land with grass and trees, for example around a large house in the country

par·kour /pɑrˈkʊr/ *noun* [U] the sport of moving through a city by running, jumping, and climbing under, around, and through things **ORIGIN** From French *parcours du combatant*, a type of military training.

park·way /ˈpɑrkweɪ/ *noun* (*abbr.* **Pkwy**) a wide road with trees and grass along the sides or middle

par·lance /ˈpɑrləns/ *noun* [U] (*formal*) a particular way of using words or expressing yourself, for example one used by a particular group: *in common/legal/modern parlance*

par·lay /ˈpɑrleɪ, -li/ *verb*
PHR V **parlay sth into sth** to use or develop something such as money or a skill to make it more successful or worth more: *She hopes to parlay her success as a model into an acting career.*

par·ley /ˈpɑrli/ *noun, verb*
• *noun* (*old-fashioned*) a discussion between enemies or people who disagree, in order to try and find a way of solving a problem
• *verb* [I] ~ **(with sb)** (*old-fashioned*) to discuss something with someone in order to solve a disagreement

par·lia·ment 🔑 /ˈpɑrləmənt/ *noun*
1 [C] the group of people who are elected to make and change the laws of a country: *The German parliament is called the "Bundestag."* **2** **Parliament** [U] the parliament of the United Kingdom, consisting of the House of Commons and the House of Lords ♦ *a Member of Parliament* ♦ *The issue was debated in Parliament.* **3** also **Parliament** [C, U] a particular period during which a parliament is working; Parliament as it exists between one GENERAL ELECTION and the next: *to dissolve Parliament* (= formally end its activities) *and call an election*

par·lia·men·tar·i·an /ˌpɑrləmənˈtɛriən/ *noun* a member of a parliament, especially one with a lot of skill and experience

par·lia·men·ta·ry /ˌpɑrləˈmɛntri, -təri/ *adj.* [usually before noun] connected with a parliament; having a parliament: *parliamentary elections* ♦ *a parliamentary democracy*

par·lor (*CanE usually* **par·lour**) /ˈpɑrlər/ *noun* **1** (in compounds) a store that provides particular goods or services: *a beauty/an ice-cream parlor* ➔ see also MASSAGE PARLOR **2** (*old-fashioned*) a room in a private house for sitting in, entertaining visitors, etc.

parlor game (*CanE usually* **parlour game**) *noun* (*old-fashioned*) a game played in the home, especially a word game or guessing game

par·lor·maid (*CanE usually* **par·lour·maid**) /ˈpɑrlərˌmeɪd/

noun (*old use*) a female servant who was employed in the past to serve food at the dinner table

par·lous /ˈpɑːləs/ *adj.* (*formal*) (of a situation) very bad and very uncertain; dangerous **SYN** PERILOUS

Par·me·san /ˈpɑːməˌzæn; -ˌʒæn; -zən/ (also ˌParmesan ˈcheese) *noun* [U] a type of very hard Italian cheese that is usually GRATED and eaten on Italian food

pa·ro·chi·al /pəˈroʊkiəl/ *adj.* **1** [usually before noun] (*formal*) connected with a church PARISH: *a member of the parochial church council* **2** (*disapproving*) only concerned with small issues that happen in your local area and not interested in more important things ▶ **pa·ro·chi·al·ism** /pəˈroʊkiəˌlɪzəm/ *noun* [U]: *the parochialism of a small community*

pa·rochial ˌschool *noun* a private school supported by a particular Christian church

par·o·dist /ˈpærədɪst/ *noun* a person who writes parodies (parody)

par·o·dy /ˈpærədi/ *noun, verb*
• *noun* (*pl.* par·o·dies) ~ (of sth) **1** [C, U] a piece of writing, music, acting, etc. that deliberately copies the style of someone or something in order to be amusing: *a parody of a horror film* **2** [C] (*disapproving*) something that is such a bad or unfair example of something that it seems ridiculous **SYN** TRAVESTY: *The trial was a parody of justice.*
• *verb* (par·o·dies, par·o·dy·ing, par·o·died, par·o·died) ~ sb/sth to copy the style of someone or something in an exaggerated way, especially in order to make people laugh **SYN** LAMPOON

pa·role /pəˈroʊl/ *noun, verb*
• *noun* [U] **1** permission that is given to a prisoner to leave prison before the end of their SENTENCE on condition that they behave well: *to be eligible for parole* ◆ *She was released on parole.* ⊃ collocations at JUSTICE **2** (*linguistics*) language considered as the words individual people use, rather than as the communication system of a particular community ⊃ compare LANGUE
• *verb* [usually passive] ~ sb to give a prisoner permission to leave prison before the end of their SENTENCE on condition that they behave well: *She was paroled after two years.*

par·ox·ysm /ˈpærəkˌsɪzəm/ *noun* ~ (of sth) **1** a sudden strong feeling or expression of an emotion that cannot be controlled: *paroxysms of hate* ◆ *a paroxysm of laughter* **2** (*medical*) a sudden short attack of pain, causing physical shaking that cannot be controlled

par·quet /pɑːrˈkeɪ/ *noun* [U] a floor covering made of flat pieces of wood fixed together in a pattern: *parquet flooring* ⊃ compare WOODBLOCK

par·ri·cide /ˈpærəˌsaɪd/ *noun* [U, C] (*formal*) the crime of killing your father, mother, or a close relative; a person who is guilty of this crime ⊃ compare FRATRICIDE, MATRICIDE, PATRICIDE

par·rot /ˈpærət/ *noun, verb*
• *noun* a tropical bird with a curved beak. There are several types of parrots, most of which have bright feathers. Some are kept as pets and can be trained to copy human speech.
• *verb* ~ sb/sth (*disapproving*) to repeat what someone else has said without thinking about what it means

par·ry /ˈpæri/ *verb* (par·ries, par·ry·ing, par·ried, par·ried) **1** [T, I] ~ (sth) to defend yourself against someone who is attacking you by pushing their arm, weapon, etc. to one side **SYN** DEFLECT: *He parried a blow to his head.* ◆ *The shot was parried by the goalie.* **2** [T] ~ sth | + speech to avoid having to answer a difficult question, criticism, etc., especially by replying in the same way **SYN** FEND OFF: *She parried all questions about their relationship.* ▶ **par·ry** *noun* (*pl.* par·ries)

parse /pɑːrs/ *verb* ~ sth (*grammar*) to divide a sentence into parts and describe the grammar of each word or part

Par·see (also Par·si) /ˈpɑːrsi; ˌpɑːrˈsi/ *noun* a member of a religious group whose ANCESTORS originally came from Persia and whose religion is Zoroastrianism

par·si·mo·ni·ous /ˌpɑːrsəˈmoʊniəs/ *adj.* (*formal*) extremely unwilling to spend money **SYN** MEAN ▶ **par·si·mo·nious·ly** *adv.*

par·si·mo·ny /ˈpɑːrsəˌmoʊni/ *noun* [U] (*formal*) the fact of being extremely unwilling to spend money **SYN** MEANNESS

pars·ley /ˈpɑːrsli/ *noun* [U] a plant with curly green leaves that are used in cooking as an HERB and to decorate food: *fish with parsley sauce* ⊃ picture at HERB

pars·nip /ˈpɑːrsnɪp/ *noun* [C, U] a long, pale yellow root vegetable ⊃ picture at FRUIT

par·son /ˈpɑːrsn/ *noun* (*old-fashioned*) **1** an Anglican VICAR or PARISH priest **2** (*informal*) a Protestant CLERGYMAN

par·son·age /ˈpɑːrsənɪdʒ/ *noun* a parson's house

ˌparson's ˈnose *noun* = POPE'S NOSE

part 🔑 /pɑːrt/ *noun, verb, adv.*
• *noun*
▷ SOME **1** [U] ~ of sth some but not all of a thing: *We spent part of the time in the museum.* ◆ *Part of the building was destroyed in the fire.* ◆ *Voters are given only part of the story* (= only some of the information). ◆ *Part of me feels sorry for him* (= I feel partly, but not entirely, sorry for him).
▷ PIECE **2** [C] a section, piece, or feature of something: *The early part of her life was spent in Paris.* ◆ *The novel is good in parts.* ◆ *We've done the difficult part of the job.* ◆ *The procedure can be divided into two parts.* ◆ *The worst part was having to wait three hours in the rain.*
▷ MEMBER **3** [U] a member of something; a person or thing that, together with others, makes up a single unit: *You need to be able to work as part of a team.*
▷ OF MACHINE **4** [C] a piece of a machine or structure: *aircraft parts* ◆ *the working parts of the machinery* ◆ *spare parts*
▷ OF BODY/PLANT **5** [C] a separate piece or area of a human or animal body or of a plant: *the parts of the body* ⊃ see also PRIVATE PARTS
▷ REGION/AREA **6** [C] an area or a region of the world, a country, a town, etc.: *the northern part of the country* ◆ *a plant that grows in many parts of the world* ◆ *Which part of Japan do you come from?* ◆ *Come and visit us if you're ever in our part of the world.* **7** parts [pl.] (*old-fashioned, informal*) a region or an area: *She's not from these parts.* ◆ *He's just arrived back from foreign parts.*
▷ OF BOOK/SERIES **8** [C] (*abbr.* pt.) a section of a book, television series, etc., especially one that is published or broadcast separately: *an encyclopedia published in 25 weekly parts* ◆ *Henry IV, Part II* ◆ *The final part will be shown next Sunday evening.*
▷ FOR ACTOR **9** [C] a role played by an actor in a play, movie, etc.; the words spoken by an actor in a particular role: *She was very good in the part.* ◆ *Have you learned your part yet?* ◆ (*figurative*) *He's always playing a part* (= pretending to be something that he is not).
▷ INVOLVEMENT **10** [C, usually sing., U] the way in which someone or something is involved in an action or situation: *He had no part in the decision.*
▷ IN MUSIC **11** [C] music for a particular voice or instrument in a group singing or playing together: *the clarinet part* ◆ *four-part harmony*
▷ EQUAL PORTION **12** [C] a unit of measurement that allows you to compare the different amounts of substances in something: *Add three parts wine to one part water.*
▷ IN HAIR **13** [C] a line on a person's head where the hair is divided with a COMB ⊃ picture at HAIR

IDM the best/better part of sth most of something, especially a period of time; more than half of something: *The trip took her the better part of an hour.* for the most part mostly; usually: *The contributors are, for the most part, professional scientists.* ⊃ language bank at GENERALLY for my, his, their, etc. part speaking for myself, etc. **SYN** PERSONALLY have a part to play (in sth) to be able to help something: *We all have a part to play in the fight against crime.* have/play a part (in sth) to be involved in something: *She plays an active part in local politics.* have/play/take/want no part in/of sth to not be involved or

---

1068   h **hat**   m **man**   n **no**   ŋ **sing**   l **leg**   r **red**   y **yes**   w **wet**

refuse to be involved in something, especially because you disapprove of it: *I want no part of this sordid business.* **in part** partly; to some extent: *Her success was due in part to luck.* **look/dress the part** to have an appearance or wear clothes suitable for a particular job, role, or position **a man/woman of (many) parts** a person with many skills **on the part of sb/on sb's part** made or done by someone: *It was an error on my part.* **part and parcel of sth** an essential part of something: *Keeping the accounts is part and parcel of my job.* **part of the furniture** a person or thing that you are so used to seeing that you no longer notice them: *I worked there so long that I became part of the furniture.* **take part (in sth)** to be involved in something **SYN** PARTICIPATE: *to take part in a discussion/demonstration/fight/celebration* ◆ *How many countries took part in the last Olympic Games?* ⊃ **more at** DISCRETION, LARGE, SUM

● **verb**

> **LEAVE SOMEONE 1** [I] (*formal*) if a person **parts** from another person, or two people **part**, they leave each other: *We parted at the airport.* ◆ *I hate to part on such bad terms.* ◆ **~ from sb** *He has recently parted from his wife* (= they have started to live apart). ⊃ see also PARTING *adj.*

> **KEEP APART 2** [T, often passive] **~ sb (from sb)** (*formal*) to prevent someone from being with someone else: *I hate being parted from the children.* ◆ *The puppies were parted from their mother at birth.*

> **MOVE AWAY 3** [I, T] if two things or parts of things **part** or you **part** them, they move away from each other: *The crowd parted in front of them.* ◆ *The elevator doors parted and out stepped the President.* ◆ **~ sth** *Her lips were slightly parted.* ◆ *She parted the curtains a little and looked out.*

> **HAIR 4** [T] **~ sth** to divide your hair into two sections with a COMB, creating a line that goes from the back of your head to the front: *He parts his hair in the middle.*

IDM **part company (with/from sb) 1** to leave someone; to end a relationship with someone: *This is where we part company* (= go in different directions). ◆ *The band have parted company with their manager.* ◆ *The band and their manager have parted company.* **2** to disagree with someone about something: *Weber parted company with Marx on a number of important issues.* ⊃ **more at** FOOL **PHR V** **'part with sth** to give something to someone else, especially something that you would prefer to keep: *Make sure you read the contract before parting with any money.*

● **adv.** (often in compounds) consisting of two things; to some extent but not completely: *She's part French, part English.* ◆ *His feelings were part anger, part relief.* ◆ *The work was part funded by grants from the National Geographic Society.* ◆ *He is part owner of a farm in France.*

par·take /pɑr'teɪk/ *verb* (**par·took** /-'tʊk/, **par·tak·en** /-'teɪkən/) (*formal*) **1** [I] **~ (of sth)** (*old-fashioned or humorous*) to eat or drink something, especially something that is offered to you: *Would you care to partake of some refreshment?* **2** [I] **~ (in sth)** (*old-fashioned*) to take part in an activity: *They preferred not to partake in the social life of the town.*
PHR V **par'take of sth** (*formal*) to have some of a particular quality: *His work partakes of the aesthetic fashions of his time.*

par·terre /pɑr'ter/ *noun* (from *French*) **1** a flat area in a garden, with plants arranged in a formal design **2** the lower level in a theater where the audience sits, especially the area underneath the BALCONY

par·the·no·gen·e·sis /ˌpɑrθənoʊ'dʒɛnəsəs/ *noun* [U] (*biology*) the process of producing new plants or animals from an OVUM that has not been FERTILIZED ▶ **par·the·no·ge·net·ic** /ˌpɑrθənoʊdʒə'nɛtɪk/ *adj.*: *parthenogenetic species* **par·the·no·ge·net·i·cally** /-kli/ *adj.*: *These organisms reproduce parthenogenetically.*

par·tial /'pɑrʃl/ *adj.* **1** not complete or whole: *It was only a partial solution to the problem.* ◆ *a partial eclipse of the sun* **2** [not before noun] **~ to sb/sth** (*old-fashioned*) liking someone or something very much: *I'm not partial to mushrooms.* **3** [not usually before noun] **~ (toward sb/sth)** (*disapproving*) showing or feeling too much support for one

person, team, idea, etc., in a way that is unfair **SYN** BIASED **ANT** IMPARTIAL

par·ti·al·i·ty /ˌpɑrʃi'æləti/ *noun* (*formal*) **1** [U] (*disapproving*) the unfair support of one person, team, idea, etc. **SYN** BIAS **2** [sing.] **~ for sth/sb** a feeling of liking something or someone very much **SYN** FONDness: *She has a partiality for exotic flowers.*

par·tial·ly /'pɑrʃəli/ *adv.* partly; not completely: *The road was partially blocked by a fallen tree.* ◆ *a society for the blind and partially sighted* (= people who can see very little) ⊃ **note at** PARTLY

par·tic·i·pant **AWL** /pɑr'tɪsəpənt/ *noun* **~ (in sth)** a person who is taking part in an activity or event: *He has been an active participant in the discussion.*

par·tic·i·pate **AWL** /pɑr'tɪsəˌpeɪt/ *verb* [I] **~ (in sth)** (*somewhat formal*) to take part in or become involved in an activity: *She didn't participate in the discussion.* ◆ *We encourage students to participate fully in the running of the college.* ◆ *Details of the competition are available at all participating stores.*

par·tic·i·pa·tion **AWL** /pɑrˌtɪsə'peɪʃn/ *noun* [U] the act of taking part in an activity or event: *a show with lots of audience participation* ◆ **~ in sth** *A back injury prevented active participation in any sports for a while.*

par·tic·i·pa·to·ry **AWL** /pɑr'tɪsəpəˌtɔri/ *adj.* [usually before noun] allowing everyone in a society, business, etc. to give their opinions and to help make decisions: *Participatory democracy is a fundamental principle of cooperative businesses.*

par·ti·ci·ple /'pɑrtəˌsɪpl/ *noun* (in English) a word formed from a verb, ending in *-ing* (= the PRESENT PARTICIPLE) or *-ed, -en*, etc. (= the PAST PARTICIPLE) ▶ **par·ti·cip·i·al** /ˌpɑrtə'sɪpiəl/ *adj.*

par·ti·cle /'pɑrtɪkl/ *noun* **1** a very small piece of something: *particles of dust* ◆ *dust particles* ◆ *There was **not a particle of** evidence* (= no evidence at all) *to support the case.* **2** (*physics*) a very small piece of matter, such as an ELECTRON or a PROTON, that is part of an atom ⊃ see also ALPHA PARTICLE, ELEMENTARY PARTICLE **3** (*grammar*) an adverb or a preposition that can combine with a verb to make a phrasal verb: *In "She tore up the letter," the word "up" is a particle.* ⊃ see also ADVERBIAL PARTICLE

par·ti·cle·board /'pɑrtɪklˌbɔrd/ *noun* [U] a type of board that is used for building, made of small pieces of wood that are pressed together and stuck with glue

'particle ˌphysics *noun* [U] the scientific study of very small pieces of matter that are parts of an atom

par·tic·u·lar /pər'tɪkyələr/ *adj., noun*

● **adj. 1** [only before noun] used to emphasize that you are referring to one individual person, thing, or type of thing and not others **SYN** SPECIFIC: *There is one particular patient I'd like you to see.* ◆ *Is there a particular type of book he enjoys?* **2** [only before noun] greater than usual; special: *We must pay particular attention to this point.* ◆ *These documents are of particular interest.* **3** **~ (about/over sth)** very definite about what you like and careful about what you choose **SYN** FUSSY: *She's very particular about her clothes.*
IDM **in particular 1** especially or particularly: *He loves science fiction in particular.* ⊃ language bank at EMPHASIS **2** special or specific: *Peter was lying on the sofa doing nothing in particular.* ◆ *Is there anything in particular you'd like for dinner?* ◆ *She directed the question at no one in particular.*

● **noun 1** [usually pl.] a fact or detail, especially one that is officially written down: *The police officer noted all the particulars of the burglary.* ◆ *The nurse asked me for my particulars* (= personal details such as your name, address, etc.). ◆ *The new contract will be the same in every particular as the old one.* **2** **particulars** [pl.] written information and details about a property, business, job, etc.: *Application forms and further particulars are available from the Personnel Office.*

---

par·tic·u·lar·i·ty /pərˌtɪkyəˈlærəti/ noun (pl. **par·tic·u·lar·i·ties**) (formal) **1** [U] the quality of being individual or unique: *the particularity of each human being* **2** [U] attention to detail; being exact **3 particularities** [pl.] the special features or details of something

par·tic·u·lar·ize /pərˈtɪkyələˌraɪz/ verb [I, T] ~ (sth) (formal) to give details of something, especially one by one; to give particular examples of something

par·tic·u·lar·ly /pərˈtɪkyələrli/ adv.

especially; more than usual or more than others: *particularly good/important/useful* ◆ *Traffic is bad, particularly downtown.* ◆ *I enjoyed the play, particularly the second half.* ◆ *The lecture was not particularly* (= not very) *interesting.* ◆ *"Did you enjoy it?" "No, not particularly* (= not very much).*"*

par·tic·u·late /pərˈtɪkyələt/ adj., noun (chemistry)
● *adj.* relating to, or in the form of, PARTICLES: *particulate pollution*
● *noun* **particulates** [pl.] matter in the form of PARTICLES

part·ing /ˈpɑrtɪŋ/ noun, adj.
● *noun* **1** [U, C] the act or occasion of leaving a person or place: *the moment of parting* ◆ *We had a tearful parting at the airport.* **2** [U, C] the act or result of dividing something into parts: *the parting of the clouds*
  IDM **a/the parting of the ways** a point at which two people or groups of people decide to separate
● *adj.* [only before noun] said or done by someone as they leave: *a parting kiss* ◆ *His parting words were "I love you."*
  IDM **parting shot** a final remark, especially an unkind one, that someone makes as they leave

par·ti·san /ˈpɑrtəzən; -sn/ adj., noun
● *adj.* (often disapproving) showing too much support for one person, group, or idea, especially without considering it carefully **SYN** ONE-SIDED: *Most newspapers are politically partisan.*
● *noun* **1** a person who strongly supports a particular leader, group, or idea **SYN** FOLLOWER **2** a member of an armed group that is fighting secretly against enemy soldiers who have taken control of its country ► **par·ti·san·ship** /-ˌʃɪp/ noun [U]

par·ti·tion /pɑrˈtɪʃn/ noun, verb
● *noun* **1** [C] a wall or screen that separates one part of a room from another: *a glass partition* ◆ *partition walls* **2** [U] the division of one country into two or more countries: *the partition of Germany after the war*
● *verb* [often passive] to divide something into parts: ~ **sth** *to partition a country* ◆ ~ **sth into sth** *The room is partitioned into three sections.*
  PHR V **par·tition sth**↔**'off** to separate one area, one part of a room, etc. from another with a wall or screen

par·ti·tive /ˈpɑrtətɪv/ noun (grammar) a word or phrase that shows a part or quantity of something: *In "a spoonful of sugar," the word "spoonful" is a partitive.* ► **par·ti·tive** adj.

part·ly /ˈpɑrtli/ adv.

to some extent; not completely: *Some people are unwilling to attend the classes **partly because** of the cost involved.* ◆ *He was only **partly** responsible for the accident.*

> **WHICH WORD?**
>
> **partly ◆ partially**
>
> ▪ **Partly** and **partially** both mean "not completely": *The road is partly/partially finished.* **Partly** is especially used to talk about the reason for something, often followed by *because* or *due to*: *I didn't enjoy the trip very much, partly because of the weather.* **Partially** should be used when you are talking about physical conditions: *His mother is partially blind.*

part·ner **AWL** /ˈpɑrtnər/ noun, verb
● *noun* **1** the person that you are married to or having a sexual relationship with: *Come to the New Year disco and bring your partner!* ◆ *a marriage partner* ⊃ collocations at MARRIAGE ⊃ see also DOMESTIC PARTNER **2** one of the people who owns a business and shares the profits, etc.: *a partner in a law firm* ◆ *a junior/senior partner* **3** a person that you are doing an activity with, such as dancing or playing a game: *a dancing/tennis, etc. partner* ⊃ see also SPARRING PARTNER **4** a country or an organization that has an agreement with another country: *a trading partner* ⊃ see also SILENT PARTNER
● *verb* ~ **sb** to be someone's partner in a dance, game, etc.: *Gerry offered to partner me at tennis.*

part·ner·ship **AWL** /ˈpɑrtnərˌʃɪp/ noun
1 [U] the state of being a partner in business: *to be in/to go into partnership* ◆ ~ **with sb/sth** *He developed his own program **in partnership** with an American expert.* **2** [C, U] a relationship between two people, organizations, etc.; the state of having this relationship: *Marriage should be an equal partnership.* ◆ ~ **with sb/sth** *the school's partnership with parents* ◆ ~ **between A and B** *a partnership between the United States and Europe* **3** [C] a business owned by two or more people who share the profits: *a junior member of the partnership*

part of 'speech noun (grammar) one of the classes into which words are divided according to their grammar, such as noun, verb, adjective, etc. **SYN** WORD CLASS

par·took pt of PARTAKE

par·tridge /ˈpɑrtrɪdʒ/ noun (pl. **par·tridg·es** or **par·tridge**) [C, U] a brown bird with a round body and a short tail, which people hunt for sport or food; the meat of this bird

part-'time adj. (abbr. PT) for part of the day or week in which people work: *She's looking for a part-time job.* ◆ *to study on a part-time basis* ◆ *part-time workers* ◆ *I'm only part-time at the moment.* ▶ **part-'time** adv.: *Liz works part-time from 10 till 2.* ⊃ compare FULL-TIME

part-'timer noun a person who works part-time

par·tu·ri·tion /ˌpɑrtʃəˈrɪʃn; ˌpɑrtə-/ noun [U] (technical) the act of giving birth

part-'way adv. some of the way: *They were part-way through the speeches when he arrived.*

par·ty /ˈpɑrti/ noun, verb
● *noun* (pl. **par·ties**) **1** (especially in compounds) a social occasion, often in a person's home, at which people eat, drink, talk, dance, and enjoy themselves: *a birthday/dinner/garden, etc. party* ◆ *to give/have/throw a party* ◆ *Did you go to the party?* ◆ *party games* ⊃ see also BACHELOR PARTY, HOUSE PARTY **2** also **Party** a political organization that you can vote for in elections and whose members have the same aims and ideas: *the Democratic and Republican Parties* ◆ *She belongs to the Green Party.* ◆ *the ruling/opposition party* ◆ *the party leader/manifesto/policy* ⊃ collocations at POLITICS **3** a group of people who are doing something together, such as traveling or visiting somewhere: *The guide took a party of 40 tourists to France.* ◆ *The theater gives a 10% discount to parties of more than ten.* ⊃ see also SEARCH PARTY **4** (formal) one of the people or groups of people involved in a legal agreement or argument: *the guilty/innocent party* ◆ *The contract can be terminated by either party with three months' notice.* ⊃ see also INJURED PARTY, THIRD PARTY
  IDM **be (a) party to sth** (formal) to be involved in an agreement or action: *to be party to a dispute* ◆ *He refused to be a party to any violence.* **bring sth to the party/table** to contribute something useful to a discussion, project, etc.: *What Alvarez brought to the party was real commitment and energy.*
● *verb* (**par·ties, par·ty·ing, par·tied, par·tied**) [I] (informal) to enjoy yourself, especially by eating, drinking alcohol, and dancing: *They were out partying every night.*

'party ˌanimal noun (informal) a person who likes to go to parties, often drinks a lot of alcohol, and tends to behave in a loud and noisy way

party ˌfavors *noun* [pl.] small gifts that are often given to children at a party

party-ˌgoer *noun* a person who enjoys going to parties or who is a guest at a particular party

ˌparty ˈline¹ *noun* the official opinions and policies of a political party, which members are expected to support **IDM** see TOE *v.*

ˈparty line² *noun* a telephone line that is shared by two or more customers

ˌparty ˈpolitics *noun* [U] political activity that involves political parties: *The President should stand above party politics.* ♦ *Many people think that party politics should not enter into local government.*

par·ty-poop·er /ˈpɑrti ˌpupər/ *noun* (*informal*) a person who does not want to take part in an enjoyable activity and spoils the fun for other people

ˈparty ˌschool *noun* (*informal*) a college or university that has a reputation for attracting students who like to have parties and enjoy themselves rather than being serious about their studies

ˌparty ˈwall *noun* a wall that divides two buildings or rooms and belongs to both owners

par·ve·nu /ˈpɑrvəˌnu/ *noun* (*pl.* **par·ve·nus**) (*formal*, *disapproving*) a person from a low social or economic position who has suddenly become rich or powerful

pas·cal *noun* **1** /ˈpæskl; pæˈskæl/ (*abbr.* **Pa**) the standard unit for measuring pressure **2 Pascal, PASCAL** /pæˈskæl/ a language used for writing programs for computer systems

pas·chal /ˈpæskl/ *adj.* (*formal*) **1** relating to Easter **2** relating to the Jewish Passover

pas de deux /ˌpɑ də ˈdʊ/ *noun* (*pl.* **pas de deux**) (from French) a dance, often part of a BALLET, that is performed by two people

pash·mi·na /pæʃˈminə/ *noun* a long piece of cloth made of fine soft wool from a type of GOAT and worn by a woman around the shoulders

Pash·to /ˈpʌʃtoʊ/ *noun* [U] the official language of Afghanistan, also spoken in northern Pakistan

pass 🔑 /pæs/ *verb, noun*

● *verb*

> MOVE **1** [I, T] to move past or to the other side of someone or something: *Several people were passing but nobody offered to help.* ♦ *I hailed a passing taxi.* ♦ *The road was so narrow that cars were unable to pass.* ♦ ~ *sb/sth to pass a barrier/sentry/checkpoint* ♦ *You'll pass a bank on the way to the train station.* ♦ *She passed me in the street without even saying hello.* ♦ *There was a truck behind that was trying to pass me.* **2** [I] + *adv./prep.* to go or move in the direction mentioned: *The procession passed slowly along the street.* ♦ *A plane passed low overhead.* **3** [T] ~ *sth + adv./prep.* to make something move in the direction or into the position mentioned: *He passed the rope around the post three times to secure it.*

> GIVE **4** [T] to give something to someone by putting it into their hands or in a place where they can easily reach it: ~ *sth (to sb) Pass the salt, please.* ♦ *Pass that book over.* ♦ ~ *sb sth Pass me over that book.*

> BALL **5** [T, I] (in ball games) to kick, hit, or throw the ball to a player of your own side: ~ *sth (to sb) He passed the ball to Reggie Miller.* ♦ ~ *(to sb) Why do they keep passing back to the goalie?*

> AFTER DEATH **6** [I] ~ *to sb* to be given to another person after first belonging to someone else, especially after the first person has died: *On his death, the estate passed to his eldest son.*

> BECOME GREATER **7** [T] ~ *sth* (of an amount) to become greater than a particular total **SYN** EXCEED: *Unemployment has now passed the three million mark.*

> CHANGE **8** [I] ~ *from sth to/into sth* to change from one state or condition to another: *She had passed from childhood to early womanhood.*

> TIME **9** [I] when time *passes*, it goes by: *Six months passed and we still had no news from them.* ♦ *We grew more anxious*

with every passing day. **10** [T] ~ *sth* to spend time, especially when you are bored or waiting for something: *We sang songs to* **pass the time.** ♦ *How did you pass the evening?*

> END **11** [I] to come to an end; to be over: *They waited for the storm to pass.*

> TEST/EXAM **12** [I, T] to achieve the required standard in an exam, a test, etc.: *I'm not really expecting to pass first time.* ♦ ~ *sth She hasn't passed her driving test yet.* **ANT** FAIL **13** [T] ~ *sb* to test someone and decide that they are good enough, according to an agreed standard: *The examiners passed all the candidates.* **ANT** FAIL

> LAW/PROPOSAL **14** [T] ~ *sth* to accept a proposal, law, etc. by voting: *The bill was passed by 285 votes to 150.*

> HAPPEN **15** [I] to be allowed: *I don't like it, but I'll* **let it pass** (= will not object). ♦ *Her remarks passed without comment* (= people ignored them). **16** [I] to happen; to be said or done: ~ *(between A and B) They'll never be friends again after all that has passed between them.* ♦ + *adj. His departure passed unnoticed.*

> NOT KNOW **17** [I] ~ *(on sth)* to say that you do not know the answer to a question, especially during a QUIZ: *"What's the capital of Peru?" "I'll have to pass on that one."* ♦ *"Who wrote 'Catch-22'?" "Pass* (= I don't know)."

> NOT WANT **18** [I] ~ *(on sth)* to say that you do not want something that is offered to you: *Thanks. I'm going to pass on dessert, if you don't mind.*

> SAY/STATE SOMETHING **19** [T] ~ *sth (on sb/sth)* to say or state something, especially officially: *The court waited in silence for the judge to* **pass sentence.** ♦ *It's not for me to* **pass judgment** *on your behavior.* ♦ *The man smiled at the girl and passed a friendly remark.*

> BELIEF/UNDERSTANDING **20** [T] ~ **belief, understanding,** etc. (*formal*) to go beyond the limits of what you can believe, understand, etc.: *It passes belief* (= is impossible to believe) *that she could do such a thing.*

> IN CARD GAMES **21** [I] to refuse to play a card or make a BID¹ when it is your turn

> FROM THE BODY **22** [T] ~ *sth* to send something out from the body as or with waste matter: *If you're passing blood, you ought to see a doctor.*

IDM **come to pass** (*old use*) to happen **not pass your lips 1** if words do **not pass your lips,** you say nothing **2** if food or drink does **not pass your lips,** you eat or drink nothing **pass the hat around** (*informal*) to collect money from a number of people, for example to buy a present for someone **pass muster** to be accepted as of a good enough standard **pass the time of day (with sb)** to say hello to someone and have a short conversation with them **pass water** (*formal*) to URINATE

PHR V ˌpass sth↔aˈround to give something to another person, who gives it to someone else, etc. until everyone has seen it: *Can you pass these pictures around for everyone to look at, please?* ˈpass as sb/sth = PASS FOR/AS SB/STH ˌpass aˈway **1** (also ˌpass ˈon) to die. People say "pass away" to avoid saying "die.": *His mother passed away last year.* **2** to stop existing: *civilizations that have passed away* ˌpass ˈby (sb/sth) to go past: *The procession passed right by my front door.* ˌpass sb/sth ˈby to happen without affecting someone or something: *She feels that life is passing her by* (= that she is not enjoying the opportunities and pleasures of life). ˌpass sth↔ˈdown [often passive] to give or teach something to your children or people younger than you, who will then give or teach it to those who live after them, and so on **SYN** HAND DOWN ˈpass for/as sb/sth to be accepted as someone or something: *He speaks the language so well he could easily pass for a German.* ♦ *We had some wine—or what passes for wine in that area.* ˈpass into sth to become a part of something: *Many foreign words have passed into the English language.* ˌpass sb/yourself/sth ˈoff as sb/sth to pretend that someone or something is something they are not: *He escaped by passing himself off as a guard.* ˌpass ˈon = PASS AWAY ˌpass sth↔ˈon (to sb) to give something to someone else, especially after receiving it or using it yourself: *Pass the book on to me when you've finished with it.* ♦ *I passed your message on to my mother.* ♦ *Much of the discount is pocketed by retailers instead of being passed on to customers.*

,pass 'out to become unconscious **SYN** FAINT **,pass sb↔'over** to not consider someone for promotion in a job, especially when they deserve it or think that they deserve it: *He was passed over in favor of a younger man.* **,pass 'over sth** to ignore or avoid something **SYN** OVERLOOK: *They chose to pass over her rude remarks.* **,pass 'through…** to go through a town, etc., stopping there for a short time but not staying: *We were passing through, so we thought we'd come and say hello.* **,pass sth↔'up** (*informal*) to choose not to make use of a chance, an opportunity, etc.: *Imagine passing up an offer like that!*

● *noun*
▷ **OFFICIAL DOCUMENT 1** an official document or ticket that shows that you have the right to enter or leave a place, to travel on a bus or train, etc.: *a boarding pass* (= for a plane) ◆ *There is no admittance without a security pass.* ⊃ **see also** BUS PASS
▷ **OF BALL 2** (in some sports) an act of hitting or throwing the ball to another player in your team: *a long pass to the corner* ◆ *a back pass to the goalkeeper*
▷ **IN EXAM 3** a successful result in an exam: *The exams are graded honors, pass or fail.*
▷ **THROUGH MOUNTAINS 4** a road or way over or through mountains: *a mountain pass*
▷ **MOVING PAST/OVER 5** an act of going or moving past or over something: *The helicopter made several passes over the village before landing.*
▷ **STAGE IN PROCESS 6** a stage in a process, especially one that involves separating things from a larger group: *In the first pass all the addresses are loaded into the database.*
IDM **come to such a pass| come to a pretty pass** (*old-fashioned or humorous*) to reach a sad or difficult state **make a pass at sb** (*informal*) to try to start a sexual relationship with someone

pass·a·ble /ˈpæsəbl/ *adj.* **1** fairly good but not excellent **SYN** SATISFACTORY **2** [not usually before noun] if a road or a river is **passable**, it is not blocked and you can travel along or across it **ANT** IMPASSABLE

pass·a·bly /ˈpæsəbli/ *adv.* in a way that is acceptable or good enough **SYN** REASONABLY: *He speaks passably good French.*

pas·sage /ˈpæsɪdʒ/ *noun*
▷ **LONG NARROW WAY 1** (also **pas·sage·way** /ˈpæsɪdʒweɪ/) [C] a long narrow area with walls on either side that connects one room or place with another **SYN** CORRIDOR: *a secret underground passage* ◆ *A dark narrow passage led to the main hall.*
▷ **IN THE BODY 2** [C] a tube in the body through which air, liquid, etc. passes: *blocked nasal passages*
▷ **SECTION FROM BOOK 3** [C] a short section from a book, piece of music, etc. **SYN** EXCERPT, EXTRACT: *Read the following passage and answer the questions below.* ⊃ **collocations at** LITERATURE
▷ **OF TIME 4** [sing.] **the ~ of time** (*literary*) the process of time passing: *Her confidence grew with the passage of time.*
▷ **OF BILL/LEGISLATION 5** [sing.] the process of discussing a BILL in a law-making body so that it can become law: *The bill is now guaranteed an easy passage through the House of Representatives.*
▷ **JOURNEY BY SHIP 6** [sing.] a journey from one place to another by ship: *Her grandfather had **worked his passage*** (= worked on a ship to pay for the journey) *to America.*
▷ **GOING THROUGH 7** [sing.] **a ~ (through sth)** a way through something: *The officers forced a passage through the crowd.* **8** [U] (*formal*) the action of going across, through, or past something: *Large trees may obstruct the passage of light.* **9** [U, C, usually sing.] the permission to travel across a particular area of land: *We were promised (a) safe passage through the occupied territory.* ⊃ **see also** BIRD OF PASSAGE, RITE OF PASSAGE

pass·book /ˈpæsbʊk/ *noun* a small book containing a record of the money you put into and take out of a savings account, for example at a bank

pas·sé /pæˈseɪ/ *adj.* [not usually before noun] (from *French, disapproving*) no longer fashionable **SYN** OUTMODED

pas·sen·ger 🔊 /ˈpæsəndʒər/ *noun* a person who is traveling in a car, bus, train, plane, or ship and who is not driving it or working on it: *a passenger train* (= carrying passengers, not goods)

passenger ,seat *noun* the seat in a car that is next to the driver's seat ⊃ **picture at** CAR

pass·er·by (also **passer-by**) /ˌpæsərˈbaɪ/ *noun* (*pl.* **pass·ers·by, passers-by**) a person who is going past someone or something by chance, especially when something unexpected happens: *Police asked passersby if they had seen the accident.* ⊃ **thesaurus box at** WITNESS

,pass-'fail *adj.* connected with a grading system for school classes, etc. in which a student passes or fails rather than receiving a grade as a letter (for example, A or B) ▶ **,pass-'fail** *adv.*: *to take a class pass-fail*

pas·sim /ˈpæsəm/ *adv.* (from *Latin*) used in the notes to a book or an article to show that a particular name or subject appears in several places in it

pass·ing 🔊 /ˈpæsɪŋ/ *noun, adj.*
● *noun* [U] **1** **the ~ of time/the years** the process of time going by **2** (*formal*) the fact of something ending or of someone dying: *When the government is finally brought down, no one will mourn its passing.* ◆ *the passing of the old year* (= on New Year's Eve) ◆ *Many will mourn her passing* (= her death, when you do not want to say this directly). **3** **the ~ of sth** the act of making something become a law: *the passing of a resolution/law*
IDM **in passing** done or said while you are giving your attention to something else **SYN** CASUALLY: *He only mentioned it in passing and didn't give any details.*
● *adj.* [only before noun] **1** lasting only for a short period of time and then disappearing **SYN** BRIEF: *a passing phase/thought/interest* ◆ *He makes only a **passing reference** to the theory in his book* (= it is not the main subject of his book). ◆ *She bears more than a **passing resemblance** to* (= looks very like) *your sister.* **2** going past: *I love him more with each passing day.* ◆ *the noise of passing cars* **3** **~ grade** a grade/mark that achieves the required standard in an exam, a test, etc.

passing ,lane *noun* the part of a major road, such as an INTERSTATE, nearest the middle of the road, where vehicles drive fastest and can go past vehicles ahead

passing ,shot *noun* (in TENNIS) a shot that goes past your opponent, and that they cannot reach

pas·sion 🔊 /ˈpæʃn/ *noun*
1 [C, U] a very strong feeling of love, hatred, anger, enthusiasm, etc.: *He's a man of violent passions.* ◆ *a crime of passion* ◆ *She argued her case with considerable passion.* ◆ *Passions were running high* (= people were angry and emotional) *at the meeting.* **2** [sing.] (*formal*) a state of being very angry **SYN** RAGE: *She flies into a passion if anyone even mentions his name.* **3** [U] **~ (for sb)** a very strong feeling of sexual love: *His passion for her made him blind to everything else.* **4** [C] **~ (for sth)** a very strong feeling of liking something; a hobby, an activity, etc. that you like very much: *Americans have a passion for sports.* ◆ *Music is a passion with him.* **5** **the Passion** [sing.] (in Christianity) the suffering and death of Jesus Christ

pas·sion·ate /ˈpæʃənət/ *adj.* **1** having or showing strong feelings of sexual love or of anger, etc.: *to have a passionate nature* **2** having or showing strong feelings of enthusiasm for something or belief in something: *a passionate interest in music* ◆ *a passionate defender of civil liberties* ▶ **pas·sion·ate·ly** *adv.*: *He took her in his arms and kissed her passionately.* ◆ *They are all passionately interested in environmental issues.*

passion ,flower *noun* a tropical climbing plant with large brightly colored flowers

passion ,fruit *noun* (*pl.* **pas·sion fruit**) [C, U] a small tropical fruit with thick purple skin and many seeds inside,

t **tea**	ţ **butter**	d **did**	k **cat**	g **got**	tʃ **chin**	dʒ **June**	f **fall**

produced by some types of passion flowers ⭢ picture at FRUIT

pas·sion·less /'pæʃnləs/ adj. without emotion or enthusiasm

'passion ˌplay noun a play about the suffering and death of Jesus Christ

pas·sive AWL /'pæsɪv/ adj., noun
- adj. **1** accepting what happens or what people do without trying to change anything or oppose them: He played a passive role in the relationship. ◆ a passive observer of events **2** (grammar) connected with the form of a verb used when the subject is affected by the action of the verb, for example "He was bitten by a dog." is a passive sentence ⭢ compare ACTIVE ▶ **pas·sive·ly** AWL adv.
- noun (also ˌpassive 'voice) [sing.] (grammar) the form of a verb used when the subject is affected by the action of the verb ⭢ compare ACTIVE

ˌpassive-agˈgressive adj. being angry without expressing your anger openly, but resisting people in authority by refusing to do what they want or to accept responsibility for your actions: He exhibited passive-aggressive tendencies.

ˌpassive reˈsistance noun [U] a way of opposing a government or an enemy by peaceful means, often by refusing to obey laws or orders

ˌpassive 'smoking noun [U] the act of breathing in smoke from other people's cigarettes

pas·siv·i·ty AWL /pæ'sɪvəti/ noun [U] the state of accepting what happens without reacting or trying to fight against it

pas·siv·ize /'pæsə,vaɪz/ verb ~ sth (grammar) to put a verb into the passive form

'pass key (also 'master ˌkey) noun a key that can be used to open many different locks in a building

Pass·o·ver /'pæs,oʊvər/ noun [U, C] the Jewish religious festival and holiday in memory of the escape of the Jews from Egypt

'pass ˌplay (also 'passing ˌplay) noun (in football) a play in which a player passes the ball forward to another member of the team ⭢ compare RUN PLAY

pass·port 🖉 /'pæsport/ noun
1 an official document that identifies you as a citizen of a particular country, and that you may have to show when you enter or leave a country: a valid passport ◆ a United States passport ◆ I was stopped as I went through passport control (= where passports are checked). ◆ a passport photo **2** ~ to sth a thing that makes something possible or enables you to achieve something SYN KEY: The only passport to success is hard work.

pass·word /'pæswərd/ noun **1** a secret word or phrase that you need to know in order to be allowed into a place **2** (computing) a series of letters and/or numbers that you must type into a computer or computer system in order to be able to use it: Enter a username and password to get into the system.

past 🖉 /pæst/ adj., noun, prep., adv.
- adj. **1** gone by in time: in past years/centuries/ages ◆ in times past ◆ The time for discussion is past. **2** [only before noun] gone by recently; just ended: I haven't seen much of her in the past few weeks. ◆ The past month has been really busy at work. **3** [only before noun] belonging to an earlier time: past events ◆ From past experience I'd say he's probably forgotten the time. ◆ past and present students of the college ◆ Let's forget about who was more to blame—it's all past history. **4** [only before noun] (grammar) connected with the form of a verb used to express actions in the past
- noun **1** the past [sing.] the time that has gone by; things that happened in an earlier time: I used to go there often in the past. ◆ the recent/distant past ◆ She looked back on the past without regret. ◆ Writing letters seems to be a thing of the past. **2** [C] a person's past life or career: We don't know anything about his past. ◆ They say she has a "past" (= bad things in her

past life that she wishes to keep secret). **3** the past [sing.] (grammar) = PAST TENSE IDM see BLAST, DISTANT, LIVE¹
- prep. **1** on or to the other side of someone or something: We live in the house just past the church. ◆ He hurried past them without stopping. ◆ He just walked **straight past** us! **2** above or further than a particular point or stage: Unemployment is now past the 3 million mark. ◆ The flowers are past their best. ◆ He's past his prime. ◆ She's long past retirement age. ◆ Honestly, I'm **past caring** what happens (= I can no longer be bothered to care). **3** later than something: half past two ◆ It was past midnight when we got home. ◆ His rent is **past due** (= it has not been paid for by the time it should have been).
- adv. **1** from one side of something to the other: I called out to him as he ran past. **2** used to describe time passing SYN BY: A week went past and nothing had changed.

pas·ta /'pɑstə/ noun [U] an Italian food made from flour, water, and sometimes eggs, formed into different shapes and usually served with a sauce. It is hard when dry and soft when cooked.

paste /peɪst/ noun, verb
- noun **1** [sing.] a soft wet mixture, usually made of a powder and a liquid: She mixed the flour and water to a smooth paste. **2** [C] (especially in compounds) a smooth mixture of crushed meat, fish, etc. that is spread on bread or used in cooking **3** [U] a type of glue that is used for sticking paper to things: wallpaper paste **4** [U] a substance like glass, that is used for making artificial JEWELS, for example diamonds
- verb **1** [T] ~ sth + adv./prep. to stick something to something else using glue or paste: He pasted the pictures into his scrapbook. ◆ Paste the two pieces together. ◆ Paste down the edges. **2** [T] ~ sth to make something by sticking pieces of paper together: The children were busy cutting and pasting paper hats. **3** [T, I] ~ (sth) (computing) to copy or move text into a document from another place or another document: This function allows you to **cut and paste** text. ◆ It's quicker to cut and paste than to retype.

paste·board /'peɪstbɔrd/ noun [U] a type of thin board made by sticking sheets of paper together

pas·tel /pæ'stɛl/ noun **1** [U] soft colored CHALK, used for drawing pictures: drawings in pastel **2** pastels [pl.] small sticks of CHALK: a box of pastels **3** [C] a picture drawn with pastels ⭢ collocations at ART **4** [C] a pale delicate color: The whole house was painted in soft pastels.

pas·tern /'pæstərn/ noun (anatomy) the part of a horse's foot between the FETLOCK and the HOOF

pas·teur·ize /'pæstʃə,raɪz/ verb ~ sth to heat a liquid, especially milk, to a particular temperature and then cool it, in order to kill harmful bacteria ▶ **pas·teur·i·za·tion** /,pæstʃərə'zeɪʃn/ noun [U]

pas·tiche /pæ'stiʃ/ noun **1** [C] a work of art, piece of writing, etc. that is created by deliberately copying the style of someone or something else: a pastiche of the classic detective story **2** [C] a work of art, etc. that consists of a variety of different styles **3** [U] the art of creating a pastiche

pas·time /'pæstaɪm/ noun something that you enjoy doing when you are not working SYN HOBBY ⭢ thesaurus box at INTEREST

past·ing /'peɪstɪŋ/ noun [sing.] a heavy defeat in a game or competition

ˌpast 'master noun ~ (at sth/at doing sth) a person who is very good at something because they have a lot of experience in it SYN EXPERT: She's a past master at getting what she wants.

pas·tor /'pæstər/ noun a minister in charge of a church or group in some Christian Protestant Churches

pas·to·ral /'pæstərəl/ adj. **1** relating to the work of a priest or teacher in giving help and advice on personal matters, not just those connected with religion or education: pastoral care **2** showing country life or the countryside, especially in a romantic way: a pastoral scene/poem/

symphony **3** relating to the farming of animals: *agricultural and pastoral practices*

pas·to·ral·ism /ˈpæstərəˌlɪzəm/ *noun* [U] a way of keeping animals such as CATTLE, sheep, etc. that involves moving them from place to place to find water and food ▶ **pas·to·ral·ist** /-lɪst/ *noun, adj.*

past 'participle *noun* (*grammar*) the form of a verb that in English ends in *-ed, -en,* etc. and is used with the verb *have* to form PERFECT tenses such as *I have eaten,* with the verb *be* to form passive sentences such as *It was destroyed,* or sometimes as an adjective, as in *an upset stomach* ⊃ compare PRESENT PARTICIPLE

the ˌpast 'perfect (also the ˌpast ˌperfect 'tense, the pluperfect) *noun* [sing.] (*grammar*) the form of a verb that expresses an action completed before a particular point in the past, formed in English with *had* and the past participle

pas·tra·mi /pəˈstrɑmi/ *noun* [U] cold, spicy, smoked beef

pas·try /ˈpeɪstri/ *noun* (*pl.* **pas·tries**) **1** [U] a mixture of flour, fat, and water or milk that is rolled out flat and baked as a base or covering for PIES, etc. ⊃ see also FILO PASTRY, PUFF PASTRY **2** [C] a small cake made using pastry ⊃ see also DANISH

'pastry ˌchef *noun* a professional cook whose main job is to make pastry, cakes, etc.

the ˌpast 'tense (also the 'past) *noun* [sing.] (*grammar*) the form of a verb used to describe actions in the past: *The past tense of "take" is "took."*

pas·tur·age /ˈpæstʃərɪdʒ/ *noun* [U] (*technical*) land covered with grass for animals to eat

pas·ture /ˈpæstʃər/ *noun, verb*
● *noun* **1** [U, C] land covered with grass that is suitable for feeding animals on: *an area of permanent/rough/rich pasture* ◆ *high mountain pastures* ◆ *The cattle were put out to pasture.* **2 pastures** [pl.] the circumstances of your life, work, etc.: *I felt we were off to greener pastures* (= a better way of life). **IDM** **put sb out to pasture/grass** (*informal*) to force someone to stop doing their job, especially because they are old
● *verb* ~ **sth** to put animals in a field to feed on grass

pas·ture·land /ˈpæstʃərˌlænd/ *noun* [U] (also **pas·ture·lands** [pl.]) land where animals can feed on grass

past·y /ˈpeɪsti/ *adj.* pale and not looking healthy **SYN** PALLID: *a pasty face/complexion*

pat /pæt/ *verb, noun, adj., adv.*
● *verb* (**-tt-**) to touch someone or something gently several times with your hand flat, especially as a sign of affection: ~ **sth** *She patted the dog on the head.* ◆ *He patted his sister's hand consolingly.* ◆ ~ **sth + adj.** *Pat your face dry with a soft towel.* **IDM** **pat sb/yourself on the back** to praise someone or yourself for doing something well **PHR V** ˌpat sb↔ˈdown to pass your hands over someone's body to search them for hidden weapons, drugs, etc.
● *noun* **1** a gentle friendly touch with your open hand or with a flat object: *He gave her knee an affectionate pat.* **2** ~ **of butter** a small, soft, flat lump of butter **IDM** **a pat on the back (for sth/for doing sth)** praise or approval for something that you have done well: *He deserves a pat on the back for all his hard work.*
● *adj.* (usually *disapproving*) (of an answer, a comment, etc.) too quick, easy, or simple; not seeming natural or realistic **SYN** GLIB: *The ending of the novel is a little too pat to be convincing.* ◆ *There are no pat answers to these questions.*
● *adv.* **IDM** **have/know sth down pat** to know something perfectly so that you can repeat it at any time without having to think about it: *He had all the answers down pat.* **stand pat** to refuse to change your mind about a decision you have made or an opinion you have

patch /pætʃ/ *noun, verb*
● *noun*
> SMALL AREA **1** a small area of something, especially one that is different from the area around it: *a black dog with a white patch on its back* ◆ *a bald patch on the top of his head* ◆ *damp patches on the wall* ◆ *patches of dense fog*
> PIECE OF MATERIAL **2** a small piece of material that is used to cover a hole in something or to make a weak area stronger, or as decoration: *I sewed patches on the knees of my jeans.* **3** a piece of material that you wear over an eye, usually because the eye is damaged: *He had a black patch over one eye.* ⊃ see also EYEPATCH **4** a piece of material that you sew onto clothes as part of a uniform **5** a piece of material that people can wear on their skin to help them to stop smoking: *nicotine patches*
> IN COMPUTING **6** a small piece of code (= instructions that a computer can understand) that can be added to a computer program to improve it or to correct a fault: *Follow the instructions below to download and install the patch.*
> PIECE/AREA OF LAND **7** a small piece of land, especially one used for growing vegetables or fruit: *a vegetable patch*
> DIFFICULT TIME **8** (*informal*) a period of time of the type mentioned, usually a difficult or unhappy one: *to go through a bad/difficult/rough patch* ⊃ see also PURPLE PATCH

THESAURUS

patch

dot ◆ mark ◆ spot

These are all words for a small part on a surface that is a different color from the rest.

patch an area of something, especially one which is different from the area around it: *a white dog with a black patch around its eye* ◆ *patches of dense fog*

dot a small round mark on something, especially one that is printed: *The letters "i" and "j" have dots over them.* ◆ *The island is a small green dot on the map.* **NOTE** Periods and decimal points are often referred to as "dots," especially when talking about computers: *The file is called "my essay dot doc."* ◆ *The IP address is "192 dot 168 dot zero dot zero."*

mark a noticeable area of color on the body of a person or an animal: *The horse had a white mark on his head.*

spot a small round area that is a different color or feels different from the surface it is on: *Which one has spot—a leopard or a tiger?*

PATTERNS
- a patch/dot/mark/spot **on** sth
- **with** patches/dots/marks/spots
- a **blue/black/red, etc.** patch/dot/mark/spot

● *verb* ~ **sth (with sth)** to cover a hole or a worn place, especially in clothes, with a piece of cloth or other material **SYN** MEND: *patched jeans* ◆ *to patch a hole in the roof* **PHR V** ˌpatch sb/sth 'through (to sb/sth) to connect telephone or electronic equipment temporarily: *She was patched through to New York on the satellite link.* ˌpatch sth↔to'gether to make something from several different parts, especially in a quick and careless way: *They hope to be able to patch together a temporary settlement.* ˌpatch sth/sb↔'up **1** to repair something, especially in a temporary way, by adding a new piece of material or a patch: *Just to patch the boat up will cost $10,000.* **2** to treat someone's injuries, especially quickly or temporarily: *The doctor will soon patch you up.* **3** to try to stop arguing with someone and be friends again: *They've managed to patch up their differences.* ◆ *Have you tried patching things up with her?* **4** to agree on something, especially after long discussions and even though the agreement is not exactly what everyone wants: *They managed to patch up a deal.*

patch·ou·li /pəˈtʃuli/ *noun* [U] a PERFUME made with oil from the leaves of a S.E. Asian bush

---

h **hat**   m **man**   n **no**   ŋ **sing**   l **leg**   r **red**   y **yes**   w **wet**

patch·work /ˈpætʃwərk/ *noun* **1** [U] a type of NEEDLEWORK in which small pieces of cloth of different colors or designs are sewn together: *a patchwork quilt* ➔ compare CRAZY QUILT ➔ picture at BED **2** [sing.] a thing that is made up of many different pieces or parts: *a patchwork of different styles and cultures* ◆ *From the plane, the landscape was just a patchwork of fields.*

patch·y /ˈpætʃi/ *adj.* **1** existing or happening in some places and not others SYN UNEVEN: *patchy fog* ◆ *The grass was dry and patchy.* **2** not complete; good in some parts, but not in others: *a patchy knowledge of Spanish* ◆ *It was a patchy performance.* ▶ **patch·i·ly** /-tʃəli/ *adv.* **patch·i·ness** /-tʃinəs/ *noun* [U]

pate /peɪt/ *noun* (*old use* or *humorous*) the top part of the head, especially when there is no hair on it: *The sun beat down on his bald pate.*

pâ·té /pɑˈteɪ; pæ-/ *noun* [U] a soft mixture of very finely chopped meat or fish, served cold and used for spreading on bread, etc.

pâ·té de foie gras /ˌpɑ teɪ də fwɑ ˈgrɑ; pæˌteɪ-/ (also **foie ˈgras**) *noun* [U] (from *French*) an expensive type of pâté made from the LIVER of a GOOSE

pa·tel·la /pəˈtɛlə/ *noun* (*pl.* **pa·tel·lae** /-li/) (*anatomy*) the KNEECAP ➔ picture at BODY

pat·ent /ˈpætnt/ *noun, adj., verb*
● *noun* [C, U] an official right to be the only person to make, use, or sell a product or an invention; a document that proves this: *to apply for/obtain a patent on an invention* ◆ *The device was protected by patent.*
IDM **patent pending** used to show that an application for a patent has been made for a particular product or invention, but has not yet been approved

● *adj.* [only before noun] **1** connected with a patent: *patent applications/laws* ◆ *the U.S. Patent Office* **2** (*old-fashioned*) (of a product) made or sold by a particular company: *patent medicines* **3** /ˈpeɪtnt; ˈpætnt/ (*formal*) used to emphasize that something bad is very clear and obvious SYN BLATANT: *It was a patent lie.*

● *verb* ~ sth to obtain a patent for an invention or a process

pat·ent·ee /ˌpætnˈti/ *noun* a person or an organization that holds the patent for something

patent leath·er /ˌpætnt ˈlɛðər; ˌpætn-/ *noun* [U] a type of leather with a hard shiny surface, used especially for making shoes and bags

pat·ent·ly /ˈpeɪtntli; ˈpæt-/ *adv.* (*formal*) without doubt SYN CLEARLY: *Her explanation was patently ridiculous.* ◆ *It was patently obvious that she was lying.*

pa·ter·fa·mil·i·as /ˌpɑtərfəˈmiliəs; ˌpeɪtər-; ˌpætər-/ *noun* [sing.] (*formal* or *humorous*) the man who is the head of a family

pa·ter·nal /pəˈtərnl/ *adj.* **1** connected with being a father; typical of a kind father: *paternal love* ◆ *He gave me a piece of paternal advice.* **2** related through the father's side of the family: *my paternal grandmother* (= my father's mother) ➔ compare MATERNAL ▶ **pa·ter·nal·ly** /-nəli/ *adv.*: *He smiled paternally at them.*

pa·ter·nal·ism /pəˈtərnəˌlɪzəm/ *noun* [U] (sometimes *disapproving*) the system in which a government or an employer protects the people who are governed or employed by providing them with what they need, but does not give them any responsibility or freedom of choice ▶ **pa·ter·nal·is·tic** /pəˌtərnəˈlɪstɪk/ (also **pa·ter·nal·ist**) *adj.*: *a paternalistic employer*

pa·ter·ni·ty /pəˈtərnəti/ *noun* [U] the fact of being the father of a child: *He refused to admit paternity of the child.* ➔ compare MATERNITY

paˈternity ˌleave *noun* time that the father of a new baby is allowed to have away from work ➔ see also MATERNITY LEAVE, PARENTAL LEAVE ➔ collocations at CHILD

paˈternity ˌsuit (also **paˈternity ˌcase**) *noun* a court case that is intended to prove who a child's father is, especially so that he can be ordered to give the child financial support

path /pæθ/ (*pl.* **paths** /pæðz; pæθs/) (also **path·way**) *noun* **1** a way or track that is built or is made by the action of people walking: *a concrete path* ◆ *the garden path* ◆ *Follow the path through the woods.* ◆ *to walk along a path* ◆ *The path led up a steep hill.* ◆ *a coastal path* ➔ see also FOOTPATH **2** a line along which someone or something moves; the space in front of someone or something as they move SYN WAY: *He threw himself into the path of an oncoming vehicle.* ◆ *The avalanche forced its way down the mountain, crushing everything in its path.* ◆ *Three men blocked her path.* ➔ see also FLIGHT PATH **3** a plan of action or a way of achieving something: *a career path* ◆ *the path to success* **IDM** see BEAT *v.*, CROSS *v.*, LEAD¹ *v.*, PRIMROSE, RESISTANCE, SMOOTH *v.*, STRAY *v.*

pa·thet·ic /pəˈθɛtɪk/ *adj.* **1** making you feel sympathy or sadness SYN PITIFUL: *a pathetic and lonely old man* ◆ *The starving children were a pathetic sight.* **2** (*informal, disapproving*) weak and not successful SYN FEEBLE: *a pathetic excuse* ◆ *She made a pathetic attempt to smile.* ◆ *You're pathetic!* ▶ **pa·thet·i·cally** /-kli/ *adv.*: *He cried pathetically.* ◆ *a pathetically shy woman*

paˌthetic ˈfallacy *noun* [U, sing.] (in art and literature) the act of describing animals and things as having human feelings

path·find·er /ˈpæθˌfaɪndər/ *noun* **1** a person, group, or thing that goes before others and shows the way over unknown land **2** a person, group, or thing that finds a new way of doing something SYN TRAILBLAZER: *The company is a pathfinder in computer technology.*

patho- /ˈpæθoʊ; -θə/ *combining form* (in nouns, adjectives, and adverbs) connected with disease: *pathogenesis* (= the development of a disease) ◆ *pathophysiology*

path·o·gen /ˈpæθədʒən/ *noun* (*technical*) a thing that causes disease ▶ **path·o·gen·ic** /ˌpæθəˈdʒɛnɪk/ *adj.*

path·o·gen·e·sis /ˌpæθəˈdʒɛnəsəs/ *noun* (*medical*) the way in which a disease develops

path·o·log·i·cal /ˌpæθəˈlɑdʒɪkl/ *adj.* **1** not reasonable or sensible; impossible to control: *pathological fear/hatred/violence* ◆ *a pathological liar* (= a person who cannot stop telling lies) **2** caused by, or connected with, disease or illness: *pathological depression* **3** (*technical*) connected with PATHOLOGY ▶ **path·o·log·i·cally** /-kli/ *adv.*: *pathologically jealous*

pa·thol·o·gist /pəˈθɑlədʒɪst/ *noun* a doctor who studies pathology and examines dead bodies to find out the cause of death ➔ compare MEDICAL EXAMINER

pa·thol·o·gy /pəˈθɑlədʒi/ *noun* **1** [U] the scientific study of diseases **2** [C] an aspect of someone's behavior that is extreme and unreasonable and that they cannot control

pa·thos /ˈpeɪθɑs; -θoʊs/ *noun* [U] (in writing, speech, and plays) the power of a performance, description, etc. to produce feelings of sadness and sympathy

path·way /ˈpæθweɪ/ *noun* **1** a path that you can walk on: *There was a narrow pathway leading down the cliff.* **2** a series of nerves that information travels along: *neural pathways*

pa·tience /ˈpeɪʃns/ *noun* [U]
1 ~ (with sb/sth) the ability to stay calm and accept a delay or something annoying without complaining: *She has little patience with* (= will not accept or consider) *such views.* ◆ *People have lost patience with* (= have become annoyed about) *the slow pace of reform.* ◆ *My patience is wearing thin.* ◆ *Teaching children with special needs requires patience and understanding.* **2** the ability to spend a lot of time doing something difficult that needs a lot of attention and effort: *It takes time and patience to photograph wildlife.* ◆ *I don't have the patience to do jigsaw puzzles.* **IDM** see JOB, TRY *v.*

pa·tient /ˈpeɪʃnt/ *noun, adj.*
● *noun* **1** a person who is receiving medical treatment, especially in a hospital: *cancer patients* **2** a person who receives treatment from a particular doctor, dentist, etc.: *He's one of Dr. Shaw's patients.* **3** (*grammar*) the person or

thing that is affected by the action of the verb. In the sentence "I started the car," the patient is *car*. ⟳ compare AGENT

● **adj.** ~ **(with sb/sth)** able to wait for a long time or accept annoying behavior or difficulties without becoming angry: *She's very patient with young children.* ◆ *You'll just have to be patient and wait till I'm finished.* ▶ **pa·tient·ly** *adv.: She sat patiently waiting for her turn.*

pat·i·na /pə'tinə; 'pætn·ə/ *noun* [usually sing.] **1** a green, black, or brown layer that forms on the surface of some metals **2** a thin layer that forms on other materials; the shiny surface that develops on wood or leather when it is polished: (*figurative*) *He looked relaxed and elegant and had the patina of success.*

pat·i·na·tion /ˌpætn'eɪʃn/ *noun* [U, C] (*technical*) a shiny layer on the surface of metal, wood, etc.; the process of covering something with a shiny layer

pat·i·o /'pætiˌoʊ/ *noun* (*pl.* **pat·i·os**) a flat hard area outside, and usually behind, a house where people can sit: *Let's have lunch out on the patio.*

'patio ˌdoor *noun* [usually pl.] a large glass sliding door that leads to a patio

pa·tis·se·rie /pə'tɪsəri/ *noun* (from *French*) **1** [C] a store that sells cakes, etc. **2** [U] (also **pa·tis·se·ries** [pl.]) (*formal*) cakes

pat·ois /'pætwɑ; 'pɑ-/ *noun* (*pl.* **pat·ois** /-twɑz/) a form of a language, spoken by people in a particular area, that is different from the standard language of the country

pa·tri·arch /'peɪtriˌɑrk/ *noun* **1** the male head of a family or community ⟳ compare MATRIARCH **2** an old man that people have a lot of respect for **3 Patriarch** the title of a most senior BISHOP (= a senior priest) in the Orthodox or Roman Catholic Church

pa·tri·ar·chal /ˌpeɪtri'ɑrkl/ *adj.* **1** ruled or controlled by men; giving power and importance only to men: *a patriarchal society* **2** connected with a patriarch ⟳ compare MATRIARCHAL

pa·tri·arch·ate /'peɪtriˌɑrkət/ *noun* (*formal*) **1** the title, position, or period of office of a patriarch **2** the area governed by a patriarch

pa·tri·arch·y /'peɪtriˌɑrki/ *noun* (*pl.* **pa·tri·arch·ies**) [C, U] a society, system, or country that is ruled or controlled by men ⟳ compare MATRIARCHY

pa·tri·cian /pə'trɪʃn/ *adj.* (*formal*) connected with or typical of the highest social class **SYN** ARISTOCRATIC ▶ **pa·tri·cian** *noun* ⟳ compare PLEBEIAN

pat·ri·cide /'pætrəˌsaɪd/ *noun* [U, C] (*formal*) the crime of killing your father; a person who is guilty of this crime ⟳ compare FRATRICIDE, MATRICIDE, PARRICIDE

pat·ri·lin·e·al /ˌpætrə'lɪniəl/ *adj.* (*formal*) used to describe the relationship between father and child that continues in a family with each generation, or something that is based on this relationship: *In that society, inheritance of land is patrilineal* (= the children get the land that their father owned). ⟳ compare MATRILINEAL

pat·ri·mo·ny /'pætrəˌmoʊni/ *noun* [sing.] (*formal*) **1** property that is given to someone when their father dies **SYN** INHERITANCE **2** the works of art and TREASURES of a nation, church, etc. **SYN** HERITAGE

pa·tri·ot /'peɪtriət/ *noun* a person who loves their country and who is ready to defend it against an enemy

pa·tri·ot·ic /ˌpeɪtri'ɑtɪk/ *adj.* having or expressing a great love of your country: *a patriotic man who served his country well* ◆ *patriotic songs* ▶ **pa·tri·ot·i·cally** *adv.* /-kli/

pa·tri·ot·ism /'peɪtriəˌtɪzəm/ *noun* [U] love of your country and willingness to defend it

pa·trol /pə'troʊl/ *verb, noun*
● **verb** (-ll-) **1** [T, I] ~ **(sth)** to go around an area or a building at regular times to check that it is safe and that there is no trouble: *Troops patrolled the border day and night.* ◆ *Guards can be seen patrolling everywhere.* **2** [T] ~ **sth** to drive or walk

around a particular area, especially in a threatening way: *Gangs of youths patrol the streets at night.*

● **noun** **1** [C, U] the act of going to different parts of a building, an area, etc. to make sure that there is no trouble or crime: *Security guards make regular patrols at night.* ◆ *a police car on patrol* **2** [C] a group of soldiers, vehicles, etc. that patrol an area: *a naval/police patrol* ◆ *a patrol car/boat* **3** a group of about six BOY SCOUTS or GIRL SCOUTS that forms part of a larger group

pa·trol·man /pə'troʊlmən/, **pa·trol·wom·an** /pə'troʊl-ˌwʊmən/ *noun* (*pl.* **pa·trol·men** /-mən/, **pa·trol·wom·en** /-ˌwɪmɪn/) a police officer who walks or drives around an area to make sure that there is no trouble or crime: *Patrolman Don Lilly*

pa'trol ˌwagon (also *informal* **'paddy ˌwagon**) *noun* a police van for transporting prisoners in

pa·tron /'peɪtrən/ *noun* **1** a person who gives money and support to artists and writers: *Peggy Guggenheim was the patron of many artists.* **2** a famous person who supports an organization such as a charity and whose name is used in the advertisements, etc. for the organization **3** (*formal*) a person who uses a particular store, restaurant, etc.: *Patrons are requested not to smoke.*

pa·tron·age /'peɪtrənɪdʒ; 'pæ-/ *noun* [U] **1** the support, especially financial, that is given to a person or an organization by a patron: *Patronage of the arts comes from businesses and private individuals.* **2** the system by which an important person gives help or a job to someone in return for their support **3** the support that a person gives a store, restaurant, etc. by spending money there

pa·tron·ess /'peɪtrənəs/ *noun* a female PATRON

pa·tron·ize /'peɪtrəˌnaɪz; 'pæ-/ *verb* **1** [T, I] ~ **(sb)** (*disapproving*) to treat someone in a way that seems friendly, but that shows that you think that they are not very intelligent, experienced, etc.: *Some television programs tend to patronize children.* **2** [T] ~ **sth** (*formal*) to be a regular customer of a store, restaurant, etc.: *The club is patronized by students and locals alike.* **3** [T] ~ **sb/sth** to help a particular person, organization, or activity by giving them money: *She patronizes many contemporary American artists.*

pa·tron·iz·ing /'peɪtrəˌnaɪzɪŋ; 'pæ-/ *adj.* (*disapproving*) showing that you feel better or more intelligent than someone else **SYN** SUPERIOR: *a patronizing smile* ◆ *I was only trying to explain; I didn't want to sound patronizing.* ▶ **pa·tron·iz·ing·ly** *adv.: He patted her hand patronizingly.*

ˌpatron 'saint *noun* a Christian SAINT who is believed to protect a particular place or group of people: *St. Patrick, Ireland's patron saint* ◆ *St. Christopher, patron saint of travelers*

pat·ro·nym·ic /ˌpætrə'nɪmɪk/ *noun* (*technical*) a name formed from the name of your father or a male ANCESTOR, especially by adding something to the beginning or end of their name ⟳ compare MATRONYMIC

pat·sy /'pætsi/ *noun* (*pl.* **pat·sies**) (*informal*) a weak person who is easily cheated or tricked, or who is forced to take the blame for something that someone else has done wrong

pat·ter /'pætər/ *noun, verb*
● **noun** **1** [sing.] the sound that is made by something repeatedly hitting a surface quickly and lightly: *the patter of feet/footsteps* ◆ *the patter of rain on the roof* **2** [U, sing.] fast continuous talk by someone who is trying to sell you something or entertain you: *sales patter*
   IDM **the patter of tiny feet** (*informal* or *humorous*) a way of referring to children when someone wants, or is going to have, a baby: *We can't wait to hear the patter of tiny feet.*
● **verb** **1** [I] + **adv./prep.** to make quick, light sounds as a surface is being hit several times: *Rain pattered against the window.* **2** [I] + **adv./prep.** to walk with light steps in a particular direction: *I heard her feet pattering along the corridor.*

pat·tern 🔊 /'pætərn/ *noun, verb*
● **noun** **1** the regular way in which something happens or is done: *changing patterns of behavior* ◆ *an irregular sleeping*

pattern ♦ *The murders all seem to follow a (similar) pattern* (= happen in the same way). **2** [usually sing.] an excellent example to copy: *This system **sets the pattern** for others to follow.* **3** a regular arrangement of lines, shapes, colors, etc. as a design on material, carpets, etc.: *a pattern of diamonds and squares* ♦ *a shirt with a floral pattern* **4** a design, set of instructions, or shape to cut around that you use in order to make something: *a knitting pattern* ♦ *She bought a dress pattern and some material.* **5** a small piece of material, paper, etc. that helps you choose the design of something **SYN** SAMPLE: *wallpaper patterns*

• **verb 1 ~ sth** to form a regular arrangement of lines or shapes on something: *Frost patterned the window.* ♦ *a landscape patterned by vineyards* **2 ~ sth** (*technical*) to cause a particular type of behavior to develop: *Adult behavior is often patterned by childhood experiences.*
PHRV 'pattern sth after sth (also 'pattern sth on sth) [usually passive] to use something as a model for something; to copy something: *a new approach patterned after Japanese ideas*

pat·terned /ˈpætərnd/ *adj.* decorated with a pattern: *patterned wallpaper* ♦ **~ with sth** *cups patterned with yellow flowers*

pat·tern·ing /ˈpætərnɪŋ/ *noun* [U] **1** (*technical*) the forming of fixed ways of behaving by copying or repeating something: *cultural patterning* ♦ *the patterning of husband-wife roles* **2** the arrangement of shapes or colors to make patterns: *a red fish with black patterning*

pat·ty /ˈpæti/ *noun* (*pl.* **pat·ties**) finely chopped meat, fish, etc. formed into a small, round, flat shape: *a hamburger patty*

pau·ci·ty /ˈpɔsəti/ *noun* [sing.] **~ (of sth)** (*formal*) a small amount of something; less than enough of something: *a paucity of information*

paunch /pɔntʃ; pɑntʃ/ *noun* a fat stomach on a man ▶ **paunch·y** *adj.*

pau·per /ˈpɔpər/ *noun* (*old use*) a very poor person

pause 🔑 /pɔz/ *verb, noun*
• **verb 1** [I] to stop talking or doing something for a short time before continuing: *Anita paused for a moment, then said, "All right."* ♦ *The woman spoke almost without **pausing for breath** (= very quickly).* ♦ *I paused at the door and looked back.* ♦ *Pausing only to pull on a sweater, he ran out of the house.* **2** [T] **~ sth** to stop a tape, CD, etc. for a short time using the pause button: *She paused the DVD and went to answer the phone.*
• **noun 1** [C] **~ (in sth)** a period of time during which someone stops talking or stops what they are doing: *There was a long pause before she answered.* ♦ *David waited for a pause in the conversation so he could ask his question.* ♦ *After a brief pause, they continued climbing.* ♦ *The rain fell **without pause**.* **2** [C] (also **fer·ma·ta**) (*music*) a sign (⌢) over a note or a REST to show that it should be longer than usual **3** [U] (also 'pause button) a control that allows you to stop a CD player, TAPE RECORDER, etc. for a short time: *Press pause to stop the tape.*
IDM give (sb) pause (also give (sb) pause for thought) (*formal*) to make someone think seriously about something or hesitate before doing something ⸰ more at PREGNANT

pa·vane (also **pa·van**) /pəˈvɑn; -ˈvæn/ *noun* a slow dance popular in the 16th and 17th centuries; a piece of music for this dance

pave /peɪv/ *verb* [often passive] **~ sth (with sth)** to cover a surface with flat stones or bricks: *a paved area near the back door*
IDM pave the way (for sb/sth) to create a situation in which someone will be able to do something or something can happen: *This decision paved the way for changes in employment rights for women.* ⸰ more at ROAD, STREET

pave·ment /ˈpeɪvmənt/ *noun* **1** [C, U] any area of flat stones on the ground: *a mosaic pavement* **2** [U] the surface of a road: *Two cars skidded on the icy pavement.* **IDM** see POUND *v.*

pa·vil·ion /pəˈvɪlyən/ *noun* **1** a temporary building used at public events and exhibitions: *the U.S. pavilion at the Trade Fair* **2** a large building used for sports or entertainment: *Pauley Pavilion, home of the university's basketball team* **3** a building that is meant to be more beautiful than useful, built as a shelter in a park or used for concerts and dances

pav·ing /ˈpeɪvɪŋ/ *noun* [U] **1** a surface of flat stones or material like stone on the ground: *Weeds grew through the cracks in the paving.* **2** the stones or material that are used to make a flat surface on the ground: *We'll use concrete paving.*

'paving ˌstone *noun* a flat, usually square, piece of stone that is used to make a hard surface for walking on **SYN** FLAGSTONE

Pav·lov·i·an /pævˈloʊviən/ *adj.* (of an animal's or a human's reaction) happening in response to a particular STIMULUS: *Her yawn was a Pavlovian response to my yawn.* **ORIGIN** From the name of the Russian scientist, I. P. Pavlov, who carried out experiments on dogs, showing how they could be conditioned to react to certain stimuli.

paw /pɔ/ *noun, verb*
• **noun 1** the foot of an animal that has CLAWS or nails ⸰ picture at ANIMAL **2** (*informal*) a person's hand: *Take your filthy paws off me!*
• **verb 1** [I, T] (of an animal) to scratch or touch something repeatedly with a paw: **~ at sth** *The dog pawed at my sleeve.* ♦ **~ sth** *The stallion pawed the ground impatiently.* **2** [T] **~ sb** (sometimes *humorous*) to touch someone in a rough sexual way that they find offensive

pawn /pɔn/ *noun, verb*
• **noun 1** a CHESS piece of the smallest size and least value. Each player has eight pawns at the start of a game. ⸰ picture at TOY **2** a person or group whose actions are controlled by more powerful people: *The hostages are being used as political pawns.*
IDM in pawn if something is **in pawn**, it has been pawned: *All her jewelry was in pawn.*
• **verb ~ sth** to leave an object with a pawnbroker in exchange for money. The object is returned to the owner if they pay back the money within an agreed period of time. If not, it can be sold.

pawn·brok·er /ˈpɔnˌbroʊkər/ *noun* a person who lends money in exchange for articles left with them. If the money is not paid back by a particular time, the pawnbroker can sell the article.

Paw·nee /pɔˈni/ *noun* (*pl.* **Paw·nee** or **Paw·nees**) a member of a Native American people, many of whom live in the state of Oklahoma

pawn·shop /ˈpɔnʃɑp/ *noun* a pawnbroker's store

pay 🔑 /peɪ/ *verb, noun*
• **verb** (paid, paid /peɪd/) **1** [I, T] to give someone money for work, goods, services, etc.: **~ (for sth)** *I'll pay for the tickets.* ♦ *Are you **paying in cash** or by credit card?* ♦ *My company **pays well** (= pays high salaries).* ♦ **~ for sb to do sth** *Her parents paid for her to go to Jamaica.* ♦ **~ sth** *to pay cash* ♦ **~ sth for sth** *She pays $875 a month for this apartment.* ♦ **~ sb (for sth)** *Would you mind paying the taxi driver?* ♦ **~ sb sth** *He still hasn't paid me the money he owes me.* ♦ *I'm paid $100 a day.* ♦ **~ sb/ sth to do sth** *I don't pay you to sit around all day doing nothing!* ⸰ see also LOW-PAID, PREPAID, WELL-PAID **2** [T] to give someone money that you owe them: **~ sth** *to pay a bill/ debt/fine/ransom, etc.* ♦ **~ sth to sb** *Membership fees should be paid to the secretary.* ♦ **~ sb sth** *Have you paid him the rent yet?* **3** [I] (of a business, etc.) to produce a profit: *It's hard to make farming pay.* **4** [I, T] to result in some advantage or profit for someone: *Crime doesn't pay.* ♦ **it pays to do sth** *It pays to keep up to date with your work.* ♦ **it pays sb to do sth** *It would probably pay you to hire an accountant.* **5** [I] to suffer or be punished for your beliefs or actions: **~ (for sth)** *You'll pay for that remark!* ♦ **~ (with sth)** *Many people paid with their lives* (= they died). **6** [T] used with some nouns to show that you are giving or doing the thing mentioned: **~ sth** *I didn't **pay attention** to what she was saying.* ♦ *The director **paid tribute***

to all she had done for the charity. ♦ *I'll **pay a call on** (= visit) my friends.* ♦ *~ **sb sth** I'll pay you a call when I'm in town.* ♦ *He's always **paying me compliments.***

IDM **the devil/hell to pay** (*informal*) a lot of trouble: *There'll be hell to pay when he finds out.* **he who pays the piper calls the tune** (*saying*) the person who provides the money for something can also control how it is spent **pay sb (back) with interest** to do the same thing to someone as they have done to you, but with more force, enthusiasm, etc. **pay court to sb** (*old-fashioned*) to treat someone with great respect in order to gain favor in them **pay dividends** to produce great advantages or profits: *Exercising regularly will pay dividends in the end.* **pay for itself** (of a new system, something you have bought, etc.) to save as much money as it cost: *The rail pass will pay for itself after about two trips.* **pay good money for sth** used to emphasize that something cost(s) a lot of money, especially if the money is wasted: *I paid good money for this jacket, and now look at it—it's ruined!* **pay its way** (of a business, etc.) to make enough money to pay what it costs to keep it going: *The bridge is still not paying its way.* **pay the penalty (for sth/for doing sth)| pay a/the price (for sth/for doing sth)** to suffer because of bad luck, a mistake, or something you have done: *He looked terrible this morning. I think he's paying the penalty for all those late nights.* ♦ *They're now paying the price for past mistakes.* **sb pays their debt to society** used to say that someone is being punished for a crime, usually by being put in prison: *He paid his debt to society for his previous convictions and is now a free man.* **pay through the nose (for sth)** (*informal*) to pay much too much money for something **pay your dues** to work hard and experience difficulties before achieving success: *She paid her dues singing in the chorus for very little money before becoming a star.* **pay your respects (to sb)** (*formal*) to visit someone or to send a message of good wishes as a sign of respect for them: *Many came to **pay their last respects** (= by attending someone's funeral).* **pay your way** to pay for everything yourself without having to rely on anyone else's money ➔ more at ARM *n.*, HEED *n.*, ROB

PHR V **,pay sb 'back (sth) | ,pay sth↔'back (to sb)** to return money that you borrowed from someone **SYN** REPAY: *I'll pay you back next week.* ♦ *You can pay back the loan over a period of three years.* ♦ *Did he ever pay you back that $100 he owes you?* **,pay sb 'back (for sth)** to punish someone for making you or someone else suffer: *I'll pay him back for making me look like a fool in front of everyone.* ➔ related noun PAYBACK **,pay sth↔'down** to reduce an amount of money that you owe by paying some of it: *She used the money to pay down her mortgage.* **,pay sth↔'in | ,pay sth 'into sth** to put money into a bank account: *She has a savings account for vacations, and she pays in $75 a week.* ♦ *I'd like to pay some more money into my pension fund.* **,pay 'off** (*informal*) (of a plan or an action, especially one that involves risk) to be successful and bring good results: *The gamble paid off.* **,pay sb↔'off 1** to pay someone what they have earned and tell them to leave their job: *The crew were paid off as soon as the ship docked.* **2** (*informal*) to give someone money to prevent them from doing something or talking about something illegal or dishonest that you have done: *All the witnesses had been paid off.* ➔ related noun PAYOFF **,pay sth↔'off** to finish paying money owed for something: *We paid off our mortgage after fifteen years.* **,pay sth↔'out 1** to pay a large sum of money for something: *I had to pay out $500 to get my car repaired.* ➔ related noun PAYOUT **2** to pass a length of rope through your hands **,pay 'up** to pay all the money that you owe to someone, especially when you do not want to or when the payment is late: *I had a hard time getting him to pay up.*

● **noun** [U] the money that someone gets for doing regular work: *Her job is hard work, but the pay is good.* ♦ *a **pay increase** ♦ a **pay raise** ♦ a 3% **pay offer** ♦ **vacation pay** ♦ to make a **pay claim** (= to officially ask for an increase in pay)* ➔ see also SICK PAY ➔ thesaurus box at INCOME

IDM **in the pay of sb/sth** (usually *disapproving*) working for someone or for an organization, often secretly

pay·a·ble /'peɪəbl/ *adj.* [not before noun] **1** that must be paid or can be paid: *A 10% deposit is payable in advance.* ♦ *The price is payable in monthly instalments.* **2** when a check, etc. is made **payable** to someone, their name is written on it and they can then deposit it to their bank account

,pay-as-you-'go *adj.* connected with a system of paying for a service just before you use it rather than paying for it later: *pay-as-you-go phones*

pay·back /'peɪbæk/ *noun* [C, U] **1** the money that you receive back on money that you have invested (especially when this is equal to the amount that you invested to start with); the time that it takes to get your money back: *a 10-year payback* **2** the advantage or reward that someone receives for something they have done; the act of paying something back: *His victory was seen as payback for all the hard work he'd put in during training.* ♦ (*informal*) *It's **payback time!*** (= a person will have to suffer for what they have done)

'pay ,channel *noun* a television channel that you must pay for separately in order to watch it

pay·check (*CanE* **pay·cheque**) /'peɪtʃɛk/ *noun* **1** the check that you are given when your wages are paid to you **2** a way of referring to the amount of money that you earn: *a huge paycheck*

pay·day /'peɪdeɪ/ *noun* [U, C] the day on which you get your wages or salary: *Friday is payday.*

'pay dirt *noun* [U] earth that contains valuable minerals or metal such as gold
IDM **hit/strike pay dirt** (*informal*) to suddenly be in a successful situation, especially one that makes you rich

pay·ee /ˌpeɪˈiː/ *noun* (*technical*) a person that money or a check is paid to

'pay ,envelope *noun* an envelope containing your wages; the amount a person earns

pay·er /'peɪər/ *noun* a person who pays or who has to pay for something: *mortgage payers* ♦ *The company are not very good payers* (= they are slow to pay their bills, or they do not pay their employees well).

,pay-for-per'formance *adj.* [only before noun] paying more or less money depending on how well a person does their job: *There has been an increase in pay-for-performance plans all over the U.S.* ➔ compare PERFORMANCE, PERFOR-MANCE-RELATED

,paying 'guest *noun* a person who pays to live in someone's house with them, usually for a short time

pay·load /'peɪloʊd/ *noun* (*technical*) **1** the passengers and goods on a ship or an aircraft for which payment is received **2** the goods that a vehicle, for example a truck, is carrying; the amount it is carrying **3** the EXPLOSIVE power of a bomb or a MISSILE **4** the equipment carried by a SPACECRAFT or SATELLITE

pay·mas·ter /'peɪˌmæstər/ *noun* **1** (usually *disapproving*) a person or group of people that pays another person or organization and therefore can control their actions **2** an official who pays the wages in the army, a factory, etc.

pay·ment 🔑 /'peɪmənt/ *noun*
1 [U] *~* **(for sth)** the act of paying someone or something or of being paid: *payment in installments/in advance/by check/in cash* ♦ *There will be a penalty for late payment of bills.* **2** [C] *~* **(for sth)** a sum of money paid or expected to be paid: *a cash payment* ♦ *They are finding it difficult to **meet the payments** on their car.* ♦ *He agreed to make ten **monthly payments** of $150.* ➔ see also BALANCE OF PAYMENTS, DOWN PAYMENT **3** [U, sing.] *~* **(for sth)** a reward or an act of thanks for something you have done **SYN** RECOMPENSE: *We'd like you to accept this gift **in payment for** your kindness.* ♦ *Is this all the payment I get for my efforts?*
IDM **on payment of sth** when something has been paid: *Attendance is only allowed on payment of the full registration fee.*

payment

premium ◆ contribution ◆ subscription ◆ repayment ◆ deposit ◆ installments

These are all words for an amount of money that you pay or are expected to pay, or for the act of paying.

payment an amount of money that you pay or are expected to pay; the act of paying: *ten monthly payments of $50 ◆ payment in advance*

premium an amount of money that you pay once or regularly for an insurance policy; an extra payment added to the basic rate; a higher amount of money than usual: *an insurance premium ◆ a premium for express delivery*

contribution a sum of money that you pay regularly, often to your employer or the government, for benefits such as health insurance, a retirement plan, etc: *You can increase your monthly contributions to your savings account.*

subscription an amount of money you pay in advance to receive regular copies of a newspaper or magazine, or to receive a service: *a subscription to "Newsweek"*

repayment money that you pay to a bank, etc. until you have returned all the money that you owe; the act of paying this money: *to set up a repayment plan*

deposit an amount of money that you pay as the first part of a larger payment; money that you put into a bank account: *We've put down a 5% deposit on the house. ◆ I made a $500 deposit into my checking account.*

installments one of a number of payments that you make regularly over a period of time until you have paid for something: *We paid for the car by/in installments.*

PATTERNS

- (a/an) **annual/monthly/regular** payment/ premium/contributions/subscription/deposit/ installments
- payment/repayment **in full**
- to **pay** a premium/a contribution/a subscription fee/ a deposit/installments
- to **make** (a) payment/deposit
- to **meet/keep up (with)** (the) payment(s)/the premiums

pay·off /'peɪɔf; -ɑf/ *noun* (*informal*) **1** a payment of money to someone so that they will not cause you any trouble, or to make them keep a secret **SYN** BRIBE **2** a payment of money to someone to persuade them to leave their job **3** an advantage or a reward for something you have done

pay·o·la /peɪˈoʊlə/ *noun* [U] (*informal*) the practice of giving or taking payments for doing something illegal, especially for illegally influencing the sales of a particular product **SYN** BRIBERY

pay·out /'peɪaʊt/ *noun* a large amount of money that is given to someone: *an insurance payout ◆ a lottery payout*

pay-per-'view *noun* [U] a system of television broadcasting in which you pay an extra sum of money to watch a particular program, such as a movie or a sports event

'pay phone *noun* a telephone, usually in a public place, that is operated using coins or a card

pay·roll /'peɪroʊl/ *noun* **1** a list of people employed by a company showing the amount of money to be paid to each of them: *We have 500 people on the payroll.* **2** [usually sing.] the total amount paid in wages by a company

'payroll ,tax *noun* [C, U] a tax that is based on the wages paid to employees and is paid either by employers or partly by employers and partly by employees

'pay stub *noun* a piece of paper given to an employee that shows how much money they have been paid and how much has been taken away for tax, etc.

pay T'V (also ,pay 'television) *noun* [U] a system of television broadcasting in which you pay extra money to watch particular television programs or channels

PBS /,pi bi 'ɛs/ *abbr.* Public Broadcasting Service (an organization that broadcasts television programs to local stations that do not show advertisements)

PC /,pi 'si/ *abbr.* **1** personal computer (a small computer that is designed for one person to use at work or at home) ⊃ picture at COMPUTER **2** POLITICALLY CORRECT

PCB /,pi si 'bi/ *abbr.*, *noun*
- *adj.* printed circuit board
- *noun* (*chemistry*) any of a group of harmful chemicals used in the past in industry

P'C card *noun* (*computing*) a plastic card with a PRINTED CIRCUIT on it that can be put into a computer to allow it to work with other devices

PCP /,pi si 'pi/ *abbr.* **1** PRIMARY CARE PHYSICIAN **2** PRIMARY CARE PROVIDER

pct. *abbr.* percent

pd *abbr.* paid

PDA /,pi di 'eɪ/ *noun* the abbreviation for "personal digital assistant" (a very small computer that is used for storing personal information and creating documents, and that may include other functions such as telephone, FAX, connection to the Internet, etc.) ⊃ picture at COMPUTER

PD day /,pi 'di deɪ/ *noun* (*especially CanE*) = PROFESSIONAL DEVELOPMENT DAY

PDF /,pi di 'ɛf/ (also PD'F file) *noun* (*computing*) the abbreviation for "portable document format" (a type of computer file that can contain words or pictures. It can be read using any system, can be sent from one computer to another, and will look the same on any computer.): *I'll send it to you as a PDF.*

p.d.q. /,pi di 'kyu/ *abbr.* (*informal*) pretty damn/damned quick (= very fast): *Make sure you get here p.d.q.*

P.E. /,pi 'i/ *noun* [U] the abbreviation for "physical education" (sport and exercise that is taught in schools): *a P.E. class*

pea /pi/ *noun* a small, round, green seed, eaten as a vegetable. Several peas grow together inside a long thin POD on a climbing plant also called a pea: *frozen peas ◆ pea soup* ⊃ picture at FRUIT ⊃ see also CHICKPEA, SPLIT PEA, SWEET PEA

peace ◆ peacefulness

- The noun **peace** can be used to talk about a peaceful state or situation: *world peace ◆ I just need some peace and quiet.* **Peacefulness** is not a common word. It means "the quality of being peaceful."

peace /pis/ *noun*
1 [U, sing.] a situation or a period of time in which there is no war or violence in a country or an area: *war and peace ◆ peace talks/negotiations ◆ The negotiators are trying to make peace between the warring factions. ◆ A UN force has been sent to keep the peace (= to prevent people from fighting). ◆ After years of war, the people long for a lasting peace. ◆ the Peace of Utrecht, 1713 (= the agreement ending the war) ◆ The two communities live together in peace. ◆ The countries have been at peace for more than a century. ◆ the peace movement (= that tries to prevent war by protesting, persuading politicians, etc.)* ⊃ collocations at WAR **2** [U] the state of being calm or quiet: *She lay back and enjoyed the peace of the summer evening. ◆ I would work better if I had some peace and quiet. ◆ He just wants to be left in peace (= not to be disturbed). ◆ I need to check that she is all right, just for my own peace of mind (= so that I do not have to worry). ◆ He never felt really at peace with himself.* **3** [U] the state of living in friendship with someone without

arguing: *They simply can't seem to live in peace with each other.* ♦ *She felt **at peace with** the world.* ⊃ see also JUSTICE OF THE PEACE

IDM hold your peace/tongue (*old-fashioned*) to say nothing although you would like to give your opinion make (your) peace with sb to end an argument with someone, usually by saying you are sorry ⊃ more at WICKED *n.*

peace·a·ble /'pisəbl/ *adj.* **1** not involving or causing argument or violence **SYN** PEACEFUL: *A peaceable settlement has been reached.* **2** not liking to argue; wishing to live in peace with others **SYN** CALM, PEACEFUL: *a peaceable character* ▸ **peace·a·bly** /-bli/ *adv.*

the 'Peace Corps *noun* [sing.] a U.S. organization that sends young Americans to work in other countries in order to create international friendship

'peace ˌdividend *noun* [usually sing.] money previously spent on weapons and the defense of a country and now available to be used for other things because of a reduction in the country's military forces

peace·ful 🔑 /'pisfl/ *adj.*
1 not involving a war, violence, or argument: *a peaceful protest/demonstration/solution* ♦ *They hope for a peaceful settlement of the dispute.* **2** quiet and calm; not worried or disturbed in any way **SYN** TRANQUIL: *a peaceful atmosphere* ♦ *peaceful sleep* ♦ *It's so peaceful out here in the country.* ♦ *He had a peaceful life.* **3** trying to create peace or to live in peace; not liking violence or disagreement **SYN** PEACEABLE: *a peaceful society* ♦ *The aims of the organization are wholly peaceful.* ▸ **peace·ful·ly** /-fəli/ *adv.*: *The siege has ended peacefully.* ♦ *The baby slept peacefully.* **peace·ful·ness** *noun* [U] ⊃ note at PEACE

peace·keep·er /'pis,kipər/ *noun* **1** a member of a military force who has been sent to help stop people fighting in a place where war or violence is likely **2** a person who tries to stop people arguing or fighting: *She's the peacekeeper in that family.*

peace·keep·ing /'pis,kipɪŋ/ *adj.* [only before noun] intended to help stop people fighting and prevent war or violence in a place where this is likely: *peacekeeping operations* ♦ *a United Nations peacekeeping force* ⊃ collocations at WAR

'peace-ˌloving *adj.* preferring to live in peace and to avoid arguments and fighting **SYN** PEACEABLE

peace·mak·er /'pis,meɪkər/ *noun* a person who tries to persuade people or countries to stop arguing or fighting and to make peace

peace·nik /'pisnɪk/ *noun* (*informal*, usually *disapproving*) someone who believes war and violence are always wrong and refuses to fight **SYN** PACIFIST

'peace ˌoffering *noun* a present given to someone to show that you are sorry for something or want to make peace after an argument

'peace pipe *noun* a TOBACCO pipe offered and smoked as a symbol of peace by Native Americans

'peace ˌprocess *noun* [usually sing.] a series of talks and agreements designed to end war or violence between two groups

peace·time /'pistaɪm/ *noun* [U] a period of time when a country is not at war ⊃ compare WARTIME

peach /pitʃ/ *noun, adj.*
● *noun* **1** [C] a round fruit with soft red and yellow skin, yellow flesh, and a large rough seed inside: *a peach tree* ⊃ picture at FRUIT ⊃ compare NECTARINE **2** [sing.] ~ (of a...) (*old-fashioned, informal*) a particularly good or attractive person or thing **3** [U] a pinkish-orange color
IDM peaches and cream **1** (of a person's face) having smooth, pale skin with pink cheeks: *a peaches and cream complexion* **2** (of a situation) progressing well, with few problems: *In spite of outward appearances, all was not peaches and cream in their relationship.*
● *adj.* pinkish-orange in color

peach Mel·ba /ˌpitʃ 'mɛlbə/ *noun* [U, C] a cold DESSERT (= a sweet dish) made from half a PEACH, ice cream, and RASPBERRY sauce

peach·y /'pitʃi/ *adj.* **1** like a peach in color, taste, or appearance: *pale peachy skin* **2** (*informal*) fine; very nice: *Everything is just peachy.*

'pea coat (also **'pea ˌjacket**) *noun* a type of thick short coat

pea·cock /'pikɑk/ *noun* a large male bird with long blue and green tail feathers that it can spread out like a fan: *as proud as a peacock* ⊃ see also PEAHEN

ˌpeacock 'blue *adj.* deep greenish-blue in color
▸ ˌpeacock 'blue *noun* [U]

pea·fowl /'pifaʊl/ *noun* (*pl.* pea·fowl) a large PHEASANT found mainly in Asia. The male is called a PEACOCK and the female is called a PEAHEN.

ˌpea-'green *adj.* bright green in color, like PEAS

pea·hen /'pihɛn/ *noun* a large brown bird, the female of the peacock

'pea ˌjacket *noun* = PEA COAT

peak 🔑 /pik/ *noun, verb, adj.*
● *noun* **1** [usually sing.] the point when someone or something is best, most successful, strongest, etc. **SYN** HEIGHT: *Traffic **reaches its peak** between 8 and 9 in the morning.* ♦ *She's **at the peak** of her career.* **2** a boxer well past his peak ♦ *the **peaks and valleys** of married life* ⊃ compare OFF-PEAK **2** the pointed top of a mountain; a mountain with a pointed top: *a mountain peak* ♦ *snow-capped/jagged peaks* ♦ *The climbers made camp halfway up the peak.* **3** any narrow and pointed shape, edge, etc.: *Whisk the egg whites into stiff peaks.*
● *verb* [I] to reach the highest point or value: *Oil production peaked in the early 1980s.* ♦ *Unemployment peaked at 17%.* ♦ *an athlete who peaks* (= produces his or her best performance) *at just the right time*
● *adj.* [only before noun] used to describe the highest level of something, or a time when the greatest number of people are doing something or using something: *It was a time of **peak demand** for the product.* ♦ *March is one of the peak periods for our business.* ♦ *The athletes are all in **peak condition**.* ♦ *We need extra help during the **peak season**.* ⊃ compare OFF-PEAK

peak·ed *adj.* **1** /'pikt/ having a pointed top: *a peaked roof* **2** /'pikəd/ sick or pale: *You're looking a little peaked. Are you OK?*

ˌpeak 'oil *noun* [U] the point in time when world oil production reaches its highest rate, after which it goes into permanent decline

ˌpeak 'rate *noun* the busiest time, which is therefore charged at the highest rate: *peak-rate phone calls*

peal /pil/ *noun, verb*
● *noun* **1** ~ (of sth) a loud sound or series of sounds: *She burst into peals of laughter.* **2** the loud ringing sound of a bell: *a peal of bells rang out* **3** a set of bells that all have different notes; a musical pattern that can be rung on a set of bells
● *verb* **1** [I] ~ (out) (of bells) to ring loudly: *The bells of the city began to peal out.* **2** [I] ~ (with sth) to suddenly laugh loudly: *Ellen pealed with laughter.*

pea·nut /'pinʌt/ *noun* **1** [C] a nut that grows underground in a thin shell: *a packet of salted peanuts* ♦ *peanut oil* ⊃ picture at NUT **2** peanuts [pl.] (*informal*) a very small amount of money: *He gets paid peanuts for doing that job.*

ˌpeanut 'butter *noun* [U] a thick, soft substance made from very finely chopped PEANUTS, usually eaten spread on bread: *a peanut butter and jelly sandwich*

'peanut ˌgallery *noun* (*informal*) **1** the cheapest seats in a theater, usually very high up and farthest from the stage **2** the people who sit in the peanut gallery : *You could hear shrieks of laughter coming from the peanut gallery.*

pear /pɛr/ *noun* a yellow or green fruit that is narrow at the top and wide at the bottom: *a pear tree* ⊃ picture at FRUIT ⊃ see also PRICKLY PEAR

pearl /pɜrl/ *noun* **1** [C] a small, hard, shiny, white ball that forms inside the shell of an OYSTER and is of great value as a JEWEL: *a string of pearls* ♦ *a pearl necklace* ♦ *She was wearing her pearls* (= a NECKLACE of pearls). ➔ **picture at** JEWELRY ➔ **see also** SEED PEARL **2** [C] a copy of a pearl that is made artificially **3** [U] = MOTHER-OF-PEARL: *pearl buttons* **4** [C, usually sing.] a thing that looks like a pearl in shape or color: *pearls of dew on the grass* **5** [C] a thing that is very highly valued: *She is a pearl among women.*
IDM **cast, throw, etc. pearls before swine** to give or offer valuable things to people who do not understand their value **a pearl of wisdom** (usually *ironic*) a wise remark: *Thank you for those pearls of wisdom.*

ˌpearl ˈbarley *noun* [U] smooth grains of BARLEY, which are added to soups and other dishes

pearl·y /ˈpɜrli/ *adj.* of or like a pearl: *pearly white teeth*
IDM **pearly whites** (*humorous*) your teeth: *Remember to brush your pearly whites before you go to bed.*

the ˌPearly ˈGates *noun* [pl.] (*humorous*) the gates of heaven

ˈpear-shaped *adj.* **1** shaped like a pear **2** a **pear-shaped** person is wider around their waist and hips than around the top part of their body

peas·ant /ˈpɛznt/ *noun* **1** (especially in the past, or in poorer countries) a farmer who owns or rents a small piece of land: *peasant farmers* **2** (*informal, disapproving*) a person who is rude, behaves badly, or has little education **SYN** LOUT

peas·ant·ry /ˈpɛzntri/ *noun* [sing.] all the peasants in a region or country: *the local peasantry*

pea·shoot·er /ˈpiˌʃutər/ *noun* a small tube that children use to blow small objects such as dried PEAS at someone or something, in order to hit them or it

peat /pit/ *noun* [U] a soft black or brown substance formed from decaying plants just under the surface of the ground, especially in cool wet areas. It is burned as a fuel or used to improve garden soil: *peat bogs* ▶ **peat·y** /ˈpiti/ *adj.*: *peaty soils*

ˈpeat moss (also sphag·num) *noun* [U] a type of MOSS that grows in wet areas, used especially for planting plants in pots, making FERTILIZER, etc.

peb·ble /ˈpɛbl/ *noun* a smooth, round stone that is found in or near water

peb·bly /ˈpɛbli/ *adj.* covered with pebbles: *a pebbly beach*

pe·can /pɪˈkan; -ˈkæn; ˈpikæn/ *noun* the nut of the **pecan tree** with a smooth pinkish-brown shell ➔ **picture at** NUT

pec·ca·dil·lo /ˌpɛkəˈdɪloʊ/ *noun* (*pl.* pec·ca·dil·loes or pec·ca·dil·los) a small unimportant thing that someone does wrong

pec·ca·ry /ˈpɛkəri/ (*pl.* pec·ca·ries) *noun* an animal like a pig, which lives in the southern U.S., Mexico, and Central and S. America

peck /pɛk/ *verb, noun*
● *verb* **1** [I] (of birds) to move the beak forward quickly and hit or bite something: ~ **(at sth)** *A robin was pecking at crumbs on the ground.* ♦ ~ **sth** *A bird had pecked a hole in the sack.* ♦ ~ **sth out** *Vultures had pecked out the dead goat's eyes.* **2** [T] (*informal*) to kiss someone lightly and quickly: ~ **sb on sth** *He pecked her on the cheek as he went out.* ♦ ~ **sth** *She pecked his cheek.*
IDM **a/the pecking order** (*informal, often humorous*) the order of importance in relation to one another among the members of a group **SYN** HIERARCHY: *The Lakers are at the top of the pecking order of NBA teams.*
PHR V ˈpeck at sth to eat only a very small amount of a meal because you are not hungry **SYN** PICK AT
● *noun* **1** (*informal*) a quick kiss: *He gave her a friendly peck on the cheek.* **2** an act of pecking someone or something: *The canary gave a quick peck at the seed.* **3** a unit for measuring grain and fruit, equal to a quarter of a BUSHEL or 8 QUARTS: *a peck of apples*

pecs /pɛks/ *noun* [pl.] (*informal*) = PECTORALS

pec·tin /ˈpɛktən/ *noun* [U] (*chemistry*) a substance similar to sugar that forms in fruit that is ready to eat, and is used to make JAM firm as it is cooked

pec·to·ral /ˈpɛktərəl/ *adj., noun*
● *adj.* (*anatomy*) relating to or connected with the chest or breast: *pectoral muscles*
● *noun* **pectorals** (also *informal* **pecs**) [pl.] the muscles of the chest

pe·cu·liar /pɪˈkyulyər/ *adj.* **1** strange or unusual, especially in a way that is unpleasant or worrying **SYN** ODD: *a peculiar smell/taste* ♦ *There was something peculiar in the way he smiled.* ♦ *I had a peculiar feeling we'd met before.* ♦ *For some peculiar reason, she refused to come inside.* **2** ~ **(to sb/sth)** belonging or relating to one particular place, situation, person, etc., and not to others: *a species of bird peculiar to Asia* ♦ *He has his own peculiar style, which you'll soon get used to.* ♦ *the peculiar properties of mercury*

pe·cu·li·ar·i·ty /pɪˌkyuliˈærəti/ *noun* (*pl.* pe·cu·li·ar·i·ties) **1** [C] a strange or unusual feature or habit: *a physical peculiarity* **2** [C] a feature that only belongs to one particular person, thing, place, etc. **SYN** CHARACTERISTIC: *the cultural peculiarities of Americans* **3** [U] the quality of being strange or unusual

pe·cu·liar·ly /pɪˈkyulyərli/ *adv.* **1** very; more than usually **SYN** ESPECIALLY, PARTICULARLY: *These plants are peculiarly prone to disease.* **2** in a way that relates to or is especially typical of one particular person, thing, place, etc.: *He seemed to believe that it was a peculiarly Western problem.* **3** in a strange or unusual way

pe·cu·ni·ar·y /pɪˈkyuniˌɛri/ *adj.* (*formal*) relating to or connected with money: *pecuniary advantage*

ped- /pid/ *combining form* (in nouns and adjectives) connected with children: *pediatrician*

ped·a·gog·ic /ˌpɛdəˈgadʒɪk/ (also ped·a·gog·i·cal /ˌpɛdəˈgadʒɪkl/) *adj.* (*formal*) concerning teaching methods: *pedagogic principles* ▶ **ped·a·gog·i·cally** /-kli/ *adv.*

ped·a·gogue /ˈpɛdəˌgag/ *noun* (*old use* or *formal*) a teacher; a person who likes to teach people things, especially because they think they know more than other people

ped·a·go·gy /ˈpɛdəˌgoʊdʒi; -ˌgadʒi/ *noun* [U] (*technical*) the study of teaching methods

ped·al /ˈpɛdl/ *noun, verb*
● *noun* **1** a flat bar on a machine such as a bicycle, car, etc. that you push down with your foot in order to make parts of the machine move or work: *I couldn't reach the pedals on her bike.* ♦ *She pressed her foot down sharply on the brake pedal.* ➔ **picture at** BICYCLE **2** a bar on a musical instrument such as a piano or an organ that you push with your foot in order to control the sound
● *verb* (-l-) **1** [I, T] to ride a bicycle somewhere: + **adv./prep.** *I saw her pedaling along the path.* ♦ *He jumped on his bike and pedaled off.* ♦ ~ **sth** + **adv./prep.** *She pedaled her bicycle up the track.* **2** [I, T] to turn or press the pedals on a bicycle or other machine: (+ **adv./prep.**) *You'll have to pedal hard up this hill.* ♦ ~ **sth** *She had been pedaling her exercise bike all morning.* ➔ **see also** BACKPEDAL, SOFT-PEDAL

ˈpedal ˌpushers *noun* [pl.] women's pants that reach just below the knee

ped·ant /ˈpɛdnt/ *noun* (*disapproving*) a person who is too concerned with small details or rules, especially when learning or teaching

pe·dan·tic /pəˈdæntɪk/ *adj.* (*disapproving*) too worried about small details or rules ▶ **pe·dan·ti·cally** /-kli/ *adv.*

ped·ant·ry /ˈpɛdntri/ *noun* [U] (*disapproving*) too much attention to small details or rules

ped·dle /ˈpɛdl/ *verb* **1** ~ **sth** to try to sell goods by going from house to house or from place to place: *He worked as a door-to-door salesman peddling cloths and brushes.* ♦ *to peddle illegal drugs* **2** ~ **sth** to spread an idea or story in order to get people to accept it: *to peddle malicious gossip* ♦ *This line*

(= publicly stated opinion) *is being peddled by all the government spokesmen.*

ped·dler /ˈpɛdlər/ *noun* **1** (also **drug ˌpeddler**) a person who sells illegal drugs **2** a person who in the past traveled from place to place trying to sell small objects

ped·er·ast /ˈpɛdəˌræst/ *noun* (*formal*) a man who has sex with a boy ▶ **ped·er·as·ty** /ˈpɛdəˌræsti/ *noun* [U]

ped·es·tal /ˈpɛdəstl/ *noun* the base that a column, statue, etc. rests on: *a pedestal sink* (= a SINK supported by a column) ◆ *I replaced the vase carefully on its pedestal.* ⊃ **picture at ARCHITECTURE**
IDM **to put/place sb on a pedestal** to admire someone so much that you do not see their faults ⊃ **more at KNOCK**

pe·des·tri·an /pəˈdɛstriən/ *noun, adj.*
● *noun* a person walking in the street and not traveling in a vehicle ⊃ **compare MOTORIST**
● *adj.* **1** [only before noun] used by, or for the use of, pedestrians; connected with pedestrians: *pedestrian areas* ◆ *Pedestrian accidents are down by 5%.* **2** without any imagination or excitement; dull **SYN** UNIMAGINATIVE

peˌdestrian ˈcrossing *noun* = CROSSWALK

pe·des·tri·an·ize /pəˈdɛstriəˌnaɪz/ *verb* ~ **sth** to make a street or part of a town into an area that is only for people who are walking, not for vehicles ▶ **pe·des·tri·an·i·za·tion** /pəˌdɛstriənəˈzeɪʃn/ *noun* [U]

peˌdestrian ˈmall *noun* a part of a town, especially a shopping area, that vehicles are not allowed to enter

pe·di·a·tri·cian /ˌpidiəˈtrɪʃn/ *noun* a doctor who studies and treats the diseases of children

pe·di·at·rics /ˌpidiˈætrɪks/ *noun* [U] the branch of medicine concerned with children and their diseases ▶ **pe·di·at·ric** *adj.*: *pediatric surgery*

ped·i·cure /ˈpɛdɪˌkyʊr/ *noun* [C, U] the care and treatment of the feet and TOENAILS ⊃ **compare MANICURE**

ped·i·gree /ˈpɛdəgri/ *noun, adj.*
● *noun* **1** [C] knowledge of or an official record of the animals from which an animal has been bred: *dogs with good pedigrees* (= their ANCESTORS are known and of the same breed) **2** [C, U] a person's family history or the background of something, especially when this is impressive: *She was proud of her long pedigree.* ◆ *The product has a pedigree going back to the last century.*
● *adj.* = PEDIGREED

ped·i·greed /ˈpɛdəgrid/ (also **ped·i·gree**) *adj.* [only before noun] (of an animal) coming from a family of the same breed that has been officially recorded for a long time and is thought to be of a good quality: *pedigreed sheep*

ped·i·ment /ˈpɛdəmənt/ *noun* (*architecture*) the part in the shape of a triangle above the entrance of a building in the ancient Greek style

pe·dom·e·ter /pəˈdɑmətər/ *noun* an instrument for measuring how far you have walked

pe·do·phile /ˈpɛdəˌfaɪl/ *noun* a person who is sexually attracted to children

pe·do·phil·i·a /ˌpɛdəˈfɪliə/ *noun* [U] the condition of being sexually attracted to children; sexual activity with children

pee /pi/ *verb, noun*
● *verb* (**peed, peed**) [I] (*informal*) to pass waste liquid from your body **SYN** URINATE: *I need to pee.*
● *noun* (*informal*) **1** [sing.] an act of passing liquid waste from your body: *to take a pee* **2** [U] liquid waste passed from your body; URINE

peek /pik/ *verb* **1** [I] to look at something quickly and secretly because you should not be looking at it **SYN** PEEP: *No peeking!* ◆ **+ adv./prep.** *She peeked at the audience from behind the curtain.* ◆ *I couldn't resist peeking in the drawer.* **2** [I] ~ **out/over/through, etc.** to be just visible: *Her feet peeked out from the end of the blanket.* ▶ **peek** *noun* [sing.]: *I took a quick peek inside.*

peek·a·boo /ˈpikəˌbu/ *noun* [U] a simple game played to amuse young children, in which you keep hiding your face and then showing it again, saying "Peekaboo!"

peel /pil/ *verb, noun*
● *verb* **1** [T] ~ **sth** to take the skin off fruit, vegetables, etc.: *to peel an orange/a banana* ◆ *Have you peeled the potatoes?* ⊃ **collocations at COOKING** **2** [T, I] ~ **(sth) away/off/back** to remove a layer, covering, etc. from the surface of something; to come off the surface of something: *Carefully peel away the lining paper.* ◆ *The label will peel off if you soak it in water.* **3** [I] ~ **(off)** (of a covering) to come off in strips or small pieces: *The wallpaper was beginning to peel.* **4** [I] (of a surface) to lose strips or small pieces of its covering: *Put on some cream to keep your nose from peeling.* ◆ *The walls have begun to peel.* **IDM** **see EYE**
PHR V **ˌpeel ˈoff** to leave a group of vehicles, aircraft, etc. and turn to one side: *The leading car in the motorcade peeled off to the right.* **ˌpeel sth↔ˈoff** (*informal*) to remove some or all of your clothes: *He peeled off his shirt.* **ˌpeel ˈout** (*informal*) to leave quickly and in a noisy way, especially in a car, on a motorcycle, etc.
● *noun* **1** [U, C] the thick skin of some fruits and vegetables: *orange/lemon peel* ◆ *an orange/a lemon peel* ⊃ **picture at FRUIT** ⊃ **compare RIND, SKIN, ZEST 2 peels** [pl.] = PEELINGS

peel·er /ˈpilər/ *noun* (usually in compounds) a special type of knife for taking the skin off fruit and vegetables: *a potato peeler* ⊃ **picture at KITCHEN**

peel·ings /ˈpilɪŋz/ (also **peels**) *noun* [pl.] the skin of fruit or vegetables that has been removed

peep /pip/ *verb, noun*
● *verb* **1** [I] (**+ adv./prep.**) to look quickly and secretly at something, especially through a small opening: *We caught her peeping through the keyhole.* ◆ *Could I just peep inside?* ◆ *He was peeping at her through his fingers.* **2** [I] **+ adv./prep.** to be just visible: *The tower peeped above the trees.* ◆ *The sun peeped out from behind the clouds.* **3** [I, T] ~ **(sth)** to make a short high sound; to make something make this sound
● *noun* **1** [C, usually sing.] a quick or secret look at something: *Dave took a quick peep at the last page.* **2** [sing.] (*informal*) something that someone says or a sound that someone makes: *We did not hear a peep out of the baby all night.* **3** [C] a short high sound like the one made by a young bird or by a whistle

peep·er /ˈpipər/ (also **ˈspring ˈpeeper**) *noun* a small N. American frog with gray-brown skin, the males of which make a short, high sound in the spring

peep·hole /ˈpiphoʊl/ *noun* a small opening in a wall, door, etc. that you can look through

ˌPeeping ˈTom *noun* (*disapproving*) a person who likes to watch people secretly when they are taking off their clothes **SYN** VOYEUR

ˈpeep show *noun* **1** a series of moving pictures in a box that you look at through a small opening **2** a type of show in which someone pays to watch a woman take off her clothes in a small room

peer /pɪr/ *noun, verb*
● *noun* **1** [usually pl.] a person who is the same age or who has the same social status as you: *She enjoys the respect of her peers.* ◆ *Children are worried about failing in front of their peers.* **2** a member of the British NOBILITY
● *verb* [I] (**+ adv./prep.**) to look closely or carefully at something, especially when you cannot see it clearly: *We peered into the shadows.* ◆ *He went to the window and peered out.* ◆ *She kept peering over her shoulder.* ◆ *He peered closely at the photograph.* ⊃ **thesaurus box at STARE**

ˈpeer group *noun* a group of people of the same age or social status: *She gets on well with her peer group.* ◆ *peer-group pressure*

peer·less /ˈpɪrləs/ *adj.* better than all others of its kind **SYN** UNSURPASSED: *a peerless performance*

peer pressure noun [U] pressure from people of your age or social group to behave like them in order to be liked or accepted: *Teenagers are highly influenced by peer pressure.*

peer review noun [U, C] a judgment on a piece of scientific or other professional work by others working in the same area: *All research proposals are subject to peer review before selection.* ▶ **peer-reviewed** adj.: *peer-reviewed journals*

peer-to-peer adj. [only before noun] (*computing*) (of a computer system) in which each computer can act as a SERVER for the others, allowing data to be shared without the need for a central server ⊃ compare CLIENT-SERVER

peeve /piv/ noun IDM see PET adj.

peeved /pivd/ adj. ~ **(about sth)** (*informal*) annoyed: *He sounded peeved about not being told.*

peev·ish /'piviʃ/ adj. easily annoyed by unimportant things; bad-tempered SYN IRRITABLE ▶ **peev·ish·ly** adv.

pee·wee /'piwi/ noun, adj.
• *noun* (*informal*) a person or thing that is very small or smaller than usual: *I was a real peewee until I turned 13, and then I shot up to 6 feet.*
• *adj.* (*informal*) very small or relating to small children: *Our 8-year-old is in a peewee baseball league.* ◆ *We got him a peewee version of his brother's bike.*

pegs

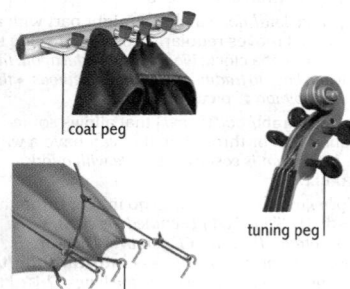

coat peg

tuning peg

tent peg

peg /pɛg/ noun, verb
• *noun* 1 a short piece of wood, metal, or plastic used for holding things together, hanging things on, marking a position, etc.: *There's a peg near the door to hang your coat on.* 2 (also **tent peg**) a small pointed piece of wood or metal that you attach to the ropes of a tent and push into the ground in order to hold the tent in place 3 (also **tuning peg**) a wooden, metal, or plastic screw used for making the strings of a musical instrument tighter or looser IDM **bring/take sb down a peg (or two)** to make someone realize that they are not as good, important, etc. as they think they are: *He needed to be taken down a peg or two.* **a peg to hang sth on** something that gives you an excuse or opportunity to discuss or explain something ⊃ more at SQUARE
• *verb* (-gg-) 1 to fasten something with a peg: ~ **sth + adv./prep.** *Peg down the edges of the net.* ◆ ~ **sth to sth** *She was busy pegging her tent to the ground.* 2 [usually passive] to fix or keep prices, wages, etc. at a particular level: ~ **sth (at sth)** *Pay increases will be pegged at 5%.* ◆ ~ **sth (to sth)** *Loan repayments are pegged to your income.* 3 ~ **sb as sth** (*informal*) to think of someone in a particular way: *She pegged him as a big spender.* 4 (*informal*) to throw something: *He pegged the ball to second base.*

peg·board /'pɛgbɔrd/ noun 1 a small board with a pattern of holes to put pegs in, used in some games: *a cribbage pegboard* 2 a board with holes to put pegs or hooks in, used to hang things on: *a pegboard for tools*

peg leg noun (*informal*) an artificial leg, especially one made of wood

pe·jo·ra·tive /pɪ'dʒɔrətɪv; -'dʒɑr-/ adj. (*formal*) a word or remark that is **pejorative** expresses disapproval or criticism SYN DEROGATORY: *I'm using the word "academic" here in a pejorative sense.* ▶ **pe·jo·ra·tive·ly** adv.

Pe·king·ese (also **Pe·kin·ese**) /,pikə'niz; -'nis/ noun (pl. **Pe·king·ese** or **Pe·king·es·es**) a very small dog with long soft hair, short legs, and a flat nose

pe·lag·ic /pə'lædʒɪk/ adj. (*technical*) connected with, or living in, the parts of the ocean that are far from land

pel·i·can /'pɛlɪkən/ noun a large bird that lives near water, with a bag of skin under its long beak for storing food

pel·la·gra /pə'lægrə; -'leɪ-/ noun [U] a disease caused by a lack of good food, that causes the skin to crack and may lead to mental illness

pel·let /'pɛlət/ noun 1 a small hard ball of any substance, often of soft material that has become hard: *food pellets for chickens* 2 a very small metal ball that is fired from a gun

pell-mell /,pɛl 'mɛl/ adv. (*old-fashioned*) very quickly and in a way that is not controlled

pel·lu·cid /pə'lusɪd/ adj. (*literary*) extremely clear SYN TRANSPARENT

pe·lo·ta /pə'loutə/ noun 1 [U] a game from Spain in which players hit a ball against a wall using a kind of BASKET attached to their hand 2 [C] the ball used in the game of pelota

the pel·o·ton /'pɛlə,tɑn/ noun [sing.] (from *French*) the main group of riders in a bicycle race

pelt /pɛlt/ verb, noun
• *verb* 1 [T] ~ **sb (with sth)** to attack someone by throwing things at them: *The children pelted him with snowballs.* 2 [I] ~ **(down)** (of rain) to fall very heavily 3 [I] + **adv./prep.** (*informal*) to run somewhere very fast SYN DASH: *We pelted down the hill after the car.*
• *noun* the skin of an animal, especially with the fur or hair still on it

pelvic floor noun (*anatomy*) the muscles at the base of the ABDOMEN, attached to the pelvis

pel·vis /'pɛlvəs/ noun the wide, curved set of bones at the bottom of the body that the legs and SPINE are connected to ⊃ picture at BODY ▶ **pel·vic** /'pɛlvɪk/ adj. [only before noun]: *the pelvic bones*

pem·mi·can /'pɛmɪkən/ noun [U] a food made from crushed dried meat, originally made by Native Americans

pen 🖉 /pɛn/ noun, verb
• *noun* 1 (often in compounds) an instrument made of plastic or metal used for writing with ink: *pen and ink* ◆ *a new book from the pen of John Grisham* ⊃ see also FELT-TIP PEN, FOUNTAIN PEN 2 a small piece of land surrounded by a fence in which farm animals are kept: *a sheep pen* 3 (*slang*) = PENITENTIARY IDM **the pen is mightier than the sword** (*saying*) people who write books, poems, etc. have a greater effect on history and human affairs than soldiers and wars **put pen to paper** to write or start to write something ⊃ more at SLIP n.
• *verb* (-nn-) 1 ~ **sth** (*formal*) to write something: *He penned a letter to the local paper.* 2 ~ **sb/sth (in/up)** to shut an animal or a person in a small space: *At clipping time sheep need to be penned.* ◆ *The whole family was penned up in one room for a month.*

pe·nal /'pinl/ adj. [usually before noun] 1 connected with or used for punishment, especially by law: *penal reforms* ◆ *the penal system* ◆ *Criminals could at one time be sentenced to penal servitude* (= prison with hard physical work). ◆ *a penal colony* (= a place where criminals were sent as a punishment in the past) 2 that can be punished by law: *a penal offense* 3 very severe: *penal rates of interest*

penal code noun a system of laws connected with crime and punishment

pe·nal·ize /'pinl,aɪz; 'pɛn-/ verb 1 ~ **sb (for sth)** to punish someone for breaking a rule or law by making them suffer a disadvantage: *You will be penalized for poor spelling.* **2** to punish someone for breaking a rule in a sport or game by giving an advantage to their opponent: **~ sb (for sth)** *He was penalized for high-sticking.* ◆ **~ sth** *Foul play will be severely penalized.* **3 ~ sb** to put someone at a disadvantage by treating them unfairly: *The new law appears to penalize the poorest members of society.*

pen·al·ty 🔑 /'penlti/ *noun* (*pl.* **pen·al·ties**)
1 a punishment for breaking a law, rule, or contract: *to impose a penalty* ◆ *Assault **carries** a maximum **penalty** of seven years' imprisonment.* ◆ **~ (for sth)** *The penalty for traveling without a ticket is $200.* ◆ *Contractors who fall behind schedule incur heavy financial penalties.* ◆ *a penalty clause in a contract* ◆ *You can withdraw money from the account at any time **without penalty.*** ⊃ see also DEATH PENALTY **2 ~ (of sth)** a disadvantage suffered as a result of something: *One of the penalties of fame is the loss of privacy.* **3** (in sports and games) a disadvantage given to a player or a team when they break a rule: *He incurred a ten-second penalty in the first round.* **4** (in SOCCER and some other similar sports) a chance to score a goal or point without any defending players, except the GOALKEEPER, trying to stop it. This chance is given because the other team has broken the rules; the goal or point that is given if it is successful: *We **were awarded a penalty** after a late tackle.* ◆ *I volunteered to **take the penalty** (= be the person who tries to score the goal/point).* ◆ *He **missed a penalty** in the last minute of the game.* **IDM** see PAY *v.*

penalty ˌarea *noun* (in SOCCER) the area in front of the goal. If the defending team breaks the rules within this area, the other team is given a penalty.

penalty ˌbox *noun* (in HOCKEY) an area next to the ice where a player who has broken the rules must wait for a short time

penalty ˌkick *noun* a kick that is taken as a PENALTY in the game of SOCCER

ˌpenalty ˈshoot-out *noun* (in SOCCER) a way of deciding the winner when both teams have the same score at the end of a game. Each team is given a number of chances to kick the ball into the goal and the team that scores the most goals wins.

pen·ance /'penəns/ *noun* **1** [C, usually sing., U] (especially in particular religions) an act that you give yourself to do, or that a priest gives you to do, in order to show that you are sorry for something you have done wrong: *an act of penance* ◆ **~ for sth** *to do penance for your sins* ⊃ collocations at RELIGION **2** [sing.] something that you have to do even though you do not like doing it: *She regards living in New York as a penance; she hates big cities.*

ˌpen-and-ˈink *adj.* [usually before noun] drawn with a pen: *pen-and-ink drawings*

pen·chant /'pentʃənt/ *noun* **~ for sth** a special liking for something **SYN** FONDNESS: *She **has a penchant** for champagne.*

pen·cil 🔑 /'pensl/ *noun, verb*
● *noun* [C, U] a narrow piece of wood, or a metal or plastic case, containing a black or colored substance, used for drawing or writing: *a pencil drawing* ◆ *I'll get a pencil and paper.* ◆ *She scribbled a note **in pencil**.* ◆ *colored pencils* ⊃ picture at STATIONERY ⊃ see also EYEBROW PENCIL, MECHANICAL PENCIL
● *verb* (-l-) **~ sth** to write, draw, or mark something with a pencil: *a penciled portrait* ◆ *A previous owner had penciled "First Edition" inside the book's cover.*
PHR V ˌpencil sth/sb↔ˈin to write down someone's name or details of an arrangement with them that you know might have to be changed later: *We've penciled in a meeting for Tuesday afternoon.* ◆ *Shall I pencil you in (= for a meeting) for Friday?*

ˈpencil ˌcase *noun* a small bag, etc. for holding pencils and pens

ˈpencil-ˌpusher *noun* (*informal, disapproving*) a person with

a boring job, especially in an office, that involves a lot of writing

ˈpencil ˌsharpener *noun* a small device with a blade inside, used for making pencils sharp ⊃ picture at STATIONERY

ˈpencil ˌskirt *noun* a narrow straight skirt

ˌpencil-ˈthin *adj.* very thin: *a pencil-thin mustache* ◆ *All the models had pencil-thin figures.*

pend·ant /'pendənt/ *noun* a piece of jewelry that you wear around your neck on a chain ⊃ picture at JEWELRY

pen·dent /'pendənt/ *adj.* hanging down from above or over the edge of something: *a set of pendent lights* ◆ *pendent plants spilling over the edge of the cliff*

pend·ing /'pendɪŋ/ *prep., adj.*
● *prep.* (*formal*) while waiting for something to happen; until something happens: *He was released on bail pending further investigation.*
● *adj.* (*formal*) **1** waiting to be decided or settled: *Nine cases are still pending.* ◆ *a pending file/tray* (= where you put letters, etc. you are going to deal with soon) **2** going to happen soon **SYN** IMMINENT: *A presidential election is pending.* ◆ *his pending departure*

ˈpen drive *noun* = FLASH DRIVE

pen·du·lous /'pendʒələs/ *adj.* (*formal*) hanging down loosely and swinging from side to side

pen·du·lum /'pendʒələm/ *noun* a long straight part with a weight at the end that moves regularly from side to side to control the movement of a clock: (*figurative*) *In education, the pendulum has swung back to traditional teaching methods.* ◆ *the pendulum of public opinion* ⊃ picture at CLOCK

pen·e·tra·ble /'penətrəbl/ *adj.* (*formal*) that allows something to be pushed into or through it; that can have a way made through it: *soil that is easily penetrable with a fork* **ANT** IMPENETRABLE

pen·e·trate /'penəˌtreɪt/ *verb* **1** [T, I] to go into or through something: **~ sth** *The knife had penetrated his chest.* ◆ *The sun's radiation penetrates the skin.* ◆ (*figurative*) *The war penetrates every area of the nation's life.* ◆ **~ into/through/to sth** *These fine particles penetrate deep into the lungs.* **2** [T, I] to succeed in entering or joining an organization, a group, etc. especially when this is difficult to do: **~ sth** *They had penetrated airport security.* ◆ *The party has been penetrated by extremists.* ◆ *This year the company has been trying to penetrate new markets* (= to start selling their products there). ◆ **~ into sth** *The troops had penetrated deep into enemy lines.* **3** [T] **~ sth** to see or show a way into or through something: *Our eyes could not penetrate the darkness.* ◆ *The flashlights barely penetrated the gloom.* **4** [T] **~ sth** to understand or discover something that is difficult to understand or is hidden: *Science can penetrate many of nature's mysteries.* **5** [I, T] to be understood or realized by someone: *I was at the door before his words penetrated.* ◆ **~ sth** *None of my advice seems to have penetrated his thick skull* (= he has not listened to any of it).

pen·e·trat·ing /'penəˌtreɪtɪŋ/ *adj.* **1** (of someone's eyes or the way they look at you) making you feel uncomfortable because the person seems to know what you are thinking: *penetrating blue eyes* ◆ *a penetrating gaze/look/stare* **2** (of a sound or voice) loud and hard **SYN** PIERCING: *Her voice was shrill and penetrating.* **3** showing that you have understood something quickly and completely: *a penetrating comment/ criticism/question* **4** spreading deeply or widely: *a penetrating smell* ◆ *the penetrating cold/damp*

pen·e·tra·tion /ˌpenəˈtreɪʃn/ *noun* [U] the act or process of making a way into or through something: *The floor is sealed to prevent water penetration.* ◆ *the company's successful penetration of overseas markets*

pen·e·tra·tive /'penəˌtreɪtɪv/ *adj.* **1** able to make a way into or through something: *penetrative weapons* **2** deep and thorough: *a penetrative survey*

pen·guin /'peŋgwən/ *noun* a black and white bird that lives in the Antarctic. Penguins cannot fly but use their wings for

t tea	ţ butter	d did	k cat	g got	tʃ chin	dʒ June	f fall

swimming. There are several types of penguins, some of them very large but some of them quite small.

penguin

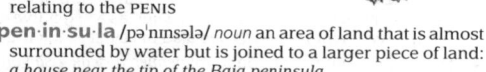

pen·i·cil·lin /ˌpenəˈsɪlən/ *noun* [U] a substance obtained from MOLD, used as a drug to treat or prevent infections caused by bacteria; a type of ANTIBIOTIC

pe·nile /ˈpinaɪl/ *adj.* [only before noun] (*technical*) relating to the PENIS

pen·in·su·la /pəˈnɪnsələ/ *noun* an area of land that is almost surrounded by water but is joined to a larger piece of land: *a house near the tip of the Baja peninsula*

pen·in·su·lar /pəˈnɪnsələr/ *adj.* on or connected with a peninsula: *peninsular Spanish* (= that is spoken in Spain, not in Latin America)

pe·nis /ˈpinəs/ *noun* the organ on the body of a man or male animal that is used for urinating (URINATE) and sex

pen·i·tence /ˈpenətəns/ *noun* [U] a feeling of being sorry because you have done something wrong

pen·i·tent /ˈpenətənt/ *adj.*, *noun*
- *adj.* feeling or showing that you are sorry for having done something wrong
- *noun* a person who shows that they are sorry for doing something wrong, especially a religious person who wants God to forgive them

pen·i·ten·tial /ˌpenəˈtenʃl/ *adj.* (*formal*) showing that you are sorry for having done something wrong

pen·i·ten·tia·ry /ˌpenəˈtenʃəri/ *noun* (*pl.* pen·i·ten·tia·ries) (also *informal* pen) a prison

pen·knife /ˈpennaɪf/ *noun* (*pl.* pen·knives /-naɪvz/) = POCKETKNIFE

pen·light /ˈpenlaɪt/ *noun* a small FLASHLIGHT shaped like a pen: *She keeps a penlight in the glove compartment of her car.*

pen·man·ship /ˈpenmənˌʃɪp/ *noun* [U] (*formal*) the art of writing by hand; skill in doing this

pen-name *noun* a name used by a writer instead of their real name SYN NOM DE PLUME ⊃ compare PSEUDONYM

pen·nant /ˈpenənt/ *noun* **1** a long, narrow, pointed flag, for example one used on a ship to give signals **2** a flag given to the winning team in a sports league, especially in baseball

pen·ni·less /ˈpenɪləs/ *adj.* having no money; very poor SYN DESTITUTE ⊃ thesaurus box at POOR

Penn·syl·va·nia Dutch /ˌpensl̩ˌveɪnyə ˈdʌtʃ/ *noun* **1** the Pennsylvania Dutch [pl.] a group of people originally from Germany and Switzerland who settled in Pennsylvania in the 17th and 18th centuries **2** [U] a type of German mixed with English spoken by the Pennsylvania Dutch

pen·ny /ˈpeni/ *noun*
1 (*pl.* pen·nies) a cent ⊃ picture at MONEY **2** (*pl.* pence) a small British coin and unit of money equal to 1/100th of one pound (£1): *That will be 45 pence, please.*
IDM **every penny** all of the money: *We collected $700 and every penny went to charity.* **in for a penny, in for a pound** (*saying*) used to say that since you have started to do something, it is worth spending as much time or money as you need to in order to complete it **not a penny** no money at all: *It didn't cost a penny.* **a penny for your thoughts** (*saying*) used to ask someone what they are thinking about **a penny saved is a penny earned** (*saying*) used to say that it is important to save money whenever possible **penny wise and pound foolish** (*saying*) used to say that someone does not spend their money well, paying too much for large purchases and trying to save money on small things **turn up like a bad penny** (*informal*) (of a person) to appear when they are not welcome or not

wanted, especially when this happens regularly ⊃ more at LAST¹ *det.*, PINCH *v.*, PRETTY *adj.*

penny-ante *adj.* (*informal*, *disapproving*) not very important or valuable: *Theirs was a penny-ante organization of small-time criminals.*

penny candy *noun* [C, U] candy that is sold in small individual pieces that cost only a few cents each

penny-pinching *adj.* (*disapproving*) unwilling to spend money ▶ **penny-pinching** *noun* [U]

penny whistle *noun* = TIN WHISTLE

Pe·nob·scot /pəˈnɑbskɑt; -skət/ *noun* (*pl.* Pe·nob·scot) **1** [C] a member of a group of Native Americans originally from Maine **2** [U] the language of the Penobscot people

pe·nol·o·gy /piˈnɑlədʒi/ *noun* [U] the scientific study of the punishment of criminals and the operation of prisons ▶ **pe·nol·o·gist** /-dʒɪst/ *noun*

pen pal *noun* a person that you make friends with by writing letters, often someone you have never met

pen·sion¹ /ˈpenʃn/ *noun* an amount of money paid regularly by a company or government to someone who is considered to be too old or too sick to work: *to receive a retirement pension* ◆ *a disability/widow's pension* ◆ *a state pension* ◆ *to live on a pension* ◆ *to draw a personal/private pension* ◆ *a pension fund* ⊃ collocations at AGE

pen·sion² /pɑnˈsyoun/ *noun* (from French) a small, usually cheap, hotel in some European countries, especially France

pen·sion·er /ˈpenʃənər/ *noun* a person who is receiving a PENSION¹, especially from the government ⊃ see also SENIOR CITIZEN

pension plan (also **retirement plan**) *noun* a system in which you, and usually your employer, pay money regularly into a fund while you are employed. You are then paid a PENSION¹ when you retire.

pen·sive /ˈpensɪv/ *adj.* thinking deeply about something, especially because you are sad or worried: *a pensive mood* ◆ *to look pensive* ▶ **pen·sive·ly** *adv.*

penta- /ˈpentə/ *combining form* (in nouns, adjectives, and adverbs) five; having five: *pentagon* ◆ *pentathlon*

pen·ta·gon /ˈpentəˌgɑn/ *noun* **1** [C] (*geometry*) a flat shape with five straight sides and five angles ⊃ picture at SHAPE **2** the Pentagon [sing.] the building near Washington D.C. that is the HEADQUARTERS of the Department of Defense and military leaders: *a spokesman for the Pentagon*

pen·tag·o·nal /penˈtægənl/ *adj.* (*geometry*) having five sides

pen·ta·gram /ˈpentəˌgræm/ *noun* a flat shape of a star with five points, formed by five straight lines. Pentagrams are often used as magic symbols.

pen·tam·e·ter /penˈtæmətər/ *noun* [C, U] (*technical*) a line of poetry with five stressed syllables; the rhythm of poetry with five stressed syllables to a line

pen·tath·lon /penˈtæθlən; -lɑn/ *noun* a sporting event in which people compete in five different sports (running, riding, swimming, shooting, and FENCING) ⊃ compare BIATHLON, DECATHLON, HEPTATHLON, TETRATHLON, TRIATHLON

pen·ta·ton·ic /ˌpentəˈtɑnɪk/ *adj.* (*music*) related to or based on a SCALE of five notes

Pen·te·cost /ˈpentɪˌkɑst; -ˌkɔst/ *noun* [U, C] **1** (in the Christian Church) the 7th Sunday after Easter when Christians celebrate the Holy Spirit coming to the APOSTLES **2** = SHAVUOTH

Pen·te·cos·tal /ˌpentɪˈkɑstl; -ˈkɔstl/ *adj.* connected with a group of Christian Churches that emphasize the gifts of the Holy Spirit, such as the power to heal the sick ▶ **Pen·te·cos·tal·ist** /-təˌlɪst/ *noun*

pent·house /ˈpenthaʊs/ *noun* an expensive and comfortable apartment or set of rooms at the top of a tall building

pent-up /ˌpɛnt ˈʌp/ adj. **1** (of feelings, energy, etc.) that cannot be expressed or released: *pent-up frustration/energy* **2** having feelings that you cannot express: *She was too pent-up to speak.*

pe·nul·ti·mate /pɪˈnʌltəmət/ adj. [only before noun] immediately before the last one: *the penultimate chapter/day/stage*

pe·num·bra /pəˈnʌmbrə/ noun (technical) **1** an area of shadow that is between fully dark and fully light **2** (astronomy) the shadow made by the earth or the moon during a PARTIAL ECLIPSE ➔ compare UMBRA

pe·nu·ri·ous /pəˈnuriəs/ adj. (formal) very poor SYN DESTITUTE, PENNILESS

pen·u·ry /ˈpɛnyəri/ noun [U] (formal) the state of being very poor SYN POVERTY

pe·on /ˈpiɑn/ noun **1** a worker on a farm in Latin America **2** (humorous) a person with a hard or boring job that is not well paid and not considered important

pe·o·ny /ˈpiəni/ noun (pl. **pe·o·nies**) a garden plant with large round white, pink, or red flowers

peo·ple 🔊 /ˈpipl/ noun, verb
• **noun 1** [pl.] persons; men, women, and children: *At least ten people were killed in the crash.* ✦ *There were a lot of people at the party.* ✦ *Many young people are out of work.* **2** [pl.] persons in general or everyone: *He doesn't care what people think of him.* ✦ *She tends to annoy people.* **HELP** Use **everyone** or **everybody** instead of "all people." **3** [C] all the persons who live in a particular place or belong to a particular country, race, etc.: *the American people* ✦ *the native peoples of the Great Plains* ➔ see also TOWNSPEOPLE **4 the people** [pl.] the ordinary men and women of a country rather than those who govern or have a special position in society: *the life of the common people* ✦ *It was felt that the government was no longer in touch with the people.* ➔ see also LITTLE PEOPLE **5** [pl.] men and women who work in a particular type of job or are involved in a particular area of activity: *a meeting with business people and bankers* ✦ *These garments are intended for professional sports people.* **6** [pl.] (literary) the men, women, and children that a person leads: *The king urged his people to prepare for war.* **7** [pl.] the men and women who work for you or support you: *I've had my people watching the house for a few days.* **8** [pl.] (informal) guests or friends: *I'm having people to dinner this evening.* **9** [pl.] (old-fashioned) the men, women, and children that you are closely related to, especially your parents, grandparents, etc.: *She's spending the holidays with her people.* **10** [pl.] (informal) used when trying to get a group of people to listen to you: *Look, people, you've got to quiet down or we'll be here all night.* ➔ see also BOAT PEOPLE, STREET PEOPLE, TRADES-PEOPLE
IDM **of all people** when you say **of all people**, you are emphasizing that someone is the person you would most or least expect to do something: *She of all people should know the answer to that.* **people (who live) in glass houses shouldn't throw stones** (saying) you should not criticize other people, because they will easily find ways of criticizing you **you people** used when addressing a group of people: *Would you people please move on?* ➔ more at MAN n., THING
• **verb** [usually passive] **~ sth (with sth)** to live in a place or fill it with people: *The town was peopled largely by workers from the car factory and their families.* ✦ *The ballroom was peopled with guests.*

people person noun (informal) a person who enjoys, and is good at, being with and talking to other people

people-watching noun [U] the act of spending time looking at different kinds of people in a public place because you find this interesting: *At this super-trendy bistro, both the food and the people-watching get high marks.*

Pe·or·i·a /piˈɔriə/ noun a small city in Illinois. The opinions of the people who live there are considered to be typical of opinions in the whole of the U.S.: *Ask yourself what the folks in Peoria will think of it.*

pep /pɛp/ verb, noun
• **verb** (-pp-)
PHR V **pep sb/sth↔up** (informal) to make someone or something more interesting or full of energy: *Pep up meals by adding more unusual spices.* ✦ *A walk in the fresh air will pep you up.*
• **noun** [U] energy and enthusiasm

pep·per 🔊 /ˈpɛpər/ noun, verb
• **noun 1** [U] a powder made from dried berries (BERRY) (called PEPPERCORNS), used to give a hot flavor to food: *Season with salt and pepper* ✦ *freshly ground pepper* ➔ picture at FRUIT ➔ see also BLACK PEPPER, CAYENNE, WHITE PEPPER **2** [C, U] a hollow fruit, usually red, green, or yellow, with a sweet or spicy flavor, eaten as a vegetable or used to give flavor to food ➔ see also BELL PEPPER, CHILI
• **verb ~ sth** to put pepper on food: *peppered steak* ✦ *Salt and pepper the potatoes.*
PHR V **pepper sb/sth with sth** [usually passive] to hit someone or something with a series of small objects, especially bullets SYN SPRAY **pepper sth with sth** [often passive] to include large numbers of something in something: *He peppered his speech with jokes.*

pepper-and-salt adj. = SALT-AND-PEPPER

pep·per·corn /ˈpɛpərˌkɔrn/ noun a dried BERRY from a tropical plant, that is crushed to make pepper ➔ picture at HERB

pepper mill noun a small device for crushing PEPPER-CORNS to make pepper ➔ picture at KITCHEN

pep·per·mint /ˈpɛpərˌmɪnt/ noun **1** [U] a type of MINT (= a plant used to give flavor to food that produces an oil with a strong flavor) ➔ compare SPEARMINT **2** [C] a candy flavored with peppermint oil

pep·per·o·ni /ˌpɛpəˈrouni/ noun [U] a type of spicy SAUSAGE: *a pepperoni pizza*

pepper shaker noun a small container with holes in the top, used for putting pepper on food

pepper spray noun [C, U] a chemical substance made from hot peppers that causes a person's eyes, nose, and throat to sting when it is sprayed on them

pep·per·y /ˈpɛpəri/ adj. **1** tasting of pepper **2** bad-tempered: *a peppery old man*

pep pill noun (informal) a pill containing a drug that gives you more energy or makes you happy for a short time

pep·py /ˈpɛpi/ adj. (pep·pi·er, pep·pi·est) (informal) lively and full of energy or enthusiasm: *a peppy advertising jingle*

pep rally noun (informal) a meeting of school students before a sports event to encourage support for the team: *(figurative) The Democrats held a pep rally on Capitol Hill yesterday.*

pep·sin /ˈpɛpsən/ noun [U] (biology) a substance in the stomach that breaks down PROTEINS in the process of DIGESTION

pep talk noun (informal) a short speech intended to encourage someone to work harder, try to win, have more confidence, etc.

pep·tic ul·cer /ˌpɛptɪk ˈʌlsər/ noun an ULCER in the DIGESTIVE SYSTEM, especially in the stomach

pep·tide /ˈpɛptaɪd/ noun (chemistry) a chemical consisting of two or more AMINO ACIDS joined together

per 🔊 /pər/ prep.
used to express the cost or amount of something for each person, number used, distance traveled, etc.: *Rooms cost $50 per person, per night.* ✦ *60 miles per hour*
IDM **as per sth** following something that has been decided: *The work was carried out as per instructions.* **as per normal/usual** (informal) in the way that is normal or usual; as often happens: *Everyone blamed me, as per usual.*

per·am·bu·la·tion /pəˌræmbyəˈleɪʃn/ noun [C] (formal or humorous) a slow walk or journey around a place, especially

| h hat | m man | n no | ŋ sing | l leg | r red | y yes | w wet |

one made for pleasure ▶ **per·am·bu·late** *verb* /pəˈræm-bjəˌleɪt/ [I, T] ~ **(sth)**

per an·num /pər ˈænəm/ *adv.* (*abbr.* p.a.) (from *Latin*) for each year: *earning $30,000 per annum*

per·cale /pərˈkeɪl/ *noun* [U] a type of cotton or POLYESTER cloth used for making sheets

per cap·i·ta /pər ˈkæpətə/ *adj.* (from *Latin*) for each person: *Per capita income rose sharply last year.* ▶ **per cap·i·ta** *adv.*: *average earnings per capita*

per·ceive **AWL** /pərˈsiv/ *verb* **1** to notice or become aware of something: ~ *sth I perceived a change in his behavior.* ◆ ~ *that... She perceived that all was not well.* ◆ ~ *sb/sth to be/have sth The patient was perceived to have difficulty in breathing.* **HELP** This pattern is usually used in the passive. **2** to understand or think of someone or something in a particular way **SYN** SEE: ~ *sb/sth/yourself (as sth) This discovery was perceived as a major breakthrough.* ◆ *She did not perceive herself as disabled.* ◆ ~ *sb/sth to be/have sth They were widely perceived to have been unlucky.* **HELP** This pattern is usually used in the passive.

> **WORD FAMILY**
> perceive *verb*
> perception *noun*
> perceptive *adj.*
> perceptible *adj.* (≠ imperceptible)

per·cent /pərˈsɛnt/ (*abbr.* pct.) (*symb.* %) *noun, adj., adv.*
- **noun** (*pl.* **per·cent**) one part in every hundred: *Poor families spend 80 to 90 percent of their income on food.* ◆ *It is often stated that we use only 10 percent of our brain.* ◆ *What percent of the population is overweight?*
- **adj., adv.** by, in, or for every hundred: *a 15 percent rise in price* ◆ *House prices rose five percent last year.*

GRAMMAR

expressing percentages
- Percentages (= numbers of percent) are written in words as *twenty-five percent* and in numbers as *25%*.
- If a percentage is used with an uncountable or a singular noun, the verb is generally singular: *90% of the land is cultivated.*
- If the noun is singular but represents a group of people, the verb is singular: *Eighty percent of the work force is against the strike.*
- If the noun is plural, the verb is plural: *65% of children play computer games.*

per·cent·age **AWL** /pərˈsɛntɪdʒ/ *noun* **1** the number, amount, or rate of something, expressed as if it is part of a total which is 100; a part or share of a whole: *What percentage of the population is overweight?* ◆ *A high percentage of the female staff works part-time.* ◆ *Interest rates are expected to rise by one percentage point (= one percent).* ◆ *The figure is expressed as a percentage.* ◆ *The results were analyzed in percentage terms.* **2** [usually sing.] a share of the profits of something: *He gets a percentage for every car sold.*

per·cen·tile /pərˈsɛntaɪl/ *noun* (technical) one of the 100 equal groups that a larger group of people can be divided into, according to their place on a scale measuring a particular value: *Overall these students rank in the 21st percentile on the tests—that is, they did worse than 79 percent of all children taking the test.*

per·cep·ti·ble /pərˈsɛptəbl/ *adj.* (formal) **1** great enough for you to notice it **SYN** NOTICEABLE: *a perceptible change/increase/decline/impact* ◆ *The price increase has had no perceptible effect on sales.* ◆ *Her foreign accent was barely perceptible.* **2** (technical) that you can notice or feel with your senses: *the perceptible world* **ANT** IMPERCEPTIBLE ▶ **per·cep·ti·bly** /-bli/ *adv.*: *Income per head rose perceptibly.* ◆ *It was perceptibly colder.*

per·cep·tion **AWL** /pərˈsɛpʃn/ *noun* **1** [U] (formal or technical) the way you notice things, especially with the senses: *our perception of reality* ◆ *visual perception* ⊃ see also EXTRASENSORY PERCEPTION **2** [U] (formal) the ability to understand the true nature of something **SYN** INSIGHT: *She showed great perception in her assessment of the family situation.* **3** [U, C] (formal) an idea, a belief, or an image you have as a result of how you see or understand something: *a campaign to change public perception of the police* ◆ ~ *that... There is a general perception that standards in schools are falling.*

per·cep·tive /pərˈsɛptɪv/ *adj.* **1** (approving) having or showing the ability to see or understand things quickly, especially things that are not obvious: *a highly perceptive comment* ◆ *It was very perceptive of you to notice that.* **2** connected with seeing, hearing, and understanding: *our innate perceptive abilities* ▶ **per·cep·tive·ly** *adv.* **per·cep·tive·ness** *noun* [U]

per·cep·tu·al /pərˈsɛptʃuəl/ *adj.* [only before noun] (technical) relating to the ability to PERCEIVE things or the process of perceiving: *perceptual skills*

perch /pərtʃ/ *verb, noun*
- **verb 1** [I] ~ **(on sth)** (of a bird) to land and stay on a branch, etc.: *A robin was perching on the fence.* **2** [I, T] (informal) to sit or to make someone sit on something, especially on the edge of it **SYN** SIT: ~ **(on sth)** *We perched on a couple of high stools at the bar.* ◆ ~ **sb/yourself (on sth)** *She perched herself on the edge of the bed.* **3** [I] ~ **(on sth)** to be placed on the top or the edge of something: *The hotel perched precariously on a steep hillside.*
- **noun 1** a place where a bird rests, especially a branch or bar for this purpose, for example in a bird's CAGE **2** a high seat or position: *He watched the game from his precarious perch on top of the wall.* **3** (*pl.* **perch**) a FRESHWATER fish that is sometimes used for food **IDM** see KNOCK *v.*

per·chance /pərˈtʃæns/ *adv.* (old use) perhaps

perched /pərtʃt/ *adj.* ~ **on, etc. sth 1** (especially of a bird) sitting or resting on something: *There was a bird perched on the roof.* **2** placed in a high and/or dangerous position: *a hotel perched high on the cliffs*

per·cip·i·ent /pərˈsɪpiənt/ *adj.* (formal) having or showing the ability to understand things, especially things that are not obvious **SYN** PERCEPTIVE

per·co·late /ˈpərkəˌleɪt/ *verb* **1** [I] (of a liquid, gas, etc.) to move gradually through a surface that has very small holes or spaces in it: *Water had percolated down through the rocks.* **2** [I] to gradually become known or spread through a group or society: *It had percolated through to us that something interesting was about to happen.* **3** [T, I] ~ **(sth)** to make coffee in a percolator; to be made in this way ▶ **per·co·la·tion** /ˌpərkəˈleɪʃn/ *noun* [U]

per·co·la·tor /ˈpərkəˌleɪtər/ *noun* a pot for making coffee, in which boiling water is forced up a central tube and then comes down again through the coffee

per·cus·sion /pərˈkʌʃn/ *noun* **1** [U] musical instruments that you play by hitting them with your hand or with a stick, for example drums: *percussion instruments* ◆ *The track features Joey Langton on percussion.* **2** the percussion [sing.] (also **per·cussion ˌsection** [C]) the players of percussion instruments in an ORCHESTRA ⊃ compare BRASS, STRING, WOODWIND

per·cus·sion·ist /pərˈkʌʃənɪst/ *noun* a person who plays percussion instruments

per·cus·sive /pərˈkʌsɪv/ *adj.* (technical) connected with sounds made by hitting things, especially PERCUSSION instruments

per·cu·ta·ne·ous /ˌpərkjuˈteɪniəs/ *adj.* (medical) made or done through the skin: *a percutaneous injection*

per di·em /pər ˈdiəm/ *adj., noun* (from *Latin*)
- **adj.** [only before noun] (of money) for each day: *a per diem allowance* ▶ **per di·em** *adv.*: *He agreed to pay at specified rates per diem.*
- **noun** [U, C] money paid, for example to employees, for

things they need to buy every day: *He will get $14,000 a year in per diem to help with the higher costs of living in Washington.*

per·di·tion /pərˈdɪʃn/ *noun* [U] (*formal*) **1** punishment that lasts for ever after death **2** (*literary*) loss of the soul and punishment after death; hell **3** (*old-fashioned*) complete loss, failure, or destruction: *His mother felt that his behavior was leading him down the path to perdition.*

per·e·gri·na·tion /ˌpɛrəɡrəˈneɪʃn/ *noun* [usually pl.] (*literary* or *humorous*) a journey, especially a long slow one

per·e·grine /ˈpɛrəɡrən; -ˌɡrɪn/ (also ˌperegrine ˈfalcon) *noun* a gray and white BIRD OF PREY (= a bird that kills other creatures for food) that can be trained to hunt

per·emp·to·ri·ly /pəˈrɛmptərəli/ *adv.* (*formal*) in a way that allows no discussion or refusal: *She peremptorily rejected the request.*

per·emp·to·ry /pəˈrɛmptəri/ *adj.* (*formal, disapproving*) (especially of someone's manner or behavior) expecting to be obeyed immediately and without question or refusal: *a peremptory summons* ♦ *The letter was peremptory in tone.*

per·en·ni·al /pəˈrɛniəl/ *adj., noun*
● *adj.* **1** continuing for a very long time; happening again and again: *the perennial problem of water shortages* ♦ *that perennial favorite, the hamburger* **2** (of plants) living for two years or more ▶ **per·en·ni·al·ly** *adv.*: *a perennially popular subject*
● *noun* any plant that lives for more than two years
➔ compare ANNUAL, BIENNIAL

per·fect 🔊 *adj., verb, noun*
● *adj.* /ˈpərfɪkt/ **1** having everything that is necessary; complete and without faults or weaknesses: *in perfect condition* ♦ *a perfect set of teeth* ♦ *Well I'm sorry—but nobody's **perfect*** (= used when someone has criticized you). **2** completely correct; exact and accurate: *She speaks perfect English.* ♦ *a perfect copy/fit/match* ♦ *What perfect timing!* ➔ see also WORD-PERFECT **3** the best of its kind: *a perfect example of the painter's early style* ♦ *the perfect crime* (= one in which the criminal is never discovered) **4** excellent; very good: *The weather was perfect.* ➔ thesaurus box at EXCELLENT **5** ~ **for sb/sth** exactly right for someone or something **SYN** IDEAL: *It was a perfect day for a picnic.* ♦ *She's the perfect candidate for the job.* ♦ *"Will 2:30 be OK for you?" "Yes, that will be perfect."* **6** [only before noun] total; complete: *I don't know him—he's a perfect stranger.* **7** (*grammar*) connected with the form of a verb that consists of part of the verb *have* with the past participle of the main verb, used to express actions completed by the present or a particular point in the past or future: *"I have eaten" is the present perfect tense of the verb "to eat," "I had eaten" is the past perfect, and "I will have eaten" is the future perfect.* ➔ see also FUTURE PERFECT, PAST PERFECT, PRESENT PERFECT **IDM** see PRACTICE *n.*, TEN, WORLD
● *verb* /pərˈfɛkt/ ~ **sth** to make something perfect or as good as you can: *As a musician, she has spent years perfecting her technique.*
● *noun* /ˈpərfɪkt/ **the perfect** (also **the ˌperfect ˈtense**) [sing.] (*grammar*) the form of a verb that expresses actions completed by the present or a particular point in the past or future, formed in English with part of the verb *have* and the past participle of the main verb ➔ see also FUTURE PERFECT, PAST PERFECT, PRESENT PERFECT

per·fec·tion /pərˈfɛkʃn/ *noun* [U, sing.] **1** the state of being perfect: *physical perfection* ♦ *The fish was cooked to perfection.* ♦ *The novel achieves a perfection of form that is quite new.* ♦ *His performance was perfection* (= something perfect). **2** the act of making something perfect by doing the final improvements: *They have been working on the perfection of the new model.*

per·fec·tion·ist /pərˈfɛkʃənɪst/ *noun* (sometimes *disapproving*) a person who likes to do things perfectly and is not satisfied with anything less ▶ **per·fec·tion·ism** /-ʃəˌnɪzəm/ *noun* [U]

per·fect·ly 🔊 /ˈpərfɪktli/ *adv.*
1 completely: *It's perfectly normal to feel like this.* ♦ *It's perfectly good as it is* (= it doesn't need changing). ♦ *You know perfectly well what I mean.* ♦ *To be perfectly honest, I didn't want to go anyway.* ♦ *He stood perfectly still until the danger had passed.* ♦ *"Do you understand?" "Perfectly."* ♦ (*old-fashioned*) *How perfectly awful!* **2** in a perfect way: *The TV works perfectly now.* ♦ *It fits perfectly.*

ˌperfect ˈpitch *noun* [U] (*music*) the ability to identify or sing a musical note correctly without the help of an instrument

ˌperfect ˈstorm *noun* [sing.] an occasion when several bad things happen at the same time, creating a situation that could not be worse

per·fid·i·ous /pərˈfɪdiəs/ *adj.* (*literary*) that cannot be trusted **SYN** TREACHEROUS

per·fi·dy /ˈpərfədi/ *noun* [U] (*literary*) unfair treatment of someone who trusts you **SYN** TREACHERY

per·fo·rate /ˈpərfəˌreɪt/ *verb* ~ **sth** to make a hole or holes through something: *The explosion perforated his eardrum.* ♦ *a perforated line* (= a row of small holes in paper, made so that a part can be torn off easily)

per·fo·ra·tion /ˌpərfəˈreɪʃn/ *noun* **1** [C, usually pl., U] a small hole in a surface, often one of a series of small holes: *Tear the sheet of stamps along the perforations.* **2** [U] (*medical*) the process of splitting or tearing in such a way that a hole is left: *Excessive pressure can lead to perforation of the stomach wall.*

per·force /pərˈfɔrs/ *adv.* (*old use* or *formal*) because it is necessary or cannot be avoided **SYN** NECESSARILY

per·form 🔊 /pərˈfɔrm/ *verb*
1 [T] ~ **sth** to do something, such as a piece of work, task, or duty **SYN** CARRY OUT: *to perform an experiment/a miracle/a ceremony* ♦ *She performs an important role in our organization.* ♦ *This operation has never been performed in this country.* ♦ *A computer can perform many tasks at once.* **2** [T, I] ~ **(sth)** to entertain an audience by playing a piece of music, acting in a play, etc.: *to perform somersaults/magic tricks* ♦ *The play was first performed in 2007.* ♦ *I'd like to hear it performed live.* ♦ *to perform on the flute* ♦ *I'm looking forward to seeing you perform.* **3** [I] ~ **(well/badly/poorly)** to work or function well or badly: *The engine seems to be performing well.* ♦ *The company has been performing poorly over the past year.* **IDM** see MIRACLE

per·for·mance 🔊 /pərˈfɔrməns/ *noun*
1 [C] the act of performing a play, concert, or some other form of entertainment: *The performance starts at seven.* ♦ *an evening performance* ♦ *a performance of Ravel's String Quartet* ♦ *a series of performances by the Kirov Ballet* ♦ *one of the band's rare live performances* ➔ collocations at MUSIC **2** [C] the way a person performs in a play, concert, etc.: *She gave the greatest performance of her career.* ♦ *an Oscar-winning performance from Al Pacino* **3** [U, C] how well or badly you do something; how well or badly something works: *the country's economic performance* ♦ *It was an impressive performance by the French team.* ♦ *The new management techniques aim to improve performance.* ♦ *He criticized the recent poor performance of the company.* ♦ *high-performance* (= very powerful) *cars* ♦ *performance indicators* (= things that show how well or badly something is working) ➔ compare PAY-FOR-PERFORMANCE, PERFORMANCE-RELATED **4** [U, sing.] (*formal*) the act or process of performing a task, an action, etc.: *She has shown enthusiasm in the performance of her duties.* ♦ *He did not want a repeat performance of the humiliating defeat he had suffered.* **5** [sing.] (*informal*) a display of exaggerated behavior or a process involving a great deal of unnecessary time and effort: *He stopped to tie his shoe and seemed to be making quite a performance of it.*

perˈformance ˌart *noun* [U] an art form in which an artist gives a performance, rather than producing a physical work of art ▶ **perˈformance ˌartist** *noun*

perˈformance-enˌhancing *adj.* [only before noun] (of a substance, especially a drug) that people take so that they will be more successful in a sports competition: *steroids and other performance-enhancing drugs*

per·formance-re·lated *adj.* [only before noun] depending on how well a person does their job: *Is there any evidence that performance-related pay actually improves performance?* ⟳ compare PERFORMANCE, PAY-FOR-PERFORMANCE

per·for·ma·tive /pərˈfɔrmətɪv/ *adj.* (*grammar*) when someone uses a performative word or expression, for example "I promise" or "I apologize," they are also doing something (promising or apologizing) ⟳ see also CONSTATIVE

per·form·er /pərˈfɔrmər/ *noun*
1 a person who performs for an audience in a show, concert, etc.: *a brilliant/polished/seasoned performer* **2** a person or thing that behaves or works in the way mentioned: *He was a poor performer at school and left without graduating.* ♦ *The new model is the **star performer** of the motor industry this year.*

the per·forming 'arts *noun* [pl.] arts such as music, dance, and drama that are performed for an audience

per·fume /ˈpərfyum/ *noun, verb*
● *noun* [C, U] **1** a liquid, often made from flowers, that you put on your skin to make yourself smell nice: *a bottle of expensive perfume* ♦ *We carry a wide range of perfumes.* ♦ *the perfume counter of the store* ♦ *She was wearing too much perfume.* **2** a pleasant, often sweet, smell SYN SCENT: *the heady perfume of the roses*
● *verb* [often passive] **1** ~ sth (with sth) (*literary*) (especially of flowers) to make the air in a place smell pleasant SYN SCENT: *The garden was perfumed with the smell of roses.* **2** ~ sth (with sth) to put perfume in or on something: *She perfumed her bath with fragrant oils.* ▶ **per·fumed** *adj.*: *perfumed soap*

per·fum·er·y /pərˈfyuməri/ *noun* (*pl.* **per·fum·er·ies**) **1** [C] a place where perfumes are made and/or sold **2** [U] the process of making perfume

per·func·to·ry /pərˈfʌŋktəri/ *adj.* (*formal*) (of an action) done as a duty or habit, without real interest, attention, or feeling: *a perfunctory nod/smile* ♦ *They only made a perfunctory effort.* ▶ **per·func·to·ri·ly** /-tərəli/ *adv.*: *to nod/smile perfunctorily*

per·go·la /ˈpərgələ/ *noun* an ARCH in a garden or yard with a frame for plants to grow over and through

---

LANGUAGE BANK

perhaps

making an opinion sound less definite

- Most cybercrime involves traditional crimes, such as theft and fraud, being committed in new ways. Phishing is **perhaps/possibly/probably** the best-known example of this.

- It **seems/appears** that the more personal data that organizations collect, the more opportunity there is for this information to be lost or stolen.

- **It seems clear that** the widespread use of Social Security numbers to identify people contributes to the problem of identity theft.

- **It could be argued that** the widespread use of Social Security numbers to identify people contributes to the problem of identity theft.

- **It is possible that/It may be that** the only way to protect ourselves against DNA identity theft is to avoid the creation of national DNA databases.

⟳ Language Banks at IMPERSONAL, OPINION

---

per·haps /pərˈhæps/ *adv.*
1 possibly SYN MAYBE: *"Are you going to come?" "Perhaps. I'll see how I feel."* ♦ *Perhaps he's forgotten.* **2** used when you want to make a statement or an opinion less definite: *This is*

perhaps his best novel to date. **3** used when making a rough estimate: *a change that could affect perhaps 20% of the population* **4** used when you agree or accept something unwillingly, or do not want to say strongly that you disapprove: *"You could do it yourself." "Yeah, perhaps."* **5** used when making a polite request, offer, or suggestion: *Perhaps it would be better if you came back tomorrow.* ♦ *I think perhaps you've had enough to drink tonight.*

per·i·gee /ˈpɛrədʒi/ *noun* (*astronomy*) the point in the ORBIT of the moon, a planet, or other object in space when it is nearest the planet, for example the earth, around which it turns ⟳ compare APOGEE

per·il /ˈpɛrəl/ *noun* (*formal* or *literary*) **1** [U] serious danger: *The country's economy is now in grave peril.* **2** [C, usually pl.] ~ (of sth) the fact of something being dangerous or harmful: *a warning about the perils of drug abuse*
IDM **do sth at your (own) peril** used to warn someone that if they do something, it may be dangerous or cause them problems

per·il·ous /ˈpɛrələs/ *adj.* (*formal* or *literary*) very dangerous SYN HAZARDOUS ▶ **per·il·ous·ly** *adv.*: *We came perilously close to disaster.*

pe·rim·e·ter /pəˈrɪmətər/ *noun* **1** the outside edge of an area of land: *Guards patrol the perimeter of the estate.* ♦ *a perimeter fence/track/wall* **2** (*mathematics*) the total length of the outside edge of an area or a shape ⟳ compare CIRCUMFERENCE

per·i·na·tal /ˌpɛrəˈneɪtl/ *adj.* (*technical*) at or around the time of birth: *perinatal care* ♦ *perinatal mortality*

per·i·ne·um /ˌpɛrəˈniəm/ *noun* (*pl.* **per·i·ne·a** /-ˈniə/) (*anatomy*) the area between the ANUS and the SCROTUM or VULVA

pe·ri·od AWL /ˈpɪriəd/ *noun, adv., adj.*
● *noun*
▷ LENGTH OF TIME **1** a particular length of time: *a period of consultation/mourning/uncertainty* ♦ *The factory will be closed down over a 2-year period/a period of two years.* ♦ *This compares with a 4% increase for the same period last year.* ♦ *This offer is available for a limited period only.* ♦ *All these changes happened over a period of time.* ♦ *The aim is to reduce traffic at peak periods.* ♦ *You can have it for a trial period* (= in order to test it). ⟳ see also COOLING-OFF PERIOD **2** a length of time in the life of a particular person or in the history of a particular country: *What period of history would you most like to have lived in?* ♦ *the post-war period* ♦ *Like Picasso, she too had a blue period.* ♦ *Most teenagers go through a period of rebelling.* **3** (*geology*) a length of time that is a division of an ERA. A period is divided into EPOCHS: *the Jurassic period*
▷ LESSON **4** any of the parts that a day is divided into at a school, college, etc. for study: *"What do you have next period?" "French."* ♦ *a free/study period* (= for private study)
▷ WOMAN **5** the flow of blood each month from the body of a woman who is not pregnant: *period pains* ♦ *monthly periods* ♦ *When did you last have a period?* ⟳ compare MENSTRUATION
▷ PUNCTUATION **6** the mark (.) used at the end of a sentence and in some abbreviations, for example *e.g.*
● *adv.* (*informal*) used at the end of a sentence to emphasize that there is nothing more to say about a subject: *The answer is no, period!*
● *adj.* [only before noun] having a style typical of a particular time in history: *period costumes/furniture*

pe·ri·od·ic AWL /ˌpɪriˈɑdɪk/ (also *less frequent* **pe·ri·od·i·cal** /ˌpɪriˈɑdɪkl/) *adj.* [usually before noun] happening fairly often and regularly: *Periodic checks are carried out on the equipment.* ▶ **pe·ri·od·i·cal·ly** AWL /-kli/ *adv.*: *Mailing lists are updated periodically.*

pe·ri·od·i·cal AWL /ˌpɪriˈɑdɪkl/ *noun* a magazine that is published every week, month, etc., especially one that is concerned with an academic subject

the periodic 'table *noun* [sing.] (*chemistry*) a list of all the chemical elements, arranged according to their ATOMIC NUMBER

---

per·i·o·don·tal /ˌperiəˈdɑntl/ *adj.* (*medical*) related to or affecting the parts of the mouth that surround and support the teeth

per·i·o·don·ti·tis /ˌperioudɑnˈtaɪtəs/ (also **py·or·rhe·a**) *noun* [U] (*medical*) a condition in which the area around the teeth becomes sore and swollen, which may make the teeth fall out

'period ˌpiece *noun* **1** a play, movie, etc. that is set in a particular period of history **2** a decorative object, piece of furniture, etc. that was made during a particular period of history and is typical of that period

per·i·pa·tet·ic /ˌperəpəˈtɛtɪk/ *adj.* (*formal*) going from place to place, for example in order to work: *a peripatetic music teacher*

pe·riph·er·al /pəˈrɪfərəl/ *adj., noun*
- *adj.* **1** (*formal*) not as important as the main aim, part, etc. of something: *peripheral information* ♦ **~ to sth** *Fund-raising is peripheral to their main activities.* **2** (*technical*) connected with the outer edge of a particular area: *the peripheral nervous system* ♦ *peripheral vision* **3** (*computing*) (of equipment) connected to a computer: *a peripheral device* ▶ **pe·riph·er·al·ly** *adv.*
- *noun* (*computing*) a piece of equipment that is connected to a computer: *monitors, printers, and other peripherals*

pe·riph·er·y /pəˈrɪfəri/ *noun* [usually sing.] (*pl.* **pe·riph·er·ies**) (*formal*) **1** the outer edge of a particular area: *industrial development on the periphery of the town* ♦ *The condition makes it difficult for patients to see objects at the periphery of their vision.* **2** the less important part of something, for example of a particular activity or of a social or political group: *minor parties on the periphery of American politics*

pe·riph·ra·sis /pəˈrɪfrəsəs/ *noun* [U] **1** (*technical*) the use of an indirect way of speaking or writing **2** (*grammar*) the use of separate words to express a GRAMMATICAL relationship, instead of verb endings, etc. ▶ **per·i·phras·tic** /ˌperəˈfræstɪk/ *adj.*

per·i·scope /ˈperəˌskoup/ *noun* a device like a long tube, containing mirrors that enable the user to see over the top of something, used especially in a SUBMARINE (= a ship that can operate underwater) to see above the surface of the ocean

per·ish /ˈperɪʃ/ *verb* **1** [I] (*formal or literary*) (of people or animals) to die, especially in a sudden violent way: *A family of four perished in the fire.* **2** [I] (*formal*) to be lost or destroyed: *Early buildings were made of wood and have perished.* **IDM** **perish the thought** (*informal*) used to say that you find a suggestion unacceptable or that you hope that something will never happen: *Me get married? Perish the thought!*

per·ish·a·ble /ˈperɪʃəbl/ *adj.* (especially of food) likely to decay or go bad quickly: *perishable goods/foods*

per·ish·a·bles /ˈperɪʃəblz/ *noun* [pl.] (*technical*) types of food that decay or go bad quickly

per·i·stal·sis /ˌperəˈstɔlsəs; -ˈstɑl-; -ˈstæl-/ *noun* [U] (*biology*) the wave-like movements of the INTESTINE, etc. caused when the muscles contract and relax

per·i·to·ne·um /ˌperətəˈniəm/ *noun* (*pl.* **per·i·to·ne·ums** or **per·i·to·ne·a** /-ˈniə/) (*anatomy*) the MEMBRANE (= very thin layer of TISSUE) on the inside of the ABDOMEN that covers the stomach and other organs

per·i·to·ni·tis /ˌperətəˈnaɪtəs/ *noun* [U] (*medical*) a serious condition in which the inside wall of the body becomes swollen and infected

per·i·win·kle /ˈperɪˌwɪŋkl/ *noun* **1** [C, U] a small plant with light blue or white flowers that grows along the ground **2** [C] a small SHELLFISH, like a SNAIL, that you can eat **3** (also **periwinkle 'blue**) [U] a color that is between light blue and light purple

per·jure /ˈpərdʒər/ *verb* **~ yourself** (*law*) to tell a lie in court after you have sworn to tell the truth ▶ **per·jur·er** *noun*

per·ju·ry /ˈpərdʒəri/ *noun* [U] (*law*) the crime of telling a lie in court

perk /pərk/ *noun, verb*
- *noun* (also *formal* **per·qui·site**) [usually pl.] something you receive as well as your wages for doing a particular job: *Perks offered by the company include a car and free health insurance.* ♦ (*figurative*) *Not having to get up early is just one of the perks of being retired.*
- *verb* [T, I] **~ (sth)** (*informal*) to make coffee in a PERCOLATOR; coffee made in this way: *It'll just take a minute for me to perk some coffee.* ♦ *Once the coffee perks, we can have breakfast.* **PHR V** **ˌperk 'up** | **ˌperk sb↔'up** (*informal*) to become or to make someone become more cheerful or lively, especially after they have been sick or sad **SYN** BRIGHTEN: *He soon perked up when his friends arrived.* **ˌperk 'up** | **ˌperk sth↔'up** (*informal*) to increase, or to make something increase in value, etc.: *Share prices had perked up slightly by close of trading.* **ˌperk sth↔'up** (*informal*) to make something more interesting, more attractive, etc. **SYN** LIVEN: *ideas for perking up bland food*

perk·y /ˈpərki/ *adj.* (**perk·i·er, perk·i·est**) (*informal*) cheerful and full of energy ▶ **perk·i·ness** *noun* [U]

perm /pərm/ *noun, verb*
- *noun* a way of changing the style of your hair by using chemicals to create curls that last for several months: *to have a perm* ⊃ picture at HAIR
- *verb* **~ sth** to give someone's hair a perm: *to have your hair permed* ♦ *a shampoo for permed hair*

per·ma·frost /ˈpərməˌfrɔst/ *noun* [U] (*technical*) a layer of soil that is permanently frozen, in very cold regions of the world

per·ma·nence /ˈpərmənəns/ (also *less frequent* **per·ma·nen·cy** /ˈpərmənənsi/) *noun* [U] the state of lasting for a long time or for all time in the future: *The spoken word is immediate but lacks permanence.* ♦ *We no longer talk of the permanence of marriage.*

per·ma·nent 🔑 /ˈpərmənənt/ *adj., noun*
- *adj.* lasting for a long time or for all time in the future; existing all the time: *a permanent job* ♦ *permanent staff* ♦ *They are now living together on a permanent basis.* ♦ *The accident has not done any permanent damage.* ♦ *a permanent fixture* (= a person or an object that is always in a particular place) **ANT** IMPERMANENT, TEMPORARY ▶ **per·ma·nent·ly** *adv.*: *The stroke left his right side permanently damaged.* ♦ *She had decided to settle permanently in France.*
- *noun* (*old-fashioned*) = PERM

ˌpermanent 'resident *noun* (*CanE*) someone from another country who is allowed to live and work in Canada

ˌpermanent 'wave *noun* (*old-fashioned*) = PERM

per·ma·tan /ˈpərməˌtæn/ *noun* (*informal, humorous*) the brown skin color that a person with pale skin gets from being in the sun, when they have this skin color all year

per·me·a·ble /ˈpərmiəbl/ *adj.* **~ (to sth)** (*technical*) allowing a liquid or gas to pass through: *The skin of amphibians is permeable to water.* ♦ *permeable rocks* **ANT** IMPERMEABLE ▶ **per·me·a·bil·i·ty** /ˌpərmiəˈbɪləti/ *noun* [U]

per·me·ate /ˈpərmiˌeɪt/ *verb* (*formal*) **1** [T, I] (of a liquid, gas, etc.) to spread to every part of an object or a place: **~ sth** *The smell of leather permeated the room.* ♦ **+ adv./prep.** *rainwater permeating through the ground* **2** [T, I] (of an idea, an influence, a feeling, etc.) to affect every part of something: **~ sth** *a belief that permeates all levels of society* ♦ **+ adv./prep.** *Dissatisfaction among the managers soon permeated down to members of the workforce.* ▶ **per·me·a·tion** /ˌpərmiˈeɪʃn/ *noun* [U] (*formal*)

per·mis·si·ble /pərˈmɪsəbl/ *adj.* (*formal*) acceptable according to the law or a particular set of rules: *permissible levels of nitrates in water* ♦ **~ (for sb) (to do sth)** *It is not permissible for employers to discriminate on grounds of age.*

per·mis·sion 🔑 /pərˈmɪʃn/ *noun*
1 [U] the act of allowing someone to do something, especially when this is done by someone in a position of authority: **~ (for sth)** *You must ask permission for all major*

t tea ṱ butter d did k cat g got tʃ chin dʒ June f fall

expenditures. ◆ ~ **(for sb/sth) (to do sth)** *The school has been refused permission to expand.* ◆ *No official* **permission** *has been* **given** *for the event to take place.* ◆ *She took the car* **without permission.** ◆ *poems reprinted* **by kind permission** *of the author* ◆ (*formal*) *With your permission, I'd like to say a few words.* **2** [C, usually pl.] an official written statement allowing someone to do something: *The publisher is responsible for obtaining the necessary permissions to reproduce illustrations.*

per·mis·sive /pərˈmɪsɪv/ *adj.* allowing or showing a freedom of behavior that many people do not approve of, especially in sexual matters: *permissive attitudes* ◆ *permissive parents* (= who allow their children a lot of freedom) ▶ **per·mis·sive·ness** *noun* [U]

the per·mis·sive so·ci·ety *noun* [sing.] (often *disapproving*) the changes toward greater freedom in attitudes and behavior that happened in many countries in the 1960s and 1970s, especially the greater freedom in sexual matters

per·mit 🔑 *verb, noun*
● *verb* /pərˈmɪt/ (**-tt-**) (*formal*) **1** [T] to allow someone to do something or to allow something to happen: ~ **sth** *Cell phones are not permitted in the library.* ◆ *There are fines for exceeding permitted levels of noise pollution.* ◆ ~ **sb/yourself sth** *We were not permitted any contact with each other.* ◆ *Jim permitted himself a wry smile.* ◆ ~ **sb/yourself to do sth** *Visitors are not permitted to take photographs.* ◆ *She would not permit herself to look at them.* ◆ (*formal*) *Permit me to offer you some advice.* **2** [I, T] to make something possible: *We hope to visit the cathedral, if time permits.* ◆ *I'll come tomorrow,* **weather permitting** (= if the weather is fine). ◆ ~ **sth** *The password permits access to all files on the network.* ◆ ~ **sb/sth to do sth** *ATMs permit you to withdraw money at any time.*
● *noun* /ˈpərmɪt/ an official document that gives someone the right to do something, especially for a limited period of time: *a fishing/residence/parking, etc. permit* ◆ *to apply for a* **permit** ◆ *to issue a permit* ⊃ see also LEARNER'S PERMIT, WORK PERMIT

per·mu·ta·tion /ˌpərmyuˈteɪʃn/ *noun* [usually pl.] any of the different ways in which a set of things can be ordered: *The possible permutations of x, y, and z are xyz, xzy, yxz, yzx, zxy, and zyx.*

per·ni·cious /pərˈnɪʃəs/ *adj.* (*formal*) having a very harmful effect on someone or something, especially in a way that is gradual and not easily noticed

per·o·ra·tion /ˌpɛrəˈreɪʃn/ *noun* (*formal*) **1** the final part of a speech in which the speaker gives a summary of the main points **2** (*disapproving*) a long speech that is not very interesting

per·ox·ide /pəˈrɑksaɪd/ (also **hydrogen perˈoxide**) *noun* [U] a clear liquid used to kill bacteria and to BLEACH hair (= make it lighter): *a woman with peroxide blonde hair*

per·pen·dic·u·lar /ˌpərpənˈdɪkyələr/ *adj., noun*
● *adj.* **1** ~ **(to sth)** (*technical*) forming an angle of 90° with another line or surface; vertical and going straight up: *Are the lines perpendicular to each other?* ◆ *The staircase was almost perpendicular* (= very steep). **2 Perpendicular** (*architecture*) connected with a style of ARCHITECTURE common in England in the 14th and 15th centuries, that makes use of vertical lines and wide ARCHES
● *noun* **the perpendicular** [sing.] a line, position, or direction that is exactly perpendicular: *The wall is a little out of the perpendicular.*

per·pe·trate /ˈpərpəˌtreɪt/ *verb* (*formal*) to commit a crime or do something wrong or evil: ~ **sth** *to perpetrate a crime/fraud/massacre* ◆ ~ **sth against/upon/on sb** *violence perpetrated against women and children* ▶ **per·pe·tra·tion** /ˌpərpəˈtreɪʃn/ *noun* [U]

per·pe·tra·tor /ˈpərpəˌtreɪtər/ *noun* a person who commits a crime or does something that is wrong or evil: *the perpetrators of the crime*

per·pet·u·al /pərˈpɛtʃuəl/ *adj.* **1** [usually before noun] continuing for a long period of time without interruption

SYN CONTINUOUS: *the perpetual noise of traffic* ◆ *We lived for years in a perpetual state of fear.* **2** [usually before noun] frequently repeated, in a way that is annoying **SYN** CONTINUAL: *How can I work with these perpetual interruptions?* **3** [only before noun] (of a job or position) lasting for the whole of someone's life: *He was elected perpetual president.* ◆ (*humorous*) *She's a perpetual student.* ▶ **per·pet·u·al·ly** *adv.*

per·petual ˈmotion *noun* [U] a state in which something moves continuously without stopping, or appears to do so: *We're all in a state of* **perpetual motion** *in this office* (= we're always moving around or changing things).

per·pet·u·ate /pərˈpɛtʃueɪt/ *verb* ~ **sth** (*formal*) to make something such as a bad situation, a belief, etc. continue for a long time: *to perpetuate injustice* ◆ *This system perpetuated itself for several centuries.* ◆ *Comic books tend to perpetuate the myth that "boys don't cry."* ▶ **per·pet·u·a·tion** /pərˌpɛtʃuˈeɪʃn/ *noun* [U]

per·pe·tu·i·ty /ˌpərpəˈtuəti/ *noun* [U]
IDM **in perpetuity** (*formal*) for all time in the future **SYN** FOREVER: *They do not own the land in perpetuity.*

per·plex /pərˈplɛks/ *verb* [usually passive] ~ **sb** | **it perplexes sb that...** if something **perplexes** you, it makes you confused or worried because you do not understand it: *They were perplexed by her response.* ▶ **per·plex·ing** /pərˈplɛksɪŋ/ *adj.*: *a perplexing problem*

per·plexed /pərˈplɛkst/ *adj.* confused and anxious because you are unable to understand something; showing that you feel this way: *a perplexed expression* ◆ *She looked perplexed.* ▶ **per·plex·ed·ly** /pərˈplɛksədli/ *adv.*

per·plex·i·ty /pərˈplɛksəti/ *noun* (pl. **per·plex·i·ties**) (*formal*) **1** [U] the state of feeling confused and anxious because you do not understand something **SYN** CONFUSION: *Most of them just stared at her in perplexity.* **2** [C, usually pl.] something that is difficult to understand: *the perplexities of life*

per·qui·site /ˈpərkwəzət/ *noun* (*formal*) **1** [usually pl.] = PERK **2** ~ **(of sb)** something to which someone has a special right because of their social position: *Politics used to be the perquisite of the property-owning classes.*

per se /pər ˈseɪ/ *adv.* (from *Latin*) used meaning "by itself" to show that you are referring to something on its own, rather than in connection with other things: *The drug is not harmful per se, but is dangerous when taken with alcohol.*

per·se·cute /ˈpərsəˌkyut/ *verb* [often passive] **1** ~ **sb (for sth)** to treat someone in a cruel and unfair way, especially because of their race, religion, or political beliefs: *Throughout history, people have been persecuted for their religious beliefs.* ◆ *persecuted minorities* **2** ~ **sb** to deliberately annoy someone all the time and make their life unpleasant **SYN** HARASS: *Why are the media persecuting him like this?* ▶ **per·se·cu·tion** /ˌpərsəˈkyuʃn/ *noun* [U, C]: *the victims of religious persecution*

perseˈcution ˌcomplex *noun* a type of mental illness in which someone believes that other people are trying to harm them

per·se·cu·tor /ˈpərsəˌkyutər/ *noun* a person who treats another person or group of people in a cruel and unfair way

per·se·ver·ance /ˌpərsəˈvɪrəns/ *noun* [U] (*approving*) the quality of continuing to try to achieve a particular aim despite difficulties: *They showed great perseverance in the face of difficulty.* ◆ *The only way to improve is through hard work and dogged perseverance.*

per·se·vere /ˌpərsəˈvɪr/ *verb* [I] (*approving*) to continue trying to do or achieve something despite difficulties: ~ **(in sth/in doing sth)** *Despite a number of setbacks, they persevered in their attempts to fly around the world in a balloon.* ◆ ~ **(with sth/sb)** *She persevered with her violin lessons.* ◆ *You have to persevere with difficult students.*

per·se·ver·ing /ˌpərsəˈvɪrɪŋ/ *adj.* [usually before noun] (*approving*) showing determination to achieve a particular aim despite difficulties

Per·sian /ˈpɜːʒən/ *noun* **1** [C] a person from ancient Persia, or modern Persia, now called Iran **2** (also **Far·si**) [U] the official language of Iran **3** [C] = PERSIAN CAT ▶ **Per·sian** *adj.*

ˌPersian ˈcarpet (also ˌPersian ˈrug) *noun* a carpet of traditional design from the Near East, made by hand from silk or wool

ˌPersian ˈcat (also Per·sian) *noun* a breed of cat with long hair, short legs, and a round flat face

per·si·flage /ˈpɜːsəˌflɑːʒ/ *noun* [U] (*formal*) comments and jokes in which people laugh at each other in a fairly unkind but not serious way

per·sim·mon /pərˈsɪmən/ *noun* a sweet fruit that looks like a large orange tomato

per·sist ![AWL] /pərˈsɪst/ *verb* **1** [I, T] to continue to do something despite difficulties or opposition, in a way that can seem unreasonable: ~ **(in doing sth)** *Why do you persist in blaming yourself for what happened?* ◆ ~ **(in sth)** *She persisted in her search for the truth.* ◆ ~ **(with sth)** *He persisted with his questioning.* ◆ + **speech** *"So, did you agree or not?" he persisted.* **2** [I] to continue to exist: *If the symptoms persist, consult your doctor.*

per·sist·ence ![AWL] /pərˈsɪstəns/ *noun* [U] **1** the fact of continuing to try to do something despite difficulties, especially when other people are against you and think that you are being annoying or unreasonable: *His persistence was finally rewarded when the insurance company agreed to pay for the damage.* ◆ *It was her sheer persistence that wore them down in the end.* **2** the state of continuing to exist for a long period of time: *the persistence of unemployment in the 1970s and 1980s*

per·sist·ent ![AWL] /pərˈsɪstənt/ *adj.* **1** determined to do something despite difficulties, especially when other people are against you and think that you are being annoying or unreasonable: *How do you deal with persistent salesmen who won't take no for an answer?* ◆ *a persistent offender* (= a person who continues to commit crimes after they have been caught and punished) ◆ *She was persistent in her efforts to find a job.* ◆ *She can be very persistent when she wants something.* **2** continuing for a long period of time without interruption, or repeated frequently, especially in a way that is annoying and cannot be stopped **SYN** UNRELENTING: *persistent rain* ◆ *a persistent cough* ▶ **per·sist·ent·ly** ![AWL] *adv.*: *They have persistently denied claims of illegal trading.* ◆ *persistently high interest rates*

perˌsistent ˌvegetative ˈstate *noun* (*medical*) a condition in which a person's body is kept working by medical means but the person shows no sign of brain activity

per·snick·et·y /pərˈsnɪkəti/ *adj.* (*informal, disapproving*) worrying too much about unimportant details; showing this **SYN** FUSSY

per·son ♪ /ˈpɜːsn/ *noun* (*pl.* peo·ple /ˈpiːpl/ or, especially in formal use, **persons**)
1 a human as an individual: *What sort of person would do a thing like that?* ◆ *He's a fascinating person.* ◆ *What is she like as a person?* ◆ *He's just the person we need for the job.* ◆ *I had a letter from the people who used to live next door.* ◆ *I'm not really a city person* (= I don't really like cities). **HELP** Use everyone or everybody instead of "all people." ➔ see also PEOPLE **PERSON 2** (*formal* or *disapproving*) a human, especially one who is not identified: *A certain person* (= somebody that I do not wish to name) *told me about it.* ◆ *The price is $40 per person.* ◆ *This vehicle is licensed to carry 4 persons.* (= on a notice) ◆ (*law*) *The verdict was murder by a person or persons unknown.* ➔ see also VIP **3** -**person** (in compounds) a person working in the area of business mentioned; a person concerned with the thing mentioned: *a salesperson* ◆ *a spokesperson* **4** (*grammar*) any of the three classes of personal pronouns. The **first person** (*I/we*) refers to the person(s) speaking; the **second person** (*you*) refers to the person(s) spoken to; the **third person** (*he/she/it/they*) refers to the person(s) or thing(s) spoken about.
IDM **about/on your person** if you have or carry something **about/on your person**, you carry it about with you, for example in your pocket **in person** if you do something **in person**, you go somewhere and do it yourself, instead of doing it by mail, asking someone else to do it, etc. **in the person of sb** (*formal*) in the form or shape of someone: *Help arrived in the person of his mother.* ➔ more at RESPECTER

per·so·na /pərˈsoʊnə/ *noun* (*pl.* per·so·nae /-niː; -naɪ/ or per·so·nas) (*formal*) the aspects of a person's character that they show to other people, especially when their real character is different: *His public persona is quite different from the family man described in the book.* ➔ see also DRAMATIS PERSONAE

per·son·a·ble /ˈpɜːsənəbl/ *adj.* (of a person) attractive to other people because of having a pleasant appearance and character

per·son·age /ˈpɜːsənɪdʒ/ *noun* (*formal*) an important or famous person: *a royal personage*

per·son·al ♪ /ˈpɜːsənl/ *adj.*
▸ **YOUR OWN 1** [only before noun] your own; not belonging to or connected with anyone else: *personal effects/belongings/possessions* ◆ *personal details* (= your name, age, etc.) ◆ *Of course, this is just a personal opinion.* ◆ *The novel is written from personal experience.* ◆ *Use stencils to add a few personal touches to walls and furniture.* ◆ *All rental cars are for personal use only.*
▸ **FEELINGS/CHARACTER/RELATIONSHIPS 2** [only before noun] connected with individual people, especially their feelings, characters, and relationships: *Having good personal relationships is the most important thing for me.* ◆ *He was popular as much for his personal qualities as for his management skills.*
▸ **NOT OFFICIAL 3** not connected with a person's job or official position: *The letter was marked "Personal."* ◆ *I'd like to talk to you about a personal matter.* ◆ *I try not to let work interfere with my personal life.* ◆ *She's a personal friend of mine* (= not just somebody I know because of my job).
▸ **DONE BY PERSON 4** [only before noun] done by a particular person rather than by someone who is acting for them: *The President made a personal appearance at the event.* ◆ *I shall give the matter my personal attention.*
▸ **DONE FOR PERSON 5** [only before noun] made or done for a particular person rather than for a large group of people or people in general: *We offer a personal service to all our customers.* ◆ *a personal pension plan* (= a pension offered by a private company to one particular person)
▸ **OFFENSIVE 6** referring to a particular person's character, appearance, opinions, etc. in a way that is offensive: *Try to avoid making personal remarks.* ◆ *There's no need to get personal!* ◆ *Nothing personal* (= I do not wish to offend you), *but I do have to go now.*
▸ **CONNECTED WITH BODY 7** [only before noun] connected with a person's body: *personal cleanliness/hygiene*

ˈpersonal ˌad *noun* a private advertisement in a newspaper, etc., especially from someone who is looking for a romantic or sexual partner

ˌpersonal asˈsistant *noun* a person who works as a secretary or an assistant for one person

ˌpersonal ˈbest *noun* the best result that you have ever had in an event such as a race or other competition: *His personal best is a 3.5-minute mile.*

ˌpersonal ˈcheck (*CanE* personal ˈcheque) *noun* a check that an individual writes to pay for something out of their own bank account ➔ compare CASHIER'S CHECK

ˌpersonal comˈputer *noun* (*abbr.* PC) a small computer that is designed for one person to use at work or at home ➔ compare MAINFRAME, MICROCOMPUTER, MINICOMPUTER

ˈpersonal ˌday *noun* a day that you take off work for personal reasons, but not because you are sick or on vacation

ˌpersonal ˌdigital asˈsistant *noun* = PDA

ˌpersonal exˈemption *noun* the amount of money you are allowed to earn each year before you have to pay INCOME TAX ıpersonal inforˈmation ˌmanager *noun* (*abbr.* PIM) a computer program in which you write names, addresses, things that you have to do, etc.

ıpersonal ˈinjury *noun* [U] (*law*) physical injury, rather than damage to property or to someone's reputation

per·son·al·i·ty 🔑 /ˌpɜrsəˈnæləti/ *noun* (*pl.* per·son·al·i·ties)

1 [C, U] the various aspects of a person's character that combine to make them different from other people: *His wife has a strong personality.* ◆ *The children all have very different personalities.* ◆ *He maintained order by sheer force of personality.* ◆ *There are likely to be tensions and **personality clashes** in any social group.* **2** [U] the qualities of a person's character that make them interesting and attractive: *We need someone with lots of personality to head the project.* **3** [C] a famous person, especially one who works in entertainment or sports **SYN** CELEBRITY: *personalities from the world of music* ◆ *a TV/sports personality* **4** [C] a person whose strong character makes them noticeable: *Their son is a real personality.* **5** [U] the qualities of a place or thing that make it interesting and different **SYN** CHARACTER: *The problem with many modern buildings is that they lack personality.*

persoˈnality ˌcult (also ˌcult of personˈality) *noun* (*disapproving*) a situation in which people are encouraged to show extreme love and admiration for a famous person, especially a political leader

persoˈnality disˌorder *noun* (*technical*) a serious mental condition in which someone's behavior makes it difficult for them to have normal relationships with other people or a normal role in society

per·son·al·ize /ˈpɜrsənəˌlaɪz/ *verb* **1** [usually passive] ~ sth to mark something in some way to show that it belongs to a particular person: *All the towels were personalized with their initials.* **2** ~ sth to design or change something so that it is suitable for the needs of a particular person: *All our courses are personalized to the needs of the individual.* **3** ~ sth to refer to particular people when discussing a general subject: *The mass media tends to personalize politics.* ▶ per·son·al·i·za·tion *noun* [U, sing.] per·son·al·ized *adj.*: *a highly personalized service* ◆ *a personalized license plate* (= on a car)

per·son·al·ly 🔑 /ˈpɜrsənəli/ *adv.*

1 used to show that you are giving your own opinion about something: *Personally, I prefer the second option.* ◆ *"Is it worth the effort?" "Personally speaking, yes."* **2** by a particular person rather than by someone acting for them: *All letters will be answered personally.* ◆ *Do you know him personally* (= have you met him, rather than just knowing about him from other people)? **3** in a way that is connected with one particular person rather than a group of people **SYN** INDIVIDUALLY: *He was personally criticized by inspectors for his incompetence.* ◆ *You will be held personally responsible for any loss or breakage.* **4** in a way that is intended to be offensive: *I'm sure she didn't mean it personally.* **5** in a way that is connected with someone's personal life rather than with their job or official position: *Have you had any contact with any of the suspects, either personally or professionally?* **IDM** take sth personally to be offended by something: *I'm afraid he took your remarks personally.*

ıpersonal ˈorganizer *noun* a small file with loose sheets of paper in which you write down information, addresses, what you have arranged to do, etc.; a very small computer for the same purpose

ıpersonal ˈpronoun *noun* (*grammar*) any of the pronouns *I, you, he, she, it, we, they, me, him, her, us, them*

per·son·als /ˈpɜrsənlz/ *noun* [pl.] a part of a newspaper or magazine for private messages or small advertisements

ıpersonal ˈshopper *noun* a person whose job is to help someone else buy things, either by going with them around a store or by doing their shopping for them

ıpersonal ˈspace *noun* [U] the space directly around where you are standing or sitting: *He leaned toward her and she stiffened at this invasion of her personal space.*

ıpersonal ˈstereo *noun* a small CD player or radio with HEADPHONES that you carry with you and use while you are moving around

ıpersonal ˈtrainer *noun* a person who is paid by someone to help them exercise, especially by deciding what types of exercise are best for them

per·so·na non gra·ta /pərˌsoʊnə nɑn ˈgrɑtə/ *noun* [U] (from *Latin*) a person who is not welcome in a particular place because of something they have said or done, especially one who is told to leave a country by the government

per·son·i·fi·ca·tion /pərˌsɑnəfəˈkeɪʃn/ *noun* **1** [C, usually sing.] ~ of sth a person who has a lot of a particular quality or characteristic **SYN** EPITOME: *She was the personification of elegance.* **2** [U, C] the practice of representing objects, qualities, etc. as humans, in art and literature; an object, quality, etc. that is represented in this way: *the personification of autumn in Keats's poem*

per·son·i·fy /pərˈsɑnəˌfaɪ/ *verb* (per·son·i·fies, per·son·i·fy·ing, per·son·i·fied, per·son·i·fied) **1** ~ sth to be an example of a quality or characteristic, or to have a lot of it **SYN** TYPIFY: *These children personify all that is wrong with the education system.* ◆ *He is kindness personified.* **2** [usually passive] ~ sth (as sb) to show or think of an object, quality, etc. as a person: *The river was personified as a goddess.*

per·son·nel /ˌpɜrsəˈnɛl/ *noun* **1** [pl.] the people who work for an organization or one of the armed forces: *skilled personnel* ◆ *sales/technical/medical/security/military, etc. personnel* **2** [U] the department in a company that deals with employing and training people **SYN** HUMAN RESOURCES: *the personnel department/manager* ◆ *She works in personnel.* ◆ *Personnel is currently reviewing pay scales.*

personˈnel ˌcarrier *noun* a military vehicle for carrying soldiers

ıperson-to-ˈperson *adj.* [usually before noun] **1** happening between two or more people who deal directly with each other rather than through another person: *Technical support is offered on a person-to-person basis.* **2** (of a telephone call) made by calling the OPERATOR (= a person who works at a telephone exchange) and asking to speak to a particular person. If that person is not available, the call does not have to be paid for: *a person-to-person call*

per·spec·tive 🔑 ▣ AWL /pərˈspɛktɪv/ *noun*

1 [C] a particular attitude toward something; a way of thinking about something **SYN** VIEWPOINT: *a global perspective* ◆ *Try to see the issue from a different perspective.* ◆ *a report that looks at the education system from the perspective of deaf people* ◆ ~ on sth *His experience abroad provides a wider perspective on the problem.* **2** [U] the ability to think about problems and decisions in a reasonable way without exaggerating their importance: *She was aware that she was losing all sense of perspective.* ◆ *Try to keep these issues in perspective.* ◆ *Talking to others can often help to put your own problems into perspective.* ◆ *It is important not to let things get out of perspective.* **3** [U] the art of creating an effect of depth and distance in a picture by representing people and things that are far away as being smaller than those that are nearer the front: *We learned how to draw buildings in perspective.* ◆ *The tree on the left is out of perspective.* **4** [C] a view, especially one in which you can see far into the distance: *a perspective of the whole valley*

per·spi·ca·cious /ˌpɜrspɪˈkeɪʃəs/ *adj.* (*formal*) able to understand someone or something quickly and accurately; showing this: *a perspicacious remark* ▶ per·spi·cac·i·ty /ˌpɜrspɪˈkæsəti/ *noun* [U]

per·spi·ra·tion /ˌpɜrspəˈreɪʃn/ *noun* [U] **1** drops of liquid that form on your skin when you are hot **SYN** SWEAT: *Beads of perspiration stood out on his forehead.* ◆ *Her skin was damp with perspiration.* **2** the act of perspiring: *Perspiration cools the skin in hot weather.*

per·spire /pərˈspaɪər/ *verb* [I] (*formal*) to produce sweat on your body **SYN** SWEAT

per·suade 🔊 /pərˈsweɪd/ verb
1 to make someone do something by giving them good reasons for doing it: ~ **sb to do sth** *Try to persuade him to come.* ♦ ~ **sb** *Please try and persuade her.* ♦ *She's always easily persuaded.* ♦ *I'm sure he'll come with a bit of persuading.* ♦ ~ **sb into sth/into doing sth** *I allowed myself to be persuaded into entering the competition.* **2** to make someone believe that something is true **SYN** CONVINCE: ~ **sb/yourself that...** *It will be difficult to persuade them that there's no other choice.* ♦ *She had persuaded herself that life was not worth living.* ♦ ~ **sb** *No one was persuaded by his arguments.* ♦ ~ **sb of sth** (*formal*) *I am still not fully persuaded of the plan's merits.*

WHICH WORD?

persuade ♦ convince

- The main meaning of **persuade** is to make someone agree to do something by giving them good reasons for doing it: *I tried to persuade her to see a doctor.* The main meaning of **convince** is to make someone believe that something is true: *He convinced me that he was right.*
- It is quite common, however, for each of these words to be used with both meanings, especially for **convince** to be used as a synonym for **persuade**: *I persuaded/convinced her to see a doctor.*

per·sua·sion /pərˈsweɪʒn/ *noun* **1** [U] the act of persuading someone to do something or to believe something: *It didn't take much persuasion to get her to tell us where he was.* ♦ *After a little gentle persuasion, he agreed to come.* ♦ *She has great powers of persuasion.* **2** [C, U] a particular set of beliefs, especially about religion or politics: *politicians of all persuasions* ♦ *every shade of religious persuasion*

per·sua·sive /pərˈsweɪsɪv/ *adj.* able to persuade someone to do or believe something: *persuasive arguments* ♦ *He can be very persuasive.* ▶ **per·sua·sive·ly** *adv.*: *They argue persuasively in favor of a total ban on handguns.* **per·sua·sive·ness** *noun* [U]

pert /pərt/ *adj.* **1** (of a part of the body) small, firm, and attractive: *a pert nose* ♦ *pert features* **2** (especially of a girl or young woman) showing a lack of respect, especially in a cheerful and amusing way **SYN** IMPUDENT: *a pert reply* ▶ **pert·ly** *adv.*

per·tain /pərˈteɪn/ *verb* [I] (*formal*) to exist or to apply in a particular situation or at a particular time: *Living conditions are vastly different from those pertaining in their country of origin.* ♦ *Those laws no longer pertain.*
PHR V **per·tain to sth/sb** (*formal*) to be connected with something or someone: *the laws pertaining to adoption*

per·ti·na·cious /ˌpərtnˈeɪʃəs/ *adj.* (*formal*) determined to achieve a particular aim despite difficulties or opposition ▶ **per·ti·nac·i·ty** /ˌpərtnˈæsəti/ *noun* [U]

per·ti·nent /ˈpərtn·ənt/ *adj.* (*formal*) appropriate to a particular situation **SYN** RELEVANT: *a pertinent question/fact* ♦ ~ **to sth** *Please keep your comments pertinent to the topic under discussion.* ▶ **per·ti·nent·ly** *adv.* **per·ti·nence** /-əns/ *noun* [U]

per·turb /pərˈtərb/ *verb* ~ **sb** (*formal*) to make someone worried or anxious **SYN** ALARM: *Her sudden appearance did not seem to perturb him in the least.* ▶ **per·turbed** *adj.*: *a perturbed young man* ♦ ~ **at/about sth** *She didn't seem perturbed at the change of plan.* **ANT** UNPERTURBED

per·tur·ba·tion /ˌpərtərˈbeɪʃn/ *noun* **1** [U] (*formal*) the state of feeling anxious about something that has happened **SYN** ALARM **2** [C, U] (*technical*) a small change in the quality, behavior, or movement of something: *temperature perturbations*

per·tus·sis /pərˈtʌsəs/ *noun* [U] (*medical*) = WHOOPING COUGH

pe·ruse /pəˈruːz/ *verb* ~ **sth** (*formal or humorous*) to read something, especially in a careful way: *A copy of the report is available for you to peruse at your leisure.* ▶ **pe·rus·al** /pə-**

ˈruːzl/ *noun* [U, sing.]: *The agreement was signed after careful perusal.*

perv (also **perve**) /pərv/ *noun* (*informal*) = PERVERT

per·vade /pərˈveɪd/ *verb* ~ **sth** (*formal*) to spread through and be noticeable in every part of something **SYN** PERMEATE: *a pervading mood of fear* ♦ *the sadness that pervades most of her novels* ♦ *The entire house was pervaded by a sour smell.*

per·va·sive /pərˈveɪsɪv/ *adj.* existing in all parts of a place or thing; spreading gradually to affect all parts of a place or thing: *a pervasive smell of damp* ♦ *A sense of social change is pervasive in her novels.* ▶ **per·va·sive·ly** *adv.* **per·va·sive·ness** *noun* [U]

per·verse /pərˈvərs/ *adj.* showing deliberate determination to behave in a way that most people think is wrong, unacceptable, or unreasonable: *a perverse decision* (= one that most people do not expect and think is wrong) ♦ *She finds a perverse pleasure in upsetting her parents.* ♦ *Do you really mean that or are you just being **deliberately perverse**?* ▶ **per·verse·ly** *adv.*: *She seemed perversely proud of her criminal record.* **per·ver·si·ty** /pərˈvərsəti/ *noun* [U]: *He refused to attend out of sheer perversity.*

per·ver·sion /pərˈvərʒn/ *noun* [U, C] **1** behavior that most people think is not normal or acceptable, especially when it is connected with sex; an example of this type of behavior: *sexual perversion* **2** the act of changing something that is good or right into something that is bad or wrong; the result of this: *the perversion of justice* ♦ *Her account was a perversion of the truth.*

per·vert *verb, noun*
● *verb* /pərˈvərt/ **1** ~ **sth** to change a system, process, etc. in a bad way so that it is not what it used to be or what it should be: *Some scientific discoveries have been perverted to create weapons of destruction.* **2** ~ **sb/sth** to affect someone in a way that makes them act or think in an immoral or unacceptable way **SYN** CORRUPT: *Some people believe that television can pervert the minds of children.*
● *noun* /ˈpərvərt/ (also *informal* **perv**) a person whose sexual behavior is not thought to be normal or acceptable by most people **SYN** DEVIANT: *a sexual pervert*

per·vert·ed /pərˈvərtəd/ *adj.* not thought to be normal or acceptable by most people: *sexual acts, normal and perverted* ♦ *She was having difficulty following his perverted logic.* ♦ *They clearly take a perverted delight in watching others suffer.*

pe·se·ta /pəˈseɪtə/ *noun* the former unit of money in Spain (replaced in 2002 by the euro)

pes·ky /ˈpeski/ *adj.* [only before noun] (*informal*) annoying: *pesky insects*

pe·so /ˈpeɪsoʊ/ *noun* (*pl.* **pe·sos**) the unit of money in many Latin American countries and the Philippines

pes·sa·ry /ˈpesəri/ *noun* (*pl.* **pes·sa·ries**) **1** a small piece of solid medicine that is placed inside a woman's VAGINA and left to dissolve, used to cure an infection or to prevent her from becoming pregnant ⭘ see also SUPPOSITORY **2** a device that is placed inside a woman's VAGINA to support the WOMB

pes·si·mism /ˈpesəˌmɪzəm/ *noun* [U] ~ **(about/over sth)** a feeling that bad things will happen and that something will not be successful; the tendency to have this feeling: *There is a mood of pessimism in the company about future job prospects.* **ANT** OPTIMISM

pes·si·mist /ˈpesəmɪst/ *noun* a person who always expects bad things to happen: *You don't have to be a pessimist to realize that we're in trouble.* **ANT** OPTIMIST

pes·si·mis·tic /ˌpesəˈmɪstɪk/ *adj.* ~ **(about sth)** expecting bad things to happen or something not to be successful; showing this: *They appeared surprisingly pessimistic about their chances of winning.* ♦ *a pessimistic view of life* ♦ *I think you're being far too pessimistic.* **ANT** OPTIMISTIC ▶ **pes·si·mis·ti·cally** /-kli/ *adv.*

pest /pest/ *noun* **1** an insect or animal that destroys plants,

ʌ **cup**   ə **about**   eɪ **say**   aɪ **five**   ɔɪ **boy**   aʊ **now**   oʊ **go**   ər **bird**

food, etc.: *pest control* ✦ *insect/plant/garden pests* **2** (*informal*) an annoying person or thing: *That child is being a real pest.*

pes·ter /'pɛstər/ *verb* [T, I] to annoy someone, especially by asking them something many times **SYN** BADGER: *~ sb for sth Journalists pestered neighbors for information.* ✦ *~ sb with sth He has been pestering her with phone calls for over a week.* ✦ *~ sb/sth The horses were continually pestered by flies.* ✦ *~ (sb to do sth) The kids kept pestering me to read to them.*

pes·ti·cide /'pɛstəˌsaɪd/ *noun* [C, U] a chemical used for killing pests, especially insects: *vegetables grown without the use of pesticides* ✦ *crops sprayed with pesticide* ➔ see also HERBICIDE, INSECTICIDE

pes·ti·lence /'pɛstələns/ *noun* [U, sing.] (*old use* or *literary*) any infectious disease that spreads quickly and kills a lot of people

pes·ti·len·tial /ˌpɛstə'lɛnʃl/ *adj.* **1** [only before noun] (*literary*) extremely annoying **2** (*old use*) connected with or causing a pestilence

pes·tle /'pɛsl; 'pɛstl/ *noun* a small heavy tool with a round end used for crushing things in a special bowl called a MORTAR ➔ picture at KITCHEN, LABORATORY

pes·to /'pɛstoʊ/ *noun* [U] an Italian sauce made of BASIL leaves, PINE NUTS, cheese, and oil

PET *noun* [U] **1** /ˌpi i 'ti/ the abbreviation for "polyethylene terephthalate" (an artificial substance used to make materials for packaging food, including plastic drinks bottles) **2** /pɛt/ (*medical*) the abbreviation for "positron emission tomography" (a process that produces an image of your brain or of another part inside your body): *a PET scan*

pet /pɛt/ *noun, verb, adj.*
● *noun* **1** an animal, a bird, etc. that you have at home for pleasure, rather than one that is kept for work or food: *Do you have any pets?* ✦ *a pet dog/hamster, etc.* ✦ *a family/domestic pet* ✦ *pet food* ✦ *a pet store* (= where animals are sold as pets) **2** (usually *disapproving*) a person who is given special attention by someone, especially in a way that seems unfair to other people **SYN** FAVORITE: *She's the teacher's pet.*
● *verb* (-tt-) **1** [T] *~ sb/sth* to touch or move your hand gently over an animal or a child in a kind and loving way **2** [I] (*informal*) (of two people) to kiss and touch each other in a sexual way ➔ see also PETTING
● *adj.* [only before noun] that you are very interested in: *his pet subject/theory/project, etc.* ➔ see also PET NAME
   IDM *sb's pet peeve* something that you particularly dislike

pet·al /'pɛtl/ *noun* a delicate colored part of a flower. The head of a flower is usually made up of several petals around a central part. ➔ picture at PLANT

pe·tard /pə'tɑrd/ *noun* **IDM** see HOIST v.

Pete /pit/
   IDM *for Pete's sake* (*informal, old-fashioned*) used to show that you are annoyed about something: *For Pete's sake turn down that music!* ✦ *Oh, for Pete's sake, why can't I get this thing to work!*

Pe·ter /'pitər/ *noun* **IDM** see ROB

pe·ter /'pitər/ *verb*
   PHRV *peter 'out* to gradually become smaller, quieter, etc. and then end: *The campaign petered out for lack of support.* ✦ *The road petered out into a dirt track.*

Peter 'Pan *noun* a person who looks unusually young for their age, or who behaves in a way that would be more appropriate for someone younger **ORIGIN** From a story by J.M. Barrie about a boy with magic powers who never grew up.

Pe·ters pro·jec·tion /'pitərz prə'dʒɛkʃn/ *noun* [sing.] a map of the world on which the relative size, but not the shape of countries, is more accurate than on more traditional maps ➔ compare MERCATOR PROJECTION

pet·i·ole /'pɛtiˌoʊl/ *noun* (*biology*) the thin part at the base of a leaf that supports it and joins it to the STEM of a plant

petit bourgeois /ˌpɛti bur'ʒwɑ; pə'ti-; -'burʒwɑ/ (also **pet·ty bour·geois**) *noun* (*pl.* **pet·its/pet·ty bour·geois**) (*disapproving*) a member of the lower middle class in society, especially one who thinks that money, work, and social position are very important ▶ **petit bourgeois** (also **petty bourgeois**) *adj.* [usually before noun]

pe·tite /pə'tit/ *adj.* (*approving*) (of a girl, woman, or her figure) small and thin: *a petite blonde*

the pe·tite bourgeoi·sie (also **petty bourgeoi·sie**) *noun* [sing.] the lower middle class in society

pe·tit four /ˌpɛti 'fɔr/ *noun* [usually pl.] (*pl.* **petits fours** /ˌpɛti 'fɔrz/) (from *French*) a very small decorated cake or cookie that is served with coffee or tea

pe·ti·tion /pə'tɪʃn/ *noun, verb*
● *noun* **1** *~ (against/for sth)* a written document signed by a large number of people that asks someone in a position of authority to do or change something: *a petition against experiments on animals* ✦ *The workers are circulating a petition for tighter safety standards.* **2** (*law*) an official document asking a court to take a particular course of action **3** (*formal*) a formal prayer to God or request to someone in authority
● *verb* **1** [I, T] to make a formal request to someone in authority, especially by sending them a petition: *~ for/against sth Local residents have successfully petitioned against prison building in their area.* ✦ *~ sb/sth (for sth) The group intends to petition Congress for reform of the law.* ✦ *~ sb/sth to do sth Parents petitioned the school to review its admissions policy.* **2** [I, T] *~ (sb) (for sth)* | *~ sb/sth to do sth* to formally ask for something in court: *to petition for divorce*

pe·ti·tion·er /pə'tɪʃənər/ *noun* **1** a person who organizes or signs a petition **2** (*law*) a person who asks a court to take a particular course of action **3** (*formal*) a person who makes a formal request to someone in authority

pe·tit mal /ˌpɛti 'mɑl/ *noun* [U] a form of EPILEPSY that is not very serious, in which someone becomes unconscious only for very short periods

pet 'name *noun* a name you use for someone instead of their real name, as a sign of affection

pet·rel /'pɛtrəl/ *noun* a black and white bird that can fly over the ocean a long way from land

Pe·tri dish /'pitri ˌdɪʃ/ *noun* a shallow covered dish used for growing bacteria, etc. in ➔ picture at LABORATORY

pet·ri·fied /'pɛtrəˌfaɪd/ *adj.* **1** extremely frightened **SYN** TERRIFIED: *a petrified expression* ✦ *~ (of sth) I'm petrified of snakes.* ✦ *They were petrified with fear* (= so frightened that they were unable to move or think). ✦ *~ (that...) She was petrified that the police would burst in at any moment.* **2** [only before noun] **petrified** trees, insects, etc. have died and been changed into stone over a very long period of time: *a petrified forest*

pet·ri·fy /'pɛtrəˌfaɪ/ *verb* (pet·ri·fies, pet·ri·fy·ing, pet·ri·fied, pet·ri·fied) **1** [T] *~ sb* to make someone feel extremely frightened **SYN** TERRIFY **2** [I, T] *~ (sth)* to change or to make something change into a substance like stone

petro- /'pɛtroʊ/ *combining form* (in nouns, adjectives, and adverbs) **1** connected with rocks: *petrology* **2** connected with gas: *petrochemical*

pet·ro·chem·i·cal /ˌpɛtroʊ'kɛmɪkl/ *noun* any chemical substance obtained from PETROLEUM oil or natural gas: *the petrochemical industry*

pet·ro·dol·lar /'pɛtroʊˌdɑlər/ *noun* a unit of money that is used for calculating the money earned by countries that produce and sell oil

pe·tro·le·um /pə'troʊliəm/ *noun* [U] oil that is found under the ground or the ocean and is used to produce gasoline, PARAFFIN, DIESEL oil, etc.

pe·troleum 'jelly (also **pet·ro·la·tum** /ˌpɛtrəˈleɪtəm/) *noun* [U] a soft clear substance obtained from petroleum, used to heal injuries on the skin or to make machine parts move together more smoothly **SYN** VASELINE™

pe·trol·o·gy /pəˈtrɑlədʒi/ *noun* [U] the scientific study of how rocks are made and what they are made of

pet·ti·coat /ˈpɛtiˌkoʊt/ *noun* (*old-fashioned*) a piece of women's underwear like a thin dress or skirt, worn under a dress or skirt **SYN** SLIP

pet·ti·fog·ging /ˈpɛtiˌfɔɡɪŋ; -ˌfɑɡɪŋ/ *adj.* [only before noun] (*old-fashioned*) paying too much attention to unimportant details; concerned with unimportant things **SYN** PETTY

pet·ting /ˈpɛtɪŋ/ *noun* [U] the activity of kissing and touching someone, especially in a sexual way: *heavy petting* (= sexual activity which avoids PENETRATION)

'petting ˌzoo *noun* a zoo with animals that children can touch

pet·ty /ˈpɛti/ *adj.* (usually *disapproving*) **1** [usually before noun] small and unimportant **SYN** MINOR: *petty squabbles* ♦ *petty crime/theft* (= that is not very serious) ♦ *a petty criminal/thief* ♦ *a petty bureaucrat/official* (= who does not have much power or authority, although they might pretend to) **2** caring too much about small and unimportant matters, especially when this is unkind to other people **SYN** SMALL-MINDED: *How could you be so petty?* ▶ **pet·ti·ness** *noun* [U]

ˌpetty bourˈgeois = PETIT BOURGEOIS

the ˌpetty bourgeoiˈsie *noun* [sing.] = PETITE BOURGEOISIE

ˌpet·ty ˈcash *noun* [U] a small amount of money kept in an office for small payments

ˌpetty ˈlarceny *noun* [U] (*law*) the crime of stealing something that is not worth a lot of money ⊃ compare GRAND LARCENY

ˌpetty ˈofficer *noun* (*abbr.* PO) a sailor of middle rank in the navy

pet·u·lant /ˈpɛtʃələnt/ *adj.* bad-tempered and unreasonable, especially because you cannot do or have what you want ▶ **pet·u·lant·ly** *adv.* **pet·u·lance** /-ləns/ *noun* [U]

pe·tu·nia /pəˈtunyə/ *noun* a garden plant with white, pink, purple, or red flowers

pew /pyu/ *noun* a long wooden seat in a church

pew·ter /ˈpyutər/ *noun* [U] a gray metal made by mixing tin with LEAD¹, used especially in the past for making cups, dishes, etc.; objects made from pewter

PFD /ˌpi ɛf ˈdi/ *noun* a LIFE JACKET or similar device that is designed to help you float in water (the abbreviation for "personal flotation device")

PG /ˌpi ˈdʒi/ *abbr.* used to show that some scenes in a particular movie may not be suitable for young children (the abbreviation for "parental guidance") ⊃ compare G, NC-17, PG-13 , R

PG-13 /ˌpi dʒi θərˈtin/ *symbol* used to show that some scenes in a particular movie may not be suitable for children under the age of 13 (the symbol for "parental guidance under 13") ⊃ compare G, NC-17, PG, R

pH /ˌpi ˈeɪtʃ/ *noun* [sing.] (*chemistry*) a measurement of the level of acid or ALKALI in a SOLUTION or substance. In the pH range of 0 to 14 a reading of below 7 shows an acid and of above 7 shows an alkali: *a pH of 7.5* ♦ *to test the pH level of the soil*

phag·o·cyte /ˈfæɡəˌsaɪt/ *noun* (*biology*) a type of cell present in the body that is able to absorb bacteria and other small cells

pha·lanx /ˈfeɪlæŋks/ *noun* (*formal*) a large group of people or things standing very close together

phal·lic /ˈfælɪk/ *adj.* of or like a phallus: *phallic symbols*

phal·lo·cen·tric /ˌfæloʊˈsɛntrɪk/ *adj.* (*formal*) related to men, male power, or the phallus as a symbol of male power ▶ **phal·lo·cen·trism** /ˌfæloʊˈsɛntrɪzəm/ *noun* [U]

phal·lus /ˈfæləs/ *noun* **1** (*technical*) the male sexual organ **2** a model or an image of the male sexual organ that represents power and FERTILITY

phan·tasm /ˈfæntæzəm/ *noun* (*formal*) a thing seen in the imagination **SYN** ILLUSION

phan·tas·ma·go·ri·a /fænˌtæzməˈɡɔriə/ *noun* [sing.] (*formal*) a changing scene of real or imagined figures, for example as seen in a dream or created as an effect in a movie ▶ **phan·tas·ma·gor·i·cal** /-ˈɡɔrɪkl; -ˈɡɑrɪkl/ *adj.*

phan·ta·sy /ˈfæntəsi/ *noun* [C, U] (*old use*) = FANTASY

phan·tom /ˈfæntəm/ *noun, adj.*
• *noun* **1** a GHOST: *the phantom of his dead father* **2** a thing that exists only in your imagination
• *adj.* [only before noun] **1** like a GHOST: *a phantom horseman* **2** existing only in your imagination: *phantom profits* ♦ *phantom illnesses* ♦ *a phantom pregnancy* (= a condition in which a woman seems to be pregnant but in fact is not)

phar·aoh /ˈfɛroʊ/ *noun* a ruler of ancient Egypt

Phar·i·see /ˈfærəsi/ *noun* **1** a member of an ancient Jewish group who followed religious laws very strictly **2** (*disapproving*) a person who is very proud of the fact that they have high religious and moral standards, but who does not care enough about other people **SYN** HYPOCRITE

phar·ma·ceu·ti·cal /ˌfɑrməˈsutɪkl/ *adj., noun*
• *adj.* [only before noun] connected with making and selling drugs and medicines: *pharmaceutical products* ♦ *the pharmaceutical industry*
• *noun* [usually pl.] (*technical*) a drug or medicine: *the development of new pharmaceuticals*

phar·ma·cist /ˈfɑrməsɪst/ *noun* (also **drug·gist**) a person whose job is to prepare medicines and sell or give them to the public in a store or in a hospital: *We had to wait for the pharmacist to make up her prescription.* ⊃ see also PHARMACY

phar·ma·col·o·gist /ˌfɑrməˈkɑlədʒɪst/ *noun* a scientist who studies pharmacology

phar·ma·col·o·gy /ˌfɑrməˈkɑlədʒi/ *noun* [U] the scientific study of drugs and their use in medicine ▶ **phar·ma·co·log·i·cal** /ˌfɑrməkəˈlɑdʒɪkl/ *adj.*: *pharmacological research*

phar·ma·co·poe·ia (also **phar·ma·co·pe·ia**) /ˌfɑrməkəˈpiə/ *noun* (*technical*) an official book containing a list of medicines and drugs and instructions for their use

phar·ma·cy /ˈfɑrməsi/ *noun* (*pl.* **phar·ma·cies**) **1** [C] a store, or part of one, that sells medicines and drugs ⊃ compare DRUGSTORE **2** [C] a place in a hospital where medicines are prepared ⊃ see also DISPENSARY **3** [U] the study of how to prepare medicines and drugs

pharm·ing /ˈfɑrmɪŋ/ *noun* [U] **1** the process of changing the GENES of an animal or a plant so that it produces large quantities of a substance, especially for use in medicine **ORIGIN** From "farming" and "pharmaceutical." **2** the practice of secretly changing computer files or software so that visitors to a popular Web site are sent to a different Web site instead, without their knowledge, where their personal details are stolen and used to steal money from them ⊃ compare PHISHING

pha·ryn·ge·al /fəˈrɪndʒəl; -dʒiəl; ˌfærənˈdʒiəl/ *adj., noun*
• *adj.* (*medical*) relating to the pharynx
• *noun* (also **pha·ryngeal ˈconsonant**) (*phonetics*) a speech sound produced by the root of the tongue using the PHARYNX

phar·yn·gi·tis /ˌfærənˈdʒaɪtɪs/ *adj.* *noun* [U] (*medical*) a condition in which the throat is red and sore

phar·ynx /ˈfærɪŋks/ *noun* (*pl.* **pha·ryn·ges** /fəˈrɪndʒiz/) (*anatomy*) the soft area at the top of the throat where the passages to the nose and mouth connect with the throat

phase 🔑 **AWL** /feɪz/ *noun, verb*
• *noun* **1** a stage in a process of change or development: *during the first/next/last phase* ♦ *the initial/final phase of the*

t **tea**   ţ **butter**   d **did**   k **cat**   g **got**   tʃ **chin**   dʒ **June**   f **fall**

project ♦ *a critical/decisive phase* ♦ *the design phase* ♦ *His anxiety about the work was just a passing phase.* ♦ *She's going through a difficult phase.* ♦ *The wedding marked the beginning of a new phase in Emma's life.* **2** each of the shapes of the moon as we see it from the earth at different times of the month

IDM **in phase/out of phase (with sth)** **1** working/not working together in the right way: *The traffic lights were out of phase.* **2** (*physics*) if two or more light or sound wave cycles are **in phase**, their high and low points occur at the same time; if they are **out of phase**, they occur at different times

● *verb* [usually passive] **~ sth** to arrange to do something gradually in stages over a period of time: *the phased withdrawal of troops from the area* ♦ *Closure of the hospitals was phased over a three-year period.*

PHRV **phase sth↔in** to introduce or start using something gradually in stages over a period of time: *The new tax will be phased in over two years.* **phase sth↔out** to stop using something in stages over a period of time: *Subsidies to farmers will be phased out by next year.*

phat /fæt/ *adj.* (*slang*) very good

phat·ic *adj.* /'fætɪk/ *adj.* (*linguistics*) relating to language used for social purposes rather than to give information or ask questions: *phatic communication*

Ph.D. /ˌpi eɪtʃ 'di/ *noun* **1** a university degree of a very high level that is given to someone who has done research in a particular subject (the abbreviation for "Doctor of Philosophy"): *to be/have/do a Ph.D.* ♦ *Anne Thomas, Ph.D.* ⊃ collocations at EDUCATION **2** a person who has a Ph.D.

pheas·ant /'fɛznt/ *noun* [C, U] (*pl.* pheas·ants or pheas·ant) a large bird with a long tail, the male of which is brightly colored. People sometimes shoot pheasants for sport or food. Meat from this bird is also called pheasant: *to hunt pheasant* ♦ *roast pheasant* ⊃ picture at ANIMAL

phe·nol·o·gy /fə'nɑlədʒi/ *noun* [U] the study of patterns of events in nature, especially in the weather and in the behavior of plants and animals

phe·nom /'finɑm; fə'nɑm/ *noun* (*informal*) a person or thing that is very successful or impressive **SYN** PHENOMENON

phe·nom·e·nal **AWL** /fə'nɑmənl/ *adj.* very great or impressive **SYN** EXTRAORDINARY: *The product has been a phenomenal success.*

phe·nom·e·nal·ly /fə'nɑmənəli/ *adv.* **1** in a very great or impressive way **SYN** EXTRAORDINARILY: *This product has been phenomenally successful* **2** extremely; very: *phenomenally bad weather*

phe·nom·e·nol·o·gy /fəˌnɑmə'nɑlədʒi/ *noun* [U] the branch of philosophy that deals with what you see, hear, feel, etc. in contrast to what may actually be real or true about the world ▶ **phe·nom·e·no·log·i·cal** /fəˌnɑmənə'lɑdʒɪkl/ *adj.*

phe·nom·e·non **AWL** /fə'nɑmə,nɑn; -nən/ *noun* (*pl.* phe·nom·e·na /-nə/) **1** a fact or an event in nature or society, especially one that is not fully understood: *cultural/natural/social phenomena* ♦ *Globalization is a phenomenon of the 21st century.* **2** (*pl.* phe·nom·e·nons) a person or thing that is very successful or impressive

phe·no·type /'finə,taɪp/ *adj., noun* (*biology*) the set of characteristics of a living thing, resulting from its combination of GENES and the effect of its environment ⊃ compare GENOTYPE

pher·o·mone /'fɛrə,moʊn/ *noun* (*biology*) a substance produced by an animal as a chemical signal, often to attract another animal of the same SPECIES

phew /fyu/ *exclamation* a sound that people make to show that they are hot, tired, or happy that something bad has finished or did not happen: *Phew, it's hot in here!* ♦ *Phew, I'm glad that's all over.* ⊃ compare WHEW

phi /faɪ/ *noun* the 21st letter of the Greek alphabet (Φ, φ)

phi·al /'faɪəl/ *noun* (*formal*) = VIAL

Phi ˌ**Beta** ˈ**Kappa** *noun* a society for college and university students who are very successful in their studies

phi·lan·der·er /fə'lændərər/ *noun* (*old-fashioned, disapproving*) a man who has sexual relationships with many different women

phi·lan·der·ing /fə'lændərɪŋ/ *noun* [U] (*old-fashioned, disapproving*) (of a man) the fact of having sexual relationships with many different women **SYN** WOMANIZING ▶ **phi·lan·der·ing** *adj.* [only before noun]

phi·lan·thro·pist /fə'lænθrəpɪst/ *noun* a rich person who helps the poor and those in need, especially by giving money

phi·lan·thro·py /fə'lænθrəpi/ *noun* [U] the practice of helping the poor and those in need, especially by giving money ▶ **phil·an·throp·ic** /ˌfɪlən'θrɑpɪk/ *adj.*: *philanthropic work* **phil·an·throp·i·cally** /ˌfɪlən'θrɑpɪkli/ *adv.*

phi·lat·e·list /fə'lætl·ɪst/ *noun* (*technical*) a person who collects or studies stamps

phi·lat·e·ly /fə'lætli/ *noun* [U] (*technical*) the collection and study of stamps **SYN** STAMP COLLECTING ▶ **phil·a·tel·ic** /ˌfɪlə'tɛlɪk/ *adj.*

-phile /faɪl/ *combining form* (in nouns and adjectives) liking a particular thing; a person who likes a particular thing: *Francophile* ♦ *bibliophile* ⊃ compare -PHOBE

phil·har·mon·ic /ˌfɪlər'mɑnɪk; ˌfɪlhɑr-/ *adj.* used in the names of ORCHESTRAS, music societies, etc.: *the Boston Philharmonic (Orchestra)*

-philia /'fɪliə/ *combining form* (in nouns) love of something, especially connected with a sexual attraction that is not considered normal: *pedophilia* ⊃ compare -PHOBIA

phil·is·tine /'fɪlə,stin/ *noun* (*disapproving*) a person who does not like or understand art, literature, music, etc. ▶ **phil·is·tine** *adj.*: *philistine attitudes* **phil·is·tin·ism** /'fɪləsti,nɪzəm/ *noun* [U]: *the philistinism of the tabloid press*

Phil·lips™ /'fɪləps/ *adj.* (of a screw or SCREWDRIVER) with a cross-shaped part for turning ⊃ compare SLOTTED

philo- /'fɪloʊ; -lə/ (also **phil-**) *combining form* (in nouns, adjectives, verbs, and adverbs) liking: *philanthropy*

phi·lol·o·gist /fə'lɑlədʒɪst/ *noun* a person who studies philology

phi·lol·o·gy /fə'lɑlədʒi/ *noun* [U] the scientific study of the development of language or of a particular language ▶ **phil·o·log·i·cal** /ˌfɪlə'lɑdʒɪkl/ *adj.*

phi·los·o·pher **AWL** /fə'lɑsəfər/ *noun* **1** a person who studies or writes about philosophy: *the Greek philosopher Aristotle* **2** a person who thinks deeply about things: *He seems to be a bit of a philosopher.*

the phiˈ**losopher's** ˌ**stone** *noun* [sing.] an imaginary substance that, in the past, people believed could change any metal into gold or silver, or could make people live for ever

phil·o·soph·i·cal **AWL** /ˌfɪlə'sɑfɪkl/ (also **phil·o·soph·ic** /ˌfɪlə'sɑfɪk/) *adj.* **1** connected with philosophy: *the philosophical writings of Kant* ♦ *philosophic debate* **2** **~ (about sth)** (*approving*) having a calm attitude toward a difficult or disappointing situation **SYN** STOIC: *He was philosophical about losing and said that he'd be back next year to try again.* ▶ **phil·o·soph·i·cally** **AWL** /-kli/ *adv.*: *This kind of evidence is philosophically unconvincing.* ♦ *She took the bad news philosophically.*

phi·los·o·phize **AWL** /fə'lɑsə,faɪz/ *verb* [I] **~ (about/on sth)** to talk about something in a serious way, especially when other people think this is boring: *He spent the evening philosophizing on the meaning of life.* ▶ **phi·los·o·phiz·ing** **AWL** *noun* [U]

phi·los·o·phy 🖉 **AWL** /fə'lɑsəfi/ *noun*
1 [U] the study of the nature and meaning of the universe and of human life: *moral philosophy* ♦ *the philosophy of science* ♦ *a professor of philosophy* ♦ *a degree in philosophy*
2 [C] a particular set or system of beliefs resulting from the

search for knowledge about life and the universe: *the philosophy of Jung* **3** [C] a set of beliefs or an attitude to life that guides someone's behavior: *Her philosophy of life is to take every opportunity that presents itself.*

phil·ter (*CanE usually* **phil·tre**) /ˈfɪltər/ *noun* (*literary*) a magic drink that is supposed to make people fall in love

phish·ing /ˈfɪʃɪŋ/ *noun* [U] the activity of tricking people by getting them to give their identity, bank account numbers, etc. over the Internet or by e-mail, and then using these to steal money from them ➲ compare PHARMING

phle·bi·tis *adj.* /fləˈbaɪtəs/ *noun* [U] (*medical*) a condition in which the walls of a VEIN become sore and swollen

phle·bot·o·my *adj.* /fləˈbɑtəmi/ *noun* [C, U] (*pl.* **phle·bot·o·mies**) (*medical*) the opening of a VEIN in order to remove blood or put another liquid in

phlegm /flɛm/ *noun* [U] **1** the thick substance that forms in the nose and throat, especially when you have a cold **2** the ability to remain calm in a situation that is difficult or upsetting

phleg·mat·ic /flɛgˈmætɪk/ *adj.* not easily made angry or upset **SYN** CALM: *a phlegmatic temperament* ▶ **phleg·mat·i·cally** /-kli/ *adv.*

phlo·em /ˈfloʊəm; -ɛm/ *noun* [U] (*biology*) the material in a plant containing very small tubes that carry sugars produced in the leaves around the plant ➲ compare XYLEM

phlox /flɑks/ *noun* **1** a tall garden plant with groups of white, blue, or red flowers with a sweet smell **2** a low, spreading plant with small white, blue, or pink flowers

-phobe /foʊb/ *combining form* (in nouns) a person who dislikes a particular thing or particular people: *Anglophobe* ♦ *xenophobe* ➲ compare -PHILE

pho·bi·a /ˈfoʊbiə/ *noun* **1** a strong unreasonable fear of something: *He has a phobia about flying.* **2** **-phobia** (in nouns) a strong unreasonable fear or hatred of a particular thing: *claustrophobia* ♦ *xenophobia* ➲ compare -PHILIA

pho·bic /ˈfoʊbɪk/ *noun* a person who has a strong unreasonable fear or hatred of something: *cat phobics* **2** **-phobic** (in adjectives) having a strong unreasonable fear or hatred of a particular thing: *claustrophobic* ♦ *xenophobic* ▶ **pho·bic** *adj.*: *phobic anxiety*

phoe·nix /ˈfiːnɪks/ *noun* (in stories) a magic bird that lives for several hundred years before burning itself and then being born again from its ASH: *to rise like a phoenix from the ashes* (= to be powerful or successful again)

phone 🔑 /foʊn/ *noun, verb*
- *noun* **1** [U, C] a system for talking to someone else over long distances using wires or radio; a machine used for this; a telephone: *I have to make a phone call.* ♦ *The phone rang and Pat answered it.* ♦ *They like to do business by phone/over the phone.* ♦ *His phone must be switched off.* ♦ *I don't have my phone with me.* ♦ *a phone bill* ➲ see also CAR PHONE, CELL PHONE, PAY PHONE, TELEPHONE **2** [C] the part of a phone that you hold in your hand and speak into; a telephone: *to pick up the phone* ♦ *He left the phone off the hook as he didn't want to be disturbed.* ➲ see also TELEPHONE **3** **-phone** (in nouns) an instrument that uses or makes sound: *dictaphone* ♦ *xylophone* **4** **-phone** (in adjectives and nouns) speaking a particular language; a person who does this: *anglophone* ♦ *francophone* **5** (*phonetics*) a sound made in speech, especially when not considered as part of the sound system of a particular language ➲ compare PHONEME
  IDM be on the phone to be using the telephone: *He's been on the phone with Kate for more than an hour.*
- *verb* [I, T] to make a telephone call to someone **SYN** CALL: *~ sb/sth Could you phone the restaurant and make a reservation?*
  PHR V phone ˈin 1 to make a telephone call to a place, for example to the place where you work: *+ adj. Three people have phoned in sick already this morning.* **2** to make a telephone call to a radio or television station: *Listeners are invited to phone in with their comments.* **phone sth⟷ˈin 1** to make a telephone call in order to give someone some

information: *I need you to phone the story in before five.* **2** to report something, give an opinion, order something, etc. by using the telephone: *Contributions to the relief fund can be phoned in day or night.*

TOPIC COLLOCATIONS

Phones

making and receiving phone calls
- the phone/telephone **rings**
- **answer/pick up/hang up** the phone/telephone
- **lift/pick up/hold/replace** the receiver
- **dial** a phone number/an extension number/a wrong number/an area code
- **call sb/talk (to sb)/speak (to sb)** on the phone/telephone; **from home/work/the office**
- **make/get/receive** a phone call
- take the phone **off the hook** (= remove the receiver so that the phone does not ring)
- the line is **busy**
- the phones have been **ringing off the hook** (= ringing frequently)
- **put sb through/get through** to the person you want to speak to
- **put sb on hold** (= so that they must wait for the person they want to speak to)
- **call from/use** a landline

cell phones
- **be/talk** on a cell phone/(*informal*) cell
- **use/answer/call (sb on)/get a message on** your cell phone/cell
- **switch/turn on/off** your cell phone/cell
- **charge/recharge** your cell phone/cell
- a cell phone **is on/is off/rings/goes off/is on vibrate/is on silent/is in silent mode**
- **send/receive** a text (message)/a picture message
- **insert/remove/change** a SIM card

phone book *noun* = TELEPHONE DIRECTORY

phone booth (also **ˈtelephone ˌbooth**) *noun* a place that is partly separated from the surrounding area, containing a public telephone, in a hotel, restaurant, on the street, etc.

phone call *noun* = CALL

phone card *noun* = CALLING CARD

pho·neme /ˈfoʊnim/ *noun* (*phonetics*) any one of the set of smallest units of speech in a language that distinguish one word from another. In English, the /s/ in *sip* and the /z/ in *zip* represent two different phonemes. ▶ **pho·ne·mic** /fəˈnimɪk/ *adj.*

phone ˌnumber *noun* = TELEPHONE NUMBER

phone tag (also **ˈtelephone ˌtag**) *noun* [U] (*informal*) a situation in which two people repeatedly call each other on the phone and leave messages, but never actually speak to each other: *We played phone tag for several days before I was able to reach him.*

phone ˌtapping *noun* the practice of connecting a piece of equipment to a telephone in order to listen secretly to other people's telephone conversations

pho·net·ic /fəˈnɛtɪk/ *adj.* **1** using special symbols to represent each different speech sound: *the International Phonetic Alphabet* ♦ *a phonetic symbol/transcription* **2** (of a spelling or spelling system) that closely matches the sounds represented: *Spanish spelling is phonetic, unlike English spelling.* **3** connected with the sounds of human speech ▶ **pho·net·i·cally** /-kli/ *adv.*

pho·net·ics /fəˈnɛtɪks/ *noun* [U] the study of speech sounds and how they are produced ▶ **pho·ne·ti·cian** /ˌfoʊnəˈtɪʃn/ *noun*

phone tree *noun* a list of the names and telephone numbers of the people in an organization, arranged in a way that shows who should call whom in case of an emergency, etc.: *They used the phone tree to notify everyone that the building was closed due to a snowstorm.*

h hat   m man   n no   ŋ sing   l leg   r red   y yes   w wet

pho·ney = PHONY

phon·ic /ˈfɑnɪk/ *adj.* **1** (*technical*) relating to sound; relating to sounds made in speech **2 -phonic** (in adjectives) connected with an instrument that uses or makes sound: *telephonic*

phon·ics /ˈfɑnɪks/ *noun* [U] a method of teaching people to read based on the sounds that letters represent

phono- /ˈfoʊnoʊ; -nə/ (also **phon-**) *combining form* (in nouns, adjectives, and adverbs) connected with sound or sounds: *phonetic*

pho·no·graph /ˈfoʊnəˌɡræf/ *noun* (*old-fashioned*) = RECORD PLAYER

pho·nol·o·gy /fəˈnɑlədʒi/ *noun* [U] (*linguistics*) the speech sounds of a particular language; the study of these sounds ▸ **pho·no·log·i·cal** /ˌfoʊnəˈlɑdʒɪkl/ *adj.*: *phonological analysis* **pho·nol·o·gist** /fəˈnɑlədʒɪst/ *noun*

pho·ny (also **pho·ney**) /ˈfoʊni/ *adj., noun*
• *adj.* (**pho·ni·er, pho·ni·est**) (*informal, disapproving*) not real or true; false, and trying to trick people **SYN** FAKE: *She spoke with a phony Russian accent.*
• *noun* (*pl.* **pho·nies** or **pho·neys**) (*informal*) a person who is not honest or sincere; a thing that is not real or true

phony ˈwar *noun* [sing.] a period of time when two groups are officially at war but not actually fighting

phoo·ey /ˈfui/ *exclamation* used when you think someone or something is wrong or silly ▸ **phoo·ey** *noun* [U]: *It's all phooey!*

phos·gene /ˈfɑzdʒin/ *noun* [U] a poisonous gas, used as a CHEMICAL WEAPON, for example during the First World War

phos·phate /ˈfɑsfeɪt/ *noun* [C, U] (*chemistry*) any COMPOUND containing phosphorus, used in industry or for helping plants to grow: *phosphate-free detergent*

phos·pho·res·cent /ˌfɑsfəˈrɛsnt/ *adj.* (*technical*) **1** producing a faint light in the dark ➋ compare FLUORESCENT **2** producing light without heat or with so little heat that it cannot be felt ▸ **phos·pho·res·cence** /-ˈrɛsns/ *noun* [U]

phos·phor·ic ac·id /ˌfɑsˌfɔrɪk ˈæsɪd/ *noun* [U] an acid used in FERTILIZERS and in the production of DETERGENTS and food

phos·pho·rus /ˈfɑsfərəs/ *noun* [U] (*symb.* **P**) a chemical element. Phosphorus is found in several different forms, including as a poisonous, pale yellow substance that shines in the dark and starts to burn as soon as it is placed in air.

pho·tic /ˈfoʊtɪk/ *adj.* (*technical*) **1** relating to, or caused by, light **2** relating to the part of the ocean that receives enough light for plants to grow: *the photic zone*

pho·to 🔊 /ˈfoʊtoʊ/ *noun* (*pl.* **pho·tos**)
= PHOTOGRAPH: *a color/black-and-white photo* ♦ *a passport photo* ♦ *a photo album* (= a book for keeping your photos in) ➋ thesaurus box at PHOTOGRAPH

photo- /ˈfoʊtoʊ; -tə/ *combining form* (in nouns, adjectives, verbs, and adverbs) **1** connected with light: *photosynthesis* **2** connected with photography: *photogenic*

ˈphoto ˌbooth *noun* a small structure with walls and a roof where you can put money in a machine and get a photograph of yourself in a few minutes

pho·to·cell /ˈfoʊtoʊˌsɛl/ *noun* = PHOTOELECTRIC CELL

pho·to·chem·i·cal /ˌfoʊtoʊˈkɛmɪkl/ *adj.* (*chemistry*) caused by or relating to the chemical action of light: *photochemical smog*

pho·to·cop·i·er /ˈfoʊtəˌkɑpiər/ (also **cop·i·er**) *noun* a machine that makes copies of documents, etc. by photographing them

pho·to·cop·y 🔊 /ˈfoʊtəˌkɑpi/ *noun, verb*
• *noun* (*pl.* **photocopies**) (also **copy**) a copy of a document, etc. made by the action of light on a specially treated surface: *Make as many photocopies as you need.*

• *verb* (**photocopies, photocopying, photocopied, photocopied**) (also **copy**) **1** [T, I] **~ (sth)** to make a photocopy of something: *a photocopied letter* ♦ *Can you get these photocopied for me by 5 o'clock?* ♦ *I seem to have spent most of the day photocopying.* **2** [I] **~ well/badly** (of printed material) to produce a good/bad photocopy: *The comments in pencil didn't photocopy very well.*

pho·to·e·lec·tric /ˌfoʊtoʊˈlɛktrɪk/ *adj.* using an electric current that is controlled by light

ˌphotoeˌlectric ˈcell (also **pho·to·cell**) *noun* an electric device that uses a stream of light. When the stream is broken it shows that someone or something is present, and can be used to control alarms, machinery, etc.

ˌphoto ˈfinish *noun* [usually sing.] the end of a race in which the leading runners or horses are so close together that only a photograph of them passing the finish line can show which is the winner

pho·to·gen·ic /ˌfoʊtəˈdʒɛnɪk/ *adj.* looking attractive in photographs: *I'm not very photogenic.*

pho·to·graph 🔊 /ˈfoʊtəˌɡræf/ *noun, verb*
• *noun* (also **pho·to**) a picture that is made by using a camera: *aerial/satellite photographs* ♦ *color photographs* ♦ *Please enclose a recent passport-sized photograph of yourself.* ♦ *I spent the day **taking photographs** of the city.*
• *verb* **1** [T] to take a photograph of someone or something: **~ sb/sth** *He has photographed some of the world's most beautiful women.* ♦ *a beautifully photographed book* (= with good photographs in it) ♦ **~ sb/sth + adj.** *She refused to be photographed nude.* ♦ **~ sb/sth doing sth** *They were photographed playing with their children.* **2** [I] **~ well, badly, etc.** to look or not look attractive in photographs: *Some people just don't photograph well.*

THESAURUS

photograph

picture ♦ photo ♦ shot ♦ snapshot ♦ print

These are all words for a picture that has been made using a camera.

photograph a picture that has been made using a camera: *a photograph of the house* ♦ *Can I take a photograph?*

picture a photograph: *We had our picture taken in front of the hotel.*

photo a photograph: *a passport photo*

PHOTOGRAPH, PICTURE, OR PHOTO?

Photograph is slightly more formal and **photo** is slightly less formal. **Picture** is used especially in the context of photographs in newspapers, magazines, and books.

shot a photograph: *I tried to get a shot of him in the water.*
 NOTE Shot often places more emphasis on the process of taking the photograph than on the finished picture.

snapshot an informal photograph that is taken quickly, and not by a professional photographer: *holiday snapshots*

print a copy of a photograph that is produced from film or from a digital camera: *a set of prints*

PATTERNS
▪ a color photograph/picture/photo/snapshot/print
▪ to take a photograph/picture/photo/shot/snapshot

---

pho·tog·ra·pher 🔊 /fəˈtɑɡrəfər/ *noun* a person who takes photographs, especially as a job: *a wildlife/fashion/portrait photographer*

pho·to·graph·ic /ˌfoʊtəˈɡræfɪk/ *adj.* connected with photographs or photography: *photographic equipment/film/images* ♦ *They produced a photographic record of the event.*

• *His paintings are almost photographic in detail.* ▶ **pho·to·graph·i·cally** /-kli/ *adv.*

photographic memory *noun* [usually sing.] the ability to remember things accurately and in great detail after seeing them

pho·tog·ra·phy 🔑 /fə'tɑgrəfi/ *noun* [U]
the art, process, or job of taking photographs or filming something: *color/flash/aerial, etc. photography* ◆ *fashion photography* by David Burn ◆ *Her hobbies include hiking and photography.* ◆ *the director of photography* (= the person who is in charge of the actual filming of a movie, TV program, etc.) ◆ *Did you see the movie about Antarctica? The photography was amazing!* ⊃ picture at HOBBY

pho·to·jour·nal·ism /ˌfoʊtoʊˈdʒɚnəˌlɪzəm/ *noun* [U] the work of giving news using mainly photographs ▶ **pho·to·jour·nal·ist** *noun*

pho·to·mon·tage /ˌfoʊtoʊmɑnˈtɑʒ; -moʊn-/ *noun* [C, U] a picture that is made up of different photographs put together; the technique of producing these pictures

pho·ton /'foʊtɑn/ *noun* (*physics*) a unit of ELECTROMAGNETIC energy

photo opportunity (also informal **'photo op**) *noun* an occasion when a famous person arranges to be photographed doing something that will impress the public

pho·to·re·al·ism /ˌfoʊtoʊˈriəˌlɪzəm/ *noun* [U] an artistic style that represents a subject in an accurate and detailed way, like a photograph

pho·to·re·cep·tor /ˌfoʊtoʊrɪˈsɛptər/ *noun* (*biology*) a cell or an organ that is sensitive to light

pho·to·sen·si·tive /ˌfoʊtoʊˈsɛnsətɪv/ *adj.* (*technical*) reacting to light, for example by changing color or producing an electrical signal

photo shoot *noun* an occasion when a photographer takes pictures of someone, for example a famous person, fashion model, etc. for use in a magazine, etc.: *I went on a photo shoot to Rio with him.*

Pho·to·stat™ /'foʊtəˌstæt/ *noun* a photocopy or a machine that produces them

pho·to·syn·the·sis /ˌfoʊtoʊˈsɪnθəsəs/ *noun* [U] (*biology*) the process by which green plants turn CARBON DIOXIDE and water into food using energy obtained from light from the sun ⊃ collocations at LIFE

pho·to·syn·the·size /ˌfoʊtoʊˈsɪnθəˌsaɪz/ *verb* [I, T] ~ **(sth)** (*biology*) (of plants) to make food by means of PHOTOSYNTHESIS

pho·tot·ro·pism /ˌfoʊtəˈtroʊpɪzəm; foʊˈtɑtrəˌpɪzəm/ *noun* [U] (*biology*) the action of a plant turning toward or away from light ▶ **pho·to·trop·ic** /ˌfoʊtəˈtroʊpɪk; -'trɑpɪk/ *adj.*

pho·to·vol·ta·ic /ˌfoʊtoʊvɑlˈteɪk; -voʊl-/ *adj.* (*physics*) relating to the production of electricity at the meeting point of two substances that have been exposed to light: *a photovoltaic cell*

phras·al /'freɪzl/ *adj.* of or connected with a phrase

phrasal 'verb *noun* (*grammar*) a verb combined with an adverb or a preposition, or sometimes both, to give a new meaning, for example *go in for, win over,* and *see to*

phrase 🔑 /freɪz/ *noun, verb*
• *noun* **1** (*grammar*) a group of words without a FINITE verb, especially one that forms part of a sentence. "The green car" and "on Friday morning" are phrases. ⊃ see also NOUN PHRASE ⊃ thesaurus box at WORD **2** a group of that which have a particular meaning when used together: *a memorable phrase* ◆ *She was, in her own favorite phrase, "a woman without a past."* ⊃ see also CATCHPHRASE **3** (*music*) a short series of notes that form within a longer passage in a piece of music **IDM** see COIN *v.*, TURN *n.*
• *verb* **1** [T] to say or write something in a particular way: ~ **sth (+ adv./prep.)** *a carefully phrased remark* ◆ *I agree with what he says, but I'd have phrased it differently.* ◆ ~ **sth as sth**

Her order was phrased as a suggestion. **2** [I, T] ~ **(sth)** to divide a piece of music into small groups of notes; to play or sing these in a particular way, especially in an effective way

phrase book *noun* a book containing lists of common expressions translated into another language, especially for people visiting a foreign country

phra·se·ol·o·gy /ˌfreɪziˈɑlədʒi/ *noun* [U] (*formal*) the particular way in which words and phrases are arranged when saying or writing something

phras·ing /'freɪzɪŋ/ *noun* [U] **1** the words used to express something: *The phrasing of the report is ambiguous.* **2** (*music*) the way in which a musician or singer divides a piece of music into phrases by pausing in suitable places

phreak·ing /'frikɪŋ/ *noun* [U] (*informal*) the act of getting into a communications system illegally, usually in order to make telephone calls without paying ▶ **phreak·er** *noun*

phre·nol·o·gy /frəˈnɑlədʒi/ *noun* [U] the study of the shape of the human head, which some people think is a guide to a person's character ▶ **phre·nol·o·gist** /-dʒɪst/ *noun*

phy·lum /'faɪləm/ *noun* (*pl.* **phy·la** /-lə/) (*biology*) a group into which animals, plants, etc. are divided, smaller than a KINGDOM and larger than a CLASS ⊃ compare GENUS

phys. ed. /ˌfɪz ˈɛd/ *noun* [U] = PHYSICAL EDUCATION

phys·i·cal 🔑 **AWL** /'fɪzɪkl/ *adj., noun*
• *adj.*
▷ THE BODY **1** [usually before noun] connected with a person's body rather than their mind: *physical fitness* ◆ *physical appearance* ◆ *The ordeal has affected both her mental and physical health.* ◆ *He tends to avoid all physical contact.*
▷ REAL THINGS **2** [only before noun] connected with things that actually exist or are present and can be seen, felt, etc. rather than things that only exist in a person's mind: *the physical world/universe/environment* ◆ *the physical properties* (= the color, weight, shape, etc.) *of copper*
▷ NATURE/SCIENCE **3** [only before noun] according to the laws of nature: *It is a physical impossibility to be in two places at once.* **4** [only before noun] connected with the scientific study of forces such as heat, light, sound, etc. and how they affect objects: *physical laws*
▷ SEX **5** involving sex: *physical love* ◆ *They are having a physical relationship.*
▷ PERSON **6** (*informal*) (of a person) liking to touch other people a lot: *She's not very physical.*
▷ VIOLENT **7** (*informal*) violent (used to avoid saying this in a direct way): *Are you going to cooperate or do we have to get physical?*
• *noun* (also **physical exami'nation**) a medical examination of a person's body, for example to check that they are healthy enough to do a particular job: *an annual physical*

TOPIC COLLOCATIONS

Physical Appearance

A person may be described as **having**:

eyes
- (bright) blue/green/(dark/light) brown/hazel **eyes**
- deep-set/sunken/bulging/protruding **eyes**
- small/beady/sparkling/twinkling/shifty **eyes**
- piercing/penetrating/steely **eyes**
- bloodshot/watery/puffy **eyes**
- bushy/thick/dark/raised/arched **eyebrows**
- long/dark/thick/curly/false **eyelashes/lashes**

face
- a flat/bulbous/pointed/sharp/snub **nose**
- a straight/a pointy/a Roman/an aquiline **nose**
- full/thick/thin/pouty **lips**
- dry/chapped/cracked **lips**
- flushed/rosy/red/ruddy/pale **cheeks**
- soft/chubby/sunken **cheeks**
- white/perfect/crooked/protruding **teeth**
- a large/high/broad/wide **forehead**

- a strong/weak/pointed/double **chin**
- a long/full/bushy/wispy **beard**
- a full/thin **goatee**
- a long/thin/bushy/droopy/handlebar/pencil **mustache**

hair and skin

- pale/fair/olive/dark/tanned **skin**
- dry/oily/smooth/rough/leathery/wrinkled **skin**
- a dark/pale/light/sallow/ruddy/olive/swarthy/clear **complexion**
- deep/fine/small/facial **wrinkles**
- blonde/blond/fair/(light/dark) brown/(jet-)black/auburn/red/ginger/gray **hair**
- straight/curly/wavy/frizzy/spiky **hair**
- thick/thin/fine/bushy/thinning **hair**
- dyed/bleached/soft/silky/dry/greasy/shiny **hair**
- long/short/shoulder-length/cropped **hair**
- a bald/balding/shaved **head**
- a receding **hairline**
- a bald **patch/spot**
- a side/center **part**

body

- a long/short/thick/slender/(disapproving) scrawny **neck**
- broad/narrow/sloping/rounded/hunched **shoulders**
- a bare/broad/muscular/small/large **chest**
- a flat/round/swollen/bulging **stomach**
- a small/tiny/narrow/slim/slender/28-inch **waist**
- big/wide/narrow/slim **hips**
- a straight/bent/arched/broad/hairy **back**
- thin/slender/muscular **arms**
- big/large/small/manicured/calloused/gloved **hands**
- long/short/fat/slender/delicate/bony **fingers**
- long/muscular/hairy/shapely/(both informal, often disapproving) skinny/spindly **legs**
- muscular/chubby/(informal, disapproving) flabby **thighs/calves**
- big/little/small/dainty/wide/narrow/bare **feet**
- a good/slim/slender/hourglass **figure**
- be of slim/medium/average/large/athletic/stocky **build**

ˌphysical eduˈcation (also phys. ed.) noun (abbr. P.E.) [U] sports and exercise that are taught in schools

ˌphysical geˈography noun [U] **1** the scientific study of the natural features on the surface of the earth, for example mountains and rivers **2** the way in which the natural features of a place are arranged: *the physical geography of Colorado*

phys·i·cal·i·ty /ˌfɪzɪˈkæləti/ noun [U] (formal) the quality of being physical rather than emotional or spiritual

phys·i·cally 🔑 **AWL** /ˈfɪzɪkli/ adv.
1 in a way that is connected with a person's body rather than their mind: *mentally and physically handicapped* ◆ *physically and emotionally exhausted* ◆ *I felt physically sick before the exam.* ◆ *I don't find him physically attractive.* ◆ *They were physically prevented from entering the building.*
2 according to the laws of nature or what is possible: *It's physically impossible to finish by the end of the week.*

ˌphysical ˈscience noun [U] (also the physical sciences [pl.]) the areas of science concerned with studying natural forces and things that are not alive, for example physics and chemistry ⟳ compare LIFE SCIENCES

ˌphysical ˈtherapist noun a person whose job is to give patients physical therapy

ˌphysical ˈtherapy noun [U] the treatment of disease, injury, or weakness in the joints or muscles by exercises, MASSAGE, and the use of light and heat

ˌphysical ˈtraining noun = PT

phy·si·cian /fəˈzɪʃn/ noun a doctor, especially one who is a specialist in general medicine and not SURGERY ⟳ compare SURGEON

phyˌsician's asˈsistant (also phyˌsician asˈsistant) noun (abbr. PA) a person who is qualified to assist a doctor and to do basic medical procedures

phys·i·cist /ˈfɪzəsɪst/ noun a scientist who studies physics: *a nuclear physicist*

phys·ics 🔑 /ˈfɪzɪks/ noun [U]
the scientific study of matter and energy and the relationships between them, including the study of forces, heat, light, sound, electricity, and the structure of atoms: *a degree in physics* ◆ *particle/nuclear/theoretical physics* ◆ *the laws of physics* ◆ *a school physics department* ◆ *to study the physics of the electron* ⟳ see also ASTROPHYSICS, GEOPHYSICS

physio- /ˈfɪziou/ combining form (in nouns, adjectives, and adverbs) **1** connected with nature **2** connected with PHYSIOLOGY

phys·i·og·no·my /ˌfɪziˈɑgnəmi; -ˈɑnəmi/ noun (pl. phys·i·og·no·mies) (formal) the shape and features of a person's face

phys·i·ol·o·gist /ˌfɪziˈɑlədʒɪst/ noun a scientist who studies physiology

phys·i·ol·o·gy /ˌfɪziˈɑlədʒi/ noun **1** [U] the scientific study of the normal functions of living things: *the department of anatomy and physiology* **2** [U, sing.] the way in which a particular living thing functions: *plant physiology* ◆ *the physiology of the horse* ▶ phys·i·o·log·i·cal /ˌfɪziəˈlɑdʒɪkl/ adj.: *the physiological effect of space travel* phys·i·o·log·i·cally /-kli/ adv.

phy·sique /fəˈzik/ noun [C, U] the size and shape of a person's body **SYN** BUILD: *He has the physique of a football player.* ◆ *a powerful physique*

pi /paɪ/ noun **1** (geometry) the symbol π used to show the RATIO of the CIRCUMFERENCE of (= distance around) a circle to its DIAMETER (= distance across), that is about 3.14159 **2** the 16th letter of the Greek alphabet (Π, π)

pi·a·nis·si·mo /ˌpiəˈnɪsəˌmou/ adv. (abbr. pp) (music) played or sung very quietly **ANT** FORTISSIMO ▶ pi·a·nis·si·mo adj.

pi·an·ist /piˈænɪst; ˈpiənɪst/ noun a person who plays the piano: *a concert pianist* ◆ *a jazz pianist*

pi·a·no 🔑 noun, adv.
• noun /piˈænou/ (pl. pi·a·nos) (also old-fashioned, formal pi·a·no·forte /piˌænəˈfɔrteɪ; piˈænəˌfɔrt/) a large musical instrument played by pressing the black and white keys on the keyboard. The sound is produced by small HAMMERS hitting the metal strings inside the piano: *to play the piano* ◆ *playing jazz on the piano* ◆ *piano music* ◆ *a piano teacher/lesson* ◆ *Ravel's piano concerto in G* ⟳ picture at INSTRUMENT ⟳ see also GRAND PIANO, UPRIGHT PIANO
• adv. /piˈɑnou/ (abbr. p.) (music) played or sung quietly **ANT** FORTE ▶ pi·a·no adj.

piˈano acˌcordion noun a type of ACCORDION that you press buttons and keys on to produce the different notes

Pi·a·no·la™ /ˌpiəˈnoulə/ noun a piano that plays automatically by means of a PIANO ROLL **SYN** PLAYER PIANO

piˈano ˌroll noun a roll of paper full of very small holes that controls the movement of the keys in a Pianola™

pi·az·za /piˈɑtsə/ noun a public square, especially in an Italian town

pic /pɪk/ noun (informal) a picture or movie

pi·ca /ˈpaɪkə/ noun (technical) a unit for measuring the size of printed letters and the length of a line of printed text

pi·can·te /pɪˈkɑnteɪ/ adj. (from Spanish) (of food) hot and spicy: *tortilla chips dipped in a picante sauce*

pic·a·resque /ˌpɪkəˈrɛsk/ adj. (formal) connected with literature that describes the adventures of a person who is sometimes dishonest but easy to like: *a picaresque novel*

pic·co·lo /ˈpɪkəˌlou/ noun (pl. pic·co·los) a musical instrument of the WOODWIND group, like a small FLUTE that plays high notes ➔ picture at INSTRUMENT

pick 🔑 /pɪk/ *verb, noun*

● *verb* **1** [T] to choose someone or something from a group of people or things: ~ *sb/sth Pick a number from one to twenty.* ◆ *She picked the best cake for herself.* ◆ *He* **picked his words** *carefully.* ◆ *Have I picked a bad time to talk to you?* ◆ ~ *sb/sth to do sth He has been picked to play in this week's game.* ➔ see also HANDPICKED ➔ thesaurus box at CHOOSE **2** [T] ~ *sth* to take flowers, fruit, etc. from the plant or the tree where they are growing: *to pick grapes* ◆ *flowers freshly picked from the garden* ◆ *to go blackberry picking* **3** [T] to pull or remove something or small pieces of something from something else, especially with your fingers: ~ *sth + adv./ prep. She picked bits of fluff from his sweater.* ◆ *He picked the nuts off the top of the cake.* ◆ ~ *sth to* **pick your nose** (= put your finger inside your nose to remove dried MUCUS) ◆ *to* **pick your teeth** (= use a small sharp piece of wood to remove pieces of food from your teeth) ◆ ~ *sth + adj. The dogs picked the bones clean* (= ate all the meat from the bones). **4** [I, T] ~ *(sth)* = PLUCK

IDM **pick and choose** to choose only those things that you like or want very much: *You have to take any job you can get— you can't pick and choose.* **pick sb's brains** (*informal*) to ask someone a lot of questions about something because they know more about the subject than you do **pick a fight/ quarrel (with sb)** to deliberately start a fight or an argument with someone **pick a lock** to open a lock without a key, using something such as a piece of wire **pick sb's pocket** to steal something from someone's pocket without them noticing ➔ related noun PICKPOCKET **pick up the bill, tab, etc. (for sth)** (*informal*) to pay for something: *The company picked up the tab for his hotel room.* **pick up the pieces** to return or to help someone return to a normal situation, particularly after a shock or a disaster: *You cannot live your children's lives for them; you can only be there to pick up the pieces when things go wrong.* **pick up speed** to go faster **pick up steam 1** (*informal*) to become gradually more powerful, active, etc.: *His election campaign is beginning to pick up steam.* **2** (of a vehicle) to increase speed gradually **pick up the threads** to return to an earlier situation or way of life after an interruption **pick your way (across, along, among, over, through sth)** to walk carefully, choosing the safest, driest, etc. place to put your feet: *She picked her way delicately over the rough ground.* **pick a winner 1** to choose a horse, etc. that you think is most likely to win a race **2** (*informal*) to make a very good choice ➔ more at BONE *n.*, HOLE *n.*, PIECE *n.*, SHRED *n.*

PHR V **'pick at sth 1** to eat food slowly, taking small amounts or bites because you are not hungry **2** to pull or touch something several times: *He tried to undo the knot by picking at it with his fingers.*

,**pick sb↔'off** (*informal*) to aim carefully at a person, an animal, or an aircraft, especially one of a group, and then shoot them: *Snipers were picking off innocent civilians.* ,**pick sth↔'off** to remove something from something such as a tree, a plant, etc.: *Pick off all the dead leaves.*

'**pick on sb/sth 1** to treat someone unfairly, by blaming, criticizing, or punishing them: *The other girls picked on her because of her size.* **2** to choose someone or something: *He picked on two of her statements that he said were untrue.*

,**pick sb/sth↔'out 1** to choose someone or something carefully from a group of people or things **SYN** SELECT: *She was picked out from dozens of applicants for the job.* ◆ *He picked out the ripest peach for me.* **2** to recognize someone or something from among other people or things: *See if you can pick me out in this photo.* ,**pick sth↔'out 1** to play a tune on a musical instrument slowly without using written music: *He picked out the tune on the piano with one finger.* **2** to discover or recognize something after careful study: *Read the play again and pick out the major themes.* **3** to make something easy to see or hear: *a sign painted yellow, with the lettering picked out in black*

,**pick sth↔'over** | ,**pick 'through sth** to examine a group of things carefully, especially to choose the ones you want:

Pick over the lentils and remove any little stones. ◆ *I picked over the facts of the case.*

,**pick 'up 1** to get better, stronger, etc. **SYN** IMPROVE: *Trade usually picks up in the spring.* ◆ *The wind is picking up now.* ◆ *Sales have picked up 14% this year.* ➔ related noun PICKUP **2** (*informal*) to start again; to continue: *Let's* **pick up where we left off** *yesterday.* **3** (*informal*) to put things away and make things neat, especially for someone else: *All I seem to do is cook, wash, and pick up after the kids.* ,**pick 'up** | ,**pick sth 'up** to answer a phone: *The phone rang and rang and nobody picked up.* ,**pick sb↔'up 1** to go somewhere in your car and get someone who is waiting for you: *I'll pick you up at five.* **2** to allow someone to get into your vehicle and take them somewhere: *The bus picks up passengers outside the airport.* **3** to rescue someone from the ocean or from a dangerous place, especially one that is difficult to reach: *A lifeboat picked up survivors.* **4** (*informal*, often *disapproving*) to start talking to someone you do not know because you want to have a sexual relationship with them: *He goes to clubs to pick up girls.* ➔ related noun PICKUP **5** (*informal*) (of the police) to arrest someone: *He was picked up by police and taken to the station for questioning.* **6** to make someone feel better: *Try this—it will pick you up.* ➔ related noun PICK-ME-UP ,**pick sb/ sth↔'up 1** to take hold of someone or something and lift them/it up: *She went over to the crying child and picked her up.* **2** to receive an electronic signal, sound, or picture: *We were able to pick up Voice of America.* 🔑 ,**pick sth↔'up 1** to get information or a skill by chance rather than by making a deliberate effort: *to pick up bad habits* ◆ *Here's a tip I picked up from my mother.* ◆ *She picked up Spanish when she was living in Mexico.* **2** to identify or recognize something: *Scientists can now pick up early signs of the disease.* **3** to get something from a place: *I picked up my coat from the cleaners.* ➔ related noun PICKUP **4** to buy something, especially cheaply or by chance: *We managed to pick up a few bargains at the auction.* **5** to get or obtain something: *I seem to have picked up a terrible cold from somewhere.* ◆ *I picked up $30 in tips today.* **6** to find and follow a route: *to pick up the scent of an animal* ◆ *We can pick up the interstate in a few miles.* **7** to return to an earlier subject or situation in order to continue it **SYN** TAKE UP: *He picks up this theme again in later chapters of the book.* **8** to notice something that is not very obvious; to see something that you are looking for: *I picked up the faint sound of a car in the distance.* **9** to put things away neatly: *Will you pick up all your toys?* **10** to put things away and make a room neat: *to pick up a room* ,**pick 'up on sth 1** to notice something and perhaps react to it: *She failed to pick up on the humor in his remark.* **2** to return to a point that has already been mentioned or discussed: *If I could just pick up on a question you raised earlier.* ,**pick yourself 'up** to stand up again after you have fallen: *He just picked himself up and went on running.* ◆ (*figurative*) *She didn't waste time feeling sorry for herself—she just picked herself up and carried on.*

● *noun* **1** [sing.] an act of choosing something: *Take your pick* (= choose). ◆ *The winner gets first pick of the prizes.* **2** [C] a person or thing that is chosen: *She was his pick for best actress.* ➔ thesaurus box at CHOICE **3** [sing.] **the ~ of sth** the best thing or things in a group: *We're reviewing the pick of this month's new books.* ◆ *I think we got* **the pick of the bunch** (= the best in the group). **4** [C] = PICKAX: *picks and shovels* **5** [C] a small piece of metal, plastic, etc. used for PLUCKING the strings of a GUITAR or similar instrument **SYN** PLECTRUM ➔ see also ICE PICK, TOOTHPICK

pick·ax (also **pick·axe**) /'pɪkæks/ *noun* a large heavy tool that has a curved metal bar with sharp ends fixed at the center to a wooden handle. It is used for breaking rocks or hard ground.

pick·er /'pɪkər/ *noun* a person or machine that picks flowers, vegetables, etc.: *cotton pickers*

pick·et /'pɪkət/ *noun, verb*
● *noun* **1** a group of people who stand outside the entrance to a building in order to protest about something, especially in order to stop people from entering a factory, etc. during a strike: *I was on picket duty at the time.* **2** = PICKETER: *Five pickets were arrested by police.* **3** a

| t tea | t̬ butter | d did | k cat | g got | tʃ chin | dʒ June | f fall |

soldier or group of soldiers guarding a military base **4** a pointed piece of wood that is fixed in the ground, especially as part of a fence: *a picket fence*

● **verb** [T, I] **~ (sth)** to stand outside somewhere such as your place of work to protest about something or to try and persuade people to join a strike: *200 workers were picketing the factory.* ◆ *Striking workers picketed outside the gates.*

pick·et·er /ˈpɪkətər/ *noun* a person who is picketing

pick·et·ing /ˈpɪkətɪŋ/ *noun* [U] the activity of standing outside the entrance to a building in order to protest about something and stop people from entering the building: *mass picketing of the factory*

ˈpicket ˌline *noun* a line or group of picketers: *Fire crews refused to cross the picket line.*

pick·ings /ˈpɪkɪŋz/ *noun* [pl.] something, especially money, that can be obtained from a particular situation in an easy or a dishonest way: *There were only **slim pickings** (= few opportunities and not much money) to be made at the fair.* ◆ *There are **rich pickings** (= financial benefits) to be had by investing in this sort of company.* ◆ *The strike affecting the country's largest airline is producing **easy pickings** for smaller companies.*

pick·le /ˈpɪkl/ *noun, verb*
● **noun** a small CUCUMBER that has been preserved in VINEGAR before being eaten
  IDM **in a pickle** (*informal*) in a difficult or unpleasant situation
● **verb** **~ sth** to preserve food in VINEGAR or salt water

pick·led /ˈpɪkld/ *adj.* **1** (of food) preserved in VINEGAR: *pickled cabbage/herring/onions* **2** (*old-fashioned, informal*) drunk

ˈpick-me-ˌup *noun* (*informal*) something that makes you feel better, happier, healthier, etc., especially medicine or an alcoholic drink: (*figurative*) *This deal would offer the best possible pick-me-up to the town's ailing economy.*

pick-off /ˈpɪkɔf; -ɑf/ *noun* (in baseball) a situation in which a player running out a BASE is out because a FIELDER or the PITCHER suddenly throws the ball to that base

pick·pock·et /ˈpɪkˌpɑkət/ *noun* a person who steals money, etc. from other people's pockets, especially in crowded places

pick·up /ˈpɪkʌp/ *noun, adj.*
● **noun** **1** (also **ˈpickup ˌtruck**) [C] a vehicle with low sides and no roof at the back, used, for example, by farmers ⇨ picture at TRUCK **2** [U, C] an occasion when someone or something is collected: *Goods are delivered not later than noon on the day after pickup.* **3** [C] **~ (in sth)** an improvement: *a pickup in the housing market* **4** [U] a vehicle's ability to ACCELERATE (= increase in speed) **5** [C] a person someone meets for the first time, for example in a bar, with whom they start a sexual relationship: *casual pickups* **6** [C] the part of a record player or musical instrument that changes electrical signals into sound, or sound into electrical signals
● **adj.** [only before noun] (of a sports game) often not planned in advance and that anyone who wants to can join in: *A group of kids started a pickup game of basketball on the street outside.*

pick·y /ˈpɪki/ *adj.* (*informal*) (of a person) liking only particular things and difficult to please **SYN** FUSSY: *a picky eater* ◆ *She's very picky about her clothes.*

ˌpick-your-ˈown *adj.* [only before noun] (of fruit or vegetables) picked by the customer on the farm where they are grown: *pick-your-own strawberries*

pic·nic /ˈpɪknɪk/ *noun, verb*
● **noun** **1** an occasion when people pack a meal and take it to eat outdoors, especially in the countryside: *It's a nice day. Let's go for a picnic.* ◆ *We had a picnic beside the river.* **2** the meal, usually consisting of SANDWICHES, salad, and fruit, etc. that you take with you when you go on a picnic: *Let's eat our picnic by the lake.* ◆ *a picnic lunch* ◆ *a picnic basket*
  IDM **be no picnic** (*informal*) to be difficult and cause a lot of

problems: *Bringing up a family when you're unemployed is no picnic.*

● **verb** (**-ck-**) [I] to have a picnic: *No picnicking allowed* (= on a sign)

pic·nick·er /ˈpɪknɪkər/ *noun* a person who is having a picnic

pico- /ˈpikoʊ/ /ˈpaɪkoʊ-/ *combining form* (in nouns; used in units of measurement) 10⁻¹²; one million millionth

pic·to·graph /ˈpɪktəˌgræf/ (also **pic·to·gram** /ˈpɪktəˌgræm/) *noun* **1** a picture representing a word or phrase **2** a diagram that uses pictures to represent amounts or numbers of a particular thing

pic·to·ri·al /pɪkˈtɔriəl/ *adj.* [usually before noun] **1** using or containing pictures: *a pictorial account/record of the expedition* **2** connected with pictures: *pictorial traditions*
  ▸ **pic·to·ri·al·ly** *adv.*

pic·ture ✎ /ˈpɪktʃər/ *noun, verb*
● **noun**
> **PAINTING/DRAWING 1** [C] a painting or drawing, etc. that shows a scene, person, or thing: *A picture of flowers hung on the wall.* ◆ *The children were **drawing pictures** of their pets.* ◆ *She wanted a famous artist to **paint her picture** (= a picture of herself).* ◆ *a book with lots of pictures in it*
> **PHOTOGRAPH 2** [C] a photograph: *We had our **picture taken** in front of the hotel.* ◆ *The picture shows the couple together on their yacht.* ◆ *Do you have any pictures of your trip?* ⇨ thesaurus box at PHOTOGRAPH
> **ON TV 3** [C] an image on a television screen: *harrowing television pictures of the famine* ◆ *satellite pictures* ◆ *The picture isn't very clear tonight.*
> **DESCRIPTION 4** [C, usually sing.] a description that gives you an idea in your mind of what something is like: *The writer paints a gloomy picture of the economy.* ◆ *The police are trying to **build up a picture** of what happened.*
> **MENTAL IMAGE 5** [C, usually sing.] a mental image or memory of something: *I have a vivid picture of my grandfather smiling down at me when I was very small.*
> **GENERAL SITUATION 6 the picture** [sing.] the general situation concerning someone or something: *Just a few years ago the picture was very different.* ◆ *The overall picture for farming is encouraging.*
> **MOVIE 7** [C] a movie: *The movie won nine Academy Awards, including Best Picture.* ◆ *I believe her husband's **in pictures** (= he acts in movies or works in the industry).* ⇨ see also MOTION PICTURE **8 the pictures** [pl.] (*old-fashioned, informal*) the movies: *Shall we go to the pictures tonight?*
  IDM **be/look a picture** to look very beautiful or special **be the picture of health/guilt/misery, etc.** (*informal*) to look extremely healthy, guilty, etc. **get the picture** (*informal*) to understand a situation, especially one that someone is describing to you: *"I pretended that I hadn't heard." "I get the picture."* **in/out of the picture** (*informal*) involved/not involved in a situation: *Morris is likely to win, with Jones out of the picture now.* **put/keep sb in the picture** (*informal*) to give someone the information they need in order to understand a situation: *Just to put you in the picture—there have been a number of changes here recently.* ⇨ more at BIG *adj.*, PAINT *v.*, PRETTY *adj.*

● **verb**
> **IMAGINE 1** to imagine someone or something; to create an image of someone or something in your mind: **~ sb/sth** *I can still picture the house I grew up in.* ◆ **~ sb/sth as sth** *We found it hard to picture him as the father of teenage sons.* ◆ **~ sb/sth doing sth** *When he did not come home she pictured him lying dead on the roadside somewhere.* ◆ **~ what, how, etc....** *I tried to picture what it would be like to live alone.*
> **DESCRIBE 2** [often passive] **~ sb/sth as sth** to describe or present someone or something in a particular way **SYN** PORTRAY: *Before the trial Liz had been pictured as a frail woman dominated by her husband.*
> **SHOW IN PHOTOGRAPH 3** [usually passive] to show someone or something in a photograph or picture: **~ sb/sth (+ adv./prep/adj.)** *She is pictured here with her parents.* ◆ **~ sb/sth**

doing sth *The team is pictured setting off on their European tour.*

THESAURUS

picture

painting ♦ drawing ♦ portrait ♦ print ♦ sketch

These are all words for a scene, person, or thing that has been represented on paper by drawing, painting, etc.

picture a scene, person, or thing that has been represented on paper using a pencil, a pen, or paint: *The children were drawing pictures of their pets.*

painting a picture that has been made using paint: *a collection of paintings by Native American artists*

drawing a picture that has been made using a pencil or a pen, not paint: *a pencil/charcoal drawing*

portrait a painting, drawing, or photograph of a person, especially of the head and shoulders: *Vermeer's "Portrait of the Artist in his Studio"* ♦ *a self-portrait* (= a painting that you do of yourself)

print a picture that has been copied from a painting using photography: *a Renoir print*

sketch a simple picture that is drawn quickly and does not have many details: *I usually do a few very rough sketches before I start on a painting.*

PATTERNS

- to **draw** a picture/portrait/sketch
- to **paint** a picture/portrait
- to **make** a painting/drawing/portrait/print/sketch
- to **do** a painting/drawing/portrait/sketch

'picture ˌbook *noun* a book with a lot of pictures, especially one for children

'picture ˌmessaging *noun* [U] a system of sending images from one cell phone to another **SYN** EMS

ˌpicture-'perfect *adj.* exactly right in appearance or in the way things are done

ˌpicture 'postcard *noun* (*old-fashioned*) a POSTCARD with a picture on one side

ˌpicture-'postcard *adj.* [only before noun] (of places) very pretty: *a picture-postcard village*

'picture ˌrail *noun* a narrow strip of wood attached to the walls of a room below the ceiling and used for hanging pictures from

pic·tur·esque /ˌpɪktʃəˈrɛsk/ *adj.* **1** (of a place, building, scene, etc.) pretty, especially in a way that looks old-fashioned **SYN** QUAINT: *a picturesque cottage/setting/village* **2** (of language) producing strong mental images by using unusual words: *a picturesque description of life at sea* ▸ **pic·tur·esque·ly** *adv.*: *The inn is picturesquely situated on the banks of the river.*

ˌpicture 'window *noun* a very large window made of a single piece of glass

pid·dle /ˈpɪdl/ *verb* [I] (*old-fashioned, informal*) to URINATE

pid·dling /ˈpɪdlɪŋ/ *adj.* [only before noun] (*informal, disapproving*) small and unimportant **SYN** TRIVIAL

pidg·in /ˈpɪdʒən/ *noun* [U] **1** a simple form of a language, especially English, Portuguese, or Dutch, with a limited number of words, which are used together with words from a local language. It is used when people who do not speak the same language to talk to each other. **2** Pidgin = TOK PISIN **3** ~ **English, French, Japanese, etc.** a way of speaking a language that uses simple words and forms, used when a person does not speak the language well, or when they are talking to someone who does not speak the language well: *I tried to get my message across in my pidgin Italian.*

pie /paɪ/ *noun* [C, U] a baked dish of fruit or meat and vegetables with PASTRY on the bottom, sides, and top: *a*

slice of apple pie ♦ Help yourself to some more pie. ♦ a pie dish ⊃ see also CUSTARD PIE, POT PIE, SHEPHERD'S PIE
IDM **a piece/slice/share of the pie** a share of something such as money, profits, etc. **pie in the sky** (*informal*) an event that someone talks about that seems very unlikely to happen: *This talk of moving to Australia is all just pie in the sky.* ⊃ more at AMERICAN *adj.*, EASY *adj.*, EAT, FINGER *n.*, NICE

pie·bald /ˈpaɪbɔld/ *adj.* (of a horse) with areas on it of two colors, usually black and white **SYN** PINTO ⊃ compare SKEWBALD

piece 🔑 /pis/ *noun, verb*

● *noun*

▸ SEPARATE AMOUNT **1** [C] ~ **(of sth)** (used especially with *of* and uncountable nouns) an amount of something that has been cut or separated from the rest of it; a standard amount of something: *a piece of string/wood* ♦ *She wrote something on a small piece of paper.* ♦ *a large piece of land* ♦ *a piece of cake/cheese/meat* ♦ *He cut the pizza into bite-sized pieces.* ♦ *I've got a piece of grit in my eye.*

▸ PART **2** [C, usually pl.] one of the bits or parts that something breaks into: *There were tiny pieces of glass all over the road.* ♦ *The boat had been smashed to pieces on the rocks.* ♦ *The vase lay in pieces on the floor.* **3** [C] one of the parts that something is made of: *He took the clock to pieces.* ♦ *a missing piece of the puzzle* ♦ *The bridge was taken down piece by piece.* ♦ *a 500-piece jigsaw puzzle* ⊃ see also ONE-PIECE, TWO-PIECE, THREE-PIECE

▸ SINGLE ITEM **4** [C] (used especially with *of* and uncountable nouns) a single item of a particular type, especially one that forms part of a set: *a piece of clothing/furniture/luggage* ♦ *a piece of equipment/machinery* ♦ *a 28-piece dinner service* **5** [C] ~ **of sth** used with many uncountable nouns to describe a single example or an amount of something: *a piece of advice/information/news* ♦ *an interesting piece of research* ♦ *Isn't that a piece of luck?* **6** [C] ~ **(of sth)** a single item of writing, art, music, etc. that someone has produced or created: *a piece of art/music/poetry, etc.* ♦ *They performed pieces by Bach and Handel.* ♦ (*formal*) *They have some beautiful pieces* (= works of art, etc.) *in their home.* ⊃ see also MASTER-PIECE, MUSEUM PIECE, PARTY PIECE, PERIOD PIECE, SHOW-PIECE

▸ NEWS ARTICLE **7** [C] an article in a newspaper or magazine, or a broadcast on television or radio: *Did you see her piece about the Internet in the paper today?* ⊃ see also SET PIECE

▸ COIN **8** [C] a coin of the value mentioned: *a five-cent piece*

▸ IN CHESS, ETC. **9** [C] one of the small figures or objects that you move around in games such as CHESS

▸ SHARE OF SOMETHING **10** [sing.] ~ **of sth** a part or share of something: *companies seeking a piece of the market*

▸ GUN **11** [C] (*slang*) a gun

▸ DISTANCE **12** **a piece** [sing.] (*old-fashioned, informal*) a short distance: *She lives down the road a piece from here.* **HELP** You will find other compounds ending in **piece** at their place in the alphabet.

IDM **a/some piece of work** (*informal*) used to express the fact that you admire someone or find them amusing, often when they have done something that surprises you: *She's a real piece of work.* ♦ *You're some piece of work, Jack, do you know that?* **fall to pieces 1** (usually used in the progressive tenses) (of things) to become very old and in bad condition because of long use **SYN** FALL APART: *Our car is falling to pieces, we've had it so long.* **2** (of a person, an organization, a plan, etc.) to stop working; to be destroyed: *He's worried the business will fall to pieces without him.* **give sb a piece of your mind** (*informal*) to tell someone that you disapprove of their behavior or are angry with them **go to pieces** (*informal*) (of a person) to be so upset or afraid that you cannot manage to live or work normally **(all) in one piece** (*informal*) safe; not damaged or hurt, especially after a journey or dangerous experience: *They were lucky to get home in one piece.* **(all) of a piece** (*formal*) **1** all the same or similar: *The houses are all of a piece.* **2** all at the same time: *The house was built all of a piece in 1854.* **pick/pull/tear sb/sth to pieces/shreds** (*informal*) to criticize someone, or their work or ideas, very severely **a piece of the action**

(*informal*) a share or role in an interesting or exciting activity, especially in order to make money: *Foreign firms will all want a piece of the action if the new airport goes ahead.* **a piece of cake** (*informal*) a thing that is very easy to do ⊃ more at BIT, PICK *v.*, PIE, SAY *v.*, VILLAIN

VOCABULARY BUILDING

Pieces of things

If you want to talk about a small amount or one example of something that is normally an uncountable noun, there is a range of words you can use. You must choose the right one to go with the substance you are talking about.

- **Piece** is a very general word and can be used with most uncountable nouns: *a piece of paper/wood/string/cake/fruit/meat/work/research/advice*
- **Bit** can be used with abstract uncountable nouns: *a bit of luck/confidence/attention*
- A **slice** is a thin, flat piece: *a slice of bread/cake/salami/cheese/pie/apple* ♦ (*figurative*) *a slice of life*
- A **chunk** is a thick, solid piece: *a chunk of cheese/bread/rock* ♦ *a chunk of land* (= a fairly large piece)
- A **lump** is a piece of something solid without any particular shape: *a lump of coal/clay*
- A **fragment** is a very small piece of something that is broken or damaged: *fragments of glass* ♦ (*figurative*) *fragments of conversation*. It can also be used with countable nouns to mean a small part of something: *a fragment of the story*
- A **speck** is a tiny piece of powder: *a speck of dust/dirt* You can also say: *a speck of light*
- **Drop** is used with liquids: *a drop of water/rain/blood/milk/whiskey*
- A **pinch** is as much as you can hold between your finger and thumb: *a pinch of salt/cinnamon*
- A **portion** is enough for one person: *a portion of chicken*

● **verb**
PHR V ˌpiece sth↔toˈgether **1** to understand a story, situation, etc. by taking all the facts and details about it and putting them together: *Police are trying to piece together the last hours of her life.* **2** to put the separate parts of something together to make a complete whole **SYN** ASSEMBLE: *to piece together a jigsaw puzzle*

pi·èce de ré·sist·ance /ˌpyes də ˌreɪzɪ'stɑns/ *noun* [usually sing.] (*pl.* **pi·èces de ré·sist·ance** /ˌpyes də ˌreɪzɪ'stɑns/) (from *French*) the most important or impressive part of a group or series of things

piece·meal /'pismil/ *adj.* [usually before noun] (often *disapproving*) done or happening gradually at different times and often in different ways, rather than carefully planned at the beginning: *a piecemeal approach to dealing with the problem* ♦ *piecemeal changes* ▶ **piece·meal** *adv.*: *The reforms were implemented piecemeal.*

ˌpiece of ˈeight *noun* (*pl.* ˌpieces of ˈeight) an old Spanish coin

ˌpiece rate *noun* an amount of money paid for each thing or amount of something that a worker produces

piece·work /'piswɜrk/ *noun* [U] work that is paid for by the amount done and not by the hours worked ▶ **piece·work·er** *noun*

ˈpie chart *noun* a diagram consisting of a circle that is divided into sections to show the size of particular amounts in relation to the whole ⊃ picture at GRAPH

ˈpie crust (also **pie·crust** /'paɪkrʌst/) *noun* [C, U] the baked PASTRY that is under and sometimes over the contents of a pie

pied /paɪd/ *adj.* (especially of birds) of two or more different colors, especially black and white

pied-à-terre /ˌpyeɪd ə 'ter/ *noun* (*pl.* **pieds-à-terre** /ˌpyeɪd ə-/) (from *French*) a small apartment, usually in a city, that you do not live in as your main home but keep for use when necessary

ˌPied ˈPiper *noun* a person who persuades a lot of other people to follow them or do something with them **ORIGIN** From the old German story of the Pied Piper of Hamelin, who made first rats and later children follow him by playing beautiful music on his pipe.

ˈpie-eyed *adj.* (*informal*) very drunk

pier /pɪr/ *noun* **1** a long low structure built in a lake, river, or the ocean and joined to the land at one end, used by boats to allow passengers to get on and off **SYN** DOCK **2** a long structure built in the ocean and joined to the land at one end, often with places of entertainment on it **3** (*technical*) a large strong piece of wood, metal, or stone that is used to support a roof, wall, bridge, etc.

pierce /pɪrs/ *verb* **1** [T, I] to make a small hole in something, or to go through something, with a sharp object: **~ sth** *The arrow pierced his shoulder.* ♦ *He pierced another hole in his belt with his knife.* ♦ *to have your ears/nose, etc. pierced* (= to have a small hole made in your ears/nose so that you can wear jewelry there) ♦ **~ sb** (*figurative*) *She was pierced to the heart with guilt.* ♦ **~ through sth** *The knife pierced through his coat.* **2** [T, I] **~ (through) sth** (*literary*) (of light, sound, etc.) to be suddenly seen or heard: *Sirens pierced the silence of the night.* ♦ *Shafts of sunlight pierced the heavy mist.* **3** [T, I] **~ (through) sth** to force a way through a barrier **SYN** PENETRATE: *They failed to pierce the Steelers defense.*

pierc·ing /'pɪrsɪŋ/ *adj., noun*
● *adj.* **1** [usually before noun] (of eyes or the way they look at someone) seeming to notice things about another person that would not normally be noticed, especially in a way that makes that person feel anxious or embarrassed: *She looked at me with piercing blue eyes.* ♦ *a piercing look* **2** [usually before noun] (of sounds) very high, loud, and unpleasant **SYN** SHRILL: *a piercing shriek* ♦ *She has such a piercing voice.* **3** [only before noun] (of feelings) affecting you very strongly, especially in a way that causes you pain: *piercing sadness* **4** (of the wind or cold) very strong and feeling as if it can pass through your clothes and skin **5** [only before noun] sharp and able to make a hole in something: *The animal is covered in long piercing spines.* ▶ **pierc·ing·ly** *adv.*: *His eyes were piercingly blue.* ♦ *The weather remained piercingly cold.*
● *noun* **1** [U] = BODY PIERCING **2** [C] the hole that is made in your ear, nose, or some other part of your body so that you can wear jewelry there: *She has a tongue piercing.*

Pi·er·rot /ˌpiə'rou/ *noun* a male character in traditional French plays, with a sad white face and a pointed hat

pie·tà /pyer'tɑ/ *noun* (*art*) a picture or SCULPTURE of the Virgin Mary holding the dead body of Christ

pi·e·ty /'paɪəti/ *noun* [U] the state of having or showing a deep respect for someone or something, especially for God and religion; the state of being PIOUS

pig /pɪg/ *noun, verb*

● *noun* **1** (also **hog**) an animal with pink, black, or brown skin, short legs, a broad nose, and a short tail which curls around itself. Pigs are kept on farms for their meat (called PORK) or live in the wild: *a pig farmer* ♦ *Pigs were grunting and squealing in the yard.* ⊃ see also BOAR, GUINEA PIG, PIGLET, SOW², SWINE **2** (*informal, disapproving*) an unpleasant or offensive person; a person who is dirty or GREEDY: *Arrogant pig!* ♦ *Don't be such a pig!* ♦ *The greedy pig's eaten all the cookies!* ♦ *She made a pig of herself with the ice cream* (= ate too much). ♦ *He's a real male chauvinist pig* (= a man who does not think women are equal to men). **3** (*slang*) an offensive word for a police officer
IDM (buy) a pig in a poke if you **buy a pig in a poke**, you buy something without seeing it or knowing if it is good enough **when pigs fly** (*ironic, saying*) used to show that you do not believe something will ever happen: *"With any luck, we'll be finished tomorrow." "Yeah, when pigs fly!"*
● *verb* (-gg-)
PHR V ˌpig ˈout (on sth) (*informal*) to eat too much food: *They pigged out on pizza.*

---

pi·geon /ˈpɪdʒən/ *noun* a fat gray and white bird with short legs. Pigeons are common in cities and also live in woods and fields where people shoot them for sport or food: *the sound of pigeons cooing* ➔ compare DOVE¹ ➔ see also CARRIER PIGEON, HOMING PIGEON

pigeon

pi·geon·hole /ˈpɪdʒən-ˌhoʊl/ *noun, verb*
- **noun 1** one of a set of small boxes that are fixed on a wall and open at the front, used for putting letters, messages, etc. in; one of a similar set of boxes that are part of a desk, used for keeping papers, documents, etc. in **2** (*disapproving*) a group or type that someone or something is considered or described as belonging to, even when this is not accurate or not fair and does not take account of their individual qualities: *She doesn't fit into a convenient musical pigeonhole.* ♦ *Those were the ethnic pigeonholes we put people in then.*
- **verb** ~ **sb (as sth)** (*disapproving*) to decide that someone belongs to a particular group or type without thinking deeply enough about it and considering what other qualities they might have **SYN** CATEGORIZE, LABEL: *He has been pigeonholed as a children's writer.*

pigeon-ˌtoed *adj.* having feet that point toward each other and not straight forward

pig·ger·y /ˈpɪɡəri/ *noun* (*pl.* **pig·ger·ies**) a place where pigs are kept or bred

pig·gy /ˈpɪɡi/ *noun* (*pl.* **pig·gies**) a child's word for a pig

pig·gy·back /ˈpɪɡiˌbæk/ *noun, verb*
- **noun** a ride on someone's back, while he or she is walking: *Give me a piggyback, Daddy!* ♦ *a piggyback ride* ▶ **pig·gy·back** *adv.: to ride piggyback*
- **verb**
  PHR V **ˈpiggyback on sb/sth** to use something that already exists as a support for your own work; to use a larger organization, etc. for your own advantage

ˈpiggy ˌbank *noun* a container in the shape of a pig, with a narrow opening in the top for putting coins in, used by children to save money

pig·head·ed /ˈpɪɡˌhɛdəd/ *adj.* unwilling to change your opinion about something, in a way that other people think is annoying and unreasonable **SYN** OBSTINATE, STUBBORN ▶ **pig·head·ed·ness** *noun* [U]

ˌpig-ˈignorant *adj.* (*informal*) very stupid or badly educated

ˈpig ˌiron *noun* [U] a form of iron that is not pure

pig·let /ˈpɪɡlət/ *noun* a young pig

pig·ment /ˈpɪɡmənt/ *noun* [U, C] **1** a substance that exists naturally in people, animals, and plants and gives their skin, leaves, etc. a particular color **2** a colored powder that is mixed with a liquid to produce paint, etc.

pig·men·ta·tion /ˌpɪɡmənˈteɪʃn/ *noun* [U] the presence of pigments in skin, hair, leaves, etc. that causes them to be a particular color

pig·men·ted /ˈpɪɡmɛntəd/ *adj.* (especially of skin) having a natural color

pig·my = PYGMY

pig·pen /ˈpɪɡpɛn/ (also **pig·sty** /ˈpɪɡstaɪ/ *pl.* **pig·sties**) *noun* **1** [C] a small building or a closed-in area where pigs are kept **2** [sing.] (*informal*) a very dirty or messy place

pig·skin /ˈpɪɡskɪn/ *noun* **1** [sing.] (*informal*) the ball used in football **2** [U] leather made from the skin of a pig

pig·tail /ˈpɪɡteɪl/ *noun* hair that is tied together into two bunches and sometimes twisted into BRAIDS, worn one on each side of the head: *She wore her hair in pigtails.* ➔ picture at HAIR ➔ compare PONYTAIL

pike /paɪk/ *noun* **1** (*pl.* **pike**) a large FRESHWATER fish with

very sharp teeth **2** a weapon with a sharp blade on a long wooden handle, used in the past by soldiers on foot **3** = TURNPIKE

IDM **come down the pike** (*informal*) to happen; to become noticeable: *We're hearing a lot about new inventions coming down the pike.*

pi·laf /ˈpilaf; pɪˈlaf/ *noun* [U, C] a hot, spicy, Eastern dish of rice and vegetables, and often pieces of meat or fish

pi·las·ter /pəˈlæstər/ *noun* (*technical*) a flat column that sticks out from the wall of a building, used as decoration

Pi·la·tes /pəˈlɑtiz/ *noun* [U] a system of stretching and pushing exercises using special equipment, which help make your muscles stronger and make you able to bend parts of your body more easily

pile /paɪl/ *noun, verb*
- **noun 1** [C] a number of things that have been placed on top of each other: *a pile of books/clothes/bricks* ♦ *He arranged the documents in neat piles.* ♦ *She looked in horror at the mounting pile of letters on her desk.* **2** [C] a mass of something that is high in the middle and wider at the bottom than at the top **SYN** HEAP: *a pile of sand* ♦ *piles of dirty laundry* **3** [C, usually pl.] ~ **of sth** (*informal*) a lot of something: *I have piles of work to do.* ♦ *He walked out leaving a pile of debts behind him.* **4** [U, sing.] the short threads, pieces of wool, etc. that form the soft surface of carpets and some types of cloth such as VELVET: *a deep-pile carpet* **5** [C] a large wooden, metal, or stone post that is fixed into the ground and used to support a building, bridge, etc.

IDM **(at the) bottom/top of the pile** in the least/most important position in a group of people or things **make a pile (of money)/make your pile** (*informal*) to make a lot of money
- **verb 1** [T] to put things one on top of another; to form a pile: ~ **sth** *She piled the boxes one on top of the other.* ♦ *The clothes were piled high on the chair.* ♦ ~ **sth up** *Snow was piled up against the door.* **2** [T] to put something on/into something; to load something with something: ~ **A with B** *The sofa was piled high with cushions.* ♦ *He piled his plate with as much food as he could.* ♦ ~ **B on(to) A** *He piled as much food as he could onto his plate.* ♦ ~ **B in(to) A** *She piled everything into her suitcase.* ➔ see also STOCKPILE **3** [I] + **adv./prep.** (*informal*) (of a number of people) to go somewhere quickly without order or control: *The coach finally arrived and we all piled on.*
  PHR V **ˈpile on** (especially of a person's weight) to increase quickly: *The weight just piled on while I was abroad.* **ˌpile sth↔ˈon 1** to make something increase rapidly: *The team piled on the points in the first half of the game.* ♦ *I've been piling on the pounds* (= I have put on weight) *recently.* **2** to express a feeling in a much stronger way than is necessary: *Don't pile on the drama!* ♦ *Things aren't really that bad—she does tend to pile it on.* **3** to give someone more or too much of something: *The Canadian team piled on the pressure in the last 15 minutes.* **ˌpile sth ˈon(to) sb** to give someone a lot of something to do, carry, etc.: *He felt his boss was piling too much work on him.* **ˌpile ˈup** to become larger in quantity or amount **SYN** ACCUMULATE: *Work always piles up at the end of the year.*

ˈpile ˌdriver *noun* **1** (*informal*) a very heavy kick or blow **2** a machine for forcing heavy posts into the ground

pile·up /ˈpaɪlʌp/ *noun* a road accident involving several vehicles crashing into one another: *Three people died in a multiple pileup in freezing fog.*

pil·fer /ˈpɪlfər/ *verb* [I, T] to steal things of little value or in small quantities, especially from the place where you work: ~ **(from sb/sth)** *He was caught pilfering.* ♦ ~ **sth (from sb/sth)** *She regularly pilfered stamps from work.* ▶ **pil·fer·age** /ˈpɪlfərɪdʒ/ *noun* [U] (*formal*): *pilferage of goods* **pil·fer·er** *noun*: *Certain types of goods are preferred by pilferers.* **pil·fer·ing** *noun* [U]: *We know that pilfering goes on.*

pil·grim /ˈpɪlɡrəm/ *noun* **1** a person who travels to a holy place for religious reasons: *Muslim pilgrims on their way to Mecca* ♦ *Christian pilgrims visiting Lourdes* **2 Pilgrim** a member of the group of English people (**the Pilgrim**

Fathers) who sailed to America on the ship *The Mayflower* in 1620 and started a COLONY in Massachusetts

pil·grim·age /'pɪlgrəmɪdʒ/ *noun* [C, U] **1** a journey to a holy place for religious reasons: *to go on/make a pilgrimage* ⊃ collocations at RELIGION **2** a journey to a place that is connected with someone or something that you admire or respect: *His grave has become a **place of pilgrimage.***

pill /pɪl/ *noun, verb*
• *noun* **1** [C] a small round piece of medicine that you swallow without chewing it: *a vitamin pill* ⊃ see also PEP PILL, SLEEPING PILL **2 the pill** or **the Pill** [sing.] a pill that some women take to prevent them becoming pregnant: *the contraceptive pill* ◆ *to be/go **on the pill*** ⊃ see also MORNING-AFTER PILL **3** [C] (*informal*) an annoying person
  IDM **sugar/sweeten the pill** to do something that makes an unpleasant situation seem less unpleasant SYN SUGAR-COAT ⊃ more at BITTER
• *verb* [I] (of a piece of clothing, especially one made of wool) to become covered in very small balls of FIBER

pil·lage /'pɪlɪdʒ/ *verb* [I, T] to steal things from a place or region, especially in a war, using violence SYN PLUNDER: *The rebels went looting and pillaging.* ◆ *~ sth The town had been pillaged and burned.* ◆ *~ sth from sth Works of art were pillaged from churches and museums.* ▶ **pil·lage** *noun* [U]: *They brought back horrific accounts of murder and pillage.*
pil·lag·er *noun* ⊃ compare LOOT, PLUNDER

pil·lar /'pɪlər/ *noun* **1** a large round stone, metal, or wooden post that is used to support a bridge, the roof of a building, etc., especially when it is also decorative **2** a large round stone, metal, or wooden post that is built to remind people of a famous person or event SYN COLUMN **3** *~ of sth* a mass of something that is shaped like a pillar: *a pillar of smoke/rock* **4** *~ of sth* a strong supporter of something; an important member of something: *a pillar of the Church* ◆ *a pillar of society* **5** *~ of sth* a person who has a lot of a particular quality: *She is a **pillar of strength** in a crisis.* **6** a basic part or feature of a system, organization, belief, etc.: *the central pillar of this theory*
  IDM **be driven, pushed, etc. from pillar to post** to be forced to go from one person or situation to another without achieving anything

pil·lared /'pɪlərd/ *adj.* [only before noun] (of a building or part of a building) having pillars

pill·box /'pɪlbɑks/ *noun* **1** a small shelter for soldiers, often partly underground, from which a gun can be fired **2** a small box for storing pills: *When she travels, she takes a few aspirin in a pillbox.*

pil·lion /'pɪlyən/ *noun* a seat for a passenger behind the driver of a motorcycle: *a pillion passenger/seat* ▶ **pil·lion** *adv.*: *to ride pillion*

pil·lo·ry /'pɪləri/ *verb, noun*
• *verb* (pil·lo·ries, pil·lo·ry·ing, pil·lo·ried, pil·lo·ried) [often passive] *~ sb* to criticize someone strongly in public: *He was regularly pilloried by the press for his radical ideas.*
• *noun* (*pl.* pil·lo·ries) a wooden frame, with holes for the head and hands, which people were locked into in the past as a punishment ⊃ compare STOCK

pil·low /'pɪloʊ/ *noun, verb*
• *noun* **1** a square or rectangular (RECTANGLE) piece of cloth filled with soft material, used to rest your head on in bed: *She lay back against the pillows.* ◆ *pillow talk* (= conversations in bed between lovers) ◆ *He lay on the grass using his backpack as a pillow.* **2** = CUSHION ⊃ see also THROW PILLOW
• *verb ~ sth* (+ *adv./prep.*) (*literary*) to rest something, especially your head, on an object: *She lay on the grass, her head pillowed on her arms.*

pil·low·case /'pɪloʊˌkeɪs/ (also pil·low·slip /'pɪloʊˌslɪp/) *noun* a cloth cover for a PILLOW, that can be removed

pi·lot /'paɪlət/ *noun, verb, adj.*
• *noun* **1** a person who operates the controls of an aircraft, especially as a job: *an airline pilot* ◆ *a fighter pilot* ◆ *The*

accident was caused by pilot error. ⊃ see also AUTOPILOT , CO-PILOT, TEST PILOT **2** a person with special knowledge of a difficult area of water, for example the entrance to a HARBOR, whose job is to guide ships through it **3** a single television program that is made in order to find out whether people will like it and want to watch further programs **4** = PILOT LIGHT
• *verb* **1** *~ sth* to fly an aircraft or guide a ship; to act as a pilot: *The plane was piloted by the instructor.* ◆ *The captain piloted the boat into a mooring.* **2** *~ sth (through sth)* to guide someone or something somewhere, especially through a complicated place or system: *She piloted a bill on the rights of part-time workers through Congress.* **3** *~ sth* to test a new product, idea, etc. with a few people or in a small area before it is introduced everywhere
• *adj.* [only before noun] done on a small scale in order to see if something is successful enough to do on a large scale: *a pilot project/study/survey* ◆ *a pilot episode* (= of a radio or television series)

'pilot ˌlight (also pilot) *noun* a small flame that burns all the time, for example on a gas BOILER, and lights a larger flame when the gas is turned on

'pilot ˌwhale *noun* a small WHALE that lives in warm seas

Pilsner (also Pilsener) /'pɪlznər; 'pɪls-/ (also Pils /pɪlz; pɪls/) *noun* [U] a type of strong, light-colored beer originally made in what is now the Czech Republic

PIM /pɪm/ /ˌpi aɪ ˈɛm/ *abbr.* PERSONAL INFORMATION MANAGER

Pi·ma /'pimə/ *noun* (*pl.* Pi·ma or Pi·mas) *noun* a member of a Native American people, many of whom live in the state of Arizona

pi·men·to /pə'mɛntoʊ/ *noun* (*pl.* pi·men·tos) a small red PEPPER with a mild taste

pimp /pɪmp/ *noun, verb*
• *noun* a man who controls PROSTITUTES and lives on the money that they earn
• *verb* **1** [I] *~ (for sb)* to get customers for a PROSTITUTE **2** [T] (*informal*) to add things to something to make it look or sound better, especially by making it more individual: *~ sth Pimp your car with stylish custom wheels!* ◆ *~ sth up I would love to pimp the songs up.*

pim·per·nel /'pɪmpərˌnɛl/ *noun* a small wild plant with red, white, or blue flowers

pim·ple /'pɪmpl/ *noun* a small, raised, red spot on the skin ⊃ compare SPOT ⊃ see also GOOSE PIMPLES ▶ **pim·ply** /'pɪmpli/ *adj.*: *pimply skin* ◆ *a pimply youth*

PIN /pɪn/ (also 'PIN ˌnumber) *noun* the abbreviation for "personal identification number" (a number given to you, for example by a bank, so that you can use a plastic card to take out money from an ATM (= a cash machine))

pin /pɪn/ *noun, verb*
• *noun*
  ⟩ FOR FASTENING/JOINING **1** a short thin piece of stiff wire with a sharp point at one end and a round head at the other, used especially for fastening together pieces of cloth when sewing ⊃ see also BOBBY PIN, HAIRPIN, HATPIN, LINCHPIN, PINS AND NEEDLES, SAFETY PIN
  ⟩ JEWELRY **2** a piece of jewelry with a pin on the back of it, that can be fastened to your clothes SYN BROOCH **3** a short thin piece of stiff wire with a sharp point at one end and an item of decoration at the other, worn as jewelry: *a diamond pin* ⊃ picture at JEWELRY ⊃ see also TIEPIN
  ⟩ BADGE **4** a type of BADGE that is fastened with a pin at the back: *He supports the group and wears its pin on his lapel.*
  ⟩ MEDICAL **5** a piece of steel used to support a bone in your body when it has been broken
  ⟩ ELECTRICAL **6** one of the metal parts that stick out of an electric plug: *a 2-pin plug*
  ⟩ IN GAMES **7** a wooden or plastic object that is shaped like a bottle and that players try to knock down in games such as BOWLING ⊃ picture at HOBBY ⊃ see also TENPIN
  ⟩ IN GOLF **8** a stick with a flag on top of it, placed in a hole so that players can see where they are aiming for

> LEGS **9** pins [pl.] (*informal*) a person's legs
> ON SMALL BOMB **10** a small piece of metal on a HAND GRENADE that stops it from exploding and is pulled out just before the HAND GRENADE is thrown **IDM** see HEAR

● ***verb*** (-nn-)
> FASTEN/JOIN **1** ~ sth + adv./prep. to attach something onto another thing or fasten things together with a pin, etc.: *She pinned the ribbon onto her shirt.* ◆ *A message had been pinned to the noticeboard.* ◆ *Pin all the pieces of material together.* ◆ *She always wears her hair pinned back.*
> PREVENT MOVEMENT **2** ~ sb/sth + adv./prep. to make someone unable to move by holding them or pressing them against something: *They pinned him against a wall and stole his wallet.* ◆ *He grabbed her arms and pinned them to her sides.* ◆ *They found him pinned under the wreckage of the car.* **IDM** **pin (all) your hopes on sb/sth | pin your faith in sb/sth** to rely on someone or something completely for success or help: *The company is pinning its hopes on the new project.*
> **PHRV** ,pin sb↔'down **1** to make someone unable to move by holding them firmly: *Two men pinned him down until the police arrived.* **2** to find someone and make them answer a question or tell you something you need to know: *I need the up-to-date sales figures but I can never pin him down at the office.* ,pin sb↔'down (to sth/doing sth) to make someone make a decision or say clearly what they think or what they intend to do: *It's difficult to pin her down to fixing a date for a meeting.* ,pin sth↔'down to explain or understand something exactly: *The cause of the disease is difficult to pin down precisely.* 'pin sth on sb to make someone be blamed for something, especially for something they did not do: *No one would admit responsibility. They all tried to pin the blame on someone else.* ◆ *You can't pin this one on me—I wasn't even there!*

pi·ña co·la·da /ˌpinyə kəˈlɑdə/ *noun* [C, U] (from *Spanish*) an alcoholic drink made by mixing RUM with PINEAPPLE juice and COCONUT

pin·a·fore /ˈpɪnəˌfɔr/ *noun* a loose piece of clothing like a dress without sleeves, worn by children over their clothes to keep them clean, or by young girls over a dress

pi·ña·ta /pinˈyɑtə; pɪn-/ *noun* (from *Spanish*) a brightly decorated container, often a figure of a person or an animal, filled with toys and candy, which children try to hit with a stick with their eyes covered in order to break it open, as a party game

pin·ball /ˈpɪnbɔl/ *noun* [U] a game played on a **pinball machine**, in which the player sends a small metal ball up a sloping board and scores points as it BOUNCES off objects. The player tries to prevent the ball from reaching the bottom of the machine by pressing two buttons at the side.

pince-nez /ˌpæns ˈneɪ/ *noun* (*pl.* pince-nez) (from *French*) a pair of glasses, worn in the past, with a spring that fits on the nose, instead of parts at the sides that fit over the ears

pin·cer /ˈpɪnsər/ *noun* **1** pincers [pl.] a tool made of two crossed pieces of metal, used for holding things firmly and pulling things, for example nails out of wood: *a pair of pincers* **2** [C] one of a pair of curved CLAWS of some types of animals, for example CRABS and LOBSTERS ⊃ picture at ANIMAL

'pincer ˌmovement *noun* [usually sing.] a military attack in which an army attacks the enemy from two sides at the same time

pinch /pɪntʃ/ *verb, noun*
● ***verb***
> WITH THUMB AND FINGER **1** [T] ~ sb/sth/yourself to take a piece of someone's skin between your thumb and first finger and squeeze hard, especially to hurt the person: *My sister's always pinching me and it really hurts.* ◆ *He pinched the baby's cheek playfully.* ◆ (*figurative*) *She had to pinch herself to make sure she was not dreaming.* **2** [T] ~ sth (+ adv./prep.) to hold something tightly between the thumb and finger or between two things that are pressed together: *Pinch the*

nostrils together between your thumb and finger to stop the bleeding. ◆ *a pinched nerve in the neck*
> OF A SHOE **3** [I, T] ~ (sb/sth) if something such as a shoe pinches part of your body, it hurts you because it is too tight: *These new shoes pinch.*
> COST TOO MUCH **4** [T] ~ sb/sth to cost a person or an organization a lot of money or more than they can spend: *Higher interest rates are already pinching the housing industry.* **IDM** **pinch pennies** (*informal*) to try to spend as little money as possible
> **PHRV** ,pinch sth↔'off/'out to remove something by pressing your fingers together and pulling

● ***noun***
> WITH THUMB AND FINGER **1** an act of squeezing a part of someone's skin tightly between your thumb and finger, especially in order to hurt them: *She gave him a pinch on the arm to wake him up.*
> SMALL AMOUNT **2** the amount of something that you can hold between your finger and thumb: *a pinch of salt* **IDM** **in a pinch** used to say that something could be done or used in a particular situation if it is really necessary: *We can get six people around this table in a pinch.* ⊃ more at FEEL *v.*, SALT *n.*

pinched /pɪntʃt/ *adj.* (of a person's face) pale and thin, especially because of illness, cold, or worry

pinch-'hit *verb* **1** [I] (in baseball) to hit the ball for another player **2** [I] ~ (for sb) (*informal*) to do something for someone else who is suddenly unable to do it

pinch-'run *verb* [I] (in baseball) to take the place of a player who is on a BASE: *Gordon pinch-ran for Gomez.*

pin·cush·ion /ˈpɪnˌkʊʃn/ *noun* a small thick PAD made of cloth, used for sticking pins in when they are not being used

pine /paɪn/ *noun, verb*
● ***noun*** **1** [C, U] (also 'pine tree) an EVERGREEN forest tree with leaves like needles: *pine forests* ◆ *pine needles* **2** (also pine·wood) [U] the pale soft wood of the pine tree, used in making furniture, etc.: *a pine table*
● ***verb*** [I] to become very sad because someone has died or gone away: *She pined for months after he'd gone.*
> **PHRV** ,pine a'way to become very sick and weak because you miss someone or something very much: *After his wife died, he just pined away.* 'pine (away) for sb/sth to want or miss someone or something very much: *She was pining for the mountains of her native country.*

pin·e·al /ˈpaɪniəl; paɪˈniəl; ˈpɪniəl/ (also pineal ˌgland) *noun* (*anatomy*) a small organ in the brain that releases a HORMONE

pine·ap·ple /ˈpaɪˌnæpl/ *noun* [C, U] a large tropical fruit with thick rough skin, sweet yellow flesh with a lot of juice, and stiff leaves on top: *fresh pineapple* ◆ *a can of pineapple chunks* ◆ *pineapple juice* ⊃ picture at FRUIT

'pine cone *noun* the hard dry fruit of the PINE tree

'pine ˌmarten *noun* a small wild animal with a long body, short legs, and sharp teeth. Pine martens live in forests and eat animals.

'pine nut *noun* the white seed of some PINE trees, used in cooking

pine·wood /ˈpaɪnwʊd/ *noun* = PINE

ping /pɪŋ/ *noun, verb*
● ***noun*** a short, high sound made when a hard object hits something that is made of metal or glass
● ***verb*** **1** [I, T] ~ (sth) to make a short, high, ringing sound; to make something produce this sound **2** [I] (of a car engine) to make knocking sounds because the fuel is not burning correctly **3** [T] ~ sth to test whether an Internet connection is working by sending a signal to a computer and waiting for a reply **4** [T] ~ sth (to sb) (*informal*) to send an e-mail or a TEXT MESSAGE to someone: *I'll ping it to you later.*

Ping-Pong™ /ˈpɪŋ pɔŋ; -pɑŋ/ *noun* [U] = TABLE TENNIS ⊃ picture at SPORT

pin·head /ˈpɪnhɛd/ *noun* the very small surface at one end of a pin

pin·hole /ˈpɪnhoʊl/ *noun* a very small hole, especially one made by a pin

pin·ion /ˈpɪnyən/ *verb* ~ **sb/sth** + **adv./prep.** to hold or tie someone or something, especially by their arms, so that they cannot move: *His arms were pinioned to his sides.* ◆ *They were pinioned against the wall.*

pink 🔑 /pɪŋk/ *adj., noun, verb*
- *adj.* pale red in color: *pale pink roses* ◆ *She went bright pink with embarrassment.* ▶ **pink·ness** *noun* [U] **IDM** see TICKLE
- *noun* **1** [U, C] the color that is produced when you mix red and white together: *She was dressed in pink.* ◆ *The bedroom was decorated in pale pinks.* **2** [C] a garden plant with pink, red, or white flowers that have a sweet smell

pink-ˈcollar *adj.* [only before noun] connected with low-paid jobs done mainly by women, for example in offices and restaurants: *pink-collar workers* ⊃ compare BLUE-COLLAR, WHITE-COLLAR

pink·eye /ˈpɪŋkaɪ/ *noun* [U] a disease that causes the eyes to become red and swollen and that is easily passed to others **SYN** CONJUNCTIVITIS

pink·ie (also **pink·y**) /ˈpɪŋki/ *noun* (*pl.* **pink·ies**) the smallest finger of the hand **SYN** LITTLE FINGER: *a pinkie ring* (= worn on the smallest finger)

ˈpinking ˌshears *noun* [pl.] special scissors used for cutting cloth so that it will not FRAY at the edges

pink·ish /ˈpɪŋkɪʃ/ *adj.* fairly pink in color

pink·o /ˈpɪŋkoʊ/ *noun* (*pl.* **pink·os** or **pink·oes**) (*informal, disapproving*) a COMMUNIST or a SOCIALIST ▶ **pink·o** *adj.*

ˈpink slip *noun* (*informal*) a letter given to someone to say that they must leave their job ▶ **ˈpink-slip** *verb* [T] to fire someone from their job

ˈpin ˌmoney *noun* [U] (*old-fashioned*) a small amount of money that you earn, especially when this is used to buy things that you want rather than things that you need

pin·na·cle /ˈpɪnəkl/ *noun* **1** [usually sing.] ~ **of sth** the most important or successful part of something: *the pinnacle of her career* **2** a small, pointed, stone decoration built on the roof of a building **3** a high pointed piece of rock, especially at the top of a mountain

Pinocchio /pəˈnoʊkiˌoʊ/ *noun* a character in a children's story who changes from a wooden figure into a boy. Whenever he tells a lie, his nose grows longer: *Cartoons showed the senator as a long-nosed Pinocchio.*

pi·noch·le /ˈpinʌkl; -nɑkl/ *noun* [U] a card game for two or more people that uses a special set of 48 cards

pin·point /ˈpɪnpɔɪnt/ *verb, adj., noun*
- *verb* **1** ~ **sth** to find and show the exact position of someone or something or the exact time that something happened: *He was able to pinpoint on the map the site of the medieval village.* **2** ~ **sth** to be able to give the exact reason for something or to describe something exactly: *The report pinpointed the areas most in need of help.*
- *adj.* if something is done with **pinpoint accuracy**, it is done exactly, and in exactly the right position: *The pilots bombed strategic targets with pinpoint accuracy.*
- *noun* a very small area of something, especially light

pin·prick /ˈpɪnprɪk/ *noun* **1** a very small area of something, especially light: *His eyes narrowed to two small pinpricks of black.* **2** a very small hole in something, especially one that has been made by a pin **3** something that annoys you even though it is small and unimportant

ˌpins and ˈneedles *noun* [U] an uncomfortable feeling in a part of your body, caused when a normal flow of blood returns after it has been partly blocked, especially because you have been sitting or lying in an awkward position: *to have pins and needles*
   IDM **on pins and needles** (*informal*) very nervous, worried, or anxious, especially when you are waiting to find out something: *Everyone was on pins and needles waiting for the results.*

pin·stripe /ˈpɪnstraɪp/ *noun* **1** [C] one of the white vertical lines printed on dark cloth that is used especially for making business suits **2** [U, C] dark cloth with white vertical lines printed on it; a suit made from this cloth: *a pinstripe suit* ▶ **pin·striped** /-straɪpt/ *adj.* [only before noun]: *a pinstriped suit* ◆ *a pinstriped official* (= who is wearing a pinstriped suit)

pint 🔑 /paɪnt/ *noun* (*abbr.* **pt.**)
   1 (in the U.S.) a unit for measuring liquids and some dry goods, equal to 0.473 of a liter. There are 8 pints in a gallon: *a pint of milk* **2** (in Canada and some other countries) a unit for measuring liquids, equal to 0.568 of a liter

pin·to /ˈpɪntoʊ/ *adj.* (of a horse) with areas on it of two colors, usually black and white **SYN** PIEBALD ▶ **pin·to** *noun* (*pl.* **pin·tos**)

ˈpinto ˌbean *noun* a type of curved BEAN with colored marks on the skin

ˈpint-sized (also **ˈpint-size**) *adj.* (*informal*) (of people) very small

pin·up /ˈpɪnʌp/ *noun* **1** a picture of an attractive person, especially one who is not wearing many clothes, that is put on a wall for people to look at **2** a person who appears in a pinup

pin·wheel /ˈpɪnwil/ *noun* **1** a toy with curved plastic parts that form the shape of a flower, which turns around on the end of a stick when you blow on it **2** a round flat FIREWORK that spins around when lit

Pin·yin /ˌpɪnˈyɪn/ *noun* [U] the standard system of ROMAN spelling in Chinese

pi·o·neer /ˌpaɪəˈnɪr/ *noun, verb*
- *noun* **1** ~ **(in/of sth)** a person who is the first to study and develop a particular area of knowledge, culture, etc. that other people then continue to develop **SYN** TRAILBLAZER: *a pioneer in the field of microsurgery* ◆ *a computer pioneer* ◆ *a pioneer aviator* ◆ *a pioneer design* (= one that introduces new ideas, methods, etc.) **2** one of the first people to go to a particular area in order to live and work there: *the pioneer spirit*
- *verb* ~ **sth** when someone **pioneers** something, they are one of the first people to do, discover, or use something new: *a new technique pioneered by surgeons in a Chicago hospital*

pi·o·neer·ing /ˌpaɪəˈnɪrɪŋ/ *adj.* [usually before noun] introducing ideas and methods that have never been used before: *pioneering work on infant mortality* ◆ *the pioneering days of radio*

pi·ous /ˈpaɪəs/ *adj.* **1** having or showing a deep respect for God and religion **SYN** DEVOUT: *pious acts* **ANT** IMPIOUS ⊃ see also PIETY **2** (*disapproving*) pretending to be religious, moral, or good in order to impress other people **SYN** SANCTIMONIOUS: *pious sentiments* **3** ~ **hope** something that you want to happen but is unlikely to be achieved: *Such reforms seem likely to remain little more than pious hopes.* ▶ **pi·ous·ly** *adv.*

pip /pɪp/ *noun, verb*
- *noun* **1** one of the dots showing the value on DICE and DOMINOES; one of the marks showing the value of SUIT of a PLAYING CARD **2** a small hard seed that is found in some types of fruit
- *verb* (**-pp-**) ~ **sb** (*informal*) to beat someone in a race, competition, etc. by only a small amount or at the last moment: *She pipped her rival for the gold medal.*

pipe 🔑 /paɪp/ *noun, verb*
- *noun* **1** [C, U] a tube through which liquids and gases can flow: *hot and cold water pipes* ◆ *a leaking gas pipe* ◆ *Copper pipe is sold in lengths.* ◆ *a burst pipe* ⊃ collocations at DECORATE ⊃ see also DRAINPIPE, EXHAUST, WASTE PIPE, WINDPIPE **2** [C] a narrow tube with a bowl at one end, used for smoking TOBACCO: *to smoke a pipe*

◆ *He puffed on his pipe.* ◆ *pipe tobacco* **3** [C] a musical instrument in the shape of a tube, played by blowing ⊃ see also PAN PIPES **4** [C] any of the tubes from which sound is produced in an organ **5 pipes** [pl.] = BAGPIPES

● **verb 1** [T] **~ sth (+ adv./prep.)** to send water, gas, oil, etc. through a pipe from one place to another: *to pipe oil across the desert* ◆ *Water is piped from the reservoir to the city.* **2** [T] **~ sth (+ adv./prep.)** [usually passive] to send sounds or signals through a wire or cable from one place to another: *The speech was piped over a public address system.* **3** [T, I] **~ (sb)** to play music on a pipe or the BAGPIPES, especially to welcome someone who has arrived: *Passengers were piped aboard ship at the start of the cruise.* ◆ *a prize for piping and drumming* **4** [I, T] **(+ speech)** to speak or sing in a high voice or with a high sound: *Outside a robin piped.* **5** [T] **~ sth (on sth)** to decorate food, especially a cake, with thin lines of ICING, etc. by squeezing it out of a special bag or tube: *The cake had "Happy Birthday" piped on it.*
PHR V pipe 'down (*informal*) used especially in orders, to tell someone to stop talking or to be less noisy ,**pipe 'up (with sth)** (*informal*) to begin to speak: *The person next to me piped up with a silly comment.* ◆ *+ speech "I know the answer," piped up a voice at the back of the room.*

,**pipe band** *noun* a marching band consisting of BAGPIPES and drums

,**pipe ,cleaner** *noun* a short piece of wire, covered with soft material, used for cleaning inside a TOBACCO pipe

,**piped 'music** *noun* [U] recorded music that is played continuously in stores, restaurants, etc.

,**pipe dream** *noun* a hope or plan that is impossible to achieve or not practical

pipe·line /'paɪplaɪn/ *noun* a series of pipes that are usually underground and are used for carrying oil, gas, etc. over long distances
IDM in the pipeline/works something that is **in the pipeline** or **in the works** is being discussed, planned, or prepared and will happen or exist soon

,**pipe ,organ** *noun* = ORGAN

pip·er /'paɪpər/ *noun* a person who plays music on a pipe or the BAGPIPES **IDM see PAY** *v.*

pi·pette /paɪ'pɛt/ *noun* (*technical*) a narrow tube used in a laboratory for measuring or transferring small amounts of liquids ⊃ **picture at LABORATORY**

pipe·work /'paɪpwərk/ *noun* [U] the pipes used for carrying oil, gas, or water around a machine, building, etc.

pip·ing /'paɪpɪŋ/ *noun, adj.*
● *noun* [U] **1** a pipe or pipes of the type or length mentioned: *ten feet of lead piping* **2** a folded strip of cloth, often with a length of string inside, used to decorate a piece of clothing, a CUSHION, etc.: *a uniform with gold piping* **3** lines of cream or FROSTING as decoration on a cake **4** the sound of a pipe or pipes being played
● *adj.* (of a person's voice) high

,**piping 'hot** *adj.* (of liquids or food) very hot

pip·it /'pɪpɪt/ *noun* (often in compounds) a small brown bird with a pleasant song: *a meadow/rock/tree pipit*

pip·squeak /'pɪpskwik/ *noun* (*old-fashioned, informal*) a person that you think is unimportant or does not deserve respect because they are small or young

pi·quan·cy /'pikənsi/ *noun* [U] the quality of being piquant: *The tart flavor of the cranberries adds piquancy.* ◆ *The situation has an added piquancy since the two men are also rivals in love.*

pi·quant /'pikənt; pi'kɑnt/ *adj.* **1** having a pleasantly strong or spicy taste **2** exciting and interesting

pi·qué /pi'keɪ/ *noun* [U] a type of stiff cloth with a raised pattern

pique /pik/ *noun, verb*
● *noun* [U] (*formal*) annoyed or bitter feelings that you have, usually because your pride has been hurt: *When he realized no one was listening to him, he left in a fit of pique.*

● *verb* **~ sb/sth** (*formal*) to make someone annoyed or upset **SYN** WOUND[1] ▸ **piqued** *adj.* [not before noun]: *She couldn't help feeling a little piqued by his lack of interest.*
IDM pique sb's interest, curiosity, etc. to make someone very interested in something

pi·ra·cy /'paɪrəsi/ *noun* [U] **1** the crime of attacking ships at sea in order to steal from them **2** the act of making illegal copies of DVDs, computer programs, books, etc., in order to sell them: *software piracy* ⊃ **see also PIRATE**

pi·ra·nha /pə'rɑnə; -'rɑnyə; -'rænə/ *noun* a small S. American FRESHWATER fish that attacks and eats live animals

pi·rate /'paɪrət/ *noun, verb*
● *noun* **1** (especially in the past) a person on a ship that attacks other ships at sea in order to steal from them: *a pirate ship* **2** (often used as an adjective) a person who makes illegal copies of DVDs, computer programs, books, etc., in order to sell them: *a pirate edition* ◆ *software pirates* **3** (often used as an adjective) a person or an organization that broadcasts illegally: *a pirate radio station* ⊃ **see also** PIRACY ▸ **pi·rat·i·cal** /paɪ'rætɪkl; pə-/ *adj.*
● *verb* **~ sth** to copy and use or sell someone's work or a product without permission and without having the right to do so: *pirated computer games*

pir·ou·ette /ˌpɪru'ɛt/ *noun* a fast turn or spin that a person, especially a BALLET dancer, makes on one foot ▸ **pir·ou·ette** *verb* [I]: *She pirouetted across the stage.*

pis·ca·to·ri·al /ˌpɪskə'tɔriəl/ (also **pis·ca·to·ry** /'pɪskə,tɔri/) *adj.* (*formal*) relating to fishing or to FISHERMEN

Pis·ces /'paɪsiz/ *noun* **1** [U] the 12th sign of the ZODIAC, the Fishes **2** [sing.] a person born under the influence of this sign, that is between February 20 and March 20 ▸ **Pis·ce·an** /'paɪsiən/ *noun, adj.*

pis·cine /'paɪsin; 'pɪsin; 'pɪsaɪn/ *adj.* (*formal or technical*) of or related to fish

pis·tach·i·o /pə'stæʃi,oʊ/ *noun* (*pl.* **pis·tach·i·os**) **1** (also **pi'stachio nut**) [C] the small green nut of an Asian tree ⊃ **picture at NUT 2** [U] a pale green color

piste /pist/ *noun* a track of firm snow prepared for SKIING on ⊃ **see also OFF-PISTE**

pis·til /'pɪstl/ *noun* (*biology*) the female organs of a flower, which receive the POLLEN and produce seeds

pis·tol /'pɪstl/ *noun* a small gun that you can hold and fire with one hand: *an automatic pistol* ◆ *a starting pistol* (= used to signal the start of a race) ⊃ **see also WATER PISTOL**

,**pistol-,whip** *verb* **~ sb** to hit someone with the BUTT of a pistol many times

pis·ton /'pɪstən/ *noun* a part of an engine that consists of a short CYLINDER that fits inside a tube and moves up and down or backward and forward to make other parts of the engine move

piston

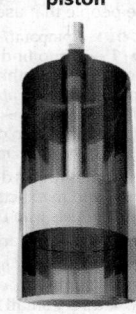

pit /pɪt/ *noun, verb*
● *noun*
▸ DEEP HOLE **1** [C] a large deep hole in the ground: *We dug a deep pit in the yard.* ◆ *The body had been dumped in a pit.* **2** [C] (especially in compounds) a deep hole in the ground from which minerals are dug out: *a chalk/gravel pit*
▸ IN SKIN **3** [C] a small shallow hole in the surface of something, especially a mark left on the surface of the skin by some disease, such as CHICKEN POX ⊃ **see also PITTED**
▸ IN FRUIT **4** [C] a hard shell containing the nut or seed in the middle of some types of fruit: *a peach pit* ⊃ **picture at FRUIT**
▸ IN MOTOR RACING **5 the pit** [sing.] (also **the pits** [pl.]) a place near the track where cars can stop for fuel, new tires, etc. during a race ⊃ **see also PIT STOP**

> **IN THEATER** 6 [sing.] = ORCHESTRA PIT
> **PART OF BODY** 7 [C] (*informal*) = ARMPIT
> **IN BUSINESS** 8 [C] the area of a STOCK EXCHANGE where a particular product is traded: *the corn pit* ⊃ compare FLOOR
IDM **be the pits** (*informal*) to be very bad or the worst example of something **the pit of your/the stomach** the bottom of the stomach, where people say they feel strong feelings, especially fear: *He had a sudden sinking feeling in the pit of his stomach.* ⊃ more at BOTTOMLESS

● *verb* (-tt-) [usually passive]
> **MAKE HOLES** 1 ~ sth to make marks or holes on the surface of something: *The surface of the moon is pitted with craters.* ◆ *Smallpox scars had pitted his face.*
> **FRUIT** 2 ~ sth to remove the hard seed from the inside of a fruit: *pitted olives*
PHR V **pit sb/sth against sth** to test someone or their strength, intelligence, etc. in a struggle or contest against someone or something else: *Lawyers and accountants felt that they were being pitted against each other.* ◆ *a chance to pit your wits against the world champions* (= in a test of your intelligence)

pi·ta /'pitə/ *noun* (also **pita bread**) [U, C] a type of flat bread in the shape of an OVAL that can be split open and filled

pit-a-pat /'pɪtə,pæt/ *adv., noun* = PITTER-PATTER

pit bull (also **pit bull terrier**) *noun* a very strong dog with short legs, sometimes used in dog fights where people bet on which dog will win

pitch 🔧 /pɪtʃ/ *noun, verb*
● *noun*
> **IN BASEBALL** 1 [C] an act of throwing the ball; the way in which it is thrown ⊃ thesaurus box at THROW
> **TO SELL SOMETHING** 2 [C, usually sing.] talk or arguments used by a person trying to sell things or persuade people to do something: *an aggressive sales pitch* ◆ *the candidate's campaign pitch* ◆ *Each company was given ten minutes to make its pitch.*
> **OF SOUND** 3 [sing., U] how high or low a sound is, especially a musical note: *A basic sense of rhythm and pitch is essential in a music teacher.* ⊃ see also PERFECT PITCH
> **DEGREE/STRENGTH** 4 [sing., U] the degree or strength of a feeling or activity; the highest point of something: *a frenetic pitch of activity* ◆ *Speculation has reached such a pitch that a decision will have to be made immediately.*
> **BLACK SUBSTANCE** 5 [U] a black sticky substance made from oil or coal, used on roofs or the wooden boards of a ship to stop water from coming through
> **OF SHIP/AIRCRAFT** 6 [U] (*technical*) the movement of a ship up and down in the water or of an aircraft in the air ⊃ compare ROLL
> **OF ROOF** 7 [sing., U] (*technical*) the degree to which a roof slopes
IDM **make a pitch for sb/sth | make a pitch to sb** to make a determined effort to get something or to persuade someone of something

● *verb*
> **THROW** 1 [T] ~ sb/sth + adv./prep. to throw someone or something with force: *The explosion pitched her violently into the air.* ◆ (*figurative*) *The new government has already been pitched into a crisis.*
> **IN SPORTS** 2 [I, T] ~ (sth) (in baseball) to throw the ball to the person who is BATTING ⊃ note at BASEBALL 3 [T, I] ~ (sth) (in GOLF) to hit the ball in a high curve
> **FALL** 4 [I] + adv./prep. to fall heavily in a particular direction: *With a cry, she pitched forward.*
> **TRY TO SELL** 5 [T] to aim or direct a product or service at a particular group of people: ~ sth (at sb) *The new software is being pitched at banks.* ◆ ~ sth (as sth) *Orange juice is to be pitched as an athlete's drink.* 6 [T, I] to try to persuade someone to buy something, to give you something, or to make a business deal with you: ~ sth *Representatives went to Japan to pitch the company's newest products.* ◆ ~ (for sth) *We were pitching against a much larger company for the contract.*
> **SET LEVEL** 7 [T] to set something at a particular level: ~ sth

(+ adv./prep.) *They have pitched their prices too high.* ◆ ~ sth (at sth) *The test was pitched at too low a level for the students.*
> **SOUND/MUSIC** 8 [T] ~ sth + adj. to produce a sound or piece of music at a particular level: *You pitched that note a little flat.* ◆ *The song was pitched too low for my voice.* ⊃ see also HIGH-PITCHED, LOW-PITCHED
> **TENT** 9 [T] ~ sth to set up a tent or a camp for a short time: *We could pitch our tent in that field.* ◆ *They pitched camp for the night near the river.* ⊃ see also PITCHED
> **OF SHIP/AIRCRAFT** 10 [I] to move up and down on the water or in the air: *The sea was rough and the ship pitched and rolled all night.*
IDM **pitch a story/line/yarn (to sb)** (*informal*) to tell someone a story or make an excuse that is not true
PHR V **pitch in (with sb/sth)** (*informal*) to join in and help with an activity, by doing some of the work or by giving money, advice, etc.: *Everyone pitched in with the work.* ◆ *Local companies pitched in with building materials and labor.* **pitch sth↔'in** to give a particular amount of money in order to help with something: *We all pitched in $10 to buy her a gift.* **pitch 'into sth** (*informal*) to start an activity with enthusiasm: ~ doing sth *I rolled up my sleeves and pitched into cleaning the kitchen.*

pitch and putt *noun* [U] GOLF played on a very small course
pitch-'black *adj.* completely black or dark
pitch-'dark *adj.* completely dark
pitched /pɪtʃt/ *adj.* (of a roof) sloping; not flat
pitched 'battle *noun* 1 a fight that involves a large number of people: *The demonstration escalated into a pitched battle with the police.* 2 a military battle fought with soldiers arranged in prepared positions

pitcher · jug

pitch·er /'pɪtʃər/ *noun* 1 a container with a handle and a LIP, for holding and pouring liquids: *a pitcher of water* 2 (in baseball) the player who throws the ball to the BATTER ⊃ picture at BASEBALL ⊃ note at BASEBALL
pitch·fork /'pɪtʃfɔrk/ *noun* a farm tool in the shape of a large fork with a long handle and two or three sharp metal points, used especially for lifting and moving HAY (= dried grass), etc.
pitch·out /'pɪtʃaʊt/ *noun* 1 (in baseball) a BALL deliberately thrown so that it is too far away to hit, so that the CATCHER can throw it to get a player who is running between BASES out 2 (in football) a ball thrown sideways
pit·e·ous /'pɪtiəs/ *adj.* [usually before noun] (*literary*) deserving pity or causing you to feel pity SYN PATHETIC: *a piteous cry/sight* ▶ **pit·e·ous·ly** *adv.*
pit·fall /'pɪtfɔl/ *noun* a danger or difficulty, especially one that is hidden or not obvious at first: *the potential pitfalls of buying a house*
pith /pɪθ/ *noun* [U] 1 a soft, dry, white substance inside the skin of oranges and some other fruits 2 the essential or most important part of something: *the pith of her argument*
pith helmet *noun* a light hard hat worn to give protection from the sun in very hot countries
pith·y /'pɪθi/ *adj.* (*approving*) (pith·i·er, pith·i·est) (of a comment, piece of writing, etc.) short but expressed well and full of meaning ▶ **pith·i·ly** /'pɪθəli/ *adv.*: *pithily expressed*
pit·i·a·ble /'pɪtiəbl/ *adj.* (*formal*) 1 deserving pity or causing you to feel pity: *The refugees were in a pitiable state.* 2 not

deserving respect: *a pitiable lack of talent* ▶ **pit·i·a·bly** /-əbli/ *adv.*

pit·i·ful /'pɪtɪfl/ *adj.* **1** deserving pity or causing you to feel pity **SYN** PATHETIC: *The horse was a **pitiful sight** (= because it was very thin or sick).* **2** not deserving respect **SYN** POOR: *a pitiful effort/excuse/performance* ▶ **pit·i·ful·ly** /-fli/ *adv.*: *The dog was whining pitifully.* ◆ *She was pitifully thin.* ◆ *The fee is pitifully low.*

pit·i·less /'pɪtɪləs/ *adj.* **1** showing no pity; cruel **SYN** CALLOUS: *a pitiless killer/tyrant* **2** very cruel or severe, and never ending **SYN** RELENTLESS: *a scorching, pitiless sun* ▶ **pit·i·less·ly** *adv.*

pi·ton /'pitɑn/ *noun* a short pointed piece of metal used in rock-climbing. The piton is fixed into the rock and has a rope attached to it through a ring at the other end.

'pit stop *noun* **1** (in motor racing) an occasion when a car stops during a race for more fuel, etc. **2** (*informal*) a short stop during a long trip for a rest, a meal, etc.

pit·tance /'pɪtns/ *noun* [usually sing.] a very small amount of money that someone receives, for example as their pay, and that is hardly enough to live on: *to pay someone a pittance* ◆ *to work for a pittance*

pit·ted /'pɪtəd/ *adj.* **1** having small marks or holes in the surface **2** (of fruit) having had the large hard seed (= the PIT) removed: *pitted olives*

pit·ter-pat·ter /'pɪtər ˌpætər/ (also ˌpit-a-'pat, ˌpitter-'pat) *adv.* with quick light steps or beats: *Her heart went pitter-patter.* ◆ **pit·ter-pat·ter** (also ˌpit-a-'pat, ˌpitter-'pat) *noun* [sing.]: *I could hear the pitter-patter of feet in the corridor.*

pi·tu·i·tar·y /pə'tuəˌteri/ (also pi'tuitary ˌgland) *noun* a small organ at the base of the brain that produces HORMONES that influence growth and sexual development

pit·y /'pɪti/ *noun, verb*

• *noun* **1** [U] ~ **(for sb/sth)** a feeling of sympathy and sadness caused by the suffering and troubles of others: *I could only feel pity for what they were enduring.* ◆ *a **look/feeling/surge of pity*** ◆ *I **took pity on** her and lent her the money.* ◆ (*formal*) *I beg you to **have pity on** him.* ◆ *I don't want your pity.* **2** [sing.] used to show that you are disappointed about something **SYN** SHAME: **a ~ (that…)** *It's a pity that you can't stay longer.* ◆ *"I've lost it!" "Oh, what a pity."* ◆ *What a pity that she didn't tell me earlier.* ◆ **a ~ (to do sth)** *It seems a pity to waste this food.* ◆ *This dress is really nice. Pity it's so expensive.* ◆ *Oh, **that's a pity.*** ◆ *It would be **a great pity** if you gave up now.* **IDM** **more's the pity** (*informal*) unfortunately: *"Was the bicycle insured?" "No, more's the pity!"*

WORD FAMILY
pity *noun, verb*
pitiful *adj.*
pitiless *adj.*
pitiable *adj.*
piteous *adj.*

• *verb* (pit·ies, pit·y·ing, pit·ied, pit·ied) (not used in the progressive tenses) to feel sorry for someone because of their situation; to feel pity for someone: **~ sb** *He pitied people who were stuck in dead-end jobs.* ◆ *Compulsive gamblers are more **to be pitied** than condemned.* ◆ **~ sb doing sth** *I pity her having to work such long hours.*

pit·y·ing /'pɪtiɪŋ/ *adj.* [usually before noun] showing pity for someone, often in a way that shows that you think you are better than them: *a pitying look/smile* ▶ **pit·y·ing·ly** *adv.*

piv·ot /'pɪvət/ *noun, verb*

• *noun* **1** the central point, pin, or column on which something turns or balances **2** the central or most important person or thing: *The chapel was the pivot of community life.* ◆ *The pivot on which the old system turned had disappeared.*

• *verb* [I, T] ~ **(sth) (+ adv./prep.)** to turn or balance on a central point (= a pivot); to make something do this: *Windows that pivot from a central point are easy to clean.* ◆ *She pivoted around and walked out.* **PHR V** **'pivot on/around sth** (of an argument, a theory, etc.) to depend completely on something **SYN** HINGE ON

piv·ot·al /'pɪvətl/ *adj.* of great importance because other things depend on it: *a pivotal role in world affairs*

pix /pɪks/ *noun* [pl.] (*informal*) pictures, photographs, or movies: *They showed us their wedding pix.*

pix·el /'pɪksl/ *noun* (*computing*) any of the small individual areas on a computer screen, which together form the whole display

pix·el·ate (also pix·el·late) /'pɪksəˌleɪt/ *verb* **1** ~ **sth** to divide an image into pixels **2** ~ **sth** to show an image on television as a small number of large pixels, especially in order to hide someone's identity

pix·ie (also pix·y) /'pɪksi/ *noun* (*pl.* pix·ies) (in stories) a creature like a small person with pointed ears, who has magic powers

piz·za /'pitsə/ *noun* [C, U] an Italian dish consisting of a flat round bread base with cheese, tomatoes, vegetables, meat, etc. on top: *a ham and mushroom pizza* ◆ *Is there any pizza left?*

piz·zazz /pə'zæz/ *noun* [U] (*informal*) a lively and exciting quality or style **SYN** FLAIR: *We need someone with youth, glamor, and pizzazz.*

piz·ze·ri·a /ˌpitsə'riə/ (also 'pizza ˌparlor) *noun* a restaurant that serves mainly pizza

piz·zi·ca·to /ˌpɪtsɪ'kɑtoʊ/ *adj., adv.* (*music*) played using the fingers instead of a BOW[1] to pull at the strings of a musical instrument such as a VIOLIN

pj's (also PJ's) /'pidʒeɪz/ *noun* [pl.] (*informal*) PAJAMAS

Pk. *abbr.* (used in written addresses) = PARK

pkg. *abbr.* (in writing) = PACKAGE *n.* (1)

Pkwy *abbr.* (in writing) = PARKWAY

Pl. *abbr.* (used in written addresses) PLACE: *College Pl.*

pl. *abbr.* (in writing) plural

plac·ard /'plækərd; -kɑrd/ *noun* a large written or printed notice that is put in a public place or carried on a stick in a march: *They were carrying placards and banners demanding that he resign.*

pla·cate /'pleɪkeɪt/ *verb* ~ **sb** to make someone feel less angry about something **SYN** PACIFY: *a placating smile* ◆ *The concessions did little to placate the students.*

pla·ca·to·ry /'pleɪkəˌtɔri/ *adj.* (*formal*) designed to make someone feel less angry by showing that you are willing to satisfy or please them: *a placatory remark/smile/gesture*

place ⚷ /pleɪs/ *noun, verb*

• *noun*
▸ POSITION/POINT/AREA **1** [C] a particular position, point, or area: *Is this the place where it happened?* ◆ *This would be a good place for a picnic.* ◆ *I can't be in two places at once.*
▸ CITY/TOWN/BUILDING **2** [C] a particular city, town, building, etc.: *I can't remember all the places we visited in Thailand.* ◆ *I used to live in Seattle, and I'm still fond of the place.* ◆ *The police searched the place.* ◆ *We were looking for a place to eat.* ◆ *Let's get out of this place!* **3** [C] (especially in compounds or phrases) a building or an area of land used for a particular purpose: *a meeting place* ◆ *The town has many excellent eating places.* ◆ *churches and other places of worship* ◆ *He can usually be contacted at his place of work.* ⊃ see also RESTING PLACE
▸ HOME **4** [sing.] a house or apartment; a person's home: *What about dinner at my place?* ◆ *I'm fed up with living with my parents, so I'm looking for a place of my own.*
▸ AREA ON SURFACE **5** [C] a particular area on a surface, especially on a person's body: *He broke his arm in three places.* ◆ *The paint was peeling off the wall in places.*
▸ IN BOOK/SPEECH, ETC. **6** [C] a point in a book, speech, piece of music, etc., especially one that someone has reached at a particular time: *She had marked her place with a bookmark.* ◆ *Excuse me, I seem to have lost my place.*
▸ SEAT **7** [C] a position, seat, etc., especially one that is available for or being used by a person or vehicle: *Come and sit here—I've saved you a place.* ◆ *I don't want to lose my place in the line.* ◆ *Would you like to change places with me so you can see better?* ◆ *I've set a place for you at the table.*
▸ ROLE/IMPORTANCE **8** [sing.] ~ **(in sth)** the role or importance of someone or something in a particular situation, usually in relation to others: *He is assured of his place in*

Λ cup   ə about   eɪ say   aɪ five   ɔɪ boy   aʊ now   oʊ go   ər bird history. ◆ *Accurate reporting **takes second place** to lurid detail.* ◆ *My father believed that people should **know their place*** (= behave according to their social position). ◆ *It's **not your place*** (= your role) *to give advice.* ◆ *Anecdotes **have no place in*** (= are not acceptable in) *an academic essay.*

> **ON TEAM/IN ACTIVITY 9** [C] an opportunity to play for a team or take part in something: *She has **won a place** on the Olympic team.* ◆ *He **lost his place** on the team.*

> **CORRECT POSITION 10** [C] the natural or correct position for something: *Is there a place on the form to put your address?* ◆ *Put it back in its place when you've finished with it.*

> **SAFE AREA 11** [C] (usually with a negative) a suitable or safe area for someone to be: *These streets are **no place for** a child to be out alone at night.*

> **IN RACE/COMPETITION 12** [C, usually sing.] a position among the winners of a race or competition: *He finished in third place.*

> **STREET/SQUARE 13 Place** [sing.] (*abbr.* **Pl.**) used as part of a name for a short street or square: *66 Portland Place*

> **MATHEMATICS 14** [C] the position of a figure after a DECIMAL POINT: *The number is correct to three decimal places.*

IDM **all over the place/lot** (*informal*) **1** everywhere: *New restaurants are appearing all over the place.* **2** not neat or clean; not well organized: *Your calculations are all over the place* (= completely wrong). **change/swap places (with sb)** (usually used in negative sentences) to be in someone else's situation: *I'm perfectly happy—I wouldn't change places with anyone.* **fall into place** if something complicated or difficult to understand **falls into place**, it becomes organized or clear in your mind **be going places** to be getting more and more successful in your life or career: *a young architect who's really going places* **if I was/were in your place** used to introduce a piece of advice you are giving to someone: *If I were in your place, I'd resign immediately.* **in the first place** used at the end of a sentence to talk about why something was done or whether it should have been done or not: *I still don't understand why you chose that name in the first place.* ◆ *I should never have taken that job in the first place.* **in the first, second, etc. place** used at the beginning of a sentence to introduce the different points you are making in an argument: *Well, in the first place, he has all the right qualifications.* **in my, your, etc. place** in my, your, etc. situation: *I wouldn't want to be in your place.* **in place 1** (also **into place**) in the correct position; ready for something: *Carefully lay each slab in place.* ◆ *The receiver had already clicked into place.* **2** working or ready to work: *All the arrangements are now in place for their visit.* **3** in one exact place, without moving in any direction: *Running in place is good exercise.* **in place of sb/sth | in sb's/sth's place** instead of someone or something: *You can use milk in place of cream in this recipe.* ◆ *He was unable to come to the ceremony, but he sent his son to accept the award in his place.* **out of place 1** not in the correct place: *Some of these files seem to be out of place.* **2** not suitable for a particular situation: *Her remarks were out of place.* ◆ *I felt completely out of place among all these successful people.* **a place in the sun** a position in which you are comfortable or have an advantage over other people **put yourself in sb else's/sb's place** to imagine that you are in someone else's situation: *Of course I was upset—just put yourself in my place.* **put sb in their place** to make someone feel stupid or embarrassed for showing too much confidence: *At first she tried to take charge of the meeting but I soon put her in her place.* **take place** to happen, especially after previously being arranged or planned: *The film festival takes place in October.* ◆ *We may never discover what took place that night.* **take sb's/sth's place | take the place of sb/sth** to replace someone or something: *She couldn't attend the meeting so her assistant took her place.* ◆ *Computers have taken the place of typewriters in today's offices.* **take your place 1** to go to the physical position that is necessary for an activity: *Take your places for the race.* **2** to take or accept the status in society that is correct or that you deserve ⊃ more at HAIR, HEART, PRIDE *n.*, ROCK *n.*

● **verb**

> **IN POSITION 1** [T] ~ sth + adv./prep. to put something in a particular place, especially when you do it carefully or deliberately: *He placed his hand on her shoulder.* ◆ *A bomb had been placed under the seat.* ◆ *The parking lots in the town are few, but strategically placed.*

> **IN SITUATION 2** [T] ~ sb/yourself + adv./prep. (more formal than *put*) to put someone/yourself in a particular situation: *to place someone in command* ◆ *She was placed in the care of an uncle.* ◆ *His resignation placed us in a difficult position.* ◆ *The job places great demands on me.*

> **ATTITUDE 3** [T] ~ sth (on sth/doing sth) used to express the attitude someone has toward someone or something: *Great emphasis is placed on education.* ◆ *They place a high value on punctuality.*

> **RECOGNIZE 4** [T] ~ sb/sth (usually used in negative sentences) to recognize someone or something and be able to identify them/it: *I've seen her before but I just can't place her.* ◆ *His accent was impossible to place.*

> **BET/ORDER/ADVERTISEMENT 5** [T] ~ sth to give instructions about something or make a request for something to happen: *to place a bet/an order* ◆ *We placed an advertisement for a housekeeper in the local paper.*

> **FIND HOME/JOB 6** [T] to find a suitable home, job, etc. for someone: ~ sb (with sb/sth) *The children were placed with foster parents.* ◆ ~ sb (in sth) *The agency placed about 2,000 secretaries last year.*

> **GIVE RANK 7** [T] ~ sb/sth + adv./prep. to decide that someone or something has a particular position or rank compared with other people or things: *I would place her among the top five tennis players in the world.* ◆ *Nursing attracts people who place relationships high on their list of priorities.*

> **IN RACE 8** [I] ~ first, second, third, etc. used to describe a person, a team, or a horse, etc. finishing in a particular position in a race: *He placed fifth in last Saturday's race.* **9** [I] (used about a horse) to be among the first three to finish the race, usually in second place: *His horse placed in the last race.*

IDM **be well, ideally, uniquely, better, etc. placed for sth/to do sth 1** to be in a good, very good, etc. position or have a good, etc. opportunity to do something: *Engineering majors are well placed for a wide range of jobs.* ◆ *The company is ideally placed to take advantage of the new legislation.* **2** to be located in a pleasant or convenient place: *The hotel is well placed for restaurants, bars, and clubs.* ⊃ more at PEDESTAL, PREMIUM *n.*

THESAURUS

place

site ◆ **area** ◆ **position** ◆ **point** ◆ **location** ◆ **scene** ◆ **spot** ◆ **venue**

These are all words for a particular area or part of an area, especially one used for a particular purpose or where something is situated or happens.

place a particular point, area, city, town, building, etc., especially one used for a particular purpose or where a particular thing happens: *This would be a good place for a picnic.*

site the place where something, especially a building, is or will be situated; a place where something happened or that is used for a particular purpose: *They've chosen a site for the new school.*

area a part of a room, building, or particular space that is used for a special purpose; a particular place on an object: *the hotel reception area* ◆ *Move the cursor to a blank area on the screen.*

position the place where a person or thing is situated; the place where someone or something is meant to be: *From his position at the top of the hill, he could see the harbor.* **NOTE** The **position** of someone or something is often temporary: the place where the person or thing is at a particular time.

point a particular place within an area, where something happens or is supposed to happen: *the point at which the river divides*

location a place where something happens or exists,

especially a place that is not named or not known: *The company is moving to a new location.*

scene a place where something happens, especially something unpleasant: *the scene of the accident*

spot a particular point or area, especially one that has a particular character or where something particular happens: *I proposed to your mother on this very spot 50 years ago.*

venue the place where people meet for an organized event such as a performance or a sports event: *Please note the change of venue for this event.*

PATTERNS

- **at** a/the place/site/position/point/location/scene/spot/venue
- **in** a(n) place/area/position/location/venue
- **the** place/site/point/location/spot/venue **where...**
- **the right** place/site/position/location/spot/venue
- **a central** site/position/location/venue
- **the**/sth's **exact/precise** place/site/position/point/location/spot

pla·ce·bo /pləˈsiːboʊ/ *noun* (*pl.* **pla·ce·bos**) a substance that has no physical effects, given to patients who do not need medicine but think that they do, or used when testing new drugs: *the placebo effect* (= the effect of taking a placebo and feeling better)

place card *noun* a small card with a person's name on it, placed on a table to show where they are to sit

placed /pleɪst/ *adj.* [after noun] (of a horse, in a race) finishing among the winners (usually second or third)

place·hold·er /ˈpleɪsˌhoʊldər/ *noun* **1** (*technical*) a symbol or piece of text that replaces something that is missing **2** (*linguistics*) an item that is necessary in a sentence, but does not have real meaning, for example the word "it" in "It's a pity she left."

place·kick /ˈpleɪskɪk/ *noun* (in football and RUGBY) a kick made by putting the ball on the ground first

place mat (also **place·mat**) /ˈpleɪsmæt/ *noun* a small MAT on a table on which a person's plate is put

place·ment /ˈpleɪsmənt/ *noun* [U] **1** the act of finding someone a suitable job or place to live: *a job placement service* ◆ *placement with a foster family* **2** the act of placing something somewhere: *This procedure ensures correct placement of the catheter.* ➔ see also ADVANCED PLACEMENT, PRODUCT PLACEMENT

placement test *noun* a test that is designed to find the appropriate level for students in a course or program of study

place name *noun* a name of a town or other place

pla·cen·ta /pləˈsɛntə/ *noun* usually **the placenta** (*anatomy*) the material that comes out of a woman's or female animal's body after a baby has been born, and that was necessary to feed and protect the baby SYN AFTERBIRTH

pla·cen·tal /pləˈsɛntl/ *adj.* **1** (*medical*) of or related to the PLACENTA **2** (*biology*) having a PLACENTA: *placental mammals*

placer mining *noun* [U] the process of getting gold or other valuable minerals, usually from a river or lake, by washing away the sand that surrounds it

place setting *noun* a set or an arrangement of knives, forks, and spoons, and/or plates and dishes, for one person

plac·id /ˈplæsɪd/ *adj.* **1** (of a person or an animal) not easily excited or irritated: *a placid baby/horse* ANT HIGH-SPIRITED **2** calm and peaceful, with very little movement SYN TRANQUIL: *the placid waters of the lake* ▶ **pla·cid·i·ty** /pləˈsɪdəti/ *noun* [U] **plac·id·ly** /ˈplæsɪdli/ *adv.*

pla·gia·rism /ˈpleɪdʒəˌrɪzəm/ *noun* [U, C] (*disapproving*) an act of plagiarizing something; something that has been

plagiarized: *There were accusations of plagiarism.* ◆ *a text full of plagiarisms* ▶ **pla·gia·rist** /-rɪst/ *noun*

pla·gia·rize /ˈpleɪdʒəˌraɪz/ *verb* [T, I] **~ (sth)** (*disapproving*) to copy another person's ideas, words, or work and pretend that they are your own: *He was accused of plagiarizing his colleague's results.*

plague /pleɪg/ *noun, verb*

- *noun* **1** also **the plague** [U] = BUBONIC PLAGUE: *an outbreak of plague* **2** [C] any infectious disease that kills a lot of people SYN EPIDEMIC: *the plague of AIDS* **3** [C] **~ of sth** large numbers of an animal or insect that come into an area and cause great damage: *a plague of locusts/rats* IDM see AVOID

- *verb* **1** **~ sb/sth (with sth)** to cause pain or trouble to someone or something over a period of time SYN TROUBLE: *to be plagued by doubt* ◆ *Financial problems are plaguing the company.* ◆ *The team has been plagued by injury this season.* **2** **~ sb (with sth)** to annoy someone or create problems, especially by asking for something, demanding attention, etc. SYN HOUND: *Rock stars have to get used to being plagued by autograph hunters.*

plaid /plæd/ *noun* [U] a pattern on cloth of lines and squares of different colors and widths, especially a TARTAN pattern ➔ picture at CLOTHES

plain 🔊 /pleɪn/ *adj., noun, adv.*

- *adj.* (**plain·er**, **plain·est**) **1** easy to see or understand SYN CLEAR: *He made it plain that we should leave.* ◆ *She made her annoyance plain.* ◆ *The facts were plain to see.* ◆ *It was a rip-off, plain and simple.* ➔ thesaurus box at CLEAR **2** not trying to trick anyone; honest and direct: *The plain fact is that nobody really knows.* ◆ *a politician with a reputation for plain speaking* **3** not decorated or complicated; simple: *a plain but elegant dress* ◆ *plain vanilla* ◆ *The interior of the church was plain and simple.* ◆ *plain yogurt* (= without sugar or fruit) ➔ compare FANCY **4** without marks or a pattern on it: *curtains in plain or printed cotton* ◆ *Write on plain paper* (= without lines). **5** [only before noun] used to emphasize that something is very ordinary, not special in any way SYN EVERYDAY: *You don't need any special skills for this job, just plain common sense.* **6** (especially of a woman) not beautiful or attractive **7** describing a simple STITCH used in KNITTING ▶ **plain·ness** /ˈpleɪnnəs/ *noun* [U]

  IDM **in plain English** simply and clearly expressed, without using technical language **in plain sight/view** in a place that is very obvious; not hidden: *His laptop was stolen when he left it in plain sight in his car.* **(as) plain as the nose on your face** very obvious **plain old (sb/sth)** not special or complicated: *Avoid antibiotics and try plain old soap and water.*

- *noun* [C] (also **plains** [pl.]) a large area of flat land: *the flat coastal plain of Thassos* ◆ *the Great Plains*

- *adv.* (*informal*) used to emphasize how bad, stupid, etc. something is: *plain stupid/wrong*

THESAURUS

plain

simple ◆ stark ◆ bare ◆ unequivocal

These words all describe statements, often about something unpleasant, that are very clear, not trying to hide anything, and not using more words than necessary.

plain used for talking about a fact that other people may not like to hear; honest and direct in way that other people may not like: *The plain truth is that nobody really knows.*

simple [only before noun] used for talking about a fact that other people may not like to hear; very obvious and not complicated by anything else: *The simple facts of the case proved that she was wrong.*

PLAIN OR SIMPLE?

When it is being used to emphasize facts that other people may not like to hear, **plain** is usually used in the

t **tea**   ṭ **butter**   d **did**   k **cat**   g **got**   tʃ **chin**   dʒ **June**   f **fall**

expression *the plain fact/truth is that…* **Simple** can be used in this way too, but it can also be used in a wider variety of structures and collocations (such as *reason* and *matter*): *The problem was due to the simple fact that…* ◆ ~~The problem was due to the plain fact that…~~ ◆ ~~for the plain reason that…~~ Expressions with **simple** often suggest impatience with other people's behavior.

stark (*somewhat formal*) used for describing an unpleasant fact or difference that is very obvious: *He had to face the stark reality of the situation.* **NOTE** *The simple/plain truth* may be something that some people do not want to hear, but it may be good for them to hear it anyway. *The stark truth* is something particularly unpleasant and painful to accept.

bare [only before noun] the most basic or simple, with nothing extra: *She gave me only a bare outline of the plan.*

unequivocal (*formal*) expressing your opinion or intention very clearly and firmly: *The reply was an unequivocal "no."*

PATTERNS
- the plain/simple/stark/bare/unequivocal **truth**
- a(n) plain/simple/stark/unequivocal **fact/statement**
- a(n) plain/simple/unequivocal **answer**

plain·chant /ˈpleɪntʃænt/ *noun* [U] = PLAINSONG

plain clothes *noun* [pl.] ordinary clothes, not uniform, when worn by police officers on duty: *officers in plain clothes* ▸ **plain-ˈclothes** *adj.* [only before noun]: *plain-clothes police officers*

plain ˈJane *noun* a woman who is not beautiful, or who does not use a lot of makeup or try to make herself look fashionable

plain-Jane *adj.* [only before noun] very simple and not particularly attractive: *They bought an inexpensive plain-Jane house and turned it into a gorgeous home.*

plain·ly /ˈpleɪnli/ *adv.* **1** in a way that is easy to see, hear, understand, or believe **SYN** CLEARLY: *The ocean was plainly visible in the distance.* ◆ *The lease plainly states that all damage must be paid for.* ◆ *She had no right to interfere in what was plainly a family matter.* ◆ *Plainly* (= obviously), *something was wrong.* **2** using simple words to say something in a direct and honest way: *To put it plainly, he's a crook.* **3** in a simple way, without decoration: *She was plainly dressed and wore no makeup.*

plain·song /ˈpleɪnsɔŋ/ (also **plain·chant**) *noun* [U] a type of church music for voices alone, used since the Middle Ages

plain-ˈspoken (also **plain·spo·ken**) /ˌpleɪnˈspoʊkən/ *adj.* saying what you think in very simple, direct language: *a plain-spoken man*

plaint /pleɪnt/ *noun* (*literary*) a sad cry or sound

plain text *noun* [U] (*computing*) data that is stored in the form of ASCII (= a standard code used so that data can be moved between computers that use different programs). Plain text cannot be FORMATTED (= displayed in a particular way on the screen).

plain·tiff /ˈpleɪntəf/ (also **com·plain·ant**) *noun* (*law*) a person who makes a formal complaint against someone in court ⊃ compare DEFENDANT

plain·tive /ˈpleɪntɪv/ *adj.* sounding sad, especially in a weak, complaining way **SYN** MOURNFUL: *a plaintive cry/voice* ▸ **plain·tive·ly** *adv.*

plan 🔑 /plæn/ *noun, verb*
● *noun*
▷ INTENTION **1** something that you intend to do or achieve: ~ **(for sth)** *Do you have any plans for the summer?* ◆ ~ **(to do sth)** *There are no plans to build new offices.* ◆ *Your best plan* (= the best thing to do) *would be to go by car.* ◆ *There's been a change of plan.* ◆ *We can't change our plans now.* ⊃ thesaurus box at PURPOSE
▷ ARRANGEMENT **2** a set of things to do in order to achieve

something, especially one that has been considered in detail in advance: ~ **(for sth)** *Both sides agreed to a detailed plan for keeping the peace.* ◆ ~ **(to do sth)** *The government has announced plans to create one million new training places.* ◆ *a development/business/peace, etc. plan* ◆ *a five-point plan* ◆ *a three-year plan* ◆ *We need to make plans for the future.* ◆ *a plan of action/campaign* ◆ *Let's hope everything will go according to plan.* ⊃ see also MASTER PLAN
▷ MAP **3** a detailed map of a building, town, etc.: *a plan of the museum* ◆ *a street plan of the city*
▷ DRAWING **4** [usually pl.] ~ **(for/of sth)** (*technical*) a detailed drawing of a machine, building, etc. that shows its size, shape, and measurements: *The architect is drawing up plans for the new offices.* ⊃ compare ELEVATION, GROUND PLAN **5** a diagram that shows how something will be arranged: *a seating plan* (= showing where each person will sit, for example at a dinner) ◆ *a floor plan* (= showing how furniture is arranged)
▷ MONEY **6** (especially in compounds) a way of investing money for the future: *a savings plan* **IDM** see SOUND *v.*

● *verb* (-nn-)
▷ MAKE ARRANGEMENTS **1** [T, I] to make detailed arrangements for something you want to do in the future: ~ **sth** *to plan a trip* ◆ *Everything went exactly as planned.* ◆ *We planned the day down to the last detail.* ◆ ~ **sth for sth** *A meeting has been planned for early next year.* ◆ ~ **(for sth)** *to plan for the future* ◆ ~ **how, what, etc.…** *I've been planning how I'm going to spend the day.* ◆ ~ **that…** *They planned that the two routes would connect.*
▷ INTEND/EXPECT **2** [I, T] to intend or expect to do something: ~ **on sth/on doing sth** *We hadn't planned on going anywhere this evening.* ◆ ~ **to do sth** *They plan to arrive some time after three.* ◆ ~ **sth** *We're planning a trip to the Dominican Republic in the spring—are you interested?*
▷ DESIGN **3** [T] ~ **sth** to make a design or an outline for something: *to plan an essay/a garden* ◆ *a well-planned campaign*
PHR V ˌplan sth↔ˈout to plan carefully and in detail something that you are going to do in the future: *Plan out your route before you go.* ◆ *She has her career all planned out.*

ˌPlan ˈA *noun* [sing.] the thing or things someone intends to do if everything happens as they expect

pla·nar /ˈpleɪnər/ *adj.* (*technical*) of or related to a flat surface

ˌPlan ˈB *noun* [sing.] the thing or things someone intends to do if their first plan is not successful: *If Plan A fails, go to Plan B.*

plane 🔑 /pleɪn/ *noun, adj., verb*
● *noun* **1** = AIRPLANE: *She left by plane for Albany.* ◆ *a plane crash* ◆ *I caught the next plane to Philadelphia.* ◆ *The plane took off an hour late.* ◆ *The plane landed in San Juan.* ⊃ picture on page 1116 ⊃ collocations at TRAVEL **2** (*geometry*) any flat or level surface, or an imaginary flat surface through or joining material objects: *the horizontal/vertical plane* **3** a level of thought, existence, or development: *to reach a higher plane of achievement* **4** a tool with a blade set in a flat surface, used for making the surface of wood smooth by shaving very thin layers off it ⊃ picture at TOOL
● *adj.* [only before noun] (*technical*) completely flat; level: *a plane surface*
● *verb* **1** [T] to make a piece of wood smoother or flatter with a plane *n.* (4): ~ **sth** *Plane the surface down first.* ◆ ~ **sth + adj.** *Then plane the wood smooth.* **2** [I] (of a bird) to fly without moving the wings, especially high up in the air **3** [I] (of a boat, etc.) to move quickly across water, only just touching the surface

plane·load /ˈpleɪnloʊd/ *noun* the number of people or the amount of goods that can be carried in a plane: *two planeloads of refugees*

plan·er /ˈpleɪnər/ *noun* an electric tool for making wooden surfaces smooth

plan·et 🔑 /ˈplænət/ *noun*
1 [C] a large round object in space that moves around a star

Planes and Aircraft

plane (also airplane)

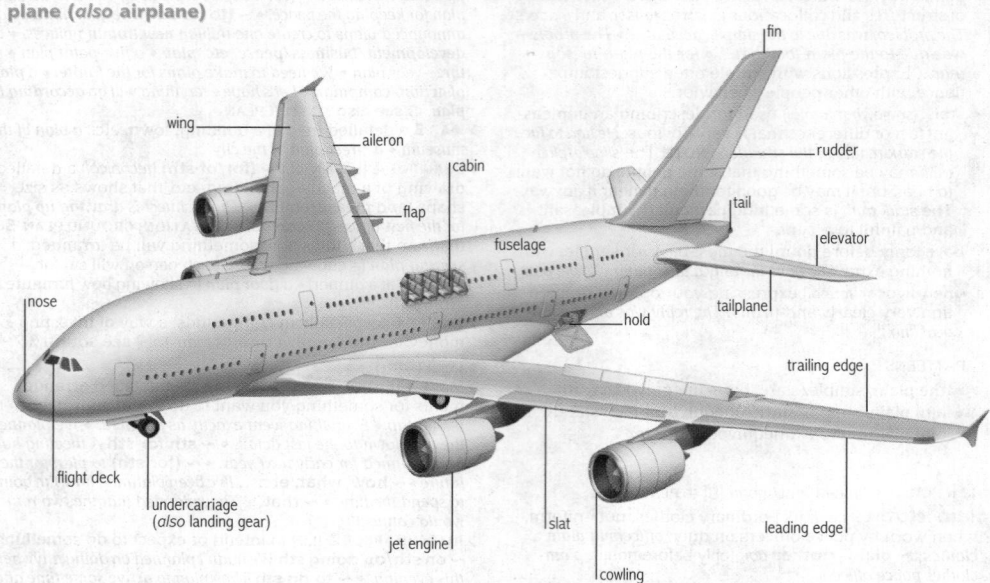

fin · wing · aileron · cabin · rudder · flap · tail · fuselage · elevator · nose · tailplane · hold · trailing edge · flight deck · undercarriage (also landing gear) · jet engine · slat · leading edge · cowling

aircraft

fighter

helicopter

rotor blade

cockpit · propeller

light aircraft

glider

blimp

biplane

N526 · skid

seaplane

basket

hot-air balloon

G-CBMZ

(such as the sun) and receives light from it: *the planets of our solar system* ♦ *the planet Earth/Venus/Mars* **2 the planet** [sing.] used to mean "the world," especially when talking about the environment: *the battle to save the planet* **IDM to be on another planet| what planet is sb on?** (*informal, humorous*) used to suggest that someone's ideas are not realistic or practical: *He thinks being a father is easy. What planet is he on?*

plan·e·tar·i·um /ˌplænəˈtɛriəm/ *noun* a building with a curved ceiling to represent the sky at night, with moving images of the planets and stars, used to educate and entertain people

plan·e·tar·y /ˈplænəˌtɛri/ *adj.* [only before noun] (*technical*) relating to a planet or planets: *a planetary system*

plane tree *noun* a tree with spreading branches and broad leaves, that is often found in towns in northern countries

plan·gent /ˈplændʒənt/ *adj.* **1** (*formal*) (of sounds) loud, with a strong beat **2** (*literary*) (of sounds or images) expressing sadness **SYN PLAINTIVE**: *the plangent sound of the harpsichord*

plank /plæŋk/ *noun* **1** a long, narrow, flat piece of wood that is used for making floors, etc.: *a plank of wood* ♦ *a wooden plank* **2** a main point in the policy of an organization, especially a political party: *The central plank of the bill was rural development.* **IDM see WALK** *v.*

plank·ing /ˈplæŋkɪŋ/ *noun* [U] planks used to make a floor, etc.

plank·ton /ˈplæŋktən/ *noun* [U] the very small forms of plant and animal life that live in water

planned e·con·o·my (also com·mand e·con·o·my) *noun* an economy in which production, prices, and incomes are decided and fixed by the central government

plan·ner /ˈplænər/ *noun* **1** = CITY PLANNER **2** a person who makes plans for a particular area of activity: *curriculum planners* ➔ see also CERTIFIED FINANCIAL PLANNER **3** a book, computer program, etc. that contains dates and is used for recording information, arranging meetings, etc.

plan·ning ✎ /ˈplænɪŋ/ *noun* [U]

1 the act or process of making plans for something: *financial planning* ➔ see also FAMILY PLANNING **2** = CITY PLANNING

plant ✎ /plænt/ *noun, verb*

● *noun*

> LIVING THING **1** [C] a living thing that grows in the earth and usually has a STEM, leaves, and roots, especially one that is smaller than a tree or bush: *All plants need light and water.* ♦ *flowering/garden/indoor plants* ♦ *a tomato/potato plant* ♦ *the animal and plant life of the area* ➔ picture on page 1118 ➔ collocations at LIFE ➔ see also BEDDING PLANT, HOUSE-PLANT, RUBBER PLANT

> FACTORY **2** [C] a factory or place where power is produced or an industrial process takes place: *a nuclear reprocessing plant* ♦ *Japanese car plants* ♦ *a chemical plant* ➔ see also SEWAGE TREATMENT PLANT ➔ thesaurus box at FACTORY

> MACHINERY **3** [U] the large machinery that is used in industrial processes: *The company has been investing in new plant and equipment.*

> SOMETHING ILLEGAL **4** [C, usually sing.] (*informal*) something that someone has deliberately placed among another person's clothes or possessions in order to make them appear guilty of a crime

> PERSON **5** [C] a person who joins a group of criminals or enemies in order to get and secretly report information about their activities

● *verb*

> SEEDS/PLANTS **1** ~ sth to put plants, seeds, etc. in the ground to grow: *to plant and harvest rice* ♦ *Plant these shrubs in full sun.* **2** to cover or supply a garden, yard, area of land, etc. with plants: ~ sth *a densely planted orange grove* ♦ ~ sth **with sth** *The field had been plowed and planted with corn.*

> PUT IN POSITION **3** ~ sth/yourself + adv./prep. to place something or yourself firmly in a particular place or

position: *They planted a flag on the summit.* ♦ *He planted himself squarely in front of us.*

> BOMB **4** ~ sth (+ adv./prep.) to hide something such as a bomb in a place where it will not be found

> SOMETHING ILLEGAL **5** ~ sth (on sb) to hide something, especially something illegal, in someone's clothing, possessions, etc. so that when it is found, it will look as though they committed a crime: *He claims that the drugs were planted on him.*

> PERSON **6** ~ sb (in sth) to send someone to join a group, etc., especially in order to make secret reports on its members

> THOUGHT/IDEA **7** ~ sth (in sth) to make someone think or believe something, especially without them realizing that you gave them the idea: *He planted the first seeds of doubt in my mind.*

PHR V ˌplant sth↔ˈout to put plants in the ground so that they have enough room to grow

plan·tain /ˈplæntən; -teɪn/ *noun* **1** [C, U] a fruit like a large BANANA, but less sweet, that is cooked and eaten as a vegetable **2** [C] a wild plant with small green flowers and broad flat leaves that spread out close to the ground

plan·tar /ˈplæntər/ *adj.* (*anatomy*) of or related to the bottom of the foot

plantar ˌwart *noun* a small hard lump like a WART on the bottom of the foot, which can be easily spread from person to person

plan·ta·tion /plænˈteɪʃn/ *noun* **1** a large area of land, especially in a hot country, where crops such as coffee, sugar, rubber, etc. are grown: *a banana plantation* **2** (in the past) a large farm in the southern U.S. on which cotton or TOBACCO was grown by SLAVES **3** a large area of land that is planted with trees to produce wood: *conifer/forestry plantations*

plant·er /ˈplæntər/ *noun* **1** an attractive container to grow a plant in **2** a person who owns or manages a PLANTATION in a tropical country: *a tea planter* **3** a machine that plants seeds, etc.

plant·ing /ˈplæntɪŋ/ *noun* [U, C] an act of planting something; something that has just been planted: *Tree City U.S.A. promotes tree planting.* ♦ *These bushes are fairly recent plantings.*

plants·man /ˈplæntsmən/, **plants·wom·an** /ˈplæntsˌwʊmən/ *noun* (*pl.* **plants·men** /-mən/, **plants·wom·en** /-ˌwɪmɪn/) an expert in garden plants and GARDENING

plaque /plæk/ *noun* **1** [C] a flat piece of stone, metal, etc., usually with a name and dates on, attached to a wall in memory of a person or an event **2** [U] a soft substance that forms on teeth and encourages the growth of harmful bacteria ➔ compare SCALE

plas·ma /ˈplæzmə/ (also **plasm** /ˈplæzəm/) *noun* [U] **1** (*biology* or *medical*) the clear liquid part of blood, in which the blood cells, etc. float **2** (*physics*) a gas that contains approximately equal numbers of positive and negative electric charges and is present in the sun and most stars

plasma ˌscreen *noun* a type of television or computer screen that uses plasma with electrical charges to produce a very clear image

plasma ˈTV *noun* a television set with a plasma screen

plas·ter /ˈplæstər/ *noun, verb*

● *noun* **1** [U] a substance made of LIME, water, and sand that is put on walls and ceilings to give them a smooth hard surface: *an old house with crumbling plaster and a leaking roof* **2** (also *less frequent* **plaster of Paris**) [U] a white powder that is mixed with water and becomes very hard when it dries, used especially for making copies of statues or holding broken bones in place: *a plaster bust of Julius Caesar*

● *verb* **1** ~ sth to cover a wall, etc. with plaster ➔ collocations at DECORATE **2** ~ sb/sth/yourself in/with sth to cover someone or something with a wet or sticky substance: *She plastered herself in suntan lotion.* ♦ *We were plastered from head*

Plants and Flowers

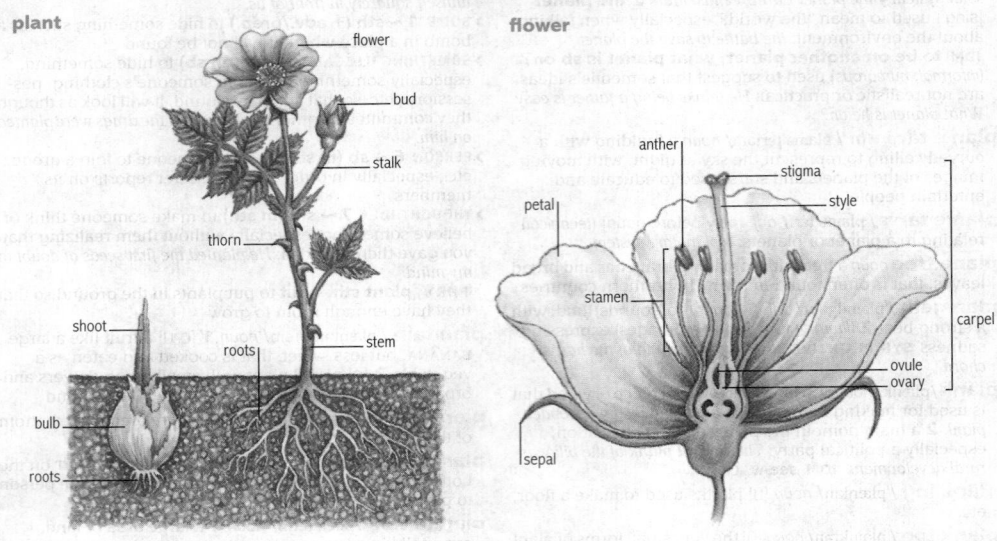

plant

- flower
- bud
- stalk
- thorn
- shoot
- roots
- stem
- bulb
- roots

flower

- anther
- stigma
- style
- petal
- stamen
- carpel
- ovule
- ovary
- sepal

types of plants

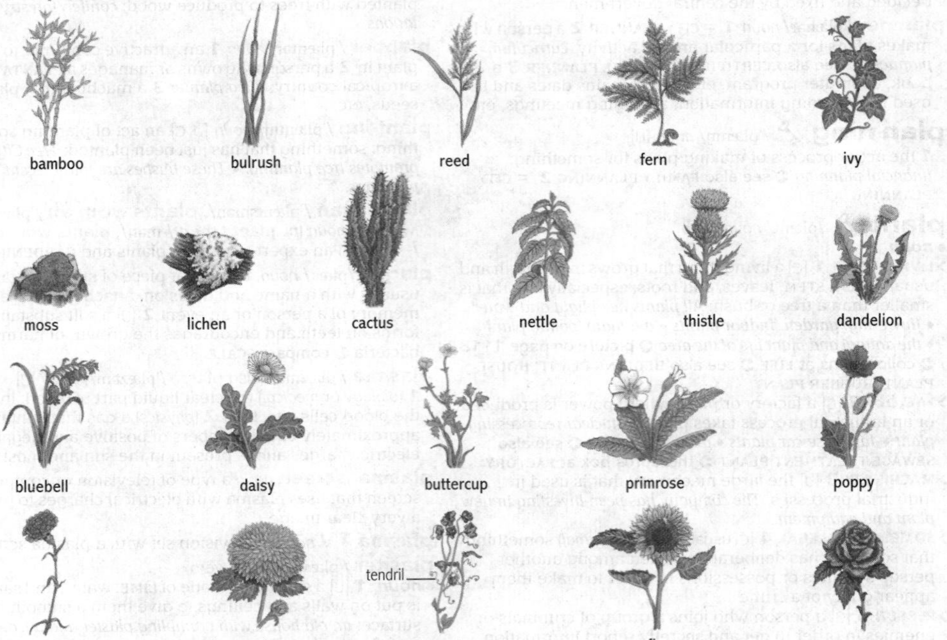

bamboo

bulrush

reed

fern

ivy

moss

lichen

cactus

nettle

thistle

dandelion

bluebell

daisy

buttercup

primrose

poppy

carnation

chrysanthemum

tendril

sweet pea

sunflower

rose

trumpet

daffodil

tulip

iris

lily

orchid

lotus

ʌ **cup**   ə **about**   eɪ **say**   aɪ **five**   ɔɪ **boy**   aʊ **now**   oʊ **go**   ər **bird**

to foot with mud. **3 ~ sth + adv./prep.** to make your hair flat and stick to your head: *His wet hair was plastered to his head.* **4 ~ sth + adv./prep.** to completely cover a surface with pictures or POSTERS: *She had plastered her bedroom wall with photos of him.* ◆ *She had photos of him plastered all over her bedroom wall.* ◆ *The next day, their picture was plastered all over the newspapers.*

PHR V ˌplaster ˈover sth to cover something such as a crack or an old wall with plaster

plas·ter·board /ˈplæstərˌbɔrd/ (also **dry·wall**) *noun* [U] a building material made of sheets of heavy paper with plaster between them, used for inside walls and ceilings

ˌplaster ˈcast *noun* **1** a copy of something, made from PLASTER OF PARIS: *They took a plaster cast of the teeth for identification purposes.* **2** = CAST n. (2)

plas·tered /ˈplæstərd/ *adj.* [not before noun] (*informal*) drunk: *to be/get plastered*

plas·ter·er /ˈplæstərər/ *noun* a person whose job is to put plaster on walls and ceilings

plas·ter of Par·is /ˌplæstər əv ˈpærəs/ *noun* [U] = PLASTER (2)

plas·ter·work /ˈplæstərˌwərk/ *noun* [U] the dry PLASTER on ceilings when it has been formed into shapes and patterns for decoration

plas·tic 🔑 /ˈplæstɪk/ *noun, adj.*
• *noun* **1** [U, C, usually pl.] a light, strong material that is produced by chemical processes and can be formed into shapes when heated. There are many different types of plastic, used to make different objects and FABRICS: *The pipes should be made of plastic.* ◆ *a sheet of clear plastic* ◆ *the plastic industry* **2** plastics [U] the science of making plastics **3** [U] (*informal*) a way of talking about CREDIT CARDS: *Do they take plastic?*
• *adj.* **1** made of plastic: *a plastic bag/cup/toy* **2** (of a material or substance) easily formed into different shapes **SYN** MALLEABLE: *Clay is a plastic substance.* **3** (*disapproving*) that seems artificial; not real or sincere **SYN** FALSE: *TV game show hosts with their banal remarks and plastic smiles*

ˌplastic ˈarts *noun* [pl.] (*technical*) art forms that involve making models or representing things so that they seem solid: *The plastic arts include sculpture, pottery, and painting.*

ˌplastic ˈbullet *noun* a bullet that is made of plastic, and intended to injure but not to kill people

ˌplastic ex·plo·sive *noun* [U, C] an EXPLOSIVE that is used to make bombs

plas·tic·i·ty /plæˈstɪsəti/ *noun* [U] (*technical*) the quality of being easily made into different shapes

plas·ti·cize /ˈplæstəˌsaɪz/ *verb* ~ **sth** (*technical*) to add something to a substance so that it becomes easy to bend and form into different shapes

ˌplastic ˈsurgeon *noun* a doctor who is qualified to perform plastic surgery

ˌplastic ˈsurgery *noun* [U] medical operations to repair injury to a person's skin, or to improve a person's appearance

ˌplastic ˈwrap (also **Saran Wrap™**) *noun* [U] a thin, transparent, plastic material that sticks to a surface and to itself, used especially for wrapping food

plate 🔑 /pleɪt/ *noun, verb*
• *noun*
▷ FOOD **1** [C] a flat, usually round, dish that you put food on: *sandwiches on a plate* ◆ *a pile of dirty plates* ◆ *dinner plates* **2** [C] the amount of food that you can put on a plate: *a plate of sandwiches* ◆ *two large plates of pasta* ⊃ compare PLATEFUL **3** [C] a whole main course of a meal, served on one plate: *Try the seafood plate.*
▷ FOR STRENGTH **4** [C] a thin flat piece of metal, used especially to join things or make something stronger: *The tanks were mainly constructed of steel plates.* ◆ *She had a metal plate inserted in her arm.*

▷ FOR INFORMATION **5** [C] a flat piece of metal with some information on it, for example someone's name: *A brass plate beside the door said "Dr. Alan Tate."* ⊃ see also NAME-PLATE
▷ ON VEHICLE **6** [usually pl.] the pieces of metal or plastic at the front and back of a vehicle with numbers and letters on them ⊃ see also LICENSE PLATE, VANITY PLATE
▷ IN BASEBALL **7** [sing.] = HOME PLATE
▷ SILVER/GOLD **8** [U] ordinary metal that is covered with a thin layer of silver or gold: *The cutlery is plate, not solid silver.* ⊃ see also GOLD PLATE, SILVER PLATE, TINPLATE **9** [U] dishes, bowls, etc. that are made of silver or gold
▷ IN CHURCH **10** usually the plate [sing.] a flat dish that is used to collect money from people in a church
▷ ON ANIMAL **11** [C] (*biology*) one of the thin flat pieces of horn or bone that cover and protect an animal: *the armadillo's protective shell of bony plates*
▷ GEOLOGY **12** [C] one of the very large pieces of rock that form the earth's surface and move slowly: *the Pacific plate* ◆ *Earthquakes are caused by two tectonic plates bumping into each other.* ⊃ see also PLATE TECTONICS
▷ PRINTING/PHOTOGRAPHY **13** [C] a photograph that is used as a picture in a book, especially one that is printed on a separate page on high-quality paper: *The book includes 55 color plates.* ◆ *See plate 4.* **14** [C] a sheet of metal, plastic, etc. that has been treated so that words or pictures can be printed from it: *a printing plate* **15** [C] a thin sheet of glass, metal, etc. that is covered with chemicals so that it reacts to light and can form an image, used in larger or older cameras
▷ IN MOUTH **16** [C] a thin piece of plastic that fits inside your mouth, and has artificial teeth attached to it, or wire, etc. to make the teeth straight ⊃ compare BRACE n. (2) ⊃ see also BOOKPLATE, BREASTPLATE, FOOTPLATE, HOTPLATE
IDM have enough/a lot/too much on your plate (*informal*) to have a lot of work or problems, etc. to deal with ⊃ more at HAND v., STEP v.
• *verb* [usually passive] **1 ~ sth (with sth)** to cover a metal with a thin layer of another metal, especially gold or silver: *a silver ring plated with gold* ⊃ see also GOLD-PLATED, SILVER PLATE **2 ~ sth (with sth)** to cover something with sheets of metal or another hard substance: *The walls of the vault were plated with steel.* ⊃ see also ARMOR-PLATED

pla·teau /plæˈtoʊ/ *noun, verb*
• *noun* (*pl.* **pla·teaus** or **pla·teaux** /-ˈtoʊz/) **1** an area of flat land that is higher than the land around it **2** a time of little or no change after a period of growth or progress: *Inflation has reached a plateau.*
• *verb* [I] ~ **(out)** to stay at a steady level after a period of growth or progress: *Unemployment has at last plateaued out.*

plate·ful /ˈpleɪtfʊl/ *noun* the amount that a plate holds: *She ate three platefuls of spaghetti.*

ˌplate ˈglass *noun* [U] very clear glass of good quality, made in thick sheets, used for doors, windows of stores, etc.

plate·let /ˈpleɪtlət/ *noun* a very small part of a cell in the blood, shaped like a disk. Platelets help to CLOT the blood from a cut or wound.

ˌplate tec·tonics *noun* [U] (*geology*) the movements of the large sheets of rock (called PLATES) that form the earth's surface; the scientific study of these movements

plat·form 🔑 /ˈplætfɔrm/ *noun*
▷ AT TRAIN STATION **1** the raised flat area beside the track at a train station, where you get on or off the train: *The man fell from the platform and onto the tracks.* ⊃ compare TRACK
▷ FOR PERFORMERS **2** a flat surface raised above the level of the ground or floor, used by public speakers or performers so that the audience can see them **SYN** ROSTRUM: *Coming onto the platform now is tonight's conductor, Marin Alsop.* ◆ *Representatives of both parties shared a platform* (= they spoke at the same meeting).
▷ RAISED SURFACE **3** a raised level surface, for example one that equipment stands on or is operated from: *an oil/gas*

platform ♦ *a launch platform* (= for SPACECRAFT) ♦ *a viewing platform with stunning views over the valley*
‣ POLITICS/OPINIONS **4** [usually sing.] the aims of a political party and the things that they say they will do if they are elected to power: *They are campaigning on an anti-immigration platform.* **5** an opportunity or a place for someone to express their opinions publicly or make progress in a particular area: *She used the newspaper column as a platform for her feminist views.*
‣ COMPUTING **6** the type of computer system or the software that is used: *an IBM platform* ♦ *a multimedia platform*
‣ SHOES **7** a high thick SOLE of a shoe: *platform shoes*
⊃ picture at SHOE

ˈplatform ˌgame (also **platˈform·er** /ˈplætfɔrmər/) *noun* a computer game in which the player controls a character who jumps and climbs between platforms at different positions on the screen

plat·ing /ˈpleɪtɪŋ/ *noun* [U] **1** a thin covering of a metal, especially silver or gold, on another metal **2** a layer of coverings, especially of metal plates: *armor plating*

plat·i·num /ˈplætn·əm/ *noun* [U] (*symb.* **Pt**) a chemical element. Platinum is a silver-gray PRECIOUS METAL, used in making expensive jewelry and in industry.

ˌplatinum ˈblonde *noun* (*informal*) a woman whose hair is a very pale silver color, especially because it has been colored with chemicals; this color of hair ▶ **platinum ˈblonde** *adj.*

ˌplatinum ˈdisc *noun* a platinum record in a frame, given to a singer, etc. who has sold a very high number of records

plat·i·tude /ˈplætə·tud/ *noun* (*disapproving*) a comment or statement that has been made very often before and is therefore not interesting ▶ **plat·i·tu·di·nous** /ˌplætə-ˈtudn·əs/ *adj.* (*formal*)

pla·ton·ic /pləˈtɑnɪk/ *adj.* (of a relationship) friendly but not involving sex: *platonic love* ♦ *Their relationship is strictly platonic.*

Pla·to·nism /ˈpleɪtn·ɪzəm/ *noun* [U] (*philosophy*) the ideas of the ancient Greek PHILOSOPHER Plato and those who followed him ▶ **Pla·to·nist** /ˈpleɪtn·ɪst/ *adj., noun*

pla·toon /pləˈtun/ *noun* a small group of soldiers that is part of a COMPANY and commanded by a LIEUTENANT

plat·ter /ˈplætər/ *noun* a large plate that is used for serving food: *a silver platter* ♦ *I'll have the fish platter* (= several types of fish and other food served on a large plate). **IDM see SILVER**

plat·y·pus /ˈplætəpəs/ (also ˌduck-billed ˈplatypus) *noun* an Australian animal that is covered in fur and has a beak like a DUCK, WEBBED feet (= with skin between the toes), and a flat tail. Platypuses lay eggs but give milk to their young.

plau·dits /ˈplɔdɪts/ *noun* [pl.] (*formal*) praise and approval: *His work won him plaudits from the critics.*

plau·si·ble /ˈplɔzəbl/ *adj.* **1** (of an excuse or explanation) reasonable and likely to be true: *Her story sounded perfectly plausible.* ♦ *The only plausible explanation is that he forgot.* **ANT** IMPLAUSIBLE **2** (*disapproving*) (of a person) good at sounding honest and sincere, especially when trying to trick people: *She was a plausible liar.* ▶ **plau·si·bil·i·ty** /ˌplɔzəˈbɪləti/ *noun* [U] **plau·si·bly** /ˈplɔzəbli/ *adv.*: *He argued very plausibly that the claims were true.*

play /pleɪ/ *verb, noun*
● *verb*
‣ OF CHILDREN **1** [I, T] to do things for pleasure, as children do; to enjoy yourself, rather than work: *You'll have to play inside today.* ♦ *There's a time to work and a time to play.* ♦ *~ with sb/sth Some kids were playing with a ball in the street.* ♦ *I haven't got anybody to play with!* ♦ *~ sth Let's play a different game.* ⊃ thesaurus box at ENTERTAINMENT **2** [T, no passive, I] *~ (sth)* to pretend to be or do something for fun: *Let's play pirates.*
‣ TRICK **3** [T] *~ a trick/tricks (on sb)* to trick someone for fun
‣ SPORTS/GAMES **4** [T, I] to be involved in a game; to compete against someone in a game: *~ sth to play football/chess/cards, etc.* ♦ *~ sb The Patriots are playing the Steelers*

tomorrow. ♦ *~ sb at sth Have you played her at squash yet?* ♦ *~ for sb He plays for Cleveland.* ♦ *~ against sb The Patriots are playing against the Steelers on Saturday.* ♦ *+ adv./prep. Evans played very well.* **5** [I] *+ noun* to take a particular position in a sports team: *Who's playing shortstop?* ♦ *I've never played right wing before.* **6** [T] *~ sb (+ adv./prep.)* to include someone in a sports team: *I think we should play Matt at center.* **7** [T] *~ sth* to make contact with the ball and hit or kick it in the way mentioned: *She played the ball and ran forward.* ♦ *He played a backhand volley.* **8** [T] *~ sth* to move a piece in CHESS, etc.: *She played her bishop.* **9** [T, I] *~ (sth)* (in card games) to put a card face upward on the table, showing its value: *to play your ace/a trump* ♦ *He played out of turn!*
‣ MUSIC **10** [T, I] to perform on a musical instrument; to perform music: *~ (sth) to play the piano/violin/flute, etc.* ♦ *In the distance a band was playing.* ♦ *~ sth (on sth) He played a tune on his harmonica.* ♦ *~ sth to sb Play that new piece to us.* ♦ *~ sb sth Play us that new piece.* **11** [T, I] to make a tape, CD, etc. produce sound: *~ sth (for sb) Play their new CD for me, please.* ♦ *~ (sb sth) Play me their new CD, please.* ♦ *My favorite song was playing on the radio.*
‣ ACT/PERFORM **12** [T] *~ sth* to act in a play, movie, etc.; to act the role of someone: *The part of Elizabeth was played by Gwyneth Paltrow.* ♦ *He had always wanted to play Othello.* **13** [I] to pretend to be something that you are not: *+ adj. I decided it was safer to play dead.* ♦ *+ noun She enjoys playing the wronged wife.* **14** [I] *~ (to sb)* to be performed: *A production of "Carmen" was playing to packed houses.*
‣ HAVE EFFECT **15** [T] *~ a part/role (in something)* to have an effect on something: *The media played an important part in the last election.*
‣ SITUATION **16** [T] *~ sth + adv./prep.* to deal with a situation in the way mentioned: *He played the situation carefully for maximum advantage.*
‣ OF LIGHT/A SMILE **17** [I] *+ adv./prep.* to move or appear quickly and lightly, often changing direction or shape: *Sunlight played on the surface of the lake.*
‣ OF FOUNTAIN **18** [I] when a FOUNTAIN plays, it produces a steady stream of water
IDM Most idioms containing **play** are at the entries for the nouns and adjectives in the idioms. For example, **play the game** is at **game.** **have money, time, etc. to play with** (*informal*) to have plenty of money, time, etc. for doing something
PHR V ˌplay aˈround (with sb/sth) **1** to behave or treat something in a careless way: *Don't play around with my tools!* **2** (*informal*) to have a sexual relationship with someone, usually with someone who is not your usual partner ˌplay aˈlong (with sb/sth) to pretend to agree with someone or something: *I decided to play along with her idea.* ˈplay at sth/at doing sth (often *disapproving*) to do something without being serious about it or putting much effort into it ˌplay aˈway (from home) (of a sports team) to play a game at the opponent's field or STADIUM ˌplay sthↄˈback (to sb) to play music, video, etc. that has been recorded on a tape, DVD, etc.: *Play that last section back to me again.* ⊃ related noun PLAYBACK ˌplay sthↄˈdown to try to make something seem less important than it is **SYN** DOWNPLAY **ANT** PLAY UP ˌplay off sth to use something in order to get an advantage: *She plays off her resemblance to the president's daughter.* ˌplay off sth/sb to act with something or someone in a way that produces a good result: *The yellow and purple play off each other nicely.* ˌplay A off against B to put two people or groups in competition with each other, especially in order to get an advantage for yourself: *She played her two rivals off against each other and got the job herself.* ⊃ related noun PLAYOFF ˌplay ˈon (*sports*) to continue to play; to start playing again: *The referee made his decision and told the teams to play on.* ˈplay on/upon sth to take advantage of someone's feelings, etc. **SYN** EXPLOIT: *Advertisements often play on people's fears.* ˌplay sthↄˈout when an event is played out, it happens **SYN** ENACT: *Their love affair was played out against the backdrop of war.* ˌplay yourself/itself ˈout to become weak and no longer useful or important ˌplay sthↄˈup to try to make something seem

more important than it is **SYN** OVERPLAY **ANT** PLAY DOWN 'play with sb/sth to treat someone who is emotionally attached to you in a way that is not serious and that can hurt their feelings: *She tends to play with men's emotions.* ◆ *She realized that Patrick was merely playing with her.* 'play with sth **1** to keep touching or moving something: *She was playing with her hair.* ◆ *Stop playing with your food!* **2** to use things in different ways to produce an interesting or humorous effect, or to see what effect they have: *In this poem, Fitch plays with words that sound alike.* ◆ *The composer plays with the exotic sounds of Japanese instruments.*

● *noun*

> CHILDREN **1** [U] things that people, especially children, do for pleasure rather than as work: *the happy sounds of children at play* ◆ *the importance of learning through play* ◆ *a play area*
> IN THEATER **2** [C] a piece of writing performed by actors in a theater or on television or radio: *to put on* (= perform) *a play* ◆ *a play by Shakespeare* ◆ *a radio play* ⊃ see also MYSTERY PLAY, PASSION PLAY
> IN SPORTS **3** [U] the playing of a game: *Rain stopped play.* ◆ *There was some excellent play in yesterday's match.* ⊃ see also FAIR PLAY **4** [C] an action or move in a game: *a defensive play* ⊃ see also PASS PLAY, RUN PLAY
> IN ROPE **5** [U] the possibility of free and easy movement: *We need more play in the rope.*
> ACTIVITY/INFLUENCE **6** [U] the activity or operation of something; the influence of something on something else: *the free play of market forces* ◆ *The financial crisis has brought new factors into play.* ◆ *Personal feelings should not come into play when you are making business decisions.*
> OF LIGHT/A SMILE **7** [U] (*literary*) a light, quick movement that keeps changing: *the play of sunlight on water*
IDM in/out of play (*sports*) (of a ball) inside/outside the area allowed by the rules of the game: *She just managed to keep the ball in play.* make a play for sb/sth to try to obtain something; to do things that are intended to produce a particular result: *She was making a play for the sales manager's job.* a play on words the humorous use of a word or phrase that can have two different meanings **SYN** PUN ⊃ more at CALL v., CHILD, WORK n.

play·a·ble /'pleɪəbl/ *adj.* **1** (of a piece of music or a computer game) easy to play **2** (of a sports field) in good condition and suitable for playing on **ANT** UNPLAYABLE

play·act·ing /'pleɪˌæktɪŋ/ *noun* [U] behavior that seems to be honest and sincere when in fact the person is pretending ▶ play·act *verb* [I]: *He thought she was playacting but in fact she had really hurt herself.*

play·back /'pleɪbæk/ *noun* [U, C, usually sing.] the act of playing music, showing a movie, or listening to a telephone message that has been recorded before; a recording that you listen to or watch again

play·bill /'pleɪbɪl/ *noun* **1** a printed notice advertising a play **2** a theater program

play·book /'pleɪbʊk/ *noun* (*sports*) a book or set of notes, used especially in football, with descriptions and diagrams of the various PLAYS (= actions or moves in a game) that a team can make: (*figurative*) *The competition took their sales approach right out of our playbook.*

play·boy /'pleɪbɔɪ/ *noun* a rich man who spends his time enjoying himself

play-by-'play *noun* [usually sing.] a report on what is happening in a sports game, given as the game is being played

'play date *noun* an arrangement that parents make for their children to play together at a particular time and place: *Cleo has a play date tomorrow afternoon at Charlotte's house.*

Play-Doh™ /'pleɪdoʊ/ *noun* [U] a soft substance like clay that is made in different colors, used by children for making models

played 'out *adj.* [not before noun] (*informal*) no longer having any influence or effect

play·er 🔑 /'pleɪər/ *noun*
1 a person who takes part in a game or sport: *a tennis/soccer/chess, etc. player* ◆ *a game for four players* ◆ *a midfield player* **2** a company or person involved in a particular area of business or politics: *The company has emerged as a major player in the Los Angeles property market.* ⊃ see also TEAM PLAYER **3** (in compounds) a machine for reproducing sound or pictures that have been recorded on CDs, etc.: *a CD/DVD/cassette/record player* **4** (usually in compounds) a person who plays a musical instrument: *a trumpet player* **5** (*old-fashioned*) (especially in names) an actor: *The Phoenix Players present "Romeo and Juliet."*

'player pi·ano *noun* a piano that plays automatically by means of a PIANO ROLL **SYN** PIANOLA™

play·ful /'pleɪfl/ *adj.* **1** full of fun; wanting to play: *a playful puppy* **2** (of a remark, an action, etc.) made or done in fun; not serious **SYN** LIGHTHEARTED: *He gave her a playful punch on the arm.* ▶ play·ful·ly /-fəli/ *adv.* play·ful·ness *noun* [U]

play·go·er /'pleɪˌgoʊər/ *noun* = THEATERGOER

play·ground /'pleɪgraʊnd/ *noun* **1** an outdoor area where children can play, especially at a school or in a park ⊃ compare SCHOOLYARD **2** a place where a particular type of people go to enjoy themselves: *The resort is a playground of the rich and famous.*

'play group *noun* an organized group of young children and their parents that meets regularly so that the children can play together ⊃ compare NURSERY SCHOOL

play·house /'pleɪhaʊs/ *noun* **1** used in names of theaters: *the Tryon Playhouse* **2** a model of a house large enough for children to play in

play·ing /'pleɪɪŋ/ *noun* **1** [U] the way in which someone plays something, especially a musical instrument: *The orchestral playing is superb.* **2** [C] the act of playing a piece of music: *repeated playings of the National Anthem*

playing cards

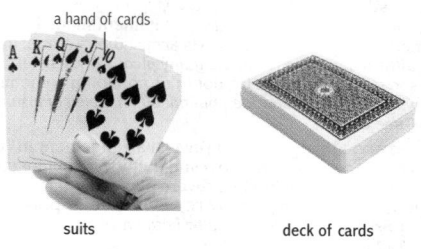

a hand of cards

suits

deck of cards

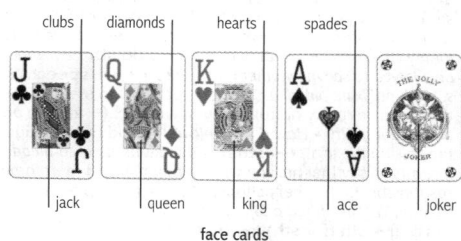

clubs | diamonds | hearts | spades

jack | queen | king | ace | joker

face cards

'playing ˌcard (also card) *noun* any one of a set of 52 cards with numbers and pictures printed on one side, that are used to play various card games: *a deck of (playing) cards*

'playing ˌfield *noun* a large area of grass, usually with lines marked on it, where people play sports and games: *the school playing fields* **IDM** see LEVEL *adj.*

play·let /'pleɪlət/ *noun* a short play

play·list /'pleɪlɪst/ *noun* **1** a list of all the songs and pieces of music that are played by a radio station or on a radio

program 2 a list of songs that you arrange and play on personal digital equipment, such as an **iPod™**

play·mak·er /ˈpleɪˌmeɪkər/ *noun* a player in a team game who starts attacks, or brings other players on the same side into positions from which they could score

play·mate /ˈpleɪmeɪt/ *noun* a friend with whom a child plays

play·off /ˈpleɪɔf; -ɑf/ *noun* a game or a series of games between two players or teams with equal points or scores to decide who the winner is: *They lost to Chicago in the playoffs.*

play·pen /ˈpleɪpɛn/ *noun* a frame with wooden bars or NETTING that surrounds a small area in which a baby or small child can play safely

play·room /ˈpleɪrum; -rʊm/ *noun* a room in a house for children to play in

play·thing /ˈpleɪθɪŋ/ *noun* **1** a person or thing that you treat like a toy, without really caring about them or it: *She was an intelligent woman who refused to be a rich man's plaything.* **2** (*old-fashioned*) a toy: *The teddy bear was his favorite plaything.*

play·time /ˈpleɪtaɪm/ *noun* [U] a time for playing and having fun: *With so much homework to do, her playtime is now very limited.*

play·wright /ˈpleɪraɪt/ *noun* a person who writes plays for the theater, television, or radio SYN DRAMATIST ⊃ compare SCREENWRITER, SCRIPTWRITER

pla·za /ˈplɑzə; ˈplæzə/ *noun* **1** a public outdoor square with buildings around it **2** a small shopping center, sometimes also with offices: *a downtown shopping plaza* **3** (also ˈservice ˌplaza) a place beside a highway where you can stop to use the bathroom, get a meal, and buy gas for your car ⊃ see also TOLL PLAZA

plea /pli/ *noun* **1** (*formal*) an urgent emotional request: ~ **(for sth)** *She made an impassioned plea for help.* ◆ ~ **(to sb) (to do sth)** *a plea to industries to stop pollution* ◆ *He refused to listen to her tearful pleas.* **2** (*law*) a statement made by someone or for someone who is accused of a crime: *a plea of guilty/not guilty* ◆ *to enter a guilty plea* **3** ~ **of sth** (*law*) a reason given to a court for doing or not doing something: *He was charged with murder, but got off on a plea of insanity.* **IDM** see COP *v.*

ˌplea ˈbargaining *noun* [U] (*law*) an arrangement in court by which a person admits to being guilty of a smaller crime in the hope of receiving less severe punishment for a more serious crime ⊃ compare STATE'S EVIDENCE ▶ ˈplea ˌbargain *noun*: *He reached a plea bargain with the authorities.*

plead /plid/ *verb* (plead·ed, plead·ed or pled, pled /plɛd/) **1** [I, T] to ask someone for something in a very strong and serious way SYN BEG: ~ **(with sb) (to do sth)** *She pleaded with him not to go.* ◆ ~ **(with sb) (for sth)** *I was forced to plead for my child's life.* ◆ *pleading eyes* ◆ ~ **to do sth** *He pleaded to be allowed to see his mother one more time.* ◆ + speech *"Do something!" she pleaded.* **2** [I, T, no passive] to state in court that you are guilty or not guilty of a crime: **(+ adj.)** *to plead guilty/not guilty* ◆ *How do you plead?* (= said by the judge at the start of the trial) ◆ ~ **sth** *He advised his client to plead insanity* (= say that he/she was mentally ill and therefore not responsible for his/her actions). **3** [T] ~ **sth** to present a case to a court: *They hired a top lawyer to plead their case.* **4** [T, no passive] ~ **sth (for sth)** | ~ **that…** to give something as an explanation or excuse for something: *He pleaded family problems for his lack of concentration.* **5** [T, I] to argue in support of someone or something: ~ **sth** *She appeared on television to plead the cause of political prisoners everywhere.* ◆ ~ **for sb/sth** *The United Nations has pleaded for a halt to the bombing.*

plead·ing /ˈplidɪŋ/ *noun* **1** [C, U] an act of asking for something that you want very much, in an emotional way: *He refused to give in to her pleadings.* **2** [C, usually pl.] (*law*) a formal statement of someone's case in court ⊃ see also SPECIAL PLEADING

plead·ing·ly /ˈplidɪŋli/ *adv.* in an emotional way that shows that you want something very much but are not certain that someone will give it to you: *He looked pleadingly at her.*

pleas·ant /ˈplɛznt/ *adj.* (**pleas·ant·er**, **pleas·ant·est**) HELP **more pleasant** and **most pleasant** are more common

1 enjoyable, pleasing, or attractive: *a pleasant climate/ evening/place* ◆ *What a pleasant surprise!* ◆ *to live in pleasant surroundings* ◆ *music that is pleasant to the ear* ◆ *a pleasant environment to work in* ◆ *It was pleasant to be alone again.* **2** friendly and polite: *a pleasant young man* ◆ *a pleasant smile/voice/manner* ◆ ~ **to sb** *Please try to be pleasant to our guests.* **ANT** UNPLEASANT ▶ **pleas·ant·ly** *adv.*: *a pleasantly cool room* ◆ *I was pleasantly surprised by my exam results.* ◆ *"Can I help you?" he asked pleasantly.* **pleas·ant·ness** *noun* [U]: *She remembered the pleasantness of the evening.*

pleas·ant·ry /ˈplɛzntri/ *noun* (*pl.* **pleas·ant·ries**) [usually pl.] (*formal*) a friendly remark made in order to be polite: *After exchanging the usual pleasantries, they got down to serious discussion.*

please /pliz/ *exclamation, verb*

● **exclamation 1** used as a polite way of asking for something or telling someone to do something: *Please sit down.* ◆ *Two coffees, please.* ◆ *Quiet please!* ◆ *Please could I leave early today?* **2** used to add force to a request or statement: *Please don't leave me here alone.* ◆ *Please, please don't forget.* ◆ *Please, I don't understand what I have to do.* **3** used as a polite way of accepting something: *"Would you like some help?" "Yes, please."* ◆ *"Coffee?" "Please."* **4** **Please!** (*informal*, often *humorous*) used to ask someone to stop behaving badly: *Children, please! I'm trying to work.* ◆ *John! Please!* **5** **Please/ P-lease** /pəˈliz/ used when you are replying to someone who has said something that you think is stupid: *Oh, please! You cannot be serious.*

● **verb 1** [T, I] ~ **(sb)** | **it pleases sb to do sth** to make someone happy: *You can't please everybody.* ◆ *He's a difficult man to please.* ◆ *There's just no pleasing some people* (= some people are impossible to please). ◆ *I did it to please my parents.* ◆ *She's always very eager to please.* **ANT** DISPLEASE **2** [I] often used after *as* or *what, where*, etc. to mean "to want," "to choose," or "to like" to do something: *You may stay as long as you please.* ◆ *She always does exactly as she pleases.* ◆ *I'm free now to live wherever I please.* **IDM as… as you please** (*informal*) used to emphasize the manner in which someone does something, especially when this is surprising: *She walked right up to the president and shook his hand, as calm as you please.* **if you please** (*old-fashioned, formal*) used when politely asking someone to do something: *Take a seat, if you please.* **please the eye** to be very attractive to look at **please God** used to say that you very much hope or wish that something will happen: *Please God, don't let him be dead.* **please yourself** (*informal*) used to tell someone that you are annoyed with them and do not care what they do: *"I don't think I'll bother finishing this." "Please yourself."* **please yourself** | **do as you please** to be able to do whatever you like: *There were no children to cook for, so we could just please ourselves.*

pleased /plizd/ *adj.*

1 feeling happy about something: ~ **(with sb/sth)** *She was very pleased with her exam results.* ◆ *The boss should be pleased with you.* ◆ ~ **(that…)** *I'm really pleased that you're feeling better.* ◆ ~ **(to hear, know, etc. sth)** *I'm pleased to hear about your news.* ◆ *You're coming? I'm so pleased.* ◆ *He did not look too pleased when I told him.* ⊃ thesaurus box at GLAD **2** ~ **to do sth** happy or willing to do something: *We are always pleased to be able to help.* ◆ *I was pleased to hear you've been promoted.* ◆ *Aren't you pleased to see me?* ◆ *Pleased to meet you* (= said when you are introduced to someone). ◆ *Thank you for your invitation, which I am very pleased to accept.* ◆ *I am pleased to inform you that the book you ordered has arrived.* **IDM (as) pleased as Punch** very pleased **far from pleased** | **none too pleased** not pleased; angry: *She was*

| h **hat** | m **man** | n **no** | ŋ **sing** | l **leg** | r **red** | y **yes** | w **wet** |

none too pleased at having to do it all again. **only too pleased (to do sth)** very happy or willing to do something: *We're only too pleased to help.* **pleased with yourself** (often *disapproving*) too proud of something you have done: *He was looking very pleased with himself.*

pleas·ing /'plizɪŋ/ *adj.* that gives you pleasure or satisfaction: *a pleasing design* ♦ *~ to sb/sth The new building was pleasing to the eye.* ⊃ thesaurus box at SATISFYING
▶ **pleas·ing·ly** *adv.*: *She had a pleasingly direct manner.*

pleas·ur·a·ble /'plɛʒərəbl/ *adj.* giving pleasure **SYN** ENJOYABLE: *a pleasurable experience* ♦ *We do everything we can to make your trip pleasurable.*

pleas·ur·a·bly /'plɛʒərəbli/ *adv.* with pleasure: *He sipped his coffee pleasurably.*

THESAURUS

pleasure

delight ♦ joy ♦ privilege ♦ treat ♦ honor

These are all words for things that make you happy or bring you enjoyment.

pleasure a thing that brings you enjoyment or satisfaction: *the pleasures and pains of everyday life* ♦ *It's been a pleasure talking with you.*

delight a thing or person that brings you great enjoyment or satisfaction: *the delights of living in the country*

joy a thing or person that brings you great enjoyment or happiness: *the joys and sorrows of childhood*

PLEASURE, DELIGHT, OR JOY?

A **delight** or a **joy** is greater than a **pleasure**; a person, especially a child, can be a **delight** or **joy**, but not a **pleasure**; **joys** are often contrasted with **sorrows**, but **delights** are not.

privilege (*somewhat formal*) something that you are proud and lucky to have the opportunity to do: *It was a great privilege to hear her sing.*

treat (*informal*) a thing that someone enjoyed or is likely to enjoy very much: *You've never been to this area before? Then you're in for a real treat.*

honor (*formal*) something that you are very pleased or proud to do because people are showing you great respect: *It was a great honor to be invited to speak here today.*

PATTERNS
■ the pleasures/delights/joys **of** something
■ It's a great pleasure/joy **to** me that…
■ It's a pleasure/delight/joy/privilege/treat/honor **to** do sth
■ It's a pleasure/delight/joy **to** see/find…
■ a pleasure/delight/joy **to** behold/watch
■ a **real** pleasure/delight/joy/privilege/treat
■ a **great** pleasure/joy/privilege/honor
■ a **rare** joy/privilege/treat/honor

---

pleas·ure /'plɛʒər/ *noun*
1 [U] a state of feeling or being happy or satisfied **SYN** ENJOYMENT: *to read for pleasure* ♦ *~ (in sth/in doing sth) He takes no pleasure in his work.* ♦ *~ (of sth/of doing sth) She had the pleasure of seeing him look surprised.* ♦ (*formal*) *We request the pleasure of your company at the marriage of our daughter Lisa.* ♦ *It gives me great pleasure to introduce our guest speaker.* ⊃ thesaurus box at FUN **2** [U] the activity of enjoying yourself, especially in contrast to working: *Are you in Paris on business or pleasure?* ⊃ thesaurus box at ENTERTAINMENT **3** [C] a thing that makes you happy or satisfied: *the pleasures and pains of everyday life* ♦ *the simple pleasures of the countryside* ♦ *It's a pleasure to meet you.* ♦ *"Thanks for doing that." "It's a pleasure."* ⊃ compare DISPLEASURE
IDM **at your/sb's pleasure** (*formal*) as you want; as

someone else wants: *The land can be sold at the owner's pleasure.* **my pleasure** used as a polite way of replying when someone thanks you for doing something, to show that you were happy to do it **with pleasure** used as a polite way of accepting or agreeing to something: *"May I sit here?" "Yes, with pleasure."*

pleasure ,boat (also **pleasure ,craft**) *noun* a boat used for short pleasure trips

pleat /plit/ *noun* a permanent fold in a piece of cloth, made by sewing the top or side of the fold

pleat·ed /'plitəd/ *adj.* having pleats: *a pleated skirt*

pleath·er /'plɛðər/ *noun* [U] a plastic material that looks like leather: *a pleather jacket* **ORIGIN** From "plastic" and "leather."

plebe /plib/ *noun* (*informal*) a first-year student, especially at a military or NAVAL college

ple·be·ian /plə'biən/ *adj., noun*
● *adj.* **1** connected with ordinary people or people of the lower social classes **2** (*disapproving*) lacking in culture or education: *plebeian tastes*
● *noun* (usually *disapproving*) a person from a lower social class (used originally in ancient Rome) ⊃ compare PATRICIAN

pleb·i·scite /'plɛbə,saɪt/ *noun* *~ (on sth)* (*politics*) a vote by the people of a country or a region on an issue that is very important **SYN** REFERENDUM: *to hold a plebiscite on the country's future system of government*

plec·trum /'plɛktrəm/ *noun* (*pl.* **plec·trums** or **plec·tra** /-trə/) a small piece of metal, plastic, etc. used for PLUCKING the strings of a GUITAR or similar instrument **SYN** PICK

pled *pt, pp* OF PLEAD

pledge /plɛdʒ/ *noun, verb*
● *noun* **1** a serious promise **SYN** COMMITMENT: *~ (of sth) a pledge of support* ♦ *~ (to do sth) Will the government honor its campaign pledge not to raise taxes?* ♦ *~ (that…) Management has given a pledge that there will be no layoffs this year.* **2** a sum of money or something valuable that you leave with someone to prove that you will do something or pay back money that you owe
IDM **sign/take the pledge** (*old-fashioned*) to make a promise never to drink alcohol
● *verb* **1** [T] to formally promise to give or do something: *~ sth Japan has pledged $100 million in humanitarian aid.* ♦ *The government pledged their support for the plan.* ♦ *~ sth to sb/sth We all had to pledge allegiance to the flag (= state that we are loyal to our country).* ♦ *~ to do sth The group has pledged to continue campaigning.* ♦ *~ (that)… The group has pledged that they will continue campaigning.* **2** [T] to make someone or yourself formally promise to do something **SYN** SWEAR: *~ sb/yourself (to sth) They were all pledged to secrecy.* ♦ *~ sb/yourself to do sth The government has pledged itself to root out corruption.* **3** [T] *~ sth* to leave something with someone as a pledge **4** [I, T] to promise to become a junior member of a FRATERNITY or SORORITY: *Do you think you'll pledge this semester?* ♦ *~ sth My brother pledged Sigma Nu.*

the ,Pledge of Al'legiance *noun* [sing.] a formal promise to be loyal to the U.S., which citizens make standing in front of the flag with their right hand on their heart

ple·na·ry /'plɛnəri; 'pli-/ *adj., noun*
● *adj.* [only before noun] (*formal*) **1** (of meetings, etc.) to be attended by everyone who has the right to attend: *The new committee holds its first plenary session this week.* **2** without any limit; complete: *The Council has plenary powers to administer the agreement.*
● *noun* (*pl.* **ple·na·ries**) a plenary meeting

plen·i·po·ten·ti·ar·y /,plɛnəpə'tɛnʃi,ɛri; -ʃəri/ *noun* (*pl.* **plen·i·po·ten·ti·ar·ies**) (*technical*) a person who has full powers to take action, make decisions, etc. on behalf of their government, especially in a foreign country
▶ **plen·i·po·ten·ti·ar·y** *adj.*: *plenipotentiary powers*

---

plen·i·tude /ˈplɛnəˌtud/ *noun* [sing., U] (*formal*) a large amount of something **SYN** ABUNDANCE

plen·te·ous /ˈplɛntiəs/ *adj.* (*literary*) = PLENTIFUL

plen·ti·ful /ˈplɛntɪfl/ (also **plen·te·ous**) *adj.* available or existing in large amounts or numbers **SYN** ABUNDANT: *a plentiful supply of food* ◆ *In those days jobs were plentiful.* ▶ **plen·ti·fully** /-fli/ *adv.*: *Evidence is plentifully available.* ◆ *She kept them plentifully supplied with gossip.*

plen·ty 🔑 /ˈplɛnti/ *pron., adv., noun, det.*
- *pron.* ~ (**of sth**) a large amount; as much or as many as you need: *plenty of eggs/money/time* ◆ *"Do we need more milk?" "No, there's plenty in the fridge."* ◆ *They always gave us plenty to eat.* ◆ *We had plenty to talk about.* ⊃ note at MANY, MUCH
- *adv.* **1** ~ **more (of) (something)** a lot: *We have plenty more of them in the warehouse.* ◆ *There's plenty more paper if you need it.* **2** ~ **big, long, etc. enough (to do something)** (*informal*) more than big, long, etc. enough: *The rope was plenty long enough to reach the ground.* **3** (*informal*) a lot; very: *We talked plenty about our kids.* ◆ *You can be married and still be plenty lonely.*
- *noun* [U] (*formal*) a situation in which there is a large supply of food, money, etc.: *Everyone is happier in times of plenty.* ◆ *We had food and drink in plenty.*
- *det.* (*informal*) a lot of: *There's plenty room for all of you!*

ple·num /ˈplɛnəm; ˈpli-/ *noun* a meeting attended by all the members of a committee, etc.; a PLENARY meeting

ple·o·nasm /ˈpliəˌnæzəm/ *noun* [U, C] (*technical*) the use of more words than are necessary to express a meaning. For example, "see with your eyes" is a pleonasm because the same meaning can be expressed using "see." ▶ **ple·o·nas·tic** /ˌpliəˈnæstɪk/ *adj.*

pleth·o·ra /ˈplɛθərə/ *noun* [sing.] (*formal*) an amount that is greater than is needed or can be used **SYN** EXCESS

pleu·ra /ˈplʊrə/ *noun* (*anatomy*) (*pl.* **pleu·rae** /ˈplʊri/) (*anatomy*) one of the two MEMBRANES that surround the lungs

pleu·ri·sy /ˈplʊrəsi/ *noun* [U] a serious illness that affects the inner covering of the chest and lungs, causing severe pain in the chest or sides

Plex·i·glas™ /ˈplɛksiˌglæs/ *noun* [U] a strong, transparent, plastic material that is often used instead of glass

plex·us ⊃ SOLAR PLEXUS

pli·a·ble /ˈplaɪəbl/ *adj.* **1** easy to bend without breaking **SYN** FLEXIBLE **2** (of people) easy to influence or control **SYN** IMPRESSIONABLE

pli·ant /ˈplaɪənt/ *adj.* **1** soft and able to bend easily: *the pliant body of a dancer* ◆ *pliant materials* **2** (sometimes *disapproving*) willing to accept change; easy to influence or control: *He was deposed and replaced by a more pliant successor.* ▶ **pli·an·cy** /ˈplaɪənsi/ *noun* [U] **pli·ant·ly** *adv.*

pli·ers /ˈplaɪərz/ *noun* [pl.] a metal tool with handles, used for holding things firmly, and twisting and cutting wire: *a pair of pliers* ⊃ picture at TOOL

plight /plaɪt/ *noun, verb*
- *noun* [sing.] a difficult and sad situation: *the plight of the homeless* ◆ *The African elephant is in a desperate plight.*
- *verb*
  IDM plight your troth (*old use* or *humorous*) to make a promise to a person saying that you will marry them; to marry someone

Plim·soll line /ˈplɪmsəl ˌlaɪn; -soul-/ (also **ˈload line**) *noun* a line on the side of a ship showing the highest point that the water can safely reach when the ship is loaded

plinth /plɪnθ/ *noun* a block of stone on which a column or statue stands ⊃ picture at ARCHITECTURE

plod /pladʒ/ *verb* (-dd-) [I, T] to walk slowly with heavy steps, especially because you are tired **SYN** TRUDGE: + *adv./prep. Our horses plodded down the muddy track.* ◆ *We plodded*

on through the rain. ◆ ~ **your way** + *adv./prep. I watched her plodding her way across the field.* ▶ **plod** *noun* [sing.]
PHR V ˌplod aˈlong/ˈon to make very slow progress, especially with difficult or boring work **SYN** SLOG

plod·der /ˈplɑdər/ *noun* a person who works slowly and steadily but without imagination

plod·ding /ˈplɑdɪŋ/ *adj.* working or doing something slowly and steadily, especially in a way that other people think is boring

plonk /plɑŋk/ *verb* ⊃ see also PLUNK

plop /plɑp/ *noun, verb*
- *noun* [usually sing.] a short sound like that of a small object dropping into water
- *verb* (-pp-) **1** [I] + *adv./prep.* to fall, making a plop: *The frog plopped back into the water.* ◆ *A tear plopped down onto the page she was reading.* **2** [T] ~ **sth** + *adv./prep.* to drop something into something, especially a liquid, so that it makes a plop: *Can you just plop some ice in my drink?* **3** [T, I] ~ (**yourself**) (**down**) to sit or lie down heavily or in a relaxed way

plo·sive /ˈploʊsɪv/ *noun* (*phonetics*) a speech sound made by stopping the flow of air coming out of the mouth and then suddenly releasing it, for example /t/ and /p/ in *top* ▶ **plo·sive** *adj.*

plot 🔑 /plɑt/ *noun, verb*
- *noun* **1** [C, U] the series of events that form the story of a novel, play, movie, etc.: *a conventional plot about love and marriage* ◆ *The book is well organized in terms of plot.* ⊃ collocations at LITERATURE **2** [C] ~ (**to do sth**) a secret plan made by a group of people to do something wrong or illegal **SYN** CONSPIRACY **3** [C] a small piece of land that is used or intended for a special purpose: *She bought a small plot of land to build a house on.* ◆ *a vegetable plot* ⊃ thesaurus box at LAND
  IDM the plot thickens used to say that a situation is becoming more complicated and difficult to understand
- *verb* (-tt-) **1** [I, T] to make a secret plan to harm someone, especially a government or its leader **SYN** CONSPIRE: ~ (**with sb**) (**against sb**) *They were accused of plotting against the state.* ◆ ~ **sth** *Military officers were suspected of plotting a coup.* ◆ ~ **to do sth** *They were plotting to overthrow the government.* **2** [T] ~ **sth** (**out**) (**on sth**) to mark something on a map, for example the position or course of something: *The earthquake centers had been plotted (out) on a world map.* **3** [T] ~ **sth** (**out**) (**on sth**) to make a diagram or chart from some information: *We carefully plotted each patient's response to the drug on a chart.* **4** [T] ~ **sth** (**on sth**) to mark points on a GRAPH and draw a line or curve connecting them: *First, plot the temperature curve on the graph.* **5** [T] ~ **sth** to write the plot of a novel, play, etc.: *a tightly-plotted thriller*

plot·ter /ˈplɑtər/ *noun* **1** a person who makes a secret plan to harm someone **SYN** CONSPIRATOR **2** a device that turns data from a computer into a GRAPH, usually on paper

plov·er /ˈplʌvər; ˈploʊ-/ *noun* a bird with long legs and a short tail that lives on wet ground

plow /plaʊ/ *noun, verb*
- *noun* a large piece of farming equipment with one or several curved blades, pulled by a TRACTOR or by animals. It is used for digging and turning over soil, especially before seeds are planted. ⊃ see also SNOWPLOW
- *verb* [T, I] **1** ~ (**sth**) to use a SNOWPLOW to clean snow from roads: *We hired someone to plow the driveway while we're away.* ◆ *I hope they plow before I have to go to work tomorrow.* **2** ~ (**sth**) to dig and turn over a field or other area of land with a plow: *plowed fields* ⊃ collocations at FARMING
  PHR V ˌplow sth↔ˈback (in/into sth) | ˌplow sth↔ˈback ˈin **1** to turn over growing crops, grass, etc. with a plow and mix them into the soil to improve its quality **2** to put money made as profit back into a business in order to improve it: *The money was all plowed back into the company.* ˈplow into sb/sth (especially of a vehicle or its driver) to crash violently into something, especially because you are

driving too fast or not paying enough attention: *A truck plowed into the back of the bus.* **,plow sth 'into sth** to invest a large amount of money in a company or project: *The government has plowed more than $20 billion into building new schools.* **,plow 'on (with sth)** to continue doing something that is difficult or boring: *No one was listening to her, but she plowed on regardless.* **,plow (your way) 'through sth 1** to force a way through something: *She plowed her way through the waiting crowds.* **2** (of a vehicle or an aircraft) to go violently through something, out of control: *The plane plowed through the trees.* **3** to make slow progress through something difficult or boring, especially a book, a report, etc.: *I had to plow through dozens of legal documents.* **,plow sth↔'up 1** to turn over a field or other area of land with a plow to change it from grass, for example, to land for growing crops **2** to break up the surface of the ground by walking or driving across it again and again: *The paths get all plowed up by motorbikes.*

plow·man /ˈplaʊmən/ *noun* (pl. **plow·men** /-mən/) a man whose job is guiding a plow, especially one pulled by animals

plow·share /ˈplaʊʃer/ (also **share**) *noun* the broad curved blade of a PLOW **IDM** see SWORD

ploy /plɔɪ/ *noun* words or actions that are carefully planned to get an advantage over someone else **SYN** MANEUVER: *a clever marketing ploy* ◆ **~ to do sth** *It was all a ploy to distract attention from his real aims.*

pluck /plʌk/ *verb, noun*
● *verb*
> HAIR **1** [T] **~ sth (out)** to pull out hairs with your fingers or with TWEEZERS: *She plucked out a gray hair.* ◆ *expertly plucked eyebrows*
> CHICKEN, ETC. **2** [T] **~ sth** to pull the feathers off a dead bird, for example a chicken, in order to prepare it for cooking
> MUSICAL INSTRUMENT **3** (also **pick**) [T, I] **~ (at) sth** to play a musical instrument, especially a GUITAR, by pulling the strings with your fingers: *to pluck the strings of a violin* ◆ *He took the guitar and plucked at the strings.*
> REMOVE SOMEONE OR SOMETHING **4** [T] **~ sb (from sth) (to sth)** to remove someone from a place or situation, especially one that is unpleasant or dangerous: *Police plucked a drowning girl from the river yesterday.* ◆ *Survivors of the wreck were plucked to safety by a helicopter.* ◆ *She was plucked from obscurity to instant stardom.* **5** [T] **~ sth (from sth)** to take hold of something and remove it by pulling it: *He plucked the wallet from the man's grasp.*
> FRUIT/FLOWER **6** [T] **~ sth (from sth)** (*old-fashioned* or *literary*) to pick a fruit, flower, etc. from where it is growing: *I plucked an orange from the tree.*
IDM **pluck sth out of the air** to say a name, number, etc. without thinking about it, especially in answer to a question: *I just plucked a figure out of the air and said, "Would $1,000 seem reasonable to you?"* **pluck up (the) courage (to do sth)** to make yourself do something even though you are afraid to do it: *I finally plucked up the courage to ask her for a date.*
PHR V **'pluck at sth** to hold something with the fingers and pull it gently, especially more than once **SYN** TUG: *The child kept plucking at his mother's sleeve.* ◆ (*figurative*) *The wind plucked at my jacket.*
● *noun* [U] (*informal*) courage and determination: *It takes a lot of pluck to do what she did.*

pluck·y /ˈplʌki/ *adj.* (*informal*) (**pluck·i·er, pluck·i·est**) having a lot of courage and determination **SYN** BRAVE
▶ **pluck·i·ly** /ˈplʌkəli/ *adv.*

plug /plʌg/ *noun, verb*
● *noun*
> ELECTRICAL EQUIPMENT **1** a small plastic object with two or three metal pins that connects a piece of electrical equipment to the main supply of electricity: *a three-pin plug* **2** a small object that connects a wire from one piece of electrical equipment to an opening in another: *the plug from the computer to the printer*
> IN ENGINE **3** = SPARK PLUG

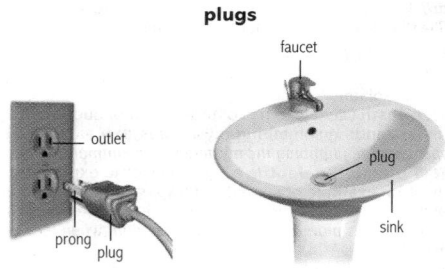
plugs

faucet

outlet

plug

prong
plug

sink

> IN BATH/SINK **4** a thick round piece of plastic, rubber, or metal that you put in the hole in a BATHTUB or a SINK to stop the water from flowing out: *She pulled out the plug and let the water drain away.* ➔ thesaurus box at LID
> IN HOLE **5** a round piece of material that fits into a hole and blocks it: *She took the plug of cotton from her ear.* ➔ see also EARPLUG **6** = STOPPER
> FOR SCREW **7** a small plastic tube that you put into a hole in a wall so that it will hold a screw
> FOR BOOK/MOVIE **8** (*informal*) praise or attention that someone gives to a new book, movie, etc. in order to encourage people to buy or see it: *He managed to get in a plug for his new book.* **IDM** see PULL *v.*
● *verb* (**-gg-**)
> FILL HOLE **1** **~ sth (up)** to fill a hole with a substance or piece of material that fits tightly into it: *He plugged the hole in the pipe with an old rag.*
> PROVIDE SOMETHING MISSING **2** **~ sth** to provide something that has been missing from a particular situation and is needed in order to improve it: *A cheaper range of products was introduced to plug the gap at the lower end of the market.*
> BOOK/MOVIE **3** **~ sth** to give praise or attention to a new book, movie, etc. in order to encourage people to buy or see it **SYN** PROMOTE: *She came on the show to plug her latest album.*
> SHOOT **4** **~ sb** (*old-fashioned, informal*) to shoot someone
PHR V **,plug a'way (at sth)** to continue working hard at something, especially something that you find difficult
,plug sth↔'in | **,plug sth 'into sth** to connect a piece of electrical equipment to the main supply of electricity or to another piece of electrical equipment: *Is the printer plugged in?* **ANT** UNPLUG **,plug sth 'into sth 1** = TO PLUG STH IN **2** to connect a computer to a computer system: *All our computers are plugged into the main network.* **,plug 'into sth 1** (of a piece of electrical equipment) to be able to be connected to the main supply of electricity or to another piece of electrical equipment: *The DVD player plugs into the back of the television.* **2** to become involved with a particular activity or group of people: *The company has doubled its profits since plugging into lucrative overseas markets.*

,Plug and 'Play *noun* [U] (*computing*) a system that makes it possible for a piece of equipment, such as a printer, to be connected to a computer and to work immediately, without the user needing to do anything ▶ **,plug-and-'play** *adj.*: *plug-and-play peripherals*

'plug-in *adj., noun*
● *adj.* **1** able to be connected using a plug: *a plug-in griddle* **2** (*computing*) able to be added to a computer system so that it can do more things: *a plug-in graphics card*
● *noun* **1** (*computing*) a piece of computer software that can be added to a system so that it can do more things **2** (*CanE*) a connection to an electricity supply in a garage, etc. so that you can use an electric HEATER to warm the engine of a car, so that it starts more easily

plum /plʌm/ *noun, adj.*
● *noun* **1** [C] a soft round fruit with smooth red or purple skin, sweet flesh, and a large flat seed inside: *a plum tree* ➔ picture at FRUIT **2** [U, C] a dark red-purple color

●**adj.** (of a job, etc.) considered very good and worth having: *She's landed a plum job at an advertising agency.*

plum·age /ˈpluːmɪdʒ/ *noun* [U] the feathers covering a bird's body

plumb /plʌm/ *verb, adv.*
●**verb** ~ **sth** (*literary*) to try to understand or succeed in understanding something mysterious **SYN** FATHOM: *She spent her life plumbing the mysteries of the human psyche.* **IDM plumb the depths of sth** to be or to experience an extreme example of something unpleasant: *His latest novel plumbs the depths of horror and violence.* ◆ *The team's poor performances* **plumbed new depths** *last night when they lost 10–2.*
●**adv. 1** (used before prepositions) exactly: *He was standing plumb in the middle of the road.* **2** (*old-fashioned*, *informal*) completely: *He's plumb crazy.*

plumb·er /ˈplʌmər/ *noun* a person whose job is to fit and repair things such as water pipes, toilets, etc.

plumb·ing /ˈplʌmɪŋ/ *noun* [U] **1** the system of pipes, etc. that supply water to a building ⟳ **collocations** at DECORATE **2** the work of a plumber

'**plumb line** *noun* a piece of thick string with a weight attached to one end, used to find the depth of water or to test whether a wall, etc. is straight

plume /pluːm/ *noun* **1** a cloud of something that rises and curves upward in the air: *a plume of smoke* **2** a large feather: *a black hat with an ostrich plume* **3** a group of feathers or long thin pieces of material tied together and often used as a decoration ⟳ **see also** NOM DE PLUME

plumed /pluːmd/ *adj.* having or decorated with a plume or plumes: *a plumed helmet*

plum·met /ˈplʌmət/ *verb* [I] to fall suddenly and quickly from a high level or position **SYN** PLUNGE: *Share prices plummeted to an all-time low.* ◆ *Her spirits plummeted at the thought of meeting him again.* ◆ *The jet plummeted into a row of houses.*

plum·my /ˈplʌmi/ *adj.* like a plum in color, taste, etc.

plump /plʌmp/ *adj.*, *verb*
●**adj.** (**plump·er**, **plump·est**) **1** having a soft round body; slightly fat: *a short plump woman* ◆ *a plump face* **2** looking soft, full, and attractive to use or eat: *plump cushions* ◆ *plump tomatoes* ▸ **plump·ness** *noun* [U]
●**verb** ~ **sth** (**up**) to make something larger, softer, and rounder: *He leaned forward while the nurse plumped up his pillows.* **PHR V** '**plump for sb/sth** (*informal*) to choose someone or something from a number of people or things, especially after thinking carefully

'**plum to·mato** *noun* an Italian variety of tomato that is long and thin, rather than round

plun·der /ˈplʌndər/ *verb, noun*
●**verb** [I, T] to steal things from a place, especially using force during a time of war **SYN** LOOT: *The troops crossed the country, plundering and looting as they went.* ◆ ~ **sth (of sth)** *The abbey had been plundered of its valuables.* ◆ ~ **sth (from sth)** *Only a small amount of the money that he plundered from his companies has been recovered.* ⟳ **compare** PILLAGE ▸ **plun·der·er** *noun*
●**noun** [U] **1** the act of plunder **2** things that have been stolen, especially during a war, etc. ⟳ **compare** PILLAGE

plunge /plʌndʒ/ *verb, noun*
●**verb 1** [I, T] to move or make someone or something move suddenly forward and/or downward: + adv./prep. *She lost her balance and plunged 100 feet to her death.* ◆ ~ **sb/sth** + adv./prep. *The earthquake plunged entire towns over the edge of the cliffs.* **2** [I] (of prices, temperatures, etc.) to decrease suddenly and quickly **SYN** PLUMMET: *Stock markets plunged at the news of the coup.* **3** [I] + adv./prep. (of a road, surface, etc.) to slope down steeply: *The track plunged down into the valley.* **4** [I] to move up and down suddenly and violently: *The horse plunged and reared.* ◆ (*figurative*) *His heart plunged* (= because of a strong emotion).

PHR V ,**plunge** '**in** | ,**plunge** 'into sth **1** to jump into something, especially with force: *The pool was declared open and eager swimmers plunged in.* **2** to start doing something in an enthusiastic way, especially without thinking carefully about what you are doing: *She was about to plunge into her story when the phone rang.* ◆ *He's always plunging in at the deep end* (= becoming involved in difficult situations without being well enough prepared). ,**plunge sth** 'in | ,**plunge sth** 'into sth to push something quickly and with force into something else: *He plunged his sword into the giant's body.* ,**plunge** 'into sth **1** = PLUNGE IN **2** to experience something unpleasant: *The country plunged deeper into recession.* ,**plunge sb/sth** 'into sth to make someone or something experience something unpleasant: *The news plunged them into deep depression.* ◆ *There was a flash of lightning and the house was* **plunged into darkness**.
●**noun** [usually sing.] **1** a sudden movement downward or away from something **SYN** DROP: *The calm water ends there and the river begins a headlong plunge.* **2** ~ **(in sth)** a sudden decrease in an amount or the value of something **SYN** DROP: *a dramatic plunge in profits* **3** ~ **into sth** the act of becoming involved in a situation or activity: *The company is planning a deeper plunge into the commercial market.* **4** an act of jumping or, in DIVING into water; a quick swim: *He took the plunge into the deep end.* ◆ *She went for a plunge.* **IDM take the plunge** (*informal*) to decide to do something important or difficult, especially after thinking about it for a long time

'**plunge pool** *noun* a small, deep, artificial pool filled with cold water, especially one that you jump into in order to get cooler after a SAUNA

plung·er /ˈplʌndʒər/ *noun* **1** a part of a piece of equipment that can be pushed down ⟳ **picture** at COFFEE, LABORATORY **2** a piece of equipment used for clearing kitchen and bathroom pipes, which consists of a rubber cup fastened to a handle ⟳ **picture** at TOOL

plung·ing /ˈplʌndʒɪŋ/ *adj.* (of a dress, BLOUSE, etc.) cut in a deep V shape at the front: *a plunging neckline*

plunk /plʌŋk/ *verb* (*informal*) **1** (also **plonk**) [T] ~ **sth + adv./ prep.** to put something down on something, especially noisily or carelessly: *He plunked the package down on the desk.* **2** (also **plonk**) [T, I] ~ **(yourself) down** to sit down heavily or carelessly: *He just plunked himself down and turned on the TV.* **3** [T] ~ **sth** to play a GUITAR, a keyboard, etc. with your fingers and produce a rough, unpleasant sound ▸ **plunk** *noun*: *the plunk, plunk of the banjo* **PHR V** '**plunk sth↔down** to pay money for something, especially a large amount: *Some people plunk down $20 every week for lottery tickets.*

plu·per·fect /ˌpluːˈpɜːrfɪkt/ *noun* (*grammar*) = PAST PERFECT

plu·ral /ˈplʊrəl/ *noun, adj.*
●**noun** (*abbr. pl.*) (*grammar*) a form of a noun or verb that refers to more than one person or thing: *The plural of "child" is "children."* ◆ *The verb should be* **in the plural**. ⟳ **compare** SINGULAR
●**adj. 1** (*abbr. pl.*) (*grammar*) connected with or having the plural form: *Most plural nouns in English end in "s."* **2** relating to more than one: *a plural society* (= with more than one RACIAL, religious, etc. group)

plu·ral·ism /ˈplʊrəlɪzəm/ *noun* [U] (*formal*) **1** the existence of many different groups of people in one society, for example people of different races, or of different political or religious beliefs: *cultural pluralism* **2** the belief that it is possible and good for different groups of people to live together in peace in one society **3** (usually *disapproving*) the fact of having more than one job or position at the same time, especially in the Christian Church

plu·ral·ist /ˈplʊrəlɪst/ *adj.*, *noun*
●**adj.** (also **plu·ral·is·tic** /ˌplʊrəˈlɪstɪk/) **1** (of a society) having many different groups of people and different political parties in it: *a pluralist democracy* **2** (*philosophy*) not based on a single set of principles or beliefs: *a pluralist approach to politics*

t **tea** ţ **butter** d **did** k **cat** g **got** tʃ **chin** dʒ **June** f **fall**

• **noun 1** a person who believes that it is possible and good for different groups of people to live together in peace in our society **2** a person who has more than one job or position at the same time, especially in the Christian Church

plu·ral·i·ty /pluˈrælət̬i/ *noun* (*pl.* **plu·ral·i·ties**) **1** [C, usually sing.] (*formal*) a large number: *a plurality of influences* **2** [C, usually sing.] (*politics*) the number of votes given to one person, political party, etc. when this number is less than 50% but more than any other single person, etc. receives: *In order to be elected, a candidate needs only a plurality of the votes cast.* ⊃ compare MAJORITY **3** [U] (*grammar*) the state of being plural

plu·ral·ize /ˈplʊrəˌlaɪz/ *verb* ~ **sth** to make a word plural ▸ **plu·ral·i·za·tion** /ˌplʊrələˈzeɪʃn/ *noun* [U]

plus¹ ✏ [AWL] /plʌs/ *prep., noun, adj., conj.*

• **prep. 1** used when the two numbers or amounts mentioned are being added together: *Two plus five is seven.* ✦ *The cost is $22, plus $1.50 for postage.* **ANT** MINUS **2** as well as something or someone; and also: *We have to fit five of us plus all our gear in the car.* **ANT** MINUS

IDM plus or minus used when the number mentioned may actually be more or less by a particular amount **SYN** GIVE OR TAKE: *The margin of error was plus or minus three percentage points.*

• **noun 1** (*informal*) an advantage; a good thing: *Knowledge of French is a plus in her job.* ✦ *There were a lot of pluses in the performance.* **2** (also **plus sign**) the symbol (+), used in mathematics: *He put a plus instead of a minus.* **ANT** MINUS

• **adj. 1** used after a number to show that the real number or amount is more than the one mentioned: *The work will cost $10,000 plus.* **2** above zero: *The temperature is plus four degrees.* **ANT** MINUS **3** [only before noun] used to describe an aspect of something that you consider to be a good thing: *One of the hotel's **plus points** is that it is very central.* ✦ *On the plus side, all the staff are enthusiastic.* **ANT** MINUS **4** [not before noun] (used in a system of grades) slightly higher than the grade A, B, etc.: *I got a B plus (B+) on the test.* **ANT** MINUS

• **conj.** (*informal*) used to add more information **SYN** FURTHERMORE: *I have too much to do at work. Plus my father is not well.*

plus² /plu/
IDM plus ça change /ˌplu sɑ ˈʃɑ̃ʒ/ (*saying, from French*) used as a way of saying that people and situations never really change over time, although they may appear to

plush /plʌʃ/ *adj., noun*
• **adj.** (*informal*) very comfortable; expensive and of good quality **SYN** LUXURIOUS: *a plush hotel*
• **noun** [U] a type of silk or cotton cloth with a thick soft surface made of a mass of threads: *red plush armchairs*

Plu·to /ˈplutoʊ/ *noun* one of a number of round objects in space that are not as large as planets but that go around the sun. In August 2006, the International Astronomical Union declared that Pluto should be called a DWARF PLANET because it is smaller and has different characteristics from the other planets in our SOLAR SYSTEM; in 2008 it declared that DWARF PLANETS farther from the sun than Neptune could also be called plutoids.

plu·toc·ra·cy /pluˈtɑkrəsi/ *noun* (*pl.* **plu·toc·ra·cies**) **1** [U] government by the richest people of a country **2** [C] a country governed by the richest people in it

plu·to·crat /ˈplutəˌkræt/ *noun* (*often disapproving*) a person who is powerful because of their wealth

plu·toid /ˈplutɔɪd/ *noun* any DWARF PLANET that is farther from the sun than the planet Neptune

plu·to·ni·um /pluˈtoʊniəm/ *noun* [U] (*symb.* **Pu**) a chemical element. Plutonium is RADIOACTIVE and is used in nuclear weapons and in producing nuclear energy.

ply /plaɪ/ *verb, noun*
• **verb** (**plies, ply·ing, plied, plied**) **1** [I, T] (*literary*) (of ships,

buses, etc.) to travel regularly along a particular route or between two particular places: + **adv./prep.** *Ferries ply across a narrow strait to the island.* ✦ *Buses ply regularly to and from these places.* ✦ ~ **sth** *canals plied by gondolas and steamboats* **2** [T] ~ **sth** (*formal*) to use a tool, especially in a skillful way: *The tailor delicately plied his needle.*
IDM ply your trade to do your work or business
PHR V 'ply sb with sth 1 to keep giving someone large amounts of something, especially food and/or drink **2** to keep asking someone questions: *He plied me with questions from the moment he arrived.*

• **noun** [U] (especially in compounds) a measurement of wool, rope, wood, etc. that tells you how thick it is: *four-ply knitting yarn*

ply·wood /ˈplaɪwʊd/ *noun* [U] board made by sticking thin layers of wood on top of each other: *plywood furniture*

PM /ˌpi ˈɛm/ *noun* (*informal*) the abbreviation for "prime minister": *an interview with the PM*

p.m. ✏ (also **P.M.**) /ˌpi ˈɛm/ *abbr.*
after 12 o'clock NOON (from Latin "post meridiem"): *The appointment is at 3 p.m.* ⊃ compare A.M.

PMP /ˌpi ɛm ˈpi/ *noun* the abbreviation for "portable media player" (a piece of equipment that stores and plays sound and pictures)

PMS /ˌpi ɛm ˈɛs/ *noun* [U] physical and emotional problems, such as pain and feeling depressed, that many women experience before their PERIOD (= flow of blood) each month. PMS is an abbreviation for "premenstrual syndrome." ⊃ see also PREMENSTRUAL

pneu·mat·ic /nuˈmæt̬ɪk/ *adj.* [usually before noun] **1** filled with air: *a pneumatic tire* **2** worked by air under pressure: *pneumatic tools*

pneuˌmatic 'drill *noun* = JACKHAMMER

pneu·mo·nia /nuˈmoʊnyə/ *noun* [U] a serious illness affecting one or both lungs that makes breathing difficult

PO /ˌpi ˈoʊ/ *abbr.* POST OFFICE ⊃ see also PO BOX

poach /poʊtʃ/ *verb* **1** [T] ~ **sth** to cook food, especially fish, gently in a small amount of liquid: *poached salmon* **2** [T] ~ **sth** to cook an egg gently in nearly boiling water after removing its shell **3** [T, I] ~ **(sth)** to illegally hunt birds, animals, or fish on someone else's property or without permission: *The elephants are poached for their tusks.* **4** [T, I] ~ **(sb/sth) (from sb/sth)** to take and use someone or something that belongs to someone or something else, especially in a secret, dishonest, or unfair way: *The company poached the contract from their main rivals.* ✦ *Several of our employees have been poached by a rival firm.* ✦ *I hope I'm not poaching on your territory* (= doing something that is actually your responsibility).

poach·er /ˈpoʊtʃər/ *noun* **1** a person who illegally hunts birds, animals, or fish on someone's else's property **2** a special pan for POACHING eggs

ˌPO box (also **ˌpost office ˌbox**) *noun* used as a kind of address, so that mail can be sent to a post office where it is kept until it is collected: *Write to PO Box 8189, Phoenix, AZ*

pocked /pakt/ *adj.* having holes or hollow marks on the surface **SYN** PITTED

pock·et ✏ /ˈpakət/ *noun, verb*
• **noun**
▸ IN CLOTHING **1** a small piece of material like a small bag sewn into or onto a piece of clothing so that you can carry things in it: *a coat pocket* ✦ *I put the note in my pocket.* ✦ *Turn out your pockets* (= empty your pockets). ✦ *Take your hands out of your pockets!* ✦ *a pocket dictionary* (= one that is small enough to fit in your pocket) ⊃ picture at CLOTHES
▸ SMALL CONTAINER **2** a small bag or container fastened to something so that you can put things in it, for example, in a car door or in a bag: *Information about safety procedures is in the pocket in front of you* (= on a plane).
▸ MONEY **3** [usually sing.] used to talk about the amount of money that you have to spend: *We have vacations to suit*

every pocket. ♦ *He had no intention of paying for the meal out of his own pocket.* ⊃ see also DEEP POCKETS

> SMALL GROUP/AREA **4** a small group or area that is different from its surroundings: *There are still a few isolated pockets of resistance to the new regime.* ♦ *a pocket of air* ⊃ see also AIR POCKET

> IN POOL, ETC. **5** (in the game of POOL and some other similar games) any of the holes or nets around the edges of the table that you have to hit the ball into ⊃ picture at HOBBY **IDM** be in sb's pocket to be controlled or strongly influenced by someone have sb in your pocket to have influence or power over someone, for example a police officer or a politician, especially by threatening them or by offering them money have sth in your pocket to be certain to win something out of pocket having lost money as a result of something: *That one mistake left him thousands of dollars out of pocket.* ⊃ compare OUT-OF-POCKET ⊃ more at BURN v., DIP v., PICK v.

● *verb*

> PUT INTO POCKET **1** ~ sth to put something into your pocket: *She paid for the drink and pocketed the change without counting it.*

> MONEY **2** ~ sth to take or keep something, especially an amount of money, that does not belong to you: *He regularly charges passengers more than the normal fare and pockets the difference.* **3** ~ sth to earn or win an amount of money: *Last year, she pocketed over $1 million in advertising contracts.*

> IN POOL, ETC. **4** ~ sth (in the game of POOL and some other similar games) to hit a ball into a POCKET

pock·et·book /ˈpakətˌbʊk/ *noun* **1** used to refer to the financial situation of a person or country: *Many foreign goods are too expensive for American pocketbooks.* ♦ *The increase is likely to hit the pocketbooks of consumers.* **2** = PURSE *n.* (1) **3** (in the past) a small flat case for carrying papers or money

pock·et·ful /ˈpakətˌfʊl/ *noun* the amount a pocket holds: *a pocketful of coins*

pock·et·knife /ˈpakətˌnaɪf/ *noun* (*pl.* -knives /-ˌnaɪvz/) (also **pen·knife**) a small knife with one or more blades that fold down into the handle ⊃ picture at TOOL

pocket money *noun* [U] a small amount of money that you can spend on things you need or want ⊃ compare SPENDING MONEY

pocket-sized (also **pocket-size**) *adj.* small enough to fit into your pocket or to be carried easily

pocket veto *noun* a method by which the president can stop a new law from being introduced by not signing it and keeping it until a session of Congress has finished

pock·mark /ˈpakmɑrk/ *noun* a hollow mark on the skin, often caused by disease or infection

pock·marked /ˈpakmɑrkt/ *adj.* covered with hollow marks or holes: *a pockmarked face* ♦ *The district is pockmarked with caves.*

pod /pad/ *noun* **1** a long thin case filled with seeds that develops from the flowers of some plants, especially PEAS and BEANS: *a pea pod* ♦ *a vanilla pod* ⊃ picture at FRUIT **2** a long narrow container that is hung under an aircraft and used to carry fuel, equipment, weapons, etc. **3** part of a SPACECRAFT or a boat that can be separated from the main part **4** [C] a small group of sea animals, such as DOLPHINS or WHALES, swimming together: *a pod of adult dolphins*

pod·cast /ˈpadkæst/ *noun* a recording of a radio broadcast or a video that can be taken from the Internet: *To listen to the podcast, click on the link below.* ⊃ collocations at E-MAIL ▸ **pod·cast·er** *noun*: *The U.S. has an estimated 60 million podcasters.* **pod·cast·ing** *noun* [U]: *Podcasting could turn into an audio form of blogging.*

po·di·a·trist /pəˈdaɪətrɪst/ *noun* a person whose job is the care and treatment of people's feet

po·di·a·try /pəˈdaɪətri/ *noun* [U] the work of a podiatrist

po·di·um /ˈpoʊdiəm/ *noun* **1** a small platform that a person

stands on when giving a speech or CONDUCTING an ORCHESTRA, etc. **SYN** ROSTRUM **2** = LECTERN

Po·dunk /ˈpoʊdʌŋk/ *adj.* (*informal*) (of a town) small, dull, and not important **ORIGIN** From a place name of southern New England.

po·em 🔊 /ˈpoʊəm/ *noun*
a piece of writing in which the words are chosen for their sound and the images they suggest, not just for their obvious meanings. The words are arranged in separate lines, usually with a repeated rhythm, and often the lines RHYME at the end. ⊃ collocations at LITERATURE

po·e·sy /ˈpoʊəzi; -si/ *noun* [U] (*literary*) poetry

po·et /ˈpoʊət/ *noun* a person who writes poems

po·et·ess /ˈpoʊətəs/ *noun* (*old-fashioned*) a woman who writes poems

po·et·ic /poʊˈɛtɪk/ (also *less frequent* **po·et·i·cal** /poʊˈɛtɪkl/) *adj.* **1** [only before noun] connected with poetry; being poetry: *poetic language* ♦ *Byron's Poetical Works* **2** (*approving*) like or suggesting poetry, especially because it shows imagination and deep feeling **SYN** LYRICAL: *There is a poetic quality to her playing.* ▸ **po·et·i·cally** /-kli/ *adv.*

poetic justice *noun* [U] a situation in which something bad happens to someone, and you think that this is what they deserve

poetic license (CanE **poetic licence**) *noun* [U] the freedom to change facts, the normal rules of language, etc. in a special piece of writing or speech in order to achieve a particular effect

po·et·ics /poʊˈɛtɪks/ *noun* [U] **1** the art of writing poetry **2** the study of poetry, literature, etc.

poet laureate *noun* a poet who is chosen for an official position in a country or region, or one who is UNOFFICIALLY considered to be the best or most typical of their country or region: *the New York State poet laureate* ♦ *the poet laureate of young America*

po·et·ry 🔊 /ˈpoʊətri/ *noun*
1 [U] a collection of poems; poems in general **SYN** VERSE: *epic/lyric/pastoral, etc. poetry* ♦ *Maya Angelou's poetry* ♦ *a poetry reading* ⊃ collocations at LITERATURE ⊃ compare PROSE **2** [U, sing.] (*approving*) a beautiful and elegant quality: *There was poetry in all her gestures.*

po·go stick /ˈpoʊgoʊ ˌstɪk/ *noun* a pole with a bar to stand on and a spring at the bottom, that you jump around on for fun

po·grom /pəˈgram; -ˈgrʌm/ *noun* the organized killing of large numbers of people, because of their race or religion (originally the killing of Jews in Russia)

poign·ant /ˈpɔɪnyənt/ *adj.* having a strong effect on your feelings, especially in a way that makes you feel sad **SYN** MOVING: *a poignant image/moment/memory, etc.* ♦ *Her face was a poignant reminder of the passing of time.* ▸ **poign·an·cy** /ˈpɔɪnyənsi/ *noun* [U]: *the poignancy of parting and separation* ♦ *Of particular poignancy was the photograph of their son with his sisters, taken the day before he died.* **poign·ant·ly** *adv.*

poin·set·ti·a /pɔɪnˈsɛtə; -ˈsɛtiə/ *noun* a tropical plant with large red or pink leaves that grow to look like flowers, often grown indoors in pots

point 🔊 /pɔɪnt/ *noun, verb*
● *noun*
> OPINION/FACT **1** [C] a thing that someone says or writes giving their opinion or stating a fact: *She made several interesting points in the article.* ♦ *I take your point* (= understand and accept what you are saying). ♦ *He's just saying that to prove a point* (= to show his idea is right). ♦ *OK, you've made your point!* ⊃ see also TALKING POINT

> MAIN IDEA **2** [C] usually **the point** the main or most important idea in something that is said or done: *The point is you shouldn't have to wait so long to see a doctor.* ♦ *I wish he would get to the point* (= say it quickly). ♦ *I'll come straight to*

| h hat | m man | n no | ŋ sing | l leg | r red | y yes | w wet |

the point: we need more money. ✦ *Do you **see my point*** (= understand)*?* ✦ *I think I **missed the point*** (= did not understand).* ✦ *You **have a point*** (= your idea is right) —*it would be better to wait till this evening.* ✦ *"There won't be anywhere to park." "Oh, **that's a (good) point*** (= I had not thought of that).*"* ✦ *It just isn't true. **That's the whole point*** (= the only important fact).* ✦ *"He's been married before." "**That's beside the point*** (= not important)."* ✦ *I know it won't cost very much but **that's not the point*** (= not the important thing).*
> PURPOSE **3** [U, sing.] the purpose or aim of something: *What's the **point** of all this violence?* ✦ *There's **no point** in getting angry.* ✦ *I **don't see the point** of doing it all again.* ✦ *The point of the lesson is to compare the two countries.* ➾ thesaurus box at PURPOSE
> DETAIL **4** [C] a particular detail or fact: *Here are the **main points** of the news.* ✦ *Can you explain that point again?*
> QUALITY **5** [C] a particular quality or feature that someone or something has: *Tact is not one of her **strong points**.* ✦ *Read the manual to learn the program's **finer points*** (= small details).* ✦ *Living in Portland **has its good points**, but the weather is not one of them.* ➾ see also SELLING POINT
> TIME **6** [C] a particular time or stage of development: *The climber was **at/on the point** of death when they found him.* ✦ *We were **on the point** of giving up.* ✦ *Many people suffer from mental illness **at some point** in their lives.* ✦ *We had **reached the point** when there was no money left.* ✦ *At this point in time, we just have to wait.* ✦ *At this point, I don't care what you decide to do.* ➾ see also HIGH POINT, LOW POINT, SATURATION POINT, STARTING POINT, STICKING POINT, TURNING POINT
> PLACE **7** [C] a particular place or area: *I'll wait for you at the meeting point in the arrivals hall.* ✦ *the point at which the river divides* ✦ *Draw a line from point A to point B.* ✦ *No parking beyond this point.* ➾ thesaurus box at PLACE ➾ see also FOCAL POINT, JUMPING-OFF POINT, THREE-POINT TURN, VANISHING POINT, VANTAGE POINT
> DIRECTION **8** [C] one of the marks of direction around a COMPASS: *the points of the compass* (= N., S., E., W., etc.)
> IN COMPETITION **9** [C] (*abbr.* **pt.**) an individual unit that adds to a score in a game or sports competition: *to **win/lose a point*** ✦ *Australia finished 20 points ahead.* ✦ *They won **on points*** (= by scoring more points rather than by completely defeating their opponents).* ➾ see also BROWNIE POINT, MATCH POINT
> MEASUREMENT **10** [C] a mark or unit on a scale of measurement: *The party's share of the vote fell by ten percentage points.* ➾ see also BOILING POINT, FREEZING POINT, MELTING POINT
> PUNCTUATION **11** [C] a small dot used in writing, especially the dot that separates a whole number from the part that comes after it: *two point six (2.6)* ✦ *a decimal point* ✦ *We broadcast on ninety-five point nine (95.9) FM.* ➾ see also BULLET POINT
> SHARP END **12** [C] the sharp thin end of something: *the point of a pencil/knife/pin* ➾ picture at KITCHEN ➾ see also BALL-POINT, GUNPOINT, KNIFEPOINT
> LAND **13** also **Point** [C] a narrow piece of land that stretches into the ocean: *The ship sailed around the point.* ✦ *Orient Point*
> OF LIGHT/COLOR **14** [C] a very small dot of light or color: *The stars were points of light in the sky.*
> IN BALLET **15** **points** [pl.] = POINTE
> SIZE OF LETTERS **16** [U] a unit of measurement for the size of letters in printing or on a computer screen, etc.: *Change the text to 10 point.*
   IDM **beside the point** to not be important or closely related to the main thing you are talking about: *Yes, I know it was an accident, but that's beside the point.* ✦ *They took my words out of context, but that's beside the point.* **in point of fact** used to say what is true in a situation: *In point of fact, she is their adopted daughter.* **make a point of doing sth** to be or make sure you do something because it is important or necessary: *I made a point of closing all the windows before leaving the house.* **more to the point** used to say that something is more important than something else: *I couldn't do the job—I've never been to Spain and, more to the point, I don't speak Spanish.* **on point** appropriate or relevant to the situation: *The quotation was directly on point.* ✦ *Let's stay on point.* **point of contact** a place where you go or a person

that you speak to when you are dealing with an organization: *The receptionist is the first point of contact most people have with the clinic.* **a point of departure 1** a place where a trip starts **2** (*formal*) an idea, a theory, or an event that is used to start a discussion, an activity, etc. **a point of honor** a thing that someone considers to be very important for their honor or reputation **the point of no return** the time when you must continue with what you have decided to do, because it is not possible to get back to an earlier situation **point taken** used to say that you accept that someone else is right when they have disagreed with you or criticized you: *Point taken. Let's drop the subject.* **to the point** expressed in a simple, clear way without any extra information or feelings **SYN** PERTINENT: *The letter was short and to the point.* **to the point of (doing) sth** to a degree that can be described as something: *He was rude to the point of being aggressive.* **up to a (certain) point** to some extent; to some degree but not completely: *I agree with you up to a point.* ➾ more at BELABOR, CASE *n.*, FINE *adj.*, LABOR *v.*, MOOT, SCORE *v.*, SORE *adj.*, STRETCH *v.*

● *verb*
> SHOW WITH FINGER **1** [I, T, no passive] to stretch out your finger or something held in your hand toward someone or something in order to show someone where a person or thing is: *~ (at/to/toward sb/sth)* *"What's your name?" he asked, pointing at the child with his pen.* ✦ *He pointed to the spot where the house used to stand.* ✦ *She pointed in my direction.* ✦ *It's rude to point!* ✦ *~ sth* *She pointed her finger in my direction.*
> AIM **2** [T] *~ sth (at sb/sth)* to aim something at someone or something: *He pointed the gun at her head.*
> FACE DIRECTION **3** [I] *+ adv./prep.* to face in or be directed toward a particular direction: *The telescope was pointing in the wrong direction.* ✦ *The signpost pointed straight ahead.* ✦ *A compass needle points north.*
> LEAD TO **4** [I, T] to lead to or suggest a particular development or logical argument: *+ adv./prep. The evidence seems to point in that direction.* ✦ *~ the way + adv./prep. The fans are looking to the new players to point the way to victory.*
> SHOW THE WAY **5** [T] to show someone which way to go: *~ sb + adv./prep. I wonder if you could point me in the right direction for the bus station.* ✦ *~ the way + adv./prep. A series of yellow arrows pointed the way to reception.*
> WALL **6** [T] *~ sth* to put MORTAR between the bricks of a wall
   IDM **point the/a finger (at sb)** to accuse someone of doing something: *We often point the finger at someone else when things go wrong.* ✦ *The article points an accusing finger at the authorities.*
   PHR V **,point sb/sth↔'out (to sb)** to stretch your finger out toward someone or something in order to show someone which person or thing you are referring to: *I'll point him out to you next time he comes in.* | **,point 'out (to sb)** | **,point sth↔'out (to sb)** to mention something in order to give someone information about it or make them notice it: *She tried in vain to point out to him the unfairness of his actions.* ✦ *He pointed out the dangers of driving alone.* ✦ *~ that... I should point out that not one of these paintings is original.* ✦ *+ speech "It's not very far," she pointed out.* ➾ language bank at ARGUE **'point to sth 1** to mention something that you think is important and/or the reason why a particular situation exists: *The board of directors pointed to falling productivity to justify their decision.* **2** to suggest that something is true or likely: *All the signs point to a successful year ahead.* **,point sth↔'up** (*formal*) to emphasize something so that it becomes more noticeable **SYN** HIGHLIGHT: *The conference merely pointed up divisions in the party.*

,**point-and-'click** *adj.* (*computing*) able to be used with a mouse

,**point-and-'shoot** *adj.* (of a camera) easy to use, without a person needing to adjust controls on it

,**point-'blank** *adj.* [only before noun] **1** (of a shot) fired with the gun touching or very close to the person or thing it is aimed at: *The officer was shot dead **at point-blank range**.* **2** (of something that is said) very definite and direct, and not very polite **SYN** BLUNT: *a point-blank refusal*

▶ **point-ˈblank** *adv.*: *She fired point-blank at his chest.* ◆ *He refused point-blank to be photographed.*

pointe /pɔɪnt; pwænt/ *noun* [U] (also **pointes** /pwænt/ [pl.]) a position in BALLET in which a dancer balances on the TIPS (= ends) of his/her toes

point·ed 🖋 /ˈpɔɪntəd/ *adj.*
1 having a sharp end: *a pointed chin* ◆ *pointed teeth* ◆ *a pointed instrument* ➔ see also POINTY **2** aimed in a clear and often critical way against a particular person or their behavior: *a pointed comment/remark* ◆ *His words were a pointed reminder of her position.*

point·ed·ly /ˈpɔɪntədli/ *adv.* in a way that is clearly intended to show what you mean or to express criticism: *She yawned and looked pointedly at her watch.*

point·er /ˈpɔɪntər/ *noun* **1** (*informal*) a piece of advice: *Here are some pointers on how to go about the writing task.* **2** ~ (**to sth**) a sign that something exists; a sign that shows how something may develop in the future: *The surge in car sales was regarded as an encouraging pointer to an improvement in the economy.* **3** a thin strip of metal that points to the numbers on a DIAL on a piece of equipment for measuring something **4** a stick used to point to things on a map or picture on a wall **5** (*computing*) a small symbol, for example an arrow, that marks a point on a computer screen **6** a large dog used in hunting, trained to stand still with its nose pointing toward the birds that are being hunted

ˈpointer ˌfinger *noun* a child's word for the INDEX FINGER

ˈpoint guard *noun* (in basketball) the player who directs the team's offensive players

poin·til·lism /ˈpɔɪntəˌlɪzəm/ *noun* [U] a style of painting that was developed in France in the late 19th century in which very small dots of color are used to build up the picture
▶ **poin·til·list** /-lɪst/ *adj.* **poin·til·list** *noun*: *Seurat, the French pointillist*

point·ing /ˈpɔɪntɪŋ/ *noun* [U] the MORTAR that is put in the spaces between the bricks or stones in a wall; the method of filling in the spaces with MORTAR

ˈpointing deˌvice *noun* (*computing*) a mouse or other device that allows you to move the CURSOR on a computer screen

point·less /ˈpɔɪntləs/ *adj.* having no purpose; not worth doing: *We searched until we knew it would be pointless to continue.* ▶ **point·less·ly** *adv.*: *He argued pointlessly with his parents.* **point·less·ness** *noun* [U]: *the pointlessness of war*

ˈpoint man *noun* a soldier who goes in front of the others to look for danger: (*figurative*) *the President's point man on education* (= the person who is responsible for it)

ˌpoint of ˈorder *noun* (*pl.* **points of order**) (*formal*) a question about whether the rules of behavior in a formal discussion or meeting are being followed correctly

ˌpoint of ˈreference *noun* (*pl.* **points of reference**) something that you already know that helps you understand a situation or explain something to someone

ˌpoint of ˈsale *noun* [sing.] the place where a product is sold: *More information on healthy foods should be provided at the point of sale.*

ˌpoint of ˈuse *noun* [sing.] the place where a product or a service is actually used: *In some countries medical care is free at the point of use.*

ˌpoint of ˈview *noun* (*pl.* **points of view**) **1** the particular attitude or opinion that someone has about something: *Why can't you ever see my point of view?* ◆ *There are a number of different points of view on this issue.* ◆ *From my point of view* (= as far as I was concerned), *the party was a complete success.* **2** a particular way of considering or judging a situation SYN ANGLE: *These statistics are important from an ecological point of view.* ◆ *The book is written from the father's point of view.*

point·y /ˈpɔɪnti/ *adj.* (*informal*) with a point at one end SYN POINTED: *pointy ears* ◆ (*humorous*) *Don't try to argue when*

you find yourself at the *pointy end* of a knife (= when someone is threatening you with a knife).

poise /pɔɪz/ *noun, verb*
● *noun* [U] **1** a calm and confident manner with control of your feelings or behavior **2** the ability to move or stand in an elegant way with good control of your body
● *verb* [I, T] to be or hold something steady in a particular position, especially above something else: + *adv./prep. The hawk poised in mid-air ready to swoop.* ◆ ~ **sth/yourself to do sth** *He was poising himself to launch a final attack.* ◆ ~ **sth/yourself + adv./prep.** *She poised the javelin in her hand before the throw.*

poised /pɔɪzd/ *adj.* **1** [not before noun] in a position that is completely still but is ready to move at any moment: ~ (**on, above, over, etc. sth**) *Tina was tense, her hand poised over the telephone.* ◆ *He stopped writing and looked at me, pen poised.* ◆ ~ **to do sth** *The cat crouched in the grass, poised to jump.* **2** [not before noun] ~ (**in, on, above, etc. sth**) in a position that is balanced but likely to change in one direction or another: *The cup was poised on the edge of the chair.* ◆ (*figurative*) *The world stood poised between peace and war.* **3** [not before noun] completely ready for something or to do something SYN SET: ~ **for sth** *The economy is poised for recovery.* ◆ ~ **to do sth** *She is poised to become the highest-paid supermodel in the fashion world.* **4** having a calm and confident manner and in control of your feelings and behavior: *He is a remarkably poised young man.* SYN ASSURED

poi·son 🖋 /ˈpɔɪzn/ *noun, verb*
● *noun* [C, U] **1** a substance that causes death or harm if it is swallowed or absorbed into the body: *Some mushrooms contain a deadly poison.* ◆ *How did he die? Was it poison?* ◆ *The dog was killed by rat poison* (= poison intended to kill RATS). ◆ *to hunt with poison arrows* ◆ *bombs containing poison gas* **2** an idea, a feeling, etc. that is extremely harmful: *the poison of racial hatred*
IDM **what's your poison?** (*informal, humorous*) used to ask someone what alcoholic drink they would like ➔ more at MAN *n.*
● *verb* **1** ~ **sb/yourself (with sth)** to harm or kill a person or an animal by giving them poison **2** ~ **sth** to put poison in or on something: *a poisoned arrow* ◆ *Someone had been poisoning his food.* ◆ *Large sections of the river have been poisoned by toxic waste from factories.* **3** ~ **sth** to have a bad effect on something: *His comment served only to poison the atmosphere still further.* ◆ *She succeeded in poisoning their minds against me.*

poi·son·er /ˈpɔɪzənər/ *noun* a person who murders someone by using poison

poi·son·ing /ˈpɔɪzənɪŋ/ *noun* [U, C] **1** the fact or state of having swallowed or absorbed poison: *a series of deaths caused by carbon monoxide poisoning* ◆ *At least 10,000 children are involved in accidental poisonings every year.* **2** the act of killing or harming someone or something by giving them poison: *The police suspected poisoning.* ◆ *The rats were controlled by poisoning.* ➔ see also BLOOD POISONING, FOOD POISONING

ˌpoison ˈivy *noun* [U] a climbing plant that causes painful ITCHY spots on the skin when you touch it

ˌpoison ˈoak *noun* [U] a bush that causes painful ITCHY spots on the skin when you touch it

poi·son·ous 🖋 /ˈpɔɪzənəs/ *adj.*
1 causing death or illness if swallowed or absorbed into the body SYN TOXIC: *poisonous chemicals/plants* ◆ *This gas is highly poisonous.* ◆ *The leaves of certain trees are poisonous to cattle.* **2** (of animals and insects) producing a poison that can cause death or illness if the animal or insect bites you SYN VENOMOUS: *poisonous snakes* **3** extremely unpleasant or unfriendly: *the poisonous atmosphere in the office*

ˌpoison-ˈpen ˌletter *noun* an unpleasant letter that is not signed and is intended to upset the person who receives it

'poison ,pill noun (informal, business) a form of defense used by a company to prevent, or to reduce the effect of, a TAKEOVER BID that they do not want, for example by selling some of their important possessions

poke /poʊk/ verb, noun

• verb **1** [T] to quickly push your fingers or another object into someone or something SYN PROD: ~ sb/sth with sth *She poked him in the ribs with her elbow.* ◆ ~ sth into sth *She poked her elbow into his ribs.* ◆ ~ sb/sth *I'm sick of being poked and prodded by doctors.* ◆ *She got up and poked the fire* (= to make it burn more strongly). **2** [T] ~ sth + adv./prep. to push something somewhere or move it in a particular direction with a small quick movement: *He poked his head around the corner to check that nobody was coming.* ◆ *Someone had poked a message under the door.* ◆ *Don't poke her eye out with that stick!* **3** [I] ~ + adv./prep. if an object is **poking out of, through, etc.** something, you can see a part of it that is no longer covered by something else: *The end of the cable was left poking out of the wall.* ◆ *Clumps of grass poked up through the snow.* **4** [T] ~ a hole in something (with something) to make a hole in something by pushing your finger or another object into it: *The kids poked holes in the ice with sticks.*
  IDM **poke fun at sb/sth** to say unkind things about someone or something in order to make other people laugh at them SYN RIDICULE: *Her novels poke fun at the upper class.* ⊃ more at NOSE *n.*
  PHR V **,poke a'round** (informal) to look for something, especially something that is hidden among other things that you have to move: *The police spent the day poking around in his office but found nothing.* ◆ (figurative) *We've had journalists poking around and asking a lot of questions.* **'poke at sth** to push a pointed object, your finger, etc. at something repeatedly with small quick movements: *He poked at the spaghetti with a fork.*

• noun [C, usually sing.] the action of quickly pushing your fingers or another object into someone or something: *to give the fire a poke* ◆ *He gave me a poke in the ribs to wake me up.*
  IDM **have a poke around** (informal) to look carefully around a place to see what you can find; to try to find out information about someone or something **take a poke at sb/sth** (old-fashioned, informal) to make an unkind remark about someone or something; to laugh at someone or something ⊃ more at PIG *n.*

pok·er /'poʊkər/ noun **1** [U] a card game for two or more people, in which the players bet on the values of the cards they hold **2** [C] a metal stick for moving or breaking up coal in a fire

'poker-,faced adj. (informal) with an expression on your face that does not show what you are thinking or feeling ▶ **'poker ,face** noun: *He maintained a poker face.*

pok·y (also **poke·y**) /'poʊki/ adj. (informal) (**pok·i·er, pok·i·est**) extremely slow and annoying

pol /pɑl/ noun (informal) = POLITICIAN

po·lar /'poʊlər/ adj. [only before noun] **1** connected with, or near the North or South Pole: *the polar regions* ◆ *polar explorers* **2** (technical) connected with the POLE (= the positive and negative ends) of a MAGNET: *polar attraction* **3** (formal) used to describe something that is the complete opposite of something else: *The parents' position is often the polar opposite of the child's.*

'polar ,bear noun a white BEAR that lives near the North Pole

po·lar·i·ty /pə'lærəti/ noun [U] **1** ~ (between A and B) (formal) the situation when two tendencies, opinions, etc. oppose each other: *the growing polarity between the left and right wings of the party* **2** [U, C] (physics) the condition of having two POLES with opposite qualities

po·lar·ize /'poʊlə,raɪz/ verb **1** [I, T] to separate or make people separate into two groups with completely opposite opinions: *Public opinion has polarized on this issue.* ◆ ~ sth *The issue has polarized public opinion.* **2** [T] ~ sth (physics) to make waves of light, etc. VIBRATE in a single direction **3** [T] ~ sth (physics) to give polarity to something: *to polarize a magnet* ▶ **po·lar·i·za·tion** /,poʊlərə'zeɪʃn/ noun [U, C]

Po·lar·oid™ /'poʊlə,rɔɪd/ noun **1** (also **,Polaroid 'camera**) [C] a camera that can produce a photograph within a few seconds **2** [C] a photograph that has been taken with a Polaroid camera **3** [U] a transparent substance that is put on SUNGLASSES and car windows to make the sun seem less bright: *Polaroid sunglasses* **4** Polaroids (also **,Polaroid 'sunglasses**) [pl.] SUNGLASSES that have a layer of Polaroid on them

pole /poʊl/ noun, verb

• noun **1** a long, thin, straight piece of wood or metal, especially one with the end placed in the ground, used as a support: *a tent pole* ◆ *a ski pole* ◆ *a curtain pole* ⊃ picture at SPORT ⊃ see also FLAGPOLE, TELEPHONE POLE, TOTEM POLE **2** either of the two points at the opposite ends of the line on which the earth or any other planet turns: *the North/South Pole* ⊃ see also MAGNETIC POLE (1) **3** (physics) either of the two ends of a MAGNET, or the positive or negative points of an electric battery ⊃ see also MAGNETIC POLE (2) **4** either of two opposite or contrasting extremes: *Their opinions were at opposite poles of the debate.*
  IDM **be poles apart** to be widely separated; to have no interests that you share ⊃ more at GREASY, TOUCH

• verb [T, I] ~ (sth) + adv prep. to move a boat by pushing on the bottom of a river, etc. with a pole

pole·ax /'poʊlæks/ verb ~ sb to hit someone very hard so that they fall down and cannot stand up again

pole·cat /'poʊlkæt/ noun **1** (informal) = SKUNK **2** a small, European, wild animal with a long thin body, dark brown fur, and a strong unpleasant smell

po·lem·ic /pə'lemɪk/ noun (formal) **1** [C] a speech or a piece of writing that argues very strongly for or against something or someone **2** [U] (also **po·lem·ics** [pl.]) the practice or skill of arguing strongly for or against something or someone: *Her speech was memorable for its polemic rather than its substance.*

po·lem·i·cal /pə'lemɪkl/ (also less frequent **po·lem·ic**) adj. (formal) involving strong arguments for or against something, often in opposition to the opinion of others

po·lem·i·cist /pə'lemɪsɪst/ noun (formal) a person who makes skillful use of polemic

po·len·ta /pə'lentə/ noun [U] **1** a yellow food made with CORNMEAL (= special flour), used in Italian cooking **2** the special flour used to make polenta

'pole po,sition noun [U, C] the leading position at the start of a race involving cars or bicycles

the 'Pole Star noun [sing.] the star that is above the North Pole in the sky

the 'pole vault noun [sing.] a sports event in which people try to jump over a high bar, using a long pole to push themselves off the ground ▶ **'pole-,vaulter** noun **'pole-,vaulting** noun [U]

po·lice /pə'liːs/ noun, verb

• noun often **the police** [pl.] an official organization whose job is to make people obey the law and to prevent and solve crime; the people who work for this organization: *A man was arrested by the police and held for questioning.* ◆ *Get out of the house or I'll call the police.* ◆ *Police suspect a local gang.* ◆ *a police car* ◆ *Hundreds of police in riot gear struggled to control the violence.* ⊃ see also KITCHEN POLICE, SECRET POLICE

• verb **1** ~ sth (of the police, army, etc.) to go around a particular area to make sure that no one is breaking the law there: *The border will be policed by UN officials.* **2** ~ sth (of a committee, etc.) to make sure that a particular set of rules is obeyed SYN MONITOR: *The profession is policed by its own regulatory body.*

po'lice com,missioner noun = COMMISSIONER

po·lice de·part·ment *noun* the police organization of a particular city or town

po·lice dog *noun* a dog that is trained to find or attack suspected criminals

po·lice force *noun* the police organization of a country, district, city, or town

po·lice·man /pə'lismən/ *noun* (*pl.* **po·lice·men** /-mən/) a male police officer ⊃ note at GENDER

po·lice of·fi·cer (also **of·fi·cer**) *noun* a member of the police

po·lice state *noun* (*disapproving*) a country where people's freedom, especially to travel and to express political opinions, is controlled by the government, with the help of the police

po·lice sta·tion (also **station house**) *noun* the office of a local police force: *The suspect was taken to the nearest police station for questioning.*

po·lice·wom·an /pə'lis,wumən/ *noun* (*pl.* **po·lice·wom·en** /-,wimən/) a female police officer ⊃ note at GENDER

po·lic·ing /pə'lisɪŋ/ *noun* [U] **1** the activity of keeping order in a place with police: *community policing* **2** the activity of controlling an industry, an activity, etc. to make sure that people obey the rules

pol·i·cy 🔑 **AWL** /'pɑləsi/ *noun* (*pl.* **pol·i·cies**)
1 [C, U] ~ **(on sth)** a plan of action agreed or chosen by a political party, a business, etc.: *the present government's policy on education* ◆ *The company has adopted a firm policy on shoplifting.* ◆ *We have tried to pursue a policy of neutrality.* ◆ *U. S. foreign/domestic policy* ◆ *They have had a significant change in policy on paternity leave.* ◆ *a policy document* ⊃ collocations at POLITICS **2** [C, U] (*formal*) a principle that you believe in that influences how you behave; a way in which you usually behave: *She is following her usual policy of ignoring all offers of help.* ◆ (*saying*) *Honesty is the best policy.* **3** [C] a written statement of a contract of insurance: *Check the terms of the policy before you sign.*

pol·i·cy·hold·er /'pɑləsi,houldər/ *noun* (*formal*) a person or group that holds an insurance policy

po·li·o /'pouliou/ (also *formal* **po·li·o·my·e·li·tis** /,pouliou,maɪə'laɪtɪs/) *noun* [U] an infectious disease that affects the central nervous system and can cause temporary or permanent PARALYSIS (= loss of control or feeling in part or most of the body)

pol·ish 🔑 /'pɑlɪʃ/ *noun, verb*
● *noun* **1** [U, C] a substance used when rubbing a surface to make it smooth and shiny: *furniture/floor/shoe/silver polish* ◆ *wax polish* ⊃ see also NAIL POLISH **2** [sing.] an act of polishing something: *I give it a polish now and again.* **3** [sing.] the shiny appearance of something after it has been polished **SYN** LUSTER, SHEEN **4** [U] a high quality of performance achieved with great skill: *She played the cello with the polish of a much older musician.* **5** [U] high standards of behavior; being polite **SYN** REFINEMENT **IDM** see SPIT *n.*
● *verb* **1** [T, I] to make something smooth and shiny by rubbing it: ~ **(sth)** *Polish shoes regularly to protect the leather.* ◆ ~ **sth (up) (with sth)** *He polished his glasses with a handkerchief.* **2** [T] to make changes to something in order to improve it: ~ **sth** *The statement was carefully polished and checked before release.* ◆ ~ **sth up** *The hotel has polished up its act* (= improved its service) *since last year.*
PHR V **polish sb↔off** (*informal*) to kill someone **polish sth↔off** (*informal*) to finish something, especially food, quickly: *He polished off the remains of the apple pie.*

pol·ished /'pɑlɪʃt/ *adj.* **1** shiny as a result of polishing **SYN** GLEAMING **2** elegant, confident, and/or highly skilled **SYN** FINE

pol·ish·er /'pɑlɪʃər/ *noun* a machine for polishing something: *a floor polisher*

po·lit·bu·ro /'pɑlət,byurou; 'poulət-/ *noun* (*pl.* **po·lit·bu·ros**) the most important committee of a Communist party, with the power to decide on policy

po·lite 🔑 /pə'laɪt/ *adj.* (**po·lit·er, po·lit·est**) **HELP** more **polite** and **most polite** are also common
1 having or showing good manners and respect for the feelings of others **SYN** COURTEOUS: *Please be polite to our guests.* ◆ *We were all too polite to object.* **ANT** IMPOLITE
2 socially correct but not always sincere: *I don't know how to make polite conversation.* ◆ *The performance was greeted with polite applause.* **3** [only before noun] from a class of society that believes it is better than others: *"Butt" is not a word we use in polite company.* ▶ **po·lite·ly** *adv.* **po·lite·ness** *noun* [U]

pol·i·tesse /,pɑlə'tɛs/ *noun* [U] (from *French, formal, literary*) POLITENESS

pol·i·tic /'pɑlə,tɪk/ *adj.* (*formal*) (of actions) based on good judgment **SYN** PRUDENT, WISE: *It seemed politic to say nothing.* ⊃ see also BODY POLITIC

po·lit·i·cal 🔑 /pə'lɪtɪkl/ *adj.*
1 connected with the state, government, or public affairs: *a monarch without political power* ◆ *He was a political prisoner* (= one who was put in prison because he was thought to be harmful to the state). **2** connected with the different groups working in politics, especially their policies and the competition between them: *a political debate/party/leader* ◆ *What are your political sympathies?* **3** (of people) interested in or active in politics: *She became very political at college.* ◆ *I'm not a political animal* (= a person who is interested in politics). **4** concerned with power, status, etc. within an organization, rather than with matters of principle: *I suspect that he was dismissed for political reasons.* ⊃ see also POLITICALLY

po·lit·i·cal ac·tion com·mit·tee *noun* (*abbr.* PAC) a group of people who collect money to support the candidates and policies that will help them achieve their political and social aims

po·lit·i·cal a·sy·lum *noun* [U] (*formal*) = ASYLUM

po·lit·i·cal cor·rect·ness *noun* [U] (sometimes *disapproving*) the principle of avoiding language and behavior that may offend particular groups of people ⊃ see also POLITICALLY CORRECT

po·lit·i·cal e·con·omy *noun* [U] the study of how nations organize the production and use of wealth

po·lit·i·cal ge·og·ra·phy *noun* [U] the way in which the world is divided into different countries, especially as a subject of study

po·lit·i·cal·ly 🔑 /pə'lɪtɪkli/ *adv.*
in a way that is connected with politics: *a politically sensitive issue* ◆ *It makes sense politically as well as economically.*

po·lit·i·cal·ly cor·rect *adj.* (*abbr.* PC) used to describe language or behavior that deliberately tries to avoid offending particular groups of people ⊃ see also POLITICAL CORRECTNESS

po·lit·i·cal·ly in·cor·rect *adj.* failing to avoid language or behavior that may offend particular groups of people

po·lit·i·cal sci·ence (also **pol·i·tics**) *noun* [U] the study of government and politics

po·lit·i·cal sci·en·tist *noun* an expert in political science

pol·i·ti·cian 🔑 /,pɑlə'tɪʃn/ *noun*
1 (also *informal* **pol**) a person whose job is concerned with politics, especially as an elected member of a LEGISLATURE (= governing body) **2** (*disapproving*) a person who is good at using different situations in an organization to try to get power or advantage for himself or herself

po·lit·i·cize /pə'lɪtə,saɪz/ *verb* [often passive] **1** ~ **sth** to make something a political issue: *the highly politicized issue of unemployment* **2** ~ **sb/sth** to make someone or something become more involved in politics: *The rural population has become increasingly politicized in recent years.* ▶ **po·lit·i·ci·za·tion** /pə,lɪtəsə'zeɪʃn/ *noun* [U]: *the politicization of education*

| t **tea** | t̬ **butter** | d **did** | k **cat** | g **got** | tʃ **chin** | dʒ **June** | f **fall** |

pol·i·tick·ing /ˈpɑləˌtɪkɪŋ/ *noun* [U] (often *disapproving*) political activity, especially to win support for yourself

po·lit·i·co /pəˈlɪtɪˌkoʊ/ *noun* (*pl.* **po·lit·i·cos**) (*informal, disapproving*) a politician; a person who is active in politics

Politics

power

- **create/form/be the leader of** a political party
- **gain/take/win/lose/regain** control of Congress
- **start/spark/lead/be on the brink of** a revolution
- **be engaged/locked in** an internal power struggle
- **lead/form** a rival/breakaway faction
- **seize/take** control of power/the government
- **bring down/overthrow/topple** the government/president/regime
- **abolish/overthrow/restore** the monarchy
- **establish/install** a military dictatorship/a stable government
- **be forced/removed/driven from** office/power
- **resign/step down as** party leader/president/prime minister/governor/a senator
- **enter/retire from/return to** political life

political debate

- **spark/provoke** a heated/hot/intense/lively debate
- **engage in/participate in/contribute to** (the) political/public debate (on/over sth)
- **get involved in/feel excluded from** the political process
- **launch/start/lead/spearhead** a campaign/movement
- **join/be linked with** the peace/anti-war/feminist/civil rights movement
- **criticize/speak out against/challenge/support** the government
- **lobby/put pressure on** the government (to do sth)
- **come under fire/pressure from** opposition parties

policy

- **call for/demand/propose/push for/advocate** democratic/political/land reform(s)
- **formulate/implement** domestic economic policy
- **change/influence/shape/have an impact on** government/economic/public policy
- **be consistent with/be in line with/go against/be opposed to** government policy
- **reform/restructure/modernize** the tax system
- **privatize/improve/deliver/make cuts in** public services
- **invest (heavily) in/spend sth on** schools/education/public services/(the) infrastructure
- **nationalize** the banks/the oil industry
- **promise/propose/deliver/give** ($80 billion in/significant/substantial/massive) tax cuts
- **a/the budget is approved/passed** by Congress/the House/the Senate

making laws

- **have a majority in/have seats in** Congress/the House/the Senate
- **propose/sponsor** a bill/legislation/a resolution/an amendment
- **introduce/bring in/draw up/draft/adopt/pass** a bill/a law/a resolution/an amendment/legislation/measures
- **amend/repeal** an act/a law/legislation
- **veto/vote against/oppose** a bill/legislation/a measure/a proposal/a resolution
- **get/require/be decided by** a majority vote
- ➲ more collocations at ECONOMY, VOTE

pol·i·tics 🔊 /ˈpɑləˌtɪks/ *noun*

1 [U] the activities involved in getting and using power in public life, and being able to influence decisions that affect a country or a society: *party politics* ♦ *local politics* ♦ *He's thinking of going into politics* (= trying to become a member of Congress, etc.) ♦ *a major figure in Canadian politics* **2** [U] (*disapproving*) matters concerned with getting or using power within a particular group or organization: *I don't want to get involved in office politics.* ♦ *the internal politics of the legal profession* ♦ *sexual politics* (= concerning relationships of power between the sexes) **3** [pl.] a person's political views or beliefs: *His politics are extreme.* **4** Politics [U] = POLITICAL SCIENCE: *a degree in Politics* **5** [sing.] a system of political beliefs; a state of political affairs: *A politics of the future has to engage with new ideas.*

pol·i·ty /ˈpɑləti/ *noun* (*pl.* **pol·i·ties**) (*technical*) **1** [C] a society as a political unit **2** [U] the form or process of government

pol·ka /ˈpoʊlkə; ˈpoʊkə/ *noun* a fast dance for two people together that was popular in the 19th century; a piece of music for this dance

pol·ka dot /ˈpoʊkə ˌdɑt/ *noun* one of many dots that together form a pattern, especially on cloth: *a polka-dot tie* ➲ picture at CLOTHES

poll /poʊl/ *noun, verb*

● *noun* **1** (also oˈpinion ˌpoll) [C] the process of questioning people who are representative of a larger group in order to get information about the general opinion **SYN** SURVEY: *to carry out/conduct a poll* ♦ *A recent poll suggests some surprising changes in public opinion.* **2 the polls** [pl.] (*politics*) places where people go to vote in an election: *Tuesday is the day America goes to the polls* (= when elections are held). ♦ *Polls close* (= voting ends) *at 9 p.m.* **3** [C, usually pl.] the number of votes recorded in an election **SYN** BALLOT: *Davis is ahead in the polls.* ➲ see also EXIT POLL, STRAW POLL

● *verb* **1** [T, I] to receive a particular number of votes in an election: ~ **sth** *They polled 39% of the vote in the last election.* ♦ **+ adv./prep.** *The Republicans have polled well* (= received many votes) *in recent elections.* **2** [T, usually passive] ~ **sb** to ask a large number of members of the public what they think about something **SYN** SURVEY: *Over 50% of those polled were against the proposed military action.*

pol·lard /ˈpɑlərd/ *verb* [usually passive] ~ **sth** (*technical*) to cut off the branches at the top of a tree so that the lower branches will grow more thickly

pol·len /ˈpɑlən/ *noun* [U] fine powder, usually yellow, that is formed in flowers and carried to other flowers of the same kind by the wind or by insects, to make those flowers produce seeds ➲ collocations at LIFE

ˈpollen ˌcount *noun* [usually sing.] a number that shows the amount of pollen in the air, used to warn people whose health is affected by it

ˈpollen ˌtube *noun* (*biology*) a tube that grows when pollen lands on the STIGMA (= a part of the female organ) of a flower, in order to carry the male cell to the OVULE (= the part that contains the female cell)

pol·li·nate /ˈpɑləˌneɪt/ *verb* ~ **sth** to put pollen into a flower or plant so that it produces seeds: *flowers pollinated by bees/the wind* ► **pol·li·na·tion** /ˌpɑləˈneɪʃn/ *noun* [U]

poll·ing /ˈpoʊlɪŋ/ *noun* [U] **1** the activity of voting: *Polling has been heavy since 8 a.m.* **2** the act of asking questions as part of an opinion poll

ˈpolling ˌplace (also **ˈpolling ˌstation**) *noun* a building where people go to vote in an election

pol·li·wog (also **pol·ly·wog**) /ˈpɑliˌwɑg/ *noun* = TADPOLE

poll·ster /ˈpoʊlstər/ *noun* a person who makes or asks the questions in an opinion POLL

ˈpoll tax *noun* a tax that must be paid at the same rate by every person or every adult in a particular area

pol·lu·tant /pəˈlutnt/ *noun* (*formal*) a substance that pollutes something, especially air and water

pol·lute /pəˈlut/ *verb* to add dirty or harmful substances to land, air, water, etc. so that it is no longer pleasant or safe to use: **~ sth** *the exhaust fumes that are polluting our cities* ◆ **~ sth by/with sth** *The river has been polluted with toxic waste from local factories.* ◆ (*figurative*) *a society polluted by racism* ⊃ collocations at ENVIRONMENT

pol·lut·er /pəˈluːtər/ *noun* a person, company, country, etc. that causes pollution

pol·lu·tion /pəˈluːʃn/ *noun* [U]
1 the process of making air, water, soil, etc. dirty; the state of being dirty: *air/water pollution* ◆ *to reduce levels of environmental pollution* ⊃ collocations at ENVIRONMENT
2 substances that make air, water, soil, etc. dirty: *beaches covered with pollution* **3 noise/light ~** harmful or annoying levels of noise, or of artificial light at night

Pol·ly·an·na /ˌpɑliˈænə/ *noun* [usually sing.] a person who is always cheerful and expects only good things to happen
ORIGIN From the name of a character in a children's story by Eleanor Hodgman Porter.

pol·ly·wog = POLLIWOG

po·lo /ˈpoʊloʊ/ *noun* [U] a game in which two teams of players riding on horses try to hit a ball into a goal using long wooden hammers (called MALLETS) ⊃ see also WATER POLO

pol·o·naise /ˌpɑləˈneɪz/ *noun* a slow Polish dance that was popular in the 19th century; a piece of music for this dance

po·lo·ni·um /pəˈloʊniəm/ *noun* [U] (*symb.* **Po**) a chemical element. Polonium is a RADIOACTIVE metal that is present in nature when URANIUM decays.

'polo ˌshirt *noun* an informal shirt with short sleeves, a COLLAR, and a few buttons at the neck ⊃ picture at CLOTHES

pol·ter·geist /ˈpoʊltərˌɡaɪst/ *noun* a GHOST that some people believe makes loud noises and throws objects

poly- /ˈpɑli/ *combining form* (in nouns, adjectives, and adverbs) many: *polygamy* ◆ *polyphonic*

pol·y·an·dry /ˈpɑliˌændri/ *noun* [U] (*technical*) the custom of having more than one husband at the same time ⊃ compare POLYGAMY ▶ **pol·y·an·drous** /ˌpɑliˈændrəs/ *adj.*

pol·y·car·bon·ate /ˌpɑliˈkɑrbənət; -ˌneɪt/ *noun* [U, C] (*technical*) a very strong transparent plastic used, for example, in windows and LENSES

pol·y·es·ter /ˌpɑliˈɛstər/ *noun* [U] a strong material made of FIBERS (called polyesters) that are produced by chemical processes, often mixed with other materials and used especially for making clothes: *a cotton and polyester shirt*

pol·y·eth·yl·ene /ˌpɑliˈɛθəˌlin/ *noun* [U] a strong, thin, plastic material, used especially for making bags or for wrapping things in

po·lyg·a·my /pəˈlɪɡəmi/ *noun* [U] (*technical*) the custom of having more than one wife at the same time ⊃ compare POLYANDRY ▶ **po·lyg·a·mist** /pəˈlɪɡəmɪst/ *noun* **po·lyg·a·mous** /pəˈlɪɡəməs/ *adj.*: *a polygamous marriage/society*

pol·y·glot /ˈpɑliˌɡlɑt/ *adj.* (*formal*) knowing, using, or written in more than one language **SYN** MULTILINGUAL: *a polyglot nation* ▶ **pol·y·glot** *noun*

pol·y·gon /ˈpɑliˌɡɑn/ *noun* (*geometry*) a flat shape with at least three straight sides and angles, and usually five or more ▶ **po·lyg·o·nal** /pəˈlɪɡənl/ *adj.*

pol·y·graph /ˈpɑliˌɡræf/ *noun* (*technical*) (*formal*) = LIE DETECTOR

pol·y·he·dron /ˌpɑliˈhidrən/ *noun* (*pl.* **pol·y·he·dra** /-drə/ or **pol·y·he·drons**) (*geometry*) a solid shape with many flat sides, usually more than six ▶ **pol·y·he·dral** /-ˈhidrəl/ *adj.*

pol·y·math /ˈpɑliˌmæθ/ *noun* (*formal, approving*) a person who knows a lot about many different subjects

pol·y·mer /ˈpɑləmər/ *noun* (*chemistry*) a natural or artificial substance consisting of large MOLECULES (= groups of atoms) that are made from combinations of small simple MOLECULES

po·lym·er·ize /pəˈlɪməˌraɪz; ˈpɑləməˌraɪz/ *verb* [I, T] **~ (sth)** (*chemistry*) to combine, or to make units of a chemical

combine, to make a POLYMER: *The substance polymerizes to form a hard plastic.* ▶ **po·lym·er·i·za·tion** /pəˌlɪmərəˈzeɪʃn; ˌpɑləmərə-/ *noun* [U]

pol·y·mor·phous /ˌpɑliˈmɔrfəs/ (also **pol·y·mor·phic** /ˌpɑliˈmɔrfɪk/) *adj.* (*formal* or *technical*) having or passing through many stages of development

po·ly·no·mi·al /ˌpɑliˈnoʊmiəl/ *noun* an ALGEBRAIC expression that has more than one group of numbers or letters, joined by the sign + or − ⊃ compare BINOMIAL ▶ **po·ly·no·mi·al** *adj.*

pol·yp /ˈpɑləp/ *noun* **1** (*medical*) a small lump growing inside the body that is caused by disease but is usually harmless **2** a small and very simple sea creature with a body shaped like a tube

po·lyph·o·ny /pəˈlɪfəni/ *noun* [U] (*music*) the combination of several different patterns of musical notes sung together to form a single piece of music **SYN** COUNTERPOINT ▶ **pol·y·phon·ic** /ˌpɑliˈfɑnɪk/ *adj.*

pol·y·pro·pyl·ene /ˌpɑliˈproʊpəˌlin/ *noun* [U] a strong plastic often used for objects such as toys or chairs that are made in a MOLD

po·ly·se·mous /ˌpɑliˈsiməs; pəˈlɪsəməs/ *adj.* (*linguistics*) (of a word) having more than one meaning

po·ly·se·my /pəˈlɪsəmi/ *noun* [U] (*linguistics*) the fact of having more than one meaning

pol·y·sty·rene /ˌpɑliˈstaɪrin/ (also **Sty·ro·foam**™) *noun* [U] a very light soft plastic that is usually white, used especially for making containers that prevent heat loss: *polystyrene cups*

pol·y·syl·la·ble /ˈpɑliˌsɪləbl/ *noun* (*technical*) a word of several (usually more than three) syllables ▶ **pol·y·syl·lab·ic** /ˌpɑlisɪˈlæbɪk/ *adj.*

pol·y·tech·nic /ˌpɑliˈtɛknɪk/ *noun* a school for higher education in technical and other practical subjects

pol·y·the·ism /ˈpɑliθiˌɪzəm/ *noun* [U] the belief that there is more than one god ⊃ compare MONOTHEISM ▶ **pol·y·the·is·tic** /ˌpɑliθiˈɪstɪk/ *adj.*

pol·y·tun·nel /ˈpɑliˌtʌnl/ *noun* a long low structure covered with plastic used for growing seeds or young plants outdoors

pol·y·un·sat·u·rat·ed fat /ˌpɑliʌnˌsætʃəreɪtəd ˈfæt/ *noun* [C, U] (also **pol·y·un·sat·u·rates** /ˌpɑliʌnˈsætʃərəts/ [pl.]) a type of fat found, for example, in seeds and vegetable oils, that does not encourage the harmful development of CHOLESTEROL: *foods that are high in polyunsaturated fats* ⊃ see also MONOUNSATURATED FAT, SATURATED FAT, TRANS-FATTY ACID, UNSATURATED FAT

pol·y·u·re·thane /ˌpɑliˈyʊrəˌθeɪn/ *noun* [U] (*technical*) a type of plastic material used in making paints, glues, etc.

pol·y·va·lent /ˌpɑliˈveɪlənt/ *adj.* **1** (*chemistry*) having a VALENCY of 3 or more **2** (*formal*) having many different functions or forms: *polyvalent managerial skills* ▶ **pol·y·va·lence** /-ləns/ *noun* [U]

pol·y·vi·nyl chlo·ride /ˌpɑlivaɪnl ˈklɔraɪd/ *noun* [U] (*technical*) = PVC

po·made /pəˈmeɪd; poʊ-/ *noun* (*old-fashioned*) [U, C] a liquid that is put on the hair to make it look shiny and smell nice

po·man·der /ˈpɑmændər; ˈpoʊ-/ *noun* a round container filled with dried flowers, leaves, etc. that is used to give a pleasant smell to rooms or clothes

pome·gran·ate /ˈpɑməˌɡrænət/ *noun* a round fruit with thick smooth skin and red flesh full of large seeds ⊃ picture at FRUIT

pom·e·lo /pəˈmɛloʊ; ˈpɑməˌloʊ/ (also **pum·me·lo**) *noun* (*pl.* **pom·e·los**, **pum·me·los**) a large CITRUS fruit that has thick yellow skin and that tastes similar to a GRAPEFRUIT, but sweeter

pom·mel /ˈpʌml; ˈpɑml/ *noun* **1** the higher front part of a SADDLE on a horse **2** the round part on the end of the handle of a SWORD

ˈpommel ˌhorse *noun* a large object on four legs with two handles on top, which GYMNASTS put their hands on and swing their body and legs around

pomp /pɑmp/ *noun* [U] the impressive clothes, decorations, music, etc. and traditional customs that are part of an official occasion or ceremony: *all the pomp and ceremony of a royal wedding*
IDM **pomp and circumstance** formal and impressive ceremony

pom·pa·dour /ˈpɑmpəˌdɔr/ *noun* **1** a men's hairstyle in which a piece of hair at the front of the head is brushed upward and backward **2** a women's hairstyle in which the hair at the front of the head is turned upward and backward in a roll

pom·pom /ˈpɑmpɑm/ (also **pom·pon** /ˈpɑmpɑn/) *noun* **1** a small ball made of wool, used for decoration, especially on a hat ⊃ picture at HAT **2** a large round bunch of strips of plastic, tied to a handle, used by CHEERLEADERS

pomp·ous /ˈpɑmpəs/ *adj.* (*disapproving*) showing that you think you are more important than other people, especially by using long and formal words **SYN** PRETENTIOUS: *a pompous official* ▶ **pom·pos·i·ty** /pɑmˈpɑsəti/ *noun* [U]: *The prince's manner was informal, without a trace of pomposity.* **pomp·ous·ly** *adv.*

pon·cho /ˈpɑntʃou/ *noun* (*pl.* **pon·chos**) a type of coat without sleeves, made from one large piece of cloth with a hole in the middle for the head to go through

pond /pɑnd/ *noun* a small area of still water, especially one that is artificial: *a fish pond*
IDM **across the pond** (*informal*) on the other side of the Atlantic Ocean from the U.S./Britain ⊃ more at BIG

pon·der /ˈpɑndər/ *verb* [I, T] (*formal*) to think about something carefully for a period of time **SYN** CONSIDER: ~ **(about/on/over sth)** *She pondered over his words.* ◆ *They were left to ponder on the implications of the announcement.* ◆ ~ **sth** *The senator pondered the question for a moment.* ◆ ~ **whether, what, etc.…** *They are pondering whether the money could be better used elsewhere.* ◆ **+ speech** *"I wonder why," she pondered aloud.*

pon·der·ous /ˈpɑndərəs/ *adj.* (*formal*) **1** (*disapproving*) (of speech and writing) too slow and careful; serious and boring **SYN** TEDIOUS **2** moving slowly and heavily; able to move only slowly **SYN** LABORED: *She watched the cow's ponderous progress.* ▶ **pon·der·ous·ly** *adv.* **pon·der·ous·ness** *noun* [U]

pone /poun/ *noun* [U] = CORN PONE

pon·tiff /ˈpɑntəf/ *noun* (*formal*) the POPE (= the leader of the Roman Catholic Church)

pon·tif·i·cal /pɑnˈtɪfɪkl/ *adj.* (*formal*) connected with a POPE

pon·tif·i·cate *verb, noun*
● *verb* /pɑnˈtɪfəˌkeɪt/ [I] ~ **(about/on sth)** (*disapproving*) to give your opinions about something in a way that shows that you think you are right
● *noun* /pɑnˈtɪfəkət/ the official position or period in office of a POPE

pon·toon /pɑnˈtun/ *noun* **1** a temporary floating platform built across several boats or hollow structures, especially one used for tying boats to **2** a boat or hollow structure that is one of several used to support a floating platform or bridge: *a pontoon bridge*

po·ny /ˈpouni/ *noun, verb*
● *noun* (*pl.* **po·nies**) a type of small horse ⊃ see also SHETLAND PONY **IDM** see DOG
● *verb* (**po·nies, po·ny·ing, po·nied, po·nied**)
PHR V **pony 'up sth** (*informal*) to pay money for something: *Each guest had to pony up $40 for the meal.*

po·ny·tail /ˈpouniˌteɪl/ *noun* a bunch of hair tied at the back of the head so that it hangs like a horse's tail ⊃ picture at HAIR ⊃ compare PIGTAIL

Ponzi scheme /ˈpɑnzi ˌskim/ *noun* a plan for making money that involves encouraging people to invest by offering them a high rate of interest and using their money to pay earlier INVESTORS. When there are not enough new INVESTORS, people who have recently invested lose their money. **ORIGIN** From Charles Ponzi, who organized the first scheme of this kind in the U.S. in 1919.

pooch /putʃ/ *noun* (*informal*) a dog

poo·dle /ˈpudl/ *noun* a dog with thick curly hair that is sometimes cut into special shapes

poof /puf; puf/ *exclamation* used when talking about something disappearing suddenly: *He walked through—and vanished. Poof! Like that.*

pooh /pu/ *exclamation* used to say that you think someone's idea, suggestion, etc. is not very good or that you do not believe what someone has said: *"I might lose my job for this." "Oh, pooh, no one will care."*

pooh-bah /ˈpu bɑ/ *noun* (*informal*, usually *disapproving*) a person who has a lot of power or authority, especially someone who behaves as though they are more important than other people: *telecommunications pooh-bahs*

ˌpooh-ˈpooh *verb* ~ **sth** (*informal*) to say that a suggestion, an idea, etc. is not true or not worth thinking about

pool /pul/ *noun, verb*
● *noun*
▷ FOR SWIMMING **1** [C] = SWIMMING POOL: *Does the hotel have a pool?* ◆ *relaxing by the pool* ⊃ see also PLUNGE POOL
▷ OF WATER **2** [C] a small area of still water, especially one that has formed naturally: *freshwater pools* ◆ *a tide pool* (= between rocks by the ocean)
▷ OF LIQUID/LIGHT **3** [C] ~ **(of sth)** a small amount of liquid or light lying on a surface: *The body was lying in a pool of blood.* ◆ *a pool of light*
▷ GROUP OF THINGS/PEOPLE **4** [C] ~ **(of sth)** a supply of things or money that is shared by a group of people and can be used when needed: *a pool of cars used by the firm's sales force* **5** [C] ~ **(of sth)** a group of people available for work when needed: *a pool of cheap labor*
▷ GAME **6** [U] a game for two people played with 16 balls on a table, often in bars. Players use CUES (= long sticks) to try to hit the balls into pockets at the edge of the table: *a pool table* ◆ *to shoot* (= play) *pool* ⊃ picture at HOBBY ⊃ compare BILLIARDS **7** [C] an amount of money that is bet by a group of individuals, often on a sports event, by putting money into a fund that is given to the winner; the group of individuals who bet this money: *He won the pool by correctly guessing the final score.* ◆ *Would you like to join the office pool on the NBA finals?* ⊃ see also GENE POOL
● *verb* ~ **sth** to collect money, information, etc. from different people so that it can be used by all of them: *The students work individually, then pool their ideas in groups of six.* ◆ *Police forces across the country are pooling resources in order to solve this crime.*

pool·room /ˈpulrum; -rʊm/ *noun* a place for playing a game of POOL

pool·side /ˈpulsaɪd/ *noun* [sing.] the area around a swimming pool: *lazing at the poolside* ◆ *a poolside bar*

poop /pup/ *noun, verb*
● *noun* **1** (also ˈpoop deck) [C] the raised part at the back end of a ship ⊃ compare STERN **2** [U] (*informal*) the solid waste that is passed through the BOWELS: *dog poop on the sidewalk* **3** [U] (*old-fashioned, informal*) information about something, especially the most recent news
● *verb* (*informal*) **1** [I] to pass solid waste from the BOWELS: *The dog just pooped in the kitchen!* **2** [T] ~ **sb (out)** to make someone very tired
PHR V **poop 'out** to stop working or functioning

pooped /pupt/ (also ˌpooped 'out) *adj.* [not before noun] (*informal*) very tired

poop·er scoop·er /ˈpupər ˌskupər/ (also ˈpoop scoop) *noun* (*informal*) a tool used by dog owners for removing their dogs' solid waste from the streets

poor

disadvantaged ⬩ needy ⬩ low-income ⬩ impoverished ⬩ deprived ⬩ penniless ⬩ hard up

These words all describe someone who has very little or no money and therefore cannot satisfy their basic needs.

poor having very little money; not having enough money for basic needs: *They were too poor to buy shoes for the kids.*

disadvantaged having less money and fewer opportunities than most people in society: *economically disadvantaged areas of the city*

needy poor: *It's a charity that provides assistance to needy children.*

low-income having less money to live on than most people in society: *Our agency helps low-income families pay their heating bills.*

impoverished (*journalism*) poor: *Thousands of impoverished families in rural areas are desperate to move to the cities.*

deprived [usually before noun] without enough food, education, and all the things that are necessary for people to live a happy and comfortable life

WHICH WORD?

Poor is the most general of these words and can be used to describe yourself, another individual person, people as a group, or a country or an area. **Needy** is mostly used to describe people considered as a group. It is not used to talk about yourself or individual people: *poor/needy/low-income children/families* ⬩ ~~They were too needy to buy shoes for the kids.~~ **Low-income** is a polite way to describe people who are poor. **Impoverished** is used, especially in journalism, to talk about poor countries and the people who live there. To talk about poor areas in rich countries, use **deprived**.

penniless (*literary*) having no money; very poor: *He died penniless in Paris.*

hard up (*informal*) having very little money, especially for a short period of time: *I was always hard up as a student.*

PATTERNS

- poor/disadvantaged/needy/low-income/impoverished/deprived/penniless/hard-up **people/families**
- poor/disadvantaged/needy/low-income/impoverished/deprived **areas**
- poor/disadvantaged/low-income/impoverished **countries**
- a(n) poor/disadvantaged/impoverished/deprived **background**

poor 🔑 /pʊr; pɔr/ *adj.* (**poor·er, poor·est**)
> HAVING LITTLE MONEY **1** having very little money; not having enough money for basic needs: *They were too poor to buy shoes for the kids.* ⬩ *We aim to help the poorest families.* ⬩ *It's among the poorer countries of the world.* **ANT** RICH **2 the poor** *noun* [pl.] people who have very little money: *They provided food and shelter for the poor.* **ANT** RICH
> UNFORTUNATE **3** [only before noun] deserving sympathy: *Have you heard about poor old Harry? His wife's left him.* ⬩ *It's hungry—the poor little thing.* ⬩ *"I have tons of homework to do." "Oh, you poor thing."*
> NOT GOOD **4** not good; of a quality that is low or lower than expected: *the party's poor performance in the election* ⬩ *to be in poor health* ⬩ *It was raining heavily and visibility was poor.* ⬩ *poor food/light/soil* ⬩ *to have a poor opinion of someone* (= to not think well of someone) **5** (of a person) not good or skilled at something: *a poor swimmer* ⬩ *a poor judge of character*

⬩ *She's a good teacher but a poor manager.* ⬩ *a poor sailor* (= someone who easily gets sick at sea)
> HAVING LITTLE OF SOMETHING **6** ~ **in sth** having very small amounts of something: *a country poor in natural resources* ⬩ *soil poor in nutrients* **ANT** RICH
IDM **the poor man's sb/sth** a person or thing that is similar to, but of a lower quality than, a particular famous person or thing: *Sparkling white wine is the poor man's champagne.* ⊃ more at ACCOUNT *n.*

poor·house /'pʊrhaʊs; 'pɔr-/ *noun* (in the past) a building where very poor people were sent to live and given work to do

poor·ly /'pʊrli; 'pɔr-/ *adv.* in a way that is not good enough **SYN** BADLY: *a poorly attended meeting* (= at which there are not many people) ⬩ *poorly designed* ⬩ *The job is relatively poorly paid.* ⬩ *Our candidate fared poorly in the election* (= did not get many votes).

poor·ness /'pʊrnəs; 'pɔr-/ *noun* [U] the state of lacking a good quality or feature: *The poorness of the land makes farming impossible.*

ˌ**poor reˈlation** *noun* something that is not treated with as much respect as other similar things because it is not thought to be as good, important, or successful

pop 🔑 /pɑp/ *noun, verb, adj., adv.*
● *noun*
> MUSIC **1** (also ˌ**pop ˈmusic**) [U] popular music that usually has a strong rhythm and simple tunes, often contrasted with other forms of popular music: *rock, pop, and soul* ⊃ collocations at MUSIC
> FATHER **2** (also **pops**) [sing.] (*old-fashioned, informal*) used as a word for "father," especially as a form of address: *Hi, Pop!*
> SOUND **3** [C] a short, sharp, EXPLOSIVE sound: *The cork came out of the bottle with a loud pop.*
> DRINK **4** [U] (*informal*) = SODA
IDM **...a pop** (*informal*) costing a particular amount for each one: *We can charge $50 a pop.*
● *verb* (**-pp-**)
> MAKE SOUND **1** [I, T] ~ **(sth)** to make a short EXPLOSIVE sound; to cause something to make this sound: *the sound of corks popping* **2** [T, I] ~ **(sth)** to burst, or make something burst, with a short EXPLOSIVE sound: *She jumped as someone popped a balloon behind her.*
> GO QUICKLY **3** [I] + **adv./prep.** (*informal*) to go somewhere quickly, suddenly, or for a short time: *I'll pop over and see you this evening.* ⬩ *Why don't you pop in* (= visit us) *for a drink next time you're in the area?*
> PUT QUICKLY **4** [T] ~ **sth** + **adv./prep.** (*informal*) to put something somewhere quickly, suddenly, or for a short time: *He popped his head around the door and said hello.*
> APPEAR SUDDENLY **5** [I] + **adv./prep.** to suddenly appear, especially when not expected: *The window opened and a dog's head popped out.* ⬩ *An idea suddenly popped into his head.* ⬩ (*computing*) *The menu pops up when you click twice on the mouse.*
> OF EARS **6** [I] if your ears **pop** when you are going up or down in a plane, etc., the pressure in them suddenly changes
> OF EYES **7** [I] if your eyes **pop** or **pop out**, they suddenly open fully because you are surprised or excited: *Her eyes nearly popped out of her head when she saw them.*
> TAKE DRUGS **8** [T] ~ **sth** (*informal*) to take a lot of a drug, regularly: *She's been popping pills for months.*
> OPEN HOOD **9** [T] ~ **the hood** to open the HOOD of a car
IDM **pop the question** (*informal*) to ask someone to marry you
PHR V ˌ**pop 'off** (*informal*) to die ˌ**pop sth**↔ˈ**on** (*informal*) to put on a piece of clothing: *I'll just pop on a sweater and meet you outside.*
● *adj.* [only before noun]
> MUSIC/STYLE **1** connected with modern popular music: *a pop song* ⬩ *a pop band/group* ⬩ *a pop star* ⬩ *a pop concert*
2 made in a modern popular style: *pop fashions of the 1960s*

● *adv.*

IDM **go pop** to burst or explode with a sudden, short sound: *The balloon went pop.*

pop. *abbr.* population: *pop. 200,000*

pop 'art *noun* also **Pop Art** [U] a style of art, developed in the 1960s, that was based on popular culture and used material such as advertisements, movie images, etc.

pop·corn *noun* /'papkɔrn/ [U] a type of food made from grains of CORN that are heated until they burst, forming light balls that are then covered with salt and butter

'pop ,culture *noun* [U] (sometimes *disapproving*) TV shows, books, toys, etc. that are popular among ordinary people in a particular society: *Mickey Mouse has become a part of American pop culture.*

pope /poʊp/ *noun* often **the Pope** the leader of the Roman Catholic Church, who is also the Bishop of Rome: *the election of a new pope* ◆ *Pope John Paul II* ◆ *a visit from the Pope* ⊃ see also PAPACY, PAPAL

IDM **Is the Pope a Catholic?** (*humorous*) used to say that there is no doubt that something is true: *"Will they arrive late?" "Is the Pope a Catholic?"*

'pope's 'nose (also **,parson's 'nose**) *noun* the piece of flesh at the tail end of a cooked bird, usually a chicken

'pop-eyed *adj.* (*informal*) having eyes that are wide open, especially because you are very surprised, excited, or frightened

'pop 'fly (also **'pop-up**) *noun* (*sports*) (in baseball) a ball that is hit high into the air but does not go far, making it easy to catch

pop·gun /'papgʌn/ *noun* a toy gun that fires small objects such as CORKS and makes a short sharp noise

pop·lar /'paplər/ *noun* a tall straight tree with soft wood

pop·lin /'paplən/ *noun* [U] a type of strong cotton cloth used for making clothes

'pop ,music *noun* = POP

pop·o·ver /'pap,oʊvər/ *noun* a type of food made from a mixture of eggs, milk, and flour that rises to form a hollow shell when it is baked

pop·pa /'papə/ *noun* (*informal*) used by children to talk about or to address their father ⊃ see also PAPA, POP

,pop psy'chology *noun* [U] the use by ordinary people of simple or fashionable ideas from PSYCHOLOGY in order to understand or explain people's feelings and emotional problems

pop·py /'papi/ *noun* (*pl.* **pop·pies**) a wild or garden plant, with a large delicate flower that is usually red, and small black seeds. OPIUM is obtained from one type of poppy: *poppy fields/seeds* ⊃ picture at PLANT

pop·py·cock /'papi,kak/ *noun* [U] (*old-fashioned*, *informal*) nonsense

,pop 'quiz *noun* a short test that is given to students without any warning

Pop·si·cle™ /'papsɪkl/ *noun* a piece of ice flavored with fruit, served on a stick

pop·u·lace /'papyələs/ *noun* usually **the populace** [sing.] (*formal*) all the ordinary people of a particular country or area: *He had the support of large sections of the local populace.* ◆ *The populace at large is opposed to sudden change.*

pop·u·lar ♪ /'papyələr/ *adj.*
1 liked or enjoyed by a large number of people: *a hugely/immensely popular singer* ◆ *This is one of our most popular designs.* ◆ *Skiing has become very popular recently.* ◆ **~ (with sb)** *These policies are unlikely to prove popular with middle-class voters.* ◆ *I'm not very popular with my parents* (= they are annoyed with me) *at the moment.* ◆ (*ironic*) *"Our dog got into the neighbor's yard again!" "You'll be popular."* **ANT** UNPOPULAR **2** [only before noun] (sometimes *disapproving*) suited to the taste and knowledge of ordinary people: *popular music/culture/fiction* ◆ *the popular press* **3** [only before noun] (of

ideas, beliefs, and opinions) shared by a large number of people: *a popular misconception* ◆ **Contrary to popular belief**, *women cause fewer road accidents than men.* ◆ **Popular opinion** *was divided on the issue.* ◆ **By popular demand**, *the tour has been extended by two weeks.* **4** [only before noun] connected with the ordinary people of a country: *The party still has widespread popular support.*

,popular ety'mology *noun* = FOLK ETYMOLOGY

,popular 'front *noun* a political group or party that has SOCIALIST aims

pop·u·lar·i·ty /,papyə'lærəti/ *noun* [U] the state of being liked, enjoyed, or supported by a large number of people: *the increasing popularity of biking* ◆ *Her novels have gained in popularity over recent years.* ◆ **~ with/among sb** *to win/lose popularity with the students*

pop·u·lar·ize /'papyələ,raɪz/ *verb* **1 ~ sb/sth** to make a lot of people know about something and enjoy it: *The program did much to popularize little-known writers.* **2 ~ sth** to make a difficult subject easier to understand for ordinary people: *He spent his life popularizing natural history.* ▶ **pop·u·lar·i·za·tion** /,papyələrə'zeɪʃn/ *noun* [U]

pop·u·lar·ly /'papyələrli/ *adv.* **1** by a large number of people **SYN** COMMONLY: *a popularly held belief* ◆ *the UN Conference on Environment and Development, popularly known as the "Earth Summit"* **2** by the ordinary people of a country **SYN** DEMOCRATICALLY: *a popularly elected government*

pop·u·late /'papyə,leɪt/ *verb* **1** [often passive] **~ sth** to live in an area and form its population **SYN** INHABIT: *a heavily/densely/sparsely/thinly populated country* ◆ *The island is populated largely by sheep.* ◆ (*figurative*) *the amazing characters that populate her novels* **2 ~ sth** to move people or animals to an area to live there: *The French began to populate the island in the 15th century.* **3 ~ sth** (*computing*) to add data to a document

pop·u·la·tion ♪ /,papyə'leɪʃn/ *noun*
1 [C, U] all the people who live in a particular area, city, or country; the total number of people who live there: *One third of the world's population consumes two thirds of the world's resources.* ◆ *The entire population of the town was at the meeting.* ◆ *countries with aging populations* ◆ *Muslims make up 55% of the population.* ◆ *an increase in population* ◆ *areas of dense/sparse population* (= where many/not many people live) ◆ *The population is increasing at about 6% per year.* ◆ *Oregon has a population of nearly 4 million.* **2** [C] a particular group of people or animals living in a particular area: *the adult/working/rural, etc. population of the country*

popu'lation ex,plosion *noun* a sudden large increase in the number of people in an area

pop·u·lism /'papyə,lɪzəm/ *noun* [U] a type of politics that claims to represent the opinions and wishes of ordinary people ▶ **pop·u·list** /-lɪst/ *noun*: *a party of populists* **pop·u·list** *adj.* [usually before noun]: *a populist leader*

pop·u·lous /'papyələs/ *adj.* (*formal*) where a large number of people live: *one of America's most populous states*

'pop-up *adj.*, *noun*
● *adj.* [only before noun] **1** (of a book, etc.) containing a picture that stands up when the pages are opened: *a pop-up birthday card* **2** (of an electric TOASTER) that pushes the bread quickly upward when it is ready **3** (of a computer menu, etc.) that can be brought to the screen quickly while you are working on another document: *a pop-up menu/window*
● *noun* **1** (*computing*) a window that appears suddenly on the screen and covers another window, usually with an advertisement: *I was distracted by the pop-ups that kept appearing on their Web site.* **2** = POP FLY

por·ce·lain /'pɔrslən; -sələn/ *noun* [U, C] a hard, white, shiny substance made by baking CLAY and used for making delicate cups, plates, and decorative objects; objects that are made of this: *a porcelain figure*

porch /pɔrtʃ/ *noun* **1** a platform with an open front and a roof, built onto the side of a house on the ground floor ⊃ picture at HOUSE **SYN** VERANDA **2** a small area at the entrance to a building, such as a house or a church, that is covered by a roof and often has walls

por·cine /'pɔrsaɪn/ *adj.* (*formal*) like a pig; connected with pigs

por·cu·pine /'pɔrkyə,paɪn/ *noun* an animal covered with long stiff parts like needles (called QUILLS), that it can raise to protect itself when it is attacked

porcupine

pore /pɔr/ *noun, verb*
● *noun* one of the very small holes in your skin that sweat can pass through; one of the similar small holes in the surface of a plant or a rock ⊃ see also POROUS

● *verb*
PHR V 'pore over sth to look at or read something very carefully **SYN** EXAMINE: *His lawyers are poring over the fine print in the contract.*

pork /pɔrk/ *noun* [U] meat from a pig that has not been CURED (= preserved using salt or smoke): *roast pork* ♦ *pork chops* ♦ *a leg of pork* ⊃ compare BACON, HAM

'pork ,barrel *noun* [U] (*slang*) local projects that are given a lot of government money in order to win votes; the money that is used

pork·er /'pɔrkər/ *noun* a pig that is made fat and used as food

'pork rinds *noun* [pl.] crisp pieces of pig skin that are fried and eaten cold, often sold in bags as a SNACK

pork·y /'pɔrki/ *adj.* (*informal, disapproving*) (of people) fat

por·nog·ra·pher /pɔr'nɑgrəfər/ *noun* (*disapproving*) a person who produces or sells pornography

por·no·graph·ic /,pɔrnə'græfɪk/ *adj.* [usually before noun] (*disapproving*) intended to make people feel sexually excited by showing naked people or sexual acts, usually in a way that many other people find offensive: *pornographic movies/ magazines*

por·nog·ra·phy /pɔr'nɑgrəfi/ (also *informal* **porn** /pɔrn/, **por·no**) *noun* [U] (*disapproving*) books, magazines, videos, etc. that describe or show naked people and sexual acts in order to make people feel sexually excited, especially in a way that many other people find offensive

po·ros·i·ty /pə'rɑsəti/ *noun* [U] (*technical*) the quality or state of being porous

po·rous /'pɔrəs/ *adj.* having many small holes that allow water or air to pass through slowly: *porous material/rocks/ surfaces*

por·phyr·i·a /pɔr'fɪriə/ *noun* [U] (*medical*) a disease of the blood that causes mental problems and makes the skin sensitive to light

por·poise /'pɔrpəs/ *noun* a sea animal that looks like a large fish with a pointed mouth. Porpoises are similar to DOLPHINS but smaller.

por·ridge /'pɔrɪdʒ; 'pɑr-/ *noun* [U] a type of soft thick food made by boiling CEREAL in milk or water

port /pɔrt/ *noun, verb*
● *noun* **1** [C] a town or city with a HARBOR, especially one where ships load and unload goods: *fishing ports* ♦ *Rotterdam is a major port.* **2** [C, U] (*abbr.* **Pt.**) a place where ships load and unload goods or shelter from storms: *a naval port* ♦ *The ship spent four days in port.* ♦ *They reached port at last.* ♦ *port of entry* (= a place where people or goods can enter a country) ⊃ see also AIRPORT, FREE PORT, HELIPORT, SEAPORT **3** [U] the side of a ship or aircraft that is on the left when you are facing forward: *the port side* **ANT** STARBOARD **4** [C] (*computing*) a place on a computer where you can attach another piece of equipment, often using a cable:

the modem port **5** (also **port 'wine**) [U] a strong sweet wine, usually dark red, that is made in Portugal. It is usually drunk at the end of a meal. **6** [C] a glass of port
IDM any port in a storm (*saying*) if you are in great trouble, you take any help that is offered

● *verb* **1** ~ sth (to sth) (*computing*) to copy software from one system or machine to another **2** ~ sth (to sth) to continue to use the same number when you change from one phone company to another: *how to port your number to a new cell phone*

port·a·ble /'pɔrtəbl/ *adj., noun*
● *adj.* that is easy to carry or to move: *a portable TV* ♦ (*figurative*) *a portable loan/pension* (= that can be moved if you change banks, jobs, etc.) ♦ *portable software* ▶ **port·a·bil·i·ty** /,pɔrtə'bɪləti/ *noun* [U]: *The new light cover increases this model's portability.*
● *noun* a small type of machine that is easy to carry, especially a computer or a television

por·tage /'pɔrtɪdʒ/ *noun* [U] the act of carrying boats or goods between two rivers

Por·ta John™ /'pɔrtə ,dʒɑn/ *noun* = PORTA POTTI™

por·tal /'pɔrtl/ *noun* **1** [usually pl.] (*formal* or *literary*) a large impressive gate or entrance to a building **2** (*computing*) a Web site that is used as a point of entry to the Internet, where information has been collected that will be useful to a person interested in particular kinds of things: *a business/ news/shopping portal*

Por·ta Pot·ti™ (also **por·ta-pot·ty**) /'pɔrtə ,pɑti/ *noun* (pl. **Por·ta Pot·ties**) (also **Por·ta John™**) a toilet inside a small light building that can be moved from place to place

port·cul·lis /pɔrt'kʌləs/ *noun* a strong, heavy, iron gate that can be raised or let down at the entrance to a castle

por·tend /pɔr'tɛnd/ *verb* ~ sth (*formal*) to be a sign or warning of something that is going to happen in the future, especially something bad or unpleasant **SYN** FORESHADOW

por·tent /'pɔrtɛnt/ *noun* (*literary*) a sign or warning of something that is going to happen in the future, especially when it is something unpleasant **SYN** OMEN

por·ten·tous /pɔr'tɛntəs/ *adj.* **1** (*literary*) important as a sign or warning of something that is going to happen in the future, especially when it is something unpleasant: *a portentous sign* **2** (*formal, disapproving*) very serious and intended to impress people **SYN** POMPOUS: *a portentous remark* ▶ **por·ten·tous·ly** *adv.* **por·ten·tous·ness** *noun* [U]

por·ter /'pɔrtər/ *noun* **1** a person whose job is carrying people's bags and other loads, especially at a train station, at an airport, or in a hotel **2** a person whose job is helping passengers on a train, especially in a SLEEPING CAR

port·fo·li·o /pɔrt'fouli,ou/ *noun* (pl. **port·fo·li·os**) **1** a thin flat case used for carrying documents, drawings, etc. **2** a collection of photographs, drawings, etc. that you use as an example of your work, especially when applying for a job **3** (*finance*) a set of shares owned by a particular person or organization: *an investment/share portfolio* **4** (*formal*) the particular area of responsibility of a government official: *She resigned her portfolio.* **5** the range of products or services offered by a particular company or organization: *a portfolio of wines*

port·hole /'pɔrthoul/ *noun* a round window in the side of a ship or an aircraft

por·ti·co /'pɔrtɪ,kou/ *noun* (pl. **por·ti·coes** or **por·ti·cos**) (*formal*) a roof that is supported by columns, especially one that forms the entrance to a large building ⊃ picture at ARCHITECTURE

por·tion **AWL** /'pɔrʃn/ *noun, verb*
● *noun* **1** one part of something larger: *a substantial/ significant portion of the population* ♦ *Only a small portion of the budget is spent on books.* ♦ *The central portion of the bridge collapsed.* **2** an amount of food that is large enough for one person: *a generous portion of meat* ♦ *She cut the cake into six small portions.* **3** [usually sing.] a part of something that is

shared with other people **SYN** SHARE: *You must accept a portion of the blame for this crisis.*
- *verb* to divide something into parts or portions: ~ **sth** *The factory portions and packs over 12,000 meals a day.* ♦ ~ **sth out** *Land was portioned out among the clans.*

port·ly /ˈpɔrtli/ *adj.* [usually before noun] (especially of an older man) somewhat fat

port·man·teau /pɔrtˈmæntoʊ; ˌpɔrtmænˈtoʊ/ *noun, adj.*
- *noun* (*pl.* port·man·teaus or port·man·teaux) (*old-fashioned*) a large heavy SUITCASE that opens into two parts
- *adj.* [only before noun] consisting of a number of different items that are combined into a single thing: *a portmanteau course* ♦ *"Depression" is a portmanteau condition.*

port·manteau ˌword *noun* a word that is invented by combining the beginning of one word and the end of another and keeping the meaning of each. For example, *motel* is a portmanteau word that is a combination of *motor* and *hotel*.

por·to·bel·lo /ˌpɔrtəˈbɛloʊ/ *noun* (*pl.* por·to·bel·los) (also **portoˈbello ˌmushroom**) a very large brown MUSHROOM used in cooking

ˌport of ˈcall *noun* (*pl.* ports of call) **1** a port where a ship stops during a journey **2** (*informal*) a place where you go or stop for a short time, especially when you are going to several places: *My first port of call in town was the bank.*

por·trait /ˈpɔrtrət/ *noun, adj.*
- *noun* **1** a painting, drawing, or photograph of a person, especially of the head and shoulders: *He had his portrait painted in uniform.* ♦ *a full-length portrait* ♦ *a portrait painter* Ͻ see also SELF-PORTRAIT Ͻ thesaurus box at PICTURE Ͻ collocations at ART **2** a detailed description of someone or something **SYN** DEPICT: *a portrait of life at the French court*
- *adj.* (*computing*) (of a page of a document, etc.) printed so that the top of the page is one of the shorter sides Ͻ compare LANDSCAPE

por·trait·ist /ˈpɔrtrətɪst/ *noun* a person who makes portraits

por·trai·ture /ˈpɔrtrətʃər; -ˌtʃʊr/ *noun* [U] the art of making portraits; the portraits that are made

por·tray /pɔrˈtreɪ/ *verb* **1** ~ **sb/sth** to show someone or something in a picture; to describe someone or something in a piece of writing **SYN** DEPICT **2** ~ **sb/sth (as sb/sth)** to describe or show someone or something in a particular way, especially when this does not give a complete or accurate impression of what they are like **SYN** REPRESENT: *Throughout the trial, he portrayed himself as the victim.* **3** ~ **sb/sth** to act a particular role in a movie or play **SYN** PLAY: *Her father will be portrayed by Robert De Niro.*

por·tray·al /pɔrˈtreɪəl/ *noun* [C, U] the act of showing or describing someone or something in a picture, play, book, etc.; a particular way in which this is done: *The article examines the portrayal of older women in the media.* ♦ *He is best known for his chilling portrayal of Hannibal Lecter.*

Por·tu·guese /ˌpɔrtʃəˈgiz; -ˈgis; ˈpɔrtʃəˌgiz; -ˌgis/ *adj., noun*
- *adj.* from or connected with Portugal
- *noun* **1** (*pl.* Por·tu·guese) [C] a person from Portugal **2** [U] the language used in Portugal, Brazil, and some other countries

pose 🔑 **AWL** /poʊz/ *verb, noun*
- *verb* **1** [T] ~ **sth** to create a threat, problem, etc. that has to be dealt with: *to pose a threat/challenge/danger/risk* ♦ *The task poses no special problems.* **2** [T] ~ **a question** (*formal*) to ask a question, especially one that needs serious thought **3** [I] ~ **(for sb/sth)** to sit or stand in a particular position in order to be painted, drawn, or photographed: *The delegates posed for a group photograph.* **4** [I] ~ **as sb** to pretend to be someone in order to trick other people: *The gang entered the building posing as workmen.* **5** [I] (usually used in the progressive tenses) (*disapproving*) to dress or behave in a way that is intended to impress other people: *I saw him out posing in his new sports car.*

- *noun* **1** a particular position in which someone stands, sits, etc., especially in order to be painted, drawn, or photographed: *He adopted a relaxed pose for the camera.* **2** (*disapproving*) a way of behaving that is not sincere and is only intended to impress other people **SYN** AFFECTATION **IDM** see STRIKE *v.*

pos·er /ˈpoʊzər/ *noun* **1** (also **pos·eur**) (*disapproving*) a person who behaves or dresses in a way that is intended to impress other people and is not sincere **2** (*informal*) a difficult question or problem **SYN** PUZZLER

po·seur /poʊˈzər/ *noun* = POSER

posh /pɑʃ/ *adj.* (**posh·er, posh·est**) (*informal*) elegant and expensive: *a posh hotel* ♦ *You look very posh in your new suit.*

pos·it /ˈpɑzət/ *verb* ~ **sth** | ~ **that...** (*formal*) to suggest or accept that something is true so that it can be used as the basis for an argument or discussion **SYN** POSTULATE: *Most religions posit the existence of life after death.*

po·si·tion 🔑 /pəˈzɪʃn/ *noun, verb*
- *noun*
> PLACE **1** [C] the place where someone or something is located: *From his position on the cliff top, he had a good view of the harbor.* ♦ *Where would be the best position for the lights?* Ͻ thesaurus box at PLACE **2** [U] the place where someone or something is meant to be; the correct place: *Is everybody in position?* ♦ *He took up his position by the door.*
> WAY SOMEONE OR SOMETHING IS PLACED **3** [C, U] the way in which someone is sitting or standing, or the way in which something is arranged: *a sitting/kneeling/lying position* ♦ *Keep the box in an upright position.* ♦ *Make sure that you are working in a comfortable position.* ♦ *My arms were aching so I shifted (my) position slightly.*
> SITUATION **4** [C, usually sing.] the situation that someone is in, especially when it affects what they can and cannot do: *to be in a position of power/strength/authority* ♦ *What would you do in my position?* ♦ *This put him and his colleagues in a difficult position.* ♦ *The company's financial position is not certain.* ♦ ~ **to do sth** *I'm afraid I am not in a position to help you.* Ͻ thesaurus box at SITUATION
> OPINION **5** [C] ~ **(on sth)** an opinion on or an attitude toward a particular subject: *to declare/reconsider/shift/change your position* ♦ *the party's position on education reforms* ♦ *She has made her position very clear.* ♦ *My parents always took the position that early bedtimes meant healthy children.*
> LEVEL OF IMPORTANCE **6** [C, U] a person or organization's level of importance when compared with others: *the position of women in society* ♦ *the company's dominant position in the world market* ♦ *Wealth and position* (= high social status) *were not important to her.*
> JOB **7** [C] (*formal*) a job **SYN** POST: *He held a senior position in a large company.* ♦ *I would like to apply for the position of Sales Director.* Ͻ thesaurus box at JOB
> IN RACE/COMPETITION **8** [C] a place in a race, competition, or test, when compared with others: *He was able to work his way up to third position in the race.*
> IN SPORTS **9** [C] the place where someone plays and the responsibilities they have in some team games: *What position does he play?*
> IN WAR **10** [C, usually pl.] a place where a group of people involved in fighting have put men and guns: *They attacked the enemy positions at dawn.*

- *verb* ~ **sth** (+ adv./prep.) to put someone or something in a particular position **SYN** PLACE: *Large television screens were positioned at either end of the stadium.* ♦ *She quickly positioned herself behind the desk.* ♦ *The company is now well positioned to compete in foreign markets.* ▸ **po·si·tion·ing** /pəˈzɪʃnɪŋ/ *noun* [U]

po·si·tion·al /pəˈzɪʃənl/ *adj.* [only before noun] (*technical* or *sports*) connected with the position of someone or something: *The team has made some positional changes because two players are injured.*

poˈsition ˌpaper *noun* a written report from an organization or a government department that explains or recommends a particular course of action

pos·i·tive ⚲ **AWL** /'pazətɪv/ *adj., noun*

● *adj.*

> CONFIDENT **1** thinking about what is good in a situation; feeling confident and sure that something good will happen: *a positive attitude/outlook* ◆ *the power of positive thought* ◆ **~ (about sth)** *She tried to be more positive about her new job.* ◆ **On the positive side**, *profits have increased.* ◆ *The report ended on a positive note.* **ANT** NEGATIVE

> EFFECTIVE/USEFUL **2** directed at dealing with something or producing a successful result: *We must take positive steps to deal with the problem.* ◆ *It will require positive action by all in the industry.* **ANT** NEGATIVE **3** expressing agreement or support: *We've had a very positive response to the idea.* **ANT** NEGATIVE **4** good or useful: *to make a positive contribution to a discussion* ◆ *His family has been a very positive influence on him.* ◆ *Overseas investment has had a positive effect on exports.* **ANT** NEGATIVE

> SURE/DEFINITE **5** [not before noun] (of a person) completely sure that something is correct or true: **~ (about sth)** *I can't be positive about what time it happened.* ◆ **~ (that...)** *She was positive that he had been there.* ◆ *"Are you sure?" "Positive."* ⊃ thesaurus box at SURE **6** [only before noun] (*informal*) complete and definite **SYN** ABSOLUTE: *He has a positive genius for upsetting people.* ◆ *It was a positive miracle that we survived.* **7** giving clear and definite proof or information **SYN** CONCLUSIVE: *We have no positive evidence that she was involved.* ◆ (*formal*) *This is proof positive that he stole the money.*

> SCIENTIFIC TEST **8** showing clear evidence that a particular substance or medical condition is present: *a positive pregnancy test* ◆ *The athlete tested positive for steroids.* ◆ *to be HIV positive* **ANT** NEGATIVE

> NUMBER/QUANTITY **9** greater than zero **ANT** NEGATIVE

> ELECTRICITY **10** (*technical*) containing or producing the type of electricity that is carried by a PROTON: *a positive charge* ◆ *the positive terminal of a battery* **ANT** NEGATIVE

● *noun*

> GOOD QUALITY **1** [C, U] a good or useful quality or aspect: *Take your weaknesses and translate them into positives.*

> IN PHOTOGRAPHY **2** [C] (*technical*) a developed film showing light and dark areas and colors as they actually were, especially one printed from a NEGATIVE

> RESULT OF TEST **3** [C] the result of a test or an experiment that shows that a substance or condition is present **ANT** NEGATIVE

pos·i·tive·ly **AWL** /'pazətɪvli/ *adv.* **1** /'pazətɪvli/ ,pazə'tɪvli/ used to emphasize the truth of a statement, especially when this is surprising or when it contrasts with a previous statement: *The instructions were not just confusing, they were positively misleading.* **2** in a way that shows you are thinking of the good things about a situation, not the bad: *Very few of those interviewed spoke positively about their childhood.* ◆ *Thinking positively is one way of dealing with stress.* **ANT** NEGATIVELY **3** in a way that shows you approve of or agree with something or someone: *Investors reacted positively to news of the takeover.* **ANT** NEGATIVELY **4** in a way that leaves no possibility of doubt **SYN** CONCLUSIVELY: *Her attacker has now been positively identified by police.* **5** (*technical*) in a way that contains or produces the type of electricity that is opposite to that carried by an ELECTRON: *positively charged protons* **ANT** NEGATIVELY

pos·i·tiv·ism /'pazətɪ,vɪzəm/ *noun* [U] a system of philosophy based on things that can be seen or proved, rather than on ideas ▶ **pos·i·tiv·ist** /-vɪst/ *noun* **pos·i·tiv·ist** *adj.*: *a positivist approach*

pos·i·tron /'pazə,tran/ *noun* (*physics*) a PARTICLE in an atom that has the same mass as an ELECTRON and an equal but positive charge

pos·se /'pasi/ *noun* **1** (in the past) a group of people who were brought together by a SHERIFF (= an officer of the law) in order to help him catch a criminal **2** (*informal*) a group of people who are similar in some way, or who spend time together: *a little posse of helpers* **3** (*informal*) a group of young men involved in crime connected with drugs

pos·sess ⚲ /pə'zɛs/ *verb* (not used in the progressive tenses)

1 ~ sth (*formal*) to have or own something: *He was charged with possessing a shotgun without a license.* ◆ *The gallery possesses a number of the artist's early works.* **2 ~ sth** (*formal*) to have a particular quality or feature: *I'm afraid he doesn't possess a sense of humor.* **3** [usually passive] **~ sb** (*literary*) (of a feeling, an emotion, etc.) to have a powerful effect on someone and control the way that they think, behave, etc. **4 ~ sb to do sth** (used in negative sentences and questions) to make someone do something that seems strange or unreasonable: *What possessed him to say such a thing?*

pos·sessed /pə'zɛst/ *adj.* [not before noun] **~ (by sth)** (of a person or their mind) controlled by an evil spirit: *She has convinced herself that she is possessed by the devil.*

IDM **be possessed of sth** (*formal*) to have a particular quality or feature: *She was possessed of exceptional powers of concentration.* **like a man/woman possessed | like one possessed** with a lot of force or energy: *He flew out of the room like a man possessed.*

pos·ses·sion ⚲ /pə'zɛʃn/ *noun*

> HAVING/OWNING **1** [U] (*formal*) the state of having or owning something: *The manuscript is just one of the treasures in their possession.* ◆ *The gang was caught in possession of stolen goods.* ◆ *The possession of a passport is essential for foreign travel.* ◆ *On her father's death, she came into possession of* (= received) *a vast fortune.* ◆ *You cannot legally take possession of the property* (= start using it after buying it) *until three weeks after the contract is signed.* **2** [C, usually pl.] something that you own or have with you at a particular time **SYN** BELONGINGS: *personal possessions* ◆ *The ring is one of her most treasured possessions.* ⊃ thesaurus box at THING

> IN SPORTS **3** [U] the state of having control of the ball: *to win/get/lose possession of the ball*

> LAW **4** [U] the state of having illegal drugs or weapons with you at a particular time: *She was charged with possession.*

> COUNTRY **5** [C] (*formal*) a country that is controlled or governed by another country

> BY EVIL SPIRIT **6** [U] the situation when someone's mind is believed to be controlled by the DEVIL or by an evil spirit

IDM **possession is nine tenths of the law** (*saying*) if you already have or control something, it is difficult for someone else to take it away from you, even if they have the legal right to it ⊃ more at FIELD *n.*

pos·ses·sive /pə'zɛsɪv/ *adj., noun*

● *adj.* **1 ~ (of/about sb/sth)** demanding total attention or love; not wanting someone to be independent: *Some parents are too possessive of their children.* **2 ~ (of/about sth)** not liking to lend things or share things with others: *Jimmy's very possessive about his toys.* **3** (*grammar*) showing that something belongs to someone or something: *possessive pronouns* (= yours, his, etc.) ▶ **pos·ses·sive·ly** *adv.*: *"That's mine!" she said possessively.* **pos·ses·sive·ness** *noun* [U]: *I couldn't stand his jealousy and possessiveness.*

● *noun* (*grammar*) **1** [C] an adjective, a pronoun, or a form of a word that expresses the fact that something belongs to someone or something: *"Ours" and "their" are possessives.* **2 the possessive** [sing.] the special form of a word that expresses belonging ⊃ compare GENITIVE

pos·ses·sor /pə'zɛsər/ *noun* (*formal* or *humorous*) a person who owns or has something **SYN** OWNER: *He is now the proud possessor of a driver's license.*

pos·si·bil·i·ty ⚲ /,pasə'bɪləti/ *noun* (*pl.* **pos·si·bil·i·ties**)

1 [U, C] the fact that something might exist or happen, but is not certain to: **~ (that...)** *There is now no possibility that she will make a full recovery.* ◆ **~ (of sth/of doing sth)** *He refused to rule out the possibility of a tax increase.* ◆ *It is not beyond the bounds of possibility that we'll all meet again one day.* ◆ *Bankruptcy is a real possibility if sales don't improve.* ◆ *What had seemed impossible now seemed a distinct possibility.* **2** [C, usually pl.] one of the different things that you can do in

| h hat | m man | n no | ŋ sing | l leg | r red | y yes | w wet |

a particular situation: *to **explore/consider/investigate** a wide range of possibilities* ♦ *to **exhaust** all the possibilities* ♦ *Selling the house is just one possibility that is open to us.* ♦ **The possibilities are endless.** ◐ **thesaurus box at** OPTION **3** [C, usually pl.] something that gives you a chance to achieve something **SYN** OPPORTUNITY: *The course offers a range of exciting possibilities for developing your skills.* **4 possibilities** [pl.] if something **has possibilities**, it can be improved or made successful **SYN** POTENTIAL: *The house is in a bad state of repair but it has possibilities.*

pos·si·ble 🔑 /ˈpɑsəbl/ adj., noun

● **adj. 1** [not usually before noun] that can be done or achieved: *It is possible to get there by bus.* ♦ *Would it be possible for me to leave a message for her?* ♦ *This wouldn't have been possible without you.* ♦ *Try to avoid losing your temper **if at all possible** (= if you can).* ♦ *Use public transportation **whenever possible** (= when you can).* ♦ *It's just not **physically possible** to finish all this by the end of the week.* ♦ *We spent every possible moment on the beach.* **ANT** IMPOSSIBLE **2** that might exist or happen but is not certain to: *a possible future president* ♦ *the possible side effects of the drug* ♦ *Frost is possible, although unlikely, at this time of year.* ♦ *It's just possible that I gave them the wrong directions.* ♦ *With the possible exception of the Beatles, no other band has become so successful so quickly.* ◐ **language bank at** PERHAPS **3** reasonable or acceptable in a particular situation: *There are several possible explanations.* **4** used after adjectives to emphasize that something is the best, worst, etc. of its type: *It was the **best possible** surprise anyone could have given me.* ♦ *Don't leave your packing until the **last possible** moment.*

IDM as quickly, much, soon, etc. as possible as quickly, much, soon, etc. as you can: *We will get your order to you as soon as possible.* ◐ **more at** WORLD

● **noun** a person or thing that is suitable for a particular job, purpose, etc. and might be chosen: *Out of all the people interviewed, there are only five possibles.*

pos·si·bly 🔑 /ˈpɑsəbli/ adv.

1 used to say that something might exist, happen, or be true, but you are not certain **SYN** PERHAPS: *It was possibly their worst performance ever.* ♦ *She found it difficult to get along with her, possibly because of the difference in their ages.* ♦ *"Will you be around next week?" "Possibly."* ◐ **language bank at** PERHAPS **2** used to emphasize that you are surprised, annoyed, etc. about something: *You can't possibly mean that!* **3** used to ask someone politely to do something: *Could you possibly open that window?* **4** used to say that someone will do or has done as much as they can in order to make something happen: *I will come as soon as I possibly can.* ♦ *They tried everything they possibly could to improve the situation.* **5** used with negatives, especially "can't" and "couldn't," to say strongly that you cannot do something or that something cannot or could not happen or be done: *I can't possibly tell you that!* ♦ *You can't possibly carry all those bags.* ♦ *"Let me buy it for you." "That's very kind of you, but I couldn't possibly (= accept)."*

pos·sum /ˈpɑsəm/ noun (informal) = OPOSSUM

IDM play possum (*informal*) to pretend to be asleep or not aware of something, in order to trick someone

post 🔑 /poʊst/ noun, verb

● **noun**
> WOOD/METAL **1** [C] (often in compounds) a piece of wood or metal that is set in the ground in a vertical position, especially to support something or to mark a position: *corner posts (= that mark the corners of a sports field)* ◐ **picture at** BAR ◐ **see also** BEDPOST, GATEPOST, SIGNPOST
> JOB **2** [C] (*formal*) an important job, especially one in government **SYN** POSITION: *a government/an academic post* ♦ *He has **held the post** for three years.* ♦ *She was offered a key post in the new government.* ◐ **thesaurus box at** JOB **3** [C] an act of sending someone to a particular place to do their job, especially for a limited period of time: *an overseas post*
> FOR SOLDIER/GUARD **4** [C] the place where someone, especially a soldier, does their job: *a police/customs/military post*

♦ *an observation post* ♦ *The guards were ordered not to leave their posts.* ◐ **see also** COMMAND POST, STAGING POST, TRADING POST
> INTERNET **5** (also **post·ing**) [C] (*computing*) a message sent to a discussion group on the Internet; a piece of writing that forms part of a BLOG: *That forum does not allow posts from nonmembers.*
> END OF RACE **6 the post** [sing.] the place where a race finishes, especially in horse racing ◐ **see also** FIRST-PAST-THE-POST
> IN SPORTS **7** [C, usually sing.] = GOALPOST: *The ball hit the post and bounced in.* **IDM see** DEAF, PILLAR

● **verb**
> PUBLIC NOTICE **1** [T, often passive] **~ sth + adv./prep.** to put a notice, etc. in a public place so that people can see it **SYN** DISPLAY: *A copy of the letter was posted on the bulletin board.*
> GIVE INFORMATION **2** [T] to announce something publicly or officially, especially financial information or a warning: **~ sth** *The company posted a $1.1 billion loss.* ♦ *A snow warning was posted for Ohio.* ♦ **~ sb/sth + adj.** *The aircraft and its crew were **posted missing**.* **3** [T, I] to put information or pictures on a Web site: **~ sth (on sth)** *The results will be posted on the Internet.* ♦ **~ (on sth)** *The photos have been provided by fans who post on the message board.*
> PAY MONEY TO COURT **4** [T] **~ bail/(a) bond** to pay money to a court so that a person accused of a crime can go free until their trial: *She was released after posting a $100 cash bond and her driver's license.*
> SOMEONE FOR JOB **5** [T, usually passive] **~ sb + adv./prep.** to send someone to a place for a period of time as part of their job: *She's been posted to Washington for two years.* ♦ *Most of our employees get posted abroad at some stage.*
> SOLDIER/GUARD **6** [T] **~ sb + adv./prep.** to put someone, especially a soldier, in a particular place so that they can guard a building or area: *Guards have been posted along the border.*

IDM keep sb posted (about/on sth) to regularly give someone the most recent information about something and how it is developing

post- /poʊst/ *prefix* (in nouns, verbs, and adjectives) after: *a post-Impressionist* ♦ *the post-1945 period* ♦ *postgraduate* ◐ **compare** ANTE-, PRE-

post·age /ˈpoʊstɪdʒ/ noun [U] the cost of sending a letter, etc. by mail: *an increase in postage rates* ♦ *How much was the postage on that letter?* ♦ *All prices include **postage and handling**.*

postage ˌmeter noun a machine that prints an official mark on a letter to show that the cost of posting it has been paid, or does not need to be paid

postage ˌstamp noun (*formal*) = STAMP

post·al /ˈpoʊstl/ adj. [only before noun] connected with the official system for sending and delivering letters, etc.: *the **postal service/system*** ♦ *postal charges*
IDM go postal (*informal*) to become very angry: *He went postal when he found out.*

postal ˌcode noun (CanE) a group of six letters and numbers that you put at the end of an address. The postal code helps the post office to sort letters by machine.

postal ˌservice noun **1** a system of collecting and delivering letters, etc.: *a good postal service* **2 the Postal Service** the national organization in many countries that is responsible for collecting and delivering letters, etc.

post·card /ˈpoʊstkɑrd/ (also **card**) noun a card used for sending messages by mail without an envelope, especially one that has a picture on one side: *colorful postcards of California* ♦ *Send us a postcard from Venice!* ◐ **see also** PICTURE POSTCARD

post·date /ˌpoʊstˈdeɪt/ verb **1 ~ sth** to write a date on a check that is later than the actual date so that the check cannot be CASHED (= exchanged for money) until that date ◐ **compare** BACKDATE **2 ~ sth** to happen, exist, or be made at a later date than something else in the past **ANT** PREDATE

post·doc /ˈpoʊstdɑk/ *noun* (*informal*) a person who is doing advanced research or study after completing a PH.D.

post·doc·tor·al /ˌpoʊstˈdɑktərəl/ *adj.* connected with advanced research or study that is done after a PH.D. has been completed ⊃ compare POSTGRADUATE

post·er /ˈpoʊstər/ *noun* **1** a large notice, often with a picture on it, that is put in a public place to advertise something: *election posters* ◆ *a poster campaign* (= an attempt to educate people about something by using posters) **2** a large picture that is printed on paper and put on a wall as decoration: *posters of her favorite movie stars* **3** a person who posts a message on a MESSAGE BOARD (= a place on a Web site where people can read or write messages)

ˈposter ˌchild (also **ˈposter ˌboy**, **ˈposter ˌgirl**) *noun* **1** a child with a particular illness or other problem whose picture appears on a poster advertising an organization that helps children with that illness or problem **2** (often *humorous*) a person who is seen as representing a particular quality or activity: *He is the poster child for incompetent government.*

pos·te·ri·or /pɑˈstɪriər; poʊ-/ *adj., noun*
● *adj.* [only before noun] (*technical*) located behind something or at the back of something **ANT** ANTERIOR
● *noun* (*humorous*) the part of your body that you sit on; your behind

posteriori ⊃ A POSTERIORI

pos·ter·i·ty /pɑˈstɛrəti/ *noun* [U] (*formal*) all the people who will live in the future: *Their music has been preserved for posterity.* ◆ *Posterity will remember him as a great man.*

ˈposter ˌpaint *noun* [U, C] a thick paint used especially for children's paintings

ˈpost exˌchange *noun* = PX

post·grad·u·ate /ˌpoʊstˈɡrædʒuət/ (also *informal* post-grad /ˈpoʊstɡræd/) *adj.* connected with further studies that someone does at a university after receiving their first degree: *postgraduate studies/research* ◆ *a postgraduate course* ⊃ compare POSTDOCTORAL ⊃ note at STUDENT ▶ **post·grad·u·ate** *noun*

post·haste /ˌpoʊstˈheɪst/ *adv.* (*literary*) as quickly as you can: *to depart posthaste*

post hoc /ˌpoʊst ˈhɑk/ *adj.* (from Latin, *formal*) (of an argument, etc.) stating that one event is the cause of another because it happened first: *a post hoc explanation*

post·hu·mous /ˈpɑstʃəməs/ *adj.* [usually before noun] happening, done, published, etc. after a person has died: *a posthumous award for bravery* ▶ **post·hu·mous·ly** *adv.*

post-inˈdustrial *adj.* [only before noun] (of a place or society) no longer relying on heavy industry (= the production of steel, large machinery, etc.)

post·ing /ˈpoʊstɪŋ/ *noun* = POST *n.* (5)

Post-it™ (also **ˈPost-it ˌnote**) *noun* a small piece of colored sticky paper that you use for writing a note on, and that can be easily removed ⊃ picture at STATIONERY

post·mark /ˈpoʊstmɑrk/ *noun* an official mark placed over the stamp on a letter, etc. that shows when and where it was mailed and makes it impossible to use the stamp again ▶ **post·mark** *verb* [usually passive]: **~ sth** *The card was postmarked Tokyo, March 9.*

post·mas·ter /ˈpoʊstˌmæstər/, **post·mis·tress** /ˈpoʊstˌmɪstrəs/ *noun* a person who is in charge of a post office

post·mod·ern /ˌpoʊstˈmɑdərn/ *adj.* connected with or influenced by postmodernism

post·mod·ern·ism /ˌpoʊstˈmɑdərˌnɪzəm/ *noun* [U] a style and movement in art, ARCHITECTURE, literature, etc. in the late 20th century that reacts against modern styles, for example by mixing features from traditional and modern styles ⊃ compare MODERNISM ▶ **post·mod·ern·ist** /-nɪst/ *noun, adj.* [usually before noun]

post·mod·i·fi·er /ˌpoʊstˈmɑdəˌfaɪər/ *noun* (*grammar*) a word, such as an adjective or adverb, that describes another word or group of words, or restricts its/their meaning in some way, and is placed after it/them: *In "run fast," the adverb "fast" is a postmodifier.* ⊃ compare MODIFIER, PREMODIFIER

post·mor·tem /ˌpoʊstˈmɔrtəm/ *noun* **1** (also **post mortem examiˈnation**) a medical examination of the body of a dead person in order to find out how they died **SYN** AUTOPSY: *to do/conduct/carry out a postmortem* ◆ **~ on sb** *The postmortem on the child revealed that she had been poisoned.* **2 ~ (on sth)** a discussion or an examination of an event after it has happened, especially in order to find out why it failed: *to hold a postmortem on the candidate's election defeat*

post·na·tal /ˌpoʊstˈneɪtl/ *adj.* [only before noun] connected with the period after the birth of a child: *postnatal care* ⊃ compare PRENATAL

ˈpost ˌoffice *noun*
1 [C] a place where you can buy stamps, mail letters, etc.: *Where's the main post office?* ◆ *You can buy your stamps at the post office.* ◆ *a post office counter* **2 the Post Office** [sing.] (*abbr.* PO) the national organization in many countries that is responsible for collecting and delivering mail: *He works for the Post Office.* **3** [U] a children's game in which imaginary letters are exchanged for kisses

ˈpost office ˌbox *noun* = PO BOX

post·op·er·a·tive /ˌpoʊstˈɑpərətɪv; -ˈɑprətɪv/ *adj.* [only before noun] (*medical*) connected with the period after a medical operation: *postoperative complications/pain/care*

post·paid /ˌpoʊstˈpeɪd/ *adj.* [only before noun] that you can send free because the charge has already been paid: *a postpaid envelope* ▶ **post·paid** *adv.*

post·par·tum /ˌpoʊstˈpɑrtəm/ *adj.* [only before noun] connected with the period after the birth of a child: *postpartum care* ⊃ compare PRENATAL

ˌpostpartum deˈpression *noun* [U] a medical condition in which a woman feels very sad and anxious in the period after her baby is born

post·pone /poʊˈspoʊn/ *verb* to arrange for an event, etc. to take place at a later time or date **SYN** PUT OFF: **~ sth** *The game has already been postponed three times.* ◆ **~ sth to/until sth** *We'll have to postpone the meeting until next week.* ◆ **~ doing sth** *It was an unpopular decision to postpone building the new hospital.* ⊃ compare CANCEL ▶ **post·pone·ment** *noun* [U, C]: *Riots led to the postponement of local elections.*

post·po·si·tion /ˌpoʊstpəˈzɪʃn/ *noun* (*grammar*) a word or part of a word that comes after the word it relates to, for example, "-ish" in "greenish" ▶ **post·po·si·tion·al** /-ʃənl/ *adj.*

post·pran·di·al /ˌpoʊstˈprændiəl/ *adj.* [usually before noun] (*formal* or *humorous*) happening immediately after a meal

post·pro·duc·tion /ˌpoʊstprəˈdʌkʃn/ *adj.* [usually before noun] postproduction work on music or on movies is done after recording or filming: *postproduction editing* ▶ **post·pro·duc·tion** *noun* [U]: *The movie is now in postproduction and will be released next month.*

post·script /ˈpoʊstskrɪpt; ˈpoʊsskrɪpt/ *noun* **1** (*abbr.* P.S.) **~ (to sth)** an extra message that you add at the end of a letter after your signature **2 ~ (to sth)** extra facts or information about a story, an event, etc. that are added after it has ended

post·sea·son /ˈpoʊstˌsizn/ *adj., noun*
● *adj.* [only before noun] (*sports*) taking place after the end of the regular sports season, when teams play additional games to decide which team is best in a particular sport: *The postseason games, leading up to the finals, should be very exciting.*
● *noun* [usually sing.] (*sports*) the period of time after the regular sports season: *The team is expected to do well in the postseason.*

post·synch /ˌpoʊstˈsɪŋk/ *verb* **~ sth** (*technical*) to add sound to a movie after it has been filmed

---

ʌ **cup**   ə **about**   eɪ **say**   aɪ **five**   ɔɪ **boy**   aʊ **now**   oʊ **go**   ər **bird**

post-trau·matic 'stress dis·order *noun* [U] (*medical*) a medical condition in which a person suffers mental and emotional problems resulting from an experience that shocked them very much

pos·tu·late *verb, noun*
- *verb* /ˈpɑstʃəˌleɪt/ ~ sth | ~ that... (*formal*) to suggest or accept that something is true so that it can be used as the basis for a theory, etc. **SYN** POSIT: *They postulated a 500-year lifespan for a plastic container.*
- *noun* /ˈpɑstʃələt/ (*formal*) a statement that is accepted as true, that forms the basis of a theory, etc.

pos·tur·al /ˈpɑstʃərəl/ *adj.* (*formal*) connected with the way you hold your body when sitting or standing

pos·ture /ˈpɑstʃər/ *noun, verb*
- *noun* **1** [U, C] the position in which you hold your body when standing or sitting: *a comfortable/relaxed posture ◆ upright/sitting/supine postures ◆ Good posture is essential when working at the computer. ◆ Back pain can be the result of bad posture.* **2** [C, usually sing.] your attitude to a particular situation or the way in which you deal with it: *The administration has adopted an aggressive posture on immigration.*
- *verb* [I] ~ (as sth) (*formal*) to pretend to be something that you are not by saying and doing things in order to impress or trick people

pos·tur·ing /ˈpɑstʃərɪŋ/ *noun* [U, C] (*disapproving*) behavior that is not natural or sincere but is intended to attract attention or to have a particular effect

post·war /ˌpoʊstˈwɔr/ *adj.* [usually before noun] existing, happening, or made in the period after a war, especially World War II: *the postwar years*

po·sy /ˈpoʊzi/ *noun* (*pl.* **po·sies**) a small bunch of flowers

pot 🔑 /pɑt/ *noun, verb*
- *noun*
  ▷ FOR COOKING **1** [C] a deep round container used for cooking things in: *pots and pans* ⟳ picture at COOKING
  ▷ CONTAINER **2** [C] (especially in compounds) a container of various kinds, made for a particular purpose: *a coffee pot ◆ a teapot ◆ Is there any more coffee in the pot?* ⟳ picture at COFFEE ⟳ see also CHAMBER POT, CHIMNEY POT, FLOWERPOT, LOBSTER POT, MELTING POT, POTTED **3** [C] the amount contained in a pot: *They drank a pot of coffee.* **4** [C] a bowl, etc. that is made by a POTTER
  ▷ MONEY **5** the pot [sing.] the total amount of money that is bet in a card game **6** the pot [sing.] all the money given by a group of people in order to do something together, for example to buy food ⟳ see also KITTY
  ▷ DRUG **7** [U] (*informal*) = MARIJUANA
  ▷ SHOT **8** [C] = POTSHOT: *He took a pot at the neighbour's cat with his air rifle.*
  ▷ STOMACH **9** [C] (*informal*) a large stomach that sticks out; a potbelly
  ▷ TOILET **10** the pot [sing.] (*informal*) a toilet
  IDM go to pot (*informal*) to be spoiled because people are not working hard or taking care of things the pot calling the kettle black (*saying, informal*) used to say that you should not criticize someone for a fault that you have yourself ⟳ more at GOLD *n.*, QUART, WATCH *v.* ⟳ see also POTLUCK
- *verb* (-tt-) ~ sth to put a plant into a FLOWERPOT filled with soil

po·ta·ble /ˈpoʊtəbl/ *adj.* (*formal*) (of water) safe to drink

pot·ash /ˈpɑtæʃ/ *noun* [U] a chemical containing potassium, used to improve soil for farming and in making soap

po·tas·si·um /pəˈtæsiəm/ *noun* [U] (*symb.* **K**) a chemical element. Potassium is a soft silver-white metal that exists mainly in COMPOUNDS that are used in industry and farming.

po·ta·to 🔑 /pəˈteɪtoʊ; -tə/ *noun* [C, U] (*pl.* **po·ta·toes**) a round white vegetable with a brown or red skin that grows underground as part of a plant also called a potato: *Will you peel the potatoes for me? ◆ baked/boiled/fried/roast*

potatoes ⟳ picture at FRUIT ⟳ see also COUCH POTATO, HOT POTATO, MASHED POTATOES, MEAT AND POTATOES, SWEET POTATO

po'tato ˌchip *noun* a thin round slice of potato that is fried until hard, then dried and eaten cold. Potato chips are sold in bags and have many different flavors: *salt-and-vinegar potato chips*

po'tato ˌmasher *noun* a kitchen UTENSIL (= tool) for MASHING potatoes ⟳ picture at COOKING, KITCHEN

pot·bel·lied /ˈpɑtˌbɛlid/ *adj.* (of people and animals) having a large stomach that sticks out ▶ **pot·bel·ly** /ˈpɑtˌbɛli/ (also *informal* pot) *noun*

ˌpotbelly 'stove (also *ˌpotbellied 'stove*) *noun* a stove that burns wood or coal and has a short, round shape

pot·boil·er /ˈpɑtˌbɔɪlər/ *noun* (*disapproving*) a book, a play, etc. that is produced only to earn money quickly

pot·bound /ˈpɑtbaʊnd/ (also *root·bound*) *adj.* (of a plant) having roots that fill the pot, with no more room for them to grow

pot cheese *noun* [U] a type of soft white cheese with lumps in it

po·ten·cy /ˈpoʊtnsi/ *noun* (*pl.* **po·ten·cies**) [U, C] **1** the power that someone or something has to affect your body or mind: *the potency of desire ◆ If you keep a medicine too long, it may lose its potency.* **2** the ability of a man to have sex

po·tent /ˈpoʊtnt/ *adj.* **1** having a strong effect on your body or mind: *a potent drug ◆ a very potent alcoholic brew ◆ a potent argument* **2** powerful: *a potent force* ⟳ see also IMPOTENT ▶ **po·tent·ly** *adv.*

po·ten·tate /ˈpoʊtnˌteɪt/ *noun* (*literary, often disapproving*) a ruler who has a lot of power, especially when this is not restricted by anyone else in the government

po·ten·tial 🔑 **AWL** /pəˈtɛnʃl/ *adj., noun*
- *adj.* [only before noun] that can develop into something or be developed in the future **SYN** POSSIBLE: *potential customers ◆ a potential source of conflict ◆ a potential governor ◆ First we need to identify actual and potential problems.* ▶ **po·ten·tial·ly** **AWL** /-ʃəli/ *adv.*: *a potentially dangerous situation*
- *noun* **1** [U] the possibility of something happening or being developed or used: ~ (for) *the potential for change ◆* ~ (for doing sth) *The South American marketplace offers excellent potential for increasing sales.* **2** [U] qualities that exist and can be developed **SYN** PROMISE: *All children should be encouraged to realize their full potential. ◆ She has great potential as an artist. ◆ He has the potential to become a world-class musician. ◆ The house has a lot of potential.* **3** [U, C] (*physics*) the difference in VOLTAGE between two points in an electric field or CIRCUIT

po,tential 'energy *noun* [U] (*physics*) the form of energy that an object gains as it is lifted

po·ten·ti·al·i·ty /pəˌtɛnʃiˈæləti/ *noun* (*pl.* **po·ten·ti·al·i·ties**) (*formal*) a power or a quality that exists and is capable of being developed: *We often underestimate our potentialities.*

po·ten·ti·om·e·ter /pəˌtɛnʃiˈɑmətər/ *noun* **1** a device for measuring differences in electrical POTENTIAL **2** a device for varying electrical RESISTANCE, used, for example, in volume controls

pot·hold·er /ˈpɑtˌhoʊldər/ *noun* a piece of thick cloth for handling hot dishes and pans

pot·hole /ˈpɑthoʊl/ *noun* **1** a large rough hole in the surface of a road that is formed by traffic and bad weather **2** a deep hole that is formed in rock, especially by the action of water

po·tion /ˈpoʊʃn/ *noun* (*literary*) a drink of medicine or poison; a liquid with magic powers: *a magic/love potion ◆* (*humorous*) *I've tried all kinds of drugs, creams, pills, and potions.*

pot ˌliquor *noun* [U] the liquid in which meat, fish, or vegetables have been cooked

---

pot·luck /ˌpɑt'lʌk; 'pɑtlʌk/ *noun* **1** a meal to which each guest brings some food, which is then shared out among the guests **2** used to talk about a situation in which you have to choose something or go somewhere without knowing very much about it, and hope that it will be good, pleasant, etc: *It's potluck whether you get good advice or not.* ◆ *You're welcome to stay to supper, but you'll have to take **potluck** (= eat whatever is available).* ▶ **pot·luck** *adj.* [only before noun]: *a potluck supper*

ˌpot **'pie** *noun* [C, U] meat, vegetables, etc. baked in a deep dish with PASTRY on top: *a chicken pot pie*

pot·pour·ri /ˌpoʊpʊ'ri/ *noun* (from French) **1** [U, C] a mixture of dried flowers and leaves used for making a room smell pleasant **2** [sing.] a mixture of various things that were not originally intended to form a group: *a potpourri of tunes*

pot roast *noun* a piece of meat cooked with vegetables in a pot

pot·shot /'pɑtʃɑt/ (also **pot**) *noun* (*informal*) a shot that someone fires without aiming carefully: *Somebody took a potshot at him as he drove past.* ◆ (*figurative*) *The newspapers took constant potshots at* (= criticized) *the president.*

pot·tage /'pɑtɪdʒ/ *noun* [U] (*old use*) soup or STEW

pot·ted /'pɑtəd/ *adj.* [only before noun] planted in a pot: *potted plants*

pot·ter /'pɑtər/ *noun* a person who makes CLAY pots by hand

ˌpotter's ˌwheel *noun* a piece of equipment with a flat disk that goes around, on which potters put wet CLAY in order to shape it into pots ⊃ picture at HOBBY

pot·ter·y /'pɑtəri/ *noun* (*pl.* **pot·ter·ies**) **1** [U] pots, dishes, etc. made with CLAY that is baked in an oven, especially when they are made by hand ◆ *a piece of pottery* ⊃ picture at HOBBY **2** [U] the CLAY that some dishes and pots are made of: *a jug made of blue-glazed pottery* **3** [U] the skill of making pots and dishes from CLAY, especially by hand: *a pottery class* **4** [C] a place where CLAY pots and dishes are made

ˌpotting ˌshed *noun* a small building where seeds and young plants are grown in pots before they are planted outside

ˌpotting ˌsoil *noun* [U] good quality soil, used for growing plants in pots

pot·to /'pɑtoʊ/ *noun* (*pl.* **pot·tos**) an animal like a MONKEY with a pointed face, found in tropical W. Africa

pot·ty /'pɑti/ *noun* (*pl.* **pot·ties**) (*informal*) **1** a pot that very young children use when they are too small to use a toilet **2** (used especially by and to small children) a toilet: *Do you need to go potty* (= go to the toilet) *before we leave?*

ˌpotty-ˌmouthed *adj.* (*informal*) using rude, offensive language: *a potty-mouthed comedian*

ˌpotty-ˌtrain *verb* ~ sb to teach a small child to use a potty or toilet ▶ ˌpotty-ˌtrained *adj.* ˌpotty-ˌtraining *noun* [U]

POTUS *abbr.* (in writing) President of the United States

pouch /paʊtʃ/ *noun* **1** a small bag, usually made of leather, and often carried in a pocket or attached to a belt: *a tobacco pouch* ◆ *She kept her money in a pouch around her neck.* **2** a large bag for carrying letters, especially official ones ⊃ see also DIPLOMATIC POUCH **3** a pocket of skin on the stomach of some female MARSUPIAL animals, such as KANGAROOS, in which they carry their young ⊃ picture at ANIMAL **4** a pocket of skin in the cheeks of some animals, such as HAMSTERS, in which they store food

poul·tice /'poʊltəs/ *noun* a soft substance spread on a cloth, sometimes heated, and put on the skin to reduce pain or swelling

poul·try /'poʊltri/ *noun* **1** [pl.] chickens, TURKEYS, DUCKS, and GEESE, kept for their meat or eggs: *to keep poultry* ◆ *poultry farming* **2** [U] meat from chickens, TURKEYS, DUCKS, and GEESE: *Eat plenty of fish and poultry.*

pounce /paʊns/ *verb* [I] to move forward suddenly in order to attack or catch someone or something: *The lion crouched, ready to pounce.* ◆ ~ **on/upon sb/sth** *The muggers pounced on her as she got out of the car.* ◆ *Kobe pounced on the loose ball and scored.*

PHR V 'pounce on sth to quickly notice something that someone has said or done, especially in order to criticize it **SYN** SEIZE ON: *The press immediately pounced on his comments.*

pound 🔑 /paʊnd/ *noun, verb*

● *noun*
> **WEIGHT 1** [C] (*abbr.* **lb.**) a unit for measuring weight, 16 ounces, equal to 0.454 of a kilogram: *half a pound of butter* ◆ *They cost two dollars a pound.* ◆ *I've lost six and a half pounds since I started my diet.*
> **MONEY 2** [C] (*symb.* £) the unit of money in the U.K. and several other countries: *a ten-pound note* ◆ *I prefer to be paid in pounds sterling* (= U.K. pounds). **3 the pound** [sing.] (*finance*) the value of the British pound compared with the value of the money of other countries
> **FOR DOGS 4** [C] a place where dogs that have been found in the street without their owners are kept until their owners claim them
> **FOR CARS 5** [C] a place where vehicles that have been parked illegally are kept until their owners pay to get them back
> **SYMBOL 6** [U] = POUND SIGN: *Press pound/the pound key.*
> **IDM (have, get, want, etc.) your pound of flesh** the full amount that someone owes you, even if this will cause them trouble or suffering **ORIGIN** From Shakespeare's *The Merchant of Venice*, in which the moneylender Shylock demanded a pound of flesh from Antonio's body if he could not pay back the money he borrowed. ⊃ more at OUNCE, PENNY

● *verb*
> **HIT 1** [I, T] to hit something or someone hard many times, especially in a way that makes a lot of noise **SYN** HAMMER: ~ **at/against/on sth** *Heavy rain pounded on the roof.* ◆ *Someone was pounding at the door.* ◆ ~ **away (at/against/on sth)** *The factory's machinery pounded away day and night.* ◆ ~ **sb/sth (with sth)** *She pounded him with her fists.* ⊃ thesaurus box at BEAT
> **WALK NOISILY 2** [I] + **adv./prep.** to move with noisy steps: *She pounded down the corridor after him.*
> **OF HEART/BLOOD 3** [I] to beat quickly and loudly: *Her heart was pounding with excitement.* ◆ *The blood was pounding* (= making a beating noise) *in his ears.* ◆ *Her head began to pound.* ◆ *a pounding headache*
> **BREAK INTO PIECES 4** [T] ~ **sth (to/into sth)** to hit something many times in order to break it into smaller pieces: *The seeds were pounded to a fine powder.*
> **ATTACK WITH BOMBS 5** [T] ~ **sth** to attack an area with a large number of bombs over a period of time: *The area is still being pounded by rebel guns.*
> **OF MUSIC 6** [I] ~ **(out)** to be played loudly: *Rock music was pounding out from the jukebox.*
> **IDM pound the pavement/streets** to spend a lot of time going from place to place looking for something, especially a job: *With the country's jobless rate increasing, the number of people pounding the pavement had become a growing worry.*
> **PHR V** ˌpound sth↔'out to play music loudly on a musical instrument: *to pound out a tune on the piano*

pound·age /'paʊndɪdʒ/ *noun* [U] **1** (*technical*) a charge that is made for every pound in weight of something **2** (*informal*) weight: *to carry extra poundage*

pound cake *noun* [C, U] a plain yellow cake made with eggs, butter, flour, and sugar

pound·er /'paʊndər/ *noun* (in compounds) **1** something that weighs the number of pounds mentioned: *a three-pounder* (= a fish, for example, that weighs 3 pounds) **2** a gun that fires a SHELL that weighs the number of pounds mentioned: *an eighteen-pounder*

pound·ing /'paʊndɪŋ/ *noun* **1** a very loud repeated noise, such as the sound of something hitting something else hard; the sound or the feeling of your heart beating strongly: *We were awoken by a pounding at the door.* ◆ *There was a pounding in his head.* **2** an occasion when something is hit hard or attacked and severely damaged **SYN** BATTERING: *The boat took a pounding in the gale.* ◆ *(figurative) The team took a pounding* (= was badly defeated).

pound sign *noun* **1** the symbol (#), especially one on a keyboard or a telephone **2** the symbol (£) that represents a pound in British money

pour /pɔr/ *verb*

1 [T] ~ **sth** (+ *adv./prep.*) to make a liquid or other substance flow from a container in a continuous stream, especially by holding the container at an angle: *Pour the sauce over the pasta.* ◆ *Although I poured it carefully, I still spilled some.* **2** [I] + *adv./prep.* (of liquid, smoke, light, etc.) to flow quickly in a continuous stream: *Tears poured down his cheeks.* ◆ *Thick black smoke was pouring out of the roof.* **3** [T, I] to serve a drink by letting it flow from a container into a cup or glass: ~ **(sth)** *Will you pour the coffee?* ◆ *Should I pour?* ◆ ~ **sth out** *I was in the kitchen, pouring out drinks.* ◆ ~ **sth for sb** *I poured a cup of tea for you.* ◆ ~ **sb sth** *I poured you a cup of tea.* **4** [I, T] when rain **pours** down or when **it's pouring rain**, rain is falling heavily: ~ **(down)** *The rain continued to pour down.* ◆ *It's pouring outside.* ◆ ~ **rain** *It's pouring rain.* **5** [I] + *adv./prep.* to come or go somewhere continuously in large numbers **SYN** FLOOD: *Letters of complaint continue to pour in.* ◆ *Commuters came pouring out of the station.* **IDM** see COLD *adj.*, HEART, RAIN *v.*, SCORN *n.* **PHR V** ,**pour sth** '**into sth** to provide a large amount of money for something: *The government has poured millions into the education system.* ,**pour** '**out** when feelings or someone's words **pour out**, they are expressed, usually after they have been kept hidden for some time: *The whole story then came pouring out.* ,**pour sth**↔'**out** to express your feelings or give an account of something, especially after keeping it secret or hidden: *She poured out her troubles to me over a cup of coffee.* ⟳ related noun OUTPOURING

pout /paʊt/ *verb* [I, T] ~ **(sth)** | + *speech* if you **pout**, **pout** your lips, or if your lips **pout**, you push out your lips to show you are annoyed or to look attractive: *He pouted angrily.* ◆ *Her lips pouted invitingly.* ◆ *models pouting their lips for the camera* ▶ **pout** *noun*: *Her lips were set in a pout of annoyance.* **pout·y** *adj.*: *pouty lips*

pou·tine /puˈtin; -ˈtin/ *noun* [U] (*CanE*) a dish of FRENCH FRIES with melted cheese on top, served with a sauce (usually GRAVY)

pov·er·ty /ˈpɑvərti/ *noun*

1 [U] the state of being poor: *conditions of abject/extreme poverty* ◆ *to alleviate/relieve poverty* ◆ *Many elderly people live in poverty.* ⟳ collocations at INTERNATIONAL **2** [U, sing.] a lack of something; poor quality: *There is a poverty of color in her work.*

the '**poverty** ,**line** (also **the** '**poverty** ,**level**) *noun* [sing.] the official level of income that is necessary to be able to buy the basic things you need, such as food and clothes, and to pay for somewhere to live: *A third of the population is living at or below the poverty line.*

poverty-,**stricken** *adj.* extremely poor; with very little money

poverty ,**trap** *noun* [usually sing.] a situation in which poor people stay poor in spite of political and social changes

POW /ˌpi oʊ ˈdʌblyu; -ˈdʌbəyu/ *noun* PRISONER OF WAR: *a POW camp*

pow /paʊ/ *exclamation* used to express the sound of an explosion, a gun firing, or someone hitting someone else

pow·der /ˈpaʊdər/ *noun*, *verb*

● *noun* **1** [U, C] a dry mass of very small fine pieces or grains: *chili powder* ◆ *lumps of chalk crushed to (a) fine white powder* ◆ *The snow was like powder.* ◆ *A wide range of cleaning fluids and powders is available.* ⟳ see also BAKING POWDER, CURRY POWDER, TALCUM POWDER **2** [U] a very fine, soft, dry substance that you can put on your face to make it look

smooth and dry ⟳ picture at MAKEUP **3** [U] = GUNPOWDER **IDM** keep your powder dry (*old-fashioned*) to remain ready for a possible emergency take a powder (*informal*) to leave suddenly; to run away

● *verb* ~ **sth** to put powder on something: *She powdered her face and put on her lipstick.* **IDM** powder your nose (*old-fashioned*) a polite way of referring to the fact that a woman is going to the bathroom: *I'm just going to powder my nose.*

powder '**blue** *adj.* very pale blue in color ▶ **powder** '**blue** *noun* [U]

pow·dered /ˈpaʊdərd/ *adj.* **1** (of a substance that is naturally liquid) dried and made into powder: *powdered milk* **2** crushed and made into a powder: *powdered chalk* **3** covered with powder: *her powdered cheeks*

powdered '**milk** *noun* [U] = DRY MILK

powdered '**sugar** *noun* [U] = CONFECTIONER'S SUGAR

powder ,**keg** *noun* a dangerous situation that may suddenly become very violent

powder ,**puff** *noun* a small round piece of soft material that you use for putting powder on your face

powder ,**room** *noun* **1** a small room in a house containing a SINK and a toilet, usually for guests to use **SYN** HALF-BATH **2** a polite word for a women's bathroom in a public building

pow·der·y /ˈpaʊdəri/ *adj.* like powder; covered with powder: *a light fall of powdery snow* ◆ *powdery cheeks*

pow·er /ˈpaʊər/ *noun*, *verb*

● *noun*
▷ CONTROL **1** [U] the ability to control people or things: ~ **(over sb/sth)** *The aim is to give people more power over their own lives.* ◆ ~ **(to do sth)** *He has the power to make things very unpleasant for us.* ◆ *to have someone in your power* (= to be able to do what you like with someone) **2** [U] political control of a country or an area: *to take/seize/lose power* ◆ *The present regime has been in power for two years.* ◆ *The Republicans came to power in the last election.* ◆ *They are hoping to return to power.* ◆ *a power struggle between rival factions within the party* ⟳ collocations at POLITICS ⟳ see also BALANCE OF POWER
▷ ABILITY **3** [U] (in people) the ability or opportunity to do something: *It is not within my power* (= I am unable or not in a position) *to help you.* ◆ *I will do everything in my power to help you.* **4** [U] (also **powers** [pl.]) a particular ability of the body or mind: *He had lost the power of speech.* ◆ *The drug may affect your powers of concentration.* ◆ *He had to use all his powers of persuasion.* **5 powers** [pl.] all the abilities of a person's body or mind: *At 26, he is at the height of his powers and ranked fourth in the world.*
▷ AUTHORITY **6** [U, C, usually pl.] the right or authority of a person or group to do something: ~ **(to do sth)** *The Secretary of State has the power to approve the proposals.* ◆ *The powers of the police must be clearly defined.* ◆ ~ **(of sth)** *The President has the power of veto over all new legislation.* ⟳ see also POWER OF ATTORNEY
▷ COUNTRY **7** [C] a country with a lot of influence in world affairs, or with great military strength: *world powers* ◆ *an allied/enemy power* ⟳ see also SUPERPOWER
▷ INFLUENCE **8** [U] (in compounds) strength or influence in a particular area of activity: *economic power* ◆ *air/sea power* (= military strength in the air/at sea) ◆ *purchasing power* **9** [U] the influence of a particular thing or group within society: *the power of the media* ◆ *black power*
▷ ENERGY **10** [U] the strength or energy contained in something: *The ship was helpless against the power of the storm.* ◆ *It was a performance of great power.* ⟳ see also FIREPOWER, STAYING POWER **11** [U] physical strength used in action; physical strength that someone possesses and might use: *He hit the ball with as much power as he could.* ◆ *the sheer physical power of the man* **12** [U] energy that can be collected and used to operate a machine, to make electricity, etc.: *nuclear/wind/solar power* ◆ *engine power* ⟳ see also HORSEPOWER

> ELECTRICITY **13** [U] the public supply of electricity: *They switched off the power.* ◆ *a power failure*
> MATHEMATICS **14** [C, usually sing.] the number of times that an amount is to be multiplied by itself: *4 to the third power/ to the power of 3 is 4^3 (= 4×4×4=64).*
> OF LENS **15** [U] the amount by which a LENS can make objects appear larger: *the power of a microscope/telescope*
> GOOD/EVIL SPIRIT **16** [C] a good or evil spirit that controls the lives of others: *the powers of darkness* (= the forces of evil)
  IDM **the (real) power behind the throne** the person who really controls an organization, a country, etc. in contrast to the person who is legally in charge **the powers that be** (often *ironic*) the people who control an organization, a country, etc. ⊃ more at CORRIDOR,

● *verb*
> SUPPLY ENERGY **1** [T, usually passive] **~ sth** to supply a machine or vehicle with the energy that makes it work: *The aircraft is powered by a jet engine.*
> MOVE QUICKLY **2** [I, T] to move or move something very quickly and with great power in a particular direction: **+ adv./prep.** *He powered through the water.* ◆ **~ sth + adv./prep.** *She powered her way into the lead.* ◆ *He powered the ball into the basket.*
  PHR V **power 'down** | **power sth↔'down** to stop a machine, especially a computer, by turning off the electricity supply: *We were told to power down at 9:45.* ◆ *Log off or power down your system.* **ANT** POWER STH UP **power sth↔'up** to prepare a machine to start working by supplying it with electricity **ANT** POWER STH DOWN ⊃ related noun POWER-UP

'power ˌbase *noun* the area or the people that provide the main support for a politician or a political party

pow·er·boat /'paʊərˌboʊt/ *noun* a fast boat with a powerful engine that is used especially for racing

ˌpower 'breakfast *noun* a meeting that business people have early in the morning while they eat breakfast

ˌpower 'broker *noun* a person who has a strong influence on who has political power in an area

ˌpower ˌdressing *noun* [U] a style of dressing in which people in business wear formal and expensive clothes to emphasize how important they and their jobs are

pow·ered /'paʊərd/ *adj.* (usually in compounds) operated by a form of energy such as electricity or by the type of energy mentioned: *a powered wheelchair* ◆ *a solar-powered calculator* ⊃ see also HIGH-POWERED

pow·er·ful 🔑 /'paʊərfl/ *adj.*
1 (of people) being able to control and influence people and events **SYN** INFLUENTIAL: *an immensely powerful organization* ◆ *a rich and powerful man* ◆ *Only the intervention of powerful friends obtained her release.* **2** having great power or force; very effective: *powerful weapons* ◆ *a powerful engine* ◆ *a powerful voice* **3** having a strong effect on your mind or body: *a powerful image/drug/speech* **4** (of a person or an animal) physically strong **SYN** MUSCULAR: *a powerful body* ◆ *a powerful athlete* ▶ **pow·er·ful·ly** /-fli/ *adv.*: *a powerfully emotive song* ◆ *He is powerfully built* (= he has a large strong body). ◆ *She argued powerfully for reform.*

pow·er·house /'paʊərˌhaʊs/ *noun* **1** a group or an organization that has a lot of power: *China has been described as an "emerging economic powerhouse."* **2** a person or team that is very successful, especially in sports; a place that produces successful players and teams: *He helped transform the team into a powerhouse.* ◆ *Cornell was a collegiate hockey powerhouse.* **3** a person who is very strong and full of energy **4** a type of food that provides a lot of energy: *Chicken turns this pizza into a protein powerhouse.*

pow·er·less /'paʊərləs/ *adj.* **1** without power to control or to influence someone or something **SYN** HELPLESS: *powerless minorities* ◆ *When the enemy attacked, we were completely powerless against them.* **2 ~ to do sth** completely unable to do something: *I saw what was happening, but I was powerless to help.* ▶ **pow·er·less·ness** *noun* [U]: *a feeling/sense of powerlessness*

ˌpow·er·lift·ing /'paʊərˌlɪftɪŋ/ *noun* [U] the sport of lifting weights in three different ways, in a set order ▶ **pow·er·lift·er** *noun*

'power ˌline *noun* a thick wire that carries electricity: *overhead power lines*

'power ˌnap *noun* a short sleep that someone has during the day in order to get back their energy

ˌpower of at'torney *noun* (*pl.* powers of attorney) [U, C] (*law*) the right to act as the representative of someone in business or financial matters; a document that gives someone this right

'power ˌoutage *noun* an interruption in the supply of electricity; a period of time when this happens

'power ˌplant *noun* a building or group of buildings where electricity is produced: *a hydroelectric/nuclear power plant*

'power ˌplay *noun* **1** [U] (in HOCKEY) a situation in which one team has more players than another because a player is off the ice as a punishment **2** [C] a powerful move by someone to get or achieve what they want: *She made a series of power plays to take over his job.*

ˌpower 'politics *noun* [U] a situation in which a country tries to achieve its aims by using or threatening to use its military or economic power against another country

power-ˌsharing *noun* [U] a policy or system in which different groups or political parties share responsibility for making decisions, taking political action, etc.

ˌpower 'steering *noun* [U] (in a vehicle) a system that uses power from the engine to help the driver change direction

'power ˌtrip *noun* [usually sing.] (*informal*) an action or way of behaving in which a person gets great pleasure from having control over others: *Barnes has been on a power trip ever since he was promoted to head coach.*

power-ˌup *noun* **1** [U] the moment when a machine is switched on and starts working: *Does the computer beep on power-up?* **2** [C] in computer games, an advantage that a character can get if a player wins a certain number of points, for example more strength

'power ˌuser *noun* (*computing*) someone who needs computer products that are fastest and have the most features

'power ˌwalking *noun* [U] the activity of walking very quickly as a form of exercise

pow·wow /'paʊwaʊ/ *noun* **1** a meeting of Native Americans **2** (*informal* or *humorous*) a meeting for discussion

pox /pɑks/ *noun* **the pox** [sing.] (*old use*) **1** = SMALLPOX **2** an infectious disease spread by sexual contact **SYN** SYPHILIS ⊃ see also CHICKEN POX

pp *abbr.* very quietly (from Italian "pianissimo")

pp. *abbr.* pages: *See pp. 100–117.*

ppi /ˌpi pi 'aɪ/ *abbr.* (*computing*) pixels per inch (a measure of the quality of images)

PPO /ˌpi pi 'oʊ/ *abbr.* preferred-provider organization (a company that provides medical treatment for large organizations such as insurance companies and employers)

PPV /ˌpi pi 'vi/ *abbr.* PAY-PER-VIEW

PR /ˌpi 'ar/ *noun* [U] **1** the abbreviation for PUBLIC RELATIONS: *a PR department/agency/campaign* ◆ *The article is very good PR for the theater.* **2** the abbreviation for PROPORTIONAL REPRESENTATION

prac·ti·ca·ble /'præktɪkəbl/ *adj.* (*formal*) able to be done; likely to be successful **SYN** FEASIBLE, WORKABLE: *at the earliest practicable opportunity* ◆ *as soon as (is) practicable* ◆ *The only practicable alternative is to postpone the meeting.* ◆ *Employers should provide a safe working environment, as far as is reasonably practicable.* ⊃ compare IMPRACTICABLE ▶ **prac·ti·ca·bil·i·ty** /ˌpræktɪkə'bɪləti/ *noun* [U]: *We were doubtful about the practicability of the plan.* **prac·ti·ca·bly** /'præktɪkəbli/ *adv.*: *Please reply as soon as is practicably possible.*

prac·ti·cal /ˈpræktɪkl/ adj.

> CONNECTED WITH REAL THINGS **1** connected with real situations rather than with ideas or theories: *to have gained* ***practical experience*** *of the work* ◆ ***practical advice/help/support*** ◆ *practical problems* ◆ *There are some obvious practical applications of the research.* ◆ ***In practical terms,*** *it means spending less.* ◆ *From a practical point of view, it isn't a good place to live.* ⊃ compare THEORETICAL

> LIKELY TO WORK **2** (of an idea, a method, or a course of action) right or sensible; likely to be successful **SYN** WORKABLE: *It wouldn't be practical for us to go all that way just for the weekend.* **ANT** IMPRACTICAL

> USEFUL **3** (of things) useful or suitable: *a practical little car, ideal for the city* **ANT** IMPRACTICAL

> SENSIBLE **4** (of a person) sensible and realistic: *Let's be practical and work out the cost first.* **ANT** IMPRACTICAL

> GOOD AT MAKING THINGS **5** (of a person) good at making or repairing things **SYN** HANDY: *Bob's very practical. He does all the odd jobs around the house.*

> ALMOST TOTAL **6** [only before noun] almost complete or total **SYN** VIRTUAL: *She married a practical stranger.*

IDM for (all) practical purposes used when you are stating what the reality of a situation is: *There's still another ten minutes of the game to go, but for practical purposes it's already over.*

prac·ti·cal·i·ty /ˌpræktɪˈkæləti/ noun **1** [U] the quality of being suitable or likely to be successful: *I have doubts about the practicality of their proposal.* **2** [U] the quality of being sensible and realistic: *I was impressed by her practicality.* **3** **practicalities** [pl.] the real facts and circumstances rather than ideas or theories: *It sounds like a good idea; let's look at the practicalities and work out the costs.*

ˌpractical ˈjoke noun a trick that is played on someone to make them look stupid and to make other people laugh ▶ ˌpractical ˈjoker noun

prac·ti·cal·ly /ˈpræktɪkli/ adv.

1 almost; very nearly **SYN** VIRTUALLY: *The theater was practically empty.* ◆ *I meet famous people practically every day.* ◆ *My essay is practically finished now.* ◆ *There's practically no difference between the two options.* ⊃ note at ALMOST **2** in a realistic or sensible way; in real situations: *Practically speaking, we can't afford it.* ◆ *It sounds like a good idea, but I don't think it will work practically.*

ˌpractical ˈnurse noun a nurse with practical experience but less training than a REGISTERED NURSE

prac·tice /ˈpræktəs/ verb, noun

● **verb** (CanE usually **prac·tise**) **1** [I, T] to do an activity or train regularly so that you can improve your skill: *You need to practice every day.* ◆ **~ for sth** *The team is practicing for their big game on Friday.* ◆ **~ sth** *to practice the piano every day* ◆ *They practiced the dance until it was perfect.* ◆ **~ (sth) on sb/sth** *He usually wants to practice his English on me.* ◆ **~ doing sth** *I practiced backing the car into the garage.* **2** [T] **~ sth** to do something regularly as part of your normal behavior: *to practice self-restraint* ◆ *Do you still practice your religion?* **3** [I, T] to work as a doctor, lawyer, etc.: *There are over 5,000 corporate lawyers practicing in the city.* ◆ **~ as sth** *She practiced as a trial lawyer for many years.* ◆ **~ sth** *She's practicing medicine in Philadelphia.*

IDM practice what you preach to do the things yourself that you tell other people to do

● **noun** (CanE also **prac·tise**)

> ACTION NOT IDEAS **1** [U] action rather than ideas: *the theory and practice of teaching* ◆ *She's determined to put her new ideas into practice.*

> WAY OF DOING SOMETHING **2** [U, C] a way of doing something that is the usual or expected way in a particular organization or situation: *common/current/standard practice* ◆ *guidelines for good practice* ◆ *a review of pay and working practices* ◆ *religious practices* ⊃ see also BEST PRACTICE, CODE OF PRACTICE

> HABIT/CUSTOM **3** [C] a thing that is done regularly; a habit or a custom: *the American practice of giving workers two weeks of vacation a year* ◆ *It is his practice to read several books a week.*

> FOR IMPROVING SKILL **4** [U] training or doing an activity regularly so that you can improve your skill; the time you spend doing this: *English conversation practice* ◆ *It takes a lot of practice to play the violin well.* ◆ *There's basketball practice every Wednesday night.* ◆ *She does an hour of piano practice every day.*

> OF DOCTOR/LAWYER **5** [U, C] the work or the business of some professional people such as doctors, dentists, and lawyers; the place where they work: *the practice of medicine* ◆ *Students should have prior experience of veterinary practice.* ◆ *My lawyer is no longer in practice.* ◆ *a successful medical/dental/law practice* ⊃ see also FAMILY PRACTICE, GENERAL PRACTICE, GROUP PRACTICE, PRIVATE PRACTICE

IDM in practice in reality: *Prisoners have legal rights, but in practice these rights are not always respected.* be/get/out of practice to be/become less good at doing something than you were because you have not spent time doing it recently: *Don't ask me to speak French! I'm out of practice.* practice makes perfect (saying) a way of encouraging people by telling them that if you do an activity regularly and try to improve your skill, you will become very good at it

prac·ticed /ˈpræktəst/ adj. good at doing something because you have been doing it regularly: *She's only 18 but she's already a practiced composer.* ◆ *It took a practiced eye to spot the difference.* ◆ **~ in sth** *He has good ideas but he isn't practiced in the art of marketing.*

prac·tic·ing /ˈpræktəsɪŋ/ adj. [only before noun] taking an active part in a particular religion, profession, etc.: *a practicing Christian/teacher*

prac·tise (CanE) = PRACTICE

prac·ti·tion·er **AWL** /prækˈtɪʃənər/ noun **1** (technical) a person who works in a profession, especially medicine or law: *health care practitioners* ◆ *a qualified practitioner* ⊃ see also GENERAL PRACTITIONER **2** (formal) a person who regularly does a particular activity, especially one that requires skill: *one of the greatest practitioners of science fiction*

prag·mat·ic /prægˈmætɪk/ adj. solving problems in a practical and sensible way rather than by having fixed ideas or theories **SYN** REALISTIC: *a pragmatic approach to management problems* ▶ **prag·mat·i·cally** /-kli/ adv.

prag·mat·ics /prægˈmætɪks/ noun [U] (linguistics) the study of the way in which language is used to express what someone really means in particular situations, especially when the actual words used may appear to mean something different

prag·ma·tism /ˈprægmə tɪzəm/ noun [U] (formal) thinking about solving problems in a practical and sensible way rather than by having fixed ideas and theories ▶ **prag·ma·tist** /-tɪst/ noun

prai·rie /ˈprɛri/ noun [C, U] **1** a flat wide area of land in N. America, without many trees and originally covered with grass **2** the Prairies the Canadian PROVINCES (= government divisions) of Manitoba, Saskatchewan, and Alberta

ˈprairie ˌdog noun a small brown animal of the SQUIRREL family that lives in holes on the prairies

ˈprairie ˌwolf noun = COYOTE

praise /preɪz/ noun, verb

● **noun** [U] **1** (also less frequent **praises** [pl.]) words that show approval of or admiration for someone or something: *His teachers are full of praise for the progress he's making.* ◆ *She wrote poems in praise of freedom.* ◆ *His latest movie has won high praise from the critics.* ◆ *We have nothing but praise for the way they handled the investigation.* ◆ *The team coach singled out two players for special praise.* ◆ *She left with their praises ringing in her ears.* ◆ *They always sing his praises* (= praise him very highly). **2** the expression of worship to God: *hymns/songs of praise* ◆ *Praise be (to God)!* (= expressing belief or joy)

IDM see DAMN v.

verb 1 to express your approval or admiration for someone or something **SYN** COMPLIMENT: *~ sb/sth She praised his cooking.* ◆ *~ sb/sth for sth/for doing sth He praised his team for their performance.* ◆ *~ sb/sth as sth Critics praised the work as highly original.* **2** *~ sb* to express your thanks to or your respect for God: *Praise the Lord.* ◆ *Allah be praised.*
IDM praise sb/sth to the skies to praise someone or something a lot

praise·wor·thy /ˈpreɪzˌwɜrði/ *adj.* (*formal*) deserving praise **SYN** COMMENDABLE: *a praiseworthy achievement*

pra·line /ˈprɑlin/ *noun* [U] a candy made of nuts and boiled sugar

pra·na /ˈprɑnə/ *noun* [U] (in Hindu philosophy) the force that keeps all life in existence

prance /præns/ *verb* **1** [I] + **adv./prep.** to move quickly with exaggerated steps so that people will look at you: *The lead singer was prancing around with the microphone.* **2** [I] (of a horse) to move with high steps

prank /præŋk/ *noun* a trick that is played on someone as a joke: *a childish prank* ▶ **prank·ster** /ˈpræŋkstər/ *noun*: *Student pranksters did considerable damage to the school buildings.*

pra·se·o·dym·i·um /ˌpreɪzioʊˈdɪmiəm/ *noun* [U] (*symb.* **Pr**) a chemical element. Praseodymium is a soft silver-white metal used in ALLOYS and to color glass.

prat·fall /ˈprætfɔl/ *noun* **1** an embarrassing mistake **2** a fall on your bottom

prat·tle /ˈprætl/ *verb* [I] *~ (on/away) (about sb/sth)* (*old-fashioned*, often *disapproving*) to talk a lot about unimportant things: *She prattled on about her vacation all evening.* ▶ **prat·tle** *noun* [U]

prawn /prɔn/ *noun* a SHELLFISH like a large SHRIMP

prax·is /ˈpræksəs/ *noun* [U] (*philosophy*) a way of doing something; the use of a theory or a belief in a practical way

pray /preɪ/ *verb, adv.*
● *verb* **1** [I, T] to speak to God, especially to give thanks or ask for help: *They knelt down and prayed.* ◆ *~ for sb/sth I'll pray for you.* ◆ *to pray for peace* ◆ *~ to sb (for sb/sth) She prayed to God for an end to her sufferings.* ◆ *~ (that) We prayed (that) she would recover from her illness.* ◆ *~ to do sth He prayed to be forgiven.* ◆ *+ speech "Please God, don't let it happen," she prayed.* **2** [I, T] to hope very much that something will happen: *~ (for sth) We're praying for good weather on Saturday.* ◆ *~ that... I prayed that nobody would notice my mistake.*
● *adv.* (*old use* or *ironic*) used to mean "please" when you are asking a question or telling someone to do something: *What, pray, is the meaning of this?* ◆ *Pray continue.*

prayer /prɛr/ *noun*
1 [C] *~ (for sb/sth)* words that you say to God giving thanks or asking for help: *to say your prayers* ◆ *prayers for the sick* ◆ *He arrived at that very moment, as if in answer to her prayer.* ◆ *Their prayers were answered and the child was found safe and well.* ⊃ collocations at RELIGION **2** [C] a fixed form of words that you can say when you speak to God: *It was a prayer she had learned as a child.* ⊃ see also THE LORD'S PRAYER **3** [U] the act or habit of praying: *They knelt in prayer.* ◆ *We believe in the power of prayer.* **4** prayers [pl.] a religious meeting that takes place regularly in which people say prayers **5** [C, usually sing.] a thing that you hope for very much: *My prayer is that one day he will walk again.*
IDM not have a prayer (of doing sth) to have no chance of succeeding (in doing something) ⊃ more at WING *n.*

prayer book *noun* a book that contains prayers, for using in religious services

prayer meeting *noun* a religious meeting when people say prayers to God

prayer rug (also **prayer mat**) *noun* a small carpet on which Muslims rest their knees when they are saying prayers

prayer wheel *noun* (in Tibetan Buddhism) an object that is turned as a way of saying a prayer

praying mantis (also **man·tis**) *noun* a large green insect that eats other insects. The female praying mantis often eats the male.

pre- /pri/ *prefix* (in verbs, nouns, and adjectives) before: *preheat* ◆ *precaution* ◆ *prewar* ◆ *preseason training* (= before a sports season starts) ⊃ compare ANTE-, POST-

preach /pritʃ/ *verb* **1** [I, T] to give a religious talk in a public place, especially in a church during a service: *She preached to the congregation about forgiveness.* ◆ *~ sth The minister preached a sermon on the parable of the lost sheep.* **2** [T, I] to tell people about a particular religion, way of life, system, etc. in order to persuade them to accept it: *~ sth to preach the word of God* ◆ *He preached the virtues of capitalism to us.* ◆ *~ (about sth) She preached about the benefits of a healthy lifestyle.* ⊃ collocations at RELIGION **3** [I] (*disapproving*) to give someone advice on moral standards, behavior, etc., especially in a way that they find annoying or boring: *I'm sorry, I didn't mean to preach.* ◆ *~ at sb You're preaching at me again!*
IDM preach to the converted to speak to people in support of views that they already hold ⊃ more at PRACTICE *v.*

preach·er /ˈpritʃər/ *noun* a person, often a member of the CLERGY, who gives religious talks and often performs religious ceremonies, for example in a church: *a preacher famous for her inspiring sermons* ◆ *a lay preacher* (= who is not a priest, etc. but who has been trained to give religious talks)

preach·y /ˈpritʃi/ *adj.* (*informal*, *disapproving*) trying to give advice or to persuade people to accept an opinion on what is right and wrong

pre·am·ble /priˈæmbl; ˈpriˌæmbl/ *noun* [C, U] (*formal*) an introduction to a book or a written document; an introduction to something you say: *The aims of the treaty are stated in its preamble.* ◆ *She gave him the bad news without preamble.*

pre·ar·ranged /ˌpriəˈreɪndʒd/ *adj.* planned or arranged in advance

pre·but·tal /ˌpriˈbʌtl/ *noun* [C, U] (*informal*) a statement saying or proving that a criticism is false or unfair before the criticism has actually been made

pre·can·cer·ous /ˌpriˈkænsərəs/ *adj.* (*medical*) that will develop into cancer if not treated: *precancerous cells*

pre·car·i·ous /prɪˈkɛriəs/ *adj.* **1** (of a situation) not safe or certain; dangerous: *He earned a precarious living as an artist.* ◆ *The museum is in a financially precarious position.* **2** likely to fall or cause someone to fall: *That ladder looks very precarious.* ◆ *The path down to the beach is very precarious in wet weather.* ▶ **pre·car·i·ous·ly** *adv.*: *The economy is precariously close to recession.* ◆ *He balanced the glass precariously on the arm of his chair.* **pre·car·i·ous·ness** *noun* [U]

pre·cast /ˌpriˈkæst/ *adj.* (of some building materials) made into shapes that are ready to use: *precast concrete slabs*

pre·cau·tion /prɪˈkɔʃn/ *noun* [usually pl.] **1** *~ (against sth)* something that is done in advance in order to prevent problems or to avoid danger: *safety precautions* ◆ *precautions against fire* ◆ *You must take all reasonable precautions to protect yourself and your family.* ◆ *I'll keep the letter as a precaution.* **2** precautions [pl.] a way of referring to CONTRACEPTION: *They didn't take any precautions and she got pregnant.* ▶ **pre·cau·tion·ar·y** /prɪˈkɔʃəˌnɛri/ *adj.*: *He was kept in the hospital overnight as a precautionary measure.*

pre·cede **AWL** /prɪˈsid/ *verb* **1** [T, I] *~ (sb/sth)* to happen before something or come before something or someone in order: *the years preceding the war* ◆ *His resignation was preceded by weeks of speculation.* ◆ *She preceded me in the job.* ◆ *See the preceding chapter.* **2** [T] *~ sb + adv./prep.* to go in front of someone: *She preceded him out of the room.*
PHR V pre·cede sth with sth to do or say something to introduce something else: *She preceded her speech with a vote of thanks to the committee.*

prec·e·dence **AWL** /ˈprɛsədəns/ *noun* [U] *~ (over sb/sth)*

ʌ **cup**   ə **about**   eɪ **say**   aɪ **five**   ɔɪ **boy**   aʊ **now**   oʊ **go**   ər **bird**

the condition of being more important than someone else and therefore coming or being dealt with first **SYN** PRIORITY: *She had to learn that her wishes did not take precedence over other people's needs.* ◆ *The speakers came on to the platform in order of precedence* (= the most important one first).

prec·e·dent **AWL** /ˈpresədənt/ *noun* **1** [C, U] an official action or decision that has happened in the past and that is seen as an example or a rule to be followed in a similar situation later: *The ruling set a precedent for future libel cases.* **2** [C, U] a similar action or event that happened earlier: *historical precedents* ◆ *There is no precedent for a disaster of this scale.* ◆ *Such protests are without precedent in recent history.* **3** [U] the way that things have always been done **SYN** TRADITION: *to break with precedent* (= to do something in a different way) ⊃ see also UNPRECEDENTED

pre·cept /ˈpriːsept/ *noun* [C, U] (*formal*) a rule about how to behave or what to think **SYN** PRINCIPLE

pre·cinct /ˈpriːsɪŋkt/ *noun* **1** one of the parts into which a town or city is divided in order to organize elections **2** a part of a city that has its own police station; the police station in this area: *Detective Hennessy of the 44th precinct* ◆ *The murder occurred just a block from the precinct.* **3** [usually pl.] the area around a place or a building, sometimes surrounded by a wall: *the university/cathedral precincts* ◆ *within the precincts of the castle*

pre·cious /ˈpreʃəs/ *adj., adv.*
● *adj.* **1** rare and worth a lot of money: *a precious vase* ◆ *The necklace was set with precious jewels—diamonds, rubies, and emeralds.* ⊃ see also PRECIOUS METAL, PRECIOUS STONE ⊃ thesaurus box at VALUABLE **2** valuable or important and not to be wasted: *Clean water is a precious commodity in that part of the world.* ◆ *You're wasting precious time!* **3** loved or valued very much **SYN** TREASURED: *precious memories/possessions* **4** (*informal*) very attractive and easy to feel love for: *Isn't their new baby precious?* **5** [only before noun] (*informal*) used to show you are angry that another person thinks something is very important: *I didn't touch your precious car!* **6** (*disapproving*) (especially of people and their behavior) very formal, exaggerated, and not natural in what you say and do **SYN** AFFECTED ▶ **pre·cious·ness** *noun* [U]: *the preciousness of an old friendship* ◆ *His writings reveal an unattractive preciousness of style.*
● *adv.* ~ **little/few** (*informal*) used to emphasize the fact that there is very little of something or that there are very few of something: *There's precious little to do in this town.*

ˌprecious ˈmetal *noun* [C, U] a very valuable metal such as gold or silver

ˌprecious ˈstone (also stone) *noun* a rare valuable stone, such as a diamond, that is used in jewelry ⊃ see also SEMI-PRECIOUS

prec·i·pice /ˈpresəpəs/ *noun* a very steep side of a high CLIFF, mountain, or rock: (*figurative*) *The country was now on the edge of a precipice* (= very close to disaster). ⊃ see also PRECIPITOUS

pre·cip·i·tate *verb, adj., noun*
● *verb* /prɪˈsɪpəˌteɪt/ (*formal*) **1** ~ **sth** to make something, especially something bad, happen suddenly or sooner than it should **SYN** BRING ON, SPARK OFF: *His resignation precipitated a leadership crisis.* **2** ~ **sb/sth into sth** to suddenly force someone or something into a particular state or condition: *The assassination of the president precipitated the country into war.*
● *adj.* /prɪˈsɪpətət/ (*formal*) (of an action or a decision) happening very quickly or suddenly and usually without enough care and thought ▶ **pre·cip·i·tate·ly** *adv.*: *to act precipitately*
● *noun* /prɪˈsɪpəˌteɪt; -tət/ (*chemistry*) a solid substance that has been separated from a liquid in a chemical process

pre·cip·i·ta·tion /prɪˌsɪpəˈteɪʃn/ *noun* **1** [U] (*technical*) rain, snow, etc. that falls; the amount of this that falls: *an increase in annual precipitation* **2** [U, C] (*chemistry*) a chemical process in which solid material is separated from a liquid

pre·cip·i·tous /prɪˈsɪpətəs/ *adj.* (*formal*) **1** very steep, high, and often dangerous **SYN** SHEER: *precipitous cliffs* ◆ *a precipitous drop at the side of the road* **2** sudden and great **SYN** ABRUPT: *a precipitous decline in exports* **3** done very quickly, without enough thought or care **SYN** HASTY: *a precipitous action* ▶ **pre·cip·i·tous·ly** *adv.*: *The land dropped precipitously down to the rocky shore.* ◆ *The dollar plunged precipitously.* ◆ *We don't want to act precipitously.* ⊃ see also PRECIPICE

pré·cis /ˈpreɪsi; preɪˈsi/ *noun* [C, U] (*pl.* **pré·cis** /-siz; -ˈsiz/) a short version of a speech or a piece of writing that gives the main points or ideas **SYN** SUMMARY: *to write/give/make a précis of a report* ▶ **pré·cis** *verb* (**pré·cises** /-siz; -ˈsiz/, **pré·cis·ing** /-sɪŋ; -ˈsiŋ/, **pré·cised**, **pré·cised** /-sid; -ˈsid/): ~ **sth** *to précis a scientific report*

pre·cise 🔑 **AWL** /prɪˈsaɪs/ *adj.*
1 clear and accurate **SYN** EXACT: *precise details/instructions/measurements* ◆ *Can you give a more precise definition of the word?* ◆ *I can be reasonably precise about the time of the incident.* **2** [only before noun] used to emphasize that something happens at a particular time or in a particular way: *We were just talking about her when, at that precise moment, she walked in.* ◆ *Doctors found it hard to establish the precise nature of her illness.* **3** taking care to be exact and accurate, especially about small details **SYN** METICULOUS: *a skilled and precise worker* ◆ *small, precise movements*
IDM **to be (more) precise** used to show that you are giving more detailed and accurate information about something you have just mentioned: *The shelf is about a yard long—well, 35 inches, to be precise.*

pre·cise·ly 🔑 **AWL** /prɪˈsaɪsli/ *adv.*
1 exactly: *They look precisely the same to me.* ◆ *That's precisely what I meant.* ◆ *It's not clear precisely how the accident happened.* ◆ *The meeting starts precisely at 2 o'clock.* **2** accurately; carefully: *to describe something precisely* ◆ *She pronounced the word very slowly and precisely.* **3** used to emphasize that something is very true or obvious: *It's precisely because I care about you that I don't like you staying out late.* **4** used to emphasize that you agree with a statement, especially because you think it is obvious or is similar to what you have just said: *"It's not that easy, is it?" "No, precisely."*
IDM **more precisely** used to show that you are giving more detailed and accurate information about something you have just mentioned: *The problem is due to discipline, or, more precisely, the lack of discipline, in schools.* ⊃ language bank at I.E.

pre·ci·sion **AWL** /prɪˈsɪʒn/ *noun* [U] the quality of being exact, accurate, and careful **SYN** ACCURACY: *done with mathematical precision* ◆ *Historians can't estimate the date with any (degree of) precision.* ◆ *He chose his words with precision.* ◆ *precision instruments/tools*

pre·clude /prɪˈkluːd/ *verb* (*formal*) to prevent something from happening or someone from doing something; to make something impossible: ~ **sth** *Lack of time precludes any further discussion.* ◆ ~ **sb from doing sth** *My lack of interest in the subject precluded me from gaining much enjoyment out of it.*

pre·co·cious /prɪˈkoʊʃəs/ *adj.* (sometimes *disapproving*) (of a child) having developed particular abilities and ways of behaving at a much younger age than usual: *a precocious child who started her acting career at the age of 5* ◆ *From an early age, she displayed a precocious talent for music.* ▶ **pre·co·cious·ly** *adv.*: *a precociously talented child* **pre·co·cious·ness** (also **pre·coc·i·ty** /prɪˈkɑsəti/) *noun* [U]: *his unusual precociousness*

pre·cog·ni·tion /ˌprikɑɡˈnɪʃn/ *noun* [U] (*formal*) the knowledge of something that will happen in the future, that someone has because of a dream or a sudden feeling

pre-Co·lum·bi·an /ˌpri kəˈlʌmbiən/ *adj.* connected with the history and the cultures of the Americas before the arrival of Columbus in 1492

pre·con·ceived /ˌprikənˈsivd/ *adj.* [only before noun] (of ideas, opinions, etc.) formed before you have enough information or experience of something: *Before I started the job, I had no preconceived notions of what it would be like.*

pre·con·cep·tion /ˌprikənˈsɛpʃn/ *noun* [C, usually pl., U] an idea or opinion that is formed before you have enough information or experience **SYN** ASSUMPTION: *a book that will challenge your preconceptions about rural life* ➔ compare MISCONCEPTION

pre·con·di·tion /ˌprikənˈdɪʃn/ *noun* ~ (for/of sth) something that must exist or exist before something else can exist or be done **SYN** PREREQUISITE: *A ceasefire is an essential precondition for negotiation.*

pre·con·scious /ˌpriˈkɑnʃəs/ *adj.* (*psychology*) associated with a part of the mind from which memories and thoughts that have not been REPRESSED can be brought to the surface

pre·cooked /ˌpriˈkʊkt/ *adj.* (of food) prepared and partly cooked in advance so that it can be quickly heated and eaten later

pre·cur·sor /priˈkərsər; ˈpriˌkərsər/ *noun* ~ (of/to sth) (*formal*) a person or thing that comes before someone or something similar and that leads to or influences its development **SYN** FORERUNNER

pre·cut /ˌpriˈkʌt/ *adj.* cut in advance and ready to use

pre·date /ˌpriˈdeɪt/ (also **an·te·date**) *verb* ~ sth to be built or formed, or to happen, at an earlier date than something else in the past: *Few of the town's fine buildings predate the earthquake of 1755.* **ANT** POSTDATE

pre·da·tion /prɪˈdeɪʃn/ *noun* [U] (*technical*) the act of an animal killing and eating other animals

pred·a·tor /ˈprɛdətər/ *noun* **1** an animal that kills and eats other animals: *the relationship between predator and prey* **2** (*disapproving*) a person or an organization that uses weaker people for their own advantage: *to protect domestic industry from foreign predators*

pred·a·to·ry /ˈprɛdəˌtɔri/ *adj.* **1** (*technical*) (of animals) living by killing and eating other animals **2** (of people) using weaker people for their own financial or sexual advantage: *a predatory insurance salesman* ◆ *a predatory look*

pred·a·to·ry ˈlend·ing *noun* [U] the practice of lending money to people who cannot afford to pay it back, often by hiding the true cost of the loan: *Many people say that the collapse of the housing market was due to predatory lending.*

predatory ˈpricing *noun* [U] (*business*) the practice of a business company selling goods at such a low price that other companies can no longer compete and have to stop selling similar goods

pre·de·cease /ˌpridɪˈsis/ *verb* ~ sb (*law*) to die before someone: *His wife predeceased him.*

pred·e·ces·sor /ˈprɛdəˌsɛsər/ *noun* **1** a person who did a job before someone else: *The new president reversed many of the policies of his predecessor.* **2** a thing, such as a machine, that has been followed or replaced by something else ➔ compare SUCCESSOR

pre·des·ti·na·tion /ˌpridɛstəˈneɪʃn/ *noun* [U] the theory or the belief that everything that happens has been decided or planned in advance by God or by FATE and that humans cannot change it

pre·des·tined /ˌpriˈdɛstənd/ *adj.* ~ (to do sth) (*formal*) already decided or planned by God or by FATE: *It seems she was predestined to be famous.*

pre·de·ter·mine /ˌpridɪˈtərmən/ *verb* ~ sth (*formal*) to decide something in advance so that it does not happen by chance: *The sex of the embryo is predetermined at fertilization.* ▶ **pre·de·ter·mined** *adj.*: *An alarm sounds when the temperature reaches a predetermined level.*

pre·de·ter·min·er /ˌpridɪˈtərmənər/ *noun* (*grammar*) a word that can be used before a determiner, such as *all* in *all the students* or *twice* in *twice the price*

pre·dic·a·ment /prɪˈdɪkəmənt/ *noun* a difficult or unpleasant situation, especially one where it is difficult to know what to do **SYN** QUANDARY: *the club's financial predicament* ◆ *I'm in a terrible predicament.*

pred·i·cate *noun*, *verb*
• *noun* /ˈprɛdɪkət/ (*grammar*) a part of a sentence containing a verb that makes a statement about the subject of the verb, such as *went home* in *John went home.* ➔ compare OBJECT
• *verb* /ˈprɛdɪˌkeɪt/ (*formal*) **1** [usually passive] ~ sth on/upon sth to base something on a particular belief, idea, or principle: *Democracy is predicated on the rule of law.* **2** ~ that... | ~ sth to state that something is true: *The article predicates that the market collapse was caused by weakness of the dollar.*

pred·i·ca·tive /ˈprɛdɪkətɪv; -ˌkeɪtɪv/ *adj.* (*grammar*) (of an adjective) coming after a verb such as *be, become, get, seem, look*. Many adjectives, for example *old*, can be either predicative as in *The man is very old*, or ATTRIBUTIVE as in *an old man*. Some, like *asleep*, can only be predicative. ▶ **pred·i·ca·tive·ly** *adv.*

pre·dict 🔑 **AWL** /prɪˈdɪkt/ *verb* to say that something will happen in the future **SYN** FORECAST: ~ sth *a reliable method of predicting earthquakes* ◆ *Nobody could predict the outcome.* ◆ ~ **what, whether, etc....** *It is impossible to predict what will happen.* ◆ ~ **(that)...** *She predicted that the election result would be close.* ◆ **it is predicted that...** *It was predicted that inflation would continue to fall.* ◆ **sb/sth is predicted to do sth** *The trial is predicted to last for months.* ➔ language bank at EXPECT ▶ **pre·dict·ed** **AWL** *adj.*

AWL COLLOCATIONS

predict

predict *verb*

■ accurately, correctly, confidently, reliably
Even very sophisticated computer models cannot accurately predict the course of a storm.

■ impossible to, difficult to
There are always events, such as political or natural disasters, that are impossible to predict and that affect the economy.

■ outcome | future | behavior | likelihood, probability
Historians are better at reading the past than predicting the future.
The computer model uses data from midsummer winds to predict the likelihood of hurricanes striking the United States later in the season.

■ hypothesis, model, theory | analyst, economist, expert, forecaster
The hypothesis predicts that fathers who come from families that were more nurturing will have stronger attitudes about fatherhood.

■ as predicted by
As predicted by previous research, dark-colored roof surfaces were shown to be absorbing solar radiation.

prediction *noun*

■ dire | accurate | testable | theoretical | qualitative, quantitative
Dire predictions were made about the fate of the Antarctic ecosystem.
These results support the theoretical predictions.
Ecologists often need to make quantitative predictions about how animal and plant populations will change.

■ test | confirm, validate, verify | contradict | make
The results confirm the prediction and support the hypothesis.

---

pre·dict·a·ble **AWL** /prɪˈdɪktəbl/ *adj.* **1** if something is
predictable, you know in advance that it will happen or
what it will be like: *a predictable result* ♦ *The ending of the book
was totally predictable.* ♦ *In March and April, the weather is
much less predictable.* ➲ collocations at PREDICT **2** (often
disapproving) behaving or happening in a way that you
would expect, and therefore boring: *He's very nice, but I find
him a little dull and predictable.* ▶ **pre·dict·a·bil·i·ty** **AWL**
/prɪˌdɪktəˈbɪləti/ *noun* [U] **pre·dict·a·bly** **AWL** /prɪˈdɪktəbli/
adv.: *Prices were predictably high.* ♦ *Predictably, the new
regulations proved unpopular.*

pre·dic·tion **AWL** /prɪˈdɪkʃn/ *noun* [C, U] a statement that
says what you think will happen; the act of making such a
statement: *Not many people agree with the administration's
prediction that the economy will improve.* ♦ *The results of the
experiment confirmed our predictions.* ♦ *Skilled readers make
use of context and prediction.* ♦ *It's difficult to make accurate
predictions about the effects on the environment.* ➲ collocations
at PREDICT, SCIENTIFIC ➲ language bank at EXPECT

pre·dic·tive /prɪˈdɪktɪv/ *adj.* [usually before noun] **1** (*formal*)
connected with the ability to show what will happen in the
future: *the predictive power of science* **2** (of a computer
program) allowing you to enter text on a computer or a cell
phone more quickly by using the first few letters of each
word to predict what you want to say: *predictive text input*
♦ *predictive messaging*

pre·dic·tor /prɪˈdɪktər/ *noun* (*formal*) something that can
show what will happen in the future: *Cholesterol level is not a
strong predictor of heart disease in women.*

pre·di·gest·ed /ˌpriːdaɪˈdʒɛstəd; -dɪˈdʒɛs-/ *adj.* (of information) put in a simple form that is easy to understand

pre·di·lec·tion /ˌprɛdlˈɛkʃn/ *noun* [usually sing.] ~ **(for sth)**
(*formal*) if you **have a predilection for** something, you like it
very much **SYN** LIKING, PREFERENCE

pre·dis·pose /ˌpriːdɪˈspoʊz/ *verb* (*formal*) **1** to influence
someone so that they are likely to think or behave in a
particular way: ~ **sb to sth** *He believes that some people are
predisposed to criminal behavior.* ♦ ~ **sb to do sth** *Her good
mood predisposed her to enjoy the play.* **2** ~ **sb to sth** to make
it likely that you will suffer from a particular illness: *Stress
can predispose people to heart attacks.*

pre·dis·po·si·tion /ˌpriːdɪspəˈzɪʃn/ *noun* [C, U] ~ **(to/
toward sth)** | ~ **(to do sth)** (*formal*) a condition that makes
someone or something likely to behave in a particular way
or to suffer from a particular disease: *a genetic predisposition
to liver disease*

pre·dom·i·nance **AWL** /prɪˈdɑmənəns/ *noun* **1** [sing.] the
situation of being greater in number or amount than other
things or people **SYN** PREPONDERANCE: *a predominance of
female teachers in elementary schools* **2** [U] the state of having
more power or influence than others **SYN**

pre·dom·i·nant **AWL** /prɪˈdɑmənənt/ *adj.* **1** most obvious
or noticeable: *a predominant feature* ♦ *Yellow is the predominant color this spring in the fashion world.* **2** having more
power or influence than others **SYN** DOMINANT: *a predominant culture*

pre·dom·i·nant·ly **AWL** /prɪˈdɑmənəntli/ (also *less
frequent* **pre·dom·i·nate·ly** /prɪˈdɑmənətli/) *adv.* mostly;
mainly: *She works in a predominantly male environment.*
➲ language bank at GENERALLY

pre·dom·i·nate **AWL** /prɪˈdɑməˌneɪt/ *verb* **1** [I] to be
greater in amount or number than something or someone
else in a place, group, etc.: *a color scheme in which red
predominates* ♦ *Women predominated in the audience.* **2** [I]
~ **(over sb/sth)** to have the most influence or importance:
*Private interest was not allowed to predominate over the public
good.*

pre·ec·lamp·si·a /ˌpriːɪˈklæmpsiə/ *noun* [U] (*medical*) a condition in which a pregnant woman has high BLOOD
PRESSURE, which can become serious if it is not treated

pree·mie /ˈpriːmi/ *noun* (*informal*) a PREMATURE baby

pre·em·i·nent /priˈɛmənənt/ *adj.* (*formal*) more important,
more successful, or of a higher standard than others
SYN OUTSTANDING: *Dickens was preeminent among English
writers of his day.* ▶ **pre·em·i·nence** /-nəns/ *noun* [U]: *to
achieve preeminence in public life*

pre·em·i·nent·ly /priˈɛmənəntli/ *adv.* to a very great
degree; especially

pre·empt /priˈɛmpt/ *verb* **1** ~ **sth** to prevent something
from happening by taking action to stop it: *A good training
course will preempt many problems.* **2** ~ **sb/sth** to do or say
something before someone else does: *She was just about to
apologize when he preempted her.* **3** ~ **sth** to replace a
planned program on the television: *The scheduled program
will be preempted by a special news bulletin.*

pre·emp·tion /priˈɛmpʃn/ *noun* [U] (*business*) the opportunity given to one person or group to buy goods, shares, etc.:
Existing shareholders will have preemption rights.

pre·emp·tive /priˈɛmptɪv/ *adj.* done to stop someone from
taking action, especially action that will be harmful to
yourself: *a preemptive attack/strike on the military base*

preen /priːn/ *verb* **1** [T, I] ~ **(yourself)** (usually *disapproving*)
to spend a lot of time making yourself look attractive and
then admiring your appearance: *Will you stop preening
yourself in front of the mirror?* **2** [T] ~ **yourself (on sth)**
(usually *disapproving*) to feel very pleased with yourself
about something and show other people how pleased you
are **3** [I, T] ~ **(itself)** (of a bird) to clean itself or make its
feathers smooth with its beak

pre·ex·ist /ˌpriːɪɡˈzɪst/ *verb* [I] to exist from an earlier time: *a
preexisting medical condition* ▶ **pre·ex·ist·ent** /ˌpriːɪɡˈzɪstənt/
adj.

pre·fab /ˈpriːfæb/ *noun* (*informal*) a prefabricated building:
They live in a prefab house.

pre·fab·ri·cat·ed /ˌpriːˈfæbrəˌkeɪtəd/ *adj.* (especially of a
building) made in sections that can be put together later
▶ **pre·fab·ri·ca·tion** /ˌpriːˌfæbrəˈkeɪʃn/ *noun* [U]

pref·ace /ˈprɛfəs/ *noun, verb*
● *noun* an introduction to a book, especially one that
explains the author's aims ➲ compare FOREWORD
● *verb* **1** ~ **sth (with sth)** to provide a book or other piece of
writing with a preface: *He prefaced the diaries with a short
account of how they were discovered.* **2** ~ **sth by/with sth** |
~ **sth by doing sth** (*formal*) to say something before you
start making a speech, answering a question, etc.: *I must
preface my remarks with an apology.*

pref·a·to·ry /ˈprɛfəˌtɔri/ *adj.* [only before noun] (*formal*)
acting as a PREFACE or an introduction to something: *a
prefatory note*

pre·fect /ˈpriːfɛkt/ *noun* **1** also **Prefect** an officer responsible for an area of local government in some countries, for
example France, Italy, and Japan **2** (in some British
schools) an older student with some authority over
younger students and some other responsibilities and
advantages

---

pre·fec·ture /ˈprifɛktʃər/ *noun* an area of local government in some countries, for example France, Italy, and Japan

pre·fer 🖉 /prɪˈfər/ *verb* (-rr-) (not used in the progressive tenses)
to like one thing or person better than another; to choose one thing rather than something else because you like it better: **~ sth** *"Coffee or tea?" "I'd prefer tea, thanks."* ◆ *I much prefer jazz to rock music.* ◆ *I would prefer it if you didn't tell anyone.* ◆ *A local firm is to be preferred.* ◆ **~ sth + adj.** *I prefer my coffee black.* ◆ **~ to do sth** *The donor prefers to remain anonymous.* ◆ *I prefer not to think about it.* ◆ **~ sb/sth to do sth** *Would you prefer me to stay?* ◆ **~ doing sth** *I prefer playing doubles.* ◆ **~ that…** (*formal*) *I would prefer that you did not mention my name.*

pref·er·a·ble /ˈprɛfərəbl; ˈprɛfrə-/ *adj.* more attractive or more suitable; to be preferred to something: **~ (to sth)** *Anything was preferable to the tense atmosphere at home.* ◆ **~ (to doing sth)** *He finds country life infinitely preferable to living in the city.* ◆ **~ (to do sth)** *It would be preferable to employ two people, not one.* ▶ **pref·er·a·bly** /-bli/ *adv.*: *We're looking for a new house, preferably one near the school.*

pref·er·ence 🖉 /ˈprɛfrəns; -fərəns/ *noun*
1 [U, sing.] **~ (for sb/sth)** a greater interest in or desire for someone or something than someone or something else: *It's a matter of personal preference.* ◆ *Many people expressed a strong preference for the original plan.* ◆ *I can't say that I have any particular preference.* ◆ *Let's make a list of possible speakers, in order of preference.* **2** [C] a thing that is liked better or best: *a study of consumer preferences* ➋ thesaurus box at CHOICE
IDM **give preference to sb/sth** to treat someone or something in a way that gives them an advantage over other people or things: *Preference will be given to graduates of this university.* **in preference to sb/sth** rather than someone or something: *She was chosen in preference to her sister.*

pref·er·en·tial /ˌprɛfəˈrɛnʃl/ *adj.* [only before noun] giving an advantage to a particular person or group: *Don't expect to get preferential treatment.* ▶ **pref·er·en·tial·ly** /-ʃəli/ *adv.*

pre·fer·ment /prɪˈfərmənt/ *noun* [U] (*formal*) the fact of being given a more important job or a higher rank **SYN** PROMOTION

pre·fig·ure /ˌpriˈfɪgyər/ *verb* **~ sth** (*formal*) to suggest or show something that will happen in the future

pre·fix /ˈprifɪks/ *noun, verb*
• *noun* **1** (*grammar*) a letter or group of letters added to the beginning of a word to change its meaning, such as *un-* in *unhappy* and *pre-* in *preheat* ➋ compare AFFIX, SUFFIX **2** a word, letter, or number that is put before another: *Our car insurance policies have the prefix AYN.* **3** (*old-fashioned*) a title such as *Dr.* or *Mrs.* used before a person's name
• *verb* to add letters or numbers to the beginning of a word or number: **~ A to B** *Out-of-state members have additional letters prefixed to their code numbers.* ◆ **~ B with A** *Their code numbers are prefixed with additional letters.*

preg·nan·cy /ˈprɛgnənsi/ *noun* (*pl.* **preg·nan·cies**) [U, C] the state of being pregnant: *Many women experience morning sickness during pregnancy.* ◆ *a pregnancy test* ◆ *unplanned/unwanted pregnancies* ◆ *the increase in teenage pregnancies* ➋ collocations at CHILD

preg·nant 🖉 /ˈprɛgnənt/ *adj.*
1 (of a woman or female animal) having a baby or young animal developing inside her/its body: *My wife is pregnant.* ◆ *I was pregnant with our third child at the time.* ◆ *a heavily pregnant woman* (= one whose baby is nearly ready to be born) ◆ *to get/become pregnant* ◆ *He got his girlfriend pregnant and they're getting married.* ◆ *She's six months pregnant.* ➋ collocations at CHILD **2 ~ with sth** (*formal*) full of a quality or feeling: *Her silences were pregnant with criticism.*
IDM **a pregnant pause/silence** an occasion when nobody speaks, although people are aware that there are feelings or thoughts to express

pre·heat /ˌpriˈhit/ *verb* **~ sth** to heat an oven to a particular temperature before you put food in it to cook

pre·hen·sile /priˈhɛnsl/ *adj.* (*technical*) (of a part of an animal's body) able to hold things: *the monkey's prehensile tail*

pre·his·tor·ic /ˌprihɪˈstɔrɪk; -ˈstɑr-/ *adj.* connected with the time in history before information was written down: *in prehistoric times* ◆ *prehistoric man/remains/animals/burial sites*

pre·his·to·ry /ˌpriˈhɪstəri; -ˈhɪstri/ *noun* **1** [U] the period of time in history before information was written down **2** [sing.] the earliest stages of the development of something: *the prehistory of capitalism*

pre·in·stall /ˌpriɪnˈstɔl/ *verb* = PRELOAD

pre·judge /ˌpriˈdʒʌdʒ/ *verb* **~ sth** (*formal*) to make a judgment about a situation before you have all the necessary information: *They took care not to prejudge the issue.*

prej·u·dice /ˈprɛdʒədəs/ *noun, verb*
• *noun* [U, C] an unreasonable dislike of or preference for a person, group, custom, etc., especially when it is based on their race, religion, sex, etc.: *a victim of racial prejudice* ◆ *Their decision was based on ignorance and prejudice.* ◆ **~ against sb/sth** *There is much less prejudice today against women in the medical profession.* ◆ **~ in favor of sb/sth** *I must admit to a prejudice in favor of Ivy League universities.*
IDM **without prejudice (to sth)** (*law*) without affecting any other legal matter: *They agreed to pay compensation without prejudice* (= without admitting GUILT).
• *verb* **1 ~ sb (against sb/sth)** to influence someone so that they have an unfair or unreasonable opinion about someone or something **SYN** BIAS: *The prosecution lawyers have been trying to prejudice the jury against her.* **2 ~ sth** (*formal*) to have a harmful effect on something: *Any delay will prejudice the child's welfare.*

prej·u·diced /ˈprɛdʒədəst/ *adj.* having an unreasonable dislike of or preference for someone or something, especially based on their race, religion, sex, etc.: *Few people will admit to being racially prejudiced.* ◆ **~ (against/in favor of sb/sth)** *They are prejudiced against older applicants.* ◆ (*humorous*) *I think it's an excellent article, but then I'm prejudiced—I wrote it.*

prej·u·di·cial /ˌprɛdʒəˈdɪʃl/ *adj.* **~ (to sth)** (*formal*) harming or likely to harm someone or something **SYN** DAMAGING: *developments prejudicial to the company's future*

prel·ate /ˈprɛlət/ *noun* (*formal*) a priest of high rank in the Christian Church, such as a BISHOP or CARDINAL

pre·lim /ˈprilɪm/ *noun* [usually pl.] (*informal*) a game, race, etc. in the early stages of a sports competition that determines who will continue to compete: *He finished second in the prelims and will advance to the finals.*

pre·lim·i·nar·y **AWL** /prɪˈlɪməˌnɛri/ *adj., noun*
• *adj.* happening before a more important action or event **SYN** INITIAL: *After a few preliminary remarks he announced the winners.* ◆ *preliminary results/findings/inquiries* ◆ *the preliminary rounds of the contest* ◆ **~ to sth** *pilot studies preliminary to a full-scale study*
• *noun* (*pl.* **pre·lim·i·nar·ies**) **~ (to sth)** an action or event that is done in preparation for something: *Research will be needed as a preliminary to making a decision.* ◆ *I'll skip the usual preliminaries and come straight to the point.* ◆ *Our team was lucky to get through the preliminaries* (= the preliminary stages in a sports competition).

pre·load /ˌpriˈloud/ (also **pre·in·stall**) *verb* **~ sth** (*computing*) to load something in advance: *The PC comes with office software preloaded.* ▶ **pre·load** *noun*

prel·ude /ˈpreɪlud; ˈprɛlyud/ *noun* **1** a short piece of music, especially an introduction to a longer piece **2 ~ (to sth)** an action or event that happens before another more important one and forms an introduction to it

pre·mar·i·tal /ˌpriˈmærətl/ *adj.* [only before noun] happening before marriage: *premarital sex*

pre·ma·ture /ˌpriːməˈtʃʊr; -ˈtʊr/ adj. **1** happening before the normal or expected time: *his premature death at the age of 37* **2** (of a birth or a baby) happening or being born before the normal length of PREGNANCY has been completed: *The baby was four weeks premature.* ◆ *a premature birth after only thirty weeks* **3** happening or made too soon: *a premature conclusion/decision/judgment* ◆ *It is premature to talk about success at this stage.* ▶ **pre·ma·ture·ly** adv.: *The child was born prematurely.* ◆ *Her hair became prematurely white.*

pre·med /ˌpriːˈmɛd/ noun (*informal*) **1** [U] a course or set of classes that students take in preparation for medical school **2** [C] a student who is taking classes in preparation for medical school **3** [U] = PREMEDICATION

pre·med·i·ca·tion /ˌpriːˌmɛdəˈkeɪʃn/ (also *informal* **pre·med**) noun [U] drugs given to someone in preparation for an operation or other medical treatment

pre·med·i·tat·ed /ˌpriːˈmɛdəˌteɪtəd/ adj. (of a crime or bad action) planned in advance: *a premeditated attack* ◆ *The killing was not premeditated.* **ANT** UNPREMEDITATED ▶ **pre·med·i·ta·tion** /ˌpriːmɛdəˈteɪʃn/ noun [U]

pre·men·stru·al /ˌpriːˈmɛnstruəl; -strəl/ adj. happening or experienced before MENSTRUATION: *Many women suffer from premenstrual syndrome/tension, causing headaches and depression.* ⊃ see also PMS

pre·mier /prɪˈmɪr; -ˈmyɪr; ˈprimɪr/ adj., noun
● **adj.** [only before noun] most important, famous, or successful: *one of the country's premier chefs*
● **noun 1** used especially in newspapers, etc. to mean "prime minister" **2** (in Canada) the first minister of a PROVINCE or TERRITORY

pre·miere /prɪˈmɪr; -ˈmyɛr; -ˈmyɪr/ noun, verb
● **noun** the first public performance of a movie or play: *the world premiere of his new play* ◆ *The movie will have its premiere in July.* ⊃ see also SEASON PREMIERE
● **verb** [T, I] **~ (sth)** to perform a play or piece of music or to show a movie to an audience for the first time; to be performed or shown to an audience for the first time: *The play was premiered at the Indiana Rep in 2008.* ◆ *His new movie premieres in New York this week.*

pre·mier·ship /prɪˈmɪrʃɪp; -ˈmyɪr-/ noun [sing.] the period or position of being prime minister: *during Stephen Harper's premiership*

prem·ise /ˈprɛməs/ noun (*formal*) a statement or an idea that forms the basis for a reasonable line of argument: *the basic premise of her argument* ◆ *a false premise* ◆ *His reasoning is based on the premise that all people are equally capable of good and evil.*

prem·ised /ˈprɛməst/ adj. **~ on/upon sth** (*formal*) based on a particular idea or belief that is considered to be true: *Traditional economic analysis is premised on the assumption that more is better.*

prem·is·es 🔑 /ˈprɛməsəz/ noun [pl.] (*formal*) the building and land near to it that a business owns or uses: *business/commercial/industrial premises* ◆ *No alcohol may be consumed on the premises.* ◆ *Police were called to escort her off the premises.* ⊃ thesaurus box at BUILDING

pre·mi·um /ˈprimiəm/ noun, adj.
● **noun 1** an amount of money that you pay once or regularly for an insurance policy: *a monthly premium of $11.50* ⊃ thesaurus box at PAYMENT **2** an extra payment added to the basic rate: *You have to pay a high premium for express delivery.* ◆ *A premium of 10% is paid out after 20 years.* **IDM at a premium 1** if something is **at a premium**, there is little of it available and it is difficult to get: *Space is at a premium in a one-bedroom apartment.* **2** at a higher than normal price: *Shares are selling at a premium.* **put/place/set a premium on sb/sth** to think that someone or something is particularly important or valuable
● **adj.** [only before noun] very high (and higher than usual); of high quality: *premium prices/products*

pre·mod·i·fi·er /ˌpriːˈmɑːdəˌfaɪər/ noun (*grammar*) a word,

such as an adjective or adverb, that describes another word or group of words, or restricts its/their meaning in some way, and is placed before it/them: *In "a loud noise," the adjective "loud" is a premodifier.* ⊃ compare MODIFIER, POSTMODIFIER

pre·mo·ni·tion /ˌprɛməˈnɪʃn/ noun a feeling that something is going to happen, especially something unpleasant: **~ (of sth)** *a premonition of disaster* ◆ **~ (that…)** *He had a premonition that he would never see her again.* ▶ **pre·mon·i·to·ry** /prɪˈmɑːnəˌtɔri/ adj. (*formal*): *a premonitory dream*

pre·na·tal /ˌpriːˈneɪtl/ adj. relating to the medical care given to pregnant women: *prenatal care/diagnosis/screening/testing* ⊃ compare POSTNATAL

pre·nup·tial a·gree·ment /ˌpriˌnʌpʃl əˈgrimənt/ (also *informal* **pre·nup** /ˈprinʌp/) noun an agreement made by a couple before they get married in which they say how their money and property is to be divided if they get divorced

pre·oc·cu·pa·tion /priˌɑːkyəˈpeɪʃn/ noun **1** [U, C] **~ (with sth)** a state of thinking about something continuously; something that you think about frequently or for a long time **SYN** OBSESSION: *She found his preoccupation with money irritating.* ◆ *His current preoccupation is the hiring of a new manager.* **2** [U] a mood created by thinking or worrying about something and ignoring everything else: *She spoke slowly, in a state of preoccupation.*

pre·oc·cu·pied /priˈɑːkyəˌpaɪd/ adj. **~ (with sth)** thinking and/or worrying continuously about something so that you do not pay attention to other things: *He was too preoccupied with his own thoughts to notice anything wrong.*

pre·oc·cu·py /priˈɑːkyəˌpaɪ/ verb (pre·oc·cu·pies, pre·oc·cu·py·ing, pre·oc·cu·pied, pre·oc·cu·pied) **~ sb** if something is **preoccupying** you, you think or worry about it very often or all the time

pre·op·er·a·tive /priˈɑːpərətɪv; -ˈɑːprətɪv/ (also **pre-op**, *informal*) adj. [only before noun] connected with the period before a medical operation: *Please schedule a preoperative appointment seven days before surgery.*

pre·or·dained /ˌpriɔːrˈdeɪnd/ adj. (*formal*) already decided or planned by God or by FATE **SYN** PREDESTINED: *Is everything we do preordained?* ◆ **~ to do sth** *They seemed preordained to meet.*

pre-ˈowned adj. not new; owned by someone else before: *pre-owned automobiles* **SYN** SECONDHAND

prep /prɛp/ noun, verb
● **noun** [U] (*informal*) preparation: *The meal requires a lot of prep, but not much time to cook.* ◆ *She's taking a college prep course.*
● **verb** (-pp-) **1** [T, I] (*informal*) to prepare (something): **~ sth** *Prep the vegetables in advance.* ◆ **~ (for sth)** *They're prepping for the SATs.* **2** [T] **~ sb** (*technical*) to prepare someone for a medical operation

pre·pack·aged (also **pre·packed** /ˌpriˈpækt/) adj. (of goods, especially food) put into packages before being sent to stores to be sold: *prepackaged cheese and crackers*

pre·paid /ˌpriˈpeɪd/ adj. paid for in advance: *a prepaid debit card* ◆ *A prepaid envelope is enclosed (= so you do not have to pay the cost of sending a letter).*

prep·a·ra·tion 🔑 /ˌprɛpəˈreɪʃn/ noun **1** [U] **~ (for sth)** the act or process of getting ready for something or making something ready: *These skills are good preparation for a career in teaching.* ◆ *food preparation* ◆ *Careful preparation for the final exam is essential.* ◆ *The third book in the series is currently in preparation.* ◆ *The team has been training hard in preparation for the big game.* **2** [C, usually pl.] things that you do to get ready for something or make something ready: **~ (for sth)** *The country is making preparations for war.* ◆ *Was going to college a good preparation for your career?* ◆ **~ (to do sth)** *We made preparations to move to new offices.* ◆ *wedding preparations* **3** [C] a substance that has been specially prepared for use as a medicine, COSMETIC, etc.: *a pharmaceutical preparation* ◆ *preparations for the hair and skin*

pre·par·a·to·ry /prɪˈpɛrəˌtɔri; ˈprɛpərəˌtɔri/ adj. (*formal*) done in order to prepare for something: *preparatory meetings* ♦ *Security checks had been carried out* **preparatory to** (= to prepare for) *the President's visit.*

pre'paratory ˌschool *noun* = PREP SCHOOL

pre·pare 🔑 /prɪˈpɛr/ *verb*
1 [T] to make something or someone ready to be used or to do something: **~ sth/sb** *to prepare a report* ♦ **~ sth/sb for sb/sth** *A hotel room is being prepared for them.* ♦ *The college prepares students for a career in business.* **2** [I, T] to make yourself ready to do something or for something that you expect to happen: *I had no time to prepare.* ♦ **~ for sth** *The whole class is working hard preparing for the test.* ♦ **~ yourself (for sth)** *The police are preparing themselves for trouble at the demonstration.* ♦ **~ to do sth** *I was preparing to leave.* ♦ **~ yourself to do sth** *The troops prepared themselves to go into battle.* **3** [T] **~ sth** to make food ready to be eaten: *He was in the kitchen preparing lunch.* **4** [T] **~ sth (from sth)** to make a medicine or chemical substance, for example by mixing other substances together: *remedies prepared from herbal extracts*
IDM **prepare the ground (for sth)** to make it possible or easier for something to be achieved: *The committee will prepare the ground for further investigation of the issue.*

pre·pared 🔑 /prɪˈpɛrd/ *adj.*
1 [not before noun] **~ (for sth)** ready and able to deal with something: *I was not prepared for all the problems it caused.* ♦ *We'll be better prepared next time.* ♦ *When they set out they were well prepared.* **ANT** UNPREPARED ⊃ see also ILL-PREPARED **2 ~ to do sth** willing to do something: *We are not prepared to accept these conditions.* ♦ *How much are you prepared to pay?* **ANT** UNWILLING **3** done, made, written, etc. in advance: *The police officer read out a prepared statement.*

pre·par·ed·ness /prɪˈpɛrədnəs/ *noun* [U] **~ (to do sth)** (*formal*) the state of being ready or willing to do something: *I was surprised by his preparedness to break the law.* ♦ *The troops are in a state of preparedness.*

pre·pay·ment /ˌpriːˈpeɪmənt/ *noun* [U] payment in advance: *a prepayment plan*

pre·pon·der·ance /prɪˈpɑndərəns/ *noun* [sing.] if there is a **preponderance** of one type of people or things in a group, there are more of them than others **SYN** PREDOMINANCE

pre·pon·der·ant /prɪˈpɑndərənt/ *adj.* [usually before noun] (*formal*) larger in number or more important than other people or things in a group ▶ **pre·pon·der·ant·ly** *adv.*

prep·o·si·tion /ˌprɛpəˈzɪʃn/ *noun* (*grammar*) a word or group of words, such as *in, from, to, out of,* and *on behalf of,* used before a noun or pronoun to show place, position, time, or method ▶ **prep·o·si·tion·al** /-ʃənl/ *adj.*: *a prepositional phrase* (= a preposition and the noun following it, for example *at night* or *after breakfast*)

pre·pos·sess·ing /ˌpriːpəˈzɛsɪŋ/ *adj.* (especially after a negative) (*formal*) attractive in appearance **SYN** APPEALING: *He was not a prepossessing sight.* ⊃ compare UNPREPOSSES-SING

pre·pos·ter·ous /prɪˈpɑstərəs/ *adj.* (*formal*) **1** completely unreasonable, especially in a way that is shocking or annoying **SYN** OUTRAGEOUS: *These claims are absolutely preposterous!* **2** unusual in a silly or shocking way **SYN** OUTRAGEOUS: *The band members were famous for their preposterous clothes and haircuts.* ▶ **pre·pos·ter·ous·ly** *adv.*: *a preposterously expensive bottle of wine*

prep·py (also **prep·pie**) /ˈprɛpi/ *noun* (*pl.* **prep·pies**) (*informal*) a young person who goes or went to an expensive private school and who dresses and acts in a way that is thought to be typical of such a school ▶ **prep·py** (also **prep·pie**) *adj.*: *a preppy image* ♦ *preppy clothes*

pre·pran·di·al /ˌpriːˈprændiəl/ *adj.* [only before noun] (*formal* or *humorous*) happening immediately before a meal: *a preprandial drink*

pre·pro·duc·tion /ˌpriːprəˈdʌkʃn/ *adj.* [usually before noun]

done before the process of producing something, especially a movie, begins: *the preproduction script* ▶ **pre·pro·duc·tion** *adv.* **pre·pro·duc·tion** *noun* [U]

ˈprep school (also **preˈparatory ˌschool**) *noun* a high school, usually a private one, that prepares students for college

pre·quel /ˈpriːkwəl/ *noun* a book or movie about events that happened before those in a popular book or movie: *Fans waited for years for the first Star Wars prequel.* ⊃ compare SEQUEL

Pre-Raph·a·el·ite /ˌpriː ˈræfiəˌlaɪt/ *noun, adj.*
● *noun* a member of a group of British 19th-century artists who painted in a style similar to Italian artists of the 14th and 15th centuries, before the time of Raphael
● *adj.* **1** connected with or in the style of the Pre-Raphaelites: *Pre-Raphaelite paintings* **2** (especially of a woman) looking like a person in a painting by one of the Pre-Raphaelites, for example with pale skin and long, thick, dark red hair

pre·re·cord /ˌpriːrɪˈkɔrd/ *verb* **~ sth** to record music, a television program, etc. in advance, so that it can be broadcast or used later

pre·reg·is·ter /ˌpriːˈrɛdʒəstər/ *verb* [I] **~ (for sth)** to register for something before the usual time or before something starts ▶ **pre·reg·is·tra·tion** /ˌpriːˌrɛdʒəˈstreɪʃn/ *noun* [U]

pre·req·ui·site /ˌpriːˈrɛkwəzət/ *noun* [usually sing.] **~ (for/of/to sth)** (*formal*) something that must exist or happen before something else can happen or be done **SYN** PRECONDITION: *A college degree is an essential prereq-uisite for employment at this level.* ⊃ compare REQUISITE ▶ **pre·req·ui·site** *adj.* [only before noun]: *prerequisite knowledge*

pre·rog·a·tive /prɪˈrɑgətɪv/ *noun* (*formal*) a right or advan-tage belonging to a particular person or group because of their importance or social position: *In many countries education is still the prerogative of the rich.* ♦ *One of the* **presidential prerogatives** (= the special rights of a president) *is the use of Air Force One.*

pres·age /ˈprɛsɪdʒ; prɪˈseɪdʒ/ *verb* **~ sth** (*literary*) to be a warning or sign that something will happen, usually something unpleasant ▶ **pres·age** /ˈprɛsɪdʒ/ *noun: the first presages of winter*

Pres·by·te·ri·an /ˌprɛzbəˈtɪriən; ˌprɛs-/ *noun* a member of a branch of the Christian Protestant Church that is based on the teachings of John Calvin and is governed by ELDERS who are all equal in rank. ▶ **Pres·by·te·ri·an** *adj.* **Pres·by·te·ri·an·ism** /ˌprɛzbəˈtɪriəˌnɪzəm; ˌprɛs-/ *noun* [U]

pres·by·ter·y /ˈprɛzbəˌtɛri; ˈprɛs-/ *noun* (*pl.* **pres·by·ter·ies**) **1** a local council of the Presbyterian Church **2** a house where a Roman Catholic priest lives **3** part of a church, near the east end, beyond the CHOIR

pre·school /ˈpriːskul/ *noun* a school for children between the ages of about two and five **SYN** NURSERY SCHOOL ▶ **pre·school·er** *noun*

pre·scient /ˈprɛʃnt; -ʃiənt/ *adj.* (*formal*) knowing or appear-ing to know about things before they happen ▶ **pre·science** /ˈprɛʃns; -ʃiəns/ *noun* [U]

pre·scribe /prɪˈskraɪb/ *verb* **1** (of a doctor) to tell someone to take a particular medicine or have a particular treatment; to write a PRESCRIPTION for a particular medicine, etc.: **~ sth** *Valium is usually prescribed to treat anxiety.* ♦ **~ sth (for sth/sb)** *She may be able to prescribe something for that cough.* **2** (of a person or an organization with authority) to say what should be done or how something should be done **SYN** STIPULATE: **~ sth** *The prescribed form must be completed and returned to this office.* ♦ **~ that...** *Police regulations prescribe that an officer's badge must be clearly visible.* ♦ **~ which, what, etc....** *The syllabus prescribes precisely which books should be read.*

pre·scrip·tion /prɪˈskrɪpʃn/ *noun* **1** [C] **~ (for sth)** an official piece of paper on which a doctor writes the type of medicine you should have, and that enables you to get it from a PHARMACY: *The doctor gave me a prescription for antibiotics.* ◆ *Antibiotics are only available by prescription.* ◆ *They are not available without a prescription.* ◆ *prescription drugs/medication(s)* **2** [C] medicine that your doctor has ordered for you: *The pharmacist will make up your prescription.* **3** [U] the act of prescribing medicine: *The prescription of drugs is a doctor's responsibility.* **4** [C] **~ (for sth)** (*formal*) a plan or a suggestion for making something happen or for improving it: *a prescription for happiness*

pre·scrip·tive /prɪˈskrɪptɪv/ *adj.* **1** (*formal*) telling people what they should do: *prescriptive methods of teaching* **2** (*linguistics*) telling people how a language should be used, rather than describing how it is used **ANT** DESCRIPTIVE **3** (*technical*) (of rights and institutions) made legal or acceptable because they have existed for a long time: *prescriptive powers*

pre·se·lect /ˌpriːsəˈlekt/ *verb* **~ sth** to choose something in advance so it is ready to be used: *You can preselect programs you want to watch, and program your DVR to record them.*

pre·sell /ˌpriːˈsel/ *verb* (**pre·sold, pre·sold** /-ˈsoʊld/) **1 ~ sth** to help sell a product, service, etc., especially one that is not yet available, by using advertising and other techniques to attract consumers' attention: *Putting a trial version on your Web site is a great way of preselling your product.* **2 ~ sth** to sell something in advance of when it is available: *These farmers presell their crops.*

pres·ence 🔑 /ˈprezns/ *noun*
1 [U] (of a person) the fact of being in a particular place: *He hardly seemed to notice my presence.* ◆ *Her presence during the crisis had a calming effect.* ◆ (*formal*) *Your presence is requested at the meeting.* **ANT** ABSENCE **2** [U] (of a thing or a substance) the fact of being in a particular place or thing: *The test can identify the presence of abnormalities in the unborn child.* **ANT** ABSENCE **3** [sing.] a group of people, especially soldiers, who have been sent to a place to deal with a particular situation: *The government is maintaining a heavy police presence in the area.* ◆ *a military presence* **4** [C, usually sing.] (*literary*) a person or spirit that you cannot see but that you feel is near: *She felt a presence behind her.* **5** [U] (*approving*) the quality of making a strong impression on other people by the way you talk or behave: *a man of great presence*
IDM **in the presence of sb | in sb's presence** with someone in the same place: *The document was signed in the presence of two witnesses.* ◆ *She asked them not to discuss the matter in her presence.* **in the presence of sth** when something exists in a particular place: *Litmus paper turns red in the presence of an acid.* **make your presence felt** to do something to make people very aware of the fact that you are there; to have a strong influence on a group of people or a situation

ˌpresence of ˈmind *noun* [U] the ability to react quickly and stay calm in a difficult or dangerous situation: *The boy had the presence of mind to turn off the gas.*

pre·sent 🔑 *adj., noun, verb*
● *adj.* /ˈprezNt/ **1** [only before noun] existing or happening now: *in the present situation* ◆ *the present owner of the house* ◆ *a list of all club members, past and present* ◆ *We do not have any more information at the present time.* ◆ *A few brief comments are sufficient for present purposes.* ⊃ note at ACTUAL ⊃ see also THE PRESENT DAY **2** [not before noun] **~ (at sth)** (of a person) being in a particular place: *There were 200 people present at the meeting.* **ANT** ABSENT **3** [not before noun] **~ (in sth)** (of a thing or a substance) existing in a particular place or thing: *Levels of pollution present in the atmosphere are increasing.* ◆ *Analysis showed that traces of arsenic were present in the body.* **ANT** ABSENT
IDM **all present and accounted for** used to say that all the things or people who should be there are now there **present company excepted** (*informal*) used after being rude or critical about someone to say that the people you are talking to are not included in the criticism
● *noun* /ˈprezNt/ **1** a thing that you give to someone as a gift:

birthday/Christmas/wedding, etc. presents ◆ *What can I get him for a birthday present?* **2** usually **the present** [sing.] the time now: *You've got to forget the past and start living in the present.* ◆ *I'm sorry, he's not here at present* (= now). **3** **the present** [sing.] (*grammar*) = THE PRESENT TENSE **IDM** see MOMENT, TIME *n.*
● *verb* /prɪˈzent/
▷ GIVE **1** to give something to someone, especially formally at a ceremony: **~ sth** *The mayor will start the race and present the prizes.* ◆ **~ sb with sth** *On his retirement, colleagues presented him with a set of golf clubs.* ◆ **~ sth to sb** *The sword was presented by the family to the museum.*
▷ SOMETHING TO BE CONSIDERED **2** to show or offer something for other people to look at or consider: **~ sth (to sb)** *The committee will present its final report to Congress in June.* ◆ **~ sth (for sth)** *Eight options were presented for consideration.* ◆ *Are you presenting a paper at the conference?*
▷ SOMETHING IN PARTICULAR WAY **3** to show or describe something or someone in a particular way: **~ sth** *The company decided that it needed to present a more modern image.* ◆ *It is essential that we present a united front* (= show that we all agree). ◆ **~ yourself + adv./prep.** *You need to present yourself better.* ◆ **~ sth/sb/yourself as sth** *He likes to present himself as a radical politician.* ◆ *The article presents these proposals as misguided.*
▷ CAUSE A PROBLEM **4** to cause something to happen or be experienced: **~ sb with sth** *Your request shouldn't present us with any problems.* ◆ **~ sth** *Use of these chemicals may present a fire risk.*
▷ ITSELF **5** (of an opportunity, a solution, etc.) to suddenly happen or become available **SYN** ARISE: **~ itself** *One major problem did present itself, though.* ◆ *As soon as the opportunity presented itself, she would get another job.* ◆ **~ itself to sb** *Thankfully, a solution presented itself to him surprisingly soon.*
▷ PLAY/BROADCAST **6 ~ sth** to produce a show, play, broadcast, etc. for the public: *Compass Theater Company presents a new production of "King Lear."*
▷ INTRODUCE SOMEONE **7 ~ sb (to sb)** (*formal*) to introduce someone formally, especially to someone of higher rank or status: *I'd like to present my fiancé to you.*
▷ YOURSELF **8 ~ yourself at, for, in, etc.** (*formal*) to officially appear somewhere: *You will be asked to present yourself for an interview.* ◆ *She was ordered to present herself in court on May 20.*
▷ EXPRESS SOMETHING **9 ~ sth (to sb)** (*formal*) to offer or express something in speech or writing: *Please allow me to present my views on the subject.*
▷ CHECK/BILL **10 ~ sth** to give someone a check or bill that they should pay: *Several checks presented by the defendant were returned by the bank.* ◆ *The builders presented a bill for several thousand dollars.*
IDM **present arms** (of soldiers) to hold a RIFLE vertical in front of the body as a mark of respect

pre·sent·a·ble /prɪˈzentəbl/ *adj.* **1** looking clean and attractive, and suitable to be seen in public: *I've got to make myself presentable before the guests arrive.* **2** acceptable: *You're going to have to do a lot more work on this essay before it's presentable.*

pres·en·ta·tion 🔑 /ˌprezNˈteɪʃn; ˌpriː-/ *noun*
1 [U] the act of showing something or of giving something to someone: *The trial was adjourned following the presentation of new evidence to the court.* ◆ *The presentation of prizes began after the speeches.* ◆ *The Mayor will make the presentation* (= hand over the gift) *herself.* ◆ *Members will be admitted on/upon presentation of a membership card.* **2** [U] the way in which something is offered, shown, explained, etc. to others: *Improving the product's presentation* (= the way it is wrapped, advertised, etc.) *should increase sales.* ◆ *I admire the clear, logical presentation of her arguments.* **3** [C] a meeting at which something, especially a new product or idea, or piece of work, is shown to a group of people: *The sales manager will give a presentation on the new products.* **4** [C] the series of computer SLIDES (= images) that accompany the talk when someone gives a presentation at a meeting: *I put*

my presentation on a memory stick. **5** [C] a ceremony or formal occasion during which a gift or prize is given **6** [C] a performance of a play, etc. in a theater **7** [C, U] (*medical*) the position in which a baby is lying in the mother's body just before birth

pres·en·ta·tion·al /ˌprɛznˈteɪʃənl; ˌpri-/ *adj.* [only before noun] connected with the act of showing, explaining, or offering something to other people, especially a new product, a policy, or a performance: *a course on developing presentational skills*

the ˌpresent ˈday *noun* [sing.] the situation that exists in the world now, rather than in the past or the future: *a study of European drama, from Ibsen to the present day* ▶ **present-ˈday** *adj.* [only before noun]: *present-day fashions* ◆ *present-day America*

pre·sent·er /prɪˈzɛntər/ *noun* **1** a person who makes a speech or talks to an audience about a particular subject: *conference presenters* **2** a person who gives someone a prize at a ceremony

pre·sen·ti·ment /prɪˈzɛntəmənt/ *noun* (*formal*) a feeling that something is going to happen, especially something unpleasant **SYN** FOREBODING: *a presentiment of disaster*

pres·ent·ly /ˈprɛzntli/ *adv.* **1** at the time you are speaking or writing; now **SYN** CURRENTLY: *The crime is presently being investigated by the police.* ◆ *These are the courses presently available.* **HELP** In this meaning **presently** usually comes before the verb, adjective, or noun that it refers to. **2** used to show that something happened after a short time: *Presently, the door opened again and three men stepped out.* **HELP** In this meaning **presently** usually comes at the beginning of a sentence. **3** used to show that something will happen soon **SYN** SHORTLY: *She'll be here presently.* **HELP** In this meaning **presently** usually comes at the end of a sentence.

ˌpresent ˈparticiple *noun* (*grammar*) the form of the verb that in English ends in *-ing* and is used with the verb *to be* to form progressive tenses such as *I was running* or sometimes as an adjective as in *running water* ⊃ compare PAST PARTI-CIPLE

the ˌpresent ˈperfect *noun* [sing.] (*grammar*) the form of a verb that expresses an action done in a time period up to the present, formed in English with the present tense of *have* and the past participle of the verb, as in *I have eaten*

ˌpresent ˈtense (also **the present**) *noun* [usually sing.] (*grammar*) the form of a verb that expresses an action that is happening now or at the time of speaking

pres·er·va·tion /ˌprɛzərˈveɪʃn/ *noun* [U] **1** the act of keeping something in its original state or in good condition: *architectural/environmental/food preservation* ◆ *a preservation group/society* **2** the act of making sure that something is kept: *The central issue in the strike was the preservation of jobs.* **3** the degree to which something has not been changed or damaged by age, weather, etc.: *The paintings were in an excellent state of preservation.* ⊃ see also SELF-PRESERVATION

pres·er·va·tion·ist /ˌprɛzərˈveɪʃənɪst/ *noun* a person who works to keep old buildings or areas of land in their original condition and to prevent them from being destroyed

pre·serv·a·tive /prɪˈzərvətɪv/ *noun* [C, U] a substance used to prevent food or wood from decaying: *The juice contains no artificial preservatives.* ◆ *(a) wood preservative* ⊃ collocations at DIET ▶ **pre·serv·a·tive** *adj.* [only before noun]

pre·serve ↗ /prɪˈzərv/ *verb, noun*
• *verb* **1** ~ sth to keep a particular quality, feature, etc.; to make sure that something is kept: *He was anxious to preserve his reputation.* ◆ *Efforts to preserve the peace have failed.* **2** [often passive] to keep something in its original state in good condition: ~ sth/sb *a perfectly preserved 17th-century house* ◆ (*humorous*) *Is he really 60? He's remarkably well preserved.* ◆ ~ sth + adj. *This vase has been preserved intact.* **3** ~ sth to prevent something, especially food, from decaying by treating it in a particular way: *olives preserved in*

brine ◆ *Wax polish preserves wood and leather.* **4** ~ sb/sth (from sth) to keep someone or something alive, or safe from harm or danger **SYN** SAVE: *The society was set up to preserve endangered species from extinction.* ⊃ compare CON-SERVE
• *noun* **1** [C] = RESERVE (2) **2** [sing.] ~ (of sb) an activity, a job, an interest, etc. that is thought to be suitable for one particular person or group of people: *Football is no longer the preserve of men.* ◆ *in the days when nursing was a female preserve* **3** [C, usually pl., U] a sweet food made by boiling fruit with a large amount of sugar **4** [C] an area of private land or water where animals and fish are kept for people to hunt

pre·serv·er /prɪˈzərvər/ *noun* [C] a person who makes sure that a particular situation does not change: *The police are the preservers of law and order.* ⊃ see also LIFE PRESERVER

pre·set /ˌpriˈsɛt/ *verb* (**pre·set·ting, pre·set, pre·set**) **1** to set the controls of a piece of electrical equipment so that it will start to work at a particular time: ~ sth to do sth *You can preset the thermostat to make the heat come on when you want it to.* ◆ ~ sth *to preset TV channels/radio stations* (= to set the controls so that particular channels are selected when you press particular buttons) **2** [usually passive] ~ sth to decide something in advance: *They kept to the preset route.*

pre·side /prɪˈzaɪd/ *verb* [I] to lead or be in charge of a meeting, ceremony, etc.: *the presiding judge* ◆ ~ at/over sth *They asked if I would preside at the committee meeting.* ◆ (*figurative*) *His administration presided over one of the worst economic declines in the country's history* (= he was in power when the decline happened).

pres·i·den·cy /ˈprɛzədənsi/ *noun* [usually sing.] (*pl.* **pres·i·den·cies**) the job of being president of a country or an organization; the period of time someone holds this job: *the current holder of the university presidency* ◆ *He was a White House official during the Bush presidency.*

pres·i·dent ↗ /ˈprɛzədənt; -dɛnt/ *noun*
1 also **President** the leader of a REPUBLIC, especially the U.S.: *Several presidents attended the funeral.* ◆ *the President of the United States* ◆ *President Obama is due to visit the country next month.* ◆ *Do you have any comment, Mr. President?* ⊃ collocations at POLITICS **2** also **President** the person in charge of some organizations, clubs, colleges, etc.: *to be made president of the student council* **3** the person in charge of a bank or a commercial organization: *the bank president* ◆ *the president of Columbia Pictures* ▶ **pres·i·den·tial** /ˌprɛzəˈdɛnʃl/ *adj.*: *a presidential campaign/candidate/election* ◆ *a presidential system of government*

ˌpresident-eˈlect *noun* (*pl.* **presidents-elect**) a person who has been elected to be president but who has not yet begun the job

Presiˌdential ˌMedal of ˈFreedom *noun* a MEDAL in the U.S. that is the highest award a person can be given during a time of peace

ˈPresidents' ˌDay *noun* a legal holiday in the U.S. that falls on the third Monday in February, in memory of the birthdays of George Washington and Abraham Lincoln

pre·sid·i·um (also **prae·sid·i·um**) /prɪˈsɪdiəm/ *noun* a per-manent committee that makes important decisions as part of a government or large political organization, especially in COMMUNIST countries

press ↗ /prɛs/ *noun, verb*
• *noun*
> NEWSPAPERS **1** [sing.] newspapers and magazines: *the local/national/foreign press* ◆ *the tabloid press* (= smaller newspapers with a lot of pictures and stories of famous people) ◆ *The story was reported in the press and on television.* ◆ *the business/music/sports press* (= newspapers and maga-zines about business/music/sports) ◆ *freedom of the press/press freedom* (= the freedom to report any events and express opinions) ◆ *The event is bound to attract wide press coverage* (= it will be written about in many newspapers). **2 the press** [sing.] the journalists and photographers who work for

t tea   t̬ butter   d did   k cat   g got   tʃ chin   dʒ June   f fall

newspapers and magazines: *Members of the press were not allowed to attend the trial.* **3** [U] the type or amount of reports that newspapers write about someone or something: *The airline has **had a lot of bad press** recently* (= journalists have written unpleasant things about it).
▷ **PUBLISHING/PRINTING 4** [C, U] a machine for printing books, newspapers, etc.; the process of printing them: *We were able to watch the pages rolling off the presses.* ◆ *These prices are correct at **press time**.* ◆ *a story that is **hot off the press*** (= has just appeared in the newspapers) ➔ see also **PRINTING PRESS**
5 [C] a business that prints and publishes books: *Oxford University Press*
▷ **EQUIPMENT FOR PRESSING 6** [C] (especially in compounds) a piece of equipment that is used for creating pressure on things, to make them flat, or to get liquid from them: *a pants press* ◆ *a garlic press*
▷ **ACT OF PUSHING 7** [C, usually sing.] an act of pushing something with your hand or with a tool that you are holding: *He gave the bell another press.*
▷ **CROWD 8** [sing.] a large number of people or things competing for space or movement **SYN** THRONG: *the press of bodies all moving in the same direction* **IDM** see STOP v.

● *verb*
▷ **PUSH/SQUEEZE 1** [T, I] to push something closely and firmly against something; to be pushed in this way: *~ sth/sb/ yourself against sth She pressed her face against the window.* ◆ *~ sth to sth He pressed a handkerchief to his nose.* ◆ *~ sth together She pressed her lips together.* ◆ *~ against sth His body was pressing against hers.* ➔ picture at SQUEEZE **2** [T, I] to push or squeeze part of a device, etc. in order to make it work: *~ sth to press a button/switch/key* ◆ *~ sth + adj. He pressed the lid firmly shut.* ◆ *(+ adv./prep.) Press here to open.* ◆ *She pressed down hard on the gas pedal.* **3** [T] *~ sth into/ onto sth* to put something in a place by pushing it firmly: *He pressed a coin into her hand and moved on.* **4** [T] *~ sth* to squeeze someone's hand or arm, especially as a sign of affection **5** [I] *+ adv./prep.* (of people in a crowd) to move in the direction mentioned by pushing: *The photographers pressed around the celebrities.* ◆ *(figurative) A host of unwelcome thoughts were pressing in on him.*
▷ **TRY TO PERSUADE 6** [T] to make strong efforts to persuade or force someone to do something **SYN** PUSH, URGE: *~ sb If pressed, he will admit that he knew about the affair.* ◆ *~ sb for sth The bank is pressing us for repayment of the loan.* ◆ *~ sb to do sth They are pressing us to make a quick decision.* ◆ *~ sb into sth/into doing sth Don't let yourself be pressed into doing something you don't like.*
▷ **POINT/CLAIM/CASE 7** [T] *~ sth* to express or repeat something with force: *I hate to **press the point**, but you do owe me $200.* ◆ *She is still **pressing her claim** for compensation.* ◆ *They were determined to **press their case** at the highest level.*
▷ **MAKE FLAT/SMOOTH 8** [T] to make something flat or smooth by using force or putting something heavy on top: *~ sth pressed flowers* (= pressed between the pages of a book) ◆ *~ sth + adj. Press the soil flat with the back of a spade.* **9** [T] *~ sth* to make clothes smooth using a hot iron **SYN** IRON: *My suit needs pressing.*
▷ **FRUIT/VEGETABLES 10** [T] *~ sth* to squeeze the juice out of fruit or vegetables by using force or weight
▷ **METAL 11** [T] to make something from a material, using pressure: *~ sth to press a CD* ◆ *~ sth from/out of sth The car bodies are pressed out of sheets of metal.*
IDM **press (the) flesh** (*informal*) (of a famous person or politician) to say hello to people by shaking hands **press sth home** to get as much advantage as possible from a situation by attacking or arguing in a determined way: *press home an attack/an argument/a point* ◆ *Simone saw her opponent was hesitating and pressed home her advantage.* **press sb/sth into service** to use someone or something for a purpose that they were not trained or intended for because there is nobody or nothing else available: *Every type of boat was pressed into service to rescue passengers from the sinking ferry.* ➔ more at CHARGE, PANIC BUTTON
PHRV **press a'head/'on (with sth)** to continue doing something in a determined way; to hurry forward: *The company is pressing ahead with its plans for a new warehouse.*

◆ *"Should we stop here for the night?" "No, let's press on."* **press for sth** to keep asking for something **SYN** DEMAND, PUSH FOR: *They continued to press for a change in the law.* **press sth on sb** to try to make someone accept something, especially food or drink, although they may not want it: *She kept pressing more food on us.*

'press ,agency *noun* = NEWS AGENCY

'press ,agent (also *informal* **flack**) *noun* a person whose job is to supply information and advertising material about a particular actor, musician, theater, etc. to newspapers, radio, or television

'press box *noun* a special area or a room at a sports event where sports journalists sit

'press ,clipping *noun* = CLIPPING

'press ,conference (also **'news ,conference**) *noun* a meeting at which someone talks to a group of reporters in order to answer their questions or to make an official statement: *to hold/give a press conference*

'press corps *noun* (*pl.* **press corps**) a group of journalists who work in or go to a particular place to report on an event

pressed /prest/ *adj.* **1** [not before noun] *~ (for sth)* not having enough of something, especially time or money: *I'm really pressed for cash right now.* ➔ see also HARD-PRESSED **2** made flat using force or a heavy object: *pictures made with pressed flowers* ◆ *neatly pressed slacks*

'press ,gallery *noun* an area in a court of law for journalists to sit in

'press gang *noun* a group of people who were employed in the past to force men to join the army or navy

'press-gang *verb* *~ sb (into sth/into doing sth)* (*informal*) to force someone to do something that they do not want to do

press·ing /'presɪŋ/ *adj.*, *noun*
● *adj.* [usually before noun] **1** needing to be dealt with immediately **SYN** URGENT: *I have some pressing business to attend to.* **2** difficult to refuse or to ignore: *a pressing invitation*
● *noun* an object, for example a CD, made by using pressure or weight to shape a piece of metal, plastic, etc.; a number of such objects that are made at one time: *the latest pressing of the CD*

'press ,office *noun* the office of a large organization, political party, or government department that answers questions from journalists and provides them with information

'press ,officer *noun* a person who is in charge of or works for a press office

'press re,lease *noun* an official statement made to reporters by a large organization, a political party, or a government department

'press ,secretary *noun* a person who works for a politician or a political organization and gives information about them to reporters, the newspapers, etc.

pres·sure ✏ /'preʃər/ *noun*, *verb*
● *noun*
▷ **WHEN SOMETHING PRESSES 1** [U] the force or weight with which something presses against something else: *The nurse applied pressure to his arm to stop the bleeding.* ◆ *The barriers gave way under the pressure of the crowd.*
▷ **OF GAS/LIQUID 2** [U, C] the force produced by a particular amount of gas or liquid in a confined space or container; the amount of this: *air/water pressure* ◆ *Check the tire pressure* (= the amount of air in a tire) *regularly.* ➔ see also BLOOD PRESSURE
▷ **OF ATMOSPHERE 3** [U] the force of the atmosphere on the earth's surface: *A band of high/low pressure is moving across the Great Lakes region.* ➔ see also ATMOSPHERIC
▷ **PERSUASION/FORCE 4** [U] the act of trying to persuade or force someone to do something: *~ (for sth) The pressure for change continued to mount.* ◆ *~ (on sb) (to do sth) There is a great deal of pressure on young people to conform.* ◆ *The*

government eventually bowed to **popular pressure** (= they agreed to do what people were trying to get them to do). ⟹ **see also** PEER PRESSURE

▷ STRESS **5** [U] (also **pressures** [pl.]) difficulties and feelings of anxiety that are caused by the need to achieve or to behave in a particular way: *She was unable to attend because of the pressure of work.* ◆ *You need to be able to handle pressure in this job.* ◆ *How can anyone enjoy the pressures of city life?* **IDM** **put pressure on sb (to do sth)** to force or to try to persuade someone to do something **under pressure 1** if a liquid or a gas is kept **under pressure**, it is forced into a container so that when the container is opened, the liquid or gas escapes quickly **2** being forced to do something: *The director is under increasing pressure to resign.* **3** made to feel anxious about something you have to do: *The team performs well under pressure.*

● **verb** [often passive] **~ sb (into sth/into doing sth)** | **~ sb to do sth** to persuade someone to do something, especially by making them feel that they have to or should do it: *Don't let yourself be pressured into making a hasty decision.*

THESAURUS

pressure

stress ◆ **tension** ◆ **strain**

These are all words for the feelings of anxiety caused by the problems in someone's life.

pressure difficulties and feelings of anxiety that are caused by the need to achieve something or to behave in a particular way: *She was losing sleep over the pressure of her work.*

stress pressure or anxiety caused by the problems in someone's life: *stress-related illness*

PRESSURE OR STRESS?

It is common to say that someone *is suffering from stress*, while **pressure** may be the thing that causes **stress**.

tension a feeling of anxiety and stress that makes it impossible to relax: *nervous tension*

strain pressure on someone because they have too much to do or manage; the problems, worry, or anxiety that this produces: *I found it a strain staying home with four children.*

PATTERNS

- to be **under** pressure/stress/strain
- **considerable** pressure/stress/tension/strain
- to **cause** stress/tension/strain
- to **cope with** the pressure/stress/tension/strain
- to **relieve/release** the pressure/stress/tension
- to be **suffering from** stress/tension

---

pressure ˌcooker *noun* **1** a strong metal pot with a tight lid, that cooks food quickly by steam under high pressure **2** a situation that is difficult or dangerous because people are likely to become anxious or violent

pressure ˌgroup *noun* a group of people who try to influence the government and ordinary people's opinions in order to achieve the action they want, for example a change in a law: *the environmental pressure group "Greenpeace"* ⟹ **compare** ADVOCACY GROUP ⟹ **see also** INTEREST GROUP

pressure ˌhose *noun* a long tube that is strong enough for liquid to pass through it at high pressure

pressure ˌpoint *noun* **1** a place on the surface of the body that is sensitive to pressure, for example where an artery can be pressed against a bone to stop the loss of blood **2** a place or situation where there is likely to be trouble

pressure ˌsuit *noun* a suit that can be filled with air, used to protect the person wearing it from low air pressure, for example while flying a plane very high in the atmosphere

pressure ˌwasher *noun* a machine that cleans things by spraying them with water under high pressure

pres·sur·ize /ˈprɛʃəˌraɪz/ *verb* [usually passive] **~ sth** to keep the air pressure in a SUBMARINE, an aircraft, etc. the same as it is on earth ▶ **pres·sur·i·za·tion** /ˌprɛʃərəˈzeɪʃn/ *noun* [U]

pres·tige /prɛˈstiʒ; -ˈstidʒ/ *noun, adj.*
● *noun* [U] the respect and admiration that someone or something has because of their social position or what they have done **SYN** STATUS: *personal prestige* ◆ *There is a lot of prestige attached to owning a car like this.* ◆ *jobs with low prestige*
● *adj.* [only before noun] **1** that brings respect and admiration; important: *a prestige job* **2** admired and respected because it looks important and expensive **SYN** LUXURY: *a prestige car*

pres·tig·ious /prɛˈstɪdʒəs; -ˈsti-/ *adj.* [usually before noun] respected and admired as very important or of very high quality: *a prestigious award* ◆ *a prestigious university*

pres·to /ˈprɛstoʊ/ *exclamation, adv., adj., noun*
● *exclamation* **1** something that people say when they have just done something so quickly and easily that it seems to have been done by magic: *You just press the button and, presto, a perfect cup of coffee!* **2** something that people say just before they finish a magic trick
● *adv., adj.* (used as an instruction in a piece of music) very quickly
● *noun* (pl. **pres·tos**) a piece of music that should be performed very quickly

pre·sum·a·bly 🔑 **AWL** /prɪˈzuməbli/ *adv.* used to say that you think that something is probably true: *Presumably, this is where the accident happened.* ◆ *You'll be taking the car, presumably?* ◆ *I couldn't concentrate, presumably because I was so tired.*

pre·sume **AWL** /prɪˈzum/ *verb* **1** [I, T] to suppose that something is true, although you do not have actual proof **SYN** ASSUME: *They are very expensive, I presume?* ◆ *"Is he still abroad?" " I presume so."* ◆ **~ (that)…** *I presumed (that) he understood the rules.* ◆ **it is presumed that…** *Little is known of the youngest son; it is presumed that he died young.* ◆ **~ sb/sth to be/have sth** *I presumed him to be her husband.* **2** [T] to accept that something is true until it is shown not to be true, especially in court: **~ sb/sth + adj.** *Twelve passengers are missing, presumed dead.* ◆ *In English law, a person is presumed innocent until proved guilty.* ◆ **~ sth** *We must presume innocence until we have proof of guilt.* ◆ **~ sb/sth to be/have sth** *We must presume them to be innocent until we have proof of guilt.* **3** [T] **~ sth** (*formal*) to accept something as true or existing and to act on that basis: *The course seems to presume some previous knowledge of the subject.* **4** [I] **~ to do sth** (*formal*) to behave in a way that shows a lack of respect by doing something that you have no right to do: *I wouldn't presume to tell you how to run your own business.*
PHR V **pre'sume on/upon sb/sth** (*formal*) to make use of someone's friendship by asking them for more than you should: **~ to do sth** *I felt it would be presuming on our personal relationship to keep asking her for help.*

pre·sump·tion **AWL** /prɪˈzʌmpʃn/ *noun* **1** [C] something that people think is probably true: *There is a general presumption that the doctor knows best.* **2** [U] (*formal*) behavior that is too confident and shows a lack of respect for other people **3** [U, C] (*law*) the act of supposing that something is true, although it has not yet been proved or is not certain: *Everyone is entitled to the presumption of innocence until they are proven to be guilty.*

pre·sump·tive /prɪˈzʌmptɪv/ *adj.* [usually before noun] (*formal* or *technical*) likely to be true, based on the facts that are available ⟹ **see also** HEIR PRESUMPTIVE

pre·sump·tu·ous **AWL** /prɪˈzʌmptʃuəs/ *adj.* [not usually before noun] too confident, in a way that shows a lack of respect for other people

pre·sup·pose /ˌprisəˈpoʊz/ *verb* (*formal*) **1 ~ sth** to accept

---

h **hat**   m **man**   n **no**   ŋ **sing**   l **leg**   r **red**   y **yes**   w **wet**

something as true or existing, and act on that basis before it has been proved to be true **SYN** PRESUME: *Teachers sometimes presuppose a fairly high level of knowledge by the students.* **2** ~ **that...** | ~ **sth** to depend on something in order to exist or be true **SYN** ASSUME: *His argument presupposes that it does not matter who is in power.*

pre·sup·po·si·tion /ˌpriːsʌpəˈzɪʃn/ *noun* [C, U] (*formal*) something that you believe to be true and use as the beginning of an argument even though it has not been proved; the act of believing it is true **SYN** ASSUMPTION: *theories based on presupposition and coincidence*

pre·tax /ˌpriːˈtæks/ *adj.* [only before noun] before the tax has been taken away: *pretax profits/losses/income*

pre·teach /ˌpriːˈtiːtʃ/ *verb* ~ **sth** to teach something, especially new words, to students before a test, homework, etc.

pre·teen /ˌpriːˈtiːn/ *noun* a young person of about 11 or 12 years of age ▶ **pre·teen** *adj.* [usually before noun]: *the preteen years*

pre·tend 🔊 /prɪˈtɛnd/ *verb, adj.*
- *verb* **1** [I, T] to behave in a particular way, in order to make other people believe something that is not true: *I'm tired of having to pretend all the time.* ♦ *Of course I was wrong; it would be hypocritical to pretend otherwise.* ♦ ~ **(to sb) (that...)** *He pretended to his family that everything was fine.* ♦ ~ **to do sth** *He pretended not to notice.* ♦ *She didn't love him, though she pretended to.* ♦ ~ **sth** (*formal*) *She pretended an interest she did not feel.* **2** [I, T] (especially of children) to imagine that something is true as part of a game: *They didn't have any real money so they had to pretend.* ♦ ~ **(that)...** *Let's pretend (that) we're astronauts.* **3** [I, T] (usually used in negative sentences and questions) to claim to be, do, or have something, especially when this is not true: ~ **to sth** *I can't pretend to any great musical talent.* ♦ ~ **(that)...** *I don't pretend (that) I know much about the subject, but...* ♦ ~ **to be/do/have sth** *The book doesn't pretend to be a great work of literature.*
- *adj.* [usually before noun] (*informal*) (often used by children) not real; imaginary: *pretend cakes*

pre·tend·er /prɪˈtɛndər/ *noun* ~ **(to sth)** a person who claims they have a right to a particular title even though other people disagree with them

pre·tense /ˈpriːtens; prɪˈtens/ *noun* **1** [U, sing.] the act of behaving in a particular way, in order to make other people believe something that is not true: *Their friendliness was only pretense.* ♦ ~ **of doing sth** *By the end of the evening she had abandoned all pretense of being interested.* ♦ ~ **of sth** *He made no pretense of great musical knowledge.* ♦ ~ **that...** *She was unable to keep up the pretense that she loved him.* **2** [U, C, usually sing.] (*formal* or *literary*) a claim that you have a particular quality or skill: ~ **(to sth)** *a woman with some pretense to beauty* ♦ ~ **(to doing sth)** *I make no pretense to being an expert on the subject.* **IDM** see FALSE

pre·ten·sion /prɪˈtɛnʃn/ *noun* [C, usually pl., U] **1** the act of trying to appear more important, intelligent, etc. than you are in order to impress other people: *intellectual pretensions* ♦ *The play mocks the pretensions of the new middle class.* ♦ *He spoke without pretension.* **2** a claim to be or to do something: ~ **(to sth/to doing sth)** *a building with no pretensions to architectural merit* ♦ ~ **(to do sth)** *The movie makes no pretension to reproduce life.*

pre·ten·tious /prɪˈtɛnʃəs/ *adj.* (*disapproving*) trying to appear important, intelligent, etc. in order to impress other people; trying to be something that you are not, in order to impress: *That's a pretentious name for a dog!* ♦ *It was just an ordinary house—nothing pretentious.* ♦ *He's so pretentious!* ⊃ compare UNPRETENTIOUS ▶ **pre·ten·tious·ly** *adv.* **pre·ten·tious·ness** *noun* [U]

the pret·er·ite (also **pret·er·it**) /ˈprɛtərət/ *noun* [sing.] (*grammar*) a form of a verb that expresses the past

pre·term /ˌpriːˈtɜːrm/ *adj.* born or happening after a short PREGNANCY, especially one that is less than 37 weeks: *caring for low birthweight and preterm babies* ♦ *a preterm birth/*

delivery ▶ **pre·term** *adv.*: *Babies born preterm are at greater risk of needing hospitalization.*

pre·ter·nat·u·ral /ˌpriːtərˈnætʃrəl; -ˈnætʃərəl/ *adj.* [only before noun] (*formal*) that does not seem natural; that cannot be explained by natural laws ▶ **pre·ter·nat·u·ral·ly** *adv.*: *The city was preternaturally quiet.*

pre·test /ˈpriːtest/ *noun* a test that you take to find out how much you already know or can do before learning or doing something ▶ **pre·test** *verb* ~ **sb**

pre·text /ˈpriːtekst/ *noun* ~ **(for sth/for doing sth)** | ~ **(to do sth)** a false reason that you give for doing something, usually something bad, in order to hide the real reason; an excuse: *The incident was used as a pretext for intervention in the area.* ♦ *He left the party early on the pretext of having work to do.* ⊃ thesaurus box at REASON

pret·ti·fy /ˈprɪtɪfaɪ/ *verb* (pret·ti·fies, pret·ti·fy·ing, pret·ti·fied, pret·ti·fied) ~ **sth** (usually *disapproving*) to try to make something pretty, often with the result that it looks worse or false

pret·ty 🔊 /ˈprɪti/ *adv., adj.*
- *adv.* (with adjectives and adverbs) **1** to some extent; fairly: *I'm pretty sure I'll be going.* ♦ *The game was pretty good.* ♦ *It's pretty hard to explain.* ♦ *I'm going to have to find a new apartment pretty soon.* **2** very: *That performance was pretty impressive.* ♦ *Things are looking pretty good!* **IDM** **pretty much/near/well** (*informal*) almost; almost completely: *One dog looks pretty much like another to me.*
- *adj.* (pret·ti·er, pret·ti·est) **1** (especially of a woman, or a girl) attractive without being very beautiful: *a pretty face* ♦ *a pretty little girl* ♦ *You look so pretty in that dress!* ⊃ thesaurus box at BEAUTIFUL **2** (of places or things) attractive and pleasant to look at or to listen to without being large, beautiful, or impressive: *pretty clothes* ♦ *a pretty garden* ♦ *a pretty name* ▶ **pret·ti·ly** /ˈprɪtɪli/ *adv.*: *The rooms are simply but prettily furnished.* **pret·ti·ness** /ˈprɪtinəs/ *noun* [U]: **IDM** **as pretty as a picture** (*old-fashioned*) very pretty **not just a pretty face** (*humorous*) used to emphasize that you have particular skills or qualities: *"I didn't know you could play the piano." "I'm not just a pretty face, you know!"* **not a pretty sight** (*humorous*) not pleasant to look at: *You should have seen him in his swimming trunks—not a pretty sight!* **a pretty penny** (*old-fashioned*) a lot of money ⊃ more at PASS n.

pret·zel /ˈprɛtsl/ *noun* a crisp salty type of bread in the shape of a knot or stick

pre·vail /prɪˈveɪl/ *verb* **1** [I] ~ **(in/among sth)** to exist or be very common at a particular time or in a particular place: *We were horrified at the conditions prevailing in local prisons.* ♦ *Those beliefs still prevail among certain social groups.* **2** [I] ~ **(against/over sth)** (*formal*) (of ideas, opinions, etc.) to be accepted, especially after a struggle or an argument **SYN** TRIUMPH: *Justice will prevail over tyranny.* ♦ *Fortunately, common sense prevailed.* **3** [I] ~ **(against/over sb)** (*formal*) to defeat an opponent, especially after a long struggle **PHR V** **pre·vail on/upon sb to do sth** (*formal*) to persuade someone to do something: *I'm sure he could be prevailed upon to give a talk.*

pre·vail·ing /prɪˈveɪlɪŋ/ *adj.* [only before noun] **1** existing or most common at a particular time **SYN** CURRENT, PRE-DOMINANT: *the prevailing economic conditions* ♦ *the attitude toward science prevailing at the time* ♦ *The prevailing view seems to be that they will find her guilty.* **2** the **prevailing wind** in an area is the one that blows over it most frequently

prev·a·lent /ˈprɛvələnt/ *adj.* ~ **(among sb)** | ~ **(in sb/sth)** that exists or is very common at a particular time or in a particular place **SYN** COMMON, WIDESPREAD: *a prevalent view* ♦ *These prejudices are particularly prevalent among people living in the North.* ▶ **prev·a·lence** /-ləns/ *noun* [U]

pre·var·i·cate /prɪˈværəˌkeɪt/ *verb* [I, T] (+ **speech**) (*formal*) to avoid giving a direct answer to a question in order to hide the truth: *Stop prevaricating and come to the point.* ▶ **pre·var·i·ca·tion** /prɪˌværəˈkeɪʃn/ *noun* [U, C]

pre·vent 🔑 /prɪˈvɛnt/ verb
to stop someone from doing something; to stop something from happening: ~ sth/sb *The accident could have been prevented.* ◆ ~ **sb/sth from doing sth** *He is prevented by law from holding a license.* ◆ *Nothing would prevent him from speaking out against injustice.* ▶ **pre·vent·a·ble** /prɪˈvɛntəbl/ adj.: *preventable diseases/accidents*

pre·ven·tion /prɪˈvɛnʃn/ noun [U] the act of stopping something bad from happening: *accident/crime prevention* ◆ *the prevention of disease* ◆ *a fire prevention officer* **IDM** see OUNCE

pre·ven·tive /prɪˈvɛntɪv/ (also **pre·ven·ta·tive** /prɪˈvɛntə-tɪv/) adj. [only before noun] intended to try to stop something that causes problems or difficulties from happening: *preventive medicine* ◆ *The police were able to take preventive action and avoid a possible riot.* ⟳ compare CURATIVE

pre·ver·bal /ˌpriˈvərbl/ adj. [usually before noun] (technical) connected with the time before a child learns to speak: *a preverbal communication*

pre·view /ˈprivyu/ noun, verb
• *noun* **1** an occasion at which you can see a movie, a show, etc. before it is shown to the general public: *a press preview* (= for journalists only) ◆ *a special preview of our winter fashion collection* ⟳ see also SNEAK PREVIEW **2** a description in a newspaper or a magazine that tells you about a movie, a television program, etc. before it is shown to the public: *Turn to page 12 for a preview of next week's programs.* **3** a series of short scenes from a movie or television program, shown in advance to advertise it **SYN** TRAILER ⟳ thesaurus box at ADVERTISEMENT
• *verb* **1** ~ sth to see a movie, a television program, etc. before it is shown to the general public and write an account of it for a newspaper or magazine: *The exhibition was previewed in last week's issue.* **2** ~ sth to give someone a short account of something that is going to happen, be studied, etc.: *The professor previewed the course for us.*

pre·vi·ous 🔑 **AWL** /ˈpriviəs/ adj. [only before noun]
1 happening or existing before the event or object that you are talking about **SYN** PRIOR: *No previous experience is necessary for this job.* ◆ *The car has only had one previous owner.* ◆ *She is his daughter from a previous marriage.* ◆ *I was unable to attend because of a previous engagement.* ◆ *The judge will take into consideration any previous convictions.* **2** immediately before the time you are talking about: *I couldn't believe it when I heard the news. I'd only seen him the previous day.*
▶ **previous to** prep.: *Previous to this, she'd always been well.*

pre·vi·ous·ly 🔑 **AWL** /ˈpriviəsli/ adv.
before the time that you are talking about: *The building had previously been used as a hotel.* ◆ *I had visited them three days previously.*

pre·war /ˌpriˈwɔr/ adj. [usually before noun] happening or existing before a war, especially before World War II: *the prewar years* ◆ *prewar Europe*

ˌpre-ˈwash verb, noun
• *verb* **1** ~ sth to wash cloth before it is used, or clothing before it is sold **2** ~ sth to give clothing an extra wash before the main wash, especially in a machine
• *noun* ˈpre-wash **1** [C] an extra wash before the main wash **2** [U] a substance that is applied to clothing before washing, in order to make it cleaner

prey /preɪ/ noun, verb
• *noun* [U, sing.] **1** an animal, a bird, etc. that is hunted, killed, and eaten by another: *The lion will often stalk its prey for hours.* ◆ **birds of prey** (= birds that kill for food) ⟳ collocations at LIFE **2** a person who is harmed or tricked by someone, especially for dishonest purposes: *Elderly people are easy prey for dishonest salesmen.*
IDM be/fall prey to sth (formal) **1** (of an animal) to be killed and eaten by another animal or bird **2** (of a person) to be harmed or affected by something bad

• *verb*
IDM prey on sb's mind (of a thought, problem, etc.) to make someone think and worry about it all the time
PHR V ˈprey on/upon sb/sth **1** (of an animal or a bird) to hunt and kill another animal for food **2** to harm someone who is weaker than you, or make use of them in a dishonest way to get what you want: *Bogus social workers have been preying on old people living alone.*

prez /prɛz/ noun (informal) = PRESIDENT

price

cost ◆ value ◆ expense ◆ worth

These words all refer to the amount of money that you have to pay for something.

price the amount of money that you have to pay for an item or a service: *house prices* ◆ *These shoes don't have a price on them.* ◆ *I can't afford it at that price.*

cost the amount of money that you need in order to buy, make, or do something: *A new computer system has been installed at a cost of $180,000.*

value how much something is worth in money or other goods for which it can be exchanged: *Sports cars tend to hold their value well.* **NOTE** Value can also mean how much something is worth compared with its price: *This restaurant is an excellent value* (= is worth the money it costs).

PRICE, COST, OR VALUE?
The **price** is what someone asks you to pay for an item or service: *to ask/charge a high price* ◆ *to ask/charge a high cost/value.* Obtaining or achieving something may have a **cost**; the **value** of something is how much other people would be willing to pay for it: *house prices* ◆ *the cost of changing jobs* ◆ *The house now has a market value of one million dollars.*

expense the money that you spend on something; something that makes you spend money: *The garden was expanded at great expense.* ◆ *Owning a car is a major expense.*

worth the financial value of someone or something: *He has a personal net worth of $10 million.* **NOTE** Worth is more often used to mean the practical or moral value of something.

PATTERNS
■ the **high** price/cost/value
■ the **real/true** price/cost/value/worth
■ to **put/set** a price/value **on** something
■ to **increase/reduce** the price/cost/value/expense
■ to **raise/double/lower** the price/cost/value
■ to **cut** the price/cost

price 🔑 /praɪs/ noun, verb
• *noun* **1** [C, U] the amount of money that you have to pay for something: *Boat for sale, price $4,000* ◆ *house/retail/oil/share prices* ◆ *to charge a high/reasonable/low price for something* ◆ *The price of cigarettes is set to rise again.* ◆ *He managed to get a good price for the car.* ◆ *rising/falling prices* ◆ *Can you give me a price for the work* (= tell me how much you will charge)? ◆ *I'm only buying it if it's the right price* (= a price that I think is reasonable). ◆ *Children over five must pay (the) full price for the ticket.* ◆ *How much are these? They don't have a price on them.* ◆ *It's amazing how much computers have come down in price over the past few years.* ◆ *price rises/increases/cuts* ◆ *a price list* ⟳ see also ASKING PRICE, COST PRICE, HALF-PRICE, LIST PRICE, MARKET PRICE, PURCHASE PRICE, SELLING PRICE **2** [sing.] the unpleasant things that you must do or experience in order to achieve something or as a result of achieving something: ~ (of sth) *Criticism is part of the price of leadership.* ◆ ~ (for sth/for doing sth) *Loneliness is a high price to pay for independence in your old age.* ◆ *Giving up his job*

ʌ cup   ə about   eɪ say   aɪ five   ɔɪ boy   aʊ now   oʊ go   ər bird

was *a small price to pay* for his children's happiness. **3** [C] (in horse racing) the numbers that tell you how much money you will receive if the horse that you bet on wins the race **SYN** ODDS: *Six to one is a good price for that horse.* ⟳ see also STARTING PRICE

IDM at any price whatever the cost or the difficulties may be: *We want peace at any price.* **at a price 1** (also for a price) costing a lot of money: *You can buy strawberries all year round, but for a price.* **2** involving something unpleasant: *Her generosity comes at a price.* ♦ *He'll help you—at a price!* **beyond price** (*formal* or *literary*) extremely valuable or important **everyone has their price** (*saying*) you can persuade anyone to do something by giving them more money or something that they want **not at any price** used to say that no amount of money would persuade you to do or to sell something: *I wouldn't work for her again—not at any price!* **a price on sb's head** an amount of money that is offered for capturing or killing someone **put a price on sth** to say how much money something valuable is worth: *They haven't yet put a price on the business.* ♦ *You can't put a price on that sort of loyalty.* **what price...?** (*informal*) used to say that you think that something you have achieved may not be worth all the problems and difficulties it causes: *What price fame and fortune?* ⟳ more at CHEAP, PAY v.

● **verb 1** [usually passive] to fix the price of something at a particular level: **~ sth + adv./prep.** *a reasonably priced house* ♦ *These goods are priced too high.* ♦ **~ sth at sth** *The tickets are priced at $100 each.* **2 ~ sth (up)** to write or stick tickets on goods to show how much they cost **3 ~ sth** to compare the prices of different types of the same thing: *We priced various models before buying this one.*

IDM price yourself/sth out of the market to charge such a high price for your goods, services, etc. that no one wants to buy them

price con·trols *noun* [pl.] (*economics*) restrictions that a government puts on the price of goods at particular times, such as when there is a war, when there is not enough of something, there is a war, etc.

price-·fixing *noun* [U] the practice of companies agreeing not to sell goods below a particular price

price index *noun* ⟳ CONSUMER PRICE INDEX

price·less /'praɪsləs/ *adj.* **1** extremely valuable or important: *a priceless collection of antiques* ♦ *priceless information* ⟳ thesaurus box at VALUABLE **2** (*informal*) extremely amusing: *You should have seen his face—it was priceless!*

price tag *noun* a label on something that shows how much you must pay: (*figurative*) *There is a $2 million price tag on the team's star player.* ⟳ picture at LABEL

price war *noun* a situation in which companies or stores keep reducing the prices of their products and services in order to attract customers away from their COMPETITORS

pric·ey /'praɪsi/ *adj.* (pric·i·er, pric·i·est) (*informal*) expensive ⟳ thesaurus box at EXPENSIVE

pric·ing /'praɪsɪŋ/ *noun* [U] the act of deciding how much to charge for something: *competitive pricing* ♦ *pricing policy*

prick /prɪk/ *verb, noun*
● **verb 1** [T] to make a very small hole in something with a sharp point: **~ sth** *He pricked the balloon and popped it.* ♦ **~ sth with sth** *Prick holes in the paper with a pin.* **2** [T] **~ sth (on sth)** to make a small hole in the skin so that it hurts or blood comes out: *She pricked her finger on a needle.* **3** [I, T] to make someone feel a slight pain as if they were being pricked: *He felt a pricking sensation in his throat.* ♦ **~ sth** *Tears pricked her eyes.*

IDM prick your conscience| your conscience pricks you to make you feel guilty about something; to feel guilty about something: *Her conscience pricked her as she lied to her sister.* **prick (up) your ears 1** (of an animal, especially a horse or dog) to raise the ears **2** (also **your ears prick up**) (of a person) to listen carefully, especially because you have just heard something interesting: *Her ears pricked up at the sound of his name.*

● **noun 1** an act of making a very small hole in something with a sharp point: *I'm going to give your finger a little prick with this needle.* **2** a slight pain caused by a sharp point or something that feels like a sharp point: *You will feel a tiny prick in your arm.* ♦ (*figurative*) *He could feel the hot prick of tears in his eyes.*

prick·le /'prɪkl/ *verb, noun*
● **verb 1** [T, I] **~ (sth)** to give someone an unpleasant feeling on their skin, as if a lot of small sharp points are pushing into it: *The rough cloth prickled my skin.* ♦ *His mustache prickled when he kissed me.* **2** [I] **~ (with sth)** (of skin, eyes, etc.) to sting or feel strange and unpleasant because you are frightened, angry, excited, etc.: *Her eyes prickled with tears.* ♦ *The hairs on the back of my neck prickled when I heard the door open.* ♦ (*figurative*) *He prickled* (= became angry) *at the suggestion that it had been his fault.*

● **noun 1** a small sharp part on the STEM or leaf of a plant or on the skin of some animals: *a cactus covered in prickles* **2** a slight stinging feeling on the skin: *a prickle of fear/excitement*

prick·ly /'prɪkli/ *adj.* (prick·li·er, prick·li·est) **1** covered with prickles: *a prickly bush* **2** causing you to feel as if your skin is touching something that is covered with prickles: *a prickly feeling* **3** (*informal*) (of a person) easily annoyed or offended **SYN** TOUCHY **4** (of a decision, an issue, etc.) difficult to deal with because people have very different ideas about it **SYN** THORNY: *Let's move on to the prickly subject of tax reform.*

prickly heat *noun* [U] a skin condition, common in hot countries, that causes small red spots that ITCH

prickly pear *noun* **1** a type of CACTUS with PRICKLES (= sharp parts like needles) and yellow flowers **2** the fruit of the prickly pear. It is shaped like a PEAR and can be eaten.

pride 🔑 /praɪd/ *noun, verb*
● **noun**
▷ PLEASURE/SATISFACTION **1** [U, sing.] a feeling of pleasure or satisfaction that you get when you or people who are connected with you have done something well or own something that other people admire: *The sight of her son graduating filled her with pride.* ♦ **~ (in sth)** *I take (a) pride in my work.* ♦ **~ (in doing sth)** *We take great pride in offering the best service in town.* ♦ *I looked* **with pride** *at what I had achieved.* ♦ *Success in sports is a source of national pride.* ⟳ thesaurus box at SATISFACTION **2** [sing.] **the ~ of sth** a person or thing that gives people a feeling of pleasure or satisfaction: *The new sports stadium is the pride of the town.*
▷ RESPECT FOR YOURSELF **3** [U] the feeling of respect that you have for yourself: *Pride would not allow him to accept the money.* ♦ *Her pride was hurt.* ♦ *Losing his job was a real* **blow to his pride.** ♦ *It's time to* **swallow your pride** (= hide your feelings of pride) *and ask for your job back.* **4** [U] (*disapproving*) the feeling that you are better or more important than other people: *Male pride forced him to suffer in silence.* ⟳ see also PROUD
▷ LIONS **5** [C] a group of LIONS
IDM sb's pride and joy a person or thing that causes someone to feel great pleasure or satisfaction **pride comes/goes before a fall** (*saying*) if you have too high an opinion of yourself or your abilities, something will happen to make you look stupid **pride of place** the position in which something is most easily seen that is given to the most important thing in a particular group

● **verb**
PHR V pride yourself on sth/on doing sth [no passive] to be proud of something: *She had always prided herself on her appearance.*

priest 🔑 /prist/ *noun*
1 a person who is qualified to perform religious duties and ceremonies in the Roman Catholic, Anglican, and Orthodox Churches: *a parish priest* ♦ *the ordination of women priests* ⟳ compare CHAPLAIN, CLERGYMAN, MINISTER, VICAR

2 (*feminine* priest·ess /ˈpriːstəs/) a person who performs religious ceremonies in some religions that are not Christian

priest·hood /ˈpriːsthʊd/ *noun* **1** the priesthood [sing.] the job or position of being a priest: *to enter the priesthood* (= to become a priest) ⊃ collocations at RELIGION **2** all the priests of a particular religion or country

priest·ly /ˈpriːstli/ *adj.* [usually before noun] connected with a priest; like a priest

prig /prɪɡ/ *noun* (*disapproving*) a person who behaves in a morally correct way and who shows that they disapprove of what other people do ▶ **prig·gish** /ˈprɪɡɪʃ/ *adj.* **prig·gish·ness** *noun* [U]

prim /prɪm/ *adj.* (**prim·mer, prim·mest**) (*disapproving*) **1** (of a person) always behaving in a careful and formal way, and easily shocked by anything that is offensive: *You can't tell her that joke—she's much too **prim and proper**.* **2** formal and neat **SYN** DEMURE: *a prim suit with a high-necked collar* ▶ **prim·ly** *adv.*: *"You're not supposed to say that," she said primly.*

pri·ma bal·le·ri·na /ˌpriːmə ˌbæləˈriːnə/ *noun* the main woman dancer in a BALLET company

pri·ma·cy **AWL** /ˈpraɪməsi/ *noun* (*pl.* **pri·ma·cies**) (*formal*) **1** [U] the fact of being the most important person or thing: *a belief in the primacy of the family* **2** [C] the position of an ARCHBISHOP

pri·ma don·na /ˌprɪmə ˈdɒnə/ ; /ˌpriːmə-/ *noun* **1** the main woman singer in an OPERA performance or an OPERA company **2** (*disapproving*) a person who thinks they are very important because they are good at something, and who behaves badly when they do not get what they want

pri·ma fa·ci·e /ˌpraɪmə ˈfeɪʃi ; -ˈfeɪʃə ; ˌpriːmə-/ *adj.* [only before noun] (from *Latin, law*) based on what at first seems to be true, although it may be proved false later: *prima facie evidence* ▶ **pri·ma fa·ci·e** *adv.*: *Prima facie, there is a strong case against him.*

pri·mal /ˈpraɪml/ *adj.* [only before noun] (*formal*) connected with the earliest origins of life; very basic **SYN** PRIMEVAL: *the primal hunter-gatherer* ◆ *a primal urge/fear*

pri·ma·ri·ly 🔑 **AWL** /praɪˈmɛrəli/ *adv.*

mainly **SYN** CHIEFLY: *a course designed primarily for specialists* ◆ *The problem is not primarily a financial one.*

pri·ma·ry 🔑 **AWL** /ˈpraɪˌmɛri ; -məri/ *adj., noun*

● *adj.* **1** [usually before noun] main; most important; basic **SYN** PRIME: *The primary aim of this course is to improve your spoken English.* ◆ *Our primary concern must be the children.* ◆ *Good healthcare is of primary importance.* **2** [usually before noun] developing or happening first; earliest: *primary causes* ◆ *The disease is still in its primary stage.* **3** [only before noun] connected with the education of children between the ages of about five and eleven: *primary teachers* ⊃ compare ELEMENTARY, SECONDARY

● *noun* (*pl.* **pri·ma·ries**) (also **primary e·lection**) an election in which people in a particular area vote to choose a candidate for a future important election: *the Illinois primary* ◆ *the presidential primaries*

primary 'care (also **primary 'healthcare**) *noun* [U] the medical treatment that you receive first when you are sick, from a doctor who might then recommend that you visit a specialist

primary 'care phy·si·cian *noun* (*abbr.* PCP) a doctor who provides primary care

primary 'care pro·vider *noun* (*abbr.* PCP) a company or organization that provides primary care

primary 'color (CanE usually **primary 'colour**) *noun* one of the three colors, red, yellow, and blue, which can be mixed together to make all other colors

primary 'healthcare *noun* = PRIMARY CARE

primary 'industry *noun* [U, C] (*economics*) the section of industry that provides RAW MATERIALS to be made into goods, for example farming and MINING ⊃ compare SECONDARY INDUSTRY, TERTIARY INDUSTRY

primary 'school *noun* (*old-fashioned*) = ELEMENTARY SCHOOL ⊃ compare SECONDARY SCHOOL

primary 'source *noun* a document, etc. that contains information obtained by research or observation, not taken from other books, etc. ⊃ compare SECONDARY SOURCE

primary 'stress *noun* [C, U] (*phonetics*) the strongest stress that is put on a syllable in a word or a phrase when it is spoken ⊃ compare SECONDARY STRESS

pri·mate *noun* **1** /ˈpraɪmeɪt/ any animal that belongs to the group of MAMMALS that includes humans, APES, and MONKEYS **2** /ˈpraɪmət/ ; /ˈpraɪmeɪt/ an ARCHBISHOP (= a priest of very high rank in the Christian Church): *the Primate of Canada*

prime **AWL** /praɪm/ *adj., noun, verb*

● *adj.* [only before noun] **1** main; most important; basic: *My prime concern is to protect my property.* ◆ *Winning is not the prime objective in this sport.* ◆ *The care of the environment is of prime importance.* ◆ *He's the police's **prime suspect** in this case.* ⊃ thesaurus box at MAIN **2** of the best quality; excellent: *prime (cuts of) beef* ◆ *The store has a prime position in the mall.* **3** a **prime example** of something is one that is typical of it: *The building is a prime example of 1960s architecture.* **4** most likely to be chosen for something; most suitable: *The house is isolated and a prime target for burglars.* ◆ *He's a prime candidate for promotion.*

● *noun* [sing.] the time in your life when you are strongest or most successful: *a young woman in her prime* ◆ *He was barely 30 and **in the prime of (his) life**.* ◆ *These flowers are long past their prime.*

● *verb* **1** to prepare someone for a situation so that they know what to do, especially by giving them special information **SYN** BRIEF: **~ sb (with sth)** *They had been primed with good advice.* ◆ **~ sb (for sth)** *She was ready and primed for action.* ◆ **~ sb to do sth** *He had primed his friends to give the journalists as little information as possible.* **2 ~ sth** to make something ready for use or action: *The bomb was primed, ready to explode.* **3 ~ sth** to prepare wood, metal, etc. for painting by covering it with a special paint that helps the next layer of paint to stay on **IDM prime the pump** to encourage the growth of a new or weak business or industry by putting money into it

prime 'minister 🔑 (also Prime 'Minister) *noun* (*abbr.* PM)

the main minister and leader of the government in some countries

prime 'mover *noun* a person or thing that starts something and has an important influence on its development

prime 'number *noun* (*mathematics*) a number that can be divided exactly only by itself and 1, for example 7, 17, and 41

prim·er[1] /ˈpraɪmər/ *noun* [U, C] a type of paint that is put on wood, metal, etc. before it is painted to help the paint to stay on the surface

prim·er[2] /ˈprɪmər/ *noun* **1** a book that contains basic instructions: *The President doesn't need a primer on national security.* **2** (*old-fashioned*) a book for teaching children how to read, or containing basic facts about a school subject

prime 'rate *noun* the lowest rate of interest at which business customers can borrow money from banks

prime 'rib *noun* [U] a piece of BEEF that is cut from the RIB section of the animal

prime 'time *noun* [U] the time when the greatest number of people are watching television or listening to the radio: *the most popular show on prime-time television*

pri·me·val /praɪˈmiːvl/ *adj.* [usually before noun] **1** from the earliest period of the history of the world; very ancient: *primeval forests* **2** (*formal*) (of a feeling or a desire) very

t tea	ṭ butter	d did	k cat	ɡ got	tʃ chin	dʒ June	f fall

strong and not based on reason, as if from the earliest period of human life: *primeval urges*

prim·i·tive /ˈprɪmətɪv/ *adj., noun*

● *adj.* **1** [usually before noun] belonging to a very simple society with no industry, etc.: *primitive tribes* ◆ *primitive beliefs* **2** [usually before noun] belonging to an early stage in the development of humans or animals: *primitive man* **3** very simple and old-fashioned, especially when something is also not convenient and comfortable **SYN** CRUDE: *The methods of communication used during the war were primitive by today's standards.* ◆ *The facilities on the campsite were very primitive.* **4** [usually before noun] (of a feeling or a desire) very strong and not based on reason, as if from the earliest period of human life: *a primitive instinct* ▶ **prim·i·tive·ly** *adv.* **prim·i·tive·ness** *noun* [U]

● *noun* **1** an artist of the period before the Renaissance; an example of work from this period **2** an artist who paints in a very simple style like a child; an example of the work of such an artist

prim·i·tiv·ism /ˈprɪmətɪˌvɪzəm/ *noun* [U] a belief that simple forms and ideas are the most valuable, expressed as a philosophy or in art or literature

pri·mo·gen·i·ture /ˌpraɪmoʊˈdʒenətʃər; -ˌtʃʊr/ *noun* [U] **1** (*formal*) the fact of being the first child born in a family **2** (*law*) the system in which the oldest son in a family receives all the property when his father dies

pri·mor·di·al /praɪˈmɔrdiəl/ *adj.* [usually before noun] (*formal*) **1** existing at or from the beginning of the world **SYN** PRIMEVAL **2** (of a feeling or a desire) very basic **SYN** PRIMORDIAL: *primordial impulses*

primp /prɪmp/ *verb* [I, T] **~ (sth/yourself)** (often *disapproving*) to make yourself look attractive by arranging your hair, putting on makeup, etc.

prim·rose /ˈprɪmroʊz/ *noun* **1** [C] a small wild plant that produces pale yellow flowers in spring ⊃ picture at PLANT **2** (also ˌprimrose ˈyellow) [U] a pale yellow color ▶ **prim·rose** (also ˌprimrose ˈyellow) *adj.* **IDM** **the primrose path** (*literary*) an easy life that is full of pleasure but that causes you harm in the end

Pri·mus™ /ˈpraɪməs/ (also **ˈPrimus ˌstove**) *noun* a small stove that you can move around that burns oil. It is used especially by people who are camping.

prince 🔑 /prɪns/ *noun*

1 a male member of a royal family who is not king, especially the son or grandson of the king or queen: *the royal princes* ◆ *the Prince of Wales* **2** the male ruler of a small country or state that has a royal family; a male member of this family, especially the son or grandson of the ruler: *Prince Albert of Monaco* **3** (in some European countries) a NOBLEMAN **4** **~ of/among sth** (*literary*) a man who is thought to be one of the best in a particular field: *the prince of comedy*

ˌPrince ˈCharming *noun* [sing.] (usually *humorous*) a man who seems to be a perfect boyfriend or husband because he is very attractive, kind, etc. **ORIGIN** From the hero of some European fairy tales, for example *Cinderella* and *Sleeping Beauty*.

ˌprince ˈconsort *noun* a title sometimes given to the husband of a queen, who is himself a prince: *Prince Albert, the Prince Consort*

prince·ling /ˈprɪnslɪŋ/ *noun* (usually *disapproving*) a prince who rules a small or unimportant country

prince·ly /ˈprɪnsli/ *adj.* [usually before noun] **1** (usually *ironic*) if you say that an amount of money is **princely**, you are usually saying the opposite, meaning that it is not very large: *I bought a bike for the princely sum of $20!* **2** (*old-fashioned, formal*) very grand; generous: *princely buildings* ◆ *a princely gift* **3** connected with a prince; like a prince

the ˌPrince of ˈDarkness *noun* a name for the DEVIL

the ˌPrince of ˈPeace *noun* a name for Jesus Christ

prin·cess 🔑 /ˈprɪnsəs; -sɛs/ *noun*

1 a female member of a royal family who is not a queen, especially the daughter or granddaughter of the king or queen: *the royal princesses* ◆ *Princess Anne* **2** the wife of a prince: *the Princess of Wales* **3** (*disapproving*) a young woman who has always been given everything that she wants, and who thinks that she is better than other people

prin·ci·pal 🔑 **AWL** /ˈprɪnsəpl/ *adj., noun*

● *adj.* [only before noun] most important; main: *The principal reason for this omission is lack of time.* ◆ *New roads will link the principal cities of the area.* ⊃ thesaurus box at MAIN

● *noun* **1** a teacher who is in charge of a school: *Principal Ray Smith* **2** [usually sing.] (*finance*) an amount of money that you lend to someone or invest to earn interest **3** the person who has the most important part in a play, an OPERA, etc. **4** (*technical*) a person that you are representing, especially in business or law **5** the most important person in a company or organization

prin·ci·pal·i·ty /ˌprɪnsəˈpæləti/ *noun* (*pl.* **prin·ci·pal·i·ties**) a country that is ruled by a prince: *the principality of Monaco*

prin·ci·pally **AWL** /ˈprɪnsəpli/ *adv.* mainly **SYN** CHIEFLY: *The book is aimed principally at beginners.* ◆ *No new power stations have been built, principally because of the cost.*

ˌprincipal ˈparts *noun* [pl.] (*grammar*) the forms of a verb from which all the other forms can be made. In English these are the infinitive (for example *swim*), the past tense (*swam*), and the past participle (*swum*).

prin·ci·ple 🔑 /ˈprɪnsəpl/ *noun*

1 [C, usually pl., U] a moral rule or a strong belief that influences your actions: *He has high moral principles.* ◆ *I refuse to lie about it; it's against my principles.* ◆ *Stick to your principles and tell him you won't do it.* ◆ *She refuses to allow her family to help her as a matter of principle.* ◆ *He doesn't invest in the arms industry on principle.* **2** [C] a law, a rule, or a theory that something is based on: *the principles and practice of writing reports* ◆ *The principle behind it is very simple.* ◆ *There are three fundamental principles of teamwork.* ◆ *Discussing all these details will get us nowhere; we must get back to first principles* (= the most basic rules). **3** [C] a belief that is accepted as a reason for acting or thinking in a particular way: *the principle that free education should be available for all children* **4** [sing.] a general or scientific law that explains how something works or why something happens: *the principle that heat rises*

IDM **in principle 1** if something can be done **in principle**, there is no good reason why it should not be done, although it has not yet been done and there may be some difficulties: *In principle there is nothing that a human can do that a machine might not be able to do one day.* **2** in general but not in detail: *They have agreed to the proposal in principle, but we still have to negotiate the terms.*

prin·ci·pled **AWL** /ˈprɪnsəpld/ *adj.* **1** having strong beliefs about what is right and wrong; based on strong beliefs: *a principled woman* ◆ *to take a principled stand against abortion* **ANT** UNPRINCIPLED **2** based on rules or truths: *a principled approach to language teaching*

print 🔑 /prɪnt/ *verb, noun*

● *verb*
▷ **LETTERS/PICTURES 1** [T, I] **~ (sth)** to produce letters, pictures, etc. on paper using a machine that puts ink on the surface: *Do you want your address printed at the top of the letter?* ◆ *I'm printing a copy of the document for you.* ◆ *Each card is printed with a different message.* ◆ (*computing*) *Click on the icon when you want to print.*
▷ **BOOKS/NEWSPAPERS 2** [T] **~ sth** to produce books, newspapers, etc. by printing them in large quantities: *They printed 30,000 copies of the book.*
▷ **PUBLISH 3** [T] **~ sth** to publish something in printed form: *The photo was printed in all the national newspapers.*
▷ **PHOTOGRAPH 4** [T] **~ sth** to produce a photograph from film or a digital file: *I'm having the pictures developed and printed.*

> WRITE **5** [I, T] to write without joining the letters together: *In some countries children learn to print when they first go to school.* ◆ **~ sth** *Print your name and address clearly in the space provided.*
> MAKE MARK **6** [T] **~ sth (in/on sth)** to make a mark on a soft surface by pressing: *The tracks of the large animal were clearly printed in the sand.* ◆ (*figurative*) *The memory of that day was indelibly printed on his brain.*
> MAKE DESIGN **7** [T] to make a design on a surface or cloth by pressing a surface that has been colored with ink or DYE against it: *They had printed their own design on the T-shirt.*
  IDM **the printed word/page** what is published in books, newspapers, etc.: *the power of the printed word* ◆ more at LICENSE *n.*, WORTH *adj.*
  PHR V ,print sth↔'out to produce a document or information from a computer in printed form ◆ related noun PRINTOUT

● **noun**
> LETTERS/NUMBERS **1** [U] letters, words, numbers, etc. that have been printed onto paper: *in large/small/bold print* ◆ *The print quality of the new laser printer is superb.* ◆ see also THE SMALL PRINT
> NEWSPAPERS/BOOKS **2** [U] used to refer to the business of producing newspapers, magazines, and books: *the print media* ◆ *print unions*
> MARK **3** [C, usually pl.] a mark left by your finger, foot, etc. on the surface of something: *His prints were found on the gun.* ◆ see also FINGERPRINT, FOOTPRINT
> PICTURE **4** [C] a picture that is cut into wood or metal then covered with ink and printed onto paper; a picture that is copied from a painting using photography: *a framed set of prints* ◆ thesaurus box at PICTURE ◆ collocations at ART
> PHOTOGRAPH **5** [C] a photograph produced from film: *How many sets of prints would you like?* ◆ *a color print* ◆ thesaurus box at PHOTOGRAPH ◆ see also BLUEPRINT
> CLOTH **6** [U, C] cotton cloth that has a pattern printed on it; this pattern: *a cotton dress* ◆ *a floral print*
  IDM **get into print** to be published: *By the time this gets into print, they'll already have left the country.* **in print** **1** (of a book) still available from the company that publishes it **2** (of a person's work) printed in a book, newspaper, etc.: *It was the first time he had seen his name in print.* **out of print** (of a book) no longer available from the company that publishes it

print·a·ble /'prɪntəbl/ *adj.* (usually used with a negative) suitable to be repeated in writing and read by people: *His comment when he heard the news was not printable* (= was very offensive). **ANT** UNPRINTABLE

,printed 'circuit *noun* a CIRCUIT for electricity that uses thin strips of metal instead of wires to carry the current

print·er 🔍 /'prɪntər/ *noun*
  1 a machine for printing text on paper, especially one connected to a computer: *a color/laser printer* ◆ picture at COMPUTER **2** a person or a company whose job is printing books, etc.

print·ing /'prɪntɪŋ/ *noun* **1** [U] the act of producing letters, pictures, patterns, etc. on something by pressing a surface covered with ink against it: *the invention of printing* ◆ *the printing trade* ◆ *color printing* **2** [C] the act of printing a number of copies of a book at one time: *The book is in its sixth printing.* **3** [U] a type of writing when you write all the letters separately and do not join them together

'printing ,press *noun* a machine that produces books, newspapers, etc. by pressing a surface covered in ink onto paper

print·mak·er /'prɪnt,meɪkər/ *noun* an artist who prints pictures or designs

,print on de'mand *noun* (*abbr.* POD) [U] a system of printing books only when a customer wants one: *The titles are available through print on demand.* ◆ *This is a print-on-demand title.*

print·out /'prɪntaʊt/ *noun* [U, C] a page or set of pages containing information in printed form from a computer: *a*

printout of text downloaded from the Internet ◆ compare READOUT

'print run *noun* (*technical*) the number of copies of a book, magazine, etc. printed at one time

pri·on /'priɒn/ *noun* (*biology*) a very small unit of PROTEIN that is believed to be the cause of brain diseases such as BSE, CJD, and SCRAPIE

pri·or 🔍 **AWL** /'praɪər/ *adj.*, *noun*
● **adj.** [only before noun] **1** happening or existing before something else or before a particular time: *Although not essential, some **prior knowledge** of statistics is desirable.* ◆ *This information must not be disclosed without **prior written consent**.* ◆ *Visits are by **prior arrangement**.* ◆ *Please give us **prior notice** if you need to check in early.* ◆ *She will be unable to attend because of a **prior engagement**.* **2** already existing and therefore more important: *They have a **prior claim** to the property.* **3** 'prior to (*formal*) before something: *during the week prior to the meeting*
● **noun** (feminine pri·or·ess /'praɪərəs/) **1** a person who is in charge of a group of MONKS or NUNS living in a PRIORY **2** (in an ABBEY) a person next in rank below an ABBOT or ABBESS

priori ◆ A PRIORI

pri·or·i·tize **AWL** /praɪ'ɔrə,taɪz; -'ar-/ *verb* **1** [T, I] **~ (sth)** to put tasks, problems, etc. in order of importance, so that you can deal with the most important first: *You should make a list of all the jobs you have to do and prioritize them.* **2** [T] **~ sth** (*formal*) to treat something as being more important than other things: *The organization was formed to prioritize the needs of older people.* ▶ **pri·or·i·ti·za·tion** **AWL** /praɪ,ɔrətə-'zeɪʃn; -,arə-/ *noun* [U]

pri·or·i·ty 🔍 **AWL** /praɪ'ɔrəti; -'ar-/ *noun* (*pl.* pri·or·i·ties)
  1 [C] something that you think is more important than other things and should be dealt with first: *a high/low priority* ◆ *Education is a **top priority**.* ◆ *Our first priority is to improve standards.* ◆ *Financial security was high on his **list of priorities**.* ◆ *You need to **get your priorities right/straight*** (= decide what is important to you). **2** [U] **~ (over sth)** the most important place among various things that have to be done or among a group of people **SYN** PRECEDENCE: *Club members will be **given priority**.* ◆ *The search for a new vaccine will **take priority over** all other medical research.* ◆ *Priority cases, such as homeless families, get dealt with first.*

pri·o·ry /'praɪəri/ *noun* (*pl.* pri·o·ries) a building where a community of MONKS or NUNS lives, that is smaller and less important than an ABBEY

prism /'prɪzəm/ *noun* **1** (*geometry*) a solid figure with ends that are parallel and of the same size and shape, and with sides whose opposite edges are equal and parallel ◆ picture at SHAPE **2** a transparent glass or plastic object, often with ends in the shape of a triangle, which separates light that passes through it into the colors of the RAINBOW

pris·mat·ic /prɪz'mætɪk/ *adj.* **1** (*technical*) using or containing a prism; in the shape of a prism **2** (*literary*) (of colors) formed by a prism; very bright and clear

pris·on 🔍 /'prɪzn/ *noun*
  1 [C, U] a building where people are kept as a punishment for a crime they have committed, or while they are waiting for trial **SYN** JAIL: *He was **sent to prison** for five years.* ◆ *She is **in prison**, awaiting trial.* ◆ *to be **released from prison*** ◆ *a **maximum-security prison*** ◆ *the **prison population*** (= the total number of prisoners in a country) ◆ *the problem of overcrowding in prisons* ◆ *Ten prison officers and three inmates needed hospital treatment following the riot.* ◆ collocations at JUSTICE ◆ note at SCHOOL **2** [U] the system of keeping people in prisons: *the **prison system*** ◆ *The government insists that "prison works" and plans to introduce a tougher sentencing policy for people convicted of violent crime.* **3** [C] a place or situation from which someone cannot escape: *His hospital room had become a prison.*

h **hat**   m **man**   n **no**   ŋ **sing**   l **leg**   r **red**   y **yes**   w **wet**

'prison ,camp noun a guarded camp where prisoners, especially prisoners of war or political prisoners, are kept

pris·on·er ✎ /'prɪzənər/ noun
1 a person who is kept in prison as a punishment, or while they are waiting for trial: *The number of prisoners serving life sentences has fallen.* ◆ *They are demanding the release of all political prisoners.* **2** a person who has been captured, for example by an enemy, and is being kept somewhere: *He was taken prisoner by rebel soldiers.* ◆ *They are holding her prisoner and demanding a large ransom.* ◆ (*figurative*) *She is afraid to go out and has become a virtual prisoner in her own home.*

,prisoner of 'conscience noun (*pl.* prisoners of conscience) a person who is kept in prison because of their political or religious beliefs

,prisoner of 'war noun (*pl.* prisoners of war) (*abbr.* POW) a person, usually a member of the armed forces, who is captured by the enemy during a war and kept in a prison camp until the war has finished

pris·sy /'prɪsi/ adj. (*informal*, *disapproving*) too careful to always behave correctly and appearing easily shocked by offensive behavior, etc. **SYN** PRUDISH

pris·tine /'prɪstin; prɪ'stin/ adj. **1** fresh and clean, as if new **SYN** IMMACULATE: *The car is in pristine condition.* **2** not developed or changed in any way; left in its original condition **SYN** UNSPOILED: *pristine, pollution-free beaches*

prith·ee /'prɪði/ exclamation (*old use*) used when asking someone politely to do something

pri·va·cy /'praɪvəsi/ noun [U] **1** the state of being alone and not watched or disturbed by other people: *She was longing for some peace and privacy.* ◆ *I value my privacy.* ◆ *He read the letter later in the privacy of his own room.* **2** the state of being free from the attention of the public: *freedom of speech and the right to privacy*

pri·vate ✎ /'praɪvət/ adj., noun
● **adj.**
▷**NOT PUBLIC 1** [usually before noun] belonging to or for the use of a particular person or group; not for public use: *The sign said, "Private property. Keep out."* ◆ *Those are my father's private papers.* ◆ *The hotel has 110 bedrooms, all with private bathrooms.*
▷**CONVERSATION/MEETING 2** intended for or involving a particular person or group of people, not for people in general or for others to know about: *a private conversation* ◆ *They were sharing a private joke.* ◆ *Senior defense officials held private talks.*
▷**FEELINGS/INFORMATION 3** that you do not want other people to know about **SYN** SECRET: *her private thoughts and feelings*
▷**NOT OWNED/RUN BY GOVERNMENT 4** [usually before noun] owned or managed by an individual person or independent company rather than by the government: *private industries/hospitals* ◆ *a program to return many of the state-owned companies to private ownership* **ANT** PUBLIC
▷**NOT WORK 5** [usually before noun] not connected with your work or official position: *a politician's private life*
▷**QUIET 6** where you are not likely to be disturbed; quiet: *Let's go somewhere a bit more private.* **ANT** PUBLIC
▷**PERSON 7** [usually before noun] not wanting to share thoughts and feelings with other people: *He's a very private person.*
▷**CLASSES 8** [usually before noun] given by a teacher, etc. to one person or a small group of people for payment: *She gives private English classes on weekends.*
▷**MONEY 9** that you receive from property or other sources but do not have to earn: *He has a private income.*

▶ **pri·vate·ly** adv.: *Can we speak privately?* ◆ *In public he supported the official policy, but privately he was sure it would fail.* ◆ *a privately owned company* ◆ *Their children were educated privately.* ◆ *She smiled, but privately she was furious.*
● **noun 1** [C] (*abbr.* Pvt.) a soldier of the lowest rank in the

army: *Private (John) Smith* **2** **privates** [pl.] (*informal*) = PRIVATE PARTS
IDM **in private** with no one else present: *Is there somewhere we can discuss this in private?* ➔ compare IN PUBLIC

,private de'tective (also ,private in'vestigator, *informal* ,private 'eye) (also) noun a DETECTIVE who is not in the police, but who can be employed to find out information, find a missing person, follow someone, etc.

,private 'enterprise noun [U] the economic system in which industry or business is owned by independent companies or individual people and is not controlled by the government ➔ compare FREE ENTERPRISE

,private 'equity noun [U] (*finance*) investment made in a company, usually a small one, whose shares are not bought and sold by the public

pri·va·teer /,praɪvə'tɪr/ noun a ship used in the past for attacking and stealing from other ships

,private 'parts (also *informal* **pri·vates**) noun [pl.] a polite way of referring to the sexual organs without saying their names

,private 'practice noun [U] (of a profession) the fact of working on your own or in a small independent company rather than as an employee of the government or a large company: *He is a lawyer in private practice.*

'private ,school noun a school that receives no money from the government and where the education of the students is paid for by their parents ➔ compare PUBLIC SCHOOL

,private 'secretary noun a secretary whose job is to deal with the more important and personal affairs of a person in business, or of a public figure

the ,private 'sector noun [sing.] the part of the economy of a country that is not under the direct control of the government ➔ collocations at ECONOMY ➔ compare THE PUBLIC SECTOR

,private 'viewing noun an occasion when a few people are invited to look at an exhibition of paintings, a movie, etc. before the public is allowed to see it

pri·va·tion /praɪ'veɪʃn/ noun [C, usually pl., U] (*formal*) a lack of the basic things that people need for living **SYN** HARDSHIP: *the privations of poverty* ◆ *They endured years of suffering and privation.*

pri·va·tize /'praɪvə,taɪz/ verb ~ sth to sell a business or an industry so that it is no longer owned by the government **SYN** DENATIONALIZE **ANT** NATIONALIZE ▶ **pri·va·ti·za·tion** /,praɪvətə'zeɪʃn/ noun [U]: *There were fears that privatization would lead to job losses.*

priv·et /'prɪvət/ noun [U] a bush with small dark green leaves that remain on the bush and stay green all year, often used for HEDGES: *a privet hedge*

priv·i·lege /'prɪvəlɪdʒ; 'prɪvlɪdʒ/ noun, verb
● **noun 1** [C] a special right or advantage that a particular person or group of people has: *Education should be a universal right and not a privilege.* ◆ *You can enjoy all the benefits and privileges of club membership.* **2** [U] (*disapproving*) the rights and advantages that rich and powerful people in a society have: *As a member of the nobility, his life had been one of wealth and privilege.* **3** [sing.] something that you are proud and lucky to have the opportunity to do **SYN** HONOR: *I hope to have the privilege of working with them again.* ◆ *It was a great privilege to hear her sing.* ➔ thesaurus box at PLEASURE **4** [C, U] (*technical*) a special right to do or say things without being punished: *Congressional privilege* (= the special right of members of Congress to say particular things without risking legal action)
● **verb** ~ sb/sth (*formal*) to give someone or something special rights or advantages that others do not have **SYN** FAVOR: *education policies that privilege the children of wealthy parents*

priv·i·leged /'prɪvəlɪdʒd; 'prɪvlɪdʒd/ adj. **1** (sometimes *disapproving*) having special rights or advantages that most people do not have: *Those in authority were in a privileged* position. ◆ *She comes from a privileged background.* ◆ *In those days, only a privileged few had the vote.* **2** [not before noun] having an opportunity to do something that makes you feel proud **SYN** HONOR: *We are privileged to welcome you as our speaker this evening.* **3** (*law*) (of information) known only to a few people and legally protected so that it does not have to be made public **SYN** CONFIDENTIAL

priv·y /ˈprɪvi/ *adj., noun*
● *adj.* (*formal*) **~ to sth** allowed to know about something secret: *She was not privy to any information contained in the letters.*
● *noun* (*pl.* **pri·vies**) (*old-fashioned*) a toilet, especially an outdoor one

prize 🔑 /praɪz/ *noun, adj., verb*
● *noun* **1** an award that is given to a person who wins a competition, race, etc. or who does very good work: *She was awarded the Nobel Peace prize.* ◆ *He won first prize in the woodwind section.* ◆ *There are no prizes for guessing* (= it is very easy to guess) *who she was with.* ◆ *I won $500 in prize money.* ◆ *Win a car in our grand prize draw!* ⊃ see also CONSOLATION PRIZE, DOOR PRIZE **2** something very important or valuable that is difficult to achieve or obtain: *World peace is the greatest prize of all.*
● *adj.* [only before noun] **1** (especially of an animal, a flower, or a vegetable) good enough to win a prize in a competition: *prize cattle* **2** being a very good example of its kind: *a prize student* ◆ *a prize catch* (= a big fish).
● *verb* **1** [usually passive] to value something highly **SYN** TREASURE: **~ sth** *an era when honesty was prized above all other virtues* ◆ **~ sth for sth** *Oil of cedarwood is highly prized for its use in perfumery.* **2** = PRY

prized /praɪzd/ *adj.* [only before noun] very valuable to someone: *I lost some of my most prized possessions in the fire.*

prize·fight /ˈpraɪzfaɪt/ *noun* a BOXING competition that is fought for money ▶ **prize·fight·er** *noun* **prize·fight·ing** *noun* [U]

prize·win·ner /ˈpraɪzˌwɪnər/ *noun* a person who has won a prize ▶ **prize·win·ning** *adj.* [only before noun]: *a prizewinning story*

pro /proʊ/ *noun, adj., prep.*
● *noun* (*pl.* **pros**) (*informal*) a person who works as a professional, especially in a sport: *a golf pro* ◆ *a young boxer who's just turned pro* ◆ *He handled the situation like an old pro* (= someone who has a lot of experience).
    IDM **the pros and cons** the advantages and disadvantages of something: *We weighed up the pros and cons.*
● *adj.* [only before noun] (in sports) professional: *a pro wrestler* ◆ *pro football*
● *prep.* (*informal*) if someone is **pro** someone or something, they are in favor of or support that person or thing: *He has always been pro the environment.* ⊃ compare ANTI

pro- /proʊ/ *prefix* (in adjectives) in favor of; supporting: *pro-democracy* ⊃ compare ANTI-

pro·ac·tive /proʊˈæktɪv/ *adj.* (of a person or policy) controlling a situation by making things happen rather than waiting for things to happen and then reacting to them ⊃ compare REACTIVE ▶ **pro·ac·tive·ly** *adv.*

pro-am /ˌproʊ ˈæm/ *adj.* [only before noun] (in sports) involving both professional and AMATEUR players: *a pro-am golf tournament* ▶ **pro-am** *noun: to play in a pro-am*

prob /prɑb/ *noun* (*informal*) a problem
    IDM **no prob** (also **no probs**) (*informal*) used to mean "there is no problem": *I can let you have it by next week. No prob.*

prob·a·bi·lis·tic /ˌprɑbəbəˈlɪstɪk/ *adj.* [usually before noun] (*technical*) (of methods, arguments, etc.) based on the idea that, as we cannot be certain about things, we can base our beliefs or actions on what is likely

prob·a·bil·i·ty /ˌprɑbəˈbɪləti/ *noun* (*pl.* **prob·a·bil·i·ties**) **1** [U, C] how likely something is to happen **SYN** LIKELIHOOD: *The probability is that prices will rise rapidly.* ◆ *There seemed to be a high probability of success.* **2** [C] a thing

that is likely to happen: *A fall in interest rates is a strong probability in the present economic climate.* ◆ *It now seems a probability rather than just a possibility.* **3** [C, U] (*mathematics*) a RATIO showing the chances that a particular thing will happen: *There is a 60% probability that the population will be infected with the disease.*
    IDM **in all probability...** it is very likely that: *In all probability he failed to understand the consequences of his actions.* ⊃ more at BALANCE *n.*

prob·a·ble /ˈprɑbəbl/ *adj., noun*
● *adj.* likely to happen, to exist, or to be true: *the probable cause/explanation/outcome* ◆ *highly/quite/most probable* ◆ *It is probable that the disease has a genetic element.* ⊃ compare IMPROBABLE
● *noun* **~ (for sth)** a person or an animal that is likely to win a race or to be chosen for a team

probable ˈcause *noun* [U] (*law*) good reason to think that a crime has been committed: *You must have probable cause to arrest someone.* ◆ *The police cannot search a suspect without probable cause and a warrant*

prob·a·bly 🔑 /ˈprɑbəbli/ *adv.*
used to say that something is likely to happen or to be true: *You're probably right.* ◆ *It'll probably be OK.* ◆ *It was the best known and probably the most popular of her songs.* ◆ *"Is he going to be there?" "Probably."* ◆ *"Do we need the car?" "Probably not."* ◆ *As you probably know, I'm going to be changing jobs soon.* ◆ *The two cases are most probably connected.* ⊃ language bank at PERHAPS

pro·bate /ˈproʊbeɪt/ *noun, verb*
● *noun* [U] (*law*) the official process of proving that a WILL (= a legal document that says what is to happen to a person's property when they die) is valid
● *verb* **~ sth** (*law*) to prove that a WILL is valid

pro·ba·tion /proʊˈbeɪʃn/ *noun* [U] **1** (*law*) a system that allows a person who has committed a crime not to go to prison if they behave well and if they see an official (called a PROBATION OFFICER) regularly for a fixed period of time: *The prisoner was put on probation.* ◆ *He was given two years' probation.* **2** a time of training and testing when you start a new job to see if you are suitable for the work: *a period of probation* **3** a fixed period of time during which a student who has behaved badly or not worked hard must improve their work or their behavior ▶ **pro·ba·tion·ar·y** /proʊˈbeɪʃəˌneri/ *adj.: a probationary period* ◆ *young probationary teachers*

pro·ba·tion·er /proʊˈbeɪʃənər/ *noun* **1** a person who is new in a job and is being watched to see if they are suitable **2** a person who is seeing a PROBATION OFFICER because of having committed a crime

proˈbation ˌofficer *noun* a person whose job is to check on people who are on probation and help them

probe /proʊb/ *verb, noun*
● *verb* **1** [I, T] to ask questions in order to find out secret or hidden information about someone or something **SYN** INVESTIGATE: **~ (into sth)** *He didn't like the media probing into his past.* ◆ **~ sth** *a TV program that probed government scandals in the 1990s* ◆ **+ speech** *"Then what happened?" he probed.* **2** [T] **~ sth** to touch, examine, or look for something, especially with a long thin instrument: *The doctor probed the wound for signs of infection.* ◆ *Searchlights probed the night sky.*
● *noun* **1** **~ (into sth)** (used especially in newspapers) a thorough and careful investigation of something: *a police probe into the financial affairs of the company* **2** (also ˈspace probe) a SPACECRAFT without people on board that obtains information and sends it back to earth **3** (*technical*) a long, thin, metal tool used by doctors for examining inside the body **4** (*technical*) a small device put inside something and used by scientists to test something or record information

prob·ing /ˈproʊbɪŋ/ *adj.* **1** intended to discover the truth: *They asked a lot of probing questions.* **2** examining someone or something closely: *She looked away from his dark probing eyes.* ▶ **prob·ing** *noun: the journalist's unwanted probings*

pro·bi·ot·ic /ˌprəʊbaɪˈɒtɪk/ *adj.* [only before noun] encouraging the growth of bacteria that have a good effect on the body: *probiotic products/yogurt/cheese*

pro·bi·ty /ˈprəʊbəti/ *noun* [U] (*formal*) the quality of being completely honest: *financial probity*

prob·lem /ˈprɒbləm/ *noun, adj.*

● *noun* **1** a thing that is difficult to deal with or to understand: *big/major/serious problems ◆ health/family, etc. problems ◆ financial/practical/technical problems ◆ to address/tackle/solve a problem ◆ to fix a problem ◆ the problem of drug abuse ◆ If he chooses Mary, it's bound to cause problems. ◆ Let me know if you have any problems. ◆ Most students face the problem of supporting themselves while they are studying. ◆ The problem first arose in 2008. ◆ Unemployment is a very real problem for graduates now. ◆ It's a nice table. The only problem is (that) it's too big for our room. ◆ Stop worrying about their marriage—it isn't your problem. ◆ There's no history of heart problems* (= disease connected with the heart) *in our family.* **2** a question that can be answered by using logical thought or mathematics: *mathematical problems ◆ to find the answer to the problem*

IDM **have a problem with sth** to disagree with or object to something: *I have no problem with you working at home tomorrow. ◆ (informal) We are going to do this my way. Do you have a problem with that?* (= showing that you are impatient with the person to whom you are speaking) **no problem** (*informal*) **1** (also **not a problem**) used to show that you are happy to help someone or that something will be easy to do: *"Can I pay by credit card?" "Yes, no problem."* **2** used after someone has thanked you or said they are sorry for something: *"Thanks for the ride." "No problem."* **it's/that's not my problem** (*informal*) used to show that you do not care about someone else's difficulties **that's her/his/their/your problem** (*informal*) used to show that you think a person should deal with their own difficulties **what's your problem?** (*informal*) used to show that you think someone is being unreasonable: *What's your problem? I only asked if you could help me for ten minutes.*

● *adj.* [only before noun] causing problems for other people: *She was a problem child, always in trouble.*

prob·lem·at·ic /ˌprɒbləˈmætɪk/ (also *less frequent* **prob·lem·at·i·cal** /ˌprɒbləˈmætɪkl/) *adj.* difficult to deal with or to understand; full of problems; not certain to be successful **ANT** UNPROBLEMATIC

'problem-ˌsolving *noun* [U] the act of finding ways of dealing with problems

pro bono /ˌprəʊ ˈbəʊnəʊ/ *adj.* [only before noun] (from *Latin*) (especially of legal work) done without asking for payment

pro·bos·cis /prəˈbɒsɪs; -ˈbɒskəs/ *noun* (*pl.* **pro·bos·ces** /-ˈbɒsiz/ or **pro·bos·cis·es**) (*technical*) **1** the long FLEXIBLE nose of some animals, such as an ELEPHANT **2** the long thin mouth, like a tube, of some insects **3** (*humorous*) a large human nose

pro·caine /ˈprəʊkeɪn/ (also **no·vo·caine**) *noun* [U] (*medical*) a substance used to stop someone from feeling pain in a particular part of their body, especially by a dentist

pro·ce·dure /prəˈsiːdʒər/ *noun*
1 [C, U] ~ **(for sth)** a way of doing something, especially the usual or correct way: *maintenance procedures ◆ emergency/safety/disciplinary procedures ◆ to follow normal/standard/accepted procedure ◆ Making a complaint is quite a simple procedure.* **2** [U] the official or formal order or way of doing something, especially in business, law, or politics: *court/legal/parliamentary procedure* **3** [C] (*medical*) a medical operation: *to perform a routine surgical procedure* ▸ **pro·ce·dur·al** /prəˈsiːdʒərəl/ *adj.* (*formal*): *procedural rules*

pro·ceed /prəˈsiːd; prəʊ-/ *verb*
1 [I] ~ **(with sth)** to continue doing something that has already been started; to continue being done: *We're not sure whether we still want to proceed with the sale. ◆ Work is proceeding slowly.* **2** [I] ~ **to do sth** to do something next,

after having done something else first **SYN** GO ON: *He outlined his plans and then proceeded to explain them in more detail. ◆ (humorous) Having said she wasn't hungry, she then proceeded to order a three-course meal.* **3** [I] **+ adv./prep.** (*formal*) to move or travel in a particular direction: *The marchers proceeded slowly along the street. ◆ Passengers for Rome should proceed to Gate 32 for boarding.*
PHR V **pro·ceed against sb** (*law*) to start a court case against someone **pro·ceed from sth** (*formal*) to be caused by or be the result of something

pro·ceed·ing **AWL** /prəˈsiːdɪŋ; prəʊ-/ *noun* (*formal*)
1 [C, usually pl.] ~ **(against sb) (for sth)** the process of using a court to settle a disagreement or to deal with a complaint: *bankruptcy/divorce/extradition, etc. proceedings ◆ to bring legal proceedings against someone* **2** **proceedings** [pl.] an event or a series of actions: *The mayor will open the proceedings at City Hall tomorrow. ◆ We watched the proceedings from the balcony.* **3** **proceedings** [pl.] the official written report of a meeting, etc.

pro·ceeds **AWL** /ˈprəʊsiːdz/ *noun* [pl.] ~ **(of/from sth)** the money that you receive when you sell something or organize a performance, etc.; profits: *She sold her car and bought a piano with the proceeds. ◆ The proceeds of the concert will go to charity.*

LANGUAGE BANK

process
describing a process

- This diagram **illustrates the process of** paper-making. / This diagram **shows how** paper is made.
- **First/First of all**, logs are delivered to a paper mill, where the bark is removed and the wood is cut into small chips.
- **Next/Second**, the wood chips are pulped, either using chemicals or in a pulping machine.
- Pulping breaks down the internal structure of the wood and **enables/allows** the natural oils **to** be removed.
- **Once/After** the wood has been pulped, the pulp is bleached **in order to** remove impurities. / …is bleached **so that** impurities **can** be removed.
- **The next stage is to** feed the pulp into the paper machine, where it is mixed with water **and then** poured onto a wire conveyor belt.
- **As** the pulp travels along the conveyor belt, the water drains away. **This causes** the solid material **to** sink to the bottom, forming a layer of paper.
- **At this point** the new paper is still wet, **so** it is passed between large heated rollers, which press out the remaining water and **simultaneously** dry the paper. / …dry the paper **at the same time**.
- **The final stage is to** wind the paper onto large rolls. / **Finally**, the paper is wound onto large rolls.

⊃ notes at FIRST, LASTLY
⊃ Language Banks at CONCLUSION, FIRST

---

pro·cess¹ **AWL** /ˈprəʊses/ *noun, verb* ⊃ see also PROCESS²

● *noun* **1** a series of things that are done in order to achieve a particular result: *a consultation process ◆ to begin the difficult process of reforming the education system ◆ I'm afraid getting things changed will be a slow process. ◆ Coming off the drug was a long and painful* (= difficult) *process for him. ◆ Find which food you are allergic to by process of elimination. ◆ We're in the process of selling our house. ◆ I was moving some furniture and I twisted my ankle in the process* (= while I was doing it). ⊃ see also PEACE PROCESS **2** a series of things that happen, especially ones that result in natural changes: *the aging process ◆ It's a normal part of the learning process.* **3** a method of doing or making something, especially one that is used in industry: *manufacturing processes*

• **verb 1 ~ sth** to treat raw material, food, etc. in order to change it, preserve it, etc.: *Most of the food we buy is processed in some way.* ✦ *processed cheese* ✦ *a sewage processing plant* **2 ~ sth** to deal officially with a document, request, etc.: *It will take a week for your application to be processed.* **3 ~ sth** (*computing*) to perform a series of operations on data in a computer ▶ **pro·cess·ing** AWL *noun* [U]: *the food processing industry* ⊃ see also DATA PROCESSING, WORD PROCESSING

pro·cess² /prə'sɛs/ *verb* [I] **+ adv./prep.** (*formal*) to walk or move along slowly in, or as if in, a procession ⊃ see also PROCESS¹

pro·ces·sion /prə'sɛʃn/ *noun* **1** [C, U] a line of people or vehicles that move along slowly, especially as part of a ceremony; the act of moving in this way: *a funeral procession* ✦ *a torchlight procession* ✦ *The procession made its way down the hill.* ✦ *Groups of unemployed people from all over the country marched* **in procession** *to the capital.* **2** [C] a number of people who come one after the other: *A procession of waiters appeared bearing trays of food.*

pro·ces·sion·al /prə'sɛʃənl/ *adj.* [only before noun] used in a procession, especially a religious one; connected with a procession

pro·ces·sor /'prɑsɛsər/ *noun* **1** a machine or person that processes things **2** (*computing*) a part of a computer that controls all the other parts of the system **SYN** CENTRAL PROCESSING UNIT ⊃ see also FOOD PROCESSOR, MICRO-PROCESSOR, WORD PROCESSOR

¡**pro-'choice** (also **pro·choice**) /,proʊ'tʃɔɪs/ *adj.* believing that a pregnant woman should be able to choose to have an ABORTION if she wants ⊃ compare ANTICHOICE, PRO-LIFE, RIGHT-TO-LIFE

pro·claim /prə'kleɪm; proʊ-/ *verb* **1** to publicly and officially tell people about something important **SYN** DECLARE: **~ sth** *The president proclaimed a state of emergency.* ✦ **~ that...** *The charter proclaimed that all states would have their own government.* ✦ **~ sb/sth/yourself + noun** *He proclaimed himself emperor.* ✦ **~ sb/sth/yourself to be/have sth** *Steve checked the battery and proclaimed it to be dead.* ✦ **~ how, what, etc....** *The senator proclaimed how shocked he was at the news.* ✦ **+ speech** *"We will succeed," she proclaimed.* **2** (*formal*) to show something clearly; to be a sign of something: **~ sth** *This building, more than any other, proclaims the character of the town.* ✦ **~ sb/sth + noun** *His accent proclaimed him a Southerner.* ✦ **~ sb/sth to be/have sth** *His accent proclaimed him to be a Southerner.*

proc·la·ma·tion /,prɑklə'meɪʃn/ *noun* [C, U] an official statement about something important that is made to the public; the act of making an official statement

pro·cliv·i·ty /prə'klɪvəti; proʊ-/ *noun* (*pl.* **pro·cliv·i·ties**) **~ (for sth/for doing sth)** (*formal*) a natural tendency to do something or to feel something, often something bad **SYN** PROPENSITY: *his sexual/criminal proclivities* ✦ *the government's proclivity for spending money*

pro·cras·ti·nate /prə'kræstə,neɪt/ *verb* [I] (*formal, disapproving*) to delay doing something that you should do, usually because you do not want to do it ▶ **pro·cras·ti·na·tion** /prə,kræstə'neɪʃn/ *noun* [U]

pro·cre·ate /'proʊkri,eɪt/ *verb* [I, T] **~ (sth)** (*formal*) to produce children or baby animals **SYN** REPRODUCE ▶ **pro·cre·a·tion** /,proʊkri'eɪʃn/ *noun* [U]: *They believe that sex should be only for procreation.*

Pro·crus·te·an /proʊ'krʌstiən/ *adj.* (of a system, a set of rules, etc.) treating all people or things as if they are the same, without considering individual differences and in a way that is too strict and unreasonable **ORIGIN** From the Greek story of **Procrustes**, a robber who forced people to lie on a bed and made them fit it by stretching their bodies or cutting off part of their legs.

proc·tor /'prɑktər/ *noun* a person who watches people while they are taking an exam to make sure that they have everything they need, that they keep to the rules, etc. ▶ **proc·tor** *verb* [T, I] **~ (sth)**

pro·cure /prə'kyʊr; proʊ-/ *verb* **1** [T] (*formal*) to obtain something, especially with difficulty: **~ sth (for sb/sth)** *She managed to procure a ticket for the concert.* ✦ *They procured a copy of the report for us.* ✦ **~ sb sth** *They procured us a copy of the report.* **2** [T, I] **~ (sb)** to provide a PROSTITUTE for someone

pro·cure·ment /prə'kyʊrmənt; proʊ-/ *noun* [U] (*formal*) the process of obtaining supplies of something, especially for a government or an organization

prod /prɑd/ *verb, noun*
• *verb* (**-dd-**) **1** [T, I] to push someone or something with your finger or with a pointed object **SYN** POKE: **~ sb/sth (+ adv./prep.)** *She prodded him in the ribs to wake him up.* ✦ **~ at sb/sth** *He prodded at his breakfast with a fork.* **2** [T] **~ sb (into sth/into doing sth)** to try to make someone do something, especially when they are unwilling: *She finally prodded him into action.*
• *noun* **1** the act of pushing someone with your finger or with a pointed object **SYN** DIG: *She gave him a sharp prod with her umbrella.* **2** (*informal*) an act of encouraging someone or of reminding someone to do something: *If they haven't replied by next week, you'll have to call them and give them* **a prod**. **3** an instrument like a stick that is used for prodding animals

prod·ding /'prɑdɪŋ/ *noun* [U] encouragement to do something: *He needed no prodding.*

prod·i·gal /'prɑdɪgl/ *adj.* (*formal, disapproving*) too willing to spend money or waste time, energy, or materials **SYN** EXTRAVAGANT ▶ **prod·i·gal·i·ty** /,prɑdə'gæləti/ *noun* [U]
IDM **the/a prodigal (son)** a person who leaves home and wastes their money and time on a life of pleasure, but who later is sorry about this and returns home

pro·di·gious /prə'dɪdʒəs/ *adj.* [usually before noun] (*formal*) very large or powerful and causing surprise or admiration **SYN** COLOSSAL, ENORMOUS: *a prodigious achievement/memory/talent* ✦ *DVDs can store* **prodigious amounts** *of information.* ▶ **pro·di·gious·ly** *adv.*: *a prodigiously talented musician*

prod·i·gy /'prɑdədʒi/ *noun* (*pl.* **prod·i·gies**) a young person who is unusually intelligent or skillful for their age: *a child prodigy* ✦ *a musical prodigy*

pro·duce 🔑 *verb, noun*
• *verb* /prə'dus/
▷ GOODS **1 ~ sth** to make things to be sold, especially in large quantities **SYN** MANUFACTURE: *a factory that produces microchips* ⊃ see also MASS-PRODUCE ⊃ thesaurus box at MAKE, PRODUCT
▷ MAKE NATURALLY **2 ~ sth** to grow or make something as part of a natural process; to have a baby or young animal: *The region produces over 50% of the country's wheat.* ✦ *Our cat produced kittens last week.* ✦ *Her duty was to produce an heir to the throne.*
▷ CREATE WITH SKILL **3 ~ sth** to create something, especially when skill is needed: *She produced a delicious meal out of a few leftovers.*
▷ RESULT/EFFECT **4 ~ sth** to cause a particular result or effect **SYN** BRING ABOUT: *A phone call to the manager produced the result she wanted.* ✦ *The drug produces a feeling of excitement.*
▷ SHOW/BRING OUT **5 ~ sth (from/out of sth)** to show or make something appear from somewhere: *He produced a letter from his pocket.* ✦ *At the meeting the finance director produced the figures for the previous year.*
▷ PERSON **6 ~ sb** if a town, country, etc. **produces** someone with a particular skill or quality, the person comes from that town, country, etc.: *He is the greatest athlete this country has ever produced.*

WORD FAMILY
produce *verb*
producer *noun*
production *noun*
productive *adj.* (≠ unpro-ductive)
productively *adv.*
product *noun*
produce *noun*

> MOVIE/PLAY **7** ~ sth to be in charge of preparing a movie, play, etc. for the public to see: *She produced a TV series about adopted children.*

• **noun** /ˈproʊdus/ [U] things that have been made or grown, especially things connected with farming: *farm produce* ◆ *The store sells only fresh local produce.* ◆ *It says on the label "Produce of Chile."*

pro·duc·er /prəˈdusər/ noun

1 a person, a company, or a country that grows or makes food, goods, or materials: *French wine producers* ◆ *Libya is a major oil producer.* ⊃ compare CONSUMER **2** a person who is in charge of the practical and financial aspects of making a movie or a play: *Hollywood screenwriters, actors, and producers* ⊃ compare DIRECTOR **3** a person or company that arranges for someone to make a program for radio or television, or a record, CD, etc.: *an independent television producer*

prod·uct /ˈprɑdʌkt/ noun

1 [C, U] a thing that is grown or produced, usually for sale: *dairy/meat/pharmaceutical, etc. products* ◆ *investment in product development* ◆ *to launch a new product onto the market* ◆ (*business*) *We need new product to sell* (= a new range of products). ⊃ see also END PRODUCT, GROSS NATIONAL PRODUCT ⊃ collocations at BUSINESS **2** [C] a thing produced during a natural, chemical, or industrial process: *the products of the reaction* ⊃ see also BYPRODUCT, WASTE PRODUCT **3** ~ of sth a person or thing that is the result of something: *The child is the product of a broken home.* **4** [C, U] a cream, jelly, or liquid that you put on your hair or skin to make it look better: *This product can be used on wet or dry hair.* **5** (*mathematics*) a quantity obtained by multiplying one number by another: *The product of 21 and 16 is 336.*

THESAURUS

product

goods ◆ commodity ◆ merchandise ◆ produce

These are all words for things that are produced to be sold.

product a thing that is produced or grown, usually to be sold: *to create/develop/launch a new product*

goods things that are produced to be sold: *cotton/leather goods* ◆ *electrical/sporting goods*

commodity (*economics*) a product or raw material that can be bought and sold, especially between countries: *rice, flour, and other basic commodities*

merchandise goods that are bought or sold; things that you can buy that are connected with or that advertise a particular event or organization: *official Olympic merchandise*

GOODS OR MERCHANDISE?

Choose **goods** if the emphasis is on what the product is made of or what it is for: *leather/household goods.* Choose **merchandise** if the emphasis is less on the product itself and more on its brand or the fact of buying/selling it.

produce things that have been grown or made, especially things connected with farming: *We sell only fresh local produce.*

PATTERNS

- **consumer/industrial** products/goods/commodities
- **household** products/goods
- **farm** products/produce
- **luxury** products/goods/commodities
- to **sell/market** a product/goods/a commodity/merchandise/produce
- to **export** a product/goods/a commodity/merchandise
- to **buy/purchase** a product/goods/a commodity/merchandise/produce

---

pro·duc·tion /prəˈdʌkʃn/ noun

1 [U] the process of growing or making food, goods, or materials, especially in large quantities: *wheat/oil/car, etc. production* ◆ *land available for food production* ◆ *The new model will be in production by the end of the year.* ◆ *Production of the new aircraft will start next year.* ◆ *The car went out of production in 2007.* ◆ *production costs* ◆ *a production process* **2** [U] the quantity of goods that is produced: *a decline/an increase in production* ◆ *It is important not to let production levels fall.* **3** [U] the act or process of making something naturally: *drugs to stimulate the body's production of hormones* **4** [C, U] a movie, a play, or a broadcast that is prepared for the public; the act of preparing a movie or a play, etc.: *a new production of "King Lear"* ◆ *He wants a career in movie production.*

IDM **on production of sth** (*formal*) when you show something: *Discounts only on production of your student ID card.*

pro·duc·tion line (also as·sem·bly line) *noun* a line of workers and machines in a factory that a product passes along, and where parts are made, put together, or checked at each stage until the product is finished: *Cars are checked as they come off the production line.*

pro·duc·tion num·ber *noun* a scene in a musical play or a movie where a lot of people sing and dance

pro·duc·tive /prəˈdʌktɪv/ *adj.* **1** making goods or growing crops, especially in large quantities: *highly productive farming land* ◆ *productive workers* ANT UNPRODUCTIVE **2** doing or achieving a lot SYN FRUITFUL: *a productive meeting* ◆ *My time spent in the library was very productive.* ⊃ compare COUNTERPRODUCTIVE **3** ~ of sth (*formal*) resulting in something or causing something: *a play productive of the strongest emotions* ▶ **pro·duc·tive·ly** *adv.*: *to use land more productively* ◆ *It's important to spend your time productively.*

pro·duc·tiv·i·ty /ˌproʊdʌkˈtɪvəti; ˌprɑ-/ *noun* [U] the rate at which a worker, a company, or a country produces goods, and the amount produced, compared with how much time, work, and money is needed to produce them: *high/improved/increased productivity* ◆ *Pay rates depend on levels of productivity.*

product place·ment *noun* [U, C] the use of particular products in movies, videos, or television programs in order to advertise them

Prof. *abbr.* (in writing) Professor: *Prof. Mike Harrison*

prof /prɑf/ *noun* (*informal*) = PROFESSOR: *a college prof*

pro·fane /proʊˈfeɪn; prə-/ *adj., verb*

• *adj.* **1** (*formal*) having or showing a lack of respect for God or holy things: *profane language* **2** (*technical*) not connected with religion or holy things SYN SECULAR: *songs of sacred and profane love*

• *verb* ~ sth (*formal*) to treat something holy with a lack of respect

pro·fan·i·ty /proʊˈfænəti; prə-/ *noun* (*pl.* **pro·fan·i·ties**) (*formal*) **1** [U] behavior that shows a lack of respect for God or holy things **2** [C, usually pl.] SWEAR WORDS, or religious words used in a way that shows a lack of respect for God or holy things: *He uttered a stream of profanities.*

pro·fess /prəˈfɛs/ *verb* (*formal*) **1** to claim that something is true or correct, especially when it is not: ~ sth *She still professes her innocence.* ◆ ~ to be/have sth *I don't profess to be an expert on this subject.* **2** to state openly that you have a particular belief, feeling, etc. SYN DECLARE: ~ sth *He professed his admiration for their work.* ◆ ~ yourself + adj. *She professed herself satisfied with the progress so far.* **3** ~ sth to belong to a particular religion: *to profess Christianity/Islam/Judaism*

pro·fessed /prəˈfɛst/ *adj.* [only before noun] (*formal*) **1** used to describe a belief or a position that someone has publicly made known: *a professed Christian/anarchist* **2** used to describe a feeling or an attitude that someone says they have but that may not be sincere: *These, at least, were their professed reasons for pulling out of the deal.*

---

pro·fes·sion /prəˈfɛʃn/ *noun*
1 [C] a type of job that needs special training or skill, especially one that needs a high level of education: *the medical/legal/teaching, etc. profession* ♦ *to enter/go into/join a profession* ♦ *He was an electrician by profession.* ♦ *She was at the very top of her profession.* ⊃ **thesaurus box** at WORK ⊃ **collocations** at JOB **2 the profession** [sing.] all the people who work in a particular type of profession: *The legal profession has always resisted change.* **3 the profes·sions** [pl.] (*old-fashioned*) the traditional jobs that need a high level of education and training, such as being a doctor or a lawyer: *employment in industry and the professions* **4** [C] *~ of sth* a statement about what you believe, feel, or think about something, which is sometimes made publicly **SYN** DECLARATION: *a profession of faith*

pro·fes·sion·al 🔑 **AWL** /prəˈfɛʃənl/ *adj., noun*
● *adj.* **1** [only before noun] connected with a job that needs special training or skill, especially one that needs a high level of education: *professional qualifications/skills* ♦ *professional standards/practice* ♦ *an opportunity for professional development* ♦ *If it's a legal matter, you need to seek professional advice.* **2** (of people) having a job that needs special training and a high level of education: *Most of the people taking the course were professional women.* **3** showing that someone is well trained and extremely skilled **SYN** COMPETENT: *He dealt with the problem in a highly professional way.* **ANT** AMATEUR **4** suitable or appropriate for someone working in a particular profession: *professional conduct/misconduct* **ANT** UNPROFESSIONAL **5** (*abbr.* **pro**) doing something as a paid job rather than as a hobby: *a professional golfer* ♦ *After he won the amateur championship he turned professional.* **ANT** AMATEUR **6** (*abbr.* **pro**) (of sports) done as a paid job rather than as a hobby: *the world of professional football* **ANT** AMATEUR ⊃ **compare** NONPROFESSIONAL
● *noun* **1** a person who does a job that needs special training and a high level of education: *the terms that doctors and other health professionals use* **2** (also *informal* **pro**) a person who does a sport or other activity as a paid job rather than as a hobby: *a top golf professional* **ANT** AMATEUR **3** (also *informal* **pro**) a person who has a lot of skill and experience: *This was clearly a job for a real professional.* **ANT** AMATEUR

pro·fessional de·velopment day (also **PD day**) *noun* (*especially CanE*) a day on which classes at schools are canceled so that teachers can get further training in their subjects

pro·fes·sion·al·ism **AWL** /prəˈfɛʃənəˌlɪzəm/ *noun* [U]
1 the high standard that you expect from a person who is well trained in a particular job: *We were impressed by the professionalism of the staff.* **2** great skill and ability: *the power and professionalism of her performance* **3** the practice of using professional players in sports: *Increased professionalism has changed the game radically.*

pro·fes·sion·al·ize /prəˈfɛʃənəˌlaɪz/ *verb* [usually passive] *~ sth* to make an activity more professional, for example by paying people who take part in it ▶ **pro·fes·sion·al·i·za·tion** /prəˌfɛʃənələˈzeɪʃn/ *noun* [U]: *the increasing professionalization of sports*

pro·fes·sion·al·ly **AWL** /prəˈfɛʃənəli/ *adv.* **1** in a way that is connected with a person's job or training: *You need a complete change, both professionally and personally.* **2** in a way that shows skill and experience: *The product has been marketed very professionally.* **3** by a person who has the right skills and qualifications: *The burglar alarm should be professionally installed.* **4** as a paid job, not as a hobby: *After the injury, he never played professionally again.*

pro·fes·sor 🔑 /prəˈfɛsər/ (also *informal* **prof**) *noun* (*abbr.* **Prof.**)
a teacher at a university or college, especially one with a high rank: *Professor (Ann) Williams* ♦ *a chemistry professor* ⊃ **see also** ASSISTANT PROFESSOR, ASSOCIATE PROFESSOR, FULL PROFESSOR, VISITING PROFESSOR

pro·fes·so·ri·al /ˌproʊfəˈsɔriəl; ˌprɑ-/ *adj.* connected with a professor; like a professor: *professorial duties* ♦ *His tone was almost professorial.*

pro·fes·sor·ship /prəˈfɛsərˌʃɪp/ *noun* the rank or position of a university professor: *a visiting professorship* ♦ *She was appointed to a professorship in economics at Princeton.*

prof·fer /ˈprɑfər/ *verb* (*formal*) **1** *~ sth (to sb)* | *~ sb sth* to offer something to someone, by holding it out to them: *"Try this," she said, proffering a plate.* **2** to offer something such as advice or an explanation: *~ sth (to sb)* *What advice would you proffer to someone starting up in business?* ♦ *~ sb sth* *What advice would you proffer her?* ♦ *~ itself* *A solution proffered itself.*

pro·fi·cient /prəˈfɪʃnt/ *adj.* able to do something well because of training and practice: *I'm a reasonably proficient driver.* ♦ *~ in sth/in doing sth* *She's proficient in several languages.* ♦ *~ at sth/at doing sth* *He's proficient at his job.* ▶ **pro·fi·cien·cy** /prəˈfɪʃnsi/ *noun* [U]: *to develop proficiency* ♦ *a certificate of language proficiency* ♦ *~ in sth/in doing sth* *a high level of oral proficiency in English*

pro·file 🔑 /ˈproʊfaɪl/ *noun, verb*
● *noun* **1** the outline of a person's face when you look from the side, not the front: *his strong profile* ♦ *a picture of the president in profile* **2** a description of someone or something that gives useful information: *a job/employee profile* ♦ *We first build up a detailed profile of our customers and their requirements.* ♦ *You can update your Facebook profile (= your description of yourself on a SOCIAL NETWORKING Web site).* **3** the general impression that someone or something gives to the public and the amount of attention they receive: *The deal will certainly raise the company's international profile.* **4** the edge or outline of something that you see against a background: *the profile of the tower against the sky* **IDM** **a high/low profile** the amount of attention someone or something has from the public: *This issue has had a high profile in recent months.* ♦ *I advised her to keep a low profile for the next few days (= not to attract attention).*
● *verb* *~ sb/sth* to give or write a description of someone or something that gives the most important information: *His career is profiled in this month's journal.*

pro·fil·ing /ˈproʊfaɪlɪŋ/ *noun* [U] the act of collecting useful information about someone or something so that you can give a description of them or it: *customer profiling* ♦ *offender profiling* ⊃ **see also** RACIAL PROFILING ▶ **pro·fil·er** /ˈproʊfaɪlər/ *noun*

prof·it 🔑 /ˈprɑfət/ *noun, verb*
● *noun* **1** [C, U] the money that you make in business or by selling things, especially after paying the costs involved: *a rise/an increase/a drop/a fall in profits* ♦ *~ (on sth)* *The company made a healthy profit on the deal.* ♦ *~ (from sth)* *Profit from exports rose 7.3%.* ♦ *Net profit (= after you have paid costs and tax) was up 16.1%.* ♦ *The sale generated record profits.* ♦ *We should be able to sell the house at a profit.* ♦ *The agency is voluntary and not run for profit.* **ANT** LOSS ⊃ **collocations** at BUSINESS **2** [U] (*formal*) the advantage that you get from doing something: *Future lawyers could study this text with profit.*
● *verb* [I, T] (*formal*) to get something useful from a situation; to be useful to someone or give them an advantage: *~ (from sth)* *Farmers are profiting from the new legislation.* ♦ *~ (by sth)* *We tried to profit by our mistakes (= learn from them).* ♦ *~ sth* *Many local people believe the development will profit them.*

prof·it·a·ble /ˈprɑfətəbl/ *adj.* **1** that makes or is likely to make money: *a highly profitable business* ♦ *It is usually more profitable to sell direct to the public.* ⊃ **thesaurus box** at SUCCESSFUL **2** that gives someone an advantage or a useful result **SYN** REWARDING: *She spent a profitable afternoon in the library.* ▶ **prof·it·a·bil·i·ty** /ˌprɑfətəˈbɪləti/ *noun* [U]: *to increase profitability* **prof·it·a·bly** /ˈprɑfətəbli/ *adv.*: *to run a business profitably* ♦ *He spent the weekend profitably.*

| h hat | m man | n no | ŋ sing | l leg | r red | y yes | w wet |

profit and loss account *noun* (*business*) a list that shows the amount of money that a company has earned and the total profit or loss that it has made in a particular period of time

prof·it·eer·ing /ˌprɑfəˈtɪrɪŋ/ *noun* [U] (*disapproving*) the act of making a lot of money in an unfair way, for example by asking very high prices for things that are hard to get ▶ **prof·it·eer** /ˌprɑfəˈtɪr/ *noun*

pro·fit·er·ole /prəˈfɪtəˌroʊl/ *noun* = CREAM PUFF (1)

prof·it·less /ˈprɑfətləs/ *adj.* (*formal*) producing no profit or useful result

profit-making *adj.* [usually before noun] (of a company or a business) that makes or will make a profit

profit margin (also **mar·gin**) *noun* (*business*) the difference between the cost of buying or producing something and the price that it is sold for

profit-sharing *noun* [U] the system of dividing all or some of a company's profits among its employees

profit-taking *noun* [U] (*business*) the sale of shares in companies whose value has increased

prof·li·gate /ˈprɑflɪgət/ *adj.* (*formal, disapproving*) using money, time, materials, etc. in a careless way **SYN** WASTEFUL: *profligate spending* ▶ **prof·li·ga·cy** /ˈprɑflɪgəsi/ *noun* [U]

pro-form *noun* (*grammar*) a word that depends on another part of the sentence or text for its meaning, for example "her" in "I like Ruth but I don't love her."

pro for·ma /ˌproʊ ˈfɔrmə/ *adj.* (from *Latin*) [usually before noun] **1** (especially of a document) prepared in order to show the usual way of doing something or to provide a standard method: *a pro forma letter* ◆ *pro forma instructions* **2** (of a document) sent in advance: *a pro forma invoice* (= a document that gives details of the goods being sent to a customer) **3** done because it is part of the usual way of doing something, although it has no real meaning: *a pro forma debate* ▶ **pro forma** *noun: I enclose a pro forma for you to complete, sign, and return.*

pro·found /prəˈfaʊnd/ *adj.* **1** very great; felt or experienced very strongly: *profound changes in the earth's climate* ◆ *My father's death had a profound effect on us all.* **2** showing great knowledge or understanding: *profound insights* ◆ *a profound book* **3** needing a lot of study or thought: *profound questions about life and death* **4** (*medical*) very serious; complete: *profound disability*

pro·found·ly /prəˈfaʊndli/ *adv.* **1** in a way that has a very great effect on someone or something: *We are profoundly affected by what happens to us in childhood.* **2** (*medical*) very seriously; completely: *profoundly deaf*

pro·fun·di·ty /prəˈfʌndəti/ *noun* (*pl.* **pro·fun·di·ties**) (*formal*) **1** [U] the quality of understanding or dealing with a subject at a very serious level **SYN** DEPTH: *He lacked profundity and analytical precision.* **2** [U] the quality of being very great, serious, or powerful: *the profundity of her misery* **3** [C, usually pl.] something that someone says that shows great understanding: *His profundities were lost on the young audience.*

pro·fuse /prəˈfyus/ *adj.* produced in large amounts: *profuse apologies/thanks* ◆ *profuse bleeding* ▶ **pro·fuse·ly** /prəˈfyusli/ *adv.: to bleed profusely* ◆ *to apologize profusely*

pro·fu·sion /prəˈfyuʒn/ *noun* [sing., U] (*formal or literary*) a very large quantity of something **SYN** ABUNDANCE: *a profusion of colors* ◆ *Roses grew in profusion against the old wall.*

pro·gen·i·tor /proʊˈdʒɛnətər/ *noun* (*formal*) **1** a person or thing from the past that a person, an animal, or a plant that is alive now is related to **SYN** ANCESTORS: *He was the progenitor of a family of distinguished actors.* **2** a person who starts an idea or a movement: *the progenitors of modern art*

prog·e·ny /ˈprɑdʒəni/ *noun* [pl.] (*formal or humorous*) a person's children; the young of animals and plants: *He was surrounded by his numerous progeny.*

pro·ges·ter·one /proʊˈdʒɛstəˌroʊn/ *noun* [U] a HORMONE produced in the bodies of women and female animals that prepares the body to become pregnant and is also used in CONTRACEPTION ↭ compare ESTROGEN, TESTOSTERONE

prog·no·sis /prɑgˈnoʊsəs/ *noun* (*pl.* **prog·no·ses** /-siz/) **1** (*medical*) an opinion, based on medical experience, of the likely development of a disease or an illness **2** (*formal*) a judgment about how something is likely to develop in the future **SYN** FORECAST: *The prognosis is for more people to work part-time in the future.* ▶ **prog·nos·tic** /prɑgˈnɑstɪk/ *adj.*

prog·nos·ti·ca·tion /prɑgˌnɑstəˈkeɪʃn/ *noun* (*formal*) a thing that someone says will happen in the future: *gloomy prognostications*

pro·gram /ˈproʊgræm; -grəm/ *noun, verb*
● *noun*
> PLAN /COURSE OF STUDY **1** a plan of things that will be done or included in the development of something: *to launch a research program* ◆ *a training program for new staff* ◆ *a program of economic reform* **2** a course of study: *a school program*
> FOR COMPUTER **3** (*computing*) a set of instructions in CODE that control the operations or functions of a computer: *Load the program into the computer.*
> ON TV/RADIO **4** something that people watch on television or listen to on the radio: *a news program* ◆ *Did you see that program about the space lab last night?* ↭ collocations at TELEVISION
> FOR PLAY/CONCERT **5** a thin book or a piece of paper that gives you information about a play, a concert, etc.: *a theater program*
> ORDER OF EVENTS **6** an organized order of performances or events: *an exciting musical program* ◆ *a week-long program of lectures* ◆ *What's the program for* (= What are we going to do) *tomorrow?*
> OF MACHINE **7** a series of actions done by a machine, such as a WASHING MACHINE: *Select a cool program for woolen clothes.*
> **IDM get with the program** (*informal*) (usually in orders) used to tell someone that they should change their attitude and do what they are supposed to be doing
● *verb* (-mm- or, -m-)
> COMPUTER **1** [I, T] (*computing*) to give a computer, etc. a set of instructions to make it perform a particular task: *In this class, students will learn how to program.* ◆ **~ sth (to do sth)** *The computer is programmed to warn users before information is deleted.*
> MACHINE **2** [T] **~ sth (to do sth)** to give a machine instructions to do a particular task: *She programmed the oven to come on at eight.*
> PLAN **3** [T, usually passive] **~ sth (for sth)** to plan for something to happen, especially as part of a series of planned events: *The final section of road is programmed for completion next month.*
> PERSON/ANIMAL **4** [T, usually passive] **~ sb/sth to do sth** to make a person, an animal, etc. behave in a particular way, so that it happens automatically: *Human beings are genetically programmed to learn certain kinds of language.*

pro·gram·ma·ble /ˈproʊˌgræməbl/ *adj.* (of a computer or an electrical device) able to accept instructions that control how it operates or functions

pro·gram·mat·ic /ˌproʊgrəˈmætɪk/ *adj.* [usually before noun] (*formal*) connected with, suggesting, or following a plan: *programmatic reforms*

programmed learning *noun* [U] a method of study in which a subject is divided into very small parts and the student must be successful in one part before they can go on to the next

pro·gram·mer /ˈproʊgræmər/ *noun* a person whose job is writing programs for computers

pro·gram·ming /ˈproʊgræmɪŋ/ *noun* [U] **1** the process of writing and testing programs for computers: *a high-level programming language* **2** the planning of which television or radio programs to broadcast: *politically balanced programming*

prog·ress 🔑 *noun, verb*

● **noun** /ˈprɑːgrɛs; -grəs/ [U] **1** the process of improving or developing, or of getting nearer to achieving or completing, something: *to make progress* ◆ *slow/steady/rapid/good progress* ◆ *We have made great progress in controlling inflation.* ◆ *economic/scientific/technical progress* ◆ *They asked for a progress report on the project.* **2** movement forward or toward a place: *She watched his slow progress down the steep slope.* ◆ *There wasn't much traffic so we made good progress.* **IDM in progress** (*formal*) happening at this time: *Work on the new offices is now in progress.* ◆ *Please be quiet—examination in progress.*

● **verb** /prəˈgrɛs/ **1** [I] to improve or develop over a period of time; to make progress **SYN** ADVANCE: *The course allows students to progress at their own speed.* ◆ *Work on the new road is progressing slowly.* **2** [I] + adv./prep. (*formal*) to move forward: *The line of traffic progressed slowly through the town.* ◆ (*figurative*) *Cases can take months to progress through the courts.* **3** [I] to go forward in time **SYN** GO ON: *The weather became colder as the day progressed.* **PHR V pro·gress to sth** to move on from doing one thing to doing something else: *She started off playing the recorder and then progressed to the clarinet.*

pro·gres·sion /prəˈgrɛʃn/ *noun* **1** [U, C] the process of developing gradually from one stage or state to another: *opportunities for career progression* ◆ *the rapid progression of the disease* ◆ *~ (from sth) (to sth) the natural progression from childhood to adolescence* **2** [C] a number of things that come in a series ⊃ see also ARITHMETIC PROGRESSION, GEOMETRIC PROGRESSION

pro·gres·sive /prəˈgrɛsɪv/ *adj., noun*

● **adj. 1** in favor of new ideas, modern methods, and change: *progressive schools* **ANT** RETROGRESSIVE **2** happening or developing steadily: *a progressive reduction in the size of the workforce* ◆ *a progressive muscular disease* **3** (also con·tin·u·ous) (*grammar*) connected with the form of a verb (for example *I am waiting* or *It is raining*) that is made from a part of *be* and the present participle. Progressive forms are used to express an action that continues for a period of time. ▶ **pro·gres·siv·ism** /prəˈgrɛsɪˌvɪzəm/ *noun* [U]: *political progressivism*

● **noun** [usually pl.] a person who is in favor of new ideas, modern methods, and change: *political battles between progressives and conservatives*

pro·gres·sive·ly /prəˈgrɛsɪvli/ *adv.* (often with a comparative) steadily and continuously: *The situation was becoming progressively more difficult.* ◆ *The pain got progressively worse.*

pro·hib·it **AWL** /prəˈhɪbət; proʊ-/ *verb* (*formal*) **1** [often passive] to stop something from being done or used, especially by law **SYN** FORBID: *~ sth a law prohibiting the sale of alcohol* ◆ *~ sb from doing sth Trademark law prohibits companies from using marks similar to existing ones.* **2** *~ sth/sb from doing sth* to make something impossible to do **SYN** PREVENT: *The high cost of equipment prohibits many people from taking up this sport.*

pro·hi·bi·tion **AWL** /ˌproʊəˈbɪʃn/ *noun* **1** [U] the act of stopping something from being done or used, especially by law: *the prohibition of smoking in public areas* **2** [C] *~ (against/on sth)* a law or a rule that stops something being done or used: *a prohibition against selling alcohol to people under the age of 18* **3** Prohibition [U] (in the U.S.) the period of time from 1920 to 1933 when it was illegal to make and sell alcoholic drinks

pro·hi·bi·tion·ist /ˌproʊəˈbɪʃənɪst/ *noun* a person who supports the act of making something illegal, especially the sale of alcoholic drinks

pro·hib·i·tive **AWL** /prəˈhɪbətɪv; proʊ-/ *adj.* **1** (of a price or a cost) so high that it prevents people from buying something or doing something **SYN** EXORBITANT: *prohibitive costs* ◆ *The price of property in the city is prohibitive.* **2** preventing people from doing something by law: *prohibitive legislation* **3** (of a person taking part in an election or a competition) extremely likely to win: *Miami began the day*

a prohibitive Super Bowl favorite. ▶ **pro·hib·i·tive·ly** *adv.*: *Car insurance can be prohibitively expensive for young drivers.*

proj·ect 🔑 **AWL** *noun, verb*

● **noun** /ˈprɑːdʒɛkt; -dʒɪkt/
> **PLANNED WORK 1** a planned piece of work that is designed to find information about something, to produce something new, or to improve something: *a research project* ◆ *a building project* ◆ *to set up a project to computerize the library system*
> **SCHOOL/COLLEGE WORK 2** a piece of work involving careful study of a subject over a period of time, done by school or college students: *a history project* ◆ *More emphasis is being placed on collaborative project work at all levels of schooling.*
> **SET OF AIMS/ACTIVITIES 3** a set of aims, ideas, or activities that someone is interested in or wants to bring to people's attention: *The party attempted to assemble its aims into a focused political project.*
> **HOUSING 4** [usually pl.] = HOUSING PROJECT: *Going into the projects alone is dangerous.*

● **verb** /prəˈdʒɛkt/
> **PLAN 1** [T, usually passive] *~ sth* to plan an activity, a project, etc. for a time in the future: *The next edition of the book is projected for publication in March.* ◆ *The projected housing development will go ahead next year.*
> **ESTIMATE 2** [T, usually passive] to estimate what the size, cost, or amount of something will be in the future based on what is happening now **SYN** FORECAST: *~ sth A growth rate of 4% is projected for next year.* ◆ *it is projected that... It is projected that the unemployment rate will fall.* ◆ *~ sth to do sth The unemployment rate has been projected to fall.* **HELP** This pattern is usually used in the passive.
> **LIGHT/IMAGE 3** [T] *~ sth (on/onto sth)* to make light, an image, etc. fall onto a flat surface or screen: *Images are projected onto the retina of the eye.*
> **STICK OUT 4** [I] + adv./prep. to stick out beyond an edge or a surface **SYN** PROTRUDE: *a building with balconies projecting out over the street*
> **PRESENT YOURSELF 5** [T] to present someone, something, or yourself to other people in a particular way, especially one that gives a good impression: *~ sth They sought advice on how to project a more positive image of their company.* ◆ *She projects an air of calm self-confidence.* ◆ *~ sb/sth/yourself (as sb/sth) He projected himself as a man worth listening to.*
> **SEND/THROW UP OR AWAY 6** [T] *~ sth/sb (+ adv./prep.)* to send or throw something up or away from yourself: *Actors must learn to project their voices.* ◆ (*figurative*) *the powerful men who would project him into the White House* **PHR V pro·ject sth onto sb** (*psychology*) to imagine that other people have the same feelings, problems, etc. as you, especially when this is not true

pro·jec·tile /prəˈdʒɛktəl; -taɪl/ *noun, adj.*

● **noun** (*formal* or *technical*) **1** an object, such as a bullet, that is fired from a gun or other weapon **2** any object that is thrown as a weapon

● **adj.** (*formal* or *technical*) very fast and with a lot of force: *projectile motion* ◆ *The virus causes projectile* (= sudden and violent) *vomiting.*

pro·jec·tion **AWL** /prəˈdʒɛkʃn/ *noun*
> **ESTIMATE 1** [C] an estimate or a statement of what figures, amounts, or events will be in the future, or what they were in the past, based on what is happening now: *to make forward/backward projections of population figures* ◆ *Sales have exceeded our projections.*
> **OF IMAGE 2** [U, C] the act of putting an image of something onto a surface; an image that is shown in this way: *the projection of three-dimensional images on a computer screen* ◆ *laser projections*
> **OF SOLID SHAPE 3** [C] (*technical*) a solid shape or object as represented on a flat surface: *map projections*
> **SOMETHING THAT STICKS OUT 4** [C] something that sticks out from a surface: *tiny projections on the cell*
> **OF VOICE/SOUND 5** [U] the act of making your voice, a sound, etc. AUDIBLE (= able to be heard) at a distance: *voice projection*

ʌ cup   ə about   eɪ say   aɪ five   ɔɪ boy   aʊ now   oʊ go   ər bird

> PSYCHOLOGY **6** [U] the act of imagining that someone else is thinking the same as you and is reacting in the same way

> OF THOUGHTS/FEELINGS **7** [C,U] the act of giving a form and structure to inner thoughts and feelings: *The story is a projection of the writer's personal spiritual struggle.*

pro·jec·tion·ist /prəˈdʒɛkʃənɪst/ *noun* a person whose job is to show movies by operating a PROJECTOR

pro·jec·tor /prəˈdʒɛktər/ *noun* a piece of equipment for projecting photographs, movies, or computer images onto a screen ⊃ see also DATA PROJECTOR, OVERHEAD PROJECTOR, SLIDE PROJECTOR

pro·lapse /ˈproʊlæps/ *noun* (*medical*) a condition in which an organ of the body has slipped forward or down from its normal position

pro·le·tar·i·an /ˌproʊləˈtɛriən/ *adj.* connected with ordinary people who earn money by working, especially those who do not own any property ⊃ compare BOURGEOIS ▶ **pro·le·tar·i·an** *noun*

the pro·le·tar·i·at /ˌproʊləˈtɛriət/ *noun* [sing.] (*technical*) (used especially when talking about the past) the class of ordinary people who earn money by working, especially those who do not own any property ⊃ compare BOURGEOISIE

pro-ˈlife *adj.* [usually before noun] opposed to ABORTION: *the pro-life movement* ♦ *a pro-life campaigner* ⊃ compare ANTICHOICE, PRO-CHOICE ▶ **pro-ˈlifer** *noun*

pro·lif·er·ate /prəˈlɪfəˌreɪt/ *verb* [I] to increase rapidly in number or amount **SYN** MULTIPLY: *Books and articles on the subject have proliferated over the last year.*

pro·lif·er·a·tion /prəˌlɪfəˈreɪʃn/ *noun* [U, sing.] the sudden increase in the number or amount of something; a large number of a particular thing: *attempts to prevent cancer cell proliferation* ♦ *a proliferation of personal computers*

pro·lif·ic /prəˈlɪfɪk/ *adj.* **1** (of an artist, a writer, etc.) producing many works, etc.: *a prolific author* ♦ *a prolific goalscorer* ♦ *one of the most prolific periods in her career* **2** (of plants, animals, etc.) producing a lot of fruit, flowers, young, etc. **3** able to produce enough food, etc. to keep many animals and plants alive: *prolific rivers* **4** existing in large numbers: *a pop star with a prolific following of teenage fans* ▶ **pro·lif·i·cal·ly** /-kli/ *adv.*: *to write prolifically* ♦ *animals that breed prolifically*

pro·lix /proʊˈlɪks; ˈproʊlɪks/ *adj.* (*formal*) (of writing, a speech, etc.) using too many words and therefore boring ▶ **pro·lix·i·ty** /proʊˈlɪksəti/ /proʊˈlɪksəti/ *noun* [U]

pro·logue /ˈproʊlɔɡ; -lɑɡ/ *noun* a speech, etc. at the beginning of a play, book, or movie that introduces it ⊃ compare EPILOGUE

pro·long /prəˈlɔŋ/ *verb* ~ sth to make something last longer **SYN** EXTEND: *The operation could prolong his life by two or three years.* ♦ *Don't prolong the agony* (= of not knowing something) —*just tell us who won!*

pro·lon·ga·tion /ˌproʊlɔŋˈɡeɪʃn/ *noun* [U, sing.] (*formal*) the act of making something last longer: *the artificial prolongation of human life*

pro·longed /prəˈlɔŋd/ *adj.* continuing for a long time: *a prolonged illness* ♦ *a prolonged period of dry weather*

prom /prɑm/ *noun* a formal dance that is held at a high school, especially at the end of the school year: *the senior prom*

prom·e·nade /ˌprɑməˈneɪd; -ˈnɑd/ *noun, verb*
● *noun* **1** (becoming *old-fashioned*) a public place for walking, usually a wide path beside the ocean **2** (*old-fashioned*) a walk that you take for pleasure or exercise, especially by the ocean, in a public park, etc.
● *verb* [I] (*old-fashioned*) to walk up and down in a relaxed way, by the ocean, in a public park, etc.

Pro·me·the·an /prəˈmiθiən/ *adj.* doing things in an individual and original way and showing no respect for authority and rules **ORIGIN** From the Greek myth in which

Prometheus, a Titan, stole fire from the gods and gave it to humans.

pro·me·thi·um /prəˈmiθiəm/ *noun* [U] (*symb.* **Pm**) a chemical element. Promethium is a RADIOACTIVE metal that was first produced artificially in a nuclear REACTOR and is found in small amounts in nature.

prom·i·nence /ˈprɑmənəns/ *noun* [U, sing.] the state of being important, well known, or noticeable: *a young actor who has recently risen to prominence* ♦ *The newspapers have given undue prominence to the story.* ♦ *She has achieved a prominence she hardly deserves.*

prom·i·nent /ˈprɑmənənt/ *adj.* **1** important or well known: *a prominent politician* ♦ *He played a prominent part in the campaign.* ♦ *She was prominent in the fashion industry.* **2** easily seen **SYN** NOTICEABLE: *The church tower was a prominent feature in the landscape.* ♦ *The story was given a prominent position on the front page.* **3** sticking out from something: *a prominent nose* ♦ *prominent cheekbones* ▶ **prom·i·nent·ly** *adv.*: *The photos were prominently displayed on her desk.* ♦ *Problems of family relationships feature prominently in her novels.*

pro·mis·cu·ous /prəˈmɪskyuəs/ *adj.* (*disapproving*) **1** having many sexual partners: *promiscuous behavior* ♦ *a promiscuous lifestyle* ♦ *to be sexually promiscuous* **2** (*formal*) taken from a wide range of sources, especially without careful thought: *promiscuous reading* ♦ *a stylistically promiscuous piece of music* ▶ **prom·is·cu·i·ty** /ˌprɑməˈskyuəti/ *noun* [U]: *sexual promiscuity* **prom·is·cu·ous·ly** /prəˈmɪskyuəsli/ *adv.*

prom·ise 🔑 /ˈprɑməs/ *verb, noun*
● *verb* **1** [I, T] to tell someone that you will definitely do or not do something, or that something will definitely happen: ~ **(to do sth)** *The college principal promised to look into the matter.* ♦ *"Promise not to tell anyone!" "I promise."* ♦ *They arrived at 7:30 as they had promised.* ♦ ~ **sth** *The government has promised a full investigation into the disaster.* ♦ *I'll see what I can do but I can't promise anything.* ♦ ~ **(that)** ... *The brochure promised (that) the local food would be excellent.* ♦ ~ **sb (that)...** *You promised me (that) you'd be home early tonight.* ♦ ~ **sth to sb** *He promised the money to his grandchildren.* ♦ ~ **sb sth** *He promised his grandchildren the money.* ♦ ~ **yourself sth** *I've promised myself some fun when the exams are over.* ♦ ~ **(sb) + speech** *"I'll be back soon," she promised.* **2** [T] to make something seem likely to happen; to show signs of something: **it promises to be sth** *It promises to be an exciting few days.* ♦ ~ **sth** *There were dark clouds overhead promising rain.*
IDM **I (can) promise you** (*informal*) used as a way of encouraging or warning someone about something: *I can promise you, you'll have a wonderful time.* ♦ *If you don't take my advice, you'll regret it, I promise you.* **promise (sb) the earth/moon/world** (*informal*) to make promises that will be impossible to keep ⊃ more at LICK *n.*
● *noun* **1** [C] a statement that tells someone that you will definitely do or not do something: *to make/keep/break a promise* ♦ ~ **(to do sth)** *She kept her promise to visit her aunt regularly.* ♦ ~ **(of sth)** *The government failed to keep its promise of lower taxes.* ♦ ~ **(that...)** *Do I have your promise that you won't tell anyone about this?* ♦ *You haven't gone back on your promise, have you?* **2** [U] a sign that someone or something will be successful **SYN** POTENTIAL: *Her work shows great promise.* ♦ *He failed to fulfill his early promise.* ♦ *Their future was full of promise.* **3** [U, sing.] ~ **of sth** a sign, or a reason to hope, that something may happen, especially something good: *The day dawned bright and clear, with the promise of warm sunny weather.*

the Promised Land *noun* [sing.] a place or situation where you expect to be happy, safe, etc.

prom·is·ing /ˈprɑməsɪŋ/ *adj.* showing signs of being good or successful: *He was voted the most promising new actor for his part in the movie.* ♦ *The weather doesn't look very promising.* ▶ **prom·is·ing·ly** *adv.*: *The day began promisingly with bright sunshine.*

prom·is·so·ry note /ˈprɑməsɔri ˌnoʊt/ *noun* (*technical*) a signed document containing a promise to pay a stated amount of money before a particular date

pro·mo /ˈproʊmoʊ/ *adj.* [only before noun] (*informal*) connected with promoting (= advertising) someone or something, especially a new music single: *a promo video* ▶ **pro·mo** *noun* (*pl.* **pro·mos**): *to make rock promos*

prom·on·to·ry /ˈprɑmənˌtɔri/ *noun* (*pl.* **prom·on·tor·ies**) a long narrow area of high land that goes out into the ocean **SYN** HEADLAND

pro·mote 🔑 **AWL** /prəˈmoʊt/ *verb*
1 ~ sth to help something to happen or develop **SYN** ENCOURAGE: *policies to promote economic growth* ♦ *a campaign to promote awareness of environmental issues* **2** to help sell a product, service, etc. or make it more popular by advertising it or offering it at a special price: ~ **sth** *The band has gone on tour to promote their new album.* ♦ ~ **sth as sth** *The area is being promoted as a tourist destination.* **3** [often passive] to move someone to a higher rank or more senior job: ~ **sb** *She worked hard and was soon promoted.* ♦ ~ **sb (from sth) (to sth)** *He has been promoted to sergeant.* **ANT** DEMOTE

pro·mot·er **AWL** /prəˈmoʊtər/ *noun* **1** a person or company that organizes or provides money for an artistic performance or a sports event **2** ~ **of sth** a person who tries to persuade others about the value or importance of something **SYN** CHAMPION: *He has been a huge promoter of alternative energy and new technology.*

pro·mo·tion 🔑 **AWL** /prəˈmoʊʃn/ *noun*
1 [U, C] ~ **(to sth)** a move to a more important job or rank in a company or an organization: *Her promotion to Sales Manager took everyone by surprise.* ♦ *The new job is a promotion for him.* ♦ *a job with excellent promotion prospects* ⊃ collocations at JOB **2** [U, C] activities done in order to increase the sales of a product or service; a set of advertisements for a particular product or service: *Her job is mainly concerned with sales and promotion.* ♦ *We are doing a special promotion of Chilean wines.* ⊃ see also CROSS-PROMOTION ⊃ thesaurus box at ADVERTISEMENT **3** [U] ~ **of sth** (*formal*) activity that encourages people to believe in the value or importance of something, or that helps something to succeed: *a society for the promotion of religious tolerance*

pro·mo·tion·al /prəˈmoʊʃənl/ *adj.* connected with advertising: *promotional material*

prompt 🔑 /prɑmpt/ *adj., verb, noun, adv.*
• *adj.* **1** done without delay **SYN** IMMEDIATE: *Prompt action was required as the fire spread.* ♦ *Prompt payment of the invoice would be appreciated.* **2** [not before noun] (of a person) acting without delay; arriving at the right time **SYN** PUNCTUAL: *Please be prompt when attending these meetings.* ▶ **prompt·ness** *noun* [U]
• *verb* **1** [T] to make someone decide to do something; to cause something to happen **SYN** PROVOKE: ~ **sth** *The discovery of the bomb prompted an increase in security.* ♦ *His speech prompted an angry outburst from a man in the crowd.* ♦ ~ **sb to do sth** *The thought of her daughter's wedding day prompted her to lose some weight.* **2** [T] to encourage someone to speak by asking them questions or suggesting words that they could say: ~ **sb** *She was too nervous to speak and had to be prompted.* ♦ ~ **sb to do sth** (*computing*) *The program will prompt you to enter data where required.* ♦ ~ **(sb) + speech** *"And then what happened?" he prompted.* **3** [T, I] ~ **(sb)** to follow the text of a play and remind the actors what the words are if they forget their lines
• *noun* **1** a word or words said to an actor, to remind them what to say next when they have forgotten **2** (*computing*) a sign on a computer screen that shows that the computer has finished doing something and is ready for more instructions
• *adv.* exactly at the time mentioned: *The meeting will begin at ten o'clock prompt.*

prompt·er /ˈprɑmptər/ *noun* a person who prompts actors in a play

prompt·ing /ˈprɑmptɪŋ/ *noun* [U] also **promptings** [pl.] an act of persuading someone to do something: *He wrote the letter without further prompting.* ♦ *Never again would she listen to the promptings of her heart.*

prompt·ly 🔑 /ˈprɑmptli/ *adv.*
1 without delay: *She deals with all the correspondence promptly and efficiently.* **2** exactly at the correct time or at the time mentioned **SYN** PUNCTUALLY: *They arrived promptly at two o'clock.* **3** (always used before the verb) immediately: *She read the letter and promptly burst into tears.*

prom·ul·gate /ˈprɑmlˌgeɪt/ *verb* (*formal*) **1** [usually passive] ~ **sth** to spread an idea, a belief, etc. among many people **2** ~ **sth** to announce a new law or system officially or publicly ▶ **prom·ul·ga·tion** /ˌprɑmlˈgeɪʃn/ *noun* [U]

prone /proʊn/ *adj.* **1** likely to suffer from something or to do something bad **SYN** LIABLE: ~ **to sth** *prone to injury* ♦ *Working without a break makes you more prone to error.* ♦ ~ **to do sth** *Tired drivers were found to be particularly prone to ignore warning signs.* **2** -**prone** (in adjectives) likely to suffer or do the thing mentioned: *error-prone* ♦ *injury-prone* ⊃ see also ACCIDENT-PRONE **3** (*formal*) lying flat with the front of your body touching the ground **SYN** PROSTRATE: *The victim lay prone without moving.* ♦ *He was found lying in a prone position.* ⊃ compare SUPINE ▶ **prone·ness** /ˈproʊnnəs/ *noun* [U]: *proneness to depression*

prong /prɔŋ; prɑŋ/ *noun* **1** each of the two or more long pointed parts of a fork **2** each of the separate parts of an attack, argument, etc., that move toward a place, subject, etc. from different positions **3** -**pronged** (in adjectives) having the number or type of prongs mentioned: *a two-pronged fork* ♦ *a three-pronged attack*

pro·nom·i·nal /proʊˈnɑmənl/ *adj.* (*grammar*) relating to a pronoun

pro·noun /ˈproʊnaʊn/ *noun* (*grammar*) a word that is used instead of a noun or noun phrase, for example *he, it, hers, me, them*, etc.: *demonstrative/interrogative/possessive/ relative pronouns* ⊃ see also PERSONAL PRONOUN

pro·nounce 🔑 /prəˈnaʊns/ *verb*
1 ~ **sth** to make the sound of a word or letter in a particular way: *Very few people can pronounce my name correctly.* ♦ *The "b" in lamb is not pronounced.* ⊃ see also PRONUNCIATION, UNPRONOUNCEABLE **2** to say or give something formally, officially, or publicly: ~ **sth** *to pronounce an opinion* ♦ *The judge will pronounce sentence today.* ♦ ~ **sb/sth + noun** *She pronounced him the winner of the competition.* ♦ *I now pronounce you husband and wife* (= in a marriage ceremony). ♦ ~ **sb/sth + adj.** *She was pronounced dead on arrival at the hospital.* ♦ ~ **sb/sth to be/have sth** *He pronounced the country to be in a state of war.* ♦ ~ **that...** *She pronounced that an error had been made.* ♦ **+ speech** *"It's pneumonia," he pronounced gravely.*
PHR V **pro'nounce for/against sb** (*law*) to give a judgment in court for or against someone: *The judge pronounced for* (= in favor of) *the defendant.* **pro'nounce on/ upon sth** (*formal*) to state your opinion on something, or give a decision about something: *The police chief will pronounce on further security measures later today.*

> WORD FAMILY
> pronounce *verb*
> pronunciation *noun*
> unpronounceable *adj.*
> mispronounce *verb*

pro·nounce·a·ble /prəˈnaʊnsəbl/ *adj.* (of sounds or words) that can be pronounced **ANT** UNPRONOUNCEABLE

pro·nounced /prəˈnaʊnst/ *adj.* very noticeable, obvious, or strongly expressed **SYN** DEFINITE: *He walked with a pronounced limp.* ♦ *She has very pronounced views on art.*

pro·nounce·ment /prəˈnaʊnsmənt/ *noun* ~ **(on sth)** (*formal*) a formal public statement

pron·to /ˈprɑntoʊ/ *adv.* (*informal*) quickly; immediately: *I expect to see you back here, pronto!*

pro·nun·ci·a·tion 🔊 /prəˌnʌnsiˈeɪʃn/ *noun*
1 [U, C] the way in which a language or a particular word or sound is pronounced: *a guide to English pronunciation* ◆ *There is more than one pronunciation of "progress."* **2** [sing.] the way in which a particular person pronounces the words of a language: *Your pronunciation is excellent.*

proof 🔊 /pruf/ *noun, adj., verb*
● *noun* **1** [U, C] information, documents, etc. that show that something is true **SYN** EVIDENCE: *positive/conclusive proof* ◆ *~ of sth Can you provide any proof of identity?* ◆ *Keep the receipt as proof of purchase.* ◆ *These results are a further proof of his outstanding ability.* ◆ *~ that... There is no proof that the knife belonged to her.* **2** [U] the process of testing whether something is true or a fact: *What is the method of proof?* ⊃ see also BURDEN OF PROOF **3** [C] (*mathematics*) a way of proving that a statement is true or that what you have calculated is correct **4** [C, usually pl.] a copy of printed material that is produced so that mistakes can be corrected: *She was checking the proofs of her latest novel.* **5** [U] a standard used to measure the strength of alcoholic drinks
IDM **the proof of the pudding (is in the eating)** (*saying*) you can only judge if something is good or bad when you have tried it ⊃ more at LIVING
● *adj.* **1** *~ against sth* (*formal*) that can resist the damaging or harmful effects of something: *The sea wall was not proof against the strength of the waves.* **2** (in compounds) that can resist or protect against the thing mentioned: *rainproof/windproof clothing* ◆ *The car has childproof locks on the rear doors.* ◆ *an inflation-proof pension plan*
● *verb* **1** *~ sth* to put a special substance on something, especially cloth, to protect it against water, fire, etc.: *proofed canvas* **2** *~ sth* to produce a test copy of a piece of printed work so that mistakes can be corrected: *color proofing*

proof·read /ˈprufrid/ *verb* (**proof·read, proof·read** /-rɛd/) [T, I] *~ (sth)* to read and correct a piece of written or printed work: *Has this document been proofread?* ▶ **proof·read·er** /-ˌridər/ *noun*: *to work as a proofreader for a publishing company*

prop /prɑp/ *noun, verb*
● *noun* **1** a piece of wood, metal, etc. used to support something or keep it in position: *Rescuers used props to stop the roof of the tunnel from collapsing.* **2** a person or thing that gives help or support to someone or something that is weak **3** [usually pl.] a small object used by actors during the performance of a play or in a movie: *He is responsible for all the stage props and lighting.*
IDM **give props to sb** (*informal*) used to say that people should appreciate what someone has done because it is good: *I gotta give props to the bass player.* **ORIGIN** Props here means "proper respect or recognition."
● *verb* (-pp-) **1** to support an object by leaning it against something, or putting something under it etc.; to support a person in the same way: *~ sth/sb/yourself (up) (against sth) He propped his bike against the wall.* ◆ *She propped herself up on one elbow.* ◆ *He lay propped against the pillows.* ◆ *~ sth + adj. The door was propped open.*
PHR V **ˌprop sth↔ˈup 1** to prevent something from falling by putting something under it to support it **SYN** SHORE UP **2** (often *disapproving*) to help something that is having difficulties: *The government was accused of propping up declining industries.*

prop·a·gan·da /ˌprɑpəˈgændə/ *noun* [U] (usually *disapproving*) ideas or statements that may be false or exaggerated and that are used in order to gain support for a political leader, party, etc.: *enemy propaganda* ◆ *a propaganda campaign*

prop·a·gan·dist /ˌprɑpəˈgændɪst/ *noun* (*formal*, usually *disapproving*) a person who creates or spreads propaganda ▶ **prop·a·gan·dist** *adj.* [only before noun]: *a propagandist organization*

prop·a·gan·dize /ˌprɑpəˈgændaɪz/ *verb* [I, T] *~ sb/sth* (*formal*, *disapproving*) to spread propaganda; to influence people using propaganda

prop·a·gate /ˈprɑpəˌgeɪt/ *verb* **1** [T] *~ sth* (*formal*) to spread an idea, a belief, or a piece of information among many people: *Television advertising propagates a false image of the ideal family.* **2** [T, I] *~ (sth)* (*technical*) to produce new plants from a parent plant: *The plant can be propagated from seed.* ◆ *Plants won't propagate in these conditions.* ▶ **prop·a·ga·tion** /ˌprɑpəˈgeɪʃn/ *noun* [U]

prop·a·ga·tor /ˈprɑpəˌgeɪtər/ *noun* a box for propagating plants in

pro·pane /ˈproʊpeɪn/ *noun* [U] a gas found in natural gas and PETROLEUM, and used as a fuel for cooking and heating: *a propane gas cylinder*

pro·pel /prəˈpɛl/ *verb* (-ll-) [often passive] **1** *~ sth* (+ adv./prep.) to move, drive, or push something forward or in a particular direction: *mechanically propelled vehicles* ◆ *He succeeded in propelling the ball across the line.* **2** *~ sb* + adv./prep. to force someone to move in a particular direction or to get into a particular situation: *She grabbed him from behind and propelled him through the door.* ◆ *Fury propelled her into action.* ⊃ see also PROPULSION

pro·pel·lant /prəˈpɛlənt/ *noun* [C, U] **1** a gas that forces out the contents of an AEROSOL **2** a thing or substance that propels something, for example the fuel that fires a ROCKET

pro·pel·ler /prəˈpɛlər/ *noun* a device with two or more blades that turn quickly and cause a ship or an aircraft to move forward ⊃ picture at PLANE

pro·pen·si·ty /prəˈpɛnsəti/ *noun* (pl. **pro·pen·si·ties**) (*formal*) a tendency to a particular kind of behavior **SYN** INCLINATION: *~ (for sth/for doing sth) He showed a propensity for violence.* ◆ *~ (to do sth) She has a propensity to exaggerate.*

prop·er 🔊 /ˈprɑpər/ *adj.*
1 [only before noun] right, appropriate, or correct; according to the rules: *We should have had a proper discussion before voting.* ◆ *Please follow the proper procedures for dealing with complaints.* ◆ *Nothing is in its proper place.* **2** socially and morally acceptable: *It is right and proper that parents take responsibility for their children's attendance at school.* ◆ *The development was planned without proper regard to the interests of local people.* ◆ *He is always perfectly proper in his behavior.* **ANT** IMPROPER ⊃ see also PROPRIETY **3** [after noun] according to the most exact meaning of the word: *The celebrations proper always begin on the last stroke of midnight.* **4** *~ to sth* (*formal*) belonging to a particular type of thing; natural in a particular situation or place: *They should be treated with the dignity proper to all individuals created by God.*

ˌproper ˈfraction *noun* (*mathematics*) a FRACTION that is less than one, with the bottom number greater than the top number, for example $\frac{1}{4}$ or $\frac{2}{3}$

prop·er·ly /ˈprɑpərli/ *adv.* **1** in a way that is correct and/or appropriate: *How much money do we need to do the job properly?* ◆ *The television isn't working properly.* ◆ *Make sure the letter is properly addressed.* **2** in a way that is socially or morally acceptable: *You acted perfectly properly in approaching me first.* ◆ *When will these kids learn to behave properly?* **3** really; in fact: *He had usurped powers that properly belonged to the head of state.* ◆ *The subject is not, properly speaking* (= really), *a science.*

ˌproper ˈnoun (also **ˌproper ˈname**) *noun* (*grammar*) a word that is the name of a person, a place, an institution, etc. and is written with a capital letter, for example *Tom, Mrs. Jones, Rome, Texas, the Rhine, the White House* ⊃ compare ABSTRACT NOUN, COMMON NOUN

prop·er·tied /ˈprɑpərtid/ *adj.* [only before noun] (*formal*) owning property, especially land

prop·er·ty 🔊 /ˈprɑpərti/ *noun* (pl. **prop·er·ties**)
1 [U] a thing or things that are owned by someone; a possession or possessions: *This building is government property.* ◆ *Be careful not to damage other people's property.* ⊃ see also INTELLECTUAL PROPERTY, PUBLIC PROPERTY ⊃ thesaurus box at THING **2** [U] land and buildings: *The price of property has risen enormously.* ◆ *property prices* ◆ *a*

property developer ⊃ thesaurus box at BUILDING **3** [C] a building or buildings and the surrounding land: *There are a lot of empty properties in the area.* ⊃ thesaurus box at BUILDING **4** [C, usually pl.] (*formal*) a quality or characteristic that something has: *Compare the physical properties of the two substances.* ◆ *a plant with medicinal properties*

proph·e·cy /ˈprɑfəsi/ *noun* (*pl.* **proph·e·cies**) **1** [C] a statement that something will happen in the future, especially one made by someone with religious or magic powers: *to fulfill a prophecy* (= make it come true) **2** [U] (*formal*) the power of being able to say what will happen in the future: *She was believed to have the gift of prophecy.*

proph·e·sy /ˈprɑfəˌsaɪ/ *verb* (**proph·e·sies**, **proph·e·sy-ing**, **proph·e·sied**, **proph·e·sied**) to say what will happen in the future (done in the past using religious or magic powers): ~ **sth** *to prophesy war* ◆ ~ **that...** *She prophesied that she would win a gold medal.* ◆ + **speech** *"It will end in disaster," he prophesied.*

proph·et /ˈprɑfət/ *noun* **1** [C] (in the Christian, Jewish, and Muslim religions) a person sent by God to teach the people and give them messages from God **2 the Prophet** [sing.] Muhammad, who founded the religion of Islam **3** a person who claims to know what will happen in the future **4** ~ **(of sth)** a person who teaches or supports a new idea, theory, etc.: *They had known Lincoln as a prophet of human freedom and brotherhood.* **5 the Prophets** [pl.] the name used for some books of the Old Testament and the Hebrew Bible **IDM** see DOOM *n.*

proph·et·ess /ˈprɑfətəs/ *noun* a woman who is a prophet

pro·phet·ic /prəˈfɛtɪk/ *adj.* (*formal*) **1** correctly stating or showing what will happen in the future: *Many of his warnings proved prophetic.* **2** like or connected with a prophet or prophets: *the prophetic books of the Old Testament* ▸ **pro·phet·i·cally** /-kli/ *adv.*

pro·phy·lac·tic /ˌproʊfəˈlæktɪk/ *adj., noun*
● *adj.* (*medical*) done or used in order to prevent a disease: *prophylactic treatment* ▸ **pro·phy·lac·ti·cally** /-kli/ *adv.*
● *noun* **1** (*medical*) a medicine, device, or course of action that prevents disease **2** (*formal*) = CONDOM

pro·phy·lax·is /ˌproʊfəˈlæksəs/ *noun* [U] (*medical*) action that is taken in order to prevent disease

pro·pin·qui·ty /prəˈpɪŋkwəti/ *noun* [U] (*formal*) the state of being near in space or time **SYN** PROXIMITY

pro·pi·ti·ate /prəˈpɪʃiˌeɪt/ *verb* ~ **sb** (*formal*) to stop someone from being angry by trying to please them **SYN** PLACATE: *Sacrifices were made to propitiate the gods.* ▸ **pro·pi·ti·a·tion** /prəˌpɪʃiˈeɪʃn/ *noun* [U]

pro·pi·ti·a·to·ry /prəˈpɪʃiəˌtɔri/ *adj.* (*formal*) intended to win back the friendship and approval of an angry or aggressive person: *She saw the flowers as a propitiatory offering.*

pro·pi·tious /prəˈpɪʃəs/ *adj.* ~ **(for sth/sb)** (*formal*) likely to produce a successful result: *It was not a propitious time to start a new business.*

pro·po·nent /prəˈpoʊnənt/ *noun* ~ **(of sth)** (*formal*) a person who supports an idea or a course of action **SYN** ADVOCATE

pro·por·tion 🔑 **AWL** /prəˈpɔrʃn/ *noun*
> PART OF WHOLE **1** [C] a part or share of a whole: *Water covers a large proportion of the earth's surface.* ◆ *Loam is a soil with roughly equal proportions of clay, sand, and silt.* ◆ *The proportion of regular smokers increases with age.* ◆ *An exceptionally high proportion of young people now enter college after graduating from high school.*
> RELATIONSHIP **2** [U] ~ **(of sth to sth)** the relationship of one thing to another in size, amount, etc. **SYN** RATIO: *The proportion of men to women in the college has changed dramatically over the years.* ◆ *The basic ingredients are limestone and clay in the proportion 2:1.* ◆ *The room is very long in proportion to* (= relative to) *its width.* **3** [U, C, usually pl.] the correct relationship in size, degree, importance, etc. between one thing and another or between the parts of a whole: *You haven't drawn the figures in the foreground in proportion.* ◆ *The head is out of proportion with the body.* ◆ *an*

impressive building with fine proportions ◆ *Always try to keep a* **sense of proportion** (= a sense of the relative importance of different things).
> SIZE/SHAPE **4 proportions** [pl.] the measurements of something; its size and shape: *This method divides the task into more manageable proportions.* ◆ *a food shortage that could soon* **reach crisis proportions** ◆ *a room of fairly generous proportions*
> MATHEMATICS **5** [U] the equal relationship between two pairs of numbers, as in the statement "4 is to 8 as 6 is to 12" **IDM keep sth in proportion** to react to something in a sensible way and not think it is worse or more serious than it really is **out of (all) proportion (to sth)** larger, more serious, etc. in relation to something than is necessary or appropriate: *They earn salaries out of all proportion to their ability.* ◆ *The media has blown the incident up out of all proportion.*

GRAMMAR

proportion

- If **proportion** is used with an uncountable or a singular noun, the verb is generally singular: *A proportion of the land is used for agriculture.*
- If **the proportion of** is used with a plural countable noun, or a singular noun that represents a group of people, the verb is usually singular, but with **a (large, small, etc.) proportion of**, a plural verb is often used: *The proportion of small cars on America's roads is increasing.* ◆ *A high proportion of five-year-olds have teeth in poor condition.*

LANGUAGE BANK

proportion
describing fractions and proportions

- According to this pie chart, **a third of** students' leisure time is spent watching TV.
- **One in five** hours is spent socializing.
- Socializing **accounts for/makes up/comprises** about 20% of leisure time.
- Students spend **twice as much** time playing computer games as playing sports.
- **Three times as many** hours are spent playing computer games as reading.
- The figure for playing computer games is **three times higher than** the figure for reading.
- **The largest proportion of** time is spent playing computer games.
- ⊃ note at HALF
- ⊃ Thesaurus at CONSIST
- ⊃ Language Banks at EXPECT, FALL, ILLUSTRATE, INCREASE

---

pro·por·tion·al **AWL** /prəˈpɔrʃənl/ *adj.* ~ **(to sth)** of an appropriate size, amount, or degree in comparison with something: *Salary is proportional to years of experience.* ◆ *to be* **directly/inversely proportional** *to something* ▸ **pro·por·tion·ally** **AWL** /-ʃənəli/ *adv.*: *Families with children spend proportionally less per person than families without children.*

pro·por·tion·al·i·ty /prəˌpɔrʃəˈnæləti/ *noun* [U] (*formal*) the principle that an action, a punishment, etc. should not be more severe than is necessary

pro·por·tional represen·ta·tion *noun* [U] (*abbr.* PR) a system that gives each party in an election a number of seats in relation to the number of votes its candidates receive

pro·por·tion·ate **AWL** /prəˈpɔrʃənət/ *adj.* ~ **(to sth)** (*formal*) increasing or decreasing in size, amount, or degree according to changes in something else **SYN** PROPORTIONAL: *The number of accidents is proportionate*

| h **hat** | m **man** | n **no** | ŋ **sing** | l **leg** | r **red** | y **yes** | w **wet** |

to the increased volume of traffic. ➔ compare DISPROPOR-TIONATE ▸ **pro·por·tion·ate·ly** [AWL] *adv.*: *Prices have risen but wages have not risen proportionately.*

pro·por·tioned /prə'pɔrʃənd/ *adj.* (used especially after an adverb) having parts that relate in size to other parts in the way that is described: *a well-proportioned living room* ◆ *She was tall and perfectly proportioned.*

pro·pos·al 🔖 /prə'poʊzl/ *noun*
1 [C, U] a formal suggestion or plan; the act of making a suggestion: *to submit/consider/accept/reject a proposal* ◆ *~ to do sth a proposal to build more offices* ◆ *~ that... His proposal that the system should be changed was rejected.* ◆ *~ for sth They judged that the time was right for the proposal of new terms for the trade agreement.* **2** [C] an act of formally asking someone to marry you

pro·pose 🔖 /prə'poʊz/ *verb*
▸ SUGGEST PLAN **1** [T] (*formal*) to suggest a plan, an idea, etc. for people to think about and decide on: *~ sth The government proposed changes to the voting system.* ◆ *What would you propose?* ◆ *~ that... She proposed that the book be banned.* ◆ *it is proposed that... It was proposed that the president be elected for a period of two years.* ◆ *~ doing sth He proposed changing the name of the company.* ◆ *it is proposed to do sth It was proposed to pay the money from public funds.*
▸ INTEND **2** [T] to intend to do something: *~ to do sth What do you propose to do now?* ◆ *~ doing sth How do you propose getting home?*
▸ MARRIAGE **3** [I, T] to ask someone to marry you: *He was afraid that if he proposed she might refuse.* ◆ *~ to sb She proposed to me!* ◆ *~ sth (to sb) to propose marriage*
▸ AT FORMAL MEETING **4** [T] to suggest something at a formal meeting and ask people to vote on it: *~ sb (for/as sth) I propose Tom Ellis for chairman.* ◆ *~ sth to propose a motion* (= to be the main speaker in support of an idea at a formal debate) ➔ compare OPPOSE, SECOND
▸ SUGGEST EXPLANATION **5** [T] *~ sth* (*formal*) to suggest an explanation of something for people to consider **SYN** PROPOUND: *She proposed a possible solution to the mystery.*
IDM **propose a toast (to sb)| propose sb's health** to ask people to wish someone health, happiness, and success by raising their glasses and drinking: *I'd like to propose a toast to the bride and the groom.*

pro·pos·er /prə'poʊzər/ *noun* a person who formally suggests something at a meeting

prop·o·si·tion /ˌprɑpə'zɪʃn/ *noun, verb*
● *noun* **1** an idea or a plan of action that is suggested, especially in business: *I'd like to put a business proposition to you.* ◆ *He was trying to make it look like an **attractive proposition*.* **2** a thing that you intend to do; a problem or task to be dealt with **SYN** MATTER: *Getting a work permit is not always a simple proposition.* **3** also **Proposition** (*informal*) (*abbr.* **Prop**) a suggested change to the law that people can vote on: *One of the propositions up for vote in California is proposition 1-A.* ◆ *Vote "No" to Prop 16* (= on a sign). **4** (*formal*) a statement that expresses an opinion: *Her assessment is based on the proposition that power corrupts.* **5** (*mathematics*) a statement of a THEOREM, and an explanation of how it can be proved ▸ **prop·o·si·tion·al** /-ʃənl/ *adj.*
● *verb ~ sb* to say in a direct way to someone that you would like to have sex with them: *She was propositioned by a strange man in the bar.*

pro·pound /prə'paʊnd/ *verb ~ sth* (*formal*) to suggest an idea or explanation of something for people to consider **SYN** PROPOSE, PUT FORWARD: *the theory of natural selection, first propounded by Charles Darwin*

pro·pri·e·tar·y /prə'praɪəˌteri/ *adj.* [usually before noun] **1** (of goods) made and sold by a particular company and protected by a REGISTERED TRADEMARK: *a proprietary medicine* ◆ *proprietary brands* ◆ *a proprietary name* **2** relating to an owner or to the fact of owning something: *The company has a proprietary right to the property.* **3** behaving as

if you owned someone or something: *He looked about him with a proprietary air.*

pro·pri·e·tor /prə'praɪətər/ *noun* (*formal*) the owner of a business, a hotel, etc.: *newspaper proprietors* ▸ **pro·pri·e·tor·ship** /-ˌʃɪp/ *noun* [U] ➔ see also PROPRIETRESS

pro·pri·e·to·ri·al /prəˌpraɪə'tɔriəl/ *adj.* (*formal*) relating to an owner or to the fact of owning something: *proprietorial rights* ◆ *He laid a proprietorial hand on her arm* (= as if he owned her). ▸ **pro·pri·e·to·ri·al·ly** *adv.*

pro·pri·e·tress /prə'praɪətrəs/ *noun* (*old-fashioned*) a woman who owns a business, hotel, etc. ➔ see also PROPRIETOR

pro·pri·e·ty /prə'praɪəti/ *noun* (*formal*) **1** [U] moral and social behavior that is considered to be correct and acceptable: *Nobody questioned the propriety of her being there alone.* **ANT** IMPROPRIETY **2** **the proprieties** [pl.] the rules of correct behavior **SYN** ETIQUETTE: *They were careful to observe the proprieties.*

pro·pul·sion /prə'pʌlʃn/ *noun* [U] (*technical*) the force that drives something forward: *wind/steam/jet propulsion* ➔ see also PROPEL ▸ **pro·pul·sive** /prə'pʌlsɪv/ *adj.*

pro ra·ta /ˌproʊ 'reɪtə/ *adj.* (from *Latin, formal*) (of a payment or share of something) calculated according to how much of something has been used, the amount of work done, etc. **SYN** PROPORTIONATE: *If costs go up, there will be a pro rata increase in prices.* ▸ **pro rata** *adv.*: *Prices will increase pro rata.*

prorate *verb* [T] to calculate a payment according to how much of something has been used, the amount of work done, etc.: *The bonus will be prorated according to salaries.*

pro·sa·ic /proʊ'zeɪɪk/ *adj.* (usually *disapproving*) **1** ordinary and not showing any imagination **SYN** UNIMAGINATIVE: *a prosaic style* **2** dull; not romantic **SYN** MUNDANE: *the prosaic side of life* ▸ **pro·sa·i·cally** /-kli/ *adv.*

pro·sce·ni·um /prə'siniəm/ *noun* the part of the stage in a theater that is in front of the curtain: *a traditional theater with a **proscenium** arch* (= one that forms a frame for the stage where the curtain is opened)

pro·sciut·to /prə'ʃutoʊ/ *noun* [U] a type of Italian HAM that is served in very thin slices

pro·scribe /proʊ'skraɪb/ *verb ~ sth* (*formal*) to say officially that something is banned: *proscribed organizations* ▸ **pro·scrip·tion** /proʊ'skrɪpʃn/ *noun* [U, C]

prose /proʊz/ *noun* [U] writing that is not poetry: *the author's clear elegant prose* (= style of writing)

pros·e·cute /'prɑsəˌkyut/ *verb* **1** [T, I] *~ (sb/sth) (for sth/doing sth)* to officially charge someone with a crime in court: *The company was prosecuted for breaching the Occupational Safety and Health Act.* ◆ *Trespassers will be prosecuted* (= a notice telling people to keep out of a particular area). ◆ *The police decided not to prosecute.* **2** [I, T] *~ (sb)* to be a lawyer in a court case for a person or an organization that is charging someone with a crime: *the prosecuting counsel/lawyer/attorney* ◆ *James Spencer, prosecuting, claimed that the witness was lying.* **3** [T] *~ sth* (*formal*) to continue taking part in or doing something: *They had overwhelming public support to prosecute the war.*

pros·e·cu·tion /ˌprɑsə'kyuʃn/ *noun* **1** [U, C] the process of trying to prove in court that someone is guilty of a crime (= of prosecuting them); the process of being officially charged with a crime in court: *Prosecution for a first minor offense rarely leads to imprisonment.* ◆ *He threatened to bring a private prosecution against the doctor.* ➔ collocations at JUSTICE **2** **the prosecution** [sing.] a person or an organization that prosecutes someone in court, together with the lawyers, etc.: *He was a **witness for the prosecution**.* ◆ *The prosecution has failed to prove its case.* ◆ *defense and prosecution* ◆ *a prosecution lawyer* **3** [U] (*formal*) the act of making something happen or continue

pros·e·cu·tor /'prɑsəˌkyutər/ *noun* **1** a public official who charges someone officially with a crime and prosecutes them in court: *the state prosecutor* **2** a lawyer who leads the case against a DEFENDANT in court

pros·e·lyt·ize /ˈprɑsələˌtaɪz/ *verb* [I] (*formal*, often *disapproving*) to try to persuade other people to accept your beliefs, especially about religion or politics

prose poem *noun* a piece of writing that uses the language and ideas associated with poetry, but is not in VERSE form

pro shop *noun* a store at a GOLF CLUB that sells or repairs golf equipment, usually run by a professional player who works at that club

pros·o·dy /ˈprɑsədi/ *noun* [U] **1** (*technical*) the patterns of sounds and rhythms in poetry; the study of this **2** (*phonetics*) the part of PHONETICS that is concerned with stress and INTONATION as opposed to individual speech sounds ▶ **pro·sod·ic** /prəˈsɑdɪk/ *adj.*

pros·pect ⚒ **AWL** /ˈprɑspɛkt/ *noun, verb*
● *noun* **1** [U, sing.] the possibility that something will happen: ~ **(of sth/of doing sth)** *There is no immediate prospect of peace.* ◆ *A place in the semifinals is in prospect* (= likely to happen). ◆ ~ **(that…)** *There's a reasonable prospect that his debts will be paid.* **2** [sing.] an idea of what might or will happen in the future: *an exciting prospect* ◆ *Traveling alone around the world is a daunting prospect.* ◆ ~ **(of sth/of doing sth)** *The prospect of becoming a father filled him with alarm.* **3 prospects** [pl.] the chances of being successful: *good job/employment/career prospects* ◆ *At 25 he was an unemployed musician with no prospects.* ◆ ~ **for sth** *Long-term prospects for the economy have improved.* ◆ ~ **of sth** *What are the prospects of promotion in this job?* **4** [C] ~ **(for sth)** a person who is likely to be successful in a competition: *She is one of Canada's best prospects for a gold medal.* **5** [C] (*formal*) a wide view of an area of land, etc.: *a delightful prospect of the lake*
● *verb* [I] ~ **(for sth)** to search an area for gold, minerals, oil, etc.: *Thousands moved to the area to prospect for gold.* ◆ (*figurative*) *to prospect for new clients*

pros·pec·tive **AWL** /prəˈspɛktɪv/ *adj.* [usually before noun] **1** expected to do something or to become something SYN POTENTIAL: *a prospective buyer* **2** expected to happen soon SYN FORTHCOMING: *They are worried about prospective changes in the law.*

pros·pec·tor /ˈprɑspɛktər/ *noun* a person who searches an area for gold, minerals, oil, etc.

pro·spec·tus /prəˈspɛktəs/ *noun* **1** a book or printed document that gives information about a school, college, etc. in order to advertise it **2** (*business*) a document that gives information about a company's shares before they are offered for sale

pros·per /ˈprɑspər/ *verb* [I] to develop in a successful way; to be successful, especially in making money SYN THRIVE

pros·per·i·ty /prɑˈspɛrəti/ *noun* [U] the state of being successful, especially in making money: *Our future prosperity depends on economic growth.* ◆ *The country is enjoying a period of peace and prosperity.*

pros·per·ous /ˈprɑspərəs/ *adj.* rich and successful SYN AFFLUENT: *prosperous countries* ⊃ thesaurus box at RICH

pros·tate /ˈprɑsteɪt/ (also **prostate gland**) *noun* a small organ in men, near the BLADDER, that produces a liquid in which SPERM is carried

pros·the·sis /prɑsˈθisəs/ *noun* (*pl.* **pros·the·ses** /-siz/) (*medical*) an artificial part of the body, for example a leg, an eye, or a tooth ▶ **pros·thet·ic** /prɑsˈθɛtɪk/ *adj.*: *a prosthetic arm*

pros·thet·ics /prɑsˈθɛtɪks/ *noun* **1** [pl.] artificial parts of the body **2** [U] the activity of making or attaching artificial body parts

pros·ti·tute /ˈprɑstəˌtut/ *noun, verb*
● *noun* a person who has sex for money
● *verb* **1** ~ **sth/yourself** to use your skills, abilities, etc. to do something that earns you money but that other people do

not respect because you are capable of doing something better: *Many felt he was prostituting his talents by writing Hollywood scripts.* **2** ~ **yourself** to work as a prostitute

pros·ti·tu·tion /ˌprɑstəˈtuʃn/ *noun* [U] **1** the work of a prostitute: *Many women were forced into prostitution.* ◆ *child prostitution* **2** ~ **of sth** (*formal*) the use of your abilities on something of little value

pros·trate /ˈprɑstreɪt/ *adj., verb*
● *adj.* (*formal*) **1** lying on the ground and facing downward: *They fell prostrate in worship.* ◆ *He stumbled over Luke's prostrate body.* **2** ~ **(with sth)** so shocked, upset, etc. that you cannot do anything: *She was prostrate with grief after her son's death.*
● *verb* **1** ~ **yourself** to lie on your front with your face looking downward, especially as an act of worship **2** [usually passive] ~ **sb** to make someone feel weak, shocked, and unable to do anything SYN OVERCOME: *He was expecting to find her prostrated by the tragedy.* ◆ *For months he was prostrated with grief.*

pros·tra·tion /prɑˈstreɪʃn/ *noun* [U] (*formal*) **1** extreme physical weakness: *a state of prostration brought on by the heat* **2** the action of lying with your face downward, especially in worship

prot·ac·tin·i·um /ˌproʊtækˈtɪniəm/ *noun* [U] (*symb.* **Pa**) a chemical element. Protactinium is a RADIOACTIVE metal found naturally when URANIUM decays.

pro·tag·o·nist /proʊˈtægənɪst/ *noun* (*formal*) **1** the main character in a play, movie, or book ⊃ compare HERO **2** one of the main people in a real event, especially a competition, battle, or struggle **3** an active supporter of a policy or movement, especially one that is trying to change something SYN CHAMPION: *a leading protagonist of the conservation movement*

pro·te·an /ˈproʊtiən; proʊˈtiən/ *adj.* (*literary*) able to change quickly and easily: *a protean character*

pro·te·ase /ˈproʊtiˌeɪz; -ˌeɪs/ *noun* (*biology*) a substance in the body that breaks down PROTEINS and PEPTIDES

pro·tect ⚒ /prəˈtɛkt/ *verb*
1 [T, I] to make sure that someone or something is not harmed, injured, damaged, etc.: ~ **sb/sth/yourself (against/from sth)** *Troops have been sent to protect aid workers against attack.* ◆ *They huddled together to protect themselves from the wind.* ◆ *Each company is fighting to protect its own commercial interests.* ◆ ~ **(against/from sth)** *a paint that helps protect against rust* **2** [T, usually passive] ~ **sth** to introduce laws that make it illegal to kill, harm, or damage a particular animal, area of land, building, etc.: *a protected area/species* **3** [T, usually passive] ~ **sth** to help an industry in your own country by taxing goods from other countries so that there is less competition: *protected markets* **4** [T, I] ~ **(sb/sth) (against sth)** to provide someone or something with insurance against fire, injury, damage, etc.: *Many policies do not protect you against personal injury.*

pro·tec·tion ⚒ /prəˈtɛkʃn/ *noun*
1 [U] ~ **(for/of sb/sth) (against/from sth)** the act of protecting someone or something; the state of being protected: *Wear clothes that provide adequate protection against the wind and rain.* ◆ *He asked to be put under police protection.* ◆ *the conservation and protection of the environment* ◆ *data protection laws* **2** [C] ~ **(against sth)** a thing that protects someone or something against something: *They wore the charm as a protection against evil spirits.* **3** [U] ~ **(against sth)** insurance against fire, injury, damage, etc.: *Our policy offers complete protection against fire and theft.* **4** [U] the system of helping an industry in your own country by taxing foreign goods: *The government is ready to introduce protection for the car industry.* **5** [U] the system of paying criminals so that they will not attack your business or property: *to pay protection money* ◆ *to run a protection racket*

pro·tec·tion·ism /prəˈtɛkʃəˌnɪzəm/ *noun* [U] the principle or practice of protecting a country's own industry by taxing foreign goods ▶ **pro·tec·tion·ist** /-ʃənɪst/ *adj.*: *protectionist policies*

pro·tec·tive /prəˈtɛktɪv/ *adj.* **1** [only before noun] providing or intended to provide protection: *Workers should wear full **protective clothing**.* ◆ *a protective layer of varnish* ◆ *a protective barrier against the sun's rays* **2** having or showing a wish to protect someone or something: **~ (toward sb/sth)** *She had been fiercely protective toward him as a teenager.* ◆ **~ (of sb/sth)** *He was extremely protective of his role as advisor.* ◆ *He put a protective arm around her shoulders.* **3** intended to give an advantage to your own country's industry: *protective tariffs* ▶ **pro·tec·tive·ly** *adv.*: *She clutched her bag protectively.* **pro·tec·tive·ness** *noun* [U]

pro₁tective 'custody *noun* [U] the state of being kept in prison for your own safety

pro·tec·tor /prəˈtɛktər/ *noun* a person, an organization, or a thing that protects someone or something: *I regarded him as my friend and protector.* ◆ *the company's image as a protector of the environment* ◆ *Hard hats and ear protectors are provided.* ➷ see also SURGE PROTECTOR

pro·tec·tor·ate /prəˈtɛktərət/ *noun* **1** [C] a country that is controlled and protected by a more powerful country ➷ compare COLONY **2** [U] the state or period of being controlled and protected by another country

pro·té·gé (*feminine* **pro·té·gée**) /ˈproʊtəˌʒeɪ; ˌproʊtəˈʒeɪ/ *noun* (from *French*) a young person who is helped in their career and personal development by a more experienced person: *a protégé of the great violinist Yehudi Menuhin*

pro·tein /ˈproʊtin/ *noun* [C, U] a natural substance found in meat, eggs, fish, some vegetables, etc. There are many different proteins and they are an essential part of what humans and animals eat to help them grow and stay healthy: *essential proteins and vitamins* ◆ *protein deficiency* ◆ *Peas, beans, and lentils are a good source of vegetable protein.*

pro tem /ˌproʊ ˈtɛm/ *adv.* (from *Latin*) for now, but not for a long time: *A new manager will be appointed pro tem.* ▶ **pro tem** *adj.*: *A pro tem committee was formed from existing members.*

pro·test 🔊 *noun, verb*

● **noun** /ˈproʊtɛst/ [U, C] the expression of strong disagreement with or opposition to something; a statement or an action that shows this: *The director resigned in protest at the decision.* ◆ *The announcement raised a storm of protest.* ◆ *a protest march* ◆ *She accepted the charge without protest.* ◆ **~ (against sth)** *The workers staged a protest against the proposed changes in their contracts.* ◆ *The building work will go ahead, despite protests from local residents.* ◆ *The riot began as a peaceful protest.*
IDM **under protest** unwillingly and after expressing disagreement: *She wrote a letter of apology but only under protest.*

● **verb** /prəˈtɛst; ˈproʊtɛst/ **1** [I, T] to say or do something to show that you disagree with or disapprove of something, especially publicly: **~ (about/against/at sth)** *Students took to the streets to protest against the decision.* ◆ *The victim's widow protested at the leniency of the sentence.* ◆ *There's no use protesting, I won't change my mind.* ◆ **~ sth** *They fully intend to protest the decision.* ➷ thesaurus box at COMPLAIN **2** [T] to say firmly that something is true, especially when you have been accused of something or when other people do not believe you: **~ sth** *She has always protested her innocence.* ◆ **~ that…** *He protested that the trip was too far by car.* ◆ **+ speech** *"That's not what you said earlier!" Jane protested.*

Prot·es·tant /ˈprɑtəstənt/ *noun* a member of a part of the Western Christian Church that separated from the Roman Catholic Church in the 16th century: *He's a Protestant.* ▶ **Prot·es·tant** *adj.*: *The majority of the population is Protestant.* ◆ *a Protestant church/country* **Prot·es·tant·ism** /ˈprɑtəstənˌtɪzəm/ *noun* [U]

₁Protestant 'ethic (also **₁Protestant 'work ₁ethic**) *noun* [sing.] the idea that a person has a duty to work hard and spend their time and money in a careful, responsible way, sometimes thought to be typical of Protestants

prot·es·ta·tion /ˌprɑtəˈsteɪʃn; ˌproʊ-/ *noun* [C, U] (*formal*) a strong statement that something is true, especially when other people do not believe you: *She repeated her protestation of innocence.* ◆ *Despite his protestation to the contrary, he was extremely tired.*

pro·test·er /ˈproʊtɛstər; prəˈtɛs-/ *noun* a person who makes a public protest **SYN** DEMONSTRATOR: *Thousands of protesters marched through the city.*

proto- /ˈproʊtoʊ/ *combining form* (in nouns and adjectives) original; from which others develop: *prototype* ◆ *proto-modernist painters*

pro·to·col **AWL** /ˈproʊtəˌkɔl; -ˌkɑl/ *noun* **1** [U] a system of fixed rules and formal behavior used at official meetings, usually between governments: *a breach of protocol* ◆ *the protocol of diplomatic visits* **2** [C] (*technical*) the first or original version of an agreement, especially a TREATY between countries, etc.; an extra part added to an agreement or TREATY: *the first Geneva Protocol* ◆ *It is set out in a legally binding protocol which forms part of the treaty.* **3** [C] (*computing*) a set of rules that control the way data is sent between computers **4** [C] (*technical*) a plan for performing a scientific experiment or medical treatment

₁Proto-₁Indo-Euro'pean *noun* [U] the ancient language on which all Indo-European languages are thought to be based. There are no written records of Proto-Indo-European, but experts have tried to construct it from the evidence of modern languages.

pro·ton /ˈproʊtɑn/ *noun* (*physics*) a very small piece of matter (= a substance) with a positive electric charge that forms part of the NUCLEUS (= central part) of an atom ➷ picture at ATOM ➷ see also ELECTRON, NEUTRON

pro·to·plasm /ˈproʊtəˌplæzm/ *noun* [U] (*biology*) a clear substance like jelly that forms the living part of an animal or plant cell ➷ compare CYTOPLASM

pro·to·type /ˈproʊtəˌtaɪp/ *noun* **~ (for/of sth)** the first design of something from which other forms are copied or developed: *the prototype of the modern bicycle* ▶ **pro·to·typ·i·cal** /ˌproʊtəˈtɪpɪkl/ *adj.*

pro·to·zo·an /ˌproʊtəˈzoʊən/ *noun* (*pl.* **pro·to·zo·ans** or **pro·to·zo·a** /-ˈzoʊə/) (*biology*) a very small living thing, usually with only one cell, which can only be seen under a MICROSCOPE ▶ **protozoan** *adj.*

pro·tract·ed /prəˈtræktəd; proʊ-/ *adj.* lasting longer than expected or longer than usual: *protracted delays/disputes/negotiations* **SYN** PROLONGED

pro·trac·tor /ˈproʊtræktər; proʊˈtræk-/ *noun* an instrument for measuring and drawing angles, usually made from a half circle of clear plastic with degrees (0° to 180°) marked on it

pro·trude /prəˈtrud; proʊ-/ *verb* [I] (*formal*) to stick out from a place or a surface: *protruding teeth* ◆ **~ from sth** *He hung his coat on a nail protruding from the wall.*

pro·tru·sion /prəˈtruʒn; proʊ-/ *noun* [C, U] (*formal*) a thing that sticks out from a place or surface; the fact of doing this: *a protrusion on the rock face*

pro·tu·ber·ance /prəˈtubərəns; proʊ-/ *noun* (*formal*) a round part that sticks out from a surface **SYN** BULGE

pro·tu·ber·ant /prəˈtubərənt; proʊ-/ *adj.* (*formal*) curving or swelling out from a surface **SYN** BULGING: *protuberant eyes*

proud 🔊 /praʊd/ *adj., adv.*

● *adj.* (**proud·er**, **proud·est**)
> PLEASED **1** feeling pleased and satisfied about something that you own or have done, or are connected with: *proud parents* ◆ **the proud owner** *of a new car* ◆ **~ of sb/sth/yourself** *Your achievements are something to be proud of.* ◆ *He was proud of himself for not giving up.* ◆ **~ to be/have sth** *I feel very proud to be a part of the team.* ◆ **~ that…** *She was proud that her daughter had so much talent.* ➷ thesaurus box at GLAD **2** [only before noun] causing someone to feel pride: *This is*

the proudest moment of my life. ◆ The car had been his **proudest possession**.

> FEELING TOO IMPORTANT **3** (*disapproving*) feeling that you are better and more important than other people **SYN** ARROGANT: *She was too proud to admit she could be wrong.*

> HAVING SELF-RESPECT **4** having respect for yourself and not wanting to lose the respect of others: *They were a proud and independent people.* ◆ *Don't be too proud to ask for help.*

> BEAUTIFUL/TALL **5** (*literary*) beautiful, tall, and impressive: *The sunflowers stretched tall and proud to the sun.* ➔ see also PRIDE

● *adv.*

IDM **do yourself/sb proud** to do something that makes you proud of yourself or that makes other people proud of you

proud·ly ✎ /ˈpraʊdli/ adv.

1 in a way that shows that someone is proud of something: *She proudly displayed her prize.* **2** (*literary*) in a way that is large and impressive: *The Rockies rose proudly in the background.*

prov·a·ble /ˈpruːvəbl/ adj. that can be shown to be true

prove ✎ /pruːv/ verb

(proved, proved or proved, prov·en /ˈpruːvn/)

> SHOW SOMETHING IS TRUE **1** [T] to use facts, evidence, etc. to show that something is true: ~ **sth** *They hope this new evidence will prove her innocence.* ◆ *"I know you're lying." "Prove it!"* ◆ *He felt he needed to prove his point* (= show other people that he was right). ◆ *Are you just doing this to prove a point?* ◆ *What are you trying to prove?* ◆ *I certainly don't have anything to prove* —*my record speaks for itself.* ◆ ~ **sth to sb** *Just give me a chance and I'll prove it to you.* ◆ ~ **(that)…** *This proves (that) I was right.* ◆ ~ **sb/sth/yourself + adj./noun** *She was determined to prove everyone wrong.* ◆ *In this country, you are innocent until proven guilty.* ◆ ~ **sb/sth/yourself to be/ have sth** *You've just proved yourself to be a liar.* ◆ ~ **what, how, etc.…** *This just proves what I have been saying for some time.* ◆ **it is proven that…** *Can it be proven that he did commit these offenses?* **ANT** DISPROVE ➔ language bank at EVIDENCE ➔ see also PROOF, PROVEN

> BE **2** linking verb if something **proves** dangerous, expensive, etc. or if it **proves to be** dangerous, expensive, etc., you discover that it is dangerous, etc. over a period of time **SYN** TURN OUT: + **adj.** *The opposition proved too strong for him.* ◆ + **noun** *Shares in the industry proved a poor investment.* ◆ ~ **to be sth** *The promotion proved to be a turning point in his career.*

> YOURSELF **3** [T] ~ **yourself (to sb)** to show other people how good you are at doing something or that you are capable of doing something: *He constantly feels he has to prove himself to others.* **4** [T] ~ **yourself + adj/noun** | ~ **yourself to be sth** to show other people that you are a particular type of person or that you have a particular quality: *He proved himself determined to succeed.*

> OF BREAD **5** [I] to swell before being baked because of the action of YEAST **SYN** RISE

prov·en /ˈpruːvn/ adj. [only before noun] tested and shown to be true: *a student of proven ability* ◆ *It is a proven fact that fluoride strengthens growing teeth.* **ANT** UNPROVEN ➔ see also PROVE

prov·e·nance /ˈprɑvənəns; -ˌnɑns/ noun [U, C] (*technical*) the place that something originally came from **SYN** ORIGIN: *All the furniture is of English provenance.* ◆ *There's no proof about the provenance of the painting* (= whether it is genuine or not).

ˈpro-verb noun (*grammar*) a verb that depends on another verb for its meaning, for example "do" in "She likes chocolate and so do I."

pro·verb /ˈprɑvɜrb/ noun a well-known phrase or sentence that gives advice or says something that is generally true, for example "Waste not, want not."

pro·ver·bi·al /prəˈvɜrbiəl/ adj. **1** [only before noun] used to show that you are referring to a particular proverb or well-known phrase: *Let's not count our proverbial chickens.* **2** [not usually before noun] well known and talked about by a lot of people **SYN** FAMOUS: *Their hospitality is proverbial.* ▶ **pro·ver·bi·al·ly** adv.

pro·vide ✎ /prəˈvaɪd/ verb

1 to give something to someone or make it available for them to use **SYN** SUPPLY: ~ **sth** *The hospital has a commitment to provide the best possible medical care.* ◆ *The report was not expected to provide any answers.* ◆ *Please answer questions in the space provided.* ◆ ~ **sth for sb** *We are here to provide a service for the public.* ◆ ~ **sb with sth** *We are here to provide the public with a service.* **2** ~ **that…** (*formal*) (of a law or rule) to state that something will or must happen **SYN** STIPULATE: *The final section provides that any work produced for the company is thereafter owned by the company.* ➔ see also PROVISION

PHR V **pro·vide against sth** (*formal*) to make preparations to deal with something bad or unpleasant that might happen in the future **pro·vide for sb** to give someone the things that they need to live, such as food, money, and clothing **pro·vide for sth** (*formal*) **1** to make preparations to deal with something that might happen in the future **2** (of a law, rule, etc.) to make it possible for something to be done: *The legislation provides for the detention of suspected terrorists for up to seven days.*

pro·vid·ed ✎ /prəˈvaɪdəd/ (also **pro·vid·ing**) conj.

~ **(that)…**

used to say what must happen or be done to make it possible for something else to happen **SYN** IF: *We'll buy everything you produce, provided of course the price is right.* ◆ *Provided that you have the money in your account, you can withdraw up to $100 a day.*

prov·i·dence /ˈprɑvədəns/ also **Providence** noun [U] God, or a force that some people believe controls our lives and the things that happen to us, usually in a way that protects us **SYN** FATE: *to trust in divine providence*

prov·i·dent /ˈprɑvədənt/ adj. (*formal*) careful in planning for the future, especially by saving money **SYN** PRUDENT **ANT** IMPROVIDENT

prov·i·den·tial /ˌprɑvəˈdɛnʃl/ adj. (*formal*) lucky because it happens at the right time, but without being planned **SYN** TIMELY ▶ **prov·i·den·tial·ly** /-ʃəli/ adv.

pro·vid·er /prəˈvaɪdər/ noun a person or an organization that supplies someone with something they need or want: *training providers* ◆ *We are one of the largest providers of employment in the area.* ◆ *The eldest son is the family's sole provider* (= the only person who earns money). ➔ see also SERVICE PROVIDER

pro·vid·ing /prəˈvaɪdɪŋ/ conj. = PROVIDED

prov·ince /ˈprɑvəns/ noun **1** [C] one of the areas that some countries are divided into, with its own local government: *the provinces of Canada* **2 the provinces** [pl.] all the parts of a country except the capital city: *a shy young man from the provinces* [sing.] (*formal*) a person's particular area of knowledge, interest, or responsibility: *Such decisions are normally the province of higher management.* ◆ *I'm afraid the matter is outside my province* (= I cannot or need not deal with it).

pro·vin·cial /prəˈvɪnʃl/ adj., noun

● *adj.* **1** [only before noun] connected with one of the large areas that some countries are divided into, with its own local government: *provincial assemblies/elections* **2** [only before noun] (sometimes *disapproving*) connected with the parts of a country that do not include the capital city: *a provincial town* **3** (*disapproving*) unwilling to consider new or different ideas or things **SYN** NARROW-MINDED ▶ **pro·vin·cial·ly** /-ʃəli/ adv.

● *noun* (often *disapproving*) a person who lives in or comes from a part of the country that is not near the capital city

pro·vin·cial·ism /prəˈvɪnʃəˌlɪzəm/ noun [U] (disapproving) the attitude of people who are unwilling to consider new or different ideas or things

proving ground noun a place where something such as a new machine, vehicle, or weapon can be tested: *It's an ideal proving ground for the new car.* ◆ (figurative) *The club is the proving ground for young boxers.*

pro·vi·sion /prəˈvɪʒn/ noun, verb
● **noun 1** [U, C, usually sing.] the act of supplying someone with something that they need or want; something that is supplied: *housing provision* ◆ *The government is responsible for the provision of healthcare.* ◆ *There is no provision for anyone to sit down here.* ◆ *The provision of specialist teachers is being increased.* **2** [U, C] preparations that you make for something that might or will happen in the future: ~ **for sb/sth** *He had already made provisions for* (= planned for) *the financial future of) his wife and children before the accident.* ◆ *You should make provision for things going wrong.* ◆ ~ **against sth** *Small businesses are advised to make adequate provisions against bad debts.* **3 provisions** [pl.] supplies of food and drinks, especially for a long journey **4** [C] a condition or an arrangement in a legal document: *Under the provisions of the lease, the tenant is responsible for repairs.* ⊃ see also PROVIDE
● **verb** [often passive] ~ **sb/sth (with sth)** (formal) to supply someone or something with enough of something, especially food, to last for a particular period of time

pro·vi·sion·al /prəˈvɪʒənl/ adj. **1** arranged for the present time only and likely to be changed in the future **SYN** TEMPORARY: *a provisional government* ◆ *provisional arrangements* **2** arranged, but not yet definite: *The reservation is only provisional.* ▸ **pro·vi·sion·al·ly** /-ʒənəli/ adv.: *The meeting has been provisionally arranged for Friday.*

pro·vi·so /prəˈvaɪzoʊ/ noun (pl. **pro·vi·sos**) a condition that must be accepted before an agreement can be made **SYN** PROVISION: *Their participation is subject to a number of important provisos.* ◆ *He agreed to their visit with the proviso that they should stay no longer than one week.*

pro·vo·ca·teur /proʊˌvɑkəˈtər/ noun = AGENT PROVOCATEUR

prov·o·ca·tion /ˌprɑvəˈkeɪʃn/ noun [U, C] the act of doing or saying something deliberately in order to make someone angry or upset; something that is done or said to cause this: *He reacted violently only under provocation.* ◆ *The terrorists can strike at any time without provocation.* ◆ *She bursts into tears at the slightest provocation.* ◆ *So far the police have refused to respond to their provocations.*

pro·voc·a·tive /prəˈvɑkətɪv/ adj. **1** intended to make people angry or upset; intended to make people argue about something: *a provocative remark* ◆ *He doesn't really mean that—he's just being deliberately provocative.* **2** intended to make someone sexually excited: *a provocative smile* ▸ **pro·voc·a·tive·ly** adv.

pro·voke /prəˈvoʊk/ verb **1** ~ **sth** to cause a particular reaction or have a particular effect: *The announcement provoked a storm of protest.* ◆ *The article was intended to provoke discussion.* ◆ *Dairy products may provoke allergic reactions in some people.* **2** ~ **sb (into sth/into doing sth)** | ~ **sb to do sth** to say or do something that you know will annoy someone so that they react in an angry way **SYN** GOAD: *The lawyer claimed his client was provoked into acts of violence by the defendant.* ◆ *Be careful what you say—he's easily provoked.*

pro·vost /ˈproʊvoʊst/ also **Provost** noun **1** a senior official who manages the affairs of some colleges and universities **2** the head of a group of priests belonging to a particular CATHEDRAL

prow /praʊ/ noun (formal or literary) the pointed front part of a ship or boat

prow·ess /ˈpraʊəs/ noun [U] (formal) great skill at doing something: *academic/athletic prowess*

prowl /praʊl/ verb, noun
● **verb 1** [I, T] (+ adv./prep.) | ~ **sth** (of an animal) to move quietly and carefully around an area, especially when hunting: *The tiger prowled through the undergrowth.* **2** [I, T] (+ adv./prep.) | ~ **sth** to move quietly and carefully around an area, especially with the intention of committing a crime: *A man was seen prowling around outside the factory just before the fire started.* **3** [T, I] ~ **sth** | (+ adv./prep.) to walk around a room, an area, etc., especially because you are bored, anxious, etc., and cannot relax: *He prowled the empty rooms of the house at night.*
● **noun**
IDM **(be/go) on the prowl** (of an animal or a person) moving quietly and carefully, hunting or looking for something: *There was a fox on the prowl near the chickens.* ◆ *an intruder on the prowl*

prowl·er /ˈpraʊlər/ noun a person who follows someone or who moves around quietly outside their house, especially at night, in order to frighten them, harm them, or steal something from them

prox·i·mal /ˈprɑksəməl/ adj. (anatomy) located toward the center of the body

prox·i·mate /ˈprɑksəmət/ adj. [usually before noun] (technical) nearest in time, order, etc. to something

prox·im·i·ty /prɑkˈsɪməti/ noun [U] ~ **(of sb/sth) (to sb/sth)** (formal) the state of being near someone or something in distance or time: *a house in the proximity of* (= near) *the highway* ◆ *The proximity of the college to a big city makes it very popular.* ◆ *The area has a number of schools in close proximity to each other.* ◆ *the death of two members of her family in close proximity*

prox·y /ˈprɑksi/ noun (pl. **prox·ies**) **1** [U] the authority that you give to someone to do something for you, when you cannot do it yourself: *You can vote either in person or by proxy.* ◆ *a proxy vote* **2** [C, U] a person who has been given the authority to represent someone else: *Your proxy will need to sign the form on your behalf.* ◆ *They were like proxy parents to me.* ◆ ~ **for sb** *She is acting as proxy for her husband.* **3** [C] ~ **for sth** (formal or technical) something that you use to represent something else that you are trying to measure or calculate: *The number of patients on a doctor's list was seen as a good proxy for assessing how hard they work.*

Pro·zac™ /ˈproʊzæk/ noun a drug used to treat the illness of DEPRESSION: *She's been on Prozac for two years.*

prude /prud/ noun (disapproving) a person that you think is too easily shocked by things connected with sex

pru·dent /ˈprudnt/ adj. sensible and careful when you make judgments and decisions; avoiding unnecessary risks: *a prudent businessman* ◆ *a prudent decision/investment* ◆ *It might be more prudent to get a second opinion before going ahead.* **ANT** IMPRUDENT ▸ **pru·dence** /ˈprudns/ noun [U] ⊃ thesaurus box at CARE **pru·dent·ly** adv.

prud·er·y /ˈprudəri/ noun [U] (formal, disapproving) the attitude or behavior of people who seem very easily shocked by things connected with sex

prud·ish /ˈprudɪʃ/ adj. (disapproving) very easily shocked by things connected with sex **SYN** STRAIT-LACED ▸ **prud·ish·ness** noun [U]

prune /prun/ noun, verb
● **noun** a dried PLUM that is often eaten cooked: *stewed prunes* ◆ *prune juice*
● **verb 1** to cut off some of the branches from a tree, bush, etc. so that it will grow better and stronger: ~ **sth** *When should you prune apple trees?* ◆ *He pruned the longer branches off the tree.* ◆ ~ **sth back** *The hedge needs pruning back.* **2** ~ **sth (back)** to make something smaller by removing parts; to cut out parts of something: *Staff numbers have been pruned back to 175.* ◆ *Prune out any unnecessary details.* ▸ **prun·ing** noun [U]: *All roses require annual pruning.* ◆ *The company would benefit from a little pruning here and there.*

pruning shears noun [pl.] a garden tool like a pair of strong scissors, used for cutting plant STEMS and small branches: *a pair of pruning shears*

---

pru·ri·ent /ˈprʊriənt/ adj. (formal, disapproving) having or showing too much interest in things connected with sex ▶ **pru·ri·ence** /-əns/ noun [U]

Prus·sian blue /ˌprʌʃn ˈbluː/ noun [U] a deep blue color used in paints

pry /praɪ/ verb (pries, pry·ing, pried, pried /praɪd/) **1** (also **prize**) to use force to separate something from something else: ~ **sth** + **adv./prep.** He pried her fingers from the bag and took it from her. ◆ ~ **sth** + **adj.** She used a knife to pry open the lid. **2** [I] ~ **(into sth)** to try to find out information about other people's private lives in a way that is annoying or rude: I'm sick of you prying into my personal life! ◆ I'm sorry. I didn't mean to pry. ◆ She tried to keep the children away from the prying eyes of the world's media.
PHR V ˌpry sth↔ˈout (of sb) | ˈpry sth from sb to force someone to give you information about someone or something

P.S. /ˌpiː ˈɛs/ noun something written at the end of a letter to introduce some more information or something that you have forgotten. P.S. is the abbreviation for "postscript.": P.S. Could you send me your fax number again? ◆ She added a P.S. asking me to water the plants.

psalm /sɑm; sɑlm/ noun a song, poem, or prayer that praises God, especially one in the Bible: the Book of Psalms

psal·ter /ˈsɔltər; ˈsɑl-/ noun a book containing a collection of songs and poems (called psalms) with their music, which is used in a church

pse·phol·o·gy /siˈfɑlədʒi/ noun [U] the study of how people vote in elections ▶ **pse·phol·o·gist** /-dʒɪst/ noun

pseudo- /ˈsudoʊ/ combining form (in nouns, adjectives, and adverbs) not genuine; false or pretended: pseudointellectual ◆ pseudoscience

pseu·do·nym /ˈsudnˌɪm/ noun a name used by someone, especially a writer, instead of their real name: She writes under a pseudonym. ⊃ compare PEN-NAME ▶ **pseu·don·y·mous** /suˈdɑnəməs/ adj.

psi /saɪ; psaɪ/ noun the 23rd letter of the Greek alphabet (Ψ, ψ)

p.s.i. /ˌpiː ɛs ˈaɪ/ abbr. pounds per square inch (used for giving the pressure of tires, etc.)

psit·ta·co·sis /ˌsɪtəˈkoʊsəs/ noun [U] (medical) a disease of birds, especially PARROTS, which causes PNEUMONIA (= a disease of the lungs) in humans

pso·ri·a·sis /səˈraɪəsəs/ noun [U] (medical) a skin disease that causes rough red areas where the skin comes off in small pieces

psst /pst/ exclamation the way of writing the sound people say when they want to attract someone's attention quietly: Psst! Let's get out now before they see us!

PST /ˌpiː ɛs ˈtiː/ abbr. provincial sales tax (a tax that is added to the price of goods in some parts of Canada)

psych (also **psy·che**) /saɪk/ verb
PHR V ˌpsych sb↔ˈout (of sth) (informal) to make an opponent feel less confident by saying or doing things that make you seem better, stronger, etc. than them ˌpsych sb/ yourself ˈup (for sth) (informal) to prepare someone/ yourself mentally for something difficult or unpleasant: I'd got myself all psyched up for the interview and then it was called off at the last minute. ⊃ see also PSYCHED

psy·che noun, verb
● **noun** /ˈsaɪki/ (formal) the mind; your deepest feelings and attitudes: the human psyche ◆ She knew, at some deep level of her psyche, that what she was doing was wrong.
● **verb** /saɪk/ = PSYCH

psyched /saɪkt/ adj. [not before noun] (informal) excited, especially about something that is going to happen

psych·e·de·lia /ˌsaɪkəˈdilyə/ noun [U] music, art, fashion, etc. that is created as a result of the effects of psychedelic drugs

psy·che·del·ic /ˌsaɪkəˈdɛlɪk/ adj. [usually before noun] **1** (of drugs) causing the user to see and hear things that are not there or that do not exist (= to HALLUCINATE) **2** (of art, music, clothes, etc.) having bright colors, strange sounds, etc. like those that are experienced when taking psychedelic drugs

psy·chi·at·ric /ˌsaɪkiˈætrɪk/ adj. relating to psychiatry or to mental illness: a psychiatric hospital/nurse ◆ psychiatric treatment ◆ psychiatric disorders ⊃ compare MENTAL

psy·chi·a·trist /saɪˈkaɪətrɪst; sə-/ noun a doctor who studies and treats mental illnesses

psy·chi·a·try /saɪˈkaɪətri; sə-/ noun [U] the study and treatment of mental illness

psy·chic /ˈsaɪkɪk/ adj., noun
● **adj.** **1** (also less frequent **psy·chi·cal** /ˈsaɪkɪkl/) connected with strange powers of the mind and not able to be explained by natural laws **SYN** PARANORMAL: psychic energy/forces/phenomena/powers ◆ psychic healing **2** (of a person) seeming to have strange mental powers and to be able to do things that are not possible according to natural laws: She claims to be psychic and helps people to contact the dead. ◆ How am I supposed to know? I'm not psychic! **3** (also less frequent **psy·chi·cal**) (formal) connected with the mind rather than the body ▶ **psy·chi·cally** /-kli/ adv.
● **noun** a person who claims to have strange mental powers so that they can do things that are not possible according to natural laws, such as predicting the future and speaking to dead people

psy·cho /ˈsaɪkoʊ/ noun (pl. psy·chos) (informal) a person who is mentally ill and who behaves in a very strange violent way ▶ **psycho** adj.

psycho- /ˈsaɪkoʊ/ (also **psych-**) combining form (in nouns, adjectives, and adverbs) connected with the mind: psychology ◆ psychiatric

psy·cho·ac·tive /ˌsaɪkoʊˈæktɪv/ adj. (technical) (of a drug) affecting the mind

psy·cho·anal·y·sis /ˌsaɪkoʊəˈnæləsəs/ (also **a·nal·y·sis**) noun [U] a method of treating someone who is mentally ill by asking them to talk about past experiences and feelings in order to try to find explanations for their present problems ▶ **psy·cho·an·a·lyt·ic** /ˌsaɪkoʊˌænlˈɪtɪk/ adj. [only before noun]: a psychoanalytic approach **psy·cho·an·a·lyt·i·cally** /-kli/ adv.

psy·cho·an·a·lyst /ˌsaɪkoʊˈænlˌɪst/ (also **an·a·lyst**) noun a person who treats patients using psychoanalysis

psy·cho·an·a·lyze (also **an·a·lyze**) verb ~ **sb** to treat or study someone using psychoanalysis

psy·cho·bab·ble /ˈsaɪkoʊˌbæbl/ noun [U] (informal, disapproving) the language that people use when they talk about feelings and emotional problems, which sounds very scientific, but really has little meaning

psy·cho·dra·ma /ˈsaɪkoʊˌdrɑmə/ noun **1** a way of treating people who are mentally ill by encouraging them to act events from their past to help them understand their feelings **2** a play or movie that makes the minds and feelings of the characters more important than the events

psy·cho·ki·ne·sis /ˌsaɪkoʊkɪˈnisəs/ noun [U] the supposed ability to move an object by using the power of the mind

psy·cho·lin·guis·tics /ˌsaɪkoʊlɪŋˈgwɪstɪks/ noun [U] the study of how the mind processes and produces language ▶ **psy·cho·lin·guis·tic** adj.

psy·cho·log·i·cal **AWL** /ˌsaɪkəˈlɑdʒɪkl/ adj. **1** [usually before noun] connected with a person's mind and the way in which it works: the psychological development of children ◆ Abuse can lead to both psychological and emotional problems. ◆ Her symptoms are more psychological than physical (= imaginary rather than real). ◆ Victory in the last game gave them **a psychological advantage** over their opponents. ◆ a psychological novel (= one that examines the minds of the characters) **2** [only before noun] connected with the study of PSYCHOLOGY: psychological research ▶ **psy·cho·log·i·cally** **AWL** /-kli/ adv.: psychologically harmful ◆ Psychologically, the defeat was devastating.

IDM **the psychological moment** the best time to do something in order for it to be successful

ˌpsychological ˈwarfare *noun* [U] things that are said and done in order to make an opponent believe that they cannot win a war, a competition, etc.

psy·chol·o·gist **AWL** /saɪˈkɑlədʒɪst/ *noun* a scientist who studies and is trained in psychology: *an educational psychologist* ◆ *a clinical psychologist* (= one who treats people with mental DISORDERS or problems)

psy·chol·o·gy **AWL** /saɪˈkɑlədʒi/ *noun* **1** [U] the scientific study of the mind and how it influences behavior: *social/educational/child psychology* ⊃ compare POP PSYCHOLOGY **2** [sing.] the kind of mind that someone has that makes them think or behave in a particular way: *the psychology of small boys* **3** [sing.] how the mind influences behavior in a particular area of life: *the psychology of interpersonal relationships*

psy·cho·met·ric /ˌsaɪkəˈmɛtrɪk/ *adj.* [only before noun] (*technical*) used for measuring mental abilities and processes: *psychometric testing*

psy·cho·path /ˈsaɪkəˌpæθ/ *noun* a person suffering from a serious mental illness that causes them to behave in a violent way toward other people ▸ **psy·cho·path·ic** /ˌsaɪkəˈpæθɪk/ *adj.*: *a psychopathic disorder/killer*

psy·cho·pa·thol·o·gy /ˌsaɪkoupəˈθɑlədʒi/ *noun* [U] **1** the scientific study of mental DISORDERS **2** a DISORDER that affects someone's mind or their behavior

psy·cho·sis /saɪˈkousəs/ *noun* [C, U] (*pl.* **psy·cho·ses** /-siz/) a serious mental illness that affects the whole personality ⊃ see also PSYCHOTIC

psy·cho·so·mat·ic /ˌsaɪkousəˈmætɪk/ *adj.* **1** (of an illness) caused by mental problems, such as stress and worry, rather than physical problems **2** (*technical*) connected with the relationship between the mind and the body

psy·cho·ther·a·py /ˌsaɪkouˈθɛrəpi/ (also **ther·a·py**) *noun* [U] the treatment of mental illness by discussing someone's problems with them rather than by giving them drugs ▸ **psy·cho·ther·a·pist** /-ˈθɛrəpɪst/ (also **ther·a·pist**) *noun*

psy·chot·ic /saɪˈkɑtɪk/ *noun* (*medical*) a person suffering from severe mental illness ▸ **psy·chot·ic** *adj.*: *a psychotic disorder/illness* ◆ *a psychotic patient* ⊃ see also PSYCHOSIS ⊃ thesaurus box at MENTALLY ILL

psy·cho·tro·pic /ˌsaɪkəˈtroʊpɪk/ *adj.* [usually before noun] (*medical*) relating to drugs or substances that affect a person's mental state: *psychotropic medication/drugs*

PT /ˌpi ˈti/ *abbr.* **1** (also **P/T**) (in writing) PART-TIME: *PT secretary wanted for small company.* **2** PHYSICAL THERAPY or PHYSICAL THERAPIST: *My doctor says I need three weeks of PT.* **3** physical training (sports and physical exercise taught in the army, etc.)

pt. 🔑 (also **pt**) *abbr.* **1** part: *Shakespeare's Henry IV Pt. 2* **2** pint **3** point: *The winner scored 10 pts.* **4** Pt. (especially on a map) port: *Pt. Charleston*

PTA /ˌpi ti ˈeɪ/ *noun* the abbreviation for "parent-teacher association" (a group run by parents and teachers in a school that organizes social events and helps the school in different ways)

ptar·mi·gan /ˈtɑrmɪɡən/ *noun* a type of GROUSE (= a bird with a fat body and feathers on its legs), found in mountain areas and in Arctic regions

pter·o·dac·tyl /ˌtɛrəˈdæktl/ *noun* a flying REPTILE that lived millions of years ago

PTO /ˌpi ti ˈoʊ/ a group of parents and teachers that is similar to a PTA (the abbreviation for "parent-teacher organization")

pub /pʌb/ *noun* (especially in the U.K. and Ireland) a building where people go to drink and meet their friends. Pubs serve alcoholic and other drinks, and often also food: *We met in an old Irish pub.* ⊃ compare BAR

pu·ber·ty /ˈpyubərti/ *noun* [U] the period of a person's life during which their sexual organs develop and they become capable of having children: *to reach puberty* ⊃ collocations at AGE ⊃ see also ADOLESCENCE

pu·bes /ˈpyubiz/ *noun* (*pl.* **pu·bes**) the lower front part of the body, above the legs, covered by hair in adults

pu·bes·cent /pyuˈbɛsnt/ *adj.* [usually before noun] (*formal*) in the period of a person's life when they are changing physically from a child to an adult

pu·bic /ˈpyubɪk/ *adj.* [only before noun] connected with the part of a person's body near their sexual organs: *pubic hair* ◆ *the pubic bone*

pu·bis /ˈpyubəs/ *noun* (*pl.* **pu·bes** /-biz/) one of the two bones that form the sides of the PELVIS

pub·lic 🔑 /ˈpʌblɪk/ *adj., noun*

● *adj.*
▸ OF ORDINARY PEOPLE **1** [only before noun] connected with ordinary people in society in general: *The campaign is designed to increase public awareness of the issues.* ◆ *Levels of waste from the factory may be a danger to public health.* ◆ *Why would the closure of hospitals be in the public interest* (= useful to ordinary people)*?* ◆ *The government had to bow to public pressure.*
▸ FOR EVERYONE **2** [only before noun] provided, especially by the government, for the use of people in general: *a public education system* ◆ *a public library* **ANT** PRIVATE ⊃ see also PUBLIC SCHOOL
▸ OF GOVERNMENT **3** [only before noun] connected with the government and the services it provides: *public money/spending/funding/expenditure* ◆ *He spent much of his career in public office* (= working in the government)*.* ◆ *The rail industry is no longer in public ownership* (= controlled by the government)*.* **ANT** PRIVATE
▸ SEEN/HEARD BY PEOPLE **4** known to people in general: *a public figure* (= a person who is well known because they are often on the television, radio, etc.) ◆ *Details of the government report have not yet been made public.* ◆ *She entered public life* (= started a job in which she became known to the public) *at the age of 25.* **5** open to people in general; intended to be seen or heard by people in general: *a public apology* ◆ *The painting will be put on public display next week.* ◆ *This may be the band's last public appearance together.*
▸ PLACE **6** where there are a lot of people who can see and hear you: *Let's go somewhere a little less public.* **ANT** PRIVATE

▸ **pub·lic·ly** /-kli/ *adv.*: *a publicly owned company* ◆ *He later publicly apologized for his comments.* ◆ *This information is not publicly available.*

IDM **go public 1** to tell people about something that is a secret **2** (of a company) to start selling shares on the STOCK EXCHANGE **in the public eye** well known to many people through newspapers and television: *She doesn't want her children growing up in the public eye.* ⊃ more at KNOWLEDGE

● *noun* [sing.]
▸ ORDINARY PEOPLE **1** the public ordinary people in society in general: *The museum is now open to the public.* ◆ *There have been many complaints from members of the public.* ◆ *The public has a right to know what is contained in the report.* ⊃ see also THE GENERAL PUBLIC
▸ GROUP OF PEOPLE **2** a group of people who share a particular interest or who are involved in the same activity: *the theater-going public* ◆ *She knows how to keep her public* (= for example, the people who buy her books) *satisfied.*

IDM **in public** when other people, especially people you do not know, are present: *She doesn't like to be seen in public without her makeup on.* ⊃ compare IN PRIVATE

ˌpublic ˈaccess *noun* [U] **1** the right of people in general to go into particular buildings or areas of land, or to obtain particular information: *public access to the countryside* **2** the right of people in general to use television or radio channels to present their own programs: *a public access channel*

public ad·dress ˌsystem noun (abbr. ˌPˈA ˌsystem) an electronic system that uses MICROPHONES and LOUDSPEAKERS to make music, voices, etc. louder so that they can be heard by everyone in a particular place or building

public af·fairs noun [pl.] issues and questions about social, economic, political, or business activities, etc. that affect ordinary people in general

pub·li·ca·tion 🔑 **AWL** /ˌpʌbləˈkeɪʃn/ noun
1 [U, C] the act of printing a book, a magazine, etc. and making it available to the public; a book, a magazine, etc. that has been published: *the publication date* ♦ *the publication of his first novel* ♦ *specialist publications* **2** [U] the act of printing something in a newspaper, report, etc. so that the public knows about it: *a delay in the publication of the exam results* ♦ *The newspaper continues to defend its publication of the photographs.*

public corpo·ra·tion noun a company that sells shares in itself to the public

public de·fender noun (*law*) a lawyer who is paid by the government to defend people in court if they cannot pay for a lawyer themselves

public do·main noun [sing.] something that is in the **public domain** is available for everyone to use or to discuss and is not secret: *The information has been placed in the public domain.* ♦ *public domain software*

public enemy noun a person who has done, or is believed to have done, a very bad thing, especially something that is harmful to society: *public enemy number one* (= the person or thing that is most frightening or that is most hated)

public holiday noun a day on which most of the stores, businesses, and schools in a country are closed, often to celebrate a particular event

public housing noun [U] houses and apartments that are built by the government for people who do not have much money

pub·li·cist /ˈpʌbləsɪst/ noun a person whose job is to make something known to the public, for example a new product, actor, etc.

pub·lic·i·ty 🔑 /pʌˈblɪsəti/ noun [U]
1 the attention that is given to someone or something by newspapers, television, etc.: *good/bad/adverse publicity* ♦ *There has been a great deal of publicity surrounding his disappearance.* ♦ *The trial took place amid a blaze of* (= a lot of) *publicity.* **2** the business of attracting the attention of the public to something or someone; the things that are done to attract attention: *She works in publicity.* ♦ *There has been a lot of advance publicity for her new movie.* ♦ *publicity material* ♦ *a publicity campaign* ♦ *The band dressed up as the Beatles as a publicity stunt.* ⊃ thesaurus box at ADVERTISEMENT

pub·li·cize /ˈpʌbləsaɪz/ verb ~ sth to make something known to the public; to advertise something: *They flew to Europe to publicize the plight of the refugees.* ♦ *a much/highly/widely publicized speech* (= that has received a lot of attention on television, in newspapers, etc.) ♦ *He was in town publicizing his new biography of Kennedy.*

public nuisance noun **1** [sing., U] (*law*) an illegal act that causes harm to people in general: *The defendants could be held liable for creating a public nuisance in New York State.* **2** [C, usually sing.] (*informal*) a person or thing that annoys a lot of people

public o·pinion noun [U] the opinions that people in society have about an issue: *The media has a powerful influence on public opinion.*

public property noun [U] **1** (*law*) land, buildings, etc. that are owned by the government and can be used by everyone **2** a person or thing that everyone has a right to know about: *statesmen and others who are already public property*

public radio noun [U] a radio network that receives funds from both the government and the public

public re·lations noun **1** [U] (abbr. PR) the business of giving the public information about a particular organization or person in order to create a good impression: *She works in public relations.* **2** [pl.] the state of the relationship between an organization and the public: *Sponsoring the local team is good for public relations.*

public school noun [C, U] a free local school paid for by the government ⊃ compare PREPARATORY SCHOOL, PRIVATE SCHOOL, PAROCHIAL SCHOOL

the public sector noun [sing.] (*economics*) the part of the economy of a country that is owned or controlled by the government ⊃ compare THE PRIVATE SECTOR

public servant noun a person who is employed by the state or in local government, or who is an elected representative: *pay increases for public servants* ♦ *a long and outstanding career as a public servant*

public service noun **1** [C] a service such as transportation or healthcare that a government or an official organization provides for people in general in a particular society: *to improve public services in the area* ♦ *a public service broadcast* **2** [C, U] something that is done to help people rather than to make a profit: *to perform a public service* **3** [U] the government and government departments: *to work in public service* ♦ *public service workers*

public-spirited adj. willing to do things that will help other people in society: *a public-spirited act* ♦ *That was very public-spirited of you.* ▶ **public spirit** noun [U]

public television noun [U] a television service that shows mainly EDUCATIONAL programs and is paid for by the government, the public, and some companies

public transit noun [U] = MASS TRANSIT

public transpor·tation noun [U] the system of buses, trains, etc. provided by the government or by companies, which people use to travel from one place to another: *to travel on/by public transportation* ♦ *Most of us use public transportation to get to work.* ⊃ collocations at TOWN

public u·tility noun (*formal*) a private company that must obey government rules, which supplies essential services such as gas, water, and electricity to the public

public works noun [pl.] building work, such as that of hospitals, schools, and roads, which is paid for by the government

pub·lish 🔑 **AWL** /ˈpʌblɪʃ/ verb
1 [T] ~ sth to produce a book, magazine, CD-ROM, etc. and sell it to the public: *The first edition was published in 2007.* ♦ *He works for a company that publishes reference books.* ♦ *Most of our titles are also published on CD-ROM.* **2** [T] ~ sth to print a letter, an article, etc. in a newspaper or magazine: *Pictures of the suspect were published in all the daily papers.* **3** [T] ~ sth to make something available to the public on the Internet: *The report will be published on the Internet.* **4** [T, I] ~ (sth) (of an author) to have your work printed and sold to the public: *She hasn't published anything for years.* ♦ *University professors are under pressure to publish.* **5** [T] ~ sth (*formal*) to make official information known to the public **SYN** RELEASE: *The findings of the committee will be published on Friday.*

pub·lish·er **AWL** /ˈpʌblɪʃər/ noun a person or company that prepares and prints books, magazines, newspapers, or electronic products and makes them available to the public

pub·lish·ing 🔑 **AWL** /ˈpʌblɪʃɪŋ/ noun [U]
the profession or business of preparing and printing books, magazines, CD-ROMS, etc. and selling or making them available to the public: *a publishing house* (= company) ⊃ see also DESKTOP PUBLISHING

puce /pyus/ adj. red-purple in color: *His face was puce with rage.* ▶ **puce** noun [U]

puck /pʌk/ noun **1** a hard, flat, rubber disk that is used as a ball in HOCKEY ⊃ picture at SPORT **2** (*computing*) a pointing device that looks like a computer mouse and is used to control the movement of the CURSOR on a computer screen

ʌ cup   ə about   eɪ say   aɪ five   ɔɪ boy   aʊ now   oʊ go   ər bird

puck·er /ˈpʌkər/ verb [I, T] ~ (sth) (up) to form or to make something form small folds or lines: *His face puckered, and he was ready to cry.* ◆ *She puckered her lips.* ◆ *puckered fabric*

puck·ish /ˈpʌkɪʃ/ adj. [usually before noun] (*literary*) enjoying playing tricks on other people **SYN** MISCHIEVOUS

pud·ding /ˈpʊdɪŋ/ noun [U, C] **1** a cold DESSERT (= a sweet dish) like cream, flavored with fruit, vanilla, chocolate, etc.: *chocolate pudding* **2** a hot DESSERT (= a sweet dish), made with rice, bread, etc. and eggs and milk: *bread/rice pudding* **IDM** see PROOF n.

pud·dle /ˈpʌdl/ noun a small amount of water or other liquid, especially rain, that has collected in one place on the ground

pu·den·da /pyuˈdɛndə/ noun [pl.] (*old-fashioned, formal*) the sexual organs that are outside the body, especially those of a woman

pudg·y /ˈpʌdʒi/ adj. (*informal*, usually *disapproving*) slightly fat

Pueb·lo /ˈpwɛbloʊ/ noun (pl. **Pueb·lo** or **Pueb·los**) noun a member of a group of Native American people who live in the states of Arizona and New Mexico

pueb·lo /ˈpwɛbloʊ/ noun (pl. **pueb·los**) (from *Spanish*) a town or VILLAGE in Latin America or the S.W. part of the U. S., especially one with traditional buildings

pu·er·ile /ˈpyʊrəl/ adj. (*formal, disapproving*) silly; suitable for a child rather than an adult **SYN** CHILDISH

puff /pʌf/ verb, noun
● **verb 1** [I, T] to smoke a cigarette, pipe, etc.: ~ (at/on sth) *He puffed (away) on his pipe.* ◆ ~ **sth** *I sat puffing my cigar.* **2** [T, I] to make smoke or steam blow out in clouds; to blow out in clouds: ~ **sth (out)** *Chimneys were puffing out clouds of smoke.* ◆ ~ **(out)** *Steam puffed out.* **3** [I, T] (+ speech) (*informal*) to breathe loudly and quickly, especially after you have been running **SYN** GASP: *I was starting to puff a little from the climb.* **4** [I] + **adv./prep.** to move in a particular direction, sending out small clouds of smoke or steam: *The train puffed into the station.* **IDM** be puffed up with pride, etc. to be too full of pride, etc. puff and pant (also *informal* puff and blow) to breathe quickly and loudly through your mouth after physical effort ⊃ more at HUFF **PHR V** ,puff sth↔ 'out to make something bigger and rounder, especially by filling it with air: *She puffed out her cheeks.* ,puff 'up | ,puff sth↔ 'up to swell or to make something swell: *Her cheeks puffed up.* ◆ *The frog puffed itself up.*

● **noun 1** [C] an act of breathing in something such as smoke from a cigarette, or drugs: *He had a few puffs at the cigar.* ◆ *Take two puffs on the inhaler every four hours.* **2** [C] a small amount of air, smoke, etc. that is blown from somewhere: *a puff of wind* ◆ *Puffs of white smoke came from the chimney.* ◆ *Any chance of success seemed to vanish in a puff of smoke* (= to disappear quickly). **3** [C] a hollow light PASTRY that is filled with cream, jelly, etc. ⊃ see also CREAM PUFF **4** (also 'puff piece) [C] (*informal*, usually *disapproving*) a piece of writing or speech that praises someone or something too much ⊃ see also POWDER PUFF

puff·ball /ˈpʌfbɔl/ noun a FUNGUS with a round brown head that bursts when it is ready to release its seeds

puff·er /ˈpʌfər/ noun = PUFFERFISH

puff·er·fish /ˈpʌfərˌfɪʃ/ noun (pl. **puff·er·fish** or **puff·er·fish·es**) (also **puff·fer**) a poisonous fish that lives in warm seas and fills with air when it is in danger

puf·fin /ˈpʌfən/ noun a black and white bird with a large, brightly colored beak that lives near the ocean, common in the N. Atlantic

,puff 'pastry noun [U] a type of light DOUGH that forms many thin layers when baked, used for making PIES, cakes, etc.

'puff piece noun = PUFF

,puff 'sleeve (also ,puffed 'sleeve) noun a short sleeve that fits close to the body at the shoulder and the lower edge, and is wider in the middle

puff·y /ˈpʌfi/ adj. (puff·i·er, puff·i·est) **1** (of eyes, faces, etc.) looking swollen (= larger, rounder, etc. than usual): *Her eyes were puffy from crying.* **2** (of clouds, etc.) looking soft, round, and white ▶ **puff·i·ness** noun [U]

pug /pʌg/ noun a small dog with short hair and a wide flat face with deep folds of skin

pu·gi·list /ˈpyudʒəlɪst/ noun (*old-fashioned*) a BOXER ▶ **pu·gi·lism** /-ˌlɪzəm/ noun [U] **pu·gi·lis·tic** /ˌpyudʒəˈlɪstɪk/ adj.

pug·na·cious /pʌgˈneɪʃəs/ adj. (*formal*) having a strong desire to argue or fight with other people **SYN** BELLICOSE ▶ **pug·na·cious·ly** adv. **pug·nac·i·ty** /pʌgˈnæsəti/ noun [U]

pu·is·ance /ˈpwisɑns; -sns/ noun [U] (*literary*) great power or influence

puke /pyuk/ verb [I, T] ~ (sth) (up) (*informal*) to VOMIT: *The baby puked all over me this morning.* ◆ *That guy makes me puke* (= makes me angry)! ◆ *I puked up my dinner.* ▶ **puke** noun [U]: *to be covered in puke*

pul·chri·tude /ˈpʌlkrəˌtud/ noun [U] (*literary*) beauty

Pu·litz·er Prize /ˈpʊlɪtsər ˌpraɪz; ˈpyu-/ noun [C, usually sing.] (in the U.S.) one of a number of prizes that are given each year for excellent work in literature, music, or JOURNALISM

pull 🔑 /pʊl/ verb, noun
● **verb**
> **MOVE/REMOVE SOMETHING 1** [I, T] to hold something firmly and use force in order to move it or try to move it toward yourself: *You push and I'll pull.* ◆ *Don't pull so hard or the handle will come off.* ◆ ~ **at/on sth** *I pulled on the rope to see if it was secure.* ◆ ~ **sth** *Stop pulling her hair!* ◆ ~ **sb/sth + adv./ prep.** *She pulled him gently toward her.* ◆ ~ **sth + adj.** *Pull the door shut.* **2** [T] ~ **sth (+ adv./prep.)** to remove something from a place by pulling: *Pull the plug out.* ◆ *She pulled off her boots.* ◆ *He pulled a gun on me* (= took out a gun and aimed it at me). **3** [T] ~ **sb/sth + adv./prep.** to move someone or something in a particular direction by pulling: *Pull your chair closer to the table.* ◆ *He pulled on his sweater.* ◆ *She took his arm and pulled him along.* **4** [T] ~ **sth** to hold or be attached to something and move it along behind you: *In this area oxen are used to pull carts.*
> **BODY 5** [I, T] to move your body or a part of your body in a particular direction, especially using force: + **adv./prep.** *He tried to kiss her but she pulled away.* ◆ ~ **sth/yourself + adv./prep.** *The dog snapped at her and she quickly pulled back her hand.* ◆ ~ **sth/yourself + adj.** *John pulled himself free and ran off.*
> **CURTAINS 6** [T] ~ **sth** to open or close curtains, etc. **SYN** DRAW: *Pull the curtains—it's dark outside.*
> **MUSCLE 7** [T] ~ **sth** to damage a muscle, etc. by using too much force: *to pull a muscle/ligament/tendon* ⊃ thesaurus box at INJURE
> **SWITCH 8** [T] ~ **sth** to move a switch, etc. toward yourself or down in order to operate a machine or piece of equipment: *Pull the lever to start the motor.* ◆ *Don't pull the trigger!*
> **VEHICLE/ENGINE 9** [I, T] ~ **(something) to the right/the left/one side** to move or make a vehicle move sideways: *The wheel is pulling to the left.* ◆ *She pulled the car to the right to avoid the dog.* **10** [I] (of an engine) to work hard and use a lot of power: *The old car pulled hard as we drove slowly up the hill.*
> **BOAT 11** [I, T] ~ **(sth) (+ adv./prep.)** to use OARS to move a boat along: *They pulled toward the shore.*
> **CROWD/SUPPORT 12** [T] ~ **sb/sth (in)** to attract the interest or support of someone or something: *They pulled in huge crowds on their latest tour.*
> **TRICK/CRIME 13** [T] ~ **sth** (*informal*) to succeed in playing a trick on someone, committing a crime, etc.: *He's pulling some sort of trick on you.*
> **CANCEL 14** [T] ~ **sth** (*informal*) to cancel an event; to stop showing an advertisement, etc.: *The gig was pulled at the last moment.*

IDM **pull a fast one (on sb)** (*slang*) to trick someone **pull in different/opposite directions** to have different aims that cannot be achieved together without causing problems **pull sb's leg** (*informal*) to play a joke on someone, usually by making them believe something that is not true **pull out all the stops** (*informal*) to make the greatest effort possible to achieve something **pull the plug on sb/sth** (*informal*) to put an end to someone's project, a plan, etc. **pull your punches** (*informal*) (usually used in negative sentences) to express something less strongly than you are able to, for example to avoid upsetting or shocking someone: *Her articles certainly don't pull any punches.* **pull sth/a rabbit out of the hat** (*informal*) to suddenly produce something as a solution to a problem **pull rank (on sb)** to make use of your place or status in society or at work to make someone do what you want **pull the rug (out) from under sb's feet** (*informal*) to take help or support away from someone suddenly **pull strings (for sb)** (also **pull wires**) (*informal*) to use your influence in order to get an advantage for someone **pull the strings** to control events or the actions of other people **pull up stakes** to suddenly move from your house and go to live somewhere else **pull your weight** to work as hard as everyone else in a job, an activity, etc. **pull the wool over sb's eyes** (*informal*) to try to trick someone; to hide your real actions or intentions from someone ⊃ more at BOOTSTRAP, HORN, PIECE *n.*, SHRED *n.*

PHR V ,**pull a'head (of sb/sth)** to move in front of someone or something: *The bikers were together until the bend, when Tyler pulled ahead.* ,**pull sb/sth a'part** to separate people or animals that are fighting ,**pull sth a'part** to separate something into pieces by pulling different parts of it in different directions ,**pull at sth** = PULL ON STH ,**pull a'way (from sth)** (of a vehicle) to start moving: *They waved as the bus pulled away.* ,**pull 'back 1** (of an army) to move back from a place **SYN** WITHDRAW **2** to decide not to do something that you were intending to do, because of possible problems **SYN** WITHDRAW: *Their sponsors pulled back at the last minute.* ,**pull sb↔'back** to make an army move back from a place ,**pull sb 'down** to make someone less happy, healthy or successful ,**pull sth↔'down 1** to destroy a building completely **SYN** DEMOLISH **2** = PULL STH IN ,**pull sb↔'in** (*informal*) to bring someone to a police station in order to ask them questions about a crime ,**pull sth↔'in/'down** (*informal*) to earn the large amount of money mentioned **SYN** MAKE: *I think she's pulling in over $100,000.* ,**pull 'in (to sth)** (of a train) to enter a station and stop ,**pull 'off** | ,**pull 'off sth** (of a vehicle or its driver) to leave the road in order to stop for a short time ,**pull sth↔'off** (*informal*) to succeed in doing something difficult: *We pulled off the deal.* ◆ *I never thought you'd pull it off.* '**pull on/at sth** to take long deep breaths from a cigarette, etc. ,**pull 'out** (of a vehicle or its driver) to move away from the side of the road, etc.: *A car suddenly pulled out in front of me.* ,**pull 'out (of sth) 1** (of a train) to leave a station **2** to move away from something or stop being involved in it **SYN** WITHDRAW: *The project became so expensive that we had to pull out.* ,**pull sb/sth 'out (of sth)** to make someone or something move away from something or stop being involved in it **SYN** WITHDRAW: *They are pulling their troops out of the war zone.* ⊃ related noun PULL-OUT ,**pull 'over** (of a vehicle or its driver) to move to the side of the road in order to stop or let something pass ,**pull sb/sth↔'over** (of the police) to make a driver or vehicle move to the side of the road ,**pull 'through** | ,**pull 'through sth 1** to get better after a serious illness, operation, etc.: *The doctors think she will pull through.* **2** to succeed in doing something very difficult: *It's going to be tough but we'll pull through it together.* ,**pull sb 'through** | ,**pull sb 'through sth 1** to help someone get better after a serious illness, operation, etc. **2** to help someone succeed in doing something very difficult: *I relied on my instincts to pull me through.* ,**pull to'gether** to act, work, etc. together with other people in an organized way and without fighting ,**pull yourself to'gether** to take control of your feelings and behave in a calm way: *Stop crying and pull yourself*

together! ,**pull 'up** (of a vehicle or its driver) to stop: *He pulled up at the traffic lights.*

● *noun*
▷ **TRYING TO MOVE SOMETHING 1** [C] an act of trying to make something move by holding it firmly and bringing it toward you: *I gave the door a sharp pull and it opened.*
▷ **PHYSICAL FORCE 2** [sing.] **the ~ (of sth)** a strong physical force that makes something move in a particular direction: *the earth's gravitational pull*
▷ **ATTRACTION 3** [C, usually sing.] **the ~ (of sth)** the fact of something attracting you or having a strong effect on you: *The magnetic pull of the city was hard to resist.*
▷ **INFLUENCE 4** [U] (*informal*) power and influence over other people: *people who have a lot of pull with the media*
▷ **ON CIGARETTE/DRINK 5** [C] **~ (at/on sth)** an act of taking a deep breath of smoke from a cigarette, etc. or a deep drink of something: *She took a long pull on her cigarette.*
▷ **MUSCLE INJURY 6** [C] an injury to a muscle caused by using too much force
▷ **HANDLE/ROPE 7** [C] (especially in compounds) something such as a handle or rope that you use to pull something: *a bell/door pull*

pull
drag ◆ **draw** ◆ **haul** ◆ **tow** ◆ **tug**
These words all mean to move something in a particular direction, especially toward or behind you.

pull to hold something and move it in a particular direction; to hold or be attached to a vehicle and move it along behind you: *Pull the chair closer to the table.* ◆ *They use horses to pull their carts.*

drag to pull someone or something in a particular direction or behind you, usually along the ground, and especially with effort: *The sack is too heavy to lift—you'll have to drag it.*

draw (*formal*) to move someone or something by pulling them/it gently; to pull a vehicle such as a carriage: *I drew my chair closer to the fire.* ◆ *a horse-drawn carriage*

haul to pull someone or something to a particular place with a lot of effort: *Liz hauled her suitcase up the stairs.*

DRAG OR HAUL?
You usually **drag** something behind you along the ground; you usually **haul** something toward you, often upward toward you. **Dragging** something often needs effort, but **hauling** always does.

tow to pull a car, boat, or light plane behind another vehicle, using a rope or chain: *Our car was towed away by the police.*

tug to pull someone or something hard in a particular direction: *The boy tugged at his father's sleeve.*

PATTERNS
- to pull/drag/draw/haul/tow sb/sth **along/down/ toward** sth
- to pull/drag/draw/haul/tow sb/sth **behind you**
- to pull/drag/draw/haul a **cart/sled**
- to pull/draw a **coach/carriage**
- to pull/haul/tow a **trailer**
- **horses** pull/draw/haul sth
- **dogs** pull/drag/haul sth

'**pull·back** /'pʊlbæk/ *noun* **1** an act of taking soldiers away from an area **2** a time when prices are reduced, or when fewer people want to buy something

'**pull date** *noun* = SELL-BY DATE

'**pull-down** *adj.* **1** designed to be used by being pulled down: *a pull-down bed* **2** **~ menu** (*computing*) a list of possible choices that appears on a computer screen below a menu title

t **tea**   ţ **butter**   d **did**   k **cat**   ɡ **got**   tʃ **chin**   dʒ June   f **fall**

pulled 'pork *noun* [U] meat from a pig that is cooked very slowly, often with smoke, until it is so soft you can pull it into small pieces with your hands

pul·let /ˈpʊlət/ *noun* a young chicken, especially one that is less than one year old

pul·ley /ˈpʊli/ *noun* a wheel or set of wheels over which a rope or chain is pulled in order to lift or lower heavy objects: *a system of ropes and pulleys* ⟳ picture at BLOCK AND TACKLE

Pull·man /ˈpʊlmən/ *noun* (pl. **Pull·mans**) a type of very comfortable car on a train

pull-out *noun, adj.*
• *noun* **1** a part of a magazine, newspaper, etc. that can be taken out easily and kept separately: *an eight-page pull-out on health* ◆ *a pull-out guide* **2** an act of taking an army away from a particular place; an act of taking an organization out of a system
• *adj.* [only before noun] a **pull-out** bed, COUCH, etc. can be kept hidden when not in use and pulled out when it is needed

pull·o·ver /ˈpʊlˌoʊvər/ *noun* a piece of clothing made of wool or cotton for the upper part of the body, with long sleeves and no buttons ⟳ compare SWEATER

pull tab (also **tab**) *noun* a small piece of metal with a ring attached that is pulled to open cans of food, drinks, etc. ⟳ picture at PACKAGING

pul·lu·late /ˈpʌlyəˌleɪt/ *verb* (*formal*) **1** [I] to breed or spread quickly **2** [I] to be full of life or activity ▶ **pul·lu·lat·ing** *adj.*: *a pullulating mass of people*

pull-up (also **'chin-up**) *noun* [usually pl.] an exercise in which you hold onto a high bar above your head and pull yourself up toward it

pul·mo·nar·y /ˈpʊlməˌnɛri; ˈpʌl-/ *adj.* [only before noun] (*medical*) connected with the lungs

pulp /pʌlp/ *noun, verb, adj.*
• *noun* **1** [sing., U] a soft wet substance that is made especially by crushing something: *Cook the fruit gently until it forms a pulp.* ◆ *His face had been **beaten to a pulp** (= very badly beaten).* **2** [U] a soft substance that is made by crushing wood, cloth, or other material, and then used to make paper: *paper/wood pulp* **3** [U] the soft part inside some fruit and vegetables SYN FLESH: *I prefer orange juice with pulp.* ▶ **pulp·y** *adj.*: *Cook the fruit slowly until soft and pulpy.*
• *verb* ~ sth to crush or beat something so that it becomes soft and wet: *Unsold copies of the novel had to be pulped.*
• *adj.* [only before noun] (of books, magazines, etc.) badly written and often intended to shock people: *pulp fiction*

pul·pit /ˈpʊlpɪt; ˈpʌl-/ *noun* a small platform in a church that is like a box and is high above the ground, where a priest, etc. stands to speak to the people

pul·sar /ˈpʌlsɑr/ *noun* (*astronomy*) a star that cannot be seen but that sends out regular rapid radio signals ⟳ compare QUASAR

pul·sate /ˈpʌlseɪt/ *verb* **1** [I] to make strong regular movements or sounds: *pulsating rhythms* ◆ *a pulsating headache* ◆ *Lights were pulsating in the sky.* **2** [I] to be full of excitement or energy SYN BUZZ: *a pulsating game* ◆ ~ with sth *The streets were pulsating with life.* ▶ **pul·sa·tion** /pʌlˈseɪʃn/ *noun* [C, U]

pulse /pʌls/ *noun, verb*
• *noun* **1** [usually sing.] the regular beat of blood as it is sent around the body, which can be felt in different places, especially on the inside part of the wrist; the number of times the blood beats in a minute: *a strong/weak pulse* ◆ *an abnormally high pulse rate* ◆ *The doctor took/felt my pulse.* ◆ *Fear sent her **pulse racing** (= made it beat very quickly).* **2** a strong regular beat in music SYN RHYTHM: *the throbbing pulse of the drums* **3** a single short increase in the amount of light, sound, or electricity produced by a machine, etc.: *pulse waves* ◆ *sound pulses* IDM see FINGER *n.*

• *verb* **1** [I] to move, beat, or flow with strong regular movements or sounds SYN THROB: *A vein pulsed in his temple.* ◆ *the pulsing rhythm of the music* **2** [I] ~ (with sth) to be full of a feeling such as excitement or energy SYN BUZZ: *The auditorium pulsed with excitement.*

pul·ver·ize /ˈpʌlvəˌraɪz/ *verb* **1** ~ sth (*formal*) to crush something into a fine powder **2** ~ sb/sth (*informal*) to defeat or destroy someone or something completely SYN CRUSH: *We pulverized the opposition.*

pu·ma /ˈpumə/ *noun* = COUGAR

pum·ice /ˈpʌməs/ (also **'pumice ˌstone**) *noun* [U] a type of gray stone that comes from VOLCANOES and is very light in weight. It is used in powder form for cleaning and polishing, and in pieces for rubbing on the skin to make it softer.

pum·mel /ˈpʌml/ *verb* (-l-) [T, I] to keep hitting someone or something hard, especially with your FISTS (= tightly closed hands): ~ sb/sth (with sth) *He pummeled the pillow with his fists.* ◆ (*figurative*) *She pummeled (= strongly criticized) her opponents.* ◆ ~ (at sth) *Her fists pummeled at his chest.*

pum·me·lo /ˈpʌməˌloʊ/ *noun* = POMELO

pump /pʌmp/ *noun, verb*
• *noun* **1** a machine that is used to force liquid, gas, or air into or out of something: *Some gas stations have the same kind of pump and nozzle.* ◆ *a gas pump* ◆ *a foot/hand pump (= that you work by using your foot or hand)* ◆ *a bicycle pump* ⟳ picture at BED, BICYCLE ⟳ see also STOMACH PUMP **2** a woman's formal shoe that is plain and does not cover the top of the foot ⟳ picture at SHOE IDM see PRIME *v.*
• *verb* **1** [T, I] to make water, air, gas, etc. flow in a particular direction by using a pump or something that works like a pump: ~ (sth) (+ adv./prep.) *The engine is used for pumping water out of the mine.* ◆ *The heart pumps blood around the body.* ◆ ~ sth + adj. *The lake had been pumped dry.* **2** [I] + adv./prep. (of a liquid) to flow in a particular direction as if it is being forced by a pump: *Blood was pumping out of his wound.* **3** [T] ~ sth (+ adv./prep.) to move something quickly up and down or in and out: *He kept pumping my hand up and down.* ◆ *I pumped the handle like crazy.* **4** [I] to move quickly up and down or in and out: *She sprinted for the line, legs pumping.* ◆ *My heart was pumping with excitement.* **5** [T] ~ sb (for sth) (*informal*) to try to get information from someone by asking them a lot of questions: *See if you can pump him for more details.*
IDM **pump bullets, shots, etc. into sb** to fire a lot of bullets into someone **pump sb full of sth** to fill someone with something, especially with drugs: *They pumped her full of painkillers.* **pump iron** (*informal*) to do exercises in which you lift heavy weights in order to make your muscles stronger **pump sb's stomach** to remove the contents of someone's stomach using a pump, because they have swallowed something harmful
PHR V **ˌpump sth ˈinto sth** | **ˌpump sth ˈin** to put a lot of money into something: *He pumped all his savings into the business.* **ˌpump sth ˈinto sb** to force a lot of something into someone: *It's difficult to pump facts and figures into tired students.* **ˌpump sth↔ˈout** (*informal*) to produce something in large amounts: *loudspeakers pumping out rock music* ◆ *Our cars pump out thousands of tons of poisonous fumes every year.* **ˌpump sb↔ˈup** [usually passive] to make someone feel more excited or determined **ˌpump sth↔ˈup 1** to fill a tire, etc. with air using a pump **2** (*informal*) to increase the amount, value, or volume of something: *Interest rates were pumped up last week.*

ˌpump-ˌaction *adj.* [only before noun] (of a gun or other device) worked by quickly pulling or pressing part of it in and out or up and down: *a pump-action shotgun* ◆ *a pump-action spray*

pumped /pʌmpt/ (also **ˌpumped ˈup**) *adj.* (*informal*) filled with excitement or enthusiasm: *We're really pumped for the game tonight!*

pum·per·nick·el /ˈpʌmpərˌnɪkl/ *noun* [U] (from *German*) a type of heavy, dark brown bread made from RYE, originally from Germany and often sold in slices

pump·kin /ˈpʌmpkɪn/ *noun* [U, C] a large round vegetable with thick orange skin. The seeds can be dried and eaten and the soft flesh can be cooked as a vegetable or in sweet PIE: *Pumpkin pie is a traditional American dish served on Thanksgiving.* ⟳ see also JACK-O'-LANTERN ⟳ picture at FRUIT

pump-ˌpriming *noun* [U] the act of investing money to encourage growth in an industry or a business, especially by a government

ˈpump room *noun* (especially in the past) the room at a SPA where people go to drink the special water

pun /pʌn/ *noun, verb*
• *noun* ~ (on sth) the smart or humorous use of a word that has more than one meaning, or of words that have different meanings but sound the same: *We're banking on them lending us the money— no pun intended!* ⟳ compare WORD-PLAY
• *verb* (-nn-) [I] to make a pun

Punch /pʌntʃ/ *noun* IDM see PLEASED

punch ✎ /pʌntʃ/ *verb, noun*

• *verb* **1** to hit someone or something hard with your FIST (= closed hand): *~ sb/sth He was kicked and punched as he lay on the ground.* ◆ *He was **punching the air** in triumph.* ◆ *~ sb/sth in/on sth She punched him on the nose.* **2** ~ sth (in/through sth) to make a hole in something with a PUNCH or some other sharp object: *~ sth to punch a time card* ◆ *~ sth in/through sth The machine punches a row of holes in the metal sheet.* **3** ~ sth to press buttons or keys on a computer, telephone, etc. in order to operate it: *I punched the button to summon the elevator.* ▶ **punch·er** *noun: He's one of boxing's strongest punchers.*
IDM **punch above your weight** to be or try to be more successful than others in doing something that normally requires more skill, experience, money, etc. than you have: *This player seems to be able to constantly punch above his weight.* ⟳ more at HOLE *n.*
PHR V **ˌpunch ˈin/ˈout** to record the time you arrive at/leave work by putting a card into a special machine ⟳ see also CLOCK IN, CLOCK OUT **ˌpunch sth↔ˈin | ˌpunch sth ˈinto sth** to put information into a computer by pressing the keys: *He punched in the security code.* **ˌpunch sb ˈout** (*informal*) to hit someone so hard that they fall down **ˌpunch sth↔ˈout 1** to press a combination of buttons or keys on a computer, telephone, etc.: *He picked up the telephone and punched out his friend's number.* **2** to make a hole in something or knock something out by hitting it very hard: *I felt as if all my teeth had been punched out.* **3** to cut something from paper, wood, metal, etc. with a special tool
• *noun* **1** [C] a hard hit made with the FIST (= closed hand): *a punch in the face* ◆ *Hill threw a punch at the police officer.* ◆ *a knockout punch* ◆ *He shot out his right arm and landed a punch on Lorrimer's nose.* ⟳ see also RABBIT PUNCH **2** [U] the power to interest people: *It's a well-constructed crime story, told with speed and punch.* **3** [C] a tool or machine for cutting holes in paper, leather, or metal: *a hole punch* ⟳ picture at STATIONERY **4** [U] a drink made by mixing water, fruit juice, spices, and sometimes wine or another alcoholic drink: *a recipe for fruit punch* IDM see BEAT *v.*, PACK *v.*, PULL *v.*, ROLL *v.*

punch·ball /ˈpʌntʃbɔl/ *noun* a heavy leather ball, fixed on a spring, which is punched, especially by BOXERS as a part of training, or as a form of exercise

punch·bowl /ˈpʌntʃboʊl/ *noun* a bowl used for serving PUNCH

punch·card /ˈpʌntʃkɑrd/ (also ˌpunched ˈcard) *noun* a card on which, in the past, information was recorded as lines of holes and used for giving instructions, etc. to computers and other machines

ˈpunch–drunk (also ˈslap-ˌhappy) *adj.* **1** (of a BOXER) confused as a result of being punched on the head many

times **2** (also **punchy**) unable to think clearly; in a confused state

ˈpunching ˌbag *noun* a heavy leather bag, hung on a rope, which is punched, especially by BOXERS as part of training, or as a form of exercise

punch·line /ˈpʌntʃlaɪn/ (also *informal* ˈtag line) *noun* the last few words of a joke that make it funny

punch·y /ˈpʌntʃi/ *adj.* (punch·i·er, punch·i·est) **1** (of a speech, song, etc.) having a strong effect because it expresses something clearly in only a few words **2** = PUNCH-DRUNK (2)

punc·til·i·ous /pʌŋkˈtɪliəs/ *adj.* (*formal*) very careful to behave correctly or to perform your duties exactly as you should: *a punctilious host* ▶ **punc·til·i·ous·ly** *adv.* **punc·til·i·ous·ness** *noun* [U]

punc·tu·al /ˈpʌŋktʃuəl/ *adj.* happening or doing something at the arranged or correct time; not late: *She has been reliable and punctual.* ◆ *a punctual start at 9 o'clock* ▶ **punc·tu·al·i·ty** /ˌpʌŋktʃuˈæləti/ *noun* [U] **punc·tu·al·ly** /ˈpʌŋktʃuəli/ *adv.*: *They always pay punctually.*

punc·tu·ate /ˈpʌŋktʃueɪt/ *verb* **1** [T, often passive] ~ sth (with sth) to interrupt something at intervals: *Her speech was punctuated by bursts of applause.* **2** [I, T] ~ (sth) to divide writing into sentences and phrases by using special marks, for example commas, question marks, etc.

punc·tu·a·tion /ˌpʌŋktʃuˈeɪʃn/ *noun* [U] the marks used in writing that divide sentences and phrases; the system of using these marks

punctuˈation ˌmark *noun* a sign or mark used in writing to divide sentences and phrases

punc·ture /ˈpʌŋktʃər/ *noun, verb*
• *noun* a small hole, especially in the skin, made by a sharp point ⟳ see also LUMBAR PUNCTURE
• *verb* **1** [T, I] ~ (sth) to make a small hole in something; to get a small hole: *to puncture a tire* ◆ *She was taken to the hospital with broken ribs and a punctured lung.* ◆ *One of the front tires had punctured.* **2** [T] ~ sth to suddenly make someone feel less confident, proud, etc.: *to puncture someone's confidence*

pun·dit /ˈpʌndət/ *noun* a person who knows a lot about a particular subject and who often talks about it in public SYN EXPERT

pun·gent /ˈpʌndʒənt/ *adj.* **1** having a strong taste or smell: *the pungent smell of burning rubber* ⟳ thesaurus box at BITTER **2** direct and having a strong effect: *pungent criticism* ▶ **pun·gen·cy** /-dʒənsi/ *noun* [U] **pun·gent·ly** *adv.*

pun·ish ✎ /ˈpʌnɪʃ/ *verb*

1 to make someone suffer because they have broken the law or done something wrong: *~ sb Those responsible for this crime will be severely punished.* ◆ *My parents used to punish me by not letting me watch TV.* ◆ *~ sb for sth/for doing sth He was punished for refusing to answer their questions.* **2** ~ sth (by/with sth) to set the punishment for a particular crime: *In those days murder was always punished with the death penalty.* **3** ~ yourself (for sth) to blame yourself for something that has happened

pun·ish·a·ble /ˈpʌnɪʃəbl/ *adj.* ~ (by/with sth) (of a crime) that can be punished, especially by law: *a crime punishable by/with imprisonment* ◆ *Giving false information to the police is a punishable offense.*

pun·ish·ing /ˈpʌnɪʃɪŋ/ *adj.* [usually before noun] long and difficult and making you work hard so you become very tired: *The President has a punishing schedule for the next six months.*

pun·ish·ment ✎ /ˈpʌnɪʃmənt/ *noun*

1 [U, C] an act or a way of punishing someone: *to inflict/impose/mete out punishment* ◆ *~ (for sth) What is the punishment for murder?* ◆ *There is little evidence that harsher punishments deter any better than more lenient ones.* ◆ *The punishment should fit the crime.* ◆ *He was sent to his room as a* *punishment.* ⊃ see also CAPITAL PUNISHMENT, CORPORAL PUNISHMENT **2** [U] rough treatment: *The carpet by the door takes the most punishment.*

pu·ni·tive /'pyunətɪv/ *adj.* [usually before noun] (*formal*) **1** intended as punishment: *There are calls for more punitive measures against people who drink and drive.* ◆ *He was awarded punitive damages* (= in a court of law). **2** very severe and that people find very difficult to pay: *punitive taxes* ▶ **pu·ni·tive·ly** *adv.*

Pun·ja·bi /pʌn'dʒabi; pʊn-/ *noun* **1** [C] a person from the Punjab area in N.W. India and Pakistan **2** [U] the language of people from the Punjab ▶ **Pun·ja·bi** *adj.*

punk /pʌŋk/ *noun* **1** (also ˌpunk ˈrock) [U] a type of loud and aggressive ROCK music popular in the late 1970s and early 1980s: *a punk band* **2** (also ˌpunk ˈrocker) [C] a person who likes punk music and dresses like a punk musician, for example by wearing metal chains, leather clothes, and having brightly colored hair: *a punk haircut* **3** [C] (*informal*) a young man or boy who behaves in a rude or violent way

pun·ster /'pʌnstər/ *noun* a person who often makes PUNS

punt¹ /pʌnt/ *noun, verb* ⊃ see also PUNT²
● *noun* **1** (in football or RUGBY) a long kick made after dropping the ball from your hands **2** a long shallow boat with a flat bottom and square ends, which is moved by pushing the end of a long pole against the bottom of a river
● *verb* **1** [T] ~ sth (+ adv./prep.) to kick a ball hard so that it goes a long way, sometimes after it has dropped from your hands and before it reaches the ground **2** [I, T] ~ (sth) (+ adv./prep.) to travel in a punt, especially for pleasure: *We spent the day punting on the river.* ◆ *to go punting*

punt² /pʊnt/ *noun* the former unit of money in the Republic of Ireland (replaced in 2002 by the EURO) ⊃ see also PUNT¹

pu·ny /'pyuni/ *adj.* (pun·i·er, pun·i·est) (*disapproving*) **1** small and weak **SYN** FEEBLE: *The lamb was a puny little thing.* **2** not very impressive: *They laughed at my puny efforts.*

pup /pʌp/ *noun* **1** = PUPPY **2** a young animal of various SPECIES (= types): *a seal pup*

pu·pa /'pyupə/ *noun* (*pl.* pu·pae /-pi/) an insect in the stage of development between a LARVA and an adult insect ⊃ compare CHRYSALIS ▶ **pu·pal** /'pyupəl/ *adj.* [usually before noun]

pu·pate /'pyupeɪt/ *verb* [I] (*biology*) to develop into a pupa

pu·pil /'pyupl/ *noun* **1** the small, round, black area at the center of the eye: *Her pupils were dilated.* ⊃ picture at BODY ⊃ compare IRIS **2** a person who is being taught, especially a child in a school: *How many pupils does the school have?* ◆ *She now teaches only private pupils.* **3** a person who is taught artistic, musical, etc. skills by an expert: *The painting is by a pupil of Rembrandt.*

pup·pet /'pʌpət/ *noun* **1** a model of a person or an animal that can be made to move, for example by pulling strings attached to parts of its body or by putting your hand inside it. A puppet with strings is also called a MARIONETTE: *a hand puppet* ◆ *a puppet show* **2** (usually *disapproving*) a person or group whose actions are controlled by another: *The occupying forces set up a puppet government.*

pup·pet·eer /ˌpʌpə'tɪr/ *noun* a person who performs with puppets

pup·pet·ry /'pʌpətri/ *noun* [U] the art and skill of making and using puppets

pup·py /'pʌpi/ *noun* (*pl.* pup·pies) (also pup) a young dog: *a Labrador puppy* ◆ *a litter of puppies*

ˈpuppy ˌlove *noun* [U] feelings of love that a young person has for someone else and that adults do not think is very serious

ˈpup tent *noun* a small tent for one or two people

pur·chase 🖊 **AWL** /'pərtʃəs/ *noun, verb*
● *noun* (*formal*) **1** [U, C] the act or process of buying something: *to make a purchase* (= buy something) ◆ *Keep your receipt as proof of purchase.* ◆ *The company has just announced*

its $27 million purchase of Park Hotel. ⊃ **collocations** at SHOPPING **2** [C] something that you have bought: *major purchases, such as a new car* ◆ *If you are not satisfied with your purchase we will give you a full refund.* **3** [U, sing.] (*technical*) a firm hold on something with the hands or feet, for example when you are climbing **SYN** GRIP: *She tried to get a purchase on the slippery rock.*
● *verb* ~ sth (from sb) (*formal*) to buy something: *The equipment can be purchased from your local supplier.* ◆ *They purchased the land for $1 million.* ◆ (*figurative*) *Victory was purchased* (= achieved) *at too great a price.*

ˈpurchase ˌprice *noun* [usually sing.] (*formal*) the price that is paid for something you buy

pur·chas·er **AWL** /'pərtʃəsər/ *noun* (*formal*) a person who buys something ⊃ compare BUYER

pur·chas·ing **AWL** /'pərtʃəsɪŋ/ *noun* [U] (*business*) the activity of buying things, especially for a company

ˈpurchasing ˌpower *noun* [U] **1** money that people have available to buy goods with **2** the amount that a unit of money can buy: *the peso's purchasing power*

pur·dah /'pərdə/ *noun* [U] the system in some Muslim societies by which women live in a separate part of a house or cover their faces so that men do not see them: *to be in purdah* ◆ *He kept his daughters in virtual purdah.*

pure 🖊 /pyʊr/ *adj.*
(pur·er /'pyʊrər/, pur·est /'pyʊrəst/)
‣ NOT MIXED **1** [usually before noun] not mixed with anything else; with nothing added: *pure gold/silk, etc.* ◆ *These shirts are 100% pure cotton.* ◆ *Classical dance in its purest form requires symmetry and balance.* ◆ *One movie is classified as pure art, the other as entertainment.*
‣ CLEAN **2** clean and not containing any harmful substances: *a bottle of pure water* ◆ *The air was sweet and pure.* **ANT** IMPURE
‣ COMPLETE **3** [only before noun] complete and total: *They met by pure chance.* ◆ *She laughed with pure joy.*
‣ MORALLY GOOD **4** without evil thoughts or actions, especially sexual ones; morally good: *to lead a pure life* ◆ *His motives were pure.* ◆ (*literary*) *to be pure in body and mind* **ANT** IMPURE
‣ COLOR/SOUND/LIGHT **5** very clear; perfect: *beaches of pure white sand* ◆ *a pure voice*
‣ SUBJECT YOU STUDY **6** [only before noun] concerned with increasing knowledge of the subject rather than with using knowledge in practical ways: *pure mathematics* ◆ *technology as opposed to pure science subjects* ⊃ compare APPLIED
‣ BREED/RACE **7** not mixed with any other breed or race, etc.: *These cattle are one of the purest breeds.* ⊃ see also PURE-BRED
⊃ see also PURIFY, PURITY
IDM ˌpure and ˈsimple used after the noun that it refers to in order to emphasize that there is nothing but the thing you have just mentioned involved in something: *It's laziness, pure and simple.*

ˌpure-ˈbred *adj.* (of an animal) born from parents of the same breed, not from a mix of two or more breeds

pu·rée /pyʊ'reɪ/ *noun, verb*
● *noun* [U, C] food in the form of a thick liquid made by crushing fruit or cooked vegetables in a small amount of water: *apple purée*
● *verb* (pu·réed, pu·réed) ~ sth to make food into a purée

pure·ly 🖊 /'pyʊrli/ *adv.* only; completely: *I saw the letter purely by chance.* ◆ *The charity is run on a purely voluntary basis.* ◆ *She took the job purely and simply for the money.*

pur·ga·tive /'pərgətɪv/ *noun* a substance, especially a medicine, that causes your BOWELS to empty ▶ **pur·ga·tive** *adj.*

pur·ga·to·ry /'pərgəˌtɔri/ *noun* [U] **1** usually **Purgatory** (in Roman Catholic teaching) a place or state in which the souls of dead people suffer for the bad things they did when they were living, so that they can become pure enough to go to heaven **2** (*informal, humorous*) any place or state of suffering: *Getting up at four o'clock every morning is sheer purgatory.*

purge /pɜrdʒ/ *verb, noun*
- **verb 1** to remove people from an organization, often violently, because their opinions or activities are unacceptable to the people in power: **~ sth (of sb)** *His first act as leader was to purge the party of extremists.* ◆ **~ sb (from sth)** *He purged extremists from the party.* **2** (*formal*) to make yourself/someone or something pure, healthy, or clean by getting rid of bad thoughts or feelings: **~ yourself/sb/sth (of sth)** *We need to purge our sport of racism.* ◆ **~ sth (from sth)** *Nothing could purge the guilt from her mind.* **3** to get rid of something from the body: *a diet to purge the body of toxins*
- **noun** the act of removing people, often violently, from an organization because their views are unacceptable to the people who have power

pu·ri·fi·er /ˈpjʊrəˌfaɪər/ *noun* a device that removes substances that are dirty, harmful, or not wanted: *an air/water purifier*

pu·ri·fy /ˈpjʊrəˌfaɪ/ *verb* (**pu·ri·fies, pu·ri·fy·ing, pur·i·fied, pu·ri·fied**) **1 ~ sth** to make something pure by removing substances that are dirty, harmful, or not wanted: *One tablet will purify a quart of water.* **2 ~ sb/sth/yourself** to make someone pure by removing evil from their souls: *Hindus purify themselves by bathing in the river Ganges.* **3 ~ sth (from sth)** (*technical*) to take a pure form of a substance out of another substance that contains it ▶ **pu·ri·fi·ca·tion** /ˌpjʊrəfəˈkeɪʃn/ *noun* [U]: *a water purification plant*

Pu·rim /ˈpʊrɪm; pʊˈrɪm/ *noun* [U] a Jewish festival that is celebrated in the spring

pur·ist /ˈpjʊrɪst/ *noun* a person who thinks things should be done in the traditional way and who has strong opinions on what is correct in language, art, etc. ▶ **pur·ism** /ˈpjʊrɪzəm/ *noun* [U]

pu·ri·tan /ˈpjʊrətn/ *noun, adj.*
- **noun 1** (*usually disapproving*) a person who has very strict moral attitudes and who thinks that pleasure is bad **2 Puritan** a member of a Protestant group of Christians in England and North America in the 16th and 17th centuries who wanted to worship God in a simple way
- **adj. 1 Puritan** connected with the puritans and their beliefs **2** = PURITANICAL

pu·ri·tan·i·cal /ˌpjʊrəˈtænɪkl/ (also **pu·ri·tan**) *adj.* (*usually disapproving*) having very strict moral attitudes: *Their parents had a puritanical streak and didn't approve of dancing.*

pu·ri·tan·ism /ˈpjʊrətnˌɪzəm/ *noun* [U] **1 Puritanism** the beliefs and practices of the puritans **2** very strict moral attitudes

pu·ri·ty /ˈpjʊrəti/ *noun* [U] the state or quality of being pure: *The purity of the water is tested regularly.* ◆ *spiritual purity* **ANT** IMPURITY

purl /pɜrl/ *noun* [U] a STITCH used in KNITTING ▶ **purl** *verb* [I]

pur·lieus /ˈpɜrluz/ *noun* [pl.] (*literary*) the area near or surrounding a place

pur·loin /pərˈlɔɪn/ *verb* **~ sth (from sb/sth)** (*formal or humorous*) to steal something or use it without permission

pur·ple 🔊 /ˈpɜrpl/ *adj.*
1 having the color of blue and red mixed together: *a purple flower* ◆ *His face was purple with rage.* **2 prose/passage** writing or a piece of writing that is too grand in style ▶ **pur·ple** *noun* [U, C]: *She was dressed in purple.*

Purple 'Heart *noun* a MEDAL given to a member of the armed forces of the U.S. who has been wounded in battle

pur·plish /ˈpɜrpəlɪʃ; -plɪʃ/ *adj.* similar to purple in color: *purplish lips*

pur·port *verb, noun*
- **verb** /pərˈpɔrt/ **~ to be/have sth** (*formal*) to claim to be something or to have done something, when this may not be true **SYN** PROFESS: *The book does not purport to be a complete history of the period.*
- **noun** /ˈpɜrpɔrt/ [sing.] **the ~ of sth** (*formal*) the general meaning of something

pur·port·ed /pərˈpɔrtəd/ *adj.* [only before noun] (*formal*) that has been stated to have happened or to be true, when this might not be the case: *the scene of the purported crime* ▶ **pur·port·ed·ly** *adv.*: *documents purportedly written by famous people such as President John F. Kennedy*

purpose
aim ◆ intention ◆ plan ◆ point ◆ idea
These are all words for talking about what someone intends to do or achieve.
purpose what something is supposed to achieve; what someone is trying to achieve: *The purpose of the visit was to see the campus in person.*
aim what someone is trying to achieve; what something is supposed to achieve: *Our main aim is to increase sales in the Northwest.*

PURPOSE OR AIM?
Your **purpose** for doing something is your reason for doing it; your **aim** is what you want to achieve. Aim can suggest that you are only trying to achieve something; **purpose** gives a stronger sense of achievement being certain. Aim can be *someone's aim* or *the aim of something*. **Purpose** is more usually *the purpose of something*; you can talk about *someone's purpose* but that is more formal.
intention what you intend to do: *I have no intention of going to the wedding.* ◆ *She's full of good intentions but things rarely work out for her.*
plan what you intend to do or achieve: *There are no plans to build new offices.*

INTENTION OR PLAN?
Your **intentions** are what you want to do, especially in the near future; your **plans** are what you have decided or arranged to do, often, but not always, in the longer term.
point (*somewhat informal*) the purpose or aim of something: **What's the point** of all this violence? ◆ *The point of the lesson is to compare the two countries.*
idea (*somewhat informal*) the purpose of something; someone's aim: *The whole idea of going was so that we could meet her new boyfriend.* ◆ **What's the idea** behind this assignment?

POINT OR IDEA?
Point is a more negative word than **idea**. If you say *What's the point...?* you are suggesting that there is no point; if you say *What's the idea...?* you are genuinely asking a question. **Point**, but not **idea**, is used to talk about things you feel annoyed or unhappy about: *There's no idea in... ◆ I don't see the idea of....*

PATTERNS
- with the aim/intention/idea of doing sth
- sb's intention/plan to do sth
- to have a(n) purpose/aim/intention/plan/point
- to achieve a(n) purpose/aim

pur·pose 🔊 /ˈpɜrpəs/ *noun*
1 [C] the intention, aim, or function of something; the thing that something is supposed to achieve: *Our campaign's main purpose is to raise money.* ◆ *The purpose of the book is to provide a complete guide to the university.* ◆ *A meeting was called for the purpose of appointing a new treasurer.* ◆ *The experiments serve no useful purpose* (= are not useful). ◆ *The building is used for religious purposes.* **2 purposes** [pl.] what is needed in a particular situation: *These gifts count as income for tax purposes.* ◆ *For the purposes of this study, the three groups have been combined.* **3** [C, U] meaning that is important and

valuable to you: *Volunteer work gives her life (a sense of) purpose.* **4** [U] the ability to plan something and work successfully to achieve it **SYN** DETERMINATION: *He has enormous confidence and strength of purpose.* ⊃ see also CROSS PURPOSES

IDM **on purpose** not by accident; deliberately: *He did it on purpose, knowing it would annoy her.* **to little/no purpose** (formal) with little/no useful effect or result ⊃ more at INTENT, PRACTICAL

pur·pose·ful /ˈpərpəsfl/ adj. having a useful purpose; acting with a clear aim and with determination: *Purposeful work is an important part of the regime for young offenders.* ◆ *She looked purposeful and determined.* ▶ **pur·pose·ful·ly** /-fəli/ adv. **pur·pose·ful·ness** noun [U]

pur·pose·less /ˈpərpəsləs/ adj. having no meaning, use, or clear aim **SYN** MEANINGLESS, POINTLESS: *purposeless destruction*

pur·pose·ly /ˈpərpəsli/ adv. on purpose; deliberately: *He sat down, purposely avoiding her gaze.*

pur·pos·ive /ˈpərpəsɪv/ adj. (formal) having a clear and definite purpose **SYN** PURPOSEFUL

purr /pər/ verb **1** [I] when a cat **purrs**, it makes a low continuous sound in the throat, especially when it is happy or comfortable **2** [I] (of a machine or vehicle) to make a low continuous sound; to move making such a sound: *a purring engine* ◆ *The car purred away.* **3** [I, T] **(+ speech)** to speak in a low and gentle voice, for example to show you are happy or satisfied, or because you want to attract someone or get them to do something: *He was purring with satisfaction.* ▶ **purr** (also **pur·ring**) noun [sing.]: *the purr of a cat/a car engine*

purse /pərs/ noun, verb
• noun **1** (also **hand·bag, pock·et·book**) [C] a small bag for money, keys, etc., carried especially by women ⊃ picture at BAG **2** [C] = CHANGE PURSE **3** [sing.] the amount of money that is available to a person, an organization, or a government to spend: *We have vacations to suit every purse.* **4** [C] (sports) a sum of money given as a prize in a sports event such as a BOXING match or horse race **IDM** see SILK
• verb ~ **your lips** to form your lips into a small, tight, round shape, for example to show disapproval

purs·er /ˈpərsər/ noun an officer on a ship who is responsible for taking care of the passengers, and for the accounts

the ˈpurse strings noun [pl.] a way of referring to money and how it is controlled or spent: *Who holds the purse strings in your house?* ◆ *The government will have to tighten the purse strings* (= spend less).

pur·su·ance /pərˈsuəns/ noun
IDM **in pursuance of sth** (formal or law) in order to do something; in the process of doing something: *They may need to borrow money in pursuance of their legal action.*

pur·su·ant /pərˈsuənt/ adj. ~ **to sth** (formal or law) according to or following something, especially a rule or law **SYN** IN ACCORDANCE WITH

pur·sue ⚓ **AWL** /pərˈsu/ verb (formal)
1 ~ **sth** to do something or try to achieve something over a period of time: *to pursue a goal/an aim/an objective* ◆ *We intend to pursue this policy with determination.* ◆ *She wishes to pursue a medical career.* **2** to continue to discuss, find out about, or be involved in something: *~ sth | + speech to pursue legal action* ◆ *We have decided not to pursue the matter.* **3** ~ **sb/sth** to follow or chase someone or something, especially in order to catch them: *She left the theater, hotly pursued by the press.* ◆ *Police pursued the car at high speed.*

pur·su·er /pərˈsuər/ noun a person who is following or chasing someone

pur·suit **AWL** /pərˈsut/ noun **1** [U] ~ **of sth** the act of looking for or trying to find something: *the pursuit of happiness/knowledge/profit* ◆ *She traveled the world in pursuit of her dreams.* **2** [U] the act of following or chasing someone: *We drove away with two police cars in pursuit* (= following). ◆ *I galloped off on my horse with Rosie in hot*

pursuit (= following quickly behind). **3** [C, usually pl.] an activity that you do regularly, often for pleasure **SYN** HOBBY, PASTIME: *outdoor/leisure/artistic pursuits*

pu·ru·lent /ˈpyʊrələnt; ˈpyʊryə-/ adj. (medical) containing or producing PUS: *a purulent discharge from the wound*

pur·vey /pərˈveɪ/ verb ~ **sth** (formal) to supply food, services, or information to people

pur·vey·or /pərˈveɪər/ noun (formal) a person or company that supplies something

pur·view /ˈpərvyu/ noun [U]
IDM **within/outside the purview of sth** (formal) within the limits of what a person, an organization, etc. is responsible for; dealt with by a document, law, etc.

pus /pʌs/ noun [U] a thick yellowish or greenish liquid that is produced in an infected wound

push ⚓ /pʊʃ/ verb, noun
• verb
> USING HANDS/ARMS/BODY **1** [I, T] to use your hands, arms, or body in order to make someone or something move forward or away from you; to move part of your body into a particular position: *We pushed and pushed but the piano wouldn't move.* ◆ *Push hard when I tell you to.* ◆ *You push and I'll pull.* ◆ ~ **at sth** *She pushed at the door but it wouldn't budge.* ◆ ~ **sth** *He walked slowly up the hill pushing his bike.* ◆ ~ **sb/sth + adv./prep.** *She pushed the cup toward me.* ◆ *He pushed his chair back and stood up.* ◆ *He tried to kiss her but she pushed him away.* ◆ *She pushed her face toward him.* ◆ ~ **sth + adj.** *I pushed the door open.* **2** [I, T] to use force to move past someone or something using your hands, arms, etc.: *People were pushing and shoving to get to the front.* ◆ + **adv./prep.** *The fans pushed against the barrier.* ◆ ~ **your way + adv./prep.** *Try and push your way through the crowd.*
> AFFECT SOMETHING **3** [T] ~ **sth + adv./prep.** to affect something so that it reaches a particular level or state: *This development could push the country into recession.* ◆ *The rise in interest rates will push prices up.*
> SWITCH/BUTTON **4** [T] ~ **sth** to press a switch, button, etc., for example in order to make a machine start working: *I pushed the button for the top floor.*
> PERSUADE **5** [T] to persuade or encourage someone to do something that they may not want to do: ~ **sb (into sth/ into doing sth)** *My teacher pushed me into entering the competition.* ◆ ~ **sb to do sth** *No one pushed you to take the job, did they?*
> WORK HARD **6** [T] ~ **sb/yourself** to make someone work hard: *The music teacher really pushes her students.* ◆ *Lucy should push herself a little harder.*
> PUT PRESSURE ON SOMEONE **7** [T] ~ **sb (+ adv./prep.)** (informal) to put pressure on someone and make them angry or upset: *Her parents are very tolerant, but sometimes she pushes them too far.*
> NEW IDEA/PRODUCT **8** [T] ~ **sth** (informal) to try hard to persuade people to accept or agree with a new idea, buy a new product, etc.: *The interview gave him a chance to push his latest movie.* ◆ *She didn't want to push the point any further at that moment.*
> SELL DRUGS **9** [T] ~ **sth** (informal) to sell illegal drugs
> OF ARMY **10** [I] + **adv./prep.** to move forward quickly through an area: *The army pushed (on) toward the capital.*
IDM **be pushing 40, 50, etc.** (informal) to be nearly 40, 50, etc. years old **be pushing up (the) daisies** (old-fashioned, humorous) to be dead and in a grave **push all the (right) buttons** (informal) to do exactly the right things to please someone: *a new satirical comedy show that pushes all the right buttons* **push sb's buttons** (informal) to make someone react in either a positive or a negative way: *I've known him for years, but I still don't know what pushes his buttons.* **push the envelope** (informal) to go beyond the limits of what is allowed or thought to be possible: *He is a performer who consistently pushes the envelope of TV comedy.* **push your luck| push it/things** (informal) to take a risk because you have successfully avoided problems in the past: *You didn't get caught last time, but don't push your luck!* **push sth to the back of your mind** to try to forget about something

unpleasant: *I tried to push the thought to the back of my mind.* ➔ more at PANIC BUTTON

PHR V ,push a'head/'forward (with sth) to continue with a plan in a determined way: *The government is pushing ahead with its electoral reforms.* ,push sb a'round to give orders to someone in a rude or unpleasant way ,push sth↔'aside to avoid thinking about something: *He pushed aside the feelings of fear.* ,push sth 'back to make the time or date of a meeting, etc. later than originally planned: *The start of the game was pushed back from 2 p.m. to 4 p.m.* 'push for sth | 'push sb for sth to repeatedly ask for something or try to make something happen because you think it is very important.: *The pressure group is pushing for a ban on GM foods.* ◆ *I'm going to have to push you for an answer.* ,push 'forward to continue moving or traveling somewhere, especially when it is a long distance or difficult ,push yourself/sb 'forward to make other people think about and notice you or someone else: *She had to push herself forward to get a promotion.* ,push 'off to move away from land in a boat, or from the side of a swimming pool, etc. ,push 'on to continue with a journey or an activity: *We rested for a while then pushed on to the next camp.* ,push sb↔'out to make someone leave a place or an organization ,push sb/sth↔'out to make something less important than it was; to replace something ,push sth↔'out to produce something in large quantities: *factories pushing out cheap cotton shirts* ,push sb/sth 'over to make someone or something fall to the ground by pushing them: *Sam pushed me over in the playground.* ➔ see also PUSHOVER ,push sth↔'through to get a new law or plan officially accepted: *The government is pushing the changes through before the election.*

● **noun**
▷ USING HANDS/ARMS/BODY **1** an act of pushing something or someone: *She gave him a gentle push.* ◆ *The car won't start. Can you give it a push?* ◆ **At the push of a button** (= very easily) he could get a whole list of names.
▷ OF ARMY **2** a large and determined military attack: *a final push against the enemy* ◆ (*figurative*) *The firm has begun a major push into the European market.*
▷ EFFORT **3** ~ for sth a determined effort to achieve something: *The push for reform started in 2009.* **4** encouragement to do something: *He wants to open his own business, but needs a push in the right direction to get him started.*

IDM when push comes to shove (*informal*) when there is no other choice; when everything else has failed

push·back /'pʊʃbæk/ *noun* [U] opposition or resistance to a plan, an idea, or a change: *The plan was abandoned because the pushback from the military was so strong.*

'push-,button *adj.* [only before noun] operated by pressing buttons with your fingers: *a push-button phone*

push·cart /'pʊʃkɑrt/ *noun* a small CART (= a vehicle like a box on wheels) pushed by a person, often used for selling something outdoors: *Vendors with their pushcarts were selling hot dogs and ice cream at the zoo.*

push·er /'pʊʃər/ *noun* (*informal*) a person who sells illegal drugs: *drug pushers* ➔ see also PAPER-PUSHER, PENCIL-PUSHER

push·o·ver /'pʊʃ,oʊvər/ *noun* (*informal*) **1** a person who is easy to persuade or influence: *I don't think she'll agree—she's no pushover.* **2** a thing that is easy to do or win: *The game will be a pushover.*

push·pin /'pʊʃpɪn/ *noun* a type of THUMBTACK with a colored plastic head that is not flat ➔ picture at STATIONERY

'push poll *noun* (*politics*) a way of trying to influence the way people vote by giving them information, often something bad about an opposing candidate, while seeming to be asking their opinion ▶ 'push ,polling *noun* [U]: *allegations of push polling*

'push-up *noun* [usually pl.] an exercise in which you lie on your stomach and raise your body off the ground by pressing down on your arms until your arms are straight ➔ picture at EXERCISE

push·y /'pʊʃi/ *adj.* (push·i·er, push·i·est) (*informal, disapproving*) trying hard to get what you want, especially in a way that seems rude: *a pushy salesman* ▶ **push·i·ness** *noun* [U]

pu·sil·lan·i·mous /,pyusə'lænəməs/ *adj.* (*formal*) frightened to take risks

puss /pʊs/ *noun* (*informal*) a person's face or mouth

pus·sy /'pʊsi/ *noun* (*pl.* pus·sies) a child's word for a cat

pus·sy·cat /'pʊsi,kæt/ *noun* (*informal*) **1** a child's word for a cat **2** a person who is kind and friendly, especially when you would not expect them to be like this: *He's just a pussycat really, once you get to know him.*

pus·sy·foot /'pʊsi,fʊt/ *verb* [I] ~ (around) (*informal*, usually *disapproving*) to be careful or anxious about expressing your opinion in case you upset someone

'pussy ,willow *noun* a small tree with flowers in spring that are like soft fur

pus·tule /'pʌstʃʊl/ *noun* (*formal* or *medical*) a spot on the skin containing PUS

put 🔧 /pʊt/ *verb* (put·ting, put, put)

▷ IN PLACE/POSITION **1** ~ sth + adv./prep. to move something into a particular place or position: *Put the suitcases down there, please.* ◆ *Did you put sugar in my coffee?* ◆ *Put your hand up if you need more paper.* **2** ~ sth + adv./prep. to move something into a particular place or position using force: *He put his fist through a glass door.* **3** ~ sb/sth + adv./prep. to cause someone or something to go to a particular place: *Her family put her into a nursing home.* ◆ *It was the year that we put a man on the moon.*
▷ ATTACH **4** ~ sth + adv./prep. to attach or fix something to something else: *We had to put new locks on all the doors.*
▷ WRITE **5** ~ sth (+ adv./prep.) to write something or make a mark on something: *Put your name here.* ◆ *Friday at 11? I'll put it in my calendar.* ◆ *I couldn't read what she had put.*
▷ PRINT/PUBLISH **6** ~ sth + adv./prep. to have something printed in a newspaper or listed online: *He put an ad for a housemate in the paper.*
▷ INTO STATE/CONDITION **7** ~ sb/sth + adv./prep. to bring someone or something into the state or condition mentioned: *I was put in charge of the office.* ◆ *The incident put her in a bad mood.* ◆ *Put yourself in my position. What would you have done?* ◆ *I tried to put the matter into perspective.* ◆ *Don't go putting yourself at risk.* ◆ *It was time to put their suggestion into practice.* ◆ *This new injury will put him out of action for several weeks.*
▷ AFFECT SOMEONE OR SOMETHING **8** ~ sth on/onto/to sth to make someone or something feel something or be affected by something: *Her new job has put a great strain on her.* ◆ *They put pressure on her to resign.* ◆ *It's time you put a stop to this childish behavior.*
▷ GIVE VALUE/RANK **9** ~ sth on sth to give or attach a particular level of importance, trust, value, etc. to something: *Our company puts the emphasis on quality.* ◆ *He put a limit on the amount we could spend.* **10** ~ sb/sth + adv./prep. to consider someone or something to belong to the class or level mentioned: *I'd put her in the top rank of modern novelists.*
▷ EXPRESS **11** ~ sth + adv./prep. to express or state something in a particular way: *She put it very tactfully.* ◆ *Put simply, we accept their offer or go bankrupt.* ◆ *I was, to put it mildly, annoyed* (= I was extremely angry). ◆ *He was too trusting—or, to put it another way, he had no head for business.* ◆ *The meat was — how shall I put it?* —*a little overdone.* ◆ *As T.S. Eliot puts it...* ◆ *She had never tried to put this feeling into words.* ◆ *Can you help me put this letter into good English, please?*
▷ IN SPORTS **12** ~ sth to throw the SHOT (=a type of heavy ball)

IDM Most idioms containing **put** are at the entries for the nouns and adjectives in the idioms. For example, **put your foot down** is at **foot**. **I wouldn't put it past sb (to do sth)** (*informal*) used to say that you think someone is capable of doing something wrong, illegal, etc. **put it to sb that...** to suggest something to someone to see if they can argue against it: *I put it to you that you are the only person who had a motive for the crime.* **put one over on sb** (*informal*) to persuade someone to believe something that is not true: *Don't try to put one over on me!* **put together** used when comparing or contrasting someone or something with a group of other people or things to mean "combined" or "in total": *Your department spent more last year than all the others put together.* **put up or shut up** used to tell someone to stop just talking about something and actually do it, show it, etc.

PHR V 'put sth a'bove sth = PUT STH BEFORE STH

,put yourself/sth↔a'cross/'over (to sb) to communicate your ideas, feelings, etc. successfully to someone: *She's not very good at putting her views across.*

,put sth↔a'side **1** to ignore or forget something, usually a feeling or difference of opinion **SYN** DISREGARD: *They decided to put aside their differences.* **2** to save something or keep it available to use: *We put some money aside every month for our retirement.* ♦ *I put aside half an hour every day to write my diary.*

'put sb/sth at sth to calculate someone or something to be a particular age, weight, amount, etc.: *They put the damage to the building at over $1 million.*

,put sb↔a'way [often passive] (*informal*) to send someone to prison, to a mental hospital, etc. ,put sth↔a'way **1** to put something in the place where it is kept because you have finished using it: *I'm just going to put the car away* (= in the garage). **2** to save money to spend later: *She has a few thousand dollars put away for her retirement.* **3** (*informal*) to eat or drink large quantities of something: *He must have put away a bottle of whiskey last night.*

,put sth↔'back **1** to return something to its usual place or to the place where it was before it was moved: *If you use something, put it back!* **2** to move something to a later time or date **SYN** POSTPONE: *The meeting has been put back to next week.* **3** to cause something to be delayed: *Poor trading figures put back our plans for expansion.* **4** to move the hands of a clock so that they show the correct earlier time: *Remember to put your clocks back tonight* (= because the time has officially changed).

'put sth be,fore sb to present something to a person or a group of people so that they can consider it: *The proposal was put before the committee and rejected.*

'put sth before/above sth to treat something as more important than something else

,put sth be'hind you to try to forget about an unpleasant experience and think about the future

,put sb↔'down (*informal*) to make someone look or feel stupid, especially in front of other people ⊃ related noun PUT-DOWN ,put sth↔'down **1** to stop holding something and place it on a table, shelf, etc.: *Put that knife down before you hurt somebody!* ♦ *It's a great book. I couldn't put it down.* ⊃ see also UNPUTDOWNABLE **2** to write something; to make a note of something: *The meeting's on the 22nd. Put it down in your calendar.* **3** to pay part of the cost of something: *We put a 5% deposit down on the house.* **4** to stop something by force **SYN** CRUSH: *to put down a rebellion* ♦ *The military government is determined to put down all opposition.* **5** [often passive] to kill an animal, usually by giving it a drug, because it is old or sick: *We had to have our cat put down.* **6** to put a baby to bed: *Can you be quiet—I've just put the baby down.* ,put sb 'down as sth to consider or judge someone to be a particular type of person: *I'd put them both down as retired teachers.* ,put sb 'down for sth to put someone's name on a list, etc. for something: *Put me down for three tickets for Saturday.* ♦ *They've put their son down for the local school.* 'put sth down to sth to consider that something is caused by something **SYN** ATTRIBUTE: *What do you put her success down to?*

,put sth↔'forth (*formal*) = PUT sth out

,put yourself/sb↔'forward to suggest yourself/someone as a candidate for a job or position: *Can I put you/your name forward for club secretary?* ,put sth↔'forward **1** to move something to an earlier time or date: *We've put the wedding forward by one week.* **2** to move the hands of a clock to the correct later time: *Remember to put your clocks forward tonight*

(= because the time has officially changed). **3** to suggest something for discussion: *to put forward a suggestion* ,put sth↔'in **1** to place equipment or furniture into position so that it can be used **SYN** INSTALL: *We're having a new shower put in.* **2** to include something in a letter, story, etc. **3** to interrupt another speaker in order to say something: *Could I put in a word?* ♦ **+ speech** *"But what about us?" he put in.* **4** to officially make a claim, request, etc.: *The company has put in a claim for damages.* **5 ~ a (...) performance** to give a performance of something, especially one of a particular kind: *All the actors put in great performances.* **6** (also ,put sth into sth) to spend a lot of time or make a lot of effort doing something: *She often puts in twelve hours' work a day.* ♦ **~ doing sth** *He's putting a lot of work into improving his French.* ⊃ related noun INPUT **7** (also ,put sth 'into sth) to use or give money: **~ doing sth** *He's put all his savings into buying that house.* ,put sb 'in (at...) | 'put into... (of a boat or its sailors) to enter a port: *We put in at Syracuse and stayed there for three days.* ,put 'in for sth to officially ask for something: *Are you going to put in for that job?* ,put yourself/sb/sth 'in for sth to enter yourself/someone or something for a competition

,put sth 'into sth **1** to add a quality to something: *He put as much feeling into his voice as he could.* **2** = PUT in (6), PUT (7)

,put sb↔'off **1** to cancel a meeting or an arrangement that you have made with someone: *It's too late to put them off now.* **2** to make someone dislike someone or something or not trust them/it: *She's very smart but her manner does tend to put people off.* ♦ *Don't be put off by how it looks—it tastes delicious.* ⊃ see also OFF-PUTTING **3** (also ,put sb 'off sth) to disturb someone who is trying to give all their attention to something that they are doing: *Don't put me off when I'm trying to concentrate.* ♦ *The sudden noise put her off her game.* ,put sb 'off sth/sb to make someone lose interest in or enthusiasm for something or someone: *He was put off science by bad teaching.* ♦ **~ doing sth** *The accident put her off driving for life.* ,put sth↔'off to change something to a later time or date **SYN** DELAY, POSTPONE: *We've had to put off our wedding until September.* ♦ **~ doing sth** *He keeps putting off going to the dentist.*

,put sb 'on to give someone the telephone so that they can talk to the person at the other end: *Hi, Dad—can you put Nicky on?* ,put sth↔'on **1** to dress yourself in something: *Hurry up! Put your coat on!* **ANT** TAKE OFF **2** to apply something to your skin, face, etc.: *She's just putting on her makeup.* **3** to switch on a piece of equipment: *Before you start making the pie, put the oven on at 350 degrees.* ♦ *She put on the brakes suddenly.* **4** to make a tape, CD, DVD, etc. begin to play: *Do you mind if I put some music on?* ♦ *He put some jazz on the stereo.* **5** to become heavier, especially by the amount mentioned **SYN** GAIN: *She looks like she's put on weight.* ♦ *He must have put on several pounds.* **6** to provide something specially: *The city is putting on extra buses during the summer.* **7** to produce or present a play, a show, etc.: *The local drama club is putting on "Macbeth."* **8** to pretend to have a particular feeling, quality, way of speaking, etc.: *He put on a British accent.* ♦ *I don't think she was hurt. She was just putting it on.* put sth on sth **1** to add an amount of money or a tax to the cost of something: *The government has put fifty cents on the price of a pack of cigarettes.* **2** to bet money on something: *I've never put money on a horse.* ♦ *I put $5 on him to win.*

,put sb 'onto sb/sth **1** to tell the police, etc. about where a criminal is or about a crime: *What first put the police onto the scam?* **2** to tell someone about someone or something that they may like or find useful: *Who put you onto this restaurant? It's great!*

,put yourself 'out (for sb) (*informal*) to make a special effort to do something for someone: *Please don't put yourself out on my account.* ,put sb 'out **1** to cause someone trouble, extra work, etc. **SYN** INCONVENIENCE: *I hope our arriving late didn't put them out.* **2 be put out** to be upset or offended: *He was really put out.* **3** to make someone unconscious: *These pills should put him out for a few hours.* **4** [usually passive] to cause a baseball player to stop hitting or running because of a play made by the other team: *He was put out just before he got to third base.* **5** [usually passive] to defeat someone in a sports competition so that they can no longer compete: *She was put out by Serena Williams in the fourth round.* ,put **sth**↔'out **1** to take something out of your house and leave it, for example for someone to collect: *to put the garbage/ trash out* **2** to place something where it will be noticed and used: *Have you put out clean towels for the guests?* **3** to stop something from burning or shining: *to put out a candle/ cigarette/light* ◆ *Firefighters soon put the fire out.* **4** to produce something, especially for sale: *The factory puts out 500 new cars a week.* ⊃ related noun OUTPUT **5** to publish or broadcast something: *Police have put out a description of the man they wish to question.* **6** to make a figure, result, etc. wrong: *The rise in interest rates put our estimates out by several thousands.* **7** (also *formal* ,put **sth**↔'forth) to develop or produce new leaves, SHOOTS, etc. ,put 'out (to.../from...) (of a boat or its sailors) to leave a port: *to put out to sea* ◆ *We put out from Bayonne.*

,put yourself/**sth** 'over (to **sb**) = PUT YOURSELF/**STH** ACROSS (TO **SB**)

,put **sth**↔'through to continue with and complete a plan, program, etc.: *We managed to put the deal through.* ,put **sth** 'through **sth** **1** to make someone experience something very difficult or unpleasant: *You have put your family through a lot recently.* **2** to arrange or pay for someone to attend a school, college, etc.: *He put all his children through college.* ,put **sb/sth** 'through (to **sb/...**) to connect someone by telephone: *Could you put me through to the manager, please?* 'put **sb** to **sth** to cause someone trouble, difficulty, etc.: *I hope we're not putting you to too much trouble.* 'put **sth** to **sb** **1** to offer a suggestion to someone so that they can accept or reject it: *Your proposal will be put to the board of directors.* **2** to ask someone a question: *The audience is now invited to put questions to the speaker.*

,put **sth**↔to'gether to make or prepare something by fitting or collecting parts together: *to put together a model plane/an essay/a meal* ◆ *I think we can put together a very strong case for the defense.* ⊃ thesaurus box at BUILD 'put **sth** toward **sth** to give money to pay part of the cost of something: *Here's $100 to put toward your ski trip.* ,put **sb** 'under to use a drug to make someone unconscious: *The anesthetic will put him under shortly.* ,put 'up **sth** **1** to show a particular level of skill, determination, etc. in a fight or contest: *They surrendered without putting up much of a fight.* ◆ *The team put up a great performance* (= played very well). **2** to suggest an idea, etc. for other people to discuss: *to put up an argument/a case/a proposal* ,put **sb**↔'up **1** to let someone stay at your home: *We can put you up for the night.* **2** to suggest or present someone as a candidate for a job or position: *The Green Party hopes to put up more candidates in the next election.* ,put **sth**↔'up **1** to raise something or put it in a higher position: *to put up a flag* ◆ *She's put her hair up.* **2** to build something or place something somewhere: *to put up a building/fence/ memorial/tent* ⊃ thesaurus box at BUILD **3** to fix something in a place where it will be seen SYN DISPLAY: *to put up a notice* **4** to raise or increase something: *They've put up the rent by $100 a month.* **5** to provide or lend money: *A local businessman has put up the $500,000 needed to save the club.* ,put 'up (at...) to stay somewhere for the night: *We put up at a motel.* ,put **sb** 'up to **sth** (*informal*) to encourage or persuade someone to do something wrong or stupid: *Some of the older boys must have put him up to it.* ,put 'up with **sb/ sth** to accept someone or something that is annoying, unpleasant, etc. without complaining SYN TOLERATE: *I don't know how she puts up with him.* ◆ *I'm not going to put up with their smoking any longer.*

pu·ta·tive /'pyutətɪv/ *adj.* [only before noun] (*formal or law*) believed to be the person or thing mentioned SYN PRESUMED: *the putative father of this child*

'**put-down** *noun* (*informal*) a remark or criticism that is intended to make someone look or feel stupid

'**put-on** *noun* [usually sing.] something that is done to trick or cheat people

pu·tre·fac·tion /ˌpyutrəˈfækʃn/ *noun* [U] (*formal*) the process of decaying, especially that of a dead body

pu·tre·fy /'pyutrəˌfaɪ/ *verb* (**pu·tre·fies, pu·tre·fy·ing, pu·tre·fied, pu·tre·fied**) [I] (*formal*) to decay and smell very bad SYN ROT

pu·trid /'pyutrəd/ *adj.* **1** (of dead animals or plants) decaying and therefore smelling very bad SYN FOUL: *the putrid smell of rotten meat* **2** (*informal*) very unpleasant: *a putrid pink color*

putsch /pʊtʃ/ *noun* (from *German*) a sudden attempt to remove a government by force

putt /pʌt/ *verb* [I, T] ~ (**sth**) (in GOLF) to hit the ball gently when it is on the short grass near the hole, so that it rolls across the ground a short distance into or toward the hole ▶ **putt** *noun*

put·ter /'pʌtər/ *verb, noun*
• *verb* **1** [I] (of a boat or vehicle) to make a repeated low sound as it moves slowly: *the puttering of the engine as it reduced speed* **2** [I] (**+ adv./prep.**) to do things or move without hurrying, especially when you are doing something that you enjoy and that is not important: *I spent the morning puttering around the house.*
• *noun* (in GOLF) the type of CLUB that is used for putting (= hitting the ball short distances)

putt·ing green /'pʌtɪŋ ˌgrin/ *noun* a small GOLF COURSE on an area of smooth short grass where people can practice PUTTING

put·ty /'pʌti/ *noun* [U] a soft sticky substance that becomes hard when it is dry and that is used for fastening glass into window frames
IDM (**like**) **putty in sb's hands** easily controlled or influenced by another person: *She'll persuade him. He's like putty in her hands.*

'**put-up ˌjob** *noun* [usually sing.] (*informal*) a plan or an event that has been arranged secretly in order to trick or cheat someone

'**put-up·on** *adj.* treated in an unfair way by someone because they take advantage of your kindness or willingness to do things: *his much put-upon wife*

putz /pʌts/ *verb, noun*
• [I] ~ **around** (*informal*) to waste time not doing anything useful or important
• *noun* (*informal*) a stupid person

puzzles

sudoku

AKEHJOMNBALNIMZ
ALSKDJFHQPWOMNB
HGEFIGJLEPQMWZB
PEAPQRGLIKWZBTR
ITRBINWOMRINWJE
AKCHJOMNBALNIMZ
ALHKDJFHQPWOMNB
HGJFIGJLEPQMWZB
PEVPQRGLIKWZBTR

wordsearch

crossword puzzle

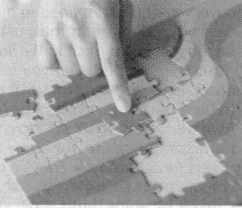

jigsaw puzzle

puz·zle /'pʌzl/ *noun, verb*
• *noun* **1** a game, etc. that you have to think about carefully in order to answer it or do it: *a crossword puzzle* ◆ *a book of puzzles for children* **2** = JIGSAW PUZZLE **3** [usually sing.] something that is difficult to understand or explain SYN MYSTERY

• *verb* ~ **sb** to make someone feel confused because they do not understand something **SYN** BAFFLE: *What puzzles me is why he left the country without telling anyone.* ▸ **puz·zling** /ˈpʌzlɪŋ/ *adj.*: *one of the most puzzling aspects of the crime* **PHR V** **'puzzle over/about sth** to think hard about something in order to understand or explain it ˌ**puzzle sth**↔**'out** to find the answer to a difficult or confusing problem by thinking carefully **SYN** WORK OUT: ~ **why, what, etc....** *He was trying to puzzle out why he had been brought to the house.*

puz·zled /ˈpʌzld/ *adj.* unable to understand something or the reason for something **SYN** BAFFLED: *She had a puzzled look on her face.* ◆ *Scientists are puzzled as to why the whale had swum to the shore.* ◆ *He looked puzzled so I repeated the question.*

puz·zle·ment /ˈpʌzlmənt/ *noun* [U] (*formal*) a feeling of being confused because you do not understand something: *She frowned in puzzlement.*

puz·zler /ˈpʌzlər/ *noun* (*informal*) something that makes you feel confused **SYN** POSER (2)

PVC /ˌpi vi ˈsi/ *noun* [U] the abbreviation for "polyvinyl chloride" (a strong plastic material used for a wide variety of products, such as clothing, pipes, floor coverings, etc.)

PVR /ˌpi vi ˈar/ *noun* the abbreviation for personal video recorder (a device that records video onto a hard disk or other memory device, using digital technology) **SYN** DVR

Pvt. *abbr.* (in writing) PRIVATE: *Pvt. John Smith*

PX /ˌpi ˈɛks/ (*pl.* **PXs** /ˌpi ˈɛksəz/) *noun* post exchange (a store at a military base that sells food, clothes, and other things)

pyg·my (also **pig·my**) /ˈpɪgmi/ *noun, adj.*
• *noun* (*pl.* **pyg·mies**) **1** **Pygmy** a member of a race of very short people living in parts of Africa and S.E. Asia **2** (*disapproving*) a very small person or thing, or one that is weak in some way: *He regarded them as intellectual pygmies.*
• *adj.* [only before noun] used to describe a plant or SPECIES (= type) of animal that is much smaller than other similar kinds: *a pygmy shrew*

py·lon /ˈpaɪlɑn/ *noun* **1** a tall metal structure that is used for carrying electricity wires high above the ground **2** a plastic object shaped like a CONE and often red and white, or yellow, in color, used on roads to show where vehicles are not allowed to go, for example while repairs are being done **SYN** TRAFFIC CONE **3** a tall structure that is used to support something heavy: *Pylons are often used as support structures for suspension bridges.*

py·or·rhea /ˌpaɪəˈriə/ *noun* [U] (*medical*) = PERIODONTITIS

pyr·a·mid /ˈpɪrəmɪd/ *noun* **1** a large building with a square or TRIANGULAR base and sloping sides that meet in a point at the top. The ancient Egyptians built stone pyramids as

places to bury their kings and queens. ᴐ picture at BUILDING, SHAPE **2** (*geometry*) a solid shape with a square or TRIANGULAR base and sloping sides that meet in a point at the top **3** an image, an object, or a pile of things that has the shape of a pyramid: *a pyramid of cans in a shop window* ◆ *The food pyramid shows you the food you should eat for a healthy diet.* **4** an organization or a system in which there are fewer people at each level as you get near the top: *a management pyramid* ▸ **py·ram·i·dal** /pəˈræmədl; ˈpɪrəˌmɪdl/ *adj.*

'pyramid ˌscheme *noun* an illegal way of making money, in which people are persuaded to invest money or sell a product and to persuade others to do the same, with the later INVESTORS paying money to the earlier INVESTORS, until the payment structure collapses and most people lose their money

pyre /ˈpaɪər/ *noun* a large pile of wood on which a dead body is placed and burned in a funeral ceremony

Py·rex™ /ˈpaɪrɛks/ *noun* [U] a type of hard glass that does not break at high temperatures, and is often used to make dishes for cooking food in

py·rite /ˈpaɪraɪt; ˈpaɪraɪt/ *noun* [U] a shiny yellow mineral that is made up of SULFUR and a metal such as iron: *copper/iron pyrite*

py·ro /ˈpaɪroʊ/ *noun* (*pl.* **py·ros**) (*informal*) a PYROMANIAC

py·ro·ma·ni·a /ˌpaɪroʊˈmeɪniə/ *noun* [U] (*technical*) a mental illness that causes a strong desire to set fire to things

py·ro·ma·ni·ac /ˌpaɪroʊˈmeɪniˌæk/ *noun* **1** (*technical*) a person who suffers from pyromania **2** (*informal, humorous*) a person who enjoys making or watching fires

py·ro·tech·nics /ˌpaɪrəˈtɛknɪks/ *noun* **1** [U, pl.] (*technical*) FIREWORKS or a display of FIREWORKS **2** [pl.] (*formal*) a skillful and complicated display of skill, for example by a musician, writer, or speaker: *guitar pyrotechnics* ▸ **py·ro·tech·nic** *adj.* [usually before noun]

Pyr·rhic vic·to·ry /ˌpɪrɪk ˈvɪktəri/ *noun* a victory that is not worth winning because the winner has suffered or lost so much in winning it **ORIGIN** From **Pyrrhus**, the king of Epirus, who defeated the Romans in 279 B.C.E. but lost many of his own men.

Py·thag·o·re·an the·o·rem /pəˌθæɡəˌriən ˈθɪrəm; -ˈθiərəm/ *noun* (*geometry*) the rule that, in a RIGHT TRIANGLE, the SQUARE of the HYPOTENUSE (= the side opposite the right angle) is equal to the squares of the other two sides added together

py·thon /ˈpaɪθɑn/ *noun* a large tropical snake that kills animals for food by winding its long body around them and crushing them

Qq

Q /kyu/ *noun, abbr.*
- *noun* also **q** [C, U] (*pl.* Qs, Q's, q's /kyuz/) the 17th letter of the English alphabet: *"Queen" begins with (a) Q/"Q."*
- *abbr.* question **IDM** see MIND *v.*

QA /ˌkyu ˈeɪ/ *abbr.* QUALITY ASSURANCE

Qa·ba·lah = KABBALAH

QB *abbr.* (in writing) QUARTERBACK

QED (also **Q.E.D.**) /ˌkyu i ˈdi/ *abbr.* that is what I wanted to prove and I have proved it (from Latin "quod erat demonstrandum")

qib·la (also **kib·lah**) /ˈkɪblə/ *noun* [sing.] the direction of the Kaaba (the holy building at Mecca), toward which Muslims turn when they are PRAYING

qt *abbr.* (in writing) QUART

Q-tip™ *noun* (also **ˌcotton ˈswab**) a small stick with COTTON at each end, used for cleaning inside the ears, etc.

qtr. *abbr.* (in writing) quarter

qua /kwɑ/ *prep.* (from *Latin, formal*) as something; in the role of something: *The soldier acted qua soldier, not as a human being.* ➾ see also SINE QUA NON

quack /kwæk/ *noun, verb*
- *noun* **1** the sound that a DUCK makes **2** (*informal, disapproving*) a person who dishonestly claims to have medical knowledge or skills: *quack doctors and their remedies* ◆ *She exposed Dr. Jones as a quack.*
- *verb* [I] when a DUCK **quacks**, it makes the noise that is typical of ducks

quack·er·y /ˈkwækəri/ *noun* [U] the methods or behavior of someone who pretends to have medical knowledge

quad /kwɑd/ *noun* **1** = QUADRANGLE **2** = QUADRUPLET **3** = QUADRICEPS

quad·ran·gle /ˈkwɑˌdræŋgl/ (also **quad**) *noun* an open square area that has buildings all around it, especially in a school or college

quad·ran·gu·lar /kwɑˈdræŋgyələr/ *adj.* (of a shape) having four sides and flat rather than solid (*geometry*)

quad·rant /ˈkwɑdrənt/ *noun* **1** (*geometry*) a quarter of a circle or of its CIRCUMFERENCE (= the distance around it) ➾ picture at SHAPE **2** an instrument for measuring angles, especially to check your position at sea or to look at stars

quad·ra·phon·ic (also **quad·ro·phon·ic**) /ˌkwɑdrəˈfɑnɪk/ *adj.* (of a system of recording or broadcasting sound) coming from four different SPEAKERS at the same time ➾ compare STEREO

quad·rat·ic /kwɑˈdrætɪk/ *adj.* (*mathematics*) involving an unknown quantity that is multiplied by itself once only: *a quadratic equation*

quadri- /ˈkwɑdrə/ (also **quadr-**) *combining form* (in nouns, adjectives, and adverbs) four; having four: *quadrilateral* ◆ *quadruplet*

quad·ri·ceps /ˈkwɑdrəˌsɛps/ (also **quad**) *noun* (*pl.* **quad·ri·ceps** *anatomy*) the large muscle at the front of the THIGH

quad·ri·lat·er·al /ˌkwɑdrəˈlætərəl/ *noun* (*geometry*) a flat shape with four straight sides ▸ **quad·ri·lat·er·al** *adj.*

quad·rille /kwɑˈdrɪl/ *noun* a dance for four or more couples in a square, popular in the past

quad·ril·lion /kwɑˈdrɪlyən/ *number* the number 10^{15}, or 1 followed by 15 zeros

quad·ri·ple·gic /ˌkwɑdrəˈplidʒɪk/ *noun* a person who is permanently unable to use their arms and legs ▸ **quad·ri·ple·gic** *adj.* **quad·ri·ple·gi·a** /ˌkwɑdrəˈplidʒə/ *noun* [U]

quad·ro·phon·ic *adj.* = QUADRAPHONIC

quad·ru·ped /ˈkwɑdrəˌpɛd/ *noun* (*technical*) any creature with four feet ➾ compare BIPED

quad·ru·ple *verb* /kwɑˈdrupl/ *adj., det.*
- *verb* [I, T] **~ (sth)** to become four times bigger; to make something four times bigger: *Sales have quadrupled in the last five years.*
- *adj.* [only before noun], *det.* **1** consisting of four parts, people, or groups: *a quadruple alliance* **2** being four times as much or as many: *This year we produced quadruple the amount produced in 2010.*

quad·ru·plet /kwɑˈdruplət/ (also **quad**) *noun* one of four children born at the same time to the same mother

quaff /kwɑf; kwæf/ *verb* **~ sth** (*old-fashioned* or *literary*) to drink a large amount of something quickly

quag·mire /ˈkwæɡˌmaɪər/ *noun* **1** an area of soft wet ground **SYN** BOG **2** a difficult or dangerous situation **SYN** MORASS

qua·hog /ˈkoʊhɔɡ; ˈkwɔ-; -hɑɡ/ *noun* a large N. Atlantic CLAM that is used for food

quail /kweɪl/ *noun, verb*
- *noun* [C, U] (*pl.* **quails** or **quail**) a small brown bird, whose meat and eggs are used for food; the meat of this bird
- *verb* [I] **~ (at/before sb/sth)** (*literary*) to feel frightened or to show that you are frightened

quaint /kweɪnt/ *adj.* attractive in an unusual or old-fashioned way: *quaint old customs* ◆ *a quaint seaside village* ▸ **quaint·ly** *adv.* **quaint·ness** *noun* [U]

quake /kweɪk/ *verb, noun*
- *verb* **1** [I] **~ (with sth)** (of a person) to shake because you are very frightened or nervous **SYN** TREMBLE: *Quaking with fear, Polly slowly opened the door.* **2** [I] (of the earth or a building) to move or shake violently: *The ground quaked as the bomb exploded.*
- *noun* (*informal*) = EARTHQUAKE

Quak·er /ˈkweɪkər/ *noun* a member of the Society of Friends, a Christian religious group that meets without any formal ceremony and is strongly opposed to violence and war ▸ **Quak·er** *adj.*: *a Quaker school*

qual·i·fi·ca·tion /ˌkwɑləfəˈkeɪʃn/ *noun*
1 [C] a skill or type of experience that you need for a particular job or activity: *Previous teaching experience is a necessary qualification for this job.* ◆ *Does he have the qualifications to be a congressman?* **2** [C, U] information that you add to a statement to limit the effect that it has or the way it is applied **SYN** PROVISO: *I accept his theories, but not without certain qualifications.* ◆ *The plan was approved without qualification.* **3** [U] the fact of passing an exam, completing a course of training, or reaching the standard necessary to do a job or take part in a competition: *Nurses in training should be given a guarantee of employment following qualification.* ◆ *A victory in this game will earn them qualification for the World Cup.*

qual·i·fied /ˈkwɑlɑˌfaɪd/ *adj.*
1 having passed the exams or completed the training that is necessary in order to do a particular job; having the experience to do a particular job: *a qualified teacher, etc.* ◆ *to be highly/suitably/fully qualified* ◆ **~ for sth** *She's extremely well qualified for the job.* **2** [not before noun] **~ (to do sth)** having the practical knowledge or skills to do something: *I don't know much about it, so I don't feel qualified to comment.* **3** [usually before noun] (of approval, support, etc.) limited in some way: *The plan was given only qualified support.* ◆ *The project was only a qualified success.*

qual·i·fi·er /ˈkwɑləˌfaɪər/ *noun* **1** a person or team that has defeated others in order to enter a particular competition **2** a game or match that a person or team has to win in order to enter a particular competition: *a qualifier for the championship* **3** (*grammar*) a word, especially an adjective or

---

ʌ **cup**   ə **about**   eɪ **say**   aɪ **five**   ɔɪ **boy**   aʊ **now**   oʊ **go**   ər **bird**

adverb, that describes another word in a particular way: *In "the open door," "open" is a qualifier, describing the door.*

qual·i·fy /'kwɑlə,faɪ/ *verb* (qual·i·fies, qual·i·fy·ing, qual·i·fied, qual·i·fied)

> GIVE SKILLS/KNOWLEDGE **1** [T] to give someone the skills and knowledge they need to do something: ~ **sb (for sth)** *This training course will qualify you for a better job.* ◆ ~ **sb to do sth** *The test qualifies you to drive heavy vehicles.*

> HAVE/GIVE RIGHT **2** [I, T] to have or give someone the right to do something: ~ **(for sth)** *If you live in the area, you qualify for a parking permit.* ◆ *To qualify, you must have lived in this country for at least three years.* ◆ ~ **sb (for sth)** *Paying a fee doesn't automatically qualify you for membership.*

> FOR JOB **3** [I] to reach the standard of ability or knowledge needed to do a particular job, for example by completing a course of study or passing exams: *How long does it take to qualify?* ◆ ~ **as sth** *He qualified as a doctor last year.*

> FOR COMPETITION **4** [I] to be of a high enough standard to enter a competition; to defeat another person or team in order to enter or continue in a competition: *He failed to qualify.* ◆ ~ **for sth** *They qualified for the World Cup.*

> FIT DESCRIPTION **5** [I, T] to have the right qualities to be described as a particular thing: ~ **(as sth)** *Do you think this dress qualifies as evening wear?* ◆ ~ **sth (as sth)** *It's an old building, but that doesn't qualify it as an ancient monument!*

> STATEMENT **6** [T] ~ **sth** | ~ **what...** to add something to a previous statement to make the meaning less strong or less general: *I want to qualify what I said earlier—I didn't mean he couldn't do the job, only that he would need supervision.*

> GRAMMAR **7** [T] ~ **sth** (of a word) to describe another word in a particular way: *In "the open door," "open" is an adjective qualifying "door."*

qual·i·ta·tive ‹AWL› /'kwɑlə,teɪtɪv/ *adj.* [usually before noun] connected with how good something is, rather than with how much of it there is: *qualitative analysis/research* ◆ *There are qualitative differences between the two products.* ↻ compare QUANTITATIVE ▶ **qual·i·ta·tive·ly** ‹AWL› *adv.*: *qualitatively different*

qual·i·ty /'kwɑləti/ *noun, adj.*
• *noun* (pl. qual·i·ties) **1** [U, C] the standard of something when it is compared to other things like it; how good or bad something is: *to be of good/poor/top quality* ◆ *materials of a high quality* ◆ *high-quality materials* ◆ *a decline in water quality* ◆ *When costs are cut, product quality suffers.* ◆ *Their quality of life improved dramatically when they moved to North Carolina.* **2** [U] a high standard SYN EXCELLENCE: *contemporary writers of quality* ◆ *We aim to provide quality at reasonable prices.* **3** [C] a thing that is part of a person's character, especially something good: *personal qualities such as honesty and generosity* ◆ *to have leadership qualities* **4** [C, U] a feature of something, especially one that makes it different from something else: *the special quality of light and shade in her paintings*
• *adj.* [only before noun] used especially by people trying to sell goods or services to say that something is of a high quality: *We specialize in quality furniture.* ◆ *quality service at a competitive price*

quality as·sur·ance *noun* [U] (abbr. **QA**) the practice of managing the way goods are produced or services are provided to make sure they are kept at a high standard

quality con·trol *noun* [U] the practice of checking goods as they are being produced, to make sure that they are of a high standard

quality time *noun* [U] time spent giving your full attention to someone, especially to your children after work

qualm /kwɑm/ *noun* [usually pl.] ~ **(about sth)** a feeling of doubt or worry about whether what you are doing is right SYN MISGIVING: *He had been working very hard so he had no qualms about taking a few days off.*

quan·da·ry /'kwɑndri/ *noun* (pl. quan·da·ries) [usually sing.] the state of not being able to decide what to do in a difficult situation SYN DILEMMA: *George was in a quandary—should he go or shouldn't he?*

quan·ta pl. of QUANTUM

quan·ti·fi·er /'kwɑntə,faɪər/ *noun* (grammar) a determiner or pronoun that expresses quantity, for example "all" or "both"

quan·ti·fy /'kwɑntə,faɪ/ *verb* (quan·ti·fies, quan·ti·fy·ing, quan·ti·fied, quan·ti·fied) ~ **sth** to describe or express something as an amount or a number: *The risks to health are impossible to quantify.* ▶ **quan·ti·fi·a·ble** /ˌkwɑntə'faɪəbl; 'kwɑntə,faɪ-/ *adj.*: *quantifiable data* **quan·ti·fi·ca·tion** /ˌkwɑntəfə'keɪʃn/ *noun* [U]

quan·ti·ta·tive /'kwɑntə,teɪtɪv/ *adj.* connected with the amount or number of something rather than with how good it is: *quantitative analysis/research* ◆ *There is no difference between the two in quantitative terms.* ↻ compare QUALITATIVE ▶ **quan·ti·ta·tive·ly** *adv.*

quan·ti·ty /'kwɑntəti/ *noun* (pl. quan·ti·ties) **1** [C, U] an amount or a number of something: *a large/small quantity of something* ◆ *enormous/vast/huge quantities of food* ◆ *a product that is cheap to produce in large quantities* ◆ *Is it available in sufficient quantity?* **2** [U] the measurement of something by saying how much of it there is: *The data is limited in terms of both quality and quantity.* **3** [C, U] a large amount or number of something: *The police found a quantity of drugs at his home.* ◆ *It's cheaper to buy goods in quantity.* ◆ *I was overwhelmed by the sheer quantity of information available.* IDM see UNKNOWN

quan·tum /'kwɑntəm/ *noun* (pl. qua·nta /-tə/) (physics) a very small quantity of ELECTROMAGNETIC energy

quantum leap (also less frequent **quantum jump**) *noun* a sudden, great, and important change, improvement, or development

quantum me·chanics *noun* [U] (physics) the branch of MECHANICS that deals with movement and force in pieces of matter smaller than atoms

quantum theory *noun* [U] (physics) a theory based on the idea that energy exists in units that cannot be divided

quar·an·tine /'kwɔrən,tin; 'kwɑr-/ *noun, verb*
• *noun* [U] a period of time when an animal or a person that has or may have a disease is kept away from others in order to prevent the disease from spreading: *The dog was kept in quarantine for six months.* ◆ *quarantine regulations*
• *verb* ~ **sth/sb** to put an animal or a person into quarantine

quark /kwɔrk; kwɑrk/ *noun* (physics) a very small part of matter (= a substance). There are several types of quarks and it is thought that PROTONS, NEUTRONS, etc. are formed from them.

quar·rel /'kwɔrəl; 'kwɑr-/ *noun, verb*
• *noun* **1** [C] ~ **(with sb/between A and B) (about/over sth)** an angry argument or disagreement between people, often about a personal matter: *a family quarrel* ◆ *He did not mention the quarrel with his wife.* ◆ *They had a quarrel about money.* ◆ *Were you at any time aware of a quarrel between the two of them?* **2** [U] ~ **(with sb/sth)** (especially in negative sentences) a reason for complaining about someone or something or for disagreeing with someone or something: *We have no quarrel with his methods.* IDM see PICK v.
• *verb* (-l- CanE usually -ll-) [I] to have an angry argument or disagreement: *My sister and I used to quarrel all the time.* ◆ ~ **(with sb) (about/over sth)** *She quarreled with her brother over their father's will.* PHR V **quarrel with sb/sth** to disagree with someone or something: *Nobody could quarrel with your conclusions.*

quar·rel·some /'kwɔrəlsəm; 'kwɑr-/ *adj.* (of a person) liking to argue with other people SYN ARGUMENTATIVE

quar·ry /'kwɔri; 'kwɑri/ *noun, verb*
• *noun* (pl. quar·ries) **1** [C] a place where large amounts of stone, etc. are dug out of the ground: *a slate quarry* ◆ *the site of a disused quarry* ↻ compare MINE **2** [sing.] an animal or a person that is being hunted or followed SYN PREY: *The*

hunters lost sight of their quarry in the forest. ◆ The photographers pursued their quarry through the streets.

● *verb* (quar·ries, quar·ry·ing, quar·ried, quar·ried) [T, I] to take stone, etc. out of a quarry: ~ **sth (from/out of sth)** *The local rock is quarried from the hillside.* ◆ ~ **(for) sth** *The area is being quarried for limestone.* ▶ **quar·ry·ing** *noun* [U]: *There has been quarrying in the area for centuries.*

'quarry ,tile *noun* a floor TILE made from stone that has not been GLAZED

quart /kwɔrt/ *noun* (*abbr.* qt) a unit for measuring liquids, equal to 2 pints or about 0.94 of a liter

quar·ter 🔑 /'kwɔrtər/ *noun, verb*
● *noun* (*abbr.* qtr.)
> 1 OF 4 PARTS **1** (also **fourth**) [C] one of four equal parts of something: *a quarter of a mile* ◆ *The program lasted an hour and a quarter.* ◆ *Cut the apple into quarters.* ◆ *The theater was about three quarters full.* ⊃ note at HALF
> 15 MINUTES **2** [C] a period of 15 minutes either before or after every hour: *It's quarter of four now—I'll meet you at quarter after.*
> 25 CENTS **3** [C] a coin of the U.S. and Canada worth 25 cents ⊃ picture at MONEY
> IN SPORTS **4** [C] one of the four periods of time into which a game of football is divided
> 3 MONTHS **5** [C] a period of three months, used especially as a period for which bills are paid or a company's income is calculated
> PART OF ACADEMIC YEAR **6** [C] one of four equal divisions within an academic year in some schools, usually about 12 weeks long: *I'm taking a course in South American literature this quarter.* ⊃ compare SEMESTER, TRIMESTER
> PART OF TOWN **7** [C, usually sing.] a district or part of a town: *the Latin quarter* ◆ *the historic quarter of the city*
> PERSON/GROUP **8** [C] a person or group of people, especially as a source of help, information, or a reaction: *Support for the plan came from an unexpected quarter.* ◆ *The news was greeted with dismay in some quarters.*
> ROOMS TO LIVE IN **9** quarters [pl.] rooms that are provided for soldiers, servants, etc. to live in: *We were moved to more comfortable living quarters.* ◆ *married quarters*
> OF MOON **10** [C] the period of time twice a month when we can see a quarter of the moon: *The moon is in its first quarter.*
> WEIGHT **11** [C] a unit for measuring weight, 25 pounds; a quarter of a HUNDREDWEIGHT
> PITY **12** [U] (*old-fashioned* or *literary*) a kind or forgiving attitude that someone shows toward an enemy or opponent who is in their power **SYN** MERCY: *His rivals knew that they could expect no quarter from such a ruthless adversary.*
IDM see CLOSE² *adj.*
● *verb*
> DIVIDE INTO 4 **1** ~ **sth** to cut or divide something into four parts: *She peeled and quartered an apple.*
> PROVIDE ROOMS **2** ~ **sb (+ adv./prep.)** (*formal*) to provide someone with a place to eat and sleep: *The soldiers were quartered in the town.*

quar·ter·back /'kwɔrtər,bæk/ *noun, verb*
● *noun* (*abbr.* QB) (in football) the player who directs the team's offensive play and passes the ball to other players at the start of each play
● *verb* **1** [I] (in football) to play as a quarterback **2** [T] ~ **sth** to direct or organize something

quar·ter·deck /'kwɔrtər,dɛk/ *noun* a part of the upper level of a ship, at the back, that is used mainly by officers

,quarter-'final *noun* (in sports or competitions) one of the four games or matches to decide the players or teams for the SEMIFINALS of a competition

'Quarter ,Horse *noun* a small breed of horse that can run very fast over short distances

quar·ter·ly /'kwɔrtərli/ *adj., adv., noun*
● *adj.* produced or happening every three months: *a quarterly meeting of the board* ▶ **quar·ter·ly** *adv.*: *to pay the rent quarterly*

● *noun* (*pl.* quar·ter·lies) a magazine, etc. published four times a year

quar·ter·mas·ter /'kwɔrtər,mæstər/ *noun* an officer in the army who is in charge of providing food, uniforms, and a place to live

'quarter ,note *noun* (*music*) a note that lasts half as long as a HALF NOTE ⊃ picture at MUSIC

'quarter-,tone *noun* (*music*) a quarter of a TONE on a musical SCALE, for example half of the INTERVAL (= the difference) between the notes E and F

quar·tet /kwɔr'tɛt/ *noun* **1** a group of four musicians or singers who play or sing together: *the Amadeus Quartet* **2** a piece of music for four musicians or singers: *a Beethoven string quartet* **3** a set of four people or things: *the last in a quartet of novels*

quar·tile /'kwɔrtaɪl; 'kwɔrtl̩/ *noun* (*statistics*) one of four equal groups into which a set of things can be divided according to the DISTRIBUTION of a particular VARIABLE: *women in the fourth quartile of height* (= the shortest 25% of women) ⊃ compare QUINTILE

quar·to /'kwɔrtoʊ/ *noun* (*pl.* quar·tos) (*technical*) **1** [U] a size of page made by folding a standard sheet of paper twice to make eight pages **2** [C] a book with pages in quarto size

quartz /kwɔrts/ *noun* [U] a hard mineral, often in CRYSTAL form, that is used to make very accurate clocks and watches

qua·sar /'kweɪzɑr/ *noun* (*astronomy*) a large object like a star, that is far away and that shines very brightly and occasionally sends out strong radio signals ⊃ compare PULSAR

quash /kwɑʃ/ *verb* **1** ~ **sth** (*law*) to officially say that a decision made by a court is no longer valid or correct **SYN** OVERTURN: *His conviction was later quashed by the State Supreme Court.* **2** ~ **sth** to take action to stop something from continuing **SYN** SUPPRESS: *The rumors were quickly quashed.*

quasi- /'kweɪzaɪ; 'kwɑzi/ *combining form* (in adjectives and nouns) **1** that appears to be something but is not really so: *a quasi-scientific explanation* **2** partly; almost: *a quasi-official body*

quat·er·cen·ten·ar·y /ˌkwɑtərsɛn'tɛnəri; -'sɛntə,nɛri/ *noun* (*pl.* quat·er·cen·ten·ar·ies) a 400th anniversary: *to celebrate the quatercentenary of Shakespeare's birth*

quat·rain /'kwɑtreɪn/ *noun* (*technical*) a poem, or VERSE of a poem, that has four lines

qua·ver /'kweɪvər/ *verb, noun*
● *verb* [I, T] (+ **speech**) if someone's voice quavers, it is unsteady, usually because the person is nervous or afraid: *"I'm not safe here, am I?" she asked in a quavering voice.* ▶ **qua·ver·y** /'kweɪvəri/ *adj.*: *a quavery voice*
● *noun* [usually sing.] a shaking sound in someone's voice

quay /ki; keɪ/ *noun* a platform in a HARBOR where boats come in to load, etc.: *A crowd was waiting on the quay.*

quay·side /'kisaɪd; 'keɪ-; 'kweɪ-/ *noun* [usually sing.] a quay and the area near it: *crowds waiting on/at the quayside to welcome them*

quea·sy /'kwizi/ *adj.* **1** feeling sick; wanting to VOMIT **SYN** NAUSEOUS **2** slightly nervous or worried about something ▶ **quea·si·ly** /-zəli/ *adv.* **quea·si·ness** /-zinəs/ *noun* [U]

Quech·ua /'kɛtʃwə/ *noun* [U] a language originally spoken by the Quechua people of S. America, now spoken in Peru, Bolivia, Chile, Colombia, and Ecuador

queen 🔑 /kwin/ *noun*
> FEMALE RULER **1** the female ruler of an independent state that has a royal family: *to be crowned queen* ◆ *kings and queens* ◆ *the Queen of Norway* ◆ *Queen Victoria* **2** (also ,queen 'consort) the wife of a king
> BEST IN GROUP **3** ~ **(of sth)** a woman, place, or thing that is thought to be one of the best in a particular group or area:

the queen of fashion ◆ *a movie queen* ◆ *Venice, queen of the Adriatic*

> **AT FESTIVAL 4** a woman or girl chosen to perform official duties at a festival or celebration: *the queen of the annual Artichoke Festival* ◆ *a homecoming queen* ➔ see also BEAUTY QUEEN

> **IN CHESS 5** the most powerful piece used in the game of CHESS that can move any number of squares in any direction ➔ picture at TOY

> **IN CARDS 6** a PLAYING CARD with the picture of a queen on it ➔ picture at PLAYING CARD

> **INSECT 7** a large female insect that lays eggs for the whole group: *a queen bee* **IDM** see UNCROWNED

ˌqueen ˈbee *noun* **1** a female BEE that produces eggs for the whole group of bees in a HIVE ➔ compare DRONE, WORKER **2** a woman who behaves as if she is the most important person in a particular place or group

queen·ly /ˈkwinli/ *adj.* of, like, or suitable for a queen

ˌqueen ˈmother *noun* a title given to the wife of a king who has died and who is the mother of the new king or queen: *Queen Elizabeth, the Queen Mother*

ˌQueen's ˈBirthday *noun* (*CanE*) = VICTORIA DAY

queen-size (also ˈqueen-sized) *adj.* (of beds, sheets, etc.) larger than a standard size but not as big as KING-SIZE

queer /kwɪr/ *adj., noun*
● *adj.* (queer·er, queer·est) **1** (*old-fashioned*) strange or unusual **SYN** ODD: *His face was a queer pink color.* **2** (*usually offensive*) an offensive way of describing a HOMOSEXUAL, especially a man, which is, however, also used by some homosexuals about themselves
● *noun* (*usually offensive*) an offensive word for a HOMOSEXUAL, especially a man, which is, however, also used by some homosexuals about themselves

queer·ly /ˈkwɪrli/ *adv.* (*old-fashioned*) in a strange or unusual way: *He looked at me queerly.*

quell /kwɛl/ *verb* **1** ~ sth/sb to stop something such as violent behavior or protests: *Extra police were called in to quell the disturbances.* ◆ (*figurative*) *She started to giggle, but Bob quelled her with a look.* **2** ~ sth to stop or reduce strong or unpleasant feelings **SYN** CALM: *to quell your fears*

quench /kwɛntʃ/ *verb* **1** ~ your thirst to drink so that you no longer feel thirsty **SYN** SLAKE **2** ~ sth (*formal*) to stop a fire from burning **SYN** EXTINGUISH: *Firefighters tried to quench the flames raging through the building.*

quer·u·lous /ˈkwɛrələs/ *adj.* (*formal, disapproving*) complaining; showing that you are annoyed **SYN** PEEVISH
▶ **quer·u·lous·ly** *adv.*

que·ry /ˈkwɪri; ˈkwɛri/ *noun, verb*
● *noun* (*pl.* que·ries) a question, especially one asking for information or expressing a doubt about something: *Our assistants will be happy to answer your queries.* ◆ *If you have a query about your insurance policy, contact our customer service department.*
● *verb* (que·ries, que·ry·ing, que·ried, que·ried) **1** ~ sth | ~ what, whether, etc.... to express doubt about whether something is correct or not: *We queried the bill because it seemed much too high.* ◆ *I'm not in a position to query their decision.* **2** + speech to ask a question: *"Who will be leading the team?" queried Steve.*

ˈquery ˌlanguage *noun* [C, U] (*computing*) a system of words and symbols that you type in order to ask a computer to give you information

que·sa·dil·la /ˌkeɪsəˈdiə/ *noun* a spicy Mexican dish consisting of a TORTILLA (= flat round bread) filled with a mixture of cheese, meat, or other ingredients, folded in half, and fried

quest /kwɛst/ *noun, verb*
● *noun* ~ (for sth) (*formal* or *literary*) a long search for something, especially for some quality such as happiness: *the quest for happiness/knowledge/truth* ◆ *He set off in quest of adventure.*

● *verb* [I] ~ (for sth) (*formal* or *literary*) to search for something that is difficult to find

ques·tion 🔑 /ˈkwɛstʃən/ *noun, verb*
● *noun* **1** [C] a sentence, phrase, or word that asks for information: *to ask/answer a question* ◆ *The question is, how much are they going to pay you?* ◆ (*formal*) *The question arises as to whether or not he knew of the situation.* ◆ *The key question of what caused the leak remains unanswered.* ◆ (*formal*) *He put a question to the Vice President about the recent reforms.* ◆ *I hope the police don't ask any tough questions.* ◆ *In an interview, try to ask open questions that don't just need "Yes" or "No" as an answer.* **2** [C] a task or request for information that is intended to test your knowledge or understanding, for example in an exam or a competition: *Question 3 was very difficult.* ◆ *On the exam there's sure to be a question on energy.* **3** [C] ~ (of sth) a matter or topic that needs to be discussed or dealt with: *Let's look at the question of security.* ◆ *The question which needs to be addressed is one of funding.* ◆ *Which route is better remains an open question* (= it is not decided). **4** [U] doubt or confusion about something: *Her honesty is beyond question.* ◆ *His suitability for the job is open to question.* ◆ *Her version of events was accepted without question.* **IDM** **bring/throw sth into question** to cause something to become a matter for doubt and discussion: *This case brings into question the whole purpose of the law.* **come into question** to become a matter for doubt and discussion **good question!** (*informal*) used to show that you do not know the answer to a question: *"How much is all this going to cost?" "Good question!"* **in question 1** that is being discussed: *On the day in question we were in Miami.* **2** in doubt; uncertain: *The future of public transport is not in question.* **just/merely/only a question of (sth/doing sth)** used to say that something is not difficult to predict, explain, do, etc.: *It's merely a question of time before the business collapses.* ◆ *It's just a question of deciding what you really want.* **out of the question** impossible or not allowed, and therefore not worth discussing: *Another trip abroad this year is out of the question.* **there is/was no question of (sth happening/sb doing sth)** there is/was no possibility of something: *There was no question of his/him canceling the trip so near the departure date.* ➔ more at BEG, CALL *v.*, MOOT *adj.*, POP *v.*
● *verb* **1** ~ sb (about/on sth) | + speech to ask someone questions about something, especially officially: *She was arrested and questioned about the fire.* ◆ *The students were questioned on the books they had been studying.* ◆ *Over half of those questioned said they rarely got any exercise.* **2** to have or express doubts or suspicions about something: ~ sth *I just accepted what he told me. I never thought to question it.* ◆ *No one has ever questioned her judgment.* ◆ ~ whether, what, etc.... *He questioned whether the accident was solely the truck driver's fault.*

ques·tion·a·ble /ˈkwɛstʃənəbl/ *adj.* **1** that you have doubts about because you think it is not accurate or correct **SYN** DEBATABLE: *The conclusions that they come to are highly questionable.* ◆ *It is questionable whether this is a good way of solving the problem.* **2** likely to be dishonest or morally wrong **SYN** SUSPECT: *Her motives for helping are questionable.* ▶ **ques·tion·a·bly** /-bli/ *adv.*

ques·tion·er /ˈkwɛstʃənər/ *noun* a person who asks questions, especially in a broadcast program or a public debate

ques·tion·ing /ˈkwɛstʃənɪŋ/ *noun, adj.*
● *noun* [U] the activity of asking someone questions: *He was taken to the police station for questioning.* ◆ *They faced some hostile questioning over the cost of the project.*
● *adj.* showing that you need information, or that you have doubts: *a questioning look* ◆ *She raised a questioning eyebrow.* ▶ **ques·tion·ing·ly** *adv.*

ˈquestion ˌmark *noun* the mark (?) used in writing after a question **IDM** **a question mark over/against sth** used to say that something is not certain: *There's still a big question mark hanging over his future with the team.*

ques·tion·naire /ˌkwɛstʃəˈnɛr/ *noun* ~ (on/about sth) a written list of questions that are answered by a number of people so that information can be collected from the answers: *to complete a questionnaire* ♦ *to fill out a questionnaire*

'question ,tag (also **'tag ,question**) *noun* (*grammar*) a phrase such as *isn't it?* or *don't you?* that you add to the end of a statement in order to turn it into a question or check that the statement is correct, as in *You like chocolate, don't you?*

queue /kyu/ *noun, verb*
• *noun* (*computing*) a list of items of data stored in a particular order: *a printer queue*
• *verb* (**queu·ing** or **queue·ing**) [T, I] ~ (**sth**) (*computing*) to add tasks to other tasks so that they are ready to be done in order; to come together to be done in order: *The system queues the jobs before they are processed.*

quib·ble /'kwɪbl/ *verb, noun*
• *verb* [I] ~ (**about/over sth**) to argue or complain about a small matter or an unimportant detail: *It isn't worth quibbling over such a small amount.*
• *noun* a small complaint or criticism, especially one that is not important: *minor quibbles*

quiche /kiʃ/ *noun* [C, U] an open PIE filled with a mixture of eggs and milk with meat, vegetables, cheese, etc. ➔ compare TART

WHICH WORD?

quick ♦ quickly ♦ fast

- **Quickly** is the usual adverb from **quick**: *I quickly realized that I was on the wrong train.* ♦ *My heart started to beat more quickly.*
- **Quick** is sometimes used as an adverb in very informal language, especially as an exclamation: *Come on! Quick! They'll see us!* **Quicker** is used more often: *My heart started to beat much quicker.* ♦ *The quicker I get you away from here, the better.*
- **Fast** is more often used when you are talking about the speed that someone or something moves at: *How fast can a cheetah run?* ♦ *Can't you drive any faster?* ♦ ~~You're driving too quickly.~~ There is no word **fastly**.

---

quick 🖋 /kwɪk/ *adj., adv., noun*
• *adj.* (**quick·er**, **quick·est**) **1** done with speed; taking or lasting a short time: *She gave him a quick glance.* ♦ *These cakes are very quick and easy to make.* ♦ *Would you like a quick drink?* ♦ *The doctor said she'd make a quick recovery.* ♦ *It's quicker by train.* ♦ *Are you sure this is the quickest way?* ♦ *Have you finished already? That was quick!* ♦ *His quick thinking saved her life.* ♦ *He fired three shots in quick succession.* **2** moving or doing something fast: *a quick learner* ♦ ~ (**to do sth**) *The kids were quick to learn.* ♦ *She was quick* (= too quick) *to point out the mistakes I'd made.* ♦ *Her quick hands suddenly stopped moving.* ♦ *Try to be quick! We're late already.* ♦ *Once again, his quick wits* (= quick thinking) *got him out of an awkward situation.* ♦ (*informal*) *He's a quick study* (= he learns quickly). **3** [only before noun] happening very soon or without delay: *We need to make a quick decision.* ♦ *The company wants quick results.* ➔ note at FAST
IDM to have a quick temper to become angry easily **quick and dirty** (*informal*) used to describe something that is usually complicated, but is being done quickly and simply in this case: *Read our quick-and-dirty guide to creating a Web site.* ➔ more at BUCK *n.*, DRAW *n.*, MARK *n.*, UPTAKE
• *adv.* (**quick·er**, **quick·est**) **1** quickly; fast: *Come as quick as you can!* ♦ *Let's see who can get there quickest.* ♦ *It's another of his schemes to get rich quick.* **2** **quick-** (in adjectives) doing the thing mentioned quickly: *quick-thinking* ♦ *quick-growing*
IDM (as) quick as a flash/wink very quickly: *Quick as a wink she was at his side.*
• *noun* the quick [sing.] the soft, sensitive flesh that is under your nails: *She has bitten her nails down to the quick.*

IDM cut sb to the quick to upset someone very much by doing or saying something unkind

quick·en /'kwɪkən/ *verb* (*formal*) **1** [I, T] to become quicker or make something quicker: *She felt her heartbeat quicken as he approached.* ♦ ~ **sth** *He quickened his pace to catch up with them.* **2** [I, T] ~ (**sth**) to become more active; to make something more active: *His interest quickened as he heard more about the plan.*

quick·ie /'kwɪki/ *noun* (*informal*) a thing that only takes a short time: *I've got a question—it's just a quickie.* ♦ *a quickie divorce*

quick·lime /'kwɪklaɪm/ *noun* [U] = LIME *n.* (3)

quick·ly 🖋 /'kwɪkli/ *adv.*
1 fast: *She walked quickly away.* ♦ *We'll repair it as quickly as possible.* ♦ *The last few weeks have gone quickly* (= the time seems to have passed quickly). **2** soon; after a short time: *He replied to my letter very quickly.* ♦ *It quickly became clear that she was dying.* ➔ note at QUICK, SOON

quick·ness /'kwɪknəs/ *noun* [U] the quality of being fast, especially at thinking, etc.: *She was known for the quickness of her wit.* ♦ *He amazes me with his quickness and eagerness to learn.*

quick·sand /'kwɪksænd/ *noun* [U] (also **quick·sands** [pl.]) **1** deep wet sand that you sink into if you walk on it **2** a situation that is dangerous or difficult to escape from

quick·sil·ver /'kwɪk,sɪlvər/ *noun, adj.*
• *noun* [U] (*old use*) = MERCURY
• *adj.* [only before noun] (*literary*) changing or moving very quickly: *his quicksilver temperament*

quick·step /'kwɪkstɛp/ *noun* a dance for two people together, with a lot of fast steps; a piece of music for this dance

,quick-'tempered *adj.* likely to become angry very quickly: *a quick-tempered woman*

,quick-'witted *adj.* able to think quickly; intelligent: *a quick-witted student/response* **ANT** SLOW-WITTED

quid pro quo /,kwɪd prou 'kwou/ *noun* [sing.] (from *Latin*) a thing given in return for something else

qui·es·cent /kwi'ɛsnt; kwaɪ-/ *adj.* **1** (*formal*) quiet; not active **2** (*medical*) (of a disease, etc.) not developing, especially when this is probably only a temporary state **SYN** DORMANT ▶ **qui·es·cence** /-'ɛsns/ *noun* [U]

qui·et 🖋 /'kwaɪət/ *adj., noun, verb*
• *adj.* (**qui·et·er**, **qui·et·est**) **1** making very little noise: *her quiet voice* ♦ *a quieter, more efficient engine* ♦ *Could you keep the kids quiet while I'm on the phone?* ♦ *He got very quiet* (= did not say much) *so I knew he was upset.* ♦ *"Be quiet," said the teacher.* ♦ *She crept downstairs (as) quiet as a mouse.* **2** without many people or much noise or activity: *a quiet street* ♦ *They lead a quiet life.* ♦ *Business is usually quieter at this time of year.* ♦ *They had a quiet wedding.* ♦ *a quiet sea* **3** not disturbed; peaceful: *to have a quiet drink* ♦ *I was looking forward to a quiet evening at home.* **4** (of a person) tending not to talk very much: *She was quiet and shy.* **5** (of a feeling or an attitude) definite but not expressed in an obvious way: *He had an air of quiet authority.* ▶ **qui·et·ly** *adv.*: *to speak/move quietly* ♦ *I spent a few hours quietly relaxing.* ♦ *He is quietly confident that they can succeed* (= he is confident, but he is not talking about it too much). ♦ *a quietly-spoken woman* **qui·et·ness** *noun* [U]: *the quietness of the countryside* ♦ *His quietness worried her.*
IDM keep quiet about sth | keep sth quiet to say nothing about something; to keep something secret: *I've decided to resign, but I'd like to keep quiet about it.*
• *noun* [U] the state of being calm and without much noise: *the quiet of his own room* ♦ *the quiet of the early morning* ♦ *I go to the library for a little peace and quiet.*
IDM on the quiet without telling anyone **SYN** SECRETLY
• *verb* [I, T] to become calmer or less noisy; to make someone or something calmer or less noisy **SYN** CALM (SB) DOWN:

| h **hat** | m **man** | n **no** | ŋ **sing** | l **leg** | r **red** | y **yes** | w **wet** |

~ (down) *The demonstrators quieted down when the police arrived.* ◆ **~ sb/sth (down)** *He's very good at quieting the kids.*

qui·et·ism /ˈkwaɪəˌtɪzəm/ *noun* [U] (*formal*) an attitude to life which makes you calmly accept things as they are rather than try to change them ▶ **qui·et·ist** /-tɪst/ *noun, adj.*

qui·e·tude /ˈkwaɪəˌtud/ *noun* [U] (*literary*) the state of being still and quiet SYN CALM

qui·e·tus /kwaɪˈitəs/ *noun* [C, U] (*literary*) **1** death, or something that causes death, considered as a welcome end to life **2** something that makes a person or situation calm

quill /kwɪl/ *noun* **1** (also **ˈquill ˌfeather**) a large feather from the wing or tail of a bird **2** (also **ˌquill ˈpen**) a pen made from a quill feather **3** one of the long sharp stiff SPINES on a PORCUPINE

quilt /kwɪlt/ *noun* a decorative cover for a bed, made of two layers with soft material between them, held in place with lines of STITCHING: *a patchwork quilt* ⊃ picture at BED ⊃ compare COMFORTER

quilt·ed /ˈkwɪltəd/ *adj.* (of clothes, etc.) made of two layers of cloth with soft material between them, held in place by lines of STITCHES: *a quilted jacket*

quilt·ing /ˈkwɪltɪŋ/ *noun* [U] the work of making a quilt; cloth that is used for this

quince /kwɪns/ *noun* a hard, bitter, yellow fruit used for making jelly, JAM, etc. It grows on a tree, also called a quince: *quince jelly* ◆ *a flowering quince*

quin·cen·ten·ar·y /ˌkwɪnsɛnˈtɛnəri; -ˈsɛntəˌnɛri/ *noun* (*pl.* **quin·cen·ten·ar·ies**) a 500th anniversary: *the quincentenary of Columbus's voyage to America*

qui·nine /ˈkwaɪnaɪn/ *noun* [U] a drug made from the BARK of a S. American tree, used in the past to treat MALARIA

qui·noa /ˈkinwɑ/ *noun* [U] a S. American plant, grown for its seeds, used as food and to make alcoholic drinks; the seeds of this plant

quint /kwɪnt/ *noun* (*informal*) = QUINTUPLET

quin·tes·sence /kwɪnˈtɛsns/ *noun* [sing.] **the ~ of sth** (*formal*) **1** the perfect example of something: *It was the quintessence of a Cape Cod beach house.* **2** the most important features of something SYN ESSENCE: *a painting that captures the quintessence of Viennese elegance* ▶ **quin·tes·sen·tial** /ˌkwɪntəˈsɛnʃl/ *adj.*: *He was the quintessential tough guy.* **quin·tes·sen·tial·ly** /-ʃəli/ *adv.*

quin·tet /kwɪnˈtɛt/ *noun* **1** a group of five musicians or singers who play or sing together: *the Miles Davis Quintet* **2** a piece of music for five musicians or singers: *a string quintet*

quin·tile /ˈkwɪntaɪl/ *noun* (*statistics*) one of five equal groups into which a set of things can be divided according to the DISTRIBUTION of a particular VARIABLE: *men in the first quintile of weight* (= the heaviest 20% of men) ⊃ compare QUARTILE

quin·tu·ple /kwɪnˈtupl; -ˈtʌpl/ *adj., det., verb*
● *adj.* [only before noun], *det.* **1** consisting of five parts, people, or groups **2** being five times as much or as many
● *verb* [I, T] **~ (sth)** to become five times bigger; to make something five times bigger: *Sales have quintupled over the past few years.*

quin·tu·plet /kwɪnˈtʌplət/ (also *informal* **quint**) *noun* one of five children born at the same time to the same mother

quip /kwɪp/ *noun, verb*
● *noun* a smart and amusing remark: *to make a quip*
● *verb* (-pp-) **+ speech** to make a smart and amusing remark

quire /ˈkwaɪər/ *noun* (*old-fashioned*) four sheets of paper folded to make eight LEAVES (= 16 pages)

quirk /kwərk/ *noun, verb*
● *noun* **1** an aspect of someone's personality or behavior that is a little strange SYN PECULIARITY **2** a strange thing that happens, especially by accident: *By a strange quirk of fate they had reserved rooms at the same hotel.* ▶ **quirk·y** *adj.*: *a quirky sense of humor*

● *verb* [T, I] **~ (sth)** to twist your mouth or EYEBROWS suddenly; (of your mouth or EYEBROWS) to move in this way: *David quirked an eyebrow and smirked slightly.* ◆ *Her lips quirked suddenly.*

quis·ling /ˈkwɪzlɪŋ/ *noun* (*disapproving*) a person who helps an enemy that has taken control of his or her country SYN COLLABORATOR

quit /kwɪt/ *verb* (**quit·ting**, **quit**, **quit**) **1** [I, T] (*informal*) to leave your job, school, etc.: *If I don't get more money I'll quit.* ◆ **~ as sth** *He has decided to quit as manager of the team.* ◆ **~ sth** *He quit the show last year because of bad health.* **2** [T, I] (*informal*) to stop doing something: **~ doing sth** *I've quit smoking.* ◆ **~ (sth)** *Just quit it!* ◆ *We only just started. We're not going to quit now.* **3** [T, I] **~ (sth)** to leave the place where you live: *The landlord gave them all* **notice to quit.** ◆ *We decided it was time to quit the city.* **4** [I, T] **~ (sth)** to close a computer program or application

quite 🖉 /kwaɪt/ *adv.*

1 to a great degree; very; really: *You'll be quite comfortable here.* ◆ *I can see it quite clearly.* ◆ *"You don't have any intention of coming back?" "I'm quite sorry, but no, I don't."* **2** to the greatest possible degree SYN COMPLETELY, ABSOLUTELY, ENTIRELY: *This is quite a different problem.* ◆ *I'm* **quite happy** *to wait for you here.* ◆ *It wasn't quite as simple as I thought it would be.* ◆ *Quite frankly, I don't blame you.* ◆ *I've had* **quite enough** *of your tantrums.* ◆ *Are you* **quite sure?** ◆ *I* **quite agree.** ◆ *I don't quite know what to do next.* ◆ *Quite apart from all the work, he had financial problems.* ◆ *"I almost think she prefers animals to people." "* **Quite right, too,** *" said Bill.* ◆ *"I'm sorry to be so difficult." "* **That's quite all right.** *"* **3 not quite** used to show that something is nearly right or suitable, or almost happens: *There's not quite enough bread for breakfast.* ◆ *It's like being in the Alps, but not quite.* ◆ *I can't quite reach it—can you give it to me?* ◆ *The theater was not quite full.* ◆ *These shoes don't quite fit.*

IDM **quite a/the sth** (also *informal* **quite some sth**) used to show that a person or thing is particularly impressive or unusual in some way: *She's quite a beauty.* ◆ *We found it quite a change when we moved to Boston.* ◆ *He's quite the little gentleman, isn't he?* ◆ *It must be quite some car.* **quite something** impressive; (of an event) major: *The alumni will join the cast of 42nd Street onstage. It will be quite something to see.* **quite a lot (of sth)** a large number or amount of something: *They drank quite a lot of wine.* **quite some sth** **1** a large amount of something: *She hasn't been seen for quite some time.* **2** (*informal*) = QUITE a/the sth ⊃ more at CONTRARY[1], FEW *pron.*

quits /kwɪts/ *adj.* IDM see CALL *v.*

quit·ter /ˈkwɪtər/ *noun* (often *disapproving*) a person who gives up easily and does not finish a task they have started

quiv·er /ˈkwɪvər/ *verb, noun*
● *verb* [I] to shake slightly; to make a slight movement SYN TREMBLE: *Her lip quivered and then she started to cry.*
● *noun* **1** an emotion that has an effect on your body; a slight movement in part of your body: *He felt a quiver of excitement run through him.* ◆ *Jane couldn't help the quiver in her voice.* **2** a case for carrying arrows

quix·ot·ic /kwɪkˈsɑtɪk/ *adj.* (*formal*) having or involving ideas or plans that show imagination but are usually not practical ORIGIN From the character Don Quixote in the novel by Miguel de Cervantes, whose adventures are a result of him trying to achieve or obtain things that are impossible.

quiz /kwɪz/ *noun, verb*
● *noun* (*pl.* **quiz·zes**) **1** an informal test given to students: *a reading comprehension quiz* ⊃ see also POP QUIZ **2** a competition or game in which people try to answer questions to test their knowledge: *a general knowledge quiz* ◆ *a television quiz show* ⊃ note at EXAM
● *verb* (-zz-) **1** to ask someone a lot of questions about something in order to get information from them SYN QUESTION: **~ sb (about sb/sth)** *Four men are being quizzed by police about the murder.* ◆ **~ sb (on/over sth)** *We were quizzed on our views about education.* **2 ~ sb** to give

students an informal test: *You will be quizzed on chapter 6 tomorrow.*

quiz show *noun* a radio or television show in which people answer a series of questions and compete with each other to see who can win the most money or prizes **SYN** GAME SHOW

quiz·zi·cal /ˈkwɪzɪkl/ *adj.* (of an expression) showing that you are slightly surprised or amused: *a quizzical expression* ▶ **quiz·zi·cal·ly** /-kli/ *adv.*: *She looked at him quizzically.*

quoit /kɔɪt; kwɔɪt/ *noun* **1** [C] a ring that is thrown onto a small post in the game of quoits **2 quoits** [U] a game in which rings are thrown onto a small post

Quonset hut™ /ˈkwɑnsət ˌhʌt/ *noun* a shelter made of metal with curved walls and roof

quo·rum /ˈkwɔrəm/ *noun* [sing.] the smallest number of people who must be at a meeting before it can begin or decisions can be made

quo·ta /ˈkwoʊt̬ə/ *noun* **1** [C] the limited number or amount of people or things that is officially allowed: *to introduce a strict import quota on grain* ◆ *a quota system for accepting refugees* **2** [C] an amount of something that someone expects or needs to have or achieve: *I'm going home now— I've done my quota of work for the day.* **3** [sing.] (*politics*) a fixed number of votes that a candidate needs in order to be elected: *He was 76 votes short of the quota.*

quot·a·ble /ˈkwoʊt̬əbl/ *adj.* (of a statement) interesting or amusing and worth repeating

quota ˌsystem *noun* **1** (*politics*) a system that limits the number of immigrants from any one country who may officially enter the U.S. each year **2** a policy of either limiting the number of students, employees, etc. of minority groups in a school or business, or of requiring a certain number or percentage to be hired or admitted: *The school had a quota system in place for many years.* **3** (*economics*) a system that limits the amount of particular goods that can enter or leave a country

quo·ta·tion **AWL** /kwoʊˈteɪʃn/ *noun* **1** (also *informal* **quote**) [C] a group of words or a short piece of writing taken from a book, play, speech, etc. and repeated because it is interesting or useful: *The book began with a quotation from Goethe.* ◆ *a dictionary of quotations* **2** [U] the act of repeating something interesting or useful that another person has written or said: *The writer illustrates his point by quotation from a number of sources.* **3** [C] (also *informal* **quote**) a statement of how much money a particular piece of work will cost **SYN** ESTIMATE: *You need to get a written quotation before they start work.* **4** [C] (*finance*) a statement of the current value of goods or shares: *the latest quotations from the Stock Exchange*

quoˈtation ˌmarks (also *informal* **quotes**) *noun* [pl.] a pair of marks ("") placed around a word, sentence, etc. to show that it is what someone said or wrote, that it is a title, or that you are using it in an unusual way

quote 🔑 **AWL** /kwoʊt/ *verb, noun*
● *verb*
▷ REPEAT EXACT WORDS **1** [T, I] to repeat the exact words that another person has said or written: ~ **sth (from sb/sth)** *He quoted a passage from the minister's speech.* ◆ *to quote Shakespeare* ◆ *Quote this reference number in all correspondence.* ◆ ~ **(sb) (as doing sth)** *The President was quoted in the press as saying that he disagreed with the decision.* ◆ "*It will all be gone tomorrow.*" " *Can I quote you on that?* " ◆ *Don't quote me on this* (= this is not an official statement), *but I think he is going to resign.* ◆ *She said, and I quote, "Life is meaningless without love."* ◆ **+ speech** "*New York is the biggest collection of villages in the world ,*" *he quoted.* ➔ see also MISQUOTE
▷ GIVE EXAMPLE **2** [T] ~ **(sb) sth** to mention an example of something to support what you are saying: *Can you quote me an instance of when this happened?* ➔ thesaurus box at MENTION
▷ GIVE PRICE **3** [T, I] ~ **(sb) (sth) (for sth/for doing sth)** to tell a customer how much money you will charge them for a job, service, or product: *They quoted us $300 for installing a shower unit.* **4** [T] ~ **sth (at sth)** (*finance*) to give a market price for shares, gold, or foreign money: *Yesterday the euro was quoted at $1,178.53, unchanged from Monday.* **5** [T] ~ **sth** (*finance*) to give the prices for a business company's shares on a STOCK EXCHANGE: *Several cosmetic companies are quoted on the New York Stock Exchange.*
IDM **quote (… unquote)** (*informal*) used to show the beginning (and end) of a word, phrase, etc. that has been said or written by someone else: *It was quote, "the hardest decision of my life," unquote, and one that he lived to regret.*
● *noun* (*informal*)
▷ EXACT WORDS **1** = QUOTATION (1): *The essay was full of quotes.*
▷ PRICE **2** = QUOTATION (3): *Their quote for the job was way too high.*
▷ PUNCTUATION **3 quotes** [pl.] = QUOTATION MARKS: *If you take text from other sources, place it in quotes.*

quoth /kwoʊθ/ *verb* **+ speech** (*old use* or *humorous*) used meaning "said" before "I," "he," or "she."

quo·tid·i·an /kwoʊˈtɪdiən/ *adj.* (*formal*) ordinary; typical of what happens every day **SYN** DAY-TO-DAY

quo·tient /ˈkwoʊʃnt/ *noun* (*mathematics*) a number which is the result when one number is divided by another ➔ see also INTELLIGENCE QUOTIENT

Qu·r'an = KORAN

q.v. /ˌkyu ˈvi/ *abbr.* used in books to tell a reader that there is more information in another part of the book (from Latin "quod vide")

qwer·ty (also **QWERTY**) /ˈkwɜrt̬i/ *adj.* [usually before noun] (of a keyboard) with the keys arranged in the way that is usual for English, with Q, W, E, R, T, and Y on the left of the top row of letters

Rr

R /ɑr/ *noun, abbr.*

● **noun** also **r** (*pl.* **Rs, R's, r's** /ɑrz/) [C, U] the 18th letter of the English alphabet: *"Rose" begins with (an) R/"R."* **IDM** see **THREE**

● **abbr. 1 R.** (especially on maps) River: *R. Trask* **2** (also **R.**) (in politics in the U.S.) **REPUBLICAN 3** used to show that no one younger than 17 will be allowed to see a particular movie unless an adult goes with them (the abbreviation for "restricted") ⊃ compare G *abbr.* (1), NC-17, PG, PG-13 **4** **ROENTGEN** ⊃ see also **R & B, R & D, R & R**

rab·bi /'ræbaɪ/ *noun* a Jewish religious leader or a teacher of Jewish law: *the Chief Rabbi* (= the leader of Jewish communities in a particular country) ◆ *Rabbi Sacks*

rab·bin·i·cal /rə'bɪnɪkl/ (also **rab·bin·ic**) *adj.* connected with rabbis or Jewish law or teaching

rabbit

hare

rab·bit /'ræbət/ *noun*

● **noun 1** [C] a small animal with soft fur, long ears, and a short tail. Rabbits live in holes in the ground or are kept as pets or for food.: *a rabbit hutch* ⊃ compare **HARE 2** [U] meat from a rabbit **IDM** see **PULL** *v.*

'rabbit ,punch *noun* a sharp hit made with the edge of your hand to the back of someone's neck or head: *The rabbit punch is illegal in boxing because it is so dangerous.*

'rabbit ,warren (also **war·ren**) *noun* **1** a system of holes and underground tunnels where wild rabbits live **2** (*disapproving*) a building or part of a city with many narrow passages or streets

rab·ble /'ræbl/ *noun* [sing.] (*disapproving*) **1** a large group of noisy people who are or may become violent **SYN** **MOB**: *a drunken rabble* **2 the rabble** ordinary people, or people who are considered to have a low social position **SYN** **THE MASSES**: *a speech that appealed to the rabble*

'rabble-,rouser *noun* a person who makes speeches to crowds of people intending to make them angry or excited, especially for political aims ▶ **'rabble-,rousing** *adj.* **'rabble-,rousing** *noun* [U]

Rab·e·lai·si·an /,ræbə'leɪʒn/ *adj.* dealing with sex and the human body in a crude but humorous way **ORIGIN** From the French writer François Rabelais, whose works dealt with sex and the body in this way.

rab·id /'ræbəd/ **1** [usually before noun] (*disapproving*) (of a type of person) having very strong feelings about something and acting in an unacceptable way: *rabid right-wing fanatics* ◆ *the rabid tabloid press* **2** [usually before noun] (*disapproving*) (of feelings or opinions) violent or extreme: *rabid speculation* **3** suffering from rabies: *a rabid dog* ▶ **rab·id·ly** *adv.*

ra·bies /'reɪbiz/ *noun* [U] a disease of dogs and other animals that causes **INSANITY** and death. Infected animals can pass the disease to humans by biting them.

rac·coon (also **ra·coon**) /ræ'kun/ *noun* **1** [C] a small N. American animal with grayish-brown fur, black marks on its face, and black rings around its tail **2** [U] the fur of the raccoon

raccoon

race /reɪs/ *noun, verb*

● **noun**
▷ COMPETITION **1** [C] **~ (between A and B)** | **~ (against sb)** a competition between people, animals, vehicles, etc. to see which one is the faster or fastest: *a race between the two best runners of the club* ◆ *Who won the race?* ◆ *He's already in training for the big race against Bailey.* ◆ *Their horse finished third in the race last year.* ◆ *a boat/horse/road, etc. race* ◆ *a five-kilometer race* ◆ *Let's have a race to the end of the beach!* ⊃ see also **DRAG RACE, HORSE RACE 2** [sing.] a situation in which a number of people, groups, organizations, etc. are competing, especially for political power or to achieve something first: **~ (for sth)** *the race for the presidency* ◆ **~ (to do sth)** *The race is on* (= has begun) *to find a cure for the disease.* ⊃ see also **RAT RACE**
▷ FOR HORSES **3 the races** [pl.] a series of horse races that happen at one place on a particular day: *to go to the races*
▷ PEOPLE **4** [C] one of the main groups that humans can be divided into according to their physical differences, for example the color of their skin: *the Caucasian/Mongolian, etc. race* ◆ *people of mixed race* ◆ *This custom is found in people of all races throughout the world.* ◆ *legislation against discrimination on the grounds of race or sex* **5** [C] a group of people who share the same language, history, culture, etc.: *the Nordic races* ◆ *He admired Canadians as a hardy and determined race.* ⊃ see also **HUMAN RACE**
▷ ANIMALS/PLANTS **6** [C] a breed or type of animal or plant: *a race of cattle*
IDM **a race against time/the clock** a situation in which you have to do something or finish something very fast before it is too late ⊃ more at **HORSE** *n.*

● **verb**
▷ COMPETE **1** [I, T] to compete against someone or something to see who can go faster or the fastest, do something first, etc.; to take part in a race or races: **~ (against sb/sth)** *Who will he be racing against in the next round?* ◆ *They raced to a thrilling victory in the relay.* ◆ *She'll be racing for the senior team next year.* ◆ **~ sb/sth** *We raced each other back to the car.* ◆ **~ to do sth** *Television companies are racing to be the first to show his life story.* **2** [T] **~ sth** to make an animal or a vehicle compete in a race: *to race dogs/horses* ◆ *to race dirt bikes*
▷ MOVE FAST **3** [I, T] to move very fast; to move someone or something very fast: **+ adv./prep.** *He raced up the stairs.* ◆ *The days seemed to race past.* ◆ **~ sb/sth + adv./prep.** *The injured man was raced to the hospital.* ◆ *She raced her car through the narrow streets of the town.*
▷ OF HEART/MIND/THOUGHTS **4** [I] to function very quickly because you are afraid, excited, etc.: *My mind raced as I tried to work out what was happening.* ◆ *She took a deep breath to calm her racing pulse.*
▷ OF ENGINE **5** [I] to run too fast: *The truck came to rest against a tree, its engine racing.*

TOPIC COLLOCATIONS

Race and Immigration

prejudice and racism

- **experience/encounter** racism/discrimination/prejudice/anti-Semitism
- **face/suffer from** persecution/discrimination
- **fear/escape from/flee** racial/political/religious persecution
- **constitute/be a form of** racial discrimination
- **reflect/reveal/show/have** a racial/cultural bias
- **be biased/be prejudiced against** people of color/African Americans/Latinos/Native Americans/Asians, etc.
- **discriminate against** minority groups/minorities
- **perpetuate/conform to/fit/defy** a common/popular/traditional/negative stereotype

---

- overcome/be blinded by deep-seated/racial prejudice
- entrench/perpetuate racist attitudes
- hurl/shout a(n) racist/racial/ethnic slur
- challenge/confront racism/discrimination/prejudice
- combat/fight (against)/tackle blatant/overt/covert/subtle/institutional/systemic racism

race and society
- damage/improve race relations
- practice (racial/religious) tolerance/segregation
- overcome/bridge/break down/transcend cultural/racial barriers
- encourage/promote social integration
- outlaw/end discrimination/slavery/segregation
- promote/embrace/celebrate cultural/ethnic diversity
- conform to/challenge/violate (accepted/established/prevailing/dominant) social/cultural norms
- live in a multicultural society/a cosmopolitan city
- attack/criticize multiculturalism
- fight for/struggle for/promote racial equality
- perpetuate/reinforce economic and social inequality
- introduce/be for/be against affirmative action
- accuse sb of reverse discrimination
- support/be active in/play a leading role in the civil rights movement

immigration
- control/restrict/limit/encourage immigration
- attract/draw a wave of immigrants
- assist/welcome refugees
- house/shelter refugees and asylum seekers
- smuggle illegal immigrants into the U.S.
- deport/repatriate illegal immigrants/those denied refugee status
- assimilate/integrate new immigrants
- employ/hire migrant workers
- exploit/rely on (cheap/illegal) migrant/foreign labor/workers
- apply for/gain/obtain/be granted/be denied (full) citizenship
- have/hold dual citizenship

'**race car** (also 'racing ,car) *noun* a car that has been specially designed for motor racing

'**race card** *noun*
  IDM play the race card to bring the issue of race into a debate in order to gain political advantage, especially during an election

race·course /ˈreɪskɔrs/ *noun* = RACETRACK

race·horse /ˈreɪshɔrs/ *noun* a horse that is bred and trained to run in races ⊃ picture at SPORT

rac·er /ˈreɪsər/ *noun* **1** a person or an animal that competes in races: *Italy's champion downhill racer* **2** a car, boat, etc. designed for racing: *an ocean racer*

'**race re,lations** *noun* [pl.] the relationships between people of different races who live in the same community

'**race ,riot** *noun* violent behavior between people of different races living in the same community

race·track /ˈreɪstræk/ *noun* **1** a track for races between runners, cars, bicycles, etc.: *You can't cross the road—it's like a racetrack.* ⊃ picture at SPORT **2** (also **race·course**) a track where horses race and the buildings, etc. that are connected with it

race·way /ˈreɪsweɪ/ *noun* a track for racing cars or horses

ra·cial /ˈreɪʃl/ *adj.* **1** [only before noun] happening or existing between people of different races: *racial hatred/prejudice/tension/violence* ♦ *racial equality* ♦ *They have pledged to end racial discrimination in areas such as employment.* **2** [usually before noun] connected with a person's race: *racial minorities* ♦ *a person's racial origin* ▶ **ra·cial·ly**

/-ʃəli/ *adv.: The attacks were not racially motivated.* ♦ *racially mixed schools*

,**racial 'profiling** *noun* [U] (*disapproving*) the fact of police officers, etc. suspecting that someone has committed a crime based on the color of their skin or their race rather than on any evidence

rac·ing 🔑 /ˈreɪsɪŋ/ *noun* [U]
  1 (also '**horse ,racing**) the sport of racing horses: *a racing stable* ⊃ see also FLAT RACING **2** (usually in compounds) any sport that involves competing in races: *motor/drag, etc. racing* ♦ *a racing driver*

'**racing ,car** *noun* = RACE CAR

rac·ism /ˈreɪsɪzəm/ *noun* [U] (*disapproving*) **1** the unfair treatment of people who belong to a different race; violent behavior toward them: *a victim of racism* ♦ *ugly outbreaks of racism* **2** the belief that some races of people are better than others: *irrational racism* ▶ **rac·ist** /ˈreɪsɪst/ *noun: He's a racist.* **rac·ist** *adj.: racist thugs* ♦ *racist attitudes/attacks/remarks*

racks

plate rack

wine rack

vegetable rack

toast rack

magazine rack

luggage rack

roof rack (*also* luggage rack)

rack /ræk/ *noun, verb*
● *noun* **1** (often in compounds) a piece of equipment, usually made of metal or wooden bars, that is used for holding things or for hanging things on: *a wine/plate/magazine rack* ♦ *I looked through a rack of clothes at the back of the store.* ⊃ see also LUGGAGE RACK, ROOF RACK, TOWEL RACK **2** usually **the rack** an instrument of TORTURE, used in the past for punishing and hurting people. Their arms and legs were tied to the wooden frame and then pulled in opposite directions, stretching the body. **3** ~ **of lamb** a piece of lamb that includes the front RIBS and is cooked in the oven **4** a part of a machine that consists of a bar with parts that a wheel or gear can fit into
  IDM go to rack and ruin to get into a bad condition: *They let the house go to rack and ruin.* **off the rack** (of clothes) made to a standard average size and not made especially to fit you: *He buys his clothes off the rack.* ♦ *an off-the-rack suit* **on the rack** feeling extreme pressure, anxiety, or pain
● *verb* (also *less frequent* **wrack**) [often passive] ~ **sb/sth** to make someone suffer great physical or mental pain: *to be racked with/by guilt* ♦ *Her face was racked with pain.* ♦ *Violent sobs racked her whole body.*
  IDM rack your brain(s) to think very hard or for a long time about something: *She racked her brains, trying to remember exactly what she had said.*
  PHR V rack 'up sth to collect something, such as profits or losses in a business, or points in a competition: *The*

company racked up $200 million in losses in two years. ◆ *In ten years of boxing he racked up a record 176 wins.*

rack·et /'rækət/ *noun* **1** (also **rac·quet**) [C] a piece of sports equipment used for hitting the ball, etc. in the games of TENNIS, SQUASH or BADMINTON. It has an OVAL frame, with strings stretched across and down it. ⟳ **picture at SPORT** ⟳ **compare BAT** *n.* (1) **2** [sing.] (*informal*) a loud unpleasant noise **SYN** DIN: *Stop making that terrible racket!* **3** [C] (*informal*) a dishonest or illegal way of getting money: *a protection/extortion/drugs, etc. racket* **4** [C] (*informal*) a type of activity or business: *How long have you been in the journalism racket?*

rack·et·eer /ˌrækə'tɪr/ *noun* (*disapproving*) a person who makes money through dishonest or illegal activities ▶ **rack·et·eer·ing** *noun* [U]

rack rate *noun* the standard price of a hotel room

rac·on·teur /ˌrækɒn'tɜr/ *noun* a person who is good at telling stories in an interesting and amusing way

ra·coon = RACCOON

rac·quet = RACKET

rac·quet·ball /'rækət,bɔl/ *noun* [U] a game played by two or four players on a COURT with four walls, using RACKETS and a small, hollow, rubber ball

rac·y /'reɪsi/ *adj.* (**rac·i·er**, **rac·i·est**) having a style that is exciting and amusing, sometimes in a way that is connected with sex: *a racy novel*

rad /ræd/ *adj., noun*
● *adj.* (*old-fashioned, slang*) very good
● *noun* (*physics*) a unit for measuring the effect of RADIATION

ra·dar /'reɪdɑr/ *noun* [U] a system that uses radio waves to find the position and movement of objects, for example planes and ships, when they cannot be seen: *They located the ship by radar.* ◆ *a radar screen* ⟳ **compare SONAR** **IDM** **below/under the radar** used to say that people are not aware of something: *Experts say a lot of corporate crime stays under the radar.* **on/off the radar (screen)** used to say that people's attention is on or not on something: *The issue of terrorism is back on the radar screen.* ⟳ **more at BUBBLE** *v.*

radar ˌtrap *noun* = SPEED TRAP

ra·di·al /'reɪdiəl/ *adj., noun*
● *adj.* having a pattern of lines, etc. that go out from a central point toward the edge of a circle: *the radial pattern of public transportation facilities* ▶ **ra·di·al·ly** *adv.*
● *noun* (also ˌradial 'tire) a car tire with strong parts inside that point away from the outside part and make the tire stronger and safer

ra·di·an /'reɪdiən/ *noun* (*geometry*) a unit used to measure an angle, equal to the angle at the center of a circle whose ARC is the same length as the circle's RADIUS

ra·di·ance /'reɪdiəns/ *noun* [U] **1** a special bright quality that shows in someone's face, for example because they are very happy or healthy **2** warm light shining from something

ra·di·ant /'reɪdiənt/ *adj.* **1** showing great happiness, love, or health: *a radiant smile* ◆ *The bride looked radiant.* ◆ *~ with sth She was radiant with health.* **2** giving a warm bright light: *The sun was radiant in a clear blue sky.* **3** [only before noun] (*technical*) sent out in RAYS from a central point: *the radiant heat/energy of the sun* ▶ **ra·di·ant·ly** *adv.*: *radiantly happy* ◆ *He smiled radiantly.*

ra·di·ate /'reɪdiˌeɪt/ *verb* **1** [T, I] ~ (**sth**) | ~ (**from sb**) if a person **radiates** a particular quality or emotion, or if it **radiates** from them, people can see it very clearly: *He radiated self-confidence and optimism.* **2** [I, T] ~ (**from sth**) | ~ (**sth**) if something **radiates** heat, light, or energy, or if heat, etc. **radiates** from it, the heat is sent out in all directions **SYN** GIVE (STH) OFF: *Heat radiates from the stove.* **3** [I] + *adv./prep.* (of lines, etc.) to spread out in all directions from a central point: *Five roads radiate from the square.* ◆ *The pain started in my stomach and radiated all over my body.*

ra·di·a·tion /ˌreɪdi'eɪʃn/ *noun* **1** [U, C] powerful and very dangerous RAYS that are sent out from RADIOACTIVE substances: *high levels/doses of radiation that damage cells* ◆ *the link between exposure to radiation and childhood cancer* ◆ *a radiation leak from a nuclear power station* ◆ *radiation sickness* ◆ *the radiations emitted by radium* **2** [U] heat, energy, etc. that is sent out in the form of RAYS: *ultraviolet radiation* ◆ *electromagnetic radiation from power lines* **3** (also radi-ˈation ˌtherapy) [U] the treatment of cancer and other diseases using radiation ⟳ **compare CHEMOTHERAPY, RADIOTHERAPY**

ra·di·a·tor /'reɪdiˌeɪtər/ *noun* **1** a hollow metal device for heating rooms. Radiators are usually connected by pipes through which hot water is sent.: *a central heating system with a radiator in each room* **2** a device for cooling the engine of a vehicle or an aircraft

rad·i·cal **AWL** /'rædɪkl/ *adj., noun*
● *adj.* [usually before noun] **1** concerning the most basic and important parts of something; thorough and complete **SYN** FAR-REACHING: *the need for radical changes in education* ◆ *demands for radical reform of the law* ◆ *radical differences between the sexes* **2** new, different, and likely to have a great effect: *radical ideas* ◆ *a radical solution to the problem* ◆ *radical proposals* **3** in favor of thorough and complete political or social change: *the radical wing of the party* ◆ *radical politicians/students/writers* **4** (*old-fashioned, slang*) very good ▶ **rad·i·cally** **AWL** /-kli/ *adv.*: *The new methods are radically different from the old.* ◆ *Attitudes have changed radically.*
● *noun* **1** a person with radical opinions: *political radicals* **2** (*chemistry*) a group of atoms that behave as a single unit in a number of COMPOUNDS ⟳ **see also FREE RADICAL**

ˌradical 'chic *noun* [U] fashionable LEFT-WING views; the people, behavior, and way of life connected with these views

rad·i·cal·ism /'rædɪkəˌlɪzəm/ *noun* [U] belief in RADICAL ideas and principles

rad·i·cal·ize /'rædɪkəˌlaɪz/ *verb* ~ **sb/sth** to make people more willing to consider new and different policies, ideas, etc.; to make people more RADICAL in their political opinions: *Recent events have radicalized opinion on educational matters.*

ra·dic·chi·o /rə'diki,oʊ/ *noun* [U] a type of CHICORY (= a leaf vegetable) with dark red leaves

ra·di·i pl. of RADIUS

ra·di·o 🔊 /'reɪdi,oʊ/ *noun, verb*
● *noun* **1** often **the radio** [U, sing.] the activity of broadcasting programs for people to listen to; the programs that are broadcast: *The interview was broadcast on radio and television.* ◆ *The play was written especially for radio.* ◆ *I listen to the radio on the way to work.* ◆ *Did you hear the interview with him on the radio?* ◆ *local/national radio* ◆ *a radio program/station* ◆ *satellite radio* **2** [C] a piece of equipment used for listening to programs that are broadcast to the public: *to turn the radio on/off* ◆ *a car radio* ⟳ **see also CLOCK RADIO** **3** [U] the process of sending and receiving messages through the air using ELECTROMAGNETIC waves: *He was unable to contact Blake by radio.* ◆ *to keep in radio contact* ◆ *radio signals/waves* **4** [C] a piece of equipment, for example on ships or planes, for sending and receiving radio signals: *to hear a gale warning on/over the ship's radio*
● *verb* (ra·di·o·ing, ra·di·oed, ra·di·oed) [I, T] ~ (**sth**) | ~ **that...** to send a message to someone by radio: *The police officer radioed for help.* ◆ *The warning was radioed to headquarters.*

radio– /'reɪdioʊ/ *combining form* (in nouns, adjectives, and adverbs) **1** connected with radio waves or broadcasting: *radio-controlled* **2** connected with radioactivity or RADIATION: *radiotherapy*

ra·di·o·ac·tive /ˌreɪdioʊ'æktɪv/ *adj.* sending out harmful RADIATION caused when the nuclei (NUCLEUS) (= central part) of atoms are broken up ▶ **ra·di·o·ac·tiv·i·ty**

/-æk'tɪvəti/ noun [U]: *the study of radioactivity* ♦ *a rise in the level of radioactivity*

radio as'tronomy noun [U] the part of ASTRONOMY that studies radio waves sent out by objects in space

'radio ˌbutton noun (*computing*) a small circle on a computer screen that you click on in order to make a particular choice. The radio button is then marked with a dot to show that it has been selected.

ra·di·o·car·bon /ˌreɪdiou'kɑrbən/ noun [U] (*technical*) a RADIOACTIVE form of CARBON that is present in the materials of which living things are formed, used in CARBON DATING: *radiocarbon analysis*

radio'carbon ˌdating noun [U] (*formal*) = CARBON DATING

ra·di·o·chem·is·try /ˌreɪdiou'kɛməstri/ noun [U] the area of chemistry that is concerned with RADIOACTIVE substances ▶ **ra·di·o·chem·i·cal** /ˌreɪdiou'kɛmɪkl/ *adj.*

ˌradio-con'trolled *adj.* controlled from a distance by radio signals

ra·di·og·ra·pher /ˌreɪdi'ɑɡrəfər/ noun a person working in a hospital whose job is to take X-RAY photographs or to use X-RAYS to treat some illnesses, such as cancer

ra·di·og·ra·phy /ˌreɪdi'ɑɡrəfi/ noun [U] the process or job of taking X-RAY photographs

ra·di·o·iso·tope /ˌreɪdiou'aɪsəˌtoup/ noun (*chemistry*) a form of a chemical element that sends out RADIATION

ra·di·ol·o·gist /ˌreɪdi'ɑlədʒɪst/ noun a doctor who is trained in radiology

ra·di·ol·o·gy /ˌreɪdi'ɑlədʒi/ noun [U] the study and use of different types of RADIATION in medicine, for example to treat diseases

ra·di·o·met·ric /ˌreɪdiou'mɛtrɪk/ *adj.* relating to a measurement of radioactivity (RADIOACTIVE) ▶ **ra·di·o·met·ri·cally** /-kli/ *adv.*: *These rocks have been dated radiometrically at two billion years old.*

ra·di·o·tel·e·phone /ˌreɪdiou'tɛləˌfoun/ noun a telephone that works by sending and receiving radio signals, used especially in cars, boats, etc.

ˌradio 'telescope noun a piece of equipment that receives radio waves from space and is used for finding stars and the position of SPACECRAFT, etc.

ra·di·o·ther·a·py /ˌreɪdiou'θɛrəpi/ noun [U] the treatment of disease by RADIATION: *a course of radiotherapy* ⊃ compare CHEMOTHERAPY ▶ **ra·di·o·ther·a·pist** /-pɪst/ noun

'radio ˌwave noun a low-energy ELECTROMAGNETIC wave, especially when used for long-distance communication

rad·ish /'rædɪʃ/ noun [C, U] a small, crisp, red or white root vegetable with a strong taste, eaten raw in salads: *a bunch of radishes* ⊃ picture at FRUIT

ra·di·um /'reɪdiəm/ noun [U] (*symb.* **Ra**) a chemical element. Radium is a white RADIOACTIVE metal used in the treatment of diseases such as cancer.

ra·di·us /'reɪdiəs/ noun (pl. ra·di·i /'reɪdiˌaɪ/) **1** a straight line between the center of a circle and any point on its outer edge; the length of this line ⊃ picture at SHAPE ⊃ compare DIAMETER **2** a round area that covers the distance mentioned from a central point: *They deliver to within a 5-mile radius of the store.* **3** (*anatomy*) the shorter bone of the two bones in the lower part of the arm between the elbow and the wrist, on the same side as the thumb ⊃ picture at BODY ⊃ see also ULNA

ra·don /'reɪdɑn/ noun [U] (*symb.* **Rn**) a chemical element. Radon is a RADIOACTIVE gas used in the treatment of cancer.

raf·fi·a /'ræfiə/ noun [U] soft material that looks like string and is made from the leaves of a type of PALM tree, used for making BASKETS, MATS, etc. or for tying things

raff·ish /'ræfɪʃ/ *adj.* (of someone's behavior, clothes, etc.) not very acceptable according to some social standards, but interesting and attractive

raf·fle /'ræfl/ noun, verb
● **noun** a way of making money for a particular project or organization. People buy tickets with numbers on them and some of these numbers are later chosen to win prizes. ⊃ compare LOTTERY
● **verb** ~ sth to give something as a prize in a raffle

raft /ræft/ noun **1** a flat structure made of pieces of wood tied together and used as a boat or floating platform **2** a small boat made of rubber or plastic that is filled with air: *an inflatable raft* ⊃ picture at BOAT **3** [usually sing.] ~ of sth (*informal*) a large number or amount of something: *a whole raft of new proposals*

raft·er /'ræftər/ noun [usually pl.] one of the sloping pieces of wood that support a roof

raft·ing /'ræftɪŋ/ noun [U] the sport or activity of traveling down a river on a raft: *We went **white-water rafting** on the Colorado River.*

rag /ræɡ/ noun, verb
● **noun 1** [C, U] a piece of old, often torn, cloth used especially for cleaning things ⊃ see also GLAD RAGS **2** [C] (*informal*, usually *disapproving*) a newspaper that you believe to be of low quality: *the local rag* **3** a piece of RAGTIME music
  IDM **in rags** wearing very old torn clothes: *The children were dressed in rags.* **(from) rags to riches** from being extremely poor to being very rich: *a rags-to-riches story* ♦ *Hers was a classic tale of rags to riches.*
● **verb** (-gg-) ~ sb (about sth) (*old-fashioned*) to laugh at and/or play tricks on someone SYN TEASE
  PHR V **'rag on sb** (*informal*) to complain to someone about their behavior, work, etc.

ra·ga /'rɑɡə/ noun a traditional pattern of notes used in Indian music; a piece of music based on one of these patterns

rag·a·muf·fin /'ræɡəˌmʌfɪn/ noun a person, usually a child, who is wearing old clothes that are torn and dirty

rag·bag /'ræɡbæɡ/ noun [sing.] a collection of things that appear to have little connection with each other: *a ragbag of ideas*

'rag doll noun a soft DOLL made from pieces of cloth ⊃ picture at TOY

rage /reɪdʒ/ noun, verb
● **noun 1** [U, C] a feeling of violent anger that is difficult to control: *His face was dark with rage.* ♦ *to be shaking/trembling/speechless with rage* ♦ *Sue stormed out of the room in a rage.* ♦ *He flies into a rage if you even mention the subject.* **2** [U] (in compounds) anger and violent behavior caused by a particular situation: *a case of **air rage** on our flight home* ⊃ see also ROAD RAGE
  IDM **be all the rage** (*informal*) to be very popular and fashionable
● **verb 1** [I, T] to show that you are very angry about something or with someone, especially by shouting SYN RAIL: ~ (at/against/about sb/sth) *He raged against the injustice of it all.* ♦ + speech *"That's unfair!" she raged.* **2** [I] ~ (on) (of a storm, a battle, an argument, etc.) to continue in a violent way: *The riots raged for three days.* ♦ *The blizzard was still raging outside.* **3** [I] (+ adv./prep.) (of an illness, a fire, etc.) to spread very quickly: *Forest fires were raging out of control.* ♦ *A flu epidemic raged through the local schools.*

rag·ged /'ræɡəd/ *adj.* **1** (of clothes) old and torn SYN SHABBY **2** (of people) wearing old or torn clothes: *ragged children* **3** having an outline, an edge, or a surface that is not straight or even: *ragged clouds* ♦ *a ragged coastline* **4** not smooth or controlled: *I could hear the sound of his ragged breathing.* ♦ *Their performance was still very ragged.* **5** (*informal*) very tired, especially after physical effort ▶ **rag·ged·ly** *adv.*: *raggedly dressed* ♦ *She was breathing raggedly.* **rag·ged·ness** noun [U]
  IDM **run sb ragged** (*informal*) to make someone do a lot of work or make a big effort so that they become tired

rag·ged·y /'ræɡədi/ *adj.* (*informal*) **1** old and torn, or wearing old and torn clothes: *raggedy beggars* **2** having edges or ends that are not straight or even: *a photo with a raggedy border*

rag·ing /ˈreɪdʒɪŋ/ *adj.* [only before noun] **1** (of feelings or emotions) very strong: *a raging appetite/thirst* ♦ *raging jealousy* **2** (of natural forces) very powerful: *a raging storm* ♦ *The stream had become a raging torrent.* ♦ *The building was now a raging inferno.* **3** (of a pain or an illness) very strong or painful: *a raging headache* **4** very serious and causing strong feelings: *His speech has provoked a raging debate.*

rag·lan /ˈræɡlən/ *adj.* [only before noun] **1** (of a sleeve) sewn to the front and back of a coat, sweater, etc. in a line that slopes down from the neck to under the arm **2** (of a coat, sweater, etc.) having raglan sleeves

ra·gout /ræˈɡuː/ *noun* [C, U] (from *French*) a hot dish of meat and vegetables cooked together with various spices **SYN** STEW

rag·tag /ˈræɡtæɡ/ *adj.* [usually before noun] (*informal*) (of a group of people or an organization) not well organized; giving a bad impression: *a ragtag band of rebels*

rag·time /ˈræɡtaɪm/ *noun* [U] an early form of JAZZ, especially for the piano, first played by African American musicians in the early 1900s

the ˈrag trade *noun* [sing.] (*old-fashioned, informal*) the business of designing, making, and selling clothes

rag·weed /ˈræɡwiːd/ *noun* [U] a N. American plant with small green flowers that contain a lot of POLLEN, which causes HAY FEVER in some people

rag·wort /ˈræɡwɜːrt; -wɔːrt/ *noun* [U] a wild plant with yellow flowers, poisonous to cows and horses

rah-rah /ˌrɑ ˈrɑ/ *adj.* [only before noun] (*informal*, usually *disapproving*) very enthusiastic about something, often without thinking much about it: *her rah-rah support of the proposal*

raid /reɪd/ *noun, verb*
● *noun* **1** ~ (on sth) a short surprise attack on an enemy by soldiers, ships, or aircraft: *They carried out a bombing raid on enemy bases.* ➔ collocations at WAR ➔ see also AIR RAID **2** ~ (on sth) a surprise visit by the police looking for criminals or for illegal goods or drugs: *They were arrested during a **dawn raid**.* **3** an attempt to buy enough of a company's shares to gain control over the company: *Their business has become a target for a corporate raid.*
● *verb* **1** ~ sth (of police) to visit a person or place without warning to look for criminals, illegal goods, drugs, etc. **2** ~ sth (of soldiers, fighting planes, etc.) to attack a place without warning: *Villages along the border are regularly raided.* ♦ *a **raiding party** (= a group of soldiers, etc. that attack a place)* **3** ~ sth to enter a place, usually using force, and steal from it **SYN** PLUNDER, RANSACK: *Many treasures were lost when the tombs were raided in the last century.* ♦ (*humorous*) *I caught him raiding the fridge again (= taking food from it).*

raid·er /ˈreɪdər/ *noun* a person who makes a criminal raid on a place: *armed/masked raiders*

rail ♪ /reɪl/ *noun, verb*
● *noun* **1** [C] a wooden or metal bar placed around something as a barrier or to provide support: *She leaned on the ship's rail and gazed out to sea.* ➔ see also GUARD RAIL, HANDRAIL **2** [C] a bar attached to the wall for hanging things on: *a picture/curtain rail* **3** [C, usually pl.] each of the two metal bars that form the track that trains run on **4** [U] (often before another noun) railroads as a means of transport: *to travel by rail* ♦ *rail travel/services/fares* ♦ *a rail link/network*
IDM **get back on the rails** (*informal*) to become successful again after a period of failure, or to begin functioning normally again **go off the rails** (*informal*) **1** to start behaving in a strange or unacceptable manner, for example, drinking a lot of alcohol or taking drugs **2** to lose control and stop functioning correctly: *The company has gone off the rails in recent years.*
● *verb* [I, T] ~ (at/against sth/sb) | + speech (*formal*) to complain about something or someone in a very angry way **SYN** RAGE: *She railed against the injustice of it all.*
PHR V **ˌrail sth ˈin/ˈoff** to separate an area or object from others by placing rails around it

rail·car /ˈreɪlkɑr/ *noun* = CAR (2)

rail·head /ˈreɪlhɛd/ *noun* (*technical*) the point at which a railroad ends

rail·ing /ˈreɪlɪŋ/ *noun* [usually pl.] a fence made of vertical metal or wooden bars; one of these bars: *iron railings* ♦ *I chained my bike to the park railings.* ♦ *She leaned out over the railing.*

rail·ler·y /ˈreɪləri/ *noun* [U] (*formal*) friendly joking about a person

rail·road ♪ /ˈreɪlroʊd/ *noun, verb*
● *noun* **1** a track with rails on which trains run: *railroad tracks* **2** a system of tracks, together with the trains that run on them, and the organization and people needed to operate them: *This town got a lot bigger when the railroad came in the 1860s.*
● *verb* **1** ~ sb (into sth/into doing sth) to force someone to do something before they have had enough time to decide whether or not they want to do it **2** ~ sth (through/through sth) to make a group of people accept a decision, law, etc. quickly by putting pressure on them: *The bill was railroaded through the House.* **3** ~ sb to decide that someone is guilty of a crime, without giving them a fair trial

ˈrailroad ˌcrossing *noun* a place where a road crosses a railroad line

rail·road·er /ˈreɪlˌroʊdər/ *noun* a person who works for a rail company

rail·way /ˈreɪlweɪ/ *noun* (*especially CanE*) a railroad

rai·ment /ˈreɪmənt/ *noun* [U] (*old use*) clothing

VOCABULARY BUILDING

rain and storms

rain

- **Drizzle** is fine light rain.
- A **shower** is a short period of rain.

- A **downpour** or a **cloudburst** is a heavy fall of rain that often starts suddenly.
- When it is raining very hard, you can say that it is **pouring** or **pouring rain**. You can also say: **The heavens opened.** or **It's raining cats and dogs.**
- A **flood** is a lot of water moving into an area.
- A **flash flood** moves into an area very quickly and is extremely dangerous.

storms

- A **thunderstorm** is a storm with thunder and lightning and usually very heavy rain.
- A **hurricane** has very strong winds and begins at sea.
- A **monsoon** is a period of very heavy rain in particular countries, or the wind that brings this rain.
- A **cyclone** and a **typhoon** are types of violent tropical storms with very strong winds.
- A **squall** is a sudden strong, violent wind, usually in a rain or snow storm.
- A **tornado** (or *informal* **twister**) has very strong winds that move in a circle, often with a long narrow cloud.
- A **whirlwind** moves very fast in a spinning movement and causes a lot of damage.
- A **dust storm** carries clouds of dust in the wind over a wide area.
- A **blizzard** is a snow storm with very strong winds.
- A **whiteout** is a blizzard in which you cannot see anything around you.
- **Tempest** is used mainly in literary language to describe a violent storm.

rain /reɪn/ *noun, verb*

● *noun* **1** [U, sing.] water that falls from the sky in separate drops: *There will be rain across the region tomorrow.* ◆ *Rain is forecast for the weekend.* ◆ *Don't go out in the rain.* ◆ *It's pouring rain* (= raining very hard). ◆ *heavy/torrential/driving rain* ◆ *The rain poured down.* ◆ *It looks like rain* (= as if it is going to rain). ◆ *A light rain began to fall.* ◆ *I think I felt a drop of rain.* ⊃ collocations at WEATHER ⊃ see also ACID RAIN, RAINY ⊃ note on page 1207 **2 the rains** [pl.] the season of heavy continuous rain in tropical countries: *The rains come in September.* **3** [sing.] **~ of sth** a large number of things falling from the sky at the same time: *a rain of arrows/stones* **IDM come rain, come shine| (come) rain or shine** whether there is rain or sun; whatever happens: *He goes jogging every morning, rain or shine.* ⊃ more at RIGHT *adj.*

● *verb* **1** [I] when it rains, water falls from the sky in drops: *Is it raining?* ◆ *It had been raining hard all night.* ◆ *It hardly rained at all last summer.* ◆ *It started to rain.* **2** [I, T] to fall or to make something fall on someone or something in large quantities: **~ (down) (on sb/sth)** *Bombs rained (down) on the city's streets.* ◆ *Falling debris rained on us from above.* ◆ *He covered his face as the blows rained down on him* (= he was hit repeatedly). ◆ **~ sth (down) (on sb/sth)** *The volcano erupted, raining hot ash over a wide area.* **IDM be raining cats and dogs** (*informal*) to be raining heavily **when it rains, it pours** (*saying*) used to say that when one bad thing happens to you, other bad things happen soon after **rain on sb's parade** (*informal*) to spoil something for someone **PHR V be ˌrained ˈout** (of an event) to be canceled or to have to stop because it is raining: *The game has been rained out again.*

ˈrain ˌbarrel *noun* a large BARREL (= container) for collecting rain as it flows off a roof

rain·bow /ˈreɪnboʊ/ *noun* a curved band of different colors that appears in the sky when the sun shines through rain: *all the colors of the rainbow*

ˌrainbow coaˈlition *noun* a political group formed by different parties who agree to work together, especially one that includes one or more very small parties

ˌrainbow ˌtrout *noun* [C, U] type of TROUT (= a fish that is often eaten as food, and often caught in the sport of fishing)

ˈrain check *noun* **1** a ticket that can be used later if a game, show, etc. is stopped or canceled **2** a printed piece of paper allowing you to buy an item later at the same reduced price, because it is temporarily not available: *If the store is out of the brand on sale, don't forget to get a rain check.* **IDM take a rain check (on sth)** (*informal*) to refuse an offer or invitation but say that you might accept it later: *"Are you coming for a drink?" "Can I take a rain check? I must get this finished tonight."*

rain·coat /ˈreɪnkoʊt/ *noun* a long light coat that keeps you dry in the rain ⊃ picture at CLOTHES

ˈrain date *noun* an alternative date when an event will take place if it has to be canceled on the original date because of rain: *July 15 is our annual family fun day (rain date July 22).*

rain·drop /ˈreɪndrɑp/ *noun* a single drop of rain

rain·fall /ˈreɪnfɔl/ *noun* [U, sing.] the total amount of rain that falls in a particular area in a particular amount of time; an occasion when rain falls: *There has been below average rainfall this month.* ◆ *an average annual rainfall of 10 in.*

rain·for·est /ˈreɪnˌfɔrəst; -ˌfɑr-/ *noun* [C, U] a thick forest in tropical parts of the world that have a lot of rain: *the Amazon rainforest* ⊃ compare CLOUD FOREST

rain·mak·er /ˈreɪnˌmeɪkər/ *noun* **1** (*business*) a person who makes a business grow and become successful **2** a person who is believed to have the power to make rain fall, especially among Native Americans

rain·out /ˈreɪnaʊt/ *noun* an occasion when bad weather prevents an event from starting or finishing

rain·proof /ˈreɪnpruf/ *adj.* that can keep rain out: *a rainproof jacket*

rain·storm /ˈreɪnstɔrm/ *noun* a heavy fall of rain

rain·wa·ter /ˈreɪnˌwɔtər; -ˌwɑtər/ *noun* [U] water that has fallen as rain: *a barrel for collecting rainwater*

rain·y /ˈreɪni/ *adj.* (rain·i·er, rain·i·est) having or bringing a lot of rain: *a rainy day* ◆ *the rainy season* ◆ *the rainiest place in the continental U.S.* **IDM save, keep, etc. sth for a rainy day** to save something, especially money, for a time when you will really need it

raise /reɪz/ *verb, noun*

● *verb*
> MOVE UPWARD **1 ~ sth** to lift or move something to a higher level: *She raised the gun and fired.* ◆ *He raised a hand in greeting.* ◆ *She raised her eyes from her work.* **ANT LOWER[1]** ⊃ note at RISE **2 ~ sth/sb/yourself (+ adv./prep.)** to move something/someone/yourself to a vertical position: *Somehow we managed to raise her to her feet.* ◆ *He raised himself up on one elbow.* **ANT LOWER[1]**
> INCREASE **3 ~ sth (to sth)** to increase the amount or level of something: *to raise salaries/prices/taxes* ◆ *They raised their offer to $500.* ◆ *How can we raise standards in schools?* ◆ *Don't tell her about the job until you know for sure—we don't want to raise her hopes* (= make her hope too much). ◆ *I've never heard him even raise his voice* (= speak louder because he was angry). ⊃ thesaurus box at SHOUT
> CHILD/ANIMAL **4** to care for a child or young animal until it is able to take care of itself: **~ sb/sth** *They were both raised in the South.* ◆ *kids raised on a diet of junk food* ◆ **~ sb/sth as sth** | **~ sb/sth + noun** *They raised her (as) a Catholic.* ◆ *I was born and raised a city boy.* ⊃ compare BRING UP
> COLLECT MONEY/PEOPLE **5 ~ sth** to bring or collect money or people together; to manage to get or form something: *to raise a loan* ◆ *We are raising money for charity.* ◆ *He began raising an army.* ⊃ see also FUND-RAISER
> MENTION SUBJECT **6 ~ sth** to mention something for people to discuss or someone to deal with **SYN BROACH**: *The book raises many important questions.* ◆ *I'm glad you raised the subject of money.*
> CAUSE **7 ~ sth** to cause or produce something; to make something appear: *to raise doubts in people's minds* ◆ *The plans for the new development have raised angry protests from local residents.* ◆ *It wasn't an easy audience, but he raised a laugh with his joke.* ◆ *It had been a difficult day but she managed to raise a smile.* ◆ *The horses' hooves raised a cloud of dust.* ⊃ see also CURTAIN RAISER
> FARM ANIMALS/CROPS **8 ~ sth** to breed particular farm animals; to grow particular crops: *to raise cattle/corn*
> END SOMETHING **9 ~ sth** to end a restriction on someone or something: *to raise a blockade/a ban/an embargo/a siege*
> IN CARD GAMES **10 ~ sb** to make a higher bet than another player in a card game: *I'll raise you another hundred dollars.*
> DEAD PERSON **11 ~ sb (from sth)** to make someone who has died come to life again **SYN RESURRECT**: *Christians believe that God raised Jesus from the dead.*
> ON RADIO/PHONE **12 ~ sb** to contact someone and speak to them by radio or telephone: *We managed to raise him on his cell phone.*
> MATHEMATICS **13 ~ sth to the power of sth** to multiply an amount by itself a particular number of times: *3 raised to the power of 3 is 27* (= 3×3×3).
IDM raise a/your hand against/to sb to hit, or threaten to hit, someone **raise the bar** to set a new, higher standard of quality or performance: *The factory has raised the bar on productivity, food safety, and quality.* **raise your eyebrows (at sth)** [often passive] to show that you disapprove of or are surprised by something: *Eyebrows were raised when he arrived without his wife.* **raise your glass (to sb)** to hold up your glass and wish someone happiness, good luck, etc. before you drink **raise hell** (*informal*) to protest angrily, especially in a way that causes trouble for someone **raise the roof** to produce or make someone produce a lot of noise in a building, for example by shouting or CHEERING **raise sb's spirits** to make someone feel more cheerful or

ʌ **cup**   ə **about**   eɪ **say**   aɪ **five**   ɔɪ **boy**   aʊ **now**   oʊ **go**   ər **bird**

brave **SYN** CHEER SB UP ⮯ more at ANTE, HACKLES, SIGHT *n.*, TEMPERATURE

PHR V 'raise sth to sb/sth to build or place a statue, etc. somewhere in honor or memory of someone or something: *The town raised a memorial to those killed in the war.*

- **noun** an increase in the money you are paid for the work you do: *Every time a worker gets a raise, her 401(k) contribution rate increases.*

raised /reɪzd/ *adj.* **1** higher than the area around: *a raised platform* **2** at a higher level than normal: *the sound of raised voices*

rai·sin /'reɪzn/ *noun* a dried GRAPE

rais·ing /'reɪzɪŋ/ *noun* [U, sing.] the act of raising something: *consciousness raising* ◆ *a raising of standards in schools* ⮯ see also FUND-RAISER

rai·son d'ê·tre /ˌreɪzoʊn 'dɛtrə/ *noun* [sing.] (from *French*) the most important reason for someone's or something's existence: *Work seems to be her sole raison d'être.*

rai·ta /'raɪtə/ *noun* [U] a S. Asian dish of finely chopped raw vegetables mixed with YOGURT

ra·ja (also **ra·jah**) /'rɑdʒə/ *noun* an Indian king or prince who ruled over a state in the past

rake /reɪk/ *noun, verb*
- **noun** **1** [C] a garden tool with a long handle and a row of metal pieces with points at the end, used for gathering fallen leaves and making soil smooth ⮯ picture at TOOL **2** [C] (*old-fashioned*) a man, especially a rich and fashionable one, who is thought to have low moral standards, for example because he drinks or gambles a lot or has sex with a lot of women **3** [sing.] (*technical*) the amount by which something, especially the stage in a theater, slopes
- **verb** **1** [T, I] to pull a rake over a surface in order to make it level or to remove something: ~ **(sth) (+ adv./prep.)** *We raked the leaves into a pile.* ◆ (*figurative*) *She raked a comb through her hair.* ◆ ~ **sth + adj.** *First rake the soil smooth.* **2** [T] ~ **sth (with sth)** to point a camera, light, gun, etc. at someone or something and move it slowly from one side to the other: *They raked the streets with machine-gun fire.* ◆ *Searchlights raked the grounds.* **3** [I] + **adv./prep.** to search a place carefully for something: *She raked around in her bag for her keys.* **4** [T, I] ~ **(sth)** to scratch the surface of something with a sharp object, especially your nails **IDM** **rake sb over the coals** to criticize someone severely because they have done something wrong **PHR V** ˌrake 'in sth (*informal*) to earn a lot of money, especially when it is done easily: *The movie raked in more than $300 million.* ◆ *She's been raking it in since she started her new job.* ˌrake 'over sth (*informal, disapproving*) to examine something that happened in the past in great detail and keep talking about it, when it should be forgotten: *She had no desire to rake over the past.* ˌrake sth↔'up (*informal, disapproving*) to mention something unpleasant that happened in the past and that other people would like to forget

raked /reɪkt/ *adj.* (*technical*) placed on a slope: *raked seating*

rak·ish /'reɪkɪʃ/ *adj.* **1** (of a man) acting like a RAKE (= in an immoral, etc. way) **SYN** DISSOLUTE **2** if you wear a hat at a **rakish angle**, it is not straight on your head and it makes you look relaxed and confident **SYN** JAUNTY ▶ **rak·ish·ly** *adv.*

ral·ly /'ræli/ *noun, verb*
- **noun** **1** [C] a large public meeting, especially one held to support a particular idea or political party: *to attend/hold a rally* ◆ *a peace/protest, etc. rally* ◆ *a mass rally in support of the strike* ⮯ see also PEP RALLY **2** [C] a race for cars, motorcycles, etc. over public roads: *the Monte Carlo rally* ◆ *rally driving* **3** [C] (in TENNIS and similar sports) a series of hits of the ball before a point is scored **4** [sing.] (in sports or on a stock exchange) an act of returning to a strong position after a period of difficulty or weakness **SYN** RECOVERY: *After a furious late rally, they finally scored.* ◆ *a rally in shares on the stock market*

- **verb** (**ral·lies, ral·ly·ing, ral·lied, ral·lied**) **1** [I, T] to come together or bring people together in order to help or support someone or something: ~ **(around/behind/to sb/sth)** *The party rallied behind the President.* ◆ *Many national newspapers rallied to his support.* ◆ ~ **sb/sth (around/behind/to sb/sth)** *They have rallied a great deal of support for their campaign.* **2** [I] to become healthier, stronger, etc. after a period of illness, weakness, etc. **SYN** RECOVER: *He never really rallied after the operation.* ◆ *The champion rallied to win the second set 6–3.* **3** [I] (*finance*) (especially of share prices or a country's money) to increase in value after falling in value **SYN** RECOVER: *The company's shares had rallied slightly by the close of trading.* ◆ *The pound rallied against the dollar.* **PHR V** ˌrally a'round | ˌrally a'round sb (of a group of people) to work together in order to help someone who is in a difficult or unpleasant situation

rallying ˌcry *noun* a phrase or an idea that is used to encourage people to support someone or something

rallying ˌpoint *noun* a person, a group, an event, etc. that makes people come together in support of something

RAM /ræm/ *noun* [U] computer memory in which data can be changed or removed and can be looked at in any order (the abbreviation for "random-access memory"): *256 megabytes of RAM*

ram /ræm/ *verb, noun*
- **verb** (**-mm-**) **1** ~ **sth** (of a vehicle, a ship, etc.) to drive into or hit another vehicle, ship, etc. with force, sometimes deliberately: *Two passengers were injured when their taxi was rammed from behind by a bus.* **2** ~ **sth + adv./prep.** to push something somewhere with force: *She rammed the key into the lock.* ◆ (*figurative*) *The spending cuts had been rammed through Congress.* **IDM** **ram sth↔home** to emphasize an idea, argument, etc. very strongly to make sure people listen to it ⮯ more at THROAT **PHR V** ˌram 'into sth | ˌram sth 'into sth to hit against something, or to make something hit against something, with force: *He rammed his truck into the back of the one in front.*
- **noun** **1** a male sheep ⮯ compare EWE **2** a part in a machine that is used for hitting something very hard or for lifting or moving things: *hydraulic rams* ⮯ see also BAT-TERING RAM

Ram·a·dan /'rɑmədɑn; ˌrɑmə'dɑn/ *noun* [U, C] the 9th month of the Muslim year, when Muslims do not eat or drink between SUNRISE and SUNSET

ram·ble /'ræmbl/ *verb, noun*
- **verb** **1** [I] + **adv./prep.** to walk for pleasure, especially in the countryside: *We spent the afternoon rambling in the woods.* **2** [I] to talk about someone or something in a confused way, especially for a long time: *He had lost track of what he was saying and began to ramble.* ◆ ~ **(on) (about sb/sth)** *What is she rambling on about now?* **3** [I] (+ **adv./prep.**) (of plants) to grow in many different directions, especially over other plants or objects: *Climbing plants rambled over the front of the house.* ⮯ see also RAMBLING
- **noun** **1** a long walk for pleasure: *to go for a ramble in the country* **2** a long confused speech or piece of writing: *She went into a long ramble about the evils of television.*

ram·bler /'ræmblər/ *noun* **1** a plant, especially a ROSE, that grows up walls, fences, etc. **2** a person who walks in the countryside for pleasure, especially as part of an organized group

ram·bling /'ræmblɪŋ/ *adj., noun*
- **adj.** **1** (of a building) spreading in various directions with no particular pattern **SYN** SPRAWLING **2** (of a speech or piece of writing) very long and confused **SYN** INCOHERENT: *a rambling letter* **3** (of a plant) growing or climbing in all directions, for example up a wall: *a rambling rose*
- **noun** **1** [U] the activity of walking for pleasure in the countryside **2** **ramblings** [pl.] speech or writing that continues for a long time without saying much and seems very confused: *the ramblings of a madman*

Ram·bo /'ræmboʊ/ *noun* (*informal*) a way of referring to a very strong and aggressive man **ORIGIN** From the name of the main character in David Morrell's novel *First Blood*, which was made popular in three movies in the 1980s.

ram·bunc·tious /ræm'bʌŋkʃəs/ *adj.* (*informal*) full of energy in a cheerful and noisy way **SYN** BOISTEROUS

ram·bu·tan /'ræmbʊˌtæn; 'rɑmbʊˌtan/ *noun* a red tropical fruit with soft pointed parts on its skin and a slightly sour taste

ram·e·kin /'ræməkən/ *noun* a small dish for baking and serving food for one person ⊃ picture at KITCHEN

ra·men /'rɑmən/ *noun* [U] thin Asian NOODLES, usually served in a light soup

ram·i·fi·ca·tion /ˌræməfə'keɪʃn/ *noun* [usually pl.] one of the large number of complicated and unexpected results that follow an action or a decision **SYN** COMPLICATION: *These changes are bound to have widespread social ramifications.*

ram·i·fy /'ræməˌfaɪ/ *verb* (ram·i·fies, ram·i·fy·ing, ram·i·fied, ram·i·fied) [I] (*formal*) to spread out and form branches: *A system of canals was built, ramifying throughout the country.*

ramp /ræmp/ *noun, verb*
• *noun* **1** a slope that joins two parts of a road, path, building, etc. when one is higher than the other: *Ramps should be provided for wheelchair users.* **2** a road used for driving onto or off a major road such as a HIGHWAY: *a freeway exit ramp* ⊃ see also OFF-RAMP, ON-RAMP **3** a slope or set of steps that can be moved, used for loading a vehicle or getting on or off a plane: *a loading ramp*
• *verb*
  PHR V ˌramp sth↔'up to make something increase in amount

ram·page *noun, verb*
• *noun* /'ræmpeɪdʒ/ [usually sing.] a sudden period of wild and violent behavior, often causing damage and destruction: *Gangs of youths went on the rampage in the city yesterday.*
• *verb* /'ræmpeɪdʒ; ræm'peɪdʒ/ [I] + adv./prep. (of people or animals) to move through a place in a group, usually breaking things and causing damage: *a herd of rampaging elephants*

ramp·ant /'ræmpənt/ *adj.* **1** (of something bad) existing or spreading everywhere in a way that cannot be controlled **SYN** UNCHECKED: *rampant inflation* ♦ *Unemployment is now rampant in most of the Midwest.* **2** (of plants) growing thickly and very fast in a way that cannot be controlled ► ramp·ant·ly *adv.*

ram·part /'ræmpɑrt/ *noun* [usually pl.] a high wide wall of stone or earth with a path on top, built around a castle, town, etc. to defend it

ram·rod /'ræmrɑd/ *noun* a long straight piece of iron used in the past to push EXPLOSIVES into a gun
  IDM ramrod straight (of a person) with a very straight back and looking serious and formal

ram·shack·le /'ræmˌʃækl/ *adj.* **1** (of buildings, vehicles, furniture, etc.) in a very bad condition and needing repair **SYN** TUMBLEDOWN **2** (of an organization or a system) badly organized or designed and not likely to last very long **SYN** RICKETY

ran *pt of* RUN

ranch /ræntʃ/ *noun* **1** a large farm, especially in the western U.S. or Canada, where cows, horses, sheep, etc. are bred: *a cattle/sheep ranch* ♦ *ranch hands* (= the people who work on a ranch) ⊃ see also DUDE RANCH **2** = RANCH HOUSE (2)

ˌranch 'dressing *noun* [U, C] a thick white mixture of MAYONNAISE, BUTTERMILK, etc. used to add flavor to a salad

ranch·er /'ræntʃər/ *noun* a person who owns, manages, or works on a ranch: *a cattle rancher*

'ranch house *noun* **1** a house on a ranch **2** (also ranch) a house built all on one level, that is very wide but not very deep from front to back and has a roof that is not very steep ⊃ compare BUNGALOW

ranch·ing /'ræntʃɪŋ/ *noun* [U] the activity of running a RANCH: *cattle/sheep ranching*

ran·cid /'rænsəd/ *adj.* if food containing fat is **rancid**, it tastes or smells unpleasant because it is no longer fresh

ran·cor (*CanE usually* **ran·cour**) /'ræŋkər/ *noun* [U] (*formal*) feelings of hatred and a desire to hurt other people, especially because you think that someone has done something unfair to you **SYN** BITTERNESS: *She learned to accept criticism without rancor.* ► ran·cor·ous /'ræŋkərəs/ *adj.*: *a rancorous legal battle*

rand /rænd; rɑnt/ *noun* (*pl.* rand) the unit of money in the Republic of South Africa

R & B /ˌɑr ən 'bi/ *abbr.* RHYTHM AND BLUES

R & D /ˌɑr ən 'di/ *abbr.* RESEARCH AND DEVELOPMENT

ran·dom **AWL** /'rændəm/ *adj., noun*
• *adj.* **1** [usually before noun] done, chosen, etc. without someone deciding in advance what is going to happen, or without any regular pattern: *the random killing of innocent people* ♦ *a random sample/selection* (= in which each thing has an equal chance of being chosen) ♦ *The information is processed in a random order.* ♦ *He grabbed a random pair of jeans and an old red shirt.* ♦ *She dodged the random items that were on the concrete floor.* **2** [only before noun] (*informal*) (especially of a person) not known or not identified: *Some random guy gave me a hundred bucks.* **3** (*informal*) a thing or person that is **random** is strange and does not make sense, often in a way that amuses or interests you: *Mom, you are so random!* ♦ *The humor is great because it's just so random and unhinged from reality.* ► ran·dom·ly **AWL** *adv.*: *The winning numbers are randomly selected by computer.* ♦ *My phone seems to turn itself off randomly.* ran·dom·ness **AWL** *noun* [U]: *It introduced an element of randomness into the situation.*
• *noun*
  IDM at random without deciding in advance what is going to happen, or without any regular pattern: *She opened the book at random* (= not at any particular page) *and started reading.* ♦ *The terrorists fired into the crowd at random.* ♦ *Names were chosen at random from a list.*

ˌrandom 'access *noun* [U] (*computing*) the ability in a computer to go straight to data items without having to read through items stored previously

ˌrandom-ˌaccess 'memory *noun* [U] (*computing*) = RAM

ran·dom·ize /'rændəˌmaɪz/ *verb* ~ sth (*technical*) to use a method in an experiment, a piece of research, etc. that gives every item an equal chance of being considered; to put things in a RANDOM order

R & R /ˌɑr ən 'ɑr/ *abbr.* **1** rest and recreation (doing things for enjoyment rather than working) **2** (*medical*) rescue and resuscitation

rang *pt of* RING²

range 🔑 **AWL** /reɪndʒ/ *noun, verb*
• *noun*
  ❯ VARIETY **1** [C, usually sing.] ~ (of sth) a variety of things of a particular type: *The hotel offers a wide range of facilities.* ♦ *There is a full range of activities for kids.*
  ❯ LIMITS **2** [C, usually sing.] the limits between which something varies: *Most of the students are in the 17-20 age range.* ♦ *There will be an increase in the range of 0 to 3 percent.* ♦ *It's difficult to find a house in our price range* (= that we can afford). ♦ *This was outside the range of his experience.*
  ❯ DISTANCE **3** [C, U] the distance over which something can be seen or heard: *The child was now out of her range of vision* (= not near enough for her to see). **4** [C, U] the distance over which a gun or other weapon can hit things: *These missiles have a range of 300 miles.* ⊃ see also CLOSE-RANGE, LONG-RANGE, SHORT-RANGE **5** [C] the distance that a vehicle will travel before it needs more fuel
  ❯ MUSIC **6** [C, usually sing.] all of the notes that a person's voice or a musical instrument can produce, from high to low: *She was gifted with an incredible vocal range.*
  ❯ ABILITY **7** [C, usually sing.] the full extent of a person's

t tea   ṭ butter   d did   k cat   g got   tʃ chin   dʒ June   f fall

knowledge or abilities: *Those two movies give some indication of his range as an actor.*
> OF MOUNTAINS **8** [C] a line or group of mountains or hills: *the great mountain range of the Alps*
> FOR SHOOTING **9** [C] an area of land where people can practice shooting or where bombs, etc. can be tested: *a shooting range* ⊃ see also DRIVING RANGE, RIFLE RANGE
> OF PRODUCTS **10** [C] a set of products of a particular type **SYN** LINE: *our new range of hair products* ⊃ see also MIDRANGE, TOP OF THE LINE
> STOVE **11** a large piece of equipment for cooking food, containing an oven and gas or electric rings on top **SYN** STOVE: *Cook the meat on a low heat on top of the range.*
> FOR COWS **12 the range** [sing.] a large open area for keeping cows, etc. ⊃ see also FREE-RANGE
IDM in/within range (of sth) near enough to be reached, seen, or heard: *He shouted angrily at anyone within range.* **out of range (of sth)** too far away to be reached, seen, or heard: *The cat stayed well out of range of the children.*

● *verb*
> VARY **1** [I] to vary between two particular amounts, sizes, etc., including others between them: ~ **from A to B** *to range in size/length/price from A to B* ◆ *Accommodations range from tourist class to luxury hotels.* ◆ ~ **between A and B** *Estimates of the damage range between $1 million and $5 million.* **2** [I] to include a variety of different things in addition to those mentioned: ~ **from A to B** *She has had a number of different jobs, ranging from chef to swimming instructor.* ◆ + **adv./prep.** *The conversation ranged widely* (= covered a lot of different topics). ⊃ see also WIDE-RANGING
> ARRANGE **3** [T, usually passive] ~ **sb/sth/yourself + adv./prep.** (*formal*) to arrange people or things in a particular position or order: *The delegates ranged themselves around the table.* ◆ *Spectators were ranged along the whole route of the procession.*
> MOVE AROUND **4** [I, T] to move around an area: + **adv./prep.** *He ranges far and wide in search of inspiration for his paintings.* ◆ ~ **sth** *Her eyes ranged the room.*
PHRV **range yourself/sb a'gainst/'with sb/sth** [usually passive] to join with other people to oppose or support someone or something: *The whole family seemed ranged against him.* **'range over sth** to include a variety of different subjects: *His lecture ranged over a number of topics.*

range·find·er /ˈreɪndʒˌfaɪndər/ *noun* an instrument for estimating how far away an object is, used with a camera or gun

rang·er /ˈreɪndʒər/ *noun* **1** a person whose job is to take care of a park, a forest, or an area of countryside **2 Ranger** a soldier who is trained to make quick attacks in enemy areas ⊃ compare COMMANDO

rang·y /ˈreɪndʒi/ *adj.* (of a person or an animal) having long thin arms and/or legs

rank ✏ /ræŋk/ *noun, verb, adj.*
● *noun*
> POSITION IN ORGANIZATION/ARMY, ETC. **1** [U, C] the position, especially a high position, that someone has in a particular organization, society, etc.: *She was not used to associating with people of high social rank.* ◆ *He rose through the ranks to become managing director.* ◆ *Within months she was elevated to ministerial rank.* ⊃ see also RANKING **2** [C, U] the position that someone has in the army, navy, police, etc.: *He was soon promoted to the rank of captain.* ◆ *officers of junior/senior rank* ◆ *a campaign to attract more women into the military ranks* ◆ *officers, and other ranks* (= people who are not officers) ◆ *The colonel was stripped of his rank* (= was given a lower position, especially as a punishment). **3 the ranks** [pl.] the position of ordinary soldiers rather than officers: *He served in the ranks for most of the war.* ◆ *He rose from the ranks* (= from being an ordinary soldier) *to become a captain.*
> QUALITY **4** [sing.] the degree to which someone or something is of high quality: *a painter of the first rank* ◆ *a country that is no longer in the front rank of world powers* ◆ *The findings are arranged in rank order according to performance.*
> MEMBERS OF GROUP **5 the ranks** [pl.] the members of a

particular group or organization: *We have a number of international players in our ranks.* ◆ *At 50, he was forced to join the ranks of the unemployed.* ◆ *There were serious divisions within the party's own ranks.*
> LINE/ROW **6** [C] a line or row of soldiers, police, etc. standing next to each other: *They watched as ranks of marching infantry passed the window.* **7** [C] a line or row of people or things: *massed ranks of spectators* ◆ *The trees grew in serried ranks* (= very closely together).
IDM break ranks 1 (of soldiers, police, etc.) to fail to remain in line **2** (of the members of a group) to refuse to support the group or the organization of which they are members ⊃ more at CLOSE¹ *v.*, PULL *v.*
● *verb* (not used in the progressive tenses)
> GIVE POSITION **1** [T, I] to give someone or something a particular position on a scale according to quality, importance, success, etc.; to have a position of this kind: ~ **sb/sth (+ adv./prep.)** *The tasks have been ranked in order of difficulty.* ◆ *She is currently the highest ranked player in the world.* ◆ *top-ranked players* ◆ ~ **sb/sth as sth** *Voters regularly rank education as being more important than defense.* ◆ ~ **(sb/sth) + adj.** *At the height of her career she ranked second in the world.* ◆ ~ **sb/sth + noun** *The university is ranked number one in the country for engineering.* ◆ ~ **as sth** *It certainly doesn't rank as his greatest win.* ◆ **(+ adv./prep.)** *The restaurant ranks among the finest in town.* ◆ *This must rank with* (= be as good as) *the greatest movies ever made.*
> PUT IN LINE/ROW **2** [T, usually passive] ~ **sth** to arrange objects in a line or row
● *adj.* **1** having a strong unpleasant smell: *The house was full of the rank smell of urine.* **2** [only before noun] used to emphasize a particular quality, state, etc.: *an example of rank stupidity* ◆ *The winning horse was a rank outsider.* **3** (of plants, etc.) growing too thickly

the ˌrank and 'file *noun* [sing.] **1** the ordinary soldiers who are not officers **2** the ordinary members of an organization: *the rank and file of the workforce* ◆ *rank-and-file members*

'rank correˌlation *noun* [U] (*statistics*) a method for finding to what extent two sets of numbers, each arranged in order, are connected or have an effect on each other

rank·ing /ˈræŋkɪŋ/ *noun, adj.*
● *noun* **1** the position of someone or something on a scale that shows how good or important they are in relation to other similar people or things, especially in sports: *He has improved his ranking this season from 67th to 30th.* ◆ *She has retained her No.1 world ranking.* **2 the rankings** [pl.] an official list showing the best players of a particular sport in order of how successful they are
● *adj.* **1** having a high or the highest rank in an organization, etc.: *a ranking diplomat* ◆ *He was the ranking officer* (= the most senior officer present at a particular time). **2** (in compounds) having the particular rank mentioned: *high-ranking/low-ranking police officers* ◆ *a top-ranking player*

ran·kle /ˈræŋkl/ *verb* [I, T] if something such as an event or a remark **rankles**, it makes you feel angry or upset for a long time: ~ **(sb)** *Her comments still rankled.* ◆ ~ **with sb** *His decision to sell the land still rankled with her.*

ran·sack /ˈrænsæk/ *verb* ~ **sth (for sth)** to make a place messy, causing damage, because you are looking for something **SYN** TURN UPSIDE DOWN: *The house had been ransacked by burglars.*

ran·som /ˈrænsəm/ *noun, verb*
● *noun* [C, U] money that is paid to someone so that they will set free a person who is being kept as a prisoner by them: *The kidnappers demanded a ransom of $50,000 from his family.* ◆ *a ransom demand/note* ◆ *ransom money* ◆ *They are refusing to pay ransom for her release.*
IDM hold sb for ransom 1 to keep someone as a prisoner and demand that other people pay you an amount of money before you set them free **2** (*disapproving*) to take action that puts someone in a very difficult situation in order to force them to do what you want ⊃ more at KING

- **verb ~ sb** to pay money to someone so that they will set free the person that they are keeping as a prisoner: *The kidnapped children were all ransomed and returned home unharmed.*

rant /rænt/ *verb* [I, T] **~ (on) (about sth)** | **~ at sb** | **+ speech** (*disapproving*) to speak or complain about something in a loud and/or angry way ▶ **rant** *noun* **IDM** **rant and rave** (*disapproving*) to show that you are angry by shouting or complaining loudly for a long time

rant·ings /ˈræntɪŋz/ *noun* [pl.] loud or angry comments or speeches that continue for a long time

rap /ræp/ *noun, verb*
- **noun** **1** [C] a quick sharp hit or knock: *There was a sharp rap on the door.* **2** [U] a type of popular music with a fast strong rhythm and words that are spoken fast, not sung: *a rap song/artist* **3** [C] a rap song **4** [C] (*informal*) a criminal CONVICTION (= the fact of being found guilty of a crime) **5** [sing.] (*informal*) an unfair judgment on something or someone: *He denounced the criticisms as "just one bum rap after another."* ◆ *Wolves get a bad rap, says a woman who owns three.*
  IDM **(give sb/get) a rap on/over/across the knuckles** (*informal*) (to give sb/receive) gentle criticism for something: *We got a rap over the knuckles for being late.* **take the rap (for sb/sth)** (*informal*) to be blamed or punished, especially for something you have not done **SYN** TAKE THE BLAME: *She was prepared to take the rap for the shoplifting, though it had been her sister's idea.* ⊃ more at BEAT *v.*
- **verb** (-pp-) **1** [I, T] to hit a hard object or surface several times quickly, making a noise: **(+ adv./prep.)** *She rapped angrily on the door.* ◆ **~ sth (+ adv./prep.)** *He rapped the table with his pen.* **2** [T] **~ sth (out)** | **+ speech** to say something suddenly and quickly in a loud, angry way: *He walked through the store, rapping out orders to his staff.* **3** [I, T] **~ (sth)** (*music*) to say the words of a rap ⊃ see also RAPPER **4** [T] **~ sb/sth (for sth/for doing sth)** (used mainly in newspapers) to criticize someone severely, usually publicly: *Some of the teachers were rapped for poor performance.*
  IDM **rap sb on/over the knuckles** | **rap sb's knuckles** to criticize someone gently for something

ra·pa·cious /rəˈpeɪʃəs/ *adj.* (*formal, disapproving*) wanting more money or goods than you need or have a right to have **SYN** GRASPING ▶ **ra·pa·cious·ly** *adv.* **ra·pac·i·ty** /rəˈpæsəti/ *noun* [U]: *the rapacity of landowners seeking greater profit*

rape /reɪp/ *verb, noun*
- **verb ~ sb** to force someone to have sex with you when they do not want to by threatening or using violence ⊃ see also RAPIST
- **noun** **1** [U, C] the crime of forcing someone to have sex with you, especially using violence: *He was charged with rape.* ◆ *a rape victim* ◆ *an increase in the number of reported rapes* ⊃ see also DATE RAPE, RAPIST **2** [sing.] **~ (of sth)** (*literary*) the act of destroying or spoiling an area in a way that seems unnecessary **3** [U] a plant with bright yellow flowers, grown as food for farm animals and for its seeds that are used to make oil

rape·seed /ˈreɪpsiːd/ *noun* [U] seeds of the rape plant, used mainly for cooking oil ⊃ see also CANOLA

rap·id 🔑 /ˈræpəd/ *adj.*
1 [usually before noun] happening in a short period of time: *rapid change/expansion/growth* ◆ *a rapid rise/decline in sales* ◆ *The patient made a rapid recovery.* **2** done or happening very quickly: *a rapid pulse/heartbeat* ◆ *The guard fired four shots in rapid succession.* ◆ *The disease is spreading at a rapid rate.* ⊃ note at FAST ▶ **ra·pid·i·ty** /rəˈpɪdəti/ *noun* [U]: *the rapidity of economic growth* ◆ *The disease is spreading with alarming rapidity.* 🔑 **rap·id·ly** /ˈræpədli/ *adv.*: *a rapidly growing economy* ◆ *Crime figures are rising rapidly.*

rapid-'fire *adj.* [only before noun] **1** (of questions, comments, etc.) spoken very quickly, one after the other **2** (of a gun) able to shoot bullets very quickly, one after the other

rapid-re'sponse *adj.* [only before noun] having the necessary training and equipment to be able to act quickly when there is an emergency such as an accident, an attack, or a natural disaster: *a U.N. rapid-response unit* ◆ *rapid-response systems for early detection of the virus*

rap·ids /ˈræpədz/ *noun* [pl.] part of a river where the water flows very fast, usually over rocks: *to shoot the rapids* (= to travel quickly over them in a boat)

rapid 'transit *noun* [U] the system of fast public transportation in cities, especially the SUBWAY ⊃ compare MASS TRANSIT ⊃ see also TRANSIT

ra·pi·er /ˈreɪpiər/ *noun* a long, thin, light SWORD that has two sharp edges: (*figurative*) *rapier wit* (= very quick and sharp)

rap·ist /ˈreɪpɪst/ *noun* a person who RAPES someone (= forces someone to have sex when they do not want to)

rap·pel /rəˈpɛl; ræ-/ *verb* (-ll-) [I] **~ (down, off, etc. sth)** to go down a steep CLIFF or rock while attached to a rope, pushing against the slope or rock with your feet ⊃ picture at SPORT ▶ **rap·pel** *noun*

rap·per /ˈræpər/ *noun* a person who speaks the words of a RAP song

rap·port /rəˈpɔr; ræ-/ *noun* [sing., U] **~ (with sb)** | **~ (between A and B)** a friendly relationship in which people understand each other very well: *She understood the importance of establishing a close rapport with clients.*

rap·proche·ment /ˌræproʊʃˈmɑ̃; -ˈmɑn/ *noun* [sing., U] (from French, *formal*) a situation in which the relationship between two countries or groups of people becomes more friendly after a period during which they were enemies: **~ (with sb)** *policies aimed at bringing about a rapprochement with China* ◆ **~ (between A and B)** *There now seems little chance of rapprochement between the warring factions.*

'rap sheet *noun* (*informal*) a record kept by the police of the crimes that someone has committed

rapt /ræpt/ *adj.* so interested in one particular thing that you are not aware of anything else: *a rapt audience* ◆ *She listened to the speaker with rapt attention.* ▶ **rapt·ly** *adv.*

rap·tor /ˈræptər/ *noun* (*technical*) any BIRD OF PREY (= a bird that kills other creatures for food)

rap·ture /ˈræptʃər/ *noun* [U] (*formal*) a feeling of extreme pleasure and happiness **SYN** DELIGHT: *Charles listened with rapture to her singing.* ◆ *The children gazed at her in rapture.* **IDM** **be in, go into, etc. raptures (about/over sb/sth)** to feel or express extreme pleasure or enthusiasm for someone or something: *The critics went into raptures about her performance.* ◆ *The last-minute goal sent the fans into raptures.*

rap·tur·ous /ˈræptʃərəs/ *adj.* [usually before noun] expressing extreme pleasure or enthusiasm for someone or something **SYN** ECSTATIC: *rapturous applause* ⊃ thesaurus box at EXCITED ▶ **rap·tur·ous·ly** *adv.*

rare 🔑 /rɛr/ *adj.* (rar·er, rar·est)
1 not done, seen, happening, etc. very often: *a rare disease/occurrence/sight* ◆ **~ (for sb/sth to do sth)** *It's extremely rare for it to be this hot in April.* ◆ **~ (to do sth)** *It is rare to find such loyalty these days.* ◆ *On the rare occasions when they met he hardly even dared speak to her.* ◆ *It was a rare (= very great) honor to be made a fellow of the college.* **2** existing only in small numbers and therefore valuable or interesting: *a rare book/coin/stamp* ◆ *a rare breed/plant* ◆ *This species is extremely rare.* **3** (of meat) cooked for only a short time so that the inside is still red ⊃ compare WELL DONE ⊃ see also RARITY

rare·bit /ˈrɛrbɪt/ *noun* = WELSH RAREBIT

rare 'earth *noun* (also **rare 'earth element**) any one of a group of chemical elements that have similar properties and tend to occur together in nature

rar·e·fac·tion /ˌrɛrəˈfækʃn/ *noun* [U] a decrease in the DENSITY of air or a gas: *rarefaction at higher levels in the atmosphere*

rar·e·fied /ˈrɛrəˌfaɪd/ adj. [usually before noun] **1** (often disapproving) understood or experienced by only a very small group of people who share a particular area of knowledge or activity: the rarefied atmosphere of academic life **2** (of air) containing less OXYGEN than usual

'**rare gas** noun (chemistry) = NOBLE GAS

rare·ly ✏ /ˈrɛrli/ adv.
not very often: She is rarely seen in public nowadays. ◆ We rarely agree on what to do. ◆ a rarely performed play ◆ (formal) Rarely has a debate attracted so much media attention.

rar·ing /ˈrɛrɪŋ/ adj. ~ **to do sth** (informal) very enthusiastic about starting to do something: The new recruits arrived early, all dressed up and **raring to go** (= to start). ◆ She is raring to get back to work after her operation.

rar·i·ty /ˈrɛrəti/ noun (pl. rar·i·ties) **1** [C] a person or thing that is unusual and is therefore often valuable or interesting: Women are still something of a rarity in senior positions in business. ◆ His collection of plants contains many rarities. **2** (also less frequent rare·ness) [U] the quality of being rare: The value of antiques will depend on their condition and rarity.

ras·cal /ˈræskl/ noun **1** (humorous) a person, especially a child or man, who shows a lack of respect for other people and enjoys playing tricks on them: Come here, you little rascal! **2** (old-fashioned) a dishonest man ▶ **ras·cal·ly** /-kəli/ adj. (old-fashioned)

rash /ræʃ/ noun, adj.
● **noun 1** [C, usually sing.] an area of red spots on a person's skin, caused by an illness or a reaction to something: I woke up covered in a rash. ◆ I break out in a rash (= a rash appears on my skin) if I eat chocolate. ◆ The sun brought her out in (= caused) an itchy rash. ◆ a heat rash (= caused by heat) ⊃ compare SPOT ⊃ see also DIAPER RASH **2** [sing.] ~ (of sth) a lot of something; a series of unpleasant things that happen over a short period of time **SYN** SPATE: a rash of movies about life in prison ◆ There has been a rash of burglaries in the area over the last month.
● **adj.** (of people or their actions) doing something that may not be sensible without first thinking about the possible results; done in this way **SYN** IMPULSIVE, RECKLESS: a rash young man ◆ ~ **(to do sth)** It would be rash to assume that everyone will agree with you on this. ◆ Think twice before doing anything rash. ◆ This is what happens when you make rash decisions. ▶ **rash·ly** adv.: She had rashly promised to lend him the money. **rash·ness** noun [U]: He bitterly regretted his rashness.

rasp /ræsp/ noun, verb
● **noun 1** [sing.] a rough unpleasant sound **2** [C] a metal tool with a long blade covered with rows of sharp points, used for making rough surfaces smooth
● **verb 1** [T, I] to say something in a rough unpleasant voice **SYN** CROAK: + speech "Where have you been?" she rasped. ◆ ~ **(sth) (out)** He rasped out some instructions. **2** [I] to make a rough unpleasant sound **SYN** GRATE: a rasping cough/voice **3** [T] ~ **sth** to rub a surface with a rasp or with something rough that works or feels like a rasp: The wind rasped his face.

rasp·ber·ry /ˈræzˌbɛri/ noun (pl. rasp·ber·ries) **1** a small dark red soft fruit that grows on bushes: raspberry jam ⊃ picture at FRUIT **2** (also Bronx cheer) (informal) a rude sound made by sticking out the tongue and blowing: to blow a raspberry at someone

rasp·y /ˈræspi/ adj. (of someone's voice) having a rough sound, as if the person has a sore throat **SYN** CROAKY

Ras·ta·far·i·an /ˌræstəˈfɛriən; ˌrɑstəˈfɑr-/ (also informal Rast·a) noun a member of a Jamaican religious group that worships the former Emperor of Ethiopia, Haile Selassie, and that believes that black people will one day return to Africa. Rastafarians often wear DREADLOCKS and have other distinguishing patterns of behavior and dress. ▶ **Ras·ta·far·i·an** (also informal Ras·ta) adj. **Ras·ta·far·i·an·ism** /-iəˌnɪzəm/ noun [U]

ras·ter·ize /ˈræstəˌraɪz/ (also rip) verb ~ **sth** (computing) to change text or images into a form in which they can be printed

rat /ræt/ noun, verb
● **noun 1** a small animal with a long tail, that looks like a large mouse, usually considered a PEST (= an animal that is disliked because it destroys food or spreads disease): rat poison ⊃ picture at RODENT ⊃ compare RUG RAT **2** (informal, disapproving) an unpleasant person, especially one who is not loyal or who tricks someone **IDM** see SINK v., SMELL v.
● **verb** (-tt-)
PHR V '**rat on sb** (also rat sb↔**out (to sb)**) (informal, disapproving) to tell someone in authority about something wrong that someone else has done: Where I come from, you don't rat on your friends. ◆ Someone ratted us out to the police.

rat-a-tat /ˌræt ə ˈtæt/ (also ˌrat-a-ˌtat-ˈtat, ˌrat-ˌtat-ˈtat) noun [sing.] a series of short loud sounds like those made by knocking on a door or shooting bullets one after the other quickly: the rat-a-tat-tat of drums

ra·ta·touille /ˌrætəˈtui/ noun [U, C] (from French) a dish of onions, BELL PEPPERS, EGGPLANTS, ZUCCHINI, and tomatoes cooked together

ratch·et /ˈrætʃət/ noun, verb
● **noun** a wheel or bar with teeth along the edge and a metal piece that fits between the teeth, allowing movement in one direction only

ratchet

● **verb**
PHR V ˌratchet (sth)↔ˈup to increase, or make something increase, repeatedly and by small amounts: Overuse of credit cards has ratcheted up consumer debt to unacceptable levels.

rate ✏ /reɪt/ noun, verb
● **noun 1** a measurement of the speed at which something happens: Most people walk at an average rate of 2 miles an hour. ◆ The number of reported crimes is increasing at an alarming rate. ◆ Figures published today show another fall in the rate of inflation. ◆ At the rate you work, you'll never finish! **2** a measurement of the number of times something happens or exists during a particular period: Local businesses are closing at a/the rate of three a year. ◆ a high/low/rising rate of unemployment ◆ the annual crime/divorce rate ◆ His pulse rate dropped suddenly. ◆ a high success/failure rate ⊃ see also BIRTH RATE, DEATH RATE **3** a fixed amount of money that is charged or paid for something: advertising/insurance/postal, etc. rates ◆ to pay someone a low/high hourly rate ◆ We offer special reduced rates for students. ◆ a fixed-rate mortgage (= one in which the amount of money paid back each month is fixed for a particular period) ◆ the basic rate of tax (= the lowest amount that is paid by everyone) ◆ exchange/interest rates ◆ rates of exchange/interest ⊃ see also FLAT RATE, PRIME RATE, RACK RATE, FIRST-RATE, SECOND-RATE, THIRD-RATE **IDM** at any rate (informal) **1** used to say that a particular fact is true despite what has happened in the past or what may happen in the future: Well, that's one good piece of news at any rate. ◆ I may be away on business next week but at any rate I'll be back by Friday. **2** used to show that you are being more accurate about something that you have just said: He said he'll be coming tomorrow. At any rate, I think that's what he said. **3** used to show that what you have just said is not as important as what you are going to say: There were maybe 60 or 70 people there. At any rate, the room was packed. at this/that rate (informal) used to say what will happen if a particular situation continues to develop in the same way: At this rate, we'll be bankrupt soon. ⊃ more at GOING adj.
● **verb** (not used in the progressive tenses) **1** [T, I] to have or think that someone or something has a particular level of quality, value, etc.: ~ sb/sth (+ adv./prep.) The university is highly rated for its research. ◆ They rated him highly as a colleague. ◆ ~ sb/sth + adj. Voters continue to rate education

---

i see   ɪ sit   ɛ ten   æ cat   ɑ hot   ɔ saw   ʊ put   u too

high on their list of priorities. ◆ ~ **sb/sth (as) sth** | ~ **sb/sth**
+ **noun** *The show was rated (as) a success by critics and
audiences.* ◆ ~ **as sth** *The game rated as one of their worst
defeats.* ◆ + **adj.** *I'm afraid our needs do not rate very high with
this administration.* **2** [T, usually passive] to place someone or
something in a particular position on a scale in relation to
similar people or things **SYN** RANK: ~ **sb/sth (+ adv./
prep.)** *The schools were rated according to their exam results.*
◆ *a top-rated program* ◆ ~ **sb/sth + noun** *She is currently rated
number two in the world.* **3** [T] ~ **sth** to be good, important,
etc. enough to be treated in a particular way **SYN** MERIT:
The incident didn't even rate a mention in the press.
4 [T, usually passive] ~ **sth (+ noun)** to state that a movie,
video, or computer game is suitable for a particular
audience ⊃ see also X-RATED

THESAURUS

rate

charge ◆ **fee** ◆ **rent** ◆ **fine** ◆ **fare** ◆ **toll**

These are all words for an amount of money that is
charged or paid for something.

rate a fixed amount of money that is asked or paid for
something: *a low hourly rate* ◆ *interest rates*

charge an amount of money that is asked for goods or
services: *an admission charge* ◆ *a rental charge*

fee (*somewhat formal*) an amount of money that you have
to pay for professional advice or services, to go to a
school or college, or to join an organization: *legal fees*
◆ *an annual membership fee*

rent an amount of money that you regularly have to pay
for use of a home or an office

fine a sum of money that must be paid as punishment
for breaking a law or rule: *a parking fine*

fare the money that you pay to travel by bus, plane, taxi,
etc.

toll an amount of money that you have to pay to use a
particular road or bridge.

PATTERNS

- (a) rate/charge/fee/rent/fine/fare/toll **for** sth
- (a) rate/charge/fee/rent/toll **on** sth
- at a rate/charge/fee/rent/fare **of**...
- **for** a charge/fee
- to **pay** (a) rate/charge/fee/rent/fine/fare/toll
- to **charge** (a) rate/fee/rent/fare/toll

'rate cap *noun* a limit placed on the amount of interest
banks, etc. may charge

rath·er 🔊 /'ræðər/ *adv.*
1 used to mean "fairly" or "to some degree," often when
you are expressing slight criticism, disappointment, or
surprise: *The instructions were rather complicated.* ◆ *She fell
and hurt her leg rather badly.* ◆ *I didn't fail the exam; in fact I did
rather well!* ◆ *It was a rather difficult question.* ◆ *It was rather a
difficult question.* **2** used to correct something you have
said, or to give more accurate information: *She worked as a
secretary, or rather, a personal assistant.* ◆ *In the end he had to
walk—or rather run—to the office.* ⊃ language bank at I.E.
3 used to introduce an idea that is different or opposite to
the idea that you have stated previously: *The walls were not
white, but rather a sort of dirty gray.*
IDM 🔊 **rather than** instead of someone or something: *I
think I'll have a cold drink rather than coffee.* ◆ *Why didn't you
ask for help, rather than trying to do it on your own?* **would
rather... (than)** (usually reduced to *'d rather*) would prefer
to: *She'd rather die than give a speech.* ◆ *"Do you want to come
with us?" "No, I'd rather not."* ◆ *Would you rather walk or take
the bus?* ◆ *"Do you mind if I smoke?" "Well, I'd rather you didn't."*

rat·i·fy /'ræt̮ə,faɪ/ *verb* (rat·i·fies, rat·i·fying, rat·i·fied,
rat·i·fied) ~ **sth** to make an agreement officially valid by
voting for or signing it: *The treaty was ratified by all the
member states.* ▶ **rat·i·fi·ca·tion** /,ræt̮əfə'keɪʃn/ *noun* [U]

rat·ing /'reɪt̮ɪŋ/ *noun* **1** [C] a measurement of how good,
popular, important, etc. someone or something is, especially in relation to other people or things: *The poll gave a
popular approval rating of 39% for the President.* ◆ *Education
has been given a high-priority rating by the new administration.*
⊃ see also CREDIT RATING **2 the ratings** [pl.] a set of
figures that show how many people watch or listen to a
particular television or radio program, used to show how
popular a program is: *The show has gone up in the ratings.*
⊃ collocations at TELEVISION **3** [C] a number or letter that
shows which groups of people a particular movie is
suitable for: *The movie has an R rating.*

ra·tio **AWL** /'reɪʃi,oʊ; 'reɪʃoʊ/ *noun* (*pl.* ra·tios) ~ **(of A to B)**
the relationship between two groups of people or things
that is represented by two numbers showing how much
larger one group is than the other: *What is the ratio of men to
women in the department?* ◆ *The school has a very high teacher-
student ratio.* ◆ *The ratio of applications to available positions
currently stands at 100:1.*

ra·ti·oc·i·na·tion /,ræʃi,oʊsə'neɪʃn; -,ɑsə-/ *noun* [U] (*formal*)
the process of thinking or arguing about something in a
logical way

ra·tion /'ræʃn; 'reɪ-/ *noun, verb*
● *noun* **1** [C] a fixed amount of food, fuel, etc. that you are
officially allowed to have when there is not enough for
everyone to have as much as they want, for example during
a war: *the weekly butter ration* **2 rations** [pl.] a fixed amount
of food given regularly to a soldier or to someone who is in
a place where there is not much food available: *We're on
short rations* (= allowed less than usual) *until fresh supplies
arrive.* ◆ *Once these latest rations run out, the country will again
face hunger and starvation.* **3** [sing.] ~ **(of sth)** an amount of
something that is thought to be normal or fair: *As part of the
diet, allow yourself a small daily ration of sugar.* ◆ *I've had my
ration of problems for one day—you deal with it!*
● *verb* [often passive] to limit the amount of something that
someone is allowed to have, especially because there is not
enough of it available: ~ **sth** *Eggs were rationed during the
war.* ◆ ~ **sb to sth** *The villagers were rationed to two liters of
water a day.* ⊃ see also RATIONING

ra·tion·al **AWL** /'ræʃənl/ *adj.* **1** (of behavior, ideas, etc.)
based on reason rather than emotions: *a rational argument/
choice/decision* ◆ *rational analysis/thought* ◆ *There is no
rational explanation for his actions.* **2** (of a person) able to
think clearly and make decisions based on reason rather
than emotions **SYN** REASONABLE: *No rational person would
ever behave like that.* **ANT** IRRATIONAL ▶ **ra·tion·al·i·ty**
AWL /,ræʃə'næləti/ *noun* [U]: *the rationality of his argument*
ra·tion·al·ly **AWL** /'ræʃənəli/ *adv.*: *to act/behave/think rationally* ◆ *She argued her case calmly and rationally.*

ra·tion·ale /,ræʃə'næl/ *noun* ~ **(behind/for/of sth)** (*formal*)
the principles or reasons that explain a particular decision,
course of action, belief, etc. **SYN** REASON: *What is the
rationale behind these new exams?*

ra·tion·al·ism **AWL** /'ræʃənə,lɪzəm/ *noun* [U] (*philosophy*)
the belief that all behavior, opinions, etc. should be based
on reason rather than on emotions or religious beliefs

ra·tion·al·ist /'ræʃənəlɪst/ *noun* a person who believes in
rationalism ▶ **ra·tion·al·ist** (also **ra·tion·al·is·tic** /,ræʃənə-
'lɪstɪk/) *adj.* [usually before noun]: *a rationalistic position*

ra·tion·al·ize **AWL** /'ræʃənə,laɪz/ *verb* [T, I] ~ **(sth)** to find
or try to find a logical reason to explain why someone
thinks, behaves, etc. in a way that is difficult to understand:
an attempt to rationalize his violent behavior ▶ **ra·tion·al·i·
za·tion** **AWL** /,ræʃənələ'zeɪʃn/ *noun* [U, C]: *No amount of
rationalization could justify his actions.*

ˌrational ˈnumber *noun* (*mathematics*) a number that can
be expressed as the RATIO of two whole numbers

ra·tion·ing /'ræʃənɪŋ; 'reɪ-/ *noun* [U] the policy of limiting
the amount of food, fuel, etc. that people are allowed to
have when there is not enough for everyone to have as
much as they want

the ˈrat race *noun* [sing.] (*disapproving*) the way of life of people living and working in a large city where people compete in an aggressive way with each other in order to be more successful, earn more money, etc. ⊃ collocations at TOWN

rats /ræts/ *exclamation* (*informal*) used to show that you are annoyed about something: *Rats! I forgot my glasses.*

rat·tan /rəˈtæn; ræ-/ *noun* [U] a S.E. Asian climbing plant with long, thin, strong STEMS, used especially for making furniture: *a rattan chair*

rat-tat-tat /ˌræt tæt ˈtæt/ *noun* [sing.] = RAT-A-TAT

rat·tle /ˈrætl/ *verb, noun*
● *verb* (*informal*) **1** [I, T] ~ (sth) to make a series of short loud sounds when hitting against something hard; to make something do this: *Every time a bus went past, the windows rattled.* **2** [I] + adv./prep. (of a vehicle) to make a series of short loud sounds as it moves somewhere: *A convoy of trucks rattled by.* **3** [T] ~ sb to make someone nervous or frightened **SYN** UNNERVE: *He was clearly rattled by the question.* ⊃ see also SABER-RATTLING
 IDM **rattle sb's cage** (*informal*) to annoy someone: *Who's rattled his cage?*
 PHR V ˌrattle aˈround | ˌrattle aˈround sth (*informal*) to be living, working, etc. in a room or building that is too big: *She spent the last few years alone, rattling around the old family home.* ˌrattle sth↔ˈoff to say something from memory without having to think too hard: *She can rattle off the names of all the presidents of the U.S.* ˌrattle ˈon (about sth) (*informal*) to talk continuously about something that is not important or interesting, especially in an annoying way
● *noun* **1** (also **rat·tling**) [usually sing.] a series of short loud sounds made when hard objects hit against each other: *the rattle of gunfire* ◆ *From the kitchen came a rattling of cups and saucers.* ⊃ see also DEATH RATTLE **2** a baby's toy that makes a series of short loud sounds when it is shaken **3** a wooden object that is held in one hand and makes a series of short loud sounds when you spin it around, used, for example, by people watching a sports game

rat·tle·snake /ˈrætlˌsneɪk/ (also *informal* **rat·tler** /ˈrætlər; ˈrætl.ər/) *noun* a poisonous snake that makes a noise like a rattle with its tail when it is angry or afraid

rat·ty /ˈræti/ *adj.* **1** (*informal*) in bad condition **SYN** SHABBY: *long ratty hair* ◆ *a ratty old pair of jeans* **2** looking like a RAT

rau·cous /ˈrɔkəs/ *adj.* sounding loud and rough: *raucous laughter* ◆ *a raucous voice* ◆ *a group of raucous young men* ▶ **rau·cous·ly** *adv.* **rau·cous·ness** *noun* [U]

raun·chy /ˈrɔntʃi; ˈran-/ *adj.* (*informal*) **1** intended to be sexually exciting **SYN** SEXY: *a raunchy magazine* ◆ *Their stage act is a little too raunchy for television.* **2** looking dirty and messy: *a raunchy old man*

rav·age /ˈrævɪdʒ/ *verb* [usually passive] ~ sth to damage something badly **SYN** DEVASTATE: *a country ravaged by civil war*

rav·ag·es /ˈrævɪdʒəz/ *noun* [pl.] **the ~ of sth** (*formal*) the destruction caused by something: *the ravages of war* ◆ *Her looks had not survived the ravages of time.*

rave /reɪv/ *verb, noun*
● *verb* **1** [I, T] ~ (about sb/sth) | + speech to talk or write about something in a very enthusiastic way: *The critics raved about his performance in "Hamlet."* **2** [I, T] ~ (at sb) | + speech to shout in a loud and emotional way at someone because you are angry with them: *She was shouting and raving at them.* **3** [I, T] ~ (at sb) | + speech to talk or shout in a way that is not logical or sensible: *He wandered the streets raving at passers-by.* **IDM** see RANT
● *noun* **1** a large party, held outside or in an empty building, at which people dance to fast electronic music and often take illegal drugs: *an all-night rave* **2** = RAVE REVIEW

rav·el /ˈrævl/ *verb* (-l-, *CanE usually* -ll-) ~ sth to make a situation or problem more complicated

ra·ven /ˈreɪvən/ *noun, adj.*
● *noun* a large bird of the CROW family, with shiny black feathers and a rough unpleasant cry

● *adj.* [only before noun] (*literary*) (of hair) shiny and black: *raven-haired*

rav·en·ing /ˈrævənɪŋ/ *adj.* (*literary*) (especially of animals) aggressive and hungry: *He says the media are ravening wolves.*

rav·en·ous /ˈrævənəs/ *adj.* **1** (of a person or an animal) extremely hungry **SYN** STARVE: *What's for lunch? I'm absolutely ravenous.* **2** [only before noun] (of HUNGER) very great: *a ravenous appetite* ▶ **rav·en·ous·ly** *adv.*

ˌrave reˈview (also **rave**) *noun* an article in a newspaper or magazine that is very enthusiastic about a particular movie, book, etc.

ra·vine /rəˈvin/ *noun* a deep and very narrow valley with steep sides

rav·ing /ˈreɪvɪŋ/ *adj., adv.*
● *adj.* [only before noun] **1** (of a person) talking or behaving in a way that shows they are crazy: *The man's a raving lunatic.* **2** used to emphasize a particular state or quality: *She's no raving beauty.*
● *adv.*
 IDM **(stark) raving mad** (*informal*) completely crazy

rav·ings /ˈreɪvɪŋz/ *noun* [pl.] words that have no meaning, spoken by someone who is crazy: *He dismissed her words as the ravings of a hysterical woman.*

ra·vi·o·li /ˌræviˈouli/ *noun* [U] PASTA in the shape of small squares filled with meat, cheese, etc., usually served with a sauce

rav·ish /ˈrævɪʃ/ *verb* (*literary*) **1** ~ sb (of a man) to force a woman to have sex **SYN** RAPE **2** [usually passive] ~ sb to give someone great pleasure

rav·ish·ing /ˈrævɪʃɪŋ/ *adj.* extremely beautiful **SYN** GORGEOUS: *a ravishing blonde* ▶ **rav·ish·ing·ly** *adv.*: *ravishingly beautiful*

raw 🔑 /rɔ/ *adj., noun*
● *adj.*
> **FOOD 1** not cooked: *raw meat* ◆ *These fish are often eaten raw.*
> **MATERIALS 2** [usually before noun] in its natural state; not yet changed, used, or made into something else: *raw sugar*
> **INFORMATION 3** [usually before noun] not yet organized into a form in which it can be easily used or understood: *This information is only raw data and will need further analysis.*
> **EMOTIONS/QUALITIES 4** [usually before noun] powerful and natural; not controlled or trained: *songs full of raw emotion* ◆ *He started with nothing but raw talent and determination.*
> **PART OF BODY 5** red and painful because the skin has been damaged: *There were raw patches on her feet where the shoes had rubbed.* ⊃ thesaurus box at PAINFUL
> **PERSON 6** [usually before noun] new to a job or an activity, and therefore without experience or skill: *a raw beginner* ◆ *raw recruits* (= for example, in the army)
> **WEATHER 7** very cold: *a raw north wind* ◆ *It had been a wet raw winter.*
> **DESCRIPTION 8** honest, direct, and sometimes shocking: *a raw portrayal of working-class life* ◆ *raw language* (= containing many sexual details)
 ▶ **raw·ness** *noun* [U]
 IDM **a raw deal** the fact of someone being treated unfairly: *Older workers often get a raw deal.*
● *noun*
 IDM **in the raw 1** in a way that does not hide the unpleasant aspects of something: *He spent a couple of months on the streets to experience life in the raw.* **2** with no clothes on **SYN** NAKED ⊃ more at NERVE *n.*

ˈraw bar *noun* a part of a restaurant where raw OYSTERS and other SHELLFISH are sold

raw·boned /ˈrɔbound/ *adj.* (of a person) having such a thin body that bones can be seen under the skin

raw·hide /ˈrɔhaɪd/ *noun* [U] natural leather that has not had any special treatment

ˌraw maˈterial *noun* [C, U] a basic material that is used to make a product: *We have had problems with the supply of raw* materials to the factory. ◆ *These trees provide the raw material for high-quality paper.* ◆ *(figurative) The writer uses her childhood as raw material for this novel.*

ray /reɪ/ *noun* **1** a narrow line of light, heat, or other energy: *the sun's rays* ◆ *ultraviolet rays* ◆ *The windows were shining in the reflected rays of the setting sun.* ⊃ see also COSMIC RAYS, X-RAY **2** ~ **of sth** a small amount of something good, or of something that you are hoping for **SYN** GLIMMER: *There was just one small ray of hope.* **3** a sea fish with a large, broad, flat body and a long tail, that is used for food
IDM a ray of sunshine (*informal*) a person or thing that makes life brighter or more cheerful **catch/get/grab some rays** (*informal*) to sit or lie in the sun, especially in order to get a SUNTAN

'ray gun *noun* (in SCIENCE FICTION stories) a gun that kills or injures people by sending out harmful RAYS

ray·on /'reɪɑn/ *noun* [U] a FIBER made from CELLULOSE; a smooth material made from this, used for making clothes

raze /reɪz/ *verb* [usually passive] ~ **sth** to completely destroy a building, town, etc. so that nothing is left: *The village was razed to the ground.*

ra·zor /'reɪzər/ *noun* an instrument that is used for shaving: *an electric razor* ◆ *a safety/disposable/straight razor* ⊃ compare SHAVER
IDM be on the razor's edge | be on a razor edge to be in a difficult situation where any mistake may be very dangerous

ra·zor·bill /'reɪzərˌbɪl/ *noun* a black and white bird with a beak that looks like an old-fashioned RAZOR, found in the N. Atlantic and the Baltic Sea

'razor ˌblade *noun* a thin sharp piece of metal that is used in a razor, especially one that can be thrown away when it is no longer sharp ⊃ picture at BLADE

ˌrazor-'sharp *adj.* **1** extremely sharp: *razor-sharp teeth* **2** showing that someone is extremely intelligent: *a razor-sharp mind*

ˌrazor-'thin *adj.* (of a victory in an election, etc.) won by a very small number of votes

'razor ˌwire *noun* [U] strong wire with sharp blades sticking out, placed on top of walls and around areas of land to keep people out

razz /ræz/ *verb* ~ **sb** (*old-fashioned, informal*) to TEASE someone by saying or doing things to make people laugh at them

ˌrazzle-'dazzle /ˌræzl 'dæzl/ *noun* [U] (*informal*) **1** = RAZZMATAZZ **2** (especially in football) unusual and complicated movements that are intended to confuse an opponent: *A bit of razzle-dazzle by Smith sent them to a 35-14 victory.*

razz·ma·tazz /'ræzməˌtæz; ˌræzmə'tæz/ (also ˌrazzle-'dazzle) *noun* [U] (*informal*) a lot of noisy exciting activity that is intended to attract people's attention: *The documentary focuses on the razzmatazz of an American political campaign.*

RBI /ˌɑr bi 'aɪ/ *abbr.* (in baseball) run batted in (a run scored by a player in the field as a result of another player who has hit the ball and who gets credit for the run): *He finished the season with five RBIs.*

RC /ˌɑr 'si/ *abbr.* ROMAN CATHOLIC

RCMP /ˌɑr si ɛm 'pi/ *abbr.* Royal Canadian Mounted Police (the national police force of Canada)

Rd. *abbr.* (used in written addresses) Road: *112 Meetinghouse Rd.*

RDA /ˌɑr di 'eɪ/ *abbr.* recommended daily allowance (the amount of a chemical, for example a VITAMIN or a mineral, that you should have every day)

re¹ /reɪ/ *noun* the second note in a MAJOR SCALE

re² /ri; reɪ/ *prep.* used at the beginning of a business letter, etc. to introduce the subject that it is about; used on an e-mail that you are sending as a reply: *Re your letter of September 1...* ◆ *Re: travel expenses*

re- 🔑 /ri/ *prefix*
(in verbs and related nouns, adjectives, and adverbs) again: *reapply* ◆ *reincarnation* ◆ *reassuring*

reach 🔑 /ritʃ/ *verb, noun*

● *verb*
▷ ARRIVE **1** [T] ~ **sth/sb** to arrive at the place that you have been traveling to: *They didn't reach the motel until after dark.* ◆ *I hope this letter reaches you.* **2** [T] ~ **sb** to come to someone's attention: *The rumors eventually reached the president.*
▷ LEVEL/SPEED/STAGE **3** [T] ~ **sth** to increase to a particular level, speed, etc. over a period of time: *The conflict has now reached a new level of intensity.* ◆ *Daytime temperatures can reach 90°F.* **4** [T] ~ **sth** to arrive at a particular point or stage of something after a period of time: *He first reached the finals in 2008.* ◆ *The negotiations have reached a deadlock.*
▷ ACHIEVE AIM **5** [T] ~ **sth** to achieve a particular aim **SYN** ARRIVE AT: *to reach a conclusion/decision/verdict/ compromise* ◆ *Politicians again failed to reach an agreement.* ⊃ see also FAR-REACHING
▷ WITH HAND/ARM **6** [I, T] to stretch your hand toward something in order to touch it, pick it up, etc.: + **adv./prep.** *She reached inside her bag for a pen.* ◆ ~ **sth** + **adv./prep.** *He reached out his hand to touch her.* **7** [I, T] to be able to stretch your hand far enough in order to touch something, pick something up, etc.: (+ **adv./prep.**) *"Grab the end of the rope." "I can't reach that far!"* ◆ ~ **sth** *Can you reach the light switch from where you're sitting?* **8** [T] to stretch your hand out or up in order to get something for someone: ~ **sth for sb** *Can you reach that box for me?* ◆ ~ **sb sth** *Can you reach me that box?*
▷ BE LONG ENOUGH **9** [I, T] to be big enough, long enough, etc. to arrive at a particular point: + **adv./prep.** *The rug only reached halfway across the room.* ◆ ~ **sth** *Is the cord long enough to reach the socket?*
▷ CONTACT SOMEONE **10** [T] ~ **sb** to communicate with someone, especially by telephone: *Do you know where I can reach him?*
▷ BE SEEN/HEARD BY SOMEONE **11** [T] ~ **sb** to be seen or heard by someone: *Through television and radio we are able to reach a wider audience.*
IDM reach for the stars to try to be successful at something that is difficult ⊃ more at EAR
PHR V reach 'out to sb to show someone that you are interested in them and/or want to help them: *The church needs to find new ways of reaching out to young people.*

● *noun*
▷ OF ARMS **1** [sing., U] the distance over which you can stretch your arms to touch something; the distance over which a particular object can be used to touch something else: *As a boxer, his long reach gives him a significant advantage.* ◆ *The ball was well **beyond the reach of** the outfielder.* ◆ *Cleaning fluids should be kept **out of the reach of** children.* ◆ *He lashed out angrily, hitting anyone **within his reach**.* ◆ *Use shears with a long reach for cutting high hedges.*
▷ OF POWER/INFLUENCE **2** [sing., U] the limit to which someone or something has the power or influence to do something: *Such matters are **beyond the reach of** the law.* ◆ *Victory is now **out of her reach**.* ◆ *The basic model is priced well **within the reach of** most people.* ◆ *The company has now overtaken IBM in terms of size and reach.*
▷ OF RIVER **3** [C, usually pl.] a straight section of water between two bends on a river: *the **upper/lower reaches of** the Mississippi* (= the part that is farthest from/nearest to the ocean)
▷ PLACE FAR FROM CENTER **4** reaches [pl.] **the outer, further, etc.** ~ **of something** the parts of an area or a place that are a long way from the center: *the outer reaches of space* ◆ *(figurative) an exploration of the deepest reaches of the human mind*
▷ SECTIONS OF ORGANIZATION **5** reaches [pl.] **the higher, lower, etc.** ~ **of something** the higher, etc. sections of an organization, a system, etc.: *There are still few women in the upper reaches of business.* ◆ *Many franchises in the lower reaches of the league are in financial difficulty.*

IDM **within (easy) reach (of sth)** close to something: *The house is within easy reach of schools and sports facilities.*

reach·a·ble /ˈriːtʃəbl/ *adj.* [not before noun] that is possible to reach: *Many parts of Alaska are only reachable by plane.*

re·ac·quaint /ˌriːəˈkweɪnt/ *verb* **~ sb/yourself with sb/sth** to let someone/yourself find out about something again or get used to something again: *I need to reacquaint myself with this program—it's been a long time since I used it.* ◆ *I hadn't seen him since high school, and we spent all afternoon getting reacquainted.*

re·act ✎ **AWL** /riˈækt/ *verb*
1 [I] **~ (to sth) (by doing sth)** to change or behave in a particular way as a result of or in response to something: *Local residents reacted angrily to the news.* ◆ *I nudged her but she didn't react.* ◆ *You never know how he is going to react.* ◆ *The market reacted by falling a further two points.* **2** [I] **(+ adv./prep.)** to become ill after eating, breathing, etc. a particular substance: *People can react badly to certain food additives.* **3** [I] **~ (with sth)** | **~ (together)** (*chemistry*) (of substances) to experience a chemical change when coming into contact with another substance: *Iron reacts with water and air to produce rust.*
PHR V **re·act a·gainst sb/sth** to show dislike or opposition in response to something, especially by deliberately doing the opposite of what someone wants you to do: *He reacted strongly against the artistic conventions of his time.*

re·ac·tance /riˈæktəns/ *noun* [U, C] (*physics*) (*symb.* **X**) the opposition of a piece of electrical equipment, etc. to the flow of an ALTERNATING CURRENT ⊃ compare RESISTANCE

re·ac·tant /riˈæktənt/ *noun* (*chemistry*) a substance that takes part in and is changed by a chemical reaction

re·ac·tion ✎ **AWL** /riˈækʃn/ *noun*
> **TO EVENT/SITUATION 1** [C, U] **~ (to sb/sth)** what you do, say, or think as a result of something that has happened: *What was his reaction to the news?* ◆ *My **immediate reaction** was one of shock.* ◆ *A spokesman said the changes were not **in reaction to** the company's recent losses.* ◆ *There has been a **mixed reaction** to her appointment as director.* ◆ *The decision provoked an angry reaction from local residents.* ◆ *I tried shaking him but there was no reaction.*
> **CHANGE IN ATTITUDES 2** [C, usually sing., U] **~ (against sth)** a change in people's attitudes or behavior caused by disapproval of the attitudes, etc. of the past: *The return to traditional family values is a reaction against the permissiveness of recent decades.*
> **TO DRUGS 3** [C, U] a response by the body, usually a bad one, to a drug, chemical substance, etc.: *to have an **allergic reaction** to a drug*
> **TO DANGER 4** **re·ac·tions** [pl.] the ability to move, or do something, quickly in response to something, especially if in danger: *a skilled driver with quick reactions*
> **AGAINST PROGRESS 5** [U] opposition to social or political progress or change: *The forces of reaction made change difficult.*
> **SCIENCE 6** [C, U] (*chemistry*) a chemical change produced by two or more substances acting on each other: *a chemical/nuclear reaction* ⊃ see also CHAIN REACTION **7** [U, C] (*physics*) a force shown by something in response to another force, which is of equal strength and acts in the opposite direction

re·ac·tion·ary **AWL** /riˈækʃəˌnɛri/ *noun* (*pl.* **re·ac·tion·ar·ies**) (*disapproving*) a person who is opposed to political or social change ▶ **re·ac·tion·ary** *adj.*: *a reactionary government*

re·ac·ti·vate **AWL** /riˈæktəˌveɪt/ *verb* **~ sth** to make something start working or happening again after a period of time ▶ **re·ac·ti·va·tion** **AWL** *noun* [U]

re·ac·tive **AWL** /riˈæktɪv/ *adj.* **1** (*formal*) showing a reaction or response: *The police presented a reactive rather than preventive strategy against crime.* ⊃ compare PROACTIVE **2** (*chemistry*) tending to show chemical change when mixed with another substance: *highly reactive substances*

re·ac·tiv·i·ty /ˌriːækˈtɪvəti/ *noun* [U, C] (*chemistry*) the degree

to which something reacts, or is likely to react: *Oxygen has high reactivity.*

re·ac·tor **AWL** /riˈæktər/ (also **nuclear re·actor**) *noun* a large structure used for the controlled production of nuclear energy

read ✎ *verb, noun, adj.*
● *verb* /riːd/ (**read, read** /rɛd/)
> **WORDS/SYMBOLS 1** [I, T] (not used in the progressive tenses) to understand the meaning of written or printed words or symbols by looking at them: *She's still learning to read.* ◆ *Some children can read and write before they go to kindergarten.* ◆ **~ sth** *I can't read your writing.* ◆ *Can you read music?* ◆ *I'm trying to read the map.* **2** [I, T] to go through written or printed words, etc. in silence or speaking them to other people: *I'm going to go to bed and read.* ◆ **~ to sb/yourself** *He liked reading to his grandchildren.* ◆ **~ sth** *to read a book/a magazine/the newspaper* ◆ *Have you read any Steinbeck* (= novels by him)? ◆ *He read the poem aloud.* ◆ **~ sth to sb/yourself** *Go on—read it to us.* ◆ **~ sb sth** *She read us a story.* ⊃ see also PROOFREAD **3** [T] **~ sth** (not used in the progressive tenses) to understand the meaning of BRAILLE symbols by touching them: *Soon she may need to read Braille.*
> **DISCOVER BY READING 4** [I, T] (not used in the progressive tenses) to discover or find out about someone or something by reading: **~ about/of sth** *I read about the accident in the local paper.* ◆ **~ that...** *I read that he had resigned.* ◆ **~ sth** *Don't believe everything you read on the Internet.*
> **SOMEONE'S MIND/THOUGHTS 5** [T] **~ someone's mind/thoughts** to guess what someone else is thinking
> **SOMEONE'S LIPS 6** [T] **~ someone's lips** to look at the movements of someone's lips to learn what they are saying ⊃ see also LIP-READ
> **UNDERSTAND 7** [T] to understand something in a particular way **SYN** INTERPRET: **~ sth** *How do you read the present situation?* ◆ **~ sth as sth** *Silence must not always be read as consent.*
> **OF A PIECE OF WRITING 8** [T] **+ speech** to have something written on it; to be written in a particular way: *The sign read "No admittance."* ◆ *I changed the last paragraph. It now reads as follows...* **9** [I] **+ adv./prep.** to give a particular impression when read: *Generally, the article reads very well.* ◆ *The poem reads like* (= sounds as if it is) *a translation.*
> **MEASURING INSTRUMENT 10** [T] **~ sth** (of measuring instruments) to show a particular weight, pressure, etc.: *The thermometer reads 75 degrees.* **11** [T] **~ sth** to get information from a measuring instrument: *A man came to read the gas meter.*
> **HEAR 12** [T] **~ sb** to hear and understand someone speaking on a radio set: *"Do you read me?" "I'm reading you loud and clear."*
> **REPLACE WORD 13** [T] **~ A for B** | **~ B as A** to replace one word, etc. with another when correcting a text: *For "madam" in line 3 read "madman."*
> **COMPUTING 14** [T] (of a computer or the person using it) to take information from a disk etc: **~ sth** *My computer can't read the attachment you sent.* ◆ **~ sth into sth** *to read a file into a computer*
> **IDM** **read between the lines** to look for or discover a meaning in something that is not openly stated: *Reading between the lines, I think Christy needs money.* **read sb like a book** to understand easily what someone is thinking or feeling **read my lips** (*informal*) used to tell someone to listen carefully to what you are saying: *Read my lips: no new taxes* (= I promise there will be no new taxes). **read (sb) the riot act** to tell someone with force that they must not do something
> **PHR V** **read sth↔'back** to read a message, etc. to others in order to check that it is correct: *I'll read the list back to you to make sure we've included everyone.* **read sth 'into sth** to think that something means more than it really does: *Don't read too much into what she says.* **read 'on** to continue reading: *That's the story so far. Now read on...* **read sth↔'out** to read something using your voice, especially to other people: *I'll read out the assignments so everyone will know what to do.* **read sth↔'over/'through** to read

something carefully from beginning to end to look for mistakes or check details ,read 'up on sb/sth to read a lot about a subject: *I'll need to read up on the case before the meeting.*

• **noun** /riːd/ [sing.] (*informal*) **a good, interesting, etc. ~** a book, an article, etc. that is good, etc.: *His thrillers are always a good read.*

• **adj.** /rɛd/ (used after an adverb) (of a person) having knowledge that has been gained from reading books, etc.: *She's very widely read in law.* ➔ see also WELL READ

read·a·ble /ˈriːdəbl/ *adj.* **1** (of a book, an article, etc.) that is easy, interesting and enjoyable to read **2** (of written or printed words) clear and easy to read **SYN** LEGIBLE ➔ see also MACHINE-READABLE ▶ **read·a·bil·i·ty** /ˌriːdəˈbɪləti/ *noun* [U]

re·ad·dress /ˌriːəˈdrɛs/ *verb* **~ sth** to change the address written on an envelope because the person the letter is for does not live at the address it has been delivered to

read·er /ˈriːdər/ *noun*
1 a person who reads, especially one who reads a lot or in a particular way: *an avid reader of science fiction* ◆ *a fast/slow reader* ◆ *The reader is left to draw his or her own conclusions.* ➔ collocations at LITERATURE **2** a person who reads a particular newspaper, magazine, etc.: *readers' letters* ◆ *Are you a "New York Times" reader?* **3** an easy book that is intended to help people learn to read their own or a foreign language: *a series of graded English readers* **4** (*computing*) an electronic device that reads data stored in one form and changes it into another form so that a computer can perform operations on it **5** (*technical*) a machine that produces on a screen a large image of a text stored on a MICROFICHE or MICROFILM ➔ see also MIND READER

read·er·ship /ˈriːdərʃɪp/ *noun* [usually sing.] the number or type of people who read a particular newspaper, magazine, etc.: *a readership of around 10,000* ◆ *In its new format, the magazine hopes to attract a much wider readership.*

read·i·ly /ˈrɛdli/ *adv.* **1** quickly and without difficulty **SYN** FREELY: *All ingredients are readily available from your local supermarket.* **2** in a way that shows you do not object to something **SYN** WILLINGly: *Most people readily accept the need for laws.*

read·i·ness /ˈrɛdinəs/ *noun* **1** [U] **~ (for sth)** the state of being ready or prepared for something: *Everyone has doubts about their readiness for parenthood.* **2** [U, sing.] **~ (of sb) (to do sth)** the state of being willing to do something: *Over half the people interviewed expressed their readiness to die for their country.*

read·ing /ˈriːdɪŋ/ *noun*
▷ ACTIVITY **1** [U] the activity of someone who reads: *My hobbies include reading and painting.* ◆ *He needs more help with his reading.* ◆ *Are you any good at map reading?* ◆ *reading glasses* (= worn when reading) ◆ *a reading lamp/light* (= one that can be moved to shine light onto something that you are reading) **2** [sing.] an act of reading something: *A closer* (= more detailed) *reading of the text reveals just how desperate he was feeling.*
▷ BOOKS/ARTICLES **3** [U] books, articles, etc. that are intended to be read: *reading matter/material* ◆ *a series of reading books* (= books that teach children how to read) *for children* ◆ *further reading* (= at the end of a book, a list of other books that give more information about the same subject) ◆ *The report makes for interesting reading* (= it is interesting to read) ◆ *The article is not exactly light reading* (= it is not easy to read). **4** [C] a chapter or part of a book that is read in class or set for homework, etc
▷ WAY OF UNDERSTANDING **5** [C] **~ (of sth)** the particular way in which you understand a book, situation, etc. **SYN** INTERPRETATION: *a literal reading of the text* ◆ *My own reading of events is less optimistic.*
▷ MEASUREMENT **6** [C] the amount or number shown on an instrument used for measuring something: *Meter readings are taken every three months.*

▷ EVENT **7** [C] an event at which someone reads something to an audience for entertainment; a piece of literature that is read at such an event: *a poetry reading* ◆ *The evening ended with a reading from her latest novel.*
▷ FROM BIBLE/KORAN/TORAH **8** [C] a short section from the Bible, Koran, Torah, etc. that someone reads to people as part of a religious service: *The reading today is from the Book of Daniel.*
▷ IN PARLIAMENT OR CONGRESS **9** [C] one of the stages during which a BILL (= a proposal for a new law) must be discussed and accepted by a parliament or congress before it can become law

'**reading ˌage** *noun* a person's ability to read, measured by comparing it with the average ability of children of a particular age: *a 30-year-old man with a reading age of eight*

'**reading ˌgroup** *noun* = BOOK GROUP

'**reading ˌlist** *noun* a list of books, etc. that students are expected to read for a particular subject

'**reading ˌroom** *noun* a place, especially a room in a library, club, etc., where people can read or study

re·ad·just **AWL** /ˌriːəˈdʒʌst/ *verb* **1** [I] to get used to a changed or new situation: *Children are highly adaptable—they just need time to readjust.* ◆ **~ to sth/doing sth** *Once again he had to readjust to living alone.* **2** [T] **~ sth** to change or move something slightly: *She got out of the car and readjusted her dress.* ▶ **re·ad·just·ment** **AWL** *noun* [C, U]: *He has made a number of readjustments to his technique.* ◆ *a painful period of readjustment*

re·ad·mit /ˌriːədˈmɪt/ *verb* (-tt-) [often passive] **1 ~ sb (to sth)** to allow someone to join a group, an organization or an institution again **2 ~ sb (to sth)** to take someone into a hospital again after they had been allowed to leave: *He was readmitted only a week after being discharged.* ▶ **re·ad·mis·sion** /ˌriːədˈmɪʃn/ *noun* [U, C] **~ (to sth)**

ˌ**read–only 'memory** *noun* [U] (*computing*) = ROM

read·out /ˈriːdaʊt/ *noun* (*computing*) a display of information on a computer screen ➔ compare PRINTOUT

read·through /ˈriːdθruː/ *noun* an occasion when the words of a play are spoken by members of a theater group, before they begin practicing acting it

ready /ˈrɛdi/ *adj., verb, noun*
• **adj.** (**read·i·er, read·i·est**)
▷ PREPARED/AVAILABLE **1** [not before noun] fully prepared for what you are going to do: *Are you almost ready?* ◆ *"Let's go!" "I'm ready when you are!"* ◆ **~ for sth** *I'm just getting the kids ready for school.* ◆ *I was twenty years old and ready for anything.* ◆ **~ to do sth** *We're ready to go.* ◆ *Volunteers were ready and waiting to pack the food in boxes.* **2** [not before noun] completed and available to be used: *Come on, dinner's ready!* ◆ *The new building should be ready by 2015.* ◆ **~ for sth** *Can you help me get everything ready for the party?* ◆ **~ to do sth** *The contract will be ready to sign in two weeks.* **3** available to be used easily and immediately: *All the relevant records are easily available ready to hand.* ◆ *a ready supply of wood* ◆ *a ready source of income* ➔ see also READILY, READINESS, ROUGH-AND-READY
▷ WILLING **4** [not before noun] willing and quick to do or give something: **~ for sth** *I was very angry and ready for a fight.* ◆ **~ with sth** *She's always ready with advice.* ◆ **~ to do sth** *He's always ready to help his friends.* ◆ *Don't be so ready to believe the worst about people.*
▷ LIKELY TO DO SOMETHING **5 ~ to do sth** likely to do something very soon **SYN** ON THE POINT OF: *She looked ready to collapse at any minute.*
▷ NEEDING SOMETHING **6 ~ for sth** needing something as soon as possible: *I'm ready for bed.* ◆ *After the long walk, we were all ready for something to drink.*
▷ QUICK/SMART **7** [only before noun] quick and smart: *She has great charm and a ready wit.*
IDM **make ready (for sth)** (*formal*) to prepare: *to make ready for the president's visit* **(get) ready, (get) set, go!** what you say to tell people to start a race **ready to roll** (*informal*) ready to start **ready, willing, and able** capable of doing

h **h**at   m **m**an   n **n**o   ŋ si**ng**   l **l**eg   r **r**ed   y **y**es   w **w**et

something and very willing to act: *Are you ready, willing, and able to work?*

● **verb** (read·ies, read·y·ing, read·ied, read·ied) ~ sb/yourself/sth (for sth) | ~ sb/yourself/sth (to do sth) (*formal*) to prepare someone/yourself/something for something: *Western companies were readying themselves for the challenge from Eastern markets.*

● **noun**
> **IDM** **at the ready** available to be used immediately: *We all had our cameras at the ready.*

ready-'made *adj.* **1** prepared in advance so that you can eat or use it immediately: *ready-made pie crust* **2** (*old-fashioned*) (especially of clothes) made in standard sizes, not to the measurements of a particular customer: *a ready-made suit* **3** already provided for you so you do not need to produce or think about it yourself: *When he married her, he also took on a ready-made family.*

ready-'mixed *adj.* already mixed and ready to use: *ready-mixed concrete*

ready 'money (also ,ready 'cash) *noun* [U] (*informal*) money in the form of coins and bills that you can spend immediately

ready-to-'wear *adj.* (of clothes) made in standard sizes, not to the measurements of a particular customer

re·af·firm /ˌriːəˈfɜːrm/ *verb* ~ sth to state something again in order to emphasize that it is still true ► **re·af·fir·ma·tion** /ˌriːæfərˈmeɪʃn/ *noun* [C, U]

re·a·gent /riˈeɪdʒənt/ *noun* (*chemistry*) a substance used to cause a chemical reaction, especially in order to find out if another substance is present

real 🔊 /riːl; ˈriːəl/ *adj., adv.*

● **adj.**
> EXISTING/NOT IMAGINED **1** actually existing or happening and not imagined or pretended: *It wasn't a ghost; it was a real person.* ◆ *pictures of animals, both real and mythological* ◆ *In the movies guns kill people instantly, but it's not like that in real life.* ◆ *Politicians seem to be out of touch with* **the real world.** ◆ *The growth of violent crime is a very real problem.* ◆ *There's no real possibility of them changing their minds.* ◆ *We have a real chance of success.*
> TRUE/GENUINE **2** genuine and not false or artificial: *Are those real flowers?* ◆ *real leather* **3** [only before noun] actual or true, rather than what appears to be true: *Tell me the real reason.* ◆ *Bono's real name is Paul Hewson.* ◆ *See the real Africa on one of our walking safaris.* ◆ *I couldn't resist the opportunity to meet a* **real** *wine celebrity.* **4** [only before noun] having all the important qualities that it should have to deserve to be called what it is called: *She never had any real friends in school.* ◆ *his first real kiss* ◆ *I had no real interest in politics.* ◆ *He was making a real effort to be nice to her.* ◆ *She has not shown any real regret for what she did.*
> FOR EMPHASIS **5** [only before noun] used to emphasize a state or quality: *He looks like a real idiot.* ◆ *This accident could have produced a real tragedy.* ◆ *Her next play was a real contrast.*
> MONEY/INCOME **6** [only before noun] when the effect of such things as price increases on the power of money to buy things is included in the sums: *Real wage costs have risen by 10% in the past year.* ◆ *This represents a reduction of 5%* **in real terms.**
> **IDM** **for real** genuine or serious: *This is not a fire drill—it's for real.* ◆ *He managed to convince voters that he was for real.* **get real!** (*informal*) used to tell someone that they are behaving in a stupid or unreasonable way **keep it real** (*informal*) to act in an honest and natural way **the real thing** (*informal*) the genuine thing: *Are you sure it's the real thing* (= love), *not just infatuation?* ⊃ more at McCoy, POWER *n.*

● **adv.** (*informal*) very: *That tastes real good.* ◆ *He's a real nice guy.* ◆ *I'm real sorry.*

real es,tate *noun* [U] **1** (also **re·al·ty**) property in the form of land or buildings: *My father sold real estate.* **2** the business of selling houses or land for building: *to work in real estate*

real estate ,agent *noun* a person whose job is to sell houses and land for people ⊃ compare REALTOR™

re·a·lign /ˌriːəˈlaɪn/ *verb* **1** ~ sth to change the position or direction of something slightly: *The road was realigned to improve visibility.* **2** ~ sth to make changes to something in order to adapt it to a new situation: *The company has been forced to realign its overseas operations.* **3** ~ yourself (with sb/sth) to change your opinions, policies, etc. so that they are the same as those of another person, group, etc.: *Some conservative Democrats have realigned themselves with the right.* ► **re·a·lign·ment** *noun* [U, C]: ~ (of sth) *the realignment of personal goals* ◆ *political realignments*

re·al·ism /ˈriːəlɪzəm/ *noun* [U] **1** a way of seeing, accepting, and dealing with situations as they really are without being influenced by your emotions or false hopes: *There was a new mood of realism among the leaders at the peace talks.* **2** (in novels, paintings, movies, etc.) the quality of being very like real life **3** also **Realism** a style in art or literature that shows things as they are in real life ⊃ compare IDEALISM, ROMANTICISM

re·al·ist /ˈriːəlɪst/ *noun* **1** a person who accepts and deals with a situation as it really is and does not try to pretend that it is different: *I'm a realist—I know you can't change people overnight.* **2** a writer, painter, etc. whose work represents things as they are in real life

re·al·is·tic 🔊 /ˌriːəˈlɪstɪk/ *adj.*
1 accepting in a sensible way what it is actually possible to do or achieve in a particular situation: *a realistic assessment* ◆ *We have to* **be realistic** *about our chances of winning.* ◆ *It is not realistic to expect people to spend so much money.* **2** sensible and appropriate; possible to achieve **SYN** FEASIBLE, VIABLE: *We must set realistic goals.* ◆ *a realistic target* ◆ *to pay a realistic salary* **3** representing things as they are in real life: *a realistic drawing* ◆ *We try to make these training courses as realistic as possible.* **ANT** UNREALISTIC

re·al·is·ti·cally /ˌriːəˈlɪstɪkli/ *adv.* **1** used to say what you think can actually be achieved in a particular situation: *Realistically, there is little prospect of a ceasefire.* **2** in a way that shows someone accepts in a sensible way what it is actually possible to do or achieve: *How many can you realistically hope to sell?* ◆ *Kate spoke realistically about the task ahead.* **3** in a way that represents things as they are in real life: *a fireplace with realistically glowing logs*

re·al·i·ty 🔊 /riˈæləti/ *noun*
(*pl.* re·al·i·ties) **1** [U] the true situation and the problems that actually exist in life, in contrast to how you would like life to be: *She refuses to* **face reality.** ◆ *You're* **out of touch with reality.** ◆ *The reality is that there is not enough money to pay for this project.* **2** [C] a thing that is actually experienced or seen, in contrast to what people might imagine: *the harsh realities of life* ◆ *This decision reflects the realities of the political situation.* ◆ *Will time travel ever* **become a reality**? **3** [U] ~ **television/TV/shows/series/contestants** television/shows, etc. that use real people (not actors) in real situations, presented as entertainment: *the reality show "American Idol"*
> **IDM** **in reality** used to say that a situation is different from what has just been said or from what people believe: *Outwardly she seemed confident but in reality she felt extremely nervous.* ⊃ see also VIRTUAL REALITY

re'ality ,check *noun* [usually sing.] (*informal*) an occasion when you are reminded of how things are in the real world, rather than how you would like things to be

re,ality T'V *noun* [U] television shows that are based on real people (not actors) in real situations, presented as entertainment: *a reality TV star*

re·al·i·za·ble /ˈriːəlaɪzəbl/ *adj.* **1** possible to achieve or make happen: *realizable objectives* **2** that can be sold and turned into money: *realizable assets*

re·al·i·za·tion /ˌriːələˈzeɪʃn/ *noun* **1** [sing.] the act or process of becoming aware of something **SYN** AWARENESS: ~ (of sth) *the sudden realization of what she had done* ◆ ~ (that...)

There is a growing realization that changes must be made. **2** [C, usually sing.] **~ (of sth)** the process of achieving a particular aim, etc. **SYN** ACHIEVEMENT: *It was the realization of his greatest ambition.* **3** [U] **~ of your asset(s)** (*formal*) the act of selling something that you own, such as property, in order to get the money that you need for something **4** [U, C] **~ (of sth)** (*formal*) the act of producing a sound, play, design, etc.; or the thing that is produced

re·al·ize 🔑 /ˈriːəˌlaɪz/ *verb*
▸ BE/BECOME AWARE **1** [T, I] (not used in the progressive tenses) to understand or become aware of a particular fact or situation: **~ (that)…** *I didn't realize (that) you were so unhappy.* ◆ *The moment I saw her, I realized something was wrong.* ◆ **~ how, what, etc. …** *I don't think you realize how important this is to her.* ◆ **~ (sth)** *I hope you realize the seriousness of this crime.* ◆ *Only later did she realize her mistake.* ◆ *The situation was more complicated than they had at first realized.* ◆ *They were able to leave without any of us realizing their absence.* ◆ **it is realized that…** *There was a cheer when it was realized that everyone was safely back.*
▸ ACHIEVE SOMETHING **2** [T] **~ sth** to achieve something important that you very much want to do: *She never realized her ambition of becoming a professional singer.* ◆ *We try to help all students realize their full potential* (= be as successful as they are able to be).
▸ HAPPEN **3** [T, usually passive] **~ sth** if someone's fears **are realized**, the things that they are afraid will happen, do happen: *His worst fears were realized when he saw that the door had been forced open.*
▸ SELL **4** [T] **~ your asset(s)** (*formal*) to sell things that you own, for example property, in order to get the money that you need for something **SYN** CONVERT **5** [T] **~ sth** (*formal*) (of goods, etc.) to be sold for a particular amount of money **SYN** MAKE: *The paintings realized $2 million at auction.*
▸ MAKE SOMETHING REAL **6** [T] **~ sth** (*formal*) to produce something that can be seen or heard, based on written information or instructions: *The stage designs have been beautifully realized.*

real-life *adj.* [only before noun] actually happening or existing in life, not in books, stories, or movies: *a novel based on real-life events* ◆ *a real-life Romeo and Juliet* **ANT** FICTIONAL

re·al·lo·cate /ˌriˈæləˌkeɪt/ *verb* **~ sth (to sb/sth)** to change the way in which money or materials are shared between different people, groups, projects, etc. **SYN** REDISTRIBUTE ▶ **re·al·lo·ca·tion** /ˌriˌæləˈkeɪʃn/ *noun* [U]

real·ly 🔑 /ˈrili; ˈriːli; ˈriːəli/ *adv.*
1 used to say what is actually the fact or the truth about something: *What do you really think about it?* ◆ *Tell me what really happened.* ◆ *They are not really my aunt and uncle.* ◆ *I can't believe I am really going to meet the President.* **2** used to emphasize something you are saying or an opinion you are giving: *I want to help, I really do.* ◆ *Now I really must go.* ◆ *I really don't mind.* ◆ *He really likes you.* ◆ *I really and truly am in love this time.* **3** used to emphasize an adjective or adverb: *a really hot fire* ◆ *I'm really sorry.* **4** used, often in negative sentences, to reduce the force of something you are saying: *I don't really agree with that.* ◆ *It doesn't really matter.* ◆ *"Did you enjoy the book?" "Not really."* (= "No" or "not very much.") **HELP** The position of **really** can change the meaning of the sentence. **I don't really know** means that you are not sure about something; **I really don't know** emphasizes that you do not know. (Look at sense 2.) **5** used in questions and negative sentences when you want someone to say "no": *Do you really expect me to believe that?* ◆ *I don't really need to go, do I?* **6** used to express interest in or surprise at what someone is saying: *"We're going to Japan next month." "Oh, really?"* ◆ *"She's resigned." "Really? Are you sure?"* **7** used to show that you disapprove of something someone has done: *Really, you could have told us before.*

realm /rɛlm/ *noun* **1** an area of activity, interest, or knowledge: *in the realm of literature* ◆ *At the end of the speech he seemed to be moving into the realms of fantasy.* **2** (*formal*) a

country ruled by a king or queen **SYN** KINGDOM: *the defense of the realm*
IDM **beyond/within the realm of possibility** not possible/possible: *A successful outcome is not beyond the realm of possibility.*

real 'number *noun* (*mathematics*) any number that is not an IMAGINARY NUMBER ➔ compare COMPLEX NUMBER

re·al·po·li·tik /reɪˈɑlˌpoʊlɪˌtik/ *noun* [U] (from *German*) a system of politics that is based on the actual situation and needs of a country or political party rather than on moral principles

real time *noun* [U] (*computing*) the fact that there is only a very short time between a computer system receiving information and dealing with it: *To make the training realistic the simulation operates in real time.* ◆ *real-time missile guidance systems*

Re·al·tor™ (also **re·al·tor**) /ˈriltər; ˈriəl-/ *noun* a real estate agent who is a member of the National Association of Realtors, an agency that licenses them

re·al·ty /ˈrilti; ˈriəl-/ *noun* [U] = REAL ESTATE

real-world *adj.* existing in the real world and not specially invented for a particular purpose: *Teachers need to prepare their students to deal with real-world situations outside the classroom.*

ream /rim/ *noun, verb*
● *noun* **1** [C] (*technical*) 500 sheets of paper **2** reams [pl.] (*informal*) a large quantity of writing: *He always took reams of notes in class.*
● *verb* **~ sb** (*informal*) to treat someone unfairly or cheat them: *We got reamed on that deal.*
PHR V **ream sb↔'out** (*informal*) to criticize someone strongly because they have done something wrong

re·an·i·mate /ˌriˈænəˌmeɪt/ *verb* **~ sb/sth** (*formal*) to give someone or something new life or energy: *With the election of a new mayor, the whole project was reanimated.*

reap /rip/ *verb* **1** [T] **~ sth** to obtain something, especially something good, as a direct result of something that you have done: *They are now reaping the rewards of all their hard work.* **2** [I, T] **~ (sth)** to cut and collect a crop, especially WHEAT, from a field **SYN** HARVEST
IDM **you reap what you sow** (*saying*) you have to deal with the bad effects or results of something that you originally started

reap·er /ˈripər/ *noun* a person or a machine that cuts and collects crops on a farm ➔ see also THE GRIM REAPER

re·ap·pear /ˌriəˈpɪr/ *verb* [I] to appear again after not being heard of or seen for a period of time: *She went upstairs and did not reappear until morning.* ▶ **re·ap·pear·ance** /ˌriəˈpɪrəns/ *noun* [U, sing.]

re·ap·ply /ˌriəˈplaɪ/ *verb* (re·ap·plies, re·ap·ply·ing, re·ap·plied, re·ap·plied) **1** [T] **~ sth** to put another layer of a substance on a surface: *Sunblock should be reapplied after swimming.* **2** [I] **~ (for sth)** to make another formal request for something: *If you don't get accepted this year, you can always reapply.* **3** [T] **~ sth** to use something again, especially in a different situation: *Students are taught a number of skills that can be reapplied throughout their studies.* ▶ **re·ap·pli·ca·tion** *noun* [C, U]

re·ap·point /ˌriəˈpɔɪnt/ *verb* **~ sb (as) sth | ~ sb + noun | ~ sb (to sth)** to give someone the job that they used to have in the past: *After the trial he was reappointed (as) treasurer.* ▶ **re·ap·point·ment** *noun* [U]

re·ap·prais·al /ˌriəˈpreɪzl/ *noun* [C, usually sing., U] the act of examining something again to see if it needs to be changed

re·ap·praise /ˌriəˈpreɪz/ *verb* **~ sth** (*formal*) to think again about the value or nature of something to see if your opinion about it should be changed **SYN** REASSESS

rear 🔑 /rɪr/ *noun, adj., verb*
● *noun* **1** usually **the rear** [sing.] the back part of something: *A trailer was attached to the rear of the truck.* ◆ *There are toilets at the front and rear of the plane.* ◆ *They instructed us to deliver*

the goods *to the rear* of the building. ➔ note at BACK **2** [C]
(*informal*) the part of the body that you sit on **SYN** BACKSIDE:
He was kicked in the rear.

IDM **bring up the rear** to be at the back of a line of people,
or last in a race

● *adj.* [only before noun] at or near the back of something:
front and rear windows ◆ *the rear entrance to the building*

● *verb* **1** [T] ~ *sb/sth* [often passive] to care for young
children or animals until they are fully grown **SYN** RAISE:
She reared a family of five on her own. **2** [T] ~ *sth* to breed or
keep animals or birds, for example on a farm: *to rear cattle*
3 [I] ~ **(up)** (of an animal, especially a horse) to raise itself
on its back legs, with the front legs in the air: *The horse
reared, throwing its rider.* **4** [I] ~ **(up)** (of something large) to
seem to lean over you, especially in a threatening way: *The
great bulk of the building reared up against the night sky.*

IDM **sth rears its (ugly) head** if something unpleasant
rears its head or rears its ugly head, it appears or happens
PHR V **'rear sb/sth on sth** [usually passive] to give a person
or an animal a particular type of food, entertainment, etc.
while they are young: *I'm the son and grandson of sailors and
was reared on stories of life at sea.*

ˌrear ˈadmiral *noun* an officer of very high rank in the navy:
Rear Admiral Baines

ˌrear ˈend *noun* **1** (*informal*) the part of the body that you sit
on **SYN** BACKSIDE: *He sits on his rear end all day.* **2** the back
end of something, especially a vehicle: *repairs to the rear end
of the truck*

ˌrear-ˈend *verb* ~ *sth/sb* (*informal*) (of a vehicle or driver) to
drive into the back of another vehicle

rear·guard /'rɪrgɑrd; 'rɪr'gɑrd/ *noun* usually **the rearguard**
[sing.] a group of soldiers that protect the back part of an
army especially when the army is RETREATING after it has
been defeated **ANT** VANGUARD

ˌrearguard ˈaction *noun* [usually sing.] a struggle to
change or stop something even when it is not likely that
you will succeed: *They have been **fighting a rearguard action**
for two years to stop their house from being demolished.*

rear·ing /'rɪrɪŋ/ *noun* [U] **1** the process of caring for
children as they grow up, teaching them how to behave as
members of society **2** the process of breeding animals or
birds and caring for them as they grow: *livestock rearing*

re·arm /ˌriˈɑrm/ *verb* [I, T] to obtain, or supply someone with,
new or better weapons, armies, etc.: *The country was
forbidden to rearm under the terms of the treaty.* ◆ ~ *sb Rebel
troops were being rearmed.* ▶ re·ar·ma·ment /ˌriˈɑrməmənt/
noun [U]

rear·most /'rɪrmoʊst/ *adj.* (*formal*) farthest back: *the rearmost
section of the aircraft*

re·ar·range /ˌriəˈreɪndʒ/ *verb* **1** ~ *sth* to change the
position or order of things; to change your position: *We
rearranged the furniture in the bedroom.* ◆ *She rearranged
herself in another pose.* **2** ~ *sth* to change the time, date, or
place of an event **SYN** RESCHEDULE: *Can you rearrange your
schedule so that you're free on Tuesday?* ▶ re·ar·range·ment
noun [C, U]

rear·view mir·ror /'rɪrvyu ˈmɪrər/ *noun* a mirror in which a
driver can see the traffic behind ➔ picture at CAR

rear·ward /'rɪrwərd/ *adj.* (*formal*) at, near, or toward the
back of something: *a rearward movement* ▶ rear·ward (also
rear·wards) *adv.*

ˌrear-wheel ˈdrive *noun* [U] a system in which power from
the engine is sent to the back wheels of a vehicle
➔ compare FRONT-WHEEL DRIVE

rea·son 🔑 /'rizn/ *noun, verb*

● *noun* **1** [C] a cause or an explanation for something that
has happened or that someone has done: ~ **(why...)** *I'd like
to know the reason why you're so late.* ◆ *Give me **one good
reason** why I should help you.* ◆ ~ **(that...)** *We're not going for
the **simple reason** that we can't afford it.* ◆ ~ **(for sth)** *She gave
no reasons for her decision.* ◆ ~ **(for doing sth)** *I have no*

particular reason for doubting him. ◆ *He said no but he didn't
give a reason.* ◆ ***For some reason*** *(= one that I don't know or
don't understand) we all have to come in early tomorrow.* ◆ *The
man attacked me **for no apparent reason.*** ◆ *She resigned for
personal reasons.* ◆ ***For reasons of** security the door is always
kept locked.* ◆ *He wants to keep them all in his office **for reasons
best known to himself.*** ◆ *people who, **for whatever reason**, are
unable to support themselves* ◆ "*Why do you want to know?*"
"***No reason.***" (= I do not want to say why.) ◆ "*Why did she do
that?*" "*She **must have her reasons.***" (= secret reasons which
she does not want to tell) ◆ (*formal*) *She was found not guilty **by
reason of** (= because of) insanity.* ➔ language bank at
THEREFORE **2** [U] a fact that makes it right or fair to do
something: ~ **(to do sth)** *They have reason to believe that he is
lying.* ◆ *We **have every reason** (= have very good reasons) to feel
optimistic.* ◆ ~ **(why...)** *There is no reason why we should agree
to this.* ◆ ~ **(for sth/for doing sth)** *This result gives us **all the
more reason** for optimism.* ◆ *She complained, **with reason**
(= rightly), that she had been underpaid.* **3** [U] the power of
the mind to think in a logical way, to understand and have
opinions, etc.: *Only human beings are capable of reason* (= of
thinking in a logical way, etc.). ◆ *to lose your reason* (= become
mentally ill) **4** [U] what is possible, practical, or right: *I can't
get her to **listen to reason**.* ◆ *Why can't they **see reason**?* ◆ *to be
open to reason* (= to be willing to accept sensible advice) ◆ *He's
looking for a job and he's willing to do anything **within reason**.*

IDM **it stands to reason** (*informal*) it must be clear to any
sensible person who thinks about it: *It stands to reason that
they'll leave if you don't pay them enough.* ➔ more at RHYME *n.*

● *verb* **1** [T, I] ~ **(that...)** | + **speech** to form a judgment
about a situation by considering the facts and using your
power to think in a logical way: *She reasoned that she must
have left her bag on the train.* ◆ *They couldn't fire him, he
reasoned. He was the only one who knew how the system
worked.* **2** [I] to use your power to think and understand: *the
human ability to reason*

PHR V ˌreason sth ˈout to try and find the answer to a
problem by using your power to think in a logical way
SYN FIGURE OUT ˈreason with sb to talk to someone in
order to persuade them to be more sensible: *I tried to reason
with him, but he wouldn't listen.*

THESAURUS

reason

**explanation ◆ grounds ◆ basis ◆ excuse ◆ motive
◆ justification ◆ pretext**

These are all words for a cause or an explanation for
something that has happened or that someone has
done.

reason a cause or an explanation for something that has
happened or that someone has done; a fact that makes
it right or fair to do something: *She refused our request,
but she didn't give a reason.*

explanation a statement, fact, or situation that tells you
why something has happened; a reason given for
something: *The most likely explanation is that his plane
was delayed.* ◆ *She left the room abruptly without explanation.*

grounds (*somewhat formal*) a good or true reason for
saying, doing, or believing something: *You have no
grounds for your accusation.*

basis (*somewhat formal*) the reason why people make a
particular choice: *On what basis will this decision be
made?*

excuse a reason, either true or invented, that you give to
explain or defend your behavior; a good reason that
you give for doing something that you want to do for
other reasons: *Late again! What's your excuse this time?*
◆ *It gave me an excuse to drive instead of walking.*

motive a reason that explains someone's behavior:
There seemed to be no motive for the murder.

justification (*somewhat formal*) a good reason why something exists or is done: *I can see no possible justification for any further tax increases.*

GROUNDS OR JUSTIFICATION?

Justification is used to talk about finding or understanding reasons for actions, or trying to explain why it is a good idea to do something. It is often used with words like *little, no, some, every, without,* and *not any.* **Grounds** is used more for talking about reasons that already exist, or that have already been decided, for example by law: *moral/economic grounds.*

pretext (*somewhat formal*) a false reason that you give for doing something, usually something bad, in order to hide the real reason: *He left the party early on the pretext of having to work.*

PATTERNS

- (a/an) reason/explanation/grounds/basis/excuse/motive/justification/pretext **for** sth
- the reason/motive **behind** sth
- **on the** grounds/basis/pretext **of/that…**
- (a) **valid** reason/explanation/grounds/excuse/motive/justification
- a **good** reason/explanation/basis/excuse/motive

rea·son·a·ble 🔊 /'riːznəbl; 'riznə-/ *adj.*
1 ~ (to do sth) fair, practical, and sensible: *It is reasonable to assume that he knew beforehand that this would happen.* ◆ *Be reasonable! We can't work late every night.* ◆ *Any reasonable person would have done exactly as you did.* ◆ *The prosecution has to prove beyond reasonable doubt that he is guilty of murder.* **ANT** UNREASONABLE **2** acceptable and appropriate in a particular situation: *He made us a reasonable offer for the car.* ◆ *You must submit your claim within a reasonable time.* **3** (of prices) not too expensive **SYN** FAIR: *We sell good-quality food at reasonable prices.* ⊃ thesaurus box at CHEAP **4** [usually before noun] fairly good, but not very good **SYN** AVERAGE: *a reasonable standard of living* ◆ *The quality of service was reasonable, I suppose* (= but not excellent). ▸ **rea·son·a·ble·ness** *noun* [U]

rea·son·a·bly 🔊 /'riːznəbli; 'riznə-/ *adv.*
1 to a degree that is fairly good but not very good: *The instructions are reasonably straightforward.* ◆ *She seems reasonably happy in her new job.* **2** in a logical and sensible way: *We tried to discuss the matter calmly and reasonably.* **3** in a fair way: *He couldn't reasonably be expected to pay back the loan all at once.* ◆ *The apartments are reasonably priced* (= not too expensive).

rea·soned /'riːznd/ *adj.* [only before noun] (of an argument, opinion, etc.) presented in a logical way that shows careful thought

rea·son·ing /'riːznɪŋ/ *noun* [U] the process of thinking about things in a logical way; opinions and ideas that are based on logical thinking: *What is the reasoning behind this decision?* ◆ *This line of reasoning is faulty.*

re·as·sem·ble /ˌriːə'sɛmbl/ *verb* **1** [T] **~ sth** to fit the parts of something together again after it has been taken apart: *We had to take the table apart and reassemble it upstairs.* **2** [I] to meet together again as a group after a break: *The class reassembled after lunch.*

re·as·sert /ˌriːə'sɜːrt/ *verb* **1 ~ sth** to make other people recognize again your right or authority to do something, after a period when this has been in doubt: *She found it necessary to reassert her position.* **2 ~ itself** to start to have an effect again, after a period of not having any effect: *He thought about giving up his job, but then common sense reasserted itself.* **3** to state again, clearly and firmly, that something is true: **~ that…** *He reasserted that all parties should be involved in the talks.* ◆ **~ sth** *Traditional values have been reasserted.* ▸ **re·as·ser·tion** /ˌriːə'sɜːrʃn/ *noun* [sing., U]

re·as·sess **AWL** /ˌriːə'sɛs/ *verb* **~ sth** to think again about something to decide if you need to change your opinion of it **SYN** REAPPRAISE ▸ **re·as·sess·ment** **AWL** *noun* [U, C]

re·as·sign **AWL** /ˌriːə'saɪn/ *verb* [often passive] **1 ~ sb (to sth)** to give someone a different duty, position, or responsibility: *After his election defeat he was reassigned to the diplomatic service.* **2 ~ sth (to sb/sth)** to give something to a different person or organization; to change the status of something: *The case was reassigned to a different court.* ▸ **re·as·sign·ment** *noun* [U]

re·as·sur·ance /ˌriːə'ʃʊrəns/ *noun* **1** [U] **~ (that…)** the fact of giving advice or help that takes away a person's fears or doubts: *to give/provide/offer reassurance* **2** [C] **~ (that…)** something that is said or done to take away a person's fears or doubts: *We were given reassurances that the water was safe to drink.*

re·as·sure /ˌriːə'ʃʊr/ *verb* to say or do something that makes someone less frightened or worried **SYN** SET SB'S MIND AT REST: **~ sb (about sth)** *They tried to reassure her, but she still felt anxious.* ◆ **~ sb that…** *The doctor reassured him that there was nothing seriously wrong.*

re·as·sur·ing /ˌriːə'ʃʊrɪŋ/ *adj.* making you feel less worried or uncertain about something: *a reassuring smile* ◆ *It's reassuring (to know) that we've got the money if necessary.* ▸ **re·as·sur·ing·ly** *adv.*

re·a·wak·en /ˌriːə'weɪkən/ *verb* **~ sth** to make you feel a particular emotion again or to make you remember something again **SYN** REKINDLE: *The place reawakened childhood memories.*

re·bar·ba·tive /rɪ'bɑːrbətɪv/ *adj.* (*formal*) not attractive **SYN** OBJECTIONABLE

re·bate /'riːbeɪt/ *noun* **1** an amount of money that is paid back to you because you have paid too much: *a tax rebate* **2** an amount of money that is taken away from the cost of something, before you pay for it **SYN** DISCOUNT: *Buyers are offered a cash rebate.*

reb·el *noun, verb*
● *noun* /'rɛbl/ **1** a person who fights against the government of their own country: *rebel forces* ◆ *Armed rebels advanced toward the capital.* **2** a person who opposes someone in authority over them within an organization, a political party, etc. **3** a person who does not like to obey rules or who does not accept normal standards of behavior, dress, etc.: *I've always been the rebel of the family.*
● *verb* /rɪ'bɛl/ (-ll-) [I] **~ (against sb/sth)** to fight against or refuse to obey an authority, for example a government, a system, your parents, etc.: *He later rebelled against his strict religious upbringing.* ◆ *Most teenagers find something to rebel against.*

re·bel·lion /rɪ'bɛljən/ *noun* **~ (against sb/sth)** **1** [U, C] an attempt by some of the people in a country to change their government, using violence **SYN** UPRISING: *In the American Civil War, the Confederacy rose in rebellion against the Union.* ◆ *The army put down the rebellion.* ⊃ collocations at WAR **2** [U, C] opposition to authority within an organization, a political party, etc.: *Some members are in rebellion against proposed cuts in spending.* **3** [U] opposition to authority; being unwilling to obey rules or accept normal standards of behavior, dress, etc.: *teenage rebellion*

re·bel·lious /rɪ'bɛljəs/ *adj.* **1** unwilling to obey rules or accept normal standards of behavior, dress, etc.: *rebellious teenagers* ◆ *He has always had a rebellious streak.* **2** opposed to the government of a country; opposed to those in authority within an organization: *rebellious cities/factions* ▸ **re·bel·lious·ly** *adv.*: *"I don't care!" she said rebelliously.* **re·bel·lious·ness** *noun* [U]

re·birth /ˌriː'bɜːrθ; 'riːbɜːrθ/ *noun* [U, sing.] **1** a period of new life, growth, or activity: *the seasonal cycle of death and rebirth* **2** a spiritual change when a person's faith becomes stronger or they convert to another religion

re·birth·ing /ˌriː'bɜːrθɪŋ/ *noun* [U] a type of PSYCHOTHERAPY

t **t**ea	ṭ bu**tt**er	d **d**id	k **c**at	g **g**ot	tʃ **ch**in	dʒ **J**une	f **f**all

that involves reproducing the experience of being born using controlled breathing

re·boot /ˌriˈbut/ verb [T, I] ~ **(sth)** (computing) if you **reboot** a computer or it **reboots**, you switch it off and then start it again immediately

re·born /ˌriˈbɔrn/ verb, adj.
• **verb** be **reborn** (used only in the passive without by) **1** to become active or popular again **2** to be born again: *If you were reborn as an animal, which animal would you be?*
• **adj. 1** having become active again: *a reborn version of social democracy* **2** having experienced a complete spiritual change: *reborn evangelical Christians* ➲ see also BORN-AGAIN

re·bound verb, noun
• **verb** /rɪˈbaʊnd/ **1** [I] ~ **(from/off sth)** to BOUNCE back after hitting something: *The ball rebounded off the rim and Schultz dunked it in.* **2** [I] ~ **(on sb)** (formal) if something that you do **rebounds** on you, it has an unpleasant effect on you, especially when the effect was intended for someone else **SYN** BACKFIRE **3** [I] (business) (of prices, etc.) to rise again after they have fallen **SYN** BOUNCE BACK
• **noun** /ˈribaʊnd/ **1** (sports) a ball that hits something and BOUNCES back **2** (in basketball) the act of catching the ball after a player has thrown it at the BASKET and has not scored a point: *Their team leads in rebounds this year.* **3** (business) a positive reaction that happens after something negative
IDM **on the rebound** while you are sad and confused, especially after a relationship has ended

re·brand /ˌriˈbrænd/ verb ~ **sth/yourself** to change the image of a company or an organization, or one of its products or services, for example by changing its name or by advertising it in a different way: *In the 1990s the company rebranded itself as a leader of the green movement.*
▶ **re·brand·ing** noun [sing., U]: *a rebranding exercise* ♦ *a $10 million rebranding*

re·buff /rɪˈbʌf/ noun (formal) an unkind refusal of a friendly offer, request, or suggestion **SYN** REJECTION: *Her offer of help was met with a sharp rebuff.* ▶ **re·buff** verb: ~ **sth** *They rebuffed her request for help.*

re·build /ˌriˈbɪld/ verb (re·built, re·built /-ˈbɪlt/) **1** ~ sth to build or put something together again: *After the earthquake, the people set about rebuilding their homes.* ♦ *He rebuilt the engine using parts from cars that had been scrapped.* **2** ~ sth to make something or someone complete and strong again: *When she lost her job, she had to rebuild her life completely.* ♦ *attempts to rebuild the shattered postwar economy*

re·buke /rɪˈbyuk/ verb [often passive] ~ **sb (for sth/for doing sth)** (formal) to speak severely to someone because they have done something wrong **SYN** REPRIMAND: *The company was publicly rebuked for having neglected safety procedures.* ▶ **re·buke** noun [C, U]: *He was silenced by her stinging rebuke.*

to be or not to be

re·bus /ˈribəs/ noun a combination of pictures and letters that represent a word whose meaning has to be guessed

re·but /rɪˈbʌt/ verb (-tt-) ~ **sth** (formal) to say or prove that a statement or criticism is false **SYN** REFUTE ▶ **re·but·tal** /rɪˈbʌtl/ noun [C, U]: *He issued a firm rebuttal to the accusations.*

re·cal·ci·trant /rɪˈkælsətrənt/ adj. (formal) unwilling to obey rules or follow instructions; difficult to control ▶ **re·cal·ci·trance** /-trəns/ noun [U]

re·call ♪ verb, noun
• **verb** /rɪˈkɔl/ **1** [T, I] (formal) (not used in the progressive

tenses) to remember something **SYN** RECOLLECT: ~ sth *She could not recall his name.* ♦ **(+ adv./prep.)** *If I recall correctly, he lives in Atlanta.* ♦ ~ **(sb/sth) doing sth** *I can't recall meeting her before.* ♦ ~ **that…** *He recalled that she always came home late on Wednesdays.* ♦ ~ **what, when, etc. …** *Can you recall exactly what happened?* ♦ **+ speech** *"It was on a Thursday in March," he recalled.* **2** [T] ~ sth (not used in the progressive tenses) to make someone think of something **SYN** EVOKE: *The poem recalls Eliot's "The Waste Land."* **3** [T] to order someone to return: ~ **sb** *Both countries recalled their ambassadors.* ♦ ~ **sb to sth** *He was recalled to military duty.* **4** [T] ~ sth (business) to ask for something to be returned, often because there is something wrong with it: *The company has recalled all the faulty hairdryers.*
• **noun 1** /ˈrikɔl; rɪˈkɔl/ [U] the ability to remember something that you have learned or something that happened in the past: *She has amazing powers of recall.* ♦ *to have **instant recall*** (= to be able to remember something immediately) ♦ *to have **total recall*** (= to be able to remember all the details of something) **2** /ˈrikɔl/ [sing.] (business) a request or order from a company to return a product because of a possible problem **3** /ˈrikɔl/ [sing.] the act of removing a public official from office by a vote **4** /ˈrikɔl/ [sing.] an official order for someone to return to a place: *Thomas's recall to the swim team.* ♦ *the recall of their ambassador from Peru*
IDM **beyond recall** impossible to bring back to the original state; impossible to remember

re·cant /rɪˈkænt/ verb [T, I] ~ **(sth)** (formal) to say, often publicly, that you no longer have the same belief or opinion that you had before ▶ **re·can·ta·tion** /ˌrikænˈteɪʃn/ noun [C, U]

re·cap /ˈrikæp/ verb (-pp-) [I, T] = RECAPITULATE: *Let me just recap what we've decided on so far.*

re·ca·pit·u·late /ˌrikəˈpɪtʃəleɪt/ verb (formal) (also **re·cap**) [I, T] ~ **(on sth)** | ~ **sth** | ~ **what, where, etc.…** to repeat or give a summary of what has already been said, decided, etc.: *To recapitulate briefly, the three main points are these…* ▶ **re·ca·pit·u·la·tion** /ˌrikəˌpɪtʃəˈleɪʃn/ noun [C, U] (formal) (also **re·cap**)

re·cap·ture /ˌriˈkæptʃər/ verb **1** ~ sth to win back a place, position, etc. that was previously taken from you by an enemy or a rival: *Government troops soon recaptured the island.* **2** ~ **sb/sth** to catch a person or an animal that has escaped **3** ~ sth to bring back a feeling or repeat an experience that you had in the past: *He was trying to recapture the happiness of his youth.* ▶ **re·cap·ture** noun [U]: *the recapture of towns occupied by the rebels*

re·cast /ˌriˈkæst/ verb (re·cast, re·cast) **1** ~ **sth (as sth)** to change something by organizing or presenting it in a different way: *She recast her lecture as a radio talk.* **2** ~ **sb (as sth)** to change the actors or the role of a particular actor in a play, etc.

re·cede /rɪˈsid/ verb **1** [I] to move gradually away from someone, or away from a previous position: *The sound of the truck receded into the distance.* ♦ *She watched his receding figure.* **2** [I] (especially of a problem, feeling, or quality) to become gradually weaker or smaller: *The prospect of bankruptcy had now receded* (= it was less likely). ♦ *The pain was receding slightly.* **3** [I] (of hair) to stop growing at the front of the head: *a middle-aged man with **receding hair/a receding hairline*** ➲ picture at HAIR **4** [I] **a** ~ **chin** a chin that slopes backward toward the neck

re·ceipt ♪ /rɪˈsit/ noun
1 (also **sales slip**) [C] ~ **(for sth)** a piece of paper that shows that goods or services have been paid for: *Can I have a receipt, please?* ♦ *to **make out*** (= write) *a receipt* ➲ collocations at SHOPPING **2** [U] ~ **(of sth)** (formal) the act of receiving something: *to acknowledge receipt of a letter* ♦ *The goods will be dispatched **on receipt of** an order form.* ♦ *Are you **in receipt of** any payments from them?* **3** **receipts** [pl.] (business) money that a business, bank, or government receives: *net/gross receipts*

re·ceiv·a·ble /rɪˈsivəbl/ adj. (business) (usually following a noun) (of bills, accounts, etc.) for which money has not yet been received: *accounts receivable*

re·ceiv·a·bles /rɪˈsivəblz/ *noun* [pl.] (*business*) money that is owed to a business

re·ceive 🔑 /rɪˈsiv/ *verb*

> GET/ACCEPT **1** [T] (somewhat *formal*) to get or accept something that is sent or given to you: ~ **sth** *to receive a letter/present/phone call* ♦ *to receive information/payment/thanks* ♦ ~ **sth from sb/sth** *He received an award for bravery from the police department.*

> TREATMENT/INJURY **2** [T] to experience or be given a particular type of treatment or an injury: ~ **sth from sb** *We received a warm welcome from our hosts.* ♦ ~ **sth** *Emergency cases will receive professional attention immediately.* ♦ *to receive severe injuries*

> REACT TO SOMETHING **3** [T, usually passive] to react to something new in a particular way: ~ **sth + adv./prep.** *The play was well received by the critics.* ♦ ~ **sth with sth** *The statistics were received with concern.*

> GUESTS **4** [T, often passive] ~ **sb (with sth)** | ~ **sb (as sth)** (*formal*) to welcome or entertain a guest, especially formally: *He was received as an honored guest at the White House.*

> AS MEMBER OF SOMETHING **5** [T] ~ **sb (into sth)** to officially recognize and accept someone as a member of a group: *Three young people were received into the church at Easter.*

> TV/RADIO **6** [T] ~ **sth** to change broadcast signals into sounds or pictures on a television, radio, etc.: *to receive programs via satellite* **7** [T] ~ **sth/sb** to be able to hear a radio message that is being sent by someone: *I'm receiving you loud and clear.*

> IN SPORTS **8** [I, T] ~ **(sth)** (in TENNIS, etc.) to be the player that the SERVER hits the ball to: *She won the toss and chose to receive.*

IDM **be at/on the receiving end (of sth)** (*informal*) to be the person that an action, etc. is directed at, especially an unpleasant one: *She found herself on the receiving end of a lot of criticism.*

re·ceived /rɪˈsivd/ *adj.* [only before noun] (*formal*) accepted by most people as being correct: *The received wisdom is that they cannot win.*

re·ceiv·er /rɪˈsivər/ *noun* **1** the part of a telephone that you hold close to your mouth and ear: *to pick up/lift/put down/replace the receiver* ➔ collocations at PHONE ➔ compare HANDSET **2** a piece of radio or television equipment that changes broadcast signals into sound or pictures: *a satellite receiver* ➔ compare TRANSMITTER **3** (*law*) a person who is chosen by a court to be in charge of a company that is BANKRUPT: *to call in the receivers* **4** a person who receives something: *Molly's more of a giver than a receiver.* **5** a person who buys or accepts stolen goods, knowing that they have been stolen **6** (in football) a player who is allowed to catch the ball when it is passed forward by the QUARTERBACK

re·ceiv·er·ship /rɪˈsivərˌʃɪp/ *noun* [U] (*law*) the state of a business being controlled by a receiver because it has no money: *to go into receivership*

re·cent 🔑 /ˈrisnt/ *adj.* [usually before noun] that happened or began only a short time ago: *a recent development/discovery/event* ♦ *his most recent visit to Poland* ♦ *There have been many changes in recent years.*

re·cent·ly 🔑 /ˈrisntli/ *adv.* not long ago: *We received a letter from him recently.* ♦ *Until recently they were living in New York. I haven't seen them recently* (= it is some time since I saw them). ♦ *Have you used it recently* (= in the recent past)?

re·cep·ta·cle /rɪˈsɛptəkl/ *noun* **1** ~ **(for sth)** (*formal*) a container for putting something in: (*figurative*) *a trash receptacle* **2** = OUTLET (5)

re·cep·tion 🔑 /rɪˈsɛpʃn/ *noun* **1** [C, usually sing.] the type of welcome that is given to someone or something: *Her latest album has met with a mixed*

reception *from fans.* ♦ *Delegates gave him a warm reception as he called for more spending on education.* **2** [C] a formal social occasion to welcome someone or celebrate something: *a wedding reception* **3** [U] the act of receiving or welcoming someone: *the reception of refugees from the war zone* **4** [U] the quality of radio and television signals that are broadcast: *good/bad reception* ♦ *There was very poor reception on my phone.* **5** [U] the area inside the entrance of a hotel, an office building, etc. where guests or visitors go first when they arrive: *the reception area* ♦ *We arranged to meet in reception at 6.30.* ♦ *You can leave a message with reception.* ♦ *the reception desk* ➔ compare FRONT DESK **6** [C] (in football) the act of catching a ball when it is being passed forward: *a 33-yard reception*

reˈception ˌcenter (*CanE usually* **reˈception ˌcentre**) *noun* a place where people, for example those without a home, can get help and temporary housing: *a reception center for refugees*

re·cep·tion·ist /rɪˈsɛpʃənɪst/ *noun* a person whose job is to deal with people arriving at or telephoning a hotel, a place of business, a doctor's office, etc.

re·cep·tive /rɪˈsɛptɪv/ *adj.* ~ **(to sth)** willing to listen to or to accept new ideas or suggestions **SYN** RESPONSIVE: *She was always receptive to new ideas.* ♦ *He gave an impressive speech to a receptive audience.* ▸ **re·cep·tive·ness**, **re·cep·tiv·i·ty** /ˌrisɛpˈtɪvəti/ *noun* [U]: *receptivity to change*

re·cep·tor /rɪˈsɛptər/ *noun* (*biology*) a sense organ or nerve ending in the body that reacts to changes such as heat or cold and makes the body react in a particular way

re·cess *noun*, *verb* /ˈrisɛs; rɪˈsɛs/
● *noun* **1** [C, U] a period of time during the year when a group of people who make laws, the members of a committee, etc. do not meet **2** [C] a short break in a trial in court: *The judge called a short recess.* **3** [U] a period of time between classes at school when children can play **4** [C] a part of a wall that is set further back than the rest of the wall, forming a space **SYN** ALCOVE: *a recess for books* **5** [C, usually pl.] the part of a place that is furthest from the light and hard to see or get to: *He stared into the dark recesses of the room.* ♦ (*figurative*) *The doubt was still there, in the deep recesses of her mind.*

● *verb* [often passive] **1** [T, I] ~ **(sth)** to take or to order a recess: *The hearing was recessed for the weekend.* **2** [T] ~ **sth (in/into sth)** to put something in a position that is set back into a wall, etc.: *recessed shelves*

re·ces·sion /rɪˈsɛʃn/ *noun* **1** [C, U] a difficult time for the economy of a country, when there is less trade and industrial activity than usual and more people are unemployed: *the impact of the current recession on manufacturing* ♦ *The economy is in deep recession.* ♦ *policies to pull the country out of recession* ➔ collocations at ECONOMY **2** [U] (*formal*) the movement backward of something from a previous position: *the gradual recession of the floodwaters*

re·ces·sion·ar·y /rɪˈsɛʃəˌnɛri/ *adj.* [only before noun] connected with a recession or likely to cause one

re·ces·sive /rɪˈsɛsɪv/ *adj.* (*biology*) a **recessive** physical characteristic only appears in a child if it has two GENES for this characteristic, one from each parent. It does not appear if a DOMINANT gene is also present.

re·charge /ˌriˈtʃɑrdʒ/ *verb* **1** [T, I] ~ **(sth)** to fill a battery with electrical power; to be filled with electrical power: *He plugged his razor in to recharge it.* ♦ *The drill takes about three hours to recharge.* **2** [I] (*informal*) to get back your strength and energy by resting for a time: *We needed the break in order to recharge.* ▸ **re·charge·a·ble** /ˌriˈtʃɑrdʒəbl/ *adj.*: *rechargeable batteries*

IDM **recharge your batteries** to get back your strength and energy by resting for a while

re·cher·ché /rəˌʃɛrˈʃeɪ/ *adj.* (from *French*, *formal*, usually *disapproving*) unusual and not easy to understand, chosen in order to impress people

re·cid·i·vist /rɪˈsɪdəvɪst/ *noun* (*formal*) a person who continues to commit crimes, and seems unable to stop, even after being punished ▶ **re·cid·i·vism** /-ˌvɪzəm/ *noun* [U]

rec·i·pe /ˈresəpi/ *noun* **1** ~ **(for sth)** a set of instructions that tells you how to cook something and the **INGREDIENTS** (= items of food) you need for it: *a recipe for chicken soup* ◆ *vegetarian recipes* ◆ *a recipe file* **2** ~ **for sth** a method or an idea that seems likely to have a particular result **SYN** FORMULA: *His plans are* ***a recipe for disaster***. ◆ *What's her recipe for success?*

re·cip·i·ent /rɪˈsɪpiənt/ *noun* (*formal*) a person who receives something: *recipients of awards*

re·cip·ro·cal /rɪˈsɪprəkl/ *adj.* involving two people or groups who agree to help each other or behave in the same way to each other: *The two colleges have a reciprocal agreement whereby students from one college can attend classes at the other.* ▶ **re·cip·ro·cally** /-kli/ *adv.*

reˌciprocal ˈverb *noun* (*grammar*) a verb that expresses the idea of an action that is done by two or more people or things to each other, for example "kiss" in the sentence "Paul and Claire kissed."

re·cip·ro·cate /rɪˈsɪprəˌkeɪt/ *verb* **1** [T, I] to behave or feel toward someone in the same way as they behave or feel toward you: ~ **sth (with sth)** *Her passion for him was not reciprocated.* ◆ *He smiled but his smile was not reciprocated.* ◆ ~ **(with sth)** *I wasn't sure whether to laugh or to reciprocate with a remark of my own.* **2** [I] (*technical*) to move backward and forward in a straight line: *a reciprocating action* ▶ **re·cip·ro·ca·tion** /rɪˌsɪprəˈkeɪʃn/ *noun* [U]

rec·i·proc·i·ty /ˌresəˈprɒsəti/ *noun* [U] (*formal*) a situation in which two people, countries, etc. provide the same help or advantages to each other

re·cit·al /rɪˈsaɪtl/ *noun* **1** a public performance of music or poetry, usually given by one person or a small group: *to give a piano recital* ➔ **collocations at** MUSIC **2** a spoken description of a series of events, etc. that is often long and boring

rec·i·ta·tion /ˌresəˈteɪʃn/ *noun* **1** [C, U] an act of saying a piece of poetry or literature that you have learned to an audience **2** [C] an act of talking or writing about a series of things: *She continued her recitation of the week's events.*

rec·i·ta·tive /ˌresətəˈtiːv/ *noun* [C, U] (*music*) a passage in an OPERA or ORATORIO that is sung in the rhythm of ordinary speech with many words on the same note

re·cite /rɪˈsaɪt/ *verb* **1** [T, I] ~ **(sth) (to sb)** | ~ **what…** | + **speech** to say a poem, piece of literature, etc. that you have learned, especially to an audience: *Each child had to recite a poem to the class.* **2** [T] ~ **sth (to sb)** | ~ **what…** | + **speech** to say a list or series of things: *They recited all their grievances to me.* ◆ *She could recite a list of all the presidents.*

reck·less /ˈrekləs/ *adj.* showing a lack of care about danger and the possible results of your actions **SYN** RASH: *He showed* ***a reckless disregard for*** *his own safety.* ◆ *She was a good rider, but reckless.* ◆ *He had always been reckless with money.* ◆ *The accident was caused by* ***reckless driving*** **ANT** CAUTIOUS ▶ **reck·less·ly** *adv.*: *He admitted driving recklessly.* **reck·less·ness** *noun* [U]

reck·on /ˈrekən/ *verb* **1** [T, I] ~ **(that)…** (*informal*) to think something or have an opinion about something: *I reckon (that) I'm going to get that job.* ◆ *It's worth a lot of money, I reckon.* **2** **be reckoned** [T] (not used in the progressive tenses) to be generally considered to be something: ~ **to be/have sth** *Children are reckoned to be more sophisticated nowadays.* ◆ + **noun/adj.** *It was generally reckoned a success.* **3** [T] to calculate an amount, a number, etc.: ~ **sth (at sth)** *The age of the earth is reckoned at about 4,600 million years.* ◆ ~ **(that)…** *They reckon (that) their profits are down by at least 20%.* ◆ **be reckoned to do sth** *The journey was reckoned to take about two hours.* **IDM** see NAME *n.* **PHR V** **ˈreckon on sth** to expect something to happen or to rely on something happening: *They hadn't reckoned on a rebellion.* ◆ ~ **doing sth** *Unfortunately, we reckoned on having good weather.* **ˈreckon with sb/sth 1** [usually passive] to consider or treat someone or something as a serious opponent, problem, etc.: *They were already a political force to*

be reckoned with. **2** (usually used in negative sentences) to consider something as a possible problem that you should be prepared for **SYN** TAKE STH INTO ACCOUNT: ~ **doing sth** *I didn't reckon with getting caught up in so much traffic.*

reck·on·ing /ˈrekənɪŋ/ *noun* **1** [U, C] the act of calculating something, especially in a way that is not very exact: *By my reckoning you still owe me $10.* **2** [C, usually sing., U] a time when someone's actions will be judged to be right or wrong and they may be punished: *In the* ***final reckoning*** *truth is rewarded.* ◆ *Officials concerned with environmental policy predict that* ***a day of reckoning*** *will come.*

re·claim /rɪˈkleɪm/ *verb* **1** to get something back or to ask to have it back after it has been lost, taken away, etc.: ~ **sth** *You'll have to go to the police station to reclaim your wallet.* ◆ ~ **sth from sb/sth** *The team reclaimed the title from their rivals.* **2** ~ **sth (from sth)** to make land that is naturally either too wet or too dry suitable to be built on, farmed, etc.: *The site for the airport will be reclaimed from the swamp.* ◆ *reclaimed marshland* **3** [usually passive] ~ **sth** if a piece of land **is reclaimed by** desert, forest, etc., it turns back into desert, etc. after being used for farming or building **4** ~ **sth (from sth)** to obtain materials from waste products so that they can be used again ➔ see also RECYCLE **5** ~ **sb (from sth)** to rescue someone from a bad or criminal way of life ▶ **rec·la·ma·tion** /ˌrekləˈmeɪʃn/ *noun* [U]: *land reclamation*

re·clas·si·fy /ˌriːˈklæsəˌfaɪ/ *verb* (**re·clas·si·fies**, **re·clas·si·fy·ing**, **re·clas·si·fied**, **re·clas·si·fied**) ~ **sth** to put something in a different class or category: *The drug is to be reclassified after trials showed it to be more harmful than previously thought.*

re·cline /rɪˈklaɪn/ *verb* **1** [I] ~ **(against/in/on sth)** (*formal*) to sit or lie in a relaxed way, with your body leaning backward: *She was reclining on a sofa.* ◆ *a reclining figure* (= for example in a painting) **2** [I, T] ~ **(sth)** when a seat **reclines** or when you **recline** a seat, the back of it moves into a comfortable sloping position: *a reclining chair*

re·clin·er /rɪˈklaɪnər/ *noun* (also **reˈcliner ˌchair**) *noun* a soft comfortable chair with a back that can be pushed back at an angle so that you can lean back in it ➔ **picture at** CHAIR

rec·luse /ˈreklus/ *noun* a person who lives alone and likes to avoid other people: *to lead the life of a recluse* ▶ **re·clu·sive** /rɪˈklusɪv/ *adj.*: *a reclusive millionaire*

rec·og·ni·tion 🔑 /ˌrekəɡˈnɪʃn/ *noun* **1** [U] the act of remembering who someone is when you see them, or of identifying what something is: *He glanced briefly toward her but there was no sign of recognition.* ◆ *the automatic recognition of handwriting and printed text by a computer* **2** [sing., U] ~ **(that…)** the act of accepting that something exists, is true, or is official: *a growing recognition that older people have potential too* ◆ *There is a general recognition of the urgent need for reform.* ◆ *to seek* ***international/official/formal recognition*** *as a sovereign state* **3** [U] ~ **(for sth)** public praise and reward for someone's work or actions: *She gained only minimal recognition for her work.* ◆ *He received the award* ***in recognition of*** *his success over the past year.* **IDM** **to change, alter, etc. beyond recognition** to change so much that you can hardly recognize it: *The town has changed beyond recognition since I was last here.*

rec·og·niz·a·ble /ˈrekəɡˌnaɪzəbl; ˌrekəɡˈnaɪ-/ *adj.* ~ **(as sth/sb)** easy to know or identify: *The building was easily recognizable as a prison.* ◆ *After so many years she was still instantly recognizable.* **ANT** UNRECOGNIZABLE ▶ **rec·og·niz·a·bly** /-bli/ *adv.*

re·cog·ni·zance /rɪˈkɒɡnəzəns; -ˈkɒnə-/ *noun* [U] (*law*) a promise by someone who is accused of a crime to appear in court on a particular date; a sum of money paid as a guarantee of this promise

rec·og·nize 🔑 /ˈrekəɡˌnaɪz/ *verb* (not used in the progressive tenses) **1** to know who someone is or what something is when you see or hear them, because you have seen or heard them or it before: **~ sb/sth** *I recognized him as soon as he entered the room.* ◆ *Do you recognize this tune?* ◆ **~ sb/sth by/from sth** *I recognized her by her red hair.* ⊃ thesaurus box at IDENTIFY **2** to admit or to be aware that something exists or is true **SYN** ACKNOWLEDGE: **~ sth** *They recognized the need to take the problem seriously.* ◆ **~ sth as sth** *Drugs were not recognized as a problem then.* ◆ **~ how, what, etc. ...** *Nobody recognized how urgent the situation was.* ◆ **~ that...** *We recognized that the task was not straightforward.* ◆ **it is recognized that...** *It was recognized that this solution could only be temporary.* ◆ **~ sb/sth to be/have sth** *Drugs were not recognized to be a problem then.* ⊃ thesaurus box at ADMIT **3** to accept and approve of someone or something officially: **~ sb/sth (as sth)** *recognized qualifications* ◆ *Most countries have refused to recognize the new regime.* ◆ **be recognized to be/have sth** *He is recognized to be their natural leader.* **4 be recognized (as sth)** to be thought of as very good or important by people in general: *The book is now recognized as a classic.* ◆ *She's a recognized authority on the subject.* **5 ~ sb/sth** to give someone official thanks for something that they have done or achieved: *His service to the country was recognized with the award of the Medal of Honor.*

re·coil *verb, noun*
● *verb* /rɪˈkɔɪl/ **1** [I] to move your body quickly away from someone or something because you find them or it frightening or unpleasant **SYN** FLINCH: **~ (from sb/sth)** *She recoiled from his touch.* ◆ **~ (at sth)** *He recoiled in horror at the sight of the corpse.* **2** [I] **~ (from sth/from doing sth)** | **~ (at sth)** to react to an idea or a situation with strong dislike or fear **SYN** SHRINK: *She recoiled from the idea of betraying her own brother.* **3** [I] (of a gun) to move suddenly backward when you fire it
● *noun* /ˈriːkɔɪl/ [U, sing.] a sudden movement backward, especially of a gun when it is fired

rec·ol·lect /ˌrekəˈlekt/ *verb* [T, I] (not used in the progressive tenses) (somewhat *formal*) to remember something, especially by making an effort to remember it **SYN** RECALL: **~ (sth)** *She could no longer recollect the details of the letter.* ◆ *As far as I can recollect, she wasn't there on that occasion.* ◆ **~ what, how, etc. ...** *I don't recollect what he said.* ◆ **~ that...** *I recollect that we were all gathered in the kitchen.* ◆ **~ (sb/sth) doing sth** *I recollect him/his saying that it was dangerous.* ◆ **+ speech** *"It was just before the war," she recollected.*

rec·ol·lec·tion /ˌrekəˈlekʃn/ *noun* (*formal*) **1** [U] the ability to remember something; the act of remembering something **SYN** MEMORY: **~ (of doing sth)** *I have no recollection of meeting her before.* ◆ **~ (of sth)** *My recollection of events differs from his.* ◆ **To the best of my recollection** (= if I remember correctly) *I was not present at that meeting.* **2** [C] a thing that you remember from the past **SYN** MEMORY: *to have a clear/ vivid/dim/vague recollection of something*

re·com·mence /ˌriːkəˈmens/ *verb* [I, T] (*formal*) to begin again; to start doing something again: *Work on the bridge will recommence next month.* ◆ **~ (doing) sth** *The two countries agreed to recommence talks the following week.*

rec·om·mend 🔑 /ˌrekəˈmend/ *verb*
1 to tell someone that something is good or useful, or that someone would be suitable for a particular job, etc.: **~ sb/ sth** *Can you recommend a good hotel?* ◆ **~ sb/sth (to sb) (for/ as sth)** *I recommend the book to all my students.* ◆ *She was recommended for the job by a colleague.* ◆ *The hotel's new restaurant comes* **highly recommended** (= a lot of people have praised it). **2** to advise a particular course of action; to advise someone to do something: **~ sth** *The report recommended a 10% pay increase.* ◆ *It is dangerous to exceed the recommended dose.* ◆ *a recommended price of $50* ◆ **~ (that)...** *I recommend (that) he see a lawyer.* ◆ **it is recommended that...** *It is strongly recommended that the machines be checked every year.* ◆ **~ sb to do sth** *Passengers are recommend to arrive at the airport early.* ◆ **~ (sb) doing sth** *He recommended reading the book before seeing the movie.* ◆ **~ how, what, etc....** *Can you recommend how much we should charge?* **3 ~ sb/sth (to sb)** to make someone or

something seem attractive or good **SYN** COMMEND: *This system has* **much to recommend it.**

rec·om·men·da·tion 🔑 /ˌrekəmenˈdeɪʃn/ *noun* **1** [C] an official suggestion about the best thing to do: *to accept/reject a recommendation* ◆ **~ (to sb) (for/on/about sth)** *The committee* **made recommendations** *to the board on teachers' pay and conditions.* ◆ *I had the operation* **on the recommendation** *of my doctor.* **2** [U, C] the act of telling someone that something is good or useful or that someone would be suitable for a particular job, etc.: *We chose the hotel* **on their recommendation** (= because they recommended it). ◆ *It's best to find a builder through* **personal recommendation***.* ◆ *Here's a list of my top CD recommendations.* **3** [C] a formal letter or statement that someone would be suitable for a particular job, etc. **SYN** TESTIMONIAL: *to write somebody a recommendation*

rec·om·pense /ˈrekəmˌpens/ *noun, verb*
● *noun* [U] **~ (for sth/sb)** (*formal*) something, usually money, that you are given because you have suffered in some way, or as a payment for something: *There must be adequate recompense for workers who lose their jobs.* ◆ *I received $1,000* **in recompense** *for loss of earnings.*
● *verb* **~ sb (for sth)** (*formal*) to do something for someone or give them a payment for something that they have suffered **SYN** COMPENSATE: *There was no attempt to recompense the miners for the loss of their jobs.*

re·con /ˈriːkɑn/ *noun* [C, U] (*informal*) = RECONNAISSANCE

rec·on·cile /ˈrekənˌsaɪl/ *verb* **1 ~ sth (with sth)** to find an acceptable way of dealing with two or more ideas, needs, etc. that seem to be opposed to each other: *an attempt to reconcile the need for industrial development with concern for*

ʌ cup   ə about   eɪ say   aɪ five   ɔɪ boy   aʊ now   oʊ go   ər bird

the environment ♦ *It was hard to reconcile his career ambitions with the needs of his children.* **2** [usually passive] to make people become friends again after an argument or a disagreement: **~ sb** *The pair were reconciled after Jackson made a public apology.* ♦ **~ sb with sb** *He has recently been reconciled with his wife.* **3 ~ sb/yourself (to sth)** to make someone/yourself accept an unpleasant situation because it is not possible to change it **SYN** **RESIGN YOURSELF TO:** *He could not reconcile himself to the prospect of losing her.* ▶ **rec·on·cil·a·ble** /ˌrɛkənˈsaɪləbl/ *adj.*

rec·on·di·a·tion /ˌrɛkənˌsɪliˈeɪʃn/ *noun* **1** [sing., U] **~ (between A and B)** | **~ (with sb)** an end to a disagreement and the start of a good relationship again: *The change of policy brought about a reconciliation with their former enemy.* **2** [U] **~ (between A and B)** | **~ (with sth)** the process of making it possible for two different ideas, facts, etc. to exist together without being opposed to each other: *the reconciliation between environment and development*

rec·on·dite /ˈrɛkənˌdaɪt/ *adj.* (*formal*) not known about or understood by many people **SYN** **OBSCURE**

re·con·di·tion /ˌrikənˈdɪʃn/ *verb* [often passive] **~ sth** to repair a machine so that it is in good condition and works well **SYN** **OVERHAUL**

re·con·fig·ure /ˌrikənˈfɪɡyər/ *verb* **~ sth** to make changes to the way that something is arranged to work, especially computer equipment or a program: *You may need to reconfigure the firewall if you add a new machine to your network.*

re·con·firm /ˌrikənˈfərm/ *verb* **~ sth** to check again that something is definitely correct or as previously arranged: *You have to reconfirm your flight 24 hours before traveling.*

re·con·nais·sance /rɪˈkɑnəsəns; -zəns/ (*also informal* **re·con**) *noun* [C, U] the activity of getting information about an area for military purposes, using soldiers, planes, etc.: *to make an aerial reconnaissance of the island* ♦ *a reconnaissance aircraft/mission/satellite* ⊃ collocations at **WAR**

re·con·nect /ˌrikəˈnɛkt/ *verb* [T, I] **1** to connect something again; to connect to something again: **~ sth (to sth)** *I replaced the faucets and reconnected the water supply.* ♦ **~ (to sth)** *Once you have removed the virus, it is safe to reconnect to the Internet.* **2 ~ (with sb)** to get to know someone again: *I hadn't seen her since high school, but we recently reconnected.*

re·con·noi·ter /ˌrikəˈnɔɪtər/ *verb* [I, T] **~ (sth)** to get information about an area, especially for military purposes, by using soldiers, planes, etc.

re·con·quer /ˌriˈkɑŋkər/ *verb* **~ sth** to take control again of a country or city by force, after having lost it

re·con·sid·er /ˌrikənˈsɪdər/ *verb* [T, I] **~ (sth)** | **~ what, how, etc. …** to think about something again, especially because you might want to change a previous decision or opinion: *to reconsider your decision/position* ♦ *Recent information may persuade the board to reconsider.* ▶ **re·con·sid·er·a·tion** /ˌrikənˌsɪdəˈreɪʃn/ *noun* [U, sing.]

re·con·sti·tute /ˌriˈkɑnstəˌtut/ *verb* **1 ~ sth/itself (as sth)** (*formal*) to form an organization or a group again in a different way: *The group reconstituted itself as a political party.* **2** [usually passive] **~ sth** to bring dried food, etc. back to its original form by adding water ▶ **re·con·sti·tu·tion** /ˌriˌkɑnstəˈtuʃn/ *noun* [U]

re·con·struct **AWL** /ˌrikənˈstrʌkt/ *verb* **1 ~ sth (from sth)** to build or make something again that has been damaged or that no longer exists: *They have tried to reconstruct the settlement as it would have been in pre-Columbian times.* **2 ~ sth** to be able to describe or show exactly how a past event happened, using the information you have gathered: *Investigators are trying to reconstruct the circumstances of the crash.*

re·con·struc·tion **AWL** /ˌrikənˈstrʌkʃn/ *noun* **1** [U] the process of changing or improving the condition of something or the way it works; the process of putting something back into the state it was in before: *the post-war reconstruction of Germany* ♦ *a reconstruction period* **2** [U] the activity of

building again something that has been damaged or destroyed: *the reconstruction of the sea walls* **3** [C] a copy of something that no longer exists: *A modern reconstruction of Shakespeare's Globe Theater opened in 1997.* **4** [C] a short film showing events that are known to have happened in order to try and get more information or better understanding, especially about a crime: *Last night police staged a reconstruction of the incident.* **5 Reconstruction** [U] the period after the American Civil War when the southern states returned to the U.S. and laws were passed that gave rights to African Americans

re·con·struc·tive /ˌrikənˈstrʌktɪv/ *adj.* [only before noun] (of medical treatment) that involves **RECONSTRUCTING** part of a person's body because it has been badly damaged or because the person wants to change its shape: *reconstructive surgery*

re·con·vene /ˌrikənˈvin/ *verb* [I, T] **~ (sth)** if a meeting, congress, parliament, etc. **reconvenes** or if someone **reconvenes** it, it meets again after a break

record 🔑 *noun, verb*

● ***noun*** rec·ord /ˈrɛkərd/

> **WRITTEN ACCOUNT** **1** [C] **~ (of sth)** a written account of something that is kept so that it can be looked at and used in the future: *You should keep a record of your expenses.* ♦ *medical/dental records* ♦ *Last summer was the wettest on record.* ♦ *It was the worst flood since records began.*

> **MUSIC** **2** [C] a thin round piece of plastic on which music, etc. was recorded: *to play a record* ♦ *a record collection* ♦ *a record company* (= one that produces and sells records) ⊃ collocations at **MUSIC**

> **HIGHEST/BEST** **3** [C] the best result or the highest or lowest level that has ever been reached, especially in sports: *She holds the world record for the 100 meters.* ♦ *to break the record* (= to achieve a better result than there has ever been before) ♦ *to set a new record* ♦ *There was a record number of candidates for the position.* ♦ *I got to work in record time.* ♦ *record profits* ♦ *Unemployment has reached a record high* (= the highest level ever).

> **OF SOMEONE/SOMETHING'S PAST** **4** [sing.] **~ (on sth)** the facts that are known about someone/something's past behavior, character, achievements, etc.: *The report criticizes the government's record on housing.* ♦ *The airline has a good safety record.* ♦ *He has an impressive record of achievement.* ⊃ see also **TRACK RECORD**

> **OF CRIMES** **5** (also ˌcriminal ˈrecord) [C] the fact of having committed crimes in the past: *Does he have a record?*

IDM **(just) for the record 1** used to show that you want what you are saying to be officially written down and remembered **2** used to emphasize a point that you are making, so that the person you are speaking to takes notice: *And, for the record, he would be the last person I'd ask.* **off the record** if you tell someone something **off the record**, it is not yet official and you do not want them to repeat it publicly **put sth on (the) record** | **be/go on (the) record (as saying…)** to say something publicly or officially so that it may be written down and repeated: *He didn't want to go on the record as either praising or criticizing the proposal.* **put/set the record straight** to give people the correct information about something in order to make it clear that what they previously believed to be right was, in fact, wrong ⊃ more at **MATTER** *n.*

● ***verb*** re·cord /rɪˈkɔrd/

> **KEEP ACCOUNT** **1** [T] to keep a permanent account of facts or events by writing them down, filming them, storing them in a computer, etc.: **~ sth** *Her childhood is recorded in the diaries of those years.* ♦ *You should record all your expenses during your trip.* ♦ **~ how, what, etc. …** *His job is to record how politicians vote on major issues.* ♦ **~ that…** *She recorded in her diary that they crossed the Equator on June 15.* ♦ **it is recorded that…** *It is recorded that, by the year 630, 1,500 monks were attached to the monastery.*

> **MAKE COPY** **2** [T, I] to make a copy of music, a movie, etc. by storing it on tape or a disk so that you can listen to or watch it again: **~ (sth)** *Did you remember to record that program for*

me. ♦ *a recorded concert* ♦ **~ sb/sth doing sth** *He recorded the class rehearsing before the performance.*
▸ MUSIC **3** [T, I] **~ (sth)** to perform music so that it can be copied onto and kept on tape or a disk: *The band is back in the U.S. recording their new album.*
▸ MAKE OFFICIAL STATEMENT **4** [T] **~ sth | ~ that…** to make an official or legal statement about something: *The coroner recorded a verdict of accidental death.*
▸ OF MEASURING INSTRUMENT **5** [T] **~ sth | ~ what, how, etc. …** to show a particular measurement or amount: *The thermometer recorded a temperature of 100°F.*

ˈrecord-ˌbreaker *noun* a person or thing that achieves a better result or higher level than has ever been achieved before ▶ ˈrecord-ˌbreaking *adj.* [only before noun]: *a record-breaking jump*

re·cord·er /rɪˈkɔrdər/ *noun* **1** (in compounds) a machine for recording sound, or pictures, or both: *a tape/cassette/ video/DVD recorder* **2** a musical instrument in the shape of a pipe that you blow into, with holes that you cover with your fingers ⟳ picture at INSTRUMENT **3** a person who keeps a record of events or facts

ˈrecord ˌholder *noun* a person who has achieved the best result that has ever been achieved in a sport or other activity

re·cord·ing 🗝 /rɪˈkɔrdɪŋ/ *noun*
1 [C] sound or pictures that have been recorded on tape, video, etc.: *a video recording of the wedding* **2** [U] the process of making a record, tape, movie, etc.: *during the recording of the show* ♦ *recording equipment* ♦ *a recording studio* **3** [U] the process or act of writing down and storing information for official purposes: *the recording of financial transactions*

reˈcording engiˌneer (also re·cord·ist) *noun* a person whose job is making sound recordings, especially in a recording studio

re·cord·ist /rɪˈkɔrdɪst/ *noun* = RECORDING ENGINEER

ˈrecord ˌplayer *noun* a piece of equipment for playing records in order to listen to the music, etc. on them

re·count¹ /rɪˈkaʊnt/ *verb* (*formal*) to tell someone about something, especially something that you have experienced: **~ sth (to sb)** *She was asked to recount the details of the conversation to the court.* ♦ **~ what, how, etc. …** *They recounted what had happened during those years.* ♦ **+ speech** *"It was before the Vietnam War," he recounted.*

re·count² /ˈrikaʊnt/ *noun* an act of counting something again, especially votes: *The defeated candidate demanded a recount.* ▶ re·count /ˌriˈkaʊnt/ *verb* **~ sth**

re·coup /rɪˈkup/ *verb* **~ sth** to get back an amount of money that you spent or lost SYN RECOVER: *We hope to recoup our initial investment in the first year.*

re·course /ˈrikɔrs; rɪˈkɔrs/ *noun* [U] (*formal*) the fact of having to, or being able to, use something that can provide help in a difficult situation: *Your only recourse is legal action.* ♦ *She made a complete recovery without recourse to surgery.* ♦ *The government, when necessary, has recourse to the armed forces.*

re·cov·er 🗝 AWL /rɪˈkʌvər/ *verb*
▸ FROM ILLNESS **1** [I] **~ (from sth)** to get well again after being sick, hurt, etc.: *He's still recovering from his operation.*
▸ FROM SOMETHING UNPLEASANT **2** [I] **~ (from sth)** to return to a normal state after an unpleasant or unusual experience or a period of difficulty: *It can take many years to recover from the death of a loved one.* ♦ *The economy is at last beginning to recover.*
▸ MONEY **3** [T] **~ sth (from sb/sth)** to get back the same amount of money that you spent or that is owed to you SYN RECOUP: *He is unlikely to ever recover his legal costs.*
▸ SOMETHING LOST/STOLEN **4** [T] to get back or find something that was lost, stolen, or missing: **~ sth** *The police eventually recovered the stolen paintings.* ♦ **~ sth from sb/sth** *Six bodies were recovered from the wreckage.*
▸ POSITION/STATUS **5** [T] **~ sth** to win back a position, level, status, etc. that has been lost SYN REGAIN: *The team recovered its lead in the second half.*

▸ SENSES/EMOTIONS **6** [T] to get back the use of your senses, control of your emotions, etc. SYN REGAIN: **~ sth** *It took her a few minutes to recover consciousness.* ♦ *to recover your sight* ♦ **~ yourself** *She seemed upset but quickly recovered herself.*
▶ re·cov·ered AWL *adj.* [not before noun]: *She is now fully recovered from her injuries.*

re-cov·er /ˌriˈkʌvər/ *verb* **~ sth** to put a new cover on something

re·cov·er·a·ble AWL /rɪˈkʌvərəbl/ *adj.* **1** that you can get back after it has been spent or lost: *Travel expenses will be recoverable from the company.* **2** that can be obtained from the ground: *recoverable oil reserves*

re·cov·er·y 🗝 AWL /rɪˈkʌvəri/ *noun*
(*pl.* re·cov·er·ies) **1** [C, usually sing., U] **~ (from sth)** the process of becoming well again after an illness or injury: *My father made a full recovery from the operation.* ♦ *to make a remarkable/quick/speedy/slow, etc. recovery* ♦ *She is on the road to* (= making progress toward) *recovery.* **2** [C, usually sing., U] **~ (in sth)** the process of improving or becoming stronger again: *The government is forecasting an economic recovery.* ♦ *a recovery in consumer spending* ♦ *The economy is showing signs of recovery.* **3** [U] **~ (of sth)** the action or process of getting something back that was lost or stolen: *There is a reward for information leading to the recovery of the missing diamonds.*

reˈcovery ˌroom *noun* the room in a hospital where patients are kept immediately after an operation

rec·re·ant /ˈrɛkriənt/ *adj.* (*literary*) not brave SYN COWARDly

re·cre·ate AWL /ˌrikriˈeɪt/ *verb* **~ sth** to make something that existed in the past exist or seem to exist again: *The movie recreates the glamor of 1940s Hollywood.* ▶ re·cre·a·tion /ˌrikriˈeɪʃn/ *noun* [C, U]: *The writer attempts a recreation of the sights and sounds of his childhood.*

rec·re·a·tion /ˌrɛkriˈeɪʃn/ *noun* **1** [U] the fact of people doing things for enjoyment, when they are not working: *the need to improve facilities for leisure and recreation* ♦ *the increasing use of land for recreation* **2** [C] a particular activity that someone does when they are not working SYN HOBBY, PASTIME: *His recreations include golf, football, and fishing.* ⟳ thesaurus box at ENTERTAINMENT

rec·re·a·tion·al /ˌrɛkriˈeɪʃənl/ *adj.* connected with activities that people do for enjoyment when they are not working: *recreational activities/facilities* ♦ *These areas are set aside for public recreational use.*

recreˌational ˈvehicle *noun* = RV

recreˈation ˌroom *noun* (*formal*) = REC ROOM

re·crim·i·na·tion /rɪˌkrɪməˈneɪʃn/ *noun* [C, usually pl., U] an angry statement that someone makes accusing someone else of something, especially in response to a similar statement from them: *bitter recriminations* ▶ re·crim·i·na·to·ry /rɪˈkrɪmənəˌtɔri/ *adj.*

rec room /ˈrɛk rum; -rʊm/ (also *formal* recreˈation room) *noun* a room in a home, school, hospital, office building, etc. in which people can relax, play games, etc.

re·cruit /rɪˈkrut/ *verb, noun*
● *verb* **1** [T, I] **~ (sb) (to sth) | ~ sb to do sth** to find new people to join a company, an organization, the armed forces, etc.: *The police are trying to recruit more officers from ethnic minorities.* ♦ *They recruited several new members to the team.* ♦ *He's responsible for recruiting at all levels.* ⟳ collocations at JOB **2 ~ sb to do sth** to persuade someone to do something, especially to help you: *We were recruited to help peel the vegetables.* **3 ~ sth** to form a new army, team, etc. by persuading new people to join it: *to recruit a task force* ▶ re·cruit·er *noun* re·cruit·ment *noun* [U]: *the recruitment of new members* ♦ *a recruitment drive*
● *noun* **1** a person who has recently joined the armed forces or the police: *the training of new recruits* ♦ *He spoke of us scornfully as raw recruits* (= people without training or experience). **2** a person who joins an organization, a

t **t**ea   ţ bu**tt**er   d **d**id   k **c**at   g **g**ot   tʃ **ch**in   dʒ **J**une   f **f**all

company, etc.: *attempts to attract new recruits to the nursing profession*

rec·tal /'rɛktəl/ *adj.* (*anatomy*) relating to the RECTUM

rec·tan·gle /'rɛk,tæŋgl/ *noun* a flat shape with four straight sides, two of which are usually longer than the other two, and four angles of 90° ⊃ picture at SHAPE ▶ **rec·tan·gu·lar** /rɛk'tæŋgyələr/ *adj.*

rec·ti·fy /'rɛktə,faɪ/ *verb* (**rec·ti·fies, rec·ti·fy·ing, rec·ti·fied, rec·ti·fied**) ~ **sth** (*formal*) to put right something that is wrong **SYN** CORRECT: *to rectify a fault* ◆ *We need to start thinking about how to rectify the situation.* ▶ **rec·ti·fi·a·ble** /,rɛktə'faɪəbl/ *adj.*: *The damage will be easily rectifiable.* **rec·ti·fi·ca·tion** /,rɛktəfə'keɪʃn/ *noun* [U]

rec·ti·lin·e·ar /,rɛktə'lɪniər/ *adj.* (*technical*) **1** in a straight line: *rectilinear motion* **2** having straight lines: *rectilinear forms*

rec·ti·tude /'rɛktə,tud/ *noun* [U] (*formal*) the quality of thinking or behaving in a correct and honest way **SYN** UPRIGHTNESS

rec·to /'rɛktoʊ/ *noun* (*pl.* **rec·tos**) (*technical*) the page on the right side of an open book **ANT** VERSO

rec·tor /'rɛktər/ *noun* **1** an Anglican priest who is in charge of a particular area, (called a PARISH) ⊃ compare VICAR **2** the head of certain universities, colleges, or schools

rec·to·ry /'rɛktəri/ *noun* (*pl.* **rec·to·ries**) *noun* a house where the priest or minister of a church lives, or lived in the past

rec·tum /'rɛktəm/ *noun* (*pl.* **rec·tums** or **rec·ta** /-tə/) (*anatomy*) the end section of the tube where food waste collects before leaving the body through the ANUS ⊃ picture at BODY

re·cum·bent /rɪ'kʌmbənt/ *adj.* [usually before noun] (*formal*) (of a person's body or position) lying down

re·cu·per·ate /rɪ'kupə,reɪt/ *verb* (*formal*) **1** [I] ~ **(from sth)** to get back your health, strength, or energy after being sick, tired, injured, etc. **SYN** RECOVER: *He's still recuperating from his operation.* **2** [T] ~ **sth** to get back money that you have spent or lost **SYN** RECOUP, RECOVER: *He hoped to recuperate at least some of his losses.* ▶ **re·cu·per·a·tion** /rɪ,kupə'reɪʃn/ *noun* [U]: *It was a period of rest and recuperation.*

re·cu·per·a·tive /rɪ'kupərətɪv; -pə,reɪtɪv/ *adj.* (*formal*) helping you to get better after you have been sick, very tired, etc.

re·cur /rɪ'kər/ *verb* (**-rr-**) [I] to happen again or a number of times: *This theme recurs several times throughout the book.* ◆ *a recurring illness/problem/nightmare, etc.*

re·cur·rence /rɪ'kərəns/ *noun* [C, usually sing., U] if there is a **recurrence** of something, it happens again: *attempts to prevent a recurrence of the problem*

re·cur·rent /rɪ'kərənt/ *adj.* that happens again and again: *recurrent infections* ◆ *Poverty is a recurrent theme in her novels.*

re·cur·sion /rɪ'kərʒn/ *noun* [U] (*mathematics*) the process of repeating a FUNCTION, each time applying it to the result of the previous stage

re·cur·sive /rɪ'kərsɪv/ *adj.* (*technical*) involving a process that is applied repeatedly

rec·u·sant /'rɛkyəzənt; rɪ'kyuzənt/ *noun* (*formal*) a person who refuses to do what a rule or person in authority says they should do ▶ **rec·u·san·cy** /-zənsi/ *noun* [U]

re·cuse /rɪ'kyuz/ *verb* ~ **sb/yourself (from sth)** to excuse a judge, lawyer, or member of a jury from a case in court because they may not be able to act fairly: *The judge recused himself from the case because he knew a member of the family.*

re·cy·cla·ble /ri'saɪkləbl/ *adj.* able to be RECYCLED

re·cy·cle /ri'saɪkl/ *verb* **1** ~ **sth** to treat things that have already been used so that they can be used again: *The company recycles about 85% of the paper it uses.* ◆ *recycled paper* ⊃ collocations at ENVIRONMENT **2** ~ **sth** to use the same ideas, methods, jokes, etc. again: *He recycled all his old jokes.* ▶ **re·cy·cling** *noun* [U]: *the recycling of glass* ◆ *a recycling plant*

réd 🔊 /rɛd/ *adj., noun*

● *adj.* (**red·der, red·dest**) **1** having the color of blood or fire: *a red car* ◆ *The light* (= traffic light) *changed to red before I could get across.* **2** (of the eyes) BLOODSHOT (= with thin lines of blood in them) or surrounded by red or very pink skin: *Her eyes were red from crying.* **3** (of the face) bright red or pink, especially because you are angry, embarrassed, or ashamed: *He babbled something and got very red in the face.* ◆ *She was red as a beet.* **4** (of hair or an animal's fur) red-brown in color: *a red-haired girl* ◆ *red deer* ⊃ see also REDHEAD **5** (*informal*, sometimes *disapproving, politics*) having very LEFT-WING political opinions ⊃ compare PINK **6** (*politics*) (of an area in the U.S.) having more people who vote for the Republican candidate than the Democratic one: *red states/counties* **ANT** BLUE ▶ **red·ness** *noun* [U, sing.]: *You may notice redness and swelling after the injection.* **IDM** see PAINT *v.*, WAVE *v.*

● *noun* **1** [C, U] the color of blood or fire: *She often wears red.* ◆ *the reds and browns of the woods in the fall* (= of the leaves) ◆ *I marked the corrections in red* (= in red ink). ◆ *The traffic light was red.* **2** [U, C] red wine: *Would you prefer red or white?* ◆ *an Italian red* **3** [C] (*informal, disapproving, politics*) a person with very LEFT-WING political opinions ⊃ compare PINKO **IDM** be in the red (*informal*) to owe money because you have spent more than you have: *The company has plunged $37 million into the red.* ⊃ compare BE IN THE BLACK see red (*informal*) to become very angry

re·dact /rɪ'dækt/ *verb* ~ **sth (from sth)** to remove information from a document because you do not want the public to see it: *All sensitive personal information has been redacted from the public documents.*

red a'lert *noun* [U, sing.] a situation in which you are prepared for something dangerous to happen; a warning of this: *Following the bomb blast, local hospitals were put on red alert.*

red 'blood cell (also **red cell**, *biology* **e·ryth·ro·cyte**) *noun* any of the red-colored cells in the blood that carry OXYGEN

red-'blooded *adj.* [usually before noun] (*informal*) full of strength and energy: *red-blooded young males*

red·breast /'rɛdbrɛst/ *noun* (*literary*) a ROBIN

red·brick /'rɛdbrɪk/ *adj.* [usually before noun] (of buildings, walls, etc.) built with bricks of a color that is between red and brown: *redbrick row houses*

red 'card *noun* (in SOCCER) a card shown by the REFEREE to a player who has broken the rules of the game and is not allowed to play for the rest of the game ⊃ compare YELLOW CARD

red 'carpet usually **the red carpet** *noun* [sing.] a strip of red carpet laid on the ground for an important visitor to walk on when he or she arrives: *I didn't expect to be given the red carpet treatment!*

red cell *noun* = RED BLOOD CELL

red 'cent *noun* [sing.] (especially after a negative) a very small amount of money: *I didn't get a red cent for all my work.*

red·coat /'rɛdkoʊt/ *noun* a British soldier in the past, especially during the American Revolution

the Red 'Crescent *noun* [sing.] the name used by national branches in Muslim countries of the International Movement of the Red Cross and the Red Crescent, an organization that takes care of people who are suffering because of war or natural disasters

the Red 'Cross *noun* [sing.] an international organization that takes care of people who are suffering because of war or natural disasters. Its full name is the International Movement of the Red Cross and the Red Crescent.

red 'deer *noun* (*pl.* **red deer**) a DEER with large ANTLERS (= horns shaped like branches) that has a red-brown coat in summer

red·den /'rɛdn/ *verb* [I, T] ~ **(sth)** to become red; to make something red: *The sky was reddening.* ◆ *He could feel his face* reddening with embarrassment. ◆ *He stared at her and she reddened.*

red·dish /'rɛdɪʃ/ *adj.* fairly red in color

red 'dwarf *noun* (*astronomy*) a small, old star that is not very hot

re·dec·o·rate /,ri'dɛkə,reɪt/ *verb* [I, T] to change the way a room or the inside of a house looks by putting new paint and/or paper on the walls, getting new furniture and curtains etc.: *We just redecorated.* ◆ *~ sth My dad and I are going to redecorate my room.* ▶ **re·dec·o·ra·tion** /,ri,dɛkə-'reɪʃn/ *noun* [U]

re·deem /rɪ'dim/ *verb* **1 ~ sb/sth** to make someone or something seem less bad **SYN** COMPENSATE FOR: *The excellent acting wasn't enough to redeem a weak plot.* ◆ *The only redeeming feature of the job* (= good thing about it) *is the salary.* **2 ~ yourself** to do something to improve the opinion that people have of you, especially after you have done something bad: *He has a chance to redeem himself after last week's mistakes.* **3 ~ sb** to save someone from the power of evil: *Christians believe that Jesus Christ came to redeem us from sin.* **4 ~ sth** to pay the full sum of money that you owe someone; to pay a debt: *to redeem a loan/ mortgage* **5 ~ sth** to exchange something such as shares or VOUCHERS for money or goods: *This voucher can be redeemed at any of our branches.* **6 ~ sth** to get back a valuable object from someone by paying them back the money you borrowed from them in exchange for the object: *He was able to redeem his watch from the pawnshop.* **7 ~ a pledge/ promise** (*formal*) to do what you promised you would do

re·deem·a·ble /rɪ'diməbl/ *adj.* **~ (against sth)** that can be exchanged for money or goods: *This store credit is redeemable for up to a year.*

the Re·deem·er /rɪ'dimər/ *noun* [sing.] (*literary*) Jesus Christ

re·de·fine **AWL** /,ridɪ'faɪn/ *verb* to change the nature or limits of something; to make people consider something in a new way: **~ sth** *The new constitution redefined the powers of the president.* ◆ **~ what, how, etc. ...** *We need to redefine what we mean by democracy.* ▶ **re·def·i·ni·tion** /,ri,dɛfə'nɪʃn/ *noun* [U, C]

re·demp·tion /rɪ'dɛmpʃn/ *noun* [U] **1** (*formal*) the act of saving or state of being saved from the power of evil; the act of REDEEMING: *the redemption of the world from sin* **2** (*finance*) the act of exchanging shares or VOUCHERS for money or goods (= of REDEEMING them) **IDM** **beyond/past redemption** too bad to be saved or improved

re·demp·tive /rɪ'dɛmptɪv/ *adj.* (*formal*) that saves you from the power of evil: *the redemptive power of love*

re·de·ploy /,ridɪ'plɔɪ/ *verb* to move someone or something to a new position or job: **~ sb/sth** *Our troops will be redeployed elsewhere.* ◆ **~ sb/sth to sth** *Most of the employees will be redeployed to other parts of the company.* ▶ **re·de·ploy·ment** *noun* [U]: *the redeployment of staff/resources*

re·de·sign /,ridɪ'zaɪn/ *verb* **~ sth** to design something again, in a different way ▶ **re·de·sign** *noun* [U, C]

re·de·vel·op /,ridɪ'vɛləp/ *verb* [T, I] **~ (sth)** to change an area by building new roads, houses, factories, etc.: *The city has plans to redevelop the site.* ▶ **re·de·vel·op·ment** *noun* [U, C]: *inner-city redevelopment*

'red-eye *noun* **1** (also **'red-eye flight**) [C] (*informal*) a flight in a plane at night, on which you cannot get enough sleep: *We took the red-eye to Boston.* **2** [U] the appearance of having red eyes that people sometimes have in photographs taken using flash

'red-faced *adj.* with a red face, especially because you are embarrassed or angry

red 'flag *noun* **1** a flag used to warn people of danger **2** a red flag as a symbol of revolution or COMMUNISM

red 'giant *noun* (*astronomy*) a large star toward the end of its life that is relatively cool and gives out a light that is somewhat red

red-'handed *adj.* **IDM** see CATCH *v.*

red·head /'rɛdhɛd/ *noun* a person who has red hair ▶ **'red-headed** *adj.*: *a red-headed girl*

red 'herring *noun* an unimportant fact, idea, event, etc. that takes people's attention away from something important **ORIGIN** From the custom of using the smell of a smoked, dried herring (which was red) to train dogs to hunt.

red-'hot *adj.* **1** (of metal or something burning) so hot that it looks red: *Red-hot coals glowed in the fire.* **2** showing strong feeling: *her red-hot anger* **3** (*informal*) new, exciting, and of great interest to people: *a red-hot issue* **4** used to describe the person, animal, or team that is considered almost certain to win a competition, etc.: *The race was won by the red-hot favorite.*

re·di·al *verb, noun*
● *verb* /,ri'daɪəl; 'ri,daɪəl/ (-l-, CanE also -ll-) **1** [I, T] **~ (sth)** to call a telephone number again by pressing all of the individual numbers again **2** [I] to call a telephone number again, using the button that automatically calls the last number that was called
● *noun* /'ri,daɪəl/ **1** [U] the ability to redial a telephone number automatically **2** (also **'redial button**) [sing.] the button that automatically calls the last number that was called

re·did pt of REDO

re·di·rect /,ridə'rɛkt; -daɪ-/ *verb* **1 ~ sth (to sth)** to use something, for example money, in a different way or for a different purpose: *We are redirecting resources to this important new project.* **2 ~ sth (to sth)** to send something to a different address or in a different direction: *Questions are being redirected to the press office.* ◆ *Make sure you get your mail redirected to your new address.* ▶ **re·di·rec·tion** /,ridə'rɛkʃn; -daɪ-/ *noun* [sing., U]: *a sudden redirection of economic policy* ◆ *the redirection of mail*

re·dis·cov·er /,ridɪ'skʌvər/ *verb* **~ sth** to find again something that had been forgotten or lost ▶ **re·dis·cov·er·y** /,ridɪ'skʌvri; -'skʌvri/ *noun* (*pl.* **re·dis·cov·er·ies**) [U, C]

re·dis·tri·bute **AWL** /,ridɪ'strɪbyut; -yət/ *verb* **~ sth (from sb/sth) (to sb/sth)** to share something out among people in a different way: *Wealth needs to be redistributed from the rich to the poor.* ▶ **re·dis·tri·bu·tion** **AWL** /,ri,dɪstrə'byuʃn/ *noun* [U, sing.]: *the redistribution of wealth* **re·dis·trib·u·tive** /,ridɪ'strɪbyətɪv/ *adj.*

re·dis·trict /,ri'dɪstrɪkt/ *verb* [T, I] **~ (sth)** to change the official borders between districts

red-'letter ,day *noun* an important day, or a day that you will remember, because of something good that happened then **ORIGIN** From the custom of using red ink to mark holidays and festivals on a calendar.

red 'light *noun* a signal telling the driver of a vehicle to stop: *to go through a red light* (= not stop at one)

red-'light ,district *noun* a part of a town where there are many PROSTITUTES

red·line /'rɛdlaɪn/ *verb* **~ sth** to refuse to give loans or insurance to people in an area that is considered to be a bad financial risk: *The neighborhood was redlined in the 1970s because of the high percentage of poor people living there.* ▶ **red·lin·ing** *noun* [U]: *Redlining is illegal.*

red 'meat *noun* [U] meat that is red in color before it has been cooked, especially beef ⊃ compare WHITE MEAT (1)

red·neck /'rɛdnɛk/ *noun* (*informal*) an offensive word for a person who lives in a rural area, especially in the southern United States, and who has conservative political opinions and little education

re·do /,ri'du/ *verb* (**re·does** /-'dʌz/, **re·did** /-'dɪd/, **re·done** /-'dʌn/) **~ sth** to do something again or in a different way: *A whole day's work had to be redone.* ◆ *We just redid the bathroom* (= decorated it again).

red·o·lent /'rɛdl·ənt/ *adj.* [not before noun] **~ of/with sth** (*literary*) **1** making you think of the thing mentioned: *an* atmosphere redolent of the sea **2** smelling strongly of the thing mentioned: *a kitchen redolent with the smell of baking* ▸ **red·o·lence** /-əns/ *noun* [U]

re·dou·ble /ˌriˈdʌbl/ *verb* **~ sth** to increase something or make it stronger: *The townspeople are* **redoubling their efforts** *to find the missing child.* ◆ *redoubled enthusiasm*

re·doubt /rɪˈdaʊt/ *noun* **1** (*literary*) a place or situation in which someone or something is protected when they are being attacked or threatened **2** a small building from which soldiers can fight and defend themselves

re·doubt·a·ble /rɪˈdaʊtəbl/ *adj.* (*formal*) if a person is **redoubtable**, they have very strong qualities that make you respect them and perhaps feel afraid of them **SYN** FORMIDABLE

re·dound /rɪˈdaʊnd/ *verb*
PHR V re'dound to sth (*formal*) to improve the impression that people have of you: *Their defeat redounds to the glory of those whom they attacked.*

ˌred ˈpanda *noun* = PANDA (2)

ˌred ˈpepper *noun* **1** [C, U] a hollow red fruit that is eaten, raw or cooked, as a vegetable **2** [U] = CAYENNE

re·draft **AWL** /ˌriˈdræft/ *verb* **~ sth** to write an article, a letter, etc. again in order to improve it or make changes ▸ **re·draft** /ˈriˈdræft/ *noun*

re·draw /ˌriˈdrɔ/ *verb* (**re·drew** /-ˈdru/, **re·drawn** /-ˈdrɔn/) **~ sth** to make changes to something such as the borders of a country or region, a plan, an arrangement, etc.: *After the war the map of Europe was redrawn.* ◆ *to* **redraw the boundaries** *between male and female roles in the home*

re·dress *verb, noun*
● *verb* **~ sth** (*formal*) to correct something that is unfair or wrong **SYN** PUT RIGHT: *to redress an injustice* **IDM** **redress the balance** to make a situation equal or fair again
● *noun* /ˈridrɛs; rɪˈdrɛs/ [U] **~ (for/against sth)** (*formal*) payment, etc. that you should get for something wrong that has happened to you or harm that you have suffered **SYN** COMPENSATION: *to seek legal redress for unfair dismissal* ◆ *to have little prospect of redress*

red·shirt /ˈrɛdʃərt/ *noun* a college sports player who does not play for one year in order to be allowed to play for an extra year later ▸ **red·shirt** [T, I]: **~ (sb)** *He was redshirted in his freshman season at Florida State.* ◆ *He redshirted this past year.*

ˌred-tailed ˈhawk *noun* an American HAWK with a red tail

ˌred ˈtape *noun* [U] (*disapproving*) official rules that seem more complicated than necessary and prevent things from being done quickly **ORIGIN** From the custom of tying up official documents with red or pink tape.

re·duce 🔑 /rɪˈdus/ *verb*
1 [T] to make something less or smaller in size, quantity, price, etc.: **~ sth** *Reduce speed now* (= on a sign). ◆ *Giving up smoking reduces the risk of heart disease.* ◆ **~ sth by sth** *Costs have been reduced by 20% over the past year.* ◆ **~ sth (from sth) (to sth)** *The number of employees was reduced from 40 to 25.* ◆ *The skirt was reduced to $30 in the sale.* **2** [T, I] **~ (sth)** if you **reduce** a liquid or a liquid **reduces**, you boil it so that it becomes less in quantity **3** [I] (*informal*) to lose weight by limiting the amount and type of food that you eat: *a reducing plan* **4** [T] **~ sth (to sth)** to change a FRACTION to the form with the lowest numbers: *The fraction 2/10 can be reduced to 1/5.* **5** [T] **~ sth** (*chemistry*) to add one or more ELECTRONS to a substance, or to remove OXYGEN from a substance ⊃ compare OXIDIZE **IDM** see CIRCUMSTANCE
PHR V re'duce sb/sth (from sth) to sth/to doing sth [usually passive] to force someone or something into a particular state or condition, usually a worse one: *a beautiful building* **reduced to rubble** ◆ *She was* **reduced to tears** *by their criticisms.* ◆ *They were* **reduced to begging** *in the streets.* re'duce sth to sth to change something to a more general or more simple form: *We can reduce the problem to two main issues.*

re·duc·i·ble /rɪˈdusəbl/ *adj.* **~ to sth** (*formal*) that can be described or considered simply as something: *The problem is not reducible to one of money.*

re·duc·ti·o ad ab·sur·dum /rɪˌdʌktioʊ æd əbˈsərdəm/ *noun* [U, C] (*philosophy*) (from *Latin*) a method of proving that something is not true by showing that its result is not logical or sensible

re·duc·tion 🔑 /rɪˈdʌkʃn/ *noun*
1 [C, U] **~ (in sth)** an act of making something less or smaller; the state of being made less or smaller: *a 33% reduction in the number of hospital beds available* ◆ *There has been some reduction in unemployment.* ◆ *a slight/significant/substantial/drastic reduction in costs* **2** [C] an amount of money by which something is made cheaper: *There are reductions for children sharing a room with two adults.* **3** [C] a copy of a photograph, map, picture, etc. that is made smaller than the original one **ANT** ENLARGEMENT **4** [U, C] (*chemistry*) the fact of adding one or more ELECTRONS to a substance, or of removing OXYGEN from a substance

re·duc·tion·ism /rɪˈdʌkʃəˌnɪzəm/ *noun* [U] (*formal*, often *disapproving*) the belief that complicated things can be explained by considering them as a combination of simple parts ▸ **re·duc·tion·ist** /-nɪst/ *adj., noun*

re·duc·tive /rɪˈdʌktɪv/ *adj.* (*formal*, often *disapproving*) that tries to explain something complicated by considering it as a combination of simple parts

re·dun·dan·cy /rɪˈdʌndənsi/ *noun* [U] (*formal* or *technical*) the state of not being necessary or useful: *Natural language is characterized by redundancy* (= words are used that are not really necessary for someone to understand the meaning).

re·dun·dant /rɪˈdʌndənt/ *adj.* not needed or useful: *The picture has too much redundant detail.* ▸ **re·dun·dant·ly** *adv.*

re·du·pli·cate /rɪˈduplə̩keɪt/ *verb* [I, T] **~ (sth/itself)** to make a copy of something in order to form another of the same kind: *These cells are able to reduplicate themselves.*

re·dux /ˈridʌks/ *adj.* [after noun] brought back into use or made popular again: *The 1980s were far more than just the 1950s redux.*

ˌred ˈwine *noun* **1** [U, C] wine that gets its red color from the skins of the GRAPES **2** [C] a glass of red wine ⊃ compare BLUSH WINE, ROSÉ, WHITE WINE

red·wood /ˈrɛdwʊd/ *noun* **1** [C] a very tall type of tree that grows especially in California and Oregon: *giant redwoods* ⊃ picture at TREE **2** [U] the red-brown wood of the redwood tree

ˈred zone *noun* [sing.] (in football) the area within 20 YARDS of a team's GOAL LINE

ˌre-ˈecho *verb* [I, T] to be repeated many times; to repeat something many times: *Their shouts re-echoed through the darkness.* ◆ *Her words re-echoed in his mind.* ◆ **~ sth** *He has constantly re-echoed the main theme of his acceptance speech: "We want to be proud again!."*

reed /rid/ *noun* **1** a tall plant like grass with a hollow STEM that grows in or near water: *reed beds* (= where they grow) ⊃ picture at PLANT **2** a small thin piece of CANE, metal, or plastic in some musical instruments such as the OBOE or the CLARINET that moves very quickly when air is blown over it, producing a sound

re·ed·u·cate (also **re-educate**) /ˌriˈɛdʒə̩keɪt/ *verb* **~ sb** to teach someone to think or behave in a new or different way ▸ **re·ed·u·ca·tion** (also **re-education**) /ˌriˌɛdʒəˈkeɪʃn/ *noun* [U]

reed·y /ˈridi/ *adj.* [usually before noun] **1** (of a voice or sound) high and not very pleasant **2** full of reeds: *reedy river banks*

reef /rif/ *noun, verb*
● *noun* **1** a long line of rocks or sand near the surface of the ocean: *a coral reef* **2** a part of a sail that can be tied or rolled up to make the sail smaller in a strong wind
● *verb* **~ sth** (*technical*) to make a sail smaller by tying or rolling up part of it

reef·er /ˈriːfər/ noun **1** (*informal*) a truck, railroad car, or ship specially designed to carry goods that need to be in a refrigerator: *reefers carrying fresh fruit from California* **2** (*old-fashioned, slang*) a cigarette containing MARIJUANA

reek /riːk/ verb, noun
- **verb 1** [I] ~ (**of sth**) to smell very strongly of something unpleasant: *His breath reeked of tobacco.* **2** [I] ~ (**of sth**) (*disapproving*) to suggest very strongly that something unpleasant or suspicious is involved in a situation: *Her denials reeked of hypocrisy.*
- **noun** [sing.] a strong unpleasant smell **SYN** STENCH

reel /riːl/ noun, verb
- **noun 1** a round object around which you wind such things as wire or film; a reel together with the film, wire, etc. that is wound around it: *a reel on a fishing rod* ◆ *reels of magnetic tape* ◆ *a new reel of film* ⊃ compare SPOOL **2** a fast Scottish, Irish, or American dance, usually for two or four couples; a piece of music for this dance
- **verb 1** [I] (+ adv./prep.) to move in a very unsteady way, for example because you are drunk or have been hit **SYN** STAGGER: *I punched him on the chin, sending him reeling backward.* **2** [I] ~ (**at/from/with sth**) to feel very shocked or upset about something: *I was still reeling from the shock.* **3** [I] to seem to be spinning around and around: *When he opened his eyes, the room was reeling.*
  PHRV ,**reel sth**↔︎'**in/**'**out** to wind something on/off a reel: *I slowly reeled the fish in.* ,**reel sth**↔︎'**off** to say or repeat something quickly without having to stop or think about it: *She immediately reeled off several names.*

re·e·lect (also **re-e·lect**) /ˌriːɪˈlɛkt/ verb ~ **sb (to sth)** to elect someone again: ~ **sb (to sth)** *She was reelected to the Senate.* ◆ ~ **sb (as) sth** | ~ **sb + noun** *The committee voted to reelect him (as) chairman.* ▶ **re·e·lec·tion** (also **re-e·lec·tion**) /ˌriːɪˈlɛkʃn/ noun [U]: *to run for reelection*

re·e·merge (also **re-e·merge**) /ˌriːɪˈmɜːrdʒ/ verb [I] to appear somewhere again: *The cancer may reemerge years later.*

re·en·act (also **re-en·act**) /ˌriːɪˈnækt/ verb ~ **sth** to repeat the actions of a past event: *Members of the American Civil War Society will reenact the battle.* ▶ **re·en·act·ment** (also **re-en·act·ment**) /ˌriːɪˈnæktmənt/ noun

,**re-**'**enter** (also **re-en·ter**) /ˌriːˈɛntər/ verb [T, I] ~ (**sth**) to return to a place or to an area of activity that you used to be in

,**re-**'**entry** (also **re-en·try**) /ˌriːˈɛntri/ noun ~ (**into sth**) **1** [U] the act of returning to a place or an area of activity that you used to be in: *She feared she would not be granted re-entry into the U.S.* ◆ *a re-entry program for nurses* (= for nurses returning to work after a long time doing something else) **2** [U, C] the return of a SPACECRAFT into the earth's atmosphere

re·e·val·u·ate **AWL** (also **re-e·val·u·ate**) /ˌriːɪˈvælyuˌeɪt/ verb ~ **sth** to think about something again, especially in order to form a new opinion about it ⊃ collocations at EVALUATE ▶ **re·e·val·u·a·tion** **AWL** (also **re-e·val·u·a·tion**) noun [C, U]

re·ex·am·ine (also **re-ex·am·ine**) /ˌriːɪɡˈzæmən/ verb ~ **sth** to examine or think about something again, especially because you may need to change your opinion **SYN** REASSESS: *All the evidence needs to be reexamined.* ▶ **re·ex·am·i·na·tion** (also **re-ex·am·i·na·tion**) /ˌriːɪɡˌzæmə'neɪʃn/ noun [U, sing.]

ref /rɛf/ noun, verb (*informal*)
- **noun** = REFEREE: *The game's not over till the ref blows the whistle.*
- **verb** (**-ff-**) ~ **sth** = REFEREE: *The game was badly reffed.*

ref. /rɛf/ abbr. reference (used especially in business as a way of identifying something such as a document): *our ref.: 3498*

re·fec·to·ry /rɪˈfɛktəri/ noun (*pl.* **re·fec·to·ries**) a large room in which meals are served, especially in a religious institution, and in some schools and colleges in Britain

re·fer 🔑 /rɪˈfɜːr/ verb (**-rr-**)
PHRV **re**'**fer to sb/sth** (**as sth**) to mention or speak about someone or something: *The victims were not referred to by name.* ◆ *Her mother never referred to him again.* ◆ *You know who I'm referring to.* ◆ *She always referred to Ben as "that nice man."* ◆ *I promised not to refer to the matter again.* ⊃ thesaurus box at MENTION **re**'**fer to sb/sth 1** to describe or be connected to someone or something: *The star refers to items which are intended for the advanced learner.* ◆ *The term "Arts" usually refers to humanities and social sciences.* ◆ *This paragraph refers to the events of last year.* ⊃ language bank at DEFINE **2** to look at something or ask a person for information **SYN** CONSULT: *You may refer to your notes if you want.* ◆ *to refer to a dictionary* **re**'**fer sb/sth to sb/sth** to send someone or something to someone or something for help, advice, or a decision: *My doctor referred me to a specialist.* ◆ *The case was referred to the Court of Appeals.* ◆ (*formal*) *May I refer you to my letter of May 14?*

ref·er·a·ble /rɪˈfɜːrəbl; ˈrɛfərəbl/ adj. ~ **to sth** (*formal*) that can be related to something else: *These symptoms may be referable to virus infection rather than parasites.*

ref·er·ee /ˌrɛfəˈriː/ noun, verb
- **noun 1** (also *informal* **ref**) the official who controls the game in some sports: *He was sent off for arguing with the referee.* ⊃ compare UMPIRE **2** a person who is asked to settle a disagreement: *to act as a referee between the parties involved* **3** a person who reads and checks the quality of a technical article before it is published
- **verb 1** (also *informal* **ref**) [I, T] to act as the referee in a game: *a refereeing decision* ◆ ~ **sth** *Who refereed the final?* **2** [T] ~ **sth** to read and check the quality of a technical article before it is published

,**referee's as**'**sistant** noun = ASSISTANT REFEREE

ref·er·ence 🔑 /ˈrɛfrəns/ noun, verb
- **noun**
  ⟩ **MENTIONING SOMEONE OR SOMETHING 1** [C, U] ~ (**to sb/sth**) a thing you say or write that mentions someone or something else; the act of mentioning someone or something: *The book is full of references to growing up in India.* ◆ *She made no reference to her illness but only to her future plans.* ◆ *the President's passing reference to* (= brief mention of) *the end of the war*
  ⟩ **LOOKING FOR INFORMATION 2** [U] the act of looking at something for information: *Keep the list of numbers near the phone for easy reference.* ◆ *I wrote down the name of the hotel for future reference* (= because it might be useful in the future). ◆ *The library contains many popular works of reference* (= reference books).
  ⟩ **ASKING FOR ADVICE 3** [U] ~ (**to sb/sth**) (*formal*) the act of asking someone for help or advice: *The emergency nurse can treat minor injuries without reference to a doctor.*
  ⟩ **NUMBER/WORD/SYMBOL 4** [C] (*abbr.* **ref.**) a number, word, or symbol that shows where something is on a map, or where you can find a piece of information: *The map reference is Y4.* ◆ *Please quote your reference number when making an inquiry.*
  ⟩ **FOR NEW JOB 5** [C] a letter written by someone who knows you, giving information about your character and abilities, especially to a new employer: *We will check references after the interview.* **6** [C] a person who agrees to write a reference, for you, for example when you are applying for a job: *My previous boss will act as a reference for me.*
  ⟩ **IN BOOK 7** [C] a note in a book that tells you where a particular piece of information comes from: *There is a list of references at the end of each chapter.* ⊃ see also CROSS REFERENCE, FRAME OF REFERENCE, TERMS OF REFERENCE **IDM** **in/with reference to** (*formal*) used to say what you are talking or writing about: *With reference to your letter of July 22...*
- **verb** (*formal*) **1** ~ **sth** to refer to something: *The following is a guide to locating some of the information referenced in this publication.* **2** ~ **sth** to provide a book, etc. with references: *Each chapter is referenced, citing literature up to 2010.*

'**reference** ,**book** noun a book that contains facts and information, that you look at when you need to find out something particular

'reference ˌlibrary *noun* a library containing books that can be read in the library but cannot be borrowed ⊃ compare LENDING LIBRARY

'reference ˌpoint *noun* a standard by which something can be judged or compared

ref·er·en·dum /ˌrefəˈrendəm/ *noun* (*pl.* ref·er·en·dums or ref·er·en·da /-də/) [C, U] **~ (on sth)** an occasion when all the people of a country or state can vote on an important issue: *Switzerland decided to hold a referendum on joining the EU.* ♦ *The changes were approved by referendum.* ⊃ collocations at VOTE ⊃ thesaurus box at ELECTION

re·fer·ral /rɪˈfɜːrəl/ *noun* [U, C] **~ (to sb/sth)** the act of sending someone who needs professional help to a person or place that can provide it: *illnesses requiring referral to hospitals* ♦ *to make a referral*

re·fill *verb, noun*
• *verb* /ˌriːˈfɪl/ **~ sth (with sth)** to fill something again: *He refilled her glass.* ▶ **re·fill·a·ble** /ˌriːˈfɪləbl/ *adj.*: *a refillable gas cylinder*
• *noun* /ˈriːfɪl/ **1** another drink of the same type: *Would you like a refill?* **2** an amount of something, sold in a cheap container, that you use to fill up a more expensive container that is now empty

re·fi·nance /ˌriːˈfaɪnæns; ˌriːfəˈnæns/ *verb* [T, I] **~ (sth)** (*finance*) to borrow money in order to pay a debt

re·fine **AWL** /rɪˈfaɪn/ *verb* **1 ~ sth** to make a substance pure by taking other substances out of it: *the process of refining oil/sugar* **2 ~ sth** to improve something by making small changes to it

re·fined **AWL** /rɪˈfaɪnd/ *adj.* **1** [usually before noun] (of a substance) made pure by having other substances taken out of it: *refined sugar* **2** (of a person) polite, well educated, and able to judge the quality of things; having the kind of manners that are considered typical of a high social class **SYN** CULTURED, GENTEEL **ANT** UNREFINED

re·fine·ment **AWL** /rɪˈfaɪnmənt/ *noun* **1** [C] a small change to something that improves it: *This particular model has a further refinement.* **2** [C] **~ of sth** a thing that is an improvement on an earlier, similar thing: *The new plan is a refinement of the one before.* **3** [U] the process of improving something or of making something pure: *the refinement of industrial techniques* ♦ *the refinement of uranium* **4** [U] the quality of being polite and well educated and able to judge the quality of things; the state of having the kind of manners that are considered typical of a high social class **SYN** GENTILITY: *an atmosphere of refinement*

re·fin·er /rɪˈfaɪnər/ *noun* a person or company that refines substances such as sugar or oil: *oil refiners*

re·fin·er·y /rɪˈfaɪnəri/ *noun* (*pl.* re·fin·er·ies) a factory where a substance such as oil is refined (= made pure)

re·fit /ˌriːˈfɪt/ *verb* (-tt-) **~ sth** to repair or fit new parts, equipment, etc. to something: *He spent $70,000 refitting his yacht.* ▶ **re·fit** /ˈriːfɪt/ *noun*: *The ship has undergone a complete refit.*

re·flate /ˌriːˈfleɪt/ *verb* [T, I] **~ (sth)** (*economics*) to increase the amount of money that is used in a country, usually in order to increase the demand for goods ⊃ compare DEFLATE, INFLATE ▶ **re·fla·tion** /ˌriːˈfleɪʃn/ *noun* [U] **re·fla·tion·ar·y** /ˌriːˈfleɪʃəˌneri/ *adj.*: *reflationary policies*

re·flect ✐ /rɪˈflekt/ *verb*
1 [T, usually passive] **~ sb/sth (in sth)** to show the image of someone or something on the surface of something such as a mirror, water, or glass: *His face was reflected in the mirror.* ♦ *She could see herself reflected in his eyes.* **2** [T] **~ sth** to throw back light, heat, sound, etc. from a surface: *The windows reflected the bright afternoon sunlight.* ♦ *When the sun's rays hit the earth, a lot of the heat is reflected back into space.* **3** [T] **~ sth** to show or be a sign of the nature of something or of someone's attitude or feeling: *Our newspaper aims to reflect the views of the local community.* **4** [I, T] to think carefully and deeply about something: *Before I decide, I need time to reflect.*

♦ **~ on/upon sth** *She was left to reflect on the implications of her decision.* ♦ **~ that…** *On the way home he reflected that the interview had gone well.* ♦ **~ how, what, etc.…** *She reflected how different it could have been.* ♦ **+ speech** *"It could all have been so different," she reflected.*
IDM **reflect well, badly, etc. on sb/sth** to make someone or something appear to be good, bad, etc. to other people: *This incident reflects badly on everyone involved.*

re·flect·ance /rɪˈflektəns/ *noun* [U, C] (*physics*) a measure of how much light is reflected off a surface, considered as a part of the total light that shines onto it

reˌflected ˈglory *noun* [U] admiration or praise that is given to someone, not because of something that they have done, but because of something that someone connected with them has done: *She basked in the reflected glory of her daughter's success.*

re·flec·tion /rɪˈflekʃn/ *noun* **1** [C] an image in a mirror, on a shiny surface, on water, etc.: *He admired his reflection in the mirror.* **2** [U] the action or process of sending back light, heat, sound, etc. from a surface **3** [C] a sign that shows the state or nature of something: *Your clothes are often a reflection of your personality.* ♦ *The increase in crime is a sad reflection on* (= shows something bad about) *our society today.* **4** [U] careful thought about something, sometimes over a long period of time: *She decided on reflection to accept his offer after all.* ♦ *A week off would give him time for reflection.* **5** [C, usually pl.] your written or spoken thoughts about a particular subject or topic: *a book of her reflections on childhood* **6** [C] an account or a description of something: *The article is an accurate reflection of events that day.* **IDM** see MATURE *adj.*

re·flec·tive /rɪˈflektɪv/ *adj.* **1** (*formal*) thinking deeply about things **SYN** THOUGHTFUL: *a quiet and reflective man* **2** reflective surfaces send back light or heat: *reflective car license plates* ♦ *On dark nights children should wear reflective clothing.* **3 ~ of sth** typical of a particular situation or thing; showing the state or nature of something: *His abilities are not reflective of the team as a whole.* ♦ *Everything you do or say is reflective of your personality.* ▶ **re·flec·tive·ly** *adv.*: *She sipped her wine reflectively.*

re·flec·tiv·i·ty /ˌriːflekˈtɪvəti/ *noun* [U] (*physics*) the degree to which a material reflects light or RADIATION

re·flec·tor /rɪˈflektər/ *noun* **1** a surface that reflects light **2** a small piece of special glass or plastic that is put on a bicycle, or on clothing, so that it can be seen at night when light shines on it ⊃ picture at BICYCLE

re·flex /ˈriːfleks/ *noun* an action or a movement of your body that happens naturally in response to something and that you cannot control; something that you do without thinking: *The doctor tested her reflexes.* ♦ *to have quick/slow reflexes* ♦ *a reflex response/reaction* ♦ *Only the goalie's quick reflexes* (= his ability to react quickly) *stopped the ball from going in.* ♦ *Almost as a reflex action, I grab my pen as the phone rings.*

'reflex ˌangle *noun* an angle of more than 180° ⊃ picture at SHAPE ⊃ compare ACUTE ANGLE, OBLIQUE ANGLE, OBTUSE ANGLE, RIGHT ANGLE

re·flex·ive /rɪˈfleksɪv/ *adj.* a **reflexive** word or form of a word shows that the action of the verb affects the person who performs the action: *In "He cut himself," "cut" is a reflexive verb and "himself" is a reflexive pronoun.*

re·flex·ol·o·gy /ˌriːflekˈsɒlədʒi/ *noun* [U] a type of alternative treatment in which someone's feet are rubbed in a particular way in order to heal other parts of their body or to make the person feel mentally relaxed ▶ **re·flex·ol·o·gist** /-dʒɪst/ *noun*

re·float /ˌriːˈfloʊt/ *verb* **~ sth** to make a boat or ship float again, for example after it has become stuck on the bottom in shallow water

re·flow /ˈriːfloʊ/ *noun* [U] (*technical*) **1** a method of joining metals together by heating and melting SOLDER (= a soft metal mixture) **2** the fact of changing text on a computer screen so that it takes more or less space

re·flux /ˈriflʌks/ noun [U] the flowing back of the liquid contents of the stomach into the ESOPHAGUS: *He has acid reflux.*

re·fo·cus AWL /ˌriˈfoukəs/ verb **1** [I, T] to give attention, effort, etc. to something new or different: ◆ **~ (on/upon sb/sth)** *Policy must refocus on people instead of places.* ◆ **~ sth (on/upon sb/sth)** *We need to refocus attention on the real issues facing this country.* **2** [I, T] (of your eyes, a camera, etc.) to adapt or be adjusted again so that things can be seen clearly; to adjust something again so that you can see things clearly

re·for·est·a·tion /ˌrifɔrəˈsteɪʃn; -far-/ noun (*technical*) the act of planting new trees in an area where there used to be a forest ⟳ compare DEFORESTATION

re·form 🔑 /rɪˈfɔrm/ verb, noun
● **verb 1** [T] **~ sth** to improve a system, an organization, a law, etc. by making changes to it: *proposals to reform Social Security* ◆ *The law needs to be reformed.* **2** [I, T] to improve your behavior; to make someone do this: *He has promised to reform.* ◆ **~ sb** *She thought she could reform him.* ▶ **re·formed** adj.: *a reformed character*
● **noun** [U, C] change that is made to a social system, an organization, etc. in order to improve or correct it: *a government committed to reform* ◆ *economic/electoral/constitutional, etc. reform* ◆ *the reform of the educational system* ◆ *reforms in education* ◆ *far-reaching/major/sweeping reforms*

re-form /ˌriˈfɔrm/ verb [I, T] to form again or form something again, especially into a different group or pattern: *The band is re-forming after 23 years.* ◆ **~ sth** *The party has recently been re-formed.*

re·for·mat /ˌriˈfɔrmæt/ verb (-tt-) **~ sth** (*computing*) to give a new FORMAT to a computer disk

ref·or·ma·tion /ˌrefərˈmeɪʃn/ noun **1** [U] (*formal*) the act of improving or changing someone or something **2 the Reformation** [sing.] new ideas in religion in 16th century Europe that led to attempts to reform the Roman Catholic Church and to the forming of the Protestant Churches; the period of time when these changes were taking place

re·form·a·to·ry /rɪˈfɔrmətɔri/ noun (*pl.* re·form·a·to·ries) (also re'form school) a type of school that young criminals are sent to instead of prison

Re,formed 'Church noun [sing.] a church that has accepted the principles of the REFORMATION, especially a Calvinist one

re·form·er /rɪˈfɔrmər/ noun a person who works to achieve political or social change

re·form·ist /rɪˈfɔrmɪst/ adj. wanting or trying to change political or social situations ▶ **re·form·ist** noun

re·for·mu·late AWL /ˌriˈfɔrmyəˌleɪt/ verb **1 ~ sth** to create or prepare something again: *It is never too late to reformulate your goals.* **2 ~ sth** to say or express something in a different way: *Let me try to reformulate the problem.* ▶ **re·for·mu·lation** AWL noun [U, C]

re·fract /rɪˈfrækt/ verb **~ sth** (*physics*) (of water, air, glass, etc.) to make light change direction when it goes through at an angle: *Light is refracted when passed through a prism.* ▶ **re·frac·tion** /rɪˈfrækʃn/ noun [U]

re·frac·tive /rɪˈfræktɪv/ adj. (*physics*) causing, caused by, or relating to refraction

re,fractive 'index noun (*physics*) a measurement of how much an object or a substance refracts light (= causes it to change direction)

re·frac·tom·e·ter /ˌrifrækˈtɑmətər/ noun (*physics*) an instrument for measuring a refractive index

re·frac·tor /rɪˈfræktər/ noun (*physics*) something such as a LENS which REFRACTS light (= causes it to change direction)

re·frac·to·ry /rɪˈfræktəri/ adj. **1** (*formal*) (of a person) difficult to control; behaving badly **2** (*medical*) (of a disease or medical condition) difficult to treat or cure

re·frain /rɪˈfreɪn/ verb, noun
● **verb** [I] (*formal*) to stop yourself from doing something, especially something that you want to do SYN DESIST FROM: **~ (from sth)** *Please refrain from smoking.* ◆ **~ (from doing sth)** *He has refrained from criticizing the government in public.*
● **noun 1** a comment or complaint that is often repeated: *Complaints about unhealthy food in schools have become a familiar refrain.* **2** the part of a song or a poem that is repeated after each VERSE SYN CHORUS

re·fresh /rɪˈfrɛʃ/ verb **1** [T] **~ sb/yourself** to make someone feel less tired or less hot: *The long sleep had refreshed her.* ◆ *He refreshed himself with a cool shower.* **2** [T] **~ sth** (*informal*) to fill someone's glass or cup again: *Let me refresh your glass.* **3** [T] **~ your/someone's memory** to remind yourself/someone of something, especially with the help of something that can be seen or heard SYN JOG: *He had to refresh his memory by looking at his notes.* **4** [T, I] (*computing*) to get the most recent information, for example on an Internet page, by clicking on a button on the screen: *Click here to refresh this document.* ◆ *The page refreshes automatically.*

re'fresher ,course /rɪˈfrɛʃər ˌkɔrs/ (also re·fresh·er) noun a short period of training to improve your skills or to teach you about new ideas and developments in your job

re·fresh·ing /rɪˈfrɛʃɪŋ/ adj. **1** pleasantly new or different: *It made a refreshing change to be taken seriously for once.* **2** making you feel less tired or hot: *a refreshing drink/shower* ▶ **re·fresh·ing·ly** adv.: *refreshingly different* ◆ *The house was refreshingly cool inside.*

re·fresh·ment /rɪˈfrɛʃmənt/ noun **1 refreshments** [pl.] drinks and small amounts of food that are provided or sold to people in a public place or at a public event: *Light refreshments will be served during the break.* **2** [U] (*formal*) food and drinks: *In Waterbury, we made a short stop for refreshment.* ◆ *Can we offer you some refreshment?* ◆ *a refreshment room/ kiosk/tent* ◆ (*humorous*) *liquid refreshment* (= alcoholic drink) **3** [U] (*formal*) the fact of making someone feel stronger or less tired or hot: *a place to rest and find refreshment for mind and body*

re·fried beans /ˌrifraɪd ˈbinz/ noun [pl.] BEANS that have been boiled and fried in advance and are heated again when needed, used especially in Mexican cooking

re·frig·er·ate /rɪˈfrɪdʒəˌreɪt/ verb **~ sth** to make food, etc. cold in order to keep it fresh or preserve it: *Once opened, this product should be kept refrigerated.* ◆ *a refrigerated truck* ▶ **re·frig·er·a·tion** /rɪˌfrɪdʒəˈreɪʃn/ noun [U]: *Keep all meat products under refrigeration.*

re·frig·er·a·tor 🔑 /rɪˈfrɪdʒəˌreɪtər/ (also informal fridge) noun
a piece of electrical equipment in which food is kept cold so that it stays fresh: *This dessert can be served straight from the refrigerator.*

re·fu·el /ˌriˈfyuəl/ verb (-l-, CanE -ll-) [T, I] **~ (sth)** to fill something, especially a plane, with fuel in order to continue a journey; to be filled with fuel: *to refuel a plane* ◆ *The planes needed to refuel before the next mission.* ◆ *a refueling stop*

ref·uge /ˈrɛfyudʒ/ noun **1** [U] shelter or protection from danger, trouble, etc.: *A further 300 people have taken refuge in the U.S. embassy.* ◆ **~ (from sb/sth)** *They were forced to seek refuge from the fighting.* ◆ *a place of refuge* ◆ *As the situation at home got worse she increasingly took refuge in her work.* **2** [C] **~ (from sb/sth)** a place, person, or thing that provides shelter or protection for someone or something: *He regarded the room as a refuge from the outside world.* ◆ *a wetland refuge for birds* **3** [C] a building that provides a temporary home for people in need of shelter or protection from someone or something: *a women's refuge* ◆ *a refuge for the homeless*

ref·u·gee /ˌrɛfyuˈdʒi; ˈrɛfyudʒi/ noun a person who has been forced to leave their country or home, because there is a

t tea   ţ butter   d did   k cat   g got   tʃ chin   dʒ June   f fall

war or for political, religious, or social reasons: *a steady flow of refugees from the war zone* ♦ *political/economic refugees* ♦ *a refugee camp* ⊃ collocations at WAR

re·ful·gent /rɪˈfʌldʒənt/ *adj.* (*formal*) very bright

re·fund *noun, verb*
● *noun* /ˈriːfʌnd/ a sum of money that is paid back to you, especially because you paid too much or because you returned goods to a store: *a tax refund* ♦ *to claim/demand/ receive a refund* ♦ *If there is a delay of 12 hours or more, you will receive a full refund of the price of your trip.* ⊃ collocations at SHOPPING
● *verb* /rɪˈfʌnd; ˈriːfʌnd/ to give someone their money back, especially because they have paid too much or because they are not satisfied with something they bought **SYN** REIMBURSE: ~ *sth Tickets cannot be exchanged or money refunded.* ♦ ~ **sth to sb** *We will refund your money to you in full if you are not entirely satisfied.* ♦ ~ *sb sth We will refund you your money in full.* ▸ **re·fund·a·ble** /rɪˈfʌndəbl/ *adj.*: *a refundable deposit* ♦ *Tickets are not refundable.*

re·fur·bish /ˌriːˈfɜːrbɪʃ/ *verb* ~ **sth** to clean and decorate a room, building, etc. in order to make it more attractive, more useful, etc. ⊃ collocations at DECORATE ▸ **re·fur·bish·ment** *noun* [U, C]: *The hotel is closed for refurbishment.*

re·fus·al /rɪˈfjuːzl/ *noun* [U, C]
an act of saying or showing that you will not do, give, or accept something: ~ **(of sth)** *the refusal of a request/an invitation/an offer* ♦ *a blunt/flat/curt refusal* ♦ ~ **to do sth** *His refusal to discuss the problem is very annoying.* ⊃ see also FIRST REFUSAL

re·fuse¹ /rɪˈfjuːz/ *verb*
1 [I, T] to say that you will not do something that someone has asked you to do: *Go on, ask her; she can hardly refuse.* ♦ ~ **to do sth** *He flatly refused to discuss the matter.* ♦ *She refused to accept that there was a problem.* **2** [T] ~ **sth** to say that you do not want something that has been offered to you **SYN** TURN DOWN: *I politely refused their invitation.* ♦ *The job offer was simply too good to refuse.* **3** [T] to say that you will not allow something; to say that you will not give or allow someone something that they want or need **SYN** DENY: ~ **sth** *The bank refused his demand for a full refund.* ♦ *The authorities refused permission for the new housing development.* ♦ ~ **sb sth** *They refused him a visa.* ♦ *She would never refuse her kids anything.*

ref·use² /ˈrefjuːs/ *noun* [U] waste material that has been thrown away **SYN** GARBAGE: *domestic/household refuse* ♦ *the city refuse dump* ♦ *refuse collection/disposal*

re·fuse·nik /rɪˈfjuːznɪk/ *noun* a person who refuses to obey an order or law as a protest

re·fute /rɪˈfjuːt/ *verb* (*formal*) **1** ~ **sth** to prove that something is wrong **SYN** REBUT: *to refute an argument/a theory, etc.* **2** ~ **sth** to say that something is not true or fair **SYN** DENY: *She refutes any suggestion that she behaved unprofessionally.* ▸ **re·fut·a·ble** /rɪˈfjuːtəbl/ *adj.* **ref·u·ta·tion** /ˌrefjuˈteɪʃn/ *noun* [C, U]: *a refutation of previously held views*

re·gain /rɪˈɡeɪn; ˌriː-/ *verb* **1** ~ **sth** to get back something you no longer have, especially an ability or a quality: *I struggled to regain some dignity.* ♦ *The party has regained control of the region.* ♦ *She paused on the edge, trying to regain her balance.* ♦ *He did not regain consciousness* (= wake up after being unconscious) *for several days.* **2** ~ **sth** (*literary*) to get back to a place that you have left: *They finally managed to regain the beach.*

re·gal /ˈriːɡl/ *adj.* typical of a king or queen, and therefore impressive: *regal power* ♦ *the regal splendor of the palace* ♦ *She dismissed him with a regal gesture.* ⊃ compare ROYAL ▸ **re·gal·ly** /-ɡəli/ *adv.*

re·gale /rɪˈɡeɪl/ *verb*
PHRV **re·ˈgale sb with sth** to amuse or entertain someone with stories, jokes, etc.: *He regaled us with tales of his days as a jazz pianist.*

re·ga·li·a /rɪˈɡeɪliə/ *noun* [U] the special clothes that are worn or objects that are carried at official ceremonies

re·gard /rɪˈɡɑːrd/ *verb, noun*
● *verb* **1** to think about someone or something in a particular way: ~ **sb/sth (+ adv./prep.)** *Her work is very highly regarded.* ♦ ~ **sb/sth/yourself as sth** *Capital punishment was regarded as inhuman and immoral.* ♦ *He regards himself as a patriot.* ♦ *She is widely regarded as the current leader's natural successor.* **2** ~ **sb/sth (+ adv./prep.)** (*formal*) to look at someone or something, especially in a particular way **SYN** CONTEMPLATE: *He regarded us suspiciously.*
IDM **as regards sb/sth** (*formal*) concerning or in connection with someone or something: *I have little information as regards her fitness for the post.* ♦ *As regards the first point in your letter…*
● *noun* **1** [U] (*formal*) attention to, or thought and care for, someone or something: ~ **for sb/sth** *to do something with little/no regard for other people's opinions* ♦ *to have/show little regard for other people's property* ♦ ~ **to sb/sth** *He was driving without regard to speed limits.* **2** [U] (*formal*) respect or admiration for someone: *He held her in high regard* (= had a good opinion of her). ♦ ~ **for sb/sth** *I had great regard for his abilities.* **3 re·gards** [pl.] used to send good wishes to someone at the end of a letter, or when asking someone to give your good wishes to another person who is not present: *With kind regards, Yours…* ♦ *Give your brother my regards when you see him.*
IDM **have regard to sth** (*law*) to remember and think carefully about something: *It is always necessary to have regard to the terms of the contract.* **in this/that regard** (*formal*) concerning what has just been mentioned: *I have nothing further to say in this regard.* **in/with regard to sb/sth** (*formal*) concerning someone or something: *a country's laws in regard to human rights* ♦ *The company's position with regard to overtime is made clear in their contracts.* ⊃ more at AS *conj.*

THESAURUS

regard

call ♦ **find** ♦ **consider** ♦ **see** ♦ **view**

These words all mean to think about someone or something in a particular way.

regard to think of someone or something in a particular way: *He seemed to regard the whole thing as a joke.*

call to say that someone or something has particular qualities or characteristics: *I wouldn't call German an easy language.*

find to have a particular feeling or opinion about something: *You may find his story hard to believe.*

consider to think of someone or something in a particular way: *Whom do you consider (to be) responsible for the accident?*

REGARD OR CONSIDER?

These two words have the same meaning, but they are used in different patterns and structures. In this meaning, **consider** must be used with a complement or clause: you can *consider sb/sth to be sth* or *consider sb/sth as sth*, although very often the *to be* or *as* is left out: *He considers himself an expert.* ♦ *They are considered a high-risk group.* You can also *consider that sb/sth is sth* and again, the *that* can be left out. **Regard** is used in a narrower range of structures. The most frequent structure is *regard sb/sth as sth*; the *as* cannot be left out: ~~I regard him a close friend.~~ You cannot ~~regard sb/sth to be sth~~ or ~~regard that sb/sth is sth.~~ However, **regard** (but not **consider** in this meaning) can also be used without a noun or adjective complement but with just an object and adverb (*sb/sth is highly regarded*) or adverbial phrase (*regard sb/sth with suspicion/jealousy/admiration*).

see to have an opinion of something: *Try to see things from her point of view.*

re·gard·ing 🔑 /rɪˈɡɑrdɪŋ/ *prep.* concerning someone or something; about someone or something: *She has said nothing regarding your request.* ♦ *Call me if you have any problems regarding your work.*

re·gard·less /rɪˈɡɑrdləs/ *adv.* paying no attention, even if the situation is bad or there are difficulties: *The weather was terrible but we carried on regardless.*

re·gardless of *prep.* paying no attention to something or someone; treating something or someone as not being important: *The club welcomes all new members regardless of age.* ♦ *He went ahead and did it, regardless of the consequences.* ♦ *The amount will be paid to everyone regardless of whether they have children or not.*

re·gat·ta /rɪˈɡɑtə, -ˈɡætə/ *noun* a sports event in which races between ROWBOATS or SAILBOATS are held

Re·gen·cy /ˈridʒənsi/ *adj.* [usually before noun] of or in the style of the period 1811–20 in Britain, when George, Prince of Wales, was regent (= ruled the country in place of the king, his father): *Regency architecture*

re·gen·cy /ˈridʒənsi/ *noun* (*pl.* **re·gen·cies**) a period of government by a REGENT (= a person who rules a country in place of the king or queen)

re·gen·er·ate /rɪˈdʒɛnəˌreɪt/ *verb* **1** [T] ~ **sth** to make an area, institution, etc. develop and grow strong again: *The money will be used to regenerate the commercial heart of the town.* **2** [I, T] (*biology*) to grow again; to make something grow again: *Once destroyed, brain cells do not regenerate.* ♦ ~ **sth/itself** *If the woodland is left alone, it will regenerate itself in a few years.* ▶ **re·gen·er·a·tion** /rɪˌdʒɛnəˈreɪʃn; ˌri-/ *noun* [U]: *economic regeneration* ♦ *the regeneration of cells in the body* **re·gen·er·a·tive** /rɪˈdʒɛnərətɪv; -nəˌreɪtɪv/ *adj.*: *the regenerative powers of nature*

re·gent /ˈridʒənt/ *noun* also **Re·gent** a person who rules a country because the king or queen is too young, old, sick, etc.: *to act as regent* ▶ **re·gent** *adj.* also **Re·gent** [after noun]: *the Prince Regent*

reg·gae /ˈrɛɡeɪ/ *noun* [U] a type of popular music with strong rhythms, developed in Jamaica from the 1960s

reg·i·cide /ˈrɛdʒəˌsaɪd/ *noun* [U, C] (*formal*) the crime of killing a king or queen; a person who is guilty of this crime

re·gime **AWL** /rɪˈʒim; reɪ-/ *noun* **1** a government, especially one that has not been elected in a fair way: *a fascist/totalitarian/military, etc. regime* ♦ *an oppressive/brutal regime* ⊃ collocations at POLITICS **2** a method or system of organizing or managing something: *a social regime of individual freedom* **3** = REGIMEN: *a dietary regime*

reg·i·men /ˈrɛdʒəmən/ (also **re·gime**) *noun* (*medical* or *formal*) a set of rules about food and exercise or medical treatment that you follow in order to stay healthy or to improve your health

reg·i·ment /ˈrɛdʒəmənt/ *noun* **1** a large group of soldiers that is commanded by a COLONEL **2** (*formal*) a large number of people or things

reg·i·men·tal /ˌrɛdʒəˈmɛntl/ *adj.* [only before noun] connected with a particular regiment of soldiers: *a regimental flag* ♦ *regimental headquarters*

reg·i·ment·ed /ˈrɛdʒəˌmɛntəd/ *adj.* (*disapproving*) **1** involving strict discipline and/or organization: *The school imposes a very regimented lifestyle on its students.* **2** arranged in strict groups, patterns, etc.: *regimented lines of trees* ▶ **reg·i·men·ta·tion** /ˌrɛdʒəmənˈteɪʃn/ *noun* [U]: *She rebelled against the regimentation of school life.*

re·gion 🔑 **AWL** /ˈridʒən/ *noun* **1** a large area of land, usually without exact limits or borders: *the Arctic/tropical/desert, etc. regions* ♦ *one of the most densely populated regions of North America* **2** one of the areas that a country is divided into, that has its own customs and/or its own government: *the Basque region of Spain* **3** a part of the body, usually one that has a particular character or problem: *pains in the abdominal region* **IDM** **in the region of** used when you are giving a number, price, etc. to show that it is not exact **SYN** APPROXIMATELY: *He earns somewhere in the region of $50,000.*

re·gion·al 🔑 **AWL** /ˈridʒənl/ *adj.* [usually before noun] of or relating to a region: *regional variations in pronunciation* ♦ *the conflict between regional and national interests* ♦ *regional councils/elections/newspapers* ▶ **re·gion·al·ly** **AWL** /-nəli/ *adv.*: *regionally based television stations*

re·gion·al·ism /ˈridʒənəˌlɪzəm/ *noun* **1** [C] a feature of a language that exists in a particular part of a country, and is not part of the standard language **2** [U] the desire of the people who live in a particular region of a country to have more political and economic independence

reg·is·ter 🔑 **AWL** /ˈrɛdʒəstər/ *verb, noun*

● *verb*

▷ **PUT NAME ON LIST** **1** [T, I] to record your/someone's/something's name on an official list: ~ **sth** *to register a birth/marriage/death* ♦ *to register a company/trademark* ♦ ~ **sth in sth** *The ship was registered in Panama.* ♦ ~ **sb + adj.** *She is officially registered (as) disabled.* ♦ ~ **(sb) as sth** *7,500 people were registered as exhibitors.* ♦ ~ **(with sb/sth)** *You need to register with our office by December 1.* ♦ ~ **(at/for sth)** *to register at a hotel*

▷ **OFFICIALLY JOIN CLASS** **2** [I, T] to arrange for yourself or for someone else to officially join a class in school **SYN** ENROLL: ~ **(for sth)** *When do you register for the spring semester?* ♦ ~ **sb (at sth)** *Tommy's mother registered him at the local elementary school.*

▷ **GIVE OPINION PUBLICLY** **3** [T] ~ **sth** (*formal*) to make your opinion known officially or publicly: *China has registered a protest over foreign intervention.*

▷ **ON MEASURING INSTRUMENT** **4** [I] (+ *noun*) if a measuring instrument **registers** an amount or something **registers** an amount on a measuring instrument, the instrument shows or records that amount: *The thermometer registered 32°F.* ♦ *The earthquake registered 3 on the Richter scale.* ♦ *The stock exchange has registered huge losses this week.*

▷ **SHOW FEELING** **5** [T, no passive, I] ~ **(sth)** (*formal*) to show or express a feeling: *Her face registered disapproval.* ♦ *Shock registered on everyone's face.*

▷ **NOTICE SOMETHING** **6** [T, no passive, I] (often used in negative sentences) ~ **(sth)** to notice something and remember it; to be noticed: *He barely registered our presence.* ♦ *I told her my name, but it obviously didn't register.*

▷ **LETTER/PACKAGE** **7** [T, usually passive] ~ **sth** to send something by mail, paying extra money to protect it against loss or damage: *Can I register this, please?* ♦ *a registered letter*

● *noun*

▷ **LIST OF NAMES** **1** [C] an official list or record of names, items, etc.; a book that contains such a list: *a church register* (= of births, marriages, and deaths) ♦ *to be on the register of voters* ♦ *Could you sign the hotel register please, sir?*

▷ **OF VOICE/INSTRUMENT** **2** [C] (*technical*) the range, or part of a range, of a human voice or a musical instrument: *in the upper/middle/lower register*

▷ **OF WRITING/SPEECH** **3** [C, U] (*linguistics*) the level and style of

a piece of writing or speech, that is usually appropriate to the situation that it is used in: *The essay suddenly switches from a formal to an informal register.*
> **FOR HOT/COLD AIR 4** [C] an opening, with a cover that you can have open or shut, that allows hot or cold air from a heating or cooling system into a room つ compare VENT
> **MACHINE 5** [C] = CASH REGISTER

ˌregistered ˈmail *noun* [U] a method of sending a letter or package in which the person sending it pays extra money to protect it against loss or damage

ˌregistered ˈnurse *noun* (*abbr.* RN) a nurse who has a degree in NURSING and who has passed an exam to be allowed to work in a particular state

ˌregistered ˈtrademark *noun* (*symb* ®) the sign or name of a product, etc. that is officially recorded and protected so that no one else can use it

reg·is·trar /ˈrɛdʒəˌstrɑr/ *noun* **1** a person whose job is to keep official records, especially of births, marriages, and deaths **2** the senior officer in a school, college, or university who keeps student grade reports and other records

reg·is·tra·tion **AWL** /ˌrɛdʒəˈstreɪʃn/ *noun* **1** [U, C] the act of making an official record of something or someone: *the registration of letters and packages ♦ the registration of students for a course ♦ registration fees ♦ vehicle registrations ♦ the registration of a child's birth* **2** [U, C] a document showing that an official record has been made of something つ compare LOGBOOK

reg·is·try /ˈrɛdʒəstri/ *noun* (*pl.* reg·is·tries) **1** [C] a place where official records are kept **2** [U] the act of making an official record of something **3** [C] an official list or record or names, items, etc.; a book that contains such a list: *a gift registry* (= a list in a store of gifts that someone would like to receive, for example for their wedding)

re·gress /rɪˈɡrɛs/ *verb* [I] ~ **(to sth)** (*formal*, usually *disapproving*) to return to an earlier or less advanced form or way of behaving

re·gres·sion /rɪˈɡrɛʃn/ *noun* [U, C] ~ **(to sth)** the process of going back to an earlier or less advanced form or state

re·gres·sive /rɪˈɡrɛsɪv/ *adj.* **1** becoming or making something less advanced: *The policy has been condemned as a regressive step.* **2** (*technical*) (of taxes) having less effect on the rich than on the poor

re·gret ♪ /rɪˈɡrɛt/ *verb, noun*
● *verb* (-tt-) **1** to feel sorry about something you have done or about something that you have not been able to do: ~ **sth** *If you don't do it now, you'll only regret it. ♦ The decision could be one he lives to regret. ♦ "I've had a wonderful life," she said, "I don't regret a thing." ♦* ~ **doing sth** *He bitterly regretted ever having mentioned it. ♦* ~ **what, how, etc. ...** *I deeply regret what I said. ♦* ~ **that...** *I regret that I never got to meet him in person.* **2** (*formal*) used to say in a polite or formal way that you are sorry or sad about a situation: ~ **sth** *The airline regrets any inconvenience. ♦* ~ **that...** *I regret that I am unable to accept your kind invitation. ♦* ~ **to do sth** *We regret to inform you that your application has not been successful.* **it is regretted that...**
● *noun* [U, C] a feeling of sadness or disappointment that you have because of something that has happened, or something that you have done or not done: *It is with great regret that I accept your resignation. ♦ She expressed her regret at the decision. ♦ a pang/twinge of regret ♦ I have no regrets about leaving New Jersey* (= I do not feel sorry about it). *♦ What is your greatest regret* (= the thing that you are most sorry about doing or not doing)? *♦ He gave up teaching in 2009,* **much to the regret of** *his students.*

re·gret·ful /rɪˈɡrɛtfl/ *adj.* feeling or showing sadness or disappointment because of something that has happened or something that you have done or not done **SYN** RUEFUL: *a regretful look*

re·gret·ful·ly /rɪˈɡrɛtfəli/ *adv.* **1** in a way that shows you are sad or disappointed about something: *"I'm afraid not," he said regretfully. ♦ Emma shook her head regretfully.* **2** used

to show that you are sorry that something is the case and you wish the situation were different: *Regretfully, mounting costs have forced the museum to close.* つ note at REGRETTABLE

re·gret·ta·ble /rɪˈɡrɛtəbl/ *adj.* ~ **(that...)** that you are sorry about and wish had not happened: *It is regrettable that the police were not informed sooner. ♦ The loss of jobs is highly regrettable.* ▶ re·gret·ta·bly /-bli/ *adv.*: *Regrettably, crime has been increasing in this area.*

WHICH WORD?

regrettably ♦ regretfully

- **Regrettably** is used as a sentence adverb to show that you are sorry about something and wish the situation were different: *Regrettably, some jobs will be lost.*
- **Regretfully** can be used in the same way, but is more frequently used to mean "in a way that shows you are sad or disappointed about something": *He sighed regretfully.*

---

re·group /ˌriˈɡrup/ *verb* **1** [T, I] ~ **(sth) (for sth)** to arrange the way people or soldiers work together in a new way, especially in order to continue fighting or attacking someone: *They regrouped their forces and renewed the attack. ♦ After its election defeat, the party needs to regroup.* **2** [I] (of a person) to return to a normal state after an unpleasant experience or a period of difficulty, and become ready to make an effort again with new enthusiasm or strength: *Summer is a time to relax, regroup, and catch up on all those things you've been putting off all year.*

reg·u·lar ♪ /ˈrɛɡyələr/ *adj., noun*
● *adj.*
> **FOLLOWING PATTERN 1** following a pattern, especially with the same time and space in between each thing and the next: *regular breathing ♦ a regular pulse/heartbeat ♦ A light flashed at regular intervals. ♦ There is a regular bus service to the airport. ♦ regular meetings/visits ♦ The equipment is checked on a regular basis.* **ANT** IRREGULAR
> **FREQUENT 2** done or happening often: *Do you get regular exercise? ♦ Domestic violence is a regular occurrence in some families.* **ANT** IRREGULAR **3** [only before noun] (of people) doing the same thing or going to the same place often: *our regular customers ♦ regular offenders* (= against the law) *♦ He was a regular visitor to her house.*
> **USUAL 4** [only before noun] usual: *I couldn't see my regular doctor today. ♦ On Monday he would have to return to his regular duties. ♦ It's important to follow the regular procedure.*
> **ORDINARY 5** [only before noun] ordinary; without any special or extra features: *Do you want regular or diet cola? ♦* (*approving*) *He's just a regular guy who loves his dog.*
> **EVEN 6** having an even shape: *a face with regular features ♦ a regular geometric pattern* **ANT** IRREGULAR
> **PERMANENT 7** lasting or happening over a long period: *a regular income ♦ She couldn't find any regular employment.*
> **STANDARD SIZE 8** of a standard size: *Regular or large fries?*
> **SOLDIER 9** [only before noun] belonging to or connected with the permanent armed forces or police force of a country: *a regular army/soldier* **ANT** IRREGULAR
> **GRAMMAR 10** (especially of verbs or nouns) changing their form in the same way as most other verbs and nouns: *The past participle of regular verbs ends in "-ed."* **ANT** IRREGULAR
> **FOR EMPHASIS 11** (*informal*) used for emphasis to show that someone or something is an exact or clear example of the thing mentioned: *The whole thing was a regular disaster.*
● *noun*
> **CUSTOMER 1** a customer who often goes to a particular store, bar, restaurant, etc.: *He's one of our regulars.*
> **MEMBER OF TEAM 2** a person who often plays in a particular team, takes part in a particular television show, etc.: *We are missing six regulars because of injury.*
> **SOLDIER 3** a professional soldier who belongs to a country's permanent army

reg·u·lar·i·ty /ˌrɛgjəˈlærəti/ noun **1** [U] the fact that the same thing happens again and again, and usually with the same length of time between each time it happens: *Aircraft passed overhead with monotonous regularity.* **2** [U] the fact that something is arranged in an even way or in an organized pattern: *the striking regularity of her features* **3** [C] something that has a pattern to it: *They had observed regularities in the behavior of the animals.* ⊃ compare IRREG-ULARITY

reg·u·lar·ize /ˈrɛgjələˌraɪz/ verb ~ sth to make a situation that already exists legal or official: *Illegal immigrants were given the opportunity to regularize their position.* ▶ **reg·u-lar·i·za·tion** noun [U]

reg·u·lar·ly 🔑 /ˈrɛgjələrli/ adv.
1 at regular intervals or times: *We meet regularly to discuss the progress of the project.* **2** often: *I go there quite regularly.* **3** in an even or balanced way: *The plants were spaced regularly, about 20 inches apart.*

reg·u·late [AWL] /ˈrɛgjəˌleɪt/ verb **1** ~ sth to control something by means of rules: *The activities of credit companies are regulated by law.* ♦ *It is up to the regulating authority to put the measures into effect.* **2** [T] ~ sth to control the speed, pressure, temperature, etc. in a machine or system: *This valve regulates the flow of water.*

reg·u·la·tion 🔑 [AWL] /ˌrɛgjəˈleɪʃn/ noun, adj.
• noun **1** [C, usually pl.] an official rule made by a government or some other authority: *too many rules and regulations* ♦ *fire/safety/building, etc. regulations* ♦ *to comply with the regulations* ♦ *Under the new regulations spending on office equipment will be strictly controlled.* ♦ *the strict regulations governing the sale of weapons* ♦ *The new regulation will come into force on January 1.* **2** [U] controlling something by means of rules: *the voluntary regulation of the press*
• adj. [only before noun] that must be worn or used according to the official rules: *in regulation uniform*

reg·u·la·tor [AWL] /ˈrɛgjəˌleɪtər/ noun **1** a person or an organization that officially controls an area of business or industry and makes sure that it is operating fairly **2** a device that automatically controls something such as speed, temperature, or pressure

reg·u·la·to·ry [AWL] /ˈrɛgjələˌtɔri/ adj. [usually before noun] having the power to control an area of business or industry and make sure that it is operating fairly: *regulatory bodies/authorities/agencies*

re·gur·gi·tate /rɪˈgərdʒəˌteɪt/ verb **1** ~ sth (formal) to bring food that has been swallowed back up into the mouth again **2** ~ sth (disapproving) to repeat something you have heard or read without really thinking about it or under-standing it ▶ **re·gur·gi·ta·tion** /rɪˌgərdʒəˈteɪʃn/ noun [U]

re·hab /ˈrihæb/ noun [U] **1** the process of helping to cure someone who has a problem with drugs or alcohol: *to go into rehab* ♦ *a rehab clinic* **2** the process of helping someone become healthy again after an injury or a serious illness

re·ha·bil·i·tate /ˌriəˈbɪləˌteɪt; ˌrihə-/ verb **1** ~ sb to help someone to have a normal, useful life again after they have been very sick or in prison for a long time: *a unit for rehabilitating drug addicts* **2** ~ sb (as sth) to begin to consider that someone is good or acceptable after a long period during which they were considered bad or unac-ceptable: *He played a major role in rehabilitating Magritte as an artist.* **3** ~ sth to return a building or an area to its previous good condition ▶ **re·ha·bil·i·ta·tion** /ˌriəˌbɪləˈteɪʃn; ˌrihə-/ noun [U]: *a drug rehabilitation center* ♦ *the rehabilitation of the steel industry*

re·hash /ˌriˈhæʃ/ verb ~ sth (disapproving) to arrange ideas, pieces of writing, or pieces of film into a new form but without any great change or improvement: *He just rehashes songs from the 60s.* ▶ **re·hash** /ˈrihæʃ/ noun [sing.] (disap-proving): *The movie is just a rehash of the best TV episodes.*

re·hear /ˌriˈhɪr/ verb (re·heard, re·heard /-ˈhərd/) ~ sth (law) to hear or consider again a case in court

re·hear·ing /ˌriˈhɪrɪŋ/ noun (law) an opportunity for a case to be heard or considered again in court

re·hears·al /rɪˈhərsl/ noun **1** [C, U] time that is spent practicing a play or piece of music in preparation for a public performance: *to have a rehearsal* ♦ *We only had six days of rehearsal.* ♦ *Our new production of "Hamlet" is currently in rehearsal.* ♦ *a rehearsal room* ⊃ see also DRESS REHEARSAL **2** [C, usually sing.] ~ (for sth) an experience or event that helps to prepare you for something that is going to happen in the future: *These training exercises are designed to be a rehearsal for the invasion.* **3** [C, usually sing.] ~ of sth (formal) the act of repeating something that has been said before: *We listened to his lengthy rehearsal of the arguments.*

re·hearse /rɪˈhərs/ verb **1** [I, T] to practice or make people practice a play, piece of music, etc. in preparation for a public performance: ~ (for sth) *We were given only two weeks to rehearse.* ♦ ~ sth/sb *Today, we'll just be rehearsing the final scene.* ♦ *The actors were poorly rehearsed.* **2** [T] ~ sth to prepare in your mind or practice privately what you are going to do or say to someone: *She walked along rehearsing her excuse for being late.* **3** [T] ~ sth (formal, usually disap-proving) to repeat ideas or opinions that have often been expressed before

re·heat /ˌriˈhit/ verb ~ sth to heat cooked food again after it has been left to go cold

re·home /ˌriˈhoʊm/ verb ~ sth to find a new owner for a pet, especially a dog or cat: *The organization rescues stray dogs and rehomes them.*

re·house /ˌriˈhaʊz/ verb ~ sb to provide someone with a different home to live in: *Thousands of earthquake victims are still waiting to be rehoused.*

reign /reɪn/ noun, verb
• noun **1** the period during which a king, queen, EMPEROR, etc. rules: *in/during the reign of Charles II* **2** the period during which someone is in charge of an organization, a team, etc.
• verb **1** [I] to rule as king, queen, EMPEROR, etc.: *the reigning monarch* ♦ *Queen Victoria reigned from 1837 to 1901.* ♦ ~ over sb/sth *Herod reigned over Palestine at that time.* **2** [I] ~ (over sb/sth) to be the best or most important in a particular situation or area of skill: *the reigning champion* ♦ *In the field of classical music, he still reigns supreme.* **3** [I] (literary) (of an idea, a feeling, or an atmosphere) to be the most obvious feature of a place or moment: *At last silence reigned* (= there was complete silence).

re·ig·nite /ˌriɪgˈnaɪt/ verb [I, T] to start burning again; to make something start burning again: *The oven burners reignite automatically if blown out.* ♦ ~ sth *You may need to reignite the pilot light.* ♦ (figurative) *Their passion was reignited by a romantic trip to Venice.*

reign of ˈterror noun (pl. reigns of terror) a period during which there is a lot of violence and many people are killed by the ruler or people in power

rei·ki /ˈreɪki/ noun [U] (from Japanese) a method of healing based on the idea that energy can be directed into a person's body by touch

re·im·burse /ˌriɪmˈbərs/ verb (formal) to pay back money to someone that they have spent or lost: ~ sth *We will reimburse any expenses incurred.* ♦ ~ sb (for sth) *You will be reimbursed for any loss or damage caused by our company.* ▶ **re·im·burse·ment** noun [U]

rein /reɪn/ noun, verb
• noun **1** [C, usually pl.] a long, narrow, leather band that is attached to a BIT (= a metal bar in a horse's mouth) and is held by the rider in order to control the horse: *She pulled gently on the reins.* ⊃ picture at HORSE **2** the reins [pl.] the state of being in control or the leader of something: *It was time to hand over the reins of power* (= to give control to someone else). ♦ *The vice president was forced to take up the reins of office.*
    IDM give/allow sb/sth free/full rein | give/allow free/full rein to sth to give someone complete freedom of action; to allow a feeling to be expressed freely: *The designer*

ʌ cup   ə about   eɪ say   aɪ five   ɔɪ boy   aʊ now   oʊ go   ər bird

was given free rein. ◆ *The script allows full rein to her larger-than-life acting style.* ⊃ more at TIGHT

● **verb**

 PHR V ,rein sb/sth↔'back | ,rein sth↔'in **1** to start to control someone or something more strictly **SYN** CHECK: *We need to rein back public spending.* ◆ *She kept her emotions tightly reined in.* **2** to stop a horse or make it go more slowly by pulling back the reins

re·in·car·nate /ˌriːnˈkɑːneɪt/ *verb* [T, I, often passive] **~ (sb/sth) (in/as sb/sth)** to be born again in another body after you have died; to make someone be born again in this way: *They believe humans are reincarnated in animal form.*

re·in·car·na·tion /ˌriːnkɑːˈneɪʃn/ *noun* **1** [U] the belief that after someone's death their soul lives again in a new body ⊃ collocations at RELIGION **2** [C, usually sing.] a person or an animal whose body contains the soul of a dead person

rein·deer /ˈreɪndɪr/ *noun* (*pl.* rein·deer or rein·deers) a large DEER with long ANTLERS (= horns shaped like branches), that lives in cold northern regions: *herds of reindeer*

re·in·force **AWL** /ˌriːnˈfɔːrs/ *verb* **1 ~ sth** to make a feeling, an idea, etc. stronger: *Such jokes tend to reinforce racial stereotypes.* ◆ *The climate of political confusion has only reinforced the country's economic decline.* ◆ *Success in the talks will reinforce his reputation as an international statesman.* **2 ~ sth** to make a structure or material stronger, especially by adding another material to it: *All buildings are now reinforced to withstand earthquakes.* ◆ *reinforced steel* **3 ~ sth** to send more people or equipment in order to make an army, etc. stronger: *The U.N. has undertaken to reinforce its military presence along the borders.*

,reinforced 'concrete *noun* [U] concrete with metal bars or wires inside to make it stronger

re·in·force·ment **AWL** /ˌriːnˈfɔːrsmənt/ *noun* **1 reinforce·ments** [pl.] extra soldiers or police officers who are sent to a place because more are needed: *to send in reinforcements* **2** [U, sing.] the act of making something stronger, especially a feeling or an idea

re·in·state /ˌriːnˈsteɪt/ *verb* **1 ~ sb/sth (in/as sth)** to give back a job or position that had been taken away from someone: *He was reinstated in his post.* **2 ~ sth (in/as sth)** to return something to its previous position or status **SYN** RESTORE: *There have been repeated calls to reinstate the death penalty.* ▶ **re·in·state·ment** *noun* [U]

re·in·sur·ance /ˌriːnˈʃʊrəns/ *noun* [U] (*finance*) the practice of one insurance company buying insurance from another company against any losses that result from claims that are made against it

re·in·ter·pret **AWL** /ˌriːnˈtɜːrprət/ *verb* **~ sth** to interpret something in a new or different way ▶ **re·in·ter·pre·ta·tion** **AWL** /ˌriːnˌtɜːrprəˈteɪʃn/ *noun* [C, U]

re·in·tro·duce /ˌriːntrəˈduːs/ *verb* **1 ~ sth** to start to use something again **SYN** BRING BACK: *to reintroduce the death penalty* ◆ *plans to reintroduce trams to the city* **2 ~ sth** to put a type of animal, bird, or plant back into a region where it once lived ▶ **re·in·tro·duc·tion** /ˌriːntrəˈdʌkʃn/ *noun* [U, C]

re·in·vent /ˌriːnˈvent/ *verb* **~ sth/yourself (as sth)** to present yourself/something in a new form or with a new image: *The former wild man of rock has reinvented himself as a respectable family man.*
 IDM reinvent the wheel to waste time creating something that already exists and works well

re·in·vest **AWL** /ˌriːnˈvest/ *verb* [T, I] **~ (sth)** to put profits that have been made on an investment back into the same investment or into a new one ▶ **re·in·vest·ment** **AWL** *noun* [U, C]

re·in·vig·or·ate /ˌriːnˈvɪɡəreɪt/ *verb* **~ sth/sb** to give new energy or strength to something or someone: *We need to reinvigorate the economy of the area.* ◆ *I felt reinvigorated after a rest and a shower.*

re·is·sue /ˌriːˈɪʃuː/ *verb, noun*
● **verb ~ sth (as sth)** to publish or produce again a book, record, etc. that has not been available for some time: *old jazz recordings reissued on CD* ◆ *The novel was reissued in paperback.*
● **noun** an old book or record that has been published or produced again after not being available for some time

re·it·er·ate /riˈɪtəreɪt/ *verb* (*formal*) to repeat something that you have already said, especially to emphasize it: **~ sth** *to reiterate an argument/a demand/an offer* ◆ **~ that…** *Let me reiterate that we are fully committed to this policy.* ◆ **+ speech** *"I said, "money,'" he reiterated.* ▶ **re·it·er·a·tion** /riˌɪtəˈreɪʃn/ *noun* [sing., U]: *a reiteration of her previous statement*

re·ject 🔑 **AWL** *verb, noun*
● **verb** /rɪˈdʒekt/
 › ARGUMENT/IDEA/PLAN **1 ~ sth** to refuse to accept or consider something: *to reject an argument/a claim/a decision/an offer/a suggestion* ◆ *The boss rejected any idea of reforming the system.* ◆ *The proposal was firmly rejected.* ◆ *All our suggestions were rejected out of hand.*
 › SOMEONE FOR JOB **2 ~ sb** to refuse to accept someone for a job, position, etc.: *Voters rejected the hard-line candidates.* ◆ *I've been rejected by all the universities I applied to.*
 › NOT USE/PUBLISH **3 ~ sth** to decide not to use, sell, publish, etc. something because its quality is not good enough: *Imperfect articles are rejected by our quality control.*
 › NEW ORGAN **4 ~ sth** (of the body) to not accept a new organ after a TRANSPLANT operation, by producing substances that attack the organ
 › NOT LOVE **5 ~ sb/sth** to fail to give a person or an animal enough care or affection: *The lioness rejected the smallest cub, which died.* ◆ *When her husband left home, she felt rejected and useless.*
 ▶ **re·jec·tion** **AWL** /rɪˈdʒekʃn/ *noun* [U, C]: *Her proposal met with unanimous rejection.* ◆ *a rejection letter* (= a letter in which you are told, for example, that you have not been accepted for a job) ◆ *painful feelings of rejection*
● **noun** /ˈriːdʒekt/
 › SOMETHING THAT CANNOT BE USED **1** something that cannot be used or sold because there is something wrong with it
 › PERSON **2** a person who has not been accepted as a member of a team, society, etc.: *one of society's rejects*

re·jig·ger /riːˈdʒɪɡər/ *verb* **~ sth** (*informal*) to make changes to something; to arrange something in a different way

re·joice /rɪˈdʒɔɪs/ *verb* [I, T] (*formal*) to express great happiness about something: *When the war ended, people finally had cause to rejoice.* ◆ **~ at/in/over sth** *The middle class is rejoicing over the tax cuts.* ◆ **~ to do sth** *They rejoiced to see their son well again.* ◆ **~ that…** *I rejoice that justice has prevailed.*

re·joic·ing /rɪˈdʒɔɪsɪŋ/ *noun* [U] (also **re·joic·ings** [pl.]) the happy celebration of something: *a time of great rejoicing*

re·join¹ /riˈdʒɔɪn/ *verb* [T, I] **~ (sb/sth)** to join someone or something again after leaving them or it: *to rejoin a club* ◆ *She turned off her phone and rejoined them at the table.* ◆ *The path goes through a wood before rejoining the main road.*

re·join² /rɪˈdʒɔɪn/ *verb* **+ speech** | **~ that…** (*formal*) to say something as an answer, especially something quick, critical, or amusing **SYN** RETORT: *"You're wrong!" she rejoined.*

re·join·der /rɪˈdʒɔɪndər/ *noun* [usually sing.] (*formal*) a reply, especially a quick, critical, or amusing one **SYN** RETORT

re·ju·ve·nate /rɪˈdʒuːvəneɪt/ *verb* **~ sb/sth** to make someone or something look or feel younger or more lively ▶ **re·ju·ve·na·tion** /rɪˌdʒuːvəˈneɪʃn/ *noun* [U, sing.]

re·kin·dle /ˌriːˈkɪndl/ *verb* **~ sth** (*formal*) to make something become active again **SYN** REAWAKEN: *to rekindle feelings/hopes*

re·laid *pt, pp* of RELAY²

re·lapse *noun, verb*
● **noun** /ˈriːlæps/ [C, U] the fact of becoming sick again after making an improvement: *to have/suffer a relapse* ◆ *a risk of relapse*

• **verb** /rɪˈlæps; ˈriːlæps/ [I] **~ (into sth)** to go back into a previous condition or into a worse state after making an improvement: *They relapsed into silence.* ◆ *He relapsed into his old bad habits.* ◆ *Two days after leaving the hospital she relapsed into a coma.*

re·late 🔑 /rɪˈleɪt/ *verb*
1 show or make a connection between two or more things **SYN** CONNECT: **~ sth** *I found it difficult to relate the two ideas in my mind.* ◆ **~ A to B** *In the future, pay increases will be related to productivity.* **2** (*formal*) to give a spoken or written report of something; to tell a story: **~ sth** *She relates her childhood experiences in the first chapters.* ◆ **~ sth to sb** *He related the facts of the case to journalists.* ◆ **~ how, what, etc....** *She related how he had run away from home as a boy.* ◆ **~ that...** *The story relates that an angel appeared and told him to sing.* **PHR V** **re·late to sth/sb** **1** to be connected with something or someone; to refer to something or someone: *We shall discuss the problem as it relates to our specific case.* ◆ *The second paragraph relates to the situation in the war zone.* **2** to be able to understand and have sympathy with someone or something **SYN** EMPATHIZE WITH: *Many adults can't relate to children.* ◆ *Our product needs an image that people can relate to.*

re·lat·ed 🔑 /rɪˈleɪtəd/ *adj.*
1 ~ (to sth/sb) connected with something or someone in some way: *Much of the crime in this area is related to drug abuse.* ◆ *These problems are closely related.* ◆ *a related issue/question* ◆ *a stress-related illness* **2 ~ (to sth/sb)** in the same family: *Are you related to Margaret?* ◆ *We're distantly related.* **3 ~ (to sth)** belonging to the same group: *related languages* ◆ *The llama is related to the camel.* **ANT** UNRELATED ▶ **re·lat·ed·ness** *noun* [U]

re·la·tion 🔑 /rɪˈleɪʃn/ *noun*
1 relations [pl.] the way in which two people, groups, or countries behave toward each other or deal with each other: *diplomatic/international/foreign relations* ◆ *U.S.-Chinese relations* ◆ *teacher-student relations* ◆ **~ (with sb/sth)** *Relations with neighboring countries have become strained.* ◆ **~ (between A and B)** *We seek to improve relations between our two countries.* ◆ (*formal*) *to have sexual relations* (= to have sex) ⊃ **collocations** at INTERNATIONAL ⊃ **see also** INDUSTRIAL RELATIONS, PUBLIC RELATIONS, RACE RELATIONS **2** [U, C] the way in which two or more things are connected: **~ between A and B** *the relation between rainfall and crop yields* ◆ **~ to sth** *the relation of the farmer to the land* ◆ *The fee they are offering bears no relation to the amount of work involved.* ◆ (*formal*) *I have some comments to make in relation to* (= concerning) *this matter.* ◆ *Its brain is small in relation to* (= compared with) *its body.* **3** [C] a person who is in the same family as someone else **SYN** RELATIVE: *a close/near/distant relation of mine* ◆ *a relation by marriage* ◆ *a party for friends and relations* ◆ *He's called Brady too, but we're no relation* (= not related). ◆ *Is he any relation to you?* ⊃ **see also** BLOOD RELATION, POOR RELATION

re·la·tion·al /rɪˈleɪʃənl/ *adj.* (*formal* or *technical*) existing or considered in relation to something else

re·la·tional ˈdatabase *noun* (*computing*) a DATABASE that recognizes relationships between different pieces of information

re·la·tion·ship 🔑 /rɪˈleɪʃnˌʃɪp/ *noun*
1 [C] the way in which two people, groups, or countries behave toward each other or deal with each other: **~ (between A and B)** *The relationship between the police and the local community has improved.* ◆ **~ (with sb)** *She has a very close relationship with her sister.* ◆ *I have established a good working relationship with my boss.* ◆ *a master-servant relationship* ⊃ **see also** LOVE-HATE RELATIONSHIP **2** [C] **~ (between A and B)** | **~ (with sb)** a loving and/or sexual friendship between two people: *Their affair did not develop into a lasting relationship.* ◆ *She's had a series of miserable relationships.* ◆ *Are you in a relationship?* **3** [C, U] the way in which two or more things are connected: **~ (between A and B)** *the relationship between mental and physical health* ◆

~ (to sth) *This comment bore no relationship to the subject of our conversation.* ◆ *People alter their voices in relationship to background noise.* **4** [C, U] the way in which a person is related to someone else in a family: *a father-son relationship* ◆ **~ between A and B** *I'm not sure of the exact relationship between them—I think they're cousins.*

rel·a·tive 🔑 /ˈrɛlətɪv/ *adj., noun*
• *adj.* **1** considered and judged by being compared with something else: *the relative merits of the two plans* **2 ~ (to sth)** considered according to its position or connection with something else: *the position of the sun relative to the earth* **3** [only before noun] that exists or that has a particular quality only when compared with something else **SYN** COMPARATIVE: *They now live in relative comfort* (= compared with how they lived before). ◆ *Given the failure of the previous plan, this turned out to be a relative success.* ◆ *It's all relative, isn't it? We never had any money when I was a kid so $500 was a fortune to us.* ⊃ **compare** ABSOLUTE **4 ~ to sth** (*formal*) having a connection with something; referring to something: *the facts relative to the case* **5** (*grammar*) referring to an earlier noun, sentence, or part of a sentence: *In "the man who came," "who" is a relative pronoun and "who came" is a relative clause.*
• *noun* **1** a person who is in the same family as someone else **SYN** RELATION: *a close/distant relative* ◆ *her friends and relatives* **2** a thing that belongs to the same group as something else: *The ibex is a distant relative of the mountain goat.*

relative aˌtomic ˈmass (also ˌatomic ˈmass, aˌtomic ˈweight) *noun* (*chemistry*) the average MASS of all the naturally occurring atoms of a chemical element

relative ˈdensity (also speˌcific ˈgravity) *noun* [U] (*chemistry*) the mass of a substance divided by the mass of the same volume of water or air

rel·a·tive·ly 🔑 /ˈrɛlətɪvli/ *adv.*
to a fairly large degree, especially in comparison to something else: *I found the test relatively easy.* ◆ *We had relatively few applications for the job.* ◆ *Lack of exercise is also a risk factor for heart disease but it's relatively small when compared with the others.*
IDM **relatively speaking** used when you are comparing something with similar things: *Relatively speaking, these jobs provide good salaries.*

rel·a·tiv·ism /ˈrɛlətəˌvɪzəm/ *noun* [U] (*formal*) the belief that truth is not always and generally valid, but can be judged only in relation to other things, such as your personal situation ▶ **rel·a·tiv·ist** /-vɪst/ *adj.*: *a relativist view* **rel·a·tiv·ist** *noun*

rel·a·tiv·i·ty /ˌrɛləˈtɪvəti/ *noun* [U] **1** (*physics*) Einstein's theory of the universe, based on the principle that all movement is relative and that time is a fourth DIMENSION related to space **2** (*formal*) the state of being relative and only able to be judged when compared with something else

re·launch /ˌriːˈlɔntʃ/ *verb* **~ sth** to start or present something again in a new or different way, especially a product for sale ▶ **re·launch** /ˈriːlɔntʃ/ *noun*

re·lax 🔑 **AWL** /rɪˈlæks/ *verb*
1 [I] to rest and do something enjoyable, especially after work or effort **SYN** UNWIND: *Just relax and enjoy the movie.* ◆ *I'm going to spend the weekend just relaxing.* ◆ **~ with sth** *When I get home from work I like to relax with the newspaper.* **2** [I, T] **~ (sb)** to become or make someone become calmer and less worried: *I'll only relax when I know you're safe.* ◆ *Relax! Everything will be OK.* **3** [I, T] to become or make something become less tight or stiff: *Allow your muscles to relax completely.* ◆ **~ sth** *The massage relaxed my tense back muscles.* ◆ *He relaxed his grip on her arm.* ◆ (*figurative*) *The dictator refuses to relax his grip on power.* **4** [T] to allow rules, laws, etc. to become less strict: *The council has relaxed the ban on dogs in city parks.* **5** [T] **~ sth** to allow your

attention or effort to become weaker: *You cannot afford to relax your concentration for a moment.*

re·lax·ant /rɪˈlæksənt/ *noun* (*medical*) a drug that is used to make the body relax: *a muscle relaxant*

re·lax·a·tion **AWL** /ˌrilækˈseɪʃn/ *noun* **1** [U] ways of resting and enjoying yourself; time spent resting and enjoying yourself: *I go hiking for relaxation.* ◆ *a few days of relaxation* ◆ *relaxation techniques* ➔ thesaurus box at ENTERTAINMENT **2** [C] something pleasant you do in order to rest, especially after you have been working: *Fishing is his favorite relaxation.* **3** [U, C, usually sing.] the act of making a rule or some form of control less strict or severe: *the relaxation of foreign currency controls* ◆ *a relaxation of travel restrictions*

re·laxed 🔑 **AWL** /rɪˈlækst/ *adj.*
1 ~ **(about sth)** (of a person) calm and not anxious or worried: *He appeared relaxed and confident before the match.* ◆ *She had a very relaxed manner.* **2** (of a place) calm and informal: *a family-run hotel with a relaxed atmosphere* **3** ~ **(about sth)** not caring too much about discipline or making people follow rules **SYN** LAID-BACK: *I take a fairly relaxed attitude toward what the kids wear to school.*

re·lax·ing 🔑 **AWL** /rɪˈlæksɪŋ/ *adj.*
helping you to rest and become less anxious: *a relaxing evening with friends*

re·lay¹ *verb, noun*
● *verb* /ˈrilei; rɪˈlei/ **1** ~ **sth (to sb)** to receive and send on information, news, etc. to someone: *He relayed the message to his boss.* ◆ *Instructions were relayed to him by phone.* **2** ~ **sth (to sb)** to broadcast television or radio signals: *The game was relayed by satellite to audiences all over the world.*
● *noun* /ˈrilei/ **1** (also **ˈrelay ˌrace**) a race between teams in which each member of the team runs or swims one section of the race: *the 4×100 meter relay* ◆ *a relay team* ◆ *the sprint relay* **2** a fresh set of people or animals that take the place of others that are tired or have finished a period of work: *Rescuers worked **in relays** to save the trapped miners.* **3** an electronic device that receives radio or television signals and sends them on again with greater strength: *a relay station*

re·lay² /ˌriˈlei/ *verb* (**re·laid, re·laid** /ˌriˈleɪd/) ~ **sth** to lay something such as carpet or track again: *They plan to relay about half a mile of the track.*

re·lease 🔑 **AWL** /rɪˈlis/ *verb, noun*
● *verb*
▷ SET SOMEONE OR SOMETHING FREE **1** to let someone or something come out of a place where they have been kept or trapped: ~ **sb/sth** *to release a prisoner/hostage* ◆ ~ **sb/sth from sth** *Firefighters took two hours to release the driver from the wreckage.*
▷ STOP HOLDING SOMETHING **2** ~ **sth** to stop holding something or stop it from being held so that it can move, fly, fall, etc. freely **SYN** LET GO, LET LOOSE: *He refused to release her arm.* ◆ *10,000 balloons were released at the ceremony.* ◆ *Intense heat is released in the reaction.*
▷ FEELINGS **3** ~ **sth** to express feelings such as anger or worry in order to get rid of them: *She burst into tears, releasing all her pent-up emotions.*
▷ FREE SOMEONE FROM DUTY **4** to free someone from a duty, responsibility, contract, etc.: ~ **sb** *The club is releasing some of its older players.* ◆ ~ **sb from sth** *The new law released employers from their obligation to recognize unions.*
▷ PART OF MACHINE **5** ~ **sth** to remove something from a fixed position, allowing something else to move or function: *to release the clutch/handbrake/switch, etc.*
▷ MAKE LESS TIGHT **6** ~ **sth** to make something less tight: *You need to release the tension in these shoulder muscles.*
▷ MAKE AVAILABLE **7** ~ **sth** to make something available to the public: *Police have released no further details about the accident.* ◆ *to release a movie/book/CD* ◆ *new products released onto the market* **8** ~ **sth** to make something available that had previously been restricted: *The new building program will go ahead as soon as the government releases the funds.*

● *noun*
▷ SETTING SOMEONE OR SOMETHING FREE **1** [U, sing.] ~ **(of sb) (from sth)** the act of setting a person or an animal free; the state of being set free: *The government has been working to secure the release of the hostages.* ◆ *She can expect an early release from prison.*
▷ MAKING SOMETHING AVAILABLE **2** [U, sing.] the act of making something available to the public: *The new software is planned for release in April.* ◆ *The movie's general release is next week.* **3** [C] a thing that is made available to the public, especially a new CD or movie: *the latest new releases* ➔ see also PRESS RELEASE
▷ OF GAS/CHEMICAL **4** [U, C] the act of letting a gas, chemical, etc. come out of the container where it has been safely held: *the release of carbon dioxide into the atmosphere* ◆ *to monitor radiation releases*
▷ FROM UNPLEASANT FEELING **5** [U, sing.] the feeling that you are free from pain, anxiety, or some other unpleasant feeling: *a sense of release after the exam* ◆ *I think her death was a merciful release.*

rel·e·gate /ˈrelәgeit/ *verb* ~ **sb/sth (to sth)** to give someone a lower or less important position, rank, etc. than before: *She was then relegated to the role of assistant.* ◆ *He relegated the incident to the back of his mind.* ▶ **rel·e·ga·tion** /ˌrelәˈgeiʃn/ *noun* [U]: *relegation of the footnotes to the back of the book*

re·lent /rɪˈlɛnt/ *verb* **1** [I] to finally agree to something after refusing **SYN** GIVE IN: *"Well, just for a little while then,"* she said, finally relenting. **2** [I] to become less determined, strong, etc.: *After two days the rain relented.* ◆ *The police will not relent in their fight against crime.*

re·lent·less /rɪˈlɛntlәs/ *adj.* **1** not stopping or getting less strong **SYN** UNRELENTING: *her relentless pursuit of perfection* ◆ *The sun was relentless.* **2** refusing to give up or be less strict or severe: *a relentless enemy* ▶ **re·lent·less·ly** *adv.*

rel·e·vant 🔑 **AWL** /ˈrelәvәnt/ *adj.*
1 closely connected with the subject you are discussing or the situation you are thinking about: *a relevant suggestion/question/point* ◆ *Do you have the relevant experience?* ◆ ~ **to sth/sb** *These comments are not directly relevant to this inquiry.* **ANT** IRRELEVANT **2** ~ **(to sth/sb)** having ideas that are valuable and useful to people in their lives and work: *Her novel is still relevant today.* ▶ **rel·e·vance** **AWL** /-vәns/ *noun* [U]: *I don't see the relevance of your question.* ◆ *What he said has no direct relevance to the matter in hand.* ◆ *a classic play of contemporary relevance* **rel·e·vant·ly** *adv.*: *The applicant has experience in teaching and, more relevantly, in industry.*

re·li·a·ble AWL /rɪ'laɪəbl/ adj. **1** that can be trusted to do something well; that you can rely on **SYN** DEPENDABLE: *We are looking for someone who is reliable and hard-working.* ◆ *a reliable friend* ◆ *My car's not as reliable as it used to be.* **2** that is likely to be correct or true: *Our information comes from a reliable source.* ◆ *a reliable witness* **ANT** UNRELIABLE ➾ collocations at RELY ▶ **re·li·a·bil·i·ty** AWL /rɪ,laɪə'bɪləti/ noun [U]: *The incident cast doubt on her motives and reliability.* ◆ *The reliability of these results has been questioned.* **re·li·a·bly** AWL /rɪ'laɪəbli/ adv.: *I am reliably informed* (= told by someone who knows the facts) *that the company is being sold.*

re·li·ance AWL /rɪ'laɪəns/ noun [U, sing.] ~ **(on/upon sb/sth)** the state of needing someone or something in order to survive, be successful, etc.; the fact of being able to rely on someone or something **SYN** DEPENDENCE ➾ collocations at RELY: *Heavy reliance on one client is risky when you are building up a business.* ◆ *Such learning methods encourage too great a reliance upon the teacher.* ◆ *The study program concentrates more on group work and places less reliance on* (= depends less on) *lectures.*

re·li·ant AWL /rɪ'laɪənt/ adj. ~ **on/upon sb/sth** needing someone or something in order to survive, be successful, etc. **SYN** DEPENDENT: *The hostel is heavily reliant upon charity.* ➾ see also SELF-RELIANT

rel·ic /'rɛlɪk/ noun **1** ~ **(of/from sth)** an object, a tradition, a system, etc. that has survived from the past: *The building stands as the last remaining relic of the town's cotton industry.* ◆ *Videotapes may already seem like relics of a bygone era.* **2** a part of the body or clothing of a holy person, or something that they owned, that is kept after their death and respected as a religious object: *holy relics*

re·lief 🔊 /rɪ'liːf/ noun

> REMOVAL OF ANXIETY/PAIN **1** [U, sing.] the feeling of happiness that you have when something unpleasant stops or does not happen: *a sense of relief* ◆ *We all breathed a sigh of relief when he left.* ◆ *She sighed with relief.* ◆ *Much to my relief, the car was not damaged.* ◆ *News of their safety came as a great relief.* ◆ *It was a relief to be able to talk to someone about it.* ◆ *What a relief!* **2** [U] ~ **(from/of sth)** the act of removing or reducing pain, anxiety, etc.: *modern methods of pain relief* ◆ *the relief of suffering*

> HELP **3** [U] food, money, medicine, etc. that is given to help people in places where there has been a war or natural disaster **SYN** AID: *famine/disaster relief* ◆ *a relief agency/organization/worker* **4** [U] financial help given by the government to people who need it

> ON TAX **5** [U] = TAX RELIEF: *relief on mortgage interest payments*

> SOMETHING DIFFERENT **6** [U, sing.] something that is interesting or enjoyable that replaces something boring, difficult, or unpleasant for a short period of time: *a few moments of light relief in an otherwise dull performance* ◆ *There was little*

comic relief in his speech. ◆ ~ **from sth** *The calm of the countryside came as a welcome relief from the hustle and bustle of city life.*

> WORKERS **7** [C] (often used as an adjective) a person or group of people that replaces another when they have finished working for the day or when they are sick: *The next crew relief comes on duty at 9 o'clock.* ◆ *relief drivers*

> FROM ENEMY **8** [sing.] ~ **of…** the act of freeing a town, etc. from an enemy army that has surrounded it

> IN ART **9** [U, C] a way of decorating wood, stone, etc. by cutting designs into the surface of it so that some parts stick out more than others; a design that is made in this way: *The column was decorated in high relief* (= with designs that stick out a lot) *with scenes from Greek mythology.* ◆ *The bronze doors are covered with sculpted reliefs.* ➾ picture at ARCHITECTURE

> MAKING SOMETHING NOTICEABLE **10** [U] the effect of colors, light, etc. that makes an object more noticeable than others around it: *The snow-capped mountain stood out in sharp relief against the blue sky.* **11** [U] the quality of a particular situation, problem, etc. that makes it more noticeable than before: *Their differences have been thrown into sharp relief by the present crisis.*

re'lief map noun a map that uses various colors, etc. to show the different heights of hills, valleys, etc.

re·lieve /rɪ'liːv/ verb **1** ~ **sth** to remove or reduce an unpleasant feeling or pain: *to relieve the symptoms of a cold* ◆ *to relieve anxiety/guilt/stress* ◆ *Being able to tell the truth at last seemed to relieve her.* **2** ~ **sth** to make a problem less serious **SYN** ALLEVIATE: *efforts to relieve poverty* ◆ *to relieve traffic congestion* **3** ~ **sth** to make something less boring, especially by introducing something different: *We played cards to relieve the boredom of the long wait.* ◆ *The black and white pattern is relieved by tiny colored flowers.* **4** ~ **sb** to replace someone who is on duty: *to relieve a sentry* ◆ *You'll be relieved at six o'clock.* **5** ~ **sth** to free a town, etc. from an enemy army that has surrounded it **6** ~ **yourself** a polite way of referring to going to the bathroom: *I had to relieve myself behind a bush.*
PHR V re'lieve sb of sth **1** to help someone by taking something heavy or difficult from them: *Let me relieve you of some of your bags.* ◆ *The new assistant will relieve us of some of the paperwork.* **2** (informal, ironic) to steal something from someone: *A boy with a knife relieved him of his wallet.* **3** to dismiss someone from a job, position, etc.: *General Beale was relieved of his command.*

re·lieved /rɪ'liːvd/ adj. feeling happy because something unpleasant has stopped or has not happened; showing this: *She sounded relieved.* ◆ ~ **(to see, hear, find, etc. something)** *You'll be relieved to know your jobs are safe.* ◆ ~ **(that…)** *I'm just relieved that nobody was hurt.* ◆ *They exchanged relieved glances.* ➾ thesaurus box at GLAD

TOPIC COLLOCATIONS

Religion
being religious

■ believe in God/Christ/Allah/free will/predestination/heaven and hell/an afterlife/reincarnation
■ be/become an agnostic/an atheist/a believer/a Buddhist/Christian/Hindu/Muslim, etc.
■ convert to/practice a religion/Buddhism/Catholicism/Christianity/Islam/Judaism, etc.
■ go to church/temple (= the synagogue)
■ go to the local church/mosque/synagogue
■ belong to a church/a religious community
■ join/enter the Church/a convent/a monastery/the clergy/the priesthood/a religious sect/a cult
■ praise/worship/obey/serve/glorify God

celebrations and ritual

■ attend/hold/conduct/lead a service
■ perform a ceremony/a rite/a ritual/a baptism/the Hajj/a bar mitzvah/a bat mitzvah
■ carry out/perform a sacred/burial/funeral/fertility/purification rite/the last rites

- **go on/make** a pilgrimage
- **celebrate** Christmas/Diwali/Easter/Eid/Hanukkah/Passover/Ramadan
- **observe/break** the Sabbath/a fast/Ramadan
- **deliver/preach/hear** a sermon
- **lead/address** the congregation
- **say/recite** a prayer/blessing

religious texts and ideas

- **preach/proclaim/spread** the word of God/the Gospel/the message of Islam/a message
- **study/follow** the dharma/the teachings of Buddha
- **read/study/understand/interpret** scripture/the Bible/the Koran/the Gospel/the Torah
- **be based on/derived from** divine revelation
- **commit/consider sth** heresy/sacrilege

religious belief and experience

- **seek/find/gain** enlightenment/wisdom
- **strengthen/lose/question** your faith
- **keep/practice/abandon** the faith
- **save/purify/lose** your soul
- **obey/follow/keep/break/violate** a commandment/Islamic law/Jewish law
- **be/accept/do** God's will
- **receive/experience** divine grace
- **achieve/attain** enlightenment/salvation/nirvana
- **undergo** a conversion/rebirth/reincarnation
- **hear/answer** a prayer
- **commit/confess/forgive** a sin
- **do/perform** penance

re·li·gion 🔑 /rɪˈlɪdʒən/ *noun*
1 [U] the belief in the existence of a god or gods, and the activities that are connected with the worship of them: *Is there always a conflict between science and religion?* **2** [C] one of the systems of faith that are based on the belief in the existence of a particular god or gods: *the Jewish religion* ◆ *Christianity, Islam, and other world religions* ◆ *The law states that everyone has the right to practice their own religion.* **3** [sing.] a particular interest or influence that is very important in your life: *For him, football is an absolute religion.* **IDM** **get religion** (*informal, disapproving*) to suddenly become interested in religion

re·li·gi·os·i·ty /rɪˌlɪdʒiˈɑsəti/ *noun* [U] (*formal, sometimes disapproving*) the state of being religious or too religious

re·li·gious 🔑 /rɪˈlɪdʒəs/ *adj.*
1 [only before noun] connected with religion or with a particular religion: *religious beliefs/faith* ◆ *religious education* (= education about religion) ◆ *religious instruction* (= instruction in a particular religion) ◆ *religious groups* ◆ *objects that have a religious significance* **2** (of a person) believing strongly in the existence of a god or gods **SYN** DEVOUT: *His wife is very religious.* ▶ **re·li·gious·ness** *noun* [U]

re·li·gious·ly /rɪˈlɪdʒəsli/ *adv.* **1** very carefully or regularly: *She followed the instructions religiously.* **2** in a way that is connected with religion: *Were you brought up religiously?*

reˈligious ˌschool *noun* a school supported by a SYNA-GOGUE, church, etc. and attended in addition to a regular school: *She has religious school on Sunday mornings.*

re·lin·quish /rɪˈlɪŋkwɪʃ/ *verb* (*formal*) to stop having something, especially when this happens unwillingly **SYN** GIVE UP: ~ **sth** *He was forced to relinquish control of the company.* ◆ *They had relinquished all hope that she was alive.* ◆ ~ **sth to sb** *She relinquished possession of the house to her sister.*

rel·i·quar·y /ˈrɛləˌkwɛri/ *noun* (*pl.* **rel·i·quar·ies**) a container in which a RELIC of a holy person is kept

rel·ish /ˈrɛlɪʃ/ *verb, noun*
● *verb* to get great pleasure from something; to want very much to do or have something **SYN** ENJOY: ~ **sth** *to relish a fight/challenge/debate* ◆ *to relish the idea/thought of something* ◆ *I don't relish the prospect of getting up early tomorrow.* ◆ ~ **(sb/sth) doing sth** *Nobody relishes cleaning the oven.*

● *noun* **1** [U] great enjoyment or pleasure: *She savored the moment with obvious relish.* **2** [U, C] a cold, thick, spicy sauce made from fruit and vegetables that have been boiled, that is served with meat, cheese, etc.

re·live /ˌriˈlɪv/ *verb* ~ **sth** to experience something again, especially in your imagination: *He relives the horror of the crash every night in his dreams.*

re·load /ˌriˈloʊd/ *verb* **1** [I, T] ~ **(sth)** to put more bullets into a gun, more film into a camera, etc. **2** [T] ~ **sth** to put data or a program into the memory of a computer again **3** [T] ~ **sth** to fill a container, vehicle, machine, etc. again

re·lo·cate **AWL** /ˌriˈloʊkeɪt/ *verb* [I, T] (especially of a company or workers) to move or to move someone or something to a new place to work or operate: *The firm may be forced to relocate from New York to Stamford.* ◆ ~ **sth** *The company relocated its head office to Stamford.* ▶ **re·lo·ca·tion** **AWL** /ˌriloʊˈkeɪʃn/ *noun* [U, C]: *relocation costs*

re·luc·tant **AWL** /rɪˈlʌktənt/ *adj.* hesitating before doing something because you do not want to do it or because you are not sure that it is the right thing to do: *reluctant agreement* ◆ ~ **(to do sth)** *She was reluctant to admit she was wrong.* ◆ *He finally gave a reluctant smile.* ◆ *a reluctant hero* (= a person who does not want to be called a hero) ▶ **re·luc·tance** **AWL** /-təns/ *noun* [U, sing.]: ~ **(to do sth)** *There is still some reluctance on the part of employers to become involved in this project.* ◆ *They finally agreed to our terms with a certain reluctance.* **re·luc·tant·ly** **AWL** *adv.*: *We reluctantly agreed to go with her.*

re·ly 🔑 **AWL** /rɪˈlaɪ/ *verb*
(**re·lies**, **re·ly·ing**, **re·lied**, **re·lied**)
PHR V **reˈly on/upon sb/sth** **1** to need or depend on someone or something: *As babies, we rely entirely on others for food.* ◆ ~ **to do sth** *These days we rely heavily on computers to organize our work.* ◆ ~ **doing sth** *The industry relies on the price of raw materials remaining low.* **2** to trust or have faith in someone or something: *You should rely on your own judgment.* ◆ ~ **to do sth** *You can rely on me to keep your secret.* ◆ *He can't be relied on to tell the truth.* ⊃ thesaurus box at TRUST

WORD FAMILY
rely *verb*
reliable *adj.* (≠ unreliable)
reliably *adv.*
reliability *noun* (≠ unreliability)
reliance *noun*

AWL COLLOCATIONS

rely

rely *verb*
to need something or someone and not be able to live or work well without it/him/her
- **heavily** | **entirely, exclusively, solely** | **mainly, mostly, primarily, principally** | **extensively**
  The author relies heavily on the primary sources of the literature.
- **tend to**
  Larger volume commercial fruit and vegetable growers tend to rely on migrant labor to harvest crops.

reliability *noun*
- **ascertain, assess, evaluate** | **improve** | **ensure** | **maximize**
  To ensure the reliability of the experiments, all experiments were repeated two to three times.
- **a degree of ~** | **a level of ~**
  Higher-accuracy instruments provide increased levels of reliability and confidence.

reliable *adj.*
- **scientifically, statistically** | **highly** | **fairly, reasonably, sufficiently**
  The data set used is too small to yield statistically reliable conclusions.

■ **indicator, predictor** | **estimate** | **source**
  The authors conclude that consumer credit is one of the most reliable indicators of an advanced civilization.
■ **prove**
  Tall buildings soak up radio waves, so landline communications might prove more reliable.

unreliable *adj.*

■ **inherently, intrinsically** | **notoriously** | **demonstrably** | **wholly** | **potentially** | **statistically**
  Forecasters are notoriously unreliable at predicting things like the next wave of technological change.
  These models were statistically unreliable because of the very small sample sizes.
■ **render sth**
  Technical difficulties in the design of experiments render data unreliable.
■ **prove**
  Prior efforts to identify this disorder proved unreliable and expensive.

reliance *noun*

■ **place** | **question** | **decrease, lessen, reduce** | **necessitate** | **preclude** | **entail**
  These findings suggest that new industries lessen reliance on agriculture.
■ **excessive, heavy, inordinate, undue** | **exclusive**
  The almost exclusive reliance on memoirs and letters tells us how strongly the biographical element dominates Frank's work.

REM /rem; ˌɑr i ˈem/ *abbr.* rapid eye movement (describes a period of sleep during which you dream and your eyes make many small movements)

re·made pt, pp of REMAKE

re·main 🔑 /rɪˈmeɪn/ *verb* (*formal*)
(not usually in the progressive tenses) **1** *linking verb* to continue to be something; to be still in the same state or condition: **+ adj.** *to remain silent/standing/seated/motionless* ♦ *Train fares are likely to remain unchanged.* ♦ *It remains true that sports are about competing well, not winning.* ♦ **+ noun** *In spite of their quarrel, they remain the best of friends.* ♦ *He will remain (as) manager of the club until the end of his contract.* **2** [I] to still be present after the other parts have been removed, used, etc.; to continue to exist: *Very little of the house remained after the fire.* ♦ *There were only ten minutes remaining.* **3** [I] ~ **(to do sth)** to still need to be done, said, or dealt with: *Much remains to be done.* ♦ *It remains to be seen* (= it will only be known later) *whether you are right.* ♦ *There remained one significant problem.* ♦ *Questions remain about the President's honesty.* ♦ *I feel sorry for her, but the fact remains (that) she lied to us.* ⊃ language bank at NEVERTHELESS **4** [I] **+ adv./prep.** to stay in the same place; to not leave: *They remained in Mexico until June.* ♦ *The plane remained on the ground.* ♦ *She left, but I remained behind.* **IDM** see ALOOF

re·main·der /rɪˈmeɪndər/ *noun, verb*
● *noun* **1** usually **the remainder** [usually sing.] the remaining people, things, or time **SYN** THE REST: *I kept some of his books and gave away the remainder.* **HELP** When the **remainder** refers to a plural noun, the verb is plural: *Most of our employees work in New York; the remainder are in London.* **2** [C, usually sing.] (*mathematics*) the number left after one number has been SUBTRACTED from another, or one number has been divided into another: *Divide 2 into 7, and the answer is 3, remainder 1.* **3** [C] a book that has been remaindered
● *verb* [I, T, usually passive] ~ **(sth)** to sell books at a reduced price

re·main·ing 🔑 /rɪˈmeɪnɪŋ/ *adj.* [only before noun]
still needing to be done or dealt with: *The remaining twenty patients were transferred to another hospital.* ♦ *Any remaining*

tickets for the concert will be sold on the door. ⊃ see also REMAIN

re·mains 🔑 /rɪˈmeɪnz/ *noun* [pl.]
1 ~ **(of sth)** the parts of something that are left after the other parts have been used, eaten, removed, etc.: *She fed the remains of her lunch to the dog.* **2** the parts of ancient objects and buildings that have survived and are discovered in the present day: *prehistoric remains* ♦ *the remains of a Roman fort* **3** (*formal*) the body of a dead person or animal: *They had discovered* **human remains**.

re·make *noun, verb*
● *noun* /ˈriːmeɪk/ a new or different version of an old movie or song
● *verb* /ˌriːˈmeɪk/ (**re·made, re·made** /-ˈmeɪd/) ~ **sth** to make a new or different version of something such as an old movie or song; to make something again: *"The Seven Samurai" was remade in Hollywood as "The Magnificent Seven."*

re·mand /rɪˈmænd/ *verb, noun*
● *verb* [usually passive] ~ **sb (+ adv./prep.)** to send someone away from a court to wait for their trial that will take place at a later date: *The two men were charged with burglary and* **remanded in custody** (= sent to prison until their trial). ♦ *She was* **remanded on bail** (= allowed to go free until the trial after leaving a sum of money with the court).
● *noun* [U] the process of keeping someone in prison while they are waiting for their trial: *He is currently being held on* **remand**. ♦ *a remand prisoner*

re·mark 🔑 /rɪˈmɑrk/ *noun, verb*
● *noun* **1** [C] something that you say or write which expresses an opinion, a thought, etc. about someone or something **SYN** COMMENT: *to make a remark* ♦ *He made a number of rude remarks about the food.* ♦ *What exactly did you mean by that last remark?* **2** [U] (*old-fashioned* or *formal*) the quality of being important or interesting enough to be noticed **SYN** NOTE: *The exhibition contains nothing that is worthy of remark.*
● *verb* [I, T] to say or write a comment about something or someone **SYN** COMMENT: ~ **on/upon sth/sb** *The judges remarked on the high standard of entries for the competition.* ♦ ~ **how…** *She remarked how tired I was looking.* ♦ **+ speech** *"It's much colder than yesterday," he remarked casually.* ♦ ~ **that…** *Critics remarked that the play was not original.* ♦ **be remarked on** *The similarities between the two have often been remarked on.*

re·mark·a·ble 🔑 /rɪˈmɑrkəbl/ *adj.*
unusual or surprising in a way that causes people to take notice **SYN** ASTONISHING: *a remarkable achievement/career/talent* ♦ *She was a truly remarkable woman.* ♦ ~ **for sth** *The area is remarkable for its scenery.* ♦ ~ **that…** *It is remarkable that nobody noticed sooner.* **ANT** UNREMARKABLE
▶ **re·mark·a·bly** /-bli/ *adv.*: *The car is in remarkably good condition for its age.* ♦ *Remarkably, nobody was killed.*

re·mar·ry /ˌriːˈmæri/ *verb* (**re·mar·ries, re·mar·ry·ing, re·mar·ried, re·mar·ried**) [I] to marry again after being divorced or after your husband or wife has died
▶ **re·mar·riage** /ˌriːˈmærɪdʒ/ *noun* [U, C]

re·mas·ter /ˌriːˈmæstər/ *verb* ~ **sth** to make a new MASTER copy of a recording in order to improve the sound quality: *All the tracks have been* **digitally remastered** *from the original tapes.*

re·match /ˈriːmætʃ/ *noun* [usually sing.] a match or game played again between the same people or teams, especially because neither side won the first match or game

re·me·di·a·ble /rɪˈmiːdiəbl/ *adj.* (*formal*) that can be solved or cured **SYN** CURABLE: *remediable problems/diseases*

re·me·di·al /rɪˈmiːdiəl/ *adj.* [only before noun] **1** aimed at solving a problem, especially when this involves correcting or improving something that has been done wrong: *remedial treatment* (= for a medical problem) ♦ *Remedial action must be taken now.* **2** connected with school students

ʌ **cup**   ə **about**   eɪ **say**   aɪ ə **five 19**   ɔɪ **boy**   aʊ **now**   oʊ **go**   ər **bird**

who are slower at learning than others: *remedial education* ♦ *a remedial class*

re·me·di·a·tion /rɪˌmidiˈeɪʃn/ *noun* [U] the process of improving something or correcting something that is wrong, especially changing or stopping damage to the environment or helping school students who are slower at learning than others: *remediation of contaminated soil* ▶ **re·me·di·ate** /rɪˈmidiˌeɪt/ *verb*: ~ **sth** *The problems need to be detected and remediated quickly.*

rem·e·dy /ˈrɛmədi/ *noun, verb*
• *noun* (*pl.* **rem·e·dies**) **1** a way of dealing with or improving an unpleasant or difficult situation **SYN** SOLUTION: ~ **(for sth)** *There is no simple remedy for unemployment.* ♦ ~ **(to sth)** *There are a number of possible remedies to this problem.* **2** a treatment or medicine to cure a disease or reduce pain that is not very serious: *an herbal remedy* ♦ ~ **for sth** *an excellent home remedy for sore throats* **3** ~ **(against sth)** (*law*) a way of dealing with a problem, using the processes of the law **SYN** REDRESS: *Holding copyright provides the only legal remedy against unauthorized copying.*
• *verb* (**rem·e·dies, rem·e·dy·ing, rem·e·died, re·me·died**) ~ **sth** to correct or improve something **SYN** PUT RIGHT: *to remedy a problem* ♦ *This situation is easily remedied.*

re·mem·ber 🔑 /rɪˈmɛmbər/ *verb*
(not usually used in the progressive tenses)
▷ SOMEONE OR SOMETHING FROM THE PAST **1** [T, I] to have or keep an image in your memory of an event, a person, a place, etc. from the past: ~ **(sb/sth)** *This is Carla. Do you remember her?* ♦ *I don't remember my first day at school.* ♦ *He still remembered her as the lively teenager he'd known years before.* ♦ *As far as I can remember, this is the third time we've met.* ♦ ~ **doing sth** *Do you remember turning the lights off before we came out?* ♦ *I vaguely remember hearing him come in.* ♦ ~ **sb/sth doing sth** *I can still vividly remember my grandfather teaching me to play cards.* ♦ (*formal*) *I can't remember his taking a single day off work.* ♦ ~ **(that)...** *I remember (that) we used to go and see them most weekends.*
▷ FACT/INFORMATION **2** [T, I] to bring back to your mind a fact, piece of information, etc. that you knew: ~ **(sth)** *I'm sorry—I can't remember your name.* ♦ *We were going to help me with this. Remember?* ♦ ~ **how, what,...** *Can you remember how much money we spent?* ♦ ~ **(that)...** *Remember that we're going out tonight.* **3** [T] to keep an important fact in your mind: ~ **(that)...** *Remember (that) you may feel sleepy after taking the pills.* ♦ **it is remembered that...** *It should be remembered that the majority of accidents happen in the home.*
▷ SOMETHING YOU HAVE TO DO **4** [T] to not forget to do something; to actually do what you have to do: ~ **to do sth** *Remember to call me when you arrive!* ♦ ~ **sth** *Did you remember your homework* (= to bring it)*?* **HELP** Notice the difference between **remember doing something** and **remember to do something**: *I remember mailing the letter* means "I have an image in my memory of doing it";: *I remembered to mail the letter* means "I didn't forget to do it."
▷ IN PRAYERS **5** [T] ~ **sb** to think about someone with respect, especially when saying a prayer **SYN** COMMEMORATE: *a church service to remember the war dead*
▷ GIVE PRESENT **6** [T] ~ **sb/sth** to give money, a present, etc. to someone or something: *My aunt always remembers my birthday* (= by sending a card or present)*.* ♦ *His grandfather remembered him* (= left him money) *in his will.*
IDM **be remembered for sth | be remembered as sth** to be famous or known for a particular thing that you have done in the past: *He is best remembered as the man who brought jazz to England.*
PHR V **re'member me to sb** (*old-fashioned*) used to ask someone to give your good wishes to someone else: *Remember me to your parents.*

re·mem·brance /rɪˈmɛmbrəns/ *noun* **1** [U] the act or process of remembering an event in the past or a person who is dead: *A service was held in remembrance of local soldiers killed in the war.* ♦ (*formal*) *He smiled at the remembrance of their first kiss.* **2** [C] (*formal*) an object that causes you to remember something or someone; a memory of

someone or something: *The cenotaph stands as a remembrance of those killed during the war.*

Re'membrance Day *noun* (*CanE*) a holiday in Canada on November 11 in honor of those killed in war

re·mind 🔑 /rɪˈmaɪnd/ *verb* ~ **sb (about/of sth)**
to help someone remember something, especially something important that they must do: ~ **sb** *I'm sorry, I've forgotten your name. Can you remind me?* ♦ **That** (= what you have just said, done, etc.) **reminds me,** *I must get some cash.* ♦ *"You need to finish that essay."* *"Don't remind me* (= I don't want to think about it)*."* ♦ *"Don't forget the camera." "Remind me about it nearer the time."* ♦ ~ **sb to do sth** *Remind me to phone Alan before I go out.* ♦ ~ **sb (that)...** *Passengers are reminded (that) no smoking is allowed on this train.* ♦ ~ **sb what, how, etc....** *Can someone remind me what I should do next?* ♦ ~ **sb + speech** *"You had an accident," he reminded her.*
PHR V **re'mind sb of sb/sth** if someone or something **reminds** you of someone or something else, they make you remember or think about the other person, place, thing, etc. because they are similar in some way: *You remind me of your father when you say that.* ♦ *That smell reminds me of France.*

re·mind·er /rɪˈmaɪndər/ *noun* **1** ~ **(of sb/sth)** | ~ **(that...)** something that makes you think about or remember someone or something, that you have forgotten or would like to forget: *The sheer size of the cathedral is a constant reminder of the power of religion.* ♦ *The incident served as a timely reminder of just how dangerous mountaineering can be.* ♦ *a friendly reminder* **2** a letter, an e-mail, a note, etc. informing someone that they have not done something

rem·i·nisce /ˌrɛməˈnɪs/ *verb* [I] ~ **(about sth/sb)** to think, talk, or write about a happy time in your past: *We spent a happy evening reminiscing about the past.*

rem·i·nis·cence /ˌrɛməˈnɪsns/ *noun* **1** [C, usually pl.] a spoken or written description of something that someone remembers about their past life **SYN** MEMORY: *The book is a collection of his reminiscences about the actress.* ♦ *reminiscences of a wartime childhood* **2** [U] the act of remembering things that happened in the past **SYN** RECOLLECTION **3** [C, usually pl.] something that reminds you of something similar: *Her music is full of reminiscences of African rhythms.*

rem·i·nis·cent /ˌrɛməˈnɪsnt/ *adj.* **1** ~ **of sb/sth** reminding you of someone or something: *The way he laughed was strongly reminiscent of his father.* **2** [only before noun] (*formal*) showing that you are thinking about the past, especially in a way that causes you pleasure: *a reminiscent smile*

re·miss /rɪˈmɪs/ *adj.* [not before noun] (*formal*) not giving something enough care and attention **SYN** NEGLIGENT: ~ **(of sb) (to do sth)** *It was remiss of them not to inform us of these changes sooner.* ♦ ~ **(in sth/in doing sth)** *She had clearly been remiss in her duty.*

re·mis·sion /rɪˈmɪʃn/ *noun* [U, C] **1** a period during which a serious illness improves for a time and the patient seems to get better: *The patient has been in remission for the past six months.* ♦ *The symptoms reappeared after only a short remission.* **2** (*formal*) an act of reducing or canceling the amount of money that someone has to pay: *New businesses may qualify for tax remission.* ♦ *Children of college employees are eligible to receive full remission of tuition fees.*

re·mit /rɪˈmɪt/ *verb* (**-tt-**) (*formal*) **1** to send money, etc. to a person or place **SYN** FORWARD: ~ **sth** *to remit funds* ♦ ~ **sth to sb** *Payment will be remitted to you in full.* **2** ~ **sth** to cancel or free someone from a debt, duty, punishment, etc. **SYN** CANCEL: *to remit a fine* ♦ *to remit a prison sentence* ⊃ see also UNREMITTING
PHR V **re'mit sth to sb** [usually passive] (*law*) to send a matter to an authority so that a decision can be made: *The case was remitted to the Court of Appeals.*

re·mit·tance /rɪˈmɪtns/ *noun* **1** [C] (*formal*) a sum of money that is sent to someone in order to pay for something: *Please return the completed form with your remittance.* **2** [U] the act of sending money to someone in order to pay for something **SYN** PAYMENT: *Remittance can be made by check or credit card.*

re·mix /ˌriˈmɪks/ *verb* ~ **sth** to make a new version of a recorded piece of music by using a machine to arrange the separate parts of the recording in a different way, add new parts, etc. ▶ **re·mix** /ˈrimɪks/ (also **mix**) *noun* **re·mix·er** *noun*: *the skills of remixer Tom Moulton*

rem·nant /ˈrɛmnənt/ *noun* **1** [usually pl.] a part of something that is left after the other parts have been used, removed, destroyed, etc. **SYN** REMAINS: *The woods are remnants of a huge forest that once covered the whole area.* **2** a small piece of cloth that is left when the rest has been sold

re·mod·el /ˌriˈmɑdl/ *verb* (-l-, *CanE usually* -ll-) ~ **sth** to change the structure or shape of something

re·mold /ˌriˈmoʊld/ *verb* ~ **sth** (*formal*) to change something such as an idea, a system, etc.: *attempts to remold policy to make it more acceptable*

re·mon·strance /rɪˈmɑnstrəns/ *noun* [C, U] (*formal*) a protest or complaint

re·mon·strate /ˈrɛmənˌstreɪt; rɪˈmɑnstreɪt/ *verb* [I, T] ~ **(with sb) (about sth)** | **+ speech** (*formal*) to protest or complain about something or someone: *They remonstrated with the official about the decision.*

re·morse /rɪˈmɔrs/ *noun* [U] the feeling of being extremely sorry for something wrong or bad that you have done: *I felt guilty and full of remorse.* ◆ ~ **for sth/for doing sth** *He was filled with remorse for not believing her.* ▶ **re·morse·ful** /rɪˈmɔrsfl/ *adj.* **re·morse·ful·ly** /-fəli/ *adv.*

re·morse·less /rɪˈmɔrsləs/ *adj.* **1** (especially of an unpleasant situation) seeming to continue or become worse in a way that cannot be stopped **SYN** RELENTLESS: *the remorseless increase in crime* **2** cruel, and having or showing no sympathy for other people **SYN** MERCILESS: *a remorseless killer* ▶ **re·morse·less·ly** *adv.*

re·mort·gage /ˌriˈmɔrgɪdʒ/ *verb* [I, T] ~ **(sth)** to arrange a second MORTGAGE on your house or apartment, or to increase or change your first one ▶ **re·mort·gage** *noun*

re·mote 🔑 /rɪˈmoʊt/ *adj., noun*
● *adj.* (**re·mot·er, re·mot·est**)
▷ PLACE **1** far away from places where other people live **SYN** ISOLATED: *a remote beach* ◆ *one of the remotest areas of the world* ◆ ~ **from sth** *The farmhouse is remote from any other buildings.*
▷ TIME **2** [only before noun] far away in time **SYN** DISTANT: *in the remote past/future* ◆ *a remote ancestor* (= who lived a long time ago)
▷ RELATIVES **3** [only before noun] (of people) not closely related **SYN** DISTANT: *a remote cousin*
▷ COMPUTER/SYSTEM **4** that you can connect to from far away, using an electronic link: *a remote terminal/database*
▷ DIFFERENT **5** ~ **(from sth)** very different from something: *His theories are somewhat remote from reality.*
▷ NOT FRIENDLY **6** (of people or their behavior) not very friendly or interested in other people **SYN** ALOOF, DISTANT
▷ VERY SMALL **7** not very great **SYN** SLIGHT: *There is still a remote chance that they will find her alive.* ◆ *I don't have the remotest idea what you're talking about.*

▶ **re·mote·ness** *noun* [U]: *the geographical remoteness of the island* ◆ *His remoteness made her feel unloved.*
● *noun* (*informal*) = REMOTE CONTROL

re·mote access *noun* [U] the use of a computer system, etc. that is in another place, that you can connect to when you are far away, using an electronic link

re·mote con·trol *noun* **1** [U] the ability to operate a machine from a distance using radio or electrical signals: *It works by remote control.* ◆ *a remote-control camera* **2** (also *informal* **re·mote, zap·per**) [C] a device that allows you to operate a television, etc. from a distance: *I can't find the remote control.* ▶ **re·mote-con·trolled** *adj.*: *remote-controlled equipment*

re·mote·ly /rɪˈmoʊtli/ *adv.* **1** (usually in negative sen-

tences) to a very slight degree **SYN** SLIGHTLY: *It wasn't even remotely funny* (= it wasn't at all funny). ◆ *The two incidents were only remotely connected.* **2** from a distance: *remotely operated* ◆ *Many people are working remotely.* **3** far away from places where other people live: *The church is remotely situated on the north coast of the island.*

re·mote sensing *noun* [U] the use of SATELLITES to search for and collect information about the earth

re·mount /ˌriˈmaʊnt/ *verb* **1** [I, T] ~ **(sth)** to get on a horse, bicycle, etc. again after getting off it or falling off it **2** [T] ~ **sth** to organize and begin something a second time

re·mov·a·ble **AWL** /rɪˈmuvəbl/ *adj.* [usually before noun] that can be taken off or out of something **SYN** DETACHABLE

re·mov·al 🔑 **AWL** /rɪˈmuvl/ *noun* [U]
1 ~ **(of sb/sth)** the act of taking someone or something away from a particular place: *Clearance of the site required the removal of a number of trees.* ◆ *the removal of a tumor* **2** ~ **(of sth)** the act of getting rid of something: *stain removal* ◆ *the removal of trade barriers* **3** ~ **(of sb)** the act of dismissing someone from their job **SYN** DISMISSAL: *events leading to the removal of the president from office*

re·move 🔑 **AWL** /rɪˈmuv/ *verb, noun*
● *verb* **1** to take something or someone away from a place: ~ **sth/sb** *Illegally parked vehicles will be removed.* ◆ ~ **sth/sb from sth/sb** *He removed his hand from her shoulder.* ◆ *Three children were removed from the school for persistent bad behavior.* **2** to take off clothing, etc. from the body: *She removed her glasses and rubbed her eyes.* **3** to get rid of something unpleasant, dirty, etc.; to make something disappear: ~ **sth** *She has had the tumor removed.* ◆ *to remove problems/obstacles/objections* ◆ ~ **sth from sb/sth** *The news removed any doubts about the company's future from my mind.* **4** ~ **sb from sth** to dismiss someone from their position or job: *The elections removed the government from power.*
IDM **once, twice, etc. removed** (of a cousin) belonging to a different generation: *He's my cousin's son so he's my first cousin once removed.* **be far/further/furthest removed from sth** to be very different from something; to not be connected with something: *Many of these books are far removed from the reality of the children's lives.*
● *noun* [C, U] (*formal*) an amount by which two things are separated: *Charlotte seemed to be living at one remove from reality.*

re·mov·er /rɪˈmuvər/ *noun* [U, C] (usually in compounds) a substance used for getting rid of marks, paint, etc.: *nail polish remover* ◆ *stain remover*

re·mu·ner·ate /rɪˈmyunəˌreɪt/ *verb* [usually passive] ~ **sb (for sth)** (*formal*) to pay someone for work that they have done

re·mu·ner·a·tion /rɪˌmyunəˈreɪʃn/ *noun* [U, C] (*formal*) an amount of money that is paid to someone for the work they have done

re·mu·ner·a·tive /rɪˈmyunərətɪv; -nəˌreɪtɪv/ *adj.* [usually before noun] (*formal*) paying a lot of money: *remunerative work*

ren·ais·sance /ˈrɛnəˌsɑns; -ˌzɑns/ *noun* [sing.] **1 the Renaissance** the period in Europe during the 14th, 15th, and 16th centuries when people became interested in the ideas and culture of ancient Greece and Rome and used these influences in their own art, literature, etc.: *Renaissance art* **2** a situation when there is new interest in a particular subject, form of art, etc. after a period when it was not very popular **SYN** REVIVAL: *to experience a renaissance*

Renaissance man, Renaissance woman *noun* a person who is good at a lot of things and has a lot of interests, especially writing and painting

re·nal /ˈrinl/ *adj.* [usually before noun] (*medical*) relating to or involving the KIDNEYS: *renal failure*

re·name /ˌriˈneɪm/ *verb* to give someone or something a

t **tea**   ţ **butter**   d **did**   k **cat**   g **got**   tʃ **chin**   dʒ **June**   f **fall**

new name: ~ **sth** *to rename a street* ◆ ~ **sth** + **noun** *Leningrad was renamed St. Petersburg.*

re·nas·cence /rɪˈnæsns; -ˈneɪ-/ *noun* [U, sing.] (*formal*) a situation in which there is new interest in a particular subject, form of art, etc. after a period when it was not very popular ▶ **re·nas·cent** /rɪˈnæsnt; -ˈneɪ-/ *adj.*: *renascent fascism*

rend /rend/ *verb* (**rent, rent** /rent/) ~ **sth** (*old use* or *literary*) to tear something apart with force or violence: *They rent their clothes in grief.* ◆ (*figurative*) *a country rent in two by civil war* ◆ (*figurative*) *Loud screams rent the air.* ⊃ see also HEART-RENDING

rend·er /ˈrendər/ *verb*
▷ **CAUSE SOMEONE OR SOMETHING TO BE SOMETHING** **1** ~ **sb/ sth** + **adj.** (*formal*) to cause someone or something to be in a particular state or condition **SYN** MAKE: *to render something harmless/useless/ineffective* ◆ *Hundreds of people were rendered homeless by the earthquake.*
▷ **GIVE HELP** **2** (*formal*) to give someone something, especially in return for something, or because it is expected: ~ **sth to sb/sth** *They rendered assistance to the disaster victims.* ◆ *to render a service to someone* ◆ ~ **sb sth** *to render someone a service* ◆ ~ **sth** *It was payment **for services rendered**.*
▷ **PRESENT SOMETHING** **3** ~ **sth** (*formal*) to present something, especially when it is done officially **SYN** FURNISH: *The committee was asked to render a report on the housing situation.*
▷ **EXPRESS/PERFORM** **4** ~ **sth** (*formal*) to express or perform something: *He stood up and rendered a beautiful version of "Summertime."* ◆ *The artist has rendered the stormy sea in dark greens and browns.*
▷ **TRANSLATE** **5** to express something in a different language **SYN** TRANSLATE: ~ **sth (as sth)** *The Italian phrase can be rendered as "I did my best."* ◆ ~ **sth (into sth)** *It's a concept that is difficult to render into English.*
▷ **WALL** **6** ~ **sth** (*technical*) to cover a wall with a layer of PLASTER or CEMENT
▷ **MELT** **7** ~ **sth (down)** to make fat liquid by heating it; to melt something

rend·er·ing /ˈrendərɪŋ/ *noun* **1** [C] the performance of a piece of music, a role in a play, etc.; the particular way in which something is performed **SYN** INTERPRETATION, RENDITION: *her dramatic rendering of Lady Macbeth* **2** [C] a piece of writing that has been translated into a different language; the particular way in which it has been translated: *a faithful rendering of the original text* **3** [U, C] (*technical*) a layer of PLASTER or CEMENT that is put on a brick or stone wall in order to make it smooth

ren·dez·vous /ˈrɑːndeɪˌvuː/ *noun, verb*
● *noun* (*pl.* **ren·dez·vous** /-ˌvuːz/) (from *French*) **1** ~ **(with sb)** an arrangement to meet someone at a particular time and place **2** a place where people have arranged to meet **3** a bar, etc. that is a popular place for people to meet: *a lively Paris rendezvous*
● *verb* (**ren·dez·voused, ren·dez·voused** /-ˌvuːd/) [I] (from *French*) ~ **(with sb)** to meet at a time and place that have been arranged in advance

ren·di·tion /renˈdɪʃn/ *noun* **1** the performance of something, especially a song or piece of music; the particular way in which it is performed **SYN** INTERPRETATION **2** [U] the practice of sending foreign suspects to be questioned in another country, according to an established legal procedure ⊃ see also EXTRAORDINARY RENDITION

ren·e·gade /ˈrenəˌɡeɪd/ *noun* (*formal, disapproving*) **1** (often used as an adjective) a person who leaves one political, religious, etc. group to join another that has very different views **2** a person who opposes and lives outside a group or society that they used to belong to **SYN** OUTLAW

re·nege /rɪˈneɡ; -ˈnɪɡ/ *verb* [I] ~ **(on sth)** (*formal*) to break a promise, an agreement, etc. **SYN** GO BACK ON: *to renege on a deal/debt/contract, etc.*

re·new /rɪˈnuː/ *verb* **1** ~ **sth** to begin something again after a pause or an interruption **SYN** RESUME: *The army renewed its assault on the capital.* ◆ *We have to renew our efforts to attract young players.* ◆ *The annual dinner is a chance to renew acquaintance with old friends.* **2** ~ **sth** to make something valid for a further period of time: *to **renew a license/lease/subscription/contract**, etc.* ◆ *How do I go about renewing my passport?* ◆ *I'd like to renew these library books* (= arrange to borrow them for a further period of time). **3** ~ **sth** to emphasize something by saying or stating it again **SYN** REITERATE, REPEAT: *to **renew an appeal/a request/a complaint**, etc.* ◆ *Community leaders have renewed calls for a peaceful settlement.* ◆ *The project is to go ahead following renewed promises of aid from the U.N.* **4** ~ **sth** to change something that is old or damaged and replace it with something new of the same kind: *The wiring in your house should be renewed every ten to fifteen years.*

re·new·a·ble /rɪˈnuːəbl/ *adj.* **1** [usually before noun] (of energy and natural resources) that is replaced naturally or controlled carefully and can therefore be used without the risk of finishing it all: *renewable sources of energy such as wind and solar power* ⊃ collocations at ENVIRONMENT **2** (of a contract, ticket, etc.) that can be made valid for a further period of time after it has finished: *a renewable lease* ◆ *The work permit is not renewable.* **ANT** NONRENEWABLE

re·new·a·bles /rɪˈnuːəblz/ *noun* [pl.] types of energy that can be replaced naturally such as energy produced from wind or water: *renewables such as hydroelectricity and solar energy* ◆ *investment in renewables* **HELP** Renewables are more commonly referred to as **renewable energy (sources)**.

re·new·al /rɪˈnuːəl/ *noun* [U, C] **1** ~ **(of sth)** a situation in which something begins again after a pause or an interruption: *a renewal of interest in traditional teaching methods* **2** the act of making a contract, etc. valid for a further period of time after it has finished: *The lease comes **up for renewal** at the end of the month.* ◆ *the renewal date* **3** a situation in which something is replaced, improved, or made more successful: *economic renewal* ◆ **urban renewal** (= the act of improving the buildings, etc. in a particular area)

re·newed /rɪˈnuːd/ *adj.* [usually before noun] happening again with increased interest or strength: *Renewed fighting has been reported on the border.* ◆ *with renewed enthusiasm*

ren·min·bi /ˌrenmɪnˈbiː/ *noun* (*pl.* **ren·min·bi**) **1** the **renminbi** [sing.] the money system of China **2** = YUAN

ren·net /ˈrenət/ *noun* [U] a substance that makes milk thick and sour and is used in making cheese

re·nounce /rɪˈnaʊns/ *verb* (*formal*) **1** ~ **sth** to state officially that you are no longer going to keep a title, position, etc. **SYN** GIVE UP: *to renounce a claim/title/privilege/right* **2** ~ **sth** to state publicly that you no longer have a particular belief or that you will no longer behave in a particular way: *to renounce ideals/principles/beliefs, etc.* ◆ *a joint declaration renouncing the use of violence* **3** ~ **sb/sth** to state publicly that you no longer wish to have a connection with someone or something because you disapprove of them **SYN** DISOWN: *He had renounced his former associates.* ⊃ see also RENUNCIATION

ren·o·vate /ˈrenəˌveɪt/ *verb* ~ **sth** to repair and paint an old building, a piece of furniture, etc. so that it is in good condition again ⊃ collocations at DECORATE ▶ **ren·o·va·tion** /ˌrenəˈveɪʃn/ *noun* [U, C, usually pl.]: *buildings in need of renovation* ◆ *There will be extensive renovations to the hospital.*

re·nown /rɪˈnaʊn/ *noun* [U] (*formal*) fame and respect because of something you have done that people admire: *He **won renown as** a fair judge.* ◆ *a pianist **of some/international/great** renown*

re·nowned /rɪˈnaʊnd/ *adj.* famous and respected **SYN** CELEBRATED, NOTED: *a renowned author* ◆ ~ **as sth** *It is renowned as one of the region's best restaurants.* ◆ ~ **for sth** *She is renowned for her patience.*

rent /rent/ *noun, verb* ⊃ see also REND
● *noun* **1** [U, C] an amount of money that you regularly pay so that you can use a house, etc.: *How much rent do you pay for this place?* ◆ *The landlord has raised the rent again.* ◆ *a*

month's rent in advance ◆ a high/low/fair rent ⊃ thesaurus box at RATE **2** [C] (formal) a torn place in a piece of material or clothing

IDM **for rent** (especially on printed signs) available to rent

● *verb* **1** [T, I] to regularly pay money to someone so that you can use something that they own, such as a house, some land, a machine, etc.: ~ **(sth)** *to live in rented accommodations/housing/property* ◆ ~ **sth from sb** *Who do you rent the land from?* **2** [T] to allow someone to use something that you own such as a house or some land in exchange for regular payments: ~ **sth (out) (to sb)** *He rents rooms in his house to students.* ◆ *The land is rented out to other farmers.* ◆ *She agreed to rent the room to me.* ◆ ~ **sb sth** *She agreed to rent me the room.* **3** [T] ~ **sth** to pay money to someone so that you can use something for a short period of time: *We rented a car for the week and explored the area.* ◆ *Should we rent a movie tonight?* **4** [I] ~ **rent for sth** to be available for someone to use if they pay a particular amount of money: *The apartment rents for $500 a month.*

'rent-a- combining form (informal, often humorous) (in nouns and adjectives) showing that the thing mentioned can be rented: *rent-a-car* ◆ *rent-a-crowd*

ren·tal /'rɛntl/ noun **1** [U, C, usually sing.] the amount of money that you pay to use something for a particular period of time: *Telephone charges include line rental.* **2** [U] the act of renting something or an arrangement to rent something: *the world's largest car rental company* ◆ *video rental* ◆ *a rental car* ◆ *a minimum rental period of three months* **3** [C] a house, car, or piece of equipment that you can rent: *"Is this your own car?" "No, it's a rental."*

rent·ed /'rɛntəd/ adj. that you pay rent for: *a rented studio*

rent·er /'rɛntər/ noun **1** a person who rents something: *house buyers and renters* **2** a person or an organization that provides something for people to rent: *a ski equipment renter*

rent-'free adj. for which no rent is paid: *rent-free housing* ▶ **rent-'free** adv.

rent·ier /rɑn'tyeɪ/ noun (technical) a person who lives from money earned from property and investments

re·nun·ci·a·tion /rɪˌnʌnsi'eɪʃn/ noun (formal) **1** [U, C] an act of stating publicly that you no longer believe something or that you are giving something up: *the renunciation of violence* **2** [U] the act of rejecting physical pleasures, especially for religious reasons **SYN** SELF-DENIAL ⊃ see also RENOUNCE

re·oc·cur /ˌriə'kər/ verb (-rr-) [I] to happen again or a number of times **SYN** RECUR

re·of·fend /ˌriə'fɛnd/ verb [I] to commit a crime again: *Without help, many released prisoners will reoffend.* ▶ **re·of·fend·er** noun

re·o·pen /ˌri'oʊpən/ verb **1** [T, I] ~ **(sth)** to open a store, theater, etc. again, or to be opened again, after being closed for a period of time: *The school was reopened just two weeks after the fire.* ◆ *The store will reopen at 9 a.m. on January 2.* **2** [T, I] ~ **(sth)** to deal with or begin something again after a period of time; to start again after a period of time: *to reopen a discussion* ◆ *The police have decided to reopen the case.* ◆ *Management has agreed to reopen talks with the union.* ◆ *The trial reopened on March 6.* ▶ **re·o·pen·ing** noun [U, sing.]

IDM **reopen old wounds** to remind someone of something unpleasant that happened or existed in the past

re·or·der /ri'ɔrdər/ verb **1** [T, I] ~ **(sth)** to ask someone to supply you with more of a product: *Please quote this reference number when reordering stock.* **2** [T] ~ **sth** to change the order in which something is arranged

re·or·gan·ize /ri'ɔrgəˌnaɪz/ verb [T, I] ~ **(sth)** to change the way in which something is organized or done ▶ **re·or·gan·i·za·tion** /riˌɔrgənə'zeɪʃn/ noun [U, C]: *the reorganization of the school system*

re·o·ri·ent **AWL** /ˌri'ɔriˌɛnt/ verb **1** ~ **sb/sth (to/toward/away from sb/sth)** to change the focus or direction of someone or something: *Other governments may reorient their foreign policies away from the United States.* **2** ~ **yourself** to

find your position again in relation to your surroundings ▶ **re·o·ri·en·ta·tion** **AWL** noun [U]

rep /rɛp/ noun (informal) **1** [C] = SALES REPRESENTATIVE, REPRESENTATIVE **2** [C] a person who speaks officially for a group of people, especially at work: *a union rep* **3** [U] (informal) the abbreviation for REPERTORY

Rep. abbr. (in American politics) **1** REPRESENTATIVE **2** REPUBLICAN

re·pack·age /ˌri'pækɪdʒ/ verb **1** ~ **sth** to change the boxes, bags, etc. in which a product is sold **2** ~ **sth** to present something in a new way: *She earns more since she repackaged herself as a business consultant.*

re·paid pt, pp of REPAY

re·pair ♪ /rɪ'pɛr/ verb, noun

● *verb* **1** ~ **sth** to restore something that is broken, damaged, or torn to good condition: *to repair a car/roof/road/television* ◆ *It's almost 15 years old. It isn't worth **having it repaired**.* **2** ~ **sth** to say or do something in order to improve a bad or unpleasant situation **SYN** PUT RIGHT: *It was too late to repair the damage done to their relationship.* ▶ **re·pair·er** noun: *He was the son of a watch repairer.* **PHR V** **re'pair to...** (formal or humorous) to go to a particular place

● *noun* [C, U] an act of repairing something: *They agreed to pay the costs of any repairs.* ◆ *I took my bike in **for repair**.* ◆ *The building was **in need of repair**.* ◆ *a TV repair shop* ◆ *The car was damaged **beyond repair** (= it was too badly damaged to be repaired).* ◆ *The hotel is currently **under repair** (= being repaired).* ◆ *The bridge will remain closed until essential **repair work** has been carried out.*

IDM **in good, bad, etc. repair** | **in a good, bad, etc. state of repair** (formal) in good, etc. condition

re·pair·a·ble /rɪ'pɛrəbl/ adj. [not usually before noun] that can be repaired **ANT** IRREPARABLE

re·pair·man /rɪ'pɛrmæn; -mən/ noun (pl. re·pair·men /-mɛn; -mən/) a person whose job is to repair things: *a TV repairman*

re·par·a·ble /'rɛpərəbl/ adj. adj. that can be repaired **ANT** IRREPARABLE

rep·a·ra·tion /ˌrɛpə'reɪʃn/ noun (formal) **1** **reparations** [pl.] money that is paid by a country that has lost a war, for the damage, injuries, etc. that it has caused **2** [U] the act of giving something to someone or doing something for them in order to show that you are sorry for suffering that you have caused: *Offenders should be forced to **make reparation to** the community.*

rep·ar·tee /ˌrɛpar'ti; -'teɪ/ noun [U] smart and amusing comments and replies that are made quickly **SYN** SWORDPLAY

re·past /rɪ'pæst/ noun (old-fashioned or formal) a meal

re·pa·tri·ate /ˌri'peɪtriˌeɪt/ verb **1** ~ **sb** to send or bring someone back to their own country: *The refugees were forcibly repatriated.* **2** ~ **sth** (business) to send money or profits back to your own country ▶ **re·pa·tri·a·tion** /ˌriˌpeɪtri'eɪʃn/ noun [U, C]: *the repatriation of immigrants/profits* ◆ *a voluntary repatriation program*

re·pay /rɪ'peɪ/ verb (re·paid, re·paid /-'peɪd/) **1** to pay back the money that you have borrowed from someone: ~ **sth** *to repay a debt/loan/mortgage* ◆ *I'll repay the money I owe them next week.* ◆ ~ **sth to sb** *The advance must be repaid to the publisher if the work is not completed on time.* ◆ ~ **sb** *When are you going to repay them?* ◆ ~ **sb sth** *I fully intend to repay them the money that they lent me.* **2** to give something to someone or do something for them in return for something that they have done for you **SYN** RECOMPENSE: ~ **sb (for sth)** *How can I ever repay you for your generosity?* ◆ ~ **sth (with sth)** *Their trust was repaid with fierce loyalty.* **3** ~ **sth** (formal) if something **repays** your attention, interest, study, etc., it is worth spending time to look at it, etc.: *The report repays careful reading.*

re·pay·a·ble /rɪ'peɪəbl/ adj. that can or must be paid back: *The loan is repayable in monthly installments.*

h **h**at   m **m**an   n **n**o   ŋ **s**ing   l **l**eg   r **r**ed   y **y**es   w **w**et

re·pay·ment /rɪˈpeɪmənt/ *noun* **1** [U] the act of paying back money that you have borrowed from a bank, etc.: *The loan is due for repayment by the end of the year.* **2** [C, usually pl.] money that you pay to a bank, etc. until you have returned all the money that you owe: *loan repayments* ⟳ thesaurus box at PAYMENT

re·peal /rɪˈpil/ *verb* ~ **sth** if a government, or other group, or person with authority **repeals** a law, that law is no longer valid ▶ **re·peal** *noun* [U]

re·peat 🔑 /rɪˈpit/ *verb, noun*
● *verb*

WORD FAMILY
repeat *verb, noun*
repeatable *adj.* (≠ unrepeatable)
repeated *adj.*
repeatedly *adv.*
repetition *noun*
repetitive *adj.*
repetitious *adj.*

▷ SAY/WRITE AGAIN **1** [T] to say or write something again or more than once: ~ **sth** *to repeat a question* ◆ *I'm sorry—could you repeat that?* ◆ *She kept repeating his name softly over and over again.* ◆ *The opposition has been repeating its calls for her resignation.* ◆ ~ **yourself** *Please tell me if I'm repeating myself* (= if I have already said this). ◆ ~ **that**... *He's fond of repeating that the company's success is all down to him.*
▷ DO AGAIN **2** [T, I] ~ **(sth)** to do or produce something again or more than once: *to repeat a mistake/a process/an exercise* ◆ *The treatment should be repeated every two to three hours.* ◆ *They are hoping to repeat last year's victory.* ◆ *These offers are unlikely to be repeated.* ◆ *The programs will be repeated next year.* ◆ *She was young for her class, so she repeated kindergarten.* ◆ *Lift and lower the right leg 20 times. Repeat with the left leg.*
▷ HAPPEN AGAIN **3** [T, I] ~ **(sth/itself)** to happen more than once in the same way: *History has a strange way of repeating itself.* ◆ *a repeating pattern/design*
▷ WHAT SOMEONE ELSE SAID **4** [T] to tell someone something that you have heard or been told by someone else: ~ **sth to sb** *I don't want you to repeat a word of this to anyone.* ◆ ~ **sth** *The rumor has been widely repeated in the press.* **5** [T] to say something that someone else has said, especially in order to learn it: ~ **sth (after sb)** *Listen and repeat each sentence after me.* ◆ ~ **what**... *Can you repeat what I've just said word for word?* ◆ **+ speech** *"Are you really sure?" she repeated.*
▷ FOR EMPHASIS **6** [I, T] used to emphasize something that you have already said: *The claims are, I repeat, totally unfounded.* ◆ ~ **sth** *I am not, repeat not, traveling in the same car as him!*
● *noun* **1** a television or radio program that has been broadcast before: *"Is it a new series?" "No, a repeat."* **2** an event that is very similar to something that happened before: *A repeat of the 1906 earthquake could kill up to 11,000 people.* ◆ *She didn't want a* **repeat performance** *of what had happened the night before.* ◆ *(business) a* **repeat order** (= for a further supply of the same goods) **3** *(music)* a passage that is repeated

re·peat·a·ble /rɪˈpitəbl/ *adj.* [not usually before noun] **1** (of a comment, etc.) (usually in negative sentences) polite and not offensive: *His reply was not repeatable.* **2** that can be repeated **ANT** UNREPEATABLE

re·peat·ed 🔑 /rɪˈpitəd/ *adj.* [only before noun] happening, said, or done many times: *repeated absences from work* ▶ **re·peat·ed·ly** *adv.*: *The victim had been stabbed repeatedly in the chest.*

re·peat·er /rɪˈpitər/ *noun* (*technical*) a gun that you can fire several times without having to load it again

re·pel /rɪˈpɛl/ *verb* (-ll-) **1** [T] ~ **sb/sth** (*formal*) to successfully fight someone who is attacking you, your country, etc. and drive them away: *to repel an attack/invasion/invader* ◆ *Troops repelled an attempt to infiltrate the south of the island.* ◆ *(figurative) The reptile's prickly skin repels nearly all of its predators.* **2** [T] ~ **sth** to drive, push, or keep something away: *a spray that repels insects* ◆ *The fabric has been treated to repel water.* **3** [T] ~ **sb** (not used in the progressive tenses) to make someone feel horror or disgust **SYN** DISGUST, REPULSE: *I was repelled by the smell.* **4** [T, I] ~ **(sth)** (*technical*) if one thing **repels** another, or if two things **repel** each

other, an electrical or MAGNETIC force pushes them apart: *Like poles repel each other.* **ANT** ATTRACT ⟳ see also REPULSION, REPULSIVE

re·pel·lent /rɪˈpɛlənt/ *adj., noun*
● *adj.* **1** ~ **(to sb)** (*formal*) very unpleasant; causing strong dislike **SYN** REPULSIVE: *Their political ideas are repellent to most people.* **2** (in compounds) not letting a particular substance, especially water, pass through it: *water-repellent fabrics*
● *noun* [U, C] **1** a substance that is used for keeping insects away from you: *(an) insect repellent* **2** a substance that is used on cloth, stone, etc. to prevent water from passing through it: *(a) water repellent*

re·pent /rɪˈpɛnt/ *verb* [I, T] (*formal*) to feel and show that you are sorry for something bad or wrong that you have done: *God welcomes the sinner who repents.* ◆ ~ **of sth** *She had repented of what she had done.* ◆ ~ **sth** *He came to repent his hasty decision* (= wished he had not made it).

re·pent·ance /rɪˈpɛntəns/ *noun* [U] ~ **(for sth)** the fact of showing that you are sorry for something wrong that you have done **SYN** REMORSE: *He shows no sign of repentance.*

re·pent·ant /rɪˈpɛntənt/ *adj.* feeling or showing that you are sorry for something wrong that you have done **SYN** CONTRITE, **ANT** UNREPENTANT

re·per·cus·sion /ˌripərˈkʌʃn; ˌrɛpər-/ *noun* [usually pl.] an indirect and usually bad result of an action or event, which may happen some time afterward **SYN** CONSEQUENCE, RESULT: *The collapse of the company will* **have repercussions** *for the whole industry.*

rep·er·toire /ˈrɛpərˌtwɑr/ *noun* **1** (also *formal* **rep·er·to·ry**) all the plays, songs, pieces of music, etc. that a performer knows and can perform: *a pianist with a wide repertoire* **2** all the things that a person is able to do: *a young child's growing verbal repertoire*

rep·er·to·ry /ˈrɛpərˌtɔri/ *noun* **1** (also *informal* **rep**) [U] the type of work of a theater company in which different plays are performed for short periods of time: *an actor in repertory* ◆ *a repertory company* **2** [C] (*formal*) = REPERTOIRE

rep·e·ti·tion /ˌrɛpəˈtɪʃn/ *noun* **1** [U, C] the fact of doing or saying the same thing many times: *learning by repetition* **2** [C] a thing that has been done or said before: *We do not want to see a repetition of last year's tragic events.*

rep·e·ti·tious /ˌrɛpəˈtɪʃəs/ *adj.* (often *disapproving*) involving something that is often repeated: *a long and repetitious speech* ▶ **rep·e·ti·tious·ly** *adv.* **rep·e·ti·tious·ness** *noun*

re·pet·i·tive /rɪˈpɛtətɪv/ *adj.* **1** saying or doing the same thing many times, so that it becomes boring **SYN** MONOTONOUS: *a repetitive task.* **2** repeated many times: *a repetitive pattern of behavior* ▶ **re·pet·i·tive·ly** *adv.* **re·pet·i·tive·ness** *noun* [U]

re·phrase /ˌriˈfreɪz/ *verb* ~ **sth** to say or write something using different words in order to make the meaning clearer or less offensive, etc

re·place 🔑 /rɪˈpleɪs/ *verb*
1 ~ **sth/sb** to be used instead of something or someone else; to do something instead of someone or something else **SYN** TAKE OVER FROM: *The new design will eventually replace all existing models.* ◆ *Teachers will never be replaced by computers in the classroom.* **2** to remove someone or something and put another person or thing in their place: ~ **sb/sth** *He will be difficult to replace when he leaves.* ◆ ~ **sb/sth with/by sb/sth** *It is not a good idea to miss meals and replace them with snacks.* **3** ~ **sth** to change something that is old, damaged, etc. for a similar thing that is newer or better: *All the old carpets need replacing.* ◆ *You'll be expected to replace any broken glasses.* **4** ~ **sth (+ adv./prep.)** to put something back in the place where it was before: *I replaced the cup carefully in the saucer.* ◆ *to replace the handset* (= after using the telephone).

re·place·a·ble /rɪˈpleɪsəbl/ *adj.* that can be replaced **ANT** IRREPLACEABLE

re·place·ment /rɪˈpleɪsmənt/ *noun* **1** [U] the act of replacing one thing with another, especially something that is newer or better: *the replacement of worn car parts* ♦ *replacement windows* **2** [C] a thing that replaces something, especially because the first thing is old, broken, etc.: *a hip replacement* **3** [C] ~ **(for sb)** a person who replaces another person in an organization, especially in their job: *We need to find a replacement for Sue.*

re·play *noun, verb*
• *noun* /ˈriːpleɪ/ **1** (*sports*) a game that is played again because neither side won in the previous game **2** the playing again of a short section of a movie, tape, etc., especially to look at or listen to something more carefully: *We watched a replay of the wedding on video.* ➔ see also ACTION REPLAY **3** something that is repeated or happens in exactly the same way as it did before: *This election will not be a replay of the last one.*
• *verb* /ˌriːˈpleɪ/ **1** [usually passive] ~ **sth** to play a sports game again because neither team won the first game **2** ~ **sth** to play again something that has been recorded on tape, film, etc.: *The police replayed footage of the accident over and over again.* ♦ (*figurative*) *He replayed the scene in his mind* (= he thought about it many times).

re·plen·ish /rɪˈplenɪʃ/ *verb* ~ **sth (with sth)** (*formal*) to make something full again by replacing what has been used **SYN** TOP UP: *to replenish food and water supplies* ♦ *Allow me to replenish your glass.* ▶ **re·plen·ish·ment** *noun* [U]

re·plete /rɪˈpliːt/ *adj.* **1** [not before noun] ~ **(with sth)** (*formal*) filled with something; with a full supply of something: *literature replete with drama and excitement* **2** (*old-fashioned* or *formal*) very full of food

rep·li·ca /ˈreplɪkə/ *noun* a very good or exact copy of something: *a replica of the Eiffel Tower* ♦ *The weapon used in the raid was a replica.* ♦ *replica guns*

rep·li·cate /ˈreplɪkeɪt/ *verb* **1** [T] ~ **sth** (*formal*) to copy something exactly **SYN** DUPLICATE: *Subsequent experiments failed to replicate these findings.* **2** [T, I] ~ **(itself)** (*technical*) (of a virus or a MOLECULE) to produce exact copies of itself: *The drug prevents the virus from replicating itself.* ▶ **rep·li·ca·tion** /ˌreplɪˈkeɪʃn/ *noun* [U, C]

re·ply 🔑 /rɪˈplaɪ/ *verb, noun*
• *verb* (re·plies, re·ply·ing, re·plied, re·plied) **1** [I, T] to say or write something as an answer to someone or something: ~ **(to sb/sth) (with sth)** *to reply to a question/an advertisement* ♦ *He never replied to any of my letters.* ♦ *She only replied with a smile.* ♦ **+ speech** *"I won't let you down," he replied confidently.* ♦ ~ **that…** *The senator replied that he was not in a position to comment.* ➔ note at ANSWER **2** [I] ~ **(to sth) (with sth)** to do something as a reaction to something that someone has said or done: *The terrorists replied to the government's statement with more violence.*
• *noun* [C, U] an act of replying to something or someone in speech, in writing, or by some action: *We had over 100 replies to our advertisement.* ♦ *I asked her what her name was but she* **made no reply.** ♦ (*formal*) *I am writing* **in reply to** *your letter of March 16.*

re·po man /ˈriːpoʊ ˌmæn/ *noun* (*informal*) a person whose job is to REPOSSESS (= take back) goods from people who still owe money for them and cannot pay

re·port 🔑 /rɪˈpɔːrt/ *verb, noun*
• *verb*
▷ GIVE INFORMATION **1** [T, I] to give people information about something that you have heard, seen, done, etc.: ~ **sth (to sb)** *The crash happened seconds after the pilot reported engine trouble.* ♦ *Call me urgently if you have anything to report.* ♦ ~ **(on sth) (to sb)** *The committee will report on its research next month.* ♦ ~ **(sb/sth) doing sth** *The neighbors reported seeing him leave the building around noon.* ♦ ~ **sb/sth + adj.** *The doctor reported the patient fully recovered.* ♦ ~ **sb/sth as sth/as doing sth** *The house was reported as being in excellent condition.* ♦ **be reported to be/have sth** *The house was reported to be in excellent condition.* ♦ ~ **(that)…** *Employers reported that graduates were deficient in writing and problem-*

solving skills. ♦ ~ **what, how, etc.…** *She failed to report what had occurred.* ♦ **+ speech** *"The cabin's empty," he reported back.*
▷ NEWS/STORY **2** [T, I] to present a written or spoken account of an event in a newspaper, on television, etc.: ~ **sth** *The stabbing was reported in the local press.* ♦ **it is reported that…** *It was reported that several people had been arrested.* ♦ ~ **that…** *The TV news reported that several people had been arrested.* ♦ ~ **(on sth)** *She reports on local restaurants for the magazine.* **3** **be reported** [T] used to show that something has been stated, and you do not know if it is true or not: ~ **to do sth** *She is reported to earn over $10 million a year.* ♦ ~ **as doing sth** *The President is reported as saying that he needs a break.* ♦ **it is reported that…** *It was reported that changes were being considered.*
▷ CRIME/ACCIDENT, ETC. **4** [T] to tell a person in authority about a crime, an accident, an illness, etc. or about something bad that someone has done: ~ **sth (to sb)** *Have you reported the accident to the police yet?* ♦ *a decrease in the number of reported cases of AIDS* ♦ ~ **sb (to sb) (for sth/for doing sth)** *He's already been reported twice for arriving late.* ♦ ~ **sb/sth + adj.** *She has reported her daughter missing.*
▷ ARRIVE **5** [I] ~ **(to sb/sth) (for sth)** to tell someone that you have arrived, for example for work or for a meeting with someone: *You should report for duty at 9:30 a.m.* ♦ *All visitors must report to the reception desk on arrival.*
PHR V re·port ˈback to return to a place, especially in order to work again: *Take an hour for lunch and report back at 2.* re·port ˈback (on sth) (to sb) to give someone information about something that they have asked you to find out about: *Find out as much as you can about him and report back to me.* ♦ *One person in the group should be prepared to report back to the class on your discussion.* ♦ ~ **that…** *They reported back that no laws had actually been broken.* reˈport to sb (not used in the progressive tenses) (*business*) if you **report to** a particular manager in an organization that you work for, they are officially responsible for your work and for telling you what to do
• *noun*
▷ OF NEWS **1** ~ **(on/of sth)** a written or spoken account of an event, especially one that is published or broadcast: *Are these newspaper reports true?* ♦ *a weather report*
▷ INFORMATION **2** ~ **(on sth)** a spoken or written description of something containing information that sb needs to have: *a police/medical report* ♦ *Can you give us a progress report?*
▷ OFFICIAL STUDY **3** ~ **(on sth)** an official document written by a group of people who have examined a particular situation or problem: *The committee will publish their report on the health center in a few weeks.*
▷ STORY **4** a story or piece of information that may or may not be true: *I don't believe these reports of UFO sightings.* ♦ *There are unconfirmed reports of a shooting in the capital.*
▷ OF GUN **5** the sound of an explosion or of a gun being fired **SYN** BANG, BLAST: *a loud report*
IDM of bad/good report (*formal*) talked about by people in a bad/good way

THESAURUS

report

story ♦ account ♦ version

These are all words for a written or spoken account of events.

report a written or spoken account of an event, especially one that is published or broadcast: *We're getting reports of fighting in the south of the country.*

story an account, often spoken, of what happened to someone, or of how something happened; a report of events in a newspaper, magazine, or news broadcast: *It was many years before the full story was made public.* ♦ *the front-page story*

account a written or spoken description of something that has happened: *He gave the police a full account of the incident.*

ʌ cup   ə about   eɪ say   aɪ five   ɔɪ boy   aʊ now   oʊ go   ər bird

re·port·age /rɪˈpɔrtɪdʒ; ˌrepɔrˈtɑʒ/ noun [U] (*formal*) the reporting of news or the typical style in which this is done in newspapers, or on TV and radio

re'port card noun a written statement about a student's work at a school, etc. that is sent to their parents

re·port·ed·ly /rɪˈpɔrtədli/ adv. according to what some people say: *The band has reportedly decided to split up.*

re¡ported 'question noun (*grammar*) = INDIRECT QUESTION

re¡ported 'speech (also ¡indirect 'speech) noun [U] (*grammar*) a report of what someone has said that does not use their exact words: *In reported speech, "I'll come later." becomes "He said he'd come later."*

re·port·er 🔊 /rɪˈpɔrtər/ noun
a person who collects and reports news for newspapers, radio, or television: *a reporter from the New York Times* ◆ *a crime reporter* ⭢ compare JOURNALIST ⭢ see also CUB REPORTER

re·port·ing /rɪˈpɔrtɪŋ/ noun [U] the presenting and writing about news on television and radio, and in newspapers: *accurate/balanced/objective reporting*

re·pose /rɪˈpoʊz/ noun, verb
- **noun** [U] (*literary*) a state of rest, sleep, or feeling calm
- **verb** (*literary*) **1** [I] + adv./prep. (of an object) to be or be kept in a particular place **2** [I] + adv./prep. (of a person) to lie or rest in a particular place

re·pos·i·to·ry /rɪˈpɑzəˌtɔri/ noun (pl. re·pos·i·to·ries) (*formal*) **1** a place where something is stored in large quantities **2** a person or book that is full of information: *My father is a repository of family history.*

re·pos·sess /ˌripəˈzɛs/ verb [usually passive] **~ sth** to take back property or goods from someone who has arranged to buy them but who still owes money for them and cannot pay

re·pos·ses·sion /ˌripəˈzɛʃn/ noun **1** [U, C] the act of repossessing property, goods, etc.: *families threatened with repossession* ◆ *a repossession order* **2** [C] a house, car, etc. that has been repossessed: *Auctions are the best place for buying repossessions.*

rep·re·hen·si·ble /ˌreprɪˈhɛnsəbl/ adj. (*formal*) morally wrong and deserving criticism SYN DEPLORABLE

rep·re·sent 🔊 /ˌreprɪˈzɛnt/ verb
> ACT/SPEAK FOR SOMEONE **1** [often passive] **~ sb/sth** to be a member of a group of people and act or speak on their behalf at an event, a meeting, etc.: *The competition attracted over 500 contestants representing 8 different countries.* ◆ *Local businesses are well represented on the committee* (= there are a lot of people from them on the committee). ◆ *The President was represented at the ceremony by the Vice President.* **2 ~ sb/sth** to act or speak officially for someone and defend their interests: *The union represents over 200,000 teachers.* ◆ *The association was formed to represent the interests of women artists.* ◆ *Ms. Dale is representing the defendant* (= is his/her lawyer) *in the case.*

> BE EQUAL TO **3** *linking verb* + **noun** (not used in the progressive tenses) to be something SYN CONSTITUTE: *This contract represents 20% of the company's annual revenue.* ◆ *This decision represents a significant departure from previous policy.*

> BE EXAMPLE OF **4** [no passive] **~ sth** to be an example or expression of something SYN BE TYPICAL OF: *a project representing all that is good in the community* ◆ *Those comments do not represent the views of us all.*

> BE SYMBOL **5 ~ sth** (not used in the progressive tenses) to be a symbol of something SYN SYMBOLIZE: *Each color on the chart represents a different department.* ◆ *Wind direction is represented by arrows.*

> IN PICTURE **6 ~ sb/sth (as sb/sth)** | **~ sb/sth doing sth** to show someone or something, especially in a picture SYN DEPICT: *The carvings represent a hunting scene.* ◆ *The results are represented in fig. 3 below.*

> DESCRIBE **7 ~ sb (as sth)** (*formal*) to present or describe someone or something in a particular way, especially when this may not be fair: *The king is represented as a villain in the play.* ◆ *The risks were represented as negligible.*

> MAKE FORMAL STATEMENT **8 ~ sth (to sb)** | **~ that…** (*formal*) to make a formal statement to someone in authority in order to make your opinions known or to protest: *They represented their concerns to the authorities.*

re-pre-sent /ˌri prɪˈzɛnt/ verb **~ sth** to give, show, or send something again, especially a check, bill, etc. that has not been paid

rep·re·sen·ta·tion /ˌreprɪzɛnˈteɪʃn; -zən-/ noun **1** [U, C] the act of presenting someone or something in a particular way; something that shows or describes something SYN PORTRAYAL: *the negative representation of single mothers in the media* ◆ *The snake swallowing its tail is a representation of infinity.* **2** [U] the fact of having representatives who will speak or vote for you or on your behalf: *The green movement lacks effective representation in the legislature.* ◆ *The accused was not allowed legal representation.* ⭢ see also PROPORTIONAL REPRESENTATION **3 representations** [pl.] (*formal*) formal statements made to someone in authority, especially in order to make your opinions known or to protest: *We have **made representations to** the mayor but without success.*

rep·re·sen·ta·tion·al /ˌreprɪzɛnˈteɪʃənl; -zən-/ adj. **1** (*technical*) (especially of a style of art or painting) trying to show things as they really are ⭢ compare ABSTRACT **2** involving the act of representing someone or something: *local representational democracy*

rep·re·sen·ta·tive 🔊 /ˌreprɪˈzɛntətɪv/ noun, adj.
- **noun ~ (of sb/sth)** **1** a person who has been chosen to speak or vote for someone else or on behalf of a group: *a representative of the U.N.* ◆ *our elected representatives in government* ◆ *a union representative* ◆ *The committee includes representatives from industry.* **2** (also *informal* **rep**) a person who works for a company and travels around selling its products: *a sales representative* ◆ *She's our representative in France.* **3** a person chosen to take the place of someone else: *He's the principal's representative at the ceremony.* **4** a person who is typical of a particular group: *The singer is regarded as a representative of the youth of her generation.* **5** **Representative** (*abbr.* **Rep.**) (in the U.S.) a member of the House of Representatives, the lower house of Congress; a member of the House of Representatives in the lower house of a state LEGISLATURE
- **adj. 1 ~ (of sb/sth)** typical of a particular group of people: *Is a questionnaire answered by 500 people truly representative of the population as a whole?* ANT UNREPRESENTATIVE **2** [usually before noun] containing or including examples of all the different types of people or things in a large group: *a representative sample of teachers* ANT UNREPRESENTATIVE **3 ~ (of sth)** able to be used as a typical example of something: *The painting is not representative of his work of the period.* ANT UNREPRESENTATIVE **4** (of a system of government, etc.) consisting of people who have been chosen to speak or vote on behalf of the rest of a group: *a representative democracy*

re·press /rɪˈprɛs/ *verb* **1** ~ **sth** to try not to have or show an emotion, a feeling, etc. **SYN** CONTROL: *to repress a smile* ◆ *He burst in, making no effort to repress his fury.* **2** [often passive] ~ **sb/sth** to use political and/or military force to control a group of people and restrict their freedom **SYN** SUPPRESS

re·pressed /rɪˈprɛst/ *adj.* **1** (of a person) having emotions or desires that are not allowed to be expressed **2** (of emotions) not expressed openly: *repressed anger*

re·pres·sion /rɪˈprɛʃn/ *noun* [U] **1** the act of using force to control a group of people and restrict their freedom: *government repression* **2** the act of controlling strong emotions and desires and not allowing them to be expressed, so that they no longer seem to exist: *sexual repression*

re·pres·sive /rɪˈprɛsɪv/ *adj.* **1** (of a system of government) controlling people by force and restricting their freedom **SYN** DICTATORIAL, TYRANNICAL: *a repressive regime/ measure/law* **2** controlling emotions and desires and not allowing them to be expressed ► **re·pres·sive·ly** *adv.* **re·pres·sive·ness** *noun* [U]

re·prieve /rɪˈpriv/ *verb, noun*
• *verb* [usually passive] (not usually used in the progressive tenses) **1** ~ **sb** to officially cancel or delay a punishment, especially for a prisoner who is CONDEMNED to death: *a reprieved murderer* **2** ~ **sth** to officially cancel or delay plans to close something or end something: *70 jobs have been reprieved until next April.*
• *noun* [usually sing.] **1** an official order stopping a punishment, especially for a prisoner who is CONDEMNED to death **SYN** STAY OF EXECUTION **2** a delay before something bad happens: *Campaigners have won a reprieve for the hospital threatened with closure.*

rep·ri·mand /ˈrɛprəˌmænd; ˌrɛprəˈmænd/ *verb* ~ **sb (for sth)** | **+ speech** (*formal*) to tell someone officially that you do not approve of them or their actions **SYN** REBUKE: *The officers were severely reprimanded for their unprofessional behavior.* ► **rep·ri·mand** /ˈrɛprəˌmænd/ *noun* [C, U]: *He received a severe reprimand for his behavior.*

re·print *verb, noun*
• *verb* /ˌriˈprɪnt/ [usually passive] ~ **sth** to print more copies of a book, an article, etc. with few or no changes
• *noun* /ˈriprɪnt/ **1** an act of printing more copies of a book because all the others have been sold **2** a book that has been reprinted

re·pris·al /rɪˈpraɪzl/ *noun* [C, U] a violent or aggressive act toward someone because of something bad that they have done toward you **SYN** RETALIATION: *They did not want to give evidence for fear of reprisals.* ◆ *They shot ten hostages in reprisal for the assassination of their leader.* ⊃ collocations at WAR

re·prise /rɪˈpriz/ *noun* [usually sing.] a repeated part of something, especially a piece of music

re·proach /rɪˈproʊtʃ/ *noun, verb*
• *noun* (*formal*) **1** [U] blame or criticism for something you have done: *His voice was full of reproach.* ◆ *The captain's behavior is above/beyond reproach* (= you cannot criticize it). **2** [C] a word or remark expressing blame or criticism: *He listened to his wife's bitter reproaches.* **3** [U] a state of shame or loss of honor: *Her actions brought reproach upon herself.* **4** [sing.] ~ **(to sb/sth)** a person or thing that brings shame on someone or something **SYN** DISCREDIT: *Such living conditions are a reproach to our society.*
• *verb* (*formal*) **1** ~ **sb (for sth/for doing sth)** | ~ **sb (with sth/with doing sth)** | ~ **(sb) + speech** to blame or criticize someone for something that they have done or not done, because you are disappointed in them: *She was reproached by colleagues for leaking the story to the press.* **2** ~ **yourself (for sth/for doing sth)** | ~ **yourself (with sth)** to feel guilty about something that you think you should have done in a different way: *He reproached himself for not telling her the truth.*

re·proach·ful /rɪˈproʊtʃfl/ *adj.* expressing blame or criticism: *a reproachful look* ► **re·proach·ful·ly** /-fəli/ *adv.*

rep·ro·bate /ˈrɛprəˌbeɪt/ *noun* (*formal* or *humorous*) a person who behaves in a way that society thinks is immoral ► **rep·ro·bate** *adj.* [only before noun]

re·proc·ess /ˌriˈprɑsɛs/ *verb* ~ **sth** to treat waste material so that it can be used again: *All these countries reprocess nuclear fuel.*

re·pro·duce 🔑 /ˌriprəˈdus/ *verb*
1 [T] ~ **sth** to make a copy of a picture, piece of text, etc.: *It is illegal to reproduce these worksheets without permission from the publisher.* ◆ *The photocopier reproduces colors very well.* **2** [T] ~ **sth** to produce something again; to make something happen again in the same way: *The atmosphere of the novel is successfully reproduced in the movie.* **3** [I, T] if people, plants, animals, etc. **reproduce** or **reproduce themselves**, they produce young: *Most reptiles reproduce by laying eggs on land.* ◆ ~ **itself** *cells reproducing themselves* (= making new ones) ► **re·pro·duc·i·ble** /-ˈdusəbl/ *adj.*

re·pro·duc·tion /ˌriprəˈdʌkʃn/ *noun* **1** [U] the act or process of producing babies, young animals, or plants: *sexual reproduction* **2** [U] the act or process of producing copies of a document, book, picture, etc.: *Use a black pen on white paper to ensure good reproduction.* **3** [U] the process of recording sounds onto tapes, records, videos, etc.: *Digital recording gives excellent sound reproduction.* **4** [C] a thing that has been reproduced, especially a copy of a work of art: *a catalog with color reproductions of the paintings for sale* ◆ *reproduction furniture* (= furniture made as a copy of an earlier style)

re·pro·duc·tive /ˌriprəˈdʌktɪv/ *adj.* [only before noun] connected with producing babies, young animals or plants: *reproductive organs*

re·pro·graph·ics /ˌriprəˈgræfɪks/ *noun* [U] (*technical*) the science and practice of copying documents and pictures for publishing, etc.

re·proof /rɪˈpruf/ *noun* (*formal*) **1** [U] blame or disapproval: *His words were a mixture of pity and reproof.* **2** [C] a remark that expresses blame or disapproval **SYN** REBUKE: *She received a mild reproof from the teacher.*

re·prove /rɪˈpruv/ *verb* ~ **sb (for sth/for doing sth)** | ~ **(sb) + speech** (*formal*) to tell someone that you do not approve of something that they have done **SYN** REBUKE: *He reproved her for rushing away.* ► **re·prov·ing** *adj.* [usually before noun]: *a reproving glance* **re·prov·ing·ly** *adv.*

rep·tile /ˈrɛptaɪl; -təl/ *noun* any animal that has cold blood and skin covered in SCALES, and that lays eggs. Snakes, CROCODILES, and TURTLES are all reptiles. ⊃ compare AMPHIBIAN ► **rep·til·i·an** /rɛpˈtɪliən; -ˈtɪlyən/ *adj.*: *our reptilian ancestors* ◆ (*figurative*) *He licked his lips in an unpleasantly reptilian way.*

re·pub·lic /rɪˈpʌblɪk/ *noun* a country that is governed by a president and politicians elected by the people and where there is no king or queen: *newly independent republics* ◆ *the Republic of Ireland* ⊃ compare MONARCHY

re·pub·li·can /rɪˈpʌblɪkən/ *noun, adj.*
• *noun* **1** a person who supports a form of government with a president and politicians elected by the people with no king or queen ⊃ compare ROYALIST **2** **Re·pub·li·can** (*abbr.* R, Rep.) a member or supporter of the Republican Party ⊃ compare DEMOCRAT
• *adj.* **1** connected with or like a republic; supporting the principles of a republic: *a republican government/movement* **2** also **Republican** connected with the Republican Party ► **re·pub·li·can·ism** also **Re·pub·li·can·ism** /-kəˌnɪzəm/ *noun* [U]: *a strong commitment to Republicanism*

the Re·publican ˈParty *noun* [sing.] one of the two main political parties in the U.S., usually considered to support conservative views, and to want to limit the power of central government ⊃ compare THE DEMOCRATIC PARTY

re·pu·di·ate /rɪˈpyudiˌeɪt/ *verb* (*formal*) **1** ~ **sth** to refuse to accept something **SYN** REJECT: *to repudiate a suggestion*

t tea   ţ butter   d did   k cat   g got   tʃ chin   dʒ June   f fall

2 ~ sth to say officially and/or publicly that something is not true **SYN** DENY: *to repudiate a report* **3 ~ sb** (old-fashioned) to refuse to be connected with someone any longer **SYN** DISOWN: *He repudiated his first wife and married her sister.* ▶ **re·pu·di·a·tion** /rɪˌpyudiˈeɪʃn/ *noun* [U]

re·pug·nance /rɪˈpʌgnəns/ *noun* [U] (*formal*) strong feelings of dislike or disgust about something **SYN** REPULSION: *She was trying to overcome her physical repugnance for him.*

re·pug·nant /rɪˈpʌgnənt/ *adj.* [not usually before noun] (*formal*) making you feel strong dislike or disgust **SYN** REPULSIVE: *We found his suggestion absolutely repugnant.* ◆ **~ to sb** *The idea of eating meat was repugnant to her.*

re·pulse /rɪˈpʌls/ *verb* (*formal*) **1** [usually passive] **~ sb** to make someone feel disgust or strong dislike **SYN** REPEL: *I was repulsed by the horrible smell.* ⊃ thesaurus box at SHOCK **2 ~ sb/sth** to fight someone who is attacking you and drive them away **SYN** REPEL: *to repulse an attack/invasion/offensive* **3 ~ sb/sth** to refuse to accept someone's help, attempts to be friendly, etc. **SYN** REJECT: *Each time I tried to help I was repulsed.* ◆ *She repulsed his advances.*

re·pul·sion /rɪˈpʌlʃn/ *noun* [U] **1** a feeling of very strong dislike of something that you find extremely unpleasant **2** (*physics*) the force by which objects tend to push each other away: *the forces of attraction and repulsion* ⊃ see also REPEL ⊃ compare ATTRACTION

re·pul·sive /rɪˈpʌlsɪv/ *adj.* **1** causing a feeling of strong dislike; very unpleasant **SYN** DISGUSTING: *a repulsive sight/smell/habit* ◆ *What a repulsive man!* ⊃ thesaurus box at DISGUSTING **2** (*physics*) causing repulsion (= a force that pushes away): *repulsive forces* ▶ **re·pul·sive·ly** *adv.*: *repulsively ugly*

re·pur·pose /ˌriˈpərpəs/ *verb* **~ sth** to change something slightly in order to make it suitable for a new purpose

rep·u·ta·ble /ˈrɛpyətəbl/ *adj.* that people consider to be honest and to provide a good service **SYN** RESPECTed: *a reputable dealer/company/supplier* ⊃ compare DISREPUTABLE

rep·u·ta·tion 🔑 /ˌrɛpyəˈteɪʃn/ *noun* [C, U] the opinion that people have about what someone or something is like, based on what has happened in the past: *to earn/establish/build a reputation* ◆ *to have a good/bad reputation* ◆ **~ (as sth)** *She soon acquired a reputation as a first-class cook.* ◆ **~ (for sth/for doing sth)** *I'm aware of Mark's reputation for being late.* ◆ *to damage/ruin someone's reputation* ◆ *The weather in Portland is living up to its reputation* (= is exactly as expected).

re·pute /rɪˈpyut/ *noun* [U] (*formal*) the opinion that people have of someone or something **SYN** REPUTATION: *She is a writer of international repute.* ◆ *My parents were artists of (some) repute* (= had a very good reputation).

re·put·ed /rɪˈpyutəd/ *adj.* [not usually before noun] generally thought to be something or to have done something, although this is not certain **SYN** RUMORED: **~ (to be sth)** *He is reputed to be the best heart surgeon in the country.* ◆ **~ (to have done sth)** *The house is wrongly reputed to have been the poet's birthplace.* ◆ *She sold her share of the company for a reputed $7 million.* ▶ **re·put·ed·ly** *adv.*

re·quest 🔑 /rɪˈkwɛst/ *noun, verb*
● *noun* **~ (for sth)** | **~ (that...)** **1** the action of asking for something formally and politely: *They made a request for further aid.* ◆ *He was there at the request of his manager/at his manager's request* (= because his manager had asked him to go). ◆ *The writer's name was withheld by request* (= because the writer asked for this to be done). ◆ *catalogs are available on request.* **2** a thing that you formally ask for: *My request was granted.* ◆ *a radio request program* (= a program of music, songs, etc. that people have asked for)
● *verb* (*formal*) to ask for something or ask someone to do something in a polite or formal way: **~ sth (from sb)** *She requested permission to film at the White House.* ◆ *You can request a free copy of the leaflet.* ◆ **~ sb to do sth** *You are requested not to smoke anywhere in the building.* ◆ **~ that...**

She requested that no one be told of her decision until the next meeting. ◆ **+ speech** *"Please come with me," he requested.*

req·ui·em /ˈrɛkwiəm/ (also **requiem** ˈmass) *noun* **1** a Christian ceremony for a person who has recently died, at which people say prayers for his or her soul **2** a piece of music for this ceremony

re·quire 🔑 **AWL** /rɪˈkwaɪər/ *verb* (not usually used in the progressive tenses) (*formal*)
1 to need something; to depend on someone or something: **~ sth** *These pets require a lot of care and attention.* ◆ *This condition requires urgent treatment.* ◆ *Do you require anything else?* (= in a store, for example) ◆ **~ sb/sth to do sth** *A successful marriage requires us to show trust and loyalty.* ◆ **~ that...** *The situation required that he be present.* ◆ **~ doing sth** *Lentils do not require soaking before cooking.* **2** [often passive] to make someone do or have something, especially because it is necessary according to a particular law or set of rules: **~ sth** *The wearing of seat belts is required by law.* ◆ *"Hamlet" is required reading* (= must be read) *for this course.* ◆ *Several students failed to reach the required standard.* ◆ **~ sth of sb** *What exactly is required of a receptionist* (= what are they expected to do)? ◆ **~ sb to do sth** *All candidates will be required to take a short test.* ◆ **~ that...** *We require that you comply with the following rules:...* ⊃ thesaurus box at DEMAND

re·quire·ment 🔑 **AWL** /rɪˈkwaɪərmənt/ *noun* (*formal*)
1 usually **requirements** [pl.] something that you need or want: *the basic requirements of life* ◆ *a software package to meet your requirements* ◆ *Our immediate requirement is extra staff.* **2** something that you must have in order to do something else: *to meet/fulfill/satisfy the requirements* ◆ *What is the minimum entrance requirement for this degree program?*

req·ui·site /ˈrɛkwəzət/ *adj., noun* (*formal*)
● *adj.* [only before noun] necessary for a particular purpose: *She lacks the requisite experience for the job.*
● *noun* something that you need for a particular purpose: **~ for/of sth** *A college degree has become a requisite for entry into most professions.* ⊃ compare PREREQUISITE

req·ui·si·tion /ˌrɛkwəˈzɪʃn/ *noun, verb*
● *noun* [C, U] a formal, official written request or demand for something: *the requisition of ships by the government* ◆ *a requisition form/order*
● *verb* **~ sth** to officially demand the use of a building, vehicle, etc., especially during a war or an emergency: *The school was requisitioned as a military hospital.*

re·quite /rɪˈkwaɪt/ *verb* **~ sth** (*formal*) to give something such as love, kindness, a favor, etc. in return for what someone has given you: *requited love* ⊃ compare UNREQUITED

ˌre-ˈroute *verb* **~ sth** to change the route that a road, vehicle, telephone call, etc. normally follows

re·run *noun, verb*
● *noun* /ˈrirʌn/ **1** a television program that is shown again: *reruns of old TV shows* **2** an event, such as a race or competition, that is held again **3** something that is done in the same way as something in the past: *We wanted to avoid a rerun of last year's disastrous trip.*
● *verb* /ˌriˈrʌn/ (re·run·ning, re·ran /-ˈræn/, re·run) **1 ~ sth** to show a movie, television program, etc. again **2 ~ sth** to do something again in a similar way: *to rerun an experiment* **3 ~ sth** to run a race again

re·sale /ˈriseɪl/ *noun* [U] the sale to another person of something that you have bought: *the resale value of a car*

re·sched·ule **AWL** /ˌriˈskɛdʒul; -dʒəl/ *verb* **1 ~ sth (for/to sth)** | **~ sth to do sth** to change the time at which something has been arranged to happen, especially so that it takes place later: *The meeting has been rescheduled for next week.* **2 ~ sth** (*finance*) to arrange for someone to pay back money that they have borrowed at a later date than was originally agreed ▶ **re·sched·ul·ing** *noun* [U, sing.]

re·scind /rɪˈsɪnd/ *verb* ~ **sth** (*formal*) to officially state that a law, contract, decision, etc. is no longer valid **SYN** REVOKE

re·scis·sion /rɪˈsɪʒn/ *noun* (*formal*) the act of canceling or ending a law, an order, or an agreement

res·cue 🔑 /ˈrɛskyu/ *verb, noun*

• *verb* to save someone or something from a dangerous or harmful situation: ~ **sb/sth from sth/sb** *He rescued a child from drowning.* ◆ *The house was rescued from demolition.* ◆ *You rescued me from an embarrassing situation.* ◆ ~ **sb/sth** *They were eventually rescued by helicopter.* ◆ ~ **sb/sth + adj.** *She had despaired of ever being rescued alive.* ⊃ thesaurus box at SAVE ▶ **res·cu·er** /ˈrɛskyuər/ *noun*

• *noun* **1** [U] the act of saving someone or something from a dangerous or difficult situation; the fact of being saved: *We had given up hope of rescue.* ◆ *A wealthy benefactor came to their rescue with a generous donation.* ◆ *a rescue attempt/ operation* ◆ *a mountain rescue team* ◆ *rescue workers/boats/ helicopters* **2** [C] an occasion when someone or something is saved from a dangerous or difficult situation: *Ten fishermen were saved in a daring sea rescue.*

re·search 🔑 **AWL** *noun, verb*

• *noun* /ˈrisərtʃ; rɪˈsərtʃ/ [U] a careful study of a subject, especially in order to discover new facts or information about it: *medical/historical/scientific, etc. research* ◆ *to do/ conduct/undertake research* ◆ ~ **(into/on sth/sb)** *He has carried out extensive research into renewable energy sources.* ◆ *Recent research on deaf children has produced some interesting findings about their speech.* ◆ *a research project/ grant/student* ◆ *I've done some research to find out the cheapest way of traveling there.* ⊃ collocations at SCIENTIFIC ⊃ see also MARKET RESEARCH, OPERATIONS RESEARCH

• *verb* /rɪˈsərtʃ; ˈrisərtʃ/ [I, T] to study something carefully and try to discover new facts about it: ~ **(into/in/on sth)** *They're researching into ways of improving people's diet.* ◆ ~ **sth** *to research a problem/topic/market* ◆ *She's in New York researching her new book* (= finding facts and information to put in it). ◆ ~ **how, what, etc....** *We have to research how the product will actually be used.* ▶ **re·search·er** **AWL** *noun*

research and development *noun* [U] (*abbr.* R & D) (in industry, etc.) work that tries to find new products and processes or to improve existing ones

re·sect /rɪˈsɛkt/ *verb* ~ **sth** (*medical*) to cut out part of an organ or a piece of TISSUE from the body ▶ **re·sec·tion** /rɪˈsɛkʃn/ *noun* [U, C]

re·sell /ˌriˈsɛl/ *verb* (re·sold, re·sold /-ˈsoʊld/) ~ **sth** to sell something that you have bought: *He resells the goods at a profit.*

re·sem·blance /rɪˈzɛmbləns/ *noun* [C, U] the fact of being or looking similar to someone or something **SYN** LIKENESS: *a striking/close/strong resemblance* ◆ *family resemblances* ◆ ~ **to sb/sth** *She bears an uncanny resemblance to my former boss.* ◆ *The movie bears little resemblance to the original novel.* ◆ ~ **between A and B** *The resemblance between the two signatures was remarkable.*

re·sem·ble /rɪˈzɛmbl/ *verb* [no passive] (not used in the progressive tenses) ~ **sb/sth** to look like or be similar to another person or thing: *She closely resembles her sister.* ◆ *So many hotels resemble each other.* ◆ *The plant resembles grass in appearance.*

re·sent /rɪˈzɛnt/ *verb* to feel bitter or angry about something, especially because you feel it is unfair: ~ **sth/sb** *I deeply resented her criticism.* ◆ ~ **doing sth** *He bitterly resents being treated like a child.* ◆ ~ **sb doing sth** *She resented him making all the decisions.* ◆ (*formal*) *She resented his making all the decisions.*

re·sent·ful /rɪˈzɛntfl/ *adj.* feeling bitter or angry about something that you think is unfair: *a resentful look* ◆ ~ **of/at/ about sth** *They seemed to be resentful of our presence there.* ◆ *She was resentful at having been left out of the team.* ▶ **re·sent·ful·ly** /-fəli/ *adv.*

re·sent·ment /rɪˈzɛntmənt/ *noun* [U, sing.] a feeling of anger

or unhappiness about something that you think is unfair: *to feel/harbor/bear resentment toward/against someone* ◆ *She could not conceal the deep resentment she felt at the way she had been treated.*

res·er·va·tion 🔑 /ˌrɛzərˈveɪʃn/ *noun*

1 [C] an arrangement for a seat on a plane or train, a room in a hotel, etc. to be kept for you: *I'll call the restaurant and make a reservation.* ◆ *We have a reservation in the name of Grant.* ⊃ collocations at RESTAURANT **2** [C, U] a feeling of doubt about a plan or an idea **SYN** MISGIVING: *I have serious reservations about his ability to do the job.* ◆ *They support the measures without reservation* (= completely). **3** [C] an area of land in the U.S. that is kept separate for Native Americans to live in

re·serve 🔑 /rɪˈzərv/ *verb, noun*

• *verb* **1** to ask for a seat, table, room, etc. to be available for you or someone else at a future time: ~ **sth for sb/sth** *I'd like to reserve a table for three for eight o'clock.* ◆ ~ **sth** *I've reserved a room in the name of Jones.* **2** to keep something for someone or something, so that it cannot be used by any other person or for any other reason: ~ **sth for sb/sth** *These seats are reserved for special guests.* ◆ ~ **sth** *I'd prefer to reserve (my) judgment* (= not make a decision) *until I know all the facts.* **3** ~ **sth** to have or keep a particular power: *The management reserves the right to refuse admission.* ◆ (*law*) *All rights reserved* (= no one else can publish or copy this).

• *noun*

▷ **SUPPLY** **1** [C, usually pl.] a supply of something that is available to be used in the future or when it is needed: *large oil and gas reserves* ◆ *He discovered unexpected reserves of strength.* ◆ *reserve funds*

▷ **PROTECTED LAND** **2** (also **pre·serve**) [C] a piece of land that is a protected area for animals, plants, etc.: *a wildlife reserve* ⊃ see also GAME PRESERVE, NATURE RESERVE **3** [C] (in Canada) an area of land that is kept separate for Native Canadians to live in

▷ **QUALITY/FEELING** **4** [U] the quality that someone has when they do not talk easily to other people about their ideas, feelings, etc.: *She found it difficult to make friends because of her natural reserve.* **5** [U] (*formal*) a feeling that you do not want to accept or agree to something, etc. until you are quite sure that it is all right to do so: *Any contract should be treated with reserve until it has been checked.* ◆ *She trusted him without reserve* (= completely).

▷ **IN SPORTS** **6** [C] an extra player who plays on a team when one of the other players is injured or not available to play

▷ **MILITARY FORCE** **7** **the reserve** [sing.] (also **the reserves** [pl.]) an extra military force, etc. that is not part of a country's regular forces, but is available to be used when needed: *the army reserve(s)* ◆ *the reserve police*

▷ **PRICE** **8** (also **re·serve price**) [C] the lowest price that someone will accept for something, especially something that is sold at an AUCTION

IDM **in reserve** available to be used in the future or when needed: *The money was being kept in reserve for their retirement.* ◆ *200 police officers were held in reserve.*

re·served /rɪˈzərvd/ *adj.* (of a person or their character) slow or unwilling to show feelings or express opinions **SYN** SHY ⊃ compare UNRESERVED

re·serv·ist /rɪˈzərvɪst/ *noun* a soldier, etc. who is a member of the RESERVES (= a military force that can be used in an emergency)

res·er·voir /ˈrɛzərˌvwar; -ˌvwɔr/ *noun* **1** a natural or artificial lake where water is stored before it is taken by pipes to houses, etc. **2** (*formal*) a large amount of something that is available to be used **3** (*technical*) a place in an engine or a machine where a liquid is kept before it is used

re·set /ˌriˈsɛt/ *verb* (re·set·ting, re·set, re·set) **1** ~ **sth (to sth)** | ~ **sth to do sth** to change a machine, an instrument, or a control so that it gives a different time or number or is ready to use again: *You need to reset your watch to local time.* **2** [often passive] ~ **sth** to place something in the correct position again: *to reset a broken bone* ◆ *His left arm was reset.*

'reset ,button *noun* a button that you press on a machine or instrument to make it ready to use again: *The reset button will restart the game.*

re·set·tle /ˌriˈsetl/ *verb* **1** [T, I] **~ (sb)** to help people go and live in a new country or area; to go and live in a new country or area: *Many of the refugees were resettled in Canada.* **2** [T] **~ sth** to start to use an area again as a place to live: *The region was only resettled 200 years later.* **3** [I, T] **~ (yourself)** to make yourself comfortable in a new position: *The birds flew around and then resettled on the pond.* ► **re·set·tle·ment** *noun* [U]: *the resettlement of refugees* ◆ *a resettlement agency*

re·shape /ˌriˈʃeɪp/ *verb* **~ sth** to change the shape or structure of something

re·shuf·fle /ˌriˈʃʌfl/ (also *less frequent* **shuf·fle**) *verb* [T, I] **~ (sth)** to change around the jobs that a group of people do, for example in a government: *The President eventually decided against reshuffling the Cabinet.* ► **re·shuf·fle** *noun*: *a Cabinet reshuffle*

re·side **AWL** /rɪˈzaɪd/ *verb* [I] **+ adv./prep.** (*formal*) to live in a particular place: *He returned to the U.S. in 1939, having resided abroad for many years.*
PHR V **reˈside in sb/sth** to be in someone or something; to be caused by something: *The source of the problem resides in the fact that the currency is too strong.* **reˈside in/with sb/sth** (of a power, a right, etc.) to belong to someone or something **SYN** BE VESTED IN: *The ultimate authority resides with the board of directors.*

res·i·dence **AWL** /ˈrezədəns; -ˌdens/ *noun* (*formal*) **1** [C] a house, especially a large or impressive one: *a beautiful family residence for sale* (= for example, in an advertisement) ◆ *The White House is the President's official residence.* **2** [U] the state of living in a particular place: (*formal*) *They were not able to take up residence in their new home until the spring.* ◆ *Please state your occupation and place of residence.* ◆ *The flag flies when the Queen is in residence.* **3** (also **res·i·den·cy**) [U] permission to live in a country that is not your own: *They have been denied residence in this country.* ◆ *a residence permit*
IDM **in residence** having an official position in a particular place such as a college or university: *a writer in residence*

'residence ,hall (also **hall**) *noun* = DORMITORY (1)

res·i·den·cy /ˈrezədənsi; -ˌdensi/ *noun* (*pl.* **res·i·den·cies**) (*formal*) **1** [U] = RESIDENCE: *She has been granted permanent residency in the U.S.* **2** [U] the state of living in a particular place: *a residency requirement for students* **3** [U, C] the period of time when a doctor working in a hospital receives special advanced training **4** [U, C] the period of time that an artist, a writer, or a musician spends working for a particular institution

res·i·dent 🖋 **AWL** /ˈrezədənt; -ˌdent/ *noun, adj.*
• *noun* **1** a person who lives in a particular place or who has their home there: *a resident of the United States* ◆ *There were confrontations between local residents and the police.* **2** a person who is staying in a hotel: *The hotel restaurant is open to nonresidents.* **3** a doctor working in a hospital who is receiving special advanced training
• *adj.* living in a particular place: *the town's resident population* (= not tourists or visitors) ◆ *to be resident abroad/in Greece.* ◆ *Tom's our resident expert* (= our own expert) *on foreign movies.*

,resident 'alien *noun* (*law*) a person from another country who has permission to stay in the U.S.

res·i·den·tial **AWL** /ˌrezəˈdenʃl/ *adj.* [usually before noun] **1** (of an area of a city or town) suitable for living in; consisting of houses rather than factories or offices: *a quiet residential area* **2** relating to homes rather than offices: *The gas company offers special rates for residential customers.* **3** (of a job, a course, etc.) requiring a person to live at a particular place; offering a place to live: *a residential language course* ◆ *a residential home for the elderly* ◆ *residential care for children*

,residents' associ,ation *noun* a group of people who live in a particular area and join together to discuss the problems of that area

re·sid·u·al /rɪˈzɪdʒuəl/ *adj.* [only before noun] (*formal*) remaining at the end of a process **SYN** OUTSTANDING: *There are still a few residual problems with the computer program.*

re·sid·u·ary /rɪˈzɪdʒuˌeri/ *adj.* **1** (*law*) remaining from the money and property left by a person who has died after all debts, gifts, etc. have been paid **2** (*technical*) remaining at the end of a process

res·i·due /ˈrezəˌdu/ *noun* **1** a small amount of something that remains at the end of a process: *pesticide residues in fruit and vegetables* **2** (*law*) the part of the money, property, etc. of a person who has died that remains after all the debts, gifts, etc. have been paid: *The residue of the estate was divided equally among his children.*

re·sid·u·um /rɪˈzɪdʒuəm/ *noun* (*pl.* **re·sid·u·a** /-dʒuə/) (*technical*) something that remains after a reaction or process has taken place

re·sign /rɪˈzaɪn/ *verb* [I, T] to officially tell someone that you are leaving your job, an organization, etc.: *He resigned as manager after eight years.* ◆ **~ (from sth)** *Two members resigned from the board in protest.* ◆ **~ sth** *My father resigned his directorship last year.*
PHR V **reˈsign yourself to sth** to accept something unpleasant that cannot be changed or avoided: *She resigned herself to her fate.* ◆ **~ doing sth** *We had to resign ourselves to taking a loss on the sale.*

res·ig·na·tion /ˌrezɪgˈneɪʃn/ *noun* **1** [U, C] the act of giving up your job or position; the occasion when you do this: *a letter of resignation* ◆ *There were calls for her resignation from the board of directors.* ◆ *Further resignations are expected.* ⇒ collocations at JOB **2** [C] a letter, for example to your employers, to say that you are leaving your job or position: *to offer/hand in/tender your resignation* ◆ *We haven't received his resignation yet.* **3** [U] patient willingness to accept a difficult or unpleasant situation that you cannot change: *They accepted their defeat with resignation.*

re·signed /rɪˈzaɪnd/ *adj.* being willing to calmly accept something unpleasant or difficult that you cannot change: *a resigned sigh* ◆ **~ to sth/doing sth** *He was resigned to never seeing his birthplace again.* ► **re·sign·ed·ly** /rɪˈzaɪnədli/ *adv.*: *"I suppose you're right," she said resignedly.*

re·sil·ience /rɪˈzɪlyəns/ (also *less frequent* **re·si·li·en·cy** /rɪˈzɪlyənsi/) *noun* [U] **1** the ability of people or things to feel better quickly after something unpleasant, such as shock, injury, etc. **2** the ability of a substance to return to its original shape after it has been bent, stretched, or pressed

re·sil·ient /rɪˈzɪlyənt/ *adj.* **1** able to feel better quickly after something unpleasant such as shock, injury, etc.: *He'll get over it—young people are amazingly resilient.* **2** (of a substance) returning to its original shape after being bent, stretched, or pressed ► **re·sil·ient·ly** *adv.*

res·in /ˈrezn/ *noun* [C, U] **1** a sticky substance that is produced by some trees and is used in making VARNISH, medicine, etc. **2** an artificial substance similar to resin, used in making plastics ► **res·in·ous** /ˈrezənəs/ *adj.*: *the resinous scent of pine trees*

re·sist 🖋 /rɪˈzɪst/ *verb*
1 [T, I] to refuse to accept something and try to stop it from happening **SYN** OPPOSE: **~ (sth)** *to resist change* ◆ *They are determined to resist pressure to change the law.* ◆ **~ doing sth** *The bank strongly resisted cutting interest rates.* **2** [I, T] to fight back when attacked; to use force to stop something from happening: *He tried to pin me down, but I resisted.* ◆ **~ sth** *She was charged with resisting arrest.* **3** [T, I] (usually in negative sentences) to stop yourself from having something you like or doing something you very much want to do: **~ (sth)** *I finished the cake. I couldn't resist it.* ◆ *I found the temptation to miss the class too hard to resist.* ◆ **~ doing sth** *He couldn't resist showing off his new car.* **4** [T] **~ sth** to not be harmed or damaged by something: *A healthy diet should help your body resist infection.* ◆ *This new paint is designed to resist heat.*

| i **see** | ɪ **sit** | ɛ **ten** | æ **cat** | ɑ **hot** | ɔ **saw** | ʊ **put** | u **too** | 1255 |

re·sist·ance 🔈 /rɪˈzɪstəns/ noun

1 [U, sing.] dislike of or opposition to a plan, an idea, etc.; refusal to obey: *As with all new ideas, it met with resistance.* ◆ *~ to sb/sth There has been a lot of resistance to this new law.* ◆ *Resistance to change has nearly destroyed the industry.* **2** [U, sing.] the act of using force to oppose someone or something: *armed resistance* ◆ *The defenders put up a strong resistance.* ◆ *~ to sb/sth The demonstrators offered little or no resistance to the police.* **3** [U, sing.] *~ (to sth)* the power not to be affected by something: *AIDS lowers the body's resistance to infection.* **4** [U, sing.] *~ (to sth)* a force that stops something from moving or makes it move more slowly: *wind/air resistance* (= in the design of planes or cars) **5** [U, C] (*physics*) (*symb* R) the opposition of a piece of electrical equipment, etc. to the flow of a DIRECT CURRENT ⟳ compare REACTANCE **6** often **the Resistance** [sing.] a secret organization that resists the authorities, especially in a country that an enemy has control of: *resistance fighters*
IDM **(choose, follow, take, etc.) the path/line of least resistance** (to choose, etc.) the easiest way of doing something

re·sist·ant /rɪˈzɪstənt/ adj. **1** *~ (to sth)* not affected by something; able to resist something: *plants that are resistant to disease* **2** *~ (to sth)* opposing something and trying to stop it from happening: *Elderly people are not always resistant to change.* **3** -resistant (in adjectives) not damaged by the thing mentioned: *disease-resistant plants* ◆ *fire-resistant materials* ⟳ see also HEAT-RESISTANT, WATER-RESISTANT

re·sist·er /rɪˈzɪstər/ noun a person who resists someone or something

re·sist·i·ble /rɪˈzɪstəbl/ adj. that can be resisted
ANT IRRESISTIBLE

re·sis·tive /rɪˈzɪstɪv/ adj. **1** able to survive or cope with the action or effect of something **2** (*physics*) relating to electrical RESISTANCE ▶ **re·sis·tiv·i·ty** /ˌriːzɪˈstɪvəti/ noun [U, C]

re·sis·tor /rɪˈzɪstər/ noun (*physics*) a device that has RESISTANCE to an electric current in a CIRCUIT

re·size /ˌriːˈsaɪz/ verb *~ sth* to make something bigger or smaller, especially an image on a computer screen

re·skill /ˌriːˈskɪl/ verb [I, T] *~ (sb)* to learn new skills so that you can do a new job; to teach someone new skills

res·o·lute /ˈrezəluːt; ˌrezəˈluːt/ adj. having or showing great determination **SYN** DETERMINED: *resolute leadership* ◆ *He became even more resolute in his opposition to the plan.* **ANT** IRRESOLUTE ▶ **res·o·lute·ly** adv.: *They remain resolutely opposed to the idea.* **res·o·lute·ness** noun [U]

res·o·lu·tion **AWL** /ˌrezəˈluːʃn/ noun **1** [C] a formal statement of an opinion agreed on by a committee or a council, especially by means of a vote: *to pass/adopt/carry a resolution* **2** [U, sing.] the act of solving or settling a problem, disagreement, etc. **SYN** SETTLEMENT: *The government is pressing for an early resolution of the dispute.* **3** [U] the quality of being resolute or determined **SYN** RESOLVE: *The reforms owe a great deal to the resolution of one man.* **4** [C] *~ (to do sth)* a firm decision to do or not to do something: *She made a resolution to visit her relatives more often.* ◆ *Have you made any New Year's resolutions?* (= for example, to give up smoking from January 1) **5** [U, sing.] the power of a computer screen, printer, etc. to give a clear image, depending on the size of the dots that make up the image: *high-resolution graphics*

re·solve 🔈 **AWL** /rɪˈzɑlv/ verb, noun
● **verb** (*formal*) **1** [T] *~ sth/itself* to find an acceptable solution to a problem or difficulty **SYN** SETTLE: *to resolve an issue/a dispute/a conflict/a crisis* ◆ *Both sides met in order to try to resolve their differences.* **2** [T, I] to make a firm decision to do something: *~ to do sth He resolved not to tell her the truth.* ◆ *~ (that)... She resolved (that) she would never see him again.* ◆ *~ on sth/on doing sth We had resolved on making an early start.* **3** [T] (of a committee, meeting, etc.) to reach a decision by means of a formal vote: **it is resolved that...** *It was resolved that the matter be referred to a higher authority.* ◆

~ that... They resolved that the matter be referred to a higher authority. ◆ *~ to do sth The Supreme Council resolved to resume control over the national press.*
PHR V **re·solve into sth | re·solve sth into sth** (*formal*) **1** to separate or to be separated into its parts: *to resolve a complex argument into its basic elements* **2** (of something seen or heard at a distance) to gradually turn into a different form when it is seen or heard more clearly: *The orange light resolved itself into four lanterns.* **3** to gradually become or be understood as something: *The discussion eventually resolved itself into two main issues.*
● **noun** [U] (*formal*) strong determination to achieve something **SYN** RESOLUTION: *The difficulties in her way merely strengthened her resolve.* ◆ *~ to do sth The government reiterated its resolve to uncover the truth.*

re·solved **AWL** /rɪˈzɑlvd/ adj. [not before noun] *~ (to do sth)* (*formal*) determined: *I was resolved not to see him.*

res·o·nance /ˈrezənəns/ noun **1** [U] (*formal*) (of sound) the quality of being resonant: *the strange and thrilling resonance of her voice* **2** [C, U] (*technical*) the sound or other VIBRATION produced in an object by sound or VIBRATIONS of a similar FREQUENCY from another object **3** [U, C] (*formal*) (in a piece of writing, music, etc.) the power to bring images, feelings, etc. into the mind of the person reading or listening; the images, etc. produced in this way

res·o·nant /ˈrezənənt/ adj. **1** (*formal*) (of sound) deep, clear, and continuing for a long time: *a deep resonant voice* **2** (*technical*) causing sounds to continue for a long time **SYN** RESOUNDING: *resonant frequencies* **3** (*literary*) having the power to bring images, feelings, memories, etc. into your mind: *a poem filled with resonant imagery* ▶ **res·o·nant·ly** adv.

res·o·nate /ˈrezəneɪt/ verb (*formal*) **1** [I] (of a voice, an instrument, etc.) to make a deep, clear sound that continues for a long time **2** [I] (of a place) to be filled with sound; to make a sound continue longer **SYN** RESOUND: *a resonating chamber* ◆ *~ with sth The room resonated with the chatter of 100 people.* **3** [I] *~ (with sb/sth)* to remind someone of something; to be similar to what someone thinks or believes: *These issues resonated with the voters.*
PHR V **'res·o·nate with sth** (*literary*) to be full of a particular quality or feeling: *She makes a simple story resonate with complex themes and emotions.*

res·o·na·tor /ˈrezəˌneɪtər/ noun (*technical*) a device for making sound louder and stronger, especially in a musical instrument

re·sort 🔈 /rɪˈzɔrt/ noun, verb
● **noun** **1** [C] a place where a lot of people go on vacation: *island/ski/mountain, etc. resorts* ◆ *a popular vacation resort* ◆ *the resort town of Sea Island, Georgia* ⟳ collocations at TRAVEL **2** [U] *~ to sth* the act of using something, especially something bad or unpleasant, because nothing else is possible **SYN** RECOURSE: *There are hopes that the conflict can be resolved without resort to violence.* **3** **the first/last/final** *~* the first or last course of action that you should or can take in a particular situation: *Strike action should be regarded as a last resort, when all attempts to negotiate have failed.* ◆ **In the last resort** (= in the end) *everyone must decide for themselves.*
● **verb**
PHR V **re'sort to sth** to make use of something, especially something bad, as a means of achieving something, often because there is no other possible solution **SYN** HAVE RECOURSE TO: *They felt thay had to resort to violence.* ◆ *~ doing sth We may have to resort to using untrained staff.*

re·sound /rɪˈzaʊnd/ verb (*formal*) **1** [I] *~ (through sth)* (of a sound, voice, etc.) to fill a place with sound: *Laughter resounded through the house.* ◆ (*figurative*) *The tragedy resounded around the world.* **2** [I] *~ (with/to sth)* (of a place) to be filled with sound: *The street resounded to the thud of marching feet.*

re·sound·ing /rɪˈzaʊndɪŋ/ adj. [only before noun] **1** very great **SYN** EMPHATIC: *a resounding victory/win/defeat* ◆ *The evening was a resounding success.* **2** (of a sound) very loud and continuing for a long time **SYN** RESONANT ▶ **re·sound·ing·ly** adv.

re·source ♪ **AWL** /ˈriːsɔːrs; rɪˈsɔːrs/ noun, verb
• noun **1** [C, usually pl.] a supply of something that a country, an organization, or a person has and can use, especially to increase their wealth: *the exploitation of minerals and other natural resources* ◆ *We do not have the resources (= money) to update our computer software.* ◆ *We must make the most efficient use of the available financial resources.* ◆ *We agreed to pool our resources (= so that everyone gives something).* ⊃ collocations at ENVIRONMENT ⊃ see also HUMAN RE-SOURCES **2** [C] something that can be used to help achieve an aim, especially a book, equipment, etc. that provides information for teachers and students: *The database could be used as a teaching resource in colleges.* ◆ *Time is your most valuable resource, especially in exams.* ◆ *resource books for teachers* **3** resources [pl.] personal qualities such as courage and imagination that help you deal with difficult situations: *He has no inner resources and hates being alone.*
• verb **~ sth** to provide something with the money or equipment that is needed: *Schools in the area are still inadequately resourced.*

re·source·ful **AWL** /rɪˈsɔːrsfl/ adj. (approving) good at finding ways of doing things and solving problems, etc. **SYN** ENTERPRISING ▶ **re·source·ful·ly** /-fəli/ adv. **re·source·ful·ness** noun [U]

re·spect ♪ /rɪˈspɛkt/ noun, verb
• noun **1** [U, sing.] **~ (for sb/sth)** a feeling of admiration for someone or something because of their good qualities or achievements: *I have the greatest respect for your brother.* ◆ *A two-minute silence was observed as a mark of respect.* ◆ *A deep mutual respect and understanding developed between them.* ⊃ see also SELF-RESPECT **ANT** DISRESPECT **2** [U, sing.] **~ (for sb/sth)** polite behavior toward or care for someone or something that you think is important: *to show a lack of respect for authority* ◆ *He has no respect for her feelings.* ◆ *Everyone has a right to be treated with respect.* **ANT** DISRESPECT **3** [C] a particular aspect or detail of something: *In this respect we are very fortunate.* ◆ *There was one respect, however, in which they differed.* **IDM** in respect of sth (formal or business) **1** concerning: *A writ was served on the firm in respect of their unpaid bill.* **2** in payment for something: *money received in respect of overtime worked* with respect | with all due respect used when you are going to disagree, usually quite strongly, with someone: *With all due respect, the figures simply do not support you on this.* with respect to sth (formal or business) concerning: *The two groups were similar with respect to income and status.* ⊃ more at DUE adj., PAY v.
• verb **1** (not usually used in the progressive tenses) to have a very good opinion of someone or something; to admire someone or something: *~ sb/sth I respect Jack's opinion on most subjects.* ◆ *a much loved and highly respected teacher* ◆ *~ sb/sth for sth She has always been honest with me, and I respect her for that.* **2** **~ sth** to be careful about something; to make sure you do not do something that someone would consider to be wrong: *to respect other people's property* ◆ *She promised to respect our wishes.* ◆ *He doesn't respect other people's right to privacy.* **3** **~ sth** to agree not to break a law, principle, etc.: *The new leader has promised to respect the constitution.*

re·spect·a·bil·i·ty /rɪˌspɛktəˈbɪləti/ noun [U] the fact of being considered socially acceptable

re·spect·a·ble /rɪˈspɛktəbl/ adj. **1** considered by society to be acceptable, good, or correct: *a highly respectable neighborhood* ◆ *a respectable married man* ◆ *Go and make yourself look respectable.* **ANT** DISREPUTABLE **2** fairly good; that there is not reason to be ashamed of **SYN** ACCEPTABLE: *a perfectly respectable result* ▶ **re·spect·a·bly** /-bli/ adv.: *respectably dressed*

re·spect·er /rɪˈspɛktər/ noun
IDM be no respecter of persons to treat everyone in the same way, without being influenced by their importance, wealth, etc.

re·spect·ful /rɪˈspɛktfl/ adj. showing or feeling respect: *The onlookers stood at a respectful distance.* ◆ *We were brought up to be respectful of authority.* **ANT** DISRESPECTFUL ▶ **re·spect·ful·ly** /-fəli/ adv.: *He listened respectfully.*

re·spect·ing /rɪˈspɛktɪŋ/ prep. (formal) concerning **SYN** WITH RESPECT TO: *information respecting the child's whereabouts*

re·spec·tive /rɪˈspɛktɪv/ adj. [only before noun] belonging or relating separately to each of the people or things already mentioned: *They are each recognized specialists in their respective fields.* ◆ *the respective roles of men and women in society*

re·spec·tive·ly /rɪˈspɛktɪvli/ adv. in the same order as the people or things already mentioned: *Julie and Mark, aged 17 and 19 respectively*

res·pi·ra·tion /ˌrɛspəˈreɪʃn/ noun [U] (formal) the act of breathing: *Blood pressure and respiration are also recorded.* ⊃ see also ARTIFICIAL RESPIRATION

res·pi·ra·tor /ˈrɛspəˌreɪtər/ noun **1** a piece of equipment that makes it possible for someone to breathe over a long period when they are unable to do so naturally: *She was put on a respirator.* **2** a device worn over the nose and mouth to allow someone to breathe in a place where there is a lot of smoke, gas, etc.

res·pi·ra·to·ry /ˈrɛsprəˌtɔri; rɪˈspɛrə-/ adj. connected with breathing: *the respiratory system* ◆ *respiratory diseases*

re·spire /rɪˈspaɪər/ verb [I] (technical) to breathe

res·pi·rom·e·ter /ˌrɛspəˈrɑmətər/ noun (medical) a piece of equipment for measuring how much air someone's lungs will hold

res·pite /ˈrɛspət/ noun [sing., U] **1** **~ (from sth)** a short break or escape from something difficult or unpleasant: *The medicine brought a brief respite from the pain.* ◆ *There was no respite from the suffocating heat.* ◆ *She continued to work without respite.* ◆ *respite care (= temporary care arranged for old, mentally ill, etc. people so that the people who usually care for them can have a rest)* ⊃ thesaurus box at REST **2** a short delay allowed before something difficult or unpleasant must be done **SYN** REPRIEVE: *His creditors agreed to give him a temporary respite.*

re·splen·dent /rɪˈsplɛndənt/ adj. **~ (in sth)** (formal or literary) brightly colored in an impressive way: *He glimpsed Sonia, resplendent in a red dress.* ▶ **re·splend·ent·ly** adv.

re·spond ♪ **AWL** /rɪˈspɑnd/ verb
1 [I, T] (somewhat formal) to give a spoken or written answer to someone or something **SYN** REPLY: *I asked him his name, but he didn't respond.* ◆ **~ (to sb/sth) (with sth)** *She never responded to my letter.* ◆ + speech "I'm not sure," she responded. ◆ **~ that...** *When asked about the company's future, the director responded that he remained optimistic.* ⊃ note at ANSWER **2** [I] **~ (to sth) (with sth/by doing sth)** to do something as a reaction to something that someone has said or done **SYN** REACT: *How did they respond to the news?* ◆ *The government responded by banning all future demonstrations.* **3** [I] **~ (to sth/sb)** to react quickly or in the correct way to something or someone: *The car responds very well to the controls.* ◆ *You can rely on him to respond to a challenge.* **4** [I] **~ (to sth)** to improve as a result of a particular kind of treatment: *The infection did not respond to the drugs.*

re·spond·ent **AWL** /rɪˈspɑndənt/ noun **1** a person who answers questions, especially in a survey: *60% of the respondents agreed with the suggestion.* **2** (law) a person who is accused of something

re·sponse ♪ **AWL** /rɪˈspɑns/ noun
1 [C, U] a spoken or written answer: *She made no response.* ◆ **~ to sb/sth** *In response to your inquiry...* ◆ *I received an encouraging response to my advertisement.* **2** [C, U] a reaction

to something that has happened or been said: *The news provoked an angry response.* ◆ *a positive response* ◆ *I knocked on the door but there was no response.* ◆ **~ (to sb/sth)** *The product was developed in response to customer demand.* ◆ *We sent out over 1,000 letters but the response rate has been low* (= few people replied). **3** [C, usually pl.] **~ (to sb/sth)** a part of a religious service that the people sing or speak as an answer to the part that the religious leader sings or speaks

re'sponse time *noun* the length of time that a person or system takes to react to something: *The average response time to emergency calls was 9 minutes.*

re·spon·si·bil·i·ty 🔑 /rɪˌspɑnsəˈbɪləti/ *noun*
(pl. **re·spon·si·bil·i·ties**) **1** [U, C] a duty to deal with or take care of someone or something, so that it is your fault if something goes wrong: **~ (for sth)** *We are recruiting a sales manager with responsibility for the European market.* ◆ **~ (for doing sth)** *They have responsibility for ensuring that the rules are enforced.* ◆ **~ (to do sth)** *It is their responsibility to ensure that the rules are enforced.* ◆ *parental rights and responsibilities* ◆ *to take/assume overall responsibility for personnel* ◆ *I don't feel ready to take on new responsibilities.* ◆ *to be in a position of responsibility* ◆ *I did it on my own responsibility* (= without being told to and being willing to take the blame if it had gone wrong). ⊃ see also CORPORATE RESPONSIBILITY **2** [U] **~ (for sth)** blame for something bad that has happened: *The bank refuses to accept responsibility for the mistake.* ◆ *Nobody has claimed responsibility for the bombing.* **3** [U, C] a duty to help or take care of someone because of your job, position, etc.: **~ (to/toward sb)** *She feels a strong sense of responsibility toward her employees.* ◆ **~ (to do sth)** *I think we have a moral responsibility to help these countries.*

re·spon·si·ble 🔑 /rɪˈspɑnsəbl/ *adj.*
▷ **HAVING JOB/DUTY 1** having the job or duty of doing something or taking care of someone or something, so that it is your fault if something goes wrong: **~ (for doing sth)** *Mike is responsible for designing the entire project.* ◆ **~ (for sb/sth)** *Even where parents no longer live together, they each continue to be responsible for their children.*
▷ **CAUSING SOMETHING 2** **~ (for sth)** being able to be blamed for something: *Who's responsible for this mess?* ◆ *Everything will be done to bring those responsible to justice.* ◆ *He is mentally ill and cannot be held responsible for his actions.* **3** **~ (for sth)** being the cause of something: *Cigarette smoking is responsible for about 90% of deaths from lung cancer.*
▷ **TO SOMEONE IN AUTHORITY 4** **~ to sb/sth** having to report to someone or something with authority or in a higher position and explain to them what you have done: *The CEO is responsible to the board of directors.*
▷ **RELIABLE 5** (of people or their actions or behavior) that you can trust and rely on **SYN** CONSCIENTIOUS: *Clare has a mature and responsible attitude to work.* **ANT** IRRESPONSIBLE
▷ **JOB 6** [usually before noun] needing someone who can be trusted and relied on; involving important duties: *a responsible job/position*

re·spon·si·bly /rɪˈspɑnsəbli/ *adv.* in a sensible way that shows you can be trusted: *to act responsibly*

re·spon·sive **AWL** /rɪˈspɑnsɪv/ *adj.* **1** [not usually before noun] **~ (to sb/sth)** reacting quickly and in a positive way: *Companies have to be responsive to consumer demand.* ◆ *a flu virus that is not responsive to treatment* **2** **~ (to sb/sth)** reacting with interest or enthusiasm **SYN** RECEPTIVE: *The club is responsive to new ideas.* ◆ *a responsive and enthusiastic audience* **ANT** UNRESPONSIVE ▶ **re·spon·sive·ly** *adv.* **re·spon·sive·ness** **AWL** *noun* [U]: *a lack of responsiveness to client needs*

rest 🔑 /rɛst/ *noun, verb*
● *noun*
▷ **REMAINING PART/PEOPLE/THINGS 1** [sing.] **the ~ (of sth)** the remaining part of something: *I'm not doing this job for the rest of my life.* ◆ *How would you like to spend the rest of the day?* ◆ *Take what you want and throw the rest away.* **2** [pl.] **the ~ (of sth)** the remaining people or things; the others: *Don't blame*

Alex. *He's human, like the rest of us.* ◆ *The first question was difficult, but the rest were pretty easy.*
▷ **PERIOD OF RELAXING 3** [C, U] a period of relaxing, sleeping, or doing nothing after a period of activity: *We stopped for a well-deserved rest.* ◆ **~ (from sth)** *to have/take a rest from all your hard work* ◆ *Try to get some rest —you have a busy day tomorrow.* ◆ *There are no matches tomorrow, which is a rest day, but the tournament resumes on Monday.*
▷ **SUPPORT 4** [C] (often in compounds) an object that is used to support or hold something: *an armrest* (= for example on a seat or chair)
▷ **IN MUSIC 5** [C, U] a period of silence between notes; a sign that shows a rest between notes ⊃ picture at MUSIC
IDM and (all) the rest (of it) (*informal*) used at the end of a list to mean everything else that you might expect to be on the list: *He wants a big house, and an expensive car, and all the rest of it.* **at rest 1** (*technical*) not moving: *At rest the insect looks like a dead leaf.* **2** dead and therefore free from trouble or anxiety. People say "at rest" to avoid saying "dead.": *She now lies at rest in the churchyard.* **come to rest** to stop moving: *The car crashed through the barrier and came to rest in a field.* ◆ *His eyes came to rest on Clara's face.* **give it a rest** (*informal*) used to tell someone to stop talking about something because they are annoying you **give sth a rest** (*informal*) to stop doing something for a while **lay sb to rest** to bury someone. People say "to lay someone to rest" to avoid saying "to bury someone.": *George was laid to rest beside his parents.* **lay/put sth to rest** to stop something by showing it is not true: *The announcement finally laid all the speculation about their future to rest.* **the rest is history** used when you are telling a story to say that you do not need to tell the end of it, because everyone knows it already ⊃ more at MIND *n.*, WICKED *n.*

● *verb*
▷ **RELAX 1** [I, T] to relax, sleep, or do nothing after a period of activity or illness; to not use a part of your body for some time: *The doctor told me to rest.* ◆ *I can rest easy* (= stop worrying) *knowing that she's safely home.* ◆ (*figurative*) *He won't rest* (= will never be satisfied) *until he finds her.* ◆ **~ sth** *Rest your eyes every half an hour.* ⊃ see also RESTED
▷ **SUPPORT 2** [T, I] to support something by putting it on or against something; to be supported in this way: **~ sth + adv./prep.** *Rest your head on my shoulder.* ◆ *He rested his chin in his hands.* ◆ **+ adv./prep.** *His chin rested on his hands.* ◆ *Their bikes were resting against the wall.*

t tea   ţ butter   d did   k cat   g got   tʃ chin   dʒ June   f fall

> **BE LEFT 3** [I] if you let a matter **rest**, you stop discussing it or dealing with it: *The matter cannot rest there—I intend to sue.*

> **BE BURIED 4** [I] + **adv./prep.** to be buried. People say "rest" to avoid saying "be buried.": *She rests beside her husband in the local cemetery.* ◆ *May he rest in peace.* ➲ see also RIP

IDM **rest assured (that…)** (*formal*) used to emphasize that what you say is true or will definitely happen: *You may rest assured that we will do all we can to find him.* **rest your case**

1 I rest my case (sometimes *humorous*) used to say that you do not need to say any more about something because you think that you have proved your point **2** (*law*) used by lawyers in court to say that they have finished presenting their case: *The prosecution rests its case.* ➲ more at EASY *adv.*, GOD, LAUREL

PHR V **'rest on/upon sb/sth 1** to depend or rely on someone or something: *All our hopes now rest on you.* **2** to look at someone or something: *Her eyes rested on the piece of paper in my hand.* **'rest on sth** to be based on something: *The whole argument rests on a false assumption.* **'rest with sb (to do sth)** (*formal*) if it **rests with someone to do something**, it is their responsibility to do it: *It rests with management to justify their actions.* ◆ *The final decision rests with the doctors.*

'rest ˌarea (also **'rest stop**) *noun* an area beside an important road where people can stop their cars to rest, eat, etc.

re·start /ˌriˈstɑrt/ *verb* [I, T] **~ (sth)** to start again, or to make something start again, after it has stopped: *to restart a game* ◆ *The doctors struggled to restart his heart.* ▶ **re·start** /ˈristɑrt/ *noun*

re·state /ˌriˈsteɪt/ *verb* **~ sth** (*formal*) to say something again or in a different way, especially so that it is more clearly or strongly expressed ▶ **re·state·ment** *noun* [U]

res·tau·rant 🔑 /ˈrestəˌrɑnt; ˈrestrɑnt; ˈrestərənt/ *noun* a place where you can buy and eat a meal: *an Italian restaurant* ◆ *We had dinner in a restaurant.* ◆ *We went out to a restaurant to celebrate.* ◆ *a restaurant owner* ◆ *a fast food restaurant* ➲ compare CAFE

TOPIC COLLOCATIONS

Restaurants

eating out

- eat (lunch/dinner)/dine/meet at/in a restaurant
- go (out)/take sb (out) for lunch/dinner/a meal
- have a meal with sb
- make/have a reservation (in/under the name of Baker)
- reserve a table for six
- ask for/request a table for two/a table by the window

in the restaurant

- wait to be seated
- show sb to their table
- sit in the corner/by the window/at the bar/at the counter
- hand sb/give sb the menu/wine list
- open/read/study/peruse the menu
- the restaurant has a three-course set menu/a children's menu/an extensive wine list
- taste/sample/try the wine
- the waiter takes your order
- order/choose/have the soup of the day/one of the specials/the house specialty
- serve/finish the appetizers/the first course/the main course/dessert/coffee
- complain about the food/the service/your meal
- enjoy your meal

paying

- pay/ask for the check/the bill
- pay for/treat sb to dinner/lunch/the meal
- a gratuity/a service charge is (not) included
- give sb/leave (sb) a tip

---

res·tau·ra·teur /ˌrestərəˈtər/ *noun* (*formal*) a person who owns and manages a restaurant

'rest cure *noun* a period spent resting or relaxing in order to improve your physical or mental health

rest·ed /ˈrestəd/ *adj.* feeling healthy and full of energy because you have had a rest: *I awoke feeling rested and refreshed.* ➲ see also REST

rest·ful /ˈrestfl/ *adj.* that makes you feel relaxed and peaceful **SYN** CALMing: *a hotel with a restful atmosphere*

'rest home *noun* a place where old or sick people are cared for

'resting ˌplace *noun* **1** a grave. People say "resting place" to avoid saying "grave.": *her final/last resting place* **2** a place where you can rest

res·ti·tu·tion /ˌrestəˈtuʃn/ *noun* [U] **~ (of sth) (to sb/sth)** **1** (*formal*) the act of giving back something that was lost or stolen to its owner **SYN** RESTORATION **2** (*law*) payment, usually money, for some harm or wrong that someone has suffered

res·tive /ˈrestɪv/ *adj.* (*formal*) unable to stay still, or unwilling to be controlled, especially because you feel bored or not satisfied ▶ **res·tive·ness** *noun* [U]

rest·less /ˈrestləs; ˈresləs/ *adj.* **1** unable to stay still or be happy where you are, because you are bored or need a change: *The audience was becoming restless.* ◆ *After five years in the job, he was beginning to feel restless.* **2** without real rest or sleep **SYN** DISTURBED: *a restless night* ▶ **rest·less·ly** *adv.*: *He moved restlessly from one foot to another.* **rest·less·ness** *noun* [U]: *the restlessness of youth*

re·stock /ˌriˈstɑk/ *verb* [T, I] **~ (sth) (with sth)** to fill something with new or different things to replace those that have been used, sold, etc.; to get a new supply of something

res·to·ra·tion **AWL** /ˌrestəˈreɪʃn/ *noun* **1** [U, C] the work of repairing and cleaning an old building, a painting, etc. so that its condition is as good as it originally was: *The palace is closed for restoration.* ◆ *restoration work* **2** [U, C] **~ of sth** the act of bringing back a system, a law, etc. that existed previously: *the restoration of democracy/the monarchy* **3** [U] **~ (of sth)** the act of returning something to its correct place, condition, or owner: *the restoration of the Elgin marbles to Greece*

re·stor·a·tive /rɪˈstɔrətɪv/ *adj.*, *noun*
- *adj.* **1** (*formal*) making you feel strong and healthy again: *the restorative power of fresh air* **2** (*medical*) connected with treatment that repairs the body or a part of it: *restorative dentistry/surgery*
- *noun* (*old-fashioned*) a thing that makes you feel better, stronger, etc.

re·store 🔑 **AWL** /rɪˈstɔr/ *verb*
1 ~ sth (to sb) to bring back a situation or feeling that existed before: *The measures are intended to restore public confidence in the economy.* ◆ *Order was quickly restored after the riots.* ◆ *Such kindness restores your faith in human nature* (= makes you believe most people are kind). ◆ *The operation restored his sight* (= made him able to see again). **2 ~ sb/sth to sth** to bring someone or something back to a former condition, place, or position: *He is now fully restored to health.* ◆ *We hope to restore the garden to its former glory* (= make it as beautiful as it used to be). **3 ~ sth** to repair a building, work of art, piece of furniture, etc. so that it looks as good as it did originally: *Her job is restoring old paintings.* **4 ~ sth** to bring a law, tradition, way of working, etc. back into use **SYN** REINTRODUCE: *to restore ancient traditions* ◆ *Some people argue that the death penalty should be restored.* **5 ~ sth (to sb/sth)** (*formal*) to give something that was lost or stolen back to someone: *The police have now restored the painting to its rightful owner.*

re·stor·er /rɪˈstɔrər/ *noun* a person whose job is to repair old buildings, works of art, etc. so that they look as they did when new

---

re·strain **AWL** /rɪ'streɪn/ *verb* **1** to stop someone or something from doing something, especially by using physical force: ~ **sb/sth** *The prisoner had to be restrained by the police.* ✦ *He placed a restraining hand on her arm.* ✦ ~ **sb/ sth from sth/from doing sth** *They have obtained an injunction restraining the company from selling the product.* **2** to stop yourself from feeling an emotion or doing something that you would like to do: ~ **sth** *John managed to restrain his anger.* ✦ ~ **yourself (from sth/from doing sth)** *She had to restrain herself from crying out in pain.* **3** ~ **sth** to stop something that is growing or increasing from becoming too large **SYN** KEEP UNDER CONTROL: *The government is taking steps to restrain inflation.*

re·strained **AWL** /rɪ'streɪnd/ *adj.* **1** showing calm control rather than emotion: *her restrained smile* **2** not too brightly colored or decorated **SYN** DISCREET: *The costumes and lighting in the play were restrained.*

re'straining ˌorder *noun* ~ **(against sb)** an official order given by a judge that demands that something must or must not be done. A restraining order does not require a trial in court but only lasts for a limited period of time. ↪ compare INJUNCTION

re·straint **AWL** /rɪ'streɪnt/ *noun* **1** [C, usually pl.] ~ **(on sb/ sth)** a rule, a fact, an idea, etc. that limits or controls what people can do: *The government has imposed export restraints on some products.* ↪ thesaurus box at LIMIT **2** [U] the act of controlling or limiting something because it is necessary or sensible to do so: *wage restraint* **3** [U] the quality of behaving calmly and with control **SYN** SELF-CONTROL: *The police appealed to the crowd for restraint.* ✦ *He exercised considerable restraint in ignoring the insults.* **4** [U] (*formal*) the use of physical force to control someone who is behaving in a violent way: *the physical restraint of prisoners* **5** [C] (*formal*) a type of SEAT BELT or safety device: *Children must use an approved child restraint or adult seat belt.*

re·strict 🔑 **AWL** /rɪ'strɪkt/ *verb*

1 to limit the size, amount, or range of something: ~ **sth to sth** *Speed is restricted to 30 mph in towns.* ✦ *We restrict the number of students per class to 10.* ✦ ~ **sth** *Fog severely restricted visibility.* ✦ *Having small children tends to restrict your freedom.* **2** ~ **sth** to stop someone or something from moving or acting freely **SYN** IMPEDE: *The long skirt restricted her movements.* **3** ~ **sth (to sb)** to control something with rules or laws: *Access to the club is restricted to members only.* **4** ~ **yourself/sb (to sth/to doing sth)** to allow yourself or someone to have only a limited amount of something or to do only a particular kind of activity: *I restrict myself to one cup of coffee a day.*

re·strict·ed 🔑 **AWL** /rɪ'strɪktəd/ *adj.* **1** limited or small in size or amount: *a restricted space* ✦ *a restricted range of foods* **2** limited in what you are able to do: *In those days women led fairly restricted lives.* ✦ *Her vision is restricted in one eye.* **3** controlled by rules or laws: *to allow children only restricted access to the Internet* ✦ *The tournament is restricted to players under the age of 23.* **4** [usually before noun] (of a place) only open to people with special permission, especially because it is secret or dangerous: *to enter a restricted zone* **ANT** UNRESTRICTED

re·stric·tion 🔑 **AWL** /rɪ'strɪkʃn/ *noun* **1** [C] a rule or law that limits what you can do or what can happen: *import/speed/travel, etc. restrictions* ✦ ~ **on sth** *to impose/place a restriction on something* ✦ *The government has agreed to lift restrictions on press freedom.* ↪ thesaurus box at LIMIT **2** [U] the act of limiting or controlling someone or something: *sports clothes that prevent any restriction of movement* **3** [C] a thing that limits the amount of freedom you have: *the restrictions of a prison*

re·stric·tive **AWL** /rɪ'strɪktɪv/ *adj.* **1** preventing people from doing what they want: *restrictive laws* **2** (also **de·fin·ing**) (*grammar*) (of RELATIVE CLAUSES) explaining which particular person or thing you are talking about rather than giving extra information about them. In "The books that are

on the table are mine," "that are on the table" is a restrictive relative clause. ↪ compare NONRESTRICTIVE ▶ **re·stric·tive·ly** **AWL** *adv.*

re·string /ˌriː'strɪŋ/ *verb* (**re·strung, re·strung** /-'strʌŋ/) ~ **sth** to fit new strings on a musical instrument such as a GUITAR or VIOLIN, or on a sports RACKET

rest·room /'rɛstrum; -rʊm/ (also **'rest room**) *noun* a room with a toilet in a public place, such as a theater or restaurant

re·struc·ture **AWL** /ˌriː'strʌktʃər/ *verb* [T, I] ~ **(sth)** to organize something such as a system or a company in a new and different way ▶ **re·struc·tur·ing** **AWL** *noun* [U, C, usually sing.]

'rest stop *noun* = REST AREA

re·sult 🔑 /rɪ'zʌlt/ *noun, verb*

● *noun*
> **CAUSED BY SOMETHING 1** [C, U] ~ **(of sth)** a thing that is caused or produced because of something else: *She died as a result of her injuries.* ✦ *The failure of the company was a direct result of bad management.* ✦ *He made one big mistake, and, as a result, lost his job.* ✦ *The farm was flooded, with the result that most of the harvest was lost.* ✦ *The end result* (= the final one) of *her hard work was a place in medical school.* ✦ *This book is the result of 25 years of research.* ↪ language bank at BECAUSE, CONSEQUENTLY
> **OF GAME/ELECTION 2** [C] ~ **(of sth)** the final score or the name of the winner in a sports event, competition, election, etc.: *They will announce the result of the vote tonight.* ✦ *the election results* ✦ *the football results*
> **OF TEST/RESEARCH 3** [C] ~ **(of sth)** the information that you get from a scientific test or piece of research: *the result of an experiment* ↪ collocations at SCIENTIFIC
> **SUCCESS 4** results [pl.] things that are achieved successfully: *The project is beginning to show results.* ✦ *a coach who knows how to get results from his players*

● *verb* [I] ~ **(from sth)** to happen because of something else that happened first: *job losses resulting from changes in production* ✦ *When water levels rise, flooding results.* ✦ *It was a large explosion and the resulting damage was extensive.* **PHR V** **re'sult in sth** to make something happen **SYN** LEAD TO: *The cyclone has resulted in many thousands of deaths.* ✦ ~ **sb/sth doing sth** *These millions resulted in many elderly people suffering hardship.* ↪ language bank at CAUSE

THESAURUS

result

consequence ◦ outcome ◦ repercussion

These are all words for a thing that is caused because of something else.

result a thing that is caused or produced by something else: *She died as a result of her injuries.* ✦ *This book is the result of 25 years of research.*

consequence (*somewhat formal*) a result of something that has happened, especially a bad result: *This decision could have serious consequences for the industry.* **NOTE** **Consequences** is used most frequently to talk about possible negative results of an action. It is commonly used with such words as *adverse, dire, disastrous, fatal, harmful, negative, serious, tragic,* and *unfortunate.* Even when there is no adjective, **consequences** often suggests negative results.

outcome the final result of an action or a process: *We are waiting to hear the outcome of the negotiations.*

RESULT OR OUTCOME?

Result is often used to talk about things that are caused directly by something else: *Aggression is often the result of fear.* **Outcome** is more often used to talk about what happens at the end of a process, when the exact relation of cause and effect is less clear: ~~Aggresssion is often the outcome of fear.~~ **Result** is often used after an event to talk about what happened. **Outcome** is often used

---

| 1260 | **h** hat | **m** man | **n** no | **ŋ** sing | **l** leg | **r** red | **y** yes | **w** wet |

before an action or a process to talk about what is likely to happen.

repercussion (*somewhat formal*) an indirect and usually bad result of an action or event that may happen some time afterward

PATTERNS

- to have consequences/repercussions **for** sb/sth
- **with** the result/consequence/outcome **that...**
- the **possible** result/consequences/outcome/repercussions
- the **likely/inevitable** result/consequences/outcome
- (a/an) **negative** results/consequences/outcome/repercussions
- **far-reaching/serious** results/consequences/repercussions
- to **have** a result/consequences/an outcome/repercussions

re·sult·ant /rɪˈzʌltnt/ *adj.* [only before noun] (*formal*) caused by the thing that has just been mentioned: *the growing economic crisis and resultant unemployment*

re·sult·a·tive /rɪˈzʌltətɪv/ *adj.* (*grammar*) (of verbs, conjunctions, or clauses) expressing or relating to the result of an action

re·sume /rɪˈzum/ *verb* (*formal*) **1** [T, I] if you **resume** an activity, or if it **resumes**, it begins again or continues after an interruption: ~ **(sth)** *to resume talks/negotiations* ◆ *She resumed her career after an interval of six years.* ◆ *The noise resumed, louder than before.* ◆ ~ **doing sth** *He got back in the car and resumed driving.* **2** [T] ~ **your seat/place/position** to go back to the seat or place that you had before

ré·su·mé (also **re·su·mé, re·su·me**) /ˈrɛzəˌmeɪ/ *noun* **1** a written record of your education and the jobs you have done, that you send when you are applying for a job **2** ~ **(of sth)** a short summary or account of something: *a brief résumé of events so far*

re·sump·tion /rɪˈzʌmpʃn/ *noun* [sing., U] ~ **(of sth)** (*formal*) the act of beginning something again after it has stopped: *We are hoping for an early resumption of peace talks.*

re·sup·ply /ˌrisəˈplaɪ/ *verb* ~ **sb (with sth)** to give someone new supplies of something they need; to give something to someone again in a different form ▸ **re·sup·ply** *noun*

re·sur·face /ˌriˈsɜrfəs/ *verb* **1** [I] to come to the surface again after being underwater or under the ground: *The submarine resurfaced.* ◆ (*figurative*) *All the old hostilities resurfaced when they met again.* **2** [T] ~ **sth** to put a new surface on a road, path, etc.

re·sur·gence /rɪˈsɜrdʒəns/ *noun* [sing., U] the return and growth of an activity that had stopped

re·sur·gent /rɪˈsɜrdʒənt/ *adj.* [usually before noun] (*formal*) becoming stronger or more popular again

res·ur·rect /ˌrɛzəˈrɛkt/ *verb* **1** ~ **sth** to bring back into use something, such as a belief, a practice, etc., that had disappeared or been forgotten **SYN** REVIVE **2** ~ **sb** to bring a dead person back to life **SYN** RAISE FROM THE DEAD

res·ur·rec·tion /ˌrɛzəˈrɛkʃn/ *noun* **1 the Resurrection** [sing.] (in the Christian religion) the time when Jesus Christ returned to life again after his death; the time when all dead people will become alive again, when the world ends **2** [U, sing.] a new beginning for something that is old or that had disappeared or become weak

re·sus·ci·tate /rɪˈsʌsɪˌteɪt/ *verb* ~ **sb/sth** to make someone start breathing again or become conscious again after they have almost died **SYN** REVIVE: *He had a heart attack and all attempts to resuscitate him failed.* ◆ (*figurative*) *efforts to resuscitate the economy* ▸ **re·sus·ci·ta·tion** /rɪˌsʌsɪˈteɪʃn/ *noun* [U]: *frantic attempts at resuscitation* ➡ *see also* MOUTH-TO-MOUTH RESUSCITATION

re·tail¹ /ˈriteɪl/ *noun, adv., verb* ➡ *see also* RETAIL² *verb*
- *noun* [U] the selling of goods to the public, usually through stores: *The recommended retail price is $9.99.* ◆ *department stores and other retail outlets* ◆ *the retail trade* ➡ *compare* WHOLESALE ▸ **re·tail** *adv.*: *to buy/sell retail* (= in a store)
- *verb* **1** [T] ~ **sth** to sell goods to the public, usually through stores: *The company manufactures and retails its own range of sportswear.* **2** [I] ~ **at/for sth** (*business*) to be sold at a particular price: *The book retails at $14.95.*

re·tail² /ˈriteɪl; rɪˈteɪl/ *verb* ~ **sth (to sb)** (*formal*) to tell people about something, especially about a person's behavior or private life **SYN** RECOUNT¹: *She retailed the neighbors' activities with relish.* ➡ *see also* RETAIL¹

re·tail·er /ˈriteɪlər/ *noun* a person or business that sells goods to the public

re·tail·ing /ˈriteɪlɪŋ/ *noun* [U] the business of selling goods to the public, usually through stores: *career opportunities in retailing* ➡ *compare* WHOLESALING

retail ˈtherapy *noun* [U] (*usually humorous*) the act of going shopping and buying things in order to make yourself feel more cheerful: *I was ready for a little retail therapy.* ➡ *collocations at* SHOPPING

re·tain 🔑 **AWL** /rɪˈteɪn/ *verb* (*somewhat formal*)
1 ~ **sth** to keep something; to continue to have something **SYN** PRESERVE: *to retain your independence* ◆ *He struggled to retain control of the situation.* ◆ *The house retains much of its original charm.* ◆ *She retained her tennis title for the third year.* **2** ~ **sth** to continue to hold or contain something: *a soil that retains moisture* ◆ *This information is no longer retained within the computer's main memory.* ◆ (*figurative*) *She has a good memory and finds it easy to retain facts.* **3** ~ **sb/sth** (*law*) if a member of the public **retains** someone such as a lawyer, he or she pays money regularly or in advance so the lawyer, etc. will do work for him or her when it is needed: *a retaining fee* ◆ *to retain the services of a lawyer* ➡ *see also* RETENTION, RETENTIVE

re·tain·er **AWL** /rɪˈteɪnər/ *noun* **1** a sum of money that is paid to someone to make sure they will be available to do work when they are needed: *The agency will pay you a monthly retainer.* **2** a device that keeps a person's teeth straight after they have had treatment with BRACES **3** (*old-fashioned*) a servant, especially one who has been with a family for a long time

re·tain·ing **AWL** /rɪˈteɪnɪŋ/ *adj.* [only before noun] (*technical*) intended to keep something in the correct position: *a retaining wall* (= one that keeps the earth or water behind it in position)

re·take *verb, noun*
- *verb* /ˌriˈteɪk/ (**re·took** /-ˈtʊk/, **re·tak·en** /-ˈteɪkən/) **1** ~ **sth** (especially of an army) to take control of something such as a town again: *Government forces moved in to retake the city.* ◆ (*figurative*) *Moore fought back to retake the lead later in the race.* **2** ~ **sth** to take an exam or a test again, usually after failing it the first time
- *noun* /ˈriteɪk/ **1** the act of filming a scene in a movie again, because it was not right before **2** an exam or a test that is taken for a second time: *Students are only allowed one retake.*

re·tal·i·ate /rɪˈtæliˌeɪt/ *verb* [I] to do something harmful to someone because they have harmed you first **SYN** TAKE REVENGE: ~ **(against sb/sth)** *to retaliate against an attack* ◆ ~ **(by doing sth/with sth)** *The boy hit his sister, who retaliated by kicking him.* ▸ **re·tal·i·a·to·ry** /rɪˈtæliəˌtɔri/ *adj.*: *retaliatory action*

re·tal·i·a·tion /rɪˌtæliˈeɪʃn/ *noun* [U] ~ **(against sb/sth) (for sth)** action that a person takes against someone who has harmed them in some way **SYN** REPRISAL: *retaliation against U.N. workers* ◆ *The shooting may have been in retaliation for the arrest of the terrorist suspects.*

re·tard *verb* /rɪˈtɑrd/ ~ **sth** (*formal*) to make the development or progress of something slower **SYN** DELAY, SLOW DOWN: *The progression of the disease can be retarded by early surgery.* ▸ **re·tar·da·tion** /ˌritɑrˈdeɪʃn/ *noun* [U]: *Many factors can lead to growth retardation in unborn babies.*

re·tard·ed /rɪˈtɑrdəd/ adj. (old-fashioned, offensive) less developed mentally than is normal for a particular age

retch /retʃ/ verb [I] to make sounds and movements as if you are vomiting (VOMIT) although you do not actually do so: *The smell made her retch.*

re·tell /ˌriˈtɛl/ verb (re·told, re·told /-ˈtoʊld/) ~ sth to tell a story again, often in a different way

re·ten·tion AWL /rɪˈtɛnʃn/ noun [U] (formal) **1** the action of keeping something rather than losing it or stopping it: *The company needs to improve its training and retention of staff.* **2** the action of keeping liquid, heat, etc. inside something rather than letting it escape: *Eating too much salt can cause fluid retention.* **3** the ability to remember things: *Visual material aids the retention of information.* ⊃ see also RETAIN

re·ten·tive AWL /rɪˈtɛntɪv/ adj. (of the memory) able to store facts and remember things easily ⊃ see also RETAIN

re·test /ˌriˈtɛst/ verb ~ sb/sth to test someone or something again: *Subjects were retested one month later.*

re·think /ˌriˈθɪŋk/ verb (re·thought, re·thought /-ˈθɔt/) [T, I] ~ (sth) to think again about an idea, a course of action, etc., especially in order to change it: *to rethink a plan* ▸ **re·think** /ˈriθɪŋk/ (also re·think·ing) noun [sing.]: *a radical rethink of company policy*

ret·i·cent /ˈrɛtəsnt/ adj. unwilling to tell people about things **SYN** RESERVED, UNCOMMUNICATIVE: *She was shy and reticent.* ♦ ~ **about sth** *He was extremely reticent about his personal life.* ▸ **ret·i·cence** /ˈrɛtəsns/ noun [U] (formal)

re·tic·u·lat·ed /rɪˈtɪkyəˌleɪtəd/ adj. (technical) built, arranged, or marked like a net or network, with many small squares or sections

ret·i·cule /ˈrɛtɪˌkyul/ noun (old use) a woman's small bag, usually made of cloth and with a string that can be pulled tight to close it

ret·i·na /ˈrɛtnˌə/ noun (pl. ret·i·nas or ret·i·nae /ˈrɛtnˌi/) a layer of TISSUE at the back of the eye that is sensitive to light and sends signals to the brain about what is seen ⊃ picture at BODY ▸ **ret·i·nal** /ˈrɛtnˌəl/ [usually before noun], adj.

ret·i·nue /ˈrɛtnˌu/ noun a group of people who travel with an important person to provide help and support **SYN** ENTOURAGE

re·tire 🔑 /rɪˈtaɪər/ verb
> FROM JOB **1** [I, T] to stop doing your job, especially because you have reached a particular age or because you are ill; to tell someone they must stop doing their job: ~ **(from sth)** *She was forced to retire early from teaching because of health problems.* ♦ *She retired at 65, as required by company policy.* ♦ ~ **to sth** *My dream is to retire to a villa in the Caribbean.* ♦ ~ **as sth** *He has no plans to retire as editor of the magazine.* ♦ ~ **sb** *She was retired from the civil service on medical grounds.*
> IN SPORTS **2** [I] to stop competing during a game, race, etc., usually because you are injured: ~ **(from sth)** *She fell badly, spraining her ankle, and had to retire.* ♦ + adj. *He retired injured in the first five minutes of the game.*
> FROM/TO A PLACE **3** [I] (formal) to leave a place, especially to go somewhere quieter or more private: *The jury retired to consider the evidence.* ♦ ~ **to sth** *After dinner he likes to retire to his study.*
> OF ARMY **4** [I] (formal) to move back from a battle in order to organize your soldiers in a different way
> GO TO BED **5** [I] (literary) to go to bed: *I retired late that evening.*
> IN BASEBALL **6** [T] ~ **sb** to make a player or team have to stop their turn at BATTING: *He retired twelve batters in a row.*
> FROM USE/SERVICE **7** [T] ~ **sth** to withdraw something from use or service: *The cruise ship was retired in 2001.* ♦ *Mickey Mantle's jersey number 7 was retired in 1969* (= no longer used, as a sign of respect).

re·tired 🔑 /rɪˈtaɪərd/ adj.
having retired from work: *a retired doctor* ♦ *Dad is retired now.*

re·tir·ee /rɪˌtaɪəˈri/ noun a person who has stopped working because of their age

re·tire·ment 🔑 /rɪˈtaɪərmənt/ noun
1 [U, C] the fact of stopping work because you have reached a particular age; the time when you do this: *At 60, he was approaching retirement.* ♦ *Susan is going to take early retirement* (= retire before the usual age). ♦ *retirement age* ♦ *a retirement party* ⊃ collocations at JOB **2** [U, sing.] the period of your life after you have stopped work at a particular age: *to provide for retirement* ♦ *We all wish you a long and happy retirement.* ♦ *Up to a third of one's life is now being spent in retirement.* ⊃ collocations at AGE **3** [U] ~ **(from sth)** the act of stopping a particular type of work, especially in sports, politics, etc.: *He announced his retirement from football.* ♦ *She came out of retirement to win two gold medals at the championships.*

re·tirement com·mu·nity noun a group of homes for older or retired people, with nearby facilities offering activities and services: *My parents' retirement community has its own golf course.*

re·tirement ˌhome noun a place where elderly people live and are cared for

re·tirement ˌplan noun = PENSION PLAN

re·tir·ing /rɪˈtaɪərɪŋ/ adj. preferring not to spend time with other people **SYN** SHY: *a quiet, retiring man*

re·told pt, pp of RETELL

re·tool /ˌriˈtul/ verb **1** [T, I] ~ **(sth)** to replace or change the machines or equipment in a factory so that it can produce new or better goods **2** [T] ~ **sth** (informal) to organize something in a new or different way

re·tort /rɪˈtɔrt/ verb, noun
• verb to reply quickly to a comment, in an angry, offended, or humorous way: + speech *"Don't be ridiculous!" Pat retorted angrily.* ♦ ~ **that…** *Sam retorted that it was my fault as much as his.*
• noun **1** a quick, angry, or humorous reply **SYN** REJOINDER, RIPOSTE: *She bit back* (= stopped herself from making) *a sharp retort.* **2** a closed bottle with a long, narrow, bent SPOUT that is used in a laboratory for heating chemicals ⊃ picture at LABORATORY

re·touch /ˌriˈtʌtʃ/ verb ~ sth to make small changes to a picture or photograph so that it looks better

re·trace /rɪˈtreɪs/ verb **1** ~ **sth** to go back along exactly the same path or route that you have come along: *She turned around and began to retrace her steps toward the house.* **2** ~ **sth** to make the same trip that someone else has made in the past: *They are hoping to retrace the epic voyage of Christopher Columbus.* **3** ~ **sth** to find out what someone has done or where they have been: *Detectives are trying to retrace her movements on the night she disappeared.*

re·tract /rɪˈtrækt/ verb **1** [T] ~ **sth** (formal) to say that something you have said earlier is not true or correct, or that you did not mean it: *He made a false confession, which he later retracted.* ♦ *They tried to persuade me to retract my words.* **2** [T] ~ **sth** (formal) to refuse to keep an agreement, a promise, etc.: *to retract an offer* **3** [I, T] (technical) to move back into the main part of something; to pull something back into the main part of something: *The animal retracted into its shell.* ♦ ~ **sth** *The landing gear was fully retracted.*

re·tract·a·ble /rɪˈtræktəbl/ adj. that can be moved or pulled back into the main part of something: *a knife with a retractable blade*

re·trac·tion /rɪˈtrækʃn/ noun (formal) **1** [C] a statement saying that something you previously said or wrote is not true: *He demanded a full retraction of the allegations against him.* **2** [U] (technical) the act of retracting something (= pulling it back): *the retraction of a cat's claws*

re·train /ˌriˈtreɪn/ verb [I, T] to learn, or to teach someone, a new type of work, a new skill, etc.: ~ **(sb) (as sth)** *She retrained as a teacher.* ♦ ~ **sb to do sth** *Staff have been* *retrained to use the new technology.* ▶ **re·train·ing** *noun* [U]

re·tread *noun, verb*
● **noun** /ˈriːtrɛd/ **1** a tire made by putting a new rubber surface on an old tire **2** (*disapproving*) a book, movie, song, etc. that contains ideas that have been used before
● **verb** /ˌriːˈtrɛd/ **1** (re·tread·ed, re·tread·ed) ~ **sth** to put a new rubber surface on an old tire **2** (re·tread·ed, re·tread·ed or re·trod /ˌriːˈtrɑd/, re·trod·den /ˌriːˈtrɑdn/) ~ **sth** (*disapproving*) to make a new version of a book, movie, etc., usually one that is not as interesting as the original: *The author retreads an old and familiar story.*

re·treat /rɪˈtriːt/ *verb, noun*
● **verb**
> FROM DANGER/DEFEAT **1** [I] to move away from a place or an enemy because you are in danger or because you have been defeated: *The army was forced to retreat after suffering heavy losses.* ♦ *We retreated back down the mountain.* **ANT ADVANCE**
> MOVE AWAY/BACK **2** [I] to move away or back **SYN RECEDE:** *He watched her retreating figure.* ♦ *The flood waters slowly retreated.*
> CHANGE DECISION **3** [I] + **adv./prep.** to change your mind about something because of criticism or because a situation has become too difficult **SYN BACK OFF:** *The government had retreated from its pledge to reduce class sizes.*
> TO QUIET PLACE **4** [I] (+ **adv./prep.**) to escape to a place that is quieter or safer **SYN RETIRE:** *Bored with the conversation, she retreated to her bedroom.* ♦ (*figurative*) *He retreated into a world of fantasy.*
> FINANCE **5** [I] + **noun** to lose value: *Share prices retreated sharply from yesterday's highs.*
● **noun**
> FROM DANGER/DEFEAT **1** [C, usually sing., U] a movement away from a place or an enemy because of danger or defeat: *Napoleon's retreat from Moscow* ♦ *The army was in full retreat* (= retreating very quickly). ♦ *to sound the retreat* (= to give a loud signal for an army to move away) ⊃ collocations at WAR
> ESCAPE **2** [C, usually sing., U] ~ **(from/into sth)** an act of trying to escape from a particular situation to one that you think is safer or more pleasant **SYN ESCAPE:** *Is watching television a retreat from reality?*
> CHANGE OF DECISION **3** [C, usually sing.] an act of changing a decision because of criticism or because a situation has become too difficult: *The Senator made an embarrassing retreat from his earlier position.*
> QUIET PLACE **4** [C] a quiet, private place that you go to in order to get away from your usual life: *a country retreat* **5** [U, C] a period of time when someone stops their usual activities and goes to a quiet place for prayer, thought, etc.; an organized event when people can do this: *He went into retreat and tried to resolve the conflicts within himself.* ♦ *to go on a Buddhist retreat* ♦ *a weeklong retreat to develop teamwork* **IDM** see BEAT *v.*

re·trench /rɪˈtrɛntʃ/ *verb* [I] (*formal*) (of a business, government, etc.) to spend less money; to reduce costs ▶ **re·trench·ment** *noun* [U, C]: *a period of retrenchment*

re·tri·al /ˈriːtraɪəl, ˌriːˈtraɪəl/ *noun* [usually sing.] a new trial of a person whose criminal offense has already been judged once in court

ret·ri·bu·tion /ˌrɛtrəˈbjuːʃn/ *noun* [U] ~ **(for sth)** (*formal*) severe punishment for something seriously wrong that someone has done: *People are seeking retribution for the latest terrorist outrages.* ♦ *fear of divine retribution* (= punishment from God) ▶ **re·trib·u·tive** /rɪˈtrɪbyətɪv/ *adj.* [usually before noun]: *retributive justice*

re·triev·al /rɪˈtriːvl/ *noun* [U] **1** (*formal*) the process of getting something back, especially from a place where it should not be **SYN RECOVERY:** *The ship was buried, beyond retrieval, at the bottom of the sea.* ♦ (*figurative*) *By then the situation was beyond retrieval* (= impossible to put right). **2** (*computing*) the process of getting back information that is stored on a computer: *methods of information retrieval*

re·trieve /rɪˈtriːv/ *verb* **1** (*formal*) to bring or get something back, especially from a place where it should not be **SYN RECOVER:** ~ **sth from sb/sth** *She bent to retrieve her comb from the floor.* ♦ ~ **sth** *The police have been able to retrieve some of the stolen money.* **2** (*computing*) to find and get back data or information that has been stored in the memory of a computer: ~ **sth from sb/sth** *to retrieve information from the database* ♦ ~ **sth** *The program allows you to retrieve items quickly by searching under a keyword.* **3** ~ **sth** to make a bad situation better; to get back something that was lost: *You can only retrieve the situation by apologizing.* ▶ **re·triev·a·ble** /rɪˈtriːvəbl/ *adj.* **ANT IRRETRIEVABLE**

re·triev·er /rɪˈtriːvər/ *noun* a large dog used in hunting to bring back birds that have been shot ⊃ see also GOLDEN RETRIEVER

re·tro /ˈrɛtroʊ/ *adj.* using styles or fashions from the recent past: *the current Seventies retro trend*

retro- /ˈrɛtroʊ; -trə/ *prefix* (in nouns, adjectives, and adverbs) back or backward: *retrograde* ♦ *retrospectively*

ret·ro·ac·tive /ˌrɛtroʊˈæktɪv/ (also **ret·ro·spec·tive**) *adj.* (of a new law or decision) intended to take effect from a particular date in the past rather than from the present date: *retroactive legislation* ♦ *retroactive pay increases* ▶ **ret·ro·ac·tive·ly** *adv.*: *The ruling will be applied retroactively.*

re·trod *pt of* RETREAD *v.* (2)

re·trod·den *pp of* RETREAD *v.* (2)

ret·ro·fit /ˈrɛtroʊˌfɪt/ *verb* (-tt-) ~ **sth** to put a new piece of equipment into a machine that did not have it when it was built; to provide a machine with a new part, etc.: *Voice recorders were retrofitted into planes already in service.* ♦ *They retrofitted the plane with improved seating.* ▶ **ret·ro·fit** *noun*

ret·ro·flex /ˈrɛtrəˌflɛks/ *adj.* **1** (*medical*) (of a part of the body) turned backward **2** (*phonetics*) (of a speech sound) produced with the end of the tongue turned up against the hard PALATE

ret·ro·grade /ˈrɛtrəˌgreɪd/ *adj.* (*formal, disapproving*) (of an action) making a situation worse or returning to how something was in the past: *The closure of the factory is a retrograde step.*

ret·ro·gres·sive /ˌrɛtrəˈgrɛsɪv/ *adj.* (*formal, disapproving*) returning to old-fashioned ideas or methods instead of making progress **ANT PROGRESSIVE**

ret·ro·nym /ˈrɛtrənɪm/ *noun* a new name that is given to something that has existed for a long time, in order to distinguish it from a more modern development: *The list of retronyms includes acoustic guitar, manual typewriter, silent movie and landline phone.*

ret·ro·spect /ˈrɛtrəˌspɛkt/ *noun*
IDM in retrospect thinking about a past event or situation, often with a different opinion of it from the one you had at the time: *In retrospect, I think that I was wrong.* ♦ *The decision seems extremely odd, in retrospect.*

ret·ro·spec·tion /ˌrɛtrəˈspɛkʃn/ *noun* [U] (*formal*) thinking about past events or situations

ret·ro·spec·tive /ˌrɛtrəˈspɛktɪv/ *adj., noun*
● **adj.** **1** thinking about or connected with something that happened in the past **2** = RETROACTIVE ▶ **ret·ro·spec·tive·ly** *adv.*: *She wrote retrospectively about her childhood.* ♦ *The new rule will be applied retrospectively.*
● **noun** a public exhibition of the work that an artist has done in the past, showing how his or her work has developed

ret·ro·vi·rus /ˈrɛtroʊˌvaɪrəs/ *noun* any of a group of viruses that includes HIV. Retroviruses multiply by making changes to DNA. ⊃ see also ANTI-RETROVIRAL

re·try /ˌriːˈtraɪ/ *verb* (re·tries, re·try·ing, re·tried, re·tried) **1** [T] ~ **sb/sth** to examine a person or case again in court **2** [I] to make another attempt to do something, especially on a computer

ret·si·na /rɛtˈsiːnə/ *noun* [U, C] a type of red or white wine from Greece that is given a special flavor with RESIN

re·turn /rɪˈtɜrn/ verb, noun

● **verb**

> **COME/GO BACK 1** [I] to come or go back from one place to another: *I waited a long time for him to return.* ◆ **~ (to…) (from…)** *She's returning to China after she finishes college in the United States.* ◆ *I returned from work to find the house empty.* ◆ *When did she return home from the trip?*

> **BRING/GIVE BACK 2** [T] to bring, give, put, or send something back to someone or something: **~ sb/sth to sb/sth** *We had to return the hair dryer to the store because it was faulty.* ◆ *I have to return some books to the library.* ◆ **~ sth** *Don't forget to return my pen!* ◆ **~ sb/sth + adj.** *I returned the letter unopened.*

> **OF FEELING/QUALITY 3** [I] to come back again **SYN** REAPPEAR, RESURFACE: *The following day the pain returned.* ◆ *Her suspicions returned when things started disappearing again.*

> **TO PREVIOUS SUBJECT/ACTIVITY 4** [I] **~ (to sth)** to start discussing a subject you were discussing earlier, or doing an activity you were doing earlier: *He returns to this topic later in the report.* ◆ *She looked up briefly then returned to her sewing.* ◆ *The doctor may allow her to return to work next week.*

> **TO PREVIOUS STATE 5** [I] **~ to sth** to go back to a previous state: *Train service returned to normal after the strike.*

> **DO/GIVE THE SAME 6** [T] **~ sth** to do or give something to someone because they have done or given the same to you first; to have the same feeling about someone that they have about you: *to return a favor/greeting/stare* ◆ *She phoned him several times but he was too busy to return her call.* ◆ *It's time we returned their invitation* (= invited them to something as they invited us to something first). ◆ *He did not return her love.* ◆ *"You were both wonderful!" "So were you!" we said, returning the compliment.* ◆ *to return fire* (= to shoot at someone who is shooting at you)

> **IN TENNIS, ETC. 7** [T] **~ sth** to hit the ball back to your opponent during a game: *to return a serve/shot*

> **A VERDICT 8** [T] **~ a verdict** to give a decision about something in court: *The jury returned a verdict of not guilty.*

> **PROFIT 9** [T] **~ sth** (*business*) to give or produce a particular amount of money as a profit: *to return a high rate of interest* ◆ *Last year the company returned a profit of $100 million.*

● **noun**

> **COMING BACK 1** [sing.] **~ (to…) (from…)** the action of arriving in or coming back to a place that you were in before: *He was met by his brother on his return from Italy.* ◆ *I saw the play on its return to Broadway.* ◆ *on the return flight/trip*

> **GIVING/SENDING BACK 2** [U, sing.] the action of giving, putting, or sending something or someone back: *We would appreciate the prompt return of books to the library.* ◆ *The judge ordered the return of the child to his mother.*

> **OF FEELING/STATE 3** [sing.] **~ (of sth)** the situation when a feeling or state that has not been experienced for some time starts again **SYN** REAPPEARance: *the return of spring* ◆ *a return of my doubts*

> **TO PREVIOUS SITUATION/ACTIVITY 4** [sing.] **~ to sth** the action of going back to an activity or a situation that you used to do or be in: *his return to power* ◆ *They appealed for a return to work* (= after a strike).

> **PROFIT 5** [U, C] the amount of profit that you get from something **SYN** EARNINGS, YIELD: *a high rate of return on capital* ◆ *farmers seeking to improve returns from their crops*

> **OFFICIAL REPORT 6** [C] an official report or statement that gives particular information to the government or another body: *census returns* ◆ *election returns* (= the number of votes for each candidate in an election) ⊃ see also TAX RETURN

> **TICKET 7** [C] a ticket for the theater or a sports game that was bought by someone but is given back to be sold again

> **ON COMPUTER 8** [U] (also **reˈturn key** [C]) the button that you press on a computer when you reach the end of an instruction, or to begin a new line: *To exit this option, press return.*

> **IN TENNIS, ETC. 9** [C] the action of hitting the ball, etc. back to your opponent: *a powerful return of serve*

IDM **in return (for sth) 1** as a way of thanking someone or paying them for something they have done: *Can I buy you lunch in return for your help?* **2** as a response or reaction to something: *I asked her opinion, but she just asked me a question in return.* ⊃ more at HAPPY, POINT n.

---

re·turn·a·ble /rɪˈtɜrnəbl/ adj. **1** that can or must be given back after a period of time: *A returnable deposit is payable on arrival.* ◆ *Sale merchandise is not returnable.* **2** (of bottles and containers) that can be taken back to a store in order to be used again **ANT** NONRETURNABLE

reˌturn adˈdress noun the address that a letter should be returned to if it cannot be delivered: *Write your return address in the upper left-hand corner of the envelope.*

re·turn·ee /rɪˌtərˈni/ noun [usually pl.] a person who returns to their own country, after living in another country

reˌturn ˈgame (also **reˌturn ˈmatch**) noun a second game or match between the same two players or teams

reˈturn key noun [C] = RETURN n. (8)

reˌturn ˈmail noun [U] mail that is sent as a reply or response to something: *This is where the return mail is received and read.* ◆ *Please reply to this letter by return mail* (= as soon as possible).

reˌturn ˈvisit noun a trip to a place that you have been to before, or a trip to see someone who has already come to see you: *This hotel is worth a return visit.* ◆ *The President is making a return visit to Moscow.*

re·u·ni·fy /ˌriˈyunəˌfaɪ/ verb (re·u·ni·fies, re·u·ni·fy·ing, re·u·ni·fied, re·u·ni·fied) [often passive] **~ sth** to join together two or more regions or parts of a country so that they form a single political unit again ▶ **re·u·ni·fi·ca·tion** /ˌriˌyunəfəˈkeɪʃn/ noun [U]: *the reunification of Germany*

re·un·ion /riˈyunyən/ noun **1** [C] a social occasion or party attended by a group of people who have not seen each other for a long time: *a family reunion* ◆ *the school's annual reunion* ◆ *a reunion of the class of '85* **2** [C, U] **~ (with sb)** | **~ (between A and B)** the act of people coming together after they have been apart for some time: *an emotional*

| t tea | t̬ butter | d did | k cat | g got | tʃ chin | dʒ June | f fall |

reunion between mother and son ◆ *Christmas is a time of reunion.* **3** [U] the action of becoming a single group or organization again: *Some have advocated the reunion of the Church of England with the Church of Rome.*

re·u·nite /ˌriyuˈnaɪt/ *verb* **1** [T, I, usually passive] to bring two or more people together again after they have been separated for a long time; to come together again: **~ A with/and B** *Last night she was reunited with her children.* ◆ **~ (sb)** *The family was reunited after the war.* ◆ *There have been rumors that the band will reunite for a world tour.* **2** [T, I] **~ (sth)** to join together again separate areas or separate groups within an organization, a political party, etc.; to come together again: *As leader, his main aim is to reunite the country.*

re·us·a·ble /ˌriˈyuzəbl/ *adj.* that can be used again: *reusable plastic bottles*

re·use /ˌriˈyuz/ *verb* **~ sth** to use something again: *Please reuse your envelopes.* ▶ **re·use** /ˌriˈyus/ *noun* [C, U]: *multiple reuses* ◆ *the reuse of wastewater*

rev /rɛv/ *verb, noun*
● *verb* (-vv-) [T, I] **~ (sth) (up)** when you rev an engine or it revs, it runs quickly: *The taxi driver revved up his engine.* ◆ *I could hear the car revving outside.*
● *noun* (*informal*) a complete turn of an engine, used when talking about an engine's speed **SYN** REVOLUTION: *4,000 revs per minute*

Rev. *abbr.* (used before a name) REVEREND: *Rev. Walter Johnson*

re·val·ue /ˌriˈvælyu/ *verb* **1** [T] **~ sth** to estimate the value of something again, especially giving it a higher value **2** [T, I] **~ (sth)** to increase the value of the money of a country when it is exchanged for the money of another country: *The yen is to be revalued.* **ANT** DEVALUE ▶ **re·val·u·a·tion** /ˌriˌvælyuˈeɪʃn/ *noun* [U, C, usually sing.]: *the revaluation of the dollar*

re·vamp /ˌriˈvæmp/ *verb* **~ sth** to make changes to the form of something, usually to improve its appearance ▶ **re·vamp** /ˈrivæmp/ *noun* [sing.] **re·vamp·ing** *noun* [U, sing.]: *The whole house needs a revamping if we're ever going to sell it.*

re·vanch·ism /rɪˈvænˌtʃɪzəm; -ˈvanˌʃɪzəm/ *noun* [U] a policy of attacking someone who has attacked you, especially by a country in order to get back land

re·veal 🔑 **AWL** /rɪˈvil/ *verb*
1 to make something known to someone **SYN** DISCLOSE: **~ sth (to sb)** *to reveal a secret* ◆ *Details of the murder were revealed by the local paper.* ◆ **~ (that)…** *The report reveals (that) the company experienced a loss of $50 million last year.* ◆ **it is revealed that…** *It was revealed that important evidence had been suppressed.* ◆ **~ how, what, etc.…** *Officers could not reveal how he died.* ◆ **~ sb/sth to be/have sth** *Salted peanuts were recently revealed to be the nation's favorite snack.* ⊃ language bank at EVIDENCE **2** to show something that previously could not be seen **SYN** DISPLAY: **~ sth** *He laughed, revealing a line of white teeth.* ◆ *The door opened to reveal a cozy little room.* ◆ **~ yourself** *She crouched in the dark, too frightened to reveal herself.* ⊃ see also REVELATION, REVELATORY

re·vealed re·li·gion *noun* [U, C] religion that is based on a belief that God has shown himself

re·veal·ing **AWL** /rɪˈvilɪŋ/ *adj.* **1** giving you interesting information that you did not know before: *The document provided a revealing insight into the administration's priorities.* ◆ *The answers the children gave were extremely revealing.* **2** (of clothes) allowing more of someone's body to be seen than usual: *a revealing blouse* ▶ **re·veal·ing·ly** *adv.*: *He spoke revealingly about his problems.*

rev·eil·le /ˈrɛvəli/ *noun* [U] a tune that is played to wake soldiers in the morning; the time when it is played

rev·el /ˈrɛvl/ *verb, noun*
● *verb* (-l-, CanE usually -ll-) [I] to spend time enjoying yourself in a noisy, enthusiastic way

PHR V **'revel in sth** to enjoy something very much: *She was clearly reveling in all the attention.* ◆ **~ doing sth** *Some people seem to revel in annoying others.*
● *noun* [usually pl.] (*literary*) noisy celebrations

rev·e·la·tion **AWL** /ˌrɛvəˈleɪʃn/ *noun* **1** [C] **~ (about/concerning sth)** | **~ (that…)** a fact that people are made aware of, especially one that has been secret and is surprising **SYN** DISCLOSURE: *startling/sensational revelations about her private life* **2** [U] **~ (of sth)** the act of making people aware of something that has been secret **SYN** DISCLOSURE: *The company's financial problems followed the revelation of a major fraud scandal.* **3** [C, U] something that is considered to be a sign or message from God ⊃ collocations at RELIGION ⊃ see also REVEAL
IDM **come as/be a revelation (to sb)** to be a completely new or surprising experience; to be different from what was expected

rev·el·a·to·ry /ˈrɛvələˌtɔri; rəˈvɛlə-/ *adj.* (*formal*) making people aware of something that they did not know before: *a revelatory insight* ⊃ see also REVEAL

rev·el·er (*CanE usually* **rev·el·ler**) /ˈrɛvələr/ *noun* a person who is having fun in a noisy way, usually with a group of other people and often after drinking alcohol

rev·el·ry /ˈrɛvəlri/ *noun* [U] (also **rev·el·ries** [pl.]) noisy fun, usually involving a lot of eating and drinking **SYN** FESTIVITY, MERRYMAKING: *We could hear sounds of revelry from next door.* ◆ *New Year's Eve revelries*

re·venge /rɪˈvɛndʒ/ *noun, verb*
● *noun* [C, U] **1** something that you do in order to make someone suffer because they have made you suffer: *He swore to take (his) revenge on his political enemies.* ◆ *She is seeking revenge for the murder of her husband.* ◆ *The bombing was in revenge for the assassination.* ◆ *revenge attacks/killings* **2** (*sports*) the defeat of a person or team that defeated you in a previous game: *The Yankees wanted to get revenge for their defeat earlier in the season.*
● *verb*
PHR V **re'venge yourself on sb** | **be re'venged on sb** (*literary*) to punish or hurt someone because they have made you suffer: *She vowed to be revenged on them all.* ⊃ note at AVENGE

rev·e·nue **AWL** /ˈrɛvəˌnu/ *noun* [U] (also **rev·e·nues**) the money that a government receives from taxes or that an organization, etc. receives from its business **SYN** RECEIPTS: *a shortfall in tax revenue* ◆ *a slump in oil revenues* ◆ *The company's annual revenues rose by 30%.* ⊃ collocations at BUSINESS ⊃ see also INTERNAL REVENUE SERVICE

re·verb /ˈrivərb; rɪˈvərb/ *noun* [U] a sound effect that can be adjusted by electronic means to give music more or less of an ECHO

re·ver·ber·ate /rɪˈvərbəˌreɪt/ *verb* **1** [I] (of a sound) to be repeated several times as it is reflected off different surfaces **SYN** ECHO: *Her voice reverberated around the canyon walls.* **2** [I] **~ (with/to sth)** (of a place) to seem to shake because of a loud noise: *The hall reverberated with the sound of music and dancing.* **3** [I] (*formal*) to have a strong effect on people for a long time or over a large area: *Repercussions of the case continue to reverberate through the financial world.*

re·ver·ber·a·tion /rɪˌvərbəˈreɪʃn/ *noun* **1** [C, usually pl., U] a loud noise that continues for some time after it has been produced because of the surfaces around it **SYN** ECHO **2** **reverberations** [pl.] the effects of something that happens, especially unpleasant ones that spread among a large number of people **SYN** REPERCUSSION

re·vere /rɪˈvɪr/ *verb* [usually passive] **~ sb (as sth)** (*formal*) to feel great respect or admiration for someone or something **SYN** IDOLIZE

rev·er·ence /ˈrɛvərəns; ˈrɛvrəns/ *noun* [U] **~ (for sb/sth)** (*formal*) a feeling of great respect or admiration for someone or something: *The poem conveys his deep reverence for nature.*

Rev·er·end /ˈrɛvərənd; ˈrɛvrənd/ *adj.* [only before noun]

Reverend (*abbr.* Rev.) the title of a member of the clergy that is also sometimes used to talk to or about one: *Reverend Billy Graham* ◆ *Good morning, Reverend.* ➔ see also RIGHT REVEREND

Reverend ˈMother *noun* a title of respect used when talking to or about a MOTHER SUPERIOR (= the head of a female religious community)

rev·er·ent /ˈrevərənt; ˈrevrənt/ *adj.* (*formal*) showing great respect and admiration **SYN** RESPECTFUL ▶ **rev·er·ent·ly** *adv.*

rev·er·en·tial /ˌrevəˈrenʃl/ *adj.* (*formal*) full of respect or admiration: *His name was always mentioned in almost reverential tones.* ▶ **rev·er·en·tial·ly** /-ʃəli/ *adv.*: *She lowered her voice reverentially.*

rev·er·ie /ˈrevəri/ *noun* [C, U] (*formal*) a state of thinking about pleasant things, almost as though you are dreaming **SYN** DAYDREAM: *She was jolted out of her reverie as the door opened.*

re·vers /rɪˈvɪr/ *noun* (*pl.* **re·vers** /-ˈvɪrz/) (*technical*) the edge of a coat, jacket, etc. that is turned back so that you see the opposite side of it, especially at the LAPEL

re·ver·sal **AWL** /rɪˈvɜrsl/ *noun* **1** [C, U] ~ **(of sth)** a change of something so that it is the opposite of what it was: *a complete/dramatic/sudden reversal of policy* ◆ *the reversal of a decision* ◆ *The governor suffered a total reversal of fortune(s) last week.* **2** [C] a change from being successful to having problems or being defeated: *the team's recent reversal* ◆ *The company's financial problems were only a temporary reversal.* **3** [C, U] an exchange of positions or functions between two or more people: *It's a complete role reversal/reversal of roles* (= for example when a husband takes care of the house and children while the wife works).

re·verse 🔑 **AWL** /rɪˈvɜrs/ *verb, noun, adj.*
- *verb*
> CHANGE TO OPPOSITE **1** [T] ~ **sth** to change something completely so that it is the opposite of what it was before: *to reverse a procedure/process/trend* ◆ *The government has failed to reverse the economic decline.* ◆ *It is sometimes possible to arrest or reverse the disease.* **2** [T] ~ **sth** to change a previous decision, law, etc. to the opposite one: *The Court of Appeals reversed the decision.* **3** [T] ~ **sth** to turn something the opposite way around or change the order of something around: *Writing is reversed in a mirror.* ◆ *You should reverse the order of these pages.*
> EXCHANGE TWO THINGS **4** [T] ~ **sth** to exchange the positions or functions of two things: *It felt as if we had reversed our roles of parent and child.* ◆ *She used to work for me, but our situations are now reversed.*
> YOURSELF **5** [T] ~ **yourself (on sth)** to admit you were wrong or to stop having a particular position in an argument: *He has reversed himself on a dozen issues.*
> VEHICLE **6** [I, T] when a vehicle or its driver **reverses**, or the driver **reverses** a vehicle, the vehicle goes backward: *He reversed around the corner.* ◆ *Caution! This truck is reversing.* ◆ ~ **sth** *Now reverse the car.* ➔ compare BACK *v.*
- *noun*
> OPPOSITE **1** the reverse [sing.] the opposite of what has just been mentioned: *This problem is the reverse of the previous one.* ◆ *Although I expected to enjoy living in the country, in fact the reverse is true.* ◆ *When driving south, the reverse applies.* ◆ *It wasn't easy to persuade her to come— quite the reverse.*
> BACK **2** the reverse [sing.] the back of a coin, piece of material, piece of paper, etc.
> IN VEHICLE **3** (also reˈverse ˈgear) [U] the machinery in a vehicle used to make it move backward: *Put the car in/into reverse.*
> LOSS/DEFEAT **4** [C] (*formal*) a loss or defeat; a change from success to failure **SYN** SETBACK: *Property values have suffered another reverse.* ◆ *a damaging political reverse*
IDM in reverse in the opposite order or way **SYN** BACKWARD: *The secret number is my phone number in reverse.* ◆ *We did a similar trip to yours, but in reverse.* go/put

sth **into reverse** to start to happen, or to make something happen, in the opposite way: *In 2008 economic growth went into reverse.*
- *adj.* [only before noun]
> OPPOSITE **1** opposite to what has been mentioned: *to travel in the reverse direction* ◆ *The winners were announced in reverse order* (= the person in the lowest place was announced first). ◆ *The experiment had the reverse effect of what was intended.*
> BACK **2** opposite to the front: *Iron the garment on the reverse side.*

re·verse discriˈmiˈnation *noun* [U] (*disapproving*) the practice of making sure that a particular number of jobs, etc. are given to people from groups that are often treated unfairly because of their race, sex, etc. even when this means being unfair to people from groups, such as white people, who have had advantages in the past **HELP** The term **reverse discrimination** is almost always used in a disapproving way; to describe this policy in a way that is not necessarily disapproving use **affirmative action**.

reˌverse engiˈneering *noun* [U] the copying of another company's product after examining it carefully to find out how it is made

re·vers·i·ble **AWL** /rɪˈvɜrsəbl/ *adj.* **1** (of clothes, materials, etc.) that can be turned inside out and worn or used with either side showing: *a reversible jacket* **2** (of a process, an action, or a disease) that can be changed so that something returns to its original state or situation: *Is the trend toward higher rates of bankruptcy reversible?* ◆ *reversible kidney failure* **ANT** IRREVERSIBLE ▶ **re·vers·i·bil·i·ty** /rɪˌvɜrsəˈbɪləti/ *noun* [U]

re·ver·sion /rɪˈvɜrʒn/ *noun* **1** [U, sing.] ~ **(to sth)** (*formal*) the act or process of returning to a former state or condition: *a reversion to traditional farming methods* **2** [U, C] (*law*) the return of land or property to someone: *the reversion of Hong Kong to China*

re·vert /rɪˈvɜrt/ *verb*
PHR V reˈvert to sb/sth (*law*) (of property, rights, etc.) to return to the original owner again reˈvert to sth (*formal*) **1** to return to a former state; to start doing something again that you used to do in the past: *After her divorce she reverted to her maiden name.* ◆ *His manner seems to have reverted to normal.* ◆ *Try not to revert to your old eating habits.* **2** to return to an earlier topic or subject: *So, to revert to your earlier question…* ◆ *The conversation kept reverting to the events of March 6th.*

re·vet·ment /rɪˈvetmənt/ *noun* (*technical*) stones or other material used to make a wall stronger, hold back a bank of earth, etc.

re·view 🔑 /rɪˈvyu/ *noun, verb*
- *noun* **1** [U, C] an examination of something, with the intention of changing it if necessary: *a review of the state's education policy* ◆ *The case is subject to judicial review.* ◆ *His parole application is up for review next week.* ◆ *The terms of the contract are under review.* ◆ *a wage/salary review* ◆ *a review body/date/panel* **2** [C, U] a report in a newspaper or magazine, or on the Internet, television, or radio, in which someone gives their opinion of a book, play, movie, etc.; the act of writing this kind of report: *a book review* ◆ *the review section of the paper* ◆ *good/bad/mixed/rave reviews in the press* ◆ *He submitted his latest novel for review.* ➔ collocations at LITERATURE **3** [C] a report on a subject or on a series of events: *a review of customer complaints* ◆ *to publish a review of recent cancer research* **4** [C] (*formal*) a ceremony that involves an official INSPECTION of soldiers, etc. by an important visitor **5** [C] a class or period of time in which you look again at something you have studied, especially in order to prepare for an exam
- *verb* **1** ~ **sth** to carefully examine or consider something again, especially so that you can decide whether any changes need to be made **SYN** REASSESS: *to review the evidence* ◆ *The governor will review the situation later in the year.* ➔ thesaurus box at EXAMINE **2** ~ **sth** to think about past events, for example to try to understand why they

happened **SYN** TAKE STOCK OF: *to review your failures and triumphs* ◆ *She had been reviewing the previous week on her way home.* **3** ~ **sth** to write a report of a book, play, movie, etc. in which you give your opinion of it: *The play was reviewed in the newspaper.* **4** ~ **sb/sth** to make an official INSPECTION of a group of soldiers, etc. in a military ceremony **5** ~ **sth** to look again at something you have studied, especially in order to prepare for an exam **6** ~ **sth** to check a piece of work to see if there are any mistakes

re·view·er /rɪ'vyuər/ *noun* **1** a person who writes reviews of books, movies, or plays **2** a person who examines or considers something carefully, for example to see if any changes need to be made

re·vile /rɪ'vaɪl/ *verb* [usually passive] ~ **sb (for sth/for doing sth)** (*formal*) to criticize someone or something in a way that shows how much you dislike them: *He was reviled in the press for his angry outbursts.*

re·vise 🔑 **AWL** /rɪ'vaɪz/ *verb*
1 [T] ~ **sth** to change your opinions or plans, for example because of something you have learned: *I can see I'll have to revise my opinion of his abilities now.* ◆ *The government may need to revise its policy in the light of this report.* **2** [T] ~ **sth** to change something, such as a book or an estimate, in order to correct or improve it: *a revised edition of a textbook* ◆ *I'll prepare a revised estimate for you.* ◆ *We may have to revise this figure upward.*

re·vi·sion 🔑 **AWL** /rɪ'vɪʒn/ *noun*
1 [C] a change or set of changes to something: *He made some minor revisions to the report before printing it.* **2** [U, C] the act of changing something, or of examining something with the intention of changing it: *a system in need of revision* ◆ *a revision of trade policies*

re·vi·sion·ism /rɪ'vɪʒə,nɪzəm/ *noun* [U] (often *disapproving, politics*) ideas that are different from, and want to change, the main ideas or practices of a political system, especially Marxism ▶ **re·vi·sion·ist** /-nɪst/ *noun: bourgeois revisionists* **re·vi·sion·ist** *adj.: revisionist historians*

re·vis·it /ˌri'vɪzət/ *verb* **1** ~ **sth** to visit a place again, especially after a long period of time **2** ~ **sth** to return to an idea or a subject and discuss it again: *It's an idea that may be worth revisiting at a later date.*

re·vi·tal·ize /ri'vaɪtl,aɪz/ *verb* ~ **sth** to make something stronger, more active, or more healthy: *measures to revitalize the neighborhood* ▶ **re·vi·tal·i·za·tion** /ri,vaɪtl-ə'zeɪʃn/ *noun* [U]: *the revitalization of the steel industry*

re·viv·al /rɪ'vaɪvl/ *noun* **1** [U, C] an improvement in the condition or strength of something: *the revival of trade* ◆ *an economic revival* ◆ *a revival of interest in folk music* **2** [C, U] the process of something becoming or being made popular or fashionable again: *a religious revival* ◆ *Jazz is enjoying a revival.* **3** [C] a new production of a play, etc. that has not been performed for some time: *the New York City Ballet's revival of Balanchine's "Swan Lake"*

re·viv·al·ism /rɪ'vaɪvə,lɪzəm/ *noun* [U] **1** the process of creating interest in something again, especially religion **2** the practice of using ideas, designs, etc. from the past: *revivalism in architecture*

re·viv·al·ist /rɪ'vaɪvəlɪst/ *noun* a person who tries to make something popular again, especially religion ▶ **re·viv·al·ist** *adj.: revivalist movements* ◆ *a revivalist preacher*

re·vive /rɪ'vaɪv/ *verb* **1** [I, T] to become, or to make someone or something become, conscious or healthy and strong again: *The flowers soon revived in water.* ◆ *The economy is beginning to revive.* ◆ ~ **sb/sth** *The paramedics couldn't revive her.* ◆ *This movie is intended to revive her flagging career.* **2** [T] ~ **sth** to make something start being used or done again: *This quaint custom should be revived.* ◆ *She has been trying to revive the debate over equal pay.* **3** [T] ~ **sth** to produce again a play, etc. that has not been performed for some time: *This 1930s musical is being revived at summer theaters all over the country.* ⊃ see also REVIVAL

re·viv·i·fy /ˌri'vɪvə,faɪ/ *verb* (**re·viv·i·fies, re·viv·i·fy·ing,**

re·viv·i·fied, re·viv·i·fied) ~ **sth** (*formal*) to give new life or health to something **SYN** REVITALIZE

re·vo·ca·tion /ˌrevə'keɪʃn/ *noun* [U, C] (*formal*) the act of canceling a law, etc.: *the revocation of several statutes*

re·voke /rɪ'voʊk/ *verb* ~ **sth** (*formal*) to officially cancel something so that it is no longer valid

re·volt /rɪ'voʊlt/ *noun, verb*
● *noun* [C, U] a protest against authority, especially that of a government, often involving violence; the action of protesting against authority **SYN** UPRISING: *the Peasants' Revolt of 1381* ◆ *to lead/stage a revolt* ◆ *The army quickly crushed the revolt.* ◆ *the biggest revolt this government has ever seen* ◆ *Attempts to negotiate peace ended in armed revolt.* ◆ (*formal*) *The people rose in revolt.*
● *verb* **1** [I] to take violent action against the people in power **SYN** REBEL, RISE UP: *The peasants threatened to revolt.* ◆ ~ **against sb/sth** *Finally the people revolted against the military dictatorship.* ⊃ collocations at WAR ⊃ see also REVOLUTION **2** [I] ~ **(against sth)** to behave in a way that is the opposite of what someone expects of you, especially in protest **SYN** REBEL: *Teenagers often revolt against parental discipline.* **3** [T] ~ **sb** to make you feel horror or disgust **SYN** DISGUST: *All the violence in the movie revolted me.* ◆ *The way he ate his food revolted me.* ⊃ see also REVULSION

re·volt·ing /rɪ'voʊltɪŋ/ *adj.* extremely unpleasant **SYN** DISGUSTING: *a revolting smell* ◆ *a revolting little man* ⊃ thesaurus box at DISGUSTING ▶ **re·volt·ing·ly** *adv.: The room was revoltingly dirty.*

rev·o·lu·tion 🔑 **AWL** /ˌrevə'luʃn/ *noun*
1 [C, U] an attempt, by a large number of people, to change the government of a country, especially by violent action: *a socialist revolution* ◆ *the outbreak of the American Revolution in 1776* ◆ *to start a revolution* ◆ *a country on the brink of revolution* ⊃ collocations at POLITICS ⊃ see also COUNTERREVOLU-TION, REVOLT **2** [C] a great change in conditions, ways of working, beliefs, etc. that affects large numbers of people: *a cultural/social/scientific, etc. revolution* ◆ ~ **in sth** *A revolution in information technology is taking place.* ⊃ see also INDUSTRIAL REVOLUTION **3** [C, U] ~ **(around/on sth)** a complete CIRCULAR movement around a point, especially of one planet around another: *the revolution of the earth around the sun* ⊃ see also REVOLVE **4** (also *informal* **rev**) [C] a CIRCULAR movement made by something fixed to a central point, for example in a car engine: *rotating at 300 revolutions per minute*

rev·o·lu·tion·ary **AWL** /ˌrevə'luʃə,neri/ *adj., noun*
● *adj.* **1** [usually before noun] connected with political revo-lution: *a revolutionary leader* ◆ *revolutionary uprisings* **2** involving a great or complete change: *a revolutionary idea* ◆ *a time of rapid and revolutionary change* **3** **Revolutionary** connected with the American Revolu-tion: *Revolutionary ideals of liberty and democracy*
● *noun* (*pl.* **rev·o·lu·tion·ar·ies**) a person who starts or supports a revolution, especially a political one: *socialist revolutionaries*

the Revo·lutionary War *noun* [sing.] = AMERICAN REVOLUTION

rev·o·lu·tion·ize **AWL** /ˌrevə'luʃə,naɪz/ *verb* ~ **sth** to completely change the way that something is done: *Aerial photography has revolutionized the study of archaeology.*

re·volve /rɪ'vɑlv/ *verb* [I] to go in a circle around a central point: *The fan revolved slowly.* ◆ *The earth revolves on its axis.* **PHR V** **re'volve around sth** to move around something in a circle: *The earth revolves around the sun.* **re'volve around sb/sth** to have someone or something as the main interest or subject: *His whole life revolves around surfing.* ◆ *She thinks that the world revolves around her.* ◆ *The discussion revolved around the question of changing the team's name.*

re·volv·er /rɪ'vɑlvər/ *noun* a small gun that has a container for bullets that turns around so that shots can be fired quickly without someone having to stop to put more bullets in

re·volv·ing /rɪ'vɒlvɪŋ/ adj. [usually before noun] able to turn in a circle: a revolving chair ◆ The theater has a revolving stage.

re·volving 'door noun **1** a type of door in an entrance to a large building that turns around in a circle as people go through it **2** used to talk about a place or an organization that people enter and then leave again very quickly: These schools suffer from a revolving door of young teachers who leave for higher-paying jobs.

re·vue /rɪ'vyu/ noun [C, U] a show in a theater, with songs, dances, jokes, short plays, etc., often about recent events

re·vul·sion /rɪ'vʌlʃn/ noun [U, sing.] ~ (at/against/from sth) (formal) a strong feeling of disgust or horror **SYN** REPUGNANCE: She felt a deep sense of revulsion at the violence. ◆ I started to feel a revulsion against their decadent lifestyle. ◆ Most people viewed the bombings with revulsion. ⟳ see also REVOLT

re·ward 🔑 /rɪ'wɔrd/ noun, verb
- **noun 1** [C, U] a thing that you are given because you have done something good, worked hard, etc.: a financial reward ◆ ~ (for sth/for doing sth) a reward for good behavior ◆ You deserve a reward for being so helpful. ◆ Winning the game was just reward for the effort the team made. ◆ The company is now reaping the rewards of their investments. **2** [C] an amount of money that is offered to someone for helping the police to find a criminal or for finding something that is lost: A $500 reward has been offered for the return of the necklace. **IDM** see VIRTUE
- **verb** [often passive] to give something to someone because they have done something good, worked hard, etc.: ~ sb for sth She was rewarded for her efforts with a cash bonus. ◆ ~ sb for doing sth He rewarded us handsomely (= with a lot of money) for helping him. ◆ ~ sb with sth She started singing to the baby and was rewarded with a smile. ◆ ~ sb/sth Our patience was finally rewarded.

re·ward·ing /rɪ'wɔrdɪŋ/ adj. **1** (of an activity, etc.) worth doing; that makes you happy because you think it is useful or important: a rewarding experience/job ⟳ thesaurus box at SATISFYING **2** producing a lot of money **SYN** PROFITABLE: Teaching is not very financially rewarding (= is not very well paid). **ANT** UNREWARDING

re·wind /ˌri'waɪnd/ verb (re·wound, re·wound /-'waʊnd/) [T, I] ~ (sth) to make a tape in a CASSETTE player, etc. go backward

'rewind button noun a button that you press to make a tape in a CASSETTE player, etc. go backward: Hit the rewind button and listen to the song again.

re·wire /ˌri'waɪər/ verb ~ sth to put new electrical wires into a building or piece of equipment

re·word /ˌri'wərd/ verb ~ sth to write something again using different words in order to make it clearer or more acceptable ▶ **re·word·ing** noun [C, U]

re·work /ˌri'wərk/ verb ~ sth to make changes to something in order to improve it or make it more suitable ▶ **re·work·ing** noun [C, U]: The movie is a reworking of the Frankenstein story.

re·writ·a·ble /ˌri'raɪtəbl/ adj. (computing) able to be used again for different data: a rewritable CD

re·write /ˌri'raɪt/ verb (re·wrote /-'roʊt/, re·writ·ten /-'rɪtn/) ~ sth to write something again in a different way, usually in order to improve it or because there is some new information: I intend to rewrite the story for younger children. ◆ This essay will have to be completely rewritten. ◆ an attempt to rewrite history (= to present historical events in a way that shows or proves what you want them to) ▶ **re·write** /'riraɪt/ noun

r.h. abbr. (in writing) RIGHT HAND

rhap·so·dize /'ræpsəˌdaɪz/ verb [I, T] ~ (about/over sth) | + speech (formal) to talk or write with great enthusiasm about something **SYN** GO INTO RAPTURES ABOUT

rhap·so·dy /'ræpsədi/ noun (pl. rhap·so·dies) **1** (often in titles) a piece of music that is full of feeling and is not regular in form: Liszt's Hungarian Rhapsodies **2** (formal) the expression of great enthusiasm or happiness in speech or writing ▶ **rhap·sod·ic** /ræp'sɑdɪk/ adj.

rhe·a /'riə/ noun a large S. American bird that cannot fly

rheme /rim/ noun (linguistics) the part of a sentence or clause that adds new information to what the reader or audience already knows ⟳ compare THEME

rhe·ni·um /'riniəm/ noun [U] (symb. Re) a chemical element. Rhenium is a rare silver-white metal that exists naturally in the ORES of MOLYBDENUM and some other metals.

rhe·sus fac·tor /'risəs ˌfæktər/ noun [sing.] (medical) a substance present in the red blood cells of around 85% of humans. Its presence (**rhesus positive**) or absence (**rhesus negative**) can be dangerous for babies when they are born and for people having BLOOD TRANSFUSIONS.

'rhesus ˌmonkey noun a small S. Asian MONKEY, often used in scientific experiments

rhet·o·ric /'rɛtərɪk/ noun [U] **1** (formal, often disapproving) speech or writing that is intended to influence people, but that is not completely honest or sincere: the rhetoric of political slogans ◆ empty rhetoric **2** (formal) the skill of using language in speech or writing in a special way that influences or entertains people **SYN** ORATORY

rhe·tor·i·cal /rɪ'tɔrɪkl; -'tɑr-/ adj. **1** (of a question) asked only to make a statement or to produce an effect rather than to get an answer: "Don't you care what I do?" he asked, but it was a **rhetorical question**. **2** (formal, often disapproving) (of a speech or piece of writing) intended to influence people, but not completely honest or sincere **3** (formal) connected with the art of RHETORIC: the use of rhetorical devices such as metaphor and irony ▶ **rhe·tor·i·cal·ly** /-kli/ adv.: "Do you think I'm stupid?" she asked rhetorically. ◆ a rhetorically structured essay

rhet·o·ri·cian /ˌrɛtə'rɪʃn/ noun (technical) a person who is skilled in the art of formal rhetoric

rheuˌmatic 'fever noun [U] a serious disease that causes fever with swelling and pain in the joints

rheu·ma·tism /'rumə,tɪzəm/ noun [U] a disease that makes the muscles and joints painful, stiff, and swollen ▶ **rheu·mat·ic** /ru'mætɪk/ adj.: rheumatic pains

rheu·ma·toid ar·thri·tis /ˌrumətɔɪd ɑr'θraɪtəs/ noun [U] (medical) a disease that gets worse over a period of time and causes painful swelling and permanent damage in the joints of the body, especially the fingers, wrists, feet, and ankles

rheu·ma·tol·o·gy /ˌrumə'tɑlədʒi/ noun [U] the study of the diseases of joints and muscles, such as RHEUMATISM and ARTHRITIS

rheum·y /'rumi/ adj. (of the eyes) containing a lot of water

rhine·stone /'raɪnstoʊn/ noun a clear stone that is intended to look like a diamond, used in cheap jewelry

rhi·ni·tis /raɪ'naɪtəs/ noun [U] (medical) a condition in which the inside of the nose becomes swollen and sore, caused by an infection or an ALLERGY

rhi·no /'raɪnoʊ/ noun (pl. rhi·no, rhi·nos) (informal) = RHINOCEROS: black/white rhino ◆ rhino horn

rhi·noc·er·os /raɪ'nɑsərəs/ noun (pl. rhi·noc·er·os or rhi·noc·er·os·es) (also informal rhi·no) a large heavy animal with very thick skin and either one or two horns on its nose, that lives in Africa and Asia

rhinoceros

rhi·zome /'raɪzoʊm/ noun (technical) the thick STEM of some plants, such as IRIS and MINT, that grows along or under the ground and has roots and STEMS growing from it

rho /roʊ/ noun the 17th letter of the Greek alphabet (P, ρ)

Rhodes scholar /ˌroʊdz 'skɑlər/ noun a student from the

U.S., Germany, or the Commonwealth who is given a SCHOLARSHIP to study in Britain at Oxford University from a fund that was started by Cecil Rhodes in 1902

rho·di·um /ˈroʊdiəm/ *noun* [U] (*symb.* **Rh**) a chemical element. Rhodium is a hard silver-white metal that is usually found in PLATINUM.

rho·do·den·dron /ˌroʊdəˈdɛndrən/ *noun* a bush with large red, purple, pink, or white flowers

rhom·boid /ˈrɑmbɔɪd/ *noun* (*geometry*) a flat shape with four straight sides, with only the opposite sides and angles equal to each other ➔ picture at SHAPE

rhom·bus /ˈrɑmbəs/ *noun* (*geometry*) a flat shape with four equal sides and four angles that may not be 90° ➔ picture at SHAPE

rho·tic /ˈroʊtɪk/ *adj.* (*phonetics*) (of an accent) pronouncing the /r/ after a vowel in words like *car*, *early*, etc. General American accents are rhotic.

rhu·barb /ˈrubɑrb/ *noun* [U] the thick red STEMS of a garden plant, also called rhubarb, that are cooked and eaten as a fruit: *rhubarb pie*

rhum·ba = RUMBA

rhyme /raɪm/ *noun, verb*
• *noun* **1** [C] a word that has the same sound or ends with the same sound as another word: *Can you think of a rhyme for "beauty?"* **2** [C] a short poem in which the last word in the line has the same sound as the last word in another line, especially the next one: *children's rhymes and stories* ➔ see also NURSERY RHYME **3** [U] the use of words in a poem or song that have the same sound, especially at the ends of lines: *a poem written in rhyme* • *the poet's use of rhyme* **IDM** **there's no rhyme or reason to/for sth | without rhyme or reason** if there is **no rhyme or reason to** something or it happens **without rhyme or reason**, it happens in a way that cannot be easily explained or understood
• *verb* **1** [I] ~ **(with sth)** if two words, syllables, etc. **rhyme**, or if one **rhymes** with the other, they have or end with the same sound: *"Though" rhymes with "low."* • *"Tough" and "through" don't rhyme.* • *rhyming couplets* **2** [T] ~ **sth (with sth)** to put words that sound the same together, for example when you are writing poetry: *You can rhyme "girl" with "curl."* **3** [I] (of a poem) to have lines that end with the same sound: *I prefer poems that rhyme.*

rhyming slang *noun* [U] a way of talking in which you use words or phrases that rhyme with the word you mean, instead of using that word. For example in COCKNEY rhyming slang "apples and pears" means "stairs."

rhythm 🔑 /ˈrɪðəm/ *noun* [U, C]
1 a strong, regular, repeated pattern of sounds or movements: *to dance to the rhythm of the music* • *music with a fast/slow/steady rhythm* • *jazz rhythms* • *He can't seem to play in rhythm.* • *The boat rocked up and down in rhythm with the water.* • *the rhythm of her breathing* • *a dancer with a natural sense of rhythm* (= the ability to move in time to a fixed beat) **2** a regular pattern of changes or events: *the rhythm of the seasons* • *biological/body rhythms* ➔ see also BIORHYTHM

rhythm and blues *noun* [U] (*abbr.* R & B) a type of music that is a mixture of BLUES and JAZZ and has a strong rhythm

rhythm gui·tar *noun* [U] a GUITAR style that consists mainly of CHORDS played with a strong rhythm ➔ compare LEAD GUITAR

rhyth·mic /ˈrɪðmɪk/ (also *less frequent* **rhyth·mi·cal** /ˈrɪðmɪkl/) *adj.* having a regular pattern of sounds, movements, or events: *music with a fast, rhythmic beat* • *the rhythmic ticking of the clock* ▶ **rhyth·mi·cally** /-kli/ *adv.*

the rhythm method *noun* [sing.] a method of avoiding getting pregnant that involves a woman only having sex during the time of the month when she is unlikely to get pregnant

rhythm section *noun* the part of a band that supplies the rhythm, usually consisting of drums, BASS[1], and sometimes piano

RI *abbr.* (in writing) Rhode Island

ri·a /ˈriə/ *noun* (*technical*) a long narrow area of water formed when a river valley floods

rib /rɪb/ *noun, verb*
• *noun* **1** [C] any of the curved bones that are connected to the SPINE and surround the chest: *a broken/bruised/cracked rib* • *Stop poking me in the ribs!* ➔ picture at BODY ➔ see also RIB CAGE **2** [U, C] a piece of meat with one or more bones from the ribs of an animal ➔ see also SHORT RIBS, SPARE RIB **3** [C] a curved piece of wood, metal, or plastic that forms the frame of a boat, roof, etc. and makes it stronger **4** [C] one of the raised lines in some types of KNITTING, or a pattern of these **IDM** see DIG *v.*
• *verb* (-bb-) ~ **sb (about/over sth)** (*old-fashioned*, *informal*) to laugh at someone and make jokes about them, in a friendly way **SYN** TEASE

rib·ald /ˈrɪbld; ˈraɪbɔld/ *adj.* (of language or behavior) referring to sex in an offensive but humorous way

rib·ald·ry /ˈrɪbəldri/ *noun* [U] language or behavior that refers to sex in an offensive but humorous way

ribbed /rɪbd/ *adj.* (especially of material for clothes) having raised lines: *a ribbed sweater*

rib·bing /ˈrɪbɪŋ/ *noun* **1** [U] a pattern of raised lines in KNITTING or on a surface **2** [C, U] (*old-fashioned*, *informal*) the act of making fun of someone in a friendly way: *We took a ribbing.* • *some good-natured ribbing*

rib·bon /ˈrɪbən/ *noun* **1** [U, C] a narrow strip of material, used to tie things or for decoration: *a present tied with yellow ribbon* • *lengths of velvet ribbon* • *She was wearing two blue silk ribbons in her hair.* ➔ picture at ROPE **2** [C] something that is long and narrow in shape: *The road was a ribbon of moonlight.* **3** [C] a ribbon in special colors, or tied in a special way, that is given to someone as a prize or as a military honor, or that is worn by someone to show that they support a particular cause ➔ picture at MEDAL **4** [C] a long strip of material containing ink that you put into TYPEWRITERS and some computer printers **IDM** **cut/tear, etc. sth to ribbons** to cut/tear, etc. something very badly

ribbon lake *noun* (*technical*) a long narrow lake

rib cage *noun* the structure of curved bones (called RIBS), that surrounds and protects the chest ➔ picture at BODY

rib eye (also **rib-eye steak**) *noun* a piece of beef that is cut from outside the RIBS

ri·bo·fla·vin /ˈraɪbouˌfleɪvən/ *noun* [U] a VITAMIN that is important for producing energy, found in milk, LIVER, eggs, and green vegetables

rib-tickler *noun* (*informal*) a funny joke or story ▶ **rib-tickling** *adj.*

rice 🔑 /raɪs/ *noun* [U]
short, narrow, white or brown grain grown on wet land in hot countries as food; the plant that produces this grain: *a grain of rice* • *boiled/steamed/fried rice* • *long-/short-grain rice* • *brown rice* (= without its outer covering removed) • *rice paddies* (= rice fields) ➔ picture at CEREAL

rice paper *noun* [U] **1** a type of very thin paper that is used for writing and drawing on **2** a type of very thin paper that you can eat, used in cooking, for example for wrapping other food in

rice pudding *noun* [U, C] a DESSERT (= a sweet dish) made from rice cooked with milk and sugar

rich 🔑 /rɪtʃ/ *adj.* (rich·er, rich·est)
› **WITH A LOT OF MONEY 1** having a lot of money or property: *one of the richest women in the world* • *Nobody gets rich from writing nowadays.* • (*slang*) *to be filthy/stinking* (= extremely) *rich* **ANT** POOR **2 the rich** *noun* [pl.] people who have a lot of money or property: *It's a favorite resort for the rich and famous.* **ANT** THE POOR **3** (of a country) producing a lot of wealth so

that many of its people can live at a high standard: *the richest countries/economies/nations* **ANT** POOR

> FULL OF VARIETY **4** very interesting and full of variety: *the region's rich history and culture* ◆ *She leads a rich and varied life.*

> CONTAINING/PROVIDING SOMETHING **5** ~ (in sth) (often in compounds) containing or providing a large supply of something: *Oranges are rich in vitamin C.* ◆ *The area is rich in wildlife.* ◆ *His novels are a rich source of material for the movie industry.* ◆ *iron-rich rocks* **ANT** POOR

> FOOD **6** containing a lot of fat, butter, eggs, etc. and making you feel full quickly: *a rich creamy sauce* ◆ *a rich chocolate cake*

> SOIL **7** containing the substances that make it good for growing plants in **SYN** FERTILE: *a rich well-drained soil* **ANT** POOR

> COLORS/SOUNDS **8** (of colors, sounds, smells, and tastes) strong or deep; very beautiful or pleasing: *rich dark reds*

> EXPENSIVE **9** (*literary*) expensive and beautiful **SYN** SUMPTUOUS: *The rooms were decorated with rich fabrics.*

> CRITICISM **10** (*informal*) used to say that a criticism someone makes is surprising and not reasonable, because they have the same fault: *Me? Lazy? That's rich, coming from you!* ⊃ compare RICHNESS **IDM** see STRIKE *v*.

rich·es /ˈrɪtʃəz/ *noun* [pl.] large amounts of money and valuable or beautiful possessions: *a career that brought him fame and riches* ◆ *material riches* **IDM** see EMBARRASSMENT, RAG *n*.

rich·ly /ˈrɪtʃli/ *adv.* **1** in a beautiful and expensive manner: *a richly decorated room* **2** used to express the fact that something has a pleasant strong color, taste, or smell: *a richly flavored sauce* ◆ *The polished floor glowed richly.* **3** in a

generous way: *She was richly rewarded for all her hard work.* **4** in a way that people think is right and good **SYN** THOROUGHLY: *richly deserved success* ◆ *richly earned respect* **5** used to express the fact that the quality or thing mentioned is present in large amounts: *richly varied countryside* ◆ *a richly atmospheric novel*

rich·ness /ˈrɪtʃnəs/ *noun* [U] the state of being rich in something, such as color, minerals, or interesting qualities: *the richness and variety of marine life* ⊃ compare WEALTH

the Rich·ter scale /ˈrɪktər ˌskeɪl/ *noun* [sing.] a system for measuring how strong an EARTHQUAKE is: *an earthquake measuring 7.3 on the Richter scale*

ri·cin /ˈraɪsn/ *noun* [U] a very poisonous substance obtained from the seeds of the CASTOR OIL plant

rick /rɪk/ *noun* a large pile of HAY or STRAW that is built in a regular shape and covered to protect it from rain

rick·ets /ˈrɪkəts/ *noun* [U] a disease of children caused by a lack of good food that makes the bones become soft and badly formed, especially in the legs

rick·et·y /ˈrɪkəti/ *adj.* not strong or well made; likely to break: *a rickety chair*

rick·shaw /ˈrɪkʃɔ/ *noun* a small, light vehicle with two wheels used in some Asian countries to carry passengers. The rickshaw is pulled by someone walking or riding a bicycle.

ric·o·chet /ˈrɪkəˌʃeɪ/ *verb, noun*

● *verb* (ric·o·chet·ing /-ˌʃeɪɪŋ/, ric·o·cheted, ric·o·cheted /-ˌʃeɪd/) [i] + adv./prep. (of a moving object) to hit a surface and come off it fast at a different angle: *The bullet ricocheted off a nearby wall.*

● *noun* **1** [C] a ball, bullet, or stone that ricochets: *A protester was killed by a ricochet (bullet).* **2** [U] the action of ricocheting: *the ricochet of bricks and bottles off police riot shields*

ri·cot·ta /rɪˈkɑtə/ *noun* [U] a type of soft white Italian cheese

ric·tus /ˈrɪktəs/ *noun* (*formal*) a wide twisted or smiling mouth that does not look natural or relaxed

rid /rɪd/ *verb* (rid·ding, rid, rid)

IDM **be rid of sb/sth** (*formal*) to be free of someone or something that has been annoying you or that you do not want: *She wanted to be rid of her parents and their authority.* ◆ *I was glad to be rid of the car when I finally sold it.* **get rid of sb/sth** to make yourself free of someone or something that is annoying you or that you do not want; to throw something away: *Try and get rid of your visitors before I get there.* ◆ *The problem is getting rid of nuclear waste.* ◆ *I can't get rid of this headache.* ◆ *We got rid of all the old furniture.*

PHR V **'rid sb/sth of sb/sth** (*formal*) to remove something that is causing a problem from a place, group, etc.: *We will need to take further measures to rid our streets of crime.* **'rid yourself of sb/sth** (*formal*) to make yourself free from someone or something that is annoying you or causing you a problem: *to rid yourself of guilt* ◆ *He wanted to rid himself of the burden of the secret.*

rid·dance /ˈrɪdns/ *noun* [U]

IDM **good riddance (to sb/sth)** an unkind way of saying that you are pleased that someone or something has gone: *"Goodbye and good riddance!" she said to him angrily as he left.*

rid·den /ˈrɪdn/ *adj.* (usually in compounds) full of a particular unpleasant thing: *a disease-ridden slum* ◆ *a class-ridden society* ◆ *She was guilt-ridden at the way she had treated him.* ◆ *She was ridden with guilt.* ⊃ see also RIDE *v*.

rid·dle /ˈrɪdl/ *noun, verb*

● *noun* **1** a question that is difficult to understand, and that has a surprising answer, that you ask someone as a game: *Stop talking in riddles* (= saying things that are confusing) — *say what you mean.* ◆ *to solve the riddle of the Sphinx* **2** a mysterious event or situation that you cannot explain **SYN** MYSTERY: *the riddle of her husband's murder*

● *verb* [usually passive] ~ sb/sth (with sth) to make a lot of holes in someone or something: *The car was riddled with bullets.*

IDM **be riddled with sth** to be full of something, especially something bad or unpleasant: *His body was riddled with cancer.* ◆ *Her typing was slow and riddled with mistakes.*

ride /raɪd/ *verb, noun*

● *verb* (**rode** /roʊd/, **rid·den** /ˈrɪdn/)

▷ HORSE **1** [I, T] to sit on a horse, etc. and control it as it moves: *I learned to ride as a child.* ◆ + *adv./prep.* *They rode along narrow country lanes.* ◆ *He was riding on a large black horse.* ◆ ~ *sth* *She had never ridden a horse before.* ◆ *He's ridden six winners so far this year* (= in horse racing).

▷ BICYCLE/MOTORCYCLE **2** [T, I] to sit on and control a bicycle, motorcycle, etc. or to stand on a SNOWBOARD and move on it: ~ *sth* (+ *adv./prep.*) *The boys were riding their bikes around the streets.* ◆ *He rode a Harley Davidson.* ◆ (+ *adv./prep.*) *The ground there is too rough to ride over.*

▷ IN VEHICLE **3** [I, T] to travel in a vehicle, especially as a passenger: (+ *adv./prep.*) *I walked back while the others rode in the car.* ◆ ~ *sth* (+ *adv./prep.*) *to ride the subway/an elevator, etc.* ◆ *She rode the bus to school every day.*

▷ ON WATER/AIR **4** [I, T] to float or be supported on water or air: (+ *adv./prep.*) *We watched the balloon riding high above the fields.* ◆ ~ *sth* *surfers riding the waves*

▷ GO THROUGH AREA **5** [T] ~ *sth* to go through or over an area on a horse, bicycle, etc.: *We rode the mountain trails.*

▷ CRITICIZE **6** [T] ~ *sb* to criticize or TEASE someone in an annoying way: *Why is everybody riding me today?*

IDM **be riding for a fall** to be doing something that involves risks and that may end in disaster **be riding high** to be successful or very confident **let sth ride** to decide to do nothing about a problem that you know you may have to deal with later **ride the crest of sth** to enjoy great success or support because of a particular situation or event: *The band is riding the crest of its last tour.* **ride herd on sb/sth** (*informal*) to keep watch or control over someone or something: *police riding herd on crowds of youths on the streets* **ride shotgun** (*informal*) to ride in the front passenger seat of a car or truck **ride a/the wave of sth** to enjoy or be supported by the particular situation or quality mentioned: *Schools are riding a wave of renewed public interest.* ⊃ more at WISH *n.*

PHR V ˈ**ride on sth** (usually used in the progressive tenses) to depend on something: *My whole future is riding on this interview.* ˌ**ride sth↔ˈout** to manage to survive a difficult situation or time without having to make great changes ˌ**ride ˈup** (of clothing) to move gradually upward, out of position: *Short skirts tend to ride up when you sit down.*

● *noun*

▷ IN VEHICLE **1** a short journey in a vehicle, on a bicycle, etc.: *a train ride through beautiful countryside* ◆ *It's a ten-minute bus ride from here to town.* ◆ *Steve gave me a ride on his motorcycle.* ◆ *We went for a ride on our bikes.* ◆ *a bike ride* **2** a free trip in a car, etc. to a place you want to get to: *She hitched a ride to the bus station.* ◆ *We were able to get a ride into town when we missed the bus.* **3** the kind of trip you make in a car, etc.: *a smooth/comfortable/bumpy, etc. ride* ◆ (*figurative*) *The new legislation faces a bumpy ride* (= will meet with opposition and difficulties).

▷ ON HORSE **4** a short trip on a horse, etc.: *a pony ride* ◆ *The kids had a ride on an elephant at the zoo.* ◆ *He goes for a ride almost every morning.*

▷ AT AMUSEMENT PARK/FAIR **5** a large machine at an AMUSEMENT PARK, etc. that you ride on for fun or excitement; an occasion when you go on one of these: *The rides are free.* ◆ *a roller coaster ride*

IDM **come/go along for the ride** (*informal*) to join in an activity for pleasure but without being seriously interested in it **have a rough/an easy ride | give sb a rough/an easy ride** (*informal*) to experience/not experience difficulties when you are doing something; to make things difficult/easy for someone: *He's going to have a rough ride at the board meeting next week.* **take sb for a ride** (*informal*) to cheat or trick someone: *It's not a nice feeling to discover that someone you trusted has taken you for a ride.* ⊃ more at FREE *adj.*

rid·er /ˈraɪdər/ *noun*

1 a person who rides a horse, bicycle, motorcycle, or SNOWBOARD: *Three riders* (= people riding horses) *were approaching.* ◆ *horses and their riders* ◆ *She's an experienced rider.* ◆ *The road was full of joggers and bike riders.* **2** ~ (**to sth**) an extra piece of information that is added to an official document

ridge /rɪdʒ/ *noun, verb*

● *noun* **1** a narrow area of high land along the top of a line of hills; a high pointed area near the top of a mountain: *walking along the ridge* ◆ *the northeast ridge of Mount Everest* **2** a raised line on the surface of something; the point where two sloping surfaces join: *The ridges on the soles of my boots stopped me from slipping.* ◆ *the ridge of the roof* **3** ~ (**of high pressure**) (*technical*) a long narrow area of high pressure in the atmosphere ⊃ compare TROUGH

● *verb* [usually passive] ~ *sth* to make narrow raised lines or areas on the surface of something

ridged /rɪdʒd/ *adj.* (of an object or area) with raised lines on the surface

rid·i·cule /ˈrɪdəˌkjuːl/ *noun, verb*

● *noun* [U] unkind comments that make fun of someone or something, or make them or it look silly **SYN** MOCKERY: *She is an object of ridicule in the tabloid newspapers.* ◆ *to hold someone up to ridicule* (= make fun of someone publicly)

● *verb* ~ *sb/sth* to make someone or something look silly by laughing at them or it in an unkind way **SYN** MAKE FUN OF

ri·dic·u·lous /rɪˈdɪkyələs/ *adj.*

very silly or unreasonable **SYN** ABSURD, LUDICROUS: *I look ridiculous in this hat.* ◆ *Don't be ridiculous! You can't pay $75 for a T-shirt!* ▶ **ri·dic·u·lous·ly** *adv.*: *The meal was ridiculously expensive.* **ri·dic·u·lous·ness** *noun* [U] **IDM** see SUBLIME *n.*

rid·ing /ˈraɪdɪŋ/ *noun*

1 [U] = HORSEBACK RIDING: *I'm taking riding lessons.* ◆ *riding boots* **2** (*CanE*) [C] a district that elects its own representative to a state or federal government ⊃ see also CONSTITUENCY (1)

rife /raɪf/ *adj.* [not before noun] **1** if something bad or unpleasant is **rife** in a place, it is very common there **SYN** WIDESPREAD: *It is a country where corruption is rife.* ◆ *Rumors are rife that he is going to resign.* **2** ~ (**with sth**) full of something bad or unpleasant: *Los Angeles is rife with gossip about the stars' private lives.*

riff /rɪf/ *noun* a short repeated pattern of notes in popular music or JAZZ

rif·fle /ˈrɪfl/ *verb* [I, T] to turn over papers or the pages of a book quickly and without reading them all **SYN** LEAF: ~ **through sth** *He was riffling through the papers on his desk.* ◆ ~ *sth* *to riffle the pages of a book*

riff-raff /ˈrɪf ræf/ *noun* [U] (*disapproving*) an insulting way of referring to people of low social class or people who are not considered socially acceptable

ri·fle /ˈraɪfl/ *noun, verb*

● *noun* a gun with a long BARREL that you hold to your shoulder to fire

● *verb* **1** [I, T] ~ (**through**) **sth** to search quickly through something in order to find or steal something: *She rifled through her clothes for something suitable to wear.* **2** [T] ~ *sth* if you rifle something, you steal something from it: *His wallet had been rifled.* **3** [T] ~ *sth* + *adv./prep.* to hit, throw, or kick a ball very hard and straight

ri·fle·man /ˈraɪflmən/ *noun* (*pl.* **ri·fle·men** /-mən/) a soldier who carries a rifle

ˈ**rifle ˌrange** *noun* **1** [C] a place where people practice shooting with rifles **2** [U] the distance that a bullet from a rifle will travel

rift /rɪft/ *noun* **1** a serious disagreement between people that stops their relationship from continuing **SYN** BREACH, DIVISION: *The rift within the party deepened.* ◆ *Efforts to heal the rift between the two countries have failed.* ⊃ collocations at

INTERNATIONAL **2** a large crack or opening in the ground, rocks, or clouds

'rift ˌvalley *noun* a valley with steep sides formed when two parallel cracks develop in the earth's surface and the land between them sinks

rig /rɪg/ *verb, noun*
● *verb* (-gg-) [usually passive] **1** ~ sth to arrange or influence something in a dishonest way in order to get the result that you want **SYN** FIX: *He said the election was rigged.* ◆ *to rig the market* (= to cause an artificial rise or fall in prices, in order to make a profit) **2** ~ sth (with sth) to provide a ship or boat with ropes, sails, etc.; to fit the sails, etc. in position **3** ~ sth (up) (with sth) to fit equipment somewhere, sometimes secretly: *The lights were rigged (up) but not yet tested.* ◆ *The car had been rigged with about 300 lbs of explosive.* **PHR V** ˌrig sb/sth/yourself↔'out (in/with sth) [often passive] (*old-fashioned*) to provide someone or something with a particular kind of clothes or equipment: *I was accepted for the job and rigged out in a clown costume.* ˌrig sth↔'up to make or to build something quickly, using whatever materials are available: *We managed to rig up a shelter for the night.*
● *noun* **1** (especially in compounds) a large piece of equipment that is used for taking oil or gas from the ground or the bottom of the ocean: *an oil rig* **2** the way that the MAST and sails on a boat, etc. are arranged **3** (*informal*) = TRACTOR-TRAILER **4** equipment that is used for a special purpose: *a CB radio rig*

rig·a·ma·role /'rɪgəməˌroul/ *noun* [U, sing.] = RIGMAROLE

rig·a·to·ni /ˌrɪgə'touni/ *noun* [U] PASTA in the shape of short hollow tubes with RIDGES

rig·ging /'rɪgɪŋ/ *noun* [U] **1** the ropes that support the MAST and sails of a boat or ship **2** the act of influencing something in a dishonest way in order to get the result that you want: *vote rigging*

right 🗝 /raɪt/ *adj., adv., noun, verb, exclamation*
● *adj.*
▷ **MORALLY GOOD 1** [not usually before noun] ~ (to do sth) morally good or acceptable; correct according to law or a person's duty: *You were quite right to criticize him.* ◆ *Is it ever right to kill?* ◆ *It seems only right to warn you of the risk.* ◆ *I hope we're doing the right thing.* **ANT** WRONG
▷ **TRUE/CORRECT 2** true or correct as a fact: *Did you get the answer right?* ◆ *"David, isn't it?" "Yes, that's right."* ◆ (*informal*) *It was Monday you went to see Angie, right?* ◆ *Let me get this right* (= understand correctly) —*you want us to do an extra ten hours' work for no extra pay?* **ANT** WRONG ⊃ thesaurus box at TRUE
3 correct for a particular situation or thing, or for a particular person: *Have you got the right change* (= the exact amount) *for the bus fare?* ◆ *Is this the right way to the beach?* ◆ *You're not holding it the right way.* ◆ *Next time we'll get it right.* ◆ *He's the right man for the job.* ◆ *I'm glad you split up. She wasn't right for you.* ◆ *I was waiting for the right moment to ask him.* ◆ *She knows all the right people* (= important people, for example those who can help her career). ◆ *His success was due to being in the right place at the right time* (= being able to take opportunities when they came). **ANT** WRONG **4** [not before noun] correct in your opinion or judgment: ~ (about sth) *She was right about Tom having no money.* ◆ ~ (to do sth) *You're right to be cautious.* ◆ *"It's not easy." "Yeah, you're right."* ◆ ~ (in doing sth) *Am I right in thinking we've met before?* **ANT** WRONG
▷ **NORMAL 5** [not before noun] in a normal or good enough condition: *I just don't feel right today* (= I feel sick). ◆ *That sausage doesn't smell right.* ◆ *Things aren't right between her parents.* ◆ *If only I could have helped put things right.* ◆ *He's not quite right in the head* (= not mentally normal). **ANT** WRONG
▷ **NOT LEFT 6** [only before noun] of, on, or toward the side of the body that is toward the east when a person faces north: *my right eye* ◆ *Stay on the right side of the road.* ◆ *Take a right turn at the intersection.* ⊃ see also RIGHT-WING **ANT** LEFT
⊃ see also ALL RIGHT ▸ **right·ness** *noun* [U]: *the rightness* (= justice) *of their cause* ◆ *the rightness of his decision*

IDM give your right arm for sth/to do sth (*informal*) used to say that someone is willing to give up a lot in order to have or do something that they really want: *I'd have given my right arm to be there with them.* (not) in your right mind (not) mentally normal ⊃ thesaurus box at CRAZY (as) right as rain (*informal*) in excellent health or condition right on **1** correct or true: *I think his analysis is right on.* **2** (*informal, old-fashioned*) used to express strong approval or encouragement: *Right on, man!* right side out with the part that is usually outside facing you, in the correct way for wearing: *I had to turn some of the clothes right side out after washing them.* right side up with the top part turned to the top; in the correct, normal position: *I dropped my toast, but luckily it fell right side up.* **ANT** UPSIDE DOWN ⊃ more at FOOT *n.*, HEAD *n.*, HEART, IDEA, MIGHT *n.*, MR., NOTE *n.*, PUSH *v.*, SIDE *n.*, TRACK *n.*
● *adv.*
▷ **EXACTLY 1** exactly; directly: *Lee was standing right behind her.* ◆ *The wind was right in our faces.* ◆ *The bus came right on time.*
▷ **COMPLETELY 2** all the way; completely: *The car spun right off the track.* ◆ *She kept right on swimming until she reached the other side.*
▷ **IMMEDIATELY 3** (*informal*) immediately; without delay: *I'll be right back.* ◆ *I'll be right with you* (= I am coming very soon).
▷ **CORRECTLY 4** correctly: *You guessed right.* **ANT** WRONG
▷ **SATISFACTORILY 5** in the way that things should happen or are supposed to happen: *Nothing's going right for me today.* **ANT** WRONG
▷ **NOT LEFT 6** on or to the right side: *Turn right at the end of the street.* **ANT** LEFT
IDM right and left (*informal*) everywhere or in large amounts: *They were handing out samples right and left.* right away/off immediately; without delay: *I want it sent right away.* ◆ *I told him right off what I thought of him.* right now **1** at this moment: *He's not in the office right now.* **2** immediately: *Do it right now!* right off the bat (*informal*) immediately; without delay: *We liked each other right off the bat.* ⊃ more at ALLEY, SERVE *v.*, WINDOW
● *noun*
▷ **SOMETHING MORALLY GOOD 1** [U, C] what is morally good or correct: *She doesn't understand the difference between right and wrong.* ◆ *You did right to tell me about it.* ◆ *He wouldn't apologize. He knew he was in the right* (= had justice on his side). ◆ *It was difficult to establish the rights and wrongs* (= the true facts) *of the matter.* **ANT** WRONG
▷ **MORAL/LEGAL CLAIM 2** [C, U] a moral or legal claim to have or get something or to behave in a particular way: ~ (to sth) *Everyone has a right to a fair trial.* ◆ ~ (to do sth) *You have no right to stop me from going in there.* ◆ *What gives you the right to do that?* ◆ *She had every right to be angry.* ◆ *You're quite within your rights to ask for your money back.* ◆ *By rights* (= if justice were done) *half the money should be mine.* ◆ *There is no right of appeal against the decision.* ◆ *The property belongs to her by right.* ◆ *They had fought hard for equal rights.* ⊃ see also ANIMAL RIGHTS, CIVIL RIGHTS, HUMAN RIGHT
▷ **FOR BOOK/MOVIE, ETC. 3** rights [pl.] the authority to perform, publish, film, etc. a particular work, event, etc.: *He sold the rights for $2 million.* ◆ *all rights reserved* (= protected or kept for the owners of the book, movie, etc.)
▷ **NOT LEFT SIDE 4** the/someone's right [sing.] the right side or direction: *Take the first street on the right.* ◆ *She seated me on her right.* **ANT** LEFT **5** [sing.] the first, second, etc. ~ the first, second, etc. road on the right side: *Take the first right, then the second left.* **ANT** LEFT **6** a right [sing.] a turn to the right: *to make a right* ◆ (*informal*) *to hang a right* **ANT** LEFT
▷ **POLITICS 7** the right, the Right [sing.] political groups that most strongly support traditional and conservative social, financial, and religious views ⊃ compare RIGHT WING: *He felt that the Republican Party had been taken over by the Right.* **ANT** LEFT **8** the right [sing.] the part of a political party whose members are most conservative: *He's on the right of the Democratic Party.* **ANT** LEFT
▷ **IN BOXING 9** a blow that is made with your right hand: *He hit him with a right to the jaw.* **ANT** LEFT

---

h **h**at   m **m**an   n **n**o   ŋ si**ng**   l **l**eg   r **r**ed   y **y**es   w **w**et

IDM **do right by sb** (*informal*) to treat someone fairly and make sure that they have all they need or want: *You won't have to worry about money—I'll do right by you.* **in your own right** because of your personal qualifications or efforts, not because of your connection with someone else **put/set sb/ sth to rights** to put things in their right places or right order: *It took us ages to put things to rights after the hurricane.* ⊃ more at DEAD *adj.*, WRONG *n.*

● **verb**
❯ RETURN TO POSITION **1** ~ **sb/sth/yourself** to return someone or something/yourself to the normal, vertical position: *They learned to right a capsized canoe.* ◆ *At last the plane righted itself and flew on.*
❯ CORRECT **2** ~ **sth** to correct something that is wrong or not in its normal state **SYN** PUT RIGHT: *Righting the economy will demand major cuts in expenditure.*
IDM **right a wrong** to do something to correct an unfair situation or something bad that you have done

● **exclamation** (*informal*) **1** used to show that you accept a statement or an order: *"You may find it hurts a little at first." "Right." ◆ "Barry's here." "Oh, right."* **2** used to check that someone agrees with you or has understood you: *There were twenty of them, right?* **3** used to get someone's attention, to say that you are ready to do something, or to tell them to do something: *Right! Let's get going.* **4** (*ironic*) used to say that you do not believe someone, or that you disagree with them: *"I won't be late tonight." "Yeah, right."*

right ˈ**angle** *noun* an angle of 90°: *Place the table at a right angle to the wall.* ⊃ picture at SHAPE ⊃ compare ACUTE ANGLE, OBLIQUE ANGLE, OBTUSE ANGLE, REFLEX ANGLE

ˌright-ˈangled *adj.* having or consisting of a right angle

ˌright ˈbrain *noun* [U, sing.] the right side of the human brain, which is thought to be used for creating new ideas and to be where emotions come from ⊃ compare LEFT BRAIN

ˈright-click *verb* [T, I] ~ sth | ~ (on sth) to choose a particular function or item on a computer screen, etc., by pressing the button on a mouse that is on the right side

right·eous /ˈraɪtʃəs/ *adj.* (*formal*) **1** morally right and good: *a righteous God* **2** that you think is morally acceptable or fair: *righteous anger/indignation, etc.* ⊃ see also SELF-RIGHTEOUS ▶ **right·eous·ly** *adv.* **right·eous·ness** *noun* [U]

ˌright ˈfield *noun* (in baseball) the part of the field to the right of the player who is hitting the ball (the BATTER)

ˌright ˈfielder *noun* (in baseball) the player who defends right field

right·ful /ˈraɪtfl/ *adj.* [only before noun] (*formal*) that is correct, right, or legal **SYN** PROPER: *The stolen car was returned to its rightful owner.* ▶ **right·ful·ly** /-fəli/ *adv.*: *She was only claiming what was rightfully hers.*

ˈright-hand *adj.* [only before noun] **1** on the right side of something: *on the right-hand side of the road* ◆ *the top right-hand corner of the screen* **2** intended for use by your right hand: *a right-hand glove* **ANT** LEFT-HAND

ˌright-ˈhanded *adj.* **1** a person who is **right-handed** uses their right hand for writing, using tools, etc. **2** a **right-handed** tool is designed to be used with the right hand **ANT** LEFT-HANDED ▶ ˌright-ˈhanded *adv.*

ˌright-ˈhander *noun* **1** a person who uses their right hand for writing, using tools, etc. **2** a hit with the right hand **ANT** LEFT-HANDER

ˌright-hand ˈman *noun* [sing.] a person who helps someone a lot and who they rely on, especially in an important job: *the President's right-hand man*

right·ist /ˈraɪtɪst/ *noun* a person who supports RIGHT-WING political parties and their ideas **SYN** RIGHT-WINGER **ANT** LEFTIST ▶ **right·ist** *adj.*

right·ly 🔊 /ˈraɪtli/ *adv.*
1 for a good reason: *The school was rightly proud of its many successful graduates.* ◆ *He was proud of his beautiful house, and rightly so.* ◆ *Quite rightly, the environment is of great concern.* **2** in a correct or accurate way **SYN** CORRECTLY: *Rightly or wrongly, many older people are afraid of violence in the streets.* ◆ *As she rightly pointed out, the illness can affect adults as well as children.* ◆ *I can't rightly say what happened.* ◆ *I don't rightly know where he's gone.* ◆ *If I remember rightly, there's a bus at six o'clock.* ⊃ note at RIGHT

ˌright-ˈminded (also ˌright-ˈthinking) *adj.* (of a person) having beliefs and opinions that most people approve of

right·most /ˈraɪtmoʊst/ *adj.* [only before noun] farthest to the right

ˌright-of-ˈcenter (CanE usually ˌright-of-ˈcentre) *adj.* = CENTER-RIGHT

ˌright of ˈway (also ˌright-of-ˈway) *noun* (*pl.* ˌrights of ˈway, ˌrights-of-ˈway) **1** [U] the right to drive across or into a road before another vehicle: *I had the right of way at the intersection.* ◆ *Whose right of way is it?* **2** [U] legal permission to go onto or through another person's land: *Private property—no right of way.* **3** [C] a public path that goes through private land

ˈrights ˌissue *noun* (*business*) an offer to buy shares in a company at a cheaper price to people who already own some shares in it

right·size /ˈraɪtsaɪz/ *verb* [I, T] ~ (sth) (*business*) to change the size of a company in order to reduce costs, especially by reducing the number of employees

ˌright-ˈthinking *adj.* = RIGHT-MINDED

,right-to-'life *adj.* [only before noun] opposed to ABORTION **SYN** PRO-LIFE: *protests by right-to-life groups*

,right 'triangle *noun* a triangle with a RIGHT ANGLE ⊃ picture at SHAPE

right·ward /ˈraɪtwərd/ *adj.* **1** on or to the right: *a rightward movement* **2** toward more RIGHT-WING political ideas: *a rightward shift in voting patterns* ▸ **right·ward** *adv.*

the ,right 'wing *noun* **1** [sing.] the part of a political party whose members are least in favor of social change: *He is on the right wing of the party.* **2** [C,U] an attacking player or position on the right side of the field in a sports game **ANT** LEFT WING

,right-'wing *adj.* supporting the conservative policies of the political right: *right-wing policies* **ANT** LEFT-WING

,right-'winger *noun* **1** a person on the right wing of a political party: *She is a prominent Republican right-winger.* **2** a person who plays on the right side of the field in a sports game **ANT** LEFT-WINGER

rig·id **AWL** /ˈrɪdʒəd/ *adj.* **1** (often *disapproving*) (of rules, methods, etc.) very strict and difficult to change **SYN** INFLEXIBLE: *The curriculum was too narrow and too rigid.* ♦ *His rigid adherence to the rules made him unpopular.* **2** (of a person) not willing to change their ideas or behavior **SYN** INFLEXIBLE: *rigid attitudes* **3** (of an object or substance) stiff and difficult to move or bend: *a rigid support for the tent* ♦ *She sat upright, her body* **rigid with fear.** ▸ **ri·gid·i·ty** **AWL** /rɪˈdʒɪdəti/ *noun* [U,C]: *the rigidity of the law on this issue* ♦ *the rigidity of the metal bar* **rig·id·ly** **AWL** /ˈrɪdʒədli/ *adv.*: *The speed limit must be rigidly enforced.* ♦ *She stared rigidly ahead.*

rig·ma·role /ˈrɪgməˌroʊl/ (also **rig·a·ma·role**) *noun* [U, sing.] **1** a long and complicated process that is annoying and seems unnecessary: *I couldn't face the whole rigmarole of getting a work permit again.* **2** a long and complicated story

rig·or (*CanE usually* **rig·our**) /ˈrɪgər/ *noun* **1** [U] the fact of being careful and paying great attention to detail: *academic/intellectual/scientific, etc. rigor* **2** [U] (*formal*) the fact of being strict or severe: *This crime must be treated with the full rigor of the law.* **3 the rigors of something** [pl.] the difficulties and unpleasant conditions of something: *The plants were unable to withstand the rigors of a harsh winter.*

rig·or mor·tis /ˌrɪgər ˈmɔrtəs/ *noun* [U] the process by which the body becomes stiff after death

rig·or·ous /ˈrɪgərəs/ *adj.* **1** done carefully and with a lot of attention to detail **SYN** THOROUGH: *a rigorous analysis* **2** demanding that particular rules, processes, etc. are strictly followed **SYN** STRICT: *The work failed to meet their rigorous standards.* ▸ **rig·or·ous·ly** *adv.*: *The country's press is rigorously controlled.*

the Rig Ve·da /ˌrɪg ˈveɪdə/ *noun* [sing.] the oldest and most important of the Vedas (= Hindu holy texts)

rile /raɪl/ *verb* ~ **sb** | **it riles sb that...** to annoy someone or make them angry **SYN** ANGER: *Nothing ever seemed to rile him.*

IDM be/get (all) riled up (*informal*) to be or get very annoyed

Ri·ley /ˈraɪli/ *noun* **IDM** see LIFE

rill /rɪl/ *noun* a shallow channel cut by water flowing over rock or soil

rim /rɪm/ *noun, verb*
● *noun* **1** the edge of something in the shape of a circle: *He looked at them over the rim of his glass.* ♦ *The rims of her eyes were red from crying.* ♦ *glasses with gold rims* ⊃ picture at EDGE **2** the metal edge of a wheel onto which the tire is fastened ⊃ picture at BICYCLE **3 -rimmed** *adj.* having a particular type of rim: *gold-rimmed glasses* ♦ *red-rimmed eyes* (= for example, from crying) ⊃ see also HORN-RIMMED
● *verb* (-mm-) [often passive] ~ **sth** (*formal*) to form an edge around something

rime /raɪm/ *noun* [U] (*literary*) FROST

rim·less /ˈrɪmləs/ *adj.* [only before noun] (of glasses) having

LENSES (= the transparent parts that you look through) that are not surrounded by frames

rind /raɪnd/ *noun* **1** [U] the thick outer skin of some types of fruit: *lemon rind* ⊃ compare PEEL, SKIN, ZEST **2** [U,C] the thick outer skin of some foods such as BACON and some types of cheese ⊃ see also PORK RINDS

rings

boxing ring

diamond ring   key ring

ring¹ 🔊 /rɪŋ/ *noun, verb* ⊃ see also RING²
● *noun*
▸ JEWELRY **1** [C] a piece of jewelry that you wear on your finger, consisting of a round band of gold, silver, etc., sometimes decorated with PRECIOUS STONES: *a gold ring* ♦ *A diamond glittered on her* **ring finger** (= the finger next to the little finger, especially on the left hand). ⊃ see also ENGAGEMENT RING, SIGNET RING, WEDDING RING
▸ CIRCLE **2** [C] an object in the shape of a circle with a large hole in the middle: *a key ring* ♦ *a ring of keys* ♦ *curtain rings* ⊃ picture at SPORT ⊃ see also ONION RING **3** [C] a round mark or shape: *She had dark rings around her eyes from lack of sleep.* ♦ *After the kids' bath, there was a ring of scum around the tub.*
▸ FOR PERFORMANCE/COMPETITION **4** [C] a closed area in which animals or people perform or compete, with seats around the outside for the audience: *a boxing ring* ♦ *a circus ring* ⊃ see also BULLRING
▸ GROUP OF PEOPLE **5** [C] a group of people who are working together, especially in secret or illegally: *a spy ring* ♦ *a drug ring*
IDM run rings around sb (*informal*) to be much better at doing something than someone else ⊃ more at HAT
● *verb* [often passive] (ringed, ringed) ~ **sb/sth (with sth)** to surround someone or something: *Thousands of demonstrators ringed the building.*

ring² /rɪŋ/ *verb, noun* ⊃ see also RING¹
● *verb* (rang /ræŋ/, rung /rʌŋ/)
▸ TELEPHONE **1** [I] (of a telephone) to make a sound because someone is trying to call you: *Will you answer the telephone if it rings?*
▸ BELL **2** [T,I] if you ring a bell or if a bell rings, it produces a sound: ~ **(sth)** *Someone was ringing the doorbell.* ♦ *The church bells rang.* ♦ ~ **for sb/sth** *Just ring for the nurse* (= attract the nurse's attention by ringing a bell) *if you need her.*
▸ WITH SOUND **3** [I] ~ **(with sth)** (*literary*) to be full of a sound; to fill a place with sound **SYN** RESOUND: *The house rang with children's laughter.* ♦ *Applause rang through the concert hall.*
▸ WITH QUALITY **4** [I] ~ **(with sth)** to be full of a particular quality: *His words rang with pride.*
▸ OF EARS **5** [I] to be uncomfortable and be unable to hear

ʌ **cup**   ə **about**   eɪ **say**   aɪ **five**   ɔɪ **boy**   aʊ **now**   oʊ **go**   ər **bird**

clearly, usually because you have heard a loud noise, etc.: *The music was so loud it made my ears ring.* **IDM** **ring a bell** (*informal*) to sound familiar to you, as though you have heard it before: *His name rings a bell but I can't think where we met.* **ring in your ears/head** to make you feel that you can still hear something: *His warning was still ringing in my ears.* **ring off the hook** (usually used in the progressive tenses) (of a telephone) to ring many times: *The phone has been ringing off the hook with offers of help.* **ring true/hollow/false** to give the impression of being sincere/true or not sincere/true: *It may seem like a strange story but it rings true to me.* ➔ more at ALARM *n.*, BELL **PHR V** ,ring 'in sth to ring bells to celebrate something, especially the new year ,ring 'out to be heard loudly and clearly: *A number of shots rang out.* ,ring sth↔'up to enter the cost of goods being bought in a store on a CASH REGISTER by pressing the buttons; to make sales of a particular value: *She rang up all the items on the cash register.* ◆ *The company rang up sales of $166 million last year.*

● **noun**
> OF BELL **1** [C] the sound that a bell makes; the act of ringing a bell: *There was a ring at the door.* ◆ *He gave a couple of loud rings on the doorbell.*
> SOUND **2** [sing.] a loud clear sound: *the ring of horse's hooves on the cobblestones*
> QUALITY **3** [sing.] ~ **(of sth)** a particular quality that words, sounds, etc. have: *His explanation has a ring of truth about it.* ◆ *Her protestation had a hollow ring to it* (= did not sound sincere). ◆ *The story had a familiar ring to it* (= as if I had heard it before).
IDM **give sb a ring** (*informal*) to make a telephone call to someone: *I'll give you a ring tomorrow.* ➔ more at BRASS

,ring a,round the 'rosy *noun* [U] a singing game played by children, in which the players hold hands and dance in a circle, falling down at the end of the song

'ring ,bearer *noun* a person, usually a boy, who carries the rings for the BRIDE and BRIDEGROOM at a wedding

'ring ,binder *noun* a file for holding papers, in which metal rings go through the edges of the pages, holding them in place ➔ picture at STATIONERY

ringed /rɪŋd/ *adj.* [only before noun] **1** having a ring or rings on: *a ringed finger* **2** (especially of an animal or bird) having a mark or marks like a ring on it: *a ringed plover*

ring·er /'rɪŋər/ *noun* **1** = BELL-RINGER **2** a horse or person that takes part in a race illegally, for example by using a false name **IDM** see DEAD *adj.*

ring·ette /rɪŋ'ɛt/ *noun* [U] a Canadian game similar to HOCKEY, played with a straight stick and rubber ring, especially by women

'ring ,finger *noun* the finger next to the smallest one, especially on the left hand, on which a wedding ring is traditionally worn ➔ picture at BODY

ring·ing /'rɪŋɪŋ/ *adj.*, *noun*
● **adj.** [only before noun] **1** (of a sound) loud and clear **2** (of a statement, etc.) powerful and made with a lot of force: *a ringing endorsement of her leadership*
● **noun** [sing., U] an act or a sound of ringing: *There was an unpleasant ringing in my ears.*

ring·lead·er /'rɪŋ,lidər/ *noun* (*disapproving*) a person who leads others in crime or in causing trouble

ring·let /'rɪŋlət/ *noun* [usually pl.] a long curl of hair hanging down from someone's head ➔ picture at HAIR

ring·mas·ter /'rɪŋ,mæstər/ *noun* a person in charge of a CIRCUS performance

ring·side /'rɪŋsaɪd/ *noun* [U] the area closest to the space in which a BOXING match or CIRCUS takes place: *According to law, a doctor must be present at the ringside.* ◆ *a ringside seat*

ring·tone /'rɪŋtoʊn/ *noun* the sound a telephone makes when someone is calling you. Ringtones are often short tunes, and the word is especially used to refer to the different sounds cell phones make when they ring.

ring·toss /'rɪŋtɔs/ *noun* [U] a game in which players try to throw rings over wooden sticks, or over objects in order to win them as prizes

ring·worm /'rɪŋwɜrm/ *noun* [U] an infectious skin disease that produces small red areas shaped like rings

rink /rɪŋk/ *noun* **1** = ICE RINK **2** = SKATING RINK

rink·y-dink /'rɪŋki ,dɪŋk/ *adj.* (*informal*) of poor quality; cheap and/or old-fashioned: *a rinky-dink rhinestone necklace* ◆ *a rinky-dink little town*

rinse /rɪns/ *verb*, *noun*
● **verb** **1** ~ sth to wash something with clean water only, not using soap: *Rinse the cooked pasta with boiling water.* **2** ~ sth to remove the soap from something with clean water after washing it ➔ thesaurus box at CLEAN **3** ~ sth + adv./prep. to remove dirt, etc. from something by washing it with clean water: *She rinsed the mud off her hands.* ◆ *I wanted to rinse the taste out of my mouth.*
PHR V ,rinse sth↔'out to make something clean, especially a container, by washing it with water: *Rinse the cup out before use.*
● **noun** **1** [C] an act of rinsing something: *I gave the glass a rinse.* ◆ *Fabric conditioner is added during the final rinse.* **2** [C, U] a liquid that you put on your hair when it is wet in order to change its color: *a blue rinse* **3** [C, U] a liquid used for cleaning the mouth and teeth

ri·ot /'raɪət/ *noun*, *verb*
● **noun** **1** [C] a situation in which a group of people behave in a violent way in a public place, often as a protest: *One prison guard was killed when a riot broke out in the jail.* ◆ *food/race riots* **2** [sing.] ~ **of sth** (*formal*) a collection of a lot of different types of the same thing: *The garden was a riot of color.* **3** a riot [sing.] (*old-fashioned*, *informal*) a person or an event that is very amusing and enjoyable
IDM **run riot 1** (of people) to behave in a way that is violent and/or not under control **SYN** RAMPAGE: *They let their kids run riot.* **2** if your imagination, a feeling, etc. **runs riot**, you allow it to develop and continue without trying to control it **3** (of plants) to grow and spread quickly ➔ more at READ *v.*
● **verb** [I] (of a crowd of people) to behave in a violent way in a public place, often as a protest ▶ ri·ot·er *noun*: *Rioters set fire to parked cars.* ri·ot·ing *noun* [U]: *Rioting broke out in the capital.*

'riot ,gear *noun* [U] the clothes and equipment used by the police when they are dealing with riots

ri·ot·ous /'raɪətəs/ *adj.* [usually before noun] **1** (*formal*) noisy and/or violent, especially in a public place: *riotous behavior* **2** noisy, exciting, and enjoyable in an uncontrolled way **SYN** UPROARIOUS: *a riotous party* ◆ *riotous laughter*

ri·ot·ous·ly /'raɪətəsli/ *adv.* extremely: *riotously funny*

'riot po,lice *noun* [pl.] police who are trained to deal with people RIOTING

'riot ,shield (also shield) *noun* a piece of equipment made from strong plastic, used by the police to protect themselves from angry crowds

RIP **1** *abbr.* /,ɑr aɪ 'pi/ rest in peace (often written on graves) **2** *noun* /rɪp/ (*computing*) = RASTER IMAGE PROCESSOR

rip /rɪp/ *verb*, *noun*
● **verb** (-pp-) **1** [T, I] to tear something or to become torn, often suddenly or violently: ~ **(sth)** *I ripped my jeans on the fence.* ◆ *The flags had been ripped in two.* ◆ *I heard the tent rip.* ◆ ~ **sth + adj.** *She ripped the letter open.* **2** [T] ~ **sth + adv./prep.** to remove something quickly or violently, often by pulling it: *He ripped off his tie.* ◆ *We ripped the old carpeting off the stairs.* **3** [T] ~ **sth** (*computing*) to copy sound or video files from a Web site or CD on to a computer **4** [T] (*computing*) = RASTERIZE
IDM **let rip (at sb)** (*informal*) to speak or do something with great force, enthusiasm, etc. and without control: *When she gets angry with her boyfriend, she really lets rip at him.* ◆ *The group let rip with a single from their new album.* **let rip | let sth rip** (*informal*) **1** to go or allow something such as a car to go

as fast as possible: *Once on the open road, he let rip.* ♦ *Come on Steve—let her rip.* **2** to do something or to allow something to happen as fast as possible: *This would cause inflation to let rip again.* **rip sb/sth apart/to shreds, etc.** to destroy something; to criticize someone very strongly ⊃ more at HEART, LIMB

PHR V **'rip at sth** to attack something violently, usually by tearing or cutting it ,**rip 'into sb (for/with sth)** to criticize someone and tell them that you are very angry with them ,**rip 'into/'through sb/sth** to go very quickly and violently into or through someone or something: *A bullet ripped into his shoulder.* ,**rip sb**↔**'off** [usually passive] (*informal*) to cheat someone, by making them pay too much, by selling them something of poor quality, etc.: *Tourists complain of being ripped off by local cab drivers.* ⊃ related noun RIP-OFF ,**rip sth**↔**'off** (*informal*) to steal something: *Thieves broke in and ripped off five computers.* ,**rip sth**↔**'up** to tear something into small pieces: *He ripped up the letter and threw it in the fire.*

● **noun** [usually sing.] **1** a long tear in cloth, paper, etc. **2** = RIP CURRENT

ri·par·i·an /rɪˈperiən/ *adj.* [usually before noun] **1** (*technical*) growing in, living in, or relating to areas of wet land near to a river or stream **2** (*law*) on, near, or relating to the bank of a river

rip·cord /ˈrɪpkɔrd/ *noun* the string that you pull to open a PARACHUTE

'**rip ,current** (also rip) *noun* a strong current of water that flows away from the coast

ripe /raɪp/ *adj.* (rip·er, rip·est) **1** (of fruit or crops) fully grown and ready to be eaten **ANT** UNRIPE **2** (of cheese or wine) having a flavor that has fully developed **SYN** MATURE **3** (of a smell) strong and unpleasant **4** ~ (**for sth**) ready or suitable for something to happen: *This land is ripe for development.* ♦ *The conditions were ripe for social change.* ♦ *We'll suggest these changes when the time is ripe.* ▶ **ripe·ness** *noun* [U]
   IDM a/the ripe old age (of...) an age that is considered to be very old: *He lived to the ripe old age of 91.*

rip·en /ˈraɪpən/ *verb* [I, T] ~ (**sth**) to become ripe; to make something ripe

'**rip-off** *noun* (*informal*) **1** [usually sing.] something that is not worth what you pay for it: *$70 for a T-shirt! What a rip-off!* **2** ~ (**of sth**) a copy of something, especially one that is less expensive or not as good as the original thing: *The single is a rip-off of a 70s hit.*

ri·poste /rɪˈpoʊst/ *noun* (*formal*) **1** a quick and often amusing reply, especially to criticism **SYN** RETORT: *a witty riposte* **2** a course of action that takes place in response to something that has happened: *The U.S. delivered an early riposte to the air attack.* ▶ **ri·poste** *verb* + **speech**

ripped /rɪpt/ *adj.* (*informal*) having strong muscles that you can see clearly: *Is your goal to get ripped at the gym?*

rip·per /ˈrɪpər/ *noun* (*informal*) a person who is very good at SNOWBOARDING

ripple

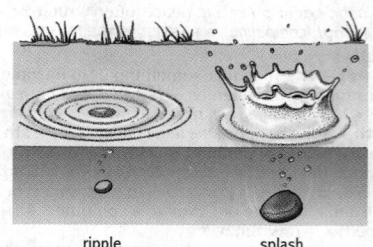

ripple   splash

rip·ple /ˈrɪpl/ *noun, verb*
● **noun** **1** a small wave on the surface of a liquid, especially water in a lake, etc.: *The air was so still that there was hardly a*

ripple on the pond's surface. **2** a thing that looks or moves like a small wave: *ripples of sand* **3** [usually sing.] ~ **of sth** a sound that gradually becomes louder and then quieter again: *a ripple of applause/laughter* **4** [usually sing.] ~ **of sth** a feeling that gradually spreads through a person or group of people: *A ripple of fear passed through him.* ♦ *The announcement sent a ripple of excitement through the crowd.*
● **verb** **1** [I, T] to move or to make something move in very small waves: *The lake rippled in the breeze.* ♦ *rippling muscles* ♦ ~ **sth** *The wind rippled the wheat in the fields.* **2** [I] + **adv./ prep.** (of a feeling, etc.) to spread through a person or a group of people like a wave: *A gasp rippled through the crowd.*

'**ripple ef,fect** *noun* a situation in which an event or action has an effect on something, which then has an effect on something else: *His resignation will have a ripple effect on the whole department.*

'**rip-,roaring** *adj.* [only before noun] (*informal*) **1** noisy, exciting, and/or full of activity: *a rip-roaring celebration* **2** ~ **drunk** extremely drunk **3** ~ **success** a great success

Rip Van Win·kle /ˌrɪp væn ˈwɪŋkl/ *noun* a person who is surprised to find how much the world has changed over a period of time **ORIGIN** From the name of a character in a short story by the American writer Washington Irving. He sleeps for 20 years and wakes up to find that the world has completely changed.

rise 🔑 /raɪz/ *noun, verb*
● **noun**
▷ INCREASE **1** [C] ~ (**in sth**) an increase in an amount, a number, or a level: *The town is seeing a rise in both residential and commercial property values.* ♦ *A sharp rise in oil prices could disrupt the economic recovery.* ⊃ language bank at INCREASE
▷ IN POWER/IMPORTANCE **2** [sing.] ~ (**of sb/sth**) the act of becoming more important, successful, powerful, etc.: *the rise of fascism in Europe* ♦ *the rise and fall of the Roman Empire* ♦ *her meteoric rise to power*
▷ UPWARD MOVEMENT **3** [sing.] an upward movement: *She watched the gentle rise and fall of his chest as he slept.*
▷ SLOPING LAND **4** [C] an area of land that slopes upward **SYN** SLOPE: *The church was built at the top of a small rise.* ⊃ see also HIGH-RISE
   IDM get a rise out of sb to make someone react in an angry way by saying something that you know will annoy them, especially as a joke **give rise to sth** (*formal*) to cause something to happen or exist: *The novel's success gave rise to a number of sequels.*
● **verb** (**rose** /rouz/, **risen** /ˈrɪzn/)
▷ MOVE UPWARD **1** [I] (+ **adv./prep.**) to come or go upward; to reach a higher level or position: *Smoke was rising from the chimney.* ♦ *The river has risen (by) several feet.*
▷ GET UP **2** [I] (+ **adv./prep.**) (*formal*) to get up from a lying, sitting, or KNEELING position: *He was accustomed to rising (= getting out of bed) early.* ♦ *They rose from the table.* ♦ *She rose to her feet.* ⊃ thesaurus box at STAND
▷ OF SUN/MOON **3** [I] when the sun, moon, etc. **rises**, it appears above the HORIZON: *The sun rises in the east.* **ANT** SET
▷ INCREASE **4** [I] to increase in amount or number: *rising fuel bills* ♦ *The price of gas rose.* ♦ *Gas rose in price.* ♦ *Unemployment rose (by) 3%.* ♦ *Air pollution has risen above an acceptable level.* ⊃ language bank at INCREASE
▷ BECOME POWERFUL/IMPORTANT **5** [I] (+ **adv./prep.**) to become more successful, important, powerful, etc.: *a rising young politician* ♦ *She rose to power in the 1970s.* ♦ *He rose to the rank of general.* ♦ *She rose through the ranks to become managing director.*
▷ OF SOUND **6** [I] if a sound **rises**, it become louder and higher: *Her voice rose angrily.*
▷ OF WIND **7** [I] if the wind **rises**, it begins to blow more strongly
▷ OF FEELING **8** [I] (*formal*) if a feeling **rises** inside you, it begins and gets stronger: *He felt anger rising inside him.* ♦ *Her spirits rose* (= she felt happier) *at the news.*

t **t**ea   ṭ **butt**er   d **d**id   k **c**at   g **g**ot   tʃ **ch**in   dʒ **J**une   f **f**all

> **OF YOUR COLOR 9** [I] (*formal*) if your color **rises**, your face becomes pink or red with embarrassment
> **OF HAIR 10** [I] if hair **rises**, it stands vertical instead of lying flat: *The hair on the back of my neck rose when I heard the scream.*
> **FIGHT 11** [I] **~ (up) (against sb/sth)** (*formal*) to begin to fight against your ruler or government or against a foreign army **SYN** REBEL: *The peasants rose in revolt.* ◆ *He called on the people to rise up against the invaders.* ⊃ related noun UPRISING
> **BECOME VISIBLE 12** [I] (*formal*) to be or become visible above the surroundings: *Mountains rose in the distance.*
> **OF LAND 13** [I] if land **rises**, it slopes upward: *The ground rose steeply all around.*
> **OF BEGINNING OF RIVER 14** [I] **+ adv./prep.** a river **rises** where it begins to flow: *The Mississippi rises in Lake Itasca in Minnesota.*
> **OF BREAD/CAKES 15** [I] when bread, cakes, etc. **rise**, they swell because of the action of YEAST or BAKING POWDER
> **OF DEAD PERSON 16** [I] **~ (from sth)** to come to life again: *to rise from the dead* ◆ (*figurative*) *Can a new political movement rise from the ashes of an old one?*
> **IDM rise and shine** (*old-fashioned*) usually used to tell someone to get out of bed and be active ⊃ more at GORGE *n.*, HACKLES, HEIGHT
> **PHR V rise aˈbove sth 1** to not be affected or limited by problems, insults, etc.: *She had the courage and determination to rise above her physical disability.* **2** to be wise enough or morally good enough not to do something wrong or not to think the same as other people: *I try to rise above prejudice.* **3** to be of a higher standard than other things of a similar kind: *His work rarely rises above the mediocre.* ˈrise to sth **1** to show that you are able to deal with an unexpected situation, problem, etc.: *Luckily, my mother rose to the occasion.* ◆ *He was determined to rise to the challenge.* **2** to react when someone is deliberately trying to make you angry or get you interested in something: *I refuse to rise to that sort of comment.* ◆ *As soon as I mentioned money he rose to the bait.*

WHICH WORD?

rise ◆ raise

verbs

- Raise is a verb that must have an object and **rise** is used without an object. When you **raise** something, you lift it to a higher position or increase it: *He raised his head from the pillow.* ◆ *We were forced to raise the price.* When people or things **rise**, they move from a lower to a higher position: *She rose from the chair.* ◆ *The helicopter rose into the air.* Rise can also mean "to increase in number or quantity": *Costs are always rising.*

nouns

- The noun **rise** means a movement upward or an increase in an amount or quantity: *a rise in interest rates.* Rise can also mean the process of becoming more powerful or important: *her dramatic rise to power.* The noun **raise** is often used to mean an increase in pay: *a three percent pay raise.*

ris·er /ˈraɪzər/ *noun* **1 early/late ~** a person who usually gets out of bed early/late in the morning **2** (*technical*) the vertical part between two steps in a set of stairs ⊃ compare TREAD **3 risers** [pl.] a set of wide steps that have several levels and are intended for performers to stand on: *The chorus went up to the stage and stood on the risers.*

ris·i·ble /ˈrɪzəbl/ *adj.* (*formal*, *disapproving*) deserving to be laughed at rather than taken seriously **SYN** LUDICROUS, RIDICULOUS

ris·ing /ˈraɪzɪŋ/ *noun* a situation in which a group of people protest against, and try to get rid of, a government, a leader, etc. **SYN** REVOLT, UPRISING

risk /rɪsk/ *noun, verb*

- **noun 1** [C, U] the possibility of something bad happening at some time in the future; a situation that could be dangerous or have a bad result: **~ (of sth/of doing sth)** *Smoking can increase the risk of developing heart disease.* ◆ *Patients should be made aware of the risks involved with this treatment.* ◆ **~ (that…)** *There is still a risk that the whole deal will fall through.* ◆ **~ (to sb/sth)** *The chemicals pose little risk* (= are not dangerous) *to human health.* ◆ *a calculated risk* (= one that you have thought about and consider to be worth taking because of the possible benefits) ◆ *Any business venture contains an element of risk.* ◆ *We could probably trust her with the information, but it's just not worth the risk.* **2** [C] **~ (to sth)** a person or thing that is likely to cause problems or danger at some time in the future: *The group was considered to be a risk to national security.* ◆ *a major health/fire risk* **3** [C] a **good/bad/poor ~** a person or business that a bank or an insurance company is willing/unwilling to lend money or sell insurance to because they are likely/unlikely to pay back the money, etc.: *With five previous claims, he's now a bad insurance risk.*
- **IDM at risk (from/of sth)** in danger of something unpleasant or harmful happening: *As with all diseases, certain groups will be more at risk than others.* ◆ *If we go to war, innocent lives will be put at risk.* **at the risk of doing sth** used to introduce something that may sound stupid or may offend someone: *At the risk of showing my ignorance, how exactly does the Internet work?* **at risk to yourself/sb/sth** with the possibility of harming yourself/someone/something: *He risked his life to save the dog, at considerable risk to his own life.* **do sth at your own risk** to do something even though you have been warned about the possible dangers and will have to take responsibility for anything bad that happens: *Persons swimming beyond this point do so at their own risk.* (= on a notice) ◆ *Valuables are left at their owner's risk.* (= on a notice) **run a risk (of sth/of doing sth)** to be in a situation in which something bad could happen to you: *People who are overweight run a risk of a heart attack or stroke.* **run the risk (of sth/ of doing sth)** | **run risks** to be or put yourself in a situation in which something bad could happen to you: *We don't want to run the risk of losing their business.* **take a risk** | **take risks** to do something even though you know that something bad could happen as a result: *That's a risk I'm not prepared to take.* ◆ *You have no right to take risks with other people's lives.*

- **verb 1 ~ sth** to put something valuable or important in a dangerous situation, in which it could be lost or damaged: *He risked his life to save her.* ◆ *She was risking her own and her children's health.* ◆ *He risked all his money on a game of cards.* **2** to do something that may cause you to get into a situation that is unpleasant for you: **~ sth** *There was no choice. If they stayed there, they risked death.* ◆ **~ (sb/sth) doing sth** *They knew they risked being arrested.* **3** to do something that you know is not really a good idea or may not succeed: **~ sth** *He risked a glance at her furious face.* ◆ *It was a difficult decision but we decided to risk it.* ◆ **~ doing sth** *We've been advised not to risk traveling in these conditions.*
- **IDM risk life and limb** | **risk your neck** to risk being killed or injured in order to do something

ˈrisk asˌsessment *noun* [C, U] (*business*) the act of identifying possible risks, calculating how likely they are to happen and estimating what effects they might have, especially in the context of a company taking responsibility for the safety of its employees or members of the public: *The employer has an obligation to carry out a risk assessment.*

ˈrisk-aˌverse *adj.* not willing to do something if it is possible that something bad could happen as a result: *We live in a risk-averse culture.* ◆ *In business you cannot be innovative and risk-averse at the same time.*

ˈrisk-ˌtaking *noun* [U] the practice of doing things that involve risks in order to achieve something ▶ **ˈrisk-ˌtaker** *noun*

risk·y /ˈrɪski/ *adj.* (**risk·i·er, risk·i·est** **HELP** You can also use **more risky** and **most risky**.) involving the possibility of something bad happening **SYN** DANGEROUS: *Life as a helicopter pilot can be a risky business* (= dangerous). ♦ *a risky investment* ♦ *It's far too risky to generalize from one set of results.* ▶ **risk·i·ly** /-kəli/ *adv.* **risk·i·ness** /-kinəs/ *noun* [U]

ri·sot·to /rɪˈsɑtoʊ; -ˈzɑ-; -ˈsoʊ-; -ˈzoʊ-/ *noun* (*pl.* **ri·sot·tos**) [C, U] an Italian dish of rice cooked with vegetables, meat, etc.

ris·qué /rɪˈskeɪ/ *adj.* a **risqué** performance, comment, joke, etc. is a little shocking, usually because it is about sex

Rit·a·lin™ /ˈrɪtl·ən/ *noun* a drug that is sometimes given to children who cannot keep quiet or still, to help them become calmer and concentrate better

rite /raɪt/ *noun* a ceremony performed by a particular group of people, often for religious purposes: *funeral rites* ♦ *initiation rites* (= performed when a new member joins a secret society) ➔ **collocations** at RELIGION ➔ **see also** THE LAST RITES

ˌrite of ˈpassage *noun* a ceremony or an event that marks an important stage in someone's life

rit·u·al /ˈrɪtʃuəl/ *noun, adj.*
● *noun* [C, U] **1** a series of actions that are always performed in the same way, especially as part of a religious ceremony: *religious rituals* ♦ *She objects to the ritual of organized religion.* ➔ **collocations** at RELIGION **2** something that is done regularly and always in the same way: *Sunday lunch with the in-laws has become something of a ritual.*
● *adj.* [only before noun] **1** done as part of a ritual or ceremony: *ritual chanting* **2** always done or said in the same way, especially when this is not sincere: *ritual expressions of sympathy* ▶ **rit·u·al·ly** *adv.*: *The goat was ritually slaughtered.*

rit·u·al·is·tic /ˌrɪtʃuəˈlɪstɪk/ *adj.* [usually before noun] **1** connected with the ritual performed as part of a ceremony: *a ritualistic act of worship* **2** always done or said in the same way, especially when this is not sincere

rit·u·al·ize /ˈrɪtʃuəˌlaɪz/ *verb* [usually passive] **~ sth** (*formal*) to do something in the same way or pattern every time: *ritualized expressions of grief*

ritz·y /ˈrɪtsi/ *adj.* (*informal*) expensive and fashionable **ORIGIN** From the Ritz, the name of several very comfortable and expensive hotels.

ri·val 🔑 /ˈraɪvl/ *noun, adj., verb*
● *noun* **~ (to sb/sth) (for sth)** a person, company, or thing that competes with another in sports, business, etc.: *The two teams have always been rivals.* ♦ *Japan was their biggest economic rival.* ♦ *This latest design has no rival/rivals* (= it is easily the best design available). ▶ **ri·val** *adj.* [only before noun]: *a rival bid/claim/offer* ♦ *fighting between rival groups* ♦ *He was shot by a member of a rival gang.*
● *verb* (-l- or -ll-) **~ sb/sth (for/in sth)** to be as good, impressive, etc. as someone or something else **SYN** COMPARE WITH: *You will find scenery to rival anything you can see in the Alps.* ➔ **see also** UNRIVALLED

ri·val·ry /ˈraɪvəlri/ *noun* (*pl.* **ri·val·ries**) [C, U] a state in which two people, companies, etc. are competing for the same thing: **~ (with sb/sth) (for sth)** *a fierce rivalry for world supremacy* ♦ **~ (between A and B) (for sth)** *There is a certain amount of friendly rivalry between the teams.* ♦ *political rivalries* ♦ *sibling rivalry* (= between brothers and sisters)

riv·en /ˈrɪvn/ *adj.* [not before noun] **~ (by/with sth)** (*formal*) **1** (of a group of people) divided because of disagreements, especially in a violent way: *a party riven by internal disputes* **2** (of an object) divided into two or more pieces

riv·er 🔑 /ˈrɪvər/ *noun*
1 (*abbr.* R.) a natural flow of water that continues in a long line across land to the ocean: *the Hudson River* ♦ *on the banks of the river* (= the ground at the side of a river) ♦ *to travel up the/down the river* (= in the opposite direction to/in the same direction as the way in which the river is flowing) ♦ *the mouth*

of the river (= where it enters the ocean) ♦ *Can we swim in the river?* ♦ *a boat on the river* ♦ *They have a house on the river* (= beside it). ➔ **picture** at OXBOW **2 ~ (of sth)** a large amount of liquid that is flowing in a particular direction: *Rivers of molten lava flowed down the mountain.* **IDM** see SELL *v.*

riv·er·bank /ˈrɪvərˌbæŋk/ *noun* the ground at the side of a river: *on the riverbank*

riv·er·bed /ˈrɪvərˌbɛd/ *noun* the area of ground over which a river usually flows: *a dried-up riverbed*

ˈriver ˌblindness *noun* [U] (*medical*) a tropical skin disease caused by a PARASITE of certain flies that breed in rivers, which can also cause a person to become blind

riv·er·front /ˈrɪvərˌfrʌnt/ *noun* an area of land next to a river with buildings, stores, restaurants, etc. on it

riv·er·ine /ˈrɪvəˌraɪn; -ˌrɪn/ *adj.* [usually before noun] (*technical*) on, near, or relating to a river or the banks of a river

riv·er·side /ˈrɪvərˌsaɪd/ *noun* [sing.] the ground along either side of a river: *a riverside path* ♦ *a walk by the riverside*

riv·et /ˈrɪvət/ *noun, verb*
● *noun* a metal pin that is used to fasten two pieces of leather, metal, etc. together
● *verb* [usually passive] **1 ~ sb/sth** to hold someone's interest or attention so completely that they cannot look away or think of anything else: *I was absolutely riveted by her story.* ♦ *My eyes were riveted on the figure lying in the road.* **2 ~ sth** to fasten something with rivets: *The steel plates were riveted together.*
IDM **be riveted to the spot/ground** to be so shocked or frightened that you cannot move

riv·et·ing /ˈrɪvətɪŋ/ *adj.* (*approving*) so interesting or exciting that it holds your attention completely **SYN** ENGROSSING

riv·i·er·a /ˌrɪviˈɛrə/ *noun* often **Riviera** an area by the ocean that is warm and popular for vacations, especially the Mediterranean coast of France: *the French/Mexican Riviera*

riv·u·let /ˈrɪvyələt/ *noun* (*formal*) a very small river; a small stream of water or other liquid

RN /ˌɑr ˈɛn/ *abbr.* REGISTERED NURSE

RNA /ˌɑr ɛn ˈeɪ/ *noun* [U] (*chemistry*) a chemical present in all living cells. Like DNA it is a type of NUCLEIC ACID.

roach /roʊtʃ/ *noun* **1** (*informal*) = COCKROACH: *The apartments were infested with rats and roaches.* **2** (*pl.* **roach**) a small European FRESHWATER fish **3** (*slang*) the end part of a cigarette containing MARIJUANA

road 🔑 /roʊd/ *noun*
1 a hard surface built for vehicles to travel on: *a main/major/back/side road* ♦ *a country/mountain road* ♦ *They live just up/down the road* (= further on the same road). ♦ *The house is on a very busy road.* ♦ *He was walking along the road when he was attacked.* ♦ *It would be better to transport the goods by rail rather than by road.* ♦ *Take the first road on the left and then follow the signs.* ♦ *We parked on a side road.* ♦ *road accidents/safety/users* **2 Road** (*abbr.* **Rd.**) used in names of roads, especially in towns: *305 Mockingbird Valley Road* **3** the way to achieving something: *to be on the road to recovery* ♦ *We have discussed breaking up the company, but we would prefer not to go down that road.*
IDM **(further) along/down the road** at some time in the future: *There are certain to be more job losses further down the road.* **one for the road** (*informal*) a last alcoholic drink before you leave a party, etc. **on the road 1** traveling, especially for long distances or periods of time: *The band has been on the road for six months.* **2** (of a car) in a condition in which it can be legally driven: *It will cost about $500 to get the car back on the road.* **3** moving from place to place, and having no permanent home: *Life on the road can be very hard.* **the road to hell is paved with good intentions** (*saying*) it is not enough to intend to do good things; you must actually do them ➔ **more at** END *n.*, HIT *v.*, RUBBER, SHOW *n.*

roads

roads and streets

- In a town or city, **street** is the most general word for a road with houses and buildings on one or both sides: *a street map of Harrisburg, Pennsylvania*. **Street** is not used for roads between towns, but streets in towns are often called **Road**: *Colesberg Street* ♦ *Old Georgetown Road*. A **road map** of a country shows you the major routes between, around, and through towns and cities.
- Other words used in the names of streets include: **Circle, Court, Crescent, Drive, Hill,** and **Way. Avenue** suggests a wide street. A **lane** is a narrow street.
- **Main Street** is used, especially as a name, for the main street of a town, where most stores, banks, etc. are, or used to be before a town got bigger.

larger roads

- The roads that connect towns and cities are called **highways, freeways,** or **interstates** (for example State Route 347, Interstate 94). These are large divided roads built so that long-distance traffic could avoid towns.
- A **beltway** is built around a city or town to reduce traffic in the center: *the D.C. beltway*. A **bypass** passes around a town or city rather than through the center: *the Richmond bypass*.

road·block /'roʊdblɑk/ noun **1** a barrier put across the road by the police or army so that they can stop and search vehicles **2** something that stops a plan from going ahead

road hog noun (*informal*, *disapproving*) a person who drives in a dangerous way without thinking about the safety of other road users

road·house /'roʊdhaʊs/ noun (*old-fashioned*) a restaurant or bar on a main road in the country

road·ie /'roʊdi/ noun (*informal*) a person who works with a band of musicians on tour, and helps move and set up their equipment

road kill noun **1** [U] an animal, or animals, that have been killed by a car on the road **2** [C, U] the killing of an animal by a car hitting it on the road

road map noun **1** a map that shows the roads of an area, especially one that is designed for a person who is driving a car **2** a set of instructions or suggestions about how to do something or find out about something

road movie noun a movie that is based on a journey taken by the main character or characters

road rage noun [U] a situation in which a driver becomes extremely angry or violent with the driver of another car because of the way they are driving

road·run·ner /'roʊdrʌnər/ noun a N. American bird of the CUCKOO family, that lives in desert areas and can run very fast

road show noun a traveling show arranged by a radio or television program, or by a magazine, company, or political party

road·side /'roʊdsaɪd/ noun [sing.] the edge of the road: *We parked by the roadside*. ♦ *a roadside café*

road sign noun a sign near a road giving information or instructions to drivers

road·ster /'roʊdstər/ noun (*old-fashioned*) a car with no roof and two seats

road test noun **1** a test to see how a vehicle functions or what condition it is in **2** the part of a DRIVING TEST that involves driving a vehicle on the road

road-test verb ~ sth to test a vehicle to see how it functions or what condition it is in

road trip noun (*informal*) a trip made in a car over a long distance

road·way /'roʊdweɪ/ noun [C, U] a road or the part of a road used by vehicles

road·work /'roʊdwərk/ noun [U] work that is done repairing roads; an area where this work is being done

road·wor·thy /'roʊd,wərði/ adj. (of a vehicle) in a safe condition to drive ▶ **road·wor·thi·ness** noun [U]

roam /roʊm/ verb **1** [I, T] to walk or travel around an area without any definite aim or direction **SYN** WANDER: **(+ adv./prep.)** *The sheep are allowed to roam freely on this land.* ♦ ~ sth *to roam the countryside/the streets, etc.* **2** [I, T] (of the eyes or hands) to move slowly over every part of someone or something: ~ **(over sth/sb)** *His gaze roamed over her.* ♦ ~ **sth/sb** *Her eyes roamed the room.*

roam·ing /'roʊmɪŋ/ noun [U] using a cell phone by connecting to a different company's network, for example when you are in a different country: *international roaming charges*

roan /roʊn/ noun an animal, especially a horse, that has hair of two colors mixed together: *a strawberry roan* (= with a mixture of brown and gray hair that looks pink) ▶ **roan** adj. [only before noun]

roar /rɔr/ verb, noun

- **verb 1** [I] to make a very loud, deep sound: *We heard a lion roar.* ♦ *The gun roared deafeningly.* ♦ *The engine* **roared to life** (= started noisily). **2** [I, T] to shout something very loudly: *The crowd roared.* ♦ ~ **sth (out)** *The fans roared (out) their approval.* ♦ **+ speech** *"Stand back," he roared.* **3** [I] to laugh very loudly: *He looked so funny, we all roared.* ♦ ~ **with laughter** *It made them roar with laughter.* **4** [I] **+ adv./prep.** (of a vehicle or its rider/driver) to move very fast, making a lot of noise: *She stepped on the gas and the car roared away.* **5** [I] (of a fire) to burn brightly with a lot of flames, heat, and noise

- **noun 1** a loud deep sound made by an animal, especially a LION, or by someone's voice: *His speech was greeted by a roar of applause.* ♦ *roars of laughter* **2** a loud continuous noise made by the wind or ocean, or by a machine: *I could barely hear above the roar of traffic.*

roar·ing /'rɔrɪŋ/ adj. [only before noun] **1** making a continuous loud, deep noise: *All we could hear was the sound of roaring water.* **2** (of a fire) burning with a lot of flames and heat
IDM do a **roaring trade (in sth)** (*informal*) to sell a lot of something very quickly **roaring drunk** (*informal*) extremely drunk and noisy **a roaring success** (*informal*) a very great success

the ˌroaring ˈforties noun [pl.] an area of rough ocean between LATITUDES 40° and 50° south

the ˌroaring ˈtwenties noun [pl.] the years from 1920 to 1929, considered as a time when people were confident and cheerful

roast /roʊst/ verb, noun, adj.

- **verb 1** [T, I] ~ **(sth)** to cook food, especially meat, without liquid in an oven or over a fire; to be cooked in this way: *to roast a chicken* ♦ *the smell of roasting meat* ⊃ collocations at COOKING **2** [T, I] ~ **(sth)** to cook nuts, BEANS, etc. in order to dry them and turn them brown; to be cooked in this way: *roasted chestnuts* **3** [T] ~ **sb** (*informal or humorous*) to be very angry with someone; to criticize someone strongly **4** [I, T] ~ **(sth)** (*informal*) to become or to make something become very hot in the sun or by a fire: *She could feel her skin beginning to roast.*

- **noun 1** a large piece of meat that is cooked whole in the oven: *He made a roast for dinner.* **2** (often in compounds) a party that takes place in someone's yard at which food is cooked over an open fire: *a hot dog roast* **3** an event, especially a meal, at which people celebrate someone's life by telling funny stories about them

- **adj.** [only before noun] cooked in an oven or over a fire: *roast chicken*

roast·ing /ˈroʊstɪŋ/ *adj., noun*
- **adj.** **1** [only before noun] used for roasting meat, vegetables, etc.: *a roasting dish* **2** (also ˌroasting ˈhot) so hot that you feel uncomfortable: *a roasting hot day*
- **noun** [sing.] (*informal*) an occasion when someone is criticized severely: *They got a roasting at the next meeting.*

rob 🔑 /rɑb/ *verb* (-bb-)
~ **sb/sth (of sth)** to steal money or property from a person or place: *to rob a bank* ◆ *The tomb had been robbed of its treasures.* ⊃ collocations at CRIME
IDM rob sb blind (*informal*) to cheat or trick someone so that they lose a lot of money **rob the cradle** (*informal*) to have a sexual relationship with a much younger person **rob Peter to pay Paul** (*saying*) to borrow money from one person to pay back what you owe to another person; to take money from one thing to use for something else
PHR V ˈrob sb/sth of sth [often passive] to prevent someone from having something that they need or deserve **SYN DEPRIVE**: *A last-minute goal robbed the team of victory.* ◆ *He had been robbed of his dignity.*

rob·ber /ˈrɑbər/ *noun* a person who steals from a person or place, especially using violence or threats: *a bank robber*

rob·ber·y /ˈrɑbəri/ *noun* (*pl.* **rob·ber·ies**) [U, C] the crime of stealing money or goods from a bank, store, person, etc., especially using violence or threats: *armed robbery* (= using a gun, knife, etc.) ◆ *There has been a spate of robberies in the area recently.* ⊃ collocations at CRIME ⊃ compare BURGLARY, THEFT **IDM see HIGHWAY**

robe /roʊb/ *noun, verb*
- **noun** **1** a long, loose piece of outer clothing, especially one worn as a sign of rank or office at a special ceremony: *a judge's robes* ◆ *cardinals in red robes* **2** = BATHROBE
- **verb** [usually passive] ~ **sb/yourself (in sth)** (*formal*) to dress someone/yourself in long, loose clothes or in the way mentioned: *a robed choir* ◆ *The priests were robed in black.*

rob·in /ˈrɑbən/ *noun* **1** a gray American bird with a red breast **2** a brown European bird with a red breast, smaller than an American robin ⊃ see also ROUND ROBIN

ˈRobin ˈHood *noun* a person who takes or steals money from rich people and gives it to poor people **ORIGIN** From the name of a character in traditional English stories who lived in a forest, robbing rich people and giving money to poor people.

ro·bo·call /ˈroʊboʊˌkɔl/ *noun* (*informal, disapproving*) a phone call from a company that is trying to sell you something, using an automatic DIALING system to call your number and a recorded message

ro·bot /ˈroʊbɑt/ *noun* **1** a machine that can perform a complicated series of tasks automatically: *These cars are built by robots.* **2** (especially in stories) a machine that is made to look like a human and that can do some things that a human can do

ro·bot·ic /roʊˈbɑtɪk/ *adj.* **1** connected with robots: *a robotic arm* **2** like a robot, making stiff movements, speaking without feeling or expression, etc.

ro·bot·ics /roʊˈbɑtɪks/ *noun* [U] the science of designing and operating ROBOTS

ro·bust /roʊˈbʌst; ˈroʊbʌst/ *adj.* **1** strong and healthy: *She was almost 90, but still very robust.* **2** strong; able to survive being used a lot and not likely to break **SYN STURDY**: *a robust piece of equipment* **3** (of a system or an organization) strong and not likely to fail or become weak: *robust economic growth* **4** strong and full of determination; showing that you are sure about what you are doing or saying **SYN VIGOROUS**: *It was a typically robust performance by the Secretary of Defense.* ▶ **ro·bust·ly** *adv.*: *The furniture was robustly constructed.* ◆ *They defended their policies robustly.* **ro·bust·ness** *noun* [U]

rock 🔑 /rɑk/ *noun, verb*
- **noun**
> **HARD MATERIAL 1** [U, C] the hard, solid material that forms part of the surface of the earth and some other planets: *They drilled through several layers of rock to reach the oil.* ◆ *a cave with striking rock formations* (= shapes made naturally from rock) ◆ *The tunnel was blasted out of solid rock.* ◆ *volcanic/igneous/sedimentary, etc. rocks* **2** [C] a mass of rock standing above the earth's surface or in the ocean: *the Rock of Gibraltar* ◆ *The ship crashed into the rocks at Point Joe, the scene of several shipwrecks.* **3** [C] a large single piece of rock: *They clambered over the rocks at the foot of the cliff.* ◆ *The sign said "Danger: falling rocks."*
> **STONE 4** [C] a small stone: *Protesters pelted the soldiers with rocks.*
> **MUSIC 5** (also ˌrock ˈmusic) [U] a type of loud popular music with a strong beat developed in the 1960s, and played on electric GUITARS and drums: *punk rock* ◆ *a rock band/star*
> **JEWEL 6** [C, usually pl.] (*informal*) a PRECIOUS STONE, especially a diamond
> **PERSON 7** [C, usually sing.] a person who is emotionally strong and who you can rely on: *He is my rock.*
IDM (caught/stuck) between a rock and a hard place in a situation where you have to choose between two things, both of which are unpleasant **on the rocks 1** a relationship or business that is **on the rocks** is having difficulties and is likely to fail soon: *Sue's marriage is on the rocks.* **2** (of drinks) served with pieces of ice but no water: *Scotch on the rocks* ⊃ more at STEADY *adj.*
- **verb**
> **MOVE GENTLY 1** [I, T] to move gently backward and forward or from side to side; to make someone or something move in this way: (+ *adv./prep.*) *The boat rocked from side to side in the waves.* ◆ *She was rocking backward and forward in her seat.* ◆ ~ **sb/sth** (+ *adv./prep.*) *He rocked the baby gently in his arms.*
> **SHOCK 2** [T, often passive] ~ **sb/sth** to shock someone or something very much or make them afraid: *The country was rocked by a series of political scandals.* ◆ *The news rocked the world.*
> **SHAKE 3** [I, T] to shake or to make something shake violently: *The house rocked when the bomb exploded.* ◆ ~ **sth** *The town was rocked by an earthquake.* ◆ (*figurative*) *The scandal rocked the government* (= made the situation difficult for it).
> **DANCE 4** [I] (*old-fashioned*) to dance to ROCK MUSIC
> **BE GOOD 5** something rocks [I] (*slang*) used to say that something is very good: *Her new movie rocks!*
IDM rock the boat (*informal*) to do something that upsets a situation and causes problems: *She was told to keep her mouth shut and not rock the boat.* ⊃ more at FOUNDATION

rock·a·bil·ly /ˈrɑkəˌbɪli/ *noun* [U] a type of American music that combines ROCK AND ROLL and country music

ˌrock and ˈroll (also ˌrock 'n' roll) *noun* [U] a type of music that started to become popular in the 1950s with a strong beat and simple tunes

ˌrock ˈbottom *noun* [U] (*informal*) the lowest point or level that is possible: *Prices hit rock bottom.* ◆ *The marriage had reached rock bottom.* ▶ ˌrock-ˈbottom *adj.*: *rock-bottom prices*

ˈrock ˌcandy *noun* [U] a type of hard candy made from sugar that is melted then allowed to form CRYSTALS

ˈrock ˌclimbing *noun* [U] the sport or activity of climbing steep rock surfaces: *to go rock climbing* ⊃ picture at SPORT

ˈrock ˌcrystal *noun* [U] a pure clear form of QUARTZ (= a hard mineral)

rock·er /ˈrɑkər/ *noun* **1** = ROCKING CHAIR **2** one of the two curved pieces of wood on the bottom of a rocking chair **3** a person who performs, dances to, or enjoys ROCK MUSIC **IDM be off your rocker** (*informal*) to be crazy

ˈrocker ˌswitch *noun* (*technical*) a type of electrical switch where you press one end down to turn it on, and the other end down to turn it off again

rock·et /ˈrɑkət/ *noun, verb*
- **noun** **1** a SPACECRAFT in the shape of a tube that is driven

by a stream of gases let out behind it when fuel is burned inside: *a space rocket* ◆ *The rocket was launched in 2007.* ◆ *The idea took off like a rocket* (= it immediately became popular). **2** a MISSILE (= a weapon that travels through the air) that carries a bomb and is driven by a stream of burning gases: *a rocket attack* **3** a FIREWORK that goes high into the air and then explodes with colored lights

- *verb* **1** [I] **(+ adv./prep.)** to increase very quickly and suddenly **SYN** SHOOT UP: *rocketing prices* ◆ *Unemployment has rocketed up again.* ◆ *The total has rocketed from 376 to 532.* **2** [I] **+ adv./prep.** to move very fast: *The car rocketed out of a side street.* **3** [I, T] to achieve or to make someone or something achieve a successful position very quickly: ~ **(sb/sth) to sth** *The band rocketed to stardom with their first single.* **4** [T] ~ **sth** to attack a place with rockets

rocket-ˌfueled *adj.* [only before noun] happening, moving, or increasing very fast: *There are already signs of rocket-fueled growth.*

rock·et·ry /ˈrɑkətri/ *noun* [U] the area of science that deals with ROCKETS and with sending rockets into space; the use of rockets

rocket ˌscience *noun* [U]
IDM it's not rocket science (*informal*) used to emphasize that something is easy to do or understand: *Go on, you can do it. It's not exactly rocket science, is it?*

rocket ˌscientist *noun* (*informal*) an extremely intelligent person: *He's a nice kid—maybe not a rocket scientist, but he's very sweet.*

rock face *noun* a vertical surface of rock, especially on a mountain

rock·fall /ˈrɑkfɔl/ *noun* the fact of rocks falling down; a pile of rocks that have fallen

rock ˌgarden *noun* a garden or part of a garden consisting of an arrangement of large stones with plants growing among them

ˌrock-ˈhard *adj.* extremely hard or strong

rocking ˌchair (also **rock·er**) *noun* a chair with two curved pieces of wood under it that make it move backward and forward ⊃ picture at CHAIR

rocking ˌhorse *noun* a wooden horse for children that can be made to ROCK backward and forward ⊃ picture at TOY

rock ˌmusic *noun* [U] = ROCK

rock 'n' roll /ˌrɑk ən ˈroʊl/ *noun* [U] = ROCK AND ROLL

rock salt *noun* [U] a kind of salt that comes from the ground

ˌrock ˈsolid *adj.* **1** that you can trust not to change or to disappear: *The support for the party was rock solid.* **2** extremely hard and not likely to break

rock·y /ˈrɑki/ *adj.* (**rock·i·er, rock·i·est**) **1** made of rock; full of rocks: *a rocky coastline* ◆ *rocky soil* **2** difficult and not certain to continue or to be successful: *a rocky marriage*

the ˌRocky ˈMountain ˌStates *noun* [pl.] the eight U.S. states in the area of the Rocky Mountains; from north to south they are: Montana, Idaho, Wyoming, Colorado, Utah, Nevada, Arizona, and New Mexico.

ro·co·co (also **Ro·co·co** /rəˈkoʊkoʊ/) *adj.* used to describe a style of ARCHITECTURE, furniture, etc. that has a lot of decoration, especially in the shape of curls; used to describe a style of literature or music that has a lot of detail and decoration. The rococo style was popular in the 18th century.

rod /rɑd/ *noun* **1** (often used in compounds) a long straight piece of wood, metal, or glass ⊃ see also LIGHTNING ROD **2** = FISHING ROD: *fishing with rod and line* **3** also **the rod** (*old-fashioned*) a stick that is used for hitting people as a punishment: *There used to be a saying: "Spare the rod and spoil the child."* **4** (*slang*) a small gun **IDM** see BEAT *v.*

rode pt of RIDE

rodents

beaver   gopher

chipmunk   squirrel

rat   mouse

ro·dent /ˈroʊdnt/ *noun* any small animal that belongs to a group of animals with strong, sharp front teeth. Mice and RATS are rodents.

ro·de·o /ˈroʊdiˌoʊ; roʊˈdeɪoʊ/ *noun* (*pl.* **ro·de·os**) a public competition, especially in the U.S., in which people show their skill at riding wild horses and catching CATTLE with ropes

roe /roʊ/ *noun* [U, C] the mass of eggs inside a female fish (**hard roe**) or the SPERM of a male fish (**soft roe**), used as food: *cod's roe*

roent·gen·i·um /rɛntˈgɛniəm; rʌnt-; -ˈdʒɛni-/ *noun* [U] (*symb.* **Rg**) a chemical element. Roentgenium is a RADIOACTIVE element that is produced artificially and has no known use.

Roe v. Wade /ˌroʊ vɜrsəs ˈweɪd/ *noun* a legal case in the U.S. Supreme Court that decided that ABORTION is allowed by the Constitution

rog·er /ˈrɑdʒər/ *exclamation* people say **Roger!** in communication by radio to show that they have understood a message

rogue /roʊg/ *noun, adj.*
- *noun* **1** (*humorous*) a person who behaves badly, but in a harmless way **SYN** SCOUNDREL: *He's a bit of a rogue, but very charming.* **2** (*old-fashioned*) a man who is dishonest and immoral **SYN** RASCAL: *a rogues' gallery* (= a collection of pictures of criminals)
- *adj.* [only before noun] **1** (of an animal) living apart from the main group, and possibly dangerous **2** behaving in a different way from other similar people or things, often causing damage: *a rogue gene* ◆ *a rogue police officer*

ro·guish /ˈroʊgɪʃ/ *adj.* (usually *approving*) (of a person) pleasant and amusing but looking as if they might do something wrong: *a roguish smile* ▶ **ro·guish·ly** *adv.*

Ro·hyp·nol™ /roʊˈhɪpnɔl/ *noun* [U] a drug that makes you want to sleep, and that can make you unable to remember what happens for a period after you take it

roil /rɔɪl/ *verb* **1** ~ **sth** to stir up the mud or other material that settles at the bottom of water: *Strong winds roil these waters.* **2** ~ **sb/sth** to disturb or upset someone or something: *The financial scandal has roiled the stock market.*

roist·er·ing /ˈrɔɪstərɪŋ/ *adj.* (*old-fashioned*) having fun in a cheerful, noisy way

role 🔑 **AWL** /roʊl/ *noun*
1 the function or position that someone has or is expected to have in an organization, in society, or in a relationship: *the role of the teacher in the classroom* ◆ *She refused to take on the traditional woman's role.* ◆ *In many marriages there has*

been a complete **role reversal** (= change of roles) *with the man staying at home and the woman going out to work.* **2** an actor's part in a play, movie, etc.: *It is one of the greatest roles she has played.* ◆ *Who is in the **lead role**?* (= the most important one) **3** the degree to which someone or something is involved in a situation or an activity and the effect that they have on it: *the role of diet in preventing disease* ◆ *The media plays a **major role** in influencing people's opinions.* ◆ *a **key/vital role***

'role ˌmodel *noun* a person that you admire and try to copy

'role-play *noun* a learning activity in which you behave in the way someone else would behave in a particular situation: *Role-play allows students to practice language in a safe situation.* ▶ **'role-play** *verb* [I, T] ~ (sth)

'role-playing ˌgame *noun* a game in which players pretend to be imaginary characters who take part in adventures, especially in situations from FANTASY literature

roll ✎ /roʊl/ *noun, verb*

● *noun*
▷ OF PAPER/CLOTH, ETC. **1** [C] ~ (of sth) a long piece of paper, cloth, film, etc. that has been wrapped around itself or a tube several times so that it forms the shape of a tube: *a roll of film* ◆ *Wallpaper is sold in rolls.* ⊃ picture at PACKAGING
▷ OF CANDY, ETC. **2** [C] ~ (of sth) a paper tube wrapped around candy, etc.: *a roll of mints*
▷ BREAD **3** [C] a small LOAF of bread for one person: *Soup and a roll: $4.50* ⊃ compare BUN ⊃ see also JELLY ROLL, SPRING ROLL
▷ OF BODY **4** [sing.] an act of rolling the body over and over: *The kittens were enjoying a roll in the sunshine.* **5** [C] a physical exercise in which you roll your body on the ground, moving your back and legs over your head: *a forward/backward roll*
▷ OF SHIP/PLANE **6** [U] the act of moving from side to side so that one side is higher than the other ⊃ compare PITCH *n.* (8)
▷ OF FAT **7** [C] an area of too much fat on your body, especially around your waist: *Rolls of fat hung over his belt.*
▷ LIST OF NAMES **8** [C] an official list of names: *The chairman called/took the roll* (= called out the names on a list to check that everyone was present). ◆ *the voter rolls* (= a list of all the people who can vote in an election) ⊃ see also PAYROLL
▷ SOUND **9** [C] ~ (of sth) a deep continuous sound: *the distant roll of thunder* ◆ *a drum roll*
▷ OF DICE **10** [C] an act of rolling a DIE: *The order of play is decided by the roll of a die.*
▷ PHONETICS **11** [C] = TRILL
IDM **be on a roll** (*informal*) to be experiencing a period of success at what you are doing: *Don't stop me now—I'm on a roll!* **a roll in the hay** (*informal*) an act of having sex with someone

● *verb*
▷ TURN OVER **1** [I, T] to turn over and over and move in a particular direction; to make a round object do this: **+ adv./prep.** *The ball rolled down the hill.* ◆ *We watched the waves rolling onto the beach.* ◆ ~ sth + adv./prep. *Deliverymen were rolling barrels across the yard.* **2** [I, T] to turn over and over or around and around while remaining in the same place; to make something do this: (**+ adv./prep.**) *a dog rolling in the mud* ◆ *Her eyes rolled.* ◆ ~ sth (+ adv./prep.) *She rolled her eyes upward* (= to show surprise or disapproval). ◆ *He was rolling a pencil between his fingers.* **3** [I, T] ~ (sb/sth) over (onto sth) | ~ (sb/sth) (over) onto sth to turn over to face a different direction; to make someone or something do this: ~ over (onto sth) *She rolled over to get some sun on her back.* ◆ ~ onto sth *He rolled onto his back.* ◆ ~ sb/sth (over) (onto sth) *I rolled the baby over onto its stomach.* ◆ *to roll a dice/die* (= in a game) ◆ *She rolled her car in a 100 mph crash.*
▷ MOVE (AS IF) ON WHEELS **4** [I, T] to move smoothly (on wheels or as if on wheels); to make something do this: (**+ adv./prep.**) *The car began to roll back down the hill.* ◆ *The traffic rolled slowly forward.* ◆ *Mist was rolling in from the sea.* ◆ ~ sth (+ adv./prep.) *He rolled the cart across the room.*
▷ MAKE BALL/TUBE **5** [T, I] ~ (sth) (up) (into sth) to make something/yourself into the shape of a ball or tube: *I rolled the string into a ball.* ◆ *We rolled up the carpet.* ◆ *a rolled-up*

newspaper ◆ *I always **roll my own*** (= make my own cigarettes). ◆ *The cat rolled up into a ball.* ⊃ compare UNROLL
▷ FOLD CLOTHING **6** [T] to fold the edge of a piece of clothing, etc. over and over on itself to make it shorter: ~ sth up *Roll up your sleeves.* ◆ ~ sth + adv./prep. *She rolled her jeans to her knees.*
▷ MAKE SOMETHING FLAT **7** [T] ~ sth (out) to make something flat by pushing something heavy over it: *Roll the dough on a floured surface.* ⊃ picture at COOKING
▷ WRAP UP **8** [T] ~ sb/sth/yourself (up) in sth to wrap or cover someone or something/yourself in something: *Roll the meat in the breadcrumbs.* ◆ *He rolled himself up in the blanket.*
▷ OF SHIP/PLANE/WALK **9** [I, T] ~ (sth) (+ adv./prep.) to move or make something move from side to side: *He walked with a rolling gait.* ◆ *The ship was rolling heavily to and fro.* ⊃ compare PITCH *v.* (6)
▷ MAKE SOUND **10** [I, T] to make a long continuous sound: *rolling drums* ◆ *Thunder rolled.* ◆ ~ sth *to roll your r's* (= by letting your tongue VIBRATE with each "r" sound)
▷ MACHINE **11** [I, T] when a machine **rolls** or someone **rolls** it, it operates: *They had to repeat the scene because the cameras weren't rolling.* ◆ ~ sth *Roll the cameras!*
IDM **be rolling in money/it** (*informal*) to have a lot of money **let's roll** (*informal*) used to suggest to a group of people that you should all start doing something or going somewhere **rolled into one** combined in one person or thing: *Banks are several businesses rolled into one.* **rolling in the aisles** (*informal*) laughing a lot: *She soon had us rolling in the aisles.* **a rolling stone gathers no moss** (*saying*) a person who moves from place to place, job to job, etc. does not have a lot of money, possessions, or friends but is free from responsibilities **roll up your sleeves** to prepare to work or fight **roll with the punches** to adapt yourself to a difficult situation ⊃ more at BALL *n.*, GRAVE¹ *n.*, HEAD *n.*, READY *adj.*, TONGUE *n.*
PHR V **ˌroll aˈround** to be laughing so much that you can hardly control yourself **ˌroll sth⟷ˈback 1** to turn or force something back or further away: *to roll back the frontiers of space* **2** to reduce prices, etc.: *to roll back inflation* **ˌroll sth⟷ˈdown 1** to open something by turning a handle: *He rolled down his car window and started shouting at them.* **2** to make a piece of clothing, etc. hang or lie flat: *to roll down your sleeves* **ˌroll ˈin** (*informal*) **1** to arrive in great numbers or amounts: *Offers of help are still rolling in.* **2** to arrive late at a place, without seeming worried or sorry: *Steve rolled in around lunchtime.* **ˌroll sth⟷ˈout 1** to make something flat by pushing something over it: *Roll out the dough.* **2** to officially make a new product available or start a new political CAMPAIGN **SYN** LAUNCH: *The new model is to be rolled out in July.* ⊃ related noun ROLL-OUT **ˌroll ˈover** (*informal*) to be easily defeated without even trying: *We can't expect them to just roll over for us.* **ˌroll sth⟷ˈover** (*technical*) to allow money that someone owes to be paid back at a later date: *The bank refused to roll over the debt.* ⊃ related noun ROLLOVER **ˌroll ˈup** (*informal*) to arrive: *Bill finally rolled up two hours late.* **ˌroll sth⟷ˈup** to close something by turning a handle: *She rolled up all the windows.*

'roll·back /'roʊlbæk/ *noun* [sing., U] **1** a reduction in a price or in pay, to a past level **2** the act of changing a situation, law, etc. back to what it was before

'roll bar *noun* a metal bar over the top of a car without a roof, used to make the car stronger and to protect passengers if the car turns over

'roll call *noun* [U, sing.] the reading of a list of names to a group of people to check who is there: *Roll call will be at 7 a.m.* ◆ *The guest list reads like a roll call of the nation's heroes.*

ˌrolled ˈgold *noun* [U] gold in the form of a thin layer that is rolled onto something to cover it

ˌrolled ˈoats *noun* [pl.] OATS that have had their shells removed before being crushed, used especially for making OATMEAL

roll·er /'roʊlər/ *noun* **1** a piece of wood, metal, or plastic, shaped like a tube, that rolls over and over and is used in

t tea ţ butter d did k cat ɡ got tʃ chin dʒ June f fall machines, for example to make something flat, or to move something: *the heavy steel rollers under the conveyor belt* **2** (often in compounds) a machine or piece of equipment with a part shaped like a tube so that it rolls backward and forward. It may be used for making something flat, crushing something, or spreading something: *Flatten the surface of the grass with a roller.* ◆ *a paint roller* ⊃ see also STEAMROLLER **3** a piece of wood or metal, shaped like a tube, that is used for moving heavy objects: *We'll need to move the piano on rollers.* **4** a long powerful wave in the ocean: *Huge Atlantic rollers crashed onto the rocks.* **5** a small plastic tube that hair is rolled around to give it curls SYN CURLER: *heated rollers* ◆ *Her hair was in rollers.* ⊃ see also HIGH ROLLER

roll·er·ball /ˈroʊlərˌbɔl/ *noun* a type of BALLPOINT pen

Roll·er·blade™ /ˈroʊlərˌbleɪd/ (also ˌin-line ˈskate) *noun* a type of boot with a line of small wheels attached to the bottom ⊃ picture at HOBBY ▶ **Roll·er·blade** *verb* [I]

roller ˌcoaster *noun* **1** a track at a FAIRGROUND or an AMUSEMENT PARK that goes up and down very steep slopes and that people ride on in a small train for fun and excitement: *a roller-coaster ride* **2** a situation that keeps changing very quickly: *The last few weeks have been a real roller coaster.*

roller ˌskate (also **skate**) *noun, verb*
● *noun* a type of boot with two pairs of small wheels attached to the bottom: *a pair of roller skates*
● *verb* [I] to move over a hard surface wearing roller skates ▶ **roller ˌskating** (also **skat·ing**) *noun* [U]

roller ˌtowel *noun* a long roll of towel, usually in a public bathroom, part of which hangs down for you to dry your hands on

rol·lick·ing /ˈrɑlɪkɪŋ/ *adj.* [only before noun] cheerful and often noisy SYN EXUBERANT: *a rollicking comedy*

roll·ing /ˈroʊlɪŋ/ *adj.* [only before noun] **1** (of hills or countryside) having gentle slopes **2** done in regular stages or at regular intervals over a period of time: *a rolling program of reform*

rolling ˌmill *noun* a machine or factory that produces flat sheets of metal

rolling ˌpin *noun* a wooden or glass kitchen UTENSIL (= a tool) in the shape of a tube, used for rolling DOUGH flat ⊃ picture at COOKING, KITCHEN

rolling ˌstock *noun* [U] the engines, trains, etc. that are used on a railroad

roll-on *adj.* [only before noun] spread or put on the body using a ball that moves around in the top of a bottle or container: *a roll-on deodorant* ▶ **roll-on** *noun*

roll-out *noun* an occasion when a company introduces or starts to use a new product

roll·o·ver /ˈroʊlˌoʊvər/ *noun* [U] **1** (*technical*) the act of allowing money that is owed to be paid at a later date **2** the turning over of a vehicle during an accident

roll-top ˈdesk *noun* a desk with a top that you roll back to open it

ro·ly-po·ly /ˌroʊli ˈpoʊli/ *adj.* [only before noun] (*informal*) (of people) short, round, and fat SYN PLUMP

ROM /rɑm/ *noun* [U] the abbreviation for "read-only memory" (computer memory that contains instructions or data that cannot be changed or removed) ⊃ compare CD-ROM

the Ro·ma /ˈroʊmə/ *noun* [pl.] the ROMANI people: *the Roma population of eastern Europe*

ro·maine /roʊˈmeɪn/ *noun* [C, U] a type of LETTUCE with long crisp leaves

ro·ma·ji /ˈroʊmədʒi/ *noun* [U] (from *Japanese*) a system of writing Japanese that uses the ROMAN ALPHABET

Ro·man /ˈroʊmən/ *adj., noun*
● *adj.* **1** connected with ancient Rome or the Roman Empire: *a Roman road/temple/villa* **2** connected with the modern city of Rome **3** connected with the Roman Catholic Church **4 roman roman** type is ordinary printing type which does not lean forward: *Definitions in this dictionary are printed in roman type.* ⊃ compare ITALIC
● *noun* **1** [C] a citizen of the ancient Roman REPUBLIC or empire **2** [C] a person from the modern city of Rome **3 roman** [U] the ordinary style of printing that uses letters that do not lean forward ⊃ compare ITALICS **IDM** see ROME

the ˌRoman ˈalphabet *noun* [sing.] the alphabet that is used in English and in most western European languages

ˌRoman ˈCatholic (also **Cath·o·lic**) *noun* (*abbr.* RC) a member of the part of the Christian Church that has the POPE as its leader ▶ **ˌRoman ˈCatholic** (also **Catholic**) *adj.* **ˌRoman Ca·ˈtholicism** (also **Ca·thol·i·cism**) *noun* [U]

Ro·mance /roʊˈmæns; ˈroʊmæns/ *adj.* [only before noun] **Romance** languages, such as French, Italian, and Spanish, are languages that developed from Latin

ro·mance *noun, verb*
● *noun* /roʊˈmæns; ˈroʊmæns/ **1** [C] an exciting, usually short, relationship between two people who are in love with each other: *a shipboard romance* ◆ *They had a whirlwind romance.* **2** [U] love or the feeling of being in love: *Spring is here and romance is in the air.* ◆ *How can you put the romance back into your marriage?* ⊃ collocations at MARRIAGE **3** [U] a feeling of excitement and adventure, especially connected to a particular place or activity: *the romance of travel* **4** [C] a story about a love affair: *She's a compulsive reader of romances.* **5** [C] a story of excitement and adventure, often set in the past: *medieval romances*
● *verb* /roʊˈmæns/ **1** [I] to tell stories that are not true or to describe something in a way that makes it seem more exciting or interesting than it really is **2** [T] ~ sb to have or to try to have a romantic relationship with someone

Ro·man·esque /ˌroʊməˈnɛsk/ *adj.* used to describe a style of ARCHITECTURE that was popular in western Europe from the 10th to the 12th centuries and that had round ARCHES, thick walls and tall PILLARS ⊃ see also NORMAN

Rom·a·ni (also **Rom·a·ny**) /ˈrɑməni; ˈroʊ-/ *noun* (*pl.* **Rom·a·nies**) **1** [C] a member of a group of people, originally from Asia, who traditionally travel from place to place instead of living in one place SYN GYPSY **2** [U] the language of Romani people ▶ **Rom·a·ni** (also **Rom·a·ny**) *adj.* [usually before noun]

ˌRoman ˈlaw *noun* the legal system of the ancient Romans, and the basis for CIVIL LAW in many countries

ˌRoman ˈnose *noun* a nose that curves out at the top

ˌRoman ˈnumeral *noun* one of the letters used by the ancient Romans to represent numbers and still used today in some situations. In this system I=1, V=5, X=10, L=50, C=100, D=500, M=1000 and these letters are used in combinations to form other numbers.: *Henry VIII* ◆ *© CNN MMIX (2009)* ⊃ compare ARABIC NUMERAL

Ro·ma·no /rəˈmɑnoʊ/ *noun* (also Ro·ˌmano ˈcheese) *noun* [U] a type of very hard Italian cheese

Romano- /rəˈmɑnoʊ; roʊ-/ *combining form* (in nouns and adjectives) Roman: *Romano-British pottery*

ro·man·tic 🔑 /roʊˈmæntɪk/ *adj., noun*
● *adj.* **1** connected or concerned with love or a sexual relationship: *a romantic candlelit dinner* ◆ *romantic stories/ fiction/comedy* ◆ *I'm not interested in a romantic relationship.* **2** (of people) showing feelings of love: *Why don't you ever give me flowers? I wish you'd be more romantic.* **3** beautiful in a way that makes you think of love or feel strong emotions: *romantic music* ◆ *romantic mountain scenery* **4** having an attitude to life where imagination and the emotions are especially important; not looking at situations in a realistic way: *a romantic view of life* ◆ *When I was younger, I had romantic ideas of becoming a writer.* **5 Romantic** [usually before noun] used to describe literature, music, or art, especially of the 19th century, that is concerned with strong feelings, imagination, and a return to nature, rather than reason, order, and intellectual ideas: *the Romantic*

movement ◆ *Keats is one of the greatest Romantic poets.*
▶ **ro·man·ti·cally** /-kli/ *adv.*: *to be romantically involved with someone* ◆ *Their names have been linked romantically.* ◆ *He talked romantically of the past and his youth.*

● **noun 1** a person who is emotional and has a lot of imagination, and who has ideas and hopes that may not be realistic: *an incurable romantic* ◆ *He was a romantic at heart and longed for adventure.* **2** Romantic a writer, a musician, or an artist who writes, etc. in the style of romanticism

ro·man·ti·cism /rou'mæntə,sızəm/ *noun* [U] (also Ro·man·ti·cism) **1** a style and movement in art, music, and literature in the late 18th and early 19th century, in which strong feelings, imagination, and a return to nature were more important than reason, order, and intellectual ideas ➔ compare REALISM **2** the quality of seeing people, events, and situations as more exciting and interesting than they really are **3** strong feelings of love; the fact of showing emotion, affection, etc.

ro·man·ti·cize /rou'mæntə,saız/ *verb* [T, I] ~ **(sth)** to make something seem more attractive or interesting than it really is: *romanticizing the past* ◆ *a romanticized picture of parenthood*

Rom·a·ny = ROMANI

rom·com /'ramkam/ *noun* (*informal*) a humorous movie or television show that is about love; a romantic comedy

Rome /roum/ *noun*
  IDM **Rome wasn't built in a day** (*saying*) used to say that a complicated task will take a long time and needs patience **when in Rome (do as the Romans do)** (*saying*) used to say that when you are in a foreign country, or a situation you are not familiar with, you should behave in the way that the people around you behave

ro·me·o /'roumi,ou/ *noun* (*pl.* ro·me·os) (also Ro·me·o) (*often humorous*) a young male lover or a man who has sex with a lot of women ORIGIN From the name of the young hero of Shakespeare's play *Romeo and Juliet.*

romp /ramp/ *verb, noun*
● **verb** [I] **(+ adv./prep.)** to play in a happy and noisy way: *kids romping around in the snow*
  IDM **romp home/to victory** to easily win a race or competition: *Their horse romped home in the 2 o'clock race.*
● **noun** (*often used in newspapers*) (*informal*) **1** [C] an amusing book, play, or movie that is full of action or adventure **2** [sing.] an easy victory in a sports competition: *They won in a 5–1 romp.*

romp·ers /'rampərz/ *noun* [pl.] (*old-fashioned*) a piece of clothing worn by a baby, that covers the body and legs

ron·do /'randou/ *noun* (*pl.* ron·dos) a piece of music in which the main tune is repeated several times, sometimes forming part of a longer piece

rood screen /'rud skrin/ *noun* (*technical*) a wooden or stone structure in some churches that divides the part near the ALTAR from the rest of the church

roof 🔑 /ruf; ruf/ *noun, verb*
● **noun** (*pl.* roofs) **1** the structure that covers or forms the top of a building or vehicle: *a flat/sloping roof* ◆ *a thatched/slate, etc. roof* ◆ *The corner of the classroom was damp where the roof had leaked.* ◆ *Tim climbed on to the garage roof.* ◆ *The roof of the car was not damaged in the accident.* ➔ picture at HOUSE ➔ see also SUNROOF **2** -roofed (in adjectives) having the type of roof mentioned: *flat-roofed buildings* **3** the top of an underground space such as a tunnel or cave **4** ~ **of your mouth** the top of the inside of your mouth
  IDM **go through the roof 1** (of prices, etc.) to rise or increase very quickly **2** (also **hit the roof**) (*informal*) to become very angry **have a roof over your head** to have somewhere to live **under one roof | under the same roof** in the same building or house: *There are a number of stores and restaurants all under one roof.* ◆ *I don't think I can live under the same roof as you any longer.* **under your roof** in your home: *I don't want her under my roof again.* ➔ more at CAT, RAISE *v.*

● **verb** [often passive] to cover something with a roof; to put a roof on a building: ~ **sth (in/over)** *The shopping center is not roofed over.* ◆ ~ **sth with/in sth** *Their cottage was roofed with green slate.*

roof·er /'rufər; 'ru-/ *noun* a person whose job is to repair or build roofs

'roof ,garden *noun* a garden on the flat roof of a building

roof·ing /'rufɪŋ; 'ru-/ *noun* [U] **1** material used for making or covering roofs **2** the process of building roofs

'roof ,rack (also **'luggage ,rack**) *noun* a metal frame fixed to the roof of a car and used for carrying bags, suitcases, and other large objects

roof·top /'ruftap; 'ruf-/ *noun* the outside part of the roof of a building: *From the hill we looked out over the rooftops of Athens.* ◆ *The prisoners staged a rooftop protest.*
  IDM **shout, etc. sth from the rooftops** to talk about something in a very public way: *He was in love and wanted to shout it from the rooftops.*

rook /ruk/ *noun* **1** a large black bird of the CROW family. Rooks build their nests in groups at the tops of trees. **2** = CASTLE (1)

rook·er·y /'rukari/ *noun* (*pl.* rook·er·ies) a group of trees with rooks' nests in them

rook·ie /'ruki/ *noun* (*informal*) **1** a person who has just started a job or an activity and has very little experience **2** a member of a sports team in his or her first full year of playing that sport

room 🔑 /rum; rum/ *noun, verb*
● **noun**
> IN BUILDING **1** [C] a part of a building that has its own walls, floor, and ceiling and is usually used for a particular purpose: *He walked out of the room and slammed the door.* ◆ *They were in the next room and we could hear every word they said.* ◆ *a dining/living room* ◆ *They had to sit in the waiting room for an hour.* ◆ *I think Simon is in his room* (= bedroom). ◆ *I don't want to watch TV. I'll be in the other room* (= a different room). HELP There are many compounds ending in **room**. You will find them at their place in the alphabet.
> -ROOM **2** (in adjectives) having the number of rooms mentioned: *a three-room apartment*
> IN HOTEL **3** [C] a bedroom in a hotel, etc.: *a double/single room* ◆ *I'd like to reserve a room with a view of the lake.* ◆ *She rents rooms to students.* ➔ collocations at TRAVEL
> SPACE **4** [U] empty space that can be used for a particular purpose: ~ **(for sb/sth)** *Is there enough room for me in the car?* ◆ *There's room for one more at the table.* ◆ *Do you have room for a computer on your desk?* ◆ *Yes, there's plenty of room.* ◆ *How can we make room for all the furniture?* ◆ *I'll move the table—it takes up too much room.* ◆ ~ **(to do sth)** *Make sure you have plenty of room to sit comfortably.* ➔ see also ELBOW ROOM, HEADROOM, LEGROOM, STANDING ROOM
> POSSIBILITY **5** [U] ~ **for sth** the possibility of something existing or happening; the opportunity to do something: *He had to be certain. There could be no room for doubt.* ◆ *There's some room for improvement in your work* (= it is not as good as it could be). ◆ *It is important to give children room to think for themselves.*
> PEOPLE **6** [sing.] all the people in a room: *The whole room burst into applause.*
  IDM **no room to swing a cat** (*informal*) when someone says there's no room to swing a cat, they mean that a room is very small and that there is not enough space **room to maneuver** the chance to change the way that something happens and influence decisions that are made ➔ more at ELEPHANT, SMOKE *n.*
● **verb** [I] ~ **(with sb)** | ~ **(together)** to rent a room somewhere; to share a rented room or apartment with someone: *She and Nancy roomed together at college.*

room·er /'rumər/ *noun* a person who rents a room in someone's house

room·ful /'rumfʊl/ noun [sing.] a large number of people or things that are in a room: *He announced his resignation to a roomful of reporters.*

room·ie /'rumi/ noun (*informal*) = ROOMMATE

'**rooming house** noun a building where rooms with furniture can be rented for living in

room·mate /'rummeɪt/ (also *informal* **room·ie**) noun **1** a person that you share a room or an apartment with, especially at a college or university **2** a person who shares an apartment with one or more others

'**room service** noun [U] a service provided in a hotel, by which guests can order food and drinks to be brought to their rooms: *He ordered coffee from room service.*

'**room temperature** noun [U] the normal temperature inside a building: *Serve the wine at room temperature.*

room·y /'rumi/ adj. (**room·i·er, room·i·est**) (*approving*) having a lot of space inside **SYN** SPACIOUS: *a surprisingly roomy car* ▶ **room·i·ness** noun [U]

roost /rust/ noun, verb
• noun a place where birds sleep **IDM** see RULE v.
• verb [I] (of birds) to rest or go to sleep somewhere **IDM** see HOME adv.

roost·er /'rustər/ noun an adult male chicken ⊃ compare HEN

root 🔑 /rut; rʊt/ noun, verb
• noun
>OF PLANT **1** [C] the part of a plant that grows under the ground and absorbs water and minerals that it sends to the rest of the plant: *deep spreading roots* ◆ *I pulled the plant up by* (= including) *the roots.* ◆ *Tree roots can cause damage to buildings.* ◆ *root crops/vegetables* (= plants whose roots you can eat, such as carrots) ⊃ collocations at LIFE ⊃ picture at PLANT ⊃ picture at TREE ⊃ see also GRASS ROOTS, TAPROOT
>OF HAIR/TOOTH/NAIL **2** [C] the part of a hair, tooth, nail, or tongue that attaches it to the rest of the body: *hair that is blonde at the ends and dark at the roots*
>MAIN CAUSE OF PROBLEM **3** [C, usually sing.] the main cause of something, such as a problem or difficult situation: *Money, or love of money, is said to be the root of all evil.* ◆ *We have to get to the root of the problem.* ◆ *What lies at the root of his troubles is a sense of insecurity.* ◆ *What would you say was the root cause of the problem?*
>ORIGIN **4** [C, usually pl.] the origin or basis of something: *Flamenco has its roots in Arabic music.*
>CONNECTION WITH PLACE **5** roots [pl.] the feelings or connections that you have with a place because you have lived there or your family came from there: *I'm proud of my Italian roots.* ◆ *After 20 years in America, I still feel my roots are in England.*
>OF WORD **6** [C] (*linguistics*) the part of a word that has the main meaning and that its other forms are based on; a word that other words are formed from: *"Walk" is the root of "walks," "walked," "walking," and "walker."*
>MATHEMATICS **7** [C] a quantity that, when multiplied by itself a particular number of times, produces another quantity ⊃ see also CUBE ROOT, SQUARE ROOT
IDM put down roots **1** (of a plant) to develop roots **2** to settle and live in one place: *After ten years traveling the world, she felt it was time to put down roots somewhere.* take root **1** (of a plant) to develop roots **2** (of an idea) to become accepted widely: *Fortunately, militarism failed to take root in Europe as a whole.*
• verb
>OF PLANTS **1** [I, T] ~ (sth) to grow roots; to make or encourage a plant to grow roots
>SEARCH **2** [I] to search for something by moving things or turning things over **SYN** RUMMAGE: ~ (about/around) for sth *pigs rooting for food* ◆ *Who's been rooting around in my desk?* ◆ ~ (through sth) (for sth) *"It must be here somewhere," she said, rooting through the suitcase.*
PHR V '**root for sb** [no passive] (usually used in the progressive tenses) (*informal*) to support or encourage someone in a sports competition or when they are in a difficult situation: *We're rooting for the Bulls.* ◆ *Good luck—I'm rooting for you!* ,**root sth/sb**↔'**out 1** to find the person or thing that is causing a problem and remove or get rid of them **2** to find someone or something after searching for a long time ,**root sb to** '**sth** to make someone unable to move because of fear, shock, etc.: *Embarrassment rooted her to the spot.* ,**root sth**↔'**up** to dig or pull up a plant with its roots

'**root beer** noun **1** [U] a sweet drink with bubbles that does not contain alcohol, made from GINGER and the roots of other plants **2** [C] a bottle, can, or glass of root beer

root·bound /'rutbaʊnd/ adj. = POTBOUND

'**root ca·nal** noun the space inside the root of a tooth

'**root di·rectory** noun (*computing*) a file that contains all the other files in a program, system, etc.

root·ed /'rutəd; 'rʊ-/ adj. **1** ~ in sth developing from or being strongly influenced by something: *His problems are deeply rooted in his childhood experiences.* **2** fixed in one place; not moving or changing: *She was rooted to her chair.* ◆ *Their life is rooted in Chicago now.* ◆ *Racism is still deeply rooted in our society.* ⊃ see also DEEP-ROOTED
IDM rooted to the spot so frightened or shocked that you cannot move

root·er /'rutər; 'rʊ-/ noun (*informal*) a person who supports a particular team or player **SYN** SUPPORTER

root·in'-toot·in' /,rutn 'tutn/ adj. [only before noun] (*informal*) enthusiastic, cheerful, and lively

root·less /'rutləs; 'rʊt-/ adj. having nowhere that you really think of as home, or as the place where you belong: *She had had a rootless childhood moving from town to town.* ▶ **root·less·ness** noun [U]

root·sy /'rutsi/ adj. (*informal*) (of music) belonging to a particular tradition, and not changed from the original style

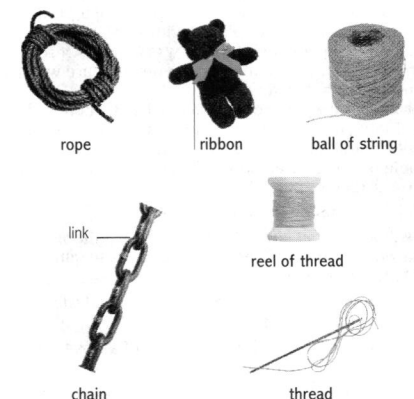

rope   ribbon   ball of string

link

reel of thread

chain   thread

rope 🔑 /roʊp/ noun, verb
• noun **1** [C, U] very strong, thick string made by twisting thinner strings, wires, etc. together: *The rope broke and she fell 150 feet onto the rocks.* ◆ *We tied his hands together with rope.* ◆ *The anchor was attached to a length of rope.* ◆ *Coils of rope lay on the dock.* ⊃ see also JUMP ROPE, TOW ROPE **2** the ropes [pl.] the fence made of rope that is around the edge of the area where a BOXING or WRESTLING match takes place ⊃ picture at SPORT **3** [C] a number of similar things attached together by a string or thread: *a rope of pearls*
IDM give sb enough rope to allow someone freedom to do what they want, especially in the hope that they will make a mistake or look silly: *The question was vague, giving the interviewee enough rope to hang herself.* jump/skip rope to jump over a rope that is held at both ends by you or by two other people and is passed again and again over your

head and under your feet: *She likes to jump rope as a warm-up.* ⊃ see also JUMP ROPE **on the ropes** (*informal*) very close to being defeated **show sb/know/learn the ropes** (*informal*) to show someone/know/learn how a particular job should be done ⊃ more at END *n.*

- **verb 1** to tie one person or thing to another with a rope: **~ A and B together** *The thieves had roped the guard's feet together.* ◆ **~ A to B** *I roped the goat to a post.* **2 ~ sth** to tie something with a rope so that it is held tightly and safely: *I closed and roped the trunk.* **3 ~ sth** to catch an animal by throwing a circle of rope around it **SYN** LASSO **PHR V** ,rope sb↔'in | ,rope sb 'into sth [usually passive] (*informal*) to persuade someone to join in an activity or to help to do something, even when they do not want to: **~ to do sth** *Everyone was roped in to help with the show.* ◆ **~ doing sth** *Ben was roped into making coffee for the whole team.* ,rope sth↔'off to separate an area from another one, using ropes, to stop people from entering it: *Police roped off the street to investigate the accident.*

,rope 'ladder *noun* a LADDER made of two long ropes connected by short pieces of wood or metal at regular intervals

Roque·fort™ /'roukfərt/ *noun* [U] a type of soft French cheese with blue marks and a strong flavor

Ror·schach test /'rɔrʃak ˌtɛst/ (also **'ink-blot ˌtest**) *noun* (*psychology*) a test in which people have to say what different shapes made by ink make them think of

ro·sa·ry /'rouzəri/ *noun* (*pl.* **ro·sa·ries**) **1** [C] a string of BEADS that are used by some Roman Catholics for counting prayers as they say them **2 the Rosary** [sing.] the set of prayers said by Roman Catholics while counting rosary BEADS

rose 🔑 /rouz/ *noun, adj.* ⊃ see also RISE *v.*
- **noun 1** [C] a flower with a sweet smell that grows on a bush with THORNS (= sharp points) on its STEM: *a bunch of red roses* ◆ *a rose bush/garden* ◆ *a climbing/rambling rose* ⊃ picture at PLANT **2** (also ,rose 'pink) [U] a pink color **3** [C] a piece of metal or plastic with small holes in it that is attached to the end of a pipe or WATERING CAN so that the water comes out in a fine spray when you are watering plants **4** [C] = CEILING ROSE **IDM** **be coming up roses** (*informal*) (of a situation) to be developing in a successful way **a rose by any other name would smell as sweet** (*saying*) what is important is what people or things are, not what they are called ⊃ more at BED *n.*, SMELL *v.*
- **adj.** (also ,rose 'pink) pink in color

ro·sé /rou'zei/ *noun* [U, C] (from *French*) a light pink wine: *a bottle of rosé* ◆ *an excellent rosé* ⊃ compare BLUSH WINE, RED WINE, WHITE WINE

ro·se·ate /'rouziət/ *adj.* [usually before noun] (*literary* or *technical*) pink in color

rose·bud /'rouzbʌd/ *noun* the flower of a ROSE before it is open

'rose-,colored (*CanE usually* 'rose-,coloured) *adj.* **1** pink in color **2** (also 'rose-,tinted) used to describe an idea or a way of looking at a situation as being better or more positive than it really is: *a rose-tinted vision of the world* ◆ *He tends to view the world through rose-colored glasses.*

'rose hip *noun* = HIP *n.* (3)

rose·mar·y /'rouz,mɛri/ *noun* [U] a bush with small narrow leaves that smell sweet and are used in cooking as an HERB ⊃ picture at HERB

Ro·set·ta Stone /rou'zɛtə ˌstoun/ *noun* [sing.] something, especially a discovery, that helps you to understand or find an explanation for a mystery or area of knowledge that not much was known about before ORIGIN From the name of an ancient stone with writing in three different languages on it that was found near Rosetta in Egypt in 1799. It has helped archaeologists to understand and translate many other ancient Egyptian texts.

ro·sette /rou'zɛt/ *noun* **1** a round decoration made of RIBBON that is worn by supporters of a political party or sports team, or to show that someone has won a prize ⊃ picture at MEDAL **2** a thing that has the shape of a ROSE: *a wedding dress with silk rosettes*

'rose ,water *noun* [U] a liquid with a sweet smell that is made from ROSES and used as a PERFUME or in cooking

,rose 'window *noun* a decorative round window in a church, often with colored glass (= STAINED GLASS) in it

rose·wood /'rouzwud/ *noun* [U] the hard red-brown wood of a tropical tree, that has a pleasant smell and is used for making expensive furniture

Rosh Ha·sha·nah (also **Rosh Ha·sha·na**) /ˌrouʃ həˈʃɔnə; ˌraʃ həˈʃɑnə/ *noun* [U] the Jewish New Year festival, held in September or October

ros·in /'razn/ *noun* [U] a substance that is used on the BOW² of a musical instrument such as a VIOLIN so that it moves across the strings more easily ▶ **ros·in** *verb* ~ **sth**

ros·ter /'rastər/ *noun* **1** a list of people's names and the jobs that they have to do at a particular time: *a duty roster* **2** a list of the names of people who are available to do a job, play on a team, etc.

ros·trum /'rastrəm/ *noun* (*pl.* **ros·trums** or **ros·tra** /-trə/) a small raised platform that a person stands on to make a speech, CONDUCT music, receive a prize, etc.

ros·y /'rouzi/ *adj.* (**ros·i·er**, **ros·i·est**) **1** pink and pleasant in appearance: *She had rosy cheeks.* **2** likely to be good or successful **SYN** HOPEFUL: *The future is looking very rosy for our company.* ◆ *She painted a rosy picture of their life together in Italy* (= made it appear to be very good and perhaps better than it really was).

rot /rat/ *verb, noun*
- **verb** (**-tt-**) [I, T] to decay, or make something decay, naturally and gradually **SYN** DECOMPOSE: *rotting leaves* ◆ **~ (away)** *The window frame had rotted away completely.* ◆ (*figurative*) *prisoners thrown in jail and left to rot* ◆ **~ sth** *Too much sugar will rot your teeth.* ⊃ see also ROTTEN
- **noun** [U] **1** the process or state of decaying and falling apart: *The wood must not get damp as rot can quickly result.* ⊃ see also DRY ROT, WET ROT **2 the rot** used to describe the fact that a situation is getting worse: *The rot set in last year when they reorganized the department.* ◆ *The team should manage to stop the rot if they play well this week.*

ro·ta·ry /'routəri/ *adj., noun*
- **adj.** [only before noun] **1** (of a movement) moving in a circle around a central fixed point: *rotary motion* **2** (of a machine or piece of equipment) having parts that move in this way: *a rotary engine*
- **noun** (*pl.* **ro·ta·ries**) = TRAFFIC CIRCLE

'Rotary ,Club *noun* a branch of an organization of business and professional people whose members meet for social reasons and to raise money for charity

ro·tate /'routeit/ *verb* **1** [I, T] to move or turn around a central fixed point; to make something do this: *Stay well away from the helicopter when its blades start to rotate.* ◆ **~ about/around sth** *winds rotating around the eye of a hurricane* ◆ **~ sth** *Rotate the wheel through 180 degrees.* **2** [I, T] if a job **rotates**, or if people **rotate** a job, they regularly change the job or regularly change who does the job: (**+ adv./prep.**) *The presidency rotates among the members.* ◆ *When I joined the company, I rotated around the different departments.* ◆ **~ sth** *We rotate the night shift so no one has to do it all the time.* ▶ **ro·tat·ing** *adj.* [only before noun]: *rotating parts* ◆ *a rotating presidency*

ro·ta·tion /rou'teiʃn/ *noun* **1** [U] the action of an object moving in a circle around a central fixed point: *the daily rotation of the earth on its axis* **2** [C] one complete movement in a circle around a fixed point: *This switch controls the number of rotations per minute.* **3** [U, C] the act of regularly changing the thing that is being used in a particular situation, or of changing the person who does a particular

ʌ cup   ə about   eɪ say   aɪ five   ɔɪ boy   aʊ now   oʊ go   ər bird

job: *crop rotation/the rotation of crops* (= changing the crop that is grown on an area of land in order to protect the soil) ◆ *Wheat, corn, and sugar beets are planted in rotation.* ◆ *The committee is chaired by all the members in rotation.* ▸ **ro·ta·tion·al** /-ʃənl/ *adj.* [only before noun]

ROTC /ˈrɑtsi; ˌɑr ou ti ˈsi/ *abbr.* Reserve Officers' Training Corps (an organization for students in the U.S. who are training to be military officers while they are studying)

rote /rout/ *noun* [U] (often used as an adjective) the process of learning something by repeating it until you remember it, rather than by understanding the meaning of it: *to learn by rote* ◆ *rote learning*

ro·tis·ser·ie /rouˈtɪsəri/ *noun* (from *French*) a piece of equipment for cooking meat that turns it around on a long straight piece of metal (called a SPIT)

ro·tor /ˈroutər/ *noun* a part of a machine that turns around a central point: *rotor blades on a helicopter* ➲ picture at PLANE

rot·ten /ˈrɑtn/ *adj., adv.*
● *adj.* **1** (of food, wood, etc.) that has decayed and cannot be eaten or used: *the smell of rotten vegetables* ◆ *The fruit is starting to go rotten.* ◆ *rotten floorboards* **2** [usually before noun] (*informal*) very bad **SYN** TERRIBLE: *I've had a rotten day!* ◆ *What rotten luck!* ◆ *She's a rotten singer.* **3** [usually before noun] (*informal*) dishonest: *The organization is rotten to the core.* **4** [not before noun] (*informal*) looking or feeling sick: *She felt rotten.* **5** [not before noun] (*informal*) feeling guilty about something you have done: *I feel rotten about leaving them behind.* **6** [only before noun] (*informal*) used to emphasize that you are angry or upset about something: *You can keep your rotten money!* ▸ **rot·ten·ness** *noun* [U]
● *adv.* (*informal*) to a large degree; very much: *She spoils the children rotten.*

Rott·wei·ler /ˈrɑtˌwaɪlər/ *noun* a large breed of dog that can be very aggressive

ro·tund /rouˈtʌnd/ *adj.* (*formal* or *humorous*) having a fat, round body **SYN** PLUMP: *the rotund figure of Mr. Stevens* ▸ **ro·tun·di·ty** /rouˈtʌndəti/ *noun* [U]

ro·tun·da /rouˈtʌndə/ *noun* a round building or hall, especially one with a curved roof (= a DOME) ➲ picture at ARCHITECTURE

rou·ble *noun* = RUBLE

rou·é /ruˈeɪ/ *noun* (*old-fashioned*) a man who drinks too much alcohol, uses illegal drugs, or is sexually immoral, especially a man who is fairly old

rouge /ruʒ/ *noun* [U] (*old-fashioned*) a red powder or cream used by women for giving color to their cheeks ▸ **rouge** *verb* ~ **sth**

rough 🔑 /rʌf/ *adj., noun, verb, adv.*
● *adj.* (**rough·er**, **rough·est**)
▹ NOT SMOOTH **1** having a surface that is not even or regular: *rough ground* ◆ *The skin on her hands was hard and rough.* ◆ *Trim rough edges with a sharp knife.* **ANT** SMOOTH
▹ NOT EXACT **2** not exact; not including all details **SYN** APPROXIMATE: *a rough calculation/estimate of the cost* ◆ *I've got a rough idea of where I want to go.* ◆ *There were about 20 people there, at a rough guess.* ◆ *a rough draft of a speech* ◆ *a rough sketch*
▹ VIOLENT **3** not gentle or careful; violent: *This watch is not designed for rough treatment.* ◆ *They complained of rough handling by the guards.* ◆ *rough kids* ◆ *Don't try any rough stuff with me!* **4** where there is a lot of violence or crime: *the roughest neighborhood in the city*
▹ SEA **5** having large and dangerous waves: *It was too rough to sail that night.*
▹ WEATHER **6** wild and with storms
▹ DIFFICULT **7** difficult and unpleasant **SYN** TOUGH: *He's had a really rough time recently* (= he's had a lot of problems). ◆ *We'll get someone in to do the rough work* (= the hard physical work).
▹ PLAIN/BASIC **8** simply made and not finished in every detail; plain or basic: *rough wooden tables* ◆ *a rough track*

▹ NOT SMOOTH **9** not smooth or pleasant to taste, listen to, etc.: *a rough wine/voice*
  ▸ **rough·ness** *noun* [U] ➲ see also ROUGHLY
  IDM **rough around the edges** having parts or qualities that are not yet as good as they should be: *She's a little rough around the edges, but she's a great neighbor.* **a rough deal** the fact of being treated unfairly **rough edges** small parts of something or of a person's character that are not yet as good as they should be: *The ballet still had some rough edges.* ◆ *He had a few rough edges knocked off at school.* ➲ more at RIDE *n.*
● *noun*
▹ IN GOLF **1** the **rough** [sing.] the part of a GOLF COURSE where the grass is long, making it more difficult to hit the ball ➲ compare FAIRWAY
▹ DRAWING/DESIGN **2** [C] (*technical*) the first version of a drawing or design that has been done quickly and without much detail
▹ VIOLENT PERSON **3** [C] (*old-fashioned*, *informal*) a violent person: *a gang of roughs*
  IDM **take the rough with the smooth** to accept the unpleasant or difficult things that happen in life as well as the good things ➲ more at DIAMOND
● *verb*
  IDM **rough it** (*informal*) to live in a way that is not very comfortable for a short time: *We can sleep on the beach. I don't mind roughing it for a night or two.*
  PHR V **rough sth↔ˈout** to draw or write something without including all the details: *I've roughed out a few ideas.* **rough sb↔ˈup** (*informal*) to hurt someone by hitting or kicking them: *He claimed that guards had roughed him up in prison.*
● *adv.* using force or violence: *Do they always play this rough?*

rough·age /ˈrʌfɪdʒ/ *noun* [U] the part of food that helps to keep a person healthy by keeping the BOWELS working and moving other food quickly through the body **SYN** FIBER

rough-and-ˈready *adj.* [usually before noun] **1** simple and prepared quickly but good enough for a particular situation: *a rough-and-ready guide to the education system* **2** (of a person) not very polite, educated, or fashionable

rough and ˈtumble *noun* [U, sing.] **1** ~ (**of sth**) a situation in which people compete with each other and are aggressive in order to get what they want: *the rough and tumble of politics* **2** noisy and slightly violent behavior when children or animals are playing together

rough·cast /ˈrʌfkæst/ *noun* [U] a type of PLASTER containing small stones that is used for covering the outside walls of buildings ▸ **rough·cast** *adj.*

ˈrough cut *noun* the first version of a movie, after the different scenes have been put together

ˈrough-cut *verb* ~ **sth** to cut something quickly, without paying attention to the exact size

rough·en /ˈrʌfn/ *verb* [I, T] to become rough; to make something rough: *His voice roughened with every word.* ◆ ~ **sth** *Cold weather roughens your skin.*

ˌrough-ˈhewn *adj.* [only before noun] **1** (of stone, wood, etc.) cut in a way that leaves it with a rough surface: *rough-hewn walls* ◆ (*figurative*) *the rough-hewn features of his face* **2** (*formal*) (of a person or their behavior) not very polite or educated

rough·house /ˈrʌfhaus; -hauz/ *verb* [I, T] ~ (**sb**) (*informal*) to fight someone or play with someone roughly: *Quit rough-housing, you two!*

rough·ing /ˈrʌfɪŋ/ *noun* [U] (in HOCKEY and football) an illegal use of force, for which a PENALTY may be given

ˌrough ˈjustice *noun* [U] **1** punishment that does not seem fair: *It was rough justice that they lost in the closing seconds of the game.* **2** treatment that is fair but not official or expected: *There was a certain amount of rough justice in his downfall.*

rough·ly /'rʌfli/ adv.

1 approximately but not exactly: *Sales are up by roughly 10%.* ◆ *We live roughly halfway between here and the coast.* ◆ *They all left at roughly the same time.* ◆ **Roughly speaking,** *we receive about fifty letters a week on the subject.* **2** using force or not being careful and gentle: *He pushed her roughly out of the way.* ◆ *"What do you want?" she demanded roughly.* **3** in a way that does not leave a smooth surface: *roughly plastered walls*

rough·neck /'rʌfnɛk/ noun (*informal*) **1** a man who is noisy, rude, and aggressive **2** a man who works on an OIL RIG

rough·shod /'rʌfʃad/ adv.

IDM **ride/run roughshod over sb/sth** to treat someone badly and not worry about their feelings; to ignore laws, people's rights, etc.: *run roughshod over local laws* (=ignore local laws)

rou·lette /ru'lɛt/ noun [U] a gambling game in which a ball is dropped onto a moving wheel that has holes with numbers on them. Players bet on which hole the ball will be in when the wheel stops. ⊃ **see also** RUSSIAN ROULETTE

round 🔑 /raʊnd/ adj., noun, verb, adv., prep.

● **adj.** (round·er, round·est) **1** shaped like a circle or a ball: *a round plate* ◆ *These glasses suit people with round faces.* ◆ *The fruit are small and round.* ◆ *Football isn't played with a round ball.* ◆ *the discovery that the world is round* ◆ *The child was watching it all with big round eyes* (= showing interest). ◆ *a T-shirt with a round neck* ⊃ **see also** ROUND-EYED, ROUND-TABLE **2** having a curved shape: *round green hills* ◆ *She had a small mouth and round pink cheeks.* **3** [only before noun] a **round** figure or amount is one that is given as a whole number, usually one ending in 0 or 5: *Make it a round figure —say forty dollars.* ◆ *Two thousand is a nice round number—put that down.* ◆ *Well, in round figures* (= not giving the exact figures) *we've spent twenty thousand so far.* ► **round·ness** noun [U]: *His face had lost its boyish roundness.*

● **noun**

➤ STAGE IN PROCESS **1** a set of events that form part of a longer process: *the next round of peace talks* ◆ *the final round of voting in the election*
➤ IN SPORTS **2** a stage in a sports competition: *the qualifying rounds of the National Championships* ◆ *Hewitt was knocked out of the tournament in the third round.* **3** a stage in a BOXING or WRESTLING match: *The fight only lasted five rounds.* **4** a complete game of GOLF; a complete way around the course in some other sports, such as SHOW JUMPING: *We played a round of golf.* ◆ *the first horse to jump a clear round*
➤ REGULAR ACTIVITIES/ROUTE **5** a regular series of activities: *the daily round of school life* ◆ *Her life is one long round of parties and fun.* **6** a regular route that someone takes when delivering or collecting something; a regular series of visits that someone makes: *Dr. Green was on her daily hospital rounds.*
➤ DRINKS **7** a number of drinks bought by one person for all the others in a group: *a round of drinks* ◆ *It's my round* (= it is my turn to pay for the next set of drinks).
➤ CIRCLE **8** a round object or piece of something: *Cut the dough into rounds.*
➤ OF APPLAUSE **9** ~ **of applause** a short period during which people show their approval of someone or something by CLAPPING, etc.: *There was a great round of applause when the dance ended.*
➤ SHOT **10** a single shot from a gun; a bullet for one shot: *They fired several rounds at the crowd.* ◆ *We only have three rounds of ammunition left.*
➤ SONG **11** (*music*) a song for two or more voices in which each sings the same tune but starts at a different time
IDM **make the rounds (of sth) 1** if news or a joke **makes the rounds,** it is passed on quickly from one person to another **2** to go around from place to place, especially when looking for work or support for a political CAMPAIGN, etc. **in the round 1** (of a work of art) made so that it can be seen from all sides: *an opportunity to see Canova's work in the round* **2** (of a theater or play) with the people watching all around a central stage

● **verb 1** [T] ~ **sth** to go around a corner of a building, a bend in the road, etc.: *The boat rounded the tip of the island.* ◆ *We rounded the bend at high speed.* **2** [T, I] ~ **(sth)** to make something into a round shape; to form into a round shape: *She rounded her lips and whistled.* ◆ *His eyes rounded with horror.* **3** [T] ~ **sth (up/down) (to sth)** to increase or decrease a number to the next highest or lowest whole number
PHR V **round sth↔'off (with sth) 1** (also **round sth↔ 'out**) to finish an activity or complete something in a good or suitable way: *She rounded off the tour with a concert at Carnegie Hall.* **2** to take the sharp or rough edges off something: *You can round off the corners with sandpaper.* **round sb/sth↔'up 1** to find and gather together people, animals, or things: *I rounded up a few friends for a party.* ◆ *The cattle are rounded up in the evenings.* **2** if police or soldiers **round up** a group of people, they find them and arrest or capture them ⊃ **related noun** ROUNDUP

● **adv.** = AROUND adv.: *The dancers went round and round.*
IDM **round about 1** in the area near a place: *in Hartford and the towns round about* **2** approximately: *We're leaving round about ten.* ◆ *A new roof will cost round about $6,000.*

● **prep.** = AROUND prep.: *The earth moves round the sun.*

round·a·bout /'raʊndə,baʊt/ adj. [usually before noun] not done or said using the shortest, simplest, or most direct way possible: *It was a difficult and roundabout trip.* ◆ *He told us, in a very roundabout way, that he was thinking of leaving.*

round·ed /'raʊndəd/ adj. [usually before noun] **1** having a round shape: *a surface with rounded edges* ◆ *rounded shoulders* **2** having a wide variety of qualities that combine to produce something pleasant, complete, and balanced: *a smooth rounded taste* ◆ *a fully rounded education* **3** (*phonetics*) (of a speech sound) produced with the lips in a narrow, round position **ANT** UNROUNDED ⊃ **see also** WELL-ROUNDED

roun·del /'raʊndl/ noun (*technical*) a round design that is used as a decoration or to identify an aircraft

'round–eyed adj. with eyes that are fully open because of surprise, fear, etc.

round·house /'raʊndhaʊs/ noun a punch where the arm moves around in a wide curve

'roundhouse ,kick noun a move in KARATE and other MARTIAL ARTS, in which you turn on one foot as you make a high kick with the other

round·ing /'raʊndɪŋ/ noun [U] (*phonetics*) the fact of producing a speech sound with the lips in a rounded position

round·ly /'raʊndli/ adv. strongly or by a large number of people: *The report has been roundly criticized.* ◆ *They were roundly defeated* (= they lost by a large number of points).

round 'robin noun (*sports*) a competition in which every player or team plays every other player or team

'round–,shouldered adj. with shoulders that are bent forward or sloping downward

rounds·man /'raʊndzmən/ noun (*pl.* **rounds·men** /-mən/) the police officer in charge of a group of officers that is moving around an area

'round–,table adj. [only before noun] (of discussions, meetings, etc.) at which everyone is equal and has the same rights: *round-table talks*

round-the-'clock (also **,round-the-'clock**) adj. [only before noun] lasting or happening all day and night: *round-the-clock nursing care* ⊃ **see also** CLOCK

round 'trip noun [C, U] a trip to a place and back again: *a 30-mile round trip to work* ◆ *It's 30 miles round trip to work.* ► **,round-'trip** adj.: *a round-trip ticket* ⊃ **compare** ONE-WAY

'round·up /'raʊndʌp/ noun [usually sing.] **1** a summary of the most important points of a particular subject, especially the news: *We'll be back after the break with a roundup of today's* *other stories.* **2** an act of bringing people or animals together in one place for a particular purpose

round·worm /ˈraʊndwɜrm/ *noun* a small WORM that lives in the INTESTINES of pigs, humans, and some other animals

rouse /raʊz/ *verb* **1** (*formal*) to wake someone up, especially when they are sleeping deeply ~ **sb from sleep/bed**: *The telephone roused me from sleep at 6 a.m.* ◆ ~ **sb** *Nicky roused her with a gentle nudge.* **2** to make someone want to start doing something when they were not active or interested in doing it: ~ **sb/yourself (to sth)** *A lot of people were roused to action by the appeal.* ◆ ~ **sb/yourself to do sth** *Richard couldn't rouse himself to say anything in reply.* **3** ~ **sth** (*formal*) to make someone feel a particular emotion: *to rouse someone's anger* ◆ *What **roused your suspicions** (= what made you suspicious)?* **4** [usually passive] ~ **sb** to make someone angry, excited, or full of emotion: *Chris is not easily roused.* ⊃ see also AROUSE

rous·ing /ˈraʊzɪŋ/ *adj.* [usually before noun] **1** full of energy and enthusiasm: *a rousing cheer* ◆ *The team was given **a rousing reception** by the fans.* **2** intended to make other people feel enthusiastic about something: *a rousing speech*

roust /raʊst/ *verb* ~ **sb (from sth)** to disturb someone or make them move from a place

roust·a·bout /ˈraʊstəˌbaʊt/ *noun* a man with no special skills who does temporary work, for example on an OIL RIG or in a CIRCUS **SYN** CASUAL LABORER

rout /raʊt/ *noun, verb*
● *noun* [sing.] a situation in which someone is defeated easily and completely in a battle or competition
IDM **put sb to rout** (*literary*) to defeat someone easily and completely
● *verb* ~ **sb** to defeat someone completely in a competition, a battle, etc.: *The Buffalo Bills routed the Atlanta Falcons 41–14.*

route 🔑 **AWL** /rut; raʊt/ *noun, verb*
● *noun* **1** a way that you follow to get from one place to another: *Which is the best route to take?* ◆ *Drivers are advised to find an alternative route.* ◆ *a coastal route* ◆ ~ **(from A to B)** *the quickest route from Florence to Rome* ◆ *an escape route* ⊃ see also EN ROUTE **2** a fixed way along which a bus, train, etc. regularly travels or goods are regularly sent: *The house is not on a bus route.* ◆ *shipping routes* ◆ *a bike route* (= a path that is only for CYCLISTS) **3** ~ **(to sth)** a particular way of achieving something: *the route to success* **4** (*abbr.* Rte.) used before the number of a main road in the U.S.: *Route 66*
● *verb* (rout·ing, rout·ed, rout·ed) ~ **sb/sth** (+ adv./prep.) to send someone or something by a particular route: *Satellites route data all over the globe.*

route·man *noun* a person who delivers things to people in a particular area

route march *noun* a long march for soldiers over a particular route, especially to improve their physical condition

rout·er /ˈraʊtər/ *noun* **1** (*computing*) a device that sends data to the appropriate parts of a computer network ⊃ picture at COMPUTER **2** an electric tool that cuts shallow lines in surfaces

rou·tine 🔑 /ruˈtin/ *noun, adj.*
● *noun* **1** [C, U] the normal order and way in which you regularly do things: *We are trying to get the baby into a routine for feeding and sleeping.* ◆ *Make exercise a part of your **daily routine**.* ◆ *We clean and repair the machines **as a matter of routine**.* **2** [U] (*disapproving*) a situation in which life is boring because things are always done in the same way: *She needed a **break from routine**.* **3** [C] a series of movements, jokes, etc. that are part of a performance: *a dance routine* **4** [C] (*computing*) a list of instructions that enable a computer to perform a particular task
● *adj.* [usually before noun] **1** done or happening as a normal part of a particular job, situation, or process: *routine inquiries/questions/tests* ◆ *The fault was discovered during a*

routine check. **2** not unusual or different in any way: *He died of a heart attack during a routine operation.* **3** (*disapproving*) ordinary and boring **SYN** DULL, HUMDRUM: *a routine job* ◆ *This type of work rapidly becomes routine.* ▶ **rou·tine·ly** *adv.*: *Visitors are routinely checked as they enter the building.*

rout·ing num·ber /ˈraʊtɪŋ ˌnʌmbər/ *noun* a number that is used to identify a particular bank

roux /ru/ *noun* [C, U] (*pl.* roux) (from French) a mixture of fat and flour heated together until they form a solid mass, used for making sauces

rove /roʊv/ *verb* **1** [I, T] (*formal*) to travel from one place to another, often with no particular purpose **SYN** ROAM: + adv./prep. *A quarter of a million refugees roved around the country.* ◆ ~ **sth** *bands of thieves who roved the countryside* **2** [I] (+ adv./prep.) if someone's eyes **rove**, the person keeps looking in different directions

rov·er /ˈroʊvər/ *noun* (*literary*) a person who likes to travel a lot rather than live in one place

rov·ing /ˈroʊvɪŋ/ *adj.* [usually before noun] traveling from one place to another and not staying anywhere permanently: *a roving reporter for ABC news* ◆ *Patrick's roving lifestyle takes him between London and Los Angeles.*
IDM **have a roving eye** (*old-fashioned*) to always be looking for the chance to have a new sexual relationship

row 🔑 /roʊ/ *noun, verb*
● *noun* **1** ~ **(of sb/sth)** a number of people standing or sitting next to each other in a line; a number of objects arranged in a line: *a row of trees* ◆ *We sat **in a row** at the back of the room.* ◆ *The vegetables were planted in neat rows.* **2** a line of seats in a movie theater, etc.: *Let's sit in the back row.* ◆ *Our seats are five rows from the front.* **3** a complete line of STITCHES in KNITTING or CROCHET ⊃ picture at HOBBY **4** Row used in the name of some roads: *Park Row* **5** [usually sing.] an act of ROWING a boat; the period of time spent doing this: *We went for a row on the lake.* ⊃ see also DEATH ROW, SKID ROW
IDM **in a row 1** if something happens several times **in a row**, it happens in exactly the same way each time, and nothing different happens in the time between: *This is her third win in a row.* **2** if something happens for several days, etc. **in a row**, it happens on each of those days: *Inflation has fallen for the third month in a row.* ⊃ more at DUCK *n.*
● *verb* **1** [I, T] to move a boat through water using OARS (= long wooden poles with flat ends): *We rowed around the island.* ◆ ~ **sth** *Grace rowed the boat out to sea again.* **2** [T] ~ **sb** (+ adv./prep.) to take someone somewhere in a boat with OARS: *The fisherman rowed us back to the shore.*

row·boat /ˈroʊboʊt/ *noun* a small open boat that you move using OARS ⊃ picture at BOAT

row·dy /ˈraʊdi/ *adj.* (row·di·er, row·di·est) (of people) making a lot of noise or likely to cause trouble **SYN** DISORDERLY: *a rowdy crowd at the football game* ▶ **row·di·ly** /ˈraʊdl-i/ *adv.* **row·di·ness** /-dinəs/ *noun* [U] **row·dy** *noun* (*pl.* row·dies): *rowdies and troublemakers*

row·dy·ism /ˈraʊdiˌɪzəm/ *noun* [U] behavior that is noisy and causes trouble

row·er /ˈroʊər/ *noun* a person who ROWS a boat

row house *noun* a house that is one of a row of houses that are joined together on each side ⊃ picture at HOUSE ⊃ compare TOWNHOUSE

row·ing /ˈroʊɪŋ/ *noun* [U] the sport or activity of traveling in a boat using OARS: *to go rowing*

rowing ma·chine *noun* a piece of sports equipment on which you make the same movements as someone who is ROWING a boat ⊃ picture at EXERCISE

roy·al 🔑 /ˈrɔɪəl/ *adj., noun*
● *adj.* [only before noun] **1** connected with or belonging to the king or queen of a country: *the royal family* ◆ *the royal household* ⊃ compare REGAL **2** used in the names of organizations that serve or are supported by a king or

queen: *the Royal Navy* ♦ *the Royal Society for the Protection of Birds* **3** impressive; suitable for a king or queen **SYN** SPLENDID: *We were given a royal welcome.*

● **noun** [usually pl.] (*informal*) a member of a royal family

,**royal** ,**blue** *adj.* deep bright blue ▶ ,**royal** ,**blue** *noun* [U]

,**royal** '**flush** *noun* [usually sing.] (in card games) a set of cards that a player has that are the five highest cards of a SUIT, the ACE, king, queen, JACK, and ten

,**Royal** '**Highness** *noun* **His/Her/Your Royal Highness** a title of respect used when talking to or about a member of the royal family: *Their Royal Highnesses, the Duke and Duchess of Kent*

roy·al·ist /'rɔɪəlɪst/ *noun* a person who believes that a country should have a king or queen **SYN** MONARCHIST ⊃ compare REPUBLICAN ▶ **roy·a·list** *adj.*

,**royal** '**jelly** *noun* [U] a substance that is produced by worker BEES and that is fed to a young QUEEN BEE: *health food products containing royal jelly*

roy·al·ly /'rɔɪəli/ *adv.* (*old-fashioned*) very well; in a very impressive way or to a great degree

the ,**royal** '"**we**" *noun* [sing.] the use of "we" instead of "I" by a single person, as used traditionally by kings and queens in the past

roy·al·ty /'rɔɪəlti/ *noun* (*pl.* **roy·al·ties**) **1** [U] one or more members of a royal family: *The gala evening was attended by royalty and politicians.* ♦ *We were treated like royalty.* **2** [C, usually pl.] a sum of money that is paid to someone who has written a book, piece of music, etc. each time that it is sold or performed: *All royalties from the album will go to charity.* ♦ *She received $2,000 in royalties.* **3** [C, usually pl.] a sum of money that is paid by an oil or mining company to the owner of the land that they are working on

rpm /,ar pi 'ɛm/ *abbr.* revolutions per minute (a measurement of the speed of an engine or a record when it is playing)

RR *abbr.* (in writing) **1** also **R.R.** RURAL ROUTE **2** = RAILROAD

'**R-** ,**rated** *adj.* (of a movie) having a rating of R, meaning that no one younger than 17 will be allowed to see it unless an adult goes with them: *R-rated films* ♦ (*figurative*) *certain R-rated activities at the hotel*

RRSP /,ar ar ɛs 'pi/ *abbr.* (*CanE*) registered retirement savings plan (a special type of savings plan, in which you can save money without paying taxes on it until you stop working when you are older)

RSI /,ar ɛs 'aɪ/ *noun* [U] the abbreviation for "repetitive strain injury" or "repetitive stress injury" (pain and swelling, especially in the arms and hands, caused by performing the same movement many times in a job or an activity)

RSS /,ar ɛs 'ɛs/ *abbr.* (*computing*) Really Simple Syndication (a standard system for the distribution of information, especially news, from an Internet Web site to Internet users)

RSVP (also **R.S.V.P.**) /,ar ɛs vi 'pi/ *abbr.* (written on invitations) please reply (from French "répondez s'il vous plaît")

Rte. *abbr.* (in writing) route: *Stay on Rte. 1 until the bridge.*

RTF /,ar ti 'ɛf/ *abbr.* (*computing*) rich text format (a type of file containing data that can be used with different programs or systems): *an RTF file*

rub ✏ /rʌb/ *verb, noun*

● **verb** (-**bb-**) **1** [T, I] to move your hand, or something such as a cloth, backward and forward over a surface while pressing firmly: *~ sth She rubbed her chin thoughtfully.* ♦ *~ sth/yourself with sth Rub the surface with sandpaper before painting.* ♦ *~ sth/yourself against sth The cat rubbed itself against my legs.* ♦ *~ at sth I rubbed at the stain on the cloth.* ♦ *~ against sth Animals had been rubbing against the trees.* ♦ *~ sth/yourself + adj. Rub the surface smooth.* **2** [T, I] to press two surfaces against each other and move them

backward and forward; to be pressed together and move in this way: *~ sth (together) She rubbed her hands in delight.* ♦ *~ (together) It sounded like two pieces of wood rubbing together.* **3** [I, T] (of a surface) to move backward and forward many times against something while pressing it, especially causing pain or damage: *The back of my shoe is rubbing.* ♦ *~ on/against sth The wheel is rubbing on the fender.* ♦ *~ sth (+ adj.) The horse's neck was rubbed raw* (= until the skin came off) *where the rope had been.* **4** [T] *~ sth + adv./prep.* to spread a liquid or other substance over a surface while pressing firmly: *She rubbed the lotion into her skin.*

IDM **rub sb's nose in it** (*informal*) to keep reminding someone in an unkind way of their past mistakes **rub salt into the wound | rub salt into sb's wounds** to make a difficult experience even more difficult for someone **rub shoulders with sb** (also **rub elbows with sb**) to meet and spend time with a famous person, socially or as part of your job **rub sb the wrong way** (*informal*) to make someone annoyed or angry, often without intending to, by doing or saying something that offends them ⊃ more at TWO **PHR V** **rub sb/oneself/sth↔'down** to rub the skin of a person, horse, etc. hard with something to make it clean and dry ,**rub sth↔'down** to make something smooth by rubbing it with a special material ,**rub it 'in | ,rub sth 'in** [no passive] to keep reminding someone of something they feel embarrassed about and want to forget: *I know I was stupid; you don't have to rub it in.* ,**rub 'off (on/onto sb)** (of personal qualities, behavior, opinions, etc.) to become part of a person's character as a result of that person spending time with someone who has those qualities, etc.: *Her sense of fun has rubbed off on her children.* ,**rub sth↔'off (sth) | ,rub 'off** to remove something or to be removed by rubbing: *She rubbed off the dead skin.* ♦ *The gold coloring had begun to rub off.* ,**rub sb↔'out** (*slang*) to murder someone

● **noun** **1** [C, usually sing.] an act of rubbing a surface: *She gave her knee a quick rub.* **2** **the rub** [sing.] (*formal* or *humorous*) a problem or difficulty: *The hotel is in the middle of nowhere and there lies the rub. We don't have a car.*

rub·ber ✏ /'rʌbər/ *noun*

1 [U] a strong substance that can be stretched and does not allow liquids to pass through it, used for making tires, boots, etc. It is made from the liquid (= SAP) inside a tropical plant or is produced using chemicals.: *a ball made of rubber* ♦ *a rubber tree* ⊃ see also FOAM RUBBER, INDIA RUBBER **2** [C] (*informal*) = CONDOM **3** [C] (in some card games or sports) a competition consisting of a series of games or matches between the same teams or players

IDM **where the rubber meets the road** the point at which something is tested and you really find out whether it is successful or true: *Here's where the rubber meets the road: will consumers actually buy the product?* ⊃ more at BURN *v.* ▶ **rub·ber** *adj.* [usually before noun]: *a rubber ball* ♦ *rubber gloves*

'**rubber** ,**band** *noun* a thin, round piece of rubber used for holding things together ⊃ picture at STATIONERY

,**rubber** '**boot** *noun* one of a pair of long boots made of rubber, usually reaching almost up to the knee, that you wear to stop your feet from getting wet ⊃ picture at SHOE

,**rubber** '**bullet** *noun* a bullet made of rubber intended to injure but not to kill people, used by the army or police to control violent crowds

rub·ber·ized /'rʌbəˌraɪzd/ *adj.* [only before noun] covered with rubber: *rubberized cloth*

rub·ber·neck /'rʌbərˌnɛk/ *verb* [I] (*informal*) to turn to look at something while you are driving past it ▶ **rub·ber·neck·er** *noun*

'**rubber** ,**plant** *noun* a plant with thick, shiny, green leaves, often grown indoors

,**rubber** '**stamp** *noun* **1** a small tool that you hold in your hand and use for printing the date, the name of an organization, etc. on a document ⊃ picture at STATIONERY

2 (*disapproving*) a person or group that automatically gives approval to the actions or decisions of others: *The committee is seen as a rubber stamp for decisions made elsewhere.*

ˌrubber-ˈstamp *verb* ~ sth (often *disapproving*) to give official approval to a law, plan, decision, etc., especially without considering it carefully

rub·ber·y /ˈrʌbəri/ *adj.* **1** looking or feeling like rubber: *The eggs were overcooked and rubbery.* **2** (of legs or knees) feeling weak and unable to support your weight

rub·bing /ˈrʌbɪŋ/ *noun* a copy of writing or a design on a piece of stone or metal that is made by placing a piece of paper over it and rubbing with CHALK, a pencil, etc. ⊃ see also BRASS RUBBING

ˈrubbing ˌalcohol *noun* [U] a clear liquid, consisting mainly of alcohol, used for cleaning wounds, etc.

rub·bish /ˈrʌbɪʃ/ *noun* [U] (*informal*) comments, ideas, etc. that you think are stupid or wrong SYN NONSENSE: *It's not rubbish—it's true!*

rub·ble /ˈrʌbl/ *noun* [U] broken stones or bricks from a building or wall that has been destroyed or damaged: *The bomb reduced the houses to rubble.*

ˈrub-down *noun* **1** the act of rubbing someone or something with a cloth or special material, for example to make a person dry or to make something dry, clean, or smooth: *You may need to give the floor a rub-down with sandpaper.* **2** the act of rubbing and pressing a person's body with the hands to reduce pain in the muscles and joints SYN MASSAGE

Rube Gold·berg /ˌrub ˈgoʊldbɜrg/ *adj.* [only before noun] (*humorous*) (of machines and devices) having a very complicated design, especially when used to perform a very simple task; not practical

ru·bel·la /ruˈbɛlə/ *noun* [U] (*medical*) = GERMAN MEASLES

Ru·ben·esque /ˌrubəˈnɛsk/ *adj.* (of a woman) having a round body with large breasts and hips ORIGIN From the name of the Flemish painter Peter Paul Rubens, who often painted women with large, fairly fat bodies.

Ru·bi·con /ˈrubɪˌkɑn/ **the Rubicon** *noun* [sing.] the point at which a decision has been taken that can no longer be changed: *Today we cross the Rubicon. There is no going back.* ORIGIN From the Rubicon, a stream that formed the border between Italy and Gaul. When Julius Caesar broke the law by crossing it with his army in 49 B.C., it led inevitably to war.

ru·bi·cund /ˈrubɪkənd/ *adj.* (*literary*) (of a person's face) having a healthy red color SYN RUDDY

ru·bid·i·um /ruˈbɪdiəm/ *noun* [U] (*symb.* **Rb**) a chemical element. Rubidium is a rare, soft, silver-colored metal that reacts strongly with water and burns when it is brought into contact with air.

Ru·bik's cube™ /ˌrubɪks ˈkyub/ *noun* a PUZZLE consisting of a plastic CUBE covered with colored squares that you turn to make each side of the cube a different color

ru·ble (also **rou·ble**) /ˈrubl/ *noun* the unit of money in Russia

ru·bric /ˈrubrɪk/ *noun* (*formal*) **1** a title or set of instructions written in a book, an exam paper, etc. **2** a statement of the purpose or function of something

ru·by /ˈrubi/ *noun* (*pl.* **ru·bies**) **1** [C] a dark red PRECIOUS STONE: *a ruby ring* **2** [U] a dark red color ▶ **ru·by** *adj.*: *ruby lips*

ruched /ruʃt/ *adj.* (of cloth, clothes, etc.) sewn so that they hang in folds: *ruched curtains*

ruck·us /ˈrʌkəs/ *noun* [sing.] (*informal*) a situation in which there is a lot of noisy activity, confusion, or argument SYN COMMOTION

rud·der /ˈrʌdər/ *noun* a piece of wood or metal at the back of a boat or an aircraft that is used for controlling its direction ⊃ picture at PLANE

rud·der·less /ˈrʌdərləs/ *adj.* (*formal*) with no one in control; not knowing what to do

rud·dy /ˈrʌdi/ *adj.* **1** (of a person's face) looking red and healthy: *ruddy cheeks* ◆ *a ruddy complexion* **2** (*literary*) red in color: *a ruddy sky*

rude 🔑 /rud/ *adj.* (**rud·er, rud·est**)
1 having or showing a lack of respect for other people and their feelings SYN IMPOLITE: *a rude comment* ◆ ~ **(to sb) (about sb/sth)** *The man was downright rude to us.* ◆ *Why are you so rude to your mother?* ◆ *She was very rude about my driving.* ◆ ~ **(to do sth)** *It's rude to speak when you're eating.* **2** [only before noun] (*formal*) sudden, unpleasant, and unexpected: *Those expecting good news will get a rude shock.* ◆ *If the players think they can win this match easily, they are in for a rude awakening.* **3** (*literary*) made in a simple, basic way SYN PRIMITIVE: *rude shacks* ▶ **rude·ness** *noun* [U]: *She was critical to the point of rudeness.*

rude·ly 🔑 /ˈrudli/ *adv.*
1 in a way that shows a lack of respect for other people and their feelings: *They brushed rudely past us.* ◆ *"What do you want?" she asked rudely.* **2** (*formal*) in a way that is sudden, unpleasant, and unexpected: *I was rudely awakened by the phone ringing.*

ru·di·men·ta·ry /ˌrudəˈmɛntri; -ˈmɛntəri/ *adj.* **1** (*formal*) dealing with only the most basic matters or ideas SYN BASIC: *They were given only rudimentary training in the job.* **2** (*formal* or *technical*) not highly or fully developed SYN BASIC: *Some dinosaurs had only rudimentary teeth.*

ru·di·ments /ˈrudəmənts/ *noun* [pl.] **the ~ (of sth)** (*formal*) the most basic or essential facts of a particular subject, skill, etc. SYN BASICS

rue /ru/ *verb* (**rue·ing** or **ru·ing**, **rued**, **rued**) ~ sth (*old-fashioned* or *formal*) to feel bad about something that happened or something that you did because it had bad results **SYN** REGRET: *He rued the day they had bought such a large house.*

rue·ful /'rufl/ *adj.* feeling or showing that you are sad or sorry: *a rueful smile* ▶ **rue·ful·ly** /-fəli/ *adv.*: *"So this is goodbye," she said ruefully.*

ruff /rʌf/ *noun* **1** a ring of colored or marked feathers or fur around the neck of a bird or an animal **2** a wide, stiff, white COLLAR with many folds in it, worn especially in the 16th and 17th centuries

ruf·fi·an /'rʌfiən/ *noun* (*old-fashioned*) a violent man, especially one who commits crimes **SYN** THUG

ruf·fle /'rʌfl/ *verb, noun*
• *verb* **1** to disturb the smooth surface of something, so that it is not even: ~ *sth She ruffled his hair affectionately.* ◆ ~ *sth up The bird ruffled up its feathers.* **2** [often passive] ~ *sb* to make someone annoyed, worried, or upset **SYN** FLUSTER: *She was obviously ruffled by his question.* ◆ *He never gets ruffled, even under pressure.*
  IDM **ruffle sb's/a few feathers** (*informal*) to annoy or upset someone or a group of people: *The senator's speech ruffled a few feathers in the business world.* ⊃ more at SMOOTH *v.*
• *noun* [usually pl.] a strip of cloth that is sewn in folds and is used to decorate a piece of clothing at the neck or wrists **SYN** FRILL

ruf·fled /'rʌfld/ *adj.* decorated with ruffles: *a ruffled blouse*

rug /rʌg/ *noun* **1** a piece of thick material like a small carpet, that is used for covering or decorating part of a floor: (= that covers part of the floor of a room) **2** (*informal*) = TOUPEE
  IDM see PULL *v.*, SWEEP *v.*

rug·by (also **Rug·by**) /'rʌgbi/ *noun* [U] a game played by two teams of 13 or 15 players, using an OVAL ball which may be kicked or carried. Teams try to put the ball over the other team's line. **ORIGIN** Named after Rugby school in England, where the game was first played.

rug·ged /'rʌgəd/ *adj.* **1** (of the landscape) not level or smooth and having rocks rather than plants or trees: *rugged cliffs* ◆ *They admired the rugged beauty of the coastline.* **2** [usually before noun] (*approving*) (of a man's face) having strong, attractive features **3** [usually before noun] (of a person) determined to succeed in a difficult situation, even if this means using force or upsetting other people: *a rugged individualist* **4** (of equipment, clothing, etc.) strong and designed to be used in difficult conditions: *A less rugged vehicle would never have made the trip.* ◆ *rugged outdoor clothing* ▶ **rug·ged·ly** *adv.*: *ruggedly handsome* **rug·ged-ness** *noun* [U]

'rug rat *noun* (*informal*) a child

ru·in /'ruɪn/ *verb, noun*
• *verb* **1** ~ *sth* to damage something so badly that it loses all its value, pleasure, etc.; to spoil something **SYN** WRECK: *The bad weather ruined our trip.* ◆ *That one mistake ruined his chances of getting the job.* ◆ *My new shoes got ruined in the mud.* **2** ~ *sb/sth* to make someone or something lose all their money, position, etc.: *If she loses the court case it will ruin her.* ◆ *The country was ruined by the war.*
• *noun* **1** [U] the state or process of being destroyed or severely damaged: *A large number of churches fell into ruin after the revolution.* **2** [U] the fact of having no money, of having lost your job, position, etc.: *The divorce ultimately led to his ruin.* ◆ *The bank stepped in to save the company from financial ruin.* **3** [sing.] something that causes a person, company, etc. to lose all their money, job, position, etc. **SYN** DOWNFALL: *Gambling was his ruin.* **4** [C] (also **ruins** [pl.]) the parts of a building that remain after it has been destroyed or severely damaged: *The old mill is now little more than a ruin.* ◆ *We visited the ruins of a Norman castle.* ◆ (*figurative*) *He was determined to build a new life out of the ruins of his career.*
  IDM **in ruins** destroyed or severely damaged: *Years of*

fighting have left the area in ruins. ◆ *The scandal left his reputation in ruins.* ⊃ more at RACK *n.*

ru·in·a·tion /,ruə'neɪʃn/ *noun* [U] (*formal*) the process of destroying something or someone, or being destroyed **SYN** DESTRUCTION: *Urban development has led to the ruination of vast areas of countryside.*

ru·ined /'ruɪnd/ *adj.* [only before noun] (of a building, town, etc.) destroyed or severely damaged so that only parts remain: *a ruined castle*

ru·in·ous /'ruənəs/ *adj.* (*formal*) **1** costing a lot of money and more than you can afford: *ruinous legal fees* **2** causing serious problems or damage **SYN** DEVASTATING: *The decision was to prove ruinous.* **3** (*formal*) (of a town, building, etc.) destroyed or severely damaged: *a ruinous chapel* ◆ *The buildings were in a ruinous state.* ▶ **ru·in·ous·ly** *adv.*: *ruinously expensive*

rule /rul/ *noun, verb*
• *noun*
  ▷ OF ACTIVITY/GAME **1** [C] a statement of what may, must, or must not be done in a particular situation or when playing a game: *to follow/obey/observe the rules* ◆ *It's against all rules and regulations.* ◆ *to break a rule* (= not follow it) ◆ *This explains the rules under which the library operates.* ◆ *Without unwritten rules civilized life would be impossible.* ⊃ see also GROUND RULES
  ▷ ADVICE **2** [C] a statement of what you are advised to do in a particular situation: *There are no **hard and fast rules** for planning healthy meals.* ◆ *The first rule is to make eye contact with your interviewer.* ⊃ see also GOLDEN RULE
  ▷ HABIT/NORMALLY TRUE **3** [C, usually sing.] a habit; the normal state of things; what is true in most cases: *He makes it a rule never to borrow money.* ◆ *I go to bed early **as a rule**.* ◆ *Cold winters here are the exception rather than the rule* (= are rare). ◆ *As a general rule, vegetable oils are better for you than animal fats.*
  ▷ OF SYSTEM **4** [C] a statement of what is possible according to a particular system, for example the grammar of a language: *the rules of grammar*
  ▷ GOVERNMENT/CONTROL **5** [U] the government of a country or control of a group of people by a particular person, group, or system: *under Communist/civilian/military, etc. rule* ◆ *majority rule* (= government by the political party that most people have voted for) ◆ *The Ottoman empire imposed direct rule from Tripoli.* ⊃ see also HOME RULE
  ▷ MEASURING TOOL **6** [C] a measuring instrument with a straight edge ⊃ see also SLIDE RULE
  IDM **bend/stretch the rules** to change the rules to suit a particular person or situation **play by sb's (own) rules** if someone **plays by their own rules** or makes other people **play by their rules**, they set the conditions for doing business or having a relationship **play by the rules** to deal fairly and honestly with people **the rules of the game** the standards of behavior that most people accept or that actually operate in a particular area of life or business **the rule of law** the condition in which all members of society, including its rulers, accept the authority of the law **a rule of thumb** a practical method of doing or measuring something, usually based on past experience rather than on exact measurement
• *verb*
  ▷ GOVERN/CONTROL **1** [T, I] to control and have authority over a country, a group of people, etc.: ~ *sth At that time John ruled England.* ◆ (*figurative*) *Eighty million years ago, dinosaurs ruled the earth.* ◆ ~ **(over sb/sth)** *Charles I ruled for eleven years.* ◆ *She once ruled over a vast empire.* ◆ (*figurative*) *After the revolution, anarchy ruled.* **2** [T, often passive] ~ *sth* (often *disapproving*) to be the main thing that influences and controls someone or something: *The pursuit of money ruled his life.* ◆ *We live in a society where we are ruled by the clock.*
  ▷ GIVE OFFICIAL DECISION **3** [I, T] to give an official decision about something **SYN** PRONOUNCE: ~ **(on sth)** *The court will rule on the legality of the action.* ◆ ~ **against/in favor of sb/ sth** *The judge ruled against/in favor of the plaintiff.* ◆ ~ *sb/sth*

+ **adj.** *The deal may be ruled illegal.* ◆ **~ sb/sth to be/have sth** *The deal was ruled to be illegal.* ◆ **it is ruled that...** *It was ruled that the women were unfairly dismissed.*
> DRAW STRAIGHT LINE **4** [T] **~ sth** to draw a straight line using something that has a firm, straight edge
IDM **rule the roost** (*informal*) to be the most powerful member of a group ⊃ more at DIVIDE *v.*, HEART
PHR V **rule sb/sth↔ˈout 1 ~ (as sth)** to state that something is not possible or that someone or something is not suitable **SYN** EXCLUDE: *Police have not ruled out the possibility that the man was murdered.* ◆ *The proposed solution was ruled out as too expensive.* **2** to prevent someone from doing something; to prevent something from happening: *His age effectively ruled him out as a possible candidate.* **rule sb ˈout of sth** [usually passive] (in sports) to state that a player, runner, etc. will not be able to take part in a sports event; to prevent a player from taking part: *He has been ruled out of the match with a knee injury.*

ˈ**rule book** *noun* usually **the rule book** the set of rules that must be followed in a particular job, organization, or game

ruled /ruld/ *adj.* **ruled** paper has lines printed across it

rul·er 🔑 /ˈrulər/ *noun*
1 a person who rules or governs **2** a straight strip of wood, plastic, or metal, marked in inches or centimeters, used for measuring or for drawing straight lines ⊃ picture at STATIONERY

rul·ing /ˈrulɪŋ/ *noun, adj.*
● *noun* **~ (on sth)** an official decision made by someone in a position of authority, especially a judge: *The court will make its ruling on the case next week.*
● *adj.* [only before noun] having control over a particular group, country, etc.: *the ruling party*

rum /rʌm/ *noun* **1** [U, C] a strong, alcoholic drink made from the juice of SUGAR CANE **2** [C] a glass of rum

rum·ba (also **rhum·ba**) /ˈrʌmbə; ˈrum-/ *noun* a fast dance originally from Cuba; a piece of music for this dance

rum·ble /ˈrʌmbl/ *verb, noun*
● *verb* **1** [I] to make a long, deep sound or series of sounds: *The machine rumbled as it started up.* ◆ *thunder rumbling in the distance* ◆ *I'm so hungry my stomach's rumbling.* **2** [I] + **adv./prep.** to move slowly and heavily, making a rumbling sound: *tanks rumbling through the streets* **3** [I] (*informal*) (of a GANG of young people) to fight against another GANG
● *noun* **1** [U, C] **~ (of sth)** a long, deep sound or series of sounds: *the rumble of thunder* ◆ *Inside, the noise of the traffic was reduced to a distant rumble.* ◆ (*figurative*) *Although an agreement was reached, there are still rumbles of resentment.* **2** [C] (*informal*) a fight in the street between two or more GANGS (= groups of young people)

ˈ**rumble ˌstrip** *noun* a raised strip across a road or along its edge that makes a loud noise when a vehicle drives over it in order to warn the driver to go slower or that he or she is too close to the edge of the road

rum·bling /ˈrʌmblɪŋ/ *noun* **1** (also used as an adjective) a long deep sound or series of sounds: *the rumblings of thunder* ◆ *a rumbling noise* ◆ (*figurative*) *the rumblings of discontent* **2** [usually pl.] things that people are saying that may not be true **SYN** RUMOR: *There are rumblings that the election may have to be postponed.*

ru·mi·nant /ˈrumənənt/ *noun* (*technical*) any animal that brings back food from its stomach and chews it again. Cows and sheep are both ruminants. ▶ **ru·mi·nant** *adj.*: *ruminant animals*

ru·mi·nate /ˈruməneɪt/ *verb* [I, T] **~ (on/over/about sth)** | + **speech** (*formal*) to think deeply about something **SYN** PONDER ▶ **ru·mi·na·tion** /ˌrumənˈeɪʃn/ *noun* [C, U]

ru·mi·na·tive /ˈrumənˌeɪtɪv/ *adj.* (*formal*) tending to think deeply and carefully about things **SYN** PENSIVE, THOUGHTFUL: *in a ruminative mood* ▶ **ru·mi·na·tive·ly** *adv.*

rum·mage /ˈrʌmɪdʒ/ *verb* [I] + **adv./prep.** to move things around carelessly while searching for something: *She was rummaging around in her bag for her keys.* ◆ *I rummaged through the contents of the box until I found the book I wanted.*

ˈ**rummage ˌsale** *noun* a sale of old or used clothes, etc. to make money for a church, school, or other organization ⊃ see also GARAGE SALE, TAG SALE, YARD SALE

rum·my /ˈrʌmi/ *noun* [U] a simple card game in which players try to collect particular combinations of cards

ru·mor 🔑 (CanE usually **ru·mour**) /ˈrumər/ *noun, verb*
● *noun* [C, U] a piece of information, or a story, that people talk about, but that may not be true: *to start/spread a rumor* ◆ **~ (of sth)** *There are widespread rumors of job losses.* ◆ **~ (about sth)** *Some malicious rumors are circulating about his past.* ◆ **~ (that...)** *I heard a rumor that they are getting married.* ◆ *Many of the stories are based on rumor.* ◆ *Rumor has it* (= people say) *that he was murdered.*
● *verb* **be rumored** to be reported as a rumor and possibly not true: **it is rumored that...** *It's widely rumored that she's getting promoted.* ◆ **~ to be/have sth** *He was rumored to be involved in the crime.* ▶ **ru·mored** (CanE usually **ru·moured**) *adj.* [only before noun]: *He denied his father's rumored love affair.*

ru·mor-mon·ger (CanE usually **ru·mour-mon·ger**) /ˈrumər ˌmɑŋgər; -ˌmʌŋ-/ *noun* a person who spreads rumors

rump /rʌmp/ *noun* **1** [C] the round area of flesh at the top of the back legs of an animal that has four legs **2** [U] a piece of good quality meat cut from the rump of a cow **3** [C, usually sing.] (*humorous*) the part of the body that you sit on **SYN** BACKSIDE

rum·ple /ˈrʌmpl/ *verb* **~ sth** to make something messy or not smooth and neat: *She rumpled his hair playfully.* ◆ *The bed was rumpled where he had slept.*

rum·pus /ˈrʌmpəs/ *noun* [usually sing.] (*informal*) a lot of noise that is made especially by people who are complaining about something **SYN** COMMOTION: *to cause a rumpus*

ˈ**rumpus ˌroom** *noun* (*old-fashioned*) a room in a house for playing games in, sometimes in the BASEMENT

run 🔑 /rʌn/ *verb, noun*
● *verb* (run·ning, ran /ræn/, run)
> MOVE FAST ON FOOT **1** [I] to move using your legs, going faster than when you walk: *Can you run as fast as Mike?* ◆ *They turned and ran when they saw us coming.* ◆ *She came running to meet us.* ◆ *The dogs ran off as soon as we appeared.* **HELP** In spoken English **run** can be used with **and** plus another verb, instead of with **to** and the infinitive, especially to tell someone to hurry and do something: *Run and get your swimsuits, kids.* ◆ *I ran and knocked on the nearest door.* **2** [T] **~ sth** to travel a particular distance by running: *Who was the first person to run a mile in under four minutes?* **3** sometimes **go running** [I] to run as a sport: *She used to run when she was at college.* ◆ *I often go running before work.*
> RACE **4** [I, T] to take part in a race: **~ (in sth)** *He will be running in the 100 meters tonight.* ◆ *There are only five horses running in the first race.* ◆ **~ sth** *to run the marathon* ◆ *Holmes ran an impressive race to take the gold medal.* ⊃ see also RUNNER **5** [T, often passive] **~ sth** to make a race take place: *The Derby will be run in spite of the bad weather.*
> HURRY **6** [I] + **adv./prep.** to hurry from one place to another: *I've spent the whole day running after the kids.*
> MANAGE **7** [T] **~ sth** to be in charge of a business, etc.: *to run a hotel/store/language school* ◆ *He has no idea how to run a business.* ◆ *Stop trying to run my life* (= organize it) *for me.* ◆ *The shareholders want more say in how the company is run.* ◆ *a badly run company* ◆ *state-run industries* ⊃ see also RUNNING
> PROVIDE **8** [T] **~ sth** to make a service, course of study, etc. available to people **SYN** ORGANIZE: *The college runs summer courses for foreign students.*
> VEHICLE/MACHINE **9** [T] **~ sth** to own and use a vehicle or machine: *I can't afford to run a car on my salary.* **10** [I, T] to operate or function; to make something do this: *Stan had the*

chainsaw running. ◆ (*figurative*) *Her life had always run smoothly before.* ◆ ~ **on sth** *Our van runs on* (= uses) *diesel.* ◆ ~ **sth** *Could you run the engine for a moment?*

> BUSES/TRAINS **11** [I] (+ *adv./prep.*) to travel on a particular route: *Buses to the shopping mall run every half-hour.* ◆ *All the trains are running late* (= are leaving later than planned). **12** [T] ~ **sth** (+ *adv./prep.*) to make buses, trains, etc. travel on a particular route: *They run extra trains during the rush hour.*

> DRIVE SOMEONE **13** [T] ~ **sb** + *adv./prep.* (*informal*) to drive someone to a place in a car: *Can I run you home?*

> MOVE SOMEWHERE **14** [I] + *adv./prep.* to move, especially quickly, in a particular direction: *The car ran off the road into a ditch.* ◆ *A shiver ran down my spine.* ◆ *The sled ran smoothly over the frozen snow.* ◆ *The old tramlines are still there but now no trams run on them.* **15** [T] ~ **sth** + *adv./prep.* to move something in a particular direction: *She ran her fingers nervously through her hair.* ◆ *I ran my eyes over the page.*

> LEAD/STRETCH **16** [I, T] to lead or stretch from one place to another; to make something do this: + *adv./prep.* *He had a scar running down his left cheek.* ◆ *The road runs parallel to the river.* ◆ ~ **sth** + *adv./prep.* *We ran a cable from the lights to the stage.*

> CONTINUE FOR TIME **17** [I] ~ **(for sth)** to continue for a particular period of time without stopping: *Her last musical ran for six months on Broadway.* **18** [I] ~ **(for sth)** to operate or be valid for a particular period of time: *The permit runs for three months.* ◆ *The lease on my house only has a year left to run.*

> HAPPEN **19** [I] (usually used in the progressive tenses) to happen at the time mentioned: + *adv./prep.* *Programs are running a few minutes behind schedule this evening.* ◆ *The murderer was given three life sentences, to run concurrently.*

> GUNS, DRUGS, ETC. **20** [T] ~ **sth** (+ *adv./prep.*) to bring or take something into a country illegally and secretly **SYN** SMUGGLE ⊃ see also RUNNER

> OF STORY/ARGUMENT **21** [I, T] to have particular words, contents, etc.: *Their argument ran something like this...* ◆ + *speech* "*Ten shot dead by gunmen," ran the newspaper headline.*

> LIQUID **22** [I] + *adv./prep.* to flow: *The tears ran down her cheeks.* ◆ *Water was running all over the bathroom floor.* **23** [T] to make liquid flow: ~ **sth (into sth)** *She ran hot water into the bucket.* ◆ *to run the hot faucet* (= to turn it so that water flows from it) ◆ ~ **sth for sb** *I'll run a bath for you.* ◆ ~ **sb sth** *I'll run you a bath.* **24** [I] to send out a liquid: *Who left the faucet running?* ◆ *Your nose is running* (= MUCUS is flowing from it). ◆ *The smoke makes my eyes run.* **25** [I] (usually used in the progressive tenses) ~ **with sth** to be covered with a liquid: *His face was running with sweat.* ◆ *The bathroom floor was running with water.*

> OF COLOR **26** [I] if the color **runs** in a piece of clothing when it gets wet, it dissolves and may come out of the clothing into other things

> MELT **27** [I] (of a solid substance) to melt: *The wax began to run.* ⊃ see also RUNNY

> BE/BECOME **28** [I] + *adj.* to become different in a particular way, especially in a bad way: *The river ran dry* (= stopped flowing) *during the drought.* ◆ *Supplies are running low.* ◆ *We're running short of milk.* ◆ *You've got your rivals running scared.* **29** [I] ~ **at sth** to be at or near a particular level: *Inflation was running at 26%.*

> OF NEWSPAPER/MAGAZINE **30** [T] ~ **sth** to print and publish an item or a story: *On advice from their lawyers they decided not to run the story.*

> A TEST/CHECK **31** [T] ~ **a test/check (on something)** to do a test/check on something: *The doctors decided to run some more tests on the blood samples.*

> IN ELECTION **32** [I] to be a candidate in an election for a political position, especially in the U.S.: *Bush ran a second time in 2004.* ◆ ~ **for sb/sth** *to run for president* ◆ ~ **in sth** *to run in the election*

> OF PANTYHOSE/STOCKINGS **33** [I] if PANTYHOSE or STOCKINGS **run**, a long, thin hole appears in them

IDM Most idioms containing **run** are at the entries for the nouns and adjectives in the idioms. For example, **run riot** is at **riot**. **come running** to be pleased to do what someone

wants: *She knew she had only to call and he would come running.* **run for it** (often used in orders) to run in order to escape from someone or something **up and running** working fully and correctly: *It will be a lot easier when we have the database up and running.*

PHR V **run across sb/sth** to meet someone or find something by chance

run 'after sb/sth to run to try to catch someone or something **SYN** PURSUE

run 'after sb (*informal*) to try to have a romantic or sexual relationship with someone **SYN** PURSUE: *He's always running after younger women.* **run a'long** (*old-fashioned, informal*) used in orders to tell someone, especially a child, to go away

run a'round with sb (also **'run with sb**) (usually *disapproving*) to spend a lot of time with someone: *She's always running around with older men.*

'run at sb [no passive] to run toward someone to attack or as if to attack them: *He ran at me with a knife.*

run a'way (from sb/...) to leave sb/a place suddenly; to escape from sb/a place: *He ran away from home at the age of thirteen.* ◆ *Looking at all the accusing faces, she felt a sudden urge to run away.* ⊃ related noun RUNAWAY **run a'way from sth** to try to avoid something because you are shy, lack confidence, etc.: *You can't just run away from the situation.*

run a'way with you if a feeling **runs away with you**, it gets out of your control: *Her imagination tends to run away with her.* **run a'way/'off with sb** | **run a'way/'off (together)** to leave home, your husband, wife, etc. in order to have a relationship with another person: *She ran away with her boss.* ◆ *She and her boss ran away together.* **run a'way with sth 1** to win something clearly or easily **2** to believe something that is not true: *I don't want you to run away with the impression that all I do is have meetings all day.*

run back 'over sth to discuss or consider something again **SYN** REVIEW: *I'll run back over the procedure once again.* **run sth 'by/'past sb** (*informal*) to show someone something or tell someone about an idea in order to see their reaction to it

run 'down to lose power or stop working: *The battery has run down.* **run sth↔'down** to make something lose power or stop working: *If you leave your headlights on, you'll soon run down the battery.* **run sb/sth↔'down 1** (of a vehicle or its driver) to hit someone or something and knock them/it to the ground **2** to criticize someone or something in an unkind way: *He's always running her down in front of other people.*

run sb↔'in (*old-fashioned, informal*) to arrest someone and take them to a police station

run 'into sb (*informal*) to meet someone by chance: *Guess who I ran into today!* **'run into sth 1** to enter an area of bad weather while traveling: *We ran into thick fog on the way home.* **2** to experience difficulties, etc.: *Be careful not to run into debt.* ◆ *to run into danger/trouble/difficulties* **3** to reach a particular level or amount: *Her income runs into six figures* (= is more than $100,000). **'run sth into sb/sth** to crash into someone or something: *The bus went out of control and ran into a line of people.* **'run sth into sb/sth** to make a vehicle crash into someone or something: *He ran his car into a tree.*

run sth↔'off to copy something on a machine: *Could you run off twenty copies of the agenda?* **run 'off with sb** | **run 'off (together)** = RUN AWAY WITH SB **run 'off with sth** to steal something and take it away: *The treasurer had run off with the club's funds.*

run 'on to continue without stopping; to continue longer than is necessary or expected: *The meeting will finish promptly—I don't want it to run on.*

run 'out 1 if a supply of something **runs out**, it is used up or finished: *Time is running out for the trapped miners.* **2** if an agreement or a document **runs out**, it becomes no longer valid **SYN** EXPIRE **run 'out (of sth)** to use up or finish a supply of something: *We ran out of gas.* ◆ *Could I have a cigarette? I seem to have run out.* **run 'out on sb** (*informal*) to leave someone that you live with, especially when they need your help

,run 'over if a container or its contents **run over**, the contents come over the edge of the container **SYN** OVERFLOW ,run sb/sth↔'over (of a vehicle or its driver) to knock a person or an animal down and drive over their body or a part of it: *Two children were run over and killed.* ,run 'over sth to read through or practice something quickly: *She ran over her notes before giving the lecture.* ,run sth 'past sb = RUN STH BY/PAST SB: *Run that past me again.* ,run sb↔'through (*literary*) to kill someone by sticking a knife, SWORD, etc. through them ,run 'through sth **1** [no passive] to pass quickly through something: *An angry murmur ran through the crowd.* ♦ *Thoughts of revenge kept running through his mind.* **2** [no passive] to be present in every part of something: *A deep melancholy runs through her poetry.* **3** to discuss, repeat, or read something quickly: *He ran through the names on the list.* ♦ *Could we run through your proposals once again?* **4** to perform, act, or practice something: *Can we run through Scene 3 again, please?* ➔ related noun RUN-THROUGH **5** to use up or spend money carelessly: *She ran through the entire amount within two years.* 'run to sth to be of a particular size or amount: *The book runs to nearly 800 pages.* ,run sth↔'up **1** to allow a bill, debt, etc. to reach a large total **SYN** ACCUMULATE: *How had he managed to run up so many debts?* **2** to make a piece of clothing quickly, especially by sewing: *to run up a blouse* **3** to raise something, especially a flag ,run 'up against sth to experience a difficulty: *The government is running up against considerable opposition to its tax reforms.* 'run with sb = RUN AWAY WITH SB 'run with sth to accept or start to use a particular idea or method: *OK, let's run with Jan's suggestion.*

● noun
> **ON FOOT 1** [C] an act of running; a period of time spent running or the distance that someone runs: *I go for a run every morning.* ♦ *a five-mile run* ♦ *Catching sight of her, he broke into a run* (= started running). ♦ *I decided to make a run for it* (= to escape by running). ♦ *She took the stairs at a run.*
> **TRIP 2** [C] a trip by car, plane, boat, etc., especially a short one or one that is made regularly: *They took the car out for a run.* ➔ see also MILK RUN
> **OF SUCCESS/FAILURE 3** [C] a period of something good or bad happening; a series of successes or failures **SYN** SPELL: *a run of good/bad luck* ♦ *Our team finally lost, ending an unbeaten run of 18 games.*
> **OF PLAY/MOVIE 4** [C] a series of performances of a play or movie: *The show had a record-breaking run on Broadway.*
> **OF PRODUCT 5** [C] the amount of a product that a company decides to make at one time: *The first print run of 6,000 copies sold out.*
> **MONEY 6** [C, usually sing.] ~ **on the dollar, etc.** a situation when many people sell dollars, etc. and the value of the money falls **7** [C, usually sing.] ~ **on a bank** a situation when many people suddenly want to take their money out of a bank
> **SUDDEN DEMAND 8** [C, usually sing.] ~ **on sth** a situation when many people suddenly want to buy something: *a run on the band's latest CD*
> **WAY THINGS HAPPEN 9** [sing.] **the ~ of sth** the way things usually happen; the way things seem to be happening on a particular occasion: *In the normal run of things the only exercise he gets is climbing in and out of taxis.*
> **IN SPORTS 10** [C] a sloping track used in SKIING and some other sports: *a ski/toboggan, etc. run* **11** [C] a point scored in the game of baseball or CRICKET: *Our team won by four runs.* ➔ see also HOME RUN ♦ note at BASEBALL
> **IN ELECTION 12** [sing.] an act of trying to get elected to public office: *He made an unsuccessful run for governor in 2008.*
> **FOR ANIMALS/BIRDS 13** [C] (often in compounds) an area surrounded by a fence or wire, in which animals or birds are kept as pets or on a farm: *a chicken run*
> **IN MUSIC 14** [C] a series of notes sung or played quickly up or down the SCALE

> **IN CARD GAMES 15** [C] a series of cards held by one player
> **IN PANTYHOSE/STOCKINGS 16** [C] a long thin hole in PANTYHOSE or STOCKINGS where some threads have broken
> **ILLNESS 17 the runs** [pl.] (*informal*) = DIARRHEA ➔ see also DRY RUN, TRIAL RUN
IDM the common, general, ordinary, usual **run (of sth)** the average type of something: *He was very different from the general run of movie stars.* **give sb/get/have the run of sth** to give sb/get/have permission to make full use of something: *Her dogs have the run of the house.* **give sb a (good) run for their money** to make someone try very hard, using all their skill and effort, in order to beat you in a game or competition **on the run 1** trying to avoid being captured: *He's on the run from the police.* **2** (*informal*) continuously active and moving around: *I've been on the run all day and I'm exhausted.* ♦ *Here are some quick recipes for when you're eating on the run* (= in a hurry). ➔ more at LONG adj., SHORT adj.

run·a·round /'rʌnəˌraʊnd/ noun
IDM **give sb the runaround** (*informal*) to treat someone badly by not telling them the truth, or by not giving them the help or the information they need, and sending them somewhere else

run·a·way /'rʌnəˌweɪ/ adj., noun
● adj. [only before noun] **1** (of a person) having left without telling anyone: *runaway children* **2** (of an animal or a vehicle) not under the control of its owner, rider, or driver: *a runaway horse/car* **3** happening very easily or quickly, and not able to be controlled: *a runaway winner/victory* ♦ *the runaway success of her first play* ♦ *runaway inflation*
● noun a person who has suddenly left or escaped from someone or something, especially a child who has left home without telling anyone: *teenage runaways living on the streets*

run·down /'rʌndaʊn/ noun [usually sing.] ~ **(on/of sth)** an explanation or a description of something: *I can give you a brief rundown on each of the applicants.*

,run-'down adj. **1** (of a building or place) in very bad condition; that has not been taken care of **SYN** NEGLECTED: *run-down inner-city areas* **2** [not before noun] (of a person) tired or slightly sick, especially from working hard: *to be run-down* **3** (of a business, etc.) not as busy or as active as it used to be: *run-down transportation services*

rune /run/ noun **1** one of the letters in an alphabet that people in northern Europe used in ancient times and cut into wood or stone **2** a symbol that has a mysterious or magic meaning ▶ **ru·nic** /'runɪk/ adj.: *runic inscriptions*

rung /rʌŋ/ noun one of the bars that forms a step in a LADDER: *He put his foot on the bottom rung to keep the ladder steady.* ♦ (*figurative*) *to get a foot on the bottom rung of the career ladder* ♦ *She was a few rungs above him on the social ladder.* ➔ see also RING¹

'run-in noun ~ **(with sb)** (*informal*) an argument or a fight: *The fiery player has had several run-ins with referees.*

run·nel /'rʌnl/ noun (*formal* or *literary*) a small stream or channel

run·ner /'rʌnər/ noun
1 a person or an animal that runs, especially one taking part in a race: *a long-distance/cross-country/marathon, etc. runner* ♦ *a list of runners* (= horses in a race) *and riders* ➔ see also FORERUNNER, FRONT RUNNER, ROADRUNNER **2** (especially in compounds) a person who takes goods illegally into or out of a place: *a drug runner* ➔ see also GUNRUNNER **3** a strip of metal, plastic, or wood that something slides on or can move along on: *the runners of a sled* **4** a plant STEM that grows along the ground and puts down roots to form a new plant **5** a long, narrow piece of cloth or carpet on a piece of furniture or on the floor **6** a person in a company or an organization whose job is to take messages, documents, etc. from one place to another **7** (*CanE*) a shoe that is used for running or doing other sports in

,runner-'up noun (pl. ,runners-'up) a person or team that finishes second in a race or competition; a person or team that has not finished first but that wins a prize: *Winner: Kay Hall. Runner-up: Chris Platts.* ♦ *The runners-up will all receive a $100 prize.*

run·ning 🔑 /'rʌnɪŋ/ noun, adj.

● **noun** [U] **1** the action or sport of running: *to go running* ♦ *running shoes* **2** the activity of managing or operating something: *the day-to-day running of a business* ♦ *the running costs of a car* (= for example of fuel, repairs, insurance) **3** -running (in compounds) the activity of bringing something such as drugs, guns, etc. into a country secretly and illegally: *drug-running*
IDM **in/out of the running (for sth)** (*informal*) having some/no chance of succeeding or achieving something
● **adj. 1** used after a number and a noun such as "year," "day," or "time," to say that something has happened in the same way several times, without a change: *She's won the championship three years running.* ♦ *It was the third day running that the train had been late.* ♦ *No party has won an election four times running.* **2 running water** is water that is flowing somewhere, or water that is supplied to a building and available to be used through faucets: *I can hear the sound of running water.* ♦ *a remote cabin without electricity or running water* **3** [only before noun] lasting a long time; continuous **SYN** ONGOING: *For years he had fought a running battle with the authorities over the land.* ♦ *a running argument* ♦ *His old raincoat became a running joke* (= people kept laughing at it). ○ see also LONG-RUNNING **4** -running (in compounds) running or flowing in the way mentioned: *a fast-running river* **IDM** see ORDER *n.*

,running ,back *noun* (in football) an offensive player whose main job is to run forward carrying the ball

,running 'commentary *noun* a continuous description of an event, especially a sports event, that someone gives as it happens: *to give a running commentary on the game*

'running ,dog *noun* **1** (*disapproving*) a person who follows a political system or set of beliefs without questioning them **2** a dog that has been bred to run, especially for racing or for pulling a SLED across snow

,running 'head *noun* (*technical*) a title or word printed at the top of each page of a book

'running ,mate *noun* [usually sing.] (*politics*) the person who is chosen by a candidate in an election, especially a PRESIDENTIAL election, to support them and to have the next highest political position if they win: *The presidential nominee was advised to choose a woman as a running mate.*

,running 'sore *noun* a small area on the body that is infected and has liquid (called PUS) coming out of it

,running 'start *noun* [sing.] a start to a race in which the runners are already running when they reach the starting line: *The racers were given a running start.* ♦ (*figurative*) *The Democratic candidate seems to be off to a running start.* ♦ (*figurative*) *Government benefits gave veterans a running start* (= an advantage).

'running ,time *noun* the amount of time that a movie, a trip, etc. lasts

,running 'total *noun* the total number or amount of things, money, etc. that changes as you add each new item

run·ny /'rʌni/ *adj.* (run·ni·er, run·ni·est) **1** (of your nose or eyes) producing a lot of liquid, for example when you have a cold **2** having more liquid than is usual; not solid: *runny honey* ♦ *I don't like my eggs too runny.*

'run-off *noun* **1** [C] a second vote or competition that is held to find a winner because two people taking part in the first competition got the same result **2** [U, C] rain, water, or other liquid that runs off land into streams and rivers

,run-of-the-'mill *adj.* (often *disapproving*) ordinary, with no special or interesting features

,run-on 'sentence *noun* two or more sentences or independent CLAUSES joined without the correct grammar

,run 'play (also ,running 'play) *noun* (in football) a play in which a player carries the ball forward from behind the LINE OF SCRIMMAGE ○ compare PASS PLAY

runt /rʌnt/ *noun* **1** the smallest, weakest animal of the young that are born from the same mother at the same time: *the runt of the litter* **2** (*informal*, *disapproving*) a rude way of referring to a small, weak, or unimportant person

'run-through *noun* a practice for a performance of a play, show, etc. **SYN** REHEARSAL

'run-time *noun* [U, C] (*computing*) **1** the amount of time that a program takes to perform a task **2** the time when a program is performing a task

'run-up *noun* ~ (to sth) a period of time leading up to an important event; the preparation for this: *an increase in spending in the run-up to Christmas* ♦ *in the run-up to the election*

run·way /'rʌnweɪ/ *noun* **1** a long narrow strip of ground with a hard surface that an aircraft takes off from and lands on ○ collocations at TRAVEL **2** a raised platform for people to walk on, especially a CATWALK (= a long stage that models walk on during a fashion show)

ru·pee /'rupi; ruˈpi/ *noun* the unit of money in India, Pakistan, and some other countries

rup·ture /'rʌptʃər/ *noun, verb*
● **noun** [C, U] **1** (*medical*) an injury in which something inside the body breaks apart or bursts: *the rupture of a blood vessel* **2** a situation when something breaks or bursts: *ruptures of oil and water pipelines* **3** (*informal*) a HERNIA of the ABDOMEN: *I nearly gave myself a rupture lifting that pile of books.* **4** (*formal*) the ending of agreement or of good relations between people, countries, etc.: *a rupture in relations between the two countries* ♦ *Nothing could heal the rupture with his father.*
● **verb 1** [T, I] ~ (sth/yourself) (*medical*) to burst or break apart something inside the body; to be broken or burst apart: *a ruptured appendix* ♦ *He ruptured himself* (= got a HERNIA) *trying to lift the piano.* **2** [T, I] ~ (sth) to make something such as a container or a pipe break or burst; to be broken or burst: *The impact ruptured both fuel tanks.* ♦ *A pipe ruptured, leaking water all over the house.* **3** [T] ~ sth to make an agreement or good relations between people or countries end: *the risk of rupturing North-South relations*

ru·ral 🔑 /'rʊrəl/ *adj.* [usually before noun]
connected with or like the countryside: *rural areas* ♦ *a rural economy* ♦ *rural America* ♦ *a rural way of life* ○ compare URBAN

'rural ,route *noun* (*abbr.* RR) a route along which mail is delivered in rural areas

ruse /ruz/ *noun* a way of doing something or of getting something by cheating someone **SYN** TRICK

rush 🔑 /rʌʃ/ *verb, noun*
● **verb**
❯ **MOVE FAST 1** [I, T] to move or to do something with great speed, often too fast: *We've got plenty of time; there's no need to rush.* ♦ *the sound of rushing water* ♦ + adv./prep. *Don't rush off, I haven't finished.* ♦ *I've been rushing around all day trying to get everything done.* ♦ *People rushed to buy shares in the company.* ♦ ~ sth *We had to rush our meal.*
❯ **TAKE/SEND QUICKLY 2** [T] ~ sb/sth + adv./prep. | ~ sb sth to transport or send someone or something somewhere with great speed: *Ambulances rushed the injured to the hospital.* ♦ *Relief supplies were rushed in.*
❯ **DO SOMETHING TOO QUICKLY 3** [I, T] to do something or to make someone do something without thinking about it carefully: ~ into sth/into doing sth *We don't want to rush into having a baby.* ♦ ~ sb *Don't rush me. I need time to think about it.* ♦ ~ sb into sth/into doing sth *I'm not going to be rushed into anything.*

h **hat**   m **man**   n **no**   ŋ **sing**   l **leg**   r **red**   y **yes**   w **wet**

▷ ATTACK **4** [T] ~ sb/sth to try to attack or capture someone or something suddenly: *A group of prisoners rushed an officer and managed to break out.* ◆ *Fans rushed the stage after the concert.*

▷ IN FOOTBALL **5** [T] ~ sb to run into someone who has the ball **6** [I] to move forward and gain ground by carrying the ball and not passing it

▷ IN COLLEGES **7** [T, I] ~ (sth) to go through the process of joining a FRATERNITY or SORORITY: *He's deciding whether to rush a fraternity.* ◆ *She plans to rush in January.* **8** [T] ~ sb to give a lot of attention to a student because you want them to join your FRATERNITY or SORORITY: *He is being rushed by Sigma Nu.* **IDM** see FOOL n., FOOT n.

PHR V ,rush sth⟷'out to produce something very quickly: *The editors rushed out an item on the crash for the late news.* ,rush sth⟷'through | ,rush sth 'through sth to deal with official business very quickly by making the usual process shorter than usual: *to rush a bill through Congress*

● *noun*

▷ FAST MOVEMENT **1** [sing.] a sudden strong movement: *Shoppers made a rush for the exits.* ◆ *She was trampled in the rush to get out.* ◆ *They listened to the rush of the ocean below.* ◆ *The door blew open, letting in a rush of cold air.* ◆ *He had a rush of blood to the head and punched the man.*

▷ HURRY **2** [sing., U] a situation in which you are in a hurry and need to do things quickly: *I can't stop—I'm in a rush.* ◆ *What's the rush?* ◆ *"I'll let you have the book back tomorrow." "There's no rush."* ◆ *The words came out in a rush.* ◆ *a rush job* (= one that has been done quickly)

▷ BUSY SITUATION **3** [sing.] a situation in which people are very busy and there is a lot of activity: *The evening rush was just starting.* ◆ *the Christmas rush*

▷ OF FEELING **4** [sing.] ~ (of sth) a sudden strong emotion or sign of strong emotion: *a sudden rush of excitement/fear/anger* **5** [sing.] a sudden feeling of extreme pleasure or excitement: *Parachuting will give you the rush of a lifetime.* ◆ *Users of the drug report experiencing a rush that lasts several minutes.*

▷ SUDDEN DEMAND **6** [sing.] ~ (on/for sth) a sudden large demand for goods, etc.: *There's been a rush on umbrellas this week.* ⊃ see also GOLD RUSH

▷ PLANT **7** [C, usually pl.] a tall plant like grass that grows near water. Its long thin STEMS can be dried and used for making BASKETS, the seats of chairs, etc.: *rush matting*

▷ OF MOVIE **8** rushes [pl.] (*technical*) the first prints of a movie before they have been EDITED

▷ IN FOOTBALL **9** [C] an occasion when a player or players run toward a player on the other team who has the ball: *There was a rush on the quarterback.* **10** [C] an occasion when a player runs forward with the ball: *Johnson carried the ball an average of 6 yards per rush.*

▷ IN COLLEGES **11** [sing.] the time when parties are held for students who want to join a FRATERNITY or SORORITY: *rush week* ◆ *a rush party* **IDM** see BUM n.

rushed /rʌʃt/ *adj.* done too quickly or made to do something too quickly: *It was a rushed decision made at the end of the meeting.* ◆ *Let's start work on it now so we're not too rushed at the end.* **IDM** see FOOT n.

'**rush hour** *noun* [C, usually sing., U] the time, usually twice a day, when the roads are full of traffic, and trains are crowded, because people are traveling to or from work: *the morning/evening rush hour* ◆ *Don't travel at rush hour/during rush hour.* ◆ *rush-hour traffic* ⊃ collocations at DRIVING

rus·set /'rʌsət/ *adj.* red-brown in color ▶ rus·set *noun* [U]: *leaves of russet and gold*

Rus·sian /'rʌʃn/ *adj., noun*
● *adj.* from or connected with Russia
● *noun* **1** [C] a person from Russia **2** [U] the language of Russia

,**Russian** '**doll** *noun* one of a set of hollow, painted figures which fit inside each other

,**Russian rou'lette** *noun* [U] a dangerous game in which a person shoots at their own head with a gun that contains a

bullet in only one of its chambers, so that the person does not know if the gun will fire or not: (*figurative*) *The airline was accused of playing Russian roulette with passenger safety.*

Russo- /'rʌsoʊ/ *combining form* (in nouns and adjectives) Russian: *Russo-Japanese relations*

rust /rʌst/ *noun, verb*
● *noun* [U] **1** a red-brown substance that is formed on some metals by the action of water and air: *pipes covered with rust* ◆ *rust spots* ◆ *a rust-colored dress* ⊃ see also RUSTY **2** a plant disease that causes red-brown spots; the FUNGUS that causes this disease
● *verb* [I, T] if metal rusts or something rusts it, it becomes covered with rust **SYN** CORRODE: *old rusting farming implements* ◆ *Brass doesn't rust.* ◆ ~ sth *Water had got in and rusted the engine.* ▶ rust·ed *adj.: rusted iron* ⊃ see also RUSTY
PHR V ,rust a'way to be gradually destroyed by rust

'**rust belt** *noun* a region that used to have a lot of industry, but that has now decreased in importance and wealth, especially parts of the northern U.S. where there were many factories that have now closed

rus·tic /'rʌstɪk/ *adj., noun*
● *adj.* **1** (*approving*) typical of the country or of country people; simple: *an old cottage full of rustic charm* **2** made very simply of rough wood: *a rustic garden seat* ◆ *a rustic fence* ▶ rus·tic·i·ty /rʌ'stɪsəti/ *noun* [U]
● *noun* (*disapproving* or *humorous*) a person who lives in or comes from the country

rus·tle /'rʌsl/ *verb, noun*
● *verb* **1** [I, T] ~ (sth) if something dry and light rustles or you rustle it, it makes a sound like paper, leaves, etc. moving or rubbing together: *the sound of the trees rustling in the breeze* **2** [T] ~ sth to steal farm animals
PHR V ,rustle sth⟷'up (for sb) (*informal*) to make or find something quickly for someone and without planning: *I'm sure I can rustle you up a sandwich.* ◆ *She's trying to rustle up some funding for the project.*
● *noun* [sing.] a light, dry sound like leaves or pieces of paper moving or rubbing against each other: *There was a rustle of paper as people turned the pages.* ◆ *I heard a faint rustle in the bushes.*

rus·tler /'rʌslər/ *noun* a person who steals farm animals

rus·tling /'rʌslɪŋ/ *noun* **1** [U, C] the sound of light, dry things moving together: *the soft rustling of leaves* **2** [U] the act of stealing farm animals

rust·proof /'rʌstpruf/ *adj.* rustproof metal has had a substance put on it so that it will not RUST

rust·y /'rʌsti/ *adj.* (rust·i·er, rust·i·est) **1** covered with RUST: *rusty metal* ◆ *a rusty old car* **2** [not usually before noun] (*informal*) (of a sport, skill, etc.) not as good as it used to be, because you have not been practicing: *My tennis is very rusty these days.* ◆ *I haven't played the piano for ages—I may be a little rusty.* ▶ rust·i·ness *noun* [U]

rut /rʌt/ *noun* **1** [C] a deep track that a wheel makes in soft ground **2** [C] a boring way of life that does not change: *I gave up my job because I felt I was stuck in a rut.* ◆ *If you don't go out and meet new people, it's easy to get into a rut.* **3** [U] also the rut the time of year when male animals, especially DEER, become sexually active ⊃ see also RUTTED, RUTTING

ru·ta·ba·ga /'rutə,beɪɡə; ,rutə'beɪɡə/ *noun* [C, U] a large, round, yellow root vegetable ⊃ picture at FRUIT

ru·the·ni·um /ru'θiniəm/ *noun* [U] (*symb* Ru) a chemical element. Ruthenium is a hard silver-white metal that breaks easily and is found in PLATINUM ORES.

ruth·er·for·di·um /,rʌðər'fɔrdiəm/ *noun* [U] (*symb.* Rf) a chemical element. Rutherfordium is RADIOACTIVE and does not exist in nature but is produced artificially when atoms COLLIDE (= crash into each other).

ruth·less /'ruθləs/ *adj.* (*disapproving*) (of people or their behavior) hard and cruel; determined to get what you want and not caring if you hurt other people: *a ruthless dictator*

◆ *The way she behaved toward him was utterly ruthless.* ◆ *He has a ruthless determination to succeed.* ▸ **ruth·less·ly** *adv.* **ruth·less·ness** *noun* [U]

rut·ted /'rʌtəd/ *adj.* (of a road or path) with deep tracks that have been made by wheels ➔ see also RUT

rut·ting /'rʌtɪŋ/ *adj.* (of male animals, especially DEER) in a time of sexual activity: *rutting deer* ◆ *the rutting season* ➔ see also RUT

RV /ˌɑr 'vi/ *noun* the abbreviation for "recreational vehicle"; a large vehicle designed for people to live and sleep in when they are traveling or on vacation ➔ **picture at** CAR

Rx /ˌɑr 'ɛks/ *noun* **1** the written abbreviation for a doctor's PRESCRIPTION **2** a solution to a problem: *There's no Rx for unemployment.*

-ry ➔ -ERY

rye /raɪ/ *noun* [U] a plant that looks like BARLEY but that produces larger grain, grown as food for animals and for making flour and WHISKEY; the grain of this plant: *rye bread* ◆ *rye whiskey* ➔ **picture at** CEREAL

rye·grass /'raɪɡræs/ *noun* [U] a type of grass that is grown as food for animals

ʌ cup   ə about   eɪ say   aɪ five   ɔɪ boy   aʊ now   oʊ go   ər bird

Ss

S /ɛs/ *noun, abbr., symbol*
- **noun** also **s** [C, U] (*pl.* **Ss, S's, s's** /ˈɛsəz/) the 19th letter of the English alphabet: *"Snow" begins with (an) S/"S."*
- **abbr.** (in writing) **1** usually **S.** (also *So.*) south; southern: *S. Boston* **2** (*pl.* **SS**) Saint **3** (especially for sizes of clothes) small **4** SIEMENS ⊃ see also S AND H
- **symbol** the symbol for ENTROPY

-'s /s; z; əz/ *suffix, short form*
- **suffix** (added to nouns) **1** belonging to: *the woman's hat* ◆ *Peter's desk* ◆ *children's clothes* **2** used to refer to someone's home: *Should we go to David's* (= David's house) *tonight?*
- **short form** (*informal*) **1** used after *he, she* or *it* and *where, what, who* or *how* to mean "is" or "has": *She's still in the bathtub.* ◆ *What's he doing now?* ◆ *It's time to go now.* ◆ *Who's taken my pen?* **2** (used after *let* when making a suggestion that includes yourself and others) us: *Let's go out for lunch.*

-s' /s; z; əz/ *suffix* (forming the end of plural nouns) belonging to: *the cats' tails* ◆ *their wives' jobs*

SA *abbr.* South Africa

sab·bath /ˈsæbəθ/ *noun* often **the Sabbath** [sing.] (in Judaism and Christianity) the holy day of the week that is used for resting and worshiping God. For Jews this day is Saturday and for Christians it is Sunday: *to keep/break the Sabbath* (= to obey/not obey the religious rules for this day)

sab·bat·i·cal /səˈbætɪkl/ *noun* [C, U] a period of time when someone, especially a teacher at a college or university, is allowed to stop their normal work in order to study or travel: *to take a year's sabbatical* ◆ *a sabbatical semester/year* ◆ *He's on sabbatical.*

sa·ber /ˈseɪbər/ *noun* **1** a heavy SWORD with a curved blade **2** a light SWORD with a thin blade used in the sport of FENCING

ˈsaber-ˌrattling *noun* [U] the act of trying to frighten someone by threatening to use force

sa·ber·tooth /ˈseɪbərˌtuθ/ (also ˌsaber-toothed ˈtiger) *noun* a large animal of the cat family with two very long curved upper teeth, that lived thousands of years ago and is now EXTINCT

sa·ble /ˈseɪbl/ *noun* **1** [C] a small animal from northern Asia with dark, yellow-brown fur **2** [U] the skin and fur of the sable, used for making expensive coats and artists' brushes

sab·o·tage /ˈsæbətɑʒ/ *noun, verb*
- **noun** [U] **1** the act of doing deliberate damage to equipment, transportation, machines, etc. to prevent an enemy from using them, or to protest about something: *an act of economic/military/industrial sabotage* ◆ *Police investigating the train derailment have not ruled out sabotage.* **2** the act of deliberately spoiling something in order to prevent it from being successful
- **verb 1** ~ sth to damage or destroy something deliberately to prevent an enemy from using it, or to protest about something: *The main electricity supply had been sabotaged by the rebels.* **2** ~ sth to prevent something from being successful or being achieved, especially deliberately: *Protesters failed to sabotage the peace talks.* ◆ *The rise in interest rates sabotaged any chance of the company's recovery.*

sab·o·teur /ˌsæbəˈtər; -ˈtʊr/ *noun* a person who does deliberate damage to something to prevent an enemy from using it, or to protest about something: *Saboteurs blew up a small section of the track.*

sac /sæk/ *noun* a part inside the body of a person, an animal, or a plant, that is shaped like a bag, has thin skin around it, and contains liquid or air

sac·cha·rin /ˈsækərən/ *noun* [U] a sweet, chemical substance used instead of sugar, especially by people who are trying to lose weight

sac·cha·rine /ˈsækərən; -ˌrin/ (also *less frequent* **sac·cha·rin**) *adj.* (*disapproving*) (of people or things) too emotional in a way that seems exaggerated **SYN** SENTIMENTAL: *a saccharine smile* ◆ *saccharine songs*

sac·er·do·tal /ˌsæsərˈdoʊtl/ *adj.* (*formal*) connected with a priest or priests

sa·chet /sæˈʃeɪ/ *noun* a small bag containing dried HERBS or flowers that you put with your clothes to make them smell pleasant

sack 🔊 /sæk/ *noun, verb*
- **noun 1** [C] a large bag with no handles, made of strong rough material, or strong paper, or plastic, used for storing and carrying, for example flour, coal, etc. **2** [C] a strong paper bag for carrying things you have bought from a store **3** [C] the contents of a sack: *They used up a sack of potatoes.* ◆ *two sacks of groceries* **4** the sack [sing.] (*informal*) being told by your employer that you can no longer continue working for a company, etc., usually because of something that you have done wrong: *He got the sack for swearing.* ◆ *Her work was so poor that she was given the sack.* ◆ *Four hundred workers face the sack.* **5** the sack [sing.] (*informal*) a bed (often referring to sexual activity): *He caught them in the sack together.* **6** usually the sack [sing.] (*formal*) the act of stealing or destroying property in a captured town: *the sack of Rome* **IDM** see HIT v.
- **verb 1** ~ sb (*informal*) to dismiss someone from a job **SYN** FIRE: *She was sacked for refusing to work on Sundays.* **2** ~ sth (of an army, etc., especially in the past) to destroy things and steal property in a town or building: *Rome was sacked by the Goths in 410.* **3** ~ sb (in football) to knock down the QUARTERBACK
  PHR V ˌsack ˈout (*informal*) to go to sleep or to bed

sack·but /ˈsækbʌt/ *noun* a type of TROMBONE used in the RENAISSANCE period

sack·cloth /ˈsækklɔθ/ (also ˈsack·ing) *noun* [U] a type of rough cloth made from JUTE, etc., used for making sacks **IDM** wear, put on, etc. sackcloth and ashes to behave in a way that shows that you are sorry for something that you have done

sack·ful /ˈsækfʊl/ *noun* the amount contained in a sack: *two sackfuls of flour*

sack·ing /ˈsækɪŋ/ *noun* **1** [C] an act of SACKING someone (= dismissing them from their job) **2** [U] = SACKCLOTH

ˈsack race *noun* a race in which the runners jump forward inside a sack

sac·ra·ment /ˈsækrəmənt/ *noun* (in Christianity) **1** [C] an important religious ceremony such as marriage, BAPTISM, or COMMUNION **2** the sacrament [sing.] the bread and wine that are eaten and drunk during the service of COMMUNION ▶ **sac·ra·men·tal** /ˌsækrəˈmɛntl/ *adj.* [usually before noun]: *sacramental wine*

sa·cred /ˈseɪkrəd/ *adj.* **1** connected with God or a god; considered to be holy: *a sacred image/shrine/temple* ◆ *sacred music* ◆ *Cows are sacred to Hindus.* **2** very important and treated with great respect **SYN** SACROSANCT: *Human life must always be sacred.* ◆ *For journalists nothing is sacred* (= they can write about anything). ▶ **sa·cred·ness** *noun* [U] ⊃ see also SANCTITY

ˌsacred ˈcow *noun* (*disapproving*) a custom, system, etc. that has existed for a long time and that many people think should not be questioned or criticized

sac·ri·fice /ˈsækrəˌfaɪs/ *noun, verb*
- **noun 1** [C, U] the fact of giving up something important or valuable to you in order to get or do something that seems more important; something that you give up in this way: *The makers of the product assured us that there had been no sacrifice of quality.* ◆ *Her parents made sacrifices so that she could have a good education.* ◆ *to make the final/supreme sacrifice* (= to die for your country, to save a friend, etc.) **2** [C, U] ~ (to sb) the act of offering something to a god,

---

especially an animal that has been killed in a special way; an animal, etc. that is offered in this way: *They offered sacrifices to the gods.* ♦ *a human sacrifice* (= a person killed as a sacrifice)

● **verb 1** [T] to give up something that is important or valuable to you in order to get or do something that seems more important for yourself or for another person: **~ sth for sb/sth** *She sacrificed everything for her children.* ♦ *The designers have sacrificed speed for fuel economy.* ♦ **~ sth** *Would you sacrifice a football game to go out with a girl?* **2** [T, I] **~ (sb/sth)** to kill an animal or a person and offer it or them to a god, in order to please the god

sac·ri·fi·cial /ˌsækrəˈfɪʃl/ *adj.* [usually before noun] offered as a sacrifice: *a sacrificial lamb*

sac·ri·lege /ˈsækrəlɪdʒ/ *noun* [U, sing.] an act of treating a holy thing or place without respect: *(figurative) It would be sacrilege to alter the composer's original score.* ⟳ collocations at RELIGION ► **sac·ri·le·gious** /ˌsækrəˈlɪdʒəs/ *adj.*

sac·ris·tan /ˈsækrəstən/ *noun* a person whose job is to take care of the holy objects in a Christian church and to prepare the ALTAR for services

sac·ris·ty /ˈsækrəsti/ *noun* (*pl.* **sac·ris·ties**) a room in a church where a priest prepares for a service by putting on special clothes and where various objects used in worship are kept **SYN** VESTRY

sac·ro·sanct /ˈsækrouˌsæŋkt/ *adj.* that is considered to be too important to change or question **SYN** SACRED: *I'll work till late in the evening, but my weekends are sacrosanct.*

sac·rum /ˈsækrəm; ˈseɪ-/ *noun* (*pl.* **sa·cra** /-krə/ or **sac·rums**) (*anatomy*) a bone in the lower back, between the two hip bones of the PELVIS

SAD /sæd/ *abbr.* SEASONAL AFFECTIVE DISORDER

sad 🔑 /sæd/ *adj.* (**sad·der, sad·dest**)
> UNHAPPY **1** unhappy or showing unhappiness: **~ (to do sth)** *We are very sad to hear that you are leaving.* ♦ **~ (that…)** *I was sad that she had to go.* ♦ **~ (about sth)** *I felt terribly sad about it.* ♦ *She looked sad and tired.* ♦ *He gave a slight, sad smile.* ♦ *The divorce left him* **sadder and wiser** (= having learned from the unpleasant experience). **2** that makes you feel unhappy: *a sad story* ♦ **~ (to do sth)** *It was sad to see them go.* ♦ **~ (that…)** *It is sad that so many of his paintings have been lost.* ♦ *We had some sad news yesterday.* ♦ *He's a sad case—his wife died last year and he can't seem to manage without her.* ♦ **Sad to say** (= unfortunately), *the house has now been demolished.*
> UNACCEPTABLE **3** unacceptable; deserving blame or criticism **SYN** DEPLORABLE: *a sad state of affairs* ♦ *It's a sad fact that many of those killed were children.*
> BORING **4** (*informal*) boring or not fashionable: *You sad old man.* ♦ *You'd have to be sad to wear a shirt like that.*
> IN POOR CONDITION **5** in poor condition: *The salad consisted of a few leaves of sad-looking lettuce.* ⟳ see also SADLY, SADNESS

sad·den /ˈsædn/ *verb* [often passive] (*formal*) to make someone sad: **~ sb** *We were deeply saddened by the news of her death.* ♦ **~ sb to do sth** *Fans were saddened to see the former champion play so badly.* ♦ **it saddens sb that…** *It saddened her that people could be so cruel.*

sad·dle /ˈsædl/ *noun, verb*
● **noun 1** a leather seat for a rider on a horse: *She swung herself into the saddle.* ⟳ picture at HORSE **2** a seat on a bicycle or motorcycle ⟳ picture at BICYCLE **3** a piece of meat from the back of an animal
 IDM in the saddle 1 in a position of authority and control **2** riding a horse: *Three weeks after the accident he was back in the saddle.*
● **verb ~ sth** to put a saddle on a horse
 PHR V ˌsaddle ˈup | ˌsaddle sth↔ˈup to put a saddle on a horse ˈsaddle sb/yourself with sth [often passive] to give someone/yourself an unpleasant responsibility, task, debt, etc.: *I've been saddled with organizing the conference.* ♦ *The company was saddled with debts of $12 million.*

sad·dle·bag /ˈsædlˌbæg/ *noun* **1** one of a pair of bags put over the back of a horse **2** a bag attached to the back of a bicycle or motorcycle saddle

ˈ**saddle ˌhorse** *noun* **1** a frame on which saddles are cleaned or stored **2** a horse that is used only for riding

sad·dler /ˈsædlər/ *noun* a person whose job is making, repairing, and selling SADDLES and other leather goods

sad·dler·y /ˈsædləri/ *noun* [U] SADDLES and leather goods for horses; the art of making these

ˈ**saddle ˌsore** *adj.* feeling sore and stiff after riding a horse

ˈ**saddle ˌstitch** *noun* a STITCH of thread or piece of wire put through the fold of a magazine, etc. to hold it together

Sa·die Haw·kins Day /ˌseɪdi ˈhɔkənz ˌdeɪ/ *noun* a day when there is a custom that women can invite men to a social event instead of waiting to be invited, especially to a **Sadie Hawkins Day** dance

sa·dism /ˈseɪdɪzəm; ˈsæd-/ *noun* [U] **1** enjoyment from watching or making someone suffer: *There's a streak of sadism in his nature.* **2** a need to hurt someone in order to get sexual pleasure ⟳ compare MASOCHISM

sa·dist /ˈseɪdɪst; ˈsæd-/ *noun* a person who gets pleasure, especially sexual pleasure, from hurting other people ► **sa·dis·tic** /səˈdɪstɪk/ *adj.*: *He took sadistic pleasure in taunting the boy.* **sa·dis·ti·cally** /-kli/ *adv.*

sad·ly 🔑 /ˈsædli/ *adv.*
1 unfortunately: *Sadly, after eight years of marriage they had grown apart.* **2** in a sad way: *She shook her head sadly.* **3** very much and in a way that makes you sad: *She will be sadly missed.* ♦ *If you think I'm going to help you again, you're* **sadly** (= completely) **mistaken.**

sad·ness 🔑 /ˈsædnəs/ *noun*
1 [U, sing.] the feeling of being sad: *memories tinged with sadness* ♦ *I felt a deep sadness.* **2** [C, usually pl.] something that makes you sad: *our joys and sadnesses*

sa·do·mas·o·chism /ˌseɪdouˈmæsəˌkɪzəm/ *noun* [U] enjoyment from hurting someone and being hurt, especially during sexual activity ► **sa·do·mas·o·chist** /-kɪst/ *noun* **sa·do·mas·o·chis·tic** /ˌseɪdouˌmæsəˈkɪstɪk/ *adj.*

sa·fa·ri /səˈfɑri/ *noun* [U, C] a trip to see or hunt wild animals, especially in east or southern Africa: *to be/go on safari*

sa·fari ˌpark *noun* a park in which wild animals move around freely and are watched by visitors from their cars

sa·fari ˌsuit *noun* a light-colored suit worn by men in hot weather, especially one with pockets on the front of the jacket

safe 🔑 /seɪf/ *adj., noun*
● **adj.** (**saf·er, saf·est**)
> PROTECTED **1** [not before noun] protected from any danger or harm: *The children are quite safe here.* ♦ *She didn't feel safe on her own.* ♦ *Will the car be safe parked in the road?* ♦ **~ (from sb/sth)** *They aimed to make the country safe from terrorist attacks.* ♦ *Your secret is safe with me* (= I will not tell anyone else). ♦ *Here's your passport. Now* **keep it safe.** **ANT** UNSAFE
> WITHOUT PHYSICAL DANGER **2** not likely to lead to any physical harm or danger: **~ (for sb) (to do sth)** *Is the water here safe to drink?* ♦ *The street is not safe for children to play in.* ♦ *It is one of the safest cars in the world.* ♦ *We watched the explosion* **from a safe distance.** ♦ *Builders were called in to make the building safe.* **ANT** UNSAFE
> NOT HARMED/LOST **3** not harmed, damaged, lost, etc.: *We were glad she let us know she was safe.* ♦ *The missing child was found* **safe and well.** ♦ *They turned up* **safe and sound.** ♦ *A reward was offered for the animal's* **safe return.**
> PLACE **4** where someone or something is not likely to be in danger or to be lost: *We all want to live in safer cities.* ♦ *Keep your passport in a safe place.* **ANT** UNSAFE
> WITHOUT RISK **5** not involving much or any risk; not likely to be wrong or to upset someone: *a safe investment* ♦ *a safe subject for discussion* ♦ **~ (to do sth)** *It's safe to assume (that) there will always be a demand for new software.* ♦ *It would be*

safer to take more money with you in case of emergency.
• (*disapproving*) *The show was well performed, but so safe and predictable.*
> PERSON **6** [usually before noun] doing an activity in a careful way **SYN** CAREFUL: *a safe driver*
> LAW **7** based on good evidence: *a safe verdict* ⊃ see also FAIL-SAFE
IDM better safe than sorry (*saying*) used to say that it is wiser to be too careful than to act too quickly and do something you may later wish you had not in safe hands| in the safe hands of sb being taken care of well by someone: *I've left the kids in safe hands—with my parents.*
• *Their problem was in the safe hands of the experts.* on the safe side being especially careful; taking no risks: *I took some extra cash just to be on the safe side.* play (it) safe to be careful; to avoid risks safe in the knowledge that confident because you know that something is true or will happen: *She went out safe in the knowledge that she looked fabulous.* ⊃ more at BET n.

• **noun** a strong metal box or cupboard with a complicated lock, used for storing valuable things in, for example, money or jewelry

ˌsafe ˈconduct (also ˌsafe ˈpassage) *noun* [U, C] official protection from being attacked, arrested, etc. when passing through an area; a document that promises this: *The guerrillas were promised safe conduct out of the country.*

ˈsafe deˌposit ˌbox (also ˈsafety deˌposit ˌbox) *noun* a metal box for storing valuable things, usually kept in a special room at a bank

ˈsafe·guard /ˈseɪfɡɑrd/ *verb, noun*
• **verb** [T, I] (*formal*) to protect something or someone from loss, harm, or damage; to keep something or someone safe: *~ sth to safeguard a person's interests* • *to safeguard jobs* • *~ sth/sb against/from sth The new card will safeguard the company against fraud.* • *~ against sth The leaflet explains how to safeguard against dangers in the home.*
• **noun** *~* (**against sth**) something that is designed to protect people from harm, risk, or danger: *Stronger legal safeguards are needed to protect the consumer.*

ˌsafe ˈhaven *noun* a place where someone can go to be safe from danger or attack

ˈsafe house *noun* a house used by people who are hiding, for example by criminals hiding from the police, or by people who are being protected by the police from other people who may wish to harm them

ˈsafe·keep·ing /ˌseɪfˈkipɪŋ/ *noun* [U] **1** the fact of something being in a safe place where it will not be lost or damaged: *She had put her watch in her pocket for safekeeping.* **2** the fact of someone or something being taken care of by someone who can be trusted: *The documents are in the safekeeping of our lawyers.*

ˈsafe·ly 🔊 /ˈseɪfli/ *adv.*
1 without being harmed, damaged, or lost: *The plane landed safely.* **2** in a way that does not cause harm or that protects someone or something from harm: *The bomb has been safely disposed of.* • *The money is safely locked in a drawer.* **3** without much possibility of being wrong: *We can safely say that he will accept the job.* **4** without any possibility of the situation changing: *I thought the kids were safely tucked up in bed.* **5** without any problems being caused; with no risk: *These recommendations can safely be ignored.*

ˈsafe mode *noun* [U] (*computing*) a way of starting a computer that makes it easier to find a problem without the risk of losing data

ˌsafe ˈpassage *noun* [U, C] = SAFE CONDUCT

the ˈsafe ˌperiod *noun* [sing.] the time just before and during a woman's PERIOD when she is unlikely to become pregnant

ˈsafe room *noun* = PANIC ROOM

ˌsafe ˈsex *noun* [U] sexual activity in which people try to protect themselves from AIDS and other sexual diseases, for example by using a CONDOM

ˈsafe·ty 🔊 /ˈseɪfti/ *noun* (*pl.* safe·ties)
1 [U] the state of being safe and protected from danger or harm: *a place where children can play in safety* • *The police are concerned for the safety of the 12-year-old boy who has been missing for three days.* • *He was kept in custody for his own safety.* **2** [U] the state of not being dangerous: *I'm worried about the safety of the treatment.* • *safety standards* • *a local campaign to improve road safety* • *The airline has an excellent safety record.* **3** [U] a place where you are safe: *I managed to swim to safety.* • *We watched the lions from the safety of the car.* • *They reached safety seconds before the building was engulfed in flames.* **4** [C] a device that stops a gun from being fired or a machine from working by accident: *Is the safety on?* **5** [C] (in football) a DEFENSIVE player who plays in a position far away from the other team
IDM safety first (*saying*) safety is the most important thing there's safety in numbers (*saying*) being in a group makes you safer and makes you feel more confident

ˈsafety ˌbelt *noun* = SEAT BELT

ˈsafety ˌcurtain *noun* a curtain that can come down across the stage in a theater, intended to stop a fire from spreading

ˈsafety deˌposit ˌbox *noun* = SAFE DEPOSIT BOX

ˈsafety ˌglass *noun* [U] strong glass that does not break into sharp pieces

ˈsafety ˌlamp *noun* a special lamp used by MINERS, with a flame that does not cause underground gases to explode

ˈsafety ˌmatch *noun* a type of match that will light only if it is rubbed against a specially prepared rough surface, often on the side of its box

ˈsafety ˌmeasure *noun* something that you do in order to prevent something bad or dangerous from happening

ˈsafety ˌnet *noun* **1** an arrangement that helps to prevent disaster if something goes wrong: *a financial safety net* • *people who have fallen through the safety net and ended up homeless on the streets* **2** a net placed underneath ACROBATS, etc. to catch them if they fall

ˈsafety ˌpin *noun* a pin with a point bent back toward the head, that is covered when closed so that it cannot hurt you ⊃ picture at CLOTHES

ˈsafety ˌrazor *noun* a RAZOR (= a tool used for shaving) with a cover over the blade to stop it from cutting the skin ⊃ compare STRAIGHT RAZOR

ˈsafety ˌvalve *noun* **1** a device that lets out steam or pressure in a machine when it becomes too great **2** a harmless way of letting out feelings of anger, excitement, etc.: *Exercise is a good safety valve for the tension that builds up at work.*

saf·flow·er /ˈsæˌflaʊər/ *noun* [C, U] a plant with orange flowers, whose seeds produce an oil that is used in cooking

saf·fron /ˈsæfrən; -frɑn/ *noun* [U] **1** a bright yellow spice made from CROCUS flowers, used in cooking to give color and flavor to food ⊃ picture at HERB **2** a bright orange-yellow color ▶ saf·fron *adj.*: *Buddhist monks in saffron robes*

SAG /sæɡ/ *abbr.* SCREEN ACTORS GUILD

sag /sæɡ/ *verb* (-gg-) **1** [I] to hang or bend down in the middle, especially because of weight or pressure: *a sagging roof* • *The tent began to sag under the weight of the rain.* • *Your skin starts to sag as you get older.* **2** [I] to become weaker or fewer: *Their share of the vote sagged badly at the last election.* ▶ sag *noun* [U, C, usually sing.]: *Weight has caused the sag.*
IDM see JAW *n.*

sa·ga /ˈsɑɡə/ *noun* **1** a long, traditional story about adventures and brave acts, especially one from Norway or Iceland **2** a long story about events over a period of many years: *a family saga* **3** a long series of events or adventures and/or a report about them: *The front page is devoted to the continuing saga of the hijack.* • (*humorous*) *the saga of how I missed the plane*

sa·ga·cious /səˈɡeɪʃəs/ *adj.* (*formal*) showing good

judgment and understanding SYN WISE ▸ sa·gac·i·ty /sə'gæsəti/ noun [U]

sage /seɪdʒ/ noun, adj.
• **noun 1** [U] a plant with flat, light green leaves that have a strong smell and are used in cooking as an HERB ⊃ picture at HERB **2** [C] (formal) a very wise person
• **adj.** (literary) wise, especially because you have a lot of experience ▸ **sage·ly** adv.: She nodded sagely.

sage·brush /'seɪdʒbrʌʃ/ noun [U] a plant with leaves that smell sweet, that grows in dry regions in the western U.S.; an area of ground covered with sagebrush

sag·gy /'sægi/ adj. (sag·gi·er, sag·gi·est) (informal) no longer firm; hanging or sinking down in way that is not attractive

Sag·it·tar·i·us /ˌsædʒə'teriəs/ noun **1** [U] the 9th sign of the ZODIAC, the ARCHER **2** [sing.] a person born under the influence of this sign, that is between November 22 and December 20, approximately ▸ **Sag·it·ta·ri·an** noun, adj.

sa·go /'seɪgoʊ/ noun [U] hard, white grains made from the soft inside of a type of PALM tree and used in cooking: sago pudding

sa·gua·ro /sə'gwaroʊ; sə'waroʊ/ noun (pl. sa·gua·ros) a very large CACTUS that grows in the southern U.S. and Mexico

said /sed/ **1** pt, pp of SAY **2** adj. [only before noun] (formal or law) = AFOREMENTIONED: the said company

sail /seɪl/ verb, noun
• **verb 1** [I, T] (of a boat or ship or the people on it) to travel on water using sails or an engine: (+ adv./prep.) to sail into harbor • The boat sailed smoothly across the lake. • The ferry sails from Port Townsend to Keystone. • one of the first people to sail around the world • ~ sth to sail the Atlantic **2** also go sailing [I, T] to control or travel on a boat with a sail, especially as a sport: We spent the weekend sailing off the south coast. • Do you go sailing often? • ~ sth She sails her own sailboat. **3** [I] (of a boat or ship or the people in it) to begin a trip on water: We sail at 2 p.m. tomorrow. • ~ for sth He sailed for the Bermudas from Rhode Island. **4** [I] + adv./prep. to move quickly and smoothly in a particular direction; (of people) to move in a confident manner: clouds sailing across the sky • The ball sailed over the goalie's head. • She sailed past me, ignoring me completely.
  IDM **sail close to the wind** to take a risk by doing something that is dangerous or that may be illegal
  PHRV **sail 'through (sth)** to pass an exam, a test, etc. without any difficulty
• **noun 1** [C, U] a sheet of strong cloth that the wind blows against to make a boat or ship travel through the water: As the boat moved down the river the wind began to fill the sails. • a ship **under sail** (= using sails) • in the days of sail (= when ships all used sails) • She moved away like a ship **in full sail** (= with all its sails spread out). **2** [sing.] a trip in a boat or ship: We went for a sail. • a two-hour sail across the bay **3** [C] a set of boards attached to the arm of a WINDMILL
  IDM **set sail (from/for…)** (formal) to begin a trip by ocean: a liner setting sail from New York • We set sail (for France) at high tide. ⊃ more at TRIM v., WIND¹ n.

sail·board /'seɪlbɔrd/ (also board) noun = WINDSURFER ⊃ picture at SPORT ▸ **sail·board·er** noun **sail·board·ing** noun [U]

sail·boat /'seɪlboʊt/ noun a boat with sails ⊃ picture at BOAT

sail·cloth /'seɪlklɔθ/ noun [U] a type of strong cloth used for making sails

sail·ing /'seɪlɪŋ/ noun
1 [U] the sport or activity of traveling in a boat with sails: to go sailing • a sailing club **2** [C] one of the regular times that a ship leaves a port: There are six sailings a day.
  IDM **be clear/smooth sailing** to be simple and free from trouble

'sailing ˌship noun a ship with sails

sail·mak·er /'seɪlˌmeɪkər/ noun a person whose job is to make or repair sails ▸ **sail·mak·ing** noun [U]

sail·or /'seɪlər/ noun
1 a person who works on a ship as a member of the CREW
2 a person who sails a boat
  IDM **a good/bad sailor** a person who rarely/often becomes sick at sea

'sailor ˌsuit noun a suit for a child made in the style of an old-fashioned sailor's uniform

saint /seɪnt/ noun **1** (abbr. S., St.) a person that the Christian Church recognizes as being very holy, because of the way they have lived or died: St. John • St. Valentine's Day • The children were all named after saints. ⊃ see also PATRON SAINT, ST. BERNARD **2** a very good, kind, or patient person: She's a saint to go on living with that man. • His behavior would try the patience of a saint. ▸ **saint·hood** /-hʊd/ noun [U]

saint·ed /'seɪntəd/ adj. [usually before noun] (old-fashioned or humorous) considered or officially stated to be a saint: And how is my sainted sister?

saint·ly /'seɪntli/ adj. like a saint; very holy and good: to lead a saintly life ▸ **saint·li·ness** noun [U]

'saint's ˌday noun (in the Christian Church) a day of the year when a particular SAINT is remembered and on which, in some countries, people who are named after that SAINT have celebrations

saith /seθ; 'seɪəθ/ (old use) = SAYS

sake¹ /seɪk/ noun ⊃ see also SAKE²
  IDM **for Christ's, God's, goodness', heaven's, pity's, etc. sake** used to emphasize that it is important to do something or when you are annoyed about something: Do be careful, for goodness' sake. • Oh, for heaven's sake! • For pity's sake, help me! HELP Some people find the use of **Christ, God,** or **heaven** here offensive. **for sth's sake** because of the interest or value something has, not because of the advantages it may bring: I believe in education for its own sake. • art for art's sake **for the sake of sb/sth | for sb's/sth's sake** in order to help someone or something, or because you like someone or something: They stayed together for the sake of the children. • You can do it. Please, for my sake. • I hope you're right, for all our sakes (= because this is important for all of us). **for the sake of sth/ of doing sth** in order to get or keep something: The translation sacrifices naturalness for the sake of accuracy. • She gave up smoking for the sake of her health. • Don't get married just for the sake of it. • Let's suppose, for the sake of argument (= in order to have a discussion), that interest rates went up by 2%. ⊃ more at OLD

sa·ke² (also sa·ki) /'saki/ noun [U] a Japanese alcoholic drink made from rice ⊃ see also SAKE¹

sa·laam /sə'lam/ verb [I, T] ~ (sb) (in some Eastern countries) to say hello to someone in a formal way by bending forward from the waist and putting your right hand on your FOREHEAD ▸ **sa·laam** noun

sal·a·ble (also sale·a·ble) /'seɪləbl/ adj. good enough to be sold; that someone will want to buy: a salable product • not in salable condition ANT UNSALABLE

sa·la·cious /sə'leɪʃəs/ adj. (formal) (of stories, pictures, etc.) encouraging sexual desire or containing too much sexual detail ▸ **sa·la·cious·ness** noun [U]

sal·ad /'sæləd/ noun
1 [U, C] a mixture of raw vegetables such as LETTUCE, tomato, and CUCUMBER, usually served with other food as part of a meal: All main courses come with a salad or vegetables. • Is cold meat and salad OK for lunch? • a **side salad** (= a small bowl of salad served with the main course of a meal) • a **salad bowl** (= a large bowl for serving salad in) ⊃ collocations at COOKING ⊃ see also CAESAR SALAD, GREEN SALAD **2** [C, U] (in compounds) meat, fish, cheese, etc. served with salad: a tuna salad **3** [U, C] (in compounds) raw or cooked vegetables, etc. that are cut into small pieces, often mixed with MAYONNAISE and served cold with other

food: *potato salad* ◆ *a pasta salad* ⊃ see also FRUIT SALAD **4** [U] any green vegetable, especially LETTUCE, that is eaten raw in a salad: *salad greens*

IDM **your salad days** (*old-fashioned*) the time when you are young and do not have much experience of life

salad **dressing** *noun* [U, C] = DRESSING

sal·a·man·der /ˈsæləˌmændər/ *noun* an animal like a LIZARD, with short legs and a long tail, that lives both on land and in water (= is an AMPHIBIAN) ⊃ picture at ANIMAL

sa·la·mi /səˈlɑmi/ *noun* [U, C] (*pl.* sa·la·mis) a type of large, spicy SAUSAGE served cold in thin slices

sa·lami **slicing** *noun* [U] (*informal*) the act of removing something gradually by small amounts at a time

sal·a·ried /ˈsælərid/ *adj.* **1** (of a person) receiving a salary: *a salaried employee* **2** (of a job) for which a salary is paid: *a salaried position*

sal·a·ry 🔑 /ˈsæləri/ *noun* (*pl.* sal·a·ries) money that employees receive for doing their job, especially professional employees or people working in an office, usually paid once or twice a month: *an annual salary of $40,000* ◆ *a 9% salary increase* ◆ *She's on a salary of $55,000.* ◆ *He receives a base salary of $215,000, plus bonuses based on performance.* ⊃ compare WAGE ⊃ thesaurus box at INCOME

sal·a·ry·man /ˈsæləriˌmæn/ *noun* (*pl.* sal·a·ry·men /-ˌmɛn/) (especially in Japan) a WHITE-COLLAR worker (= one who works in an office)

sale 🔑 /seɪl/ *noun* **1** [U, C] an act or the process of selling something: *regulations governing the sale of alcoholic beverages* ◆ *I haven't made a sale all week.* ◆ *She gets 10% commission on each sale.* **2** sales [pl.] the number of items sold: *Retail sales fell in November by 10%.* ◆ *Export sales were up by 32% last year.* ◆ *the sales figures for May* ◆ *a sales drive/campaign* (= a special effort to sell more) ⊃ collocations at BUSINESS **3** sales [U] (also sales department [C]) the part of a company that deals with selling its products: *a sales and marketing director* ◆ *She works in sales/in the sales department.* ◆ *The Weldon Group has a 6,000 strong sales force.* **4** [C] an occasion when a store sells its goods at a lower price than usual: *The sale starts next week.* ◆ *Memorial Day sales* ◆ *sale prices* **5** [C] an occasion when goods are sold, especially an AUCTION: *a contemporary art sale* ⊃ see also GARAGE SALE, RUMMAGE SALE, TAG SALE, YARD SALE

IDM **for sale** available to be bought, especially from the owner: *I'm sorry, it's not for sale.* ◆ *They've put their house up for sale.* ◆ *an increase in the number of stolen vehicles being offered for sale* ◆ *a "for sale" sign* **on sale 1** available to be bought, especially in a store: *Tickets are on sale at the box office.* ◆ *The new model goes on sale next month.* **2** being offered at a reduced price: *All video equipment is on sale today and tomorrow.*

sale·a·ble = SALABLE

sales clerk (also **clerk**) *noun* a person whose job is to serve customers in a store

sales·girl /ˈseɪlzgərl/ *noun* a girl or woman who works in a store

sales·man /ˈseɪlzmən/, **sales·wom·an** /ˈseɪlzˌwumən/ *noun* (*pl.* sales·men /-mən/, sales·wom·en /-ˌwɪmən/) a man or woman whose job is to sell goods, for example, in a store: *a car salesman* ⊃ note at GENDER

sales·man·ship /ˈseɪlzmənˌʃɪp/ *noun* [U] skill in persuading people to buy things

sales·per·son /ˈseɪlzˌpərsn/ *noun* (*pl.* sales·peo·ple) a person whose job is to sell goods, for example, in a store

sales repre·sentative (also *informal* **sales rep**, **rep**) *noun* an employee of a company who travels around a particular area selling the company's goods to stores, etc.

sales·room /ˈseɪlzrum; -rʊm/ *noun* a room where goods are sold at an AUCTION

sales slip *noun* = RECEIPT

sales talk *noun* [U] talk that tries to persuade someone to buy something

sales tax *noun* [U, C] (in some countries) the part of the price you pay when you buy something that goes to the government as tax

sales·wom·an *noun* ⊃ SALESMAN

sal·i·cyl·ic ac·id /ˌsæləˌsɪlɪk ˈæsɪd/ *noun* [U] a bitter chemical found in some plants, used in ASPIRIN (= a drug used for reducing pain and making your blood thinner)

sa·li·ent /ˈseɪliənt/ *adj.* [only before noun] most important or noticeable: *She pointed out the salient features of the new design.* ◆ *He summarized the salient points.*

sa·line /ˈseɪlin/ *adj.*, *noun*
● *adj.* [usually before noun] (*technical*) containing salt: *Wash the lenses in saline solution.* ▶ **sa·lin·i·ty** /səˈlɪnəti/ *noun* [U]: *to measure the salinity of the water*
● *noun* [U] (*technical*) a mixture of salt in water

Salis·bur·y steak /ˌsɔlzbɛri ˈsteɪk; ˌsælz-/ *noun* finely chopped beef mixed with egg and onions, made into a flat, round shape, and cooked under or over a strong heat

sa·li·va /səˈlaɪvə/ *noun* [U] the liquid that is produced in your mouth that helps you to swallow food

sal·i·var·y /ˈsæləˌvɛri/ *adj.* (*technical*) of or producing saliva

sal·i·vate /ˈsæləˌveɪt/ *verb* [I] (*formal*) to produce more saliva in your mouth than usual, especially when you see or smell food: (*figurative*) *He was salivating over the thought of the million dollars.* ▶ **sal·i·va·tion** /ˌsæləˈveɪʃn/ *noun* [U]

sal·low /ˈsælou/ *adj.* (of a person's skin or face) having a slightly yellow color that does not look healthy **SYN** PASTY

sal·ly /ˈsæli/ *noun*, *verb*
● *noun* (*pl.* sal·ies) **1** a remark that is intended to entertain or amuse someone **SYN** WITTICISM **2** a sudden attack by an enemy
● *verb* (sal·lies, sal·ly·ing, sal·lied, sal·lied)
PHR V **sally** **forth/**' **out** (*old-fashioned* or *literary*) to leave a place in a determined or enthusiastic way

salm·on /ˈsæmən/ *noun* [C, U] (*pl.* salm·on) a large fish with silver skin and pink flesh that is used for food. Salmon live in the ocean but swim up rivers to lay their eggs.: *a whole salmon* ◆ *smoked salmon* ◆ *wild and farmed salmon*

sal·mo·nel·la /ˌsælməˈnɛlə/ *noun* [U] a type of bacteria that makes people sick if they eat infected food; an illness caused by this bacteria: *cases of salmonella poisoning* ◆ *an outbreak of salmonella*

salmon **pink** *adj.* orange-pink in color, like the flesh of a salmon ▶ **salmon** **pink** *noun* [U]

sa·lon /səˈlɑn/ *noun* **1** a store that gives customers hair or beauty treatment or that sells expensive clothes: *a beauty salon* ◆ *a hair/nail salon* **2** (*old-fashioned*) a room in a large house used for entertaining guests **3** (in the past) a regular meeting of writers, artists, and other guests at the house of a famous or important person: *a literary salon*

sa·loon /səˈlun/ *noun* **1** a bar where alcoholic drinks were sold in the western U.S. and Canada in the past **2** a large comfortable room on a ship, used by the passengers to sit and relax in

sal·sa /ˈsɑlsə; ˈsɔl-/ *noun* **1** [U] a type of Latin American dance music **2** [C, U] a dance performed to this music **3** [U] a sauce eaten with Mexican food: *chips and salsa*

salt 🔑 /sɔlt/ *noun*, *verb*, *adj.*
● *noun* **1** [U] a white substance that is added to food to give it a better flavor or to preserve it. Salt is obtained from mines and is also found in ocean water. It is sometimes called **common salt** to distinguish it from other chemical salts. **SYN** SODIUM CHLORIDE: *Pass the salt, please.* ◆ *a pinch of salt* (= a small amount of it) ◆ *Season with salt and pepper.* ⊃ see also ROCK SALT, SEA SALT **2** [C] (*chemistry*) a chemical formed from a metal and an acid: *mineral salts* ⊃ see also ACID SALT, EPSOM SALTS **3** salts [pl.] a substance that looks

or tastes like salt: *bath salts* (= used to give a pleasant smell to bath water) ⊃ see also SMELLING SALTS
IDM the salt of the earth a very good and honest person that you can always depend on take sth with a grain/ pinch of salt to be careful about believing that something is completely true ⊃ more at RUB *v.*, WORTH *adj.*

● *verb* **1** [usually passive] ~ sth to put salt on or in food: *salted peanuts* ◆ *a pan of boiling salted water* **2** ~ sth (down) to preserve food with salt: *salted fish* **3** ~ sth to put salt on roads to melt ice or snow
PHRV ,salt sth↔a'way to save something for the future, secretly and usually dishonestly: *She salted away the profits in foreign bank accounts.*

● *adj.* [only before noun] containing, tasting of, or preserved with salt: *salt water* ◆ *salt beef*

,salt-and-'pepper (also ,pepper-and-'salt) *adj.* (especially of hair) having two colors that are mixed together, especially a dark color and a light one

salt·box /'sɔltbɑks/ *noun* a house that has two floors at the front and one floor at the back, with a roof that slopes down between the two floors

'salt ,cellar *noun* a small open dish containing salt

'salt flats *noun* [pl.] a flat area of land, covered with a layer of salt

salt·ine /sɔl'tin/ *noun* a thin, dry CRACKER with salt on top of it **SYN** SODA CRACKER

'salt marsh *noun* an area of open land near a coast, that is regularly flooded by the ocean

'salt pan *noun* an area of low land where ocean water has EVAPORATED to leave salt

salt·pe·ter (*CanE usually* salt·pe·tre) /,sɔlt'pitər/ *noun* [U] a white powder used for preserving food and making matches and GUNPOWDER

'salt ,shaker *noun* a small container for salt, usually with one hole in the top, that is used at the table

'salt truck *noun* a large vehicle used for putting salt or sand on the roads in winter when there is ice on them

'salt ,water *noun* [U] ocean water; water containing salt
▶ salt·wa·ter /'sɔlt,wɔtər; -,wɑtər/ *adj.* [only before noun]: *saltwater fish* ⊃ compare FRESHWATER

salt·y 🔊 /'sɔlti/ *adj.* (salt·i·er, salt·i·est) **1** containing or tasting of salt: *salty food* ◆ *salty sea air* ⊃ compare SWEET **2** (*old-fashioned*) (of language or humor) amusing and sometimes slightly offensive ▶ salt·i·ness *noun* [U]: *She could taste the saltiness of her tears.*

sa·lu·bri·ous /sə'lubriəs/ *adj.* (*formal*) (of a place) pleasant to live in; clean and healthy

sal·u·tar·y /'sælyə,tɛri/ *adj.* having a good effect on someone or something, though often seeming unpleasant: *a salutary lesson/experience/warning* ◆ *The accident was a salutary reminder of the dangers of climbing.*

sal·u·ta·tion /,sælyə'teɪʃn/ *noun* **1** [C, U] (*formal*) something that you say to welcome or say hello to someone; the action of welcoming or saying hello to someone **2** [C] (*technical*) the words that are used in a letter to address the person you are writing to, for example "Dear Sir"

sa·lu·ta·to·ri·an /sə,lutə'tɔriən/ *noun* the student who has the second highest grades in a group of students and who gives a speech at a GRADUATION ceremony ⊃ compare VALEDICTORIAN

sa·lute /sə'lut/ *verb, noun*
● *verb* **1** [I, T] to touch the side of your head with the fingers of your right hand to show respect, especially in the armed forces: *The sergeant stood to attention and saluted.* ◆ ~ sb/sth *to salute an officer/the flag* **2** [T] ~ sb/sth (*formal*) to express respect and admiration for someone or something **SYN** ACKNOWLEDGE: *The players saluted the fans before leaving the field.* ◆ *The president saluted the courage of those who had fought for their country.*
● *noun* **1** [C] the action of raising your right hand to the side

of your head as a sign of respect, especially between soldiers and officers **2** [C, U] a thing that you say or do to show your admiration or respect for someone or something or to welcome someone: *He raised his hat as a friendly salute.* ◆ *His first words were a salute to the people of South Africa.* ◆ *They all raised their glasses in salute.* **3** [C] an official occasion when guns are fired into the air to show respect for an important person: *a 21-gun salute*

sal·vage /'sælvɪdʒ/ *noun, verb*
● *noun* [U] **1** the act of saving things that have been, or are likely to be, damaged or lost, especially in a disaster or an accident: *the salvage of the wrecked tanker* ◆ *a salvage company/operation/team* **2** the things that are saved from a disaster or an accident: *an exhibition of the salvage from the wreck*
● *verb* **1** to save a badly damaged ship, etc. from being lost completely; to save parts or property from a damaged ship or from a fire, etc.: ~ sth *The wreck was salvaged by a team from the U.S.* ◆ *The house was built using salvaged materials.* ◆ ~ sth from sth *We only managed to salvage two paintings from the fire.* **2** ~ sth to manage to rescue something from a difficult situation; to stop a bad situation from being a complete failure: *What can I do to salvage my reputation?* (= get a good reputation again) ◆ *He wondered what he could do to salvage the situation.* ◆ *They lost 5–2, salvaging a little pride with two late goals.*

'salvage ,yard *noun* a place where old machines, cars, etc. are broken up so that the metal can be sold or used again

sal·va·tion /sæl'veɪʃn/ *noun* [U] **1** (in Christianity) the state of being saved from the power of evil: *to pray for the salvation of the world* **2** a way of protecting someone from danger, disaster, loss, etc.: *Group therapy classes have been his salvation.*

the Sal,vation 'Army *noun* [sing.] a Christian organization whose members wear military uniforms and work to help poor people

salve /sæv/ *noun, verb*
● *noun* [U, C] a substance that you put on a wound or sore skin to help it heal or to protect it
● *verb* ~ your conscience (*formal*) to do something that makes you feel less guilty

sal·ver /'sælvər/ *noun* a large plate, usually made of metal, on which drinks or food are served at a formal event

sal·vo /'sælvoʊ/ *noun* (*pl.* sal·vos *or* sal·voes) the act of firing several guns or dropping several bombs, etc. at the same time; a sudden attack: *The first salvo exploded a short distance away.* ◆ (*figurative*) *The newspaper article was the opening salvo in what proved to be a long battle.*

sal vo·la·ti·le /,sæl və'lætl.i/ *noun* [U] a type of SMELLING SALTS

sal·war /sʌl'wɑr/ (also shal·war) *noun* light, loose pants that are tight around the ankles, sometimes worn by S. Asian women: *a salwar kameez* (= a salwar worn with a KAMEEZ)

Sa·mar·i·tan /sə'mærətn/ *noun*
IDM a good Samaritan a person who gives help and sympathy to people who need it **ORIGIN** From the Bible story of a person from Samaria who helps an injured man that no one else will help

sa·mar·i·um /sə'mɛriəm/ *noun* [U] (*symb.* Sm) a chemical element. Samarium is a hard silver-white metal used in making strong MAGNETS.

sam·ba /'sɑmbə/ *noun* a fast dance originally from Brazil; a piece of music for this dance

same 🔊 /seɪm/ *adj., pron., adv.*
● *adj.* **1** exactly the one or ones referred to or mentioned; not different: *We have lived in the same house for twenty years.* ◆ *Our children go to the same school as theirs.* ◆ *She's still the same fun-loving person that I knew at college.* ◆ *This one works in exactly the same way as the other.* ◆ *They both said pretty much the same thing.* ◆ *He used the very same* (= exactly the same) *words.* ◆ *I resigned last Friday and left that same day.*

ʌ cup   ə about   eɪ say   ɪə near   aɪ five   ɔɪ boy   aʊ now   oʊ go   ər bird

2 exactly like the one or ones referred to or mentioned: *I bought the **same** car **as** yours* (= another car of that type). ♦ *She was wearing the **same** dress **that** I had on.* ♦ *The same thing happened to me last week.*
IDM Most idioms containing **same** are at the entries for the nouns and verbs in the idioms. For example, **be in the same boat** is at **boat**. **same old, same old** (*informal*) used to say that a situation has not changed at all: *"How's it going?" "Oh, same old, same old."*

● **pron. 1** the ~ (as...) the same thing or things: *I think the same as you do about this.* ♦ *Just do the same as me* (= as I do). ♦ *His latest movie is just **more of the same**—exotic locations, car chases, and a final shoot-out.* ♦ (*informal*) *"I'll have coffee." "Same for me, please* (= I will have one too)*."* **2** the ~ (as...) having the same number, color, size, quality, etc.: *There are several brands and they're not all the same.* ♦ *I'd like one the same as yours.*
IDM **all/just the same** despite this **SYN** NEVERTHELESS: *He's not very reliable, but I like him just the same.* ♦ *"Will you stay for lunch?" "No, but thanks all the same."* ♦ *All the same, there's some truth in what she says.* **be all the same to sb** to not be important to someone: *It's all the same to me whether we eat now or later.* **one and the same** the same person or thing: *It turns out that her aunt and my cousin are one and the same.* **same here** (*informal*) used to say that something is also true of you: *"I can't wait to see it." "Same here."* **(the) same to you** (*informal*) used to answer a GREETING, an insult, etc.: *"Merry Christmas!" "And the same to you!"* ♦ *"Get lost!" "Same to you!"*

● **adv.** usually **the same** in the same way: *We treat boys exactly **the same as** girls.* ♦ (*informal*) *He gave me five dollars, **same as usual**.*

same·ness /ˈseɪmnəs/ *noun* [U] the quality of being the same; a lack of variety: *She grew tired of the sameness of the food.*

ˈsame-sex *adj.* [only before noun] **1** of the same sex: *The child's same-sex parent acts as a role model.* **2** involving people of the same sex: *a same-sex relationship*

sa·mo·sa /səˈmoʊsə/ *noun* a type of hot, spicy, S. Asian food consisting of a triangle of thin crisp PASTRY filled with meat or vegetables and fried

sam·o·var /ˈsæməˌvɑr/ *noun* a large container for heating water, used especially in Russia for making tea

sam·pan /ˈsæmpæn/ *noun* a small boat with a flat bottom used along the coast and rivers of China

sam·ple 🔑 /ˈsæmpl/ *noun, verb*

● **noun 1** a number of people or things taken from a larger group and used in tests to provide information about the group: *The interviews were given to a **random sample** of students.* ♦ *The survey covers a **representative sample** of schools.* ♦ *a sample survey* **2** a small amount of a substance taken from a larger amount and tested in order to obtain information about the substance: *a blood sample* ♦ *Samples of the water contained pesticide.* ⊃ collocations at SCIENTIFIC **3** a small amount or example of something that can be looked at or tried to see what it is like: *"I'd like to see a sample of your work," said the manager.* ♦ *a **free sample** of shampoo* **4** (*technical*) a piece of recorded music or sound that is used in a new piece of music

● **verb 1** ~ sth to try a small amount of a particular food to see what it is like; to experience something for a short time to see what it is like: *I sampled the delights of Greek cooking for the first time.* **2** ~ sb/sth (*technical*) to test, question, etc., part of something or of a group of people in order to find out what the rest is like: *12% of the children sampled said they prefer cats to dogs.* **3** ~ sth (*technical*) to record part of a piece of music, or a sound, in order to use it in a new piece of music

sam·pler /ˈsæmplər/ *noun* **1** a piece of cloth decorated with different STITCHES that people made in the past to show a person's skill at sewing **2** a collection that shows typical examples of something, especially pieces of music

sam·pling /ˈsæmplɪŋ/ *noun* [U, C] **1** the process of taking a sample; a sample that is taken: *statistical sampling* **2** (*technical*) the process of copying and recording parts of a piece of music in an electronic form so that they can be used in a different piece of music; a piece of music copied in this way

ˈsampling ˌerror *noun* (*statistics*) a situation in which a set of results or figures does not show a true situation, because the group of people or things it was based on was not typical of a wider group

sam·u·rai /ˈsæməˌraɪ/ *noun* (*pl.* **sam·u·rai**) (from *Japanese*) (in the past) a member of a powerful military class in Japan

san·a·to·ri·um /ˌsænəˈtɔriəm/ (also **san·i·tar·i·um** /ˌsænəˈteriəm/) *noun* (*pl.* **san·a·to·ri·ums** or **san·a·to·ri·a** /-ˈtɔriə/) a place like a hospital where patients who have a lasting illness or who are getting better after an illness are treated

sanc·ti·fy /ˈsæŋktəˌfaɪ/ *verb* (**sanc·ti·fies, sanc·ti·fied, sanc·ti·fy·ing, sanc·ti·fied**) [usually passive] (*formal*) **1** ~ sth to make something holy **2** ~ sth to make something seem right or legal; to give official approval to something: *This was a practice sanctified by tradition.* ▶ **sanc·ti·fi·ca·tion** /ˌsæŋktəfəˈkeɪʃn/ *noun* [U]

sanc·ti·mo·ni·ous /ˌsæŋktəˈmoʊniəs/ *adj.* (*disapproving*) giving the impression that you feel you are better and more moral than other people **SYN** SELF-RIGHTEOUS ▶ **sanc·ti·mo·ni·ous·ly** *adv.* **sanc·ti·mo·ni·ous·ness** *noun* [U]

sanc·tion /ˈsæŋkʃn/ *noun, verb*

● **noun 1** [C, usually pl.] ~ (against sb) an official order that limits trade, contact, etc. with a particular country, in order to make it do something, such as obeying international law: *Trade sanctions were imposed against any country that refused to sign the agreement.* ♦ *The economic sanctions have been lifted.* ⊃ collocations at INTERNATIONAL **2** [U] (*formal*) official permission or approval for an action or a change **SYN** AUTHORIZATION: *These changes will require the sanction of the court.* **3** [C] ~ (against sth) a course of action that can be used, if necessary, to make people obey a law or behave in a particular way **SYN** PENALTY: *The ultimate sanction will be the closure of the restaurant.*

● **verb 1** ~ sth (*formal*) to give permission for something to take place: *The government refused to sanction a further cut in interest rates.* **2** ~ sb/sth (*technical*) to punish someone or something; to impose a sanction on something

sanc·ti·ty /ˈsæŋktəti/ *noun* [U] **1** ~ (of sth) the state of being very important and worth protecting: *the sanctity of marriage* **2** (*formal*) the state of being holy: *a life of sanctity, like that of St. Francis*

sanc·tu·ar·y /ˈsæŋktʃuˌeri/ *noun* (*pl.* **sanc·tu·ar·ies**) **1** [C] an area where wild birds or animals are protected and encouraged to breed **SYN** RESERVE: *a bird/wildlife sanctuary* **2** [U] safety and protection, especially for people who are being chased or attacked: *to take sanctuary in a place* ♦ *The government offered sanctuary to 4,000 refugees.* ♦ *She longed for the sanctuary of her own home.* **3** [C, usually sing.] a safe place, especially one where people who are being chased or attacked can stay and be protected: *The church became a sanctuary for the refugees.* **4** [C] a holy building or the part of it that is considered the most holy

sanc·tum /ˈsæŋktəm/ *noun* [usually sing.] (*formal*) **1** a private room where someone can go and not be disturbed: *She once allowed me into her **inner sanctum**.* **2** a holy place

sand 🔑 /sænd/ *noun, verb*

● **noun 1** [U] a substance that consists of very small, fine grains of rock. Sand is found on beaches, in deserts, etc.: *a grain of sand* ♦ *Concrete is a mixture of sand and cement.* ♦ *His hair was the color of sand.* ♦ *The children were playing in the sand* (= for example, in a SANDBOX). **2** [U, C, usually pl.] a large area of sand on a beach: *We went for a walk along the sand.* ♦ *children playing on the sand* ♦ *miles of golden sands* ⊃ see also SANDY **IDM** see HEAD *n.*, SHIFT *v.* ⊃ thesaurus box at COAST

● **verb** ~ sth (down) to make something smooth by rubbing it with sandpaper or using a sander

---

san·dal /'sændl/ noun a type of light, open shoe that is worn in warm weather. The top part consists of leather or cloth bands that attach the SOLE to your foot. ➲ picture at SHOE

san·daled /'sændld/ adj. [only before noun] wearing sandals: *sandaled feet*

san·dal·wood /'sændl,wʊd/ noun [U] a type of oil with a sweet smell that is obtained from a hard tropical wood (also called sandalwood) and used to make PERFUME

sand·bag /'sændbæg/ noun, verb
• noun a bag filled with sand used to build a wall as a protection against floods or explosions
• verb (-gg-) **1** ~ sth to put sandbags in or around something as protection against floods or explosions **2** ~ sb (*informal*) to attack someone by criticizing them strongly; to treat someone badly

sand·bank /'sændbæŋk/ noun a raised area of sand in a river or the ocean

sand·bar /'sændbɑr/ noun a long mass of sand at the point where a river meets the ocean, that is formed by the movement of the water

sand·blast /'sændblæst/ verb [often passive] ~ sth to clean, polish, decorate, etc. a surface by firing sand at it from a special machine

sand·box /'sændbɑks/ noun an area in the ground or a shallow container, filled with sand, for children to play in ➲ picture at TOY

sand·cas·tle /'sænd,kæsl/ noun a pile of sand made to look like a castle, usually by a child on a beach

'**sand dune** noun = DUNE

sand·er /'sændər/ noun an electric tool with a rough surface used for making wood smooth

s and h (also **s & h**) abbr. (in writing) shipping and handling

S & L /,ɛs ən 'ɛl/ abbr. SAVINGS AND LOAN ASSOCIATION

sand·lot /'sændlɑt/ adj. [only before noun] (of a sport) played for enjoyment rather than as a job for money

the **sand·man** /'sændmæn/ noun [sing.] an imaginary man who is said to help children get to sleep

sand·pa·per /'sænd,peɪpər/ noun, verb
• noun [U] strong paper with a rough surface covered with sand or a similar substance, used for rubbing surfaces in order to make them smooth ➲ picture at TOOL
• verb (also sand) ~ sth (down) to make something smooth by rubbing it with sandpaper

sand·pi·per /'sænd,paɪpər/ noun a small bird with long legs and a long beak that lives near rivers and lakes

sand·stone /'sændstoʊn/ noun [U] a type of stone that is formed of grains of sand tightly pressed together, used in building

sand·storm /'sændstɔrm/ noun a storm in a desert in which sand is blown into the air by strong winds

'**sand trap** (also trap) noun = BUNKER ➲ picture at HOBBY

'**sand wedge** noun a GOLF CLUB used for hitting the ball out of sand

sand·wich /'sænwɪtʃ; 'sændwɪtʃ/ noun, verb
• noun two slices of bread with a layer of meat, cheese, etc. between them: *a ham and cheese sandwich* ➲ see also CLUB SANDWICH, OPEN SANDWICH
• verb
  PHR V '**sandwich sb/sth between sb/sth** [usually passive] to fit something or someone into a very small space between two other things or people, or between two times: *I was sandwiched between two fat men on the bus.* ,**sandwich A and B to'gether (with sth)** to put something between two things to join them: *Sandwich the cake layers together with cream.*

'**sandwich ,board** noun a pair of boards with advertisements on them that someone wears at the front and back of their body as they walk around in public

sand·y /'sændi/ adj. (sand·i·er, sand·i·est) **1** covered with

or containing sand: *a sandy beach* ♦ *sandy soil* **2** (of hair) having a light color, between yellow and red

sane /seɪn/ adj. (san·er, san·est) **1** having a normal healthy mind; not mentally ill **SYN** OF SOUND MIND: *No sane person would do that.* ♦ *Being able to get out of the city at the weekend keeps me sane.* **2** sensible and reasonable: *the sane way to solve the problem* **ANT** INSANE ➲ see also SANITY ► **sane·ly** adv.

sang pt of SING

sang·froid /sɑŋ'frwɑ; -'fwɑ/ noun [U] (from *French*) the ability to remain calm in a difficult or dangerous situation

san·gri·a /sæŋ'griə/ noun [U] (from *Spanish*) an alcoholic drink made of red wine mixed with fruit, and sometimes with SODA WATER or BRANDY added

san·gui·nar·y /'sæŋgwə,nɛri/ adj. (*formal*) involving or liking killing and blood

san·guine /'sæŋgwən/ adj. ~ (about sth) (*formal*) cheerful and confident about the future **SYN** OPTIMISTIC: *They are less sanguine about the company's long-term prospects.* ♦ *He tends to take a sanguine view of the problems involved.* ► **san·guine·ly** adv.

san·i·tar·i·um = SANATORIUM

san·i·tar·y /'sænə,tɛri/ adj. **1** [only before noun] connected with keeping places clean and healthy to live in, especially by removing human waste: *Overcrowding and poor sanitary conditions led to disease in the refugee camps.* ♦ *The hut had no cooking or sanitary facilities.* **2** clean; not likely to cause health problems **SYN** HYGIENIC: *The new houses were more sanitary than the old ones had been.* **ANT** INSANITARY

,**sanitary 'napkin** (also ,sanitary 'pad) noun a thick piece of soft material that women wear outside their body to absorb the blood during their PERIOD ➲ compare TAMPON

san·i·ta·tion /,sænə'teɪʃn/ noun [U] the equipment and systems that keep places clean, especially by removing human waste: *disease resulting from poor sanitation*

sani'tation ,worker noun (*formal*) a person whose job is to remove waste from outside houses, etc. **SYN** GARBAGE MAN

san·i·tize /'sænə,taɪz/ verb (*formal*) **1** ~ sth (*disapproving*) to remove the parts of something that could be considered unpleasant: *This sanitized account of his life does not mention his time in prison.* **2** ~ sth to clean something thoroughly using chemicals to remove bacteria **SYN** DISINFECT

san·i·ty /'sænəti/ noun [U] **1** the state of having a normal healthy mind: *His behavior was so strange that I began to doubt his sanity.* ♦ *to keep/preserve your sanity* **2** the state of being sensible and reasonable: *After a series of road accidents the police pleaded for sanity among drivers.* **ANT** INSANITY ➲ see also SANE

sank pt of SINK

sans /sænz/ prep. (*literary* or *humorous*) without: *I'm on a diet so I had a salad sans dressing.*

San·skrit /'sænskrɪt/ noun [U] an ancient language of India belonging to the Indo-European family, in which the Hindu holy texts are written and on which many modern languages are based

sans ser·if /,sæn 'sɛrəf/ noun [U] (*technical*) (in printing) a TYPEFACE in which the letters have no SERIF

San·ta Claus /'sæntə ,klɔz/ (also San·ta) noun an imaginary old man with red clothes and a long white beard. Parents tell young children that he brings them presents at Christmas.

sap /sæp/ noun, verb
• noun **1** [U] the liquid in a plant or tree that carries food to all its parts: *Maple syrup is made from sap extracted from the sugar maple tree.* **2** [C] (*informal*) a stupid person that you can easily trick, or treat unfairly
• verb (-pp-) to make something or someone weaker; to destroy something gradually: ~ sth *The hot sun sapped our energy.* ♦ ~ sb (of sth) *Years of failure have sapped him of his confidence.*

| t tea | ţ butter | d did | k cat | g got | tʃ chin | dʒ June | f fall |

sa·pi·ent /'seɪpiənt/ adj. (literary) having great intelligence or knowledge ▶ **sa·pi·ence** /-əns/ noun [U] **sa·pi·ent·ly** adv.

sap·ling /'sæplɪŋ/ noun a young tree

sap·o·dil·la /ˌsæpə'dɪlə/ noun a large tropical American tree that produces a fruit that can be eaten and CHICLE (= a substance used to make GUM)

sap·phic /'sæfɪk/ noun (formal) relating to LESBIANS ▶ **sap·phism** /'sæfɪzəm/ noun [U]

sap·phire /'sæfaɪər/ noun **1** [C, U] a clear, bright blue PRECIOUS STONE **2** [U] a bright blue color ▶ **sap·phire** adj.: sapphire eyes

sap·py /'sæpi/ adj. (sap·pi·er, sap·pi·est) **1** (informal) silly and SENTIMENTAL; full of unnecessary emotion: sappy love songs **2** (of plants) full of SAP (= liquid)

sap·wood /'sæpwʊd/ noun [U] the soft younger outer layers of the wood of a tree, inside the BARK ⊃ compare HEART-WOOD

Sa·ran Wrap™ /sə'ræn ræp/ noun [U] = PLASTIC WRAP

sar·casm /'sɑrkæzəm/ noun [U] a way of using words that are the opposite of what you mean in order to be unpleasant to someone or to make fun of them: "That will be useful," she snapped with heavy sarcasm (= she really thought it would not be useful at all). ♦ a hint/touch/trace of sarcasm in his voice

sar·cas·tic /sɑr'kæstɪk/ adj. showing or expressing sarcasm: sarcastic comments ♦ a sarcastic manner ♦ "There's no need to be sarcastic," she said. ▶ **sar·cas·ti·cally** /-kli/ adv.

sar·co·ma /sɑr'koʊmə/ noun (medical) a harmful (= MALIGNANT) lump (= a TUMOR) that grows in certain parts of the body such as muscle or bone

sar·coph·a·gus /sɑr'kɑfəgəs/ noun (pl. **sar·coph·a·gi** /-ˌdʒaɪ; -ˌgaɪ/) a stone COFFIN (= box that a dead person is buried in), especially one that is decorated, used in ancient times

sar·dine /sɑr'din/ noun a small, young, sea fish that is either eaten fresh or preserved in cans
  IDM (packed, crammed, etc.) like sardines (informal) pressed tightly together in a way that is uncomfortable or unpleasant

sar·don·ic /sɑr'dɑnɪk/ adj. (disapproving) showing that you think that you are better than other people and do not take them seriously **SYN** MOCKING: a sardonic smile ▶ **sar·don·i·cally** /-kli/ adv.

sarge /sɑrdʒ/ noun (informal) used to talk to or about a SERGEANT

sa·ri /'sɑri/ noun a long piece of cloth that is wrapped around the body and worn as the main piece of clothing by women in S. Asia

sa·rin /'sɑrən; 'sɛr-/ noun [U] a type of poisonous gas used in chemical weapons

sa·rong /sə'rɔŋ; -'rɑŋ/ noun a long piece of cloth wrapped around the body from the waist or the chest, worn by Malaysian and Indonesian men and women and sometimes by women in the West, for example on the beach

SARS /sɑrz/ noun [U] the abbreviation for "severe acute respiratory syndrome" (an illness that is easily spread from person to person, that affects the lungs, and can sometimes cause death): No new SARS cases have been reported in the region.

sar·sa·pa·ril·la /ˌsæspə'rɪlə/ noun **1** [U] a dried substance that is used to flavor drinks and medicines, obtained from a plant also called sarsaparilla **2** [U, C] a a drink made with sarsaparilla

sar·to·ri·al /sɑr'tɔriəl/ adj. [only before noun] (formal) relating to clothes, especially men's clothes, and the way they are made or worn ▶ **sar·to·ri·al·ly** adv.

SASE noun the abbreviation used in writing for "self-addressed stamped envelope" (an envelope on which you have written your name and address and put a stamp so that someone else can use it to send something to you)

sash /sæʃ/ noun **1** a long strip of cloth worn around the waist or over one shoulder, especially as part of a uniform **2** either of a pair of windows, one above the other, that are opened and closed by sliding them up and down inside the frame

sa·shay /sæ'ʃeɪ/ verb [I] + adv./prep. to walk in a very confident but relaxed way, especially in order to be noticed

'sash cord noun a string or rope with a weight at one end attached to a sash window allowing it to stay open in any position

sa·shi·mi /sə'ʃimi/ noun [U, C] (from Japanese) a Japanese dish consisting of slices of raw fish

ˌsash 'window noun a window that consists of two separate parts, one above the other, that you open by sliding one of the parts up or down

Sas·quatch /'sæskwɑtʃ/ noun = BIGFOOT

sass /sæs/ noun, verb
● **noun** [U] (informal) **1** (disapproving) behavior or talk that is rude and lacking respect **2** (approving) a confident and lively way of behaving or attitude: She has plenty of sass, wit, and intelligence.
● **verb ~ sb** (informal) to speak to someone in a rude way, without respect: Don't sass your mother!

sas·sa·fras /'sæsəˌfræs/ noun a N. American tree with pleasant-smelling leaves and BARK. Its leaves are sometimes used to make a type of tea.

sas·sy /'sæsi/ adj. (sas·si·er, sas·si·est) (informal) **1** (disapproving) (especially of children) rude; showing a lack of respect: sassy behavior ♦ a sassy remark ⊃ thesaurus box at RUDE **2** (approving) fashionable and confident: his sassy, streetwise daughter

SAT™ noun /ˌɛs eɪ 'ti/ the abbreviation for "Scholastic Aptitude Test" (a test taken by high school students who want to go to a college): to take the SAT ♦ I scored 1050 on my SATs. ♦ an SAT score

sat pt, pp of SIT

Sa·tan /'seɪtn/ noun the DEVIL

sa·tan·ic /sə'tænɪk; seɪ-/ adj. **1** often Satanic connected with the worship of the DEVIL: satanic cults **2** (formal) morally bad and evil **SYN** DEMONIC ▶ **sa·tan·i·cally** /-kli/ adv.

sa·tan·ism /'seɪtnˌɪzəm/ noun [U] the worship of Satan ▶ **sa·tan·ist** /'seɪtn-ɪst/ noun

sa·tay /sɑ'teɪ; 'sɑteɪ/ noun [U, C] a S.E. Asian dish consisting of meat or fish cooked on sticks and served with a sauce made with PEANUTS

satch·el /'sætʃəl/ noun a leather bag that you hang over your shoulder or wear on your back, that children used to use for carrying their books to school

sat·com (also **SAT.COM**) /'sætkɑm/ noun [U] satellite communications

sate /seɪt/ verb ~ **sth** (formal) to satisfy a desire

sat·ed /'seɪtəd/ adj. [not usually before noun] ~ **(with sth)** (formal) having had so much of something that you do not need any more: sated with pleasure

sat·el·lite /'sætlˌaɪt/ noun **1** an electronic device that is sent into space and moves around the earth or another planet. It is used for communicating by radio, television, etc. and for providing information.: a weather/communications satellite ♦ The interview was broadcast live by satellite from Hollywood. ♦ satellite television/TV (= broadcast using a satellite) ♦ a satellite broadcast/channel/picture ⊃ collocations at TELE-VISION **2** a natural object that moves around a larger natural object in space: The moon is a satellite of earth. **3** a town, a country, or an organization that is controlled by, and depends on, another larger or more powerful one: satellite states

'satellite ˌdish noun a piece of equipment that receives signals from a satellite, used to enable people to watch satellite television

'satellite ˌstation noun **1** a company that broadcasts television programs using a satellite **2** a place where special equipment is used to follow the movements of satellites and receive information from them

sa·ti = SUTTEE

sa·ti·ate /'seɪʃiˌeɪt/ verb [usually passive] ~ **sb/sth** (formal) to give someone so much of something that they do not feel they want any more ▶ **sa·ti·a·tion** /ˌseɪʃiˈeɪʃn/ noun [U]

sa·ti·e·ty /səˈtaɪəti/ noun [U] (formal or technical) the state or feeling of being completely full of food, or of having had enough of something

sat·in /'sætn/ noun, adj.
- **noun** [U] a type of cloth with a smooth, shiny surface: a white satin ribbon
- **adj.** [only before noun] having the smooth, shiny appearance of satin: The paint has a satin finish.

sat·in·y /'sætn·i/ adj. looking or feeling like satin: her satiny skin

sat·ire /'sætaɪər/ noun [U, C] a way of criticizing a person, an idea, or an institution in which you use humor to show their faults or weaknesses; a piece of writing that uses this type of criticism: **political/social satire** ◆ a work full of **savage/ biting satire** ◆ The novel is a stinging satire on American politics.

sa·tir·i·cal /səˈtɪrɪkl/ (also less frequent **sa·tir·ic** /səˈtɪrɪk/) adj. using satire to criticize someone or something: a satirical magazine ▶ **sa·tir·i·cally** /-kli/ adv.

sat·i·rist /'sætərɪst/ noun a person who writes or uses SATIRE

sat·i·rize /'sætəˌraɪz/ verb ~ **sb/sth** to use SATIRE to show the faults in a person, an organization, a system, etc.

sat·is·fac·tion ♪

/ˌsætəsˈfækʃn/ noun

1 [U, C] the good feeling that you have when you have achieved something or when something that you wanted to happen does happen; something that gives you this feeling: **to gain/get/derive satisfaction from something** ◆ a **look/smile of satisfaction** ◆ She looked back on her career **with great satisfaction.** ◆ He had **the satisfaction of** seeing his book become a best seller. ◆ She didn't want to **give him the satisfaction of** seeing her cry. ◆ The company is trying to improve **customer satisfaction.** ◆ He was enjoying all the satisfactions of being a parent. ⊃ see also DISSATISFACTION **2** [U] the act of FULFILLING a need or desire: the satisfaction of sexual desires ◆ the satisfaction of your ambitions **3** [U] (formal) an acceptable way of dealing with a complaint, a debt, an injury, etc.: I complained to the manager but I didn't get any satisfaction.

IDM **to sb's satisfaction 1** if you do something **to someone's satisfaction**, they are pleased with it: The case was settled **to the complete satisfaction** of the client. **2** if you prove something **to someone's satisfaction**, they believe or accept it: Can you demonstrate **to our satisfaction that** your story is true?

WORD FAMILY
satisfaction noun (≠ dissatisfaction)
satisfactory adj. (≠ unsatisfactory)
satisfy verb
satisfying adj. (≠ unsatisfying)
satisfied adj. (≠ dissatisfied) (≠ unsatisfied)

THESAURUS

satisfaction

happiness ◦ pride ◦ contentment ◦ fulfillment

These are all words for the good feeling that you have when you are happy or when you have achieved something.

satisfaction the good feeling that you have when you have achieved something or when something that you wanted to happen does happen: He derived great satisfaction from knowing that his son was happy.

happiness the good feeling that you have when you are happy: Money can't buy you happiness.

pride a feeling of pleasure or satisfaction that you get when you, or people who are connected with you, have done something well or own something that other people admire: The sight of her son graduating filled her with pride.

contentment (somewhat formal) a feeling of happiness or satisfaction with what you have: They found contentment in living a simple life.

fulfillment a feeling of happiness or satisfaction with what you do or have done: her search for personal fulfillment

SATISFACTION, HAPPINESS, CONTENTMENT, OR FULFILLMENT?

You can feel **satisfaction** at achieving almost anything, small or large; you feel **fulfillment** when you do something useful and enjoyable with your life. **Happiness** is the feeling you have when things give you pleasure and can be quite a lively feeling; **contentment** is a quieter feeling that you get when you have learned to find pleasure in things.

PATTERNS

- satisfaction/happiness/pride/contentment/fulfillment **in** sth
- **real** satisfaction/happiness/pride/contentment/fulfillment
- **true** satisfaction/happiness/contentment/fulfillment
- **great** satisfaction/happiness/pride
- **quiet** satisfaction/pride/contentment
- to **feel** satisfaction/happiness/pride/contentment
- to **bring sb** satisfaction/happiness/pride/contentment/fulfillment
- to **find** satisfaction/happiness/contentment/fulfillment

sat·is·fac·to·ry /ˌsætəsˈfæktəri/ adj. good enough for a particular purpose **SYN** ACCEPTABLE: a satisfactory explanation/answer/solution/conclusion ◆ The work is satisfactory but not outstanding. ◆ The existing law is not entirely/wholly satisfactory. **ANT** UNSATISFACTORY ▶ **sat·is·fac·to·ri·ly** /-tərəli/ adv.: Her disappearance has never been satisfactorily explained. ◆ Our complaint was dealt with satisfactorily.

sat·is·fied ♪ /'sætəsˌfaɪd/ adj.

1 pleased because you have achieved something or because something that you wanted to happen has happened: a satisfied smile ◆ a satisfied customer ◆ ~ **with sb/ sth** She's never satisfied with what she has. **ANT** DISSATISFIED ⊃ thesaurus box at HAPPY **2** ~ **(that...)** | ~ **(with sth)** believing or accepting that something is true **SYN** CONVINCED: I'm satisfied that they are telling the truth. ⊃ compare UNSATISFIED

sat·is·fy ♪ /'sætəsˌfaɪ/ verb (sat·is·fies, sat·is·fy·ing, sat·is·fied, sat·is·fied)

1 ~ **sb** (not used in the progressive tenses) to make someone pleased by doing or giving them what they want: Nothing satisfies him—he's always complaining. ◆ The proposed plan will not satisfy everyone. **2** ~ **sth** to provide what is wanted, needed, or asked for: The food wasn't enough to satisfy his hunger. ◆ to satisfy someone's curiosity ◆ The education system must satisfy the needs of all children. ◆ We cannot satisfy demand for the product. ◆ She failed to satisfy all the requirements for entry to the college. **3** (not used in the progressive tenses) to make someone certain something is true or has been done: ~ **sb** Her explanation did not satisfy the teacher. ◆ ~ **sb of sth** People need to be satisfied of the need for a new system. ◆ ~ **sb/yourself (that)...** Once I had satisfied myself (that) it was the right decision, we went ahead.

sat·is·fy·ing ♪ /'sætəsˌfaɪɪŋ/ adj.

giving pleasure because it provides something you need or want: a satisfying meal ◆ a satisfying experience ◆ It's satisfying

h **hat**	m **man**	n **no**	ŋ **sing**	l **leg**	r **red**	y **yes**	w **wet**

to play a game really well. ▶ **sat·is·fy·ing·ly** /ˈsætɪsfaɪŋli/ *adv.*

THESAURUS

satisfying

rewarding • pleasing • gratifying • fulfilling

These words all describe an experience, an activity, or a fact that gives you pleasure because it provides something you need or want.

satisfying that gives you pleasure because it provides something that you need or want: *Soup and a salad can be a satisfying meal.*

rewarding (of an experience or an activity) that makes you happy because you think it is useful or important; worth doing: *Nursing can be a very rewarding career.*

pleasing (*somewhat formal*) that gives you pleasure, especially to look at, hear, or think about: *It was a simple but pleasing design.*

gratifying (*formal*) that gives you pleasure, especially because it makes you feel that you have done well: *It is gratifying to see such good results.*

fulfilling (of an experience or an activity) that makes you happy, because it makes you feel your skills and talents are being used: *He'd like to find a more fulfilling career.*

SATISFYING, REWARDING, OR FULFILLING?

Almost any experience, important or not, can be **satisfying. Rewarding** and **fulfilling** are used more for longer, more serious activities, such as jobs or careers. **Satisfying** and **fulfilling** are more about your personal satisfaction or happiness; **rewarding** is more about your sense of doing something important and being useful to others.

PATTERNS
■ a satisfying/rewarding/gratifying/fulfilling **experience/feeling**
■ (a) satisfying/rewarding/fulfilling **job/career/work**
■ to **find sth** satisfying/rewarding/pleasing/gratifying

sat·su·ma /sætˈsumə/ *noun* a type of small orange without seeds and with loose skin that comes off easily

sat·u·rate /ˈsætʃəˌreɪt/ *verb* **1** ~ sth to make something completely wet **SYN** SOAK: *The continuous rain had saturated the soil.* **2** [often passive] ~ sth/sb (with/in sth) to fill something or someone completely with something so that it is impossible or useless to add any more: *The company had saturated the market for cell phones* (= so that no new buyers could be found).

sat·u·rat·ed /ˈsætʃəˌreɪtəd/ *adj.* **1** [not usually before noun] completely wet **SYN** SOAKED ⊃ thesaurus box at WET **2** [usually before noun] (*chemistry*) if a chemical SOLUTION (= a liquid with something dissolved in it) is **saturated**, it contains the greatest possible amount of the substance that has been dissolved in it: *a saturated solution of sodium chloride* **3** [usually before noun] (of colors) very strong: *saturated reds*

ˌsaturated ˈfat *noun* [C, U] a type of fat found, for example, in butter, fried food, and many types of meat, that encourages the harmful development of CHOLESTEROL ⊃ see also MONOUNSATURATED FAT, POLYUNSATURATED FAT, TRANS-FATTY ACID, UNSATURATED FAT

sat·u·ra·tion /ˌsætʃəˈreɪʃn/ *noun* [U] **1** (often *figurative*) the state or process that happens when no more of something can be accepted or added because there is already too much of it or too many of them: *a business beset by price wars and **market saturation*** (= the fact that no new customers can be found) ◆ ***saturation bombing** of the city* (= covering the whole city) ◆ *There was **saturation coverage*** (= so much that it was impossible to avoid it or add to it) *of the event by the media.* **2** (*chemistry*) the degree to which something is absorbed in

something else, expressed as a PERCENTAGE of the greatest possible

ˌsatuˈration point *noun* [U, sing.] **1** the stage at which no more of something can be accepted or added because there is already too much of it or too many of them: *The market for computer games has reached saturation point.* **2** (*chemistry*) the stage at which no more of a substance can be absorbed into a liquid or VAPOR

Sat·ur·day 🔑 /ˈsætərˌdeɪ; -di/ *noun* [C, U] (*abbr.* Sat.) the day of the week after Friday and before Sunday **HELP** To see how **Saturday** is used, look at the examples at **Monday**. **ORIGIN** From the Old English for "day of Saturn," translated from Latin *Saturni dies.*

Sat·urn /ˈsætərn/ *noun* a large planet in the SOLAR SYSTEM that has rings around it and is 6th in order of distance from the sun ⊃ picture at EARTH

Sat·ur·na·li·a /ˌsætərˈneɪlyə/ *noun* [U] an ancient Roman festival that took place in December, around the time that Christmas now takes place

sat·ur·na·li·an /ˌsætərˈneɪlyən/ *adj.* **1** relating to Saturnalia **2** involving wild celebrations

sat·ur·nine /ˈsætərˌnaɪn/ *adj.* (*literary*) (of a person or their face) looking serious and threatening

sa·tyr /ˈseɪtər/ *noun* (in ancient Greek stories) a god of the woods, with a man's face and body and a GOAT's legs and horns

sauce 🔑 /sɔs/ *noun* **1** [C, U] a thick liquid that is eaten with food to add flavor to it: *tomato/cranberry/cream, etc. sauce* ◆ *chicken in a white sauce* ◆ *ice cream with hot fudge sauce* ⊃ see also SOY SAUCE, TARTAR SAUCE, WHITE SAUCE **2** [U] (*old-fashioned, informal*) **the sauce** alcoholic drinks: *Her husband is **on the sauce*** (= drinking alcohol) *again.*
IDM **what's sauce for the goose is sauce for the gander** (*old-fashioned, saying*) what one person is allowed to do, another person must be allowed to do in a similar situation

sauce·boat /ˈsɔsboʊt/ *noun* a long, low container used for serving or pouring sauce at a meal

sauce·pan /ˈsɔspæn/ (*also* pot) *noun* a deep, round, metal pot with a lid and one long handle or two short handles, used for cooking things over heat ⊃ picture at COOKING

sau·cer /ˈsɔsər/ *noun* a small, shallow, round dish that a cup stands on; an object that is shaped like this: *cups and saucers* ⊃ picture at CUP ⊃ see also FLYING SAUCER

sau·cy /ˈsɔsi/ *adj.* (sau·ci·er, sau·ci·est) rude or referring to sex in a way that is amusing but not offensive: *saucy jokes* ◆ *a saucy smile* ▶ **sau·ci·ly** /-səli/ *adv.*

sau·er·kraut /ˈsaʊərˌkraʊt/ *noun* [U] (from *German*) CABBAGE (= a type of green vegetable) that is preserved in salt water and then cooked

sau·na /ˈsɔnə; ˈsaʊnə/ *noun* a period of time in which you sit or lie in a room (also called a sauna) that has been heated to a very high temperature. Some saunas involve the use of steam: *a hotel with a swimming pool and sauna* ◆ *to **have/take** a sauna*

saun·ter /ˈsɔntər/ *verb* [I] + adv./prep. to walk in a slow relaxed way **SYN** STROLL: *He sauntered by, looking as if he had all the time in the world.* ▶ **saun·ter** *noun* [sing.]: *This part of the route should be an easy saunter.*

sau·ri·an /ˈsɔriən/ *adj., noun* (*biology*)
● *adj.* relating to LIZARDS
● *noun* a large REPTILE, especially a DINOSAUR

sau·sage /ˈsɔsɪdʒ; ˈsɑ-/ *noun* [C, U] a mixture of finely chopped meat, fat, bread, etc. in a long tube of skin, cooked and eaten whole or served cold in thin slices: *beef/pork sausages* ◆ *a quarter pound of garlic sausage* ⊃ see also LIVERWURST

ˈsausage ˌlink *noun* = LINK n. (6)

sausage meat *noun* [U] the mixture of finely chopped meat, fat, bread, etc. used for making sausages

sau·té /sɔːˈteɪ; soʊ-/ *verb* (**sau·té·ing, sau·téed, sau·téed** or **sau·té·ing, sau·téd, sau·téd**) **~ sth** to fry food quickly in a little hot fat ▶ **sau·té** *adj.* [only before noun]: *sauté potatoes*

sav·age /ˈsævɪdʒ/ *adj., noun, verb*

● *adj.* **1** aggressive and violent; causing great harm **SYN** BRUTAL: *savage dogs* ◆ *She had been badly hurt in what police described as "a savage attack."* ◆ *savage public spending cuts* **2** involving very strong criticism: *The article was a savage attack on the government's record.* **3** [only before noun] (*old-fashioned*) an offensive way of referring to groups of people or customs that are considered to be simple and not highly developed **SYN** PRIMITIVE: *a savage tribe* ▶ **sav·age·ly** *adv.*: *savagely attacked/criticized* ◆ *"No!" he snarled savagely.*

● *noun* **1** (*old-fashioned*) an offensive word for someone who belongs to a people that is simple and not developed: *the development of the human race from primitive savages* **2** a cruel and violent person: *He described the attack as the work of savages.*

● *verb* [usually passive] **1 ~ sb** (of an animal) to attack someone violently, causing serious injury: *She was savaged to death by a bear.* **2 ~ sb/sth** (*formal*) to criticize someone or something severely: *Her latest novel has been savaged by the critics.*

sav·age·ry /ˈsævɪdʒri/ *noun* [U] behavior that is very cruel and violent **SYN** VIOLENCE: *The police were shocked by the savagery of the attacks.*

sa·van·nah (also **sa·van·na**) /səˈvænə/ *noun* [C, U] a wide, flat, open area of land, especially in Africa, that is covered with grass but has few trees ⊃ compare VELD

sa·vant /sæˈvɑnt; sə-/ *noun* (*formal*) **1** a person with great knowledge and ability **2** a person who is less intelligent than others but who has particular unusual abilities that other people do not have

---

THESAURUS

save

rescue ◆ bail sb out ◆ come through (for sb)

These words all mean to prevent someone from dying, losing something, being harmed, or being embarrassed.

save to prevent someone from dying, being harmed, or destroyed, or losing something: *Doctors were unable to save him.* ◆ *a campaign to save the panda from extinction*

rescue to save someone from a dangerous or harmful situation: *They were rescued by a passing cruise ship.*

bail sb out to rescue someone from a difficult situation, especially by providing money: *Don't expect me to bail you out if it all goes wrong.*

come through (for sb) (*somewhat informal*) to prevent disaster for someone: *My sister really came through for me when I lost my job.*

PATTERNS

- to save/rescue sb/sth **from** sth
- to rescue sb/bail sb out **financially**

save /seɪv/ *verb, noun, prep., conj.*

● *verb*

▷ KEEP SAFE **1** [T] to keep someone or something safe from death, harm, loss, etc.: **~ sb/sth** *to save someone's life* ◆ *Doctors were unable to save her.* ◆ *He's trying to save their marriage.* ◆ *She needs to win the next two games to save the match.* ◆ (*figurative*) *Thanks for doing that. You saved my life* (= helped me a lot). ◆ **~ sb/sth (from sth)** *to save a rare species (from extinction)* ◆ **~ sb/sth from doing sth** *She saved a little girl from falling into the water.*

▷ MONEY **2** [I, T] to keep money instead of spending it, especially in order to buy a particular thing: *I'm not very*

good at saving. ◆ **~ (up) (for sth)** *I'm saving for a new bike.* ◆ *We've been saving up to go to Argentina.* ◆ **~ sth (up) (for sth)** *You should save a little each week.* ◆ *I've saved almost $500 so far.*

▷ KEEP FOR FUTURE **3** [T] to keep something to use or enjoy in the future: **~ sth (for sth/sb)** *He's saving his strength for the last part of the race.* ◆ *We'll eat some now and save some for tomorrow.* ◆ *Save some food for me.* ◆ **~ sb sth** *Save me some food.*

▷ COMPUTING **4** [T, I] **~ (sth)** to store information in a computer by giving it a special instruction: *Don't forget to save the file before you close it.* ◆ *Save data frequently.*

▷ NOT WASTE **5** [T, I] to avoid wasting something or using more than necessary: **~ sth** *We'll take a cab to save time.* ◆ *Reserve early and save $50!* ◆ *We should try to save water.* ◆ **~ sth on sth** *The government is trying to save $100 million on defense.* ◆ **~ sb sth (on sth)** *If we go this way it will save us two hours on the trip.* ◆ **~ on sth** *I save on bus fare by walking to work.*

▷ COLLECT SOMETHING **6** [T] **~ sth** to collect something because you like it or for a special purpose: *I've been saving theater programs for years.* ◆ *If you save ten box tops, you can get a T-shirt.*

▷ AVOID SOMETHING BAD **7** [T] to avoid doing something difficult or unpleasant; to make someone able to avoid doing something difficult or unpleasant: **~ sb from doing sth** *The prize money saved her from having to find a job.* ◆ **~ sth** *She did it herself to save argument.* ◆ **~ sb sth** *Thanks for sending that letter for me—it saved me a trip.* ◆ **~ doing sth** *He's grown a beard to save shaving.* ◆ **~ sb doing (from) sth** *If you call for an appointment, it'll save you having to wait.*

▷ IN SPORTS **8** [T, I] **~ (sth)** (in SOCCER, etc.) to prevent an opponent's shot from going in the goal: *to save a penalty* ◆ *The goalie saved Johnson's long-range shot.*

IDM **not be able to do sth to save your life** (*informal*) to be completely unable to do something: *He can't interview people to save his life.* **save sb's bacon/neck** (*informal*) to rescue someone from a very difficult situation **save the day/situation** to prevent failure or defeat, when this seems certain to happen: *Orr's late goal saved the day for the Bruins.* **save face** to avoid or help someone avoid embarrassment: *She was fired, but she saved face by telling everyone she'd resigned.* **save your breath** (*informal*) used to tell someone that it is not worth wasting time and effort saying something because it will not change anything: *Save your breath—you'll never persuade her.* **save your (own) skin/hide/neck** to try to avoid death, punishment, etc., especially by leaving others in an extremely difficult situation: *To save his own skin, he lied and blamed the accident on his friend.* ⊃ more at PENNY

● *noun* (in SOCCER, etc.) an action by the GOALKEEPER that stops a goal from being scored: *He made a spectacular save.*

● *prep.* (also **save for**) (*old use* or *formal*) except something: *They knew nothing about her save her name.*

● *conj.* (*old use* or *formal*) except: *They found out nothing more save that she had borne a child.*

THESAURUS

save

budget ◆ economize ◆ tighten your belt

These words all mean to spend less money.

save to keep money instead of spending it, often in order to buy a particular thing: *I'm saving for a new car.*

budget to be careful about the amount of money you spend; to plan to spend an amount of money for a particular purpose: *I've budgeted $1,000 to furnish my new apartment.*

economize to use less money, time, etc. than you normally use

tighten your belt (*somewhat informal*) to spend less money because there is less available: *My parents really had to tighten their belts after my mother retired.*

ʌ cup   ə about   eɪ say   aɪ five   ɔɪ boy   aʊ now   oʊ go   ər bird

PATTERNS
- to save up/budget **for** sth
- to **have to** save/budget/economize/tighten our belts
- to **try to/manage to/be able to** save/budget/economize

sav·er /'seɪvər/ noun **1** a person who saves money and puts it in a bank, etc. for future use **2** (often in compounds) something that helps you spend less money or use less of the thing mentioned: *a money/time saver* ➔ see also LIFESAVER

sav·ing 🔑 /'seɪvɪŋ/ noun
1 (also **sav·ings**) [C] an amount of something such as time or money that you do not need to use or spend: *Buy three for a saving of ten dollars.* ◆ *With the new boiler you will have big savings on fuel bills.* **2** **savings** [pl.] money that you have saved, especially in a bank, etc.: *He put all his savings into buying a boat.* **3** **-saving** (in adjectives) that prevents the waste of the thing mentioned or stops it from being necessary: *energy-saving modifications* ◆ *labor-saving devices* ◆ *space-saving built-in furniture* ➔ see also FACE-SAVING

saving 'grace noun [usually sing.] the one good quality that a person or thing has that prevents them or it from being completely bad

savings ac'count noun a type of bank account that you can put money into and earn interest: *Our savings account is only paying about 2% interest.* ➔ compare CHECKING ACCOUNT

savings and 'loan association noun (abbr. **S & L**) an organization like a bank, that offers savings account s and lends money to people who want to buy a house

'savings ˌbank noun a bank that offers savings accounts

'savings ˌbond noun a type of BOND that is issued and sold by the U.S. government, mainly to individuals

'savings ˌrate noun **1** the relationship between personal income after paying taxes, and spending money on goods and services, used to measure the amount of money people are saving: *an American savings rate of only 4%* **2** the interest rate paid on a SAVINGS ACCOUNT: *The savings rate is averaging around 2%.*

sav·ior (CanE usually **sav·iour**) /'seɪvyər/ noun **1** a person who rescues someone or something from a dangerous or difficult situation: *The new manager has been hailed as the savior of the team.* **2** **the/our Savior** used in the Christian religion as another name for Jesus Christ

sav·oir faire /ˌsævwɑr 'fɛr/ noun [U] (from French, approving) the ability to behave in the appropriate way in social situations

sa·vor (CanE usually **sa·vour**) /'seɪvər/ verb, noun
● **verb 1** ~ sth to enjoy the full taste or flavor of something, especially by eating or drinking it slowly **SYN** RELISH: *He ate his meal slowly, savoring every mouthful.* **2** ~ sth to enjoy a feeling or an experience thoroughly **SYN** RELISH: *I wanted to savor every moment.*
PHR V **'savor of sth** [no passive] (formal) to seem to have an amount of something, especially something bad: *His recent comments savor of hypocrisy.*
● **noun** [usually sing.] (formal or literary) a taste or smell, especially a pleasant one: (figurative) *For Emma, life had lost its savor.*

sa·vor·y /'seɪvəri/ adj., noun
● **adj.** (CanE usually **sa·vour·y**) **1** having a taste that is salty, not sweet: *savory snacks* **2** having a pleasant taste or smell: *a savory smell from the kitchen* ➔ see also UNSAVORY
● **noun 1** [U] a plant that is related to MINT and is used in cooking as an HERB **2** (pl. **sa·vor·ies**) [C, usually pl.] (formal) a small amount of a food with a salty taste, not a sweet one, often served at a party, etc.

sav·vy /'sævi/ noun, adj.
● **noun** [U] (informal) practical knowledge or understanding of something: *political savvy*

● **adj.** (sav·vi·er, sav·vi·est) (informal) having practical knowledge and understanding of something; having COMMON SENSE: *savvy shoppers*

saw /sɔ/ noun, verb ➔ see also SEE v.
● **noun 1** (often in compounds) a tool that has a long blade with sharp points (called TEETH) along one of its edges. A saw is moved backward and forward by hand or driven by electricity, and is used for cutting wood or metal. ➔ see also CHAINSAW, CIRCULAR SAW, FRETSAW, HACKSAW, HANDSAW, JIGSAW **2** (old-fashioned) a short phrase or sentence that states a general truth about life or gives advice
● **verb** (sawed, sawed or sawed, sawn /sɔn/) **1** [I, T] to use a saw to cut something: *The workmen sawed and hammered all day.* ◆ + adv./prep. *He accidentally sawed through a cable.* ◆ ~ sth (+ adv./prep.) *She sawed the plank in half.* **2** [I, T] ~ (away) (at sth) | ~ sth to move something backward and forward on something as if using a saw: *She sawed away at her violin.* ◆ *He was sawing energetically at a loaf of bread.*
PHR V **ˌsaw sth↔'down** to cut something and bring it to the ground using a saw: *The tree had to be sawed down.* **ˌsaw sth↔'off** | **ˌsaw sth 'off** to remove something by cutting it with a saw: *We sawed the dead branches off the tree.* **ˌsaw sth↔'up (into sth)** to cut something into pieces with a saw: *We sawed the tree up into firewood.*

saw·dust /'sɔdʌst/ noun [U] very small pieces of wood that fall as powder when wood is cut with a SAW

sawed-off 'shotgun noun a SHOTGUN with part of its BARREL cut off

saw·horse /'sɔhɔrs/ noun a wooden frame that supports wood that is being cut with a SAW

sawm /soʊm/ noun [U] the Muslim practice of not eating or drinking in the day during the ninth month of the Muslim year, called RAMADAN

saw·mill /'sɔmɪl/ noun a factory in which wood is cut into boards using machinery

sax /sæks/ noun (informal) = SAXOPHONE

Sax·on /'sæksn/ noun a member of a race of people once living in N.W. Germany, some of whom settled in Britain in the 5th and 6th centuries ➔ see also ANGLO-SAXON
▶ **Sax·on** adj.: *Saxon churches/kings*

sax·o·phone /'sæksəfoʊn/ (also informal **sax**) noun a metal musical instrument that you blow into, used especially in JAZZ ➔ picture at INSTRUMENT

sax·o·phon·ist /'sæksəˌfoʊnɪst/ noun a person who plays the saxophone

say 🔑 /seɪ/ verb, noun, exclamation
● **verb** (says /sɛz/, said, said /sɛd/)
▷ **SPEAK 1** [T, I] to speak or tell someone something, using words: + speech *"Hello!" she said.* ◆ *"That was marvelous," said Daniel.* **HELP** In stories the subject often comes after said, says or say when it follows the actual words spoken, unless it is a pronoun.: ~ sth *Be quiet, I have something to say.* ◆ *I didn't believe a word she said.* ◆ *That's a terrible thing to say.* ◆ *He knew that if he wasn't back by midnight, his parents would have something to say about it* (= be angry). ◆ ~ sth to sb *She said nothing to me about it.* ◆ ~ to sb/yourself + speech *I said to myself* (= thought), *"That can't be right!"* ◆ ~ (that)… *He said (that) his name was Sam.* ◆ it is said that… *It is said that she lived to be over 100.* ◆ ~ (what, how, etc.…) *She finds it hard to say what she feels.* ◆ *"That's impossible!" "So you say* (= but I think you may be wrong)." ◆ *"Why can't I go out now?" "Because I say so."* ◆ *"What do you want it for?" "I'd rather not say."* ◆ ~ to do sth *He said to meet him here.* ◆ sb/sth is said to be/have sth *He is said to have been a brilliant scholar.*
▷ **REPEAT WORDS 2** [T] ~ sth to repeat words, phrases, etc.: *to say a prayer* ◆ *Try to say that line with more conviction.*
▷ **EXPRESS OPINION 3** [T, I] to express an opinion on something: ~ sth *Say what you like* (= although you disagree) *about her, she's a fine singer.* ◆ *I'll say this for them, they're a very efficient company.* ◆ *Anna thinks I'm lazy— what do you say* (= what is your opinion)? ◆ ~ (that)… *I can't say I blame her*

for resigning (= I think she was right). ◆ *I say* (= suggest) *we go without them*. ◆ *I wouldn't say they were rich* (= in my opinion they are not rich). ◆ *That's not to say it's a bad movie* (= it is good but it is not without faults). ◆ ~ **(what, how, etc....)** *It's hard to say what caused the accident.* ◆ *"When will it be finished?" " I couldn't say* (= I don't know)*."*

> GIVE EXAMPLE **4** [T, no passive] to suggest or give something as an example or a possibility: ~ **sth/sb** *You could learn the basics in, let's say, three months.* ◆ *Let's take any writer, say* (= for example) *Dickens...* ◆ ~ **(that)...** *Say you lose your job: what would you do then?*

> SHOW THOUGHTS/FEELINGS **5** [T] ~ **sth (to sb)** to make thoughts, feelings, etc. clear to someone by using words, looks, movements, etc.: *His angry glance said it all.* ◆ *That really says it all, doesn't it?* (= it shows clearly what is true) ◆ *Just what is the artist trying to say in her work?*

> GIVE WRITTEN INFORMATION **6** [T, no passive] (of something that is written or can be seen) to give particular information or instructions: **+ speech** *The sign said "Keep Out."* ◆ ~ **sth** *The clock said three o'clock.* ◆ ~ **(that)...** *The instructions say (that) we should leave it to set for four hours.* ◆ ~ **where, why, etc....** *The book doesn't say where he was born.* ◆ ~ **to do sth** *The guidebook says to turn left.*

IDM go without saying to be very obvious or easy to predict: *Of course I'll help you. That goes without saying.* have something, nothing, etc. to say for yourself to be ready, unwilling, etc. to talk or give your views on something: *She doesn't have much to say for herself* (= doesn't take part in conversation)*.* ◆ *He had plenty to say for himself* (= he had a lot of opinions and was willing to talk)*.* ◆ *Late again—what do you have to say for yourself* (= what is your excuse)*?* having said that (*informal*) used to introduce an opinion that makes what you have just said seem less strong: *My job is really stressful. Having said that, I enjoy the challenge.* I'll say! (*old-fashioned, informal*) used for emphasis to say "yes": *"Does she see him often?" "I'll say! Nearly every day."* I must say (*informal*) used to emphasize an opinion: *Well, I must say, that's the funniest thing I've heard all week.* it says a lot, very little, etc. for sb/sth (*informal*) it shows a good/bad quality that someone or something has: *It says a lot for her that she never lost her temper.* ◆ *It didn't say much for their efficiency that the order arrived a week late.* I wouldn't say no (to sth) (*informal*) used to say that you would like something or to accept something that is offered: *I wouldn't say no to a pizza.* ◆ *"Coffee, Brian?" "I wouldn't say no."* the less/least said the better the best thing to do is say as little as possible about something never say die (*saying*) do not stop hoping not say boo **1** to be very shy or gentle **2** to not say anything at all: *Walter looked at us, but he didn't say boo.* not to say used to introduce a stronger way of describing something: *a difficult, not to say impossible, task* say cheese used to ask someone to smile before you take their photograph say no (to sth) to refuse an offer, a suggestion, etc.: *If you don't invest in this, you're saying no to a potential fortune.* say no more (*informal*) used to say that you understand exactly what someone means or is trying to say, so it is unnecessary to say anything more: *"They went to New York together." "Say no more!"* say your piece to say exactly what you feel or think say what? (*informal*) used to express surprise at what someone has just said: *"He's getting married." "Say what?"* say when used to ask someone to tell you when you should stop pouring a drink or serving food for them because they have enough that is to say (*in other words:* *three days from now, that is to say on Friday* that's not saying much used to say that something is not very unusual or special: *She's a better player than me, but that's not saying much* (= because I am a very bad player)*.* that said used to introduce an opinion that makes what you have just said seem less strong there's no saying used to say that it is impossible to predict what might happen: *There's no saying how he'll react.* there's something, not much, etc. to be said for sth/doing sth there are/are not good reasons for doing something, believing something, or agreeing with something to say the least without exaggerating at all: *I was surprised, to say the least.* to say nothing of sth used to introduce a further fact or thing in addition to those already

mentioned **SYN** NOT TO MENTION: *It was too expensive, to say nothing of the time it wasted.* well said! (*informal*) I agree completely: *"We must stand up for ourselves." "Well said, John."* what do/would you say (to sth/doing sth) (*informal*) would you like sth/to do something?: *What do you say to eating out tonight?* ◆ *Let's go away for a weekend. What do you say?* what/whatever sb says, goes (*informal*, often *humorous*) a particular person must be obeyed: *Sarah wanted the kitchen painted green, and what she says, goes.* whatever you say (*informal*) used to agree to someone's suggestion because you do not want to argue when all is said and done when everything is considered: *I know you're upset, but when all's said and done it isn't exactly a disaster.* who can say (...)? used to say that nobody knows the answer to a question: *Who can say what will happen next year?* who says (...)? (*informal*) used to disagree with a statement or an opinion: *Who says I can't do it?* who's to say (...)? used to say that something might happen or might have happened in a particular way, because nobody really knows: *Who's to say we would not have succeeded if we'd had more time?* you can say that again (*informal*) I agree with you completely: *"He's in a bad mood today." "You can say that again!"* you don't say! (*informal*, often *ironic*) used to express surprise: *"They left without us." "You don't say!"* (= I'm not surprised) you said it! (*informal*) used to agree with someone's suggestion: *"Let's go to the movies tonight." "You said it!"* ⟳ more at DARE *v.*, EASY *adv.*, ENOUGH *pron.*, GLAD, LET *v.*, MEAN *v.*, MIND *v.*, NEEDLESS, RECORD *n.*, SOON, SORRY *adj.*, SUFFICE, UNCLE, WORD *n.*

● **noun** [sing., U] ~ **(in sth)** the right to influence something by giving your opinion before a decision is made: *We had no say in the decision to sell the company.* ◆ *People want a greater say in local government.* ◆ *The judge has the final say on the sentence.*

IDM have your say (*informal*) to have the opportunity to express yourself fully about something: *She won't be happy until she's had her say.* ⟳ see also SAY YOUR PIECE

● **exclamation** (*informal*) **1** used for showing surprise or pleasure: *Say, that's a nice haircut!* **2** used for attracting someone's attention or for making a suggestion or comment: *Say, how about going to a movie tonight?*

WHICH WORD?

say ‧ tell

- Say never has a person as the object. You **say something** or **say something to someone**. Say is often used when you are giving somebody's exact words: *"Sit down," she said.* ◆ *Anne said, "I'm tired."* ◆ *Anne said (that) she was tired.* ◆ *What did he say to you?* You cannot use "say about," but **say something about** is correct: *I want to say something/a few words/a little about my family.* Say can also be used with a clause when the person you are talking to is not mentioned: *She didn't say what she intended to do.*

- Tell usually has a person as the object and often has both a direct and an indirect object: *Have you told him the news yet?* It is often used with "that" clauses: *Anne told me (that) she was tired.* Tell is usually used when someone is giving facts or information, often with *what, where,* etc: *Can you tell me when the movie starts?* (BUT: *Can you give me some information about the school?*) Tell is also used when you are giving someone instructions: *The doctor told me to stay in bed.* ◆ *The doctor told me (that) I had to stay in bed.* OR *The doctor said (that) I had to stay in bed.* NOT ~~The doctor said me to stay in bed.~~

say‧ing /ˈseɪɪŋ/ *noun* a well-known phrase or statement that expresses something about life that most people believe is wise and true: *"Accidents will happen," as the saying goes.*

ˈ**say-so** *noun* [sing.] (*informal*) permission that someone gives to do something: *Nothing could be done without her say-so.*

IDM on sb's say-so based on a statement that someone

makes without giving any proof: *He hired and fired people on his partner's say-so.*

SC *abbr.* (in writing) South Carolina

scab /skæb/ *noun, verb*

- **noun 1** [C] a hard dry covering that forms over a wound as it heals **2** [U] a disease of plants, especially apples and potatoes, that causes a rough surface **3** [C] (*informal, disapproving*) a worker who refuses to join a strike or takes the place of someone on strike **4** [U] a skin disease of animals
- **verb** (**-bb-**) [I] (of a wound) to form a scab; to become covered with a scab: *The cut will scab over in about three days.*

scab·bard /'skæbərd/ *noun* a cover for a SWORD, that is made of leather or metal **SYN** SHEATH

scab·by /'skæbi/ *adj.* covered in scabs

sca·bies /'skeɪbiz/ *noun* [U] a skin disease that causes ITCHING and small, red, raised spots

scab·rous /'skæbrəs/ *adj.* **1** (*formal*) offensive or shocking in a sexual way **SYN** INDECENT **2** (*technical*) having a rough surface **SYN** SCALY: *scabrous skin*

scads /skædz/ *noun* [pl.] **~ (of sth)** (*informal*) large numbers or amounts of something: *scads of $20 bills*

scaf·fold /'skæfəld; -foʊld/ *noun* **1** a platform used when executing (EXECUTE) criminals by cutting off their heads or hanging them from a rope **2** a structure made of scaffolding, for workers to stand on when they are working on a building

scaf·fold·ing /'skæfəldɪŋ; -ˌfoʊl-/ *noun* [U] poles and boards that are joined together to make a structure for workers to stand on when they are working high up on the outside wall of a building

sca·lar /'skeɪlər/ *adj.* (*mathematics*) (of a quantity) having size but no direction ⊃ compare VECTOR ▶ **sca·lar** *noun*

scal·a·wag /'skælə,wæg/ (also **scal·ly·wag**) *noun* (*informal*) a person, especially a child, who behaves badly, but not in a serious way **SYN** SCAMP

scald /skɔld/ *verb, noun*

- **verb 1 ~ sth/yourself** to burn yourself or part of your body with very hot liquid or steam: *Be careful not to scald yourself with the steam.* ◆ (*figurative*) *Tears scalded her eyes.* ⊃ thesaurus box at BURN ⊃ collocations at INJURY **2 ~ sth** to heat a liquid without boiling it: *scalded milk* **3 ~ sth** to put something in boiling liquid for a short time: *Scald the tomatoes and remove the skins.*
- **noun** an injury to the skin from very hot liquid or steam

scald·ing /'skɔldɪŋ/ *adj.* hot enough to SCALD: *scalding water* ◆ (*figurative*) *Scalding tears poured down her face.* ▶ **scald·ing** *adv.*: *scalding hot*

scale 🔑 /skeɪl/ *noun, verb*

- **noun**
> SIZE **1** [sing., U] the size or extent of something, especially when compared with something else: *They entertain on a large scale* (= they hold expensive parties with a lot of guests). ◆ *Here was corruption on a grand scale.* ◆ *On a global scale, 77% of energy is created from fossil fuels.* ◆ *to achieve economies of scale in production* (= to produce many items so the cost of producing each one is reduced) ◆ **~ of sth** *It was impossible to comprehend the full scale of the disaster.* ◆ *It was not until morning that the sheer scale of the damage could be seen* (= how great it was). ⊃ see also FULL-SCALE, LARGE-SCALE, SMALL-SCALE
> RANGE OF LEVELS **2** [C] a range of levels or numbers used for measuring: *a five-point pay scale* ◆ *to evaluate performance on a scale from 1 to 10* ⊃ see also RICHTER SCALE, SLIDING SCALE, TIMESCALE **3** [C, usually sing.] the set of all the different levels of something, from the lowest to the highest: *At the other end of the scale, life is a constant struggle to get enough to eat.* ◆ *the social scale*
> OF MAP/DIAGRAM/MODEL **4** [C] the relationship between the actual size of something and its size on a map, diagram, or model that represents it: *a scale of 1:25000* ◆ *a scale model/*

scales

bathroom scale

the scale of C

scale

fish scales

kitchen scale

drawing ◆ *Both plans are drawn to the same scale.* ◆ *Is this diagram to scale* (= are all its parts the same size and shape in relation to each other as they are in the thing represented)?
> MARKS FOR MEASURING **5** [C] a series of marks at regular intervals on an instrument that is used for measuring: *How much does it read on the scale?*
> WEIGHING INSTRUMENT **6** [C] an instrument for weighing people or things: *a bathroom/a kitchen scale* ◆ (*figurative*) *the scales of justice* (= represented as the two pans on a BALANCE)
> IN MUSIC **7** [C] a series of musical notes moving upward or downward, with fixed intervals between each note, especially a series of eight starting on a particular note: *the scale of C major* ◆ *to practice scales on the piano* ⊃ compare KEY, OCTAVE
> OF FISH/REPTILE **8** [C] any of the thin plates of hard material that cover the skin of many fish and REPTILES
> IN WATER PIPES, ETC. **9** [U] a hard, greyish-white substance that is sometimes left inside water pipes and containers for heating water ⊃ see also LIMESCALE **IDM** see TIP v.

- **verb**
> CLIMB **1 ~ sth** (*formal*) to climb to the top of something very high and steep: *the first woman to scale Mount Everest* ◆ (*figurative*) *He has scaled the heights of his profession.*
> FISH **2 ~ sth** to remove the small flat hard pieces of skin from a fish
> TEETH **3 ~ sth** to remove TARTAR from the teeth by SCRAPING: *The dentist scaled and polished my teeth.*
> CHANGE SIZE **4 ~ sth (from sth) (to sth)** (*technical*) to change the size of something: *Text can be scaled from 4 points to 108 points without any loss of quality.*
PHR V ˌscale sth↔'down (also ˌscale sth↔'back) to reduce the number, size, or extent of something: *We are thinking of scaling down our training programs next year.* ◆ *The IMF has scaled back its growth forecasts for the next decade.* ⊃ thesaurus box at CUT ˌscale sth↔'up to increase the size or number of something

sca·lene tri·an·gle /ˌskeɪlin 'traɪæŋgl/ *noun* (*geometry*) a triangle whose sides are all of different lengths ⊃ picture at SHAPE

scal·lion /'skælyən/ (also ˌgreen 'onion) *noun* a type of small onion with a long green STEM and leaves. Scallions are often eaten raw in salads. ⊃ picture at FRUIT

scal·lop /'skæləp; 'skɑləp/ *noun, verb*

- **noun 1** a SHELLFISH that can be eaten, with two flat round shells that fit together: *a scallop shell* **2** any one of a series of small curves cut on the edge of a piece of cloth, PIE CRUST, etc. for decoration
- **verb** [usually passive] **~ sth** to decorate the edge of something with small curves: *a scalloped edge*

scal·ly·wag /'skæliˌwæg/ *noun* (*informal*) = SCALAWAG

scalp /skælp/ *noun, verb*

● *noun* **1** the skin that covers the part of the head where the hair grows **2** (in the past) the skin and hair that was removed from the head of a dead enemy by some Native American peoples as a sign of victory **3** (*informal*) a symbol of the fact that someone has been defeated or punished: *They have claimed some impressive scalps in their bid for the championship.*

● *verb* **1** ~ **sb** to remove the skin and hair from the top of an enemy's head as a sign of victory **2** ~ **sth** to sell tickets for a popular event illegally, at a price that is higher than the official price, especially outside a theater, STADIUM, etc.

scal·pel /'skælpəl/ *noun* a small sharp knife used by doctors in medical operations

scalp·er /'skælpər/ *noun* a person who buys tickets for concerts, sports events, etc. and then sells them to other people at a higher price: *ticket scalpers*

scal·y /'skeɪli/ *adj.* (scal·i·er, scal·i·est) (of skin) covered with SCALES, or hard and dry, with small pieces that come off

scaly anteater *noun* = PANGOLIN

scam /skæm/ *noun, verb*

● *noun* (*informal*) a dishonest plan for making money
⊃ collocations at CRIME

● *verb* (-mm-) ~ **sb (out of sth)** | ~ **sth (from sb)** (*informal*) to trick someone into giving you money: *a guy that scams the elderly out of their savings*

scamp /skæmp/ *noun* (*old-fashioned*) a child who enjoys playing tricks and causing trouble SYN SCALAWAG

scamp·er /'skæmpər/ *verb* [I] + **adv./prep.** (especially of children or small animals) to move quickly with short light steps

scam·pi /'skæmpi/ (also **shrimp scampi**) *noun* [U] a dish of large SHRIMPS (= a type of sea creature) fried in butter and GARLIC

scan /skæn/ *verb, noun*

● *verb* (-nn-) **1** [T] to look at every part of something carefully, especially because you are looking for a particular thing or person SYN SCRUTINIZE: ~ **sth for sth** *He scanned the horizon for any sign of land.* ◆ ~ **sth** *She scanned his face anxiously.* **2** [T, I] to look quickly but not very carefully at a document, etc.: ~ **sth (for sth)** *I scanned the list quickly for my name.* ◆ ~ **through sth (for sth)** *She scanned through the newspaper over breakfast.* **3** [T] ~ **sth** to get an image of an object, a part of someone's body, etc. on a computer by passing X-RAYS, ULTRASOUND waves or ELEC-TROMAGNETIC waves over it in a special machine: *Their brains are scanned so that researchers can monitor the progress of the disease.* **4** [I, T] ~ **(sth)** (*computing*) (of a program) to examine a computer program or document in order to look for a virus: *This software is designed to scan all new files for viruses.* **5** [T] ~ **sth** (*computing*) to pass light over a picture or document using a SCANNER in order to copy it and put it in the memory of a computer: *How do I scan a photo and attach it to an e-mail?* **6** [T] ~ **sth** (of a light, RADAR, etc.) to pass across an area: *Concealed video cameras scan every part of the compound.* **7** [I] (of poetry) to have a regular rhythm according to fixed rules: *This line doesn't scan.*
PHR V ,scan sth 'into sth | ,scan sth 'in (*computing*) to pass light over a picture or document using a SCANNER in order to copy it and put it in the memory of a computer: *Text and pictures can be scanned into the computer.*

● *noun* **1** [C] a medical test in which a machine produces a picture of the inside of a person's body on a computer screen after taking X-RAYS: *to have a brain scan* **2** [sing.] the act of looking quickly through something written or printed, usually in order to find something

scan·dal /'skændl/ *noun* **1** [C, U] behavior or an event that people think is morally or legally wrong and that causes public feelings of shock or anger: *a series of sex scandals* ◆ to *cause/create a scandal* ◆ *The scandal broke* (= became known to the public) *in May.* ◆ *There has been no hint of scandal during his time in office.* **2** [U] talk or reports about the shocking or

immoral things that people have done or are thought to have done: *to spread scandal* ◆ *newspapers full of scandal* **3** [sing.] ~ **(that...)** an action, attitude, etc. that you think is shocking and not at all acceptable SYN DISGRACE: *It is a scandal that such a large town has no orchestra.*

scan·dal·ize /'skændl,aɪz/ *verb* ~ **sb** to do something that people find very shocking SYN OUTRAGE: *She scandalized her family with her extravagant lifestyle.*

scan·dal·mon·ger /'skændl,mɑŋgər; -,mʌŋgər/ *noun* (*disapproving*) a person who spreads stories about the shocking or immoral things that other people have done

scan·dal·ous /'skændl·əs/ *adj.* **1** shocking and unacceptable SYN DISGRACEFUL: *a scandalous waste of money* ◆ **it is scandalous that...** *It is scandalous that he has not been punished.* **2** [only before noun] containing talk about the shocking or immoral things that people have done or are thought to have done: *scandalous stories* ▶ **scan·dal·ous·ly** *adv.*: *scandalously low pay*

scandal sheet *noun* (*disapproving*) a newspaper or magazine that is mainly concerned with shocking stories about the immoral behavior and private lives of famous or important people

Scan·di·na·vi·a /,skændə'neɪviə/ *noun* [U] a cultural region in N.W. Europe consisting of Norway, Sweden, and Denmark and sometimes also Iceland, Finland, and the Faroe Islands ▶ **Scan·di·na·vi·an** /-viən/ *adj.*, *noun*

scan·di·um /'skændiəm/ *noun* [U] (*symb.* **Sc**) a chemical element. Scandium is a silver-white metal found in various minerals.

scan·ner /'skænər/ *noun* **1** a device for examining something or recording something using light, sound, or X-RAYS: *The identity cards are examined by an electronic scanner.* **2** (*computing*) a device that copies pictures and documents so that they can be stored on a computer: *a document scanner* ⊃ see also FLATBED SCANNER **3** a machine used by doctors to produce a picture of the inside of a person's body on a computer screen: *a body scanner* **4** a piece of equipment for receiving and sending RADAR signals

scan·sion /'skænʃn/ *noun* [U] (*technical*) the rhythm of a line of poetry

scant /skænt/ *adj.* [only before noun] **1** hardly any; not very much and not as much as there should be: *I paid scant attention to what she was saying.* ◆ *The firefighters went back into the house with scant regard for their own safety.* **2** a little less than the amount or measure stated: *Add a scant teaspoon of salt.*

scant·y /'skænti/ *adj.* (scant·i·er, scant·i·est) **1** too little in amount for what is needed: *Details of his life are scanty.* **2** (of clothes) very small and not covering much of your body: *a scanty bikini* ▶ **scant·i·ly** /-təli/ *adv.*: *scantily dressed models*

-scape /skeɪp/ *combining form* (in nouns) a view or scene of: *landscape* ◆ *seascape* ◆ *moonscape*

scape·goat /'skeɪpgoʊt/ *noun* a person who is blamed for something bad that someone else has done or for some failure SYN FALL GUY: *She felt she had been made a scapegoat for her boss's incompetence.* ▶ **scape·goat** *verb* ~ **sb/sth**

scap·u·la /'skæpyələ/ *noun* (*pl.* scap·u·lae /-li/ or scap·u·las) (*anatomy*) the SHOULDER BLADE ⊃ picture at BODY

scar /skɑr/ *noun, verb*

● *noun* **1** a mark that is left on the skin after a wound has healed: *a scar on his cheek* ◆ *Will the operation leave a scar?* ◆ *scar tissue* **2** a permanent feeling of great sadness or mental pain that is left with after an unpleasant experience: *His years in prison have left deep scars.* **3** something unpleasant or ugly that spoils the appearance or public image of something: *The town still bears the scars of war.* ◆ *Racism has been a scar on the game.*

● *verb* (-rr-) [often passive] **1** ~ **sb/sth** (of a wound, etc.) to leave a mark on the skin after it has healed: *His face was badly scarred.* **2** ~ **sb** (of an unpleasant experience) to leave someone with a feeling of sadness or mental pain: *The*

h **hat**   m **man**   n **no**   ŋ **sing**   l **leg**   r **red**   y **yes**   w **wet**

experience left her **scarred for life. 3 ~ sth** to spoil the appearance of something: *The hills are scarred by quarries.* ◆ *battle-scarred buildings*

scar·ab /ˈskærəb/ (also **ˈscarab beetle**) *noun* a large black BEETLE (= an insect with a hard shell); a design showing a scarab beetle

scarce /skers/ *adj., adv.*
● *adj.* (**scarc·er, scarc·est**) if something is **scarce**, there is not enough of it and it is only available in small quantities: *scarce resources* ◆ *Details of the accident are scarce.* ◆ *Food was becoming scarce.*
  IDM **make yourself scarce** (*informal*) to leave somewhere and stay away for a time in order to avoid an unpleasant situation
● *adv.* (*literary*) only just; almost not: *I can scarce remember him.*

scarce·ly /ˈskersli/ *adv.* **1** only just; almost not: *I can scarcely believe it.* ◆ *We scarcely ever meet.* ◆ *Scarcely a week goes by without some new scandal in the papers.* **2** used to say that something happens immediately after something else happens: *He had scarcely hung up the phone when the doorbell rang.* ◆ *Scarcely had the game started when it began to rain.* **3** used to suggest that something is not at all reasonable or likely: *It was scarcely an occasion for laughter.* ◆ *She could scarcely complain, could she?* ⊃ note at HARDLY

scar·ci·ty /ˈskersəti/ *noun* [U, C] (*pl.* **scar·ci·ties**) if there is a **scarcity of** something, there is not enough of it and it is difficult to obtain it **SYN** SHORTAGE: *a time of scarcity* ◆ *a scarcity of resources*

THESAURUS

scare

frighten ◆ alarm ◆ terrify

These words all mean to make someone afraid.

scare to make someone feel afraid: *They managed to scare away the bears.*

frighten to make someone feel afraid, often suddenly: *She brought out a gun and frightened them off.*

SCARE OR FRIGHTEN?

Frighten is slightly more formal than **scare**.

alarm to make someone anxious or afraid: *I am alarmed at how quickly this decision was made.* **NOTE** Alarm is used when someone has a feeling that something unpleasant or dangerous might happen in the future; the feeling is often more one of worry than actual fear.

terrify to make someone feel extremely afraid: *Flying terrified her.*

PATTERNS

■ to scare/frighten sb/sth **away/off**
■ to scare/frighten/terrify sb **into** doing sth
■ It scares/frightens/alarms/terrifies me **that…**
■ It scares/frightens/alarms/terrifies me **to** think, see, etc.

---

scare /sker/ *verb, noun*
● *verb* **1** [T] to frighten someone: *~ sb You scared me.* ◆ *it scares sb to do sth It scared me to think I was alone in the building.* **2** [I] to become frightened: *He doesn't scare easily.* ⊃ see also SCARY **IDM** See DAYLIGHTS, DEATH, LIFE **PHR V** ˌscare sb↔aˈway/ˈoff to make someone go away by frightening them: *They managed to scare the bears away.* ˈscare sb into doing sth to frighten someone in order to make them do something: *Local businesses were scared into paying protection money.* ˌscare sb↔'off to make someone afraid of or nervous about doing something, especially without intending to: *Rising prices are scaring customers off.* ˌscare ˈup sth (*informal*) to find or make something by using whatever is available: *I'll see if I can scare up enough chairs for us all.*
● *noun* **1** [C] (used especially in newspapers) a situation in which a lot of people are anxious or frightened about something: *a bomb/health scare* ◆ *recent scares about pesticides in food* ◆ *a scare story* (= a news report that spreads more anxiety or fear about something than is necessary) ◆ *to cause a major scare* ◆ *scare tactics* (= ways of persuading people to do something by frightening them) **2** [sing.] a sudden feeling of fear: *You gave me a scare!* ◆ *We've had quite a scare.* ⊃ see also SCARY

scare·crow /ˈskerkroʊ/ *noun* a figure made to look like a person, that is dressed in old clothes and put in a field to frighten birds away

scared /skerd/ *adj.*
frightened of something or afraid that something bad might happen: *a scared look* ◆ *~ (of doing sth) She is scared of going out alone.* ◆ *~ (of sb/sth) He's scared of heights.* ◆ *~ (to do sth) People are scared to use the buses late at night.* ◆ *~ (that…) I'm scared (that) I'm going to fall.* ◆ *The thieves got scared and ran away.* ◆ *a scared look* ◆ *I was scared to death* (= very frightened). ◆ *We were scared stiff* (= very frightened). **IDM** See SHADOW *n.*, WIT, WITLESS ⊃ thesaurus box at AFRAID

scared·y-cat /ˈskerdi ˌkæt/ (also **fraid·y cat**) *noun* (*informal, disapproving*) a children's word for a person who is easily frightened

scare·mon·ger /ˈskerˌmɑŋgər; -ˌmʌŋgər/ *noun* (*disapproving*) a person who spreads stories deliberately to make people frightened or nervous ▶ **scare·mon·ger·ing** *noun* [U]

ˈscare quotes *noun* [pl.] QUOTATION MARKS that a writer puts around a word or phrase to show that it is used in an unusual way, usually one that the writer does not agree with: *This pronunciation came from the organization's "scientific" committee (the scare quotes are mine).*

scarf /skarf/ *noun, verb*
● *noun* (*pl.* **scarves** /skarvz/ or *less frequent* **scarfs**) a piece of cloth that is worn around the neck, for example for warmth or decoration. Women also wear scarves over their shoulders or hair: *a wool/silk scarf* ⊃ picture at CLOTHES
● *verb* (also) [I, T] *~ (sth down)* (*informal*) to eat a lot of something quickly

scar·i·fy /ˈskerəˌfaɪ/ *verb* (**scar·i·fies, scar·i·fy·ing, scar·i·fied, scar·i·fied**) (*technical*) **1 ~ sth** to break up an area of grass, etc. and remove pieces of material from it that are not wanted **2 ~ sth** to make cuts in the surface of something, especially skin

scar·let /ˈskarlət/ *adj.* bright red in color: *scarlet berries* ◆ *She went scarlet with embarrassment.* ▶ **scar·let** *noun* [U]

ˌscarlet ˈfever *noun* [U] a serious infectious disease that causes fever and red marks on the skin

ˌscarlet ˈwoman *noun* (*old-fashioned*) a woman who has sexual relationships with many different people

scarp /skarp/ *noun* (*technical*) a very steep slope

scarves pl. of SCARF

scar·y /ˈskeri/ *adj.* (**scar·i·er, scar·i·est**) (*informal*) frightening: *It was a really scary moment.* ◆ *a scary movie* ⊃ see also SCARE *v.*

scat /skæt/ *noun, exclamation*
● *noun* [U] **1** a style of JAZZ singing in which the voice is made to sound like a musical instrument **2** the solid waste matter of wild animals
● *exclamation* used to tell an animal to go away: *Get out of here! Scat!*

scath·ing /ˈskeɪðɪŋ/ *adj.* criticizing someone or something very severely **SYN** WITHERING: *a scathing attack on the new management* ◆ *~ about sb/sth He was scathing about the government's performance.* ▶ **scath·ing·ly** *adv.*: *"Oh, she's just a kid," he said scathingly.*

scat·o·log·i·cal /ˌskætlˈɑdʒɪkl/ *adj.* (*formal*) connected with human waste from the body in an unpleasant way: *scatological humor*

---

scat·ter /ˈskætər/ *verb, noun*
- *verb* **1** [T] to throw or drop things in different directions so that they cover an area of ground: ~ *sth They scattered his ashes at sea.* ◆ ~ *sth* **on/over/around** *sth Scatter the grass seed over the lawn.* ◆ ~ *sth* **with sth** *Scatter the lawn with grass seed.* **2** [I, T] to move or to make people or animals move very quickly in different directions **SYN** DISPERSE: *At the first gunshot, the crowd scattered.* ◆ ~ *sb/sth The explosion scattered a flock of birds roosting in the trees.*
- *noun* [usually sing.] (also **scat·ter·ing** [sing.]) a small amount or number of things spread over an area: *a scattering of houses*

scat·ter·brain /ˈskætərˌbreɪn/ *noun* (*informal*) a person who is always losing or forgetting things and cannot think in an organized way ▶ **scat·ter·brained** *adj.*

scatter diagram (also **scat·ter·gram** /ˈskætərˌɡræm/) *noun* (*statistics*) a diagram that shows the relationship between two VARIABLES by creating a pattern of dots

scat·tered /ˈskætərd/ *adj.* spread far apart over a wide area or over a long period of time: *a few scattered settlements* ◆ *sunshine with scattered showers* ◆ *Her family is scattered around the world.*

scat·ter·shot /ˈskætərˌʃɑt/ (also **scat·ter·gun** /ˈskætərˌɡʌn/) *adj.* [only before noun] referring to a way of doing or dealing with something by considering many different possibilities, people, etc. in a way that is not well organized: *The scattershot approach to marketing means that the campaign is not targeted at particular individuals.*

scav·enge /ˈskævɪndʒ/ *verb* **1** [T, I] (of a person, an animal or a bird) to search through waste for things that can be used or eaten: ~ **sth (from sth)** *Much of their furniture was scavenged from other people's garbage.* ◆ ~ **(through sth) (for sth)** *Dogs scavenged through the trash cans for something to eat.* **2** [T, I] (of animals or birds) to eat dead animals that have been killed by another animal, by a car, etc.: ~ *sth Crows scavenge carrion left on the roads.* ◆ ~ **(on sth)** *Some animals scavenge on dead fish in the wild.*

scav·eng·er /ˈskævɪndʒər/ *noun* an animal, a bird, or a person that scavenges

scavenger hunt *noun* a game in which players have to find various objects

sce·nar·i·o **AWL** /səˈnɛriˌoʊ/ *noun* (*pl.* **sce·nar·i·os**) **1** a description of how things might happen in the future: *Let me suggest a possible scenario.* ◆ *The worst-case scenario* (= the worst possible thing that could happen) *would be for the factory to be closed down.* ◆ *a nightmare scenario* **2** a written outline of what happens in a movie or play **SYN** SYNOPSIS

scene 🔑 /sin/ *noun*
▷ PLACE **1** [C, usually sing.] ~ **(of sth)** the place where something happens, especially something unpleasant: *the scene of the accident/attack/crime* ◆ *Firefighters were on the scene immediately.* ⊃ thesaurus box at PLACE
▷ EVENT **2** [C] ~ **(of sth)** an event or a situation that you see, especially one of a particular type: *The candidate's victory produced scenes of joy all over the country.* ◆ *She witnessed some very distressing scenes.*
▷ IN MOVIE/PLAY, ETC. **3** [C] a part of a movie, play, or book in which the action happens in one place or is of one particular type: *The movie opens with a scene in a New York apartment.* ◆ *I got very nervous before my big scene* (= the one where I have a very important part). **4** [C] one of the small sections that a play or an OPERA is divided into: *Act I, Scene 2 of "Macbeth"*
▷ AREA OF ACTIVITY **5** *the scene, the… scene* [sing.] (*informal*) a particular area of activity or way of life and the people who are part of it: *After years at the top, she just vanished from the scene.* ◆ *the club/dance/music, etc. scene* ◆ *A newcomer has appeared on the fashion scene.*
▷ VIEW **6** [C] a view that you see: *a pleasant rural scene* ◆ *They went abroad for a change of scene* (= to see and experience new surroundings). ⊃ thesaurus box at VIEW

▷ PAINTING/PHOTOGRAPH **7** [C] a painting, drawing, or photograph of a place and the things that are happening there: *an exhibition of Parisian street scenes*
▷ ARGUMENT **8** [C, usually sing.] a loud, angry argument, especially one that happens in public and is embarrassing: *She had made a scene in the middle of the party.* ◆ *"Please leave," he said. "I don't want a scene."*
IDM **behind the scenes 1** in the part of a theater, etc. that the public does not usually see: *The students were able to go behind the scenes to see how programs are made.* **2** in a way that people in general are not aware of: *A lot of negotiating has been going on behind the scenes.* ◆ *behind-the-scenes work* **not sb's scene** (*informal*) not the type of thing that someone likes or enjoys doing **set the scene (for sth) 1** to create a situation in which something can easily happen or develop: *His arrival set the scene for another argument.* **2** to give someone the information and details they need in order to understand what comes next: *The first part of the program was just setting the scene.*

scen·er·y /ˈsinəri/ *noun* [U] **1** the natural features of an area, such as mountains, valleys, rivers, and forests, when you are thinking about them being attractive to look at: *The scenery is magnificent.* ◆ *to enjoy the scenery* ⊃ thesaurus box at COUNTRY **2** the painted background that is used to represent natural features or buildings on a theater stage

sce·nic /ˈsinɪk/ *adj.* **1** [usually before noun] having beautiful natural scenery: *an area of scenic beauty* ◆ *They took the scenic route back to the hotel.* ◆ *a scenic drive* **2** [only before noun] connected with scenery in a theater: *scenic designs* ▶ **sce·ni·cally** /-kli/ *adv.*: *scenically attractive areas*

scent /sɛnt/ *noun, verb*
- *noun* **1** [U, C] the pleasant smell that something has: *The air was filled with the scent of wild flowers.* ◆ *These flowers have no scent.* **2** [U, C, usually sing.] the smell that a person or an animal leaves behind and that that other animals such as dogs can follow **SYN** TRAIL: *The dogs must have lost her scent.* **3** [U] (*old-fashioned*) a liquid with a pleasant smell that you wear on your skin to make it smell nice: *a bottle of scent* **4** ~ **of sth** [sing.] the feeling that something is present or is going to happen very soon: *The scent of victory was in the air.*
IDM **put/throw sb off the scent** to do something to stop someone from finding you or discovering something **on the scent (of sth)** close to discovering something
- *verb* **1** ~ **sth** to find something by using the sense of smell: *The dog scented a rabbit.* **2** ~ **sth** to begin to feel that something exists or is about to happen **SYN** SENSE: *The press could scent a scandal.* ◆ *By then, the team was scenting victory.* **3** [often passive] ~ **sth (with sth)** to give something a particular, pleasant smell: *Roses scented the night air.*

scent·ed /ˈsɛntəd/ *adj.* having a strong, pleasant smell

scent·less /ˈsɛntləs/ *adj.* without a smell

scep·ter (*CanE usually* **scep·tre**) /ˈsɛptər/ *noun* a decorated ROD carried by a king or queen at ceremonies as a symbol of their power ⊃ compare MACE, ORB

scha·den·freu·de (also **Scha·den·freu·de**) /ˈʃɑdnˌfrɔɪdə/ *noun* [U] (from *German*) a feeling of pleasure at the bad things that happen to other people

sched·ule 🔑 **AWL** /ˈskɛdʒul; -dʒəl/ *noun, verb*
- *noun* **1** [C, U] a plan that lists all the work or other activities that you have to do and when you must do each thing: *I have a hectic schedule for the next few days.* ◆ *We're working on a tight schedule* (= we have a lot of things to do in a short time). ◆ *Filming began on schedule* (= at the planned time). ◆ *The new bridge has been finished two years ahead of schedule.* ◆ *The tunnel project has already fallen behind schedule.* ⊃ note at AGENDA **2** [C] a list showing the times at which something is due to arrive or leave: *a bus/train schedule* ◆ *a schedule of our weekend walking tours* **3** [C] a list showing the times of each class in school: *Each semester there is a new course schedule.* ◆ *I haven't printed out my class schedule yet.* **4** [C] a list of the television and radio programs that are on a particular channel and the times that they start: *The*

ʌ **cup**   ə **about**   eɪ **say**   aɪ **five**   ɔɪ **boy**   aʊ **now**   oʊ **go**   ər **bird**

channel's schedules are filled with old movies and repeats.
5 [C] a written list of things, for example prices, rates, or conditions: *tax schedules*
- **verb** to arrange for something to happen at a particular time: **~ sth (for sth)** *The meeting is scheduled for Friday afternoon.* ◆ *One of the scheduled events is a talk on alternative medicine.* ◆ *We'll be stopping here for longer than scheduled.* ◆ **~ sb/sth to do sth** *I'm scheduled to arrive in LA at 5 o'clock.*
  ▶ **sched·ul·er** /'skedʒulər/ *noun: The President's schedulers allowed 90 minutes for TV interviews.*

ˌscheduled ˈflight *noun* a plane service that leaves at a regular time each day or week **⊃ compare** CHARTER FLIGHT

sche·ma /'skimə/ *noun (pl.* **sche·mas** or **sche·ma·ta** /'skimətə; ski'mɑtə/) *(technical)* an outline of a plan or theory

sche·mat·ic 〔AWL〕/ski'mætɪk; skɪ-/ *adj.* **1** in the form of a diagram that shows the main features or relationships but not the details: *a schematic diagram* **2** according to a fixed plan or pattern: *The play has a very schematic plot.*
  ▶ **sche·mat·i·cal·ly** 〔AWL〕/-kli/ *adv.: The process is shown schematically in figure 3.*

sche·ma·tize /'skimə.taɪz/ *verb* **~ sth** *(technical)* to organize something in a system: *schematized data*

scheme 〔AWL〕/skim/ *noun, verb*
- **1 noun** a plan for getting money or some other advantage for yourself, especially one that involves cheating other people: *an elaborate scheme to avoid taxes* **2** a system for organizing or arranging things: *a classification scheme for libraries* **⊃ see also** COLOR SCHEME
  IDM **the/sb's scheme of things** the way things seem to be organized; the way someone wants everything to be organized: *My personal problems are not really important in the overall scheme of things.* ◆ *I don't think marriage figures in his scheme of things.*
- **verb** [I, T] *(disapproving)* to make secret plans to do something that will help yourself and possibly harm others **SYN** PLOT: **~ (against sb)** *She seemed to feel that we were all scheming against her.* ◆ **~ to do sth** *His colleagues, meanwhile, were busily scheming to get rid of him.* ◆ **~ sth** *Her enemies were scheming her downfall.*

schem·er /'skimər/ *noun (disapproving)* a person who plans secretly to do something for their own advantage

schem·ing 〔AWL〕/'skimɪŋ/ *adj. (formal)* often planning secretly to do something for your own advantage, especially by cheating other people

scher·zo /'skɛrtsoʊ/ *noun (pl.* **scher·zos**) *(from Italian)* a short, lively piece of music, that is often part of a longer piece

schil·ling /'ʃɪlɪŋ/ *noun* the former unit of money in Austria (replaced in 2002 by the EURO)

schism /'skɪzəm; 'sɪzəm/ *noun* [C, U] *(formal)* strong disagreement within an organization, especially a religious one, that makes its members divide into separate groups
  ▶ **schis·mat·ic** /skɪz'mætɪk/ *adj.*

schist /ʃɪst/ *noun* [U] a type of rock formed of layers of different minerals, that breaks naturally into thin, flat pieces

schiz·oid /'skɪtsɔɪd/ *adj. (technical)* similar to or suffering from schizophrenia: *schizoid tendencies*

schiz·o·phre·ni·a /ˌskɪtsə'friniə; -'frɛniə/ *noun* [U] a mental illness in which a person becomes unable to link thought, emotion, and behavior, leading to WITHDRAWAL from reality and personal relationships

schiz·o·phren·ic /ˌskɪtsə'frɛnɪk/ *noun, adj.*
- **noun** a person who suffers from schizophrenia
- **adj. 1** suffering from schizophrenia **2** *(informal)* frequently changing your mind about something or holding opinions about something that seem to oppose each other

schlep (also **schlepp**) /ʃlɛp/ *verb* (**-pp-**) *(informal)* **1** [I]
+ **adv./prep.** to go somewhere, especially if it is a slow, difficult journey, or you do not want to go **2** [T] **~ sth**
(+ **adv./prep.**) to carry or pull something heavy: *I'm not schlepping these suitcases all over town.* **ORIGIN** From Yiddish *shlepn*, "to drag." ▶ **schlep** (also **schlepp**) *noun* [sing.]

schlock /ʃlɑk/ *noun* [U] *(informal)* things that are cheap and of poor quality

schmaltz /ʃmɑlts; ʃmɔlts/ *noun* [U] *(informal, disapproving)* the quality of being too SENTIMENTAL ▶ **schmaltz·y** *adj.* (schmaltz·i·er, schmaltz·i·est)

schmo (also **shmo**) /ʃmoʊ/ *noun (pl.* **schmoes** or **shmoes**) *(informal, disapproving)* a person who is stupid or unwise in an annoying way

schmooze /ʃmuz/ *verb* [I, T] **~ (with) sb** *(informal)* to talk in an informal and friendly way with someone, especially in order to gain an advantage by persuading people to like you and do what you want ▶ **schmooz·er** *noun*

schmuck /ʃmʌk/ *noun (informal, disapproving)* a stupid person: *He's such a schmuck!*

schnapps /ʃnaps/ *noun* [U] *(from German)* a strong alcoholic drink made from grain

schnau·zer /'ʃnaʊzər/ *noun* a dog with short rough hair which forms curls

schnook /ʃnʊk/ *noun (informal, disapproving)* a stupid or unimportant person

schol·ar /'skɑlər/ *noun* **1** a person who knows a lot about a particular subject because they have studied it in detail: *a classical scholar* ◆ *He was the most distinguished scholar in his field.* **2** a student who has been given a scholarship to study at a school, college, or university: *a Rhodes scholar*

schol·ar·ly /'skɑlərli/ *adj.* **1** (of a person) spending a lot of time studying and having a lot of knowledge about an academic subject **SYN** ACADEMIC **2** connected with academic study **SYN** ACADEMIC: *a scholarly journal*

schol·ar·ship /'skɑlər.ʃɪp/ *noun* **1** [C] an amount of money given to someone by an organization to help pay for their education: *She won a scholarship to study at Stanford.* ◆ *He went to drama school on a scholarship.* **2** [U] the serious study of an academic subject and the knowledge and methods involved **SYN** LEARNING: *a magnificent work of scholarship*

scho·las·tic /skə'læstɪk/ *adj.* [only before noun] *(formal)* **1** connected with schools and education: *scholastic achievements* **2** connected with scholasticism

scho·las·ti·cism /skə'læstə.sɪzəm/ *noun* [U] a system of philosophy, based on religious principles and writing, that was taught in universities in the Middle Ages

school 🔑 /skul/ *noun, verb*
- **noun**
- ▸ **WHERE CHILDREN LEARN 1** [C] a place where children go to be educated: *My brother and I went to the same school.* ◆ *(formal)* Which school do they attend? ◆ *I'm going to the school today to talk to Kim's teacher.* ◆ *We need more money for roads, hospitals, and schools.* ◆ *school buildings* **2** [U] (used without *the* or *a*) the process of learning in a school; the time during your life when you go to a school: *to start/quit school* ◆ *Where did you go to school?* ◆ *All my kids are still in school.* ◆ *to teach school* (= teach in a school) ◆ *The transition from school to work can be difficult.* **⊃ collocations at** EDUCATION **3** [U] (used without *the* or *a*) the time during the day when children are working in a school: *Can I meet you after school today?* ◆ *School begins at 9.* ◆ *The kids are at/in school until 3:30.* ◆ *after-school activities*
- ▸ **STUDENTS AND TEACHERS 4 the school** [sing.] all the children or students and the teachers in a school: *I had to stand up in front of the whole school.*
- ▸ **FOR PARTICULAR SKILL 5** [C] (often in compounds) a place where people go to learn a particular subject or skill: *a drama/language/riding, etc. school*
- ▸ **COLLEGE/UNIVERSITY 6** [C, U] (informal) a college or university; the time that you spend there: *famous schools like Yale and Harvard* ◆ *Where did you go to school?* **⊃ see also** GRADUATE SCHOOL, PARTY SCHOOL **7** [C] a department of a

college or university that teaches a particular subject: *the business/medical/law school* ♦ *the School of Dentistry*
> OF WRITERS/ARTISTS **8** [C] a group of writers, artists, etc. whose style of work or opinions have been influenced by the same person or ideas: *the Hudson River school of painting*
> OF FISH **9** [C] a large number of fish or other sea animals, swimming together: *a school of dolphins* ⟳ compare SHOAL
HELP There are many compounds ending in **school**. You will find them at their place in the alphabet.
IDM school(s) of thought a way of thinking that a number of people share: *There are two schools of thought about how this illness should be treated.*

● *verb*
> YOURSELF/ANIMAL **1** (*formal*) to train someone/yourself/an animal to do something: **~ sb/sth/yourself (in sth)** *to school a horse* ♦ *She had schooled herself in patience.* ♦ **~ sb/sth/yourself to do sth** *I have schooled myself to remain calm under pressure.*
> CHILD **2 ~ sb** (*formal*) to educate a child: *She should be schooled with her peers.*

GRAMMAR

school
■ When a **school** is being referred to as an institution, you do not need to use *the*: *When do the children finish school?* When you are talking about a particular building, *the* is used: *I'll meet you outside the school.* **Prison**, **jail**, **court**, and **church** work in the same way: *Her husband spent three years in prison.* ♦ *She drove by the prison every day.*

ˈschool age *noun* [U] the age or period when a child normally attends school: *children of school age* ♦ *school-age children*

ˈschool board *noun* an elected committee that is in charge of all the public schools in a particular area: *School boards set policy and evaluate results.*

school·book /ˈskulbʊk/ *noun* a TEXTBOOK or other book that is used in schools

school·boy /ˈskulbɔɪ/ *noun* a boy who attends school

school·child /ˈskultʃaɪld/ *noun* (*pl.* school·child·ren /-ˌtʃɪldrən/) (also *informal* school·kid) a child who attends school

ˈschool·day (also ˈschool day) /ˈskuldeɪ/ *noun* **1** a day of the week when students go to school: *I get up very early on schooldays.* **2** the hours during which school is open: *The schoolday ends at 3:00 p.m.* **3** the part of the day that students spend at school: *Her schoolday started with a math test.* **4** school·days [pl.] the period in your life when you go to school: *She hadn't seen Laura since her schooldays.*

ˈschool ˌdistrict *noun* an area that contains several schools that are governed together

ˈschool friend (also school·mate) *noun* a friend who attends or attended the same school as you: *She met up with some of her old* (= former) *high school friends.*

school·girl /ˈskulgərl/ *noun* a girl who attends school

school·house /ˈskulhaʊs/ *noun* **1** a school building, especially a small one in a small town in the past **2** a house for a teacher next to a small school

school·ing /ˈskulɪŋ/ *noun* [U] the education you receive at school: *secondary schooling* ♦ *He had very little schooling.*

school·kid /ˈskulkɪd/ *noun* (*informal*) = SCHOOLCHILD

school·marm /ˈskulmɑrm/ *noun* (*disapproving*) a woman who teaches in a school, especially one who is old-fashioned and strict ▶ school·marm·ish /-ˌmɑrmɪʃ/ *adj.*

school·mas·ter /ˈskulˌmæstər/, school·mis·tress /ˈskulˌmɪstrəs/ *noun* (*old-fashioned*) a teacher in a school

school·mate /ˈskulmeɪt/ *noun* = SCHOOL FRIEND

school·room /ˈskulrum; -rʊm/ *noun* (*old-fashioned*) a classroom

school·teach·er /ˈskulˌtitʃər/ *noun* a person whose job is teaching in a school

school·work /ˈskulwərk/ *noun* [U] work that students do at school or for school: *She is struggling to keep up with her schoolwork.*

school·yard /ˈskulyard/ *noun* an outdoor area of a school for children to play in ⟳ compare PLAYGROUND

schoon·er /ˈskunər/ *noun* **1** a sailing ship with two or more MASTS (= posts that support the sails) **2** a tall glass for beer

schtick = SHTICK

schwa (also shwa) /ʃwɑ/ *noun* (*phonetics*) a vowel sound in parts of words that are not stressed, for example the "a" in *about* or the "e" in *moment*; the PHONETIC symbol for this, /ə/

sci·at·ic /saɪˈætɪk/ *adj.* [only before noun] (*anatomy*) of the hip or of the nerve which goes from the PELVIS to the THIGH (= the **sciatic nerve**)

sci·at·i·ca /saɪˈætɪkə/ *noun* [U] pain in the back, hip, and outer side of the leg, caused by pressure on the sciatic nerve

sci·ence 🔑 /ˈsaɪəns/ *noun*
1 [U] knowledge about the structure and behavior of the natural and physical world, based on facts that you can prove, for example by experiments: *new developments in science and technology* ♦ *the advance of modern science* ♦ *the laws of science* **2** [U] the study of science: *science students/teachers/courses* **3** [U, C] a particular branch of science: *to study one of the sciences* ⟳ compare ART, HUMANITY **4** [sing.] a system for organizing the knowledge about a particular subject, especially one concerned with aspects of human behavior or society: *a science of international politics* ⟳ see also DOMESTIC SCIENCE, EARTH SCIENCE, LIFE SCIENCES, NATURAL SCIENCE, POLITICAL SCIENCE, ROCKET SCIENCE, SOCIAL SCIENCE **IDM** see BLIND *v.*

ˈscience ˌfair *noun* a competition in which students at a school compete to present the best science project

ˌscience ˈfiction (also *informal* sci-fi) (*abbr.* SF) *noun* [U] a type of book, movie, etc. that is based on imagined scientific discoveries of the future, and often deals with space travel and life on other planets

ˈscience ˌpark *noun* an area where there are a lot of companies or organizations involved in scientific research and development

sci·en·tif·ic 🔑 /ˌsaɪənˈtɪfɪk/ *adj.* [usually before noun]
1 involving science; connected with science: *a scientific discovery* ♦ *scientific knowledge* ♦ *sites of scientific interest* **2** (of a way of doing something or thinking) careful and logical: *He took a very scientific approach to management.* ♦ *We need to be more scientific about this problem.* **ANT** UNSCIENTIFIC ⟳ compare NONSCIENTIFIC ▶ sci·en·tif·i·cally /-kli/ *adv.*

TOPIC COLLOCATIONS

Scientific Research
theory
■ **formulate/advance** a theory/hypothesis
■ **build/construct/create/develop** a simple/theoretical/mathematical model
■ **develop/establish/provide/use** a theoretical/conceptual framework/an algorithm
■ **advance/argue/develop** the thesis that…
■ **explore** an idea/a concept/a hypothesis
■ **make** a prediction/an inference
■ **base** a prediction/your calculations on sth
■ **investigate/evaluate/accept/challenge/reject** a theory/hypothesis/model

experiment

- **design** an experiment/a questionnaire/a study/a test
- **do** research/an experiment/an analysis
- **make** observations/calculations
- **take/record** measurements
- **carry out/conduct/perform** an experiment/a test/a longitudinal study/observations/clinical trials
- **run** an experiment/a simulation/clinical trials
- **repeat** an experiment/a test/an analysis
- **replicate** a study/the results/the findings
- **observe/study/examine/investigate/assess** a pattern/a process/a behavior
- **fund/support** the research/project/study
- **seek/provide/get/secure** funding for research

results

- **collect/gather/extract** data/information
- **yield** data/evidence/similar findings/the same results
- **analyze/examine** the data/soil samples/a specimen
- **consider/compare/interpret** the results/findings
- **fit** the data/model
- **confirm/support/verify** a prediction/a hypothesis/the results/the findings
- **prove** a conjecture/hypothesis/theorem
- **draw/make/reach** the same conclusions
- **read/review** the records/literature
- **describe/report** an experiment/a study
- **present/publish/summarize** the results/findings
- **present/publish/read/review/cite** a paper in a scientific journal

sci·en·tism /'saɪənˌtɪzəm/ *noun* [U] **1** a way of thinking or expressing ideas that is considered to be typical of scientists **2** complete belief in scientific methods, or in the truth of scientific knowledge

sci·en·tist 🔑 /'saɪəntɪst/ *noun*

a person who studies one or more of the NATURAL SCIENCES (= for example, physics, chemistry, and biology): *a research scientist* ◆ *nuclear scientists* ◆ *scientists and engineers* ◆ *the cartoon figure of the mad scientist working in his laboratory* ⟳ see also COMPUTER SCIENCE, POLITICAL SCIENTIST, ROCKET SCIENTIST, SOCIAL SCIENTIST

Sci·en·tol·o·gy™ /ˌsaɪən'tɒlədʒi/ *noun* [U] a religious system based on getting knowledge of yourself and spiritual fulfillment (FULFILL) through courses of study and training ▶ **Sci·ent·ol·o·gist** /-dʒɪst/ *noun*

sci-fi /ˌsaɪ 'faɪ/ *noun* [U] (*informal*) = SCIENCE FICTION

scim·i·tar /'sɪmətər; -ˌtɑr/ *noun* a short curved SWORD with one sharp edge, used especially in Eastern countries

scin·til·la /sɪn'tɪlə/ *noun* [sing.] ~ (of sth) (*formal*) (usually in negative sentences) a very small amount of something: *There is not a scintilla of truth in what she says.*

scin·til·lat·ing /'sɪntlˌeɪtɪŋ/ *adj.* very intelligent, amusing, and interesting: *a scintillating performance* ◆ *Statistics on unemployment levels hardly make for scintillating reading.*

sci·on /'saɪən/ *noun* **1** (*formal* or *literary*) a young member of a family, especially a famous or important one **2** (*technical*) a piece of a plant, especially one cut to make a new plant

sci·roc·co /ʃə'rɑkoʊ/ ⟳ SIROCCO

scissor kick (also **scissors kick**) *noun* **1** (in swimming) a strong kick with the legs moving in opposite directions **2** (in SOCCER) an action of kicking the ball while jumping sideways in the air

scis·sors 🔑 /'sɪzərz/ *noun* [pl.]

a tool for cutting paper or cloth, that has two sharp blades with handles, joined together in the middle: *a pair of scissors* ⟳ see also NAIL SCISSORS ⟳ picture at KITCHEN ⟳ picture at TOOL ▶ **scis·sor** *adj.* [only before noun]: *The legs move in a scissor action.*

scle·ra /'sklɪrə; 'sklɛrə/ (**scle·rae** /'sklɪri; 'sklɛri/ or **scle·ras**) *noun* (*anatomy*) the white part of the eye ⟳ picture at BODY

scle·ro·sis /sklə'roʊsəs/ *noun* [U] (*medical*) a condition in which soft TISSUE in the body becomes hard, in a way that is not normal ⟳ see also MULTIPLE SCLEROSIS ▶ **scle·rot·ic** /sklə'rɑtɪk/ *adj.*

scoff /skɔf; skɑf/ *verb* [I, T] ~ (at sb/sth) | + speech to talk about someone or something in a way that makes it clear that you think they are stupid or ridiculous **SYN** MOCK: *He scoffed at our amateurish attempts.* ◆ *Don't scoff—she's absolutely right.*

scoff·law /'skɑflɔ; 'skɔf-/ *noun* (*informal*) a person who often breaks the law but in a way that is not very serious

scold /skoʊld/ *verb* [T, I] ~ sb (for sth/for doing sth) | (+ speech) (*formal*) to speak angrily to someone, especially a child, because they have done something wrong **SYN** REBUKE: *He scolded them for arriving late.* ▶ **scold·ing** *noun* [usually sing.]: *I got a scolding from my mother.*

sco·li·o·sis /ˌskoʊli'oʊsəs/ *noun* [U] (*medical*) a condition in which the SPINE is curved in a way that is not normal

sconce /skɑns/ *noun* an object that is attached to a wall, used for holding a CANDLE or an electric light: *wall sconces*

scone /skoʊn/ *noun* a small cake, sometimes with dried fruit in it

scoop /skup/ *noun, verb*

● *noun* **1** [C] a tool like a large spoon with a deep bowl, used for picking up substances in powder form like flour, or for serving food like ice cream ⟳ picture at KITCHEN **2** [C] the amount picked up by a scoop: *two scoops of mashed potato* **3** [C] a piece of important or exciting news that is printed in one newspaper before other newspapers know about it **4** the scoop [U] (*informal*) the latest information about someone or something, especially details that are not generally known: *I got the inside scoop on his new girlfriend.*

● *verb* **1** to move or lift something with a scoop or something like a scoop: ~ sth (+ adv./prep.) *She scooped ice cream into their bowls.* ◆ *First, scoop a hole in the soil.* ◆ *Scoop out the melon flesh.* ◆ ~ sth up (+ adv./prep.) *He quickly scooped the money up from the desk.* **2** ~ sb/sth (up) (+ adv./prep.) to move or lift someone or something with a quick continuous movement: *She scooped the child up in her arms.* **3** ~ sb/sth to publish a story before all the other newspapers, television companies, etc.: *The paper had inside information and scooped all its rivals.*

scooped /skupt/ (also **scoop**) *adj.* [only before noun] (of the neck of a woman's dress, etc.) cut low and round: *a scooped neck/neckline*

scoot /skut/ *verb* [I] (+ adv./prep.) (*informal*) to go or leave somewhere in a hurry: *I'd better scoot or I'll be late.*

scoot·er /'skutər/ *noun* **1** (also **motor scooter**) a light motorcycle, usually with small wheels and a curved metal cover at the front to protect the rider's legs **2** a vehicle with two small wheels attached to a narrow board with a vertical handle. The rider holds the handle, puts one foot on the board, and pushes against the ground with the other. ⟳ picture at BICYCLE

scope ᴬᵂᴸ /skoʊp/ *noun, verb*

● *noun* [U] **1** the opportunity or ability to do or achieve something **SYN** POTENTIAL: ~ (for sth) *There's still plenty of scope for improvement.* ◆ *Her job offers very little scope for promotion.* ◆ ~ (for sb) (to do sth) *The extra money will give us the scope to improve our facilities.* ◆ *First try to do something that is within your scope.* **2** the range of things that a subject, an organization, an activity, etc. deals with: *Our powers are limited in scope.* ◆ *This subject lies beyond the scope of our investigation.* ◆ *These issues were outside the scope of the article.* **3** -scope (in nouns) an instrument for looking through or watching something with: *microscope* ◆ *telescope*

● *verb* **1** ~ sth (*informal*) to look at or examine something thoroughly: *His eyes scoped the room, trying to spot her in the crowd.* **2** ~ sth (out) to examine something carefully before you start work on it so that you know the size of the task: *The information helped us scope the project.*

PHR V ,scope sth↔'out to look at something carefully in order to see what it is like

scorch /skɔrtʃ/ verb **1** [T, I] ~ (sth) | ~ sth + adj. to burn and slightly damage a surface by making it too hot; to be slightly burned by heat: *I scorched my dress when I was ironing it.* ♦ *Don't stand so close to the fire—your coat is scorching!* ⟳ thesaurus box at BURN **2** [T, I] ~ (sth) to become or to make something become dry and brown, especially from the heat of the sun or from chemicals: *scorched grass* ♦ *The leaves will scorch if you water them in the sun.*

ˌscorched 'earth ˌpolicy noun (in a war) a policy of destroying anything in a particular area that may be useful to the enemy

scorch·er /'skɔrtʃər/ noun (informal) a very hot day

scorch·ing /'skɔrtʃɪŋ/ adj. (informal) **1** very hot **SYN** BAKING **2** used to emphasize how strong, powerful, etc. something is: *a scorching critique of the government's economic policy*

ˈscorch mark noun a mark made on a surface by burning

score 🎵 /skɔr/ noun, verb
● noun
▷ POINTS/GOALS, ETC. **1** [C] the number of points, goals, etc. scored by each player or team in a game or competition: *a high/low score* ♦ *What's the score now?* ♦ **The final score was 4–3.** ♦ *I'll keep (the) score.* **2** [C] the number of points someone gets for correct answers on a test: *test scores* ♦ *an IQ score of 120* ♦ *a perfect score*
▷ MUSIC **3** [C] a written or printed version of a piece of music showing what each instrument is to play or what each voice is to sing: *an orchestral score* ♦ *the score of Verdi's "Requiem"* **4** [C] the music written for a movie or play: *an award for best original score*
▷ TWENTY **5** [C] (pl. score) a set or group of 20 or approximately 20: *Several cabs and a score of cars were parked outside.* ♦ *Doyle's success brought imitators by the score* (= very many). ♦ *the biblical age of three score years and ten* (= 70)
▷ MANY **6** scores [pl.] very many: *There were scores of boxes and crates, all waiting to be checked and loaded.*
▷ CUT **7** [C] a cut in a surface, made with a sharp tool
▷ FACTS ABOUT SITUATION **8** the score [sing.] (informal) the real facts about the present situation: *What's the score?* ♦ *You don't have to lie to me. I know the score.*
IDM on that/this score as far as that/this is concerned: *You don't have to worry on that score.* ⟳ more at EVEN v., SETTLE v.
● verb
▷ GIVE/GET POINTS/GOALS **1** [I, T] to win points, goals, etc. in a game or competition: *Fraser scored again in the second half.* ♦ ~ sth *to score a goal/try/touchdown/victory* **2** [I] to keep a record of the points, goals, etc. won in a game or competition: *Who's going to score?* **3** [T, I] to gain marks for a test or an exam: ~ sth *She scored 98% on the French test.* ♦ + adv./prep. *Girls usually score highly on language exams.* **4** [T] ~ sth to give something or someone a particular number of points: *The tests are scored by psychologists.* ♦ *Score each criterion on a scale of 1 to 5.* ♦ *a scoring system* **5** [T] ~ sth to be worth a particular number of points: *Each correct answer will score two points.*
▷ SUCCEED **6** [T, I] to succeed; to have an advantage: ~ (sth) *The army continued to score successes in the south.* ♦ *She's scored again with her latest blockbuster.* ♦ ~ over sth *Bicycles score over other forms of transportation in towns.*
▷ ARRANGE/WRITE MUSIC **7** [T, usually passive] to arrange a piece of music for one or more musical instruments or for voices: ~ sth for sth *The piece is scored for violin, viola, and cello.* ♦ ~ sth *The director invited him to score the movie* (= write the music for it).
▷ CUT **8** [T] ~ sth to make a cut or mark on a surface: *Score the card first with a knife.*
▷ HAVE SEX **9** [I] ~ (with sb) (slang) (especially of a man) to have sex with a new partner: *Did you score last night?*
▷ BUY DRUGS **10** [T, I] ~ (sth) (slang) to buy or get illegal drugs
IDM score a point/points (off/against/over sb) to show

that you are better than someone, especially by making clever remarks, for example in an argument score points (with sb) to please someone, or make them like you: *Coming late to work won't score points with the boss.*

score·board /'skɔrbɔrd/ noun a large board on which the score in a game or competition is shown ⟳ picture at FOOTBALL

score·card /'skɔrkɑrd/ noun a card or piece of paper that people watching or playing a game can use to write the score on, or on which the score can be officially recorded

score·keep·er /'skɔrˌkipər/ noun a person whose job is to keep the score of a game: *the official scorekeeper at basketball games*

score·less /'skɔrləs/ adj. (of a game) without either team getting any points, goals, etc.: *a scoreless tie*

scor·er /'skɔrər/ noun **1** (in sports) a player who scores points, goals, etc.: *the Jets' top scorer* **2** a person who keeps a record of the points, goals, etc. scored in a game or competition **3 a high/low ~** a person who gets a high/low number of points on a test or exam

scorn /skɔrn/ noun, verb
● noun [U] a strong feeling that someone or something is stupid or not good enough, usually shown by the way you speak **SYN** CONTEMPT: *Her fellow teachers greeted her proposal with scorn.* ♦ ~ for sb/sth *They had nothing but scorn for his political views.*
IDM pour/heap scorn on sb/sth to speak about someone or something in a way that shows that you do not respect them or have a good opinion of them
● verb **1** ~ sb/sth to feel or show that you think someone or something is stupid and you do not respect them or it **SYN** DISMISS: *She scorned their views as old-fashioned.* **2** (formal) to refuse to have or do something because you are too proud: ~ sth *to scorn an invitation* ♦ ~ to do sth *She would have scorned to stoop to such tactics.* **IDM** see HELL

scorn·ful /'skɔrnfl/ adj. showing or feeling scorn **SYN** CONTEMPTUOUS: *a scornful laugh* ♦ ~ of sth *He was scornful of such "female" activities as cooking.* ▶ **scorn·ful·ly** /-fəli/ adv.: *She laughed scornfully.*

Scor·pi·o /'skɔrpiˌoʊ/ noun **1** [U] the 8th sign of the ZODIAC, the SCORPION **2** (pl. Scor·pi·os) [C] a person born under the influence of this sign, that is between October 23rd and November 21st, approximately

scor·pi·on /'skɔrpiən/ noun a small creature that is related to spiders, with eight legs, two front CLAWS (= curved and pointed arms) and a long tail that curves over its back and can give a poisonous sting. Scorpions live in hot countries. ⟳ picture at ANIMAL

Scot /skɑt/ noun **1** a person from Scotland **2** the Scots [pl.] the people of Scotland ⟳ note at SCOTTISH

Scotch /skɑtʃ/ noun, adj.
● noun **1** [U] the type of WHISKEY made in Scotland: *a bottle of Scotch* **2** [C] a glass of Scotch: *Do you want a Scotch?*
● adj. of or connected with Scotland

scotch /skɑtʃ/ verb ~ sth to stop something from happening; to take action to end something: *Plans for a merger have been scotched.* ♦ *rumors that he had fled the country were promptly scotched by his wife.*

ˌScotch 'bonnet noun a type of very hot CHILI

ˌScotch 'tape™ noun [U] clear plastic tape that is sticky on one side, used for sticking things together

ˌscot-'free /ˌskɑt 'fri/ adv. (informal) without receiving the punishment you deserve: *They got off scot-free because of lack of evidence.* **ORIGIN** This idiom comes from the old English word "scot" meaning "tax." People were scot-free if they didn't have to pay the tax.

Scots /skɑts/ adj., noun
● adj. of or connected with Scotland, and especially with the English language as spoken in Scotland or the Scots language: *He spoke with a Scots accent.* ♦ *She comes from an old Scots family.*

h hat   m man   n no   ŋ sing   l leg   r red   y yes   w wet

- **noun** [U] a language spoken in Scotland, closely related to English but with many differences

Scot·tie /ˈskɑti/ noun (informal) = SCOTTISH TERRIER

Scot·tish /ˈskɑtɪʃ/ adj. of or connected with Scotland or its people: the Scottish Highlands ◆ Scottish dancing

Scottish ˈterrier (also Scot·tie, informal) noun a small TERRIER (= type of dog) with rough hair and short legs

scoun·drel /ˈskaʊndrəl/ noun (old-fashioned) a man who treats other people badly, especially by being dishonest or immoral SYN ROGUE

scour /ˈskaʊər/ verb **1** ~ sth (for sb/sth) to search a place or thing thoroughly in order to find someone or something SYN COMB: We scoured the area for somewhere to pitch our tent. **2** ~ sth (out) to clean something by rubbing its surface hard with rough material: I had to scour out the pans. **3** ~ sth (away/out) | ~ sth (from/out of sth) to make a passage, hole, or mark in the ground, rocks, etc. as the result of movement, especially over a long period: The water had raced down the slope and scoured out the bed of a stream.

scourge /skɜrdʒ/ noun, verb
- **noun 1** [usually sing.] ~ (of sb/sth) (formal) a person or thing that causes trouble or suffering: the scourge of war/disease/poverty ◆ Inflation was the scourge of the 1970s. **2** a WHIP used to punish people in the past
- **verb 1** [usually passive] ~ sb (literary) to cause trouble or suffering to someone: He lay awake, scourged by his conscience. **2** ~ sb (old use) to hit someone with a scourge SYN WHIP

scouring ˌpad noun a small ball of wire or stiff plastic used for cleaning pans

scout /skaʊt/ noun, verb
- **noun 1 the Scouts** [pl.] an organization (officially called **Boy Scouts of America, Girl Scouts of the USA,** or **Scouts Canada**) that trains young people in practical skills and does a lot of activities with them, for example camping: to join the Scouts **2** a boy or girl who is a member of the Scouts: Both my brothers were scouts. ◆ a scout troop ⊃ see also BOY SCOUT, GIRL SCOUT ⊃ compare BROWNIE **3** a person, an aircraft, etc. sent ahead to get information about the enemy's position, strength, etc. **4** = TALENT SCOUT
- **verb 1** [T, I] to search an area or various areas in order to find or discover something: ~ sth (for sb/sth) They scouted the area for somewhere to stay the night. ◆ ~ (around) (for sb/sth) The kids were scouting around for wood for the fire. ◆ a military scouting party **2** [I, T] ~ (sb) to look for sports players, actors, musicians, etc. who have special ability, so you can offer them work: He scouts for the Giants. **PHRV ˌscout sthↄˈout** to find out what an area is like or where something is, by searching: We went ahead to scout out the lie of the land.

scout·ing /ˈskaʊtɪŋ/ noun [U] the activities that boy and girl scouts take part in; the Scout organization

scout·mas·ter /ˈskaʊtˌmæstər/ (also ˈscout leader) noun the adult in charge of a group of BOY SCOUTS

scowl /skaʊl/ verb, noun
- **verb** [I] ~ (at sb/sth) to look at someone or something in an angry or annoyed way SYN GLOWER
- **noun** an angry look or expression: He looked up at me with a scowl.

Scrab·ble™ /ˈskræbl/ noun [U] a board game in which players try to make words from letters printed on small plastic blocks and connect them to words that have already been placed on the board

scrab·ble /ˈskræbl/ verb [I] ~ (around) (for sth) | + adv./prep. to try to find or to do something in a hurry or with difficulty, often by moving your hands or feet around quickly, without much control: She scrabbled around in her bag for her glasses. ◆ He was scrabbling for a foothold on the steep slope. ◆ a sound like rats scrabbling on the other side of the wall

scrag·gly /ˈskrægli/ adj. (informal) thin and growing in a way that is not even: a scraggly beard

scram /skræm/ verb (-mm-) [I] (old-fashioned, informal) (usually used in orders) to go away quickly: Scram! I don't want you here.

scram·ble /ˈskræmbl/ verb, noun
- **verb**
  > WALK/CLIMB **1** [I] + adv./prep. to move quickly, especially with difficulty, using your hands to help you SYN CLAMBER: She managed to scramble over the wall. ◆ He scrambled to his feet as we came in.
  > DO SOMETHING QUICKLY **2** [I] ~ to do sth | + adv./prep. to move or do something quickly because you are in a hurry: Rescue workers scrambled to find survivors in the wreckage.
  > PUSH/FIGHT **3** [I] to push, fight, or compete with others in order to get or to reach something: ~ for sth The audience scrambled for the exits. ◆ ~ to do sth Shoppers were scrambling to get the best bargains.
  > EGGS **4** [T, usually passive] ~ sth to cook an egg by mixing the white and yellow parts together and heating them, sometimes with milk and butter: scrambled eggs
  > TELEPHONE/RADIO **5** [T, often passive] ~ sth to change the way that a telephone or radio message sounds so that only people with special equipment can understand it: scrambled satellite signals
  > CONFUSE THOUGHTS **6** [T] ~ sth to confuse someone's thoughts, ideas, etc. so that they have no order: Alcohol seemed to have scrambled his brain.
  > AIRCRAFT **7** [T, I, usually passive] ~ (sth) to order that planes, etc. should take off immediately in an emergency; to take off immediately in an emergency: A helicopter was scrambled to help rescue three young climbers. ◆ They scrambled as soon as the call came through.
  > IN FOOTBALL **8** [I] (of a QUARTERBACK in football) to run around with the ball while waiting for a chance to throw it: He scrambled left and right on the play.
- **noun**
  > DIFFICULT WALK/CLIMB **1** [sing.] a difficult walk or climb over rough ground, especially one in which you have to use your hands
  > PUSH/FIGHT **2** [sing.] ~ (for sth) a situation in which people push, fight, or compete with each other in order to get or do something SYN FREE-FOR-ALL: There was a mad scramble for the best seats.

scram·bler /ˈskræmblər/ noun a device that changes radio or telephone signals or messages so that they cannot be understood by other people

scrap /skræp/ noun, verb
- **noun 1** [C] a small piece of something, especially paper, cloth, etc.: She scribbled his phone number on a scrap of paper. ◆ (figurative) scraps of information ◆ (figurative) She was just a scrap of a thing (= small and thin). **2** [sing.] (usually with a negative) a small amount of something SYN BIT: It won't make a scrap of difference. ◆ There's not a scrap of evidence to support his claim. ◆ a barren landscape without a scrap of vegetation **3 scraps** [pl.] food left after a meal: Give the scraps to the dog. **4** [U] things that are not wanted or cannot be used for their original purpose, but that have some value for the material they are made of: We sold the car for scrap (= so that any good parts can be used again). ◆ scrap metal ◆ a scrap dealer (= a person who buys and sells scrap) **5** (informal) a short fight or disagreement SYN SCUFFLE, SQUABBLE: He was always getting into scraps at school. ⊃ see also SCRAPPY
- **verb** (-pp-) **1** [T, often passive] ~ sth to cancel or get rid of something that is no longer practical or useful: They had been forced to scrap plans for a new school building. ◆ The oldest of the aircraft were scrapped. **2** [I] (informal) to fight with someone: The bigger boys started scrapping.

scrap·book /ˈskræpbʊk/ noun a book with empty pages where you can stick pictures, newspaper articles, etc.

scrape /skreɪp/ verb, noun
- **verb**
  > REMOVE **1** [T] to remove something from a surface by moving something sharp and hard like a knife across it:

~ sth (+ adv./prep.) *She scraped the mud off her boots.* ◆ ~ sth + adj. *The kids had scraped their plates clean.*

> DAMAGE **2** [T] to rub something by accident so that it gets damaged or hurt: ~ sth *She fell and scraped her knee.* ◆ ~ sth + adv./prep. *I scraped the side of my car on the wall.* ◆ *Sorry, I've scraped some paint off the car.* ◆ *The wire had scraped the skin from her fingers.*

> MAKE SOUND **3** [I, T] to make an unpleasant noise by rubbing against a hard surface; to make something do this: (+ adv./prep.) *I could hear his pen scraping across the paper.* ◆ *We could hear her scraping away at the violin.* ◆ ~ sth (+ adv./prep.) *Don't scrape your chairs on the floor.*

> MAKE HOLE IN GROUND **4** [T] ~ sth (out) to make a hole or hollow place in the ground: *He found a suitable place, scraped a hole, and buried the bag in it.*

> PULL HAIR BACK **5** [T] ~ your hair back to pull your hair tightly back, away from your face: *Her hair was scraped back from her face in a ponytail.*

IDM **scrape (the bottom of) the barrel** (*disapproving*) to have to use whatever things or people you can get, because there is not much choice available ⊃ more at BOW¹ v.
PHR V ,scrape 'by (on sth) to manage to live on the money you have, but with difficulty: *I can just scrape by on what my parents give me.* ,scrape 'in | ,scrape 'into sth to manage to get a job, a position, a place at college, etc., but with difficulty: *He scraped in with 180 votes.* ◆ *Our team just scraped into the semi-finals.* ,scrape sth↔'out **1** to remove something from inside something else, using something sharp or hard like a knife: *Scrape out the flesh of the melon with a spoon.* **2** to win or get something with difficulty: *He scraped out a victory by only a few hundred votes.* ,scrape 'through | ,scrape 'through sth to succeed in doing something with difficulty, especially in passing an exam: *I might scrape through the exam if I'm lucky.* ,scrape sth↔to'gether/'up to obtain or collect together something, but with difficulty: *We managed to scrape together eight volunteers.*

● *noun*
> ACTION/SOUND **1** [sing.] the action or unpleasant sound of one thing rubbing roughly against another: *the scrape of iron on stone*

> DAMAGE **2** [C] an injury or a mark caused by rubbing against something rough: *She emerged from the overturned car with only a few cuts and scrapes.*

> DIFFICULT SITUATION **3** [C] (*old-fashioned*) a difficult situation that you have caused yourself: *He was always getting into scrapes as a boy.*

scrap·er /'skreɪpər/ *noun* a tool used for scraping, for example for scraping ice from a car

'scrap heap *noun* a pile of things, especially of metal, that are no longer wanted or useful
IDM **on the scrap heap** (*informal*) no longer wanted or considered useful

scrap·ie /'skreɪpi/ *noun* [U] a serious disease that affects the NERVOUS SYSTEM of sheep

scrap·ing /'skreɪpɪŋ/ *noun* [usually pl.] a small amount of something produced by scratching a surface

'scrap paper *noun* [U] loose pieces of paper used for writing notes on

scrap·py /'skræpi/ *adj.* (*informal*) (scrap·pi·er, scrap·pi·est) very determined and willing to fight or argue with people in order to achieve something: *a scrappy team* ⊃ see also SCRAP n. (5)

scrap·yard /'skræpyɑrd/ *noun* = JUNKYARD

scratch 🔊 /skrætʃ/ *verb, noun, adj.*
● *verb*
> RUB WITH YOUR NAILS **1** [T, I] to rub your skin with your nails, usually because it is ITCHING: ~ sth/yourself *John yawned and scratched his chin.* ◆ *The dog scratched itself behind the ear.* ◆ ~ (at sth) *Try not to scratch.* ◆ *She scratched at the insect bites on her arm.*

> CUT SKIN **2** [T, I] to cut or damage your skin slightly with something sharp: ~ (sb/sth/yourself) *I'd scratched my leg and it was bleeding.* ◆ *Does the cat scratch?* ◆ ~ sb/sth/ yourself on sth *She scratched herself on a nail.*

> DAMAGE SURFACE **3** [T] ~ sth to damage the surface of something, especially by accident, by making thin, shallow marks on it: *Be careful not to scratch the furniture.* ◆ *The car's paintwork is badly scratched.*

> MAKE/REMOVE MARK **4** [T] ~ sth + adv./prep. to make or remove a mark, etc. on something deliberately, by rubbing it with something hard or sharp: *They scratched lines in the dirt to mark out a goal.* ◆ *We scratched some of the dirt away.* ◆ (*figurative*) *You can scratch my name off the list.*

> MAKE SOUND **5** [I] (+ adv./prep.) to make an irritating noise by rubbing something with something sharp: *His pen scratched away on the paper.*

> A LIVING **6** [T] ~ a living to make enough money to live on, but with difficulty

> CANCEL **7** [T, I] to decide that something cannot happen, or someone or something cannot take part in something, before it starts: ~ sb/sth *to scratch a rocket launch* ◆ ~ sb/sth (from sth) *The horse was scratched from the race because of injury.*

IDM **scratch your head (over sth)** to think hard in order to find an answer to something **scratch the surface (of sth)** to deal with, understand, or find out about only a small part of a subject or problem **you scratch my back and I'll scratch yours** (*saying*) used to say that if someone helps you, you will help them, even if this is unfair to others
PHR V ,scratch a'round (for sth) to search for something, especially with difficulty ,scratch sth↔'out to remove a word, especially a name, from something written, usually by putting a line through it

● *noun*
> MARK/CUT **1** [C] a mark, a cut, or an injury made by scratching someone's skin or the surface of something: *Her hands were covered in scratches from the thorns.* ◆ *It's only a scratch* (= a very slight injury). ◆ *He escaped without a scratch* (= was not hurt at all).

> SOUND **2** [sing.] the unpleasant sound of something sharp or rough being rubbed against a surface

> WITH YOUR NAILS **3** [sing.] the act of scratching a part of your body when it ITCHES: *The dog had a good scratch.*
IDM **from scratch 1** without any previous preparation or knowledge: *I learned German from scratch in six months.* **2** from the very beginning, not using any of the work done earlier: *They decided to dismantle the machine and start again from scratch.* **up to scratch** as good as something or someone should be **SYN** SATISFACTORY: *His work just isn't up to scratch.* ◆ *It'll take months to bring the band up to scratch.*

● *adj.* (especially in GOLF) with no HANDICAP: *a scratch player*

'scratch card *noun* a card that you buy that has an area that you scratch off to find out if you have won some money or a prize

'scratch pad *noun* a small book of cheap paper for writing notes on

'scratch paper *noun* [U] cheap paper, or loose sheets of paper, for writing notes on

scratch·y /'skrætʃi/ *adj.* (scratch·i·er, scratch·i·est) **1** (of clothes or cloth) rough and unpleasant to the touch **SYN** ITCHY **2** (of a record, voice, etc.) making a rough, unpleasant sound like something being scratched across a surface: *a scratchy recording of Mario Lanza* ◆ *a scratchy pen* **3** (of writing or drawings) done without care **4** that feels sore: *a scratchy throat*

scrawl /skrɔl/ *verb, noun*
● *verb* [T, I] to write something in a careless, messy way, making it difficult to read **SYN** SCRIBBLE: ~ sth (across/in/ on/over sth) *I tried to read his directions, scrawled on a piece of paper.* ◆ ~ across/in/on/over sth *Someone had scrawled all over my notes.*

● *noun* a careless, messy way of writing; something written in this way **SYN** SCRIBBLE: *Her signature was an illegible* *scrawl.* ♦ *I can't be expected to read this scrawl!* ♦ *The paper was covered in scrawls.*

scrawn·y /ˈskrɔːni/ *adj.* (**scrawn·i·er, scrawn·i·est**) (*disapproving*) (of people or animals) very thin in a way that is not attractive

scream 🔑 /skriːm/ *verb, noun*

• *verb* **1** [I, T] to give a loud, high cry, because you are hurt, frightened, excited, etc. **SYN** SHRIEK: *He covered her mouth to stop her from screaming.* ♦ *~ in/with sth The kids were screaming with excitement.* ♦ *~ out (in/with sth) People ran for the exits, screaming out in terror.* ♦ *~ yourself + adj. The baby was screaming himself hoarse.* **2** [T, I] to shout something in a loud, high voice because of fear, anger, etc. **SYN** YELL: + speech *"Help!" she screamed.* ♦ *~ (out) (for sth/sb) Someone was screaming for help.* ♦ *~ at sb (to do sth) He screamed at me to stop.* ♦ *~ sth (out) (at sb) She screamed abuse at him.* ♦ *~ (out) that… His sister screamed out that he was crazy.* ⊃ thesaurus box at SHOUT **3** [I] to make a loud, high noise; to move fast, making this noise **SYN** SCREECH: *Lights flashed and sirens screamed.* ♦ + adv./prep. *The powerboat screamed out of the marina.*
IDM scream bloody 'murder to scream loudly and for a long time, especially in order to protest about something **PHR V** ˌscream 'out (for sth) to be in need of attention in a very noticeable way **SYN** CALL OUT: *These books scream out to be included in a list of favorites.*

• *noun* **1** [C] a loud, high cry made by someone who is hurt, frightened, excited, etc.; a loud, high noise: *She let out a scream of pain.* ♦ *He drove off with a scream of tires.* **2** [sing.] (*old-fashioned, informal*) a person or thing that causes you to laugh: *He's a scream.*

scream·ing·ly /ˈskriːmɪŋli/ *adv.* extremely: *It was screamingly obvious what we should do next.*

scree /skriː/ *noun* [U, C] an area of small loose stones, especially on a mountain, which may slide when you walk on them

screech /skriːtʃ/ *verb, noun*
• *verb* **1** [I, T] to make a loud, high, unpleasant sound; to say something using this sound: *Monkeys were screeching in the trees.* ♦ *The wind screeched in his ears.* ♦ *screeching brakes* ♦ *He screeched with pain.* ♦ *~ (sth) (at sb) He screeched something at me.* **2** [I] (+ adv./prep.) (of a vehicle) to make a loud, high, unpleasant noise as it moves: *The car screeched to a halt outside the hospital.* ♦ *A police car screeched out of a side street.*
• *noun* a loud, high, unpleasant cry or noise: *a screech of brakes/tires* ♦ *She suddenly let out a screech.*

screed /skriːd/ *noun* a long piece of writing, especially one that is not very interesting

screen 🔑 /skriːn/ *noun, verb*
• *noun*
▷ TV/COMPUTER/MOVIES **1** [C] the flat surface at the front of a television or computer, on which you see pictures or information: *a computer screen* ♦ *a monitor with a 21 inch screen* ♦ *They were staring at the television screen.* ♦ *Move your cursor to the top of the screen.* ♦ *the screen display* ♦ *Can you do a printout of this screen for me* (= of all the information on it)? ⊃ picture at COMPUTER ⊃ see also ON-SCREEN **2** [C] the large flat surface that movies or pictures are shown on: *a movie screen* ♦ *an eight-screen movie theater* ♦ *The movie will be coming to your screens shortly.* **3** often the screen [sing., U] movies or television in general: *He has adapted the play for the screen.* ♦ *Some actors never watch themselves on screen.* ♦ *She was a star of stage and screen* (= plays and movies). ♦ *a screen actor* ⊃ see also OFF-SCREEN, SILVER SCREEN, SMALL SCREEN **4** [C] the data or images shown on a computer screen: *Press the F1 key to display a help screen.*
▷ ON WINDOW/DOOR **5** [C] a wire or plastic net that is held in a frame and fastened on a window, or a door, to let in air but keep out insects
▷ PIECE OF FURNITURE **6** [C] a vertical piece of furniture or equipment, especially one that can be moved around, that is used to divide a room or to keep one area hidden or separate: *The nurse put a screen around the bed.* ⊃ see also FIRE SCREEN
▷ FOR HIDING/PROTECTING SOMETHING OR SOMEONE **7** [C] ~ (of sth) something that prevents someone from seeing or being aware of something, or that protects someone or something: *We planted a screen of tall trees.* ♦ (*figurative*) *All the research was conducted behind a screen of secrecy.* ⊃ see also SMOKESCREEN, SUNSCREEN
▷ IN CHURCH **8** [C] a wood or stone structure in a church, that partly separates the main area from the ALTAR or CHOIR
IDM see RADAR

• *verb*
▷ HIDE SOMETHING OR SOMEONE **1** ~ sth/sb (from sth/sb) to hide or protect something or someone by placing something in front of or around them **SYN** : *Dark glasses screened his eyes from the sun.*
▷ PROTECT SOMEONE **2** ~ sb from sb/sth to protect someone from something dangerous or unpleasant, especially to protect someone who has done something illegal or dishonest **SYN** SHIELD
▷ FOR DISEASE **3** [often passive] ~ sb (for sth) to examine people in order to find out if they have a particular disease or illness: *Men over 55 should be regularly screened for prostate cancer.*
▷ CHECK **4** ~ sb (of a company, an organization, etc.) to find out information about people who work or who want to work for you in order to make sure that they can be trusted: *Government employees may be screened for security purposes.* **5** ~ sth to check something to see if it is suitable or if you want it: *I use my voice mail to screen my phone calls.*
▷ SHOW MOVIE/TV PROGRAM **6** [usually passive] ~ sth to show a movie, etc. in a movie theater or on television: *a list of films to be screened as part of the festival*
PHR V ˌscreen sth↔'off [often passive] to separate part of a room, etc. from the rest of it by putting a screen around it: *Beds can be screened off to give patients more privacy.* ˌscreen sb↔'out to decide not to allow someone to join an organization, enter a country, etc. because you think they may cause trouble ˌscreen sth↔'out to prevent something harmful from entering or going through something: *The ozone layer screens out dangerous rays from the sun.*

ˈScreen Actors ˌGuild *noun* (*abbr.* SAG) an organization that protects the interests of actors in movies and television

ˈscreen door *noun* a door consisting of a screen that lets in air but keeps out insects

ˈscreen dump *noun* a copy of what is on a computer screen at a particular time; the act of printing this out

screen·er /ˈskriːnər/ *noun* a person who checks people and their bags at an airport

screen·ing /ˈskriːnɪŋ/ *noun* **1** [C] the act of showing a movie or television program: *This will be the movie's first screening in this country.* **2** [U, C] the testing or examining of a large number of people or things for disease, faults, etc.: *breast cancer screening*

screen·play /ˈskriːnpleɪ/ *noun* the words that are written for a movie (= the SCRIPT), together with instructions for how it is to be acted and filmed

screen-print *verb* [T, I] ~ (sth) to force ink or metal onto a surface through a screen of silk or artificial material to produce a picture ▶ ˈscreen print *noun*

ˈscreen ˌsaver *noun* a computer program that replaces a screen display on a computer with another, moving, display after a particular length of time, to stop the screen from being damaged

screen·shot /ˈskriːnʃɑt/ *noun* (*computing*) an image of the display on a screen, used when showing how a program works

ˈscreen test *noun* a test to see if someone is suitable to appear in a movie

screen·writ·er /ˈskriːnˌraɪtər/ *noun* a person who writes SCREENPLAYS ⊃ compare PLAYWRIGHT, SCRIPTWRITER

screw 🔧 /skru/ *noun, verb*

● *noun* **1** [C] a thin, pointed piece of metal like a nail with a raised SPIRAL line (called a THREAD) along it and a line or cross cut into its head. Screws are turned and pressed into wood, metal, etc. with a SCREWDRIVER in order to fasten two things together: *One of the screws is loose.* ◆ *Now tighten all the screws.* ⮺ picture at TOOL ⮺ collocations at DECORATE ⮺ see also CORKSCREW **2** [C] an act of turning a screw **3** [C] a PROPELLER on a ship, a boat, or an aircraft **IDM** **have a screw loose** to be slightly strange in your behavior **put the screws on (sb)** to force someone to do something by frightening and threatening them ⮺ more at TURN *n.*

● *verb* **1** [T] ~ sth + adv./prep. to fasten one thing to another or make something tight with a screw or screws: *The bookcase is screwed to the wall.* ◆ *You need to screw all the parts together.* ◆ *Now screw down the lid.* ⮺ compare UNSCREW **2** [T] to twist something around in order to fasten it in place: ~ sth + adv./prep. *She screwed the cap back on the jar.* ◆ ~ sth + adj. *Screw the bolt tight.* ⮺ compare UNSCREW **3** [I] (+ adv./prep.) to be attached by screwing: *The bulb should just screw into the socket.* ◆ *The lid simply screws on.* **4** [T] to squeeze something, especially a piece of paper, into a tight ball: ~ sth up (into sth) *I screwed up the letter and threw it into the fire.* ◆ ~ sth (up) into sth *Screw the foil into a little ball.* ⮺ see also SCREWED-UP **5** [T] (*slang*) to cheat someone, especially by making them pay too much money for something: ~ sb *We've been screwed.* ◆ ~ sb for sth *How much did they screw you for* (= how much did you have to pay)*?*
IDM **screw up your courage** to force yourself to be brave enough to do something: *I finally screwed up my courage and went to the dentist.* ⮺ more at HEAD *n.*
PHR V ,screw a'round (*slang*) to waste time instead of doing something that you should be doing: *I woke up at noon and screwed around the rest of the day.* ,screw a'round with sth (*slang*) to touch, use, or change something in a careless or foolish way: *Don't screw around with the wiring.* ,screw sth 'out of sb | ,screw sb 'out of sth to take something from someone or make them give it to you, especially by cheating or tricking them: *They screwed the money out of her by threats.* ◆ *He screwed investors out of thousands of dollars.* ,screw 'up (*slang*) to do something badly or spoil something **SYN** MESS UP: *You really screwed up there!* ⮺ related noun SCREW-UP ,screw sb↔'up (*slang*) to upset or confuse someone so much that they are not able to deal with problems in their life: *Her father's death really screwed her up.* ⮺ see also SCREWED-UP ,screw sth↔'up **1** to fasten something with screws: *to screw up a crate* **2** (*slang*) to do something badly or spoil something: *Don't screw it up this time.* ⮺ related noun SCREW-UP ,screw your 'eyes/'face↔up to contract the muscles of your eyes or face because the light is too strong, you are in pain, etc.: *He took a sip of the medicine and screwed up his face.*

screw·ball /'skrubɔl/ *noun* (*informal*) a strange or crazy person

screw·driv·er /'skru,draɪvər/ *noun* **1** a tool with a narrow blade that is specially shaped at the end, used for turning screws ⮺ picture at TOOL **2** a COCKTAIL (= an alcoholic drink) made from VODKA and orange juice

,screwed-'up *adj.* **1** (*informal*) emotionally disturbed, especially because of something bad that has happened to you in the past: *an extremely screwed-up kid* **2** twisted into a ball: *a screwed-up tissue* **3** if your face or eyes are screwed-up, the muscles are tight, because you are worried, in pain, etc., or because the light is too bright

'screw top *noun* a top for a container, especially a wine bottle, that screws onto it ⮺ picture at PACKAGING ▶ screw-top (also 'screw-topped) *adj.* [only before noun]: *screw-top bottles*

'screw-up *noun* (*pl.* screw-ups) (*slang*) an occasion when you do something badly or spoil something

screw·y /'skrui/ *adj.* (*informal*) strange or crazy

scrib·ble /'skrɪbl/ *verb, noun*
● *verb* **1** [T, I] to write something quickly and carelessly, especially because you do not have much time **SYN** SCRAWL: ~ sth *He scribbled a note to his sister before leaving.* ◆ ~ sth down *She scribbled down her phone number and pushed it into his hand.* ◆ ~ (away) *Throughout the interview the journalists scribbled away furiously.* **2** [I] (+ adv./prep.) to draw marks that do not mean anything: *Someone had scribbled all over the table in crayon.*
● *noun* **1** [U, sing.] careless and messy writing **SYN** SCRAWL: *How do you expect me to read this scribble?* **2** [C, usually pl.] marks or pictures that seem to have no meaning **SYN** SCRAWL: *The page was covered with a mass of scribbles.*

scrib·bler /'skrɪblər/ *noun* **1** (*disapproving* or *humorous*) a journalist, author, or other writer **2** (*CanE*) a book with plain paper for writing in, especially for children at school

scribe /skraɪb/ *noun* **1** a person who made copies of written documents before printing was invented **2** (*informal*) a writer, especially a journalist: *As some scribe said, the issue is very complex.*

scrim·mage /'skrɪmɪdʒ/ *noun* **1** (in football) a period of play that begins with the ball being placed on the ground ⮺ see also LINE OF SCRIMMAGE **2** a practice game of football, soccer, basketball, etc.

scrimp /skrɪmp/ *verb* [I] to spend very little money on the things that you need to live, especially so that you can save it to spend on something else: *They scrimped and saved to give the children a good education.*

scrip /skrɪp/ *noun* **1** (*business*) an extra share in a business, given out instead of a DIVIDEND **2** (*informal*) a PRESCRIPTION

script /skrɪpt/ *noun, verb*
● *noun* **1** [C] a written text of a play, movie, broadcast, talk, etc.: *That line isn't in the original script.* **2** [U] writing done by hand: *She admired his neat script.* ⮺ see also MANUSCRIPT **3** [U, C] a set of letters in which a language is written **SYN** ALPHABET: *a document in Cyrillic script* **4** [U, C] (*computing*) a series of instructions for a computer: *The bug was caused by an error in the script.*
● *verb* [often passive] ~ sth to write the script for a movie, play, etc.

script·ed /'skrɪptəd/ *adj.* read from or done according to a script: *a scripted talk* **ANT** UNSCRIPTED

scrip·to·ri·um /skrɪp'tɔriəm/ *noun* (*pl.* scrip·to·ri·ums or scrip·to·ri·a /-'tɔriə/) (*old use*) a room for writing in, especially in a MONASTERY

scrip·ture /'skrɪptʃər/ *noun* **1** Scripture [U] also the Scriptures [pl.] the Bible **2** scriptures [pl.] the holy books of a particular religion: *Hindu scriptures* ▶ scrip·tur·al /'skrɪptʃərəl/ *adj.*: *scriptural references*

script·writ·er /'skrɪpt,raɪtər/ *noun* a person who writes the words for movies, television, and radio plays ⮺ compare PLAYWRIGHT, SCREENWRITER

scrod /skrɑd/ *noun* [U] the white flesh of a young COD or HADDOCK: *The menu choices were scrod and flounder.*

scrof·u·la /'skrɑfyələ/ *noun* [U] (*medical*) a disease in which the GLANDS swell, probably a form of TUBERCULOSIS

scroll /skroʊl/ *noun, verb*
● *noun* **1** a long roll of paper for writing on **2** a decoration cut in stone or wood with a curved shape like a roll of paper
● *verb* [I, T] (*computing*) to move text on a computer screen up or down so that you can read different parts of it: + adv./prep. *Use the arrow keys to scroll through the list of files.* ◆ *Scroll down to the bottom of the document.* ◆ ~ sth *Use the arrow keys to scroll the list of files.*

'scroll bar *noun* (*computing*) a strip at the edge of a computer screen that you use to scroll through a file with, using a mouse

Scrooge /skrudʒ/ *noun* [usually sing.] (*informal, disapproving*) a person who is very unwilling to spend money **ORIGIN** From **Ebenezer Scrooge**, a character in Charles Dickens' *A Christmas Carol.*

scro·tum /ˈskroʊtəm/ *noun* (*pl.* **scro·tums** or **scro·ta** /-tə/) the bag of skin that contains the TESTICLES in men and most male animals

scrounge /skraʊndʒ/ *verb* [T, I] (*informal*, *disapproving*) to get something from someone by asking them for it rather than by paying for it: ◆ **~ (sth) (off/from sb)** *He's always scrounging free meals off us.* ◆ **~ (for sth)** *What is she scrounging for this time?* ▶ **scroung·er** *noun*: *a campaign against welfare scroungers*

scrub /skrʌb/ *verb, noun*
● *verb* (**-bb-**) **1** [T, I] to clean something by rubbing it hard, perhaps with a brush and usually with soap and water: **~ sth/yourself** *I found him in the kitchen, scrubbing the floor.* ◆ **~ sth/yourself down** *She scrubbed the counters down with bleach.* ◆ **~ (at sth)** *The woman scrubbed at her face with a tissue.* ◆ **~ sth/yourself + adj.** *Scrub the vegetables clean.* **2** [T] **~ sth** (*informal*) to cancel something that you have arranged to do
PHRV ,**scrub sth↔ˈoff** | **scrub sth off sth** to remove something from the surface of an object by rubbing it hard with a brush, etc.: *This treatment involves scrubbing off the top layer of dead skin.* ,**scrub sth↔ˈout** to clean the inside of something by rubbing it hard with a brush and usually with soap and water ,**scrub ˈup** (of a doctor, nurse, etc.) to wash your hands and arms before performing a medical operation
● *noun* **1** [sing.] an act of scrubbing something: *I've given the floor a good scrub.* **2** [U] small bushes and trees: *The bird disappeared into the scrub.* **3** (also **scrub·land**) [U] an area of dry land covered with small bushes and trees **4** **scrubs** [pl.] (*technical*) the special clothes worn by SURGEONS when they are doing medical operations

scrub·ber /ˈskrʌbər/ *noun* a brush or other object that you use for cleaning things, for example pans

ˈ**scrub brush** *noun* a stiff brush for cleaning floors and other surfaces ⊃ picture at CLEANING

scrub·by /ˈskrʌbi/ *adj.* **1** covered with small bushes and trees: *a scrubby hillside* **2** (of trees) small and not fully developed: *scrubby vegetation*

scrub·land /ˈskrʌblænd/ *noun* [U] = SCRUB n. (3)

ˈ**scrub nurse** *noun* a nurse with special training, who helps during operations

ˈ**scrub room** *noun* a place in a hospital next to an operating room, where doctors and nurses get ready for operations

scruff /skrʌf/ *noun*
IDM **by the scruff of the/sb's neck** roughly holding the back of an animal's or person's neck: *She grabbed him by the scruff of the neck and threw him out.*

scruff·y /ˈskrʌfi/ *adj.* (**scruff·i·er**, **scruff·i·est**) (*informal*) dirty or messy **SYN** SHABBY: *He looked a little scruffy.* ◆ *a scruffy pair of jeans* ▶ **scruff·i·ly** /-fəli/ *adv.* **scruff·i·ness** /-finəs/ *noun* [U]

scrum /skrʌm/ *noun* **1** a part of a RUGBY game when players from both sides link themselves together in a group, with their heads down, and push against the other side. The ball is then thrown between them and each side tries to get it. **2** the group of players who link themselves together in a scrum

scrump·tious /ˈskrʌmpʃəs/ *adj.* (*informal*) tasting very good **SYN** DELICIOUS

scrunch /skrʌntʃ/ *verb* **1** [I] to make a loud sound like the one that is made when you walk on GRAVEL (= small stones) **SYN** CRUNCH: *The snow scrunched underfoot.* **2** [T] **~ sth (up)** to squeeze something into a small round shape in your hands: *He scrunched up the note and threw it on the fire.* **3** [T] **~ sth (up)** to squeeze something into a smaller shape or into a smaller space: *The armadillo scrunched itself up into a ball.* ◆ *She scrunched up her eyes in the midday sun.* ◆ *Our coats were all scrunched up in the corner.* **4** [T] **~ sth** to create a HAIRSTYLE with loose curls by squeezing the hair with the hands ▶ **scrunch** *noun* [sing.]: *the scrunch of tires on the gravel*

,**scrunch-ˈdry** *verb* **~ sth** to create a HAIRSTYLE with loose curls by drying the hair while squeezing it with your hand

scrunch·ie (also **scrunch·y**) /ˈskrʌntʃi/ *noun* (*pl.* **scrunch·ies**) a RUBBER BAND covered in cloth used to fasten hair away from the face

scru·ple /ˈskrupl/ *noun, verb*
● *noun* [C, usually pl.] a feeling that prevents you from doing something that you think may be morally wrong: *I overcame my moral scruples.* ◆ *He had no scruples about spying on her.* ◆ *She is totally without scruple.*
● *verb* [I] **not scruple to do something** (*formal*) to be willing to do something even if it might be wrong or immoral: *Invading armies didn't scruple to resort to massacre.*

scru·pu·lous /ˈskrupjələs/ *adj.* **1** careful about paying attention to every detail **SYN** METICULOUS: *You must be scrupulous about hygiene when you're preparing a baby's bottle.* ◆ *scrupulous attention to detail* **2** **~ (in sth/in doing sth)** careful to be honest and do what is right: *He was scrupulous in all his business dealings.* **ANT** UNSCRUPULOUS ▶ **scru·pu·lous·ly** *adv.*: *Her house is scrupulously clean.* ◆ *to be scrupulously honest* **scru·pu·lous·ness** *noun* [U]

scru·ti·nize /ˈskrutn̩ˌaɪz/ *verb* **~ sb/sth** to look at or examine someone or something carefully: *She leaned forward to scrutinize their faces.* ◆ *The statement was carefully scrutinized before publication.*

scru·ti·ny /ˈskrutn̩i/ *noun* [U] (*formal*) careful and thorough examination **SYN** INSPECTION: *Her argument doesn't really stand up to scrutiny.* ◆ *Foreign policy has come under close scrutiny recently.* ◆ *The documents should be available for public scrutiny.*

scu·ba div·ing /ˈskubə ˌdaɪvɪŋ/ (also **scu·ba**) *noun* [U] the sport or activity of swimming underwater using special breathing equipment consisting of a container of air that you carry on your back and a tube through which you breathe the air: *to go scuba diving* ⊃ picture at HOBBY

scud /skʌd/ *verb* (**-dd-**) [I] **+ adv./prep.** (*literary*) (of clouds) to move quickly across the sky

scuff /skʌf/ *verb* **1** **~ sth (on sth)** to make a mark on the smooth surface of something when you rub it against something rough: *I scuffed the heel of my shoe on the stonework.* **2** **~ your feet, heels, etc.** to drag your feet along the ground as you walk ▶ **scuffed** *adj.*: *After only one day, his shoes were already scuffed and dirty.* **scuff** (also ˈ**scuff mark**) *noun*

scuf·fle /ˈskʌfl/ *noun, verb*
● *noun* **~ (with sb)** | **~ (between A and B)** a short and not very violent fight or struggle: *Scuffles broke out between police and demonstrators.* ⊃ thesaurus box at FIGHT
● *verb* **1** [I] **~ (with sb)** (of two or more people) to fight or struggle with each other for a short time, in a way that is not very serious: *She scuffled with photographers as she left her hotel.* **2** [I] **+ adv./prep.** to move quickly, making a quiet rubbing noise: *Some animal was scuffling in the bushes.*

scuf·fling /ˈskʌflɪŋ/ *noun* [U] a low noise made by something moving around: *He could hear whispering and scuffling on the other side of the door.*

scull /skʌl/ *noun, verb*
● *noun* **1** [C, usually pl.] one of a pair of small OARS used by a single person ROWING a boat, one in each hand **2** **sculls** [pl.] a race between small, light boats with pairs of sculls: *single/double sculls* (= with one/two people in each boat) **3** [C] a small, light boat used in sculls races
● *verb* [I] to ROW a boat using sculls

scul·ler /ˈskʌlər/ *noun* a person who ROWS with sculls

scul·ler·y /ˈskʌləri/ *noun* (*pl.* **scul·ler·ies**) a small room next to the kitchen in an old house, originally used for washing dishes, etc.

scul·ling /ˈskʌlɪŋ/ *noun* [U] the sport of racing with SCULLS

sculpt /skʌlpt/ *verb* [usually passive] **1** to make figures or objects by CARVING or shaping wood, stone, CLAY, metal, etc.: **~ sth (in sth)** *a display of animals sculpted in ice* ◆ **~ sth**

(from/out of sth) *The figures were sculpted from single blocks of marble.* ⊃ collocations at ART **2** ~ **sth** to give something a particular shape: *a coastline sculpted by the wind and sea*

sculp·tor /ˈskʌlptər/ *noun* a person who makes SCULPTURES

sculp·tress /ˈskʌlptrəs/ *noun* a woman who makes SCULPTURES

sculp·ture /ˈskʌlptʃər/ *noun* **1** [C, U] a work of art that is a solid figure or object made by CARVING or shaping wood, stone, CLAY, metal, etc.: *a marble sculpture of Venus* ♦ *He collects modern sculpture.* ⊃ collocations at ART **2** [U] the art of making sculptures: *the techniques of sculpture in stone* ▸ **sculp·tur·al** /ˈskʌlptʃərəl/ *adj.*: *sculptural decoration*

sculp·tured /ˈskʌlptʃərd/ *adj.* [usually before noun] **1** (of figures or objects) CARVED or shaped from wood, stone, CLAY, metal, etc. **2** (*approving*) (of part of the body) having a clear and pleasing shape: *sculptured cheekbones*

scum /skʌm/ *noun* **1** [U, sing.] a layer of bubbles or an unpleasant substance that forms on the surface of a liquid: *Skim off any scum.* ♦ *stinking water covered by a thick green scum* **2** (*informal*) [pl.] an insulting word for people that you strongly disapprove of: *Don't waste your sympathy on scum like that.* ♦ *Drug dealers are the scum of the earth* (= the worst people there are). ▸ **scum·my** /ˈskʌmi/ *adj.*: *scummy water* ♦ *scummy people dropping litter*

scum·bag /ˈskʌmbæg/ *noun* (*slang, offensive*) an unpleasant person

scur·ril·ous /ˈskərələs/ *adj.* (*formal*) very rude and insulting, and intended to damage someone's reputation: *scurrilous rumors* ▸ **scur·ril·ous·ly** *adv.*

scur·ry /ˈskəri/ *verb* (**scur·ries, scur·ry·ing, scur·ried, scur·ried**) [I] **+ adv./prep.** to run with quick, short steps **SYN** SCUTTLE: *She said goodbye and scurried back to work.* ♦ *Ants scurried around the pile of rotting food.* ▸ **scur·ry** *noun* [sing.]

scur·vy /ˈskərvi/ *noun* [U] a disease caused by a lack of VITAMIN C from not eating enough fruit and vegetables

scut·tle /ˈskʌtl/ *verb* **1** [I] **+ adv./prep.** to run with quick, short steps **SYN** SCURRY: *She scuttled off when she heard the sound of his voice.* ♦ *He held his breath as a rat scuttled past.* **2** [T] ~ **sth** to deliberately cause something to fail **SYN** FOIL: *Shareholders successfully scuttled the deal.* **3** [T] ~ **sth** to sink a ship deliberately by making holes in the side or bottom of it

scut·tle·butt /ˈskʌtlˌbʌt/ *noun* [U] (*slang*) stories about other people's private lives, that may be unkind or not true **SYN** GOSSIP

scuzz·y /ˈskʌzi/ *adj.* (**scuzz·i·er, scuzz·i·est**) (*informal*) dirty and unpleasant

Scyl·la and Cha·ryb·dis /ˌsɪlə ən kəˈrɪbdəs/ *noun* used to refer to a situation in which an attempt to avoid one danger increases the risk from another danger **ORIGIN** From ancient Greek stories in which a female sea creature (called Scylla) tried to catch and eat sailors who passed between her cave and a whirlpool (called Charybdis).

scythe /saɪð/ *noun, verb*
● *noun* a tool with a long handle and a slightly curved blade, used for cutting long grass, etc.
● *verb* [T, I] ~ **(sth)** to cut grass, etc. with a scythe: *the scent of newly scythed grass*

SD *abbr.* (in writing) South Dakota

SD card /ˌɛs ˈdi kɑrd/ *noun* the abbreviation for "secure digital card" (a type of MEMORY CARD, used with DIGITAL cameras, cell phones, music players, etc.)

SDHC card /ˌɛs di eɪtʃ ˈsi kɑrd/ *noun* the abbreviation for "secure digital high capacity card" (a type of MEMORY CARD that can store more data than an SD card)

SDI /ˌɛs di ˈaɪ/ *abbr.* STRATEGIC DEFENSE INITIATIVE

S.E. (also SE) *abbr.* (in writing) southeast; south-eastern: *S.E. Asia*

sea 🔊 /si/ *noun*
1 often **the sea** [U] (also *literary* **seas** [pl.]) the salt water that covers most of the earth's surface and surrounds its continents and islands: *to travel by sea* ♦ *We left port and headed for the open sea* (= far away from land). ♦ *the cold seas of the Arctic* ♦ *a sea voyage* ♦ *a hotel room with a sea view* ⊃ see also THE HIGH SEAS, OCEAN **2** [C] (often **Sea**, especially as part of a name) a large area of salt water that is part of an ocean or surrounded by land: *the North Sea* ♦ *the Caspian Sea* **3** [C] also **seas** [pl.] the movement of the waves of the ocean: *It was a calm sea.* ♦ *The sea was very rough.* **4** [sing.] ~ **of sth** a large amount of something that stretches over a wide area: *He looked down at the sea of smiling faces before him.*
IDM **at sea 1** on the ocean, especially in a ship, or in the ocean: *It happened on the second night at sea.* ♦ *They were lost at sea.* **2** confused and not knowing what to do: *I'm all at sea with these new regulations.* **go to sea** to become a sailor **out to sea** far away from land where the ocean is deepest: *She fell overboard and was swept out to sea.* **put (out) to sea** to leave a port or HARBOR by ship or boat ⊃ more at DEVIL, FISH *n.*

ˌsea ˈair *noun* [U] air near the ocean, thought to be good for the health: *Smell that sea air!*

ˈsea aˌnemone *noun* a simple, brightly colored sea creature that sticks onto rocks and looks like a flower

the ˈsea·bed /ˈsibɛd/ *noun* [sing.] the floor of the ocean

sea·bird /ˈsibərd/ *noun* a bird that lives close to the ocean, for example on CLIFFS or islands, and gets its food from it

sea·board /ˈsibɔrd/ *noun* the part of a country that is along its coast: *the Atlantic seaboard*

sea·bor·gi·um /siˈbɔrgiəm/ *noun* [U] (*symb.* **Sg**) a RADIOACTIVE chemical element. Seaborgium is produced when atoms COLLIDE (= crash into each other).

sea·borne /ˈsibɔrn/ *adj.* [only before noun] carried in ships: *a seaborne invasion*

ˌsea ˈbreeze *noun* a wind blowing from the ocean toward the land

ˈsea ˌcaptain *noun* the captain of a ship

ˈsea change *noun* [usually sing.] a strong and noticeable change in a situation

ˈsea ˌchantey *noun* = CHANTEY

ˌsea ˈcucumber *noun* an INVERTEBRATE animal that lives in the ocean, with a thick body that is covered with lumps

ˈsea dog *noun* (*informal*) a sailor who is old or who has a lot of experience

sea·far·er /ˈsiˌfɛrər/ *noun* (*old-fashioned* or *formal*) a sailor

sea·far·ing /ˈsiˌfɛrɪŋ/ *adj.* [only before noun] connected with work or travel on the ocean: *a seafaring nation* ▸ **sea·far·ing** *noun* [U]

sea·food /ˈsifud/ *noun* [U] fish and sea creatures that can be eaten, especially SHELLFISH: *a seafood restaurant* ♦ *a seafood cocktail*

sea·front /ˈsifrʌnt/ /= OCEANFRONT

sea·go·ing /ˈsiˌɡoʊɪŋ/ *adj.* [only before noun] (of ships) built for crossing the ocean

sea·grass /ˈsigræs/ *noun* [U] a plant like grass that grows in or close to the ocean

ˌsea-ˈgreen *adj.* bluish-green in color, like the ocean ▸ **ˌsea ˈgreen** *noun* [U]

sea·gull /ˈsigʌl/ *noun* = GULL: *A flock of seagulls flew over the lake.*

ˈsea horse *noun* a small sea fish that swims in a vertical position and has a head that looks like the head of a horse

seal 🔊 /sil/ *verb, noun*
● *verb*
▷ CLOSE ENVELOPE **1** ~ **sth (up/down)** to close an envelope, etc. by sticking the edges of the opening together: *Make sure you've signed the check before sealing the envelope.* ♦ *a sealed bid* (= one that is kept in a sealed envelope and therefore remains secret until all other bids have been received)

| h **hat** | m **man** | n **no** | ŋ **sing** | l **leg** | r **red** | y **yes** | w **wet** |

> **CLOSE CONTAINER 2** [often passive] **~ sth (up) (with sth)** to close a container tightly or fill a crack, etc., especially so that air, liquid, etc. cannot get in or out: *The organs are kept in sealed plastic bags.*

> **COVER SURFACE 3** [often passive] **~ sth (with sth)** to cover the surface of something with a substance in order to protect it: *The floors had been stripped and sealed with varnish.*

> **MAKE SOMETHING DEFINITE 4 ~ sth** to make something definite, so that it cannot be changed or argued about: *to seal a contract* ♦ *They drank a glass of wine to seal their new friendship.* ♦ *Both firms hope to seal the deal soon.* ♦ *The discovery of new evidence sealed his fate* (= nothing could prevent what was going to happen to him).

> **CLOSE BORDERS/EXITS 5 ~ sth** (of the police, army, etc.) to prevent people from passing through a place: *Troops have sealed the borders between the countries.* **IDM** see LIP, SIGN v. **PHR V** ,seal sth↔'in to prevent something that is contained in something else from escaping 'seal sth in sth to put something in an envelope, container, etc. and seal it: *The body was sealed in a lead coffin.* ,seal sth↔'off (of the police, army) to prevent people from entering a particular area

● **noun**

> **SEA ANIMAL 1** [C] a sea animal that eats fish and lives around coasts. There are many types of seals, some of which are hunted for their fur: *a colony of seals* ♦ *harbor seals basking on the rocks*

> **OFFICIAL MARK 2** [C] an official design or mark, stamped on a document to show that it is genuine and carries the authority of a particular person or organization: *The letter bore the president's seal.*

> **MAKING SOMETHING DEFINITE 3** [sing.] a thing that makes something definite: *The project has been given the government's seal of approval* (= official approval). ♦ *I looked upon the gift as a seal on our friendship.*

> **ON CONTAINERS 4** [C] a substance, strip of material, etc. used to fill a crack so that air, liquid, etc. cannot get in or out: *a jar with a rubber seal in the lid* ♦ *Only drink bottled water and check the seal isn't broken.*

> **ON LETTERS/BOXES 5** [C] a piece of WAX (= a soft substance produced by BEES), soft metal, or paper that is placed across the opening of something such as a letter or box and that has to be broken before the letter or box can be opened: *He broke the wax seal and unrolled the paper.* **6** a piece of metal, a ring, etc. with a design on it, used for stamping a WAX or metal seal

IDM **set the seal on sth** (*formal*) to make something definite or complete: *Her election to the premiership set the seal on a remarkable political career.* **under seal** (*formal*) (of a document) in a sealed envelope that cannot be opened before a particular time

'**sea lane** *noun* an official route at sea that is regularly used by ships

seal·ant /'silənt/ (also **seal·er**) *noun* [U, C] a substance that is put onto a surface to stop air, water, etc. from entering or escaping from it

'**sea legs** *noun* [pl.] the ability to walk easily on a moving ship and not to feel sick at sea: *It won't take you long to find your sea legs.*

seal·er /'silər/ *noun* **1** = SEALANT **2** a person who hunts SEALS

'**sea ,level** *noun* [U] the average height of the ocean, used as the basis for measuring the height of all places on land: *1,000 feet above sea level*

sea·lift /'silɪft/ *noun* an operation to take people, soldiers, food, etc. to or from an area by ship, especially in an emergency ▶ **sea·lift** *verb* ⊃ compare AIRLIFT

seal·ing /'silɪŋ/ *noun* [U] the activity of hunting SEALS

'**sealing ,wax** *noun* [U] a type of WAX that melts quickly when it is heated and becomes hard quickly when it cools, used in the past for SEALING letters, etc.

'**sea ,lion** *noun* a large SEAL (= a sea animal with thick fur,

that eats fish and lives around the coast) that lives by the Pacific Ocean

seal·skin /'silskɪn/ *noun* [U] the skin and fur of some types of SEALS, used for making clothes

seam /sim/ *noun* **1** a line along which two edges of cloth, etc. are joined or sewn together: *a shoulder seam* **2** a thin layer of coal or other material, between layers of rock under the ground: *They struck a rich seam of iron ore.* ♦ (*figurative*) *The book is a rich seam of information.* **3** a line where two edges meet, for example the edges of wooden boards

IDM **be bursting/bulging at the seams** (*informal*) to be very full, especially of people **be falling/coming apart at the seams** (*informal*) to be going very badly wrong and likely to stop functioning completely: *She was falling apart at the seams, spending most of her time in tears.*

sea·man /'simən/ *noun* (*pl.* **sea·men** /-mən/) a member of the navy or a sailor on a ship, below the rank of an officer: *Seaman Bates* ♦ *a merchant seaman*

sea·man·ship /'simən,ʃɪp/ *noun* [U] skill in sailing a boat or ship

seamed /simd/ *adj.* **1** having a seam or seams: *seamed stockings* **2** (*literary*) covered with deep lines: *an old man with a brown seamed face*

'**sea mile** *noun* = NAUTICAL MILE

seam·less /'simləs/ *adj.* **1** without a SEAM: *a seamless garment* **2** with no spaces or pauses between one part and the next: *a seamless flow of talk* ▶ **seam·less·ly** *adv.*

seam·stress /'simstrəs/ *noun* (*old-fashioned*) a woman who can sew and make clothes or whose job is sewing and making clothes

seam·y /'simi/ *adj.* (**seam·i·er**, **seam·i·est**) unpleasant and immoral **SYN** SORDID: *a seamy sex scandal* ♦ *the seamier side of life*

se·ance /'seɪɑns/ *noun* a meeting at which people try to make contact with and talk to the spirits of dead people

sea·plane /'siplein/ (also **hy·dro·plane**) *noun* a plane that can take off from and land on water ⊃ picture at PLANE

sea·port /'sipɔrt/ *noun* a town with a HARBOR used by large ships: *the Pacific seaports*

'**sea power** *noun* **1** [U] the ability to control the seas with a strong navy **2** [C] a country with a strong navy

sear /sɪr/ *verb* **1** [T] **~ sth** to burn the surface of something in a way that is sudden and powerful: *The heat of the sun seared their faces.* ♦ *Sear the meat first* (= cook the outside of it quickly at a high temperature) *to retain its juices.* **2** [I, T] (*formal*) to cause someone to feel sudden and great pain: *+ adv./prep. The pain seared along her arm.* ♦ **~ sb** *Feelings of guilt seared him.* ⊃ see also SEARING

search 🔍 /sərtʃ/ *noun, verb*

● **noun 1 ~ (for sth/sb)** an attempt to find someone or something, especially by looking carefully for them/it: *a long search for the murder weapon* ♦ *Detectives carried out a thorough search of the building.* ♦ *She went into the kitchen in search of* (= looking for) *a drink.* ♦ *The search for a cure goes on.* ♦ *The search is on* (= has begun) *for someone to fill the post.* ♦ *Eventually the search was called off.* ♦ *a search and rescue team* **2** (*computing*) an act of looking for information in a computer DATABASE or network: *to do a search on the Internet*

● **verb 1** [I, T] to look carefully for something or someone; to examine a particular place when looking for someone or something: **~ (for sth/sb)** *She searched in vain for her passport.* ♦ *Police searched for clues in the area.* ♦ *+ adv./prep. The customs officers searched through our bags.* ♦ *I've searched high and low for those files.* ♦ **~ sth** *His house had clearly been searched and the book was missing.* ♦ **~ sth for sth/sb** *Police searched the area for clues.* ♦ *Firefighters searched the buildings for survivors.* ♦ *searching the Web for interesting sites* **2** [T] (especially of the police) to examine someone's clothes, their pockets, etc. in order to find something that they may be hiding: **~ sb** *Visitors are regularly searched as they enter the building.* ♦ **~ sb for sth** *The youths were arrested and searched*

for anything that would incriminate them. ⊃ see also STRIP
SEARCH **3** [I] ~ **(for sth)** to think carefully about something,
especially in order to find the answer to a problem: *He
searched desperately for something to say.* ⊃ see also SOUL-
SEARCHING
IDM search me (*informal*) used to emphasize that you do
not know the answer to someone's question: *"Why didn't
she say anything?" "Search me!"*
PHR V ˌsearch sth/sb⟷ˈout to look for something or
someone until you find them **SYN** TRACK DOWN: *Fighter
pilots searched out and attacked enemy aircraft.*

search·a·ble /ˈsɜrtʃəbl/ *adj.* (of a computer DATABASE or
network) having information organized in such a way that
it can be searched for using a computer: *a searchable
database*

ˈsearch ˌengine *noun* a computer program that searches
the Internet for information, especially by looking for
documents containing a particular word or group of words

search·er /ˈsɜrtʃər/ *noun* **1** a person who is trying to find
something or someone **2** (*computing*) a program that helps
you find information in a computer DATABASE or network

search·ing /ˈsɜrtʃɪŋ/ *adj.* [usually before noun] (of a look, a
question, etc.) trying to find out the truth about something;
thorough and serious: *a searching investigation/analysis/
examination* ♦ *He gave her a long, searching look.* ♦ *The police
asked him some searching questions.* ▶ **search·ing·ly** *adv.*

search·light /ˈsɜrtʃlaɪt/ *noun* a powerful lamp that can be
turned in any direction, used, for example, for finding
people or vehicles at night

ˈsearch ˌparty *noun* an organized group of people who are
looking for a person or thing that is missing or lost

ˈsearch ˌwarrant *noun* an official document that allows
the police to search a building, for example to look for
stolen property

sear·ing /ˈsɪrɪŋ/ *adj.* [usually before noun] (*formal*) **1** so
strong that it seems to burn you: *the searing heat of a tropical
summer* ♦ *searing pain* **2** (of words or speech) powerful and
critical: *a searing attack on the government* ▶ **sear·ing·ly**
adv. ⊃ see also SEAR

ˈsea salt *noun* [U] a type of salt that is obtained from ocean
water

sea·scape /ˈsiskeɪp/ *noun* a picture or view of the ocean
⊃ compare TOWNSCAPE

sea·shell /ˈsiʃɛl/ *noun* the shell of a small creature that lives
in the ocean, often found empty when the creature has died

sea·shore /ˈsiʃɔr/ *noun* usually **the seashore** [usually sing.]
the land along the edge of the ocean, usually where there is
sand and rocks ⊃ thesaurus box at COAST

sea·sick /ˈsisɪk/ *adj.* [not usually before noun] feeling sick or
wanting to VOMIT when you are traveling on a boat or ship:
to be/feel/get seasick ▶ ˈsea·sick·ness *noun* [U]

sea·side /ˈsisaɪd/ *adj.* [only before noun] in an area near the
ocean: *a seaside resort* ♦ *a seaside vacation home*

sea·son 🔑 /ˈsizn/ *noun, verb*
● *noun* **1** any of the four main periods of the year: spring,
summer, fall, and winter: *the changing seasons* **2 the dry/
rainy/wet** ~ a period of the year in tropical countries when
it is either very dry or it rains a lot **3** a period of time during
a year when a particular activity happens or is done: *the
football/hunting/shooting, etc. season* ♦ *He scored his first
goal of the season on Saturday.* ♦ *The female changes color
during the breeding season.* ♦ *The hotels are always full during
the peak season* (= when most people are on vacation). ♦ *the
tourist season* ♦ *the holiday season* (= the time of Thanksgiving, Hanukkah, Christmas, and New Year) ⊃ see also CLOSED
SEASON[2], HIGH SEASON, OFF-SEASON **4** a period of time in
which a play is shown in one place; a series of plays,
movies, or television programs: *The play opens for a second
season in New York next week.* ♦ *a season of films by Alfred
Hitchcock* **5** a period of time during one year when a
particular style of clothes, hair, etc. is popular and

fashionable: *This season's look is soft and romantic.*
IDM **in season 1** (of fruit or vegetables) easily available
and ready to eat because it is the right time of year for them
2 (of a female animal) ready to reproduce **SYN** IN HEAT **out
of season 1** (of fruit or vegetables) not easily available
because it is not the right time of year for them **2** at the
times of year when few people go on vacation: *Hotels are
cheaper out of season.* **season's greetings** used at Christmas to wish someone an enjoyable holiday
▸ *verb* [T, I] ~ **(sth) (with sth)** to add salt, pepper, etc. to food
in order to give it more flavor: *Season the lamb with garlic.*
♦ *Add the mushrooms, and season to taste* (= add as much salt,
pepper, etc. as you think is necessary).

sea·son·a·ble /ˈsizənbl/ *adj.* usual or suitable for the time
of year: *seasonable temperatures* **ANT** UNSEASONABLE

sea·son·al /ˈsizənl/ *adj.* **1** happening or needed during a
particular season; varying with the seasons: *seasonal
workers brought in to cope with the Christmas period* ♦ *seasonal
variations in unemployment figures* **2** typical of or suitable for
the time of year, especially Christmas: *seasonal decorations*
ANT UNSEASONAL ▶ **sea·son·al·ly** /-nəli/ *adv.*: *seasonally
adjusted unemployment figures* (= not including the changes
that always happen in different seasons)

ˌseasonal afˈfective disˌorder *noun* [U] (*abbr.* SAD) a
medical condition in which a person feels sad and tired
during late fall and winter when there is not much light
from the sun

sea·son·al·i·ty /ˌsizəˈnæləti/ *noun* [U, sing.] (*technical*) the
fact of varying with the seasons: *a high degree of climatic
seasonality*

sea·soned /ˈsiznd/ *adj.* **1** [usually before noun] (of a person)
having a lot of experience of a particular activity: *a seasoned
campaigner/performer/traveler, etc.* **2** (of food) with salt,
pepper, etc. added to it: *The sausage was very highly
seasoned.* **3** (of wood) made suitable for use by being left
outside

sea·son·ing /ˈsizənɪŋ/ *noun* [U, C] a substance used to add
flavor to food, especially salt and pepper

ˌseason preˈmiere *noun* the first show of a new season for
a television series that is continuing: *The season premiere is
scheduled for September 21.*

ˌseason ˈticket *noun* a ticket that you can use many times
within a particular period for a series of sports games,
concerts, plays, etc. and that usually costs less than paying
separately each time: *a season ticket holder* ♦ *season tickets to
the opera*

seat 🔑 /sit/ *noun, verb*
● *noun*
▸ **PLACE TO SIT 1** a place where you can sit, for example a
chair: *She sat back in her seat.* ♦ *He put his bags on the seat
behind him.* ♦ *Please take a seat* (= sit down). ♦ *Ladies and
gentlemen, please take your seats* (= sit down). ♦ *a window/
corner seat* (= one near a window/in a corner) ♦ *a child seat*
(= for a child in a car) ♦ *Would you prefer a window seat or an
aisle seat?* (= on a plane) ♦ *We used the branch of an old tree as a
seat.* ♦ *We all filed back to our seats in silence.* ⊃ see also BACK
SEAT, BUCKET SEAT, EJECTION SEAT, HOT SEAT, LOVE SEAT,
PASSENGER SEAT
▸ **-SEATER 2** (in nouns and adjectives) with the number of
seats mentioned: *a ten-seater minibus*
▸ **PART OF CHAIR 3** the part of a chair, etc. on which you
actually sit: *a steel chair with a plastic seat*
▸ **IN PLANE/TRAIN/THEATER 4** a place where you pay to sit in a
plane, train, theater, etc.: *to reserve a seat* (= for a concert,
etc.) ♦ *There are no seats left on that flight.*
▸ **OFFICIAL POSITION 5** an official position as a member of a
council, committee, etc.: *a seat on the city council/in Congress*
♦ *to win/lose a seat* (= in an election) ♦ *The majority of seats on
the board will be held by business representatives.*
▸ **TOWN/CITY 6** ~ **of sth** (*formal*) a place where people are
involved in a particular activity, especially a city that has a
university or the offices of a government: *Washington is the*

seat of government of the U.S. ◆ *a university town renowned as a seat of learning*

> **PART OF BODY 7** (especially *formal*) the part of the body on which a person sits **SYN** BUTTOCKS

> **PART OF PANTS 8** the part of a pair of pants that covers a person's seat

IDM (fly) by the seat of your pants (*informal*) to act without careful thought and without a plan that you have made in advance, hoping that you will be lucky and be successful **SYN** WING IT **be in the driver's seat** to be the person in control of a situation ⊃ more at BACK SEAT, CATBIRD, EDGE *n.*

● *verb*
> **SIT DOWN 1** ~ sb/yourself (*formal*) to give someone a place to sit; to sit down in a place: *Please wait to be seated* (= in a restaurant, etc.). ◆ *Please be seated* (= sit down). ◆ *He seated himself behind the desk.* ⊃ thesaurus box at SIT

> **OF BUILDING/VEHICLE 2** ~ sb to have enough seats for a particular number of people: *The aircraft seats 200 passengers.*

seat belt (also **safety belt**) *noun* a belt that is attached to the seat in a car or a plane and that you fasten around yourself so that you are not thrown out of the seat if there is an accident: *Fasten your seat belts.* ⊃ picture at CAR ● collocations at DRIVING

seat·ing /ˈsiːtɪŋ/ *noun* [U] places to sit; seats: *The theater has seating for about 500 people.* ◆ *The room had a seating capacity of over 200.* ◆ *the seating arrangements/plan for the conference*

seat·mate /ˈsiːtmeɪt/ *noun* a person that you sit next to when you are traveling, especially on a plane

seat sale *noun* (*CanE*) a sale of flight tickets at a reduced price

sea turtle *noun* = TURTLE ⊃ picture at ANIMAL

sea urchin (also **ur·chin**) *noun* a small sea creature with a round shell that is covered with SPIKES

sea wall *noun* a large strong wall built to stop the ocean from flowing onto the land

sea·ward /ˈsiːwərd/ *adj.* toward the ocean; in the direction of the ocean: *the seaward side of the coastal road* ▶ **sea·ward** (also **sea·wards**) *adv.*: *Her gaze was focused seawards.*

sea water *noun* [U] water from the ocean, that is salty

sea·way /ˈsiːweɪ/ *noun* a passage from the ocean through the land along which large ships can travel

sea·weed /ˈsiːwiːd/ *noun* [U, C] a plant that grows in the ocean or on rocks at the edge of the ocean. There are many different types of seaweed, some of which are eaten as food.

sea·wor·thy /ˈsiːˌwɜrði/ *adj.* (of a ship) in a suitable condition to sail ▶ **sea·wor·thi·ness** *noun* [U]

se·ba·ceous /sɪˈbeɪʃəs/ *adj.* [usually before noun] (*biology*) producing a substance like oil in the body: *the sebaceous glands in the skin*

seb·or·rhe·a /ˌsɛbəˈriːə/ *noun* [U] a medical condition of the skin in which an unusually large amount of SEBUM is produced by the SEBACEOUS GLANDS ▶ **seb·or·rhe·ic** /ˌsɛbəˈriːɪk/ *adj.*

se·bum /ˈsiːbəm/ *noun* [U] an oil-like substance produced by the SEBACEOUS GLANDS

SEC /ˌɛs iː ˈsiː/ *abbr.* Securities and Exchange Commission (a U.S. government organization that controls how STOCKS and BONDS are traded to make sure that this is done in an honest way)

sec /sɛk/ *noun* **a sec** [sing.] (*informal*) a very short time; a second: *Stay there. I'll be back in a sec.* ◆ *Hang on* (= wait) *a sec.*

Sec. (also **Secy.**) *abbr.* SECRETARY

sec. *abbr.* second(s)

se·cede /sɪˈsiːd/ *verb* [I] ~ (from sth) (*formal*) (of a state, country, etc.) to officially leave an organization of states, countries, etc. and become independent: *The Republic of Panama seceded from Colombia in 1903.*

se·ces·sion /sɪˈsɛʃn/ *noun* [U, C] ~ (from sth) the fact of an area or group becoming independent from the country or larger group that it belongs to

se·ces·sion·ist /sɪˈsɛʃənɪst/ *adj.* [only before noun] supporting or connected with secession ▶ **se·ces·sion·ist** *noun*: *a military campaign against the secessionists*

se·clude /sɪˈkluːd/ *verb* ~ yourself/sb (from sb/sth) (*formal*) to keep yourself or someone away from contact with other people

se·clud·ed /sɪˈkluːdəd/ *adj.* **1** (of a place) quiet and private; not used or disturbed by other people: *a secluded garden/beach/spot, etc.* **2** without much contact with other people **SYN** SOLITARY: *to lead a secluded life*

se·clu·sion /sɪˈkluːʒn/ *noun* [U] the state of being private or of having little contact with other people: *the seclusion and peace of the island*

sec·ond 🔊 /ˈsɛkənd/ *det., ordinal number, adv., noun, verb*

● *det., ordinal number* **1** happening or coming next after the first in a series of similar things or people; 2nd: *This is the second time it's happened.* ◆ *The Panthers scored a second goal just after half-time.* ◆ *the second of June/June 2nd* ◆ *He was the second to arrive.* ◆ *We have one child and are expecting our second in July.* **2** next in order of importance, size, quality, etc. to one other person or thing: *Osaka is Japan's second-largest city.* ◆ *Chicago, America's second city* ◆ *The spreadsheet application is second only to word processing in terms of popularity.* ◆ *As a dancer, he is second to none* (= nobody is a better dancer than he is). **3** [only before noun] another; in addition to one that you already own or use: *They have a second home in Arizona.*

● *adv.* **1** after one other person or thing in order or importance: *She finished second in the marathon.* ◆ *One of the smaller parties finished a close second* (= nearly won). ◆ *I agreed to speak second.* ◆ *He is a writer first and a scientist second.* ◆ *I finished second (to) last* (= the one before the last one) *in the race.* **2** used to introduce the second of a list of points you want to make in a speech or piece of writing **SYN** SECONDLY: *She did it first because she wanted to, and second because I asked her to.* ⊃ language bank at FIRST, PROCESS[1]

● *noun* **1** [C] (*symb* ʺ) (*abbr.* sec.) a unit for measuring time. There are 60 seconds in one minute: *She can run 100 meters in just over 11 seconds.* ◆ *For several seconds he did not reply.* ◆ *The light flashes every 5 seconds.* ◆ *The water flows at about 3 feet per second.* **2** [C] (also *informal* sec) a very short time **SYN** MOMENT: *I'll be with you in a second.* ◆ *They had finished in/within seconds.* ⊃ see also SPLIT SECOND **3** [C] (*symb.* ʺ) a unit for measuring angles. There are 60 seconds in one minute: *1° 6′ 10″* (= one degree, six minutes, and ten seconds) **4 seconds** [pl.] (*informal*) a second amount of the same food that you have just eaten: *Seconds, anybody?* **5** [C, usually pl.] an item that is sold at a lower price than usual because it is not perfect **6** (also **second 'gear**) [U] one of four or five positions of the gears in a vehicle: *When it's icy, start off in second.* **7** [C] a person whose role is to help and support someone else, for example in a BOXING match or in a formal DUEL in the past **IDM** see JUST *adv.*, WAIT *v.*

● *verb* ~ sth to state officially at a meeting that you support another person's idea, suggestion, etc. so that it can be discussed and/or voted on: *Any proposal must be seconded by two other members of the committee.* ◆ (*informal*) *"Thank God that's finished." "I'll second that!"* (= I agree) ⊃ compare PROPOSE

sec·ond·ar·y 🔊 /ˈsɛkənˌdɛri/ *adj.*
1 less important than something else: *That is just a secondary consideration.* ◆ *Experience is what matters—age is of secondary importance.* ◆ ~ to sth *Raising animals was only secondary to other forms of farming.* **2** happening as a result of something else: *a secondary infection* ◆ *a secondary effect* ◆ *a secondary color* (= made from mixing two primary colors) **3** [only before noun] connected with teaching children of

11-18 years: *secondary teachers* ◆ *the secondary curriculum* ⊃ compare ELEMENTARY, PRIMARY ▶ **sec·ond·ar·i·ly** /ˌsɛkənˈdɛrəli/ *adv.*: *Their clothing is primarily functional and only secondarily decorative.*

ˌsecondary eduˈcation *noun* [U] education for children between the ages of 11 and 18: *primary and secondary education*

ˌsecondary ˈindustry *noun* [U, C] (*economics*) the section of industry that uses RAW MATERIALS to make goods ⊃ compare PRIMARY INDUSTRY, TERTIARY INDUSTRY

ˈsecondary ˌschool *noun* a school for young people between the ages of 11 and 18 ⊃ compare PRIMARY SCHOOL, HIGH SCHOOL

ˌsecondary ˈsource *noun* a book or other source of information where the writer has taken the information from some other source and not collected it himself or herself ⊃ compare PRIMARY SOURCE

ˌsecondary ˈstress *noun* [U, C] (*phonetics*) the second strongest stress that is put on a syllable in a word or a phrase when it is spoken ⊃ compare PRIMARY STRESS

ˌsecond baˈnana *noun* (*informal*) an assistant, or a person who has a less important job or position than someone else: *He was tired of always playing second banana.* ⊃ compare TOP BANANA

ˌsecond ˈbase *noun* [sing.] (in baseball) the second of the BASES that players must touch ⊃ picture at BASEBALL

ˌsecond ˈbest *adj.* **1** not as good as the best: *The two teams seemed evenly matched but in the end the Knicks were second best* (= did not win). ◆ *my second-best suit* **2** not exactly what you want; not perfect: *a second-best solution* ▶ ˌsecond ˈbest *noun* [U]: *Sometimes you have to settle for* (= be content with) *second best.*

ˌsecond ˈclass *noun* [U] **1** the system of sending newspapers and magazines by mail **2** a way of traveling on a train or ship that costs less and is less comfortable than FIRST CLASS.

ˌsecond-ˈclass *adj.* **1** (*disapproving*) (of a person) less important than other people: *Older people should not be treated as second-class citizens.* **2** of a lower standard or quality than the best: *a second-class education* **3** connected with the system of sending newspapers and magazines by mail **4** [only before noun] connected with the less expensive way of traveling on a train, ship, etc.: *second-class carriages/ compartments/passengers* ▶ ˌsecond ˈclass *adv.*: *to send a magazine second class* ◆ *to travel second class*

the ˌSecond ˈComing *noun* [sing.] a day in the future when Christians believe Jesus Christ will come back to earth

ˌsecond ˈcousin *noun* a child of a cousin of your mother or father

ˌsecond-deˈgree *adj.* [only before noun] **1** ~ **murder, assault, burglary, etc.** murder, etc. that is less serious than FIRST-DEGREE crimes **2** ~ **burns** burns of the second most serious of three kinds, causing BLISTERS but no permanent marks ⊃ compare FIRST-DEGREE, THIRD-DEGREE

ˌsecond-geneˈration *adj.* **1** used to describe people who were born in the country they live in but whose parents came to live there from another country: *She was a second-generation Japanese-American.* **2** (of a product, technology, etc.) at a more advanced stage of development than an earlier form: *second-generation hand-held computers*

ˌsecond-ˈguess *verb* **1** [T, I] ~ **(sb/sth)** to criticize someone after a decision has been made; to criticize something after it has happened **2** [T] ~ **sb/sth** to guess what someone will do before they do it: *It was impossible to second-guess the decision of the jury.*

ˈsecond ˌhand *noun* the hand on some watches and clocks that shows seconds ⊃ picture at CLOCK

sec·ond·hand /ˌsɛkəndˈhænd/ *adj.* **1** not new; owned by someone else before: *secondhand cars* ◆ *a secondhand bookshop* (= for selling secondhand books) **2** (often *disap-*

proving) (of news, information, etc.) learned from other people, not from your own experience: *secondhand opinions* ▶ sec·ond·hand *adv.*: *I bought the camera second-hand.* ◆ *I only heard about it secondhand.* ⊃ compare FIRST-HAND

ˌsecondhand ˈsmoke *noun* [U] smoke that is breathed in from other people's cigarettes

ˌsecond ˈhome *noun* **1** [C] a house or apartment that someone owns as well as their main home and uses, for example, for vacations **2** [sing.] a place where someone lives and that they know as well as, and like as much as, their home

ˌsecond in comˈmand *noun* a person who has the second highest rank in a group and takes charge when the leader is not there

ˌsecond ˈlanguage *noun* a language that someone learns to speak well and that they use for work or at school, but that is not the language they learned first: *ESL or English as a Second Language*

ˌsecond ˈlanguage acquisition *noun* [U] (*abbr.* SLA) (*linguistics*) the learning of a second language

ˌsecond lieuˈtenant *noun* an officer of lower rank in the army or AIR FORCE, just below the rank of a LIEUTENANT

sec·ond·ly /ˈsɛkəndli/ *adv.* used to introduce the second of a list of points you want to make in a speech or piece of writing: *Firstly, it's expensive, and secondly, it's too slow.*

ˌsecond ˈnature *noun* [U] ~ **(to sb) (to do sth)** something that you do very easily and naturally, because it is part of your character or you have done it so many times

the ˌsecond ˈperson *noun* [sing.] (*grammar*) the form of a pronoun or verb used when addressing someone: *In the phrase "you are," the verb "are" is in the second person and the word "you" is a second-person pronoun.* ⊃ compare THE FIRST PERSON, THE THIRD PERSON

ˌsecond-ˈrate *adj.* not very good or impressive **SYN** MEDIOCRE: *a second-rate player*

ˌsecond ˈsight *noun* [U] the ability that some people seem to have to know or see what will happen in the future or what is happening in a different place

ˌsecond-ˈstring *adj.* [only before noun] (usually of a player on a sports team) only used occasionally when someone or something else is not available: *a second-string quarterback*

sec·ond wind /ˌsɛkənd ˈwɪnd/ *noun* [sing.] (*informal*) new energy that makes you able to continue with something that had made you tired

the ˌSecond World ˈWar *noun* [sing.] = WORLD WAR II

se·cre·cy /ˈsikrəsi/ *noun* [U] the fact of making sure that nothing is known about something; the state of being secret: *the need for absolute secrecy in this matter* ◆ *Everyone involved was sworn to secrecy.* ◆ *The whole affair is still shrouded in secrecy.*

se·cret ♪ /ˈsikrət/ *adj., noun*

● *adj.* **1** known about by only a few people; kept hidden from others: *secret information/meetings/talks* ◆ ~ **(from sb)** *He tried to keep it secret from his family.* ◆ *Details of the proposals remain secret.* ◆ *a secret passage leading to the beach* ⊃ see also TOP SECRET **2** [only before noun] used to describe actions and behavior that you do not tell other people about: *He's a secret drinker.* ◆ *her secret fears* ◆ *a secret room* **3** [not usually before noun] ~ **(about sth)** (of a person or their behavior) liking to have secrets that other people do not know about; showing this **SYN** SECRETIVE: *They were so secret about everything.* ◆ *Jessica caught a secret smile flitting between the two of them.* ▶ se·cret·ly *adv.*: *The police had secretly filmed the conversations.* ◆ *She was secretly pleased to see him.*

● *noun* **1** [C] something that is known about by only a few people and not told to others: *Can you keep a secret?* ◆ *The location of the ship is a closely guarded secret.* ◆ *Shall we let him in on* (= tell him) *the secret?* ◆ *He made no secret of his ambition* (= he didn't try to hide it). ◆ *She was dismissed for revealing*

t tea   ţ butter   d did   k cat   g got   tʃ chin   dʒ June   f fall

trade secrets. ♦ *official/State secrets* **2** usually **the secret** [sing.] the best or only way to achieve something; the way a particular person achieves something: *Careful planning is the secret of success.* ♦ *She still looks so young. What's her secret?* **3** [C, usually pl.] a thing that is not yet fully understood or that is difficult to understand: *the secrets of the universe*

IDM **in secret** without other people knowing about it: *The meeting was held in secret.* ➔ more at GUILTY, OPEN *adj.*

ˌsecret ˈagent (also aˈgent) *noun* a person who is used by a government to find out secret information about other countries or governments **SYN** SPY

sec·re·tar·i·al /ˌsɛkrəˈtɛriəl/ *adj.* involving or connected with the work of a secretary: *secretarial work*

sec·re·tar·i·at /ˌsɛkrəˈtɛriət/ *noun* the department of a large international or political organization that is responsible for running it, especially the office of a SECRETARY GENERAL

sec·re·tar·y 🔑 /ˈsɛkrəˌteri/ *noun* (*pl.* sec·re·tar·ies) (*abbr.* Sec.)
1 a person who works in an office, working for another person, dealing with letters and telephone calls, typing, keeping records, arranging meetings with people, etc.: *a legal/medical secretary* ♦ *Please contact my secretary to make an appointment.* ➔ see also EXECUTIVE SECRETARY, PRIVATE SECRETARY **2** an official of a club, society, etc. who deals with writing letters, keeping records, and making business arrangements: *the membership secretary* **3** the head of a government department, chosen by the President: *Secretary of the Treasury*

ˌSecretary ˈGeneral *noun* the person who is in charge of the department that deals with the running of a large international or political organization: *the former Secretary General of NATO*

ˌSecretary of ˈState *noun* the head of the government department that deals with foreign affairs

se·crete /sɪˈkrit/ *verb* **1** ~ sth (of part of the body or a plant) to produce a liquid substance: *Insulin is secreted by the pancreas.* **2** ~ sth (in sth) (*formal*) to hide something, especially something small: *The drugs were secreted in the lining of his suitcase.*

se·cre·tion /sɪˈkriʃn/ *noun* (*technical*) **1** [U] the process by which liquid substances are produced by parts of the body or plants: *the secretion of bile by the liver* **2** [C, usually pl.] a liquid substance produced by parts of the body or plants: *bodily secretions*

se·cre·tive /ˈsikrətɪv/ *adj.* ~ (about sth) tending or liking to hide your thoughts, feelings, ideas, etc. from other people: *He's very secretive about his work.* ▶ se·cre·tive·ly *adv.* se·cre·tive·ness *noun* [U]

ˌsecret poˈlice *noun* [sing.] a police force that works secretly to make sure that citizens behave as their government wants

ˌsecret ˈservice *noun* [usually sing.] a government department that is responsible for protecting its government's military and political secrets and for finding out the secrets of other governments

sect /sɛkt/ *noun* (sometimes *disapproving*) a small group of people who belong to a particular religion but who have some beliefs or practices that separate them from the rest of the group

sec·tar·i·an /sɛkˈtɛriən/ *adj.* [usually before noun] (often *disapproving*) connected with the differences that exist between groups of people who have different religious views: *sectarian attacks/violence* ♦ *attempts to break down the sectarian divide in Northern Ireland* **ANT** NONSECTARIAN

sec·tar·i·an·ism /sɛkˈtɛriəˌnɪzəm/ *noun* [U] (often *disapproving*) strong support for one particular religious or political group, especially when this leads to violence between different groups

sec·tion 🔑 **AWL** /ˈsɛkʃn/ *noun, verb*
● *noun*
▷ PART/PIECE **1** [C] any of the parts into which something is divided: *That section of the road is still closed.* ♦ *The library has a large biology section.* ♦ *the tail section of the plane* **2** [C] a separate part of a structure from which the whole can be put together: *The kit comes in sections that you assemble yourself.*
▷ OF DOCUMENT/BOOK **3** [C] a separate part of a document, book, etc.: *These issues will be discussed more fully in the next section.* ♦ *the sports section of the newspaper* ♦ *Section 7 of the Endangered Species Act* (= the 7th part of a legal document)
▷ GROUP OF PEOPLE **4** [C] a separate group within a larger group of people: *an issue that will affect large sections of the population* ♦ *the brass section of an orchestra* ➔ see also RHYTHM SECTION
▷ OF ORGANIZATION **5** [C] a department in an organization, institution, etc. **SYN** DIVISION: *He's the director of the finance section.*
▷ DISTRICT **6** [C] a district of a town, city, or county: *the Dorchester section of Boston*
▷ MEASUREMENT **7** [C] a measure of land, equal to one square mile
▷ DIAGRAM **8** [C] a drawing or diagram of something as it would look if it were cut from top to bottom or from one side to the other: *The illustration shows a section through a leaf.* ♦ *The architect drew the house in section.* ➔ see also CROSS SECTION
▷ MEDICAL **9** [C, U] (*medical*) the act of cutting or separating something in an operation: *The surgeon performed a section* (= made a cut) *on the vein.* **10** [C] (*informal*) = CESAREAN **11** [C] (*medical, biology*) a very thin, flat piece cut from body TISSUE to be looked at under a MICROSCOPE: *to examine a section from the kidney*
● *verb*
▷ MEDICAL/BIOLOGY **1** ~ sth (*medical*) to divide body TISSUE by cutting **2** ~ sth (*biology*) to cut animal or plant TISSUE into thin slices in order to look at it under a MICROSCOPE **PHR V** ˌsection sth↔ˈoff to separate an area from a larger one: *Parts of the town had been sectioned off.*

sec·tion·al /ˈsɛkʃənl/ *adj.* [usually before noun] **1** connected with one particular group within a community or an organization: *the sectional interests of managers and workers* **2** made of separate sections: *a sectional building* **3** connected with a CROSS SECTION of something (= a surface or an image formed by cutting through something from top to bottom): *a sectional drawing*

sec·tor 🔑 **AWL** /ˈsɛktər/ *noun*
1 a part of an area of activity, especially of a country's economy: *the manufacturing sector* ♦ *service-sector jobs* (= in hotels, restaurants, etc.) ➔ collocations at ECONOMY ➔ see also THE PRIVATE SECTOR, THE PUBLIC SECTOR **2** a part of a particular area, especially an area under military control: *each sector of the war zone* **3** (*geometry*) a part of a circle lying between two straight lines drawn from the center to the edge ➔ picture at SHAPE

sec·u·lar /ˈsɛkyələr/ *adj.* **1** not connected with spiritual or religious matters: *secular music* ♦ *Ours is a secular society.* **2** (of priests) living among ordinary people rather than in a religious community

sec·u·lar·ism /ˈsɛkyələˌrɪzəm/ *noun* [U] (*technical*) the belief that religion should not be involved in the organization of society, education, etc. ▶ sec·u·lar·ist /-lərɪst/ *adj.* [usually before noun]

sec·u·lar·i·za·tion /ˌsɛkyələrəˈzeɪʃn/ *noun* [U] the process of removing the influence or power that religion has over something

sec·u·lar·ize /ˈsɛkyələˌraɪz/ *verb* [often passive] ~ sth to make something SECULAR; to remove something from the control or influence of religion: *a secularized society*

se·cure 🔑 **AWL** /sɪˈkyʊr/ *adj., verb*
● *adj.*
▷ HAPPY/CONFIDENT **1** feeling happy and confident about yourself or a particular situation: *At last they were able to feel secure about the future.* ♦ *She finished the match, secure in the*

knowledge that she was going through to the next round. **ANT** INSECURE

> CERTAIN/SAFE **2** likely to continue or be successful for a long time **SYN** SAFE: *a secure job/income* ◆ *It's not a very secure way to make a living.* ◆ *The future of the company looks secure.* **ANT** INSECURE **3** ~ **(against/from sth)** that cannot be affected or harmed by something: *Information must be stored so that it is secure from accidental deletion.*

> BUILDING/DOOR/ROOM **4** guarded and/or made stronger so that it is difficult for people to enter or leave: *Check that all windows and doors have been made as secure as possible.* ◆ *a secure unit for youth offenders* **ANT** INSECURE

> FIRM **5** not likely to move, fall down, etc. **SYN** STABLE: *The aerial doesn't look very secure to me.* ◆ *It was difficult to maintain a secure foothold on the ice.* ◆ *(figurative)* Our relationship was now on a more secure footing. **ANT** INSECURE

▶ **se·cure·ly** **AWL** *adv.*: *She locked the door securely behind her.* ◆ *Make sure the ropes are securely fastened.*

● *verb*

> GET SOMETHING **1** (*formal*) to obtain or achieve something, especially when this means using a lot of effort: ~ **sth** *to secure a contract/deal* ◆ *The team managed to secure a place in the finals.* ◆ *She secured 2,000 votes.* ◆ ~ **sth for sb/sth/ yourself** *He secured a place for himself in law school.* ◆ ~ **sb/ sth/yourself sth** *He secured himself a place in law school.*

> FASTEN FIRMLY **2** ~ **sth (to sth)** to attach or fasten something firmly: *She secured the rope firmly to the back of the car.*

> PROTECT FROM HARM **3** to protect something so that it is safe and difficult to attack or damage: ~ **sth against sth** *to secure a property against intruders* ◆ ~ **sth** *The windows were secured with locks and bars.* ◆ *(figurative)* a savings plan that will secure your child's future

> A LOAN **4** ~ **sth** to legally agree to give someone property or goods that are worth the same amount as the money that you have borrowed from them, if you are unable to pay the money back: *a loan secured against the house*

se·cu·ri·ty 🔑 **AWL** /sɪˈkyʊrəti/ *noun* (*pl.* se·cu·ri·ties)

> PROTECTION **1** [U] the activities involved in protecting a country, building, or person against attack, danger, etc.: *national security* (= the defense of a country) ◆ *airport security* ◆ *They carried out security checks at the airport.* ◆ *The visit took place amid tight security* (= the use of many police officers). ◆ *the security forces/services* (= the police, army, etc.) ◆ *a high/ maximum security prison* (= for dangerous criminals) ⊃ collocations at INTERNATIONAL ⊃ see also HIGH-SECURITY **2** [U] the department of a large company or organization that deals with the protection of its buildings, equipment, and staff: *Security was called to the incident.* **3** [U] protection against something bad that might happen in the future: *financial security* ◆ *Job security* (= the guarantee that you will keep your job) *is a thing of the past.*

> FEELING HAPPY/SAFE **4** [U] the state of feeling happy and safe from danger or worry: *the security of a loving family life* ◆ *She'd allowed herself to be lulled into a false sense of security* (= a feeling that she was safe when in fact she was in danger).

> FOR A LOAN **5** [U, C] a valuable item, such as a house, that you agree to give to someone if you are unable to pay back the money that you have borrowed from them: *His home and business are being held as security for the loan.*

> SHARES IN COMPANY **6** securities [pl.] (*finance*) documents proving that someone is the owner of shares, etc. in a particular company ⊃ see also SOCIAL SECURITY

se'curity ˌblanket *noun* **1** a BLANKET or other object that a child holds in order to feel safe **2** something that provides protection against attack, danger, etc.: *A firewall provides an essential security blanket for your computer network.*

the Se'curity ˌCouncil (also the ˌUN Se'curity ˌCouncil, the ˌUnited ˌNations Se'curity ˌCouncil) *noun* [sing.] the part of the United Nations that tries to keep peace and order in the world, consisting of representatives of fifteen countries

se'curity deˌposit *noun* [usually sing.] an amount of money you pay when you rent an apartment or house and

that is returned to you if you do not cause any damage: *The landlord requires a security deposit of one month's rent.*

se'curity ˌguard *noun* a person whose job is to guard money, valuables, a building, etc.

se'curity ˌrisk *noun* a person who cannot be given secret information because they are a danger to a particular country, organization, etc., especially because of their political beliefs

se'curity ˌservice *noun* a government organization that protects a country and its secrets from enemies

Secy. *abbr.* = SEC.

se·dan /sɪˈdæn/ *noun* a car with four doors and a TRUNK (= space at the back for carrying things) that is separated from the part where the driver and passengers sit ⊃ picture at CAR

seˌdan 'chair *noun* a box containing a seat for one person, carried on poles by two people, used in the 17th and 18th centuries

se·date /sɪˈdeɪt/ *adj., verb*

● *adj.* [usually before noun] **1** slow, calm, and relaxed **SYN** UNHURRIED: *We followed the youngsters at a more sedate pace.* **2** quiet, especially in a way that lacks excitement: *a sedate country town* **3** (of a person) quiet and serious in a way that seems formal: *a sedate, sober man* ▶ se·date·ly *adv.*

● *verb* [often passive] ~ **sb/sth** to give someone drugs in order to make them calm or to make them sleep **SYN** TRANQUILIZE: *Most of the patients are heavily sedated.*

se·da·tion /sɪˈdeɪʃn/ *noun* [U] the act of giving someone drugs in order to make them calm or to make them sleep; the state that results from this: *The victim's wife was being kept under sedation in the local hospital last night.*

sed·a·tive /ˈsɛdətɪv/ *noun* a drug that makes someone go to sleep or makes them feel calm and relaxed **SYN** TRANQUILIZER ▶ sed·a·tive *adj.* [usually before noun]: *the sedative effect of the drug*

sed·en·tar·y /ˈsɛdnˌtɛri/ *adj.* **1** (of work, activities, etc.) in which you spend a lot of time sitting down: *a sedentary job/ occupation/lifestyle* **2** (of people) spending a lot of time sitting down and not moving: *He became increasingly sedentary in later life.* **3** (*technical*) (of people or animals) that stay and live in the same place or area: *Rhinos are largely sedentary animals.* ◆ *a sedentary population*

Se·der /ˈseɪdər/ *noun* a Jewish CEREMONIAL service and dinner on the first night or first two nights of Passover

sedge /sɛdʒ/ *noun* [U] a plant like grass that grows in wet ground or near water

sed·i·ment /ˈsɛdəmənt/ *noun* [U] **1** the solid material that settles at the bottom of a liquid **2** (*geology*) sand, stones, mud, etc. carried by water or wind and left, for example, on the bottom of a lake, river, etc.

sed·i·men·ta·ry /ˌsɛdəˈmɛntri; -ˈmɛntəri/ *adj.* (*geology*) connected with or formed from the sand, stones, mud, etc. that settle at the bottom of lakes, etc.: *sedimentary rocks*

sed·i·men·ta·tion /ˌsɛdəmənˈteɪʃn/ *noun* [U] (*geology*) the process of depositing sediment

se·di·tion /sɪˈdɪʃn/ *noun* [U] (*formal*) the use of words or actions that are intended to encourage people to oppose a government **SYN** INSURRECTION ▶ se·di·tious /sɪˈdɪʃəs/ *adj.*: *seditious activity*

se·duce /sɪˈdus/ *verb* **1** ~ **sb** to persuade someone to have sex with you, especially someone who is younger or who has less experience than you **2** ~ **sb (into sth/into doing sth)** to persuade someone to do something that they would not usually agree to do by making it seem very attractive **SYN** ENTICE: *The promise of huge profits seduced him into parting with his money.*

se·duc·er /sɪˈdusər/ *noun* a person who persuades someone to have sex with them

se·duc·tion /sɪˈdʌkʃn/ *noun* **1** [U, C] the act of persuading

| h **h**at | m **m**an | n **n**o | ŋ si**ng** | l **l**eg | r **r**ed | y **y**es | w **w**et |

someone to have sex with you: *Cleopatra's seduction of Caesar* **2** [C, usually pl., U] ~ **(of sth)** the qualities or features of something that make it seem attractive: *Who could resist the seductions of the tropical island?*

se·duc·tive /sɪˈdʌktɪv/ *adj.* **1** sexually attractive: *a seductive woman* ♦ *She used her most seductive voice.* **2** attractive in a way that makes you want to have or do something **SYN** TEMPTING: *The idea of retiring to the south of France is highly seductive.* ▶ **se·duc·tive·ly** *adv.* **se·duc·tive·ness** *noun* [U]

se·duc·tress /sɪˈdʌktrəs/ *noun* a woman who persuades someone to have sex with her

sed·u·lous /ˈsɛdʒələs/ *adj.* (*formal*) showing great care and effort in your work **SYN** DILIGENT ▶ **sed·u·lous·ly** *adv.*

see /si/ *verb, noun*

● *verb* (saw /sɔ/, seen /sin/)
▷ **USE EYES 1** [T, I] (not usually used in the progressive tenses) to become aware of someone or something by using your eyes: ~ **(sb/sth)** *She looked for him but couldn't see him in the crowd.* ♦ *The opera was the place to see and be seen* (= by other important or fashionable people). ♦ ~ **(that)...** *He could see (that) she had been crying.* ♦ ~ **what, how, etc....** *Did you see what happened?* ♦ ~ **sb/sth + adj.** *I hate to see you unhappy.* ♦ ~ **sb/sth doing sth** *She was seen running away from the scene of the crime.* ♦ ~ **sb/sth do sth** *I saw you put the key in your pocket.* ♦ **sb/sth is seen to do sth** *He was seen to enter the building about the time the crime was committed.* **2** [I] (not usually used in the progressive tenses) to have or use the power of sight: *She will never see again* (= she has become blind). ♦ *On a clear day you can see for miles from here.* ♦ ~ **to do sth** *It was getting dark and I couldn't see to read.*
▷ **WATCH 3** [T] (not usually used in the progressive tenses) ~ **sth** to watch a game, television program, performance, etc.: *Did you see that program on Brazil last night?* ♦ *In the evening we went to see a movie.* ♦ *Fifty thousand people saw the championship.* ➔ thesaurus box at LOOK
▷ **LOOK UP INFORMATION 4** [T] (used in orders) ~ **sth** to look at something in order to find information: *See page 158.*
▷ **MEET BY CHANCE 5** [T] ~ **sb** (not usually used in the progressive tenses) to be near and recognize someone; to meet someone by chance: *Guess who I saw at the party last night!*
▷ **VISIT 6** [T] ~ **sb** to visit someone: *Come and see us again soon.*
▷ **HAVE MEETING 7** [T] ~ **sb (about sth)** to have a meeting with someone: *You ought to see a doctor about that cough.* ♦ *What is it you want to see me about?*
▷ **SPEND TIME 8** [T] (often used in the progressive tenses) ~ **sb** to spend time with someone: *Are you seeing anyone* (= having a romantic relationship with anyone)? ♦ *They've been seeing a lot of each other* (= spending a lot of time together) *recently.*
▷ **UNDERSTAND 9** [I, T] (not usually used in the progressive tenses) to understand something: *"It opens like this." "Oh, I see."* ♦ ~ **sth** *He didn't see the joke.* ♦ *I don't think she saw the point of the story.* ♦ *I can see both sides of the argument.* ♦ *Make Lydia see reason* (= be sensible), *will you?* ♦ ~ **(that)...** *Can't you see (that) he's taking advantage of you?* ♦ *I don't see that it matters what Josh thinks.* ♦ ~ **what, why, etc....** *"It's broken." "Oh yes, I see what you mean." "Can we go swimming?" "I don't see why not* (= yes, you can)." ♦ **be seen to do sth** *The government not only has to do something, it must be seen to be doing something* (= people must be aware that it is doing something). ➔ thesaurus box at UNDERSTAND
▷ **HAVE OPINION 10** [T] ~ **sth + adv./prep.** (not usually used in the progressive tenses) to have an opinion of something: *I see things differently now.* ♦ *Try to see things from her point of view.* ♦ *Lack of money is the main problem, as I see it* (= in my opinion). ♦ *The way I see it, you have three main problems.* ➔ thesaurus box at REGARD
▷ **IMAGINE 11** [T] (not usually used in the progressive tenses) to consider something as a future possibility; to imagine someone or something as sth: ~ **sb/sth doing sth** *I can't see her changing her mind.* ♦ ~ **sb/sth as sth** *Her colleagues see her as a future director.* ➔ thesaurus box at IMAGINE

▷ **FIND OUT 12** [I, T] (not usually used in the progressive tenses) to find out something by looking, asking, or waiting: *"Has the mail come yet?" "I'll just go and see." ♦ "Is he going to get better?" "I don't know, we'll just have to wait and see."* ♦ *We'll have a great time, you'll see.* ♦ ~ **what, how, etc.** *... Go and see what the kids are doing, will you?* ♦ *We'll have to see how it goes.* ♦ ~ **(that)** *I see (that) interest rates are going up again.* ♦ **it is seen that...** *It can be seen that certain groups are more at risk than others.* **13** [I, T] (not usually used in the progressive tenses) to find out or decide something by thinking or considering: *"Will you be able to help us?" "I don't know, I'll have to see." ♦ "Can I go to the party?" "We'll see* (= I'll decide later)." ♦ ~ **what, whether, etc....** *I'll see what I can do to help.*
▷ **MAKE SURE 14** [T] (not usually used in the progressive tenses) ~ **that...** to make sure that you do something or that something is done: *See that all the doors are locked before you leave.*
▷ **EXPERIENCE 15** [T] (not used in the progressive tenses) ~ **sth** to experience or suffer something: *He has seen a great deal in his long life.* ♦ *I hope I never live to see the day when computers finally replace books.* ♦ *It didn't surprise her—she had seen it all before.*
▷ **WITNESS EVENT 16** [T] (not used in the progressive tenses) ~ **sth** to be the time when an event happens: *This year sees the centenary of Mahler's death.* **17** [T] (not used in the progressive tenses) ~ **sth** to be the place where an event happens **SYN** WITNESS: *This stadium has seen many thrilling football games.*
▷ **HELP 18** [T] ~ **sb + adv./prep.** to go with someone to help or protect them: *I saw the old lady across* (= helped her cross) *the road.* ♦ *May I see you home* (= go with you as far as your house)? ♦ *My secretary will see you out* (= show you the way out of the building).

IDM Most idioms containing **see** are at the entries for the nouns and adjectives in the idioms. For example, **not see the forest for the trees** is at **forest**. **for all (the world) to see** clearly visible; in a way that is clearly visible **let me see/let's see** (*informal*) used when you are thinking or trying to remember something: *Now let me see—how old is she now?* **see sth coming** to realize that there is going to be a problem before it happens: *We should have seen it coming. There was no way he could keep going under all that pressure.* **see for yourself** to find out or look at something yourself in order to be sure that what someone is saying is true: *If you don't believe me, go and see for yourself!* **see sb/sth for what they are/it is** to realize that someone or something is not as good, pleasant, etc. as they/it seem **seeing that...** (also *informal* **seeing as (how)...**) because of the fact that...: *Seeing that he's been off sick all week he's unlikely to come.* **see you (around)** | **(I'll) be seeing you** | **see you later** (*informal*) goodbye: *I'd better be going now. See you!* **you see** (*informal*) used when you are explaining something: *You see, the thing is, we won't be finished before Friday.*

PHR V **'see about sth** to deal with something: *I must see about* (= prepare) *lunch.* ♦ *He says he won't help, does he? Well, we'll soon see about that* (= I will demand that he does help). ♦ [+ **-ing**] *I'll have to see about getting that roof repaired.* **'see sth in sb/sth** to find someone or something attractive or interesting: *I don't know what she sees in him.* **,see sb↔'off 1** to go to a station, an airport, etc. to say goodbye to someone who is starting a trip **2** to defeat someone in a game, fight, etc.: *The home team saw off the challengers by 68 points to 47.* **,see sth↔'out** (not used in the progressive tenses) to reach the end or last until the end of something: *They had enough fuel to see the winter out.* ♦ *He saw out his career in Denver.* **,see 'through sb/sth** (not used in the progressive tenses) to realize the truth about someone or something: *We saw through him from the start.* ♦ *I can see through your little game* (= I am aware of the trick you are trying to play on me). **,see sth 'through** (not usually used in the progressive tenses) to not give up doing a task, project, etc. until it is finished: *She's determined to see the job through.* **,see sb 'through** | **,see sb 'through sth** (not used in the progressive tenses) to give help or support to someone for a particular period of time: *Her courage and good humor saw* her through. ♦ *I only have $20 to see me through the week.* **'see to sth** to deal with something: *Will you see to the arrangements for the next meeting?* ♦ *Don't worry— I'll see to it.* ♦ *We'll have to get that door seen to* (= repaired). **'see to it that…** to make sure that…: *Can you see to it that the fax goes this afternoon?*

● *noun* (*formal*) the district or office of a BISHOP or an ARCHBISHOP: *the Holy See* (= the office of the POPE)

seed /sid/ *noun, verb*

● *noun*
> OF PLANTS/FRUIT **1** [C, U] the small hard part produced by a plant, from which a new plant can grow: *a packet of wild flower seeds* ♦ *sesame seeds* ♦ *an apple seed* ♦ *Sow the seeds outdoors in spring.* ♦ *These vegetables can be **grown from seed**.* ♦ *seed potatoes* (= used for planting) Ⓒ picture at HERB, FRUIT Ⓒ collocations at LIFE Ⓒ see also BIRDSEED
> BEGINNING **2** [C, usually pl.] ~ **(of sth)** the beginning of a feeling or a development that continues to grow: *the seeds of rebellion* ♦ *This **planted the seeds** of doubt in my mind.*
> IN SPORTS **3** [C] (in sports, especially TENNIS) one of the best players or teams in a competition. The seeds are given a position in a list to try and make sure that they do not play each other in the early parts of the competition: *The top seed won comfortably.* ♦ *the number one seed*
> OF A MAN **4** [U] (*old-fashioned* or *humorous*) SEMEN **5** [U] (*literary*) all the people who are the children, grandchildren, etc. of one man
IDM **go/run to seed 1** (especially of a vegetable plant) to produce flowers and seeds as well as leaves **2** to become much less attractive or good because of lack of attention: *After his divorce, he let himself go to seed.* Ⓒ more at SOW¹

● *verb*
> OF A PLANT **1** [I] to produce seeds **2** [T] ~ **itself** to produce other plants using its own seeds
> AREA OF GROUND **3** [T, usually passive] ~ **sth (with sth)** to plant seeds in an area of ground: *a newly seeded lawn*
> IN SPORTS **4** [T, usually passive] ~ **sb** to make a player or team a seed in a competition: *He has been seeded 14th at the U.S. Open next week.*

seed·bed /'sidbɛd/ *noun* **1** an area of soil that has been specially prepared for planting seeds in **2** [usually sing.] ~ **(of/for sth)** a place or situation in which something can develop

'seed coat *noun* the outer covering of a seed: *Barley has a hard seed coat.*

seed·corn /'sidkɔrn/ *noun* [U] **1** the grain that is kept for planting the next year's crops **2** people or things that will be successful or useful in the future

seed·ed /'sidəd/ *adj.* [usually before noun] **1** (of a sports player or team, especially in TENNIS) given a number showing that they are one of the best players or teams in a

particular competition: *a seeded player* **2** (of fruit) with the seeds removed: *seeded tomatoes*

seed·less /'sidləs/ *adj.* [usually before noun] (of fruit) having no seeds: *seedless grapes*

seed·ling /'sidlɪŋ/ *noun* a young plant that has grown from a seed

'seed ˌmoney (also **'seed ˌcapital**) *noun* [U] money to start a new business, project, etc.

'seed pearl *noun* a small PEARL

seed·y /'sidi/ *adj.* (**seed·i·er**, **seed·i·est**) (*disapproving*) dirty and unpleasant, possibly connected with immoral or illegal activities: *a seedy bar* ♦ *the seedy world of prostitution* ♦ *a seedy-looking man* ▶ **seed·i·ness** *noun* [U]

'Seeing ˈEye dog™ *noun* = GUIDE DOG

seek **AWL** /sik/ *verb* (**sought, sought** /sɔt/) (*formal*) **1** [T, I] to look for something or someone: ~ **sth/sb** *Drivers are advised to seek alternative routes.* **2** [T, I] ~ **(sth)** to try to obtain or achieve something: *to seek funding for a project* ♦ *Highly qualified secretary seeks employment.* (= in an advertisement) ♦ *We are currently seeking new ways of expanding our membership.* **3** [T] to ask someone for something: ~ **sth** *I think it's time we sought legal advice.* ♦ ~ **sth from sb** *She managed to calm him down and seek help from a neighbor.* **4** [I] ~ **to do sth** to try to do something **SYN** ATTEMPT: *They quickly sought to distance themselves from the protesters.* **5** **-seeking** (in adjectives and nouns) looking for or trying to get the thing mentioned; the activity of doing this: *attention-seeking behavior* ♦ *Voluntary work can provide a framework for job-seeking.* Ⓒ see also HEAT-SEEKING, SELF-SEEKING Ⓒ see also HIDE-AND-SEEK
IDM **seek your fortune** (*literary*) to try to find a way to become rich, especially by going to another place **PHR V** ˌseek sb/sth 'out to look for and find someone or something, especially when this means using a lot of effort

seek·er /'sikər/ *noun* (often in compounds) a person who is trying to find or get the thing mentioned: *an attention/a publicity seeker* ♦ *seekers after the truth* Ⓒ see also ASYLUM SEEKER

seem /sim/ *linking verb* **1** ~ **(to sb) (to be) sth** (not used in the progressive tenses) to give the impression of being or doing something **SYN** APPEAR: + **adj.** *You seem happy.* ♦ *Do whatever seems best to you.* ♦ ~ **like sth** *It seemed like a good idea at the time.* ♦ ~ **(as though…)** *It always seemed as though they would get married.* ♦ *"He'll be there, won't he?" "So it seems* (= people say so).*"* ♦ **it seems that…** *It seems that they know what they're doing.* ♦ ~ **to do/be/have sth** *They seem to know what they're doing.* **2** ~ **to do/be/have sth** used to make what you say about your thoughts, feelings, or actions less strong: *I seem to have left my book at home.* ♦ *I can't seem to* (= I've tried, but I can't) *get started today.* **3** **it seems** | **it would seem** used to suggest that something is true when you are not certain or when you want to be polite: ~ **(that)…** *It would seem that we all agree.* ♦ + **adj.** *It seems only reasonable to ask students to buy a dictionary.* Ⓒ language bank at OPINION

seem·ing /'simɪŋ/ *adj.* [only before noun] (*formal*) appearing to be something that may not be true **SYN** APPARENT: *a seeming impossibility* ♦ *She handled the matter with seeming indifference.*

seem·ing·ly /'simɪŋli/ *adv.* **1** in a way that appears to be true but may in fact not be: *a seemingly stupid question* ♦ *a seemingly endless journey* **2** according to what you have read or heard **SYN** APPARENTLY: *Seemingly, he borrowed the money from the bank.*

seem·ly /'simli/ *adj.* (*old-fashioned* or *formal*) appropriate for a particular social situation **ANT** UNSEEMLY

seen pp of SEE

seep /sip/ *verb* [I] + **adv./prep.** (especially of liquids) to flow slowly and in small quantities through something or into something **SYN** TRICKLE: *Blood was beginning to seep* through the bandages. ♦ *Water seeped from a crack in the pipe.* ♦ (*figurative*) *Gradually the pain seeped away.*

seep·age /ˈsipɪdʒ/ noun [U, C, usually pl.] the process by which a liquid flows slowly and in small quantities through something; the result of this process: *Water gradually escapes by seepage through the ground.* ♦ *oil seepages*

seer /sɪr/ noun (*literary*) (especially in the past) a person who claims that they can see what is going to happen in the future **SYN** PROPHET

seer·suck·er /ˈsɪrˌsʌkər/ noun [U] a type of light cotton cloth with a pattern of raised lines and squares on its surface

ˈsee-saw noun, verb
● *noun* **1** (also ˈteeter-ˌtotter) [C] a piece of equipment for children to play on consisting of a long, flat piece of wood that is supported in the middle. A child sits at each end and makes the see-saw move up and down. **2** [sing.] a situation in which things keep changing from one state to another and back again
● *verb* [I] ~ **(from A to B)** to keep changing from one situation, opinion, emotion, etc. to another and back again: *Her emotions see-sawed from anger to fear.* ♦ *Share prices see-sawed all day.*

seethe /sið/ verb **1** [I] to be extremely angry about something but try not to show other people how angry you are **SYN** FUME: *She seethed silently in the corner.* ♦ ~ **with sth** *He marched off, seething with frustration.* ♦ ~ **at sth** *Inwardly he was seething at this challenge to his authority.* **2** [I] ~ **(with sth)** (*formal*) (of a place) to be full of a lot of people or animals, especially when they are all moving around: *The resort is seething with tourists all year round.* ♦ *He became caught up in a* **seething mass** *of arms and legs.* **3** [I] (*formal*) (of liquids) to move around quickly and violently: *The gray ocean seethed beneath them.*

ˈsee-through adj. (of cloth) very thin so that you can see through it: *a see-through blouse*

seg·ment noun, verb
● *noun* /ˈsɛgmənt/ **1** a part of something that is separate from the other parts or can be considered separately: *She cleaned a small segment of the painting.* ♦ *Lines divided the area into segments.* **2** one of the sections of an orange, a lemon, etc. ➔ picture at FRUIT **3** (*geometry*) a part of a circle separated from the rest by a single line ➔ picture at SHAPE **4** (*geometry*) a part of a straight line between two points **5** (*phonetics*) the smallest speech sound that a word can be divided into
● *verb* /ˈsɛgmɛnt/ [often passive] ~ **sth** (*technical*) to divide something into different parts: *Market researchers often segment the population on the basis of age and social class.* ♦ *The worm has a segmented body* (= with different sections joined together).

seg·men·tal /sɛgˈmɛntl/ adj. (*phonetics*) relating to the individual sounds that make up speech, as opposed to features such as stress and INTONATION

seg·men·ta·tion /ˌsɛgmənˈteɪʃn/ noun [U, C, usually pl.] (*technical*) the act of dividing something into different parts; one of these parts

seg·re·gate /ˈsɛgrəˌgeɪt/ verb **1** ~ **sb (from sb)** to separate people of different races, religions, or sexes and treat them in a different way: *a culture in which women are segregated from men* ♦ *a racially segregated community* ♦ *a segregated school* (= one for students of one race or religion only) **ANT** INTEGRATE **2** ~ **sth (from sth)** to keep one thing separate from another: *In all our restaurants, smoking and non-smoking areas are segregated from each other.*

seg·re·ga·tion /ˌsɛgrəˈgeɪʃn/ noun [U] **1** the act or policy of separating people of different races, religions, or sexes and treating them in a different way: *racial/religious segregation* ♦ *segregation by age and sex* **2** (*formal*) the act of separating people or things from a larger group: *the segregation of smokers and non-smokers in restaurants*

seg·re·ga·tion·ist /ˌsɛgrəˈgeɪʃənɪst/ adj. supporting the

separation of people according to their sex, race, or religion: *segregationist policies* ▶ **seg·re·ga·tion·ist** noun

se·gue /ˈsɛgweɪ/ verb [I] + **adv./prep.** to move smoothly from one song, subject, place, etc. to another: *a spiritual that segued into a singalong chorus* ♦ *He then segued into a discussion of atheism.* ▶ **se·gue** noun

seine /seɪn/ (also ˈseine net) noun a type of fishing net that hangs down in the water and is pulled together at the ends to catch fish

seis·mic /ˈsaɪzmɪk/ adj. [only before noun] **1** connected with or caused by EARTHQUAKES: *seismic waves* **2** having a very great effect; of very great size: *a seismic shift in the political process*

seis·mo·graph /ˈsaɪzməˌgræf/ noun an instrument that measures and records information about EARTHQUAKES

seis·mol·o·gy /saɪzˈmalədʒi/ noun [U] the scientific study of EARTHQUAKES ▶ **seis·mo·log·i·cal** /ˌsaɪzməˈladʒɪkl/ adj.: *the National Seismological Institute* **seis·mol·o·gist** /saɪzˈmalədʒɪst/ noun

seize /siz/ verb **1** to take someone or something in your hand suddenly and using force **SYN** GRAB: ~ **sth from sb** *She tried to seize the gun from him.* ♦ ~ **sb/sth** *He seized her by the arm.* ♦ *She seized hold of my hand.* **2** ~ **sth (from sb)** to take control of a place or situation, often suddenly and violently: *They seized the airport in a surprise attack.* ♦ *The army has seized control of the country.* ♦ *He seized power in a military coup.* **3** ~ **sb** to arrest or capture someone: *The men were seized as they left the building.* **4** ~ **sth** to take illegal or stolen goods away from someone: *A large quantity of drugs was seized during the raid.* **5** ~ **a chance, an opportunity, the initiative, etc.** to be quick to make use of a chance, an opportunity, etc. **SYN** GRAB: *The party seized the initiative with both hands* (= quickly and with enthusiasm). **6** ~ **sb** (of an emotion) to affect someone suddenly and deeply: *Panic seized her.* ♦ *He was seized by curiosity.*
PHR V ˈseize on/upon sth to suddenly show a lot of interest in something, especially because you can use it to your advantage **SYN** POUNCE ON/UPON: *The rumors were eagerly seized upon by the local press.* ˌseize ˈup **1** (of the parts of a machine) to stop moving or working correctly **2** if a part of your body **seizes up**, you are unable to move it easily and it is often painful

sei·zure /ˈsiʒər/ noun **1** [U, C] ~ **(of sth)** the use of legal authority to take something from someone; an amount of something that is taken in this way: *The court ordered the seizure of his assets.* ♦ *the largest ever seizure of cocaine at a U.S. port* **2** [U] ~ **(of sth)** the act of using force to take control of a country, town, etc.: *the army's seizure of power* ♦ *the seizure of Burma by Japan in 1942* **3** [C] a sudden attack of an illness, especially one that affects the brain: *Her seizures are now controlled by drugs.*

sel·dom /ˈsɛldəm/ adv. not often **SYN** RARELY: *He had seldom seen a child with so much talent.* ♦ *She seldom, if ever, goes to the theater.* ♦ *They seldom watch television these days.* ♦ (*literary*) *Seldom had he seen such beauty.*

se·lect 🔑 **AWL** /səˈlɛkt/ verb, adj.
● *verb* **1** (*formal*) to choose someone or something from a group of people or things, usually according to a system: ~ **sb/sth for sth** *He hasn't been selected for the team.* ♦ *All our hotels have been carefully selected for the excellent value they provide.* ♦ ~ **sb/sth as sth** *She was selected as the state senate candidate from San Diego.* ♦ ~ **sb/sth** *a randomly selected sample of 23 schools* ♦ *selected poems of T.S. Eliot* ♦ *This model is available at selected stores only.* ♦ ~ **sb/sth to do sth** *Six theater companies have been selected to take part in this year's festival.* ♦ ~ **what, which, etc....** *Select what you want from the options available.* ➔ thesaurus box at CHOOSE **2** ~ **sth** (*computing*) to mark something on a computer screen; to choose something, especially from a menu: *Select the text you want to format by holding down the left button on your mouse.* ♦ *Select "New Mail" from the "Send" menu.*
● *adj.* **1** [only before noun] carefully chosen as the best out of a larger group of people or things: *a select wine list* ♦ *Only a*

select few (= a small number of people) *have been invited to the wedding.* **2** (of a society, club, place, etc.) used by people who have a lot of money or a high social position **SYN** EXCLUSIVE: *They live in a very select area.* ◆ *a select club*

se·lect com·mit·tee *noun* a small group of politicians or experts that have been chosen to examine a particular subject or problem

se·lect·ee /səˌlɛkˈti/ *noun* **1** a person who is chosen for something **2** a person who is chosen to do MILITARY SERVICE

se·lec·tion 🔑 **AWL** /səˈlɛkʃn/ *noun*
1 [U] the process of choosing someone or something from a group of people or things, usually according to a system: *The final team selection will be made tomorrow.* ◆ *the random selection of numbers* ◆ *selection criteria* ◆ *the selection process* **2** [C] a number of people or things that have been chosen from a larger group: *A selection of readers' comments is published below.* ⊃ **thesaurus box at** CHOICE **3** [C] a collection of things from which something can be chosen **SYN** CHOICE: *The showroom has a **wide selection** of kitchens.* ⊃ **see also** NATURAL SELECTION

se·lec·tion·al /səˈlɛkʃənl/ *adj.* (*linguistics*) used to describe the process by which each word limits what kind of words can be used with it in normal language: *"Eat" has the selectional restriction that it must be followed by a kind of food, so "I eat sky" is not possible.*

se·lection com·mit·tee *noun* a group of people who choose, for example, the members of a sports team

se·lec·tive **AWL** /səˈlɛktɪv/ *adj.* **1** [usually before noun] affecting or concerned with only a small number of people or things from a larger group: *the selective breeding of cattle* ◆ *selective work stoppage* **2** ~ **(about/in sth)** tending to be careful about what or who you choose: *You will have to be selective about which information to include in the report.* ◆ *Their admissions policy is very selective.* ◆ *a selective school* (= one that chooses which children to admit, especially according to ability) ▶ **se·lec·tive·ly** **AWL** *adv.*: *The product will be selectively marketed in the U.S.* (= only in some areas). **se·lec·tiv·i·ty** /səˌlɛkˈtɪvəti/ *noun* [U]: *Schools are tending toward greater selectivity.*

se·lec·tive service *noun* [U] a system in which people have to spend a period of time in the armed forces by law

se·lec·tor **AWL** /səˈlɛktər/ *noun* a device in an engine, a piece of machinery, etc. that allows you to choose a particular function

se·le·ni·um /səˈliniəm/ *noun* [U] (*symb.* **Se**) a chemical element. Selenium is a gray substance that is used in making electrical equipment and colored glass. A lack of selenium in the human body can lead to illnesses such as DEPRESSION.

self 🔑 /sɛlf/ *noun* (*pl.* selves /sɛlvz/)
1 [C, usually sing.] the type of person you are, especially the way you normally behave, look, or feel: *You'll soon be feeling like your old self again* (= feeling well or happy again). ◆ *He's not **his usual happy self** this morning.* ◆ *Only with a few people could she be **her real self*** (= show what she was really like rather than what she pretended to be). ◆ *his private/professional self* (= how he behaves at home/work) **2** [U] (also **the self** [sing.]) (*formal*) a person's personality or character that makes them different from other people: *Many people living in institutions have lost their sense of self* (= the feeling that they are individual people). ◆ *the inner self* (= a person's emotional and spiritual character) **3** [U] (*formal*) your own advantage or pleasure rather than that of other people: *She didn't do it for any reason of self.* **4** [C] used to refer to a person: *You didn't hurt your little self, did you?* ◆ *We look forward to seeing Mrs. Brown and **your good self** this evening.* **IDM** see FORMER

self- 🔑 /sɛlf/ *combining form*
(in nouns and adjectives) of, to, or by yourself or itself: *self-control* ◆ *self-addressed* ◆ *self-taught*

ˌself-abˈsorbed *adj.* only concerned about or interested in yourself ▶ **ˌself-abˈsorption** *noun* [U]

ˌself-aˈbuse *noun* [U] behavior by which a person does harm to himself or herself

ˌself-ˈaccess *noun* [U] a method of learning in which students choose their materials and use them to study on their own: *a **self-access center/library***

ˌself-actualiˈzation *noun* [U] the fact of using your skills and abilities and achieving as much as you can possibly achieve **SYN** SELF-REALIZATION

ˌself-adˈdressed *adj.* if an envelope is **self-addressed**, someone has written their own address on it ⊃ **see also** SASE

ˌself-adˈhesive *adj.* [usually before noun] covered on one side with a sticky substance so that it can be stuck to something without the use of glue, etc.: *self-adhesive tape*

ˌself-agˈgrandizement *noun* [U] (*formal*, *disapproving*) the process of making yourself seem more powerful or important: *Napoleon's self-aggrandizement* ▶ **self-ag·gran·diz·ing** /ˌsɛlf əˈgrændaɪzɪŋ/ *adj.*

ˌself-aˈnalysis *noun* [U] the study of your own character and behavior, especially your reasons for doing things

ˌself-apˈpointed *adj.* [usually before noun] (usually *disapproving*) giving yourself a particular title, job, etc., especially without the agreement of other people

ˌself-apˈpraisal *noun* [U, C] an act or the process of judging your own work or achievements

ˌself-asˈsertive *adj.* very confident and not afraid to express your opinions ▶ **ˌself-asˈsertion**, **ˌself-asˈsertiveness** *noun* [U]

ˌself-asˈsessment *noun* [U] the process of judging your own progress, achievements, etc.

ˌself-asˈsured *adj.* having a lot of confidence in yourself and your abilities **SYN** CONFIDENT ▶ **ˌself-asˈsurance** *noun* [U]

ˌself-aˈwareness *noun* [U] knowledge and understanding of your own character ▶ **self-aˈware** *adj.*

ˌself-ˈcentered *adj.* (*disapproving*) tending to think only about yourself and not thinking about the needs or feelings of other people ▶ **ˌself-ˈcenteredness** *noun* [U]

ˌself-conˈfessed *adj.* [only before noun] admitting that you are a particular type of person or have a particular problem, especially a bad one: *a self-confessed thief*

ˌself-ˈconfident *adj.* having confidence in yourself and your abilities **SYN** CONFIDENT: *a self-confident child* ◆ *a self-confident manner* ▶ **ˌself-ˈconfidence** *noun* [U]: *He has no self-confidence.*

ˌself-congratuˈlation *noun* [U] (usually *disapproving*) a way of behaving that shows that you think you have done something very well and are pleased with yourself ▶ **ˌself-conˈgratulatory** *adj.*: *The winners gave themselves a self-congratulatory round of applause.*

ˌself-ˈconscious *adj.* **1** ~ **(about sth)** nervous or embarrassed about your appearance or what other people think of you: *He's always been self-conscious about being so short.* **2** (often *disapproving*) done in a way that shows you are aware of the effect that is being produced: *The humor of the play is self-conscious and contrived.* **ANT** UNSELFCONSCIOUS ▶ **ˌself-ˈconsciously** *adv.*: *She was self-consciously aware of his stare.* **ˌself-ˈconsciousness** *noun* [U]

ˌself-conˈtained *adj.* **1** not needing or depending on other people: *Her father was a quiet, self-contained man.* **2** able to operate or exist without outside help or influence **SYN** INDEPENDENT: *a self-contained community* ◆ *Each chapter is self-contained and can be studied in isolation.*

ˌself-contraˈdictory *adj.* containing two ideas or statements that cannot both be true ▶ **ˌself-contraˈdiction** *noun* [U]

ˌself-conˈtrol *noun* [U] the ability to remain calm and not show your emotions even though you are feeling angry, excited, etc.: *to lose/regain your **self-control*** ◆ *It took all his self-control not to shout at them.* ▶ ˌself-conˈtrolled *adj.*

ˌself-corˈrecting *adj.* [usually before noun] that corrects or adjusts itself without outside help: *The economic market is a self-correcting mechanism that does not need regulation by government.*

ˌself-ˈcriticism *noun* [U] the process of looking at and judging your own faults or weaknesses ▶ ˌself-ˈcritical *adj.*: *Don't be too self-critical.*

ˌself-deˈception *noun* [U] the act of making yourself believe something that you know is not true

ˌself-deˈfeating *adj.* causing more problems and difficulties instead of solving them; not achieving what you wanted to achieve but having an opposite effect: *Paying too much attention to children when they misbehave can be self-defeating.*

ˌself-deˈfense *noun* [U] **1** something you say or do in order to protect yourself when you are being attacked, criticized, etc.: *The man later told police that he was acting in **self-defense**.* **2** the skill of being able to protect yourself from physical attack without using weapons: *I'm taking classes in self-defense.*

ˌself-deˈlusion *noun* [U] the act of making yourself believe something that you know is not true

ˌself-deˈnial *noun* [U] the act of not having or doing the things you like, either because you do not have enough money, or for moral or religious reasons **SYN** ABSTINENCE

ˌself-ˈdeprecating *adj.* done in a way that makes your own achievements or abilities seem unimportant: *He gave a self-deprecating shrug.* ▶ ˌself-depreˈcation /ˌsɛlf dɛprəˈkeɪʃn/ *noun* [U]

ˌself-deˈscribed *adj.* [only before noun] using particular words to describe yourself, although your description may not be true or accurate: *He's a self-described "nice guy."*

ˌself-deˈstruct /ˌsɛlf dɪˈstrʌkt/ *verb* [I] (especially of a machine, etc.) to destroy itself, usually by exploding: *This tape will self-destruct in 30 seconds.* ◆ (*figurative*) *In the last half-hour of the movie the plot rapidly self-destructs.*

ˌself-deˈstruction *noun* [U] the act of doing things to deliberately harm yourself ▶ ˌself-deˈstructive *adj.*

ˌself-determiˈnation *noun* [U] **1** the right of a country and its people to be independent and to choose their own government and political system **SYN** INDEPENDENCE **2** the right or ability of a person to control their own FATE

ˌself-deˈvelopment *noun* [U] the process by which a person's character and abilities are developed: *Staff are encouraged to use the library for professional self-development.*

ˌself-ˈdiscipline *noun* [U] the ability to make yourself do something, especially something difficult or unpleasant: *It takes a lot of self-discipline to go jogging in winter.*

ˌself-ˈdiscovery *noun* [U] the process of understanding more about yourself in order to make yourself happier: *David left his boring job to go on a **journey of self-discovery**.*

ˌself-ˈdoubt *noun* [U, C] the feeling that you are not good enough

ˌself-ˈeducated *adj.* having learned things by reading books, etc., rather than at school or college

ˌself-efˈfacing *adj.* not wanting to attract attention to yourself or your abilities **SYN** MODEST: *He was a shy, self-effacing man.* ▶ ˌself-efˈfacement *noun* [U]

ˌself-emˈployed *adj.* working for yourself and not employed by a company, etc.: *a self-employed musician* ◆ *retirement plans for the self-employed* (= people who are self-employed) ▶ ˌself-emˈployment *noun* [U]

ˌself-eˈsteem *noun* [U] a feeling of being happy with your own character and abilities **SYN** SELF-WORTH: *to have high/low self-esteem* ◆ *You need to build your self-esteem.*

ˌself-ˈevident *adj.* obvious and needing no further proof or

explanation: *The dangers of such action are self-evident.* ◆ *a self-evident truth* ▶ ˌself-ˈevidently *adv.*

ˌself-examiˈnation *noun* [U] **1** the study of your own behavior and beliefs to find out if they are right or wrong **2** the act of checking your body for any signs of illness

ˌself-exˈplanatory *adj.* easy to understand and not needing any more explanation

ˌself-exˈpression *noun* [U] the expression of your thoughts or feelings, especially through activities such as writing, painting, dancing, etc.: *You should encourage your child's attempts at self-expression.*

ˌself-fulˈfilling *adj.* [usually before noun] a **self-fulfilling** PROPHECY is one that becomes true because people expect it to be true and behave in a way that will make it happen: *If you expect to fail, you will fail. It's a self-fulfilling prophecy.*

ˌself-fulˈfillment *noun* [U] the feeling of being happy and satisfied that you have everything you want or need

ˌself-ˈgovernment *noun* [U] the government or control of a country or an organization by its own people or members, not by others ▶ ˌself-ˈgoverning *adj.*

ˌself-ˈharm *noun* [U] the practice of deliberately injuring yourself, for example by cutting yourself, as a result of having serious emotional or mental problems ▶ ˌself-ˈharm *verb* [I]: *As a teenager I was self-harming regularly.*

ˌself-ˈhelp *noun* [U] the act of relying on your own efforts and abilities in order to solve your problems, rather than depending on other people for help ▶ ˌself-ˈhelp *adj.* [only before noun]: *a self-help discussion group for people suffering from depression* (= whose members help each other)

ˈself·hood /ˈsɛlfhʊd/ *noun* [U] the quality that gives a person or thing an individual identity and makes them different from others: *to understand the nature and development of selfhood*

ˌself-ˈimage *noun* the opinion or idea you have of yourself, especially of your appearance or abilities: *to have a **positive/negative self-image***

ˌself-imˈportant *adj.* (*disapproving*) thinking that you are more important than other people **SYN** ARROGANT ▶ ˌself-imˈportance *noun* [U] ˌself-imˈportantly *adv.*

ˌself-imˈposed *adj.* [usually before noun] a **self-imposed** task, duty, etc. is one that you force yourself to do rather than one that someone else forces you to do

ˌself-imˈprovement *noun* [U] the process by which a person improves their knowledge, status, character, etc. by their own efforts

ˌself-inˈduced *adj.* (of illness, problems, etc.) caused by yourself: *self-induced vomiting*

ˌself-inˈdulgent *adj.* (*disapproving*) allowing yourself to have or do things that you like, especially when you do this too much or too often ▶ ˌself-inˈdulgence *noun* [U]

ˌself-inˈflicted *adj.* a **self-inflicted** injury, problem, etc. is one that you cause for yourself: *a self-inflicted wound*

ˌself-ˈinterest *noun* [U] (*disapproving*) the fact of someone only considering their own interests and of not caring about things that would help other people: *Not all of them were acting out of self-interest.* ▶ ˌself-ˈinterested *adj.*

ˈself·ish /ˈsɛlfɪʃ/ *adj.* caring only about yourself rather than about other people: *selfish behavior* ◆ *Do you think I'm being selfish by not letting her go?* ◆ *What a selfish thing to do!* ◆ *It was selfish of him to leave all the work to you.* **ANT** SELFLESS, UNSELFISH ▶ ˈself·ish·ly *adv.*: *She looked forward, a little selfishly, to a weekend away from her family.* ˈself·ish·ness *noun* [U]

ˌself-ˈknowledge *noun* [U] an understanding of yourself

ˈself·less /ˈsɛlfləs/ *adj.* thinking more about the needs, happiness, etc. of other people than about your own: *a life of selfless service to the community* **ANT** SELFISH ▶ ˈself·less·ly *adv.* ˈself·less·ness *noun* [U]

self-'love *noun* [U] (*approving*) the feeling that your own happiness and wishes are important

self-'made *adj.* [usually before noun] having become rich and successful through your own hard work rather than having had money given to you: *He was proud of the fact that he was a self-made man.*

self-'motivated *adj.* if a person is **self-motivated**, they are capable of hard work and effort without the need for encouragement ▶ **self-moti'vation** *noun* [U]

self-muti'lation *noun* [U] the act of wounding yourself, especially when this is a sign of mental illness

self-per'petuating *adj.* continuing without any outside influence: *Revenge leads to a self-perpetuating cycle of violence.*

self-'pity *noun* [U] (often *disapproving*) feeling sorry for yourself, especially because of something unpleasant or unfair that has happened to you: *She's not someone who likes to wallow in self-pity.* ▶ **self-'pitying** *adj.*

self-'portrait *noun* a painting, etc. that you do of yourself

self-pos'sessed *adj.* able to remain calm and confident in a difficult situation ▶ **self-pos'session** *noun* [U]: *He soon recovered his usual self-possession.*

self-preser'vation *noun* [U] the fact of protecting yourself in a dangerous or difficult situation: *She was held back by some sense of self-preservation.*

self-pro'claimed *adj.* (often *disapproving*) giving yourself a particular title, job, etc. without the agreement or permission of other people

self-pro'motion *noun* [U] (usually *disapproving*) the activity of making people notice you and your abilities, especially in a way that annoys other people: *The article was a piece of blatant self-promotion.*

self-reali'zation *noun* [U] the fact of using your skills and abilities and achieving as much as you can possibly achieve **SYN** SELF-ACTUALIZATION

self·ref·er·en·tial /ˌself refəˈrenʃl/ *adj.* (*technical*) (of a work of literature) referring to the fact of actually being a work of literature, or to the author, or to other works that the author has written

self-re'gard *noun* [U] a good opinion of yourself, which is considered bad if you have too little or too much: *He suffers from a lack of self-regard.* ▶ **self-re'garding** *adj.*: *His biography is nothing but self-regarding nonsense.*

self-'regulating *adj.* something that is **self-regulating** controls itself: *a self-regulating economy* ▶ **self-regu'lation** *noun* [U]

self-re'liant *adj.* able to do or decide things by yourself, rather than depending on other people for help **SYN** INDEPENDENT ▶ **self-re'liance** *noun* [U]

self-re'spect *noun* [U] a feeling of pride in yourself that what you do, say, etc. is right and good

self-re'specting *adj.* [only before noun] (especially in negative sentences) having pride in yourself because you believe that what you do is right and good: *No self-respecting journalist would ever work for that newspaper.*

self-re'straint *noun* [U] the ability to stop yourself doing or saying something that you want to because you know it is better not to: *She exercised all her self-restraint and kept quiet.*

self-'righteous *adj.* (*disapproving*) feeling or behaving as if what you say or do is always morally right, and other people are wrong **SYN** SANCTIMONIOUS ▶ **self-'righteously** *adv.* **self-'righteousness** *noun* [U]

self-rising 'flour *noun* [U] flour that contains BAKING POWDER ⊃ compare ALL-PURPOSE FLOUR

self-'rule *noun* [U] the governing of a country or an area by its own people

self-'sacrifice *noun* [U] (*approving*) the act of not allowing yourself to have or do something in order to help other people: *the courage and self-sacrifice of those who fought in the war* ▶ **self-'sacrificing** *adj.*

self-'same /ˈselfseɪm/ *adj.* [only before noun] **the, this, etc. selfsame…** used to emphasize that two people or things are the same **SYN** IDENTICAL: *Jane had been wondering that selfsame thing.*

self-'satisfied *adj.* (*disapproving*) too pleased with yourself or your own achievements **SYN** SMUG: *He had a self-satisfied smirk on his face.* ▶ **self-satis'faction** *noun* [U]: *a look of self-satisfaction*

self-'seeking *adj.* (*disapproving*) interested only in your own needs and interests rather than thinking about the needs of other people ▶ **self-'seeking** *noun* [U]

self-se'lection *noun* [U] a situation in which people decide for themselves to do something rather than being chosen to do it ▶ **self-se'lected** *adj.* **self-se'lecting** *adj.*: *a self-selecting group*

self-'service *adj.* [usually before noun] a **self-service** store, restaurant, etc. is one in which customers serve themselves and then pay for the goods ▶ **self-'service** *noun* [U]: *The café provides quick self-service at low prices.*

self-'serving *adj.* (*disapproving*) interested only in gaining an advantage for yourself

self-'starter *noun* (*approving*) a person who is able to work on their own and make their own decisions without needing anyone to tell them what to do

self-'storage *noun* [U] a service that provides a place where you can store things and a key so that you can get them when you need them: *self-storage facilities/units*

self-'study *noun* [U] the activity of learning about something without a teacher to help you ▶ **self-'study** *adj.*: *self-study materials*

self-'styled *adj.* [only before noun] (*disapproving*) using a name or title that you have given yourself, especially when you do not have the right to do it

self-suf'ficient *adj.* ~ **(in sth)** able to do or produce everything that you need without the help of other people: *The country is totally self-sufficient in food production.* ▶ **self-suf'ficiency** *noun* [U]

self-sup'porting *adj.* having enough money to be able to operate without financial help from other people

self-'taught *adj.* having learned something by reading books, etc., rather than by someone teaching you: *a self-taught artist*

self-'titled *adj.* [only before noun] (of a CD, record, etc.) having a title that is the same as the performer's name: *The band released a self-titled album in 1997.*

self-'willed *adj.* (*disapproving*) determined to do what you want without caring about other people **SYN** HEADSTRONG

self-'worth *noun* [U] a feeling of confidence in yourself that you are a good and useful person **SYN** SELF-ESTEEM

sell 🖉 /sel/ *verb, noun*

● *verb* (sold, sold /səʊld/)

▸ EXCHANGE FOR MONEY **1** [T, I] to give something to someone in exchange for money: ~ **sth (to sb) (for sth)** *I sold my car to James for $1,800.* ◆ ~ **sb sth (for sth)** *I sold James my car for $1,800.* ◆ ~ **(sth) (at sth)** *They sold the business at a profit/ loss* (= they gained/lost money when they sold it). ◆ *We offered them a good price but they wouldn't sell.*

▸ OFFER FOR SALE **2** [T] ~ **sth** to offer something for people to buy: *Most supermarkets sell a selection of organic products.* ◆ *Do you sell stamps?* ◆ *to sell insurance* ⊃ compare CROSS-SELLING

▸ BE BOUGHT **3** [T, I] to be bought by people in the way or in the numbers mentioned; to be offered at the price mentioned: ~ **(sth)** *The magazine sells 300,000 copies a week.* ◆ *The book sold well and was reprinted many times.* ◆ *The new design just didn't sell* (= nobody bought it). ◆ ~ **for/at sth** *The pens sell for just $1.50 each.*

▸ PERSUADE **4** [I, T] to make people want to buy something: *You may not like it but advertising sells.* ◆ ~ **sth** *It is quality not price that sells our products.* **5** [T] ~ **sth/yourself (to sb)** to persuade someone that something is a good idea, service, product, etc.; to persuade someone that you are the right person for a job, position, etc.: *Now we have to try and sell the idea to management.* ◆ *You really have to sell yourself at a job interview.*

▷ TAKE MONEY/REWARD **6** [T] ~ **yourself (to sb)** (*disapproving*) to accept money or a reward from someone for doing something that is against your principles **SYN** PROSTITUTE ➔ see also SALE

IDM **be sold on sth** (*informal*) to be very enthusiastic about something **sell your body** to have sex with someone in exchange for money **sell sb down the river** (*informal*) to give poor or unfair treatment to someone you have promised to help **ORIGIN** From the custom of buying and selling slaves on the plantations on the Mississippi river. Slaves who caused trouble for their masters could be sold to plantation owners lower down the river, where conditions would be worse. **sell sb/yourself short** to not value someone/yourself highly enough and show this by the way you treat or present them/yourself **sell your soul (to the devil)** to do anything, even something bad or dishonest, in return for money, success, or power ➔ more at HOT *adj.* **PHR V** ,sell sth↔'off **1** to sell things cheaply because you want to get rid of them or because you need the money **2** to sell all or part of an industry, a company, or land: *The Church sold off the land for housing.* 'sell sb on sth (*informal*) to persuade someone to be enthusiastic about something: *I couldn't sell him on the idea.* ,sell 'out | be ,sold 'out (of tickets for a concert, sports game, etc.) to be all sold: *The tickets sold out within hours.* ◆ *This week's performances are completely sold out.* ,sell 'out (of sth) | be ,sold 'out (of sth) to have sold all the available items, tickets, etc.: *I'm sorry, we've sold out of bread.* ◆ *We are already sold out for what should be a fantastic game.* ,sell 'out (to sb/sth) **1** (*disapproving*) to change or give up your beliefs or principles: *He's a talented screenwriter who has sold out to TV soap operas.* **2** to sell your business or a part of your business: *The company eventually sold out to a multinational media group.* ➔ related noun SELLOUT ,sell sb↔'out (*disapproving*) to disappoint or hurt someone who trusted you: *The association has sold out its members with its decision on this issue.* ➔ related noun SELLOUT

● *noun* [sing.] **a hard, tough, easy, etc. ~** something that is difficult/easy to persuade people to buy or accept: *This policy is going to be a tough sell to the public.* ➔ see also HARD SELL

'sell-by ,date (also 'pull date) *noun* the date printed on food packages, etc. after which the food must not be sold: *This milk is past its sell-by date.* ◆ (*figurative*) *These policies are way past their sell-by date.*

sell·er /'sɛlər/ *noun* **1** a person who sells something: *a flower seller* ◆ *The law is intended to protect both the buyer and the seller.* ➔ see also BOOKSELLER ➔ compare VENDOR **2 a good, poor, etc. ~** a product that has been sold in the amounts or way mentioned: *This particular model is one of our biggest sellers.* ➔ see also BEST SELLER

IDM **a seller's market** a situation in which people selling something have an advantage, because there is not a lot of a particular item for sale, and prices can be kept high

'selling ,point *noun* a feature of something that makes people want to buy or use it: *The price is obviously one of the main selling points.* ◆ *Sales departments try to identify a product's USP or "unique selling point."*

'selling ,price *noun* the price at which something is sold ➔ compare ASKING PRICE

'sell-off *noun* (*business*) the sale of a large number of STOCKS and SHARES, after which their value usually falls

'sell-out (also sell-'out) /'sɛlaʊt/ *noun* [usually sing.] **1** a play, concert, etc. for which all the tickets have been sold: *Next week's final looks like being a sellout.* ◆ *a sellout tour* **2** a situation in which someone is not loyal to a person or group who trusted them, by not doing something that they promised to do, or by doing something that they promised not to do: *The workers see the deal as a union sellout to management.* **3** someone who is not loyal to a person or group who trusted them, especially by giving up their

beliefs or principles: *The actor was accused of being a sellout to his own culture.*

selt·zer /'sɛltsər/ *noun* [U, C] water with natural bubbles and usually containing minerals, used as a drink

sel·vage (also sel·vedge) /'sɛlvɪdʒ/ *noun* an edge that is made on a piece of cloth, which stops the threads from coming apart (= stops it from FRAYING)

selves pl. of SELF

se·man·tic /sə'mæntɪk/ *adj.* [usually before noun] (*linguistics*) connected with the meaning of words and sentences ▶ se·man·ti·cally /-kli/ *adv.*: *semantically related words*

se,mantic 'field *noun* (*linguistics*) a set of words with related meanings

se·man·tics /sə'mæntɪks/ *noun* [U] (*linguistics*) **1** the study of the meanings of words and phrases **2** the meaning of words, phrases, or systems

sem·a·phore /'sɛmə,fɔr/ *noun, verb*

● *noun* [U] a system for sending signals in which you hold your arms or two flags in particular positions to represent different letters of the alphabet

● *verb* [I, T] ~ **(sth)** | ~ **that...** to send a message to someone by semaphore or a similar system of signals

sem·blance /'sɛmbləns/ *noun* [sing., U] ~ **of sth** (*formal*) a situation in which something seems to exist although this may not, in fact, be the case: *The ceasefire brought about a semblance of peace.* ◆ *Life at last returned to some semblance of normality.*

se·men /'simən/ *noun* [U] the whitish liquid containing SPERM that is produced by the sex organs of men and male animals

se·mes·ter 🔑 /sə'mɛstər/ *noun* one of the two periods that the school or college year is divided into: *the spring/fall semester* ➔ compare TRIMESTER

sem·i /'sɛmi/ *noun* (pl. sem·is) (*informal*) **1** = TRACTOR-TRAILER **2** = SEMIFINAL

semi- /'sɛmi; 'sɛməmi/ *prefix* (in adjectives and nouns) half; partly: *semicircular* ◆ *semi-final*

sem·i·an·nu·al /,sɛmi'ænyuel; ,sɛmaɪ-/ *adj.* produced or happening twice each year: *the company's semiannual report*

,semi-'arid *adj.* (*technical*) (of land or climate) dry; with little rain

,semi-auto'matic *adj.* (of a gun) able to load bullets automatically, and therefore very quickly, but not firing automatically ▶ ,semi-auto'matic *noun*

sem·i·cir·cle /'sɛmi,sərkl/ *noun* **1** (*geometry*) one half of a circle ➔ picture at SHAPE **2** the line that forms the edge of a semicircle **3** a thing, or a group of people or things, shaped like a semicircle: *a semicircle of chairs* ◆ *We sat in a semicircle round the fire.* ▶ sem·i·cir·cu·lar /,sɛmi'sərkyələr/ *adj.*: *a semicircular driveway*

sem·i·co·lon /'sɛmi,koʊlən/ *noun* the mark (;) used to separate the parts of a complicated sentence or items in a detailed list, showing a pause that is longer than a comma but shorter than a period ➔ compare COLON

sem·i·con·duc·tor /'sɛmikən,dʌktər; 'sɛmaɪ-/ *noun* (*technical*) **1** a solid substance that CONDUCTS electricity in particular conditions, better than INSULATORS but not as well as CONDUCTORS **2** a device containing a semiconductor used in ELECTRONICS

,semi-de'tached *adj.* (*CanE*) (of a house) joined to another house by a wall on one side that is shared ▶ ,semi-de'tached *noun* (*CanE*) ➔ compare DETACHED

sem·i·fi·nal /'sɛmi,faɪnl; 'sɛmaɪ-; ,sɛmi'faɪnl; ,sɛmaɪ-/ (also *informal* sem·i) *noun* one of the two games or parts of a sports competition that are held to decide who will compete in the last part (the FINAL): *He's going through to the semifinal of the men's singles.* ▶ ,semi·fi·nal·ist /,sɛmi'faɪnl,ɪst/ *noun*: *They are semifinalists for the fourth year in succession.*

---

sem·i·nal /'sɛmənl/ adj. **1** (formal) very important and having a strong influence on later developments: *a seminal work/article/study* **2** [usually before noun] (technical) of or containing SEMEN: *seminal fluid*

sem·i·nar /'sɛmə,nar/ noun **1** a class at a university or college when a small group of students and a teacher discuss or study a particular topic: *a graduate seminar* ◆ *a seminar room* ⊃ collocations at EDUCATION **2** a meeting for discussion or training: *a one-day management seminar*

sem·i·nar·i·an /,sɛmə'nɛriən/ noun a student in a seminary

sem·i·nar·y /'sɛmə,nɛri/ noun (pl. **sem·i·nar·ies**) a college where priests, ministers, or RABBIS are trained

Sem·i·nole /'sɛmə,noʊl/ noun (pl. **Sem·i·nole** or **Sem·i·noles**) a member of a Native American people, many of whom live in Oklahoma and Florida

se·mi·ot·ics /,simi'ɑtɪks, ,sɛmi-/ noun [U] the study of signs and symbols, and of their meaning and use ▶ **se·mi·ot·ic** adj.: *semiotic analysis*

ˌsemi-ˈprecious adj. [usually before noun] (of a JEWEL) less valuable than the most valuable types of JEWELS

sem·i·pri·vate /,sɛmi'praɪvət, ,sɛmaɪ-/ adj. intended for or shared with two or more people: *a semiprivate hospital room* ◆ *semiprivate tennis lessons*

sem·i·pro·fes·sion·al /,sɛmiprə'fɛʃnl, ,sɛmaɪ-/ (also **sem·i·pro** /'sɛmi,proʊ, 'sɛmaɪ-/) adj. semiprofessional musicians or sports players are paid for what they do, but do not do it as their main job ▶ **sem·i·pro·fes·sion·al** noun

ˌsemi-ˈskilled adj. [usually before noun] (of workers) having some special training or qualifications, but less than skilled people: *a semi-skilled machine operator* ◆ *semi-skilled jobs* (= for people who have some special training)

sem·i·sweet /,sɛmi'swit, ,sɛmaɪ-/ adj. slightly sweet: *semisweet chocolate*

Sem·ite /'sɛmaɪt/ noun a member of the peoples who speak Semitic languages, including Arabs and Jews

Se·mit·ic /sə'mɪtɪk/ adj. **1** of or connected with the language group that includes Hebrew and Arabic **2** of or connected with the people who speak Semitic languages, especially Hebrew and Arabic

sem·i·trail·er /'sɛmaɪ,treɪlər/ noun a TRAILER that has wheels at the back and is supported at the front by the vehicle that is pulling it

ˌsemi-ˈtropical adj. = SUBTROPICAL

sem·i·vow·el /'sɛmi,vaʊəl/ noun (phonetics) a speech sound that sounds like a vowel but functions as a consonant, for example /w/ and /y/ in the English words *wet* and *yet*

sem·i·week·ly /,sɛmi'wikli, ,sɛmaɪ-/ adj., adv. produced or happening twice each week: *a semiweekly meeting*

sem·o·li·na /,sɛmə'linə/ noun [U] large, hard grains of WHEAT used when crushed for making PASTA and sweet dishes

sem·tex /'sɛmtɛks/ noun [U] a powerful EXPLOSIVE that is used for making bombs, often illegally

Sen. abbr. SENATOR: *Sen. John K. Nordqvist*

sen·ate 🔑 /'sɛnət/ noun usually **the Senate**
1 [sing.] one of the two groups of elected politicians who make laws in some countries, for example in the U.S., Australia, Canada, and France. The Senate is smaller than the other group but higher in rank. Many states also have a Senate: *a member of the Senate* ◆ *a Senate committee* ⊃ collocations at POLITICS ⊃ compare CONGRESS, THE HOUSE OF REPRESENTATIVES **2** [C, usually sing., U] the group of people who control some universities: *the senate of Rutgers University* **3** [sing.] (in ancient Rome) the most important council of the government; the building where the council met

sen·a·tor 🔑 /'sɛnətər/ noun often **Senator** (abbr. **Sen.**) a member of a senate: *Senator McCarthy* ◆ *She has served as a Democratic senator for North Carolina since 2009.*

▶ **sen·a·to·ri·al** /,sɛnə'tɔriəl/ adj. [only before noun]: *a senatorial candidate*

send 🔑 /sɛnd/ verb (**sent, sent** /sɛnt/)
▷ BY MAIL/RADIO **1** to make something go or be taken to a place, especially by mail, e-mail, radio, etc.: ~ sth *to send a letter/package/check/fax/an e-mail* ◆ *She sent the letter by airmail.* ◆ *to send something by mail* ◆ ~ sth to sb *A radio signal was sent to the spacecraft.* ◆ *The CD player was defective so we sent it back to the manufacturers.* ◆ *Have you sent a postcard to your mother yet?* ◆ ~ sb sth *Have you sent your mother a postcard yet?* ◆ *I'll send you a text message.*
▷ MESSAGE **2** to tell someone something by sending them a message: ~ sth *My parents send their love.* ◆ ~ sth to sb *What sort of message is that sending to young people?* ◆ ~ sb sth *He sent me word to come.* ◆ ~ sth (that)… *She sent word (that) she could not come.*
▷ SOMEONE SOMEWHERE **3** to tell someone to go somewhere or to do something; to arrange for someone to go somewhere: ~ sb *Ed couldn't make it so they sent me instead.* ◆ ~ sb + adv./prep. *She sent the kids to bed early.* ◆ *to send someone to prison/boarding school* ◆ ~ sb to do sth *I sent Tom to buy some milk.*
▷ MAKE SOMETHING MOVE QUICKLY **4** to make something or someone move quickly or suddenly: ~ sth/sb doing sth *Every step he took sent the pain shooting up his leg.* ◆ *The punch sent him flying.* ◆ ~ sth/sb + adv./prep. *The report sent share prices down a further 50 cents.*
▷ MAKE SOMEONE REACT **5** to make someone behave or react in a particular way: ~ sb to sth *Her music always sends me to sleep.* ◆ ~ sb into sth *Her account of the visit sent us into fits of laughter.*
IDM **send sb packing** (informal) to tell someone firmly or rudely to go away ⊃ more at LOVE *n.*
PHR V ,send a'way (to sb) (for sth) (also ,send ,off (for sth)) to write to someone and ask them to send you something by mail: *I sent away for USC's grad school catalog.* 'send for sb to ask or tell someone to come to you, especially in order to help you: *Send for a doctor, quickly!* 'send for sth to ask someone to bring or deliver something to you: *His son found him and sent for help.* ◆ *She sent for the latest sales figures.* ,send sb 'forth (old-fashioned or literary) to send someone away from you to another place ,send 'forth sth (formal) to produce a sound, signal, etc. so that other people can hear it, receive it, etc.: *He opened his mouth and sent forth a stream of noise.* ,send sb↔'in to order someone to go to a place to deal with a difficult situation: *Troops were sent in to restore order.* ,send sth↔'in to send something by mail to a place where it will be dealt with: *Have you sent in your application yet?* ,send 'off (for sth) (also ,send a'way (to sb) (for sth)) to write to someone and ask them to send you something by mail: *I sent off for some books for my class.* ,send sth↔'off to send something to a place by mail: *I'm sending the files off to my boss tomorrow.* ,send sth↔'on **1** to send something to a place so that it arrives before you get there: *We sent our furniture on by ship.* **2** to send a letter that has been sent to someone's old address to their new address **SYN** FORWARD **3** to send something from one place/person to another: *They arranged for the information to be sent on to us.* ,send 'out for sth to ask a restaurant or store to deliver food to you at home or at work: *Let's send out for a pizza.* ,send sth↔'out **1** to send something to a lot of different people or places: *Have the invitations been sent out yet?* **2** to produce something, such as light, a signal, sound, etc. **SYN** EMIT ,send sb/sth↔'up (informal) to make people laugh at someone or something by copying them or it in a funny way: *a TV program that sends up politicians* ⊃ related noun SEND-UP ,send sb↔'up (informal) to send someone to prison

send·er /'sɛndər/ noun a person who sends something: *If undelivered, please return to sender.*

'send-off noun (informal) an occasion when people come together to say goodbye to someone who is leaving

'send-up noun (informal) an act of making someone or something look silly by copying them in a funny way

ʌ cup   ə about   eɪ say   aɪ five   ɔɪ boy   aʊ now   oʊ go   ər bird

Sen·e·ca /ˈsɛnəkə/ noun (pl. **Sen·e·ca** or **Sen·e·cas**) a member of a Native American people, many of whom now live in New York and Ohio

se·nes·cence /sɪˈnɛsns/ noun [U] (formal) the process of becoming old and showing the effects of being old ▶ **se·nes·cent** /-snt/ adj.

se·nile /ˈsinaɪl/ adj. behaving in a confused or strange way, and unable to remember things, because you are old: I think she's **going senile**. ⊃ collocations at AGE ▶ **se·nil·i·ty** /səˈnɪləti/ noun [U]: an old man on the verge of senility

senile de'mentia noun [U] a serious mental DISORDER in old people that causes loss of memory, loss of control of the body, etc.

sen·ior ✎ /ˈsinyər/ adj., noun

● **adj.**
> OF HIGH RANK **1** ~ **(to sb)** high in rank or status; higher in rank or status than others: a senior officer/manager/lecturer, etc. ◆ a senior partner in a law firm ◆ a senior post/position ◆ I have ten years' experience at senior management level. **ANT** JUNIOR
> SCHOOL/COLLEGE **2** [only before noun] connected with the last year in high school or college: the senior prom
> FATHER **3** Senior (abbr. Sr.) used after the name of a man who has the same name as his son, to avoid confusion ⊃ compare JUNIOR
> IN SPORTS **4** [only before noun] for adults or people at a more advanced level: to take part in senior competitions ◆ He won the senior men's 400 meters.

● **noun**
> IN SCHOOL/COLLEGE **1** a student in the last year at a high school or college: high school seniors ⊃ compare FRESHMAN, JUNIOR, SOPHOMORE
> OLDER PERSON **2** a person who is older than someone else: She was ten years his senior. ◆ My brother is my senior by two years. ⊃ compare JUNIOR **3** = SENIOR CITIZEN
> HIGHER RANK **4** a person who is higher in rank or status: She felt unappreciated both by her colleagues and her seniors.
> IN SPORT **5** adults or people who have reached an advanced level: tennis coaching for juniors and seniors

senior 'citizen (also **sen·ior**) noun an older person, especially someone who has retired from work. People often call someone a "senior citizen" to avoid saying that they are old.

senior 'high school (also **senior 'high**) noun a school for young people between the ages of 14 and 18 ⊃ compare JUNIOR HIGH SCHOOL

sen·ior·i·ty /ˌsinˈyɔrəti; -ˈyar-/ noun [U] **1** the fact of being older or of a higher rank than others: a position of seniority **2** the rank that you have in a company because of the length of time you have worked there: a lawyer with five years' seniority ◆ Should promotion be based on merit or seniority?

senior 'moment noun (humorous) an occasion when someone forgets something, or does not think clearly (thought to be typical of what happens when people get older): It was an important meeting and a bad time to **have a senior moment**.

sen·sa·tion /sɛnˈseɪʃn/ noun **1** [C] a feeling that you get when something affects your body: a tingling/burning, etc. sensation ◆ I had a sensation of falling, as if in a dream. **2** [U] the ability to feel through your sense of touch **SYN** FEELING: She seemed to have lost all sensation in her arm. **3** [C, usually sing.] a general feeling or impression that is difficult to explain; an experience or a memory: He had the eerie sensation of being watched. ◆ When I arrived, I had the sensation that she had been expecting me. **4** [C, usually sing., U] very great surprise, excitement, or interest among a lot of people; the person or the thing that causes this surprise: News of his arrest **caused a sensation**. ◆ The band became a sensation overnight.

sen·sa·tion·al /sɛnˈseɪʃənl/ adj. **1** causing great surprise, excitement, or interest **SYN** THRILLING: The result was a sensational 4–1 victory. **2** (disapproving) (of a newspaper, etc.) trying to get your interest by presenting facts or events as worse or more shocking than they really are **3** (informal) extremely good; wonderful **SYN** FANTASTIC: You look sensational in that dress! ▶ **sen·sa·tion·al·ly** /-ʃənəli/ adv.: They won sensationally against the best team. ◆ The incident was sensationally reported in the press. ◆ He's sensationally good-looking!

sen·sa·tion·al·ism /sɛnˈseɪʃənəˌlɪzəm/ noun [U] (disapproving) a way of getting people's interest by using shocking words or by presenting facts and events as worse or more shocking than they really are ▶ **sen·sa·tion·al·ist** /-lɪst/ adj.: sensationalist headlines

sen·sa·tion·al·ize /sɛnˈseɪʃənəˌlaɪz/ verb ~ **sth** (disapproving) to exaggerate a story so that it seems more exciting or shocking than it really is

sense ✎ /sɛns/ noun, verb

● **noun**
> SIGHT/HEARING, ETC. **1** [C] one of the five powers (sight, hearing, smell, taste, and touch) that your body uses to get information about the world around you: the five senses ◆ Dogs have a keen (= strong) **sense of smell**. ◆ the **sense organs** (= eyes, ears, nose, etc.) ◆ I could hardly believe the evidence of my own senses (= what I could see, hear, etc.). ◆ The mixture of sights, smells, and sounds around her made her senses reel. ⊃ see also SIXTH SENSE
> FEELING **2** [C] a feeling about something important: He felt an overwhelming **sense of loss**. ◆ a strong **sense of purpose/identity/duty**, etc. ◆ Helmets can give cyclists a false **sense of security**. ◆ I had the **sense that** he was worried about something.
> UNDERSTANDING/JUDGMENT **3** [sing.] an understanding about something; an ability to judge something: One of the most important things in a partner is a **sense of humor** (= the ability to find things funny or make people laugh). ◆ He has a very good **sense of direction** (= finds the way to a place easily). ◆ She has lost all sense of direction in her life. ◆ Always try to keep a **sense of proportion** (= of the relative importance of different things). ◆ a **sense of rhythm/timing** ◆ Alex doesn't have any **dress sense** (= does not know which clothes look attractive). **4** [U] good understanding and judgment; knowledge of what is sensible or practical behavior: You should **have the sense to** take advice when it is offered. ◆ **There's no sense in** (= it is not sensible) worrying about it now. ◆ Can't you **talk sense** (= say something sensible)? ◆ There's a lot of sense in what Mary says. ⊃ see also COMMON SENSE, GOOD SENSE
> NORMAL STATE OF MIND **5** senses [pl.] a normal state of mind; the ability to think clearly: If she threatens to leave, it should **bring him to his senses**. ◆ He waited for Dora to **come to her senses** and return. ◆ (old-fashioned) Are you **out of your senses**? You'll be killed! ◆ (old-fashioned) Why does she want to marry him? She must have **taken leave of her senses**.
> MEANING **6** [C] the meaning that a word or phrase has; a way of understanding sth: The word "love" is used in different senses by different people. ◆ education in its broadest sense ◆ He was a true friend, **in every sense of the word** (= in every possible way). ◆ **In a sense** (= in one way) it doesn't matter any more. ◆ **In some senses** (= in one or more ways) the criticisms were justified. ◆ (formal) **In no sense** can the issue be said to be resolved. ◆ There is a sense in which we are all to blame for the tragedy. ⊃ note at SENSIBLE

IDM **knock/talk some sense into sb** to try and persuade someone to stop behaving in a stupid way, sometimes using rough or violent methods **make sense 1** to have a meaning that you can easily understand: This sentence doesn't make sense. **2** to be a sensible thing to do: It makes sense to buy the most up-to-date version. **3** to be easy to understand or explain: John wasn't making much sense on the phone. ◆ Who would send me all these flowers? It makes no sense. **make sense of sth** to understand something that is difficult or has no clear meaning **see sense** to start to be sensible or reasonable **a sense of occasion** a feeling or understanding that an event is important or special: Candles on the table gave the evening a sense of occasion. ⊃ more at LEAVE n.

• **verb** (not used in the progressive tenses)
> BECOME AWARE **1** to become aware of something even though you cannot see it, hear it, etc.: ~ *sth Sensing danger, they started to run.* ◆ ~ **(that)…** *Lisa sensed that he did not believe her.* ◆ *Thomas, she sensed, could convince anyone of anything.* ◆ ~ **sb/sth doing sth** *He sensed someone moving around behind him.* ◆ ~ **sb/sth do sth** *He sensed something move in the bushes.* ◆ ~ **how, what, etc.…** *She could sense how nervous he was.*
> OF MACHINE **2** ~ *sth* to discover and record something: *equipment that senses the presence of toxic gases*

sense·less /'sɛnsləs/ *adj.* **1** (disapproving) having no meaning or purpose **SYN** POINTLESS: *senseless violence* ◆ *His death was a senseless waste of life.* ◆ *It's senseless to continue any further.* **2** [not before noun] unconscious: *He was beaten senseless.* ◆ *She drank herself senseless.* **3** not using good judgment: *The police blamed senseless drivers who went too fast.* ▶ **sense·less·ly** *adv.*

sen·si·bil·i·ty /ˌsɛnsə'bɪləti/ *noun* (pl. **sen·si·bil·i·ties**) **1** [U, C] the ability to experience and understand deep feelings, especially in art and literature: *a man of impeccable manners, charm, and sensibility* ◆ *artistic sensibility* **2** **sensibilities** [pl.] a person's feelings, especially when the person is easily offended or influenced by something: *The article offended her religious sensibilities.*

sen·si·ble 🔑 /'sɛnsəbl/ *adj.*
1 (of people and their behavior) able to make good judgments based on reason and experience rather than emotion **SYN** PRACTICAL (4): *She's a sensible sort of person.* ◆ *I think that's a very sensible idea.* ◆ *Say something sensible.* ◆ *I think **the sensible thing** would be to take a taxi home.* **2** (of clothes, etc.) useful rather than fashionable: *sensible shoes* **3** (formal or literary) aware of something: *I am sensible of the fact that mathematics is not a popular subject.* **ANT** INSENSIBLE
HELP Use **silly** (sense 1) or **impractical** (senses 1 and 2) as the opposite for the other senses. ▶ **sen·si·bly** /-bli/ *adv.*: *to behave sensibly* ◆ *He decided, very sensibly, not to drive when he was so tired.* ◆ *She's always very sensibly dressed.*

WHICH WORD?

sensible ◆ sensitive

- **Sensible** and **sensitive** are connected with two different meanings of **sense**.
- **Sensible** refers to your ability to make good judgments: *She gave me some very sensible advice.* ◆ *It wasn't very sensible to go out on your own so late at night.*
- **Sensitive** refers to how easily you react to things and how much you are aware of things or other people: *a soap for sensitive skin* ◆ *This movie may upset a sensitive child.*

---

sen·si·tive 🔑 /'sɛnsətɪv/ *adj.*
> TO PEOPLE'S FEELINGS **1** aware of and able to understand other people and their feelings: *a sensitive and caring man* ◆ ~ **to sth** *She is very sensitive to other people's feelings.* **ANT** INSENSITIVE ⊃ note at SENSIBLE
> TO ART/MUSIC/LITERATURE **2** able to understand art, music, and literature and to express yourself through them: *an actor's sensitive reading of the poem* ◆ *a sensitive portrait*
> EASILY UPSET **3** easily offended or upset: *You're far too sensitive.* ◆ ~ **about sth** *He's very sensitive about his weight.* ◆ ~ **to sth** *She's very sensitive to criticism.* **ANT** INSENSITIVE
> INFORMATION/SUBJECT **4** that you have to treat with great care because it may offend people or make them angry: *Health care is a politically sensitive issue.*
> TO COLD/LIGHT/FOOD, ETC. **5** reacting quickly or more than usual to something: *sensitive areas of the body* ◆ ~ **to sth** *My teeth are very sensitive to cold food.* ◆ *light-sensitive paper* **ANT** INSENSITIVE
> TO SMALL CHANGES **6** ~ **(to sth)** able to measure very small changes: *a sensitive instrument* ◆ (figurative) *The Stock Exchange is very sensitive to political change.* **ANT** INSENSITIVE

> **sen·si·tive·ly** *adv.*: *She handled the matter sensitively.* ◆ *He writes sensitively.* **IDM** see NERVE *n.*

sen·si·tiv·i·ty /ˌsɛnsə'tɪvəti/ *noun* (pl. **sen·si·tiv·i·ties**)
> TO PEOPLE'S FEELINGS **1** [U] ~ **(to sth)** the ability to understand other people's feelings: *sensitivity to the needs of children* ◆ *She pointed out with tact and sensitivity exactly where he had gone wrong.*
> TO ART/MUSIC/LITERATURE **2** [U] the ability to understand art, music, and literature and to express yourself through them: *She played with great sensitivity.*
> BEING EASILY UPSET **3** [U, C, usually pl.] a tendency to be easily offended or upset by something: *He's a mixture of anger and sensitivity.* ◆ *She was blind to the feelings and sensitivities of other people.*
> OF INFORMATION/SUBJECT **4** [U] the fact of needing to be treated very carefully because it may offend or upset people: *Confidentiality is important because of the sensitivity of the information.*
> TO FOOD/COLD/LIGHT, ETC. **5** [U, C, usually pl.] (technical) the quality of reacting quickly or more than usual to something: *food sensitivity* ◆ *allergies and sensitivities* ◆ *Some children develop a sensitivity to cow's milk.* ◆ *The eyes of some fish have a greater sensitivity to light than ours do.*
> TO SMALL CHANGES **6** [U] the ability to measure very small changes: *the sensitivity of the test*

sen·si·tize /'sɛnsə,taɪz/ *verb* [usually passive] **1** ~ **sb/sth (to sth)** to make someone or something more aware of something, especially a problem or something bad: *People are becoming more sensitized to the dangers threatening the environment.* **2** ~ **sb/sth (to sth)** (technical) to make someone or something sensitive to physical or chemical changes, or to a particular substance ▶ **sen·si·ti·za·tion** /ˌsɛnsətə'zeɪʃn/ *noun* [U]

sen·sor /'sɛnsər/ *noun* a device that can react to light, heat, pressure, etc. in order to make a machine, etc. do something or show something: *security lights with an infrared sensor* (= that come on when a person is near them)

sen·so·ry /'sɛnsəri/ *adj.* [usually before noun] (technical) connected with your physical senses: *sensory organs* ◆ *sensory deprivation*

sen·su·al /'sɛnʃuəl/ *adj.* **1** connected with your physical feelings; giving pleasure to your physical senses, especially sexual pleasure: *sensual pleasure* **2** suggesting an interest in physical pleasure, especially sexual pleasure: *sensual lips* ◆ *He was darkly sensual and mysterious.* ▶ **sen·su·al·i·ty** /ˌsɛnʃu'æləti/ *noun* [U]: *the sensuality of his poetry* **sen·su·al·ly** /'sɛnʃuəli/ *adv.*

sen·su·ous /'sɛnʃuəs/ *adj.* **1** giving pleasure to your senses: *sensuous music* ◆ *I'm drawn to the poetic, sensuous qualities of her paintings.* **2** suggesting an interest in sexual pleasure: *his full, sensuous lips* ▶ **sen·su·ous·ly** *adv.* **sen·su·ous·ness** *noun* [U]

sent pt, pp of SEND

sen·tence 🔑 /'sɛntns/ *noun, verb*
• **noun 1** [C] (grammar) a set of words expressing a statement, a question, or an order, usually containing a subject and a verb. In written English sentences begin with a capital letter and end with a period (.), a question mark (?), or an exclamation point (!). **2** [C, U] the punishment given by a court: *a jail/prison sentence* ◆ *a light/heavy sentence* ◆ *to be under sentence of death* ◆ *The judge passed sentence* (= said what the punishment would be). ◆ *He issued a light sentence to Jones.* ◆ *The prisoner has served* (= completed) *his sentence and will be released tomorrow.* ⊃ collocations at JUSTICE ⊃ see also DEATH SENTENCE, LIFE SENTENCE
• **verb** [often passive] ~ **sb (to sth)** | ~ **sb to do sth** to say officially in court that someone is to receive a particular punishment: *to be sentenced to death/life imprisonment/three years in prison*

'sentence ˌadverb *noun* (grammar) an adverb that expresses the speaker's attitude toward, or gives the subject of, the whole of the rest of the sentence: *In "Luckily, I* *didn't tell anyone" and "Financially, we have a serious problem," "luckily" and "financially" are sentence adverbs.*

sen·tenc·er /ˈsɛntnsər/ noun (formal) a person who decides on the punishment for someone who is guilty of a crime: *The judge was considered a tough sentencer.*

sen·ten·tious /sɛnˈtɛnʃəs/ adj. (formal, disapproving) trying to sound important or intelligent, especially by expressing moral judgments ▶ **sen·ten·tious·ly** adv.

sen·tient /ˈsɛnʃənt/ adj. [usually before noun] (formal) able to see or feel things through the senses: *Man is a sentient being.*

sen·ti·ment /ˈsɛntəmənt/ noun **1** [C, U] (formal) a feeling or an opinion, especially one based on emotions: *the spread of nationalist sentiments* ♦ *This is a sentiment I wholeheartedly agree with.* ♦ *Public sentiment is against any change to the law.* **2** [U] (sometimes disapproving) feelings of sympathy, romantic love, sadness, etc. that may be too strong or not appropriate: *There was no fatherly affection, no display of sentiment.* ♦ *There is no room for sentiment in business.*

sen·ti·men·tal /ˌsɛntəˈmɛntl/ adj. **1** connected with your emotions, rather than reason: *She kept the letters for sentimental reasons.* ♦ *The ring wasn't worth very much but it had great sentimental value.* **2** (often disapproving) producing emotions such as sympathy, romantic love, or sadness, that may be too strong or not appropriate; feeling these emotions too much: *a slushy, sentimental love story* ♦ *He's not the sort of man who gets sentimental about old friendships.* **ANT** UNSENTIMENTAL ▶ **sen·ti·men·tal·ly** /-təli/ adv.

sen·ti·men·tal·ist /ˌsɛntəˈmɛntəlɪst/ noun (sometimes disapproving) a person who is sentimental about things

sen·ti·men·tal·i·ty /ˌsɛntəmɛnˈtæləti/ noun [U] (disapproving) the quality of being too sentimental

sen·ti·men·tal·ize /ˌsɛntəˈmɛntəˌlaɪz/ verb [T, I] ~ (sth) (disapproving) to present something in an emotional way, emphasizing its good aspects and not mentioning its bad aspects: *Jackie was careful not to sentimentalize country life.*

sen·ti·nel /ˈsɛntənl/ noun (literary) a soldier whose job is to guard something **SYN** SENTRY: (figurative) *a tall, round tower standing sentinel over the river*

sen·try /ˈsɛntri/ noun (pl. **sen·tries**) a soldier whose job is to guard something: *to be on sentry duty*

sentry box noun a small shelter for a sentry to stand in

se·pal /ˈsipl/ noun (technical) a part of a flower, like a leaf, that lies under and supports the PETALS (= the delicate colored parts that make up the head of the flower). Each flower has a ring of sepals called a CALYX. ➔ picture at PLANT

sep·a·ra·ble /ˈsɛpərəbl; ˈsɛprəbl/ adj. **1** ~ (from sth) that can be separated from something, or considered separately: *The moral question is not entirely separable from the financial one.* **2** (grammar) (of a phrasal verb) that can be used with the object going either between the verb and the PARTICLE or after the particle: *The phrasal verb "tear up" is separable because you can say "She tore the letter up" or "She tore up the letter."* **ANT** INSEPARABLE ▶ **sep·a·ra·bil·i·ty** /ˌsɛpərəˈbɪləti; ˌsɛprə-/ noun [U]

sep·a·rate adj., verb
● adj. /ˈsɛprət/ **1** ~ (from sth/sb) forming a unit by itself; not joined to something else: *separate bedrooms* ♦ *Raw meat must be kept separate from cooked meat.* ♦ *The school is housed in two separate buildings.* **2** [usually before noun] different; not connected: *It happened on three separate occasions.* ♦ *For the past three years they have been leading totally separate lives.* ▶ **sep·a·rate·ness** noun [U, sing.]: *Japan's long-standing sense of separateness and uniqueness*
IDM **go your separate ways** **1** to end a relationship with someone **2** to go in a different direction from someone you have been travelling with ➔ more at COVER n.

WORD FAMILY
separate adj.
separately adv.
separable adj. (≠ inseparable)
separate verb
separated adj.
separation noun

● verb /ˈsɛpəˌreɪt/ **1** [I, T] to divide into different parts or groups; to divide things into different parts or groups: *Stir the sauce constantly so that it does not separate.* ♦ ~ sth *Separate the eggs* (= separate the YOLK from the white). ♦ ~ sth from/and sth *It is impossible to separate belief from emotion.* ♦ ~ sth into sth *Make a list of points and separate them into "desirable" and "essential."* **2** [I, T] to move apart; to make people or things move apart: *South America and Africa separated 200 million years ago.* ♦ ~ from sth *South America separated from Africa 200 million years ago.* ♦ ~ into sth *We separated into several different search parties.* ♦ ~ sb/sth *Police tried to separate the two men who were fighting.* ♦ *The war separated many families.* ♦ ~ sb/sth from/and sb/sth *Those suffering from infectious diseases were separated from the other patients.* **3** [T] to be between two people, areas, countries, etc. so that they are not touching or connected: ~ sb/sth *A thousand miles separates the two cities.* ♦ ~ sb/sth from/and sb *A high wall separated our back yard from the baseball diamond.* **4** [I] to stop living together as a couple with your husband, wife, or partner: *They separated last year.* ♦ ~ from sb *He separated from his wife after 20 years of marriage.* ➔ collocations at MARRIAGE **5** [T] ~ sb/sth (from sb/sth) to make someone or something different in some way from someone or something else **SYN** DIVIDE: *Politics is the only thing that separates us* (= that we disagree about). ♦ *The judges found it impossible to separate the two contestants* (= they gave them equal scores). ♦ *Only four points separate the top three teams.*
IDM **separate the men from the boys** to show or prove who is brave, skillful, etc. and who is not ➔ more at WHEAT **PHR V** **separate 'out | separate sth↔'out** to divide into different parts; to divide something into different parts: *to separate out different meanings*

sep·a·rat·ed /ˈsɛpəˌreɪtəd/ adj. no longer living with your husband, wife, or partner: *Her parents are separated but not divorced.* ♦ ~ from sb *He's been separated from his wife for a year.* ➔ collocations at MARRIAGE

sep·a·rate·ly /ˈsɛprətli/ adv. ~ (from sb/sth) as a separate person or thing; not together: *They were photographed separately and then as a group.* ♦ *Last year's figures are shown separately.*

sep·a·rates /ˈsɛprəts/ noun [pl.] individual pieces of women's clothing, for example skirts, jackets, and pants, that are designed to be worn together in different combinations

separate school noun (CanE) a public school for Catholic children in some parts of Canada

sep·a·ra·tion /ˌsɛpəˈreɪʃn/ noun **1** [U, sing.] the act of separating people or things; the state of being separate: ~ (from sb/sth) *the state's eventual separation from the federation* ♦ ~ (between A and B) *the need for a clear separation between Church and State* **2** [C] a period of time that people spend apart from each other: *They were reunited after a separation of more than 20 years.* **3** [C] a decision that a husband and wife make to live apart while they are still legally married: *a legal separation* ➔ compare DIVORCE

sepa'ration anx,iety noun [U] anxiety experienced by a young child when a parent goes away

the ,separation of 'powers noun [sing.] the principle of the Constitution that the political power of the government is divided between the President, Congress, and the Supreme Court ➔ compare CHECKS AND BALANCES

sep·a·ra·tist /ˈsɛprətɪst/ noun a member of a group of people within a country who want to separate from the rest of the country and form their own government: *Basque separatists* ▶ **sep·a·ra·tism** /ˈsɛprəˌtɪzəm/ noun [U] **sep·a·ra·tist** adj.: *a separatist movement*

sep·a·ra·tor /ˈsɛpəˌreɪtər/ noun a machine for separating things

Se·phar·di /səˈfɑrdi/ noun (pl. **Se·phar·dim**) a Jew whose ANCESTORS came from Spain or N. Africa ⊃ compare ASHKENAZI ▶ **Se·phar·dic** /-dɪk/ adj.

se·pi·a /ˈsipiə/ noun [U] **1** a brown substance used in inks and paints and used in the past for printing photographs **2** a reddish-brown color ▶ **se·pi·a** adj. [usually before noun]: *sepia ink/prints/photographs*

sep·sis /ˈsɛpsəs/ noun [U] (*medical*) an infection of part of the body in which PUS is produced

Sep·tem·ber 🔑 /sɛpˈtɛmbər/ noun [U, C] (*abbr.* Sept.) the 9th month of the year, between August and October **HELP** To see how **September** is used, look at the examples at **April**.

sep·tet /sɛpˈtɛt/ noun **1** a group of seven musicians or singers **2** a piece of music for seven musicians or singers

sep·tic /ˈsɛptɪk/ adj. (of a wound or part of the body) infected with harmful bacteria: *a septic finger* ♦ *A dirty cut may go septic.*

sep·ti·ce·mi·a /ˌsɛptəˈsimiə/ noun [U] (*medical*) infection of the blood by harmful bacteria **SYN** BLOOD POISONING

septic ˌtank noun a large container, usually underground, that holds human waste from toilets until the action of bacteria makes it liquid enough to be absorbed by the ground

sep·tu·a·ge·nar·i·an /ˌsɛptuədʒəˈnɛriən; ˌsɛptʃuə-/ noun (*formal*) a person between 70 and 79 years old

sep·tum /ˈsɛptəm/ noun (pl. **sep·ta** /-tə/) (*anatomy*) a thin part that separates two hollow areas, for example the part of the nose between the NOSTRILS

sep·ul·cher /ˈsɛpəlkər/ noun (*old use*) a place for a dead body, either cut in rock or built of stone

se·pul·chral /səˈpʌlkrəl/ adj. (*literary*) looking or sounding sad and serious; making you think of death **SYN** FUNEREAL: *He spoke in sepulchral tones.*

se·quel /ˈsikwəl/ noun ~ (to sth) **1** a book, movie, play, etc. that continues the story of an earlier one: *a sequel to the hit movie "Madagascar"* ⊃ compare PREQUEL **2** [usually sing.] something that happens after an earlier event or as a result of an earlier event: *There was an interesting sequel to these events later in the year.*

se·quence [AWL] /ˈsikwəns/ noun, verb
- **noun 1** [C] a set of events, actions, numbers, etc. that have a particular order and that lead to a particular result: *He described the sequence of events leading up to the robbery.* **2** [C, U] the order that events, actions, etc. happen in or should happen in: *The tasks had to be performed in a particular sequence.* ♦ *Number the pages in sequence.* ♦ *These pages are out of sequence.* **3** [C] a part of a movie that deals with one subject or topic or consists of one scene
- **verb 1** ~ sth (*technical*) to arrange things into a sequence **2** ~ sth (*biology*) to identify the order in which a set of GENES or parts of MOLECULES are arranged: *The human genome has now been sequenced.* ▶ **se·quenc·ing** [AWL] noun [U]: *a gene sequencing project*

the ˌsequence of ˈtenses noun [sing.] (*grammar*) the rules according to which the tense of a SUBORDINATE CLAUSE depends on the tense of a main clause, so that, for example, " *I think that you are wrong* " becomes " *I thought that you were wrong* " in the past tense

se·quenc·er /ˈsikwənsər/ noun an electronic instrument for recording and storing sounds so that they can be played later as part of a piece of music

se·quen·tial [AWL] /sɪˈkwɛnʃl/ adj. (*formal*) following in order of time or place: *sequential data processing* ▶ **se·quen·tial·ly** [AWL] /-ʃəli/ adv.: *data stored sequentially on a computer*

se·ques·ter /sɪˈkwɛstər/ verb (*law*) ~ sb to keep a JURY together in a place, in order to prevent them from talking to other people about a court case, or learning about it in the newspapers, on television, etc.

se·quin /ˈsikwən/ noun a small, round, shiny disk sewn onto clothing as decoration ▶ **se·quined** (also **se·quinned**) /ˈsikwənd/ adj. [usually before noun]

se·quoi·a /sɪˈkwɔɪə/ noun a very tall N. American tree, a type of redwood

se·ra pl. of SERUM

ser·aph /ˈsɛrəf/ noun (pl. **ser·a·ph·im** /ˈsɛrəfɪm/ or **ser·aphs**) an ANGEL of the highest rank ⊃ compare CHERUB

se·raph·ic /səˈræfɪk/ adj. (*literary*) **1** as beautiful, pure, etc. as an angel: *a seraphic child/nature* **2** extremely happy: *a seraphic smile*

ser·e·nade /ˌsɛrəˈneɪd/ noun, verb
- **noun 1** a song or tune played or sung at night by a lover outside the window of the woman he loves **2** a gentle piece of music in several parts, usually for a small group of instruments
- **verb** ~ sb to sing or play music to someone (as done in the past by a man singing under her window to the woman he loved)

ser·en·dip·i·ty /ˌsɛrənˈdɪpəti/ noun [U] the fact of something interesting or pleasant happening by chance ▶ **ser·en·dip·i·tous** /-ˈdɪpətəs/ adj.: *serendipitous discoveries*

se·rene /səˈrin/ adj. calm and peaceful: *a lake, still and serene in the sunlight* ▶ **se·rene·ly** adv.: *serenely beautiful* ♦ *She smiled serenely.* **se·ren·i·ty** /səˈrɛnəti/ noun [U, sing.]: *The hotel offers a haven of peace and serenity away from the bustle of the city.*

serf /sɜrf/ noun (in the past) a person who was forced to live and work on land that belonged to a LANDOWNER whom they had to obey

serf·dom /ˈsɜrfdəm/ noun [U] the system under which crops were grown by serfs; the state of being a serf: *the abolition of serfdom in Russia in 1861*

serge /sɜrdʒ/ noun [U] a type of strong cloth made of wool, used for making clothes: *a blue serge suit*

ser·geant /ˈsɑrdʒənt/ noun (*abbr.* Sgt.) **1** a member of one of the middle ranks in the army and the AIR FORCE, below an officer: *Sergeant Salter* ⊃ see also STAFF SERGEANT **2** a police officer just below the rank of a LIEUTENANT or CAPTAIN ⊃ see also SARGE

ˌsergeant ˈmajor noun (often used as a title) a soldier in the army of the highest rank of NONCOMMISSIONED OFFICER

se·ri·al /ˈsɪriəl/ noun, adj.
- **noun** a story on television or the radio, or in a magazine, that is broadcast or published in several separate parts
- **adj. 1** [usually before noun] (*technical*) arranged in a series: *tasks carried out in the same serial order* **2** [only before noun] doing the same thing in the same way several times: *a serial rapist* **3** [only before noun] (of a story, etc.) broadcast or published in several separate parts: *a novel in serial form* ▶ **se·ri·al·ly** /-iəli/ adv.

se·ri·al·ize /ˈsɪriəˌlaɪz/ verb ~ sth to publish or broadcast something in parts as a serial: *The novel was serialized on TV in six parts.* ▶ **se·ri·al·i·za·tion** /ˌsɪriələˈzeɪʃn/ noun [C, U]: *a newspaper serialization of the book*

ˌserial ˈkiller noun a person who murders several people one after the other in a similar way

ˌserial moˈnogamy noun [U] the fact or custom of having more than one husband, wife, or sexual partner in your life, but only one at a time

ˈserial ˌnumber noun a number put on a product, such as a camera, television, etc. in order to identify it

ˈserial ˌport noun (*computing*) a point on a computer where you connect a device such as a mouse that sends or receives data one BIT at a time

se·ries 🔑 [AWL] /ˈsɪriz/ noun (pl. **se·ries**)
1 [C, usually sing.] ~ of sth several events or things of a similar kind that happen one after the other: *The incident sparked off a whole series of events that nobody had foreseen.* ♦ *the latest in a series of articles on the nature of modern society*

2 [C] a set of radio or television programs that deal with the same subject or that have the same characters ⊃ collocations at TELEVISION **3** [C] (*sports*) a set of sports games played between the same two teams: *The team has won its first-ever playoff series.* ♦ *the World Series* (= in baseball) **4** [U, C] (*technical*) an electrical CIRCUIT in which the current passes through all the parts in the correct order

ser·if /'sɛrəf/ *noun* a short line at the top or bottom of some styles of printed letters: *a serif typeface* ⊃ compare SANS SERIF

se·ri·ous 🔑 /'sɪriəs/ *adj.*
> **BAD 1** bad or dangerous: *a serious illness/problem/offense* ♦ *to cause serious injury/damage* ♦ *They pose a serious threat to security.* ♦ *The consequences could be serious.*
> **NEEDING THOUGHT 2** needing to be thought about carefully; not only for pleasure: *a serious article* ♦ *a serious newspaper* ♦ *It's time to give serious consideration to this matter.*
> **IMPORTANT 3** that must be treated as important: *We need to get down to the serious business of calculating costs.* ♦ *The Yankees are a serious contender for the World Series this year.*
> **NOT SILLY 4** thinking about things in a careful and sensible way; not silly: *Be serious for a moment; this is important.* ♦ *I'm afraid I'm not a very serious person.*
> **NOT JOKING 5** sincere about something; not joking or meant as a joke: *Believe me, I'm deadly* (= extremely) *serious.* ♦ *Don't laugh, it's a serious suggestion.* ♦ **~ (about doing sth)** *Is she serious about wanting to sell the house?* ♦ **~ (about sb/ sth)** *He's really serious about Penny and wants to get engaged.* ♦ (*informal*) *You can't be serious!* (= you must be joking) ♦ *You think I did it? Be serious!* (= what you suggest is ridiculous)
> **LARGE AMOUNT 6** (*informal*) used to emphasize that there is a large amount of something: *You can earn serious money doing that.* ♦ *I'm ready to do some serious eating* (= I am very hungry).

THESAURUS

serious

grave • earnest • solemn

These words all describe someone who thinks and behaves carefully and sensibly, but often without much joy or laughter.

serious thinking about things in a careful and sensible way; not laughing about something: *He's really a very serious person.* ♦ *Be serious for a minute; this is important.*

grave (*somewhat formal*) (of a person) serious in manner, as if something sad, important, or worrying has just happened: *She looked very grave as she entered the room.*

earnest serious and sincere: *The earnest young doctor answered all our questions.* ♦ *an earnest attempt to communicate*

solemn looking or sounding very serious, without smiling; done or said in a very serious and sincere way: *The minister wore a solemn expression.* ♦ *I made a solemn promise that I would return.*

PATTERNS
  ▪ a(n) serious/grave/earnest/solemn **expression/face**
  ▪ a serious/solemn **mood/atmosphere**

---

se·ri·ous·ly 🔑 /'sɪriəsli/ *adv.*
1 in a serious way: *to be seriously ill/injured* ♦ *You're not seriously expecting me to believe that?* ♦ *They are seriously concerned about security.* ♦ *Smoking can seriously damage your health.* **2** used to show a change from joking to being more serious or to check that someone really means what they have said: *Seriously though, it could be really dangerous.* ♦ *Seriously? You didn't know that I had called?* **3** (*informal*) very; extremely: *They're seriously rich.*
IDM take sb/sth seriously to think that someone or something is important and deserves your attention and

respect: *We take threats of this kind very seriously.* ♦ *Why can't you ever take anything seriously?*

se·ri·ous·ness /'sɪriəsnəs/ *noun* [U, sing.] the state of being serious: *He spoke with a seriousness that was unusual in him.*
IDM in all seriousness very seriously; not as a joke

ser·mon /'sərmən/ *noun* **1** a talk on a moral or religious subject, usually given by a religious leader during a service ⊃ collocations at RELIGION ⊃ thesaurus box at SPEECH **2** (*informal*, usually *disapproving*) moral advice that a person tries to give you in a long talk

ser·mon·ize /'sərmə,naɪz/ *verb* [I] (*disapproving*) to give moral advice, especially when it is boring or not wanted
SYN MORALIZE

ser·o·to·nin /,sɛrə'tounən/ *noun* [U] a chemical in the brain that affects how messages are sent from the brain to the body, and also affects how a person feels

ser·pent /'sərpənt/ *noun* (*literary*) a snake, especially a large one

ser·pen·tine /'sərpən,tin; -,taɪn/ *adj.* (*literary*) bending and twisting like a snake **SYN** WINDING: *the serpentine course of the river*

ser·rat·ed /'sɛreɪtəd; sə'reɪtəd/ *adj.* having a series of sharp points on the edge like a SAW: *a knife with a serrated edge* ⊃ picture at KITCHEN

ser·ra·tion /sə'reɪʃn/ *noun* a part on an edge or the blade of a knife that is sharp and pointed like a SAW

ser·ried /'sɛrid/ *adj.* [usually before noun] (*literary*) standing or arranged closely together in rows or lines: *serried ranks of soldiers*

se·rum /'sɪrəm/ *noun* (*pl.* se·ra /'sɪrə/ or se·rums) **1** [U] (*biology*) the thin liquid that remains from blood when the rest has CLOTTED **2** [U, C] (*medical*) serum taken from the blood of an animal and given to people to protect them from disease, poison, etc.: *snakebite serum* **3** [U] any liquid like water in body TISSUE

serv·ant 🔑 /'sərvənt/ *noun*
1 a person who works in another person's house, and cooks, cleans, etc. for them: *a domestic servant* ♦ *They treat their mother like a servant.* **2** a person who works for a company or an organization: *a public servant* ⊃ see also CIVIL SERVANT **3** a person or thing that is controlled by something: *He was willing to make himself a servant of his art.*
IDM see OBEDIENT

serve 🔑 /sərv/ *verb, noun*
● *verb*
> **FOOD/DRINK 1** [T, I] to give someone food or drink, for example at a restaurant or during a meal: **~ (sth)** *Breakfast is served between 7 and 10 a.m.* ♦ *Pour the sauce over the pasta and serve immediately.* ♦ *Shall I serve?* ♦ **~ sth with sth** *Serve the lamb with new potatoes and green beans.* ♦ **~ sth to sb** *They served a wonderful meal to more than fifty delegates.* ♦ **~ sb with sth** *The delegates were served with a wonderful meal.* ♦ **~ sb sth** *She served us a delicious lunch.* ♦ **~ sth + adj.** *The quiche can be served hot or cold.* **2** [T] **~ sb/sth** (of an amount of food) to be enough for someone or something: *This dish will serve four hungry people.*
> **CUSTOMERS 3** [T, I] **~ (sb)** to help a customer or sell them something in a store: *Please tell us about your experience so that we can serve you better.* ♦ *She was serving behind the counter.*
> **BE USEFUL 4** [T] **~ sth/sb** to be useful to someone in achieving or satisfying something: *These experiments serve no useful purpose.* ♦ *Most of their economic policies serve the interests of big business.* ♦ *How can we best serve the needs of future generations?* ♦ *His linguistic ability served him well in his chosen profession.*
> **PROVIDE SOMETHING 5** [T] to provide an area or a group of people with a product or service: **~ sb/sth** *The center will serve the whole community.* ♦ **~ sb/sth by sth** *The town is well served by buses and major highways.*

> BE SUITABLE **6** [I] **~ (as sth)** to be suitable for a particular use, especially when nothing else is available: *The sofa will serve as a bed for a night or two.*

> HAVE PARTICULAR RESULT **7** [I] to have a particular effect or result: **~ as sth** *The judge said the punishment would serve as a warning to others.* ◆ **~ to do sth** *The attack was unsuccessful and served only to alert the enemy.*

> WORK **8** [I, T] to work or perform duties for a person, an organization, a country, etc.: **~ (as sth)** *He served as a captain in the army.* ◆ **~ in/on/with sth** *She served in the medical corps.* ◆ **~ under/with sb** *He served under Richard Nixon in the 1970s.* ◆ **~ sth** *I wanted to work somewhere where I could serve the community.* ◆ **~ sb (as sth)** *He served the family faithfully for many years* (= as a servant). **9** [T, I] to spend a period of time in a particular job or training for a job: **~ sth** *He served a one-year apprenticeship.* ◆ **~ as sth** *She was elected to serve as secretary of the local Independent Party.*

> TIME IN PRISON **10** [T] **~ sth** to spend a period of time in prison: *prisoners serving life sentences* ◆ *She is serving two years for theft.* ◆ *He has served time* (= been to prison) *before.*

> OFFICIAL DOCUMENT **11** [T] (*law*) to give or send someone an official document, especially one that orders them to appear in court: **~ sth (on sb)** *to serve a writ/summons on someone* ◆ **~ sb with sth** *to serve someone with a writ/ summons*

> IN SPORTS **12** [I, T] (in TENNIS, etc.) to start playing by throwing the ball into the air and hitting it: *Who's serving?* ◆ **~ sth** *She served an ace.*

IDM **it serves sb right (for doing sth)** used to say that something that has happened to someone is their own fault and they deserve it: *She left you? It serves you right for being so selfish.* **serve two masters** (usually used in negative sentences) to support two opposing parties, principles, etc. at the same time ⟳ more at FIRST *adv.*, MEMORY
PHR V **serve sth↔'out** to continue doing something, especially having an official position or staying in prison, for a fixed period of time that has been set: *He has three more years in prison before he's served out his sentence.* ◆ *She is determined to serve out her four-year term.* **serve sth↔'up 1** to put food onto plates and give it to people: *He served up a delicious meal.* **2** to give, offer, or provide something: *She served up the usual excuse.* ◆ *The teams served up some fantastic entertainment.*

• *noun* (in TENNIS, etc.) the action of serving the ball to your opponent

serv·er /'sɜrvər/ *noun* **1** (*computing*) a computer program that controls or supplies information to several computers connected in a network; the main computer on which this program is run ⟳ collocations at E-MAIL **2** a person who serves food in a restaurant; a waiter or waitress **3** (*sports*) a player who is serving, for example in TENNIS **4** [usually pl.] a kitchen UTENSIL (= tool) used for putting food onto someone's plate: *salad servers* ◆ *cake server* ⟳ picture at KITCHEN **5** a person who helps a priest during a church service

serv·ice 🖉 /'sɜrvəs/ *noun, verb*
• *noun*
> PROVIDING SOMETHING **1** [C] a system that provides something that the public needs, organized by the government or a private company: *the ambulance/bus/telephone, etc. service* ◆ *The government aims to improve public services, especially education.* ◆ *Essential services* (= the supply of water, gas, electricity) *will be maintained.* ⟳ see also POSTAL SERVICE **2** also **Service** [C] an organization or a company that provides something for the public or does something for the government: *the U.S. Customs Service* ◆ *the BBC World Service* ⟳ see also CIVIL SERVICE, DATING SERVICE, DIPLOMATIC SERVICE, HEALTH SERVICE, INTERNAL REVENUE SERVICE, SECRET SERVICE, SECURITY SERVICE, SOCIAL SERVICES **3** [C, U] a business whose work involves doing something for customers but not producing goods; the work that such a business does: *financial services* ◆ *the development of new goods and services* ◆ *Smith's Catering Services* (= a company) *offers the best value.* ◆ *We guarantee*

excellent service. ◆ *the service sector* (= the part of the economy involved in this type of business) ◆ *a service industry*

> IN HOTEL/STORE/RESTAURANT **4** [U] the serving of customers in hotels, restaurants, and stores: *The food was good but the service was very slow.* ◆ *Our main concern is to provide quality customer service.* ⟳ collocations at RESTAURANT ⟳ see also ROOM SERVICE, SELF-SERVICE

> WORK FOR ORGANIZATION **5** [U] **~ (to sth)** the work that someone does for an organization, etc., especially when it continues for a long time or is admired very much: *She has just celebrated 25 years' service with the company.* ◆ *The employees have good conditions of service.* ◆ *After retiring, she became involved in voluntary service in the local community.*

> OF VEHICLE/MACHINE **6** [U] the use that you can get from a vehicle or machine; the state of being used: *That computer gave us very good service.* ◆ *The ship will be taken out of service within two years.* **7** [U] an examination of a vehicle or machine followed by any work that is necessary to keep it operating well: *I took the car in for service.* ◆ *a service engineer*

> SKILLS/HELP **8** [usually pl.] the particular skills or help that a person is able to offer: **~ (of sb)** *You need the services of a good lawyer.* ◆ **~ (as sb/sth)** *He offered his services as a driver.*

> ARMY/NAVY/AIR FORCE **9** [C, usually sing., U] the army, the navy, and the AIR FORCE; the work done by people in them: *Most of the boys went straight into the service.* ◆ *He saw service in North Africa.* ◆ *a service family* ⟳ see also ACTIVE SERVICE, MILITARY SERVICE

> RELIGIOUS CEREMONY **10** [C] a religious ceremony: *morning/evening service* ◆ *to hold/attend a service* ◆ *a funeral/marriage/memorial, etc. service* ⟳ collocations at RELIGION

> BUS/TRAIN **11** [U, C, usually sing.] the fact of a bus, train, etc. going regularly to a particular place at a particular time: *small rural towns without regular bus service*

> IN TENNIS **12** [C] an act of hitting the ball in order to start playing; the way that you hit it **SYN** SERVE: *It's your service* (= your turn to start playing). ◆ *Her service has improved.*

> SET OF PLATES, ETC. **13** [C] a complete set of plates, dishes, etc. that match each other: *a tea service* (= cups, SAUCERS, a TEAPOT, and plates, for serving tea) ⟳ see also DINNER SERVICE

> BEING SERVANT **14** [U] (*old-fashioned*) the state or position of being a servant: *to be in/go into service* (= to be/become a servant)

> OF OFFICIAL DOCUMENT **15** [U] (*law*) the formal giving of an official document, etc. to someone: *the service of a demand for payment*

IDM **at the service of sb/sth | at sb's service** completely available for someone to use or to help someone: *Health care must be at the service of all who need it.* ◆ (*formal* or *humorous*) *If you need anything, I am at your service.* **be of service (to sb)** (*formal*) to be useful or helpful: *Can I be of service to anyone?* **do sb a/no service** (*formal*) to do something that is helpful/not helpful to someone: *She was doing herself no service by remaining silent.* ⟳ more at PRESS *v.*

• *verb*
> VEHICLE/MACHINE **1** [usually passive] **~ sth** to examine a vehicle or machine and repair it if necessary so that it continues to work correctly: *We need to have the car serviced.*

> PROVIDE SOMETHING **2** **~ sth/sb** to provide people with something they need, such as stores, or a transport system **SYN** SERVE: *This department services the international sales force* (= provides services for it).

> PAY INTEREST **3** **~ sth** (*technical*) to pay interest on money that has been borrowed: *The company can no longer service its debts.*

serv·ice·a·ble /'sɜrvəsəbl/ *adj.* suitable to be used: *The carpet is worn but still serviceable.*

'**service ˌcharge** *noun* **1** an amount of money that is added to a bill, as an extra charge for a service: *That will be $50, plus a service charge of $2.50.* **2** an amount of money that is paid to the owner of an apartment building for services such as putting out garbage, cleaning the stairs, etc.

ʌ **cup**   ə **about**   eɪ **say**   aɪ **five**   ɔɪ **boy**   aʊ **now**   oʊ **go**   ər **bird**

service ‚club noun an organization whose members do things to help their local community

service ‚industry noun [U, C] (*economics*) the part of a country's economy that provides services ➔ compare TERTIARY INDUSTRY

serv·ice·man /'sərvəs‚mæn; -mən/, **serv·ice·wom·an** /'sərvəs‚wumən/ noun (*pl.* **serv·ice·men** /-‚mɛn; -mən/, **serv·ice·wom·en** /-‚wɪmən/) a man or woman who is a member of the armed forces

service plaza noun = PLAZA

service pro‚vider noun a business company that provides a service to customers, especially one that connects customers to the Internet: *an Internet service provider*

service ‚road (also **frontage ‚road**) noun a side road that runs parallel to a main road, that you use to reach houses, stores, etc.

service ‚station noun = GAS STATION

serv·ic·ing /'sərvəsɪŋ/ noun [U] **1** the act of checking and repairing a vehicle, machine, etc. to keep it in good condition: *Like any other type of equipment it requires regular servicing.* **2** (*finance*) the act of paying interest on money that has been borrowed: *debt servicing*

ser·vi·ette /‚sərvi'ɛt/ noun (*CanE*) = NAPKIN

ser·vile /'sərvl; -vaɪl/ adj. (*disapproving*) wanting too much to please someone and obey them SYN FAWNING
▶ **ser·vil·i·ty** /sər'vɪləti/ noun [U]

serv·ing /'sərvɪŋ/ noun an amount of food for one person: *This recipe will be enough for four servings.*

ser·vi·tor /'sərvətər/ noun (*old use*) a male servant

ser·vi·tude /'sərvə‚tud/ noun [U] (*formal*) the condition of being a SLAVE or being forced to obey another person SYN SLAVERY

ser·vo /'sərvoʊ/ noun (*pl.* **ser·vos**) (*technical*) a part of a machine that controls a larger piece of machinery

ses·a·me /'sɛsəmi/ noun [U] a tropical plant grown for its seeds and their oil that are used in cooking: *sesame seeds* ➔ see also OPEN SESAME

ses·sion 🔊 /'sɛʃn/ noun
1 a period of time that is spent doing a particular activity: *a photo/recording/training, etc. session* ◆ *The course is made up of 12 two-hour sessions.* ➔ see also JAM SESSION **2** a formal meeting or series of meetings of a court, a parliament, etc.; a period of time when such meetings are held: *a session of the U.N. General Assembly* ◆ *The court is now in session.* ◆ *The committee met in closed session* (= with nobody else present). **3** a school or university year

session mu‚sician noun a musician who is hired to play on recordings but is not a permanent member of a band

set 🔊 /sɛt/ verb, noun, adj.
● **verb** (set·ting, set, set)
▷ PUT/START **1** [T] ~ sth/sb + adv./prep. to put something or someone in a particular place or position: *She set a tray down on the table.* ◆ *They ate everything that was set in front of them.* ◆ *The house is set* (= located) *in fifty acres of parkland.* **2** [T] to cause someone or something to be in a particular state; to start something happening: ~ sb/sth + adv./prep. *Her manner immediately set everyone at ease.* ◆ *He pulled the lever and set the machine in motion.* ◆ ~ sb/sth + adj. *The hijackers set the hostages free.* ◆ ~ sb/sth doing sth *Her remarks set me thinking.*
▷ PLAY/BOOK/MOVIE **3** [T, usually passive] ~ sth + adv./prep. to place the action of a play, novel, or movie in a particular place, time, etc.: *The novel is set in Los Angeles in the 1960s.*
▷ CLOCK/MACHINE **4** [T] ~ sth (+ adv./prep.) to prepare or arrange something so that it is ready for use or in position: *She set the camera on automatic.* ◆ *I set my watch by* (= make it show the same time as) *the TV.* ◆ *Set the alarm for 7 o'clock.*
▷ TABLE **5** [T] ~ a/the table (for sb/sth) to arrange knives, forks, etc. on a table for a meal: *Could you set the table for dinner?* ◆ *The table was set for six guests.*

▷ JEWELRY **6** [T, usually passive] to put a PRECIOUS STONE into a piece of jewelry: ~ A in B *She had the sapphire set in a gold ring.* ◆ ~ B with A *Her bracelet was set with emeralds.*
▷ ARRANGE **7** [T] ~ sth to arrange or fix something; to decide on something: *They haven't set a date for their wedding yet.* ◆ *The government has set strict limits on public spending this year.* ◆ *It is important to set realistic goals.*
▷ EXAMPLE/STANDARD, ETC. **8** [T] ~ sth to fix something so that others copy it or try to achieve it: *This could set a new fashion.* ◆ *They set high standards of customer service.* ◆ *I am unwilling to set a precedent.* ◆ *She set a new world record for the high jump.* ◆ *I rely on you to set a good example.*
▷ WORK/TASK **9** [T] to give someone a piece of work, a task, etc.: ~ sth for sb/yourself *She's set a difficult task for herself.* ◆ ~ sb/yourself sth *She's set herself a difficult task.* ◆ ~ sb to do sth *I set some people to work on the problem.*
▷ BECOME FIRM **10** [I] to become firm or hard: *Leave the concrete to set for a few hours.* ◆ + adj. *The glue had set hard.*
▷ FACE **11** [T, usually passive] ~ sth to fix your face into a firm expression: *Her jaw was set in a determined manner.*
▷ HAIR **12** [T] ~ sth to arrange someone's hair while it is wet so that it dries in a particular style: *She had her hair washed and set.*
▷ BONE **13** [T, I] ~ (sth) to put a broken bone into a fixed position and hold it there, so that it will heal; to heal in this way: *The surgeon set her broken arm.*
▷ FOR PRINTING **14** [T] ~ sth (*technical*) to use a machine or computer to arrange writing and images on pages in order to prepare a book, newspaper, etc. for printing ➔ see also TYPESETTER
▷ WORDS TO MUSIC **15** [T] ~ sth (to sth) to write music to go with words: *Schubert set many poems to music.*
▷ OF SUN/MOON **16** [I] to go down below the HORIZON: *We sat and watched the sun setting.* ANT RISE ➔ see also SUNSET
IDM Idioms containing set are at the entries for the nouns and adjectives in the idioms. For example, **set the pace** is at **pace** *n*.
PHR V **set about sth | set about doing sth** [no passive] to start doing something: *She set about the business of cleaning the house.* ◆ *We need to set about finding a solution.*
‚set sb a'gainst sb to make someone oppose a friend, relative, etc.: *She accused her husband of setting the children against her.* **‚set sth a'gainst sth | ‚set sth 'off against sth**
1 to judge something by comparing good or positive qualities with bad or negative ones: *Set against the benefits of the new technology, there is also a strong possibility that jobs will be lost.* **2** (*finance*) to record something as a business cost as a way of reducing the amount of tax you must pay: *to set capital costs off against tax*
‚set sb/sth a'part (from sb/sth) to make someone or something different from or better than others: *Her elegant style sets her apart from other journalists.* **‚set sth↔a'part (for sth)** [usually passive] to keep something for a special use or purpose: *Two rooms were set apart for use as libraries.*
‚set sth↔a'side 1 to move something to one side until you need it **2** to save or keep money or time for a particular purpose: *She tries to set aside some money every month.* **3** to not consider something, because other things are more important SYN DISREGARD: *Let's set aside my personal feelings for now.* **4** (*law*) to state that a decision made by a court is not legally valid: *The verdict was set aside by the Court of Appeals.*
‚set sth/sb↔'back to delay the progress of something or someone by a particular time: *The bad weather set back the building program by several weeks.* ➔ related noun SETBACK **‚set sb 'back sth** [no passive] (*informal*) to cost someone a particular amount of money: *The repairs could set you back over $200.* **‚set sth 'back (from sth)** [usually passive] to place something, especially a building, at a distance from something: *The house is set well back from the road.*
‚set sth↔'down 1 to write something down on paper in order to record it **2** to give something as a rule, principle, etc.: *The standards were set down by the governing body.*
‚set 'forth (*literary*) to start a journey **‚set sth↔'forth** (*formal*) to present something or make it known

SYN EXPOUND: *The President set forth his views in a television broadcast.*

,set 'in (of rain, bad weather, infection, etc.) to begin and seem likely to continue: *The rain seemed to have set in for the day.* ,set sth 'in/'into sth [usually passive] to fasten something into a flat surface so that it does not stick out from it: *a plaque set into the wall*

,set 'off to begin a journey: *We set off for Boston just after ten.* ,set sth↔'off 1 to make a bomb, etc. explode: *A gang of boys were setting off fireworks in the street.* 2 to make an alarm start ringing: *Opening this door will set off the alarm.* 3 to start a process or series of events: *Panic on the stock market set off a wave of selling.* 4 to make something more noticeable or attractive by being placed near it: *That blouse sets off the blue of her eyes.* ,set sb 'off (doing sth) to make someone start doing something such as laughing, crying, or talking ,set sth 'off against sth = SET STH AGAINST STH

'set on/upon sb [usually passive] to attack someone suddenly: *I opened the gate, and was immediately set upon by a large dog.* 'set sb/sth on sb to make a person or an animal attack someone suddenly: *The farmer threatened to set his dogs on us.*

,set 'out 1 to leave a place and begin a journey: *They set out on the last stage of their journey.* 2 to begin a job, task, etc. with a particular aim or goal: *She set out to break the world record.* ◆ *They succeeded in what they set out to do.* ,set sth↔'out 1 to arrange or display things: *Her work is always very well set out.* 2 to present ideas, facts, etc. in an organized way, in speech or writing: *He set out his objections to the plan.* ◆ *She set out the reasons for her resignation in a long letter.*

,set 'to (*old-fashioned, informal*) to begin doing something in a busy or determined way

,set sb↔'up 1 to provide someone with the money that they need in order to do something: *A bank loan helped to set him up in business.* 2 (*informal*) to make someone healthier, stronger, more lively, etc.: *The break from work really set me up for the new year.* 3 (*informal*) to trick someone, especially by making them appear guilty of something: *He denied the charges, saying the police had set him up.* ⟳ related noun SETUP ,set sth↔'up 1 to build something or put something somewhere: *The police set up roadblocks on routes out of the city.* 2 to make a piece of equipment or a machine ready for use: *She set up her stereo in her bedroom.* 3 to arrange for something to happen: *I've set up a meeting for Friday.* 4 to create something or start it: *to set up a business* ◆ *A fund will be set up for the dead men's families.* 5 to start a process or a series of events: *The slump on Wall Street set up a chain reaction in stock markets around the world.* ⟳ related noun SETUP ,set (yourself) 'up (as sb) to start running a business: *She took out a bank loan and set up on her own.* ◆ *After leaving college, he set himself up as a freelance photographer.*

● *noun*
▷ GROUP 1 [C] ~ (of sth) a group of similar things that belong together in some way: *a set of six chairs* ◆ *a complete set of her novels* ◆ *a set of false teeth* ◆ *a new set of rules to learn* ◆ *You can borrow my keys—I have a spare set.* 2 [C] a group of objects used together, for example for playing a game: *a chess set* 3 [C] (sometimes *disapproving*) a group of people who have similar interests and spend a lot of time together socially: *the smart set* (= rich, fashionable people) ◆ *New York's literary set* ⟳ see also THE JET SET
▷ TV/RADIO 4 [C] a piece of equipment for receiving television or radio signals
▷ FOR PLAY/MOVIE 5 [C] the SCENERY used for a play, movie, etc.: *We need volunteers to help build and paint the set.* 6 [C, U] a place where a play is performed or part of a movie is filmed: *The cast must all be on (the) set by 7 in the morning.*
▷ IN SPORT 7 [C] one section of a match in games such as TENNIS or VOLLEYBALL: *She won in straight sets* (= without losing a set).
▷ MATHEMATICS 8 [C] a group of things that have a shared quality: *set theory*
▷ POP MUSIC 9 [C] a series of songs or pieces of music that a musician or group performs at a concert

▷ OF FACE/BODY 10 [sing.] ~ of sth the way in which someone's face or body is fixed in a particular expression, especially one showing determination: *She admired the firm set of his jaw.*
▷ HAIR 11 [sing.] an act of arranging hair in a particular style while it is wet: *A shampoo and set costs $15.*
▷ BECOMING FIRM 12 [sing.] the state of becoming firm or solid
▷ PLANT 13 [C] a young plant, SHOOT, etc. for planting: *onion sets*

● *adj.*
▷ IN POSITION 1 in a particular position: *a house set in 40 acres of parkland* ◆ *He had close-set eyes.*
▷ PLANNED 2 [usually before noun] planned or fixed: *Each person was given set jobs to do.* ◆ *The school funds a set number of free places.* ◆ *Mornings in our house always follow a set pattern.*
▷ OPINIONS/IDEAS 3 not likely to change: *set ideas/opinions/views* on how to teach ◆ *As people get older, they get set in their ways.*
▷ MEAL 4 [only before noun] (of a meal in a restaurant) having a fixed price and a limited choice of dishes: *a set dinner/lunch/meal* ◆ *Shall we have the set menu?*
▷ LIKELY/READY 5 likely to do something; ready for something or to do something: *~ for sth The team looks set for victory.* ◆ *~ to do sth Interest rates look set to rise again.* ◆ *Be set to leave by 10 o'clock.* ⟳ language bank at EXPECT
▷ FACE 6 [usually before noun] (of a person's expression) fixed; not natural: *a set smile* ◆ *His face took on a set expression.*
IDM be (dead) set against sth/against doing sth to be strongly opposed to something: *Why are you so dead set against the idea?* be set on sth/on doing sth to want to do or have something very much; to be determined to do something ⟳ more at MARK *n*., READY *adj.*

'set-a,side *noun* [U] a system in which the government pays farmers not to use some of their land for growing crops; the land that the farmers are paid not to use

set·back /'setbæk/ *noun* a difficulty or problem that delays or prevents something, or makes a situation worse: *The team suffered a major setback when their best player was injured.* ◆ *The breakdown in talks represents a temporary setback in the peace process.*

,set 'phrase *noun* a phrase that is always used in the same form: *Don't worry about the grammar, just learn this as a set phrase.*

'set piece *noun* a part of a play, movie, piece of music, etc. that has a well-known pattern or style, and is used to create a particular effect

'set point *noun* (especially in TENNIS) a point that, if won by a player, will win them the SET

set·tee /se'ti/ *noun* a long comfortable seat with a back and arms, for two or more people to sit on **SYN** COUCH, SOFA

set·ter /'setər/ *noun* 1 a large dog with long hair, sometimes used in hunting. There are several types of setters. 2 (often in compounds) a person who sets something: *a quiz setter* ⟳ see also JET-SETTER, PACESETTER, TRENDSETTER

set·ting /'setɪŋ/ *noun* 1 a set of surroundings; the place at which something happens: *a rural/an ideal/an idyllic, etc. setting* ◆ *It was the perfect setting for a wonderful Christmas.* ⟳ thesaurus box at ENVIRONMENT 2 the place and time at which the action of a play, novel, etc. takes place: *short stories with a contemporary setting* 3 a position at which the controls on a machine can be set, to set the speed, height, temperature, etc.: *The performance of the engine was tested at different settings.* 4 (*music*) music written to go with a poem, etc.: *Schubert's setting of a poem by Goethe* 5 a piece of metal in which a PRECIOUS STONE is fixed to form a piece of jewelry 6 a complete set of equipment for eating with (knife, fork, spoon, glass, etc.) for one person, arranged on a table: *a place setting*

set·tle ✎ /'setl/ *verb, noun*
● *verb*
▷ END ARGUMENT 1 [T, I] ~ (sth) to put an end to an argument

t tea	t̬ butter	d did	k cat	g got	tʃ chin	dʒ June	f fall

or a disagreement: *to settle a dispute/an argument/a matter* ♦ *It's time you settled your differences with your father.* ♦ *There is pressure on the unions to settle.* ♦ *The company has agreed to settle out of court* (= come to an agreement without going to court). ▸ **DECIDE/ARRANGE 2** [T, often passive] to decide or arrange something finally: *~ sth It's all settled —we're leaving on the nine o'clock flight.* ♦ *Bob will be there? That settles it. I'm not coming.* ♦ *He had to settle his affairs* (= arrange all his personal business) *in Paris before he could return home.* ♦ **it is settled that...** *It's been settled that we leave on the nine o'clock flight.* ▸ **CHOOSE PERMANENT HOME 3** [I] **+ adv./prep.** to make a place your permanent home: *She settled in Vienna after her father's death.* **4** [T, usually passive, I] **~ sth I + adv./prep.** (of a group of people) to make your permanent home in a country or an area as COLONISTS: *This region was settled by the Dutch in the nineteenth century.* ▸ **INTO COMFORTABLE POSITION/STATE 5** [I, T] to make yourself or someone else comfortable in a new position: **~ (back) (+ adv./prep.)** *Ellie settled back in her seat.* ♦ **~ sb/yourself (+ adv./prep.)** *He settled himself comfortably in his usual chair.* ♦ *I settled her on the sofa and put a blanket over her.* **6** [T] **~ sth + adv./prep.** to put something carefully in a position so that it does not move: *She settled the blanket around her knees.* **7** [I, T] to become or make someone or something become calm or relaxed: *I'm waiting for my nerves to settle.* ♦ **~ sb/sth** *I took a pill to help settle my nerves.* ♦ *This should settle your stomach.* ▸ **COME TO REST 8** [I] **~ (on/over sth)** to fall from above and come to rest on something; to stay for some time on something: *Dust had settled on everything.* ♦ *Two birds settled on the fence.* ♦ *I don't think the snow will settle* (= remain on the ground without melting). ♦ *His gaze settled on her face.* ▸ **SINK DOWN 9** [I, T] **~ (sth)** to sink slowly down; to make something do this: *The contents of the package may have settled in transit.* ▸ **PAY MONEY 10** [T, I] to pay the money that you owe: **~ sth** *Please settle your bill before leaving the hotel.* ♦ *The insurance company is refusing to settle her claim.* ♦ **~ (up) (with sb)** *Let me settle with you for the meal.* ♦ *I'll pay now—we can settle up later.*

IDM settle a score/an account (with sb) | settle an old score to hurt or punish someone who has harmed or cheated you in the past: *"Who would do such a thing?" "Maybe someone with an old score to settle."* ⮕ more at DUST *n.*
PHRV settle 'down 1 to get into a comfortable position, either sitting or lying: *I settled down with a book.* **2** to start to have a quieter way of life, living in one place: *When are you going to get married and settle down?* ⮕ collocations at AGE settle 'down, settle sb↔'down to become or make someone become calm, less excited, etc.: *It always takes the class a while to settle down at the start of the lesson.* settle 'down to sth | 'settle to sth to begin to give your attention to something: *They finally settled down to a discussion of the main issues.* ♦ *He found it hard to settle to his work.* 'settle for sth to accept something that is not exactly what you want but is the best that is available: *In the end they had to settle for a tie.* ♦ *I couldn't afford the house I really wanted, so I had to settle for second best.* settle 'in | settle 'into sth to move into a new home, job, etc. and start to feel comfortable there: *How are the kids settling into their new school?* 'settle on sth to choose or make a decision about something after thinking about it: *Have you settled on a name for the baby yet?* 'settle sth on sb (*law*) to formally arrange to give money or property to someone, especially in a WILL 'settle to sth = SETTLE DOWN TO STH

● *noun* an old-fashioned piece of furniture with a long wooden seat and a high back and arms, often also with a box for storing things under the seat

set·tled /ˈsetld/ *adj.* **1** not likely to change or move: *settled weather* ♦ *a settled way of life* **2** comfortable and happy with your home, job, way of life, etc. **ANT** UNSETTLED

set·tle·ment /ˈsetlmənt/ *noun* **1** [C] an official agreement that ends an argument between two people or groups: *to negotiate a peace settlement* ♦ *The management and unions*

have reached a settlement over new working conditions. ♦ *an out-of-court settlement* (= money that is paid to someone or an agreement that is made to stop someone going to court) **2** [U] the action of reaching an agreement: *the settlement of a dispute* **3** [C] (*law*) the conditions, or a document stating the conditions, on which money or property is given to someone: *a divorce/marriage/property, etc. settlement* **4** [U] the action of paying back money that you owe: *the settlement of a debt* ♦ *a check in settlement of a bill* **5** [C] a place where people have come to live and make their homes, especially where few or no people lived before: *signs of an Iron Age settlement* **6** [U] the process of people making their homes in a place: *the settlement of the American West* **7** [U] = SUBSIDENCE

'settlement ˌhouse *noun* a public building in an area of a large city that has social problems, that provides social services such as advice and training to the people who live there

set·tler /ˈsetl.ər, ˈsetlər/ *noun* a person who goes to live in a new country or region: *white settlers in Africa*

ˌset-ˌtop 'box *noun* a device that changes a digital television signal into a form that can be seen on an ordinary television

set·up /ˈsetʌp/ *noun* [usually sing.] (*informal*) **1** a way of organizing something; a system: *I've only been here a couple of weeks and I don't really know the setup.* **2** a situation in which someone tricks you or makes it seem as if you have done something wrong: *He didn't steal the goods. It was a setup.*

sev·en /ˈsevn/ *number*
7 HELP There are examples of how to use numbers at the entry for **five**.
IDM the seven-year itch (*informal, humorous*) the desire for new sexual experience that is thought to be felt after seven years of marriage ⮕ more at SIX

the ˌseven 'seas *noun* [pl.] all of the earth's oceans

the ˌSeven 'Sisters *noun* [pl.] **1** the Pleiades, a group of seven stars **2** a group of seven traditional women's (or formerly women's) universities with high academic standards and a high social status

sev·en·teen /ˌsevnˈtiːn/ *number*
17 ▸ **sev·en·teenth** /ˌsevnˈtiːnθ/ *ordinal number, noun*
HELP There are examples of how to use ordinal numbers at the entry for **fifth**.

sev·enth /ˈsevnθ/ *ordinal number, noun*
● *ordinal number* **7th HELP** There are examples of how to use ordinal numbers at the entry for **fifth**.
IDM in seventh heaven extremely happy: *Now that he's been promoted he's in seventh heaven.*
● *noun* each of seven equal parts of something

Sev·enth-Day Ad·vent·ist /ˌsevnθ deɪ ˈædvəntɪst/ *noun* a member of a Christian religious group that believes that Christ will soon return to Earth

sev·en·ty /ˈsevnti/ **1** *number* 70 **2** *noun* the seventies [pl.] numbers, years, or temperatures from 70 to 79
▸ **sev·en·ti·eth** /ˈsevntiəθ/ *ordinal number, noun*
HELP There are examples of how to use ordinal numbers at the entry for **fifth**.
IDM in your seventies between the ages of 70 and 79

sev·er /ˈsevər/ *verb* (*formal*) **1** to cut something into two pieces; to cut something off something: **~ sth** *to sever a rope* ♦ *a severed artery* ♦ **~ sth from sth** *His hand was severed from his arm.* **2 ~ sth** to completely end a relationship or all communication with someone **SYN** BREAK OFF: *The two countries have severed all diplomatic links.*

sev·er·al 🔑 /ˈsevrəl/ *det., pron., adj.*
● *det., pron.* more than two but not very many: *Several letters arrived this morning.* ♦ *He's written several books about India.* ♦ *Several more people than usual came to the meeting.* ♦ *If you're looking for a photo of Alice you'll find several in here.* ♦ *Several of the paintings were destroyed in the fire.*

• **adj.** (formal) separate: *They said goodbye and went their several ways.*

sev·er·al·ly /ˈsɛvrəli/ adv. (formal or law) separately: *Tenants are jointly and severally liable for payment of the rent.*

sev·er·ance /ˈsɛvrəns; ˈsɛvərəns/ noun [sing., U] (formal) **1** the act of ending a connection or relationship: *the severance of diplomatic relations* **2** the act of ending someone's work contract: *employees given notice of severance* ◆ *severance pay/terms*

se·vere 🔊 /səˈvɪr/ adj. (se·ver·er, se·ver·est)
> VERY BAD **1** extremely bad or serious: *a severe handicap* ◆ *His injuries are severe.* ◆ *severe weather conditions* ◆ *a severe winter* (= one during which the weather conditions are extremely bad) ◆ *The party suffered severe losses during the last election.* ◆ *a severe shortage of qualified staff*
> PUNISHMENT **2** ~ **(on/with sb)** punishing someone in an extreme way when they break a particular set of rules **SYN** HARSH: *The courts are becoming more severe with young offenders.* ◆ *a severe punishment/sentence*
> NOT KIND **3** not kind or sympathetic and showing disapproval of someone or something **SYN** STERN: *a severe expression* ◆ *She was a severe woman who seldom smiled.*
> VERY DIFFICULT **4** extremely difficult and requiring a lot of skill or ability **SYN** STIFF: *The marathon is a severe test of stamina.*
> STYLE/APPEARANCE/CLOTHING **5** (disapproving) extremely plain and lacking any decoration: *Modern furniture is a little too severe for my taste.* ◆ *Her hair was short and severe.*

▶ **se·vere·ly** adv.: *severely disabled* ◆ *areas severely affected by unemployment* ◆ *Anyone breaking the law will be severely punished.* ◆ *a severely critical report* ◆ *Her hair was tied severely in a bun.* **se·ver·i·ty** /səˈvɛrəti/ noun [U]: *A prison sentence should match the severity of the crime.* ◆ *The chances of a full recovery will depend on the severity of her injuries.* ◆ *the severity of the problem* ◆ *He frowned with mock severity.* ◆ *The elaborate facade contrasts strongly with the severity of the interior.*

se·vi·che = CEVICHE

sew 🔊 /soʊ/ verb (sewed, sewn /soʊn/ or sewed)
1 [I, T] to use a needle and thread to make STITCHES in cloth: *My mother taught me how to sew.* ◆ *to sew by hand/machine* ◆ ~ **sth** *to sew a seam* **2** [T] to make, repair, or attach something using a needle and thread: ~ **sth** *She sews all her own clothes.* ◆ ~ **sth on** *Can you sew a button on for me?* ◆ *Surgeons were able to sew the finger back on.*
PHR V **sew sth↔ˈup 1** to join or repair something by sewing: *to sew up a seam* **2** [often passive] (informal) to arrange something in an acceptable way: *It didn't take me long to sew up the deal.* ◆ *They think they have the election sewn up* (= they think they are definitely going to win).

sew·age /ˈsuɪdʒ/ noun [U] used water and waste substances that are produced by human bodies, that are carried away from houses and factories through special pipes (= SEWERS): *a ban on the dumping of raw sewage* (= that has not been treated with chemicals) *at sea* ◆ *sewage disposal* ⊃ compare WASTEWATER

sewage ˈtreatment ˌplant (also **ˈsewage ˌplant**) noun a place where chemicals are used to clean sewage so that it can then be allowed to go into rivers, etc. or used to make MANURE

sew·er /ˈsuər/ noun an underground pipe that is used to carry sewage away from houses, factories, etc.

sew·er·age /ˈsuərɪdʒ/ noun [U] the system by which sewage is carried away from houses, factories, etc. and is cleaned and made safe by adding chemicals to it

ˈsewer ˌgrate noun a frame of metal bars over the opening to a hole in the ground that sewage goes down

sew·ing /ˈsoʊɪŋ/ noun [U] **1** the activity of making, repairing, or decorating things made of cloth using a needle and thread: *knitting and sewing* ⊃ picture at HOBBY **2** something that is being sewn: *a pile of sewing*

ˈsewing maˌchine noun a machine that is used for sewing things that are made of cloth ⊃ picture at HOBBY

sewn pp of SEW

sex 🔊 **AWL** /sɛks/ noun, verb
• **noun 1** [U, C] the state of being male or female **SYN** GENDER: *How can you tell what sex a fish is?* ◆ *a process that allows couples to choose the sex of their baby* ◆ *Please indicate your sex and date of birth below.* ◆ *sex discrimination* (= the act of treating men and women differently in an unfair way) **2** [C] either of the two groups that people, animals, and plants are divided into according to their function of producing young: *a member of the opposite sex* ◆ *single-sex schools* ⊃ see also FAIR SEX **3** [U] physical activity between two people in which they join their sexual organs, for pleasure and/or to produce a child: *It is illegal to have sex with a person under the age of 16.* ◆ *gay sex* ◆ *the sex act* ◆ *a sex attack* ◆ *a sex shop* (= one selling magazines, objects, etc. that are connected with sex) ◆ *sex education in schools* ◆ *These drugs may affect your sex drive* (= your interest in sex and the ability to have it). ⊃ see also SAFE SEX, SEXUAL INTERCOURSE **4** **-sexed** (in adjectives) having the amount of sexual activity or desire mentioned: *a highly-sexed woman*
• **verb** ~ **sth** (technical) to examine an animal in order to find out whether it is male or female
PHR V **sex sb↔ˈup** (informal) to make someone feel sexually excited **sex sth↔ˈup** (informal) to make something seem more exciting and interesting: *The profession is trying to sex up its image.*

sex·a·ge·nar·i·an /ˌsɛksədʒəˈnɛriən/ noun a person between 60 and 69 years old

ˈsex apˌpeal noun the quality of being attractive in a sexual way: *He exudes sex appeal.*

ˈsex change noun [usually sing.] a medical operation in which parts of a person's body are changed so that they become like a person of the opposite sex

ˈsex ˌchromosome noun (biology) a CHROMOSOME that decides the sex of an animal or a plant ⊃ see also X CHROMOSOME, Y CHROMOSOME

sex·ism **AWL** /ˈsɛksɪzəm/ noun [U] the unfair treatment of people, especially women, because of their sex; the attitude that causes this: *legislation designed to combat sexism in the work place* ◆ *a study of sexism in language*

sex·ist /ˈsɛksɪst/ noun (disapproving) a person who treats other people, especially women, unfairly because of their sex or who makes offensive remarks about them ▶ **sex·ist** adj.: *a sexist attitude* ◆ *sexist language*

sex·less /ˈsɛksləs/ adj. **1** that is neither male nor female, or does not seem to be either male or female: *a sexless figure* **2** in which there is no sexual desire or activity

ˈsex life noun a person's sexual activities: *ways to improve your sex life*

ˈsex ˌmaniac noun a person who wants to have sex more often than is normal and who thinks about it all the time

ˈsex ˌobject noun a person considered only for their sexual attraction and not for their character or their intelligence

ˈsex ofˌfender noun a person who has been found guilty of illegal sexual acts

sex·ol·o·gy /sɛkˈsalədʒi/ noun [U] the scientific study of human sexual behavior ▶ **sex·ol·o·gist** /-dʒɪst/ noun

sex·pot /ˈsɛkspat/ noun (informal) a person who is thought to be sexually attractive

ˈsex ˌsymbol noun a famous person who is thought by many people to be sexually attractive

sex·tant /ˈsɛkstənt/ noun an instrument for measuring angles and distances, used to calculate the exact position of a ship or an aircraft

sex·tet /sɛksˈtɛt/ noun **1** a group of six musicians or singers who play or sing together **2** a piece of music for six musicians or singers

sex·ton /ˈsɛkstən/ noun a person whose job is to take care of a church and its surroundings, ring the church bell, etc.

sex·tu·plet /sɛksˈtʌplət/ noun one of six children born at the same time to the same mother

ˈsex ˌtyping noun [U] **1** (*psychology*) the process of putting people into categories according to what people consider to be typical of each sex **2** (*biology*) the process of finding out whether a person or other living thing is male or female, especially in difficult cases when special tests are necessary

sex·u·al 🔑 AWL /ˈsɛkʃuəl/ adj. **1** [usually before noun] connected with the physical activity of sex: *sexual behavior* ◆ *They were not having a sexual relationship at the time.* ◆ *Her interest in him is purely sexual.* ◆ ***sexual orientation*** (= whether you are HETEROSEXUAL or HOMOSEXUAL) **2** [only before noun] connected with the process of producing young: *the sexual organs* (= the PENIS, VAGINA, etc.) ◆ *sexual reproduction* **3** [usually before noun] connected with the state of being male or female: *sexual characteristics* ▶ **sex·u·al·ly** /-ʃuəli; -ʃəli/ adv.: *sexually abused children* ◆ *She finds him sexually attractive.* ◆ *sexually explicit* ◆ *Girls become sexually mature earlier than boys.*

ˌsexual haˈrassment noun [U] comments about sex, physical contact, etc., usually happening at work, that a person finds annoying and offensive

ˌsexual ˈintercourse (also **in·ter·course**) (also *formal* **co·i·tus**) noun [U] (*formal*) the physical activity of sex between two people

sex·u·al·i·ty AWL /ˌsɛkʃuˈæləti/ noun [U] the feelings and activities connected with a person's sexual desires: ***male/female sexuality*** ◆ *He was confused about his sexuality.*

sex·u·al·ize /ˈsɛkʃuəˌlaɪz/ verb **~ sb/sth** to make someone or something seem sexually attractive ▶ **sex·u·al·i·za·tion** /ˌsɛkʃuələˈzeɪʃn/ noun [U]

ˌsexually transˌmitted diˈsease noun [C, U] (*abbr.* STD) any disease that is spread through sexual intercourse, such as SYPHILIS

ˈsex ˌworker noun a polite way of referring to a PROSTITUTE

sex·y /ˈsɛksi/ adj. (**sex·i·er, sex·i·est**) **1** (of a person) sexually attractive: *the sexy lead singer* ◆ *She looked shockingly sexy in a black evening gown.* **2** sexually exciting: *sexy underwear* ◆ *a sexy look* **3** (of a person) sexually excited: *The music and wine began to make him feel sexy.* **4** exciting and interesting: *a sexy new range of software* ◆ *Accountancy just isn't sexy.* ▶ **sex·i·ly** /-səli/ adv. **sex·i·ness** /-sinəs/ noun [U]

SF /ˌɛs ˈɛf/ abbr. SCIENCE FICTION

SFX /ˌɛs ɛf ˈɛks/ abbr. SPECIAL EFFECTS

SGML /ˌɛs dʒi ɛm ˈɛl/ abbr. (*computing*) Standard Generalized Mark-up Language (a system used for marking text on a computer so that the text can be read on a different computer system or displayed in different forms)

Sgt. abbr. SERGEANT: *Sgt. Williams*

sh (also **shh**) /ʃ; ʃʃ/ exclamation the way of writing the sound people make when they are telling someone to be quiet: *Sh! Keep your voice down!*

shab·by /ˈʃæbi/ adj. (**shab·bi·er, shab·bi·est**) **1** (of buildings, clothes, objects, etc.) in poor condition because they have been used a lot SYN SCRUFFY: *She wore shabby old jeans and a T-shirt.* **2** (of a person) badly dressed in clothes that have been worn a lot SYN SCRUFFY: *The old man was shabby and unkempt.* **3** (of behavior) unfair or unreasonable SYN SHODDY: *She tried to make up for her shabby treatment of him.* ▶ **shab·bi·ly** /-bəli/ adv.: *shabbily dressed* ◆ *I think you were very shabbily treated.* **shab·bi·ness** /-binəs/ noun [U]

shack /ʃæk/ noun, verb
● noun a small building, usually made of wood or metal, that has not been built well
● verb
PHR V **shack ˈup with sb** | **be ˌshacked ˈup with sb** (*slang*) to start/be living with someone that you have a

sexual relationship with, but that you are not married to: *I hear he's shacked up with some woman.*

shack·le /ˈʃækl/ verb **1 ~ sb** to put shackles on someone: *The hostage had been shackled to a radiator.* ◆ *The prisoners were kept shackled during the trial.* **2** [usually passive] **~ sb/sth** to prevent someone from behaving or speaking as they want

shack·les /ˈʃæklz/ noun [pl.] **1** two metal rings joined together by a chain and placed around a prisoner's wrists or ankles to prevent them from escaping or moving easily **2 ~ (of sth)** (*formal*) a particular state, set of conditions or circumstances, etc. that prevents you from saying or doing what you want: *a country struggling to free itself from the shackles of colonialism*

shade 🔑 /ʃeɪd/ noun, verb

● noun
▷ OUT OF SUN **1** [U] **~ (of sth)** an area that is dark and cool under or behind something, for example a tree or building, because the sun's light does not get to it: *We sat down **in the shade** of the wall.* ◆ *The temperature can reach 100°F **in the shade**.* ◆ *The trees provide shade for the animals in the summer.* ⊃ see also SHADY
▷ ON LAMP, ETC. **2** [C] a thing that you use to prevent light from coming through or to make it less bright: *I bought a new shade for the lamp.* ◆ *an eyeshade* ⊃ see also LAMPSHADE, SUNSHADE
▷ ON WINDOW **3** (also **ˈwindow ˌshade**) [C] = BLIND
▷ OF COLOR **4** [C] **~ (of sth)** a particular form of a color, that is, how dark or light it is: *a delicate/pale/rich/soft shade of red* ⊃ thesaurus box at COLOR
▷ IN PICTURE **5** [U] the dark areas in a picture, especially the use of these to produce variety: *The painting needs more **light and shade**.*
▷ OF OPINION/FEELING **6** [C, usually pl.] **~ of sth** a different kind or level of opinion, feeling, etc.: *politicians of all shades of opinion* ◆ *The word has many shades of meaning.*
▷ SLIGHTLY **7** **a shade** [sing.] a little; slightly SYN TOUCH: *He was feeling a shade disappointed.*
▷ FOR EYES **8** **shades** [pl.] (*informal*) = SUNGLASSES
▷ GHOST **9** [C] (*literary*) the spirit of a dead person; a GHOST
IDM **put sb/sth in the shade** to be much better or more impressive than someone or something: *I tried hard but her work put mine in the shade.* **shades of sb/sth** (*informal*) used when you are referring to things that remind you of a particular person, thing, or time: *short skirts and long boots— shades of the 1960s*

> **WHICH WORD?**
>
> **shade ◆ shadow**
> ■ **Shade** [U] is an area or a part of a place that is protected from the heat of the sun and so is darker and cooler: *Let's sit in the shade for a while.*
> ■ A **shadow** [C] is the dark shape made when a light shines on a person or an object: *As the sun went down, we cast long shadows on the lawn.*
> ■ **Shadow** [U] is an area of darkness in which it is difficult to distinguish things easily: *Her face was lost in shadow.*

● verb
▷ FROM DIRECT LIGHT **1** to prevent direct light from reaching something: **~ sb/sth** *The courtyard was shaded by high trees.* ◆ **~ sb/sth from/against sth** *She shaded her eyes from the sun.*
▷ LAMP **2** [usually passive] **~ sth** to provide a screen for a lamp, light, etc. to make it less bright: *a shaded lamp*

> **PART OF PICTURE 3** to make a part of a drawing, etc. darker, for example with an area of color or with pencil lines: ~ **sth** *What do the shaded areas on the map represent?* ◆ ~ **sth in** *I'm going to shade this part in.*

PHR V shade 'into sth to change gradually into something else, so that you cannot tell where one thing ends and the other thing begins: *The scarlet of the wings shades into pink at the tips.* ◆ *Distrust of foreigners can shade into racism.*

'shade tree *noun* a tree that is planted to provide shade: *Shade trees such as maple and oak will help cool your home.*

shad·ing /'ʃeɪdɪŋ/ *noun* **1** [U] the use of color, pencil lines, etc. to give an impression of light and shade in a picture or to emphasize areas of a map, diagram, etc. **2** shadings [pl.] slight differences that exist between different aspects of the same thing

shad·ow 🔑 /'ʃædoʊ/ *noun, verb*

● *noun*

> **DARK SHAPE 1** [C] the dark shape that someone or something's form makes on a surface, for example on the ground, when they or it are between the light and the surface: *The children were having fun, chasing each other's shadows.* ◆ *The ship's sail cast a shadow on the water.* ◆ *The shadows lengthened as the sun went down.* ◆ (*figurative*) *He didn't want to cast a shadow on* (= spoil) *their happiness.* ⟳ picture at SHADE ⟳ note at SHADE

> **DARKNESS 2** [U] also shadows [pl.] DARKNESS in a place or on something, especially so that you cannot easily see who or what is there: *His face was lost in in shadow, turned away from her.* ◆ *I thought I saw a figure standing in the shadows.*

> **SMALL AMOUNT 3** [sing.] ~ **of sth** a very small amount of something **SYN** HINT: *A shadow of a smile touched his mouth.* ◆ *She knew beyond a shadow of a doubt* (= with no doubt at all) *that he was lying.*

> **INFLUENCE 4** [sing.] ~ **of sb/sth** the strong (usually bad) influence of someone or something: *The new leader wants to escape from the shadow of his predecessor.* ◆ *These people have been living for years under the shadow of fear.*

> **UNDER EYES 5** shadows [pl.] dark areas under someone's eyes, because they are tired, etc.

> **SOMEONE THAT FOLLOWS SOMEONE 6** [C] a person or an animal that follows someone else all the time

> **SOMETHING NOT REAL 7** [C] a thing that is not real or possible to obtain: *You can't spend all your life chasing shadows.* ⟳ see also EYESHADOW, FIVE O'CLOCK SHADOW

IDM be afraid/scared of your own shadow to be very easily frightened; to be very nervous in/under the shadow of **1** very close to: *The new market is in the shadow of City Hall.* **2** when you say that someone is in/under the shadow of another person, you mean that they do not receive as much attention as that person ⟳ more at FORMER

● *verb*

> **FOLLOW AND WATCH 1** ~ **sb** to follow and watch someone closely and often secretly: *He was shadowed for a week by the secret police.* **2** ~ **sb** to be with someone who is doing a particular job, so that you can learn about it: *It is often helpful for teachers to shadow managers in industry.*

> **COVER WITH SHADOW 3** ~ **sth** to cover something with a shadow: *A wide-brimmed hat shadowed her face.* ◆ *The bay was shadowed by magnificent cliffs.* ⟳ see also OVERSHADOW

sha·dow·box /'ʃædoʊˌbɑks/ *verb* [I] to BOX with an imaginary opponent, especially for physical exercise or in order to train ▶ sha·dow·box·ing *noun* [U]

shad·ow·y /'ʃædoʊi/ *adj.* **1** dark and full of shadows: *Someone was waiting in the shadowy doorway.* **2** [usually before noun] difficult to see because there is not much light: *Shadowy figures approached them out of the fog.* **3** [usually before noun] that not much is known about: *the shadowy world of terrorism*

shad·y /'ʃeɪdi/ *adj.* (shad·i·er, shad·i·est) **1** protected from direct light from the sun by trees, buildings, etc.: *a shady garden* ◆ *We went to find somewhere cool and shady to have a drink.* **2** (of a tree, etc.) providing shade from the sun

3 [usually before noun] (*informal*) seeming to be dishonest or illegal: *a shady businessman/deal*

shaft /ʃæft/ *noun, verb*

● *noun* **1** (often in compounds) a long, narrow, usually vertical passage in a building or underground, used especially for an elevator or as a way of allowing air in or out: *an elevator shaft* ◆ *a mineshaft* ◆ *a ventilation shaft* **2** the long, narrow part of an arrow, HAMMER, GOLF CLUB, etc. **3** (often in compounds) a metal bar that joins parts of a machine or an engine together, enabling power and movement to be passed from one part to another ⟳ see also CAMSHAFT, CRANKSHAFT **4** [usually pl.] either of the two poles at the front of a CARRIAGE or CART between which a horse is fastened in order to pull it **5** ~ **of light, sunlight, etc.** (*literary*) a narrow strip of light: *A shaft of moonlight fell on the lake.* ◆ (*figurative*) *a shaft of inspiration* **6** ~ **of pain, fear, etc.** (*literary*) a sudden, strong feeling of pain, etc. that travels through your body: *Shafts of fear ran through her as she heard footsteps behind her.* **7** ~ **of sth** (*formal*) a remark that is intended to upset or annoy someone: *a shaft of wit* **IDM** give sb the shaft (*informal*) to treat someone unfairly

● *verb* ~ **sb** (*informal*) to treat someone unfairly or cheat them

shag /ʃæg/ *noun, adj.*

● *noun* **1** [U] a strong type of TOBACCO cut into long, thin pieces **2** [C] a large black bird with a long neck that lives near the ocean

● *adj.* [only before noun] used to describe a carpet, etc., usually made of wool, that has long threads

shag·gy /'ʃægi/ *adj.* (shag·gi·er, shag·gi·est) **1** (of hair, fur, etc.) long and messy: *a shaggy mane of hair* **2** having long messy hair, fur, etc.: *a huge, shaggy, white dog*

shaggy-'dog ˌstory *noun* a very long joke with a silly or disappointing ending

shah /ʃɑ/ *noun* the title of the kings of Iran in the past

shake 🔑 /ʃeɪk/ *verb, noun*

● *verb* (shook /ʃʊk/, shak·en /'ʃeɪkən/)

> **OBJECT/BUILDING/PERSON 1** [I, T] to move or make someone or something move with short, quick movements from side to side or up and down: *The whole house shakes when a train goes past.* ◆ ~ **sb/sth** *Shake the bottle well before use.* ◆ *He shook her violently by the shoulders.* ◆ ~ **sb/sth + adj.** *She shook her hair loose.* **2** [T] ~ **sth + adv./prep.** to move something in a particular direction by shaking: *She bent down to shake a pebble out of her shoe.*

> **YOUR HEAD 3** [T] ~ **your head** to turn your head from side to side as a way of saying "no" or to show sadness, disapproval, doubt, etc.: *She shook her head in disbelief.*

> **HANDS 4** [T] to take someone's hand and move it up and down as a way of saying "hello" or to show that you agree about something ~ **hands (with sb) (on sth)**: *Do people in Italy shake hands when they meet?* ◆ *They shook hands on the deal* (= to show that they had reached an agreement). ◆ ~ **sb's hand** *He shook my hand warmly.* ◆ ~ **sb the hand** *Our host shook each of us warmly by the hand.*

> **YOUR FIST 5** [T] ~ **your fist (at sb)** to show that you are angry with someone; to threaten someone by shaking your FIST (= closed hand)

> **OF BODY 6** [I] ~ **(with sth)** to make short, quick movements that you cannot control, for example because you are cold or afraid **SYN** TREMBLE: *He was shaking with fear.* ◆ *I was shaking like a leaf.* ◆ *Her hands had started to shake.*

> **OF VOICE 7** [I] ~ **(with sth)** (of someone's voice) to sound unsteadily, usually because you are nervous, upset, or angry

> **SHOCK SOMEONE 8** [T] (not used in the progressive tenses) to shock or upset someone very much: ~ **sb** *He was badly shaken by the news of her death.* ◆ ~ **sb up** *The accident really shook her up.*

> **BELIEF/IDEA 9** [T] ~ **sth** to make a belief or an idea less certain: *The incident had shaken her faith in him.* ◆ *This announcement is bound to shake the confidence of the industry.*

> **GET RID OF 10** [T] to get rid of something: ~ **sth off** *I can't seem to shake off this cold.* ◆ ~ **sth** *He couldn't shake the feeling that there was something wrong.*

ʌ cup   ə about   eɪ say   aɪ five   ɔɪ boy   aʊ now   oʊ go   ər bird

IDM shake in your shoes (*informal*) to be very frightened or nervous shake a leg (*old-fashioned*, *informal*) used to tell someone to start to do something or to hurry ⊃ more at FOUNDATION

PHR V ,shake sb/sth↔'down (*informal*) **1** to search a person or place in a very thorough way ⊃ related noun SHAKEDOWN **2** to threaten someone in order to get money from them ,shake sb↔'off to get away from someone who is chasing or following you 'shake on sth to shake hands in order to show that something has been agreed: *They shook on the deal.* ♦ *Let's shake on it.* ,shake sth↔'out to open or spread something by shaking, especially so that bits of dirt, dust, etc. come off it: *to shake out a duster* ,shake sb↔'up to surprise someone and make them think about something in a different way, become more active, etc. ,shake sth↔'up to make important changes in an organization, a profession, etc. in order to make it more efficient ⊃ related noun SHAKE-UP

• *noun*
> MOVEMENT **1** [C, usually sing.] an act of shaking something or someone: *Give the bottle a good shake before opening.* ♦ *He dismissed the idea with a firm shake of his head* (= turning it from side to side to mean "no"). ♦ *She gave him a shake to wake him.* ⊃ see also HANDSHAKE
> OF BODY **2** the shakes [pl.] (*informal*) a physical condition in which you cannot stop your body from shaking because of fear, illness, or because you have drunk too much alcohol: *I always get the shakes before exams.*
> DRINK **3** [C] = MILKSHAKE: *a strawberry shake*
IDM in two shakes/in a couple of shakes (*informal*) very soon ⊃ more at FAIR *adj.*, GREAT *adj.*

shake·down /'ʃeɪkdaʊn/ *noun* (*informal*) **1** a situation in which someone tries to force someone else to give them money using violence, threats, etc. **2** a thorough search of someone or something: *a police shakedown of the area* **3** a test of a vehicle to see if there are any problems before it is used generally

shak·en /'ʃeɪkən/ (also **shaken 'up**) *adj.* [not usually before noun] shocked, upset, or frightened by something

shake·out /'ʃeɪkaʊt/ *noun* [usually sing.] **1** a situation in which people lose their jobs and less successful companies are forced to close because of competition and difficult economic conditions **2** = SHAKE-UP

shak·er /'ʃeɪkər/ *noun* **1** (often in compounds) a container that is used for shaking things: *a salt shaker* ♦ *a cocktail shaker* **2 Shaker** a member of a religious group who live in a community in a very simple way and do not marry or have partners **IDM** see MOVER

'shake-up (also shake·up) (also shake·out) *noun* ~ (in/of sth) a situation in which a lot of changes are made to a company, an organization, etc. in order to improve the way in which it works: *a management shake-up*

shak·ing /'ʃeɪkɪŋ/ *noun* [sing., U] the act of shaking something or someone or the fact of being shaken

shak·y /'ʃeɪki/ *adj.* (**shak·i·er**, **shak·i·est**) **1** shaking and feeling weak because you are sick, emotional, or old **SYN** UNSTEADY: *Her voice sounded shaky on the phone.* ♦ *The old man was very shaky on his feet.* **2** not firm or safe; not certain: *That ladder looks a little shaky.* ♦ (*figurative*) *Her memories of the accident are a little shaky.* ♦ (*figurative*) *The protesters are on shaky ground* (= it is not certain that their claims are valid). **3** not seeming very successful; likely to fail **SYN** UNCERTAIN: *Business is looking shaky at the moment.* ♦ *After a shaky start, they fought back to win 3–2.* ▶ **shak·i·ly** /-kəli/ *adv.*: *"Get the doctor," he whispered shakily.*

shale /ʃeɪl/ *noun* [U] a type of soft stone that splits easily into thin, flat layers ▶ **shal·y** /'ʃeɪli/ *adj.*

shall ✎ /ʃəl; strong form ʃæl/ *modal verb* (*negative* shall not *short form* shan't /ʃænt/, *pt* should /ʃəd; strong form ʃʊd/, *negative* should not *short form* should·n't /'ʃʊdnt/)
1 (becoming *old-fashioned*) used with I and we for talking about or predicting the future: *This time next week I shall be in Scotland.* ♦ *We shan't be gone long.* ♦ *I said that I should be*

pleased to help. **2** used in questions with I and we for making offers or suggestions, or asking advice: *Shall I send you the book?* ♦ *What shall we do this weekend?* ♦ *Let's look at it again, shall we?* **3** (*old-fashioned* or *formal*) used to show that you are determined, or to give an order or instruction: *He is determined that you shall succeed.* ♦ *Candidates shall remain in their seats until all the papers have been collected.* ⊃ note at MODAL

GRAMMAR

shall • will

■ In modern English, the traditional difference between **shall** and **will** has almost disappeared, and **shall** is not used very much at all. **Shall** is now used only with I and we, and often sounds formal and old-fashioned. People are more likely to say: *I'll* (= I will) *be late* and *You'll* (= you will) *have your turn next.*
⊃ note at SHOULD

---

shal·lot /'ʃælət; ʃə'lɑt/ *noun* a vegetable like a small onion with a very strong taste ⊃ picture at FRUIT

shal·low ✎ /'ʃæloʊ/ *adj.* (**shal·low·er**, **shal·low·est**)
1 not having much distance between the top or surface and the bottom: *a shallow dish* ♦ *They were playing in the shallow end* (= of the swimming pool). ♦ *These fish are found in shallow waters around the coast.* **ANT** DEEP **2** (*disapproving*) (of a person, an idea, a comment, etc.) not showing serious thought, feelings, etc. about something **SYN** SUPERFICIAL **3 shallow breathing** involves taking in only a small amount of air each time ▶ **shal·low·ly** *adv.*: *He was breathing shallowly.* **shal·low·ness** *noun* [U]

shal·lows /'ʃæloʊz/ **the shallows** *noun* [pl.] a shallow place in a river or the ocean

sha·lom /ʃɑ'loʊm; ʃə-/ *exclamation* a Hebrew word for "hello" or "goodbye" that means "peace"

shalt /ʃælt/ *verb* **thou shalt** (*old use*) used to mean "you shall," when talking to one person

shal·war /ʃʌl'wɑr/ = SALWAR

sham /ʃæm/ *noun, adj., verb*
• *noun* (*disapproving*) **1** [sing.] a situation, feeling, system, etc. that is not as good or true as it seems to be: *The latest crime figures are a complete sham.* **2** [C, usually sing.] a person who pretends to be something that they are not **3** [U] behavior, feelings, words, etc. that are intended to make someone or something seem to be better than they really are: *Their promises turned out to be full of sham and hypocrisy.*
• *adj.* [only before noun] (usually *disapproving*) not genuine but intended to seem real **SYN** FALSE: *a sham marriage*
• *verb* (-mm-) [I, T] ~ (sth) | + adj. to pretend something: *Is he really sick or is he just shamming?*

sha·man /'ʃɑmən; 'ʃeɪ-/ *noun* a person in some religions and societies who is believed to be able to contact good and evil spirits and cure people of illnesses ▶ **sha·man·ic** /ʃə-'mænɪk; ʃeɪ-/ *adj.* **sha·man·ism** /'ʃɑmən,ɪzəm; 'ʃeɪ-/ *noun* [U]

sham·ble /'ʃæmbl/ *verb* [I] (+ adv./prep.) to walk in an awkward or lazy way, dragging your feet along the ground

sham·bles /'ʃæmblz/ *noun* [sing.] (*informal*) **1** a situation in which there is a lot of confusion **SYN** MESS: *The press conference was a complete shambles.* ♦ *What a shambles!* ♦ *The government is in a shambles over Europe.* **2** a place which is dirty or messy **SYN** MESS: *The house was a shambles.*

shame ✎ /ʃeɪm/ *noun, verb*
• *noun* **1** [U] the feelings of sadness, embarrassment, and GUILT that you have when you know that something that you have done is wrong or stupid: *His face burned with shame.* ♦ *She hung her head in shame.* ♦ *He could not live with the shame of other people knowing the truth.* ♦ *To my shame* (= I feel shame that) *I refused to listen to her side of the story.* **2** [U] (*formal*) (only used in questions and negative sentences) the ability

---

to feel shame at something you have done: *Have you no shame?* **3 a shame** [sing.] used to say that something is a cause for feeling sad or disappointed **SYN** PITY: *What a shame they couldn't come.* ◆ *It's a shame about Tim, isn't it?* ◆ *It's a shame that she wasn't here to see it.* ◆ *It would be a crying shame* (= a great shame) *not to take them up on the offer.* **4** [U] the loss of respect that is caused when you do something wrong or stupid: *There is no shame in wanting to be successful.* ◆ (*formal*) *She felt that her failure would bring shame on her family.*

IDM **put sb/sth to shame** to be much better than someone or something: *Their presentation put ours to shame.* **shame on you, him, etc.** (*informal*) used to say that someone should feel ashamed for something they have said or done

● **verb 1** ~ **sb** to make someone feel ashamed: *His generosity shamed them all.* **2** ~ **sb** (*formal*) to make someone feel that they have lost honor or respect: *You have shamed your family.*

PHR V '**shame sb into doing sth** to persuade someone to do something by making them feel ashamed not to do it: *She shamed her father into promising more help.*

shame·faced /ˈʃeɪmfeɪst/ *adj.* feeling or looking ashamed because you have done something bad or stupid **SYN** SHEEPISH: *a shamefaced smile* ▶ **shame·fac·ed·ly** /ˈʃeɪmˌfeɪsədli/ *adv.*

shame·ful /ˈʃeɪmfl/ *adj.* that should make you feel ashamed **SYN** DISGRACEFUL: *shameful behavior* ◆ *It was shameful the way she was treated.* ▶ **shame·ful·ly** /-fəli/ *adv.*

shame·less /ˈʃeɪmləs/ *adj.* (*disapproving*) not feeling ashamed of something you have done, although other people think you should **SYN** UNASHAMED ▶ **shame·less·ly** *adv.* **shame·less·ness** *noun* [U]

sham·ing /ˈʃeɪmɪŋ/ *adj.* causing someone to feel ashamed: *a shaming defeat by a less experienced team*

sham·poo /ʃæmˈpu/ *noun, verb*
● *noun* (*pl.* **sham·poos**) **1** [C, U] a liquid soap that is used for washing your hair; a similar liquid for cleaning carpets, furniture covers, or a car: *a shampoo for greasy hair* ◆ *carpet shampoo* **2** [C, usually sing.] an act of washing your hair using shampoo: *Rinse the hair thoroughly after each shampoo.* ◆ *a shampoo and set* (= an act of washing and styling someone's hair)
● *verb* (**sham·pooed, sham·pooed**) ~ **sth** to wash or clean hair, carpets, etc. with shampoo

sham·rock /ˈʃæmrɑk/ *noun* a small plant with three leaves on each STEM. The shamrock is the national symbol of Ireland.

shang·hai /ˈʃæŋhaɪ/ *verb* (**shang·hai·ing** /-ˌhaɪŋ/, **shang·haied, shang·haied** /-haɪd/) ~ **sb (into doing sth)** (*old-fashioned, informal*) to trick or force someone into doing something that they do not really want to do

Shan·gri-La /ˌʃæŋɡri ˈlɑ/ *noun* [sing.] a place that is extremely beautiful and where everything seems perfect, especially a place far away from modern life **ORIGIN** From the name of an imaginary valley in Tibet in James Hilton's novel *Lost Horizon,* where people do not grow old.

shank /ʃæŋk/ *noun* **1** the straight, narrow part between the two ends of a tool or an object **2** the part of an animal's or a person's leg between the knee and ankle **3** the lower part of the leg of an animal, cooked and eaten: *braised lamb shanks*

shan't /ʃænt/ short form of SHALL NOT

shan·ty /ˈʃænti/ *noun* (*pl.* **shan·ties**) **1** a small house, built of pieces of wood, metal, and heavy paper, where very poor people live, especially on the edge of a big city **2** = CHANTEY

'**shanty ˌtown** *noun* an area in or near a town where poor people live in shanties

shape /ʃeɪp/ *noun, verb*
● *noun* **1** [C, U] the form of the outer edges or surfaces of something; an example of something that has a particular form: *a rectangular shape* ◆ *The pool was in the shape of a heart.* ◆ *The island was originally circular in shape.* ◆ *Squares, circles, and triangles are types of shapes.* ◆ *Candles come in all shapes and sizes.* ◆ *You can recognize the fish by the shape of their fins.* ◆ *This old T-shirt has completely lost its shape.* ◆ (*figurative*) *The government provides money in the shape of* (= consisting of) *grants and student loans.* ⊃ picture on page 1355 **2** [C] a person or thing that is difficult to see clearly **SYN** FIGURE: *Ghostly shapes moved around in the dark.* **3** [U] the physical condition of someone or something: *What sort of shape was the car in after the accident?* ◆ *He's in good shape for a man of his age.* ◆ *I like to keep in shape* (= keep fit). ⊃ thesaurus box at WELL **4** [U] the particular qualities or characteristics of something: *Will new technology change the shape of broadcasting?*

IDM **get (yourself) into shape** to take exercise, eat healthy food, etc. in order to become physically fit **get/ knock/lick/whip sb into shape** to train someone so that they do a particular job, task, etc. well **get/knock/lick/ whip sth into shape** to make something more acceptable, organized, or successful: *I've got all the information together but it still needs to be knocked into shape.* **give shape to sth** (*formal*) to express or explain a particular idea, plan, etc. **in any (way,) shape or form** (*informal*) of any type: *I don't approve of violence in any shape or form.* **out of shape 1** not having the normal shape: *The wheel had been twisted out of shape.* **2** (of a person) not in good physical condition **the shape of things to come** the way things are likely to develop in the future **take shape** to develop and become more complete or organized ⊃ more at BENT *adj.*

● *verb* **1** [T] to make something into a particular shape: ~ **A into B** *Shape the dough into a ball.* ◆ ~ **sth** *This tool is used for shaping wood.* **2** [T] ~ **sb/sth** to have an important influence on the way that someone or something develops: *His ideas had been shaped by his experiences during the war.* ◆ *She had a leading role in shaping party policy.* **3** [I] ~ **to do sth** to prepare to do something, especially hit or kick something: *She was shaping to hit her second shot.*

IDM **shape up or ship out** (*informal*) used to tell someone that if they do not improve, work harder, etc. they will have to leave their job, position, etc.: *He finally faced up to his drug problem when his band told him to shape up or ship out.*

PHR V ˌ**shape 'up 1** to develop in a particular way, especially in a good way: *Our plans are shaping up nicely* (= showing signs that they will be successful). **2** (*informal*) to improve your behavior, work harder, etc.: *If he doesn't shape up, he'll soon be out of a job.*

shaped /ʃeɪpt/ *adj.* having the type of shape mentioned: *a huge balloon shaped like a giant cow* ◆ *almond-shaped eyes* ◆ *an L-shaped room* ⊃ see also PEAR-SHAPED

shape·less /ˈʃeɪpləs/ *adj.* (often *disapproving*) **1** not having any definite shape: *a shapeless sweater* **2** lacking clear organization **SYN** UNSTRUCTURED: *a shapeless and incoherent story* ▶ **shape·less·ly** *adv.* **shape·less·ness** *noun* [U]

shape·ly /ˈʃeɪpli/ *adj.* (especially of a woman's body) having an attractive curved shape

shard /ʃɑrd/ (also **sherd**) *noun* a piece of broken glass, metal, etc.: *shards of glass*

share /ʃɛr/ *verb, noun*
● *verb*
> **USE AT SAME TIME 1** [T, I] ~ **(sth) (with sb)** to have or use something at the same time as someone else: *Sue shares a house with three other students.* ◆ *There isn't an empty table. Would you mind sharing?*
> **DIVIDE BETWEEN PEOPLE 2** [T] ~ **sth (among/between sb)** to divide something between two or more people: *We shared the pizza between the four of us.* ⊃ see also JOB-SHARING, POWER-SHARING

| t tea | t̬ butter | d did | k cat | g got | tʃ chin | dʒ June | f fall |

Shapes, Solids, and Angles

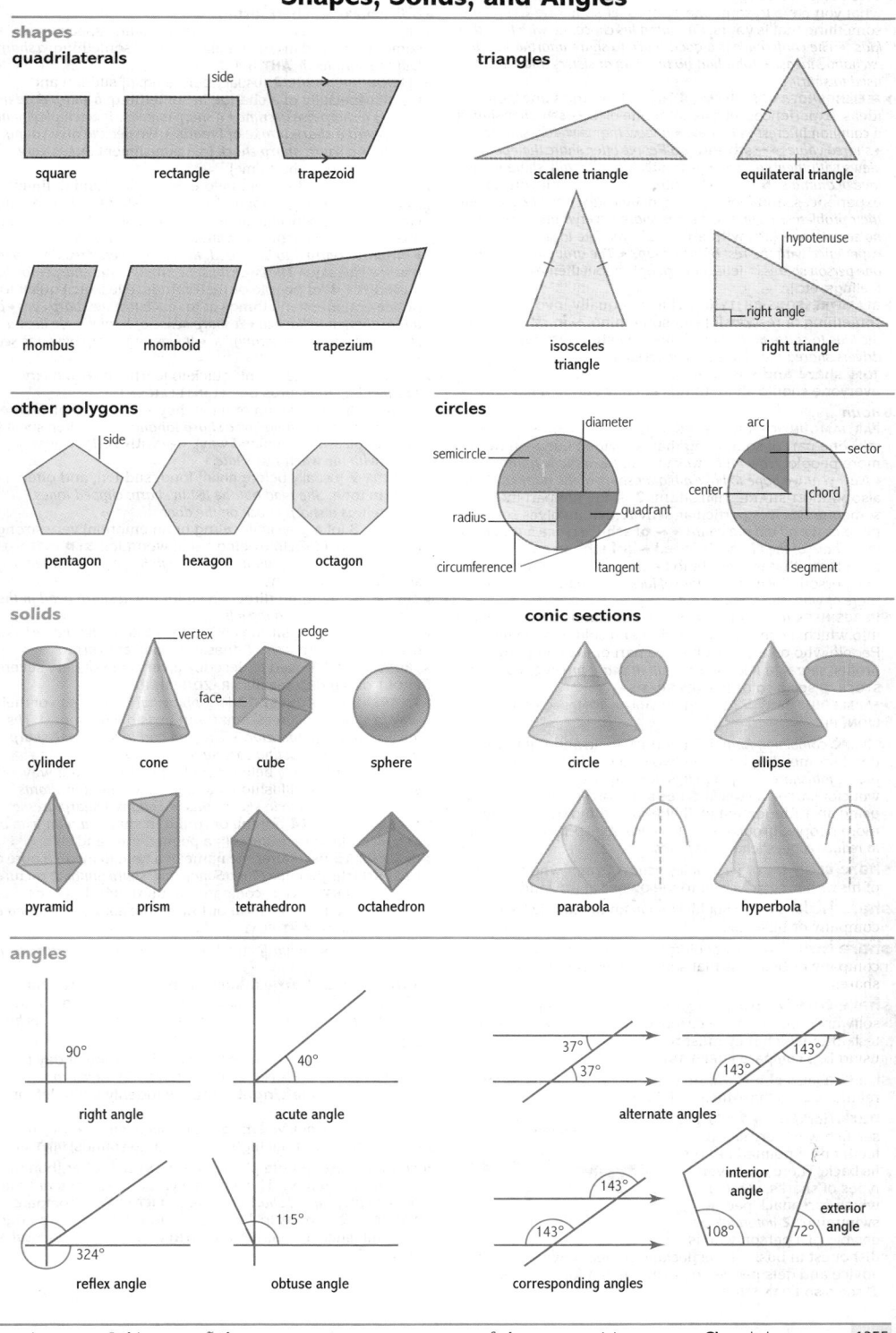

shapes

quadrilaterals

square   rectangle   side   trapezoid

rhombus   rhomboid   trapezium

triangles

scalene triangle   equilateral triangle

isosceles triangle   hypotenuse   right angle   right triangle

other polygons

side   pentagon   hexagon   octagon

circles

diameter   semicircle   radius   quadrant   circumference   tangent

arc   sector   center   chord   segment

solids

vertex   edge   face

cylinder   cone   cube   sphere

pyramid   prism   tetrahedron   octahedron

conic sections

circle   ellipse

parabola   hyperbola

angles

90° right angle

40° acute angle

37° / 37°   143° / 143° alternate angles

324° reflex angle

115° obtuse angle

143° / 143° corresponding angles

interior angle   exterior angle   108°   72°

> **GIVE SOME OF YOURS 3** [T, I] ~ **(sth) (with sb)** to give some of what you have to someone else; to let someone use something that is yours: *Eli shared his chocolate with the other kids.* ◆ *The conference is a good place to share information and exchange ideas.* ◆ *John had no brothers or sisters and wasn't used to sharing.*
> **FEELINGS/IDEAS/PROBLEMS 4** [T, I] to have the same feelings, ideas, experiences, etc. as someone else: ~ **sth** *They shared a common interest in botany.* ◆ *a view that is widely shared* ◆ *shared values* ◆ ~ **sth with sb** *People often share their political views with their parents.* ◆ ~ **in sth** *I didn't really share in her love of animals.* **5** [T, I] to tell other people about your ideas, experiences, and feelings: ~ **sth** *Men often don't like to share their problems.* ◆ *The two friends shared everything—they had no secrets.* ◆ ~ **(sth with sb)** *Would you like to share your experience with the rest of the group?* ◆ *The group listens while one person shares* (= tells other people about their experiences, feelings, etc.).
> **BLAME/RESPONSIBILITY 6** [I, T] to be equally involved in something or responsible for something: ~ **in sth** *I try to get the kids to share in the housework.* ◆ ~ **sth (with sb)** *Both drivers shared the blame for the accident.*
> **IDM** **share and share alike** (*saying*) used to say that everyone should share things equally and in a fair way
> ● **noun**
> **PART/AMOUNT OF SOMETHING 1** [C, usually sing.] ~ **(of/in sth)** one part of something that is divided between two or more people: *How much was your share of the winnings?* ◆ *Next year we hope to have a bigger share of the market.* ⊃ see also MARKET SHARE, TIMESHARE **2** [sing.] the part that someone has in a particular activity that involves several people: *We all did our share.* ◆ ~ **of sth** *Everyone must accept their share of the blame.* **3** [sing.] ~ **(of sth)** an amount of something that is thought to be normal or acceptable for one person: *I've had my share of luck in the past.* ◆ *I've done my share of worrying for one day!*
> **IN BUSINESS 4** [C] ~ **(in sth)** any of the units of equal value into which a company is divided and sold to raise money. People who own shares receive part of the company's profits: *shares in Microsoft* ◆ *a fall in share prices* ⊃ compare STOCK ⊃ see also ORDINARY SHARE
> **FARM EQUIPMENT 5** [C] = PLOWSHARE **IDM** see FAIR *adj.*, LION, PIE

-share *combining form* **1** (in nouns) an arrangement to divide something between two or more people, groups, etc.: *a job-share* (= a job that is done by two people who each work for part of the week) ⊃ see also TIMESHARE **2** (in verbs) using an arrangement to divide something between two or more people, groups, etc.: *We encourage people to rideshare to reduce congestion on the roads.*

share·crop·per /ˈʃɛrˌkrɑpər/ *noun* a farmer who gives part of his or her crop as rent to the owner of the land

share·hold·er /ˈʃɛrˌhoʊldər/ *noun* an owner of shares in a company or business

share·hold·ing /ˈʃɛrˌhoʊldɪŋ/ *noun* the amount of a company or business that someone owns in the form of shares

share·ware /ˈʃɛrwer/ *noun* [U] (*computing*) computer software (= programs, etc.) that is available free for a user to test, after which they must pay if they wish to continue using it ⊃ compare FREEWARE

sha·ri·a (also **sha·ri·ah**) /ʃaˈriə; ʃə-/ *noun* [U] the system of religious laws that Muslims follow

shark /ʃɑrk/ *noun* **1** a large sea fish with very sharp teeth and a pointed FIN on its back. There are several types of sharks, some of which can attack people swimming. **2** (*informal*, *disapproving*) a person who is dishonest in business, especially someone who gives bad advice and gets people to pay too much for something ⊃ see also LOAN SHARK

shark

fin

sharp 🔊 /ʃɑrp/ *adj., adv., noun*
● **adj.** (**sharp·er, sharp·est**)
> **EDGE/POINT 1** having a fine edge or point, especially of something that can cut or make a hole in something: *a sharp knife* ◆ *sharp teeth* **ANT** BLUNT
> **RISE/DROP/CHANGE 2** [usually before noun] sudden and rapid, especially of a change in something: *a sharp drop in prices* ◆ *a sharp rise in crime* ◆ *a sharp increase in unemployment* ◆ *He heard a sharp intake of breath.* ◆ *We need to give young criminals a short, sharp shock* (= a punishment that is very unpleasant for a short time).
> **CLEAR/DEFINITE 3** [usually before noun] clear and definite: *a sharp outline* ◆ *The photograph is not very sharp* (= there are no clear contrasts between areas of light and shade). ◆ *She drew a sharp distinction between domestic and international politics.* ◆ *In sharp contrast to her mood, the clouds were breaking up to reveal a blue sky.* ◆ *The issue must be brought into sharper focus.*
> **MIND/EYES 4** (of people or their minds, eyes, etc.) quick to notice or understand things or to react: *to have sharp eyes* ◆ *a girl of sharp intelligence* ◆ *a sharp sense of humor* ◆ *He kept a sharp lookout for any strangers.* ◆ *It was very sharp of you to see that!*
> **INTELLIGENT 5** intelligent; quick to learn: *You're a pretty sharp kid.* ⊃ thesaurus box at INTELLIGENT
> **CRITICAL 6** (of a person or what they say) critical or severe: *sharp criticism* ◆ *Emma has a sharp tongue* (= she often speaks in an unpleasant or unkind way). ◆ ~ **with sb** *He was very sharp with me when I was late.*
> **SOUNDS 7** [usually before noun] loud, sudden, and often high in tone: *She read out the list in sharp, clipped tones.* ◆ *There was a sharp knock on the door.*
> **FEELING 8** (of a physical feeling or an emotion) very strong and sudden, often like being cut or wounded **SYN** INTENSE: *He winced as a sharp pain shot through his leg.* ◆ *Polly felt a sharp pang of jealousy.*
> **CURVES 9** changing direction suddenly: *a sharp bend in the road* ◆ *a sharp turn to the left*
> **FLAVOR/SMELL 10** strong and slightly bitter: *The cheese has a distinctively sharp taste.* ⊃ thesaurus box at BITTER
> **FROST/WIND 11** used to describe a very cold or very severe FROST or wind ⊃ see also RAZOR-SHARP
> **SMART AND DISHONEST 12** (*disapproving*) (of a person or their way of doing business) smart but possibly dishonest: *His lawyer's a sharp operator.* ◆ *The firm had to face some sharp practice from competing companies.*
> **CLOTHES 13** [usually before noun] (of clothes or the way someone dresses) fashionable and new: *The consultants were a group of men in sharp suits.* ◆ *Todd is a sharp dresser.*
> **FACE/FEATURES 14** not full or round in shape: *a man with a thin face and sharp features* (= a pointed nose and chin)
> **IN MUSIC 15** used after the name of a note to mean a note a HALF STEP higher: *the Piano Sonata in C sharp minor* ⊃ picture at MUSIC **ANT** FLAT ◆ compare NATURAL **16** above the correct PITCH (= how high or low a note sounds): *That note sounded sharp.* **ANT** FLAT
> ▶ **sharp·ness** *noun* [C, U]: *There was a sudden sharpness in her voice.*
> **IDM** **not the sharpest knife in the drawer | not the sharpest tool in the shed** (*informal*, *humorous*) not intelligent: *He's not exactly the sharpest knife in the drawer, is he?*
● **adv.**
> **EXACTLY 1** used after an expression for a time of day to mean "exactly": *Please be here at seven o'clock sharp.*
> **LEFT/RIGHT 2** ~ **left/right** turning suddenly to the left or right
> **MUSIC 3** (*comparative* **sharp·er**, no *superlative*) above the correct PITCH (= how high or low a note sounds) **ANT** FLAT
● **noun 1** (*music*) a note played a HALF STEP higher than the note that is named. The written symbol is (♯): *It's a difficult piece to play, full of sharps and flats.* **ANT** FLAT ⊃ compare NATURAL **2 sharps** [pl.] (*medical*) things with a sharp edge or point, such as needles and SYRINGES: *the safe disposal of sharps*

---

sharp·en /ˈʃɑrpən/ verb **1** [T, I] ~ **(sth)** to make something sharper; to become sharper: This knife needs sharpening. ◆ The outline of the trees sharpened as it grew lighter. **2** [I, T] ~ **(sth)** if a sense or feeling sharpens or something sharpens it, it becomes stronger and/or clearer: The sea air sharpened our appetites. **3** [T] ~ sth to make a disagreement between people, or an issue on which people disagree, clearer and more likely to produce a result: There is a need to sharpen the focus of the discussion. **4** [I, T] to become or make something better, more skillful, more effective, etc. than before **SYN** IMPROVE: ~ **(up)** He needs to sharpen up before the Olympic trials. ◆ ~ sth **(up)** She's taking a class to sharpen her business skills. **5** [I, T] ~ **(sth)** if your voice sharpens or something sharpens it, it becomes high and loud in an unpleasant way

shar·pen·er /ˈʃɑrpənər/ noun (usually in compounds) a tool or machine that makes things sharp: a pencil sharpener ◆ a knife sharpener

sharp-ˈeyed adj. able to see very well and quick to notice things **SYN** OBSERVANT: A sharp-eyed reader spotted the mistake in yesterday's paper.

sharp·ly 🔑 /ˈʃɑrpli/ adv.
1 in a critical, rough, or severe way: The report was sharply critical of the police. ◆ "Is there a problem?" he asked sharply. **2** suddenly and by a large amount: Profits fell sharply following the takeover. ◆ The road fell sharply to the sea. **3** in a way that clearly shows the differences between two things: Their experiences contrast sharply with those of other children. **4** quickly and suddenly, or loudly: She moved sharply across the room to block his exit. ◆ He rapped sharply on the window. **5** used to emphasize that something has a sharp point or edge: sharply pointed

sharp·shoot·er /ˈʃɑrpˌʃutər/ noun a person who is skilled at shooting a gun

shat·ter /ˈʃætər/ verb **1** [I, T] to suddenly break into small pieces; to make something suddenly break into small pieces: ~ **(into sth)** He dropped the vase and it shattered into pieces on the floor. ◆ the sound of shattering glass ◆ ~ sth **(into sth)** The explosion shattered all the windows in the building. **2** [T, I] to destroy something completely, especially someone's feelings, hopes, or beliefs; to be destroyed in this way: ~ sth **(into sth)** Anna's self-confidence had been completely shattered. ◆ Her experience of divorce shattered her illusions about love. ◆ ~ **(into sth)** My whole world shattered into a million pieces. **3** [T] ~ sb to make someone feel extremely shocked and upset: The unexpected death of their son shattered them.

shat·tered /ˈʃætərd/ adj. very shocked and upset: The experience left her feeling absolutely shattered.

shat·ter·ing /ˈʃætərɪŋ/ adj. **1** very shocking and upsetting: a shattering experience ◆ The news of his death came as a shattering blow. **2** very loud **SYN** DEAFENING ▶ **shat·ter·ing·ly** adv.

shat·ter·proof /ˈʃætərˌpruf/ adj. designed not to shatter: shatterproof glass

shave 🔑 /ʃeɪv/ verb, noun
● **verb 1** [I, T] to cut hair from the skin, especially the face, using a RAZOR: Mike cut himself shaving. ◆ ~ sb/sth/yourself The nurse washed and shaved him. ◆ a shaved head ⊃ see also SHAVEN ⊃ picture at HAIR **2** [T] ~ sth to cut a small amount off a price, etc.: The firm had shaved profit margins.
PHR V ˌshave sth↔ˈoff | ˌshave sth ˈoff sth **1** to remove a beard or MUSTACHE by shaving: Charles decided to shave off his beard. **2** to cut very thin pieces from the surface of wood, etc.: I had to shave a few millimeters off the door to make it shut. **3** to reduce a number by a very small amount: He shaved a tenth of a second off the world record.
● **noun** an act of shaving: I need a shave. ◆ to have a shave **IDM** see CLOSE² adj.

shav·en /ˈʃeɪvn/ adj. with all the hair shaved off: a shaven head ⊃ see also CLEAN-SHAVEN ⊃ compare UNSHAVEN

shav·er /ˈʃeɪvər/ (also eˌlectric ˈrazor) noun an electric tool for shaving ⊃ compare RAZOR

ˈ**shaving ˌcream** (also ˈshaving ˌfoam) noun [U] special cream or FOAM for spreading over the face with a **shaving brush** before shaving

shav·ings /ˈʃeɪvɪŋz/ noun [pl.] thin pieces cut from a piece of wood, etc. using a sharp tool, especially a PLANE

Sha·vu·oth /ʃəˈvuʊt; ʃəˈvuəs; ˌʃɑvuˈout/ (also ˌFeast of ˈWeeks, ˌPen·te·cost) noun [U] a Jewish festival that takes place 50 days after the second day of Passover

shawl /ʃɔl/ noun a large piece of cloth worn by a woman around the shoulders or head, or wrapped around a baby

Shaw·nee /ʃɔˈni/ noun (pl. Shaw·nee or Shaw·nees) a member of a Native American people, many of whom now live in Oklahoma

she 🔑 /ʃi/ pron., noun
● **pron.** (used as the subject of a verb) a female person or animal that has already been mentioned or is easily identified: "What does your sister do?" "She's a dentist." ◆ Doesn't she (= the woman we are looking at) look like Sue? ⊃ compare HER
● **noun 1** [sing.] (informal) a female: What a sweet little dog. Is it a he or a she? **2** she- (in compound nouns) a female animal: a she-wolf

s/he /ʃi ər ˈhi; ˌʃi ˈhi/ pron. used in writing by some people when the subject of the verb could be either female (she) or male (he): If a student does not attend all the classes, s/he will not be allowed to take the exam.

shea but·ter /ˈʃeɪ ˌbʌtər; ˈʃi-/ noun [U] a type of fat obtained from the nuts of the **shea tree**, used in foods and COSMETICS

sheaf /ʃif/ noun (pl. sheaves /ʃivz/) **1** a number of pieces of paper tied or held together **2** a bunch of WHEAT tied together after being cut

shear /ʃɪr/ verb (sheared, shorn /ʃɔrn/ or sheared) **1** [T] ~ sth to cut the wool off a sheep: It was time for the sheep to be shorn. ◆ sheep shearing **2** [T] ~ sth (formal) to cut off someone's hair: shorn hair **3** [I, T] ~ **(sth) (off)** (technical) (especially of metal) to break under pressure; to cut through something and make it break: The bolts holding the wheel in place sheared off.
PHR V be ˈshorn of sth (literary) to have something important taken away from you: Shorn of his power, the deposed king went into exile.

shears /ʃɪrz/ noun [pl.] a garden tool like a very large pair of scissors, used for cutting bushes and HEDGES: a pair of garden shears ⊃ picture at TOOL ⊃ see also PINKING SHEARS, PRUNING SHEARS

shear·wa·ter /ˈʃɪrˌwɔtər; -ˌwɑtər/ noun a bird with long wings that often flies low over the ocean

sheath /ʃiθ/ noun (pl. sheaths /ʃiðz; ʃiθs/) **1** a cover that fits closely over the blade of a knife or other sharp weapon or tool ⊃ picture at SWORD **2** any covering that fits closely over something for protection: the sheath around an electric cable **3** a woman's dress that fits the body closely

sheathe /ʃið/ verb **1** ~ sth (literary) to put a knife or SWORD into a sheath **2** [usually passive] ~ sth **(in/with sth)** to cover something in a material, especially in order to protect it

ˈ**sheath knife** noun a short knife with a sheath (= cover)

sheaves pl. of SHEAF

she·bang /ʃɪˈbæŋ/ noun
IDM the whole shebang (informal) the whole thing; everything

shed /ʃed/ noun, verb
● **noun** (often in compounds) a small, simple building, usually built of wood or metal, used for keeping things in: a storage shed ◆ a garden shed ⊃ see also COWSHED, POTTING SHED, WOODSHED

• **verb** (shed·ding, shed, shed)
> GET RID OF **1** ~ sth (often used in newspapers) to get rid of something that is no longer wanted: *The factory is shedding a large number of jobs.* ♦ *a quick way to shed unwanted pounds* (= extra weight or fat on your body) ♦ *Museums have been trying hard to shed their stuffy image.*
> DROP **2** ~ sth (*formal*) to let something fall; to drop something: *Luke shed his clothes onto the floor.* ♦ *A duck's feathers shed water immediately.*
> SKIN/LEAVES **3** ~ sth if an animal **sheds** its skin, or a plant **sheds** leaves, it loses them naturally
> LIGHT **4** ~ sth (on/over sb/sth) to send light over something; to let light fall somewhere: *The candles shed a soft glow on her face.*
> TEARS **5** ~ tears (*formal* or *literary*) to cry: *She shed no tears when she heard he was dead.*
> BLOOD **6** ~ blood (*formal*) to kill or injure people, especially in a war ⊃ see also BLOODSHED **IDM** see LIGHT *n.*

she'd /ʃid/ *short form* **1** she had **2** she would

she-,devil *noun* a very cruel woman

sheen /ʃin/ *noun* [sing., U] a soft, smooth, shiny quality **SYN** SHINE: *hair with a healthy sheen*

sheep 🔊 /ʃip/ *noun* (*pl.* sheep)

sheep

an animal with a thick coat, kept on farms for its meat (called MUTTON or LAMB) or its wool: *a flock of sheep* ♦ *Sheep were grazing in the fields.* ⊃ compare EWE, LAMB, RAM ⊃ see also BLACK SHEEP
IDM **like sheep** (*disapproving*) if people behave **like** sheep, they all do what the others are doing, without thinking for themselves ⊃ more at COUNT *v.*, WOLF *n.*

sheep dip *noun* [U, C] a liquid that is used to kill insects, etc. in a sheep's coat; the container in which sheep are put to treat them with this

sheep·dog /ˈʃipdɔɡ/ *noun* **1** a dog that is trained to help control sheep on a farm **2** a dog of a breed that is often used for controlling sheep, especially a COLLIE ⊃ see also OLD ENGLISH SHEEPDOG

sheep·fold /ˈʃipfoʊld/ *noun* an area in a field surrounded by a fence or wall, where sheep are kept for safety

sheep·herd·er /ˈʃip,hɜrdər/ *noun* = SHEPHERD

sheep·ish /ˈʃipɪʃ/ *adj.* looking or feeling embarrassed because you have done something silly or wrong **SYN** SHAMEFACED: *Mary gave her a sheepish grin.* ▶ **sheep·ish·ly** *adv.*

sheep·skin /ˈʃipskɪn/ *noun* [U, C] the skin of a sheep with the wool still on it: *a sheepskin coat/rug*

sheer /ʃɪr/ *adj., adv., verb*
• *adj.* **1** [only before noun] used to emphasize the size, degree, or amount of something: *The area is under threat from the sheer number of tourists using it.* ♦ *We were impressed by the sheer size of the cathedral.* **2** [only before noun] complete and not mixed with anything else **SYN** UTTER: *The concert was sheer delight.* ♦ *I only agreed out of sheer desperation.* **3** very steep: *sheer cliffs/slopes* ♦ *Outside there was a sheer drop down to the sea below.* **4** (of cloth, etc.) thin, light, and almost transparent: *sheer nylon*
• *adv.* straight up or down: *The cliffs rise sheer from the beach.* ♦ *The ground dropped sheer away at our feet.*
• *verb*
PHR V **,sheer a'way/'off (from sth)** to change direction suddenly, especially in order to avoid hitting something: (*figurative*) *Her mind sheered away from images she did not wish to dwell on.*

sheet 🔊 /ʃit/ *noun*
> ON BED **1** a large piece of thin cloth used on a bed to lie on or lie under: *Have you changed the sheets* (= put clean sheets on the bed)? ♦ *He slid between the sheets and closed his eyes.* ⊃ picture at BED
> OF PAPER **2** a piece of paper for writing or printing on, etc. usually in a standard size: *a clean/blank sheet of paper* (= with no writing on it) ♦ *Pick up one of our free information sheets at reception.*
> FLAT, THIN PIECE **3** a flat, thin piece of any material, normally square or rectangular (RECTANGLE): *a sheet of glass/steel* ♦ *sheet metal* (= metal that has been made into thin sheets) ♦ *Place the dough on a baking sheet* (= for cooking something in an oven).
> WIDE, FLAT AREA **4** a wide, flat area of something, covering the surface of something else: *The road was covered with a sheet of ice.*
> OF FIRE/WATER **5** a large, moving mass of fire or water: *a sheet of flame* ♦ *The rain was coming down in sheets* (= very heavily).
> ON SAIL **6** (*technical*) a rope or chain fastened to the lower corner of a sail to hold it and to control the angle of the sail **HELP** There are other compounds ending **sheet**. You will find them at their place in the alphabet.

sheet ,anchor *noun* a person or thing that you can depend on in a difficult situation

sheet·ing /ˈʃitɪŋ/ *noun* [U] **1** metal, plastic, etc. made into flat, thin pieces: *metal/plastic/polythene sheeting* **2** cloth used for making sheets for beds

sheet ,lightning *noun* [U] LIGHTNING that appears as a broad area of light in the sky ⊃ compare FORKED LIGHTNING

sheet ,music *noun* [U] printed music as opposed to recorded music; printed music published on separate sheets of paper that are not fastened together to form a book

Sheet·rock™ /ˈʃitrɑk/ *noun* [U] a building material made of sheets of heavy paper with plaster between them, used for inside walls and ceilings **SYN** PLASTERBOARD

sheikh (also **sheik**) /ʃik; ʃeɪk/ *noun* **1** an Arab prince or leader; the head of an Arab family, town, etc. **2** a leader in a Muslim community or organization

sheikh·dom /ˈʃikdəm; ʃeɪk-/ *noun* an area of land ruled by a sheikh

shek·el /ˈʃɛkl/ *noun* **1** the unit of money in Israel **2** an ancient silver coin used by the Jews

shelf 🔊 /ʃɛlf/ *noun* (*pl.* shelves /ʃɛlvz/)
1 a flat board made of wood, metal, glass, etc., fixed to the wall or forming part of a cupboard, closet, BOOKCASE, etc., for things to be placed on: *I helped him put up some shelves in his bedroom.* ♦ *The book I wanted was on the top shelf.* ♦ *supermarket/library shelves* ♦ *empty shelves* **2** (*geology*) a thing shaped like a shelf, especially a piece of rock sticking out from a CLIFF or from the edge of a mass of land under the ocean: *the continental shelf* ⊃ see also SHELVE
IDM **on the shelf** (*informal*) not wanted by anyone; not used **off the shelf** that can be bought immediately and does not have to be specially designed or ordered: *I bought this package off the shelf.* ♦ *off-the-shelf software packages* ⊃ compare RACK *n.*

shelf ,life *noun* [usually sing.] the length of time that food, etc. can be kept before it is too old to be sold

shell 🔊 /ʃɛl/ *noun, verb*
• *noun* **1** [C, U] the hard outer part of eggs, nuts, some seeds, and some animals: *We collected shells on the beach.* ♦ *snail shells* ♦ *walnut shells* ♦ *earrings made out of coconut shell* ⊃ picture at ANIMAL, NUT, SHELLFISH ⊃ see also EGGSHELL, NUTSHELL, SEASHELL, TORTOISESHELL **2** [C] any object that looks like the shell of a SNAIL or sea creature: *pasta shells* **3** [C] a metal case filled with EXPLOSIVES, to be fired from a large gun **4** = CARTRIDGE **5** [C] the walls or outer structure of something, for example, an empty building or ship after a fire or a bomb attack: *The house was now a shell gutted by flames.* ♦ (*figurative*) *My life has been an empty shell since he died.* **6** [C] any structure that forms a hard outer

frame: *the body shell of a car* **7** [sing.] the outer layer of someone's personality; how they seem to be or feel: *She had developed a shell of indifference.*

IDM **come out of your shell** to become less shy and more confident when talking to other people **to go/retreat, etc. into your shell** to become shyer and avoid talking to other people

● *verb* **1** [T, I] ~ **(sth)** to fire shells at something: *They shelled the city all night.* ◆ *Just as they were leaving the rebels started shelling.* **2** [T] ~ **sth** to remove the shell or covering from nuts, PEAS, etc.

PHR V **shell 'out (for sth)** | **shell sth↔'out (for sth)** (*informal*) to pay a lot of money for something **SYN** FORK OUT: *The band shelled out $100,000 for a mobile recording studio.*

she'll /ʃil; ʃɪl/ *short form* she will

shel·lac /ʃə'læk/ *noun, verb*
● *noun* [U] a natural substance used in making varnish to protect surfaces and make them hard
● *verb* (-ck-) **1** ~ **sth** to cover something with shellac **2** [usually passive] ~ **sb** (*informal*) to defeat someone very easily: *The Republicans got shellacked in the election.*

shell·fire /'ʃel faɪər/ *noun* [U] attacks or explosions caused by SHELLS being fired from large guns

shellfish

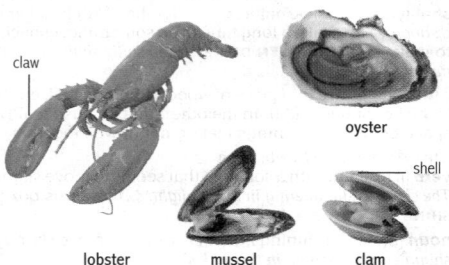

claw

lobster   mussel   clam   oyster   shell

shell·fish /'ʃelfɪʃ/ *noun* (*pl.* shell·fish) a creature with a shell, that lives in water, especially one of the types that can be eaten. OYSTERS and CRABS are shellfish. ⊃ compare CRUS-TACEAN, MOLLUSK

shell game *noun* **1 the shell game** a game in which three cups are moved around, and players must guess which is the one with a small object underneath **2** an act by an organization or a politician that tricks people in an unexpected way

shel·ling /'ʃelɪŋ/ *noun* [U] the firing of SHELLS from large guns: *We suffered weeks of heavy shelling.*

shell shock *noun* (*old-fashioned*) a mental illness that can affect soldiers who have been in battle for a long time

shell-shocked *adj.* **1** shocked, confused, or anxious because of a difficult situation, and unable to think or act normally **2** (*old-fashioned*) suffering from shell shock ⊃ compare COMBAT FATIGUE

shel·ter 🔑 /'ʃeltər/ *noun, verb*
● *noun* **1** [U] the fact of having a place to live or stay, considered as a basic human need: *Human beings need food, clothing, and shelter.* **2** [U] ~ **(from sth)** protection from rain, danger, or attack: *to take shelter from the storm* ◆ *The fox was running for the shelter of the trees.* ◆ *People were desperately seeking shelter from the gunfire.* **3** [C] (often in compounds) a structure built to give protection, especially from the weather or from attack: *They built a rough shelter from old pieces of wood.* ◆ *an air-raid shelter* ⊃ see also BUS SHELTER **4** [C] a building, usually owned by a charity, that provides a place to stay for people without a home, or protection for people or animals who have been badly treated: *a night shelter for the homeless* ◆ *an animal shelter* ◆ *a women's shelter*

● *verb* **1** [T] to give someone or something a place where they are protected from the weather or from danger; to protect someone or something: ~ **sb/sth from sb/sth** *Trees shelter the house from the wind.* ◆ ~ **sb/sth** *helping the poor and sheltering the homeless* ◆ *Perhaps I sheltered my daughter too much* (= protected her too much from unpleasant or difficult experiences). **2** [I] ~ **(from sth)** to stay in a place that protects you from the weather or from danger: *We sheltered from the rain in a doorway.*

shel·tered /'ʃeltərd/ *adj.* **1** (of a place) protected from bad weather: *a sheltered beach* **2** (sometimes *disapproving*) protected from the more unpleasant aspects or difficulties of life: *She had a very sheltered childhood.* ◆ *They both lead very sheltered lives.*

shelve /ʃelv/ *verb* **1** [T] ~ **sth** to decide not to continue with a plan, either for a short time or permanently **SYN** PUT ON ICE: *The government has shelved the idea until at least next year.* **2** [T] ~ **sth** to put books, etc. on a shelf **3** [I] (+ *adv./prep.*) (of land) to slope downward: *The beach shelved gently down to the water.*

shelves *pl.* of SHELF

shelv·ing /'ʃelvɪŋ/ *noun* [U] shelves; material for making shelves: *wooden shelving*

she·nan·i·gans /ʃə'nænɪɡənz/ *noun* [pl.] (*informal*) secret or dishonest activities that people find interesting or amusing

shep·herd /'ʃepərd/ *noun, verb*
● *noun* (also **sheep·herd·er**) a person whose job is to take care of sheep
● *verb* ~ **sb** + *adv./prep.* to guide someone or a group of people somewhere, making sure they go where you want them to go

shep·herd·ess /'ʃepərdəs/ *noun* (*old-fashioned*) a woman who takes care of sheep

shepherd's 'pie *noun* [C, U] a dish of GROUND (= finely chopped) meat covered with a layer of MASHED potatoes

sher·bet /'ʃɜrbət/ *noun* [C, U] (becoming *old-fashioned*) = SORBET

sherd /ʃɜrd/ *noun* = SHARD

sher·iff /'ʃerəf/ *noun* an elected officer responsible for keeping law and order in a county or town

Sher·lock /'ʃɜrlɑk/ (also **Sher·lock Holmes** /ˌʃɜrlɑk 'hoʊmz/) *noun* (*informal, sometimes ironic*) a person who tries to find an explanation for a crime or something mysterious, or who shows that they understand something quickly, especially something that is not obvious: *Oh, well done, Sherlock. Did you figure that out all by yourself?* **ORIGIN** From Sherlock Holmes, a very clever detective in stories by Arthur Conan Doyle, published in the late 19th and early 20th centuries.

Sher·pa /'ʃɜrpə/ *noun* a member of a Himalayan people, who often guide people in the mountains, sometimes carrying their bags, etc.

sher·ry /'ʃeri/ *noun* (*pl.* sher·ries) **1** [U, C] a strong yellow or brown wine, originally from southern Spain. It is often drunk before meals: *sweet/dry sherry* ◆ *cream sherry* (= a type of very sweet sherry) ◆ *fine quality sherries* ◆ *a sherry glass* (= a type of small, narrow wine glass) **2** [C] a glass of sherry: *I'll have a sherry.*

she's /ʃiz/ *short form* **1** she is **2** she has

Shet·land po·ny /ˌʃetlənd 'poʊni/ *noun* a very small, strong horse with a rough coat

shh = SH

Shi·a (also **Shi'a**) /'ʃiə/ *noun* (*pl.* Shi·a or Shi·as) **1** [U] one of the two main branches of the Islamic religion ⊃ compare SUNNI **2** [C] (also **Shi·ite**, **Shi'ite**) a member of the Shia branch of Islam

shi·at·su /ʃi'ɑtsu/ *noun* [U] (from *Japanese*) = ACUPRESSURE

shib·bo·leth /'ʃɪbələθ; -ˌleθ/ *noun* (*formal*) **1** an old idea, principle, or phrase that is no longer accepted by many people as important or appropriate to modern life **2** a

---

ɪr **near**   ɛr **hair**   ɑr **car**   ɔr **north**   ʊr **tour**   ɑ̃ **denouement**   p **pen**   b **bad**

custom, word, etc. that distinguishes one group of people from another **ORIGIN** From a Hebrew word meaning "ear of corn." In the Bible story, Jephthah, the leader of the Gileadites, was able to use it as a test to tell which were his own men, because others found the "sh" sound difficult to pronounce.

shied pt, pp of SHY

shield /ʃild/ noun, verb
* **noun 1** a large piece of metal or leather carried by soldiers in the past to protect the body when fighting **2** = RIOT SHIELD **3** a person or thing used to protect someone or something, especially by forming a barrier: *The gunman used the hostages as a **human shield**.* ◆ *Sunscreen may not be an effective shield against the sun's more harmful rays.* ◆ *She hid her true feelings behind a shield of cold indifference.* **4** a plate or screen that protects a machine or the person using it from damage or injury **5** an object in the shape of a shield, given as a prize in a sports competition, etc. ⊃ picture at MEDAL **6** a drawing or model of a shield showing a COAT OF ARMS **7** a police officer's BADGE
* **verb 1** to protect someone or something from danger, harm, or something unpleasant: *~ sth against sth I shielded my eyes against the glare.* ◆ *~ sb/sth from sb/sth The ozone layer shields the earth from the sun's ultraviolet rays.* ◆ *You can't shield her from the truth forever.* ◆ *~ sb/sth Police believe that somebody is shielding the killer.* **2** *~ sth* to put a shield around a piece of machinery, etc. in order to protect the person using it

shift 🔑 **AWL** /ʃift/ verb, noun
* **verb**
> MOVE **1** [I, T] to move, or move something, from one position or place to another: *Lydia shifted uncomfortably in her chair.* ◆ *~ (from…) (to…) The action of the novel shifts from Paris to London.* ◆ *~ sth We'll need to shift these tables around to make room for the band.* ◆ *~ sth (from…) (to…) He shifted his gaze from the child to her.* ◆ *She shifted her weight from one foot to the other.*
> SITUATION/OPINION/POLICY **2** [I] (of a situation, an opinion, a policy etc.) to change from one state, position, etc. to another: *Public attitudes toward marriage have shifted over the past 50 years.* ◆ *~ (from…) (to/toward/toward…) The balance of power shifted away from workers toward employers.* **3** [T] to change your opinion of or attitude toward something, or change the way that you do something: *~ sth We need to shift the focus of this debate.* ◆ *~ sth (from…) (to/toward/toward…) The new policy shifted the emphasis away from fighting inflation.*
> RESPONSIBILITY **4** [T] *~ responsibility/blame (for sth) (onto sb)* to make someone else responsible for something you should do or something bad that you have done: *He tried to shift the blame for his mistakes onto his colleagues.*
> IN VEHICLE **5** [I] to change the gears when you are driving a vehicle: *to shift into second gear*
  IDM **shift your ground** (usually *disapproving*) to change your opinion about a subject, especially during a discussion **(the) shifting sands (of sth)** used to describe a situation that changes so often that it is difficult to understand or deal with it ⊃ more at GEAR *n.*
  PHR V **shift for yourself** to do things without help from other people: *You're going to have to shift for yourself from now on.*
* **noun**
> CHANGE **1** [C] *~ (in sth)* a change in position or direction: *a dramatic shift in public opinion* ◆ *a shift of emphasis* ⊃ see also PARADIGM SHIFT
> PERIOD OF WORK **2** [C] a period of time worked by a group of workers who start work as another group finishes: *to be on the **day/night shift** at the factory* ◆ *to work an eight-hour shift* ◆ *working in shifts* ◆ **shift workers/work** ⊃ collocations at JOB ⊃ see also GRAVEYARD SHIFT, NIGHT SHIFT, SWING SHIFT **3** [C] the workers who work a particular shift
> ON COMPUTER **4** [U] the system on a computer keyboard or TYPEWRITER that allows capital letters or a different set of characters to be typed: *a shift key*

> CLOTHING **5** [C] a woman's simple, straight dress **6** [C] a simple, straight piece of clothing worn by women in the past as underwear

shift·er /ˈʃiftər/ noun the GEARSHIFT of a vehicle or the set of gears on a bicycle

shifting culti'vation noun [U] (*technical*) a way of farming in some tropical countries in which farmers use an area of land until it cannot be used for growing plants any more, then move to a new area of land

shift·less /ˈʃiftləs/ adj. (*disapproving*) lazy and having no ambition to succeed in life

shift·y /ˈʃifti/ adj. (shift·i·er, shift·i·est) (*informal*) seeming to be dishonest; looking guilty about something **SYN** FURTIVE: *shifty eyes* ◆ *to look shifty* ▶ **shift·i·ly** /-təli/ adv.

shi·i·ta·ke (also **shi·ta·ke**) /ʃɪˈtaki; ʃi-/ (also **shiitake 'mushroom**) noun (from *Japanese*) a type of Japanese or Chinese MUSHROOM

Shi·ite (also **Shi'ite**) /ˈʃiaɪt/ noun a member of the Shia branch of Islam ⊃ compare SUNNI ▶ **Shi·ite** (also **Shi'ite**) adj. [usually before noun]

shil·ling /ˈʃilɪŋ/ noun **1** a British coin in use until 1971. There were 20 shillings in one pound. **2** the unit of money in Kenya, Uganda, Tanzania, and Somalia

shil·ly-shal·ly /ˈʃili ˌʃæli/ verb (shil·ly-shal·lies, shil·ly-shal·ly·ing, shil·ly-shal·lied, shil·ly-shal·lied) [I] (*informal, disapproving*) to take a long time to do something, especially to make a decision **SYN** DITHER: *Stop shilly-shallying and make up your mind.*

shim /ʃim/ noun a thin piece of wood, rubber, metal, etc. that is thicker at one end than the other, that you use to fill a space between two things that do not fit well together

shim·mer /ˈʃimər/ verb, noun
* **verb** [I] to shine with a soft light that seems to move slightly: *The sea was shimmering in the sunlight.* ⊃ thesaurus box at SHINE
* **noun** [U, sing.] a shining light that seems to move slightly: *a shimmer of moonlight in the dark sky*

shim·my /ˈʃimi/ verb (shim·mies, shim·my·ing, shim·mied, shim·mied) [I] + adv./prep. to dance or move in a way that involves shaking your hips and shoulders

shin /ʃin/ noun the front part of the leg below the knee ⊃ picture at BODY

'shin bone noun the front and larger bone of the two bones in the lower part of the leg between the knee and the ankle ⊃ picture at BODY **SYN** TIBIA

shin·dig /ˈʃindig/ noun (*informal*) a big, noisy party

shine 🔑 /ʃaɪn/ verb, noun
* **verb** (**shone**, **shone** /ʃoʊn/) or (**shined**, **shined**) **1** [I] to produce or reflect light; to be bright: *The sun shone brightly in a cloudless sky.* ◆ *The dark polished wood shone like glass.* ◆ *(figurative) Her eyes were shining with excitement.* ◆ *Excitement was shining in her eyes.* **2** [T] *~ sth (+ adv./prep.)* to aim or point the light of a lamp, etc. in a particular direction: *He shined the flashlight around the cellar.* ◆ *(figurative) Campaigners are shining a spotlight on the world's diminishing natural resources.* **3** (**shined**, **shined**) [T] *~ sth* to polish something; to make something smooth and bright: *He shined shoes and sold newspapers to make money.* **4** [I] to be very good at something: *He failed to shine academically but he was very good at sports.* ◆ *She has set a **shining example** of loyal service over four decades.* ⊃ see also SHINY **IDM** see HAY, KNIGHT, RISE *v.*
  PHR V **shine 'through (sth)** (of a quality) to be easy to see or notice: *Her old professional skills shone through.*
* **noun** [sing.] the bright quality that something has when light is reflected on it: *a shampoo that gives your hair body and shine*
  IDM **take a shine to sb/sth** (*informal*) to begin to like someone very much as soon as you see or meet them **take**

the shine off sth (*informal*) to make something seem much less good than it did at first ➔ more at RAIN *n*.

shin·er /ˈʃaɪnər/ *noun* (*informal*) an area of dark skin that can form around someone's eye when they receive a blow to it **SYN** BLACK EYE

shin·gle /ˈʃɪŋɡl/ *noun* **1** [C, U] a small, flat piece of wood that is used to cover a wall or roof of a building ➔ picture at HOUSE **2** [U] a mass of small smooth stones on a beach or at the side of a river: *a shingle beach* **IDM** see HANG *v*.

shin·gled /ˈʃɪŋɡld/ *adj.* (of a roof, building, etc.) covered with shingles (1)

shin·gles /ˈʃɪŋɡlz/ *noun* [U] (*medical*) a disease that affects the nerves and produces a band of painful spots on the skin

shin·gly /ˈʃɪŋɡli/ *adj.* (of a beach) covered in shingle (2)

shin guard *noun* a piece of thick material that is used to protect the lower front part of the leg when playing sports

shin·ny /ˈʃɪni/ *verb, noun*
- *verb* (shin·nies, shin·ny·ing, shin·nied, shin·nied)
  PHR V ˌshinny ˈup/ˈdown sth (*informal*) to climb up or down something quickly, using your hands and legs
- *noun* (also ˈshinny ˌhockey) [U] an informal form of HOCKEY, played especially by children

ˈshin splints *noun* [pl.] sharp pain in the front parts of the lower legs caused by too much exercise, especially on a hard surface

Shin·to /ˈʃɪntoʊ/ (also **Shin·to·ism** /ˈʃɪntoʊˌɪzəm/) *noun* [U] a Japanese religion whose practices include the worship of ANCESTORS and a belief in nature spirits

shin·y /ˈʃaɪni/ *adj.* (shin·i·er, shin·i·est) smooth and bright; reflecting the light: *shiny black hair* **IDM** ˌshiny ˈnew (*approving*) very new and attractive: *shiny new stuff/software*

ship /ʃɪp/ *noun, verb*
- *noun* a large boat that carries people or goods by sea: *There are two restaurants on board the ship.* ◆ *a sailing/cargo/cruise ship* ◆ *a ship's captain/crew/company/cook* ◆ *Raw materials and labor come by ship, rail, or road.* ➔ collocations at TRAVEL ➔ see also AIRSHIP, FLAGSHIP, LIGHTSHIP **IDM** see JUMP *v.*, SINK *v.*, TIGHT
- *verb* (-pp-) **1** [T] ~ sb/sth + adv./prep. to send or transport someone or something by ship or by another means of transportation: *The company ships its goods all over the world.* ◆ *He was arrested and shipped back to the U.S. for trial.* **2** [I, T] to be available to be bought; to make something available to be bought: *The software is due to ship next month.* ◆ ~ sth *The company continues to ship more computer systems than its rivals.* **3** [T] ~ water (of a boat, etc.) to have water coming in over the sides **IDM** see SHAPE *v.*
  PHR V ˌship sb↔ˈoff (*disapproving*) to send someone to a place where they will stay: *When their parents divorced, they were shipped off to live with their grandparents.* ˌship ˈout to leave a place and go somewhere under military orders: *His unit is shipping out next week.*

-ship /ʃɪp/ *suffix* (in nouns) **1** the state or quality of: *ownership* ◆ *friendship* **2** the status or office of: *citizenship* ◆ *professorship* **3** skill or ability as: *musicianship* **4** the group of: *membership*

ship·board /ˈʃɪpbɔrd/ *adj.* [only before noun] happening on a ship: *shipboard romances*

ship·build·er /ˈʃɪpˌbɪldər/ *noun* a person or company that builds ships ▸ **ship·build·ing** *noun* [U]: *the shipbuilding industry*

ship·load /ˈʃɪploʊd/ *noun* as many goods or passengers as a ship can carry ➔ compare BOATLOAD

ship·mate /ˈʃɪpmeɪt/ *noun* sailors who are **shipmates** are sailing on the same ship as each other

ship·ment /ˈʃɪpmənt/ *noun* **1** [U] the process of sending goods from one place to another: *The goods are ready for shipment.* ◆ *the illegal shipment of arms* **2** [C] a load of goods that are sent from one place to another: *grain shipments* ◆ *a shipment of grain*

ship·own·er /ˈʃɪpˌoʊnər/ *noun* a person who owns a ship or ships

ship·per /ˈʃɪpər/ *noun* a person or company that arranges for goods to be sent from one place to another, especially by ship

ship·ping /ˈʃɪpɪŋ/ *noun* [U] **1** ships in general or considered as a group: *The canal is open to shipping.* ◆ *international shipping lanes* (= routes for ships) **2** the activity of carrying people or goods from one place to another by ship: *a shipping company* ◆ *She arranged for the shipping of her furniture to Japan.*

ˈshipping news *noun* a radio broadcast giving a report for ships on the weather conditions at sea

ˈship's ˌchandler *noun* = CHANDLER

ship·shape /ˌʃɪpˈʃeɪp; ˈʃɪpʃeɪp/ *adj.* [not usually before noun] clean and neat; in good condition and ready to use

ˌship-to-ˈshore *adj.* [only before noun] providing communication between people on a ship and people on land: *a ship-to-shore radio*

ship·wreck /ˈʃɪprɛk/ *noun, verb*
- *noun* **1** [U, C] the loss or destruction of a ship at sea

because of a storm or because it hits rocks, etc.: *They narrowly escaped shipwreck in a storm in the North Atlantic.* **2** [C] a ship that has been lost or destroyed at sea: *The contents of shipwrecks belong to the state.*

• *verb* **be shipwrecked** to be left somewhere after the ship that you have been sailing in has been lost or destroyed at sea ▶ **ship·wrecked** *adj.: a shipwrecked sailor*

ship·yard /'ʃɪpyɑrd/ *noun* a place where ships are built or repaired: *shipyard workers*

shirk /ʃɜrk/ *verb* [I, T] to avoid doing something you should do, especially because you are too lazy: *Discipline in the company was strict and no one shirked.* ◆ ~ **from sth/doing sth** *He has never shirked from taking on the big issues.* ◆ ~ **sth/ doing sth** *She never shirked her responsibilities.* ▶ **shirk·er** *noun*

shirt 🔑 /ʃɜrt/ *noun*
a piece of clothing (usually for men), worn on the upper part of the body, made of light cloth, with sleeves and usually with a COLLAR and buttons down the front: *to wear a shirt and tie* ◆ *a short-sleeved shirt* ◆ *a cotton shirt* ⊃ picture at CLOTHES ⊃ see also NIGHTSHIRT, POLO SHIRT, STUFFED SHIRT, SWEATSHIRT, T-SHIRT
IDM keep your shirt on (*informal*) used to tell someone not to get angry: *Keep your shirt on! It was only a joke.* the shirt off sb's back anything that someone has, including the things they really need themselves, that someone else takes from them or they are willing to give

shirt·front /'ʃɜrtfrʌnt/ *noun* the front part of a shirt, especially the stiff front part of a formal white shirt

shirt·sleeve /'ʃɜrtsliv/ *noun* [usually pl.] a sleeve of a shirt **IDM** in (your) shirtsleeves wearing a shirt without a jacket, etc. on top of it

shirt·tail /'ʃɜrteɪl/ *noun* the part of a shirt that is below the waist and is usually inside your pants

shish kebab /'ʃɪʃ kə,bab/ *noun* = KEBAB

shi·ta·ke = SHIITAKE

shiv·er /'ʃɪvər/ *verb, noun*
• *verb* [I] (of a person) to shake slightly because you are cold, frightened, excited, etc.: *Don't stand outside shivering—come inside and get warm!* ◆ *He shivered at the thought of the cold, dark sea.* ◆ ~ **with sth** *to shiver with cold/excitement/ pleasure, etc.*
• *noun* **1** [C] a sudden shaking movement of your body because you are cold, frightened, excited, etc.: *The sound of his voice sent shivers down her spine.* ◆ *He felt a cold shiver of fear run through him.* **2 the shivers** [pl.] shaking movements of your body because of fear or a high temperature: *I don't like him. He gives me the shivers.* ◆ *The child came in from the cold with a runny nose and the shivers.*

shiv·er·y /'ʃɪvəri/ *adj.* shaking with cold, fear, illness, etc.

shmo = SCHMO

shoal /ʃoʊl/ *noun* **1** a small hill of sand just below the surface of the ocean **2** a large number of fish swimming together as a group ⊃ compare SCHOOL *n.*(9)

shock 🔑 /ʃɑk/ *noun, verb*
• *noun*
▷ SURPRISE **1** [C, usually sing., U] a strong feeling of surprise as a result of something happening, especially something unpleasant; the event that causes this feeling: *The news of my promotion came as a shock.* ◆ *He's still in a state of shock.* ◆ *I got a terrible shock the other day.* ◆ *She still hasn't gotten over the shock of seeing him again.* ◆ (*informal*) *If you think the job will be easy, you're in for a shock.* ◆ *Losing to the worst team in the league was a more of a shock* ◆ *The team suffered a shock defeat in the first round.* ⊃ see also CULTURE SHOCK
▷ MEDICAL **2** [U] a serious medical condition, usually the result of injury in which a person has lost a lot of blood and they are extremely weak: *She was taken to the hospital suffering from shock.* ◆ *He isn't seriously injured but he is in (a*

state of) shock. ⊃ see also SHELL SHOCK, TOXIC SHOCK SYNDROME
▷ VIOLENT SHAKING **3** [C, U] a violent shaking movement that is caused by an explosion, EARTHQUAKE, etc.: *The shock of the explosion could be felt up to six miles away.* ◆ *The bumper absorbs shock on impact.*
▷ FROM ELECTRICITY **4** [C] = ELECTRIC SHOCK: *Don't touch that wire or you'll get a shock.*
▷ OF HAIR **5** a thick mass of hair on a person's head
• *verb*
▷ SURPRISE AND UPSET **1** [T] to surprise and upset someone: ~ **sb** *It shocks you when something like that happens.* ◆ *We were all shocked at the news of his death.* ◆ ~ **sb that...** *Neighbors were shocked that such an attack could happen in their area.* ◆ ~ **sb to do sth** *I was shocked to hear that he had resigned.*
▷ OFFEND/DISGUST **2** [I, T] (of bad language, immoral behavior, etc.) to make someone feel offended or disgusted: *These movies deliberately set out to shock.* ◆ ~ **sb (to do sth)** *She enjoys shocking people by saying outrageous things.*
▶ shocked *adj.: For a few minutes we stood in shocked silence.*

THESAURUS

shock
appall • horrify • disgust • sicken • repulse
These words all mean to surprise and upset someone very much.

shock [often passive] to surprise someone, usually in a way that upsets them: *We were all shocked at the news of his death.*
appall to shock and upset someone very much: *I was appalled at the way she spoke to her mother.*
horrify to make someone feel extremely shocked, upset, or frightened: *The whole country was horrified by the kidnapping.*
disgust to make someone feel shocked and almost ill because something is so unpleasant: *The level of violence in the movie really disgusted me.*
sicken to make someone feel very shocked, angry, and almost ill because something is so unpleasant: *I was sickened by the lack of concern for the child's welfare.*
repulse [often passive] (*somewhat formal*) to make someone feel disgust or strong dislike: *I was repulsed by the smell of liquor on his breath.*

PATTERNS
■ shocked/appalled/horrified/disgusted/repulsed at sb/sth
■ to shock/appall/horrify/disgust sb that...
■ to shock/appall/horrify/disgust/sicken sb to think/ see/hear...
■ sb's behavior shocks/appalls sb
■ violence/an idea shocks/appalls/horrifies/disgusts sb

shock ab·sorber *noun* a device that is fitted to each wheel of a vehicle in order to reduce the effects of traveling over rough ground, so that passengers can be more comfortable

shock·er /'ʃɑkər/ *noun* (*informal*) a movie, piece of news, or person that shocks you

shock·ing 🔑 /'ʃɑkɪŋ/ *adj.*
that offends or upsets people; that is morally wrong: *shocking behavior* ◆ *shocking news* ◆ *It is shocking that they involved children in the crime.* ◆ *a shocking waste of money* ▶ **shock·ing·ly** /'ʃɑkɪŋli/ *adv.: a shockingly high mortality rate*

shocking 'pink *noun* [U] a very bright pink color ▶ **shocking 'pink** *adj.*

shock jock *noun* (*informal*) a DISC JOCKEY on a radio show who deliberately expresses opinions or uses language that many people find offensive

shock·proof /'ʃɑkpruf/ *adj.* made so that it cannot be

shoes

strap — slingback

mule — heel

toe — pumps

flats

clogs

stiletto (*also* spike heel)

wedge

platform

kitten heels

slippers

sandal

jelly

flip-flops
(*also* thongs)

moccasins

oxfords

Loafers™

wingtips

sneakers

high-tops

boots

cowboy boot

lace — hiking boots

rubber boots

damaged if it is dropped or hit: *My watch is shockproof and waterproof.*

shock tactics *noun* [pl.] actions that are done to deliberately shock people in order to persuade them to do something or to react in a particular way

shock therapy (also **shock treatment**) *noun* [U] a way of treating mental illness by giving ELECTRIC SHOCKS or a drug that has a similar effect

shock troops *noun* [pl.] soldiers who are specially trained to make sudden attacks on the enemy

shock wave *noun* **1** a movement of very high air pressure that is caused by an explosion, EARTHQUAKE, etc. **2 shock waves** [pl.] feelings of shock that people experience when something bad happens suddenly: *The murder sent shock waves through the whole community.*

shod /ʃɑd/ *adj.* (*literary*) wearing shoes of the type mentioned: *She turned on her elegantly shod heel.* ➔ see also SHOE *v.*

shod·dy /ˈʃɑdi/ *adj.* (shod·di·er, shod·di·est) **1** (of goods, work, etc.) made or done badly and with not enough care **SYN** SECOND-RATE: *shoddy goods* ◆ *shoddy workmanship* **2** dishonest or unfair: *shoddy treatment* ▶ **shod·di·ly** /ˈʃɑdl·i/ *adv.* **shod·di·ness** /ˈʃɑdinəs/ *noun* [U]

shoe 🔑 /ʃu/ *noun, verb*

• *noun* **1** one of a pair of outer coverings for your feet, usually made of leather or plastic: *a pair of shoes* ◆ *He took his shoes and socks off.* ◆ *What's your shoe size?* ◆ *a shoe brush* ◆ *shoe polish* ➔ see also SNOWSHOE **2** = HORSESHOE
IDM **be in sb's shoes | put yourself in sb's shoes** to be in, or imagine that you are in, another person's situation, especially when it is an unpleasant or difficult one: *I wouldn't like to be in your shoes when they find out about it.* **if the shoe fits (, wear it)** if you feel that a remark applies to you, you should accept it and take it as a warning or criticism: *I didn't actually say that you were lazy, but if the shoe fits…* **if I were in your shoes** used to introduce a piece of advice you are giving to someone: *If I were in your shoes, I'd resign immediately.* **the shoe is on the other foot** used to say that a situation has changed so that someone now has power or authority over the person who used to have power or authority over them ➔ more at FILL *v.*, SHAKE *v.*, STEP *v.*

• *verb* (shoe·ing, shod, shod /ʃɑd/) ~ sth to put one or more HORSESHOES on a horse: *The horses were sent to the blacksmith to be shod.*

shoe·box /ˈʃubɑks/ *noun* **1** a box in which you take a pair of new shoes home from a store **2** (*disapproving*) a very small apartment or very small house, often with a square shape and no interesting features, especially one that is very similar to all the ones around it

shoe·horn /'ʃuhɔrn/ *noun, verb*
- *noun* a curved piece of plastic or metal, used to help your heel slide into a shoe
- *verb* ~ sth + adv./prep. to succeed in putting something into a small space or a place where it does not fit very easily: *They managed to shoehorn the material onto just one CD.*

shoe·lace /'ʃuleɪs/ (also **lace, shoe·string**) *noun* a long thin piece of material like string that goes through the holes on a shoe and is used to fasten it: *a pair of shoelaces* ♦ *to tie/untie your shoelaces* ♦ *Your shoelace is undone.* ⊃ picture at CLOTHES

shoe·mak·er /'ʃuˌmeɪkər/ *noun* a person whose job is making shoes and boots ⊃ compare COBBLER ▶ **shoe-mak·ing** *noun* [U]

shoe·shine /'ʃuʃaɪn/ *noun* [U] the activity of cleaning people's shoes for money: *a shoeshine stand on West 32nd Street*

shoe·string /'ʃustrɪŋ/ *noun, adj.*
- *noun* = SHOELACE
    IDM **on a shoestring** (*informal*) using very little money: *In the early years, they ran the business on a shoestring.*
- *adj.* [only before noun] (*informal*) that uses very little money: *The magazine exists on a shoestring budget.*

shoestring po'tatoes *noun* [pl.] potatoes cut into long thin strips and fried in oil

shoe tree *noun* an object shaped like a foot that you put inside a shoe when you are not wearing it to help the shoe keep its shape

sho·gun /'ʃoʊgən/ *noun* (in the past) a Japanese military leader

Sho·na /'ʃoʊnə/ *noun* [U] a language spoken by the Shona peoples of southern Africa, used in Zimbabwe and other parts of southern Africa

shone pt, pp of SHINE

shoo /ʃu/ *verb, exclamation*
- *verb* (shoo·ing, shooed, shooed) ~ sb/sth (+ adv./prep.) to make someone or something go away or to another place, especially by saying "shoo" and waving your arms and hands: *He shooed the dog out of the kitchen.*
- *exclamation* used to tell a child or an animal to go away

shoo·fly pie /ˌʃuflaɪ 'paɪ/ *noun* [C, U] an open PIE filled with brown sugar and MOLASSES **ORIGIN** From the need to say *shoo!* to the flies that the sugar attracts.

shoo-in *noun* ~ (for sth) | ~ (to do sth) (*informal*) a person or team that will win easily

shook pt, pp of SHAKE v.

shoot ✎ /ʃut/ *verb, noun, exclamation*
- *verb* (shot, shot /ʃɑt/)
▸ WEAPON **1** [I, T] to fire a gun or other weapon; to fire something from a weapon: *Don't shoot—I surrender.* ♦ *a serious shooting incident* ♦ ~ (sth) (at sb/sth) *troops shooting at the enemy* ♦ *The police rarely shoot to kill* (= try to kill the people they shoot at). ♦ ~ sth (from sth) *He shot an arrow from his bow.* ♦ *They shot the lock off* (= removed it by shooting). ⊃ collocations at WAR **2** [T] to kill or wound a person or an animal with a bullet, etc.: ~ sb/sth/yourself *A man was shot in the leg.* ♦ *He shot himself during an episode of depression.* ♦ *The guards were ordered to shoot on sight anyone trying to escape.* ♦ ~ sb/sth + adj. *Three people were shot dead during the robbery.* **3** [T, I] ~ (sth) (of a gun or other weapon) to fire bullets, etc.: *This is just a toy gun—it doesn't shoot real bullets.*
▸ FOR SPORT **4** [I, T] ~ (sth) to hunt and kill birds and animals with a gun as a sport: *to shoot pheasants* ♦ *They go shooting in Idaho.*
▸ MOVE QUICKLY **5** [I, T] to move suddenly or quickly in one direction; to make someone or something move in this way: + adv./prep. *A plane shot across the sky.* ♦ *His hand shot*

out to grab her. ♦ *Flames were shooting up through the roof.* ♦ (*figurative*) *The band's last single shot straight to number one on the charts.* ♦ ~ sth + adv./prep. *He shot out his hand to grab her.*
▸ OF PAIN **6** [I] to move suddenly and quickly and be very sharp: *a shooting pain in the back* ♦ + adv./prep. *The pain shot up her arm.*
▸ DIRECT AT SOMEONE **7** [T, no passive] to direct something at someone suddenly or quickly: ~ sth at sb *Journalists were shooting questions at the candidates.* ♦ *She shot an angry glance at him.* ♦ ~ sb sth *She shot him an angry glance.*
▸ MOVIE/PHOTOGRAPH **8** [I, T] to make a movie or photograph of something: *Cameras ready? OK, shoot!* ♦ ~ sth (+ adv./prep.) *Where was the movie shot?* ♦ *The movie was shot in black and white.*
▸ IN SPORTS **9** [I, T] (in basketball, HOCKEY, SOCCER, etc.) to try to kick, hit, or throw the ball into a goal or to score a point: ~ (at sth) *He should have shot instead of passing.* ♦ ~ sth *After school we'd be on the driveway shooting baskets* (= playing basketball). **10** [T] ~ sth (*informal*) (in GOLF) to make a particular score in a complete ROUND or competition: *She shot a 75 in the first round.*
▸ PLAY GAME **11** [T] ~ sth to play particular games: *to shoot pool*

IDM **have shot your wad** (*informal*) to have used all your power, money, or supplies **be like shooting fish in a barrel** (*informal*) used to emphasize how easy it is to do something: *What do you mean you can't do it? It'll be like shooting fish in a barrel!* **shoot the breeze/bull** (*informal*) to have a conversation in an informal way **SYN** CHAT: *We sat around in the bar, shooting the breeze.* **shoot from the hip** (*informal*) to react quickly without thinking carefully first **shoot yourself in the foot** (*informal*) to do or say something that will cause you a lot of trouble or harm, especially when you are trying to get an advantage for yourself **shoot it out (with sb)** (*informal*) to fight against someone with guns, especially until one side is killed or defeated: *The gang decided to shoot it out with the police.* ⊃ related noun SHOOT-OUT **shoot the messenger** to blame the person who gives the news that something bad has happened, instead of the person who is really responsible: *Don't shoot the messenger!* **shoot your mouth off (about sth)** (*informal*) **1** to talk with too much pride about something **2** to talk about something that is private or secret **shoot the rapids** to go in a boat over part of a river where the water flows very fast
PHR V **shoot sb/sth**↔**'down 1** to make someone or something fall to the ground by shooting them/it: *Several planes were shot down by enemy fire.* **2** to be very critical of someone's ideas, opinions, etc.: *His latest theory was shot down in flames.* **shoot for sth** (*informal*) to try to achieve or get something, especially something difficult: *We've been shooting for a pay raise for months.* **shoot sth**↔**'off** to light FIREWORKS and make them go off **SYN** LET STH OFF, SET STH OFF **shoot 'up 1** to grow very quickly: *Their kids have really shot up since the last time I saw them.* **2** to rise suddenly by a large amount: *Ticket prices shot up last year.* ⊃ language bank at INCREASE **3** (*slang*) to INJECT an illegal drug directly into your blood **shoot sth**↔**'up 1** to cause great damage to something by shooting **2** [no passive] (*slang*) to INJECT an illegal drug directly into your blood
- *noun*
▸ PLANT **1** the part that grows up from the ground when a plant starts to grow; a new part that grows on plants or trees: *new green shoots* ♦ *bamboo shoots* ⊃ picture at PLANT
▸ MOVIE/PHOTOGRAPHS **2** an occasion when someone takes professional photographs for a particular purpose or makes a movie: *a fashion shoot* ⊃ see also PHOTO SHOOT
- *exclamation* **1** used to show that you are annoyed when you do something stupid or when something goes wrong: *Shoot! I forgot my book!* **2** used to tell someone to say what they want to say: *You want to tell me something? OK, shoot!*

shoot-'em-up /'ʃut əm ˌʌp/ *adj.* (*informal*) a shoot-'em-up computer game, etc. is one involving a lot of violence with guns

shoot·er /'ʃutər/ noun **1** (especially in compounds) a person or weapon that shoots ⊃ see also PEASHOOTER, SHARPSHOOTER, SIX-SHOOTER, STRAIGHT SHOOTER, TROUBLESHOOTER **2** (informal) a gun **3** (used especially in news reports) a person who uses a gun to kill people

shoot·ing /'ʃutɪŋ/ noun
1 [C] a situation in which a person is shot with a gun: *Terrorist groups claimed responsibility for the shootings and bomb attacks.* **2** [U] the sport of shooting animals and birds with guns: *grouse shooting* **3** [U] the process of filming a movie: *Shooting began early this year.*

shooting gallery noun **1** a place where people shoot guns at objects for practice or to win prizes **2** (slang) a place where people go to take drugs

shooting match noun an occasion when people or groups fight or attack each other
IDM the whole shooting match (informal) everything, or a situation that includes everything

shooting star (also falling star) noun a small METEOR (= a piece of rock in outer space) that travels very fast and burns with a bright light as it enters the earth's atmosphere

shoot-out noun a fight that is fought with guns until one side is killed or defeated ⊃ see also PENALTY SHOOT-OUT

shop /ʃɑp/ noun, verb
● **noun**
> WHERE YOU BUY SOMETHING **1** [C] a small store or a department in a large store where you can buy goods or services: *a shoe shop* ◆ *There's a little gift shop around the corner.* ◆ *a butcher shop* ⊃ collocations at SHOPPING ⊃ see also COFFEE SHOP
> FOR MAKING/REPAIRING THINGS **2** (also work·shop) [C] (especially in compounds) a place where things are made or repaired, especially part of a factory where a particular type of work is done: *a repair shop* ◆ *a paint shop* (= where cars are painted) ⊃ see also BODY SHOP ⊃ thesaurus box at FACTORY
> SCHOOL SUBJECT **3** (also shop class) [U] = INDUSTRIAL ARTS
> ROOM FOR TOOLS **4** (also work·shop) [C] a room in a house where tools are kept for making repairs to the house, building things out of wood, etc.
IDM set up shop to start a business ⊃ more at BULL, TALK v.

● **verb** (-pp-)
> BUY **1** [I] ~ (for sth) to buy things in stores: *to shop for food* ◆ *He likes to shop at the local market.* ◆ *She was determined to go out and shop till she dropped.* ⊃ see also COMPARISON-SHOP **2** go shopping [I] to spend time going to stores and looking for things to buy: *There should be plenty of time to go shopping before we leave New York.* ◆ *"Where's mom?" "She went shopping."*
PHR V shop around (for sth) to compare the quality or prices of goods or services that are offered by different stores, companies, etc. so that you can choose the best: *Shop around for the best deal.*

shop·a·hol·ic /ʃɑpə'hɔlɪk; -'hɑlɪk/ noun (informal) a person who enjoys shopping very much and spends too much time or money doing it ▶ **shop·a·hol·ic** adj.

shop floor noun [sing.] **1** the area in a factory where the goods are made by the workers: *to work on the shop floor* **2** the workers in a factory, not the managers

shop·lift·ing /'ʃɑp.lɪftɪŋ/ noun [U] the crime of stealing goods from a store by deliberately leaving without paying for them ⊃ collocations at SHOPPING ▶ **shop·lift** verb [I] **shop·lift·er** noun: *Shoplifters will be prosecuted.*

shop·per /'ʃɑpər/ noun a person who buys goods from stores: *The streets were full of Christmas shoppers.* ⊃ see also MYSTERY SHOPPER, PERSONAL SHOPPER

shop·ping /'ʃɑpɪŋ/ noun [U]
the activity of going to stores and buying things: *to go shopping* ◆ *Where do you usually do your shopping?* ◆ *a*

shopping basket ◆ *a shopping cart* ⊃ see also WINDOW-SHOPPING

shopping bag noun **1** a large, strong bag made of cloth, plastic, etc. used for carrying the things you have bought **2** a paper or plastic bag for carrying shopping

shopping cart noun a large metal BASKET with wheels that you can push around a store to carry items when you are shopping

shopping center (CanE usually shopping centre) noun a group of stores built together, sometimes under one roof

shopping list noun a list that you make of all the things that you need to buy when you go shopping

shopping mall (also mall) noun a large building or covered area that has many stores, restaurants, etc. inside it

shop steward noun a person who is elected by members of a LABOR UNION in a factory or company to represent them in meetings with managers

shop talk noun [U] talk about your work or your business

shop·worn /'ʃɑpwɔrn/ adj. (of goods) dirty or not in perfect condition because they have been in a store for a long time: (figurative) *a shopworn argument* (= that is no longer new or useful)

shore /ʃɔr/ noun, verb
● **noun 1** [C, U] the land along the edge of the ocean, a lake, or another large area of water: *a rocky/sandy shore* ◆ *to swim from the boat to the shore* ◆ *a house on the shores of the lake*

2 the shore [sing.] an area that is by the ocean, especially one where people go for a day or a vacation: *Let's go to the shore.* ◆ thesaurus box at COAST **3 shores** [pl.] (especially *literary*) a country, especially one with a coast: *foreign shores* ◆ *What brings you to these shores?*

● *verb*
PHRV ,shore sth↔'up **1** to support part of a building or other large structure by placing large pieces of wood or metal against or under it so that it does not fall down **2** to help to support something that is weak or going to fail

shore·line /'ʃɔrlaɪn/ *noun* [usually sing.] the edge of the ocean or a lake: *a rocky shoreline* ◆ *The road follows the shoreline for a few miles.*

shorn *pp* of SHEAR

short 🔑 /ʃɔrt/ *adj., adv., noun, verb*

● *adj.* (short·er, short·est)
> LENGTH/DISTANCE **1** measuring or covering a small length or distance, or a smaller length or distance than usual: *He had short curly hair.* ◆ *a short walk* ◆ *a short skirt* **ANT** LONG
> HEIGHT **2** (of a person) small in height: *She was short and dumpy.* **ANT** TALL
> TIME **3** lasting or taking a small amount of time or less time than usual: *I'm going to Puerto Rico for a short break.* ◆ *Which is the shortest day of the year?* ◆ *a short book* (= taking a short time to read, because it does not have many pages) ◆ *She has a very short memory* (= remembers only things that have happened recently). ◆ (*informal*) *Life's too short to sit around moping.* ◆ *It was all over in a relatively short time.* **ANT** LONG **4** [only before noun] (of a period of time) seeming to have passed very quickly: *Just two short years ago he was the best quarterback in the country.* **ANT** LONG
> NOT ENOUGH **5** [not before noun] **~ (of sth)** not having enough of something; lacking something: *I'm afraid I'm a little short* (= of money) *this month.* ◆ *She is not short of excuses when things go wrong.* **6 ~ on sth** (*informal*) lacking or not having enough of a particular quality: *He was a big strapping guy but short on brains.* **7** [not before noun] not easily available; not supplying as much as you need: *Money was short at that time.* **8** [not before noun] **~ (of sth)** less than the number, amount, or distance mentioned or needed: *Her last throw was only three centimeters short of the world record.* ◆ *The team was two players short.* ◆ *She was just short of her 90th birthday when she died.*
> OF BREATH **9 ~ of breath** having difficulty breathing, for example because of illness
> NAME/WORD **10 ~ for sth** being a shorter form of a name or word: *Call me Jo—it's short for Joanna.* ◆ *file transfer protocol or FTP for short*
> RUDE **11** [not before noun] **~ (with sb)** (of a person) speaking to someone using few words in a way that seems rude: *I'm sorry I was short with you earlier—I had other things on my mind.*
> VOWEL **12** (*phonetics*) a **short** vowel is pronounced for a shorter time than other vowels: *Compare the short vowel in "full" and the long vowel in "fool."* **ANT** LONG ◆ see also SHORTLY ▶ **short·ness** *noun* [U]: *She suffered from shortness of breath.*

IDM get the short end of the stick to be the person in a group who is chosen or forced to perform an unpleasant duty or task: *I got the short end of the stick and had to clean the toilets.* give sb/sth/get short shrift to give sb/get little attention or sympathy have/be on a short fuse to have a tendency to get angry quickly and easily: *You may find your temper on a short fuse when confronting your teenager.* in short order quickly and without trouble in the short run concerning the immediate future: *In the short run, unemployment may fall.* in short supply not existing in large enough quantities to satisfy demand: *Basic foodstuffs were in short supply.* ◆ *Sunshine will be in short supply for most of New England.* little/nothing short of sth used when you are saying that something is almost true, or is equal to something: *Last year's figures were little short of disastrous.* ◆ *The transformation has been nothing short of a miracle.* make short work of sth/sb to defeat or deal with something or

someone quickly: *Our team made short work of the opposition* (= in a sports competition). ◆ *The kids made short work of the birthday cake* (= ate it quickly). short and sweet (*informal*) pleasant but not lasting a long time: *We don't have much time so I'll keep it short and sweet.* ◆ more at DRAW v., LIFE, LONG *adj.*, NOTICE n., TERM n.

● *adv.* (short·er, short·est) **1** if you run short of or go short of something, you do not have enough of it: *They had run short of* (= used most of their supply of) *fuel.* **2** not as far as you need or expect: *Sometimes you throw the ball short.* **3** before the time expected or arranged; before the natural time: *a career tragically cut short by illness* ◆ *I'm afraid I'm going to have to stop you short there, as time is running out.* **IDM** be caught short to be put at a disadvantage fall short of sth to fail to reach the standard that you expected or need: *The hotel fell far short of their expectations.* short of (doing) sth without something; without doing something; unless something happens: *Short of a miracle, we're certain to lose.* ◆ *Short of asking her to leave* (= and we don't want to do that) *there's not a lot we can do about the situation.* pull, bring, etc. sb up short to make someone suddenly stop what they are doing: *I was brought up short by a terrible thought.* ◆ more at SELL v., STOP v.

● *noun* (*informal*) ◆ see also SHORTS **1** a short movie, especially one that is shown before the main film **2** (*informal*) = SHORT CIRCUIT **IDM** in short in a few words: *His novels belong to a great but vanished age. They are, in short, old-fashioned.* ◆ more at LONG *adj.*

● *verb* [I, T] **~ (sth) (out)** (*informal*) = SHORT-CIRCUIT

short·age /'ʃɔrtɪdʒ/ *noun* [C, U] a situation when there is not enough of the people or things that are needed: *food/housing/water shortages* ◆ *a shortage of funds* ◆ *There is no shortage of* (= there are plenty of) *things to do in the town.*

short·bread /'ʃɔrtbrɛd/ *noun* [U] a rich, crisp cookie made with flour, sugar, and a lot of butter

short·cake /'ʃɔrtkeɪk/ *noun* [U] a type of small, plain cake with fruit and cream on top: *strawberry shortcake*

short·change /,ʃɔrt'tʃeɪndʒ/ *verb* [often passive] **1 ~ sb** to give back less than the correct amount of money to someone who has paid for something with more than the exact price: *I think the bartender short-changed me.* **2 ~ sb** to treat someone unfairly by not giving them what they have earned or deserve

,short 'circuit (also *informal* short) *noun* a failure in an electrical CIRCUIT, when electricity travels along the wrong route because of damaged wires or a fault in the connections between the wires

,short–'circuit (also *informal* short) *verb* **1** [I, T] **~ (sth)** to have a short circuit; to make something have a short circuit: *The wires had short-circuited and burned out.* **2** [T] **~ sth** to succeed in doing something more quickly than usual, without going through all the usual processes

short·com·ing /'ʃɔrt,kʌmɪŋ/ *noun* [usually pl.] a fault in someone's character, a plan, a system, etc. **SYN** DEFECT

short·cut /'ʃɔrtkʌt/ *noun* **1** a quicker or shorter way of getting to a place: *You can take a shortcut across the field.* **2** a way of doing something that is quicker than the usual way: *There are no shortcuts to economic recovery.*

short·en /'ʃɔrtn/ *verb* [T, I] to make something shorter; to become shorter: **~ (sth)** *Injury problems could shorten his career.* ◆ *a shortened version of the game* ◆ *In November the temperatures drop and the days shorten.* ◆ **~ sth to sth** *Her name's Katherine, generally shortened to Kay.* **ANT** LENGTHEN

short·en·ing /'ʃɔrtnɪŋ; 'ʃɔrtn·ɪŋ/ *noun* [U] fat that is used for making PASTRY

short·fall /'ʃɔrtfɔl/ *noun* **~ (in sth)** if there is **a shortfall in** something, there is less of it than you need or expect **SYN** DEFICIT

short·hair /'ʃɔrthɛr/ *noun* a breed of cat with short hair ◆ compare LONGHAIR

t tea ṭ butter d did k cat g got tʃ chin dʒ June f fall

short·hand /'ʃɔːthænd/ noun **1** (also **ste·nog·ra·phy**) [U] a quick way of writing using special signs or abbreviations, used especially to record what someone is saying: *typing and shorthand* ◆ *to take something down in shorthand* **2** [U, C] ~ **(for sth)** a shorter way of saying or referring to something, that may not be as accurate as the more complicated way of saying it

short-'handed adj. [not usually before noun] not having as many workers or people who can help as you need **SYN** SHORT-STAFFED

short-haul adj. [only before noun] that involves transporting people or goods over short distances, especially by plane **ANT** LONG-HAUL

short·horn /'ʃɔːthɔːn/ noun a breed of cow with short horns

short·ie = SHORTY

short list (also **short·list**) /'ʃɔːtlɪst/ noun [usually sing.] a small number of candidates for a job, etc., who have been chosen from all the people who applied: *to draw up a short list* ◆ *a short list for a literary prize* ◆ *She is on my short list of great singers.*

short-list verb [usually passive] ~ **sb/sth (for sth)** to put someone or something on a short list for a job, prize, etc.: *Candidates who are short-listed for the job will be contacted by the end of the week.*

short-lived /ˌʃɔːt'lɪvd; -'laɪvd/ adj. lasting only for a short time

short·ly 🔑 /'ʃɔːtli/ adv.
1 a short time; not long: *She arrived shortly after us.* ◆ *I saw him shortly before he died.* **2** soon: *I'll be ready shortly.* **3** in an angry and impatient way **SYN** SHARPLY

short-order 'cook noun a person who works in a restaurant cooking food that can be prepared quickly

short-range adj. [usually before noun] **1** (of weapons) designed to travel only over short distances: *short-range missiles* **2** (of plans, etc.) connected with a short period of time in the future: *a short-range weather forecast* ➪ compare LONG-RANGE

short ribs noun [pl.] a piece of beef with some of the bones from the RIBS of the cow

shorts /ʃɔːts/ noun [pl.] **1** short pants that end above or at the knee: *a pair of tennis shorts* ◆ *He was wearing a T-shirt and shorts.* ➪ picture at CLOTHES **2** = BOXER SHORTS

short·sight·ed /ˌʃɔːt'saɪtəd/ adj. not thinking carefully about the possible effects of something or what might happen in the future: *a shortsighted policy* ▶ **short·sight·ed·ness** noun [U]: *Many people accused the government of shortsightedness.* **short·sight·ed·ly** adv.

short-'staffed adj. [not usually before noun] having fewer members of staff than you need or usually have **SYN** SHORT-HANDED ➪ see also UNDERSTAFFED

short·stop /'ʃɔːtstɒp/ noun (in baseball) a player who tries to stop balls that are hit between second and third base; the position of this player ➪ picture at BASEBALL

short 'story noun a story, usually about imaginary characters and events, that is short enough to be read from beginning to end without stopping

short 'temper noun [sing.] a tendency to become angry very quickly and easily ▶ **short-'tempered** adj.

short-'term adj. **1** [usually before noun] lasting a short time; designed only for a short period of time in the future: *a short-term loan* ◆ *to find work on a short-term contract* ◆ *short-term plans* ◆ *a short-term solution to the problem* ◆ *His short-term memory* (= the ability to remember things that happened a short time ago) *is failing.* ➪ compare LONG-TERM **2** [only before noun] (of a place) where you only stay for a short time: *a short-term parking garage* ◆ *short-term patients* (= who only stay in a hospital for a short time)

short-termism /ˌʃɔːt 'tɜːmɪzəm/ noun [U] a way of thinking or planning that is concerned with the advantages or profits you could have now, rather than the effects in the future

short·wave /'ʃɔːtweɪv/ noun [C, U] (abbr. **SW**) a radio wave that has a FREQUENCY greater than 3 MEGAHERTZ ➪ compare LONG WAVE, MEDIUM WAVE

short·y (also **short·ie**) /'ʃɔːti/ noun (pl. **short·ies**) (informal) a person who is shorter than average

Sho·sho·ne /ʃoʊ'ʃoʊni/ noun (pl. **Sho·sho·ne** or **Sho·sho·nes**) a member of a Native American people many of whom now live in the state of Wyoming

shot 🔑 /ʃɒt/ noun, adj. ➪ see also SHOOT
● noun
▸ **WITH GUN 1** [C] ~ **(at sb/sth)** the act of firing a gun; the sound this makes: *The man fired several shots from his pistol.* ◆ *Someone took a shot at the car.* ◆ *We heard some shots in the distance.* ➪ see also GUNSHOT, POTSHOT **2** [C] **a good, bad, etc.** ~ a person who shoots a gun in a particular way (well, badly, etc.)
▸ **BULLETS 3** (also **lead 'shot**) [U] a large number of small metal balls that you fire together from a SHOTGUN ➪ see also BUCKSHOT **4** [C] (pl. **shot**) a large, stone or metal ball that was shot from a CANNON or large gun in the past
▸ **REMARK/ACTION 5** [C] a remark or an action that is usually one of a series, and is aimed against someone or something that you are arguing or competing with: *This statement was the opening shot in the argument.* ◆ *We're not sure which discount store fired the first shot in a price war today.*
▸ **ATTEMPT 6** [C, usually sing.] ~ **(at sth/at doing sth)** (informal) the act of trying to do or achieve something: *The team is looking good for a shot at the title.* ◆ *I've never produced a play before but I'll take a shot at it.* ◆ *I'm willing to give it a shot.* ◆ *Just give it your best shot* (= try as hard as you can) *and you'll be fine.*
▸ **IN SPORTS 7** [C] the action of hitting, kicking, or throwing the ball in order to score a point or goal in a game: *Taylor scored with a hook shot into the net.* ◆ *Good shot!* **8** often **the shot** [sing.] the heavy ball that is used in the sports competition called THE SHOT PUT
▸ **PHOTOGRAPH 9** [C] a photograph: *I got some good shots of people at the party.* ➪ see also MUGSHOT, SNAPSHOT ➪ thesaurus box at PHOTOGRAPH
▸ **SCENE IN MOVIE 10** [C] a scene in a movie that is filmed continuously by one camera: *the opening shot of a character walking across a desert*
▸ **DRUG 11** [C] (informal) a small amount of a drug that is put into your body using a SYRINGE **SYN** INJECTION: *a flu shot* (= to protect you against flu) ◆ *a shot of morphine*
▸ **DRINK 12** [C] (informal) a small amount of a drink, especially a strong alcoholic one: *a shot of whiskey*
▸ **OF SPACECRAFT 13** [C] an occasion when a SPACECRAFT is sent into space: *The space shot was shown live on television.*
▸ **HORSE/DOG IN RACE 14** [sing.] (used with numbers) a horse, dog, etc. that has the particular chance of winning a race that is mentioned: *The horse is a 10–1 shot.* **HELP** You will find other compounds ending in **shot** at their place in the alphabet.
IDM **like a shot** (informal) very quickly and without hesitating: *If I had the chance to go there, I'd go like a shot.* **a shot across the/sb's bows** something that you say or do as a warning to someone about what might happen if they do not change, etc. **a shot in the arm** something that gives someone or something the help or encouragement they need ➪ more at BIG adj., CALL v., DARK n., LONG adj., PARTING adj.
● adj. **1** ~ **(with sth)** (of cloth, hair, etc.) having another color showing through or mixed with the main color: *shot silk* **2** [not before noun] (informal) in a very bad condition; destroyed: *The brakes on this car are shot.* ◆ *I'm shot—I'm too old for this job.* ◆ *After the accident his nerves were shot to pieces.* **IDM** **shot through with sth** containing a lot of a particular color, quality, or feature: *a voice shot through with emotion*

shot·gun /'ʃɒtɡʌn/ noun a long gun that fires a lot of small metal bullets (called SHOT) and is used especially for

shooting birds or animals ⊃ see also SAWED-OFF SHOTGUN
IDM see RIDE *v.*

ˌshotgun ˈwedding (also ˌshotgun ˈmarriage) *noun* (*old-fashioned*, *informal*) a wedding that has to take place quickly, for example because the woman is pregnant

shot·mak·ing /ˈʃɒtˌmeɪkɪŋ/ *noun* [U] (in GOLF, TENNIS, etc.) a way of playing in which a player takes risks in order to win more points

Sho·to·kan /ˈʃoʊtoʊˌkɑn/ *noun* [U] (from *Japanese*) a popular form of KARATE

the ˈshot put *noun* [sing.] (also ˈshot-putting, ˌputting the ˈshot) the event or sport of throwing a heavy metal ball (called a SHOT) as far as possible

should 🔑 /ʃəd; strong form ʃʊd/ *modal verb* (*negative* should not, *short form* should·n't /ˈʃʊdnt/)
1 used to show what is right, appropriate, etc., especially when criticizing someone's actions: *You shouldn't drink and drive.* ♦ *He should have been more careful.* ♦ *A present for me? You shouldn't have!* (= used to thank someone politely)
2 used to say that you expect something is true or will happen: *We should arrive before dark.* ♦ *I should have finished the book by Friday.* ♦ *The roads should be less crowded today.*
3 used to say that something that was expected has not happened: *It should be snowing now, according to the weather forecast.* ♦ *The bus should have arrived ten minutes ago.*
4 (*formal*) used to refer to a possible event or situation: *If you should change your mind, just let me know.* ♦ *In case you should need any help, here's my number.* ♦ *Should anyone call* (= if anyone calls)*, please tell them I'm busy.* **5** used after *that* when something is suggested or arranged: *She recommended that I should take some time off.* **HELP** This idea can be expressed without "should": *She recommended that I take some time off.* **6 why, how, who, what ~ sb/sth do** used to refuse something or to show that you are annoyed at a request; used to express surprise about an event or a situation: *Why should I help him? He's never done anything for me.* ♦ *How should I know where to find you?* ♦ *I got on the bus and who should be sitting in front of me but Tony!* **7** used after *that* after many adjectives that describe feelings: *I'm anxious that we should allow plenty of time.* ♦ *I find it astonishing that he should be so rude to you.* **8** used with I and we to give opinions that you are not certain about: *I should imagine it will take about three hours.* ♦ *"Is this enough food for everyone?" "I should think so."* ♦ *"Will it matter?" "I shouldn't think so."*
9 used for expressing strong agreement: *"I know it's expensive but it will last for years." "I should hope so too!"* ♦ *"Nobody will oppose it." "I should think not!"* **10** used to tell someone that something would amuse or surprise them if they saw or experienced it: *You should have seen her face when she found out!* ⊃ note at MODAL

shoul·der 🔑 /ˈʃoʊldər/ *noun, verb*
● *noun*
▸ **PART OF BODY 1** [C] either of the two parts of the body between the top of each arm and the neck: *He slung the bag over his shoulder.* ♦ *She tapped him on the shoulder.* ♦ *He looked back over his shoulder.* ♦ *She shrugged her shoulders* (= showing that she didn't know or care). ♦ *an off-the-shoulder dress* ♦ *He carried the child on his shoulders.* ⊃ picture at BODY ⊃ collocations at PHYSICAL
▸ **-SHOULDERED 2** (in adjectives) having the type of shoulders mentioned: *broad-shouldered* ⊃ see also ROUND-SHOULDERED
▸ **CLOTHING 3** [C] the part of a piece of clothing that covers the shoulder: *a jacket with padded shoulders*
▸ **MEAT 4** [U, C] **~ (of sth)** meat from the top part of one of the front legs of an animal that has four legs
▸ **SIDE OF ROAD 5** [C] an area of ground at the side of a road where vehicles can stop in an emergency: *No shoulder for next 5 miles.* ⊃ see also SOFT SHOULDER
▸ **OF MOUNTAIN/BOTTLE, ETC. 6** [C] **~ (of sth)** a part of something, such as a bottle or mountain, that is shaped like a shoulder: *The village lay just around the shoulder of the hill.*
IDM be looking over your shoulder to be anxious and have the feeling that someone is going to do something unpleasant or harmful to you **on sb's shoulders** if blame, GUILT, etc. is on someone's shoulders, they must take responsibility for it **put your shoulder to the wheel** to start working very hard at a particular task **a shoulder to cry on** (used to describe a person who listens to your problems and gives you sympathy) **shoulder to shoulder (with sb) 1** physically close to someone **2** as one group that has the same aims, opinions, etc. ⊃ more at CHIP *n.*, COLD *adj.*, HEAD *n.*, RUB *v.*, STRAIGHT *adv.*
● *verb*
▸ **ACCEPT RESPONSIBILITY 1** [T] **~ sth** to accept the responsibility for something: *to shoulder the responsibility/blame for something* ♦ *women who shoulder the double burden of childcare and full-time work*
▸ **PUSH WITH SHOULDER 2** [T, I] to push forward with your shoulder in order to get somewhere **~ your way + adv./prep.**: *He shouldered his way through the crowd and went after her.* ♦ **+ adv./prep.** *She shouldered past a woman with a screaming baby.* **3** [T] **~ sb/sth + adv./prep.** to push someone or something out of your way with your shoulder: *He shouldered the man aside.*
▸ **CARRY ON SHOULDER 4** [T] **~ sth** to carry something on your shoulder: *She shouldered her bag and set off for home.*

ˈshoulder ˌbag *noun* a bag, especially a PURSE, that is carried over the shoulder with a long, narrow piece of leather, etc.

ˈshoulder ˌblade *noun* either of the two large, flat bones at the top of the back ⊃ picture at BODY **SYN** SCAPULA

ˌshoulder-ˈhigh *adj.* as high as a person's shoulders: *a shoulder-high wall* ► ˌshoulder-ˈhigh *adv.*: *They carried him shoulder-high through the crowd.*

ˈshoulder-ˌlength *adj.* (especially of hair) long enough to reach your shoulders ⊃ picture at HAIR

ˈshoulder ˌpad *noun* [usually pl.] **1** a small piece of thick cloth that is sewn into the shoulder of a dress, jacket, etc. to make a person's shoulders look bigger **2** a piece of hard plastic that people wear under their shirts to protect their shoulders when playing football, HOCKEY, etc. ⊃ picture at FOOTBALL

'shoulder ˌstrap *noun* **1** a strip of cloth on a dress or other piece of clothing that goes over your shoulder from the front to the back ⊃ picture at CLOTHES **2** a long strip of cloth, leather, etc. that is attached to a bag so that you can carry it over your shoulder

'shoulder ˌsurfing *noun* [U] (*informal*) the practice of watching a person who is getting money from a machine, filling out a form, etc., in order to find out their personal information

---
THESAURUS

shout

yell ◆ cry ◆ scream ◆ cheer ◆ bellow ◆ raise your voice

These words all mean to say something in a very loud voice.

shout to say something in a loud voice; to speak loudly and often angrily to someone: *Stop shouting and listen!* ◆ *"Run!" he shouted.*

yell to shout loudly, for example because you are angry, excited, afraid, or in pain: *She yelled at the boy to get down from the wall.*

cry (*somewhat formal* or *literary*) to shout loudly, especially because you are upset, afraid, excited, or very happy: *She ran over to the window and cried for help.*

scream to shout something in a loud high voice because you are afraid, angry, or excited: *He screamed at me to stop.*

cheer (especially of a crowd of people) to shout loudly to show support or praise for someone, or to give them encouragement: *We all cheered as the team came onto the field.*

bellow to shout in a loud deep voice, especially because you are angry: *My father bellowed at me from across the room.*

raise your voice to speak loudly to someone, especially because you are angry: *She never once raised her voice to us.*

PATTERNS

- to shout/yell/cry/raise your voice **to** sb
- to shout/yell/scream/bellow **at** sb
- to shout/yell/cry out/scream/bellow **in** pain/anguish/rage, etc.
- to shout/cry out/scream **for** joy/excitement/delight, etc.
- to shout/yell/cry out/scream **with** excitement/triumph, etc.
- to shout/yell/scream/bellow **at** sb **to do** sth
- to shout/yell/scream **insults**
- to shout/yell/cry/scream **for help**

---

shout 🔑 /ʃaʊt/ *verb, noun*
● *verb* **1** [I, T] to say something in a loud voice; to speak loudly/angrily to someone: *Stop shouting and listen!* ◆ ~ **for sth** *I shouted for help but nobody came.* ◆ ~ **at sb** *Then he started shouting and swearing at her.* ◆ ~ **at sb to do sth** *She shouted at him to shut the gate.* ◆ ~ **sth (at/to sb)** to shout abuse/encouragement/orders ◆ ~ **that...** *He shouted that he couldn't swim.* ◆ ~ **yourself + adj.** *She shouted herself hoarse, cheering on the team.* ◆ **+ speech** *"Run!" he shouted.* **2** [I] ~ **(out)** to make a loud noise: *She shouted out in pain when she tried to move her leg.*
PHR V ˌshout sb↔'down to shout so that someone who is speaking cannot be heard: *The speaker was shouted down by a group of protesters.* ˌshout sth↔'out to say something in a loud voice so that it can be clearly heard: *Don't shout out all the answers.* ◆ **+ speech** *"I'm over here!" I shouted out.*

● *noun* a loud cry of anger, fear, excitement, etc.: *angry shouts* ◆ *a shout of anger* ◆ *I heard her warning shout too late.*
IDM give sb a 'shout (*informal*) to tell someone something: *Give me a shout when you're ready.*

shout·ing /ʃaʊtɪŋ/ *noun* [U] loud cries from a number of people: *Didn't you hear all the shouting?*
IDM within 'shouting distance (of sth) (*informal*) very close

'shouting ˌmatch *noun* an argument or a disagreement when people shout loudly at each other

'shout-out *noun* (*informal*) a public expression of thanks or welcome: *This is a shout-out to all our sponsors and advertisers.*

shove /ʃʌv/ *verb, noun*
● *verb* **1** [I, T] to push someone or something in a rough way: *The crowd was pushing and shoving to get a better view.* ◆ **+ adv./prep.** *The door wouldn't open no matter how hard she shoved.* ◆ ~ **sb/sth (+ adv./prep.)** *He shoved her down the stairs.* **2** [T] ~ **sth (+ adv./prep.)** (*informal*) to put something somewhere roughly or carelessly: *She shoved the book into her bag and hurried off.* ◆ *He came over and shoved a piece of paper into my hand.* ◆ *Shove your suitcase under the bed.*
IDM shove it (*informal*) used to say rudely that you will not accept or do something: *"The boss wants that report now." "Yeah? Tell him he can shove it."*
PHR V ˌshove 'off (*informal*) used to tell someone rudely to go away ˌshove 'over (*informal*) to move in order to make a space for someone to sit down beside you: *Shove over! Jan wants to sit down.*

● *noun* [usually sing.] a strong push: *You have to give the door a shove or it won't close.* **IDM** see PUSH *n.*

shov·el /ʃʌvl/ *noun, verb*
● *noun* **1** a tool with a long handle and a broad blade with curved edges, used for moving earth, snow, sand, etc.: *workmen with picks and shovels* ⊃ picture at TOOL: *The children took their pails and shovels to the beach.* ⊃ compare SPADE **2** the part of a large machine or vehicle that digs or moves earth
● *verb* (-l-, *CanE usually* -ll-) ~ **sth (+ adv./prep.)** to lift and move earth, stones, coal, etc. with a shovel: *A gang of workmen were shoveling rubble onto a truck.* ◆ *They went out in freezing conditions to shovel snow.* ◆ *to shovel the sidewalk/driveway* (= to remove snow) ◆ (*figurative*) *He sat at the table, shoveling food into his mouth.*

shov·el·ful /ʃʌvlˌfʊl/ *noun* the amount that a shovel can hold

show 🔑 /ʃoʊ/ *verb, noun*
● *verb* (showed, shown /ʃoʊn/ or, rarely, showed)
▷ MAKE CLEAR **1** [T] to make something clear; to prove something: ~ **(that)...** *The figures clearly show that her claims are false.* ◆ ~ **sb that...** *Market research has shown us that people want quality, not just low prices.* ◆ ~ **sth** *a report showing the company's current situation* ◆ ~ **sb/sth to be/have sth** *His new book shows him to be a first-rate storyteller.* ◆ ~ **(sb) how, what, etc....** *This shows how people are influenced by TV advertisements.* ⊃ language bank at ILLUSTRATE
▷ LET SOMEONE SEE SOMETHING **2** [T] to let someone see something: ~ **sth** *You have to show your ticket as you go in.* ◆ ~ **sth to sb** *If there's a letter from France please show it to me.* ◆ *Have you shown your work to anyone?* ◆ ~ **sb sth** *Have you shown anyone your work?*
▷ TEACH **3** [T] to help someone to do something by letting them watch you do it or by explaining it: ~ **sth to sb** *She showed the technique to her students.* ◆ ~ **sb sth** *She showed her students the technique.* ◆ *Can you show me how to do it?*
▷ POINT **4** [T] ~ **sb sth** to point to something so that someone can see where or what it is: *He showed me our location on the map.* ◆ ~ **sb which, what, etc....** *Show me which picture you drew.*
▷ GUIDE **5** [T] to lead or guide someone to a place: ~ **sb + adv./prep.** *The attendant showed us to our seats.* ◆ *We were shown into the waiting room.* ◆ ~ **sb sth** *I'll go first and show you the way.* ⊃ thesaurus box at TAKE
▷ QUALITY/BEHAVIOR/FEELING **6** [T] to make it clear that you

have a particular quality: ~ **sth** *to show great courage* ♦ ~ **yourself + adj.** *She had shown herself unable to deal with money.* ♦ ~ **yourself to be/have sth** *He has shown himself to be ready to make compromises.* ♦ ~ **that…** *He has shown that he is ready to make compromises.* **7** [T] to behave in a particular way toward someone: ~ **sth (for/to sb)** *They showed no respect for their parents.* ♦ ~ **sb sth** *They showed their parents no respect.* **8** [I, T] if a feeling or quality **shows**, or if you **show** it, people can see it: *Fear showed in his eyes.* ♦ *She tried not to let her disappointment show.* ♦ *She's almost forty now. And it shows* (= it's obvious). ♦ ~ **sth** *Her expression showed her disappointment.* ♦ *James began to show signs of impatience.* ♦ ~ **how, what, etc.…** *She tried not to show how disappointed she was.*
> **BE VISIBLE 9** [I, T] if something **shows**, people can see it. If something **shows** a mark, dirt, etc., the mark can be seen: *She had a warm woolen hat on that left only her eyes and nose showing.* ♦ ~ **sth** *Their new white carpeting showed every mark.*
> **INFORMATION 10** [T] (not usually used in the progressive tenses) ~ **sth** to give particular information, or a time or measurement: *The map shows the principal towns and rivers.* ♦ *The clock showed midnight.* ♦ *The end-of-year statement shows a loss.*
> **OF PICTURE/PHOTOGRAPH 11** [T] ~ **sth** | ~ **sb/sth (as sth)** | ~ **sb/sth doing sth** to be of someone or something; to represent someone or something: *She objected to a photo showing her in a bikini.*
> **FOR PUBLIC TO SEE 12** [I, T] to be or make something available for the public to see: *The movie is now showing in all major cities.* ♦ ~ **sth** *The movie is being shown now.* ♦ *She plans to show her paintings early next year.*
> **PROVE 13** [T, no passive] ~ **sb (sth)** (*informal*) to prove that you can do something or are something: *They think I can't do it, but I'll show them!*
> **ARRIVE 14** [I] (*informal*) to arrive where you have arranged to meet someone or do something: *I waited an hour but he didn't show.* ◌ see also **SHOW UP**
> **ANIMAL 15** [T] ~ **sth** to enter an animal in a competition
IDM **it goes to show** used to say that something proves something: *It just goes to show what you can do when you really try.* **show sb the door** to ask someone to leave, because they are no longer welcome **show your face** to appear among your friends or in public: *She stayed at home, afraid to show her face.* **show your hand/cards** (also **tip your hand**) to make your plans or intentions known **show sb who's boss** to make it clear to someone that you have more power and authority than they have **show the way** to do something first so that other people can follow **(have) something, nothing, etc. to show for sth** (to have) something, nothing, etc. as a result of something: *All those years of hard work, and nothing to show for it!* ◌ more at **FLAG** *n.*, **PACE¹** *n.*, **ROPE** *n.*
PHR V **show sb a'round (sth)** to be a guide for someone when they visit a place for the first time to show them what is interesting: *We were shown around the school by one of the students.* ♦ *Has anyone shown you around yet?* **show 'off** (*informal, disapproving*) to try to impress others by talking about your abilities, possessions, etc.: *He's just showing off because that girl he likes is here.* ◌ related noun **SHOW-OFF** **show sb/sth↔'off 1** to show people someone or something that you are proud of: *She wanted to show off her new husband at the party.* ♦ ~ **how, what, etc.…** *He likes to show off how well he speaks French.* **2** (of clothing) to make someone look attractive, by showing their best features: *a dress that shows off her figure* **show 'through** | **show 'through sth** to be able to be seen behind or under something else: *The writing on the other side of the page shows through.* ♦ (*figurative*) *When he spoke, his bitterness showed through.* ♦ *Veins showed through her pale skin.* **show 'up** (*informal*) to arrive where you have arranged to meet someone or do something: *It was getting late when she finally showed up.* **show 'up** | **show sth↔'up** to become visible; to make something become visible: *a broken bone showed up on the X-ray* ♦ *The harsh light showed up the lines on her face.* **show sb↔'up** to make someone feel embarrassed by doing something better than them

● **noun**
> **ENTERTAINMENT 1** [C] a theater performance, especially one that includes singing and dancing: *to go to a show* ♦ *a one-woman/-man show* ♦ *to put on/stage a show* ♦ *She's the star of the show!* ◌ see also **FLOOR SHOW, ROAD SHOW 2** [C] a program on television or the radio: *to host a show* ♦ *a TV/ radio show* ♦ *a quiz show* ◌ collocations at **TELEVISION** ◌ see also **CHAT SHOW, GAME SHOW, ROAD SHOW**
> **OF COLLECTION OF THINGS 3** [C, U] an occasion when a collection of things are brought together for people to look at: *an agricultural show* ♦ *The latest computers will be on show at the exhibition.* ◌ see also **FASHION SHOW, HORSE SHOW, PEEP SHOW**
> **OF FEELING 4** [C] an action or a way of behaving that shows how you feel **SYN** DISPLAY: *a show of emotion* ♦ *a show of support* ♦ *a show of force/strength by the army.*
> **INSINCERE ACT 5** [U, sing.] something that is done only to give a good impression, but is not sincere: *He may seem charming, but it's all show!* ♦ *She pretends to be interested in opera, but it's only for show.* ♦ *He made a great show of affection, but I knew he didn't mean it.*
> **COLORFUL SIGHT 6** [C, U] a brightly colored or pleasing sight **SYN** DISPLAY: *a lovely show of spring flowers*
> **EVENT/SITUATION 7** [sing.] (*informal*) an event, a business, or a situation where something is being done or organized: *She runs the whole show.* ♦ *I won't interfere—it's your show.*
> **GOOD SHOW 8** [C, usually sing.] (*informal*) something that is done in a particular way: *The team put on a good show in the competition.*
IDM **for show** intended to be seen but not used: *These items are just for show—they're not for sale.* **get the show on the road** (*informal*) to start an activity or a journey: *Let's get this show on the road!* **a show of hands** a group of people each raising a hand to vote for or against something ◌ more at **DOG** *n.*, **STEAL**

show-and-'tell *noun* [U] an activity in which children have to bring something to show their class and talk about it to them

show-boat /'ʃoʊboʊt/ *noun, verb*
● *noun* a boat on which musical shows are performed
● *verb* [I] (*informal*, often *disapproving*) to behave in a way that tries to show people how intelligent, skillful, etc. you are ▸ **show-boat-ing** *noun* [U]

'**show business** (also *informal* **show-biz** /'ʃoʊbɪz/) *noun* [U] the business of providing public entertainment, for example in the theater, in movies, or in television: *to be in show business* ♦ *show-business people/stars* ♦ *That's showbiz!*

show-case /'ʃoʊkeɪs/ *noun* **1** [usually sing.] ~ **(for sb/sth)** an event that presents someone's abilities or the good qualities of something in an attractive way: *The festival was a showcase for young musicians.* **2** a box with a glass top or sides that is used for showing objects in a store, museum, etc. ▸ **show-case** *verb*: ~ **sth** *Jack found a film role that showcased all his talents.*

show-down /'ʃoʊdaʊn/ *noun* [usually sing.] an argument, a fight, or a test that will settle a disagreement that has lasted for a long time: *Management is facing a showdown with union members today.* ♦ *Fans gathered outside the stadium for the final showdown* (= the game that will decide the winner of the competition).

show·er 🔎 /'ʃaʊər/ *noun, verb*
● *noun* **1** a piece of equipment producing a spray of water that you stand under to wash yourself; the small room or part of a room that contains a shower: *a hotel room with bathtub and shower* ♦ *He's in the shower.* ♦ *a shower cubicle* **2** the act of washing yourself with a shower: *a hot/cold shower* ♦ *to take a shower* ♦ *shower gel* **3** a short period of rain or snow: *scattered showers* ♦ *April showers* ♦ *We were caught in a heavy shower.* ♦ *snow showers* ♦ *wintry showers* (= of snow) **4** a large number of things that arrive or fall together: *a shower of leaves* ♦ *a shower of sparks from the fire* **5** a party at which you give presents to a woman who is getting married or having a baby: *a bridal/baby shower*

ʌ **cup**   ə **about**   eɪ **say**   aɪ **five**   ɔɪ **boy**   aʊ **now**   oʊ **go**   ər **bird**

• **verb 1** [I] to wash yourself under a shower: *She showered and dressed and went downstairs.* **2** [I] ~ **(down) on sb/sth** | ~ **down** to fall onto someone or something, especially in a lot of small pieces: *Volcanic ash showered down on the town after the eruption.* **3** [T] ~ **sb with sth** to drop a lot of small things onto someone: *The bride and groom were showered with rice as they left the church.* ◆ *The roof collapsed, showering us with dust and debris.* **4** [T] to give someone a lot of something: ~ **sb with sth** *He showered her with gifts.* ◆ ~ **sth on sb** *He showered gifts on her.*

show·er·y /ˈʃaʊəri/ *adj.* (of the weather) with frequent showers of rain: *a showery day*

show·girl /ˈʃoʊɡərl/ *noun* a female performer who sings and dances in a musical show

show·ing /ˈʃoʊɪŋ/ *noun* **1** an act of showing a movie: *There are three showings a day.* **2** [usually sing.] evidence of how well or how badly someone or something is performing: *the strong/poor showing of the independent candidate in the election* ◆ *On* (= judging by) *last week's showing, the team is unlikely to win today.*

show ˌjumping *noun* [U] the sport of riding a horse and jumping over a set of fences as quickly as possible

show·man /ˈʃoʊmən/ *noun* (*pl.* **show·men** /-mən/) **1** a person who does things in an entertaining way and is good at getting people's attention **2** a person who organizes public entertainments, especially at FAIRGROUNDS

show·man·ship /ˈʃoʊmənˌʃɪp/ *noun* [U] skill in doing things in an entertaining way and getting a lot of attention

shown *pp of* SHOW

show–off *noun* (*informal, disapproving*) a person who tries to impress other people by showing how good he or she is at doing something

show·piece /ˈʃoʊpis/ *noun* an excellent example of something that people are meant to see and admire

show·place /ˈʃoʊpleɪs/ *noun* a place of great beauty, historical interest, etc. that is open to the public

show·room /ˈʃoʊrum; -rʊm/ *noun* a large store in which goods for sale, especially cars and electrical goods, are displayed: *a car showroom*

show-ˌstopper *noun* (*informal*) a performance that is very impressive and receives a lot of APPLAUSE from the audience ▶ **show-stopping** *adj.* [only before noun]: *a show-stopping performance*

show·time /ˈʃoʊtaɪm/ *noun* [U] the time that a theater performance will begin: *It's five minutes to showtime and the theater is packed.* ◆ (*figurative*) *Everybody ready? It's showtime!*

show ˌtrial *noun* an unfair trial of someone in court, organized by a government for political reasons, not in order to find out the truth

show·y /ˈʃoʊi/ *adj.* (often *disapproving*) so brightly colored, large, or exaggerated that it attracts a lot of attention SYN OSTENTATIOUS: *showy flowers* ▶ **show·i·ly** /-əli/ *adv.* **show·i·ness** /-inəs/ *noun* [U]

shrank *pt of* SHRINK

shrap·nel /ˈʃræpnəl/ *noun* [U] small pieces of metal that are thrown up and away from an exploding bomb

shred /ʃrɛd/ *verb, noun*
• *verb* (-dd-) ~ **sth** to cut or tear something into small pieces: *Serve the fish on a bed of shredded lettuce.* ◆ *He was accused of shredding documents relating to the case* (= putting them in a SHREDDER).
• *noun* **1** [usually pl.] a small thin piece that has been torn or cut from something SYN SCRAP: *shreds of paper* ◆ *His jacket had been torn to shreds by the barbed wire.* **2** [usually sing.] ~ **of sth** (used especially in negative sentences) a very small amount of something: *There is not a shred of evidence to support his claim.*
IDM **in shreds 1** very badly damaged SYN : *Her nerves were in shreds.* ◆ *The country's economy is in shreds.* **2** torn in many places: *The document was in shreds on the floor.* **pick/**

pull/tear sb/sth to pieces/shreds (*informal*) to criticize someone, or their work or ideas, very severely

shred·der /ˈʃrɛdər/ *noun* a machine that tears something into small pieces, especially paper, so that nobody can read what was printed on it

shrew /ʃru/ *noun* **1** a small animal like a mouse with a long nose **2** (*old-fashioned*) a bad-tempered, unpleasant woman

shrewd /ʃrud/ *adj.* (shrewd·er, shrewd·est) **1** very good at understanding and making judgments about a situation SYN ASTUTE: *a shrewd businessman* ◆ *She is a shrewd judge of character.* **2** showing good judgment and likely to be right: *a shrewd observation about them just now.* ▶ **shrewd·ly** *adv.* **shrewd·ness** *noun* [U]

shrew·ish /ˈʃruɪʃ/ *adj.* (*old-fashioned*) (of women) bad-tempered and always arguing

shriek /ʃrik/ *verb, noun*
• *verb* **1** [I] to give a loud, high shout, for example when you are excited, frightened, or in pain SYN SCREAM: ~ **(in sth)** *She shrieked in fright.* ◆ ~ **with sth** *The audience was shrieking with laughter.* ~ **at sb 2** [T] to say something in a loud, high voice SYN SCREAM: ~ **sth (at sb)** *She was shrieking abuse at them as they carried her off.* ◆ + **speech** *"Look out!" he shrieked.*
• *noun* a loud, high shout, for example one that you make when you are excited, frightened, or in pain: *She let out a piercing shriek.* ◆ *a shriek of delight*

shrift /ʃrɪft/ *noun* IDM see SHORT *adj.*

shrike /ʃraɪk/ *noun* a bird with a strong beak, that catches small birds and insects and sticks them on THORNS

shrill /ʃrɪl/ *adj., verb*
• *adj.* (shrill·er, shrill·est) **1** (of sounds or voices) very high and loud, in an unpleasant way SYN : *a shrill voice* **2** loud and determined but often unreasonable: *shrill demands/protests* ▶ **shril·ly** /ˈʃrɪlli/ *adv.* **shrill·ness** *noun* [U]
• *verb* **1** [I] to make an unpleasant, high, loud sound: *Behind him, the telephone shrilled.* **2** [T] + **speech** to say something in a loud, high voice SYN SHRIEK: *"Wait for me!" she shrilled.*

shrimp /ʃrɪmp/ *noun* (*pl.* **shrimp** or **shrimps**) **1** a SHELLFISH with ten legs and a long tail, that can be eaten. Shrimp turn pink when cooked: *grilled shrimp* ⊃ picture at ANIMAL **2** (*informal*) a small, physically weak person

shrimp·ing /ˈʃrɪmpɪŋ/ *noun* [U] the activity of catching shrimp: *a shrimping net* ▶ **shrimp·er** *noun*: *shrimpers and fishermen in the Gulf of Mexico*

ˌshrimp ˈscampi *noun* [U] = SCAMPI

shrine /ʃraɪn/ *noun* **1** a place where people come to worship because it is connected with a holy person or event: ~ **(to sb/sth)** *a shrine to the Virgin Mary* ◆ ~ **(of sb/sth)** *to visit the shrine of Mecca* **2** ~ **(for sb)** | ~ **(to sb/sth)** a place that people visit because it is connected with someone or something that is important to them: *Wimbledon is a shrine for all lovers of tennis.*

shrink /ʃrɪŋk/ *verb, noun*
• *verb* (shrank /ʃræŋk/ or shrunk /ʃrʌŋk/, shrunk or shrunk·en /ˈʃrʌŋkən/ **1** [I, T] ~ **(sth)** to become smaller, especially when washed in water that is too hot; to make clothes, cloth, etc. smaller in this way: *My sweater shrank in the wash.* **2** [I, T] to become or to make something smaller in size or amount: *The tumor had shrunk to the size of a pea.* ◆ *The market for their products is shrinking.* ◆ ~ **sth** *There was a movie called "Honey, I Shrunk the Kids."* ◆ *Television in a sense has shrunk the world.* ⊃ see also SHRUNKEN **3** [I] + **adv./prep.** to move back or away from something because you are frightened or shocked SYN COWER: *He shrank back against the wall as he heard them approaching.*
IDM **a shrinking violet** (*humorous*) a way of describing a very shy person
PHR V **ˈshrink from sth** to be unwilling to do something that is difficult or unpleasant: *We made it clear to them that we would not shrink from confrontation.* ◆ ~ **doing sth** *They did not shrink from doing what was right.*

- **noun** (*slang, humorous*) a PSYCHIATRIST or PSYCHOLOGIST

shrink·age /ˈʃrɪŋkɪdʒ/ *noun* [U] the process of becoming smaller in size; the amount by which something becomes smaller: *the shrinkage of heavy industry* ◆ *She bought a slightly larger size to allow for shrinkage.*

shrink-wrapped *adj.* wrapped tightly in a thin plastic covering

shriv·el /ˈʃrɪvl/ *verb* (-l-, *CanE usually* -ll-) [I, T] to become or make something dry and WRINKLED as a result of heat, cold, or being old: **~ (up)** *The leaves on the plant had shriveled up from lack of water.* ◆ **~ sth (up)** *The hot weather shriveled the grapes in every vineyard.* ▶ **shriv·eled** (*CanE usually* **shriv·elled**) *adj.*: *a shriveled old man*

shroom /ʃrum/ *noun* (*informal*) **1** a MUSHROOM **2** = MAGIC MUSHROOM

shroud /ʃraʊd/ *noun, verb*
- **noun 1** a piece of cloth that a dead person's body is wrapped in before it is buried **2 ~ of sth** (*literary*) a thing that covers, surrounds, or hides something: *The organization is cloaked in a shroud of secrecy.* ◆ *a shroud of smoke*
- **verb** [usually passive] **1 ~ sth in sth** (of DARKNESS, clouds, cloth, etc.) to cover or hide something: *The city was shrouded in mist.* **2 ~ sth in sth** to hide information or keep it secret and mysterious: *His family background is shrouded in mystery.*

Shrove Tues·day /ˌʃroʊv ˈtuzdeɪ; -ˈtuzdi/ *noun* [U, C] (in the Christian Church) the day before the beginning of Lent ⊃ compare MARDI GRAS, PANCAKE DAY ⊃ see also ASH WEDNESDAY

shrub /ʃrʌb/ *noun* a large plant that is smaller than a tree and that has several STEMS of wood coming from the ground **SYN** BUSH

shrub·ber·y /ˈʃrʌbəri/ *noun* (*pl.* **shrub·ber·ies**) [C, U] an area planted with shrubs; a group of shrubs planted together

shrub·by /ˈʃrʌbi/ *adj.* (of plants) like a SHRUB

shrug /ʃrʌg/ *verb, noun*
- **verb** (-gg-) [I, T, no passive] to raise your shoulders and then drop them to show that you do not know or care about something: *Sam shrugged and said nothing.* ◆ **~ sth** *"I don't know," Anna replied, shrugging her shoulders.* **PHR V** ,**shrug sth ˈoff/aˈside** to treat something as if it is not important **SYN** DISMISS: *Shrugging off her injury, she played on.* ◆ *He shrugged aside suggestions that he resign.* ,**shrug sb/sth ˈoff/aˈway** to push someone or something back or away with your shoulders: *Kevin shrugged off his jacket.* ◆ *She shrugged him away angrily.*
- **noun 1** [usually sing.] an act of shrugging: *Andy gave a shrug. "It doesn't matter."* **2** a very short women's sweater or jacket that is open at the front and usually has sleeves made from the same piece as the back and front

shrunk *pt, pp* of SHRINK

shrunk·en /ˈʃrʌŋkən/ *adj.* [usually before noun] that has become smaller (and less attractive) **SYN** WIZENED: *a shrunken old woman*

shtetl /ˈʃtetl; ˈʃteɪtl/ *noun* a small Jewish town in eastern Europe in the past

shtick (also **schtick**) /ʃtɪk/ *noun* [U, sing.] **1** a style of humor that is typical of a particular performer **2** a particular ability that someone has

shuck /ʃʌk/ *noun, verb*
- **noun** the outer covering of a nut, a plant such as CORN, or an OYSTER or a CLAM
- **verb ~ sth** to remove the shell or covering of nuts, CORN, SHELLFISH, etc.

shucks /ʃʌks/ *exclamation* (*old-fashioned, informal*) used to express embarrassment or disappointment

shud·der /ˈʃʌdər/ *verb, noun*
- **verb 1** [I] to shake because you are cold or frightened, or because of a strong feeling: *Just thinking about the accident*

makes me shudder. ◆ **~ with sth** *Alone in the car, she shuddered with fear.* ◆ **~ at sth** *I shuddered at the thought of all the trouble I caused.* ◆ **~ to do sth** *I shudder to think how much this is all going to cost* (= I don't want to think about it because it is too unpleasant). **2** [I] (of a vehicle, machine, etc.) to shake very hard: *The bus shuddered to a halt.*
- **noun** [usually sing.] **1** a shaking movement you make because you are cold, frightened, or disgusted: *a shudder of fear* ◆ *She gave an involuntary shudder.* **2** a strong shaking movement: *The elevator rose with a shudder.*

shuf·fle /ˈʃʌfl/ *verb, noun*
- **verb 1** [I] + **adv./prep.** to walk slowly without lifting your feet completely off the ground: *He shuffled across the room to the window.* ◆ *The line shuffled forward a little.* **2** [T, I] **~ (sth)** to move from one foot to another; to move your feet in an awkward or embarrassed way: *Jenny shuffled her feet and blushed with shame.* **3** [T, I] **~ (sth)** to mix cards up in a DECK of PLAYING CARDS before playing a game: *Shuffle the cards and deal out seven to each player.* **4** [T] **~ sth** to move paper or things into different positions or a different order: *I shuffled the documents on my desk.*
- **noun** [usually sing.] **1** a slow walk in which you take small steps and do not lift your feet completely off the ground **2** the act of mixing cards before a card game: *It's your shuffle.* **3** a type of dancing in which you take small steps and do not lift your feet completely off the ground **4** = RESHUFFLE
  IDM **lose sb/sth in the shuffle** [usually passive] to not notice someone or something or pay attention to someone or something because of a confusing situation: *Middle children tend to get lost in the shuffle.* **on shuffle** (of pieces of music stored in a music player, such as an iPod™) not in any special order: *I put the iPod on shuffle and hit play.*

shuf·fle·board /ˈʃʌflˌbɔrd/ *noun* [U] a game in which players use long sticks to push disks toward spaces with numbers on a board

shun /ʃʌn/ *verb* (-nn-) **~ sb/sth** to avoid someone or something: *She was shunned by her family when she remarried.* ◆ *an actor who shuns publicity*

shunt /ʃʌnt/ *verb, noun*
- **verb 1 ~ sb/sth** + **adv./prep.** (usually *disapproving*) to move someone or something to a different place, especially a less important one: *John was shunted sideways to a job in sales.* **2 ~ sth** to move a train or a car of a train from one track to another
- **noun** (*medical*) a small tube put in your body in a medical operation to allow the blood or other FLUID to flow from one place to another

shush /ʃʌʃ; ʃʊʃ/ *exclamation, verb*
- **exclamation** used to tell someone to be quiet
- **verb ~ sb** to tell someone to be quiet, especially by saying "shush," or by putting your finger against your lips: *Lyn shushed the children.*

shut /ʃʌt/ *verb, adj.*
- **verb** (shut·ting, shut, shut) [T, I] **~ (sth)** to make something close; to become closed: *Bob went into his room and shut the door behind him.* ◆ *I can't shut my suitcase—it's too full.* ◆ *She shut her eyes and fell asleep immediately.* ◆ *He shut his book and looked up.* ◆ *The window won't shut.* ◆ *The doors open and shut automatically.* ⊃ note at CLOSE[1]
  IDM **shut your mouth/face!** (*slang*) a rude way of telling someone to be quiet or stop talking ⊃ more at DOOR, EAR, EYE *n.*, MOUTH *n.*
  PHR V ,**shut sb/sth↔aˈway** to put someone or something in a place where other people cannot see or find them ,**shut yourself aˈway** to go somewhere where you will be completely alone ,**shut ˈdown** (of a factory, store, etc. or a machine) to stop opening for business; to stop working ⊃ related noun SHUTDOWN ,**shut sth↔ˈdown** to stop a factory, store, etc. from opening for business; to stop a machine from working: *The computer system will be shut down over the weekend.* ⊃ related noun SHUTDOWN ,**shut sb/ yourself ˈin (sth)** to put someone in a room and keep them

| t tea | ţ butter | d did | k cat | g got | tʃ chin | dʒ June | f fall |

there; to go to a room and stay there: *She shut the dog in the shed while she prepared the barbecue.* 'shut sth in sth to trap something by closing a door, lid, etc. on it: *Sam shut his finger in the car door.* ,shut 'off (of a machine, tool, etc.) to stop working: *The engines shut off automatically in an emergency.* ,shut sth↔'off **1** to stop a machine, tool, etc. from working **2** to stop a supply of gas, water, etc. from flowing or reaching a place: *A valve immediately shuts off the gas when the lid is closed.* ,shut yourself 'off (from sth) to avoid seeing people or having contact with anyone: *Martin shut himself off from the world to write his book.* ,shut sb/sth 'off from sth to separate someone or something from something: *The village was shut off from civilization by the impenetrable jungle.* ,shut sb/sth↔'out (of sth) **1** to prevent someone or something from entering a place: *Mom, Ben keeps shutting me out of the bedroom!* ◆ *sunglasses that shut out 99% of the sun's harmful rays* **2** to not allow a person to share or be part of your thoughts; to stop yourself from having particular feelings: *I wanted to shut John out of my life for ever.* ◆ *She learned to shut out her angry feelings.* ◆ *If you shut me out, how can I help you?* ,shut 'up (*informal*) to stop talking (often used as an order as a rude way of telling someone to stop talking): *Just shut up and listen!* ◆ *Will you tell Mike to shut up?* ◆ *When they finally shut up, I started again.* ,shut sb 'up to make someone stop talking **SYN** SILENCE: *She kicked Anne under the table to shut her up.* ,shut sth↔'up to close a room, house, etc. ,shut sb/sth 'up (in sth) to keep someone or something in a place and prevent them from going anywhere

● **adj.** [not before noun] not open **SYN** CLOSED: *The door was shut.* ◆ *She slammed the door shut.* ◆ *Keep your eyes shut.*

shut·down /'ʃʌtdaʊn/ *noun* the act of closing a factory or business or stopping a large machine from working, either temporarily or permanently: *factory shutdowns* ◆ *the nuclear reactor's emergency shutdown procedures*

'**shut-eye** *noun* [U] (*informal*) sleep

'**shut-in** *noun* a person who cannot leave their home very easily because they are ill or disabled

shut·out /'ʃʌtaʊt/ *noun* a game in which one team prevents the other from scoring

shut·ter /'ʃʌtər/ *noun, verb*
● **noun 1** [usually pl.] one of a pair of wooden or metal covers that can be closed over the outside of a window to keep out light or protect the windows from damage: *to open/close the shutters* ⊃ picture at HOUSE **2** the part of a camera that opens to allow light to pass through the LENS when you take a photograph
● **verb** [T] **1** to cover the outside of a window with shutters: *I shuttered all the windows and locked the doors.* **2** to close a business, store, etc. permanently or for a limited time: *The strike shuttered theaters for three weeks.* ⊃ see also SHUTTERED

shut·ter·bug /'ʃʌtərbʌg/ *noun* (*informal*) a person who likes to take a lot of photographs

shut·tered /'ʃʌtərd/ *adj.* with the shutters closed; with shutters fitted

'**shutter ,speed** *noun* the length of time that a camera's SHUTTER remains open

shut·tle /'ʃʌtl/ *noun, verb*
● **noun 1** a plane, bus, or train that travels regularly between two places: *a shuttle service between the airport and the downtown area* **2** = SPACE SHUTTLE **3** a pointed tool used in making cloth to pull a thread backward and forward over the other threads that pass along the length of the cloth
● **verb 1** [I] + adv./prep. | ~ between A and B to travel between two places frequently: *Her childhood was spent shuttling between her mother and father.* **2** [T] ~ sb (+ adv./prep.) to carry people between two places that are close, making regular trips between the two places: *A bus shuttles passengers back and forth between the international and domestic terminals.*

shut·tle·cock /'ʃʌtlkɑk/ (also **bird·ie**) *noun* the object that players hit backward and forward in the game of BADMINTON ⊃ picture at SPORT

,**shuttle di'plomacy** *noun* [U] international talks in which people travel between two or more countries in order to talk to the different governments involved

shwa *noun* = SCHWA

shy /ʃaɪ/ *adj., verb*
● **adj.** (**shy·er, shy·est**) **1** (of people) nervous or embarrassed about meeting and speaking to other people **SYN** TIMID: *a quiet, shy man* ◆ *Don't be shy—come and say hello.* ◆ *She was too shy to ask anyone for help.* ◆ *As a teenager I was painfully shy.* ◆ *She's very shy with adults.* **2** showing that someone is nervous or embarrassed about meeting and speaking to other people: *a shy smile* **3** (of animals) easily frightened and not willing to come near people: *The panda is a shy creature.* **4** [not before noun] ~ of/about (doing) sth afraid of doing something or being involved in something: *The band has never been shy of publicity.* ◆ *He disliked her and had never been shy about saying so.* ⊃ see also GUN-SHY **5** [not before noun] ~ (of sth) (*informal*) lacking the amount that is needed: *He died before Christmas, only a month shy of his 90th birthday.* ◆ *We are still two players shy (of a full team).* **6** -shy (in compounds) avoiding or not liking the thing mentioned: *camera-shy* (= not liking to be photographed) ◆ *an elusive, publicity-shy artist* ▶ **shy·ly** *adv.* **shy·ness** *noun* [U] **IDM** see ONCE
● **verb** (**shies, shy·ing, shied, shied**) [I] ~ (at sth) (especially of a horse) to turn away with a sudden movement because it is afraid or surprised: *My horse shied at the unfamiliar noise.* **PHR V** ,shy a'way (from sth) to avoid doing something because you are nervous or frightened: *Hugh never shied away from his responsibilities.* ◆ *The newspapers have shied away from investigating the story.*

shy·ster /'ʃaɪstər/ *noun* (*informal*) a dishonest person, especially a lawyer

SI /ˌɛs 'aɪ/ *abbr.* International System (used to describe units of measurement; from French "Système International"): *SI units*

Si·a·mese cat /ˌsaɪəmiz 'kæt; -mis-/ (also **Si·a·mese** /ˌsaɪə-'miz; -mis-/) *noun* a cat with short pale fur and a brown face, ears, tail, and feet

,**Siamese 'twin** = CONJOINED TWIN

sib /sɪb/ *noun* (*biology*) a brother or sister

sib·i·lant /'sɪbələnt/ *adj., noun*
● **adj.** (*formal* or *literary*) making an "s" or "sh" sound: *the sibilant sound of whispering*
● **noun** (*phonetics*) a sibilant sound made in speech, such as /s/ and /z/ in the English words *sip* and *zip*

sib·ling /'sɪblɪŋ/ *noun* (*formal*) a brother or sister: *squabbles between siblings* ◆ *sibling rivalry* (= competition between brothers and/or sisters)

sib·yl /'sɪbl/ *noun* **1** in ancient times, a woman who was thought to be able to communicate messages from a god **2** (*literary*) a woman who can predict the future

sic /sɪk/ *adv., verb*
● **adv.** (from Latin) written after a word that you have copied from somewhere, to show that you know that the word is wrongly spelled or wrong in some other way: *In the letter to parents it said: "The school is proud of it's [sic] record of excellence."*
● **verb** (-cc-) ~ sb (*informal*) to attack someone: *Sic him, Duke!* (= said to a dog) **PHR V** 'sic sth on sb (*informal*) to tell a dog to attack someone

sick /sɪk/ *adj., noun*
● **adj.**
▷ **SUFFERING FROM DISEASE 1** suffering from a disease or illness **SYN** ILL: *a sick child* ◆ *Her mother's very sick.* ◆ *Peter has*

been **out sick** (= away from work because he is sick) *for two weeks.* ◆ *Erica just* **called in sick** (= telephoned to say she will not be coming to work because she is sick). ◆ *I can't afford to* **get sick** (= become sick).

> WANTING TO VOMIT **2** [not usually before noun] feeling that you want to VOMIT: *Mom, I feel sick!* ◆ *If you eat any more candy, you'll* **make yourself sick**. ◆ *a sick feeling in your stomach*

> -SICK **3** (in compounds) feeling sick as a result of traveling on a ship, plane, etc.: *seasick* ◆ *airsick* ◆ *carsick*

> BORED **4** (*informal*) bored with or annoyed about something that has been happening for a long time, and wanting it to stop: **~ of sb/sth** *I'm sick of the way you treat me.* ◆ *I'm* **sick and tired of** *your complaining.* ◆ *I'm* **sick to death** *of all of you!* ◆ **~ of doing sth** *We're sick of waiting around like this.*

> CRUEL/STRANGE **5** (*informal*) (especially of humor) dealing with suffering, disease, or death in a cruel way that some people think is offensive: *a sick joke* ◆ *That's really sick.* **6** (*informal*) getting enjoyment from doing strange or cruel things: *a sick mind* ◆ *People think I'm sick for having a rat as a pet.* ◆ *We live in a sick society.* ⊃ see also HOMESICK, LOVESICK **IDM** **be sick** to bring food from your stomach back out through your mouth **SYN** VOMIT: *I was sick three times last night.* ◆ *She was* **violently sick. be worried sick| be sick with worry** to be extremely worried: *Where have you been? I've been worried sick about you.* **fall sick** (also *old-fashioned*) (*formal*) to become sick **make sb sick** to make someone angry or disgusted: *His hypocrisy makes me sick.* **(as) sick as a dog** (*informal*) feeling very sick; VOMIT a lot **sick at heart** (*formal*) very unhappy or disappointed **sick to your stomach** **1** feeling very angry or worried: *Nora felt sick to her stomach after hearing this news.* **2** feeling that you want to VOMIT

● *noun*
> SICK PEOPLE **the sick** [pl.] people who are sick: *All the sick and wounded were evacuated.*

TOPIC COLLOCATIONS

Being Sick

getting sick
- **catch** a cold/an infectious disease/the flu/pneumonia/a virus/(*informal*) a bug
- **get** sick/a disease/AIDS/breast cancer/a cold/the flu/a migraine
- **come down with** a cold/the flu
- **contract** a deadly disease/a serious illness/HIV/AIDS
- **be infected with** a virus/a parasite/HIV
- **develop** cancer/diabetes/a rash/an ulcer/symptoms of hepatitis
- **have** a heart attack/a stroke
- **provoke/trigger/produce** an allergic reaction
- **block/rupture** a blood vessel
- **damage/sever** a nerve/an artery/a tendon

being sick
- **feel** sick/nauseous/queasy
- **be running** a fever/a temperature
- **have** a head cold/diabetes/heart disease/lung cancer/a headache/a fever/a high temperature
- **suffer from** asthma/malnutrition/frequent headaches/bouts of depression/a mental illness
- **be in bed with/be laid up with** a cold/the flu/a migraine
- **nurse** a cold/a headache/a hangover
- **battle/fight** cancer/depression/addiction/alcoholism

treatments
- **examine** a patient
- **diagnose** a condition/disease/disorder
- **be diagnosed with** cancer/diabetes/schizophrenia
- **prescribe/be given/be on/take** drugs/medicine/medication/pills/painkillers/antibiotics
- **treat sb for** cancer/depression/shock

- **have/undergo** an examination/an operation/surgery/a kidney transplant/therapy/chemotherapy/treatment for cancer
- **have/be given** an injection/a flu shot/a blood transfusion/a scan/an X-ray
- **cure** a disease/an ailment/cancer/a headache/a patient
- **prevent** the spread of disease/further outbreaks/damage to the lungs
- **be vaccinated against** the flu/(the) measles/polio/smallpox
- **enhance/boost/confer/build up** immunity to a disease

sick·bay /ˈsɪkbeɪ/ *noun* a room or rooms, for example on a ship, with beds for people who are sick

sick·bed /ˈsɪkbɛd/ *noun* [sing.] the bed on which a person who is sick is lying: *The president left his sickbed to attend the ceremony.*

sick ˈbuilding ˌsyndrome *noun* [U] a condition that affects people who work in large offices, making them feel tired and causing headaches, sore eyes, and breathing problems, thought to be caused by, for example, the lack of fresh air or by chemicals in the air

sick day *noun* a day on which an employee is away from work because of illness, for which they receive SICK PAY

sick·en /ˈsɪkən/ *verb* **1** [T, usually passive] **~ sb** to make someone feel very shocked and angry **SYN** DISGUST ⊃ thesaurus box at SHOCK **2** [I] (*old-fashioned*) to become sick: *The baby sickened and died before his first birthday.*

sick·en·ing /ˈsɪkənɪŋ/ *adj.* **1** making you feel disgusted or shocked **SYN** REPULSIVE: *the sickening stench of burned flesh* **2** making you afraid that someone has been badly hurt or that something has been broken: *Her head hit the ground with a sickening thud.* ▸ **sick·en·ing·ly** *adv.*

sick·le /ˈsɪkl/ *noun* a tool with a curved blade and a short handle, used for cutting grass, etc. ⊃ see also HAMMER AND SICKLE

sick leave *noun* [U] permission to be away from work because of illness; the period of time spent away from work: *to be on sick leave*

sickle ˌcell aˈnemia (also **ˈsickle cell disˌease**) *noun* [U] a serious form of ANEMIA (= a disease of the blood) that is found mostly in people of African family origins, and that is passed down from parents to children

sick·ly /ˈsɪkli/ *adj.* (sick·li·er, sick·li·est) **1** often sick: *He was a sickly child.* **2** not looking healthy and strong **SYN** FRAIL: *She looked pale and sickly.* ◆ *sickly plants* **3** that makes you feel sick, especially because it is too sweet or full of false emotion: *a sickly sweet smell* ◆ *She gave me a sickly smile.* **4** (of colors) unpleasant to look at: *a sickly green color*

sick·ness /ˈsɪknəs/ *noun* **1** [U] illness; bad health: *She's been away from work because of sickness.* ◆ *insurance against sickness and unemployment* **2** [U, C, usually sing.] a particular type of illness or disease: *altitude/radiation sickness* ⊃ see also SLEEPING SICKNESS **3** [U] the feeling that you are likely to VOMIT (= bring food back up from the stomach to the mouth); the fact of VOMITING **SYN** NAUSEA: *car sickness* (= the feeling of sickness that some people get when traveling in a car) ⊃ see also MORNING SICKNESS, MOTION SICKNESS **4** [sing.] a feeling of great sadness, disappointment, or disgust

sick·o /ˈsɪkoʊ/ *noun* (pl. **sick·os**) (*informal*) a person who gets enjoyment from doing strange and cruel things: *child molesters and other sickos*

sick·out /ˈsɪkaʊt/ *noun* a strike in which all the workers at a company say they are sick and stay at home

sick pay *noun* [U] pay given to an employee who is away from work because of illness

sick·room /ˈsɪkrum; -rʊm/ *noun* a room in which a person who is sick is lying in bed

---

side /saɪd/ noun, verb

● **noun**

> **LEFT/RIGHT 1** [C, usually sing.] either of the two halves of a surface, an object, or an area that is divided by an imaginary central line: *They drive on the left side of the road in the Bahamas.* ◆ *the right side of the brain* ◆ *satellite links to the other side of the world* ◆ *She was on the far side of the room.* ◆ *They crossed from one side of the city to the other.* ◆ *Stay on your side of the bed!* **2** [C, usually sing.] a position or an area to the left or right of something: *There is a large window on either side of the front door.* ◆ *He crossed the bridge to the other side of the river.* ◆ *people on both sides of the Atlantic* ◆ *She tilted her head to one side.*

> **NOT TOP OR BOTTOM 3** [C] one of the flat surfaces of something that is not the top or bottom, front or back: *Write your name on the side of the box.* ◆ *There's a scratch on the side of my car.* ◆ *The kitchen door is at the side of the house.* ◆ *a side door/entrance/window* ◆ *Now lay the jar on its side.* **4** [C] the vertical or sloping surface around something, but not the top or bottom of it: *A path went up the side of the hill.* ◆ *Brush the sides of the pan with butter.* ⊃ see also HILLSIDE, MOUN-TAINSIDE

> **EDGE 5** [C] a part or an area of something near the edge and away from the middle: *She stood at the far side of the room, hoping not to be noticed.* ◆ *A van was parked at the side of the road.* ◆ *the south side of the lake* ⊃ see also BEDSIDE, FIRESIDE, RINGSIDE, RIVERSIDE, ROADSIDE, SEASIDE

> **OF BODY 6** [C, usually sing.] either the right or left part of a person's body, from the ARMPIT (= where the arm joins the body) to the hip: *She has a pain down her right side.* ◆ *He was lying on his side.*

> **NEAR TO SOMEONE OR SOMETHING 7** [sing.] a place or position very near to someone or something: *Stay close by my side.* ◆ *Her husband stood at her side.*

> **OF SOMETHING FLAT AND THIN 8** [C] either of two surfaces of something flat and thin, such as paper or cloth: *Write on one side of the paper only.* ◆ *Fry the steaks for two minutes on each side.*

> **PAGE 9** [C] the amount of writing needed to fill one side of a sheet of paper: *He told us not to write more than three sides.*

> **MATHEMATICS 10** [C] any of the flat surfaces of a solid object: *A cube has six sides.* ⊃ picture at SHAPE **11** [C] any of the lines that form a flat shape such as a square or triangle: *a shape with five sides* ◆ *The farm buildings form three sides of a square.*

> **-SIDED 12** used in adjectives to state the number or type of sides: *a six-sided object* ◆ *a glass-sided container*

> **IN WAR/ARGUMENT 13** [C] one of the two or more people or groups taking part in an argument, war, etc.: *We have finally reached an agreement acceptable to all sides.* ◆ *At some point during the war he seems to have changed sides.* ◆ *to be on the winning/losing side* **14** [C] one of the opinions, attitudes, or positions held by someone in an argument, a business arrangement, etc.: *We heard both sides of the argument.* ◆ *I just want you to hear my side of the story first.* ◆ *Will you keep your side of the bargain?*

> **ASPECT 15** [C] a particular aspect of something, especially a situation or a person's character: *These poems reveal her gentle side.* ◆ *This is a side of Alan that I never knew existed.* ◆ *It's good you can see the funny side of the situation.* ◆ *I'll take care of that side of things.*

> **SPORTS TEAM 16** [C] a sports team: *Their side won by 12 points.* ◆ *We were on the winning/losing side.*

> **OF FAMILY 17** [C] the part of your family that people belong to who are related either to your mother or to your father: *a cousin on my father's side* (= a child of my father's brother or sister)

> **FOOD 18** [C] (*informal*) = SIDE DISH: *Your dinner comes with a choice of two sides.*

> **MEAT 19** [C] **a ~ of beef/bacon, etc.** one of the two halves of an animal that has been killed for meat

IDM **come down on one side of the fence or the other** to choose between two possible choices **from side to side** moving to the left and then to the right and then back again: *He shook his head slowly from side to side.* ◆ *The ship rolled from side to side.* **get on the right/wrong side of sb** to make someone pleased with you/annoyed with you **have sth on your side** to have something as an advantage that will make it more likely that you will achieve something **not leave sb's side** to stay with someone, especially in order to take care of them **on/from all sides | on/from every side** in or from all directions; everywhere: *We realized we were surrounded on all sides.* ◆ *Disaster threatens on every side.* **on the big, small, high, etc. side** (*informal*) slightly too big, small, high, etc.: *These shoes are a little on the tight side.* **on the other side of the fence** in a situation that is different from the one that you are in **on the right/wrong side of 40, 50, etc.** (*informal*) younger or older than 40, 50, etc. years of age **on the side** (*informal*) **1** in addition to your main job: *a mechanic who buys and sells cars on the side* **2** secretly or illegally: *He's married but he has a girlfriend on the side.* **3** (of food in a restaurant) served at the same time as the main part of the meal, but on a separate plate; served next to something rather than on top of it: *I'd like a green salad, with the dressing on the side.* **on/to one side 1** out of your way: *I sat down and put my bags on one side.* **2** to be dealt with later: *I put his complaint to one side until I had more time.* ◆ *Leaving that to one side for now, are there any other questions?* **be on sb's side** to support and agree with someone: *I'm definitely on your side in this.* ◆ *Whose side are you on anyway?* **the other side of the coin** the aspect of a situation that is the opposite of or contrasts with the one you have been talking about **side by side 1** close together and facing in the same direction: *There were two children ahead, walking side by side.* **2** together, without any difficulties: *We have been using both systems, side by side, for two years.* ◆ *The two communities exist happily side by side.* **take sides** to express support for someone in a disagreement: *She didn't think it was wise to take sides in their argument.* **take/draw sb to one side** to speak to someone in private, especially in order to warn or tell them something about something ⊃ more at BRIGHT *adj.*, CREDIT *n.*, DISTAFF, ERR, GRASS, KNOW *v.*, RIGHT *adj.*, SAFE *adj.*, SPLIT *v.*, THORN, TIME *n.*, TWO, WRONG *adj.*

● **verb**

PHR V **'side with sb (against sb/sth)** to support one person or group in an argument against someone else: *The kids always sided with their mother against me.*

side·bar /'saɪdbɑr/ *noun* **1** a short article in a newspaper or magazine that is printed next to a main article, and gives extra information **2** a narrow area on the side of a WEB PAGE that is separate from the main part of the page

side·board /'saɪdbɔrd/ (also **buf·fet**) *noun* a piece of furniture in a DINING ROOM for putting food on before it is served, with drawers for storing knives, forks, etc.

side·burn /'saɪdbərn/ *noun* [usually pl.] hair that grows down the sides of a man's face in front of his ears ⊃ picture at HAIR

side·car /'saɪdkɑr/ *noun* a small vehicle attached to the side of a motorcycle in which a passenger can ride

'side dish (also *informal* **side**) *noun* a small amount of food, for example a salad, served with the main course of a meal **SYN** SIDE ORDER

'side ef₁fect *noun* [usually pl.] **1** an extra and usually bad effect that a drug has on you, as well as curing illness or pain **2** an unexpected result of a situation or course of action that happens as well as the result you were aiming for

'side ₁issue *noun* an issue that is less important than the main issue, and may take attention away from it

side·kick /'saɪdkɪk/ *noun* (*informal*) a person who helps another more important or more intelligent person: *Batman and his young sidekick Robin*

side·light /'saɪdlaɪt/ *noun* **~ (on sb/sth)** a piece of information, usually given by accident or in connection with another subject, that helps you to understand someone or something

side·line /'saɪdlaɪn/ *noun, verb*
- **noun 1** [C] an activity that you do as well as your main job in order to earn extra money **2 sidelines** [pl.] the lines along the two long sides of a sports field, TENNIS COURT, etc. that mark the outer edges; the area just outside these: *The coach stood on the sidelines yelling instructions to the players.*
  IDM on/from the sidelines watching something but not actually involved in it: *He was content to watch from the sidelines as his wife built up a successful business empire.*
- **verb** [usually passive] **1 ~ sb** to prevent someone from playing on a team, especially because of an injury: *The player has been sidelined by a knee injury.* **2 ~ sb** to prevent someone from having an important part in something that other people are doing: *The vice president is increasingly being sidelined.*

side·long /'saɪdlɔŋ/ *adj.* [only before noun] (of a look) out of the corner of your eye, especially in a way that is secret or disapproving: *She cast a sidelong glance at Eric to see if he had noticed her blunder.* ► **side·long** *adv.*: *She looked sidelong at him.*

side ¡order *noun* a small amount of food ordered in a restaurant to go with the main dish, but served separately **SYN SIDE DISH**: *a side order of fries*

side plate *noun* a small plate used for bread or other food that goes with a meal

si·de·re·al /saɪ'dɪriəl/ *adj.* (astronomy) related to the stars that are far away, not the sun or planets

side road *noun* a smaller and less important road leading off a main road

side·sad·dle /'saɪd,sædl/ *adv.* if you ride a horse **sidesaddle**, you ride with both your legs on the same side of the horse

side ¡salad *noun* a small salad served with the main course of a meal

side·show /'saɪdʃoʊ/ *noun* **1** a separate small show or attraction at a FAIR or CIRCUS where you pay to see a performance or take part in a game **2** an activity or event that is much less important than the main activity or event

side·split·ting /'saɪd,splɪtɪŋ/ *adj.* (informal) extremely funny; making people laugh a lot: *sidesplitting anecdotes* ► **side·split·tingly** *adv.*: *side-splittingly funny*

side·step /'saɪdstɛp/ *verb* (-pp-) **1** [T] **~ sth** to avoid answering a question or dealing with a problem: *Did you notice how she neatly sidestepped the question?* **2** [T, I] **~ (sth)** to avoid something, for example being hit, by stepping to one side: *He nimbly sidestepped the tackle and continued down the field.*

side street *noun* a smaller and less important street leading off a main street in a town

side·swipe /'saɪdswaɪp/ *verb, noun*
- **verb ~ sth** (of a vehicle) to hit the side of another vehicle that it is passing: *The bus sideswiped two parked cars.*
- **noun 1** a hit from the side: *a sideswipe by a truck* **2 ~ (at sb/ sth)** (informal) a critical comment made about someone or something while you are talking about someone or something completely different: *It was a good speech, but he couldn't resist taking a sideswipe at his opponent.*

side·track /'saɪdtræk/ *verb* [usually passive] **~ sb (into doing sth)** to make someone start to talk about or do something that is different from the main thing that they are supposed to be talking about or doing **SYN DISTRACT**: *I was supposed to be writing a letter but I got sidetracked.*

side view *noun* a view of something from the side: *The picture shows a side view of the house.*

side-view ¡mirror *noun* a mirror that sticks out from the side of a vehicle and allows the driver to see behind the vehicle ➔ picture at CAR

side·walk /'saɪdwɔk/ *noun* a flat part at the side of a road for people to walk on

sidewalk ¡artist *noun* an artist who draws pictures in CHALK on the sidewalk, hoping to get money from people who pass

side·ward /'saɪdwərd/ *adj.* to, toward, or from the side: *a sideward glance* ► **side·ward** (also **side·wards**) *adv.*: *He was blown sidewards by the wind.*

side·ways 🔑 /'saɪdweɪz/ *adv.*
1 to, toward, or from the side: *He looked sideways at her.* ♦ *The truck skidded sideways across the road.* **2** with one side facing forward: *She sat sideways on the chair.* ► **side·ways** *adj.*: *She slid him a sideways glance.* ♦ *a sideways move*

side ¡whiskers *noun* [pl.] hair growing on the sides of a man's face down to, but not on, the chin

side·wind·er /'saɪd,waɪndər/ *noun* a poisonous N. American snake that moves sideways across the desert by throwing its body in an "S" shape

sid·ing /'saɪdɪŋ/ *noun* **1** [U] material used to cover and protect the outside walls of buildings **2** [C] a short track beside a main railroad line, where trains can stand when they are not being used

si·dle /'saɪdl/ *verb* [I] **+ adv./prep.** to walk somewhere in a shy or uncertain way as if you do not want to be noticed: *She sidled up to me and whispered something in my ear.*

SIDS /saɪdz/ *noun* [U] the abbreviation for "sudden infant death syndrome" (the sudden death while sleeping of a baby that appears to be healthy) **SYN CRIB DEATH**

siege /sidʒ/ *noun* **1** a military operation in which an army tries to capture a town by surrounding it and stopping the supply of food, etc. to the people inside: *the siege of Troy* ♦ *The siege was finally lifted* (= ended) *after six months.* ♦ *The police placed the city center under a virtual state of siege* (= it was hard to get in or out). **2** a situation in which the police surround a building where people are living or hiding, in order to make them come out ➔ see also BESIEGE
  IDM under siege 1 surrounded by an army or the police in a siege **2** being criticized all the time or put under pressure by problems, questions, etc. **lay siege to sth 1** to begin a siege of a town, building, etc. **2** to surround a building, especially in order to speak to or question the person or people living or working there

siege men¡tality *noun* [sing., U] a feeling that you are surrounded by enemies and must protect yourself

sie·mens /'simənz/ *noun* (abbr. S.) (physics) the standard unit for measuring how well an object CONDUCTS electricity

si·en·na /si'ɛnə/ *noun* [U] a type of dark yellow or red CLAY used for giving color to paints, etc.

si·er·ra /si'ɛrə/ *noun* (especially in place names) a long range of steep mountains with sharp points, especially in Spain and the Americas: *the Sierra Nevada*

si·es·ta /si'ɛstə/ *noun* a rest or sleep taken in the early afternoon, especially in hot countries: *to take/have a siesta* ➔ compare NAP

sieve /sɪv/ *noun, verb*
- **noun** a tool for separating solids from liquids or larger solids from smaller solids, made of a wire or plastic net attached to a ring. The liquid or small pieces pass through the net but the larger pieces do not. ➔ picture at KITCHEN
  IDM have a memory/mind like a sieve (informal) to have a very bad memory; to forget things easily
- **verb ~ sth** to put something through a sieve

sie·vert /'sivərt/ *noun* (abbr. Sv) (physics) a unit for measuring the effect of RADIATION

sift /sɪft/ *verb* **1** [T] **~ sth** to put flour or some other fine substance through a sifter: *Sift the flour into a bowl.* **2** [T, I] to examine something very carefully in order to decide what is important or useful or to find something important: **~ sth** *We will sift every scrap of evidence.* ♦ **~ through sth** *Crash investigators have been sifting through the wreckage of the aircraft.* **3** [T] **~ sth (out) from sth** to separate something from a group of things: *She looked quickly through the papers, sifting out from the pile anything that looked interesting.*

ʌ **cup**   ə **about**   eɪ **say**   aɪ **five**   ɔɪ **boy**   aʊ **now**   oʊ **go**   ər **bird**

PHR V ˌsift sth↔'out **1** to remove something that you do not want from a substance by putting it through a sifter: *Put the flour through a sifter to sift out the lumps.* **2** to separate something, usually something you do not want, from a group of things: *We need to sift out the applications that have no chance of succeeding.*

sift·er /'sɪftər/ *noun* a tool for separating larger solids from smaller solids, made of a wire or plastic net attached to a ring, used especially for flour when you are cooking

sigh /saɪ/ *verb, noun*
● *verb* **1** [I] to take and then let out a long, deep breath that can be heard, to show that you are disappointed, sad, tired, etc.: *He sighed deeply at the thought.* ◆ *~ with sth She sighed with relief that it was all over.* **2** [T] + **speech** to say something with a sigh: *"Oh well, better luck next time," she sighed.* **3** [I] (*literary*) (especially of the wind) to make a long sound like a sigh
● *noun* an act or the sound of sighing: *to give/heave/let out a sigh* ◆ *a deep sigh* ◆ *"I'll wait," he said with a sigh.* ◆ *We all breathed a sigh of relief when it was over.*

sight 🔑 /saɪt/ *noun, verb*
● *noun*
❯ ABILITY TO SEE **1** [U] the ability to see **SYN** EYESIGHT: *to lose your sight* (= to become blind) ◆ *She has very good sight.* ◆ *The disease has affected her sight.* ◆ *He has very little sight in his right eye.*
❯ ACT OF SEEING **2** [U] *~ of sb/sth* the act of seeing someone or something: *After ten days at sea, we had our first sight of land.* ◆ *I have been known to faint at the sight of blood.* ◆ *The soldiers were given orders to shoot on sight* (= as soon as they saw someone). ◆ *She caught sight of a car in the distance.*
❯ HOW FAR YOU CAN SEE **3** [U] the area or distance within which someone can see or something can be seen: *There was no one in sight.* ◆ *At last we came in sight of a few houses.* ◆ *A bicycle came into sight on the main road.* ◆ *The end is in sight* (= will happen soon). ◆ *Leave any valuables in your car out of sight.* ◆ *Keep out of sight* (= stay where you cannot be seen). ◆ *She never lets her daughter out of her sight* (= always keeps her where she can see her). ◆ *Get out of my sight!* (= Go away!) ◆ *The boat disappeared from sight.* ◆ *The house was hidden from sight behind some trees.* ◆ *He had placed himself directly in my line of sight.*
❯ WHAT YOU CAN SEE **4** [C] a thing that you see or can see: *It's a spectacular sight as the flamingos lift into the air.* ◆ *The museum attempts to recreate the sights and sounds of 19th-century New Orleans.* ◆ *He was a sorry sight, soaked to the skin and shivering.* ◆ *The bird is now a rare sight in this country.* ⊃ thesaurus box at VIEW
❯ INTERESTING PLACES **5** sights [pl.] the interesting places, especially in a town or city, that are often visited by tourists: *We're going to San Francisco for the weekend to see the sights.*
❯ ON GUN/TELESCOPE **6** [C, usually pl.] a device that you look through to aim a gun, etc., or to look at sth through a TELESCOPE, etc.: *He had the deer in his sights now.* ◆ (*figurative*) *Even as a young actress, she always had Hollywood firmly in her sights* (= as her final goal).
IDM **at first sight 1** when you first begin to consider something: *At first sight, it may look like a generous offer, but always read the small print.* **2** when you see someone or something for the first time: *It was love at first sight* (= we fell in love the first time we saw each other). **hate, be sick of, etc. the sight of sb/sth** (*informal*) to hate, etc. someone or something very much: *I can't stand the sight of him!* **in the sight of sb/in sb's sight** (*formal*) in someone's opinion: *We are all equal in the sight of God.* **lose sight of sb/sth 1** to become no longer able to see someone or something: *They finally lost sight of land.* **2** to stop considering something; to forget something: *We don't want to lose sight of our original aim.* **out of sight, out of mind** (*saying*) used to say someone will quickly be forgotten when they are no longer with you **raise/lower your sights** to expect more/less from a situation **set your sights on sth/on doing sth** to decide that you want something and to try very hard to get it: *She's set her sights on getting into Harvard.* **a (damn, etc.)**

sight better, etc. | **a (damn, etc.) sight too good, etc.** (*informal*) very much better; much too good, etc.: *She's done a damn sight better than I did.* ◆ *It's worth a damn sight more than I thought.* **a sight for sore eyes** (*informal*) a person or thing that you are pleased to see **sight unseen** if you buy something **sight unseen**, you do not have an opportunity to see it before you buy it ⊃ more at HEAVE *v.*, KNOW *v.*, NOWHERE, PLAIN *adj.*, PRETTY *adj.*
● *verb ~ sth* (*formal*) to suddenly see something, especially something you have been looking for: *After twelve days at sea, they sighted land.*

THESAURUS

sight
view ◆ vision
These are all words for the area or distance that you can see from a particular position.

sight the area or distance that you can see from a particular position: *He looked up the street, but there was no one in sight.* ◆ *Leave any valuables in your car out of sight.*

view (*somewhat formal*) the area or distance that you can see from a particular position: *The lake soon came into view.* ◆ *Our hotel room had amazing views of the mountains.*

vision the area that you can see from a particular position: *The couple moved out of her field of vision* (= the total area you can see from a particular position).

SIGHT, VIEW, OR VISION?
View is more literary than **sight** or **vision**. It is the only word for talking about how well you can see something: ~~I didn't have a good sight/vision of the stage.~~ Vision must always be used with a possessive pronoun: *my/his/her etc. (field of) vision.* It is not used with the prepositions *in, into,* and *out of* that are very frequent with **sight** and view: ~~There was nobody in vision.~~ ◆ ~~A tall figure came into vision.~~

PATTERNS
- in/out of sight/view
- in/within sight/view of sth
- to **come into/disappear from** sight/view/sb's vision
- to **come in** sight/view of sb/sth
- to **block** sb's view/vision
- sb's **line of** sight/vision
- sb's **field of** view/vision

---

sight·ed /'saɪtəd/ *adj.* **1** able to see; not blind: *the blind parents of sighted children* **2** –sight·ed (in compounds) able to see in the way mentioned: *partially sighted* ◆ *nearsighted* ◆ *farsighted*

sight·ing /'saɪtɪŋ/ *noun* an occasion when someone sees someone or something, especially something unusual or something that lasts for only a short time: *a reported sighting of Elvis Presley*

sight·less /'saɪtləs/ *adj.* (*literary*) unable to see **SYN** BLIND: *The statue stared down at them with sightless eyes.*

'**sight line** (also **sight·line**) /'saɪtlaɪn/ *noun* = LINE OF SIGHT

'**sight-read** *verb* [T, I] *~ (sth)* to play or sing written music when you see it for the first time, without practicing it first ▶ '**sight-reader** *noun* '**sight-reading** *noun* [U]

sight·see·ing /'saɪtˌsiɪŋ/ *noun* [U] the activity of visiting interesting buildings and places as a tourist: *to go sightseeing* ◆ *Did you have a chance to do any sightseeing?* ◆ *a sightseeing tour of the city* ⊃ collocations at TRAVEL ▶ **sight·see** *verb* [I] (only used in the progressive tenses) **sight·se·er** /-ˌsiər/ *noun* **SYN** TOURIST: *New York attracts large numbers of sightseers.*

---

sig·ma /ˈsɪɡmə/ *noun* the 18th letter of the Greek alphabet (Σ, σ)

sign 🔑 /saɪn/ *noun, verb*

● *noun*

> **SHOWING SOMETHING 1** [C, U] an event, an action, a fact, etc. that shows that something exists, is happening, or may happen in the future **SYN** INDICATION: ~ **(of sth/sb)** *Headaches may be a sign of stress.* ◆ *There is no sign of John anywhere.* ◆ *Call the police at the first sign of trouble.* ◆ *There was no sign of life in the house* (= there seemed to be nobody there). ◆ *Her work is showing some signs of improvement.* ◆ ~ **(of doing sth)** *The gloomy weather shows no sign of improving.* ◆ *The fact that he didn't say "no" immediately is a good sign.* ◆ ~ **(that…)** *If an interview is too easy, it's a sure sign that you haven't got the job.* ◆ *If I had noticed the warning signs, none of this would have happened.*

> **FOR INFORMATION/WARNING 2** [C] a piece of paper, wood, or metal that has writing or a picture on it that gives you information, instructions, a warning, etc.: *a street/stop sign* ◆ *a neon/EXIT sign* ◆ *The sign on the wall said "Employees must wash hands."* ◆ *Follow the signs for the city center.*

> **MOVEMENT/SOUND 3** [C] a movement or sound that you make to tell someone something: *He gave a thumbs-up sign.* ◆ *She nodded as a sign for us to sit down.* ⭕ see also V-SIGN

> **SYMBOL 4** [C] a mark used to represent something, especially in mathematics: *a plus/minus sign* (+/−) ◆ *a dollar sign* ($)

> **STAR SIGN 5** [C] (*informal*) = STAR SIGN: *What sign are you?*

IDM **a sign of the times** something that you feel shows what things are like now, especially how bad they are

● *verb*

> **YOUR NAME 1** [I, T] to write your name on a document, letter, etc. to show that you have written it, that you agree with what it says, or that it is genuine: *Sign here, please.* ◆ ~ **sth** *Sign your name here, please.* ◆ *You haven't signed the letter.* ◆ *to sign a check* ◆ *The treaty was signed on March 24.* ◆ *The player was signing autographs for a group of fans.* ⭕ see also COSIGN

> **CONTRACT 2** [T, I] to arrange for someone, for example a sports player or musician, to sign a contract agreeing to work for your company; to sign a contract agreeing to work for a company: ~ **sb** *The team has just signed a new pitcher.* ◆ ~ **for sth** *He signed for the team yesterday.* ◆ ~ **with sth** *The band has signed with a new label.*

> **FOR DEAF PERSON 3** [I, T] to use sign language to communicate with someone: *She learned to sign to help her deaf child.* ◆ ~ **sth** *An increasing number of plays are now being signed.*

▶ **sign·er** *noun*: *the signers of the petition* ◆ *signers communicating information to deaf people*

IDM **signed and sealed | signed, sealed, and delivered** definite, because all the legal documents have been signed **sign on the dotted line** (*informal*) to sign a document to show that you have agreed to buy something or do something: *Just sign on the dotted line and the car is yours.* ⭕ more at PLEDGE *n.*

PHR V ,**sign sth**↔**a'way** to lose your rights or property by signing a document ,**sign for sth** to sign a document to show that you have received something ,**sign 'in/'out |** ,**sign sb**↔**'in/'out** to write your/someone's name when you arrive at or leave an office, a club, etc.: *All visitors must sign in on arrival.* ◆ *You must sign guests out when they leave the club.* ,**sign 'off** to end a broadcast by saying goodbye or playing a piece of music ,**sign sth**↔**'off** to give your formal approval to something, by signing your name ,**sign 'off on sth** (*informal*) to express your approval of something formally and definitely: *The President hasn't signed off on this report.* ,**sign 'up/'on |** ,**sign sb**↔**'up/'on** to sign a form or contract which says that you agree to do a job or become a soldier; to persuade someone to sign a form or contract like this **SYN** ENLIST: *He signed up for two years in the army.* ◆ *The company has signed on three top models for the fashion show.* ,**sign sth**↔**'over (to sb)** to give your rights or property to someone else by signing a document: *She signed the house over to her daughter.* ,**sign 'up (for sth)** to arrange to take a

course of study by adding your name to the list of people who are taking it ,**sign 'up to sth** to commit yourself to a project or course of action, especially one that you have agreed to with a group of other people, countries, or organizations, in which each person, country etc. agrees to do particular actions as their part of the deal: *How many countries have signed up to the Kyoto protocol on climate change?* ◆ ~ **to do sth** *We have about 100 people signed up to help so far.*

THESAURUS

sign

indication ◆ symptom ◆ symbol ◆ indicator ◆ signal

These are all words for an event, an action, or a fact that shows that something exists, is happening, or may happen in the future.

sign an event, action, or fact that shows that something exists, is happening, or may happen in the future: *Headaches may be a sign of stress.*

indication (*somewhat formal*) a remark or sign that shows that something is happening or what someone is thinking or feeling: *They gave no indication as to how the work should be done.*

SIGN OR INDICATION?

An **indication** often comes in the form of something that someone says; a **sign** is usually something that happens or something that someone does.

symptom a change in your body or mind that shows that you are not healthy; a sign that something exists, especially something bad: *A sore throat may be a symptom of an ear infection.* ◆ *The rise in inflation was just one symptom of the poor state of the economy.*

symbol a person, an object, or an event that represents a more general quality or situation: *The dove is a universal symbol of peace.*

indicator (*somewhat formal*) a sign that shows you what something is like or how a situation is changing: *the economic indicators* ◆ *Healthy skin is an indicator of overall well-being.*

signal an event, an action, or a fact that shows that something exists, is happening, or may happen in the future: *This latest decision is a signal of a major change in policy.* ◆ *Reducing prison sentences would send the wrong signals to criminals.*

SIGN OR SIGNAL?

Signal is often used to talk about an event, an action, or a fact that suggests to someone that they should do something. **Sign** is not usually used in this way: *Reducing prison sentences would send the wrong signs to criminals.*

PATTERNS

- a(n) sign/indication/symptom/symbol/indicator/signal of sth
- a(n) sign/indication/symptom/indicator/signal that…
- a clear sign/indication/symptom/symbol/indicator/signal
- an obvious sign/indication/symptom/symbol/indicator
- an early sign/indication/symptom/indicator/signal
- an outward sign/indication/symbol
- to give a(n) sign/indication/signal

sign·age /ˈsaɪnɪdʒ/ *noun* [U] (*technical*) signs, especially ones that give instructions or directions to the public

sig·nal 🔑 /ˈsɪɡnəl/ *noun, verb, adj.*

● *noun* **1** a movement or sound that you make to give someone information, instructions, a warning, etc.

| t tea | ţ butter | d did | k cat | g got | tʃ chin | dʒ June | f fall |

SYN SIGN: *a danger/warning/distress etc. signal* ◆ *At an agreed signal they left the room.* ◆ *The siren was a signal for everyone to leave the building.* ◆ *When I give the signal, run!* ◆ *All I get is a busy signal when I dial his number* (= his phone is being used). ◆ *hand signals* (= movements that CYCLISTS and drivers make with their hands to tell other people that they are going to stop, turn, etc.) **2** an event, an action, a fact, etc. that shows that something exists or is likely to happen **SYN** INDICATION: *The rise in inflation is a clear signal that the government's policies are not working.* ◆ *This latest decision is a signal of a major change in policy.* ◆ *Reducing prison sentences would send the wrong signals to criminals.* ⊃ thesaurus box at SIGN **3** a piece of equipment that uses different colored lights to tell drivers to go slower, stop, etc., used especially on railroads and roads: *traffic signals* ◆ *a stop signal* **4** a series of electrical waves that carry sounds, pictures, or messages, for example to a radio, television, or cell phone: *TV signals* ◆ *a high frequency signal* ◆ *a radar signal* ◆ *to detect/pick up signals* ◆ *to emit a signal* ◆ *I couldn't get a signal on my cell phone.*

● *verb* (-l-, *CanE usually* -ll-) **1** [I, T] to make a movement or sound to give someone a message, an order, etc.: *Don't fire until I signal.* ◆ *Did you signal before you turned right?* ◆ *~ (to sb) (for sth) He signaled to the waiter for the check.* ◆ *~ to/for sb to do sth He signaled to us to join him.* ◆ *~ sb to do sth She signaled him to follow.* ◆ *~ sth The referee signaled a foul.* ◆ *~ (that)... She signaled (that) it was time to leave.* ◆ *~ which, what, etc.... You must signal which way you are going to turn.* **2** [T] *~ sth* to be a sign that something exists or is likely to happen **SYN** INDICATE: *This announcement signaled a clear change of policy.* ◆ *The scandal surely signals the end of his political career.* **3** [T] to do something to make your feelings or opinions known: *~ sth He signaled his discontent by refusing to vote.* ◆ *~ (that)... She signaled (that) she was willing to run for office.*

● *adj.* [only before noun] (*formal*) important: *a signal honor*

sig·nal·er (*CanE usually* **sig·nal·ler**) /ˈsɪɡnələr/ *noun* = SIGNALMAN

sig·nal·ly /ˈsɪɡnəli/ *adv.* in a way that is serious and very noticeable: *They have signally failed to keep their election promises.*

sig·nal·man /ˈsɪɡnəlmən/ *noun* (*pl.* **sig·nal·men** /-mən/) (also **sig·nal·er**) **1** a person trained to give and receive signals in the army or navy **2** a person whose job is operating signals on a railroad

ˌsignal-to-ˈnoise ˌratio *noun* **1** (*technical*) the strength of an electronic signal that you want to receive, compared to the strength of the signals that you do not want **2** a measure of how much useful information you receive, compared to information which is not useful

sig·na·to·ry /ˈsɪɡnəˌtɔri/ *noun* (*pl.* **sig·na·to·ries**) *~ (to/of sth)* (*formal*) a person, a country, or an organization that has signed an official agreement: *a signatory of the Declaration of Independence* ◆ *Many countries are signatories to/of the Berne Convention.*

sig·na·ture /ˈsɪɡnətʃər/ *noun*
1 [C] your name as you usually write it, for example at the end of a letter: *Someone had forged her signature on the check.* ◆ *They collected 10,000 signatures for their petition.* ◆ *He was attacked for having put his signature to the deal.* **2** [U] (*formal*) the act of signing something: *Two copies of the contract will be sent to you for signature.* **3** [C, usually sing.] a particular quality that makes something different from other similar things and makes it easy to recognize: *Bright colors are his signature.* ⊃ see also DIGITAL SIGNATURE, KEY SIGNATURE, TIME SIGNATURE

sign·board /ˈsaɪnbɔrd/ *noun* a piece of wood that has some information on it, such as a name, and is displayed outside a store, hotel, etc.

sig·net ring /ˈsɪɡnət ˌrɪŋ/ *noun* a ring with a design cut into it, that you wear on your finger ⊃ picture at JEWELRY

sig·nif·i·cance **AWL** /sɪɡˈnɪfəkəns/ *noun* [U, C] **1** the importance of something, especially when this has an effect on what happens in the future: *a decision of major political significance* ◆ *The new drug has great significance for the treatment of the disease.* ◆ *They discussed the statistical significance of the results.* ⊃ collocations at SIGNIFICANT **2** the meaning of something: *She couldn't grasp the full significance of what he had said.* ◆ *Do these symbols have any particular significance?*

sig·nif·i·cant **AWL** /sɪɡˈnɪfəkənt/ *adj.*
1 large or important enough to have an effect or to be noticed: *a highly significant discovery* ◆ *The results of the experiment are not statistically significant.* ◆ *There are no significant differences between the two groups of students.* ◆ *Your work has shown a significant improvement.* ◆ *It is significant that girls generally do better on examinations than boys.* ⊃ compare INSIGNIFICANT **2** having a particular meaning: *It is significant that he changed his will only days before his death.* **3** [usually before noun] having a special or secret meaning that is not understood by everyone **SYN** MEANINGFUL: *a significant look/smile*

AWL COLLOCATIONS

significant
significant *adj.*
important; so large that you notice it
- change, difference, effect, impact, improvement, increase, reduction | contribution | correlation
  There were significant climatic differences, including an unusually wet season followed by dry seasons.
- statistically
  It is necessary to carry out a trial on a statistically significant number of individuals.
- highly
  The museum owns highly significant and valuable works.
- culturally, economically, historically, morally, politically, socially
  The collection includes historically significant letters from American presidents.
- prove
  The research could prove significant in medical and biotechnology fields.

insignificant *adj.*
- detail | decrease, difference, increase
  I will return to these apparently insignificant details in the last section of this paper.
- statistically
  The small sample size is statistically insignificant.
- apparently, seemingly | relatively
  Seemingly insignificant scratches in glass may cause breakage.

significance *noun*
- statistical
  In the test, high variability resulted in a lack of statistical significance.
- assess | grasp | downplay, underestimate
  There are two very different ways to assess the broader significance of these events.

significantly *adv.*
in a noticeable way
- differ, vary
  Actual markets differ significantly from perfectly competitive markets.
- lower (than)
  Significantly lower numbers of seals were observed at low tide.

sig·nif·i·cant·ly 🔑 **AWL** /sɪgˈnɪfəkəntli/ adv.
1 in a way that is large or important enough to have an effect on something or to be noticed: *The two sets of figures are not significantly different.* ◆ *Profits have increased significantly over the past few years.* ⊃ collocations at SIGNIFICANT **2** in a way that has a particular meaning: *Significantly, he did not deny that he might run for re-election.* **3** in a way that has a special or secret meaning: *She paused significantly before she answered.*

sig·nificant ˈother noun (often *humorous*) your husband, wife, partner, or someone that you have a special relationship with

sig·ni·fi·ca·tion /ˌsɪgnɪfəˈkeɪʃn/ noun (formal or linguistics) [U, C] the exact meaning of something, especially a word or phrase

sig·ni·fied **AWL** /ˈsɪgnəˌfaɪd/ noun (linguistics) the meaning expressed by a LINGUISTIC sign, rather than its form ⊃ compare SIGNIFIER

sig·ni·fi·er /ˈsɪgnəˌfaɪər/ noun (linguistics) the form of a LINGUISTIC sign, for example its sound or its printed form, rather than the meaning it expresses ⊃ compare SIGNIFIED

sig·ni·fy **AWL** /ˈsɪgnəˌfaɪ/ verb (sig·ni·fies, sig·ni·fy·ing, sig·ni·fied, sig·ni·fied) **1** [T] to be a sign of something SYN MEAN: *~ sth This decision signified a radical change in their policies.* ◆ *~ that... This mark signifies that the products conform to an approved standard.* ◆ *The white belt signifies that he's an absolute beginner.* **2** [T] to do something to make your feelings, intentions, etc. known: *~ sth She signified her approval with a smile.* ◆ *~ that... He nodded to signify that he agreed.* **3** [I] (usually used in questions or negative sentences) to be important or to matter: *His presence no longer signified.*

sign·ing /ˈsaɪnɪŋ/ noun **1** [U] the act of writing your name at the end of an official document to show that you accept it: *the signing of the Treaty of Rome* **2** [U] the act of making an official contract that arranges for someone to join a sports team or a record or film company **3** [U] the act of using sign language: *the use of signing in classrooms*

ˈsign ˌlanguage noun [U, C] a system of communicating with people who cannot hear, by using hand movements rather than spoken words

ˈsign ˌpainter noun a person who paints signs and advertisements for stores and businesses ▶ **ˈsign ˌpainting** noun [U]

sign·post /ˈsaɪnpoʊst/ noun a sign at the side of a road giving information about the direction and distance of places: *Follow the signposts to the superstore.* ◆ (figurative) *The chapter headings are useful signposts to the content of the book.*

Sikh /siːk/ noun a member of a religion (called **Sikhism**) that developed in Punjab in the late 15th century and is based on a belief that there is only one God ▶ **Sikh** adj.

si·lage /ˈsaɪlɪdʒ/ noun [U] grass or other green crops that are stored without being dried and are used to feed farm animals in winter

si·lence 🔑 /ˈsaɪləns/ noun, verb, exclamation
● **noun 1** [U] a complete lack of noise or sound SYN QUIET: *Their footsteps echoed in the silence.* ◆ *A scream broke the silence of the night.* ◆ *I need absolute silence when I'm working.* **2** [C, U] a situation when no one is speaking: *an embarrassed/awkward silence* ◆ *a moment's stunned silence* ◆ *I got used to his long silences.* ◆ *They finished their meal in total silence.* ◆ *She lapsed into silence again.* ◆ *There was a deafening silence* (= one that is very noticeable). ◆ *a two-minute silence in honor of those who had died* **3** [U, sing.] a situation in which someone refuses to talk about something or to answer questions: *She broke her public silence in a TV interview.* ◆ *~ (on sth) The company's silence on the subject has been taken as an admission of guilt.* ◆ *the right to silence* (= the legal right not to say anything when you are arrested) ◆ *There is a conspiracy of silence about what is happening* (= everyone has agreed not to discuss it). **4** [U] a situation in which people do not communicate with each other by letter or telephone:

The phone call came after months of silence.
IDM silence is golden (saying) it is often best not to say anything ⊃ more at PREGNANT
● **verb 1** *~ sb/sth* to make someone or something stop speaking or making a noise: *She silenced him with a glare.* ◆ *Our bombs silenced the enemy's guns* (= they destroyed them). **2** *~ sb/sth* to make someone stop expressing opinions that are opposed to yours: *All protest had been silenced.* ◆ *Her recent achievements have silenced her critics.*
IDM see HEAVY
● **exclamation** (formal) used to tell people to be quiet: *Silence in the court!*

si·lenc·er /ˈsaɪlənsər/ noun a device that is fixed to the end of a gun in order to reduce the amount of noise that it makes when it is fired

si·lent 🔑 /ˈsaɪlənt/ adj.
1 (of a person) not speaking: *to remain/stay/keep silent* ◆ *They huddled together in silent groups.* ◆ *As the curtain rose, the audience fell silent.* ◆ *He gave me the silent treatment* (= did not speak to me because he was angry). **2** [only before noun] (especially of a man) not talking very much SYN QUIET: *He's the strong silent type.* **3** where there is little or no sound; making little or no sound SYN QUIET: *At last the traffic fell silent.* ◆ *The streets were silent and deserted.* **4** [only before noun] not expressed with words or sound: *a silent prayer/protest* ◆ *They nodded in silent agreement.* **5** *~ (on/about sth)* not giving information about something; refusing to speak about something: *The report is strangely silent on this issue.* ◆ *the right to remain silent* (= the legal right not to say anything when you are arrested) **6** [only before noun] (of old movies) with pictures but no sound: *a silent movie/film* ◆ *stars of the silent screen* **7** (of a letter in a word) written but not pronounced: *The "b" in "lamb" is silent.*

si·lent·ly /ˈsaɪləntli/ adv. **1** without speaking: *They marched silently through the streets.* **2** without making any or much sound SYN QUIETLY: *She crept silently out of the room.* **3** without using words or sounds to express something: *She prayed silently.* ◆ *He silently agreed with much of what she had said.*
IDM sit/stand silently by to do or say nothing to help someone or deal with a difficult situation

the ˌsilent maˈjority noun [usually sing.] the large number of people in a country who think the same as each other, but do not express their views publicly

ˌsilent ˈpartner noun a person who has put money into a business company but who is not actually involved in running it

sil·hou·ette /ˌsɪluˈet/ noun, verb
● **noun 1** [C, U] the dark outline or shape of a person or an object that you see against a light background: *the silhouette of chimneys and towers* ◆ *The mountains stood out in silhouette.* **2** [C] the shape of a person's body or of an object: *The dress is fitted to give you a flattering silhouette.* **3** [C] a picture that shows someone or something as a black shape against a light background, especially one that shows the side view of a person's face
● **verb** [usually passive] *~ sb/sth (against sth)* to make something appear as a silhouette: *A figure stood in the doorway, silhouetted against the light.*

sil·i·ca /ˈsɪlɪkə/ noun [U] (symb. SiO_2) a chemical containing silicon found in sand and in rocks such as QUARTZ, used in making glass and CEMENT

ˈsilica ˌgel noun [U] a substance made from silica in the form of grains, which keeps things dry by absorbing water

sil·i·cate /ˈsɪləˌkeɪt/ noun [C, U] **1** (chemistry) any COMPOUND containing silicon and OXYGEN: *aluminum silicate* **2** a mineral that contains silica. There are many different silicates and they form a large part of the earth's CRUST.

sil·i·con /ˈsɪləˌkɑn; -kən/ noun [U] (symb. **Si**) a chemical element. Silicon exists as a gray solid or as a brown powder and is found in rocks and sand. It is used in making glass and TRANSISTORS.

,**silicon** '**chip** *noun* a very small piece of silicon used to carry a complicated electronic CIRCUIT

sil·i·cone /'sɪləˌkoʊn/ *noun* [U] a chemical containing silicon. There are several different types of silicone, used to make paint, artificial rubber, VARNISH, etc.: *a silicone breast implant*

,**Silicon** '**Valley** *noun* [U] the area in California where there are many companies connected with the computer and ELECTRONICS industries, sometimes used to refer to any area where there are a lot of computer companies

sil·i·co·sis /ˌsɪlə'koʊsəs/ *noun* [U] (*medical*) a serious lung disease caused by breathing in dust containing SILICA

silk 🔑 /sɪlk/ *noun*

1 [U] fine soft thread produced by SILKWORMS **2** [U] a type of fine smooth cloth made from silk thread: *a silk blouse* ♦ *silk stockings* ♦ *made of pure silk* ♦ *Her skin was as smooth as silk.* ⊃ picture at CLOTHES ⊃ see also WATERED SILK **3** [U] silk thread used for sewing **4** silks [pl.] clothes made of silk, especially the colored shirts worn by JOCKEYS (= people riding horses in a race)

IDM **make a silk purse out of a sow's ear** to succeed in making something good out of material that does not seem very good at all

silk·en /'sɪlkən/ *adj.* (*literary*) **1** [usually before noun] soft, smooth, and shiny like silk: *silken hair* **2** [usually before noun] smooth and gentle: *her silken voice* **3** [only before noun] made of silk: *silken ribbons*

'**silk screen** *noun* **1** [U] a method of printing in which ink is forced through a design cut in a piece of fine cloth: *silk-screen prints* **2** [C] a picture, etc. produced by this method: *Warhol's silk screen of Marilyn Monroe* ▶ '**silk-screen** *verb* ~ **sth**

silk·worm /'sɪlkwərm/ *noun* a CATERPILLAR (= a small creature like a WORM with legs) that produces silk thread

silk·y /'sɪlki/ *adj.* (**silk·i·er**, **silk·i·est**) **1** soft, smooth, and shiny like silk: *silky fur* **2** [usually before noun] smooth and gentle: *He spoke in a silky tone.* **3** made of silk or cloth that looks like silk: *a silky dress* ▶ **silk·i·ly** /-kəli/ *adv.*: *"How have I changed?" he asked silkily.* **silk·i·ness** /-kinəs/ *noun* [U] **silk·y** *adv.*: *The leaves are gray and silky smooth.*

sill /sɪl/ *noun* **1** = WINDOWSILL **2** a piece of metal that forms part of the frame of a vehicle below the doors

sil·ly 🔑 /'sɪli/ *adj., noun*

● *adj.* (**sil·li·er**, **sil·li·est**) **1** showing a lack of thought, understanding, or judgment **SYN** FOOLISH: *a silly idea* ♦ *That was a silly thing to do!* ♦ *Her work is full of silly mistakes.* ♦ *"I can walk home." "Don't be silly—it's much too far!"* ♦ *You silly boy!* **2** stupid or embarrassing, especially in a way that is more typical of a child than an adult **SYN** RIDICULOUS: *a silly sense of humor* ♦ *a silly game* ♦ *I feel silly in these clothes.* ♦ *She had a silly grin on her face.* **3** not practical or serious: *We had to wear these silly little hats.* ♦ *Why worry about a silly thing like that?* ▶ **sil·li·ness** *noun* [U]

IDM **bore, scare, beat, etc. sb silly** (*informal*) to bore, scare, beat, etc. someone so badly that they cannot think clearly: *He was scared silly by the lion's roar.* ♦ *Ryan's punch knocked me silly.* **drink, laugh, shout, etc. yourself silly** (*informal*) to drink, laugh, shout, etc. so much that you cannot behave in a sensible way

● *noun* [sing.] (*informal*) often used when speaking to children to say that they are not behaving in a sensible way: *No, silly, those aren't your shoes!*

si·lo /'saɪloʊ/ *noun* (*pl.* **si·los**) **1** a tall tower on a farm used for storing grain, etc. **2** an underground place where nuclear weapons or dangerous substances are kept **3** an underground place where SILAGE is made and stored

silt /sɪlt/ *noun, verb*

● *noun* [U] sand, mud, etc. that is carried by flowing water and is left at the mouth of a river or in a HARBOR ▶ **silt·y** *adj.*: *silty soils*

● *verb*
PHR V ,**silt sth**↔'**up** | ,**silt** '**up** to block something with silt; to become blocked with silt: *Sand has silted up the river delta.* ♦ *The harbor has now silted up.*

sil·ver 🔑 /'sɪlvər/ *noun, adj., verb*

● *noun* **1** [U] (*symb.* **Ag**) a chemical element. Silver is a gray-white PRECIOUS METAL used for making coins, jewelry, decorative objects, etc.: *a silver chain* ♦ *made of solid silver* ♦ *a silver mine* **2** [U] coins that are made of silver or a metal that looks like silver: *I need $2 in silver for the parking meter.* **3** [U] dishes, decorative objects, etc. that are made of silver: *They've had to sell the family silver to pay the bills.* **4** [U] a shiny gray-white color ⊃ see also SILVERY **5** [U, C] = SILVER MEDAL: *She won silver in last year's championships.* ♦ *The team won two silvers and a bronze.*

IDM **on a silver platter** if you are given something **on a silver platter**, you do not have to do much to get it: *These rich kids expect to have it all handed to them on a silver platter.* ⊃ more at BORN, CLOUD

● *adj.* shiny gray-white in color: *a silver car* ♦ *silver hair* ⊃ see also SILVERY

● *verb* **1** [usually passive] ~ **sth** to cover the surface of something with a thin layer of silver or something that looks like silver **2** ~ **sth** (especially *literary*) to make something become bright like silver: *Moonlight was silvering the countryside.*

,**silver anni**'**versary** *noun* the 25th anniversary of a wedding or other important event ⊃ compare DIAMOND ANNIVERSARY, GOLDEN ANNIVERSARY

sil·ver·back /'sɪlvərˌbæk/ *noun* a male adult GORILLA with white or silver hair across its back

,**silver** '**birch** *noun* [C, U] a tree with smooth, very pale gray or white BARK and thin branches, that grows in northern countries

,**silver** '**bullet** *noun* a simple solution to a complicated problem: **SYN** MAGIC BULLET *The fraud detection system by itself is not a silver bullet.*

,**silver** '**dollar** *noun* a large silver coin used in the past, that was worth one dollar, sometimes used now to describe the size of something: *a spider as big as a silver dollar*

sil·ver·fish /'sɪlvərˌfɪʃ/ *noun* (*pl.* **sil·ver·fish**) a small silver insect without wings that lives in houses and that can cause damage to materials such as cloth and paper

,**silver** '**medal** *noun* [C] (also **sil·ver** [U, C]) a MEDAL that is given to the person or the team that wins the second prize in a race or competition: *an Olympic silver medal winner* ⊃ compare BRONZE MEDAL, GOLD MEDAL ▶ ,**silver** '**medalist** *noun*: *He's an Olympic silver medalist.*

,**silver** '**plate** *noun* [U] metal that is covered with a thin layer of silver; objects that are made of this metal ▶ ,**silver-** '**plated** *adj.*

the ,**silver** '**screen** *noun* [sing.] (*old-fashioned*) the movie industry

sil·ver·smith /'sɪlvərˌsmɪθ/ *noun* a person who makes, repairs, or sells articles made of silver

,**silver** '**tongue** *noun* (*formal*) great skill at persuading people to do or to believe what you say ▶ ,**silver-**'**tongued** *adj.*

sil·ver·ware /'sɪlvərˌwɛr/ *noun* [U] **1** objects that are made of or covered with silver, especially knives, forks, dishes, etc. that are used for eating and serving food: *a piece of silverware* **2** knives, forks, and spoons, made of metal but not necessarily silver, used for eating and serving food **SYN** CUTLERY, FLATWARE

sil·ver·y /'sɪlvəri/ *adj.* [usually before noun] **1** shiny like silver; having the color of silver: *silvery light* ♦ *a silvery gray color* **2** (*literary*) (especially of a voice) having a pleasant musical sound

sim /sɪm/ *noun* (*informal*) a computer or video game that SIMULATES (= artificially creates the feeling of experienc-

ing) an activity such as flying an aircraft or playing a sport
⊃ collocations at PHONE

SIM card /'sɪm kard/ *noun* the abbreviation for "subscriber identification module" (a plastic card inside a cell phone that stores personal information about the person using the phone)

sim·i·an /'sɪmiən/ *adj.* (*technical*) like a MONKEY, especially an APE; connected with MONKEYS or APES

sim·i·lar 🔑 **AWL** /'sɪmələr/ *adj.*
like someone or something but not exactly the same: *We have very similar interests.* ◆ **~ (to sb/sth)** *My teaching style is similar to that of most other teachers.* ◆ **~ (in sth)** *The two houses are similar in size.* ◆ *The brothers look very similar.* ◆ *All our patients have broadly similar problems.* **ANT** DIFFERENT, DISSIMILAR

AWL COLLOCATIONS

similar

similar *adj.*
■ broadly, generally | highly, remarkably, strikingly | superficially | qualitatively | quantitatively | conceptually | structurally
The two methods gave qualitatively similar patterns.
■ ~ to | ~ to each other/one another | ~ to that/those of
Our results are similar to the research findings outlined in the literature review.
They spoke a language similar to that of the Aztecs.

dissimilar *adj.*
■ highly, markedly, strikingly | not entirely
If the model has too few classes, highly dissimilar plants are treated as if they were identical.
■ ~ to/from
Hayek's earliest view was not very dissimilar from Schumpeter's.

similarity *noun*
■ general | close, remarkable, significant, striking, strong | superficial | apparent | structural
This finding also bears a remarkable similarity to other studies that examined educational performance.
■ assess | find | share | bear | exhibit, reveal, show
Although the microelectronics and biotechnology industries share certain similarities, the two differ in numerous ways.
■ ~ among/between | ~ to/with
The findings of our study call attention to a striking similarity between both groups.

sim·i·lar·i·ty **AWL** /ˌsɪmə'lærəti/ *noun* (*pl.* **sim·i·lar·i·ties**)
1 [U, sing.] the state of being like someone or something but not exactly the same **SYN** RESEMBLANCE: **~ (between A and B)** *The report highlights the similarity between the two groups.* ◆ **~ (to sb/sth)** *She bears a striking similarity to her mother.* ◆ **~ (in sth)** *There is some similarity in the way they sing.* ◆ *They are both doctors but that is where the similarity ends.* **2** [C] a feature that things or people have that makes them like each other **SYN** RESEMBLANCE: *a study of the similarities and differences between the two countries* ◆ **~ in/of sth** *similarities in/of style* ◆ **~ to/with sb/sth** *The karate bout has many similarities to a boxing match.* **ANT** DIFFERENCE
⊃ collocations at SIMILAR

sim·i·lar·ly 🔑 **AWL** /'sɪmələrli/ *adv.*
1 in almost the same way: *Husband and wife were similarly successful in their chosen careers.* **2** used to say that two facts, actions, statements, etc. are like each other: *The United States won most of the track and field events. Similarly, in swimming, the top three places went to Americans.*

LANGUAGE BANK

similarly
making comparisons
■ This chart **provides a comparison of** the ways that teenage boys and girls in the U.S. spend their free time.
■ In many cases, the results for boys and girls are virtually **the same/identical**.
■ In many cases, the results for boys are virtually **the same as/identical to** the results for girls.
■ **Both** boys **and** girls spend the bulk of their free time with friends.
■ Most of the boys play more than two hours of sports a week, **as do** many of the girls.
■ **Like** many of the girls, most of the boys spend a large part of their free time using the Internet.
■ The girls particularly enjoy using social networking websites. **Similarly**, nearly all the boys said they spent at least two to three hours a week on these sites.
⊃ Language Banks at CONTRAST, ILLUSTRATE, PROPORTION, SURPRISING

sim·i·le /'sɪməli/ *noun* [C, U] (*technical*) a word or phrase that compares something to something else, using the words *like* or *as*, for example *a face like a mask* or *as white as snow*; the use of such words and phrases ⊃ compare METAPHOR

si·mil·i·tude /sɪ'mɪləˌtud/ *noun* [U] (*formal*) **~ (between A and B)** | **~ (to sb/sth)** the state of being similar to something: *the similitude between humans and gorillas*

sim·mer /'sɪmər/ *verb, noun*
● *verb* **1** [T, I] **~ (sth)** to cook something by keeping it almost at boiling point; to be cooked in this way: *Simmer the sauce gently for 10 minutes.* ◆ *Leave the soup to simmer.* ⊃ collocations at COOKING **2** [I] **~ (with sth)** to be filled with a strong feeling, especially anger, which you have difficulty controlling **SYN** SEETHE: *She was still simmering with resentment.* ◆ *Anger simmered inside him.* **3** [I] (of an argument, a disagreement, etc.) to develop for a period of time without any real anger or violence being shown: *This argument has been simmering for months.*
PHR V ˌsimmer 'down (*informal*) to become calm after a period of anger or excitement: *I left him alone until he simmered down.*
● *noun* [sing.] the state when something is almost boiling: *Bring the sauce to a simmer and cook for 5 minutes.*

Si·mon says /ˌsaɪmən 'sɛz/ *noun* [U] a children's game in which players should only do what a person says if he/she says "Simon says…" at the beginning of the instruction

sim·pa·ti·co /sɪm'pɑtɪˌkoʊ; -'pæ-/ *adj.* (*informal*, from Spanish) **1** (of a person) pleasant; easy to like **2** (of a person) with similar interests and ideas to yours **SYN** COMPATIBLE

sim·per /'sɪmpər/ *verb* [I, T] to smile in a silly and annoying way: *a silly simpering girl* ◆ **+ speech** "You're such a darling," she simpered. ▶ **sim·per** *noun* [sing.] **sim·per·ing·ly** /'sɪmpərɪŋli/ *adv.*

sim·ple 🔑 /'sɪmpl/ *adj.* (**sim·pler**, **sim·plest**)
HELP You can also use **more simple** and **most simple**.
▷ **EASY 1** not complicated; easy to understand or do **SYN** EASY: *a simple solution* ◆ *The answer is really quite simple.* ◆ *This machine is very simple to use.* ◆ *We lost because we played badly. It's as simple as that.* ◆ *Give the necessary information but keep it simple.*
▷ **BASIC/PLAIN 2** basic or plain without anything extra or unnecessary: *simple but elegant clothes* ◆ *We had a simple meal of soup and bread.* ◆ *The accommodations are simple but spacious.* **ANT** FANCY
▷ **FOR EMPHASIS 3** used before a noun to emphasize that it is exactly that and nothing else: *Nobody wanted to believe the simple truth.* ◆ *It was a matter of simple survival.* ◆ *It's nothing to worry about—just a simple headache.* ◆ *I had to do it for the*

simple reason that (= because) *I couldn't trust anyone else.*
⊃ thesaurus box at PLAIN

> **WITH FEW PARTS 4** [usually before noun] consisting of only a few parts; not complicated in structure: *simple forms of life, for example amebas ◆ a simple machine ◆* (*grammar*) *a* **simple sentence** (= one with only one verb)

> **ORDINARY 5** [only before noun] (of a person) ordinary; not special: *I'm a simple country girl.*

> **NOT INTELLIGENT 6** [not usually before noun] (of a person) not very intelligent; not mentally normal: *He's not crazy—just a little simple.*

> **GRAMMAR 7** used to describe the present or past tense of a verb that is formed without using an auxiliary verb, as in *She loves him* (= the simple present tense) or *He arrived late* (= the simple past tense) ⊃ see also SIMPLY **IDM** see PURE

simple ˈfracture *noun* an injury when a bone in your body is broken but does not come through the skin ⊃ compare COMPOUND FRACTURE

simple ˈinterest *noun* [U] (*finance*) interest that is paid only on the original amount of money that you invested, and not on any interest that it has earned ⊃ compare COMPOUND INTEREST

simple-ˈminded *adj.* (*disapproving*) not intelligent; not able to understand how complicated things are: *a simple-minded person ◆ a simple-minded approach*

sim·ple·ton /ˈsɪmpəltən/ *noun* (*old-fashioned*) a person who is not very intelligent and can be tricked easily

sim·plex /ˈsɪmplɛks/ *noun* (*linguistics*) a simple word that is not made of other words ⊃ compare COMPOUND

sim·plic·i·ty /sɪmˈplɪsəti/ *noun* (*pl.* **sim·plic·i·ties**) **1** [U] the quality of being easy to understand or use: *the relative simplicity of the new PC ◆* **For the sake of simplicity**, *let's divide the discussion into two parts.* **2** [U] (*approving*) the quality of being natural and plain: *the simplicity of the architecture ◆ the simplicity of country living* **3** [C, usually pl.] an aspect of something that is easy, natural, or plain: *the simplicities of our old way of life*
IDM **be simplicity itself** to be very easy or plain

sim·pli·fi·ca·tion /ˌsɪmpləfəˈkeɪʃn/ *noun* **1** [U, sing.] the process of making something easier to do or understand: *Complaints have led to (a) simplification of the rules.* **2** [C] the thing that results when you make a problem, statement, system, etc. easier to understand or do: *A number of simplifications have been made to the taxation system.*

sim·pli·fy /ˈsɪmpləˌfaɪ/ *verb* (**sim·pli·fies**, **sim·pli·fy·ing**, **sim·pli·fied**, **sim·pli·fied**) **~ sth** to make something easier to do or understand: *The application forms have now been simplified. ◆ I hope his appointment will **simplify matters**. ◆ a simplified version of the story for young children*

sim·plis·tic /sɪmˈplɪstɪk/ *adj.* (*disapproving*) making a problem, situation, etc. seem less difficult or complicated than it really is ▸ **sim·plis·ti·cal·ly** /-kli/ *adv.*

sim·ply 🖉 /ˈsɪmpli/ *adv.*
1 used to emphasize how easy or basic something is **SYN** JUST: *Simply add hot water and stir. ◆ The runway is simply a strip of grass. ◆ Fame is often **simply a matter of** being in the right place at the right time. ◆ You can enjoy all the water sports, or simply lie on the beach.* **2** used to emphasize a statement **SYN** ABSOLUTELY: *You simply must see the play. ◆ The view is simply wonderful! ◆ That is simply not true! ◆ I haven't seen her for simply ages.* **3** in a way that is easy to understand: *The book explains grammar simply and clearly. ◆ Anyway, **to put it simply**, we still owe them $2,000.* **4** in a way that is natural and plain: *The rooms are simply furnished. ◆ They live simply* (= they do not spend much money). **5** used to introduce a summary or an explanation of something that you have just said or done: *I don't want to be rude, **it's simply that** we have to be careful who we give this information to.*

sim·u·la·crum /ˌsɪmjəˈleɪkrəm; -ˈlæ-/ *noun* (*pl.* **sim·u·la·cra** /-krə/) (*formal*) something that looks like someone or something else or that is made to look like someone or something else **SYN** COPY

sim·u·late **AWL** /ˈsɪmjəˌleɪt/ *verb* **1 ~ sth** to pretend that you have a particular feeling **SYN** FEIGN: *I tried to simulate surprise at the news.* **2 ~ sth** to create particular conditions that exist in real life using computers, models, etc., usually for study or training purposes: *Computer software can be used to simulate conditions on the seabed.* **3 ~ sth** to be made to look like something else: *a gas heater that simulates a coal fire*

sim·u·lat·ed **AWL** /ˈsɪmjəˌleɪtəd/ *adj.* [only before noun] not real, but made to look, feel, etc. like the real thing: *simulated leather ◆ "How wonderful!" she said with simulated enthusiasm. ◆ The experiments were carried out under simulated examination conditions.*

sim·u·la·tion **AWL** /ˌsɪmjəˈleɪʃn/ *noun* **1** [C, U] a situation in which a particular set of conditions is created artificially in order to study or experience something that could exist in reality: *a computer simulation of how the planet functions ◆ a simulation model* **2** [U] the act of pretending that something is real when it is not: *the simulation of genuine concern*

sim·u·la·tor /ˈsɪmjəˌleɪtər/ *noun* a piece of equipment that artificially creates a particular set of conditions in order to train someone to deal with a situation that they may experience in reality: *a flight simulator*

si·mul·cast /ˈsaɪmlˌkæst/ *verb* (**si·mul·cast**, **si·mul·cast**) **~ sth** to broadcast something on radio and television at the same time or on both AM and FM radio ▸ **si·mul·cast** *noun*

si·mul·ta·ne·ous /ˌsaɪmlˈteɪniəs/ *adj.* happening or done at the same time as something else: *There were several simultaneous attacks by the rebels. ◆* **simultaneous translation/interpreting** ▸ **si·mul·ta·ne·i·ty** /ˌsaɪmltəˈniəti; -ˈneɪəti/ *noun* [U] **si·mul·ta·ne·ous·ly** *adv.*: *The game will be broadcast simultaneously on TV and radio.* ⊃ language bank at PROCESS

simulˌtaneous eˈquations *noun* [pl.] (*mathematics*) EQUATIONS involving two or more unknown quantities that have the same values in each EQUATION

SIN /ˌɛs aɪ ˈɛn/ *abbr.* (*CanE*) SOCIAL INSURANCE NUMBER

sin /sɪn/ *noun, verb, abbr.*
● *noun* **1** [C] an offense against God or against a religious or moral law: *to commit a sin ◆ Confess your sins to God and he will forgive you. ◆ The Bible says that stealing is a sin.* ⊃ collocations at RELIGION ⊃ see also MORTAL SIN, ORIGINAL SIN **2** [U] the act of breaking a religious or moral law: *a life of sin* **3** [C, usually sing.] (*informal*) an action that people strongly disapprove of: *It's a sin to waste taxpayers' money like that.* ⊃ see also SINFUL, SINNER
IDM **(as) guilty, miserable, ugly, etc. as sin** (*informal*) used to emphasize that someone is very guilty, etc. ⊃ more at LIVE, MULTITUDE[1]
● *verb* (-nn-) [I] to break a religious or moral law: *Forgive me, Lord, for I have sinned. ◆ **~ against sb/sth** He was more sinned against than sinning* (= although he did wrong, other people treated him even worse).
● *abbr.* (*mathematics*) SINE

ˈsin bin *noun* (*informal*) (in some sports, for example HOCKEY) a place away from the playing area where the REFEREE sends a player who has broken the rules

since 🖉 /sɪns/ *prep., conj., adv.*
● *prep.* **1** (used with the present perfect or past perfect tense) from a time in the past until a later past time, or until now: *She's been off work since Tuesday. ◆ We've lived here since 2006. ◆ I haven't eaten since breakfast. ◆ He's been working in a bank since leaving school. ◆ Since the party she had only spoken to him once. ◆ "They've split up." "**Since when?**" ◆ That was years ago. I've changed jobs **since then**.* **HELP** Use **for** not **since**, with a period of time: *I've been learning English for five years. ◆* ~~I've been learning English since five years.~~
2 ~ when? used when you are showing that you are angry about something: *Since when did he ever listen to me?*
● *conj.* **1** (used with the present perfect, past perfect, or simple present tense in the main clause) from an event in the past until a later past event, or until now: *Cath hasn't phoned since she went to Berlin. ◆ It was the first time I'd had*

visitors since I'd moved to New Haven. ◆ *It's twenty years since I've seen her.* ◆ *How long is it since we last went to the theater?* ◆ *She had been worrying **ever since** the letter arrived.* **2** because; as: *We thought that, since we were in the area, we'd stop by and see them.*

● **adv.** (used with the present perfect or past perfect tense) **1** from a time in the past until a later past time, or until now: *He left home two weeks ago and we haven't heard from him since.* ◆ *The original building has **long since** (= long before now) been demolished.* **2** at a time after a particular time in the past: *We were divorced two years ago and she has since remarried.*

sin·cere 🔑 /sɪnˈsɪr/ *adj.* (*superlative* **sin·cer·est**, no *comparative*)
1 (of feelings, beliefs, or behavior) showing what you really think or feel **SYN** GENUINE: *a sincere attempt to resolve the problem* ◆ *sincere regret* ◆ *Please accept our sincere thanks.* ◆ *a sincere apology* **2** (of a person) saying only what you really think or feel **SYN** HONEST: *He seemed sincere enough when he said he wanted to help.* ◆ **~ in sth** *She is never completely sincere in what she says about people.* **ANT** INSINCERE
▶ **sin·cer·i·ty** /sɪnˈserəti/ *noun* [U]: *She spoke with total sincerity.* ◆ *I can say **in all sincerity** that I knew nothing of these plans.*

sin·cere·ly 🔑 /sɪnˈsɪrli/ *adv.*
in a way that shows what you really feel or think about someone or something: *I sincerely believe that this is the right decision.* ◆ *"I won't let you down." "I sincerely hope not."*
IDM **Sincerely (yours)** (also **Yours sincerely**) (*formal*) used at the end of a formal letter before you sign your name, when you have addressed someone by their name

sine /saɪn/ *noun* (*abbr.* **sin**) (*mathematics*) the RATIO of the length of the side opposite one of the angles in a RIGHT TRIANGLE that are less than 90° to the length of the longest side ⊃ compare COSINE, TANGENT

si·ne·cure /ˈsaɪnəkjʊr; ˈsɪnə-/ *noun* (*formal*) a job that you are paid for even though it involves little or no work

si·ne di·e /ˌsaɪni ˈdaɪi; ˌsɪneɪ ˈdieɪ/ *adv.* (from *Latin, formal, law*) without a future date being arranged: *The case was adjourned sine die.*

si·ne qua non /ˌsɪni kwɑ ˈnɑn; -ˈnoʊn/ *noun* [sing.] **~ (of/for sth)** (from *Latin, formal*) something that is essential before you can achieve something else

sin·ew /ˈsɪnyu/ *noun* **1** [C, U] a strong band of TISSUE in the body that joins a muscle to a bone **2** [usually pl.] (*literary*) a source of strength or power **IDM** see STRAIN

sin·ew·y /ˈsɪnyui/ *adj.* (of a person or an animal) having a thin body and strong muscles **SYN** WIRY

sin·ful /ˈsɪnfl/ *adj.* morally wrong or evil **SYN** IMMORAL: *sinful thoughts* ◆ *It is sinful to lie.* ◆ (*informal*) *It's sinful to waste good food!* ▶ **sin·ful·ly** /-fəli/ *adv.* **sin·ful·ness** *noun* [U]

sing 🔑 /sɪŋ/ *verb* (**sang** /sæŋ/, **sung** /sʌŋ/)
1 [I, T] to make musical sounds with your voice in the form of a song or tune: *She usually sings in the shower.* ◆ *I just can't sing in tune!* ◆ **~ to sb** *He was singing softly to the baby.* ◆ **~ sth to sb** *Will you sing a song to us?* ◆ **~ sb sth** *Will you sing us a song?* ◆ **~ sth** *Now I'd like to sing a song by the Beatles.* ◆ **~ someone to sleep** *She sang the baby to sleep* (= sang until the baby went to sleep). ⊃ collocations at MUSIC **2** [I] (of birds) to make high musical sounds: *The birds were singing outside my window.* **3** [I] (+ adv./prep.) to make a high ringing sound like a whistle: *Bullets sang past my ears.*
IDM **sing a different tune** to change your opinion about someone or something or your attitude toward someone or something ⊃ more at FAT
PHRV **sing a·long (with sb/sth)** | **sing a·long (to sth)** to sing together with someone who is already singing or while a record, radio, or musical instrument is playing: *Do you sing along if you know the words.* ◆ **related noun** SING-ALONG **'sing of sth** (*old-fashioned* or *formal*) to mention something in a song or a poem, especially to praise it **sing 'out** to sing

or say something clearly and loudly: *A voice suddenly sang out above the rest.*

sing-a·long (also **sing·a·long**) /ˈsɪŋəˌlɔŋ/ *noun* an informal occasion at which people sing songs together

singe /sɪndʒ/ *verb* (**singe·ing**, **singed**, **singed**) [T, I] **~ (sth)** to burn the surface of something slightly, usually by mistake; to be burned in this way: *He singed his hair as he tried to light his cigarette.* ◆ *the smell of singeing fur* ⊃ thesaurus box at BURN

sing·er 🔑 /ˈsɪŋər/ *noun*
a person who sings, or whose job is singing, especially in public: *She's a wonderful singer.* ◆ *an opera singer*

sing·ing 🔑 /ˈsɪŋɪŋ/ *noun* [U]
the activity of making musical sounds with your voice: *the beautiful singing of birds* ◆ *choral singing* ◆ *There was singing and dancing all night.* ◆ *a singing teacher* ◆ *She has a beautiful singing voice.*

sin·gle 🔑 /ˈsɪŋgl/ *adj., noun, verb*
● **adj.**
> ONE **1** [only before noun] only one: *He sent her a single red rose.* ◆ *a single-sex school* (= for boys only or for girls only) ◆ *All these jobs can now be done by one single machine.* ◆ *I couldn't understand a single word she said!* ◆ *the European single currency, the euro*
> FOR EMPHASIS **2** [only before noun] used to emphasize that you are referring to one particular person or thing on its own: *Unemployment is the single most important factor in the growing crime rates.* ◆ *We eat rice every single day.*
> NOT MARRIED **3** (of a person) not married or having a romantic relationship with someone: *The apartments are ideal for single people living alone.* ◆ *Are you still single?* ⊃ see also SINGLE PARENT
> FOR ONE PERSON **4** [only before noun] intended to be used by only one person: *a single bed/room* ⊃ compare DOUBLE
IDM **(in) single file** (in) one line, one behind the other: *They made their way in single file along the cliff path.* ⊃ more at GLANCE
● **noun**
> MUSIC **1** [C] a piece of recorded music, usually popular music, that consists of one song; the CD that a single is recorded on: *The band releases its new single next week.* ⊃ compare ALBUM
> ROOM **2** [C] a room in a hotel, etc. for one person ⊃ compare DOUBLE
> MONEY **3** [C] a bill that is worth one dollar ⊃ compare DOUBLE
> UNMARRIED PEOPLE **4 singles** [pl.] people who are not married and do not have a romantic relationship with someone else: *They organize parties for singles.* ◆ *a singles bar/club*
> IN SPORTS **5 singles** [U] (especially in TENNIS) a game when only one player plays against one other; a series of two or more of these games: *the women's singles champion* ◆ *the first round of the men's singles* ◆ *a singles match* ◆ *She's won three singles titles this year.* ⊃ compare DOUBLE **6** [C] (in baseball) a hit that only allows the player to run to FIRST BASE
● **verb** [I] (in baseball) to hit the ball only far enough to be able to run to FIRST BASE: *Davis singled to center field.*
PHRV **single sb/sth↔'out (for sth/as sb/sth)** to choose someone or something from a group for special attention: *She was singled out for criticism.* ◆ *He was singled out as the outstanding performer of the games.*

single 'bed (also **twin 'bed**) *noun* a bed big enough for one person

single-'breasted *adj.* (of a jacket or coat) having only one row of buttons that fasten in the middle ⊃ compare DOUBLE-BREASTED

single 'combat *noun* [U] fighting between two people, usually with weapons

single 'figures *noun* [pl.] a number that is less than ten:

t **tea**   ţ **butter**   d **did**   k **cat**   g **got**   tʃ **chin**   dʒ **June**   f **fall**

Inflation is down to single figures. ◆ *The number of people who fail each year is now **in single figures**.*

,single-'handed *adv.* on your own with no one helping you **SYN** ALONE: *to sail around the world single-handed* ▶ ,single-'handed *adj.*: *a single-handed voyage* ,single-'handedly *adv.*

,single 'market *noun* [usually sing.] (*economics*) a group of countries that have few or no restrictions on the movement of goods, money, and people between the members of the group

,single-'minded *adj.* only thinking about one particular aim or goal because you are determined to achieve something: *the single-minded pursuit of power* ◆ *She is very single-minded about her career.* ▶ ,single-'mindedly *adv.* ,single-'mindedness *noun* [U]

sin·gle·ness /'sɪŋglnəs/ *noun* [U] **1 ~ of purpose** the ability to think about one particular aim or goal because you are determined to succeed **2** the state of not being married or having a partner

,single 'parent *noun* a person who takes care of their child or children without a husband, wife, or partner: *a single-parent family*

sin·gle·ton /'sɪŋgltən/ *noun* **1** a single item of the kind that you are talking about **2** a person who is not married or in a romantic relationship **3** a person or an animal that is not a twin, etc.

,single trans,ferable 'vote *noun* [sing.] (*politics*) a system for electing representatives in which a person's vote can be given to their second or third choice if their first choice is defeated, or if their first choice wins with more votes than they need

,single-'use *adj.* [only before noun] made to be used once only: *disposable single-use cameras*

sin·gly /'sɪŋgli/ *adv.* alone; one at a time **SYN** INDIVIDUALLY: *The stamps are available singly or in books of ten.* ◆ *Guests arrived singly or in groups.*

'sing-song *noun, adj.*
● *noun* [sing.] a way of speaking in which a person's voice keeps rising and falling
● *adj.* [only before noun] a **sing-song** voice keeps rising and falling

sin·gu·lar /'sɪŋgyələr/ *noun, adj.*
● *noun* (*grammar*) a form of a noun or verb that refers to one person or thing: *The singular of "bacteria" is "bacterium."* ◆ *The verb should be in the singular.* ⊃ compare PLURAL
● *adj.* **1** (*grammar*) connected with or having the singular form: *a singular noun/verb/ending* **2** (*formal*) very great or obvious **SYN** OUTSTANDING: *landscape of singular beauty* **3** (*literary*) unusual; strange **SYN** ECCENTRIC: *a singular style of dress*

sin·gu·lar·i·ty /ˌsɪŋgyə'lærəti/ *noun* [U] (*formal*) the quality of something that makes it unusual or strange

sin·gu·lar·ly /'sɪŋgyələrli/ *adv.* (*formal*) very; in an unusual way: *singularly beautiful* ◆ *He chose a singularly inappropriate moment to make his request.*

Sin·ha·lese /ˌsɪnhə'liz; ˌsɪnə-; -'lis/ *noun* (*pl.* Sin·ha·lese) **1** [C] a member of a race of people living in Sri Lanka **2** [U] the language of the Sinhalese ▶ Sin·ha·lese *adj.*

sin·is·ter /'sɪnəstər/ *adj.* seeming evil or dangerous; making you think something bad will happen: *There was something cold and sinister about him.* ◆ *There is another, more sinister, possibility.*

sink 🔊 /sɪŋk/ *verb, noun, adj.*
● *verb* (sank /sæŋk/, sunk /sʌŋk/) (or (less frequent sunk, sunk)
▷ IN WATER/MUD, ETC. **1** [I] to go down below the surface or toward the bottom of a liquid or soft substance: *The ship sank to the bottom of the sea.* ◆ *We're sinking!* ◆ *The wheels started to sink into the mud.* ◆ *to sink like a stone*
▷ BOAT **2** [T] **~ sth** to damage a boat or ship so that it goes

below the surface of the ocean, etc.: *a battleship sunk by a torpedo*
▷ FALL/SIT DOWN **3** [I] + adv./prep. (of a person) to move downward, especially by falling or sitting down **SYN** COLLAPSE: *I sank into an armchair.* ◆ *She sank back into her seat, exhausted.* ◆ *The old man had sunk to his knees.*
▷ MOVE DOWNWARD **4** [I] (of an object) to move slowly downward: *The sun was sinking in the west.* ◆ *The foundations of the building are starting to sink.*
▷ BECOME WEAKER **5** [I] to decrease in amount, volume, strength, etc.: *The pound has sunk to its lowest recorded level against the dollar.* ◆ *He is clearly sinking fast* (= getting weaker quickly and will soon die).
▷ OF VOICE **6** [I] to become quieter **SYN** FADE: *Her voice sank to a whisper.*
▷ DIG IN GROUND **7** [T] **~ sth** to make a deep hole in the ground **SYN** DRILL: *to sink a well/shaft/mine* **8** [T] **~ sth** (+ adv./prep.) to place something in the ground by digging: *to sink a post into the ground* ⊃ see also SUNKEN
▷ PREVENT SUCCESS **9** [T] **~ sth/sb** (*informal*) to prevent someone or someone's plans from succeeding: *I think I've just sunk my chances of getting the job.* ◆ *If the car breaks down, we'll be sunk* (= have serious problems).
▷ BALL **10** [T] **~ sth** to get a ball into a hole or BASKET in games such as GOLF or basketball: *He sank a 12-foot putt to win the match.*
▷ ALCOHOL
IDM **be sunk in sth** to be in a state of unhappiness or deep thought: *She just sat there, sunk in thought.* **(like rats) deserting/leaving a sinking ship** (*humorous, disapproving*) used to talk about people who leave an organization, a company, etc. that is having difficulties, without caring about the people who are left **sink your differences** to agree to forget about your disagreements **a/that sinking feeling** (*informal*) an unpleasant feeling that you get when you realize that something bad has happened or is going to happen **sink or swim** to be in a situation where you will either succeed by your own efforts or fail completely: *The new students were just left to sink or swim.* **sink so low | sink to sth** to have such low moral standards that you do something very bad: *Stealing from your friends? How could you sink so low?* ◆ *I can't believe that anyone would sink to such depths.* ⊃ more at HEART
PHR V ,sink 'in | ,sink 'into sth **1** (of words, an event, etc.) to be fully understood or realized: *He paused to allow his words to sink in.* ◆ *The full scale of the disaster has yet to sink in.* **2** (of liquids) to go down into another substance through the surface: *The rain sank into the dry ground.* 'sink into sth to go gradually into a less active, happy, or pleasant state: *She sank into a deep sleep.* ◆ *He sank deeper into depression.* ,sink 'into sth | ,sink sth 'into sth to go, or to make something sharp go, deep into something solid: *The dog sank its teeth into my leg* (= bit it). ◆ *I felt her nails sink into my wrist.* ,sink sth 'into sth to spend a lot of money on a business or an activity, for example in order to make money from it in the future: *We sank all our savings into the venture.*
● *noun* a large open container in a kitchen or bathroom that has faucets to supply water and that you use for washing dishes in, or for washing your face and hands in: *Don't just leave your dirty plates in the sink!* ◆ *I felt chained to the kitchen sink* (= I had to spend all my time doing jobs in the house). ◆ *the bathroom sink* ⊃ picture at PLUG **IDM** SEE KITCHEN

sink·er /'sɪŋkər/ *noun* **1** a weight that is attached to a FISHING LINE or net to keep it under the water **2** (also 'sinker ,ball) (in baseball) a type of PITCH that drops lower when it reaches the BATTER: *He kept throwing sinkers.*
IDM see HOOK *n.*

sink·hole /'sɪŋkhoʊl/ *noun* (*geology*) a large hole in the ground that a river flows into, created over a long period of time by water that has fallen as rain

sin·ner /'sɪnər/ *noun* (*formal*) a person who has committed a SIN or SINS (= broken God's law)

Sino- /'saɪnoʊ/ *combining form* (in nouns and adjectives) Chinese: *Sino-Japanese relations*

sin·u·ous /'sɪnjuəs/ *adj.* (*literary*) turning while moving, in an elegant way; having many curves: *a sinuous movement* ◆ *the sinuous grace of a cat* ◆ *the sinuous course of the river* ▶ **sin·u·ous·ly** *adv.*

si·nus /'saɪnəs/ *noun* any of the hollow spaces in the bones of the head that are connected to the inside of the nose: *blocked sinuses*

si·nus·i·tis /ˌsaɪnə'saɪtəs/ *noun* [U] the painful swelling of the sinuses

-sion /ʒn; ʃn/ ⊃ -ɪON

Sioux /su/ *noun* (*pl.* **Sioux**) a member of a Native American people from the northern central region of the U.S.

sip /sɪp/ *verb, noun*
● *verb* (-pp-) [I, T] to drink something, taking a very small amount each time: ~ **(at sth)** *She sat there, sipping at her tea.* ◆ ~ **sth** *He slowly sipped his wine.*
● *noun* a very small amount of a drink that you take into your mouth: *to have/take a sip of water*

si·phon (also **syphon**) /'saɪfn/ *noun, verb*
● *noun* a tube that is used for moving liquid from one container to another, using pressure from the atmosphere
● *verb* 1 ~ **sth** (+ **adv./prep.**) to move a liquid from one container to another, using a siphon: *I siphoned the gasoline out of the car into a can.* ◆ *The waste liquid needs to be siphoned off.* 2 ~ **sth** (+ **adv./prep.**) (*informal*) to remove money from one place and move it to another, especially dishonestly or illegally **SYN** DIVERT: *She has been accused of siphoning off thousands of dollars from the company into her own bank account.*

sip·py cup /'sɪpi ˌkʌp/ *noun* (*informal*) a cup with a lid that has holes in it so that a baby can suck liquid from it ⊃ picture at CUP

sir 🔑 /sər/ *noun*
1 used as a polite way of addressing a man whose name you do not know, for example in a store or restaurant, or to show respect: *Good morning, sir. Can I help you?* ◆ *Are you ready to order, sir?* ◆ *"Report to me tomorrow, corporal!" "Yes, sir!"* ◆ *"Thank you very much." "You're welcome, sir. Have a nice day."* ⊃ compare MA'AM ⊃ see also MADAM 2 **Dear Sir/Sirs** used at the beginning of a formal business letter when you do not know the name of the man or people that you are dealing with: *Dear Sir/Sirs* ◆ *Dear Sir or Madam* 3 **Sir** a title that is used before the first name of a man who has received one of the highest British honors (= a KNIGHT), or before the first name of a BARONET: *Sir Paul McCartney* ◆ *Thank you, Sir Paul.* ⊃ compare LADY
IDM **no sir!** | **no siree!** (*informal*) certainly not: *We will never allow that to happen! No sir!* **yes sir!** | **yes siree!** used to emphasize that something is true: *That's a fine car you have. Yes sir!*

sire /'saɪər/ *noun, verb*
● *noun* 1 (*technical*) the male parent of an animal, especially a horse ⊃ compare DAM 2 (*old use*) a word that people used when they addressed a king
● *verb* 1 ~ **sth** to be the male parent of an animal, especially a horse 2 ~ **sth** (*old-fashioned* or *humorous*) to become the father of a child

sir·ee (also **sir·ree**) /sə'ri/ *exclamation* (*informal*) used for emphasis, especially after "yes" or "no": *He's not going to do it, no siree.*

si·ren /'saɪrən/ *noun* 1 a device that makes a long loud sound as a signal or warning: *an air-raid siren* ◆ *A police car raced past with its siren wailing.* 2 (in ancient Greek stories) any of a group of sea creatures that were part woman and part bird, or part woman and part fish, whose beautiful singing made sailors sail toward them into rocks or dangerous waters 3 a woman who is very attractive or beautiful but also dangerous 4 ~ **voices/song/call** (*literary*) the TEMPTATION to do something that seems very

attractive but that will have bad results: *The government must resist the siren voices calling for tax cuts.*

sir·loin /'sərlɔɪn/ (also **sirloin 'steak**) *noun* [U, C] good quality beef that is cut from a cow's back

si·roc·co /sə'rɑkoʊ/ (also **sci·roc·co**) *noun* (*pl.* **si·roc·cos, sci·roc·cos**) a hot wind that blows from Africa into southern Europe

sis /sɪs/ *noun* (*informal*) sister (used when you are speaking to her)

si·sal /'sɪsl; 'saɪ-/ *noun* [U] strong FIBERS made from the leaves of a tropical plant also called sisal, used for making rope, floor coverings, etc.

sis·sy /'sɪsi/ *noun* (*pl.* **sis·sies**) (*informal, disapproving*) a boy that people laugh at because they think he is weak or frightened, or only interested in the kinds of things girls like **SYN** WIMP ▶ **sis·sy** *adj.*

sis·ter 🔑 /'sɪstər/ *noun*
1 a girl or woman who has the same mother and father as another person: *She's my sister.* ◆ *an older/younger sister* ◆ (*informal*) *a big/little/kid sister* ◆ *We're sisters.* ◆ *Do you have any brothers or sisters?* ◆ *My best friend has been like a sister to me* (= very close). ⊃ see also HALF-SISTER, STEPSISTER
2 used for talking to or about other members of a women's organization or other women who have the same ideas, purpose, etc. as yourself: *They supported their sisters in the dispute.* 3 **Sister** a female member of a religious group, especially a NUN: *Sister Mary* ◆ *the Sisters of Charity* 4 a member of a SORORITY (= a club for a group of female students at a college or university) 5 (*informal*) used by black people as a form of address for a black woman 6 (usually used as an adjective) a thing that belongs to the same type or group as something else: *our sister company in Italy* ◆ *a sister ship*

sister 'city (also **twin 'town**) *noun* one of two towns or cities in different countries that have a special relationship with each other: *Okayama is San Jose's sister city in Japan.*

sis·ter·hood /'sɪstər.hʊd/ *noun* 1 [U] the close loyal relationship between women who share ideas and aims 2 [C] a group of women who live in a community together, especially a religious one

sister-in-ˌlaw *noun* (*pl.* **ˌsisters-in-ˌlaw**) the sister of your husband or wife; your brother's wife; the wife of your husband or wife's brother ⊃ compare BROTHER-IN-LAW

sis·ter·ly /'sɪstərli/ *adj.* typical of or like a sister: *She gave him a sisterly kiss.*

Sis·y·phe·an /ˌsɪsə'fiən/ *adj.* (of a task) impossible to complete **ORIGIN** From the Greek myth in which Sisyphus was punished for the bad things he had done in his life with the never-ending task of rolling a large stone to the top of a hill, from which it always rolled down again.

sit 🔑 /sɪt/ *verb* (**sit·ting, sat, sat** /sæt/)
▷ **ON CHAIR, ETC. 1** [I] to be in a position on a chair, etc. in which the upper part of your body is upright and your weight is supported at the bottom of your back: *She sat and stared at the letter in front of her.* ◆ + **adv./prep.** *May I sit here?* ◆ *Just sit still!* ◆ *He went and sat beside her.* ◆ *She was sitting at her desk.* ◆ ~ **doing sth** *We sat talking for hours.* ⊃ see also 2 [T] ~ **sb** + **adv./prep.** to put someone in a sitting position: *He lifted the child and sat her on the wall.*
▷ **OF THINGS 3** [I] to be in a particular place: + **adv./prep.** *A large bus was sitting outside.* ◆ *The pot was sitting in a pool of water.* ◆ *The jacket sat beautifully on her shoulders* (= fitted well). ◆ + **adj.** *The box sat unopened on the shelf.*
▷ **HAVE OFFICIAL POSITION 4** [I] to have an official position as something or as a member of something: ~ **as sth** *He was sitting as a temporary judge.* ◆ ~ **in/on sth** *She sat on a number of committees.*
▷ **OF A GOVERNING BODY, ETC. 5** [I] (of a governing body, committee, court of law, etc.) to meet in order to do official business: *The legislature sits for less than six months of the year.*
▷ **OF BIRD 6** [I] (+ **adv./prep.**) to rest on a branch, etc. or to stay on a nest to keep the eggs warm

> **OF DOG 7** [I] to sit on the back part of its body with its front legs straight: *Rover! Sit!*
> **TAKE CARE OF CHILDREN 8** [I] ~ **(for sb)** = BABYSIT: *Who's sitting for you?* ⊃ see also HOUSE-SIT

IDM be sitting pretty (*informal*) to be in a good situation, especially when others are not sit at sb's feet to admire someone very much, especially a teacher or someone from whom you try to learn sit comfortably/easily/well, etc. (with sth) to seem right, natural, suitable, etc. in a particular place or situation: *His views did not sit comfortably with the management line.* sit in judgment (on/over/upon sb) to decide whether someone's behavior is right or wrong, when you have no right to do this: *How dare you sit in judgment on me?* sit on the fence to avoid becoming involved in deciding or influencing something: *He tends to sit on the fence at meetings.* sit tight **1** to stay where you are rather than moving away or changing position: *We sat tight and waited to be rescued.* **2** to stay in the same situation, without changing your mind or taking any action: *Shareholders are being advised to sit tight until the crisis passes.* ⊃ more at BOLT, LAUREL, SILENTLY

PHR V ,sit a'round (often *disapproving*) to spend time doing nothing very useful: *I'm far too busy to sit around here.* ◆ ~ doing sth *He just sits around watching TV.* ,sit 'back **1** to sit on something, usually a chair, in a relaxed position: *He sat back in his chair and started to read.* **2** to relax, especially by not getting too involved in or anxious about something: *She's not the kind of person who can sit back and let others do all the work.* ,sit 'by to take no action to stop something bad or wrong from happening: *We cannot just sit by and watch this tragedy happen.* ,sit 'down | ,sit yourself 'down to move from a standing position to a sitting position: *Please sit down.* ◆ *He sat down on the bed.* ◆ *They sat down to consider the problem.* ◆ *Come in and sit yourselves down.* ,sit 'down and do sth to give something time and attention in order to try to solve a problem or achieve something: *This is something that we should sit down and discuss as a team.* 'sit for sb/sth [no passive] to be a model for an artist or a photographer: *I sat for your portrait* ◆ *She sat for Augustus John.* ,sit 'in for sb to do someone's job or perform their duties while they are away, sick, etc. **SYN** STAND IN FOR ,sit 'in on sth to attend a meeting, class, etc. in order to listen to or learn from it rather than to take an active part 'sit on sth (*informal*) to have received a letter, report, etc. from someone and then not replied or taken any action concerning it: *They have been sitting on my application for a month now.* ,sit sth↔'out **1** to stay in a place and wait for something unpleasant or boring to finish: *We sat out the storm in a café.* **2** to not take part in a dance, game, or other activity 'sit through sth to stay until the end of a performance, speech, meeting, etc. that you think is boring or too long: *We had to sit through nearly two hours of speeches.* ,sit 'up **1** to be or move yourself into a sitting position, rather than lying down or leaning back: *Sit up straight—don't slouch.* **2** to not go to bed until later than usual: *We sat up half the night, talking.* ,sit 'up (and do sth) (*informal*) to start to pay careful attention to what is happening, being said, etc.: *The proposal had made his clients sit up and take notice.* ,sit sb 'up to move someone into a sitting position after they have been lying down

THESAURUS

sit

sit down ◆ be seated ◆ have/take a seat ◆ perch

These words all mean to rest your weight on your bottom with your back upright, for example on a chair.

sit to rest your weight on your bottom with your back upright, for example on a chair: *May I sit here? ◆ Sit still, will you!* **NOTE** Sit is usually used with an adverb or a prepositional phrase to show where or how someone sits, but sometimes another phrase or clause is used to show what someone does while they are sitting: *We sat talking for hours.*

sit down to move from a standing position to a sitting position: *Please sit down.*

be seated (*formal*) to be sitting: *She was seated at the head of the table.* **NOTE** Be seated is often used as a formal way of inviting someone to sit down: *Please be seated.*

have/take a seat to sit down **NOTE** Have/Take a seat is used especially as a polite way of inviting someone to sit down: *Please have a seat.*

perch (*somewhat informal*) to sit on something, especially on the edge of something: *She perched herself on the edge of the bed.* **NOTE** Perch is always used with an adverb or prepositional phrase to show where someone is perching.

PATTERNS

- to sit/sit down/be seated/have a seat/take a seat/ perch **on** sth
- to sit/sit down/be seated/have a seat/take a seat **in** sth

GRAMMAR

sit

- You can use *on*, *in*, and *at* with **sit**. You **sit on** a chair, a step, the edge of the table, etc. You **sit in** an armchair. If you are **sitting at** a table, desk, etc., you are sitting in a chair close to it, usually so that you can eat a meal, do some work, etc.

si·tar /sɪˈtɑr/ *noun* a musical instrument from S. Asia like a GUITAR, with a long neck and two sets of metal strings ⊃ picture at INSTRUMENT

sit·com /ˈsɪtkɑm/ (also *formal* ,situation 'comedy) *noun* [C, U] a regular program on television that shows the same characters in different amusing situations

'sit-down *adj.* [only before noun] **1** used to describe a meal at which you sit at a table: *a sit-down meal for 50 wedding guests* **2** used to describe a protest in which a group of people sit down in a public place and refuse to move until their demands are listened to: *a sit-down protest*

site 🔑 **AWL** /saɪt/ *noun, verb*
- *noun* **1** a place where a building, town, etc. was, is, or will be located: *the site of a sixteenth century abbey ◆ to work on a building/construction site ◆ A site has been chosen for the new school. ◆ All the materials are on site so that work can start immediately.* ⊃ thesaurus box at PLACE **2** a place where something has happened or that is used for something: *the site of the battle ◆ an archaeological site ◆ a camping site* **3** (*computing*) a place on the Internet where a company, an organization, a university, etc. puts information ⊃ collocations at E-MAIL ⊃ see also MIRROR SITE, WEB SITE
- *verb* [often passive] ~ sth + adv./prep. to build or place something in a particular position: *There was a meeting to discuss the siting of the new school. ◆ The castle is magnificently sited high up on a cliff.*

'sit-in *noun* a protest in which a group of workers, students, etc. refuse to leave their factory, college, etc. until people listen to their demands: *to hold/stage a sit-in*

sit·ter /ˈsɪtər/ *noun* **1** a person who sits or stands somewhere so that someone can paint a picture of them or photograph them **2** = BABYSITTER

sit·ting /ˈsɪtɪŋ/ *noun* **1** a period of time during which a court or a governing body deals with its business **2** a time when a meal is served in a hotel, etc. to a number of people at the same time: *A hundred people can be served at one sitting* (= at the same time). **3** a period of time that a person spends sitting and doing an activity: *I read the book in one sitting.* **4** a period of time when someone sits or stands to have their picture painted or be photographed

,sitting 'duck (also ,sitting 'target) *noun* a person or thing that is easy to attack

'sitting ,room *noun* (*old-fashioned*) = LIVING ROOM

si·tu ➔ IN SITU

sit·u·ate /ˈsɪtʃuˌeɪt/ verb (formal) **1** ~ sth + adv./prep. to build or place something in a particular position **2** ~ sth + adv./prep. to consider how an idea, event, etc. is related to other things that influence your view of it: *Let me try and situate the events in their historical context.*

sit·u·at·ed /ˈsɪtʃuˌeɪtəd/ adj. [not before noun] **1** in a particular place or position: *My bedroom was situated on the top floor of the house.* ◆ *The hotel is **beautifully situated** in a quiet spot near the river.* ◆ *All the best theaters and restaurants are situated within a few minutes' walk of each other.* **2** (formal) (of a person, an organization, etc.) in a particular situation or in particular circumstances: *Small businesses are well situated to benefit from the single market.*

sit·u·a·tion 🔑 /ˌsɪtʃuˈeɪʃn/ noun
1 all the circumstances and things that are happening at a particular time and in a particular place: *to be **in a** difficult situation* ◆ *You could get into **a** situation where you have to decide immediately.* ◆ *We have all been in similar embarrassing situations.* ◆ *the current **economic/financial/political, etc. situation*** ◆ *He could see no way out of the situation.* ◆ *In your situation, I would look for another job.* ◆ *What we have here is a crisis situation.* ◆ *I'm in a **no-win situation** (= whatever I do will be bad for me).* **2** (formal) the kind of area or surroundings that a building or town has: *The town is in a delightful situation in a wide green valley.*

THESAURUS

situation

circumstances ◆ position ◆ conditions ◆ things ◆ the case ◆ state of affairs

These are all words for the conditions and facts that are connected with and affect the way things are.

situation all the things that are happening at a particular time and in a particular place: *the current economic situation*

circumstances the facts that are connected with and affect a situation, an event, or an action; the conditions of a person's life, especially the money they have: *The ship sank in mysterious circumstances.*

position the situation that someone is in, especially when it affects what they can and cannot do: *She knew that she was in a position of power.*

conditions the circumstances in which people live, work, or do things; the physical situation that affects how something happens: *We were forced to work outside in freezing conditions.*

CIRCUMSTANCES OR CONDITIONS?

Circumstances often refers to someone's financial situation; **conditions** are things such as the quality and amount of food or shelter they have. The **circumstances** that affect an event are the facts surrounding it; the **conditions** that affect it are usually physical ones, such as the weather.

things (somewhat informal) the general situation, as it affects someone: *Hi, Jane! How are things?* ◆ *Think things over before you decide.*

the case the true situation: *If that is the case (= if the situation described is true), we need more staff.*

state of affairs a situation: *Well, this is certainly a sorry state of affairs.*

SITUATION OR STATE OF AFFAIRS?

State of affairs is mostly used with *this*. It is also used with adjectives describing how good or bad a situation is, such as *happy, sorry, shocking,* and *sad,* as well as those relating to time, such as *present* and *current.* **Situation** is much more frequent and is used in a wider variety of contexts.

▶ **sit·u·a·tion·al** /-ʃənl/ adj.

situation ˈcomedy noun [C, U] (formal) = SITCOM

ˈsit-up noun an exercise for making your stomach muscles strong, in which you lie on your back on the floor and raise the top part of your body to a sitting position ➔ picture at EXERCISE ➔ compare CRUNCH n. (4)

six /sɪks/ number
6 HELP There are examples of how to use numbers at the entry for **five**.
IDM **be six feet under** (informal) to be dead and in a grave **it's six of one and half a dozen of the other** (saying) used to say that there is not much real difference between two possible choices

six-ˈfigure adj. [only before noun] used to describe a number that is 100,000 or more: *a six-figure salary*

six·fold /ˈsɪksfoʊld; ˌsɪksˈfoʊld/ adj., adv. ➔ -FOLD

ˈsix-gun noun = SIX-SHOOTER

ˈsix-pack noun **1** a set of six bottles or cans sold together, especially of beer **2** (informal) stomach muscles that are very strong and that you can see clearly across someone's stomach ➔ see also JOE SIX-PACK

ˈsix-ˌshooter (also **ˈsix-gun**) noun a small gun that holds six bullets

six·teen /ˌsɪksˈtin/ number
16 ▶ **six·teenth** /ˌsɪksˈtinθ/ ordinal number, noun
HELP There are examples of how to use ordinal numbers at the entry for **fifth**.

ˌsix·teenth ˈnote noun (music) a note that lasts half as long as an EIGHTH NOTE ➔ picture at MUSIC

sixth /sɪksθ/ ordinal number, noun
● *ordinal number* 6th HELP There are examples of how to use ordinal numbers at the entry for **fifth**.
● *noun* each of six equal parts of something

ˌsixth ˈsense noun [sing.] a special ability to know something without using any of the five senses that include sight, touch, etc.: *My sixth sense told me to stay here and wait.*

six·ty /ˈsɪksti/ **1** number 60 **2** noun the **sixties** [pl.] numbers, years, or temperatures from 60 to 69 ▶ **six·ti·eth** /ˈsɪkstiəθ/ ordinal number, noun HELP There are examples of how to use ordinal numbers at the entry for **fifth**.
IDM **in your sixties** between the ages of 60 and 69

the ˌsixty-four ˌthousand ˌdollar ˈquestion noun (informal) the thing that people most want to know, or that is most important ORIGIN From the name of a U.S. television show of the 1950s that gave prizes of money to people who answered questions correctly. The correct answer to the last question was worth $64,000. (The original term was **the $64 question**, from a radio show of the 1940s, in which the top prize was $64.)

siz·a·ble (also **size·a·ble**) /ˈsaɪzəbl/ adj. fairly large SYN CONSIDERABLE: *The town has a sizable Sikh population.*

size 🔑 /saɪz/ noun, verb
● *noun*
> HOW LARGE/SMALL **1** [U, C] how large or small a person or thing is: *an area **the size of** (= the same size as) Rhode Island* ◆ *They complained about the size of their gas bill.* ◆ *Dogs come in all shapes and sizes.* ◆ *The facilities are excellent for a town that size.* ◆ *The kitchen is **a good size** (= not small).* ◆ *It's similar in size to a tomato.* **2** [U] the large amount or extent of

---

something: *You should have seen the size of their house!* ♦ *We were shocked at the size of his debts.*

> **OF CLOTHES/SHOES/GOODS 3** [C] one of a number of standard measurements in which clothes, shoes, and other goods are made and sold: *The jacket was the wrong size.* ♦ *It's not my size.* ♦ *They didn't have the jacket in my size.* ♦ *She's a size 12 in clothes.* ♦ *The hats are made in three sizes: small, medium and large.* ♦ *I need a bigger/smaller size.* ♦ *What size do you take/wear?* ♦ *She takes/wears a size 5 shoe.* ♦ *Do you have these shoes in (a) size 5?* ♦ *Try this one for size* (= to see if it is the correct size). ♦ *The glass can be cut to size* (= cut to the exact measurements) *for you.* **HELP** To ask about the size of something, you usually say: *How big?* You use: *What size?* to ask about something that is produced in fixed measurements.

> **-SIZED/-SIZE 4** (in adjectives) having the size mentioned: *a medium-sized house* ♦ *Cut it into bite-size pieces.* ⊃ see also KING-SIZE, MAN-SIZED, PINT-SIZED, QUEEN-SIZE

> **STICKY SUBSTANCE 5** [U] a sticky substance that is used for making material stiff or for preparing walls for WALLPAPER **IDM** **cut sb down to size** to show someone that they are not as important as they think they are **that's about the size of it** (*informal*) that's how the situation seems to be: *"So they won't pay up?" "That's about the size of it."*

● *verb*

> **GIVE SIZE 1** [usually passive] **~ sth** to mark the size of something; to give a size to something: *The screws are sized in millimeters.*

> **CHANGE SIZE 2** [usually passive] **~ sth** to change the size of something: *The fonts can be sized according to what effect you want.*

> **MAKE STICKY 3 ~ sth** to cover something with a sticky substance called size **PHRV** ˌsize sb/sth↔'up (*informal*) to form a judgment or an opinion about someone or something: *She knew that he was looking at her, sizing her up.* ♦ *He sized up the situation very quickly.*

ˌsize 'zero *noun* [U, C] the smallest size for women's clothes, used to describe women who are extremely thin: *size zero models and celebrities* ♦ *She is a size zero.*

siz·zle /ˈsɪzl/ *verb* [I] to make the sound of food frying in hot oil: *sizzling sausages* ▸ **sizzle** *noun* [sing.]

siz·zling /ˈsɪzlɪŋ/ *adj.* **1** very hot: *sizzling summer temperatures* **2** very exciting: *a sizzling love affair*

ska /skɑ/ *noun* [U] a type of fast popular music with strong rhythms, developed in Jamaica in the 1960s and that developed into REGGAE

skate /skeɪt/ *verb, noun*

● *verb* **1** [I, T] to move on skates (usually referring to ICE SKATING, if no other information is given): *Can you skate?* ♦ *It was so cold that we were able to go skating on the lake.* ♦ **~ sth** *He skated an exciting program at the American Championships.* **2** [I] to ride on a SKATEBOARD **IDM** see THIN **PHRV** ˌskate 'over sth to avoid talking about or considering a difficult subject: *He politely skated over the issue.*

● *noun* **1** = ICE SKATE, ROLLER SKATE: *a pair of skates* ⊃ picture at SPORT **2** (*pl.* skate or skates) a large flat sea fish that can be eaten

skate·board /ˈskeɪtbɔrd/ *noun* a short narrow board with small wheels at each end, which you stand on and ride as a sport: *a skateboard park/ramp* ▸ **skate·board** *verb* [I] **skate·board·er** *noun* **skate·board·ing** *noun* [U]: *a skateboarding magazine* ⊃ picture at HOBBY

skate·park /ˈskeɪtpɑrk/ *noun* an area built for people to use SKATEBOARDS, with slopes, curves, etc.

skat·er /ˈskeɪtər/ *noun* **1** a person who skates for pleasure or as a sport: *a figure/speed skater* ⊃ see also **2** = SKATE-BOARDER: *Extreme skaters perform jumps, spins, flips, etc.*

ˈskate shoe *noun* a sports shoe that is used for SKATEBOARDING

skat·ing /ˈskeɪtɪŋ/ *noun* [U] **1** (also ˈice ˌskating) the sport or activity of moving on ice on SKATES: *to go skating* ⊃ see also

FIGURE SKATING, SPEED SKATING **2** = ROLLER SKATING **IDM** see THIN

ˈskating ˌrink (also rink) *noun* **1** = ICE RINK **2** an area or a building where you can ROLLER SKATE

ske·dad·dle /skɪˈdædl/ *verb* [I] (*informal*, *humorous*) to move away or leave a place quickly, especially in order to avoid someone

skee·ter /ˈskitər/ *noun* (*informal*, *humorous*) = MOSQUITO

ˈskeet shooting /ˈskit ʃutɪŋ/ *noun* a sport in which a disk of baked clay (called a **clay pigeon**) is thrown into the air for people to shoot at

skein /skeɪn/ *noun* a long piece of wool, thread, or YARN that is loosely tied together

skel·e·tal /ˈskɛlətl/ *adj.* **1** (*technical*) connected with the skeleton of a person or an animal **2** looking like a skeleton: *skeletal figures dressed in rags* **3** that exists only in a basic form, as an outline: *He has written only a skeletal plot for the book so far.*

skel·e·ton /ˈskɛlətn/ *noun* **1** [C] the structure of bones that supports the body of a person or an animal; a model of this structure: *The human skeleton consists of 206 bones.* ♦ *a dinosaur skeleton* ⊃ picture at BODY **2** [C] (*informal*) a very thin person or animal **3** [C, usually sing.] the main structure that supports a building, etc. **SYN** FRAMEWORK: *Only the concrete skeleton of the factory remained.* **4** [C, usually sing.] the basic outline of a plan, piece of writing, etc. to which more details can be added later: *Examples were used to flesh out the skeleton of the argument.* **5** [C] **~ staff, crew, etc.** the smallest number of people, etc. that you need to do something: *There will only be a skeleton staff on duty over the holiday.* ♦ *We managed to operate a skeleton bus service during the strike.* **6** [C] (*sports*) a type of SLED (= a vehicle for sliding over ice) for racing, used by one person lying on their front with their feet pointing backward **7** [U] the sport or event of racing down a special track of ice on a skeleton: *Canada won gold and silver in the skeleton.* **IDM** **a skeleton in the closet** (*informal*) something shocking, embarrassing, etc. that has happened to you or your family in the past that you want to keep secret

ˈskeleton ˌkey *noun* a key that will open several different locks

skep·tic /ˈskɛptɪk/ *noun* a person who usually doubts that claims or statements are true, especially those that other people believe in

skep·ti·cal /ˈskɛptɪkl/ *adj.* **~ (about/of sth)** having doubts that a claim or statement is true or that something will happen: *I am skeptical about his chances of winning.* ♦ *The public remain skeptical of these claims.* ♦ *She looked highly skeptical.* ▸ **skep·ti·cal·ly** /-kli/ *adv.*

skep·ti·cism /ˈskɛptəˌsɪzəm/ *noun* [U, sing.] an attitude of doubting that claims or statements are true or that something will happen: *Such claims should be regarded with a certain amount of skepticism.*

sketch /skɛtʃ/ *noun, verb*

● *noun* **1** a simple picture that is drawn quickly and does not have many details: *The artist is making sketches for his next painting.* ⊃ thesaurus box at PICTURE ⊃ collocations at ART **2** a short funny scene on television, in the theater, etc.: *The drama group did a sketch about a couple buying a new car.* **3** a short report or story that gives only basic details about something: *a biographical sketch of the actor*

● *verb* **1** [T, I] **~ (sb/sth)** to make a quick drawing of someone or something: *He quickly sketched the view from the window.* **2** [T] **~ sth (out)** to give a general description of something, giving only the basic facts **SYN** OUTLINE: *She sketched out her plan for tackling the problem.* **PHRV** ˌsketch sth↔'in to give more information or details about something

sketch·book /ˈskɛtʃbʊk/ (also ˈsketch pad) *noun* a book of sheets of paper for drawing on

sketch·y /ˈskɛtʃi/ *adj.* (sketch·i·er, sketch·i·est) **1** not complete or detailed and therefore not very useful

SYN ROUGH: *He gave us a very sketchy account of his visit.* ◆ *sketchy notes* **2** (*informal*) likely to be dangerous: *We spotted a couple of sketchy guys down the street.* ▶ **sketch·i·ly** /-tʃəli/ *adv.* **sketch·i·ness** /-tʃinəs/ *noun* [U]

skew /skyu/ *verb* [T] **~ sth** to change or influence something with the result that it is not accurate, fair, normal, etc.: *to skew the statistics*

skew·bald /ˈskyubɔld/ *adj.* (of a horse) with areas on it of white and another color, usually not black ⊃ compare PIEBALD ▶ **skew·bald** *noun*: *He was riding a skewbald.*

skewed /skyud/ *adj.* **1** (of information) not accurate or correct **SYN** DISTORTED: *skewed statistics* **2 ~ (toward sb/ sth)** directed toward a particular place, etc. in a way that may not be accurate or fair: *The book is heavily skewed toward American readers.* **3** not straight or level: *The car had ended up skewed across the road.* ⊃ see also ASKEW

skew·er /ˈskyuər/ *noun, verb*
• *noun* a long, thin, pointed piece of metal or wood that is pushed through pieces of meat, vegetables, etc. to hold them together while they are cooking, or used to test whether something is completely cooked
• *verb* **1** to push a skewer or other thin pointed object through something **~ sb/sth | ~ sb/sth to sth 2 ~ sb/sth** (*informal*) to criticize someone or something severely: *The movie was skewered for its bad acting.*

ski /ski/ *noun, adj., verb*
• *noun* (*pl.* **skis**) **1** one of a pair of long narrow pieces of wood, metal, or plastic that you attach to boots so that you can move smoothly over snow: *a pair of skis* ⊃ picture at SPORT **2** = WATERSKI
• *adj.* [only before noun] connected with the sport of skiing: *ski boots* ◆ *the ski slopes*
• *verb* (**ski·ing, skied, skied**) **1** [I] **(+ adv./prep.)** to move over snow on skis, especially as a sport **2 go skiing** [I] to spend time skiing for pleasure: *We went skiing in France in March.* ⊃ see also SKIING, WATERSKI

skid /skɪd/ *verb, noun*
• *verb* (**-dd-**) [I] (usually of a vehicle) to slide sideways or forward in an uncontrolled way: *The car skidded on the ice and went straight into the wall.* ◆ *The taxi skidded to a halt just in time.* ◆ *Her foot skidded on the wet floor and she fell heavily.*
• *noun* **1** the movement of a vehicle when it suddenly slides sideways in an uncontrolled way: *The motorcycle went into a skid.* ◆ *The skid marks on the road showed how fast the car had been traveling.* **2** a part that is underneath some aircraft, beside the wheels, and is used for landing: *the skids of a helicopter* ⊃ picture at PLANE
  IDM put the skids on sb/sth (*informal*) to stop someone or something from being successful or making progress **be on the skids** (*informal*) to be in a bad situation that will get worse ⊃ more at HIT v.

skid·pan /ˈskɪdpæn/ *noun* an area with a surface that is especially prepared so that drivers can practice controlling skids

skid ˈrow *noun* [U] (*informal*) used to describe the poorest part of a city or town, the type of place where people who have no home or job and who drink too much alcohol live: *to be on skid row*

ski·er /ˈskiər/ *noun* a person who skis

skies pl. of SKY

skiff /skɪf/ *noun* a small light boat for ROWING or sailing, usually for one person

skif·fle /ˈskɪfl/ *noun* a type of music popular in the 1950s, that was a mixture of JAZZ and FOLK MUSIC

ski·ing /ˈskiɪŋ/ *noun* [U] the sport or activity of moving over snow on skis: *to go skiing* ◆ *downhill/cross-country skiing* ◆ *a skiing instructor/lesson/vacation, etc.*

ski·jor·ing /ˈskiˌdʒɔrɪŋ/ *noun* [U] the activity of being pulled over snow or ice on skis, by a horse or dog

ˈski jump *noun* a very steep artificial slope that ends suddenly and that is covered with snow. People ski down the slope, jump off the end and see how far they can travel through the air before landing. ▶ **ˈski ˌjumper** *noun* **ˈski ˌjumping** *noun* [U]: *Is ski jumping an Olympic sport?* ◆ *the Swiss ski-jumping team*

skil·ful *adj.* (*CanE*) = SKILLFUL

ˈski lift *noun* a machine for taking SKIERS up a slope so that they can then ski down

skill 🔑 /skɪl/ *noun*
1 [U] the ability to do something well: *The job requires skill and an eye for detail.* ◆ **~ in/at sth/doing sth** *What made him remarkable as a photographer was his skill in capturing the moment.* **2** [C] a particular ability or type of ability: *We need people with practical skills like carpentry.* ◆ *management skills*

skilled 🔑 /skɪld/ *adj.*
1 having enough ability, experience, and knowledge to be able to do something well: *a skilled engineer/negotiator/ craftsman* ◆ *a shortage of skilled labor* (= people who have had training in a skill) ◆ **~ in/at sth/doing sth** *She is highly skilled at dealing with difficult customers.* **2** (of a job) needing special abilities or training **SYN** EXPERT: *Furniture-making is very skilled work.* **ANT** UNSKILLED

skil·let /ˈskɪlət/ *noun* = FRYING PAN

skill·ful 🔑 (*CanE also* **skil·ful**) /ˈskɪlfl/ *adj.*
1 (of a person) good at doing something, especially something that needs a particular ability or special training **SYN** ACCOMPLISHED: *a skillful player/performer/teacher* **2** made or done very well **SYN** PROFESSIONAL: *Thanks to her skillful handling of the affair, the problem was averted.* ▶ **skill·ful·ly** /-fəli/ *adv.*

ˈskill set *noun* a person's range of skills or abilities

skim /skɪm/ *verb* (**-mm-**) **1** [T] to remove fat, cream, etc. from the surface of a liquid: **~ sth off/from sth** *Skim the scum off the jam and let it cool.* ◆ **~ sth** *Skim the jam and let it cool.* **2** [I, T, no passive] to move quickly and lightly over a surface, not touching it or only touching it occasionally: **~ along/over, etc. sth** *We watched the birds skimming over the lake.* ◆ **~ sth** *The speedboat took off, skimming the waves.* ◆ (*figurative*) *This report has barely skimmed the surface of the subject.* ⊃ see also SKIP **3** [I, T] to read something quickly in order to find a particular point or the main points: **~ through/over sth** *He skimmed through the article trying to find his name.* ◆ **~ sth** *I always skim the financial section of the newspaper.* **4** [T] **~ sth (from sth)** (*informal*) to steal small amounts of money frequently over a period of time **5** [I, T] **~ (sth)** to illegally copy electronic information from a credit card in order to use it without the owner's permission
  PHRV **ˌskim sth/sb↔ˈoff** to take for yourself the best part of something, often in an unfair way

ˌskim ˈmilk *noun* [U] milk that contains less fat than normal because the cream has been removed from it

ski·mo·bile /ˈskɪmouˌbil/ *noun* = SNOWMOBILE

skimp /skɪmp/ *verb* [I] **~ (on sth)** to try to spend less time, money, etc. on something than is really needed: *Older people should not skimp on food or heating.*

skimp·y /ˈskɪmpi/ *adj.* (**skimp·i·er, skimp·i·est**) **1** (of clothes) very small and not covering much of your body: *a skimpy dress* **2** (*disapproving*) not large enough in amount or size: *a skimpy meal* ◆ *They provided only skimpy details.*

skin 🔑 /skɪn/ *noun, verb*
• *noun*
  ⊳ ON BODY **1** [U, C] the layer of TISSUE that covers the body: *to have dark/fair/olive, etc. skin* ◆ *The snake sheds its skin once a year.* ◆ *cosmetics for sensitive skins* ◆ *skin cancer* ⊃ collocations at PHYSICAL ⊃ see also FORESKIN
  ⊳ -SKINNED **2** (in adjectives) having the type of skin mentioned: *dark-skinned* ◆ *fair-skinned* ⊃ see also THICK-SKINNED, THIN-SKINNED
  ⊳ OF DEAD ANIMAL **3** [C, U] (often in compounds) the skin of a dead animal with or without its fur, used for making

| t **tea** | ţ **butter** | d **did** | k **cat** | g **got** | tʃ **chin** | dʒ **June** | f **fall**

leather, etc.: *The skins are removed and laid out to dry.* ◆ *a tiger skin rug*
➤ **OF FRUIT/VEGETABLES 4** [C, U] the outer layer of some fruit and vegetables: *Remove the skins by soaking the tomatoes in hot water.* ➔ compare PEEL, RIND, ZEST
➤ **OF SAUSAGE 5** [C, U] the thin outer layer of a SAUSAGE: *Prick the skins before grilling.*
➤ **ON LIQUIDS 6** [C, U] the thin layer that forms on the surface of some liquids: *A skin had formed on the top of the milk.*
➤ **OUTSIDE LAYER 7** [C] a layer that covers the outside of something: *the outer skin of the earth* ◆ *the metal skin of the aircraft* **8** [C] a special cover for any small electronic device that you can carry with you so that you can listen to music: *You can create your own custom skin for your iPod.*
➤ **IN COMPUTER PROGRAM 9** [C] (*computing*) the INTERFACE of a computer program (= the way a computer program presents information on a screen), that the user can change to suit their particular preferences
  IDM **by the skin of your teeth** (*informal*) if you do something **by the skin of your teeth**, you only just manage to do it **get under sb's skin** (*informal*) to annoy someone: *Don't let him get under your skin.* **have sb under your skin** (*informal*) to be extremely attracted to someone **it's no skin off my, your, his, etc. nose/back** (*informal*) used to say that someone is not upset or annoyed about something because it does not affect them in a bad way **make your skin crawl** to make you feel afraid or full of disgust **(nothing but/all/only) skin and bone** (*informal*) extremely thin in a way that is not attractive or healthy ➔ more at JUMP, SAVE, THICK, THIN
● *verb* (-nn-)
➤ **ANIMAL/FRUIT/VEGETABLE 1** ~ sth to take the skin off an animal, a fruit, or a vegetable: *You'll need four ripe tomatoes, skinned and chopped.*
➤ **PART OF BODY 2** ~ sth to rub the skin off part of your body by accident: *He skinned his knees climbing down the tree.* **IDM** see WAY

skin·care /ˈskɪnker/ *noun* [U] the use of creams and special products to take care of your skin

skin-ˈdeep *adj.* [not usually before noun] (of a feeling or an attitude) not as important or strongly felt as it appears to be **SYN** SUPERFICIAL **IDM** see BEAUTY

skin-ˈdiving *noun* [U] the sport or activity of swimming underwater with simple breathing equipment but without a special suit for protection: *to go skin-diving* ▸ ˈskin-diver *noun*

skin·flint /ˈskɪnflɪnt/ *noun* (*informal, disapproving*) a person who does not like spending money **SYN** MISER

skin graft *noun* a medical operation in which healthy skin is taken from one part of someone's body and placed over another part to replace skin that has been burned or damaged; a piece of skin that is moved in this way

skin·head /ˈskɪnhed/ *noun* a young person with very short hair, especially one who is violent, aggressive, and racist (RACISM)

skink /skɪŋk/ *noun* a LIZARD with short legs or with no legs

skin·ny /ˈskɪni/ *adj., noun*
● *adj.* (skin·ni·er, skin·ni·est) **1** (*informal, usually disapproving*) very thin, especially in a way that you find unpleasant or ugly: *skinny legs* **2** (of clothes) designed to fit closely to the body: *a skinny sweater* **3** (*informal*) low in fat: *a skinny latte*
● *noun* [U] the ~ (on sb/sth) (*informal*) information about someone or something, especially details that are not generally known: *This book gives you the skinny on Hollywood.*

skinny-ˈdipping *noun* [U] (*informal*) swimming without any clothes on

skin·tight /ˌskɪnˈtaɪt/ *adj.* (of clothes) fitting very closely to the body

skip /skɪp/ *verb, noun*
● *verb* (-pp-)
➤ **MOVE WITH JUMPS 1** [I] (+ adv./prep.) to move forward lightly and quickly making a little jump with each step: *She skipped happily along beside me.*
➤ **NOT DO SOMETHING 2** [T] ~ sth to not do something that you usually do or should do: *I often skip breakfast altogether.* ◆ *She decided to skip the afternoon class.* **3** [T, I] to leave out something that would normally be the next thing that you would do, read, etc.: ~ sth *You can skip the next chapter if you have covered the topic in class.* ◆ ~ over sth *I skipped over the last part of the book.* ◆ ~ to sth *I suggest we skip to the last item on the agenda.*
➤ **CHANGE QUICKLY 4** [I] + adv./prep. to move from one place to another or from one subject to another very quickly: *She kept skipping from one topic of conversation to another.*
➤ **LEAVE SECRETLY 5** [T] ~ sth to leave a place secretly or suddenly: *The bombers skipped the country shortly after the blast.*
➤ **STONES 6** [T] ~ sth (across, over, etc. sth) to make a flat stone jump across the surface of water: *The boys were skipping stones across the pond.*
  IDM **skip it** (*informal*) used to tell someone rudely that you do not want to talk about something or repeat what you have said: *"What were you saying?" "Oh, skip it!"* **IDM** see BAIL ➔ more at HEART, ROPE *n.*
  PHR V ˌskip ˈoff/ˈout to leave secretly or suddenly ˌskip ˈout on sb to leave someone, especially when they need you
● *noun* a skipping movement: *She gave a skip and a jump and was off down the street.* **IDM** see HOP *n.*

ˈski pants *noun* [pl.] **1** pants worn for skiing **2** narrow pants made from a type of cloth that stretches and with a part that goes under the foot

ˈski-plane *noun* a plane with two parts like skis fixed to the bottom so that it can land on snow or ice

ˈski pole *noun* a stick used to push yourself forward while skiing

skip·per /ˈskɪpər/ *noun, verb*
● *noun* **1** the captain of a small ship or fishing boat **2** (*informal*) the captain or manager of a sports team
● *verb* ~ sth to be the captain of a boat, or to head a sports team, etc.: *to skipper a yacht* ◆ *He skippered the team to victory.*

skir·mish /ˈskɜrmɪʃ/ *noun, verb*
● *noun* **1** a short fight between small groups of soldiers, etc., especially one that is not planned **2** a short argument, especially between political opponents
● *verb* [I] to take part in a short fight or argument ▸ skir-mish·er *noun* skir·mish·ing *noun* [U]: *There are reports of skirmishing along the border.*

skirt /skɜrt/ *noun, verb*
● *noun* **1** [C] a piece of clothing for a woman or girl that hangs from the waist: *a long/short/straight/pleated, etc. skirt* ➔ picture at CLOTHES **2** [C] also skirts [pl.] the part of a dress, coat, etc. that hangs below the waist **3** [C] an outer covering or part used to protect the base of a vehicle or machine: *the rubber skirt around the bottom of a hovercraft* ➔ picture at BOAT
● *verb* **1** [T, I] to be or go around the edge of something: ~ sth *They followed the road that skirted the lake.* ◆ ~ around sth *I skirted around the field and crossed the bridge.* **2** [T, I] to avoid talking about a subject, especially because it is difficult or embarrassing: ~ sth *He carefully skirted the issue of where they would live.* ◆ ~ around sth *She tactfully skirted around the subject of money.*

ˈski run (also run) *noun* a track that is marked on a slope that you ski down

skit /skɪt/ *noun* ~ (on sth) a short piece of humorous writing or a performance that makes fun of someone or something by copying them: *a skit on daytime TV programs*

'ski tow *noun* **1** a machine that pulls you up the mountain on your skis **2** a rope that pulls you when you are WATER-SKIING

skit·ter /'skɪtər/ *verb* [I] + **adv./prep.** to run or move very quickly and lightly

skit·tish /'skɪtɪʃ/ *adj.* **1** (of horses) easily excited or frightened and therefore difficult to control **2** (of people) not very serious and with ideas and feelings that keep changing **3** (*business*) likely to change suddenly: *skittish financial markets* ▶ **skit·tish·ly** *adv.* **skit·tish·ness** *noun* [U]

Skiv·vies™ /'skɪviz/ *noun* [pl.] (*informal*) underwear, especially men's underwear

sku·a /'skyuə/ *noun* a large brown bird that lives near the ocean. It eats fish, which it sometimes takes from other birds.

skul·dug·ger·y (also **skull·dug·ger·y**) /skʌl'dʌgəri/ *noun* [U] (*old-fashioned* or *humorous*) dishonest behavior or activities

skulk /skʌlk/ *verb* [I] + **adv./prep.** (*disapproving*) to hide or move around secretly, especially when you are planning something bad: *There was someone skulking behind the bushes.*

skull /skʌl/ *noun* **1** the bone structure that forms the head and surrounds and protects the brain **SYN** CRANIUM ⊃ picture at BODY: *a fractured skull* **2** (*informal*) the head or the brain: *Her skull was crammed with too many thoughts.* ♦ (*informal*) *When will he get it through his thick skull that I never want to see him again!*

skull and 'crossbones *noun* [sing.] a picture of a human skull above two crossed bones, used in the past on the flags of PIRATE ships, and now used as a warning on containers with dangerous substances inside

skull·cap /'skʌlkæp/ *noun* a small round cap worn on top of the head, especially by some male Jews and by Catholic BISHOPS ⊃ see also YARMULKE

skull·dug·ger·y = SKULDUGGERY

skunk /skʌŋk/ (also *informal* **pole·cat**) *noun* a small black and white N. American animal that can produce a strong unpleasant smell to defend itself when it is attacked **IDM** see DRUNK

skunk ⟨illustration⟩

'skunk ¡cabbage *noun* [C, U] a N. American plant that grows in wet areas, the flower of which has a strong unpleasant smell

skunk·works /'skʌŋkwərks/ *noun* (*pl.* **skunk·works**) (*informal*) a small laboratory or department of a large company used for doing new scientific research or developing new products

sky ✎ /skaɪ/ *noun, verb*
• *noun* [C, U] (*pl.* **skies**) the space above the earth that you can see when you look up, where clouds and the sun, moon, and stars appear **HELP** You usually say **the sky**. When **sky** is used with an adjective, use **a… sky**. You can also use the plural form **skies**, especially when you are thinking about the great extent of the sky: *What's that in the sky?* ♦ *The sky suddenly went dark and it started to rain.* ♦ *the night sky* ♦ *a cloudless sky* ♦ *cloudless skies* ♦ *a land of blue skies and sunshine* ♦ *The skies above the river were ablaze with a spectacular firework display.* ⊃ collocations at WEATHER **IDM** the sky's the limit (*informal*) there is no limit to what someone can achieve, earn, do, etc.: *With a talent like his, the sky's the limit.* ⊃ more at GREAT, PIE, PRAISE
• *verb* (**skies, sky·ing, skied, skied**) ~ **sth** to hit a ball very high into the air: *She skied her tee shot.*

sky-'blue *adj.* bright blue in color, like the sky on a clear day ▶ ¡sky 'blue *noun* [U]

sky·box /'skaɪbɑks/ *noun* an area of expensive seats, separated from other areas, high up in a sports ground

sky·cap /'skaɪkæp/ *noun* a person whose job is to carry people's bags at an airport

sky·div·ing /'skaɪˌdaɪvɪŋ/ *noun* [U] a sport in which you jump from a plane and fall for as long as you safely can before opening your PARACHUTE: *to go skydiving* ⊃ picture at SPORT ▶ **sky·div·er** *noun*

¡sky-'high *adj.* very high; too high: *His confidence is still sky-high.* ♦ *sky-high interest rates* ▶ ¡sky-'high *adv.*: *After the election, prices went sky-high.*

sky·lark /'skaɪlɑrk/ *noun* a small bird that sings while it flies high up in the sky

sky·light /'skaɪlaɪt/ *noun* a small window in a roof ⊃ picture at HOUSE

sky·line /'skaɪlaɪn/ *noun* the outline of buildings, trees, hills, etc. seen against the sky: *the New York skyline*

'sky ¡marshal *noun* = AIR MARSHAL

Skype™ /skaɪp/ *noun* [U] a telephone system that works by direct communication between users' computers on the Internet, without the need for a central SERVER ⊃ compare VoIP

sky·rock·et /'skaɪˌrɑkət/ *verb* [I] (of prices, etc.) to rise quickly to a very high level

sky·scrap·er /'skaɪˌskreɪpər/ *noun* a very tall building in a city ⊃ picture at BUILDING

'sky ¡surfing *noun* [U] the sport of jumping from a plane and traveling through the air on a board before landing with a PARACHUTE

sky·ward /'skaɪwərd/ (also **sky·wards**) *adv.* toward the sky; up into the sky: *She pointed skyward.* ♦ *The rocket soared skywards.*

SLA /ˌɛs ɛl 'eɪ/ *abbr.* (*linguistics*) SECOND LANGUAGE ACQUISITION

slab /slæb/ *noun* **1** a thick flat piece of stone, wood, or other hard material: *a slab of marble/concrete, etc.* ♦ *The road was paved with smooth stone slabs.* ♦ *paving slabs* ♦ *a dead body on the slab* (= on a table in a MORTUARY) **2** a thick, flat slice or piece of something: *a slab of chocolate* ♦ *slabs of meat*

slack /slæk/ *adj., noun, verb*
• *adj.* (**slack·er, slack·est**) **1** not stretched tight **SYN** LOOSE: *She was staring into space, her mouth slack.* ♦ *The rope suddenly went slack.* ♦ *slack muscles* **2** (of business) not having many customers or sales; not busy: *a slack period* **3** (*disapproving*) not putting enough care, attention, or energy into something and so not doing it well enough: *He's been very slack in his work lately.* ♦ *Discipline in the classroom is very slack.* ▶ **slack·ly** *adv.*: *Her arms hung slackly by her sides.* **slack·ness** *noun* [U]
• *noun* [U] **1** the part of a rope, etc. that is hanging loosely: *There's too much slack in the tow rope.* **2** people, money, or space that should be used more fully in an organization: *There's very little slack in the budget.* **3** very small pieces of coal ⊃ see also SLACKS **IDM** cut sb some slack (*informal*) to be less critical of someone or less strict with them: *Hey, cut him some slack! He's doing his best!* take up the slack **1** to improve the way money or people are used in an organization **2** to pull on a rope, etc. until it is tight
• *verb* [I] to work less hard than you usually do or should do **PHRV** ¡slack 'off (on sth) to do something more slowly or with less energy than before

slack·en /'slækən/ *verb* **1** [I, T] to gradually become, or to make something become, slower, less active, etc. **SYN** RELAX: ~ (**off**) *We've been really busy, but things are starting to slacken off now.* ♦ ~ **sth** *She slackened her pace a little* (= walked a little more slowly). **2** [I, T] to become or to make something become less tight **SYN** LOOSEN: *His grip slackened and she pulled away from him.* ♦ ~ **sth** *He slackened the ropes slightly.*

slack·er /'slækər/ *noun* (*informal, disapproving*) a person who is lazy and avoids work

slack-jawed /'slæk dʒɔd/ adj. having your mouth open because you are shocked or confused: *She just sat there slack-jawed, with nothing to say.* ◆ *a bunch of slack-jawed idiots*

slacks /slæks/ noun [pl.] (old-fashioned or formal) pants for men or women, that are not part of a suit: *a pair of slacks*

slag /slæg/ noun [U] the waste material that remains after metal has been removed from rock

'slag heap noun a large pile of slag from a mine

slain pp of SLAY

slake /sleɪk/ verb (literary) **1 ~ your thirst** to drink so that you no longer feel thirsty **SYN** QUENCH **2 ~ sth** to satisfy a desire

sla·lom /'slɑləm/ noun a race for people on SKIS or in CANOES along a winding course marked by poles

slam /slæm/ verb, noun
● *verb* (-mm-) **1** [I, T] to shut, or to make something shut, with a lot of force, making a loud noise **SYN** BANG: *I heard the door slam behind him.* ◆ **+ adj.** *A window slammed shut in the wind.* ◆ **~ sth** *He stormed out of the house, slamming the door as he left.* ◆ **~ sth + adj.** *She slammed the lid shut.* ◆ **+ adv./prep.** *She slammed out of the room* (= went out and slammed the door behind her). **2** [T] **~ sth + adv./prep.** to put, push, or throw something into a particular place or position with a lot of force: *She slammed down the phone angrily.* ◆ *He slammed on the brakes* (= stopped the car very suddenly). **3** [T] **~ sb/sth** (used especially in newspapers) to criticize someone or something very strongly **IDM** see DOOR
PHR V ,slam 'into/a'gainst sb/sth | ,slam sth 'into/ a'gainst sb/sth to crash into something with a lot of force; to make something crash into something with a lot of force ⊃ thesaurus box at CRASH
● *noun* [usually sing.] an act of slamming something; the noise of something being slammed: *She gave the door a good hard slam.* ⊃ see also GRAND SLAM

'slam dunk noun **1** (in basketball) the act of jumping up and putting the ball through the net with a lot of force **2** (informal) something that is certain to be successful: *Politically, this issue is a slam dunk for the party.*

'slam-dunk verb **~ sth** (in basketball) to jump up and put the ball through the net with a lot of force

slam·mer /'slæmər/ noun **1 the slammer** [sing.] (slang) prison **2** [C] (also te,quila 'slammer) an alcoholic drink made by mixing TEQUILA and LEMONADE, that is drunk quickly after covering the glass and hitting it on the table to make the drink fill with bubbles

slan·der /'slændər/ noun, verb
● *noun* [C, U] a false spoken statement intended to damage the good opinion people have of someone; the legal offense of making this kind of statement: *a vicious slander on the company's good name* ◆ *He's suing them for slander.* ⊃ compare LIBEL ▶ **slan·der·ous** /'slændərəs/ adj.: *a slanderous remark*
● *verb* **~ sb/sth** to make a false spoken statement about someone that is intended to damage the good opinion that people have of them: *He angrily accused the investigators of slandering both him and his family.* ⊃ compare LIBEL

slang /slæŋ/ noun [U] very informal words and expressions that are more common in spoken language, especially used by a particular group of people, for example children, criminals, soldiers, etc.: *teenage slang* ◆ *a slang word/ expression/term* ⊃ see also RHYMING SLANG

slang·y /'slæŋi/ adj. (slang·i·er, slang·i·est) containing a lot of slang: *a slangy style*

slant /slænt/ verb, noun
● *verb* **1** [I, T] to slope or to make something slope in a particular direction or at a particular angle **+ adv./prep.** (literary): *The sun slanted through the window.* ◆ **~ sth + adv./ prep.** *Slant your skis a little more to the left.* **2** [T] **~ sth (+ adv./prep.)** (sometimes disapproving) to present information based on a particular way of thinking, especially in an unfair way: *The findings of the report had been slanted in*

favor of the manufacturers.
● *noun* **1** a sloping position: *The sofa faced the fire at a slant.* ◆ *Cut the flower stems on the slant.* **2 ~ (on sth/sb)** a way of thinking about something, especially one that shows support for a particular opinion or side in a disagreement: *She put a new slant on the play.*

slant·ed /'slæntəd/ adj. **1** sloping in one direction: *She had slanted brown eyes.* **2 ~ (toward sb/sth)** tending to be in favor of one person or thing in a way that may be unfair to others: *a biased and slanted view of events*

slant·ing /'slæntɪŋ/ adj. not straight or level; sloping: *slanting eyes/handwriting/rain*

slap /slæp/ verb, noun, adv.
● *verb* (-pp-) **1** [T] **~ sb/sth (+ adv./prep.)** to hit someone or something with the flat part of your hand **SYN** SMACK: *She slapped his face hard.* ◆ *She slapped him hard across the face.* ◆ *"Congratulations!" he said, slapping me on the back.* **2** [T] **~ sth + adv./prep.** to put something on a surface in a quick, careless, and often noisy way, especially because you are angry: *He slapped the newspaper down on the desk.* ◆ *She slapped a $10 bill into my hand.* **3** [I] **+ adv./prep.** to hit against something with the noise of someone being slapped: *The water slapped against the side of the boat.* **PHR V** ,slap sb a'round (informal) to hit someone regularly or often: *Her ex-husband used to slap her around.* ,slap sb/ sth↔'down (informal) to criticize someone in an unfair way, often in public, so that they feel embarrassed or less confident 'slap sth on sb/sth (informal) to order, especially in a sudden or an unfair way, that something must happen or someone must do something: *The company slapped a ban on using e-mail on the staff.* ,slap sth 'on sth (informal) to increase the price of something suddenly: *They've slapped 75 cents on the price of a pack of cigarettes.* ,slap sth 'on sth | ,slap sth↔'on to spread something on a surface in a quick, careless way: *Just slap some paint on the walls and it'll look fine.* ◆ *I'd better slap some makeup on before I go out.*
● *noun* **1** [C] the action of hitting someone or something with the flat part of your hand: *She gave him a slap across the face.* ◆ *He gave me a hearty slap on the back.* **2** [sing.] the noise made by hitting someone or something with the flat part of your hand; a similar noise made by something else: *the gentle slap of water against the shore*
IDM a slap in the face an action that seems to be intended as a deliberate insult to someone a slap on the wrist (informal) a warning or mild punishment
● *adv.* (also ,slap 'bang) (informal) **1** straight, and with great force: *Storming out of her room, she went slap into Luke.* **2** exactly: *Their apartment is slap bang in the middle of town.*

slap·dash /'slæpdæʃ/ adj. done, or doing something, too quickly and carelessly: *She has a very slapdash approach to keeping accounts.* ◆ *a slapdash piece of writing*

'slap-happy adj. (informal) **1** cheerful, but careless about things that should be taken seriously: *a slap-happy approach to life* **2** = PUNCH-DRUNK

slap·stick /'slæpstɪk/ noun [U] the type of humor that is based on simple actions, for example people hitting each other, falling down, etc.

slash /slæʃ/ verb, noun
● *verb* **1 ~ sth** to make a long cut with a sharp object, especially in a violent way **SYN** SLIT: *Someone had slashed the tires on my car.* ◆ *She tried to kill herself by slashing her wrists.* ◆ *We had to slash our way through the undergrowth with sticks.* **2** [often passive] **~ sth** (often used in newspapers) to reduce something by a large amount: *to slash costs/prices/ fares, etc.* ◆ *The workforce has been slashed by half.* ⊃ thesaurus box at CUT
PHR V 'slash at sb/sth (with sth) to attack someone violently with a knife, etc.
● *noun* **1** a sharp movement made with a knife, etc. in order to cut someone or something **2** a long narrow wound or cut: *a slash across his right cheek* ◆ (figurative) *Her mouth was a slash of red lipstick.* **3** the symbol (/) used to show alternatives, as in *lunch and/or dinner* and *4/5 people* and to write

---

i **see**   ɪ **sit**   ɛ **ten**   æ **cat**   ɑ **hot**   ɔ **saw**   ʊ **put**   u **too**

FRACTIONS, as in ¾ **SYN** FORWARD SLASH ⊃ see also BACKSLASH

ˌslash-and-ˈburn *adj.* **1** relating to a method of farming in which existing plants, crops, etc. are cut down and burned before new seeds are planted: *slash-and-burn agriculture* **2** aggressive and causing a lot of harm or damage

slash·er /ˈslæʃər/ (also ˈslasher movie, ˈslasher film) *noun* a frightening movie, in which an unknown person kills a lot of people

slat /slæt/ *noun* **1** one of a series of thin flat pieces of wood, metal, or plastic, used in furniture, fences, etc. **2** (*technical*) a part of the wing of an aircraft, on the front of the wing, that can be moved up or down to control upward or downward movement ⊃ picture at PLANE

slate /sleɪt/ *noun, verb*
● *noun* **1** [U] a type of dark gray stone that splits easily into thin flat layers: *a slate quarry* ♦ *The sea was the color of slate.* **2** [C] a small thin piece of slate, used for covering roofs: *A loose slate had fallen from the roof.* **3** [C] a list of the candidates in an election: *a slate of candidates* ♦ *the Democratic slate* **4** [C] a small sheet of slate in a wooden frame, used in the past in schools for children to write on **IDM** see CLEAN, WIPE
● *verb* **1** [usually passive] to plan that something will happen at a particular time in the future: *~ sth for sth The houses were first slated for demolition five years ago.* ♦ *~ sth to do sth The new store is slated to open in spring.* **2** [usually passive] (*informal*) to suggest or choose someone for a job, position, etc.: *~ sb for sth I was told that I was being slated for promotion.* ♦ *~ sb to do sth He is slated to play the lead in the new musical.*

ˌslate-ˈgray (*especially CanE* ˌslate-ˈgrey) *adj.* blue-gray in color, like slate

slath·er /ˈslæðər/ *verb*
PHR V ˈslather sth on sth | ˈslather with/in sth | ˌslather sth↔ˈon to cover something with a thick layer of a substance: *hot dogs slathered with mustard*

slat·ted /ˈslætəd/ *adj.* [usually before noun] made of slats (= thin pieces of wood): *slatted blinds*

slat·tern /ˈslætərn/ *noun* (*old-fashioned*) a messy and dirty woman ► slat·tern·ly *adj.*: *a slatternly girl*

slat·y (also slat·ey) /ˈsleɪti/ *adj.* **1** having a dark gray color: *a slaty sky* **2** containing SLATE; like SLATE: *slaty rock*

slaugh·ter /ˈslɔtər/ *noun, verb*
● *noun* [U] **1** the killing of animals for their meat: *cows taken for slaughter* **2** the cruel killing of large numbers of people at one time, especially in a war **SYN** MASSACRE: *the wholesale slaughter of innocent people* **IDM** see LAMB
● *verb* **1** *~ sth* to kill an animal, usually for its meat **SYN** BUTCHER **2** *~ sb/sth* to kill a large number of people or animals violently **SYN** MASSACRE: *Men, women and children were slaughtered and villages destroyed.* **3** *~ sb/sth* (*informal*) to defeat someone or something by a large number of points in a sports game, competition, etc.: *We were slaughtered 10–1 by the home team.*

slaugh·ter·house /ˈslɔtərˌhaʊs/ *noun* a building where animals are killed for food

Slav /slɑv/ *noun* a member of any of the races of people of central and eastern Europe who speak Slavic languages

slave /sleɪv/ *noun, verb*
● *noun* **1** (chiefly in the past) a person who is legally owned by another person and is forced to work for them: *She treated her daughter like a slave.* **2** a person who is so strongly influenced by something that they cannot live without it, or cannot make their own decisions: *~ of sth We are slaves of the automobile.* ♦ *~ to sth Sue's a slave to fashion.* **3** (*technical*) a device that is directly controlled by another one
● *verb* [I] *~ (away) (at sth)* to work very hard: *I've been slaving away all day trying to get this work finished.* ♦ *I haven't got time*

to spend hours *slaving over a hot stove* (= doing a lot of cooking).

ˈslave-ˌdriver *noun* (*disapproving*) a person who makes people work extremely hard **SYN** TYRANT

ˌslave ˈlabor *noun* [U] **1** work that is done by slaves; the slaves who do the work: *Huge palaces were built by slave labor.* **2** (*informal*) work that is very hard and very badly paid: *I left because the job was just slave labor.*

slav·er¹ /ˈslævər; ˈsleɪ-; ˈslɑ-/ *verb* [I] (usually of an animal) to let SALIVA (= the liquid produced in the mouth) run out of the mouth, especially when hungry or excited: *slavering dogs*

slav·er² /ˈsleɪvər/ *noun* **1** (in the past) a person who bought and sold SLAVES **2** a ship that was used in the past for carrying SLAVES

slav·er·y /ˈsleɪvəri/ *noun* [U] **1** the state of being a SLAVE: *to be sold into slavery* **ANT** FREEDOM **2** the practice of having SLAVES: *the abolition of slavery*

ˈslave trade *noun* [sing.] the buying and selling of people as SLAVES, especially in the 17th–19th centuries

Slav·ic /ˈslɑvɪk/ (also Slav·on·ic) *adj.* of or connected with Slavs or their languages, which include Russian, Polish, Czech, etc.

slav·ish /ˈsleɪvɪʃ/ *adj.* (*disapproving*) following or copying someone or something exactly without having any original thought at all: *a slavish adherence to the rules* ► slav·ish·ly *adv.*

Sla·von·ic /sləˈvɑnɪk/ *adj.* = SLAVIC

slay /sleɪ/ *verb* (slew /slu/, slain /sleɪn/) **1** *~ sb/sth* (old-fashioned *or* literary) to kill someone or something in a war or a fight: *St. George slew the dragon.* **2** *~ sb* (used especially in newspapers) to murder someone: *Two passengers were slain by the hijackers.* **3** *~ sb* (old-fashioned, *informal*) to have a strong effect on someone: *Those old movies still slay me!* ► slay·ing *noun*: *the drug-related slayings of five people*

sleaze /sliz/ *noun* **1** [U] dishonest or illegal behavior, especially by politicians or business people: *allegations of sleaze* ♦ *The candidate was seriously damaged by the sleaze factor.* **2** [U] behavior or conditions that are unpleasant and not socially acceptable, especially because sex is involved: *the sleaze of a town that was once a naval base* **3** [C] (also sleaze·bag, sleaze·ball /ˈslizbɔl/ *informal*) a dishonest or immoral person

slea·zy /ˈslizi/ *adj.* (slea·zi·er, slea·zi·est) (*informal*) **1** (of a place) dirty, unpleasant, and not socially acceptable, especially because sex is involved **SYN** DISREPUTABLE: *a sleazy bar* **2** (of people) immoral and unpleasant: *a sleazy reporter* ► slea·zi·ness *noun* [U]

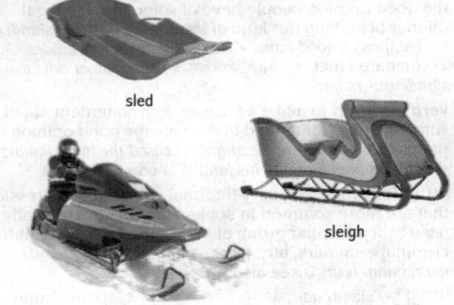

sled

sleigh

snowmobile

sled /slɛd/ *noun, verb*
● *noun* a vehicle for traveling over snow and ice, with long narrow strips of wood or metal instead of wheels. Larger sleds are pulled by horses or dogs and smaller ones are used for going down hills as a sport or for pleasure. ⊃ compare SLEIGH, TOBOGGAN
● *verb* (-dd-) [I] to ride on a sled

sled·ding /'slɛdɪŋ/ *noun* [U] the activity of riding on a sled: *to go sledding*

sledge·ham·mer /'slɛdʒˌhæmər/ *noun* a large heavy hammer with a long handle

sleek /slik/ *adj., verb*
- *adj.* (sleek·er, sleek·est) **1** (*approving*) smooth and shiny **SYN** GLOSSY: *sleek black hair* ◆ *the sleek dark head of a seal* **2** (*approving*) having an elegant smooth shape: *a sleek yacht* ◆ *the sleek lines of the new car* **3** (often *disapproving*) (of a person) looking rich, and dressed in elegant and expensive clothes: *a sleek and ambitious politician* ▶ **sleek·ly** *adv.* **sleek·ness** *noun* [U]
- *verb* ~ sth (back/down) to make something, especially hair, smooth and shiny: *His glossy hair was sleeked back over his ears.*

sleep 🔑 /slip/ *verb, noun*
- *verb* (slept, slept /slɛpt/) **1** [I] (+ adv./prep.) to rest with your eyes closed and your mind and body not active: *to sleep well/deeply/soundly/badly* ◆ *I couldn't sleep because of the noise.* ◆ *I had to sleep on the sofa.* ◆ *He slept solidly for ten hours.* ◆ *I slept at my sister's house last night* (= stayed the night there). ◆ *We both slept right through* (= were not woken up by) *the storm.* ◆ *She only sleeps for four hours a night.* ◆ *We sometimes sleep late on the weekends* (= until late in the morning). ◆ *I put the sleeping baby down gently.* ◆ *What are our sleeping arrangements here* (= where shall we sleep)? **HELP** It is more common to say that someone is asleep than to say that someone **is sleeping**. **Sleep** can only be used in the passive with a preposition such as **in** or **on**: *It was clear her bed hadn't been slept in.* **2** [T, no passive] **~ sb** to have enough beds for a particular number of people: *The apartment sleeps six.* ◆ *The hotel sleeps 120 guests.* **IDM** **let sleeping dogs lie** (*saying*) to avoid mentioning a subject or something that happened in the past, in order to avoid any problems or arguments **sleep like a log/baby** (*informal*) to sleep very well **sleep tight** (*informal*) used especially to children before they go to bed to say that you hope they sleep well: *Goodnight, sleep tight!* ◆ more at WINK **PHR V** **sleep a'round** (*informal, disapproving*) to have sex with a lot of different people **sleep 'in** to sleep until after the time you usually get up in the morning **sleep sth↔'off** to get better after something, especially drinking too much alcohol, by sleeping: *Let's leave him to sleep it off.* **sleep on sth** (*informal*) to delay making a decision about something until the next day, so that you have time to think about it: *Could I sleep on it and let you know tomorrow?* **sleep 'over** to stay the night at someone else's home: *It's very late now—why don't you sleep over?* ◆ *Can I sleep over at my friend's house?* ⊃ related noun SLEEPOVER **sleep together** | **sleep with sb** (*informal*) to have sex with someone, especially someone you are not married to: *I know he's going out with her, but I don't think they're sleeping together.* ◆ *Everyone knows she sleeps with the boss.*
- *noun* **1** [U] the natural state of rest in which your eyes are closed, your body is not active, and your mind is not conscious: *I need to get some sleep.* ◆ *I didn't get much sleep last night.* ◆ *Can you give me something to help me get to sleep* (= start sleeping)? ◆ *Go to sleep—it's late.* ◆ *He cried out in his sleep.* ◆ *Anxiety can be caused by lack of sleep.* ◆ *His talk nearly sent me to sleep* (= it was boring). ◆ *Try to go back to sleep.* **2** [sing.] a period of sleep: *Did you have a good sleep?* ◆ *Ron fell into a deep sleep.* ◆ *I'll feel better after a good night's sleep* (= a night when I sleep well). **3** [U] (*informal*) the substance that sometimes forms in the corners of your eyes after you have been sleeping **IDM** **be able to do sth in your sleep** (*informal*) to be able to do something very easily because you have done it many times before **go to sleep** (*informal*) if part of your body **goes to sleep**, you lose the sense of feeling in it, usually because it has been in the same position for too long **not lose sleep/lose no sleep over sth** to not worry much about something: *It's not worth losing sleep over.* **put sb to sleep** (*informal*) to make someone unconscious before an operation by using drugs (called an ANESTHETIC) **put sth to**

sleep to kill a sick or injured animal by giving it drugs so that it dies without pain. People say "put to sleep" to avoid saying "kill." ⊃ more at WINK

sleep·er /'slipər/ *noun* **1** (used with an adjective) a person who sleeps in a particular way: *a heavy/light/sound sleeper* **2** a person who is asleep: *Only the snores of the sleepers broke the silence of the house.* **3** a night train with beds for passengers on it: *the Washington, D.C. to Los Angeles sleeper* **4** = SLEEPING CAR **5** (*informal*) a movie, play, or book that for a long time is not very successful and then is suddenly a success **6** (also **sleeper 'agent**) a SPY who is sent to live in a country as a normal citizen and is not used until much later

sleeping ˌbag *noun* a thick warm bag that you use for sleeping in, for example when you are camping ⊃ picture at BED

Sleeping 'Beauty *noun* used to refer to someone who has been asleep for a long time: *OK, Sleeping Beauty, time to get up.* **ORIGIN** From the European fairy tale about a beautiful girl who sleeps for a hundred years and is woken up when a prince kisses her.

sleeping ˌcar (also **sleep·er**) *noun* a car on a train with beds for people to sleep in

sleeping ˌpill *noun* a pill containing a drug that helps you to sleep

sleeping ˌsickness *noun* [U] a tropical disease carried by the TSETSE FLY that causes a feeling of wanting to go to sleep and usually causes death

sleep·less /'sliplǝs/ *adj.* **1** [only before noun] without sleep: *I've had a few sleepless nights recently.* **2** [not before noun] not able to sleep: *She lay sleepless until dawn.* ▶ **sleep·less·ly** *adv.* **sleep·less·ness** *noun* [U] **SYN** INSOMNIA: *to suffer from sleeplessness*

sleep·o·ver /'slipˌoʊvər/ *noun* a party or other occasion when a child or group of children spends the night at one house ⊃ compare SLUMBER PARTY

sleep·walk /'slipwɔk/ *verb* [I] to walk around while you are asleep ▶ **sleep·walk·er** (also *formal* **som·nam·bu·list**) *noun*

sleep·y /'slipi/ *adj.* (sleep·i·er, sleep·i·est) **1** needing sleep; ready to go to sleep **SYN** DROWSY: *a sleepy child* ◆ *He had begun to feel sleepy.* ◆ *The heat and the wine made her sleepy.* **2** (of places) quiet and where nothing much happens: *a sleepy little town* ▶ **sleep·i·ly** /-pǝli/ *adv.*: *She yawned sleepily.* **sleep·i·ness** /-pinǝs/ *noun* [U]

sleep·y·head /'slipiˌhɛd/ *noun* (*informal*) a way of addressing someone who is not completely awake: *Come on sleepyhead — time to get up.*

sleet /slit/ *noun, verb*
- *noun* [U] a mixture of rain and snow

• **verb** [I] when **it is sleeting**, a mixture of rain and snow is falling from the sky

sleeve 🔑 /sliv/ *noun*
1 a part of a piece of clothing that covers all or part of your arm: *a dress with short/long sleeves* ♦ *Dan rolled up his sleeves and washed his hands.* ⟳ picture at CLOTHES ⟳ see also SHIRTSLEEVE **2** –**sleeved** (in adjectives) having sleeves of the type mentioned: *a short-sleeved shirt* **3** = JACKET (4) **4** a tube that covers a part of a machine to protect it
▸ **sleeve·less** /'slivləs/ *adj.*: *a sleeveless dress*
IDM **have/keep sth up your sleeve** to keep a plan or an idea secret until you need to use it ⟳ more at LAUGH, ROLL, TRICK, WEAR

sleigh /sleɪ/ *noun* a SLED (= a vehicle that slides over snow), especially one pulled by horses: *a sleigh ride* ⟳ picture at SLED

sleight of hand /ˌslaɪt əv 'hænd/ *noun* [U] **1** (also *formal* leg·er·de·main) skillful movements of your hand that other people cannot see: *The trick is done simply by sleight of hand.* **2** the fact of tricking people in a skillful way: *Last year's profits were more the result of financial sleight of hand than genuine growth.*

slen·der /'slɛndər/ *adj.* (slend·er·er, slend·er·est)
HELP You can also use **more slender** and **most slender**.
1 (*approving*) (of people or their bodies) thin in an attractive or elegant way **SYN** SLIM: *her slender figure* ♦ *long, slender fingers* **2** thin or narrow: *a glass with a slender stem* **3** small in amount or size and hardly enough: *to win by a slender margin/majority* ♦ *people of slender means* (= with little money) ♦ *Australia held a slender 1–0 lead at half-time.*
▸ **slen·der·ness** *noun* [U]

slept *pt, pp of* SLEEP

sleuth /sluθ/ *noun* (*old-fashioned* or *humorous*) a person who investigates crimes **SYN** DETECTIVE: *an amateur sleuth*

sleuth·ing /'sluθɪŋ/ *noun* [U] the act of investigating a crime or mysterious event: *to do some private sleuthing*

slew /slu/ *noun, verb*
• **noun** [sing.] ~ **of sth** (*informal*) a large number or amount of something
• **verb** *pt of* SLAY

slice 🔑 /slaɪs/ *noun, verb*
• **noun 1** a thin flat piece of food that has been cut off a larger piece: *a slice of bread* ♦ *Cut the meat into thin slices.* ⟳ picture at COOKING **2** (*informal*) a part or share of something: *Our firm is well placed to grab a large slice of the market.* **3** a kitchen UTENSIL (= tool) that you use to lift and serve pieces of food: *a fish slice* **4** (*sports*) (in GOLF, TENNIS, etc.) a stroke that makes the ball spin to one side rather than going straight ahead
IDM **a slice of life** a movie, play, or book that gives a very realistic view of ordinary life ⟳ more at PIE
• **verb 1** [T] ~ **sth (up)** to cut something into slices: *to slice (up) onions* ♦ *Slice the cucumber thinly.* ♦ *a sliced loaf* ⟳ collocations at COOKING ⟳ see also SALAMI SLICING **2** [I] to cut something easily with or as if with a sharp blade: + **adv./prep.** *He accidentally sliced through his finger.* ♦ *A piece of glass sliced into his shoulder.* ♦ (*figurative*) *Her speech sliced through all the confusion surrounding the situation.* ♦ ~ **sth (+ adj.)** *The knife sliced his jacket.* ♦ (*figurative*) *The ship sliced the water.* **3** [T] ~ **sth** (*sports*) to hit a ball so that it spins and does not move in the expected direction: *He managed to slice a shot over the net.* **4** [T] ~ **sth** (in GOLF) to hit the ball so that it flies away in a curve, when you do not mean to **5** [T] ~ **sth** (*informal*) to reduce something by a large amount: *The new tax has sliced annual bonuses by 30 percent.*
IDM **slice and dice (sth)** (*computing*) to divide information into small parts in order to study it more closely or to see it in different ways: *The software lets you slice and dice the data and display it in different formats.* ⟳ more at WAY
PHR V **slice sth↔'off/a'way** | **slice sth 'off sth** to cut something from a larger piece: *Slice a piece off.* ♦ (*figurative*) *He sliced two seconds off the world record.*

sliced 'bread *noun* [U] bread that is sold already cut into slices: *a loaf of sliced bread*
IDM **the best thing since sliced bread** (*informal*) if you say that something is **the best thing since sliced bread**, you think it is extremely good, interesting, etc.

slick /slɪk/ *adj., noun, verb*
• **adj.** (slick·er, slick·est) **1** (sometimes *disapproving*) done or made in a way that is smart and efficient but often does not seem to be sincere or lacks important ideas: *a slick advertising campaign* ♦ *a slick performance* **2** (sometimes *disapproving*) speaking very easily and smoothly but in a way that does not seem sincere **SYN** GLIB: *slick TV presenters* ♦ *a slick salesman* **3** done quickly and smoothly **SYN** SKILLFUL: *The crowd enjoyed the team's slick passing.* ♦ *a slick gear change* **4** smooth and difficult to hold or move on **SYN** SLIPPERY: *The roads were slick with rain.* ▸ **slick·ly** *adv.*: *The magazine is slickly produced.* **slick·ness** *noun* [U]
• **noun 1** = OIL SLICK **2** a small area of something wet and shiny: *a slick of sweat*
• **verb** [usually passive] ~ **sth + adv./prep.** to make hair very flat and smooth by putting oil, water, etc. on it: *His hair was slicked back/down with gel.*

slick·er /'slɪkər/ *noun* a long loose coat that keeps you dry in the rain ⟳ see also CITY SLICKER

slide 🔑 /slaɪd/ *verb, noun*
• **verb** (slid, slid /slɪd/)
▷ **MOVE SMOOTHLY/QUIETLY 1** [I, T] to move easily over a smooth or wet surface; to make something move in this way: (+ **adv./prep.**) *We slid down the grassy slope.* ♦ *The drawers slide in and out easily.* ♦ ~ **sth + adv./prep.** *She slid her hand along the rail.* ♦ ~ **(sth) + adj.** *The automatic doors slid open.* **2** [I, T] to move quickly and quietly, for example in order not to be noticed; to make something move in this way **SYN** SLIP: + **adv./prep.** *He slid into bed.* ♦ *She slid out while no one was looking.* ♦ ~ **sth + adv./prep.** *The man slid the money quickly into his pocket.*
▷ **BECOME LOWER/WORSE 3** [I] ~ **(from…) (to…)** to become gradually lower or of less value: *Shares slid to a 10-year low.* **4** [I] ~ **(down/into/toward sth)** to move gradually into a worse situation: *The industry has slid into decline.* ♦ *They were sliding toward bankruptcy.* ♦ *He got depressed and began to let things slide* (= failed to give things the attention they needed).
• **noun**
▷ **BECOMING LOWER/WORSE 1** [C, usually sing.] a change to a lower or worse condition: *a downward slide in the price of oil* ♦ *talks to prevent a slide into civil war* ♦ *The economy is on the slide* (= getting worse).
▷ **ON ICE 2** [sing.] a long smooth movement on ice or a smooth surface **SYN** SKID: *Her car went into a slide.*
▷ **FOR CHILDREN 3** [C] a structure with a steep slope that children use for sliding down: *to go down the slide* ⟳ picture at TOY
▷ **FALL OF ROCK 4** [C] a sudden fall of a large amount of rock or earth down a hill **SYN** LANDSLIDE: *I was afraid of starting a slide of loose stones.*
▷ **PHOTOGRAPH 5** [C] a small piece of film held in a frame that can be shown on a screen when you shine a light through it **SYN** TRANSPARENCY: *a talk with color slides*
▷ **COMPUTERS 6** [C] one page of an electronic presentation, that may contain text and images, that is usually viewed on a computer screen or projected onto a larger screen: *I'm still working on the slides for my presentation.*
▷ **FOR MICROSCOPE 7** [C] a small piece of glass that something is placed on so that it can be looked at under a MICROSCOPE ⟳ picture at LABORATORY
▷ **PART OF MUSICAL INSTRUMENT 8** [C] a part of a musical instrument or other device that slides backward and forward

slide pro·jec·tor *noun* a piece of equipment for displaying slides (= small pieces of film held in frames) on a screen ⟳ compare DATA PROJECTOR, OVERHEAD PROJECTOR

slid·er /'slaɪdər/ *noun* **1** (in baseball) a type of PITCH that suddenly curves to the side before it reaches the BATTER

2 a device for controlling something such as the volume of a radio, that you slide up and down or from side to side **3** (*computing*) an ICON that you can slide up and down or from side to side with the mouse **4** a FRESHWATER TURTLE from N. America

'**slide rule** *noun* a long narrow instrument like a ruler, with a middle part that slides backward and forward, used for calculating numbers

'**slide show** (also **slide·show**) /'slaɪdʃoʊ/ *noun* **1** a number of slides (= small pieces of film held in frames) shown to an audience using a SLIDE PROJECTOR, often during a lecture **2** (*computing*) a piece of software that shows a number of images on a computer screen in a particular order: *a slideshow presentation*

ˌ**sliding** '**door** *noun* a door that slides across an opening rather than swinging away from it

ˌ**sliding** '**scale** *noun* a system in which the rate at which something is paid varies according to particular conditions: *Fees are calculated on a sliding scale according to income* (= richer people pay more).

slight 🔑 /slaɪt/ *adj., noun, verb*
- *adj.* (slight·er, slight·est) **1** very small in degree: *a slight increase/change/delay/difference* ◆ *I woke up with a slight headache.* ◆ *The damage was slight.* ◆ *She takes offense at the slightest thing* (= is very easily offended). ◆ *There was not the slightest hint of trouble.* **2** small and thin in size: *a slight woman* **3** (*formal*) not deserving serious attention: *This is a very slight novel.*
  IDM **not in the slightest** not at all: *He didn't seem to mind in the slightest.*
- *noun* ~ **(on sb/sth)** an act or a remark that criticizes something or offends someone **SYN** INSULT: *Nick took her comment as a slight on his abilities as a manager.*
- *verb* [usually passive] ~ **sb** to treat someone rudely or without respect **SYN** INSULT: *She felt slighted because she hadn't been invited.* ▶ **slight·ing** /'slaɪtɪŋ/ *adj.* [only before noun]: *slighting remarks*

slight·ly 🔑 /'slaɪtli/ *adv.*
1 a little: *a slightly different version* ◆ *We took a slightly more direct route.* ◆ *I knew her slightly.* ◆ *"Are you worried?" "Only slightly."* **2** a **slightly built** person is small and thin

slim /slɪm/ *adj., verb*
- *adj.* (slim·mer, slim·mest) **1** (*approving*) (of a person) thin, in a way that is attractive: *a slim figure/body/waist* ◆ *She was tall and slim.* ◆ *How do you manage to stay so slim?* ◆ (*figurative*) *Many companies are a lot slimmer than they used to be* (= have fewer workers). ⊃ see also SLIMMING **2** thinner than usual: *a slim volume of poetry* **3** not as big as you would like or expect **SYN** SMALL: *a slim chance of success* ◆ *The party was returned to power with a slim majority.* ▶ **slim·ness** *noun* [U]
- *verb* (-mm-)
  PHR V ˌ**slim** '**down** to become thinner, for example as a result of eating less ⊃ collocations at DIET ˌ**slim** '**down** | ˌ**slim sth**↔'**down** to make a company or an organization smaller, by reducing the number of jobs in it; to be made smaller in this way: *They're restructuring and slimming down the workforce.* ◆ *The industry may have to slim down even further.* ◆ *the new, slimmed-down company*

slime /slaɪm/ *noun* [U] any unpleasant thick liquid substance: *The pond was full of mud and green slime.* ⊃ see also SLIMY

slime·ball /'slaɪmbɔl/ (also **slime·bag** /'slaɪmbæg/) *noun* (*informal*) an unpleasant or disgusting person

slim·line /'slɪmlaɪn/ *adj.* [only before noun] smaller or thinner in design than usual: *a slimline phone*

slim·ming /'slɪmɪŋ/ *adj.* making you look thinner than you are: *a slimming swimsuit* ⊃ see also SLIM

slim·y /'slaɪmi/ *adj.* (slim·i·er, slim·i·est) **1** like or covered with SLIME: *thick slimy mud* ◆ *The walls were black, cold and slimy.* **2** (*informal, disapproving*) (of a person or their manner) polite and extremely friendly in a way that is not sincere or honest

sling /slɪŋ/ *verb, noun*
- *verb* (slung, slung /slʌŋ/) **1** (*informal*) to throw something somewhere in a careless way **SYN** CHUCK: ~ sth + adv./prep. *Don't just sling your clothes on the floor.* ⊃ see also MUDSLINGING **2** [often passive] ~ sth + adv./prep. to put something somewhere where it hangs loosely: *Her bag was slung over her shoulder.* ◆ *We slung a hammock between two trees.* **3** [often passive] ~ sb + adv./prep. (*informal*) to put someone somewhere by force; to make someone leave somewhere: *They were slung out of the club for fighting.*
- *noun* **1** a band of cloth that is tied around a person's neck and used to support a broken or injured arm: *He had his arm in a sling.* **2** a device consisting of a band, ropes, etc. for holding and lifting heavy objects: *The engine was lifted in a sling of steel rope.* **3** a device like a bag for carrying a baby on your back or in front of you **4** (in the past) a simple weapon made from a band of leather, etc., used for throwing stones **SYN** SLINGSHOT

sling·back /'slɪŋbæk/ *noun* a woman's shoe that is open at the back with a narrow piece of leather, etc. around the heel ⊃ picture at SHOE

sling·shot /'slɪŋʃɑt/ *noun* a stick shaped like a Y with a rubber band attached to it, used by children for shooting stones

slingshot

slink /slɪŋk/ *verb* (slunk, slunk /slʌŋk/) [I] + adv./prep. to move somewhere very quietly and slowly, especially because you are ashamed or do not want to be seen **SYN** CREEP: *John was trying to slink into the house by the back door.* ◆ *The dog howled and slunk away.*

slink·y /'slɪŋki/ *adj.* (slink·i·er, slink·i·est) **1** (of a woman's clothes) fitting closely to the body in a sexually attractive way **2** (of movement or sound) smooth and slow, often in a way that is sexually attractive

slip 🔑 /slɪp/ *verb, noun*
- *verb* (-pp-)
  ▷ SLIDE/FALL **1** [I] ~ **(over)** to slide a short distance by accident so that you fall or nearly fall: *She slipped over on the ice and broke her leg.* ◆ *As I ran up the stairs, my foot slipped and I fell.*
  ▷ OUT OF POSITION **2** [I] (+ adv./prep.) to slide out of position or out of your hand: *His hat had slipped over one eye.* ◆ *The fish slipped out of my hand.* ◆ *The child slipped from his grasp and ran off.* ◆ (*figurative*) *She was careful not to let her control slip.*
  ▷ GO/PUT QUICKLY **3** [I] + adv./prep. to go somewhere quickly and quietly, especially without being noticed **SYN** CREEP: *She slipped out of the house before the others were awake.* ◆ *The ship slipped into the harbor at night.* ◆ (*figurative*) *She knew that time was slipping away.* **4** [T] to put something somewhere quickly, quietly, or secretly: ~ sth + adv./prep. *Anna slipped her hand into his.* ◆ *I managed to slip a few jokes into my speech.* ◆ *I managed to slip in a few jokes.* ◆ ~ sth to sb *They'd slipped some money to the guards.* ◆ ~ sb sth *They'd slipped the guards some money.*
  ▷ BECOME WORSE **5** [I] to fall to a lower level; to become worse: *His popularity has slipped recently.* ◆ *That's three times she's beaten me—I must be slipping!*
  ▷ INTO DIFFICULT SITUATION **6** [I] + adv./prep. to pass into a particular state or situation, especially a difficult or unpleasant one: *He began to slip into debt.* ◆ *The patient had slipped into a coma.* ◆ *We seem to have slipped behind schedule.*
  ▷ CLOTHES ON/OFF **7** [I, T] to put clothes on or to take them off quickly and easily: + adv./prep. *to slip into/out of a dress* ◆ ~ sth + adv./prep. *to slip your shoes on/off* ◆ *He slipped a coat over his sweatshirt.*
  ▷ GET FREE **8** [T] to get free; to make something or someone/ yourself free from something: ~ sth *The ship had slipped its*

---

moorings in the night. ◆ ~ (sth) + adj. *The animal had slipped free and escaped.*

IDM **let slip sth** to give someone information that is supposed to be secret: *I happened to **let it slip** that he had given me $5,000 for the car.* ◆ *She tried not to let slip what she knew.* **let sth slip (through your fingers)** to miss or fail to use an opportunity: *Don't let the chance to work abroad slip through your fingers.* **slip your mind** if something **slips your mind**, you forget it or forget to do it **slip one over on sb** (*informal*) to trick someone **slip through the net** when someone or something **slips through the net**, an organization or a system fails to find them and deal with them: *We tried to contact all former students, but one or two slipped through the net.* ⟳ more at CRACK *n.*, GEAR, TONGUE

PHR V ‚slip a'way to stop existing; to disappear or die: *Their support gradually slipped away.* ‚slip 'out when something slips out, you say it without really intending to: *I'm sorry I said that. It just slipped out.* ‚slip 'up (*informal*) to make a careless mistake: *We can't afford to slip up.* ⟳ related noun SLIP-UP

● **noun**
> SMALL MISTAKE **1** a small mistake, usually made by being careless or not paying attention: *He recited the whole poem without making a single slip.* ⟳ see also FREUDIAN SLIP ⟳ thesaurus box at MISTAKE
> PIECE OF PAPER **2** a small piece of paper, especially one for writing on or with something printed on it: *I wrote it down on a slip of paper.*
> ACT OF SLIPPING **3** an act of slipping: *One slip and you could fall to your death.*
> CLOTHING **4** a piece of women's underwear like a thin dress or skirt, worn under a dress
> PLACE FOR BOATS **5** a place in the water where boats are kept, usually between two PIERS

IDM **give sb the slip** (*informal*) to escape or get away from someone who is following or chasing you **a slip of a boy, girl, etc.** (*old-fashioned*) a small or thin, usually young, person **a slip of the pen/tongue** a small mistake in something that you write or say: *Did I call you Richard? Sorry, Robert, just a slip of the tongue.* **there's many a slip 'twixt cup and lip** (*saying*) nothing is completely certain until it really happens because things can easily go wrong

slip·case /'slɪpkeɪs/ *noun* a stiff cover that a book or other object fits into

'slip ‚cover *noun* a cover for a chair, etc. that you can take off, for example to wash it

'slip knot *noun* a knot that can slide easily along the rope, etc. on which it is tied, in order to make the LOOP or rope tighter or looser

'slip-on *noun* a shoe that you can slide your feet into without having to tie LACES: *a pair of slip-ons* ◆ *slip-on shoes*

slip·page /'slɪpɪdʒ/ *noun* [U, C, usually sing.] **1** failure to achieve an aim or complete a task by a particular date **2** a slight or gradual fall in the amount, value, etc. of something

‚slipped 'disc (also ‚slipped 'disk) *noun* a painful condition caused when one of the disks between the bones of the SPINE in a person's back moves out of place

slip·per /'slɪpər/ *noun* a loose soft shoe that you wear in the house: *a pair of slippers* ⟳ picture at SHOE

slip·pered /'slɪpərd/ *adj.* wearing slippers: *slippered feet*

slip·per·y /'slɪpəri/ *adj.* **1** (also *informal* **slip·py**) difficult to hold or to stand or move on, because it is smooth, wet, or polished: *slippery like a fish* ◆ *In places the path can be wet and slippery.* ◆ *His hand was slippery with sweat.* **2** (*informal*) (of a person) that you cannot trust: *Don't believe what he says—he's a slippery customer.* **3** (*informal*) (of a situation, subject, problem, etc.) difficult to deal with and that you have to think about carefully: *Freedom is a slippery concept* (= because its meaning changes according to your point of view).

IDM **the/a slippery slope** a course of action that is difficult to stop once it has begun, and can lead to serious problems or disaster

slip·py /'slɪpi/ *adj.* (**slip·pi·er**, **slip·pi·est**) (*informal*) = SLIPPERY

slip·shod /'slɪpʃɑd/ *adj.* done without care; doing things without care **SYN** CARELESS

slip·stream /'slɪpstrim/ *noun* [sing.] the stream of air behind a vehicle that is moving very fast

'slip-up *noun* (*informal*) a careless mistake

slip·way /'slɪpweɪ/ *noun* a sloping track leading down to water, on which ships are built or pulled up out of the water for repairs, or from which they are launched

slit /slɪt/ *noun, verb*
● *noun* a long narrow cut or opening: *a long skirt with a slit up the side* ◆ *His eyes narrowed into slits.*
● *verb* (slit·ting, slit, slit) to make a long narrow cut or opening in something: *~ sth Slit the roll with a sharp knife.* ◆ *The child's throat had been slit.* ◆ *Her skirt was slit at both sides* (= designed with an opening at the bottom on each side). ◆ *~ sth + adj. He slit open the envelope and took out the letter.*

slith·er /'slɪðər/ *verb* **1** [I] + *adv./prep.* to move somewhere in a smooth, controlled way, often close to the ground **SYN** GLIDE: *The snake slithered away as we approached.* **2** + *adv./prep.* to move somewhere without much control, for example because the ground is steep or wet: *We slithered down the slope to the road.* ◆ *They were slithering around on the ice.*

slith·er·y /'slɪðəri/ *adj.* difficult to hold or stand on because it is wet or smooth; moving in a slithering way

sliv·er /'slɪvər/ *noun* a small or thin piece of something that is cut or broken off from a larger piece: *slivers of glass* ◆ (*figurative*) *A sliver of light showed under the door.*

slob /slɑb/ *noun* (*informal, disapproving*) a person who is lazy and dirty or messy: *Get out of bed, you fat slob!*

slob·ber /'slɑbər/ *verb* [I] to let SALIVA come out of your mouth **SYN** DRIBBLE
PHR V 'slobber over sb/sth (*informal, disapproving*) to show how much you like or want someone or something without any pride or control

sloe /sloʊ/ *noun* a bitter wild fruit like a small PLUM that grows on a bush called a BLACKTHORN

'sloe-eyed *adj.* having attractive dark eyes, usually ones that are long and thin

‚sloe 'gin *noun* [U] a strong alcoholic drink made by leaving sloes in GIN so that the gin has the flavor and the color of the sloes

slog /slɑg/ *verb, noun*
● *verb* (-gg-) (*informal*) **1** [I, T] to work hard and steadily at something, especially something that takes a long time and is boring or difficult: *~ (away) (at sth) He's been slogging away at that piece of music for weeks.* ◆ *~ (through sth) The teacher made us slog through long lists of vocabulary.* ◆ *~ your way through something She slogged her way through four piles of ironing.* **2** [I, T] to walk or travel somewhere steadily, with great effort or difficulty: + *adv./prep. I've been slogging around the downtown area all day.* ◆ *~ your way through something He started to slog his way through the undergrowth.* **3** [T, I] *~ (sth) (+ adv./prep.)* to hit a ball very hard but often without skill **IDM** see GUT *n.*
● *noun* [U, C, usually sing.] a period of hard work or effort: *Writing the book took ten months of hard slog.* ◆ *It was a long slog to the top of the mountain.*

slo·gan /'sloʊgən/ *noun* a word or phrase that is easy to remember, used for example by a political party or in advertising to attract people's attention or to suggest an idea quickly **SYN** TAG LINE (2): *an advertising slogan* ◆ *a campaign slogan* ◆ *The crowd began chanting anti-government slogans.*

slo·gan·eer·ing /‚sloʊgə'nɪrɪŋ/ *noun* [U] (*disapproving*) the use of slogans in advertisements, by politicians, etc.

slo-mo /‚sloʊ 'moʊ/ *noun* [U] (*informal*) = SLOW MOTION

| h hat | m man | n no | ŋ sing | l leg | r red | y yes | w wet |

sloop /slup/ *noun* a small sailing ship with one MAST (= a post to support the sails)

slop /slɑp/ *verb, noun*
- *verb* (-pp-) **1** [I] + **adv./prep.** (of a liquid) to move around in a container, often so that some liquid comes out over the edge: *Water was slopping around in the bottom of the boat.* ♦ *As he put the glass down the beer slopped over onto the table.* **2** [T] ~ **sth** (+ **adv./prep.**) to make liquid or food come out of a container in a messy way **SYN** SPILL: *He got out of the bath, slopping water over the sides.* ♦ *She slopped some beans onto a plate.*
- *noun* [U] also **slops** [pl.] **1** waste food, sometimes fed to animals **2** liquid or partly liquid waste, for example URINE or dirty water from baths: *a slop bucket*

slope 🔑 /sloʊp/ *noun, verb*
- *noun* **1** [C] a surface or piece of land that slopes (= is higher at one end than the other) **SYN** INCLINE: *a grassy slope* ♦ *The town is built on a slope.* **2** [C, usually pl.] an area of land that is part of a mountain or hill: *the eastern slopes of the Andes* ♦ *ski slopes* ♦ *He spends all winter on the slopes* (= SKIING). **3** [sing., U] the amount by which something slopes: *a gentle/steep slope* ♦ *a slope of 45 degrees* ♦ *the angle of slope* **IDM** see SLIPPERY
- *verb* **1** [I] (+ **adv./prep.**) (of a horizontal surface) to be at an angle so that it is higher at one end than the other: *The garden slopes away toward the river.* ♦ *sloping shoulders* **2** [I] (+ **adv./prep.**) (of something vertical) to be at an angle rather than being straight or vertical: *His handwriting slopes backward.* ♦ *It was a very old house with sloping walls.*

slop·py /ˈslɑpi/ *adj.* (**slop·pi·er, slop·pi·est**) **1** that shows a lack of care, thought, or effort: *sloppy thinking* ♦ *Your work is sloppy.* ♦ *a sloppy worker* **2** (of clothes) loose and without much shape **SYN** BAGGY: *a sloppy T-shirt* **3** (*informal*) romantic in a silly or embarrassing way: *a sloppy love story* **4** containing too much liquid: *Don't make the mixture too sloppy.* ♦ (*informal*) *She gave him a big sloppy kiss.* ▶ **slop·pi·ly** /-pəli/ *adv.*: *a sloppily run department* **slop·pi·ness** /-pinəs/ *noun* [U]: *There is no excuse for sloppiness in your work.*

slop·py joe /ˌslɑpi ˈdʒoʊ/ *noun* finely chopped meat in a spicy tomato sauce, served on a BUN (= bread roll)

slosh /slɑʃ/ *verb* (*informal*) **1** [I] + **adv./prep.** (of liquid) to move around making a lot of noise or coming out over the edge of something: *The water was sloshing around under our feet.* ♦ *Some of the paint sloshed out of the can.* **2** [T] ~ **sth** + **adv./prep.** to make liquid move in a noisy way; to use liquid carelessly: *The children were sloshing water everywhere.* ♦ *She sloshed coffee into the mugs.* **3** [I] + **adv./prep.** to walk noisily in water or mud: *We all sloshed around in the puddles.*

sloshed /slɑʃt/ *adj.* (*informal*) drunk

slot /slɑt/ *noun, verb*
- *noun* **1** a long narrow opening, into which you put or fit something: *to put some coins in the slot* **2** a position, a time, or an opportunity for someone or something, for example in a list, a program of events, or a series of broadcasts: *He has a regular slot on the late-night program.* ♦ *Their album has occupied the Number One slot for the past six weeks.* ♦ *the airport's takeoff and landing slots*
- *verb* (-tt-) [T, I] to put something into a space that is available or designed for it; to fit into such a space: ~ **sth** + **adv./prep.** *He slotted a DVD into the computer.* ♦ *The bed comes in sections which can be quickly slotted together.* ♦ + **adv./prep.** *The dishwasher slots neatly between the cabinets.* **PHR V** **slot sb/sth**↔**ˈin** to manage to find a position, a time, or an opportunity for someone or something: *I can slot you in between 3 and 4.* ♦ *We slotted in some extra lessons before the exam.*

sloth /slɔθ; slɑθ/ *noun* **1** [C] a S. American animal that lives in trees and moves very slowly **2** [U] (*formal*) the bad habit of being lazy and unwilling to work

sloth·ful /ˈslɔθfl; ˈslɑθ-/ *adj.* (*formal*) lazy

ˈslot ma·chine (also ˌone-armed ˈbandit) *noun* a gambling machine that you put coins into and that gives money back if particular pictures appear together on the screen

slot·ted /ˈslɑtəd/ *adj.* [usually before noun] (*technical*) **1** having a SLOT or SLOTS in it **2** (of a screw) having a SLOT in it rather than a cross shape ⊃ compare PHILLIPS™

ˌslotted ˈspoon *noun* a large spoon with holes in it

slouch /slaʊtʃ/ *verb, noun*
- *verb* [I] (+ **adv./prep.**) to stand, sit, or move in a lazy way, often with your shoulders and head bent forward: *Sit up straight. Don't slouch.*
- *noun* [usually sing.] a way of standing or sitting in which your shoulders are not straight, so that you look tired or lazy
IDM **be no slouch** (*informal*) to be very good at something or quick to do something: *She's no slouch on the guitar.*

slouch·y /ˈslaʊtʃi/ *adj.* (**slouch·i·er, slouch·i·est**) **1** (*disapproving*) holding your body in a lazy way, often with your shoulders and head bent forward: *his slouchy posture* **2** (*approving*) (of clothes) without a firm outline; not stiff: *The slouchy suede boots look great with slim pants.*

slough¹ /slʌf/ *verb* to lose a layer of dead skin, etc.: ~ **sth** *a snake sloughing its skin* ♦ ~ **sth off** *Slough off dead skin cells by using a facial scrub.* **PHR V** **slough sth**↔**ˈoff** (*formal*) to get rid of something that you no longer want: *Responsibilities are not sloughed off so easily.*

slough² /slu; slaʊ/ *noun* (*literary*) **1** [sing.] ~ **of misery, despair, etc.** a state of sadness with no hope **2** [C] a very soft wet area of land

slov·en·ly /ˈslʌvənli/ *adj.* careless, messy, or dirty in appearance or habits: *He grew lazy and slovenly in his habits.* ▶ **slov·en·li·ness** *noun* [U]

slow 🔑 /sloʊ/ *adj., adv., verb*
- *adj.* (**slow·er, slow·est**)
  - ▷ **NOT FAST** **1** not moving, acting, or done quickly; taking a long time; not fast: *a slow driver* ♦ *Progress was slower than expected.* ♦ *The country is experiencing slow but steady economic growth.* ♦ *Collecting data is a painfully slow process.* ♦ *a slow, lingering death* ♦ *Oh you're so slow; come on, hurry up!* ♦ *The slow movement opens with a cello solo.* ♦ *She gave a slow smile.* **2** not going or allowing you to go at a fast speed: *I missed the fast train and had to get the slow one* (= the one that stops at all the stations).
  - ▷ **WITH DELAY** **3** hesitating to do something or not doing something immediately: ~ **to do sth** *She wasn't slow to realize what was going on.* ♦ ~ **in doing sth** *His poetry was slow in achieving recognition.* ♦ ~ **doing sth** *They were very slow paying me.*
  - ▷ **NOT SMART** **4** not quick to learn; finding things hard to understand: *He's the slowest in the class.*
  - ▷ **NOT BUSY** **5** not very busy; containing little action **SYN** SLUGGISH: *Sales are slow* (= not many goods are being sold).
  - ▷ **WATCH/CLOCK** **6** [not before noun] showing a time earlier than the correct time: *My watch is five minutes slow* (= it shows 1:45 when it is 1:50).
  - ▷ **IN PHOTOGRAPHY** **7** **slow** film is not very sensitive to light
  ▶ **slow·ness** *noun* [U]: *There was impatience over the slowness of reform.*
  IDM **do a slow burn** (*informal*) to slowly get angry ⊃ more at UPTAKE
- *adv.* (**slow·er, slow·est**) (used especially in the comparative and superlative forms, or in compounds) at a slow speed **SYN** SLOWLY: *Could you go a little slower?* ♦ *slow-drying paint* ♦ *slow-moving traffic* ♦ *Drive slow!* **IDM** **go slow (on sth)** to show less enthusiasm for achieving something: *The government is going slow on tax reforms.* ⊃ see also GO-SLOW
- *verb* [I, T] to go or to make something or someone go at a slower speed or be less active: *Economic growth has slowed a little.* ♦ *The bus slowed to a halt.* ♦ ~ **down/up** *The car slowed down as it approached the junction.* ♦ *The game slowed up little*

in the second half. ♦ *You must slow down* (= work less hard) *or you'll make yourself sick.* ♦ **~ sth/sb down/up** *The ice on the roads was slowing us down.* ♦ **~ sth/sb** *We hope to slow the spread of the disease.* ⊃ see also SLOWDOWN

ˌslow ˈcooker *noun* an electric pot used for cooking meat and vegetables slowly in liquid

slow·down /'sloʊdaʊn/ *noun* **1** a reduction in speed or activity: *a slowdown in economic growth* **2** a protest that workers make by doing their work more slowly than usual

ˌslow ˈfood *noun* [U] traditional food and ways of producing, cooking, and eating it ⊃ compare FAST FOOD

ˈslow lane *noun* [sing.] the part of a major road such as a HIGHWAY or INTERSTATE where vehicles drive slowest
IDM in the slow lane not making progress as fast as other people, countries, companies, etc.

slow·ly 🔊 /'sloʊli/ *adv.*
at a slow speed; not quickly: *to move slowly* ♦ *Please could you speak more slowly?* ♦ *The boat chugged slowly along.* ♦ *He found that life moved slowly in the countryside.* ♦ *Don't rush into a decision. Take it slowly.* ♦ *Slowly things began to improve.* ⊃ note at SLOW
IDM slowly but surely making slow but definite progress: *We'll get there slowly but surely.*

ˌslow ˈmotion *noun* [U] (in a movie or on television) the method of showing action at a much slower speed than it happened in real life: *Some scenes were filmed in slow motion.* ♦ *a slow-motion replay*

slow·poke /'sloʊpoʊk/ *noun* (informal) a person who moves, acts, or works too slowly

ˌslow-ˈwitted *adj.* not able to think quickly; slow to learn or understand things **ANT** QUICK-WITTED

ˈslow-worm (also ˈblind·worm) *noun* a small European REPTILE with no legs, like a snake

SLR /ˌɛs ɛl ˈɑr/ *abbr.* single-lens reflex (= used to describe a camera in which there is only one LENS which both forms the image on the film and provides the image in the VIEWFINDER)

slub /slʌb/ *noun* a lump or thick place in wool or thread
▶ **slubbed** /slʌbd/ *adj.*

sludge /slʌdʒ/ *noun* [U] **1** thick, soft, wet mud or a substance that looks like it **SYN** SLIME: *There was some sludge at the bottom of the tank.* **2** industrial or human waste that has been treated: *industrial sludge* ♦ *the use of sewage sludge as a fertilizer on farms*

slug /slʌg/ *noun, verb*
● *noun* **1** a small soft creature, like a SNAIL without a shell, that moves very slowly and often eats garden plants ⊃ picture at ANIMAL **2** (informal) a small amount of a strong alcoholic drink: *He took another slug of whiskey.* **3** (informal) a bullet **4** (informal) a piece of metal shaped like a coin used to get things from machines, etc., sometimes illegally
● *verb* (-gg-) **1 ~ sb** (informal) to hit someone hard, especially with your closed hand **2 ~ sth** (in baseball) to hit the ball hard
IDM slug it out to fight or compete until it is clear who has won

slug·fest /'slʌgfɛst/ *noun* (informal) an angry argument in

which people insult each other: *The battle between the two Democrats is turning into a nasty little slugfest.*

slug·gard /'slʌgərd/ *noun* (formal) a slow lazy person
▶ **slug·gard·ly** *adj.*

slug·ger /'slʌgər/ *noun* (informal) **1** (in baseball) a player who hits the ball, especially one who hits it very hard and for long distances **2** (approving) used when speaking to or about someone, especially a young boy, who tries really hard at something, and that you feel affection for: *Hang in there, slugger. You can do it!*

slug·gish /'slʌgɪʃ/ *adj.* moving, reacting, or working more slowly than normal and in a way that seems lazy: *sluggish traffic* ♦ *a sluggish economy* ♦ *the sluggish black waters of the canal* ♦ *He felt very heavy and sluggish after the meal.*
▶ **slug·gish·ly** *adv.* **slug·gish·ness** *noun* [U]

sluice /slus/ *noun, verb*
● *noun* (also ˈsluice gate) a sliding gate or other device for controlling the flow of water out of or into a CANAL, etc.
● *verb* **1** [T] **~ sth (down/out)** | **~ sth (with sth)** to wash something with a stream of water: *The ship's crew was sluicing down the deck.* **2** [I] **+ adv./prep.** (of water) to flow somewhere in large quantities

slum /slʌm/ *noun, verb*
● *noun* an area of a city that is very poor and where the houses are dirty and in bad condition: *a slum area* ♦ *city/urban slums* ♦ *She was brought up in the slums of Chicago.*
● *verb* (-mm-) [I] usually **be slumming** (informal) to spend time in places or conditions that are much worse than those you are used to: *There are plenty of ways you can cut costs on your trip without slumming.*
IDM slum it (often *humorous*) to accept conditions that are worse than those you are used to: *Several businessmen had to slum it in economy class.*

slum·ber /'slʌmbər/ *noun, verb*
● *noun* [U, C, usually pl.] (literary) sleep; a time when someone is asleep: *She fell into a deep and peaceful slumber.*
● *verb* [I] (literary) to sleep

ˈslumber party *noun* a party for children or young people when a group of them spend the night at one house ⊃ compare SLEEPOVER

slum·lord /'slʌmlɔrd/ *noun* (informal) a person who owns houses or apartments in a poor area and who charges very high rent for them even though they are in bad condition

slump /slʌmp/ *verb, noun*
● *verb* **1** [I] to fall in price, value, number, etc., suddenly and by a large amount **SYN** DROP: *Sales have slumped this year.* ♦ **~ by sth** *Profits slumped by over 50%.* ♦ **~ (from sth) (to sth)** *The paper's circulation has slumped to 90,000.* **2** [I] **+ adv./prep.** to sit or fall down heavily: *The old man slumped down in his chair.* ♦ *She slumped to her knees.*
● *noun* **1 ~ (in sth)** a sudden fall in sales, prices, the value of something, etc. **SYN** DECLINE: *a slump in profits* **2** a period when a country's economy or a business is doing very badly: *the slump of the 1930s* ♦ *The toy industry is in a slump.* ⊃ compare BOOM

slumped /slʌmpt/ *adj.* [not usually before noun] **~ (against/over sth)** sitting with your body leaning forward, for example because you are asleep or unconscious: *The driver was slumped exhausted over the wheel.*

slung pt, pp of SLING

slunk pt, pp of SLINK

slur /slɜr/ *verb, noun*
● *verb* (-rr-) **1 ~ sth** | **+ speech** to pronounce words in a way that is not clear so that they run into each other, usually because you are drunk or tired: *She had drunk too much and her speech was slurred.* **2 ~ sth** (music) to play or sing a group of two or more musical notes so that each one runs smoothly into the next **3 ~ sb/sth** to harm someone's reputation by making unfair or false statements about them
● *noun* **1 ~ (on sb/sth)** an unfair remark about someone or

something that may damage other people's opinion of them **SYN** INSULT: *She had dared to cast a slur on his character.* ♦ *The crowd started throwing bottles and shouting racial slurs.* **2** (*music*) a curved sign used to show that two or more notes are to be played smoothly and without a break

slurp /slɜrp/ *verb* (*informal*) **1** [T, I] to make a loud noise while you are drinking something: *~ sth He was slurping his tea.* ♦ *~ (from sth) She slurped noisily from her cup.* **2** [I] to make a noise like this: *The water slurped in the tank.* ▶ **slurp** *noun* [usually sing.]: *She took a slurp from her mug.*

slur·ry /'slɜri/ *noun* [U] a thick liquid consisting of water mixed with animal waste, CLAY, coal dust, or CEMENT

slush /slʌʃ/ *noun* [U] **1** partly melted snow that is usually dirty: *In the city the clean white snow had turned to gray slush.* **2** (*informal*, *disapproving*) stories, movies, or feelings that are considered to be silly and without value because they are too emotional and romantic ▶ **slush·y** *adj*.: *slushy pavements* ♦ *slushy romantic fiction*

'slush fund *noun* (*disapproving*) a sum of money kept for illegal purposes, especially in politics

slut /slʌt/ *noun* (*disapproving*, *offensive*) **1** a woman who has many sexual partners **2** a woman who is very messy or lazy ▶ **slut·tish** /'slʌtɪʃ/ *adj.*

sly /slaɪ/ *adj.* **1** (*disapproving*) acting or done in a secret or dishonest way, often intending to trick people **SYN** CUNNING: *a sly political move* ♦ (*humorous*) *You sly old devil! How long have you known?* **2** [usually before noun] suggesting that you know something secret that other people do not know **SYN** KNOWING: *a sly smile/grin/look/ glance, etc.* ▶ **sly·ly** *adv.*: *He glanced at her slyly.* **sly·ness** *noun* [U]
IDM **on the sly** secretly; not wanting other people to discover what you are doing: *He has to visit them on the sly.*

smack /smæk/ *verb, noun, adv.*
• *verb* **1** [T] *~ sb/sth* to hit someone with your open hand, especially as a punishment: *I think it's wrong to smack children.* ⊃ compare SPANK **2** [T] *~ sth + adv./prep.* to put something somewhere with a lot of force so that it makes a loud noise **SYN** BANG: *She smacked her hand down onto the table.* ♦ *He smacked a fist into the palm of his hand.* **3** [I] + *adv./prep.* to hit against something with a lot of force **SYN** CRASH: *Two players accidentally smacked into each other.*
IDM see LIP
PHR V **'smack of sth** to seem to contain or involve a particular unpleasant quality: *Her behavior smacks of hypocrisy.* ♦ *Today's announcement smacks of a government cover-up.*
• *noun* **1** [C] a sharp hit given with your open hand, especially to a child as a punishment: *You'll get a smack on your backside if you're not careful.* **2** [C] (*informal*) a hard hit given with a closed hand **SYN** PUNCH: *a smack on the jaw* **3** [C, usually sing.] a short loud sound: *She closed the ledger with a smack.* **4** [C] (*informal*) a loud kiss: *a smack on the lips/ cheek* **5** [U] (*slang*) the drug HEROIN: *smack addicts*
• *adv.* (*informal*) **1** (also **'smack-dab**) exactly or directly in a place: *It landed smack in the middle of the carpet.* **2** with sudden violent force, often making a loud noise: *The car drove smack into a brick wall.*

smack·er /'smækər/ *noun* **1** (*informal*) a loud kiss **2** (*slang*) a dollar

smack·ing /'smækɪŋ/ *noun* [sing., U] an act of hitting someone, especially a child, several times with your open hand, as a punishment: *He gave both of the children a good smacking.* ♦ *We don't approve of smacking.*

small 🔑 /smɔl/ *adj., adv., noun*
• *adj.* (**small·er**, **small·est**)
> **NOT LARGE 1** not large in size, number, degree, amount, etc.: *a small house/town/car/man* ♦ *A much smaller number of students passed than I had expected.* ♦ *They're having a relatively small wedding.* ♦ *That dress is too small for you.* ♦ *"I don't agree," he said in a small* (= quiet) *voice.* **2** (*abbr.* S.) used to describe one size in a range of sizes of clothes, food,

products used in the house, etc.: *small, medium, large* ♦ *This is too big—do you have a small one?* **3** not as big as something else of the same kind: *the small intestine*
> **YOUNG 4** young: *They have three small children.* ♦ *We traveled around a lot when I was small.* ♦ *As a small boy he had spent most of his time with his grandparents.*
> **NOT IMPORTANT 5** slight; not important: *I made only a few small changes to the report.* ♦ *She noticed several small errors in his work.* ♦ *Everything had been planned down to the smallest detail.* ♦ *It was no small achievement getting her to agree to the deal.*
> **BUSINESS 6** [usually before noun] not doing business on a very large scale: *a small farmer* ♦ *The government is planning to give more help to small businesses.*
> **LETTERS 7** [usually before noun] not written or printed as capitals: *Should I write "god" with a small "g" or a capital?* ♦ *She's a socialist with a small "s"* (= she has socialist ideas but is not a member of a socialist party).
> **NOT MUCH 8** [only before noun] (used with uncountable nouns) little; not much: *The government has small cause for optimism.* ♦ *They have small hope of succeeding.*
▶ **small·ness** *noun* [U]
IDM **be grateful/thankful for small mercies** to be happy that a situation that is bad is not as bad as it could have been: *Well, at least you weren't hurt. I suppose we should be grateful for small mercies.* **it's a small world** (*saying*) used to express your surprise when you meet someone you know in an unexpected place, or when you are talking to someone and find out that you both know the same person **look/feel small** to look or feel stupid, weak, ashamed, etc. ⊃ more at BIG, GREAT, HOUR, STILL, SWEAT, WAY, WONDER
• *adv.* (**small·er**, **small·est**) **1** into small pieces: *Chop the cabbage up small.* **2** in a small size: *You can fit it all in if you write very small.*
• *noun* **the ~ of the/someone's back** [sing.] the lower part of the back where it curves in ⊃ picture at BODY

small 'arms *noun* [pl.] small light weapons that you can carry in your hands

'small-bore *adj.* **1** a small-bore gun is narrow inside **2** (*informal*) not important: *small-bore issues*

small 'capitals (also **small 'caps**) *noun* [pl.] (*technical*) capital letters that are the same height as LOWER-CASE letters

small 'change *noun* [U] **1** coins of low value: *Do you have any small change for the phone?* **2** something that is of little value when compared with something else

small 'claims court *noun* a local court that deals with cases involving small amounts of money

small 'fortune *noun* [usually sing.] (*informal*) a lot of money: *That vacation cost me a small fortune.*

small 'fry *noun* (*informal*) **1** [pl.] children: *fun and games for the small fry* **2** [pl., U] people or things that are considered unimportant compared to someone or something else: *That's small fry to her.* ♦ *People like us are small fry to such a large business.*

small·ish /'smɔlɪʃ/ *adj.* fairly small: *a smallish town*

small-'minded *adj.* (*disapproving*) having fixed opinions and ways of doing things and not willing to change them or consider other people's opinions or feelings; interested in small problems and details and not in things that are really important **SYN** INTOLERANT, PETTY ▶ **small-'minded-ness** *noun* [U]

small po'tatoes *noun* [U] (*informal*) a person or thing that has no great importance or value, especially when compared with someone or something else

small·pox /'smɔlpɑks/ *noun* [U] a serious infectious disease (now extremely rare) that causes fever, leaves permanent marks on the skin, and often causes death

the 'small 'print *noun* [U] = FINE PRINT

'small-scale *adj.* [usually before noun] **1** (of an organization, activity, etc.) not large in size or extent; limited in what it does: *small-scale farming* ♦ *a small-scale study of couples in* second marriages **2** (of maps, drawings, etc.) drawn to a small scale so that not many details are shown **ANT** LARGE-SCALE

the ˌsmall ˈscreen noun [sing.] television (when contrasted with the movies): *This will be the film's first showing on the small screen.* ◆ *his first small-screen role*

ˈsmall talk noun [U] polite conversation about ordinary or unimportant subjects, especially at social occasions

ˈsmall-time adj. [only before noun] (*informal, disapproving*) (often of criminals) not very important or successful **SYN** PETTY: *a small-time crook* ⊃ compare BIG TIME

ˈsmall-town adj. [only before noun] **1** connected with a small town: *small-town America* (= people who live in small towns in America) **2** (*disapproving*) not showing much interest in new ideas or what is happening outside your own environment **SYN** NARROW-MINDED: *small-town values*

smarm·y /ˈsmɑrmi/ adj. (**smarm·i·er, smarm·i·est**) (*informal, disapproving*) too polite in a way that is not sincere **SYN** SMOOTH: *a smarmy salesman*

smart 🔑 /smɑrt/ adj., verb

● **adj.** (**smart·er, smart·est**)

> INTELLIGENT **1** intelligent; able to learn and think quickly: *She's smarter than her brother.* ◆ *He's not smart enough to be a politician.* **ANT** STUPID ⊃ thesaurus box at INTELLIGENT **2** showing good judgment: *That was a smart career move.* ◆ *OK, I admit it was not the smartest thing I ever did* (= it was a stupid thing to do). **ANT** STUPID

> RUDE **3** being rude by saying things or making jokes in a way that shows a lack of respect: *Don't get smart with me, kid.*

> COMPUTER-CONTROLLED **4** (of a device, especially of a weapon/bomb) controlled by a computer, so that it appears to act in an intelligent way: *smart bombs* ◆ *This smart washing machine will dispense an optimal amount of water for the load.*

> CLEAN/NEAT **5** (*old-fashioned*) (of people) looking clean and neat; well dressed in fashionable and/or formal clothes: *You look very smart in that suit.* **6** (*old-fashioned*) (of clothes, etc.) clean, neat, and looking new and attractive: *They were wearing their smartest clothes.*

> FASHIONABLE **7** (*old-fashioned*) connected with fashionable rich people: *smart restaurants* ◆ *She mixes with the smart set.*

> QUICK **8** (of a movement, etc.) quick and usually done with force **SYN** BRISK: *He was struck with a smart crack on the head.* ◆ *We set off at a smart pace.*

▶ **smart·ly** adv. (*old-fashioned*): *smartly dressed* ◆ *He ran off pretty smartly* (= quickly and suddenly). **smart·ness** noun [U]

● **verb 1** [I] ~ (**from sth**) to feel a sharp stinging pain in a part of your body: *His eyes were smarting from the smoke.* **2** [I] ~ (**from/over sth**) to feel upset about a criticism, failure, etc.: *They are still smarting from the 4–0 defeat last week.* ⊃ **see also** SMARTS

smart al·eck (also **smart al·ec**) /ˈsmɑrt ˌælɪk/ (also **smart-ass, ˈsmarty·ˌpants**) noun (*informal, disapproving*) a person who behaves as if they know everything and likes to show people this in an annoying way

ˈsmart bomb noun a weapon controlled by an electronic device that is intended to cause damage to the target while avoiding damage to other people, buildings, etc. that are in the area

ˈsmart card noun a small plastic card on which information is stored in electronic form ⊃ see also CHIP CARD

smart·en /ˈsmɑrtn/ verb

PHR V ˌsmarten sb/sth↔ˈup | ˌsmarten (yourself) ˈup **1** to make yourself, another person, or a place look neater or more attractive: *The hotel has been smartened up by the new owners.* **2** to make yourself, another person, or their behavior become smarter or more sensible: *You're 21, it's time you smartened up.* ◆ *He needs to smarten up his spending habits.*

the ˌsmart ˈmoney noun [U] **1** money that is invested or bet by people who have expert knowledge: *It seems the smart money is no longer in insurance* (= is no longer being invested in insurance companies). ◆ *The smart money is on him*

for the best actor award. **2** people who have expert knowledge of something: *The smart money says that he's likely to withdraw from the leadership campaign.*

smart·phone /ˈsmɑrtfoʊn/ noun a cell phone that also has some of the functions of a computer

smarts /smɑrts/ noun [U] (*informal*) intelligence: *She made it to the top on her smarts.*

smart·y-pants /ˈsmɑrti ˌpænts/ noun = SMART ALECK

smash 🔑 /smæʃ/ verb, noun

● **verb**

> BREAK **1** [T, I] ~ (**sth**) to break something, or to be broken, violently and noisily into many pieces: *Several windows had been smashed.* ◆ *He smashed the radio to pieces.* ◆ *The glass bowl smashed into a thousand pieces.*

> HIT VERY HARD **2** [I, T] to move with a lot of force against something solid; to make something do this: + **adv./prep.** *the sound of waves smashing against the rocks* ◆ *The car smashed into a tree.* ◆ ~ **sth** + **adv./prep.** *Mark smashed his fist down on the desk.* ⊃ thesaurus box at CRASH **3** [T, I] to hit something very hard and break it, in order to get through it: ~ **sth** + **adv./prep.** *They had to smash holes in the ice.* ◆ *The elephant smashed its way through the trees.* ◆ ~ **sth** + **adj.** *We had to smash the door open.* ◆ + **adv./prep.** *They had smashed through a glass door to get in.* **4** [T] ~ **sth/sb** (+ **adv./prep.**) to hit something or someone very hard **SYN** SLAM: *He smashed the ball into the goal.*

> DESTROY/DEFEAT **5** [T] ~ **sth/sb** to destroy, defeat, or put an end to something or someone: *Police say they have smashed a major drugs ring.* ◆ *She has smashed the world record* (= broken it by a large amount).

> CRASH VEHICLE **6** [T] ~ **sth (up)** to crash a vehicle: *He's smashed (up) his new car.* ⊃ note at CRASH

> IN TENNIS, ETC. **7** [T] ~ **sth** to hit a high ball downward and very hard over the net

PHR V ˌsmash sth↔ˈdown to make something fall down by hitting it hard and breaking it: *The police had to smash the door down.* ˌsmash sth↔ˈin to make a hole in something by hitting it with a lot of force: *Vandals had smashed the door in.* ◆ (*informal*) *I wanted to smash his face in* (= hit him hard in the face). ˌsmash sth↔ˈup to destroy something deliberately: *Youths had broken into the bar and smashed the place up.*

● **noun**

> ACT OF BREAKING **1** [sing.] an act of breaking something noisily into pieces; the sound this makes: *The cup hit the floor with a smash.*

> IN TENNIS, ETC. **2** [C] a way of hitting the ball downward and very hard

> SONG/MOVIE/PLAY **3** (also ˌsmash ˈhit) [C] a song, movie, or play that is very popular: *her latest smash*

smashed /smæʃt/ adj. [not before noun] (*slang*) very drunk

smash·ing /ˈsmæʃɪŋ/ adj. (*old-fashioned, informal*) very good or enjoyable **SYN** GREAT: *We had a smashing time.*

ˈsmash-up noun (*informal*) a crash in which vehicles are very badly damaged

smat·ter·ing /ˈsmætərɪŋ/ noun [sing.] ~ (**of sth**) a small amount of something, especially a little knowledge of a language: *He only has a smattering of French.*

smear /smɪr/ verb, noun

● **verb 1** [T] to spread an OILY or soft substance over a surface in a rough or careless way **SYN** DAUB: ~ **sth on/over sth** *The children had smeared mud on the walls.* ◆ ~ **sth with sth** *The children had smeared the walls with mud.* ⊃ thesaurus box at MARK **2** [T] ~ **sth** to make something dirty or GREASY: *His glasses were smeared.* ◆ *smeared windows* **3** [T] ~ **sb/sth** to damage someone's reputation by saying unpleasant things about them that are not true **SYN** SLANDER: *The story was an attempt to smear the party leader.* **4** [T, I] ~ (**sth**) to rub writing, a drawing, etc. so that it is no longer clear; to become not clear in this way **SYN** SMUDGE: *The last few words of the letter were smeared.*

● **noun 1** an OILY or dirty mark: *a smear of jam* **2** a story that is not true about someone that is intended to damage their

| t tea | ṭ butter | d did | k cat | g got | tʃ chin | dʒ June | f fall

reputation, especially in politics: *He was a victim of a smear campaign.*

smell 🔑 /smɛl/ *verb, noun*

• *verb* **1** [I] to have a particular smell: **+ adj.** *The room smelled damp.* • *Dinner smells good.* • *a bunch of sweet-smelling flowers* • **~ of sth** *His breath smelled of garlic.* • **~ like sth** *What does the perfume smell like?* **2** [T, no passive] (not used in the progressive tenses; often with *can* or *could*) to notice or recognize a particular smell: **~ sth** *He said he could smell gas when he entered the room.* • *The dog had smelled a rabbit.* • *I could smell alcohol on his breath.* • **~ sth doing sth** *Can you smell something burning?* • **~ (that)…** *I could smell that something was burning.* **3** [T] **~ sth** (not usually used in the passive) to put your nose near something and breathe in so that you can discover or identify its smell SYN SNIFF: *Smell this and tell me what you think it is.* • *I bent down to smell the flowers.* **4** [I] (not used in the progressive tenses; often with *can* or *could*) to be able to notice and recognize smells: *I can't smell because I have a bad cold.* **5** [I] (not used in the progressive tenses) to have an unpleasant smell: *The drains smell.* • *It smells in here.* • *He hadn't washed for days and was beginning to smell.* **6** [T, no passive] **~ sth** to feel that something exists or is going to happen: *He smelled danger.* • *I can smell trouble.*

IDM **come up/out of sth smelling like roses/a rose** (*informal*) to still have a good reputation, even though you have been involved in something that might have given people a bad opinion of you **smell a rat** (*informal*) to suspect that something is wrong about a situation ⊃ more at WAKE **PHR V** **ˌsmell sb/sth↔ˈout 1** to be aware of fear, danger, trouble, etc. in a situation: *He could always smell out trouble.* **2** to find something by smelling: *dogs trained to smell out drugs*

• *noun* **1** [C, U] the quality of something that people and animals sense through their noses: *a faint/strong smell* of garlic • *a sweet/fresh/musty smell* • *There was a smell of burning in the air.* • *The smells from the kitchen filled the room.* **2** [sing.] an unpleasant smell: *What's that smell? • Yuck! What a smell!* **3** [U] the ability to sense things with the nose: *Dogs have a very good sense of smell.* • *Taste and smell are closely connected.* **4** [C] the act of smelling something SYN SNIFF: *He took one smell of the liquid and his eyes began to water.*

IDM see SWEET

ˈsmelling ˌsalts *noun* [pl.] a chemical with a very strong smell, kept in a small bottle, used especially in the past for putting under the nose of a person who has become unconscious

smell·y /ˈsmɛli/ *adj.* (**smell·i·er, smell·i·est**) (*informal*) having an unpleasant smell: *smelly feet*

smelt /smɛlt/ *verb* **~ sth** to heat and melt ORE (= rock that contains metal) in order to obtain the metal it contains: *a method of smelting iron*

smelt·er /ˈsmɛltər/ *noun* a piece of equipment for smelting metal

smid·gen (also **smid·geon, smid·gin**) /ˈsmɪdʒən/ *noun* [sing.] **a ~ (of sth)** (*informal*) a small piece or amount of something: *"Sugar?" "Just a smidgen."*

smile 🔑 /smaɪl/ *verb, noun*

• *verb* **1** [I] to make a smile appear on your face: *to smile sweetly/faintly/broadly, etc.* • *He smiled with relief.* • *He never seems to smile.* • **~ at sb/sth** *She smiled at him and he smiled back.* • *I had to smile at* (= was amused by) *his optimism.* **2** [T] to say or express something with a smile: **~ sth** *She smiled her thanks.* • **+ speech** *"Perfect," he smiled.* **3** [T, no passive] **~ sth** to give a smile of a particular type: *to smile a small smile* • *She smiled a smile of dry amusement.* **IDM** see EAR **PHR V** **ˈsmile on sb/sth** (*formal*) if luck, etc. smiles on you, you are lucky or successful

• *noun* the expression that you have on your face when you are happy, amused, etc. in which the corners of your mouth turn upward: *"Oh, hello," he said, with a smile.* • *She gave a wry smile.* • *He had a big smile on his face.* • *I'm going to wipe that smile off your face* (= make you stop thinking this is funny).

IDM **all smiles** looking very happy, especially soon after you have been looking worried or sad: *Twelve hours later she was all smiles again.*

smil·ey /ˈsmaɪli/ *noun* **1** a simple picture of a smiling face that is drawn as a circle with two eyes and a curved mouth **2** a simple picture or series of keyboard symbols :-) that represents a smiling face. The symbols are used, for example, in e-mail or text messages to show that the person sending the message is pleased or is joking.

smil·ing·ly /ˈsmaɪlɪŋli/ *adv.* with a smile or smiles

smirk /smɜrk/ *verb* [I] to smile in a silly or unpleasant way that shows that you are pleased with yourself, know something that other people do not know, etc.: *It was hard not to smirk.* • *He smirked unpleasantly when we told him the bad news.* ▶ **smirk** *noun*: *She had a self-satisfied smirk on her face.*

smite /smaɪt/ *verb* (**smote** /smoʊt/, **smit·ten** /ˈsmɪtn/) (*old use* or *literary*) **1** **~ sb/sth** to hit someone or something hard; to attack or punish someone **2** **~ sb** to have a great effect on someone, especially an unpleasant or serious one ⊃ see also SMITTEN

smith /smɪθ/ *noun* = BLACKSMITH ⊃ see also GOLDSMITH, GUNSMITH, LOCKSMITH, SILVERSMITH

smith·er·eens /ˌsmɪðəˈrinz/ *noun* [pl.]
IDM **smash, blow, etc. sth to smithereens** (*informal*) to destroy something completely by breaking it into small pieces

smith·y /ˈsmɪθi/ *noun* (*pl.* **smith·ies**) a place where a BLACKSMITH works

smit·ten /ˈsmɪtn/ *adj.* [only before noun] **1** **~ (with/by sb/sth)** (especially *humorous*) suddenly feeling that you are in love with someone: *From the moment they met, he was completely smitten by her.* **2** **~ with/by sth** severely affected by a feeling, disease, etc. ⊃ see also SMITE

smock /smɑk/ *noun* **1** a loose comfortable piece of clothing like a long shirt, worn especially by women **2** a long loose piece of clothing worn over other clothes to protect them from dirt, etc.: *an artist's smock*

smock·ing /ˈsmɑkɪŋ/ *noun* [U] decoration on clothing consisting of very small tight folds which are sewn together

smog /smɑg; smɔg/ *noun* [U, C] a form of air pollution that is or looks like a mixture of smoke and FOG, especially in cities: *attempts to reduce smog caused by traffic fumes* ▶ **smog·gy** *adj.*

---

smoke

/smoʊk/ noun, verb

- **noun 1** [U] the gray, white, or black gas that is produced by something burning: *cigarette smoke* ◆ *Clouds of thick black smoke billowed from the car's exhaust.* **2** [C, usually sing.] (*informal*) an act of smoking a cigarette: *Are you coming outside for a smoke?*
  IDM go up in smoke 1 to be completely burned: *The whole house went up in smoke.* **2** if your plans, hopes, etc. **go up in smoke**, they fail completely **a smoke-filled room** (*disapproving*) a decision that people describe as being made in **a smoke-filled room** is made by a small group of people at a private meeting, rather than in an open and democratic way **where there's smoke, there's fire** (*saying*) if something bad is being said about someone or something, it usually has some truth in it

- **verb 1** [T, I] ~ (sth) to suck smoke from a cigarette, pipe, etc. into your mouth and let it out again: *He was smoking a large cigar.* ◆ *How many cigarettes do you smoke a day?* ◆ *Do you mind if I smoke?* **2** [I] to use cigarettes, etc. in this way as a habit: *Do you smoke?* ◆ *She smokes heavily.* ➔ see also CHAIN-SMOKE **3** [I] to produce smoke: *smoking factory chimneys* ◆ *the smoking remains of burned-out cars* **4** [T, usually passive] ~ sth to preserve meat or fish by hanging it in smoke from wood fires to give it a special taste: *smoked salmon*
  PHR V ,smoke sb/sth↔'out 1 to force someone or something to come out of a place by filling it with smoke: *to smoke out wasps from a nest* **2** to take action to discover where someone is hiding or to make a secret publicly known: *The police are determined to smoke out the leaders of the gang.*

'smoke a,larm (also **'smoke de,tector**) *noun* a device that makes a loud noise if smoke is in the air to warn you of a fire

'smoke bomb *noun* a bomb that produces clouds of smoke when it explodes

,smoked 'glass *noun* [U] glass that has been deliberately made dark by smoke

,smoke-'free *adj.* free from cigarette smoke; where smoking is not allowed: *a smoke-free working environment*

smoke·less /'smoʊkləs/ *adj.* [usually before noun] **1** able to burn without producing smoke: *smokeless fuels* **2** free from smoke: *a smokeless zone* (= where smoke from factories or houses is not allowed)

smok·er /'smoʊkər/ *noun* a person who smokes TOBACCO regularly: *a heavy smoker* (= someone who smokes a lot) ◆ *a smoker's cough* ◆ *a cigarette/cigar/pipe smoker* **ANT** NONSMOKER

smoke·screen /'smoʊkskrin/ *noun* **1** something that you do or say in order to hide what you are really doing or intending **2** a cloud of smoke used to hide soldiers, ships, etc. during a battle

'smoke shop *noun* a store selling cigarettes, TOBACCO, etc.

'smoke ,signal *noun* [usually pl.] **1** a signal that is sent to someone who is far away, using smoke **2** a sign of what someone is thinking or doing

smoke·stack /'smoʊkstæk/ *noun* a tall CHIMNEY that takes away smoke from a factory, ship, or engine

'smokestack ,industry *noun* a traditional industry that makes things in factories using large machines: *traditional smokestack industries like steel*

Smok·ey the Bear /,smoʊki ðə 'bɛr/ *noun* **1** the symbol used by the U.S. Forest Service on signs and advertising about preventing forest fires **2** (also **Smokey 'Bear, Smok·ey**) (*informal, old-fashioned*) (in the U.S.) a member of the police force that is responsible for the highway

smok·ing

/'smoʊkɪŋ/ *noun* [U]
the activity or habit of smoking cigarettes, etc.: *No Smoking* (= for example, on a notice) ◆ *Would you like smoking or nonsmoking?* (= for example in a restaurant) ◆ *He's trying to give up smoking.* ➔ compare NONSMOKING

,smoking 'gun *noun* [sing.] (*informal*) something that seems to prove that someone has done something wrong or illegal: *This memo could be the smoking gun that investigators have been looking for.*

'smoking ,jacket *noun* a man's comfortable jacket worn in the past, often made of VELVET

smok·y /'smoʊki/ *adj.* (**smok·i·er, smok·i·est**) **1** full of smoke: *a smoky atmosphere* ◆ *a smoky bar* **2** producing a lot of smoke: *a smoky fire* **3** tasting or smelling like smoke: *a smoky flavor* **4** having the color or appearance of smoke: *smoky blue glass* **ANT** CLEAR

smol·der /'smoʊldər/ *verb* **1** [I] to burn slowly without a flame: *The bonfire was still smoldering the next day.* ◆ *a smoldering cigarette* ◆ (*figurative*) *The feud smoldered on for years.* **2** [I] (*formal*) to be filled with a strong emotion that you do not fully express **SYN** BURN: ~ (with sth) *His eyes smoldered with anger.* ◆ ~ (in sth) *Anger smoldered in his eyes.*

smooch /smutʃ/ *verb* [I] (*informal*) to kiss and hold someone closely, especially when you are dancing slowly ▶ **smooch** *noun*

smooth

/smuð/ *adj., verb*

- **adj.** (**smooth·er, smooth·est**)
  ▷ **FLAT/EVEN 1** completely flat and even, without any lumps, holes, or rough areas: *a lotion to make your skin feel soft and smooth* ◆ *The water was as smooth as glass.* ◆ *a paint that gives a smooth, silky finish* ◆ *Over the years, the stone steps had worn smooth.* **ANT** ROUGH
  ▷ **WITHOUT LUMPS 2** (of a liquid mixture) without any lumps: *Mix the flour with the milk to form a smooth paste.*
  ▷ **WITHOUT PROBLEMS 3** happening or continuing without any problems: *They are introducing new measures to ensure the smooth running of the business.* ◆ *They could not ensure a smooth transfer of political power.*
  ▷ **MOVEMENT 4** even and regular, without sudden stops and starts: *The car's improved suspension gives you a smoother ride.* ◆ *The plane made a smooth landing.* ◆ *She swung herself over the gate in one smooth movement.*
  ▷ **MAN 5** (often *disapproving*) (of people, especially men, and their behavior) very polite and pleasant, but in a way that is often not very sincere **SYN** SMARMY: *I don't like him. He's far too smooth for me.* ◆ *He's something of a smooth operator.*
  ▷ **DRINK/TASTE 6** pleasant and not bitter: *This coffee has a smooth, rich taste.*
  ▷ **VOICE/MUSIC 7** nice to hear, and without any rough or unpleasant sounds ▶ **smooth·ness** *noun* [U]: *the smoothness of her skin* ◆ *They admired the smoothness and efficiency with which the business was run.* **IDM** see ROUGH *n.*, SAILING

- **verb** to make something smooth: ~ sth (back/down/out) *He smoothed his hair back.* ◆ *She was smoothing out the creases in her skirt.* ◆ ~ sth + adj. *He took the letter and smoothed it flat on the table.* **2** ~ sth into/onto/over sth to put a layer of a soft substance over a surface: *Smooth the icing over the top of the cake.*
  IDM smooth the path/way to make it easier for someone or something to develop or make progress: *These negotiations are intended to smooth the path to a peace treaty.* **smooth (sb's) ruffled feathers** to make someone feel less angry or offended
  PHR V ,smooth sth↔a'way/'out to make problems or difficulties disappear **,smooth sth↔'over** to make problems or difficulties seem less important or serious, especially by talking to people: *She spoke to both sides in the dispute in an attempt to smooth things over.*

smooth·ie /'smuði/ *noun* **1** (*informal*) a man who dresses well and talks very politely and confidently but who is often not honest or sincere **2** a drink made of fruit or fruit juice mixed with milk or ice cream

smooth·ly

/'smuðli/ *adv.*
1 in an even way, without suddenly stopping and starting again: *Traffic is now flowing smoothly again.* ◆ *The engine was running smoothly.* **2** without problems or difficulties: *The interview went smoothly.* **3** in a calm or confident way: *"Would you like to come this way?" he said smoothly.* **4** in a

---

h **hat**	m **man**	n **no**	ŋ **sing**	l **leg**	r **red**	y **yes**	w **wet**

way that produces a smooth surface or mixture: *The colors blend smoothly together.*

ˌsmooth ˈmuscle *noun* [U] (*anatomy*) the type of muscle found in the organs inside the body, that is not under conscious control

ˈsmooth-ˌtalking *adj.* (usually *disapproving*) talking very politely and confidently, especially to persuade someone to do something, but in a way that may not be honest or sincere

s'more /smɔr/ *noun* a cooked MARSHMALLOW eaten with chocolate between two GRAHAM CRACKERS (= a type of cookie) that is traditionally cooked over a fire when camping

smor·gas·bord /ˈsmɔrɡəsˌbɔrd/ *noun* [U, sing.] (from *Swedish*) a meal at which you serve yourself from a large range of hot and cold dishes

smote *pt of* SMITE

smoth·er /ˈsmʌðər/ *verb* **1** ~ **sb (with sth)** to kill someone by covering their face so that they cannot breathe **SYN** SUFFOCATE: *He smothered the baby with a pillow.* **2** ~ **sth/sb with/in sth** to cover something or someone thickly or with too much of something: *a rich dessert smothered in cream* ◆ *She smothered him with kisses.* **3** ~ **sth** to prevent something from developing or being expressed **SYN** STIFLE: *to smother a yawn/giggle/grin* ◆ *The voices of the opposition were effectively smothered.* **4** ~ **sb** to give someone too much love or protection so that they feel restricted: *Her husband was very loving, but she felt smothered.* **5** ~ **sth** to make a fire stop burning by covering it with something: *He tried to smother the flames with a blanket.*

SMS /ˌɛs ɛm ˈɛs/ *noun, verb*
- *noun* **1** [U] the abbreviation for "short message service" (a system for sending short written messages from one cell phone to another) **2** [C] a message sent by SMS **SYN** TEXT, TEXT MESSAGE: *I'm trying to send an SMS.* ⊃ compare EMS
- *verb* [T, I] ~ **(sb)** to send a message to someone by SMS **SYN** TEXT, TEXT MESSAGE: *He SMSed me every day.* ◆ *If you have any comments, just e-mail or SMS.* ◆ *She spends her time chatting and SMSing.*

smudge /smʌdʒ/ *noun, verb*
- *noun* a dirty mark with no clear shape: *a smudge of lipstick on a cup*
- *verb* **1** [T, I] ~ **(sth)** to touch or rub something, especially wet ink or paint, so that it is no longer clear; to become not clear in this way: *He had smudged his signature with his sleeve.* ◆ *Tears had smudged her mascara.* ◆ *Her lipstick had smudged.* **2** [T] ~ **sth** to make a dirty mark on a surface: *The mirror was smudged with fingerprints.*

smudg·y /ˈsmʌdʒi/ *adj.* **1** with dirty marks on **2** (of a picture, writing, etc.) with edges that are not clear **SYN** BLURRED

smug /smʌɡ/ *adj.* (*disapproving*) looking or feeling too pleased about something you have done or achieved **SYN** COMPLACENT: *a smug expression/smile/face, etc.* ◆ *What are you looking so smug about?* ▸ **smug·ly** *adv.* **smug·ness** *noun* [U]

smug·gle /ˈsmʌɡl/ *verb* ~ **sth/sb (+ adv./prep.)** to take, send, or bring goods or people secretly and illegally into or out of a country, etc.: *They were caught smuggling diamonds into the country.* ◆ *He managed to smuggle a gun into the prison.* ◆ *smuggled drugs* ⊃ collocations at CRIME

smug·gler /ˈsmʌɡlər/ *noun* a person who takes goods into or out of a country illegally

smug·gling /ˈsmʌɡlɪŋ/ *noun* [U] the crime of taking, sending, or bringing goods secretly and illegally into or out of a country: *drug smuggling*

smut /smʌt/ *noun* [U] (*informal*) stories, pictures, or comments about sex that deal with it in a way that some people find offensive

smut·ty /ˈsmʌti/ *adj.* [usually before noun] (*informal*) (of

stories, pictures, and comments) dealing with sex in a way that some people find offensive: *smutty jokes*

snack /snæk/ *noun, verb*
- *noun* a small meal or amount of food, usually eaten in a hurry: *a mid-morning snack* ◆ *I only have time for a snack at lunchtime.* ◆ *Do you serve bar snacks?* ◆ *a snack lunch*
- *verb* [I] ~ **on sth** to eat snacks between or instead of main meals: *It's healthier to snack on fruit rather than on chocolate.*

ˈsnack bar *noun* a place where you can buy a small quick meal, such as a SANDWICH

sna·fu /snæˈfu/ *noun* [sing.] (*informal*) a situation in which nothing happens as planned: *It was another bureaucratic snafu.*

snag /snæɡ/ *noun, verb*
- *noun* **1** a problem or difficulty, especially one that is small, hidden, or unexpected **SYN** DIFFICULTY: *There is just one small snag—where is the money coming from?* ◆ *Let me know if you run into any snags.* **2** an object or a part of an object that is rough or sharp and may cut something
- *verb* (-gg-) **1** [T, I] to catch or tear something on something rough or sharp; to become caught or torn in this way: ~ **sth on/in sth** *I snagged my sweater on the wire fence.* ◆ ~ **sth** *The fence snagged my sweater.* ◆ ~ **(on/in sth)** *The nets snagged on some rocks.* **2** [T] ~ **sth (from sb)** (*informal*) to succeed in getting something quickly, often before other people: *I snagged a ride from Joe.*

snag·gle /ˈsnæɡl/ *noun, verb*
- *noun* a messy or confused collection of things: *a snaggle of restrictions*
- *verb* [I] to become twisted, messy, or confused: *My hair snaggles when I wash it.*

ˈsnaggle-ˌtooth *noun* (*informal*) a tooth that sticks out or is a strange shape ▸ **ˈsnaggle-ˌtoothed** *adj.*

snail /sneɪl/ *noun* a small soft creature with a hard round shell on its back, that moves very slowly and often eats garden plants. Some types of snails can be eaten. ⊃ picture at ANIMAL
IDM **at a snail's pace** very slowly

ˈsnail mail *noun* [U] (*informal, humorous*) used especially by people who use e-mail to describe the system of sending letters by ordinary mail

snake /sneɪk/ *noun, verb*
- *noun* a REPTILE with a very long thin body and no legs. There are many types of snakes, some of which are poisonous: *a snake coiled up in the grass* ◆ *Venomous snakes spit and hiss when they are cornered.* ⊃ picture at ANIMAL
IDM **a snake (in the grass)** (*disapproving*) a person who pretends to be your friend but who cannot be trusted
- *verb* [I, T] to move like a snake, in long twisting curves; to go in a particular direction in long twisting curves **SYN** MEANDER: + adv./prep. *The road snaked away into the distance.* ◆ ~ **its way** + adv./prep. *The procession snaked its way through narrow streets.*

snake·bite /ˈsneɪkbaɪt/ *noun* [C, U] **1** a wound that you get when a poisonous snake bites you **2** an alcoholic drink made of equal parts of beer and CIDER

Snake·board™ /ˈsneɪkbɔrd/ *noun* ⊃ STREETBOARD

ˈsnake ˌcharmer *noun* an entertainer who seems to be able to control snakes and make them move by playing music to them

ˈsnake eyes *noun* [pl.] (*informal*) a result in a game when you throw two DICE and both show one dot

ˈsnake oil *noun* [U] (*informal*) something, for example medicine, that someone tries to sell you, but that is not effective or useful: *a snake-oil salesman*

snake·pit /ˈsneɪkpɪt/ *noun* **1** a hole in the ground in which snakes are kept **2** a place that is extremely unpleasant or dangerous

snake·skin /ˈsneɪkskɪn/ *noun* [U] the skin of a snake, used for making expensive shoes, bags, etc.

snap /snæp/ *verb, noun, adj.*

● **verb** (-pp-)

▸ BREAK **1** [T, I] to break something suddenly with a sharp noise; to be broken in this way: ~ **sth** *The wind had snapped the tree in two.* ♦ ~ **sth off (sth)** *He snapped a twig off a bush.* ♦ ~ **(off)** *Suddenly, the rope snapped.* ♦ *The branch she was standing on must have snapped off.*

▸ OPEN/CLOSE/MOVE INTO POSITION **2** [I, T] to move, or to move something, into a particular position quickly, especially with a sudden sharp noise: + **adj.** *The lid snapped shut.* ♦ *His eyes snapped open.* ♦ + **adv./prep.** *He snapped to attention and saluted.* ♦ ~ **sth + adj.** *She snapped the bag shut.*

▸ SPEAK IMPATIENTLY **3** [T, I] to speak or say something in an impatient, usually angry, voice: + **speech** *"Don't just stand there," she snapped.* ♦ ~ **(at sb)** *I was tempted to snap back angrily at him.* ♦ ~ **sth** *He snapped a reply.*

▸ OF ANIMAL **4** [I] ~ **(at sb/sth)** to try to bite someone or something SYN NIP: *The dogs snarled and snapped at our heels.*

▸ TAKE PHOTOGRAPH **5** [T, I] (*informal*) to take a photograph: ~ **sth** *A passing tourist snapped the incident.* ♦ ~ **(away)** *She seemed oblivious to the crowds of photographers snapping away.*

▸ LOSE CONTROL **6** [I] to suddenly be unable to control your feelings any longer because the situation has become too difficult: *My patience finally snapped.* ♦ *When he said that, something snapped inside her.* ♦ *And that did it. I snapped.*

▸ FASTEN CLOTHING **7** [I, T] ~ **(sth)** to fasten a piece of clothing with a snap

▸ IN FOOTBALL **8** [T] ~ **sth** to pass the ball with a quick backward movement from the ground to start a period of play: *With four seconds left, he snapped the ball for one last play.*

IDM **snap your fingers** to make a sharp noise by moving your second or third finger quickly against your thumb, to attract someone's attention, or to mark the beat of music, for example **snap out of it/sth| snap sb out of it/sth** [no passive] (*informal*) to make an effort to stop feeling unhappy or depressed; to help someone to stop feeling unhappy: *You've been depressed for weeks. It's time you snapped out of it.* **snap to it** (*informal*) used, especially in orders, to tell someone to start working harder or more quickly ⊃ more at HEAD

PHR V **snap sth↔'out** to say something in a sharp unpleasant way: *The sergeant snapped out an order.* ,**snap sth↔'up** to buy or obtain something quickly because it is cheap or you want it very much: *All the best bargains were snapped up within hours.* ♦ (*figurative*) *She's been snapped up by Hollywood to star in two major movies.*

● **noun**

▸ SHARP NOISE **1** [C] a sudden sharp noise, especially one made by something closing or breaking: *She closed her purse with a snap.* ♦ *the snap of a twig*

▸ CARD GAME **2 Snap** [U] a card game in which players take turns to put cards down and try to be the first to call out "snap" when two similar cards are put down together

▸ FASTENER **3** a type of button used for fastening clothes, consisting of two metal or plastic sections that can be pressed together ⊃ picture at CLOTHES

▸ IN FOOTBALL **4** a quick backward movement of the ball from the ground that begins a period of play

▸ COOKIE **5** a hard sweet cookie: *ginger snaps* ⊃ see also COLD SNAP

IDM **be a snap** (*informal*) to be very easy to do: *This job's a snap.*

● **adj.** [only before noun] made or done quickly and without careful thought or preparation: *It was a snap decision.* ♦ *They held a snap election.*

'**snap bean** *noun* a type of BEAN whose long crisp PODS are eaten as a vegetable

snap·drag·on /'snæp,drægən/ *noun* a small garden plant with red, white, yellow, or pink flowers that open and shut like a mouth when squeezed

snap·per /'snæpər/ *noun* [C, U] a fish that lives in warm parts of the ocean and is used for food

'**snapping** ,**turtle** *noun* a large American TURTLE with powerful JAWS

snap·py /'snæpi/ *adj.* (**snap·pi·er, snap·pi·est**) **1** (of a remark, title, etc.) smart or amusing and short: *a snappy slogan* ♦ *a snappy answer* **2** [usually before noun] (*informal*) attractive and fashionable: *a snappy outfit* ♦ *She's a snappy dresser.* **3** (of people or their behavior) tending to speak to people in a bad-tempered, impatient way **4** lively; quick: *a snappy tune* ▸ **snap·pi·ly** /-pəli/ *adv.*: *He summarized the speech snappily.* ♦ *snappily dressed* ♦ *"What?" she asked snappily.* **snap·pi·ness** /-pinəs/ *noun* [U]

IDM **make it snappy** (*informal*) used to tell someone to do something quickly or to hurry

snap·shot /'snæpʃɑt/ *noun* **1** a photograph, especially one taken quickly: *snapshots of the children* ⊃ thesaurus box at PHOTOGRAPH **2** [usually sing.] a short description or a small amount of information that gives you an idea of what something is like

snare /snɛr/ *noun, verb*

● **noun 1** a device used for catching small animals and birds, especially one that holds them by the leg or neck so that they cannot escape SYN TRAP **2** (*formal*) a situation that seems attractive but is unpleasant and difficult to escape from **3** the metal strings that are stretched across the bottom of a snare drum

● **verb** ~ **sth/sb** to catch something, especially an animal, in a snare SYN TRAP: *to snare a rabbit* ♦ (*figurative*) *Her one thought was to snare a rich husband.* ♦ (*figurative*) *He found himself snared in a web of intrigue.*

'**snare drum** *noun* a small drum with metal strings across one side that make a continuous sound when the drum is hit ⊃ picture at INSTRUMENT

snarf /snɑrf/ *verb* ~ **sth** (*informal*) to eat or drink something very quickly or in a way that people think is GREEDY: *The kids snarfed up all the cookies.*

snark·y /'snɑrki/ *adj.* (*informal*) criticizing someone in an unkind way: *a snarky remark*

snarl /snɑrl/ *verb, noun*

● **verb 1** [I] ~ **(at sb/sth)** (of dogs, etc.) to show the teeth and make a deep angry noise in the throat: *The dog snarled at us.* **2** [T] to speak in an angry or bad-tempered way: + **speech (at sb)** *"Get out of here!" he snarled.* ♦ ~ **sth (at sb)** *She snarled abuse at anyone who happened to walk past.*

PHR V ,**snarl 'up|** ,**snarl sth↔'up 1** to involve someone or something in a situation that stops their movement or progress; to become involved in a situation like this: *The accident snarled up the traffic all day.* **2** to become caught or twisted; to make something do this: *The sheets kept getting snarled up.*

● **noun 1** [usually sing.] a deep sound that an animal makes when it is angry and shows its teeth: *The dog bared its teeth in a snarl.* **2** [usually sing.] an act of speaking in an angry or bad-tempered way; the sound you make when you are angry, etc.: *a snarl of hate* **3** a situation in which traffic is unable to move: *rush-hour traffic snarls* **4** (*informal*) something that has become twisted in a messy way: *She used conditioner to remove the snarls from her hair.*

snatch /snætʃ/ *verb, noun*

● **verb 1** [T, I] to take something quickly and often rudely or roughly SYN GRAB: ~ **sth (+ adv./prep.)** *She managed to snatch the gun from his hand.* ♦ *Gordon snatched up his jacket and left the room.* ♦ **(+ adv./prep.)** *Hey, you kids! Don't all snatch!* **2** [T] ~ **sb/sth (from sb/sth)** to take someone or something away from a person or place, especially by force; to steal something SYN STEAL: *The raiders snatched $100 from the cash register.* ♦ *The baby was snatched from its parents' car.* **3** [T] ~ **sth** to take or get something quickly, especially because you do not have much time: *I managed to snatch an hour's sleep.* ♦ *The team snatched a dramatic victory in the last minute of the game.*

PHR V '**snatch at sth 1** to try to take hold of something with your hands: *He snatched at the steering wheel but I*

pushed him away. **2** to take an opportunity to do something: *We snatched at every moment we could be together.*
- **noun 1** a very small part of a conversation or some music that you hear **SYN** SNIPPET: *a snatch of music* ♦ *I only caught snatches of the conversation.* **2** an act of moving your hand very quickly to take or steal something: *a bag snatch* **IDM** **in snatches** for short periods rather than continuously: *Sleep came to him in brief snatches.*

snatch·er /'snætʃər/ *noun* (often in compounds) a person who takes something quickly with their hand and steals it: *a purse snatcher*

snaz·zy /'snæzi/ *adj.* (**snaz·zi·er, snaz·zi·est**) (*informal*) (of clothes, cars, etc.) fashionable, bright, and modern, and attracting your attention **SYN** JAZZY: *a snazzy tie*

sneak /snik/ *verb, noun, adj.*
- **verb** (**sneaked, sneaked** or *informal* **snuck, snuck** /snʌk/)
1 [I] + *adv./prep.* to go somewhere secretly, trying to avoid being seen **SYN** CREEP: *I sneaked up the stairs.* **2** [T] to do something or take someone or something somewhere secretly, often without permission: ~ *sth We sneaked a look at her diary.* ♦ ~ *sth to sb I managed to sneak a note to him.* ♦ ~ *sb sth I managed to sneak him a note.* **3** [T] ~ *sth* (*informal*) to secretly take something small or unimportant **SYN** PINCH: *I sneaked a cake when they were out of the room.* **PHR V** **,sneak 'up (on sb/sth)** to move toward someone very quietly so that they do not see or hear you until you reach them: *He sneaked up on his sister and shouted "Boo!"*
- **noun** (*old-fashioned, disapproving*) a person, especially a child, who tells someone about something wrong that another person has done **SYN** SNITCH
- **adj.** [only before noun] done without any warning: *a sneak attack*

sneak·er /'snikər/ *noun* [usually pl.] a shoe that you wear for sports or as informal clothing ⊃ picture at SHOE **SYN** TENNIS SHOE: *He wore old jeans and a pair of sneakers.*

sneak·ing /'snikɪŋ/ *adj.* [only before noun] if you have a **sneaking** feeling for someone or about something, you do not want to admit it to other people, because you feel embarrassed, or you are not sure that this feeling is right: *She had always had a sneaking admiration for him.* ♦ *I have a sneaking suspicion that she knows more than she's telling us.*

ˌsneak 'preview *noun* an opportunity to see something before it is officially shown to the public

ˈsneak thief *noun* a person who steals things without using force or breaking doors or windows

sneak·y /'sniki/ *adj.* (**sneak·i·er, sneak·i·est**) (*informal*) behaving in a secret and sometimes dishonest or unpleasant way **SYN** CRAFTY: *That was a sneaky trick!* ▶ **sneak·i·ly** /-kəli/ *adv.*

sneer /snɪr/ *verb, noun*
- **verb** [I, T] to show that you have no respect for someone by the expression on your face or by the way you speak **SYN** MOCK: ~ *(at sb/sth) He sneered at people who liked pop music.* ♦ *a sneering comment* ♦ + *speech "You? A writer?" she sneered.* ▶ **sneer·ing·ly** /'snɪrɪŋli/ *adv.*
- **noun** [usually sing.] an unpleasant look, smile, or comment that shows you do not respect someone or something: *A faint sneer of satisfaction crossed her face.*

sneeze /sniz/ *verb, noun*
- **verb** [I] to have air come suddenly and noisily out through your nose and mouth in a way that you cannot control, for example because you have a cold: *I've been sneezing all morning.*
IDM **not to be sneezed at** (*informal*) good enough to be accepted or considered seriously: *In those days, $20 was not a sum to be sneezed at.*
- **noun** the act of sneezing or the noise you make when you sneeze: *coughs and sneezes* ♦ *She gave a violent sneeze.*

snick·er /'snɪkər/ *verb* (also **snig·ger**) [I] ~ *(at sb/sth)* to laugh in a quiet unpleasant way, especially at something rude or at someone's problems or mistakes **SYN** TITTER: *What are you sniggering at?* ▶ **snick·er** (also **snig·ger**) *noun*

snide /snaɪd/ *adj.* (*informal*) criticizing someone or something in an unkind and indirect way: *snide comments/ remarks* ▶ **snide·ly** *adv.*

sniff /snɪf/ *verb, noun*
- **verb 1** [I] to breathe air in through your nose in a way that makes a sound, especially when you are crying, have a cold, etc.: *We all had colds and couldn't stop sniffing and sneezing.* **2** [T, I] to breathe air in through the nose in order to discover or enjoy the smell of something **SYN** SMELL: ~ *sth sniffing the fresh morning air* ♦ *to sniff glue* ♦ ~ *(at sth) The dog sniffed at my shoes.* ⊃ see also GLUE SNIFFING **3** [T, I] + *speech* | ~ *(sth)* to say something in a complaining or disapproving way: *"It's hardly what I'd call elegant," she sniffed.*
IDM **not to be sniffed at** (*informal*) good enough to be accepted or considered seriously: *In those days, $20 was not a sum to be sniffed at.*
PHR V **,sniff a'round** (*informal*) to try to find out information about someone or something, especially secret information: *We don't want journalists sniffing around.* **'sniff at sth** to show no interest in or respect for something **,sniff sb/ sth↔'out 1** to discover or find someone or something by using your sense of smell: *The dogs are trained to sniff out drugs.* **2** (*informal*) to discover or find someone or something by looking: *Journalists are good at sniffing out a scandal.*
- **noun 1** [C] an act or the sound of sniffing: *She took a deep sniff of the perfume.* ♦ *My mother gave a sniff of disapproval.* ♦ *His sobs soon turned to sniffs.* **2** [sing.] ~ *of sth* an idea of what something is like or that something is going to happen: *The sniff of power went to his head.* ♦ *They make threats but back down at the first sniff of trouble.* **3** [sing.] ~ *of sth* a small chance of something: *She didn't get even a sniff at a medal.*
IDM **have a (good) sniff around** to examine a place carefully

snif·fle /'snɪfl/ *verb, noun*
- **verb** [I, T] (+ *speech*) to sniff or keep sniffing, especially because you are crying or have a cold
- **noun** an act or the sound of sniffling: *After a while, her sniffles died away.*
IDM **get, have, etc. the sniffles** (*informal*) to get, have, etc. a slight cold

snif·fy /'snɪfi/ *adj.* ~ *(about sth)* (*informal*) not approving of something or someone because you think they are not good enough for you

snif·ter /'snɪftər/ *noun* a large glass used for drinking BRANDY

snig·ger /'snɪgər/ *verb, noun* = SNICKER

snip /snɪp/ *verb, noun*
- **verb** (-pp-) [T, I] to cut something with scissors using short quick strokes: ~ *sth Snip a tiny hole in the paper.* ♦ ~ *(at/ through sth) She snipped at the loose threads hanging down.* **PHR V** **,snip sth↔'off** to remove something by cutting it with scissors in short quick strokes
- **noun 1** [C] an act of cutting something with scissors; the sound that this makes: *Make a series of small snips along the edge of the fabric.* ♦ *Snip, snip, went the scissors.* **2 snips** [pl.] a tool like large scissors, used for cutting metal

snipe /snaɪp/ *verb, noun*
- **verb 1** [I] ~ *(at sb/sth)* to shoot at someone from a hiding place, usually from a distance: *Gunmen continued to snipe at people leaving their homes to find food.* **2** [I] ~ *(at sb/sth)* to criticize someone in an unpleasant way ▶ **snip·ing** *noun* [U]: *Aid workers remain in the area despite continuous sniping.*
- **noun** (*pl.* **snipe**) a bird with a long straight beak that lives on wet ground

snip·er /'snaɪpər/ *noun* a person who shoots at someone from a hidden position

snip·pet /'snɪpət/ *noun* **1** a small piece of information or news: *Do you have any interesting snippets for me?* ♦ *a snippet of information* **2** a short piece of a conversation, piece of music, etc. **SYN** EXTRACT, SNATCH

snip·py /ˈsnɪpi/ adj. (informal) rude; not showing respect

snit /snɪt/ noun

> **IDM** **be in a snit** to be bad-tempered and refuse to speak to anyone for a time because you are angry about something

snitch /snɪtʃ/ verb [I] ~ **(on sb) (to sb)** (informal, disapproving) (of a child) to tell a parent, teacher, etc. about something wrong that another child has done **SYN** **TELL ON SB**: Johnnie snitched on me to his mom. ▶ **snitch** noun: You little snitch! I'll never tell you anything again!

sniv·el /ˈsnɪvl/ verb (-l-, CanE usually -ll-) [I] to cry and complain in a way that people think is annoying **SYN** **WHINE**

sniv·el·ing (CanE usually **snivel·ling**) /ˈsnɪvəlɪŋ/ adj. [only before noun] (disapproving) tending to cry or complain a lot in a way that annoys people: a sniveling little brat

snob /snɑb/ noun (disapproving) **1** a person who admires people in the higher social classes too much and has no respect for people in the lower social classes: She's such a snob! **2** a person who thinks they are much better than other people because they are intelligent or like things that many people do not like: an intellectual snob ♦ a food/wine, etc. snob ♦ There is a snob value in driving the latest model.

snob·ber·y /ˈsnɑbəri/ noun [U] (disapproving) the attitudes and behavior of people who are snobs: intellectual snobbery

snob·bish /ˈsnɑbɪʃ/ (also informal **snob·by** /ˈsnɑbi/) adj. (disapproving) thinking that having a high social class is very important; feeling that you are better than other people because you are more intelligent or like things that many people do not like ▶ **snob·bish·ness** noun [U]

snood /snud/ noun a net or bag worn over the hair at the back of a woman's head for decoration

snook·er /ˈsnʊkər/ verb [usually passive] ~ **sb** (informal) to cheat or trick someone: Some very smart people got snookered by the bank.

snoop /snup/ verb, noun
- **verb** [I] (informal, disapproving) to find out private things about someone, especially by looking secretly around a place: ~ **(around sth)** Someone's been snooping around my apartment. ♦ ~ **(on sb)** journalists snooping on politicians ▶ **snoop·y** adj.: snoopy reporters
- **noun 1** (also **snoop·er**) a person who looks around a place secretly to find out private things about someone **2** [sing.] a secret look around a place: He had a snoop around her office.

snoot /snut/ noun (informal) **1** a person's nose **2** (disapproving) a person who treats other people as if they are not as good or as important as them

snoot·y /ˈsnuti/ (also informal **snot·ty**) adj. (snoot·i·er, snoot·i·est) (disapproving) treating people as if they are not as good or as important as you **SYN** **SNOBBISH** ▶ **snoot·i·ly** /ˈsnutl̩i/ adv. **snoot·i·ness** /ˈsnutinəs/ noun [U]

snooze /snuz/ verb [I] (informal) to have a short light sleep, especially during the day and usually not in bed: My brother was snoozing on the sofa. ᕤ thesaurus box at **SLEEP** ▶ **snooze** noun [sing.]: I often have a snooze after lunch.

snooze button noun a button on an **ALARM CLOCK** that you press when you wake up, so that you can sleep a little longer and be woken up again after a short time

snore /snɔr/ verb, noun
- **verb** [I] to breathe noisily through your nose and mouth while you are asleep: I could hear Paul snoring in the next room. ▶ **snor·er** noun **snor·ing** noun [U]: loud snoring
- **noun** noisy breathing while you are asleep: She lay awake listening to his snores.

snor·kel /ˈsnɔrkl/ noun a tube that you can breathe air through when you are swimming under the surface of the water ᕤ picture at **HOBBY** ▶ **snor·kel** verb (-l-, CanE usually -ll-) [I]

snor·kel·ing (CanE usually **snor·kel·ling**) /ˈsnɔrkəlɪŋ/ noun [U] the sport or activity of swimming underwater with a snorkel: to go snorkeling ᕤ picture at **HOBBY**

snort /snɔrt/ verb, noun
- **verb 1** [I, T] to make a loud sound by breathing air out noisily through your nose, especially to show that you are angry or amused: The horse snorted and tossed its head. ♦ ~ **with sth** to snort with laughter ♦ ~ **in sth** She snorted in disgust. ♦ + **speech** "You!" he snorted contemptuously. **2** [T] ~ **sth** to take drugs by breathing them in through the nose: to snort cocaine
- **noun 1** a loud sound that you make by breathing air out noisily through your nose, especially to show that you are angry or amused: to give a snort ♦ a snort of disgust ♦ I could hear the snort and stamp of a horse. **2** a small amount of a drug that is breathed in through the nose; an act of taking a drug in this way: to take a snort of cocaine

snot /snɑt/ noun [U] (informal) a word that some people find offensive, used to describe the liquid substance (= MUCUS) that is produced in the nose

snot·ty /ˈsnɑti/ adj. (snot·ti·er, snot·ti·est) (also **snot-nosed**) (informal) **1** = SNOOTY **2** full of or covered in snot: a snotty nose ♦ snotty kids

snout /snaʊt/ noun **1** the long nose and area around the mouth of some types of animals, such as pigs ᕤ compare MUZZLE **2** (informal, humorous) a person's nose **3** a part of something that sticks out at the front: the snout of a pistol

snow 🔑 /snoʊ/ noun, verb
- **noun 1** [U] small, soft, white pieces (called FLAKES) of frozen water that fall from the sky in cold weather; this substance when it is lying on the ground: *Snow was falling heavily.* ♦ We had snow in May this year. ♦ The snow was beginning to melt. ♦ Children were playing in the snow. ♦ 10 inches of snow were expected today. ♦ The snow didn't settle (= stay on the ground). ♦ Her skin was as white as snow. ᕤ collocations at **WEATHER** **2 snows** [pl.] (literary) an amount of snow that falls in one particular place or at one particular time: the first snows of winter ♦ the snows of Everest
  > **IDM** **as clean, pure, etc. as the driven snow** extremely clean, pure, etc.
- **verb 1** [I] when **it snows**, snow falls from the sky: It's been snowing heavily all day. **2** [T] ~ **sb** (informal) to impress someone a lot by the things you say, especially if these are not true or not sincere: He really snowed me with all his talk of buying a Porsche.
  > **IDM** **be snowed in** to be unable to leave a place because of heavy snow **be snowed under (with sth)** to have more things, especially work, than you feel able to deal with: I'd love to come but I'm completely snowed under at the moment.

snow·ball /ˈsnoʊbɔl/ noun, verb
- **noun 1** [C] a ball that you make out of snow to throw at someone or something in a game: a snowball fight **2** [sing.] (often used as an adjective) a situation that develops more and more quickly as it continues: All this publicity has had a snowball effect on the sales of their latest album. **3** [C] a COCKTAIL (= a type of alcoholic drink) that contains ADVOCAAT and LEMONADE
  > **IDM** **not have a snowball's chance in hell** (informal) to have no chance at all
- **verb** [I] if a problem, a plan, an activity, etc. **snowballs**, it quickly becomes much bigger, more serious, more important, etc.

the Snow Belt noun [sing.] (informal) the northern and northeastern states of the U.S. where the winters are very cold

snow·bird /ˈsnoʊbərd/ noun (informal) a person who spends the winter in a warmer climate, especially an old person from the north of the U.S., or from Canada, who spends the winter in the south

snow-blind adj. unable to see because of the light reflected from a large area of snow ▶ **snow-blindness** noun [U]

snow·blow·er /ˈsnoʊˌbloʊər/ noun a machine that removes snow from roads or paths by blowing it to one side

snow·board /ˈsnoʊbɔrd/ noun a long wide board that a

person stands on to move over snow in the sport of snowboarding ➲ picture at SPORT

snow·board·ing /'snoʊˌbɔrdɪŋ/ *noun* [U] the sport of moving over snow on a snowboard: *to go snowboarding* ♦ *Snowboarding is now an Olympic sport.* ➲ picture at SPORT ▸ **snow·board·er** *noun*

snow·bound /'snoʊbaʊnd/ *adj.* **1** (of a person or vehicle) trapped in a particular place and unable to move because a lot of snow has fallen **2** (of a road or building) that you cannot use or reach because a lot of snow has fallen

'snow-capped *adj.* (*literary*) (of mountains and hills) covered with snow on top

'snow chains *noun* [pl.] chains that are put on the wheels of a vehicle so that it can drive over snow

'snow cone *noun* crushed ice with a fruit flavor, served in a paper CONE

'snow-ˌcovered (also *literary* **'snow-clad**) *adj.* [usually before noun] covered with snow: *snow-covered fields*

'snow day *noun* a day when schools and/or businesses are closed because there is too much snow for people to be able to get to school or work

snow·drift /'snoʊdrɪft/ *noun* a deep pile of snow that has been blown together by the wind

snow·drop /'snoʊdrɑp/ *noun* a small white flower that appears in early spring

snow·fall /'snoʊfɔl/ *noun* [C, U] an occasion when snow falls; the amount of snow that falls in a particular place in a period of time: *a heavy/light snowfall* ♦ *an area of low snowfall* ♦ *What is the average annual snowfall for this state?*

snow·field /'snoʊfild/ *noun* a large area that is always covered with snow, for example in the mountains

snow·flake /'snoʊfleɪk/ *noun* a small soft piece of frozen water that falls from the sky as snow

'snow gun *noun* a machine that makes artificial snow and blows it onto SKI slopes

'snow job *noun* (*informal*) an attempt to trick someone or to persuade them to support something by telling them things that are not true, or by praising them too much

the 'snow line /'snoʊlaɪn/ *noun* [sing.] the level on mountains above which snow never melts completely

snow·man /'snoʊmæn/ *noun* (*pl.* **snow·men** /-mɛn/) a figure like a person that people, especially children, make out of snow for fun

snow·mo·bile /'snoʊmoʊˌbil/ (also **ski·mo·bile**) *noun* a vehicle that can move over snow and ice easily ➲ picture at SLED

'snow pea *noun* [usually pl.] a type of very small PEA that grows in long, flat, green PODS that are cooked and eaten whole

snow·plow /'snoʊplaʊ/ *noun, verb*
• *noun* a vehicle or machine for cleaning snow from roads or railroads
• *verb* [I] to bring the two points of your SKIS together, in order to go slower or to stop

snow·shoe /'snoʊʃu/ *noun* one of a pair of flat frames that you attach to the bottom of your shoes so that you can walk on deep snow without sinking in

snow·slide /'snoʊslaɪd/ *noun* = AVALANCHE

snow·storm /'snoʊstɔrm/ *noun* a very heavy fall of snow, usually with a strong wind

snow·suit /'snoʊsut/ *noun* a warm piece of clothing that covers the whole body, worn by children outdoors in cold weather

ˌsnow-'white *adj.* pure white in color: *snow-white sheets*

snow·y /'snoʊi/ *adj.* (**snow·i·er**, **snow·i·est**) **1** [usually before noun] covered with snow: *snowy fields* **2** (of a period of time) when a lot of snow falls: *a snowy weekend* **3** (*literary*) very white, like new snow: *snowy hair*

snub /snʌb/ *verb, noun*
• *verb* (**-bb-**) **1** ~ sb to insult someone, especially by ignoring them when you meet **SYN** COLD-SHOULDER: *I tried to be friendly, but she snubbed me completely.* **2** ~ sth to refuse to attend or accept something, for example as a protest **SYN** BOYCOTT: *All the country's leading players snubbed the tournament.*
• *noun* ~ (to sb) an action or a comment that is deliberately rude in order to show someone that you do not like or respect them **SYN** INSULT: *Her refusal to attend the dinner is being seen as a deliberate snub to the President.*
• *adj.* [only before noun] (of a nose) short, flat, and turned up at the end ▸ **'snub-nosed** *adj.*: *a snub-nosed child* ♦ *a snub-nosed revolver* (= with a short BARREL)

snuck pt, pp of SNEAK

snuff /snʌf/ *verb, noun*
• *verb* **1** [T] ~ sth (out) to stop a small flame from burning, especially by pressing it between your fingers or covering it with something **SYN** EXTINGUISH **2** [I, T] ~ (sth) (of an animal) to smell something by breathing in noisily through the nose: *The dogs were snuffing gently at my feet.* **PHRV** ˌsnuff sth↔'out to stop or destroy something completely: *An innocent child's life has been snuffed out by this senseless shooting.*
• *noun* [U] TOBACCO in the form of a powder that people take by breathing it into their noses **IDM** up to snuff as good as it/they should be **SYN** UP TO SCRATCH

snuff·box /'snʌfbɑks/ *noun* a small, usually decorated, box for holding snuff

snuf·fle /'snʌfl/ *verb, noun*
• *verb* **1** [I, T] (+ speech) to breathe noisily because you have a cold or you are crying **SYN** SNIFF: *I could hear the child snuffling in her sleep.* **2** [I] ~ (around) if an animal snuffles, it breathes noisily through its nose, especially while it is smelling something
• *noun* (also *less frequent* **snuf·fling**) an act or the sound of snuffling: *The silence was broken only by the snuffles of the dogs.* ♦ *His breath came in snuffles.*

snug /snʌg/ *adj.* **1** fitting someone or something closely: *The elastic at the waist gives a nice snug fit.* **2** warm, comfortable, and protected, especially from the cold **SYN** COZY: *a snug little house* ♦ *I spent the afternoon snug and warm in bed.* ▸ **snug·ly** *adv.*: *I left the children tucked up snugly in bed.* ♦ *The lid should fit snugly.* **snug·ness** *noun* [U]

snug·gle /'snʌgl/ *verb* [I, T] to get into, or to put someone or something into, a warm comfortable position, especially close to someone: + *adv./prep. The child snuggled up to her mother.* ♦ *He snuggled down under the bedclothes.* ♦ *She snuggled closer.* ♦ ~ sth + adv./prep. *He snuggled his head onto her shoulder.*

So. *abbr.* south; southern

so 🔑 /soʊ/ *adv., conj., noun*
• *adv.* **1** to such a great degree: *Don't look so angry.* ♦ *There's no need to worry so.* ♦ ~ … (that)… *She spoke so quietly (that) I could hardly hear her.* ♦ ~ … as to do sth *I'm not so stupid as to believe that.* ♦ (*formal*) *Would you be so kind as to lock the door when you leave?* **2** very; extremely: *I'm so glad to see you.* ♦ *We have so much to do.* ♦ *Their attitude is so very upper-class.* ♦ *The article was just so much* (= nothing but) *nonsense.* ♦ *He sat there ever so quietly.* ♦ *I do love it so.* **3** not ~ (as…) (used in comparisons) not to the same degree: *I haven't enjoyed myself so much for a long time.* ♦ *It wasn't so good as last time.* ♦ *It's not so easy as you'd think.* ♦ *He was not so quick a learner as his brother.* ♦ *It's not so much a hobby as a career* (= more like a career than a hobby). ♦ (*disapproving*) *Off she went without so much as* (= without even) *a "goodbye."* **4** used to show the size, amount, or number of something: *The fish was about so big* (= said when using your hands to show the size). ♦ *There are only so many* (= only a limited number of) *hours in a day.* **5** used to refer back to something that has already been mentioned: "*Is he coming?*" "*I hope so.*" ♦ "*Did they mind?*" "*I*

don't think so." ♦ If she notices, she never **says so**. ♦ I might be away next week. **If so**, I won't be able to see you. ♦ We are very busy—**so much so that** we won't be able to take time off this year. ♦ Programs are expensive, and **even more so** if you have to keep altering them. ♦ I hear that you're a writer— **is that so** (= is that true)? ♦ He thinks I dislike him but that just isn't so. ♦ George is going to help me, or **so he says** (= that is what he says). ♦ They asked me to call them and **I did so** (= I called). **6** also: Times have changed and **so have I**. ♦ "I prefer the first version." "**So do we**." **HELP** You cannot use so with negative verbs. Use **neither** or **either**: "I'm not hungry." "**Neither am I / I'm not very hungry either**." **7** used to agree that something is true, especially when you are surprised: "You were there, too." "**So I was —**I'd forgotten." ♦ "There's another one." "**So there is**." **8** (informal) used, often with a negative, before adjectives and noun phrases to emphasize something that you are saying: He is **so not** the right person for you. ♦ That is **so not** cool. **9** (informal) used, especially by children, to say that what someone says is not the case and the opposite is true: "You're not telling the truth, are you?" "I am, **so**!" **10** used when you are showing someone how to do something or telling them how something happened: Stand with your arms out, so. ♦ (literary) **So it was that** he finally returned home. **IDM** **and so forth | and so on (and so forth)** used at the end of a list to show that it continues in the same way: We discussed everything—when to go, what to see and so on. **… or so** used after a number, an amount, etc. to show that it is not exact: There were twenty or so (= about twenty) people there. ♦ We stayed for an hour or so. **so as to do sth** with the intention of doing something: We went early so as to get good seats. **so be it** (formal) used to show that you accept something and will not try to change it or cannot change it: If he doesn't want to be involved, then so be it. **so much for sth** **1** used to show that you have finished talking about something: So much for the situation in Germany. Now we turn our attention to France. **2** (informal) used to suggest that something has not been successful or useful: So much for that idea! **so… that** (formal) in such a way that: The program has been so organized that none of the talks overlap. **(all) the more so because…** used to give an important extra reason why something is true: His achievement is remarkable; all the more so because he had no help at all.

• **conj. 1** used to show the reason for something: It was still painful so I went to see a doctor. **2** ~ **(that…)** used to show the result of something: Nothing more was heard from him so that we began to wonder if he was dead. **3** ~ **(that…)** used to show the purpose of something: But I gave you a map so you wouldn't get lost! ♦ She worked hard so that everything would be ready in time. **4** used to introduce the next part of a story: So after shouting and screaming for an hour she walked out in tears. **5** (informal) used to show that you think something is not important, especially after someone has criticized you for it: So I had a couple of drinks on the way home. What's wrong with that? ♦ "You've been smoking again." "So?" **6** (informal) used to introduce a comment or a question: So, let's see. What do we need to take? ♦ So, what have you been doing today? **7** (informal) used when you are making a final statement: So, that's it for today. **8** (informal) used in questions to refer to something that has just been said: So there's nothing we can do about it? ♦ "I just got back from a trip to Rome." "So, how was it?" **9** used when stating that two events, situations, etc. are similar: Just as large companies are having to cut back, **so** small businesses are being forced to close. **IDM** **so what?** (informal) used to show that you think something is not important, especially after someone has criticized you for it: "He's fifteen years younger than you!" "So what?" ♦ So what if no one else agrees with me?

• **noun** = SOL

soak /soʊk/ verb, noun
• **verb 1** [T, I] to put something in liquid for a time so that it becomes completely wet; to become completely wet in this way: ~ **sth (in sth)** I usually soak the beans overnight. ♦ If you soak the tablecloth before you wash it, the stains should come out. ♦ ~ **(in sth)** Leave the apricots to soak for 20 minutes. ♦ I'm

going to go and soak in the bath. **2** [T] ~ **sb/sth** to make someone or something completely wet **SYN** DRENCH: A sudden shower of rain soaked the spectators. **3** [T] ~ **sb** (informal) to obtain a lot of money from someone by making them pay very high taxes or prices: He was accused of soaking his clients.
PHR V **soak 'into/'through sth | soak 'in** (of a liquid) to enter or pass through something: Blood had soaked through the bandage. **soak sth↔'off/'out** to remove something by leaving it in water **soak sth↔'up 1** to take in or absorb liquid: Use a cloth to soak up some of the excess water. **2** to absorb something into your senses, your body, or your mind: We were just sitting soaking up the atmosphere.
• **noun** (also **soak·ing**) [sing.] **1** an act of leaving something in a liquid for a period of time; an act of making someone or something wet: Give the shirt a good soak before you wash it. **2** (informal) a period of time spent taking a bath

soaked /soʊkt/ adj. **1** [not usually before noun] ~ **(with sth)** very wet **SYN** DRENCHED: He woke up soaked with sweat. ♦ You're **soaked through!** (= completely wet) ♦ They were **soaked to the skin**. ♦ You'll get soaked if you go out in this rain. ♦ Your clothes are soaked! ⊃ thesaurus box at WET **2** **-soaked** used with nouns to form adjectives describing something that is made completely wet with the thing mentioned: a blood-soaked cloth ♦ rain-soaked clothing

soak·ing /'soʊkɪŋ/ (also **soaking 'wet**) adj. completely wet **SYN** SOPPING: That coat is soaking—take it off. ♦ We arrived home soaking wet.

so-and-so /'soʊ ən ˌsoʊ/ noun (pl. **so-and-sos**) (informal) **1** [usually sing.] used to refer to a person, thing, etc. when you do not know their name or when you are talking in a general way: What would you say to Mrs. So-and-so who has called to complain about a noisy neighbor? **2** an annoying or unpleasant person. People sometimes say so-and-so to avoid using an offensive word: He's an ungrateful so-and-so.

soap 🔑 /soʊp/ noun, verb
• **noun 1** [U, C] a substance that you use with water for washing your body: soap and water ♦ a bar/piece of soap ♦ soap bubbles ⊃ picture at BAR **2** [C] (informal) = SOAP OPERA: soaps on TV ♦ She's an American soap star.
• **verb** ~ **yourself/sb/sth** to rub yourself/someone or something with soap ⊃ see also SOFT-SOAP

soap·box /'soʊpbɑks/ noun a small temporary platform that someone stands on to make a speech in a public place, usually outdoors
IDM **get/be on your soapbox** (informal) to express the strong opinions that you have about a particular subject

'soap ˌopera (also informal **soap**) noun [C, U] a story about the lives and problems of a group of people that is broadcast every day or several times a week on television or radio ⊃ collocations at TELEVISION

soap·stone /'soʊpstoʊn/ noun [U] a type of soft stone that feels like soap, used in making decorative objects

soap·suds /'soʊpsʌdz/ noun [pl.] = SUDS

soap·y /'soʊpi/ adj. [usually before noun] **1** full of soap; covered with soap **2** tasting or feeling like soap

soar /sɔr/ verb [I] **1** if the value, amount, or level of something soars, it rises very quickly **SYN** ROCKET: soaring costs/prices/temperatures ♦ Unemployment has soared to 18%. **2** ~ **(up) (into sth)** to rise quickly and smoothly up into the air: The rocket soared (up) into the air. ♦ (figurative) Her spirits soared (= she became very happy and excited). **3** to fly very high in the air or remain high in the air: an eagle soaring high above the cliffs **4** to be very high or tall: soaring mountains ♦ The building soared above us. **5** when music soars, it becomes higher or louder: soaring strings

sob /sɑb/ verb, noun
• **verb** (-bb-) **1** [I] to cry noisily, taking sudden sharp breaths: I heard a child sobbing loudly. ♦ He started to sob uncontrollably. **2** [T] to say something while you are crying: + **speech** "I hate him," she sobbed. ♦ ~ **sth (out)** He sobbed out his troubles.

h hat   m man   n no   ŋ sing   l leg   r red   y yes   w wet

IDM **sob your heart out** to cry noisily for a long time because you are very sad
- *noun* an act or the sound of sobbing: *He gave a deep sob.* ◆ *Her body was racked* (= shaken) *with sobs.*

so·ber /ˈsoʊbər/ *adj., verb*
- *adj.* **1** [not usually before noun] not drunk (= not affected by alcohol): *I promised him that I'd stay sober tonight.* ◆ *He was as sober as a judge* (= completely sober). **2** (of people and their behavior) serious and sensible: *a sober assessment of the situation* ◆ *He is honest, sober and hard-working.* ◆ *On sober reflection* (= after some serious thought), *I don't think I really need a car after all.* **3** (of colors or clothes) plain and not bright: *a sober gray suit* ▶ **so·ber·ly** *adv.* **IDM** see STONE COLD
- *verb* [T, I] ~ **(sb)** to make someone behave or think in a more serious and sensible way; to become more serious and sensible: *The bad news sobered us for a while.* ◆ *He suddenly sobered.*
  PHR V ,**sober 'up** | ,**sober sb 'up** to become or to make someone no longer drunk: *Stay here with us until you've sobered up.*

so·ber·ing /ˈsoʊbərɪŋ/ *adj.* making you feel serious and think carefully: *a sobering effect/experience/thought, etc.* ◆ *It is sobering to realize that this is not a new problem.*

so·bri·e·ty /səˈbraɪəti/ *noun* [U] (*formal*) **1** the state of being sober (= not being drunk) **2** the fact of being sensible and serious

so·bri·quet /ˈsoʊbrɪˌkeɪ/ (also **sou·bri·quet**) *noun* (*formal*) an informal name or title that you give someone or something **SYN** NICKNAME

ˈ**sob** ˌ**story** *noun* (*informal, disapproving*) a story that someone tells you just to make you feel sorry for them, especially one that does not have that effect or is not true

Soc. *abbr.* (in writing) SOCIETY

so·ca /ˈsoʊkə/ *noun* [U] a type of dance music, originally from the Caribbean, that mixes SOUL and CALYPSO

ˈ**so-called** **AWL** *adj.* **1** [only before noun] used to show that you do not think that the word or phrase that is being used to describe someone or something is appropriate: *the opinion of a so-called "expert"* ◆ *How have these so-called improvements helped the local community?* **2** [usually before noun] used to introduce the word that people usually use to describe something: *writers from the so-called "Beat Generation"*

soc·cer /ˈsɑkər/ *noun* [U] a game played by two teams of 11 players, using a round ball that players kick up and down the playing field. Teams try to kick the ball into the other team's goal: *soccer players* ◆ *a soccer field/team/match* ⊃ picture at SPORT ⊃ compare FOOTBALL

ˈ**soccer** ˌ**mom** *noun* (*informal*) a mother who spends a lot of time taking her children to activities such as sports and music lessons, used as a way of referring to a typical mother from the MIDDLE CLASSES

so·cia·ble /ˈsoʊʃəbl/ (also less frequent **so·cial**) *adj.* (of people) enjoying spending time with other people **SYN** GREGARIOUS: *She's a sociable child who'll talk to anyone.* ◆ *I'm not feeling very sociable this evening.* ◆ *We had a very sociable weekend* (= we did a lot of things with other people). **ANT** UNSOCIABLE ⊃ compare ANTISOCIAL ▶ **so·cia·bil·i·ty** /ˌsoʊʃəˈbɪləti/ *noun* [U]

so·cial 🔑 /ˈsoʊʃl/ *adj., noun*
- *adj.*
  > CONNECTED WITH SOCIETY **1** [only before noun] connected with society and the way it is organized: *social issues/problems/reforms* ◆ *a call for social and economic change* **2** [only before noun] connected with your position in society: *social class/background* ◆ *social advancement* (= improving your position in society)
  > ACTIVITIES WITH OTHERS **3** [only before noun] connected with activities in which people meet each other for pleasure: *a busy social life* ◆ *Team sports help to develop a child's social skills* (= the ability to talk easily to other people and do things

in a group). ◆ *Social events and training days are arranged for all the staff.* ◆ *Join a social club to make new friends.*
  > ANIMALS **4** [only before noun] (*technical*) living naturally in groups, rather than alone
  > FRIENDLY **5** = SOCIABLE
  ▶ **so·cial·ly** /-ʃəli/ *adv.*: *The reforms will bring benefits, socially and politically.* ◆ *This type of behavior is no longer socially acceptable.* ◆ *a socially disadvantaged family* (= one that is poor and from a low social class) ◆ *We meet at work, but never socially.* ◆ *Carnivores are usually socially complex mammals.*
- *noun* [C] (*old-fashioned*) a party that is organized by a group or club

ˌ**social 'bookmarking** *noun* [U] (*computing*) a way of BOOKMARKING (= storing and labeling) the addresses of pages on the Internet, using a special service that enables you to make them available to other Internet users

ˌ**social 'climber** *noun* (*disapproving*) a person who tries to improve their position in society by becoming friendly with people who belong to a higher social class

ˌ**social 'conscience** *noun* [sing., U] the state of being aware of the problems that affect a lot of people in society, such as being poor or having no home, and wanting to do something to help these people

ˌ**social 'contract** (also ˌ**social 'compact**) *noun* [sing.] an agreement among citizens to behave in a way that benefits everyone

ˌ**social 'Darwinism** *noun* [U] the late 19th and early 20th century theory that individuals and groups of people are affected by the same laws of NATURAL SELECTION as plants and animals: *Social Darwinism has been used to justify racist policies.*

ˌ**social de'mocracy** *noun* [U, C] a political system that combines the principles of SOCIALISM with the greater personal freedom of democracy; a country that has this political system of government ▶ ˌ**social 'democrat** *noun* ˌ**social demo'cratic** *adj.* [only before noun]

ˌ**social engi'neering** *noun* [U] the attempt to change society and to deal with social problems according to particular political beliefs, for example by changing the law

ˌ**Social In'surance** ˌ**number** *noun* (*abbr.* SIN) a number that the Canadian government uses to identify you, and that you use when you fill out official forms, apply for a job, etc.

so·cial·ism /ˈsoʊʃəˌlɪzəm/ *noun* [U] a set of political and economic theories based on the belief that everyone has an equal right to a share of a country's wealth and that the government should own and control the main industries ⊃ compare CAPITALISM, COMMUNISM, SOCIAL DEMOCRACY

so·cial·ist /ˈsoʊʃəlɪst/ *noun* a person who believes in or supports socialism; a member of a political party that believes in socialism ▶ **so·cial·ist** *adj.* [usually before noun]: *a socialist country* ◆ *socialist beliefs* ◆ *the ruling Socialist Party*

so·cial·is·tic /ˌsoʊʃəˈlɪstɪk/ *adj.* [usually before noun] (often *disapproving*) having some of the features of socialism

ˌ**socialist 'realism** *noun* [U] a theory that was put into practice in some COMMUNIST countries, especially in the Soviet Union under Stalin, that art, music, and literature should be used to show people the principles of a socialist society and encourage them to support it

so·cial·ite /ˈsoʊʃəˌlaɪt/ *noun* (sometimes *disapproving*) a person who goes to a lot of fashionable parties and is often written about in the newspapers, etc.

so·cial·i·za·tion /ˌsoʊʃələˈzeɪʃn/ *noun* [U] (*formal*) the process by which someone, especially a child, learns to behave in a way that is acceptable in their society

so·cial·ize /ˈsoʊʃəˌlaɪz/ *verb* **1** [I] ~ **(with sb)** to meet and spend time with people in a friendly way, in order to enjoy yourself **SYN** MIX: *I enjoy socializing with the other students.* ◆ *Maybe you should socialize more.* **2** [T, often passive] ~ **sb (to do sth)** (*formal*) to teach people to behave in ways that are acceptable to their society: *The family has the important* *function of socializing children.* **3** [T, usually passive] **~ sth** to organize something according to the principles of socialism

socialized 'medicine *noun* [U] medical and hospital care provided by the government for everyone by paying for it with public money

social 'media *noun* [U, pl.] websites and software programs used for social networking: *Social media is a big part of my life.* ◆ *Social media such as Facebook and Twitter are used by journalists.* ◆ *Social media advertising will boost your sales.*

social 'networking *noun* [U] communication with people who share your interests using a Web site or other service on the Internet: *a social networking site* ⊃ **collocations at** E-MAIL

social psy'chology *noun* [U] the study of people's behavior, attitudes, etc. in society ▶ **social psy'chologist** *noun*

social 'science *noun* **1** [U] the study of people in society **2** [C] a particular subject connected with the study of people in society, for example geography, economics, or SOCIOLOGY

social 'scientist *noun* a person who studies social science

social 'secretary *noun* the person who organizes social activities for an organization or for another person

Social Se'curity *noun* [U] (*abbr.* SS) a system in which people pay money regularly to the government when they are working and receive payments from the government when they are unable to work, especially when they are sick or too old to work

Social Se'curity ,number *noun* (*abbr.* SSN) an official identity number that everyone in the U.S. is given when they are born

social 'services *noun* [pl.] a system that is organized by the local government to help people who have financial or family problems; the department or the people who provide this help: *a leaflet on the range of social services available* ◆ *the local social services department*

social ,studies *noun* [U] a subject taught in schools that studies human society and that includes history, geography, government, etc.

social ,work *noun* [U] paid work that involves giving help and advice to people living in the community who have financial or family problems

social ,worker *noun* a person whose job is social work

so·ci·e·tal /sə'saɪətl/ *adj.* [only before noun] (*technical*) connected with society and the way it is organized

so·ci·e·ty 🔑 /sə'saɪəti/ *noun* (*pl.* **so·ci·e·ties**)
1 [U] people in general, living together in communities: *policies that will benefit society as a whole* ◆ *Racism exists at all levels of society.* ◆ *They carried out research into the roles of men and women in today's society* **2** [C, U] a particular community of people who share the same customs, laws, etc.: *modern industrial societies* ◆ *demand created by a consumer society* ◆ *Can Britain ever be a classless society?* ◆ *They were discussing the problems of Western society.* **3** [C] (*abbr.* Soc.) (especially in names) a group of people who join together for a particular purpose: *a member of the drama society* ◆ *the American Society of Newspaper Editors* **4** [U] the group of people in a country who are fashionable, rich, and powerful: *Their daughter married into* **high society.** ◆ *a society wedding* **5** [U] (*formal*) the state of being with other people **SYN** COMPANY: *He was a solitary man who avoided the society of others.*

socio- /'soʊsioʊ; 'soʊʃioʊ/ *combining form* (in nouns, adjectives, and adverbs) connected with society or the study of society: *socioeconomic* ◆ *sociolinguistics*

so·ci·o·cul·tur·al /ˌsoʊsioʊ'kʌltʃərəl/ *adj.* relating to society and culture

so·ci·o·ec·o·nom·ic /ˌsoʊsioʊˌɛkə'nɑmɪk; -ˌikə-/ *adj.*

relating to society and economics: *people from different socioeconomic backgrounds*

so·ci·o·lect /'soʊsioʊˌlɛkt/ *noun* (*linguistics*) a variety of a language that the members of a particular social class or social group speak

so·ci·o·lin·guis·tics /ˌsoʊsioʊlɪŋ'gwɪstɪks/ *noun* [U] the study of the way language is affected by differences in social class, region, sex, etc. ▶ **so·ci·o·lin·guis·tic** *adj.*

so·ci·ol·o·gist /ˌsoʊsi'ɑlədʒɪst/ *noun* a person who studies sociology

so·ci·ol·o·gy /ˌsoʊsi'ɑlədʒi/ *noun* [U] the scientific study of the nature and development of society and social behavior ▶ **so·ci·o·log·i·cal** /ˌsoʊsiə'lɑdʒɪkl/ *adj.*: *sociological theories* **so·ci·o·log·i·cal·ly** /-kli/ *adv.*

so·ci·o·path /'soʊsiəˌpæθ/ *noun* a person who has a mental illness and who behaves in an aggressive or dangerous way toward other people

so·ci·o·po·lit·i·cal /ˌsoʊsioʊpə'lɪtɪkl/ *adj.* relating to society and politics

sock 🔑 /sak/ *noun, verb*
• *noun* **1** a piece of clothing that is worn over the foot, ankle, and lower part of the leg, especially inside a shoe: *a pair of socks* **2** (*informal*) a strong blow, especially with the FIST: *He gave him a sock on the jaw.*
IDM **blow/knock sb's socks off** (*informal*) to surprise or impress someone very much
• *verb* **~ sb** (*informal*) to hit someone hard: *She got angry and socked him in the mouth.* ◆ (*figurative*) *The banks are socking customers with higher charges.*
IDM **sock it to sb** (*informal* or *humorous*) to do something or tell someone something in a strong and effective way: *Go in there and sock it to 'em!*
PHR V **,sock sth↔a'way** to save money

sock·et /'sakət/ *noun* **1** = OUTLET **2** a device on a piece of electrical equipment that you can fit a plug, a light BULB, etc. into: *an antenna socket on the television* **3** a curved hollow space in the surface of something that another part fits into or moves around in: *His eyes bulged in their sockets.*

sod /sad/ *noun* [sing.] (*formal* or *literary*) a layer of earth with grass growing on it; a piece of this that has been removed: *under the sod* (= in your grave)

so·da /'soʊdə/ *noun* **1** (also **'soda ,pop, pop**) [U, C] a sweet CARBONATED drink (= a drink with bubbles) made with soda water, fruit flavor, and sometimes ice cream: *He had an ice-cream soda.* **2** [U, C] = SODA WATER: *a Scotch and soda* **3** [U] a chemical substance in common use that is a COMPOUND of SODIUM: *baking/washing soda* ⊃ see also CAUSTIC SODA, SODIUM BICARBONATE, SODIUM CARBONATE

'soda ,bread *noun* [U] bread that rises because of SODIUM BICARBONATE that is added instead of YEAST

'soda ,cracker *noun* a thin dry CRACKER with salt on top of it **SYN** SALTINE

'soda ,fountain *noun* **1** (*old-fashioned*) a counter with seats in a drugstore or restaurant where you can buy soda to drink, ICE CREAM, etc. **2** a bottle containing soda water or another drink, with a device that you press to pour the drink and put bubbles into it

'soda ,pop *noun* (*old-fashioned*) = SODA

'soda ,water (also **so·da**) *noun* **1** [U] CARBONATED water (= water with bubbles) used as a drink on its own or to mix with alcoholic drinks or fruit juice (originally made with SODIUM BICARBONATE) **2** [C] a glass of soda water

sod·den /'sadn/ *adj.* **1** extremely wet **SYN** SOAKED: *sodden grass* **2 -sodden** extremely wet with the thing mentioned: *a rain-sodden jacket*

so·di·um /'soʊdiəm/ *noun* [U] (*symb.* **Na**) a chemical element. Sodium is a soft silver-white metal that is found naturally only in COMPOUNDS, such as salt.

,sodium bi'carbonate (also **bi,carbonate of 'soda, 'baking ,soda**) (also *informal* **bi·carb**) *noun* [U] (*symb.*

$NaHCO_3$) a chemical in the form of a white powder that dissolves and is used in baking to make cakes, etc. rise and become light, and in making CARBONATED drinks and some medicines

ˌsodium ˈcarbonate (also ˈwashing ˌsoda) noun [U] (symb. Na_2CO_3) a chemical in the form of white CRYSTALS or powder that dissolves and is used in making glass, soap, and paper, and for making water soft

ˌsodium ˈchloride noun [U] (symb. NaCl) common salt (a chemical made up of SODIUM and CHLORINE)

so·fa /ˈsoʊfə/ noun a long comfortable seat with a back and arms, for two or more people to sit on ➔ picture at CHAIR **SYN** COUCH

ˈsofa ˌbed noun a sofa that can be folded out to form a bed ➔ picture at BED

soft 🔊 /sɔft/ adj. (soft·er, soft·est)

>NOT HARD **1** changing shape easily when pressed; not stiff or firm: soft margarine ◆ soft feather pillows ◆ The grass was soft and springy. **2** less hard than average: soft rocks such as limestone ◆ soft cheeses **ANT** HARD
>NOT ROUGH **3** smooth and pleasant to touch: soft skin **ANT** ROUGH
>WITHOUT ANGLES/EDGES **4** not having sharp angles or hard edges: This season's fashions focus on warm tones and soft lines. ◆ The moon's pale light cast soft shadows.
>LIGHT/COLORS **5** [usually before noun] not too bright, in a way that is pleasant and relaxing to the eyes: a soft pink ◆ the soft glow of candlelight **ANT** HARSH
>RAIN/WIND **6** not strong or violent **SYN** LIGHT: A soft breeze rustled the trees.
>SOUNDS **7** not loud, and usually pleasant and gentle **SYN** QUIET: soft background music ◆ a soft voice
>SYMPATHETIC **8** kind and sympathetic; easily affected by other people's suffering: Julia's soft heart was touched by his grief. **ANT** HARD
>NOT STRICT **9** (usually disapproving) not strict or severe; not strict or severe enough **SYN** LENIENT: ~ (on sb/sth) The government is not becoming soft on crime. ◆ ~ (with sb) If you're too soft with these kids they'll never respect you. **ANT** TOUGH
>CRAZY **10** (informal, disapproving) stupid or crazy: He must be going soft in the head.
>NOT BRAVE/TOUGH ENOUGH **11** (informal, disapproving) not brave enough; wanting to be safe and comfortable: Stay in a hotel? Don't be so soft. I want to camp out under the stars.
>TOO EASY **12** (disapproving) not involving much work; too easy and comfortable: They had got too used to the soft life at home. **ANT** HARD
>WATER **13** not containing mineral salts and therefore good for washing: You won't need much soap—the water here is very soft. **ANT** HARD
>CONSONANTS **14** (phonetics) not sounding hard, for example "c" in "city" and "g" in "general" **ANT** HARD

▶ soft·ness noun [U, sing.]: the softness of her skin ◆ the softness of the water ➔ see also SOFTLY

IDM have a soft spot for sb/sth (informal) to like someone or something: She's always had a soft spot for you. ➔ more at OPTION, TOUCH

soft·ball /ˈsɔfbɔl/ noun **1** [U] a game similar to baseball but played on a smaller field with a larger softer ball **2** [C] the ball used in softball

ˌsoft-ˈboiled adj. (of eggs) boiled for a short time so that the YOLK is still soft or liquid ➔ compare HARD-BOILED

ˌsoft-ˈcore adj. [usually before noun] showing or describing sexual activity without being too detailed or shocking ➔ compare HARD-CORE

ˈsoft drink noun a cold drink that does not contain alcohol ➔ compare HARD

ˌsoft ˈdrug noun an illegal drug, such as CANNABIS, that some people take for pleasure and that is not considered as harmful as other drugs ➔ compare HARD DRUG

soft·en /ˈsɔfn/ verb **1** [I, T] to become, or to make something

softer: Fry the onions until they soften. ◆ ~ sth a lotion to soften the skin ◆ Linseed oil will soften stiff leather. **2** [I, T] ~ (sth) to become or to make something less bright, rough, or strong: Trees soften the outline of the house. **3** [I, T] to become or to make someone or something more sympathetic and less severe or critical: She felt herself softening toward him. ◆ His face softened as he looked at his son. ◆ ~ sb/sth She softened her tone a little. **4** [T] ~ sth to reduce the force or the unpleasant effects of something **SYN** CUSHION: Airbags are designed to soften the impact of a car crash. **IDM** see BLOW **PHR V** ˌsoften sb↔ˈup (informal) **1** to try to persuade someone to do something for you by being very nice to them before you ask them: Potential customers are softened up with free gifts before the sales talk. **2** to make an enemy weaker and easier to attack

soft·en·er /ˈsɔfənər/ noun **1** [C] a device that is used with chemicals to make hard water soft: a water softener **2** [U, C] a substance that you add when washing clothes to make them feel soft: fabric softener

ˌsoft ˈerror noun (computing) an error or fault that makes a program or OPERATING SYSTEM stop working, but that can often be corrected by switching the computer off then on again

ˌsoft ˈfocus noun [U] a method of producing a photograph so that the edges of the image are not clear, in order to make it look more romantic and attractive

ˈsoft goods noun [pl.] **1** things that are made of cloth, such as clothes and curtains **2** (business) any type of cloth **SYN** TEXTILES

ˌsoft-ˈhearted adj. kind, sympathetic, and emotional **SYN** KIND-HEARTED **ANT** HARD-HEARTED

soft·ie (also soft·y) /ˈsɔfti/ noun (pl. soft·ies) (informal) a kind, sympathetic, or emotional person: There's no need to be afraid of him—he's a big softie.

soft·ly 🔊 /ˈsɔftli/ adv.
in a soft way: She closed the door softly behind her. ◆ "I missed you," he said softly. ◆ The room was softly lit by a lamp. ◆ a softly tailored suit

ˈsoft ˌpedal noun (music) a PEDAL on a piano that is pressed to make the sound quieter

ˈsoft-ˌpedal verb (-l-, CanE -ll-) [T, I] ~ (on) sth (informal) to treat something as less serious or important than it really is: Television has been accused of soft-pedaling bad news.

ˌsoft ˈsell noun [sing.] a method of selling that involves persuading someone to buy something rather than using pressure or aggressive methods ➔ compare HARD SELL

ˈsoft-shoe noun, verb
• noun [U] a type of dance like TAP, performed with soft shoes that do not make a noise: a soft-shoe shuffle
• verb **1** [I] to perform a soft-shoe dance **2** [I] + adv./prep. to move somewhere very quietly, without attracting attention

ˌsoft ˈshoulder noun a strip of ground with a soft surface at the edge of a road

ˌsoft-ˈspoken adj. having a gentle and quiet voice

ˌsoft ˈtarget noun a person or thing that it is very easy to attack

ˌsoft ˈtissue noun [U, C] (anatomy) the parts of the body that are not bone, for example the skin and muscles

ˈsoft top noun a type of car that has a soft roof that can be folded down or removed; the roof of such a car ➔ see also CONVERTIBLE

soft·ware 🔊 /ˈsɔftwɛr/ noun [U]
the programs, etc. used to operate a computer: application/ system software ◆ design/educational/ music-sharing, etc. software ◆ to install/run a piece of software ◆ Will the software run on my machine? ➔ compare HARDWARE

ˈsoftware ˌengineer noun a person who writes computer programs

'software ˌpackage noun (computing) = PACKAGE

soft·wood /'sɔftwʊd/ noun [U, C] wood from trees such as PINE, that is cheap to produce and can be cut easily ➔ compare HARDWOOD

soft·y = SOFTIE

sog·gy /'sɑgi/ adj. (sog·gi·er, sog·gi·est) wet and soft, usually in a way that is unpleasant: *We squelched over the soggy ground.* ◆ *soggy bread*

soi-di·sant /ˌswɑ diˈzɑ̃/ adj. [only before noun] (from French) used to show someone's description of himself/herself, usually when you do not agree with it: *a soi-disant novelist*

soi·gnée /swɑnˈyei/ adj. (from French, formal) (of a woman) elegant; carefully and neatly dressed

soil 🗝 /sɔil/ noun, verb

● **noun** [U, C] **1** the top layer of the earth in which plants, trees, etc. grow: *poor/dry/acid/sandy/fertile, etc. soil* ◆ *the study of rocks and soils* ◆ *soil erosion* **2** (literary) a country; an area of land: *It was the first time I had set foot on African soil.*

● **verb** [often passive] **sth** (formal) to make something dirty: *soiled linen* ◆ (figurative) *I don't want you soiling your hands with this sort of work* (= doing something unpleasant or wrong). ➔ thesaurus box at DIRTY

THESAURUS

soil

dirt • mud • dust • clay • land • earth • ground

These are all words for the top layer of the earth in which plants grow.

soil the top layer of the earth in which plants grow: *Plant the seedlings in damp soil.*

dirt soil, especially loose soil: *Pack the dirt firmly around the plants.*

mud wet soil that is soft and sticky: *The car got stuck in the mud.*

dust a fine powder that consists of very small pieces of rock, earth, etc: *A cloud of dust rose as the truck pulled away.*

clay a type of heavy sticky soil that becomes hard when it is baked and is used to make things such as pots and bricks: *The tiles are made of clay.*

land an area of ground, especially of a particular type: *an area of rich, fertile land*

earth the substance that plants grow in or where people are buried after they die

ground an area of soil: *The ground was still wet from the rain.* ◆ *They drove across miles of rough, rocky ground.* **NOTE** Ground is not used for loose soil: *a handful of dry ground*

PATTERNS

■ **good/rich** soil/land/earth
■ **fertile/infertile** soil/land/ground
■ to **dig** (at/in) the soil/mud/clay/land/earth/ground
■ to **cultivate/plow** the soil/land/earth

'soil ˌscience noun [U] the study of soil, for example the study of its structure or characteristics

soi·rée /swɑˈrei/ noun (from French, formal) a formal party in the evening, especially at someone's home

so·journ /'soʊdʒɜrn/ noun (literary) a temporary stay in a place away from your home ▶ **sojourn** verb [I] + **adv./ prep.**

sol /soʊl/ (also **so**) noun (music) the fifth note of a MAJOR SCALE

sol·ace /'sɑləs/ noun [U, sing.] (formal) a feeling of emotional comfort when you are sad or disappointed; a person or thing that makes you feel better or happier when you are sad or disappointed **SYN** COMFORT: *He sought solace in the whiskey bottle.* ◆ *She turned to Rob for solace.* ◆ *His grand-*

children were a solace in his old age. ▶ **sol·ace** verb ~ **sb** (literary): *She smiled, as though solaced by the memory.*

so·lar /'soʊlər/ adj. [only before noun] **1** of or connected with the sun: *solar radiation* ◆ *the solar cycle* **2** using the sun's energy: *solar power/heating* ➔ collocations at ENVIRON-MENT

ˌsolar 'cell noun a device that converts light and heat energy from the sun into electricity

so·lar·i·um /səˈlɛriəm/ noun a room whose walls are mainly made of glass, or that has special lamps, where people go to get a SUNTAN (= make their skin go brown) using light from the sun or artificial light

ˌsolar 'panel noun a piece of equipment on a roof that uses light and heat energy from the sun to produce electricity or heating

so·lar plex·us /ˌsoʊlər 'plɛksəs/ noun [sing.] **1** (anatomy) a system of nerves at the base of the stomach **2** (informal) the part of the body at the top of the stomach, below the RIBS: *a painful punch in the solar plexus*

'solar ˌsystem noun **1 the solar system** [sing.] the sun and all the planets that move around it **2** [C] any group of planets that all move around the same star

ˌsolar 'year noun the time it takes the earth to go around the sun once, approximately 365¼ days

sold pt, pp of SELL

sol·der /'sɑdər/ noun, verb

● **noun** [U] a mixture of metals that is heated and melted and then used to join metals, wires, etc. together

● **verb** ~ **sth (to/onto sth)** | ~ **(A and B together)** to join pieces of metal or wire with solder

'soldering ˌiron noun a tool that is heated and used for joining metals and wires by soldering them

sol·dier 🗝 /'soʊldʒər/ noun, verb

● **noun** a member of an army, especially one who is not an officer: *soldiers in uniform* ◆ *soldiers on duty* ➔ see also FOOT SOLDIER

● **verb**

PHR V ˌsoldier 'on to continue with what you are doing or trying to achieve, especially when this is difficult or unpleasant

sol·dier·ing /'soʊldʒərɪŋ/ noun [U] the life or activity of being a soldier

sol·dier·ly /'soʊldʒərli/ adj. typical of a good soldier

ˌsoldier of 'fortune noun a person who fights for any country or person who will pay them **SYN** MERCENARY

sol·dier·y /'soʊldʒəri/ noun [U] (old-fashioned) a group of soldiers, especially of a particular kind

ˌsold 'out adj. **1** if a concert, game, etc. is sold out, there are no more tickets available for it **2** if a store is sold out of a product, it has no more of it left to sell

sole **AWL** /soʊl/ adj., noun, verb

● **adj.** [only before noun] **1** only; single: *the sole surviving member of the family* ◆ *My sole reason for coming here was to see you.* ◆ *This is the sole means of access to the building.* **2** belonging to one person or group; not shared: *She has sole responsibility for the project.* ◆ *the sole owner*

● **noun 1** [C] the bottom surface of the foot: *The hot sand burned the soles of their feet.* ➔ picture at BODY **2** [C] the bottom part of a shoe or sock, not including the heel: *leather soles* ➔ compare HEEL **3 -soled** (in adjectives) having the type of soles mentioned: *rubber-soled shoes* **4** [U, C] (pl. **sole**) a flat sea fish that is used for food

● **verb** [usually passive] ~ **sth** to repair a shoe by replacing the sole

sol·e·cism /'sɑləˌsɪzəm; 'soʊlə-/ noun (formal) **1** a mistake in the use of language in speech or writing **2** an example of bad manners or unacceptable behavior

sole·ly **AWL** /'soʊlli/ adv. only; not involving someone or something else: *She was motivated solely by self-interest.*

| t tea | ṭ butter | d did | k cat | g got | tʃ chin | dʒ June | f fall |

♦ *Selection is based solely on merit.* ♦ *He became solely responsible for the firm.*

sol·emn /ˈsaləm/ *adj.* **1** (of a person) not happy or smiling: SYN SERIOUS *Her face grew solemn.* ♦ *a solemn expression* ANT CHEERFUL ⊃ thesaurus box at SERIOUS **2** done, said, etc. in a very serious and sincere way: *a solemn oath/ undertaking/vow, etc.* **3** (of a religious ceremony or formal occasion) performed in a serious way: *a solemn ritual* ▶ **sol·emn·ly** *adv.*: *He nodded solemnly.* ♦ *She solemnly promised not to say a word to anyone about it.* ♦ *The choir walked solemnly past.*

so·lem·ni·ty /səˈlɛmnəti/ *noun* **1** [U] the quality of being solemn: *He was smiling, but his eyes retained a look of solemnity.* ♦ *He was buried with great pomp and solemnity.* **2 solemnities** [pl.] (*formal*) formal things that people do at a serious event or occasion: *to observe the solemnities of the occasion*

sol·em·nize /ˈsaləmˌnaɪz/ *verb* ~ **sth** (*formal*) to perform a religious ceremony, especially a marriage

so·le·noid /ˈsoʊləˌnɔɪd; ˈsalə-/ *noun* (*physics*) a piece of wire, wound into circles, that acts as a MAGNET when carrying an electric current

sol-fa /ˌsoʊl ˈfɑ; ˈsoʊl fɑ/ *noun* (*music*) a system of naming the notes of the SCALE, used in teaching singing

so·lic·it /səˈlɪsət/ *verb* **1** [T, I] (*formal*) to ask someone for something, such as support, money, or information; to try to get something or persuade someone to do something: ~ **sth (from sb)** *They were planning to solicit funds from a number of organizations.* ♦ ~ **sb (for sth)** *Historians and critics are solicited for their opinions.* ♦ ~ **(for sth)** *to solicit for money* ♦ ~ **sb to do sth** *Volunteers are being solicited to assist with the project.* **2** [I, T] ~ **(sb)** (of a PROSTITUTE) to offer to have sex with people in return for money: *Prostitutes solicited openly in the streets.* ♦ *the crime of soliciting* ▶ **so·lic·i·ta·tion** /səˌlɪsəˈteɪʃn/ *noun* [U, C]: *the solicitation of money for election funds*

so·lic·i·tor /səˈlɪsətər/ *noun* **1** a person whose job is to visit or telephone people and try to sell them something **2** the most senior legal officer of a city, town, or government department

So·licitor General *noun* (*pl.* Solicitors General) a senior legal officer, next in rank below the ATTORNEY GENERAL

so·lic·i·tous /səˈlɪsətəs/ *adj.* (*formal*) being very concerned for someone and wanting to make sure that they are comfortable, well, or happy SYN ATTENTIVE ▶ **so·lic·i·tous·ly** *adv.* (*formal*)

so·lic·i·tude /səˈlɪsəˌtud/ *noun* [U] ~ **(for sb/sth)** (*formal*) anxious care for someone's comfort, health, or happiness: *I was touched by his solicitude for the boy.*

sol·id 🔑 /ˈsaləd/ *adj., noun*
● *adj.*
▷ NOT LIQUID/GAS **1** hard or firm; not in the form of a liquid or gas: *The planet Jupiter may have no solid surface at all.* ♦ *The boat bumped against a solid object.* ♦ *She had refused all solid food.* ♦ *It was so cold that the stream had frozen solid.* ♦ *The boiler uses solid fuel.*
▷ WITHOUT HOLES OR SPACES **2** having no holes or spaces inside; not hollow: *They were drilling through solid rock.* ♦ *The stores are packed solid* (= very full and crowded) *at this time of year.*
▷ STRONG **3** strong and made well: *These chains seem fairly solid.*
▷ RELIABLE **4** that you can rely on; having a strong basis: *As yet, they have no solid evidence.* ♦ *This provided a solid foundation for their marriage.* ♦ *The team was solid as a rock in defense.*
▷ GOOD BUT NOT SPECIAL **5** definitely good and steady but perhaps not excellent or special: *2008 was a year of solid achievement.* ♦ *He's a solid player.*
▷ MATERIAL **6** [only before noun] made completely of the material mentioned (that is, the material is not only on the surface): *a solid gold bracelet*
▷ PERIOD OF TIME **7** (*informal*) without a pause; continuous:

The essay represents a solid week's work. ♦ *It rained for two hours solid this afternoon.*
▷ COLOR **8** of the color mentioned and no other color: *One cat is black and white, the other solid black.*
▷ SHAPE **9** (*geometry*) a shape that is **solid** has length, width, and height and is not flat: *A cube is a solid figure.*
▷ IN AGREEMENT **10** in complete agreement; agreed on by everyone: *The strike was solid, supported by all the members.* ⊃ see also ROCK SOLID
● *noun*
▷ NOT LIQUID/GAS **1** a substance or an object that is solid, not a liquid or a gas: *liquids and solids* ♦ *The baby is not yet on solids* (= eating solid food).
▷ SHAPE **2** (*geometry*) a shape that has length, width, and height, such as a CUBE

sol·i·dar·i·ty /ˌsaləˈdærəti/ *noun* [U] support by one person or group of people for another because they share feelings, opinions, aims, etc.: *community solidarity* ♦ ~ **with sb** *to express/show solidarity* with someone ♦ *Demonstrations were held as a gesture of solidarity with the hunger strikers.*

so·lid·i·fy /səˈlɪdəˌfaɪ/ *verb* (so·lid·i·fies, so·lid·i·fying, so·lid·i·fied, so·lid·i·fied) ~ **(into sth) 1** [I, T] to become solid; to make something solid: ~ **(into sth)** *The mixture will solidify into toffee.* ♦ ~ **sth** *solidified lava* **2** [I, T] (of ideas, etc.) to become or to make something become more definite and less likely to change: ~ **(into sth)** *Vague objections to the system solidified into firm opposition.* ♦ ~ **sth** *They solidified their position as Britain's top band.* ▶ **so·lid·i·fi·ca·tion** /səˌlɪdəfəˈkeɪʃn/ *noun* [U]

so·lid·i·ty /səˈlɪdəti/ *noun* [U] the quality or state of being solid: *the strength and solidity of Romanesque architecture* ♦ *Her writings have extraordinary depth and solidity.* ♦ *the solidity of his support for his staff*

sol·id·ly /ˈsalədli/ *adv.* **1** in a firm and strong way: *a large, solidly-built house* ♦ *He stood solidly in my path.* **2** continuously; without stopping: *It rained solidly for three hours.* **3** agreeing with or supporting someone or something completely: *The state is solidly Republican.*

solid-'state *adj.* (*technical*) using or containing solid SEMICONDUCTORS: *a solid-state radio*

so·lil·o·quy /səˈlɪləkwi/ *noun* [C, U] (*pl.* so·lil·o·quies) a speech in a play in which a character, who is alone on the stage, speaks his or her thoughts; the act of speaking thoughts in this way SYN MONOLOGUE: *Hamlet's famous soliloquy, "To be or not to be…"* ♦ *the playwright's use of soliloquy* ▶ **so·lil·o·quize** /səˈlɪləˌkwaɪz/ *verb* [I]

sol·ip·sism /ˈsaləpˌsɪzəm/ *noun* [U] (*philosophy*) the theory that only the SELF exists or can be known ▶ **sol·ip·sis·tic** /ˌsaləpˈsɪstɪk/ *adj.*

sol·i·taire /ˈsaləˌtɛr/ *noun* **1** [U] a card game for only one player **2** [C] a single PRECIOUS STONE; a piece of jewelry with a single precious stone in it

sol·i·tar·y /ˈsaləˌtɛri/ *adj., noun*
● *adj.* **1** [usually before noun] done alone; without other people: *She enjoys long solitary walks.* ♦ *He led a solitary life.* **2** (of a person or an animal) enjoying being alone; frequently spending time alone: *He was a solitary child.* ♦ *Tigers are solitary animals.* **3** (of a person, thing, or place) alone, with no other people or things around SYN SINGLE: *a solitary farm* ♦ *A solitary light burned dimly in the hall.* **4** [usually before noun] (especially in negative sentences and questions) only one SYN SINGLE: *There was not a solitary shred of evidence* (= none at all). ▶ **sol·i·tar·i·ness** *noun* [U]
● *noun* (*pl.* sol·i·tar·ies) **1** [U] (*informal*) = SOLITARY CONFINEMENT **2** [C] (*formal*) a person who chooses to live alone

solitary con'finement (also *informal* sol·i·tar·y) *noun* [U] a punishment in which a prisoner is kept alone in a separate cell: *to be in solitary confinement*

sol·i·tude /ˈsaləˌtud/ *noun* [U] the state of being alone, especially when you find this pleasant SYN PRIVACY: *She longed for peace and solitude.*

so·lo /ˈsoʊloʊ/ adj., noun
• **adj.** [only before noun] **1** done by one person alone, without anyone helping them: *his first solo flight* ◆ *a solo effort* **2** connected with or played as a musical solo: *a solo artist* (= for example a singer who sings on their own, not as part of a group) ◆ *a piece for solo violin* ▶ **so·lo** adv.: *She wanted to fly solo across the Atlantic.* ◆ *After three years with the band he decided to go solo.*
• **noun** (pl. **so·los**) **1** a piece of music, dance, or entertainment performed by only one person: *a guitar solo* ⊃ compare DUET **2** a flight in which the pilot flies alone without an INSTRUCTOR (= teacher)

so·lo·ist /ˈsoʊloʊɪst/ noun a person who plays an instrument or performs alone

Sol·o·mon /ˈsɑləmən/ noun used to talk about a very wise person: *In this job you need to exhibit the wisdom of Solomon.* **ORIGIN** From Solomon in the Bible, a king of Israel who was famous for being wise.

sol·stice /ˈsoʊlstəs; ˈsɑl-; ˈsɔl-/ noun either of the two times of the year at which the sun reaches its highest or lowest point in the sky in the middle of the day, marked by the longest and shortest days: *the summer/winter solstice* ⊃ picture at EARTH

sol·u·ble /ˈsɑlyəbl/ adj. **1** ~ (in sth) that can be dissolved in a liquid: *soluble aspirin* ◆ *Glucose is soluble in water.* **2** (formal) (of a problem) that can be solved ANT INSOLUBLE ▶ **sol·u·bil·i·ty** /ˌsɑlyəˈbɪləti/ noun [U]

so·lu·tion 🔑 /səˈluʃn/ noun
1 [C] ~ (to sth) a way of solving a problem or dealing with a difficult situation SYN ANSWER: *Attempts to find a solution have failed.* ◆ *There's no simple solution to this problem.* ◆ *Do you have a better solution?* **2** [C] ~ (to sth) an answer to a PUZZLE or to a problem in mathematics: *The solution to last week's quiz is on page 81.* **3** [C, U] a liquid in which something is dissolved: *an alkaline solution* ◆ *saline solution* **4** [U] the process of dissolving a solid or gas in a liquid: *the solution of glucose in water*

solve 🔑 /salv; sɔlv/ verb
1 ~ sth to find a way of dealing with a problem or difficult situation: *Attempts are being made to solve the problem of waste disposal.* **2** ~ sth to find the correct answer or explanation for something: *to solve an equation/a puzzle/a riddle* ◆ *to solve a crime/mystery*

sol·ven·cy /ˈsɑlvənsi/ noun [U] the state of not being in debt (= not owing money)

sol·vent /ˈsɑlvənt/ noun, adj.
• **noun** [U, C] a substance, especially a liquid, that can dissolve another substance
• **adj. 1** [not usually before noun] having enough money to pay your debts; not in debt ANT INSOLVENT **2** (technical) able to dissolve another substance, or be dissolved in another substance: *Lead is more solvent in acidic water.*

solvent a·buse noun [U] the practice of breathing in gases from glue or similar substances in order to produce a state of excitement ⊃ see also GLUE SNIFFING

solv·er /ˈsalvər; ˈsɔl-/ noun a person who finds an answer to a problem or a difficult situation: *She's a good problem solver.*

som·ber /ˈsɑmbər/ adj. **1** dark in color; dull SYN DRAB: *dressed in somber shades of gray and black* **2** sad and serious SYN MELANCHOLY: *Paul was in a somber mood.* ◆ *The year ended on a somber note.* ▶ **som·ber·ly** adv. **som·ber·ness** noun [U]

som·bre·ro /sɑmˈbreroʊ; səm-/ noun (pl. **som·bre·ros**) a Mexican hat for men that is tall with a very wide BRIM, turned up at the edges ⊃ picture at HAT

some 🔑 det., pron., adv.
• **det.** /səm; strong form sʌm/ **1** used with noncountable nouns or plural countable nouns to mean "an amount of" or "a number of," when the amount or number is not given: *There's still some wine in the bottle.* ◆ *Have some more*

vegetables. **HELP** In negative sentences and questions **any** is usually used instead of "some": *I don't want any more vegetables.* ◆ *Is there any wine left?* However, **some** is used in questions that expect a positive reply: *Would you like some milk in your coffee?* ◆ *Didn't you borrow some books of mine?* **2** /sʌm/ used to refer to certain members of a group or certain types of a thing, but not all of them: *Some people find this more difficult than others.* ◆ *I like some modern music* (= but not all of it). **3** /sʌm/ a large number or amount of something: *It was with some surprise that I heard the news.* ◆ *We've known each other for some years now.* ◆ *We're going to be working together for some time* (= a long time). **4** /sʌm/ a small amount or number of something: *There is some hope that things will improve.* **5** used with singular nouns to refer to a person, place, thing, or time that is not known or not identified: *There must be some mistake.* ◆ *He's in some kind of trouble.* ◆ *She won a competition in some newspaper or other.* ◆ *I'll see you again some time, I'm sure.* **6** /sʌm/ (informal, sometimes ironic) used to express a positive or negative opinion about someone or something: *That was some party!* ◆ *Some expert you are! You know even less than me.*
• **pron.** /sʌm/ ~ (of sb/sth) **1** used to refer to an amount of something or a number of people or things when the amount or number is not given: *Some disapprove of the idea.* ◆ *You'll find some in the drawer.* ◆ *Here are some of our suggestions.* **HELP** In negative sentences and questions **any** is usually used instead of "some": *I don't want any.* ◆ *Do you have any of the larger ones?* However, **some** is used in questions that expect a positive reply: *Would you like some?* ◆ *Weren't you looking for some of those?* **2** a part of the whole number or amount being considered: *All these students are good, but some work harder than others.* ◆ *Some of the music was weird.*
IDM ... **and then some** (informal) and a lot more than that: *We got our money's worth and then some.*
• **adv.** /sʌm/ **1** used before numbers to mean "approximately": *Some thirty people attended the funeral.* **2** (informal) to some degree: *He likes opera some.* ◆ *"Are you finding the work any easier?" "Some."*

-some /səm/ suffix **1** (in adjectives) producing; likely to: *fearsome* ◆ *quarrelsome* **2** (in nouns) a group of the number mentioned: *a foursome*

some·bod·y 🔑 /ˈsʌmˌbɑdi; -ˌbʌdi; -bədi/ pron.
= SOMEONE: *Somebody should have told me.* ◆ *She thinks she's really somebody* (= someone important) *in that car.* **ANT** NOBODY

some·day /ˈsʌmdeɪ/ adv. at some time in the future: *Someday he'll be famous.*

some·how 🔑 /ˈsʌmhaʊ/ adv.
1 (also informal **some·way**, **some·ways**) in a way that is not known or certain: *We must stop him from seeing her somehow.* ◆ *Somehow or other I must get a new job.* **2** for a reason that you do not know or understand: *Somehow, I don't feel I can trust him.* ◆ *She looked different somehow.*

some·one 🔑 /ˈsʌmwʌn/ (also **some·bod·y**) pron. **1** a person who is not known or mentioned by name: *There's someone at the door.* ◆ *Someone's left their bag behind.* ◆ *It's time for someone new* (= a new person) *to take over.* ◆ *It couldn't have been me—it must have been someone else* (= a different person). ◆ *Should we call a doctor or someone?* **HELP** The difference between **someone** and **anyone** is the same as the difference between **some** and **any**. Look at the notes there. **2** an important person: *He was a small-time lawyer eager to be someone.* ⊃ compare NOBODY

some·place /ˈsʌmpleɪs/ adv., pron. = SOMEWHERE: *It has to go someplace.* ◆ *Can't you do that someplace else?* ◆ *We need to find someplace to live.*

som·er·sault /ˈsʌmərˌsɔlt/ noun, verb
• **noun** a movement in which someone turns over completely, with their feet over their head, on the ground, or in the air: *to do/turn a somersault* ◆ *He turned back somersaults.* ◆ (figurative) *Her heart did a somersault when she saw him.*

• **verb** [I] (+ adv./prep.) to turn over completely in the air: *The car hit the curb and somersaulted into the air.*

some·thing 🔊 /ˈsʌmθɪŋ/ *pron., adv.*

• **pron.** **1** a thing that is not known or mentioned by name: *We stopped for something to eat.* ◆ *Give me something to do.* ◆ *There's something wrong with the TV.* ◆ *There's something about this place that frightens me.* ◆ *Don't just stand there. Do something!* ◆ *His name is Alan something* (= I don't know his last name). ◆ *She's a professor of something or other* (= I'm not sure what) *at Amherst.* ◆ *He's something in* (= has a job connected with) *television.* ◆ *The car hit a tree or something.* ◆ *I could just eat a little something.* **HELP** The difference between **something** and **anything** is the same as the difference between **some** and **any**. Look at the notes there. **2** (*informal*) a thing that is thought to be important or worth taking notice of: *There's something in* (= some truth or some fact or opinion worth considering in) *what he says.* ◆ *It's quite something* (= a thing that you should feel happy about) *to have a job at all these days.* ◆ *"We should finish by tomorrow." "That's something"* (= a good thing), *anyway.* **3** (*informal*) used to show that a description or an amount, etc. is not exact: *She called at something after ten o'clock.* ◆ *a new comedy aimed at thirty-somethings* (= people between thirty and forty years old) ◆ *It tastes something like melon.* ◆ *They pay twenty dollars an hour. Something like that.* ◆ *She found herself something of a* (= to some degree a) *celebrity.* ◆ *The program has something to do with* (= in some way about) *the environment.* ◆ *He gave her a wry look, something between amusement and regret.* **IDM** **make something of yourself** to be successful in life **something else** a different thing; another thing: *He said something else that I thought was interesting.* **2** (*informal*) a person, a thing, or an event that is much better than others of a similar type: *I've seen some fine players, but she's something else.*

• **adv.** (*informal*) used with an adjective to emphasize a statement: *She was swearing something terrible.*

some·time /ˈsʌmtaɪm/ *adv., adj.*

• **adv.** at a time that you do not know exactly or has not yet been decided: *I saw him sometime last summer.* ◆ *We must get together sometime.*

• **adj.** [only before noun] (*formal*) **1** used to refer to what someone used to be: *Thomas Atkins, sometime vicar of this parish* **2** used to refer to what someone does occasionally: *a sometime contributor to this magazine*

some·times 🔊 /ˈsʌmtaɪmz/ *adv.*

occasionally rather than all of the time: *Sometimes I go by car.* ◆ *He sometimes writes to me.* ◆ *I like to be on my own sometimes.*

some·way /ˈsʌmweɪ/ also some·ways *adv.* (*informal*) = SOMEHOW

some·what 🔊 **AWL** /ˈsʌmwʌt/ *adv.*

to some degree: *I was somewhat surprised to see him.* ◆ *The situation has changed somewhat since we last met.* ◆ *What happened to them remains somewhat of a mystery.*

some·where 🔊 /ˈsʌmwer/ (also some·place) *adv.*

in, at, or to a place that you do not know or do not mention by name: *I've seen him somewhere before.* ◆ *Can we go somewhere warm?* ◆ *I've already looked there—it must be somewhere else.* ◆ *He went to school in New York or somewhere* (= I'm not sure where). ◆ *They live somewhere or other in France.* **HELP** The difference between **somewhere** and **anywhere** is the same as the difference between **some** and **any**. Look at the notes there. ▶ **some·where** (also some·place) *pron.*: *We need to find somewhere to* (= a place to) *live.* ◆ *I know somewhere we can go.* **IDM** **get somewhere** (*informal*) to make progress in what you are doing **somewhere around, between, etc. sth** approximately the number or amount mentioned: *It cost somewhere around two thousand dollars.*

---

som·nam·bu·list /sɑmˈnæmbyəlɪst/ *noun* (*formal*) = SLEEPWALKER ▶ som·nam·bu·lism /-ˌlɪzəm/ *noun* [U]

som·no·lent /ˈsɑmnələnt/ *adj.* (*formal*) **1** almost asleep: *a somnolent cat* ◆ (*figurative*) *a somnolent town* **2** making you feel tired: *a somnolent Sunday afternoon* ▶ som·no·lence /-ləns/ *noun* [U]

son 🔊 /sʌn/ *noun*

1 [C] a person's male child: *We have two sons and a daughter.* ◆ *They have three grown-up sons.* ◆ *He's the son of a professor.* ◆ *Maine & Sons, Grocers* (= the name of a company on a sign) ⊃ collocations at CHILD **2** [sing.] (*informal*) a friendly form of address that is used by an older man to a young man or boy: *Well, son, how can I help you?* **3** [C] (*literary*) a man who belongs to a particular place or country, etc.: *one of France's most famous sons* **4** **my son** (*formal*) used by a priest to address a boy or man **5** **the Son** [sing.] Jesus Christ as the second member of the TRINITY: *the Father, the Son, and the Holy Spirit* **IDM** **see** FATHER, FAVORITE *adj.*, PRODIGAL

so·nar /ˈsoʊnɑr/ *noun* [U] equipment or a system for finding objects underwater using sound waves ⊃ compare RADAR

so·na·ta /səˈnɑtə/ *noun* a piece of music for one instrument or for one instrument and a piano, usually divided into three or four parts

son et lu·mière /ˌsoʊn eɪ lumˈyer/ *noun* [U] (from *French*) a performance held at night at a famous place that tells its history with special lights and sound

song 🔊 /sɔŋ/ *noun*

1 [C] a short piece of music with words that you sing: *a folk/love/pop, etc. song* ◆ *We sang a song together.* ⊃ collocations at MUSIC ⊃ see also SWAN SONG **2** [U] songs in general; music for singing: *The story is told through song and dance.* ◆ *Suddenly he burst into song* (= started to sing). ⊃ see also PLAINSONG **3** [U, C] the musical sounds that birds make: *the song of the blackbird* **IDM** **for a song** (*informal*) very cheaply; at a low price **a song and dance (about sth)** (*informal*) a long explanation about something, or excuse for something **on song** (*informal*) working or performing well ⊃ more at SING

song·bird /ˈsɔŋbərd/ *noun* a bird that has a musical call, for example a WARBLER or THRUSH

song·book /ˈsɔŋbʊk/ *noun* a book containing the music and words of different songs

song·smith /ˈsɔŋsmɪθ/ *noun* (*informal*) a person who writes popular songs

song·ster /ˈsɔŋstər/ *noun* (*old-fashioned*) **1** a word sometimes used in newspapers to mean "singer" **2** a SONGBIRD

song·stress /ˈsɔŋstrəs/ *noun* a word sometimes used in newspapers to mean "a woman singer"

song·writ·er /ˈsɔŋˌraɪtər/ *noun* a person who writes the words and usually also the music for songs: *singer-songwriter Paul Simon*

song·writ·ing /ˈsɔŋˌraɪtɪŋ/ *noun* [U] the process of writing songs

son·ic /ˈsɑnɪk/ *adj.* (*technical*) connected with sound or the speed of sound: *sonic waves*

ˌsonic ˈboom *noun* the EXPLOSIVE sound that is made when an aircraft travels faster than the speed of sound

ˈson-in-ˌlaw *noun* (*pl.* sons-in-law) the husband of your daughter ⊃ compare DAUGHTER-IN-LAW

son·net /ˈsɑnət/ *noun* a poem that has 14 lines, each containing 10 syllables, and a fixed pattern of RHYME: *Shakespeare's sonnets*

son·ny /ˈsʌni/ *noun* [sing.] (*old-fashioned*) a word used by an older person to address a young man or boy

ˌson of a ˈgun *noun* (*informal*) **1** a person or thing that you are annoyed with: *My car's at the shop—the son of a gun broke down again.* **2** used to express the fact that you are surprised or annoyed: *Well, son of a gun—and I thought the old guy couldn't dance!* **3** (*old-fashioned*) used by a man to address or talk about a male friend that he admires and

---

likes: *Frank, you old son of a gun—I haven't seen you for months.*

son·o·gram /ˈsɑnəˌgræm/ *noun* (*technical*) an image of what is inside someone's body, that is taken using a special machine **⊃** compare ULTRASOUND

so·no·rous /ˈsɑnərəs/ *adj.* (*formal*) having a pleasant, full, deep sound: *a sonorous voice* ▶ **so·nor·i·ty** /səˈnɔrəti; -ˈnɑr-/ *noun* [U, C]: *the rich sonority of the bass* **so·no·rous·ly** *adv.*

soon 🔑 /sun/ *adv.* (**soon·er, soon·est**)
1 in a short time from now; a short time after something else has happened: *We'll be home soon./We'll soon be home.* ◆ *She sold the house* **soon after** *her husband died.* ◆ *I soon realized the mistake.* ◆ *It soon became clear that the program was a failure.* ◆ (*informal*) *See you soon!* **2** early; quickly: *How soon can you get here?* ◆ *We'll deliver the goods* **as soon as** *we can.* ◆ *Please send it* **as soon as possible.** ◆ *Next Monday is* **the soonest** *we can deliver.* ◆ *They arrived home sooner than expected.* ◆ **The sooner** *we set off,* **the sooner** *we will arrive.* ◆ **All too soon** *the party was over.* **⊃** see also ASAP
IDM **no sooner said than done** used to say that something was, or will be, done immediately **no sooner… than…** used to say that something happens immediately after something else: *No sooner had she said it than she burst into tears.* **⊃** note at HARDLY **the sooner the better** very soon; as soon as possible: *"When should I tell him?" "The sooner the better."* **sooner or later** at some time in the future, even if you are not sure exactly when: *Sooner or later you will have to make a decision.* **sooner rather than later** after a short time rather than after a long time: *We urged them to sort out the problem sooner rather than later.* **I, etc. would sooner do sth (than sth else)** to prefer to do something (than do something else): *She'd sooner share a house with other students than live at home with her parents.* **⊃** more at ANYTIME, JUST

soot /sʊt/ *noun* [U] black powder that is produced when wood, coal, etc. is burned **⊃** see also SOOTY

soothe /suð/ *verb* **1** ~ **sb** to make someone who is anxious, upset, etc. feel calmer **SYN** CALM: *The music soothed her for a while.* **2** ~ **sth** to make a TENSE or painful part of your body feel more comfortable **SYN** RELIEVE: *This should soothe the pain.* ◆ *Take a warm bath to soothe tense, tired muscles.* ▶ **sooth·ing** *adj.*: *a soothing voice/lotion* **sooth·ing·ly** *adv.*: *"There's no need to worry," he said soothingly.*
PHR V **'soothe sth↔away** to remove a pain or an unpleasant feeling

sooth·er /ˈsuðər/ *noun* (*CanE*) a specially shaped rubber or plastic object for a baby to suck **SYN** PACIFIER

sooth·say·er /ˈsuθˌseɪər/ *noun* (*old use*) a person who is believed to be able to tell what will happen in the future

soot·y /ˈsʊti/ *adj.* **1** covered with SOOT **2** of the color of SOOT

sop /sɑp/ *noun* [usually sing.] ~ **(to sb/sth)** a small, not very important thing that is offered to someone who is angry or disappointed in order to make them feel better

soph·ist /ˈsɑfɪst/ *noun* **1** a teacher of philosophy in ancient Greece, especially one with an attitude of doubting that statements are true **2** a person who uses intelligent but wrong arguments

so·phis·ti·cate /səˈfɪstɪkət/ *noun* (*formal*) a sophisticated person

so·phis·ti·cat·ed /səˈfɪstəˌkeɪtəd/ *adj.* **1** having a lot of experience of the world and knowing about fashion, culture, and other things that people think are socially important: *the sophisticated pleasures of city life* ◆ *Mark is a smart and sophisticated young man.* **⊃** compare NAIVE **2** (of a machine, system, etc.) advanced and complicated in the way that it works or is presented: *highly sophisticated computer systems* ◆ *Medical techniques are becoming more sophisticated all the time.* **3** (of a person) able to understand difficult or complicated ideas: *a sophisticated audience* **ANT** UNSOPHISTICATED

so·phis·ti·ca·tion /səˌfɪstəˈkeɪʃn/ *noun* [U] the quality of being sophisticated

soph·ist·ry /ˈsɑfəstri/ *noun* (*pl.* **soph·ist·ries**) (*formal*) **1** [U] the use of intelligent arguments to persuade people that something is true when it is really false **2** [C] a reason or an explanation that tries to show that something is true when it is really false

soph·o·more /ˈsɑfmɔr/ *noun* **1** a student in the second year of a course of study at a college or university **2** a high school student in the 10th grade **⊃** compare FRESHMAN, JUNIOR, SENIOR

soph·o·mor·ic /ˌsɑfˈmɔrɪk; ˌsɑfə-/ *adj.* showing a lack of MATURITY (= the ability to behave in a sensible, adult manner): *sophomoric humor*

sop·o·rif·ic /ˌsɑpəˈrɪfɪk/ *adj.* (*formal*) making you want to go to sleep: *the soporific effect of the sun*

sop·ping /ˈsɑpɪŋ/ (also **ˌsopping ˈwet**) *adj.* (*informal*) very wet **SYN** SOAKING

so·pran·o /səˈprænoʊ/ *noun, adj.*
● *noun* (*pl.* **so·pran·os** /səˈprænoʊz; səˈprænoʊz/) a singing voice with the highest range for a woman or boy; a singer with a soprano voice **⊃** compare ALTO, MEZZO-SOPRANO, TREBLE
● *adj.* [only before noun] (of a musical instrument) with the highest range of notes in its group: *a soprano saxophone* **⊃** compare ALTO, BASS[1], TENOR

so·prano re·corder *noun* (*music*) the most common size of RECORDER (= a musical instrument in the shape of a pipe that you blow into), with a high range of notes

sor·bet /sɔrˈbeɪ/ *noun* [C, U] a sweet frozen food made from sugar, water, and fruit juice, often eaten as a DESSERT

sor·cer·er /ˈsɔrsərər/ *noun* (in stories) a man with magic powers, who is helped by evil spirits

sor·cer·ess /ˈsɔrsərəs/ *noun* (in stories) a woman with magic powers, who is helped by evil spirits

sor·cer·y /ˈsɔrsəri/ *noun* [U] magic that uses evil spirits **SYN** BLACK MAGIC

sor·did /ˈsɔrdəd/ *adj.* **1** immoral or dishonest: *It was a shock to discover the truth about his sordid past.* ◆ *I didn't want to hear the sordid details of their relationship.* **2** very dirty and unpleasant **SYN** SQUALID: *people living in sordid conditions*

sore 🔑 /sɔr/ *adj., noun*
● *adj.* **1** if a part of your body is **sore**, it is painful, and often red, especially because of infection or because a muscle has been used too much: *to have a sore throat* ◆ *His feet were sore after the walk.* ◆ *My stomach is still sore* (= painful) *after the operation.* **⊃** thesaurus box at PAINFUL **2** [not before noun] ~ **(at sb/about sth)** (*informal*) upset and angry, especially because you have been treated unfairly **SYN** ANNOYED ▶ **sore·ness** *noun* [U]: *an ointment to reduce soreness and swelling*
IDM **a sore point** a subject that makes you feel angry or upset when it is mentioned: *It's a sore point with Sue's parents that the children have not been baptized yet.* **stand/stick out like a sore thumb** to be very noticeable in an unpleasant way **⊃** more at SIGHT
● *noun* a painful, often red, place on your body where there is a wound or an infection **SYN** WOUND[1]: *open sores* **⊃** see also BEDSORE, CANKER SORE, COLD SORE

sore·ly /ˈsɔrli/ *adv.* seriously; very much: *I was sorely tempted to complain, but I didn't.* ◆ *If you don't come to the reunion you'll be sorely missed.*

sor·ghum /ˈsɔrgəm/ *noun* [U] very small grain grown as food in tropical countries; the plant that produces this grain

so·ror·i·ty /səˈrɔrəti; -ˈrɑr-/ *noun* (*pl.* **so·ror·i·ties**) a club for a group of women students at a college or university **⊃** compare FRATERNITY

sor·rel /ˈsɔrəl; ˈsɑr-/ *noun* **1** [U] a plant with leaves that taste bitter and are used in salads or in making soup or sauces **2** [C] a horse of a light reddish-brown color: *a sorrel mare*

sor·row /ˈsɑroʊ; ˈsɔr-/ *noun, verb*
- *noun* **1** [U] ~ (at/for/over sth) a feeling of great sadness because something very bad has happened **SYN** GRIEF: *He expressed his sorrow at the news of her death.* ◆ *They said that the decision was made **more in sorrow than in anger**.* **2** [C] a very sad event or situation: *the joys and sorrows of childhood*
- *verb* [I] (*literary*) to feel or express great sadness: *the sorrowing relatives*

sor·row·ful /ˈsɑroʊfl; ˈsɔr-/ *adj.* (*literary*) very sad: *her sorrowful eyes* ▶ **sor·row·ful·ly** /-fəli/ *adv.*

sor·ry /ˈsɑri; ˈsɔri/ *adj., exclamation*
- *adj.* (sor·ri·er, sor·ri·est) **HELP** You can also use more sorry and most sorry. **1** [not before noun] feeling sad and sympathetic: ~ (that)... *I'm sorry that your husband lost his job.* ◆ ~ (to see, hear, etc.) *We're sorry to hear that your father's in the hospital again.* ◆ ~ (about sth) *No one is sorrier than I am about what happened.* **2** [not before noun] feeling sad and ashamed about something that has been done: ~ (about sth) *We're very sorry about the damage to your car.* ◆ ~ (for sth/doing sth) *He says he's really sorry for taking the car without asking.* ◆ ~ (that)... *She was sorry that she'd lost her temper.* ◆ *If you **say you're sorry** we'll forgive you.* **3** [not before noun] feeling disappointed about something and wishing you had done something different or had not done something: ~ (that)... *She was sorry that she'd lost contact with Mary.* ◆ *You'll be sorry if I catch you!* ◆ ~ to do sth *I was genuinely sorry to be leaving college.* **4** [only before noun] very sad or bad, especially making you feel sympathy or disapproval: *The business is in a **sorry state**.* ◆ *They were a **sorry sight** when they eventually got off the boat.*
  IDM **be/feel sorry for sb** to feel sympathy for someone: *He decided to help Jan, as he felt sorry for her.* **feel sorry for yourself** (*informal, disapproving*) to feel unhappy; feel sympathy for yourself: *Stop feeling sorry for yourself and think about other people for a change.* **I'm sorry 1** used when you are apologizing for something: *I'm sorry, I forgot.* ◆ *Oh, I'm sorry. Have I taken the one you wanted?* ◆ *I'm sorry. I can't make it tomorrow.* **2** used for disagreeing with someone or politely saying "no": *I'm sorry, I don't agree.* ◆ *I'm sorry, I'd rather you didn't go.* **3** used for introducing bad news: *I'm sorry to have to tell you you've failed.* **I'm sorry to say** used for saying that something is disappointing: *He didn't accept the job, I'm sorry to say.* ⊃ **more at** SAFE
- *exclamation* **1** used when you APOLOGIZE for something: *Sorry I'm late!* ◆ *Did I stand on your foot? Sorry!* ◆ *Sorry to bother you, but could I speak to you for a moment?* ◆ *Sorry, we don't allow dogs in the house.* ◆ *He didn't even **say sorry**.* **2** used for asking someone to repeat something that you have not heard clearly: *Sorry? Could you repeat the question?* **3** used for correcting yourself when you have said something wrong: *Take the first turn, sorry, the third turn on the right.*

sort /sɔrt/ *noun, verb*
- *noun* **1** [C] a group or type of people or things that are similar in a particular way **SYN** KIND: *"**What sort of** music do you like?" "Oh, all sorts."* ◆ *This sort of problem is quite common./These sorts of problems are quite common.* ◆ *He's the sort of person who only cares about money.* ◆ *For dessert there's a fruit pie **of some sort** (= you are not sure what kind).* ◆ *Most people went on training courses **of one sort or another** (= of various types) last year.* ◆ (*informal*) *There were snacks— peanuts, olives, **that sort of thing**.* ◆ (*informal*) *There are **all sorts of** activities (= many different ones) for kids at the campsite.* ◆ (*informal*) ***What sort of** price did you want to pay?* (= approximately how much) ⊃ **note at** KIND **2** [C, usually sing.] (*informal*) a particular type of person: *My brother would never lie to his wife; he's not that sort.* **3** (*computing*) [sing.] the process of putting things in a particular order: *to do a sort*
  IDM **it takes all sorts (to make a world)** (*saying*) used to say that you think someone's behavior is very strange or unusual but that everyone is different and likes different things **of sorts** (*informal*) used when you are saying that something is not a good example of a particular type of thing: *He offered us an apology of sorts.* **out of sorts** sick or

upset: *She was tired and out of sorts by the time she arrived home.* **sort of** (*informal*) to some extent but in a way that you cannot easily describe: *She sort of pretends that she doesn't really care.* ◆ *"Do you understand?" "Sort of."* **a sort of sth** (*informal*) used for describing something in a not very exact way: *I had a sort of feeling that he wouldn't come.* ◆ *They're a sort of greenish-blue color.* ⊃ **more at** KIND
- *verb* to arrange things in groups or in a particular order according to their type, etc.; to separate things of one type from others: ~ sth *sorting the mail* ◆ ~ sth into sth *The computer sorts the words into alphabetical order.* ◆ *Trash can easily be separated and sorted into plastics, glass and paper.* ◆ ~ sth from sth *Women and children sorted the ore from the rock.* **IDM** see WHEAT
  PHR V ,sort itself 'out (of a problem) to stop being a problem without anyone having to take action: *It will all sort itself out in the end.* ,sort sth↔'out **1** (*informal*) to organize the contents of something; to make something neater: *The cabinets need sorting out.* **2** to organize something successfully: *If you're going to the bus station, can you sort out the tickets for tomorrow?* ,sort sth↔'out (from sth) to separate something from a larger group: *Could you sort out the toys that can be thrown away?* 'sort through sth (for sth) to look through a number of things, either in order to find something or to put them in order: *I sorted through my paperwork.* ◆ *She sorted through her suitcase for something to wear.*

sort·ie /ˈsɔrti; sɔrˈti/ *noun* **1** a flight that is made by an aircraft during military operations; an attack made by soldiers **SYN** RAID **2** a short trip away from your home or the place where you are **SYN** FORAY **3** ~ into sth an effort that you make to do or join something new **SYN** FORAY: *His first sortie into politics was unsuccessful.*

SOS /ˌɛs oʊ ˈɛs/ *noun* [sing.] **1** a signal or message that a ship or plane sends when it needs urgent help: *to send an SOS* ◆ *an SOS message* **2** an urgent request for help: *We've received an SOS from the area asking for food packages.* ⊃ **see also** MAYDAY

,so-'so *adj.* (*informal*) not particularly good or bad; average: *"How are you feeling today?" "So-so."* ▶ ,so-'so *adv.*: *I only did so-so on the exam.*

sot·to vo·ce /ˌsɑtoʊ ˈvoʊtʃi/ *adv.* (from *Italian, formal*) in a quiet voice so that not everyone can hear ▶ **sot·to vo·ce** *adj.*

sou·bri·quet /ˈsubrɪkeɪ/ *noun* = SOBRIQUET

souf·flé /suˈfleɪ/ *noun* [C, U] a dish made from egg whites, milk, and flour mixed together to make it light, flavored with cheese, fruit, etc. and baked until it rises: *a cheese soufflé*

sough /saʊ; sʌf/ *verb* [I] (*literary*) (especially of the wind) to make a soft whistling sound

sought **AWL** pt, pp of SEEK

'sought ˌafter *adj.* wanted by many people, because it is of very good quality or difficult to get or to find: *This design is the most sought after.* ◆ *a much sought-after actress*

souk /suk/ *noun* a market in an Arab country

soul /soʊl/ *noun*
> **SPIRIT OF PERSON 1** [C] the spiritual part of a person, believed to exist after death: *He believed his immortal soul was in peril.* ◆ *The howling wind sounded like the wailing of lost souls (= the spirits of dead people who are not in heaven).* ⊃ **collocations at** RELIGION
> **INNER CHARACTER 2** [C] a person's inner character, containing their true thoughts and feelings: *There was a feeling of restlessness deep in her soul.*
> **SPIRITUAL/MORAL/ARTISTIC QUALITIES 3** [sing.] the spiritual and moral qualities of humans in general **SYN** PSYCHE: *the dark side of the human soul* **4** [U, C] strong and good human feeling, especially that gives a work of art its quality or enables someone to recognize and enjoy that quality: *It was a very polished performance, but it lacked soul.* **5** [sing.] **the**

~ of sth a perfect example of a good quality: *He is the soul of discretion.*

> **PERSON 6** [C] (*becoming old-fashioned*) a person of a particular type: *She's lost all her money, poor soul.* ◆ *You're a brave soul.* **7** [C] (*especially in negative sentences*) a person: *There wasn't a soul in sight* (= no one was in sight). ◆ *Don't tell a soul* (= do not tell anyone). ◆ (*literary*) *a village of 300 souls* (= with 300 people living there)

> **MUSIC 8** (also **soul music**) [U] a type of music that expresses strong emotions, made popular by African American musicians: *a soul singer*

IDM **good for the soul** (*humorous*) good for you, even if it seems unpleasant: *"Want a ride?" "No thanks. Walking is good for the soul."* ⊃ more at BARE, BODY, GOD, HEART, SELL

soul-de,stroying *adj.* (of a job or task) very dull and boring, because it has to be repeated many times or because there will never be any improvement

soul food *noun* [U] the type of food that was traditionally eaten by African Americans in the southern U.S.

soul·ful /ˈsoʊlfl/ *adj.* expressing deep feelings, especially feelings of sadness or love: *soulful eyes* ◆ *a soulful song* ▶ **soul·ful·ly** /-fəli/ *adv.* **soul·ful·ness** *noun* [U]

soul·less /ˈsoʊləs/ *adj.* **1** (of things and places) lacking any attractive or interesting qualities that make people feel happy **SYN** DEPRESSING: *They live in soulless concrete blocks.* **2** (of a person) lacking the ability to feel emotions

soul·mate /ˈsoʊlmeɪt/ *noun* a person that you have a special friendship with because you understand each other's feelings and interests

soul music *noun* [U] = SOUL

soul-,searching *noun* [U] the careful examination of your thoughts and feelings, for example in order to reach the correct decision or solution to something

sound 🔊 /saʊnd/ *noun, verb, adj., adv.*

● *noun*

> **SOMETHING YOU HEAR 1** [C] something that you can hear **SYN** NOISE: *a high/low sound* ◆ *a clicking/buzzing/scratching, etc. sound* ◆ *the different sounds and smells of the forest* ◆ *She heard the sound of footsteps outside.* ◆ *He crept into the house trying not to make a sound.* **2** [U] continuous rapid movements (called VIBRATIONS) that travel through air or water and can be heard when they reach a person's or an animal's ear: *Sound travels more slowly than light.* ⊃ note at NOISE

> **FROM TELEVISION/RADIO 3** [U] what you can hear coming from a television, radio, etc., or as part of a movie: *Could you turn the sound up/down?* ◆ *The sound quality of the tapes was excellent.*

> **OF MUSICIANS 4** [C, U] the effect that is produced by the music of a particular singer or group of musicians: *I like their sound.*

> **IMPRESSION 5** [sing.] **the ~ of sth** the idea or impression that you get of someone or something from what someone says or what you read: *They had a wonderful time by the sound of it.* ◆ *From the sound of things you were lucky to find him.* ◆ *They're consulting a lawyer? I don't like the sound of that.*

> **WATER 6** [C] (often in place names) a narrow passage of water that joins two larger areas of water **SYN** STRAIT

IDM **like, etc. the sound of your own voice** (*disapproving*) to like talking a lot or too much, usually without wanting to listen to other people

● *verb* (not usually used in the progressive tenses)

> **GIVE IMPRESSION 1** *linking verb* to give a particular impression when heard or read about: **+ adj.** *His voice sounded strange on the phone.* ◆ *She didn't sound surprised when I told her the news.* ◆ *His explanation sounds reasonable to me.* ◆ *Leo made it sound so easy. But it wasn't.* ◆ **+ noun** *She sounds just the person we need for the job.* ◆ **~ like sb/sth** *You sounded just like your father when you said that.* ◆ **~ as if/as though…** *I hope I don't sound as if/as though I'm criticizing you.* **HELP** In spoken English people often use **like** instead of **as if** or **as though**.

> **-SOUNDING 2** (in adjectives) giving the impression of

having a particular sound: *an Italian-sounding name* ◆ *fine-sounding words*

> **PRODUCE SOUND 3** [I, T] to produce a sound; to make something such as a musical instrument produce a sound: *The bell sounded for the end of the class.* ◆ **~ sth** *Passing motorists sounded their horns in support.*

> **GIVE WARNING/SIGNAL 4** [T] **~ sth** to give a signal such as a warning by making a sound: *When I saw the smoke, I tried to sound the alarm.* ◆ (*figurative*) *Scientists have sounded a note of caution on the technique.* ◆ *Leaving him off the team may sound the death knell for our chances of winning* (= signal the end of our chances).

> **PRONOUNCE 5** [T] **~ sth** (*technical*) to pronounce something: *You don't sound the "b" in the word "comb."*

> **MEASURE DEPTH 6** [T, I] **~ (sth)** (*technical*) to measure the depth of the ocean or a lake by using a line with a weight attached, or an electronic instrument

IDM **(it) sounds like a plan to me** used to agree to a suggestion that you think is good ⊃ more at NOTE, SUSPICIOUSLY

PHR V **sound 'off (about sth)** (*informal, disapproving*) to express your opinions loudly or in an aggressive way ,**sound sb↔'out (about/on sth)** | ,**sound sth↔'out** to try to find out from someone what they think about something, often in an indirect way: *I wanted to sound him out about a job.* ◆ *They decided to sound out her interest in the project.*

● *adj.* (**sound·er, soundest**)

> **RELIABLE 1** sensible; that you can rely on and that will probably give good results: *a person of sound judgment* ◆ *He gave me some very sound advice.* ◆ *This gives the design team a sound basis for their work.* ◆ *The proposal makes sound commercial sense.* ◆ *Their policies are environmentally sound.* **ANT** UNSOUND

> **THOROUGH 2** [only before noun] good and thorough: *a sound knowledge/understanding of sth* ◆ *He has a sound grasp of the issues.*

> **NOT DAMAGED/HURT 3** in good condition; not damaged, hurt, etc.: *We arrived home safe and sound.* ◆ *to be of sound mind* (= not mentally ill) ◆ *The house needs attention but the roof is sound.* **ANT** UNSOUND

> **SLEEP 4** [usually before noun] deep and peaceful: *to have a sound night's sleep* ◆ *to be a sound sleeper*

> **GOOD, BUT NOT EXCELLENT 5** good and accurate, but not excellent: *a sound piece of writing* ◆ *a sound tennis player*

> **PHYSICAL PUNISHMENT 6** severe: *to give someone a sound beating*

▶ **sound·ness** *noun* [U]: *soundness of judgment* ◆ *financial soundness* ◆ *the soundness of the building's foundations* ⊃ see also SOUNDLY

IDM **(as) sound as a bell** (*informal*) in perfect condition

● *adv.* **~ asleep** very deeply asleep

sound·a·like /ˈsaʊndəlaɪk/ *noun* a person who sounds very similar to someone who is famous

the 'sound ,barrier *noun* [sing.] the point at which an aircraft's speed is the same as the speed of sound, causing reduced control, a very loud noise (called a SONIC BOOM) and various other effects: *to break the sound barrier* (= to travel faster than the speed of sound)

'sound bite *noun* a short phrase or sentence taken from a longer speech, especially a speech made by a politician, that is considered to be particularly effective or appropriate

'sound card *noun* (*computing*) a device that can be put into a computer to allow the use of sound with MULTIMEDIA software

'sound check *noun* a process of checking that the equipment used for recording music, or for playing music at a concert, is working correctly and producing sound of a good quality

'sound ef,fect *noun* [usually pl.] a sound that is made artificially, for example the sound of the wind or a battle, and used in a movie, play, computer game, etc. to make it more realistic

'sound engi,neer *noun* a person who works in a record-

t **tea**   t̬ **butter**   d **did**   k **cat**   g **got**   tʃ **chin**   dʒ **June**   f **fall**

ing or broadcasting studio and whose job is to control the levels and balance of sound

sound·ing /ˈsaʊndɪŋ/ noun **1 soundings** [pl.] careful questions that are asked in order to find out people's opinions about something: *They will take soundings among party members.* ◆ *What do your soundings show?* **2** [C] a measurement that is made to find out how deep water is: *They took soundings along the canal.*

ˈsounding ˌboard noun a person or group of people that you discuss your ideas with before you make them known or reach a decision

sound·less /ˈsaʊndləs/ adj. without making any sound; silent: *Her lips parted in a soundless scream.* ▶ **sound·less·ly** adv.

sound·ly /ˈsaʊndli/ adv. **1** if you sleep **soundly**, you sleep very well and very deeply **2** in a way that is sensible or can be relied on: *a soundly based conclusion* **3** completely and thoroughly: *The team was soundly defeated.* **4** strongly; firmly: *These houses are soundly built.* **5** very well, but not in an excellent way: *He played soundly.* **6** (of physical punishment) severely: *He was soundly beaten by his mother.*

sound·proof /ˈsaʊndpruf/ (also **sound·proofed**) adj. made so that sound cannot pass through it or into it: *a soundproof room* ▶ **sound·proof** verb ~ sth

sound·stage /ˈsaʊndsteɪdʒ/ noun a platform or a special area where sound can be recorded, for example for a movie

ˈsound ˌsystem noun equipment for playing recorded or live music and for making it louder

sound·track /ˈsaʊndtræk/ noun **1** all the music, speech, and sounds that are recorded for a movie: *The soundtrack of "Casablanca" took weeks to edit.* **2** the music, and sometimes some speech, from a movie or musical play that is recorded for people to buy: *I've just bought the soundtrack of the latest Miyazaki movie.*

ˈsound ˌwave noun a VIBRATION in the air, in water, etc. that we hear as sound

soup 🔑 /sup/ noun, verb
● noun [U, C] a liquid food made by boiling meat, vegetables, etc. in water, often eaten as the first course of a meal: *a bowl of soup* ◆ *chicken soup* ◆ *canned/packaged soups* ◆ *a soup spoon/plate*
IDM **from soup to nuts** (informal) from beginning to end: *She told me the whole story from soup to nuts.* **in the soup** (informal) in trouble: *We're all in the soup now.*
● verb
PHRV **soup sth↔up** (informal) to make changes to something such as a car or computer, so that it is more powerful or exciting than before

soup·çon /ˈsupsɑn; supˈsɔ̃/ noun [sing.] (from French, sometimes humorous) a very small amount

ˈsoup ˌkitchen noun a place where people who have no money can get soup and other food free

soup·y /ˈsupi/ adj. **1** similar to soup: *a soupy stew* **2** (of the air) very damp and unpleasant **3** (informal) emotional in a way that is exaggerated and embarrassing

sour 🔑 /ˈsaʊər/ adj., verb
● adj. **1** having a taste like that of a lemon or of fruit that is not ready to eat: *sour apples* ◆ *a sour flavor* **ANT** SWEET ➔ see also SWEET-AND-SOUR ➔ thesaurus box at BITTER **2** (especially of milk) having an unpleasant taste or smell because it is not fresh: *to turn/go sour* ➔ note at BITTER **3** (of people) not cheerful; bad-tempered and unpleasant: *a sour and disillusioned woman* ◆ *a sour face* ◆ *The meeting ended on a sour note with several people walking out.* ▶ **sour·ly** adv.: *"Who asked you?" he said sourly.* **sour·ness** noun [U]
IDM **go/turn sour** to stop being pleasant or working correctly: *Their relationship soon went sour.* **sour grapes** (saying) used to show that you think someone is jealous and is pretending that something is not important: *He said he didn't want the job anyway, but that's just sour grapes.*

● verb **1** [I, T] (of relationships, attitudes, people, etc.) to change so that they become less pleasant or friendly than before; to make something do this: *The atmosphere at the house soured.* ◆ ~ **sth** *The disagreement over trade tariffs has soured relations between the two countries.* **2** [I, T] ~ **(sth)** if milk **sours** or if something **sours** it, it becomes sour and has an unpleasant taste or smell

source 🔑 **AWL** /sɔrs/ noun, verb
● noun **1** a place, person, or thing that you get something from: *renewable energy sources* ◆ *Your local library will be a useful source of information.* ◆ *What is their main source of income?* **2** [usually pl.] a person, book, or document that provides information, especially for study, a piece of written work or news: *He refused to name his sources.* ◆ *Government sources indicated yesterday that cuts may have to be made.* ◆ *source material* ◆ *Historians use a wide range of primary and secondary sources for their research.* **3** a person or thing that causes something, especially a problem: *a source of violence* ◆ *a source of confusion* **4** the place where a river or stream starts: *the source of the Nile*
IDM **at source** at the place or the point that something comes from or begins: *Is your salary taxed at source* (= by your employer)?
● verb [often passive] ~ **sth (from…)** (business) to get something from a particular place: *We source all the vegetables sold in our stores from local farms.* ➔ see also OUTSOURCE

source·book /ˈsɔrsbʊk/ noun a collection of texts on a particular subject, used especially as an introduction to the subject

ˈsource code noun [U] (computing) a computer program written in text form that must be translated into MACHINE CODE before it can run on a computer

ˌsour ˈcream noun [U] cream that has been made sour by adding bacteria to it, used in cooking

sour·dough /ˈsaʊərˌdoʊ/ noun [U] DOUGH (= a mixture of flour, fat, and water) that is left to FERMENT so that it has a sour taste, used for making bread; bread made with this DOUGH

ˈsour-ˌfaced adj. [usually before noun] (of a person) having a bad-tempered or unpleasant expression

sour·puss /ˈsaʊərˌpʊs/ noun (informal) a person who is not cheerful or pleasant

sou·sa·phone /ˈsuzəˌfoʊn/ noun a BRASS instrument like a TUBA, used in marching bands

souse /saʊs/ verb ~ **sth/sb** [usually passive] to SOAK something or someone completely in a liquid

soused /saʊst/ adj. **1** [only before noun] (of fish) preserved in salt water and VINEGAR: *soused herring* **2** (old-fashioned, informal) drunk

south 🔑 /saʊθ/ noun, adj., adv.
● noun [U, sing.] (abbr. S., S, So.) **1** (also **the south**) the direction that is on your right when you watch the sun rise; one of the four main points of the COMPASS: *Which way is south?* ◆ *warmer weather coming from the south* ◆ *He lives to the south of* (= farther south than) *the city.* ➔ picture at COMPASS ➔ compare EAST, NORTH, WEST **2 the south** the southern part of a country, a region, or the world: *birds flying to the south for the winter* ◆ *They bought a villa in the South of France.* **3 the South** the southeastern states of the U.S. ➔ see also THE DEEP SOUTH **4 the South** the poorer countries in the southern half of the world
● adj. [only before noun] **1** (abbr. S., S) in or toward the south: *South Boston* ◆ *They live on the south coast.* **2** a **south wind** blows from the south ➔ compare SOUTHERLY
● adv. **1** toward the south: *This room faces south.* **2** ~ **of sth** nearer to the south than something: *They live ten miles south of Hartford.* **3** ~ **of sth** (informal or finance) less or lower than something: *The drug is achieving revenues just south of $1 billion per quarter.* **ANT** NORTH

IDM **down south** (*informal*) to or in the south, especially the southern states of the U.S.: *They've gone to live down south.*

South A'merica *noun* [U] the continent that is to the south of Central America and N. America ⊃ compare LATIN AMERICA

south·bound /ˈsaʊθbaʊnd/ *adj.* traveling or leading toward the south: *southbound traffic* ♦ *the southbound lane of the highway*

south·east /ˌsaʊθˈist/ *noun* usually **the southeast** [sing.] (*abbr.* S.E., SE) the direction or region at an equal distance between south and east ⊃ picture at COMPASS ▶ **south·east** *adv.*, *adj.*

south·east·er·ly /ˌsaʊθˈistərli/ *adj.* **1** [only before noun] in or toward the southeast **2** [usually before noun] (of winds) blowing from the southeast

south·east·ern /ˌsaʊθˈistərn/ *adj.* [only before noun] (*abbr.* S.E., SE) connected with the southeast

south·east·ward /ˌsaʊθˈistwərd/ (also **south·east·wards**) *adv.* toward the southeast ▶ **south·east·ward** *adj.*

south·er·ly /ˈsʌðərli/ *adj.*, *noun*
• *adj.* **1** [only before noun] in or toward the south: *traveling in a southerly direction* **2** [usually before noun] (of winds) blowing from the south: *a warm southerly breeze* ⊃ compare SOUTH
• *noun* (*pl.* **south·er·lies**) a wind that blows from the south

south·ern 🔑 /ˈsʌðərn/ also **Southern** *adj.* (*abbr.* S., S) [usually before noun]
located in the south or facing south; connected with or typical of the south part of the world or a region: *the southern slopes of the mountains* ♦ *southern Spain* ♦ *a southern accent*

southern 'belle *noun* (*old-fashioned*) a young attractive woman from the southern U.S.

the Southern 'Cone *noun* [sing.] the region of S. America which consists of Brazil, Paraguay, Uruguay, Argentina, and Chile

the Southern 'Cross *noun* [sing.] a group of stars in the shape of a cross that can be seen from the southern HEMISPHERE

south·ern·er /ˈsʌðərnər/ *noun* a person who comes from or lives in the southern part of a country

the Southern 'Lights *noun* [pl.] (also **au·ro·ra aus·tral·is**) bands of colored light that are sometimes seen in the sky at night in the most southern countries of the world

south·ern·most /ˈsʌðərnˌmoʊst/ *adj.* [usually before noun] furthest south: *the southernmost part of the island*

south·paw /ˈsaʊθpɔ/ *noun* (*informal*) a person who prefers to use their left hand rather than their right, especially in a sport such as baseball or BOXING

the South 'Pole *noun* [sing.] the point of the earth that is furthest south ⊃ picture at EARTH

south-south'east *noun* [sing.] (*abbr.* S.S.E., SSE) the direction at an equal distance between south and southeast ▶ **south-south'east** *adv.*

south-south'west *noun* [sing.] (*abbr.* S.S.W., SSW) the direction at an equal distance between south and southwest ▶ **south-south'west** *adv.*

south·ward /ˈsaʊθwərd/ (also **south·wards**) *adv.* toward the south: *to turn southward* ▶ **south·ward** *adj.*: *in a southward direction*

south·west /ˌsaʊθˈwɛst/ *noun* usually **the southwest** [sing.] (*abbr.* S.W., SW) the direction or region at an equal distance between south and west ⊃ picture at COMPASS ▶ **south·west** *adv.*, *adj.*

south·west·er·ly /ˌsaʊθˈwɛstərli/ *adj.* **1** [only before noun] in or toward the southwest **2** [usually before noun] (of winds) blowing from the southwest

south·west·ern /ˌsaʊθˈwɛstərn/ *adj.* [only before noun] (*abbr.* S.W., SW) connected with the southwest

south·west·ward /ˌsaʊθˈwɛstwərd/ (also **south·west·wards**) *adv.* toward the southwest ▶ **south·west·ward** *adj.*

sou·ve·nir /ˌsuvəˈnɪr; ˈsuvəˌnɪr/ *noun* a thing that you buy and/or keep to remind yourself of a place, an occasion, or a vacation; something that you bring back for other people when you have been on vacation **SYN** MEMENTO: *I bought the ring as a souvenir of Greece.* ♦ *a souvenir shop* ⊃ collocations at TRAVEL

souv·la·ki /suvˈlaki/ *noun* [U, C] a Greek dish consisting of pieces of meat cooked on sticks

sou'·west·er /ˌsaʊˈwɛstər/ *noun* **1** a hat made of shiny material that keeps out the rain, with a long wide piece at the back to protect the neck ⊃ picture at HAT **2** a strong wind or storm coming from the southwest

sov·er·eign /ˈsavrən; ˈsavərən/ *noun*, *adj.*
• *noun* (*formal*) a king or queen
• *adj.* (*formal*) **1** [only before noun] (of a country or state) free to govern itself; completely independent **SYN** AUTONOMOUS **2** having complete power or the greatest power in the country: *a sovereign ruler*

sov·er·eign·ty /ˈsavrənti; ˈsavərən-/ *noun* [U] (*formal*) **1** ~ (**over sth**) complete power to govern a country: *The country claimed sovereignty over the island.* ♦ *the sovereignty of Congress* ♦ (*figurative*) *the idea of consumer sovereignty* **2** the state of being a country with freedom to govern itself: *The declaration proclaimed the full sovereignty of the republic.* ⊃ collocations at INTERNATIONAL

So·vi·et /ˈsoʊviət; -viˌɛt/ *adj.* [usually before noun] connected with the former USSR

so·vi·et /ˈsoʊviət; -viˌɛt/ *noun* **1** [C] an elected local, district, or national council in the former USSR **2 the Soviets** [pl.] the people of the former USSR

sow¹ /soʊ/ *verb* ⊃ see also SOW¹ (**sowed, sown** /soʊn/ or **sowed, sowed**) **1** [T, I] to plant or spread seeds in or on the ground: ~ (**sth**) *Sow the seeds in rows.* ♦ *Water well after sowing.* ♦ ~ **sth with sth** *The fields around had been sown with wheat.* ⊃ collocations at FARMING **2** [T] ~ **sth (in sth)** to introduce or spread feelings or ideas, especially ones that cause trouble: *to sow doubt in someone's mind* ♦ *to sow confusion*
IDM **sow the seeds of sth** to start the process that leads to a particular situation or result **sow (your) wild oats** (of young men) to go through a period of wild behavior while young, especially having a lot of romantic or sexual relationships ⊃ more at REAP

sow² /saʊ/ *noun* a female pig ⊃ compare BOAR, HOG ⊃ see also SOW¹ **IDM** see SILK

sow·er /ˈsoʊər/ *noun* a person or machine that puts seeds in the ground

soy /sɔɪ/ *noun* [U] the plant on which soybeans grow; the food obtained from soybeans: *a soy crop* ♦ *soy flour*

soy·bean /ˈsɔɪbin/ *noun* a type of BEAN, originally from S.E. Asia, that is used instead of meat or animal PROTEIN in some types of food

'soy milk *noun* [U] a liquid made from soybeans, used instead of milk

'soy sauce *noun* [U] a thin dark-brown sauce that is made from soybeans and has a salty taste, used in Chinese and Japanese cooking

spa /spa/ *noun* **1** a place where water with minerals in it, that is considered to be good for your health, comes up naturally out of the ground; the name given to a town that has such a place and where there are, or were, places where people could drink the water: *Ballston Spa* ♦ *a spa town* ♦ *spa waters* **2** (also **'health spa**) a place where people can relax and improve their health, with, for example, a swimming pool: *a superb health spa which includes sauna, Turkish bath and fitness rooms* **3** = JACUZZI™

space 🔑 /speɪs/ *noun*, *verb*
• *noun*
▷ EMPTY AREA **1** [U] an amount of an area or of a place that is

empty or that is available for use **SYN** ROOM: *floor/office/ shelf, etc. space* ♦ *We must make good use of the available space.* ♦ *That desk takes up too much space.* ♦ *There is very little storage space in the department.* ♦ *Can we make space for an extra chair?* ♦ *How much disk space will it take up?* (= on a computer) **2** [C] an area or a place that is empty: *a large/small/narrow/ wide space* ♦ *a space two yards by three yards* ♦ *a parking space* ♦ *crowded together in a confined space* ♦ *I'll clear a space for your books.* ♦ *Put it in the space between the table and the wall.* **3** [U] the quality of being large and empty, allowing you to move freely **SYN** : *The room has been furnished and decorated to give a feeling of space.* **4** [C, U] a large area of land that has no buildings on it: *the wide open spaces of the Canadian prairies* ♦ *It's a city with fine buildings and plenty of open space.* ⟳ thesaurus box at LAND
> OUTSIDE EARTH'S ATMOSPHERE **5** (also ˌouter ˈspace) [U] the area outside the earth's atmosphere where all the other planets and stars are: *the first woman in space* ♦ *the possibility of visitors from outer space* ♦ *a space flight/mission*
> PERIOD OF TIME **6** [C, usually sing.] a period of time: *Forty-four people died in the space of five days.* ♦ *They had achieved a lot in a short space of time.* ♦ *Leave a space of two weeks between appointments.*
> IN WRITING/PRINTING **7** [U, C] the part of a line, page, or document that is empty: *Don't waste space by leaving a wide margin.* ♦ *There was not enough space to print all the letters we received.* ♦ *Leave a space after the comma.*
> FREEDOM **8** [U] the freedom and the time to think or do what you want to: *She was upset and needed space.* ♦ *You have to give teenagers plenty of space.* ⟳ see also BREATHING ROOM
> WHERE THINGS EXIST/MOVE **9** [U] the whole area in which all things exist and move: *It is quite possible that space and time are finite.*
  IDM look/stare/gaze into space to look straight in front of you without looking at a particular thing, usually because you are thinking about something ⟳ more at WASTE, WATCH *v.*
● *verb* [often passive] ~ sth (+ adv./prep.) to arrange things so that they have regular spaces between them: *evenly spaced plants* ♦ *a row of closely spaced dots* ♦ *Space the posts about a yard apart.*
  PHR V ˌspace ˈout (*informal*) to take no notice of what is happening around you, especially as a result of taking drugs ⟳ see also SPACED OUT ˌspace sth⟷ˈout to arrange things with a wide space between them: *The houses are spaced out in this area of town.*
● ˈspace-age *adj.* [usually before noun] (*informal*) (especially of design or technology) very modern and advanced: *a space-age kitchen*
ˈspace bar *noun* a bar on the keyboard of a computer or TYPEWRITER that you press to make spaces between words ⟳ picture at COMPUTER
ˈspace caˌdet *noun* (*slang*) a person who behaves strangely and often forgets things, as though he or she is using drugs
space·craft /ˈspeɪskræft/ *noun* (*pl.* space·craft) a vehicle that travels in space
ˌspaced ˈout (also spac·ey) *adj.* (*informal*) not completely conscious of what is happening, often because of taking drugs
ˈspace ˌheater *noun* an electric device for heating a room
space·man /ˈspeɪsmæn; -mən/ *noun* (*pl.* space·men /-mɛn; -mən/) **1** (*informal*) a man who travels into space; an AS-TRONAUT **2** (in stories) a creature that visits the earth from another planet **SYN** ALIEN ⟳ see also SPACEWOMAN
ˈspace probe *noun* = PROBE
the ˈspace race *noun* competition between the U.S. and the Soviet Union in the 1950s and 60s to be the first to explore space
space·ship /ˈspeɪsʃɪp/ *noun* a vehicle that travels in space, carrying people
ˈspace ˌshuttle (also shut·tle) *noun* a SPACECRAFT designed to be used, for example, for traveling between the earth and a space station

ˈspace ˌstation *noun* a large structure that is sent into space and remains above the earth as a base for people working and traveling in space
space·suit /ˈspeɪssut/ *noun* a special suit that covers the whole body and has a supply of air, allowing someone to survive and move around in space
ˌspace-ˈtime *noun* [U] (*physics*) the universe considered as a CONTINUUM with four measurements—length, width, depth, and time—inside which any event or physical object is located
space·walk /ˈspeɪswɔk/ *noun* a period of time that an ASTRONAUT spends in space outside a SPACECRAFT
space·wom·an /ˈspeɪsˌwʊmən/ *noun* (*pl.* space·wom·en /-ˌwɪmən/) a woman who travels into space
spac·ey /ˈspeɪsi/ *adj.* = SPACED OUT
spa·cial = SPATIAL
spac·ing /ˈspeɪsɪŋ/ *noun* [U] **1** the amount of space that is left between things, especially between the words or lines printed on a page: *single/double spacing* (= with one or two lines left between lines of type) **2** the amount of time that is left between things happening
spa·cious /ˈspeɪʃəs/ *adj.* (*approving*) (of a room or building) large and with plenty of space for people to move around in **SYN** ROOMY ▶ spa·cious·ly *adv.* spa·cious·ness *noun* [U]: *White walls can give a feeling of spaciousness.*
spade /speɪd/ *noun* **1** [C] a garden tool with a broad metal blade and a long handle, used for digging: *Turn the soil over with a spade.* ⟳ picture at TOOL ⟳ compare SHOVEL **2** spades [pl.] one of the four sets of cards (called SUITS) in a DECK of cards. The cards have a black design shaped like pointed leaves with short STEM: *the five/queen/ace of spades* ⟳ picture at PLAYING CARD **3** [C] a card from the set of spades: *You must play a spade if you have one.*
  IDM in spades (*informal*) in large amounts or to a great degree: *He'd got his revenge now, and in spades.* ⟳ more at CALL
spade·work /ˈspeɪdwɜrk/ *noun* [U] the hard work that has to be done in order to prepare for something
spa·ghet·ti /spəˈɡɛti/ *noun* [U] PASTA in the shape of long thin pieces that look like string when they are cooked
spaˌghetti ˈwestern *noun* a movie about COWBOYS, made in Europe by Italian companies
spake /speɪk/ (*old use*) *pt* of SPEAK
spam /spæm/ *noun*, *verb*
● *noun* [U] **1** Spam™ finely chopped cooked meat that has been pressed together in a container, usually sold in cans and served cold in slices **2** (*informal*) advertising material sent by e-mail to people who have not asked for it ⟳ collocations at E-MAIL ⟳ compare JUNK MAIL, SPIM
● *verb* ~ sb/sth (*informal*) to send the same e-mail message to a large number of people, usually in order to advertise something ▶ spam·mer *noun* spam·ming *noun* [U]
span /spæn/ *noun*, *verb*, *adj.*
● *noun* **1** the length of time that something lasts or is able to continue: *I worked with him over a span of six years.* ♦ *The project must be completed within a specific time span.* ♦ *Small children have a short attention span.* ⟳ see also LIFESPAN **2** ~ (of sth) a range or variety of something: *Managers have a wide span of control.* ♦ *These forests cover a broad span of latitudes.* **3** the part of a bridge or an ARCH between one vertical support and another: *The bridge crosses the river in a single span.* **4** the width of something from one side to the other: *The kite has a span of 1 yard.* ⟳ see also WINGSPAN
● *verb* (-nn-) **1** ~ sth to last all through a period of time or to cover the whole of it: *His acting career spanned 55 years.* ♦ *Family photos spanning five generations were stolen.* **2** ~ sth to include a large area or a lot of things: *The operation, which spanned nine countries, resulted in 200 arrests.* **3** ~ sth to stretch right across something, from one side to the other **SYN** CROSS: *a series of bridges spanning the river*
● *adj.* **IDM** see SPICK

span·dex /'spændeks/ *noun* an artificial material that stretches, used especially for making sports clothes

span·gle /'spæŋgl/ *verb, noun*
- **verb** [usually passive] ~ **sth (with sth)** to cover or to decorate something with small pieces of something shiny ⊃ see also STAR-SPANGLED BANNER
- **noun** a small piece of shiny metal or plastic used to decorate clothes **SYN** SEQUIN

Spang·lish /'spæŋglɪʃ/ *noun* [U] (*informal*) language that is a mixture of SPANISH and ENGLISH, especially a type of Spanish that includes many English words

span·iel /'spænyəl/ *noun* a dog with large soft ears that hang down. There are several types of spaniels.

Span·ish /'spænɪʃ/ *adj., noun*
- **adj.** from or connected with Spain
- **noun** [U] the language of Spain, Mexico, and most countries in Central and S. America

Spanish 'fly *noun* (*pl.* **Spanish flies**) **1** [C] a bright green insect that has a strong smell and produces a harmful substance **2** [U] a poisonous mixture made from the crushed bodies of these insects, that is said to give people a strong desire to have sex

the ,Spanish Inqui'sition *noun* [sing.] **1** the organization set up by the Roman Catholic Church in Spain in the 15th century to punish people who opposed its beliefs, known for its cruel and severe methods **2** (often *humorous*) used to say that you do not like the fact that someone is questioning you a lot about something: *What is this? The Spanish Inquisition?*

,Spanish 'moss *noun* [U] a tropical American plant that has long, thin, gray leaves and that grows over trees

spank /spæŋk/ *verb* ~ **sb/sth** to hit someone, especially a child, several times on their BUTTOCKS as a punishment ⊃ compare SMACK ▶ **spank** *noun*

spank·ing /'spæŋkɪŋ/ *noun, adv., adj.*
- **noun** [C, U] a series of hits on the BUTTOCKS, given to someone, especially a child, as a punishment: *to give someone a spanking* ◆ *I don't agree with spanking.*
- **adv.** (*informal*) when you say that something is **spanking** new, etc. you are emphasizing that it is very new, etc.
- **adj.** [only before noun] (*informal*) very fast, good, or impressive

spar /spɑr/ *verb, noun*
- **verb** (-rr-) **1** [I] ~ **(with sb)** to make the movements used in BOXING, either in training or to test the speed of your opponent's reaction **2** [I] ~ **(with sb)** to argue with someone, usually in a friendly way
- **noun 1** a strong pole used to support the sails, etc. on a ship **2** a structure that supports the wing of an aircraft

spare 🔑 /spɛr/ *adj., verb, noun*
- **adj.**
> NOT USED/NEEDED **1** [usually before noun] that is not being used or is not needed at the present time: *We have a spare bedroom, if you'd like to stay.* ◆ *I'm afraid I don't have any spare cash.*
> EXTRA **2** [only before noun] kept in case you need to replace the one you usually use; extra: *a spare key/tire* ◆ *Take some spare clothes in case you get wet.*
> TIME **3** available to do what you want with rather than work: *He's studying music in his spare time.* ◆ *I haven't had a spare moment this morning.*
> PERSON **4** thin, and usually quite tall
> WRITING **5** plain and simple but elegant: *the writer's spare prose*
- **verb**
> TIME/MONEY/ROOM/THOUGHT, ETC. **1** to make something such as time or money available to someone or for something, especially when it requires an effort for you to do this: ~ **sth/sb** *I'd love to have a break, but I can't spare the time just now.* ◆ *Could you spare one of your staff to help us out?*

◆ ~ **sth/sb for sb/sth** *We can only spare one room for you.*
◆ *You should spare a thought for* (= think about) *the person who cleans up after you.* ◆ ~ **sb sth** *Surely you can spare me a few minutes?*
> SAVE SOMEONE PAIN/TROUBLE **2** to save someone/yourself from having to go through an unpleasant experience: ~ **sb/yourself sth** *He wanted to spare his mother any anxiety.*
◆ *Please spare me* (= do not tell me) *the gruesome details.* ◆ *You could have spared yourself an unnecessary trip by phoning in advance.* ◆ ~ **sb/yourself from sth** *She was spared from the ordeal of appearing in court.*
> NOT HARM/DAMAGE **3** [usually passive] (*formal*) to allow someone or something to escape harm, damage, or death, especially when others do not escape it: ~ **sb/sth (from sth)** *They killed the men but spared the children.* ◆ *During the bombing only one house was spared* (= was not hit by a bomb). ◆ ~ **sb/sth sth** *Hong Kong was spared a direct hit, but the storm still brought heavy rains and powerful winds.*
> NO EFFORT/ EXPENSE, ETC. **4** ~ **no effort, expense, etc.** to do everything possible to achieve something or to do something well without trying to limit the time or money involved: *He spared no effort to make her happy again.* ◆ *No expense was spared in furnishing the new office.*
> WORK HARD **5** not ~ **yourself** to work as hard as possible
IDM **spare sb's feelings** to be careful not to do or say anything that might upset someone **to spare** if you have time, money, etc. to spare, you have more than you need: *I have absolutely no money to spare this month.* ◆ *We arrived at the airport with five minutes to spare.*
- **noun** an extra thing that you keep in case you need to replace the one you usually use (used especially about a tire of a car): *to get the spare out of the trunk* ◆ *I've lost my key and I don't have a spare.*

,spare 'part *noun* [usually pl.] a new part that you buy to replace an old or broken part of a car, machine, etc.

'spare rib *noun* [usually pl.] a RIB of PORK (= meat from a pig) with most of the meat cut off: *barbecued spare ribs*

,spare 'tire *noun* **1** an extra wheel for a car **2** (*humorous*) a large roll of fat around someone's waist

spar·ing /'spɛrɪŋ/ *adj.* careful to use or give only a little of something: *Doctors now advise only sparing use of such creams.* ◆ ~ **with sth** *He was always sparing with his praise.* ▶ **spar·ing·ly** *adv.*: *Use the cream very sparingly.*

spark /spɑrk/ *noun, verb*
- **noun 1** [C] a very small burning piece of material that is produced by something that is burning or by hitting two hard substances together: *A shower of sparks flew up the chimney.* **2** [C] a small flash of light produced by an electric current: *sparks from a faulty light switch* ◆ *A spark ignites the fuel in a car engine.* **3** [C, usually sing.] ~ **of sth** a small amount of a particular quality or feeling **SYN** GLIMMER: *a spark of hope* **4** [U, sing.] a special quality of energy, intelligence, or enthusiasm that makes someone very interesting, amusing, etc.: *As a writer he seemed to lack creative spark.* **5** [C] an action or event that causes something important to develop, especially trouble or violence: *the sparks of revolution* **6** [C, usually pl.] feelings of anger or excitement between people: *Sparks flew at the meeting* (= there was a lot of argument).
- **verb 1** [T] to cause something to start or develop, especially suddenly: ~ **sth** *The proposal would spark a storm of protest around the country.* ◆ *Winds brought down power lines, sparking a fire.* ◆ ~ **sth off** *The riots were sparked off by the arrest of a local leader.* **2** [I] to produce small flashes of fire or electricity: *a sparking, crackling fire* ◆ (*figurative*) *The game suddenly sparked to life.*
PHR V **,spark 'up sth** to begin a conversation, an argument, a friendship, etc., often suddenly: *I tried to spark up a conversation with her.*

spar·kle /'spɑrkl/ *verb, noun*
- **verb 1** [I] ~ **(with sth)** to shine brightly with small flashes of light: *sparkling eyes* ◆ *Her jewelry sparkled in the candlelight.* ⊃ thesaurus box at SHINE **2** [I] ~ **(with sth)** to be full of life, enthusiasm, or humor: *He always sparkles at parties.*

ʌ **cup**   ə **about**   eɪ **say**   aɪ **five**   ɔɪ **boy**   aʊ **now**   oʊ **go**   ər **bird**

• **noun** [C, U] **1** a series of flashes of light produced by light hitting a shiny surface: *the sparkle of glass* ◆ (*figurative*) *There was a sparkle of excitement in her eyes.* **2** the quality of being lively and original: *The performance lacked sparkle.*

spar·kler /ˈspɑrklər/ *noun* a type of small FIREWORK that you hold in your hand and light. It burns with many bright sparks.

spar·kling /ˈspɑrklɪŋ/ *adj.* **1** (also *less frequent, informal* **spar·kly** /ˈspɑrkli/) shining and flashing with light: *the calm and sparkling waters of the lake* ◆ *sparkling blue eyes* **2** (of drinks) containing bubbles of gas: *a sparkling wine* ◆ *sparkling mineral water* **3** interesting and amusing: *a sparkling conversation/personality* **4** excellent; of very good quality: *The champion was in sparkling form.*

'spark plug (also **plug**) *noun* a part in a car engine that produces a SPARK (= a flash of electricity) that makes the fuel burn and starts the engine

'sparring partner *noun* **1** a person that you regularly have friendly arguments or discussions with **2** (in BOXING) a person that a BOXER regularly practices with

spar·row /ˈspæroʊ/ *noun* a small brown and gray bird, common in many parts of the world

sparse /spɑrs/ *adj.* (*comparative* **spars·er**, no *superlative*) only present in small amounts or numbers and often spread over a large area: *the sparse population of the islands* ◆ *Vegetation becomes sparse higher up the mountains.* ◆ *The information available on the subject is sparse.* ▶ **sparse·ly** *adv.*: *a sparsely populated area* **sparse·ness** *noun* [U]

spar·tan /ˈspɑrtn/ *adj.* (of conditions) simple or severe; lacking anything that makes life easier or more pleasant **ORIGIN** From **Sparta**, a powerful city in ancient Greece, where the people were not interested in comfort or luxury. **ANT** LUXURIOUS

spasm /ˈspæzəm/ *noun* **1** [C, U] a sudden and often painful contracting of a muscle, that you cannot control: *a muscle spasm* ◆ *The injection sent his leg into spasm.* **2** [C] ~ (of sth) a sudden strong feeling or reaction that lasts for a short time: *a spasm of anxiety/anger/coughing/pain, etc.*

spas·mod·ic /spæzˈmɑdɪk/ *adj.* **1** happening suddenly for short periods of time; not regular or continuous: *There was spasmodic fighting in the area yesterday.* **2** (*technical*) caused by your muscles becoming tight in a way that you cannot control: *spasmodic movements* ▶ **spas·mod·i·cally** /-kli/ *adv.*

spas·tic /ˈspæstɪk/ *adj.* (*medical* or *old-fashioned*) having or caused by CEREBRAL PALSY, an illness that makes it difficult for someone to control their muscles and movements. Using this word is now often considered offensive: *spastic children* ◆ *spastic reactions* ▶ **spas·tic** *noun*

spat /spæt/ *noun* **1** (*informal*) a short argument or disagreement about something unimportant **2** [usually pl.] a cloth covering for the ankle that was worn in the past by men over the shoe and fastened with buttons at the side ⊃ see also SPIT *v.*

spate /speɪt/ *noun* [usually sing.] ~ of sth a large number of things, which are usually unpleasant, that happen suddenly within a short period of time: *The bombing was the latest in a spate of terrorist attacks.*

spa·tial (also **spa·cial**) /ˈspeɪʃl/ *adj.* (*formal* or *technical*) relating to space and the position, size, shape, etc. of things in it: *changes taking place in the spatial distribution of the population* ◆ *the development of a child's spatial awareness* (= the ability to judge the positions and sizes of objects) ▶ **spa·tial·ly** /-ʃəli/ *adv.*

spat·ter /ˈspætər/ *verb, noun*
• **verb 1** [T] to cover someone or something with drops of liquid, dirt, etc., especially by accident **SYN** SPLASH: ~ sb/sth *blood-spattered walls* ◆ ~ sb/sth with sth *As the bus passed, it spattered us with mud.* ◆ ~ sth on/over sb/sth *Oil was spattered on the floor.* **2** [I] + adv./prep. (of liquid) to fall on a surface in drops, often noisily: *We heard the rain spattering on the roof.*

• **noun** (also **spat·ter·ing**) [sing.] ~ (of sth) a number of drops of a liquid or small amounts of something that hit a surface; the noise this makes: *a spatter of rain against the window* ◆ *a spattering of blood* ◆ (*figurative*) *a spatter of applause*

spat·u·la /ˈspætʃələ/ *noun* a tool with a broad flat blade used for mixing and spreading things, especially in cooking and painting ⊃ picture at LABORATORY **2** a kitchen UTENSIL that has a broad flat blade with narrow holes in it, attached to a long handle, used for turning and lifting food when cooking ⊃ picture at KITCHEN

spawn /spɔn/ *verb, noun*
• **verb 1** [I, T] ~ (sth) (of fish, FROGS, etc.) to lay eggs **2** [T] ~ sth (often *disapproving*) to cause something to develop or be produced: *The band's album spawned a string of hit singles.*
• **noun** [U] a soft substance containing the eggs of fish, FROGS, etc. ⊃ see also FROGSPAWN

spay /speɪ/ *verb* ~ sth (*technical*) to remove the ovaries (OVARY) of a female animal, to prevent it from breeding: *Have you had your cat spayed?*

SPCA /ˌɛs pi si ˈeɪ/ *abbr.* Society for the Prevention of Cruelty to Animals

speak 🔊 /spik/ *verb*
(**spoke** /spoʊk/, **spo·ken** /ˈspoʊkən/)

WORD FAMILY
speak *verb*
speaker *noun*
speech *noun*
spoken *adj.* (≠ unspoken)

▷ **HAVE CONVERSATION 1** [I] to talk to someone about something; to have a conversation with someone: ~ (to sb) (about sth/sb) *I've spoken to the manager about it.* ◆ *The President refused to speak to the waiting journalists.* ◆ *"Can I speak to Susan?" "Speaking."* (= at the beginning of a telephone conversation) ◆ *"Do you know him?" "Not to speak to."* (= only by sight) ◆ ~ (with sb) (about sth/sb) *Can I speak with you for a minute?* ◆ *I saw her in the street but we didn't speak.* ⊃ thesaurus box at TALK
▷ **USE VOICE 2** [I] to use your voice to say something: *He can't speak because of a throat infection.* ◆ *Please speak more slowly.* ◆ *Without speaking, she stood up and went out.* ◆ *He speaks with a strange accent.* ◆ *She has a beautiful speaking voice.*
▷ **MENTION/DESCRIBE 3** [I] ~ of/about sth/sb to mention or describe something or someone: *She still speaks about him with great affection.* ◆ *Witnesses spoke of a great ball of flame.* ◆ *Speaking of traveling* (= referring back to a subject just mentioned), *are you going anywhere exciting this year?* ⊃ thesaurus box at MENTION
▷ **A LANGUAGE 4** [T] (not used in the progressive tenses) ~ sth to be able to use a particular language: *to speak several languages* ◆ *to speak a little Urdu* ◆ *Do you speak English?* **5** [T, I] to use a particular language to express yourself: ~ sth *What language is it they're speaking?* ◆ ~ in sth *Would you prefer it if we spoke in German?*
▷ **-SPEAKING 6** (in adjectives) speaking the language mentioned: *French-speaking Canada* ◆ *non-English-speaking students*
▷ **MAKE SPEECH 7** [I] (+ adv./prep.) to make a speech to an audience: *to speak in public* ◆ *to speak on the radio* ◆ *to speak at a conference* ◆ *Professor Wilson was invited to speak about the results of his research.* ◆ *She spoke in favor of the new tax.* ◆ *He has a number of speaking engagements this week.*
▷ **SAY/STATE 8** [T] ~ sth to say or state something: *She was clearly speaking the truth.* ◆ *He spoke the final words of the play.* **IDM** be on speaking terms (with sb)| be speaking (to sb) to be willing to be polite or friendly toward someone, especially after an argument: *She hasn't been on speaking terms with her uncle for years.* ◆ *Are they speaking to each other again yet?* **generally, broadly, roughly, relatively, etc. speaking** used to show that what you are saying is true in a general, etc. way: *Generally speaking, the more you pay, the more you get.* ◆ *There are, broadly speaking, two ways of doing this.* ◆ *Personally speaking, I've always preferred Italian food.* ⊃ language bank at GENERALLY **no .../nothing to speak of** such a small amount that it is not worth mentioning: *They have no friends to speak of.* ◆ *She's saved a little money but*

nothing to speak of. **so to speak** used to emphasize that you are expressing something in an unusual or amusing way: *They were all very similar. All cut from the same cloth, so to speak.* **speak for itself/themselves** to be so easy to see and understand that you do not need to say anything else about it/them: *Her success speaks for itself.* **speak for myself/herself/himself, etc.** to express what you think or want yourself, rather than someone else doing it for you: *I'm quite capable of speaking for myself, thank you!* **speak for yourself** (*informal*) used to tell someone that a general statement they have just made is not true of you: *"We didn't play very well." "Speak for yourself!"* (= I think that I played well.) **speaking as sth** used to say that you are the type of person mentioned and are expressing your opinion from that point of view: *Speaking as a parent, I'm very concerned about standards in education.* **speak your mind** to say exactly what you think, in a very direct way **speak out of turn** to say something when you should not, for example because it is not the right time or you are not the right person to say it **speak volumes (about/for sth/sb)** to tell you a lot about something or someone, without the need for words **speak well/ill of sb** (*formal*) to say good or bad things about someone ➜ more at ACTION, DEVIL, FACT, ILL, LANGUAGE, MANNER, STRICTLY, TURN *n.*

PHR V ˌspeak for sb to state the views or wishes of a person or a group; to act as a representative for someone ˌspeak of sth (*formal*) to be evidence that something exists or is present: *Everything here speaks of perfect good taste.* ˌspeak 'out (against sth) to state your opinions publicly, especially in opposition to something and in a way that takes courage ➜ see also OUTSPOKEN ˌspeak to sb (about sth) (*informal*) to talk to someone in a serious way about something wrong they have done, to try to stop them from doing it again ˌspeak 'up usually used in orders to tell someone to speak more loudly: *Please speak up—we can't hear you at the back.* ˌspeak 'up (for sb/sth) to say what you think clearly and freely, especially in order to support or defend someone or something

-speak /spik/ *combining form* (in nouns) (often *disapproving*) the language used by a particular group of people, especially when it is difficult for other people to understand or they find it annoying: *management-speak* ◆ *Visitors to Web sites don't want to read marketing-speak.*

speak·eas·y /ˈspikˌizi/ *noun* (*pl.* **speak·eas·ies**) a place in the U.S. where people could buy alcohol illegally, at the time in the 1920s and 1930s when it was illegal to make or sell alcohol

speak·er 🔑 /ˈspikər/ *noun*

1 a person who gives a talk or makes a speech: *He was a* **guest speaker** *at the conference.* ◆ *She was a brilliant* **public speaker**. **2** a person who is or was speaking: *I looked around to see who the speaker was.* **3** a person who speaks a particular language: *Chinese speakers* ◆ *a* **native speaker** *of English* **4 (the) Speaker** the title of the person whose job is to control the discussions in a LEGISLATURE: *the Speaker of the House of Representatives* **5** the part of a radio, computer, or piece of musical equipment that the sound comes out of ➜ see also LOUDSPEAKER

THESAURUS

speaker

communicator ◆ gossip ◆ talker

These are all words for a person who talks or is talking, especially in a particular way.

speaker a person who is or was speaking; a person who speaks a particular language: *I looked around to see who the speaker was.* ◆ *a fluent speaker of Arabic*

communicator (*somewhat formal*) a person who is able to describe their ideas and feelings clearly to others: *The ideal candidate will be an effective communicator.*

gossip (*disapproving*) a person who enjoys talking about other people's private lives: *Myra is a sweet person, but she's also a terrible gossip.*

talker a person who talks a lot: *He's not a talker.* ◆ *She's a big talker* (= she talks a lot).

SPEAKER OR TALKER?

Talker is used when you are talking about how much someone talks. It is not used for the person who is or was talking: ~~I looked round to see who the talker was.~~

PATTERNS

- a **good/great** speaker/communicator
- an **effective/excellent** speaker/communicator

speak·er·phone /ˈspikərˌfoʊn/ *noun* [C, U] a telephone that can be used without being held, because it contains a MICROPHONE and a LOUDSPEAKER: *Let me put you on speakerphone so that everyone can hear you.*

spear /spɪr/ *noun, verb*

● *noun* **1** a weapon with a long wooden handle and a sharp metal point used for fighting, hunting, and fishing in the past ➜ picture at SWORD **2** the long pointed STEM of some plants ➜ see ASPARAGUS

● *verb* ~ sth/sb to throw or push a spear or other pointed object through something or someone: *They were standing in the river spearing fish.* ◆ *She speared an olive with her fork.*

spear·head /ˈspɪrhɛd/ *noun, verb*

● *noun* [usually sing.] a person or group that begins an activity or leads an attack against someone or something

● *verb* ~ sth to begin an activity or lead an attack against someone or something: *He is* **spearheading a campaign** *for a new stadium in the town.*

spear·mint /ˈspɪrmɪnt/ *noun* [U] a type of MINT used especially in making candy and TOOTHPASTE: *spearmint chewing gum* ➜ compare PEPPERMINT

spec /spɛk/ *noun, verb*

● *noun* [usually pl.] a detailed description of something, especially the design and materials needed to produce something: *We want the machine manufactured to our own specs.* ➜ see also SPECIFICATION, SPECS

IDM on spec (*informal*) when you do something on spec, you are trying to achieve something without organizing it in advance, but hoping you will be lucky

● *verb* (-cc-) ~ sth to design and make something to a particular standard: *The camera is well specced at the price.*

spe·cial 🔑 /ˈspɛʃl/ *adj., noun*

● *adj.* **1** [usually before noun] not ordinary or usual; different from what is normal **SYN** EXCEPTIONAL: *The school will only allow this in special circumstances.* ◆ *Some of the officials have special privileges.* ◆ *There is* **something special** *about this place.* **2** more important than others; deserving or getting more attention than usual: *What are your special interests?* ◆ *She's a very special friend.* ◆ *Our special guest on next week's show will be... ◆ Don't lose it — it's special.* **3** organized or intended for a particular purpose: *a special event* ◆ *These teachers need special training.* **4** used by or intended for one particular person or group of people: *She has a special way of smiling.* ◆ *He sent a special message to the men.* **5** [only before noun] better or more than usual: *As an only child she got special attention.* ◆ *Please take special care of it.* ➜ compare ESPECIAL

● *noun* **1** something that is not usually available but is provided for a particular purpose or on one occasion: *an election-night special on television* ◆ *The menu changes regularly and there are daily specials to choose from.* **2** (*informal*) a price for a particular product in a store or restaurant that is lower than usual: *There's a special on coffee this week.*

IDM on special on sale at a lower price for a short period of time: *The chocolates were on special at my local store.*

ˌspecial 'agent *noun* a DETECTIVE who works for the FEDERAL government in the U.S., for example for the FBI

special de'livery *noun* [U] a service that delivers a letter, etc. faster than normal

special edu'cation (also *informal* **special ed** /ˌspɛʃl ˈɛd/) *noun* [U] the education of children who have physical or learning problems

special ef'fects (also **SFX**) *noun* [pl.] unusual or exciting pieces of action in movies or television programs, that are created by computers or skillful photography to show things that do not normally exist or happen

special 'interest ˌgroup (also ˌspecial 'interest) *noun* a group of people who work together to achieve something that they are particularly interested in, especially by putting pressure on the government, etc.

spe·cial·ist 🔑 /ˈspɛʃəlɪst/ *noun*
1 a person who is an expert in a particular area of work or study: *a specialist in Japanese history* **2** a doctor who has SPECIALIZED in a particular area of medicine: *a cancer specialist* ➲ compare GENERALIST ▶ **spe·cial·ist** *adj.* [only before noun]: *specialist magazines* ◆ *You need some specialist advice.*

spe·cial·ize /ˈspɛʃəˌlaɪz/ *verb* [I] ~ **(in sth)** to become an expert in a particular area of work, study, or business; to spend more time on one area of work, etc. than on others: *Many students prefer not to specialize too soon.* ◆ *He specialized in criminal law.* ◆ *The store specializes in handmade chocolates.* ▶ **spe·cial·i·za·tion** /ˌspɛʃələˈzeɪʃn/ *noun* [U, C]

spe·cial·ized /ˈspɛʃəˌlaɪzd/ *adj.* designed or developed for a particular purpose or area of knowledge: *specialized equipment* ◆ *specialized skills*

spe·cial·ly 🔑 /ˈspɛʃəli/ *adv.*
1 for a particular purpose, person, etc.: *The ring was specially made for her.* ◆ *a specially designed diet plan* ◆ *We came specially to see you.* **2** (*informal*) more than usual or more than other things: *It will be hard to work today—specially when it's so warm and sunny outside.* ◆ *I hate homework. Specially history.* ➲ note at ESPECIALLY

special 'needs *noun* [pl.] needs that a person has because of mental or physical problems: *She teaches children with special needs.* ◆ *a special needs teacher*

special 'offer *noun* [C, U] a product that is sold at less than its usual price, especially in order to persuade people to buy it; the act of offering goods in this way: *Shop around for special offers.* ◆ *a special offer on perfume*

special 'pleading *noun* [U] trying to persuade someone about something by mentioning only the arguments that support your opinion and ignoring the arguments that do not support it

special 'school *noun* a school for children who have physical or learning problems

spe·cial·ty /ˈspɛʃəlti/ *noun* (*pl.* **spe·cial·ties**) **1** a type of food or product that a restaurant or place is famous for because it is so good: *Seafood is a specialty on the island.* ◆ *local/regional specialties* ◆ *specialty stores* **2** an area of work or study that someone gives most of their attention to and knows a lot about; something that someone is good at: *Her specialty is taxation law.* ◆ *She is finding out about medical specialties and the training required to become a doctor.*

spe·cies 🔑 /ˈspiʃiz; -siz/ *noun*
(*pl.* **spe·cies**) a group into which animals, plants, etc. that are able to breed with each other and produce healthy young are divided, smaller than a GENUS and identified by a Latin name: *a rare species of beetle* ◆ *several species of arctic birds* ◆ *a conservation area for endangered species*

the 'species ˌbarrier *noun* [sing.] the natural system that is thought to prevent diseases spreading from one type of animal or plant to another

spe·cies·ism /ˈspiʃiˌzɪzəm; ˈspisi-/ *noun* [U] (*disapproving*) the belief that humans are more important than animals, which causes people to treat animals badly ▶ **spe·cies·ist** /-zɪst/ *adj., noun*

spe·cif·ic 🔑 AWL /spəˈsɪfɪk/ *adj.*
1 detailed and exact SYN PRECISE: *I gave you specific instructions.* ◆ *"I'd like your help tomorrow." "Can you be more specific* (= tell me exactly what you want)?" **2** [usually before noun] connected with one particular thing only SYN PARTICULAR: *children's television programs aimed at a specific age group* ◆ *The money was collected for a specific purpose.* ◆ *children with specific learning difficulties* (= in one area only) **3** ~ **to sth** (*formal*) existing only in one place or limited to one thing SYN PECULIAR: *a belief that is specific to this part of Africa*

spe·cif·i·cally 🔑 AWL /spəˈsɪfɪkli/ *adv.*
1 in a detailed and exact way: *I specifically told you not to go near the water!* **2** connected with or intended for one particular thing only: *liquid vitamins specifically designed for children* ◆ *a magazine aimed specifically at working women* **3** used when you want to add more detailed and exact information: *The newspaper, or more specifically, the editor, was taken to court for publishing the photographs.*

spec·i·fi·ca·tion AWL /ˌspɛsəfəˈkeɪʃn/ *noun* [C, U] a detailed description of how something is, or should be, designed or made: *the technical specifications of the new model* (= of car) ◆ *The house has been built exactly to our specifications.* ◆ *The office was furnished to a high specification.*

speˌcific 'gravity *noun* [U] = RELATIVE DENSITY

spec·i·fic·i·ty AWL /ˌspɛsəˈfɪsəti/ *noun* [U] (*formal*) the quality of being specific

spe·cif·ics AWL /spəˈsɪfɪks/ *noun* [pl.] the details of a subject that you need to think about or discuss: *Okay, that's the broad plan—let's get down to the specifics.*

spec·i·fy AWL /ˈspɛsəˌfaɪ/ *verb* (**spec·i·fies, spec·i·fy·ing, spec·i·fied, spec·i·fied**) to state something, especially by giving an exact measurement, time, exact instructions, etc.: ~ **sth** *Remember to specify your size when ordering clothes.* ◆ ~ **who, what, etc.…** *The contract clearly specifies who can operate the machinery.* ◆ ~ **that…** *The regulations specify that calculators may not be used in the examination.* ▶ **spec·i·fi·able** AWL *adj.*

spec·i·men /ˈspɛsəmən/ *noun* **1** a small amount of something that shows what the rest of it is like SYN SAMPLE: *Astronauts have brought back specimens of rock from the moon.* ➲ collocations at SCIENTIFIC **2** a single example of something, especially an animal or a plant: *The aquarium has some interesting specimens of unusual tropical fish.* ◆ (*humorous*) *They were fine specimens of American youth!* ➲ thesaurus box at EXAMPLE **3** a small quantity of blood, URINE, etc. that is taken from someone and tested by a doctor: *to provide/take a specimen*

spe·cious /ˈspiʃəs/ *adj.* (*formal*) seeming right or true but actually wrong or false SYN MISLEADING: *a specious argument*

speck /spɛk/ *noun* a very small spot; a small piece of dirt, etc.: *The ship was now just a speck in the distance.* ◆ *specks of dust* ➲ thesaurus box at MARK

speck·le /ˈspɛkl/ *noun* [usually pl.] a small colored mark or spot on a background of a different color

speck·led /ˈspɛkld/ *adj.* covered with small marks or spots SYN FLECK

specs /spɛks/ *noun* [pl.] (*old-fashioned, informal*) glasses (GLASS): *I need a new pair of specs.* ➲ see also SPEC

spec·ta·cle /ˈspɛktəkl/ *noun* **1** [C, U] a performance or an event that is very impressive and exciting to look at: *The carnival parade was a magnificent spectacle.* **2** [C] a sight or view that is very impressive to look at: *The sunset was a stunning spectacle.* **3** [sing.] an unusual or surprising sight or situation that attracts a lot of attention: *I remember the sad spectacle of her standing in her wedding dress, covered in mud.* **4** **spectacles** [pl.] (*old-fashioned*) = glasses (GLASS): *a pair of spectacles* ◆ *a spectacle case* (= to put your glasses in) IDM **make a spectacle of yourself** to draw attention to yourself by behaving or dressing in a ridiculous way in public

---

spec·tac·u·lar /spɛkˈtækyələr/ *adj., noun*

- *adj.* very impressive **SYN** BREATHTAKING: *spectacular scenery* ◆ *Messi scored a spectacular goal.* ◆ *It was a spectacular achievement on their part.* ▶ **spec·tac·u·lar·ly** *adv.*: *It has been a spectacularly successful year.*

- *noun* an impressive show or performance: *a Christmas TV spectacular*

spec·tate /ˈspɛkteɪt/ *verb* [I] to watch something, especially a sports event

spec·ta·tor /ˈspɛkteɪtər/ *noun* a person who is watching an event, especially a sports event

ˈspectator ˌsport *noun* a sport that many people watch; a sport that is interesting to watch

spec·ter (*CanE usually* **spec·tre**) /ˈspɛktər/ *noun* **1** ~ (of sth) something unpleasant that people are afraid might happen in the future: *The country is haunted by the specter of civil war.* ◆ *These weeks of drought have once again raised the specter of widespread famine.* **2** (*literary*) a GHOST: *Was he a specter returning to haunt her?*

spec·tra pl. of SPECTRUM

spec·tral /ˈspɛktrəl/ *adj.* **1** (*literary*) like a GHOST; connected with a ghost **2** (*technical*) connected with a SPECTRUM: *spectral bands*

spec·trom·e·ter /spɛkˈtrɑmətər/ *noun* (*technical*) a piece of equipment for measuring the WAVELENGTH of SPECTRA

spec·tro·scope /ˈspɛktrəˌskoʊp/ *noun* (*technical*) a piece of equipment for forming and looking at SPECTRA ▶ **spec·tro·scop·ic** /ˌspɛktrəˈskɑpɪk/ *adj.*: *spectroscopic analysis*

spec·tros·co·py /spɛkˈtrɑskəpi/ *noun* [U] (*chemistry, physics*) the study of forming and looking at SPECTRA using SPECTROMETERS, SPECTROSCOPES, etc.

spec·trum /ˈspɛktrəm/ *noun* (*pl.* **spec·tra** /-trə/) **1** a band of colored lights in order of their WAVELENGTHS, as seen in a RAINBOW and into which light may be separated: *A spectrum is formed by a ray of light passing through a prism.* ◆ *Red and violet are at opposite ends of the spectrum.* **2** a range of sound waves or several other types of waves: *the electromagnetic/radio/sound spectrum* **3** [usually sing.] a complete or wide range of related qualities, ideas, etc.: *a broad spectrum of interests* ◆ *We will hear views from across the political spectrum.*

spec·u·late /ˈspɛkyəˌleɪt/ *verb* **1** [I, T] to form an opinion about something without knowing all the details or facts: ~ **(about/on/as to sth)** *We all speculated about the reasons for her resignation.* ◆ ~ **why, how, etc....** *It is useless to speculate why he did it.* ◆ ~ **that...** *We can speculate that the stone circles were once used in some sort of pagan ceremony.* **2** [I] ~ **(in/on sth)** to buy goods, property, shares, etc., hoping to make a profit when you sell them, but with the risk of losing money: *He likes to speculate on the stock market.*

spec·u·la·tion /ˌspɛkyəˈleɪʃn/ *noun* **1** [U, C] the act of forming opinions about what has happened or what might happen without knowing all the facts: ~ **(that...)** *There was widespread speculation that she was going to resign.* ◆ *His private life is the subject of much speculation.* ◆ ~ **(about/over sth)** *Today's announcement ends months of speculation about the company's future.* ◆ *She dismissed the newspaper reports as pure speculation.* ◆ *Our speculations proved right.* **2** [U, C] ~ **(in sth)** the activity of buying and selling goods or shares in a company in the hope of making a profit, but with the risk of losing money

spec·u·la·tive /ˈspɛkyələtɪv; -ˌleɪtɪv/ *adj.* **1** based on guessing or on opinions that have been formed without knowing all the facts **2** showing that you are trying to guess something: *She cast a speculative look at Kate.* **3** (of business activity) done in the hope of making a profit but involving the risk of losing money ▶ **spec·u·la·tive·ly** *adv.*

spec·u·la·tor /ˈspɛkyəˌleɪtər/ *noun* a person who buys and sells goods or shares in a company in the hope of making a profit: *property speculators*

spec·u·lum /ˈspɛkyələm/ *noun* (*medical*) a metal instrument

that is used to make a hole or tube in the body wider so it can be examined

sped /spɛd/ pt, pp of SPEED

speech /spitʃ/ *noun*

1 [C] ~ **(on/about sth)** a formal talk that a person gives to an audience: *to give/make/deliver a speech on human rights* ◆ *He made the announcement in a speech on television.* ◆ *Several people made speeches at the wedding.* **2** [U] the ability to speak: *I seemed to have lost the power of speech.* ◆ *a speech defect* ◆ *freedom of speech* (= the right to say openly what you think) **3** [U] the way in which a particular person speaks: *Her speech was slurred—she was clearly drunk.* **4** [U] the language used when speaking: *This expression is used mainly in speech, not in writing.* ◆ *speech sounds* **5** [C] a group of lines that an actor speaks in a play in the theater: *She has the longest speech in the play.* ⊃ see also FIGURE OF SPEECH

THESAURUS

speech

lecture ◆ **address** ◆ **talk** ◆ **sermon**

These are all words for a talk given to an audience.

speech a formal talk given to an audience: *Several people made speeches at the wedding.*

lecture a talk given to a group of people to tell them about a particular subject, often as part of a university or college course: *a lecture on the Roman army* ◆ *a course/series of lectures*

address a formal speech given to an audience: *a televised presidential address*

SPEECH OR ADDRESS?

A **speech** can be given on a public or private occasion; an **address** is always public: ~~He gave an address at the wedding.~~

talk a fairly informal session in which someone tells a group of people about a subject: *She gave an interesting talk on her visit to China.*

sermon a talk on a moral or religious subject, usually given by a religious leader during a service: *to preach a sermon*

PATTERNS

- a **long/short** speech/lecture/address/talk/sermon
- a **keynote** speech/lecture/address
- to **prepare/give/deliver/hear** a(n) speech/lecture/address/talk/sermon
- to **write** a speech/sermon
- to **attend/go to** a lecture/talk

ˈspeech act *noun* (*linguistics*) something that someone says, considered as an action, for example "I forgive you"

ˈspeech ˌbubble *noun* a circle around the words that someone says in a CARTOON

ˈspeech comˌmunity *noun* all the people who speak a particular language or variety of a language: *the Kodava speech community in India* ◆ *speech communities such as high school students or hip hop fans*

speech·i·fy·ing /ˈspitʃəˌfaɪɪŋ/ *noun* [U] (*informal, disapproving*) the act of making speeches in a very formal way, trying to sound important

speech·less /ˈspitʃləs/ *adj.* not able to speak, especially because you are extremely angry or surprised: *Laura was speechless with rage.* ▶ **speech·less·ly** *adv.* **speech·less·ness** *noun* [U]

ˈspeech recogˌnition (also **ˈvoice recogˌnition**) *noun* [U] technology that allows a computer to understand spoken words

ˈspeech ˌsynthesis *noun* [U] the production of speech from written language by a computer

ˈspeech ˌtherapy *noun* [U] special treatment to help

| h hat | m man | n no | ŋ sing | l leg | r red | y yes | w wet |

people who have problems in speaking clearly, for example in pronouncing particular sounds ► **ˈspeech ˌtherapist** *noun*

speech·writ·er /ˈspiːtʃˌraɪtər/ *noun* a person whose job is to write speeches for a politician or public figure

speed 🔑 /spiːd/ *noun, verb*

● *noun*

> **RATE OF MOVEMENT/ACTION 1** [C, U] the rate at which someone or something moves or travels: *He reduced speed and turned sharp left.* ♦ *The train began to **pick up speed*** (= go faster). ♦ *The car was **gathering speed***. ♦ *a **speed** of 50 mph* ♦ *at **high/low/full/top speed*** ♦ *at **breakneck speed*** (= fast in a way that is dangerous) ♦ *traveling at **the speed of light/sound*** ⊃ see also AIRSPEED, GROUND SPEED **2** [C, U] the rate at which something happens or is done: *the processing speed of the computer* ♦ *This course is designed so that students can progress at their own speed.* ♦ *We aim to increase the speed of delivery* (= how quickly goods are sent). **3** [U] the quality of being quick or rapid: *The accident was due to excessive speed.* ♦ *She was overtaken by the **speed of events*** (= things happened more quickly than she expected). ♦ *(formal) A car flashed past them **at speed*** (= fast).
> **IN PHOTOGRAPHY 4** [C] a measurement of how sensitive film for cameras, etc. is to light **5** [C] the time taken by a camera SHUTTER to open and close: *shutter speeds*
> **ON BICYCLE/CAR 6** [C] (especially in compounds) a gear on a bicycle, in a car, etc.: *a four-speed gearbox* ♦ *a ten-speed mountain bike*
> **DRUG 7** [U] (*informal*) an illegal AMPHETAMINE drug that is taken to give feelings of excitement and energy
> **IDM** **full speed/steam ahead** with as much speed or energy as possible **up to speed (on sth) 1** (of a person, company, etc.) performing at an expected rate or level: *the cost of **bringing** the chosen schools **up to speed** **2** (of a person) having the most recent and accurate information or knowledge: *Are you **up to speed** yet on the latest developments?* ⊃ more at TURN *n.*

● *verb* (**speed·ed**, **speed·ed** **HELP** In senses 1 and 2 **sped** is also used for the past tense and past participle.)
> **MOVE/HAPPEN QUICKLY 1** [I] + adv./prep. (*formal*) to move along quickly: *He sped away on his bike.* **2** [T] **~ sb/sth** + adv./prep. (*formal*) to take someone or something somewhere very quickly, especially in a vehicle: *The cab speeded them into the center of the city.* **3** [T] **~ sth** (*formal*) to make something happen more quickly: *The drugs will speed her recovery.*
> **DRIVE TOO FAST 4** [I] (usually used in the progressive tenses) to drive faster than the speed that is legally allowed: *The police caught him speeding.*
> **PHR V** **ˌspeed ˈup | ˌspeed sth↔ˈup** to move or happen faster; to make something move or happen faster: *The train soon speeded up.* ♦ *Can you try and **speed things up** a bit?*

speed·boat /ˈspiːdboʊt/ *noun* a boat with a motor that can travel very fast ⊃ picture at BOAT

ˈspeed bump *noun* a raised area across a road that is put there to make traffic go slower

ˈspeed dating *noun* [U] meeting people at an event organized for single people who want to begin a romantic relationship, where you are allowed to spend only a few minutes talking to one person before you have to move on to meet the next person

ˈspeed ˌdial *noun* [U] a feature on a telephone that allows numbers to be stored so that they can be DIALED by pressing a single key ► **ˈspeed-ˌdial** *verb* (-l-, CanE also -ll-) [I, T] **~ (sth/sb)**

speed·ing /ˈspiːdɪŋ/ *noun* [U] the traffic offense of driving faster than the legal limit ⊃ collocations at DRIVING

ˈspeed ˌlimit *noun* the highest speed at which you can legally drive on a particular road: *You should always keep to the speed limit.* ♦ *to break/exceed the speed limit* ♦ *The road has a 30 mph speed limit.* ⊃ collocations at DRIVING

Speed·o™ /ˈspiːdoʊ/ *noun* (*pl.* **Speed·os**) [usually pl.] a SWIMSUIT, especially a style of tight TRUNKS for men and boys: *a pair of Speedos*

speed·om·e·ter /spɪˈdɑːmətər/ *noun* an instrument in a vehicle that shows how fast the vehicle is going ⊃ picture at CAR

ˈspeed-read *verb* [I, T] **~ (sth)** to read something very quickly, paying attention to the general meaning of sentences and phrases rather than to every word ► **ˈspeed-ˌreading** *noun* [U]

ˈspeed ˌskating *noun* [U] the sport of SKATING on ice as fast as possible ⊃ compare FIGURE SKATING

speed·ster /ˈspiːdstər/ *noun* (*informal*) **1** a person who drives a vehicle or runs very fast **2** a machine or vehicle that works well at high speeds

ˈspeed trap *noun* a place on a road where police use special equipment to catch drivers who are going too fast

speed·way /ˈspiːdweɪ/ *noun* [C] a special track for racing cars or motorcycles on

speed·well /ˈspiːdwɛl/ *noun* [U, C] a small wild plant with bright blue or pinkish-white flowers

speed·y /ˈspiːdi/ *adj.* (**speed·i·er**, **speed·i·est**) **1** happening or done quickly or without delay **SYN** **RAPID**: *We wish you a speedy recovery* (= from an illness or injury). ♦ *a speedy reply* **2** moving or working very quickly: *speedy computers* ⊃ note at FAST ► **speed·i·ly** /ˈspiːdɪli/ *adv.*: *All inquiries will be dealt with as speedily as possible.*

spe·le·ol·o·gist /ˌspiːliˈɑːlədʒɪst/ *noun* a scientist who studies CAVES or a person who goes into caves as a sport ⊃ compare SPELUNKING ► **spe·le·ol·o·gy** /ˌspiːliˈɑːlədʒi/ *noun* [U]

spell 🔑 /spɛl/ *verb, noun*

● *verb* (**spelled**, **spelled** or **spelt**, **spelt** /spɛlt/) **1** [T] **~ sth** to say or write the letters of a word in the correct order: *How do you spell your surname?* ♦ *I thought her name was Catherine, but it's Kathryn spelled with a "K."* **2** [I, T] to form words correctly from individual letters: *I've never been able to spell.* ♦ **~ sth + adj.** *You've spelled my name wrong.* ⊃ see also MISSPELL **3** [T] **~ sth** (of letters of a word) to form words when they are put together in a particular order: *C—A—T spells "cat."* **4** [T] **~ sth (for sb/sth)** to have something, usually something bad, as a result; to mean something, usually something bad: *The crop failure spelled disaster for many farmers.* **5** [T] **~ sb** (*informal*) to replace for a short time someone who is doing a particular activity so that they can rest: *Carter will be here in an hour to spell you.*
PHR V **ˌspell sth↔ˈout 1** to explain something in a simple, clear way: *You know what I mean—I'm sure I don't need to spell it out.* ♦ **~ why, what, etc....** *Let me spell out why we need more money.* **2** to say or write the letters of a word in the right order: *Could you spell that name out again?*

● *noun* **1** [C] a short period of time during which something lasts: *a spell of warm weather* ♦ *a cold/hot/wet/bright, etc. spell* ♦ *There will be rain at first, with sunny spells later.* ♦ *She went to the doctor complaining of dizzy spells.* **2** [C] a period of time doing something or working somewhere: *She had a spell as a singer before becoming an actress.* ♦ *I spent a brief spell at the Washington Post.* **3** [C] words that are thought to have magic power or to make a piece of magic work; a piece of magic that happens when someone says these magic words: *a magic spell* ♦ *a book of spells* ♦ *The wizard recited a spell.* ♦ *to cast/put a spell on someone* ♦ *to be under a spell* (= affected by magic) **4** [sing.] a quality that a person or thing has that makes them so attractive or interesting that they have a strong influence on you **SYN** **CHARM**: *I completely fell under her spell.* **IDM** see WEAVE

spell·bind·ing /ˈspɛlˌbaɪndɪŋ/ *adj.* holding your attention completely **SYN** **ENTHRALLING**: *a spellbinding performance*

spell·bound /ˈspɛlbaʊnd/ *adj.* [not usually before noun] with your attention completely held by what you are listening to or watching: *a storyteller who can hold audiences spellbound*

ˈspell-check (also **ˈspell check**) *verb* **~ sth** to use a computer program to check your writing to see if your spelling is correct ▶ **'spell–check** (also **'spell check**) noun = SPELL-CHECKER

'spell-,checker (also **'spell ,checker**) noun a computer program that checks your writing to see if your spelling is correct

spell·er /'spɛlər/ noun if someone is a **good/bad speller**, they find it easy/difficult to spell words correctly

spell·ing 🔑 /'spɛlɪŋ/ noun
1 [U] the act of forming words correctly from individual letters; the ability to do this: *a spelling mistake* ◆ *the differences between British and American spelling* ◆ *My spelling is terrible.* **2** [C] the way that a particular word is written: *a list of difficult spellings*

'spelling ,bee noun a competition in which people have to spell words

spelt /spɛlt/ pt, pp of SPELL

spe·lunk·ing /spɪ'lʌŋkɪŋ/ (also **caving**) noun [U] the sport or activity of going into CAVES under the ground ⊃ picture at HOBBY ▶ **spe·lunk·er** noun ⊃ compare SPELEOLOGIST

spend 🔑 /spɛnd/ verb, noun
• *verb* (spent, spent /spɛnt/) **1** [T, I] to give money to pay for goods, services, etc.: ~ *sth I've spent all my money already.* ◆ ~ *sth on sth/on doing sth She spent $100 on a new dress.* ◆ ~ (*sth doing sth*) *The company has spent thousands of dollars updating their computer systems.* ◆ *I just can't seem to stop spending.* **2** [T] to use time for a particular purpose; to pass time: ~ **sth + adv./prep.** *We spent the weekend in Paris.* ◆ *How do you spend your spare time?* ◆ ~ *sth on sth How long did you spend on your homework?* ◆ ~ *sth doing sth I spend too much time watching television.* ◆ ~ *sth in doing sth Most of her life was spent in caring for others.* **3** [T, often passive] to use energy, effort, etc., especially until it has all been used: ~ *sth on sth She spends too much effort on things that don't matter.* ◆ ~ *itself The storm had finally spent itself.* ⊃ see also SPENT
IDM **spend the night with sb 1** to stay with someone for a night: *My daughter's spending the night with a friend.* **2** (also **spend the night together**) to stay with someone for a night and have sex with them

spend·er /'spɛndər/ noun a person who spends money in the particular way mentioned: *a big spender* (= who spends a lot of money)

spend·ing /'spɛndɪŋ/ noun [U] the amount of money that is spent by a government or an organization: *to increase public spending* ⊃ see also DEFICIT SPENDING ⊃ thesaurus box at COST

'spending ,money noun [U] money that you can spend on personal things for pleasure or entertainment

spend·thrift /'spɛndθrɪft/ noun (*disapproving*) a person who spends too much money or who wastes money ▶ **spend·thrift** adj. [usually before noun]: *spendthrift governments*

spent /spɛnt/ adj. **1** [usually before noun] that has been used, so that it cannot be used again: *spent matches* **2** (*formal*) very tired **SYN** EXHAUSTED: *After the grueling test, he felt totally spent.*
IDM **a spent force** a person or group that no longer has any power or influence ⊃ see also SPEND

sperm /spɜrm/ noun (*pl.* **sperm** or **sperms**) **1** [C] a cell that is produced by the sex organs of a male and that can combine with a female egg to produce young: *He has a low sperm count* (= very few live male cells). **2** [U] the liquid that is produced by the male sex organs that contains these cells ⊃ collocations at LIFE **SYN** SEMEN

sper·ma·to·zo·on /,spɜrmətə'zoʊɑn; -'zoʊən/ noun (*pl.* **sper·ma·to·zo·a** /-'zoʊə/) (*biology*) a sperm

'sperm bank noun a place where sperm is kept and then used to help women become pregnant artificially

sper·mi·cide /'spɜrmə,saɪd/ noun [U, C] a substance that kills SPERM, used during sex to prevent the woman from becoming pregnant ▶ **sper·mi·cid·al** /,spɜrmə'saɪdl/ adj. [only before noun]

'sperm whale noun a large WHALE that is hunted for its oil and fat ⊃ picture at ANIMAL

spew /spyu/ verb [I, T] to flow out quickly, or to make something flow out quickly, in large amounts: + **adv./prep.** *Flames spewed from the aircraft's engine.* ◆ ~ **sth + adv./prep.** *Massive chimneys were spewing out smoke.*

SPF /,ɛs pi 'ɛf/ abbr. sun protection factor (a number that tells you how much protection a particular cream or liquid gives you from the harmful effects of the sun)

sphag·num /'sfægnəm/ noun [U] = PEAT MOSS

sphere [AWL] /sfɪr/ noun **1** (*geometry*) a solid figure that is completely round, with every point on its surface at an equal distance from the center ⊃ picture at SHAPE **2** any object that is completely round, for example a ball **3** an area of activity, influence, or interest; a particular section of society **SYN** DOMAIN: *the political sphere* ◆ *This area was formerly within the sphere of influence of the U.S.* ◆ *He and I moved in totally different social spheres.* **4** **-sphere** (in nouns) a region that surrounds a planet, especially the earth: *ionosphere* ◆ *atmosphere*

spher·i·cal [AWL] /'sfɪrɪkl; 'sfɛr-/ adj. shaped like a sphere **SYN** ROUND ▶ **spher·i·cally** [AWL] /-kli/ adv.

sphe·roid /'sfɪrɔɪd/ noun (*technical*) a solid object that is approximately the same shape as a SPHERE

sphinc·ter /'sfɪŋktər/ noun (*anatomy*) a ring of muscle that surrounds an opening in the body and can contract to close it: *the anal sphincter*

sphinx /sfɪŋks/ noun often **the Sphinx** an ancient Egyptian stone statue of a creature with a human head and the body of a LION lying down. In ancient Greek stories the Sphinx spoke in RIDDLES.

spice 🔑 /spaɪs/ noun, verb
• *noun* **1** [C, U] one of the various types of powders or seeds that come from plants and are used in cooking. Spices have a strong taste and smell: *common spices such as ginger and cinnamon* ◆ *a spice jar* **2** [U] extra interest or excitement: *We need an exciting trip to add some spice to our lives.* **IDM** see VARIETY
• *verb* **1** ~ **sth (up) (with sth)** to add spice to food in order to give it more flavor **2** ~ **sth (up) (with sth)** to add interest or excitement to something: *He exaggerated the details to spice up the story.*

spick /spɪk/ adj.
IDM **spick and span** (also **spic and span**) [not usually before noun] neat and clean: *Their house is always spick and span.*

spic·y 🔑 /'spaɪsi/ adj. (spic·i·er, spic·i·est)
1 (of food) having a strong taste because spices have been used to flavor it **SYN** HOT **2** (*informal*) (of a story, piece of news, etc.) exciting and slightly shocking ▶ **spic·i·ness** noun [U]

spi·der 🔑 /'spaɪdər/ noun
a small creature with eight thin legs. Many spiders spin webs (= nets of thin threads) to catch insects for food. ⊃ picture at ANIMAL

'spider ,monkey noun a S. American MONKEY with very long arms and legs and a long PREHENSILE tail

spi·der·web /'spaɪdər,wɛb/ (also **web**) noun a fine net of threads made by a spider to catch insects: (*figurative*) *to be caught in a spiderweb of confusion* ⊃ see also COBWEB

spi·der·y /'spaɪdəri/ adj. long and thin, like the legs of a spider: *spidery fingers* ◆ *spidery writing* (= consisting of thin lines that are not very clear)

spied pt, pp of SPY

spiel /spil; ʃpil/ noun (*informal*, usually *disapproving*) a long speech that someone has used many times, that is intended to persuade you to believe something or buy something

spies noun pl. of SPY

spiff /spɪf/ verb
PHR V ,spiff 'up | ,spiff sb/sth↔'up (informal) to make yourself/someone or something look neat and attractive

spiff·y /'spɪfi/ adj. (informal) (spiff·i·er, spiff·i·est) attractive and fashionable

spig·ot /'spɪɡət/ noun **1** (technical) a device in a FAUCET that controls the flow of liquid from a container **2** any FAUCET, especially one outdoors

spike /spaɪk/ noun, verb
● **noun 1** [C] a thin object with a sharp point, especially a pointed piece of metal, wood, etc.: a row of iron spikes on a wall ◆ Her hair stood up in spikes. ➔ see also SPIKE HEEL **2** [C, usually pl.] a metal point attached to the SOLE of a sports shoe to prevent you from slipping while running ➔ compare CLEAT **3** spikes [pl.] shoes fitted with these metal spikes, used for running: a pair of spikes **4** [C] a pointed group of flowers that grow together on a single STEM **5** [C, usually sing.] (informal) a sudden large increase in something: a spike in oil prices **6** (in the sport of VOLLEYBALL) a hard hit of the ball downward and over the net
● **verb 1** [T] ~ sb/sth (on sth) to push a sharp piece of metal, wood, etc. into someone or something; to injure something on a sharp point SYN STAB **2** [T] ~ sth (with sth) to add alcohol, poison, or a drug to someone's drink or food without them knowing: He gave her a drink spiked with tranquilizers. ◆ (figurative) Her words were spiked with malice. **3** [I] ~ (to sth) to rise quickly and reach a high value: The U. S. dollar spiked to a three-month high. **4** [T] ~ sth to reject something that a person has written or said; to prevent something from happening or being made public: The article was spiked for fear of legal action against the newspaper. **5** [T] ~ sth (in the sport of VOLLEYBALL) to hit the ball hard from a position near the net so that it moves downward and over the net **6** [T] ~ sth (in football) to throw the ball to the ground with great force, in order to celebrate a TOUCH-DOWN: He proudly spiked the ball after scoring a touchdown.

spiked /spaɪkt/ adj. with one or more spikes: spiked running shoes ◆ short spiked hair

,**spike 'heel** noun a very thin high heel on a woman's shoe; a shoe with such a heel ➔ picture at SHOE SYN STILETTO

spik·y /'spaɪki/ adj. **1** having sharp points: spiky plants, such as cacti **2** (of hair) sticking straight up from the head ➔ picture at HAIR ▸ **spik·i·ness** noun [U]

spill /spɪl/ verb, noun
● **verb** (spilled, spilled or spilt, spilt /spɪlt/) **1** [I, T] (especially of liquid) to flow over the edge of a container by accident; to make liquid do this: Water had spilled out of the bucket onto the floor. ◆ ~ sth He startled her and made her spill her drink. ◆ Thousands of gallons of crude oil were spilled into the ocean. **2** [I] + adv./prep. (of people) to come out of a place in large numbers and spread out: The doors opened and people spilled into the street. ◆ (figurative) Light spilled from the windows.
IDM spill the beans (informal) to tell someone something that should be kept secret or private spill (sb's) blood (formal or literary) to kill or wound people spill your guts (to sb) (informal) to tell someone everything you know or feel about something, because you are upset ➔ more at CRY
PHR V ,spill sth↔'out | ,spill 'out to tell someone all about a problem etc. very quickly; to come out quickly: Has she been spilling out her troubles to you again? ◆ When he started to speak, the words just spilled out. ,spill 'over (into sth) **1** to fill a container and go over the edge: She filled the glass so full that the water spilled over. ◆ (figurative) Her emotions suddenly spilled over. **2** to start in one area and then affect other areas: Unrest has spilled over into areas outside the city. ➔ related noun OVERSPILL, SPILLOVER

● **noun 1** (also formal spill·age) [C, U] an act of letting a liquid come or fall out of a container; the amount of liquid that comes or falls out: Many seabirds died as a result of the oil spill. ◆ I wiped up the coffee spills on the table. **2** [C] a long match, or a thin piece of twisted paper, used for lighting fires, oil lamps, etc. **3** [C, usually sing.] a fall, especially from a bicycle or a boat: to take a spill **IDM** see THRILL n.

spill·age /'spɪlɪdʒ/ noun [U, C] (formal) = SPILL: Put the bottle in a plastic bag in case of spillage.

spill·o·ver /'spɪlˌoʊvər/ noun [C, U] **1** something that is too large or too much for the place where it starts, and spreads to other places: A second room was needed for the spillover of staff and reporters. **2** the results or the effects of something that have spread to other situations or places

spill·way /'spɪlweɪ/ noun (technical) a passage for the extra water from a DAM (= a wall across a river that holds water back)

spim /spɪm/ noun [U] (informal) advertising sent as messages on the Internet to people who have not asked for it ➔ compare SPAM **ORIGIN** From the letters for SPam via Instant Messaging.

spin /spɪn/ verb, noun
● **verb** (spin·ning, spun, spun /spʌn/)
▸ TURN AROUND QUICKLY **1** [I, T] to turn around and around quickly; to make something do this: (+ adv./prep.) The plane was spinning out of control. ◆ a spinning ice skater ◆ My head is spinning (= I feel as if my head is going around and I can't balance). ◆ ~ (around) The dancers spun around and around. ◆ ~ sth (around) to spin a ball/coin/wheel **2** [I, T] ~ (sb) around | + adv./prep. to turn around quickly once; to make someone do this: He spun around to face her.
▸ MAKE THREAD **3** [I, T] to make thread from wool, cotton, silk, etc. by twisting it: She sat by the window spinning. ◆ ~ sth to spin and knit wool ◆ ~ A into B spinning silk into thread ◆ ~ B from A spinning thread from silk
▸ OF SPIDER/SILKWORM **4** [T] ~ sth to produce thread from its body to make a web or COCOON: a spider spinning a web
▸ DRIVE/TRAVEL QUICKLY **5** [I] + adv./prep. to drive or travel quickly: They went spinning along the roads on their bikes.
▸ PRESENT INFORMATION **6** [T] ~ sth (as sth) to present information or a situation in a particular way, especially one that makes you or your ideas seem good: An aide was already spinning the senator's defeat as "almost as good as an outright win."
IDM spin (sb) a yarn, tale, etc. to try to make someone believe a long story that is not true ➔ more at HEEL
PHR V ,spin 'off (from sth) | ,spin sth↔'off (from sth) to happen or to produce something as a new or unexpected result of something that already exists: products spinning off from favorite books ➔ related noun SPIN-OFF ,spin sth↔'off (business) to form a new company from parts of an existing one: The transportation operation will be spun off into a separate company. ➔ related noun SPIN-OFF ,spin sth↔'out to make something last as long as possible
● **noun**
▸ FAST TURNING MOVEMENT **1** [C, U] a very fast turning movement: the earth's spin ◆ the spin of a wheel **2** [C, usually sing.] if an aircraft goes into a spin, it falls and turns around rapidly
▸ IN CAR **3** [C] (informal, becoming old-fashioned) a short ride in a car for pleasure: Let's go for a spin.
▸ IN TENNIS/SOCCER **4** [U] the way you make a ball turn very fast when you throw it or hit it: She puts a lot of spin on the ball. ➔ see also TOPSPIN, BACKSPIN
▸ ON INFORMATION **5** [sing., U] (informal) a way of presenting information or a situation in a particular way, especially one that makes you or your ideas seem good: Politicians put their own spin on the economic situation.
IDM in a spin very confused, worried, or excited: Her resignation put her colleagues in a spin.

spi·na bif·i·da /ˌspaɪnə 'bɪfədə/ noun [U] a medical condition in which some bones in the SPINE have not developed normally at birth, often causing PARALYSIS (= loss of control or feeling) in the legs

spin·ach /ˈspɪnɪtʃ/ noun [U] a vegetable with large, dark green leaves that are cooked or eaten in salads ➔ picture at FRUIT

spi·nal /ˈspaɪnl/ adj. [usually before noun] (technical) connected with the SPINE (= the long bone in the back): spinal injuries

ˈspinal ˌcolumn noun the SPINE

ˈspinal ˌcord noun the mass of nerves inside the SPINE that connects all parts of the body to the brain ➔ picture at BODY

ˈspinal ˌtap noun = LUMBAR PUNCTURE

spin·dle /ˈspɪndl/ noun 1 a long straight part that turns in a machine, or that another part of the machine turns around 2 a thin pointed piece of wood used for spinning wool into thread by hand

spin·dly /ˈspɪndli/ adj. (informal, often disapproving) very long and thin and not strong: spindly legs

ˈspin ˌdoctor noun (informal) a person whose job is to present information to the public about a politician, an organization, etc. in the way that seems most positive

spine /spaɪn/ noun 1 the row of small bones that are connected together down the middle of the back ➔ picture at BODY **SYN** BACKBONE 2 any of the sharp pointed parts like needles on some plants and animals: Porcupines use their spines to protect themselves. ➔ see also SPINY 3 the narrow part of the cover of a book that the pages are joined to

ˈspine-ˌchilling adj. (of a book, movie, etc.) frightening in an exciting way ▶ **ˈspine-ˌchiller** noun

spine·less /ˈspaɪnləs/ adj. 1 (disapproving) (of people) weak and easily frightened 2 (of animals) having no spine (= the long bone in the back) 3 (of animals or plants) having no spines (= sharp parts like needles)

spin·et /ˈspɪnət/ noun 1 ~ piano/organ a small piano/electronic organ 2 a kind of HARPSICHORD (= an early type of musical instrument), played like a piano

ˈspine-ˌtingling adj. (of an event, a piece of music, etc.) enjoyable because it is very exciting or frightening

spin·na·ker /ˈspɪnəkər/ noun a large extra sail on a racing YACHT that you use when the wind is coming from behind ➔ picture at BOAT

spin·ner /ˈspɪnər/ noun 1 a person who spins thread 2 a device that spins around, used on a fishing line to attract fish

spin·ning /ˈspɪnɪŋ/ noun [U] 1 the art or the process of twisting wool, etc. to make thread 2 Spinning™ a type of exercise performed on an EXERCISE BIKE, usually in a class

ˈspinning ˌwheel noun a simple machine that people used in their homes in the past for twisting wool, etc. It has a large wheel operated with the foot.

ˈspin-off noun ~ (from/of sth) 1 an unexpected but useful result of an activity that is designed to produce something else: commercial spin-offs from medical research 2 a book, a movie, a television program, or an object that is based on a book, movie, or television series that has been very successful: The TV comedy series is a spin-off of the original movie. ◆ spin-off merchandise from the latest Disney movie 3 a new independent company formed from part of an existing one; the process of forming a new company in this way: The company is planning a spin-off of their insurance division.

spin·ster /ˈspɪnstər/ noun (old-fashioned, often disapproving) a woman who is not married, especially an older woman who is not likely to marry **HELP** This word should not now be used to mean simply a woman who is not married. ➔ compare BACHELOR ▶ **spin·ster·hood** /-ˌhʊd/ noun [U]: For most women, marriage used to bring a higher status than spinsterhood.

spin·y /ˈspaɪni/ adj. (of animals or plants) having sharp points like needles ➔ see also SPINE

ˌspiny ˈanteater noun = ECHIDNA

spi·ral /ˈspaɪrəl/ noun, adj., verb
- **noun 1** a shape or design, consisting of a continuous curved line that winds around a central point, with each curve further away from the center: The birds circled in a slow spiral above the house. **2** a continuous harmful increase or decrease in something, that gradually gets faster and faster: the destructive spiral of violence in the inner cities ◆ measures to control the inflationary spiral ◆ the **upward/downward spiral** of sales
- **adj.** moving in a continuous curve that winds around a central point: A snail's shell is spiral in form. ▶ **spi·ral·ly** adv.
- **verb** [I] **1** (+ adv./prep.) to move in continuous circles, going upward or downward: The plane spiraled down to the ground. **2** to increase rapidly: the spiraling cost of health care ◆ + adv./prep. Prices are spiraling out of control. **PHR V** ˌspiral ˈdown/ˈdownward to decrease rapidly

ˈspiral-ˌbound adj. (of a book) held together by wire that is wound through holes along one edge

ˌspiral ˈstaircase noun a set of stairs that curve upward around a central post

spi·rant /ˈspaɪrənt/ noun, adj. (phonetics) = FRICATIVE ➔ compare PLOSIVE

spire /ˈspaɪər/ noun a tall pointed structure on the top of a building, especially a church

spir·it 🔑 /ˈspɪrət/ noun, verb

- **noun**
> **MIND/FEELINGS/CHARACTER 1** [U, C] the part of a person that includes their mind, feelings, and character rather than their body: the power of the human spirit to overcome difficulties **2 spirits** [pl.] a person's feelings or state of mind: to be in **high/low spirits** ◆ You must try and **keep your spirits up** (= stay cheerful). ◆ My spirits sank at the prospect of starting all over again. **3** [C] (always with an adjective) a person of the type mentioned: a brave spirit ◆ **kindred spirits** (= people who like the same things as you) ➔ see also FREE SPIRIT
> **COURAGE/DETERMINATION 4** [U] courage, determination, or energy: Show a little **fighting spirit**. ◆ Although the team lost, they played with tremendous spirit. ◆ They took away his freedom and broke his spirit.
> **LOYAL FEELINGS 5** [U, sing.] loyal feelings toward a group, team, or society: There's not much **community spirit** around here. ➔ see also TEAM SPIRIT
> **ATTITUDE 6** [sing.] a state of mind or mood; an attitude: We approached the situation in the wrong spirit. ◆ "OK, I'll try." "That's the spirit (= the right attitude)." ◆ The party went well because everyone **entered into the spirit of things**.
> **TYPICAL QUALITY 7** [sing.] the typical or most important quality or mood of something: The exhibition captures the **spirit of the age/times**.
> **REAL MEANING 8** [U] the real or intended meaning or purpose of something: Obey the spirit, not the letter (= the narrow meaning of the words) of the law.
> **SOUL 9** [C] the soul thought of as separate from the body and believed to live on after death; a GHOST: He is dead, but his spirit lives on. ◆ It was believed that people could be possessed by evil spirits. ➔ see also THE HOLY SPIRIT
> **IMAGINARY CREATURE 10** [C] (old-fashioned) an imaginary creature with magic powers, for example, a FAIRY or an ELF
> **ALCOHOL 11** [C, usually pl.] (old-fashioned) a strong alcoholic drink: I don't drink whiskey or brandy or any other spirits. **12** [U] a special type of alcohol used in industry or medicine **IDM in spirit** in your thoughts: I will be with you in spirit (= thinking about you though not with you physically). **the spirit is willing (but the flesh is weak)** (humorous, saying) you intend to do good things but you are too lazy, weak, or busy to actually do them **as/when/if the spirit moves you** as/when/if you feel like it: I'll go for a run this evening, if the spirit moves me. ➔ more at FIGHT, RAISE
- **verb** ~ sth + adv./prep. to take someone or something away in a quick, secret, or mysterious way: After the concert, the band was **spirited away** before their fans could get near them.

spir·it·ed /ˈspɪrətəd/ *adj.* [usually before noun] full of energy, determination, or courage: *a spirited young woman* ◆ *a spirited discussion* ◆ *She put up a spirited defense in the final game.* ⊃ compare DISPIRITED ⊃ see also HIGH-SPIRITED, PUBLIC-SPIRITED ▶ **spir·it·ed·ly** *adv.*

spir·it·less /ˈspɪrətləs/ *adj.* (*formal*) without energy, enthusiasm, or determination

ˈspirit ˌlevel (also **lev·el**) *noun* a glass tube partly filled with liquid, with a bubble of air inside. Spirit levels are used to test whether a surface is level, by the position of the bubble. ⊃ picture at TOOL

spir·it·u·al 🔑 /ˈspɪrətʃuəl/ *adj., noun*
- *adj.* [usually before noun] **1** connected with the human spirit, rather than the body or physical things: *a spiritual experience* ◆ *spiritual development* ◆ *a lack of spiritual values in the modern world* ◆ *We're concerned about your spiritual welfare.* ANT MATERIAL **2** connected with religion: *a spiritual leader* ⊃ compare TEMPORAL ▶ **spir·it·u·al·ly** *adv.*: *a spiritually uplifting book*
  - IDM **your spiritual home** the place where you are happiest, especially a country where you feel you belong more than in your own country because you share the ideas and attitudes of the people who live there
- *noun* a religious song of the type originally sung by African Americans when they were SLAVES in the southern U.S.

spir·it·u·al·ism /ˈspɪrətʃuəˌlɪzəm/ *noun* [U] the belief that people who have died can send messages to living people, usually through a MEDIUM (= a person who has special powers)

spir·it·u·al·ist /ˈspɪrətʃuəlɪst/ *noun* a person who believes that people who have died can send messages to living people

spir·it·u·al·i·ty /ˌspɪrətʃuˈæləti/ *noun* [U] the quality of being concerned with religion or the human spirit

spir·it·u·al·ized /ˈspɪrətʃuəˌlaɪzd/ *adj.* (*formal*) raised to a spiritual level: *She tends to have intense, spiritualized friendships.*

spit /spɪt/ *verb, noun*
- *verb* (**spit·ting**, **spat**, **spat** /spæt/ **HELP** spit is also sometimes used for the past tense and past participle.)
  - ⟩ FROM MOUTH **1** [T] to force liquid, food, etc. out of your mouth: **~ sth (out)** *She took a mouthful of food and then suddenly spat it out.* ◆ **~ sth (from sth)** *He was spitting blood from a badly cut lip.* **2** [I] to force SALIVA (= the liquid that is produced in the mouth) out of your mouth, often as a sign of anger or lack of respect: *He coughed and spat.* ◆ **~ at/on/in sb/sth** *The prisoners were spat on by their guards.* ◆ *She spat in his face and went out.*
  - ⟩ SAY SOMETHING ANGRILY **3** [T] to say something in an angry or aggressive way: **+ speech** *"You liar!" she spat.* ◆ **~ sth (at sb)** *He was dragged out of the court, spitting abuse at the judge and jury.*
  - ⟩ OF AN ANIMAL **4** [I] to make a short angry sound: *Snakes spit and hiss when they are cornered.*
  - ⟩ OF SOMETHING COOKING/BURNING **5** [I] to make a noise and throw out fat, SPARKS, etc.: *sausages spitting in the frying pan* ◆ *The logs on the fire crackled and spat.*
  - ⟩ RAIN **6** [I] (*informal*) (only used in the progressive tenses) when **it is spitting**, it is raining lightly
  - IDM **spit it out** (*informal*) usually used in orders to tell someone to say something when they seem frightened or unwilling to speak: *If you've got something to say, spit it out!* **spit venom/blood** to show that you are very angry; to speak in an angry way
  - PHR V **ˌspit ˈup** (*informal*) (especially of a baby) to VOMIT (= bring food from the stomach back out through the mouth)
- *noun*
  - ⟩ IN/FROM MOUTH **1** [U] the liquid that is produced in your mouth SYN SALIVA **2** [C, usually sing.] the act of spitting liquid or food out of your mouth

⟩ PIECE OF LAND **3** [C] a long thin piece of land that sticks out into the ocean, a lake, etc.

⟩ FOR COOKING MEAT **4** [C] a long, thin, straight piece of metal that you put through meat to hold and turn it while you cook it over a fire
- IDM **spit and polish** (*informal*) thorough cleaning and polishing of something

spit·ball /ˈspɪtbɔl/ *noun* a piece of paper that has been inside someone's mouth and then made into a ball to throw at someone

spite 🔑 /spaɪt/ *noun, verb*
- *noun* [U] a feeling of wanting to hurt or upset someone SYN MALICE: *I'm sure he only said it out of spite.*
  - IDM 🔑 **in spite of sth** if you say that someone did something **in spite of** a fact, you mean it is surprising that that fact did not prevent them from doing it SYN DESPITE: *In spite of his age, he still leads an active life.* ◆ *They went swimming in spite of all the danger signs.* ◆ *English became the official language for business in spite of the fact that the population was largely Chinese.* ⊃ language bank at HOWEVER **in spite of yourself** if you do something **in spite of** yourself, you do it although you did not intend or expect to: *He fell asleep, in spite of himself.*
- *verb* (only used in the infinitive with *to*) **~ sb** to deliberately annoy or upset someone: *They're playing the music so loud just to spite us.* IDM see NOSE

spite·ful /ˈspaɪtfl/ *adj.* behaving in an unkind way in order to hurt or upset someone SYN MALICIOUS ▶ **spite·ful·ly** /-fəli/ *adv.*: *"I don't need you," she said spitefully.* **spite·ful·ness** *noun* [U]

spit·fire /ˈspɪtˌfaɪər/ *noun* a person who gets angry very easily

ˈspit-roast *verb* **~ sth** to cook meat on a SPIT

ˌspitting ˈimage *noun*
- IDM **be the spitting image of sb** to look exactly like someone else: *She's the spitting image of her mother.*

spit·tle /ˈspɪtl/ *noun* [U] (*old-fashioned*) the liquid that forms in the mouth SYN SALIVA, SPIT

spit·toon /spɪˈtun/ *noun* a container, used especially in the past, for people to SPIT into

splash /splæʃ/ *verb, noun*
- *verb* **1** [I] **+ adv./prep.** (of liquid) to fall noisily onto a surface: *Water splashed onto the floor.* ◆ *Rain splashed against the windows.* ⊃ picture at RIPPLE **2** [T] to make someone or something wet by making water, mud, etc. fall on them/it: **~ sth on/onto/over sb/sth** *He splashed cold water on his face.* ◆ **~ sb/sth with sth** *He splashed his face with cold water.* ◆ *My clothes were splashed with mud.* ◆ **~ sb/sth** *Stop splashing me!* **3** [I] (**+ adv./prep.**) to move through water making drops fly everywhere: *The kids were splashing through the puddles.* ◆ *People were having fun in the pool, swimming or just splashing around.* **4** [T] **~ sth with sth** [usually passive] to decorate something with areas of bright color, not in a regular pattern: *The walls were splashed with patches of blue and purple.*
  - PHR V **ˈsplash sth across/over sth** to put a photograph, news story, etc. in a place where it will be easily noticed **ˌsplash ˈdown** (of a SPACECRAFT) to land in the ocean ⊃ related noun SPLASHDOWN
- *noun* **1** [C] the sound of something hitting liquid or of liquid hitting something: *We heard the splash when she fell into the pool.* **2** [C] a small amount of liquid that falls onto something; the mark that this makes: *splashes of water on the floor* ◆ *dark splashes of mud on her skirt* **3** [C] a small area of bright color or light that contrasts with the colors around it: *These flowers will give a splash of color throughout the summer.* **4** [sing.] (*informal*) a small amount of liquid that you add to a drink: *coffee with just a splash of milk* ⊃ compare DASH **5** [sing.] an article in a newspaper, etc. that is intended to attract a lot of attention
  - IDM **make, cause, etc. a splash** (*informal*) to do something

in a way that attracts a lot of attention or causes a lot of excitement

splash·down /ˈsplæʃdaʊn/ *noun* [C, U] a landing of a SPACECRAFT in the ocean

splash·y /ˈsplæʃi/ *adj.* (**splash·i·er**, **splash·i·est**) bright and very easy to notice

splat /splæt/ *noun* [sing.] (*informal*) the sound made by something wet hitting a surface with force: *The tomato hit the wall with a splat.* ▶ **splat** *adv.*: *The omelet fell splat onto the floor.*

splat·ter /ˈsplætər/ *verb* **1** [I] (+ *adv./prep.*) (of large drops of liquid) to fall or hit something noisily: *Heavy rain splattered on the roof.* **2** [T, I] to drop or throw water, paint, mud, etc. on someone or something; to make someone or something wet or dirty by landing on them in large drops: ~ **sb/sth** (+ *adv./prep.*) *The walls were splattered with blood.* ◆ + *adv./prep. Coffee had splattered across the front of his shirt.*

splay /spleɪ/ *verb* [T, I] ~ **(sth) (out)** to make fingers, legs, etc. become further apart from each other or spread out; to be spread out wide apart: *She lay on the bed, her arms and legs splayed out.* ◆ *His long fingers splayed across her back.*

splay-foot *noun* a broad flat foot that turns away from the other foot ▶ **splay-footed** *adj.*

spleen /spliːn/ *noun* **1** [C] a small organ near the stomach that controls the quality of the blood cells: *a ruptured spleen* ⊃ picture at BODY **2** [U] (*literary*) anger: *He vented his spleen* (= shouted in an angry way) *on the assembled crowd.* ⊃ see also SPLENETIC

splen·did /ˈsplɛndəd/ *adj., exclamation*
● *adj.* **1** very impressive; very beautiful: *splendid scenery* ◆ *The hotel stands in splendid isolation, surrounded by moorland.* **2** (*old-fashioned*) excellent; very good SYN GREAT: *What a splendid idea!* ◆ *We've all had a splendid time.* ▶ **splen·did·ly** *adv.*: *You all played splendidly.*
● *exclamation* (*old-fashioned*) used to show that you approve of something, or are pleased: *You're both coming? Splendid!*

splen·dif·er·ous /splɛnˈdɪfərəs/ *adj.* (*informal, humorous*) extremely good or pleasant

splen·dor (*CanE usually* **splen·dour**) /ˈsplɛndər/ *noun* **1** [U] grand and impressive beauty SYN GRANDEUR: *a view of Rheims Cathedral, in all its splendor* ◆ *The palace has been restored to its former splendor.* **2** **splendors** [pl.] the beautiful and impressive features or qualities of something, especially a place: *the splendors of Rome* (= its fine buildings, etc.)

sple·net·ic /spləˈnɛtɪk/ *adj.* (*formal*) often bad-tempered and angry

splice /splaɪs/ *verb, noun*
● *verb* **1** ~ **sth (together)** to join the ends of two pieces of rope by twisting them together **2** ~ **sth (together)** to join the ends of two pieces of film, tape, etc. by sticking them together
● *noun* the place where two pieces of film, tape, rope, etc. have been joined

splic·er /ˈsplaɪsər/ *noun* a person or machine that joins pieces of tape, cable, etc. together

splint /splɪnt/ *noun* a long piece of wood or metal that is tied to a broken arm or leg to keep it still and in the right position

splin·ter /ˈsplɪntər/ *noun, verb*
● *noun* a small, thin, sharp piece of wood, metal, glass, etc. that has broken off a larger piece SYN SHARD
● *verb* **1** [I, T] (of wood, glass, stone, etc.) to break, or to make something break, into small, thin, sharp pieces SYN SHATTER: *The mirror cracked but did not splinter.* ◆ ~ **sth** *The impact splintered the wood.* **2** [I] (of a group of people) to divide into smaller groups that are no longer connected; to separate from a larger group: *The party began to splinter.* ◆ ~ **(off) (from sth)** *Several firms have splintered off from the original company.*

splinter group *noun* a small group of people that has separated from a larger one, especially in politics

split /splɪt/ *verb, noun*
● *verb* (**split·ting**, **split**, **split**)
▷ DIVIDE **1** [T, I] ~ **(sth)** to divide, or to make a group of people divide, into smaller groups that have very different opinions: *a debate that has split the country down the middle* ◆ *The committee split over government subsidies.* **2** [T, I] to divide, or to make something divide, into two or more parts: ~ **sth (into sth)** *She split the class into groups of four.* ◆ ~ **(into sth)** *The results split neatly into two groups.* ⊃ see also SPLIT UP **3** [T] to divide something into two or more parts and share it between different people, activities, etc.: ~ **sth (with sb)** *She split the money she won with her brother.* ◆ ~ **sth between sb/sth** *His time is split between the London and Paris offices.* ⊃ see also SPLIT UP
▷ TEAR **4** [I, T] to tear, or to make something tear, along a straight line: *Her dress had split along the seam.* ◆ ~ **(sth) open** *The cushion split open and sent feathers everywhere.* ◆ ~ **sth** *Don't tell me you've split another pair of pants!*
▷ CUT **5** [T] to cut someone's skin and make it BLEED: ~ **sth open** *She split her head open on the cupboard door.* ◆ ~ **sth** *How did you split your lip?*
▷ END RELATIONSHIP **6** [I] to leave someone and stop having a relationship with them: ~ **(with sb)** *The singer split with his wife last June.* ◆ ~ **(from sb)** *She intends to split from the band at the end of the tour.* ⊃ see also SPLIT UP
▷ LEAVE **7** [I] (*old-fashioned, informal*) to leave a place quickly: *Let's split!*
IDM **split the difference** (when discussing a price, etc.) to agree on an amount that is at an equal distance between the two amounts that have been suggested **split hairs** to pay too much attention in an argument to differences that are very small and not important **split an infinitive** to place an adverb between "to" and the infinitive of a verb, for example, to say "to strongly deny a rumor." Some people consider this to be bad English style. **split your sides (laughing/with laughter)** to laugh a lot at someone or something **split the ticket** (*politics*) to vote for candidates from more than one party ⊃ more at MIDDLE
PHR V **split a'way/'off (from sth)** | **split sth↔a'way/'off (from sth)** to separate from, or to separate something from, a larger object or group: *A rebel faction has split away from the main group.* ◆ *The storm split a branch off from the main trunk.* **split 'up (with sb)** to stop having a relationship with someone: *My parents split up last year.* ◆ *She's split up with her boyfriend.* **split sb 'up** to make two people stop having a relationship with each other: *My friend is doing her best to split us up.* **split sb 'up** | **split 'up** to divide a group of people into smaller parts; to become divided up in this way: *We were split up into groups to discuss the question.* ◆ *Let's split up now and meet again at lunchtime.* **split sth↔'up** to divide something into smaller parts: *The day was split up into 6 one-hour sessions.*
● *noun*
▷ DISAGREEMENT **1** [C] a disagreement that divides a group of people or makes someone separate from someone else: ~ **(within sth)** *a damaging split within the party leadership* ◆ ~ **(with sb/sth)** *the years following his bitter split with his wife* ◆ ~ **(between A and B)** *There have been reports of a split between the CEO and the Board of Directors.*
▷ DIVISION **2** [sing.] a division between two or more things; one of the parts that something is divided into: *He demanded a 50–50 split in the profits.*
▷ TEAR/HOLE **3** [C] a long crack or hole made when something tears: *There's a big split in the tent.*
▷ BANANA DISH **4** [C] a sweet dish made from fruit, especially a BANANA cut in two along its length, with cream, ice cream, etc. on top: *a banana split*
▷ BODY POSITION **5** **the splits** [pl.] (*also* **split** [sing.]) a position in which you stretch your legs flat across the floor in opposite directions with the rest of your body vertical: *a gymnast doing the splits*

split 'end *noun* a hair on your head that has divided into parts at the end because it is dry or in poor condition

split in'finitive *noun* (*grammar*) the form of the verb with *to*, with an adverb placed between *to* and the verb, as in *She*

| h hat | m man | n no | ŋ sing | l leg | r red | y yes | w wet |

seems to really like it. Some people consider this to be bad English style.

split-ˈlevel *adj.* (of a room, floor, etc.) having parts at different levels

split ˈpea *noun* [usually pl.] a type of dried PEA, split into halves

split-personˈality disˌorder *noun* = MULTIPLE-PERSONALITY DISORDER

split ˈscreen *noun* a way of displaying two or more pictures or pieces of information at the same time on a television, movie theater, or computer screen ▶ **split-ˈscreen** *adj.* [only before noun]: *a movie with several split-screen sequences*

split ˈsecond *noun* a very short moment of time: *Their eyes met for a split second.*

split-ˈsecond *adj.* [only before noun] done very quickly or very accurately: *She had to make a split-second decision.* ◆ *The success of the raid depended on split-second timing.*

split ˈshift *noun* two separate periods of time that you spend working in a single day, with several hours between them: *I work split shifts in a busy restaurant.*

splits·ville /ˈsplɪtsvɪl/ *noun* [sing.] (*slang*) the end of a relationship: *Within three months of the honeymoon, it was splitsville for Ron and Mimi.*

split ˈticket *noun* (in elections) a vote in which someone votes for candidates from two different parties ▶ **split-ˈticket** *adj.*: *a split-ticket vote*

split·ting /ˈsplɪtɪŋ/ *adj.* [only before noun] if you have a **splitting headache**, you have a very bad pain in your head

splotch /splɑtʃ/ *noun* a large mark or spot of ink, paint, mud, etc.; a small area of color or light ▶ **splotch·y** *adj.*: *splotchy skin*

splurge /splɜrdʒ/ *verb, noun*
- *verb* [T, I] ~ **(sth) (on sth)** (*informal*) to spend a lot of money on something that you do not really need
- *noun* [usually sing.] (*informal*) an act of spending a lot of money on something that you do not really need

splut·ter /ˈsplʌtər/ *verb, noun*
- *verb* **1** [T, I] to speak quickly and with difficulty, making soft SPITTING sounds, because you are angry or embarrassed **SYN** SPUTTER: **+ speech (out)** *"But, but…you can't!" she spluttered.* ◆ ~ **(with sth)** *Her father spluttered with indignation.* **2** [I] to make a series of short EXPLOSIVE sounds **SYN** SPUTTER: *She fled from the blaze, coughing and spluttering.*
- *noun* a short EXPLOSIVE sound: *The car started with a loud splutter.*

spoil 🔑 /spɔɪl/ *verb, noun*
- *verb* **1** [T] ~ **sth** to change something good into something bad, unpleasant, useless, etc. **SYN** RUIN: *Our camping trip was spoiled by bad weather.* ◆ *Don't let him spoil your evening.* ◆ *The tall buildings have spoiled the view.* ◆ *Don't eat too many nuts—you'll spoil your appetite* (= will no longer be hungry at the proper time to eat). **2** [T] ~ **sb** to give a child everything that they ask for and not enough discipline in a way that has a bad effect on their character and behavior **SYN** OVERINDULGE: *She spoils those kids of hers.* **3** [T] ~ **sb/yourself** to make someone/yourself happy by doing something special: *Why not spoil yourself with a weekend in a top hotel?* ◆ *He really spoiled me on my birthday.* **4** [I] (of food) to become bad so that it can no longer be eaten
  IDM **be spoiling for a fight** to want to fight with someone very much ➔ more at COOK
- *noun* **1 the spoils** [pl.] (*formal* or *literary*) goods taken from a place by thieves or by an army that has won a battle or war **2 spoils** [pl.] the profits or advantages that someone gets from being successful: *the spoils of high office* **3** [U] (*technical*) waste material that is brought up when a hole is dug, etc.

spoil·age /ˈspɔɪlɪdʒ/ *noun* [U] (*technical*) the decay of food that means that it can no longer be used

spoiled /spɔɪld/ *adj.* (of a child) rude and badly behaved because they are given everything they ask for and not enough discipline: *a spoiled brat* ◆ *He's spoiled rotten* (= a lot).

spoil·er /ˈspɔɪlər/ *noun* **1** a part of an aircraft's wing that can be raised in order to interrupt the flow of air over it and so slow the aircraft's speed **2** a raised part on a fast car that prevents it from being lifted off the road when traveling very fast **3** a candidate for a political office who is unlikely to win but who may get enough votes to prevent one of the main candidates from winning **4** a person or thing that intends or is intended to stop someone or something being successful **5** information that you are given about what is going to happen in a movie, television series etc. before it is shown to the public **6** a newspaper story, book, etc. that is produced very quickly in order to take attention away from one produced by a COMPETITOR that appears at the same time

spoil·sport /ˈspɔɪlspɔrt/ *noun* (*informal*) a person who spoils other people's enjoyment, for example by not taking part in an activity or by trying to stop other people from doing it: *Don't be such a spoilsport!*

the ˈspoils ˌsystem *noun* [sing.] the arrangement in politics that allows the President to give government jobs to supporters after winning an election

spoke /spoʊk/ *noun* one of the thin bars or long straight pieces of metal that connect the center of a wheel to its outer edge, for example on a bicycle ➔ **picture at** BICYCLE ➔ **see also** SPEAK, SPOKE, SPOKEN

spo·ken 🔑 /ˈspoʊkən/ *verb, adj.*
- *verb* pp of SPEAK
- *adj.* **1** involving speaking rather than writing; expressed in speech rather than in writing: *spoken English* ◆ *spoken commands* **2** (following an adverb) speaking in the way mentioned: *a soft spoken man* ➔ **see also** OUTSPOKEN

ˈspoken for *adj.* [not before noun] already claimed or being kept for someone: *I'm afraid you can't sit there—those seats are* spoken for. ◆ (*old-fashioned*) *Liza is already spoken for* (= she is already married or has a partner).

the ˌspoken ˈword *noun* [sing.] language expressed in speech, rather than being written or sung

spokes·man /ˈspəʊksmən/, **spokes·wom·an** /ˈspəʊks-ˌwʊmən/ *noun* (*pl.* **spokes·men** /-mən/, **spokes·wom·en** /-ˌwɪmən/) a person who speaks on behalf of a group or an organization: *a police spokesman* ◆ ~ **for sb/sth** *A spokeswoman for the government denied the rumors.* ➔ note at GENDER

spokes·per·son /ˈspəʊksˌpɜːrsn/ *noun* (*pl.* **spokes·persons** or **spokes·peo·ple** /-ˌpiːpl/) ~ **(for sb/sth)** a person who speaks on behalf of a group or an organization

spon·dee /ˈspɒndi/ *noun* (*technical*) a unit of sound in poetry consisting of two strong or long syllables

sponge /spʌndʒ/ *noun, verb*
● *noun* **1** [C] a piece of artificial or natural material that is soft and light and full of holes and can hold water easily, used for washing or cleaning: (*figurative*) *His mind was like a sponge, ready to absorb anything.* ➔ picture at CLEANING, MAKEUP **2** [C] a simple sea creature with a light body full of holes, from which natural sponge is obtained
● *verb* **1** [T] ~ **sb/yourself/sth (down)** to wash someone/yourself/something with a wet cloth or SPONGE **SYN** WIPE: *She sponged his hot face.* ◆ *Take your jacket off and I'll sponge it down with water.* **2** [T] ~ **sth + adv./prep.** to remove something using a wet cloth or SPONGE **SYN** WASH: *We tried to sponge the blood off my shirt.* **3** [I] ~ **(off/on sb)** (*informal, disapproving*) to get money, food, etc. regularly from other people without doing anything for them or offering to pay **SYN** SCROUNGE: *He spent his life sponging off his relatives.*

ˈsponge bath *noun* an act of washing the whole of someone's body when they cannot get out of bed because they are sick, injured, or old

ˈsponge cake *noun* [C, U] a light cake made from eggs, sugar, and flour, with or without fat

spong·er /ˈspʌndʒər/ *noun* (*informal*) a person who gets money, food, etc. from other people without doing anything for them or offering to pay

spon·gi·form /ˈspʌndʒɪˌfɔːrm/ *adj.* (*technical*) having or relating to a structure with holes in it like a SPONGE ➔ see also BSE

spon·gy /ˈspʌndʒi/ *adj.* soft and able to absorb water easily like a SPONGE **SYN** SPRINGY: *spongy moss* ◆ *The ground was soft and spongy.* ◆ *The bread had a spongy texture.*
▶ **spon·gi·ness** *noun* [U]

spon·sor /ˈspɒnsər/ *noun, verb*
● *noun* **1** a person or company that pays for a radio or television program, or for a concert or sporting event, usually in return for advertising: *The race organizers are trying to attract sponsors.* **2** a person who agrees to give someone money for a charity if that person succeeds in completing a particular activity: *I'm collecting sponsors for next week's charity run.* **3** a person or company that supports someone by paying for their training or education **4** a person who introduces and supports a proposal for a new law, etc.: *the sponsor of the new immigration bill* **5** a person who agrees to be officially responsible for another person **6** a person who presents a child for Christian BAPTISM or CONFIRMATION **SYN** GODPARENT
● *verb* **1** ~ **sth** (of a company, etc.) to pay the costs of a particular event, program, etc. as a way of advertising: *sports events sponsored by the tobacco industry* **2** ~ **sth** to arrange for something official to take place: *The U.S. is sponsoring negotiations between the two sides.* **3** ~ **sb (for sth/to do sth)** to agree to give someone money for a charity if they complete a particular task: *Will you sponsor me for a charity walk I'm doing?* ◆ *a sponsored swim* **4** ~ **sb (through sth)** to support someone by paying for their training or education: *She found a company to sponsor her through college.* **5** ~ **sth** to introduce a proposal for a new law, etc.: *The bill was sponsored by a Republican Senator.*

spon·sor·ship /ˈspɒnsərˌʃɪp/ *noun* **1** [U, C] financial support from a sponsor: *a $50 million sponsorship deal* ◆ *The project needs to raise $8 million in sponsorship.* ◆ *We need to find sponsorships for the expedition.* **2** [U] the act of sponsoring someone or something or being sponsored: *the senator's sponsorship of the job training legislation*

spon·ta·ne·i·ty /ˌspɒntəˈneɪəti, -ˈniːəti/ *noun* [U] the quality of being spontaneous

spon·ta·ne·ous /spɒnˈteɪniəs/ *adj.* **1** not planned but done because you suddenly want to do it: *a spontaneous offer of help* ◆ *The audience burst into spontaneous applause.* **2** often doing things without planning to, because you suddenly want to do them **3** (*technical*) happening naturally, without being made to happen: *spontaneous remission of the disease* **4** done naturally, without being forced or practiced: *a tape recording of spontaneous speech* ◆ *a wonderfully spontaneous performance of the piece* ▶ **spon·ta·ne·ous·ly** *adv.*: *We spontaneously started to dance.* ◆ *The bleeding often stops spontaneously.*

sponˌtaneous comˈbustion *noun* [U] the burning of a mineral or vegetable substance caused by chemical changes inside it and not by fire or heat from outside

spoof /spuːf/ *noun, verb*
● *noun* (*informal*) a humorous copy of a movie, television program, etc. that exaggerates its main features: *It's a spoof on horror movies.*
● *verb* **1** ~ **sth** to copy a movie, television program, etc. in an amusing way by exaggerating its main features: *It is a movie that spoofs other movies.* **2** ~ **sth** to send an e-mail that appears to come from someone else's e-mail address: *Someone has been spoofing my address.* ▶ **spoof·ing** *noun* [U]

spook /spuːk/ *noun, verb*
● *noun* (*informal*) **1** a GHOST: *a castle haunted by spooks* **2** a SPY: *a CIA spook*
● *verb* [T, usually passive, I] ~ **(sb/sth)** (*informal*) to frighten a person or an animal; to become frightened: *We were spooked by the strange noises and lights.* ◆ *The horse spooked at the siren.*

spook·y /ˈspuːki/ *adj.* (**spook·i·er**, **spook·i·est**) **HELP** You can also use **more spooky** and **most spooky**. (*informal*) strange and frightening **SYN** CREEPY: *a spooky old house* ◆ *I was just thinking about her when she phoned. Spooky!*

spool /spuːl/ *noun, verb*
● *noun* a round object around which you wind such things as thread, film, wire etc.; a spool together with the thread, film, wire, etc. that is wound around it: *a spool of thread* ➔ compare REEL
● *verb* **1** [T] ~ **sth + adv./prep.** to wind something onto or off a spool **2** [T, I] ~ **(sth)** (*computing*) to move data and store it for a short time, for example on a disk, especially before it is printed

spoon /spuːn/ *noun, verb*
● *noun* **1** a tool that has a handle with a shallow bowl at the end, used for stirring, serving, and eating food: *a soup spoon* ◆ *a wooden spoon* ➔ see also DESSERTSPOON, GREASY SPOON, MEASURING SPOON, TABLESPOON, TEASPOON **2** = SPOONFUL **IDM** see BORN
● *verb* ~ **sth + adv./prep.** to lift and move food with a spoon: *She spooned the sauce over the chicken pieces.*

spoon·bill /ˈspuːnbɪl/ *noun* a large bird with long legs, a long neck, and a beak that is wide and flat at the end

spoon·er·ism /ˈspuːnəˌrɪzəm/ *noun* a mistake in which you change around the first sounds of two words by mistake when saying them, often with a humorous result, for example *well-boiled icicle* for *well-oiled bicycle* **ORIGIN** Named after **W.A. Spooner** (1844–1930), the head of New College, Oxford, who was said to have made many mistakes like this when he spoke.

ˈspoon–feed *verb* **1** (*disapproving*) to teach people something in a way that gives them too much help and does not make them think for themselves: ~ **sb (with sth)** *The*

ʌ **cup**   ə **about**   eɪ **say**   aɪ **five**   ɔɪ **boy**   aʊ **now**   oʊ **go**   ɜːr **bird**

students here do not expect to be spoon-fed. ◆ **~ sth to sb** *They had information spoon-fed to them.* **2 ~ sb** to feed someone, especially a baby, with a spoon

spoon·ful /ˈspunful/ (also **spoon**) *noun* the amount that a spoon can hold: *two spoonfuls of sugar*

spoor /spʊr; spɔr/ *noun* [sing.] a track or smell that a wild animal leaves as it travels

spo·rad·ic /spəˈrædɪk/ *adj.* happening only occasionally or at intervals that are not regular **SYN** INTERMITTENT: *sporadic fighting/gunfire/violence, etc.* ◆ *sporadic outbreaks of the disease* ▶ **spo·rad·i·cally** /-kli/ *adv.*: *She attended lectures only sporadically.* ◆ *Fighting continued sporadically for two months.*

spore /spɔr/ *noun* (*biology*) one of the very small cells that are produced by some plants and that develop into new plants: *Ferns, mosses and fungi spread by means of spores.* ➲ collocations at LIFE

sport 🔊 /spɔrt/ *noun, verb*
• *noun* **1** [C] an activity that you do for pleasure and that needs physical effort or skill, usually done in a special area and according to fixed rules: *What's your favorite sport?* ◆ *team/water sports* ◆ *There are excellent facilities for sports and recreation.* ◆ *I'm not interested in sports.* ◆ *the use of drugs in sports* ◆ *a sports club* ➲ picture on page 1438 ➲ see also BLOOD SPORT, SPECTATOR SPORT, WINTER SPORTS **2** [U] (*formal*) enjoyment or fun: *The comments were only made in sport.* ◆ *to make sport of* (= to joke about) *someone or something* **3** [C] (*biology*) a plant or an animal that is different in a noticeable way from its usual type
IDM **be a (good) sport** (*informal*) to be generous, cheerful, and pleasant, especially in a difficult situation: *She's a good sport.* ◆ *Go on, be a sport* (= used when asking someone to help you).
• *verb* **1** [T] **~ sth** to have or wear something in a proud way **SYN** WEAR: *to sport a beard* ◆ *She was sporting a T-shirt with the company's logo on it.* **2** [I] + **adv./prep.** (*literary*) to play in a happy and lively way

sport coat (also **ˈsports coat**, **ˈsport jacket**, **ˈsports jacket**) *noun* a man's jacket that is like a suit jacket, worn on informal occasions

sport·ing /ˈspɔrtɪŋ/ *adj.* [only before noun] connected with sports: *a major sporting event* ◆ *a variety of sporting activities* ◆ *His main sporting interests are golf and tennis.* ◆ *a store selling sporting goods* ▶ **sport·ing·ly** *adv.*: *He sportingly agreed to play the point again.*
IDM **a sporting chance** a reasonable chance of success

ˈsport jacket *noun* = SPORT COAT

ˈsports car (also **ˈsport car**) *noun* a low fast car, often with a roof that can be folded back ➲ picture at CAR

sports·cast /ˈspɔrtskæst/ *noun* a television or radio broadcast of sports news or a sports event

sports·cast·er /ˈspɔrtsˌkæstər/ *noun* a person who introduces and presents a sportscast

ˈsports center (CanE usually **ˈsports centre**) *noun* a building where the public can go to play many different kinds of sports, swim, etc.

ˈsports coat *noun* = SPORT COAT

ˈsports jacket *noun* = SPORT COAT

sports·man /ˈspɔrtsmən/, **sports·wom·an** /ˈspɔrtsˌwʊmən/ *noun* (*pl.* **sports·men** /-mən/, **sports·wom·en** /-ˌwɪmən/) a person who takes part in sports, especially someone who is very good at them **SYN** ATHLETE: *a natural sportswoman* ◆ *He is one of this country's top professional sportsmen.*

sports·man·like /ˈspɔrtsmənˌlaɪk/ *adj.* behaving in a fair, generous, and polite way, especially when playing a sport or game: *a sportsmanlike attitude*

sports·man·ship /ˈspɔrtsmənˌʃɪp/ *noun* [U] fair, generous, and polite behavior, especially when playing a sport or game

ˈsports ˌmedicine *noun* [U] a branch of medicine that deals with injuries and health problems caused by playing sports

sports·per·son /ˈspɔrtsˌpɜrsn/ *noun* (*pl.* **sports·per·sons** or **sports·peo·ple**) a person who takes part in sports, especially someone who is very good at them **SYN** ATHLETE

ˈsports shirt (also **ˈsport shirt**) *noun* a man's shirt for informal occasions

sports·wear /ˈspɔrtswer/ *noun* [U] **1** clothes that are worn in informal situations **2** clothes that are worn for playing sports, or in informal situations

ˌsport uˈtility ˌvehicle *noun* = SUV

sport·y /ˈspɔrti/ *adj.* (**sport·i·er**, **sport·i·est**) (*informal*) **1** (of clothes) bright, attractive, and informal; looking suitable for wearing for sports: *a sporty cotton top* **2** (of cars) fast and elegant: *a sporty Mercedes*

spot 🔊 /spɑt/ *noun, verb, adj.*
• *noun*
> SMALL MARK **1** a small round area that has a different color or feels different from the surface it is on: *Which has spots, the leopard or the tiger?* ◆ *The male bird has a red spot on its beak.* ➲ see also BEAUTY SPOT, SUNSPOT ➲ thesaurus box at PATCH **2** a small dirty mark on something: *His jacket was covered with spots of mud.* ◆ *rust spots* ➲ thesaurus box at MARK **3** [usually pl.] a small mark or lump on a person's skin that shows that they are sick: *The baby's whole body was covered in small red spots.* ➲ compare RASH, ZIT
> PLACE **4** a particular area or place: *a quiet/secluded/lonely, etc. spot* ◆ *He showed me the exact spot where he had asked her to marry him.* ◆ *She stood rooted to the spot with fear* (= unable to move). ◆ *a tourist spot* ➲ see also BLACK SPOT, BLIND SPOT, HOT SPOT, NIGHTSPOT, TROUBLE SPOT ➲ thesaurus box at PLACE
> SMALL AMOUNT **5** [usually pl.] **~ (of sth)** a small amount of a liquid: *I felt a few spots of rain.*
> PART OF SHOW **6** a part of a television, radio, club, or theater show that is given to a particular entertainer or type of entertainment: *a guest/solo spot*
> IN COMPETITION **7** a position in a competition or an event: *two teams battling for top spot*
> LIGHT **8** (*informal*) = SPOTLIGHT
IDM **in a (tight) spot** (*informal*) in a difficult situation **on the spot 1** immediately: *He answered the question on the spot.* ◆ *an on-the-spot parking fine* **2** at the actual place where something is happening: *An ambulance was on the spot within minutes.* ◆ *an on-the-spot report* **put sb on the spot** to make someone feel awkward or embarrassed by asking them a difficult question: *The interviewer's questions really put him on the spot.* ➲ more at BRIGHT, GLUE, HIT, LEOPARD, RIVET, SOFT
• *verb* (**-tt-**) **1** (not used in the progressive tenses) to see or notice a person or thing, especially suddenly or when it is not easy to do so: **~ sb/sth** *I finally spotted my friend in the crowd.* ◆ *I just spotted a mistake on the front cover.* ◆ *Can you spot the difference between these two pictures?* ◆ **~ sb/sth doing sth** *neighbors spotted smoke coming out of the house.* ◆ **~ that…** *No one spotted that the gun was a fake.* ◆ **~ what, where, etc.…** *I soon spotted what the mistake was.* ➲ see also SPOTTER ➲ thesaurus box at SEE **2 ~ sb/sth sth** (*sports*) to give your opponent or the other team an advantage: *We spotted the opposing team two goals.*
IDM **be spotted with sth** to be covered with small round marks of something: *His shirt was spotted with oil.*
• *adj.* [only before noun] (*business*) connected with a system of trading where goods are delivered and paid for immediately after sale: *spot prices*

ˈspot check *noun* a check that is made suddenly and without warning on a few things or people chosen from a group to see that everything is as it should be: *to carry out random spot checks on vehicles*

Sports

cycling

fencing — mask, foil

golf — golf course, bunker, green, hole, fairway

archery — target, arrow, bow, archer

horse racing — jockey, racecourse, racehorse

boxing — the ropes, boxing glove

gymnastics

team sports

basketball — hoop, court, basket

soccer — crossbar, goalkeeper, goal, ball

field hockey — ball, hockey stick

hockey (*also* ice hockey) — skate, puck, ice rink

racket sports

squash

badminton — shuttlecock

tennis — court, racket, net

Ping-Pong™ — paddle

field events

the pole vault

the discus

the javelin

the hammer

the high jump

track events

sprinting

hurdling — hurdle, lane

relay (*also* relay race)

t tea   ţ butter   d did   k cat   g got   tʃ chin   dʒ June   f fall

swimming

crawl

butterfly

backstroke

breaststroke

winter sports

bobsled

the luge

goggles
pole
binding
ski
downhill skiing

cross-country skiing

snowboard
snowboarding

water sports

waterskiing

surfboard
surfing

jet-skiing
Jet Ski™

windsurfer (also sailboard)
windsurfing

extreme sports

rock climbing

rappelling

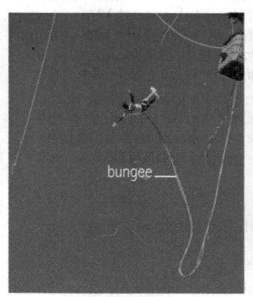
bungee
bungee jumping

hang-gliding

paragliding

skydiving

spot·less /ˈspɒtləs/ adj. perfectly clean **SYN** IMMACULATE: *a spotless white shirt* ◆ *She keeps the house spotless.* ◆ (*figurative*) *He has a spotless record so far.* ▶ **spot·less·ly** adv.: *spotlessly clean*

spot·light /ˈspɒtlaɪt/ noun, verb
- **noun 1** (also informal **spot**) [C] a light with a single, very bright BEAM that can be directed at a particular place or person: *The room was lit by spotlights.* ➔ picture at LIGHT **2 the spotlight** [U] the area of light that is made by a spotlight: *She stood alone on stage in the spotlight.* **3 the spotlight** [U] attention from newspapers, television, and the public: *Unemployment is once again in the spotlight.* ◆ *The issue will come under the spotlight when congress reconvenes.* ◆ *The report has turned the spotlight on the startling rise in street crime.*
- **verb** (spot·lit, spot·lit /-lɪt/ **HELP** Especially in sense 2, **spotlighted** is also used for the past tense and past participle.) **1** ~ **sth** to shine a spotlight on someone or something: *a spotlit stage* **2** ~ **sth** to give special attention to a problem, situation, etc. so that people notice it **SYN** HIGHLIGHT: *The program spotlights financial problems in the health service.*

spot·ted /ˈspɒtəd/ adj. having dark marks on it, sometimes in a pattern: *a leopard's spotted coat*

spot·ter /ˈspɒtər/ noun **1** (especially in compounds) a person who looks for a particular type of thing or person, as a hobby or job ➔ see also TRAINSPOTTER **2** (also ˈspotter ˌplane) a plane used for finding out what an enemy is doing

spot·ty /ˈspɒti/ adj. **1** not complete; good in some parts, but not in others: *a spotty knowledge of Spanish* ◆ *It was a spotty performance.* **2** covered with spots: *spotty bananas*

spouse /spaʊs/ noun (formal or law) a husband or wife ▶ **spous·al** /ˈspaʊzl; -sl/ adj. [only before noun] (formal): *spousal consent* ◆ *spousal abuse*

spout /spaʊt/ noun, verb
- **noun 1** a pipe or tube on a container, that you can pour liquid out through: *the spout of a teapot* **2** a stream of liquid coming out of somewhere with great force **SYN** FOUNTAIN
- **verb 1** [T, I] to send out something, especially a liquid, in a stream with great force; to come out of something in this way **SYN** POUR: ~ **sth** (**from sth**) *The wound was still spouting blood.* ◆ ~ **from/out of sth** *Clear water spouted from the fountains.* **2** [I] (of a WHALE) to send out a stream of water from a hole in its head **3** [I, T] (informal, disapproving) to speak a lot about something; to repeat something in a boring or annoying way: ~ (**off/on**) (**about sth**) *He's always spouting off about being a vegetarian.* ◆ *What are you spouting on about now?* ◆ ~ **sth** *He could spout poetry for hours.* ◆ *She could do nothing but spout insults.*

sprain /spreɪn/ verb ~ **sth** to injure a joint in your body, especially your wrist or ankle, by suddenly twisting it: *I stumbled and sprained my ankle.* ➔ collocations at INJURY ➔ thesaurus box at INJURE ▶ **sprain** noun: *a bad ankle sprain*

sprang pt of SPRING

sprat /spræt/ noun a very small European sea fish that is used for food

sprawl /sprɔl/ verb, noun
- **verb 1** [I] (+ adv./prep.) to sit or lie with your arms and legs spread out in a relaxed or awkward way: *He was sprawling in an armchair in front of the TV.* ◆ *Something hit her and sent her sprawling to the ground.* ◆ *I tripped and went sprawling.* **2** [I] + adv./prep. to spread in a messy way; to cover a large area: *The town sprawled along the side of the lake.*
- **noun 1** [C, usually sing., U] a large area covered with buildings that spreads from the city into the countryside in an ugly way: *attempts to control the fast-growing urban sprawl* **2** [C, usually sing.] an act of spreading to cover a large area in a messy way; something that spreads like this

sprawled /sprɔld/ adj. sitting or lying with your arms and legs spread out in a lazy or awkward way: *He was lying sprawled in an armchair, watching TV.*

sprawl·ing /ˈsprɔlɪŋ/ adj. [only before noun] spreading in a messy way: *a modern sprawling town*

spray /spreɪ/ noun, verb
- **noun 1** [U, C] very small drops of a liquid that are sent through the air, for example by the wind: *sea spray* ◆ *A cloud of fine spray came up from the waterfall.* ◆ (*figurative*) *a spray of machine-gun bullets* **2** [U, C] (especially in compounds) a substance that is forced out of a container such as an AEROSOL, in very small drops: *a can of insect spray* (= used to kill insects) ◆ *body spray* ➔ see also HAIRSPRAY, PEPPER SPRAY **3** [C] a device or container, for example an AEROSOL, that you use to apply liquid in fine drops: *a throat spray* **4** [C] an act of applying liquid to something in very small drops: *I gave the plants a quick spray.* **5** [C] a small branch of a tree or plant, with its leaves and flowers or berries (BERRY), that you use for decoration **SYN** SPRIG **6** [C] an attractive arrangement of flowers or jewelry, that you wear: *a spray of orchids*
- **verb 1** [T, I] to cover someone or something with very small drops of a liquid that are forced out of a container or sent through the air: ~ (**sth**) (**on/onto/over sb/sth**) *Spray the conditioner onto your wet hair.* ◆ *Champagne sprayed everywhere.* ◆ ~ **sb/sth** (**with sth**) *The crops are regularly sprayed with pesticide.* ◆ ~ **sth** + **adj.** *She's had the car sprayed blue.* **2** [T, I] to cover someone or something with a lot of small things with a lot of force: ~ **sb/sth with sth** *The gunman sprayed the building with bullets.* ◆ + **adv./prep.** *Pieces of glass sprayed all over the room.* **3** [I] (especially of a male cat) to leave small amounts of URINE to mark its own area

ˈspray can noun a small metal container that has paint in it under pressure and that you use to spray paint onto something

spray·er /ˈspreɪər/ noun a piece of equipment used for spraying liquid, especially paint or a substance used to kill insects that damage crops: *a paint/crop sprayer*

ˈspray gun noun a device for spraying paint onto a surface, that works by air pressure

ˈspray paint noun [U] paint that is kept in a container under pressure and that you can spray onto something ▶ **ˈspray-paint** verb ~ **A** (**with B**) | ~ **B** (**on A**)

spread /spred/ verb, noun
- **verb** (spread, spread)
- ▷ **OPEN/ARRANGE 1** [T] ~ **sth** (**out**) (**on/over sth**) to open something that has been folded so that it covers a larger area than before: *to spread a cloth on a table* ◆ *Sue spread the map out on the floor.* ◆ *The bird spread its wings.* **2** [T] ~ **sth** (**out**) (**on/over sth**) to arrange objects so that they cover a large area and can be seen easily: *Papers had been spread out on the desk.*
- ▷ **ARMS/LEGS 3** [T] ~ **sth** (**out**) to move your arms, legs, fingers, etc. far apart from each other: *She spread her arms and the child ran toward her.*
- ▷ **AMONG PEOPLE 4** [I, T] to affect or make something affect, be known by, or used by more and more people: (+ adv./prep.) *The disease spreads easily.* ◆ *Within weeks, his confidence had spread throughout the team.* ◆ *Use of computers spread rapidly during that period.* ◆ ~ **sth** to spread rumors/lies about someone ◆ *The disease is spread by mosquitoes.*
- ▷ **COVER LARGE AREA 5** [I, T] to cover, or to make something cover, a larger and larger area: (+ adv./prep.) *The fire rapidly spread to adjoining buildings.* ◆ *Water began to spread across the floor.* ◆ *A smile spread slowly across her face.* ◆ ~ **sth** *Using too much water could spread the stain.* **6** [T] ~ **sb/sth** to cause someone or something to be in a number of different places: *Seeds and pollen are spread by the wind.* ◆ *We have 10,000 members spread all over the country.* **7** [I] ~ (**out**) + adv./prep. to cover a large area: *The valley spread out beneath us.*
- ▷ **SOFT LAYER 8** [T, I] to put a layer of a substance onto the surface of something; to be able to be put onto a surface: ~ (**A on/over B**) *to spread butter on pieces of toast* ◆ ~ (**B with**

h **hat**   m **man**   n **no**   ŋ **sing**   l **leg**   r **red**   y **yes**   w **wet**

A) *pieces of toast spread with butter* ◆ *If the paint is too thick, it will not spread evenly.*
> **DIVIDE/SHARE 9** [T] to separate something into parts and divide them between different times or different people: **~ sth** *Why not pay monthly and spread the cost of your car insurance?* ◆ **~ sth (out) (over sth)** *A series of five interviews will be spread over two days.* ◆ **~ sth between sb/sth** *We attempted to spread the workload between the departments.*
   IDM spread like wildfire (of news, etc.) to become known by more and more people very quickly spread your net to consider a wide range of possibilities or cover a large area, especially to try to find someone or something: *They have spread their net far and wide in the search for a new team coach.* spread your wings to become more independent and confident and try new activities, etc. spread the word to tell people about something spread yourself too thin to try to do so many different things at the same time that you do not do any of them well ➔ see also MIDDLE-AGE SPREAD
   PHR V ˌspread ˈout | ˌspread yourself ˈout **1** to stretch your body or arrange your things over a large area: *There's more room to spread out in first class.* ◆ *Do you have to spread yourself out all over the sofa?* **2** to separate from other people in a group, to cover a larger area: *The searchers spread out to cover the area faster.*
● **noun**
> **INCREASE 1** [U] an increase in the amount or number of something that there is, or in the area that is affected by something: *to prevent the spread of disease* ◆ *to encourage the spread of information* ◆ *the spread of a city into the surrounding areas* ➔ see also MIDDLE-AGE SPREAD
> **RANGE/VARIETY 2** [C, usually sing.] a range or variety of people or things: *a broad spread of opinions*
> **ON BREAD 3** [C, U] a soft food that you put on bread: *Use a low-fat spread instead of butter.* ◆ *cheese spread*
> **AREA COVERED 4** [C, usually sing.] **~ (of sth)** the area that something exists in or happens in: *The company has a good geographical spread of hotels in this region.* **5** [C, usually sing.] **~ (of sth)** how wide something is or the area that something covers: *The bird's wings have a spread of nearly a yard.*
> **IN NEWSPAPER/MAGAZINE 6** [C] an article or advertisement in a newspaper or magazine, especially one that covers two opposite pages: *The story continued with a double-page spread on the inside pages.* ➔ see also CENTER SPREAD
> **MEAL 7** [C] (*informal*) a large meal, especially one that is prepared for a special occasion: *They had laid on a huge spread for the party.*
> **OF LAND/WATER 8** [C, usually sing.] **~ (of sth)** an area of land or water: *a vast spread of water* ◆ *They have a huge spread in California* (= a large farm or RANCH).
> **FINANCE 9** [U] the difference between two rates or prices
> **ON BED 10** [C] = BEDSPREAD

spread-ˌea·gled /ˈspred ˌiɡld/ (also **ˈspread-ˌeagle**) *adj.* [not usually before noun] in a position with your arms and legs spread out ▶ **ˈspread-ˌeagle** *verb* **~ sb**

spread·er /ˈspredər/ *noun* a device or machine that spreads things: *a manure spreader*

spread·sheet /ˈspredʃit/ *noun* a computer program that is used, for example, when doing financial or project planning. You enter data in rows and columns and the program calculates costs, etc. from it.

spree /spri/ *noun* **1** a short period of time that you spend doing one particular activity that you enjoy, but often too much of it: *a shopping/spending spree* ◆ *He's out on a spree.* **2** (used especially in newspapers) a period of activity, especially criminal activity: *to go on a killing spree*

sprig /sprɪɡ/ *noun* a small STEM with leaves on it from a plant or bush, used in cooking or as a decoration: *a sprig of parsley/holly/heather*

spright·ly /ˈspraɪtli/ (also *less frequent* **spry**) *adj.* (especially of older people) full of life and energy **SYN** LIVELY: *a sprightly 80-year-old* ▶ **spright·li·ness** *noun* [U]

spring

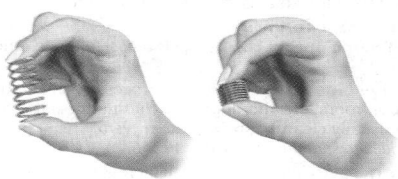

spring /sprɪŋ/ *noun, verb*
● **noun**
> **SEASON 1** [U, C] the season between winter and summer when plants begin to grow: *flowers that bloom in spring/in the spring* ◆ *He was born in the spring of 1944.* ◆ *There's a feeling of spring in the air today.* ◆ *spring flowers*
> **TWISTED WIRE 2** [C] a twisted piece of metal that can be pushed, pressed, or pulled but that always returns to its original shape or position afterward: *bed springs* **3** [U] the ability of a spring to return to its original position: *The mattress has lost its spring.*
> **WATER 4** [C] a place where water comes naturally to the surface from under the ground: *a mountain spring* ◆ *spring water*
> **CHEERFUL QUALITY 5** [U, sing.] a cheerful, lively quality: *She walked along with a spring in her step.*
> **SUDDEN JUMP 6** [C] a quick sudden jump upward or forward: *With a spring, the cat leaped on to the table.*
● **verb** (**sprang** /spræŋ/, **sprung** /sprʌŋ/ or **sprung, sprung**)
> **JUMP/MOVE SUDDENLY 1** [I] **(+ adv./prep.)** (of a person or an animal) to move suddenly and with one quick movement in a particular direction: *He turned off the alarm and sprang out of bed.* ◆ *Everyone sprang to their feet* (= stood up suddenly) *when the principal walked in.* ◆ *The cat crouched ready to spring.* ◆ (*figurative*) *to spring to someone's defense/assistance* (= to quickly defend or help someone) **2** [I] (of an object) to move suddenly and violently: **+ adv./prep.** *The branch sprang back and hit him in the face.* ◆ **+ adj.** *She turned the key and the lid sprang open.*
> **SURPRISE 3** [T] to do something, ask something, or say something that someone is not expecting: **~ sth** *She sprang a surprise by winning the tournament.* ◆ **~ sth on sb** *I'm sorry to spring it on you, but I've been offered another job.*
> **APPEAR SUDDENLY 4** [I] **+ adv./prep.** to appear or come somewhere suddenly: *Tears sprang to her eyes.*
> **FREE PRISONER 5** [T] **~ sb** (*informal*) to help a prisoner to escape: *Plans to spring the hostages have failed.*
   IDM spring into action| spring into/to life (of a person, machine, etc.) to suddenly start working or doing something: *"Let's go!" he said, springing into action.* ◆ *The town springs into life* (= becomes busy) *during the carnival.* spring a leak (of a boat or container) to develop a hole through which water or another liquid can pass spring a trap **1** to make a trap for catching animals close suddenly **2** to try to trick someone into doing or saying something; to succeed in this ➔ more at HOPE, MIND
   PHR V ˈspring for sth (*informal*) to pay for something for someone else: *I'll spring for the drinks tonight.* ˈspring from sth (*formal*) to be caused by something; to start from something: *The idea for the novel sprang from a trip to India.* ˈspring from… (*informal*) to appear suddenly and unexpectedly from a particular place: *Where on earth did you spring from?* ˌspring ˈup to appear or develop quickly and/or suddenly

spring·board /ˈsprɪŋbɔrd/ *noun* **1** a strong board that you jump on and use to help you jump high in DIVING and GYMNASTICS **2 ~ (for/to sth)** something that helps you start an activity, especially by giving you ideas: *The document provided a springboard for a lot of useful discussion.* ▶ **spring·board** *verb* [I, T]: **~ (sth) (into sth)** *The company expects that this strategic move would allow it to springboard into the foreign market.*

spring·bok /'sprɪŋbɑk/ *noun* [C] a small ANTELOPE from southern Africa that can jump high into the air

ˌspring ˈchicken *noun*
   IDM **be no spring chicken** (*humorous*) to be no longer young

ˌspring-ˈcleaning *noun* [U] the process of cleaning a house, room, etc. thoroughly, including the parts you do not usually clean ▶ **spring-ˈclean** *verb* [T, I]: **~ (sth)** *Fran decided to spring-clean the apartment.*

ˌspring ˈfever *noun* [U] a sudden increase in energy and the desire to go out and be active that some people have in the spring

ˌspring-ˈloaded *adj.* containing a metal spring that presses one part against another

ˌspring ˈpeeper *noun* = PEEPER

ˈspring roll *noun* a type of Asian food consisting of a tube of thin DOUGH, filled with vegetables and/or meat and fried until it is crisp ⊃ see also EGG ROLL

ˌspring ˈtide *noun* a TIDE in which there is a very great rise and fall of the ocean, and that happens near the new moon and the full moon each month

spring·time /'sprɪŋtaɪm/ *noun* [U] the season of spring: *a visit to New York* **in springtime/in the springtime**

ˌspring ˈtraining *noun* [U] the period in the spring when baseball players practice to prepare for their regular games: *Spring training starts February 18 this year.*

spring·y /'sprɪŋi/ (**spring·i·er**, **spring·i·est**) *adj.* **1** returning quickly to the original shape after being pushed, pulled, stretched, etc.: *We walked across the springy grass.* **2** full of energy and confidence: *She's 73, but hasn't lost that youthful, springy step.*

sprin·kle /'sprɪŋkl/ *verb, noun*
● *verb* **1** [T] to shake small pieces of something or drops of a liquid on something: **~ A on/onto/over B** *Sprinkle chocolate on top of the cake.* ◆ *She sprinkled sugar over the strawberries.* ◆ **~ B with A** *She sprinkled the strawberries with sugar.* **2** [T, usually passive] **~ sth with sth** to include a few of something in something else **SYN** STREW: *His poems are sprinkled with quotations from ancient Greek.* **3** [I] if it **sprinkles**, it rains lightly **SYN** DRIZZLE: *It's only sprinkling. We can still go out.*
● *noun* **1** [sing.] = SPRINKLING: *Add a sprinkle of cheese and serve.* **2** [C] light rain: *We've only had a few sprinkles (of rain) recently.*

sprin·kler /'sprɪŋklər/ *noun* **1** a device with holes in that is used to spray water in drops on plants, soil, or grass ⊃ picture at TOOL **2** a device inside a building that automatically sprays out water if there is a rise in temperature because of a fire

sprin·kles /'sprɪŋklz/ *noun* [pl.] extremely small pieces of colored sugar, used to decorate cakes, etc.

sprin·kling /'sprɪŋklɪŋ/ (also **sprin·kle**) *noun* a small amount of a substance that is dropped somewhere, or a number of things or people that are spread or included somewhere: *Add a sprinkling of pepper.* ◆ *Most were men, but there was also a sprinkling of young women.*

sprint /sprɪnt/ *verb, noun*
● *verb* [I, T] to run or swim a short distance very fast: **+ adv./prep.** *He sprinted for the line.* ◆ *Three runners sprinted past.* ◆ *She jumped out of the car and sprinted for the front door.* ◆ **~ sth** *I sprinted the last few yards.*
● *noun* **1** a race in which the people taking part run, swim, etc. very fast over a short distance: *a 100-meter sprint* ◆ *the world sprint champion* ⊃ picture at SPORT **2** [usually sing.] a short period of running, swimming, etc. very fast: *a sprint for the line* ◆ *a sprint for the bus* ◆ *She won in a sprint finish.* ▶ **sprint·er** *noun*

sprite /spraɪt/ *noun* (in stories) a small creature with magic powers, especially one that likes playing tricks

spritz /sprɪts/ *verb* **~ sth** to spray very small drops of liquid on something quickly: *Lightly spritz your hair with water.* ▶ **spritz** *noun*

spritz·er /'sprɪtsər/ *noun* a drink made with wine (usually white) mixed with either SODA WATER or SPARKLING mineral water (= with bubbles in it): *a white wine spritzer*

sprock·et /'sprɑkət/ *noun*
1 (also ˈsprocket ˌwheel) a wheel with a row of teeth around the edge that connect with the holes of a bicycle chain or with holes in a film, etc. in order to turn it **2** one of the teeth on such a wheel

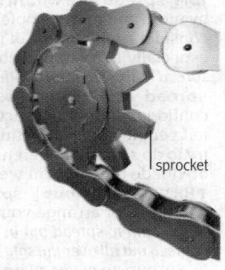
sprocket wheel
sprocket

sprout /spraʊt/ *verb, noun*
● *verb* **1** [I] (of plants or seeds) to produce new leaves or BUDS; to start to grow: *new leaves sprouting from the trees* ◆ *The seeds will sprout in a few days.* **2** [I, T] to appear; to develop something, especially in large numbers: *Hundreds of mushrooms had sprouted up overnight.* ◆ **~ sth** *The town has sprouted shopping malls, discos and nightclubs in recent years.* **3** [T, I] to start to grow something; to start to grow on someone or something: **~ sth** *Tim has sprouted a beard since we last saw him.* ◆ **~ from sth** *Hair sprouted from his chest.*
● *noun* a new part growing on a plant

spruce /sprus/ *noun, verb, adj.*
● *noun* **1** [C, U] an EVERGREEN forest tree with leaves like needles **2** [U] the soft wood of the spruce, used, for example, in making paper
● *verb*
   PHR V ˌspruce ˈup | ˌspruce sb/sth/yourself↔ˈup to make someone or something/yourself clean and neat: *She spruced up for the interview.* ◆ *The city is sprucing up its museums and galleries.*
● *adj.* (of people or places) neat and clean in appearance

sprung /sprʌŋ/ *adj.* fitted with metal springs: *a sprung mattress* ⊃ see also SPRING, SPRANG, SPRUNG

spry /spraɪ/ *adj.* = SPRIGHTLY

spud /spʌd/ *noun* (*informal*) a potato

spume /spyum/ *noun* [U] (*literary*) the mass of white bubbles that forms in waves when the ocean is rough **SYN** FOAM

spun pp of SPIN

spunk /spʌŋk/ *noun* [U] (*informal*) courage; determination

spunk·y /'spʌŋki/ *adj.* (*informal*) brave and determined; full of enthusiasm: *She is bright, tough and spunky.*

spur /spər/ *noun, verb*
● *noun* **1** a sharp pointed object that riders sometimes wear on the heels of their boots and use to encourage their horse to go faster **2** [usually sing.] **~ (to sth)** a fact or an event that makes you want to do something better or more quickly: *His speech was a powerful spur to action.* **3** an area of high ground that sticks out from a mountain or hill **4** a road or a railroad track that leads from the main road or line
   IDM **on the spur of the moment** suddenly, without planning in advance: *I phoned him up on the spur of the moment.* ◆ *a spur-of-the-moment decision* **win/earn your spurs** (*formal*) to achieve fame or success
● *verb* (**-rr-**) **1** to encourage someone to do something or to encourage them to try harder to achieve something: **~ sb/sth (on) to sth/to do sth** *Her difficult childhood spurred her on to succeed.* ◆ **~ sb/sth into sth** *I was spurred into action by the letter.* ◆ **~ sb/sth (on)** *The band has been spurred on by the success of their last single.* **2** **~ sth** to make something happen faster or sooner: *The agreement is essential to spurring economic growth around the world.* **3** **~ sth** to encourage a horse to go faster, especially by pushing the spurs on your boots into its side

spu·ri·ous /ˈspyʊriəs/ adj. **1** false, although seeming to be genuine: *He had managed to create the entirely spurious impression that the company was thriving.* **2** based on false ideas or ways of thinking: *a spurious argument* ▶ **spu·ri·ous·ly** adv.

spurn /spɜrn/ verb ~ **sb/sth** to reject or refuse someone or something, especially in a proud way **SYN** SHUN: *Eve spurned Mark's invitation.* ◆ *a spurned lover*

spurt /spɜrt/ verb, noun
● **verb 1** [I, T] (of liquid or flames) to burst or pour out suddenly; to produce sudden, powerful streams of liquid or flames: ~ **(from sth)** *Blood was spurting from her nose.* ◆ ~ **out (of/from sth)** *Red and yellow flames spurted out of the fire.* ◆ ~ **sth** *Her nose was spurting blood.* ◆ ~ **sth + adv./prep.** *The volcano spurted clouds of steam and ash high into the air.* **2** [I] **+ adv./prep.** to increase your speed for a short time to get somewhere faster: *She spurted past me to get to the line first.*
● **noun 1** an amount of liquid or flames that comes out of somewhere with great force: *a great spurt of blood* **2** a sudden increase in speed, effort, activity, or emotion for a short period of time: *Babies get very hungry during growth spurts.* ◆ *a sudden spurt of anger* ◆ *I work best in short spurts.* **IDM** **in spurts** in short periods of great activity, powerful movement, etc., rather than in a steady, continuous way: *The water came out of the tap in spurts.*

Sput·nik /ˈspʌtnɪk/ noun (from *Russian*) a SATELLITE of the type that was put into space by the Soviet Union

sput·ter /ˈspʌtər/ verb **1** [I] if an engine, a lamp, or a fire **sputters**, it makes a series of short EXPLOSIVE sounds: *sputtering fireworks* **2** [T, I] to speak quickly and with difficulty, making soft SPITTING sounds, because you are angry or shocked: *"W-What?" sputtered Anna.* ◆ ~ **(with sth)** *His rival was sputtering with rage.*

spu·tum /ˈspyuːtəm/ noun [U] (*medical*) liquid from the throat or lungs, especially when it is coughed up because of disease: *blood in the sputum*

spy /spaɪ/ noun, verb
● **noun** (*pl.* **spies**) a person who tries to get secret information about another country, organization, or person, especially someone who is employed by a government or the police: *He was denounced as a foreign spy.* ◆ *a police spy* ◆ *a spy plane/satellite* (= used to watch the activities of the enemy) ◆ *Video spy cameras are being used in public places.*
● **verb** (**spies, spy·ing, spied, spied**) **1** [I] to collect secret information about another country, organization, or person: *He spied for his government for more than ten years.* **2** [T] ~ **sb/sth** (*literary* or *formal*) to suddenly see or notice someone or something: *In the distance we spied the Pacific for the first time.*
PHR V **'spy on sb/sth** to watch someone or something secretly: *Have you been spying on me?* ,**spy sth↔'out** to get information about something

spy·glass /ˈspaɪɡlæs/ noun a small TELESCOPE

spy·mas·ter /ˈspaɪˌmæstər/ noun a person who controls a group of spies

sq. abbr. (in measurements) square: *10 sq. in.*

squab·ble /ˈskwɑbl/ verb [I] ~ **(with sb) (about/over sth)** to argue noisily about something that is not very important **SYN** BICKER: *My sisters were squabbling over what to watch on TV.* ▶ **squab·ble** noun: *family squabbles* ◆ *There were endless squabbles over who should sit where.*

squad /skwɑd/ noun **1** a section of a police force that deals with a particular type of crime: *the drug/fraud, etc. squad* **2** (in sports) a group of players, runners, etc. from which a team is chosen for a particular game or match: *the Olympic/national squad* ◆ *They still have not named their squad for the World Cup qualifier.* **3** a small group of soldiers working or being trained together つ see also FIRING SQUAD **4** a group of people who have a particular task つ see also DEATH SQUAD, HIT SQUAD

squad car noun a police car

squad·ron /ˈskwɑdrən/ noun a group of military aircraft or ships forming a section of a military force: *a bomber/fighter squadron*

squal·id /ˈskwɑləd/ adj. (*disapproving*) **1** (of places and living conditions) very dirty and unpleasant **SYN** FILTHY: *squalid housing* ◆ *squalid, overcrowded refugee camps* **2** (of situations or activities) involving low moral standards or dishonest behavior **SYN** SORDID: *It was a squalid affair involving prostitutes and drugs.*

squall /skwɔl/ noun, verb
● **noun** a sudden violent wind, often during rain or snowstorms
● **verb** [I] (usually used in the progressive tenses) (*disapproving*) to cry very loudly and noisily: *squalling kids*

squal·ly /ˈskwɔli/ adj. (of weather) involving sudden violent winds: *squally showers*

squal·or /ˈskwɑlər/ noun [U] dirty and unpleasant conditions: *the poverty and squalor of the slums* ◆ *He had lost his job and was living in squalor.*

squan·der /ˈskwɑndər/ verb ~ **sth (on sb/sth)** to waste money, time, etc. in a stupid or careless way: *He squandered all his money on gambling.*

square 🔑 /skwɛr/ adj., noun, verb, adv.
● **adj.**
▷ **SHAPE 1** (*geometry*) having four straight equal sides and four angles of 90°: *a square room* つ picture at SHAPE **2** forming an angle of 90° exactly or approximately: *The book had rounded, not square, corners.* ◆ *square shoulders* ◆ *He had a firm, square jaw.*
▷ **MEASUREMENT 3** used after a unit of measurement to say that something measures the same amount on each of four sides: *a carpet three yards square* **4** (*abbr.* **sq.**) used after a number to give a measurement of area: *an area of 36 square yards*
▷ **BROAD/SOLID 5** used to describe something that is broad or that looks solid in shape: *a man of square build* つ see also FOUR-SQUARE
▷ **LEVEL/PARALLEL 6** [not before noun] ~ **(with sth)** level with or parallel to something: *tables arranged square with the wall*
▷ **WITH MONEY 7** (*informal*) if two people are **square**, neither of them owes money to the other: *Here's the $20 I owe you—now we're square.*
▷ **IN SPORTS 8** ~ **(with sb)** if two teams are **square**, they have the same number of points: *The teams were all square at halftime.*
▷ **FAIR/HONEST 9** fair or honest, especially in business matters: *a square deal* ◆ *Are you being square with me?*
▷ **IN AGREEMENT 10** ~ **with sth** in agreement with something: *That isn't quite square with what you said yesterday.*
▷ **BORING 11** (*informal, old-fashioned, disapproving*) (of a person) considered to be boring, for example, because they are old-fashioned or work too hard at school
IDM **a square meal** a good, satisfying meal: *He looks as though he hasn't had a square meal for weeks.* **a square peg (in a round hole)** (*informal*) a person who does not feel happy or comfortable in a particular situation, or who is not suitable for it
● **noun**
▷ **SHAPE 1** [C] a shape with four straight sides of equal length and four angles of 90°; a piece of something that has this shape: *First break the chocolate into squares.* ◆ *The floor was tiled in squares of gray and white marble.* つ see also T-SQUARE
▷ **IN TOWN 2** [C] an open area in a town, usually with four sides, surrounded by buildings: *The hotel is just off the main square.* ◆ *the market/town/village square* **3** Square [sing.] (*abbr.* **Sq.**) (used in addresses): *They live at 5 Plymouth Square.*
▷ **MATHEMATICS 4** [C] the number obtained when you multiply a number by itself: *The square of 7 is 49.*
▷ **BORING PERSON 5** [C] (*informal, old-fashioned, disapproving*) a person who is considered to be boring, for example because they are old-fashioned or because they work too hard at school

IDM back to square one a return to the situation you were in at the beginning of a project, task, etc., because you have made no real progress: *If this suggestion isn't accepted, we'll be back to square one.*

● **verb**

> SHAPE **1** to make something have straight edges and corners: **~ sth** *It was like trying to square a circle. That is, it was impossible.* ◆ **~ sth off** *The boat is rounded at the front but squared off at the back.*

> MATHEMATICS **2** [usually passive] **~ sth** to multiply a number by itself: *Three squared is written 3^2.* ◆ *Four squared equals 16.*

> SHOULDERS **3 ~ yourself/your shoulders** to make your back and shoulders straight to show you are ready or determined to do something: *Bruno squared himself to face the waiting journalists.*

> PAY MONEY **4 ~ sb** (*informal*) to pay money to someone in order to get their help: *They must have squared the mayor before they got their plan underway.*

PHR V ,square sth↔a'way [usually passive] to put something in order; to finish something completely ,square 'off (against sb) to fight or prepare to fight someone ,square 'up (to sb/sth) **1** to face a difficult situation and deal with it in a determined way **2** to face someone as if you are going to fight them ,square 'up (with sb) to pay money that you owe: *Can I leave you to square up with the waiter?* 'square with sth | 'square with sth to make two ideas, facts, or situations agree or combine well with each other; to agree or be consistent with another idea, fact, or situation: *The interests of farmers need to be squared with those of consumers.* ◆ *How can you square this with your conscience?* ◆ *Your theory does not square with the facts.* 'square sth with sb to ask permission or check with someone that they approve of what you want to do: *I think I'll be able to come, but I'll square it with my parents first.*

● **adv.** (only used *after* the verb) directly; not at an angle **SYN** SQUARELY: *I looked her square in the face.* **IDM** see FAIR *adv.*

,square 'bracket noun [usually pl.] = BRACKET *n.* (2)

squared /skwɛrd/ adj. marked with squares; divided into squares: *squared paper*

'square dance noun **1** a traditional dance in which groups of four couples dance together, starting the dance by facing each other in a square **2** a social event at which people dance square dances ⟳ compare LINE DANCE

'square knot noun a type of double knot that will not come undone easily

square·ly /'skwɛrli/ adv. (usually used *after* the verb) **1** directly; not at an angle or to one side: *She looked at me squarely in the eye.* ◆ *He stood squarely in front of them, blocking the entrance.* ◆ (*figurative*) *We must meet the challenge squarely* (= not try to avoid it). **2** directly or exactly; without confusion: *The responsibility for the crisis rests squarely on the government.*

,square 'root noun (*mathematics*) a number that when multiplied by itself produces a particular number: *The square root of 64 ($\sqrt{64}$) is 8 (8×8=64).* ⟳ compare CUBE ROOT

squar·ish /'skwɛrɪʃ/ adj. almost square in shape

squash /skwaʃ; skwɔʃ/ verb, noun
● **verb 1** [T] to press something so that it becomes soft, damaged, or flat, or changes shape: **~ sth/sb** *The tomatoes at the bottom of the bag had been squashed.* ◆ **~ sth against sth** *He squashed his nose against the window.* ◆ **~ sth + adj.** *Squash your cans flat before recycling.* ⟳ picture at SQUEEZE **2** [I, T] to push someone or something or yourself into a space that is too small: **+ adv./prep.** *We all squashed into the back of the car.* ◆ **~ sb/sth + adv./prep.** *How many people are they going to try and squash into this bus?* ◆ *She was squashed between the door and the table.* **3** [T] **~ sth** to stop something from continuing; to destroy something because it is a problem for you **SYN** QUASH: *to squash a plan/an idea/a revolt* ◆ *If parents don't answer children's questions, their natural curiosity will be squashed.* ◆ *The statement was an attempt to*

squash the rumors.
PHR V ,squash 'up (against sb/sth) | ,squash sb/sth↔'up (against sb/sth) to move so close to someone or something else that it is uncomfortable: *I was squashed up against the wall.*

● **noun 1** [U] a game for two players, played in a COURT surrounded by four walls, using RACKETS and a small rubber ball: *a squash court* ◆ *to play squash* ⟳ picture at SPORT **2** (*pl.* squash or squash·es) [C, U] a type of fruit that grows on the ground and is eaten as a vegetable. **Winter squash** have hard skin and orange flesh. **Summer squash** have soft yellow or green skin and white flesh. ⟳ see also BUTTERNUT SQUASH **3** [sing.] (*informal*) if something is a squash, there is hardly enough room for everything or everyone to fit into a small space: *It's a real squash with six of us in the car.*

squash·y /'skwaʃi; 'skwɔ-/ adj. soft and easy to crush or squeeze

squat /skwat/ verb, noun, adj.
● **verb** (-tt-) **1** [I] **~ (down)** to sit on your heels with your knees bent up close to your body **2** [I, T] **~ (sth)** to live in a building or on land that is not yours, without the owner's permission: *They ended up squatting in the empty houses on the street.*
● **noun 1** a squat position of the body **2** = SQUAT THRUST
● **adj.** short and wide or fat, in a way that is not attractive: *a squat tower* ◆ *a squat muscular man with a shaven head*

squat·ter /'skwatər/ noun a person who is living in a building or on land without permission and without paying rent

'squat thrust (also squat) noun an exercise in which you start with your hands on the floor and your knees bent, and then quickly move both legs backward and forward together

squaw /skwɔ/ noun (*old use*) a word for a Native American woman that is now often considered offensive

squawk /skwɔk/ verb **1** [I] (of birds) to make a loud sharp sound: *The parrot squawked and flew away.* **2** [T, I] (+ speech) to speak or make a noise in a loud, sharp voice because you are angry, surprised, etc.: *"You did what?!" she squawked.* ▶ squawk noun: *The bird gave a startled squawk.* ◆ *a squawk of protest*

squeak /skwik/ verb, noun
● **verb 1** [I] to make a short high sound that is not very loud: *My new shoes squeak.* ◆ *The mouse ran away, squeaking with fear.* ◆ *One wheel makes a horrible squeaking noise.* **2** [T, I] (+ speech) to speak in a very high voice, especially when you are nervous or excited: *"Let go of me!" he squeaked nervously.* **3** [I] **+ adv./prep.** to only just manage to win something, pass a test, etc.: *We just squeaked into the playoffs.*
● **noun** a short high cry or sound, that is not usually very loud

squeak·er /'skwikər/ noun (*informal*) a competition or election won by only a small amount or likely to be won by only a small amount

squeak·y /'skwiki/ adj. making a short high sound; squeaking: *squeaky floorboards* ◆ *a high squeaky voice*

,squeaky 'clean adj. (*informal*) **1** completely clean, and therefore attractive: *squeaky clean hair* **2** morally correct in every way; that cannot be criticized

squeal /skwil/ verb, noun
● **verb 1** [I] to make a long high sound: *The pigs were squealing.* ◆ *The car squealed to a halt.* ◆ *Children were running around squealing with excitement.* **2** [T, I] (+ speech) to speak in a very high voice, especially when you are excited or nervous: *"Don't!" she squealed.* **3** [I] **~ (on sb)** (*informal, disapproving*) to give information, especially to the police, about something illegal that someone has done
● **noun** a long high cry or sound: *a squeal of pain* ◆ *a squeal of delight* ◆ *He stopped with a squeal of brakes.*

squeam·ish /'skwimɪʃ/ adj. **1** easily upset, or made to feel sick by unpleasant sights or situations, especially when the sight of blood is involved **2** not wanting to do something that might be considered dishonest or immoral **3** **the squeamish** noun [pl.] people who are squeamish: *This movie is not for the squeamish.* ▸ **squeam·ish·ness** noun [U]

squee·gee /'skwidʒi/ noun **1** a tool with a rubber edge and a handle, used for removing water from smooth surfaces such as windows ➜ picture at CLEANING **2** (also 'squeegee mop) a tool for washing floors, that has a long handle with two thick pieces of soft material at the end, which may be squeezed together using a piece of machinery attached to the handle

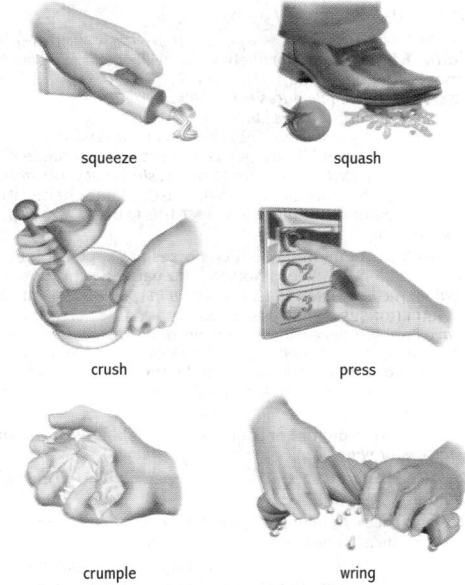

squeeze   squash

crush   press

crumple   wring

squeeze 🔑 /skwiz/ verb, noun

● **verb**

▸ **PRESS WITH FINGERS 1** [T, I] ~ (sth) to press something firmly, especially with your fingers: *to squeeze a tube of toothpaste* ◆ *to squeeze the trigger of a gun* (= to fire it) ◆ *He squeezed her hand and smiled at her.* ◆ *Just take hold of the tube and squeeze.*

▸ **GET LIQUID OUT 2** [T] to get liquid out of something by pressing or twisting it hard: ~ sth out of/from sth *to squeeze the juice from a lemon* ◆ (figurative) *She felt as if every drop of emotion had been squeezed from her.* ◆ ~ sth (out) *He took off his wet clothes and squeezed the water out.* ◆ *freshly squeezed orange juice* ◆ ~ sth + adj. *Soak the cloth in warm water and then squeeze it dry.*

▸ **INTO/THROUGH SMALL SPACE 3** [T, I] to force someone or something/yourself into or through a small space: ~ sb/sth into, through, etc. sth *We managed to squeeze six people into the car.* ◆ (figurative) *We managed to squeeze a lot into a week* (= we did a lot of different things). ◆ ~ into, through, etc. sth *to squeeze into a tight dress/a parking space* ◆ *to squeeze through a gap in the hedge* ◆ ~ through, in, past, etc. *If you move forward a little, I can squeeze past.*

▸ **THREATEN 4** [T] ~ sb (for sth) (informal) to get something by putting pressure on someone, threatening them, etc.: *He's squeezing me for $1,000.*

▸ **LIMIT MONEY 5** [T] ~ sb/sth to strictly limit or reduce the amount of money that someone or something has or can use: *High interest rates have squeezed the industry hard.*

IDM squeeze sb dry to get as much money, information, etc. out of someone as you can

PHR V ,squeeze sb/sth↔'in to give time to someone or

something, although you are very busy: *If you come this afternoon the doctor will try to squeeze you in.* ,squeeze sb/sth↔'out (of sth) to prevent someone or something from continuing to do something or be in business: *Supermarkets are squeezing out small stores.* ,squeeze sth 'out of | 'squeeze sth from sb to get something by putting pressure on someone, threatening them, etc.: *to squeeze a confession from a suspect* ,squeeze 'up (against sb/sth) | ,squeeze sb↔'up (against sb/sth) to move close to someone or something so that you are pressed against them/it: *There'll be enough room if we all squeeze up a little.* ◆ *I sat squeezed up against the wall.*

● **noun**

▸ **PRESSING WITH FINGERS 1** [C, usually sing.] an act of pressing something, usually with your hands: *He gave my hand a little squeeze.* ◆ *Give the tube another squeeze.*

▸ **OF LIQUID 2** [C] a small amount of liquid that is produced by pressing something: *a squeeze of lemon juice*

▸ **IN SMALL SPACE 3** [sing.] a situation where it is almost impossible for a number of people or things to fit into a small or restricted space: *It was a tight squeeze but we finally got everything into the case.* ◆ *Seven people in the car was a bit of a squeeze.*

▸ **REDUCTION IN MONEY 4** [C, usually sing.] a reduction in the amount of money, jobs, etc. available; a difficult situation caused by this: *a squeeze on profits* ◆ *We're really feeling the squeeze since I lost my job.* ◆ *a credit squeeze*

▸ **BOYFRIEND/GIRLFRIEND 5** [sing.] (informal) a boyfriend or girlfriend: *Who's his main squeeze?*

IDM put the squeeze on sb (to do sth) (informal) to put pressure on someone to act in a particular way; to make a situation difficult for someone

squeeze·box /'skwizbɑks/ noun (informal) an ACCORDION or a CONCERTINA

squelch /skwɛltʃ/ verb **1** [I] (+ adv./prep.) to make a wet sucking sound: *The mud squelched as I walked through it.* ◆ *Her wet shoes squelched at every step.* ◆ *We squelched across the muddy field.* **2** [T] ~ sth to stop something from growing, increasing, or developing **SYN** SQUASH: *to squelch a rumor/strike/fire* ▸ **squelch** noun [usually sing.]: *He pulled his foot out of the mud with a squelch.* **squelch·y** adj.: *squelchy ground*

squib /skwɪb/ noun a small FIREWORK

squid /skwɪd/ noun [C, U] (pl. squid or squids) a sea creature that has a long soft body, eight arms, and two TENTACLES (= long thin parts like arms) around its mouth, and that is sometimes used for food

squig·gle /'skwɪɡl/ noun a line, for example in someone's HANDWRITING, that is drawn or written in a careless way with twists and curls in it: *Are these dots and squiggles supposed to be your signature?* ▸ **squig·gly** /'skwɪɡli/ adj.

squil·lion /'skwɪlyən/ noun (informal, often humorous) a very large number: *a squillion-dollar budget*

squint /skwɪnt/ verb [I, T] to look at something with your eyes partly shut in order to keep out bright light or to see better: *to squint into the sun* ◆ *She was squinting through the keyhole.* ◆ *He squinted at the letter in his hand.* ◆ ~ sth *When he squinted his eyes, he could just make out a house in the distance.* ▸ **squint** noun [sing.]

squire /'skwaɪər/ noun **1** (in the past) a young man who was an assistant to a KNIGHT before becoming a KNIGHT himself **2** also **Squire** (in the past in England) a man of high social status who owned most of the land in a particular country area

squirm /skwɜrm/ verb **1** [I] to move around a lot making small twisting movements, because you are nervous, uncomfortable, etc. **SYN** WRIGGLE: (+ adv./prep.) *The children were squirming restlessly in their seats.* ◆ ~ + adj. *Someone grabbed him but he managed to squirm free.* **2** [I] to feel great embarrassment or shame: *It made him squirm to think how badly he'd messed up the interview.*

squir·rel /ˈskwərəl/ *noun, verb*
- *noun* a small animal with a long thick tail and red, gray, or black fur. Squirrels eat nuts and live in trees. ⊃ picture at RODENT ⊃ see also GROUND SQUIRREL
- *verb*
  PHRV ˌsquirrel sth↔aˈway to hide or store something so that it can be used later: *She had money squirreled away in various bank accounts.*

squir·rel·ly /ˈskwərəli/ *adj.* (*informal*) **1** unable to keep still or be quiet: *squirrelly kids* **2** crazy

squirt /skwərt/ *verb, noun*
- *verb* **1** [T, I] to force liquid, gas, etc. in a thin fast stream through a narrow opening; to be forced out of a narrow opening in this way **SYN** SPURT: *~ sth (+ adv./prep.) The snake can squirt poison from a distance of a yard.* ◆ *I desperately squirted water on the flames.* ◆ *(+ adv./prep.) When I cut the lemon, juice squirted in my eye.* **2** [T] to hit someone or something with a stream of water, gas, etc. **SYN** SPRAY: *~ sb/sth (with sth) The children were squirting each other with water from the hose.* ◆ *~ sth (at sb) He squirted a water pistol at me* (= made the water come out of it).
- *noun* **1** a thin fast stream of liquid that comes out of a small opening **SYN** SPRAY: *a squirt of perfume* **2** (*informal, disapproving*) a word used to refer to a short, young, or unimportant person that you do not like or that you find annoying

ˈsquirt gun *noun* = WATER PISTOL

squish /skwɪʃ/ *verb* (*informal*) **1** [I, T] *~ (sth)* if something soft **squishes** or **is squished**, it is crushed out of shape when it is pressed **2** [I] to make a soft, wet, sucking sound

squish·y /ˈskwɪʃi/ *adj.* (*informal*) soft and wet

Sr. *abbr.* SENIOR ⊃ compare JR.

SS *abbr.* **1** /ˌes ˈes/ STEAMSHIP: *the SS Titanic* **2** SOCIAL SECURITY **3** SAINTS: *SS Philip and James*

SSN /ˌes ɛs ˈɛn/ *abbr.* SOCIAL SECURITY NUMBER

St. *abbr.* **1** (used in written addresses) Street: *220 Jefferson St.* **2** State **3** SAINT

stab /stæb/ *verb, noun*
- *verb* (-bb-) **1** [T] *~ sb* to push a sharp pointed object, especially a knife, into someone, killing or injuring them: *He was stabbed to death in a racist attack.* ◆ *She stabbed him in the arm with a screwdriver.* **2** [T, I] to make a short, aggressive, or violent movement with a finger or pointed object **SYN** JAB, PROD: *~ sth (at/into/through sth) He stabbed his finger angrily at my chest.* ◆ *~ sb/sth (with sth) She stabbed the air with her fork.* ◆ *~ at/into/through sth* (*figurative*) *The pain stabbed at his chest.*
  IDM stab sb in the back to do or say something that harms someone who trusts you **SYN** BETRAY
- *noun* **1** an act of stabbing or trying to stab someone or something; a wound caused by stabbing: *He received several stabs in the chest.* ◆ *She died of a single stab wound to the heart.* **2** a sudden sharp pain or unpleasant feeling: *She felt a sudden stab of pain in the chest.* ◆ *a stab of guilt/fear/pity/jealousy, etc.* **3** [usually sing.] (*informal*) an attempt to do something: *~ (at sth) He found the test difficult but nevertheless made a good stab at it.* ◆ *~ (at doing sth) Countless people have had a stab at solving the riddle.*
  IDM a stab in the back (*informal*) an act that harms someone, done by a person they thought was a friend ⊃ more at DARK *n.*

stab·bing /ˈstæbɪŋ/ *noun, adj.*
- *noun* an occasion when a person is stabbed with a knife or other pointed object: *a fatal stabbing*
- *adj.* [usually before noun] (of pain) very sharp, sudden, and strong

sta·bil·i·ty **AWL** /stəˈbɪləti/ *noun* [U] the quality or state of being steady and not changing or being disturbed in any way (= the quality of being stable): *political/economic/social stability* ◆ *the stability of the dollar on the world's money markets* ◆ *Being back with their family should provide emotional stability for the children.* **ANT** INSTABILITY

staˈbility ˌball *noun* = EXERCISE BALL

sta·bi·lize **AWL** /ˈsteɪbəˌlaɪz/ *verb* [I, T] to become or to make something become firm, steady, and unlikely to change; to make something stable: *The patient's condition stabilized.* ◆ *~ sth government measures to stabilize prices* ◆ *Doctors stabilized the patient's condition.* ⊃ compare DESTABILIZE ▶ **sta·bi·li·za·tion** **AWL** /ˌsteɪbələˈzeɪʃn/ *noun* [U]: *economic stabilization*

sta·bi·liz·er /ˈsteɪbəˌlaɪzər/ *noun* **1** a device that keeps something steady, especially one that stops an aircraft or a ship from rolling to one side **2** (*technical*) a chemical that is sometimes added to food or paint to stop the various substances in it from separating

sta·ble 🔑 **AWL** /ˈsteɪbl/
adj., noun, verb
- *adj.* **1** firmly fixed; not likely to move, change, or fail **SYN** STEADY: *stable prices* ◆ *a stable relationship* ◆ *This ladder doesn't seem very stable.* ◆ *The patient's condition is stable* (= it is not getting worse). **2** (of a person) calm and reasonable; not easily upset **SYN** BALANCED: *Mentally, she is not very stable.* **3** (*technical*) (of a substance) staying in the same chemical or atomic state: *chemically stable* **ANT** UNSTABLE ▶ **sta·bly** /ˈsteɪbli/ *adv.*

WORD FAMILY
stable *adj.* (≠ unstable)
stability *noun* (≠ instability)
stabilize *verb*

- *noun* **1** [C] a building in which horses are kept **2** [C] an organization that keeps horses for a particular purpose: *a riding/racing stable* ◆ *His stable is near the park.* **3** [C] a group of RACEHORSES owned or trained by the same person: *There have been just three winners from his stable this season.* **4** [sing.] a group of people who work or trained in the same place; a group of products made by the same company: *actors from the same stable* ◆ *the latest printer from the Epson stable*
- *verb ~ sth* to put or keep a horse in a stable: *Where do you stable your pony?*

ˈstable ˌboy, ˈstable ˌgirl *noun* a person who works in a stable

sta·ble·man /ˈsteɪblmæn; -ˌmæn/ *noun* (*pl.* sta·ble·men /-mən; -ˌmɛn/) a person who works in a stable

sta·ble·mate /ˈsteɪblˌmeɪt/ *noun* **1** a horse, especially a racing horse, from the same stable as another horse **2** a person or product from the same organization as another person or product: *Model 90, and its stablemate Model 99.*

sta·bling /ˈsteɪblɪŋ/ *noun* [U] buildings or space where horses can be kept

stac·ca·to /stəˈkɑtoʊ/ *adj.* **1** (*music*) with each note played separately in order to produce short sharp sounds: *staccato sounds* **ANT** LEGATO **2** with short sharp sounds: *a peculiar staccato voice* ◆ *staccato bursts of gunfire* ▶ **stac·ca·to** *adv.*

stack /stæk/ *noun, verb*
- *noun* **1** [C] a pile of something, usually neatly arranged: *a stack of books* ⊃ see also HAYSTACK **2** [C] *~ (of sth)* (*informal*) a large number or amount of something; a lot of something: *stacks of money* ◆ *There's a stack of unopened mail waiting for you at the house.* ◆ *I've got stacks of work to do.* **3** [C] a tall CHIMNEY, especially on a factory ⊃ see also CHIMNEY STACK, SMOKESTACK **4 the stacks** [pl.] the part of a library, sometimes not open to the public, where books that are not often needed are stored **5** [C] (*computing*) a way of storing information in a computer in which the most recently stored item is the first to be RETRIEVED (= found or gotten back) **6** [C] (*geology*) a tall thin part of a CLIFF that has been separated from the land and stands on its own in the sea
  IDM see BLOW *v.*
- *verb* **1** [T, I] *~ (sth) (up)* to arrange objects neatly in a pile; to be arranged in this way: *to stack boxes* ◆ *logs stacked up against a wall* ◆ *Do these chairs stack?* ◆ *stacking chairs* **2** [T] *~ sth (with sth)* to fill something with piles of things: *They were busy stacking the shelves with goods.* **3** [I, T] *~ (sth) (up)* if aircraft **stack (up)** or **are stacked (up)** over an airport, there are several flying around waiting for their turn to land

| h **hat** | m **man** | n **no** | ŋ **sing** | l **leg** | r **red** | y **yes** | w **wet**

IDM ,stack it (*informal*) to fall over or off something, especially in a way that makes you look silly and makes other people laugh: *I tried a spin on the ice and stacked it.* **PHRV** ,stack 'up **1** to keep increasing in quantity until there is a large pile, a long line, etc.: *Cars quickly stacked up behind the bus.* **2** (used especially in questions or in negatives) to compare with someone or something else; to be as good as someone or something else **SYN** MEASURE UP: *Let's try him in the job and see how he stacks up.* ◆ ~ **against sb/sth** *A mobile home simply doesn't stack up against a traditional house.* **3** (used especially in negatives) to seem reasonable; to make sense: *That can't be right. It just doesn't stack up.*

stacked /stækt/ *adj.* [not usually before noun] if a surface is **stacked** with objects, there are large numbers or piles of them on it: *a table stacked with glasses* **IDM** the cards/odds are stacked against you you are unlikely to succeed because the conditions are not good for you the cards/odds are stacked in your favor you are likely to succeed because the conditions are good and you have an advantage

sta·di·um /'steɪdiəm/ *noun* (*pl.* sta·di·ums or sta·di·a /-diə/) a large sports ground surrounded by rows of seats and usually other buildings: *a football/sports stadium* ⊃ picture at FOOTBALL

staff ⚲ /stæf/ *noun, verb*
● *noun* **1** [C, usually sing., U, pl.] all the workers employed in an organization considered as a group: *medical staff* ◆ *teaching staff* ◆ *staff members* ◆ *staff development/training* ◆ *a staff meeting* ◆ *a lawyer on the staff of the Worldwide Fund for Nature* ◆ *We have around 100 part-time staff.* ⊃ collocations at JOB **2** [sing.] the people who work at a school, college, or university, but who do not teach students: *students, faculty, and staff* **3** [C] a group of senior army officers who help a commanding officer ⊃ see also CHIEF OF STAFF, GENERAL STAFF **4** [C] (*old-fashioned* or *formal*) a long stick used as a support when walking or climbing, as a weapon, or as a symbol of authority **5** (also stave) [C] (*music*) a set of five lines on which music is written ⊃ picture at MUSIC **IDM** the staff of life (*literary*) a basic food, especially bread
● *verb* [T, usually passive] ~ **sth** to work in an institution, a company, etc.; to provide people to work there: *The advice center is staffed entirely by volunteers.* ◆ *The charity provided money to staff and equip two hospitals.* ◆ *a fully staffed department* ⊃ see also OVERSTAFFED, SHORT-STAFFED, UNDERSTAFFED ▶ staff·ing *noun* [U]: *staffing levels*

GRAMMAR

staff
- Staff (sense 1) can be singular: *a staff of ten* (= a group of ten people) or plural: *I have ten staff working for me.* If it is the subject of a verb, this verb can be singular or plural: *The staff in this store is/are very helpful.*
- The plural form **staffs** is less frequent but is sometimes used to refer to more than one group of people: *the senator and her staff (singular)* ◆ *senators and their staffs (plural).*

staff·er /'stæfər/ *noun* a member of the staff of a big organization

staff ,officer *noun* a military officer who helps an officer of very high rank or who works at a military HEADQUARTERS or a government department

staff ,sergeant *noun* a member of the army or AIR FORCE just above the rank of a SERGEANT: *Staff Sergeant Bob Woods*

stag /stæg/ *noun* a male DEER ⊃ compare BUCK, DOE, HART **IDM** go stag (*old-fashioned, informal*) (of a man) to go to a party without a partner

stag ,beetle *noun* a large insect with a mouth that has parts like the horns of an animal

stage ⚲ /steɪdʒ/ *noun, verb*
● *noun*
> PERIOD/STATE **1** [C] a period or state that something or someone passes through while developing or making progress: *This technology is still in its early stages.* ◆ *The children are at different stages of development.* ◆ *The product is at the design stage.* ◆ *People tend to work hard at this stage of life.* ◆ *At one stage it looked as though they would win.* ◆ *Don't worry about the baby not wanting to leave you—it's a stage they go through.*
> PART OF PROCESS **2** [C] a separate part that a process, etc. is divided into **SYN** PHASE: *We did the first stage of the trip by train.* ◆ *The police are building up a picture of the incident stage by stage.* ◆ *The pay increase will be introduced in stages* (= not all at once). ◆ *We can take the argument one stage further.* ⊃ language bank at PROCESS¹
> THEATER **3** [C] a raised area, usually in a theater, etc. where actors, dancers, etc. perform: *The audience threw flowers onto the stage.* ◆ *There were more than 50 people on stage in one scene.* ◆ *They marched off stage to the sound of trumpets.* ⊃ see also BACKSTAGE, OFFSTAGE, ONSTAGE **4** often the stage [sing.] the theater and the world of acting as a form of entertainment: *His parents didn't want him to go on the stage* (= to be an actor). ◆ *She was a popular star of stage and screen* (= theater and movies).
> IN POLITICS **5** [sing.] an area of activity where important things happen, especially in politics: *She was forced to the center of the political stage.* ◆ *China is playing a leading role on the international stage.* ⊃ see also CENTER STAGE
> CARRIAGE **6** [C] (*old-fashioned, informal*) = STAGECOACH **IDM** set the stage for sth to make it possible for something to happen; to make something likely to happen
● *verb* **1** ~ **sth** to organize and present a play or an event for people to see: *to stage a ceremony/an event/an exhibition* ◆ *The local theater group is staging a production of "Hamlet."* ◆ *Rio de Janeiro will stage the 2016 Olympics.* **2** ~ **sth** to organize and take part in action that needs careful planning, especially as a public protest: *to stage a strike/demonstration/march/protest* **3** ~ **sth** to make something happen: *The dollar staged a recovery earlier today.* ◆ *After five years in retirement, he staged a comeback to international tennis.*

stage·coach /'steɪdʒkoʊtʃ/ *noun* a large CARRIAGE pulled by horses, that was used in the past to carry passengers, and often mail, along a regular route

stage·craft /'steɪdʒkræft/ *noun* [U] skill in presenting plays in a theater

stage di,rection *noun* a note in the text of a play telling actors when to come on to or leave the stage, what actions to perform, etc.

stage 'door *noun* the entrance at the back of a theater used by actors, staff, etc.

stage fright *noun* [U] nervous feelings felt by performers before they appear in front of an audience

stage·hand /'steɪdʒhænd/ *noun* a person whose job is to help move SCENERY, etc. in a theater, to prepare the stage for the next play or the next part of a play

stage 'left *adv.* on the left side of a stage in a theater, as seen by an actor facing the audience

stage-'manage *verb* **1** ~ **sth** to act as stage manager for a performance in a theater **2** ~ **sth** to arrange and carefully plan an event that the public will see, especially in order to give a particular impression

stage ,manager *noun* the person who is responsible for the stage, lights, SCENERY, etc. during the performance of a play in a theater

stage name *noun* a name that an actor uses instead of his or her real name

stage 'right *adv.* on the right side of a stage in a theater, as seen by an actor facing the audience

stage-struck *adj.* enjoying the theater a lot and wishing very much to become an actor

stage whisper noun **1** words that are spoken quietly by an actor to the audience and that the other people on stage are not supposed to hear **2** words that are spoken quietly by someone but that they in fact want everyone to hear: *"I knew this would happen," she said in a stage whisper.*

stag·ey = STAGY

stag·fla·tion /stægˈfleɪʃn/ noun [U] an economic situation where there is high INFLATION (= prices rising continuously) but no increase in the jobs that are available or in business activity

stag·ger /ˈstægər/ verb **1** [I, T] to walk with weak unsteady steps, as if you are about to fall SYN TOTTER: (+ adv./prep.) *The injured woman staggered to her feet.* ◆ *He staggered home, drunk.* ◆ *We seem to stagger from one crisis to the next.* ◆ (*figurative*) *The company is staggering under the weight of a $20 million debt.* ◆ *~ sth I managed to stagger the last few steps.* **2** [T] to shock or surprise someone very much SYN AMAZE: *~ sb Her remarks staggered me.* ◆ *it staggers sb that… It staggers me that Congress seems unwilling to do anything about it.* **3** [T] *~ sth* to arrange for events that would normally happen at the same time to start or happen at different times: *There were so many runners that they had to stagger the start.* ▶ **stag·ger** noun: *to walk with a stagger*

stag·gered /ˈstægərd/ adj. **1** [not before noun] *~ (at/by sth) ~ (to hear, learn, see, etc.)* very surprised and shocked at something you are told or at something that happens SYN AMAZED: *I was staggered at the amount of money the ring cost.* **2** arranged in such a way that not everything happens at the same time: *staggered working hours* (= people start and finish at different times)

stag·ger·ing /ˈstægərɪŋ/ adj. so great, shocking, or surprising that it is difficult to believe SYN ASTOUNDING ▶ **stag·ger·ing·ly** adv.: *staggeringly beautiful/expensive*

stag·ing /ˈsteɪdʒɪŋ/ noun **1** [C, U] the way a play is produced and presented on stage: *a modern staging of "King Lear"* **2** [U] a temporary platform used for standing or working on

staging area noun **1** an area where soldiers and equipment are gathered before a military operation: *a staging area for training exercises* **2** a place where people gather to organize an activity or a trip: *The church was used as a staging area for the flood relief effort.*

staging post noun a place where people, planes, ships, etc. regularly stop during a long journey

stag·nant /ˈstægnənt/ adj. **1** stagnant water or air is not moving and therefore smells unpleasant **2** not developing, growing, or changing SYN STATIC: *a stagnant economy*

stag·nate /ˈstægneɪt/ verb **1** [I] to stop developing or making progress: *Profits have stagnated.* ◆ *I feel like I'm stagnating in this job.* **2** [I] to be or become stagnant: *The water in the pond was stagnating.* ▶ **stag·na·tion** /stægˈneɪʃn/ noun [U]: *a period of economic stagnation*

stag party noun [usually sing.] = BACHELOR PARTY

stag·y (also **stag·ey**) /ˈsteɪdʒi/ adj. not natural, as if it is being acted by someone in a play

staid /steɪd/ adj. (staid·er, staid·est) not amusing or interesting; boring and old-fashioned

stain /steɪn/ verb, noun
• verb **1** [T, I] to leave a mark that is difficult to remove on something; to be marked in this way: *~ (sth) (with sth) I hope it doesn't stain the carpet.* ◆ *This carpet stains easily.* ◆ *~ sth + adj. The juice from the berries stained their fingers red.* **2** [T] to change the color of something using a colored liquid: *~ sth to stain wood* ◆ *Stain the specimen before looking at it under the microscope.* ◆ *~ sth + adj. They stained the floors dark brown.* **3** [T] *~ sth* (*formal*) to damage the opinion that people have of something: *The events had stained the city's reputation unfairly.*
• noun **1** [C] a dirty mark on something, that is difficult to remove: *a blood/a coffee/an ink, etc. stain* ◆ *stubborn stains* (= that are very difficult to remove) ◆ *How can I get this stain out?* ◆ *The carpet has been treated so that it is stain-resistant* (= it does not stain easily). ⊃ **thesaurus box at** MARK **2** [U, C] a

liquid used for changing the color of wood or cloth **3** [sing.] *a ~ on sth* (*formal*) something that damages a person's reputation, so that people think badly of them

stain·ed /steɪnd/ adj. (often in compounds) covered with stains or marked with a stain: *My dress was stained.* ◆ *paint-stained jeans* ⊃ **thesaurus box at** DIRTY

stained glass noun [U] pieces of colored glass that are put together to make windows, especially in churches

stain·less steel /ˌsteɪnləs ˈstil/ noun [U] a type of steel that does not RUST (= change color)

stair /stɛr/ noun
1 stairs [pl.] a set of steps built between two floors of a building: *We had to carry the piano up three flights of stairs.* ◆ *The children ran up/down the stairs.* ◆ *at the bottom/top of the stairs* ◆ *He remembered passing her on the stairs.* ⊃ **see also** DOWNSTAIRS, UPSTAIRS **2** [C] one of the steps in a set of stairs: *How many stairs are there up to the second floor?* **3** [sing.] (*literary*) = STAIRCASE: *The house had a panelled hall and a fine oak stair.* ▶ **stair** adj. [only before noun]: *the stair carpeting*

stair·case /ˈstɛrkeɪs/ noun a set of stairs including the posts and rails (= BANISTERS) that are fixed at the side: *a marble/stone/wooden staircase* ⊃ **see also** SPIRAL STAIRCASE

stair·lift /ˈstɛrlɪft/ noun a piece of equipment in the form of a seat that someone can sit on to be moved up and down stairs, used by people who find it difficult to walk up and down stairs without help

stair·way /ˈstɛrweɪ/ noun a set of stairs inside or outside a building

stair·well /ˈstɛrwɛl/ noun [usually sing.] the space in a building in which the stairs are built

stake /steɪk/ noun, verb
• noun **1** [C] a wooden or metal post that is pointed at one end and pushed into the ground in order to support something, mark a particular place, etc. **2** the stake [sing.] a wooden post that someone could be tied to in former times before being burned to death (= killed by fire) as a punishment: *Joan of Arc was burned at the stake.* **3** [C] money that someone invests in a company: *a 20% stake in the business* **4** [sing.] *~ in sth* a part or share in a business, plan, etc. that is important to you and that you want to be successful: *She has a personal stake in the success of the play.* ◆ *Many young people no longer feel they have a stake in society.* **5** [C] something that you risk losing, especially money, when you try to predict the result of a race, game, etc., or when you are involved in an activity that can succeed or fail: *How much was the stake* (= how much did you bet)? ◆ *They were playing cards for high stakes* (= a lot of money). **6** stakes [pl.] the money that is paid to the winners in horse racing **7** stakes [U] used in the names of some horse races **IDM** **at stake** that can be won or lost, depending on the success of a particular action: *We cannot afford to take risks when peoples' lives are at stake.* ◆ *The prize at stake is a place in the finals.* ⊃ **more at** PULL
• verb **1** *~ sth (on sth)* to risk money or something important on the result of something SYN BET: *He staked $50 on the favorite* (= for example, in horse racing). ◆ *She staked her political career on tax reform, and lost.* ◆ *That's him over there— I'd stake my life on it* (= I am completely confident). **2** *~ sth (up)* to support something with a stake: *to stake newly planted trees* **IDM** **stake (out) a/your claim (to/for/on sth)** to say or show publicly that you think something should be yours: *Adams staked his claim to a place on the Olympic team with his easy win yesterday.* **PHR V** **stake sth↔'out 1** to clearly mark the limits of something that you claim is yours **2** to state your opinion, position, etc. on something very clearly: *The President staked out his position on the issue.* **3** to watch a place secretly, especially for signs of illegal activity: *Detectives had been staking out the house for several weeks.* ⊃ **related noun** STAKEOUT

stake·hold·er /'steɪkˌhoʊldər/ noun **1** a person or company that is involved in a particular organization, project, system, etc., especially because they have invested money in it: *The candidate has said she wants to create a stakeholder economy in which all members of society feel that they have an interest in its success.* **2** a person who holds all the bets placed on a game or race and who pays the money to the winner

stake·out /'steɪkaʊt/ noun a situation in which police watch a building secretly to find evidence of illegal activities

sta·lac·tite /stə'læktaɪt/ noun a long pointed piece of rock hanging down from the roof of a CAVE (= a hollow place underground), formed over a long period of time as water containing LIME runs off the roof

sta·lag·mite /stə'lægmaɪt/ noun a piece of rock pointing upward from the floor of a CAVE (= a hollow place underground), that is formed over a long period of time from drops of water containing LIME that fall from the roof

stale /steɪl/ adj. **1** (of food, especially bread and cake) no longer fresh and therefore unpleasant to eat **2** (of air, smoke, etc.) no longer fresh; smelling unpleasant: *stale cigarette smoke* ◆ *stale sweat* **3** something that is **stale** has been said or done too many times before and is no longer interesting or exciting: *stale jokes* ◆ *Their marriage went stale long ago.* **4** a person who is **stale** has done the same thing for too long and so is unable to do it well or produce any new ideas: *After ten years in the job, she felt stale and needed a change.* ▶ **stale·ness** noun [U]

stale·mate /'steɪlmeɪt/ noun **1** [U, C, usually sing.] a disagreement or a situation in a competition in which neither side is able to win or make any progress **SYN** IMPASSE: *The talks ended in (a) stalemate.* **2** [U, sing.] (in CHESS) a situation in which a player cannot successfully move any of their pieces and the game ends without a winner ⊃ compare CHECKMATE

Sta·lin·ism /'stɑːlɪˌnɪzəm/ noun [U] the policies and beliefs of Stalin, especially that the Communist party should be the only party and that the central government should control the whole political and economic system ▶ **Sta·lin·ist** /-nɪst/ adj., noun

stalk /stɔk/ noun, verb
● **noun 1** a thin STEM that supports a leaf, flower, or fruit and joins it to another part of the plant or tree; the main STEM of a plant: *flowers on long stalks* ◆ *celery stalks* ⊃ picture at PLANT **2** a long thin structure that supports something, especially an organ in some animals, and joins it on to another part: *Crabs have eyes on stalks.*
● **verb 1** [T, I] ~ **(sth/sb)** to move slowly and quietly toward an animal or a person, in order to kill, catch, or harm it or them: *The lion was stalking a zebra.* ◆ *He stalked his victim as she walked home, before attacking and robbing her.* **2** [T] ~ **sb** to illegally follow and watch someone over a long period of time, in a way that is annoying or frightening: *She claimed that he had been stalking her over a period of three years.* **3** [I] + **adv./prep.** to walk in an angry or proud way: *He stalked off without a word.* **4** [T, I] ~ **(sth)** to move through a place in an unpleasant or threatening way: *The gunmen stalked the building, looking for victims.* ◆ *(figurative) Fear stalks the streets of the city at night.*

stalk·er /'stɔkər/ noun **1** a person who follows and watches another person over a long period of time in a way that is annoying or frightening **2** a person who follows an animal quietly and slowly, especially in order to kill or capture it

stalk·ing /'stɔkɪŋ/ noun [U] the crime of following and watching someone over a long period of time in a way that is annoying or frightening

'stalking ˌhorse noun [sing.] **1** a person or thing that is used to hide the real purpose of a particular course of action **2** a candidate for a political position who has no chance of winning, but who competes in order to divide the opposition, to see if a stronger candidate might be more successful, etc.

stall /stɔl/ noun, verb
● **noun 1** [C] a table or small shop with an open front that people sell things from, especially at a market **SYN** STAND: *a market stall* ⊃ see also BOOKSTALL **2** [C] a section inside a farm building that is large enough for one animal to be kept in **3** [C] a small area in a room, surrounded by glass, walls, etc., that contains a shower or toilet **4** [C, usually pl.] the seats at the front of a church where the CHOIR (= singers) and priests sit **5** [C, usually sing.] a situation in which a vehicle's engine suddenly stops because it is not getting enough power **6** [C, usually sing.] a situation in which an aircraft loses speed and goes steeply downward
● **verb 1** [I, T] (of a vehicle or an engine) to stop suddenly because of a lack of power or speed; to make a vehicle or engine do this: *The car stalled and refused to start again.* ◆ ~ **sth** *I stalled the car three times during my driving test.* **2** [I] ~ **(on/over sth)** to try to avoid doing something or answering a question so that you have more time: *They are still stalling on the deal.* ◆ *"What do you mean?" she asked, stalling for time.* **3** [T] ~ **sb** to make someone wait so that you have more time to do something: *See if you can stall her while I finish searching her office.* **4** [T, I] ~ **(sth)** to stop something from happening until a later date; to stop making progress: *attempts to revive the stalled peace plan* ◆ *Discussions have once again stalled.*

stal·lion /'stælyən/ noun a fully grown male horse, especially one that is used for breeding ⊃ compare COLT, GELDING, MARE

stal·wart /'stɔlwərt/ noun, adj.
● **noun** ~ **(of sth)** a loyal supporter who does a lot of work for an organization, especially a political party
● **adj.** [usually before noun] **1** loyal and able to be relied on, even in a difficult situation **SYN** FAITHFUL: *stalwart supporters* **2** (formal) physically strong

sta·men /'steɪmən/ noun (technical) a small, thin, male part in the middle of a flower that produces POLLEN and is made up of a STALK supporting an ANTHER. The center of each flower usually has several stamens. ⊃ picture at PLANT

stam·i·na /'stæmənə/ noun [U] the physical or mental strength that enables you to do something difficult for long periods of time: *It takes a lot of stamina to run a marathon.* ⊃ collocations at DIET

stam·mer /'stæmər/ verb, noun
● **verb** [I, T] to speak with difficulty, repeating sounds or words and often stopping, before saying things correctly **SYN** STUTTER: *Many children stammer but grow out of it.* ◆ + **speech** *"W-w-what?" he stammered.* ◆ ~ **sth (out)** *She was barely able to stammer out a description of her attacker.* ▶ **stam·mer·er** noun
● **noun** [sing.] a problem that someone has in speaking in which they repeat sounds or words or often pause before saying things correctly: *to have a stammer.*

stamp 🔑 /stæmp/ noun, verb
● **noun**
> **ON LETTER/PACKAGE 1** (also formal 'postage ˌstamp) [C] a small piece of paper with a design on it that you buy and stick on an envelope or a package before you post it: *a 20-cent stamp* ◆ *The U.S. postal service is raising the price for a first-class stamp by two cents.* ◆ *He has been collecting stamps since he was eight.* ◆ *a stamp album* ⊃ picture at HOBBY
> **PRINTING TOOL 2** [C] a tool for printing the date or a design or mark onto a surface: *a date stamp* ⊃ see also RUBBER STAMP
> **PRINTED DESIGN/WORDS 3** [C] a design or words made by stamping something onto a surface: *The passports, with the visa stamps, were waiting at the embassy.* ◆ *(figurative) The project has the government's stamp of approval.*
> **PROOF OF PAYMENT 4** [C] a small piece of paper, stuck on a document to show that a particular amount of money has been paid ⊃ see also FOOD STAMP

> CHARACTER/QUALITY 5 [sing.] ~ (of sth) (*formal*) the mark or sign of a particular quality or person: *All his work bears the stamp of authority.* 6 [sing.] (*formal*) a kind or class, especially of people: *men of a different stamp*
> OF FOOT 7 [sing.] an act or sound of stamping the foot: *The stamp of hooves alerted Isabel.*

• **verb**
> FOOT 1 [T, I] ~ (sth) to put your foot down heavily and noisily on the ground: *I tried stamping my feet to keep warm.* ◆ *Sam stamped his foot in anger.* ◆ *The audience was stamping and cheering.*
> WALK 2 [I] + adv./prep. to walk with loud heavy steps **SYN** STOMP: *She turned and stamped out of the room.*
> PRINT DESIGN/WORDS 3 [T, often passive] to print letters, words, a design, etc. onto something using a special tool: ~ A (with B) *The box was stamped with the maker's name.* ◆ *Wait here to have your passport stamped.* ◆ ~ B on A *I'll stamp the company name on your check.* ◆ *The maker's name was stamped in gold on the box.* ⊃ see also RUBBER-STAMP, STAMP STH ON STH
> SHOW FEELING/QUALITY 4 [T, usually passive] to make a feeling show clearly on someone's face, in their actions, etc.: ~ A with B *Their faces were stamped with hostility.* ◆ ~ B over, across, etc. A *The crime had revenge stamped all over it.* 5 [T] ~ sb as sth to show that someone has a particular quality: *Her success has stamped her as one of the country's most popular singers.*
> ON LETTER/PACKAGE 6 [T, usually passive] ~ sth to stick a stamp on a letter or package
> CUT OUT OBJECT 7 [T] ~ sth (out) (of/from sth) to cut and shape an object from a piece of metal or plastic using a special machine or tool
PHR V 'stamp on sth 1 to put your foot down with force on something: *The child stamped on the spider.* 2 to stop something from happening or stop someone from doing something, especially by using force or authority: *All attempts at modernization were stamped on by senior officials.* 'stamp sth on sth to make something have an important effect or influence on something: *She stamped her own interpretation on the role.* ,stamp sth↔'out 1 to get rid of something that is bad, unpleasant, or dangerous, especially by using force or a lot of effort **SYN** ELIMINATE: *to stamp out racism* 2 to put out a fire by bringing your foot down heavily on it

'stamp col,lecting *noun* [U] the hobby of collecting stamps from different countries ⊃ picture at HOBBY ▶ 'stamp col,lector *noun*

stam·pede /stæmˈpid/ *noun, verb*
• **noun** [C, usually sing.] 1 a situation in which a group of people or large animals such as horses suddenly start running in the same direction, especially because they are frightened or excited: *A stampede broke out when the doors opened.* 2 a situation in which a lot of people are trying to do or achieve the same thing at the same time: *Falling interest rates have led to a stampede to buy property.*
• **verb** 1 [I, T] ~ (sth) (of large animals or people) to run in a stampede; to make animals do this: *a herd of stampeding elephants* ◆ *A huge bunch of kids came stampeding down the corridor.* 2 [T, usually passive] ~ sb (into sth/into doing sth) to make someone rush into doing something without giving them time to think about it: *I refuse to be stampeded into making any hasty decisions.*

stance /stæns/ *noun* 1 ~ (on sth) the opinions that someone has about something and expresses publicly **SYN** POSITION: *What is the newspaper's stance on the war?* 2 the way in which someone stands, especially when playing a sport

stanch /stɔntʃ; stɑntʃ; stæntʃ/ (also staunch) *verb* ~ sth (*formal*) to stop the flow of something, especially blood

stan·chion /ˈstæntʃən/ *noun* (*formal*) a vertical pole used to support something

stand 🔑 /stænd/ *verb, noun*
• **verb** (stood, stood /stʊd/)
> ON FEET/BE VERTICAL 1 [I] to be on your feet; to be in a vertical position: *She was too weak to stand.* ◆ *a bird standing on one leg* ◆ *Don't just stand there —do something!* ◆ *I was standing only a few feet away.* ◆ *We all stood around in the corridor waiting.* ◆ *to stand on your head/hands* (= to be upside down, balancing on your head/hands) ◆ *After the earthquake, only a few houses were left standing.* ◆ + adj. *Stand still while I take your photo.* 2 [I] to get up onto your feet from another position: *Everyone stood when the president came in.* ◆ ~ up *We stood up in order to get a better view.*
> PUT UPRIGHT 3 [T] ~ sth/sb + adv./prep. to put something or someone in a vertical position somewhere: *Stand the ladder up against the wall.* ◆ *I stood the little girl on a chair so that she could see.*
> BE IN PLACE/CONDITION 4 [I] + adv./prep. to be in a particular place: *The castle stands on the site of an ancient battlefield.* ◆ *An old oak tree once stood here.* 5 [I] (+ adj.) to be in a particular condition or situation: *The house stood empty for a long time.* ◆ *"You're wrong about the date—it was 1988." "I stand corrected* (= accept that I was wrong).*" ◆ *You never know where you stand with her*—one minute she's friendly, the next she'll hardly speak to you.* ◆ *As things stand, there is little chance of a quick settlement of the dispute.*
> BE AT HEIGHT/LEVEL 6 [I] + noun (not used in the progressive tenses) to be a particular height: *The tower stands 60 feet high.* 7 [I] ~ at sth to be at a particular level, amount, height, etc.: *Interest rates stand at 3%.* ◆ *The world record then stood at 6.59 meters.*
> OF CAR/TRAIN, ETC. 8 [I] + adv./prep. to be in a particular place, especially while waiting to go somewhere: *The bus standing at platform 3 is for Kansas City.*
> OF LIQUID/MIXTURE 9 [I] to remain still, without moving or being moved: *Mix the batter and let it stand for twenty minutes.* ◆ *standing pools of rainwater*
> OFFER/DECISION 10 [I] if an offer, a decision, etc. made earlier stands, it is still valid: *My offer still stands.* ◆ *The world record stood for 20 years.*
> BE LIKELY TO DO SOMETHING 11 [I] ~ to do sth to be in a situation where you are likely to do something: *You stand to make a lot from this deal.*
> HAVE OPINION 12 [I] ~ (on sth) to have a particular attitude or opinion about something or towards sb: *Where do you stand on private education?*
> DISLIKE 13 [T, no passive] (not used in the progressive tenses) used especially in negative sentences and questions to emphasize that you do not like someone or something **SYN** BEAR: ~ sb/sth *I can't stand his brother.* ◆ *I can't stand the sight of blood.* ◆ *I can't stand it when you do that.* ◆ ~ doing sth *She couldn't stand being kept waiting.* ◆ ~ sb/ sth doing sth *I can't stand people interrupting constantly.* ◆ *How do you stand him being here constantly?* ⊃ thesaurus box at HATE
> SURVIVE TREATMENT 14 [T] ~ sth used especially with can/ could to say that someone or something can survive something or can TOLERATE something without being hurt or damaged: *His heart won't stand the strain much longer.* ◆ *Modern plastics can stand very high and very low temperatures.*
IDM Idioms containing **stand** are at the entries for the nouns and adjectives in the idioms. For example, **stand on ceremony** is at ceremony.
PHR V ,stand aˈside 1 to move to one side: *She stood aside to let us pass.* 2 to not get involved in something: *Don't stand aside and let others do all the work.* 3 to stop doing a job so someone else can do it
,stand ˈback (from sth) 1 to move back from a place: *The police ordered the crowd to stand back.* 2 to think about a situation as if you are not involved in it: *It's time to stand back and look at your career so far.*
,stand beˈtween sb/sth and sth to prevent someone from getting or achieving something: *Only one game stood between him and victory.*
,stand ˈby 1 to be present while something bad is happening but not do anything to stop it: *How can you stand by*

and see him accused of something he didn't do? ⊃ related noun BYSTANDER **2** to be ready for action: *The troops are standing by.* ⊃ related noun STANDBY **'stand by sb** to help someone or be friends with them, even in difficult situations: *her famous song, "Stand by your man"* **'stand by sth** to still believe or agree with something you said, decided or agreed earlier: *She still stands by every word she said.* **,stand 'down** (of a witness) to leave the WITNESS STAND in court after giving evidence

'stand for sth [no passive] **1** (not used in the progressive tenses) to be an abbreviation or symbol of something: *"The book's by T.C. Smith." "What does the "T.C." stand for?"* **2** to support something: *I hated the organization and all it stood for* (= the ideas that it supported). **3 not stand for something** to not let someone do something or something happen: *I won't stand for it any longer.*

,stand 'in (for sb) to take someone's place **SYN** DEPUTIZE: *My assistant will stand in for me while I'm away.* ⊃ related noun STAND-IN

,stand 'out (as sth) to be much better or more important than someone or something: *Four of the contestants stand out as being more talented than the rest.* ⊃ see also OUTSTANDING **,stand 'out (from/against sth)** to be easily seen; to be noticeable: *The lettering stood out well against the dark background.* ◆ *She's the sort of person who stands out in a crowd.* ◆ related noun STANDOUT

,stand 'over sb to be near someone and watch them: *I don't like you standing over me while I'm cooking.*

,stand 'up to be on your feet: *There were no seats left so I had to stand up.* ◆ *You'll look taller if you stand up straight.* **,stand sb 'up** (*informal*) to deliberately not meet someone you have arranged to meet, especially someone you are having a romantic relationship with: *I've been stood up!* **,stand 'up for sb/sth** to support or defend someone or something: *Always stand up for your friends.* ◆ *You must stand up for your rights.* ◆ *She had learned to stand up for herself.* **,stand 'up (to sth)** to remain valid even when tested, examined closely, etc.: *His argument simply doesn't stand up to close scrutiny.* ◆ *I'm afraid this document will never stand up in a court of law.* **,stand 'up to sb** to resist someone; to not accept bad treatment from someone without complaining: *It was brave of her to stand up to those bullies.* **,stand 'up to sth** (of materials, products, etc.) to remain in good condition despite rough treatment **SYN** WITHSTAND: *This carpeting is designed to stand up to a lot of wear and tear.*

● *noun*
▷ OPINION **1** [usually sing.] **~ (on sth)** an attitude toward something or an opinion that you make clear to people: *to take a firm stand on something* ◆ *He was criticized for his tough stand on immigration.*
▷ DEFENSE **2** [usually sing.] a strong effort to defend yourself or your opinion about something: *We've got to take a stand against further job losses.* ◆ *the rebels' desperate last stand*
▷ FOR SHOWING/HOLDING SOMETHING **3** a table or a vertical structure that goods are sold from, especially in the street or at a market **SYN** STALL: *a hamburger stand* ⊃ see also NEWS-STAND **4** a table or a vertical structure where things are displayed or advertised, for example at an exhibition: *a display/an exhibition stand* **5** (often in compounds) a piece of equipment or furniture that you use for holding a particular type of thing: *a bicycle/microphone/umbrella, etc. stand* ⊃ picture at BICYCLE, LABORATORY ⊃ see also HATSTAND, MUSIC STAND, WASHSTAND
▷ AT SPORTS EVENT **6 stands** [pl.] a large sloping structure at the side of a sports field or a STADIUM with rows where people sit or stand to watch the game ⊃ picture at FOOTBALL ⊃ see also GRANDSTAND
▷ IN COURT **7** [usually sing.] = WITNESS STAND: *He took the stand as the first witness.*
▷ FOR BAND/ORCHESTRA, ETC. **8** a raised platform for a band, an ORCHESTRA, a speaker, etc. ⊃ see also BANDSTAND
▷ FOR TAXIS/BUSES, ETC. **9** a place where taxis, buses, etc. park while they are waiting for passengers
▷ OF PLANTS/TREES **10 ~ (of sth)** (*technical*) a group of plants or trees of one kind: *a stand of pines* ⊃ see also HANDSTAND
IDM see FIRM

THESAURUS

stand

get up • stand up • rise • get to your feet • be on your feet

These words all mean to be in an upright position with your weight on your feet, or to put yourself in this position.

stand to be in an upright position with your weight on your feet: *She was too weak to stand.* ◆ *Stand still while the x-ray is being taken.* **NOTE Stand** is usually used with an adverb or prepositional phrase to show where or how someone stands, but sometimes another phrase or clause is used to show what someone does while they are standing: *We stood talking for a few minutes.* ◆ *He stood and gazed out the window.*

get up to get into a standing position from a sitting, kneeling, or lying position: *Please don't get up!*

stand up to be in a standing position; to stand after sitting: *Stand up straight!* ◆ *Everyone stood up when the teacher entered the classroom.*

STAND, GET UP, OR STAND UP?

Stand usually means "to be in a standing position" but can also mean "to get into a standing position". **Stand up** can be used with either of these meanings, but its use is more restricted: it is used especially when someone tells someone or a group of people to stand. **Get up** is the most frequent way of saying "get into a standing position", and this can be from a sitting, kneeling, or lying position; if you **stand up**, this is nearly always after sitting, especially on a chair. If you want to tell someone politely that they do not need to move from their chair, use **get up**: *Please don't stand up!*

rise (*formal*) to get into a standing position from a sitting, kneeling, or lying position: *Would you all rise, please, to sing the national anthem.*

get to your feet to stand up after sitting, kneeling, or lying: *I helped her to get to her feet.*

be on your feet to be standing up: *I've been on my feet all day.*

'stand-a,lone *adj.* [usually before noun] (especially of a computer) able to be operated on its own without being connected to a larger system

stand·ard 🔊 /'stændərd/ *noun, adj.*

● *noun*
▷ LEVEL OF QUALITY **1** [C, U] **~ (of sth)** a level of quality, especially one that people think is acceptable: *a fall in academic standards* ◆ *We aim to maintain high standards of customer care.* ◆ *The standard of this year's applications is very low.* ◆ *He failed to reach the required standard, and did not qualify for the race.* ◆ *Her work is not up to standard* (= of a good enough standard). ◆ *Who sets the standard for water quality?* ◆ *A number of local beaches fail to meet the county's standards for cleanliness.* ◆ *In the shanty towns there are very poor living standards.* ⊃ see also STANDARD OF LIVING, SUBSTANDARD **2** [C, usually pl.] a level of quality that is normal or acceptable for a particular person or in a particular situation: *You'd better lower your standards if you want to find somewhere cheap to live.* ◆ *It was a simple meal by Eddie's standards.* ◆ *The equipment is slow and heavy by modern standards.*
▷ LEVEL OF BEHAVIOR **3 standards** [pl.] a level of behavior that someone considers to be morally acceptable: *a man of high moral standards* ◆ *Standards aren't what they used to be.* ⊃ see also DOUBLE STANDARD
▷ UNIT OF MEASUREMENT **4** [C] a unit of measurement that is officially used; an official rule used when producing something: *a reduction in the weight standard of silver coins* ◆ *industry standards* ⊃ see also GOLD STANDARD
▷ FLAG **5** [C] a flag that is used during official ceremonies, especially one connected with a particular military group

> SONG **6** [C] a song that has been recorded by many different singers

● **adj.**

> AVERAGE/NORMAL **1** average or normal rather than having special or unusual features: *A standard letter was sent to all candidates.* ◆ *Televisions are a standard feature in most hotel rooms.* ◆ *the standard tax rate* (= paid by everyone) ◆ *It is* **standard practice** *to search visitors as they enter the building.*

> SIZE/MEASUREMENT **2** [usually before noun] following a particular standard set, for example, by an industry: *standard sizes of clothes*

> BOOK/WRITER **3** [only before noun] read by most people who are studying a particular subject

> LANGUAGE **4** [usually before noun] (of spelling, pronunciation, grammar, etc.) believed to be correct and used by most people: *Standard English* ⊃ compare NONSTANDARD, SUBSTANDARD

¦standard-¦bearer *noun* a leader in a political group or campaign

¦standard devi'ation *noun* (*statistics*) the amount by which measurements in a set vary from the average for the set

¦standard 'error *noun* (*statistics*) a method of measuring how accurate an estimate is

stand·ard·ize /'stændər¦daız/ *verb* ~ **sth** to make objects or activities of the same type have the same features or qualities; to make something standard: *a standardized contract/design/test* ▶ **stand·ard·i·za·tion** /¦stændərdə-'zeıʃn/ *noun* [U]: *the standardization of components*

¦standard of 'living *noun* (*pl.* **standards of living**) the amount of money and level of comfort that a particular person or group has: *Most people enjoy a* **high standard of living** *in this country.*

¦standard ¦time *noun* [U] the official time of a country or an area

stand·by /'stændbaı/ *noun, adj.*

● **noun** (*pl.* **stand·bys**) *noun* a person or thing that can always be used if needed, for example if someone or something else is not available or if there is an emergency: *I always keep a pizza in the freezer as a standby.* ◆ *a standby electricity generator*

   IDM **on standby 1** ready to do something immediately if needed or asked: *The emergency services were* **put on standby** *after a bomb warning.* **2** ready to travel or go somewhere if a ticket or something that is needed suddenly becomes available: *He was* **put on standby** *for the flight to New York.*

● **adj.** [only before noun] a **standby** ticket for a flight, concert, etc. cannot be bought in advance and is only available a very short time before the plane leaves or the performance starts

¦stand-down *noun* [U, C] a period when people, especially soldiers, relax after a period of duty or danger

stand·ee /stæn'di/ *noun* a person who is standing, for example in a bus or at a concert

¦stand-in *noun* **1** a person who does someone's job for a short time when they are not available **2** a person who replaces an actor in some scenes in a movie, especially dangerous ones

stand·ing /'stændıŋ/ *adj., noun*

● **adj.** [only before noun] **1** existing or arranged permanently, not formed or made for a particular situation: *a standing army* ◆ *a* **standing committee** ◆ *It's a* **standing joke** (= something that a group of people regularly laugh at). ◆ *We have a* **standing invitation** *to visit them anytime.* **2** done from a position in which you are standing rather than sitting or running: *a standing jump/start* ◆ *The speaker got a* **standing ovation** (= people stood up to clap after the speech). **3** not moving: *standing water* SYN STAGNANT ⊃ see also FREESTANDING

● **noun 1** [U] the position or reputation of someone or something within a group of people or in an organization SYN STATUS: *the* **high/low standing** *of politicians with the* public ◆ *The contract has no legal standing.* ◆ *He is a member* **in good standing** *of the Church.* **2** [U] the period of time that something has existed: *a friendship of many years' standing* ⊃ see also LONG-STANDING **3** **standings** [pl.] a list of people, teams, etc. showing their positions in a sports competition

¦standing 'order *noun* [C, U] **1** an order for something that is repeated every week, month, etc. **2** a military order that must always be obeyed

¦standing ¦room *noun* [U] space for people to stand in, especially in a theater, at a sports event, etc.: *standing room for 12,000 fans* ◆ *It was* **standing room only** *at the concert* (= all the seats were sold).

stand·off /'stændɔ:f; -ɑf/ *noun* ~ **(between A and B)** a situation in which no agreement can be reached SYN DEADLOCK

stand·off·ish /¦stænd'ɔfıʃ; -'ɑfıʃ/ *adj.* (*informal*) not friendly toward other people SYN ALOOF

stand·out /'stændaut/ *noun* (*informal*) a person or thing that is very noticeable because they are or it is better, more impressive, etc. than others in a group ▶ **stand·out** *adj.* [only before noun]: *the standout track on this album*

stand·pipe /'stændpaıp/ *noun* a pipe that is connected to a public water supply and used to provide water outside a building

stand·point /'stændpɔınt/ *noun* [usually sing.] an opinion or a way of thinking about ideas or situations SYN PERSPECTIVE: *a political/theoretical, etc. standpoint* ◆ *He is writing* **from the standpoint** *of someone who knows what prison life is like.*

stand·still /'stændstıl/ *noun* [sing.] a situation in which all activity or movement has stopped SYN HALT: *The security alert* **brought the airport to a standstill.** ◆ *Traffic in the northbound lane is* **at a complete standstill.**

¦stand-up *adj., noun*

● **adj.** [only before noun] **1 stand-up** comedy consists of one person standing in front of an audience and telling jokes **2** worn, used, etc. in a vertical position: *a stand-up collar*

● **noun 1** [U] stand-up comedy: *When did you start doing stand-up?* **2** [C] a person who performs stand-up comedy: *She started out as a stand-up.*

stank pt of STINK

stan·za /'stænzə/ *noun* (*technical*) a group of lines that forms a METRICAL unit in some types of poems SYN VERSE

staph·y·lo·coc·cus /¦stæfələ'kɑkəs/ *noun* (*medical*) (also *informal* **staph** /stæf/) a type of bacteria that can cause infections in some parts of the body such as the skin and eyes

sta·ple /'steıpl/ *adj., noun, verb*

● **adj.** [only before noun] forming a basic, large, or important part of something: *The staple crop is rice.* ◆ *Jeans are a staple part of every teenager's wardrobe.*

● **noun 1** a small piece of wire that is used in a device called a STAPLER and is pushed through pieces of paper and bent over at the ends in order to fasten the pieces of paper together ⊃ picture at STATIONERY **2** a small piece of metal in the shape of a U that is hit into wooden surfaces using a HAMMER, used especially for holding electrical wires in place **3** a basic type of food that is used a lot: *Aid workers helped distribute corn, milk, and other staples.* **4** something that is produced by a country and is important for its economy: *Rubber became the staple of the Malayan economy.* **5** ~ **(of sth)** a large or important part of something: *Celebrity gossip is a staple of the tabloid press.*

● **verb** ~ **sth** + **adv./prep.** to attach one thing to another using a staple or staples: *Staple the invoice to the receipt.* ◆ *Staple the invoice and the receipt together.*

¦staple 'diet *noun* [U, C] ~ **(of sth) 1** the food that a person or an animal normally eats: *a staple diet of meat and potatoes* ◆ *Bamboo is the panda's staple diet.* **2** something that is used

| h hat | m man | n no | ŋ sing | l leg | r red | y yes | w wet |

a lot: *Sex and violence seem to be the staple diet of television drama.*

staple gun *noun* a device for attaching paper to walls, etc. using STAPLES

sta·pler /ˈsteɪplər/ *noun* a small device used for putting staples into paper, etc. ⊃ picture at STATIONERY

staple remover *noun* a small device used for removing STAPLES from paper, etc. ⊃ picture at STATIONERY

star 🔑 /stɑr/ *noun, verb*

● *noun*
▷ IN SKY **1** [C] a large ball of burning gas in space that we see as a point of light in the sky at night: *There was a big moon and hundreds of stars were shining overhead.* ◆ *The North Star is the brightest star in the sky.* ◆ *We camped out **under the stars**.* ⊃ see also FALLING STAR, LODESTAR, POLE STAR, SHOOTING STAR, STARRY
▷ SHAPE **2** [C] an object, a decoration, a mark, etc., usually with five or six points, whose shape represents a star: *a horse with a white star on its forehead* ◆ *a sheriff's star* ◆ *I put a star by the names of the girls in the class.* ◆ *a four-star general*
▷ MARK OF QUALITY **3** [C, usually sing.] a mark that represents a star and tells you how good sth is, especially a hotel or restaurant: ***three-/four-/five-star** hotels* ◆ *What star rating does this restaurant have?*
▷ PERFORMER **4** [C] a famous and excellent singer, performer, sports player, etc.: ***pop/rock/Hollywood, etc. stars*** ◆ *a **football/tennis, etc. star*** ◆ *He's so good—I'm sure he'll be a big star.* ◆ *She acts well but she hasn't got **star quality**.* ◆ *The best models receive **star treatment**.* ⊃ see also ALL-STAR, FILM STAR, MEGASTAR, MOVIE STAR, SUPERSTAR **5** [C] a person who has the main part, or one of the main parts, in a film/ movie, play, etc.: *She was the star of a popular television series.* ◆ *The **star of the show** was a young Italian singer.* ◆ *the **star role/ part*** ⊃ see also STAR TURN
▷ BEST OF GROUP **6** [C] (often used before another noun) a person or thing that is the best of a group: *a **star student*** ◆ *Paula is the star of the class.* ◆ *He was the **star performer** at the championship.* ◆ *The **star prize** is a weekend for two in Paris.*
▷ INFLUENCE ON SOMEONE'S FUTURE **7 stars** [pl.] a description of what someone thinks is going to happen to someone in the future, based on the position of the stars and planets when they were born **SYN** HOROSCOPE: *I always like to see what the stars say before making any decisions.*
IDM **see stars** (*informal*) to see flashes of light in front of your eyes, usually because you have been hit on the head **stars in your eyes** if someone has **stars in their eyes**, they have dreams of becoming famous, especially as an entertainer ⊃ more at REACH *v.*, THANK

● *verb* (-rr-)
▷ PERFORM IN MOVIE/PLAY **1** [I] ~ **(with/opposite sb) (in sth)** to have one of the main parts in a movie, play, etc.: *She starred opposite Cary Grant in "Bringing up Baby."* ◆ *No one has yet been chosen for the **starring role** (= the main part).* **2** [T, no passive] ~ **sb** if a movie, play, etc. **stars** someone, that person has one of the main parts: *a movie starring Tom Cruise and Demi Moore* ◆ *The studio wants to star her in a sequel to last year's hit.* ⊃ see also COSTAR
▷ MARK WITH SYMBOL **3** [T, usually passive] ~ **sth** to put a symbol shaped like a star (= an ASTERISK) next to a word, etc. in order to make people notice it: *Treat the sections that have been starred as a priority.*

star anise *noun* [U, C] a small fruit in the shape of a star, used in cooking as a spice ⊃ picture at HERB

star·board /ˈstɑrbərd/ *noun* [U] the side of a ship or an aircraft that is on the right when you are facing forward ⊃ compare PORT

star·burst /ˈstɑrbərst/ *noun* a bright light in the shape of a star, or a shape that looks like a star exploding

starch /stɑrtʃ/ *noun, verb*
● *noun* **1** [U, C] a white CARBOHYDRATE food substance found in potatoes, flour, rice, etc.; food containing this: *There's too much starch in your diet.* ◆ *You need to cut down on starches.* **2** [U] starch prepared in powder form or as a

spray and used for making clothes, sheets, etc. stiff
● *verb* [usually passive] ~ **sth** to make clothes, sheets, etc. stiff using starch: *a starched white shirt*

starch·y /ˈstɑrtʃi/ *adj.* **1** (of food) containing a lot of starch **2** (*informal, disapproving*) (of a person or their behavior) very formal; not friendly or relaxed

star-crossed *adj.* (*literary*) not able to be happy because of bad luck or FATE: *Shakespeare's star-crossed lovers, Romeo and Juliet*

star·dom /ˈstɑrdəm/ *noun* [U] the state of being famous as an actor, a singer, etc.: *The group seems to be **bound for stardom** (= people say they will be famous).* ◆ *She **shot to stardom** in a Broadway musical.*

star·dust /ˈstɑrdʌst/ *noun* [U] **1** a magic quality that some famous people with a great natural ability seem to have **2** (*astronomy*) stars that are very far from the earth and appear like bright dust in the sky at night

stare 🔑 /stɛr/ *verb, noun*
● *verb* [I] ~ **(at sb/sth)** to look at someone or something for a long time: *I screamed and everyone stared.* ◆ *I stared blankly at the paper in front of me.* ◆ *He sat **staring into space** (= looking at nothing).* ◆ *She looked at them with dark staring eyes.*
IDM **be staring sb in the face 1** to be obvious or easy to see: *The answer was staring us in the face.* **2** to be certain to happen: *Defeat was staring them in the face.* **be staring sth in the face** to be unable to avoid something: *They were staring defeat in the face.*
PHR V **stare sb 'down** to look into someone's eyes for a long time until they feel embarrassed and are forced to look away

THESAURUS

stare

gaze • peer • glare

These words all mean to look at someone or something for a long time.

stare to look at someone or something for a long time, especially with surprise or fear, or because you are thinking: *I stared at the picture in shock.*

gaze (*somewhat formal*) to look steadily at someone or something for a long time, especially with surprise or love, or because you are thinking: *She gazed at Marco with affection.*

peer to look closely or carefully at someone or something, especially when you cannot see them/it clearly: *He peered at me over the top of his glasses.*

glare to look angrily at someone or something for a long time: *I looked at her and she glared back.*

PATTERNS
■ to stare/gaze/peer/glare **at** sb/sth
■ to stare/peer/glare **suspiciously**
■ to stare/peer **anxiously/intently**
■ to stare/glare **wildly/fiercely**

● *noun* an act of looking at someone or something for a long time, especially in a way that is unfriendly or that shows surprise: *She gave him a blank stare.* ⊃ thesaurus box at LOOK

star·fish /ˈstɑrfɪʃ/ *noun* (*pl.* **star·fish**) a flat sea creature in the shape of a star with five arms

star·fruit /ˈstɑrfrut/ *noun* (*pl.* **star·fruit**) a green or yellow tropical fruit with a shape like a star ⊃ picture at FRUIT

star·gaz·er /ˈstɑrˌgeɪzər/ *noun* (*informal*) a person who studies ASTROLOGY or ASTRONOMY ▶ **star·gaz·ing** *noun* [U]

stark /stɑrk/ *adj., adv.*
● *adj.* (**stark·er, stark·est**) **1** (often *disapproving*) looking severe and without any color or decoration: *I think white would be too stark for the bedroom.* ◆ *The hills stood stark against the winter sky.* **2** unpleasant; real, and impossible to

avoid **SYN** BLEAK: *The author paints a stark picture of life in a prison camp.* ◆ *a stark choice* ◆ *The remains of the building stand as a stark reminder of the fire.* ◆ *He now faces the* **stark reality** *of life in prison.* ➔ thesaurus box at PLAIN **3** very different from something in a way that is easy to see **SYN** CLEAR: *stark differences* ◆ *Social divisions in the city are stark.* ◆ *The good weather was* **in stark contrast to** *the storms of previous weeks.* **4** [only before noun] complete and total **SYN** UTTER: *The children watched in stark terror.* ▶ **stark·ly** *adv.*: *The interior is starkly simple.* ◆ *The lighthouse stood out starkly against the dark sky.* ◆ *We are starkly aware of the risks.* **stark·ness** *noun* [U]

● *adv.* ~ **naked** completely naked **IDM** see RAVING

star·less /'stɑrləs/ *adj.* with no stars in the sky: *a starless night*

star·let /'stɑrlət/ *noun* a young woman actor who plays small parts and hopes to become famous

star·light /'stɑrlaɪt/ *noun* [U] light from the stars: *We walked home by starlight.*

star·ling /'stɑrlɪŋ/ *noun* a common bird with dark, shiny feathers and a noisy call

star·lit /'stɑrlɪt/ *adj.* with light from the stars: *a starlit night*

'star ˌnetwork *noun* (*computing*) a network in which computers are connected to a central unit, rather than to each other

ˌStar of ˈDavid /ˌstɑr əv ˈdeɪvəd/ *noun* (*pl.* Stars of David) a star with six points that is used as a symbol of Judaism and the state of Israel

star·ry /'stɑri/ *noun* [usually before noun] **1** (of the sky) full of stars: *a beautiful starry night* **2** looking like a star: *starry flowers* **3** (of eyes) shining like stars

'starry-ˌeyed *adj.* (*informal*) full of emotion, hopes, or dreams about someone or something in a way that is not realistic

the ˌStars and ˈStripes *noun* [sing.] the national flag of the U.S.

star·ship /'stɑrʃɪp/ *noun* (in SCIENCE FICTION) a large SPACECRAFT in which people or other creatures travel through space

'star sign (also *informal* **sign**) *noun* one of the twelve signs of the ZODIAC: *"What's your star sign?" "Aquarius."*

the ˌStar-ˌSpangled ˈBanner *noun* [sing.] the national ANTHEM (= song) of the U.S.

'star-struck *adj.* very impressed by famous people such as actors, sports personalities, etc.

'star-ˌstudded *adj.* including many famous performers: *a star-studded cast*

start 🔧 /stɑrt/ *verb, noun*

● *verb*

> **DOING SOMETHING 1** [T, I] to begin doing or using something: ~ **sth** *I start work at nine.* ◆ *He's just started a new job.* ◆ *I only started (= began to read) this book yesterday.* ◆ *We need to start (= begin using) a new can of coffee.* ◆ *The kids start school next week.* ◆ ~ **to do sth** *It started to rain.* ◆ *Mistakes were starting to creep in.* ◆ ~ **doing sth** *She started laughing.* ◆ ~ **(on sth)** *It's a long story. Where should I start?* ◆ *It's time for you to start doing your homework.* ◆ *Can you start (= a new job) on Monday?* ◆ ~ **by doing sth** *Let's start by reviewing what we did last week.* ◆ + *adj.* *The best professional musicians* **start young.** ➔ note at BEGIN

> **HAPPENING 2** [I, T] to start happening; to make something start happening: *When does the class start?* ◆ *Have you any idea where the rumor started?* ◆ ~ **sth** *Who started the fire?* ◆ *Do you start the day with a good breakfast?* ◆ *You're always trying to start an argument.* ◆ ~ **sb/sth doing sth** *The news started me thinking.*

> **MACHINE/VEHICLE 3** [T, I] ~ **(sth)** when you **start** a machine or a vehicle or it **starts**, it begins to operate: *Start your engines!* ◆ *I can't get the car started.* ◆ *The car won't start.*

> **EXISTING 4** [I, T] to begin to exist; to make something begin

to exist: ~ **(up)** *There are a lot of small businesses starting up in that area.* ◆ ~ **sth** *They decided to start a catering business.*

> **JOURNEY 5** [I] ~ **(out)** to begin a journey; to leave **SYN** SET OFF, SET OUT: *What time are we starting tomorrow?*

> **GOING/WALKING 6** [I] + **adv./prep.** to begin to move in a particular direction: *I started after her (= began to follow her) to tell her the news.* ◆ *He started for the door, but I blocked his way.*

> **IN PARTICULAR WAY/FROM PLACE/LEVEL 7** [I, T] to begin, or to begin something such as a career, in a particular way that changed later: ~ **as sth** *She started as a secretary but ended up running the department.* ◆ ~ **out/off (as sth)** *The company started out with 30 employees.* ◆ ~ **sth (as sth)** *He started life as a teacher before turning to journalism.* **8** [I] + **adv./prep.** to begin from a particular place, amount, or situation: *The trail starts just outside the town.* ◆ *Hotel prices start at $100 a night for a double room.* ◆ *The evening started badly when the speaker failed to turn up.*

> **MOVE SUDDENLY 9** [I] to move suddenly and quickly because you are surprised or afraid **SYN** JUMP: *The sudden noise made her start.*

IDM **don't (you) start** (*informal*) used to tell someone not to complain or be critical: *Don't start! I told you I'd be late.* **get started** to begin doing something: *It's almost ten o'clock. Let's get started.* **you, he, she, etc. started it** (*informal*) you, he, she, etc. began a fight or an argument: *"Stop fighting, you two!" "He started it!"* **start something** (*informal*) to cause trouble **to start with 1** used when you are giving the first and most important reason for sth: *To start with, it's much too expensive.* **2** at the beginning: *The organization had a very small budget to start with.* ◆ *I'll have melon to start with.* ◆ *She wasn't crazy about the idea to start with.* ➔ more at ALARM, BALL, FOOT

PHR V **ˌstart ˈback** to begin to return somewhere **ˌstart ˈoff 1** to begin to move: *The horse started off at a steady trot.* **2** to begin happening; to begin doing something: *The discussion started off mildly enough.* **3** to begin by doing or being something: *Let's start off with some gentle exercises.* ◆ *We started off by introducing ourselves.* ◆ ~ **doing sth** *I started off working quite hard, but it didn't last.* **ˌstart sb ˈoff (on sth) 1** [no passive] to make someone begin doing something: *What started her off on that crazy idea?* ◆ *Don't say anything to her—you'll start her off again (= make her get angry).* ◆ ~ **doing sth** *Kevin started us all off laughing.* **2** to help someone begin doing something: *My mother started me off on the piano when I was three.* ◆ ~ **doing sth** *His father started him off farming.* **ˌstart on sb** [no passive] to attack someone physically or with words **ˌstart ˈout 1** to begin to do something, especially in business or work: *to start out in business* ◆ *She started out on her legal career in 2008.* **2** to have a particular intention when you begin something: ~ **to do sth** *I started out to write a short story, but it soon developed into a novel.* **ˌstart ˈover** to begin again: *She wasn't happy with our work and made us start over.* **ˌstart ˈup** | **ˌstart sth↔ˈup** to begin working, happening, etc.; to make something do this: *I heard his car start up.* ◆ *Start up the engines!* ➔ see also START-UP

● *noun*

> **BEGINNING 1** [C, usually sing.] the point at which something begins: *a perfect start to the day* ◆ *Things didn't look too hopeful at the start of the year.* ◆ *The meeting* **got off to a good/bad start** (= started well/badly). ◆ *The trip was a disaster* **from start to finish.** ◆ *We've had problems* **(right) from the start.** ◆ (*informal*) *This could be the start of something big.* **2** [sing.] the act or process of beginning something: *I want to get an early start in the morning.* ◆ *I'll paint the ceiling if you* **make a start** *on the walls.* ◆ *She's moving abroad to make a* **fresh start** (= to begin a new life).* ➔ see also FALSE START, KICK-START

> **OPPORTUNITY 3** [C, usually sing.] the opportunity that you are given to begin something in a successful way: *They worked hard to give their children a good start in life.* ◆ *The job gave him his start in journalism.*

> **IN RACE 4** **the start** [sing.] the place where a race begins: *The runners lined up at the start.* **5** [C, usually sing.] an amount of time or distance that someone has as an advantage over other people at the beginning of a race: *She went into the*

second round with a five-minute start on the rest of the cyclists. ♦ I gave the younger children a start. ➔ see also HEAD START **6** [C, usually pl.] (*sports*) a race or competition that someone has taken part in: *She's been beaten only once in six starts.* ▷ SUDDEN MOVEMENT **7** [C, usually sing.] an act of moving your body quickly and suddenly because you are surprised, afraid, etc.: *She woke from the dream **with a start**. ♦ You gave me quite a start!*

IDM **for a start** (*informal*) used to emphasize the first of a list of reasons, opinions, etc.: *I'm not working there—for a start, it's too far to travel.* ➔ more at FIT, FLYING START

THESAURUS

start

begin • start off • kick off • commence • open

These words are all used to talk about things happening from the beginning, or people doing the first part of something.

start to begin to happen or exist; to begin in a particular way or from a particular point: *When does the class start?*

begin to start to happen or exist; to start in a particular way or from a particular point; to start speaking: *When does the concert begin?*

START OR BEGIN?

There is not much difference in meaning between these words. **Start** is more frequent in spoken English and in business contexts; **begin** is more frequent in written English and is often used when you are describing a series of events: *The story begins on the island of Corfu.* **Start** is not used to mean "begin speaking": *"Ladies and gentlemen," he started.*

start off (*somewhat informal*) to start happening or to start doing something; to start by doing or being something: *The discussion started off mildly enough.*

kick off (*informal*) to start an event or activity, especially in a particular way; (of an event, activity, etc.) to start, especially in a particular way: *Tom will kick off with a few comments. ♦ The festival kicks off on Monday with a free concert.*

commence (*formal*) to start happening: *The negotiations are scheduled to commence at noon.*

open to start an event or activity in a particular way; (of an event, movie, or book) to start, especially in a particular way: *The story opens with a murder.*

PATTERNS

- to start/begin/start off/kick off/commence/open **with** sth
- to start/begin/start off/kick off/commence/open **by** doing sth
- to start/begin/start off **as** sth
- a **campaign/season/meeting** starts/begins/starts off/kicks off/commences/opens
- a **play/show/movie/book** starts/begins/starts off/opens

---

start·er /'stɑrtər/ *noun* **1** a person, horse, car, etc. that is in a race at the beginning: *Only 8 of the 28 starters completed the course.* ➔ compare NONSTARTER **2** a person who gives the signal for a race to start **3** a device used for starting the engine of a vehicle **4** a person who begins doing a particular activity in the way mentioned: *He was a late starter in ballet* (= older than most people when they start). ♦ a *slow starter* ➔ see also SELF-STARTER **5** (often used as an adjective) something that is intended to be used by someone who is starting to do something: *a starter home* (= a small home for someone who is buying property for the first time) ♦ *a starter kit/pack*

IDM **for starters** (*informal*) used to emphasize the first of a list of reasons, opinions, etc., or to say what happens first

starting ˌblocks (also **the blocks**) *noun* [pl.] the two blocks

on the ground that runners push their feet against at the beginning of a race

starting ˌgate *noun* a barrier that is raised or opened to let horses or dogs start running in a race

starting ˌpistol *noun* a gun used for signaling the start of a race

starting ˌpoint *noun* **1** ~ **(for sth)** a thing, an idea, or a set of facts that can be used to begin a discussion or process: *The article served as a useful starting point for our discussion.* **2** the place where you begin a trip

starting ˌprice *noun* the lowest price that starts the bidding at an AUCTION

star·tle /'stɑrtl/ *verb* to surprise someone suddenly in a way that slightly shocks or frightens them: ~ *sb/sth I didn't mean to startle you. ♦ The explosion startled the horse. ♦ I was startled by her question. ♦ **it startles sb to do sth** It startled me to find her sitting in my office.* ➔ thesaurus box at SURPRISE ▶ **star·tled** *adj.*: *She looked at him with startled eyes. ♦ He looked startled. ♦ She jumped back like a startled rabbit.*

star·tling /'stɑrtlæwːɪŋ/ *adj.* **1** extremely unusual and surprising: *a startling discovery* **2** (of a color) extremely bright: *startling blue eyes* ▶ **star·tling·ly** *adv.*

start-up *adj., noun*
● ***adj.*** [only before noun] connected with starting a new business or project: *start-up costs*
● ***noun*** a company that is just beginning to operate, especially an Internet company

ˌstar ˈturn *noun* a performance by a movie star, etc.; a performance that makes someone a star

star·va·tion /stɑr'veɪʃn/ *noun* [U] the state of suffering and death caused by having no food: *to die of/from starvation ♦ Millions will face starvation next year as a result of the drought. ♦ a starvation diet* (= one in which you do not have much to eat) ♦ *They were on starvation wages* (= extremely low wages).

starve /stɑrv/ *verb* **1** [I, T] to suffer or die because you do not have enough food to eat; to make someone suffer or die in this way: *The animals were left to starve to death. ♦ pictures of starving children ♦ The new job doesn't pay as much but we won't starve! ♦* ~ *sb/yourself She's starving herself to try to lose weight.* **2** **-starved** (in adjectives) not having something that you need: *supply-starved rebels* ➔ see also CASH-STARVED

IDM **be starving (for sth)** (also **be starved**) (*informal*) to feel very hungry: *When's dinner? I'm starving!*
PHR V **ˈstarve sb into sth/into doing sth** to force someone to do something by not allowing them to get any food or money **ˈstarve sb/sth of/for sth** [usually passive] to not give something that is needed: *I felt starved of intelligent conversation. ♦ The department has been starved for resources.* **ˌstarve sb↔ˈout (of sth)** to force someone to leave a particular building or area by not allowing them to get any food

stash /stæʃ/ *verb, noun*
● ***verb*** ~ **sth + adv./prep.** (*informal*) to store something in a safe or secret place: *She has a fortune **stashed away** in various bank accounts.*
● ***noun*** [usually sing.] (*informal*) an amount of something that is kept secretly: *a stash of money*

sta·sis /'steɪsəs/ *noun* [U, C] (*pl.* **sta·ses** /-siz/) (*formal*) a situation in which there is no change or development

stat /stæt/ *noun* (*informal*) = STATISTIC

state /steɪt/ *noun, adj., verb*
● ***noun***
▷ CONDITION OF SOMEONE OR SOMETHING **1** [C] the mental, emotional, or physical condition that a person or thing is in: *a confused state of mind ♦ He was in a state of permanent depression. ♦ anxieties about the state of the country's economy ♦ The building is in a bad state of repair* (= needs to be repaired). ♦ *She was in a state of shock.* ➔ note at CONDITION
▷ PART OF COUNTRY **2** [C] (*abbr.* **St.**) an organized political

---

community forming part of a country: *the states of Wyoming and North Dakota* ◆ *the southern states of the U.S.*

> COUNTRY **3** also **State** [C] a country considered as an organized political community controlled by one government: *the Baltic states* ◆ *European Union member states* ⊃ see also CITY STATE, NATION STATE, POLICE STATE, WELFARE STATE ⊃ note at COUNTRY

> GOVERNMENT **4** also **the state** [U, sing.] the government of a country: *matters/affairs of state* ◆ *people who are financially dependent on the state* ◆ *a state-owned company* ◆ *They wish to limit the power of the state.*

> OFFICIAL CEREMONY **5** [U] the formal ceremonies connected with high levels of government or with kings and queens: *The president was driven in state through the streets.*

> THE U.S. **6 the States** [pl.] (*informal*) the United States of America: *I've never been to the States.*

IDM **be in/get into a state** (*informal*) **1** to be/become excited or anxious: *She was in quite a state before her final exams.* **2** to be dirty or messy: *What a state this place is in!* **in a state of grace** (in the Roman Catholic Church) having been forgiven by God for the wrong or evil things you have done **a state of affairs** a situation, usually a bad one: *This state of affairs can no longer be ignored.* ⊃ thesaurus box at SITUATION

● *adj.* [only before noun] **1** connected with a particular state of a country, especially in the U.S.: *a state prison/hospital/university, etc.* ◆ *state police/troopers* ◆ *a state tax* **2** provided or controlled by the government of a country: *state secrets* (= information that could be harmful to a country if it were discovered by an enemy) **3** connected with the leader of a country attending an official ceremony: *The president is on a state visit to Moscow.*

● *verb* **1** to formally write or say something, especially in a careful and clear way: ~ **sth** *He has already stated his intention to run for election.* ◆ *The facts are clearly stated in the report.* ◆ *There is no need to **state the obvious** (= to say something that everyone already knows).* ◆ ~ **how, what, etc.…** *State clearly which option you prefer.* ◆ ~ **that…** *He stated categorically that he knew nothing about the deal.* ◆ **it is stated that…** *It was stated that standards at the hospital were dropping.* ◆ **sth is stated to be/have sth** *The contract was stated to be invalid.* ⊃ thesaurus box at DECLARE **2** [usually passive] ~ **sth** to fix or announce the details of something, especially on a written document: *This is not one of their stated aims.* ◆ *You must arrive at the time stated.* ◆ *Do not exceed the stated dose* (= of medicine).

state·craft /ˈsteɪtkræft/ *noun* [U] skill in managing state and political affairs

the ˈState Deˌpartment *noun* the U.S. government department of foreign affairs

state·hood /ˈsteɪthʊd/ *noun* [U] **1** the condition of being one of the states within a country such as the U.S. or Mexico: *West Virginia was granted statehood in 1863.* **2** the fact of being an independent country and of having the rights and powers of a country

ˈstate house (also **state·house**) /ˈsteɪthaʊs/ *noun* [usually sing.] a building in which a state LEGISLATURE (= a group of people who make the laws) meets

state·less /ˈsteɪtləs/ *adj.* not officially a citizen of any country ▸ **state·less·ness** *noun* [U]

state·let /ˈsteɪtlət/ *noun* a small state, especially one that is formed when a larger state breaks up

ˈstate ˈline *noun* the line between two states in the U.S.: *the Nevada-California state line*

state·ly /ˈsteɪtli/ *adj.* **1** impressive in size, appearance, or manner SYN MAJESTIC: *an avenue of stately chestnut trees* ◆ *a tall, stately woman* **2** slow, formal, and elegant: *a stately dance* ◆ *The procession made its stately progress through the streets of the city.* ▸ **state·li·ness** *noun* [U]

state·ment 🎵 /ˈsteɪtmənt/ *noun*

1 [C] something that you say or write that gives information or an opinion: *Are the following statements true or false?* ◆ *Your*

statement is misleading. ◆ *Is that a statement or a question?* ◆ *The play makes a strong political statement.* ⊃ see also FASHION STATEMENT **2** [C] ~ **(on/about sth)** a formal or official account of facts or opinions SYN DECLARATION: *a formal/ a public/a written/an official statement* ◆ *A government spokesperson made a statement to the press.* ◆ *The president is expected to issue a statement on the policy change this afternoon.* ◆ *The police asked me to make a statement* (= a written account of facts concerning a crime, used in court if legal action follows). **3** [C] a printed record of money paid, received, etc.: *The directors are responsible for preparing the company's financial statements.* ◆ *My bank sends me monthly statements.* ⊃ see also BANK STATEMENT **4** [U] (*formal*) the act of stating or expressing something in words SYN EXPRESSION: *When writing instructions, clarity of statement is the most important thing.*

IDM **make a statement** to express or reveal an opinion or characteristic in a very clear way, although often without words: *The housekeeping staff extended their strike mainly to make a statement about how determined they were.* ◆ *The way you dress makes a statement about you.*

ˌstate of ˈsiege *noun* a situation in which the government limits people's freedom to enter or leave a city, town, or building

ˌstate-of-the-ˈart *adj.* using the most modern or advanced techniques or methods; as good as it can be at the present time: *All the equipment here is state-of-the-art.* ◆ *a state-of-the-art system*

the ˌState of the ˈUnion Adˌdress *noun* [sing.] a speech about the achievements and plans of the government that the U.S. president gives to Congress once a year

ˈstate·room /ˈsteɪtrum; -rʊm/ *noun* a private room on a large ship

ˌstate's atˈtorney *noun* (*US*) a lawyer who represents a state in a court

ˌstate ˈschool *noun* = STATE UNIVERSITY

ˌstate's ˈevidence *noun* [U] (*law*) if a criminal **turns state's evidence**, he or she gives evidence against the people who committed a crime with him or her, in order to get a less severe punishment ⊃ compare PLEA BARGAINING

state·side /ˈsteɪtsaɪd/ *adj., adv.* (*informal*) connected with the U.S.; in or toward the U.S. (used when the person speaking is not in the U.S.): *When are you planning your next trip stateside?*

states·man /ˈsteɪtsmən/ *noun* (*pl.* **states·men** /-mən/) a wise, experienced, and respected political leader: *the party's elder statesman*

states·man·like /ˈsteɪtsmənˌlaɪk/ *adj.* having or showing the qualities and abilities of a statesman: *He was commended for his statesmanlike handling of the crisis.*

states·man·ship /ˈsteɪtsmənˌʃɪp/ *noun* [U] skill in managing state affairs

states·per·son /ˈsteɪtsˌpɜrsn/ *noun* (*pl.* **states·peo·ple**) a wise, experienced, and respected political leader

ˌstates' ˈrights *noun* [pl.] the rights of each U.S. state in relation to the national government, such as the right to make some laws and to have its own police force

ˌstate ˈtrooper (also **troop·er**) *noun* a member of the police force in any one of the U.S. states

ˌstate uniˈversity (also **ˌstate ˈschool**) *noun* a university that is managed by a state of the U.S.

state·wide /ˌsteɪtˈwaɪd/ *adj., adv.* happening or existing in all parts of a state of the U.S.: *a statewide election* ◆ *She won 10% of the vote statewide.*

stat·ic /ˈstætɪk/ *adj., noun*

● *adj.* **1** not moving, changing, or developing: *Prices on the stock market, which have been static, are now rising again.* ◆ *a static population level* **2** (*physics*) (of a force) acting as a weight but not producing movement: *static pressure* ANT DYNAMIC

stationery

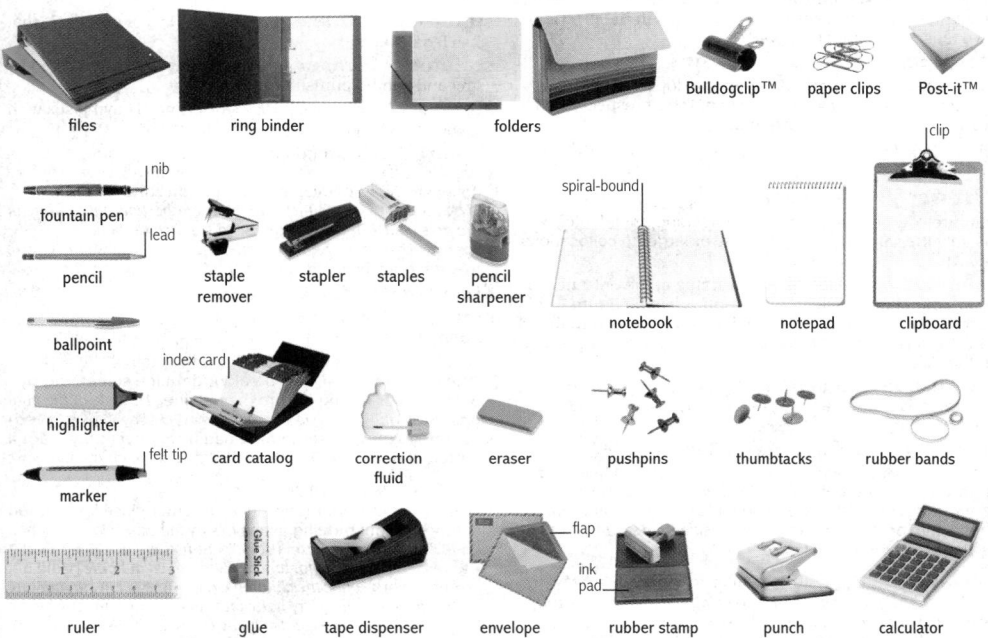

files

ring binder

folders

Bulldogclip™

paper clips

Post-it™

fountain pen — nib

pencil — lead

staple remover

stapler

staples

pencil sharpener

spiral-bound — notebook

notepad

clip — clipboard

ballpoint

index card — card catalog

highlighter

felt tip

marker

correction fluid

eraser

pushpins

thumbtacks

rubber bands

ruler

glue

tape dispenser

flap — envelope — ink pad

rubber stamp

punch

calculator

● **noun** [U] **1** noise or other effects that disturb radio or television signals and are caused by particular conditions in the atmosphere **2** (also ˌstatic elecˈtricity) electricity that gathers on or in an object that is not a CONDUCTOR of electricity: *My hair gets full of static when I brush it.* **3 statics** the science that deals with the forces that balance each other to keep objects in a state of rest ⊃ compare DYNAMIC **4** (*informal*) angry or critical comments or behavior

stat·in /ˈstætn/ *noun* a drug that people take to lower the level of CHOLESTEROL (= a substance in the body that can cause heart disease) in their blood. There are several types of statins.

sta·tion 🔑 /ˈsteɪʃn/ *noun, verb*

● **noun**

▷ FOR BUSES/TRAINS **1** a place where buses or trains stop so that passengers can get on and off; the buildings connected with this: *a train/bus station ◆ a subway station ◆ I get off at the next station. ◆ Penn Station ◆ the main station*

▷ FOR WORK/SERVICE **2** (usually in compounds) a place or building where a service is organized and provided or a special type of work is done: *a police station ◆ a gas station ◆ a fire station ◆ an agricultural research station ◆ a pollution monitoring station* ⊃ see also SPACE STATION

▷ RADIO/TV COMPANY **3** (often in compounds) a radio or television company and the programs it broadcasts: *a local radio/TV station ◆ He tuned to another station.*

▷ POSITION **4** a place where someone has to wait and watch or be ready to do work if needed: *You are not to leave your station without permission.* ⊃ see also DOCKING STATION

▷ FOR ARMY/NAVY **5** a small base for the army or navy; the people living in it: *a naval station*

● **verb**

▷ ARMED FORCES **1** [often passive] ~ sb + adv./prep. to send someone, especially from one of the armed forces, to work in a place for a period of time: *troops stationed abroad*

▷ GO TO POSITION **2** ~ sb/yourself + adv./prep. (*formal*) to go somewhere and stand or sit there, especially to wait for sth; to send someone somewhere to do this: *She stationed herself at the window to await his return.*

sta·tion·ar·y /ˈsteɪʃəˌneri/ *adj.* **1** not moving; not intended to be moved: *I remained stationary. ◆ The car collided with a stationary vehicle. ◆ a stationary exercise bike* ANT MOBILE **2** not changing in condition or quantity SYN STATIC: *a stationary population*

sta·tion·er·y /ˈsteɪʃəˌneri/ *noun* [U] **1** special paper for writing letters on, usually with matching envelopes **2** materials for writing and for using in an office, for example paper, pens, and envelopes

ˈstation ˌhouse *noun* = POLICE STATION

sta·tion·mas·ter /ˈsteɪʃnˌmæstər/ *noun* a person in charge of a train station

ˈstation ˌwagon *noun* a car with a lot of space behind the back seats and a door at the back for loading large items ⊃ picture at CAR

stat·ism /ˈsteɪtɪzəm/ *noun* [U] a political system in which the central government controls social and economic affairs ▶ **stat·ist** /ˈsteɪtɪst/ *adj., noun*

sta·tis·tic AWL /stəˈtɪstɪk/ *noun* **1 statistics** (also *informal* **stats**) [pl.] a collection of information shown in numbers: *crime/unemployment, etc. statistics ◆ According to official statistics the outbreak killed more than 500 people. ◆ Statistics show that far more people are able to ride a bicycle than can drive a car. ◆ These statistics are misleading.* ⊃ see also VITAL STATISTICS **2 statistics** (also *informal* **stats**) [U] the science of collecting and analyzing statistics: *There is a compulsory course in statistics.* **3** (also *informal* **stat**) [C] a piece of information shown in numbers: *An important statistic is that 94 percent of crime relates to property. ◆ I felt I was no longer being treated as a person but as a statistic.* ▶ **sta·tis·ti·cal** AWL /stəˈtɪstɪkl/ *adj.: statistical analysis* **sta·tis·ti·cal·ly** AWL /-kli/ *adv.: The difference between the two samples was not statistically significant.*

stat·is·ti·cian AWL /ˌstætəˈstɪʃn/ *noun* a person who studies or works with statistics

sta·tive /ˈsteɪtɪv/ *adj.* (*linguistics*) (of verbs) describing a state rather than an action. **Stative** verbs (for example *be, seem, understand, like, own*) are not usually used in the progressive tenses. ⊃ compare DYNAMIC

stats /stæts/ *noun* (*informal*) = STATISTICS

stat sheet *noun* a piece of paper or a document that gives details of something in the form of numbers, especially of a team's or a player's performance

stat·u·ar·y /ˈstætʃuˌeri/ *noun* [U] (*formal*) statues: *a collection of marble statuary*

stat·ue 🔑 /ˈstætʃu/ *noun*
a figure of a person or an animal in stone, metal, etc., usually the same size as in real life or larger ⊃ collocations at ART

the ˌStatue of ˈLiberty *noun* a statue at the entrance to New York Harbor, which represents a female figure carrying a book of laws in one hand and a TORCH in the other and is a symbol of welcome to people coming to live in the U.S.

stat·u·esque /ˌstætʃuˈɛsk/ *adj.* (*formal*) (usually of a woman) tall and beautiful in an impressive way; like a statue **SYN** IMPOSING

stat·u·ette /ˌstætʃuˈɛt/ *noun* a small statue

stat·ure /ˈstætʃər/ *noun* [U] (*formal*) **1** a person's height: *a woman of short stature* ◆ *He is small in stature.* **2** the importance and respect that a person has because of their ability and achievements: *an actress of considerable stature* ◆ *The orchestra has grown in stature.*

sta·tus 🔑 **AWL** /ˈstætəs; ˈsteɪ-/ *noun*
1 [U, C] the legal position of a person, group, or country: *They were granted refugee status.* ◆ *The party was denied legal status.* **2** [U, C, usually sing.] the social or professional position of someone or something in relation to others: *low status jobs* ◆ *to have a high social status* ◆ *Women are only asking to be given equal status with men.* ◆ *She achieved celebrity status overnight.* **3** [U] a high social position: *The job brings with it status and a high income.* **4** [U, C, usually sing.] the level of importance that is given to something: *the high status accorded to science in our culture* **5** [U] the situation at a particular time during a process: *What is the current status of our application for funds?*

status ˌbar *noun* (*computing*) an area that you see along the bottom of the computer screen or window that gives you information about the program that you are using or the document that you are working on

sta·tus quo /ˌstætəs ˈkwoʊ; ˌsteɪtəs-/ *noun* [sing.] (from *Latin*) the situation as it is now, or as it was before a recent change: *to defend/restore the status quo* ◆ *conservatives who want to maintain the status quo*

status ˌsymbol *noun* a possession that people think shows their wealth or high social status: *Exotic pets are the latest status symbol.*

stat·ute /ˈstætʃut/ *noun* **1** a law that is passed by a government and formally written down: *Penalties are laid down in the statute.* ◆ *Corporal punishment was banned by statute in 1987.* **2** a formal rule of an organization or institution: *Under the statutes of the university they had no power to dismiss him.*

statute ˌbook *noun* a collection of all the laws made by a government: *It's not yet on the statute book* (= it has not yet become law).

statute ˌlaw *noun* [U] all the written laws of a government, taken as a group ⊃ compare CASE LAW, COMMON LAW

ˌstatute of limiˈtations *noun* (*law*) the legal limit on the period of time within which action can be taken on a crime or other legal question

stat·u·to·ry /ˈstætʃəˌtɔri/ *adj.* [usually before noun] fixed by law; that must be done by law: *The authority failed to carry out its statutory duties.* ◆ *When you buy foods you have certain statutory rights.* ▶ **stat·u·to·ri·ly** /ˌstætʃəˈtɔrəli/ *adv.*

ˌstatutory ˈholiday *noun* (*CanE*) a public holiday that is fixed by law

ˌstatutory ˈinstrument *noun* (*law*) a law or other rule that has legal status

ˌstatutory ofˈfense *noun* (*law*) a crime that is described by law and can be punished by a court

ˌstatutory ˈrape *noun* [U] (*law*) the crime of having sex with someone who is not legally old enough

staunch /stɔntʃ; stɑntʃ/ *adj., verb*
● *adj.* (*superlative* **staunch·est**, no *comparative*) [usually before noun] strong and loyal in your opinions and attitude **SYN** FAITHFUL: *a staunch supporter of abortion rights* ◆ *one of the president's staunchest allies* ◆ *a staunch Catholic* ▶ **staunch·ly** *adv.*: *She staunchly defended the new policy.* ◆ *He was staunchly opposed to the war.* **staunch·ness** *noun* [U]
● *verb* (*formal*) = STANCH

stave /steɪv/ *noun, verb*
● *noun* **1** a strong stick or pole **2** = STAFF *n.* (5)
● *verb* (**staved, staved** or **stove, stove** /stoʊv/)
PHR V **ˌstave sth↔ˈin** to break or damage something by pushing it or hitting it from the outside: *The side of the boat was staved in when it hit the rocks.* **ˌstave sth↔ˈoff** (**staved, staved**) to prevent something bad from affecting you for a period of time; to delay something: *to stave off hunger*

stay 🔑 /steɪ/ *verb, noun*
● *verb* **1** [I] to continue to be in a particular place for a period of time without moving away: *to stay in bed* ◆ *"Do you want a drink?" "No, thanks, I can't stay."* ◆ *Stay there and don't move!* ◆ *We ended up staying for lunch.* ◆ *She stayed at home* (= did not go out to work) *while the children were young.* ◆ *I'm staying late at the office tonight.* ◆ *My hat won't stay on!* ◆ *Can you stay behind after they leave and help me clean up?* ◆ *We stayed to see what would happen.* ◆ **~ doing sth** *They stayed talking until well into the night.* **HELP** In spoken English **stay** can be used with **and** plus another verb, instead of with **to** and the infinitive, to show purpose or to tell somebody what to do: *I'll stay and help you.* ◆ *Can you stay and keep an eye on the baby?* **2** [I] to continue to be in a particular state or situation **SYN** REMAIN: **+ adj.** *He never stays angry for long.* ◆ *I can't stay awake any longer.* ◆ *The store stays open late on Thursdays.* ◆ **+ adv./prep.** *I don't know why they stay together* (= remain married or in a relationship). ◆ *Inflation stayed below 4% last month.* ◆ **+ noun** *We promised to stay friends forever.* **3** [I] to live in a place temporarily as a guest or visitor: *We found out we were staying in the same hotel.* ◆ *My sister's coming to stay next week.* ◆ *He's staying with friends this weekend.* ◆ *I stayed three nights at my cousin's house.*
IDM **be here to stay | have come to stay** to be accepted or used by most people and therefore a permanent part of our lives: *It looks like televised trials are here to stay.* **stay!** used to tell a dog not to move **stay the course** to continue doing something until it has finished or been completed, even though it is difficult: *Very few of the trainees have stayed the course.* **stay your hand** (*old-fashioned* or *literary*) to stop yourself from doing something; to prevent you from doing something **stay the night** to sleep at someone's house for one night: *You can always stay the night at our house.* **stay put** (*informal*) if someone or something **stays put**, they continue to be in the place where they are or where they have been put ⊃ more at ABREAST, CLEAR, LOOSE
PHR V **ˌstay aˈround** (*informal*) to not leave somewhere: *I'll stay around in case you need me.* **ˌstay aˈway (from sb/sth)** to not go near a particular person or place: *I want you to stay away from my daughter.* **ˌstay ˈin** to not go out or to remain indoors: *I feel like staying in tonight.* **ˌstay ˈon** to continue studying, working, etc. somewhere for longer than expected or after other people have left **ˌstay ˈout** to continue to be outdoors or away from your house at night **ˌstay ˈout of sth** **1** to not become involved in something that does not concern you **2** to avoid something: *to stay out of trouble* **ˌstay ˈover** to sleep at someone's house for one night **ˌstay ˈup** to go to bed later than usual: *You've got school tomorrow. I don't want you staying up late.*

---

h **hat** m **man** n **no** ŋ **sing** l **leg** r **red** y **yes** w **wet**

• **noun 1** a period of staying; a visit: *I enjoyed my stay in Puerto Rico.* • *an overnight stay* **2** a rope or wire that supports a ship's MAST, a pole, etc. ⊃ see also MAINSTAY
IDM **a stay of execution** (*law*) a legal order to delay the EXECUTION of a criminal: *to grant a stay of execution*

stay-at-home *adj.* a **stay-at-home** mother or father is one who stays at home to take care of their children instead of going out to work

stay·ca·tion /ˌsteɪˈkeɪʃn/ *noun* [U, C] a vacation that you spend at or near your home

staying power *noun* [U] the ability to continue doing something difficult or tiring until it is finished **SYN** STAMINA

St. Ber·nard /ˌseɪnt bərˈnɑrd/ *noun* a large strong dog, originally from Switzerland, where it was trained to help find people who were lost in the snow

STD /ˌɛs ti ˈdi/ *noun* the abbreviation for "sexually transmitted disease" (a disease that is passed from one person to another during sexual activity)

stead /stɛd/ *noun*
IDM **in sb's/sth's stead** (*formal*) instead of someone or something: *Coach Fox was fired and his assistant, John Smith, was appointed in his stead.* **stand sb in good stead** to be useful or helpful to someone when needed: *Your languages will stand you in good stead when it comes to finding a job.*

stead·fast /ˈstɛdfæst/ *adj.* (*literary, approving*) not changing in your attitudes or aims **SYN** FIRM: *steadfast loyalty* • *~ in sth He remained steadfast in his determination to bring the killers to justice.* ▶ **stead·fast·ly** *adv.* **stead·fast·ness** *noun* [U]

stead·y /ˈstɛdi/ *adj., verb, adv., exclamation*
• *adj.* (stead·i·er, stead·i·est) **1** developing, growing, etc. gradually and in an even and regular way **SYN** CONSTANT: *five years of steady economic growth* • *We are making slow but steady progress.* • *The gardens receive a steady stream of visitors.* **2** not changing and not interrupted **SYN** REGULAR: *His breathing was steady.* • *a steady job/income* • *She drove at a steady 50 mph.* • *They set off at a steady pace.* • *a steady boyfriend/girlfriend* (= with whom you have a serious relationship or one that has lasted a long time) • *to have a steady relationship* **3** firmly fixed, supported, or balanced; not shaking or likely to fall down: *He held the boat steady as she got in.* • *I met his steady gaze.* • *Such fine work requires a good eye and a steady hand.* **ANT** UNSTEADY **4** (of a person) sensible; who can be relied on ▶ **stead·i·ly** /ˈstɛdl·i/ *adv.*: *The company's exports have been increasing steadily.* • *The situation got steadily worse.* • *He looked at her steadily and intensely, but she didn't seem to notice.* • *The rain fell steadily.* **stead·i·ness** /ˈstɛdinəs/ *noun* [U]
IDM **(as) steady as a rock** extremely steady and calm; that you can rely on

• *verb* (stead·ies, stead·y·ing, stead·ied, stead·ied) **1** [T, I] *~ (yourself/sb/sth)* to stop yourself/someone or something from moving, shaking, or falling; to stop moving, shaking, or falling: *She steadied herself against the wall.* • *The elevator rocked slightly, steadied, and the doors opened.* **2** [I] to stop changing and become regular again: *Her heartbeat steadied.* • *~ against sth The dollar steadied against other major currencies.* **3** [T] *~ sb/sth* to make someone or something calm: *He took a few deep breaths to steady his nerves.*

• *adv.* in a way that is steady and does not change or shake: *In trading today the dollar held steady against the yen.*
IDM **go steady (with sb)** (*old-fashioned, informal*) to have a romantic or sexual relationship with someone, in which you see the other person regularly

• *exclamation* (*informal*) used to tell someone to be careful: *Steady! Don't fall off.*

steak /steɪk/ *noun* **1** (also less frequent **beef·steak**) [U, C] a thick slice of good quality beef: *fillet/sirloin steak* • *How would you like your steak done?* • *a steak knife* (= one with a special blade for cutting steak with) ⊃ see also CHICKEN-

FRIED STEAK 2 [U, C] a large thick piece of any type of fish or meat: *a swordfish steak*

steak·house /ˈsteɪkhaʊs/ *noun* a restaurant that serves mainly steak

steak tar·tare /ˌsteɪk tɑrˈtɑr/ *noun* [U, C] (from *French*) a dish made with raw chopped beef and raw eggs

steal /stil/ *verb, noun*
• *verb* (stole /stoʊl/, sto·len /ˈstoʊlən/) **1** [I, T] to take something from a person, store, etc. without permission and without intending to return it or pay for it: *~ (from sb/sth) We found out he was stealing from us for years.* • *~ sth (from sb/sth) My wallet was stolen.* • *I had my wallet stolen.* • *Thieves stole jewelry worth over $10,000.* • *It's a crime to handle stolen goods.* • (*figurative*) *to steal someone's ideas* ⊃ collocations at CRIME **2** [I] + *adv./prep.* to move secretly and quietly so that other people do not notice you **SYN** CREEP: *She stole out of the room so as not to wake the baby.* • (*figurative*) *A chill stole over her body.* **3** [T] *~ sth* (in baseball) to run to the next BASE before another player from your team hits the ball, so that you are closer to scoring: *He tried to steal second base but was out.*
IDM **steal a glance/look (at sb/sth)** to look at someone or something quickly so that no one sees you doing it **steal sb's heart** (*literary*) to make someone fall in love with you **steal a kiss (from sb)** (*literary*) to kiss someone suddenly or secretly **steal the show** [no passive] to attract more attention and praise than other people in a particular situation: *As always, the children stole the show.* **steal sb's thunder** to get the attention, success, etc. that someone else was expecting, usually by saying or doing what they had intended to say or do

• *noun* (in baseball) the act of running to another BASE while the PITCHER is throwing the ball
IDM **be a steal** to be for sale at an unexpectedly low price: *This suit is a steal at $80.*

stealth /stɛlθ/ *noun, adj.*
• *noun* [U] the fact of doing something in a quiet or secret way: *The administration was accused of trying to introduce the tax by stealth.* • *Lions rely on stealth when hunting.*
• *adj.* [only before noun] (of an aircraft) designed in a way that makes it difficult to be discovered by RADAR: *a stealth bomber*

stealth·y /ˈstɛlθi/ *adj.* doing things quietly or secretly; done quietly or secretly: *a stealthy animal* • *a stealthy movement* ▶ **stealth·i·ly** /-θəli/ *adv.*

steam /stim/ *noun, verb*
• *noun* [U] **1** the hot gas that water changes into when it boils: *Steam rose from the boiling kettle.* **2** the power that is produced from steam under pressure, used to operate engines, machines, etc.: *the introduction of steam in the 18th century* • *steam power* • *the steam age* • *a steam train/engine* **3** very small drops of water that form in the air or on cold surfaces when warm air suddenly cools **SYN** CONDENSATION: *She wiped the steam from her glasses.*
IDM **full speed/steam ahead** with as much speed or energy as possible **let/blow off (some) steam** (*informal*) to get rid of your energy, anger, or strong emotions by doing something active or noisy **run out of steam** (*informal*) to lose energy and enthusiasm and stop doing something, or do it less well **get, etc. somewhere under your own steam** (*informal*) to go somewhere without help from other people ⊃ more at PICK

• *verb* **1** [I] to send out steam: *a mug of steaming hot coffee* **2** [T, I] *~ (sth)* to place food over boiling water so that it cooks in the steam; to be cooked in this way: *steamed vegetables* ⊃ picture at COOKING ⊃ collocations at COOKING **3** [I] + *adv./prep.* (of a boat, ship, etc.) to move using the power produced by steam: *The boat steamed across the lake.* **4** [I] + *adv./prep.* (especially of a person) to go somewhere very quickly: *He spotted her steaming down the corridor toward him.* • (*figurative*) *The company is steaming ahead with its investment program.*

---

i **see**   ɪ **sit**   ɛ **ten**   æ **cat**   ɑ **hot**   ɔ **saw**   ʊ **put**   u **too**

IDM **be/get (all) steamed up (about/over sth)** (also **be steamed (about sth)**) (*informal*) to be/become very angry or excited about something

PHR V ,steam sth↔'open to open an envelope using steam to make the glue softer ,steam 'up | ,steam sth↔'up to become, or to make something become, covered with steam: *As he walked in, his glasses steamed up.*

steam·boat /'stimboʊt/ *noun* a boat driven by steam, used especially in the past on rivers and along coasts

steam·er /'stimər/ *noun* **1** a boat or ship driven by steam ⊃ see also PADDLE WHEELER **2** a metal container with small holes in it, that is placed over a pan of boiling water in order to cook food in the steam ⊃ picture at COOKING

steam·ing /'stimɪŋ/ *adj.* **1** (also ,steaming 'hot) very hot **2** (*informal*) very angry

steam·roll *verb* [T, I] ~ (sb/sth) (+ adv./prep.) to defeat someone or force them to do something, using your power or authority: *The team steamrolled their way to victory.* ♦ *She knew she let herself be steamrolled.*

steam·roll·er /'stim,roʊlər/ *noun, verb*
- *noun* a large slow vehicle with a ROLLER, used for making roads flat
- *verb* [T, I] = STEAMROLL

steam·ship /'stimʃɪp/ *noun* (*abbr.* SS) a ship driven by steam

'steam ,shovel *noun* a large machine for digging, that was originally powered by steam

steam·y /'stimi/ *adj.* (steam·i·er, steam·i·est) full of steam; covered with steam: *a steamy bathroom* ♦ *steamy windows* ♦ *the steamy heat of Houston*

steed /stid/ *noun* (*literary* or *humorous*) a horse to ride on

steel ✎ /stil/ *noun, verb*
- *noun* **1** [U] a strong, hard metal that is made of a mixture of iron and CARBON: *the iron and steel industry* ♦ *The frame is made of steel.* ♦ *The bridge is reinforced with huge steel girders.* ⊃ see also STAINLESS STEEL **2** [U] the industry that produces steel: *Steel used to be the most important industry in Pittsburgh.* ♦ *steel workers* ♦ *a steel town* **3** [C] a long, thin, straight piece of steel with a rough surface, used for rubbing knives on to make them sharp **4** [U] (*old use* or *literary*) weapons that are used for fighting: *the clash of steel* **IDM** **of steel** having a quality like steel, especially a strong, cold, or hard quality: *She felt a hand of steel* (= a strong, firm hand) *on her arm.* ♦ *You need a cool head and nerves of steel* (= great courage). ♦ *There was a hint of steel in his voice* (= he sounded cold and firm).
- *verb* to prepare yourself to deal with something unpleasant: ~ yourself (for/against sth) *As she waited, she steeled herself for disappointment.* ♦ ~ yourself to do sth *He steeled himself to tell them the truth.*

,steel 'band *noun* a group of musicians who play music on drums that are made from empty metal oil containers. Steel bands originally came from the West Indies.

,steel 'drum (also ,steel 'pan) *noun* a musical instrument used in West Indian music, made from a metal oil container that is hit in different places with two sticks to produce different notes ⊃ picture at INSTRUMENT

,steel 'wool *noun* [U] a mass of fine steel threads that you use for cleaning pots and pans, making surfaces smooth, etc.

steel·work·er /'stil,wərkər/ *noun* a person who works in a place where steel is made

steel·works /'stilwərks/ *noun* (*pl.* steel·works) a factory where steel is made

steel·y /'stili/ *adj.* **1** (of a person's character or behavior) strong, hard, and unfriendly: *a cold, steely voice* ♦ *a look of steely determination* **2** like steel in color: *steely blue eyes*
▶ **steel·i·ness** *noun* [U]

steep ✎ /stip/ *adj., verb*
- *adj.* (steep·er, steep·est) **1** (of a slope, hill, etc.) rising or falling gradually, not gradually: *a steep hill/slope/bank* ♦ *a steep climb/descent/drop* ♦ *a steep flight of stairs* ♦ *The path grew steeper as we climbed higher.* **2** [usually before noun] (of a rise or fall in an amount) sudden and very big **SYN** SHARP: *a steep decline in the birth rate* ♦ *a steep increase in unemployment* **3** (*informal*) (of a price or demand) too much; unreasonable **SYN** EXPENSIVE: *$5 for a cup of coffee seems a little steep to me.* ▶ **steep·ly** *adv.*: *a steeply sloping roof* ♦ *The path climbed steeply upward.* ♦ *Prices rose steeply.* **steep·ness** *noun* [U]
- *verb* **IDM** **be steeped in sth** (*formal*) to have a lot of a particular quality: *a city steeped in history* **PHR V** 'steep sth in sth to put food in a liquid and leave it for some time so that it becomes soft and flavored by the liquid 'steep yourself in sth (*formal*) to spend a lot of time thinking or learning about something: *They spent a month steeping themselves in Chinese culture.*

steep·en /'stipən/ *verb* [I, T] ~ (sth) to become or to make something become steeper: *After a mile, the slope steepened.*

stee·ple /'stipl/ *noun* a tall pointed tower on the roof of a church, often with a SPIRE on it

stee·ple·chase /'stipl,tʃeɪs/ *noun* **1** a long race in which horses have to jump over fences, water, etc. **2** a long race in which people run and jump over gates and water, etc. around a track

stee·ple·chas·er /'stipl,tʃeɪsər/ *noun* a horse or a person that takes part in steeplechases

stee·ple·jack /'stipl,dʒæk/ *noun* a person whose job is painting or repairing towers, tall CHIMNEYS, etc.

steer ✎ /stɪr/ *verb, noun*
- *verb* **1** [T, I] ~ (sth /sb) (+ adv./prep.) to control the direction in which a boat, car, etc. moves: *He steered the boat into the harbor.* ♦ (*figurative*) *He took her arm and steered her toward the door.* ♦ *You row and I'll steer.* **2** [T, I] ~ (sth) (+ adv./prep.) (of a boat, car, etc.) to move in a particular direction: *The ship steered a course between the islands.* ♦ *The ship steered into port.* **3** [T] ~ sth + adv./prep. to take control of a situation and influence the way in which it develops: *He managed to steer the conversation away from his divorce.* ♦ *She steered the team to victory.* ♦ *The skill is in steering a middle course between the two extremes.* **IDM** see CLEAR
- *noun* [C] a BULL (= a male cow) that has been CASTRATED (= had part of its sex organs removed), kept for its meat ⊃ compare BULLOCK, OX

steer·age /'stɪrdʒ/ *noun* [U] (in the past) the part of a ship where passengers with the cheapest tickets used to travel

steer·ing /'stɪrɪŋ/ *noun* [U] the machinery in a vehicle that you use to control the direction it goes in ⊃ see also POWER STEERING

'steering ,column *noun* the part of a car or other vehicle that the STEERING WHEEL is fitted on

'steering com,mittee *noun* a group of people that a government or an organization chooses to direct an activity and to decide how it will be done

'steering ,wheel *noun* the wheel that the driver turns to control the direction that a vehicle goes in ⊃ picture at CAR

steg·o·saur /'stɛgə,sɔr/ (also steg·o·sau·rus /,stɛgə'sɔrəs/) *noun* a DINOSAUR with a small head, four legs, and two rows of SPIKES along its back

stein /staɪn/ *noun* (from German) a large decorated cup for drinking beer, usually made of EARTHENWARE and often with a lid

stel·lar /'stɛlər/ *adj.* [usually before noun] **1** (*technical*) connected with the stars ⊃ compare INTERSTELLAR **2** (*informal*) excellent: *a stellar performance*

stem /stɛm/ *noun, verb*
- *noun* **1** the main, long, thin part of a plant above the ground from which the leaves or flowers grow; a smaller

ʌ **cup**   ə **about**   eɪ **say**   aɪ **five**   ɔɪ **boy**   aʊ **now**   oʊ **go**   ər **bird**

part that grows from this and supports flowers or leaves ➲ picture at FRUIT, PLANT **2** the long thin part of a wine glass between the bowl and the base ➲ picture at CUP **3** the thin tube of a TOBACCO pipe **4 -stemmed** (in adjectives) having one or more stems of the type mentioned: *a long-stemmed rose* **5** (*grammar*) the main part of a word that stays the same when endings are added to it: *"Writ" is the stem of the forms "writes," "writing" and "written."* **IDM** from stem to stern all the way from the front of a ship to the back

● **verb** (-mm-) **~ sth** to stop something that is flowing from spreading or increasing: *The cut was bandaged to stem the bleeding.* ◆ *They discussed ways of* **stemming the flow of** *smuggled drugs.* ◆ *The former administration had failed to* **stem the tide** *of factory closures.*
PHR V 'stem from sth (not used in the progressive tenses) to be the result of something ➲ language bank at BECAUSE

'stem cell *noun* a basic type of cell that can divide and develop into cells with particular functions. All the different kinds of cells in the human body develop from stem cells.

stem·ware /'stɛmwɛr/ *noun* [U] (*technical*) glasses and glass bowls that have a STEM

stench /stɛntʃ/ *noun* [sing.] a strong, very unpleasant smell **SYN** REEK: *an overpowering stench of rotting fish* ◆ (*figurative*) *The stench of treachery hung in the air.*

sten·cil /'stɛnsl/ *noun, verb*
● *noun* a thin piece of metal, plastic, or card with a design cut out of it, that you put onto a surface and paint over so that the design is left on the surface; the pattern or design that is produced in this way
● *verb* [T, I] **~ (sth)** to make letters or a design on something using a stencil

sten·o /'stɛnoʊ/ *noun* (*pl.* sten·os) (*informal*) **1** [C] = STENOGRAPHER **2** [U] = STENOGRAPHY

ste·nog·ra·pher /stə'nɑɡrəfər/ *noun* a person whose job is to write down what someone else says, using a quick system of signs or abbreviations

ste·nog·ra·phy /stə'nɑɡrəfi/ *noun* [U] = SHORTHAND

stent /stɛnt/ *noun* (*medical*) a small support that is put inside a BLOOD VESSEL (= tube in the body), for example in order to stop something from blocking it

sten·to·ri·an /stɛn'tɔriən/ *adj.* (*formal*) (of a voice) loud and powerful

step 🔧 /stɛp/ *noun, verb*
● *noun*
▷ MOVEMENT/SOUND **1** [C] the act of lifting your foot and putting it down in order to walk or move somewhere; the sound this makes: *a baby's first steps* ◆ *He took a step toward the door.* ◆ *We heard steps outside.* ➲ see also FOOTSTEP, GOOSE STEP
▷ WAY OF WALKING **2** [C, usually sing.] the way that someone walks: *He walked with a quick light step.*
▷ DISTANCE **3** [C] the distance that you cover when you take a step: *It's only a few steps further.* ◆ *He turned around and* **retraced his steps** (= went back the way he had come). ◆ *She moved a step closer to me.* ◆ *The hotel is only a few steps from the beach.*
▷ IN SERIES/PROCESS **4** [C] one of a series of things that you do in order to achieve something: *This was a first step toward merging the two unions.* ◆ *It's a* **big step** *giving up your job and moving halfway across the world.* ◆ *We are* **taking steps** *to prevent pollution.* ◆ *This won't solve the problem, but it's* **a step in the right direction.** ◆ *The new drug is a major* **step forward** *in the treatment of the disease.* ➲ thesaurus box at ACTION **5** [C] one of a series of things that someone does or that happen, which forms part of a process **SYN** STAGE: *Having completed the first stage, you can move on to step 2.* ◆ *I'd like to take this idea a* **step further**. ◆ *This was a big* **step up** (= to a better position) *in his career.* ◆ *I'll explain it to you* **step by step.** ◆ *a step-by-step guide to building your own home*
▷ STAIR **6** [C] a surface that you put your foot on in order to walk to a higher or lower level, especially one of a series:

She was sitting on the bottom step of the staircase. ◆ *We walked down some stone steps to the beach.* ◆ *A short* **flight of steps** *led up to the door.* ➲ picture at HOUSE ➲ see also DOORSTEP
▷ IN DANCE **7** [C, usually pl.] a series of movements that you make with your feet, that form a dance ➲ see also QUICK-STEP
▷ EXERCISE **8** [U] (often in compounds) a type of exercise that you do by stepping on and off a raised piece of equipment: *step aerobics* ◆ *a step class*
▷ IN MUSIC **9** [C] the interval between two notes that are next to each other in a SCALE ➲ compare TONE
IDM break step to change the way you are walking so that you do not walk in the same rhythm as the people you are walking or marching with fall into step (beside/with sb) to change the way you are walking so that you start walking in the same rhythm as the person you are walking with: *He caught up with her and fell into step beside her.* in/out of step (with sb/sth) **1** putting your feet on the ground in the right/wrong way, according to the rhythm of the music or the people you are moving with **2** having ideas that are the same as or different from other people's: *She was out of step with her colleagues.* one step forward, two steps back (*saying*) used to say that every time you make progress, something bad happens that makes the situation worse than before a/one step ahead (of sb/sth) when you are **one step ahead** of someone or something, you manage to avoid them or to achieve something more quickly than they do a/one step at a time when you do something **one step at a time**, you do it slowly and gradually ➲ more at WATCH

● **verb** (-pp-) [I] **+ adv./prep.** to lift your foot and move it in a particular direction or put it on or in something; to move a short distance: *to step onto/off a bus* ◆ *I stepped forward when my name was called out.* ◆ *She stepped aside to let them pass.* ◆ *We stepped carefully over the broken glass.* ◆ *I turned around quickly and stepped on his toes.* ◆ (*figurative*) *Entering into this hotel is like stepping back in time.*
IDM step into the breach to do someone's job or work when they are suddenly or unexpectedly unable to do it step into sb's shoes to continue a job or the work that someone else has started step on it (*informal*) used especially in orders to tell someone to drive faster step on sb's toes (*informal*) to offend or annoy someone, especially by getting involved in something that is their responsibility step out of line | be/get out of line to behave badly or break the rules step up to the plate to do what is necessary in order to benefit from an opportunity or deal with a crisis: *It's important for world leaders to step up to the plate and honor their commitments on global warming.*
PHR V step a'side/'down to leave an important job or position and let someone else take your place ,step 'back (from sth) to think about a situation calmly, as if you are not involved in it yourself: *We are learning to step back from ourselves and identify our strengths and weaknesses.* ,step 'forward to offer to help someone or give information ,step 'in to help someone in a disagreement or difficult situation: *A local businessman stepped in with a large donation for the school.* ◆ *The team coach was forced to step in to stop the two athletes from coming to blows.* ,step 'out to go out: *I'm stepping out for a few minutes, so please hold my calls.* ,step 'up to come forward: *She stepped up to receive her prize.* ,step sth↔'up to increase the amount, speed, etc. of something: *He has stepped up his training to prepare for the race.*

step- /stɛp/ *combining form* (in nouns) related as a result of one parent marrying again: *stepmother*

step·broth·er /'stɛp,brʌðər/ *noun* the son from an earlier marriage of your STEPMOTHER or STEPFATHER ➲ compare HALF-BROTHER

step·child /'stɛptʃaɪld/ *noun* (*pl.* step·child·ren /-,tʃɪldrən/) a child of your husband or wife by an earlier marriage

step·daugh·ter /'stɛp,dɔtər/ *noun* a daughter that your husband or wife has from an earlier marriage to another person

step·fam·i·ly /'stɛp,fæmli; -,fæməli/ *noun* (*pl.* step·fam·i-lies) the family that is formed when someone marries a person who already has children

step·fa·ther /ˈstɛpˌfaðər/ *noun* the man who is married to your mother but who is not your real father

step·lad·der /ˈstɛpˌlædər/ *noun* a short LADDER that is made of two parts, one with steps, that are joined together at the top, so that it can stand on its own or be folded flat for carrying or storing ⊃ **picture at** TOOL

step·moth·er /ˈstɛpˌmʌðər/ *noun* the woman who is married to your father but who is not your real mother

step·parent /ˈstɛpˌpɛrənt/ *noun* a stepmother or stepfather

steppe /stɛp/ *noun* [C, usually pl., U] a large area of land with grass but few trees, especially in S.E. Europe and Siberia: *the vast Russian steppes*

stepping stone *noun* **1** one of a line of flat stones that you step on in order to cross a stream or river **2** something that allows you to make progress or begin to achieve something: *a stepping stone to a more lucrative career*

step·sis·ter /ˈstɛpˌsɪstər/ *noun* the daughter from an earlier marriage of your STEPMOTHER or STEPFATHER ⊃ **compare** HALF-SISTER

step·son /ˈstɛpsʌn/ *noun* a son that your husband or wife has from an earlier marriage to another person

step·wise /ˈstɛpwaɪz/ *adj.* **1** in a series of steps, rather than continuously **2** (*music*) (of a MELODY) moving in a way that uses only the notes that are next to each other in a SCALE

-ster /stər/ *suffix* (in nouns) a person who is connected with or has the quality of a particular thing: *gangster* ♦ *youngster*

ster·e·o /ˈstɛriˌoʊ/ *noun* (pl. **ster·e·os**) **1** (also **stereo system**) [C] a machine that plays CDs, etc., sometimes with a radio, that has two separate SPEAKERS so that you hear different sounds from each: *a car/personal stereo* ♦ *Let's put some music on the stereo.* **2** [U] the system for playing recorded music, speech, etc. in which the sound is directed through two channels: *to broadcast in stereo* ▶ **ster·e·o** (also *formal* **ster·e·o·phon·ic** /ˌstɛriəˈfanɪk/) *adj.* [only before noun]: *stereo sound* ⊃ **compare** QUADRAPHONIC

ster·e·o·scop·ic /ˌstɛriəˈskapɪk/ *adj.* **1** (*technical*) able to see objects with length, width, and depth, as humans do: *stereoscopic vision* **2** (of a picture, photograph, etc.) that is made so that you see the objects in it with length, width, and depth when you use a special machine **SYN** THREE-D

ster·e·o·type /ˈstɛriəˌtaɪp/ *noun, verb*
● *noun* a fixed idea or image that many people have of a particular type of person or thing, but which is often not true in reality: *cultural/gender/racial stereotypes* ♦ *He doesn't conform to the usual stereotype of the businessman with a dark suit and briefcase.* ▶ **ster·e·o·typ·i·cal** /ˌstɛriəˈtɪpɪkl/ *adj.*: *the stereotypical image of feminine behavior* **ster·e·o·typ·i·cally** /-kli/ *adv.*
● *verb* [often passive] to form a fixed idea about a person or thing that may not really be true: ~ *sb Children from certain backgrounds tend to be stereotyped by their teachers.* ♦ ~ *sb as sth Why are professors stereotyped as absentminded?* ▶ **ster·e·o·typed** *adj.*: *a play full of stereotyped characters* **ster·e·o·typ·ing** *noun* [U]: *sexual stereotyping*

ster·ile /ˈstɛrəl/ *adj.* **1** (of humans or animals) not able to produce children or young animals **SYN** INFERTILE ⊃ **compare** FERTILE **2** completely clean and free from bacteria: *sterile bandages* ♦ *sterile water* **3** (of a discussion, an argument, etc.) not producing any useful result **SYN** FRUITLESS: *a sterile debate* **4** lacking individual personality, imagination, or new ideas: *The room felt cold and sterile.* ♦ *He felt creatively and emotionally sterile.* **5** (of land) not good enough to produce crops ▶ **ste·ril·i·ty** /stəˈrɪləti/ *noun* [U]: *The disease can cause sterility in men and women.* ♦ *the meaningless sterility of statistics* ♦ *She contemplated the sterility of her existence.*

ster·i·lize /ˈstɛrəˌlaɪz/ *verb* **1** [often passive] ~ *sth* to kill the bacteria in or on something: *to sterilize surgical instruments* ♦ *sterilized milk/water* **2** [usually passive] ~ *sb/sth* to make a person or an animal unable to have babies, especially by

removing or blocking their sex organs ▶ **ster·i·li·za·tion** /ˌstɛrələˈzeɪʃn/ *noun* [U, C]

ster·i·liz·er /ˈstɛrəˌlaɪzər/ *noun* a machine or piece of equipment that you use to make objects or substances completely clean and free from bacteria

ster·ling /ˈstərlɪŋ/ *noun, adj.*
● *noun* [U] the money system of Britain, based on the pound: *the value of sterling* ♦ *You can be paid in pounds sterling or American dollars.*
● *adj.* [usually before noun] (*formal*) of excellent quality: *He has done sterling work on the finance committee.*

sterling silver *noun* [U] silver of a particular standard of PURITY

stern /stərn/ *adj., noun*
● *adj.* (**stern·er, stern·est**) **1** serious and often disapproving; expecting someone to obey you **SYN** STRICT: *a stern face/expression/look* ♦ *a stern warning* ♦ *Her voice was stern.* ♦ *The police are planning sterner measures to combat crime.* **2** serious and difficult: *We face stern opposition.* ▶ **stern·ly** *adv.* **stern·ness** /ˈstərnnəs/ *noun* [U]
IDM **be made of sterner stuff** to have a stronger character and to be more determined in dealing with problems than other people
● *noun* the back end of a ship or boat ⊃ **picture at** BOAT ⊃ **compare** BOW¹, POOP **IDM** **see** STEM

ster·num /ˈstərnəm/ *noun* (pl. **ster·nums** or **ster·na** /-nə/) (*anatomy*) the BREASTBONE ⊃ **picture at** BODY

ste·roid /ˈstɛrɔɪd; ˈstɪr-/ *noun* a chemical substance produced naturally in the body. There are several different steroids and they can be used to treat various diseases and are also sometimes used illegally by people playing sports to improve their performance.

steth·o·scope /ˈstɛθəˌskoʊp/ *noun* an instrument that a doctor uses to listen to someone's heart and breathing

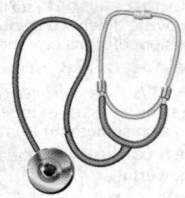

stethoscope

Stet·son™ /ˈstɛtsn/ *noun* a tall hat with a wide BRIM, worn especially by American COWBOYS

ste·ve·dore /ˈstivəˌdɔr/ *noun* a person whose job is moving goods on and off ships ⊃ **see also** DOCKER

stew /stu/ *noun, verb*
● *noun* [U, C] a dish of meat and vegetables cooked slowly in liquid in a container that has a lid: *beef stew and dumplings* ♦ *I'm making a stew for lunch.* ⊃ **picture at** COOKING
IDM **get (yourself)/be in a stew (about/over sth)** (*informal*) to become/feel very anxious or upset about something
● *verb* **1** [T, I] ~ (*sth*) to cook something slowly, or allow something to cook slowly, in liquid in a closed dish: *stewed apricots* ♦ *The meat needs to stew for two hours.* ⊃ **see also** STEWED **2** [I] **(+ adv./prep.)** to think or worry about something: *I've been stewing over the problem for a while.* ♦ *If you're feeling upset, try not to stew.*
IDM **let sb stew (in their own juice)** (*informal*) to leave someone to worry and suffer the unpleasant effects of their own actions

stew·ard /ˈstuərd/ *noun* **1** a man whose job is to take care of passengers on a ship, an aircraft, or a train and who brings them meals, etc. **2** a person employed to manage another person's property, especially a large house or land ⊃ **see also** SHOP STEWARD

stew·ard·ess /ˈstuərdəs/ *noun* **1** (*old-fashioned*) a female FLIGHT ATTENDANT **2** a woman whose job is to take care of the passengers on a ship or train

stew·ard·ship /ˈstuərdˌʃɪp/ *noun* [U] (*formal*) the act of taking care of or managing something, for example

t **tea**   ţ **butter**   d **did**   k **cat**   g **got**   tʃ **chin**   dʒ **June**   f **fall**

property, an organization, money, or valuable objects: *The organization certainly prospered under his stewardship.*

STI /ˌɛs tiː ˈaɪ/ *noun* the abbreviation for "sexually transmitted infection" (an infection that is passed from one person to another during sexual activity)

stick 🔧 /stɪk/ *noun, verb*

● *noun*

> **FROM TREE** **1** [C] a thin piece of wood that has fallen or been broken from a tree: *We collected dry sticks to start a fire.* ◆ *The boys were throwing sticks and stones at the dog.* ◆ *Her arms and legs were like sticks* (= very thin).

> **IN SPORTS** **2** [C] a long thin object that is used in some sports to hit or control the ball: *a hockey/lacrosse stick* ⊃ picture at SPORT

> **LONG THIN PIECE** **3** [C] (often in compounds) a long thin piece of something: *a stick of dynamite* ◆ *carrot sticks* ◆ *a stick of butter* ⊃ picture at PACKAGING **4** [C] (often in compounds) a thin piece of wood or plastic that you use for a particular purpose: *a candied apple on a stick* ⊃ see also CHOPSTICK, COCKTAIL STICK, DRUMSTICK, MATCHSTICK, WALKING STICK (1), YARDSTICK

> **OF GLUE, ETC.** **5** [C] a quantity of a substance, such as solid glue, that is sold in a small container with round ends and straight sides, and can be pushed further out of the container as it is used ⊃ see also LIPSTICK

> **IN PLANE/VEHICLE** **6** [C] (*informal*) the control stick of a plane ⊃ see also JOYSTICK **7** [C] (*informal*) a handle used to change the gears of a vehicle ⊃ see also GEARSHIFT, STICK SHIFT

> **FOR ORCHESTRA** **8** [C] a BATON, used by the person who CONDUCTS an ORCHESTRA

> **COUNTRY AREAS** **the sticks** [pl.] (*informal*) country areas, a long way from cities: *We live out in the sticks.* **HELP** There are many other compounds ending in **stick**. You will find them at their place in the alphabet. **IDM** see BEAT *v.*, BIG *adj.*, CARROT, SHORT *adj.*

● *verb* (stuck, stuck /stʌk/)

> **PUSH SOMETHING IN** **1** [T, I] to push something, usually a sharp object, into something; to be pushed into something: **~ sth + adv./prep.** *The nurse stuck the needle into my arm.* ◆ *Don't stick your fingers through the bars of the cage.* ◆ **+ adv./prep.** *I found a nail sticking in the tire.*

> **ATTACH** **2** [T, I] to attach something to something else, usually with a sticky substance; to become attached to something in this way: **~ sth + adv./prep.** *He stuck a stamp on the envelope.* ◆ *We used glue to stick the broken pieces together.* ◆ *I stuck the photos into an album.* ◆ **+ adv./prep.** *Her wet clothes were sticking to her body.* ◆ *The glue's useless—the pieces just won't stick.*

> **PUT** **3** [T] **~ sth + adv./prep.** (*informal*) to put something in a place, especially quickly or carelessly: *Stick your bags down there.* ◆ *He stuck his hands in his pockets and strolled off.* ◆ *Can you stick this on the noticeboard?* ◆ *Peter stuck his head around the door and said, "Coffee, anyone?"* ◆ (*informal*) *Stick 'em up!* (= put your hands above your head — I have a gun)

> **BECOME FIXED** **4** [I] **~ (in sth)** to become fixed in a position and impossible to move **SYN** JAM: *The key is stuck in the lock.* ◆ *This drawer keeps sticking.*

> **BECOME ACCEPTED** **5** [I] to become accepted: *The police couldn't make the charges stick* (= show them to be true). ◆ *His friends called him Bart and the name has stuck* (= has become the name that everyone calls him).

> **IN CARD GAMES** **6** [I] to not take any more cards ⊃ see also STUCK

IDM **stick in your mind** (of a memory, an image, etc.) to be remembered for a long time: *One of his paintings in particular sticks in my mind.* **stick in your throat/craw** (*informal*) **1** (of words) to be difficult or impossible to say **2** (of a situation) to be difficult or impossible to accept; to make you angry **stick your neck out** (*informal*) to do or say something when there is a risk that you may be wrong **stick to your guns** (*informal*) to refuse to change your mind about something even when other people are trying to persuade you that you are wrong ⊃ more at HEAD *n.*, KNIFE, MILE, NOSE, SORE, TELL

PHR V **stick aˈround** (*informal*) to stay in a place, waiting for something to happen or for someone to arrive: *Stick around; we'll need you to help us later.* **ˈstick by sb** [no passive] to be loyal to a person and support them, especially in a difficult situation **ˈstick by sth** [no passive] to do what you promised or planned to do: *They stuck by their decision.* **ˌstick ˈout** to be noticeable or easily seen: **SYN** STAND OUT *They wrote the notice in big red letters so that it would stick out.* **ˌstick ˈout (of sth)** | **ˌstick sth↔ˈout (of sth)** to be further out than something else or come through a hole; to push something further out than something else or through a hole: *His ears stick out.* ◆ *She stuck her tongue out at me.* ◆ *Don't stick your arm out of the car window.* **ˌstick it/sth ˈout** (*informal*) to continue doing something to the end, even when it is difficult or boring: *She didn't like the course but she stuck it out to get the certificate.* **ˈstick to sth** **1** to continue doing something despite difficulties: *She finds it impossible to stick to a diet.* **2** to continue doing or using something and not want to change it: *He promised to help us and he stuck to his word* (= he did as he had promised). ◆ *"Should we meet on Friday this week?" "No, let's stick to Saturday."* ◆ *She stuck to her story.* **ˌstick toˈgether** (*informal*) (of people) to stay together and support each other **ˌstick ˈup** to point upward or be above a surface: *The branch was sticking up out of the water.* **ˌstick ˈup for sb/yourself/sth** [no passive] to support or defend someone/yourself/something: *Stick up for what you believe.* ◆ *She taught her children to stick up for themselves at school.* ◆ *Don't worry—I'll stick up for you.* **ˈstick with sb/sth** [no passive] (*informal*) **1** to stay close to someone so that they can help you **2** to continue with something or continue doing something: *They decided to stick with their original plan.*

stick·ball /ˈstɪkbɔl/ *noun* an informal game similar to baseball, played with a stick and a rubber ball

stick·er /ˈstɪkər/ *noun* a sticky label with a picture or message on it, that you stick onto something: *bumper stickers* (= on cars) ◆ *a sticker album* (= to collect stickers in) ⊃ thesaurus box at LABEL

ˈsticker ˌprice *noun* the price that is marked on something, especially a car

ˈsticker ˌshock *noun* [U] the unpleasant feeling that people experience when they find that something is much more expensive than they expected

ˈstick ˌfigure *noun* a picture of a person drawn only with thin lines for the arms and legs, a circle for the head, etc.

ˈsticking ˌpoint *noun* something that people do not agree on and that prevents progress in a discussion: *This was one of the major sticking points in the negotiations.*

stick-in-the-ˌmud *noun* (*informal, disapproving*) a person who refuses to try anything new or exciting

stick·le·back /ˈstɪklˌbæk/ *noun* a small FRESHWATER fish with sharp points on its back

stick·ler /ˈstɪklər/ *noun* **~ (for sth)** a person who thinks that a particular quality or type of behavior is very important and expects other people to think and behave in the same way: *a stickler for punctuality*

ˈstick-on *adj.* [only before noun] (of an object) with glue on one side so that it sticks to something: *stick-on labels*

stick·pin /ˈstɪkpɪn/ *noun* a decorative pin that is worn on a tie to keep it in place, or as a piece of jewelry

ˈstick shift *noun* **1** (also **gear·shift**) a handle used to change the gears of a vehicle **2** a vehicle that has a stick shift ⊃ compare AUTOMATIC

stick-to-it·ive·ness /ˌstɪk ˈtu ɪtəvnəs/ *noun* [U] (*informal*) the ability to keep doing something, even if it is sometimes boring: **SYN** PERSISTENCE *The long list of jobs on her résumé suggests a lack of stick-to-itiveness.*

stick·up /ˈstɪkʌp/ *noun* (*informal*) = HOLDUP: *This is a stickup!*

stick·y 🔧 /ˈstɪki/ *adj., noun*

● *adj.* (stick·i·er, stick·i·est) **1** made of or covered in a substance that sticks to things that touch it: *sticky fingers covered in jam* ◆ *Stir in the milk to make a soft but not sticky*

dough. **2** (of paper, labels, etc.) with glue on one side so that you can stick it to a surface **3** (*informal*) (of the weather) hot and damp **4** (*informal*) (of a person) feeling hot and uncomfortable **SYN** SWEATY **5** (*informal*) difficult or unpleasant: *a sticky situation* **6** (*computing*) (of a website) so interesting and well organized that the people who visit it stay there for a long time ▶ **stick·i·ly** /-kəli/ *adv.* **stick·i·ness** /-kinəs/ *noun* [U]
> **IDM** **have sticky fingers** (*informal*) to be likely to steal something

● *noun* (*pl.* **stick·ies**) (also **sticky note**) a small piece of sticky paper that you use for writing a note on, and that can be easily removed ➲ compare POST-IT™

stiff 🔑 /stɪf/ *adj., adv., noun, verb*

● *adj.* (**stiff·er, stiff·est**)
> **DIFFICULT TO BEND/MOVE** **1** firm and difficult to bend or move: *stiff cardboard* ◆ *a stiff brush* ◆ *This once-pliable plastic had become **stiff as a board**.*
> **MUSCLES** **2** when a person is **stiff**, their muscles hurt when they move them: *I'm really stiff after that bike ride yesterday.* ◆ *I've got a **stiff neck**.*
> **MIXTURE** **3** thick and almost solid; difficult to stir: *Whisk the egg whites until stiff.*
> **DIFFICULT/SEVERE** **4** more difficult or severe than usual: *It was a **stiff climb** to the top of the hill.* ◆ *The company faces **stiff competition** from its rivals.* ◆ *The new proposals have met with **stiff opposition**.* ◆ *There are **stiff fines** for breaking the rules.* ◆ *a **stiff breeze/wind** (= one that blows strongly)*
> **NOT FRIENDLY** **5** (of a person or their behavior) not friendly or relaxed: *The speech he made to welcome them was stiff and formal.*
> **PRICE** **6** (*informal*) costing a lot or too much: *There's a stiff $15 entrance fee to the exhibit.*
> **ALCOHOLIC DRINK** **7** [only before noun] strong; containing a lot of alcohol: *a stiff whiskey*
   ▶ **stiff·ly** *adv.* **stiff·ness** *noun* [U]: *pain and stiffness in her legs*
   IDM **(keep) a stiff upper lip** to keep calm and hide your feelings when you are in pain or in a difficult situation

● *adv.* **1** (*informal*) very much; to an extreme degree: *be bored/scared/worried stiff* **2** **frozen ~** (of wet material) very cold and hard because the water has become ice: *The laundry on the clothesline was frozen stiff.* ◆ *I came home from the game frozen stiff (= very cold).*

● *noun* (*slang*) the body of a dead person ➲ see also WORKING STIFF

● *verb* **~ sb** (*informal*) to cheat someone or not pay them what you owe them, especially by not leaving any money as a tip

stiff-arm *verb* = STRAIGHT-ARM

stiff·en /'stɪfn/ *verb* **1** [I, T] to make yourself or part of your body firm, straight, and still, especially because you are angry or frightened: **~ (with sth)** *She stiffened with fear.* ◆ **~ sth (with sth)** *I stiffened my back and faced him.* **2** [I, T] (of part of the body) to become, or to make something become, difficult to bend or move: **~ (up)** *My muscles had stiffened up after the climb.* ◆ **~ sth** *stiffened muscles* **3** [T, I] **~ (sth)** to make an attitude or idea stronger or more powerful; to become stronger **SYN** STRENGTHEN: *The threat of punishment has only **stiffened their resolve** (= made them even more determined to do something).* **4** [T] **~ sth (with sth)** to make something, such as cloth, firm and unable to bend

stiff-'necked *adj.* proud and refusing to change

sti·fle /'staɪfl/ *verb* **1** [T] **~ sth** to prevent something from happening; to prevent a feeling from being expressed **SYN** SUPPRESS: *She was unable to stifle a yawn.* ◆ *They hope the new rules will not stifle creativity.* ◆ *The government failed to stifle the unrest.* **2** [I, T] to feel unable to breathe, or to make someone unable to breathe, because it is too hot and/or there is no fresh air **SYN** SUFFOCATE: *I felt I was stifling in the airless room.* ◆ **~ sb** *Most of the victims were stifled by the fumes.* ▶ **sti·fling** /'staɪflɪŋ/ *adj.*: *a stifling room* ◆ "*It's stifling in here—can we open a window?*" ◆ *At 25, she found family life stifling.* **sti·fling·ly** *adv.*: *The room was stiflingly hot.*

stig·ma /'stɪɡmə/ *noun* **1** [U, C, usually sing.] feelings of disapproval that people have about particular illnesses or ways of behaving: *the social stigma of alcoholism* ◆ *There is no longer any stigma attached to being divorced.* **2** [C] (*biology*) the part in the middle of a flower where POLLEN is received ➲ picture at PLANT

stig·ma·ta /stɪɡ'mɑtə; 'stɪɡmətə/ *noun* [pl.] marks that look like the wounds made by nails on the body of Jesus Christ, believed by some Christians to have appeared as holy marks on the bodies of some SAINTS

stig·ma·tize /'stɪɡmə,taɪz/ *verb* [usually passive] **~ sb/sth** (*formal*) to treat someone in a way that makes them feel that they are very bad or unimportant ▶ **stig·ma·ti·za·tion** /,stɪɡmətə'zeɪʃn/ *noun* [U]

stile   turnstile

stile /staɪl/ *noun* a set of steps that help people climb over a fence or gate in a field, etc.

sti·let·to /stɪ'lɛtoʊ/ *noun* (*pl.* **sti·let·tos** or **sti·let·toes**) **1** (also **stiletto 'heel**) a woman's shoe with a very high, narrow heel; the heel on such a shoe ➲ picture at SHOE **SYN** SPIKE HEEL **2** a small knife with a narrow pointed blade

still 🔑 /stɪl/ *adv., adj., noun, verb*

● *adv.* **1** continuing until a particular point in time and not finishing: *I wrote to them last month and I'm still waiting for a reply.* ◆ *Mom, I'm still hungry!* ◆ *Do you still live at the same address?* ◆ *There's still time to change your mind.* ◆ *It was, and still is, my favorite movie.* **2** despite what has just been said: *We searched everywhere but we still couldn't find it.* ◆ *The weather was cold and wet. Still, we had a great time.* **3** used for making a comparison stronger: *The next day was warmer still.* ◆ *If you can manage to get two tickets that's better still.* **4** **~ more/another** even more: *There was still more bad news to come.*

● *adj.* **1** not moving; calm and quiet: *still water* ◆ *Keep still while I brush your hair.* ◆ *The kids found it hard to **stay still**.* ◆ *Can't you **sit still**? ◆ We stayed in a village where **time has stood still** (= life has not changed for many years).* **2** with no wind: *a still summer's day* ◆ *the still night air*
   IDM **the still of the night** (*literary*) the time during the night when it is quiet and calm **a/the still small voice** (*literary*) the voice of God or your CONSCIENCE, that tells you to do what is morally right **still waters run deep** (*saying*) a person who seems to be quiet or shy may surprise you by knowing a lot or having deep feelings

● *noun* **1** a photograph of a scene from a movie or video: *a publicity still from his new movie* **2** a piece of equipment that is used for making strong alcoholic drinks: *a whiskey still* ➲ see also DISTILL

● *verb* [I, T] (*literary*) to become calm and quiet; to make something calm and quiet: *The wind stilled.* ◆ **~ sb/sth** *She spoke quietly to still the frightened child.* ◆ (*figurative*) *to still someone's doubts/fears*

still·birth /'stɪlbərθ/ *noun* [C, U] a birth in which the baby is born dead

still·born /'stɪlbɔrn/ *adj.* **1** born dead: *a stillborn baby* **2** not successful; not developing

still 'life *noun* [U, C] (*pl.* **still lifes**) the art of painting or drawing arrangements of objects such as flowers, fruit, etc.; a painting, etc. like this

still·ness /'stɪlnəs/ *noun* [U] the quality of being quiet and not moving: *The sound of footsteps on the path broke the stillness.*

stilt /stɪlt/ *noun* [usually pl.] **1** one of a set of posts that support a building so that it is high above the ground or water **2** one of two long pieces of wood that have a step on the side that you can stand on, so that you can walk above the ground: *a circus performer* **on stilts**

stilt·ed /ˈstɪltəd/ *adj.* (*disapproving*) (of a way of speaking or writing) not natural or relaxed; too formal: *We made stilted conversation for a few moments.* ▶ **stilt·ed·ly** *adv.*

Stil·ton™ /ˈstɪltn/ *noun* [U, C] a type of English cheese with blue lines of MOLD running through it and a strong flavor

stim·u·lant /ˈstɪmyələnt/ *noun* **1** a drug or substance that makes you feel more awake and gives you more energy: *Coffee and tea are mild stimulants.* **2** ~ **(to sth)** an event or activity that encourages more activity

stim·u·late /ˈstɪmyəˌleɪt/ *verb* **1** ~ **sth** to make something develop or become more active; to encourage something: *The exhibit has stimulated interest in her work.* ◆ *The article can be used to stimulate discussion among students.* **2** to make someone interested and excited about something: ~ **sb** *Parents should give children books that stimulate them.* ◆ ~ **sb to do sth** *The conference stimulated him to study the subject in more depth.* **3** ~ **sth** (*technical*) to make a part of the body function: *The women were given fertility drugs to stimulate the ovaries.* ▶ **stim·u·la·tion** /ˌstɪmyəˈleɪʃn/ *noun* [U]: *sensory/intellectual/sexual/visual/physical stimulation*

stim·u·lat·ing /ˈstɪmyəˌleɪtɪŋ/ *adj.* **1** full of interesting or exciting ideas; making people feel enthusiastic **SYN** INSPIRING: *a stimulating discussion* ◆ *a stimulating teacher* ⊃ thesaurus box at INTERESTING **2** making you feel more active and healthy: *shower gel containing plant extracts that have a stimulating effect on the skin*

stim·u·lus /ˈstɪmyələs/ *noun* (*pl.* **stim·u·li** /-ˌlaɪ/) ~ **(to/for sth)** | ~ **(to do sth) 1** [usually sing.] something that helps someone or something to develop better or more quickly: *Books provide children with ideas and a stimulus for play.* ◆ *The new tax laws should act as a stimulus to exports.* **2** something that produces a reaction in a human, an animal, or a plant: *sensory/verbal/visual stimuli* ◆ *The animals were conditioned to respond to auditory stimuli* (= sounds).

sting 🔑 /stɪŋ/ *verb, noun*

● *verb* (stung, stung /stʌŋ/) **1** [T, I] ~ **(sb/sth)** (of an insect or plant) to touch your skin or make a very small hole in it so that you feel a sharp pain: *I was stung on the arm by a wasp.* ◆ *Be careful of the nettles—they sting!* **2** [I, T] to feel, or to make someone feel, a sharp pain in a part of their body: *I put some antiseptic on the cut and it stung for a moment.* ◆ *My eyes were stinging from the smoke.* ◆ ~ **sth** *Tears stung her eyes.* ⊃ thesaurus box at HURT **3** [T] to make someone feel angry or upset: ~ **sb** *He was stung by their criticism.* ◆ *They launched a stinging attack on the government.* ◆ ~ **sb to/into sth** *Their cruel remarks stung her into action.* ◆ ~ **sb into doing sth** *He was stung into answering in his defense.* **4** [T, often passive] ~ **sb (for sth)** (*informal*) (especially in business) to treat someone unfairly and make them pay money that they did not expect to pay: *He trusted his business partner implicitly, but in the end he got stung.* ◆ *I got stung for a $200 meal.*

● *noun* **1** [C] a wound that is made when an insect, a creature, or a plant stings you: *A wasp or bee sting is painful but not necessarily serious.* **2** [C, U] any sharp pain in your body or mind: *the sting of salt in a wound* ◆ *He smiled at her, trying to* **take the sting out of** *his words* (= trying to make the situation less painful or difficult). **3** [C] a complicated secret plan by the police to catch criminals: *a sting operation to catch heroin dealers in Detroit* **4** [C] a complicated plan by criminals to cheat people out of a lot of money

sting·er /ˈstɪŋər/ *noun* the sharp pointed part of an insect or creature that can go into the skin leaving a small painful wound, sometimes with poison in it: *The scorpion has a stinger in its tail.* ◆ *a bee's stinger* ⊃ picture at ANIMAL

stinging nettle *noun* = NETTLE

sting·ray /ˈstɪŋreɪ/ *noun* a large, wide, flat sea fish that has a long tail with a sharp sting in it that can cause serious wounds

stin·gy /ˈstɪndʒi/ *adj.* (stin·gi·er, stin·gi·est) (*informal*) not given or giving willingly; not generous, especially with money: *You're stingy!* (= not willing to spend money) ◆ *Don't be so stingy with the ice cream!* **ANT** GENEROUS (1)
▶ **stin·gi·ness** *noun* [U]

stink /stɪŋk/ *verb, noun*

● *verb* (stank /stæŋk/, stunk /stʌŋk/) or (stunk, stunk) (*informal*) **1** [I] ~ **(of sth)** to have a strong, unpleasant smell **SYN** REEK: *Her breath stank of garlic.* ◆ *It stinks of smoke in here.* **2** [I] ~ **(of sth)** to seem very bad, unpleasant, or dishonest: *The whole business stank of corruption.* ◆ *"What do you think of the idea?" "I think it stinks."*
PHR V ˌstink sth↔ˈup to fill a place with a strong unpleasant smell

● *noun* (*informal*) **1** [C, usually sing.] a very unpleasant smell **SYN** REEK: *the stink of sweat and urine* **2** [sing.] a lot of trouble and anger about something: *The whole business caused quite a stink.* ◆ *We'll* **kick up a stink** (= complain a lot and cause trouble) *if they try to close the school down.*

stink bomb *noun* a container that produces a very bad smell when it is broken. Stink bombs are used for playing tricks on people.

stink·er /ˈstɪŋkər/ *noun* (*informal*) a person or thing that is very annoying or difficult

stink·ing /ˈstɪŋkɪŋ/ *adj., adv.*
● *adj.* having a very strong unpleasant smell: *I was pushed into a filthy, stinking room.*
● *adv.* (*informal*, usually *disapproving*) extremely: *They must be* **stinking rich.** ◆ *When this is over we're going to go out and get stinking drunk.*

stink·y /ˈstɪŋki/ *adj.* (stink·i·er, stink·i·est) (*informal*) **1** having an extremely bad smell **2** extremely unpleasant or bad

stint /stɪnt/ *noun, verb*
● *noun* ~ **(as sth)** a period of time that you spend working somewhere or doing a particular activity: *He did a stint abroad early in his career.* ◆ *a two-year stint in the Navy*
● *verb* [I] (usually used in negative sentences) to provide or use only a small amount of something: ~ **(on sth)** *She never stints on the food at her parties.* ⊃ see also UNSTINTING

sti·pend /ˈstaɪpɛnd; -pənd/ *noun* (*formal*) an amount of money that is paid regularly to someone, especially a priest, as wages or money to live on: *a monthly stipend* ◆ *a summer internship with a small stipend*

stip·ple /ˈstɪpl/ *verb* [often passive] ~ **sth** (*technical*) to paint or draw something using small dots or marks ▶ **stip·pling** /ˈstɪplɪŋ/ *noun* [U]

stip·u·late /ˈstɪpyəˌleɪt/ *verb* (*formal*) to state clearly and firmly that something must be done, or how it must be done **SYN** SPECIFY: ~ **sth** *A delivery date is stipulated in the contract.* ◆ ~ **that...** *The job advertisement stipulates that the applicant must have three years' experience.* ◆ ~ **what, how, etc....** *The policy stipulates what form of consent is required.* ▶ **stip·u·la·tion** /ˌstɪpyəˈleɪʃn/ *noun* [C, U]: *The only stipulation is that the topic you choose must be related to your studies.*

stir 🔑 /stər/ *verb, noun*
● *verb* (-rr-)
▷ MIX **1** [T] to move a liquid or substance around, using a spoon or something similar, in order to mix it thoroughly: ~ **sth** *She stirred her tea.* ◆ ~ **sth into sth** *The vegetables are stirred into the rice while it is hot.* ◆ ~ **sth in** *Stir in the milk until the sauce thickens.* ⊃ thesaurus box at MIX ⊃ collocations at COOKING
▷ MOVE **2** [I, T] to move, or to make something move, slightly: *She heard the baby stir in the next room.* ◆ ~ **sth/sb** *A slight breeze was stirring the branches.* ◆ *A noise stirred me from sleep.* **3** [I, T] to move, or to make someone move, in order to do something: *You haven't stirred from that chair all evening!*

♦ ~ **yourself/sb** *Their complaints have finally stirred him into action.*

> FEELINGS **4** [T] ~ **sb (to sth)** to make someone excited or make them feel something strongly: *a book that really stirs the imagination* ♦ *She was stirred by his sad story.* **5** [I] (of a feeling or a mood) to begin to be felt: *A feeling of guilt began to stir in her.*

IDM **stir the blood** to make someone excited
PHRV **stir sb↔'up** to encourage someone to do something; to make someone feel they must do something **stir sth↔'up 1** to make people feel strong emotions: *to stir up hatred* **2** to try to cause arguments or problems: *to stir up a debate* ♦ *Whenever he's around, he always manages to stir up trouble.* ♦ *We have enough problems without you trying to stir things up.* **3** to make something move around in water or air: *The wind stirred up a lot of dust.*

● *noun* **1** [sing.] excitement, anger, or shock that is felt by a number of people **SYN** COMMOTION: *Her resignation caused quite a stir.* **2** [C, usually sing.] the action of stirring something: *Could you give the rice a stir?*

'**stir-crazy** *adj.* (*informal*) showing signs of mental illness because of being kept in prison: (*figurative*) *I'm going to go stir-crazy if I stay in all weekend!*

'**stir-fry** *verb, noun*
● *verb* ~ **sth** to cook thin strips of vegetables or meat quickly by stirring them in very hot oil: *stir-fried chicken* ⊃ *picture at* COOKING ⊃ *collocations at* COOKING
● *noun* (*pl.* stir-fries) a hot dish made by stir-frying small pieces of meat, fish, and/or vegetables

stir·ring /'stɜrɪŋ/ *noun, adj.*
● *noun* ~ **(of sth)** the beginning of a feeling, an idea, or a development: *She felt a stirring of anger.*
● *adj.* [usually before noun] causing strong feelings; exciting: *a stirring performance* ♦ *stirring memories*

stir·rup /'stɜrəp/ *noun* one of the metal rings that hang down on each side of a horse's SADDLE, used to support the rider's foot ⊃ *picture at* HORSE

'**stirrup pants** *noun* [pl.] women's tight pants with a narrow strip of cloth at the bottom of each leg that fits under the foot

stitch /stɪtʃ/ *noun, verb*
● *noun* **1** [C] one of the small lines of thread that you can see on a piece of cloth after it has been sewn; the action that produces this: *Try to keep the stitches small and straight.* **2** [C] one of the small circles of wool that you make around the needle when you are knitting: *to drop a stitch* (= to lose one that you have made) **3** [C, U] (especially in compounds) a particular style of sewing or knitting that you use to make the pattern you want: *chain stitch* **4** [C] a short piece of thread, etc. that doctors use to sew the edges of a wound together: *The cut needed eight stitches.* ⊃ *collocations at* INJURY **5** [C, usually sing.] a sudden pain in the side of your body, usually caused by running or laughing: *Can we slow down? I have a stitch.*

IDM **in stitches** (*informal*) laughing a lot: *The play had us in stitches.* **not have a stitch on | not be wearing a stitch** (*informal*) to be naked **a stitch in time (saves nine)** (*saying*) it is better to deal with something immediately because if you wait it may become worse or more difficult and cause extra work

● *verb* **1** ~ **sth (+ adv./prep.)** to use a needle and thread to repair, join, or decorate pieces of cloth **SYN** SEW: *Her wedding dress was stitched by hand.* ♦ (*figurative*) *An agreement was hastily stitched together* (= made very quickly). **2** ~ **sth (up)** to sew the edges of a wound together: *The cut will need to be stitched.*

PHRV **,stitch sth↔'up 1** to use a needle and thread to join things together **2** (*informal*) to arrange or complete something: *to stitch up a deal* ♦ *They think they have the U.S. market stitched up.*

stitch·ing /'stɪtʃɪŋ/ *noun* [U] a row of stitches

St. John's Wort /seɪnt 'dʒɑnz ˌwɜrt; -ˌwɔrt/ *noun* [U, C] an HERB with yellow flowers, used in medicines

stoat /stoʊt/ *noun* a small wild animal with a long body and brown fur that, in northern areas, turns white in winter. The white fur is called ERMINE.

stock 🔑 /stɑk/ *noun, verb, adj.*
● *noun*
> SUPPLY **1** [U, C] a supply of goods that is available for sale in a store: *We have a fast turnover of stock.* ♦ *That particular model is not currently in stock.* ♦ *I'm afraid we're temporarily out of stock.* ♦ *We don't carry a large stock of pine furniture.* ⊃ *collocations at* SHOPPING **2** [C, U] ~ **(of sth)** a supply of something that is available for use: *She's built up a good stock of teaching materials over the years.* ♦ *Food stocks are running low.* ♦ *a country's housing stock* (= all the houses available for living in)
> FINANCE **3** [U] the value of the shares in a company that have been sold **4** [C, usually pl.] a share that someone has bought in a company or business: *stock prices* ♦ *to invest in stocks and bonds*
> FOOD **5** [U, C] a liquid made by cooking bones, meat, etc. in water, used for making soups and sauces: *vegetable stock*
> FARM ANIMALS **6** [U] farm animals, such as cows and sheep, that are kept for their meat, wool, etc.: *breeding stock* ⊃ *see also* LIVESTOCK
> FAMILY/ANCESTORS **7** [U] of farming, noble, French, etc. ~ having the type of family or ANCESTOR mentioned **SYN** DESCENT
> FOR PUNISHMENT **8** stocks [pl.] a wooden structure with holes for the feet, used in the past to lock criminals in as a form of punishment, especially in a public place ⊃ *compare* PILLORY
> RESPECT **9** [U] (*formal*) the degree to which someone is respected or liked by other people: *Their stock is high/low.*
> OF GUN **10** [C] the part of a gun that you hold against your shoulder when firing it
> PLANT **11** [U, C] a garden plant with brightly colored flowers with a sweet smell
> THEATER **12** [C] = STOCK COMPANY ⊃ *see also* LAUGHING STOCK, ROLLING STOCK

IDM **put stock in sth** to have a particular amount of belief in something: *She no longer puts much stock in their claims.* **take stock (of sth)** to stop and think carefully about the way in which a particular situation is developing in order to decide what to do next ⊃ *more at* LOCK

● *verb* **1** ~ **sth** (of a store) to keep a supply of a particular type of goods to sell: *Do you stock green tea?* **2** [often passive] ~ **sth (with sth)** to fill something with food, books, etc.: *The pond was well stocked with fish.* ♦ *a well-stocked library*
PHRV **,stock sth↔'up** to fill something with goods, food, etc.: *We need to stock up the freezer.* **,stock 'up (on/with sth)** to buy a lot of something so that you can use it later: *We ought to stock up on film before our trip.*

● *adj.* [only before noun] **1** (*disapproving*) a **stock** excuse, answer, etc. is one that is often used because it is easy and convenient, but that is not very original: *"No comment," was the actor's stock response.* **2** usually available for sale in a store: **SYN** STANDARD *stock sizes*

stock·ade /stɑ'keɪd/ *noun* a line or wall of strong wooden posts built to defend a place

stock·brok·er /'stɑk,broʊkər/ (*also* bro·ker) *noun* a person or an organization that buys and sells stocks for other people

stock·brok·ing /'stɑk,broʊkɪŋ/ *noun* [U] the work of a stockbroker

'**stock car** *noun* an ordinary car that has been made stronger for use in racing

'**stock ,company** *noun* **1** a company owned by people who have shares in it **2** (*also* stock) a theater company that does several different plays in a season; a REPERTORY company

'**stock ex,change** *noun* [usually sing.] a place where shares in companies are bought and sold; all of the business activity involved in doing this: *the New York Stock Exchange* ♦ *to lose money on the stock exchange*

| ʌ cup | ə about | eɪ say | aɪ five | ɔɪ boy | aʊ now | oʊ go | ɜr bird |

stock·hold·er /ˈstɑkˌhoʊldər/ noun a person who owns STOCKS and shares in a business

stock index noun [usually sing.] a list that shows the current value of shares on the STOCK MARKET, based on the prices of shares of particular companies: *The S&P 500 stock index includes 500 large companies.*

stock·ing /ˈstɑkɪŋ/ noun **1** either of a pair of thin pieces of clothing that fit closely over a woman's legs and feet: *a pair of silk stockings* ➔ compare TIGHTS ➔ see also BODY STOCKING **2** = CHRISTMAS STOCKING
IDM in your stocking feet wearing socks or stockings but not shoes

stocking cap noun a soft KNITTED hat, often with a decorative TASSEL (= bunch of threads) at the top

stocking stuffer noun a small present that is put in a CHRISTMAS STOCKING

stock-in-trade noun [U] a person's **stock-in-trade** is something that they do, say, or use very often or too often: *Famous people and their private lives are the stock-in-trade of gossip columns.*

stock·man /ˈstɑkmən/ noun (pl. **stock·men** /-mən/) **1** a man whose job is to take care of farm animals **2** a man who owns farm animals **3** a man who is in charge of the goods in a WAREHOUSE, etc.

stock market (also mar·ket) noun the business of buying and selling shares in companies and the place where this happens; a STOCK EXCHANGE: *to make money on the stock market* ♦ *a stock market crash* (= when prices of shares fall suddenly and people lose money) ➔ collocations at ECONOMY

stock option noun a right given to employees to buy shares of stock in their company at a fixed price

stock·pile /ˈstɑkpaɪl/ noun, verb
• noun a large supply of something that is kept to be used in the future if necessary: *the world's stockpile of nuclear weapons*
• verb ~ sth to collect and keep a large supply of something

stock·pot /ˈstɑkpɑt/ noun a pot in which meat, fish, vegetables, or bones are cooked to make STOCK

stock·room /ˈstɑkrum; -rʊm/ noun a room for storing things in a store, an office, etc.

stock-still adv. without moving at all: *We stood stock-still, watching the animals.*

stock·y /ˈstɑki/ adj. (stock·i·er, stock·i·est) (of a person) short, with a strong solid body SYN THICKSET ▶ stock·i·ly /-kəli/ adv.

stock·yard /ˈstɑkyɑrd/ noun a place where farm animals are kept for a short time before they are sold at a market

stodg·y /ˈstɑdʒi/ adj. (informal, old-fashioned) serious and boring; not exciting

sto·gie (also sto·gy) /ˈstoʊgi/ noun (pl. sto·gies) a cheap cigar

sto·ic /ˈstoʊɪk/ noun (formal) a person who is able to suffer pain or trouble without complaining or showing what they are feeling ▶ stoic (also sto·i·cal /ˈstoʊɪkl/) adj.: *her stoic endurance* ♦ *his stoical acceptance of death* sto·i·cally /-kli/ adv. ORIGIN From the Stoics, a group of ancient Greek philosophers, who believed that wise people should not allow themselves to be affected by painful or pleasant experiences.

sto·i·cism /ˈstoʊəˌsɪzəm/ noun [U] (formal) the fact of not complaining or showing what you are feeling when you are suffering: *She endured her long illness with stoicism.*

stoke /stoʊk/ verb **1** ~ sth (up) (with sth) to add fuel to a fire, etc.: *to stoke up a fire with more coal* ♦ *to stoke a furnace* **2** ~ sth (up) to make people feel something more strongly: *to stoke up envy* **3** ~ sth (up) to make something increase or develop more quickly: *They were accused of stoking the crisis.* PHRV **stoke up (on/with sth)** (informal) to eat or drink a lot of something, especially so that you do not feel hungry later: *Stoke up for the day on a good breakfast.*

stoked /stoʊkt/ adj. (informal) excited and pleased about something: *I'm really stoked that they chose me for the team.*

stok·er /ˈstoʊkər/ noun a person whose job is to add coal or other fuel to a fire, etc., especially on a ship or a steam train

stole /stoʊl/ verb, noun
• verb pt of STEAL
• noun a piece of clothing consisting of a wide band of cloth or fur, worn by a woman around the shoulders; a similar piece of clothing worn by a priest

sto·len verb pp of STEAL

stol·id /ˈstɑləd/ adj. (usually disapproving) not showing much emotion or interest; remaining always the same and not reacting or changing ▶ stol·id·ly adv. sto·lid·i·ty /stəˈlɪdəti/ noun [U]

sto·ma /ˈstoʊmə/ noun **1** (biology) a tiny PORE (= hole) in the outer layer of a plant's leaf or STEM **2** (biology) a small opening like a mouth, in some animals **3** (medical) an artificial opening made in an organ of the body, especially in the COLON or TRACHEA

stom·ach 🔑 /ˈstʌmək/ noun, verb
• noun the organ inside the body where food goes when you swallow it; the front part of the body below the chest: *stomach pains* ♦ *an upset stomach* ♦ *It's not a good idea to drink* (= alcohol) *on an empty stomach* (= without having eaten anything). ♦ *You shouldn't exercise on a full stomach.* ♦ *The attacker kicked him in the stomach.* ♦ *Lie on your stomach with your arms by your side.* ➔ picture at BODY ➔ collocations at PHYSICAL ➔ see also TUMMY
IDM have no stomach for sth 1 to not want to eat something: *She had no stomach for the leftover stew.* **2** to not have the desire or courage to do something: *They had no stomach for a fight.* **turn your stomach** to make you feel upset, sick, or disgusted: *Pictures of the burned corpses turned my stomach.* ➔ more at BUTTERFLY, EYE, FEEL, STRONG
• verb (especially in negative sentences or questions) **1** ~ sth to approve of something and be able to enjoy it; to enjoy being with a person: *I can't stomach violent films.* ♦ *I find him very hard to stomach.* **2** ~ sth to be able to eat something without feeling sick: *She couldn't stomach any breakfast.*

stom·ach·ache /ˈstʌməkˌeɪk/ noun [C, U] pain in or near your stomach

stomach pump noun a machine with a tube that doctors use to remove poisonous substances from someone's stomach through their mouth

stomp /stɑmp/ verb [I] + adv./prep. (informal) to walk, dance, or move with heavy steps: *She stomped angrily out of the office.*

stomping ground noun (informal) a place that someone likes and where they often go SYN HAUNT

stone 🔑 /stoʊn/ noun, verb
• noun
> HARD SUBSTANCE **1** [U] (often used before nouns or in compounds) a hard, solid mineral substance that is found in the ground, often used for building: *Most of the houses are built of stone.* ♦ *stone walls* ♦ *a stone floor* ♦ *a flight of stone steps* ➔ see also DRYSTONE WALL, LIMESTONE, SANDSTONE, SOAPSTONE **2** [C] a small piece of rock of any shape: *a pile of stones* ♦ *Some children were throwing stones into the lake.* ➔ see also HAILSTONE, PHILOSOPHER'S STONE **3** [C] (usually in compounds) a piece of stone shaped for a particular purpose: *These words are carved on the stone beside his grave.* ➔ see also CORNERSTONE, FOUNDATION STONE, GRAVESTONE, HEADSTONE, LODESTONE, MILLSTONE, PAVING STONE, STEPPING STONE, TOMBSTONE
> JEWEL **4** [C] = PRECIOUS STONE
> IN BODY **5** [C] (often in compounds) a small piece of hard material that can form in the BLADDER or KIDNEY and cause pain: *kidney stones* ➔ see also GALLSTONE
IDM carved/set in stone (of a decision, plan, etc.) unable to be changed: *People should remember that our proposals*

aren't set in stone. **leave no stone unturned** to try every possible course of action in order to find or achieve something **a stone's throw** a very short distance away: *We live just a stone's throw from here.* ◆ *The hotel is within a stone's throw of the beach.* ⊃ more at BLOOD, HEART, KILL, PEOPLE, ROLL

◆ **verb** [usually passive] **~ sb/sth** to throw stones at someone or something: *Stores were looted and vehicles stoned.* ◆ *to be stoned to death* (= as a punishment)

the 'Stone Age *noun* [sing.] the very early period of human history when tools and weapons were made of stone: *(figurative) My dad's taste in music is from the Stone Age* (= very old-fashioned). ▶ **'stone-age** *adj.* [only before noun] *(figurative)*: *stone-age* (= very out-of-date) *computers*

ˌstone ˈcold *adj.* completely cold, when it should be warm or hot: *The soup was stone cold.*
  IDM **stone-cold sober** having drunk no alcohol at all

stoned /stoʊnd/ *adj.* [not usually before noun] *(informal)* not behaving or thinking normally because of the effects of a drug such as MARIJUANA

ˌstone ˈdead *adj.* completely dead or completely destroyed

ˌstone ˈdeaf *adj.* completely unable to hear

ˈstone-faced (also ˈstony-ˌfaced) *adj.* not showing any friendly feelings

stone·ground /ˈstoʊngraʊnd/ *adj.* (of flour for bread, etc.) made by being crushed between heavy stones

stone·ma·son /ˈstoʊnˌmeɪsn/ *noun* a person whose job is cutting and preparing stone for buildings

stone·wall /ˈstoʊnwɔl/ *verb* [T, I] **~ (sth)** (especially in politics) to delay a discussion or decision by refusing to answer questions or by talking a lot

stone·ware /ˈstoʊnwɛr/ *noun* [U] pots, dishes, etc. made from CLAY that contains a small amount of the hard stone called FLINT

stone·washed /ˈstoʊnwɑʃt; -wɔʃt/ *adj.* (of jeans, etc.) washed in a special way so that the cloth loses some color and looks older

stone·work /ˈstoʊnwɜrk/ *noun* [U] the parts of a building that are made of stone

ston·i·ly /ˈstoʊnl̩i/ *adv.* in a way that shows a lack of feeling or sympathy: *She stared stonily at him for a minute.*

ston·y /ˈstoʊni/ *adj.* (ston·i·er, ston·i·est) **1** having a lot of stones on it or in it: *stony soil* **2** showing a lack of feeling or sympathy **SYN** COLD: *They listened to him in stony silence.*
  IDM **fall on stony ground** to fail to produce the result or the effect that you hope for; to have little success

ˈstony-ˌfaced *adj.* = STONE-FACED

stood *pt, pp of* STAND

stooge /studʒ/ *noun* **1** *(informal, usually disapproving)* a person who is used by someone to do things that are unpleasant or dishonest **2** a performer in a show whose role is to appear silly so that the other performers can make jokes about him or her

stool /stul/ *noun* **1** (often in compounds) a seat with legs but with nothing to support your back or arms: *a bar stool* ◆ *a piano stool* ⊃ picture at CHAIR **2** *(medical)* a piece of solid waste from your body

ˈstool ˌpigeon *noun* *(informal)* a person, especially a criminal, who helps the police to catch another criminal, for example by spending time with them and getting secret information **SYN** INFORMER

stoop /stup/ *verb, noun*
◆ **verb 1** [I] **~ (down)** to bend your body forward and downward: *She stooped down to pick up the child.* ◆ *The doorway was so low that he had to stoop.* **2** [I] to stand or walk with your head and shoulders bent forward: *He tends to stoop because he's so tall.*
  IDM **stoop so low (as to do sth)** *(formal)* to drop your moral standards far enough to do something bad or unpleasant: *She was unwilling to believe anyone would stoop so low as to steal a ring from a dead woman's finger.*
  PHR V 'stoop to sth to drop your moral standards to do something bad or unpleasant: *You can't really think I'd stoop to that!* ◆ **~ doing sth** *I didn't think he'd stoop to cheating.*
◆ **noun 1** [sing.] if someone has a **stoop**, their shoulders are always bent forward **2** [C] a raised area outside the door of a house with steps leading up to it

stooped /stupt/ *adj.* **1** standing or walking with your head and shoulders bent forward **2 stooped shoulders** are bent forward

stop 🔑 /stɑp/ *verb, noun*
◆ **verb** (-pp-)
▷ **NOT MOVE 1** [I, T] to no longer move; to make someone or something no longer move: *The car stopped at the traffic lights.* ◆ *We stopped for the night in Tampa.* ◆ **~ sb/sth** *He was stopped by the police for speeding.*
▷ **NOT CONTINUE 2** [I, T] to no longer continue to do something; to make someone or something no longer do something: **~ (doing sth)** *That phone never stops ringing!* ◆ *Please stop crying and tell me what's wrong.* ◆ *She criticizes everyone and the trouble is, she **doesn't know when to stop**.* ◆ *Can't you just stop?* ◆ **~ sb/sth** *(= make me stop talking) if I'm boring you.* ◆ *Stop it! You're hurting me.* ◆ **~ what...** *Mike immediately stopped what he was doing.*
  HELP Notice the difference between **stop doing something** and **stop to do something**: *We stopped taking pictures* means "We were no longer taking pictures.": *We stopped to take pictures* means "We stopped what we were doing so that we could start taking pictures."
▷ **END 3** [I, T] to end or finish; to make something end or finish: *When is this fighting going to stop?* ◆ *The bus service stops at midnight.* ◆ **~ doing sth** *Has it stopped raining yet?* ◆ **~ sth** *Doctors couldn't stop the bleeding.* ◆ *The umpire was forced to stop the game because of heavy rain.*
▷ **PREVENT 4** [T] to prevent someone from doing something; to prevent something from happening: **~ sb/sth** *I want to go and you can't stop me.* ◆ *We need more laws to stop pollution.* ◆ *There's no stopping us now* (= nothing can prevent us from achieving what we want to achieve). ◆ **~ sb/sth from doing sth** *There's nothing to stop you from accepting the offer.* ◆ *You can't stop people from saying what they think.* ◆ **~ sb/sth doing sth** *You can't stop people saying what they think.*
▷ **FOR SHORT TIME 5** [I] to end an activity for a short time in order to do something: **~ for sth** *I'm hungry. Let's stop for lunch.* ◆ **~ to do sth** *We stopped to admire the scenery.* ◆ *People just don't stop to think about the consequences.* **HELP** In spoken English, **stop** can be used with **and** plus another verb, instead of with **to** and the infinitive, to show purpose: *He stopped and bought some flowers.* ◆ *Let's stop and look at the map.*
▷ **NOT FUNCTION 6** [I, T] to no longer work or function; to make something no longer work or function: *Why has the engine stopped?* ◆ *I felt as if my heart had stopped.* ◆ **~ sth** *I stopped the DVD and pressed reverse.*
▷ **MONEY 7** [T] to prevent money from being paid: **~ sth** *to stop a check* (= tell the bank not to pay it)
▷ **CLOSE HOLE 8** [T] **~ sth (up) (with sth)** to block, fill, or close a hole, an opening, etc.: *Stop up the other end of the tube, will you?* ◆ *I stopped my ears but still heard her cry out.*
  IDM **stop at nothing** to be willing to do anything to get what you want, even if it is dishonest or wrong **stop the clock** to stop measuring time in a game or an activity that has a time limit **stop the presses 1** to stop PRINTING PRESSES while a newspaper is being printed because late news needs to be added: *The editor stopped the presses because the headline was wrong.* ⊃ see also STOP PRESS **2** used before telling someone important or shocking news: *Stop the presses! Jon and Julia are getting married!* **stop short| stop sb short** to suddenly stop, or make someone suddenly stop, doing something: *He stopped short when he heard his name.* **stop short of sth/of doing sth** to be unwilling to do something because it may involve a risk,

but to nearly do it: *She stopped short of calling the president a liar.* ⊃ more at BUCK *n.*, TRACK *n.*

PHR V ˌstop 'by (sth) to make a short visit somewhere: *I'll stop by this evening to see you.* ◆ *Could you stop by the store on the way home for some bread?* ˌstop 'off (at/in…) to make a short visit somewhere during a trip in order to do something: *We stopped off at a hotel for the night.* ˌstop 'over (at/in…) to stay somewhere for a short time during a long journey: *I wanted to stop over in India on the way to Australia.* ⊃ related noun STOPOVER

● noun
> ACT OF STOPPING **1** an act of stopping or stopping something; the state of being stopped: *The trip included an overnight stop in St. Louis.* ◆ *She brought the car to a stop.* ◆ *Work has temporarily come to a stop while the funding is reviewed.* ◆ *It is time to put a stop to the violence.* ◆ *Babies do not grow at a steady rate but in stops and starts.* ⊃ see also NONSTOP, WHISTLE-STOP
> OF BUS/TRAIN **2** a place where a bus or train stops regularly for passengers to get on or off: *I get off at the next stop.* ◆ *Is this your stop?* ⊃ see also BUS STOP, PIT STOP
> MUSIC **3** a row of pipes on an organ that produce the different sounds **4** a handle on an organ that the player pushes in or pulls out to control the sound produced by the pipes
> PHONETICS **5** a speech sound made by stopping the flow of air coming out of the mouth and then suddenly releasing it, for example /p, k, t/ **SYN** PLOSIVE ⊃ see also GLOTTAL STOP
> MONEY **6** [usually sing.] (also stop payment) an order telling your bank not to pay a check you have written: *I put a stop on the check because it was lost in the mail.* **IDM** see FULL STOP, PULL *v.*

ˌstop-and-ˈgo *adj.* [usually before noun] (*disapproving*) starting and then stopping: *stop-and-go traffic*

stop·cock /ˈstɑpkɑk/ (also **cock**) *noun* a tap that controls the flow of liquid or gas through a pipe

stop·gap /ˈstɑpɡæp/ *noun* something that you use or do for a short time while you are looking for something better: *The arrangement was only intended as a stopgap.* ◆ *a stopgap measure*

stop·light /ˈstɑplaɪt/ (also **stoplights**) *noun* = TRAFFIC LIGHT

stop·o·ver /ˈstɑpˌoʊvər/ *noun* **1** a short stay somewhere between two parts of a trip **SYN** LAYOVER: *We had a two-day stopover in Fiji on the way to Australia.* ⊃ collocations at TRAVEL **2** a place where you spend a short time between two parts of a trip: *an interesting stopover between Quebec City and Montreal*

stop·page /ˈstɑpɪdʒ/ *noun* [C] **1** a situation in which people stop working as part of a protest or strike **2** (*sports*) an interruption in the game for a particular reason: *Play resumed quickly after the stoppage.* **3** a situation in which something does not move forward or is blocked: *a stoppage of blood to the heart*

stop·per /ˈstɑpər/ (also **plug**) *noun* an object that fits into the top of a bottle to close it ⊃ picture at LABORATORY
▶ **stopper** *verb* ~ sth

stop·watch /ˈstɑpwɑtʃ; -wɒtʃ/ *noun* a watch that you can stop and start by pressing buttons, in order to time a race, etc. accurately

stor·age /ˈstɔrɪdʒ/ *noun* [U] **1** the process of keeping something in a particular place until it is needed; the space where things can be kept: *tables that fold flat for storage* ◆ *There's a lot of storage space in the attic.* ◆ *food storage facilities* ◆ *We need more storage now.* ⊃ see also COLD STORAGE **2** (*computing*) the process of keeping information, etc. on a computer; the way it is kept: *the storage and retrieval of information* ◆ *data storage* **3** the process of paying to keep furniture, etc. in a special building until you want it: *When we moved we had to put our furniture in storage for a while.*

ˈstorage ˌbattery *noun* a large battery that you can fill with electrical power (= that you can RECHARGE)

store 🔑 /stɔr/ *noun, verb*
● noun **1** [C] a building or part of a building where things are bought or sold: *a health food store* ◆ *a liquor store* ◆ *a big department store* ⊃ collocations at SHOPPING ⊃ see also CHAIN STORE, CONVENIENCE STORE, GENERAL STORE, PACKAGE STORE, VARIETY STORE **2** [C] a quantity or supply of something that you have and use: *her secret store of chocolate* ◆ *a vast store of knowledge* **3** [pl.] **stores** goods of a particular kind or for a particular purpose: *medical stores* **4** [C] often **stores** a place where goods of a particular kind are kept: *a grain store* ◆ *weapons stores*
IDM in store (for sb) waiting to happen to someone: *We don't know what life holds in store for us.* ◆ *If she had known what lay in store for her, she would never have agreed to go.* ◆ *They think it'll be easy but they have a surprise in store.* set/put (great, etc.) store by sth to consider something to be important: *She sets great store by her appearance.* ◆ *It is unwise to put too much store by these statistics.* ⊃ more at HIT, MIND
● verb **1** ~ sth (away/up) to put something somewhere and keep it there to use later: *animals storing up food for the winter* ◆ *He hoped the electronic equipment was safely stored away.* **2** ~ sth to keep information or facts in a computer or in your brain: *Thousands of pieces of data are stored in a computer's memory.*
PHR V ˌstore sth↔ˈup to not express strong feelings or deal with problems when you have them, especially when this causes problems later: *She had stored up all her anger and eventually snapped.* ◆ *By ignoring your feelings you are only storing up trouble for yourself.*

ˈstore-bought *adj.* [only before noun] bought from a store and not made at home: *store-bought cookies*

ˈstore-brand *adj.* used to describe goods that are marked with the name of the store in which they are sold rather than with the name of the company that produced them

ˈstore card *noun* a card that a particular store provides for regular customers so that they can use it to buy goods that they will pay for later ⊃ compare CREDIT CARD

ˈstore deˌtective *noun* a person employed by a large store to watch customers and make sure they do not steal goods

store·front /ˈstɔrfrʌnt/ *noun* **1** the outside of a store that faces the street **2** a room at the front of a store: *They run their business from a small storefront.* ◆ *a storefront office* **3** a place on the Internet where you can buy goods and services: *Welcome to our online storefront.*

store·house /ˈstɔrhaʊs/ *noun* **1** a building where things are stored **SYN** WAREHOUSE **2** ~ of information, knowledge, etc. a place or thing that has or contains a lot of information

store·keep·er /ˈstɔrˌkipər/ *noun* a person who owns or manages a store, usually a small one

store·room /ˈstɔrrum; -rʊm/ *noun* a room used for storing things

ˈstore ˌwindow (also ˈwin·dow) *noun* the glass at the front of a store and the area behind it where goods are shown to the public

sto·ried /ˈstɔrid/ *adj.* **1** [only before noun] mentioned in stories; famous; well known: *the rock star's storied career* **2** -storied (in adjectives) (of a building) having the number of levels mentioned: *a four-storied building*

stork /stɔrk/ *noun* a large black and white bird with a long beak and neck and long legs, that lives near water but often builds its nest on the top of a high building. There is a tradition that says that it is storks that bring people their new babies.

storm 🔑 /stɔrm/ *noun, verb*
● noun **1** very bad weather with strong winds and rain, and often THUNDER and LIGHTNING: *fierce/heavy/violent storms* ◆ *A few minutes later the storm broke* (= began). ◆ *I think we're in for a storm* (= going to have one). ◆ *storm damage* ⊃ collocations at WEATHER ⊃ note at RAIN **2** (in compounds) very bad weather of the type mentioned: *a thunderstorm/snowstorm/sandstorm* ⊃ see also ELECTRICAL

STORM, RAINSTORM **3** ~ **(of sth)** a situation in which a lot of people suddenly express very strong feelings about something: *a storm of protest* ◆ *A political **storm is brewing** over the President's comments.* **4** ~ **of sth** a sudden loud noise that is caused by emotion or excitement **SYN** ROAR: *a storm of applause* ➔ see also BRAINSTORM

IDM **cook, dance, etc. up a storm** (*informal*) to cook, dance, etc. with great energy and enthusiasm: *That band can play up a storm!* **take sth/sb by storm 1** to be extremely successful very quickly in a particular place or among particular people: *The play took New York by storm.* **2** to attack a place suddenly and capture it ➔ more at CALM, PORT

- **verb 1** [T, I] to suddenly attack a place: ~ **sth** *Police stormed the building and captured the gunman.* ◆ ~ **into sth** *Soldiers stormed into the city at dawn.* **2** [I] + **adv./prep.** to go somewhere quickly and in an angry, noisy way: *She stormed into my office waving a newspaper.* ◆ *He burst into tears and stormed off.* **3** [T] + **speech** to say something in a loud angry way: *"Don't you know who I am?" she stormed.*

'storm cloud *noun* [usually pl.] a dark cloud that you see when bad weather is coming: (*figurative*) *The storm clouds of revolution were gathering.*

'storm door *noun* an extra door that is fitted to the outside door of a house, etc. to give protection from bad weather

'storm surge *noun* an unusual rise in the level of the ocean near the coast, caused by wind from a severe storm

'storm-tossed *adj.* [only before noun] (*literary*) affected or damaged by storms

'storm ,trooper *noun* a soldier who is specially trained for violent attacks, especially one in Nazi Germany in the 1930s and 1940s

'storm ,water *noun* [U] water covering the ground in large quantities because of heavy rain

'storm ,window *noun* an extra window that is fitted to a window of a house to give protection from bad weather

storm·y /'stɔrmi/ *adj.* (storm·i·er, storm·i·est) **1** with strong winds and heavy rain or snow: *a dark and stormy night* ◆ *stormy weather* ◆ *stormy seas* (= with big waves) **2** full of strong feelings and angry arguments: *a stormy debate* ◆ *a stormy relationship*

sto·ry 🔑 /'stɔri/ *noun* (*pl.* sto·ries)

▸ **DESCRIPTION OF EVENTS 1** ~ **(about/of sth/sb)** a description of events and people that the writer or speaker has invented in order to entertain people: ***adventure/detective/love, etc. stories*** ◆ *a story about time travel* ◆ *Would you like me to **tell you a story**?* ◆ *He read the children a story.* ◆ *a bedtime story* ➔ collocations at LITERATURE ➔ see also GHOST STORY, SHORT STORY **2** ~ **(about/of sth/sb)** an account, often spoken, of what happened to someone or of how something happened: *It was many years before **the full story** was made public.* ◆ *The police didn't believe her story.* ◆ *We must stick to our story about the accident.* ◆ *I can't decide until I've heard **both sides of the story**.* ◆ *It's a story of courage.* ◆ *Many years later I returned to Africa, but **that's another story** (= I am not going to talk about it now).* ➔ see also COCK AND BULL STORY, HARD-LUCK STORY, LIFE STORY, SHAGGY-DOG STORY, SOB STORY, SUCCESS STORY ➔ note at REPORT **3** an account of past events or of how something has developed: *He told us the story of his life.* ◆ *the story of the Grateful Dead* ◆ *the story of the building of the bridge* **4** a report in a newspaper, magazine, or news broadcast: *a front-page story* ◆ *Now for a summary of tonight's main news stories.* ➔ see also COVER STORY, LEAD STORY **5** (also sto·ry·line) the series of events in a book, movie, play, etc. **SYN** PLOT: *Her novels always have the same basic story.*

▸ **SOMETHING THAT IS NOT TRUE 6** (*informal*) something that someone says that is not true

▸ **LEVEL OF BUILDING 7** a level of a building; a floor: *the **upper/lower story** of the house* ◆ *a **single-story/two-story** building*

IDM **the story goes (that)…** | **so the story goes** used to describe something that people are saying although it may not be correct: *She never saw him again—or so the story goes.*

---

that's the story of my life (*informal*) when you say that's the story of my life about an unfortunate experience you have had, you mean you have had many similar experiences ➔ more at LIKELY, LONG, OLD, PITCH *v.*, TELL

WHICH WORD?

story ◆ floor

- You use **story** mainly when you are talking about the number of levels a building has: *a two-story house* ◆ *The office building is five stories high.*
- **Floor** is used mainly to talk about which particular-level in the building someone lives on, goes to, etc: *His office is on the fifth floor.*

sto·ry·board /'stɔri,bɔrd/ *noun* a series of drawings or pictures that show the outline of the story of a movie, etc.

sto·ry·book /'stɔri,bʊk/ *noun* a book of stories for children: *a picture in a storybook* ◆ *storybook characters* ◆ *storybook adventures* (= like the ones in stories for children)

sto·ry·line /'stɔri,laɪn/ *noun* the basic story in a novel, play, movie, etc. **SYN** PLOT

sto·ry·tell·er /'stɔri,tɛlər/ *noun* a person who tells or writes stories ▸ **sto·ry·tell·ing** *noun* [U]

stoup /stup/ *noun* (*technical*) a stone container for holy water in a church

stout /staʊt/ *adj.*, *noun*

- *adj.* (stout·er, stout·est) **1** (of a person) somewhat fat **SYN** PLUMP **2** [usually before noun] strong and thick: *a stout pair of shoes* **3** [usually before noun] (*formal*) brave and determined: *He put up a stout defense in court.* ▸ **stout·ly** *adv.*: *He was tall and stoutly built.* ◆ *"I disagree," said Polly stoutly.* **stout·ness** *noun* [U]

- *noun* [U, C] strong dark beer made with MALT or BARLEY

'stout-,hearted *adj.* (*old-fashioned*, *literary*) brave and determined

stove 🔑 /stoʊv/ *noun*

1 a large piece of equipment for cooking food, containing an oven and gas or electric rings on top **SYN** RANGE: *She put a pan of water on the stove.* ◆ *Most people don't want to spend hours slaving over a hot stove* (= cooking). **2** a piece of equipment that can burn various fuels and is used for heating rooms: *a gas/wood-burning stove* ➔ see also POTBELLY STOVE, STAVE

stove·top /'stoʊvtɑp/ *noun* the top part of a stove where food is cooked in pans; a similar surface that is built into a kitchen unit and is separate from the oven: *stovetop cooking*

stow /stoʊ/ *verb* ~ **sth (away) (in sth)** to put something in a safe place: *She found a seat, stowed her backpack, and sat down.*

PHR V **,stow a·way** to hide in a ship, plane, etc. in order to travel secretly ➔ related noun STOWAWAY

stow·age /'stoʊɪdʒ/ *noun* [U] space provided for stowing things away, in a boat or a plane

stow·a·way /'stoʊə,weɪ/ *noun* a person who hides in a ship or plane before it leaves, in order to travel without paying or being seen

St. Patrick's Day /,seɪnt 'pætrɪks ,deɪ/ *noun* March 17, a Christian festival of the national SAINT of Ireland, when many people wear green

strad·dle /'strædl/ *verb* **1** ~ **sth/sb** to sit or stand with one of your legs on either side of someone or something: *He swung his leg over the motorcycle, straddling it easily.* **2** ~ **sth** to cross, or exist on both sides of, a river, a road, or an area of land: *The mountains straddle the California-Nevada state line.* **3** ~ **sth** to exist within, or include, different periods of time, activities, or groups of people: *a writer who straddles two cultures*

strafe /streɪf/ *verb* ~ **sth** to attack a place with bullets or bombs from an aircraft flying low

---

strag·gle /ˈstræɡl/ *verb* **1** [I] (+ *adv./prep.*) to grow, spread, or move in a messy way in different directions: *The town straggled to an end and the fields began.* **2** [I] (+ *adv./prep.*) to move slowly behind a group of people that you are with so that you become separated from them: *On the way the kids straggled behind us.*

strag·gler /ˈstræɡlər/ *noun* [usually pl.] a person or an animal that is among the last or the slowest in a group to do something, for example, to finish a race or leave a place

strag·gly /ˈstræɡli/ *adj.* growing or hanging in a way that does not look clean or attractive: *a thin woman with gray, straggly hair*

straight 🔑 /streɪt/ *adv., adj., noun*

● *adv.* (straight·er, straight·est)

> **NOT IN CURVE 1** not in a curve or at an angle; in a straight line: *Keep straight on for two miles.* ◆ *Can you stretch your arms out straighter?* ◆ *He was too tired to walk straight.* ◆ *I can't shoot straight* (= accurately). ◆ *She looked me straight in the eye.* ⟳ picture at LINE

> **IMMEDIATELY 2** by a direct route; immediately: *Come straight home after school.* ◆ *I was so tired I went straight to bed.* ◆ *She went straight from college to a high-level job.* ◆ *I'm going to the library **straight after** the class.* ◆ *I'll come **straight to the point**—your work isn't good enough.*

> **IN LEVEL/CORRECT POSITION 3** in or into a level or vertical position; in or into the correct position: *Sit up straight!* ◆ *She pulled her hat straight.*

> **HONESTLY 4** honestly and directly: *I told him straight that I didn't like him.* ◆ *Are you **playing straight** with me?*

> **WITHOUT INTERRUPTION 5** continuously without interruption: *They had been working for 16 hours straight.*

IDM go straight (*informal*) to stop being a criminal and live an honest life **play it straight** to be honest and not try to trick someone **straight away** immediately; without delay **SYN** AT ONCE: *I'll do it straight away.* **straight from the shoulder** if you say something **straight from the shoulder**, you are being very honest and direct, even if what you are saying is critical **straight off** (*informal*) without hesitating: *When asked about her change of plans, she answered straight off.* **straight out** (*informal*) honestly and directly: *She told him straight out that he was a bore.* ⟳ more at THINK v.

● *adj.* (straight·er, straight·est)

> **WITHOUT CURVES 1** without a bend or curve; going in one direction only: *a straight line* ◆ *a straight road* ◆ *long straight hair* (= without curls) ◆ *a boat sailing **in a straight line*** ◆ *straight-backed chairs*

> **CLOTHING 2** not fitting close to the body and not curving away from the body: *a straight skirt*

> **AIM/BLOW 3** going directly to the correct place: *a straight punch to the face*

> **IN LEVEL/CORRECT POSITION 4** positioned in the correct way; level, vertical, or parallel to something: *Is my tie straight?*

> **CLEAN/NEAT 5** [not usually before noun] clean and neat, with everything in the correct place: *It took hours to get the house straight.*

> **HONEST 6** honest and direct: *a straight answer to a straight question* ◆ *I don't think you're being straight with me.* ◆ *It's time for some **straight talk**.* ⟳ thesaurus box at HONEST

> **SEX 7** (*informal*) HETEROSEXUAL **ANT** GAY

> **CHOICE 8** [only before noun] simple; involving only two clear choices: *It was a **straight choice** between taking the job and staying out of work.*

> **ACTOR/PLAY 9** [only before noun] (of an actor or a play) not connected with comedy or musical theater, but with serious theater

> **WITHOUT INTERRUPTION 10** [only before noun] one after another in a series, without interruption **SYN** CONSECUTIVE: *The team has had five straight wins.*

> **ALCOHOLIC DRINK 11** not mixed with water or anything else

> **NORMAL/BORING 12** (*informal*) you can use **straight** to describe a person who is normal and ordinary, but who you consider dull and boring

> **NOT USING DRUGS 13** (*informal*) not using drugs: *That's the longest she's been straight in six years!*

> **NOT OWING MONEY 14** (*informal*) [not usually before noun] (of two people) not owing each other any money: *Give me $10 and we'll be straight.*

▶ **straight·ness** *noun* [U]

IDM get sth straight to make a situation clear; to make sure that you or someone else understands the situation: *Let's get this straight—you really had no idea where he was?* **put/set sb straight (about/on sth)** to correct someone's mistake; to make sure that someone knows the correct facts when they have had the wrong idea or impression **(earn/get) straight A's** (to get) the best grades in all your classes: *a straight A student* **the straight and narrow** (*informal*) the honest and morally acceptable way of living: *His wife is trying to keep him on the straight and narrow.* **a straight face** if you keep a **straight face**, you do not laugh or smile, although you find something funny ⟳ see also STRAIGHT-FACED ⟳ more at HEAD n., RAMROD, RECORD n.

● *noun*

> **SEX 1** (*informal*) a person who has sexual relationships with people of the opposite sex, rather than the same sex: *gays and straights*

> **OF ROAD/TRACK 2** (also straight·a·way) a straight part of a RACETRACK or road

ˈstraight-arm (also ˈstiff-arm) *verb* ~ **sb** (in sports) to push away a player who is trying to stop you, with your arm straight

ˌstraight ˈarrow *noun* (*informal*) a person who is very honest or who never does anything exciting or different

straight·a·way *adv., noun*
● *adv.* /ˌstreɪtəˈweɪ/ ⟳ STRAIGHT *adv.*
● *noun* /ˈstreɪtəˌweɪ/ = STRAIGHT *n.* (2)

ˈstraight edge *noun* a strip of wood, metal, or plastic with a straight edge used for drawing accurate straight lines, or checking them

straight·en /ˈstreɪtn/ *verb* **1** [T, I] to become straight; to make something straight: *~ sth (out) I straightened my tie and walked in.* ◆ *~ (out) The road bends here then straightens out.* **2** [T, I] to make your body straight and vertical: *~ sth He stood up and straightened his shoulders.* ◆ *~ sth/yourself up I straightened myself up to answer the question.* ◆ *~ (up) Straighten up slowly, then repeat the exercise ten times.*

PHR V ˌstraighten sb↔ˈout to help someone to deal with problems or understand a confused situation **ˌstraighten sth↔ˈout** to deal with a confused situation by organizing things that are causing problems: *I need time to straighten out my finances.* **ˌstraighten sth↔ˈup** to make something neat and clean

ˌstraight-ˈfaced *adj.* without laughing or smiling, even though you may be amused

straight·for·ward **AWL** /ˌstreɪtˈfɔrwərd/ *adj.* **1** easy to do or to understand; not complicated **SYN** EASY: *a straightforward process* ◆ *It's quite straightforward to get here.* **2** (of a person or their behavior) honest and open; not trying to trick someone or hide something ▶ **straight·for·ward·ly** *adv.*: *Let me put it more straightforwardly.* **straight·for·ward·ness** *noun* [U]

straight·jack·et *noun* = STRAITJACKET

ˌstraight-ˈlaced *adj.* = STRAIT-LACED

ˈstraight man *noun* a person in a show whose role is to provide the main entertainer with opportunities to make jokes

ˌstraight-ˈout *adj.* honest and direct: *a straight-out refusal*

ˈstraight ˌrazor *noun* a RAZOR (= a tool used for shaving) with a long sharp blade ⟳ compare SAFETY RAZOR

ˌstraight ˈshooter *noun* a person who is honest and direct: *He's a straight shooter who will tell you exactly what he thinks.*

ˌstraight ˈticket *noun* (in elections) a vote in which someone chooses all the candidates from the same party ⟳ compare SPLIT TICKET ▶ **ˌstraight-ˈticket** *adj.*: *straight-ticket voting*

---

strain 🔑 /streɪn/ noun, verb

● **noun**

> WORRY/ANXIETY **1** [U, C] pressure on someone or something because they have too much to do or manage, or something very difficult to deal with; the problems, worry, or anxiety that this produces: *Their marriage is under great strain at the moment.* ◆ *These repayments are putting a strain on our finances.* ◆ *Relax, and let us take the strain (= do things for you).* ◆ *The transit service cannot cope with the strain of so many additional passengers.* ◆ *You will learn to cope with the stresses and strains of public life.* ◆ *I found it a strain having to concentrate for so long.* ⟳ note at PRESSURE

> PHYSICAL PRESSURE **2** [U, C] the pressure that is put on something when a physical force stretches, pushes, or pulls it: *The rope broke under the strain.* ◆ *You should try not to place too much strain on muscles and joints.* ◆ *The ground here cannot take the strain of a large building.* ◆ *The cable has a 300lb. breaking strain (= it will break when it is stretched or pulled by a force greater than this).*

> INJURY **3** [C, U] an injury to a part of your body, such as a muscle, that is caused by using it too much or by twisting it: *a calf/groin/leg strain* ◆ *muscle strain*

> TYPE OF PLANT/ANIMAL/DISEASE **4** [C] a particular type of plant or animal, or of a disease caused by bacteria, etc.: *a new strain of mosquitoes resistant to the poison* ◆ *This is only one of the many strains of the disease.*

> IN SOMEONE'S CHARACTER **5** [C, usually sing.] a particular tendency in the character of a person or group, or a quality in their manner SYN STREAK: *He had a definite strain of snobbery in him.*

> OF MUSIC **6** [C, usually pl.] (formal) the sound of music being played or sung: *She could hear the strains of Mozart through the window.*

● **verb**

> INJURE **1** [T] ~ sth/yourself to injure yourself or part of your body by making it work too hard: *to strain a muscle* ⟳ collocations at INJURY ⟳ thesaurus box at INJURE

> MAKE EFFORT **2** [T, I] to make an effort to do something, using all your mental or physical strength: ~ sth to do sth *I strained my ears (= listened very hard) to catch what they were saying.* ◆ ~ sth *Necks were strained for a glimpse of the stranger.* ◆ ~ to do sth *People were straining to see what was going on.* ◆ ~ (sth) (for sth) *He burst to the surface, straining for air.* ◆ *Bend gently to the left without straining.*

> STRETCH TO LIMIT **3** [T] ~ sth to try to make something do more than it is able to do: *The sudden influx of visitors is straining hotels in the town to the limit.* ◆ *His constant complaints were straining our patience.* ◆ *The dispute has strained relations between the two countries (= made them difficult).*

> PUSH/PULL HARD **4** [I] + adv./prep. to push hard against something; to pull hard on something: *She strained against the ropes that held her.* ◆ *The dogs were straining at the leash, eager to get to the park.*

> SEPARATE SOLID FROM LIQUID **5** [T] to pour food, etc. through something with very small holes in it, for example a SIEVE, in order to separate the solid part from the liquid part: ~ sth *Use a colander to strain the vegetables.* ◆ ~ sth off *Strain off any excess liquid.*

IDM **strain at the leash** (informal) to want to do something very much: *Like all youngsters, he's straining at the leash to leave home.* **strain every nerve/sinew (to do sth)** (formal) to try as hard as you can to do something

strained /streɪnd/ adj. **1** showing the effects of worry or pressure SYN TENSE: *Her face looked strained and weary.* ◆ *He spoke in a low, strained voice.* **2** (of a situation) not relaxed or friendly SYN TENSE: *There was a strained atmosphere throughout the meeting.* ◆ *Relations between the two families are strained.* **3** not natural; produced by a deliberate effort SYN FORCED: *She gave a strained laugh.*

strain·er /ˈstreɪnər/ noun a kitchen UTENSIL (= a tool) with a lot of small holes in it, used for separating solids from liquids: *a tea-strainer*

strait /streɪt/ noun **1** also **straits** [pl.] (especially in the names of places) a narrow passage of water that connects two seas or large areas of water: *the Strait(s) of Gibraltar*

2 straits [pl.] a very difficult situation especially because of lack of money: *The factory is in dire straits.* ◆ *She found herself in desperate financial straits.*

strait·ened /ˈstreɪtnd/ adj. [only before noun] (formal) without enough money or as much money as there was before: *The family of eight was living in straitened circumstances.*

strait·jack·et (also **straight·jack·et**) /ˈstreɪtˌdʒækət/ noun **1** a piece of clothing like a jacket with long arms that are tied to prevent the person wearing it from behaving violently. Straitjackets are sometimes used to control people who are mentally ill. **2** (disapproving) a thing that stops something from growing or developing: *the straitjacket of taxation*

strait-laced (also **straight-laced**) /ˌstreɪt ˈleɪst/ adj. (disapproving) having strict or old-fashioned ideas about people's moral behavior

strand /strænd/ noun, verb

● **noun 1** a single thin piece of thread, wire, hair, etc.: *a strand of wool* ◆ *a few strands of dark hair* ◆ *She wore a single strand of pearls around her neck.* **2** one of the different parts of an idea, a plan, a story, etc.: *We heard every strand of political opinion.* ◆ *The author draws the different strands of the plot together in the final chapter.* **3** (literary) the land along the edge of the ocean, or of a lake or river

● **verb** [usually passive] **1** ~ sb to leave someone in a place from which they have no way of leaving: *The strike left hundreds of tourists stranded at the airport.* **2** ~ sth to make a boat, fish, WHALE, etc. be left on land and unable to return to the water: *The ship was stranded on a sandbank.*

strange 🔑 /streɪndʒ/ adj. (stran·ger, stran·gest)

1 unusual or surprising, especially in a way that is difficult to understand: *A strange thing happened this morning.* ◆ *She was looking at me in a very strange way.* ◆ ~ (that)... *It's strange (that) we haven't heard from him.* ◆ ~ (how...) *It's strange how childhood impressions linger.* ◆ *That's strange — the front door's open.* ◆ *I'm looking forward to the exam, strange as it may seem.* ◆ *There was something strange about her eyes.* ◆ *Strange to say, I don't really enjoy television.* **2** not familiar because you have not been there before or met the person before: *a strange city* ◆ *to wake up in a strange bed* ◆ *Never accept rides from strange men.* ◆ ~ to sb *At first the place was strange to me.* ▶ **strange·ness** noun [U]: *We all felt the strangeness of being in a ghost town.*

IDM **feel strange** to not feel comfortable in a situation; to have an unpleasant physical feeling: *She felt strange sitting at her father's desk.* ◆ *It was terribly hot and I started to feel strange.* ⟳ more at TRUTH

strange·ly 🔑 /ˈstreɪndʒli/ adv.

in an unusual or surprising way: *She's been acting very strangely lately.* ◆ *The house was strangely quiet.* ◆ *strangely shaped rocks* ◆ *Strangely enough, I don't feel at all nervous.*

stran·ger 🔑 /ˈstreɪndʒər/ noun

1 a person that you do not know: *There was a complete stranger sitting at my desk.* ◆ *They got along well although they were total strangers.* ◆ *We've told our daughter not to speak to strangers.* ◆ ~ to sb *She remained a stranger to me.* **2** a person who is in a place that they have not been in before: *Sorry, I don't know where the bank is. I'm a stranger here myself.* ◆ ~ to... *He must have been a stranger to the town.*

IDM **be no/a stranger to sth** (formal) to be familiar/not familiar with something because you have/have not experienced it many times before: *He is no stranger to controversy.* **don't be a stranger** used to tell someone that you want them to visit you more often: *Don't be a stranger—you're welcome to come by anytime.* **hello, stranger** (humorous) used to say hello to someone you have not seen for a long time: *Hello, stranger! How've you been?*

stran·gle /ˈstræŋɡl/ verb **1** ~ sb to kill someone by squeezing or pressing on their throat and neck: *to strangle someone to death* ◆ *He strangled her with her own scarf.* **2** ~ sth

ʌ **cup**   ə **about**   eɪ **say**   aɪ **five**   ɔɪ **boy**   aʊ **now**   oʊ **go**   ər **bird**

to prevent something from growing or developing: *The current monetary policy is strangling the economy.*

stran·gled /ˈstræŋɡld/ *adj.* (of a cry, someone's voice, etc.) not clear because it stops before it has completely finished: *There was a strangled cry from the other room.*

stran·gle·hold /ˈstræŋɡlˌhoʊld/ *noun* [sing.] **1** a strong hold around someone's neck that makes it difficult for them to breathe **2** ~ **(on sth)** complete control over something that makes it impossible for it to grow or develop well: *The company now had a stranglehold on the market.*

stran·gler /ˈstræŋɡlər/ *noun* a person who kills someone by squeezing their throat tightly

stran·gu·la·ted /ˈstræŋɡyəˌleɪtəd/ *adj.* **1** (*medical*) (of a part of the body) squeezed so tightly that blood etc. cannot pass through it **2** (*formal*) (of a voice) sounding as though the throat is tightly squeezed, usually because of fear or worry: *He gave a strangulated squawk.*

stran·gu·la·tion /ˌstræŋɡyəˈleɪʃn/ *noun* [U] **1** the act of killing someone by squeezing their throat tightly; the state of being killed in this way: *to die of slow strangulation* **2** (*disapproving*) the act of preventing something from growing or developing: *the strangulation of the human spirit*

strap /stræp/ *noun, verb*
- *noun* a strip of leather, cloth, or other material that is used to fasten something, keep something in place, carry something, or hold onto something: *the shoulder straps of her dress* ◆ *a watch with a leather strap* ➔ picture at BAG
- *verb* (-pp-) ~ **sth** + **adv./prep.** to fasten someone or something in place using a strap or straps: *He strapped the knife to his leg.* ◆ *Everything had to be strapped down to stop it from sliding around.* ◆ *Are you strapped in* (= wearing a seat belt in a car, plane, etc.)?

strap·less /ˈstræpləs/ *adj.* (especially of a dress or BRA) without straps

strapped /stræpt/ *adj.* ~ **(for cash, funds, etc.)** (*informal*) having little or not enough money

strap·ping /ˈstræpɪŋ/ *adj.* [only before noun] (*informal*) (of people) big, tall, and strong: *a strapping lad*

strap·py /ˈstræpi/ *adj.* (**strap·pi·er, strap·pi·est**) (*informal*) (of shoes or clothes) having straps: *white strappy sandals*

stra·ta pl. of STRATUM

strat·a·gem /ˈstrætədʒəm/ *noun* (*formal*) a trick or plan that you use to gain an advantage or to trick an opponent

stra·te·gic ᴀᴡʟ /strəˈtidʒɪk/ (also *less frequent* **stra·te·gi·cal** /strəˈtidʒɪkl/) *adj.* [usually before noun] **1** done as part of a plan that is meant to achieve a particular purpose or to gain an advantage: *strategic planning* ◆ *a strategic decision to sell off part of the business* ◆ *Cameras were set up at strategic points* (= in places where they would be most effective) *along the route.* **2** connected with getting an advantage in a war or other military situation: *Guam was of vital strategic importance during the war.* **3** (of weapons, especially nuclear weapons) intended to be fired at an enemy's country rather than used in a battle ➔ compare TACTICAL ▶ **stra·te·gi·cally** ᴀᴡʟ /-kli/ *adv.*: *a strategically placed microphone* ◆ *a strategically important target*

the Stra·tegic De·fense In·itiative *noun* (*abbr.* SDI) a military plan in which it was intended to use technology in space to defend against MISSILES

strat·e·gist ᴀᴡʟ /ˈstrætədʒɪst/ *noun* a person who is skilled at planning things, especially military activities

strat·e·gy ✎ ᴀᴡʟ /ˈstrætədʒi/ *noun* (*pl.* **strat·e·gies**) **1** [C] a plan that is intended to achieve a particular purpose: *the government's economic strategy* ◆ ~ **for doing sth** *to develop a strategy for dealing with unemployment* ◆ ~ **to do sth** *It's all part of an overall strategy to gain promotion.* **2** [U] the process of planning something or putting a plan into operation in a skillful way: *marketing strategy* **3** [U, C] the skill of planning the movements of armies in a battle or war; an example of doing this: *military strategy* ◆ *defense strategies* ➔ collocations at WAR ◆ compare TACTIC

strat·i·fi·ca·tion /ˌstrætəfəˈkeɪʃn/ *noun* [U] (*technical*) the division of something into different layers or groups: *social stratification*

strat·i·fy /ˈstrætəˌfaɪ/ *verb* (**strat·i·fies, strat·i·fy·ing, strat·i·fied, strat·i·fied**) [usually passive] ~ **sth** (*formal* or *technical*) to arrange something in layers or STRATA: *a highly stratified society* ◆ *stratified rock*

strat·o·sphere /ˈstrætəˌsfɪr/ *noun* **the stratosphere** [sing.] the layer of the earth's atmosphere between about 6 and 31 miles above the surface of the earth ➔ compare IONO-SPHERE ▶ **strat·o·spher·ic** /ˌstrætəˈsfɪrɪk; -ˈsfɛrɪk/ *adj.*: *stratospheric clouds*
    IDM **in/into the stratosphere** at or to an extremely high level: *The technology boom sent share prices into the strato-sphere.*

stra·tum /ˈstreɪtəm; ˈstræ-/ *noun* (*pl.* **stra·ta** /-tə/) **1** (*geology*) a layer or set of layers of rock, earth, etc. **2** (*formal*) a class in a society: *people from all social strata*

stra·tus /ˈstrætəs/ *noun* [U] (*technical*) a type of cloud that forms a continuous gray sheet covering the sky

straw /strɔ/ *noun* **1** [U] STEMS of WHEAT or other grain plants that have been cut and dried. Straw is used for making MATS, hats, etc., for packing things to protect them, and as food for animals or for them to sleep on: *a mattress filled with straw* ◆ *a straw hat* ➔ compare HAY **2** [C] a single STEM or piece of straw: *He was leaning over the gate chewing on a straw.* **3** (also **drinking straw**) a thin tube of plastic or paper that you suck a drink through ➔ picture at PACKAGING
    IDM **clutch/grasp at straws** to try all possible means to find a solution or some hope in a difficult or unpleasant situation, even though this seems very unlikely **the last/final straw** | **the straw that breaks the camel's back** the last in a series of bad events, etc. that makes it impossible for you to accept a situation any longer ➔ more at BRICK, DRAW

straw·ber·ry /ˈstrɔˌbɛri/ *noun* (*pl.* **straw·ber·ries**) a soft red fruit with very small yellow seeds on the surface, that grows on a low plant: *strawberries and cream* ◆ *strawberry plants* ➔ picture at FRUIT

strawberry blonde (also **strawberry blond**) *adj.* (of hair) a light reddish-yellow color

straw-colored (CanE usually **straw-coloured**) *adj.* light yellow in color: *straw-colored hair*

straw man *noun* a weak, imaginary opponent or argument that is set up in order to be defeated easily

straw poll (also **straw vote**) *noun* an occasion when a number of people are asked in an informal way to give their opinion about something or to say how they are likely to vote in an election

stray /streɪ/ *verb, adj., noun*
- *verb* **1** [I] (+ **adv./prep.**) to move away from the place where you should be, without intending to: *He strayed into the path of an oncoming car.* ◆ *Her eyes kept straying over to the clock on the wall.* **2** [I] (+ **adv./prep.**) to begin to think about or discuss a different subject from the one you should be thinking about or discussing: *My mind kept straying back to our last talk together.* ◆ *We seem to be straying from the main theme of the debate.* **3** [I] (of a person who is married or in a relationship) to have a sexual relationship with someone who is not your usual partner
    IDM **stray from the path** to behave or think in ways that are not acceptable to the people around you: *He's an artist who chose to stray from the path.*
- *adj.* [only before noun] **1** (of animals normally kept as pets) away from home and lost; having no home: *stray dogs* **2** separated from other things or people of the same kind: *A civilian was killed by a stray bullet.* ◆ *a few stray hairs*
- *noun* **1** an animal that has gotten lost or separated from its owner or that has no owner ➔ see also WAIF **2** a person or thing that is not in the right place or is separated from others of the same kind

streak /strik/ *noun, verb*

● **noun 1** a long thin mark or line that is a different color from the surface it is on: *streaks of gray in her hair* ◆ *dirty streaks on the window* ⊃ **thesaurus box at MARK 2** a part of a person's character, especially an unpleasant part: *a ruthless/vicious/mean streak* ◆ *a streak of cruelty* **3** a series of successes or failures, especially in a sport or in gambling: *a streak of good luck* ◆ *to hit* (= have) *a winning streak* ◆ *to be on a winning/losing streak* ◆ *a lucky/unlucky streak*

● **verb 1** [T] to mark or cover something with streaks: **~ sth** *Tears streaked her face.* ◆ *She's had her hair streaked* (= had special chemicals put on her hair so that it has attractive colored lines in it). ◆ **~ sth with sth** *His face was streaked with mud.* **2** [I] **+ adv./prep.** to move very fast in a particular direction **SYN SPEED**: *A car pulled out and streaked off down the road.* **3** [I] **(+ adv./prep.)** (*informal*) to run through a public place with no clothes on as a way of getting attention

streak·er /'strikər/ *noun* a person who runs through a public place with no clothes on as a way of getting attention

streak·y /'striki/ *adj.* **1** marked with lines of a different color: *streaky blonde hair* ◆ *The wallpaper was streaky with grease.* **2** not consistent in quality or performance, especially in a sport: *He's always been a streaky hitter.*

stream 🔊 /strim/ *noun, verb*

● **noun 1** a small narrow river: *mountain streams* ⊃ see also DOWNSTREAM, UPSTREAM, THE GULF STREAM **2 ~ (of sth)** a continuous flow of liquid or gas: *A stream of blood flowed from the wound.* ⊃ see also BLOODSTREAM **3 ~ (of sth/sb)** a continuous flow of people or vehicles: *I've had a steady stream of visitors.* ◆ *Cars filed past in an endless stream.* **4 ~ of sth** a large number of things that happen one after the other: *a constant stream of inquiries* ◆ *The agency provided me with a steady stream of work.* **5** video or sound that you play on a computer by receiving it as a continuous stream from the Internet, rather than needing to wait until the whole of the material has been DOWNLOADED: *You can listen to a live stream of the speech at 10:00 a.m.*

● **verb 1** [I, T] (of liquid or gas) to move or pour out in a continuous flow; to produce a continuous flow of liquid or gas: **(+ adv./prep.)** *Tears streamed down his face.* ◆ **~ with sth** *Her head was streaming with blood.* ◆ **~ from sth** *Blood was streaming from her head.* ◆ *Black smoke streamed from the exhaust.* ◆ **~ sth** *The exhaust streamed black smoke.* **2** [I] **+ adv./prep.** (of people or things) to move somewhere in large numbers, one after the other: *People streamed across the bridge.* **3** [I] to move freely, especially in the wind or water: *Her scarf streamed behind her.* **4** [T] **~ sth** (*computing*) to play video or sound on a computer by receiving it as a continuous stream from the Internet

stream·er /'strimər/ *noun* **1** a long narrow piece of colored paper, used to decorate a place for a party or other celebration **2** a long narrow piece of cloth or other material

stream·line /'strimlaɪn/ *verb* [usually passive] **1 ~ sth** to give something a smooth, even shape so that it can move quickly and easily through air or water: *The cars all have a new streamlined design.* **2 ~ sth** (*business*) to make changes to a business or system, in order to make it more efficient, especially by spending less money: *The production process is to be streamlined.* ⊃ **thesaurus box at CUT**

,stream of 'consciousness *noun* [U] a continuous flow of ideas, thoughts, and feelings, as they are experienced by a person; a style of writing that expresses this without using the usual methods of description and conversation

street 🔊 /strit/ *noun, adj.*

● **noun 1** [C] (*abbr.* St.) a public road in a city or town that has houses and buildings on one side or both sides: *The bank is just across the street.* ◆ *to walk along/down/up the street* ◆ *the town's narrow cobbled streets* ◆ *92nd Street* ◆ *1600 Pennsylvania Avenue* ◆ *He is used to being recognized in the street.* ◆ *a street map/plan* of New York ◆ *street theater/musicians* ◆ *My office is at street level* (= on the ground floor). ◆ *It's not safe to walk the streets at night.* ⊃ see also BACKSTREET, MAIN

STREET, SIDE STREET ⊃ note at ROAD **2** [sing.] the ideas and opinions of ordinary people, especially people who live in cities, which are considered important: *The feeling I get from the street is that we have a good chance of winning this election.* ◆ *The word on the street is that it's not going to happen.* **IDM** **back on the streets/street** released from prison: *He was back on the streets after spending less than six years behind bars.* **(out) on the streets/street** (*informal*) without a home; outside, not in a house or other building: *the problems of young people living on the streets* ◆ *If it had been left to me I would have put him out on the street long ago.* **on/walking the streets** working as a PROSTITUTE **the streets are paved with gold** (*saying*) used to say that it seems easy to make money in a place ⊃ more at EASY, HIT, MAN, POUND

● **adj.** [only before noun] informal and based on the daily life of ordinary people in cities: *street sports such as skateboarding and skating* ◆ *street newspapers sold by the homeless* ◆ *street culture/dance/law*

street·board /'stritbɔrd/ (also Snake·board™) *noun* two small boards joined with a short pole and with wheels on, which you stand on and ride as a sport ▶ **street·board·ing** (also snake·board·ing) *noun* [U]

street·car /'stritkɑr/ (also trol·ley, 'trolley ,car) *noun* a vehicle driven by electricity, that runs on rails along the streets of a city or a town and carries passengers ⊃ picture at TRAIN

'street clothes *noun* [pl.] ordinary clothes that people wear in public: *She took off her costume and changed into street clothes.*

'street cred (also cred) (*informal*) (also less frequent 'street credi,bility) *noun* [U] a way of behaving and dressing that is acceptable to young people, especially those who live in cities and have experienced the problems of real life: *Those clothes do nothing for your street cred.*

'street ,hockey *noun* [U] a game like HOCKEY that is played on a hard surface, wearing IN-LINE SKATES

street·light /'stritlaɪt/ (also street·lamp) *noun* a light at the top of a tall post in the street ⊃ compare LAMPPOST

'street ,people *noun* people who have no home and who live outside in a town **SYN** THE HOMELESS

street·scape /'stritskeɪp/ *noun* a picture or view of a particular street or area of streets: *streetscape photos*

'street-smart *adj.* = STREETWISE ⊃ compare BOOK-SMART

'street smarts *noun* [pl.] (*informal*) the knowledge and experience that is needed to deal with the difficulties and dangers of life in a big city

'street ,theater (*CanE usually* 'street ,theatre) *noun* [U] plays or other performances that are done in the street

'street ,value *noun* [usually sing.] a price for which something that is illegal or has been obtained illegally can be sold: *drugs with a street value of over $1 million*

street·walk·er /'stritwɔkər/ *noun* (*old-fashioned*) a PROSTITUTE who looks for customers on the streets

street·wise /'stritwaɪz/ (also 'street-smart) *adj.* (*informal*) having the knowledge and experience that is needed to deal with the difficulties and dangers of life in a big city

strength 🔊 /strɛŋkθ; strɛŋθ/ *noun*

▷ BEING PHYSICALLY STRONG **1** [U, sing.] the quality of being physically strong: *He pushed against the rock with all his strength.* ◆ *It may take a few weeks for you to build up your strength again.* ◆ *He had a physical strength that matched his outward appearance.* ◆ *That kid doesn't know his own strength* (= does not realize how strong he really is). ◆ **~ to do sth** *She didn't have the strength to walk any further.* **2** [U] the ability that something has to resist force or hold heavy weights without breaking or being damaged: *the strength of a rope* ⊃ see also INDUSTRIAL-STRENGTH

▷ BEING BRAVE **3** [U, sing.] the quality of being brave and determined in a difficult situation: *During this ordeal he was able to draw strength from his faith.* ◆ *She has a remarkable inner strength.* ◆ *You have shown great strength of character.*

t **t**ea   ţ **butter**   d **d**id   k **c**at   g **g**ot   tʃ **ch**in   dʒ **J**une   f **f**all

> **POWER/INFLUENCE 4** [U] the power and influence that someone or something has: *Political power depends upon economic strength.* ◆ *Their superior military strength gives them a huge advantage.* ◆ *to negotiate from a position of strength* ◆ *The rally was intended to be a show of strength by the opposition.*
> **OF OPINION/FEELING 5** [U] how strong or deeply felt an opinion or a feeling is: *the strength of public opinion* ◆ *This view has recently gathered strength* (= become stronger or more widely held). ◆ *I was surprised by the strength of her feelings.*
> **ADVANTAGE 6** [C] a quality or an ability that a person or thing has that gives them an advantage: *The ability to keep calm is one of her many strengths.* ◆ *the strengths and weaknesses of an argument*
> **OF NATURAL FORCE 7** [U] how strong a natural force is: *the strength of the sun* ◆ *wind strength* ◆ *the strength and direction of the tide*
> **OF FLAVOR 8** [U, C] how strong a particular flavor or substance is: *Add more curry powder depending on the strength required.* ◆ *a selection of beers with different strengths* (= with different amounts of alcohol in them)
> **OF CURRENCY 9** [U] how strong a country's CURRENCY (= unit of money) is in relation to other countries' currencies: *the strength of the dollar*
> **NUMBER IN GROUP 10** [U] the number of people in a group, a team, or an organization: *The strength of the workforce is about to be doubled from 3,000 to 6,000.* ◆ *The team will be back at full strength* (= with all the best players) *for the next game.* ◆ *The protesters turned out in strength* (= in large numbers). ◆ *These cuts have left the local police force under strength* (= with fewer members than it needs).
> **IDM** go from strength to strength to become more and more successful: *Since her appointment the department has gone from strength to strength.* on the strength of sth because someone has been influenced or persuaded by something: *I got the job on the strength of your recommendation.* ⊃ more at TOWER

strength·en /ˈstrɛŋkθən; ˈstrɛŋθən/ *verb* [I, T] to become stronger; to make someone or something stronger: *Her position in the party has strengthened in recent weeks.* ◆ *Yesterday the yen strengthened against the dollar.* ◆ *The wind had strengthened overnight.* ◆ *~ sb/sth Repairs are necessary to strengthen the bridge.* ◆ *The exercises are designed to strengthen your stomach muscles.* ◆ *The move is clearly intended to strengthen the President's position.* ◆ *The new manager has strengthened the team by bringing in several younger players.* ◆ *Their attitude only strengthened his resolve to fight on.* ◆ *The new evidence will strengthen their case.* **ANT** WEAKEN

stren·u·ous /ˈstrɛnyuəs/ *adj.* **1** needing great effort and energy **SYN** ARDUOUS: *a strenuous climb* ◆ *Avoid strenuous exercise immediately after a meal.* ◆ *How about a stroll in the park? Nothing too strenuous.* **2** showing great energy and determination: *The ship went down although strenuous efforts were made to save it.* ▶ **stren·u·ous·ly** *adv.*: *He still works out strenuously every morning.* ◆ *The government strenuously denies the allegations.*

strep throat /ˌstrɛp ˈθroʊt/ *noun* (*informal*) an infection of the throat

strep·to·coc·cus /ˌstrɛptəˈkɑkəs/ *noun* (*pl.* **strep·to·coc·ci** /-ˈkɑkaɪ/) (*medical*) a type of bacteria, some types of which can cause serious infections and illnesses

stress 🔑 **AWL** /strɛs/ *noun, verb*
● *noun*
> **MENTAL PRESSURE 1** [U, C] pressure or worry caused by the problems in someone's life: *Things can easily go wrong when people are under stress.* ◆ *to suffer from stress* ◆ *coping with stress* ◆ *She failed to withstand the stresses and strains of public life.* ◆ *stress-related illnesses* ◆ *emotional/mental stress* ◆ *Stress is often a factor in the development of long-term sickness.* ◆ *stress management* (= dealing with stress) ⊃ thesaurus box at PRESSURE ⊃ collocations at DIET
> **PHYSICAL PRESSURE 2** [U, C] ~ (on sth) pressure put on something that can damage it or make it lose its shape: *When you have an injury you start putting stress on other parts of*

your body. ◆ *a stress fracture of the foot* (= one caused by such pressure)
> **EMPHASIS 3** [U] ~ (on sth) special importance given to something: *She lays great stress on punctuality.* ◆ *I think the company places too much stress on cost and not enough on quality.*
> **ON WORD/SYLLABLE 4** [U, C] (*phonetics*) an extra force used when pronouncing a particular word or syllable: *We worked on pronunciation, stress, and intonation.* ◆ *primary/secondary stress* ◆ *In "strategic" the stress falls on the second syllable* ⊃ compare INTONATION
> **IN MUSIC 5** [U, C] extra force used when making a particular sound in music
> **ILLNESS 6** [U] illness caused by difficult physical conditions: *Those most vulnerable to heat stress are the elderly.*
● *verb*
> **EMPHASIZE 1** [T] to emphasize a fact, an idea, etc.: ~ sth *He stressed the importance of a good education.* ◆ ~ that... *I must stress that everything I've told you is strictly confidential.* ◆ **+ speech** *"There is," Johnson stressed, "no real alternative."* ◆ **it is stressed that...** *It must be stressed that this disease is very rare.* ◆ ~ how, what, etc.... *I cannot stress too much how important this is.*
> **WORD/SYLLABLE 2** [T] ~ sth to give extra force to a word or syllable when saying it: *You stress the first syllable in "happiness."* **3** [I, T] to become or make someone become too anxious or tired to be able to relax: ~ out *I try not to stress out when things go wrong.* ◆ ~ sb (out) *Driving in cities really stresses me (out).*

THESAURUS

stress
emphasize
These words both mean to give extra force to a syllable, word, or phrase when you are saying it.
stress to give extra force to a word or syllable when saying it: *You stress the first syllable in "happiness."*
emphasize to give extra force to a word or phrase when saying it, especially to show that it is important: *Shylock repeatedly emphasizes the word "bond" in his speech.*

stressed 🔑 **AWL** /strɛst/ *adj.*
1 (*also informal* stressed out) [not before noun] too anxious and tired to be able to relax **2** (of a syllable) pronounced with emphasis **ANT** UNSTRESSED **3** [only before noun] (*technical*) that has had a lot of physical pressure put on it: *stressed metal*
stress·ful **AWL** /ˈstrɛsfl/ *adj.* causing a lot of anxiety and worry: *a stressful job* ◆ *It was a stressful time for all of us.*
stress mark *noun* a mark used to show where the stress is placed on a particular word or syllable ⊃ see also PRIMARY STRESS, SECONDARY STRESS
stress-timed *adj.* (*phonetics*) (of a language) having a regular rhythm of PRIMARY STRESSES. English is considered to be a stress-timed language. ⊃ compare SYLLABLE-TIMED

stretch 🔑 /strɛtʃ/ *verb, noun*
● *verb*
> **MAKE BIGGER/LOOSER 1** [T, I] ~ (sth) to make something longer, wider, or looser, for example by pulling it; to become longer, etc. in this way: *Is there any way of stretching shoes?* ◆ *This sweater has stretched.* **2** [I] (of cloth) to become bigger or longer when you pull it and return to its original shape when you stop: *The jeans stretch to provide a perfect fit.*
> **PULL TIGHT 3** [T] to pull something so that it is smooth and tight: ~ sth *Stretch the fabric tightly over the frame.* ◆ ~ sth **+ adj.** *Make sure that the rope is stretched tight.*
> **YOUR BODY 4** [I, T] to put your arms or legs out straight and contract your muscles: *He stretched and yawned lazily.* ◆ ~ sth *The exercises are designed to stretch and tone your leg muscles.*

> **REACH WITH ARM 5** [I, T] to put out an arm or a leg in order to reach something: **+ adv./prep.** *She stretched across the table for the butter.* ◆ **~ sth + adv./prep.** *I stretched out a hand and picked up the book.*

> **OVER AREA 6** [I] **+ adv./prep.** to spread over an area of land **SYN** EXTEND: *Fields and hills stretched out as far as we could see.*

> **OVER TIME 7** [I] **+ adv./prep.** to continue over a period of time: *The town's history stretches back to before 1500.* ◆ *The talks look set to stretch into a second week.*

> **MONEY/SUPPLIES/TIME 8** [I] **~ (to sth)** (used in negative sentences and questions about an amount of money) to be enough to buy or pay for something: *I need a new car, but my savings won't stretch to it.* **9** [T] **~ sb/sth** to make use of a lot of your money, supplies, time, etc.: *The influx of refugees has* **stretched** *the country's resources* **to the limit.** ◆ *We can't take on any more work—we're fully stretched as it is.*

> **SOMEONE'S SKILL/INTELLIGENCE 10** [T] **~ sb/sth** to make use of all someone's skill, intelligence, etc.: *I need a job that will stretch me.*

> **TRUTH/BELIEF 11** [T] **~ sth** to use something in a way that would not normally be considered fair, acceptable, etc.: *He admitted that he had maybe* **stretched the truth** *a little* (= not been completely honest). ◆ *The play's plot* **stretches** *credulity* **to the limit**.

IDM **stretch your legs** (*informal*) to go for a short walk after sitting for some time: *It was good to get out of the car and stretch our legs.* **stretch a/the point** to exaggerate slightly ⊃ more at RULE

PHR V **stretch 'out | ,stretch yourself 'out** to lie down, usually in order to relax or sleep: *He stretched himself out on the sofa and fell asleep.*

● *noun*
> **AREA OF LAND/WATER 1** [C] **~ (of sth)** an area of land or water, especially a long one: *an unspoiled stretch of coastline* ◆ *a particularly dangerous stretch of road* ◆ *You rarely see boats on this stretch of the river.*

> **PERIOD OF TIME 2** [C] a continuous period of time **SYN** SPELL: *They worked in four-hour stretches.* ◆ *She used to read for hours* **at a stretch** (= without stopping). **3** [C, usually sing.] (*informal*) a period of time that someone spends in prison: *He did a ten-year stretch for fraud.*

> **CHALLENGE 4** [sing.] something that requires great effort to do, imagine, or believe: *It's* **not much of a stretch** *to think this team can win seven games.*

> **OF BODY 5** [C, U] an act of stretching out your arms or legs or your body and contracting the muscles; the state of being stretched: *We got out of the car and* **had a good stretch.** ◆ *Only do these more difficult stretches when you are warmed up.* ◆ *Stay in this position and feel the stretch in your legs.*

> **OF FABRIC 6** [U] the ability to be made longer or wider without breaking or tearing: *You need a material with plenty of stretch in it.* ◆ *stretch jeans*

> **ON RACETRACK 7** [C, usually sing.] a straight part at the end of a racing track **SYN** STRAIGHT: *the final/home stretch* ◆ (*figurative*) *The campaign has entered its final stretch.*

IDM **not by any stretch of the imagination | by no stretch of the imagination** used to say strongly that something is not true, even if you try to imagine or believe it: *She could not, by any stretch of the imagination, be called beautiful.*

stretch·er /'strɛtʃər/ *noun, verb*
● *noun* a long piece of strong cloth with a pole on each side, used for carrying someone who is sick or injured and who cannot walk: *He was carried off on a stretcher.* ◆ *stretcher cases* (= people too badly injured to be able to walk)
● *verb* **~ sb + adv./prep.** [usually passive] to carry someone somewhere on a stretcher: *He was stretchered off the field with a broken leg.*

'stretcher-,bearer *noun* a person who helps to carry a stretcher, especially in a war or when there is a very serious accident

,stretch 'limo *noun* (also *formal* ,stretch 'limousine) a very

large car that has been made longer so that it can have extra seats

'stretch marks *noun* [pl.] the marks that are left on a person's skin after it has been stretched, particularly after a woman has been pregnant

stretch·y /'strɛtʃi/ *adj.* (stretch·i·er, stretch·i·est) that can easily be made longer or wider without tearing or breaking: *stretchy fabric*

strew /struː/ *verb* (strewed, strewed or strewed, strewn /struːn/) **1** [usually passive] to cover a surface with things **SYN** SCATTER: **~ A on, over, across, etc.** **B** *Clothes were strewn across the floor.* ◆ **~ B with A** *The floor was strewn with clothes.* ◆ (*figurative*) *The way ahead is strewn with difficulties.* **2** **~ sth** to be spread or lying over a surface: *Leaves strewed the path.*

stri·at·ed /'straɪeɪtəd/ *adj.* marked on the surface with thin lines, stripes, or RIDGES: *striated muscle fiber* ◆ *striated rock*

stri·a·tion /straɪˈeɪʃn/ *noun* [usually pl.] (*technical*) a striped pattern on something, especially on a muscle

strick·en /'strɪkən/ *adj., verb*
● *adj.* (*formal*) **1** seriously affected by an unpleasant feeling or disease or by a difficult situation: *She raised her stricken face and begged for help.* ◆ *We went to the aid of the stricken boat.* ◆ **~ with/by sth** *Whole villages were stricken with the disease.* ◆ *He was stricken by a heart attack on his fiftieth birthday.* **2** (in compounds) seriously affected by the thing mentioned: *poverty-stricken families* ⊃ see also GRIEF-STRICKEN, PANIC-STRICKEN
● *verb* pp of STRIKE *v.* (10)

strict /strɪkt/ *adj.* (strict·er, strict·est)
1 that must be obeyed exactly: *strict rules/regulations/discipline* ◆ *She left* **strict instructions** *that she was not to be disturbed.* ◆ *He told me* **in the strictest confidence** (= on the understanding that I would tell nobody else). ◆ *She's on a very strict diet.* **2** demanding that rules, especially rules about behavior, should be obeyed: *a strict teacher/parent/disciplinarian* ◆ *She's very strict about things like homework.* ◆ *They were always very strict with their children.* **3** obeying the rules of a particular religion, belief, etc. exactly: *a strict Muslim* ◆ *a strict vegetarian* **4** [usually before noun] very exact and clearly defined: *It wasn't illegal* **in the strict sense** *(of the word).* ▶ **strict·ness** *noun* [U]

strict·ly /'strɪktli/ *adv.*
1 with a lot of control and rules that must be obeyed: *She was brought up very strictly.* ◆ *The industry is strictly regulated.* **2** used to emphasize that something happens or must happen in all circumstances **SYN** ABSOLUTELY: *Smoking is strictly forbidden.* ◆ *My letter is, of course, strictly private and confidential.* **3** in all details; exactly: *This is not strictly true.* **4** used to emphasize that something only applies to one particular person, thing, or situation **SYN** PURELY: *We'll look at the problem from a strictly legal point of view.* ◆ *I know we're friends, but this is strictly business.*
IDM **strictly speaking** if you are using words or rules in their exact or correct sense: *Strictly speaking, the book is not a novel, but a short story.*

stric·ture /'strɪktʃər/ *noun* (*formal*) **1** [usually pl.] **~ (on sb/sth)** a severe criticism, especially of someone's behavior **2** **~ (against/on sth)** a rule or situation that restricts your behavior **SYN** RESTRICTION: *strictures against civil servants expressing political opinions*

stride /straɪd/ *verb, noun*
● *verb* (*pt* strode /stroʊd/) [I] (not used in the perfect tenses) **+ adv./prep.** to walk with long steps in a particular direction: *We strode across the snowy fields.* ◆ *She came striding along to meet me.*
● *noun* **1** one long step; the distance covered by a step **SYN** PACE[1]: *He crossed the room in two strides.* ◆ *I was gaining on the other runners* **with every stride.** **2** your way of walking or running: *his familiar, purposeful stride* ◆ *She did not slow her stride until she was face to face with us.* **3** an improvement in

| h **hat** | m **man** | n **no** | ŋ **sing** | l **leg** | r **red** | y **yes** | w **wet** |

the way something is developing: *We're **making great strides** in the search for a cure.*

IDM **hit (your) stride** to begin to do something with confidence and at a good speed after a slow, uncertain start **put sb off their stride** to make someone take their attention off what they are doing and stop doing it so well **(match sb) stride for stride** to keep doing something as well as someone else, even though they keep making it harder for you **take sth in stride** to accept and deal with something difficult without letting it worry you too much **without breaking stride** without stopping what you are doing

stri·dent /'straɪdnt/ *adj.* **1** having a loud, rough, and unpleasant sound: *a strident voice* ◆ *strident music* **2** aggressive and determined: *He is a strident advocate of nuclear power.* ◆ *strident criticism* ▶ **stri·den·cy** /'straɪdnsi/ *noun* [U] **stri·dent·ly** *adv.*

strife /straɪf/ *noun* [U] (*formal* or *literary*) angry or violent disagreement between two people or groups of people **SYN** CONFLICT: *civil strife* ◆ *The country was torn apart by strife.*

strike 🔑 /straɪk/ *verb, noun*

● **verb** (struck, struck /strʌk/) **HELP** In sense 10 the past participle is **strick·en** /'strɪkən/

▷ **HIT SOMEONE OR SOMETHING** **1** [T] ~ sb/sth (*formal*) to hit someone or something hard or with force: *The ship struck a rock.* ◆ *The child ran into the road and was struck by a car.* ◆ *The tree was struck by lightning.* ◆ *He fell, striking his head on the edge of the table.* ◆ *The stone struck her on the forehead.* ⊃ thesaurus box at HIT **2** [T] ~ sb/sth (sth) (*formal*) to hit someone or something with your hand or a weapon: *She struck him in the face.* ◆ *He struck the table with his fist.* ◆ *Who struck the first blow (= started the fight)?*

▷ **KICK/HIT BALL** **3** [T] ~ sth (*formal*) to hit or kick a ball, etc.: *He walked up to the penalty spot and struck the ball firmly into the back of the net.*

▷ **ATTACK** **4** [I] to attack someone or something, especially suddenly: *The lion crouched ready to strike.* ◆ *Police fear that the killer may strike again.*

▷ **OF DISASTER/DISEASE** **5** [I, T] to happen suddenly and have a harmful or damaging effect on someone or something: *Two days later tragedy struck.* ◆ ~ sb/sth *The area was struck by an outbreak of cholera.*

▷ **THOUGHT/IDEA/IMPRESSION** **6** [T] (not used in the progressive tenses) (of a thought or an idea) to come into someone's mind suddenly: ~ sb *An awful thought has just struck me.* ◆ *I was struck by her resemblance to my aunt.* ◆ **it strikes sb how, what, etc....** *It suddenly struck me how we could improve the situation.* **7** [T] to give someone a particular impression: ~ sb (as sth) *His reaction struck me as odd.* ◆ *How does the idea strike you?* ◆ *She strikes me as a very efficient person.* ◆ **it strikes sb that...** *It strikes me that nobody is really in favor of the changes.*

▷ **OF LIGHT** **8** [T] ~ sth to fall on a surface: *The windows sparkled as the sun struck the glass.*

▷ **DUMB/DEAF/BLIND** **9** [T] ~ sb + adj. [usually passive] to put someone suddenly into a particular state: *to be struck dumb/deaf/blind*

▷ **REMOVE** **10** (struck, strick·en) [T] ~ sb/sth from/off sth to remove someone or something from something written, such as a list or record: *Strike his name from the list.*

▷ **OF WORKERS** **11** [I] ~ (for sth) to refuse to work as a protest: *The union has voted to strike for a pay increase of 6%.* ◆ *Striking workers picketed the factory.*

▷ **MATCH** **12** [T, I] ~ (sth) to rub something such as a match against a surface so that it produces a flame; to produce a flame when rubbed against a rough surface: *to strike a match on a wall* ◆ *The sword struck sparks off the stone floor.* ◆ *The matches were damp and he couldn't make them strike.*

▷ **OF CLOCK** **13** [I, T] to show the time by making a ringing noise, etc. **SYN** CHIME: *Did you hear the clock strike?* ◆ ~ sth *The clock has just struck three.*

▷ **MAKE SOUND** **14** [T] ~ sth to produce a musical note, sound, etc. by pressing a key or hitting something: *to strike a chord on the piano*

▷ **GOLD/OIL, ETC.** **15** [T] ~ sth to discover gold, oil, etc. by digging or DRILLING: *They had struck oil!*

▷ **GO WITH PURPOSE** **16** [I] ~ (off/out) to go somewhere with great energy or purpose: *We left the road and struck off across the fields.*

▷ **MAKE COIN** **17** [T, usually passive] ~ sth to make a coin: *Those gold coins were struck in 1907.*

▷ **TENTS/SAILS, ETC.** **18** [T] ~ sth to take down tents, sails, etc.: *It took many hours to strike camp (= take down the tents that people live in).* ◆ *The ship struck her flag and surrendered.*

IDM **be struck by/with sb/sth** (*informal*) to be impressed or interested by someone or something: *I was struck by her youth and enthusiasm.* **strike a balance (between A and B)** to manage to find a way of being fair to two opposing things; to find an acceptable position that is between two things **strike a bargain/deal** to make an agreement with someone in which both sides have an advantage **strike a blow for/against/at sth** to do something in support of/ against a belief, principle, etc.: *He felt that they had struck a blow for democracy.* **strike fear, etc. into sb/sb's heart** (*formal*) to make someone afraid, etc. **strike gold** to find or do something that brings you a lot of success or money: *He has struck gold with his latest novel.* **strike it rich** (*informal*) to get a lot of money, especially suddenly or unexpectedly **strike (it) lucky** (*informal*) to have good luck **strike a pose** to hold your body in a particular way to create a particular impression **strike while the iron is hot** (*saying*) to make use of an opportunity immediately **ORIGIN** This expression refers to a blacksmith making a shoe for a horse. He has to strike/hammer the iron while it is hot enough to bend into the shape of the shoe. **within striking distance (of sth)** near enough to be reached or attacked easily; near enough to reach or attack something easily: *The beach is within striking distance.* ◆ *The cat was now within striking distance of the duck.* ⊃ more at CHORD, FANCY *n.*, HARD *adj.*, HOME *adv.*, LIGHTNING *n.*, NOTE *n.*, PAY DIRT

PHR V **'strike at sb/sth** **1** to try to hit someone or something, especially with a weapon: *He struck at me repeatedly with a stick.* **2** to cause damage or have a serious effect on someone or something: *to strike at the root of the problem* ◆ *criticisms that strike at the heart of the party's policies* **strike 'back (at/against sb)** to try to harm someone in return for an attack or injury you have received **strike sb 'down** [usually passive] **1** (of a disease, etc.) to make someone unable to lead an active life; to make someone seriously ill; to kill someone: *He was struck down by cancer at the age of thirty.* **2** to hit someone very hard, so that they fall to the ground **strike sth ↔ 'down** to decide that a law is illegal and should not apply: *The Supreme Court struck down a Texas state law.* **strike sth↔'off** to remove something with a sharp blow; to cut something off: *He struck off the rotten branches with an ax.* **strike 'out** **1** to start being independent: *I knew it was time I struck out on my own.* **2** (*informal*) to fail or be unsuccessful: *The movie struck out and didn't win a single Oscar.* **strike 'out (at sb/sth)** **1** to aim a sudden violent blow at someone or something: *He lost his temper and struck out wildly.* **2** to criticize someone or something, especially in a public speech or in a book or newspaper: *In a recent article she strikes out at her critics.* **strike 'out** | **strike sb↔'out** (in baseball) to fail to hit the ball three times and therefore not be allowed to continue hitting; to make someone do this ⊃ related noun STRIKEOUT **strike sth↔'out/'through** to remove something by drawing a line through it **SYN** CROSS OUT: *The editor struck out the whole paragraph.* **strike 'out (for/toward sth)** to move in a determined way (toward something): *He struck out (= started swimming) toward the shore.* **strike 'up (with sth)** | **strike 'up sth** (of a band, an ORCHESTRA, etc.) to begin to play a piece of music: *The orchestra struck up and the curtain rose.* ◆ *The band struck up a waltz.* **strike 'up sth (with sb)** to begin a friendship, a relationship, a conversation, etc.: *He would often strike up conversations with complete strangers.*

● **noun**

▷ **OF WORKERS** **1** a period of time when an organized group of employees of a company stops working because of a disagreement over pay or conditions: *the bus drivers' strike*

---

i see   ɪ sit   ɛ ten   æ cat   ɑ hot   ɔ saw   ʊ put   u too

◆ *a strike by teachers* ◆ *an **unofficial/a one-day strike*** ◆ *Air traffic controllers are threatening to **go on strike**.* ◆ *Half the workforce is now **(out) on strike**.* ◆ *The train drivers have voted to **take strike action**.* ◆ *The student union has called for a **rent strike*** (= a refusal to pay rent as a protest).* ⊃ see also GENERAL STRIKE, HUNGER STRIKE

▷ **ATTACK 2** a military attack, especially by aircraft dropping bombs: *an air strike* ◆ *They decided to launch a **pre-emptive strike**.*

▷ **HITTING/KICKING 3** [usually sing.] an act of hitting or kicking something or someone: *His spectacular strike in the second half made the score 2–0.* ⊃ see also BIRD STRIKE, LIGHTNING STRIKE

▷ **IN BASEBALL 4** an unsuccessful attempt to hit the ball ⊃ note at BASEBALL

▷ **IN BOWLING 5** a situation in TENPIN BOWLING when a player knocks down all the pins with the first ball

▷ **THROW 6** (especially in football) a perfectly thrown ball: *He threw a strike to Davis for a touchdown.*

▷ **DISCOVERY OF OIL 7** [usually sing.] a sudden discovery of something valuable, especially oil

▷ **BAD THING/ACTION 8 ~ (against sb/sth)** a bad thing or action that damages someone's/something's reputation: *The amount of fuel that this car uses is a big strike against it.*
IDM **three strikes and you're out| the three strikes rule** used to describe a law that says that people who commit three crimes will automatically go to prison **ORIGIN** From baseball, in which a batter who misses the ball three times is out.

strike·bound /ˈstraɪkbaʊnd/ *adj.* unable to operate because employees have stopped working as a protest: *a strikebound airport*

strike-breaker *noun* a person who continues to work while other employees are on strike; a person who is employed to replace people who are on strike ▶ **strike-breaking** *noun* [U]

strike force *noun* a military or police force that is ready to act quickly when necessary

strike·out /ˈstraɪkaʊt/ *noun* (in baseball) a situation in which the player who is supposed to be hitting the ball has to stop because he or she has tried to hit the ball three times and failed

strik·er /ˈstraɪkər/ *noun* **1** a worker who has stopped working because of a disagreement over pay or conditions **2** (in SOCCER) a player whose main job is to attack and try to score goals

strike zone *noun* (in baseball) the area between a BATTER'S upper arms and their knees, to which the ball must be PITCHED

strik·ing 🔑 /ˈstraɪkɪŋ/ *adj.*
1 interesting and unusual enough to attract attention **SYN** MARKED: *a striking feature* ◆ *She bears a **striking resemblance** to her older sister.* ◆ *In **striking contrast** to their brothers, the girls were both intelligent and charming.* ⊃ language bank at SURPRISING **2** very attractive, often in an unusual way **SYN** STUNNING: *striking good looks* ⊃ see also STRIKE v.
▶ **strik·ing·ly** *adv.*: *The two polls produced strikingly different results.* ◆ *She is strikingly beautiful.*

string 🔑 /strɪŋ/ *noun, verb, adj.*
● *noun*
▷ **FOR TYING/FASTENING 1** [U, C] material made of several threads twisted together, used for tying things together; a piece of string used to fasten or pull something or keep something in place: *a piece/length of string* ◆ *He wrapped the package in brown paper and tied it with string.* ◆ *The key is hanging on a string by the door.* ⊃ see also DRAWSTRING, G-STRING, THE PURSE STRINGS

▷ **THINGS JOINED 2** [C] a set or series of things that are joined together, for example on a string: *a string of pearls* ◆ *The molecules join together to form long strings.*

▷ **SERIES 3** [C] a series of things or people that come closely one after another: *a string of hits* ◆ *He owns a string of racing stables.*

▷ **COMPUTING 4** [C] a series of characters (= letters, numbers, etc.)

▷ **MUSICAL INSTRUMENTS 5** [C] a tightly stretched piece of wire, NYLON, or CATGUT on a musical instrument, that produces a musical note when the instrument is played **6** **the strings** [pl.] the group of musical instruments in an ORCHESTRA that have strings, for example VIOLINS, the people who play them: *The opening theme is taken up by the strings.* ⊃ picture at INSTRUMENT ⊃ compare BRASS, PERCUSSION, WOODWIND

▷ **ON TENNIS RACKET 7** [C] any of the tightly stretched pieces of NYLON, etc. in a RACKET, used for hitting balls in TENNIS and some other games

▷ **CONDITIONS 8** **strings** [pl.] special conditions or restrictions: *Major loans like these always come with strings.* ◆ *It's a business proposition, pure and simple. No strings attached.*

▷ **IN SPORT 9** usually -**string** ⊃ FIRST-STRING, SECOND-STRING, THIRD-STRING
IDM **have/keep sb/sth on a string** (informal) to be able to control someone or something and make them do what you want: *He doesn't even know I have him on a string.* ⊃ more at APRON, PULL v.

● *verb* (strung, strung /strʌŋ/)
▷ **HANG DECORATION 1** to hang or tie something in place, especially as decoration: **~ sth + adv./prep.** *We strung paper lanterns up in the trees.* ◆ **~ A on, along, in, etc. B** *Flags were strung out along the route.* ◆ **~ B with A** *The route was strung with flags.*

▷ **JOIN THINGS 2 ~ sth + adv./prep.** to put a series of small objects on string, etc.; to join things together with string, etc. **SYN** THREAD: *She had strung the shells on a silver chain.* ◆ (figurative) *carbon atoms strung together to form giant molecules*

▷ **RACKET/MUSICAL INSTRUMENT 3 ~ sth** to put a string or strings on a RACKET or musical instrument ⊃ see also HIGH-STRUNG
PHR V **string sb aˈlong** (informal) to allow someone to believe something that is not true, for example that you love them, intend to help them, etc.: *She has no intention of giving you a divorce; she's just stringing you along.* **string sth↔ˈout** to make something last longer than expected or necessary: *They seem determined to string the talks out for an indefinite period.* ⊃ see also STRUNG OUT **string sth↔toˈgether** to combine words or phrases to form sentences: *I can barely string two words together in Japanese.* **string sb↔up** (informal) to kill someone by hanging them, especially illegally

● *adj.* [only before noun]
▷ **MUSICAL INSTRUMENT 1** consisting of musical instruments that have strings; connected with these musical instruments: *a string quartet* ◆ *a string player*

▷ **MADE OF STRING 2** made of string or something like string: *a string bag*

string bass *noun* a word for a DOUBLE BASS, used especially by JAZZ musicians

string bean *noun* **1** = GREEN BEAN **2** (informal) a very tall, thin person

string cheese *noun* [U] MOZZARELLA cheese in a tube shape that you eat by pulling off strips of it

stringed instrument *noun* any musical instrument with strings that you play with your fingers or with a BOW ²

strin·gent /ˈstrɪndʒənt/ *adj.* (formal) **1** (of a law, rule, regulation, etc.) very strict and that must be obeyed: *stringent air quality regulations* **2** (of financial conditions) difficult and very strictly controlled because there is not much money: *the government's stringent economic policies* ▶ **strin·gen·cy** /-dʒənsi/ *noun* [U]: *a period of financial stringency* **strin·gent·ly** *adv.*: *The rules are stringently enforced.*

string·er /ˈstrɪŋər/ *noun* a journalist who is not on the regular staff of a newspaper, but who often supplies stories for it

string·y /ˈstrɪŋi/ *adj.* (disapproving) **1** (of hair) long and thin and looking as if it has not been washed **2** (of food) containing long thin pieces like string and difficult to chew: *tough, stringy meat* **3** (of a person or part of their body) thin so that you can see the muscles: *a stringy neck*

strip 🔑 /strɪp/ *verb, noun*

● **verb** (-pp-)

> **TAKE OFF CLOTHES** **1** [I, T] to take off all or most of your clothes or another person's clothes **SYN** UNDRESS: *I stripped and washed myself all over.* ◆ **~ down to sth** *She stripped down to her underwear.* ◆ **~ sth off** | **~ sb (to sth)** *He stood there* **stripped to the waist** (= he had no clothes on the upper part of his body). ◆ **~ sb + adj.** *He was* **stripped naked** *and left in a cell.* **2** [I] to take off your clothes as a form of entertainment; to perform a STRIPTEASE

> **REMOVE LAYER** **3** [T] to remove a layer from something, especially so that it is completely exposed: **~ sth (off)** *Strip off all the existing paint.* ◆ *After the guests had gone, I stripped all the beds* (= removed all the sheets in order to wash them). ◆ **~ A off/from B** *Deer had stripped all the bark off the tree.* ◆ **~ B of A** *Deer had stripped the tree of its bark.*

> **REMOVE EVERYTHING** **4** [T] to remove all the things from a place and leave it empty: **~ sth (out)** *We had to strip out all the old wiring and start again.* ◆ **~ sth + adj.** *Thieves had stripped the house bare.*

> **MACHINE** **5** [T] **~ sth (down)** to separate a machine, etc. into parts so that they can be cleaned or repaired **SYN** DISMANTLE: *They taught us how to strip down a car engine and put it back together again.*

> **PUNISHMENT** **6** [T] **~ sb of sth** to take away property or honors from someone, as a punishment: *He was disgraced and stripped of his title.*

> **SCREW/GEAR** **7** [T] **~ sth** to damage a screw or gear: *It's possible that the gears are stripped on the motor.*

PHR V **strip sth↔a·way** **1** to remove a layer from something: *First, you need to strip away all the old plaster.* **2** to remove anything that is not true or necessary: *The movie aims to strip away the lies surrounding Kennedy's life.*

● **noun**

> **LONG NARROW PIECE** **1** a long narrow piece of paper, metal, cloth, etc.: *a strip of material* ◆ *Cut the meat into strips.* ⊃ see also RUMBLE STRIP **2** a long narrow area of land, ocean, etc.: *the Gaza Strip* ◆ *The islands are separated by a narrow strip of water.* ⊃ see also AIRSTRIP, LANDING STRIP

> **STREET** **3** a street that has many shops, stores, restaurants, etc. along it: *Sunset Strip*

> **PICTURE STORY** **4** = COMIC STRIP

strip club (also **strip joint**) *noun* a club where people go to watch performers take their clothes off in a sexually exciting way

stripe 🔑 /straɪp/ *noun*

1 a long narrow line of color, that is a different color from the areas next to it: *a zebra's black and white stripes* ◆ *a white tablecloth with red stripes* ⊃ picture at CLOTHES ⊃ see also PINSTRIPE, THE STARS AND STRIPES **2** a narrow piece of cloth, often in the shape of a V, that is worn on the uniform of a soldier or police officer to show their rank **3** a type, category, or opinion: *politicians* **of every stripe** ◆ *commentators* **of all** *political* **stripes** ◆ *She's an educator* **of a very different stripe.**

striped 🔑 /straɪpt/ *adj.*

marked with a pattern of stripes: *a striped shirt* ◆ *a blue and white striped jacket*

strip light *noun* a light consisting of a long glass tube that is used especially in offices, kitchens, etc. ▶ **strip lighting** *noun* [U]

strip·ling /ˈstrɪplɪŋ/ *noun* (*old-fashioned* or *humorous*) a young man who is older than a boy but who does not seem to be a real man yet

strip mall *noun* a line of stores and restaurants beside a main road

strip mining *noun* [U] a type of mining in which coal is taken out of the ground near the surface ⊃ see also OPEN-PIT

stripped-down *adj.* [usually before noun] **1** keeping only the most basic or essential features, with everything else removed: *a stripped-down version of the song* **2** (of a machine or vehicle) taken to pieces, with all the parts removed

strip·per /ˈstrɪpər/ *noun* **1** [C] a performer who takes his or her clothes off in a sexually exciting way in front of an audience: *a male stripper* **2** [U, C] (especially in compounds) a substance or tool that is used for removing paint, etc. from something: *paint stripper*

strip search *noun* an act of searching a person for illegal drugs, weapons, etc., for example at an airport or in a prison, after they have been made to take off all their clothes ▶ **strip-search** *verb* **~ sb**

strip·tease /ˈstrɪptiz/ *noun* [C, U] a form of entertainment, for example in a bar or club, when a performer removes his or her clothes in a sexually exciting way, usually to music, in front of an audience

strive /straɪv/ *verb* (**strove** /stroʊv/, **striv·en** /ˈstrɪvn/) (or (*less frequent* **strived**, **strived**) [I] (*formal*) to try very hard to achieve something: **~ (for sth)** *We encourage all members to strive for the highest standards.* ◆ **~ (against sth)** *striving against corruption* ◆ **~ to do sth** *Newspaper editors all strive to be first with a story.* ▶ **striv·ing** *noun* [U, sing.]: *our striving for perfection*

strobe /stroʊb/ (also **strobe light**) *noun* a bright light that flashes rapidly on and off, used especially at DISCOS

strob·ing /ˈstroʊbɪŋ/ *noun* [U] (*technical*) the effect, sometimes seen in the lines and stripes in a television picture, of sudden movements or flashing

strode *pt of* STRIDE

stroke 🔑 /stroʊk/ *noun, verb*

● **noun**

> **HITTING MOVEMENT** **1** an act of hitting a ball, for example with a GOLF CLUB or RACKET: *What a beautiful stroke!* ◆ *He won by two strokes* (= in GOLF, by taking two fewer strokes than his opponent). **2** a single movement of the arm when hitting someone or something: *His punishment was six strokes of the cane.*

> **IN SWIMMING/ROWING** **3** any of a series of repeated movements in swimming or ROWING: *She took a few more strokes to reach the bank.* **4** (often in compounds) a style of swimming: *Butterfly is the only stroke I can't do.* ⊃ see also BACKSTROKE, BREASTSTROKE **5** the person who sets the speed at which everyone in a boat ROWS

> **ILLNESS** **6** a sudden serious illness when a blood VESSEL (= tube) in the brain bursts or is blocked, which can cause death or the loss of the ability to move or to speak clearly: *to* **have/suffer a stroke** ◆ *The stroke left him partly paralyzed.*

> **GENTLE TOUCH** **7** [usually sing.] an act of moving your hand gently over a surface, usually several times: *He gave the cat a stroke.* ⊃ see also PET

> **OF PEN/BRUSH** **8** a mark made by moving a pen, brush, etc. once across a surface: *to paint with fine brush strokes* ◆ *At the* **stroke of a pen** (= by signing something) *they removed thousands of people from the welfare system.*

> **ACTION** **9** **~ (of sth)** a single successful action or event: *Your idea was a* **stroke of genius.** ◆ *It was a* **stroke of luck** *that I found you here.* ◆ *It was a* **bold stroke** *to reveal the identity of the murderer on the first page.* ◆ *She* **never does a stroke (of work)** (= never does any work). ⊃ see also MASTERSTROKE

> **OF CLOCK** **10** each of the sounds made by a clock or bell giving the hours: *At the first stroke it will be 9 o'clock exactly.* ◆ **on the stroke of three** (= at 3 o'clock exactly)

IDM **at a (single) stroke** | **at one stroke** with a single immediate action: *They threatened to cancel the whole project at a stroke.*

● **verb**

> **TOUCH GENTLY** **1** **~ sth** to move your hand gently and slowly over an animal's fur or hair: *He's a beautiful dog. Can I stroke him?* ⊃ see also PET **2** **~ sth/sb** to move your hand gently over a surface, someone's hair, etc.: *He stroked her hair affectionately.*

> MOVE SOMETHING GENTLY **3** ~ sth + adv./prep. to move something somewhere with a gentle movement: *She stroked away his tears.* ◆ *He stroked the ball between the posts.*
> BE NICE TO SOMEONE **4** ~ **sb** (*informal*) to be very nice to someone, especially to get them to do what you want

stroke play (also **'medal ,play**) *noun* [U] a way of playing GOLF in which your score depends on the number of times you hit the ball in the whole game, rather than on the number of holes that you win ⊃ compare MATCH PLAY

stroll /stroʊl/ *verb, noun*
• *verb* [I] (+ adv./prep.) to walk somewhere in a slow relaxed way: *People were strolling along the beach.*
• *noun* a slow relaxed walk: *We went for a stroll in the park.*

canopy

stroller   baby carriage

stroll·er /'stroʊlər/ *noun* **1** a small folding seat on wheels in which a small child sits and is pushed along ⊃ compare BABY CARRIAGE **2** a person who is enjoying a slow relaxed walk

strong 🔊 /strɔŋ/ *adj.*
(**strong·er** /'strɔŋɡər/, **strong·est** /'strɔŋɡəst/)

WORD FAMILY
strong *adj.*
strongly *adv.*
strength *noun*
strengthen *verb*

> HAVING PHYSICAL POWER **1** (of people, animals, etc.) having a lot of physical power so that you can lift heavy weights, do hard physical work, etc.: *strong muscles* ◆ *She wasn't a strong swimmer* (= she could not swim well). ◆ *He's strong enough to lift a car!* **2** (of a natural or physical force) having great power: *Stay indoors in the middle of the day, when the sun is strongest.* ◆ *a strong wind/current* ◆ *a strong magnet* **3** having a powerful effect on the body or mind: *a strong drug*
> HAVING POWER OVER PEOPLE **4** having a lot of power or influence: *a strong leader/government* **5** **the strong** [pl.] people who are rich or powerful
> HARD TO RESIST/DEFEAT/ATTACK **6** very powerful and difficult for people to fight against or defeat: *a strong team* ◆ (*figurative*) *The temptation to tell her everything was very strong.* **7** (of an argument, evidence, etc.) difficult to attack or criticize: *There is strong evidence of a link between exercise and a healthy heart.* ◆ *You have a strong case for getting your job back.*
> OPINION/BELIEF/FEELING **8** [only before noun] (of a person) holding an opinion or a belief very firmly and seriously **SYN** FIRM: *a strong supporter/opponent of the government* **9** (of an opinion, a belief, or a feeling) very powerful: *strong support for the government* ◆ *People have strong feelings about this issue.*
> NOT EASILY BROKEN **10** (of objects) not easily broken or damaged; made well: *a strong chair*
> NOT EASILY UPSET **11** not easily upset or frightened; not easily influenced by other people: *You need strong nerves to ride a bike in San Francisco.* ◆ *It's difficult, I know. But be strong!* ◆ *a strong personality* ⊃ see also HEADSTRONG, STRONG-MINDED, STRONG-WILLED
> LIKELY TO SUCCEED **12** likely to succeed or happen: *a strong candidate for the job* ◆ *You're in a strong position to negotiate a deal.* ◆ *There's a strong possibility that we'll lose the game.*

> GOOD AT SOMETHING **13** good at something: *The play has a very strong cast.* ◆ *Mathematics was never my strong point* (= I was never very good at it).
> NUMBER **14** great in number: *There was a strong police presence at the demonstration.* **15** used after numbers to show the size of a group: *a 5,000-strong crowd* ◆ *The crowd was 5,000 strong.*
> HEALTHY **16** (of a person) not easily affected by disease; healthy: *Are you feeling stronger now after your rest?* ⊃ thesaurus box at WELL
> FIRMLY ESTABLISHED **17** firmly established; difficult to destroy: *a strong marriage* ◆ *The college has strong links with local industry.*
> BUSINESS **18** (of prices, an economy, etc.) having a value that is high or increasing: *strong share prices* ◆ *The euro is getting stronger against the dollar.* **19** (of a business or an industry) in a safe financial position: *Their catering business remained strong despite the recession.*
> EASY TO SEE/HEAR/FEEL/SMELL **20** easy to see, feel, or smell; very great or INTENSE: *a strong smell* ◆ *a strong feeling of nausea* ◆ *a strong voice* (= loud) ◆ *strong colors* ◆ *a face with strong features* (= large and noticeable) ◆ *She spoke with a strong mid-western accent.* ◆ *He was under strong pressure to resign.*
> FOOD **21** having a lot of flavor: *strong cheese*
> DRINKS **22** containing a lot of a substance: *strong black coffee*
> WORDS **23** (of words or language) having a lot of force, often causing offense to people: *The movie has been criticized for strong language* (= swearing).
> GRAMMAR **24** [usually before noun] (of a verb) forming the past tense and past participle by changing a vowel, not by adding a regular ending, for example *sing, sang*
> PHONETICS **25** [usually before noun] used to describe the way some words are pronounced when they have stress. For example, the strong form of *and* is /ænd/. **ANT** WEAK
▶ **strong·ly** *adv.*: *a strongly built boat* ◆ *a light shining strongly* ◆ *a strongly worded protest* ◆ *He was strongly opposed to the idea.* ◆ *This is an issue I feel strongly about* (= I have firm opinions about). ◆ *The room smelled strongly of polish.*
IDM **be strong on sth 1** to be good at something: *I'm not very strong on dates* (= I can't remember the dates of important events). **2** to have a lot of something: *The report was strong on criticism, but short on practical suggestions.* **be sb's strong suit** to be a subject that someone knows a lot about: *I'm afraid geography is not my strong suit.* **come on strong** (*informal*) to make your feelings clear in an aggressive way, especially your sexual feelings toward someone **going strong** (*informal*) to continue to be healthy, active, or successful: *My grandmother is 90 and still going strong.* **have a strong stomach** to be able to see or do unpleasant things without feeling sick or upset **strong medicine** something extreme or severe that is used to deal with a bad situation or problem: *The policy is strong medicine, but it will save us millions.* ⊃ more at CARD *n.*

strong-arm *adj.* [only before noun] (*disapproving*) using threats or violence in order to make people do what you want: *to use strong-arm tactics against your political opponents* ▶ **'strong-arm** *verb*: **~ sb (into doing sth)** *We don't want people to feel strong-armed into buying these products.*

strong·box /'strɔŋbɑks/ *noun* a strong, usually metal, box for keeping valuable things in

strong force *noun* (*physics*) one of the four FUNDAMENTAL FORCES in the universe, that holds the parts of the NUCLEUS of an atom together ⊃ see also ELECTROMAGNETISM, GRAVITY, WEAK FORCE

strong·hold /'strɔŋhoʊld/ *noun* **1** an area in which there is a lot of support for a particular belief or group of people, especially a political party: *a Republican stronghold/a stronghold of Republicanism* **2** a castle or a place that is strongly built and difficult to attack **3** an area where there are a large number of a particular type of animal: *This valley is one of the last strongholds of the Siberian tiger.*

t tea   ṭ butter   d did   k cat   ɡ got   tʃ chin   dʒ June   f fall

strong·man /ˈstrɔŋmæn/ noun (pl. **strong·men** /-mɛn/) **1** a leader who uses threats or violence to rule a country **2** a physically very strong man, especially someone who performs in a CIRCUS

strong-ˈminded adj. having strong opinions that are not easily influenced by what other people think or say **SYN** DETERMINED

strong·room /ˈstrɔŋrum/; -rʊm/ noun a room, for example in a bank, with thick walls and a strong, solid door, where valuable items are kept

strong ˈsafety noun (in football) a DEFENSIVE player who plays opposite the attacking team's strongest side

strong-ˈwilled adj. determined to do what you want to do, even if other people advise you not to

stron·ti·um /ˈstrɑntiəm; -ʃiəm/ noun [U] (symb. **Sr**) a chemical element. Strontium is a soft silver-white metal.

strop /strɑp/ noun a strip of leather used to make a RAZOR sharp

stro·phe /ˈstroʊfi/ noun (technical) a group of lines forming a section of a poem ⊃ compare STANZA ▶ **stroph·ic** /ˈstroʊfɪk; ˈstrɑ-/ adj.

strove pt of STRIVE

struck pt, pp of STRIKE

struc·tur·al **AWL** /ˈstrʌktʃərəl/ adj. [usually before noun] connected with the way in which something is built or organized: *Storms have caused structural damage to hundreds of homes.* ◆ *structural changes in society* ▶ **struc·tur·al·ly** **AWL** adv.: *The building is structurally sound.* ◆ *The languages are structurally different.*

structural engiˈneer noun a person whose job is to plan large buildings, bridges, etc.

struc·tur·al·ism /ˈstrʌktʃərə,lɪzəm/ noun [U] (in literature, language, and social science) a theory that considers any text as a structure whose various parts only have meaning when they are considered in relation to each other ⊃ compare DECONSTRUCTION ▶ **struc·tur·al·ist** /-lɪst/ noun, adj.: *a structuralist approach*

structural linˈguistics noun [U] the part of LINGUISTICS that deals with language as a system of related structures

struc·ture 🔑 **AWL** /ˈstrʌktʃər/ noun, verb
● **noun 1** [U, C] the way in which the parts of something are connected together, arranged, or organized; a particular arrangement of parts: *the structure of the building* ◆ *changes in the social and economic structure of society* ◆ *the grammatical structures of a language* ◆ *a salary structure* **2** [C] a thing that is made of several parts, especially a building: *a stone/brick/wooden structure* ⊃ thesaurus box at BUILDING **3** [U, C] the state of being well organized or planned with all the parts linked together; a careful plan: *Your essay needs (a) structure.*
● **verb** [usually passive] to arrange or organize something into a system or pattern: **~ sth** *How well does the teacher structure the lessons?* ◆ *Make use of the toys in structured group activities.* ◆ **~ sth around sth** *The exhibition is structured around the themes of work and leisure.*

THESAURUS

structure

framework • form • composition • construction • fabric

These are all words for the way the different parts of something combine together or the way that something has been made.

structure the way in which the parts of something are connected together or arranged; a particular arrangement of parts: *the structure of the building/human body* ◆ *the social structure of society* ◆ *the grammatical structures of a language* ◆ *a salary structure*

framework a set of beliefs, ideas, or rules that forms the basis of a system or society: *The report provides a framework for further research.*

form the arrangement of parts in a whole, especially in a work of art or piece of writing: *As a photographer, shape and form were more important to him than color.*

composition (somewhat formal) the different parts or people that combine to form something; the way in which they combine: *recent changes in the composition of our workforce*

construction the way that something has been built or made: *He blamed the accident on shoddy construction.*

fabric (somewhat formal) the basic structure of a society or an organization that enables it to function successfully: *This is a trend that threatens the very fabric of society.*

PATTERNS
- the **basic** structure/framework/form/composition/construction/fabric of sth
- a **simple/complex** structure/framework/form
- the **economic/political/social** structure/framework/composition/fabric of sth
- the **chemical/genetic** structure/composition of sth

stru·del /ˈstrudl/ noun [U, C] (from German) a cake made from pieces of fruit, especially apple, rolled in thin PASTRY and baked

strug·gle 🔑 /ˈstrʌgl/ verb, noun
● **verb 1** [I] to try very hard to do something when it is difficult or when there are a lot of problems: **~ (for sth)** *a country struggling for independence* ◆ *Shona* **struggled for breath**. ◆ *life as a struggling artist* (= one who is very poor) ◆ **~ to do sth** *They struggled just to pay their bills.* **2** [I] + **adv./prep.** to move somewhere or do something with difficulty: *I struggled up the hill with the heavy bags.* ◆ *Paul struggled out of his wheelchair.* **3** [I] to fight against someone or something in order to prevent a bad situation or result: **~ (against sb/sth)** *He struggled against cancer for two years.* ◆ **~ (with sb/sth)** *Lisa struggled with her conscience before talking to the police.* **4** [I] to fight someone or try to get away from them: *I struggled and screamed for help.* ◆ **~ together** *Ben and Jack struggled together on the grass.* ◆ **~ with sb** *James was hit in the mouth as he struggled with the raiders.* ◆ **+ adj.** *How did she manage to* **struggle free?** **5** [I] **~ (with sb) (for sth)** to compete or argue with someone, especially in order to get something: *rival leaders struggling for power*
PHR V **struggle aˈlong/ˈon** to continue despite problems
● **noun 1** [C] a hard fight in which people try to obtain or achieve something, especially something that someone else does not want them to have: *a power/leadership struggle* ◆ **~ (with sb) (for/against sth)** *a struggle for independence* ◆ **~ (with sb) (to do sth)** *He is engaged in a bitter struggle with his rival to get control of the company.* ◆ **~ (between A and B)** *the struggle between good and evil* ◆ *She will not give up her children without a struggle.* ⊃ thesaurus box at CAMPAIGN **2** [C] a physical fight between two people or groups of people, especially when one of them is trying to escape, or to get something from the other: *There were no signs of a struggle at the murder scene.* ⊃ thesaurus box at FIGHT **3** [sing.] **~ (to do sth)** something that is difficult for you to do or achieve **SYN** EFFORT: *It was a real struggle to be ready on time.*

strum /strʌm/ verb (-mm-) [I, T] **~ (on) sth** to play a GUITAR or similar instrument by moving your fingers up and down across the strings: *As she sang, she strummed on a guitar.*

strum·pet /ˈstrʌmpət/ noun (old use, disapproving) a PROSTITUTE, or a woman who looks and behaves like one

strung pt, pp of STRING

strung ˈout adj. [not before noun] **1** spread out in a line: *a group of riders strung out along the beach* **2** **~ (on sth)** (slang) strongly affected by an illegal drug such as HEROIN

strut /strʌt/ *verb, noun*

● *verb* (-tt-) [I] to walk proudly with your head up and chest out to show that you think you are important: *The players strutted and posed for the cameras.*
IDM **strut your stuff** (*informal*) to proudly show your ability, especially at dancing or performing

● *noun* **1** a long thin piece of wood or metal used to support part of a vehicle or building or make it stronger **2** [sing.] (*disapproving*) an act of walking in a proud and confident way

strych·nine /'strɪknaɪn; -nən; -nin/ *noun* [U] a poisonous substance used in very small amounts as a medicine

stub /stʌb/ *noun, verb*

● *noun* **1** a short piece of a cigarette, pencil, etc. that is left when the rest of it has been used **2** the small part of a ticket, check, etc. that you keep as a record when you have given the main part to someone ➔ see also PAY STUB

● *verb* (-bb-) **~ your toe (against/on something)** to hurt your toe by accident by hitting it against something hard **PHR V** **stub sth↔'out** to stop a cigarette, etc. from burning by pressing the end against something hard

stub·ble /'stʌbl/ *noun* [U] **1** the lower, short, stiff part of the STEMS of crops such as WHEAT that are left in the ground after the top part has been cut and collected **2** the short stiff hairs that grow on a man's face when he has not shaved recently ➔ picture at HAIR ▶ **stub·bly** /'stʌbli; -bl·i/ *adj.*

stub·born /'stʌbərn/ *adj.* **1** (*often disapproving*) determined not to change your opinion or attitude **SYN** OBSTINATE: *He was too stubborn to admit that he was wrong.* ♦ *She can be as* ***stubborn as a mule.*** ♦ *stubborn pride* ♦ *a stubborn resistance to change* ♦ *a stubborn refusal to listen* **2** difficult to get rid of or deal with **SYN** PERSISTENT: *a **stubborn cough/stain*** ♦ *a stubborn problem* ▶ **stub·born·ly** /'stʌbərnli/ *adv.*: *She stubbornly refused to pay.* ♦ *Unemployment remains stubbornly high.* **stub·born·ness** *noun* [U]

stub·by /'stʌbi/

● *adj.* [usually before noun] short and thick: *stubby fingers*

stuc·co /'stʌkoʊ/ *noun* [U] a type of PLASTER that is used for covering ceilings and the outside walls of buildings ▶ **stuc·coed** /'stʌkoʊd/ *adj.*: *a stuccoed wall*

stuck /stʌk/ *adj.* [not before noun] ➔ see also STICK **1** unable to move or to be moved: *The wheels were stuck in the mud.* ♦ *This drawer keeps **getting stuck**.* ♦ *She got the key stuck in the lock.* ♦ *I can't get out—I'm stuck.* **2** in an unpleasant situation or place that you cannot escape from: *We were stuck in traffic for over an hour.* ♦ *I hate being stuck at home all day.* **3 ~ (on sth)** unable to answer or understand something: *I got stuck on the first question.* ♦ *I'll help you if you're stuck.* **4 ~ (for sth)** not knowing what to do in a particular situation: *If you're stuck for something to do tonight, come out with us.* ♦ *I've never known him to be stuck for words before.* **5 ~ with sb/sth** (*informal*) unable to get rid of someone or something that you do not want: *I was stuck with him for the whole journey.* **IDM** see ROCK, TIME WARP

stuck-'up *adj.* (*informal, disapproving*) thinking that you are more important than other people and behaving in an unfriendly way toward them **SYN** SNOBBISH

stud /stʌd/ *noun* **1** [C] a small piece of jewelry with a part that is pushed through a hole in your ear, nose, etc.: *diamond studs* **2** [C] a small round piece of metal that is attached to the surface of something, especially for decoration: *a leather jacket with studs on the back* **3** [C] a small metal object used in the past for fastening a COLLAR onto a shirt **4** [C, U] an animal, especially a horse, that is kept for breeding; a place where animals, especially horses, are kept for breeding: *a stud farm* ♦ *The horse was retired from racing and **put out to stud** (= kept for breeding).* **5** [C] (*informal*) a man who has many sexual partners and who is thought to be sexually attractive **6** [C] a small metal piece set into the tire of a vehicle to prevent slipping in bad weather **7** [C] a vertical board in the wall of a building that forms part of the building's frame

stud·ded /'stʌdəd/ *adj.* **1** decorated with small raised pieces of metal: *a studded leather belt* **2 ~ with sth** having a lot of something on or in it: *The sky was clear and studded with stars.* ♦ *an essay studded with quotations* ➔ see also STAR-STUDDED ▶ **stud** *verb* (-dd-): *~ sth Stars studded the sky.*

stu·dent 🔑 /'studnt/ *noun*

1 a person who is studying at a university or college: *a* ***medical/science, etc. student*** ♦ *a **graduate/postgraduate/ research student*** ♦ *a **student teacher/nurse*** ♦ *a **student grant/ loan** (= money that is given/lent to students to pay for their studies)* ♦ ***student fees** (= to pay for the cost of teaching)* ♦ *She's a student at Indiana University.* **2** a person who is studying at a school, especially a SECONDARY SCHOOL: *a 15-year-old high school student* ➔ compare PUPIL ➔ see also A STUDENT **3 ~ of sth** a person who is very interested in a particular subject: *a keen student of human nature*

MORE ABOUT

students

- A **student** is a person who is studying at a school, college, university, etc.
- An **undergraduate** is a student who is studying for their first degree at a university or college.
- **Graduate** is usually used with another noun and can describe a person who has completed a first degree at a university or college, or a person who has finished high school: *a college graduate* ♦ *a high school graduate*
- A **graduate student** is a person who has finished a first degree and is doing advanced study or research.

student 'body *noun* all the students in a high school or college: *The university has a student body of just over 30,000.*

student 'council *noun* [C, U] a student government, especially in a high school: *She served on student council for four years.*

student 'government *noun* [C, U] an elected group of students who plan school activities and deal with various student issues: *He's the faculty advisor to the student government.*

student 'teaching *noun* [U] the part of a course for people who are training to become teachers that involves teaching classes of students

student 'union *noun* a building where students at a university or college can go to meet socially

stud·ied /'stʌdid/ *adj.* [only before noun] (*formal*) deliberate and carefully planned: *She introduced herself with studied casualness.*

stu·di·o 🔑 /'studi,oʊ/ *noun* (*pl.* **stu·di·os**)

1 a room where radio or television programs are recorded and broadcast from, or where music is recorded: *a television studio* ♦ *a studio audience* (= one in a studio, which can be seen or heard as a program is broadcast) ♦ *a recording studio* **2** a place where movies are made or produced **3** a company that makes movies: *She works for a major Hollywood studio.* ♦ *a studio executive* **4** a room where an artist works: *a sculptor's studio* ♦ *a photography studio* **5** a place where dancing is taught or where dancers practice: *a dance studio* **6** (also **studio a'partment**) a small apartment with one main room for living and sleeping in and usually a kitchen and bathroom

stu·di·ous /'studiəs/ *adj.* spending a lot of time studying or reading **SYN** SCHOLARLY: *a studious young man*

stu·di·ous·ly /'studiəsli/ *adv.* in a way that is carefully planned and deliberate: *He studiously avoided answering the question.*

stud·muf·fin /'stʌd,mʌfən/ *noun* (*informal*) a man who is considered sexually attractive

| h hat | m man | n no | ŋ sing | l leg | r red | y yes | w wet |

stud·y /'stʌdi/ noun, verb

● **noun** (pl. **stud·ies**)
> ACTIVITY OF LEARNING **1** [U] the activity of learning or gaining knowledge, either from books or by examining things in the world: *a room set aside for private study* ◆ *academic/literary/scientific, etc. study* ◆ *It is important to develop good study skills.* ◆ *Physiology is the study of how living things work.* **2 studies** [pl.] (*formal*) a particular person's learning activities, for example at a college or university: *to continue your studies*
> ACADEMIC SUBJECT **3 studies** [U] used in the names of some academic subjects: *business/media/American studies*
> DETAILED EXAMINATION **4** [U] the act of considering or examining something in detail: *These proposals deserve careful study.* **5** [C] a piece of research that examines a subject or question in detail: *to make/carry out/conduct a study* ◆ *This study shows/confirms/suggests that...* ◆ *a detailed study of how animals adapt to their environment* ➔ collocations at SCIENTIFIC ➔ see also CASE STUDY
> ROOM **6** [C] a room, especially in someone's home, used for reading and writing
> ART **7** [C] a drawing or painting of something, especially one done for practice or before doing a larger picture: *a study of Chartres Cathedral* ◆ *a nude study*
> MUSIC **8** [C] = ÉTUDE
> PERFECT EXAMPLE **9** [sing.] **~ (in sth)** (*formal*) a perfect example of something: *His face was a study in concentration.*

● **verb** (**stud·ies, stud·y·ing, stud·ied, stud·ied**)
> LEARN **1** [T, I] **~ (for sth)** to spend time learning about a subject by reading, going to college, etc.: **~ (sth)** *How long have you been studying English?* ◆ *Don't disturb Jane, she's studying for her exams.* ◆ **~ (sth) at...** *My brother studied at the Pasadena College of Art.* ◆ **~ (sth) under...** *a composer who studied under Nadia Boulanger* (= was taught by Nadia Boulanger) ◆ **~ to do/be sth** *Nina is studying to be an architect.* ➔ collocations at EDUCATION
> EXAMINE CAREFULLY **2** [T] **~ sth** to watch, or look at, someone or something carefully in order to find out something: *Scientists are studying photographs of the planet for signs of life.* ◆ *He studied her face thoughtfully.* ◆ *Fran was studying the menu.* **3** [T] to examine something carefully in order to understand it: **~ sth** *We will study the report carefully before making a decision.* ◆ **~ how, what, etc....** *The group will study how the region coped with the loss of thousands of jobs.* ➔ thesaurus box at EXAMINE

study hall noun [U] a period of time during the school day when students study quietly on their own, usually with a teacher present

stuff /stʌf/ noun, verb

● **noun** [U] **1** (*informal*, sometimes *disapproving*) used to refer to a substance, material, group of objects, etc. when you do not know the name, when the name is not important, or when it is obvious what you are talking about: *What's all that sticky stuff on the carpet?* ◆ *The chairs were covered in some sort of plastic stuff.* ◆ *This wine is good stuff.* ◆ (*disapproving*) *I don't know how you can eat that stuff!* ◆ *They sell stationery and stuff (like that).* ◆ *Where's all my stuff* (= my possessions)? ◆ (*disapproving*) *Could you move all that stuff off the table?* ➔ see also FOODSTUFF ➔ thesaurus box at THING **2** (*informal*) used to refer in a general way to things that people do, say, think, etc.: *I have lots of stuff to do today.* ◆ *I like reading and stuff.* ◆ *The band did some great stuff on their first album.* ◆ *This is all good stuff. Well done!* ◆ *What's all this "Mrs. Smith" stuff? Call me Anna.* ◆ *I don't believe in all that stuff about ghosts.* **3 ~ (of sth)** (*formal* or *literary*) the most important feature of something; something that something else is based on or is made from: *The trip was magical, the stuff of dreams.* ◆ *Let's see what stuff you're made of* (= what sort of person you are). ➔ see also HOT STUFF
  IDM **do your stuff** (*informal*) to do what you are good at or what you have been trained to do: *Some members of the team are just not doing their stuff* (= doing as well as they should). ◆ (*figurative*) *The medicine has clearly done its stuff.* **stuff and nonsense** *exclamation* (*old-fashioned*, *informal*) used by some people to say that they think that something is stupid or not true ➔ more at KID n., KNOW v., STERN adj., STRUT v., SWEAT v.

● **verb** **1** to fill a space or container tightly with something: **~ A with B** *She had 500 envelopes to stuff with leaflets.* ◆ **~ B in, into, under, etc. A** *She had 500 leaflets to stuff into envelopes.* ◆ **~ sth** *The fridge is stuffed to bursting.* ◆ **~ sth + adj.** *All the drawers were stuffed full of letters and papers.* **2 ~ sth + adv./prep.** to push something quickly and carelessly into a small space **SYN** SHOVE: *She stuffed the money under a cushion.* ◆ *His hands were stuffed in his pockets.* **3 ~ sth** to fill a vegetable, chicken, etc. with another type of food: *Are you going to stuff the turkey?* ◆ *stuffed peppers* **4** (*informal*) to eat a lot of food or too much food; to give someone a lot or too much to eat: **~ sb/yourself** *He sat at the table stuffing himself.* ◆ **~ sb/yourself with sth** *Don't stuff the kids with chocolate before their dinner.* **5** [usually passive] **~ sth** to fill the dead body of an animal with material and preserve it, so that it keeps its original shape and appearance: *They had their pet dog stuffed.*
  IDM **stuff it** (*informal*) used to show that you have changed your mind about something or do not care about something: *I didn't want a part in the play, then I thought—stuff it—why not?* **you, etc. can stuff sth** (*informal*) used to tell someone in a rude and angry way that you do not want something: *I told them they could stuff their job.* ➔ more at FACE n.

stuffed /stʌft/ adj. [not before noun] (*informal*) having eaten so much that you cannot eat anything else **SYN** FULL

stuffed animal noun **1** a toy in the shape of an animal, made of cloth and filled with a soft substance ➔ picture at TOY **2** a dead animal that has been STUFFED: *stuffed animals in glass cases*

stuffed shirt noun (*informal, disapproving*) a person who is very serious, formal, or old-fashioned

stuffed up adj. if you are **stuffed up**, your nose is blocked and you are not able to breathe easily

stuff·ing /'stʌfɪŋ/ noun [U] **1** (also **dress·ing**) a mixture of finely chopped food, such as bread, onions, and HERBS, placed inside a chicken, etc. before it is cooked to give it flavor **2** soft material used to fill CUSHIONS, toys, etc. **SYN** FILLING **IDM** see KNOCK

stuff·y /'stʌfi/ adj. (**stuff·i·er, stuff·i·est**) **1** (of a building, room, etc.) warm in an unpleasant way and without enough fresh air: *a stuffy room* ◆ *It gets very hot and stuffy in here in summer.* **2** (*informal, disapproving*) very serious, formal, boring, or old-fashioned: *a stuffy, formal family* ◆ *plain, stuffy clothes* **3** if you have a **stuffy** nose, your nose is blocked because you have a cold ▶ **stuff·i·ness** noun [U]

stul·ti·fy·ing /'stʌltəˌfaɪɪŋ/ adj. (*formal*) making you feel very bored and unable to think of new ideas: *the stultifying effects of work that never varies* ▶ **stul·ti·fy** verb (**stul·ti·fies, stul·ti·fy·ing, stul·ti·fied, stul·ti·fied**) **~ sb** **stul·ti·fy·ing·ly** adv.

stum·ble /'stʌmbl/ verb **1** [I] to hit your foot against something while you are walking or running, and almost fall **SYN** TRIP: *The child stumbled and fell.* ◆ **~ over/on sth** *I stumbled over a rock.* **2** [I] **+ adv./prep.** to walk or move in an unsteady way: *We were stumbling around in the dark looking for a candle.* **3** [I] **~ (over/through sth)** to make a mistake or mistakes and stop while you are speaking, reading to someone, or playing music: *In her nervousness she stumbled over her words.* ◆ *I stumbled through the piano piece with difficulty.* ▶ **stumble** noun
  PHR V **stumble across/on/upon sth/sb** to discover something or someone unexpectedly: *Police have stumbled across a huge drug ring.* **stumble into sth** to become involved in something by chance: *I stumbled into acting when I left college.*

stumbling block noun **~ (to sth)** | **~ (to doing sth)** something that causes problems and prevents you from achieving your aim **SYN** OBSTACLE

stump /stʌmp/ *noun, verb*

- **noun 1** [C] the bottom part of a tree left in the ground after the rest has fallen or been cut down **2** [C] the end of something, or the part that is left after the main part has been cut, broken off, or worn away: *the stump of a pencil* **3** [C] the short part of someone's leg or arm that is left after the rest has been cut off **4 the stump** [sing.] (*informal*) the fact of a politician before an election going to different places and trying to get people's support by making speeches: *The senator gave his standard stump speech.* ◆ *politicians on the stump*
- **verb 1** [T, usually passive] ~ **sb** (*informal*) to ask someone a question that is too difficult for them to answer, or give them a problem that they cannot solve **SYN** BAFFLE: *I'm stumped. I don't know how they got here before us.* ◆ *Kate was stumped for words* (= unable to answer). **2** [I, T] + **adv./prep.** | ~ **sth** to travel around making political speeches, especially before an election: *He stumped around the country trying to build up support.* **3** [I] + **adv./prep.** to walk in a noisy, heavy way, especially because you are angry or upset **SYN** STOMP: *He stumped off, muttering under his breath.*

stump·y /ˈstʌmpi/ *adj.* (*disapproving*) short and thick **SYN** STUBBY: *stumpy fingers* ◆ *a stumpy tail*

stun /stʌn/ *verb* (-nn-) **1** ~ **sb/sth** to make a person or an animal unconscious for a short time, especially by hitting them on the head **SYN** KNOCK OUT: *The fall stunned me for a moment.* ◆ *The animals are stunned before slaughter.* **2** ~ **sb** to surprise or shock someone so much that they cannot think clearly or speak **SYN** ASTOUND ⊃ **thesaurus box at** SURPRISE **3** ~ **sb** to impress someone very much **SYN** AMAZE: *They were stunned by the view from the summit.* ▶ **stunned** *adj.*: *She was too stunned to speak.* ◆ *There was a* **stunned silence** *when I told them the news.*

stung *pt, pp of* STING

stun gre·nade *noun* a small bomb that shocks people so that they cannot do anything, without seriously injuring them

stun gun *noun* a weapon that makes a person or an animal unconscious or unable to move for a short time, usually by giving them a small electric shock

stunk *pp of* STINK

stun·ner /ˈstʌnər/ *noun* (*informal*) **1** a person (especially a woman) or a thing that is very attractive or exciting to look at **2** something, such as a piece of news, that is very surprising or shocking

stun·ning /ˈstʌnɪŋ/ *adj.* **1** extremely attractive or impressive **SYN** BEAUTIFUL: *You look absolutely stunning!* ◆ *a stunning view of the lake* **2** extremely surprising or shocking: *He suffered a stunning defeat in the election.* ▶ **stun·ning·ly** *adv.*: *stunningly beautiful* ◆ *a stunningly simple idea*

stunt /stʌnt/ *noun, verb*

- **noun 1** a dangerous and difficult action that someone does to entertain people, especially as part of a movie: *He did all his own stunts.* ◆ *a stunt pilot* **2** (sometimes *disapproving*) something that is done in order to attract people's attention: *a publicity stunt* **3** (*informal*) a stupid or dangerous act: *I've had enough of her childish stunts.* ◆ *Don't you ever* **pull a stunt** *like that again!*
- **verb** ~ **sb/sth** to prevent someone or something from growing or developing as much as they/it should: *The constant winds had stunted the growth of plants and bushes.* ◆ *His illness had not stunted his creativity.*

stunt·ed /ˈstʌntəd/ *adj.* that has not been able to grow or develop as much as it should: *stunted trees* ◆ *the stunted lives of children deprived of education*

stunt·man /ˈstʌntmæn/, **stunt·wom·an** /ˈstʌntˌwʊmən/ *noun* (*pl.* **stunt·men** /-mɛn/, **stunt·wom·en** /-ˌwɪmən/) a person whose job is to do dangerous things in place of an actor in a movie, etc.; a person who does dangerous things in order to entertain people

stu·pe·fy /ˈstupəˌfaɪ/ *verb* (**stu·pe·fies**, **stu·pe·fy·ing**, **stu·pe·fied**, **stu·pe·fied**) [often passive] ~ **sb** to surprise or shock someone; to make someone unable to think clearly: *He was stupefied by the amount they had spent.* ◆ *She was stupefied with cold.* ▶ **stu·pe·fac·tion** /ˌstupəˈfækʃn/ *noun* [U]

stu·pe·fy·ing /ˈstupəˌfaɪɪŋ/ *adj.* **1** making you unable to think clearly: *stupefying boredom* **2** very surprising or shocking ▶ **stu·pe·fy·ing·ly** *adv.*: *The party was stupefyingly dull.*

stu·pen·dous /stuˈpɛndəs/ *adj.* extremely large or impressive, especially greater or better than you expect **SYN** STAGGERING: *stupendous achievements* ◆ *stupendous costs* ▶ **stu·pen·dous·ly** *adv.*

stu·pid /ˈstupəd/ *adj., noun*

- **adj.** (**stu·pid·er**, **stu·pid·est**) **HELP** more stupid and most stupid are also common **1** showing a lack of thought or good judgment **SYN** FOOLISH, SILLY: *a stupid mistake* ◆ *It was a pretty stupid thing to do.* ◆ *I was* **stupid enough** *to believe him.* ◆ *It was stupid of you to get involved.* **2** (*disapproving*) (of a person) slow to learn or understand things; not intelligent: *He'll manage—he isn't stupid.* ◆ *Forgetting my notes made me* **look stupid**. **3** [only before noun] (*informal*) used to emphasize that you are annoyed with someone or something: *I can't get the stupid thing open!* ◆ *Get your stupid feet off the chair!* ▶ **stu·pid·ly** *adv.*: *I stupidly agreed to lend him the money.* ◆ *Todd stared stupidly at the screen.*
- **noun** [sing.] (*informal*) if you call someone **stupid**, you are telling them that you think they are not being very intelligent: *Yes, stupid, it's you I'm talking to!*

stu·pid·i·ty /stuˈpɪdəti/ *noun* (*pl.* **stu·pid·i·ties**) **1** [U, C, usually pl.] behavior that shows a lack of thought or good judgment: *I couldn't believe my own stupidity.* ◆ *the errors and stupidities of youth* **2** [U] the state or quality of being slow to learn and not intelligent

stu·por /ˈstupər/ *noun* [sing., U] a state in which you are unable to think, hear, etc. clearly, especially because you have drunk too much alcohol, taken drugs, or had a shock: *He drank himself into a stupor.* ◆ *a drunken stupor*

stur·dy /ˈstərdi/ *adj.* (**stur·di·er**, **stur·di·est**) **1** (of an object) strong and not easily damaged **SYN** ROBUST: *a sturdy pair of boots* ◆ *a sturdy table* **2** (of people and animals, or their bodies) physically strong and healthy: *a man of sturdy build* ◆ *sturdy legs* ◆ *a sturdy breed of cattle* **3** not easily influenced or changed by other people **SYN** FIRM, DETERMINED: *The town has always maintained a sturdy independence.* ▶ **stur·di·ly** /ˈstərdl·i/ *adv.*: *The boat was sturdily made.* ◆ *a sturdily built young man* ◆ *a sturdily independent community* **stur·di·ness** /-dinəs/ *noun* [U]

stur·geon /ˈstərdʒən/ *noun* (*pl.* **stur·geon** or **stur·geons**) [C, U] a large sea and FRESHWATER fish that lives in northern regions. Sturgeon are used for food and the eggs (called CAVIAR) are also eaten.

stut·ter /ˈstʌtər/ *verb, noun*

- **verb 1** [T, I] to have difficulty speaking because you cannot stop yourself from repeating the first sound of some words several times **SYN** STAMMER: **+ speech** *"W-w-what?"* he stuttered. ◆ ~ **(sth)** *I managed to stutter a reply.* **2** [I] (of a vehicle or an engine) to move or start with difficulty, making short sharp noises or movements: *The car stuttered along in first gear.*
- **noun** [sing.] a speech problem in which a person finds it difficult to say the first sound of a word and repeats it several times: *He had a terrible stutter.*

St. Val·en·tine's Day /ˌseɪnt ˈvæləntaɪnz ˌdeɪ/ *noun* ⊃ VALENTINE'S DAY

sty /staɪ/ *noun* **1** (*pl.* **sties**) = PIGPEN **2** (also **stye**) (*pl.* **sties** or **styes**) an infection of the EYELID (= the skin above or below the eye) that makes it red and sore

Styg·i·an /ˈstɪdʒiən/ *adj.* [usually before noun] (*literary*) very dark, and therefore frightening: *Stygian gloom* **ORIGIN** From the **Styx**, the river in the underworld that the souls of the dead had to cross in Greek myth.

ʌ **cup**   ə **about**   eɪ **say**   aɪ **five**   ɔɪ **boy**   aʊ **now**   oʊ **go**   ər **bird**

style ♒ AWL /staɪl/ *noun, verb*

● *noun*

▷ **WAY SOMETHING IS DONE 1** [C, U] **~ (of sth)** the particular way in which something is done: *a style of management* ◆ *a management style* ◆ *furniture to suit your style of living* ◆ *a study of different teaching styles* ◆ *I like your style* (= I like the way you do things). ◆ *Caution was not her style* (= not the way she usually behaved). ◆ *I'm surprised he rides a motorcycle—I'd have thought big cars were more his style* (= what suited him). ⟳ see also LIFESTYLE

▷ **DESIGN OF CLOTHES/HAIR 2** [C] a particular design of something, especially clothes: *We stock a wide variety of styles and sizes.* ◆ *Have you thought about wearing your hair in a shorter style?* ⟳ collocations at FASHION ⟳ see also HAIRSTYLE **3** [U] the quality of being fashionable in the clothes that you wear: *style-conscious teenagers* ◆ *Short skirts are back in style* (= fashionable).

▷ **BEING ELEGANT 4** [U] the quality of being elegant and made to a high standard: *The hotel has been redecorated but it's lost a lot of its style.* ◆ *She does everything with style and grace.*

▷ **OF BOOK/PAINTING/BUILDING 5** [C, U] the features of a book, painting, building, etc. that make it typical of a particular author, artist, historical period, etc.: *a style of architecture* ◆ *a fine example of Gothic style* ◆ *a parody written in the style of Molière*

▷ **USE OF LANGUAGE 6** [U, C] the correct use of language: *It's not considered good style to start a sentence with "but."* ◆ *Please follow house style* (= the rules of spelling, etc. used by a particular publishing company).

▷ **-STYLE 7** (in adjectives) having the type of style mentioned: *Italian-style gardens* ◆ *a buffet-style breakfast* ⟳ see also OLD-STYLE

▷ **IN A PLANT 8** (*biology*) the long thin part of a flower that carries the STIGMA ⟳ picture at PLANT [C]

IDM **in (great, grand, etc.) style** in an impressive way: *She always celebrates her birthday in style.* ◆ *He won the championship in great style.* ⟳ more at CRAMP *v.*

● *verb*

▷ **CLOTHES/HAIR, ETC. 1 ~ sth** to design, make, or shape something in a particular way: *an elegantly styled jacket* ◆ *He'd had his hair styled at an expensive salon.*

▷ **GIVE NAME/TITLE 2 ~ sb/sth/yourself (as) + noun** (*formal*) to give someone or something/yourself a particular name, title, or description: *He styled himself Major Carter.* ◆ *She likes to style herself as a champion of free speech.*

PHR V **'style sth/yourself after/on sth/sb** to copy the style, manner, or appearance of someone or something **SYN** MODEL: *a coffee bar styled after a Parisian café* ◆ *He styled himself on Elvis Presley.*

'style sheet *noun* (*computing*) a file which is used for creating documents in a particular style

sty·li pl. of STYLUS

styl·ing AWL /'staɪlɪŋ/ /-lɪn/ *noun* [U] **1** the act of cutting and/or shaping hair in a particular style: *styling gel* **2** the way in which something is designed: *The car has been criticized for its outdated body styling.*

sty·lish AWL /'staɪlɪʃ/ *adj.* (*approving*) fashionable; elegant and attractive **SYN** CLASSY: *his stylish wife* ◆ *a stylish restaurant* ◆ *It was a stylish performance by both artists.* ▶ **styl·ish·ly** *adv.* **styl·ish·ness** *noun* [U]

styl·ist /'staɪlɪst/ *noun* **1** a person whose job is cutting and shaping people's hair **2** a writer who takes great care to write or say something in an elegant or unusual way **3** a person whose job is to create or design a particular style or image for a product, a person, an advertisement, etc. **4** a person who designs fashionable clothes **5** (in sports or music) a person who performs with style

sty·lis·tic /staɪˈlɪstɪk/ *adj.* [only before noun] connected with the style an artist uses in a particular piece of art, writing, or music: *stylistic analysis* ◆ *stylistic features* ▶ **styl·is·ti·cally** /-kli/ *adv.*

sty·lis·tics /staɪˈlɪstɪks/ *noun* [U] the study of style and the methods used in written language

styl·ized AWL /'staɪəˌlaɪzd; 'staɪlaɪzd/ *adj.* drawn, written, etc. in a way that is not natural or realistic: *a stylized drawing of a house* ◆ *the highly stylized form of acting in Japanese theater* ▶ **styl·i·za·tion** /ˌstaɪləˈzeɪʃn/ *noun* [U]

sty·lus /'staɪləs/ *noun* (*pl.* **sty·lus·es** or **sty·li** /-laɪ/) **1** (*computing*) a special pen used to write text or draw an image on a special computer screen ⟳ picture at COMPUTER **2** a device on a RECORD PLAYER that looks like a small needle and is placed on the record in order to play it

sty·mie /'staɪmi/ *verb* (**sty·mie·ing** or **sty·my·ing, sty·mied, sty·mied**) **~ sb/sth** (*informal*) to prevent someone from doing something that they have planned or want to do; to prevent something from happening **SYN** FOIL

styp·tic /'stɪptɪk/ *adj.* (*medical*) able to stop the loss of blood from a wound: *I use a styptic pencil on shaving cuts.*

Sty·ro·foam™ /'staɪrəˌfoʊm/ *noun* [U] = POLYSTYRENE: *Styrofoam cups*

sua·sive /'sweɪsɪv/ *adj.* (*linguistics*) (of verbs) having a meaning that includes the idea of persuading ▶ **sua·sion** /'sweɪʒn/ *noun* [U]

suave /swav/ *adj.* (especially of a man) confident, elegant, and polite, sometimes in a way that does not seem sincere ▶ **suave·ly** *adv.*

sub /sʌb/ *noun, verb*

● *noun* (*informal*) **1** = SUBMARINE *n.* (1) **2** a substitute who replaces another player in a team: *He came on as sub.* **3** (*informal*) a SUBSTITUTE TEACHER **4** = SUBMARINE SANDWICH

● *verb* (**-bb-**) **1** [T] **~ sb** to replace a sports player with another player during a game **SYN** SUBSTITUTE: *He was subbed after just five minutes because of a knee injury.* **2** [I] **~ (for sb)** to do someone else's job for them for a short time **SYN** SUBSTITUTE **3** [T] **~ sth for sth** to use something instead of something else, especially instead of the thing you would normally use **SYN** SUBSTITUTE: *For a lower-calorie version of the recipe, try subbing milk for cream.*

sub– /sʌb/ *prefix* **1** (in nouns and adjectives) below; less than: *subfreezing temperatures* ◆ *a subtropical* (= almost tropical) *climate* ◆ *substandard* **2** (in nouns and adjectives) under: *subway* ◆ *submarine* **3** (in verbs and nouns) a smaller part of something: *subdivide* ◆ *subset*

sub·a·tom·ic /ˌsʌbəˈtɑmɪk/ *adj.* [usually before noun] (*physics*) smaller than, or found in, an atom: *subatomic particles*

sub·clause /'sʌbklɔz/ *noun* (*law*) one of the parts of a clause (= section) in a legal document

sub·com·mit·tee /'sʌbkəˌmɪti/ *noun* a smaller committee formed from a main committee in order to study a particular subject in more detail

sub·com·pact /ˌsʌbˈkɑmpækt/ *noun* a small car, smaller than a COMPACT

sub·con·scious /ˌsʌbˈkɑnʃəs/ *adj., noun*

● *adj.* [usually before noun] connected with feelings that influence your behavior even though you are not aware of them: *subconscious desires* ◆ *the subconscious mind* ⟳ compare CONSCIOUS, UNCONSCIOUS ▶ **sub·con·scious·ly** *adv.*: *Subconsciously, she was looking for the father she had never known.*

● *noun* **the/your subconscious** [sing.] the part of your mind that contains feelings that you are not aware of ⟳ compare THE UNCONSCIOUS

sub·con·ti·nent /ˌsʌbˈkɑntənənt; -ˈkɑntn̩-ənt/ *noun* [usually sing.] a large land mass that forms part of a continent, especially the part of Asia that includes India, Pakistan, and Bangladesh: *the Indian subcontinent*

sub·con·tract /ˌsʌbˈkɑntrækt/ *verb, noun*

● *verb* to pay a person or company to do some of the work that you have been given a contract to do: **~ sth (to sb/sth)** *We subcontracted the work to a small engineering firm.* ◆ **~ sb/sth (to do sth)** *We subcontracted a small engineering firm to do the work.* ▶ **sub·con·tract·ing** *noun* [U]

• *noun* a contract to do part of the work that has been given to another person or company

sub·con·trac·tor /ˌsʌbˈkɑntræktər/ *noun* a person or company that does part of the work given to another person or company

sub·cul·ture /ˈsʌbˌkʌltʃər/ *noun* (sometimes *disapproving*) the behavior and beliefs of a particular group of people in society that are different from those of most people: *the criminal/drug/youth, etc. subculture*

sub·cu·ta·ne·ous /ˌsʌbkyuˈteɪniəs/ *adj.* [usually before noun] (*technical*) under the skin: *a subcutaneous injection* ▶ **sub·cu·ta·ne·ous·ly** *adv.*

sub·di·rec·to·ry /ˈsʌbdəˌrɛktəri; -daɪ-/ *noun* (*pl.* **sub·di·rec·to·ries**) (*computing*) a DIRECTORY (= list of files or programs) that is inside another directory

sub·di·vide /ˌsʌbdəˈvaɪd; ˌsʌbdəˈvaɪd/ *verb* [T, often passive, I] **~ (sth) (into sth)** to divide something into smaller parts; to be divided into smaller parts

sub·di·vi·sion /ˈsʌbdəˌvɪʒn/ *noun* **1** [U] the act of dividing a part of something into smaller parts **2** [C] one of the smaller parts into which a part of something has been divided: *a political subdivision of the state* ◆ *subdivisions within the Hindu caste system* **3** [C] an area of land that has been divided up for building houses on

sub·due /səbˈdu/ *verb* (somewhat *formal*) **1 ~ sb/sth** to bring someone or something under control, especially by using force **SYN** DEFEAT: *Troops were called in to subdue the rebels.* **2 ~ sth** to calm or control your feelings **SYN** SUPPRESS: *Julia had to subdue an urge to stroke his hair.*

sub·dued /səbˈdud/ *adj.* **1** (of a person) unusually quiet, and possibly unhappy: *He seemed a bit subdued to me.* ◆ *She was in a subdued mood.* ◆ *The reception was a subdued affair.* **2** (of light or colors) not very bright: *subdued lighting* **3** (of sounds) not very loud: *a subdued conversation* **4** (of business activity) not very busy; with not much activity: *a period of subdued trading*

sub·freez·ing /ˌsʌbˈfrizɪŋ/ *adj.* [only before noun] colder than 32° Fahrenheit or 0° Celsius: *subfreezing temperatures*

sub·group /ˈsʌbɡrup/ *noun* a smaller group made up of members of a larger group

sub·head·ing /ˈsʌbˌhɛdɪŋ/ *noun* a title given to any of the sections into which a longer piece of writing has been divided

sub·hu·man /ˌsʌbˈhyumən/ *adj.* (*disapproving*) not working or behaving like a normal human; not fit for humans: *subhuman behavior* ◆ *They were living in subhuman conditions.* ⊃ compare INHUMAN, SUPERHUMAN

sub·ject ✎ *noun, adj., verb*

• *noun* [C] /ˈsʌbdʒɛkt; -dʒɪkt/
❯ OF CONVERSATION/BOOK **1** a thing or person that is being discussed, described, or dealt with: *an unpleasant subject of conversation* ◆ *books on many different subjects* ◆ *a magazine article on the subject of space travel* ◆ *I have nothing more to say on the subject.* ◆ *I wish you'd change the subject* (= talk about sth else). ◆ *How did we get onto the subject of marriage?* ◆ *We seem to have gotten off the subject we're meant to be discussing.* ◆ *Nelson Mandela is the subject of a new biography.* ◆ *Climate change is still very much a subject for debate.*
❯ AT SCHOOL/COLLEGE **2** an area of knowledge studied in a school, college, etc.: *Biology is my favorite subject.*
❯ OF PICTURE/PHOTOGRAPH **3** a person or thing that is the main feature of a picture or photograph, or that a work of art is based on: *Focus the camera on the subject.* ◆ *Classical landscapes were a popular subject with many 18th century painters.*
❯ OF EXPERIMENT **4** a person or thing being used to study something, especially in an experiment: *We need male subjects between the ages of 18 and 25 for the experiment.*
❯ GRAMMAR **5** a noun, noun phrase, or pronoun representing the person or thing that performs the action of the verb (*I* in *I sat down*), about which something is stated (*the house* in *the house is very old*), or, in a passive sentence, that is

affected by the action of the verb (*the tree* in *the tree was blown down in the storm*) ⊃ compare OBJECT, PREDICATE
❯ OF COUNTRY **6** a person who has the right to belong to a particular country, especially one with a king or queen: *a British subject*

• *adj.* /ˈsʌbdʒɛkt; -dʒɪkt/ **1 ~ to sth** likely to be affected by something, especially something bad: *Flights are subject to delay because of the fog.* **2 ~ to sth** depending on something in order to be completed or agreed: *The article is ready to publish, subject to your approval.* ◆ *All specially-priced vacation packages are subject to availability.* **3 ~ to sth/sb** under the authority of something or someone: *All nuclear installations are subject to international safeguards.* **4** [only before noun] (*formal*) controlled by the government of another country: *subject peoples*

• *verb* /səbˈdʒɛkt/ **~ sth (to sth)** (*formal*) to bring a country or group of people under your control, especially by using force: *The Roman Empire subjected most of Europe to its rule.* ▶ **sub·jec·tion** /səbˈdʒɛkʃn/ *noun* [U]
PHR V **sub'ject sb/sth to sth** [often passive] to make someone or something experience, suffer, or be affected by something, usually something unpleasant: *to be subjected to ridicule* ◆ *The city was subjected to heavy bombing.* ◆ *The defense lawyers claimed that the prisoners had been subjected to cruel and degrading treatment.*

sub·jec·tive /səbˈdʒɛktɪv/ *adj.* **1** based on your own ideas or opinions rather than facts, and therefore sometimes unfair: *a highly subjective point of view* ◆ *Everyone's opinion is bound to be subjective.* **2** (of ideas, feelings, or experiences) existing in someone's mind rather than in the real world **3** [only before noun] (*grammar*) the **subjective** case is the one that is used for the subject of a sentence **ANT** OBJECTIVE ▶ **sub·jec·tive·ly** *adv.*: *People who are less subjectively involved are better judges.* ◆ *subjectively perceived changes* **sub·jec·tiv·i·ty** /ˌsʌbdʒɛkˈtɪvəti/ *noun* [U]: *There is an element of subjectivity in her criticism.*

sub·jec·tiv·ism /səbˈdʒɛktəˌvɪzəm/ *noun* [U] (*philosophy*) the theory that all knowledge and moral values are subjective rather than based on truth that actually exists in the real world

ˈsubject ˌmatter *noun* [U] the ideas or information contained in a book, speech, painting, etc.: *The artist was revolutionary in both subject matter and technique.* ◆ *She's searching for subject matter for her new book.*

sub·ju·gate /ˈsʌbdʒəˌɡeɪt/ *verb* [usually passive] **~ sb/sth** (*formal*) to defeat someone or something; to gain control over someone or something: *a subjugated race* ◆ *Her personal ambitions had been subjugated to* (= considered less important than) *the needs of her family.* ▶ **sub·ju·ga·tion** /ˌsʌbdʒəˈɡeɪʃn/ *noun* [U] (*formal*): *the subjugation of Native Americans by European settlers*

sub·junc·tive /səbˈdʒʌŋktɪv/ *noun* (*grammar*) the form (or MOOD) of a verb that expresses wishes, possibility, or UNCERTAINTY; a verb in this form: *The verb is in the subjunctive.* ◆ *In "I wish I were taller," "were" is a subjunctive.* ▶ **sub·junc·tive** *adj.*: *the subjunctive mood*

sub·lease /ˈsʌblis/ *noun* a LEASE that allows you to rent to someone else a property that you rent from the owner ▶ **sub·lease** /ˌsʌbˈlis/ *verb* [T, I]

sub·let /ˈsʌblɛt; ˌsʌbˈlɛt/ *verb* (**sub·let·ting, sub·let, sub·let**) [T, I] **~ (sth) (to sb)** to rent to someone else all or part of a property that you rent from the owner

sub·li·mate /ˈsʌbləˌmeɪt/ *verb* **~ sth** (*psychology*) to direct your energy, especially sexual energy, to socially acceptable activities such as work, exercise, art, etc. **SYN** CHANNEL ▶ **sub·li·ma·tion** /ˌsʌbləˈmeɪʃn/ *noun* [U]

sub·lime /səˈblaɪm/ *adj., noun*
• *adj.* **1** of very high quality and causing great admiration: *sublime beauty* ◆ *a sublime combination of flavors* **2** (*formal*, often *disapproving*) (of a person's behavior or attitudes) extreme, especially in a way that shows they are not aware of what they are doing or are not concerned about what happens because of it: *the sublime confidence of youth*

| t tea | ṭ butter | d did | k cat | g got | tʃ chin | dʒ June | f fall |

▶ **sub·lime·ly** *adv.*: *sublimely beautiful* ◆ *She was sublimely unaware of the trouble she had caused.* **sub·lim·i·ty** /sə-ˈblɪməti/ *noun* [U]

● *noun* **the sublime** [sing.] something that is sublime: *He transforms the most ordinary subject into the sublime.*
IDM **from the sublime to the ridiculous** used to describe a situation in which something serious, important, or of high quality is followed by something silly, unimportant, or of poor quality

sub·lim·i·nal /səˈblɪmənl/ *adj.* affecting your mind even though you are not aware of it: *subliminal advertising*
▶ **sub·lim·i·nal·ly** /-nəli/ *adv.*

sub·mach·ine gun /ˌsʌbməˈʃin ɡʌn/ *noun* a light MACHINE GUN that you can hold in your hands to fire

sub·ma·rine /ˈsʌbməˌrin/ *noun, adj.*
● *noun* (also *informal* **sub**) **1** a ship that can travel under-water: *a nuclear submarine* ◆ *a submarine base* ⊃ picture at BOAT **2** = SUBMARINE SANDWICH
● *adj.* [only before noun] (*technical*) existing or located under the ocean: *submarine plant life* ◆ *submarine cables*

sub·ma·rin·er /ˌsʌbməˈrinər/ *noun* a sailor who works on a submarine

ˌ**submarine ˈsandwich** (also **submarine, sub, grind·er, he·ro, hoa·gie**) *noun* a long bread roll split open along its length and filled with various types of food

sub·merge /səbˈmərdʒ/ *verb* **1** [I, T] to go under the surface of water or liquid; to put something or make something go under the surface of water or liquid: *The submarine had had time to submerge before the warship could approach.* ◆ **~ sth** *The fields had been submerged by floodwater.* **2** **~ sth** to hide ideas, feelings, opinions, etc. completely: *Doubts that had been submerged in her mind suddenly resurfaced.* ▶ **sub·merged** *adj.*: *Her submerged car was discovered in the river by police divers.* **sub·mer·sion** /səbˈmərʒn/ *noun* [U]

sub·mers·i·ble /səbˈmərsəbl/ *adj., noun*
● *adj.* (also **sub·merg·i·ble** /səbˈmərdʒəbl/) that can be used underwater: *a submersible camera*
● *noun* a SUBMARINE (= a ship that can travel underwater) that goes underwater for short periods

sub·mis·sion **AWL** /səbˈmɪʃn/ *noun* **1** [U] the act of accepting that someone has defeated you and that you must obey them **SYN** SURRENDER: *a gesture of submission* ◆ *to beat/force/starve someone into submission* **2** [U, C] the act of giving a document, proposal, etc. to someone in authority so that they can study or consider it; the document, etc. that you give: *When is the final date for the submission of proposals?* ◆ *They prepared a report for submission to the city council.* ◆ *All parties will have the opportunity to make submissions relating to this case.* **3** [C] (*law*) a statement that is made to a judge in court

sub·mis·sive /səbˈmɪsɪv/ *adj.* too willing to accept someone else's authority and to obey them without questioning anything they want you to do: *He expected his daughters to be meek and submissive.* ◆ *She followed him like a submissive child.* **ANT** ASSERTIVE ▶ **sub·mis·sive·ly** *adv.*: *"You're right and I was wrong," he said submissively.* **sub·mis·sive·ness** *noun* [U]

sub·mit **AWL** /səbˈmɪt/ *verb* (-tt-) **1** [T] **~ sth (to sb/sth)** to give a document, proposal, etc. to someone in authority so that they can study or consider it: *to submit an application/a claim/a complaint* ◆ *Completed projects must be submitted by March 10th.* **2** [I, T] to accept the authority, control, or greater strength of someone or something; to agree to something because of this **SYN** GIVE IN TO SB/STH, YIELD: **~ (to sb/sth)** *She refused to submit to threats.* ◆ **~ yourself (to sb/sth)** *He submitted himself to a search by the guards.* **3** [T] **~ that…** (*law* or *formal*) to say or suggest something: *Counsel for the defense submitted that the evidence was inadmissible.*

sub·or·di·nate **AWL** *adj., noun, verb*
● *adj.* /səˈbɔrdn̩ət/ **1 ~ (to sb)** having less power or authority than someone else in a group or an organization: *In many societies women are subordinate to men.* **2 ~ (to sth)**

less important than something else **SYN** SECONDARY: *All other issues are subordinate to this one.*
● *noun* /səˈbɔrdn̩ət/ a person who has a position with less authority and power than someone else in an organization **SYN** INFERIOR: *the relationship between subordinates and superiors*
● *verb* /səˈbɔrdn̩eɪt/ **~ sb/sth (to sb/sth)** to treat someone or something as less important than someone or something else: *Safety considerations were subordinated to commercial interests.* ▶ **sub·or·di·na·tion** /səˌbɔrdn̩ˈeɪʃn/ *noun* [U]

su·bordinate ˈclause (also de·pendent ˈclause) *noun* (*grammar*) a group of words that is not a sentence but adds information to the main part of a sentence, for example *when it rang* in *She answered the phone when it rang.* ⊃ compare COORDINATE CLAUSE, MAIN CLAUSE

su·bordinating conˈjunction *noun* (*grammar*) a word that begins a subordinate clause, for example "although" or "because" ⊃ compare COORDINATING CONJUNCTION

sub·orn /səˈbɔrn/ *verb* (*law*) to pay or persuade someone to do something illegal, especially to tell lies in court: *to suborn a witness*

sub·par /ˌsʌbˈpar/ *adj.* below a level of quality that is usual or expected: *a subpar performance*

sub·plot /ˈsʌbplɑt/ *noun* a series of events in a play, novel, etc. that is separate from but linked to the main story

sub·poe·na /səˈpinə/ *noun, verb*
● *noun* (*law*) a written order to attend court as a witness to give evidence
● *verb* **~ sb (to do sth)** (*law*) to order someone to attend court and give evidence as a witness: *The court subpoenaed her to appear as a witness.* ⊃ collocations at JUSTICE

sub·prime /ˌsʌbˈpraɪm/ *adj.* (*finance*) connected with the practice of lending money, usually at a high rate of interest, to people who may not be able to pay the money back, because they have a bad CREDIT RATING: *subprime mortgages/loans/lending* ◆ *subprime lenders/borrowers*

sub·rou·tine /ˈsʌbruˌtin/ (also **sub·pro·gram** /ˈsʌbˌproʊɡræm/) *noun* (*computing*) a set of instructions that repeatedly perform a task within a program

sub–Sa·har·an /ˌsʌb səˈhærən; -ˈhɛrən/ *adj.* [only before noun] from or relating to areas in Africa that are south of the Sahara Desert: *sub-Saharan Africa*

sub·scribe /səbˈskraɪb/ *verb* **1** [I] **~ (to sth)** to pay an amount of money regularly in order to receive or use something: *Which journals does the library subscribe to?* ◆ *We subscribe to several sports channels (= on TV).* ◆ *He subscribed to a newsgroup (= on the Internet).* ⊃ see also UNSUBSCRIBE **2** [I] **~ (to sth)** to pay money regularly to be a member of an organization or to support a charity: *He subscribes regularly to Amnesty International.* **3** [I] **~ (for sth)** (*finance*) to apply to buy shares in a company ⊃ see also OVERSUBSCRIBED **PHR V** **subˈscribe to sth** (*formal*) to agree with or support an opinion, a theory, etc.: *The authorities no longer subscribe to the view that disabled people are unsuitable as teachers.*

sub·scrib·er /səbˈskraɪbər/ *noun* **1** a person who pays money, usually once a year, to receive regular copies of a magazine or newspaper **2** a person who pays to receive a service: *subscribers to cable television* **3** a person who gives money regularly to help the work of an organization such as a charity

sub·scrip·tion /səbˈskrɪpʃn/ *noun* [C, U] **1** an amount of money you pay, usually once a year, to receive regular copies of a newspaper or magazine, etc.; the act of paying this money: *an annual subscription* ◆ **~ (to/for sth)** *to take out a subscription to "Newsweek"* ◆ *to cancel/renew a subscription* ◆ *Copies are available by subscription.* **2** a sum of money that you pay regularly to a charity, or to be a member of a club, or to receive a service; the act of paying this money **SYN** DONATION **3** the act of people paying money for something to be done: *A statue in his memory was erected by public subscription.* ⊃ thesaurus box at PAYMENT

---

sub·sec·tion /ˈsʌbˌsɛkʃn/ *noun* a part of a section, especially of a legal document

sub·se·quent **AWL** /ˈsʌbsəkwənt/ *adj.* (*formal*) happening or coming after something else **ANT** PREVIOUS: *subsequent generations* ♦ *Subsequent events confirmed our doubts.* ♦ *Developments on this issue will be dealt with in a subsequent report.*

sub·se·quent·ly **AWL** /ˈsʌbsəkwəntli; -ˌkwɛntli/ *adv.* (*formal*) afterward; later; after something else has happened: *The original interview notes were subsequently lost.* ♦ *Subsequently, new guidelines were issued to all employees.*

subsequent to *prep.* (*formal*) after; following: *There have been further developments subsequent to our meeting.*

sub·ser·vi·ent /səbˈsərviənt/ *adj.* **1** ~ **(to sb/sth)** (*disapproving*) too willing to obey other people: *The press was accused of being subservient to the government.* **2** ~ **(to sth)** (*formal*) less important than something else: *The needs of individuals were subservient to those of the group as a whole.* ▶ **sub·ser·vi·ence** /-viəns/ *noun* [U]

sub·set /ˈsʌbsɛt/ *noun* (*technical*) a smaller group of people or things formed from the members of a larger group

sub·side /səbˈsaɪd/ *verb* **1** [I] to become calmer or quieter: *She waited nervously for his anger to subside.* ♦ *I took an aspirin and the pain gradually subsided.* **2** [I] (of water) to go back to a normal level: *The flood waters gradually subsided.* **3** [I] (of land or a building) to sink to a lower level; to sink lower into the ground: *Weak foundations caused the house to subside.*

sub·sid·ence /səbˈsaɪdns; ˈsʌbsədəns/ *noun* [U] the process by which an area of land sinks to a lower level than normal, or by which a building sinks into the ground

sub·sid·i·ar·i·ty /səbˌsɪdiˈɛrəti; ˌsʌbsɪdi-/ *noun* [U] the principle that a central authority should not be very powerful, and should only control things which cannot be controlled by local organizations

sub·sid·i·ar·y **AWL** /səbˈsɪdiˌɛri/ *adj., noun*
● *adj.* **1** ~ **(to sth)** connected with something but less important than it **SYN** ADDITIONAL: *subsidiary information* ♦ *a subsidiary matter* **2** (of a business company) owned or controlled by another company
● *noun* (*pl.* **sub·sid·i·ar·ies**) a business company that is owned or controlled by another larger company

sub·si·dize **AWL** /ˈsʌbsəˌdaɪz/ *verb* ~ **sb/sth** to give money to someone or an organization to help pay for something; to give a subsidy **SYN** FUND: *The housing projects are subsidized by the government.* ♦ *She's not prepared to subsidize his gambling any longer.* ▶ **sub·si·di·za·tion** /ˌsʌbsədəˈzeɪʃn/ *noun* [U]

sub·si·dy **AWL** /ˈsʌbsədi/ *noun* (*pl.* **sub·si·dies**) [C, U] money that is paid by a government or an organization to reduce the costs of services or of producing goods, so that the prices can be kept low: *agricultural subsidies* ♦ *to reduce the level of subsidy*

sub·sist /səbˈsɪst/ *verb* **1** [I] ~ **(on sth)** to manage to stay alive, especially with limited food or money: *Old people often subsist on very small incomes.* **2** [I] (*formal*) to exist; to be valid: *The terms of the contract subsist.*

sub·sist·ence /səbˈsɪstəns/ *noun* [U] the state of having just enough money or food to stay alive: *Many families are living below the level of subsistence.* ♦ *to live below (the) subsistence level* ♦ *They had no visible means of subsistence.* ♦ *subsistence agriculture/farming* (= growing enough only to live on, not to sell) ♦ *subsistence crops* ♦ *He worked a 16-hour day for a subsistence wage* (= enough money to buy only basic items).

sub·soil /ˈsʌbsɔɪl/ *noun* [U] the layer of soil between the surface of the ground and the hard rock underneath it ➪ compare TOPSOIL

sub·son·ic /ˌsʌbˈsɑnɪk/ *adj.* less than the speed of sound; flying at less than the speed of sound ➪ compare SUPERSONIC

sub·spe·cies /ˈsʌbˌspiʃiz; -ˌspisiz/ *noun* (*pl.* **sub·spe·cies**) a group into which animals, plants, etc. that have similar characteristics are divided, smaller than a SPECIES

sub·stance 🖉 /ˈsʌbstəns/ *noun*
1 [C] a type of solid, liquid, or gas that has particular qualities: *a chemical/radioactive, etc. substance* ♦ *banned/illegal substances* (= drugs) ♦ *a sticky substance* **2** [U] the quality of being based on facts or the truth: *It was malicious gossip, completely without substance.* ♦ *The commission's report gives substance to these allegations.* ♦ *There is some substance in what he says.* **3** [U] the most important or main part of something: *Love and guilt form the substance of his new book.* ♦ *I agreed with what she said in substance, though not with every detail.* **4** [U] (*formal*) importance **SYN** SIGNIFICANCE: *matters of substance* ♦ *Nothing of any substance was achieved in the meeting.*
IDM **a man/woman of substance** (*formal*) a rich and powerful man or woman

substance a·buse *noun* [U] the practice or habit of taking too much of a harmful drug or drinking too much alcohol: *a treatment center for substance abuse*

sub·stand·ard /ˌsʌbˈstændərd/ *adj.* not as good as normal; not acceptable **SYN** INFERIOR: *substandard goods*

sub·stan·tial 🖉 /səbˈstænʃl/ *adj.*
1 large in amount, value, or importance **SYN** CONSIDERABLE: *substantial sums of money* ♦ *a substantial change* ♦ *Substantial numbers of people support the reforms.* ♦ *He ate a substantial breakfast.* **2** [usually before noun] (*formal*) large and solid; strongly built: *a substantial house*

sub·stan·tial·ly 🖉 /səbˈstænʃəli/ *adv.*
1 very much; a lot **SYN** CONSIDERABLY: *The costs have increased substantially.* ♦ *The plane was substantially damaged in the crash.* **2** (*formal*) mainly; in most details, even if not completely: *What she says is substantially true.*

sub·stan·ti·ate /səbˈstænʃiˌeɪt/ *verb* ~ **sth** (*formal*) to provide information or evidence to prove that something is true: *The results of the tests substantiated his claims.* ▶ **sub·stan·ti·a·tion** /səbˌstænʃiˈeɪʃn/ *noun* [U]

sub·stan·tive /ˈsʌbstəntɪv/ *adj., noun*
● *adj.* (*formal*) dealing with real, important, or serious matters: *substantive issues* ♦ *The report concluded that no substantive changes were necessary.*
● *noun* (*old-fashioned, grammar*) a noun

sub·sta·tion /ˈsʌbˌsteɪʃn/ *noun* a place where the strength of electric power from a POWER PLANT is reduced before it is passed on to homes and businesses

sub·sti·tute 🖉 **AWL** /ˈsʌbstəˌtut/ *noun, verb*
● *noun* **1** a person or thing that you use or have instead of the one you normally use or have: *a meat substitute* ♦ *a substitute family* ♦ ~ **for sb/sth** *Paul's father only saw him as a substitute for his dead brother.* ♦ *The course teaches you the theory, but there's no substitute for practical experience.* ♦ *The local bus service was a poor substitute for their car.* **2** (also *informal* **sub**) a player who replaces another player in a sports game: *He was brought on as (a) substitute after half-time.*
● *verb* [I, T] to take the place of someone or something else; to use someone or something instead of someone or something else: ~ **for sb/sth** *Nothing can substitute for the advice your doctor is able to give you.* ♦ ~ **A for B** *Margarine can be substituted for butter in this recipe.* ♦ ~ **B with/by A** *Butter can be substituted with margarine in this recipe.* ♦ ~ **sb/sth** *Brady was substituted in the second half after a knee injury* (= somebody else played instead of Brady in the second half). **HELP** When *for, with,* or *by* are not used, as in the last example, it can be difficult to tell whether the person or thing mentioned is being used, or has been replaced by somebody or something else. The context will usually make this clear. ▶ **sub·sti·tu·tion** **AWL** /ˌsʌbstəˈtuʃn/ *noun* [U, C]: *the substitution of low-fat spreads for butter* ♦ *Two substitutions were made during the game.*

substitute 'teacher (also informal **sub**) noun a teacher employed to do the work of another teacher who is away because of illness, etc.

sub·strate /ˈsʌbstreɪt/ noun (technical) a substance or layer that is under something or on which something happens, for example the surface on which a living thing grows and feeds

sub·stra·tum /ˈsʌbˌstreɪtəm; -ˌstrætəm/ noun (pl. **sub·stra·ta** /-tə/) (technical) a layer of something, especially rock or soil, that is below another layer

sub·struc·ture /ˈsʌbˌstrʌktʃər/ noun a base or structure that is below another structure and that supports it: a substructure of timber piles ◆ (figurative) the substructure of national culture ➔ compare SUPERSTRUCTURE

sub·sume /səbˈsum/ verb [usually passive] ~ **sth** + **adv./prep.** (formal) to include something in a particular group and not consider it separately: All these different ideas can be subsumed under just two broad categories.

sub·tend /səbˈtend/ verb ~ **sth** (geometry) (of a line or CHORD) to be opposite to an ARC or angle

sub·ter·fuge /ˈsʌbtərˌfyudʒ/ noun [U, C] (formal) a secret, usually dishonest, way of behaving

sub·ter·ra·ne·an /ˌsʌbtəˈreɪniən/ adj. [usually before noun] (formal) under the ground: a subterranean cave

sub·text /ˈsʌbtɛkst/ noun a hidden meaning or reason for doing something

sub·ti·tle /ˈsʌbˌtaɪtl/ noun, verb
• **noun 1** [usually pl.] words that translate what is said in a movie into a different language and appear on the screen at the bottom. Subtitles are also used, especially on television, to help deaf people (= people who cannot hear well): a Polish movie with English subtitles ◆ Is the movie dubbed or are there subtitles? **2** a second title of a book that appears after the main title and gives more information
• **verb** [usually passive] to give a subtitle or subtitles to a book, movie, etc.: ~ **sth** a Spanish movie subtitled in English ◆ ~ **sth** + **noun** The book is subtitled "New language for new times." ➔ compare DUB

sub·tle /ˈsʌtl/ adj. (**sub·tler, sub·tlest**) **HELP** more subtle is also common **1** (often approving) not very noticeable or obvious: subtle colors/flavors/smells, etc. ◆ There are subtle differences between the two versions. ◆ She's been dropping subtle hints about what she'd like as a present. **2** (of a person or their behavior) behaving in a smart and skillful way, and using indirect methods, in order to achieve something: I decided to try a more subtle approach. **3** organized in a smart and skillful way: a subtle plan ◆ a subtle use of lighting in the play **4** good at noticing and understanding things: The job required a subtle mind. ▶ **sub·tly** /ˈsʌtl·i/ adv.: Her version of events is subtly different from what actually happened. ◆ Not very subtly, he raised the subject of money.

sub·tle·ty /ˈsʌtlti/ noun (pl. **sub·tle·ties**) **1** [U] the quality of being subtle: It's a thrilling movie even though it lacks subtlety. **2** [C, usually pl.] the small but important details or aspects of something: the subtleties of language

sub·to·tal /ˈsʌbˌtoʊtl/ noun the total of a set of numbers that is then added to other totals to give a final number

sub·tract /səbˈtrækt/ verb [T, I] ~ **(sth) (from sth)** to take a number or an amount away from another number or amount **SYN** TAKE AWAY: 6 subtracted from 9 is 3. **ANT** ADD ▶ **sub·trac·tion** /səbˈtrækʃn/ noun [U, C] ➔ compare ADDITION

sub·trop·i·cal /ˌsʌbˈtrɑpɪkl/ (also ˌsemi-ˈtropical) adj. in or connected with regions that are near tropical parts of the world

the sub·trop·ics /ˌsʌbˈtrɑpɪks/ noun [pl.] the regions of the earth which are near the TROPICS

sub·urb /ˈsʌbərb/ noun (also informal **the burbs** [pl.]) an area where people live that is outside the center of a city: a suburb of Atlanta ◆ an Atlanta suburb ◆ They live **in the suburbs**. ➔ collocations at TOWN

sub·ur·ban /səˈbərbən/ adj. **1** in or connected with a suburb: suburban areas ◆ a suburban street ◆ life in suburban New York **2** (disapproving) boring and ordinary: a suburban lifestyle

sub·ur·ban·ite /səˈbərbəˌnaɪt/ noun (often disapproving) a person who lives in the SUBURBS of a city

sub·ur·bi·a /səˈbərbiə/ noun [U] (often disapproving) the SUBURBS and the way of life, attitudes, etc. of the people who live there

sub·ven·tion /səbˈvɛnʃn/ noun (formal) an amount of money that is given by a government, etc. to help an organization

sub·ver·sive /səbˈvərsɪv/ adj. trying or likely to destroy or damage a government or political system by attacking it secretly or indirectly ▶ **sub·ver·sive** noun: He was a known political subversive. **sub·ver·sive·ly** adv. **sub·ver·sive·ness** noun [U]

sub·vert /səbˈvərt/ verb (formal) **1** [T, I] ~ **(sth)** to try to destroy the authority of a political, religious, etc. system by attacking it secretly or indirectly **SYN** UNDERMINE **2** [T] ~ **sth** to try to destroy a person's belief in something or someone **SYN** UNDERMINE ▶ **sub·ver·sion** /səbˈvərʒn/ noun [U]

sub·way /ˈsʌbweɪ/ noun an underground railroad system in a city: the New York subway ◆ a **subway station/train** ◆ a downtown subway stop ◆ to **ride/take the subway** ➔ note at UNDERGROUND

sub·woof·er /ˈsʌbˌwʊfər/ noun (technical) a part of a LOUDSPEAKER that produces very low sounds

ˌsub-ˈzero adj. [usually before noun] (of temperatures) below zero

suc·ceed ♪ /səkˈsid/ verb
1 [I] to achieve something that you have been trying to do or get; to have the result or effect that was intended: Our plan succeeded. ◆ ~ **in doing sth** He succeeded in being accepted to art school. ◆ I tried to discuss it with her but only succeeded in making her angry (= I failed and did the opposite of what I intended). ➔ see also SUCCESS **2** [I] to be successful in your job, earning money, power, respect, etc.: You will have to work hard if you want to succeed. ◆ ~ **in sth** She doesn't have the ruthlessness required to succeed in business. ◆ ~ **as sth** He had hoped to succeed as a violinist. ➔ see also SUCCESS **3** [T] ~ **sb/sth** to come next after someone or something and take their/its place or position **SYN** FOLLOW: Who succeeded Kennedy as President? ◆ Their early success was succeeded by a period of miserable failure. ◆ Strands of DNA are reproduced through succeeding generations. ➔ see also SUCCESSION **4** [I] ~ **(to sth)** to gain the right to a title, property, etc. when someone dies: She succeeded to the throne (= became queen) in 1558. ➔ see also SUCCESSION
IDM nothing succeeds like success (saying) when you are successful in one area of your life, it often leads to success in other areas

suc·cess ♪ /səkˈsɛs/ noun
1 [U] the fact that you have achieved something that you want and have been trying to do or get; the fact of becoming rich or famous or of getting a high social position: What's the secret of your success? ◆ ~ **(in doing sth)** I didn't have much success in finding a job. ◆ ~ **(in sth)** They didn't have much success in life. ◆ Confidence is **the key to success**. ◆ economic success ◆ Their plan will probably **meet with little success**. ◆ She was surprised by the book's success (= that it had sold a lot of copies). **2** [C] a person or thing that has achieved a good result and been successful: The party was a big success. ◆ He's proud of his daughter's successes. ◆ She wasn't a success as a teacher. ◆ He was determined to **make a success** of the business. **ANT** FAILURE **IDM** see ROARING, SUCCEED, SWEET adj.

suc·cess·ful ♪ /səkˈsɛsfl/ adj.
1 achieving your aims or what was intended: ~ **(in sth/in doing sth)** They were successful in winning the contract. ◆ ~ **(at sth/at doing sth)** I wasn't very successful at keeping the

news secret. ◆ *We congratulated them on the successful completion of the project.* **2** having become popular and/or made a lot of money: *The play was very successful on Broadway.* ◆ *a successful actor* ◆ *The company has had another successful year.* **ANT** UNSUCCESSFUL ▶ **suc·cess·ful·ly** /-fəli/ *adv.*

suc·ces·sion **AWL** /sək'sɛʃn/ *noun* **1** [C, usually sing.] a number of people or things that follow each other in time or order **SYN** SERIES: *a succession of visitors* ◆ *He's been hit by a succession of injuries since he joined the team.* ◆ *She has won the award for the third year* **in succession**. ◆ *They had three children* **in quick succession**. ◆ *The gunman fired three times* **in rapid succession**. **2** [U] the regular pattern of one thing following another thing: *the succession of the seasons* **3** [U] the act of taking over an official position or title; the right to take over an official position or title, especially to become the king or queen of a country: *He became chairman* **in succession to** *Howard Dean.* ◆ *She's third* **in order of succession** *to the throne.* ⊃ see also SUCCEED

suc'cession planning *noun* [U] (*business*) the process of training and preparing employees in a company or an organization so that there will always be someone to replace a senior manager who leaves

suc·ces·sive **AWL** /sək'sɛsɪv/ *adj.* [only before noun] following immediately one after the other **SYN** CONSECUTIVE: *This was their fourth successive win.* ◆ *Successive governments have tried to tackle the problem.* ▶ **suc·ces·sive·ly** **AWL** *adv.*: *This concept has been applied successively to painting, architecture, and sculpture.*

suc·ces·sor **AWL** /sək'sɛsər/ *noun* ~ **(to sb/sth)** a person or thing that comes after someone or something else and takes their/its place: *Who's the likely successor to him as party leader?* ◆ *Their latest release is a* **worthy successor** *to their popular debut album.* ⊃ compare PREDECESSOR

suc'cess story *noun* a person or thing that is very successful

suc·cinct /sək'sɪŋkt/ *adj.* (*approving*) expressed clearly and in a few words **SYN** CONCISE: *Keep your answers as succinct as possible.* ◆ *a succinct explanation* ▶ **suc·cinct·ly** *adv.*: *You put that very succinctly.* **suc·cinct·ness** *noun* [U]

suc·cor (*CanE usually* **suc·cour**) /'sʌkər/ *noun, verb*
- *noun* [U] (*literary*) help that you give to someone who is suffering or having problems
- *verb* ~ **sb** (*literary*) to help someone who is suffering or having problems

suc·co·tash /'sʌkə,tæʃ/ *noun* [U] a dish of CORN and BEANS cooked together

suc·cu·bus /'sʌkyəbəs/ *noun* (*pl.* **suc·cu·bi** /-ˌbaɪ/) (*literary*) a female evil spirit, supposed to have sex with a sleeping man ⊃ compare INCUBUS

suc·cu·lent /'sʌkyələnt/ *adj., noun*
- *adj.* **1** (*approving*) (of fruit, vegetables, and meat) containing a lot of juice and tasting good **SYN** JUICY: *a succulent pear/steak* **2** (*technical*) (of plants) having leaves and STEMS that are thick and contain a lot of water ▶ **suc·cu·lence** /-ləns/ *noun* [U]
- *noun* (*technical*) any plant with leaves and STEMS that are thick and contain a lot of water, for example a CACTUS

suc·cumb /sə'kʌm/ *verb* [I] to not be able to fight an attack, an illness, a TEMPTATION, etc.: *The town succumbed after a short siege.* ◆ ~ **to sth** *His career was cut short when he succumbed to cancer.* ◆ *He finally succumbed to Lucy's charms and agreed to her request.*

such /sʌtʃ/ *det., pron.*
1 of the type already mentioned: *They had been invited to a Hindu wedding and were not sure what happened on such occasions.* ◆ *He said he didn't have time, or made* **some such** *excuse.* ◆ *She longed to find somebody who understood her problems, and in him she thought she had found such a person.* ◆ *We were second-class citizens and they treated us* **as such**. ◆ *Accountants were boring. Such (= that) was her opinion before meeting Juan!* **2** of the type that you are just going to mention: **There is no such thing** *as a free lunch.* ◆ *Such advice as he was given* (= it was not very much) *has proved almost worthless.* ◆ *The knot was fastened* **in such a way** *that it was impossible to undo.* ◆ *The damage was such that it would cost thousands to repair.* **3** ~ **(is, was, etc.) sth that…** used to emphasize the great degree of something: *This issue was of such importance that we could not afford to ignore it.* ◆ *Why are you in such a hurry?* ◆ (*informal*) *It's such a beautiful day!* ◆ (*formal*) *Such is the elegance of this typeface that it is still a favorite of designers.*
IDM … **and such** and similar things or people: *The center offers activities like canoeing and sailing and such.* **as such** as the word is usually understood; in the exact sense of the word: *The new job is not a promotion as such, but it has good prospects.* ◆ *"Well, did they offer it to you?" "No, not as such, but they said I had a good chance."* **such as 1** for example: *Wild flowers such as primroses are becoming rare.* ◆ *"There are loads of things to do." "Such as?"* (= give me an example) **2** of a kind that; like: *Opportunities such as this did not come every day.* ⊃ language bank at E.G. **such as it is/they are** used to say that there is not much of something or that it is of poor quality: *The food, such as it was, was served at nine o'clock.*

such-and-such *pron., det.* (*informal*) used for referring to something without saying exactly what it is: *Always say at the start of an application that you're applying for such-and-such a job because…*

such·like /'sʌtʃlaɪk/ *pron.* things of the type mentioned: *You can buy brushes, paint, varnish, and suchlike there.* ▶ **such·like** *det.*: *food, drink, clothing, and suchlike provisions*

suck /sʌk/ *verb, noun*
- *verb* **1** [T] ~ **sth** (+ **adv./prep.**) to take liquid, air, etc. into your mouth by using the muscles of your lips: *to suck the juice from an orange* ◆ *She was noisily sucking up milk through a straw.* **2** [I, T] to keep something in your mouth and pull on it with your lips and tongue: ~ **at/on sth** *The baby sucked at its mother's breast.* ◆ *She sucked on a mint.* ◆ ~ **sth** *She sucked a mint.* ◆ *Stop sucking your thumb!* **3** [T] to take liquid, air, etc. out of something: ~ **sth** + **adv./prep.** *The pump sucks air out through the valve.* ◆ ~ **sth** + **adj.** *Greenfly can literally suck a plant dry.* **4** [T] ~ **sb/sth** + **adv./prep.** to pull someone or something with great force in a particular direction: *The canoe was sucked down into the whirlpool.* **5** something **sucks** [I] (*slang*) used to say that something is very bad: *Their new album sucks.* ⊃ compare ROCK
IDM **suck it up** (*informal*) to accept something bad and deal with it well, controlling your emotions ⊃ more at DRY
PHR V **suck sb 'in** | **suck sb 'into sth** [usually passive] to involve someone in an activity or a situation, especially one they do not want to be involved in **suck 'up (to sb)** (*informal, disapproving*) to try to please someone in authority

ʌ cup   ə about   eɪ say   aɪ five   ɔɪ boy   aʊ now   oʊ go   ər bird

by praising them too much, helping them, etc., in order to gain some advantage for yourself
● **noun** [usually sing.] an act of sucking

suck·er /'sʌkər/ noun, verb
● **noun 1** (informal) a person who is easily tricked or persuaded to do something **2 ~ for sb/sth** (informal) a person who cannot resist someone or something, or likes someone or something very much: I've always been a sucker for men with green eyes. **3** a special organ on the body of some animals that enables them to stick to a surface ⊃ picture at ANIMAL **4** a disk shaped like a cup, usually made of rubber or plastic, that sticks to a surface when you press it against it **5** a part of a tree or bush that grows from the roots rather than from the main STEM or the branches, and can form a new tree or bush **6** (slang) used to refer in a general way to a person or thing, especially for emphasis: The pilot said, "I don't know how I got the sucker down safely." **7** (informal) = LOLLIPOP
● **verb**
　PHRV sucker sb 'into sth/into 'doing sth (informal) to persuade someone to do something that they do not really want to do, especially by using their lack of knowledge or experience: I was suckered into helping.

'sucker ˌpunch noun a blow that the person who receives it is not expecting ▶ 'sucker ˌpunch verb ~ sb

suck·le /'sʌkl/ verb **1** [T] ~ sb/sth (of a woman or female animal) to feed a baby or young animal with milk from the breast or UDDER: a cow suckling her calves ♦ (old-fashioned) a mother suckling a baby **2** [I] (of a baby or young animal) to drink milk from its mother's breast or UDDER

suck·ling /'sʌklɪŋ/ noun (old-fashioned) a baby or young animal that is still drinking milk from its mother

ˌsuckling 'pig noun [U, C] a young pig still taking milk from its mother, that is cooked and eaten

suck·y /'sʌki/ adj. (suck·i·er, suck·i·est) (slang) very bad or unpleasant: a really sucky job

su·crose /'sukroʊs/ noun [U] (chemistry) the form of sugar that is obtained from SUGAR CANE and SUGAR BEET

suc·tion /'sʌkʃn/ noun [U] the process of removing air or liquid from a space or container so that something else can be sucked into it, or so that two surfaces can stick together: Vacuum cleaners work by suction. ♦ a suction cup/pump/pad ▶ suc·tion verb ~ sth (technical)

sud·den /'sʌdn/ adj.
happening or done quickly and unexpectedly: a sudden change ♦ Don't make any sudden movements. ♦ His death was very sudden. ♦ It was only decided yesterday. It's all been very sudden. ▶ sud·den·ness /'sʌdn·nəs/ noun [U]
　IDM all of a sudden quickly and unexpectedly: All of a sudden someone grabbed me around the neck.

ˌsudden 'death noun [U] a way of deciding the winner of a game when the scores are equal at the end. The players or teams continue playing and the game ends as soon as one of them gains the lead: a sudden-death play-off in golf

sud·den·ly /'sʌdnli/ adv.
quickly and unexpectedly: "Listen!" said Doyle suddenly. ♦ I suddenly realized what I had to do. ♦ It all happened so suddenly.

su·do·ku /su'doʊku/ noun [C, U] a number PUZZLE with nine squares, each containing nine smaller squares, in which you have to put the numbers one to nine so that a number appears only once in each of the nine squares and in each row of nine across and down the PUZZLE: He passes the time doing sudokus. ⊃ picture at PUZZLE

suds /sʌdz/ (also soap·suds) noun **1** [pl.] a mass of very small bubbles that forms on top of water that has soap in it **SYN** LATHER: She was up to her elbows in suds. **2** [U] (old-fashioned) beer

sue /su/ verb **1** [T, I] ~ (sb) (for sth) to make a claim against someone in court about something that they have said or done to harm you: to sue someone for breach of contract ♦ to

sue someone for $10 million (= in order to get money from someone) ♦ to sue someone for damages ♦ They threatened to sue if the work was not completed. **2** [I] ~ for sth (formal) to formally ask for something, especially in court: to sue for divorce ♦ The rebels were forced to sue for peace.

suede /sweɪd/ noun [U] soft leather with a surface like VELVET on one side, used especially for making clothes and shoes: a suede jacket

su·et /'suət/ noun [U] hard fat from around the KIDNEYS of cows, sheep, etc., used in cooking

suf·fer /'sʌfər/ verb
1 [I] to be badly affected by a disease, pain, sadness, a lack of something, etc.: I hate to see animals suffering. ♦ ~ from sth He suffers from asthma. ♦ traffic accident victims suffering from shock ♦ Many companies are suffering from a shortage of skilled staff. ♦ ~ for sth He made a rash decision and now he is suffering for it. **2** [T] ~ sth to experience something unpleasant, such as injury, defeat, or loss: He suffered a massive heart attack. ♦ The party suffered a humiliating defeat in the congressional elections. ♦ The company suffered huge losses in the last financial year. **3** [I] to become worse: His school work is suffering because of family problems.
　IDM not suffer fools gladly to have very little patience with people that you think are stupid

suf·fer·ance /'sʌfərəns/ noun [U]
　IDM on sufferance if you do something on sufferance, someone allows you to do it although they do not really want you to: He's only staying here on sufferance.

suf·fer·er /'sʌfərər/ noun a person who suffers, especially someone who is suffering from a disease: cancer sufferers ♦ She received many letters of support from fellow sufferers.

suf·fer·ing /'sʌfərɪŋ; 'sʌfrɪŋ/ noun
1 [U] physical or mental pain: Death finally brought an end to her suffering. ♦ This war has caused widespread human suffering. **2** sufferings [pl.] feelings of pain and unhappiness: The hospice aims to ease the sufferings of the dying.

suf·fice /sə'faɪs/ verb [I] (formal) (not used in the progressive tenses) to be enough for someone or something: Generally a brief note or a phone call will suffice. ♦ ~ to do sth One example will suffice to illustrate the point.
　IDM suffice (it) to say (that)… used to suggest that although you could say more, what you do say will be enough to explain what you mean

suf·fi·cien·cy **AWL** /sə'fɪʃnsi/ noun [sing.] ~ (of sth) (formal) an amount of something that is enough for a particular purpose

suf·fi·cient **AWL** /sə'fɪʃnt/ adj.
enough for a particular purpose; as much as you need: Allow sufficient time to get there. ♦ ~ to do sth These reasons are not sufficient to justify the ban. ♦ ~ for sth/sb Is $100 sufficient for your expenses? **ANT** INSUFFICIENT ⊃ see also SELF-SUFFICIENT ▶ suf·fi·cient·ly **AWL** adv.: The following day she felt sufficiently well to go to work.

suf·fix /'sʌfɪks/ noun (grammar) a letter or group of letters added to the end of a word to make another word, such as -ly in quickly or -ness in sadness ⊃ compare AFFIX, PREFIX

suf·fo·cate /'sʌfəkeɪt/ verb **1** [I, T] to die because there is no air to breathe; to kill someone by not letting them breathe air: Many dogs have suffocated in hot cars. ♦ ~ sb/sth The couple were suffocated by fumes from a faulty gas heater. ♦ He put the pillow over her face and suffocated her. ♦ (figurative) She felt suffocated by all the rules and regulations. **2** [I] be suffocating if it is suffocating, it is very hot and there is little fresh air: Can I open a window? It's suffocating in here! ▶ suf·fo·ca·tion /ˌsʌfə'keɪʃn/ noun [U]: to die of suffocation

suf·fo·cat·ing /'sʌfəˌkeɪtɪŋ/ adj. **1** making it difficult to breathe normally **SYN** STIFLING: The afternoon heat was suffocating. **2** restricting what someone or something can do: Some marriages can sometimes feel suffocating.

suf·fra·gan /ˈsʌfrəgən/ (also **suffragan ˈbishop**) *noun* a BISHOP who is an assistant to a bishop of a particular DIOCESE

suf·frage /ˈsʌfrɪdʒ/ *noun* [U] the right to vote in political elections: *universal suffrage* (= the right of all adults to vote) ♦ *women's suffrage*

suf·fra·gette /ˌsʌfrəˈdʒet/ *noun* a member of a group of women who, in Britain and the U.S. in the early part of the 20th century, worked to get the right for women to vote in political elections

suf·fra·gist /ˈsʌfrədʒɪst/ *noun* (especially in the past) a person who works to extend the right to vote in political elections to a particular group of people

suf·fuse /səˈfyuz/ *verb* [often passive] **~ sb/sth (with sth)** (*literary*) (especially of a color, light, or feeling) to spread all over or through someone or something: *Her face was suffused with color.* ♦ *Color suffused her face.*

Su·fi /ˈsufi/ *noun* a member of a Muslim group who try to become united with God through prayer and MEDITATION, and by living a very simple, strict life ▶ **Su·fism** /ˈsufɪzəm/ *noun* [U]

sug·ar 🔑 /ˈʃʊgər/ *noun, verb, exclamation*
● *noun* **1** [U] a sweet substance, often in the form of white or brown CRYSTALS, made from the juices of various plants, used in cooking or to make tea, coffee, etc. sweeter: *a sugar plantation/refinery/bowl* ♦ *This juice contains no added sugar.* ♦ *Do you take sugar* (= have it in your tea, coffee, etc.)*?* ⊃ see also BROWN SUGAR, CANE SUGAR, CONFECTIONER'S SUGAR, GRANULATED SUGAR, MAPLE SUGAR **2** [C] the amount of sugar that a small spoon can hold or that is contained in a small CUBE, added to tea, coffee, etc.: *How many sugars do you take in coffee?* **3** [C, usually pl.] (*technical*) any of various sweet substances that are found naturally in plants, fruit, etc.: *fruit sugars* ♦ *a person's blood sugar level* (= the amount of GLUCOSE in their blood) **4** [U] (*informal*) a way of addressing someone that you like or love: *See you later, sugar.*
● *verb* **~ sth** to add sugar to something; to cover something in sugar: *sugared soft drinks* ♦ *sugared cereals* **IDM** see PILL
● *exclamation* used to show that you are annoyed when you do something stupid or when something goes wrong: *Oh sugar! I've forgotten my book!*

ˈsugar ˌbeet *noun* [U] a plant with a large round root, from which sugar is made

ˈsugar ˌcane *noun* [U] a tall tropical plant with thick STEMS from which sugar is made

ˈsugar-ˌcoat *verb* **~ sth** to do something that makes an unpleasant situation seem less unpleasant

ˈsugar-ˌcoated *adj.* **1** covered with sugar **2** (*disapproving*) made to seem attractive, in a way that tricks people: *a sugar-coated promise*

ˈsugar ˌcube (also *informal* **lump**) *noun* a small CUBE of sugar, used in cups of tea or coffee

ˈsugar ˌdaddy *noun* (*informal*) a rich older man who gives presents and money to a much younger woman, usually in return for sex

ˌsugar-ˈfree *adj.* (also **sug·ar·less** /ˈʃʊgərləs/) not containing any sugar: *sugar-free yogurt*

sug·ar·ing /ˈʃʊgərɪŋ/ *noun* [U] **1** a way of removing hair from your skin using a mixture of sugar and water **2** the process of boiling juice from a MAPLE tree until it becomes sugar

ˈsugar ˌmaple (also **ˈsugar maple ˌtree**) *noun* [C, U] a North American MAPLE tree whose SAP (= liquid in the tree) is used to make MAPLE SYRUP

sug·ar·plum /ˈʃʊgərˌplʌm/ *noun* a small round candy

ˈsugar ˌsnap (also **ˈsugar snap ˌpea**, **ˈsugar ˌpea**) *noun* a type of PEA which is eaten while still in its POD

sug·ar·y /ˈʃʊgəri/ *adj.* **1** containing sugar; tasting of sugar: *sugary snacks* **2** (*disapproving*) seeming too full of emotion in a way that is not sincere **SYN** SENTIMENTAL: *a sugary smile* ♦ *sugary pop songs*

sug·gest 🔑 /səgˈdʒest; səˈdʒest/ *verb*
1 to put forward an idea or a plan for other people to think about **SYN** PROPOSE: **~ sth (to sb)** *May I suggest a white wine with this dish, Sir?* ♦ **~ itself (to sb)** *A solution immediately suggested itself to me* (= I immediately thought of a solution). ♦ **~ (that)…** *I suggest (that) we go out to eat.* ♦ **~ doing sth** *I suggested going in my car.* ♦ **it is suggested that…** *It has been suggested that bright children take their exams early.* ⊃ language bank at ARGUE **2** to tell someone about a suitable person, thing, method, etc. for a particular job or purpose **SYN** RECOMMEND: **~ sb/sth for sth** *Who would you suggest for the job?* ♦ **~ sb/sth as sth** *She suggested Denver as a good place for the conference.* ♦ **~ sb/sth** *Can you suggest a good dictionary?* **HELP** You cannot "suggest somebody something": ~~Can you suggest me a good dictionary?:~~ **~ how, what, etc.…** *Can you suggest how I might contact him?* **3** to put an idea into someone's mind; to make someone think that something is true **SYN** INDICATE: **~ (that)…** *All the evidence suggests (that) he stole the money.* ♦ **~ sth** *The symptoms suggest a minor heart attack.* ♦ **~ sth to sb** *What do these results suggest to you?* **4** to state something indirectly **SYN** IMPLY: **~ (that)…** *Are you suggesting (that) I'm lazy?* ♦ **~ sth** *I would never suggest such a thing.*

sug·gest·i·ble /səgˈdʒestəbl; səˈdʒes-/ *adj.* easily influenced by other people: *He was young and highly suggestible.*

sug·ges·tion 🔑 /səgˈdʒestʃən; səˈdʒes-/ *noun*
1 [C] an idea or a plan that you mention for someone else to think about: *Can I make a suggestion?* ♦ **~ (for/about/on sth)** *I'd like to hear your suggestions for ways of raising money.* ♦ *Are there any suggestions about how best to tackle the problem?* ♦ *We welcome any comments and suggestions on these proposals.* ♦ **~ (that…)** *He agreed with my suggestion that we should change the date.* ♦ *We are open to suggestions* (= willing to listen to ideas from other people). ♦ *We need to get it there by four. Any suggestions?* **2** [U, C, usually sing.] a reason to think that something, especially something bad, is true **SYN** HINT: **~ of sth** *A spokesman dismissed any suggestion of a boardroom rift.* ♦ **~ that…** *There was no suggestion that he was doing anything illegal.* **3** [C, usually sing.] a slight amount or sign of something **SYN** TRACE: *She looked at me with just a suggestion of a smile.* **4** [U] putting an idea into people's minds by connecting it with other ideas: *Most advertisements work through suggestion.* ♦ *the power of suggestion*
IDM **at/on sb's suggestion** because someone suggested it: *At his suggestion, I bought the more expensive printer.*

sug·ges·tive 🔑 /səgˈdʒestɪv; səˈdʒes-/ *adj.* **1 ~ (of sth)** reminding you of something or making you think about something: *music that is suggestive of warm summer days* **2** making people think about sex: *suggestive jokes* ▶ **sug·ges·tive·ly** *adv.*: *He leered suggestively.*

su·i·cid·al /ˌsuəˈsaɪdl/ *adj.* **1** people who are **suicidal** feel that they want to kill themselves: *On bad days I even felt suicidal.* ♦ *suicidal tendencies* **2** very dangerous and likely to lead to death; likely to cause very serious problems or disaster: *a suicidal leap into the swollen river* ♦ *It would be suicidal to risk going out in this weather.* ♦ *The new economic policies could prove suicidal for the party.* ▶ **su·i·cid·al·ly** /-ˈsaɪdl·i/ *adv.*: *suicidally depressed*

su·i·cide /ˈsuəˌsaɪd/ *noun* **1** [U, C] the act of killing yourself deliberately: *to commit suicide* ♦ *an attempted suicide* (= one in which the person survives) ♦ *a suicide bomber* (= who expects to die while trying to kill other people with a bomb) ♦ *a suicide letter/note* (= written before someone tries to commit suicide) ⊃ see also ASSISTED SUICIDE **2** [U] a course of action that is likely to ruin your career, position in society, etc.: *It would have been political suicide for him to challenge the allegations in court.* **3** [C] (*formal*) a person who commits suicide

t **tea**   t̯ **butter**   d **did**   k **cat**   g **got**   tʃ **chin**   dʒ **June**   f **fall**

'suicide ˌpact *noun* an agreement between two or more people to kill themselves at the same time

su·i ge·ne·ris /ˌsu:i ˈdʒenərəs/ *adj.* (from *Latin, formal*) different from all other people or things **SYN** UNIQUE

suit 🔑 /su:t/ *noun, verb*

● *noun* **1** a set of clothes made of the same cloth, including a jacket and pants or a skirt: *a business suit* ◆ *a pinstripe suit* ◆ *a two-/three-piece suit* (= of two/three pieces of clothing) ⟳ picture at CLOTHES ⟳ see also JUMPSUIT, LEISURE SUIT, PANTSUIT, SAILOR SUIT, SWEATSUIT, TRACKSUIT **2** a set of clothing worn for a particular activity: *a diving suit* ◆ *a suit of armor* ⟳ see also SPACESUIT, SWIMSUIT, WETSUIT **3** any of the four sets that form a DECK of cards: *The suits are called hearts, clubs, diamonds, and spades.* **4** = LAWSUIT: *to file/bring a suit* against someone ◆ *a divorce suit* ⟳ see also PATERNITY SUIT **5** [usually pl.] (*informal*) a person with an important job as a manager in a company or an organization, especially one thought of as being mainly concerned with financial matters or as having a lot of influence **IDM** see BIRTHDAY, FOLLOW, STRONG

● *verb* [no passive] (not used in the progressive tenses) **1** to be convenient or useful for someone: *~ sb/sth Choose a computer to suit your particular needs.* ◆ *If we met at 2, would that suit you?* ◆ *If you want to go by bus, that suits me fine.* ◆ *He can be very helpful, but only when it suits him.* ◆ **it suits sb to do sth** *It suits me to start work at a later time.* **2 ~ sb** (especially of clothes, colors, etc.) to make you look attractive: *Blue suits you. You should wear it more often.* ◆ *I don't think this coat really suits me.* **3 ~ sb/sth** (usually used in negative sentences) to be right or good for someone or something: *This hot weather doesn't suit me.* **IDM** **suit yourself** (*informal*) **1** to do exactly what you would like: *I choose my assignments to suit myself.* **2** usually used in orders to tell someone to do what they want, even though it annoys you: *"I think I'll stay in this evening." "Suit yourself!"* **PHR V** **'suit sth to sth/sb** to make something appropriate for something or someone: *He can suit his conversation to whoever he's with.* **ˌsuit 'up** to put on special clothes for an activity: *The divers took about five minutes to suit up.*

suit·a·ble 🔑 /ˈsu:təbl/ *adj.*
right or appropriate for a particular purpose or occasion: *a suitable candidate* ◆ **~ for sth/sb** *This program is not suitable for children.* ◆ *a suitable place for a picnic* ◆ **~ to do sth** *I don't have anything suitable to wear for the party.* ◆ *Would now be a suitable moment to discuss my report?* **ANT** UNSUITABLE
▶ **suit·a·bil·i·ty** /ˌsu:təˈbɪləti/ *noun* [U]: *There is no doubt about her suitability for the job.*

suit·a·bly /ˈsu:təbli/ *adv.* **1** in a way that is right or appropriate for a particular purpose or occasion: *I am not really suitably dressed for a party.* ◆ *suitably qualified candidates* **2** showing the feelings, etc. that you would expect in a particular situation: *He was suitably impressed when I told him I'd won.*

suit·case /ˈsu:tkeɪs/ (also **case**) *noun* a case with flat sides and a handle, used for carrying clothes, etc. when you are traveling: *to pack/unpack a suitcase* ⟳ picture at BAG

suite /swi:t/ *noun* **1** a set of rooms, especially in a hotel: *a hotel/private/honeymoon suite* ◆ *a suite of rooms/offices* **2** a piece of music made up of three or more related parts, for example pieces from an OPERA: *Stravinsky's Firebird Suite* **3** (*computing*) a set of related computer programs: *a suite of software development tools* **4** a set of matching pieces of furniture: *a bathroom/bedroom suite*

suit·ed /ˈsu:təd/ *adj.* [not before noun] **1** right or appropriate for someone or something: **~ (to sb/sth)** *She was ideally suited to the part of Eva Peron.* ◆ *This diet is suitable to anyone who wants to lose weight fast.* ◆ **~ (for sb/sth)** *He is not really suited for a teaching career.* **ANT** UNSUITED ⟳ compare ILL-SUITED **2** if two people are **suited** or **well suited**, they are likely to make a good couple: *Jo and I are very well suited.* ◆ *They were not suited to one another.* **ANT** UNSUITED

3 wearing a suit, or a suit of the type mentioned: *sober-suited city businessmen*

suit·ing /ˈsu:tɪŋ/ *noun* [U] cloth made especially of wool, used for making suits: *men's suiting*

suit·or /ˈsu:tər/ *noun* **1** (*old-fashioned*) a man who wants to marry a particular woman **2** (*business*) a company that wants to buy another company

Suk·kot (also **Suc·coth**) /suˈkoʊt; ˈsʊkəs/ (also ˌFeast of ˈTabernacles) *noun* [U] a Jewish festival that takes place in the fall, during which shelters are made using natural materials

sul·fate (*CanE usually* **sul·phate**) /ˈsʌlfeɪt/ *noun* [C, U] (*chemistry*) a COMPOUND of SULFURIC ACID and a chemical element: *copper sulfate*

sul·fide (*CanE usually* **sul·phide**) /ˈsʌlfaɪd/ *noun* [C, U] (*chemistry*) a COMPOUND of sulfur and another chemical element

sul·fur (*CanE usually* **sul·phur**) /ˈsʌlfər/ *noun* [U] (*symb.* **S.**) a chemical element. Sulfur is a pale yellow substance that produces a strong, unpleasant smell when it burns, and is used in medicine and industry. ▶ **sul·fur·ous** (*CanE usually* **sul·phur·ous**) /ˈsʌlfərəs/ *adj.*: *sulfurous fumes*

ˌsulfur diˈoxide (*CanE usually* ˌsulphur diˈoxide) *noun* [U] (*chemistry*) (*symb.* SO_2) a poisonous gas with a strong smell, that is used in industry and causes air pollution

sul·fu·ric ac·id (*CanE usually* **sul·phu·ric ac·id**) /sʌlˌfyʊrɪk ˈæsɪd/ *noun* [U] (*chemistry*) (*symb.* H_2SO_4) a strong clear acid

sulk /sʌlk/ *verb, noun*

● *verb* [I] (*disapproving*) to look angry and refuse to speak or smile because you want people to know that you are upset about something: *He went off to sulk in his room.*

● *noun* a period of not speaking and being bad-tempered because you are angry about something: *Jo was in a sulk upstairs.*

sulk·y /ˈsʌlki/ *adj.* (*disapproving*) bad-tempered or not speaking because you are angry about something: *Sarah had looked sulky all morning.* ◆ *a sulky child* ▶ **sulk·i·ly** /-kəli/ *adv.* **sulk·i·ness** /-kinəs/ *noun* [U]

sul·len /ˈsʌlən/ *adj.* (*disapproving*) **1** bad-tempered and not speaking, either on a particular occasion or because it is part of your character: *Bob looked pale and sullen.* ◆ *She gave him a sullen glare.* ◆ *sullen teenagers* **2** (*literary*) (of the sky or weather) dark and unpleasant ▶ **sul·len·ly** *adv.* **sul·len·ness** /ˈsʌlənnəs/ *noun* [U]

sul·ly /ˈsʌli/ *verb* (**sul·lies, sul·ly·ing, sul·lied, sul·lied**) (*formal* or *literary*) **1 ~ sth** to spoil or reduce the value of something **2 ~ sth** to make something dirty

sul·phate, sul·phide, sul·phur, ˌsulphur diˈoxide, sul·phu·ric ac·id (*CanE*) = SULFATE, SULFIDE, SULFUR, SULFUR DIOXIDE, SULFURIC ACID

sul·phur (*CanE*) = SULFUR

sul·tan /ˈsʌltn/ *noun* the title given to Muslim rulers in some countries: *the Sultan of Brunei*

sul·tan·a /sʌlˈtænə/ *noun* the wife, mother, sister, or daughter of a sultan

sul·tan·ate /ˈsʌltəˌneɪt/ *noun* **1** the rank or position of a SULTAN **2** an area of land that is ruled over by a SULTAN: *the Sultanate of Oman* **3** the period of time during which someone is a SULTAN

sul·try /ˈsʌltri/ *adj.* (**sul·tri·er, sul·tri·est**) **1** (of the weather or air) very hot and uncomfortable **SYN** MUGGY: *a sultry summer afternoon* **2** (*formal*) (of a woman or her appearance) sexually attractive; seeming to have strong sexual feelings **SYN** SEXY: *a sultry smile* ◆ *a sultry singer* ▶ **sul·tri·ness** *noun* [U]

sum 🔑 **AWL** /sʌm/ *noun, verb*

● *noun* **1** [C] **~ (of sth)** an amount of money: *You will be fined the sum of $200.* ◆ *a large sum of money* ◆ *a six-figure sum* ⟳ see also LUMP SUM **2** [C, usually sing.] **~ (of sth)** the number you get when you add two or more numbers together: *The sum of 7 and 12 is 19.* **3** (also ˌsum ˈtotal) [sing.] **the ~ of sth** all of something, especially when you think that it is not very much: *This is the sum of my achievements so far.* **4** [C] a simple problem that involves calculating numbers: *If I have my sums right, I should be able to afford the rent.*

IDM **be greater/more than the sum of its parts** to be better or more effective as a group than you would think just by looking at the individual members of the group **in sum** (*formal*) used to introduce a short statement of the main points of a discussion, speech, etc.

- *verb* (-mm-)
PHR V ˌsum ˈup | ˌsum sth⟷ˈup **1** to state the main points of something in a short and clear form **SYN** SUMMARIZE: *To sum up, there are three main ways of tackling the problem…* ◆ **~ what…** *Can I just sum up what we've agreed to so far?* ⊃ language bank at CONCLUSION **2** (of a judge) to give a summary of the main facts and arguments in a legal case, near the end of a trial ˌsum sb/sth⟷ˈup **1** to describe or show the most typical characteristics of someone or something, especially in a few words: *Totally lazy—that just about sums him up.* **2** to form or express an opinion of someone or something **SYN** SIZE UP: *She quickly summed up the situation and took control.* ⊃ related noun SUMMING-UP

sum·ma cum lau·de /ˌsʊmə kʊm ˈlaʊdə; ˌsʌmə kʌm ˈlɔːdeɪ; -di/ *adv., adj.* (from *Latin*) at the highest level of achievement that students can reach when they finish their studies at college: *He graduated summa cum laude from Harvard.* ⊃ compare CUM LAUDE, MAGNA CUM LAUDE

sum·ma·rize **AWL** /ˈsʌməˌraɪz/ *verb* [T, I] **~ (sth)** to give a summary of something (= a statement of the main points): *The results of the research are summarized at the end of the chapter.* ⊃ collocations at SUMMARY ⊃ language bank at CONCLUSION

AWL COLLOCATIONS

summary

summary noun
- contain, give, offer, present, provide
  The last section provides a summary of the key findings.
- brief, concise, succinct | descriptive, detailed | excellent
  See Nord, 1997, for a more detailed summary.
  The well-respected historian Frederick Hodge presented a succinct summary of this argument.
- ~ of findings
  The paper concludes with a summary of findings and recommendations for future research.

summarize verb
- accurately | briefly, concisely, succinctly
  A study of this scope must accurately summarize the ideas of numerous philosophers.
  In the next section of this article we will briefly summarize our methodology.
- data, finding, result | literature | argument | recommendation | conclusion
  In a recent report, UNICEF summarized the global data by regions.
  This article summarizes recent literature on the diagnosis of pneumonia.

---

sum·ma·ry 🔑 **AWL** /ˈsʌməri/ *noun, adj.*
- *noun* (*pl.* sum·ma·ries) a short statement that gives only the main points of something, not the details: *The following is a summary of our conclusions.* ◆ *a news summary* ◆ *a two-page summary of a government report* ◆ **In summary,** *this was a disappointing performance.*

- *adj.* [only before noun] **1** (*formal*) giving only the main points of something, not the details: *a summary financial statement* ◆ *I made a summary report for the records.* **2** (sometimes *disapproving*) done immediately, without paying attention to the normal process that should be followed: ***summary justice/execution*** ◆ *a summary judgment* ▶ **sum·mar·i·ly** /səˈmerəli/ *adv.*: *to be summarily dismissed/executed*

sum·ma·tion **AWL** /sʌˈmeɪʃn/ *noun* **1** [usually sing.] (*formal*) a summary of what has been done or said: *What he said was a fair summation of the discussion.* **2** (*formal*) a collection of different parts that forms a complete account or impression of someone or something: *The exhibition presents a summation of the artist's career.* **3** (*law*) a final speech that a lawyer makes near the end of a trial in court, after all the evidence has been given

sum·mer 🔑 /ˈsʌmər/ *noun, verb*
- *noun*
[U, C] the warmest season of the year, coming between spring and fall: *We're going away in the summer.* ◆ *It's very hot here in summer.* ◆ *in the summer of 2011* ◆ *late/early summer* ◆ *this/next/last summer* ◆ *a cool/hot/wet summer* ◆ *It is now* **high summer** (= the hottest part of summer). ◆ *a summer's day* ◆ *a summer dress* ◆ *the summer vacation* ◆ *two summers ago* ⊃ see also INDIAN SUMMER **IDM** see SWALLOW *n.*
- *verb* [I] to spend the summer somewhere: *We summered in Maine when I was child.*

ˈsummer ˌcamp *noun* [C, U] a place where children go during the summer and take part in sports and other activities

ˈsummer ˌhouse *noun* **1** a small building in a yard, for sitting in in good weather **2** (also **ˈsummer home**) a house that someone lives in only during the summer

ˈsummer ˌschool *noun* [C, U] courses that are held in the summer at a university or college, or at a school

ˈsummer ˌstock *noun* [U] the production of special plays and other entertainment in areas where people are on vacation

ˈsummer ˌstudent *noun* (*CanE*) a student, especially a university student, who is working at a job for the summer

sum·mer·time /ˈsʌmərˌtaɪm/ *noun* [U] the season of summer: *It's beautiful here in (the) summertime.*

sum·mer·y /ˈsʌməri/ *adj.* typical of or suitable for the summer: *summery weather* ◆ *a light summery dress* **ANT** WINTRY

ˌsumming-ˈup *noun* (*pl.* summings-up) **1** a speech that the judge makes near the end of a trial in court, in which he or she reminds the jury about the evidence and the most important points in the case before the jury makes its decision **2** an occasion when someone states the main points of an argument, etc.

sum·mit /ˈsʌmət/ *noun* **1** the highest point of something, especially the top of a mountain: *We reached the summit at noon.* ◆ *This path leads to the summit.* ◆ (*figurative*) *the summit of his career* **2** an official meeting or series of meetings between the leaders of two or more governments, at which they discuss important matters: *a summit in Moscow* ◆ *a summit conference* ⊃ collocations at INTERNATIONAL

sum·mon /ˈsʌmən/ *verb* **1 ~ sb (to do sth)** (*formal*) to order someone to appear in court **SYN** SUMMONS: *He was summoned to appear before the magistrates.* **2 ~ sb (to sth)** | **~ sb to do sth** (*formal*) to order someone to come to you: *In May 1688 he was urgently summoned to London.* ◆ *She summoned the waiter.* **3 ~ sth** (*formal*) to arrange an official meeting **SYN** CONVENE: *to summon a meeting* **4 ~ sth** (*formal*) to call for or try to obtain something: *to summon assistance/help/reinforcements* **5 ~ sth (up)** to make an effort to produce a particular quality in yourself, especially when you find it difficult **SYN** MUSTER: *She was trying to summon up the courage to leave him.* ◆ *I couldn't even summon the energy to get out of bed.*

---

h **hat**   m **man**   n **no**   ŋ **sing**   l **leg**   r **red**   y **yes**   w **wet**

PHR V ˌsummon sth↔'up to make a feeling, an idea, a memory, etc. come into your mind **SYN** EVOKE: *The book summoned up memories of my childhood.*

sum·mons /'sʌmənz/ *noun, verb*

● **noun** (*pl.* **sum·mons·es** /-zəz/) **1** (also ci·ta·tion) an order to appear in court: *to issue a summons against someone* ◆ *The police were unable to* **serve a summons on him.** ◆ *She received a summons to appear in court the following week.* **2** an order to come and see someone: *to obey a royal summons*

● **verb** to order someone to appear in court **SYN** SUMMON: *~ sb (for sth)* *She was summoned for speeding.* ◆ *~ sb to do sth* *He was summoned to appear in court.*

su·mo /'suːməʊ/ (also **sumo** 'wrestling) *noun* [U] a Japanese style of WRESTLING, in which the people taking part are extremely large: *a sumo wrestler*

sump /sʌmp/ *noun* a hole or hollow area in which liquid waste collects

sump·tu·ous /'sʌmptʃuəs/ *adj.* (*formal*) very expensive and looking very impressive: *a sumptuous meal* ◆ *We dined in sumptuous surroundings.* ▶ **sump·tu·ous·ly** *adv.* **sump·tu·ous·ness** *noun* [U]

ˌsum 'total *noun* [sing.] (sometimes *disapproving*) the whole of something; everything: *A photo, a book of poems, and a gold ring—this was the sum total of his possessions.*

Sun. *abbr.* = SUNDAY

sun /sʌn/ *noun, verb*

● **noun 1 the sun, the Sun** [sing.] the star that shines in the sky during the day and gives the earth heat and light: *the sun's rays* ◆ *the rising/setting sun* ◆ *The sun was shining and birds were singing.* ◆ *The sun was just setting.* ⊃ picture at EARTH ⊃ collocations at WEATHER **2** usually **the sun** [sing., U] the light and heat from the sun **SYN** SUNSHINE: *the warmth of the afternoon sun* ◆ *This room gets the sun in the mornings.* ◆ *We sat* **in the sun.** ◆ *The sun was blazing hot.* ◆ *Too much sun ages the skin.* ◆ *We did our best to keep* **out of the sun.** ◆ *They always take a winter vacation* **in the sun** (= in a place where it is warm and the sun shines a lot). ◆ *I see you* **got some sun** (= became red or brown) *while you were away.* ◆ *I didn't see the car coming around the corner because* **I had the sun in my eyes** (= the sun was shining in my eyes). ⊃ see also SUNNY **3** [C] (*technical*) any star around which planets move **IDM** **under the sun** used to emphasize that you are talking about a very large number of things: *We talked about everything under the sun.* **with the sun** when the sun rises or sets: *I get up with the sun.* ⊃ more at HAY, PLACE *n.*

● **verb** (-nn-) **~ yourself** to sit or lie in a place where the sun is shining on you: *We lay sunning ourselves on the deck.*

ˈsun-baked *adj.* **1** made hard and dry by the heat of the sun: *sun-baked earth* **2** receiving a lot of light and heat from the sun: *sun-baked beaches*

sun·bathe /'sʌnbeɪð/ *verb* [I] to sit or lie in the sun, especially in order to turn brown (= get a SUNTAN) ⊃ note at BATH

sun·beam /'sʌnbiːm/ *noun* a stream of light from the sun

sun·bed /'sʌnbed/ *noun* a bed for lying on under a SUNLAMP

the Sun·belt /'sʌnbelt/ *noun* [sing.] the southern and south-western parts of the U.S. that are warm for most of the year

sun·block /'sʌnblɑk/ *noun* [U, C] a cream that you put on your skin to protect it completely from the harmful effects of the sun

sun·burn /'sʌnbɜːrn/ *noun* [U] the condition of having painful red skin after spending too much time in the sun ⊃ compare SUNTAN

sun·burned /'sʌnbɜːrnd/ (also **sun·burnt** /'sʌnbɜːrnt/) *adj.* suffering from sunburn: *Her shoulders were badly sunburned.*

sun·burst /'sʌnbɜːrst/ *noun* **1** an occasion when the sun appears from behind the clouds and sends out bright streams of light **2** a design in the shape of a central disk with narrow lines coming out of it

sun·dae /'sʌndeɪ; -di/ *noun* a cold DESSERT (= a sweet dish) of ice cream covered with a sweet sauce, nuts, pieces of fruit, etc., usually served in a tall glass

Sun·day /'sʌndeɪ; -di/ *noun* (*abbr.* **Sun.**) [C, U] the day of the week after Saturday and before Monday, thought of as either the first or the last day of the week **HELP** To see how **Sunday** is used, look at the examples at **Monday.** **ORIGIN** From the Old English for "day of the sun," translated from Latin *dies solis.* **IDM** **your Sunday best** (*informal, humorous*) your best clothes ⊃ more at MONTH

ˈSunday ˌschool *noun* [C, U] a class that is organized by a church or SYNAGOGUE, where children can go for a short time on Sundays to learn about the Christian or Jewish religion

ˈsun deck *noun* the part of a ship where passengers can sit to enjoy the sun, or a similar area beside a restaurant or swimming pool

sun·der /'sʌndər/ *verb* **~ sth/sb (from sth/sb)** (*formal* or *literary*) to split or break something or someone apart, especially by force ⊃ see also ASUNDER

sun·di·al /'sʌnˌdaɪəl; -ˌdaɪl/ *noun* a device used outdoors, especially in the past, for telling the time when the sun is shining. A pointed piece of metal throws a shadow on a flat surface that is marked with the hours like a clock, and the shadow moves around as the sun moves across the sky.

sundial

sun·down /'sʌndaʊn/ *noun* [U] the time when the sun goes down and night begins **SYN** SUNSET

ˈsun-drenched *adj.* [only before noun] (*approving*) having a lot of hot sun: *sun-drenched Caribbean beaches*

sun·dress /'sʌndres/ *noun* a dress that does not cover the arms, neck, or shoulders, worn in hot weather

ˈsun-dried *adj.* [only before noun] (especially of food) dried naturally by the heat of the sun: *sun-dried tomatoes*

sun·dries /'sʌndriz/ *noun* [pl.] various items, especially small ones, that are not important enough to be named separately

sun·dry /'sʌndri/ *adj.* [only before noun] (*formal*) various; not important enough to be named separately: *a watch, a diary, and sundry other items* **IDM** **all and sundry** (*informal*) everyone, not just a few special people: *She was known to all and sundry as Bella.* ◆ *The club is open to all and sundry.*

sun·flow·er /'sʌnˌflaʊər/ *noun* a very tall plant with large yellow flowers, grown in gardens or for its seeds and their oil that are used in cooking: *sunflower oil* ⊃ picture at PLANT

sung *pp of* SING

sun·glass·es /'sʌnˌglæsəz/ (also *informal* **shades**) *noun* [pl.] a pair of glasses with dark glass in them that you wear to protect your eyes from bright light from the sun: *a pair of sunglasses* ⊃ see also DARK GLASSES, SUNSHADE

ˈsun hat *noun* a hat worn to protect the head and neck from the sun ⊃ picture at HAT

sunk *pp of* SINK

sunk·en /'sʌŋkən/ *adj.* **1** [only before noun] that has fallen to the bottom of the ocean, or of a lake or river **SYN** SUBMERGED: *a sunken ship* ◆ *sunken treasure* **2** (of eyes or cheeks) hollow and deep as a result of disease, getting old, or not having enough food **3** [only before noun] at a lower level than the area around: *a sunken garden*

ˈsun-kissed *adj.* [usually before noun] made warm or brown by the sun: *sun-kissed bodies on the beach*

sun·lamp /ˈsʌnlæmp/ *noun* a lamp that produces ULTRA-VIOLET light that has the same effect as the sun and can turn the skin brown

sun·less /ˈsʌnləs/ *adj.* without any sun; receiving no light from the sun **SYN** GLOOMY: *a sunless day* **ANT** SUNNY

sun·light /ˈsʌnlaɪt/ *noun* [U] the light from the sun: *a ray/pool of sunlight* ♦ *shafts of bright sunlight* ♦ *The morning sunlight flooded into the room.*

sun·lit /ˈsʌnlɪt/ *adj.* [usually before noun] receiving light from the sun: *a cheery sunlit kitchen*

Sun·ni /ˈsʊni/ *noun* (*pl.* Sun·ni or Sun·nis) **1** [U] one of the two main branches of the Islamic religion ⊃ compare SHIA **2** [C] a member of the Sunni branch of Islam ⊃ compare SHIITE ▶ **Sun·nite** /ˈsʊnaɪt/ *adj.* [usually before noun]

sun·ny /ˈsʌni/ *adj.* (sun·ni·er, sun·ni·est) **1** with a lot of bright light from the sun: *a sunny day* ♦ *sunny weather* ♦ *The outlook for the weekend is hot and sunny.* ♦ *a sunny garden* ♦ *Mexico was at its sunniest.* **2** cheerful and happy: *a sunny disposition*

ˈ**sunny** ˌ**side** *noun* the side of something that receives most light from the sun: (*figurative*) *the sunny side of life* (= the more cheerful aspects of life)
> **IDM** **sunny-side up** (of an egg) fried on one side only

sun·rise /ˈsʌnraɪz/ *noun* **1** [U] the time when the sun first appears in the sky in the morning **SYN** DAWN: *We got up at sunrise.* **2** [C, usually sing.] the colors in the part of the sky where the sun first appears in the morning: *the pinks and yellows of the sunrise* **ANT** SUNSET

sun·roof /ˈsʌnruf; -rof/ *noun* (*pl.* **sun·roofs**) a part of the roof of a car that you can open to let air and light in

sun·room /ˈsʌnrum; -rʊm/ *noun* a room with large windows, and often a glass roof, that lets in a lot of light

sun·screen /ˈsʌnskrin/ *noun* [C, U] a cream or liquid that you put on your skin to protect it from the harmful effects of the sun: *a high factor* (= strong) *sunscreen*

sun·set /ˈsʌnsɛt/ *noun*, *adj.*
- *noun* **1** [U] the time when the sun goes down and night begins **SYN** SUNDOWN: *Every evening at sunset, the flag was lowered.* **2** [C] the colors in the part of the sky where the sun slowly goes down in the evening: *a spectacular sunset* **ANT** SUNRISE
- *adj.* [only before noun] **1** used to describe a color that is like one of the colors in a sunset: *sunset yellow* **2** used to describe something that is near its end, or that happens at the end of something: *This is his sunset tour after fifty years as a singer.*

ˈ**sunset pro**ˌ**vision** (also ˈ**sunset** ˌ**clause**) *noun* (*law*) part of a law, a rule, or an agreement that states that it will no longer apply from a particular date: *a two-year sunset provision in the new law*

sun·shade /ˈsʌnʃeɪd/ *noun* **1** a light umbrella or other object such as an AWNING, that is used to protect people from hot sun: *a stroller with a sunshade* ⊃ compare PARASOL **2** sunshades [pl.] a pair of dark glasses that you wear to protect your eyes from bright light from the sun, especially ones that fix on to your ordinary glasses

sun·shine /ˈsʌnʃaɪn/ *noun* [U] **1** the light and heat of the sun: *the warm spring sunshine* ⊃ collocations at WEATHER **2** (*informal*) happiness: *She brought sunshine into our dull lives.*
> **IDM** see RAY

ˈ**sunshine** ˌ**law** *noun* a law that forces government organizations to make certain types of information available to the public

sun·spot /ˈsʌnspɑt/ *noun* a dark area that sometimes appears on the sun's surface

sun·stroke /ˈsʌnstroʊk/ *noun* [U] an illness with fever, weakness, headache, etc. caused by too much direct sun, especially on the head

sun·tan /ˈsʌntæn/ *noun* [usually sing.] = TAN: *Where did you go to get that suntan?* ⊃ compare SUNBURN ▶ **sun·tan** *adj.*

[only before noun]: *suntan lotion/oil* **sun·tanned** /-tænd/ *adj.* = TANNED: *a suntanned face*

sun·up /ˈsʌnʌp/ *noun* [U] the time when the sun rises and day begins **SYN** SUNRISE

ˈ**sun** ˌ**worshiper** (CanE usually ˈ**sun** ˌ**worshipper**) *noun* (*informal*) a person who enjoys lying in the sun very much

sup /sʌp/ *verb* (-pp-) [I] (*old-fashioned*) to eat SUPPER

su·per /ˈsupər/ *adj.*, *adv.*, *noun*
- *adj.* (*informal*, becoming *old-fashioned*) extremely good: *a super meal* ♦ *We had a super time in Las Vegas.* ♦ *She was super* (= very kind) *when I was having problems.*
- *adv.* (*informal*) especially; particularly: *He's been super understanding.*
- *noun* a SUPERINTENDENT of a building

super- /ˈsupər/ *combining form* **1** (in adjectives, adverbs, and nouns) extremely; more or better than normal: *super-rich* ♦ *superhuman* ♦ *superglue* **2** (in nouns and verbs) above; over: *superstructure* ♦ *superimpose*

su·per·a·bun·dance /ˌsupərəˈbʌndəns/ *noun* [sing., U] (*formal*) much more than enough of something ▶ **su·per·a·bun·dant** /-dənt/ *adj.*

su·per·an·nu·at·ed /ˌsupərˈænyuˌeɪtəd/ *adj.* [usually before noun] (*formal* or *humorous*) (of people or things) too old for work or to be used for their original purpose: *superannuated rock stars*

su·perb /suˈpərb/ *adj.* (*formal*) excellent; of very good quality: *a superb player* ♦ *The car is in superb condition.* ♦ *His performance was absolutely superb.* ♦ *You look superb.* ⊃ thesaurus box at EXCELLENT ▶ **su·perb·ly** *adv.*: *a superbly illustrated book* ♦ *She plays superbly.*

the ˈ**Super** ˌ**Bowl** *noun* a football game played every year to decide the winner of the National Football League

su·per·bug /ˈsupərˌbʌg/ *noun* a type of bacteria that cannot easily be killed by ANTIBIOTICS ⊃ see also MRSA

su·per·cen·ter (CanE usually **su·per·cen·tre**) /ˈsupərˌsɛntər/ *noun* a very large store that sells food, clothing, furniture, and many other goods

su·per·charged /ˈsupərˌtʃɑrdʒd/ *adj.* **1** (of an engine) powerful because it is supplied with air or fuel at a pressure that is higher than normal **2** (*informal*) stronger, more powerful, or more effective than usual: *supercharged words, like "terrorism" or "fascism"* ▶ **su·per·charg·er** /-ˌtʃɑrdʒər/ *noun*: *VW's supercharger for its 16-valve engine*

su·per·cil·i·ous /ˌsupərˈsɪliəs/ *adj.* (*disapproving*) behaving toward other people as if you think you are better than they are **SYN** SUPERIOR ▶ **su·per·cil·i·ous·ly** *adv.* **su·per·cil·i·ous·ness** *noun* [U]

su·per·com·put·er /ˈsupərkəmˌpyutər/ *noun* a powerful computer with a large amount of memory and a very fast CENTRAL PROCESSING UNIT

su·per·con·duc·tiv·i·ty /ˌsupərˌkɑndʌkˈtɪvəti/ *noun* [U] (*physics*) the property (= characteristic) of some substances at very low temperatures to let electricity flow with no RESISTANCE

su·per·con·duc·tor /ˈsupərkənˌdʌktər/ *noun* (*physics*) a substance that has SUPERCONDUCTIVITY

su·per·con·ti·nent /ˈsupərˌkɑntənənt; -ˌkɑntn̩·ənt/ *noun* (*geology*) any of the very large areas of land, for example Gondwana or Laurasia, that existed millions of years ago

su·per-du·per /ˌsupər ˈdupər/ *adj.* (*old-fashioned*, *informal*) excellent

su·per·e·go /ˌsupərˈigoʊ/ *noun* [usually sing.] (*pl.* **su·per·e·gos**) (*psychology*) the part of the mind that makes you aware of right and wrong and makes you feel guilty if you do wrong ⊃ compare EGO

su·per·fi·cial /ˌsupərˈfɪʃl/ *adj.* **1** (often *disapproving*) not studying or looking at something thoroughly; seeing only what is obvious: *a superficial analysis* ♦ *The book shows only a superficial understanding of the historical context.* **2** appearing to be true, real, or important until you look at it more carefully: *superficial differences/similarities* ◆ *When you first meet her, she gives a superficial impression of warmth and friendliness.* **3** (of a wound or damage) only affecting the surface and therefore not serious: *a superficial injury* ◆ *superficial burns* **4** (*disapproving*) not concerned with anything serious or important and lacking any depth of understanding or feeling **SYN** SHALLOW: *a superficial friendship* ◆ *The guests engaged in superficial chatter.* ◆ *She's so superficial!* **5** (*technical*) of or on the surface of something: *superficial veins* ◆ *a superficial deposit of acidic soils* ▶ **su·per·fi·ci·al·i·ty** /ˌsupərˌfɪʃiˈæləti/ *noun* [U] **su·per·fi·cial·ly** /ˌsupərˈfɪʃəli/ *adv.*

su·per·fine /ˌsupərˈfaɪn; ˈsupərˌfaɪn/ *adj.* (*technical*) **1** extremely light or thin; made of extremely small pieces: *superfine fibers* ◆ *superfine sugar* **2** of extremely good quality: *superfine cloth*

su·per·flu·ous /suˈpərfluəs/ *adj.* more than you need or want **SYN** UNNECESSARY: *She gave him a look that made words superfluous.* ▶ **su·per·flu·i·ty** /ˌsupərˈfluəti/ *noun* [U, sing.] (*formal*) **su·per·flu·ous·ly** /suˈpərfluəsli/ *adv.*

su·per·food *noun* /ˈsupərˌfud/ a type of food that some people think is very good for you and helps to prevent disease: *the health benefits of so-called superfoods*

Su·per·fund /ˈsupərˌfʌnd/ *noun* [U, sing.] a U.S. government system for finding and cleaning up places where dangerous waste has been thrown away: *The area has been designated as a Superfund site.*

su·per·glue /ˈsupərˌglu/ *noun* [U] a very strong glue that sticks very quickly and is used in small quantities for repairing things

su·per·group /ˈsupərˌgrup/ *noun* a very successful and very famous band that plays ROCK music, especially one whose members have already become famous in other bands

su·per·heat·ed /ˌsupərˈhitəd/ *adj.* (*physics*) **1** (of a liquid) that has been heated under pressure above its boiling point without becoming a gas **2** (of a gas) that has been heated above its temperature of SATURATION (= below which it becomes a liquid)

su·per·he·ro /ˈsupərˌhɪroʊ; -ˌhiroʊ/ *noun* (*pl.* **su·per·he·roes**) a character in a story, movie, etc. who has unusual strength or power and uses it to help people; a real person who has done something unusually brave to help someone **ANT** SUPERVILLAIN

su·per·high·way /ˌsupərˈhaɪweɪ/ *noun* **1** (*old-fashioned*) = INTERSTATE **2** = INFORMATION SUPERHIGHWAY

su·per·hu·man /ˌsupərˈhyumən/ *adj.* having much greater power, knowledge, etc. than is normal **SYN** HEROIC: *superhuman strength* ◆ *It took an almost superhuman effort to contain his anger.* ⊃ compare SUBHUMAN

su·per·im·pose /ˌsupərɪmˈpoʊz/ *verb* **1** ~ sth (on/onto sth) to put one image on top of another so that the two can be seen combined: *A diagram of the new road layout was superimposed on a map of the city.* **2** ~ sth (on/onto sth) to add some of the qualities of one system or pattern to another one in order to produce something that combines the qualities of both: *She has tried to superimpose her own attitudes onto this ancient story.* ▶ **su·per·im·po·si·tion** /ˌsupərˌɪmpəˈzɪʃn/ *noun* [U]

su·per·in·tend /ˌsupərɪnˈtɛnd/ *verb* ~ sth (*formal*) to be in charge of something and make sure that everything is working, being done, etc. as it should be **SYN** SUPERVISE ▶ **su·per·in·tend·ence** /-ˈtɛndəns/ *noun* [U]

su·per·in·tend·ent /ˌsupərɪnˈtɛndənt; ˌsuprɪn-/ *noun* **1** a person who has a lot of authority, and manages and controls an activity, a place, a group of workers, etc.: *a park superintendent* ◆ *the superintendent of schools in Dallas* **2** the head of a police department **3** a person whose job is to be in charge of a building and make small repairs, etc. to it

su·pe·ri·or 🔑 /səˈpɪriər/ *adj.*, *noun*
- *adj.* **1** ~ (to sb/sth) better in quality than someone or something else; greater than someone or something else: *vastly superior* ◆ *superior intelligence* ◆ *This model is technically superior to its competitors.* ◆ *Miami was clearly the superior team.* ◆ *The enemy won because of their superior numbers* (= there were more of them). **ANT** INFERIOR **2** ~ (to sb) higher in rank, importance, or position: *my superior officer* ◆ *superior status* ◆ *a superior court of law* **ANT** INFERIOR **3** (*disapproving*) showing by your behavior that you think you are better than others **SYN** ARROGANT: *a superior manner* ◆ *He always looks so superior.* **4** (used especially in advertisements) of very good quality; better than other similar things: *superior lakefront condominiums*
- *noun* **1** a person of higher rank, status, or position: *Among ballet dancers of the time, only Pavlova was her superior.* ◆ *He's my immediate superior* (= the person directly above me). ◆ *I'm going to complain to your superiors.* **ANT** INFERIOR **2** used in titles for the head of a religious community: *Mother Superior*

su·pe·ri·or·i·ty /səˌpɪriˈɔrəti; -ˈɑr-/ *noun* [U] **1** ~ (in sth) | ~ (to/over sth/sb) the state or quality of being better, more skillful, more powerful, greater, etc. than others: *the superiority of this operating system* ◆ *to have naval/air superiority* (= more ships/planes than the enemy) **2** behavior that shows that you think you are better than other people: *an air of superiority* **ANT** INFERIORITY

superi'ority ˌcomplex *noun* a feeling that you are better or more important than other people, often as a way of hiding your feelings of failure

su·per·la·tive /səˈpərlətɪv/ *adj.*, *noun*
- *adj.* **1** excellent **SYN** FIRST-RATE: *a superlative performance* **2** (*grammar*) relating to adjectives or adverbs that express the highest degree of something, for example *best*, *worst*, *slowest*, and *most difficult* ⊃ compare COMPARATIVE ▶ **su·per·la·tive·ly** *adv.*
- *noun* (*grammar*) the form of an adjective or adverb that expresses the highest degree of something: *It's hard to find enough superlatives to describe this book.* ⊃ compare COMPARATIVE

su·per·man /ˈsupərˌmæn/ *noun* (*pl.* **su·per·men** /-ˌmɛn/) a man who is unusually strong or intelligent or who can do something extremely well ⊃ compare SUPERWOMAN

su·per·mar·ket 🔑 /ˈsupərˌmɑrkət/ *noun* a large store that sells food, drinks, and goods used in the home. People choose what they want from the shelves and pay for it as they leave. ⊃ compare GROCERY STORE

su·per·max /ˈsupərˌmæks/ *noun* a maximum security prison, intended for very dangerous prisoners

su·per·mod·el /ˈsupərˌmɑdl/ *noun* a very famous and highly paid fashion model

su·per·nat·u·ral /ˌsupərˈnætʃrəl; -ˈnætʃərəl/ *adj.* **1** that cannot be explained by the laws of science and that seems to involve gods or magic **SYN** PARANORMAL: *supernatural powers* ◆ *supernatural strength* ⊃ compare NATURAL **2 the supernatural** *noun* [sing.] events, forces, or powers that cannot be explained by the laws of science and that seem to involve gods or magic **SYN** THE PARANORMAL: *a belief in the supernatural* ▶ **su·per·nat·u·ral·ly** *adv.*

su·per·no·va /ˌsupərˈnoʊvə; ˌsupərˈnoʊvə/ *noun* (*pl.* **su·per·no·vae** /-vi/ or **su·per·no·vas**) (*astronomy*) a star that suddenly becomes much brighter because it is exploding ⊃ compare NOVA

su·per·nu·mer·ar·y /ˌsupərˈnuməˌrɛri/ *adj.* (*formal*) more than you normally need; extra

su·per·or·di·nate /ˌsupərˈɔrdnət/ (also **hy·per·nym**) *noun* (*linguistics*) a word with a general meaning that includes the meanings of other particular words, for example "fruit" is the superordinate of "apple," "orange," etc. ⊃ compare HYPONYM ▶ **su·per·or·di·nate** *adj.* ⊃ compare SUBORDINATE

su·per·pose /ˌsupərˈpoʊz/ *verb* ~ **sth** to put something on or above something else: *They had superposed a picture of his head onto someone else's body.* ▶ **su·per·po·si·tion** /-pəˈzɪʃn/ *noun*

su·per·pow·er /ˈsupərˌpaʊər/ *noun* one of the countries in the world that has very great military or economic power and a lot of influence, for example the U.S.

su·per·script /ˈsupərˌskrɪpt/ *adj.* (*technical*) written or printed above the normal line of writing or printing ▶ **su·per·script** *noun*

su·per·sede /ˌsupərˈsid/ *verb* ~ **sth/sb** [often passive] to take the place of something or someone that is considered to be old-fashioned or no longer the best available: *The theory has been superseded by more recent research.*

su·per·size /ˈsupərˌsaɪz/ *adj.*, *verb*
- *adj.* (also **su·per·sized**) bigger than normal: *supersize portions of fries* ◆ *supersized clothing*
- *verb* [T, I] ~ **(sb/sth)** to make someone or something bigger; to become bigger: *We are being supersized into obesity* (= made very fat) *by the fast food industry.* ◆ *TV ads encourage kids to supersize.*

su·per·son·ic /ˌsupərˈsɑnɪk/ *adj.* faster than the speed of sound: *a supersonic aircraft* ◆ *supersonic flight* ➔ compare SUBSONIC

su·per·star /ˈsupərˌstɑr/ *noun* a very famous performer, for example an actor, a singer, or a sports player

su·per·state /ˈsupərˌsteɪt/ *noun* a very powerful state, especially one that is formed by several nations joining or working together: *Some people advocate a European superstate.*

su·per·sti·tion /ˌsupərˈstɪʃn/ *noun* [U, C] (often *disapproving*) the belief that particular events happen in a way that cannot be explained by reason or science; the belief that particular events bring good or bad luck: *According to superstition, breaking a mirror brings bad luck.*

su·per·sti·tious /ˌsupərˈstɪʃəs/ *adj.* believing in superstitions: *superstitious beliefs* ◆ *I'm superstitious about the number 13.* ▶ **su·per·sti·tious·ly** *adv.*

su·per·store /ˈsupərˌstɔr/ *noun* a very large supermarket or a large store that sells a wide variety of one type of goods: *a computer superstore*

su·per·struc·ture /ˈsupərˌstrʌktʃər/ *noun* **1** a structure that is built on top of something, for example the upper parts of a ship or the part of a building above the ground ➔ compare SUBSTRUCTURE **2** (*formal*) the systems and beliefs in a society that have developed from more simple ones

su·per·tank·er /ˈsupərˌtæŋkər/ *noun* a very large ship for carrying oil, etc.

ˌSuper ˈTuesday *noun* [sing.] (*informal*) a day on which several U.S. states hold PRIMARY elections

su·per·vene /ˌsupərˈvin/ *verb* [I] (*formal*) to happen, especially unexpectedly, and have a powerful effect on the existing situation

su·per·vil·lain /ˈsupərˌvɪlən/ *noun* a very bad character in a story, especially one with magic powers **ANT** SUPERHERO

su·per·vise /ˈsupərˌvaɪz/ *verb* [T, I] to be in charge of someone or something and make sure that everything is done correctly, safely, etc.: ~ **(sb/sth)** *to supervise a building site* ◆ ~ **sb doing sth** *She supervised the children playing near the pool.* ▶ **su·per·vi·sion** /ˌsupərˈvɪʒn/ *noun* [U]: *Very young children should not be left to play without supervision.* ◆ *The drug should only be used under medical supervision.*

su·per·vi·sor /ˈsupərˌvaɪzər/ *noun* a person who supervises someone or something: *I have a meeting with my supervisor about my research topic.* ▶ **su·per·vi·so·ry** /ˌsupərˈvaɪzəri/ *adj.*: *She has a supervisory role on the project.*

su·per·wom·an /ˈsupərˌwʊmən/ *noun* (pl. **su·per·wom·en** /-ˌwɪmən/) a woman who is unusually strong or intelligent or who can do something extremely well, especially a woman who has a successful career and also takes care of her home and family ➔ compare SUPERMAN

su·pine /ˈsupaɪn; suˈpaɪn/ *adj.* (*formal*) **1** lying flat on your back: *a supine position* ➔ compare PRONE **2** (*disapproving*) not willing to act or disagree with someone because you are lazy or morally weak ▶ **su·pine·ly** *adv.*

sup·per /ˈsʌpər/ *noun* **1** [U, C] an informal meal that people eat in the evening: *I'll do my homework after supper.* ◆ *What's for supper?* ◆ *We'll have an early supper tonight.* **2** [C] a social event at which an evening meal is served, often for the purpose of raising money: *a church supper*

sup·plant /səˈplænt/ *verb* ~ **sb/sth** (*formal*) to take the place of someone or something (especially someone or something older or less modern) **SYN** REPLACE

sup·ple /ˈsʌpl/ *adj.* **1** able to bend and move parts of your body easily into different positions **SYN** LIMBER: *her slim, supple body* ◆ *These exercises will help to keep you supple.* **2** soft and able to bend easily without cracking: *Moisturizing cream helps to keep your skin soft and supple.* ▶ **sup·ple·ness** *noun* [U]

sup·ple·ment **AWL** *noun*, *verb*
- *noun* /ˈsʌpləmənt/ **1** a thing that is added to something else to improve or complete it: *vitamin/dietary supplements* (= VITAMINS and other foods eaten in addition to what you usually eat) ◆ ~ **to sth** *Industrial sponsorship is a supplement to government funding.* **2** an extra separate section, often in the form of a magazine, that is sold with a newspaper: *the Sunday literary supplement* **3** ~ **(to sth)** a book or a section at the end of a book that gives extra information or deals with a special subject: *the supplement to the Oxford English Dictionary*
- *verb* /ˈsʌpləˌmɛnt/ to add something to something in order to improve it or make it more complete: ~ **sth with sth** *a diet supplemented with vitamin pills* ◆ ~ **sth** *He supplements his income by giving private lessons.* ▶ **sup·ple·men·ta·tion** /ˌsʌpləmɛnˈteɪʃn/ *noun* [U]

sup·ple·men·ta·ry **AWL** /ˌsʌpləˈmɛntri; -ˈmɛntəri/ (also **sup·ple·men·tal** /ˌsʌpləˈmɛntl/) *adj.* provided in addition to something else in order to improve or complete it **SYN** ADDITIONAL: *supplementary information*

ˌsupplementary ˈangle *noun* (*mathematics*) either of two angles which together make 180° ➔ compare COMPLE-MENTARY ANGLE

sup·ple·tion /səˈpliʃn/ *noun* [U] (*linguistics*) the use of a word as a particular form of a verb when the word is not related to the main form of the verb, for example "went" as the past tense of "go" ▶ **sup·ple·tive** /səˈplitɪv; ˈsʌplətɪv/ *adj.*

sup·pli·cant /ˈsʌplɪkənt/ (also **sup·pli·ant** /ˈsʌpliənt/) *noun* (*formal*) a person who asks for something in a HUMBLE way, especially from God or a powerful person

sup·pli·ca·tion /ˌsʌpləˈkeɪʃn/ *noun* [U, C] (*formal*) the act of asking for something with a very HUMBLE request or prayer: *She knelt in supplication.*

sup·pli·er /səˈplaɪər/ *noun* a person or company that supplies goods: *a leading supplier of computers in the U.S. and abroad*

sup·ply 🔑 /səˈplaɪ/ *noun*, *verb*
- *noun* **1** [C] an amount of something that is provided or available to be used: *The water supply is unsafe.* ◆ *Supplies of food are almost exhausted.* ◆ *We cannot guarantee adequate supplies of raw materials.* ◆ *Books were in short supply* (= there were not enough of them). **2** **supplies** [pl.] the things such as food, medicines, fuel, etc. that are needed by a group of people, for example an army or EXPEDITION: *Our supplies were running out.* ◆ *a transport plane carrying food and medical supplies for refugees* **3** [U] the act of supplying something: *The U.N. has agreed to allow the supply of emergency aid.* ◆ *A stroke can disrupt the supply of oxygen to the brain.* ◆ *The electricity supply* (= the system supplying electricity) *had been cut off.*

t **tea**   t̬ **butter**   d **did**   k **cat**   g **got**   tʃ **chin**   dʒ **June**   f **fall**

• **verb** (sup·plies, sup·ply·ing, sup·plied, sup·plied) to provide someone or something with something that they need or want, especially in large quantities: ~ **sth to sb/sth** *Foreign governments supplied arms to the rebels.* ◆ ~ **sb/sth with sth** *Foreign governments supplied the rebels with arms.* ◆ ~ **sb/sth** *Local schools supply many of the volunteers.* ◆ *foods supplying our daily vitamin needs*

sup|ply and de|mand *noun* [U] (*economics*) the relationship between the amount of goods or services that are available and the amount that people want to buy, especially when this controls prices

sup|ply chain *noun* [usually sing.] (*business*) the series of processes involved in the production and supply of goods, from when they are first made, grown, etc. until they are bought or used

sup|ply line *noun* a route along which food, equipment, etc. is transported to an army during a war

sup|ply-side *adj.* [only before noun] (*economics*) connected with the policy of reducing taxes in order to encourage economic growth

sup·port 🔑 /sə'pɔrt/ *verb, noun*
• **verb**
> ENCOURAGE/GIVE HELP **1** to help or encourage someone or something by saying or showing that you agree with them/it **SYN** BACK: ~ **sb/sth** *to support a proposal* ◆ *These measures are strongly supported by environmental groups.* ◆ *If you raise it at the meeting, I'll support you.* ◆ ~ **sb/sth in sth** *The students supported the workers in their demand for higher wages.* **2** ~ **sb** to give or be ready to give help to someone if they need it: *an organization that supports people with AIDS* ◆ *The company is committed to supporting all its customers* (= solving their problems with a product).
> PROVIDE MONEY, ETC. **3** ~ **sth** to help or encourage something to be successful by giving it money **SYN** SPONSOR: *Several major companies are supporting the project.* **4** ~ **sb/sth/yourself** to provide everything necessary, especially money, so that someone or something can live or exist: *Mark has two children to support from his first marriage.* ◆ *He turned to crime to support his drug habit.* ◆ *The atmosphere of Mars could not support life.*
> HOLD IN POSITION **5** ~ **sb/sth** to hold someone or something in position; to prevent someone or something from falling: *a platform supported by concrete pillars* ◆ *Support the baby's head when you hold it.*
> HELP PROVE SOMETHING **6** ~ **sth** to help to show that something is true **SYN** CORROBORATE: *The witness's story was not supported by the evidence.* ⟳ language bank at EVIDENCE
> COMPUTER **7** ~ **sth** (of a computer or computer system) to allow a particular program, language, or device to be used with it: *This digital audio player supports multiple formats.*
• **noun**
> ENCOURAGEMENT/MONEY **1** [U] ~ **(for sth)** encouragement and help that you give to someone or something because you approve of them and want them to be successful: *There is strong public support for the change.* ◆ *Can I rely on your support* (= will you vote for me) *in the election?* ◆ *Only a few people spoke in support of the proposal.* ◆ *Local businesses have provided financial support.* ◆ *She has no visible means of support* (= no work, income, etc.). ⟳ see also CHILD SUPPORT
> HELP **2** [U] sympathy and help that you give to someone who is in a difficult or unhappy situation: *Her family and friends have given her lots of support.* ⟳ see also MORAL SUPPORT
> HOLDING IN POSITION **3** [C] a thing that holds something and prevents it from falling: *The supports under the bridge were starting to bend.* ◆ (*figurative*) *When my father died, Jim was a real support.* **4** [U] the act of holding something firmly in position or preventing it from falling: *I wrapped a bandage around my ankle to give it some support.* ◆ *She held on to his arm for support.* **5** [C] something you wear to hold an injured or weak part of your body firmly in position: *a knee/back support*

> PROOF **6** [U] evidence that helps to show that something is true or correct: *The statistics offer further support for our theory.*
> TECHNICAL HELP **7** [U] technical help that a company gives to customers using their computers or other products: *We offer free technical support.*

sup·port·er 🔑 /sə'pɔrtər/ *noun*
a person who supports a political party, an idea, etc.: *a strong/loyal/staunch supporter* ◆ *the mayor's supporters* ◆ *a supporter of civil rights* ⟳ see also ATHLETIC SUPPORTER

sup'port group *noun* a group of people who meet to help each other with a particular problem: *a support group for single parents*

sup·port·ing /sə'pɔrtɪŋ/ *adj.* [only before noun] **1** a **supporting** actor in a play or movie has an important part but not the leading one: *He played many supporting roles before becoming a star.* **2** (*formal*) helping to show that something is true: *There was a wealth of supporting evidence.* **3** carrying the weight of something: *a supporting wall*

sup·port·ive /sə'pɔrtɪv/ *adj.* giving help, encouragement, or sympathy to someone: *a supportive family* ◆ *She was very supportive during my father's illness.*

sup·pose 🔑 /sə'pouz/ *verb*
1 [I, T] to think or believe that something is true or possible (based on the knowledge that you have): *Getting a good job isn't as easy as you might suppose.* ◆ *Prices will go up, I suppose.* ◆ ~ **sb/sth to be/have sth** (*formal*) *This combination of qualities is generally supposed to be extremely rare.* ◆ ~ **sb/sth + adj.** (*formal*) *She had supposed him* (*to be*) *very rich.* ◆ ~ **sb/sth + noun** (*formal*) *I had supposed his wife a younger woman.* ◆ ~ **(that)…** *I don't suppose for a minute that he'll agree* (= I'm sure that he won't). ◆ *Why do you suppose he resigned?* ◆ *There is no reason to suppose she's lying.* ◆ *I suppose you think it's funny, don't you?* (= showing anger) **HELP** "That" is nearly always left out, especially in speech. **2** [T] to pretend that something is true; to imagine what would happen if something were true: ~ **(that)…** *Suppose flights are full on that day—which other day could we go?* ◆ *Let us suppose, for example, that you are married with two children.* ◆ ~ **sth** (*formal*) *The theory supposes the existence of life on other planets.* ◆ ~ **sb/sth (to be/have) sth** | ~ **sb/sth + adj./noun** (*formal*) *They supposed him* (*to be*) *dead—but what if he wasn't?* **3** [I, T] used to make a statement, request, or suggestion less direct or less strong: *I could take you in the car, I suppose* (= but I don't really want to). ◆ *"Can I borrow the car?" "I suppose so"* (= Yes, but I'm not happy about it). ◆ ~ **(that)…** *I don't suppose (that) I could have the day off, could I?* ◆ *Suppose we take a later flight?* **IDM** be sup·posed to do/be sth **1** to be expected or required to do/be something according to a rule, a custom, an arrangement, etc.: *You're supposed to buy a ticket, but not many people do.* ◆ *I thought we were supposed to be paid today.* ◆ *The engine doesn't sound like it's supposed to.* ◆ *You were supposed to be here an hour ago!* ◆ *How was I supposed to know you were waiting for me?* ◆ *"Yes and no." "What is that supposed to mean?"* (= showing that you are annoyed) **2** to be generally believed or expected to be/do something: *I haven't seen it myself, but it's supposed to be a great movie.* **not be supposed to do sth** to not be allowed to do something: *You're not supposed to walk on the grass.*

sup·posed /sə'pouzd; -'pouzd/ *adj.* [only before noun] used to show that you think that a claim, statement, or way of describing someone or something is not true or correct, although it is generally believed to be **SYN** ALLEGED: *This is the opinion of the supposed experts.* ◆ *When did this supposed accident happen?*

sup·pos·ed·ly /sə'pouzədli/ *adv.* according to what is generally thought or believed but not known for certain **SYN** ALLEGEDly: *The novel is supposedly based on a true story.*

sup·pos·ing /sə'pouzɪŋ/ *conj.* ~ **(that)** used to ask someone to pretend that something is true or to imagine that something will happen: *Supposing (that) you are wrong, what will you do then?* ◆ *But supposing he sees us?*

sup·po·si·tion /ˌsʌpəˈzɪʃn/ noun (formal) **1** [C] **~ (that...)** an idea that you think is true although you may not be able to prove it **SYN** ASSUMPTION: *The police are working on the supposition that he was murdered.* **2** [U] the act of believing or claiming that something is true even though it cannot be proved: *The report is based entirely on supposition.*

sup·pos·i·to·ry /səˈpɑzəˌtɔri/ noun (pl. **sup·pos·i·to·ries**) a small piece of solid medicine that is placed in the RECTUM or VAGINA and left to dissolve gradually

sup·press /səˈprɛs/ verb **1 ~ sth** (usually *disapproving*) (of a government, ruler, etc.) to put an end, often by force, to a group or an activity that is believed to threaten authority **SYN** QUASH: *The rebellion was brutally suppressed.* **2 ~ sth** (usually *disapproving*) to prevent something from being published or made known: *The police were accused of suppressing vital evidence.* **3 ~ sth** to prevent yourself from having or expressing a feeling or an emotion: *to suppress a smile* ◆ *She was unable to suppress her anger.* **4 ~ sth** to prevent something from growing, developing, or continuing: *drugs that suppress the appetite*

sup·pres·sant /səˈprɛsnt/ noun a drug that is used to prevent one of the body's functions from working normally: *an appetite suppressant*

sup·pres·sion /səˈprɛʃn/ noun [U] the act of SUPPRESSING something: *the suppression of a rebellion* ◆ *the suppression of emotion*

sup·pres·sor /səˈprɛsər/ noun a thing or person that SUPPRESSES someone or something: *the body's pain suppressors*

sup·pu·rate /ˈsʌpyəˌreɪt/ verb [I] (formal) (of a cut, wound, etc.) to produce a thick yellow liquid (called PUS) because of infection ► **sup·pu·ra·tion** /ˌsʌpyəˈreɪʃn/ noun [U]

su·pra·na·tion·al /ˌsuprəˈnæʃənl/ adj. (formal) involving more than one country

su·pra·seg·men·tal /ˌsuprəsɛɡˈmɛntl/ adj. (phonetics) relating to features of speech such as stress and INTONATION as opposed to individual speech sounds

su·prem·a·cist /səˈprɛməsɪst/ noun a person who believes that their own race is better than others and should be in power ➋ see also WHITE SUPREMACIST

su·prem·a·cy /səˈprɛməsi/ noun [U] a position in which you have more power, authority, or status than anyone else: *the battle for supremacy in the region* ◆ *the dangerous notion of white supremacy* (= that white races are better than others and should control them) ◆ **~ over sb/sth** *The company has established total supremacy over its rivals.*

su·preme /səˈprim/ adj. [usually before noun] **1** highest in rank or position: *The case will probably go to the Supreme Court.* ◆ *the supreme champion* ◆ *It is an event in which she reigns supreme.* **2** very great or the greatest in degree: *to make the supreme sacrifice* (= die for what you believe in) ◆ *a supreme effort* ◆ *She smiled with supreme confidence.*

the Su·preme ˈBeing noun [sing.] (formal) God

the Su·preme ˈCourt noun [sing.] the highest court in a country or state

su·preme·ly /səˈprimli/ adv. extremely: *supremely confident* ◆ *They managed it all supremely well.*

su·ra (also **su·rah**) /ˈsʊrə/ noun a chapter or section of the Koran

sur·charge /ˈsɜrtʃɑrdʒ/ noun, verb
● noun **~ (on sth)** an extra amount of money that you must pay in addition to the usual price
● verb **~ sb (sth)** to make someone pay a surcharge: *The airline surcharges passengers for any checked luggage.*

sur·coat /ˈsɜrkoʊt/ noun a piece of clothing without sleeves, worn in the past over a suit of ARMOR

sure 🔑 /ʃʊr; ʃər/ adj., adv.
● adj. (**sur·er**, **sur·est**) **HELP** You can also use **more sure** and **most sure**, especially in sense 1. **1** [not before noun] confident that you know something or that you are right

SYN CERTAIN: *"Is that John over there?" "I'm not sure."* ◆ *You don't sound very sure.* ◆ **~ (that)...** *I'm pretty sure (that) he'll agree.* ◆ *Are you sure you don't mind?* ◆ **~ of sth** *I hope you are sure of your facts.* ◆ **~ about sth** *Are you sure about that?* ◆ **~ how, whether, etc....** *Ask me if you're not sure how to do it.* ◆ *I'm not sure whether I should tell you this.* **ANT** UNSURE **2** [not before noun] certain that you will receive something or that something will happen: **~ of sth** *You're always sure of a warm welcome there.* ◆ **~ of doing sth** *The team must win this game to be sure of qualifying for the finals.* **3 ~ to do sth** certain to do something or to happen: *The exhibition is sure to be popular.* ◆ *It's sure to rain.* ➋ note at CERTAIN **4** [usually before noun] that can be trusted or relied on: *It's a sure sign of economic recovery.* ◆ *There's only one sure way to do it.* ◆ *He is a sure bet for the presidential nomination* (= certain to succeed). ➋ note at CERTAIN **5** [usually before noun] steady and confident: *We admired her sure touch at the keyboard.*
IDM **be sure to do sth** used to tell someone to do something: *Be sure to give your family my regards.* **HELP** In spoken English **and** plus another verb can be used instead of **to** and the infinitive: *Be sure and call me tomorrow.* **for sure** (informal) without doubt: *No one knows for sure what happened.* ◆ *I think he'll be back on Monday, but I can't say for sure.* ◆ *I know one thing for sure —it's not going to be easy.* ◆ *"Will you be there?" "For sure."* **make sure (of sth/that...)** **1** to do something in order to be certain that something else happens: *Make sure (that) no one finds out about this.* ◆ *They scored another run, making sure of a win.* ◆ *Our staff will do their best to make sure you enjoy your visit.* **2** to check that something is true or has been done: *She looked around to make sure that she was alone.* ◆ *I think the door's locked, but I'll make sure.* **sure of yourself** (sometimes *disapproving*) very confident: *She seems very sure of herself.* **sure thing** (informal) used to say "yes" to a suggestion or request: *"Are you coming?" "Sure thing."* **to be sure** (formal) used to admit that something is true: *He is intelligent, to be sure, but he's also very lazy.*
● adv. (informal) **1** used to say "yes" to someone: *"Will you open the wine?" "Sure, where is it?"* ◆ *Did it hurt? Sure it hurt.* **2** used to emphasize something that you are saying: *Boy, it sure is hot.* ◆ *"Amazing view." "Sure is."* ◆ *That song sure as hell sounds familiar.* ◆ *He sure looked unhappy.* **3** used to reply to someone who has just thanked you for something: *"Thanks for the ride." "Sure—anytime."*
IDM **sure enough** used to say that something happened as expected: *I said he'd forget, and sure enough he did.*

THESAURUS

sure

confident ◆ convinced ◆ certain ◆ positive ◆ clear

These words all describe someone who knows without doubt that something is true or will happen.

sure [not before noun] without any doubt that you are right, that something is true, that you will get something, or that something will happen: *I'm not sure whether John is coming or not.* ◆ *Are you sure about that?* ◆ *The Orioles are sure to win this weekend.* **NOTE** Sure is often used in negative statements and questions, because there is some doubt or anxiety over the matter. If there is no doubt, people often use *know*: *I know (that) I left my bag here* (= I have no doubt about it).

confident completely sure that something will happen in the way that you want or expect: *I'm confident that you'll get the job.* ◆ *The team is confident that they will win.* **NOTE** Confident is a stronger and more definite word than **sure** and is more often used in positive statements, when you feel no anxiety.

convinced [not before noun] completely sure that something is true or right, especially because the evidence seems to prove it or someone else has persuaded you to believe it: *I'm convinced that she's innocent.*

certain [not usually before noun] sure that you are right or that something is true: *Are you absolutely certain about this?*

SURE OR CERTAIN?

Like **sure**, **certain** is often used in negative statements and questions. It is slightly more formal than **sure**; **sure** is more frequent, especially in spoken English.

positive [not before noun] (*somewhat informal*) completely sure that something is true: *She was positive that he'd been there.* ◆ *"Are you sure?" "Positive."*

clear (often used in negative statements and questions) having no doubt or confusion about something: *I'm still not clear what the job involves.*

PATTERNS
- sure/confident/convinced/certain/positive/clear **about** sth
- sure/confident/convinced/certain **of** sth
- sure/confident/convinced/certain/positive/clear **that…**
- **not** sure/certain/clear **who/what/how**, etc.
- **to feel** sure/confident/convinced/certain/positive
- **quite/absolutely/completely/fairly/pretty** sure/confident/convinced/certain/positive/clear
- **not altogether** sure/confident/convinced/certain/clear

ˈsure-ˈfire *adj.* [only before noun] (*informal*) certain to be successful or to happen as you expect: *a sure-fire success*

ˌsure-ˈfooted (also **sure-foot-ed** /ˌʃʊrˈfʊtəd/) *adj.* **1** not likely to fall when walking or climbing on rough ground **2** confident and unlikely to make mistakes, especially in difficult situations

sure·ly 🔑 /ˈʃʊrli; ˈʃər-/ *adv.*
1 used to show that you are almost certain of what you are saying and want other people to agree with you: *Surely we should do something about it?* ◆ *It's surely only a matter of time before he is found, isn't it?* **2** used with a negative to show that something surprises you and you do not want to believe it: *Surely you don't think I was responsible for this?* ◆ *"They're getting married." "Surely not!"* ◆ *They won't go, surely?* **3** (*formal*) without doubt; certainly: *He knew that if help did not arrive soon, they would surely die.* **4** (*old-fashioned, informal*) used to say "yes" to someone or to agree to something **IDM** see **SLOWLY**

WHICH WORD?

surely ◆ certainly
- You can use **surely** to show that you are almost certain about what you are saying and you want other people to agree with you. It usually comes at the beginning of the sentence: *Surely this can't be right?* **Surely** in negative sentences shows that something surprises you and you do not want to believe it: *Surely you're not thinking of going, are you?*
- **Certainly** is more formal and usually means "without doubt" or "definitely," and is used to show that you strongly believe something or to emphasize that something is really true: *I'll certainly remember this trip!* In informal English, this would be: *I'll sure remember this trip!*
- Compare: *She's certainly too busy to see you this week* (= there is no doubt about it) and *Surely she's too busy to see you this week* (= that is my opinion. Don't you agree?).
- In formal language only, **surely** can be used to mean "without doubt": *This will surely end in disaster.*
⊃ note at **COURSE**

sure·ness /ˈʃʊrnəs; ˈʃər-/ *noun* [U] the quality of being confident and steady; not hesitating or doubting: *an artist's sureness of touch* ◆ *her sureness that she had done the right thing*

sur·e·ty /ˈʃʊrəti/ *noun* [C, U] (*pl.* **sur·e·ties**) (*law*) **1** money given as a promise that you will pay a debt, appear in court, etc.: *She was granted bail with a surety of $500.* **2** a person who accepts responsibility if someone else does not pay a debt, appear in court, etc.: *to act as surety for someone*

surf /sərf/ *noun, verb*
- **noun** [U] large waves in the ocean, and the white FOAM that they produce as they fall on the beach, on rocks, etc.: *the sound of surf breaking on the beach*
- **verb 1** often **go surfing** [I, T] **~ (sth)** to take part in the sport of riding on waves on a SURFBOARD: *She is learning to surf.* ◆ *He has built a career out of surfing big waves.* **2** [T] **~ the Net/Internet** to use the Internet: *I was surfing the Net looking for information on ski resorts.*

sur·face 🔑 /ˈsərfəs/ *noun, verb*
- **noun 1** [C] the outside or top layer of something: *an uneven road surface* ◆ *We need a flat surface to play this game on.* ◆ *Teeth have a hard surface layer called enamel.* ◆ *a broad leaf with a large surface area* **2** [C, usually sing.] the top layer of an area of water or land: *the earth's surface* ◆ *These plants float on the surface of the water.* **3** [C] the flat upper part of a piece of furniture, that is used for working on: *a work surface* ◆ *She cleaned all the kitchen surfaces.* **4** [sing.] the outer appearance of a person, thing, or situation; the qualities that you see or notice, that are not hidden: *Rage bubbled just below the surface of his mind.*
IDM **on the surface** when not thought about deeply or thoroughly; when not looked at carefully: *It seems like a good idea on the surface, but there will no doubt be problems.* ◆ *On the surface, he appeared unchanged.* ⊃ more at **SCRATCH** v.
- **verb 1** [I] to come up to the surface of water **SYN** EMERGE: *The ducks dived and surfaced again several yards away.* **2** [I] to suddenly appear or become obvious after having been hidden for a while **SYN** EMERGE: *Doubts began to surface.* ◆ *She surfaced again years later in Los Angeles.* **3** [I] (*informal*) to wake up or get up after being asleep: *He finally surfaced around noon.* **4** [T] **~ sth** to put a surface on a road, path, etc.

ˈsurface ˌmail *noun* [U] letters, etc. carried by road, rail, or ocean, not by air

ˌsurface ˈtension *noun* [U] (*technical*) the property (= characteristic) of liquids by which they form a layer at their surface, and which makes sure that this surface covers as small an area as possible

ˌsurface-to-ˈair *adj.* [only before noun] (especially of MISSILES) fired from the ground or from ships and aimed at aircraft

ˌsurface-to-ˈsurface *adj.* [only before noun] (especially of MISSILES) fired from the ground or from ships and aimed at another point on the ground or at a ship

sur·fac·tant /sərˈfæktənt/ *noun* [C, U] **1** (*technical*) a substance that reduces the SURFACE TENSION of a liquid, often forming bubbles in the liquid **2** (*medical*) a substance that keeps the lungs working well to prevent breathing problems

surf·board /ˈsərfbɔrd/ (also **board**) *noun* a long, narrow board used for SURFING

sur·feit /ˈsərfət/ *noun* [usually sing.] **~ (of sth)** (*formal*) an amount that is too large **SYN** EXCESS

surf·er /ˈsərfər/ *noun* **1** a person who goes SURFING **2** (*informal*) a person who spends a lot of time using the Internet: *a web surfer*

surf·ing /ˈsərfɪŋ/ *noun* [U] **1** the sport of riding on waves while standing on a narrow board called a SURFBOARD: *to go surfing* ⊃ picture at SPORT **2** the activity of looking at different things on the Internet in order to find something interesting, or of changing between TV channels in order to find an interesting program

surf 'n' turf /ˌsɜrf ən ˈtɜrf/ *noun* [U] SEAFOOD and STEAK served together as a meal

surge /sɜrdʒ/ *verb, noun*
- *verb* **1** [I] + *adv./prep.* to move quickly and with force in a particular direction: *The gates opened and the crowd surged forward.* ◆ *Flood waters surged into their homes.* **2** [I] (+ *adv./prep.*) to fill someone with a strong feeling **SYN** SWEEP: *Relief surged through her.* **3** [I] (of prices, profits, etc.) to suddenly increase in value: *Share prices surged.* ⊃ related noun UPSURGE **4** [I] (of the flow of electrical power) to increase suddenly
- *noun* **1** ~ (of sth) a sudden increase of a strong feeling **SYN** RUSH: *She felt a sudden surge of anger.* ◆ *a surge of excitement* ⊃ see also UPSURGE **2** a sudden increase in the amount or number of something; a large amount of something: ~ (in sth) *a surge in consumer spending* ◆ *We are having trouble keeping up with the recent surge in demand.* ◆ ~ (of sth) *After an initial surge of interest, there has been little call for our services.* ⊃ see also UPSURGE **3** ~ (of sth) a sudden, strong forward or upward movement: *a tidal surge* ⊃ see also STORM SURGE **4** a sudden increase in the flow of electrical power through a system: *An electrical surge damaged the computer's disk drive.*

sur·geon /ˈsɜrdʒən/ *noun* a doctor who is trained to perform surgery (= medical operations that involve cutting open a person's body): *a brain/heart, etc. surgeon* ⊃ compare PHYSICIAN

Surgeon 'General *noun* (*pl.* Surgeons General) the chief medical officer of the U.S. Public Health Service or of a medical service in the armed forces: *Surgeon General's warning: cigarette smoking causes cancer.*

surge pro·tector *noun* a device used to protect computers and other electrical equipment from a sudden increase in the flow of electrical power

sur·ger·y 🔊 /ˈsɜrdʒəri/ *noun* (*pl.* sur·ger·ies) [U, C] medical treatment of injuries or diseases that involves cutting open a person's body and often removing or replacing some parts; the branch of medicine connected with this treatment: *major/minor surgery* ◆ *He will require surgery on his left knee.* ◆ *to undergo heart surgery*: *She had three surgeries over ten days.* ⊃ see also OPEN-HEART SURGERY, PLASTIC SURGERY

sur·gi·cal /ˈsɜrdʒɪkl/ *adj.* [only before noun] **1** used in or connected with surgery: *surgical instruments* ◆ *a surgical procedure* (= an operation) **2** used to describe something done very precisely, especially a very accurate military attack: *a bridge destroyed by a surgical strike* (= military attack against a specific target) ◆ *Our advertising targets customers with surgical precision.* ▶ **sur·gi·cal·ly** /-kli/ *adv.*: *The tumor will need to be surgically removed.*

sur·ly /ˈsɜrli/ *adj.* (sur·li·er, sur·li·est) bad-tempered and rude: *a surly youth* ▶ **sur·li·ness** *noun* [U]

sur·mise /sərˈmaɪz/ *verb, noun*
- *verb* [T, I] ~ (sth) | ~ (that)... | ~ what, where, etc.... | + speech (*formal*) to guess or suppose something using the evidence you have, without definitely knowing **SYN** CONJECTURE: *From the looks on their faces, I surmised that they had had an argument.*
- *noun* [U, C, usually sing.] (*formal*) a guess based on some facts that you know already: *This is pure surmise on my part.*

sur·mount /sərˈmaʊnt/ *verb* (*formal*) **1** ~ sth to deal successfully with a difficulty **SYN** OVERCOME: *She was well aware of the difficulties that had to be surmounted.* **2** [usually passive] ~ sth to be placed on top of something: *a high column surmounted by a statue*

sur·name /ˈsɜrneɪm/ *noun* = LAST NAME

sur·pass /sərˈpæs/ *verb* [T, I] ~ (sb/sth/yourself) (*formal*) to do or be better than someone or something: *He hopes someday to surpass the world record.* ◆ *The success of the show surpassed all expectations.* ◆ *Her cooking was always good, but this time she had surpassed herself* (= done better than her own high standards). ◆ *scenery of surpassing beauty*

sur·plice /ˈsɜrpləs/ *noun* a loose white piece of clothing with wide sleeves worn by priests and singers in the CHOIR during church services

sur·plus /ˈsɜrplʌs/ *noun, adj.*
- *noun* [C, U] **1** an amount that is extra or more than you need: *food surpluses* ◆ *Wheat was in surplus that year.* **2** the amount by which the amount of money received is greater than the amount of money spent: *a trade surplus of $400 million* ◆ *The balance of payments was in surplus last year* (= the value of exports was greater than the value of imports). ⊃ collocations at INTERNATIONAL ⊃ compare DEFICIT
- *adj.* more than is needed or used: *surplus cash* ◆ *Surplus grain is being sold for export.*

THESAURUS

surprise

startle ◆ **amaze** ◆ **stun** ◆ **astonish** ◆ **take sb aback** ◆ **astound**

These words all mean to make someone feel surprised.

surprise to give someone the feeling that you get when something happens that you do not expect or do not understand, or something that you do expect does not happen; to make someone feel surprised: *The outcome didn't surprise me at all.*

startle to surprise someone suddenly in a way that slightly shocks or frightens them: *Sorry, I didn't mean to startle you.* ◆ *The explosion startled the horse.*

amaze to surprise someone very much: *The size of the Grand Canyon amazed us all.*

stun (*somewhat informal*) to surprise or shock someone so much that they cannot think clearly or speak: *He stunned us with his announcement.*

astonish to surprise someone very much: *The news astonished everyone.*

AMAZE OR ASTONISH?

These two words have the same meaning and in most cases you can use either. If you are talking about something that both surprises you and makes you feel ashamed, use **astonish**: *He was astonished by his own stupidity.*

take sb aback [usually passive] (especially of something negative) to surprise or shock someone: *We were taken aback by her hostile reaction.*

astound to surprise or shock someone very much: *His arrogance astounded her.*

PATTERNS

- It surprises sb/startles sb/amazes sb/astonishes sb/takes sb aback/astounds sb
- to be surprised/startled/amazed/stunned/astonished/astounded **that**...
- to surprise/amaze sb **what/how**...
- It surprises/startles/amazes/stuns/astonishes/astounds sb **to know/find/learn/see/hear that**...
- to be surprised/startled/stunned **into** (doing) sth

---

sur·prise 🔊 /sərˈpraɪz; səˈpraɪz/ *noun, verb*
- *noun* **1** [C] an event, a piece of news, etc. that is unexpected or that happens suddenly: *What a nice surprise!* ◆ *a surprise attack* ◆ *There are few surprises in this year's budget.* ◆ *I have a surprise for you!* ◆ *It comes as no surprise to learn that they broke their promises.* ◆ *Her letter came as a complete surprise.* ◆ *There are lots of surprises in store for visitors to the new exhibit.* ◆ *Visitors to the new exhibit are in for a few surprises.* **2** [U, C] a feeling caused by something happening suddenly or unexpectedly: *a look of surprise* ◆ *She looked up in surprise.* ◆ ~ (at sth) *He gasped with surprise at her strength.* ◆ ~ (at seeing, hearing, etc.) *They couldn't conceal their surprise at seeing us together.* ◆ *I got a surprise when I saw the bill.* ◆ *Much to my surprise, I passed.* ◆ *To everyone's*

ʌ cup   ə about   eɪ say   aɪ five   ɔɪ boy   aʊ now   oʊ go   ər bird

surprise, the plan succeeded. ◆ *Imagine our surprise when he walked into the room!* **3** [U] the use of methods that cause feelings of surprise: *A successful campaign should have **an element of surprise**.*

IDM **surprise, surprise** (*informal*) **1** (*ironic*, often *disapproving*) used to show that something is not a surprise to you, as you could easily have predicted that it would happen or be true: *One of the candidates was the manager's niece, and surprise, surprise, she got the job.* **2** used when giving someone a surprise: *Surprise, surprise! Look who's here!* **take sb/sth by surprise** to attack or capture someone or something unexpectedly or without warning: *The police took the burglars by surprise.* **take sb by surprise** to happen unexpectedly so that someone is slightly shocked; to surprise someone: *His frankness took her by surprise.*

● *verb* **1** to make someone feel surprised: ~ **sb** *It wouldn't surprise me if they got married soon.* ◆ ~ **sb how, what, etc.…** *It always surprises me how popular he is.* ◆ ~ **sb that** *It surprises me that you've never sung professionally.* ◆ **it surprises sb to do sth** *Would it surprise you to know that I'm thinking of leaving?* **2** ~ **sb** to attack, discover, etc., someone suddenly and unexpectedly: *The army attacked at night to surprise the rebels.* ◆ *We arrived home early and surprised a burglar trying to break in.*

sur·prised /sər'praɪzd; sə'praɪzd/ *adj.*
feeling or showing surprise: *a surprised look* ◆ *She looked surprised when I told her.* ◆ ~ **(at/by sb/sth)** *I was surprised at how quickly she agreed.* ◆ *I'm surprised at you, behaving like that in front of the kids.* ◆ ~ **(to see, hear, etc.)** *They were surprised to find that he'd already left.* ◆ ~ **(that…)** *You shouldn't be surprised (that) he didn't come.* ◆ **Don't be surprised if** *I pretend not to recognize you.* ◆ *"Will she cancel the party?" "I wouldn't be surprised."* ➔ compare UNSURPRISED

sur·pris·ing /sər'praɪzɪŋ; sə'praɪ-/ *adj.*
causing surprise: *It's not surprising (that) they lost.* ◆ *We had a surprising amount in common.* ◆ *It's surprising what people will do for money.* ▶ **sur·pris·ing·ly** /sər'praɪzɪŋli/ *adv.*: *She looked surprisingly well.* ◆ *Surprisingly, he agreed right away.* ◆ *Not surprisingly on such a hot day, the beach was crowded.*

LANGUAGE BANK

surprising
highlighting interesting data

- What is **surprising** about these results **is that** boys are more likely than girls to be left-handed.
- **Surprisingly**, boys are more likely than girls to be left-handed.
- **Interestingly**, even when both parents are left-handed, there is still only a 26% chance of their children being left-handed.
- **One of the most interesting** findings **is that** only 2% of the left-handers surveyed have two left-handed parents.
- **It is interesting to note that** people are more likely to be left-handed if their mother is left-handed than if their father is.
- **The most striking** feature of these results **is that** left-handed mothers are more likely than left-handed fathers to have left-handed children.

➔ Language Banks at CONTRAST, EMPHASIS, ILLUSTRATE, SIMILARLY

---

sur·re·al /sə'ril; -'riəl/ (also *less frequent* **sur·re·al·is·tic**) *adj.* very strange; more like a dream than reality, with ideas and images mixed together in a strange way

sur·re·al·ism /sə'riə,lɪzəm/ *noun* [U] a 20th-century style and movement in art and literature in which images and events that are not connected are put together in a strange or impossible way, like a dream, to try to express what is happening deep in the mind ▶ **sur·re·al·ist** /-lɪst/ *adj.*

[usually before noun]: *a surrealist painter/painting* **sur·re·al·ist** *noun*: *the surrealist Salvador Dali*

sur·re·al·is·tic /sə,riə'lɪstɪk/ *adj.* **1** = SURREAL **2** connected with surrealism: *a surrealistic painting*

sur·ren·der /sə'rɛndər/ *verb, noun*
● *verb* **1** [I, T] to admit that you have been defeated and want to stop fighting; to allow yourself to be caught, taken prisoner, etc. **SYN** GIVE IN: ~ **(to sb)** *The rebel soldiers were forced to surrender.* ◆ ~ **yourself (to sb)** *The hijackers eventually surrendered themselves to the police.* **2** [T] (*formal*) to give up something or someone when you are forced to **SYN** RELINQUISH: ~ **sth/sb to sb** *He agreed to surrender all claims to the property.* ◆ *They surrendered their guns to the police.* ◆ ~ **sth/sb** *The defendant was released to await trial but had to surrender her passport.*
PHR V **sur'render to sth** | **sur'render yourself to sth** (*formal*) to stop trying to prevent yourself from having a feeling, habit, etc. and allow it to control what you do: *He finally surrendered to his craving for drugs.*
● *noun* [U, sing.] **1** ~ **(to sb/sth)** an act of admitting that you have been defeated and want to stop fighting: *They demanded (an) unconditional surrender.* ➔ collocations at WAR **2** the fact of allowing yourself to be controlled by something: *They accused the government of a surrender to business interests.* **3** ~ **of sth (to sb)** an act of giving something to someone else even though you do not want to, especially after a battle, etc.: *They insisted on the immediate surrender of all weapons.*

sur'render ,value *noun* the amount of money that you get if you end a life insurance policy before its official end date

sur·rep·ti·tious /,sɛrəp'tɪʃəs/ *adj.* done secretly or quickly, in the hope that other people will not notice **SYN** FURTIVE: *She sneaked a surreptitious glance at her watch.* ▶ **sur·rep·ti·tious·ly** *adv.*

sur·ro·ga·cy /'sɛrəgəsi/ *noun* [U] the practice of giving birth to a baby for another woman who is unable to have babies herself

sur·ro·gate /'sɛrəgət/ *adj.* (*formal*) used to describe a person or thing that takes the place of, or is used instead of, someone or something else: *She saw him as a sort of surrogate father.* ▶ **sur·ro·gate** *noun*

surrogate 'mother *noun* a woman who gives birth to a baby for another woman who is unable to have babies herself

sur·round /sə'raʊnd/ *verb, noun*
● *verb* **1** to be all around something or someone: ~ **sth/sb** *Tall trees surround the lake.* ◆ *the membranes surrounding the brain* ◆ *As a child I was surrounded by love and kindness.* ◆ ~ **sth/sb with sth** *The lake is surrounded with/by trees.* **2** to move into position all around someone or something, especially so as to prevent them from escaping; to move someone or something into position in this way: ~ **sb/sth** *Police surrounded the building.* ◆ ~ **sb/sth with sb/sth** *They surrounded the building with police.* **3** ~ **sth/sb** to be closely connected with something or someone: *publicity surrounding the divorce* **4** ~ **yourself with sb/sth** to choose to have particular people or things near you all the time: *I like to surround myself with beautiful things.*
● *noun* **1** a border or an area around the edge of something, especially one that is decorated **2 surrounds** [pl.] the area surrounding a place: *Cleveland and its surrounds*

sur·round·ing /sə'raʊndɪŋ/ *adj.* [only before noun]
that is near or around something: *San Francisco and the surrounding area*

sur·round·ings /sə'raʊndɪŋz/ *noun* [pl.]
everything that is around or near someone or something **SYN** ENVIRONMENT: *to work in pleasant surroundings* ◆ *The buildings have been designed to blend in with their surroundings.* ➔ thesaurus box at ENVIRONMENT

sur'round sound *noun* [U] a system for reproducing

---

sound using several SPEAKERS (= the pieces of equipment that the sound comes out of) placed around the person listening in order to produce a more realistic sound

sur·tax /ˈsɜrtæks/ *noun* [U] an extra tax on something that has already been taxed, for example tax that is charged at a higher rate than the normal rate, on income above a particular level

Sur·ti·tles™ /ˈsɜrˌtaɪtlz/ *noun* [pl.] words that translate what is being sung in an OPERA, or spoken in a play in the theater, into a different language and appear on a screen above or beside the stage

sur·veil·lance /sərˈveɪləns/ *noun* [U] the act of carefully watching a person suspected of a crime or a place where a crime may be committed **SYN** OBSERVATION: *The police are keeping the suspects **under** constant **surveillance**.* ♦ *surveillance cameras/equipment*

sur·vey 🔑 **AWL** *noun, verb*

● *noun* /ˈsɜrveɪ/ **1** an investigation of the opinions, behavior, etc. of a particular group of people, that is usually done by asking them questions: *A recent survey showed 75% of those questioned were in favor of the plan.* ♦ *The **survey** revealed that...* ♦ *to **conduct/carry out** a **survey*** **2** the act of examining and recording the measurements, features, etc. of an area of land in order to make a map or plan of it: *an aerial survey* (= made by taking photographs from an aircraft) ♦ *a geological survey* **3** a general study, view, or description of something: *a comprehensive survey of modern music*

● *verb* /sərˈveɪ; ˈsɜrveɪ/ **1** ~ **sth** to look carefully at the whole of something, especially in order to get a general impression of it **SYN** INSPECT: *The next morning we surveyed the damage caused by the fire.* ♦ *He surveyed himself in the mirror before going out.* **2** ~ **sth** to study and give a general description of something: *This chapter briefly surveys the current state of American politics.* **3** ~ **sth** to measure and record the features of an area of land, for example in order to make a map or in preparation for building **4** ~ **sb/sth** to investigate the opinions or behavior of a group of people by asking them a series of questions **SYN** INTERVIEW: *We surveyed 500 smokers and found that over three quarters would like to give it up.*

ˈsurvey ˌcourse *noun* a college course that gives an introduction to a subject for people who are thinking about studying it further

sur·vey·or /sərˈveɪər/ *noun* a person whose job is to examine and record the details of a piece of land

sur·viv·a·ble /sərˈvaɪvəbl/ *adj.* (of an accident or experience) able to be survived: *a survivable car/plane crash*

sur·viv·al **AWL** /sərˈvaɪvl/ *noun* **1** [U] the state of continuing to live or exist, often despite difficulty or danger: *the **struggle/battle/fight for survival*** ♦ *His only **chance of survival** was a heart transplant.* ♦ *Exporting is necessary for our economic survival.* **2** [C] ~ **(from sth)** something that has continued to exist from an earlier time **SYN** RELIC: *The ceremony is a survival from pre-Christian times.*
  IDM the sur·viv·al of the fit·test the principle that only the people or things that are best adapted to their surroundings will continue to exist

sur·viv·al·ist /sərˈvaɪvəlɪst/ *noun* a person who prepares for a dangerous or unpleasant situation such as a war by learning how to survive outdoors, practicing how to use weapons, storing food, etc. ▶ **sur·viv·al·ism** /sərˈvaɪvəˌlɪzəm/ *noun* [U]

surˈvival ˌkit *noun* a set of emergency equipment, including food, medical supplies, and tools

sur·vive 🔑 **AWL** /sərˈvaɪv/ *verb*
  1 [I] to continue to live or exist: *She was the last surviving member of the family.* ♦ *Of the six people injured in the crash, only two survived.* ♦ *(humorous)* "*How are you these days?*" "*Oh, surviving.*" ♦ *Don't worry, it's only a scratch—you'll survive.* ♦ ~ **from sth** *Some strange customs have survived from earlier times.* ♦ ~ **on sth** *I can't survive on $75 a week* (= it is not enough for my basic needs). ♦ ~ **as sth** *He survived as mayor*

until the city fell on hard times. **2** [T] to continue to live or exist despite a dangerous event or time: ~ **sth** *The company was able to survive the crisis.* ♦ *Many birds didn't survive the severe winter.* ♦ ~ **sth + adj.** *Few buildings survived the war intact.* **3** [T] ~ **sb/sth** to live or exist longer than someone or something **SYN** OUTLIVE: *She survived her husband by ten years.*

sur·vi·vor **AWL** /sərˈvaɪvər/ *noun* a person who continues to live, especially despite being nearly killed or experiencing great danger or difficulty: *the **sole/only survivor** of the massacre* ♦ *The plane crashed in an area of dense jungle. There were no survivors.* ♦ *There are only a few survivors from the original team* (= members who remain on it while others have been replaced). ♦ *She'll cope. She's one of life's great survivors* (= someone who deals very well with difficult situations).

sus·cep·ti·bil·i·ty /səˌsɛptəˈbɪləti/ *noun* (pl. sus·cep·ti·bil·i·ties) (formal) **1** [U, sing.] ~ **(to sth)** the state of being very likely to be influenced, harmed, or affected by something: *susceptibility to disease* **2** **susceptibilities** [pl.] a person's feelings that are likely to be easily hurt **SYN** SENSIBILITY: *It was all carried out without any consideration for the susceptibilities of the bereaved family.*

sus·cep·ti·ble /səˈsɛptəbl/ *adj.* **1** [not usually before noun] ~ **(to sb/sth)** very likely to be influenced, harmed, or affected by someone or something: *He's highly susceptible to flattery.* ♦ *Some of these plants are more susceptible to frost damage than others.* ♦ *Salt intake may lead to high blood pressure in susceptible adults.* **2** easily influenced by feelings and emotions **SYN** IMPRESSIONABLE: *She was both charming and susceptible.* **3** ~ **(of sth)** (formal) allowing something; capable of something: *Is this situation not susceptible of improvement by legislation?*

su·shi /ˈsuʃi/ *noun* [U] a Japanese dish of small cakes of cold cooked rice, flavored with VINEGAR and served with raw fish, etc. on top: *a sushi bar*

sus·pect 🔑 *verb, noun, adj.*

● *verb* /səˈspɛkt/ (not used in the progressive tenses) **1** [T, I] to have an idea that something is probably true or likely to happen, especially something bad, but without having definite proof: ~ **(sth)** *If you suspect a gas leak, do not strike a match or even turn on an electric light.* ♦ *Suspecting nothing, he walked right into the trap.* ♦ *As I had suspected all along, he was not a real policeman.* ♦ ~ **(that)...** *I began to suspect (that) they were trying to get rid of me.* ♦ **it is suspected that...** *It was suspected that the drugs had been brought into the country by boat.* ♦ ~ **sb/sth to be/have sth** *She suspected him to be an impostor.* **2** [T] ~ **sth** to be suspicious about something; to not trust something: *I suspected her motives in offering to help.* **3** [T] to have an idea that someone is guilty of something, without having definite proof: ~ **sb/sth of sth** *He resigned after being suspected of theft.* ♦ ~ **sb/sth of doing sth** *The drug is suspected of causing over 200 deaths.* ♦ ~ **sb/sth** *Whom do the police suspect?* ▶ **sus·pect·ed** *adj.*: *a suspected outbreak of smallpox* ♦ *suspected tax evasion* ♦ *suspected terrorists*

● *noun* /ˈsʌspɛkt/ a person who is suspected of a crime or of having done something wrong: *a murder suspect* ♦ *He is the prime suspect in the case.*

● *adj.* /ˈsʌspɛkt/ **1** that may be false and that cannot be relied on **SYN** QUESTIONABLE: *Some of the evidence they produced was highly suspect.* **2** that you suspect to be dangerous or illegal **SYN** SUSPICIOUS: *a suspect package* (= one that may contain drugs, a bomb, etc.)

sus·pend **AWL** /səˈspɛnd/ *verb* **1** ~ **sth/sb (from sth) (by/on sth)** to hang something from something else: *A lamp was suspended from the ceiling.* ♦ *Her body was found suspended by a rope.* **2** ~ **sth** to officially stop something for a time; to prevent something from being active, used, etc. for a time: *Production has been suspended while safety checks are carried out.* ♦ *The constitution was suspended as the fighting*

t **t**ea   ţ **bu**tter   d **d**id   k **c**at   g **g**ot   tʃ **ch**in   dʒ **J**une   f **f**all

grew worse. ◆ *In the theater we willingly* **suspend disbelief** (= temporarily believe that the characters, etc. are real). **3** ~ **sth** to officially delay something; to arrange for something to happen later than planned: *The introduction of the new system has been suspended until next year.* ◆ *to suspend judgment* (= delay forming or expressing an opinion) **4** [usually passive] ~ **sb (from sth)** to officially prevent someone from doing their job, going to school, etc. for a time: *The police officer was suspended while the complaint was being investigated.* **5 be suspended in something** (*technical*) to float in liquid or air without moving ⊃ see also SUSPENSION

su·spended ani·mation *noun* [U] **1** the state of being alive but not conscious or active **2** a feeling that you cannot do anything because you are waiting for something to happen

su·spended 'sentence *noun* a punishment given to a criminal in court that means that they will only go to prison if they commit another crime within a particular period of time

sus·pend·ers /səˈspɛndərz/ *noun* [pl.] long narrow pieces of cloth, leather, etc. for holding pants up. They are fastened to the top of the pants at the front and back and passed over the shoulders. ⊃ **picture at** CLOTHES

sus·pense /səˈspɛns/ *noun* [U] a feeling of worry or excitement that you have when you feel that something is going to happen, someone is going to tell you some news, etc.: *a tale of mystery and suspense* ◆ *Don't* **keep us in suspense.** *Tell us what happened!* ◆ *I couldn't bear the suspense a minute longer.*

sus·pen·sion **AWL** /səˈspɛnʃn/ *noun* **1** [U, C] the act of officially removing someone from their job, school, team, etc. for a period of time, usually as a punishment: *suspension from school* ◆ *The two players are appealing against their suspensions.* **2** [U, sing.] the act of delaying something for a period of time, until a decision has been taken: *These events have led to the suspension of talks.* **3** [U, C] the system by which a vehicle is supported on its wheels and that makes it more comfortable to ride in when the road surface is not even **4** [C, U] (*technical*) a liquid with very small pieces of solid matter floating in it; the state of such a liquid ⊃ see also SUSPEND

su'spension ˌbridge *noun* a bridge that hangs from steel cables that are supported by towers at each end

sus·pi·cion 🔑 /səˈspɪʃn/ *noun*
1 [U, C] a feeling that someone has done something wrong, illegal, or dishonest, even though you have no proof: *They drove away slowly to avoid arousing suspicion.* ◆ *He was arrested* **on suspicion of** *murder.* ◆ ~ **(that...)** *I have* **a sneaking suspicion** *that she's not telling the truth.* ⊃ see also SUSPECT **2** [C] ~ **(that...)** a feeling or belief that something is true, even though you have no proof: *I have a horrible suspicion that we got off at the wrong stop.* **3** [U, C] the feeling that you cannot trust someone or something: *Their offer was greeted with some suspicion.* **4** [sing.] ~ **of sth** (*formal*) a small amount of something **SYN** HINT: *His mouth quivered in the suspicion of a smile.*
IDM **above/beyond suspicion** too good, honest, etc. to have done something wrong, illegal, or dishonest: *Nobody who was near the scene of the crime is above suspicion.* **under suspicion (of sth)** suspected of doing something wrong, illegal, or dishonest: *The whole family is currently under suspicion of her murder.* ◆ *A number of doctors* **came under suspicion** *of unethical behavior.* ⊃ more at FINGER *n.*

sus·pi·cious 🔑 /səˈspɪʃəs/ *adj.*
1 ~ **(of/about sb/sth)** feeling that someone has done something wrong, illegal, or dishonest, without having any proof: *They became suspicious of his behavior and contacted the police.* ◆ *a suspicious look* ◆ *You have a very* **suspicious mind** (= you always think that people are behaving in an illegal or dishonest way).* **2** making you feel that something is wrong, illegal, or dishonest: *Didn't you notice anything suspicious in his behavior?* ◆ *She died under suspicious*

circumstances. ◆ *Police are not treating the fire as suspicious.* ◆ *It was all very suspicious.* **3** ~ **(of sb/sth)** not willing or able to trust someone or something **SYN** SKEPTICAL: *I was suspicious of his motives.* ◆ *Many were suspicious of reform.* ⊃ see also SUSPECT

sus·pi·cious·ly /səˈspɪʃəsli/ *adv.* **1** in a way that shows you think someone has done something wrong, illegal, or dishonest: *The man looked at her suspiciously.* **2** in a way that makes people think something wrong, illegal, or dishonest is happening: *Let me know if you see anyone acting suspiciously.* **3** in a way that shows you think there may be something wrong with something: *She eyed the fish on her plate suspiciously.*
IDM **look/sound suspiciously like sth** (often *humorous*) to be very similar to something: *Their latest single sounds suspiciously like the last one.*

suss /sʌs/ *verb* [T, I] ~ **(sb/sth) (out)** (*informal*) to realize something; to understand the important things about someone or something: *If you want to succeed in business you have to suss out the competition.*

sus·tain **AWL** /səˈsteɪn/ *verb* **1** ~ **sb/sth** to provide enough of what someone or something needs in order to live or exist: *Which planets can sustain life?* ◆ *The love and support of his family sustained him during his time in prison.* **2** ~ **sth** to make something continue for some time without becoming less **SYN** MAINTAIN: *a period of sustained economic growth* ◆ *a sustained attack* ◆ *She managed to sustain everyone's interest until the end of her speech.* **3** ~ **sth** (*formal*) to experience something bad **SYN** SUFFER: *to* **sustain damage/an injury/a defeat** ◆ *The company* **sustained losses** *of millions of dollars.* **4** ~ **sth** to provide evidence to support an opinion, a theory, etc. **SYN** UPHOLD: *The evidence is not detailed enough to sustain his argument.* **5** ~ **sth** (*formal*) to support a weight without breaking or falling **SYN** BEAR: *The ice will not sustain your weight.* **6** ~ **sth** (*law*) to decide that a claim, etc. is valid **SYN** UPHOLD: *The court sustained his claim that the contract was illegal.* ◆ ***Objection sustained!*** (= said by a judge when a lawyer makes an OBJECTION in court)

sus·tain·a·ble **AWL** /səˈsteɪnəbl/ *adj.* **1** involving the use of natural products and energy in a way that does not harm the environment: *sustainable forest management* ◆ *an environmentally sustainable society* **2** that can continue or be continued for a long time: *sustainable economic growth* **ANT** UNSUSTAINABLE ▸ **sus·tain·a·bil·i·ty** **AWL** /səˌsteɪnəˈbɪləti/ *noun* [U] **sus·tain·a·bly** /səˈsteɪnəbli/ *adv.*

sus·te·nance **AWL** /ˈsʌstənəns/ *noun* [U] (*formal*) **1** the food and drink that people, animals, and plants need to live and stay healthy: *There's not much sustenance in a bowl of soup.* ◆ (*figurative*) *Arguing would only give further sustenance to his allegations.* **2** ~ **(of sth)** the process of making something continue to exist: *Free and fair elections are essential for the sustenance of a democratic society.*

su·tra /ˈsutrə/ *noun* **1** a rule or statement in Sanskrit literature, or a set of rules **2** a Buddhist or Jainist holy text

sut·tee (also sa·ti) /sʌˈti; ˈsʌti/ *noun* **1** [U] the former practice in Hinduism of a wife burning herself with the body of her dead husband **2** [C] a wife who did this

su·ture /ˈsutʃər/ *noun, verb*
● *noun* (*medical*) a STITCH or stitches made when sewing up a wound, especially after an operation
● *verb* ~ **sth** (*medical*) to sew up a wound

SUV /ˌɛs yu ˈvi/ *noun* a type of large car, often with FOUR-WHEEL DRIVE and made originally for traveling over rough ground (the abbreviation for SPORT UTILITY VEHICLE) ⊃ picture at CAR

su·ze·rain·ty /ˈsuzərənti; -ˌreɪnti/ *noun* [U] (*formal*) the right of a country to rule over another country

Sv *abbr.* SIEVERT

svelte /svɛlt; sfɛlt/ *adj.* (*approving*) (of a person, especially a woman) thin and attractive

Sven·ga·li /svɛnˈɡɑli; sfɛn-/ *noun* a person who has the power to control another person's mind, make them do bad things, etc. **ORIGIN** From the name of a character in George du Maurier's novel *Trilby*.

SW *abbr.* (in writing) **1** usually **S.W.** southwest; southwestern: *S.W. Australia* **2** SHORTWAVE: *SW and LW radio*

swab /swɑb/ *noun, verb*
- *noun* **1** a piece of soft material used by a doctor, nurse, etc. for cleaning wounds or taking a sample from someone's body for testing **2** an act of taking a sample from someone's body, with a swab: *to take a throat swab*
- *verb* (-bb-) **1** ~ sth to clean or remove liquid from a wound, etc., using a swab **2** ~ sth (down) to clean or wash a floor, surface, etc. using water and a cloth, etc.

swad·dle /'swɑdl/ *verb* ~ sb/sth (*old-fashioned*) to wrap someone or something, especially a baby, tightly in clothes or a piece of cloth

swaddling clothes *noun* [pl.] strips of cloth used in the past for wrapping a baby tightly

swag /swæg/ *noun* **1** [C, usually pl.] cloth that is hung in large curved folds as decoration, especially above a window **2** [C, usually pl.] a bunch of flowers, fruit, green branches, etc. that is used as a decoration, or a CARVING on a wall of something like this **3** [U] (*old-fashioned, informal*) goods that have been stolen **SYN** LOOT

swag·ger /'swæɡər/ *verb, noun*
- *verb* [I] (+ adv./prep.) (usually *disapproving*) to walk in an extremely proud and confident way **SYN** STRUT
- *noun* [sing.] (*disapproving*) a way of walking or behaving that seems too confident

Swa·hi·li /swɑˈhili/ (also Ki·swa·hi·li) *noun* [U] a language widely used in E. Africa, especially between people who speak different first languages

swain /sweɪn/ *noun* (*old use* or *humorous*) a young man who is in love

swal·low 🔑 /'swɑloʊ/ *verb, noun*
- *verb*
- ▷ FOOD/DRINK **1** [T, I] to make food, drink, etc. go down your throat into your stomach: ~ (sth) *Always chew food well before swallowing it.* ◆ *I had a sore throat and it hurt to swallow.* ◆ ~ sth + adj. *The pills should be swallowed whole.*
- ▷ MOVE THROAT MUSCLES **2** [I] to move the muscles of your throat as if you were swallowing something, especially because you are nervous: *She swallowed hard and told him the bad news.*
- ▷ COMPLETELY COVER **3** [T, often passive] to take someone or something in or completely cover them, so that they cannot be seen or no longer exist separately: ~ sb/sth *I watched her walk down the road until she was swallowed by the darkness.* ◆ ~ sb/sth up *Large areas that were formerly rural have been swallowed up by towns.*
- ▷ USE UP MONEY **4** [T] ~ sb/sth (up) to use up something completely, especially an amount of money: *Most of my salary gets swallowed (up) by the rent and bills.*
- ▷ BELIEVE **5** [T] to accept that something is true; to believe something: ~ sth *I found her excuse very hard to swallow.* ◆ ~ sth + adj. *He told her a pack of lies, but she swallowed it whole.*
- ▷ FEELINGS **6** [T] ~ sth to hide your feelings: *to swallow your doubts* ◆ *You're going to have to swallow your pride and ask for your job back.*
- ▷ ACCEPT INSULTS **7** [T] ~ sth to accept insults, criticisms, etc. without complaining or protesting: *I was surprised that he just sat there and swallowed all their remarks.* **IDM** see BITTER
- *noun*
- ▷ BIRD **1** a small bird with long pointed wings and a tail with two points, that spends the winter in warm parts of the world but flies to northern countries for the summer
- ▷ OF FOOD/DRINK **2** an act of swallowing; an amount of food or drink that is swallowed at one time
  IDM one swallow doesn't make a summer (*saying*) you must not take too seriously a small sign that something is

happening or will happen in the future, because the situation could change

swal·low·tail /'swɑloʊˌteɪl/ *noun* a BUTTERFLY that has a thin tail on each back wing

swam pt of SWIM

swa·mi /'swɑmi/ *noun* (also used as a title) a Hindu religious teacher: *Swami Vivekanand*

swamp /swɑmp/ *noun, verb*
- *noun* [C, U] an area of ground that is very wet or covered with water and in which plants, trees, etc. are growing **SYN** MARSH: *tropical swamps* ▶ **swamp·y** *adj.*: *swampy ground*
- *verb* [often passive] **1** to make someone have more of something than they can deal with **SYN** INUNDATE: ~ sb/sth with sth *The department was swamped with job applications.* ◆ ~ sb/sth *In summer visitors swamp the island.* **2** ~ sth to fill or cover something with a lot of water **SYN** ENGULF: *The little boat was swamped by the waves.*

swamp fever *noun* [U] **1** a serious disease that affects horses **2** (*old-fashioned*) = MALARIA

swamp·land /'swɑmplænd/ *noun* [U, pl.] a large area of SWAMP

swan /swɑn/ *noun, verb*
- *noun* a large bird that is usually white and has a long thin neck. Swans live on or near water.
- *verb* (-nn-) [I] + adv./prep. (*informal, disapproving*) to go around enjoying yourself in a way that annoys other people or makes them jealous: *They've gone swanning off to Paris for the weekend.*

swan

swan dive *noun* a DIVE performed with your arms stretched out sideways until you are close to the water

swank·y /'swæŋki/ (swank·i·er, swank·i·est) (also swank) *adj.* (*informal, approving*) fashionable and expensive in a way that is intended to impress people: *a swanky new hotel*

swan song *noun* [sing.] the last piece of work produced by an artist, a musician, etc. or the last performance by an actor, ATHLETE, etc.

swap (also **swop**) /swɑp/ *verb, noun*
- *verb* (-pp-) **1** [I, T] to give something to someone and receive something in exchange: ~ (sth) (with sb) *I'm finished with this magazine. Can I swap with you?* ◆ ~ sth for sth *I swapped my red scarf for her blue one.* ◆ ~ sth *Can we swap places? I can't see the screen.* ◆ *We spent the evening swapping stories* (= telling each other stories) *about our travels.* ◆ ~ sb sth for sth *I swapped him my CD for his posters.* **2** [I] to start doing someone else's job, etc. while they do yours: *I'll drive there, and then we'll swap on the way back.* **3** [T] to replace one person or thing with another: ~ sb/sth (for sb/sth) *I think I'll swap this sweater for one in another color.* **IDM** see PLACE *n.*
- *noun* [usually sing.] an act of exchanging one thing or person for another: *Let's do a swap. You work Friday night and I'll do Saturday.*

swap meet *noun* an occasion at which people buy and sell or exchange items that interest them: *a swap meet for collectors of Star Trek memorabilia*

sward /swɔrd/ *noun* [C, U] (*literary*) an area of grass

swarm /swɔrm/ *noun, verb*
- *noun* ~ (of sth) **1** a large group of insects, especially BEES, moving together in the same direction: *a swarm of bees/locusts/flies* **2** a large group of people, especially when they are all moving quickly in the same direction **SYN** HORDE
- *verb* **1** [I] + adv./prep. (often *disapproving*) (of people, animals, etc.) to move around in a large group: *Tourists were*

swarming all over the island. **2** [I] (of BEES and other flying insects) to move around together in a large group, looking for a place to live

PHR V 'swarm with sb/sth to be full of people or things: *The conference venue was swarming with police.*

swarth·y /'swɔrði/ adj. (especially of a person or their face) having dark skin

swash /swɑʃ; swɔʃ/ noun [sing.] (*technical*) the flow of water up the beach after a wave has BROKEN

swash·buck·ling /'swɑʃˌbʌklɪŋ; 'swɔʃ-/ adj. [only before noun] (especially of movies) set in the past and full of action, adventure, fighting with SWORDS, etc.: *a swashbuckling tale of adventure on the high seas* ◆ *the swashbuckling hero of Hollywood epics*

swas·ti·ka /'swɑstɪkə/ noun an ancient symbol in the form of a cross with its ends bent at an angle of 90°, used in the 20th century as the symbol of the German Nazi party

swat /swɑt/ verb (-tt-) ~ sth to hit something, especially an insect, using your hand or a flat object ▶ **swat** noun

swatch /swɑtʃ/ noun a small piece of cloth used to show people what a larger piece would look or feel like

swath /swɑθ/ (also **swathe**) noun (*formal*) **1** a long strip of land, especially one on which the plants or crops have been cut: *The combine had cut a swath around the edge of the field.* ◆ *Development has affected vast swaths of our countryside.* **2** a large strip or area of something: *The mountains rose above a swath of thick clouds.*

IDM cut a swath through sth (of a person, fire, etc.) to pass through a particular area, destroying a large part of it

swathe /swɑð; sweɪð/ verb, noun
● **verb** [usually passive] ~ sb/sth (in sth) (*formal*) to wrap or cover someone or something in something: *He was lying on the hospital bed, swathed in bandages.*
● **noun** = SWATH

SWAT team /'swɑt tim/ noun a group of police officers who are especially trained to deal with violent situations. SWAT stands for "Special Weapons and Tactics."

sway /sweɪ/ verb, noun
● **verb 1** [I, T] to move slowly from side to side; to move something in this way: **(+ adv./prep.)** *The branches were swaying in the wind.* ◆ *Vicky swayed and fell.* ◆ ~ sth **(+ adv./prep.)** *They danced rhythmically, swaying their hips to the music.* **2** [T, often passive] ~ sb to persuade someone to believe something or do something SYN INFLUENCE: *He's easily swayed.* ◆ *She wasn't swayed by his good looks or his glib talk.*
● **noun** [U] **1** a movement from side to side **2** (*literary*) power or influence over someone: *Rebel forces hold sway over much of the island.* ◆ *He was quick to exploit those who fell under his sway.*

swear /swɛr/ verb (**swore** /swɔr/, **sworn** /swɔrn/)
1 [I] to use rude or offensive language, usually because you are angry: *She fell down and swore loudly.* ◆ ~ at sb/sth *Why did you let him swear at you like that?* **2** [T, no passive] to make a serious promise to do something SYN VOW: ~ sth *He swore revenge on the man who had killed his father.* ◆ ~ (that)... *I swear (that) I'll never leave you.* **HELP** "That" is usually left out, especially in speech.: ~ to do sth *She made him swear not to tell anyone.* **3** [T] to promise that you are telling the truth: ~ (that)... *She swore (that) she'd never seen him before.* ◆ *I could have sworn* (= I am sure) *I heard the phone ring.* ◆ ~ to sb/on sth (that)... *I swear to God I had nothing to do with it.* **4** [I, T] to make a public or official promise, especially in court: ~ (on sth) *Witnesses were required to swear on the Bible.* ◆ ~ that... *Are you willing to stand up in court and swear that you don't recognize him?* ◆ ~ to do sth *Remember, you have sworn to tell the truth.* ◆ ~ sth *Barons had to swear an oath of allegiance to the king.* **5** [T] ~ someone to secrecy/silence to make someone promise not to tell something to anyone: *Everyone was sworn to secrecy about what had happened.* ⊃ see also SWORN
PHR V 'swear by sb/sth **1** to name someone or some-

thing to show that you are making a serious promise: *I swear by almighty God that I will tell the truth.* **2** (not used in the progressive tenses) to be certain that something is good or useful: *She swears by meditation as a way of relieving stress.* ,swear sb↔'in | ,swear sb 'into sth [often passive] to make someone promise to do a job correctly, to be loyal to an organization, a country, etc.: *He was sworn in as president.* ◆ *The new senator was sworn into office.* ⊃ related noun SWEARING-IN ,swear 'off sth (*informal*) to promise that you will not do or use something again: *I decided to swear off burgers forever.* 'swear to sth (*informal*) to say that something is definitely true: *I think I put the keys back in the drawer, but I couldn't swear to it* (= I'm not completely sure).

swear·ing /'swɛrɪŋ/ noun [U] rude or offensive language: *I was shocked at the swearing.*

,swearing-'in noun [U, sing.] the act of publicly asking someone to promise to be loyal and perform their duties well when they start a new job, etc.: *the swearing-in of the new president*

'swear word noun a rude or offensive word, used, for example, to express anger SYN EXPLETIVE

sweat /swɛt/ noun, verb
● **noun**
➤ LIQUID ON SKIN **1** [U] drops of liquid that appear on the surface of your skin when you are hot, sick, or afraid SYN PERSPIRATION: *beads of sweat* ◆ *She wiped the sweat from her face.* ◆ *By the end of the game, the sweat was pouring off him.* ⊃ see also SWEATY **2** [usually sing.] the state of being covered with sweat: *I woke up in a sweat.* ◆ *She completed the routine without even working up a sweat.* ◆ *He breaks out in a sweat just at the thought of flying.* ◆ *He started having night sweats.* ⊃ see also COLD SWEAT
➤ HARD WORK **3** [U] hard work or effort: (*literary*) *She achieved success by the sweat of her brow* (= by working very hard).
➤ CLOTHES **4** sweats [pl.] (*informal*) a SWEATSUIT or SWEATPANTS: *I hung around the house all day in my sweats.*
IDM be/get in a sweat (about sth) to be/become anxious or frightened about something break a sweat (*informal*) to use a lot of physical effort: *He hardly needed to break a sweat to reach the final.* no sweat (*informal*) used to tell someone that something is not difficult or a problem when they thank you or ask you to do something: *"Thanks for everything." "Hey, no sweat!"* ⊃ more at BLOOD
● **verb**
➤ PRODUCE LIQUID ON SKIN/SURFACE **1** [I, T] when you sweat, drops of liquid appear on the surface of your skin, for example when you are hot, sick, or afraid SYN PERSPIRE: *to sweat heavily* ◆ ~ sth *He was sweating buckets* (= a lot). **2** [I] if something sweats, the liquid that is contained in it appears on its surface: *The cheese was beginning to sweat.*
➤ WORK HARD **3** [I] ~ (over sth) to work hard at something: *Are you still sweating over that report?*
➤ WORRY **4** [I] (*informal*) to worry or feel anxious about something: *They really made me sweat during the interview.*
IDM don't sweat it (*informal*) used to tell someone to stop worrying about something don't sweat the small stuff (*informal*) used to tell someone not to worry about small details or unimportant things sweat blood (*informal*) to work very hard ⊃ more at GUT n.
PHR V ,sweat sth↔'off to lose weight by doing a lot of hard exercise to make yourself sweat ,sweat it 'out (*informal*) to be waiting for something difficult or unpleasant to end, and be feeling anxious about it

sweat·band /'swɛtbænd/ noun a band of cloth worn around the head or wrist, for absorbing sweat

sweat·er /'swɛtər/ noun
a piece of warm clothing made of wool or cotton for the upper part of the body. A sweater can have long or short sleeves and be pulled over your head or have buttons like a jacket. ⊃ compare PULLOVER

sweat·pants /'swɛtpænts/ (also *informal* sweats) noun [pl.] loose warm pants, usually made of thick cotton and worn for relaxing or playing sports in

sweat·shirt /'swɛtʃərt/ *noun* a piece of clothing for the upper part of the body, with long sleeves, usually made of thick cotton and often worn for sports

sweat·shop /'swɛtʃɑp/ *noun* (*disapproving*) a place where people work for low wages in poor conditions

sweat·suit /'swɛtsut/ *noun* (also informal **sweats** [pl.]) a sweatshirt and SWEATPANTS worn together, for relaxing or playing sports in

sweat·y /'swɛti/ *adj.* (**sweat·i·er**, **sweat·i·est**) **1** covered or damp with sweat: *sweaty feet* ◆ *He felt all hot and sweaty.* **2** [only before noun] making you become hot and covered with sweat: *It was sweaty work, under the hot sun.*

sweep 🔑 /swip/ *verb, noun*

● *verb* (**swept**, **swept** /swɛpt/)
▷ WITH BRUSH OR HAND **1** [T, I] to clean a room, surface, etc. using a BROOM (= a type of brush on a long handle): **~ (sth)** *to sweep the floor* ◆ **~ sth + adj.** *The showroom had been emptied and swept clean.* **2** [T] **~ sth + adv./prep.** to remove something from a surface using a brush, your hand, etc.: *She swept the crumbs into the wastebasket.* ◆ *He swept the leaves up into a pile.*
▷ MOVE QUICKLY/WITH FORCE **3** [T] **~ sb/sth + adv./prep.** to move or push someone or something suddenly and with a lot of force: *The little boat was swept out to sea.* ◆ *She let herself be swept along by the crowd.* **4** [I, T] (of weather, fire, etc.) to move suddenly and/or with force over an area or in a particular direction: **+ adv./prep.** *Rain swept in through the broken windows.* ◆ **~ sth** *Strong winds regularly sweep the islands.*
▷ OF A PERSON **5** [I] **+ adv./prep.** to move quickly and/or smoothly, especially in a way that impresses or is intended to impress other people: *Without another word she swept out of the room.* ◆ (*figurative*) *He swept into the lead with an almost perfect performance.* **6** [T] **~ sth + adv./prep.** to move something, especially your hand or arm, quickly and smoothly in a particular direction: *He rushed to greet her, sweeping his arms wide.*
▷ OF FEELINGS **7** [I] **+ adv./prep.** to suddenly affect someone strongly: *A wave of tiredness swept over her.* ◆ *Memories came sweeping back.*
▷ OF IDEAS/FASHIONS **8** [I, T] to spread quickly: **+ adv./prep.** *Rumors of his resignation swept through the company.* ◆ **~ sth** *the latest craze sweeping America*
▷ LOOK/MOVE OVER AREA **9** [I, T] to move over an area, especially in order to look for something: **+ adv./prep.** *His eyes swept around the room.* ◆ *Searchlights swept the sky.*
▷ TOUCH SURFACE **10** [T] **~ sth** to move, or move something, over a surface, touching it lightly: *Her dress swept the ground as she walked.*
▷ HAIR **11** [T] **~ sth + adv./prep.** to brush, COMB, etc. your hair in a particular direction: *Her hair was swept back from her face.*
▷ OF LANDSCAPE **12** [I] **+ adv./prep.** to form a long smooth curve: *The hotel lawn sweeps down to the beach.*
▷ IN SPORT **13** [T] **~ sth** to win all the games in a series of games against another team or all the parts of a contest: *The Blue Jays have a chance to sweep the series.* ◆ *New Jersey swept Detroit last season.*
IDM **sweep the board** to win all the prizes, etc. in a competition **sweep sb off their feet** to make someone fall suddenly and deeply in love with you **sweep (sb) to power** to win an election by a large number of votes; to make someone win an election with a large number of votes **sweep to victory** to win a contest easily: *The Democrats swept to victory in 2008.* **sweep sth under the rug** to try to stop people from finding out about something wrong, illegal, embarrassing, etc. that has happened or that you have done
PHR V **sweep sb a'long/a'way** [usually passive] to make someone very interested or involved in something, especially in a way that makes them forget everything else: *They were swept along by the force of their emotions.* ,**sweep sth↔a'side** to ignore something completely: *She swept aside all their advice.* ,**sweep sth↔a'way** to get rid of

something completely: *Any doubts had long since been swept away.* ,**sweep sth↔'out** to remove all the dust, dirt, etc. from a room or building using a brush ,**sweep sb↔'up** to lift someone up with a sudden smooth movement: *He swept her up into his arms.*

● *noun*
▷ WITH BRUSH **1** [C, usually sing.] an act of cleaning a room, surface, etc. using a BROOM: *He gave the room a quick sweep before they arrived.*
▷ CURVING MOVEMENT **2** [C] a smooth, curving movement: *He indicated the door with a sweep of his arm.*
▷ LANDSCAPE **3** [C, usually sing.] a long, often curved, piece of road, river, coast, etc.: *the broad sweep of white cliffs around the bay*
▷ RANGE **4** [U] the range of an idea, a piece of writing, etc. that considers many different things: *Her book covers the long sweep of the country's history.*
▷ MOVEMENT/SEARCH OVER AREA **5** [C] a movement over an area, for example in order to search for something or attack something: *The rescue helicopter made another sweep over the bay.*
▷ CHIMNEY **6** [C] = CHIMNEY SWEEP
▷ GAMBLING **7** [C] (also **sweeps**) (*informal*) = SWEEPSTAKES
▷ IN SPORTS **8** [C] a series of games that a team wins against another team; the fact of winning all the parts of a contest: *a World Series sweep*
▷ TELEVISION **9** **the sweeps** [pl.] a time when television companies examine their programs to find out which ones are the most popular, especially in order to calculate advertising rates **IDM** see CLEAN *adj.*

sweep·er /'swipər/ *noun* **1** a person who sweeps something **2** a thing that sweeps something: *a carpet/street sweeper* ⊃ see also MINESWEEPER **3** (in SOCCER) a player who plays behind the other defending players in order to try and stop anyone who passes them

sweep·ing /'swipɪŋ/ *adj.* **1** [usually before noun] having an important effect on a large part of something: *sweeping reforms/changes* ◆ *Security forces were given sweeping powers to search homes.* **2** [usually before noun] (*disapproving*) too general and failing to think about or understand particular examples: *a sweeping generalization/statement* **3** **~ victory** a victory by a large number of votes, etc. **4** [only before noun] forming a curved shape: *a sweeping gesture* (= with your hand or arm) ◆ *a sweeping staircase*

sweep·stakes /'swipsteiks/ *noun* (*pl.* **sweep·stakes**) [usually sing.] **1** a type of betting in which the winner gets all the money bet by everyone else; a race or contest on which money is bet in this way: *The horse was entered in a sweepstakes for colts.* **2** a contest in which you can win a prize if your name is picked: *I entered the sweepstakes to win a trip to Italy.* **3** a competition, election, etc. whose result you cannot guess: *the college admission sweepstakes*

sweet 🔑 /swit/ *adj., noun*

● *adj.* (**sweet·er**, **sweet·est**)
▷ FOOD/DRINK **1** containing, or tasting as if it contains, a lot of sugar: *He likes his coffee sweet.* ◆ *sweet food* ◆ *I had a craving for something sweet.* ◆ *This apple pie is too sweet for me.* **ANT** SOUR ⊃ compare BITTER, SALTY
▷ SMELL **2** having a pleasant smell **SYN** FRAGRANT: *a sweet-smelling rose* ◆ *The air was sweet with incense.*
▷ SOUND **3** having a pleasant sound: *a sweet voice*
▷ PURE **4** pleasant and not containing any harmful substances: *the sweet air of a mountain village*
▷ SATISFYING **5** making you feel happy and/or satisfied: *Goodnight. Sweet dreams.* ◆ *I can't tell you how sweet this victory is.*
▷ KIND **6** having or showing a kind character: *She gave him her sweetest smile.* ◆ *It was sweet of them to offer to help.*
▷ ATTRACTIVE **7** (especially of children or small things) attractive **SYN** CUTE: *The kids look sweet in this photograph.*
▷ GOOD **8** **Sweet!** (*informal*) used to show that you approve of something: *Free tickets? Sweet!*
IDM **be sweet on sb** (*old-fashioned, informal*) to like someone very much in a romantic way **have a sweet**

| ʌ cup | ə about | eɪ say | aɪ five | ɔɪ boy | aʊ now | oʊ go | ər bird |

tooth (*informal*) to like food that contains a lot of sugar **in your own sweet time/way** how and when you want to, even though this might annoy other people: *He always does the work, but in his own sweet time.* **sweet nothings** romantic words: *to whisper sweet nothings in someone's ear* **the sweet smell of success** (*informal*) the pleasant feeling of being successful ⊃ more at HOME *n.*, SHORT *adj.*

• **noun**

▷ FOOD **1** **sweets** [pl.] candy or other sweet foods: *We don't let the kids eat sweets between meals.*

▷ PERSON **2** [U] (*old-fashioned*) a way of addressing someone that you like or love: *Don't you worry, my sweet.*

sweet-and-'sour *adj.* [only before noun] (of food) cooked in a sauce that contains sugar and VINEGAR or lemon: *Chinese sweet-and-sour pork*

sweet·bread /'switbrɛd/ *noun* [usually pl.] the THYMUS (= an organ in the neck) or the PANCREAS (= an organ near the stomach) of a young cow or sheep, eaten as food

'sweet corn *noun* [U] a type of CORN with grains that have a lot of sugar; the grains of this plant eaten as a vegetable

sweet·en /'switn/ *verb* **1** ~ **sth** to make food or drinks taste sweeter by adding sugar, etc. **2** ~ **sb (up)** (*informal*) to try to make someone more willing to help you, agree to something, etc. by giving them money, praising them, etc. **3** ~ **sth** to make something more pleasant or acceptable **IDM see** PILL

sweet·en·er /'switn·ər; 'switnər/ *noun* **1** [U, C] a substance used to make food or drink taste sweeter, used instead of sugar: *artificial sweetener(s)* ⊃ **collocations at** DIET **2** [C] (*informal*) something that is given to someone in order to persuade them to do something, especially when this is done in a secret or dishonest way

sweet·heart /'swithɑrt/ *noun* **1** [sing.] used to address someone in a way that shows affection: *Do you want some ice cream, sweetheart?* **2** [C] (*becoming old-fashioned*) a person with whom someone is having a romantic relationship: *They were childhood sweethearts.*

sweet·ie /'switi/ *noun* (*informal*) **1** [C] a person who is kind and easy to like: *He's a real sweetie.* **2** (also **'sweetie pie**) [sing.] used to address someone in a way that shows affection

sweet·ish /'switɪʃ/ *adj.* fairly sweet

sweet·ly /'switli/ *adv.* **1** in a pleasant way: *She smiled sweetly at him.* **2** in a way that smells sweet: *a sweetly scented flower*

sweet·meat /'switmit/ *noun* (*old use*) a candy; any food preserved in sugar

sweet·ness /'switnəs/ *noun* [U] **1** the quality of being pleasant: *a smile of great sweetness* **2** the quality of tasting or smelling sweet: *The air was filled with the sweetness of mimosa.* **IDM** **be (all) sweetness and light 1** (of a person) to be pleasant, friendly, and polite **2** (of a situation) to be enjoyable and easy to deal with

'sweet pea *noun* **1** [C] a climbing garden plant with pale flowers that have a sweet smell ⊃ **picture at** PLANT **2** [sing.] (*informal*) used to address someone in a way that shows affection: *Yes, my sweet pea!*

'sweet 'pepper = BELL PEPPER

'sweet po·tato *noun* [C, U] a vegetable that looks like a red potato, but that is orange inside and tastes sweet ⊃ **picture at** FRUIT

'sweet spot *noun* **1** the area on a BAT that hits the ball in the most effective way **2** a location or combination of characteristics that produces the best results: *This series aims to hit a sweet spot between romantic comedy and thriller.*

'sweet-talk *verb* ~ **sb (into sth/into doing sth)** (*disapproving*) to try to persuade someone to do something by praising them and telling them things they like to hear: *I can't believe you let him sweet-talk you into working for him!* ▶ **'sweet talk** *noun* [U]

sweet wil·liam (also **sweet Wil·liam**) /ˌswit ˈwɪlyəm/ *noun* a garden plant with groups of red, pink, or white flowers that smell sweet

swell 🔊 /swɛl/ *verb, noun, adj.*

• **verb** (**swelled**, **swol·len** /'swoʊlən/ or **swelled**, **swelled**) **1** [I] ~ **(up)** to become bigger or rounder: *Her arm was beginning to swell up where the bee had stung her.* **2** [I, T] to curve out or make something curve out: ~ **(out)** *The sails swelled (out) in the wind.* ♦ ~ **sth (out)** *The wind swelled (out) the sails.* **3** [T, I] to increase or make something increase in number or size: ~ **sth (to sth)** *Last year's profits were swelled by a fall in production costs.* ♦ *We are looking for more volunteers to* **swell the ranks** (= increase the number) *of those already helping.* ♦ ~ **(to sth)** *Membership has swelled to over 20,000.* **ANT** SHRINK **4** [I] (of a sound) to become louder: *The cheering swelled through the arena.* **5** [I] ~ **(with sth)** to be filled with a strong emotion: *to swell with pride* ⊃ **see also** SWOLLEN

• **noun** **1** [C, usually sing.] the movement of the ocean when it rises and falls without the waves breaking: *The boat was caught in a heavy* (= strong) *swell.* **2** [sing.] (*formal*) the curved shape of something, especially a part of the body: *the firm swell of her breasts* **3** [sing.] a situation in which something increases in size, number, strength, etc.: *a growing swell of support* ♦ *a swell of pride* ⊃ **see also** GROUNDSWELL **4** [sing.] (of music or noise) a gradual increase in the volume of something **SYN** CRESCENDO **5** (*old-fashioned, informal*) an important or fashionable person

• **adj.** (*old-fashioned, informal*) very good, enjoyable, etc.: *We had a swell time.*

swell·ing 🔊 /'swɛlɪŋ/ *noun* **1** [U] the condition of being larger or rounder than normal (= of being SWOLLEN): *Use ice to reduce the swelling.* **2** [C] a place on your body that has become larger or rounder than normal as the result of an illness or injury: *The fall left her with a painful swelling above her eye.*

swel·ter /'swɛltər/ *verb* [I] to be very hot in a way that makes you feel uncomfortable: *Passengers sweltered in temperatures of over 90°F.* ▶ **swel·ter·ing** *adj.*: *sweltering heat* **swel·ter·ing·ly** *adv.*: *swelteringly hot*

swept *pt, pp of* SWEEP

swept-'back *adj.* [only before noun] **1** (of an aircraft wing) pointing backward **2** (of hair) pulled back from your face

swerve /swɜrv/ *verb* [I] (especially of a vehicle) to change direction suddenly, especially in order to avoid hitting someone or something: *She swerved sharply to avoid a cyclist.* ♦ *The bus suddenly swerved into his path.* ♦ *The ball swerved into the net.* ▶ **swerve** *noun*

swift /swɪft/ *adj., noun*

• **adj.** (**swift·er, swift·est**) **1** happening or done quickly and immediately; doing something quickly: *swift action* ♦ *a swift decision* ♦ ~ **to do sth** *The White House was swift to deny the rumors.* **2** moving very quickly; able to move very quickly: *a swift current* ♦ *a swift runner* ⊃ **note at** FAST ▶ **swift·ly** *adv.*: *She moved swiftly to the rescue.* **swift·ness** *noun* [U, sing.]

• **noun** a small bird with long, narrow wings, similar to a SWALLOW

swig /swɪg/ *verb* (-gg-) ~ **sth** (*informal*) to take a large, quick drink of something, especially alcohol: *They sat around swigging beer from bottles.* ▶ **swig** *noun*: *She took a swig of Scotch and winced.*

swill /swɪl/ *verb, noun*

• **verb** **1** [T] ~ **sth (down)** (*informal*) to drink something quickly and/or in large quantities **2** [T, I] to move, or to make a liquid move, in a particular direction or around a particular place: ~ **sth + adv./prep.** *He swilled the juice around in his glass.* ♦ **+ adv./prep.** *Water swilled around in the bottom of the boat.*

• **noun** **1** [U] a mixture of waste food and water that is given to pigs to eat **2** [U] (*informal*) drink or food that is unpleasant or of a poor quality **3** [C, usually sing.] (*informal*) a large amount of a drink that you take into your mouth: *He had a quick swill of cider to wash down the sausage.*

swim 🔑 /swɪm/ *verb, noun*

● *verb* (swim·ming, swam /swæm/, swum /swʌm/) **1** [I, T] (of a person) to move through water in a horizontal position using the arms and legs: *I can't swim.* ◆ *The boys swam across the lake.* ◆ *They spent the day swimming and sunbathing.* ◆ **~ sth** *Can you swim the backstroke yet?* ◆ *How long will it take her to swim the length of the lake?* ➔ note at BATH **2** [I] **go swimming** to spend time swimming for pleasure: *I go swimming twice a week.* **3** [I] (**+ adv./prep.**) (of a fish, etc.) to move through or across water: *A shoal of fish swam past.* ◆ *Ducks were swimming around on the river.* **4** [I] usually **be swimming** to be covered with a lot of liquid: **~ (in sth)** *The main course was swimming in oil.* ◆ **~ (with sth)** *Her eyes were swimming with tears.* **5** [I] (of objects, etc.) to seem to be moving around, especially when you are sick or drunk: *The pages swam before her eyes.* **6** [I] to feel confused and/or as if everything is spinning around: *His head swam and he swayed dizzily.* **IDM** see SINK *v.*

● *noun* **1** [sing.] a period of time during which you swim: *Let's go for a swim.* **2** (in compounds) related to or used for swimming: *a swim meet* (= swimming competition between teams) ◆ *swim trunks*
IDM **in the swim (of things)** (*informal*) involved in things that are happening in society or in a particular situation

swim·mer /'swɪmər/ *noun* a person who can swim; a person who is swimming: *a good/strong swimmer* ◆ *They watched the swimmers splashing through the water.* ◆ *a shallow pool for non-swimmers*

swim·ming 🔑 /'swɪmɪŋ/ *noun* [U]
the sport or activity of swimming: *Swimming is a good form of exercise.*

swim·ming·ly /'swɪmɪŋli/ *adv.* (*informal*) without any problems or difficulties: *We hope everything will go swimmingly.*

swimming pool 🔑 (also **pool**) *noun*
1 an area of water that has been created for people to swim in: *an indoor/outdoor swimming pool* ◆ *a heated swimming pool* ◆ *an open-air swimming pool* **2** the building that contains a public swimming pool: *She trained five times a week at her local swimming pool.*

swimming trunks (also **trunks**, **swim trunks**) *noun* [pl.] a piece of clothing covering the lower part of the body and sometimes the top part of the legs, worn by men and boys for swimming: *a pair of swimming trunks*

swim·suit /'swɪmsut/ (also **bathing suit**) *noun* a piece of clothing worn for swimming, especially the type worn by women and girls

swim·wear /'swɪmwɛr/ *noun* [U] clothing that you wear for swimming

swin·dle /'swɪndl/ *verb, noun*
● *verb* to cheat someone in order to get something, especially money, from them: **~ sb (out of sth)** *They swindled him out of hundreds of dollars.* ◆ **~ sth (out of sb)** *They swindled hundreds of dollars out of him.* ▶ **swin·dler** /'swɪndlər/ *noun* **SYN** CONMAN
● *noun* [usually sing.] a situation in which someone uses dishonest or illegal methods in order to get money from a company, another person, etc. **SYN** CON: *an insurance swindle*

swine /swaɪn/ *noun* (*pl.* swine) **1** swine [pl.] (*old use* or *technical*) pigs: *a herd of swine* ◆ *swine fever* (= a disease of pigs) **IDM** see PEARL **2** [C] (*informal*) an unpleasant person: *He's an arrogant little swine!*

swine flu *noun* [U] **1** a serious illness that affects pigs **2** a serious illness spread between humans, that is genetically (GENETIC) similar to swine flu in pigs and that in some cases causes death

swine·herd /'swaɪnhərd/ *noun* (*old use*) a person whose job is to take care of pigs

swing 🔑 /swɪŋ/ *verb, noun*

● *verb* (swung, swung /swʌŋ/)
▷ **HANG AND MOVE 1** [I, T] to move backward or forward or from side to side while hanging from a fixed point; to make something do this: *His arms swung as he walked.* ◆ *As he pushed her, she swung higher and higher* (= while sitting on a swing). ◆ **~ from sth** *A set of keys swung from her belt.* ◆ **~ sth** *He sat on the stool, swinging his legs.* **2** [I, T] to move from one place to another by holding something that is fixed and pulling yourself along, up, etc.: **+ adv./prep.** *The gunshot sent monkeys swinging away through the trees.* ◆ **~ yourself + adv./prep.** *He swung himself out of the car.*
▷ **MOVE IN CURVE 3** [I, T] to move or make something move with a wide, curved movement: **+ adv./prep.** *A line of cars swung out of the White House driveway.* ◆ **~ sth** *He swung his legs over the side of the bed.* ◆ **+ adj.** *The door swung open.* ◆ **~ sth + adj.** *She swung the door open.*
▷ **TURN QUICKLY 4** [I, T] to turn or change direction suddenly; to make something do this: **+ adv./prep.** *The bus swung sharply to the left.* ◆ **~ sth + adv./prep.** *He swung the camera around to face the opposite direction.*
▷ **TRY TO HIT 5** [I, T] to try to hit someone or something: **~ at sb/sth** *She swung at me with the iron bar.* ◆ **~ sth (at sb/sth)** *He swung another punch in my direction.*
▷ **CHANGE OPINION/MOOD 6** [I, T] to change or make someone or something change from one opinion, mood, etc. to another: **~ (from A) (to B)** *The state swung from Republican to Democrat in the last election.* ◆ **~ (between A and B)** *His emotions swung between fear and curiosity.* ◆ *The game could swing either way* (= either side could win it). ◆ **~ sb/sth (to sth)** *I managed to swing them around to my point of view.*
▷ **DO/GET SOMETHING 7** [T] (*informal*) to succeed in getting or achieving something, sometimes in a slightly dishonest way: **~ sth** *We're trying to swing it so that we can travel on the same flight.*
▷ **OF MUSIC 8** [I] to have a strong rhythm
▷ **OF PARTY 9** [I] (*informal*) if a party, etc. **is swinging**, there are a lot of people there having a good time
IDM **swing the balance** = TIP *v.* **swing for the fences** to really try to achieve something great, even when it is not reasonable to expect to be so successful: *entrepreneurs who think big and swing for the fences* **swing into action** to start doing something quickly and with a lot of energy ➔ more at HIGH GEAR, ROOM
PHR V **swing 'by** | **'swing by sth** (*informal*) to visit a place or person for a short time **SYN** DROP BY: *I'll swing by your house on the way home from work.*

● *noun*
▷ **MOVEMENT 1** [C] a swinging movement or rhythm: *He took a wild swing at the ball.* ◆ *the swing of her hips*
▷ **OF OPINION/MOOD 2** [C] a change from one opinion or situation to another; the amount by which something changes: *He's subject to abrupt mood swings* (= for example from being very happy to being very sad). ◆ *Voting showed a 10% swing to the Republican party.*
▷ **HANGING SEAT 3** [C] a seat for swinging on, hung from above on ropes or chains: *The kids were playing on the swings.* ➔ picture at TOY
▷ **IN GOLF 4** [sing.] the swinging movement you make with your arms and body when you hit the ball in the game of GOLF: *I need to work on my swing.*
▷ **MUSIC 5** [U] a type of JAZZ with a smooth rhythm, played especially by big dance bands in the 1930s
▷ **JOURNEY 6** [sing.] a quick trip, especially one made by a politician, in which someone visits several different places in a short time: *a three-day campaign swing through California*
IDM **get in/into the swing (of sth)** (*informal*) to get used to an activity or a situation and become fully involved in it **in full swing** having reached a very lively level: *When we arrived the party was already in full swing.*

swing bridge *noun* a bridge that can be moved to one side to allow tall ships to pass

t tea	ţ butter	d did	k cat	g got	tʃ chin	dʒ June	f fall

swing·er /ˈswɪŋər/ noun (old-fashioned, informal) **1** a person who is fashionable and has an active social life **2** a person who has sex with many different people

swing·ing /ˈswɪŋɪŋ/ adj. [usually before noun] (old-fashioned, informal) lively and fashionable

swinging ˈdoor noun a door that you can open in either direction and that closes itself when you stop holding it open

ˈswing set noun a frame for children to play on including one or more SWINGS and often a SLIDE

ˈswing shift noun (informal) the SHIFT (= period of time worked each day) from 3 or 4 o'clock in the afternoon until 11 or 12 at night; the workers who work this SHIFT

ˈswing state noun (politics) (in an election for president in the U.S.) a state where none of the candidates can be certain of getting the most support

ˈswing vote noun [C, sing.] the votes of people who do not always vote for the same political party and have not decided which party to vote for in an election

swing ˈvoter noun a person who does not always vote for the same political party and who has not decided which party to vote for in an election

ˈswing-wing adj. [only before noun] used to describe an aircraft wing that can be moved forward for landing, etc. and backward for rapid flight

swipe /swaɪp/ verb, noun
- **verb 1** [I, T] ~ (at) sb/sth to hit or try to hit someone or something with your hand or an object by swinging your arm: *He swiped at the ball and missed.* **2** [T] (informal) to steal something SYN PINCH **3** [T] ~ sth to pass a plastic card, such as a credit card, through a special machine that is able to read the information that is stored on it
- **noun** ~ (at sb/sth) (informal) **1** an act of hitting or trying to hit someone or something by swinging your arm or something that you are holding: *She took a swipe at him with her umbrella.* **2** an act of criticizing someone or something: *He used the interview to take a swipe at his critics.*

ˈswipe card noun a special plastic card with information recorded on it that can be read by an electronic device: *Access to the building is by swipe card only.* ⊃ compare KEY CARD

swirl /swɜrl/ verb, noun
- **verb** [I, T] to move around quickly in a circle; to make something do this: **(+ adv./prep.)** *The water swirled down the drain.* ◆ *A long skirt swirled around her ankles.* ◆ *swirling mists* ◆ ~ sth **(+ adv./prep.)** *He took a mouthful of water and swirled it around in his mouth.*
- **noun 1** the movement of something that twists and turns in different directions and at different speeds **2** a pattern or an object that twists in circles

swish /swɪʃ/ verb, noun
- **verb** [I, T] to move quickly through the air in a way that makes a soft sound; to make something do this: **(+ adv./prep.)** *A large car swished past them and turned into the embassy gates.* ◆ *The pony's tail swished.* ◆ ~ sth **(+ adv./prep.)** *The pony swished its tail.* ◆ *She swished her racket aggressively through the air.*
- **noun** [sing.] the movement or soft sound made by something moving quickly, especially through the air

Swiss /swɪs/ adj., noun
- **adj.** from or connected with Switzerland
- **noun** (pl. Swiss) a person from Switzerland

Swiss ˈarmy ˌknife™ noun a small knife with several different blades and tools, such as scissors, that fold into the handle

Swiss ˈchard noun [U] = CHARD

Swiss ˈcheese noun [U, C] any hard cheese with holes in it

switch /swɪtʃ/ noun, verb
- **noun 1** a small device that you press or move up and down in order to turn a light or piece of electrical

equipment on and off: *a light switch* ◆ *an on-off switch* ◆ *That was in the days before electricity was available at the flick of a switch.* ◆ *Which switch do I press to turn it off?* ◆ *to throw a switch* (= to move a large switch) **2** a change from one thing to another, especially when this is sudden and complete: ~ **(in/of sth)** *a switch of priorities* ◆ ~ **(from A to B)** *She made the switch from full-time to part-time work when her first child was born.* ◆ *a policy switch* **3** the piece of track at a place where a railroad line divides that can be moved to allow a train to change tracks **4** a thin stick that bends easily: *a riding switch*
- **verb 1** [I, T] to change or make something change from one thing to another: ~ **(over) (from sth) (to sth)** *We're in the process of switching over to a new system of invoicing.* ◆ ~ **between A and B** *Press these two keys to switch between documents on the screen.* ◆ ~ **sth (over) (from sth) (to sth)** *When did you switch jobs?* **2** [T] to exchange one thing for another SYN SWAP: ~ **sth** *The dates of their next two games have been switched.* ◆ ~ **sth over/around** *I see you've switched the furniture around* (= changed its position). ◆ ~ **sth with sth** *Do you think she'll notice if I switch my glass with hers?* ◆ **switch sth (with sb)** *Can I switch places with you?* **3** [I, T] to do someone else's job for a short time or work during different hours so that they can do your job or work during your usual hours SYN SWAP: ~ **(with sb)** *I can't work next weekend—will you switch with me?* ◆ ~ **sth (with sb)** *Have you been able to switch your shift with anyone?* ◆ ~ **(sth) (over/around)** *Can we switch our shifts around?* IDM see HORSE n. PHRV ˌswitch ˈoff (informal) to stop thinking about something or paying attention to something: *When I hear the word "football" I switch off* (= because I am not interested in it). ◆ *The only time he really switches off* (= stops thinking about work, etc.) *is when we're on vacation.* ˌswitch ˈoff/ˈon | ˌswitch sth↔ˈoff/ˈon to turn a light, machine, etc. off/on by pressing a button or switch: *Please switch the lights off when you leave.* ◆ *How do you switch this thing on?*

switch·back /ˈswɪtʃbæk/ noun **1** a road or railroad track that has many sharp bends as it goes up a steep hill, or one that rises and falls steeply many times **2** a 180 degree bend in a road that is going up a steep hill

switch·blade /ˈswɪtʃbleɪd/ noun a knife with a blade inside the handle that jumps out quickly when a button is pressed

switch·board /ˈswɪtʃbɔrd/ noun the central part of a telephone system used by a company, etc., where telephone calls are answered and PUT THROUGH (= connected) to the appropriate person or department; the people who work this equipment: *a switchboard operator* ◆ *Call the switchboard and ask for extension 410.* ◆ *Hundreds of fans jammed the switchboard for over an hour.*

ˌswitched ˈon adj. ~ **(to sth)** aware of new things that are happening: *We're trying to get people switched on to the benefits of healthy eating.* ◆ *an organization for switched-on young people*

switch·er·oo /ˌswɪtʃəˈru/ noun [usually sing.] (informal) a situation in which something is changed or switched unexpectedly or secretly: *The magician did a switcheroo.*

ˌswitch-ˈhitter noun (in baseball) a player who can hit with the BAT on either side of their body

ˈswitch ˌover (also **switch·o·ver**) /ˈswɪtʃˌoʊvər/ noun a change from one system, method, policy, etc. to another

swiv·el /ˈswɪvl/ noun, verb
- **noun** (often used as an adjective) a device used to connect two parts of an object together, allowing one part to turn around without moving the other: *a swivel chair* (= one on which the seat turns around without moving the base) ⊃ picture at CHAIR
- **verb** (-l-, CanE usually -ll-) **1** [T, I] ~ **(sth) (+ adv./prep.)** to turn or make something turn around a fixed central point SYN SPIN: *She swiveled the chair around to face them.* **2** [I, T] ~ **(sth) (+ adv./prep.)** to turn or move your body, eyes, or head around quickly to face another direction SYN SWING: *He swiveled around to look at her.*

swiz·zle stick /ˈswɪzl ˌstɪk/ *noun* a small stick that is used to stir drinks

swol·len 🗝 /ˈswoʊlən/ *adj.*

1 (of a part of the body) larger than normal, especially as a result of a disease or an injury: *swollen glands* ♦ *Her eyes were red and swollen from crying.* **2** (of a river) containing more water than normal ➲ see also SWELL

swoon /swun/ *verb* **1** [I] **~ (over sb)** to feel very excited, emotional, etc. about someone that you think is sexually attractive, so that you almost become unconscious: *He's used to having women swooning over him.* **2** [I] (*old-fashioned*) to become unconscious **SYN** FAINT ▶ **swoon** *noun* [sing.] (*old-fashioned*): *to go into a swoon*

swoop /swup/ *verb, noun*

• *verb* **1** [I] **(+ adv./prep.)** (of a bird or plane) to fly quickly and suddenly downward, especially in order to attack someone or something **SYN** DIVE: *The aircraft swooped down over the buildings.* **2** [I] **~ (in) (on sb/sth)** (especially of police or soldiers) to visit or attack someone or something suddenly and without warning
PHR V **swoop sth↔up** to pick something up quickly and carry it away: *She swooped up her things and rushed out of the room.*

• *noun* **1** an act of moving suddenly and quickly through the air in a downward direction, as a bird does **SYN** DIVE **2** **~ (on sth/sb)** an act of arriving somewhere or attacking something or someone in a way that is sudden and unexpected **SYN** RAID: *Large quantities of drugs were found during a police swoop on the star's New York home.* **IDM** see FELL *adj.*

swoosh /swuʃ; swuʒ/ *verb* [I] **+ adv./prep.** to move quickly through the air in a way that makes a sound: *Cars and trucks swooshed past.* ▶ **swoosh** *noun* [sing.]

swop = SWAP

sword /sɔrd/ *noun* a weapon with a long metal blade and a handle: *to draw/sheathe a sword* (= to take it out/put it into its cover)
IDM **put sb to the sword** (*old-fashioned* or *literary*) to kill someone with a sword **a/the sword of Damocles** (*literary*) a bad or unpleasant thing that might happen to you at any time and that makes you feel worried or frightened **ORIGIN** From the legend in which **Damocles** had to sit at a meal at the court of Dionysius with a sword hanging by a single hair above his head. He had praised Dionysius' happiness, and Dionysius wanted him to understand how quickly happiness can be lost. **turn swords into plowshares** (*literary*) to stop fighting and return to peaceful activities ➲ more at CROSS *v.*, DOUBLE-EDGED, PEN *n.*

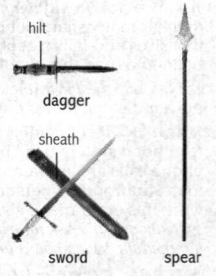

hilt
dagger
sheath
sword   spear

sword dance *noun* a dance performed with swords, especially one in which people dance between and over SWORDS that are placed on the ground

sword·fish /ˈsɔrdfɪʃ/ *noun* [C, U] (*pl.* **sword·fish**) a large sea fish with a very long, thin, pointed upper JAW

sword·play /ˈsɔrdpleɪ/ *noun* [U] the sport or skill of fighting with swords **SYN** FENCING

swords·man /ˈsɔrdzmən/ *noun* (*pl.* **swords·men** /-mən/) (usually used with an adjective) a person who fights with a SWORD: *a fine swordsman*

swords·man·ship /ˈsɔrdzmənʃɪp/ *noun* [U] skill in fighting with a SWORD

swore pt of SWEAR

sworn /swɔrn/ *adj.* [only before noun] **1** made after you have promised to tell the truth, especially in court: *a sworn*

statement **2 ~ enemies** people, countries, etc. that have a strong hatred for each other ➲ see also SWEAR

SWOT a·nal·y·sis /ˈswɑt əˌnæləsəs/ *noun* a study done by an organization in order to find its strengths and weaknesses, and what problems or opportunities it should deal with. SWOT is formed from the initial letters of "strengths," "weaknesses," "opportunities," and "threats."

swum pp of SWIM

swung pt, pp of SWING

syb·a·rit·ic /ˌsɪbəˈrɪtɪk/ *adj.* [usually before noun] (*formal*) connected with a desire for pleasure: *his sybaritic lifestyle*

syc·a·more /ˈsɪkəˌmɔr/ *noun* **1** [C, U] an American tree with spreading branches and broad leaves; the wood of this tree **2** [C, U] a European tree of the MAPLE family, with leaves that have five points and seeds shaped like a pair of wings; the wood of this tree

syc·o·phant /ˈsɪkəfənt; -ˌfænt/ *noun* (*formal, disapproving*) a person who praises important or powerful people too much and in a way that is not sincere, especially in order to get something from them ▶ **syc·o·phan·cy** /ˈsɪkəfənsi; -ˌfænsi/ *noun* [U] **syc·o·phan·tic** /ˌsɪkəˈfæntɪk/ *adj.*: *a sycophantic review*

syl·la·bar·y /ˈsɪləˌbɛri/ *noun* (*pl.* **syl·la·bar·ies**) (*technical*) a set of written characters representing syllables and used as an alphabet in some languages

syl·lab·ic /sɪˈlæbɪk/ *adj.* (*phonetics*) **1** based on syllables: *syllabic stress* **2** (of a consonant) forming a whole syllable, for example /l/ in *settle*

syl·la·ble /ˈsɪləbl/ *noun* any of the units into which a word is divided, containing a vowel sound and usually one or more consonants: *a word with two syllables* ♦ *a two-syllable word* ♦ *"Potato" is stressed on the second syllable.*

ˈsyllable-ˌtimed *adj.* (*phonetics*) (of a language) having a regular rhythm of syllables ➲ compare STRESS-TIMED

syl·la·bus /ˈsɪləbəs/ *noun* (*pl.* **syl·la·bus·es** or *less frequent* **syl·la·bi** /-ˌbaɪ/) a list of the topics, books, etc. that students should study in a particular subject at school or college ➲ collocations at EDUCATION ➲ compare CURRICULUM

syl·lo·gism /ˈsɪləˌdʒɪzəm/ *noun* (*technical*) a way of arguing in which two statements are used to prove that a third statement is true, for example: "All humans must die; I am a human; therefore I must die." ▶ **syl·lo·gis·tic** /ˌsɪləˈdʒɪstɪk/ *adj.* [only before noun]

sylph /sɪlf/ *noun* **1** an imaginary spirit **2** a girl or woman who is thin and attractive

sylph·like /ˈsɪlflaɪk/ *adj.* (of a woman or girl) thin in an attractive way

syl·van /ˈsɪlvən/ *adj.* (*literary*) connected with forests and trees

sym·bi·o·sis /ˌsɪmbiˈoʊsəs; -baɪ-/ *noun* (*pl.* **sym·bi·o·ses** /-ˈoʊsiz/) [U, C] **1** (*biology*) the relationship between two different living creatures that live close together and depend on each other in particular ways, each getting particular benefits from the other **2** a relationship between people, companies, etc. that is to the advantage of both ▶ **sym·bi·ot·ic** /ˌsɪmbiˈɑtɪk; -baɪ-/ *adj.*: *a symbiotic relationship* **sym·bi·ot·i·cally** /-kli/ *adv.*

sym·bol 🗝 **AWL** /ˈsɪmbl/ *noun*

1 ~ (of sth) a person, an object, an event, etc. that represents a more general quality or situation: *White has always been a symbol of purity in Western cultures.* ♦ *Nelson Mandela became a symbol of the anti-apartheid struggle.* ➲ thesaurus box at SIGN **2 ~ (for sth)** a sign, number, letter, etc. that has a fixed meaning, especially in science, mathematics, and music: *What is the chemical symbol for copper?* ♦ *A list of symbols used on the map is given in the index.* ➲ see also SEX SYMBOL, STATUS SYMBOL

sym·bol·ic **AWL** /sɪmˈbɑlɪk/ *adj.* **~ (of sth)** containing symbols, or being used as a symbol: *The dove is symbolic of peace.* ♦ *The election of Barack Obama had enormous symbolic* significance for the idea of a post-racial society. ◆ *The new regulations are largely symbolic* (= they will not have any real effect). ▶ **sym·bol·i·cally** AWL /-kli/ *adv.*: *a symbolically significant gesture*

sym·bol·ism AWL /ˈsɪmbəˌlɪzəm/ *noun* [U] the use of symbols to represent ideas, especially in art and literature ⊃ collocations at LITERATURE ▶ **sym·bol·ist** /-lɪst/ *adj., noun*: *the symbolist poet Rimbaud*

sym·bol·ize AWL /ˈsɪmbəˌlaɪz/ *verb* ~ sth to be a symbol of something SYN REPRESENT: *The use of light and dark symbolizes good and evil.* ◆ *He came to symbolize his country's struggle for independence.*

sym·met·ri·cal /sɪˈmɛtrɪkl/ (also **sym·met·ric** /sɪˈmɛtrɪk/) *adj.* (of a body, a design, an object, etc.) having two halves, parts, or sides that are the same in size and shape: *a symmetrical pattern* ANT ASYMMETRIC ▶ **sym·met·ri·cally** /-kli/ *adv.*

sym·me·try /ˈsɪmətri/ *noun* [U] **1** the exact match in size and shape between two halves, parts, or sides of something: *the perfect symmetry of the garden design* **2** the quality of being very similar or equal: *the increasing symmetry between men's and women's jobs*

sym·pa·thet·ic 🔑 /ˌsɪmpəˈθɛtɪk/ *adj.*
1 ~ (to/toward sb) kind to someone who is hurt or sad; showing that you understand and care about their problems: *a sympathetic listener* ◆ *I did not feel at all sympathetic toward Kate.* ◆ *I'm here if you need a sympathetic ear* (= someone to talk to about your problems). **2** ~ (to/toward sb/sth) showing that you approve of someone or something or that you share their views and are willing to support them: *to be sympathetic to youthful rebellion* ◆ *Russian newspapers are largely sympathetic to the president.* **3** (of a person) easy to like: *a sympathetic character in a novel* ◆ *I don't find her a very sympathetic person.* ANT UNSYMPATHETIC ▶ **sym·pa·thet·i·cally** /-kli/ *adv.*: *to smile at someone sympathetically*

sym·pa·thize /ˈsɪmpəˌθaɪz/ *verb* **1** [I, T] ~ (with sb/sth) | + speech to feel sorry for someone; to show that you understand and feel sorry about someone's problems: *I find it very hard to sympathize with him.* **2** [I] ~ with sb/sth to support someone or something: *He has never really sympathized with the aims of animal rights activists.*

sym·pa·thiz·er /ˈsɪmpəˌθaɪzər/ *noun* a person who supports or approves of someone or something, especially a political cause or party: *communist sympathizers*

sym·pa·thy 🔑 /ˈsɪmpəθi/ *noun* (pl. **sym·pa·thies**)
1 [U, C, usually pl.] the feeling of being sorry for someone; showing that you understand and care about someone's problems: *to express/feel sympathy for someone* ◆ *I have no sympathy for Jen; it's all her own fault.* ◆ *I wish he'd show me a little more sympathy.* ◆ *Our heartfelt sympathy goes out to the victims of the war.* ◆ (formal) *May we offer our deepest sympathies on the death of your wife.* **2** [U, C, usually pl.] the act of showing support for or approval of an idea, a cause, an organization, etc.: *The seamen went on strike in sympathy with* (= to show their support for) *the dockworkers.* ◆ *Her sympathies lie with the anti-vivisection lobby.* **3** [U] friendship and understanding between people who have similar opinions or interests: *There was no personal sympathy between them.* IDM **in sympathy with sth** happening because something else has happened: *Share prices slipped in sympathy with the discouraging economic news.* **out of sympathy with sb/sth** not agreeing with or not wanting to support someone or something

sym·pho·ny /ˈsɪmfəni/ *noun* (pl. **sym·pho·nies**) a long, complicated piece of music for a large ORCHESTRA, in three or four main parts (called MOVEMENTS): *Beethoven's Fifth Symphony* ⊃ collocations at MUSIC ▶ **sym·phon·ic** /sɪmˈfɑnɪk/ *adj.*: *Mozart's symphonic works*

symphony orchestra *noun* a large ORCHESTRA that plays CLASSICAL music: *the Boston Symphony Orchestra*

sym·po·si·um /sɪmˈpoʊziəm/ *noun* (pl. **sym·po·si·a** /-ziə/ or sym·po·si·ums) ~ (on sth) a meeting at which experts have discussions about a particular subject; a small conference

symp·tom /ˈsɪmptəm/ *noun* **1** a change in your body or mind that shows that you are not healthy: *flu symptoms* ◆ *Look out for symptoms of depression.* ◆ *Symptoms include a headache and sore throat.* **2** a sign that something exists, especially something bad SYN INDICATION: *The rise in inflation was just one symptom of the poor state of the economy.* ⊃ thesaurus box at SIGN

symp·to·mat·ic /ˌsɪmptəˈmætɪk/ *adj.* being a sign of an illness or a problem: *a symptomatic infection* ◆ ~ of sth *These disagreements are symptomatic of the tensions within the administration.*

symp·tom·ize /ˈsɪmptəˌmaɪz/ *verb* ~ sth to be a sign or SYMPTOM of something

syn·a·gogue /ˈsɪnəˌgɑg/ *noun* a building where Jews meet for religious worship and teaching

syn·apse /ˈsɪnæps/ *noun* (biology) a connection between two nerve cells ▶ **syn·ap·tic** /sɪˈnæptɪk/ *adj.*: *the synaptic membranes*

sync (also **synch**) /sɪŋk/ *noun* [U] (informal)
IDM **in sync 1** moving or working at exactly the same time and speed as someone or something else: *The soundtrack is not in sync with the picture.* **2** in agreement with someone or something; working well with someone or something: *His opinions were in sync with those of his colleagues.* **out of sync 1** not moving or working at exactly the same time and speed as someone or something else **2** not in agreement with someone or something; not working well with someone or something ⊃ see also LIP-SYNC

syn·chron·ic /sɪŋˈkrɑnɪk/ *adj.* (linguistics) relating to a language as it is at a particular point in time ⊃ compare DIACHRONIC

syn·chro·nic·i·ty /ˌsɪŋkrəˈnɪsəti/ *noun* [U] (technical) the fact of two or more things happening at exactly the same time

syn·chro·nize /ˈsɪŋkrəˌnaɪz/ *verb* [I, T] to happen at the same time or to move at the same speed as something; to make something do this: ~ (with sth) *The sound track doesn't synchronize with the action.* ◆ ~ sth (with sth) *Let's synchronize our watches* (= make them show exactly the same time). ▶ **syn·chro·ni·za·tion** /ˌsɪŋkrənəˈzeɪʃn/ (also informal **sync**) *noun* [U]

synchronized swimming *noun* [U] a sport in which groups of SWIMMERS move in patterns in the water to music

syn·chro·nous /ˈsɪŋkrənəs/ *adj.* (technical) happening or existing at the same time

syn·cline /ˈsɪnklaɪn/ *noun* (geology) an area of ground where layers of rock in the earth's surface have been folded into a curve that is lower in the middle than at the ends ⊃ compare ANTICLINE

syn·co·pat·ed /ˈsɪŋkəˌpeɪtəd/ *adj.* (music) in syncopated rhythm the strong beats are made weak and the weak beats are made strong ▶ **syn·co·pa·tion** /ˌsɪŋkəˈpeɪʃn/ *noun* [U]

syn·co·pe /ˈsɪŋkəpi/ *noun* [U] (phonetics) the dropping of a sound or sounds in the middle of a word when it is spoken, for example when *probably* is pronounced /ˈprɑbli/ ⊃ compare APOCOPE

syn·cre·tism /ˈsɪŋkrəˌtɪzəm/ *noun* [U] **1** (technical) the mixing of different religions, philosophies, or ideas **2** (linguistics) the mixing of different forms of the same word during the development of a language

syn·di·cal·ism /ˈsɪndɪkəˌlɪzəm/ *noun* [U] the belief that factories, businesses, etc. should be owned and managed by all the people who work in them

syn·di·cal·ist /ˈsɪndɪkəlɪst/ *noun* a person who believes in syndicalism ▶ **syn·di·cal·ist** *adj.*

syn·di·cate *noun, verb*
● *noun* /ˈsɪndɪkət/ a group of people or companies who work together and help each other in order to achieve a particular aim

• **verb** /'sɪndəˌkeɪt/ [usually passive] ~ **sth** to sell an article, a photograph, a television program, etc. to several different newspapers, etc.: *His column is syndicated throughout the world.* ► **syn·di·ca·tion** /ˌsɪndə'keɪʃn/ *noun* [U]

syn·drome /'sɪndroʊm/ *noun* **1** a set of physical conditions that show you have a particular disease or medical problem: *PMS or premenstrual syndrome ◆ This syndrome is associated with frequent coughing.* ⊃ see also AIDS, DOWN'S SYNDROME, SICK BUILDING SYNDROME, TOURETTE'S SYNDROME **2** a set of opinions or a way of behaving that is typical of a particular type of person, attitude, or social problem: *With teenagers, be prepared for the "Me, me, me!" syndrome* (= they think of themselves first).

syn·ec·do·che /sɪ'nɛkdəki/ *noun* [U, C] (*technical*) a word or phrase in which a part of something is used to represent a whole, or a whole is used to represent a part of something. For example, in "Chicago lost by three points," *Chicago* is used to represent the Chicago team.

syn·er·gy /'sɪnərdʒi/ *noun* (*pl.* **syn·er·gies**) [U, C] (*technical*) the extra energy, power, success, etc. that is achieved by two or more people or companies working together, instead of on their own ► **syn·er·gis·tic** /ˌsɪnər'dʒɪstɪk/ *adj.* **syn·er·gis·ti·cally** /-kli/ *adv.*

syn·es·the·sia /ˌsɪnəs'θiʒə/ *noun* [U] (*biology*) the fact of experiencing some things in a different way from most other people, for example experiencing colors as sounds or shapes as tastes, or feeling something in one part of the body when a different part is STIMULATED

syn·od /'sɪnəd/ *noun* an official meeting of church leaders and sometimes church members to discuss religious matters and make important decisions

syn·o·nym /'sɪnənɪm/ *noun* a word or expression that has the same or nearly the same meaning as another in the same language: *"Big" and "large" are synonyms.* ⊃ compare ANTONYM

syn·on·y·mous /sɪ'nɑnəməs/ *adj.* **1** (of words or expressions) having the same, or nearly the same, meaning **2** ~ **(with sth)** so closely connected with something that the two things appear to be the same: *Wealth is not necessarily synonymous with happiness.* ► **syn·on·y·mous·ly** *adv.*

syn·on·y·my /sɪ'nɑnəmi/ *noun* [U] the fact of two or more words or expressions having the same meaning

syn·op·sis /sɪ'nɑpsəs/ *noun* (*pl.* **syn·op·ses** /-siz/) a summary of a piece of writing, a play, etc. ► **syn·op·tic** /sɪ'nɑptɪk/ *adj.* (*formal*)

syn·o·vi·al /sɪ'noʊviəl/ *adj.* (*biology*) (of a joint) having a MEMBRANE (= a piece of very thin skin) containing liquid between the bones, which allows the joint to move freely

syn·tac·tic /sɪn'tæktɪk/ *adj.* (*linguistics*) connected with SYNTAX ► **syn·tac·ti·cally** /-kli/ *adv.*: *to be syntactically correct*

syn·tagm /'sɪntæm/ *noun* (also **syn·tag·ma** /sɪn'tægmə/ *pl.* **syn·tag·mas** or **syn·tag·ma·ta**) (*linguistics*) a unit of language consisting of sets of PHONEMES, words, or phrases that are arranged in order ► **syn·tag·mat·ic** /ˌsɪntæg'mætɪk/ *adj.*

syn·tax /'sɪntæks/ *noun* [U] **1** (*linguistics*) the way that words and phrases are put together to form sentences in a language; the rules of grammar for this ⊃ compare MORPHOLOGY **2** (*computing*) the rules that state how words and phrases must be used in a computer language

synth /sɪnθ/ *noun* (*informal*) = SYNTHESIZER

syn·the·sis /'sɪnθəsəs/ *noun* (*pl.* **syn·the·ses** /-siz/) **1** [U, C] ~ **(of sth)** the act of combining separate ideas, beliefs, styles, etc.; a mixture or combination of ideas, beliefs, styles, etc.: *the synthesis of art with everyday life ◆ a synthesis of traditional and modern values* **2** [U] (*technical*) the natural chemical production of a substance in animals and plants: *protein synthesis* **3** [U] (*technical*) the artificial production of a substance that is present naturally in animals and plants: *the synthesis of penicillin* **4** [U] (*technical*) the

production of sounds, music, or speech by electronic means: *speech synthesis*

syn·the·size /'sɪnθəˌsaɪz/ *verb* **1** ~ **sth** (*technical*) to produce a substance by means of chemical or BIOLOGICAL processes **2** ~ **sth** to produce sounds, music, or speech using electronic equipment **3** ~ **sth** to combine separate ideas, beliefs, styles, etc.

syn·the·siz·er /'sɪnθəˌsaɪzər/ (also *informal* **synth**) *noun* an electronic machine for producing different sounds. Synthesizers are used as musical instruments, especially for copying the sounds of other instruments, and for copying speech sounds.: *a speech synthesizer* ⊃ compare KEYBOARD

syn·thet·ic /sɪn'θɛtɪk/ *adj.*, *noun*
• **adj.** **1** artificial; made by combining chemical substances rather than being produced naturally by plants or animals **SYN** MAN-MADE: *synthetic drugs/fabrics* ⊃ thesaurus box at ARTIFICIAL **2** (also **ag·glu·ti·na·tive**) (*linguistics*) (of languages) using changes to the ends of words rather than separate words to show the functions of words in a sentence ⊃ compare ANALYTIC ► **syn·thet·i·cally** /-kli/ *adv.*
• **noun** an artificial substance or material: *cotton fabrics and synthetics*

syph·i·lis /'sɪfələs/ *noun* [U] a disease that gets worse over a period of time, spreading from the sexual organs to the skin, bones, muscles, and brain. It is caught by having sex with an infected person. ► **syph·i·lit·ic** /ˌsɪfə'lɪtɪk/ *adj.*

sy·phon = SIPHON

sy·ringe /sə'rɪndʒ/ *noun*, *verb*
• **noun** **1** (also **hy·po·der·mic, hypodermic sy·ringe**) a plastic or glass tube with a long, hollow needle that is used for putting drugs, etc. into a person's body or for taking a small amount of blood from a person ⊃ picture at LABORATORY **2** a plastic or glass tube with a rubber part at the end, used for sucking up liquid and then pushing it out
• **verb** ~ **sth** to clean something by spraying liquid into it with a syringe, or to put liquid into something using a syringe: *The doctor syringed my ears.*

syr·up /'sɪrəp; 'sər-/ *noun* [U] **1** a sweet liquid made from sugar and water, often used in cans of fruit: *peaches in syrup* **2** any thick sweet liquid made with sugar and other ingredients, used especially as a sauce: *butterscotch syrup* ⊃ see also CORN SYRUP, COUGH SYRUP, MAPLE SYRUP

syr·up·y /'sɪrəpi; 'sər-/ *adj.* **1** thick and sticky like syrup; containing syrup **2** (*disapproving*) extremely emotional and romantic and therefore unpleasant; too SENTIMENTAL: *a syrupy romantic novel*

sys·tem ♪ /'sɪstəm/ *noun*
1 [C] an organized set of ideas or theories or a particular way of doing something: *the American educational system ◆ ~ for doing sth a new system for assessing property taxes ◆ ~ of sth a system of government* ⊃ see also BINARY, METRIC SYSTEM **2** [C] a group of things, pieces of equipment, etc. that are connected or work together: *a transportation system ◆ heating systems ◆ a stereo system ◆ a security system* ⊃ see also ECOSYSTEM, EXPERT SYSTEM, OPERATING SYSTEM, PUBLIC ADDRESS SYSTEM, SOLAR SYSTEM **3** [C] a human or an animal body, or a part of it, when it is being thought of as the organs and processes that make it function: *You have to wait until the drugs have passed out of your system. ◆ the male reproductive system* ⊃ see also CENTRAL NERVOUS SYSTEM, DIGESTIVE SYSTEM, IMMUNE SYSTEM **4** **the system** [sing.] (*informal*, usually *disapproving*) the rules or people that control a country or an organization, especially when they seem to be unfair because you cannot change them: *You can't beat the system* (= you must accept it). *◆ young people rebelling against the system*
IDM **get sth out of your system** (*informal*) to do something so that you no longer feel a very strong emotion or have a strong desire: *I was very angry with him, but I think I finally got it out of my system.*

sys·tem·at·ic /ˌsɪstəˈmætɪk/ *adj.* done according to a system or plan, in a thorough, efficient, or determined way: *a systematic approach to solving the problem* ♦ *a systematic attempt to destroy the organization* ♦ *The prisoner was subjected to systematic torture.* **ANT** UNSYSTEMATIC ▶ **sys·tem·at·i·cally** /-kli/ *adv.*: *The search was carried out systematically.*

sys·tem·a·tize /ˈsɪstəməˌtaɪz/ *verb* ~ **sth** (*formal*) to arrange something according to a system **SYN** ORGANIZE ▶ **sys·tem·a·ti·za·tion** /ˌsɪstəmətəˈzeɪʃn/ *noun* [U]

sys·tem·ic /sɪˈstɛmɪk/ *adj.* (*technical*) **1** affecting or connected with the whole of something, especially the human body **2** systemic chemicals or drugs that are used to treat diseases in plants or animals enter the body of the plant or animal and spread to all parts of it: *systemic weed killers* ▶ **sys·tem·i·cally** /-kli/ *adv.*

system operator (also **systems operator**) *noun* (*computing*) a person who manages a computer system or electronic communication service

systems analyst *noun* a person whose job is to analyze the needs of a business or an organization and then design processes for working efficiently using computer programs ▶ **systems analysis** *noun* [U]

system unit *noun* (*computing*) the main part of a computer, separate from the keyboard and monitor, that contains the unit that controls all the other parts of the system

sys·to·le /ˈsɪstəli/ *noun* (*medical*) the part of the heart's rhythm when the heart PUMPS blood ⊃ **compare** DIASTOLE ▶ **sys·tol·ic** /sɪˈstɑlɪk/ *adj.*

Tt

T also **t** /tiː/ noun (pl. **Ts, T's, t's** /tiːz/) [C, U] the 20th letter of the English alphabet: *"Tin" begins with (a) T/"T."* ⊃ see also T-BONE STEAK, T-INTERSECTION, T-SHIRT, T-SQUARE
IDM to a T/tee (*informal*) used to say that something is exactly right for someone, succeeds in doing something in exactly the right way, etc.: *Her new job suits her to a T.* ♦ *The novel captures the feeling of the prewar period to a T.* ⊃ more at DOT

T4 /ˌtiː ˈfɔːr/ (also **T4 slip**) noun (*CanE*) a piece of paper your employer gives you that you attach to your INCOME TAX form that states how much money you earned and how much INCOME TAX you paid

TA /ˌtiː ˈeɪ/ abbr. TEACHING ASSISTANT

tab /tæb/ noun, verb
● **noun 1** a small piece of paper, cloth, metal, etc. that sticks out from the edge of something, and that is used to give information about it, or to hold it, fasten it, etc.: *Insert tab A into slot 1* (= for example to make a model, box, etc.). **2** = TAB STOP **3** = PULL TAB **4** a bill for goods you receive but pay for later, especially for food or drinks in a restaurant or bar; the price or cost of something: *a bar tab* ♦ *Can I put it on my tab?* ♦ *The tab for the meeting could be $3,000.* **5** (*informal*) a small solid piece of an illegal drug: *a tab of Ecstasy* **6** = TABLATURE: *guitar tabs*
IDM keep (close) tabs on sb/sth (*informal*) to watch someone or something carefully in order to know what is happening so that you can control a particular situation: *It's not always possible to keep tabs on everyone's movements.* ⊃ more at PICK
● **verb** (-bb-) **1 ~ sb (as) sth** to say that someone is suitable for a particular job or role or describe them in a particular way: *He has been tabbed by many people as a future champion.* **2 ~ sth** to use the TAB KEY when you are using a keyboard

tab·ard /ˈtæbərd/ noun a simple piece of clothing consisting of back and front sections without sleeves, and a hole for the head

Ta·bas·co™ /təˈbæskoʊ/ noun [U] a red spicy sauce made from PEPPERS

tab·bou·leh /təˈbuːli; -lə/ (also **ta·bou·li**) noun [U] an Arab dish consisting of crushed WHEAT with chopped tomatoes, onions, and HERBS

tab·by /ˈtæbi/ noun (pl. **tab·bies**) (also **'tabby cat**) a cat with brown or gray fur marked with dark lines or spots

tab·er·nac·le /ˈtæbərˌnækl/ noun **1** [C] a place of worship for some groups of Christians: *the Mormon Tabernacle Choir* **2 the tabernacle** [sing.] a small place of worship that could be moved, used by the Jews in ancient times when they were traveling in the desert

'tab key (also **tab**, *formal* **tab·u·la·tor**) noun a button on a keyboard that you use to move to a certain fixed position in a line of a document that you are typing

tab·la·ture /ˈtæblətʃər/ (also **tab**) noun [U, C] a way of representing musical notes on paper by showing the position of the fingers on a musical instrument rather than the actual notes; an example of this: *The book contains lyrics and guitar tablatures for over 100 songs.*

ta·ble ♪ /ˈteɪbl/ noun, verb
● **noun**
▷ FURNITURE **1** a piece of furniture that consists of a flat top supported by legs: *a kitchen table* ♦ *A table for two, please* (= in a restaurant). ♦ *I'd like to reserve a table* for tonight (= in a restaurant). ♦ *to set the table* (= to put the plates, knives, etc. on it for a meal) ♦ *to clear the table* (= take away the dirty plates, etc. at the end of a meal) ♦ *He questioned her next morning over the breakfast table* (= during breakfast). ♦ *a pool/billiard table*

⊃ picture at HOBBY **HELP** There are many compounds ending in **table**. You will find them at their place in the alphabet.
▷ PEOPLE **2** the people sitting at a table for a meal or to play cards, etc.: *He kept the whole table entertained with his jokes.* ⊃ see also ROUND-TABLE
▷ LIST OF FACTS/NUMBERS **3** a list of facts or numbers arranged in a special order, usually in rows and columns: *a table of contents* (= a list of the main points or information in a book, usually at the front of the book) ♦ *Table 2 shows how prices and earnings have increased over the past 20 years.* ⊃ see also MULTIPLICATION TABLE, THE PERIODIC TABLE, TURN-TABLE, WATER TABLE
IDM bring sth to the party/table to contribute something useful to a discussion, project, etc.: *What our new chairman brings to the table is real commitment and energy.* **on the table 1** (of a plan, suggestion, etc.) offered to people so that they can consider or discuss it: *Management has put several new proposals on the table.* **2** (of a plan, suggestion, etc.) not going to be discussed or considered until a future date: *We're leaving Conner's suggestion on the table until next week.* **turn the tables (on sb)** to change a situation so that you are now in a stronger position than the person who used to be in a stronger position than you ⊃ more at DRINK, WAIT
● **verb ~ sth** to leave an idea, a proposal, etc. to be discussed at a later date: *They voted to table the proposal until the following meeting.*

tab·leau /tæˈbloʊ; ˈtæbloʊ/ noun (pl. **tab·leaux** /tæˈbloʊz; ˈtæbloʊz/) **1** a work of art, especially a set of statues, showing a group of people, animals, etc. **2** a scene showing, for example, events and people from history, that is presented by a group of actors who do not move or speak: *historical tableaux of the Civil War* ♦ (*figurative*) *She stood at the door observing the peaceful domestic tableau around the fire.*

ta·ble·cloth /ˈteɪblˌklɔθ/ noun a cloth that you use for covering a table, especially when you have a meal

ta·ble d'hôte /ˌtɑbl ˈdoʊt/ adj. a **table d'hôte** meal in a restaurant costs a fixed price and there are only a limited number of dishes to choose from: *the table d'hôte menu*

'table lamp noun a small lamp that you can put on a table, etc. ⊃ picture at LIGHT

ta·ble·land /ˈteɪblˌlænd/ noun a large area of high flat land **SYN** PLATEAU

'table ˌlinen noun [U] the cloths that you use during a meal, for example TABLECLOTHS and NAPKINS

'table ˌmanners noun [pl.] the behavior that is considered correct while you are having a meal at a table with other people

ta·ble·spoon /ˈteɪblˌspun/ noun **1** a large spoon, used especially for serving food **2** (also **ta·ble·spoon·ful** /-ful/) (*abbr.* tbsp., tbs., T.) a measurement in cooking, equal to half a FLUID OUNCE or three TEASPOONS: *Add two tablespoons of water.*

tab·let ♪ /ˈtæblət/ noun
1 a flat piece of stone, CLAY, etc. that has words written on it, especially one that has been fixed to a wall in memory of an important person or event **SYN** PLAQUE **2** a small, round, solid piece of medicine that you swallow **SYN** PILL: *an aspirin tablet* ♦ *Take two tablets with water before meals.* **3** an amount of another substance in a small, round, solid piece: *water purification tablets* **4** a number of pieces of paper for writing or drawing on, that are fastened together at one edge ⊃ see also GRAPHICS TABLET

'table ˌtennis (also **'Ping-Pong™**) noun [U] a game played like TENNIS with PADDLES and a small plastic ball on a table with a net across it

ta·ble·top /ˈteɪblˌtɑp/ noun the top or the surface of a table ▸ **ta·ble·top** adj. [only before noun]: *a tabletop machine* (= that can be used on a table)

ˈtablet PˈC noun a small computer that is easy to carry, with

| t tea | ţ butter | d did | k cat | g got | tʃ chin | dʒ June | f fall |

a large touch screen and sometimes without a physical keyboard

ta·ble·ware /ˈteɪblˌwɛr/ *noun* [U] the word used in stores, etc. for items that you use for meals, such as plates, glasses, knives, and forks

ˈ**table** ˌ**wine** *noun* [U, C] a fairly cheap wine, suitable for drinking with meals

tab·loid /ˈtæblɔɪd/ *noun* a newspaper with small pages (usually half the size of those in larger papers) with short articles and a lot of pictures and stories about famous people, often thought of as less serious than other newspapers: *The story made the front page in all the tabloids.* ⊃ compare BROADSHEET ▶ **tab·loid** *adj.* [only before noun]: *tabloid journalists* ♦ *a tabloid newspaper* ♦ *the tabloid press*

ta·boo /təˈbu; tæ-/ *noun* (*pl.* **ta·boos**) ~ **(against/on sth) 1** a cultural or religious custom that does not allow people to do, use, or talk about a particular thing as people find it offensive or embarrassing: *an incest taboo* ♦ *a taboo against working on Sunday* ♦ *to break/violate a taboo* ♦ *Death is one of the great taboos in our culture.* **2** a general agreement not to do something or talk about something: *The subject is still a taboo in our family.* ▶ **ta·boo** *adj.*: *in the days when sex was a taboo subject*

ta·boo word *noun* a word that many people consider offensive or shocking, for example because it refers to sex, the body, or people's race

ta·bor /ˈteɪbər/ *noun* a musical instrument like a small drum, used in the past

ta·bou·li = TABBOULEH

ˈ**tab stop** (also **tab**) *noun* a fixed position in a line of a document that you are typing that shows where a piece of text or a column of figures, etc. will begin

tab·u·lar /ˈtæbyələr/ *adj.* [usually before noun] presented or arranged in a TABLE (= in rows and columns): *tabular data* ♦ *The results are presented in tabular form.*

ta·bu·la ra·sa /ˌtæbyələ ˈrɑzə; -ˈrɑsə/ *noun* (*pl.* **ta·bu·lae ra·sae** /ˌtæbyəli ˈrɑzi; -ˈrɑsi/) (from *Latin, formal*) **1** a situation in which there are no fixed ideas about how something should develop **2** the human mind as it is at birth, with no ideas or thoughts in it

tab·u·late /ˈtæbyəˌleɪt/ *verb* ~ **sth** to arrange facts or figures in columns or lists so that they can be read easily ▶ **tab·u·la·tion** /ˌtæbyəˈleɪʃn/ *noun* [U, C]

tab·u·la·tor /ˈtæbyəˌleɪtər/ *noun* = TAB KEY

tach·o·graph /ˈtækəˌgræf/ *noun* a device that is used in vehicles such as large trucks and some types of buses to measure their speed, how far they have traveled, and when the driver has stopped to rest

ta·chom·e·ter /tæˈkɑmətər; tə-/ *noun* a device that measures the rate that something turns and is used to measure the speed of an engine in a vehicle

tac·it /ˈtæsət/ *adj.* [usually before noun] that is suggested indirectly or understood, rather than said in words: *tacit approval/support/knowledge* ♦ *By tacit agreement, the subject was never mentioned again.* ▶ **tac·it·ly** *adv.*

tac·i·turn /ˈtæsəˌtərn/ *adj.* tending not to say very much, in a way that seems unfriendly ▶ **tac·i·tur·ni·ty** /ˌtæsəˈtərnəti/ *noun* [U]

tack /tæk/ *noun, verb*
• *noun* **1** [C] = THUMBTACK **2** [C] a small nail with a sharp point and a flat head, used especially for attaching a carpet to the floor: *a carpet tack* ⊃ compare NAIL **3** [C, U] (*technical*) the direction that a boat with sails takes as it sails at an angle to the wind in order to fill its sails: *They were sailing on (a) port/starboard tack* (= with the wind coming from the left/ right side). **4** [U, sing.] the way in which you deal with a particular situation; the direction of your words or thoughts: *a complete change of tack* ♦ *It was a brave decision to change tack in the middle of the project.* ♦ *When threats failed, she decided to try/take a different tack.* **5** [C] a long loose STITCH used for holding pieces of cloth together tempora-

rily, before you sew them finally **6** [U] (*technical*) the equipment that you need for riding a horse, such as a SADDLE and BRIDLE **IDM** see BRASS
• *verb* **1** [T] ~ **sth + adv./prep.** to fasten something in place with a tack or tacks **SYN** NAIL: *He tacked a notice on the bulletin board.* **2** [I] (*technical*) to change the direction of a sailing boat so that the wind blows onto the sails from the opposite side; to do this several times in order to travel in the direction that the wind is coming from **3** [T] ~ **sth (+ adv./prep.)** to fasten pieces of cloth together temporarily with long loose STITCHES before sewing them finally
PHR V ˌ**tack sth**↔ˈ**on** | ˌ**tack sth** ˈ**onto sth** (*informal*) to add something to something that already exists, especially in a careless way: *The poems were tacked on at the end of the book.*

tack·le /ˈtækl/ *verb, noun*
• *verb* **1** [T] ~ **sb** to deal with someone who is violent or threatening you by grabbing them and gaining control over them: *He tackled a masked intruder at his home.* **2** [I, T] ~ **(sb)** (in football) to make an opponent fall to the ground in order to stop them from running **3** [T, I] ~ **(sb)** (in SOCCER OR HOCKEY) to try and take the ball from an opponent: *He was tackled just outside the penalty area.* **4** [T] ~ **sth** to make a determined effort to deal with a difficult problem or situation: *The administration is determined to tackle inflation.* **5** [T] ~ **sb (about sth)** to speak to someone about a problem or difficult situation **SYN** CONFRONT: *I tackled him about the money he owed me.*
• *noun* **1** [U] the equipment used to do a particular sport or activity, especially fishing ⊃ see also BLOCK AND TACKLE **2** [C] an act of knocking an opponent to the ground in football; an act of trying to take the ball from an opponent in SOCCER OR HOCKEY **3** [C] (in football) a player whose job is to stop opponents by knocking them to the ground

tack·y /ˈtæki/ *adj.* (**tack·i·er**, **tack·i·est**) **1** (*informal*) cheap, badly made, and/or lacking in taste: *tacky souvenirs* ♦ *The movie had a really tacky ending.* **2** (of paint, glue, etc.) not dry and therefore slightly sticky ▶ **tack·i·ness** *noun* [U]

ta·co /ˈtɑkoʊ/ *noun* (*pl.* **ta·cos**) (from *Spanish*) a type of Mexican food consisting of a TORTILLA (= a crisp fried PANCAKE made of CORN) that is folded over and filled with meat, BEANS, etc.

tact /tækt/ *noun* [U] the ability to deal with difficult or embarrassing situations carefully and without doing or saying anything that will annoy or upset other people **SYN** SENSITIVITY: *Settling the dispute required great tact and diplomacy.* ♦ *She is not exactly known for her tact.*

tact·ful /ˈtæktfl/ *adj.* careful not to say or do anything that will annoy or upset other people **SYN** DIPLOMATIC: *That wasn't a very tactful thing to say!* ♦ *I tried to find a tactful way of telling her the truth.* **ANT** TACTLESS ▶ **tact·ful·ly** /-fəli/ *adv.*: *a tactfully worded reply* ♦ *I tactfully suggested that he should see a doctor.*

tac·tic /ˈtæktɪk/ *noun* **1** [C, usually pl.] the particular method you use to achieve something: *They tried all kinds of tactics to get us to go.* ♦ *This was just the latest in a series of delaying tactics.* ♦ *The manager discussed tactics with his team.* ♦ *Confrontation is not always the best tactic.* ♦ *It's time to change tactics.* **2 tactics** [pl.] the art of moving soldiers and military equipment around during a battle or war in order to use them in the most effective way ⊃ compare STRATEGY

tac·ti·cal /ˈtæktɪkl/ *adj.* **1** [usually before noun] connected with the particular method you use to achieve something **SYN** STRATEGIC: *tactical planning* ♦ *to have a tactical advantage* ♦ *Telling your boss you were looking for a new job was a tactical error* (= it was the wrong thing to do at that time). **2** [usually before noun] carefully planned in order to achieve a particular aim **SYN** STRATEGIC: *a tactical decision* **3** [only before noun] (especially of weapons) used or having an effect over short distances or for a short time: *tactical weapons/missiles* ⊃ compare STRATEGIC **4** [only before noun] connected with military tactics: *He was given tactical command of the operation.* ▶ **tac·ti·cally** /-kli/ *adv.*: *At the* time, it was tactically the right thing to do. ◆ *The enemy was tactically superior.*

tac·ti·cian /tæk'tɪʃn/ *noun* a person who is very skilled at planning the best way to achieve something

tac·tile /'tæktl/ *adj.* [usually before noun] connected with the sense of touch; using your sense of touch: *tactile stimuli* ◆ *visual and tactile communication* ◆ *tactile fabric* (= pleasant to touch) ◆ *tactile maps* (= that you can touch and feel) ◆ *He's a very tactile man* (= he enjoys touching people).

tact·less /'tæktləs/ *adj.* saying or doing things that are likely to annoy or to upset other people **SYN** INSENSITIVE: *a tactless remark* ◆ *It was tactless of you to comment on his hair!* **ANT** TACTFUL ▶ **tact·less·ly** *adv.* **tact·less·ness** *noun* [U]

tad /tæd/ *noun* **a tad** [sing.] (*informal*) a very small amount: *Could you turn the sound down just a tad?* ▶ **a tad** *adv.*: *It's a tad too expensive for me.*

tad·pole /'tædpoʊl/ (also **pol·li·wog** /pɒl·li·wog/ *noun* a small creature with a large head and a small tail, that lives in water and is the young form of a FROG or TOAD ➔ **picture at** ANIMAL

tae kwon do /ˌtaɪ ˌkwɑn 'doʊ/ *noun* [U] a Korean system of fighting without weapons, similar to KARATE

taf·fe·ta /'tæfətə/ *noun* [U] a type of stiff shiny cloth made from silk or a similar material, used especially for making dresses

taf·fy /'tæfi/ *noun* (*pl.* **taf·fies**) [U, C] a type of soft candy made of brown sugar boiled until it is very thick and given different shapes and colors

tag /tæg/ *noun, verb*
● *noun* **1** [C] (often in compounds) a small piece of paper, cloth, plastic, etc. attached to something to identify it or give information about it: *He put name tags on all his shirts.* ◆ *a gift tag* (= tied to a present) ◆ *The police use electronic tags to monitor the whereabouts of some offenders.* ➔ **see also** PRICE TAG ➔ **thesaurus box at** LABEL **2** [C, usually sing.] a name or phrase that is used to describe a person or thing in some way: *They are finally ready to drop the tag "the new Beatles."* ◆ *The "slim" tag stuck with him for years, even after he had grown much heavier.* **3** [C] (*linguistics*) a word or phrase that is added to a sentence for emphasis, for example *I do* in *Yes, I do* ➔ **see also** QUESTION TAG **4** [C] (*computing*) a set of letters or symbols that are put before and after a piece of text or data in order to identify it or show that it is to be treated in a particular way **5** [C] a short QUOTATION or saying in a foreign language: *the Latin tag "Si vis pacem, para bellum."* (= if you want peace, prepare for war) **6** [U] a children's game in which one child chases the others and tries to touch one of them ➔ **see also** PHONE TAG **7** **tags** [pl.] (*informal*) LICENSE PLATES on a vehicle: *Someone stole my tags!* **8** [C] a symbol or name used by a GRAFFITI writer and painted in a public place
● *verb* (-gg-) **1** ~ sth/sb to fasten a tag onto something or someone: *Each animal was tagged with a number for identification.* **2** ~ sb/sth as sth to give someone or something a name that describes what they are or do **SYN** LABEL: *The country no longer wanted to be tagged as a Third World nation.* **3** ~ sth (*computing*) to add a set of letters or symbols to a piece of text or data in order to identify it or show that it is to be treated in a particular way
PHR V **tag a·long (behind/with sb)** to go somewhere with someone, especially when you have not been asked or invited ,tag sth↔'on | ,tag sth 'onto sth to add something to the end of something that already exists, especially in a careless way: *An apology was tagged onto the end of the letter.*

Ta·ga·log /tə'gɑlɑg; -lɔg/ *noun* [U] the national language spoken in the Philippines

ta·gine /tə'ʒin/ *noun* **1** [C, U] a hot dish made with meat and vegetables, cooked with liquid and spices in a closed container **2** [C] a container made of CLAY, with a pointed lid, for cooking and serving tagine, originally used in North Africa

ta·gli·a·tel·le /ˌtɑlyə'tɛli/ *noun* [U] (from *Italian*) PASTA in the shape of long, flat strips

'tag line *noun* (*informal*) **1** = PUNCHLINE **2** a phrase used in an advertisement that is the most important and easy to remember **SYN** SLOGAN

'tag ˌquestion *noun* (*grammar*) = QUESTION TAG

'tag sale *noun* a sale of used things, held at someone's house ➔ **see also** GARAGE SALE, RUMMAGE SALE, YARD SALE

'tag team *noun* **1** a team of two WRESTLERS who take turns to fight in the same match **2** (*informal*) two people working or performing together: *The show used a tag team of interviewers.*

ta·hi·ni /tə'hini/ (also **ta·hi·na** /tə'hinə/) *noun* [U] a thick mixture made with crushed SESAME SEEDS, eaten in the Middle East

t'ai chi ch'uan /ˌtaɪ tʃi 'tʃwɑn; -dʒi-/ (also **t'ai ˈchi**) *noun* [U] (from *Chinese*) a Chinese system of exercises consisting of sets of very slow controlled movements

tai·ga /'taɪgə/ *noun* [sing., U] forest that grows in wet ground in far northern regions of the earth: *the Siberian taiga*

tail 🔑 /teɪl/ *noun, verb*
● *noun*
▷ OF BIRD/ANIMAL/FISH **1** [C] the part that sticks out and can be moved at the back of the body of a bird, an animal, or a fish: *The dog ran up, wagging its tail.* ◆ *The male has beautiful tail feathers.* ➔ **picture at** ANIMAL, HORSE ➔ **see also** PONYTAIL
▷ -TAILED **2** (in adjectives) having the type of tail mentioned: *a white-tailed eagle*
▷ OF PLANE/SPACECRAFT **3** [C] the back part of a plane, SPACECRAFT, etc.: *the tail wing* ➔ **picture at** PLANE
▷ BACK/END OF SOMETHING **4** [C] ~ (of sth) a part of something that sticks out at the back like a tail: *the tail of a kite* **5** [C] ~ (of sth) the last part of something that is moving away from you: *the tail of the procession* ➔ **see also** TAIL END
▷ JACKET **6** **tails** [pl.] = TAILCOAT: *He was wearing a top hat and tails.* ➔ **see also** COATTAILS, SHIRTTAIL
▷ SIDE OF COIN **7** **tails** [U] the side of a coin that does not have a picture of the head of a person on it, used as one choice when a coin is TOSSED to decide something ➔ **compare** HEADS at HEAD *n.* (6)
▷ PERSON WHO FOLLOWS SOMEONE **8** [C] (*informal*) a person who is sent to follow someone secretly and find out information about where that person goes, what they do, etc.: *The police have put a tail on him.*
▶ **tail·less** /'teɪlləs/ *adj.*: *Manx cats are tailless.*
IDM **on sb's tail** (*informal*) following behind someone very closely, especially in a car **the tail (is) wagging the dog** used to describe a situation in which the most important aspect is being influenced and controlled by someone or something that is not as important **turn tail** to run away from a fight or dangerous situation **with your tail between your legs** (*informal*) feeling ashamed or unhappy because you have been defeated or punished ➔ **more at** BRIGHT-EYED, CHASE, HEAD, NOSE
● *verb* ~ sb to follow someone closely, especially in order to watch where they go and what they do **SYN** SHADOW: *A private detective had been tailing them for several weeks.*
PHR V **tail 'off** to become smaller or weaker: *The number of tourists tails off in October.*

tail·back /'teɪlbæk/ *noun* [C, U] = HALFBACK

tail·bone /'teɪlboʊn/ *noun* the small bone at the bottom of the SPINE **SYN** COCCYX ➔ **picture at** BODY

tail·coat /'teɪlkoʊt/ (also **tails**) *noun* a long jacket divided at the back below the waist into two pieces that become narrower at the bottom, worn by men at formal events ➔ **compare** MORNING COAT, DINNER JACKET

,tail 'end *noun* [sing.] the very last part of something: *the tail end of the line*

tail·gate /'teɪlgeɪt/ *noun, verb*
• *noun* **1** a door at the back of a truck that opens downward and that you can open or remove when you are loading or unloading the vehicle **2** the door that opens upward at the back of a car that has three or five doors (called a HATCH-BACK)
• *verb* **1** [I, T] ~ **(sb/sth)** (*informal*) to drive too closely behind another vehicle **2** [I] to eat food and drinks outdoors, served from the tailgate of a car

tailgate party *noun* a party that a group of sports fans has before a sports event, usually a football game, in which food and alcohol are brought to the PARKING LOT of the place where the game will be played, and eaten and drunk there

tail·light /'teɪllaɪt/ *noun* a red light at the back of a car, bicycle, or train ➔ picture at CAR

tai·lor /'teɪlər/ *noun, verb*
• *noun* a person whose job is to make men's clothes, especially someone who makes suits, etc. for individual customers
• *verb* to make or adapt something for a particular purpose, a particular person, etc.: ~ **sth to/for sb/sth** *Special programs of study are tailored to the needs of specific groups.* ◆ ~ **sth to do sth** *Most travel agents are prepared to tailor travel arrangements to meet individual requirements.*

tai·lored /'teɪlərd/ *adj.* **1** (of clothes) made to fit well or closely: *a tailored jacket* **2** made for a particular person or purpose **SYN** TAILOR-MADE

tai·lor·ing /'teɪlərɪŋ/ *noun* [U] **1** the style or the way in which a suit, jacket, etc. is made: *Appropriate tailoring can flatter your figure.* **2** the job of making men's clothes

tailor-'made *adj.* **1** ~ **(for sb/sth)** | ~ **(to sth/to do sth)** made for a particular person or purpose, and therefore very suitable: *a tailor-made course of study* ◆ *a trip that's tailor-made just for you* ◆ *That job is tailor-made for her* (= perfectly suited for her). **2** (of clothes) made by a TAILOR for a particular person **SYN** BESPOKE: *a tailor-made suit*

tail·piece /'teɪlpis/ *noun* **1** ~ **(to sth)** a part that you add to the end of a piece of writing to make it longer or complete **2** (*music*) a piece of wood that the lower ends of the strings of some musical instruments are attached to

tail·pipe /'teɪlpaɪp/ *noun* = EXHAUST ➔ picture at CAR

tail·spin /'teɪlspɪn/ *noun* [sing.] **1** a situation in which a pilot loses control of an aircraft and it spins as it falls quickly toward the ground, with the back making larger circles than the front **2** a situation that suddenly becomes much worse and is not under control: *Following the announcement, share prices went into a tailspin.*

tail·wind /'teɪlwɪnd/ *noun* a wind that blows from behind a moving vehicle, a runner, etc. ➔ compare HEADWIND

taint /teɪnt/ *verb, noun*
• *verb* [often passive] ~ **sth (with sth)** (*formal*) to damage or spoil the quality of something or the opinion that people have of someone or something: *The administration was tainted with scandal.* ▶ **taint·ed** *adj.*: *tainted drinking water*
• *noun* [usually sing.] the effect of something bad or unpleasant that spoils the quality of someone or something: *to be free from the taint of corruption*

tai·pan /'taɪpæn/ *noun* (from *Chinese*) **1** a foreign person who is in charge of a business in China **2** an extremely poisonous Australian snake

take 🔑 /teɪk/ *verb, noun*
• *verb* (took /tʊk/, tak·en /'teɪkən/)
▷ CARRY/LEAD **1** [T] to carry or move something from one place to another: ~ **sth (with you)** *I forgot to take my bag with me when I got off the bus.* ◆ ~ **sth to sb/sth** *Take this to the bank for me, would you?* ◆ *Should I take a gift to my host family?* ◆ ~ **sb sth** *Should I take my host family a gift?* **2** [T] to go with someone from one place to another, especially to guide or lead them: ~ **sb** *It's too far to walk—I'll take you by car.* ◆ ~ **sb**

to sth *A boy took us to our room.* ◆ ~ **sb doing sth** *I'm taking the kids swimming later.* ◆ ~ **sb to do sth** *She took the boys to see their grandparents most weekends.* **3** [T] ~ **sb/sth + adv./prep.** to make someone or something go from one level, situation, etc. to another: *Her energy and talent took her to the top of her profession.* ◆ *The new loan takes the total debt to $100,000.* ◆ *I'd like to take my argument a stage further.* ◆ *He believes he has the skills to take the team forward.* ◆ *We'll take this matter up again at our next meeting* (= discuss it further).
▷ REACH AND HOLD **4** [T] ~ **sb/sth** to put your hands or arms around someone or something and hold them/it; to reach for someone or something and hold them/it: *I passed him the rope and he took it.* ◆ *Free newspapers; please take one.* ◆ *Can you take* (= hold) *the baby for a minute?* ◆ *He took her hand/took her by the hand* (= held her hand, for example to lead her somewhere). ◆ *She took the child in her arms and kissed him.*
▷ REMOVE **5** [T] ~ **sth/sb + adv./prep.** to remove something or someone from a place or a position: *Will you take your books off the table?* ◆ *The sign must be taken down.* ◆ *He took some keys out of his pocket.* ◆ *My name had been taken off the list.* ◆ *She was playing with a knife, so I took it away from her.* ◆ (*figurative*) *The new gym will take the pressure off the old one.* **6** [T] ~ **sth** to remove something without permission or by mistake: *Someone took my scarf.* ◆ *Did the burglars take anything valuable?* ◆ (*figurative*) *The storms took the lives of 50 people.* **7** [T] to get something from a particular source: ~ **sth from sth** *The scientists are taking water samples from the river.* ◆ *The machine takes its name from its inventor.* ◆ ~ **sth out of sth** *Part of her article is taken straight* (= copied) *out of my book.*
▷ CAPTURE **8** [T] to capture a place or person; to get control of something: ~ **sth (from sb)** *The rebels succeeded in taking the town.* ◆ *The government has taken control of the company.* ◆ ~ **sb + noun** *The rebels took him prisoner.* ◆ *He was taken prisoner by the rebels.*
▷ CHOOSE/BUY **9** [T] ~ **sth** to choose, buy, or rent something: *I'll take the gray jacket.* ◆ *We took a room at the hotel for two nights.* **10** [T] ~ **sth** (*formal*) to buy a newspaper or magazine regularly: *We take the "Chicago Tribune."*
▷ EAT/DRINK **11** [T] ~ **sth** to eat, drink, etc. something: *Do you take sugar in your coffee?* ◆ *The doctor gave me some medicine to take for my cough.* ◆ *He started taking drugs* (= illegal drugs) *in college.*
▷ MATHEMATICS **12** [T] ~ **A (away) from B** | ~ **A away** (not used in the progressive tenses) to reduce one number by the value of another **SYN** SUBTRACT: *Take 5 from 12 and you're left with 7.* ◆ (*informal*) *80 take away 5 is 75*.
▷ WRITE DOWN **13** [T] ~ **sth** to find out and record something; to write something down: *The police officer took my name and address.* ◆ *Did you take notes in the class?*
▷ PHOTOGRAPH **14** [T] ~ **sth** to photograph someone or something: *to take a photograph/picture/snapshot of someone or something* ◆ *to have your picture/photo taken*
▷ MEASUREMENT **15** [T] ~ **sth** to test or measure something: *to take someone's temperature* ◆ *I need to have my blood pressure taken.*
▷ SEAT **16** [T] ~ **sth** to sit down in or use a chair, etc.: *Are these seats taken?* ◆ *Come in; take a seat.* ➔ note at SIT
▷ GIVE EXAMPLE **17** [T] ~ **sb/sth** used to introduce someone or something as an example: *Lots of couples have problems in the first year of marriage. Take Ann and Paul.*
▷ ACCEPT/RECEIVE **18** [T] (not usually used in the progressive tenses or in the passive) ~ **sth** to accept or receive something: *If they offer me the job, I'll take it.* ◆ *She was accused of taking bribes.* ◆ *Does the hotel take credit cards?* ◆ *I'll take the call in my office.* ◆ *Why should I take the blame for somebody else's mistakes?* ◆ *If you take my advice you won't have anything more to do with him.* ◆ *Will you take $10 for the book* (= will you sell it for $10)? ◆ *The store took in* (= sold goods worth) *$100,000 last week.* **19** [T] (not usually used in the progressive tenses) ~ **sb** to accept someone as a customer, patient, etc.: *The school doesn't take boys* (= only has girls). ◆ *The dentist can't take any new patients.* **20** [T] (not usually used in the progressive tenses) ~ **sth** to experience or be affected by something: *The school took the full force of the*

explosion. ◆ *Can the ropes take the strain* (= not break)? ◆ *The team took a terrible beating.* **21** [T, no passive] **~ sth** (not usually used in the progressive tenses) to be able to bear something: *She can't take criticism.* ◆ *I don't think I can take much more of this heat.* ◆ *I find his attitude a little hard to take.* **22** [T] **~ sth/sb + adv./prep.** to react to something or someone in a particular way: *He took the criticism surprisingly well.* ◆ *These threats are not to be taken lightly.* ◆ *I wish you'd take me seriously.* ◆ *She took it in the spirit in which it was intended.*

▷ **CONSIDER 23** [T] (not used in the progressive tenses) to understand or consider something in a particular way: **~ sth (as sth)** *She took what he said as a compliment.* ◆ *How am I supposed to take that remark?* ◆ *Taken overall, the project was a success.* ◆ **~ sth to do sth** *What did you take his comments to mean?* **24** [T] (not used in the progressive tenses) to consider someone or something to be someone or something, especially when you are wrong: **~ sb/sth for sb/sth** *Even the experts took the painting for a genuine Van Gogh.* ◆ *Of course I didn't do it! What do you take me for* (= what sort of person do you think I am)? ◆ **~ sb/sth to be sb/sth** *I took the man with him to be his father.*

▷ **HAVE FEELING/OPINION 25** [T] (not usually used in the progressive tenses) **~ sth** to have a particular feeling, opinion, or attitude: *My parents always took an interest in my hobbies.* ◆ *Don't take offense* (= be offended) *at what I said.* ◆ *I took a dislike to him.* ◆ *He takes the view that children are responsible for their own actions.*

▷ **ACTION 26** [T] **~ sth** to use a particular course of action in order to deal with or achieve something: *The school system is taking action to combat drug abuse.* ◆ *We need to take a different approach to the problem.* **27** [T] **~ sth** used with nouns to say that someone is doing something, performing an action, etc.: *to take a step/walk/stroll* ◆ *to take a bath/shower* ◆ *to take a dip/swim* ◆ *to take a look/glance* ◆ *to take a bite/drink/sip* ◆ *to take a deep breath* ◆ *to take a break/rest*

▷ **FORM/POSITION 28** [T] **~ sth** to have a particular form, position, or state: *Our next class will take the form of a debate.* ◆ *The new president takes office in January.*

▷ **TIME 29** [T, no passive, I] to need or require a particular amount of time: **~ sth** *The ride to the airport takes about half an hour.* ◆ **~ sth to do sth** *It takes about half an hour to get to the airport.* ◆ *That cut is taking a long time to heal.* ◆ **~ sb (to do sth)** *It took her three hours to repair her bike.* ◆ *It'll take her some time to recover from the illness.* ◆ **~ sth for sb to do sth** *It'll take time* (= take a long time) *for her to recover from the illness.* ◆ **+ adv.** *I need a shower—I won't take long.* ➋ note at LAST¹

▷ **NEED 30** [T, no passive] to need or require something in order to happen or be done: **~ sb/sth to do sth** *It only takes one careless driver to cause an accident.* ◆ *It doesn't take much to make her angry.* ◆ **~ sth** (informal) *He didn't take much persuading* (= he was easily persuaded). **31** [T, no passive] (not used in the progressive tenses) **~ sth** (of machines, etc.) to use something in order to work: *All new cars take unleaded gas.*

▷ **SIZE OF SHOES/CLOTHES 32** [T, no passive] (not used in the progressive tenses) **~ sth** to wear a particular size in shoes or clothes: *What size shoe do you take?*

▷ **HOLD/CONTAIN 33** [T, no passive] (not used in the progressive tenses) **~ sth/sb** to have enough space for something or someone; to be able to hold or contain a particular quantity: *The bus can take 60 passengers.* ◆ *The tank takes 20 gallons.*

▷ **TEACH/LEAD 34** [T] **~ sb (for sth)** | **~ sth** to be the teacher or leader in a class or a religious service: *Mrs. Cameron will take the class if her colleague has to be away.*

▷ **STUDY 35** [T] **~ sth** to study a subject at school, college, etc.: *She is planning to take a computer course.* ◆ *How many subjects are you taking this year?*

▷ **EXAM 36** [T] **~ sth** to complete an exam or a test: *When did you take your driving test?*

▷ **TRANSPORTATION/ROAD 37** [T] **~ sth** to use a form of transportation, a road, a path, etc. to go to a place: *to take the bus/plane/train* ◆ *to take a cab* ◆ *Take the second road on the right.* ◆ *It's more interesting to take the coast road.*

▷ **GO OVER/AROUND 38** [T] **~ sth (+ adv./prep.)** to go over or around something: *The horse took the first fence well.* ◆ *He takes dangerous curves much too fast.*

▷ **IN SPORTS 39** [T] **~ sth** (of a player in a sports game) to kick or throw the ball from a fixed or agreed position: *to take a penalty/free kick/foul shot*

▷ **VOTE/SURVEY 40** [T] **~ sth** to use a particular method to find out people's opinions: *to take a vote/poll/survey*

▷ **BE SUCCESSFUL 41** [I] to be successful; to work: *The skin graft failed to take.*

▷ **GRAMMAR 42** [T] (not used in the progressive tenses) **~ sth** (of verbs, nouns, etc.) to have or require something when used in a sentence or other structure: *The verb "rely" takes the preposition "on."*

IDM Most idioms containing **take** are at the entries for the nouns and adjectives in the idioms. For example, **take a rain check (on sth)** is at **rain check**. **I, you, etc. can't take sb anywhere** (informal, often humorous) used to say that you cannot trust someone to behave well in public **have (got) what it takes** (informal) to have the qualities, ability, etc. needed to be successful **take sth as it comes** | **take sb as they come** to accept something or someone without wishing it/them to be different or without thinking about it/them very much in advance: *She takes life as it comes.* **take it (that…)** to suppose; to assume: *I take it you won't be coming to the party?* **take it from me (that…)** (informal) used to emphasize that what you are going to say is the truth: *Take it from me—he'll be a millionaire before he's 30.* **take it on/upon yourself to do sth** to decide to do something without asking permission or advice **sb can take it or leave it 1** used to say that you do not care if someone accepts or rejects your offer **2** used to say that someone does not have a strong opinion about something: *Dancing? I can take it or leave it.* **take a lot out of sb** to make someone physically or mentally tired: *Taking care of small children takes a lot out of you.* **take some/a lot of doing** (informal) to need a lot of effort or time; to be very difficult to do **take that!** (informal) used as an exclamation when you are hitting someone or attacking them in some other way

PHR V **take sb a'back** [usually passive] to shock or surprise someone very much ➋ thesaurus box at SURPRISE
,**take 'after sb** [no passive] **1** (not used in the progressive tenses) to look or behave like an older member of your family, especially your mother or father: *Your daughter doesn't take after you at all.* **2** (informal) to follow someone quickly: *I was afraid that if I started running the man would take after me.*
,**take sb/sth↔a'part** (informal) **1** to criticize someone or something severely **2** to defeat someone easily in a game or competition ,**take sth↔a'part** to separate a machine or piece of equipment into the different parts that it is made of **SYN** DISMANTLE
,**take sth↔a'way** to make a feeling, pain, etc. disappear: *They gave me some pills to take away the pain.* ,**take a'way from sth** [no passive] to make the effort or value of something seem less **SYN** DETRACT FROM: *I don't want to take away from his achievements, but he couldn't have done it without my help.*
,**take sb↔'back** to allow someone, such as your husband, wife, or partner, to come home after they have left because of a problem ,**take sb 'back (to…)** to make someone remember something: *The smell of the sea took him back to his childhood.* ,**take sth↔'back 1** if you **take** something **back** to a store, or a store **takes** something **back**, you return something that you have bought there, for example because it is the wrong size or does not work **2** to admit that something you said was wrong or that you should not have said it: *OK, I take it all back!*
,**take sth↔'down 1** to remove a structure, especially by separating it into pieces: *to take down a tent* **2** to pull down a piece of clothing worn below the waist without completely removing it: *to take down your pants* **3** to write something down: *Reporters took down every word of his speech.*
,**take sb↔'in 1** to allow someone to stay in your home: *to take in roommates* ◆ *He was homeless, so we took him in.* **2** [often passive] to make someone believe something that

is not true **SYN** DECEIVE: *Don't be taken in by his charm—he's ruthless.* ,take sth↔'in **1** to absorb something into the body, for example by breathing or swallowing: *Fish take in oxygen through their gills.* ⊃ related noun INTAKE **2** to make a piece of clothing narrower or tighter **ANT** LET OUT **3** [no passive] to include or cover something: *The tour takes in six European capitals.* **4** [no passive] to go to see or visit something such as a movie: *I generally take in a show when I'm in New York.* **5** to take notice of something with your eyes: *He took in every detail of her appearance.* **6** to understand or remember something that you hear or read: *Halfway through the chapter I realized I hadn't taken anything in.*

,take 'off **1** (of an aircraft, etc.) to leave the ground and begin to fly: *The plane took off an hour late.* ⊃ related noun TAKEOFF **ANT** LAND **2** (*informal*) to leave a place, especially in a hurry: *When he saw me coming he took off in the opposite direction.* **3** (of an idea, a product, etc.) to become successful or popular very quickly or suddenly: *The new magazine has really taken off.* ,take sb↔'off **1** to copy someone's voice, actions, or manner in an amusing way **SYN** IMPERSONATE **2** (in sports, entertainment, etc.) to make someone stop playing, acting, etc. and leave the field or the stage: *He was taken off after twenty minutes.* ,take sth↔'off **1** to remove something, especially a piece of clothing from your/someone's body: *to take off your coat* ◆ *He took off my wet boots and made me sit by the fire.* **ANT** PUT ON **2** to have a period of time as a break from work: *I've decided to take a few days off next week.* **3** [often passive] to stop a public service, television program, performances of a show, etc.: *The show was taken off because of poor ratings.* **4** to remove some of someone's hair, part of someone's body, etc.: *The hairdresser asked me how much she should take off.* ◆ *The explosion nearly took his arm off.* ,take yourself/sb 'off (to…) (*informal*) to leave a place; to make someone leave a place ,take sb 'off sth [often passive] to remove someone from something such as a job, position, piece of equipment, etc.: *The officer leading the investigation has been taken off the case.* ◆ *After three days she was taken off the ventilator.* ,take sth 'off sth **1** to remove an amount of money or a number of marks, points, etc. in order to reduce the total: *The manager took $10 off the bill.* ◆ *That experience took ten years off my life* (= made me feel ten years older). **2** [often passive] to stop something from being sold: *The diet pills were taken off the market.*

,take sb↔'on **1** to employ someone: *to take on new staff* ◆ *They took her on as a trainee.* **2** [no passive] to play against someone in a game or contest; to fight against someone: *to take someone on at tennis* ◆ *The rebels took on the entire Roman army.* ,take sth↔'on [no passive] to begin to have a particular quality, appearance, etc.: *The chameleon can take on the colors of its background.* ◆ *His voice took on a more serious tone.* ,take sth/sb↔'on **1** to decide to do something; to agree to be responsible for something or someone: *I can't take on any extra work.* ◆ *We're not taking on any new clients at present.* **2** (of a bus, plane, or ship) to allow someone or something to enter: *The bus stopped to take on more passengers.* ◆ *The ship took on more fuel at Freetown.*

,take sb↔'out to go to a restaurant, theater, club, etc. with someone you have invited ,take sb/sth↔'out (*informal*) to kill someone or destroy something: *They took out two enemy bombers.* ,take sth↔'out **1** to remove something from inside someone's body, especially a part of it: *How many teeth did the dentist take out?* **2** to obtain an official document or service: *to take out an insurance policy/a mortgage/a loan* ◆ *to take out an ad in a newspaper* **3** to buy cooked food at a restaurant and carry it away to eat, for example at home: *Would you like to eat your sandwich here or take it out?* ⊃ related noun TAKEOUT ,take sth↔'out (against sb) to start legal action against someone by means of an official document: *She took out a restraining order against her former boyfriend.* ,take sth↔'out (of sth) to obtain money by removing it from your bank account ,take sth 'out of sth to remove an amount of money from a larger amount, especially as a payment: *The fine will be*

taken out of your wages. ,take it/sth 'out on sb to behave in an unpleasant way toward someone because you feel angry, disappointed, etc., although it is not their fault: *OK, so you had a bad day. Don't take it out on me.* ◆ *She tended to take her frustrations out on her family.* ,take sb 'out of himself/ herself to make someone forget their worries and become less concerned with their own thoughts and situation

,take 'over (from sth) to become bigger or more important than something else; to replace sth: *Try not to let negative thoughts take over.* ◆ *It has been suggested that mammals took over from dinosaurs 65 million years ago.* ,take 'over (from sb) | ,take sth↔'over (from sb) **1** to begin to have control of or responsibility for something, especially in place of someone else **2** to gain control of a political party, a country, etc.: *The army is threatening to take over if civil unrest continues.* ,take sth↔'over to gain control of a business, a company, etc., especially by buying shares: *CBS Records was taken over by Sony.* ⊃ related noun TAKEOVER ,take sb 'through sth to help someone learn or become familiar with something, for example by talking about each part in turn: *The director took us through the play scene by scene.*

'take to sth [no passive] **1** to go away to a place, especially to escape from danger: *The rebels took to the hills.* **2** to begin to do something as a habit: *~ doing sth I've taken to waking up very early.* **3** to develop an ability for something: *She took to tennis as if she'd been playing all her life.* 'take to sb/sth [no passive] to start liking someone or something: *I took to my new boss immediately.* ◆ *He hasn't taken to his new school.*

,take 'up to continue, especially starting after someone or something else has finished: *The band's new album takes up where their last one left off.* ,take 'up sth to fill or use an amount of space or time: *The table takes up too much room.* ◆ *I won't take up any more of your time.* ,take sth↔'up **1** to make something such as a piece of clothing shorter: *I need to take this skirt up a couple of inches.* **ANT** LET DOWN **2** to learn or start to do something, especially for pleasure: *They took up golf when they moved to Florida.* ◆ *She has taken up the oboe* (= started to learn to play). **3** to start or begin something such as a job: *He takes up his duties next week.* **4** to join in singing or saying something: *to take up the chorus* ◆ *Their protests were later taken up by other groups.* **5** to continue something that someone else has not finished, or that has not been mentioned for some time: *She took up the story where Tim had left off.* ◆ *I'd like to take up the point you raised earlier.* **6** to move into a particular position: *I took up my position by the door.* **7** to accept something that is offered or available: *to take up a challenge* ◆ *She took up his offer of a drink.* ,take 'up with sb (*informal*) to begin to be friendly with someone, especially someone with a bad reputation ,take sb 'up on sth (*informal*) to accept an offer, a bet, etc. from someone: *Thanks for the invitation—we'll take you up on it some time.* ,take sth 'up with sb to speak or write to someone about something that they may be able to deal with or help you with: *They decided to take the matter up with their state representative.* be ,taken 'up with sth/sb to be giving all your time and energy to something or someone be 'taken with sb/sth to find someone or something attractive or interesting: *We were all very taken with his girlfriend.* ◆ *I think he's quite taken with the idea.*

● *noun* **1** a scene or part of a movie that is filmed at one time without stopping the camera: *We managed to get it right in just two takes.* **2** [usually sing.] (*informal*) an amount of money that someone receives, especially the money that is earned by a business during a particular period of time **SYN** TAKINGS: *How much is my share of the take?* **3** ~ on sth (*informal*) the particular opinion or idea that someone has about something: *What's his take on the plan?* ◆ *a new take on the Romeo and Juliet story* (= a way of presenting it) ⊃ see also DOUBLE TAKE

IDM be on the take (*informal*) to accept money from someone for helping them in a dishonest or illegal way

take

lead ◆ escort ◆ drive ◆ show ◆ walk ◆ guide ◆ usher ◆ direct

These words all mean to go with someone from one place to another.

take to go with someone from one place to another, for example in order to show them something or to show them the way to a place: *I'll take you to the party tomorrow.*

lead to go with or go in front of someone in order to show them the way or to make them go in the right direction: *Firefighters led the survivors to safety.*

escort to go with someone in order to protect or guard them or to show them the way: *The president was escorted by twelve bodyguards.*

drive to take someone somewhere in a car, taxi, etc: *My mother drove us to the airport.*

show to take someone to a particular place, in the right direction, or along the correct route: *The attendant showed us to our seats.*

walk to go somewhere with someone on foot, especially in order to make sure that they get there safely; to take an animal, especially a dog, for a walk or make an animal walk somewhere: *He always walked her home.* ◆ *Have you walked the dog yet today?*

guide to show someone the way to a place, often by going with them; to show someone a place that you know well: *She guided us through the busy streets.* ◆ *We were guided around the museums.*

usher (*somewhat formal*) to politely take or show someone where you want them to be, especially within a building: *She ushered her guests to their seats.*

direct (*somewhat formal*) to tell or show someone how to get somewhere or where to go: *A young woman directed them to the station.*

PATTERNS

- to take/lead/escort/drive/show/walk/guide/usher/direct sb **to/out of/into** sth
- to take/lead/escort/drive/show/walk/guide/usher sb **around**
- to take/lead/escort/drive/walk sb **home**
- to take/lead/escort/guide/usher sb **to safety**
- to lead/show **the way**

take·down /ˈteɪkdaʊn/ *noun* a move in which a WRESTLER quickly gets his/her opponent down to the floor from a standing position

take-home ˌpay *noun* [U] the amount of money that you earn after you have paid taxes, etc.

take·off /ˈteɪkɔf; -ɑf/ *noun* **1** [U, C] the moment at which an aircraft leaves the ground and starts to fly: *The plane is ready for takeoff.* ◆ *takeoff speed* ◆ (*figurative*) *The local economy is poised for takeoff.* **ANT** LANDING **2** [C, U] the moment at which your feet leave the ground when you jump **3** [C] if you do a **takeoff** of someone, you copy the way they speak or behave, in a humorous way to entertain people

take·out /ˈteɪkaʊt/ *noun* **1** (also **ˈcarry- out**) [U] food that is cooked and sold by a store or restaurant that you take away and eat somewhere else: *I don't want to cook tonight, let's just get some takeout.* **2** [C] a restaurant that sells food that is cooked and that you take away and eat somewhere else ▶ **take·out** *adj.*: *a takeout restaurant* ◆ *a takeout dinner*

take·o·ver /ˈteɪkˌoʊvər/ *noun* [C, U] **1** an act of taking control of a company by buying most of its shares: *a takeover bid for the company* ➔ collocations at BUSINESS **2** an act of taking control of a country, an area, or a political organization by force

tak·er /ˈteɪkər/ *noun* **1** [usually pl.] a person who is willing to accept something that is being offered: *They won't find many takers for the house at that price.* **2** (often in compounds) a person who takes something: *drug takers* ◆ *It is better to be a giver than a taker.*

tal·cum pow·der /ˈtælkəm ˌpaʊdər/ (also *informal* **talc** /tælk/) *noun* [U] a fine soft powder, usually with a pleasant smell, that you put on your skin to make it feel smooth and dry

tale 🔑 /teɪl/ *noun*

1 a story created using the imagination, especially one that is full of action and adventure: *Dickens' "A Tale of Two Cities"* ◆ *a fairy/moral/romantic, etc. tale* ➔ see also FOLK TALE, TALL TALE **2** an exciting spoken description of an event, which may not be completely true: *I love listening to his tales of life at sea.* ◆ *I've heard tales of people seeing ghosts in that house.* ◆ *The team's tale of woe continued on Saturday* (= they lost another game). ◆ *Her experiences provide a cautionary tale* (= a warning) *for us all.* ➔ see also TATTLETALE **IDM** see OLD, TELL

tal·ent 🔑 /ˈtælənt/ *noun*

1 [C, U] a natural ability to do something well: *to have great artistic talent* ◆ *a man of many talents* ◆ **~ (for sth/for doing sth)** *She showed considerable talent for getting what she wanted.* ◆ *a talent competition/contest/show* (= in which people perform, to show how well they can sing, dance, etc.) **2** [U, C] people or a person with a natural ability to do something well: *There is a wealth of talent in regional theaters around the country.* ◆ *He is a great talent.*

tal·ent·ed /ˈtæləntəd/ *adj.* having a natural ability to do something well: *a talented player*

ˈtalent ˌscout (also **scout**) *noun* a person whose job is to find people who are good at singing, acting, sport, etc. in order to give them work

tal·is·man /ˈtælɪsmən; ˈtæləz-/ *noun* an object that is thought to have magic powers and to bring good luck

talk 🔑 /tɔk/ *verb, noun*

● *verb*

▷ SPEAK TO SOMEONE **1** [I, T] to say things; to speak in order to give information or to express feelings, ideas, etc.: *Stop talking and listen!* ◆ *We talked on the phone for over an hour.* ◆ **~ (to/with sb) (about sb/sth)** *Who were you talking to just now?* ◆ *We looked around the school and talked with the principal.* ◆ *Ann and Joe aren't talking to each other right now* (= they refuse to speak to each other because they have argued). ◆ *When they get together, all they talk about is baseball.* ◆ *What are you talking about?* (= used when you are surprised, annoyed, and/or worried by something that someone has just said) ◆ *I don't know what you're talking about* (= used to say that you did not do something that someone has accused you of). ◆ **~ of sth** *Mary is talking of looking for another job.* ◆ **~ yourself + adj.** *We talked ourselves hoarse, catching up on all the news.*

▷ DISCUSS **2** [I, T] to discuss something, usually something serious or important: *This situation can't go on. We need to talk.* ◆ *The two sides in the dispute say they are ready to talk.* ◆ **~ (to/with sb) (about sth)** *Talk to your doctor if you're still worried.* ◆ **~ sth** *to talk business* ➔ thesaurus box at DISCUSSION

▷ SAY WORDS **3** [I, T] to say words in a language: *The baby is just starting to talk.* ◆ **~ in sth** *We couldn't understand them because they were talking in Chinese.* ◆ **~ sth** *Are they talking Swedish or Danish?*

▷ SENSE/NONSENSE **4** [T] **~ sth** to say things that are/are not sensible: *She talks a lot of sense.* ◆ *See if you can talk some sense into him* (= persuade him to be sensible).

▷ FOR EMPHASIS **5** [T] **be talking something** (*informal*) used to emphasize an amount of money, how serious something is, etc.: *We're talking $800 for three hours' work.*

▷ ABOUT PRIVATE LIFE **6** [I] to talk about a person's private life **SYN** GOSSIP: *Don't call me at work— people will talk.*

▷ GIVE INFORMATION **7** [I] to give information to someone,

| t tea | ţ butter | d did | k cat | g got | tʃ chin | dʒ June | f fall |

especially unwillingly: *The police questioned him but he refused to talk.*

IDM **look who's talking| you're a fine one to talk| you should talk** (*informal*) used to tell someone that they should not criticize someone else for something because they do the same things too: *"George is so careless with money." "Look who's talking!"* **now you're talking** (*informal*) used when you like what someone has suggested very much **talk about...** (*informal*) used to emphasize something: *Talk about mean! She didn't even buy me a card.* **talk a good game** to talk in a way that sounds convincing, but may not be sincere **talk shop** (usually *disapproving*) to talk about your work with the people you work with, especially when you are also with other people who are not connected with or interested in it **talk the talk** (*informal*, sometimes *disapproving*) to be able to talk in a confident way that makes people think you are good at what you do: *You can talk the talk, but can you walk the walk?* (= can you act in a way that matches your words?) **talk tough (on sth)** (*informal*) to tell people very strongly what you want **talk turkey** (*informal*) to talk about something seriously **talk your way out of sth/of doing sth** to make excuses and give reasons for not doing something; to manage to get yourself out of a difficult situation: *I managed to talk my way out of having to give a speech.* **you're a fine one to talk** (*informal*) = LOOK WHO'S TALKING **you should talk** (*informal*) = LOOK WHO'S TALKING ⊃ more at DEVIL, KNOW *v.*, LANGUAGE, MONEY, SENSE *n.*, TURN *n.*

PHR V **talk a'round sth** to talk about something in a general way without ever dealing with the most important parts of it **'talk at sb** to speak to someone without listening to what they say in reply **,talk 'back (to sb)** to answer someone rudely, especially someone in authority **,talk sb/sth↔'down** to help a pilot of a plane to land by giving instructions from the ground **,talk sth↔'down** to make something seem less important or successful than it really is: *You shouldn't talk down your own achievements.* **,talk 'down to sb** to speak to someone as if they were less important or intelligent than you **,talk sb 'into/'out of sth** to persuade someone to do/not to do something: *I didn't want to move abroad but Bill talked me into it.* ♦ **~ doing sth** *She tried to talk him out of leaving.* **,talk sth↔'out** to discuss something thoroughly in order to make a decision, solve a problem, etc. **,talk sth↔'over (with sb)** to discuss something thoroughly, especially in order to reach an agreement or make a decision: *You'll find it helpful to talk things over with a friend.* **,talk sb 'through sth** to explain to someone how something works so that they can do it or understand it: *Can you talk me through the various investment options?* **,talk sth ↔'through** to discuss something thoroughly until you are sure you understand it **,talk sb/sth 'up** to describe someone or something in a way that makes them sound better than they really are

● *noun*

▷ **CONVERSATION 1** [C] **~ (with sb) (about sth)** a conversation or discussion: *I had a long talk with my boss about my career prospects.* ♦ *I had to have a heart-to-heart talk with her.* ⊃ note at DISCUSSION

▷ **FORMAL DISCUSSIONS 2 talks** [pl.] formal discussions between governments or organizations: *arms/peace, etc. talks* ♦ *to hold talks* ♦ **~ (between A and B) (on/over sth)** *Talks between management and workers* **broke down** over the issue of sick pay. ♦ *A further* **round of talks** will be needed if the dispute is to be resolved.

▷ **SPEECH 3** [C] **~ (on sth)** a speech or lecture on a particular subject: *She gave a talk on her visit to China.* ⊃ thesaurus box at SPEECH

▷ **WORDS WITHOUT ACTIONS 4** [U] (*informal*) words that are spoken, but without the necessary facts or actions to support them: *It's just talk. He'd never carry out his threats.* ♦ *Don't pay any attention to her—she's* **all talk**.

▷ **STORIES/RUMORS 5** [U] **~ (of sth/of doing sth)** | **~ (that...)** stories that suggest a particular thing might happen in the future: *There was talk in Washington of sending in troops.* ♦ *She dismissed the stories of her resignation as media talk.*

▷ **TOPIC/WAY OF SPEAKING 6** [U] (often in compounds) a topic

of conversation or a way of speaking: *business talk* ♦ *She said it was just* **girl talk** *that a man wouldn't understand.* ♦ *The book teaches you how to understand Spanish* **street talk** (= slang). ♦ *It was tough talk, coming from a man who had begun the year in a hospital bed.* ⊃ see also SMALL TALK, TRASH TALK

IDM **the talk of sth** the person or thing that everyone is talking about in a particular place: *Overnight, she became* **the talk of the town** (= very famous).

talk·a·tive /ˈtɔkətɪv/ *adj.* liking to talk a lot: *He's not very talkative, is he?* ♦ *She was in a talkative mood.*

talk·back /ˈtɔkbæk/ *noun* [U] (*technical*) a system that allows people working in a recording or broadcasting studio to talk to each other without their voices being recorded or heard on the radio

talk·er /ˈtɔkər/ *noun* a person who talks a lot: *She's a big talker* (= she talks a lot). ♦ *He's more a talker than a doer* (= he talks instead of doing things). ⊃ thesaurus box at SPEAKER
IDM see FAST *adj.*

talk·ie /ˈtɔki/ *noun* [usually pl.] (*old-fashioned*) a movie that has sounds and not just pictures ⊃ see also WALKIE-TALKIE

,talking 'head *noun* (*informal*) a person on television who talks straight to the camera: *The election broadcast consisted largely of talking heads.*

'talking point *noun* an item that someone will speak about at a meeting, often one that supports a particular argument

'talking-to *noun* [sing.] (*informal*) a serious talk with someone who has done something wrong: *to give someone a good talking-to*

talk radio *noun* [U] radio programs in which someone discusses a particular subject with people who telephone the radio station to give their opinions

'talk show *noun* **1** a television or radio program in which famous people are asked questions and talk in an informal way about their work and opinions on various topics: *a talk-show host* **2** a television or radio program in which a PRESENTER introduces a particular topic that is then discussed by the audience

'talk time *noun* [U] the amount of time that a cell phone can be used for calls without needing more power or more payments

talk·y /'tɔki/ *adj.* (*informal*) **1** containing too much talking: *a dull, talky movie* **2** liking to talk a lot **SYN** TALKATIVE

tall /tɔl/ *adj.* (**tall·er, tall·est**)
1 (of a person, building, tree, etc.) having a greater than average height: *She's tall and thin.* ♦ *tall chimneys* ♦ *the tallest building in the world* ♦ *a tall glass of iced tea* **ANT** SHORT **2** used to describe or ask about the height of someone or something: *How tall are you?* ♦ *He's six feet tall and weighs 200 pounds.* ᴐ note at HIGH ▶ **tall·ness** *noun* [U]
IDM **stand tall** to show that you are proud and able to deal with anything **be a tall order** (*informal*) to be very difficult to do ᴐ more at OAK, WALK

tal·low /'tæloʊ/ *noun* [U] animal fat used for making CANDLES, soap, etc.

tall 'tale (also **tall 'story**) *noun* a story that is difficult to believe because what it describes seems exaggerated and not likely to be true

tal·ly /'tæli/ *noun, verb*
● *noun* (*pl.* **tal·lies**) a record of the number or amount of something, especially one that you can keep adding to: *He hopes to improve on his tally of three home runs in the past nine games.* ♦ *Keep a tally of how much you spend while you're away.*
● *verb* (**tal·lies, tal·ly·ing, tal·lied, tal·lied**) **1** [I] ~ (**with sth**) to be the same as or to match another person's account of something, another set of figures, etc. **SYN** MATCH UP: *Her report of what happened tallied exactly with the story of another witness.* **2** [T] ~ **sth** (**up**) to calculate the total number, cost, etc. of something

the Tal·mud /'talmʊd; 'tæl-/ *noun* [sing.] a collection of ancient writings on Jewish law and traditions ▶ **Tal·mud·ic** /tal'mʊdɪk; tæl-; -'mudɪk/ *adj.*

tal·on /'tælən/ *noun* a long, sharp, curved nail on the feet of some birds, especially BIRDS OF PREY (= birds that kill other creatures for food) ᴐ picture at ANIMAL

ta·ma·le /tə'mɑli/ *noun* a Mexican dish of meat or beans wrapped in DOUGH made from CORNMEAL, then put in corn HUSKS and steamed or baked

tam·a·rind /'tæmərɪnd/ *noun* a tropical tree that produces fruit, also called tamarinds, that are often preserved and used in Asian cooking

tam·bour /'tæmbʊr/ *noun* a type of drum

tam·bou·rine /ˌtæmbə'rin/ *noun* a musical instrument that has a round wooden frame, sometimes covered with plastic or skin, with metal disks around the edge. To play it you shake it or hit it with your hand. ᴐ picture at INSTRUMENT

tame /teɪm/ *adj., verb*
● *adj.* (**tam·er, tam·est**) **1** (of animals, birds, etc.) not afraid of people, and used to living with them **ANT** WILD **2** (*informal*) not interesting or exciting: *You'll find life here pretty tame after New York.* **3** (*informal*) (of a person) willing

to do what other people ask: *Her boyfriend's very tame and does whatever she wants.* ▶ **tame·ly** *adv.* **tame·ness** *noun* [U]
● *verb* ~ **sth** to make something tame or easy to control: *Lions can never be completely tamed.* ♦ *She made strenuous efforts to tame her anger.*

tam·er /'teɪmər/ *noun* (usually in compounds) a person who trains wild animals: *a lion-tamer*

Tam·il /'tæm; 'taml/ *noun* **1** [C] a member of a race of people living in Tamil Nadu in southern India and in Sri Lanka **2** [U] the language of the Tamils ▶ **Tamil** *adj.*

Tam·ma·ny Hall /ˌtæməni 'hɔl/ *noun* a dishonest political organization that had a lot of influence in New York City in the 19th and early 20th centuries (sometimes used to refer to any dishonest political organization)

tam-o'-shanter /ˌtæm ə 'ʃæntər/ *noun* a round hat made of wool with a small ball made of wool in the center, originally worn in Scotland

ta·mox·i·fen /tə'mɑksəfən/ *noun* [U] (*medical*) a drug that is used especially to treat breast cancer

tamp /tæmp/ *verb* ~ **sth** (**down**) to press something down firmly, especially into a closed space

Tam·pax™ /'tæmpæks/ *noun* (*pl.* **Tam·pax**) [C, U] a type of TAMPON

tam·per /'tæmpər/ *verb*
PHR V **'tamper with sth** to make changes to something without permission, especially in order to damage it **SYN** INTERFERE WITH: *Someone had obviously tampered with the brakes of my car.*

'tamper-proof *adj.* something that is **tamper-proof** is specially designed so that it cannot be easily changed or damaged: *a tamper-proof identity card*

tam·pon /'tæmpɑn/ *noun* a specially shaped piece of cotton material that a woman puts inside her VAGINA to absorb blood during her PERIOD ᴐ compare SANITARY NAPKIN

tan /tæn/ *verb, noun, adj., abbr.*
● *verb* (**-nn-**) **1** [I, T] ~ (**sb/sth**) if a person or their skin **tans** or is **tanned**, they become brown as a result of spending time in the sun **2** [T] ~ **sth** to make animal skin into leather by treating it with chemicals **IDM** see HIDE *n.*
● *noun* **1** [U] a yellowish-brown color **2** (also **sun·tan**) [C] the brown color that someone with pale skin becomes when they have been in the sun: *to get a tan*
● *adj.* yellowish brown in color
● *abbr.* (*mathematics*) TANGENT

tan·dem /'tændəm/ *noun* a bicycle for two riders, one behind the other ᴐ picture at BICYCLE
IDM **in tandem (with sb/sth)** a thing that works or happens **in tandem** with something else works together with it or happens at the same time as it

tan·door·i /tæn'dʊri; tan-/ *noun* [U] (often used as an adjective) a method of cooking meat on a long, straight piece of metal (called a SPIT) in a CLAY oven, originally used in S. Asia: *tandoori chicken*

tang /tæŋ/ *noun* [usually sing.] a strong, sharp taste or smell: *the tang of lemons* ▶ **tang·y** /'tæŋi/ *adj.*: *a refreshing tangy lemon flavor*

tan·gent /'tændʒənt/ *noun* **1** (*geometry*) a straight line that touches the outside of a curve but does not cross it ᴐ picture at SHAPE **2** (*abbr.* **tan**) (*mathematics*) the RATIO of the length of the side opposite an angle in a RIGHT TRIANGLE to the length of the side next to it ᴐ compare COSINE, SINE
IDM **go off on a tangent** (*informal*) to suddenly start saying or doing something that does not seem to be connected to what has gone before

tan·gen·tial /tæn'dʒenʃl/ *adj.* **1** (*formal*) having only a slight or indirect connection with something: *a tangential argument* **2** (*geometry*) of or along a tangent ▶ **tan·gen·tial·ly** /-ʃəli/ *adj.*

tan·ge·rine /ˌtændʒə'rin; 'tændʒəˌrin/ *noun* **1** [C] a type of small sweet orange with loose skin that comes off easily **2** [U] a deep orange-yellow color ▶ **tan·ge·rine** *adj.*: *a tangerine evening gown*

tan·gi·ble /'tændʒəbl/ *adj.* **1** [usually before noun] that can be clearly seen to exist: *tangible benefits/improvements/ results, etc.* ◆ *tangible assets* (= a company's buildings, machinery, etc.) **2** that you can touch and feel: *The tension between them was almost tangible.* **ANT** INTANGIBLE ▶ **tan·gi·bly** /-bli/ *adv.*

tan·gle /'tæŋgl/ *noun, verb*
• *noun* **1** a twisted mass of threads, hair, etc. that cannot be easily separated: *a tangle of branches* ◆ *Her hair was a mass of tangles.* **2** a state of confusion or lack of order: *His financial affairs are in a tangle.* **3** (*informal*) a disagreement or fight
• *verb* [T, I] **~ (sth) up** to twist something into a mass; to become twisted in this way: *She had tangled up the sheets on the bed as she lay tossing and turning.*
PHR V **'tangle with sb/sth** to become involved in an argument or a fight with someone or something

tan·gled /'tæŋgld/ *adj.* **1** twisted together in a messy way: *tangled hair/bedding* **2** complicated, and not easy to understand: *tangled financial affairs*

tan·go /'tæŋgoʊ/ *noun, verb*
• *noun* (*pl.* **tan·gos** /-goʊz/) a fast S. American dance with a strong beat, in which two people hold each other closely; a piece of music for this dance
• *verb* (**tan·go·ing, tan·goed, tan·goed**) [I] to dance the tango
IDM **it takes two to tango** (*informal*) used to say that two people or groups, and not just one, are responsible for something that has happened (usually something bad)

tank /tæŋk/ *noun, verb*
• *noun* **1** a large container for holding liquid or gas: *a hot water tank* ◆ *a fuel tank* ◆ *a fish tank* (= for keeping fish in) ⊃ **picture at** HOBBY ⊃ **picture at** BICYCLE ⊃ **see also** SEPTIC TANK, THINK TANK **2** (*also* **tank·ful** /'tæŋkfʊl/) the contents of a tank or the amount it will hold: *We drove there and back on one tank of gas.* **3** a military vehicle covered with strong metal and armed with guns. It can travel over very rough ground using wheels that move inside metal belts.
• *verb* **1** [I] (of a company or a product) to fail completely: *The company's shares tanked on Wall Street.* **2** [T, I] **~ (sth)** (*sports*) to lose a game, especially deliberately: *She was accused of tanking the match.*
PHR V **tank (sth) 'up** to fill a car with gas: *He tanked up and drove off.* ◆ *We stopped to tank the car up.*

tan·kard /'tæŋkərd/ *noun* a large, usually metal, cup with a handle, that is used for drinking beer from

tanked /tæŋkt/ (*also* **tanked 'up**) *adj.* (*informal*) very drunk

tank·er /'tæŋkər/ *noun* a ship or truck that carries oil, gas, or other liquids in large quantities: *an oil tanker* ⊃ **picture at** TRUCK ⊃ **see also** SUPERTANKER

tank·i·ni /tæŋ'kini/ *noun* a SWIMSUIT in two pieces, consisting of a short top without sleeves and the bottom half of a BIKINI

'tank top *noun* a piece of clothing like a tight T-SHIRT without sleeves

tanned /tænd/ (*also* **sun·tanned**) *adj.* having a brown skin color as a result of being in the sun

tan·ner /'tænər/ *noun* a person whose job is to TAN animal skins to make leather

tan·ner·y /'tænəri/ *noun* (*pl.* **tan·ner·ies**) a place where animal skins are TANNED and made into leather

tan·nin /'tænən/ (*also* **tannic 'acid**) *noun* [U] a yellow-brown substance found in the BARK of some trees and the fruit of many plants, used especially in making leather, ink, and wine ▶ **tan·nic** /'tænɪk/ *adj.*

tan·ta·lize /'tæntlˌaɪz/ *verb* **~ sb/sth** to make a person or an animal want something that they cannot have or do ▶ **tan·ta·liz·ing** *adj.*: *The tantalizing aroma of fresh coffee*

wafted toward them. ◆ *a tantalizing glimpse of the future* **tan·ta·liz·ing·ly** *adv.*: *The branch was tantalizingly out of reach.*

tan·ta·lum /'tæntl·əm/ *noun* [U] (*symb.* **Ta**) a chemical element. Tantalum is a hard silver-gray metal used in the production of electronic parts and of metal plates and pins for connecting broken bones.

tan·ta·mount /'tæntəˌmaʊnt/ *adj.* **~ to sth** (*formal*) having the same bad effect as something else: *If he resigned it would be tantamount to admitting that he was guilty.*

Tan·tra /'tʌntrə; 'tæn-/ *noun* **1** [C] an ancient Hindu or Buddhist text **2** [U] behavior based on these texts, including prayer and MEDITATION ▶ **tan·tric** /'tʌntrɪk; 'tæn-/ *adj.*

tan·trum /'tæntrəm/ *noun* a sudden short period of angry, unreasonable behavior, especially in a child: *Children often have **temper tantrums** at the age of two or thereabout.* ◆ *to have/ throw a tantrum*

Tao·ism /'daʊɪzəm/ *noun* [U] a Chinese philosophy based on the writings of Lao-tzu ▶ **Tao·ist** /'daʊɪst/ *noun, adj.*

tap /tæp/ *verb, noun*
• *verb* (**-pp-**) **1** [I, T] to hit someone or something quickly and lightly: **~ (away) (at sth)** *Someone tapped at the door.* ◆ *He was busy tapping away at his computer.* ◆ **~ sb/sth** *Ralph tapped me on the shoulder.* **2** [T, I] **~ (sth)** if you **tap** your fingers, feet, etc. or they **tap**, you hit them gently against a table, the floor, etc., for example to the rhythm of music: *He kept tapping his fingers on the table.* ◆ *The music set everyone's feet tapping.* **3** [I, T] to make use of a source of energy, knowledge, etc. that already exists: **~ sth** *We need to tap the expertise of the people we already have.* ◆ **~ into sth** *The movie seems to tap into a general sentimentality about animals.* **4** [T] **~ sth** to fit a device to a telephone so that someone's calls can be listened to secretly: *He was convinced his phone was being tapped.* ⊃ **see also** WIRETAPPING **5** [T] **~ sth** to cut into a tree in order to get liquid from it **6** [T, usually passive] **~ sb** to choose someone to do a particular job: *Richards has been tapped to replace the retiring chairperson.* **7** [T] **~ sth** (*phonetics*) to produce a TAP **SYN** FLAP
PHR V **tap sth↔'in/'out** to put information, numbers, letters, etc. into a machine by pressing buttons: *Tap in your PIN number.* **tap sth↔'out 1** to hit a surface gently to the rhythm of music: *She tapped out the beat on the table.* **2** to write something using a computer or a cell phone: *I tapped out a text message to Mandy.*
• *noun* **1** [C] = FAUCET: *Turn the tap on/off.* ⊃ **see also** TAP WATER **2** [C] a device for controlling the flow of liquid or gas from a pipe or container: *a gas tap* ◆ *beer taps* **3** [C] a light hit with your hand or fingers: *a tap at/on the door* ◆ *He felt a tap on his shoulder and turned around.* **4** [C] an act of fitting a device to a telephone so that someone's telephone calls can be listened to secretly: *a phone tap* **5** [U] = TAP DANCE **6** [C] (*phonetics*) a speech sound that is produced by striking the tongue quickly and lightly against the part of the mouth behind the upper front teeth. The /t/ in *later* in American English and the /r/ in *very* in some British accents are examples of taps. **SYN** FLAP **7** **taps** [U] or [pl.] a tune played on a BUGLE at military funerals and at the end of the day in military camps
IDM **on tap 1** available to be used at any time: *We have this sort of information on tap.* **2** beer that is **on tap** is in a BARREL with a tap on it **3** (*informal*) something that is **on tap** is being discussed or prepared and will happen soon

ta·pas /'tɑpəs/ *noun* [pl.] (from *Spanish*) small amounts of a variety of Spanish dishes, served with drinks in a bar

'tap dance *noun* [U, C] a style of dancing in which you tap the rhythm of the music with your feet, wearing special shoes with pieces of metal on the heels and toes ▶ **'tap-dance** *verb* [I] **'tap ˌdancer** *noun* **'tap ˌdancing** (*also* **tap**) *noun* [U]

tape /teɪp/ **AWL** /teɪp/ *noun, verb*
• *noun* **1** [U] a long, narrow strip of material with a sticky substance on one side that is used for sticking things

together: *adhesive tape* ➲ see also DUCT TAPE, INSULATING TAPE, MASKING TAPE, SCOTCH TAPE™ **2** [U] a long, narrow strip of MAGNETIC material that is used for recording sounds, pictures, or information ➲ see also MAGNETIC TAPE, VIDEOTAPE **3** [C] a CASSETTE that contains sounds, or sounds and pictures, that have recorded: *a blank tape* (= a tape that has nothing recorded on it) ◆ *I lent her my Bob Marley tapes.* ◆ *Police seized various books and tapes.* **4** [C] a long, narrow strip of material that is stretched across the place where a race will finish: *the finishing tape* **5** [C] = TAPE MEASURE **6** [C, U] a narrow strip of material that is used for tying things together or as a label: *The papers were in a pile, tied together with a tape.* ➲ see also RED TAPE, TICKER TAPE
- *verb* **1** ~ sb/sth to record someone or something on MAGNETIC tape using a special machine: *Private conversations between the two had been taped and sent to a newspaper.* **2** ~ sth (up) to fasten something by sticking or tying it with tape: *Put it in a box and tape it up securely.* **3** ~ sth + adv./ prep. to stick something onto something else using sticky tape: *Someone had taped a message on the door.* **4** ~ sth (up) to tie a bandage firmly around an injury: *You've sprained your ankle, so I'm going to tape it up.*

'tape ,measure (also tape, 'measuring ,tape) *noun* a long, narrow strip of plastic, cloth, or FLEXIBLE metal that has measurements marked on it and is used for measuring the length of something ➲ picture at TOOL

ta·per /'teɪpər/ *verb, noun*
- *verb* [I, T] to become gradually narrower; to make something become gradually narrower: *The tail tapered to a rounded tip.* ◆ ~ sth *The pots are wide at the base and tapered at the top.*
  PHR V ,taper 'off to become gradually less in number, amount, degree, etc.: *The number of applicants for teaching positions has tapered off.* ,taper sth↔'off to make something become gradually less in number, amount, degree, etc.: *They are gradually tapering off production of the older models.*
- *noun* **1** a long, thin piece of wood, paper, etc. that is used for lighting fires or lamps **2** a long, thin CANDLE **3** [usually sing.] the way that something gradually decreases in size, becoming thinner

'tape-re,cord *verb* ~ sth to record something on tape: *a tape-recorded interview*

'tape re,corder *noun* a machine that is used for recording and playing sounds on tape

'tape recording *noun* something that has been recorded on tape: *a tape recording of the interview*

tap·es·try /'tæpəstri/ *noun* (pl. tap·es·tries) [C, U] **1** a picture or pattern that is made by weaving (WEAVE) colored wool onto heavy cloth; the art of doing this: *medieval tapestries* ◆ *tapestry cushions* ◆ *crafts such as embroidery and tapestry* **2** a complex combination of events, people, or things: *All living things are part of the rich tapestry of life.* ◆ *a tapestry of history and culture* ▶ tap·es·tried *adj.*: *tapestried walls*

tape·worm /'teɪpwərm/ *noun* a long flat WORM that lives in the INTESTINES of humans and animals

'tap-in *noun* (in sports) an easy light hit of the ball into the goal or hole from a close position: *Mickelson made an easy tap-in on the 16th hole.*

tap·i·o·ca /,tæpi'oʊkə/ *noun* [U] hard white grains obtained from the CASSAVA plant, often cooked with milk to make a DESSERT (= a sweet dish)

ta·pir /'teɪpər/ *noun* an animal like a pig with a long nose, that lives in Central and S. America and S.E. Asia

tap·root /'tæprut; -rʊt/ *noun* the main root of a plant that grows straight downward and produces smaller side roots

'tap ,water *noun* [U] water supplied through pipes to a building: *Is the tap water safe to drink?*

tar /tɑr/ *noun, verb*
- *noun* [U] **1** a thick, black, sticky liquid that becomes hard when cold. Tar is obtained from coal and is used especially in making roads **2** a substance similar to tar that is formed by burning TOBACCO: *low-tar cigarettes*
- *verb* (-rr-) ~ sth to cover something with tar: *a tarred road*
  IDM tar and feather sb to put tar on someone then cover them with feathers, as a punishment be tarred with the same brush (as sb) to be thought to have the same faults, etc. as someone else

ta·ran·tu·la /tə'ræntʃələ/ *noun* a large spider covered with hair that lives in tropical regions. Some types of tarantulas have a poisonous bite.

tarantula

tar·dy /'tɑrdi/ *adj.* ~ (in doing sth) (*formal*) slow to act, move, or happen; late in happening or arriving: *The law is often tardy in reacting to changing attitudes.* ◆ *people who are tardy in paying their bills* ◆ *to be tardy for school* ▶ tar·di·ly /'tɑrdl·i/ *adv.* tar·di·ness /-dinəs/ *noun* [U]

tare /tɛr/ *noun* (*literary* or *technical*) a plant growing where you do not want it SYN WEED

tar·get **AWL** /'tɑrgət/ *noun, verb*
- *noun* **1** a result that you try to achieve: *business goals and targets* ◆ *sales targets* ◆ *Set yourself targets that you can reasonably hope to achieve.* ◆ *to meet/achieve a target* ◆ *a target date of April 2012* ◆ *The university will reach its target of 5,000 students next September.* ◆ *The new sports complex is on target to open in June.* ◆ *a target area/audience/group* (= the particular area, audience, etc. that a product, program, etc. is aimed at) ➲ collocations at BUSINESS **2** an object, a person, or a place that people aim at when attacking: *They bombed military and civilian targets.* ◆ ~ for sb/sth *Doors and windows are an easy target for burglars.* ◆ *It's a prime target* (= an obvious target) *for terrorist attacks.* ◆ ~ of sth (*figurative*) *He's become the target of a lot of criticism recently.* **3** an object that people practice shooting at, especially a round board with circles on it: *to aim at a target* ◆ *to hit/miss the target* ◆ *target practice* ➲ picture at SPORT
- *verb* (tar·get·ing, tar·get·ed, tar·get·ed) [usually passive] **1** ~ sb/sth to aim an attack or a criticism at someone or something: *The missiles were mainly targeted at the United States.* ◆ *The company has been targeted by animal rights groups for its use of dogs in drug trials.* **2** ~ sb to try to have an effect on a particular group of people: *The campaign is clearly targeted at the young.* ◆ *a new magazine that targets single men*

THESAURUS

target

objective ◆ **goal** ◆ **object** ◆ **end**

These are all words for something that you are trying to achieve.

target a result that you try to achieve: *Set targets that you can reasonably hope to achieve.* ◆ *sales targets*

objective (*somewhat formal*) something that you are trying to achieve: *What are the objectives of this project?*

goal something that you hope to achieve: *He continued to pursue his goal of becoming an actor.*

TARGET, OBJECTIVE, OR GOAL?

A **target** is usually officially recorded in some way, for example by an employer. It is often specific, and in the form of figures, such as number of sales, exam scores, or a date. People often set their own **objectives**: these are things that they wish to achieve, often as part of a project or a talk they are giving. **Goals** are often long-term, and relate to people's life and career plans or the long-term plans of a company or organization.

object the purpose of something; something that you

ʌ cup ə about eɪ say aɪ five ɔɪ boy aʊ now oʊ go ər bird

plan to achieve: *The object of the campaign is to educate people about highway safety.*

end something that you plan to achieve: *She used her family for political ends.* ◆ *That's only OK if you believe that the end justifies the means* (= bad methods of doing something are acceptable if the final result is good).

NOTE End is usually used in the plural or in particular fixed expressions.

PATTERNS

- to work **toward** a(n) target/objective/goal
- a(n) **ambitious/major/long-term/short-term/ future** target/objective/goal
- **economic/financial/business** targets/objectives/ goals
- to **set/agree on/identify/reach/meet/exceed** a(n) target/objective/goal
- to **achieve** a(n) target/objective/goal/end

ˈtarget ˌlanguage *noun* (*linguistics*) **1** (also **ˈobject ˌlanguage**) a language into which a text is being translated **2** a foreign language that someone is learning

tar·iff /'tærəf/ *noun* **1** a tax that is paid on goods coming into or going out of a country ➔ thesaurus box at TAX ➔ collocations at INTERNATIONAL **2** a list of fixed prices that are charged by a hotel or restaurant for rooms, meals, etc., or by a company for a particular service

Tar·mac™ /'tɑrmæk/ *noun* [U] **1** (also *less frequent* **tar·mac·ad·am** /ˌtɑrməˈkædəm/) (also **black·top**) a black material used for making road surfaces, that consists of small stones mixed with TAR **2 the tarmac** an area with a Tarmac surface, especially at an airport: *Three planes were standing on the tarmac, waiting to take off.*

tarn /tɑrn/ *noun* a small lake in the mountains

tar·na·tion /tɑrˈneɪʃn/ *exclamation* (*old-fashioned*) a word that people use to show that they are annoyed with someone or something

tar·nish /'tɑrnɪʃ/ *verb, noun*

- *verb* **1** [I, T] if metal **tarnishes** or something **tarnishes** it, it no longer looks bright and shiny: *The mirrors had tarnished with age.* ◆ **~ sth** *The silver candlesticks were tarnished and dusty.* **2** [T] **~ sth** to spoil the good opinion people have of someone or something **SYN** TAINT: *He hopes to improve the newspaper's somewhat tarnished public image.*
- *noun* [sing., U] a thin layer on the surface of a metal that makes it look dull and not bright

ta·rot /'tærəʊ/ *noun* [sing., U] a set of special cards with pictures on them, used for telling someone what will happen to them in the future

tarp /tɑrp/ (also *formal* **tar·pau·lin** /tɑrˈpɔlən; ˈtɑrpələn/) *noun* [C, U] a large sheet made of heavy WATERPROOF material, used to cover things with and to keep rain off

tar·ra·gon /'tærəˌgɑn; -gən/ *noun* [U] a plant with leaves that have a strong taste and are used in cooking as an HERB ➔ picture at HERB

tar·ry /'tæri/ *verb* (**tar·ries, tar·ry·ing, tar·ried, tar·ried**) [I] (*old use* or *literary*) to stay in a place, especially when you ought to leave; to delay coming to or going from a place **SYN** LINGER

tar·sal /'tɑrsl/ *noun* (*anatomy*) one of the small bones in the ankle and upper foot

tart /tɑrt/ *adj., noun*

- *adj.* **1** having a sour taste, but often in a pleasant way: *tart apples* ➔ thesaurus box at BITTER **2** [usually before noun] (of remarks, etc.) quick and unkind: *a tart reply* **SYN** SHARP ▸ **tart·ly** *adv.*: *"Too late!" said my mother tartly.* **tart·ness** *noun* [U]
- *noun* [C, U] a small open PIE filled with sweet food such as fruit: *a strawberry tart* ➔ compare QUICHE

tar·tan /'tɑrtn/ *noun* **1** [U, C] a pattern of squares and lines of different colors and widths that cross each other at an angle of 90°, used especially on cloth, and originally from

Scotland: *a tartan rug* **2** [C] a tartan pattern connected with a particular group of families (= a CLAN) in Scotland: *the MacLeod tartan* **3** [U] cloth, especially made of wool, that has a tartan pattern ➔ compare PLAID

tar·tar /'tɑrtər/ *noun* [U] a hard substance that forms on teeth

tar·tar·ic ac·id /tɑrˌtærɪk ˈæsɪd/ *noun* [U] (*chemistry*) a type of acid that is found in GRAPES that are not ready to eat

ˈtartar ˌsauce *noun* [U] a thick, cold, white sauce made from MAYONNAISE, chopped onions, and CAPERS, usually eaten with fish

Tar·zan /'tɑrzæn/ *noun* a man with a very strong body **ORIGIN** From the novel *Tarzan of the Apes* by Edgar Rice Burroughs about a man who lived with wild animals.

Ta·ser™ /'teɪzər/ *noun* a gun that fires DARTS that give a person a small electric shock and makes them unable to move for a short time

task 🔑 **AWL** /tæsk/ *noun, verb*

- *noun* **1** a piece of work that someone has to do, especially a hard or unpleasant one: *to perform/carry out/complete/ undertake a task* ◆ *a daunting/an impossible/a formidable/an unenviable, etc. task* ◆ *a thankless task* (= an unpleasant one that nobody wants to do and nobody thanks you for doing) ◆ *Our first task is to set up a communications system.* ◆ *Detectives are now faced with the task of identifying the body.* ◆ *Getting hold of this information was no easy task* (= was difficult). **2** an activity that is designed to help achieve a particular learning goal, especially in language teaching: *task-based learning*

IDM **take sb to task (for/over sth)** to criticize someone strongly for something they have done

- *verb* [usually passive] **~ sb (with sth)** (*formal*) to give someone a task to do

THESAURUS

task

duties ◆ mission ◆ job ◆ chore

These are all words for a piece of work that someone has to do.

task a piece of work that someone has to do, especially a difficult or unpleasant one: *Our first task is to set up a communications system.*

duties tasks that are part of your job: *Your duties include data entry and record keeping.*

mission an important official job that a person or group of people is given to do, especially when they are sent to another country: *They went on a fact-finding mission to learn more about it.*

job a piece of work that someone has to do: *I've got various jobs around the house.*

TASK OR JOB?

A **task** may be more difficult than a **job** and require you to think carefully about how you are going to do it. A **job** may be something small that is one of several things that you have to do, especially in the home; or a **job** can be something that takes a long time and is boring and/ or needs a lot of patience.

chore a task that you have to do regularly, especially one that you do in the home and find unpleasant or boring: *household chores*

PATTERNS

- the task/mission/job/chore **of (doing)** sth
- (a) **daily/day-to-day** task/duties/job/chore
- (a) **routine** task/duties/mission/job/chore
- a/an **easy/difficult** task/mission/job/chore
- (a) **household/domestic** task/duties/job/chore
- to **do** a task/a job/the chores
- to **finish** a task/a mission/a job/the chores
- to **give sb** a task/their duties/a mission/a job/a chore

task force *noun* **1** a military force that is brought together and sent to a particular place **2** a group of people who are brought together to deal with a particular problem

task·mas·ter /ˈtæsk ˌmæstər/ *noun* a person who gives other people work to do, often work that is difficult: *She was a hard taskmaster.*

tas·sel /ˈtæsl/ *noun* a bunch of threads that are tied together at one end and hang from CUSHIONS, curtains, clothes, etc. as a decoration

tas·seled (*CanE usually* **tas·selled**) /ˈtæsld/ *adj.* decorated with tassels

taste 🔑 /teɪst/ *noun, verb*

● ***noun***
> **FLAVOR 1** [C, U] the particular quality that different foods and drinks have that allows you to recognize them when you put them in your mouth: *a **salty/bitter/sweet, etc. taste*** ◆ *I don't like the taste of olives.* ◆ *This dish has an unusual combination of tastes and textures.* ◆ *The soup has very little taste.*
> **SENSE 2** [U] the sense you have that allows you to recognize different foods and drinks when you put them in your mouth: *I've lost my sense of taste.*
> **SMALL QUANTITY 3** [C, usually sing.] a small quantity of food or drink that you try in order to see what it is like: *Just have a taste of this cheese.*
> **SHORT EXPERIENCE 4** [sing.] a short experience of something: *This was my **first taste** of live theater.* ◆ *Although we didn't know it, this incident was **a taste of things to come**.*
> **ABILITY TO CHOOSE WELL 5** [U] a person's ability to choose things that people recognize as being of good quality or appropriate: *He has very **good taste** in music.* ◆ *They've got more money than taste.* ◆ *The room was furnished with taste.*
> **WHAT YOU LIKE 6** [C, U] what a person likes or prefers: **~ (for sth)** *That trip gave me a taste for foreign travel.* ◆ **~ (in sth)** *She has very expensive tastes in clothes.* ◆ *The color and style is **a matter** of personal taste.* ◆ *Modern art is not **to everyone's taste**.* ◆ *There are trips to suit all tastes.*
> **IDM** **be in bad, poor, the worst possible, etc. taste** to be offensive and not at all appropriate: *Most of his jokes were in very poor taste.* **be in good, the best possible, etc. taste** to be appropriate and not at all offensive **leave a bad/ nasty taste in the mouth** (of events or experiences) to make you feel disgusted or ashamed afterward **to taste** in the quantity that is needed to make something taste the way you prefer: *Add salt and pepper to taste.* ➔ **more at** ACCOUNT, ACQUIRE, MEDICINE

● ***verb*** (not used in the progressive tenses)
> **HAVE FLAVOR 1** *linking verb* to have a particular flavor: **+ adj.** *It tastes sweet.* ◆ **~ of sth** *The ice cream tasted of peppermint.* ◆ **~ like sth** *This drink tastes like sherry.* **2** **-tasting** (in adjectives) having a particular flavor: *foul-tasting medicine*
> **RECOGNIZE FLAVOR 3** [T] **~ sth** (often used with *can* or *could*) to be able to recognize flavors in food and drink: *You can taste the garlic in this stew.*
> **TEST FLAVOR 4** [T] **~ sth** to test the flavor of something by eating or drinking a small amount of it **SYN** TRY: *Taste it and see if you think there's enough salt in it.*
> **EAT/DRINK 5** [T] **~ sth** to eat or drink food or liquid: *I've never tasted anything like it.*
> **HAVE SHORT EXPERIENCE 6** [T] **~ sth** to have a short experience of something, especially something that you want more of: *He had tasted freedom only to lose it again.*

taste bud *noun* [usually pl.] one of the small structures on the tongue that allow you to recognize the flavors of food and drink

taste·ful /ˈteɪstfl/ *adj.* (especially of clothes, furniture, decorations, etc.) attractive and of good quality and showing that the person who chose them can recognize good things ▶ **taste·ful·ly** /-fəli/ *adv.*: *The bedroom was tastefully furnished.*

taste·less /ˈteɪstləs/ *adj.* **1** offensive and not appropriate: *tasteless jokes* **2** having little or no flavor: *tasteless soup*

3 showing a lack of the ability to choose things that people recognize as attractive and of good quality: *tasteless jewelry* ▶ **taste·less·ly** *adv.* **taste·less·ness** *noun* [U]

tast·er /ˈteɪstər/ *noun* a person whose job is to judge the quality of wine, tea, etc. by tasting it

tast·ing /ˈteɪstɪŋ/ *noun* an event at which people can try different kinds of food and drink, especially wine, in small quantities: *a wine tasting*

tast·y /ˈteɪsti/ *adj.* (**tast·i·er, tast·i·est**) (*approving*) having a strong and pleasant flavor: *a tasty meal* ◆ *something tasty to eat* ▶ **tast·i·ness** *noun* [U]

ta·ta·mi /təˈtɑmi/ *noun* (from *Japanese*) a traditional Japanese floor covering made from dried RUSHES

ta·ter /ˈteɪtər/ *noun* [usually pl.] (*slang*) a potato

tat·tered /ˈtætərd/ *adj.* old and torn; in bad condition: *tattered clothes* ◆ (*figurative*) *tattered relationships* ◆ (*figurative*) *the hotel's tattered reputation*

tat·ters /ˈtætərz/ *noun* [pl.] clothes or pieces of cloth that are badly torn
IDM **in tatters 1** torn in many places: *His clothes were in tatters.* **2** ruined or badly damaged **SYN** IN SHREDS: *Her reputation was in tatters.* ◆ *The state's attempt at fiscal reform lies in tatters.*

tat·tle /ˈtætl/ *verb* [I] **~ (on sb) (to sb)** (*informal, disapproving*) to tell someone, especially someone in authority, about something bad that someone else has done **SYN** TELL ON SB

tat·tle·tale /ˈtætlˌteɪl/ *noun* (*informal, disapproving*) a child who tells an adult what another child has done wrong

tat·too /tæˈtu/ *noun, verb*
● ***noun*** (*pl.* **tat·toos**) **1** a picture or design that is marked permanently on a person's skin by making small holes in the skin with a needle and filling them with colored ink: *His arms were covered in tattoos.* ➔ **collocations at** FASHION **2** [usually sing.] a rapid and continuous series of taps or hits, especially on a drum as a military signal
● ***verb*** to mark someone's skin with a tattoo: **~ A on B** *He had a heart tattooed on his shoulder.* ◆ **~ B (with A)** *His shoulder was tattooed with a heart.*

tat·too·ist /tæˈtuɪst/ *noun* a person who draws tattoos on people's skin, as a job

tat·ty /ˈtæti/ *adj.* (**tat·ti·er, tat·ti·est**) (*informal*) in a bad condition because it has been used a lot or has not been cared for well **SYN** SHABBY: *a tatty old jacket*

tau /taʊ/ *noun* the 19th letter of the Greek alphabet (T, τ)

taught *pt, pp* of TEACH

taunt /tɔnt/ /tɑnt/ *verb, noun*
● ***verb*** **~ sb** to try to make someone angry or upset by saying unkind things about them, laughing at their failures, etc.: *The other kids continually taunted him about his size.*
● ***noun*** an insulting or unkind remark that is intended to make someone angry or upset: *Black players often had to endure racist taunts.*

taupe /toʊp/ *noun* [U] a color that is between brown and gray ▶ **taupe** *adj.*

tau·rine /ˈtɔrin/ *noun* [U] an acid substance that is sometimes used in drinks that are designed to make you feel more active

Tau·rus /ˈtɔrəs/ *noun* **1** [U] the second sign of the ZODIAC, the BULL **2** [sing.] a person born under the influence of this sign, that is between April 21 and May 21 ▶ **Tau·re·an** /ˈtɔriən/ *noun, adj.*

taut /tɔt/ *adj.* **1** stretched tightly: *Keep the rope taut.* **2** showing that you are anxious or TENSE: *Her face was taut and pale.* **3** (of a person or their body) with firm muscles; not fat: *His body was solid and taut.* **4** (of a piece of writing, etc.) tightly controlled, with no unnecessary parts in it ▶ **taut·ly** *adv.* **taut·ness** *noun* [U]

taut·en /ˈtɔtn/ *verb* [I, T] **~ (sth)** to become taut; to make something taut

tau·tol·o·gy /tɔˈtɑlədʒi/ noun [U, C] a statement in which you say the same thing twice in different words, when this is unnecessary, for example "They spoke in turn, one after the other." ▶ **tau·to·log·i·cal** /ˌtɔtlˈɑdʒɪkl/ adj. **tau·tol·o·gous** /tɔˈtɑləgəs/ adj.

tav·ern /ˈtævərn/ noun (old use or literary) a bar or an INN

taw·dry /ˈtɔdri/ adj. (disapproving) **1** intended to be bright and attractive but cheap and of low quality: tawdry jewelry **2** involving low moral standards; extremely unpleasant or offensive: a tawdry affair ▶ **taw·dri·ness** noun [U]

taw·ny /ˈtɔni/ adj. between brown and yellow in color: the lion's tawny mane

tax 🔑 /tæks/ noun, verb
• **noun** [C, U] money that you have to pay to the government so that it can pay for public services. People pay tax according to their income, and businesses pay tax according to their profits. Tax is also often paid on goods and services: to raise/cut taxes ◆ tax increases/cuts ◆ changes in tax rates ◆ to pay over $1,000 in taxes ◆ profits before/after taxes ◆ ~ on sth a tax on cigarettes ⊃ collocations at ECONOMY ⊃ see also DIRECT TAX, ESTATE TAX, INDIRECT TAX, INHERITANCE TAX, PAYROLL TAX, POLL TAX, SALES TAX, WITHHOLDING TAX
• **verb 1** ~ sb/sth to put a tax on someone or something; to make someone pay tax: Any interest payments are taxed as part of your income. ◆ His declared aim was to tax the rich. **2** ~ sb/sth to need a great amount of physical or mental effort: The questions did not tax me. ◆ The problem is currently taxing the brains of the nation's experts (= making them think very hard).
PHR V ˈtax sb with sth (formal) to accuse someone of doing something wrong: I taxed him with avoiding his responsibility as a parent.

THESAURUS

tax

duty ◆ **customs duty/charge** ◆ **tariff**

These are all words for money that you have to pay to the government.

tax money that you have to pay to the government so that it can pay for public services: income tax ◆ sales tax ◆ tax cuts

duty a tax that you pay on things that you buy, especially those that you bring into a country: The company has to pay duty on all imported merchandise.

customs duty/charge tax that is paid when goods are brought in from other countries

tariff a tax that is paid on goods coming into or going out of a country, often in order to protect industry from cheap imports: A general tariff was imposed on foreign imports.

PATTERNS
- (a) tax/duty/tariff **on** sth
- to pay an amount of money **in** tax/duty/customs duty
- to **pay** (a) tax/duty/customs duty/tariff/rates
- to **collect** taxes/duties
- to **increase/raise/reduce** taxes/duty/tariffs
- to **cut** taxes/duties
- to **impose** a tax/duty/tariff
- to **put** a tax/duty **on** sth

---

tax·a·ble /ˈtæksəbl/ adj. (of money) that you have to pay tax on: taxable income

tax·a·tion /tækˈseɪʃn/ noun [U] **1** money that has to be paid as taxes: to reduce taxation **2** the system of collecting money by taxes: changes in the taxation structure

ˈtax aˌvoidance noun [U] ways of paying only the smallest amount of tax that you legally have to ⊃ compare TAX EVASION

ˈtax ˌbracket noun a range of different incomes on which the same rate of tax must be paid: Your accountant will determine which tax bracket you are in.

ˈtax break noun a special advantage or reduction in taxes that the government gives to particular people or organizations

ˈtax colˌlector noun a person whose job is collecting the tax that people must pay on the money they earn

ˈtax ˌcredit noun money that is taken off your total tax bill

ˌtax-deˈductible adj. (of costs) that can be taken off your income before the amount of tax that you have to pay is calculated

ˌtax-deˈferred adj. that you only pay tax on later: a tax-deferred savings plan

ˈtax dodge noun (informal) a way of paying less tax, legally or illegally ▶ ˈtax dodger noun

ˈtax eˌvasion noun [U] the crime of deliberately not paying all the taxes that you should pay ⊃ compare TAX AVOIDANCE

ˌtax-eˈxempt adj. that is not taxed: tax-exempt bonds

ˈtax ˌexile noun a rich person who has left their own country and gone to live in a place where the taxes are lower

ˌtax-ˈfree adj. (of money, goods, etc.) that you do not have to pay tax on: a tax-free allowance ▶ ˌtax-ˈfree adv.

ˈtax ˌhaven noun a place where taxes are low and where people choose to live or officially register their companies because taxes are higher in their own countries

tax·i 🔑 /ˈtæksi/ noun, verb
• **noun** (also **cab**, **tax·i·cab** /ˈtæksiˌkæb/) a car with a driver that you pay to take you somewhere. Taxis usually have METERS that show how much money you have to pay: a taxi driver/ride ◆ We'd better take a taxi. ◆ I came home by taxi. ◆ to order/hail/call a taxi ⊃ picture at CAR
• **verb** (tax·i·ing, tax·ied, tax·ied) [I] (of a plane) to move slowly along the ground before taking off or after landing

tax·i·der·mist /ˈtæksəˌdərmɪst/ noun a person whose job is taxidermy

tax·i·der·my /ˈtæksəˌdərmi/ noun [U] the art of STUFFING dead animals, birds, and fish with a special material so that they look like living ones and can be displayed

tax·ing /ˈtæksɪŋ/ adj. needing a great amount of physical or mental effort **SYN** DEMANDING: a taxing job ◆ This shouldn't be too taxing for you. ⊃ thesaurus box at DIFFICULT

ˈtaxi ˌsquad noun (in football and other team sports) **1** a group of players who practice with the first team but who do not play in games **2** four extra players on a team who play when other players are injured

ˈtaxi ˌstand noun a place where taxis park while they are waiting for passengers

tax·i·way /ˈtæksiˌweɪ/ noun the hard path that a plane uses as it moves to and from the RUNWAY (= the hard surface where planes take off and land)

tax·man /ˈtæksmæn/ noun (pl. tax·men /-mɛn/) **1** the **taxman** [sing.] (informal) a way of referring to the government department that is responsible for collecting taxes: He had been cheating the taxman for years. **2** [C] a person whose job is to collect taxes

tax·on·o·mist /tækˈsɑnəmɪst/ noun a person who studies or is skilled in taxonomy

tax·on·o·my /tækˈsɑnəmi/ noun (pl. tax·on·o·mies) **1** [U] the scientific process of CLASSIFYING things (= arranging them into groups): plant taxonomy **2** [C] a particular system of CLASSIFYING things ▶ **tax·o·nom·ic** /ˌtæksəˈnɑmɪk/ adj.

tax·pay·er /ˈtæksˌpeɪər/ noun a person who pays tax to the government, especially on the money they earn

ˈtax reˌlief (also reˌlief) noun [U] a reduction in the amount of tax you have to pay

---

'tax re,turn *noun* an official document in which you give details of the amount of money that you have earned and calculate how much tax you have to pay

'tax ,shelter *noun* a way of using or investing money so that you can legally avoid paying tax on it

TB *abbr.* **1** /,ti 'bi/TUBERCULOSIS **2** (in writing) TERABYTE

TBA /,ti bi 'eɪ/ *abbr.* (used in notices about events) to be announced: *party with live band (TBA)*

'T-ball = TEE BALL™

'T-bar (also **'T-bar lift**) *noun* a machine that pulls two people up a mountain on SKIS together

TBC /,ti bi 'si/ *abbr.* (used in notices about events) to be confirmed: *The four-day course will run from March 8 - 11 (TBC).*

'T-bill *abbr.* (*informal*) = TREASURY BILL

'T-bone steak *noun* a thick slice of beef containing a bone in the shape of a T

tbsp. (also **tbs.**) *abbr.* (*pl.* **tbsp.** or **tbsps.**) TABLESPOON: *Add 3 tbsp. sugar.*

TCP/IP /,ti si ,pi aɪ 'pi/ *abbr.* (*computing*) transmission control protocol/Internet protocol (a system that controls the connection of computers to the Internet)

tea 🔊 /ti/ *noun*
1 [U] the dried leaves (called tea leaves) of the tea bush ᕋ see also GREEN TEA **2** [U] a hot drink made by pouring boiling water onto tea leaves. It may be drunk with milk or lemon and/or sugar added: *a cup/mug/pot of tea* ♦ *iced/hot tea* ♦ *Would you like tea or coffee?* ♦ *Do you take sugar in your tea?* **3** [C] a cup of tea: *Two teas, please.* **4** [U, C] a hot drink made by pouring boiling water onto the leaves of other plants: *chamomile/mint/herb, etc. tea* **5** [U, C] a light meal eaten in the afternoon or early evening, usually with SANDWICHES and/or cookies and cakes and with tea to drink
IDM **not for all the tea in China** (*old-fashioned*) not even for a great reward: *I wouldn't do your job. Not for all the tea in China!* ᕋ more at CUP

'tea bag *noun* a small, thin paper bag containing tea leaves, that you pour boiling water onto in order to make tea

'tea ,biscuit *noun* (*CanE*) a small baked food made of a bread-like mixture, usually containing dried fruit

tea·cart /'tikɑrt/ *noun* a small table on wheels that is used for serving drinks and food

teach 🔊 /titʃ/ *verb* (taught, taught /tɔt/)
1 [I, T] to give lessons to students in a school, college, university, etc.; to help someone learn something by giving information about it: *She teaches at our local high school.* ♦ *He taught for several years before becoming a writer.* ♦ *~ sth I'll be teaching history and sociology next semester.* ♦ *to teach school* (= teach in a school) ♦ *~ sth to sb He teaches English to advanced students.* ♦ *~ sb sth He teaches them English.* **2** [T] to show someone how to do something so that they will be able to do it themselves: *~ (sb to do) sth Could you teach me to do that?* ♦ *~ sb how, what, etc.... My father taught me how to ride a bike.* **3** [T] to make someone feel or think in a different way: *~ sb to do sth She taught me to be less critical of other people.* ♦ *~ (sb) that... My parents taught me that honesty was always the best policy.* ♦ *~ sb sth Our experience as refugees taught us many valuable lessons.* **4** [T, no passive] (*informal*) to persuade someone not to do something again by making them suffer so much that they are afraid to do it: *~ sb to do sth Lost all your money? That'll teach you to gamble.* ♦ *I'll teach you to call* (= punish you for calling) *me a liar!* ♦ *~ sb sth The accident taught me a lesson I'll never forget.*
IDM **(you can't) teach an old dog new tricks** (*saying*) (you cannot) successfully make people change their ideas, methods of work, etc., when they have had them for a long time

teach and teachers

verbs
- **teach** *John teaches French at the local school.* ♦ *She taught me how to change a tire.*
- **educate** *Our priority is to educate people about the dangers of drugs.*
- **instruct** *Members of staff should be instructed in the use of fire equipment.*
- **train** *She's a trained midwife.* ♦ *He's training the U.S. Olympic swim team.*
- **coach** *He's the best football player I've ever coached.* ♦ *She coaches some of the local children in singing.*
- **tutor** *She tutors some of the local children in math.*
- **mentor** *She's been mentoring me ever since I started at the company.*

nouns
- **teacher** *school/college teachers*
- **instructor** *a swimming/science instructor*
- **trainer** *a horse trainer* ♦ *Do you have a personal trainer?*
- **coach** *a football coach*
- **tutor** *tutors working with migrant children*
- **mentor** *He's been my mentor for two years now.*

teach·a·ble /'titʃəbl/ *adj.* **1** (of a subject) that can be taught **2** (of a person) able to learn by being taught

teach·er 🔊 /'titʃər/ *noun*
a person whose job is teaching, especially in a school: *a history/science, etc. teacher* ♦ *high school teachers* ♦ *There is a growing need for qualified teachers of Business English.* ᕋ note at TEACH

,teacher 'training *noun* [U] the process of teaching or learning the skills you need to be a teacher in a school ▶ **,teacher 'trainer** *noun: experienced teachers and teacher trainers*

'teach-in *noun* an informal lecture and discussion on a subject of public interest

teach·ing 🔊 /'titʃɪŋ/ *noun*
1 [U] the work of a teacher: *She wants to go into teaching* (= make it a career). ♦ *the teaching profession* **2** [C, usually pl., U] the ideas of a particular person or group, especially about politics, religion, or society, that are taught to other people: *the teachings of Lenin* ♦ *views that go against traditional Christian teaching*

'teaching as,sistant (*abbr.* TA) (also **'teaching ,fellow**) *noun* a graduate student who teaches UNDERGRADUATE classes at a university or college, marks written work, etc.

'tea ,cozy *noun* a cover placed over a TEAPOT in order to keep the tea warm

tea·cup /'tikʌp/ *noun* a cup in which tea is served

'tea dance *noun* a social event held in the afternoon, especially in the past, at which people dance, drink tea, and eat a small meal

tea·house /'tihaʊs/ *noun* a Chinese or Japanese restaurant where tea is served, often as part of a special ceremony

teak /tik/ *noun* [U] the strong hard wood of a tall Asian tree, used especially for making furniture

tea·ket·tle /'ti,kɛtl/ *noun* a metal container with a lid, handle, and a SPOUT, used for boiling water ᕋ picture at COFFEE

teal /til/ *noun* **1** (*pl.* teal) [C] a small wild DUCK **2** [U] a blue-green color

'tea leaf *noun* a small piece of a dried leaf of the tea bush; used especially in the plural to describe what is left at the bottom of a cup or pot after the tea has been drunk

tea·light /'tilaɪt/ *noun* a small CANDLE that is used for decoration and which often gives off a pleasant smell

team 🔑 **AWL** /tiːm/ *noun, verb*

• *noun* **1** a group of people who play a particular game or sport against another group of people: *a football/baseball, etc. team* ◆ *a team event* (= one played by groups of people rather than individual players) ◆ *Whose team are you on?* ◆ *The team is not playing very well this season.* **2** a group of people who work together at a particular job: *the sales team* ◆ *a team leader/member* ◆ *A team of experts has/have been called in to investigate.* **3** two or more animals that are used together to pull a CART, etc.

• *verb* [usually passive] **~ sb/sth (with sb/sth)** to put two or more things or people together in order to do something or to achieve a particular effect: *He was teamed with his brother in the doubles.*
PHR V ˌteam ˈup (with sb) to join with another person or group in order to do something together ˌteam sb/sth ˈup (with sb) to put two or more people or things together in order to do something or to achieve a particular effect

ˌteam ˈhandball *noun* [U] = HANDBALL

team·mate /ˈtiːmmeɪt/ *noun* a member of the same team or group as yourself

ˌteam ˈplayer *noun* a person who is good at working as a member of a team, usually in their job

ˌteam ˈspirit *noun* [U] (*approving*) the desire and willingness of people to work together and help each other as part of a team

team·ster /ˈtiːmstər/ *noun* a person whose job is driving a truck **SYN** TRUCK DRIVER

team·work /ˈtiːmwɜːrk/ *noun* [U] the activity of working well together as a team: *She stressed the importance of good teamwork.*

ˈtea ˌparty *noun* a social event at which people eat cake, drink tea, etc. in the afternoon

tea·pot /ˈtiːpɑt/ *noun* a container with a SPOUT, a handle, and a lid, used for making and serving tea **IDM** see TEMPEST

tear¹ 🔑 /ter/ *verb, noun* ⊃ see also TEAR²

• *verb* (tore /tɔr/, torn /tɔrn/)
▷ DAMAGE **1** [T, I] to damage something by pulling it apart or into pieces, or by cutting it on something sharp; to become damaged in this way **SYN** RIP: **~ (sth) (+ adv./prep.)** *I tore my jeans on the fence.* ◆ *I tore a hole in my jeans.* ◆ *He tore the letter in two.* ◆ *a torn handkerchief* ◆ *Careful—the fabric tears very easily.* ◆ **~ sth + adj.** *I tore the package open.* **2** [T] **~ sth in sth** to make a hole in something by force **SYN** RIP: *The blast tore a hole in the wall.*
▷ REMOVE FROM SOMETHING OR SOMEONE **3** [T] **~ sth + adv./prep.** to remove something from something else by pulling it roughly or violently **SYN** RIP: *The storm nearly tore the roof off.* ◆ *I tore another sheet from the pad.* ◆ *He tore his clothes off* (= took them off quickly and carelessly) *and dived into the lake.* **4** [T] to pull yourself/someone away by force from someone or something that is holding you or them: **~ yourself/sb from sb/sth** *She tore herself from his grasp.* ◆ **~ yourself/sb + adj.** *He tore himself free.*
▷ INJURE MUSCLE **5** [T] **~ sth** to injure a muscle, etc. by stretching it too much: *a torn ligament*
▷ MOVE QUICKLY **6** [I] **+ adv./prep.** to move somewhere very quickly or in an excited way: *He tore off down the street.* ◆ *A truck tore past the gates.*
▷ -TORN **7** (in adjectives) very badly affected or damaged by something: *to bring peace to a strife-torn country* ◆ *a strike-torn industry* ⊃ see also WAR-TORN
IDM ˌtear sb/sth aˈpart, to ˈshreds, to ˈbits, etc. to destroy or defeat someone or something completely or criticize them or it severely: *We tore the other team apart in the second half.* ◆ *The critics tore his last movie to shreds.* ˌtear at your ˈheart| ˌtear your ˈheart out (*formal*) to strongly affect you in an emotional way ˌtear your ˈhair (out) (*informal*) to show that you are very angry or anxious about something: *She's keeping very calm—anyone else would be tearing their hair out.* be ˌtorn (between A and B) to be unable to decide or

choose between two people, things, or feelings: *I was torn between my parents and my friend.* ⊃ more at HEART, LIMB, LOOSE
PHR V ˌtear sb↔aˈpart/ˈup to make someone feel very unhappy or worried **SYN** RIP SB APART: *It tears me apart to think I might have hurt her feelings.* ˌtear sth↔aˈpart **1** to destroy something violently, especially by pulling it to pieces: *The dogs tore the fox apart.* **2** to make people in a country, an organization, or other place fight or argue with each other: *Racial strife is tearing our country apart.* **3** to search a place, making it look messy and causing damage: *They tore the room apart, looking for money.* **SYN** RIP STH APART ˈtear at sth to pull or cut something violently so that it tears: *He tore at the meat with his bare hands.* ˌtear yourself aˈway (from sth) | ˌtear sth aˈway (from sth) to leave somewhere even though you would prefer to stay there; to take something away from somewhere: *Dinner's ready, if you can tear yourself away from the TV.* ◆ *She was unable to tear her eyes away from him* (= could not stop looking at him). ˌtear sth↔ˈdown to pull or knock down a building, wall, etc. **SYN** DEMOLISH ˌtear ˈinto sb/sth **1** to attack someone or something physically or with words **2** to start doing something with a lot of energy: *They tore into their food as if they were starving.* ˌtear sb↔ˈup = TEAR SB APART ˌtear sth↔ˈup to destroy a document, etc. by tearing it into pieces **SYN** RIP STH UP: *She tore up all the letters he had sent her.* ◆ (*figurative*) *He accused the leader of tearing up the party's manifesto* (= of ignoring it).

• *noun* a hole that has been made in something by tearing: *This sheet has a tear in it.* **IDM** see WEAR n.

tear² 🔑 /tɪr/ *noun* [usually pl.] ⊃ see also TEAR¹
a drop of liquid that comes out of your eye when you cry: *A tear rolled down his face.* ◆ *She left the room in tears* (= crying). ◆ *He suddenly burst into tears* (= began to cry). ◆ *As he listened to the music, his eyes filled with tears.* ◆ *Their story will move you to tears* (= make you cry). ◆ *They reduced her to tears* (= made her cry, especially by being cruel or unkind). ◆ *Ann wiped a tear from her eye.* ◆ *The memory brought a tear to her eye* (= made her cry). ◆ *Most of the audience was on the verge of tears.* ◆ *I was close to tears as I told them the news.* ◆ *Desperately she fought back the tears* (= tried not to cry). ◆ *to shed tears of happiness* ◆ *tears of pain, joy, etc.* ◆ *The tears welled up in his eyes.* ▶ tear·y /ˈtɪri/ *adj.*: *teary eyes* ◆ *a teary smile/goodbye* **IDM** see BLOOD, BORED, CROCODILE

tear·drop /ˈtɪrdrɑp/ *noun* a single tear that comes from your eye

ˈtear duct /ˈtɪr dʌkt/ *noun* a tube through which tears pass from the tear GLAND to the eye, or from the eye to the nose ⊃ picture at BODY

tear·ful /ˈtɪrfl/ *adj.* **1** (of a person) crying, or about to cry: *She suddenly became very tearful.* **2** (of an event, etc.) at which people feel emotional and cry: *a tearful farewell* ▶ tear·ful·ly /-fəli/ *adv.* tear·ful·ness *noun* [U]

ˈtear gas /ˈtɪr gæs/ *noun* [U] a gas that makes your eyes sting and fill with tears, used by the police or army to control crowds

tear·jerker /ˈtɪrˌdʒɜːrkər/ *noun* (*informal*) a movie, story, etc. that is designed to make people feel sad **SYN** WEEPY

tear-off /ˈter ɔf; -ɑf/ *adj.* [only before noun] relating to something that can be removed by being torn off, especially part of a sheet of paper: *a tear-off slip*

tea·room /ˈtiːrum; -rʊm/ *noun* a restaurant in which tea, coffee, cakes, and SANDWICHES are served

tear-stained /ˈtɪr steɪnd/ *adj.* (especially of someone's face or cheeks) wet with tears

tease /tiːz/ *verb, noun*
• *verb* **1** [I, T] **~ (sb)** | **~ (sb) + speech** to laugh at someone and make jokes about them, either in a friendly way or in order to annoy or embarrass them: *Don't get upset—I was only teasing.* ◆ *I used to be teased about my name.* **2** [T] **~ sth** to annoy an animal, especially by touching it, pulling its tail, etc. **3** [T] **~ sth (+ adv./prep.)** to pull something

gently apart into separate pieces: *to tease wool into strands* **4** [T] **~ sth** to COMB your hair in the opposite direction to the way it grows so that it looks thicker

PHR V ˌtease sth↔ˈout **1** to remove knots from hair, wool, etc. by gently pulling or brushing it **2** to spend time trying to find out information or the meaning of something, especially when this is complicated or difficult: *The teacher helped them tease out the meaning of the poem.*

• *noun* [usually sing.] **1** a person who likes to play tricks and jokes on other people, especially by telling them something that is not true or by not telling them something that they want to know **2** an act that is intended as a trick or joke

tea·sel (also **tea·zle**) /ˈtiːzl/ *noun* a plant which has large flowers with SPIKES, used in the past for brushing cloth to give it a smooth surface

teas·er /ˈtiːzər/ *noun* **1** (*informal*) a difficult problem or question ⊃ see also BRAIN-TEASER **2** (also ˈteaser ˌad) an advertisement for a product that does not mention the name of the product or say much about it but is intended to make people interested and likely to pay attention to later advertisements

ˈtea ˌservice (also ˈtea set) *noun* a set consisting of a TEAPOT, sugar bowl, cups, plates, etc., used for serving tea

teas·ing·ly /ˈtiːzɪŋli/ *adv.* **1** in a way that is intended to make someone feel embarrassed, annoyed, etc. **2** in a way that suggests something and makes someone want to know more **3** in a way that is intended to make someone sexually excited

tea·spoon /ˈtiːspuːn/ *noun* **1** a small spoon for putting sugar into tea and other drinks **2** (also **tea·spoon·ful** /-ˌfʊl/) (*abbr.* t., tsp.) a measurement in cooking, equal to one sixth of a FLUID OUNCE or one third of a TABLESPOON: *Add two teaspoons of salt.*

teat /tiːt/ *noun* one of the parts of a female animal's body that the young animals suck in order to get milk

ˈtea ˌtowel *noun* (*CanE*) = DISH TOWEL

ˈtea tree *noun* a small Australian and New Zealand tree. The oil from its leaves can be used to treat wounds and skin problems.

tea·zle = TEASEL

tech /tɛk/ *noun* a college or university where students study technical subjects such as science, engineering, technology, and computer science ⊃ see also HIGH-TECH, LOW-TECH

tech·ie (also **tech·y**) /ˈtɛki/ *noun* (*pl.* **tech·ies** *informal*) a person who is expert in or enthusiastic about technology, especially computers ▶ **tech·ie** (also **tech·y**) *adj.*: *techie stuff*

tech·ne·ti·um /tɛkˈniːʃiəm; -ʃəm/ *noun* [U] (*symb.* Tc) a chemical element. Technetium is found naturally as a product of URANIUM or made artificially from MOLYBDENUM.

tech·ni·cal ✦ **AWL** /ˈtɛknɪkl/ *adj.*
1 [usually before noun] connected with the practical use of machinery, methods, etc. in science and industry: *We offer free technical support for those buying our software.* ♦ *a technical education* ♦ *technical drawing* (= especially taught as a school subject) **2** [usually before noun] connected with the skills needed for a particular job, sport, art, etc.: *Skaters score extra points for technical complexity.* **3** connected with a particular subject and therefore difficult to understand if you do not know about that subject: *The article is full of technical terms.* ♦ *The guide is too technical for a nonspecialist.* **4** [only before noun] connected with the details of a law or set of rules: *Their lawyers spent days arguing over technical details.*

ˈtechnical ˈcollege (also ˈtechnical ˌschool) *noun* a college where students can study mainly practical subjects

ˌtechnical ˈfoul *noun* (in basketball) an act of breaking certain rules of the game, especially ones relating to fair play

ˌtech·ni·cal·i·ty /ˌtɛknɪˈkæləti/ *noun* (*pl.* **tech·ni·cal·i·ties**)
1 technicalities [pl.] the small details of how to do something or how something works **2** [C] a small detail in a law or set of rules, especially one that does not seem fair: *She was released on a technicality* (= because of a small detail in the law).

ˌtechnical ˈknockout *noun* (in BOXING) a victory when the opponent is still standing but is unable to continue fighting

tech·ni·cally **AWL** /ˈtɛknɪkli/ *adv.* **1** according to the exact meaning, facts, etc.: *Technically (speaking), the two countries are still at war.* ♦ *It is still technically possible for them to win* (= but it seems unlikely). **2** in a way that is connected with the skills needed for a particular job, sport, art, etc.: *As a musician, she is technically accomplished.* **3** in a way that is connected with the practical use of machinery, methods, etc. in science and industry: *a technically advanced society* ♦ *In those days recording sound was not technically possible.*

ˈtechnical ˌschool *noun* = TECHNICAL COLLEGE

ˌtechnical supˈport (also *informal* ˈtech supˌport) *noun* [U] **1** technical help that a company gives to customers using their computers or other products: *All our software licenses include technical support.* **2** a department in a company that provides technical help to its workers or customers: *I called tech support and they fixed it.*

tech·ni·cian /tɛkˈnɪʃn/ *noun* **1** a person whose job is keeping a particular type of equipment or machinery in good condition: *laboratory technicians* **2** a person who is very skilled at the technical aspects of an art, a sport, etc.

Tech·ni·col·or™ /ˈtɛknɪˌkʌlər/ *noun* [U] a process of producing color film, as used in movies

tech·ni·color (*CanE usually* **tech·ni·col·our**) /ˈtɛknɪˌkʌlər/ *noun* [U] (*informal*) the state of having many bright colors: *The rooms were painted in glorious technicolor.*

tech·nique ✦ **AWL** /tɛkˈniːk/ *noun*
1 [C] a particular way of doing something, especially one in which you have to learn special skills: *The artist combines different techniques in the same painting.* ♦ *marketing techniques* **2** [U, sing.] the skill with which someone is able to do something practical: *Her technique has improved a lot over the past season.*

tech·no /ˈtɛknoʊ/ *noun* [U] a type of fast, electronic, dance music, typically with little or no singing

techno- /ˈtɛknoʊ/ *combining form* (in nouns, adjectives, and adverbs) connected with technology: *technophobe* (= a person who is afraid of technology)

tech·no·bab·ble /ˈtɛknoʊˌbæbl/ *noun* [U] (*informal, disapproving*) words or expressions connected with computers and technology that are difficult for ordinary people to understand

tech·noc·ra·cy /tɛkˈnɑkrəsi/ *noun* (*pl.* **tech·noc·ra·cies**) [U, C] a social or political system in which people with scientific knowledge have a lot of power

tech·no·crat /ˈtɛknəˌkræt/ *noun* an expert in science, engineering, etc. who has a lot of power in politics and/or industry ▶ **tech·no·crat·ic** /ˌtɛknəˈkrætɪk/ *adj.* [usually before noun]

tech·nol·o·gist /tɛkˈnɑlədʒɪst/ *noun* an expert in technology

tech·nol·o·gy ✦ **AWL** /tɛkˈnɑlədʒi/ *noun* (*pl.* **tech·nol·o·gies**)
1 [U, C] scientific knowledge used in practical ways in industry, for example in designing new machines: *science and technology* ♦ *recent advances in medical technology* ♦ *to make use of the most modern technologies* ⊃ see also HIGH TECHNOLOGY, INFORMATION TECHNOLOGY **2** [U] machinery or equipment designed using technology: *The company has invested in the latest technology.* ▶ **tech·no·log·i·cal** **AWL** /ˌtɛknəˈlɑdʒɪkl/ *adj.*: *technological advances* ♦ *technological change* ♦ *a major technological breakthrough* **tech·no·log·i·cally** **AWL** /-kli/ *adv.*: *technologically advanced*

tech·no·phile /'tɛknəˌfaɪl/ *noun* a person who is enthusiastic about new technology

tech·no·phobe /'tɛknəˌfoʊb/ *noun* a person who is afraid of, dislikes, or avoids new technology

tech sup·port *noun* (*informal*) = TECHNICAL SUPPORT

tech·y = TECHIE

tec·ton·ic /tɛk'tɑnɪk/ *adj.* [only before noun] (*geology*) connected with the structure of the earth's surface ⊃ see also PLATE TECTONICS

ted·dy /'tɛdi/ *noun* (*pl.* **ted·dies**) **1** = TEDDY BEAR **2** a piece of women's underwear that combines a BRA and PANTIES

teddy bear (also **ted·dy**) *noun* a soft toy BEAR ⊃ picture at TOY

te·di·ous /'tidiəs/ *adj.* lasting or taking too long and not interesting SYN BORING: *The journey soon became tedious.* ◆ *We had to listen to the tedious details of his operation.* ⊃ thesaurus box at BORING ▶ **te·di·ous·ly** *adv.* **te·di·ous·ness** *noun* [U]

te·di·um /'tidiəm/ *noun* [U] the quality of being boring SYN BOREDOM: *She longed for something to relieve the tedium of everyday life.*

tee /ti/ *noun, verb*
● *noun* **1** a flat area on a GOLF COURSE from which players hit the ball: *to drive off from the first tee* ◆ *a tee shot* **2** a small piece of plastic or wood that you stick in the ground to support a GOLF ball before you hit it **3** a stand used in Tee Ball™ to hold a baseball before it is hit with a bat IDM see T
● *verb* (**teed, teed**)
PHR V **tee 'off** to hit a GOLF ball from a tee, especially at the start of a game ,**tee sb↔'off** (*informal*) to make someone angry or annoyed ,**tee sth↔'up** | ,**tee 'up** to prepare to hit a GOLF ball by placing it on a tee

Tee Ball™ (also **T-ball**) *noun* a form of baseball for young children in which the ball is hit off a stand (= a **tee**)

,**teed 'off** *adj.* (*informal*) annoyed or angry

tee-hee /ˌti 'hi/ *noun* used to represent the sound of a quiet laugh

teem /tim/ *verb* [I] usually **be teeming** (of rain) to fall heavily SYN POUR: *The rain was teeming down.*
PHR V '**teem with sth** usually **be 'teeming with something** to be full of people, animals, etc. moving around: *The streets were teeming with tourists.* ◆ *a river teeming with fish*

teem·ing /'timɪŋ/ *adj.* present in large numbers; full of people, animals, etc. that are moving around: *teeming insects* ◆ *the teeming streets of the city*

teen·age /'tineɪdʒ/ (also *informal* **teen** /tin/) *adj.* [usually before noun] between 13 and 19 years old; connected with people of this age: *teenage girls/boys* ◆ *teenage rebellion* ◆ *teen magazines*

teen·aged /'tineɪdʒd/ *adj.* between 13 and 19 years old: *They have two teenaged daughters.*

teen·ag·er /'tinˌeɪdʒər/ (also *informal* **teen**) *noun* a person who is between 13 and 19 years old: *a magazine aimed at teenagers*

teens /tinz/ *noun* [pl.] the years of a person's life when they are between 13 and 19 years old: *She began writing poetry in her teens.* ◆ *to be in your early/late teens*

tee·ny /'tini/ *adj.* (*informal*) (**tee·ni·er, tee·ni·est**) (also **tee·ny-wee·ny** /ˌtini 'wini/, **teen·sy** /'tinsi/, **teen·sy-ween·sy** /ˌtinsi 'winsi/) very small SYN TINY

tee·ny·bopper /'tiniˌbɑpər/ *noun* (*old-fashioned, informal*) a young girl between the ages of about 10 and 13, who is very interested in pop music, fashionable clothes, etc.

tee·pee = TEPEE

'**tee shirt** = T-SHIRT

tee·ter /'titər/ *verb* [I] to stand or move in an unsteady way so that you look as if you are going to fall: *She teetered after him in her high-heeled shoes.*
IDM **teeter on the brink/edge of sth** to be very close to a

very unpleasant or dangerous situation: *The country is teetering on the brink of civil war.*

'**teeter-ˌtotter** *noun* = SEE-SAW

teeth *pl.* of TOOTH

teethe /tið/ *verb* [I] when a baby **is teething**, its first teeth are starting to grow

'**teething ˌpains** (also '**teething ˌproblems**) *noun* [pl.] small problems that a company, product, system, etc. has at the beginning

tee·to·tal /'tiˌtoʊtl/ *adj.* never drinking alcohol: *He's strictly teetotal.* ▶ **tee·to·tal·ism** /-ˌɪzəm/ *noun* [U]

tee·to·tal·er /'tiˌtoʊtlæˌwər/ *noun* a person who does not drink alcohol

Tef·lon™ /'tɛflɑn/ *noun, adj.*
● *noun* [U] a substance used especially to cover the inside of cooking pans, that stops food from sticking to them
● *adj.* (especially of a politician) still having a good reputation after making a mistake or doing something that is not legal: *The Teflon President has survived another crisis.*

tel. (also **Tel.**) *abbr.* (in writing) telephone number

tel·co /'tɛlkoʊ/ *noun* (*pl.* **tel·cos**) (used especially in newspapers) a TELECOMMUNICATIONS company: *Telcos were struggling to make money from broadband services.*

tele- /'tɛlə/ *combining form* (in nouns, verbs, adjectives, and adverbs) **1** over a long distance; far: *telepathy* ◆ *telescopic* **2** connected with television: *telethon* **3** done using a telephone: *telesales*

tel·e·bank·ing /'tɛləˌbæŋkɪŋ/ *noun* [U] = TELEPHONE BANKING

tel·e·cam·er·a /'tɛləˌkæmrə; -ˌkæmərə/ *noun* a video camera used in VIDEOCONFERENCING

tel·e·cast /'tɛləˌkæst/ *noun* a broadcast on television ▶ **telecast** *verb* (**tel·e·cast, tel·e·cast**) [usually passive]: ~ **sth** *The event will be telecast simultaneously to nearly 150 cities.* **tel·e·cast·er** *noun*

tel·e·com /'tɛləˌkɑm/ *noun* **1** [U] = TELECOMMUNICATIONS: *the telecom industry* ◆ *telecom services* **2** [C] a telecommunications company

tel·e·com·mu·ni·ca·tions /ˌtɛləkəˌmyunəˈkeɪʃnz/ (also *informal* **tel·e·com**) *noun* [U] the technology of sending signals, images, and messages over long distances by radio, telephone, television, SATELLITE, etc.: *technological developments in telecommunications* ◆ *the telecommunications industry* ▶ **tel·e·com·mu·ni·ca·tion** (also *informal* **tel·e·com**) *adj.* [only before noun]: *a telecommunication company*

tel·e·com·mute /'tɛləkəˌmyut/ *verb* [I] to work from home, communicating with your office, customers, and others by telephone, e-mail, etc. ▶ **tel·e·com·mut·er** *noun* **tel·e·com·mut·ing** *noun* [U]

tel·e·con·fer·ence /'tɛləˌkɑnfrəns/ *noun* a conference or discussion at which members are in different places and speak to each other using telephone and video connections ▶ **tel·e·con·fer·ence** *verb* [I] **tel·e·con·fer·enc·ing** *noun* [U]

tel·e·film /'tɛləˌfɪlm/ *noun* a movie that is made specially to be shown on television

tel·e·gen·ic /ˌtɛləˈdʒɛnɪk/ *adj.* a **telegenic** person looks good on television

tel·e·gram /'tɛləˌgræm/ *noun* a message sent by TELEGRAPH and then printed and given to someone

tel·e·graph /'tɛləˌgræf/ *noun, verb*
● *noun* [U] a method of sending messages over long distances, using wires that carry electrical signals
● *verb* **1** [I, T] ~ (**sth**) to send a message by telegraph **2** [T] ~ **sth** to make it clear to people what you are going to do, often without intending to

tel·e·graph·ic /ˌtɛləˈgræfɪk/ *adj.* connected with sending messages by telegraph: *You will need to arrange a telegraphic transfer from your bank to ours.*

te·leg·ra·phy /təˈlɛgrəfi/ *noun* [U] the process of sending messages by telegraph

tel·e·ki·ne·sis /ˌtɛləkɪˈnisəs/ *noun* [U] the ability to move objects without touching them, using mental powers

tel·e·mark /ˈtɛləˌmɑrk/ *noun* [U] (in SKIING or SKI JUMPING) a style of turning or landing with one SKI forward and bent knees

tel·e·mar·ket·ing /ˌtɛləˈmɑrkətɪŋ; ˈtɛləˌmɑr-/ *noun* [U] a method of selling things and taking orders for sales by telephone ▶ **tel·e·mar·ket·er** *noun*

tel·e·mat·ics /ˌtɛləˈmætɪks/ *noun* [U] the use or study of technology that allows information to be sent over long distances using computers

te·le·me·ter /ˈtɛləˌmitər; təˈlɛmətər/ *noun* (*technical*) a device for sending, receiving, and measuring scientific data over a long distance ▶ **te·le·me·ter** /ˈtɛləˌmitər/ *verb*: ~ **sth (to sth)** *Data from these instruments is telemetered to the laboratory.*

te·lem·e·try /təˈlɛmətri/ *noun* [U] (*technical*) the process of using special equipment to send, receive, and measure scientific data over long distances

tel·e·ol·o·gy /ˌtili'ɑlədʒi/ˌteli-/ *noun* [U, sing.] (*philosophy*) the theory that events and developments are meant to achieve a purpose and happen because of that ▶ **tel·e·o·log·i·cal** /ˌtiliəˈlɑdʒɪkl/ˌteli-/ *adj.*

tel·e·op·er·ate /ˌtɛləˈɑpəˌreɪt/ *verb* ~ **sth (from sth)** to operate a machine that is not in the same place as you: *Equipment on the space station is teleoperated from earth.*

tel·e·path·ic /ˌtɛləˈpæθɪk/ *adj.* **1** using telepathy: *telepathic communication* **2** (of a person) able to communicate by telepathy: *How do I know what he's thinking? I'm not telepathic!* ▶ **tel·e·path·i·cally** /-kli/ *adv.*

te·lep·a·thy /təˈlɛpəθi/ *noun* [U] the direct communication of thoughts or feelings from one person to another without using speech, writing, or any other normal method

tel·e·phone 🔔 /ˈtɛləˌfoʊn/ *noun, verb*
- *noun* **1** [C, U] a system for talking to someone else over long distances, using wires or radio; a machine used for this: *The telephone rang and Pat answered it.* ♦ *You can reserve seats over the telephone.* ♦ *I need to make a telephone call.* ♦ *telephone lines/networks/services* ⊃ collocations at PHONE **2** [C] the part of the telephone that you hold in your hand and speak into **SYN** HANDSET, RECEIVER ⊃ see also PHONE

  IDM **be on the telephone** to be using the telephone: *He's on the telephone at the moment.* ♦ *You're wanted* (= someone wants to speak to you) *on the telephone.*
- *verb* [I, T] (*formal*) to speak to someone by telephone **SYN** CALL, PHONE: *Please write or telephone for details.* ♦ *He telephoned to say he'd be late.* ♦ ~ **sth** *You can telephone your order 24 hours a day.* ♦ *I was about to telephone the police.* ⊃ note at PHONE

telephone banking (also **tel·e·bank·ing**) *noun* [U] activities relating to your bank account, which you do using the telephone

telephone booth *noun* = PHONE BOOTH

telephone di·rectory (also **phone book, telephone book**) *noun* a book that lists the names, addresses, and telephone numbers of people in a particular area: *to look up a number in the telephone directory*

telephone ex·change (also **ex·change**) *noun* a place where telephone calls are connected so that people can speak to each other

telephone number (also **phone number**) *noun* the number of a particular telephone, that you use when you make a call to it

telephone pole *noun* a tall wooden pole used for carrying telephone wires high above the ground

telephone tag *noun* [U] = PHONE TAG

te·leph·o·ny /təˈlɛfəni/ *noun* [U] the process of sending messages and signals by telephone

tel·e·pho·to lens /ˌtɛləˌfoʊtoʊ ˈlɛnz/ *noun* a camera LENS that produces a large image of an object that is far away and allows you to take photographs of it

tel·e·port /ˈtɛləˌpɔrt/ *verb* [I, T] ~ **(sb/sth)** (usually in SCIENCE FICTION) to move someone or something immediately from one place to another a distance away, using special equipment; to be moved in this way: *The search party was teleported down to the planet's surface.* ▶ **tel·e·por·ta·tion** /ˌtɛləpɔrˈteɪʃn/ *noun* [U]

tel·e·promp·ter /ˈtɛləˌprɑmptər/ *noun* a device used by people who are speaking in public, especially on television, that displays the words they have to say

tel·e·scope /ˈtɛləˌskoʊp/ *noun, verb*
- *noun* a piece of equipment shaped like a tube, containing LENSES, that you look through to make objects that are far away appear larger and nearer: *to look at the stars through a telescope* ⊃ picture at BINOCULARS ⊃ see also RADIO TELESCOPE
- *verb* **1** [I, T] ~ **(sth)** to become shorter, or make something shorter, by sliding sections inside one another **2** [T] ~ **sth (into sth)** to reduce something so that it happens in less time: *Three episodes have been telescoped into a single program.*

tel·e·scop·ic /ˌtɛləˈskɑpɪk/ *adj.* **1** connected with or using a telescope; making things look larger as a telescope does: *a rifle with a telescopic sight* **2** made of sections that can slide into each other to make the object longer or shorter: *a telescopic antenna* ▶ **tel·e·scop·i·cally** /-kli/ *adv.*

tel·e·shop·ping /ˈtɛləˌʃɑpɪŋ/ *noun* [U] shopping that is done using the telephone or television

tel·e·thon /ˈtɛləˌθɑn/ *noun* a very long television show, broadcast to raise money for charity

tel·e·type·writ·er /ˌtɛləˈtaɪpˌraɪtər/ *noun* a machine that prints out TELEX messages that have been typed in another place and sent by telephone lines

tel·e·van·ge·list /ˌtɛləˈvændʒəlɪst/ *noun* a person who appears regularly on television to try to persuade people to become Christians and to give money ▶ **tel·e·van·ge·lism** /-ˌlɪzəm/ *noun* [U]

tel·e·vise /ˈtɛləˌvaɪz/ *verb* [usually passive] ~ **sth** to broadcast something on television: *a televised debate* ♦ *to televise a novel* ♦ *The speech will be televised live.*

tel·e·vi·sion 🔔 /ˈtɛləˌvɪʒn/ *noun* (*abbr.* TV)
1 (also **television set**) [C] a piece of electrical equipment with a screen on which you can watch programs with moving pictures and sounds: *a color television* ♦ *a wide-screen television* ♦ *a plasma screen television* ♦ *to turn the television on/off* **2** [U] the programs broadcast on television: *We don't do much in the evenings except watch television.* **3** [U] the system, process, or business of broadcasting television programs: *satellite/terrestrial/cable/digital television* ♦ *the television news* ♦ *a television documentary* ♦ *a television company/presenter* ♦ *I'd like to work in television* (= for a television company). ⊃ see also CABLE TELEVISION, CLOSED-CIRCUIT TELEVISION

IDM **on television** (also *informal* **on TV**) being broadcast by television; appearing in a television program: *What's on television tonight?* ♦ *It was on TV yesterday.* ♦ *I recognize you. Aren't you on television?*

TOPIC COLLOCATIONS

Television

watching
- watch television/TV/a show/a program/a documentary/a pilot/a rerun/a repeat
- see an ad/a commercial/the news/the weather
- catch/miss a show/a program/an episode/the news
- pick up/reach for/grab/lose the remote (control)

| t tea | ţ butter | d did | k cat | g got | tʃ chin | dʒ June | f fall |

- **change** channels
- **surf (through)/flip through** the channels
- **sit in front of/turn on/turn off** the television/the TV/ the TV set
- **have/install** satellite (TV)/cable (TV)/a satellite dish

showing

- **show** a program/a documentary/an ad/a commercial/a prime-time sitcom/drama
- **run** an ad/a commercial/a movie
- **broadcast/air/repeat** a show/a program/a documentary/an episode/a series
- **go out/air/be recorded** live
- **attract/draw (in)/pull (in)** viewers
- **be a hit with** viewers/audiences/critics
- **get (low/high)** ratings

appearing

- **be on/appear on** television/TV/a TV show
- **take part in** a call-in/a game show/a quiz show/a reality TV show
- **host** a show/a program/a series/a game show/a quiz show/a (late-night/daytime) talk show
- **be/become/work as** a talk-show host/sports commentator/news anchor
- **present** the news
- **appear/perform** live (on TV)

program-making

- **do/film/make** a show/a program/a documentary/an episode/a pilot/a series/an ad/a commercial
- **work on** a soap (opera)/a pilot (episode)/a sitcom
- **write/produce** a drama/sitcom/spin-off/comedy series

tel·e·vis·u·al /ˌtelə'vɪʒuəl/ *adj.* relating to or suitable for television: *a major televisual event*

tel·ex /'teleks/ *noun, verb*
- *noun* **1** [U] an international system of communication in which messages are typed on a special machine and sent by the telephone system **2** [C] a message sent or received by telex **3** [C] (*informal*) a machine for sending and receiving messages by telex
- *verb* [I, T] ~ (sth) to send a message by telex

tell /tel/ *verb* (told, told /tould/)

> **GIVE INFORMATION 1** [T] (of a person) to give information to someone by speaking or writing: ~ **sth to sb** *He told the news to everyone he saw.* ◆ ~ **sb sth** *He told everyone he saw the news.* ◆ *Did she tell you her name?* ◆ *What did I tell you?* (= you should have listened to my advice) ◆ ~ **sb (about sth)** *Why wasn't I told about the accident?* ◆ ~ **sb/yourself (that)...** *They've told us (that) they're not coming.* ◆ *I kept telling myself (that) everything was OK.* ◆ *Are you telling me you didn't have any help with this?* (= I don't believe what you have said) ◆ ~ **sb where, what, etc....** *Tell me where you live.* ◆ ~ **sb + speech** *"I'm ready to go now," he told her.* ◆ note at SAY **2** [T] (of some writing, an instrument, a sign, etc.) to give information about something: ~ **sb sth** *The advertisement told us very little about the product.* ◆ ~ **sb how, where, etc....** *This gauge tells you how much fuel you have left.* ◆ ~ **sb (that)...** *The sound of his breathing told her (that) he was asleep.*
> **EXPRESS IN WORDS 3** [T] to express something in words: ~ **sth** *to tell stories/jokes/lies* ◆ *Are you sure you're telling the truth?* ◆ ~ **sb how, what, etc....** *I can't tell you how happy I am.*
> **SECRET 4** [I] to let someone know a secret: *Promise you won't tell.* ◆ *"Who are you going out with tonight?" "That would be telling!"* (= it's a secret)
> **ORDER 5** [T] to order or advise someone to do something: ~ **sb/yourself to do sth** *He was told to sit down and wait.* ◆ *There was a sign telling motorists to slow down.* ◆ *I kept telling myself to keep calm.* ◆ ~ **sb sth** *Do what I tell you.* ◆ ~ **sb** *Children must do as they're told.* ◆ ~ **sb what, when, etc....** *Don't tell me what to do!* ◆ ~ **sb (that)...** *The doctor told me*

(that) I should eat less fat. ⊃ thesaurus box at ORDER ⊃ note at SAY
> **KNOW/JUDGE 6** [I, T] (not used in the progressive tenses) to know, see, or judge something correctly: *I think he's happy. It's hard to tell.* ◆ *As far as I can tell, she's enjoying the course.* ◆ ~ **(that)...** *I could tell (that) he was angry from his expression.* ◆ ~ **how, if, etc....** *"That's not an original." "How can you tell?"* ◆ *The only way to tell if you like something is by trying it.*
> **DISTINGUISH 7** [T] (not used in the progressive tenses or in the passive) to distinguish one thing or person from another: ~ **sth** *It was hard to tell the difference between the two versions.* ◆ ~ **A from B** *Can you tell Tom from his twin brother?* ◆ ~ **A and B apart** *It's difficult to tell them apart.* ◆ ~ **which, what, etc....** *The kittens look exactly alike—how can you tell which is which?*
> **HAVE EFFECT 8** [I] ~ **(on sb)** to have an effect on someone or something, especially a bad one: *The strain was beginning to tell on the rescue team.*

IDM **all told** with all people, etc. counted and included: *There are 52 people coming, all told.* **don't tell me** (*informal*) used to say that you know or can guess what someone is going to say, especially because it is typical of them: *Don't tell me you were late again!* **I/I'll tell you** (*informal*) used to introduce a suggestion: *I'll tell you what—let's stay in instead.* **I tell you| I can tell you| I'm telling you** (*informal*) used to emphasize what you are saying, especially when it is surprising or difficult to believe: *It isn't cheap, I can tell you!* ◆ *I'm telling you, that's exactly what she said.* **I told you (so)** (*informal*) used when something bad has happened, to remind someone that you warned them about it and they did not listen to you **live, etc. to tell the tale** to survive a difficult or dangerous experience so that you can tell others what really happened **tell a different story/tale** to give some information that is different from what you expect or have been told **tell its own tale/story** to explain itself, without needing any further explanation or comment: *Her face told its own story.* **tell me** (*informal*) used to introduce a question: *Tell me, have you had lunch yet?* **tell me about it** (*informal*) used to say that you understand what someone is talking about and have had the same experience: *"I get so annoyed with Steve!" "Tell me about it. He drives me crazy."* **tell me another!** (*informal*) used to tell someone that you do not believe what they have said **tell tales (about sth/on sb)** to tell someone about something that another person has done wrong **tell time** to read the time from a clock, etc.: *She's only five—she hasn't learned to tell time yet.* **tell sb where to put/stick sth| tell sb what they can do with sth** (*informal*) to make it clear to someone that you are angry and are rejecting what they are offering you **there's no telling** used to say that it is impossible to know what happened or will happen: *There's no telling how they'll react.* **to tell (you) the truth** (*informal*) used when admitting something: *To tell the truth, I fell asleep in the middle of her talk.* **you can never tell| you never can tell** (*saying*) you can never be sure, for example because things are not always what they appear to be **you're telling me!** (*informal*) I completely agree with you ⊃ more at HEAR, KISS *v.*, LITTLE *adj.*, THING, TIME *n.*, TRUTH

PHR V **'tell of sth** (*formal* or *literary*) to make something known; to give an account of something: *notices telling of the proposed job cuts* **tell sb↔'off (for sth/for doing sth)** (*informal*) to speak angrily to someone for doing something wrong **SYN** SCOLD: *I told the boys off for making so much noise.* ◆ *Did you get told off?* **'tell on sb** (*informal*) to tell a person in authority about something bad that someone has done: *Promise not to tell on me!*

tell-'all *adj.* [only before noun] (of a book, an interview in a newspaper or magazine, etc.) in which someone, usually someone famous, admits something that may shock people: *a tell-all book/memoir/autobiography*

tell·er /'telər/ *noun* **1** a person whose job is to receive and pay out money in a bank **2** a machine that pays out money automatically: *automatic teller machines* **3** a person whose job is to count votes, especially in a LEGISLATURE **4** (usually in compounds) a person who tells stories, etc.: *a foul-*

mouthed teller of lies ➲ see also FORTUNE-TELLER, STORY-TELLER

tell·ing /'tɛlɪŋ/ adj. **1** having a strong or important effect; effective: a telling argument **2** showing effectively what someone or something is really like, but often without intending to: The number of homeless people is a telling comment on the state of society. ▶ **tell·ing·ly** adv.

tell·tale /'tɛlteɪl/ adj. [only before noun] showing that something exists or has happened: telltale clues/marks/signs/sounds ◆ The telltale smell of cigarettes told her that he had been in the room.

tel·lu·ri·um /tə'lʊriəm/ noun [U] (symb. **Te**) a chemical element. Tellurium is a shiny silver-white substance that breaks easily, found in SULFIDE ORES.

tem·blor /'tɛmblər/ noun an EARTHQUAKE (= a sudden, violent shaking of the earth's surface)

te·mer·i·ty /tə'mɛrəti/ noun [U] (formal) extremely confident behavior that people are likely to consider rude: He had the temerity to call me a liar!

temp /tɛmp/ noun, verb, abbr.
• noun a temporary employee in an office
• verb [I] (informal) to do a temporary job or a series of temporary jobs: I've been temping for an employment agency. ➲ collocations at JOB
• abbr. (also temp.) temperature: Max temp 63°F

tem·peh /'tɛmpeɪ/ noun [U] an Indonesian dish made from FERMENTED SOYBEANS

tem·per /'tɛmpər/ noun, verb
• noun **1** [C, usually sing., U] if someone has a **temper**, they become angry very easily: a violent/short/quick, etc. temper ◆ He must learn to **control his temper**. ◆ She broke the plates in a **fit of temper**. ◆ After an hour of waiting, **tempers began to fray** (= people began to get angry). **2** [C, usually sing.] a short period of feeling very angry: to **fly into a temper 3** [C] the way that you are feeling at a particular time **SYN** MOOD: Come back when you're in a better temper. ◆ to be in a bad, foul, etc. temper **4** -tempered (in adjectives) having a particular type of temper: good-/bad-tempered ◆ a sweet-tempered child **HELP** You will find other compounds ending in -tempered at their place in the alphabet.
  IDM lose/keep your temper (with sb) to fail/manage to control your anger: She lost her temper with a customer and shouted at him. ◆ I struggle to keep my temper with the kids when they misbehave. ➲ more at QUICK
• verb **1** ~ sth (with sth) (formal) to make something less severe by adding something that has the opposite effect: Justice must be tempered with mercy. **2** ~ sth (technical) to make metal as hard as it needs to be by heating and then cooling it

tem·per·a /'tɛmpərə/ noun [U] a kind of paint in which the color is mixed with egg and water; a method of painting that uses this kind of paint

tem·per·a·ment /'tɛmprəmənt; -pərmənt/ noun **1** [C, U] a person's or an animal's nature as shown in the way they behave or react to situations or people: to have an artistic temperament ◆ a horse with an excellent temperament ◆ She's a dreamer and a romantic by temperament. **2** [U] the tendency to get emotional and excited very easily and behave in an unreasonable way: an actor given to displays of temperament

tem·per·a·men·tal /ˌtɛmprə'mɛntl; -pər'mɛntl/ adj. **1** (usually disapproving) having a tendency to become angry, excited, or upset easily, and to behave in an unreasonable way: You never know what to expect with her. She's so temperamental. ◆ (figurative) The printer's being temperamental this morning. **2** connected with someone's nature and personality: They are firm friends in spite of temperamental differences. ▶ **tem·per·a·men·tal·ly** /-'mɛntl·i/ adv.: I'm temperamentally unsuited to this job.

tem·per·ance /'tɛmprəns; -pərəns/ noun [U] **1** (old-fashioned) the practice of not drinking alcohol because of your moral or religious beliefs **2** (formal) the practice of controlling your behavior, the amount you eat, etc., so that it is always reasonable **SYN** MODERATION

tem·per·ate /'tɛmprət; -pərət/ adj. **1** [usually before noun] (technical) (of a climate or region) having a mild temperature without extremes of heat or cold **2** (formal) behaving in a calm and controlled way **ANT** INTEMPERATE ▶ **tem·per·ate·ly** adv.

temperate ˌzone noun [C, usually sing.] (technical) an area of the Earth that is not near the EQUATOR or the South or North Pole

tem·per·a·ture /'tɛmprətʃər/ noun (abbr. temp) [C, U]
1 the measurement of degrees of how hot or cold a thing or place is: high/low temperatures ◆ a fall/drop in temperature ◆ a rise in temperature ◆ The temperature has risen (by) five degrees. ◆ Heat the oven to a temperature of 400°F (= degrees FAHRENHEIT). ◆ Some places have had temperatures in the 100s (= over 100° FAHRENHEIT). ➲ see also ABSOLUTE TEMPERATURE, ROOM TEMPERATURE **2** the measurement of how hot someone's body is: to **take someone's temperature** (= measure the temperature of someone's body using a special instrument) ➲ compare FEVER
  IDM raise/lower the temperature to increase/decrease the amount of excitement, emotion, etc. in a situation: His angry refusal to agree raised the temperature of the meeting.

tem·pest /'tɛmpəst/ noun (formal or literary) a violent storm
  IDM a tempest in a teapot a lot of anger or worry about something that is not important

tem·pes·tu·ous /tɛm'pɛstʃuəs/ adj. **1** (formal) full of extreme emotions **SYN** STORMY: a tempestuous relationship **2** (formal or literary) caused by or affected by a violent storm **SYN** STORMY: tempestuous seas

tem·plate /'tɛmplət/ noun **1** a shape cut out of a hard material, used as a model for producing exactly the same shape many times in another material **2** a thing that is used as a model for producing other similar examples: If you need to write a lot of similar letters, set up a template on your computer.

tem·ple /'tɛmpl/ noun **1** a building used for the worship of a god or gods, especially in religions other than Christianity: the Temple of Diana at Ephesus ◆ a Buddhist/Hindu/Sikh temple ◆ to go to temple (= to a service in a SYNAGOGUE, where Jews worship) ➲ collocations at RELIGION **2** each of the flat parts at the sides of the head, at the same level as the eyes and higher: He had black hair, greying at the temples. ➲ picture at BODY

tem·po /'tɛmpoʊ/ noun (pl. tem·pos or, in sense 1, technical tem·pi /'tɛmpi/) [C, U] **1** the speed or rhythm of a piece of music: a slow/fast tempo ◆ It's a difficult piece, with numerous changes of tempo. **2** the speed of any movement or activity **SYN** PACE[1]: the increasing tempo of life in Western society

tem·po·ral /'tɛmpərəl/ adj. **1** (formal) connected with the real physical world, not spiritual matters: Although spiritual leader of millions of people, the Pope has no temporal power. **2** (formal) connected with or limited by time: a universe which has spatial and temporal dimensions **3** (anatomy) near the TEMPLE(S) at the side of the head: the right temporal lobe of the brain

tem·po·rar·y /'tɛmpəˌrɛri/ AWL adj. lasting or intended to last or be used only for a short time; not permanent: temporary relief from pain ◆ I'm looking for some temporary work. ◆ They had to move into temporary accommodations. ◆ a temporary measure/solution/arrangement ◆ More than half the staff are temporary. **ANT** PERMANENT ▶ **tem·po·rar·i·ly** AWL /ˌtɛmpə'rɛrəli/ adv.: We regret this service is temporarily unavailable. **tem·po·rar·i·ness** /'tɛmpəˌrɛrinəs/ noun [U]

tem·po·rize /'tɛmpəˌraɪz/ verb [I] (formal) to delay making a decision or giving a definite answer, in order to gain time

tempt /tɛmpt/ verb **1** to attract someone or make someone want to do or have something, even if they know it is wrong: ~ sb (into sth/into doing sth) I was tempted by the

dessert menu. ◆ *Don't tempt thieves by leaving valuables clearly visible.* ◆ **~ sb to do sth** *I was tempted to take the day off.* **2** to persuade or try to persuade someone to do something that you want them to do, for example by offering them something: **~ sb (into sth/into doing sth)** *How can we tempt young people into engineering?* ◆ **~ sb to do sth** *Nothing would tempt me to live here.*
IDM **tempt fate** to do something too confidently in a way that might mean that your good luck will come to an end

temp·ta·tion /tɛmpˈteɪʃn/ *noun* **1** [C, U] the desire to do or have something that you know is bad or wrong: *the temptation of easy profits* ◆ *to* **give in to/yield to/succumb to temptation** ◆ *I couldn't* **resist the temptation** *to open the letter.* **2** [C] a thing that makes someone want to do or have something that they know is bad or wrong: *An expensive bicycle is a temptation to thieves.*

tempt·er /ˈtɛmptər/ *noun* a person who tries to persuade someone to do something, especially something bad or wrong

tempt·ing /ˈtɛmptɪŋ/ *adj.* something that is **tempting** is attractive, and makes people want to have it, do it, etc.: *It was a tempting offer.* ◆ *That cake looks very tempting.* ◆ *It's tempting to speculate about what might have happened.* ▶ **tempt·ing·ly** *adv.*

tempt·ress /ˈtɛmptrəs/ *noun* (*old-fashioned* or *humorous*) a woman who **tempts** someone, especially one who deliberately makes a man want to have sex with her

tem·pu·ra /tɛmˈpʊrə/ /tɛmˈpuːrə/ *noun* [U, C] a Japanese dish consisting of pieces of vegetables or fish that have been fried in **BATTER** (= a mixture of flour, egg, and water)

ten /tɛn/ *number* 10 **HELP** There are examples of how to use numbers at the entry for **five**.
IDM **a (perfect) ten** (*informal*) used to praise someone by giving them the highest mark on a scale of one to ten: *I'd give them a ten for all the work they did.* ◆ *She's gorgeous—definitely a ten!* **ten to one** very probably: *Ten to one he'll be late.*

ten·a·ble /ˈtɛnəbl/ *adj.* **1** (of a theory, an opinion, etc.) easy to defend against attack or criticism: *a tenable position* ◆ *The old idea that this work was not suitable for women was no longer tenable.* **ANT** **UNTENABLE** **2** [not before noun] (of a job, position, etc., especially in a university) that can be held for a particular period of time: *The lectureship is tenable for a period of three years.*

te·na·cious /təˈneɪʃəs/ *adj.* (*formal*) **1** that does not stop holding something or give up something easily; determined: *a tenacious grip* ◆ *She's a tenacious woman. She never gives up.* ◆ *The party has kept its tenacious hold on power for more than twenty years.* **2** continuing to exist, have influence, etc. for longer than you might expect
SYN **PERSISTENT**: *a tenacious illness* ▶ **te·na·cious·ly** *adv.*: *Though seriously ill, he still clings tenaciously to life.* **te·nac·i·ty** /təˈnæsəti/ *noun* [U]: *They competed with skill and tenacity.*

ten·an·cy /ˈtɛnənsi/ *noun* (*pl.* **ten·an·cies**) **1** [C] a period of time that you rent a house, land, etc. for: *a three-month tenancy* ◆ *a tenancy agreement* **2** [C, U] the right to live or work in a building or on land that you rent: *They had taken over the tenancy of the farm.*

ten·ant /ˈtɛnənt/ *noun, verb*
● *noun* a person who pays rent for the use of a room, building, land, etc. to the person who owns it: *They had evicted their tenants for non-payment of rent.* ◆ *The decorating was done by a previous tenant.* ◆ *tenant farmers* (= ones who do not own their own farms)
● *verb* [usually passive] **~ sth** to live or work in a place as a tenant: *a tenanted farm*

tend /tɛnd/ *verb*
1 [I] **~ to do sth** to be likely to do something or to happen in a particular way because this is what often or usually happens: *Women tend to live longer than men.* ◆ *When I'm tired, I tend to make mistakes.* ◆ *It tends to get very cold here in the winter.* ◆ *People* **tend to think** *that the problem will never*

affect them. ⊃ language bank at **GENERALLY** **2** [I] **~ (to/toward sth)** to take a particular direction or often have a particular quality: *His views tend toward the extreme.* ◆ *Prices have tended downward over recent years.* **3** [T, I] to care for someone or something: **~ sb/sth** *a shepherd tending his sheep* ◆ *Doctors and nurses tended the injured.* ◆ *well-tended gardens* ◆ **~ to sb/sth** *Ambulance crews were tending to the injured.* **4** [T] **~ sth** to serve customers in a store, bar, etc.: *He had a job* **tending bar** *in San Francisco.*

ten·den·cy /ˈtɛndənsi/ *noun* (*pl.* **ten·den·cies**) **1** if someone or something has a particular **tendency**, they are likely to behave or act in a particular way: *to display artistic, etc. tendencies* ◆ **~ (for sb/sth) (to do sth)** *I have a tendency to talk too much when I'm nervous.* ◆ *There is a tendency for this disease to run in families.* ◆ **~ (to/toward sth)** *She has a strong natural tendency toward caution.* **2 ~ (for sb/sth) (to do sth)** | **~ (to/toward sth)** a new custom that is starting to develop **SYN** **TREND**: *There is a growing tendency among employers to hire casual staff.*

ten·den·tious /tɛnˈdɛnʃəs/ *adj.* (*formal*, usually *disapproving*) (of a speech, piece of writing, theory, etc.) expressing a strong opinion that people are likely to disagree with **SYN** **CONTROVERSIAL** ▶ **ten·den·tious·ly** *adv.* **ten·den·tious·ness** *noun* [U]

ten·der /ˈtɛndər/ *adj., noun, verb*
● *adj.* (**ten·der·er**, **ten·der·est**) **HELP** more **tender** and most **tender** are also common **1** kind, gentle, and loving: *tender words* ◆ *What he needs now is a lot of* **tender loving care** (= sympathetic treatment). **2** (of food) easy to bite through and cut: *This meat is extremely tender.* **ANT** **TOUGH** **3** (of part of the body) painful when you touch it **SYN** **SORE** **4** easily hurt or damaged **SYN** **DELICATE**: *tender young plants* ▶ **ten·der·ly** *adv.* **ten·der·ness** *noun* [U]
IDM **at a tender age** | **at the tender age of…** used in connection with someone who is still young and does not have much experience: *He left home at the tender age of 15.* ◆ *She shouldn't be having to deal with problems like this* **at such a tender age**.
● *noun* **1** a formal offer to supply goods or do work at a stated price **SYN** **BID**[1]: *Cleaning services have been* **put out to tender** (= companies have been asked to make offers to supply these services). ◆ *a competitive tender* **2** a truck attached to a steam engine, carrying fuel and water **3** a small boat, used for carrying people or goods between a larger boat and land
● *verb* **1** [I] **~ (for sth)** to make a formal offer to supply goods or do work at a stated price: *Local firms were invited to tender for the building contract.* **2** [T] **~ sth (to sb)** (*formal*) to offer or give something to someone: *He has* **tendered his resignation** *to the President.*

ten·der·foot /ˈtɛndərˌfʊt/ *noun* (*pl.* **ten·der·feet** or **ten·der·foots**) (*informal*) a person who is new to something and not experienced **SYN** **GREENHORN**

tender-ˈhearted *adj.* having a kind and gentle nature

ten·der·ize /ˈtɛndəˌraɪz/ *verb* **~ sth** to make meat softer and easier to cut and eat by preparing it in a particular way ▶ **ten·der·iz·er** *noun*

ten·der·loin /ˈtɛndərˌlɔɪn/ *noun* [U] good quality meat from the back or side of a cow or pig

ten·di·ni·tis (also **ten·do·ni·tis**) /ˌtɛndəˈnaɪtəs/ *noun* [U] pain and swelling in a tendon of the body: *tendinitis of the shoulder*

ten·don /ˈtɛndən/ *noun* a strong band of **TISSUE** in the body that joins a muscle to a bone ⊃ collocations at **INJURY**

ten·dril /ˈtɛndrəl/ *noun* **1** a thin, curling **STEM** that grows from a climbing plant. A plant uses tendrils to attach itself to a wall or other support. **2** (*literary*) a thin, curling piece of something such as hair

ten·e·ment /ˈtɛnəmənt/ *noun* a large building divided into apartments, especially in a poor area of a city: *a tenement building/house*

ten·et /ˈtɛnət/ noun (formal) one of the principles or beliefs that a theory or larger set of beliefs is based on: *one of the basic/central tenets of Christianity*

ten·fold /ˈtɛnfoʊld; ˌtɛnˈfoʊld/ adj., adv. ➔ -FOLD

ten-gallon ˈhat noun a large hat with a broad BRIM, traditionally worn by COWBOYS

ten·nis /ˈtɛnəs/ noun [U] a game in which two or four players use RACKETS to hit a ball backward and forward across a net on a specially marked COURT: *to play tennis* ♦ *a tennis player/ match/tournament/club/court* ➔ picture at SPORT

ˈtennis ˌelbow noun [U] painful swelling of the elbow caused by too much repeated twisting of the arm

ˈtennis ˌracket (also **ˈtennis ˌracquet**) noun the RACKET that you use when you play tennis

ˈtennis ˌshoe noun [usually pl.] a shoe that you wear for sports or as informal clothing **SYN** SNEAKER

ten·on /ˈtɛnən/ noun (technical) an end of a piece of wood that has been cut to fit into a MORTISE so that the two are held together

ten·or /ˈtɛnər/ noun, adj.
• noun **1** [C] a man's singing voice with a range just below the lowest woman's voice; a man with a tenor voice ➔ compare ALTO, BARITONE, BASS¹ **2** [sing.] a musical part written for a tenor voice **3** [sing.] **the ~ of sth** (formal) the general character or meaning of something: *I was encouraged by the general tenor of his remarks.*
• adj. [only before noun] (of a musical instrument) with a range of notes similar to that of a tenor voice: *a tenor saxophone* ➔ compare ALTO, BASS¹, SOPRANO

ten·pin /ˈtɛnpɪn/ noun **1** [C] any of the ten bottle-shaped objects that players try to knock over in the game of TENPIN BOWLING **2** tenpins [U] = TENPIN BOWLING

ˌtenpin ˈbowling (also **ten·pins**) noun [U] a game in which players try to knock over tenpins by rolling a heavy ball at them, played indoors, especially in a BOWLING ALLEY ➔ compare SKITTLES

tense **AWL** /tɛns/ adj., noun, verb
• adj. **1** (of a person) nervous or worried, and unable to relax: *He's a very tense person.* ♦ *She sounded tense and angry.* **2** (of a situation, an event, a period of time, etc.) in which people have strong feelings such as worry, anger, etc. that often cannot be expressed openly: *I spent a tense few weeks waiting for the results of the tests.* ♦ *The atmosphere in the meeting was getting more and more tense.* **3** (of a muscle or other part of the body) tight rather than relaxed: *A massage will relax those tense muscles.* **4** (of wire, etc.) stretched tightly **SYN** TAUT **5** (phonetics) (of a speech sound) produced with the muscles of the speech organs stretched tight **ANT** LAX ▸ **tense·ly** **AWL** adv. **tense·ness** noun [U]
• noun (grammar) any of the forms of a verb that may be used to show the time of the action or state expressed by the verb: *the past/present/future tense*
• verb [T, I] if you **tense** your muscles, or you or your muscles tense, they become tight and stiff, especially because you are not relaxed: **~ sth/yourself (up)** *She tensed her muscles in anticipation of the blow.* ♦ *He tensed himself, listening to see if anyone had followed him.* ♦ **~ (up)** *His muscles tensed as he got ready to run.* ♦ *She tensed, hearing the strange noise again.* **IDM** **be/get tensed up** to become or feel nervous or worried so that you cannot relax

ten·sile /ˈtɛnsl/ adj. (technical) **1** [only before noun] used to describe the extent to which something can stretch without breaking: *the tensile strength of rope* **2** that can be drawn out or stretched: *tensile cable*

ten·sion 🔑 **AWL** /ˈtɛnʃn/ noun, verb
• noun **1** [U, C, usually pl.] **~ (between A and B)** a situation in which people do not trust each other, or feel unfriendly toward each other, and which may cause them to attack each other: *There is mounting tension along the border.* ♦ *international/racial/political tensions* **2** [C, U] **~ (between A and B)** a situation in which the fact that there are different needs or interests causes difficulties: *There is often a tension between the aims of the company and the wishes of the employees.* **3** [U] a feeling of anxiety and stress that makes it impossible to relax: *nervous tension* ♦ *We laughed and that helped ease the tension.* ➔ thesaurus box at PRESSURE **4** [U] the feeling of fear and excitement that is created by a writer or a movie director: *dramatic tension* ♦ *As the movie progresses the tension builds.* **5** [U] the state of being stretched tight; the extent to which something is stretched tight: *muscular tension* ♦ *Adjust the string tension of your tennis racket to suit your style of playing.* ➔ see also SURFACE TENSION
• verb **~ sth** (technical) to make a wire, sail, etc. tight and stretched

ten·sor /ˈtɛnsər; -sɔr/ noun (anatomy) a muscle that TIGHTENS or stretches part of the body

tent 🔑 /tɛnt/ noun
a shelter made of a large sheet of CANVAS, NYLON, etc. that is supported by poles and ropes fixed to the ground, and is used especially for camping: *to put up/take down a tent* ♦ *to pitch* (= put up) *a tent* ♦ *Food will be served in the hospitality tent* (= for example at an outdoor show). ➔ see also A-FRAME TENT, DOME TENT, FRAME TENT, OXYGEN TENT, PUP TENT

ten·ta·cle /ˈtɛntɪkl/ noun **1** [C] a long, thin part of the body of some creatures, such as SQUID, used for feeling or holding things, for moving, or for getting food: (figurative) *Tentacles of fear closed around her body.* ➔ picture at ANIMAL, JELLYFISH **2** tentacles [pl.] (usually disapproving) the influence that a large place, organization, or system has and that is hard to avoid: *The tentacles of satellite television are spreading even wider.*

ten·ta·tive /ˈtɛntətɪv/ adj. **1** (of an arrangement, agreement, etc.) not definite or certain because you may want to change it later: *We made a tentative arrangement to meet on Friday.* ♦ *tentative conclusions* **2** not behaving or done with confidence **SYN** HESITANT: *a tentative greeting* ♦ *I'm taking the first tentative steps toward fitness.* ▸ **ten·ta·tive·ly** adv. **ten·ta·tive·ness** noun [U]

tent·ed /ˈtɛntəd/ adj. consisting of tents; like a tent: *a tented village*

ten·ter·hooks /ˈtɛntərˌhʊks/ noun [pl.]
IDM **(be) on tenterhooks** (to be) very anxious or excited while you are waiting to find out something or see what will happen: *I've been on tenterhooks all week waiting for the results.* **ORIGIN** From **tenterhook**, a hook that in the past was used to keep material stretched on a drying frame during manufacture.

tenth /tɛnθ/ ordinal number, noun
• ordinal number 10th **HELP** There are examples of how to use ordinal numbers at the entry for **fifth**.
• noun each of ten equal parts of something **IDM** see POSSESSION

ˈtent peg noun = PEG ➔ picture at PEG

ten·u·ous /ˈtɛnyuəs/ adj. **1** so weak or uncertain that it hardly exists: *a tenuous hold on life* ♦ *His links with the organization turned out to be, at best, tenuous.* **2** extremely thin and easily broken ▸ **ten·u·ous·ly** adv.

ten·ure /ˈtɛnyər/ noun [U] **1** the period of time when someone holds an important job, especially a political one; the act of holding an important job: *his four-year tenure as President* ♦ *She knew that tenure of high political office was beyond her.* **2** the right to stay permanently in your job, especially as a teacher at a university: *It's still extremely difficult to get tenure.* **3** the legal right to live in a house or use a piece of land

ten·ured /ˈtɛnyərd/ adj. [usually before noun] **1** (of an official job) that you can keep permanently: *a tenured post* **2** (of a person, especially a teacher at a university) having the right to keep their job permanently: *a tenured professor*

te·pee (also **tee·pee**) /ˈtipi/ noun a type of tall tent shaped like a CONE, used by Native Americans in the past ➔ see also WIGWAM

tep·id /ˈtɛpəd/ adj. **1** slightly warm, sometimes in a way that is not pleasant **SYN** LUKEWARM: *tepid tea* ◆ *a tepid bath* ⊃ thesaurus box at COLD **2** not enthusiastic **SYN** LUKEWARM: *The play was greeted with tepid applause.*

te·qui·la /təˈkilə/ noun **1** [U] a strong alcoholic drink made in Mexico from a tropical plant **2** [C] a glass of tequila

te·ra- /ˈtɛrə/ prefix used in units of measurement to mean 10^{12}

ter·a·byte /ˈtɛrəˌbaɪt/ noun (abbr. TB) (computing) a unit of computer memory equal to one million million, or 10^{12} BYTES

ter·bi·um /ˈtɜrbiəm/ noun [U] (symb. Tb) a chemical element. Terbium is a silver-white metal used in LASERS, X-RAYS, and television TUBES.

ter·cen·ten·ar·y /ˌtɜrsɛnˈtɛnəri; -ˈsɛntəˌnɛri/ noun (pl. ter·cen·ten·ar·ies) the 300th anniversary of something: *the tercentenary of the school's foundation* ◆ *tercentenary celebrations*

ter·gi·ver·sate /tərˈdʒɪvərˌseɪt; ˈtɜrdʒəvərˌseɪt/ verb (formal) **1** [I] to make statements that deliberately hide the truth or that avoid answering a question directly **2** [I] to stop being loyal to one person, group, or religion and begin to support another ▶ **ter·gi·ver·sa·tion** /tərˌdʒɪvərˈseɪʃn; ˌtɜrdʒəvər-/ noun [U]

ter·i·ya·ki /ˌtɛriˈyaki/ noun [U, C] a Japanese dish consisting of meat or fish that has been left in a sweet sauce and then cooked

term 🔑 /tɜrm/ noun, verb

● **noun**

▷ **WORDS 1** [C] a word or phrase used as the name of something, especially one connected with a particular type of language: *a technical/legal/scientific, etc. term* ◆ *a term of abuse* ◆ *"Register" is the term commonly used to describe different levels of formality in language.* ⊃ thesaurus box at WORD ⊃ language bank at DEFINE **2** terms [pl.] a way of expressing yourself or of saying something: *We wish to protest in the strongest possible terms* (= to say we are very angry). ◆ *I'll try to explain in simple terms.* ◆ *The letter was brief, and couched in very polite terms.* ⊃ thesaurus box at LANGUAGE

▷ **CONDITIONS 3** terms [pl.] the conditions that people offer, demand, or accept when they make an agreement, an arrangement, or a contract: *peace terms* ◆ *Under the terms of the agreement, their funding of the project will continue until 2015.* ◆ *They failed to agree on the terms of a settlement.* ◆ *These are the terms and conditions of your employment.* **4** terms [pl.] conditions that you agree to when you buy, sell, or pay for something; a price or cost: *to buy something on easy terms* (= paying for it over a long period) ◆ *My terms are $20 a lesson.*

▷ **PERIOD OF TIME 5** [C] a period of time for which something lasts; a fixed or limited time: *during the president's first term of/in office* ◆ *He faces a maximum prison/jail term of 25 years.* ◆ *a long term of imprisonment* **6** [C, U] one of the two or three periods in the year during which classes are held in schools, colleges, etc.: *the spring/summer/fall term* ◆ *the end of the term* ⊃ see also SEMESTER, TRIMESTER **7** [sing.] (formal) the end of a particular period of time, especially one for which an agreement, etc. lasts: *the term of the loan* ◆ *His life had reached its natural term.* ◆ *(medical) The pregnancy went to full term* (= lasted the normal length of time).

▷ **IN MATH 8** [C] (mathematics) each of the various parts in a series, an EQUATION, etc.

IDM be on good, friendly, bad, etc. **terms (with sb)** to have a good, friendly, etc. relationship with someone: *I had no idea that you and he were on such intimate terms* (= were such close friends). ◆ *He is still on excellent terms with his ex-wife.* ◆ *I'm on first-name terms with my boss now* (= we call each other by our first names). **come to terms (with sb)** to reach an agreement with someone; to find a way of living or working together **come to terms with sth** to accept something unpleasant by learning to deal with it: *She is still coming to terms with her son's death.* **in terms of sth| in... terms** used to show what aspect of a subject you are talking about or how you are thinking about it: *The job is great in terms of salary, but it has its disadvantages.* ◆ *What does this mean in terms of cost?* ◆ *In practical terms this law may be difficult to enforce.* ◆ *The decision was disastrous in political terms.* ◆ *He's talking in terms of starting a completely new career.* **in the long/short/medium term** used to describe what will happen a long, short, etc. time in the future: *Such a development seems unlikely, at least in the short term* (= it will not happen for quite a long time). ⊃ see also LONG-TERM, MEDIUM-TERM, SHORT-TERM **on your own terms| on sb's terms** according to the conditions that you or someone else decides: *I'll only take the job on my own terms.* ◆ *I'm not doing it on your terms.* ⊃ more at CONTRADICTION, EQUAL adj., SPEAK, UNCERTAIN

● **verb** [often passive] ~ **sb/sth + noun/adj.** (formal) to use a particular name or word to describe someone or something: *At his age, he can hardly be termed a young man.* ◆ *REM sleep is termed "active" sleep.*

ter·ma·gant /ˈtɜrməgənt/ noun (formal) a woman who is very strict or who tries to tell people what to do, in an unpleasant way

ter·mi·nal **AWL** /ˈtɜrmənl/ noun, adj.

● **noun 1** a building or set of buildings at an airport where air passengers arrive and leave: *A second terminal was opened in 2008.* **2** a place, building, or set of buildings where journeys by train, bus, or boat begin or end: *a railway/bus/ferry terminal* **3** (computing) a piece of equipment, usually consisting of a keyboard and a screen, that joins the user to a central computer system **4** (technical) a point at which connections can be made in an electric CIRCUIT: *a positive/negative terminal*

● **adj. 1** (of an illness or a disease) that cannot be cured and will lead to death, often slowly: *He has terminal lung cancer.* ◆ *The illness is usually terminal.* ◆ *(figurative) She's suffering from terminal* (= very great) *boredom.* **2** (of a person) suffering from an illness that cannot be cured and will lead to death: *a terminal patient* **3** certain to get worse and come to an end: *The industry is in terminal decline.* **4** [only before noun] (formal or technical) at the end of something: *a terminal branch of a tree* ◆ *terminal examinations* (= at the end of a course, etc.) ▶ **ter·mi·nal·ly** /-nəli/ adv.: *a hospice for the terminally ill* ◆ *a terminally dull film*

ter·mi·nate **AWL** /ˈtɜrməˌneɪt/ verb (formal) **1** [I, T] to end; to make something end: *Your contract of employment terminates in December.* ◆ *~ sth The agreement was terminated immediately.* ◆ *to terminate a pregnancy* (= to perform or have an ABORTION) **2** [I] (of a bus or train) to end a journey/trip: *This train terminates at Grand Central.*

ter·mi·na·tion **AWL** /ˌtɜrməˈneɪʃn/ noun [U, C] (formal) the act of ending something; the end of something: *Failure to comply with these conditions will result in termination of the contract.*

ter·mi·nol·o·gy /ˌtɜrməˈnɑlədʒi/ noun (pl. ter·mi·nol·o·gies) **1** [U, C] the set of technical words or expressions used in a particular subject: *medical terminology* ⊃ thesaurus box at LANGUAGE **2** [U] words used with particular meanings: *The disagreement arose over a different use of terminology.* ⊃ note at LANGUAGE ▶ **ter·mi·no·log·i·cal** /ˌtɜrmənəˈlɑdʒɪkl/ adj.

ter·mi·nus /ˈtɜrmənəs/ noun (pl. ter·mi·ni /-ˌnaɪ/) the last station at the end of a railroad line or the last stop on a bus route

ter·mite /ˈtɜrmaɪt/ noun an insect that lives in organized groups, mainly in hot countries. Termites do a lot of damage by eating the wood of trees and buildings: *a termite colony*

ˈterm ˌpaper noun a long piece of written work that a student does on a subject that is part of a course of study

ˌterms of ˈreference noun [pl.] the limits that are set on what an official committee or report has been asked to do: *The matter, they decided, lay outside the commission's terms of reference.*

tern /tɜrn/ *noun* a bird with long pointed wings and a tail with two points that lives near the ocean

ter·race /'tɛrəs/ *noun* **1** a flat, hard area, especially outside a house or restaurant, where you can sit, eat, and enjoy the sun: *a sun terrace ♦ a roof terrace ♦ All rooms have a balcony or terrace.* ⊃ **see also** PATIO **2** one of a series of flat areas of ground that are cut into the side of a hill like steps so that crops can be grown there

ter·raced /'tɛrəst/ *adj.* (of a slope or the side of a hill) having a series of flat areas of ground like steps cut into it

ter·rac·ing /'tɛrəsɪŋ/ *noun* [U] a slope or the side of a hill that has had flat areas like steps cut into it

ter·ra·cot·ta /ˌtɛrə'kɑtə/ *noun* [U] **1** reddish-brown CLAY that has been baked but not GLAZED, used for making pots, etc. **2** a reddish-brown color

ter·ra fir·ma /ˌtɛrə 'fərmə/ *noun* [U] (from *Latin*, usually *humorous*) safe dry land, as contrasted with water or air **SYN** DRY LAND: *After two days at sea, it was good to be back on terra firma again.*

ter·ra·form /'tɛrəˌfɔrm/ *verb* **~ sth** to make a planet more like Earth, so that people can live on it

ter·rain /tə'reɪn/ *noun* [C, U] used to refer to an area of land when you are mentioning its natural features, for example, if it is rough, flat, etc.: *difficult/rough/mountainous, etc. terrain* ⊃ thesaurus box at COUNTRY

ter'rain park *noun* an outdoor area with special features designed for winter sports, especially SNOWBOARDING (= moving over snow on a special board)

ter·ra·pin /'tɛrəpən/ *noun* a small TURTLE (= a REPTILE with a hard round shell), that lives in warm rivers and lakes ⊃ compare TORTOISE

ter·rar·i·um /tə'rɛriəm/ *noun* a glass container for growing plants in or for keeping small animals such as TURTLES or snakes in

ter·res·tri·al /tə'rɛstriəl/ *adj.* **1** (*technical*) (of animals and plants) living on the land or on the ground, rather than in water, in trees, or in the air **2** connected with the planet Earth: *terrestrial life* ⊃ compare CELESTIAL, EXTRATERRES-TRIAL **3** (of television and broadcasting systems) operating on Earth rather than from a SATELLITE

ter·ri·ble 🔑 /'tɛrəbl/ *adj.*
1 very unpleasant; making you feel very unhappy, upset, or frightened: *a terrible experience ♦ What terrible news! ♦ I've just had a terrible thought.* **2** causing great harm or injury; very serious: *a terrible accident ♦ He had suffered terrible injuries.* **3** [not before noun] unhappy or sick: *I feel terrible—I think I'll go to bed.* **4** (*informal*) of very bad quality; very bad: *a terrible meal ♦ Your driving is terrible!* **5** [only before noun] used to show the great extent or degree of something bad: *a terrible mistake ♦ to be in terrible pain ♦ The room was in a terrible mess.*

THESAURUS

terrible

awful ♦ horrible ♦ dreadful ♦ foul ♦ horrendous

These words all describe something that is very unpleasant.

terrible very bad or unpleasant; making you feel unhappy, frightened, upset, ill, guilty, or disapproving: *What terrible news! ♦ That's a terrible thing to say!*

awful (*somewhat informal*) very bad or unpleasant; used to describe something that you do not like or that makes you feel depressed, ill, guilty, or disapproving: *That's an awful color. ♦ The weather last summer was awful.*

horrible (*somewhat informal*) very unpleasant; used to describe something that you do not like: *The coffee tasted horrible.*

dreadful (*somewhat informal*) very bad or unpleasant; used to describe something that you do not like or that

you disapprove of: *My schedule is dreadful this week.*

foul extremely bad or unpleasant: *A foul odor came from the kitchen. ♦ He was in a foul mood.*

horrendous (*somewhat informal*) extremely unpleasant and unacceptable: *The traffic around the city was horrendous.*

PATTERNS
- terrible/awful/horrible/dreadful **for** sb
- a(n) terrible/awful/horrible/dreadful/foul **thing**
- a(n) terrible/awful/horrible/foul **smell**
- terrible/awful/horrible/dreadful/vile/horrendous **conditions**
- terrible/awful/horrible/dreadful/foul **weather**
- terrible/awful/dreadful **news**

ter·ri·bly 🔑 /'tɛrəbli/ *adv.*
1 very: *I'm terribly sorry—did I hurt you? ♦ It's terribly important for parents to be consistent.* **2** very much; very badly: *I miss him terribly. ♦ They suffered terribly when their son was killed. ♦ The experiment went terribly wrong.*

ter·ri·er /'tɛriər/ *noun* a small active dog. There are many types of terriers. ⊃ see also BULL TERRIER, JACK RUSSELL, PIT BULL, YORKSHIRE TERRIER

ter·rif·ic /tə'rɪfɪk/ *adj.* **1** (*informal*) excellent; wonderful: *I feel absolutely terrific today! ♦ She's doing a terrific job.* ⊃ thesaurus box at GREAT **2** (*informal*) very large; very great: *I've got a terrific amount of work to do. ♦ We drove along at a terrific speed.*

ter·rif·i·cally /tə'rɪfɪkli/ *adv.* (*informal*) extremely (usually used about positive qualities): *terrifically exciting*

ter·ri·fied /'tɛrəˌfaɪd/ *adj.* very frightened: **~ (of sb/sth)** *to be terrified of spiders ♦* **~ (of doing sth)** *I'm terrified of losing you. ♦* **~ (that...)** *He was terrified (that) he would fall. ♦* **~ (at sth)** *She was terrified at the thought of being alone.* ⊃ thesaurus box at AFRAID **IDM** see WIT

ter·ri·fy /'tɛrəˌfaɪ/ *verb* (**ter·ri·fies, ter·ri·fy·ing, ter·ri·fied, ter·ri·fied**) **~ sb** to make someone feel extremely frightened: *Flying terrifies her.* ⊃ thesaurus box at SCARE ▶ **ter·ri·fy·ing** *adj.*: *It was a terrifying experience.* **ter·ri·fy·ing·ly** *adv.*

ter·rine /tə'rin/ *noun* [U, C] a soft mixture of finely chopped meat, fish, etc. pressed into a container and served cold, especially in slices as the first course of a meal

ter·ri·to·ri·al /ˌtɛrə'tɔriəl/ *adj.* **1** connected with the land or ocean that is owned by a particular country: *territorial disputes ♦ Both countries feel they have territorial claims to* (= have a right to own) *the islands.* **2** (of animals, birds, etc.) guarding and defending an area of land that they believe to be their own: *territorial instincts ♦ Cats are very territorial.* ▶ **ter·ri·to·ri·al·i·ty** /ˌtɛrəˌtɔri'æləti/ *noun* [U]: *the instinctive territoriality of some animals* **ter·ri·to·ri·al·ly** /ˌtɛrə'tɔriəli/ *adv.*: *The country was trying to expand territorially.*

ter·ri·to·ri·al 'waters *noun* [pl.] the parts of an ocean which are near a country's coast and are legally under its control

ter·ri·to·ry 🔑 /'tɛrəˌtɔri/ *noun* (*pl.* **ter·ri·to·ries**)
1 [C, U] land that is under the control of a particular country or ruler: *enemy/disputed/foreign territory ♦ occupied territories ♦ They have refused to allow U.N. troops to be stationed in their territory.* ⊃ collocations at WAR **2** [C, U] an area that one person, group, animal, etc. considers as their own and defends against others who try to enter it: *Mating blackbirds will defend their territory against intruders. ♦* (*figurative*) *This type of work is* **uncharted territory** *for us. ♦* (*figurative*) *Legal problems are Andy's territory* (= he deals with them). **3** [C, U] an area of a town, country, etc. that someone has responsibility for in their work or another activity: *Our representatives cover a very large territory.* **4** [U] a particular type of land: *unexplored territory* **5** also **Territory** [C] a country or an area that is part of the U.S., Canada, or Australia but is not a state or PROVINCE: *Guam and American Samoa are U.S. territories.*

IDM come/go with the territory to be a normal and accepted part of a particular job, situation, etc.: *She has to work late most days, but in her kind of job that goes with the territory.* ➔ more at NEUTRAL *adj.*

ter·ror 🔑 /ˈtɛrər/ *noun*

1 [U, sing.] a feeling of extreme fear: *a feeling of sheer/pure terror* ◆ *Her eyes were wild with terror.* ◆ *People fled from the explosion in terror.* ◆ *She lives in terror of* (= is constantly afraid of) *losing her job.* ◆ *Some women have a terror of losing control in the birth process.* ◆ (*literary*) *The very name of the enemy struck terror into their hearts.* ➔ thesaurus box at FEAR **2** [C] a person, situation, or thing that makes you very afraid: *These street gangs have become the terror of the neighborhood.* ◆ *Death holds no terrors for* (= does not frighten or worry) *me.* ◆ *The terrors of the night were past.* **3** [U] violent action or the threat of violent action that is intended to cause fear, usually for political purposes **SYN** TERRORISM: *a campaign of terror* ◆ *terror tactics* ➔ see also REIGN OF TERROR **4** [C] (*informal*) a person (usually a child) or an animal that causes you trouble or is difficult to control: *Their kids are real little terrors.*

ter·ror·ism 🔑 /ˈtɛrəˌrɪzəm/ *noun* [U]
the use of violent action in order to achieve political aims or to force a government to act: *an act of terrorism* ➔ collocations at CRIME

ter·ror·ist 🔑 /ˈtɛrərɪst/ *noun*
a person who takes part in terrorism: *The terrorists are threatening to blow up the plane.* ◆ *a terrorist attack/bomb/ group*

ter·ror·ize /ˈtɛrəˌraɪz/ *verb* to frighten and threaten people so that they will not oppose something or will do as they are told: *~ sb drug dealers terrorizing the neighborhood* ◆ *~ sb into doing sth People were terrorized into leaving their homes.*

ˈterror-ˌstricken *adj.* extremely frightened

ter·ry /ˈtɛri/ (also **ˈterry ˌcloth**) *noun* [U] a type of soft cotton cloth that absorbs liquids and has a surface covered with raised LOOPS of thread, used especially for making towels

terse /tərs/ *adj.* using few words and often not seeming polite or friendly: *a terse style* ◆ *The President issued a terse statement denying the charges.* ▶ **terse·ly** *adv.* **terse·ness** *noun* [U]

ter·ti·ar·y /ˈtərʃiˌɛri/ *adj.* third in order, rank, or importance: *the tertiary sector* (= the area of industry that deals with services rather than materials or goods)

ˌtertiary ˈindustry (also **ˈservice ˌindustry**) *noun* [U, C] (*economics*) the part of a country's economy that provides services ➔ compare PRIMARY INDUSTRY, SECONDARY INDUSTRY

TESL /ˈtɛsl/ *abbr.* teaching English as a second language

TESOL /ˈtisɔl; -sɑl/ /ˈtɛsɑl; ˈtɛsɔl/ *abbr.* **1** teaching English to speakers of other languages **2** teachers of English to speakers of other languages (an organization of teachers)

tes·sel·lat·ed /ˈtɛsəˌleɪtəd/ *adj.* (*technical*) made from small flat pieces arranged in a pattern: *a tessellated pavement*

test 🔑 /tɛst/ *noun, verb*

● *noun*

▷ OF KNOWLEDGE/ABILITY **1** an examination of someone's knowledge or ability, consisting of questions for them to answer or activities for them to perform: *an IQ/intelligence/ aptitude test* ◆ *to take a test* ◆ *~ (on sth) a test on irregular verbs* ◆ *to pass/fail a test* ◆ *a good grade on the test* ➔ collocations at EDUCATION ➔ see also DRIVING TEST ➔ note at EXAM

▷ OF HEALTH **2** a medical examination to discover what is wrong with you or to check the condition of your health: *a test for AIDS* ◆ *an eye test* ◆ *a pregnancy test* ◆ *When can I get my test results?* ➔ see also BLOOD TEST, BREATH TEST

▷ OF MACHINE/PRODUCT, ETC. **3** an experiment to discover whether or how well something works, or to find out more information about it: *laboratory tests* ◆ *a nuclear test* ◆ *Tests have shown high levels of pollutants in the water.* ◆ *I'll run a*

diagnostic test to see why the server keeps crashing. ➔ see also ACID TEST, BLIND TEST, MEANS TEST

▷ OF STRENGTH, ETC. **4** a situation or an event that shows how good, strong, etc. someone or something is: *The local elections will be a good test of the government's popularity.*

IDM put sb/sth to the test to put someone or something in a situation which will show what their or its true qualities are: *His theories have never really been put to the test.* stand the test of time to prove to be good, popular, etc. over a long period of time

● *verb*

▷ KNOWLEDGE/ABILITY **1** [T, I] to find out how much someone knows, or what they can do, by asking them questions or giving them activities to perform: *~ sb (on sth) Children are tested on core subjects at ages 7, 11, and 14.* ◆ *~ (sth) We test your English before deciding which class to put you in.* ◆ *Schools use various methods of testing.* **2** [I] *~ well/badly* to perform well/badly in a test of knowledge or ability: *students who tested well in reading*

▷ HEALTH **3** [T, I] to examine the blood, a part of the body, etc. to find out what is wrong with a person, or to check the condition of their health: *~ sb/sth to test someone's eyesight/ hearing* ◆ *~ sb/sth for sth The doctor tested him for hepatitis.* ◆ *+ adj. (for sth) to test positive/negative* ◆ *Two athletes tested positive for steroids.*

▷ MACHINE/PRODUCT, ETC. **4** [T] to use or try a machine, substance, etc. to find out how well it works or to find out more information about it: *~ sth Test your brakes regularly.* ◆ *~ sth on sb/sth Our beauty products are not tested on animals.* ◆ *~ sth for sth The water is regularly tested for purity.* ◆ *~ sth out They opened a single store in Europe to test out the market.* ➔ see also FIELD-TEST **5** [I] *~ well/badly* (of a machine or product) to perform well/badly in a test of how well it works: *The ad had tested badly with consumers.*

▷ STRENGTH, ETC. **6** [T] *~ sb/sth* to be difficult and therefore need all your strength, ability, etc.: *The long climb tested our fitness and stamina.* ➔ see also TESTING

IDM test the waters to find out what the situation is before doing something or making a decision

PHR V ˈtest for sth | ˈtest sth for sth to examine something to see if a particular substance, etc. is present: *testing for oil* ◆ *The software has been tested for viruses.*

test·a·ble /ˈtɛstəbl/ *adj.* that can be tested: *testable hypotheses*

tes·ta·ment /ˈtɛstəmənt/ *noun* (*formal*) **1** [C, usually sing., U] *~ (to sth)* a thing that shows that something else exists or is true **SYN** TESTIMONY: *The new model is a testament to the skill and dedication of the workforce.* **2** [C] = WILL: *This is the last will and testament of…* ➔ see also NEW TESTAMENT, OLD TESTAMENT

ˈtest ban *noun* an agreement between countries to stop testing nuclear weapons: *a test ban treaty*

ˈtest bed *noun* a piece of equipment used for testing new machinery, especially aircraft engines: (*figurative*) *The country is an ideal test bed for emerging technologies.*

ˈtest case *noun* a legal case or other situation whose result will be used as an example when decisions are being made on similar cases in the future

ˈtest drive *noun* an occasion when you drive a vehicle that you are thinking of buying so that you can see how well it works and if you like it ▶ **ˈtest-drive** *verb* ~ sth

test·er /ˈtɛstər/ *noun* **1** a person or thing that tests something: *testers of new software* **2** a small container of a product, such as PERFUME, that you can try in a store to see if you like it

tes·tes pl. of TESTIS

ˈtest flight *noun* a flight during which an aircraft or part of its equipment is tested

tes·ti·cle /ˈtɛstɪkl/ *noun* either of the two organs that produce SPERM, located in a bag of skin below the PENIS ▶ **tes·tic·u·lar** /tɛˈstɪkyələr/ *adj.* [only before noun]: *testicular cancer*

tes·ti·fy /ˈtɛstəˌfaɪ/ verb (tes·ti·fies, tes·ti·fy·ing, tes·ti·fied, tes·ti·fied) **1** [I, T] to make a statement that something happened or that something is true, especially as a witness in court: ~ **(against/for sb)** *She refused to testify against her husband.* ♦ *There are several witnesses who will testify for the defense.* ♦ ~ **about sth** *He was summoned to testify before a grand jury about his role in the affair.* ♦ ~ **to sth/to doing sth** *Evans testified to receiving $200,000 in bribes.* ♦ ~ **(that)…** *He testified (that) he was at the theater at the time of the murder.* ♦ **+ speech** *"I was approached by a man I did not recognize," she testified.* **2** [T] ~ **(that)…** to say that you believe something is true because you have evidence of it: *Too many young people are unable to write or spell well, as employers will testify.* **3** [I] to express your belief in God publicly **PHR V** ˈtestify to sth (*formal*) to show or be evidence that something is true **SYN** EVIDENCE: *The film testifies to the courage of ordinary people during the war.*

tes·ti·mo·ni·al /ˌtɛstəˈmoʊniəl/ noun **1** a formal written statement, often by a former employer, about someone's abilities, qualities, and character; a formal written statement about the quality of something: *a glowing testimonial* ♦ *The catalog is full of testimonials from satisfied customers.* **2** a thing that is given or done to show admiration for someone or to thank someone: *a testimonial dinner*

tes·ti·mo·ny /ˈtɛstəˌmoʊni/ noun (*pl.* tes·ti·mo·nies) **1** [U, sing.] ~ **(to sth)** a thing that shows that something else exists or is true **SYN** TESTAMENT: *This increase in exports bears testimony to the successes of industry.* ♦ *The pyramids are an eloquent testimony to the ancient Egyptians' engineering skills.* **2** [C, U] a formal written or spoken statement saying what you know to be true, usually in court: *a sworn testimony* ♦ *Can I refuse to give testimony?*

test·ing /ˈtɛstɪŋ/ noun, adj.
● *noun* [U] the activity of testing someone or something in order to find something out, see if it works, etc.: *nuclear testing* ♦ *testing and assessment in education*
● *adj.* (of a problem or situation) difficult to deal with and needing particular strength or abilities

ˈtesting ˌground noun **1** a place or situation used for testing new ideas and methods to see if they work **2** a place used for testing machines, etc. to see if they work correctly: *a piece of land in use as a tank testing ground*

tes·tis /ˈtɛstəs/ noun (*pl.* tes·tes /-tiz/) (*anatomy*) a TESTICLE

tes·tos·ter·one /tɛˈstɑstəˌroʊn/ noun a HORMONE (= chemical substance produced in the body) that causes men to develop the physical and sexual features that are characteristic of the male body ⊃ compare ESTROGEN, PROGESTERONE

ˈtest ˌpilot noun a pilot whose job is to fly aircraft in order to test their performance

ˈtest run noun = TRIAL RUN

ˈtest tube noun a small glass tube, closed at one end, that is used in scientific experiments ⊃ picture at LABORATORY

ˈtest-tube ˌbaby noun a baby that grows from an egg that is FERTILIZED outside the mother's body and then put back inside to continue developing normally ⊃ see also IN VITRO

tes·ty /ˈtɛsti/ adj. easily annoyed or irritated **SYN** IRRITABLE ▶ **tes·ti·ly** /-tɑli/ adv.: *"Leave me alone," she said testily.*

tet·a·nus /ˈtɛtn̩·əs; ˈtɛtnəs/ noun [U] a disease in which the muscles, especially the JAW muscles, become stiff, caused by bacteria entering the body through cuts or wounds

tête-à-tête /ˌtɛt ə ˈtɛt; ˌteɪt ə ˈteɪt/ noun (from *French*) a private conversation between two people

teth·er /ˈtɛðər/ verb, noun
● *verb* ~ **sth (to sth)** to tie an animal to a post so that it cannot move very far
● *noun* a rope or chain used to tie an animal to something, allowing it to move around in a small area

tet·ra·he·dron /ˌtɛtrəˈhidrən/ noun (*geometry*) a solid shape with four flat sides that are triangles ⊃ picture at SHAPE

te·tral·o·gy /tɛˈtralədʒi; -ˈtræ-/ noun (*pl.*) a group of four books, movies, etc. that have the same subject or characters

Teu·ton·ic /tuˈtɑnɪk/ adj. [usually before noun] (*informal*, often *disapproving*) showing qualities considered typical of German people: *The preparations were made with Teutonic thoroughness.*

Tex-Mex /ˌtɛks ˈmɛks/ adj. [only before noun] connected with the variety of Mexican cooking, music, etc. that is found in Texas and the southwestern part of the U.S. ▶ **Tex-Mex** noun [U]: *The menu includes Tex-Mex.* ♦ *The music will feature a home-grown hybrid of Tex-Mex and polka.*

text 🔑 **AWL** /tɛkst/ noun, verb
● *noun* **1** [U] the main printed part of a book or magazine, not the notes, pictures, etc.: *My job is to lay out the text and graphics on the page.* **2** [U] any form of written material: *a computer that can process text* ♦ *printed text* **3** [C] = TEXT MESSAGE **4** [C] the written form of a speech, a play, an article, etc.: *The newspaper had printed the full text of the president's speech.* ⊃ collocations at LITERATURE **5** [C] a piece of writing that you have to answer questions about in an exam or a lesson **SYN** PASSAGE: *Read the text carefully and then answer the questions.* **6** [C] = TEXTBOOK: *medical texts* **7** [C] a sentence or short passage from the Bible that is read out and discussed by someone, especially during a religious service
● *verb* [T, I] to send someone a written message using a cell phone: ~ **(sb)** *Text me when you're on your way.* ♦ *Kids seem to be texting non-stop these days.* ♦ ~ **sb sth** *I'll text you the final score.* ⊃ see also SMS ▶ **text·ing** noun [U]: *Too much texting can cause serious injury to the hands.*

text·book /ˈtɛkstbʊk/ noun, adj.
● *noun* (also text) a book that teaches a particular subject and that is used especially in schools and colleges: *a school/medical/history, etc. textbook*
● *adj.* [only before noun] used to describe something that is done exactly as it should be done, in the best possible way: *a textbook example of how the game should be played*

ˈtext ˌeditor noun (*computing*) a system or program that allows you to make changes to text

text·er /ˈtɛkstər/ noun a person who sends TEXT MESSAGES

tex·tile /ˈtɛkstaɪl/ noun **1** [C] any type of cloth made by weaving (WEAVE) or KNITTING: *a factory producing a range of textiles* ♦ *the textile industry* ♦ *a textile designer* ⊃ thesaurus box at FABRIC **2 textiles** [pl.] the industry that makes cloth

ˈtext ˌmessage (also text) noun a written message that you send using a cell phone: *Send a text message to this number to vote.* ▶ **ˈtext-ˌmessage** (also text) verb [T, I]: ~ **(sb) (sth)** *I text-messaged him to say we were waiting in the bar.* ⊃ collocations at PHONE **ˈtext-ˌmessaging** (also text·ing) noun [U]

ˌtext-to-ˈspeech noun (*abbr.* TTS) [U] (*computing*) a computer program that converts text into spoken language: *text-to-speech software* ♦ *a TTS package*

tex·tu·al **AWL** /ˈtɛkstʃuəl/ adj. [usually before noun] connected with or contained in a text: *textual analysis* ♦ *textual errors*

tex·tur·al /ˈtɛkstʃərəl/ adj. (*technical*) relating to texture: *the textural characteristics of the rocks*

tex·ture /ˈtɛkstʃər/ noun [C, U] **1** the way a surface, substance, or piece of cloth feels when you touch it, for example how rough, smooth, hard, or soft it is: *the soft texture of velvet* ♦ *She uses a variety of different colors and textures in her wall hangings.* **2** the way food or drink tastes or feels in your mouth, for example whether it is rough, smooth, light, heavy, etc.: *The two cheeses were very different in both taste and texture.* **3** the way that different parts of a piece of music or literature are combined to create a final impression: *the rich texture of the symphony*

tex·tured /ˈtɛkstʃərd/ adj. with a surface that is not smooth, but has a particular texture: *textured wallpaper*

textured 'vegetable ,protein noun (abbr. TVP) a substance that looks like meat, but which is made from SOYBEANS

TFT /ˌti ɛf ˈti/ noun a piece of technology used to make flat screens for computers, cell phones, etc. (the abbreviation for thin film transistor): *a 32in. TFT screen*

TG /ˌti ˈdʒi/ abbr. TRANSFORMATIONAL GRAMMAR

TGIF /ˌti dʒi aɪ ˈɛf/ abbr. (informal) thank God it's Friday (used to say that you are glad the working week is nearly over)

-th /θ/ suffix **1** (in ordinal numbers): *sixth* ◆ *fifteenth* ◆ *hundredth* **2** (in nouns) the action or process of: *growth*

tha·lid·o·mide /θəˈlɪdəˌmaɪd/ noun [U] a SEDATIVE drug which was given to pregnant women until, in the 1960s, it was found to have prevented some babies from developing normal arms and legs

thal·li·um /ˈθæliəm/ noun [U] (symb. Tl) a chemical element. Thallium is a soft silver-white metal whose COMPOUNDS are very poisonous.

than 🔑 /ðən; strong form ðæn; ðɛn/ prep., conj.
1 used to introduce the second part of a comparison: *I'm older than her.* ◆ *There was more whiskey in it than soda.* ◆ *He loves me more than you do.* ◆ *It was much better than I'd expected.* ◆ *You should know better than to behave like that.* ◆ *I'd rather e-mail than phone, if that's OK by you.* **2** more/less/fewer, etc. ~ used for comparing amounts, numbers, distances, etc.: *It never takes more than an hour.* ◆ *It's less than a mile to the beach.* ◆ *There were fewer than twenty people there.* **3** used in expressions showing that one thing happens right after another: *No sooner had I sat down **than** there was a loud knock on the door.* ◆ *Hardly had we arrived **than** the problems started.* **IDM** see OTHER

thang /θæŋ/ noun (informal) a way of saying or writing the word "thing," that represents the pronunciation of the southern U.S.

thank 🔑 /θæŋk/ verb
to tell someone that you are grateful for something: ~ **sb for sth** *I must write and thank Mary for the present.* ◆ *In his speech, he thanked everyone for all their hard work.* ◆ ~ **sb for doing sth** *She said goodbye and thanked us for coming.* ◆ ~ **sb** *There's no need to thank me—I enjoyed doing it.* **IDM** have sb to thank (for sth) used when you are saying who is responsible for something: *I have my parents to thank for my success.* **I'll thank you for sth/to do sth** (formal) used to tell someone that you are annoyed and do not want them to do something: *I'll thank you to mind your own business.* **thank God/goodness/heaven(s) (for sth)** used to say that you are pleased about something: *Thank God you're safe!* ◆ *"Thank goodness for that!" she said with a sigh of relief.* **HELP** Some people find the phrase **thank God** offensive. **thank your lucky stars** to feel very grateful and lucky about something **sb won't thank you for sth** used to say that someone will not be pleased or will be annoyed about something: *John won't thank you for interfering.*

thank·ful /ˈθæŋkfl/ adj. [not usually before noun] pleased about something good that has happened, or something bad that has not happened: ~ **(to do sth)** *I was thankful to see they'd all arrived safely.* ◆ ~ **(for sth)** *He wasn't badly hurt—that's something to be thankful for.* ◆ ~ **(that…)** *I was thankful that he hadn't been hurt.* **IDM** see SMALL

thank·ful·ly /ˈθæŋkfəli/ adv. **1** used to show that you are pleased that something good has happened or that something bad has been avoided **SYN** FORTUNATELY: *There was a fire in the building, but thankfully no one was hurt.* **2** in a pleased or grateful way: *I accepted the invitation thankfully.*

thank·less /ˈθæŋkləs/ adj. unpleasant or difficult to do and unlikely to bring you any rewards or thanks from anyone: *Sometimes being a mother and a housewife felt like **a thankless task**.*

thanks 🔑 /θæŋks/ exclamation, noun
● **exclamation** ⊃ see also THANK YOU **1** used to show that you are grateful to someone for something they have done:

~ **(for doing sth)** *Thanks for lending me the money.* ◆ ~ **(for sth)** *Many thanks for your support.* ◆ *"How are you?" "Fine, thanks."* (= thanks for asking) **2** a polite way of accepting something that someone has offered you: *"Would you like a coffee?" "Oh, thanks."* ◆ *"Here's the change." ◆ Thanks very much."* **3** no thanks a polite way of refusing something that someone has offered you: *"Would you like some more?" "No thanks."*
● **noun** [pl.] ~ **(to sb) (for sth)** words or actions that show that you are grateful to someone for something **SYN** GRATITUDE: *How can I ever express my thanks to you for all you've done?* ◆ *Thanks are due to all those who worked so hard for so many months.* ◆ *She murmured her thanks.* ⊃ see also VOTE OF THANKS **IDM** no thanks to sb/sth despite someone or something; with no help from someone or something: *We managed to get it finished in the end—no thanks to him* (= he didn't help). **thanks a lot 1** used to show that you are very grateful to someone for something they have done: *Thanks a lot for all you've done.* **2** (ironic) used to show that you are annoyed that someone has done something because it causes trouble or difficulty for you: *"I'm afraid I've finished all the milk." "Well, thanks a lot!"* **thanks to sb/sth** (sometimes ironic) used to say that something has happened because of someone or something: *It was all a great success—thanks to a lot of hard work.* ◆ *Everyone knows about it now, thanks to you!*

thanks·giv·ing /ˌθæŋksˈɡɪvɪŋ/ noun **1 Thanksgiving (Day)** [U, C] a public holiday that is celebrated in the U.S. on the fourth Thursday in November, and in Canada on the second Monday in October. Its original purpose was to give thanks to God for the HARVEST and for health: *Are you going home for Thanksgiving?* ⊃ compare HARVEST FESTIVAL **2** [U] (formal) the expression of thanks to God

thank you 🔑 exclamation, noun
● **exclamation** ⊃ see also THANKS **1** used to show that you are grateful to someone for something they have done: ~ **(for sth)** *Thank you for your letter.* ◆ ~ **(for doing sth)** *Thank you so/very much for sending the photos.* **2** a polite way of accepting something that someone has offered you: *"Would you like some help with that?" "Oh, thank you."* **3** no thank you a polite way of refusing something that someone has offered you: *"Would you like some more cake?" "No thank you."* **4** used at the end of a sentence to tell someone firmly that you do not need their help or advice: *"I can do that for you." "I can do it myself, thank you."*
● **noun** [usually sing.] ~ **(to sb) (for sth)** an act, a gift, a comment, etc. intended to thank someone for something they have done: *The actor sent a big thank you to all his fans for their letters of support.* ◆ *She took the money without so much as a thank you.* ◆ *a thank-you letter*

that 🔑 det., pron., conj., adv.
● **det.** /ðæt/ (pl. those /ðoʊz/) **1** used for referring to a person or thing that is not near the speaker or as near to the speaker as another: *Look at that man over there.* ◆ *How much are those apples at the back?* **2** used for referring to someone or something that has already been mentioned or is already known about: *I was living with my parents at that time.* ◆ *That incident changed their lives.* ◆ *Have you forgotten about that money I lent you last week?* ◆ *That dress of hers is too short.*
● **pron.** /ðæt/ (pl. those /ðoʊz/) **1** used for referring to a person or thing that is not near the speaker, or not as near to the speaker as another: *Who's that?* ◆ *That's Peter over there.* ◆ *Hello. Is that Jo?* ◆ *That's a nice dress.* ◆ *Those look riper than these.* **2** used for referring to someone or something that has already been mentioned, or is already known about: *What can I do about that?* ◆ *Do you remember when we went to Norway? That was a good trip.* ◆ *That's exactly what I think.* **3** (formal) used for referring to people or things of a particular type: *Those present were in favor of change.* ◆ *There are those who say* (= some people say) *she should not have gotten the job.* ◆ *Salaries are higher here than those in my country.* **4** /ðət; strong form ðæt/ (pl. that) used as a relative

pronoun to introduce a part of a sentence which refers to the person, thing, or time you have been talking about: *Where's the letter that came yesterday?* ◆ *Who was it that won the U.S. Open?* ◆ *The watch (that) you gave me keeps perfect time.* ◆ *The people (that) I spoke to were very helpful.* ◆ *It's the best novel (that) I've ever read.* ◆ *We moved here the year (that) my mother died.* **HELP** In spoken and informal written English **that** is nearly always left out when it is the object of the verb or is used with a preposition. **IDM** **that is (to say)** used to say what something means or to give more information: *He's a local government administrator, that is to say a civil servant.* ◆ *You'll find her very helpful—if she's not too busy, that is.* ⊃ language bank at I.E. **that's it** (*informal*) **1** used to say that someone is right, or is doing something right: *No, the other one… that's it.* ◆ *That's it, carry on!* **2** used to say that something is finished, or that no more can be done: *That's it, the fire's out now.* ◆ *That's it for now, but if I get any news I'll let you know.* ◆ *A week to go, and that's it!* **3** used to say that you will not accept something any longer: *That's it, I've had enough!* **4** used to talk about the reason for something: *So that's it—the fuse had gone.* ◆ *You don't love me any more, is that it?* **that's that** (*informal*) used to say that your decision cannot be changed: *Well I'm not going, and that's that.*

● **conj.** /ðət; *strong form* ðæt/ **1** used after some verbs, adjectives, and nouns to introduce a new part of the sentence: *She said (that) the story was true.* ◆ *It's possible (that) he has not received the letter.* ◆ *The fact (that) he's older than me is not relevant.* **HELP** In spoken and informal written English **that** is usually left out after reporting verbs and adjectives. It is less often left out after nouns. **2 so… that…** used to express a result: *She was so tired (that) she couldn't think straight.* **HELP** In informal English **that** is often left out. **3** (*literary*) used for expressing a hope or a wish: *Oh that I could see him again!*

● **adv.** /ðæt/ **1** used when saying how much or showing how long, big, etc. something is with your hands: *I can't walk that far* (= as far as that). ◆ *It's about that long.* **2 not (all) ~** not very, or not as much as has been said: *It isn't all that cold.* ◆ *There aren't that many people here.*

that·a·way /'ðætəˌweɪ/ *adv.* (*informal*) in that direction: *They went thataway!*

thatch /θætʃ/ *noun, verb*
● **noun 1** [U, C] dried STRAW, REEDS, etc. used for making a roof; a roof made of this material: *a roof made of thatch* ◆ *The thatch was badly damaged in the storm.* **2** [sing.] **~ of hair** (*informal*) thick hair on someone's head
● **verb ~ sth** to cover the roof of a building with thatch ▶ **thatched** *adj.*: *They live in a thatched cottage.*

thatch·er /'θætʃər/ *noun* a person whose job is thatching roofs

thaw /θɔ/ *verb, noun*
● **verb 1** [I] **~ (out)** (of ice and snow) to turn back into water after being frozen **SYN** MELT **ANT** FREEZE **2** [I] when it **thaws** or **is thawing**, the weather becomes warm enough to melt snow and ice: *It's starting to thaw.* **3** [I, T] **~ (sth) (out)** to become, or to let frozen food become, soft or liquid ready for cooking ⊃ compare DEFROST, DE-ICE, UNFREEZE: *Leave the meat to thaw completely before cooking.* **4** [I, T] **~ (sth) (out)** to become, or make something become, a normal temperature after being very cold: *I could feel my ears and toes start to thaw out.* **5** [I] **~ (out)** to become more friendly and less formal: *Relations between the two countries thawed a little after the talks.*
● **noun 1** [C, usually sing.] a period of warmer weather following one of cold weather, causing snow and ice to melt **2** [sing.] **~ (in sth)** a situation in which the relations between two enemy countries become more friendly

the 🔑 /ðə; *strong form and usually before vowels* ði/ *definite article*
1 used to refer to someone or something that has already been mentioned or is easily understood: *There were three*

questions. *The first two were relatively easy but the third one was hard.* ◆ *There was an accident here yesterday. A car hit a tree and the driver was killed.* ◆ *The heat was getting to be too much for me.* ◆ *The nights are getting longer.* **2** used to refer to someone or something that is the only, normal, or obvious one of their kind: *the Mona Lisa* ◆ *the Nile* ◆ *the Queen* ◆ *What's the matter?* ◆ *The phone rang.* ◆ *I patted her on the back.* ◆ *How's the* (= your) *baby?* **3** used when explaining which person or thing you mean: *the house at the end of the street* ◆ *The people I met there were very friendly.* ◆ *It was the best day of my life.* ◆ *You're the third person to ask me that.* ◆ *Friday the thirteenth* ◆ *Alexander the Great* **4** used to refer to a thing in general rather than a particular example: *He taught himself to play the violin.* ◆ *The dolphin is an intelligent animal.* ◆ *They placed the African elephant on their endangered list.* ◆ *I heard it on the radio.* ◆ *I'm usually out during the day.* **5** used with adjectives to refer to a thing or a group of people described by the adjective: *With him, you should always expect the unexpected.* ◆ *the unemployed* ◆ *the French* **6** used before the plural of someone's last name to refer to a whole family or a married couple: *Don't forget to invite the Jordans.* **7** enough of something for a particular purpose: *I wanted it but I didn't have the money.* **8** used with a unit of measurement to mean "every": *My car does forty miles to the gallon.* ◆ *You get paid by the hour.* **9** used with a unit of time to mean "the present": *Why not have the dish of the day?* ◆ *She's the flavor of the month with him.* **10** /ði/ used, stressing *the*, to show that the person or thing referred to is famous or important: *Sheryl Crow? Not 'the Sheryl Crow?* ◆ *At that time London was 'the place to be.*
IDM **the more, less, etc.…, the more, less, etc.…** used to show that two things change to the same degree: *The more she thought about it, the more depressed she became.* ◆ *The less said about the whole thing, the happier I'll be.*

the·a·ter 🔑 (*CanE usually* **the·a·tre**) /'θiətər/ *noun*
1 [C] a building or an outdoor area where plays and similar types of entertainment are performed: *Broadway theaters* ◆ *an open-air theater* ◆ *How often do you go to the theater?* ⊃ see also LECTURE HALL **2** (also **'movie theater**, **cin·e·ma**) [C] a building in which movies are shown **3** [U] plays considered as entertainment: *an evening of live music and theater* ◆ *current ideas about what makes good theater* (= what makes good entertainment when performed) **4** [U] also **the theater** [sing.] the work of writing, producing, and acting in plays: *I want to work in theater.* ◆ *He was essentially a man of the theater.* **5** [C, usually sing.] **~ (of war, etc.)** (*formal*) the place in which a war or fighting takes place

the·a·ter·go·er /'θiətərˌɡoʊər/ (also **play·go·er**) *noun* a person who goes regularly to the theater ▶ **the·a·ter·go·ing** *adj.*: *the theatergoing public*

theater-in-the-'round *noun* [U] a way of performing plays on a stage which is surrounded by the audience

the·at·ri·cal /θi'ætrɪkl/ *adj.* **1** [only before noun] connected with the theater: *a theatrical agent* **2** (often *disapproving*) (of behavior) exaggerated in order to attract attention or create a particular effect: *a theatrical gesture* ▶ **the·at·ri·cal·ly** /-kli/ *adv.*

the·at·ri·cal·i·ty /θiˌætrəˈkæləti/ *noun* [U] the exaggerated quality of something that is intended to attract attention or create a particular effect

the·at·ri·cals /θi'ætrɪklz/ *noun* [pl.] performances of plays: *amateur theatricals*

the·at·rics /θi'ætrɪks/ *noun* [pl.] behavior that is exaggerated and emotional in order to attract attention

thee /ði/ *pron.* (*old use* or *dialect*) a word meaning "you," used when talking to only one person who is the object of the verb: *We beseech thee, O Lord.* ⊃ compare THOU

theft /θɛft/ *noun* [U, C] **~ (of sth)** the crime of stealing something from a person or place: *car theft* ◆ *Police are investigating the theft of computers from the company's offices.* ⊃ compare BURGLARY, ROBBERY ⊃ see also IDENTITY THEFT, THIEF

their 🔑 /ðər; ðer/ det.
(the possessive form of *they*) **1** of or belonging to them: *Their parties are always fun.* ◆ *Which is their house?* **2** used instead of *his* or *her* to refer to a person whose sex is not mentioned or not known: *If anyone calls, ask for their number so I can call them back.*

theirs 🔑 /ðerz/ pron.
(the possessive form of *they*) of or belonging to them: *Theirs are the children with very fair hair.* ◆ *It's a favorite game of theirs.*

the·ism /ˈθiːɪzəm/ noun [U] belief in the existence of God or gods **ANT** ATHEISM

them 🔑 /ðəm; əm; strong form ðem/ pron.
(the object form of *they*) **1** used when referring to people, animals, or things as the object of a verb or preposition, or after the verb *be*: *Tell them the news.* ◆ *What are you doing with those matches? Give them to me.* ◆ *Did you eat all of them?* ◆ *It's them.* **2** used instead of *him* or *her* to refer to a person whose sex is not mentioned or not known: *If anyone comes in before I get back, ask them to wait.*

the·mat·ic **AWL** /θɪˈmætɪk/ adj. [usually before noun] connected with the theme or themes of something: *the thematic structure of a text* ▶ **the·mat·i·cally** **AWL** /-kli/ adv.: *The books have been grouped thematically.*

theˌmatic ˈrole (also ˈtheta ˌrole) noun (linguistics) the function that a noun phrase has in relation to a verb, for example AGENT or PATIENT

theme 🔑 **AWL** /θiːm/ noun, adj.
● noun **1** the subject or main idea in a talk, piece of writing, or work of art: *North American literature is the main theme of this year's festival.* ◆ *The President stressed a favorite campaign theme—greater emphasis on education.* ◆ *The naked male figure was always the central theme of Greek art.* ◆ *The stories are all variations on the theme of unhappy marriage.* ⊃ collocations at LITERATURE **2** (music) a short tune that is repeated or developed in a piece of music **3** = THEME MUSIC: *the theme from "The Godfather"* **4** (old-fashioned) a short piece of writing on a particular subject, done for school **5** (linguistics) the part of a sentence or clause that contains information that is not new to the reader or audience ⊃ compare RHEME
● adj. **~ bar/restaurant, etc.** a bar, restaurant, etc. that is designed to reflect a particular subject or period of history: *an Irish theme bar*

ˈtheme ˌmusic noun [U] (also theme, ˈtheme song, ˈtheme tune [C]) music that is played at the beginning and end and/or is often repeated in a movie, television program, etc.

ˈtheme park noun a large park where people go to enjoy themselves, for example by riding on large machines such as ROLLER COASTERS, and where much of the entertainment is connected with one subject or idea: *a western-style theme park* ⊃ compare AMUSEMENT PARK

them·self /ðəmˈself; ðem-/ pron. (the reflexive form of *they*) used instead of *himself* or *herself* to refer to a person whose sex is not mentioned or not known: *Does anyone here consider themself a good cook?* **HELP** Although **themself** is fairly common, especially in spoken English, many people think it is not correct.

them·selves 🔑 /ðəmˈselvz; ðem-/ pron.
1 (the reflexive form of *they*) used when people or animals performing an action are also affected by it: *They seemed to be enjoying themselves.* ◆ *The children were arguing amongst themselves.* ◆ *They've bought themselves a new car.* **2** used to emphasize *they* or a plural subject: *They themselves had had a similar experience.* ◆ *Don and Julie paid for it themselves.* **3** used instead of *himself* or *herself* to refer to a person whose sex is not mentioned or not known: *There wasn't anyone who hadn't enjoyed themselves.* **HELP** Although this use of **themselves** is fairly common, especially in spoken English, many people think it is not correct.
IDM **(all) by themselves 1** alone; without anyone else:

They wanted to spend the evening by themselves. **2** without help: *They did the cooking by themselves.* **(all) to themselves** for them alone; not shared with anyone

then 🔑 /ðen/ adv., adj.
● adv. **1** used to refer to a particular time in the past or future: *Life was harder then because neither of us had a job.* ◆ *Things were very different back then.* ◆ *She grew up in Zimbabwe, or Rhodesia as it then was.* ◆ *I saw them at Christmas but haven't heard a thing since then.* ◆ *I've been invited too, so I'll see you then.* ◆ *There's a room free in Bob's house next week but you can stay with us until then.* ◆ *Call again next week. They should have reached a decision by then.* ◆ *Just then* (= at that moment) *there was a knock at the door.* ◆ *She left in 1984 and from then on he lived alone.* ◆ *I took one look at the car and offered to buy it there and then/then and there* (= immediately). **2** used to introduce the next item in a series of actions, events, instructions, etc.: *He drank a glass of whiskey, then another, and then another.* ◆ *First cook the onions, then add the mushrooms.* ◆ *We lived in France and then Italy before coming back to the United States.* ⊃ language bank at PROCESS¹ **3** used to show the logical result of a particular statement or situation: *If you miss that train then you'll have to get a taxi.* ◆ *"My wife got a job in Chicago." "I take it you'll be moving, then."* ◆ *"You haven't done anything to upset me." "So what's wrong, then?"* ◆ *Why don't you rent a car? Then you'll be able to visit more of the area.* **4** used to introduce additional information: *She's been very busy at work and then there was all that trouble with her son.* **5** (formal) used to introduce a summary of something that has just been said: *These, then, are the main areas of concern.* **6** used to show the beginning or end of a conversation, statement, etc.: *Right then, where do you want the table to go?* ◆ *"I really have to go." "OK. Bye, then."* ◆ *OK then, I think we've just about covered everything on the agenda.*
IDM **…and then some** (informal) used to emphasize the large amount or number of something, and to say that you have not mentioned everything: *There are Indian, Chinese, Mexican, Thai restaurants… and then some!* **but then | but then again | but then again** (informal) used to introduce additional information or information that contrasts with something that has just been said: *She was early, but then again, she always is.* ◆ *"So you might accept their offer?" "Yes, then again I might not."* ⊃ more at NOW
● adj. [only before noun] used to describe someone who had a particular title, job, etc. at the time in the past that is being discussed: *That decision was taken by the then president.*

thence /ðens/ adv. (old use or formal) from that place; following that: *They made their way from Spain to France and thence to England.* ◆ *He was promoted to manager, thence to a partnership in the firm.*

thence·forth /ˈðensfɔːrθ; ðensˈfɔːrθ/ (also thence·for·ward /ˌðensˈfɔːrwərd/) adv. (old use or formal) starting from that time

theo- /ˈθiːoʊ; ˈθiːə/ combining form (in nouns, adjectives, and adverbs) connected with God or a god

the·oc·ra·cy /θiˈɑːkrəsi/ noun (pl. the·oc·ra·cies) **1** [U] government of a country by religious leaders **2** [C] a country that is governed by religious leaders ▶ **the·o·crat·ic** /ˌθiːəˈkrætɪk/ adj.: *theocratic rule*

the·o·crat /ˈθiːəˌkræt/ noun one of the religious leaders in a theocracy

the·od·o·lite /θiˈɑːdlˌaɪt/ noun a piece of equipment used by SURVEYORS for measuring angles

the·o·lo·gian /ˌθiːəˈloʊdʒən/ noun a person who studies theology

the·ol·o·gy /θiˈɑːlədʒi/ noun (pl. the·ol·o·gies) **1** [U] the study of religion and beliefs: *a degree in Theology* ◆ *a theology student* **2** [C] a set of religious beliefs: *the theologies of the East* ▶ **the·o·log·i·cal** /ˌθiːəˈlɑːdʒɪkl/ adj.: *a theological seminary* **the·o·log·i·cally** /-kli/ adv.

the·o·rem /ˈθiːrəm; ˈθiːərəm/ noun (technical) a rule or principle, especially in mathematics, that can be proved to be true ⊃ collocations at SCIENTIFIC

the·o·ret·i·cal AWL /ˌθiəˈretɪkl/ adj. [usually before noun] **1** concerned with the ideas and principles on which a particular subject is based, rather than with practice and experiment: *a theoretical approach* ◆ *theoretical physics* ◆ *The first year provides students with a sound theoretical basis for later study.* **ANT** EXPERIMENTAL, PRACTICAL ➾ collocations at THEORY **2** that could possibly exist, happen, or be true, although this is unlikely: *It's a theoretical possibility.* ▸ **the·o·ret·i·cal·ly** AWL /-kli/ adv.: *theoretically sound conclusions* ◆ *It is theoretically possible for him to overrule their decision, but highly unlikely.*

the·o·rist AWL /ˈθiərɪst; ˈθɪr-/ (also **the·o·re·ti·cian** /ˌθiərəˈtɪʃn; ˌθɪr-/) noun a person who develops ideas and principles about a particular subject in order to explain why things happen or exist

the·o·rize /ˈθiəˌraɪz/ verb [I, T] ~ **(about/on sth)** | ~ **sth** | ~ **that…** to suggest facts and ideas to explain something; to form a theory or theories about something: *The study theorizes about the role of dreams in peoples' lives.* ▸ **the·o·riz·ing** noun [U]

the·o·ry 🔑 AWL /ˈθiri; ˈθiəri/ noun (pl. **the·o·ries**) **1** [C, U] a formal set of ideas that is intended to explain why something happens or exists: *According to the theory of relativity, nothing can travel faster than light.* ➾ collocations at SCIENTIFIC **2** [U] the principles on which a particular subject is based: *the theory and practice of language teaching* **3** [C] ~ **(that…)** an opinion or idea that someone believes is true but that is not proved: *I have this theory that most people prefer being at work to being at home.*

IDM in theory used to say that a particular statement is supposed to be true but may in fact be wrong: *In theory, these machines should last for ten years or more.* ◆ *That sounds fine in theory, but have you really thought it through?*

AWL COLLOCATIONS

theory

theory noun

- **develop, formulate | advance, expound, propound | disprove, refute | support | test**
  In this study, the empirical data do not support current theories.
  New facts and observations test established theories.

- **hypothesize, posit, postulate, predict, suggest**
  The theory posits that some character types are better prepared for the challenges of being president.
  The results of our experiment aligned very closely with that predicted by theory.

- **economic, literary, political, scientific, social**
  In economic theory, when there is more competition prices are lower.

- **based on**
  Based on the theory developed in this paper, it is predicted that...

theoretical adj.

- **highly | largely | merely, purely**
  Although some purely theoretical work has been done, there is a need for empirical research.

- **concept, construct, framework, model | approach, perspective | prediction | study**
  The next section outlines the theoretical framework and reviews the prior literature.

theoretically adv.

- **defensible, informed, sound | unsound**
  These scientific hypotheses have to be logically and theoretically defensible.

---

the·os·o·phy /θiˈɑsəfi/ noun **1** [U, C] a religious system of thought that tries to know God by means of MEDITATION, prayer, etc. **2 Theosophy** [U] the belief of a religious

group, the Theosophical Society, started in New York in 1875

ther·a·peu·tic /ˌθerəˈpyutɪk/ adj. **1** [usually before noun] designed to help treat an illness: *the therapeutic properties of herbs* **2** helping you to relax: *Painting can be very therapeutic.* ▸ **ther·a·peu·ti·cally** /-kli/ adv.

ther·a·peu·tics /ˌθerəˈpyutɪks/ noun [U] the branch of medicine concerned with the treatment of diseases

ther·a·pist /ˈθerəpɪst/ noun **1** (especially in compounds) a specialist who treats a particular type of illness or problem, or who uses a particular type of treatment: *a speech therapist* ◆ *a beauty therapist* ➾ see also OCCUPATIONAL THERAPIST, PHYSICAL THERAPIST **2** = PSYCHOTHERAPIST

ther·a·py /ˈθerəpi/ noun (pl. **ther·a·pies**) **1** [U, C] the treatment of a physical problem or an illness: *Most leukemia patients undergo some sort of drug therapy* (= treatment using drugs). ◆ *alternative/complementary/natural therapies* (= treatments that do not use traditional drugs) **2** [U] = PSYCHOTHERAPY: *a therapy group* ◆ *She's in therapy.* ➾ see also CHEMOTHERAPY, GROUP THERAPY, HORMONE REPLACEMENT THERAPY, OCCUPATIONAL THERAPY, PHYSICAL THERAPY, RADIOTHERAPY, RETAIL THERAPY, SPEECH THERAPY

Ther·a·va·da /ˌθerəˈvɑdə/ (also ˌThera·vada ˈBuddhism) noun [U] one of the two major forms of Buddhism ➾ compare MAHAYANA

there 🔑 /ðer/ adv., exclamation

● **adv. 1** /ðer; weak form ðər/ **there is, are, was, were, etc.** used to show that something exists or happens: *There's a restaurant around the corner.* ◆ *There are two people waiting outside.* ◆ *Has there been an accident?* ◆ *I don't want there to be any misunderstanding.* ◆ *There seemed to be no doubt about it.* ◆ *There comes a point where you give up.* ◆ *There remains the problem of finance.* ◆ *Suddenly there was a loud bang.* ◆ (informal) *There are only four days left.* ◆ (literary) *There once was a poor farmer who had four sons.* **2** in, at, or to that place or position: *We went on to Paris and stayed there eleven days.* ◆ *I hope we get there in time.* ◆ *It's there, right in front of you!* ◆ *There it is —just behind the chair.* ◆ *"Have you seen my pen?" "Yes, it's over there."* ◆ *There are a lot of people back there* (= behind) *waiting to get in.* ◆ *I'm not going in there —it's freezing!* ◆ *We're almost there* (= we have almost arrived). ◆ *Can I get there and back in a day?* ◆ *I left in 2008 and I haven't been back there since.* ◆ *Hello, is Bob there please?* (= used when calling someone on the phone) ◆ *I took one look at the car and offered to buy it there and then/then and there* (= immediately). **3** existing or available: *I went to see if my old school was still there.* ◆ *The money's there if you need it.* **4** at that point (in a story, an argument, etc.): *"I feel…" There she stopped.* ◆ *I don't agree with you there.* **5** used to attract someone's attention: *Hello, there!* ◆ *You there! Come back!* ◆ *There you are! I've been looking for you everywhere.* **6** used to attract someone's attention to a particular person, thing, or fact: *There's the statue I was telling you about.* ◆ *That woman there is the boss's wife.* ◆ *There goes the last bus* (= we've just missed it). ◆ *There goes the phone* (= it's ringing). ◆ (humorous) *There goes my career!* (= my career is ruined) ◆ *So, there you have it: that's how it all started.* **7** ~ **to do sth** used to show the role of a person or thing in a situation: *The fact is, they're there to make money.* **IDM been there, done that** (informal) used to show that you think a place or an activity is not very interesting or impressive because you have already experienced it: *Not New York again! Been there, done that, got the T-shirt.* **be there for sb** to be available if someone wants to talk to you or if they need help: *You know I'll always be there for you.* **have been there before** (informal) to know all about a situation because you have experienced it **not all there** (informal) not very intelligent, especially because of mental illness **so there!** (informal) used to show that you are determined not to change your attitude or opinion: *Well, you can't have it, so there!* **there it is** (informal) that is the situation: *It's crazy, I know, but there it is.* **there's a good boy, girl, dog, etc.** (informal) used to praise or encourage small children or animals: *Finish your lunch, there's a good boy.* **there's sth for you** (informal) used to say that something is a very good

| t tea | ţ butter | d did | k cat | g got | tʃ chin | dʒ June | f fall |

example of something: *She visited him every day he was in the hospital. There's devotion for you.* ♦ (*ironic*) *He didn't even say thank you. There's gratitude for you!* **there, there!** (*informal*) used to persuade a small child to stop crying or being upset: *There, there! Never mind, you'll soon feel better.* **there you are** (also **there you go**) (*informal*) **1** used when giving someone a thing they want or have asked for: *There you are —that'll be $3.80, please.* ♦ *OK, there you go.* **2** used when explaining or showing something to someone: *You switch on, push in the DVD, and there you are!* ♦ *There you are! I told you it was easy.* **3** used when you are talking about something that happens in a typical way or about a situation that cannot be changed: *There you go—that's what they're like.* ♦ *I know it's not ideal but there you go...* **there you go again** (*informal*) used to criticize someone when they behave in a way that is typical of them: *There you go again—jumping to conclusions.* ⊃ more at HERE

● *exclamation* used to express satisfaction that you were right about something or to show that something annoys you: *There now! What did I tell you?* (= you can see that I was right) ♦ *There! That didn't hurt too much, did it?* ♦ *There! You've gone and woken the baby!*

there·a·bouts /ˌðɛrəˈbaʊts/ *adv.* (usually used after *or*) **1** near the place mentioned: *He comes from Miami or thereabouts.* **2** used to say that a particular number, quantity, time, etc. is not exact: *They paid $100,000 or thereabouts for the house.*

there·af·ter /ˌðɛrˈæftər/ *adv.* (*formal*) after the time or event mentioned: *She married at 17 and gave birth to her first child shortly thereafter.* ⊃ compare HEREAFTER

there·by AWL /ˌðɛrˈbaɪ; ˈðɛrbaɪ/ *adv.* (*formal*) used to introduce the result of the action or situation mentioned: *Regular exercise strengthens the heart, thereby reducing the risk of heart attack.*

there·fore 🔑 /ˈðɛrfɔr/ *adv.*
used to introduce the logical result of something that has just been mentioned: *He's only 17 and therefore not eligible to vote.* ♦ *There is still much to discuss. We shall, therefore, return to this item at our next meeting.*

LANGUAGE BANK

therefore

ways of saying "for this reason..."

- Children who grow up on a diet of junk food find it difficult to change this habit later in life. It is essential, **therefore**, that parents encourage healthy eating from an early age.
- Children who grow up on a diet of junk food find it difficult to change this habit later in life. **For this reason,** /**This is why** it is essential that children eat healthily from an early age.
- Eating habits formed in childhood tend to continue into adult life. **Thus,** the best way to prevent heart disease among adults is to encourage healthy eating from an early age.
- Eating habits formed in childhood tend to continue into adult life, **hence** the importance of encouraging healthy eating from an early age.
⊃ Language Banks at BECAUSE OF, CAUSE, CONSEQUENTLY, EMPHASIS, VITAL

---

there·from /ˌðɛrˈfrʌm; -ˈfrɑm/ *adv.* (*formal* or *law*) from the thing mentioned: *The committee will examine the agreement and any problems arising therefrom.*

there·in /ˌðɛrˈɪn/ *adv.* (*formal* or *law*) in the place, object, document, etc. mentioned: *The insurance policy covers the building and any fixtures contained therein.*
IDM **therein lies...** used to emphasize the result or consequence of a particular situation: *He works extremely hard and therein lies the key to his success.*

there·of /ˌðɛrˈʌv/ *adv.* (*formal* or *law*) of the thing mentioned: *Is the property or any part thereof used for commercial activity?*

there·on /ˌðɛrˈɑn; -ˈɔn/ *adv.* (*formal* or *law*) on the thing mentioned: *a meeting to discuss the annual accounts and the auditors' report thereon*

there's /ðɛrz; ðərz/ *short form* **1** there is **2** there has

there·to /ˌðɛrˈtu/ *adv.* (*formal* or *law*) to the thing mentioned: *The lease entitles the holder to use the buildings and any land attached thereto.*

there·un·der /ˌðɛrˈʌndər/ *adv.* (*formal* or *law*) under the thing mentioned: *the act and the regulations made thereunder*

there·up·on /ˌðɛrəˈpɑn; -ˈpɔn/ *adv.* (*formal*) **1** immediately after the situation mentioned; as a direct result of the situation mentioned: *The audience thereupon rose cheering to their feet.* **2** on the thing mentioned: *a large notice with black letters printed thereupon*

there·with /ˌðɛrˈwɪθ; -ˈwɪð/ *adv.* (*old use* or *formal*) **1** with or in the thing mentioned **2** soon or immediately after that

ther·mal /ˈθɜrml/ *adj.*, *noun*
● *adj.* [only before noun] **1** (*technical*) connected with heat: *thermal energy* **2** (of clothing) designed to keep you warm by preventing heat from escaping from the body: *thermal underwear* **3** (of streams, lakes, etc.) in which the water has been naturally heated by the earth: *thermal springs* ▸ **ther·mal·ly** /-məli/ *adv.*
● *noun* **1** [C] a rising current of warm air used, for example, by a GLIDER to gain height **2 thermals** [pl.] warm underwear that prevents heat from escaping from the body

thermal ˈimaging *noun* [U] (*technical*) the process of producing an image of something or finding out where something is, using the heat that comes from it: *Rescue teams are using thermal imaging to locate survivors of the earthquake.*

thermo- /ˈθɜrmoʊ/ *combining form* (in nouns, adjectives, and adverbs) connected with heat: *thermonuclear* ♦ *thermometer*

ther·mo·dy·nam·ics /ˌθɜrmoʊdaɪˈnæmɪks/ *noun* [U] the science that deals with the relations between heat and other forms of energy: *the laws of thermodynamics* ▸ **ther·mo·dy·nam·ic** *adj.*

ther·mom·e·ter /θərˈmɑmətər/ *noun* an instrument used for measuring the temperature of the air, a person's body, etc.: *a thermometer reading*

thermometers

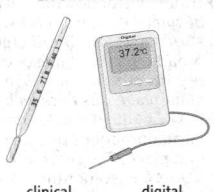

clinical   digital
thermometer   thermometer

ther·mo·nu·cle·ar /ˌθɜrmoʊˈnukliər/ *adj.* connected with nuclear reactions that only happen at very high temperatures

ther·mo·plas·tic /ˌθɜrməˈplæstɪk/ *noun* [U] (*technical*) a plastic material that can be easily shaped and bent when it is heated, and that becomes hard when it is cooled

Ther·mos™ /ˈθɜrməs/ (also ˈThermos bottle) *noun* a particular kind of VACUUM BOTTLE (= a container like a bottle with double walls with a VACUUM between them, used for keeping liquids hot or cold)

the ther·mo·sphere /ˈθɜrməˌsfɪr/ *noun* [sing.] (*technical*) the region of the atmosphere above the MESOSPHERE

ther·mo·stat /ˈθɜrməˌstæt/ *noun* a device that measures and controls the temperature of a machine or room, by switching the heating or cooling system on and off as necessary ▸ **ther·mo·stat·ic** /ˌθɜrməˈstætɪk/ *adj.* [only before noun] **ther·mo·stat·i·cally** /-kli/ *adv.*

the·sau·rus /θɪˈsɔrəs/ *noun* (pl. **the·sau·ri** /-ˈsɔraɪ/ or **the·sau·rus·es** /-ˈsɔrəsəz/) a book that lists words in groups that have similar meanings

these ⊃ THIS

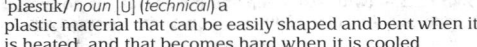

the·sis AWL /ˈθiːsəs/ noun (pl. **the·ses** /ˈθiːsiːz/) **1** ~ **(on sth)** a long piece of writing completed by a student as part of a university degree, based on their own research **2** a statement or an opinion that is discussed in a logical way and presented with evidence in order to prove that it is true: *She concluded that there was no archaeological data to support the thesis that the town had been surrounded by a wall.* ⊃ collocations at SCIENTIFIC

thes·pi·an /ˈθespiən/ noun (often *humorous*) an actor ▶ **thespian** adj.

the·ta /ˈθiːtə/ noun the 8th letter of the Greek alphabet (Θ, θ)

ˈtheta ˌrole noun = THEMATIC ROLE

they 🔑 /ðeɪ/ pron. (used as the subject of a verb) **1** people, animals, or things that have already been mentioned or are easily identified: *"Where are John and Liz?" "They went for a walk."* ◆ *They* (= the things you are carrying) *go on the bottom shelf.* **2** used instead of *he* or *she* to refer to a person whose sex is not mentioned or not known: *If anyone arrives late they'll have to wait outside.* **3** people in general: *The rest, as they say, is history.* **4** people in authority or experts: *They cut my water off.* ◆ *They now say that red wine is good for you.*

they'd /ðeɪd/ short form **1** they had **2** they would

they'll /ðeɪl; ðel/ short form they will

they're /ðer; ðər/ short form they are

they've /ðeɪv/ short form they have

thi·a·mine (also **thi·a·min**) /ˈθaɪəmən/ noun [U] a VITAMIN of the B group, found in grains, BEANS, and LIVER

thick 🔑 /θɪk/ adj., noun, adv.
● **adj. (thick·er, thick·est)**
▷ DISTANCE BETWEEN SIDES **1** having a larger distance between opposite sides or surfaces than other similar objects or than normal: *a thick slice of bread* ◆ *a thick book* (= one that has a lot of pages) ◆ *a thick coat* (= one made of heavy cloth) ◆ *thick fingers* ◆ *Everything was covered with a thick layer of dust.* **2** used to ask about or state the distance between opposite sides or surfaces: *How thick are the walls?* ◆ *They're two feet thick.*
▷ HAIR/FUR/TREES **3** growing closely together in large numbers: *thick dark hair* ◆ *a thick forest*
▷ LIQUID **4** not flowing very easily: *thick soup* ◆ *The effect will be ruined if the paint is too thick.*
▷ FOG/SMOKE/AIR **5** difficult to see through; difficult to breathe in: *The plane crashed in thick fog.* ◆ *thick smoke* ◆ ~ **with sth** *The air was thick with dust.* ◆ (figurative) *The atmosphere was thick with tension.*
▷ WITH LARGE NUMBER/AMOUNT **6** ~ **with sb/sth** having a large number of people or a large amount of something in one place: *The beach was thick with sunbathers.*
▷ ACCENT **7** (sometimes *disapproving*) easily recognized as being from a particular country or area SYN STRONG: *a thick Brooklyn accent*
▷ VOICE **8** ~ **(with sth)** deep and not as clear as normal, especially because of illness or emotion: *His voice was thick with emotion.*
▷ STUPID **9** (informal) (of a person) slow to learn or understand things: *He's too thick to realize what's going on.*
▷ FRIENDLY WITH SOMEONE **10** ~ **(with sb)** (informal) very friendly with someone, especially in a way that makes other people suspicious: *You seem to be very thick with the boss!* ⊃ see also THICKLY, THICKNESS
IDM (as) thick as thieves (informal) (of two or more people) very friendly, especially in a way that makes other people suspicious **your thick head** (informal) used to show that you are annoyed that someone does not understand something: *When will you get it into your thick head that I don't want to see you again!* **a thick skin** the ability to accept criticism, insults, etc. without becoming upset ANT A THIN SKIN ⊃ see also THICK-SKINNED ⊃ more at BLOOD
● **noun** [U]
IDM in the thick of sth involved in the busiest or most active part of something **through thick and thin** even

when there are problems or difficulties: *He's supported the team for over ten years through thick and thin.*
● **adv. (thick·er, thick·est)** in a way that produces a wide piece or deep layer of something: *Make sure you cut the bread nice and thick.*
IDM lay it on thick (informal) to talk about someone or something in a way that makes them or it seem much better or much worse than they really are; to exaggerate something: *Praise them when necessary, but don't lay it on too thick.* **thick and fast** quickly and in large quantities: *Questions were coming at them thick and fast.*

thick·en /ˈθɪkən/ verb [I, T] to become thicker; to make something thicker: *Stir until the sauce has thickened.* ◆ *It was a dangerous journey through thickening fog.* ◆ ~ **sth** *Thicken the stew with flour.* **IDM** see PLOT n.

thick·en·er /ˈθɪkənər/ noun a substance used to make a liquid thicker: *paint thickeners*

thick·et /ˈθɪkət/ noun **1** a group of bushes or small trees growing closely together **2** a large number of things that are not easy to understand or separate

thick·head·ed /ˈθɪkˌhedəd/ adj. stupid

thick·ly 🔑 /ˈθɪkli/ adv.
1 in a way that produces a wide piece or deep layer of something: *thickly sliced bread* ◆ *Apply the paint thickly in even strokes.* **2** ~ **wooded, populated, etc.** having a lot of trees, people, etc. close together **3** in a deep voice that is not as clear as normal, especially because of illness or emotion

thick·ness 🔑 /ˈθɪknəs/ noun
1 [U, C] the size of something between opposite surfaces or sides SYN WIDTH: *Use wood of at least 5in. thickness.* ◆ *The board is available in four thicknesses.* **2** [C] ~ **(of sth)** a layer of something: *The jacket was lined with a double thickness* (= two layers) *of fabric.*

thick·set /ˈθɪkset/ adj. (especially of a man) having a strong heavy body

thick-ˈskinned adj. **1** (of a person) not easily upset by criticism or unkind comments **2** (of fruit) having a thick skin ANT THIN-SKINNED

thief 🔑 /θiːf/ noun (pl. **thieves** /θiːvz/)
a person who steals something from another person or place: *a car/jewel, etc. thief* ⊃ see also THEFT **IDM** see HONOR n., THICK

thiev·er·y /ˈθiːvəri/ noun [U] (formal) the crime of stealing things

thiev·ing /ˈθiːvɪŋ/ noun [U] (informal) the act of stealing things ▶ **thieving** adj. (informal): *You don't have any right to take that, you thieving swine!*

thigh /θaɪ/ noun **1** the top part of the leg between the knee and the hip ⊃ picture at BODY ⊃ collocations at PHYSICAL **2** the top part of the leg of a chicken, etc., cooked and eaten

ˈthigh bone noun the large thick bone in the top part of the leg between the hip and the knee SYN FEMUR ⊃ picture at BODY

thim·ble /ˈθɪmbl/ noun a small metal or plastic object that you wear on the end of your finger to protect it when sewing

thim·ble·ful /ˈθɪmblˌfʊl/ noun a very small amount of a liquid, especially alcohol

thin 🔑 /θɪn/ adj., adv., verb
● **adj. (thin·ner, thin·nest)**
▷ NOT THICK **1** having a smaller distance between opposite sides or surfaces than other similar objects or than normal: *Cut the vegetables into thin strips.* ◆ *A number of thin cracks appeared in the wall.* ◆ *The body was hidden beneath a thin layer of soil.* ◆ *a thin blouse* (= of light cloth) ⊃ see also PAPER-THIN ⊃ note at NARROW
▷ NOT FAT **2** (of a person or part of the body) (sometimes *disapproving*) not covered with much flesh: *He was tall and*

thin, with dark hair. ◆ She was looking pale and thin. ◆ He is as **thin as a rail** (= very thin). ◆ thin legs
> HAIR **3** not growing closely together or in large amounts: thin gray hair
> LIQUID **4** containing more liquid than is normal or expected **SYN** RUNNY: The sauce was thin and tasteless.
> SMOKE **5** fairly easy to see through: They fought their way through where the smoke was thinner.
> AIR **6** containing less OXYGEN than normal
> SOUND **7** (disapproving) high and weak: Her thin voice trailed off into silence.
> SMILE **8** not sincere or enthusiastic: He gave a thin smile.
> LIGHT **9** not very bright: the thin gray light of dawn
> POOR QUALITY **10** of poor quality; lacking an important quality: a thin excuse (= one that people are not likely to believe) ◆ Their arguments all sound a little thin to me.

▶ **thin·ness** /ˈθɪnnəs/ noun [U] ⊃ see also THINLY
IDM be skating/walking on thin ice to be taking a risk **disappear, vanish, etc. into thin air** to disappear suddenly in a mysterious way **out of thin air** from nowhere or nothing, as if by magic **thin on top** (informal) without much hair on the head: He's starting to get a little thin on top (= he's losing his hair). **a thin skin** the lack of ability to accept criticism, insults, etc. without becoming upset **ANT** A THICK SKIN ⊃ see also THIN-SKINNED ⊃ more at LINE n., SPREAD v., THICK n., WEAR v.

saying that someone is thin

Thin is the most usual word: Steve is tall and thin and has brown hair. It is sometimes used with a negative meaning: My mother looked thin and tired after her long illness.
The following words all express praise or admiration:
- **Slim** means pleasantly thin. It is often used to describe women who have controlled their weight by diet or exercise: She has a strikingly slim figure.
- A **slender** girl or woman is thin and graceful.
- A **lean** man is thin and fit.
- **Willowy** describes a woman who is attractively tall and thin.
The following words are more negative in their meaning:
- **Skinny** means very thin, often in a way that is not attractive: a skinny little kid
- **Bony** describes parts of the body when they are so thin that the bones can be seen: the old man's bony hands
- **Scrawny** suggests that a person is thin, weak, and not attractive: a scrawny old woman
- **Gaunt** describes a person who is a little too thin and looks sad or ill.
- **Underweight** is used in medical contexts to describe people who are too thin because they are ill or have not had enough food: Women who smoke risk giving birth to underweight babies.
- **Emaciated** describes a serious condition resulting from illness or lack of food.
- **Anorexic** is a medical term, but is now also used informally to describe a girl or woman who is so thin that you are worried about them.
It is much more acceptable to talk to someone about how thin or slim they are than about how fat they are.
⊃ note at FAT

● **adv.** (thin·ner, thin·nest) in a way that produces a thin piece or layer of something: Don't spread it too thin. ◆ I like my bread sliced thin.
● **verb** (-nn-)
> LIQUID **1** [T] ~ sth (down) (with sth) to make a liquid less thick or strong by adding water or another substance: Thin the paint with water.

> OF HAIR **2** [I] to become less thick: a middle-aged man with thinning hair
> BECOME LESS THICK **3** [I, T] to become less thick or fewer in number; to make something less thick or fewer, for example by removing some things or people: The clouds thinned and the moon shone through. ◆ ~ **out** The crowd thinned out and only a few people were left. ◆ ~ **sth (out)** Thin out the seedlings to about 4 inches apart.

thine /ðaɪn/ pron., det. (old use)
● **pron.** a word meaning "yours," used when talking to only one person
● **det.** the form of thy that is used before a vowel or "h," meaning "your"

other words for "thing"

Instead of using the word **thing**, try to use more precise and interesting words, especially in formal written English.
- **aspect** That was the most puzzling aspect of the situation. (…the most puzzling thing about…)
- **attribute** Curiosity is an essential attribute for a journalist. (…an essential thing for a journalist to have.)
- **characteristic** This bird has several interesting characteristics. (There are several interesting things about this bird.)
- **detail** I want to know every detail of what happened. (…everything about…)
- **feature** Noise is a familiar feature of city life. (…a familiar thing in city life.)
- **issue** She has campaigned on many controversial issues. (…many controversial things.)
- **matter** We have several important matters to deal with at this meeting. (…several important things…)
- **point** That's a very interesting point you made. (…a very interesting thing you said.)
- **subject** The book covers a number of subjects. (…a number of things.)
- **topic** We discussed a wide range of topics. (…a wide range of things.)
- **trait** Her generosity is one of her most attractive traits. (…one of the most attractive things about her.)
- Don't use **thing** after an adjective when the adjective can be used on its own: Having your own computer is very useful. ◆ Having your own computer is a very useful thing.
- It is often more natural to use words like **something**, **anything**, etc. instead of **thing**: I have something important to tell you. ◆ I have an important thing to tell you. ◆ Do you want anything else? ◆ Do you want any other thing?
- It is more natural to say **a lot**, **a great deal**, **much**, etc. rather than **many things**: I have so much to tell you. ◆ I have so many things to tell you. ◆ She knows a lot about basketball. ◆ She knows many things about basketball.

thing /θɪŋ/ noun
> OBJECT **1** [C] an object whose name you do not use because you do not need to or want to, or because you do not know it: Can you pass me that thing over there? ◆ She's very fond of sweet things (= sweet foods). ◆ He's just bought one of those exercise things. ◆ Turn that thing off while I'm talking to you!
2 [C] an object that is not alive in the way that people and plants are: Don't treat her like that—she's a person, not a thing! ◆ He's good at making things with his hands. ◆ She took no interest in the people and things around her.
> POSSESSIONS/EQUIPMENT **3** things [pl.] objects, clothing, or tools that belong to someone or are used for a particular purpose: Can I help you pack your things? ◆ This box is full of camping things. ◆ I'll just clear away the breakfast things. ◆ Put your things (= coat, etc.) on and let's go.
> ANYTHING **4** a thing [sing.] used with negatives to mean "anything" in order to emphasize what you are saying: I

don't have a thing to wear! ◆ There wasn't a thing we could do to help. ◆ Ignore what he said—it **doesn't mean a thing**.

> FACT/EVENT/SITUATION/ACTION **5** [C] a fact, an event, a situation, or an action; what someone says or thinks: *There are a lot of things she doesn't know about me.* ◆ *There's another thing I'd like to ask you.* ◆ *A terrible thing happened last night.* ◆ *He found* **the whole thing** (= the situation) *very boring.* ◆ *I have loads of things to do today.* ◆ *The main thing to remember is to switch off the burglar alarm.* ◆ *I like camping, climbing, and that sort of thing.* ◆ *She said* **the first thing** *that came into her head.* ◆ *"Why did you tell her our secret?" "I did* **no such thing**!*" ◆ Let's forget* **the whole thing** (= everything). **6 things** [pl.] the general situation, as it affects someone: *Things haven't gone entirely to plan.* ◆ (*informal*) *Hi, Jane!* **How are things?** ◆ **Think things over** *before you decide.* ◆ **As things stand** *at present, he seems certain to win.* ◆ **All things considered** (= considering all the difficulties or problems), *she's done very well.* ◆ *Why do you make things so difficult for yourself?* ➔ thesaurus box at SITUATION

> WHAT IS NEEDED/RIGHT **7** [C, usually sing.] what is needed or socially acceptable: *You need something to cheer you up—I know just the thing!* ◆ *to say* **the right/wrong thing** ◆ *The best thing to do is to apologize.*

> THINGS OF PARTICULAR TYPE **8 things** [pl.] (*formal*) (followed by an adjective) all that can be described in a particular way: *She loves all things Japanese.*

> CREATURE **9** [C] (used with an adjective) a living creature: *All living things are composed of cells.*

> PERSON/ANIMAL **10** [C] (with an adjective) (*informal*) used to talk to or about a person or an animal, to show how you feel about them: *You silly thing!* ◆ *You must be starving, you poor things.* ◆ *The cat's very ill, poor old thing.*

IDM **A is one thing, B is another** | **it's one thing to do A, it's another thing to do B** B is very different from A, for example it is more difficult, serious, or important: *Romance is one thing, marriage is quite another.* ◆ *It's one thing to tease your sister, but it's another to hit her.* **all/other things being equal** if the conditions stay the same; if other conditions are the same: *All things being equal, we should finish the job tomorrow.* **and things (like that)** (*informal*) used when you do not want to complete a list: *She likes nice clothes and things like that.* ◆ *I've been busy shopping and things.* **be all things to all men/people 1** (of people) to please everyone by changing your attitudes or opinions to suit different people **2** (of things) to be understood or used in different ways by different people **the best, fastest, etc. thing going** (*informal*) the best, fastest, etc. thing of its kind currently available: *It's a little expensive, but this computer is the best thing going right now.* **come to/be the same thing** to have the same result or meaning **be a good thing (that)…** to be lucky that…: *It's a good thing we got here early.* **be no bad thing (that)…** used to say that although something seems to be bad, it could have good results: *We didn't want the press to get hold of the story, but it might be no bad thing.* **be onto a good thing** to have found a job, situation, or style of life that is pleasant or easy **do things to sb** (*informal*) to have a powerful emotional effect on someone: *That song just does things to me.* **do your own thing** (*informal*) to do what you want to do or what interests you, without thinking about other people; to be independent **first/last thing** early in the morning/late in the evening: *I need the report on my desk first thing Monday morning.* **first things first** (often *humorous*) the most important matters must be dealt with first: *We have a lot to discuss, but, first things first, let's have a cup of coffee!* **for one thing** used to introduce one of two or more reasons for doing something: *"Why don't you get a car?" "Well, for one thing, I can't drive!"* **have a thing about sb/sth** (*informal*) to have a strong like or dislike of someone or something in a way that seems strange or unreasonable: *She has a thing about men with beards.* **it isn't my, his, etc. thing** it is not something that you really enjoy or are interested in **it's a… thing** (*informal*) it is something that only a particular group understands: *You wouldn't know what it means—it's a girl thing.* **know/tell sb a thing or two (about sb/sth)** (*informal*) to know/tell someone some useful, interesting, or

surprising information about someone or something: *She's been married five times, so she knows a thing or two about men!* **make a (big) thing of/about sth** (*informal*) to make something seem more important than it really is **not know, etc. the first thing about sth/sb** to know nothing at all about something or someone **not quite the thing 1** not considered socially acceptable: *It wouldn't be quite the thing to turn up in running gear.* **2** (*old-fashioned*) not healthy or normal **(just) one of those things** used to say that you do not want to discuss or think about something bad or unpleasant that has happened, but just accept it: *It wasn't your fault. It was just one of those things.* **one thing after another** (*informal*) used to complain that a lot of unpleasant things keep happening to you **one thing leads to another** used to suggest that the way one event or action leads to others is so obvious that it does not need to be stated: *He offered me a ride home one night, and, well, one thing led to another and now we're married!* **be seeing/hearing things** (*informal, humorous*) to imagine that you can see or hear something that is in fact not there **there's only one thing for it** there is only one possible course of action **the thing is** (*informal*) used to introduce an important fact, reason, or explanation: *I'm sorry my assignment isn't finished. The thing is, I've had a lot of other work this week.* **the thing (about/with sth/sb) is** used to introduce a problem about something or someone: *The thing with Karl is, he's always late.* **the (whole)… thing** (*informal*) a situation or an activity of the type mentioned: *She really didn't want to be involved in the whole family thing.* **things that go bump in the night** (*informal, humorous*) used to refer to GHOSTS and other SUPERNATURAL things that cannot be explained **too much of a good thing** used to say that, although something is pleasant, you do not want to have too much of it **(what) with one thing and another** (*informal*) because you have been busy with various problems, events, or things you had to do: *I completely forgot her birthday, what with one thing and another.* ➔ more at DAY, DECENT, EASY *adv.*, NATURE, NEAR *adj.*, ONLY *adj.*, OVERDO, PUSH *v.*, REAL, SCHEME *n.*, SHAPE *n.*, SURE *adj.*, TURN *v.*, WAY *n.*, WORK *v.*

THESAURUS

things

stuff ◆ property ◆ possessions ◆ junk ◆ belongings ◆ goods ◆ valuables

These are all words for objects or items, especially ones that you own or have with you at a particular time.

things (*somewhat informal*) objects, clothing, or tools that you own or that are used for a particular purpose: *Can I help you pack your things?* ◆ *This box is full of camping things.*

stuff (*informal*) used to refer to a group of objects when you do not know their names, when the names are not important, or when it is obvious what you are talking about: *Where's all my stuff?* ◆ *Don't forget your swimming stuff.*

THINGS OR STUFF?

These words are similar and often you can use either. Use **things** when the items might be used individually as tools (*sewing things* ◆ *gardening things*). Use **stuff** to refer to all the equipment necessary for one particular activity or project.

property (*somewhat formal*) a thing or things that are owned by someone: *This building is government property.* ◆ *Be careful not to damage other people's property.*

possessions things that you own, especially something that can be moved: *Prisoners were allowed no personal possessions except letters and photographs.*

junk things that are considered useless or of little value: *I've cleared out all that old junk from the attic.*

belongings possessions that can be moved, especially ones that you have with you at a particular time: *Please* *make sure you have all your belongings with you when leaving the plane.*

goods (*somewhat formal* or *technical*) possessions that can be moved: *She was found guilty of* **trading in stolen goods.**

valuables things that are worth a lot of money, especially small personal things such as jewelry or cameras: *Never leave cash or other valuables lying around.*

PATTERNS

- **personal** things/stuff/property/possessions/belongings
- to **collect/gather/pack** (up) your things/stuff/possessions/belongings
- to **search** sb's/your/the things/stuff/property/belongings
- to **go through** sb's/your/the things/stuff/belongings

thing·a·ma·jig /ˈθɪŋəmədʒɪɡ/ *noun* (also **thing·a·ma·bob** /ˈθɪŋəməˌbɑb/, **thing·y**) (*informal*) used to refer to a thing whose name you do not know or have forgotten, or which you do not want to mention: *It's one of those thingamajigs for keeping papers together.*

thing·y /ˈθɪŋi/ *noun* (*pl.* **thing·ies**) = THINGAMAJIG

think 🔑 /θɪŋk/ *verb, noun*

● **verb** (**thought, thought** /θɔt/)

▷ **HAVE OPINION/BELIEF 1** [T, I] (not used in the progressive tenses) to have a particular idea or opinion about something or someone; to believe sth: **~ (that)…** *Do you think (that) they'll come?* ♦ *I thought I heard a scream.* ♦ *I didn't think you liked sports.* ♦ **Am I right in thinking** *that you used to live here?* ♦ *I think this is their house, but I'm not sure.* ♦ *He ought to resign, I think.* ♦ *We'll need about 20 chairs,* **I would think.** ♦ **it is thought that…** *It was once thought that the sun traveled around the earth.* ♦ **~ sth (about sth)** *What did you think about the idea?* ♦ *Well, I like it.* **What do you think?** ♦ **~ so** *"Will we make it in time?" "I think so."* ♦ *"Is he any good?" "I don't think so."* ♦ **~ sb/sth + adj.** *I think it highly unlikely that I'll get the job.* ♦ *She thought him kind and generous.* ♦ **sb/sth is thought to be sb/sth** *He's thought to be one of the richest men in America.* **HELP** This pattern is not usually used unless **think** is in the passive. ➔ language bank at OPINION

▷ **USE MIND 2** [I, T] to use your mind to consider something, to form connected ideas, to try to solve problems, etc.: *Are animals able to think?* ♦ *Let me think* (= give me time before I answer). ♦ **~ (about sth)** *I can't tell you now—I'll have to* **think about it.** ♦ *She had thought very* **deeply** *about this problem.* ♦ *All he ever thinks about is money.* ♦ *I'm sorry,* **I wasn't thinking** (= said when you have upset or offended someone accidentally). ♦ **~ what, how, etc.…** *He was trying to think what to do.* **3** [T] (usually used in the progressive tenses) to have ideas, words, or images in your mind: **~ sth** *You're very quiet. What are you thinking?* ♦ **~ what, how, etc.…** *I was just thinking what a long way it is.* ♦ **+ speech** *"I must be crazy," she thought.*

▷ **IMAGINE 4** [T, no passive, I] to form an idea of something; to imagine something: **~ where, how, etc.…** *We couldn't think where you'd gone.* ♦ *Just think how nice it would be to see them again.* ♦ **~ (that)…** *I can't think (that) he would be so stupid.* ♦ **~ (sth)** *Just think* —we'll be lying on the beach this time tomorrow. ♦ *If I'm late getting home, my mother always* **thinks the worst.** ♦ *Try to* **think yourself into** *the role.*
➔ thesaurus box at IMAGINE

▷ **EXPECT 5** [T] to expect something: **~ (that)…** *I never thought (that) I'd see her again.* ♦ *The job took longer than we thought.* ♦ *You'd think she'd have been grateful for my help* (= but she wasn't). ♦ **~ to do sth** (*formal*) *Who would have thought to find you here?*

▷ **IN A PARTICULAR WAY 6** [I, T] (*informal*) [no passive] to think in a particular way or on a particular subject: **+ adj.** *Let's think positive.* ♦ *You need to* **think big** (= aim to achieve a lot). ♦ **~ sth** *If you want to make money, you have to think money.*

▷ **SHOWING ANGER/SURPRISE 7** [T] **~ (that)…** used in questions to show that you are angry or surprised: *What do you think you're doing?*

▷ **BEING LESS DEFINITE/MORE POLITE 8** [T, I] used to make something you say sound less definite or more polite: **~ (that)…** *I thought we could go out tonight.* ♦ *Twenty guests are enough, I would have thought.* ♦ *Do you think you could open the window?* ♦ **~ so** *"You've made a mistake." "I don't think so."*

▷ **INTEND 9** [T, I] **~ (that…)** to intend something; to have a plan about something: *I think I'll go for a swim.* ♦ *I'm thinking in terms of about 70 guests at the wedding.*

▷ **REMEMBER 10** [T] to remember something; to have something come into your mind: **~ to do sth** *I didn't think* (= it did not occur to me) *to tell her.* ♦ **~ where, what, etc.…** *I can't think where I put the keys.*

IDM **come to think of it** used when you suddenly remember something or realize that it might be important: *Come to think of it, he did mention seeing you.* **I don't think so** (*informal*) used to say very strongly that you do not agree with something, or that something is not possible: *Me? Fail? I don't think so.* **if/when you think about it** used to draw attention to a fact that is not obvious or has not previously been mentioned: *It was a difficult situation, when you think about it.* **I think not** (*formal*) used to say very strongly that you believe something is not true, possible, etc.: *Was their meeting a coincidence? I think not.* **I thought as much** that is what I expected or suspected: *"He said he'd forgotten." "I thought as much."* **think again** to consider a situation again and perhaps change your idea or intention **think aloud/ out loud** to say what your thoughts are as you have them **think better of it/of doing sth** to decide not to do something after thinking further about it **SYN** RECONSIDER: *Rosie was about to protest but thought better of it.* **think (the) better of sb** to have a higher opinion of someone: *She has behaved appallingly—I must say I thought better of her.* **think nothing of it** (*formal*) used as a polite response when someone has said sorry to you or thanked you **think nothing of sth/of doing sth** to consider an activity to be normal and not particularly unusual or difficult: *She thinks nothing of walking thirty miles a day.* **think on your feet** to be able to think and react to things very quickly and effectively without any preparation **think outside (of) the box** to think about something, or how to do something, in a way that is new, different, or shows imagination **think straight** to think in a clear or logical way **think twice about sth/ about doing sth** to think carefully before deciding to do something: *You should think twice about employing someone you've never met.* **think the world, highly, a lot, not much, poorly, little, etc. of sb/sth** to have a very good, poor, etc. opinion of someone or something: *He thinks the world of his daughter.* ♦ *I don't think much of her idea.* **to think (that…)** used to show that you are surprised or shocked by something: *To think that my mother wrote all those books and I never knew!* ➔ more at **FIT, GREAT, ILL, LET, LIKE, OWN**

PHR V **ˈthink about/of sb/sth 1** to consider someone or something when you are doing or planning something: *Don't you ever think about other people?* **2** to consider doing something **SYN** CONTEMPLATE: **~ doing sth** *She's thinking of changing her job.* **think aˈhead (to sth)** to think about a future event or situation and plan for it **think ˈback (to sth)** to think about something that happened in the past: *I keep thinking back to the day I arrived here.* **think for yourˈself** to form your own opinions and make decisions without depending on others **think of sth/sb 1** to have an image or idea of something or someone in your mind: *When I said that I wasn't thinking of anyone in particular.* **2** to create an idea in your imagination: *Can anybody think of a way to raise money?* ♦ *Have you thought of a name for the baby yet?* **3** [no passive] (used especially with *can*) to remember something or someone: *I can think of at least three occasions when he arrived late.* ♦ *I can't think of her name at the moment.* **think ˈof sb/sth as sb/sth** to consider someone or something in a particular way: *I think of this place as my home.* ♦ *She is thought of as a possible director.* ➔ see also **WELL-THOUGHT-OF** **ˈthink**

of sth to imagine an actual or a possible situation: *Just think of the expense!* ◆ **~ doing sth** *I couldn't think of letting you take the blame* (= I would not allow that to happen). ,**think sth↔'out** to consider or plan something carefully: *It's a very well thought out plan.* ,**think sth↔'over** to consider something carefully, especially before reaching a decision: *He'd like more time to think things over.* ,**think sth↔'through** to consider a problem or a possible course of action fully ,**think sth↔'up** (*informal*) to create something in your mind **SYN** DEVISE, INVENT: *Can't you think up a better excuse than that?*

● *noun* [sing.]
IDM **have a think (about sth)** (*informal*) to think carefully about something in order to make a decision about it: *I'll have a think and let you know tomorrow.* **you've got another think coming** (*informal*) used to tell someone that they are wrong about something and must change their plans or opinions

think

believe ● feel ● be under the impression

These words all mean to have an idea that something is true or possible or to have a particular opinion about someone or something.

think to have an idea that something is true or possible, although you are not completely certain; to have a particular opinion about someone or something: *Do you think (that) they'll come?* ◆ *What do you think about Matt's new girlfriend?*

believe to have an idea that something is true or possible, although you are not completely certain; to have a particular opinion about someone or something: *Police believe (that) the man may be armed.*

THINK OR BELIEVE?

When you are expressing an idea that you have or that someone has of what is true or possible, **believe** is more formal than **think**. It is used especially for talking about ideas that other people have; **think** is used more often for talking about your own ideas: *Police believe... ◆ I think...* When you are expressing an opinion, **believe** is stronger than **think** and is used especially for matters of principle; **think** is used more for practical matters or matters of personal taste.

feel to have a particular opinion about something that has happened or about what you/someone ought to do: *We all felt (that) we had been cheated.*

be under the impression that... to have an idea that something is true: *I was under the impression that the work had already been completed.*

PATTERNS
- to think/believe/feel/be under the impression **that...**
- It is thought/believed/felt **that...**
- to **be** thought/believed/felt **to be** sth
- to think/believe/feel sth **about** sb/sth
- to **sincerely/honestly/seriously/mistakenly** think/believe/feel

think·a·ble /ˈθɪŋkəbl/ *adj.* [not before noun] that you can imagine as a possibility: *Such an idea was scarcely thinkable ten years ago.* **ANT** UNTHINKABLE

think·er /ˈθɪŋkər/ *noun* **1** a person who thinks seriously, and often writes about important things, such as philosophy or science: *Einstein was one of the greatest thinkers of the 20th century.* **2** a person who thinks in a particular way: *a clear thinker*

think·ing 🔑 /ˈθɪŋkɪŋ/ *noun, adj.*
● *noun* [U] **1** the process of thinking about something: *I had to do some quick thinking.* ⊃ see also WISHFUL THINKING

2 ideas or opinions about something: *What is the current thinking on this question?* ◆ *She explained the thinking behind the campaign.* **IDM** see WAY *n.*
● *adj.* [only before noun] intelligent and able to think seriously about things: *the thinking woman's magazine*

'**thinking** ,**cap** *noun*
IDM **put your thinking cap on** (*informal*) to try to solve a problem by thinking about it

'**think tank** *noun* a group of experts who provide advice and ideas on political, social, or economic issues

thin·ly /ˈθɪnli/ *adv.* **1** in a way that produces a thin piece or layer of something: *Slice the potatoes thinly.* **2** with only a few things or people spread over a place so that there is a lot of space between them: *a thinly populated area* **3** in a way that is not sincere or enthusiastic: *She smiled thinly.* **4** in a way that does not hide the truth very well **SYN** BARELY: *The novel is a thinly disguised autobiography.*

thin·ner /ˈθɪnər/ *noun* [U, C] a substance that is added to paint, VARNISH, etc. to make it less thick

'**thin-skinned** *adj.* **1** easily upset by criticism or insults **2** (of fruit) having a thin skin **ANT** THICK-SKINNED

third /θərd/ *ordinal number, noun*
● *ordinal number* 3rd **HELP** There are examples of how to use ordinal numbers at the entry for **fifth**.
IDM **third time is the charm** used when you have failed to do something twice and hope that you will succeed the third time
● *noun* each of three equal parts of something ⊃ language bank at PROPORTION

,**third 'base** *noun* [sing.] (in baseball) the third of the BASES that players must touch ⊃ picture at BASEBALL

,**third 'class** *noun* **1** [U] the class of mail used for sending advertisements, etc. **2** [U, sing.] (especially in the past) the cheapest and least comfortable part of a train, ship, etc.

,**third-'class** *adj.* **1** connected with the class of mail used to send advertisements, etc. **2** (especially in the past) connected with the cheapest and least comfortable way of traveling on a train, ship, etc. **3** (*disapproving*) (of people) less important than other people: *They are treated as third-class citizens.* ▶ ,**third 'class** *adv.*: *to travel third class*

,**third de'gree** *noun* [sing.]
IDM **give sb the third degree** (*informal*) to question someone for a long time and in a thorough way; to use threats or violence to get information from someone

,**third-de'gree** *adj.* **1 ~ burns** burns of the most serious kind, affecting TISSUE below the skin **2 ~ murder, assault, robbery, etc.** murder, etc. of the least serious of three kinds ⊃ compare FIRST-DEGREE, SECOND-DEGREE

,**third-gene'ration** *adj.* (*abbr.* 3G) **1** used to describe technology that has been developed to send data to cellphones, etc. at much higher speeds than were possible before **2** used to describe any technology that is being developed that is more advanced than the earlier two stages

third·ly /ˈθərdli/ *adv.* used to introduce the third of a list of points you want to make in a speech or piece of writing: *Thirdly, I would like to say that...*

,**third 'party** *noun* (*formal or law*) a person who is involved in a situation in addition to the two main people involved

,**third-party in'surance** *noun* [U] insurance that COVERS (= protects) you if you injure someone or damage someone's property

the ,**third 'person** *noun* [sing.] **1** (*grammar*) a set of pronouns and verb forms used by a speaker to refer to other people and things: *"They are" is the third person plural of the verb "to be."* **2** a way of writing a novel, etc. as the experience of someone else, using third person forms: *a book written in the third person* ⊃ compare THE FIRST PERSON, THE SECOND PERSON

,**third-'rate** *adj.* of very poor quality **SYN** INFERIOR: *a third-rate actor*

| t tea | ţ butter | d did | k cat | g got | tʃ chin | dʒ June | f fall |

the Third Reich /ˌθɜrd ˈraɪk; -ˈraɪx/ *noun* [sing.] the Nazi rule of Germany between 1933 and 1945

ˌthird-ˈstring *adj.* [only before noun] (usually of a player on a sports team) only used very occasionally when someone or something else is not available: *a third-string quarterback*

ˌthird ˈway *noun* [sing.] a course of action or political policy that is between two extreme positions

the ˌThird ˈWorld *noun* [sing.] a way of referring to the poor or developing countries of Africa, Asia, and Latin America, which is sometimes considered offensive: *the causes of poverty and injustice in the Third World* ◆ *Third-World debt* ⊃ compare FIRST WORLD

thirst /θɜrst/ *noun, verb*
• *noun* **1** [U, sing.] the feeling of needing or wanting a drink: *He quenched his thirst with a long drink of cold water.* ◆ *She woke up with a raging thirst and a headache.* **2** [U] the state of not having enough water to drink: *Thousands are dying of thirst.* **3** [sing.] **~ (for sth)** a strong desire for something **SYN** CRAVING: *a thirst for knowledge*
• *verb* [I] (*old use*) to be thirsty
PHR V ˈthirst for sth (*literary*) to feel a strong desire for something **SYN** CRAVE: *She thirsted for power.*

thirst·y /ˈθɜrsti/ *adj.* (thirst·i·er, thirst·i·est) **1** needing or wanting to drink: *We were hungry and thirsty.* ◆ *Digging is thirsty work* (= makes you thirsty). **2 ~ for sth** having a strong desire for something: *He is thirsty for power.* **3** (of plants, fields, etc.) dry; in need of water ▸ thirst·i·ly /-stəli/ *adv.*: *Paul drank thirstily.*

thir·teen /ˌθɜrˈtin/ *number* 13 ▸ thir·teenth /ˌθɜrˈtinθ/ *ordinal number, noun*
HELP There are examples of how to use ordinal numbers at the entry for fifth.

thir·ty /ˈθɜrti/ **1** *number* 30 **2** *noun* the thir·ties [pl.] numbers, years, or temperatures from 30 to 39 ▸ thir·ti·eth /ˈθɜrtiəθ/ *ordinal number, noun* **HELP** There are examples of how to use ordinal numbers at the entry for fifth.
IDM in your thirties between the ages of 30 and 39

this /ðɪs/ *det., pron., adv.*
• *det., pron.* (*pl.* these /ðiz/) **1** used to refer to a particular person, thing, or event that is close to you, especially compared with another: *How long have you been living in this country?* ◆ *Well, make up your mind. Which do you want? This one or that one?* ◆ *I think you'll find these more comfortable than those.* ◆ *Is this your bag?* **2** used to refer to something or someone that has already been mentioned: *There was a court case resulting from this incident.* ◆ *The boy was afraid and the dog had sensed this.* ◆ *What's this I hear about you getting married?* **3** used for introducing something to someone or showing something to someone: *Hello, this is Maria Diaz* (= on the telephone). ◆ *Jo, this is Kate* (= when you are introducing them). ◆ *This is the captain speaking.* ◆ *Listen to this.* ◆ *Do it like this* (= in the way I am showing you). **4** used with periods of time related to the present: *this week/month/year* ◆ *I saw her this morning* (= today in the morning). ◆ *Do you want me to come this Tuesday* (= Tuesday of this week) *or next Tuesday?* ◆ *Do it this minute* (= now). ◆ *He never comes to see me these days* (= now, as compared with the past). **5 ~ sth of sb's** (*informal*) used to refer to someone or something that is connected with a person, especially when you have a particular attitude toward it or them: *These new friends of hers are supposed to be very rich.* **6** (*informal*) used when you are telling a story or telling someone about something: *There was this strange man sitting next to me on the plane.* ◆ *I've been getting these pains in my chest.*
IDM this and that| this, that, and the other (*informal*) various things or activities: *"What did you talk about?" "Oh, this and that."*
• *adv.* to this degree; so: *It's about this high* (= as high as I am showing you with my hands). ◆ *I didn't think we'd get this far.*

this·tle /ˈθɪsl/ *noun* a wild plant with leaves with sharp points and purple, yellow, or white flowers made up of a

mass of narrow PETALS pointing upward. ⊃ picture at PLANT

this·tle·down /ˈθɪslˌdaʊn/ *noun* [U] a very light soft substance that contains THISTLE seeds and is blown from THISTLES by the wind

thith·er /ˈθɪðər; ˈðɪðər/ *adv.* (*old use*) to or toward that place
IDM see HITHER

tho' /ðoʊ/ *adv.* an informal spelling of "though"

thong /θɔŋ; θɑŋ/ *noun* **1** a narrow strip of leather that is used to fasten something or as a WHIP **2** a pair of women's PANTIES or men's UNDERPANTS, or the bottom part of a BIKINI, that has only a very narrow strip of cloth, like a string, at the back **3** = FLIP-FLOP

tho·rax /ˈθɔræks/ *noun* (*pl.* tho·rax·es or tho·ra·ces /ˈθɔrəsiz/) **1** (*anatomy*) the part of the body that is surrounded by the RIBS, between the neck and the waist **2** the middle section of an insect's body, to which the legs and wings are attached ▸ tho·rac·ic /θɔˈræsɪk/ *adj.* [only before noun]

tho·ri·um /ˈθɔriəm/ *noun* [U] (*symb.* Th) a chemical element. Thorium is a white RADIOACTIVE metal used as a source of nuclear energy.

thorn /θɔrn/ *noun* **1** a small, sharp, pointed part on the STEM of some plants, such as ROSES ⊃ picture at PLANT **2** a tree or bush that has thorns ⊃ see also BLACKTHORN, HAWTHORN **3** (*phonetics*) the letter that was used in Old English and Icelandic to represent the sounds /θ/ and /ð/ and later written as th
IDM a thorn in sb's side a person or thing that repeatedly annoys someone or stops them from doing something

thorn·y /ˈθɔrni/ *adj.* (thorn·i·er, thorn·i·est) **1** [usually before noun] causing difficulty or disagreement **SYN** KNOTTY: *a thorny question/issue/problem* **2** having thorns: *a thorny bush*

thor·ough /ˈθɜroʊ/ *adj.* **1** done completely; with great attention to detail: *a thorough knowledge of the subject* ◆ *The police carried out a thorough investigation.* **2** [not usually before noun] (of a person) doing things very carefully and with great attention to detail: *She's very thorough and conscientious.* ▸ thor·ough·ness *noun* [U]: *I was impressed by the thoroughness of the report.* ◆ *I admire his thoroughness.*

thor·ough·bred /ˈθɜroʊˌbrɛd; ˈθɜrə-/ *noun* an animal, especially a horse, of high quality, that has parents that are both of the same breed ▸ thor·ough·bred *adj.*: *a thoroughbred mare*

thor·ough·fare /ˈθɜroʊˌfɛr; ˈθɜrə-/ *noun* a public road or street used by traffic, especially a main road in a city or town

thor·ough·go·ing /ˈθɜroʊˌgoʊɪŋ; ˈθɜrə-/ *adj.* [only before noun] **1** very thorough; looking at every detail: *a thoroughgoing revision of the text* **2** complete: *a thoroughgoing commitment to change*

thor·ough·ly /ˈθɜrəli; ˈθɜroʊ-/ *adv.* **1** very much; completely: *We thoroughly enjoyed ourselves.* ◆ *I'm thoroughly confused.* ◆ *a thoroughly professional performance* **2** completely and with great attention to detail: *Wash the fruit thoroughly before use.* ◆ *The work had not been done very thoroughly.*

those ⊃ THAT

thou /ðaʊ/ *pron.* (*old use* or *dialect*) a word meaning "you," used when talking to only one person who is the subject of the verb ⊃ compare THEE

though /ðoʊ/ *conj., adv.*
• *conj.* **1** despite the fact that **SYN** ALTHOUGH: *Anne was fond of Tim, though he often annoyed her.* ◆ *Though she gave no sign, I was sure she had seen me.* ◆ *His clothes, though old and worn, looked clean and of good quality.* ◆ *Strange though it may sound, I was pleased it was over.* **2** used to add a fact or an opinion that makes the previous statement less strong or less important: *They're very different, though they did seem to get on*

well when they met. ◆ He'll probably say no, though it's worth asking. ⊃ note at ALTHOUGH **IDM** see AS, EVEN *adv.*

● **adv.** used especially at the end of a sentence to add a fact or an opinion that makes the previous statement less strong or less important: *Our team lost. It was a good game though.* ◆ *"Have you ever been to Australia?" "No. I'd like to, though."*

thought 🔑 /θɔt/ noun

> SOMETHING YOU THINK **1** [C] ~ (of sth/of doing sth) | ~ (that...) something that you think of or remember: *I don't like the thought of you walking home alone.* ◆ *She was struck by the sudden thought that he might already have left.* ◆ *The very thought of it makes me feel sick.* ◆ *I've just had a thought* (= an idea). ◆ *Would Mark be able to help? It's just a thought.* ◆ *"Why don't you try the other key?" "That's a thought!"* ◆ *I'd like to hear your thoughts on the subject.*
> MIND/IDEAS **2** thoughts [pl.] a person's mind and all the ideas that they have in it when they are thinking: *My thoughts turned to home.*
> PROCESS/ACT OF THINKING **3** [U] the power or process of thinking: *A good teacher encourages independence of thought.* ◆ *She was lost in thought* (= concentrating so much on her thoughts that she was not aware of her surroundings). **4** [U] the act of thinking seriously and carefully about something **SYN** CONSIDERATION: *I've given the matter careful thought.* ◆ *Not enough thought has gone into this essay.*
> CARE/WORRY **5** [C] ~ (for sb/sth) a feeling of care or worry: *Spare a thought for those without enough to eat this winter.* ◆ *Don't give it another thought* (= to tell someone not to worry after they have said they are sorry). ◆ *It's the thought that counts* (= used to say that someone has been very kind even if they have only done something small or unimportant).
> INTENTION **6** [U, C] ~ (of sth/of doing sth) an intention or a hope of doing something: *She had given up all thought of changing her job.* ◆ *He acted with no thoughts of personal gain.*
> IN POLITICS/SCIENCE, ETC. **7** [U] ideas in politics, science, etc. connected with a particular person, group, or period of history: *feminist thought* ⊃ see also THINK
> **IDM** have second thoughts to change your opinion after thinking about something again on second thought used to say that you have changed your opinion: *I'll wait here. No, on second thought, I'll come with you.* without a second thought immediately; without stopping to think about something further: *He dived in after her without a second thought.* ⊃ more at COLLECT, FOOD, PAUSE, PENNY, PERISH, SCHOOL, TRAIN, WISH

thought·crime /ˈθɔtkraɪm/ *noun* [U, C] an idea or opinion that is considered socially unacceptable or criminal **ORIGIN** From George Orwell's novel *Nineteen Eighty-Four.*

thought·ful /ˈθɔtfl/ *adj.* **1** quiet, because you are thinking: *He looked thoughtful.* ◆ *They sat in thoughtful silence.* **2** *(approving)* showing that you think about and care for other people **SYN** CONSIDERATE, KIND: *It was very thoughtful of you to send the flowers.* **3** showing signs of careful thought: *a player who has a thoughtful approach to the game* ▶ **thought·ful·ly** /-fəli/ *adv.*: *Martin looked at her thoughtfully.* ◆ *She used the towel thoughtfully provided by her host.* **thought·ful·ness** *noun* [U]

thought·less /ˈθɔtləs/ *adj.* *(disapproving)* not caring about the possible effects of your words or actions on other people **SYN** INCONSIDERATE: *a thoughtless remark* ▶ **thought·less·ly** *adv.* **thought·less·ness** *noun* [U]

ˈthought poˌlice *noun* [pl.] a group of people who are seen as trying to control people's ideas and stop them from having their own opinions

ˈthought-proˌvoking *adj.* making people think seriously about a particular subject or issue

thou·sand /ˈθaʊznd/ *number (plural verb) (abbr. K)* **1** 1,000 **HELP** You say a, one, two, etc. thousand without a final "s" on "thousand". Thousands (of...) can be used if there is no number or quantity before it. Always use a plural verb with thousand or thousands, except when an amount of money is mentioned: *Four thousand (people) are expected to attend.* ◆ *Two thousand (dollars) was withdrawn from the account.* **2** a thousand or thousands (of...) *(usually informal)* a large number: *There were thousands of people there.* **3** the thousands the numbers from 1,000 to 9,999: *The cost ran into the thousands.* **HELP** There are more examples of how to use numbers at the entry for **hundred**. **IDM** see BAT *v.*

thou·sandth /ˈθaʊznθ/ *ordinal number, noun*

● **ordinal number** 1,000th: *the city's thousandth anniversary*
● **noun** each of one thousand parts of something: *a/one thousandth of a second*

thrall /θrɔl/ *noun* **IDM** in (sb's/sth's) thrall | in thrall to sb/sth *(literary)* controlled or strongly influenced by someone or something

thrash /θræʃ/ *verb, noun*

● **verb 1** [T] ~ sb/sth to hit a person or an animal many times with a stick, etc. as a punishment **SYN** BEAT **2** [I, T] to move or make something move in a violent or uncontrolled way: ~ (about/around) *Someone was thrashing around in the water, obviously in trouble.* ◆ ~ sth (about/around) *A whale was thrashing the water with its tail.* ◆ *She thrashed her head from side to side.* **3** [T] ~ sb/sth *(informal)* to defeat someone very easily in a game: *The Flyers thrashed the Islanders 5–1.* ⊃ compare WHIP
PHRV ˌthrash sth↔ˈout to discuss a situation or problem thoroughly in order to decide something
● **noun** [U] a type of loud ROCK music

thrash·ing /ˈθræʃɪŋ/ *noun* **1** an act of hitting someone very hard, especially with a stick: *to give someone/get a thrashing* **2** *(informal)* a severe defeat in a game

thread 🔑 /θrɛd/ noun, verb

● **noun 1** [U, C] a thin string of cotton, wool, silk, etc. used for sewing or making cloth: *a needle and thread* ◆ *a robe embroidered with gold thread* ◆ *the delicate threads of a spiderweb* ⊃ picture at ROPE **2** [C] an idea or a feature that is part of something greater; an idea that connects the different parts of something: *A common thread runs through these discussions.* ◆ *The author skillfully draws together the different threads of the plot.* ◆ *I lost the thread of the argument* (= I could no longer follow it). **3** [C] ~ (of sth) a long thin line of something: *A thread of light emerged from the keyhole.* **4** [C] *(computing)* a series of connected messages on a MESSAGE BOARD on the Internet which have been sent by different people **5** [C] the raised line that runs around the length of a screw and that allows it to be attached by twisting **6** threads [pl.] *(old-fashioned, slang)* clothes **IDM** see HANG, PICK
● **verb 1** [T] ~ sth (+ adv./prep.) to pass something long and thin, especially thread, through a narrow opening or hole: *to thread a needle (with cotton)* ◆ *to thread cotton through a needle* ◆ *A tiny wire is threaded through a vein to the heart.* **2** [I, T] to move or make something move through a narrow space, avoiding things that are in the way **SYN** PICK YOUR WAY: + adv./prep. *The waiters threaded between the crowded tables.* ◆ ~ your way + adv./prep. *It took me a long time to thread my way through the crowd.* **3** [T] ~ sth (onto sth) to join two or more objects together by passing something long and thin through them: *to thread beads (onto a string)* **4** [T] ~ sth to pass film, tape, string, etc. through parts of a piece of equipment so that it is ready to use **5** [T, usually passive] ~ sth (with sth) to sew or twist a particular type of thread into something: *a robe threaded with gold and silver*

thread·bare /ˈθrɛdbɛr/ *adj.* **1** (of cloth, clothing, etc.) old and thin because it has been used a lot: *a threadbare carpet* **2** (of an argument, excuse, etc.) that does not have much effect, especially because it has been used too much

thread·ed /ˈθrɛdəd/ *adj. (technical)* (of a screw, etc.) having a THREAD

ˈthread vein *noun* a very thin VEIN, especially one that can be seen through the skin

threat 🔑 /θrɛt/ noun

1 [C, U] ~ (to do sth) a statement in which you tell someone that you will punish or harm them, especially if they do not do what you want: *to make threats against someone* ♦ *She is prepared to* **carry out her threat** *to resign.* ♦ *He received* **death threats** *from right-wing groups.* ♦ *crimes involving violence or the threat of violence* **2** [U, C, usually sing.] the possibility of trouble, danger, or disaster: *These ancient woodlands are* **under threat** *from new housing developments.* ♦ *There is a real* **threat of war. 3** [C, usually sing.] ~ **(to sth)** a person or thing that is likely to cause trouble, danger, etc.: *He is unlikely to be a threat to the Spanish player in the final.* ♦ *Drugs* **pose a major threat** *to our society.*

threat·en 🖉 /ˈθrɛtn/ *verb*
1 [T] to say that you will cause trouble, hurt someone, etc. if you do not get what you want: ~ **sb** *They broke my windows and threatened me.* ♦ ~ **sb with sth** *The attacker threatened them with a gun.* ♦ *He was threatened with dismissal if he continued to turn up late for work.* ♦ ~ **sth** *The threatened strike has been called off.* ♦ ~ **to do sth** *The hijackers threatened to kill one passenger every hour if their demands were not met.* ♦ ~ **that...** *They threatened that passengers would be killed.* **2** [I, T] to seem likely to happen or cause something unpleasant: *A storm was threatening.* ♦ ~ **to do sth** *This dispute threatens to split the party.* ♦ ~ **sth** *The clouds threatened rain.* **3** [T] ~ **sth** to be a danger to something **SYN** ENDANGER, PUT AT RISK: *Pollution is threatening marine life.*

threat·en·ing 🖉 /ˈθrɛtnæw·ɪŋ/ *adj.*
1 expressing a threat of harm or violence **SYN** MENACING: *threatening letters* ♦ *threatening behavior*
ANT NONTHREATENING **2** (of the sky, clouds, etc.) showing that bad weather is likely: *The sky was dark and threatening.*
▸ **threat·en·ing·ly** *adv.*: *He glared at her threateningly.*

three /θri/ *number*
3 HELP There are examples of how to use numbers at the entry for **five**.
IDM the three Rs (*old-fashioned*) reading, writing, and ARITHMETIC, thought to be the most important parts of a child's education ⊃ **more at** TWO

three-card ˈtrick *noun* a game in which players bet money on which is the queen out of three cards lying face down

three-ˈcornered *adj.* [usually before noun] **1** having three corners: *a three-cornered hat* **2** involving three people or groups: *a three-cornered contest*

three-ˈD (also ˌ3-ˈD) *noun* [U] the quality of having, or appearing to have, length, width, and depth (= three DIMENSIONS): *These glasses allow you to see the film in three-D.* ♦ *a three-D image*

three-diˈmensional *adj.* having, or appearing to have, length, width, and depth: *three-dimensional objects*

three·fold /ˈθrifould; ˌθriˈfould/ *adj., adv.* ⊃ -FOLD

three ˈfourths *noun* [pl.] = THREE QUARTERS

three-leg·ged race /ˌθri lɛɡəd ˈreɪs/ *noun* a race in which people taking part run in pairs, the right leg of one runner being tied to the left leg of the other

three-ˈpeat /ˈθri pit/ *noun* (used especially in newspapers) an occasion when a person or team wins a competition for the third time, especially in sport ▸ **three-peat** *verb* [I]

three-piece *adj.* [only before noun] consisting of three separate parts or pieces: *a three-piece suit* (= a set of clothes consisting of pants, a jacket, and a VEST)

three-point ˈturn *noun* a method of turning a car in a small space so that it faces in the opposite direction, by driving forward, then backward, then forward again, in a series of curves

three-ˈquarter *adj.* [only before noun] used to describe something which is three quarters of the usual size: *a three-quarter length coat*

three ˈquarters (also ˌthree ˈfourths) *noun* ~ **(of sth)** three of the four equal parts into which something may be divided: *three quarters of an hour*

three-ring ˈcircus *noun* [sing.] (*informal*) a place or situation with a lot of confusing or amusing activity

three·some /ˈθrisəm/ *noun* **1** a group of three people **2** an occasion when three people have sex together

three-star *adj.* [usually before noun] **1** having three stars in a system that measures quality. The highest standard is usually represented by four or five stars: *a three-star hotel* **2** having the third-highest military rank, and wearing a uniform that has three stars on it: *a three-star general*

three-way *adj.* [only before noun] happening or working in three ways or directions, or between three people: *a three-way switch* ♦ *a three-way discussion*

thren·o·dy /ˈθrɛnədi/ *noun* (pl. **thren·o·dies**) (*technical*) a song, poem, or other expression of great sadness for someone who has died or for something that has ended

thresh /θrɛʃ/ *verb* **1** [T] ~ **sth** to separate grains of rice, WHEAT, etc. from the rest of the plant using a machine or, especially in the past, by hitting it with a special tool ⊃ **collocations at** FARMING **2** [I, T] ~ **(sth)** to make, or cause something to make, uncontrolled movements **SYN** THRASH ▸ **thresh·ing** *noun* [U]: *a threshing machine*

thresh·old /ˈθrɛʃhould; -ʃould/ *noun* **1** the floor or ground at the bottom of a DOORWAY, considered as the entrance to a building or room: *She stood hesitating on the threshold.* ♦ *He stepped across the threshold.* **2** the level at which something starts to happen or have an effect: *He has a low* **boredom threshold** (= he gets bored easily). ♦ *I have a* **high pain threshold** (= I can suffer a lot of pain before I start to react). ♦ *My earnings are just above the* **tax threshold** (= more than the amount at which you start paying tax). **3** [usually sing.] the point just before a new situation, period of life, etc. begins: *She felt as though she was* **on the threshold of** *a new life.*

threw *pt of* THROW

thrice /θraɪs/ *adv.* (old use or formal) three times

thrift /θrɪft/ *noun* [U] **1** (approving) the habit of saving money and spending it carefully so that none is wasted ⊃ **see also** SPENDTHRIFT **2** a wild plant with bright pink flowers that grows by the ocean

thrift shop (also **thrift store**) *noun* a store that sells clothes and other goods given by people to raise money for a charity

thrift·y /ˈθrɪfti/ *adj.* (approving) careful about spending money and not wasting things **SYN** FRUGAL

thrill /θrɪl/ *noun, verb*
● *noun* **1** ~ **(to do sth)** | ~ **(of doing sth)** a strong feeling of excitement or pleasure; an experience that gives you this feeling: *It gave me a big* **thrill** *to meet my favorite author in person.* ♦ *the thrill of catching a really big fish* ♦ *She gets an obvious thrill out of performing.* **2** a sudden strong feeling that produces a physical effect: *A thrill of alarm ran through him.*
IDM (the) thrills and chills/spills (*informal*) the excitement that is involved in dangerous or scary activities or movies: *a slickly paced thriller that provides viewers with multiple thrills and chills*
● *verb* ~ **sb** to excite or please someone very much: *This band has thrilled audiences all over the world.* ♦ *I was thrilled by your news.*
PHR V ˈthrill to sth (formal) to feel very excited at something

thrilled /θrɪld/ *adj.* ~ **(about/at/with sth)** | ~ **(to do sth)** | ~ **(that...)** very excited and pleased: *He was thrilled at the prospect of seeing them again.* ♦ *I was thrilled to be invited.* ♦ *"Are you pleased?" "I'm thrilled."* ⊃ **thesaurus box at** GLAD

thrill·er /ˈθrɪlər/ *noun* a book, play, or movie with an exciting story, especially one about crime or SPYING

thrill·ing /ˈθrɪlɪŋ/ *adj.* exciting and enjoyable: *a thrilling experience/finish* ⊃ **thesaurus box at** EXCITING ▸ **thrill·ing·ly** *adv.*

thrill ride *noun* a ride at an AMUSEMENT PARK that makes you feel very excited and frightened at the same time

thrive /θraɪv/ *verb* [I] to become, and continue to be, successful, strong, healthy, etc. **SYN** FLOURISH: *New businesses thrive in this area.* ◆ *These animals rarely thrive in captivity.* ▶ **thriv·ing** *adj.*: *a thriving industry*
PHR V **'thrive on sth** to enjoy something or be successful at something, especially something that other people would not like: *He thrives on hard work.*

throat 🔑 /θroʊt/ *noun*
1 a passage in the neck through which food and air pass on their way into the body; the front part of the neck: *a sore throat* ◆ *A sob caught in his throat.* ◆ *He held the knife to her throat.* ◆ *Their throats had been cut.* **2** **-throated** (in adjectives) having the type of throat mentioned: *a deep-throated roar* ◆ *a red-throated diver* ⊃ see also CUTTHROAT
IDM **be at each other's throats** (of two or more people, groups, etc.) to be fighting or arguing with each other **cut your own throat** to do something that is likely to harm you, especially when you are angry and trying to harm someone else **force/thrust/ram sth down sb's throat** (*informal*) to try to force someone to listen to and accept your opinions in a way that they find annoying ⊃ more at CLEAR, FROG, JUMP, LUMP, STICK

throat·y /θroʊti/ *adj.* sounding low and rough: *a throaty laugh* ◆ *the throaty roar of the engines* ▶ **throat·i·ly** /θroʊtl·i/ *adv.*

throb /θrɑb/ *verb, noun*
● *verb* (-bb-) **1** [I] ~ **(with sth)** (of a part of the body) to feel a series of regular painful movements: *His head throbbed painfully.* ◆ *My feet were throbbing after the long walk home.* ⊃ thesaurus box at HURT **2** [I] to beat or sound with a strong, regular rhythm **SYN** PULSATE: *The ship's engines throbbed quietly.* ◆ *a throbbing drumbeat* ◆ *The blood was throbbing in my veins.* ◆ ~ **with sth** (*figurative*) *His voice was throbbing with emotion.*
● *noun* (also **throb·bing**) [sing.] a strong, regular beat; a feeling of pain that you experience as a series of strong beats: *the throb of the machines* ◆ *My headache faded to a dull throbbing.* ⊃ see also HEARTTHROB

throes /θroʊz/ *noun* [pl.] violent pains, especially at the moment of death: *The creature went into its death throes.*
IDM **in the throes of sth/of doing sth** in the middle of an activity, especially a difficult or complicated one: *The country was in the throes of revolutionary change.*

throm·bo·sis /θrɑmˈboʊsəs/ *noun* [C, U] (*pl.* **throm·bo·ses** /-siz/) (*medical*) a serious condition caused by a blood CLOT (= a thick mass of blood) forming in a blood VESSEL (= tube) or in the heart ⊃ see also CORONARY THROMBOSIS, DEEP VEIN THROMBOSIS

throne /θroʊn/ *noun* **1** [C] a special chair used by a king or queen to sit on at ceremonies **2** **the throne** [sing.] the position of being a king or queen: *Queen Elizabeth came/succeeded to the throne in 1952.* ◆ *when Henry VIII was on the throne* (= was king) **IDM** see POWER *n.*

throng /θrɔŋ; θrɑŋ/ *noun, verb*
● *noun* (*literary*) a crowd of people: *We pushed our way through the throng.*
● *verb* [I, T] (*literary*) to go somewhere or be present somewhere in large numbers: + **adv./prep.** *The children thronged into the classroom.* ◆ ~ **to do sth** *People are thronging to see his new play.* ◆ ~ **sth** *Crowds thronged the stores.*
PHR V **'throng with sb/sth | be 'thronged with sb/sth** to be full of people, cars, etc.: *The cafés were thronging with students.* ◆ *The streets were thronged with people.*

throt·tle /θrɑtl/ *verb, noun*
● *verb* ~ **sb** to attack or kill someone by squeezing their throat in order to stop them from breathing **SYN** STRANGLE: *He throttled the guard with his bare hands.* ◆ (*humorous*) *I like her, although I could cheerfully throttle her at times* (= because she is annoying). ◆ (*figurative*) *The city is being throttled by traffic.*
PHR V **,throttle (sth) 'back/'down/'up** to control the supply of fuel or power to an engine in order to reduce/

increase the speed of a vehicle: *I throttled back as we approached the runway.*
● *noun* a device that controls the amount of fuel that goes into the engine of a vehicle, for example the ACCELERATOR in a car: *He drove along at full throttle* (= as fast as possible).

through 🔑 /θru/ *prep., adv., adj.*
● *prep.* **HELP** For the special uses of **through** in phrasal verbs, look at the entries for the verbs. For example, **get through sth** is in the phrasal verb section at **get**. **1** from one end or side of something or someone to the other: *The burglar got in through the window.* ◆ *The bullet went straight through him.* ◆ *Her knees had gone through* (= made holes in) *her jeans.* ◆ *The sand ran through* (= between) *my fingers.* ◆ *The path led through the trees to the river.* ◆ *The doctor pushed his way through the crowd.* ◆ *The Charles River flows through Boston.* **2** **see, hear, etc.** ~ **sth** to see, hear, etc. something from the other side of an object or a substance: *I couldn't hear their conversation through the wall.* ◆ *He could just make out three people through the mist.* **3** from the beginning to the end of an activity, a situation, or a period of time: *The children are too young to sit through a concert.* ◆ *He will not live through the night.* ◆ *I'm halfway through* (= reading) *her second novel.* **4** past a barrier, stage, or test: *Go through this gate, and you'll see the house on your left.* ◆ *He drove through a red light* (= passed it when he should have stopped). ◆ *First I have to get through the exams.* ◆ *The bill had a difficult passage through Congress.* ◆ *I'd never have gotten through it all* (= a difficult situation) *without you.* **5** (also *informal* **thru**) until, and including: *We'll be in New York Tuesday through Friday.* ⊃ note at INCLUSIVE **6** by means of; because of: *You can only achieve success through hard work.* ◆ *It was through him* (= as a result of his help) *that I got the job.* ◆ *The accident happened through no fault of mine.*
● *adv.* **HELP** For the special uses of **through** in phrasal verbs, look at the entries for the verbs. For example, **carry sth through** is in the phrasal verb section at **carry**. **1** from one end or side of something to the other: *Put the coffee in the filter and let the water run through.* ◆ *The tire's flat—the nail has gone right through.* ◆ *The onlookers stood aside to let the paramedics through.* ◆ *The flood was too deep to drive through.* **2** from the beginning to the end of a thing or period of time: *Don't tell me how it ends—I haven't read it all the way through yet.* ◆ *I expect I'll struggle through until payday.* **3** past a barrier, stage, or test: *The lights were red but he drove straight through.* ◆ *Our team is through to* (= has reached) *the semi-finals.* **4** traveling through a place without stopping or without people having to get off one train and onto another: *"Did you stop in Baltimore on the way?" "No, we drove straight through."* ◆ *This train goes straight through to New York.* **5** connected by telephone: *Ask to be put through to me personally.* ◆ *I tried to call you but I couldn't get through.* **6** used after an adjective to mean "completely": *We got wet through.*
IDM **through and through** completely; in every way: *He's Texan through and through.*
● *adj.* **1** [only before noun] **through** traffic travels from one side of a place to the other without stopping **2** [only before noun] a **through** train takes you to the final place you want to get to and you do not have to get off and get on another train **3** [only before noun] a **through** road or route is open at both ends and allows traffic to travel from one end to the other: *The town lies on a busy through road.* ◆ *No through road* (= the road is closed at one end). **4** [not before noun] ~ **(with sth/sb)** used to show that you have finished using something or have ended a relationship with someone: *Are you through with that newspaper?* ◆ *Todd and I are through.*

through·out 🔑 /θruˈaʊt/ *prep.*
1 in or into every part of something: *They export their products to markets throughout the world.* **2** during the whole period of time of something: *The museum is open daily throughout the year.* ▶ **through·out** *adv.*: *The house was painted white throughout.* ◆ *The ceremony lasted two hours and we had to stand throughout.*

ʌ **cup**   ə **about**   eɪ **say**   aɪ **five**   ɔɪ **boy**   aʊ **now**   oʊ **go**   ər **bird**

through·put /ˈθruːpʊt/ *noun* [U, C, usually sing.] (*technical*) the amount of work that is done, or the number of people that are dealt with, in a particular period of time

through·way = THRUWAY

THESAURUS

throw

toss • hurl • fling • chuck • lob • pitch

These words all mean to send something from your hand through the air.

throw to send something from your hand or hands through the air: *Some kids were throwing rocks at the window.* ♦ *She threw the ball and he caught it.*

toss to throw something lightly or carelessly: *She tossed her jacket onto the bed.*

hurl to throw something violently in a particular direction: *Rioters hurled a brick through the car's windshield.*

fling to throw something somewhere with a lot of force, especially because you are angry or in a hurry: *She flung the letter down onto the table.*

chuck (*informal*) to throw something carelessly: *I chucked him the keys.*

lob (*informal*) to throw something so that it goes high through the air: *She lobbed the ball over the net.*

pitch (in baseball) to throw the ball to the batter

PATTERNS
- to throw/toss/hurl/fling/chuck/lob/pitch sth at/to sb/sth
- to throw/toss/fling/chuck sth **aside/away**
- to throw/toss/hurl/fling/chuck/lob/pitch a **ball**
- to throw/toss/hurl/fling/chuck **rocks/a brick**
- to throw/toss/hurl/fling sth **angrily**
- to throw/toss sth **casually/carelessly**

---

throw 🔑 / θroʊ/ *verb, noun*

• *verb* (threw /θruː/, thrown /θroʊn/)

▷ **WITH HAND 1** [T, I] to send something from your hand through the air by moving your hand or arm quickly: **~ (sth)** *Stop throwing rocks at the window!* ♦ *She threw the ball up and caught it again.* ♦ *They had a competition to see who could throw the furthest.* ♦ **~ sth to sb** *Don't throw it to him, give it to him!* ♦ **~ sb sth** *Can you throw me that towel?*

▷ **PUT CARELESSLY 2** [T] **~ sth + adv./prep.** to put something in a particular place quickly and carelessly: *Just throw your bag down over there.*

▷ **MOVE WITH FORCE 3** [T] to move something suddenly and with force: **~ sth + adv./prep.** *The boat was thrown onto the rocks.* ♦ *The sea throws up all kinds of debris on the beach.* ♦ **~ sth + adj.** *I threw open the windows to let the smoke out.*

▷ **PART OF BODY 4** [T] **~ sth/yourself + adv./prep.** to move your body or part of it quickly or suddenly: *He threw back his head and roared with laughter.* ♦ *I ran up and threw my arms around him.* ♦ *Jenny threw herself onto the bed.*

▷ **MAKE SOMEONE FALL 5** [T] **~ sb** to make someone fall quickly or violently to the ground: *Two riders were thrown* (= off their horses) *in the second race.*

▷ **INTO PARTICULAR STATE 6** [T, usually passive] **~ sb/sth + adv./prep.** to make someone or something be in a particular state: *Hundreds were thrown out of work.* ♦ *We were thrown into confusion by the news.* ♦ *The problem was suddenly thrown into sharp focus.*

▷ **DIRECT SOMETHING AT SOMEONE OR SOMETHING 7** [T] **~ sth on/at sb/sth** to direct something at someone or something: *to throw doubt on the verdict* ♦ *to throw the blame on someone* ♦ *to throw accusations at someone* ♦ *He threw the question back at me* (= expected me to answer it myself).

▷ **UPSET 8** [T] **~ sb** (*informal*) to make someone feel upset, confused, or surprised: *The news of her death really threw me.*

▷ **DICE 9** [T] **~ sth** to roll a DICE or let it fall after shaking it; to obtain a particular number in this way: *Throw the dice!* ♦ *He threw three sixes in a row.*

▷ **CLAY POT 10** [T] **~ sth** (*technical*) to make a CLAY pot, dish, etc. on a POTTER'S WHEEL: *a hand-thrown vase*

▷ **LIGHT/SHADE 11** [T] **~ sth (+ adv./prep.)** to send light or shade onto something: *The trees threw long shadows across the lawn.*

▷ **YOUR VOICE 12** [T] **~ your voice** to make your voice sound as if it is coming from another person or place

▷ **A PUNCH 13** [T] **~ a punch** to hit, or try to hit, someone with your FIST

▷ **SWITCH/HANDLE 14** [T] **~ sth** to move a switch, handle, etc. to operate something

▷ **BAD-TEMPERED BEHAVIOR 15** [T] **~ sth** to have a sudden period of bad-tempered behavior, violent emotion, etc.: *She'll throw a fit if she finds out.* ♦ *Children often throw tantrums at this age.*

▷ **A PARTY 16** [T] **~ a party** (*informal*) to give a party

▷ **IN SPORTS/COMPETITIONS 17** [T] **~ sth** (*informal*) to deliberately lose a game or contest that you should have won: *He was accused of having thrown the game.*

IDM Idioms containing **throw** are at the entries for the nouns and adjectives in the idioms. For example, **throw your hat into the ring** is at **hat**.

PHR V ,throw sth↔a'side to reject something such as an attitude, a way of life, etc. 'throw yourself at sth/sb **1** to rush violently at something or someone **2** (*informal, disapproving*) (usually of a woman) to be too enthusiastic in trying to attract a sexual partner ,throw sth↔a'way **1** (also ,throw sth↔'out) to get rid of something that you no longer want: *I don't need that—you can throw it away.* ♦ *That old chair should be thrown away.* **2** to fail to make use of something; to waste something: *to throw away an opportunity* ⊃ see also THROWAWAY ,throw sth 'back at sb to remind someone of something they have said or done in the past, especially to upset or annoy them ,throw sb 'back on sth [usually passive] to force someone to rely on something because nothing else is available: *There was no TV so we were thrown back on our own resources* (= had to entertain ourselves). ,throw sth↔'in **1** to include something with what you are selling or offering, without increasing the price: *You can have the piano for $200, and I'll throw in the stool as well.* **2** to add a remark to a conversation: *Jack threw in the odd encouraging comment.* ,throw yourself/sth 'into sth to begin to do something with energy and enthusiasm ,throw sth/sb↔'off **1** to manage to get rid of something or someone that is making you suffer, annoying you, etc.: *to throw off a cold/your worries/your pursuers* **2** to take off a piece of clothing quickly and carelessly: *She entered the room and threw off her wet coat.* ,throw sth↔'on to put on a piece of clothing quickly and carelessly: *She just threw on the first skirt she found.* ,throw sth↔'open (to sb) **1** to allow people to enter or visit a place where they could not go before **2** to allow people to discuss something, take part in a competition, etc.: *The debate will be thrown open to the audience.* ,throw sb↔'out (of…) to force someone to leave a place: *You'll be thrown out if you don't pay the rent.* ,throw sth↔'out **1** to say something in a way that suggests you have not given it a lot of thought: *to throw out a suggestion* **2** to decide not to accept a proposal, an idea, etc. **3** = THROW STH AWAY **4** to produce smoke, light, heat, etc.: *a small fire that threw out a lot of heat* **5** to confuse something or make it wrong: *Our calculations of the cost of our trip were thrown out by changes in the exchange rate.* ,throw sb 'over (*old-fashioned*) to stop being friends with someone or having a romantic relationship with them ,throw sb↔to'gether [often passive] to bring people into contact with each other, often unexpectedly: *Fate had thrown them together.* ,throw sth↔to'gether to make or produce something in a hurry: *I threw together a quick meal.* ,throw 'up to VOMIT: *The smell made me want to throw up.* ,throw sth↔'up **1** to VOMIT food: *The baby's thrown up her dinner.* **2** to make people notice something: *Her research has thrown up some interesting facts.* **3** to build something suddenly or in a hurry: *They're throwing up new housing developments all over the place.*

---

noun 1 the act of throwing something, especially a ball or DICE: *a well-aimed throw* ◆ *It's your throw* (= it's your turn to throw the dice). ◆ *He threw me to the ground with a judo throw.* **2** the distance which something is thrown: *a javelin throw of 57 meters* **3** a loose cloth cover that can be thrown over a SOFA, etc.
IDM **$100, etc. a throw** (*informal*) used to say how much items cost each: *The tickets for the dinner were $50 a throw.* ➔ more at STONE *n.*

throw·a·way /ˈθroʊəˌweɪ/ *adj.* [only before noun] **1** ~ **line/ remark/comment** something you say quickly without careful thought, sometimes in order to be funny: *She was very upset at what to him was just a throwaway remark.* **2** (of goods, etc.) produced cheaply and intended to be thrown away after use **SYN** DISPOSABLE: *throwaway products* ◆ *We live in a throwaway society* (= a society in which things are not made to last a long time).

throw·back /ˈθroʊbæk/ *noun* [usually sing.] ~ **(to sth)** a person or thing that is similar to someone or something that existed in the past: *The car's design is a throwback to the 1960s.*

throw·er /ˈθroʊər/ *noun* a person who throws something: *a discus thrower* ➔ see also FLAMETHROWER

throw-in *noun* (in SOCCER and RUGBY) the act of throwing the ball back onto the playing field after it has gone outside the area

thrown *pp* of THROW

throw ˌpillow *noun* a small CUSHION that can be placed on furniture, on the floor, etc. for decoration

thru /θru/ (*informal*) = THROUGH

thrush /θrʌʃ/ *noun* **1** [C] a bird with a brown back and brown spots on its chest: *a song thrush* **2** [U] an infectious disease that affects the mouth and throat

thrust /θrʌst/ *verb, noun*
verb (thrust, thrust) **1** [T, I] to push something or someone suddenly or violently in a particular direction; to move quickly and suddenly in a particular direction: ~ **sth/sb/ yourself + adv./prep.** *He thrust the baby into my arms and ran off.* ◆ *She thrust her hands deep into her pockets.* ◆ (*figurative*) *He tends to thrust himself forward too much.* ◆ **+ adv./prep.** *She thrust past him angrily and left.* **2** [I, T] ~ **(at sb) (with sth)** | ~ **(sth at sb)** to make a sudden strong forward movement at someone with a weapon, etc.: *He thrust at me with a knife.* ◆ *a thrusting movement* **IDM** see THROAT
PHR V **ˌthrust sth↔aˈside** to refuse to listen to someone's complaints, comments, etc.: *All our objections were thrust aside.* **ˌthrust sth/sb on/upon sb** to force someone to accept or deal with something or someone that they do not want: *She was annoyed at having three extra guests suddenly thrust on her.*
noun 1 the thrust [sing.] the main point of an argument, a policy, etc.: *The thrust of his argument was that change was needed.* **2** [C] a sudden strong movement that pushes something or someone forward: *He killed her with a thrust of the knife.* **3** [U] (*technical*) the force that is produced by an engine to push a plane, ROCKET, etc. forward

thrust·er /ˈθrʌstər/ *noun* a small engine used to provide extra force, especially on a SPACECRAFT

thru·way (also **through·way**) /ˈθruweɪ/ *noun* used in the names of some FREEWAYS (= important roads across or between states): *the New York State Thruway*

thud /θʌd/ *noun, verb*
noun a sound like the one which is made when a heavy object hits something else: *His head hit the floor with a dull thud.*
verb (-dd-) **1** [I, T] ~ **(sth) + adv./prep.** to fall or hit something with a low, dull sound: *His arrow thudded into the target.* **2** [I] (*literary*) (especially of the heart) to beat strongly

thug /θʌg/ *noun* a violent person, especially a criminal: *a gang of thugs* ▶ **thug·gish** /ˈθʌgɪʃ/ *adj.*: *thuggish brutality*

thug·ger·y /ˈθʌgəri/ *noun* [U] (*formal*) violent, usually criminal, behavior

thu·li·um /ˈθuliəm/ *noun* [U] (*symb.* **Tm**) a chemical element. Thulium is a soft silver-white metal.

thumb 🖉 /θʌm/ *noun, verb*
noun 1 the short thick finger at the side of the hand, slightly apart from the other four: *She still sucks her thumb when she's worried.* ➔ picture at BODY **2** the part of a glove that covers the thumb: *There's a hole in the thumb.*
IDM **be all thumbs** to be awkward with your hands so that you drop things or are unable to do something **thumbs up/ down** used to show that something has been accepted/ rejected or that it is/is not a success: *Their proposals were given the thumbs down.* ◆ *It looks like it's thumbs up for their latest album.* **ORIGIN** In contests in ancient Rome, the public put their thumbs up if they wanted a GLADIATOR to live, and down if they wanted him to be killed. **under sb's thumb** (of a person) completely controlled by someone ➔ more at RULE, SORE, TWIDDLE
verb 1 [I, T] to make a signal with your thumb to passing drivers to ask them to stop and take you somewhere: **+ adv./prep.** *He had thumbed all across Europe.* ◆ ~ **a ride** *We managed to thumb a ride with a truck driver.* **2** [T] ~ **sth (+ adv./prep.)** to touch or move something with your thumb: *She thumbed off the safety catch of her pistol.* ➔ see also WELL-THUMBED
IDM **thumb your nose at sb/sth** to make a rude sign with your thumb on your nose; to show that you have no respect for someone or something: *The company just thumbs its nose at the legislation on pollution.*
PHR V **ˌthumb through sth** to turn the pages of a book quickly in order to get a general idea of what is in it

thumb drive *noun* = FLASH DRIVE

thumb ˌindex *noun* a series of cuts in the edge of a book, with letters of the alphabet on them, to help you to find the section that you want more easily

thumb·nail /ˈθʌmneɪl/ *noun* **1** the nail on the thumb **2** (also ˌthumbnail ˈimage) (*computing*) a very small picture on a computer screen which shows you what a larger picture looks like, or what a page of a document will look like when you print it

ˌthumbnail ˈsketch *noun* a short description of something, giving only the main details

thumb·print /ˈθʌmprɪnt/ *noun* the mark made by the pattern of lines on the top of a person's thumb

thumb·screw /ˈθʌmskru/ *noun* an instrument that was used in the past for torturing (TORTURE) people by crushing their thumbs

thumb·tack /ˈθʌmtæk/ (also **tack**) *noun* a short pin with a large, round, flat head, used especially for fastening paper to a board or wall ➔ picture at STATIONERY

thump /θʌmp/ *verb, noun*
verb 1 [T, I] ~ **(sb/sth) (+ adv./prep.)** to hit someone or something hard, especially with your closed hand: *He thumped the table angrily.* ◆ *She couldn't get her breath and had to be thumped on the back.* ◆ (*informal*) *I'll thump you if you say that again.* ◆ (*figurative*) *He thumped out a tune* (= played it very loudly) *on the piano.* **2** [I, T] to fall on or hit a surface hard, with a loud dull sound; to make something do this: **+ adv./ prep.** *A bird thumped against the window.* ◆ ~ **sth + adv./ prep.** *He thumped the report down on my desk.* **3** [I] to beat strongly: *My heart was thumping with excitement.*
noun 1 the sound of something heavy hitting the ground or another object: *There was a thump as the truck hit the bank.* **2** (*informal*) an act of hitting someone or something hard: *She gave him a thump on the back.*

thun·der /ˈθʌndər/ *noun, verb*
noun 1 [U] the loud noise that you hear after a flash of LIGHTNING, during a storm: *the rumble of distant thunder* ◆ *a clap/crash/roll of thunder* ◆ *Thunder crashed in the sky.* ➔ collocations at WEATHER **2** a loud noise like thunder: *the thunder of hooves* **IDM** see STEAL *v.*

| | t tea | ṭ butter | d did | k cat | g got | tʃ chin | dʒ June | f fall |

• **verb** 1 [I] when it **thunders**, there is a loud noise in the sky during a storm 2 [I] to make a very loud deep noise **SYN** ROAR: *A voice thundered in my ear.* ♦ *thundering traffic* 3 [I] + adv./prep. to move very fast and with a loud deep noise **SYN** ROAR: *Heavy trucks kept thundering past.* 4 [T] ~ sth + adv./prep. (*informal*) to make something move somewhere very fast: *Essien thundered the puck past the goalie.* 5 [I, T] (*literary*) to shout, complain, etc. very loudly and angrily: ~ (sth) *He thundered against the evils of television.* ♦ + **speech** *"Sit still!" she thundered.*

thun·der·bolt /'θʌndər,boʊlt/ *noun* a flash of LIGHTNING that comes at the same time as the noise of THUNDER and that hits something: *The news hit them like a thunderbolt* (= was very shocking).

thun·der·clap /'θʌndər,klæp/ *noun* a loud crash made by THUNDER

thun·der·cloud /'θʌndər,klaʊd/ *noun* a large dark cloud that produces THUNDER and LIGHTNING during a storm

thun·der·ous /'θʌndərəs/ *adj.* (*formal*) 1 very loud **SYN** DEAFENING: *thunderous applause* 2 looking very angry: *his thunderous expression* ▶ **thun·der·ous·ly** *adv.*

thun·der·storm /'θʌndər,stɔrm/ *noun* a storm with THUNDER and LIGHTNING and usually very heavy rain

thun·der·struck /'θʌndər,strʌk/ *adj.* [not usually before noun] (*formal*) extremely surprised and shocked **SYN** AMAZED

thun·der·y /'θʌndəri/ *adj.* (of weather) with THUNDER; suggesting that THUNDER is likely

Thurs·day 🔑 /'θɜrzdeɪ; -di/ *noun* [C, U] (*abbr.* Thur., Thurs.)
the day of the week after Wednesday and before Friday **HELP** To see how **Thursday** is used, look at the examples at **Monday**. **ORIGIN** From the Old English for "day of thunder," translated from Latin *Jovis dies* "Jupiter's day." Jupiter was the god associated with thunder.

thus 🔑 /ðʌs/ *adv.* (*formal*)
1 as a result of something just mentioned **SYN** HENCE, THEREFORE: *He is the eldest son and thus heir to the estate.* ♦ *We do not own the building. Thus, it would be impossible for us to make any major changes to it.* 2 in this way; like this: *Many scholars have argued thus.* ♦ *The universities have expanded, thus allowing many more people the chance of higher education.* **IDM** see FAR ➾ language bank at THEREFORE

thwack /θwæk/ *verb* ~ sb/sth to hit someone or something hard, making a short loud sound ▶ **thwack** *noun: the thwack of bat on ball*

thwart /θwɔrt/ *verb* [often passive] to prevent someone from doing what they want to do **SYN** FRUSTRATE: ~ sth *to thwart someone's plans* ♦ ~ sb (in sth) *She was thwarted in her attempt to take control of the party.*

thy /ðaɪ/ (also **thine** before a vowel) *det.* (*old use*) a word meaning "your," used when talking to only one person: *Honor thy father and thy mother.*

thyme /taɪm/ *noun* [U] a plant with small leaves that have a sweet smell and are used in cooking as an HERB ➾ picture at HERB

thy·mus /'θaɪməs/ (also **'thymus ,gland**) *noun* (*anatomy*) an organ in the neck that produces LYMPHOCYTES (= cells to fight infection)

thy·roid /'θaɪrɔɪd/ (also **'thyroid ,gland**) *noun* (*anatomy*) a small organ at the front of the neck that produces HORMONES that control the way in which the body grows and functions

thy·self /ðaɪ'sɛlf/ *pron.* (*old use* or *dialect*) a word meaning "yourself," used when talking to only one person

ti /ti/ *noun* (*music*) the 7th note of a MAJOR SCALE

ti·ar·a /ti'ɑrə; -'ɛrə/ *noun* a piece of jewelry like a small crown decorated with PRECIOUS STONES, worn by a woman, for example a princess, on formal occasions

tib·i·a /'tɪbiə/ *noun* (*pl.* **tib·i·ae** /-bii/) (*anatomy*) the SHIN BONE ➾ see also FIBULA ➾ picture at BODY

tic /tɪk/ *noun* a sudden quick movement of a muscle, especially in your face or head, that you cannot control

tick /tɪk/ *verb, noun*
• **verb** [I] (of a clock, etc.) to make short, light, regular repeated sounds to mark time passing: *In the silence we could hear the clock ticking.* ♦ *a ticking bomb* ♦ ~ away *While we waited the taxi's meter kept ticking away.* **IDM** what makes sb tick what makes someone behave in the way that they do: *I've never really understood what makes her tick.* **PHRV** tick a'way/'by/'past (of time) to pass: *I had to get to the airport by two, and the minutes were ticking away.* tick sth↔a'way (of a clock, etc.) to mark the time as it passes: *The clock ticked away the minutes.* tick sb↔'off (*informal*) to make someone angry or annoyed ➾ see also TICKED OFF
• **noun** 1 [C] a small insect that bites humans and animals and sucks their blood. There are several types of ticks, some of which can carry diseases: *a tick bite* ➾ picture at ANIMAL 2 (also tick·ing) [U] a short, light, regularly repeated sound, especially that of a clock or watch: *The only sound was the soft tick of the clock.*

ticked 'off (also **ticked**) *adj.* (*informal*) [not before noun] annoyed or angry: *I was really ticked off when I found out the truth.*

tick·er /'tɪkər/ *noun* 1 = NEWS TICKER 2 (*old-fashioned, informal*) a person's heart

'ticker ,tape *noun* [U] long, narrow strips of paper with information, for example STOCK MARKET prices, printed on them by a special TELEGRAPH machine: *a ticker-tape parade in the streets of New York* (= an occasion when people throw pieces of paper as part of a celebration, for example in honor of a famous person)

tick·et 🔑 /'tɪkət/ *noun, verb*
• **noun** 1 ~ (for/to sth) a printed piece of paper that gives you the right to travel on a particular bus, train, etc. or to go into a theater, etc.: *a bus/theater/plane, etc. ticket* ♦ *free tickets to the show* ♦ *Tickets are available from the Arts center at $2.50.* ♦ *a ticket office/machine/collector* ♦ (*figurative*) *She hoped that getting this job would finally be her ticket to success.* ➾ see also E-TICKET, MEAL TICKET, SEASON TICKET 2 a printed piece of paper with a number or numbers on it, that you buy in order to have the chance of winning a prize if the number or numbers are later chosen: *a lottery/raffle ticket* ♦ *There are three winning tickets.* 3 a label that is attached to something in a store giving details of its price, size, etc. ➾ picture at LABEL 4 an official notice that orders you to pay a FINE because you have done something illegal while driving or parking your car **SYN** FINE: *a parking/speeding ticket* 5 [usually sing.] a list of candidates that are supported by a particular political party in an election: *She ran for office on the Democratic ticket.* ➾ see also DREAM TICKET **IDM** just the ticket (*informal, approving*) exactly what is needed in a particular situation **that's the ticket** (*old-fashioned, informal*) used to say that something is just what is needed or that everything is just right ➾ more at SPLIT *v.*
• **verb** 1 ~ sth/sb (*technical*) to produce and sell tickets for an event, a trip, etc.; to give someone a ticket: *Passengers can now be ticketed electronically.* 2 [usually passive] ~ sb to give someone an official notice that orders them to pay a FINE because they have done something illegal while driving or parking a car: *Park illegally, and you're likely to be ticketed.*

tick·et·ed /'tɪkətəd/ *adj.* [usually before noun] a **ticketed** event is one for which you need a ticket to get in: *The museum holds both free and ticketed events.* **IDM** be ticketed for sth to be intended for a particular purpose

tick·et·ing /'tɪkətɪŋ/ *noun* [U] the process of producing and selling tickets: *ticketing systems*

tick·ing /'tɪkɪŋ/ *noun* [U] a type of strong cotton cloth that is often striped, used especially for making MATTRESSES and PILLOW covers

tick·le /'tɪkl/ *verb, noun*
• *verb* **1** [T, I] ~ **(sb/sth)** to move your fingers on a sensitive part of someone's body in a way that makes them laugh: *The bigger girls used to chase me and tickle me.* ◆ *Stop tickling!* **2** [T, I] ~ **(sth)** to produce a slightly uncomfortable feeling in a sensitive part of the body; to have a feeling like this: *His beard was tickling her cheek.* ◆ *My throat tickles.* ◆ *a tickling cough* **3** [T] to amuse and interest someone: ~ *sb/sth to tickle someone's imagination* ◆ ~ *sb to do sth I was tickled to discover that we'd both done the same thing.*
IDM **be tickled pink** (*informal*) to be very pleased or amused **tickle sb's fancy** (*informal*) to please or amuse someone: *See if any of these tickle your fancy.*
• *noun* [usually sing.] **1** an act of tickling someone: *She gave the child a little tickle.* **2** a slightly uncomfortable feeling in a part of your body: *to have a tickle in your throat* (= that makes you want to cough)

tick·lish /'tɪklɪʃ/ *adj.* **1** (of a person) sensitive to being tickled: *Are you ticklish?* **2** (*informal*) (of a situation or problem) difficult to deal with, and possibly embarrassing **SYN** AWKWARD **3** (of a cough) that irritates your throat: *a dry ticklish cough*

tick-tock /ˌtɪk ˈtɑk/ *noun* [usually sing.] used to describe the sound of a large clock TICKING

tick·y-tack·y /'tɪki ˌtæki/ *noun* [U] (*informal*) building material that is cheap and of low quality ▶ **ticky-tacky** *adj.*

tic-tac-toe (also **tick-tack-toe**) /ˌtɪk tæk ˈtoʊ/ *noun* [U] a simple game in which two players take turns to write Os or Xs in a set of nine squares. The first player to complete a row of three Os or three Xs is the winner. ⊃ picture at TOY

tid·al /'taɪdl/ *adj.* connected with TIDES (= the regular rise and fall of the ocean): *tidal forces* ◆ *a tidal river*

'tidal ˌwave *noun* **1** a very large ocean wave that is caused by a storm or an EARTHQUAKE, and that destroys things when it reaches the land **2** ~ **(of sth)** a sudden increase in a particular feeling, activity, or type of behavior: *a tidal wave of crime*

tid·bit /'tɪdbɪt/ *noun* **1** a small special piece of food **SYN** MORSEL: *She had saved a few tidbits for her cat.* **2** a small but interesting piece of news **SYN** SNIPPET: *tidbits of gossip*

tid·dly·winks /'tɪdli ˌwɪŋks/ *noun* [U] a game in which players try to make small plastic disks jump into a cup by pressing them on the edge with a larger disk

tide /taɪd/ *noun, verb*
• *noun* **1** [C, U] a regular rise and fall in the level of the ocean, caused by the pull of the moon and sun; the flow of water that happens as the ocean rises and falls: *the ebb and flow of the tide* ◆ *The tide is in/out.* ◆ *Is the tide coming in or going out?* ◆ *The body was washed up on the beach by the tide.* ⊃ see also HIGH TIDE, LOW TIDE, NEAP TIDE, SPRING TIDE **2** [C, usually sing.] the direction in which the opinion of a large number of people seems to be moving: *It takes courage to speak out against the tide of opinion.* **3** [C, usually sing.] a large amount of something unpleasant that is increasing and is difficult to control: *There is anxiety about the rising tide of crime.* **4** [sing.] ~ **of sth** a feeling that you suddenly have that gets stronger and stronger: *A tide of rage surged through her.* **5** **-tide** [sing.] (*old use*) (in compounds) a time or season of the year: *Christmastide*
IDM **go, swim, etc. with/against the tide** to agree with/oppose the attitudes or opinions that most other people have **the tide turned | turn the tide** used to say that there is a change in someone's luck or in how successful they are being
• *verb*
PHRV ˌtide sb ˈover (sth) [no passive] to help someone during a difficult period by providing what they need: *Can you lend me some money to tide me over until I get paid?*

tide·line /'taɪdlaɪn/ *noun* a line left or reached by the ocean when the tide is at its highest point

tide·mark /'taɪdmɑrk/ *noun* a line that is made by the ocean on a beach at the highest point that the ocean reaches

'tide pool *noun* a small amount of water that collects between the rocks by the ocean

tide·wa·ter /'taɪdˌwɔtər; -ˌwɑtər/ *noun* **1** [C] an area of land at or near the coast **2** [U, C] water that is brought up by the TIDE

ti·dings /'taɪdɪŋz/ *noun* [pl.] (*old-fashioned* or *humorous*) news: *I am the bearer of good tidings.* ◆ *He brought glad tidings.*

ti·dy /'taɪdi/ *adj., verb*
• *adj.* (ti·di·er, ti·di·est) **1** arranged neatly and with everything in order: *a tidy desk* ◆ *She keeps her apartment very tidy.* ◆ *I like everything to be neat and tidy.* **ANT** UNTIDY **2** keeping things neat and in order: *I'm a tidy person.* ◆ *tidy habits* **ANT** UNTIDY **3** [only before noun] (*informal*) a **tidy** amount of money is fairly large **SYN** CONSIDERABLE: *It must have cost a tidy sum.* ◆ *a tidy profit* ▶ **ti·di·ly** /'taɪdl-i/ *adv.*: *The room was very tidily arranged.* **ti·di·ness** /-dinəs/ *noun* [U]
• *verb* (ti·dies, ti·dy·ing, ti·died, ti·died) [I, T] to make something look neat by putting things in the place where they belong: *I spent all morning cleaning and tidying.* ◆ ~ **up** *When you cook, could you please tidy up after yourself.* ◆ ~ **sth (up)** *to tidy (up) a room*
PHRV ˌtidy sth↔ˈup to arrange or deal with something so that it is well or correctly finished: *I tidied up the report before handing it in.*

tie 🔊 /taɪ/ *verb, noun*
• *verb* (ties, ty·ing, tied, tied)
▷ **FASTEN WITH STRING/ROPE 1** [T] ~ **sth (+ adv./prep.)** to attach or hold two or more things together using string, rope, etc.; to fasten someone or something with string, rope, etc.: *She tied the newspapers in a bundle.* ◆ *He had to tie her hands together.* ◆ *They tied him to a chair with a cord.* ◆ *Shall I tie the package or tape it?* ◆ *I tie back my hair when I'm cooking.* **2** [T] ~ **sth + adv./prep.** to fasten something to or around something else: *She tied a label on to the suitcase.* **3** [T] ~ **sth** to make a knot in a piece of string, rope, etc.: *to tie a ribbon* ◆ *Can you help me tie my tie?* ◆ *Tie up your shoelaces!* ◆ *I tied a knot in the rope.* **4** [I] (+ adv./prep.) to be closed or fastened with a knot, etc.: *The skirt ties at the waist.*
▷ **CONNECT/LINK 5** [T, usually passive] ~ **sb/sth (to sth/sb)** to connect or link someone or something closely with someone or something else: *Pay increases are tied to inflation.* ◆ *The house is tied to the job, so we'll have to move when I retire.*
▷ **RESTRICT 6** [T, usually passive] to restrict someone and make them unable to do everything they want to: ~ **sb** *to be tied by a contract* ◆ ~ **sb to sth** *I want to work but I'm tied to the house with the baby.* ◆ ~ **sb to doing sth** *I don't want to be tied to coming home at a particular time.*
▷ **IN GAME/COMPETITION 7** [I, T] (of two teams, etc.) to have the same number of points: ~ **(with sb)** *The University of Connecticut and Arizona State are tied 78–78 in the second half.* ◆ ~ **for sth** *They tied for second place.* ◆ ~ **sth** *The scores are tied at 3–3.* ◆ *Last night's vote was tied.*
▷ **MUSIC 8** [T] ~ **sth** to join notes with a tie ⊃ see also TONGUE-TIED
IDM **tie sb/yourself (up) in knots** to become or make someone very confused **tie one on** (*old-fashioned, slang*) to get very drunk **tie the knot** (*informal*) to get married ⊃ more at APRON, HAND *n.*
PHRV ˌtie sb ˈdown (to sth/to doing sth) to restrict someone's freedom, for example by making them accept particular conditions or by keeping them busy: *Kids tie you down, don't they?* ◆ *I don't want to tie myself down to coming back on a particular date.* ˌtie ˈin (with sth) to match or agree with something: *This evidence ties in closely with what we already know.* ˌtie ˈin (with sth) | ˌtie sth↔ˈin (with sth) to link something or be linked to something; to happen, or arrange for something to happen, at the same time as something else: *The concert will tie in with the festival of dance*

| h hat | m man | n no | ŋ sing | l leg | r red | y yes | w wet |

taking place the same weekend. ➔ related noun TIE-IN ˌtie
sth↔ˈoff to put a knot in the end of something; to close
something with string, thread, etc.: *to tie off a rope* ◆ *to tie off
an artery* ˌtie ˈup | ˌtie sth↔ˈup **1** to attach a boat to a
fixed object with a rope: *We tied up alongside the pier.* ◆ *We
tied the boat up.* **2** to close something with a knot; to be
closed or fastened with a knot: *to tie up a garbage bag* ˌtie
sb↔ˈup **1** to tie someone's arms and legs tightly so that
they cannot move or escape: *The gang tied up a security
guard.* **2** [usually passive] to keep someone busy so that
they have no time for other things: *I'm tied up in a meeting
until 3.* ˌtie sth↔ˈup **1** to attach an animal to something
with a rope, chain, etc.: *He left his dog tied up to a tree.*
2 [usually passive] to connect or link something to something else: *Her behavior is tied up with her feelings of guilt.*
3 [often passive] to invest money so that it is not easily
available for use: *Most of the capital is tied up in property.* **4** to
deal with all the remaining details of something: *We are
hoping to tie up the deal by tomorrow.* ◆ *I went into the office for
an hour to tie up any loose ends* (= finish remaining small jobs).

● *noun*
> CLOTHES **1** (also **neck·tie**) a long narrow piece of cloth worn
around the neck, especially by men, with a knot in front: *a
jacket/coat and tie* ◆ *a striped silk tie* ➔ picture at CLOTHES
➔ see also BLACK TIE, BOW TIE, WHITE TIE
> FOR FASTENING **2** a piece of string or wire used for fastening
or tying something: *ties for closing plastic bags*
> CONNECTION **3** [usually pl.] a strong connection between
people or organizations: *family ties* ◆ *the ties of friendship*
◆ *economic ties* ◆ *The firm has close ties with an American
corporation.*
> RESTRICTION **4** a thing that limits someone's freedom of
action: *He was still a young man and he did not want any ties.*
> IN GAME/COMPETITION **5** a situation in a game or competi-
tion when two or more players have the same score: *The
game ended in a tie.*
> MUSIC **6** a curved line written over two notes of the same
PITCH (= how high or low a note is) to show that they are to
be played or sung as one note
> ON RAILROAD **7** one of the heavy pieces of wood or concrete
on which the rails on a railroad track are laid

tie·break·er /ˈtaɪˌbreɪkər/ *noun* **1** (in TENNIS) a period of
extra play to decide who is the winner of a SET when both
players have won six games **2** an extra question in a
competition to decide who is the winner when two or more
of those taking part have equal scores

ˈtie-dye *verb* ~ *sth* to make patterns on cloth by tying knots
in it or tying string around it before you put it in a DYE, so
that some parts receive more color than others

ˈtie-in *noun* a product such as a book or toy that is connected
with a new movie, television program, etc.

ˈtie·pin /ˈtaɪpɪn/ (also ˈtie tack) *noun* a small decorative pin
that is worn on a tie to keep it in place

tier /tɪr/ *noun* **1** a row or layer of something that has several
rows or layers placed one above the other: *a wedding cake
with three tiers* ◆ *The seating is arranged in tiers.* **2** one of
several levels in an organization or a system: *We have
introduced an extra tier of administration.* ◆ *a two-tier system of
management*

tiered /tɪrd/ *adj.* **1** arranged in tiers: *tiered seating* **2** **-tiered**
(in compounds) having the number of tiers mentioned: *a
two-tiered system*

ˈtie-up *noun* a situation in which something stops working
or moving forward: *a traffic tie-up*

TIFF /tɪf/ *noun* [U, C] (*computing*) the abbreviation for "tagged
image file format" (a form in which images can be stored
and shown on a computer; an image created in this form)

tiff /tɪf/ *noun* a slight argument between close friends or
lovers: *to have a tiff with someone*

ti·ger /ˈtaɪgər/ *noun* a large wild animal of the cat family, that
has yellowish fur with black lines (= STRIPES) and lives in
parts of Asia: *She fought like a tiger to be able to keep her
children.* ➔ compare TIGRESS ➔ see also PAPER TIGER

ˌtiger eˈconomy *noun* the
economy of a country that is
growing very quickly

ti·ger·ish /ˈtaɪgərɪʃ/ *adj.* like
a tiger, especially in being
aggressive or showing
great energy

tiger

tight /taɪt/ *adj., adv.*

● *adj.* (**tight·er**, **tight·est**)
> FIRM **1** held or attached in position firmly; difficult to move
or undo: *He kept a tight grip on her arm.* ◆ *She twisted her hair
into a tight knot.* ◆ *The screw was so tight that it wouldn't move.*
> CLOTHES **2** fitting closely to your body and sometimes
uncomfortable: *She was wearing a tight pair of jeans.* ◆ *These
shoes are much too tight.* ◆ *The new sweater was a tight fit.*
ANT LOOSE ➔ see also SKINTIGHT
> CONTROL **3** very strict and firm: *to keep tight control* over
something ◆ *We need tighter security at the airport.*
> STRETCHED **4** stretched or pulled so that it cannot stretch
much further: *The rope was stretched tight.*
> CLOSE TOGETHER **5** [usually before noun] with things or
people packed closely together, leaving little space
between them: *There was a tight group of people around the
speaker.* ◆ *With six of us in the car it was a tight squeeze.*
> MONEY/TIME **6** difficult to manage with because there is not
enough: *We have a very tight budget.* ◆ *The president has a tight
schedule today.*
> EXPRESSION/VOICE **7** looking or sounding anxious, upset,
angry, etc.: *"I'm sorry," she said, with a tight smile.* ➔ see also
UPTIGHT
> PART OF BODY **8** feeling painful or uncomfortable because
of illness or emotion **SYN** CONSTRICTED: *He complained of
having a tight chest.* ◆ *Her throat felt tight, just looking at her
baby.*
> RELATIONSHIP **9** having a close relationship with someone
else or with other people: *It was a tight community and
newcomers were not welcome.* ➔ see also TIGHT-KNIT
> BEND/CURVE **10** curving suddenly rather than gradually:
The driver slowed down at a tight bend in the road. ◆ *The plane
flew around in a tight circle.*
> CONTEST/RACE **11** with runners, teams, etc. that seem to be
equally good **SYN** CLOSE²: *a tight race*
> NOT GENEROUS **12** (*informal, disapproving*) not wanting to
spend much money; not generous **SYN** STINGY: *He's very
tight with his money.*
> DRUNK **13** [not usually before noun] (*old-fashioned, informal*)
drunk **SYN** TIPSY
> -TIGHT **14** (in compounds) not allowing the substance
mentioned to enter: *measures to make your home weathertight*
➔ see also AIRTIGHT, WATERTIGHT

▶ **tight·ness** *noun* [U]

IDM **to keep a tight rein on sb/sth** to control someone or
something carefully or strictly **run a tight ship** to organize
something in a very efficient way, controlling other people
very closely **a tight spot/corner** a very difficult or
dangerous situation

● *adv.* (**tight·er**, **tight·est**) closely and firmly; tightly: *Hold
tight!* ◆ *My suitcase was packed tight.* ◆ *His fists were clenched
tight.* **IDM** see SIT, SLEEP *v.*

tight·en /ˈtaɪtn/ verb **1** [I, T] to become or make something become tight or tighter: ~ **(up)** *The rope holding the boat suddenly tightened and broke.* ◆ *His mouth tightened into a thin line.* ◆ ~ **sth (up)** *to tighten a lid/screw/rope/knot* ◆ *The nuts weren't properly tightened and the wheel came off.* ◆ *She tightened her grip on his arm.* **2** [T] ~ **sth** to make something become stricter: *to tighten security* **ANT LOOSEN**
IDM **tighten your belt** to spend less money because there is less available ⊃ see also BELT-TIGHTENING ⊃ thesaurus box at SAVE
PHR V **tighten ˈup (on sth)** to become stricter or more careful: *Laws on gambling have tightened up recently.* ◆ *The police are tightening up on under-age drinking.*

ˌtight ˈend noun (in football) an offensive player who plays close to the TACKLE

ˌtight-ˈfisted adj. not willing to spend or give much money **SYN** STINGY

ˌtight-ˈfitting adj. that fits very tightly or closely **SYN** CLOSE-FITTING: *a tight-fitting skirt*

ˌtight-ˈknit (also ˌtightly-ˈknit) adj. (of a family or community) with all the members having strong friendly relationships with one another: *a tight-knit mining community*

ˌtight-ˈlipped /ˌtaɪt ˈlɪpt/ adj. **1** not willing to talk about something **2** keeping your lips pressed firmly together, especially because you are angry about something

tight·ly 🔑 /ˈtaɪtli/ adv.
closely and firmly; in a tight manner: *Her eyes were tightly closed.* ◆ *He held on tightly to her arm.* ◆ *a tightly packed crowd of tourists* ⊃ note at TIGHT

tight·rope /ˈtaɪtroʊp/ noun a rope or wire that is stretched tightly high above the ground and that performers walk along, especially in a CIRCUS: *a tightrope walker*
IDM **tread/walk a tightrope** to be in a difficult situation in which you do not have much freedom of action and need to be extremely careful about what you do

tights /taɪts/ noun [pl.] a piece of clothing made of thin cloth that fits closely over a person's hips, legs, and feet, worn by women, girls, dancers, and actors: *a pair of tights* ⊃ compare PANTYHOSE

tight·wad /ˈtaɪtwɑd/ noun (informal) a person who hates to spend or give money **SYN** MISER

ti·gress /ˈtaɪgrəs/ noun a female TIGER

tike noun = TYKE

til, ˈtil /tɪl/ ⊃ UNTIL

ti·la·pi·a /təˈlɑpiə/ noun (pl. ti·la·pi·a or ti·la·pi·as) [C, U] a FRESHWATER fish found in hot countries that is used for food

til·de /ˈtɪldə/ noun **1** the mark (~) placed over letters in some languages to show how they should be pronounced, as in *España* and *São Paulo* **2** (also ˌswung ˈdash) the mark (~), used in this dictionary in some parts of an entry to represent the word in dark type at the top of the entry

tile /taɪl/ noun, verb
● noun **1** a flat, usually square, piece of baked CLAY, carpet, or other material that is used in rows for covering walls and floors: *ceramic floor tiles* ◆ *carpet tiles* **2** a piece of baked CLAY that is used in rows for covering roofs **3** any of the small flat pieces that are used in particular board games
● verb **1** ~ **sth** to cover a surface with tiles: *a tiled bathroom* **2** ~ **sth** (computing) to arrange several windows on a computer screen so that they fill the screen but do not cover each other

til·er /ˈtaɪlər/ noun a person whose job is to lay tiles

til·ing /ˈtaɪlɪŋ/ noun [U] **1** an area covered with tiles **2** the work of covering a floor, wall, etc. with tiles

till 🔑 /tɪl/ conj., prep., noun, verb
● conj., prep. = UNTIL: *We're open till 6 o'clock.* ◆ *Can't you wait till we get home?* ◆ *Just wait till you see it. It's great.* **HELP** Till is generally felt to be more informal than **until** and is used much less often in writing. At the beginning of a sentence, **until** is usually used.
● noun the drawer where the money is put in a CASH REGISTER
● verb ~ **sth** (old use) to prepare and use land for growing crops

till·age /ˈtɪlɪdʒ/ noun [U] (old-fashioned) **1** the process of preparing and using land for growing crops **2** land that is used for growing crops

till·er /ˈtɪlər/ noun a bar that is used to turn the RUDDER of a small boat in order to steer it ⊃ compare HELM

tilt /tɪlt/ verb, noun
● verb **1** [I, T] to move, or make something move, into a position with one side or end higher than the other **SYN** TIP: (+ adv./prep.) *Suddenly the boat tilted to one side.* ◆ *The seat tilts forward, when you press this lever.* ◆ ~ **sth** (+ adv./prep.) *His hat was tilted slightly at an angle.* ◆ *She tilted her head back and looked up at me with a smile.* **2** [T, I] ~ **(sth/ sb) (in favor of/away from sth/sb)** to make something or someone change slightly so that one particular opinion, person, etc. is preferred or more likely to succeed than another; to change in this way: *The conditions may tilt the balance in favor of the Kenyan runners.* ◆ *Popular opinion has tilted in favor of the socialists.*
IDM **tilt at windmills** to waste your energy attacking imaginary enemies **ORIGIN** From Cervantes' novel *Don Quixote,* in which the hero thought that the windmills he saw were giants and tried to fight them.
● noun **1** a position in which one end or side of something is higher than the other; an act of tilting something to one side: *The table is at a slight tilt.* ◆ *He answered with a tilt of his head.* **2** an attempt to win something or defeat someone: *She aims to have a tilt at the world championship next year.*
IDM **(at) full tilt** as fast as possible

tim·ber /ˈtɪmbər/ noun **1** [U] trees that are grown to be used in building or for making things: *the timber industry* **2** [C, usually pl.] a long heavy piece of wood used in building a house or ship: *roof timbers* **3** [U] = LUMBER: *houses built of timber* **4** **timber!** used to warn people that a tree that has been cut is about to fall

tim·bered /ˈtɪmbərd/ adj. built of timber; with a FRAME-WORK of timber ⊃ see also HALF-TIMBERED

tim·bre /ˈtæmbər, ˈtɪm-/ noun (formal) the quality of sound that is produced by a particular voice or musical instrument

Tim·buk·tu (also **Tim·buc·too**) /ˌtɪmbʌkˈtu/ noun a place that is very far away **ORIGIN** From the name of a town in northern Mali.

time 🔑 /taɪm/ noun, verb
● noun ⊃ see also TIMES
➢ MINUTES/HOURS/YEARS, ETC. **1** [U] what is measured in minutes, hours, days, etc.: *The changing seasons mark the passing of time.* ◆ *A visit to the museum will take you back in time to the 1930s.* ◆ *time and space* ◆ *As time went by we saw less and less of each other.* ◆ *Perceptions change over time* (= as time passes). ⊃ see also FATHER TIME **2** [U] the time shown on a clock in minutes and hours: *What time is it?* ◆ *Do you have the time?* ◆ *What time do you have?* ◆ *The time is now ten-thirty.* ◆ *Can she tell time yet* (= say what time it is by looking at a clock)? ◆ *My watch keeps perfect time* (= always shows the correct time). ◆ *Look at the time! We'll be late.* ◆ *This time tomorrow I'll be in Canada.* **3** [U] the time measured in a particular part of the world: *Greenwich Mean Time* ◆ *6 o'clock local time* ⊃ see also DAYLIGHT SAVING TIME, STANDARD TIME **4** [U, C] the time when something happens or when something should happen: *What time do you finish work?* ◆ *The baby loves bath time.* ◆ ~ **(to do sth)** *I think it's time to go to bed.* ◆ ~ **(for sth)** *It's time for lunch.* ◆ ~ **(that)…** *It's time the kids were in bed.* ◆ *By the time you get there the meeting will be over.* ◆ *A computer screen shows arrival and departure times.*

ʌ cup ə about eɪ say aɪ five ɔɪ boy aʊ now oʊ go ər bird

♦ *The train arrived right **on time*** (= at exactly the correct time).
♦ *You'll feel differently about it **when the time comes*** (= when it happens). ⊃ see also ANYTIME, CLOSING TIME, DRIVE TIME, NIGHTTIME

▸ PERIOD **5** [U] **~ (to do sth)** an amount of time; the amount of time available to work, rest, etc.: *Allow plenty of time to get to the airport.* ♦ *I can probably **make the time** to see them.* ♦ *It **takes time** to make changes in the law.* ♦ *We have **no time to lose*** (= we must hurry). ♦ *He spends most of his time working.* ♦ *She doesn't have much **free/spare time**.* ♦ *What a **waste of time!** ♦ I didn't finish the test— **I ran out of time**.* ♦ *Time's up* —have you figured out the answer yet? ♦ *He never takes any **time off*** (= time spent not working). ♦ *Jane's worked here **for some time*** (= for a fairly long period of time). ♦ *Do it now please—not in three hours' time* (= three hours from now). ♦ *The journey time is two hours.* ⊃ see also RESPONSE TIME **6** **a time** [sing.] a period of time, either long or short, during which you do something or something happens: *His injuries will **take a long time** to heal.* ♦ *I lived in Egypt **for a time**.* ♦ *The early morning is the best **time of day**.* ♦ *Her parents died **a long time** ago.* ♦ *At one time* (= at a period of time in the past) *Emily was my best friend.* ♦ *Mr. Curtis was the manager **in my time*** (= when I was working there). **7** [U, pl.] a period of history connected with particular events or experiences in people's lives: *The movie is set **at the time of** the Russian revolution.* ♦ *in ancient times* ♦ *the violent times we live in* (= the present period of history) ♦ *Times are hard for the unemployed.* ♦ ***Times have changed** since Grandma was young.* ⊃ see also OLD-TIME

▸ OCCASION/EVENT **8** [C] an occasion when you do something or when something happens: ***Every time** I hear that song I feel happy.* ♦ ***Next time** you're here let's have lunch together.* ♦ *He failed his driving test three times.* ♦ *He's determined to pass **this time**.* ♦ *When was the **last time** you saw her?* ♦ ***How many times*** (= how often) *do I have to tell you not to do that?* ♦ *I remember **one time*** (= once) *we had to abandon our car in the snow.* ♦ *(formal) **At no time** did I give my consent to the plan.* **HELP** To talk about the first or the last time you do something, use **the first/last time (that) I…**: *This is the first time (that) I've been to Chicago.* ♦ *This is the first time for me to go to Chicago.* ♦ *That was the last time (that) I saw her.* **9** [C] an event or occasion that you experience in a particular way: *Did you **have a good time** in Spain?* ♦ *I had an awful time in the hospital.*

▸ FOR RACE **10** [C, U] how long someone takes to run a race or complete an event: *The winner's time was 11.6 seconds.* ♦ *She completed the 500 meters **in record time*** (= faster than any previous runner). ♦ *one of the fastest times ever*

▸ IN MUSIC **11** [U] the number of beats in a BAR/MEASURE of music: *This piece is in four-four time.* ♦ *a slow waltz time* ♦ *The conductor **beat time** with a baton.* **12** [U] the correct speed and rhythm of a piece of music: *Try and dance **in time** to the music* (= with the same speed and rhythm). ♦ *Clap your hands to **keep time*** (= sing or play with the correct speed and rhythm). ♦ *to play **in/out of time*** (= follow/not follow the correct speed and rhythm) ♦ *He always plays in perfect time.* ⊃ see also BIG TIME, SMALL-TIME

IDM **about time** used to say that something should have happened before now **against time** if you do something **against time**, you do it as fast as you can because you do not have much time: *They're working against time to try and get people out of the rubble alive.* **ahead of/behind time** earlier/later than was expected: *We finished 15 minutes ahead of time.* **ahead of your time** having advanced or new ideas that other people use or copy later **all the time | the whole time 1** during the whole of a particular period of time: *The letter was in my pocket all the time* (= while I was looking for it). **2** very often; repeatedly: *She leaves the lights on all the time.* **at all times** always: *Our representatives are ready to help you at all times.* **at the best of times** even when the circumstances are very good: *He's never very happy at the best of times—he'll be much worse now!* **at the same time 1** at one time; together: *She was laughing and crying at the same time.* **2** used to introduce a contrasting fact, etc. that must be considered: *You have to be firm, but at the same time you should try and be sympathetic.* **at a time** separately or in groups of two, three, etc. on each occasion: *We had to*

go and see the principal one at a time. ♦ *She ran up the stairs two at a time.* **at my, your, his, etc. time of life** at the age you are (especially when you are not young): *Eyesight doesn't get any better at my time of life.* **at times** sometimes: *He can be really bad-tempered at times.* **before my, your, his, etc. time 1** happening before you were born or can remember or before you lived, worked, etc. somewhere: *"Were you taught by Professor Pascal?" "No, he was before my time."* **2** before the usual time in someone's life when something happens **SYN** PREMATURELY: *She got old before her time.* **behind the times** old-fashioned in your ideas, methods, etc. **do time** (*informal*) to spend time in prison **every time** whenever there is a choice: *I don't really like cities—give me the countryside every time.* **for the time being** for a short period of time but not permanently: *You can leave your suitcase here for the time being.* **from time to time** occasionally but not regularly: *She has to work on weekends from time to time.* **have no time for sb/sth | not have much time for sb/sth** (*informal*) to dislike someone or something: *I have no time for lazy people like Steve.* **have the time of your life** (*informal*) to enjoy yourself very much **have time on your hands | have time to kill** (*informal*) to have nothing to do or not be busy **in good time** early; with enough time so that you are not in a hurry **(all) in good time** (*informal*) used to say that something will be done or will happen at the appropriate time and not before: *Be patient, Emily! All in good time.* **in (less than/next to) no time** so soon or so quickly that it is surprising: *The kids will be leaving home in no time.* **in time** after a period of time when a situation has changed **SYN** EVENTUALLY: *They learned to accept their stepmother in time.* **in time (for sth/to do sth)** not late; with enough time to be able to do something: *Will we be in time for the six o'clock train?* ♦ *The ambulance got there just in time* (= to save someone's life). **in your own (good) time** (*informal*) when you are ready and not sooner: *Don't hassle him! He'll do it in his own good time.* **it's about/high time** (*informal*) used to say that you think someone should do something soon: *It's time you cleaned your room!* **keep up/move with the times** to change and develop your ideas, way of working, etc. so that you do what is modern and what is expected **make good, etc. time** to complete a journey quickly: *We made excellent time and arrived in Spain in two days.* **many a time | many's the time (that)…** (*old-fashioned*) many times; frequently **nine times out of ten | ninety-nine times out of a hundred** used to say that something is usually true or almost always happens: *Nine times out of ten she gives the right answer.* **not give sb the time of day** to refuse to speak to someone because you do not like or respect them: *Since the success of her novel, people shake her hand who once wouldn't have given her the time of day.* **(there is) no time like the present** (*saying*) now is the best time to do something, not in the future **of all time** that has ever existed: *Many rated him the best singer of all time.* ⊃ see also ALL-TIME **on your own time** in your free time and not when you usually work or study **take your time | take your time to do sth/doing sth 1** to use as much time as you need without hurrying: *There's no rush—take your time.* **2** used to say you think someone is late or is too slow in doing something: *You certainly took your time getting here!* **take time out** to spend some time away from your usual work or activity in order to rest or do something else instead: *She is taking time out from her music career for a year.* ⊃ thesaurus box at REST **time after time | time and (time) again** often; on many or all occasions: *You will get a perfect result time after time if you follow these instructions.* **time and a half** one and a half times the usual rate of pay ⊃ see also DOUBLE TIME **time flies** (*saying*) time seems to pass very quickly: *How time flies! I have to go now.* ♦ *Time has flown since the vacation began.* **ORIGIN** This phrase is a translation of the Latin "tempus fugit." **time is money** (*saying*) time is valuable, and should not be wasted **time is on your side** used to say that someone can wait for something to happen or can wait before doing something **(the) next, first, second, etc. time around** on the next, first, etc. occasion that the same thing happens: *He repeated none of the errors he'd made first time around.* ◆ *This time around it was not so easy.* **time was (when)…** (*old-fashioned*) used to say that something used to happen in the past **(only) time will tell** (*saying*) used to say that you will have to wait for some time to find out the result of a situation: *Only time will tell if the treatment has been successful.* **the whole time** = ALL THE TIME ⊃ more at BEAT *v.*, BIDE, BORROW, BUY *v.*, COURSE *n.*, DAY, DEVIL, EASY *adj.*, FIRST, FORTH, FULLNESS, GAIN *v.*, GIVE *v.*, HARD *adj.*, HIGH *adj.*, KILL *v.*, LONG *adj.*, LOST *adj.*, LUCK *n.*, MARK *v.*, MATTER *v.*, MOVE *v.*, NICK *n.*, OLD, ONCE *adv.*, PASS *v.*, RACE *n.*, SIGN *n.*, STITCH *n.*, SWEET *adj.*, THIRD, WHALE

● *verb*
> ARRANGE TIME **1** [often passive] to arrange to do something or arrange for something to happen at a particular time: *~ sth (for sth) She timed her arrival for shortly after 3.* ◆ *Their request was **badly timed** (= it was made at the wrong time).* ◆ *"I hope we're not too early." "You couldn't have timed it better!"* ◆ *~ sth to do sth Publication of his biography was **timed to coincide with** his 70th birthday celebrations.*
> MEASURE TIME **2** to measure how long it takes for something to happen or for someone to do something: *~ sth (at sth) The winner was timed at 20.4 seconds.* ◆ *~ how long… Time how long it takes you to answer the questions.*
> IN SPORTS **3** *~ sth* to hit or kick a ball at a particular moment in a sports game: *She timed the pass perfectly.* ◆ *a beautifully timed shot* ⊃ see also ILL-TIMED, MISTIME, TIMING, WELL TIMED
PHRV ˌtime ˈout | ˌtime sth ˈout (of a computer program or task) to turn off, or turn something off, automatically after a particular length of time even if the user has not finished: *My satellite connection timed out—it was so frustrating.*

ˌtime-and-ˈmotion ˌstudy *noun* a study to find out how efficient a company's working methods are

ˈtime bomb *noun* **1** a bomb that can be set to explode at a particular time **2** a situation that is likely to cause serious problems in the future: *Rising unemployment is a political time bomb for the government.*

ˈtime ˌcapsule *noun* a container that is filled with objects that people think are typical of the time they are living in. It is buried so that it can be discovered by people in the future.

ˈtime card *noun* a piece of card on which the number of hours that someone has worked are recorded, usually by a machine

ˈtime clock *noun* a special clock that records the exact time that someone starts and finishes work

ˈtime-conˌsuming *adj.* taking or needing a lot of time: *a difficult and time-consuming process*

ˈtime frame *noun* the length of time that is used or available for something

ˈtime-ˌhonored (CanE usually ˈtime-ˌhonoured) *adj.* respected because it has been used or done for a long time: *They showed their approval in the time-honored way (= by clapping, for example).*

ˈtime·keep·er /ˈtaɪmˌkipər/ *noun* a person who records the time that is spent doing something, for example at work or at a sports event

ˈtime·keep·ing /ˈtaɪmˌkipɪŋ/ *noun* [U] the activity of recording the time something takes

ˈtime lag (also ˈlag, ˈtime lapse) *noun* the period of time between two connected events: *There is a long time lag between when I do the work and when I get paid.*

ˈtime-lapse *adj.* [only before noun] (of photography) using a method in which a series of individual pictures of a process are shown together so that something that really happens very slowly is shown as happening very quickly: *a time-lapse sequence of a flower opening*

ˈtime·less /ˈtaɪmləs/ *adj.* (*formal*) **1** not appearing to be affected by the passing of time or by changes in fashion: *her*

timeless beauty **2** existing or continuing for ever **SYN** UNENDING: *timeless eternity* ▶ ˈtime·less·ly *adv.* ˈtime·less·ness *noun* [U]

ˈtime ˌlimit *noun* the length of time within which you must do or complete something: *We have to set a time limit for the work.* ◆ *The work must be completed within a certain time limit.*

ˈtime·line /ˈtaɪmlaɪn/ *noun* a horizontal line that is used to represent time, with the past toward the left and the future toward the right

ˈtime lock *noun* **1** a lock with a device which prevents it from being opened until a particular time **2** (*computing*) part of a program which stops the program operating after a particular time

ˈtime·ly /ˈtaɪmli/ *adj.* happening at exactly the right time **SYN** OPPORTUNE: *A nasty incident was prevented by the timely arrival of the police.* ◆ *This has been **a timely reminder** to us all.* **ANT** UNTIMELY ▶ ˈtime·li·ness *noun* [U]

ˈtime maˌchine *noun* (in SCIENCE FICTION stories) a machine that enables you to travel in time to the past or the future

ˈtime·out *noun* **1** /ˌtaɪmˈaʊt/ a short period of rest during a sports game **2** /ˈtaɪmaʊt/ (*computing*) an occasion when a process or program is automatically stopped after a certain amount of time because it has not worked successfully

ˈtime·piece /ˈtaɪmpis/ *noun* (*formal*) a clock or watch

ˌtime-ˈpoor *adj.* having very little or no free time because you work all the time: *products for customers who are time-poor but cash-rich*

ˈtim·er /ˈtaɪmər/ *noun* (often in compounds) a device that is used to measure the time that something takes; a device that starts or stops a machine working at a particular time: *an oven timer* ⊃ picture at KITCHEN ⊃ see also EGG TIMER, OLD-TIMER

ˈtime-reˌlease *adj.* [usually before noun] releasing an active substance, for example a drug, a little at a time

ˈtimes /taɪmz/ **1** *prep.* (*informal*) multiplied by: *Five times two is/equals ten* (= 5×2=10). **2** *noun* [pl.] used in comparisons to show how much more, better, etc. something is than something else: *three times as long as something* ◆ *three times longer than something* ◆ *three times the length of something* ⊃ language bank at PROPORTION

ˈtime-saving *adj.* [usually before noun] that reduces the amount of time it takes to do something: *time-saving devices*

ˈtime·scale /ˈtaɪmskeɪl/ *noun* the time taken by a process or sequence of events, especially a very long, slow process: *These rocks formed over geological timescales (millions to hundreds of millions of years).*

ˈtime-ˌserver *noun* (*disapproving*) a person who does as little work as possible in their job because they are just waiting until they leave for another job or retire ▶ ˈtime-ˌserving *adj.*, *noun* [U]

ˈtime·share /ˈtaɪmʃer/ *noun* **1** (also ˈtime-ˌsharing) [U] an arrangement in which several people own a vacation home together and each uses it at a different time of the year: *timeshare apartments* [C] a vacation home that you own in this way: *They have a timeshare in Florida.*

ˈtime sheet *noun* a piece of paper on which the number of hours that someone has worked are recorded

ˈtime ˌsignal *noun* a sound or sounds that show the exact time of day, especially a series of short high sounds that are broadcast on the radio

ˈtime ˌsignature *noun* (*music*) a sign at the start of a piece of music, usually in the form of numbers, showing the number of beats in each BAR/MEASURE

ˈtime span *noun* a period of time: *These changes have occurred over a long time span.*

ˈtimes ˌtable *noun* = MULTIPLICATION TABLE

ˈtime switch *noun* a switch that can be set to start and stop a machine working automatically at a particular time: *The heating is on a time switch.*

| t tea | t̬ butter | d did | k cat | g got | tʃ chin | dʒ June | f fall |

time·ta·ble 🔑 /ˈtaɪmˌteɪbl/ *noun*
1 a plan of when you expect particular events or activities to happen: *The government has established its timetable for the peace talks.* **2** a train, bus, or plane schedule

time trial *noun* (in cycle racing and some other sports) a race in which the people who are taking part race on their own in as fast a time as possible, instead of racing against each other at the same time

time warp *noun* an imaginary situation, described for example in SCIENCE FICTION, in which it is possible for people or things from the past or the future to move to the present
IDM be (stuck) in a time warp not having changed at all from a time in the past although everything else has

time-wasting *noun* [U] the act of wasting time ▶ **time-waster** *noun*

time-worn *adj.* old and used a lot, and therefore damaged, or no longer useful or interesting

time zone *noun* one of the 24 areas that the world is divided into, each with its own time that is one hour earlier than that of the time zone immediately to the east

tim·id /ˈtɪməd/ *adj.* shy and nervous; not brave: *He stopped in the doorway, too timid to go in.* ◆ *They've been rather timid in the changes they've made* (= they've been afraid to make any big changes). ◆ *a timid voice* ▶ **ti·mid·i·ty** /tɪˈmɪdəti/ *noun* [U] **tim·id·ly** /ˈtɪmədli/ *adv.*

tim·ing /ˈtaɪmɪŋ/ *noun* **1** [U, C] the act of choosing when something happens; a particular point or period of time when something happens or is planned: *The timing of the decision was a complete surprise.* ◆ *Please check your flight timings carefully.* **2** [U] the skill of doing something at exactly the right time: *an actor with a great sense of comic timing* ◆ *Your timing is perfect. I was just about to call you.* **3** [U] the repeated rhythm of something; the skill of producing this: *She played the piano confidently but her timing was not good.* **4** [U] (*technical*) the rate at which an electric SPARK is produced in a vehicle's engine in order to make it work

tim·or·ous /ˈtɪmərəs/ *adj.* (*formal* or *literary*) nervous and easily frightened **SYN** TIMID ▶ **tim·or·ous·ly** *adv.*

tim·pa·ni /ˈtɪmpəni/ (also *informal* **timps** /tɪmps/) *noun* [pl.] a set of large metal drums (also called KETTLEDRUMS) in an ORCHESTRA ▶ **tim·pa·nist** /ˈtɪmpənɪst/ *noun*

tin 🔑 /tɪn/ *noun*
1 [U] (*symb.* **Sn**) a chemical element. Tin is a soft silver-white metal that is often mixed with other metals or used to cover them to prevent them from RUSTING: *a tin mine* ◆ *a tin box* **2** [C] a metal container with a lid used for keeping food in: *a cake/cookie tin* ⟳ *picture at* PACKAGING **IDM see** CAT

tin can *noun* a metal container in which food and drink is sold

tinc·ture /ˈtɪŋktʃər/ *noun* [C, U] (*technical*) a substance dissolved in alcohol for use as a medicine

tin·der /ˈtɪndər/ *noun* [U] dry material, especially wood or grass, that burns easily and can be used to light a fire: *The fire started late Saturday in tinder-dry grass near the Snake River.*

tin·der·box /ˈtɪndərˌbɑks/ *noun* **1** a box containing dry material, used in the past for lighting a fire **2** (*formal*) a situation that is likely to become dangerous

tine /taɪn/ *noun* (*technical*) any of the points or sharp parts of, for example, a fork or the ANTLERS of a DEER

tin·foil /ˈtɪnfɔɪl/ *noun* [U] metal made into very thin sheets, that is used for wrapping food, etc.

tinge /tɪndʒ/ *verb, noun*
● *verb* [usually passive] **1** ~ **sth (with sth)** to add a small amount of color to something: *white petals tinged with blue* **2** ~ **sth (with sth)** to add a small amount of a particular emotion or quality to something: *a look of surprise tinged with disapproval*
● *noun* [usually sing.] a small amount of a color, feeling, or quality: *to feel a tinge of envy* ◆ *There was a faint pink tinge to the sky.* ⟳ *thesaurus box at* COLOR

tin·gle /ˈtɪŋgl/ *verb, noun*
● *verb* **1** [I] (of a part of your body) to feel as if a lot of small sharp points are pushing into it: *The cold air made her face tingle.* ◆ *a tingling sensation* ⟳ *thesaurus box at* HURT **2** [I] ~ **with sth** to feel an emotion strongly: *She was still tingling with excitement.*
● *noun* [usually sing.] **1** a slight stinging or uncomfortable feeling in a part of your body **2** an exciting or uncomfortable feeling of emotion: *to feel a tingle of excitement*

tin·gly /ˈtɪŋgli/ *adj.* causing or experiencing a slight feeling of tingling: *a tingly sensation*

tin·ker /ˈtɪŋkər/ *noun, verb*
● *noun* (in the past) a person who traveled from place to place, selling or repairing things
● *verb* [I] ~ **(with sth)** to make small changes to something in order to repair or improve it, especially in a way that may not be helpful

tin·kle /ˈtɪŋkl/ *noun, verb*
● *noun* [usually sing.] **1** (also **tin·kling** [sing., U]) a light, high, ringing sound: *the tinkle of glass breaking* **2** (*informal*) an act of urinating (URINATE)
● *verb* **1** [I, T] ~ **(sth)** to make a series of light, high, ringing sounds; to make something produce this sound: *A bell tinkled as the door opened.* ◆ *tinkling laughter* **2** (*informal*) to URINATE

tin·ni·tus /ˈtɪnətəs; tɪˈnaɪtəs/ *noun* [U] (*medical*) an unpleasant condition in which someone hears ringing in their ears

tin·ny /ˈtɪni/
● *adj.* (*disapproving*) **1** having a high, thin, sound like small pieces of metal hitting each other **2** having a taste like metal: *The beer tasted tinny.*

Tin Pan Alley *noun* [U] (*old-fashioned, informal*) people who write and publish popular songs **ORIGIN** From the name of the part of New York where many such people worked in the past.

tin·plate /ˈtɪnpleɪt/ *noun* [U] a metal material made from iron and steel and covered with a layer of tin

tin·pot /ˈtɪnpɑt/ *adj.* [only before noun] (*disapproving*) (especially of a leader or government) not important and of little worth or use: *a tinpot dictator*

tin·sel /ˈtɪnsl/ *noun* [U] strips of shiny material like metal, used as decorations, especially at Christmas

Tin·sel·town /ˈtɪnslˌtaʊn/ *noun* [U] (*informal*) a way of referring to Hollywood, the center of the U.S. movie industry

tint /tɪnt/ *noun, verb*
● *noun* **1** a shade or small amount of a particular color; a faint color covering a surface: *leaves with red and gold autumn tints* ◆ *the brownish tint of an old photo* ⟳ *thesaurus box at* COLOR **2** an artificial color used to change the color of your hair; the act of coloring the hair with a tint: *a blond tint* ◆ *to have a tint*
● *verb* **1** [usually passive] ~ **sth (with sth)** to add a small amount of color to something **2** ~ **sth** to change the color of someone's hair with a tint ▶ **tint·ed** *adj.*: *tinted glasses*

T-inter·section *noun* a place where one road joins another but does not cross it, so that the roads form the shape of the letter T

tin·tin·nab·u·la·tion /ˌtɪntəˌnæbyəˈleɪʃn/ *noun* [U, C] (*formal*) a ringing sound

tin whistle (also **penny whistle**) *noun* a simple musical instrument like a short pipe with six holes, that you play by blowing

ti·ny 🔑 /ˈtaɪni/ *adj.* (**ti·ni·er, ti·ni·est**) very small in size or amount: *a tiny baby* ◆ *Only a tiny minority hold such extreme views.* **IDM see** PATTER *n.*

-tion /ʃn/ ⟳ -ION

tip /tɪp/ noun, verb

● **noun**

▷ **END OF SOMETHING 1** the thin pointed end of something: *the tips of your fingers* ◆ *the tip of your nose* ◆ *the northern tip of the island* ⟳ see also FINGERTIP **2** a small part that fits on or over the end of something: *a walking stick with a rubber tip* ⟳ see also FELT-TIP PEN, FILTER TIP

▷ **ADVICE 3** a small piece of advice about something practical **SYN** HINT: **~ (on/for doing sth)** *handy tips for buying a computer* ◆ **~ (on/for sth)** *useful tips on how to save money* **4** (*informal*) a secret or expert piece of advice about what the result of a competition, etc. is likely to be, especially about which horse is likely to win a race: *a hot tip for the big race* **5** (also **'tip-off**) (*informal*) secret information that someone gives, for example to the police, to warn them about an illegal activity that is going to happen: *The man was arrested after an anonymous tip.*

▷ **EXTRA MONEY 6** a small amount of extra money that you give to someone, for example someone who serves you in a restaurant: *to leave a tip* ◆ *He gave the waiter a generous tip.*

IDM **on the tip of your tongue** if a word or name is **on the tip of your tongue**, you are sure that you know it but you cannot remember it **the tip of the iceberg** only a small part of a much larger problem

● **verb** (**-pp-**)

▷ **LEAN/POUR/PUSH AT AN ANGLE 1** [I, T] to move so that one end or side is higher than the other; to move something into this position **SYN** TILT: **(+ adv./prep.)** *The boat tipped to one side.* ◆ *The seat tips forward to allow passengers into the back.* ◆ **~ sth (+ adv./prep.)** *She tipped her head back and laughed loudly.* ◆ *We'll have to tip the sofa up to get it through the door.* **2** [T] **~ sth/sb + adv./prep.** to make something or someone come out of a container or its/their position by holding or lifting it/them at an angle: *She tipped the dirty water down the drain.* ◆ *The bus stopped abruptly, nearly tipping me out of my seat.* **3** [T] **~ sth + adv./prep.** to touch something lightly so that it moves in a particular direction: *The forward just managed to tip the ball into the net.*

▷ **GIVE EXTRA MONEY 4** [I, T] to give someone an extra amount of money to thank them for something they have done for you as part of their job: *Americans were always welcome because they tended to tip heavily.* ◆ **~ sb** *Did you remember to tip the waiter?* ◆ **~ sb sth** *She tipped the porter a dollar.*

▷ **PREDICT SUCCESS 5** [T] to say in advance that someone or something will be successful: **~ sb/sth (for sth)** *The band is being tipped for the top.* ◆ **~ sb/sth as sth** *The senator has been tipped by many as a future president.* ◆ **~ sb/sth to do sth** *The actor is tipped to win an Oscar for his performance.*

▷ **COVER END 6** [T, usually passive] **~ sth (with sth)** to cover the end or edge of something with a color, a substance, etc.: *The wings are tipped with yellow.*

IDM **tip the balance/scales** (also **swing the balance**) to affect the result of something in one way rather than another: *In an interview, smart presentation can tip the scales in your favor.* **tip your hand** (also **show your hand/cards**) to make your plans or intentions known **tip the scales at sth** to weigh a particular amount: *He tipped the scales at just over 175 pounds.* ⟳ more at HAT

PHR V **,tip sb↔'off (about sth)** (*informal*) to warn someone about something that is going to happen, especially something illegal: *Three men were arrested after police were tipped off about the raid.* ◆ **~ that…** *They were tipped off that he might be living in Arkansas.* ⟳ related noun TIP-OFF **,tip 'over** | **,tip sth↔'over** to fall or turn over; to make something do this: *The mug tipped over, spilling hot coffee everywhere.*

'tip-off noun **1** (*informal*) a sign that gives you information that is not obvious or expected: *Her silence was a tip-off that she didn't agree with us.* **2** (in basketball) a JUMP BALL (= a ball thrown into the air that a player from each team jumps and tries to catch) that begins a game: *The news of his injury came just two hours before tip-off.* **3** (also tip) (*informal*) secret information that someone gives, for example to the police, to warn them about an illegal activity that is going to happen: *The man was arrested after an anonymous tip-off.*

tip·per /'tɪpər/ noun (used with an adjective) a person who gives someone a TIP (= a small amount of extra money to thank them for doing something as part of their job) of the size mentioned: *She says that New Yorkers are usually big tippers.*

tip·pet /'tɪpət/ noun a long piece of fur worn in the past by a woman around the neck and shoulders, with the ends hanging down in front; a similar piece of clothing worn by judges, priests, etc.

'tipping ,point noun the point at which the number of small changes over a period of time reaches a level where a further small change has a sudden and very great effect on a system or leads to an idea suddenly spreading quickly among a large number of people

tip·ple /'tɪpl/ noun, verb

● **noun** [usually sing.] (*informal*) an alcoholic drink: *His favorite tipple was rum and lemon.*

● **verb** [I, T] **~ (sth)** (*informal*) to drink alcohol ▸ **tip·pler** /'tɪplər/ noun

tip·ster /'tɪpstər/ noun **1** a person who tells you, often in exchange for money, which horse is likely to win a race, so that you can bet on it and win money **2** a person who gives information to the police about a crime or criminal

tip·sy /'tɪpsi/ adj. (*informal*) slightly drunk **SYN** TIGHT

tip·toe /'tɪptoʊ/ noun, verb

● **noun**

IDM **on tiptoe/tiptoes** standing or walking on the front part of your foot, with your heels off the ground, in order to make yourself taller or to move very quietly: *She had to stand on tiptoe to reach the top shelf.* ◆ *We crept around on tiptoes so as not to disturb him.*

● **verb** [I] **(+ adv./prep.)** to walk using the front parts of your feet only, so that other people cannot hear you: *I tiptoed over to the window.*

,tip-'top adj. [usually before noun] (*informal*) excellent: *The house is in tip-top condition.*

ti·rade /'taɪreɪd/ noun **~ (against sb/sth)** a long angry speech criticizing someone or something or accusing someone of something: *She launched into a tirade of abuse against politicians.*

tir·a·mi·su /ˌtɪrəmi'su; -'misu/ noun [U] an Italian DESSERT (= sweet dish) made from layers of cake with coffee, chocolate, and MASCARPONE cheese

tire /'taɪər/ verb, noun

● **verb** [I, T] **~ (sb)** to become tired and feel as if you want to sleep or rest; to make someone feel this way: *Her legs were beginning to tire.* ◆ *He has made a good recovery but still tires easily.*

IDM **never tire of doing sth** to do something a lot, especially in a way that annoys people: *He went to Harvard—as he never tires of reminding us.*

PHR V **'tire of sth/sb** to become bored with something or someone or begin to enjoy it/them less: *They soon tired of the beach and went for a walk.* **,tire sb/yourself 'out** to make someone/yourself feel very tired ⟳ see also TIRED

● **noun** a thick rubber ring that fits around the edge of a wheel of a car, bicycle, etc.: *a front tire* ◆ *a back/rear tire* ◆ *to pump up a tire* ◆ *a flat/burst/punctured tire* ◆ *bald/worn tires* ◆ *to check your tire pressure* ⟳ picture at CAR, BICYCLE ⟳ collocations at DRIVING ⟳ see also SPARE TIRE

tired /'taɪərd/ adj.

1 feeling that you would like to sleep or rest; needing rest **SYN** WEARY: *to be/look/feel tired* ◆ *I'm too tired even to think.* ◆ *They were cold, hungry, and tired out (= very tired).* ◆ *tired feet* **2** feeling that you have had enough of someone or something because you no longer find them/it interesting or because they make you angry or unhappy: **~ of sb/sth** *I'm sick and tired of all the arguments.* ◆ **~ of doing sth** *She was tired of hearing about their trip to India.* **3** boring because it is too familiar or has been used too much: *He always comes out with the same tired old jokes.* ▸ **tired·ly** adv.: *He shook his head tiredly.* **tired·ness** noun [U] ⟳ see also DOG-TIRED

'tire ˌiron *noun* a metal tool for taking tires off wheels

tire·less /'taɪərləs/ *adj.* (*approving*) putting a lot of hard work and energy into something over a long period of time **SYN** INDEFATIGABLE: *a tireless campaigner for human rights* ▶ **tire·less·ly** *adv.*

tire·some /'taɪərsəm/ *adj.* making you feel annoyed **SYN** ANNOYING: *Buying a house can be a very tiresome business.* ◆ *The children were being very tiresome.* ▶ **tire·some·ly** *adv.*

tir·ing 🔑 /'taɪərɪŋ/ *adj.*
making you feel the need to sleep or rest **SYN** EXHAUSTING: *It had been a long tiring day.*

'tis /tɪz/ *abbr.* (*old use*) it is

tis·sue /'tɪʃu/ *noun* **1** [C] a piece of soft paper that absorbs liquids, used especially as a HANDKERCHIEF: *a box of tissues* **2** [U] (also **tis·sues** [pl.]) a collection of cells that form the different parts of humans, animals, and plants: *muscle/ brain/nerve, etc. tissue* ◆ *scar tissue* **3** (also **'tissue ˌpaper**) [U] very thin paper used for wrapping and packing things that break easily
IDM **a tissue of lies** (*literary*) a story, an excuse, etc. that is full of lies

Ti·tan /'taɪtn/ also **titan** *noun* (*formal*) a person who is very large, strong, intelligent, or important **ORIGIN** From the Titans, who in Greek mythology were the older gods who were defeated in a battle with Zeus.

ti·tan·ic /taɪ'tænɪk/ *adj.* (*formal*) very large, important, strong, or difficult: *a titanic struggle between good and evil*

ti·ta·ni·um /taɪ'teɪniəm/ *noun* [U] (*symb.* **Ti**) a chemical element. Titanium is a silver-white metal used in making various strong light materials.

ˌtit for 'tat /ˌtɪt fər 'tæt/ *noun* [U] a situation in which you do something bad to someone because they have done the same to you: *the routine tit for tat when countries expel each other's envoys* ◆ *tit-for-tat assassinations by rival gangs*

tithe /taɪð/ *noun* **1** (in the past) a tenth of the goods that someone produced or the money that they earned, that was paid as a tax to support the Church **2** (in some Christian Churches today) a tenth of a person's income, that they give to the Church

tit·il·late /'tɪtlˌeɪt/ *verb* [I, T] (often *disapproving*) to interest or excite someone, especially in a sexual way: *titillating pictures* ◆ *~ sth a story intended to titillate the imagination of the public* ▶ **tit·il·la·tion** /ˌtɪtl'eɪʃn/ *noun* [U]

ti·tle 🔑 /'taɪtl/ *noun, verb*
● *noun* **1** [C] the name of a book, poem, painting, piece of music, etc.: *His poems were published under the title of "Love and Reason."* ◆ *the title track from their latest CD* (= the song with the same title as the disk) ◆ *She has sung the title role in "Carmen"* (= the role of Carmen in that OPERA). **2** [C] a particular book or magazine: *The company publishes twenty new titles a year.* **3** [C] a word in front of a person's name to show their rank or profession, whether or not they are married, etc.: *The present duke inherited the title from his father.* ◆ *Give your name and title* (= Mr., Miss, Ms., Dr., etc.). ➲ note at NAME **4** [C] a name that describes a job: *The official title of the job is "Administrative Assistant."* **5** [C] the position of being the winner of a competition, especially a sports competition: *the world heavyweight title* ◆ *She has three world titles.* **6** [U, C] *~ (to sth/to do sth)* (*law*) the legal right to own something, especially land or property; the document that shows you have this right
● *verb* [usually passive] *~ sth + noun* to give a book, piece of music, etc. a particular name: *Their first album was titled "Made in Valmez."*

'title ˌbar *noun* (*computing*) a bar at the top of a computer screen, that shows the name of the program and file that is on the screen

ti·tled /'taɪtld/ *adj.* having a title such as Lord, LADY, etc.

'title ˌdeed *noun* [usually pl.] a legal document proving that someone is the owner of a particular house, etc.

'title-ˌholder *noun* **1** a person or team that has defeated all the other people or teams taking part in an important competition: *the current Olympic title-holder* **2** (*technical*) the legal owner of something

'title ˌpage *noun* a page at the front of a book that has the title and the author's name on it

ti·tlist /'taɪtl·ɪst/ *noun* someone who has won a sports title: *a boxing titlist* **SYN** CHAMPION

tit·mouse /'tɪtmaʊs/ *noun* (*pl.* **tit·mice** /-maɪs/) a small American SONGBIRD

ti·trate /'taɪtreɪt/ *verb* *~ sth* (*chemistry*) to find out how much of a particular substance is in a liquid by measuring how much of another substance is needed to react with it ▶ **ti·tra·tion** /taɪ'treɪʃn/ *noun* [U]

tit·ter /'tɪtər/ *verb* [I] to laugh quietly, especially in a nervous or embarrassed way **SYN** GIGGLE ▶ **tit·ter** *noun*

tit·u·lar /'tɪtʃələr/ *adj.* [only before noun] **1** (*formal*) having a particular title or status but no real power or authority **SYN** NOMINAL: *the titular head of state* **2** the **titular** character of a book, play, movie, etc. is the one mentioned in the title **SYN** EPONYMOUS

tix /tɪks/ *noun* [pl.] (*informal*) tickets: *Tix are $9 for members and $13 for guests.*

tiz·zy /'tɪzi/ (also **tizz** /tɪz/) *noun* [sing.] (*informal*) a state of nervous excitement or confusion: *She worked herself into a tizzy before the meeting.*

TLC /ˌti el 'si/ *noun* [U] (*informal*) the abbreviation for "tender loving care" (care that you give someone to make them feel better): *What he needs now is just rest and a lot of TLC.*

Tlin·git /'tlɪŋɡət/ *noun* (*pl.* **Tlin·git** or **Tlin·gits**) a member of a Native American people, many of whom live in Alaska and British Columbia, Canada

TM /ˌti 'em/ *abbr.* **1** TRADEMARK **2** (also **T.M.**) TRANSCENDENTAL MEDITATION™

TN *abbr.* (in writing) Tennessee

TNT /ˌti ɛn 'ti/ *noun* [U] a powerful EXPLOSIVE

to 🔑 /tə; *strong form and often before vowels* tu/ *prep., infinitive marker, adv.*
● *prep.* **HELP** For the special uses of **to** in phrasal verbs, look at the entries for the verbs. For example, **see to something** is in the phrasal verb section at **see**. **1** in the direction of something; toward something: *I walked to the office.* ◆ *It fell to the ground.* ◆ *It was on the way to the station.* ◆ *He's going to Paris.* ◆ *my first visit to Africa* ◆ *He pointed to something on the opposite bank.* ◆ *Her childhood was spent traveling from place to place.* **2** *~ the sth (of sth)* located in the direction mentioned from something: *Place the cursor to the left of the first word.* ◆ *There are mountains to the north.* **3** as far as something: *The meadows lead down to the river.* ◆ *Her hair fell to her waist.* **4** reaching a particular state: *The vegetables were cooked to perfection.* ◆ *He tore the letter to pieces.* ◆ *She sang the baby to sleep.* ◆ *The letter reduced her to tears* (= made her cry). ◆ *His expression changed from amazement to joy.* **5** used to show the end or limit of a range or period of time: *a drop in profits from $105 million to around $75 million* ◆ *I'd say he was 25 to 30 years old* (= approximately 25 or 30 years old). ◆ *I like all kinds of music from opera to reggae.* ◆ *We only work from Monday to Friday.* ◆ *I watched the program from beginning to end.* **6** before the start of something: *How long is it to lunch?* ◆ *It's five to ten* (= five minutes before ten o'clock). **7** used to show the person or thing that receives something: *He gave it to his sister.* ◆ *I'll explain to you where everything goes.* ◆ *I am deeply grateful to my parents.* ◆ *Who did she address the letter to?* ◆ (*formal*) *To whom did she address the letter?* **8** used to show the person or thing that is affected by an action: *She is devoted to her family.* ◆ *What have you done to your hair?* **9** used to show that two things are attached or connected: *Attach this rope to the front of the car.* **10** used to show a relationship between one person or thing and

another: *She's married to an Italian.* ◆ *the Japanese ambassador to France* ◆ *the key to the door* ◆ *the solution to this problem* **11** directed toward; concerning: *It was a threat to world peace.* ◆ *She made a reference to her recent book.* **12** used to introduce the second part of a comparison or RATIO: *I prefer walking to climbing.* ◆ *The industry today is nothing to what it once was.* ◆ *We won by six goals to three.* **13** used to show a quantity or rate: *There are 2.54 centimeters to an inch.* ◆ *This car does 30 miles to the gallon.* ⟳ compare PER **14** in honor of someone or something: *a monument to the soldiers who died in the war* ◆ *Let's drink to Julia and her new job.* **15** while something else is happening or being done: *He left the stage to prolonged applause.* **16** used after verbs of movement to mean "with the intention of giving something": *People rushed to her rescue and picked her up.* **17** used to show someone's attitude or reaction to something: *His music isn't really to my taste.* ◆ *To her astonishment, he smiled.* **18** used to show what someone's opinion or feeling about something is: *It sounded like crying to me.*

● **infinitive marker** HELP To is often used before the base form of a verb to show that the verb is in the infinitive. The infinitive is used after many verbs and also after many nouns and adjectives. **1** used to show purpose or intention: *I set out to buy food.* ◆ *I am going to tell you a story.* ◆ *She was determined to do well.* ◆ *His aim was to become president.* ◆ *To be honest with you, I don't remember what he said.* **2** used to show the result of something: *She managed to escape.* ◆ *It was too hot to go out.* ◆ *He couldn't get close enough to see.* **3** used to show the cause of something: *I'm sorry to hear that.* **4** used to show an action that you want or are advised to do: *I'd love to go to France this summer.* ◆ *The leaflet explains how to apply for a position.* ◆ *I don't know what to say.* HELP To can also be used without a verb following when the missing verb is easy to understand: *He asked her to come but she said she didn't want to.* **5** used to show something that is known or reported about a particular person or thing: *The house was said to be haunted.* **6** used to show that one action immediately follows another: *I reached the station only to find that my train had already left.* **7 am, is, are, was, were ~** used to show that you must or should do something: *You are not to talk during the exam.* ◆ *She was to be here at 8:30 but she didn't arrive.*

● **adv.** (usually of a door) in or into a closed position: *Push the door to.*

IDM **to and fro** backward and forward: *She rocked the baby to and fro.* HELP For the special uses of **to** in phrasal verbs, look at the entries for the verbs. For example, **set to** is in the phrasal verb section at **set**.

toad /toud/ *noun* **1** a small animal like a FROG but with a drier and less smooth skin, that lives on land but breeds in water (= is an AMPHIBIAN) ⟳ picture at ANIMAL **2** (*informal, disapproving*) an unpleasant person

toad·stool /'toudstul/ *noun* a FUNGUS with a round, flat, or curved head and a short STEM. Many types of toadstools are poisonous. ⟳ compare MUSHROOM

toad·y /'toudi/ *noun, verb*
● **noun** (*pl.* toad·ies) (*disapproving*) a person who treats someone more important with special kindness or respect in order to gain their favor or help SYN SYCOPHANT
● **verb** (toad·ies, toad·y·ing, toad·ied, toad·ied) [I] **~ (to sb)** (*disapproving*) to treat someone more important with special kindness or respect in order to gain their favor or help

toast /toust/ *noun, verb*
● **noun 1** [U] slices of bread that have been made brown and crisp by heating them on both sides in a toaster or under a BROILER: *cheese on toast* ◆ *a piece of toast* ◆ *two slices of toast* ⟳ see also FRENCH TOAST **2** [C] **~ (to sb/sth)** the act of a group of people wishing someone happiness, success, etc. by drinking a glass of something, especially alcohol, at the same time: *I'd like to **propose a toast** to the bride and groom.* ◆ *The committee **drank a toast** to the new project.* **3** [sing.] **the ~ of...** a person who is praised by a lot of people in a particular place because of something that they have done well: *The performance made her the toast of the festival.*

IDM **be toast** (*informal*) to be likely to die or be destroyed: *One mistake and you're toast.*
● **verb 1** [T] **~ sb/sth** to lift a glass of wine, etc. in the air and drink it at the same time as other people in order to wish someone or something success, happiness, etc.: *The happy couple were toasted in champagne.* ◆ *We toasted the success of the new company.* **2** [T, I] **~ (sth)** to make something, especially bread, turn brown by heating it in a toaster or close to heat; to turn brown in this way: *a toasted sandwich* ◆ *Place under a hot broiler until the nuts have toasted.* ⟳ picture at COOKING ⟳ collocations at COOKING **3** [T] **~ sth** to warm a part of your body by placing it near a fire

toast·er /'toustər/ *noun* an electrical machine that you put slices of bread in to make toast ⟳ picture at COOKING

toast·mas·ter /'toust,mæstər/ *noun* a person who introduces the speakers at a formal dinner and calls for people to drink something together in honor of particular people (= proposes TOASTS)

toast·y /'tousti/ *adj.* warm and comfortable

to·bac·co /tə'bækou/ *noun* (*pl.* to·bac·cos) [U, C] the dried leaves of the tobacco plant that are used for making cigarettes, smoking in a pipe, or chewing: *The government imposed a ban on tobacco advertising* (= the advertising of cigarettes and all other forms of tobacco).

to·bac·co·nist /tə'bækənɪst/ *noun* **1** a person who owns, manages, or works in a store selling cigarettes, tobacco for pipes, etc. **2 tobacconist's** (*pl.* tobacconists) a store that sells cigarettes, tobacco, etc.: *There's a tobacconist's on the corner.*

to·bog·gan /tə'bagən/ *noun, verb*
● **noun** a long, light, narrow SLED (= a vehicle that slides over snow), sometimes curved up in front, used for sliding down slopes
● **verb** [I] to travel down a slope on snow or ice using a toboggan ▶ **to·bog·gan·ing** *noun* [U]

toc·ca·ta /tə'kɑtə/ *noun* a piece of music for a keyboard instrument which includes difficult passages designed to show the player's skill

toc·sin /'taksn/ *noun* (*old use*) a warning bell or signal

to·day 🔑 /tə'deɪ/ *adv., noun*
● **adv. 1** on this day: *I have a piano lesson later today.* ◆ *The exams start a week from today.* **2** at the present period SYN NOWADAYS: *Young people today face a very difficult future at work.*
● **noun** [U] **1** this day: *Today is her tenth birthday.* ◆ *The review is in today's paper.* ◆ *I'm leaving a week from today.* **2** the present period of time: *today's young people*

tod·dle /'tadl/ *verb* **1** [I] when a young child who has just learned to walk **toddles**, he/she walks with short, unsteady steps **2** [I] **+ adv./prep.** (*informal*) to walk or go somewhere: *She toddles down to the park most afternoons.*

tod·dler /'tadlər/ *noun* a child who has only recently learned to walk

tod·dy /'tadi/ *noun* [C, U] (*pl.* tod·dies) [C, U] a drink made with strong alcohol, sugar, hot water, and sometimes spices: *a hot toddy*

to-do /tə 'du/ *noun* [sing.] (*informal*, becoming *old-fashioned*) unnecessary excitement or anger about something SYN FUSS: *What a to-do!*

to-'do list *noun* a list of tasks that you have to do: *Don't worry, it's on my to-do list.*

toe 🔑 /tou/ *noun, verb*
● **noun 1** one of the five small parts that stick out from the foot: *the big/little toe* (= the largest/smallest toe) ◆ *I stubbed my toe on the step.* ◆ *Can you touch your toes?* (= by bending over while keeping your legs straight) ⟳ picture at BODY **2** the part of a sock, shoe, etc. that covers the toes ⟳ picture at SHOE **3 -toed** (in adjectives) having the type or number of toes mentioned: *open-toed sandals* ◆ *a three-toed sloth* ⟳ see also PIGEON-TOED

ʌ **cup**   ə **about**   eɪ **say**   aɪ **five**   ɔɪ **boy**   aʊ **now**   oʊ **go**   ər **bird**

IDM **go/stand/fight toe to toe (with sb)** (used of two people or groups) to directly oppose each other: *He went toe to toe with the boss this morning.* **keep sb on their toes** to make sure that someone is ready to deal with anything that might happen by doing things that they are not expecting: *Surprise visits help to keep the staff on their toes.* **make sb's toes curl** to make someone feel embarrassed or uncomfortable ⟳ more at DIG *v.*, DIP *v.*, HEAD *n.*, STEP *v.*, TOP *n.*

● *verb*
  IDM **toe the line/mark** to say or do what someone in authority tells you to say or do, even if you do not share the same opinions, etc.: *to toe the party line*

toe·cap /ˈtoʊkæp/ *noun* a piece of metal or leather that covers the front part of a shoe or boot to make it stronger

ᵗtoe-ˌcurling *adj.* (*informal*) extremely embarrassing because of being very bad or silly ▶ **ᵗtoe-ˌcurlingly** *adv.*: *a toe-curlingly awful movie*

TOEFL™ /ˈtoʊfl/ *abbr.* Test of English as a Foreign Language (a test of a person's level of English that is taken in order to go to a university in the U.S.)

toe·hold /ˈtoʊhoʊld/ *noun* **1** a position in a place or an activity that you hope will lead to more power or success: *The company is anxious to gain a toehold in Europe.* **2** a very small hole or space on a CLIFF, just big enough to put your foot in when you are climbing

TOEIC™ /ˈtoʊɪk/ *noun* [U] the abbreviation for "Test of English for International Communication" (a test that measures your ability to read and understand English if it is not your first language)

toe·nail /ˈtoʊneɪl/ *noun* the nail on a toe ⟳ picture at BODY

ᵗtoe-ˌtapping *adj.* (*informal*) (of music) lively and making you want to move your feet

ˌtoe-to-ˈtoe *adj.* a toe-to-toe argument, etc., is one in which two people or groups are directly opposed to each other: *a toe-to-toe confrontation* ⟳ see also TOE *n.*

tof·fee /ˈtɔfi; ˈtɑ-/ *noun* [U, C] a hard, sticky candy made by heating sugar, butter, and water together and allowing it to cool

to·fu /ˈtoʊfu/ (also **ᵗbean curd**) *noun* [U] a soft white substance that is made from SOY and used in cooking, often instead of meat

tog /tɑg/
● *noun* **togs** [pl.] (*informal*, becoming *old-fashioned*) clothes, especially ones that you wear for a particular purpose: *running togs*

to·ga /ˈtoʊgə/ *noun* a loose outer piece of clothing worn by the citizens of ancient Rome

to·geth·er 🔑 /təˈgɛðər/ *adv., adj.*
● *adv.* **HELP** For the special uses of **together** in phrasal verbs, look at the entries for the verbs. For example, **pull yourself together** is in the phrasal verb section at **pull**. **1** with or near to someone or something else; with each other: *Together they climbed the dark stairs.* ◆ *Get all the ingredients together before you start cooking.* ◆ *Stay close together —I don't want anyone to get lost.* **2** so that two or more things touch or are joined to or combined with each other: *He rubbed his hands together in satisfaction.* ◆ *She nailed the two boards together.* ◆ *Mix the sand and cement together.* ◆ *He has more money than the rest of us put together.* **3** (of two people) in a close relationship, for example a marriage: *They split up after ten years together.* **4** in or into agreement: *After the meeting the two sides in the dispute were no closer together.* **5** at the same time: *They both spoke together.* ◆ (*informal*) *All together now: "Happy birthday to you…"* **6 for hours, days, etc. ~** (*formal*) for hours, days, etc. without stopping: *She sat for hours together just staring into space.*
  IDM **together with 1** including: *Together with the Johnsons, there were 12 of us in the house.* **2** in addition to; as well as: *I sent my order, together with a check for $40.*

● *adj.* (*informal*, *approving*) (of a person) well organized and confident: *He's incredibly together for someone so young.*

to·geth·er·ness /təˈgɛðərnəs/ *noun* [U] the happy feeling you have when you are with people you like, especially family and friends

tog·gle /ˈtɑgl/ *noun, verb*
● *noun* **1** a short piece of wood, plastic, etc. that is put through a LOOP of thread to fasten something, such as a coat or bag, instead of a button ⟳ picture at CLOTHES **2** (also **ᵗtoggle ˌswitch**) (*computing*) a key on a computer that you press to change from one style or operation to another, and back again
● *verb* [I, T] (*computing*) to press a key or set of keys on a computer keyboard in order to turn a feature on or off, or to move from one program, etc. to another: **~ (between A and B)** *He toggled between the two windows.* ◆ **~ sth** *This key toggles various views of the data.*

ᵗtoggle ˌswitch *noun* **1** an electrical switch that you move up and down or backward and forward **2** (*computing*) = TOGGLE

toil /tɔɪl/ *verb, noun*
● *verb* (*formal*) **1** [I] to work very hard and/or for a long time, usually doing hard physical work **SYN** SLAVE AWAY **2** [I] **+ adv./prep.** to move slowly and with difficulty **SYN** SLOG: *They toiled up the hill in the blazing sun.* ▶ **toil·er** *noun*
● *noun* [U] (*formal* or *literary*) hard unpleasant work that makes you very tired: *a life of hardship and toil* ⟳ see also TOILS

toi·let 🔑 /ˈtɔɪlət/ *noun*
1 [C] a large bowl attached to a pipe that you sit on or stand over when you get rid of waste matter from your body: *Have you flushed the toilet?* ◆ *I need to use the toilet* (= use the toilet). ◆ *a toilet seat* ◆ *toilet facilities* ◆ *Do you need the toilet?* **2** [U] (*old-fashioned*) the process of washing and dressing yourself, arranging your hair, etc.

ᵗtoilet ˌpaper (also **ᵗtoilet ˌtissue**) *noun* [U] thin soft paper used for cleaning yourself after you have used the toilet: *a roll of toilet paper*

toi·let·ries /ˈtɔɪlətriz/ *noun* [pl.] things such as soap or TOOTHPASTE that you use for washing, cleaning your teeth, etc.

ᵗtoiletry ˌbag *noun* a small bag for holding your soap, TOOTHBRUSH, etc. when you are traveling

ᵗtoilet-ˌtrain *verb* [usually passive] **~ sb** to teach a small child to use the toilet ▶ **ᵗtoilet-ˌtrained** *adj.* **ᵗtoilet-ˌtraining** *noun* [U]

ᵗtoilet ˌwater *noun* [U, C] a kind of PERFUME (= a pleasant-smelling liquid for the skin) that has water added to it and is not very expensive

toke /toʊk/ *noun* (*informal*) an act of breathing in smoke from a cigarette containing MARIJUANA ▶ **toke** *verb* [I, T]

to·ken /ˈtoʊkən/ *noun, adj.*
● *noun* **1** a round piece of metal or plastic used instead of money to operate some machines or as a form of payment: *a parking token* **2** something that is a symbol of a feeling, a fact, an event, etc. **SYN** EXPRESSION, MARK: *Please accept this small gift as a token of our gratitude.*
  IDM **by the same token** for the same reasons: *The penalty for failure will be high. But, by the same token, the rewards for success will be great.*
● *adj.* [only before noun] **1** involving very little effort or feeling and intended only as a way of showing other people that you think someone or something is important, when really you are not sincere: *The government has only made a token gesture toward helping the unemployed.* ◆ *There was one token woman on the committee* (= a woman who is included in the group to make it look as if women are always included, although that is not true). **2** done as a symbol to show that you are serious about something and will keep a promise or an agreement or do more later: *The government agreed to send a small token force to the area.* ◆ *a one-day token strike* **3** (of a small amount of money) that you pay or charge

someone only as a symbol, because a payment is expected **SYN** NOMINAL: *We charge only a token fee for use of the facilities.*

to·ken·ism /ˈtoʊkəˌnɪzəm/ *noun* [U] (*disapproving*) the fact of doing something only in order to do what the law requires or to satisfy a particular group of people, but not in a way that is really sincere: *Appointing one woman to the otherwise all-male staff could look like tokenism.*

Tok Pis·in /ˌtɔk ˈpɪzn; ˌtak-; -ˈpɪsn/ (also **Pidg·in**) *noun* [U] a CREOLE language based on English, used in Papua New Guinea

told *pt, pp of* TELL

tol·er·a·ble /ˈtɑlərəbl/ *adj.* (*formal*) **1** fairly good, but not of the best quality **SYN** REASONABLE: *a tolerable degree of success* **2** that you can accept or bear, although unpleasant or painful **SYN** BEARABLE: *At times, the heat was barely tolerable.* **ANT** INTOLERABLE ► **tol·er·a·bly** /-bli/ *adv.*: *He plays the piano tolerably (well).*

tol·er·ance /ˈtɑlərəns/ *noun* **1** [U] ~ **(of/for sb/sth)** the willingness to accept or TOLERATE someone or something, especially opinions or behavior that you may not agree with, or people who are not like you: *She had no tolerance for jokes of any kind.* ◆ *religious tolerance* ◆ *a reputation for tolerance toward refugees* ⟳ see also ZERO TOLERANCE **2** [C, U] ~ **(to sth)** the ability to suffer something, especially pain, difficult conditions, etc. without being harmed: *tolerance to cold* ◆ *Tolerance to alcohol decreases with age.* **3** [C, U] (*technical*) the amount by which the measurement of a value can vary without causing problems: *They were working to a tolerance of 0.0001 of a centimeter.*

tol·er·ant /ˈtɑlərənt/ *adj.* **1** ~ **(of/toward sb/sth)** able to accept what other people say or do even if you do not agree with it: *He has a very tolerant attitude toward other religions.* **2** ~ **(of sth)** (of plants, animals, or machines) able to survive or operate in difficult conditions: *The plants are tolerant of frost.* **ANT** INTOLERANT ► **tol·er·ant·ly** *adv.*

tol·er·ate /ˈtɑləˌreɪt/ *verb* **1** to allow someone to do something that you do not agree with or like **SYN** PUT UP WITH: ~ **sth** *Their relationship was tolerated but not encouraged.* ◆ *This sort of behavior will not be tolerated.* ◆ ~ **(sb/sth) doing/being/having sth** *She refused to tolerate being called a liar.* **2** ~ **sb/sth** to accept someone or something that is annoying, unpleasant, etc. without complaining **SYN** PUT UP WITH: *There is a limit to what one person can tolerate.* ◆ *I don't know how you tolerate that noise!* **3** ~ **sth** to be able to be affected by a drug, difficult conditions, etc. without being harmed: *She tolerated the chemotherapy well.* ◆ *Few plants will tolerate sudden changes in temperature.*

tol·er·a·tion /ˌtɑləˈreɪʃn/ *noun* [U] a willingness to allow something that you do not like or agree with to happen or continue **SYN** TOLERANCE: *religious toleration*

toll /toʊl/ *noun, verb*
● *noun* **1** [C] money that you pay to use a particular road or bridge: *motorway tolls* ◆ *a toll road/bridge* ⟳ thesaurus box at RATE **2** [C, usually sing.] the amount of damage or the number of deaths and injuries that are caused in a particular war, disaster, etc.: *The official death toll has now reached 7,000.* ◆ *the war's growing casualty toll* **3** [sing.] the sound of a bell ringing with slow, regular strokes **4** [C] a charge for a telephone call that is calculated at a higher rate than a local call
IDM **take a heavy toll (on sb/sth)** | **take its toll (on sb/sth)** to have a bad effect on someone or something; to cause a lot of damage, deaths, suffering, etc.: *Illness had taken a heavy toll on her.* ◆ *The recession is taking its toll on the housing markets.*
● *verb* [I, T] when a bell **tolls** or someone **tolls** it, it is rung slowly many times, especially as a sign that someone has died: ~ **sth** *The Abbey bell tolled for those killed in the war.* ◆ ~ **sth** *The bell tolled the hour.* ◆ (*figurative*) *The revolution tolled the death knell* (= signaled the end) *for the Russian monarchy.*

toll·booth /ˈtoʊlbuθ/ *noun* a small building by the side of a

road where you pay to drive on a road, go over a bridge, etc.

toll call *noun* a long-distance telephone call, for which you pay a toll: *She made a toll call to a store in New Jersey.* ⟳ compare TOLL-FREE

toll-free *adj.* (of a telephone call to an organization or a service) that you do not have to pay for: *a toll-free number*

toll·gate /ˈtoʊlɡeɪt/ *noun* a gate across a road where you stop and pay to drive on a road, go over a bridge, etc.

toll·house cook·ie /ˌtoʊlhaʊs ˈkʊki/ *noun* a crisp sweet cookie that contains small pieces of chocolate

toll plaza *noun* a row of TOLLBOOTHS across a road

Tom /tɑm/ *noun*
IDM **any/every Tom, Dick, or Harry** /ˌtɑm ˌdɪk ər ˈhæri/ (usually *disapproving*) any ordinary person rather than the people you know or people who have special skills or qualities: *We don't want any Tom, Dick, or Harry using the club bar.*

tom /tɑm/ *noun* = TOMCAT

tom·a·hawk /ˈtɑməˌhɔk/ *noun* a light AX used by Native Americans

to·ma·to 🔑 /təˈmeɪtoʊ/ *noun* [C, U] (*pl.* **to·ma·toes**) a soft fruit with a lot of juice and shiny red skin that is eaten as a vegetable either raw or cooked: *a bacon, lettuce, and tomato sandwich* ◆ *sliced tomatoes* ◆ *tomato plants* ⟳ picture at FRUIT

tomb /tum/ *noun* a large grave, especially one built of stone above or below the ground

tom·boy /ˈtɑmbɔɪ/ *noun* a young girl who enjoys activities and games that are traditionally considered to be for boys

tomb·stone /ˈtumstoʊn/ *noun* a large flat stone that lies over a grave or stands at one end, that shows the name, age, etc. of the person buried there ⟳ compare GRAVESTONE, HEADSTONE

tom·cat /ˈtɑmkæt/ (also **tom**) *noun* a male cat

tome /toʊm/ *noun* (*formal*) a large heavy book, especially one dealing with a serious topic

tom·fool /ˌtɑmˈful/ *noun* (*old-fashioned*) a silly person ► **tomfool** *adj.* [only before noun]

tom·fool·er·y /ˌtɑmˈfuləri/ *noun* [U] (*old-fashioned*) silly behavior **SYN** FOOLISHness

tom·my gun /ˈtɑmi ˌɡʌn/ *noun* a type of SUBMACHINE GUN

to·mog·ra·phy /təˈmɑɡrəfi/ *noun* [U] a way of producing an image of the inside of the human body or a solid object using X-RAYS or ULTRASOUND

to·mor·row 🔑 /təˈmɑroʊ; -ˈmɔroʊ/ *adv., noun*
● *adv.* on or during the day after today: *I'm going now. See you tomorrow.* ◆ *She's leaving tomorrow.* ◆ *They arrive a week from tomorrow* (= after a week, starting from tomorrow).
● *noun* [U] **1** the day after today: *Today is Tuesday, so tomorrow is Wednesday.* ◆ *tomorrow afternoon/morning/night/evening* ◆ *I'll see you the day after tomorrow.* ◆ *The announcement will appear in tomorrow's newspapers.* ◆ *I want it done by tomorrow.* **2** the future: *Who knows what changes tomorrow may bring?* ◆ *Tomorrow's workers will have to be more adaptable.*
IDM **do sth as if/like there's no tomorrow** to do something a lot or as though you do not care what effects it will have: *I ate as if there was no tomorrow.* ◆ *She spends money like there's no tomorrow.*

tom-tom *noun* a tall narrow drum that you play with your hands ⟳ picture at INSTRUMENT

ton 🔑 /tʌn/ *noun*
1 [C] (*pl.* **tons** or **ton**) a unit for measuring weight, equal to 2,000 pounds: (*informal*) *What have you got in this bag? It weighs a ton!* ⟳ compare TONNE **2** [C] a unit for measuring the size of a ship. 1 ton is equal to 100 CUBIC feet. **3 tons**

t tea   ṭ butter   d did   k cat   g got   tʃ chin   dʒ June   f fall

[pl.] (*informal*) a lot: *They have tons of money.* ◆ *I still have tons to do.*

IDM **like a ton of bricks** (*informal*) very heavily; very severely: *Disappointment hit her like a ton of bricks.* ◆ *They came down on him like a ton of bricks* (= criticized him very severely).

ton·al /ˈtoʊnl/ *adj.* **1** (*technical*) relating to tones of sound or color **2** (*music*) having a particular **KEY** **ANT** ATONAL ▸ **ton·al·ly** /-nl·i/ *adv.*

to·nal·i·ty /toʊˈnæləti/ *noun* [U, C] (*pl.* **to·nal·i·ties**) (*music*) the quality of a piece of music that depends on the **KEY** in which it is written

tone 🔑 /toʊn/ *noun, verb*

● *noun*

▹ **OF VOICE** **1** [C] the quality of someone's voice, especially expressing a particular emotion: *speaking in hushed/low/clipped/measured, etc. tones* ◆ *a conversational tone* ◆ *a tone of surprise* ◆ *Don't speak to me in that tone of voice* (= in that unpleasant way). ◆ *There's no need to take that tone with me—it's not my fault we're late.*

▹ **CHARACTER/ATMOSPHERE** **2** [sing.] the general character and attitude of something such as a piece of writing, or the atmosphere of an event: *The overall tone of the book is gently nostalgic.* ◆ *She set the tone for the meeting with a firm statement of company policy.* ◆ *Leave it to you to lower the tone of the conversation* (= for example by telling a rude joke). ◆ *The article was moderate in tone and presented both sides of the case.*

▹ **OF SOUND** **3** [C] the quality of a sound, especially the sound of a musical instrument or one produced by electronic equipment: *the full rich tone of the trumpet* ◆ *the volume and tone controls on a car stereo*

▹ **COLOR** **4** [C] a shade of a color: *a carpet in warm tones of brown and orange*

▹ **OF MUSCLES/SKIN** **5** [U] how strong and firm your muscles or skin are: *how to improve your muscle/skin tone*

▹ **ON TELEPHONE** **6** [C] a sound heard on a telephone line: *the dial tone* ◆ *Please speak after the tone* (= for example as an instruction on an answering machine).

▹ **IN MUSIC** **7** (also 'whole step) [C] one of the five longer **INTERVALS** in a musical **SCALE**, for example the **INTERVAL** between C and D or between E and F♯ ⊃ compare STEP

▹ **PHONETICS** **8** [C] the **PITCH** (= how high or low a sound is) of a syllable in speaking: *a rising/falling tone* **9** a particular **PITCH** pattern on a syllable in languages such as Chinese, that can be used to distinguish different meanings

▹ **-TONED** **10** (in adjectives) having the type of tone mentioned: *a bright-toned soprano* ◆ *olive-toned skin*

● *verb* [T] ~ **sth (up)** to make your muscles, skin, etc. firmer and stronger: *Massage will help to tone up loose skin under the chin.* ◆ *a beautifully toned body*

PHRV ,tone sth↔ˈdown **1** to make a speech, an opinion, etc. less extreme or offensive: *The language of the article will have to be toned down for the mass-market.* **2** to make a color less bright

,tone-ˈdeaf *adj.* unable to hear the difference between musical notes

'tone ,language *noun* a language in which differences in **TONE** can change the meaning of words

tone·less /ˈtoʊnləs/ *adj.* (of a voice, etc.) dull or flat; not expressing any emotion or interest ▸ **tone·less·ly** *adv.*

'tone ,poem *noun* a piece of music that is intended to describe a place or express an idea

ton·er /ˈtoʊnər/ *noun* [U, C] **1** a type of ink used in machines that print or photocopy **2** a liquid or cream used for making the skin on your face firm and smooth

'tone ,unit (also 'tone group) *noun* (*phonetics*) the basic unit of **INTONATION** in a language which consists of one or more syllables with a complete **PITCH** movement

tongs /taŋz; tɔŋz/ *noun* [pl.] a tool with two long parts that are joined at one end, used for picking up and holding things: *a pair of tongs* ⊃ picture at COOKING, KITCHEN, LABORATORY **IDM** see HAMMER *n.*

tongue 🔑 /tʌŋ/ *noun, verb*

● *noun* **1** [C] the soft part in the mouth that moves around, used for tasting, swallowing, speaking, etc.: *He clicked his tongue to attract their attention.* ◆ *She ran her tongue over her lips.* ◆ *It's very rude to stick your tongue out at people.* ⊃ picture at BODY **2** [U, C] the tongue of some animals, cooked and eaten: *a slice of ox tongue* **3** [C] (*formal* or *literary*) a language: *None of the tribes speak the same tongue.* ◆ *I tried speaking to her in her native tongue.* ⊃ see also MOTHER TONGUE **4** [sing.] a particular way of speaking: *He has a sharp tongue.* ◆ (*formal*) *I'll thank you to keep a civil tongue in your head* (= speak politely). ⊃ see also SILVER TONGUE **5** -tongued (in adjectives) speaking in the way mentioned: *sharp-tongued* **6** [C] a long narrow piece of leather under the **LACES** on a shoe **7** [C] ~ **(of sth)** (*literary*) something that is long and narrow and shaped like a tongue: *a tongue of flame*

IDM **get your tongue around/round sth** to pronounce a difficult word correctly **hold your tongue/peace** (*old-fashioned*) to say nothing although you would like to give your opinion **roll/slip/trip off the tongue** to be easy to say or pronounce: *It's not a name that exactly trips off the tongue, is it?* **set tongues wagging** (*informal*) to cause people to start talking about someone's private affairs **with your tongue in your cheek | with tongue in cheek** if you say something **with your tongue in your cheek**, you are not being serious and mean it as a joke ⊃ more at BITE *v.*, FIND *v.*, LOOSE *adj.*, LOOSEN, SLIP *n.*, TIP *n.*, WATCH *v.*

● *verb* **1** ~ **sth** to stop the flow of air into a wind instrument with your tongue in order to make a note **2** ~ **sth** to LICK something with your tongue

,tongue and 'groove *noun* [U] wooden boards that have a long cut along one edge and a long **RIDGE** along the other, that are used to connect them together

'tongue de,pressor *noun* a thin flat instrument that doctors use for pressing the tongue down when they are examining someone's throat

,tongue-in-ˈcheek *adj.* not intended seriously; done or said as a joke: *a tongue-in-cheek remark* ▸ **tongue-in-ˈcheek** *adv.*: *The offer was made almost tongue-in-cheek.*

'tongue-,lashing *noun* (*informal*) an occasion when someone speaks in an angry or critical way to someone who has done something wrong: *The banks got a tongue-lashing at the committee hearing.*

'tongue-tied *adj.* not able to speak because you are shy or nervous

'tongue-,twister *noun* a word or phrase that is difficult to say quickly or correctly, such as "She sells sea shells on the seashore."

ton·ic /ˈtɑnɪk/ *noun* **1** (also 'tonic ,water) [U, C] a clear drink with bubbles in it and a slightly bitter taste, that is often mixed with a strong alcoholic drink: *a gin and tonic* **2** [C] a medicine that makes you feel stronger and healthier, taken especially when you feel tired: *herbal tonics* **3** [C, U] a liquid that you put on your hair or skin in order to make it healthier: *skin tonic* **4** [C, usually sing.] (*old-fashioned*) anything that makes people feel healthier or happier: *The weekend break was just the tonic I needed.* **5** [C] (*music*) the first note of a **SCALE** of eight notes **6** (also ,tonic 'syllable) [C] (*phonetics*) the syllable in a **TONE UNIT** on which a change in **PITCH** takes place

ton·i·fy /ˈtoʊnəˌfaɪ/ *verb* (ton·i·fies, ton·i·fy·ing, ton·i·fied, ton·i·fied) ~ **sth** to make a part of the body firmer, smoother, and stronger, by exercise or by applying special creams, etc.

to·night 🔑 /təˈnaɪt/ *adv., noun*

● *adv.* on or during the evening or night of today: *Will you have dinner with me tonight?* ◆ *It's cold tonight.*

● *noun* [U] the evening or night of today: *Here are tonight's main headlines.* ◆ *Tonight will be cloudy.*

ton·nage /ˈtʌnɪdʒ/ *noun* [U, C] **1** the size of a ship or the amount it can carry, expressed in tons **2** the total amount that something weighs

tonne /tʌn/ noun (pl. tonnes or tonne) = METRIC TON

ton·sil /'tɒnsl/ noun either of the two small organs at the sides of the throat, near the base of the tongue: *I've had my tonsils out* (= removed).

ton·sil·lec·to·my /ˌtɒnsəˈlɛktəmi/ noun (pl. ton·sil·lec·to·mies) (*medical*) a medical operation to remove the TONSILS

ton·sil·li·tis /ˌtɒnsəˈlaɪtəs/ noun [U] an infection of the tonsils in which they become swollen and sore

ton·sure /'tɒnʃər/ noun the part of a MONK'S or priest's head that has been shaved

Ton·y /'toʊni/ noun (pl. Ton·ys) an award given in the U.S. for achievement in the theater

ton·y /'toʊni/ adj. (*informal*, becoming *old-fashioned*) fashionable and expensive

too 🔑 /tu/ adv.
1 used before adjectives and adverbs to say that something is more than is good, necessary, possible, etc.: *He's far too young to go on his own.* ◆ *This is too large a helping for me/This helping is too large for me.* ◆ *Is it too much to ask for a little quiet?* ◆ *The dress was too tight for me.* ◆ *It's too late to do anything about it now.* ◆ *Accidents like this happen all too* (= much too) *often.* **2** (usually placed at the end of a clause) also; as well: *Can I come too?* ◆ *When I've finished painting the bathroom, I'm going to do the kitchen too.* ⊃ note at ALSO ⊃ see also ME-TOO **3** used to comment on something that makes a situation worse: *She broke her leg last week—and on her birthday too!* **4** very: *I'm not too sure if this is right.* ◆ *I'm just going out—I won't be too long.* ◆ *She's none too* (= not very) *happy with the idea.* **5** used to emphasize something, especially your anger, surprise, or agreement with something: *"He did apologize eventually." "I would think so too!"* ◆ *"She gave me the money." "About time too!"*
IDM **be too much (for sb)** to need more skill or strength than you have; to be more difficult, annoying, etc. than you can bear

took pt of TAKE

tool 🔑 /tul/ noun, verb
● **noun 1** an instrument such as a hammer, SCREWDRIVER, SAW, etc. that you hold in your hand and use for making things, repairing things, etc.: *garden tools* ◆ *a cutting tool* ◆ *power tools* (= using electricity) ◆ *Always select the right tool for the job.* ⊃ picture on page 1573 **2** a thing that helps you to do your job or to achieve something: *research tools like questionnaires* ◆ *The computer is now an invaluable tool for the family doctor.* ◆ *Some of them carried the guns which were the tools of their trade* (= the things they needed to do their job). **3** a person who is used or controlled by another person or group: *The senator was an unwitting tool of the president.*
● **verb** [I] + adv./prep. (*informal*) to drive around in a vehicle
PHR V **tool 'up** | **tool sb/sth↔'up** (*technical*) to get or provide someone or something with the equipment, etc. that is necessary to do or produce something: *The factory is not tooled up to produce this type of engine.*

tool·bar /'tulbɑr/ noun (*computing*) a row of symbols (= ICONS) on a computer screen that show the different things that you can do with a particular program

tool·box /'tulbɑks/ noun a box with a lid for keeping tools in ⊃ picture at TOOL

tooled /tuld/ adj. (of leather) decorated with patterns made with a special heated tool

tool·kit /'tulkɪt/ noun **1** a set of tools in a box or bag **2** (*computing*) a set of software tools **3** the things that you need in order to achieve something

tool·mak·er /'tul.meɪkər/ noun a person or company that makes tools, used especially in industry ▶ **tool·mak·ing** /'tul.meɪkɪŋ/ noun [U]

too·nie /'tuni/ noun (*CanE*) the Canadian two-dollar coin

toot /tut/ noun, verb
● **noun** a short high sound made by a car horn or a whistle: *She gave a sharp toot on her horn.*

● **verb** [I, T] when a car horn **toots** or you **toot** it, it makes a short high sound: *the sound of horns tooting* ◆ **~ sth** *Toot your horn to let them know we're here.* **IDM** see HORN

tooth 🔑 /tuθ/ noun (pl. teeth /tiθ/)
1 any of the hard white structures in the mouth used for biting and chewing food: *I've just had a tooth out at the dentist's.* ◆ *to brush/clean your teeth* ◆ *tooth decay* ◆ *She answered through clenched teeth* (= opening her mouth only a little because of anger). ◆ *The cat sank its teeth into his finger.* ⊃ picture at BODY ⊃ collocations at PHYSICAL ⊃ see also BABY TOOTH, BUCK TEETH, FALSE TEETH, WISDOM TOOTH **2** a narrow pointed part that sticks out of an object: *the teeth on a saw* ⊃ picture at COMB ⊃ see also FINE-TOOTH COMB
IDM **cut your teeth on sth** to do something that gives you your first experience of a particular type of work **cut a tooth** (of a baby) to grow a new tooth **get your teeth into sth** (*informal*) to put a lot of effort and enthusiasm into something that is difficult enough to keep you interested: *Choose an essay topic that you can really get your teeth into.* **have teeth** (*informal*) (of an organization, a law, etc.) to be powerful and effective **in the teeth of sth 1** despite problems, opposition, etc.: *The new policy was adopted in the teeth of fierce criticism.* **2** in the direction that a strong wind is coming from: *They crossed the bay in the teeth of a howling gale.* **set sb's teeth on edge** (of a sound or taste) to make someone feel physically uncomfortable: *Just the sound of her voice sets my teeth on edge.* ⊃ more at ARMED, BARE, BIT, EYE, EYETEETH, FIGHT, GNASH, GRIT, KICK v., KICK n., LIE², LONG, SKIN, SWEET adj.

tooth·ache /'tuθeɪk/ noun [U, C, usually sing.] a pain in your teeth or in one tooth: *I have a toothache.*

tooth·brush /'tuθbrʌʃ/ noun a small brush for cleaning your teeth

toothbrush 'mustache noun a short MUSTACHE cut with square corners

toothed /tuθt; tuðd/ adj. [only before noun] **1** (*technical*) having teeth: *a toothed whale* **2** **-toothed** (in compounds) having the type of teeth mentioned: *a gap-toothed smile*

the 'tooth fairy noun [sing.] an imaginary creature that is said to take away a tooth that a small child leaves near his or her bed at night and to leave a coin there in its place

tooth·less /'tuθləs/ adj. **1** having no teeth: *a toothless old man* ◆ *She gave us a toothless grin.* **2** having no power or authority

tooth·paste /'tuθpeɪst/ noun [U] a substance that you put on a brush and use to clean your teeth

tooth·pick /'tuθpɪk/ noun a short pointed piece of wood or plastic used for removing bits of food from between the teeth

tooth·some /'tuθsəm/ adj. (*humorous*) (of food) tasting good **SYN** TASTY

tooth·y /'tuθi/ adj. a **toothy** smile shows a lot of teeth

too·tle /'tutl/ verb (*informal*) **1** [I] + adv./prep. to walk, drive, etc. somewhere without hurrying **2** [I, T] **~ (sth)** to produce a series of notes by blowing into a musical instrument

toot·sies /'tutsiz/ noun [pl.] (*informal*) (used by or when speaking to young children) toes or feet

top 🔑 /tɑp/ noun, adj., verb
● **noun**
▸ **HIGHEST POINT 1** [C] the highest part or point of something: *She was standing at the top of the stairs.* ◆ *Write your name at the top.* ◆ *The title is right at the top of the page.* ◆ *He filled my glass to the top.* ◆ *We climbed to the very top of the hill.* ◆ *Snow was falling on the mountain tops.* ◆ *The wind was blowing in the tops of the trees.* ⊃ see also ROOFTOP, TREETOP
▸ **UPPER SURFACE 2** [C] the upper flat surface of something: *Can you polish the top of the table?* ◆ *a desk top* ⊃ see also HARDTOP, ROLL-TOP DESK, TABLETOP
▸ **HIGHEST RANK 3** [sing.] **the ~ (of sth)** the highest or most important rank or position: *He's at the top of his profession.*

| h **hat** | m **man** | n **no** | ŋ **sing** | l **leg** | r **red** | y **yes** | w **wet** |

Tools

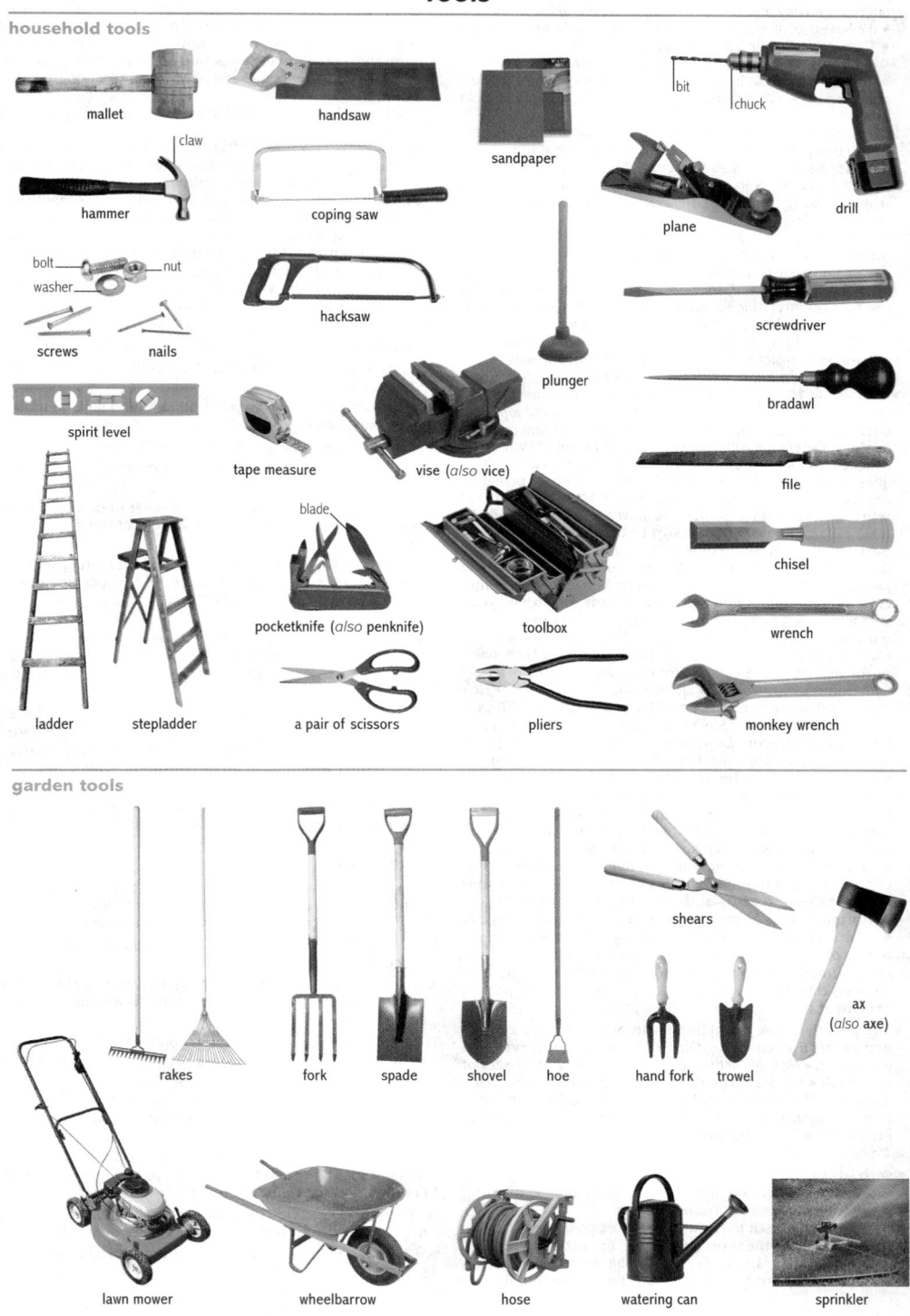

household tools

mallet

handsaw

sandpaper

claw

hammer

coping saw

bit

chuck

drill

plane

bolt — nut

washer

hacksaw

screwdriver

screws   nails

plunger

bradawl

spirit level

tape measure   vise (*also* vice)

file

blade

chisel

pocketknife (*also* penknife)

toolbox

wrench

ladder   stepladder

a pair of scissors

pliers

monkey wrench

garden tools

shears

ax
(*also* axe)

rakes

fork   spade   shovel   hoe

hand fork   trowel

lawn mower

wheelbarrow

hose

watering can

sprinkler

◆ *She is determined to make it to the top* (= achieve fame or success). ◆ *They finished the season at the top of the division.* ◆ *We have a lot of things to do, but packing is at the top of the list.* ◆ *This decision came from the top.*

▷ OF PEN/BOTTLE **4** [C] a thing that you put on the end of something to close it: *Where's the top of this pen?* ◆ *a bottle with a screw top* ⊃ picture at PACKAGING ⊃ thesaurus box at LID

▷ CLOTHING **5** [C] a piece of clothing worn on the upper part of the body: *I need a top to go with this skirt.* ◆ *a uniform/ pajama/bikini top* ⊃ see also CROP TOP

▷ LEAVES OF PLANT **6** [C, usually pl.] the leaves of a plant that is grown mainly for its root: *Remove the green tops from the carrots.*

▷ AMOUNT OF MONEY **7** tops [pl.] (*informal*) used after an amount or number to show that it is the highest possible: *It couldn't have cost more than $50, tops.*

▷ BEST **8** tops [pl.] (*old-fashioned, informal*) a person or thing of the best quality: *Among sports superstars she's (the) tops.* ◆ *In the survey New Yorkers come out tops for humor.*

▷ TOY **9** [C] a child's toy that spins on a point when it is turned around very quickly by hand or by a string: *She was so confused—her mind was spinning like a top.*

▷ BEGINNING **10** [U] (*informal*) the beginning or earliest part of something: *That was great, now let's take it from the top* (= go back to the beginning of a song, scene, etc. and practice it again). ◆ *The church bells ring at the top of the hour* (= when it is exactly 1 o'clock, 2 o'clock, etc.). ⊃ see also BIG TOP

IDM **at the top of your voice/lungs** as loudly as possible: *She was screaming at the top of her voice.* **come out on top** to win a contest or an argument: *In most boardroom disputes he tends to come out on top.* **from top to bottom** going to every part of a place in a very thorough way: *We cleaned the house from top to bottom.* **from top to toe** completely; all over **get on top of sth** to manage to control or deal with something: *How will I ever get on top of all this work?* **off the top of your head** (*informal*) just guessing or using your memory, without taking time to think carefully or check the facts: *I can't remember the name off the top of my head, but I can look it up for you.* **on top 1** on the highest point or surface: *a cake with whipped cream on top* ◆ *Stand on top and look down.* ◆ *He's going bald on top* (= on the top of his head). **2** in a leading position or in control: *She remained on top for the rest of the match.* **3** in addition: *Look, here's 30 dollars, and I'll buy you lunch on top.* **on top of sth/sb 1** on, over, or covering something or someone: *Books were piled on top of one another.* ◆ *Many people were crushed when the building collapsed on top of them.* **2** in addition to something: *He gets commission on top of his salary.* ◆ *On top of everything else, my car's been stolen.* **3** very close to something or someone: *We were all living on top of each other in that tiny apartment.* **4** in control of a situation: *Do you think he's really on top of his job?* **on top of your game | at the top of your game** (*informal*) performing at the highest level in an activity or business: *At 42, she's still on top of her game.* **on top of the world** very happy or proud **over the top** (*informal*) done to an exaggerated degree and with too much effort: *His performance is completely over the top.* ◆ *an over-the-top reaction* ⊃ more at BLOW *v.*, HEAP *n.*, PILE *n.*, THIN *adj.*

● **adj.** [usually before noun] highest in position, rank, or degree: *He lives on the top floor.* ◆ *She kept her passport in the top drawer.* ◆ *He's one of the top players in the country.* ◆ *She got the top job.* ◆ *She got top grades for her essay.* ◆ *They're top of the division.* ◆ *The athletes are all in top form* (= performing their best). ◆ *Welfare reform is a top priority for the government.* ◆ *The car was traveling at top speed.*
⊃ see also TOP-FLIGHT

● **verb** (-pp-)
▷ BE MORE **1** ~ sth to be higher than a particular amount: *Worldwide sales look set to top $1 billion.*
▷ BE THE BEST **2** ~ sth to be in the highest position on a list because you are the most successful, important, etc.: *The band topped the charts for five weeks with their first single.*
▷ PUT ON TOP **3** [usually passive] ~ sth (with sth) to put

---

something on the top of something else: *fruit salad topped with yogurt*

▷ SAY/DO SOMETHING BETTER **4** ~ sth to say or do something that is better, funnier, more impressive, etc. than something that someone else has said or done in the past: *I'm afraid the other company has topped your offer* (= offered more money).

▷ CLIMB HILL **5** ~ sth (*literary*) to reach the highest point of a hill, etc.

IDM **to top/cap it all (off)** (*informal*) used to introduce the final piece of information that is worse than the other bad things that you have just mentioned

PHR V **top sth↔'off (with sth)** to complete something successfully by doing or adding one final thing ,**top sth↔'off/up** to fill a container that already has some liquid in it with more liquid: *Top the car off with gas before you set off.* ◆ *Top the gas off before you set off.* ,**top 'out (at sth)** if something **tops out** at a particular price, speed, etc. it does not rise any higher: *Inflation topped out at 12%.*

,**Top '40** *noun* [pl.] the forty most popular songs at a particular time ▶ **Top '40** *adj.*: *a Top 40 countdown*

to·paz /ˈtoʊpæz/ *noun* [C, U] a clear, yellow, SEMI-PRECIOUS STONE: *a topaz ring*

,**top ba'nana** *noun* (*informal*) a person who has the most important job or position ⊃ compare SECOND BANANA

,**top 'brass** *noun* [sing.] (*informal*) = BRASS (3)

,**top-'class** *adj.* of the highest quality or standard: *a top-class performance*

top·coat /ˈtɑpkoʊt/ *noun* **1** the last layer of paint put on a surface ⊃ compare UNDERCOAT **2** (*old-fashioned*) an OVERCOAT

,**top 'dog** *noun* [usually sing.] (*informal*) a person, group, or country that is better than all the others, especially in a situation that involves competition

,**top 'dollar** *noun*
IDM **pay, earn, charge, etc. top dollar** (*informal*) pay, earn, charge, etc. a lot of money: *If you want the best, you have to pay top dollar.* ◆ *We can help you get top dollar when you sell your house.*

,**top-'down** *adj.* **1** (of a plan, project, etc.) starting with a general idea to which details are added later ⊃ compare BOTTOM-UP **2** starting from or involving the people who have higher positions in an organization: *a top-down management style*

,**top 'drawer** *noun* [sing.] if someone or something is from **the top drawer**, they are of the highest social class or of the highest quality ▶ **top-'drawer** *adj.*

to·pee = TOPI

,**top-'end** *adj.* [only before noun] among the best, most expensive, etc. examples of something SYN HIGH-END: *Many people are upgrading their cell phones to top-end models.*

,**top-'flight** *adj.* of the highest quality; the best or most successful

,**top 'gear** *noun* [U] the highest gear in a vehicle: *They cruised along in top gear.* ◆ (*figurative*) *Her career is moving into top gear.*

,**top-'grossing** *adj.* [only before noun] earning more money than other similar things or people: *the top-grossing movie of 2009*

,**top 'hat** (also *informal* **top·per**) *noun* a man's tall black or gray hat, worn with formal clothes on very formal occasions ⊃ picture at HAT

,**top-'heavy** *adj.* **1** too heavy at the top and therefore likely to fall **2** (of an organization) having too many senior staff compared to the number of workers

to·pi (also **to·pee**) /ˈtoʊpi; ˈtoʊpi/ *noun* a light, hard hat worn to give protection from the sun in very hot countries

to·pi·ar·y /ˈtoʊpiˌɛri/ *noun* [U] the art of cutting bushes into shapes such as birds or animals

top·ic 🔑 AWL /ˈtɑpɪk/ *noun*
a subject that you talk, write, or learn about: *The main topic of conversation was Tom's new girlfriend.* ◆ *The article covered a wide range of topics.*
IDM **on topic** appropriate or relevant to the situation: *Keep the text short and on topic.* ◆ *Let's get back on topic.*

top·i·cal AWL /ˈtɑpɪkl/ *adj.* **1** connected with something that is happening or of interest at the present time: *a topical joke/reference* ◆ **topical events** **2** (*medical*) connected with, or put directly on, a part of the body ▶ **top·i·cal·i·ty** /ˌtɑpəˈkæləti/ *noun* [U, sing.]

top·knot /ˈtɑpnɑt/ *noun* a way of arranging your hair in which it is tied up on the top of your head

top·less /ˈtɑpləs/ *adj.* (of a woman) not wearing any clothes on the upper part of the body so that her breasts are not covered: *a topless model* ◆ *a topless bar* (= where the female staff is topless) ▶ **top·less** *adv.*: *to sunbathe topless*

top-ˈlevel *adj.* [only before noun] involving the most important or best people in a company, an organization, or a sport: *a top-level meeting* ◆ *top-level tennis*

top·most /ˈtɑpmoʊst/ *adj.* [only before noun] (*formal*) highest: *the topmost branches of the tree*

top-ˈnotch *adj.* (*informal*) excellent; of the highest quality

top of the ˈline *adj.* [usually before noun] used to describe the most expensive of a group of similar products: *Our equipment is top of the line.* ◆ *our top-of-the-line model*

to·pog·ra·phy /təˈpɑgrəfi/ *noun* [U] (*technical*) the physical features of an area of land, especially the position of its rivers, mountains, etc.; the study of these features: *a map showing the topography of the island* ▶ **top·o·graph·i·cal** /ˌtɑpəˈgræfɪkl/ (also **top·o·graph·ic** /ˌtɑpəˈgræfɪk/) *adj.*: *a topographical map/feature* **top·o·graph·i·cally** /-kli/ *adv.*

to·pol·o·gy /təˈpɑlədʒi/ *noun* [U, C] (*technical*) the way the parts of something are arranged and related: *The Canadian banking topology is relatively flat, with a few large banks controlling the entire market.* ◆ *the topology of a computer network*

top·o·nym /ˈtɑpənɪm/ *noun* (*technical*) a place name

to·pos /ˈtoʊpoʊs; -pɑs/ *noun* (*pl.* **to·poi** /-pɔɪ/) (*technical*) a traditional subject or idea in literature

top·per /ˈtɑpər/ *noun* (*informal*) = TOP HAT

top·ping /ˈtɑpɪŋ/ *noun* [C, U] a layer of food that you put on top of a dish, cake, etc. to add flavor or to make it look nice

top·ple /ˈtɑpl/ *verb* **1** [I, T] to become unsteady and fall down; to make something do this: **+ adv./prep.** *The pile of books toppled over.* ◆ **~ sb/sth + adv./prep.** *He brushed past, toppling her from her stool.* **2** [T] **~ sb/sth** to make someone lose their position of power or authority **SYN** OVERTHROW: *a plot to topple the president*

top-ˈranking *adj.* [only before noun] of the highest rank, status, or importance in an organization, a sport, etc.

top-ˈrated *adj.* [only before noun] most popular with the public: *a top-rated TV show*

top·sail /ˈtɑpseɪl; ˈtɑpsl/ *noun* [usually sing.] the sail attached to the upper part of the MAST of a ship

top ˈsecret *adj.* that must be kept completely secret, especially from other governments: *This information has been classified top secret.* ◆ *top-secret documents*

top-ˈshelf *adj.* [only before noun] of the highest class: *It is a top-shelf law firm.*

top·side /ˈtɑpsaɪd/ *adv.* on or toward the upper DECKS of a ship: *We stayed topside.*

top·soil /ˈtɑpsɔɪl/ *noun* [U] the layer of soil nearest the surface of the ground ⊃ compare SUBSOIL

top·spin /ˈtɑpspɪn/ *noun* [U] (*sports*) the fast forward spinning movement that a player can give to a ball by hitting or throwing it in a special way

top·sy-tur·vy /ˌtɑpsi ˈtɜrvi/ *adj.* (*informal*) in a state of great confusion: *Everything's topsy-turvy in my life at the moment.*

the ˌtop ˈten *noun* [pl.] the ten pop records that have sold the most copies in a particular week

ˈtop-up ˌcard *noun* a card that you buy for a cell phone so that you can make more calls to the value of the card

toque *noun* **1** /toʊk/ a woman's small hat **2** (also **tuque**) /tuk/ *CanE* a close-fitting hat made of wool, sometimes with a ball of wool on the top

To·rah /ˈtɔrə; ˈtoʊrə; toʊˈrɑ/ *noun* usually **the Torah** (in Judaism) the law of God as given to Moses and recorded in the first five books of the Bible

torch /tɔrtʃ/ *noun, verb*
● *noun* **1** a long piece of wood that has material at one end that is set on fire and that people carry to give light: *a flaming torch* ◆ *the Olympic torch* ◆ (*figurative*) *They struggled to keep the torch of idealism and hope alive.* **2** = BLOWTORCH
IDM **put sth to the torch** (*literary*) to set fire to something deliberately ⊃ more at CARRY
● *verb* **~ sth** to set fire to a building or vehicle deliberately in order to destroy it

torch·bear·er /ˈtɔrtʃˌbɛrər/ *noun* **1** a person who carries a torch, for example at the Olympic Games **2** a person who leads other people, or sets an example, in working toward a valued goal: *She became a torchbearer for civil rights.*

torch·light /ˈtɔrtʃlaɪt/ *noun* [U] the light that is produced by burning torches

ˈtorch song *noun* a type of sad, romantic song about feelings of love for a person who does not share those feelings ▶ **ˈtorch ˌsinger** *noun*

tore *pt of* TEAR¹

tor·e·a·dor /ˈtɔriəˌdɔr/ *noun* a man, especially one riding a horse, who fights BULLS to entertain people, for example in Spain

tor·ment *noun, verb*
● *noun* /ˈtɔrment/ [U, C] (*formal*) extreme suffering, especially mental suffering; a person or thing that causes this **SYN** ANGUISH: *the cries of a man in torment* ◆ *She suffered years of mental torment after her son's death.* ◆ *The flies were a terrible torment.*
● *verb* /tɔrˈment; ˈtɔrment/ **1 ~ sb** (*formal*) to make someone suffer very much **SYN** PLAGUE: *He was tormented by feelings of insecurity.* **2 ~ sb/sth** to annoy a person or an animal in a cruel way because you think it is amusing **SYN** TORTURE

tor·men·tor /tɔrˈmentər/ *noun* (*formal*) a person who causes someone to suffer

torn *pp of* TEAR¹

tor·na·do /tɔrˈneɪdoʊ/ *noun* (*pl.* **tor·na·does** or **tor·na·dos**) a violent storm with very strong winds that move in a circle. There is often also a long cloud that is narrower at the bottom than the top. ⊃ collocations at WEATHER

tor·pe·do /tɔrˈpidoʊ/ *noun, verb*
● *noun* (*pl.* **tor·pe·does**) a long narrow bomb that is fired under the water from a ship or SUBMARINE and that explodes when it hits a ship, etc.
● *verb* (**tor·pe·does, tor·pe·do·ing, tor·pe·doed, tor·pe·doed**) **1 ~ sth** to attack a ship or make it sink using a torpedo **2 ~ sth** to completely destroy the possibility that something could succeed: *Her comments had torpedoed the deal.*

tor·pid /ˈtɔrpəd/ *adj.* (*formal*) not active; with no energy or enthusiasm

tor·por /ˈtɔrpər/ *noun* [U, sing.] (*formal*) the state of not being active and having no energy or enthusiasm **SYN** LETHARGY: *In the heat they sank into a state of torpor.*

torque /tɔrk/ *noun* [U] (*technical*) a twisting force that causes machinery, etc. to ROTATE (= turn around)

tor·rent /ˈtɔrənt; ˈtɑr-/ *noun* **1** a large amount of water moving very quickly: *After the winter rains, the stream becomes a raging torrent.* ◆ *The rain was coming down in torrents.* **2** a large amount of something that comes

---

suddenly and violently **SYN** DELUGE: *a torrent of abuse/criticism* ♦ *a torrent of words*

tor·ren·tial /təˈrɛnʃl/ *adj.* (of rain) falling in large amounts

tor·rid /ˈtɔrəd; ˈtar-/ *adj.* [usually before noun] **1** full of strong emotions, especially connected with sex and love **SYN** PASSIONATE: *a torrid love affair* **2** (*formal*) (of a climate or country) very hot or dry: *a torrid summer*

torrid ˌzone *noun* [sing.] (*technical*) an area of the earth near the EQUATOR **SYN** THE TROPICS

tor·sion /ˈtɔrʃn/ *noun* [U] (*technical*) twisting, especially of one end of something while the other end is held fixed

tor·so /ˈtɔrsoʊ/ *noun* (*pl.* **tor·sos**) **1** the main part of the body, not including the head, arms, or legs **SYN** TRUNK **2** a statue of a torso

tort /tɔrt/ *noun* [C, U] (*law*) something wrong that someone does to someone else that is not criminal, but that can lead to action in a CIVIL court

torte /tɔrt/ *noun* [C, U] a large cake filled with a mixture of cream, chocolate, fruit, etc.

tor·tel·li·ni /ˌtɔrtlˈini/ *noun* [pl.] small squares of PASTA that are filled with meat or cheese and then rolled and formed into small rings

tor·til·la /tɔrˈtiyə/ *noun* (from *Spanish*) a thin Mexican PANCAKE made with CORN flour or WHEAT flour, usually eaten hot and filled with meat, cheese, etc.

torˈtilla ˌchip *noun* a piece of CORN tortilla that has been fried until crisp: *The waiter brought some tortilla chips and salsa.*

tor·toise /ˈtɔrtəs/ *noun* a REPTILE with a hard round shell, that lives on land and moves very slowly. It can pull its head and legs into its shell. ➔ compare TERRAPIN, TURTLE

tor·toise·shell /ˈtɔrtəˌʃɛl; ˈtɔrtəsˌʃɛl/ *noun* **1** [U] the hard shell of a TURTLE, especially the type with orange and brown marks, used for making COMBS and small decorative objects **2** [C] = CALICO CAT **3** [C] a BUTTERFLY with orange and brown marks on its wings

tor·tu·ous /ˈtɔrtʃuəs/ *adj.* [usually before noun] (*formal*) **1** (usually *disapproving*) not simple and direct; long, complicated, and difficult to understand **SYN** CONVOLUTED: *tortuous language* ♦ *the long, tortuous process of negotiating peace* **2** (of a road, path, etc.) full of bends **SYN** WINDING ▶ **tor·tu·ous·ly** *adv.*

tor·ture /ˈtɔrtʃər/ *noun*, *verb*
● *noun* [U, C] **1** the act of causing someone severe pain in order to punish them or make them say or do something: *Many of the refugees have suffered torture.* ♦ *the use of torture* ♦ *terrible instruments of torture* ♦ *His confessions were made under torture.* ♦ *I heard stories of gruesome tortures in prisons.* **2** (*informal*) mental or physical suffering; something that causes this: *The interview was sheer torture from start to finish.*
● *verb* [often passive] **1** to hurt someone physically or mentally in order to punish them or make them tell you something: ~ **sb** *Many of the rebels were captured and tortured by secret police.* ♦ ~ **sb into doing sth** *He was tortured into giving them the information.* **2** ~ **sb** to make someone feel extremely unhappy or anxious **SYN** TORMENT: *He spent his life tortured by the memories of his childhood.* ▶ **tor·tur·er** /ˈtɔrtʃərər/ *noun*

tor·tured /ˈtɔrtʃərd/ *adj.* [only before noun] suffering severely; involving a lot of suffering and difficulty: *a tortured mind*

To·ry /ˈtɔri/ *noun* (*pl.* **To·ries**) (*CanE, informal*) a member or supporter of the Conservative party: *The Tories* (= the Tory party) *lost the election.* ▶ **To·ry** *adj.* [usually before noun]: *the Tory party* ♦ *Tory policies* **To·ry·ism** /ˈtɔriˌɪzəm/ *noun* [U]

toss /tɔs; tas/ *verb*, *noun*
● *verb*
▶ THROW **1** [T] to throw something lightly or carelessly: ~ **sth** + **adv./prep.** *I tossed the book aside and got up.* ♦ ~ **sth to sb** *He tossed the ball to Anna.* ♦ ~ **sb sth** *He tossed Anna the ball.* ➔ thesaurus box at THROW

▶ YOUR HEAD **2** [T] ~ **sth** to move your head suddenly upward, especially to show that you are annoyed or impatient: *She just tossed her head and walked off.*
▶ SIDE TO SIDE/UP AND DOWN **3** [I, T] to move or make someone or something move from side to side or up and down: *Branches were tossing in the wind.* ♦ *I couldn't sleep but kept tossing and turning in bed all night.* ♦ ~ **sb/sth** *Our boat was being tossed by the huge waves.*
▶ IN COOKING **4** [T] ~ **sth** to shake or turn food in order to cover it with oil, butter, etc.: *Drain the pasta and toss it in melted butter.*
▶ COIN **5** [T, I] to throw a coin in the air in order to decide something, especially by guessing which side is facing upward when it lands **SYN** FLIP: *Let's toss a coin.* ➔ related noun TOSS-UP
▶ THROW OUT **6** [T] ~ **sth (out)** to get rid of something: *If your T-shirt rips, just toss it.*
IDM **toss your cookies** (*informal*) to VOMIT
PHR V **toss sth↔back** (*informal*) to drink something quickly: *He tossed back a glass of wine.* **toss sth↔ in** to include something extra with what you are selling or offering, without increasing the price: *When we bought the bike, they tossed in a free basket.* **ˌtoss sth↔ˈoff** to produce something quickly and without much thought or effort
● *noun* [usually sing.]
▶ OF COIN **1** an act of throwing a coin in the air in order to decide something: *The final result was decided on/by the toss of a coin.* ♦ *to win/lose the toss* (= to guess correctly/wrongly which side of a coin will face upward when it lands on the ground after it has been thrown in the air)
▶ OF HEAD **2** ~ **of your head** an act of moving your head suddenly upward, especially to show that you are annoyed or impatient: *She dismissed the question with a toss of her head.*
▶ THROW **3** an act of throwing something, especially in a competition or game: *a toss of 10 feet*

ˌtossed ˈsalad *noun* a salad of LETTUCE and other raw vegetables mixed together **SYN** GREEN SALAD: *I'll have a tossed salad with no dressing.*

ˈtoss-up *noun* [sing.] (*informal*) a situation in which either of two choices, results, etc. is equally possible: *"Have you decided on the color yet?" "It's a toss-up between the blue and the green."*

tot /tat/ *noun* (*informal*) a very young child

to·tal 🔑 /ˈtoʊtl/ *adj.*, *noun*, *verb*
● *adj.* [usually before noun] **1** being the amount or number after everyone or everything is counted or added together: *the total profit* ♦ *This brought the total number of accidents so far this year to 113.* ♦ *The club has a total membership of 300.* **2** including everything **SYN** COMPLETE: *The room was in total darkness.* ♦ *They wanted a total ban on handguns.* ♦ *The evening was a total disaster.* ♦ *I can't believe you'd tell a total stranger about it!*
● *noun* the amount you get when you add several numbers or amounts together; the final number of people or things when they have all been counted: *You got 47 points on the written examination and 18 on the oral, making a total of 65.* ♦ *His businesses are worth a combined total of $3 billion.* ♦ *Out of a total of 15 games, they only won 2.* ♦ *The repairs came to over $500 in total* (= including everything). ➔ see also GRAND TOTAL, RUNNING TOTAL, SUM TOTAL
● *verb* (**-l-**, *CanE usually* **-ll-**) **1** ~ **sth** to reach a particular total: *Imports totaled $1.5 billion last year.* **2** ~ **sth/sb (up)** to add up the numbers of something or someone and get a total: *Each student's points were totaled and entered on a list.* **3** ~ **sth** (*informal*) to damage a car very badly, so that it is not worth repairing it

to·tal·i·tar·i·an /toʊˌtæləˈtɛriən/ *adj.* (*disapproving*) (of a country or system of government) in which there is only one political party that has complete power and control over the people ▶ **to·tal·i·tar·i·an·ism** /-ˈtɛriəˌnɪzəm/ *noun* [U]

to·tal·i·ty /toʊˈtæləti/ *noun* [C, U] (*formal*) the state of being complete or whole; the whole number or amount: *The seriousness of the situation is difficult to appreciate **in its totality**.*

to·tal·ly /ˈtoʊtl̩·i/ *adv.*

completely: *They come from totally different cultures.* ◆ *I'm still not totally convinced that he knows what he's doing.* ◆ *This behavior is totally unacceptable.* ◆ (*informal*) *"She's so cute!" "Totally!"* (= I agree) ◆ (*informal*) *It's a totally awesome experience.*

ˌtotal ˈquality ˈmanagement *noun* [U] (*abbr.* TQM) a system of management that considers that every employee in an organization is responsible for keeping the highest standards in every aspect of the company's work

tote /toʊt/ *noun, verb*
- *noun* (also **ˈtote bag**) [C] a large bag for carrying things with you ➔ picture at BAG
- *verb* **1** ~ sth (*informal*) to carry something, especially something heavy: *We arrived, toting our bags and suitcases.* **2 -toting** (in adjectives) carrying the thing mentioned: *gun-toting soldiers*

to·tem /ˈtoʊtəm/ *noun* an animal or other natural object that is chosen and respected as a special symbol of a community or family, especially among Native Americans; an image of this animal, etc. ▶ **to·tem·ic** /toʊˈtɛmɪk/ *adj.*: *totemic animals*

ˈtotem ˌpole *noun* **1** a tall wooden pole that has symbols and pictures (called TOTEMS) CARVED or painted on it, traditionally made by Native Americans **2** (*informal*) a range of different levels in an organization, etc.: *I didn't want to be **low man on the totem pole** for ever.*

to·to ➔ IN TOTO

tot·ter /ˈtɑtər/ *verb* **1** [I] (+ adv./prep.) to walk or move with weak, unsteady steps, especially because you are drunk or sick **SYN** STAGGER **2** [I] to be weak and seem likely to fall: *the tottering walls of the castle* ◆ (*figurative*) *a tottering dictatorship*

tou·can /ˈtukæn/ *noun* a tropical American bird that is black with some areas of very bright feathers, and that has a very large beak

touch /tʌtʃ/ *verb, noun*

- *verb*
- ▷ WITH HAND/PART OF BODY **1** [T] ~ sb/sth to put your hand or another part of your body onto someone or something: *Don't touch that plate—it's hot!* ◆ *Can you touch your toes?* (= bend and reach them with your hands) ◆ *I touched him lightly on the arm.* ◆ *He has hardly touched the ball all game.* ◆ (*figurative*) *I must do some more work on that article—I haven't touched it all week.*
- ▷ NO SPACE BETWEEN **2** [I, T] (of two or more things, surfaces, etc.) to be or come so close together that there is no space between: *Make sure the wires don't touch.* ◆ ~ sth *Don't let your coat touch the wet paint.* ◆ *His coat was so long it was almost touching the floor.*
- ▷ MOVE SOMETHING/HIT SOMEONE **3** [T] (often in negative sentences) ~ sth/sb to move something, especially in such a way that you damage it; to hit or harm someone: *I told you not to touch my things.* ◆ *He said I kicked him, but I never touched him!*
- ▷ EAT/DRINK/USE **4** [T] (usually in negative sentences) ~ sth to eat, drink, or use something: *You've hardly touched your food.* ◆ *He hasn't touched the money his aunt left him.*
- ▷ AFFECT SOMEONE OR SOMETHING **5** [T] ~ sb/sth (to do sth) to make someone feel upset or sympathetic: *Her story touched us all deeply.* **6** [T] ~ sb/sth (*old-fashioned* or *formal*) to affect or concern someone or something: *These are issues that touch us all.*
- ▷ EQUAL SOMEONE **7** [T] (usually in negative sentences) ~ sb to be as good as someone in skill, quality, etc.: *No one can touch him when it comes to interior design.*
- ▷ REACH LEVEL **8** [T] ~ sth to reach a particular level, etc.: *The speedometer was touching 90.*
- ▷ BE INVOLVED WITH **9** [T] ~ sth/sb to become connected with or work with a situation or person: *Everything she touches*

turns to disaster. ◆ *His last two movies have been complete flops and now no studio will touch him.*
- ▷ OF SMILE **10** [T] ~ sth to be seen on someone's face for a short time: *A smile touched the corners of his mouth.*

IDM **be ˈtouched with sth** to have a small amount of a particular quality: *His hair was touched with gray.* **not touch sb/sth with a ten-foot pole** (*informal*) to refuse to get involved with someone or something or in a particular situation **touch ˈbase (with sb)** (*informal*) to make contact with someone again **touch ˈbottom 1** to reach the ground at the bottom of an area of water **2** to reach the worst possible state or condition ➔ more at CHORD, HAIR, NERVE **PHR V** ˌtouch ˈdown (of a plane, SPACECRAFT, etc.) to land ➔ related noun TOUCHDOWN **ˈtouch sb for sth** (*informal*) to persuade someone to give or lend you something, especially money **ˌtouch sth↔ˈoff** to make something begin, especially a difficult or violent situation **ˈtouch on/upon sth** to mention or deal with a subject in only a few words, without going into detail: *In his speech he was only able to touch on a few aspects of the problem.* **ˌtouch sth↔ˈup** to improve something by changing or adding to it slightly: *She was busy touching up her makeup in the mirror.*

- *noun*
- ▷ SENSE **1** [U] the sense that enables you to be aware of things and what they are like when you put your hands and fingers on them: *the sense of touch*
- ▷ WITH HAND/PART OF BODY **2** [C, usually sing.] an act of putting your hand or another part of your body onto someone or something: *The gentle touch of his hand on her shoulder made her jump.* ◆ *All this information is readily available **at the touch of a button*** (= by simply pressing a button). ◆ *This type of engraving requires a delicate touch.*
- ▷ WAY SOMETHING FEELS **3** [sing.] the way that something feels when you put your hand or fingers on it or when it comes into contact with your body: *The body was cold **to the touch**.* ◆ *material with a smooth, silky touch* ◆ *He could not bear the touch of clothing on his sunburned skin.*
- ▷ SMALL DETAIL **4** [C] a small detail that is added to something in order to improve it or make it complete: *I spent the morning **putting the finishing touches to** the report.* ◆ *Meeting them at the airport was a nice touch.*
- ▷ WAY OF DOING SOMETHING **5** [sing.] a way or style of doing something: *She prefers to answer any fan mail herself for a more personal touch.* ◆ *Computer graphics will give your presentation the professional touch.* ◆ *He couldn't find his magic touch with the ball today* (= he didn't play well). ◆ *This meal is awful. I think I'm **losing my touch*** (= my ability to do something).
- ▷ SMALL AMOUNT **6** [C, usually sing.] ~ of sth a very small amount **SYN** TRACE: *There was a touch of sarcasm in her voice.*
- ▷ SLIGHTLY **7** **a touch** [sing.] slightly; a little: *The music was a touch too loud for my liking.*

IDM **be, get, keep, etc. in ˈtouch (with sb)** to communicate with someone, especially by writing to them or telephoning them: *Are you still in touch with your friends from college?* ◆ *Thanks for showing us your products—we'll be in touch.* ◆ *I'm trying to get in touch with Jane. Do you have her number?* ◆ *Let's keep in touch.* ◆ *I'll put you in touch with someone in your area.* **be, keep, etc. in ˈtouch (with sth)** to know what is happening in a particular subject or area: *It is important to keep in touch with the latest research.* **be out of ˈtouch (with sb)** to no longer communicate with someone, so that you no longer know what is happening to them **be, become, etc. out of ˈtouch (with sth)** to not know or understand what is happening in a particular subject or area: *Unfortunately, the people making the decisions are out of touch with the real world.* **an easy/a soft touch** (*informal*) a person that you can easily persuade to do something, especially to give you money: *Unfortunately, my father is no soft touch.* **lose ˈtouch (with sb/sth) 1** to no longer have any contact with someone or something: *I've lost touch with all my old friends.* **2** to no longer understand something, especially how ordinary people feel ➔ more at COMMON *adj.*, LIGHT *adj.*

ˌtouch-and-ˈgo *adj.* [not usually before noun] (*informal*) used to say that the result of a situation is uncertain and that there is a possibility that something bad or unpleasant will happen: *She's fine now, but it was touch-and-go for a while* (= there was a possibility that she might die).

touch·down /'tʌtʃdaʊn/ *noun* **1** [C] (in football) an act of scoring points by crossing the other team's GOAL LINE while carrying the ball, or receiving the ball when you are over the other team's GOAL LINE **2** [C, U] the moment when a plane or SPACECRAFT lands **SYN** LANDING

tou·ché /tu'ʃeɪ/ *exclamation* (from *French*) used during an argument or a discussion to show that you accept that someone has answered your comment in an intelligent way and has gained an advantage by making a good point

touched /tʌtʃt/ *adj.* [not before noun] **1** feeling happy and grateful because of something kind that someone has done; feeling emotional about something: ~ **(by sth)** *She was touched by their warm welcome.* ◆ *She was touched by the plight of the refugees.* ◆ ~ **(that…)** *I was touched that he still remembered me.* **2** (*old-fashioned, informal*) slightly crazy

touch 'football *noun* [U] a type of football in which touching is used instead of tackling (TACKLE) ⊃ compare FLAG FOOTBALL

touch·ing /'tʌtʃɪŋ/ *adj.* causing feelings of sadness or sympathy; making you feel emotional **SYN** MOVING: *It was a touching story that moved many of us to tears.* ▶ **touch·ing·ly** *adv.*

touch·line /'tʌtʃlaɪn/ *noun* a line that marks the side of a playing field, especially in SOCCER

touch pad *noun* (*computing*) a device which you touch in different places in order to operate a program

touch screen *noun* (*computing*) a computer screen which allows you to give instructions to the computer by touching areas on it

touch·stone /'tʌtʃstoʊn/ *noun* [usually sing.] ~ **(of/for sth)** (*formal*) something that provides a standard against which other things are compared and/or judged: *the touchstone for quality*

Touch-Tone™ *adj.* (of a telephone or telephone system) producing different sounds when different numbers are pushed

touch-type *verb* [I] to type without having to look at the keys of a TYPEWRITER or keyboard

touch-up *noun* a quick improvement made to the appearance or condition of something: *My lipstick needed a touch-up.*

touch·y /'tʌtʃi/ *adj.* (touch·i·er, touch·i·est) **1** [not usually before noun] ~ **(about sth)** (of a person) easily upset or offended **SYN** SENSITIVE: *He's a little touchy about his weight.* **2** [usually before noun] (of a subject) that may upset or offend people and should therefore be dealt with carefully **SYN** DELICATE, SENSITIVE ▶ **touch·i·ness** *noun* [U]

touch·y-feel·y /ˌtʌtʃi 'fili/ *adj.* (*informal*, usually *disapproving*) expressing emotions too openly

tough 🔊 /tʌf/ *adj., noun, verb*

● *adj.* (tough·er, tough·est)

▸ DIFFICULT **1** having or causing problems or difficulties: *a tough childhood* ◆ *It was a tough decision to make.* ◆ *She's been having a tough time of it* (= a lot of problems) *lately.* ◆ *He faces the toughest test of his leadership so far.* ◆ *It can be tough trying to juggle a career and a family.*

▸ STRICT/FIRM **2** demanding that particular rules be obeyed and showing a lack of sympathy for any problems or suffering that this may cause: ~ **(on sb/sth)** *Don't be too tough on him—he was only trying to help.* ◆ ~ **(with sb/sth)** *It's about time teachers started to get tough with bullies.* ◆ *The school takes a tough line on* (= punishes severely) *cheating.* **ANT** SOFT

▸ STRONG **3** strong enough to deal successfully with difficult conditions or situations: *a tough breed of cattle* ◆ *He's not tough enough for a career in sales.* ◆ *She's a tough cookie/customer* (= someone who knows what they want and is not easily influenced by other people). **4** (of a person) physically

strong and likely to be violent: *You think you're so tough, don't you?* ◆ *He plays the tough guy in the movie.*

▸ MEAT **5** difficult to cut or chew **ANT** TENDER

▸ NOT EASILY DAMAGED **6** not easily cut, broken, torn, etc.: *a tough pair of shoes* ◆ *The reptile's skin is tough and scaly.*

▸ UNFORTUNATE **7** ~ **(on sb)** (*informal*) unfortunate for someone in a way that seems unfair: *It was tough on her being dropped from the team like that.* ◆ (*ironic*) *"I can't get it finished in time." "Tough!"* (= I don't feel sorry about it.)

▶ **tough·ly** *adv.* **tough·ness** *noun* [U]

IDM **(as) tough as nails** (*informal*) **1** very strong and able to deal successfully with difficult conditions or situations **2** not feeling or showing any emotion **tough luck** (*informal*) **1** used to show sympathy for something unfortunate that has happened to someone: *"I failed by one point." "That's tough luck."* **2** (*ironic*) used to show that you do not feel sorry for someone who has a problem: *"If you take the car, I won't be able to go out." "Tough luck!"* ⊃ more at ACT *n.*, GOING *n.*, HANG *v.*, NUT, TALK *v.*

● *noun* (*old-fashioned, informal*) a person who regularly uses violence against other people

● *verb*

PHR V **tough sth↔out** to stay firm and determined in a difficult situation: *You're just going to have to tough it out.*

tough·en /'tʌfn/ *verb* **1** [T, I] ~ **(sth) (up)** to become or make something stronger, so that it is not easily cut, broken, etc.: *toughened glass* **2** [T] ~ **sth (up)** to make something such as laws or rules stricter: *The government is considering toughening up the law on censorship.* **3** [T] ~ **sb (up)** to make someone stronger and more able to deal with difficult situations

tough·ie /'tʌfi/ *noun* (*informal*) **1** a person who is determined and not easily frightened **2** a very difficult choice or question

tough 'love *noun* [U] the fact of helping someone who has problems by dealing with them in a strict way because you believe it is good for them

tough-'minded *adj.* dealing with problems and situations in a determined way without being influenced by emotions **SYN** HARDHEADED

tou·pee /tu'peɪ/ (also *informal* **rug**) *noun* a small section of artificial hair, worn by a man to cover an area of his head where hair no longer grows

tour 🔊 /tʊr/ *noun, verb*

● *noun* **1** ~ **(of/round/around sth)** a journey made for pleasure during which several different towns, countries, etc. are visited: *a walking/sightseeing, etc. tour* ◆ *a bus tour of northern California* ◆ *a tour operator* (= a person or company that organizes tours) ⊃ collocations at TRAVEL ⊃ see also PACKAGE TOUR, WHISTLE-STOP ⊃ thesaurus box at TRIP **2** an act of walking around a town, building, etc. in order to visit it: *We were given a guided tour* (= by someone who knows about the place) *of the State House.* ◆ *a tour guide* ◆ *a tour of inspection* (= an official visit of a factory, classroom, etc. made by someone whose job is to check that everything is working as expected) **3** an official series of visits made to different places by a sports team, an ORCHESTRA, an important person, etc.: *The band is currently on a one-day tour of France.* ◆ *The band is on tour in France.* ◆ *a concert tour* ◆ *The Prince will visit Boston on the last leg* (= part) *of his American tour.* ◆ *The soldiers will do a six-month tour of duty in the Mideast.*

● *verb* [T, I] to travel around a place, for example on vacation, or to perform, to advertise something, etc.: ~ **sth** *He toured America with his one-man show.* ◆ *She toured the country promoting her book.* ◆ ~ **around sth** *We spent four weeks touring around Europe.*

tour de force /ˌtʊr də 'fɔrs/ *noun* (*pl.* **tours de force** /ˌtʊr də 'fɔrs/) (from *French*) an extremely skillful performance or achievement: *a cinematic tour de force*

Tou·rette's syn·drome /tu'rets ˌsɪndroʊm/ *noun* [U] (*medical*) a DISORDER of the nerves in which a person makes a lot of small movements and sounds that they cannot control, including using swear words

tour·ism /'tʊrɪzəm/ *noun* [U] the business activity connected with providing places to stay, services, and entertainment for people who are visiting a place for pleasure: *The area is heavily dependent on tourism.* ◆ *the tourism industry* ⊃ collocations at TRAVEL ⊃ see also AGRITOURISM

tour·ist /'tʊrɪst/ *noun*
a person who is traveling or visiting a place for pleasure: *busloads of foreign tourists* ◆ *a popular **tourist attraction/ destination/resort** ◆ the **tourist industry/sector** ◆ Further information is available from the local **tourist office**.* ⊃ collocations at TRAVEL

tourist ,class *noun* [U] the cheapest type of ticket or room that is available on a plane or ship or in a hotel

tourist ,trap *noun* (*informal, disapproving*) a place that attracts a lot of tourists and where food, drink, entertainment, etc. is more expensive than normal

tour·ist·y /'tʊrɪsti/ *adj.* (*informal, disapproving*) attracting or designed to attract a lot of tourists: *Las Vegas has both touristy and high-end accommodations.* ◆ *a shop full of touristy souvenirs*

tour·na·ment /'tɔrnəmənt; 'tʊr-; 'tɔr-/ *noun* **1** (also *less frequent* **tour·ney**) a sports competition involving a number of teams or players who take part in different games and must leave the competition if they lose. The competition continues until there is only the winner left: *a golf/ basketball/tennis, etc. tournament* **2** a competition in the Middle Ages between soldiers on HORSEBACK fighting to show courage and skill

tour·ney /'tɜrni; 'tʊr-/ *noun* (used especially in newspapers) = TOURNAMENT

tour·ni·quet /'tɜrnɪkət; 'tʊr-/ *noun* a piece of cloth, etc. that is tied tightly around an arm or a leg to stop the loss of blood from a wound

tour·tière /ˌtʊr'tyɛr; ˌtɔr-/ *noun* (*CanE*) a type of meat PIE that is eaten especially at Christmas

tou·sle /'taʊzl; -sl/ *verb* [usually passive] ~ **sth** to make someone's hair messy ▶ **tou·sled** *adj.*: *a boy with blue eyes and tousled hair*

tout /taʊt/ *verb* [T] ~ **sb/sth (as sth)** to try to persuade people that someone or something is important or valuable by praising them/it: *She's being touted as the next governor.*

tow /toʊ/ *verb, noun*
● *verb* ~ **sth (away)** to pull a car or boat behind another vehicle, using a rope or chain: *Our car was towed away by the police.* ⊃ see also TOW BAR, TOW ROPE ⊃ thesaurus box at PULL
● *noun* [sing.] an act of one vehicle pulling another vehicle using a rope or chain: *The car broke down and we had to get somebody to give us a tow.* ◆ *a tow truck*
IDM **in tow 1** (*informal*) if you have someone **in tow**, they are with you and following closely behind: *She turned up with her mother in tow.* **2** if a ship is taken **in tow**, it is pulled by another ship

to·ward /tɔrd; twɔrd; 'toʊərd/ (also **to·wards**) *prep.*
1 in the direction of someone or something: *They were heading toward the Canadian border.* ◆ *She had her back toward me.* **2** getting closer to achieving something: *This is a first step toward universal health care.* **3** close or closer to a point in time: *toward the end of April* **4** in relation to someone or something: *He was warm and tender toward her.* ◆ *our attitude toward death* **5** with the aim of obtaining something, or helping someone to obtain something: *The money will go toward a new school building* (= will help pay for it).

tow bar *noun* a bar attached to the back of a vehicle for TOWING (= pulling) another vehicle

tow·el /'taʊəl/ *noun, verb*
● *noun* a piece of cloth or paper used for drying things, especially your body: *Help yourself to a clean towel.* ◆ *a hand/*

bath towel (= a small/large towel) ◆ *a **beach towel** (= a large towel used for lying on in the sun)* ⊃ see also DISH TOWEL, PAPER TOWEL
IDM **throw in the towel** (*informal*) to admit that you are defeated and stop trying
● *verb* (-l-, *CanE usually* -ll-) ~ **yourself/sb/sth (down)** to dry yourself/someone or something with a towel

towel ,bar *noun* = TOWEL RACK

tow·el·ing (also **tow·el·ling**) /'taʊəlɪŋ/ *noun* [U] a type of soft cotton cloth that absorbs liquids, used especially for making towels

towel ,rack (also **towel ,bar**) *noun* a bar or frame for hanging towels on in a bathroom

tow·er /'taʊər/ *noun, verb*
● *noun* **1** a tall, narrow building or part of a building, especially of a church or castle: *a clock/bell tower* ◆ *the Tower of London* ◆ *the Eiffel Tower* **2** (often in compounds) a tall structure used for sending television or radio signals: *a television tower* **3** (usually in compounds) a tall piece of furniture used for storing things: *a CD tower* ⊃ see also CONTROL TOWER, COOLING TOWER, IVORY TOWER, WATCHTOWER, WATER TOWER
IDM **a tower of strength** a person that you can rely on to help, protect, and comfort you when you are in trouble
● *verb*
PHRV **tower 'over/a'bove sb/sth 1** to be much higher or taller than the people or things that are near: *The cliffs towered above them.* ◆ *He towered over his classmates.* **2** to be much better than others in ability, quality, etc.: *She towers over other dancers of her generation.*

tow·er·ing /'taʊərɪŋ/ *adj.* [only before noun] **1** extremely tall or high and therefore impressive: *towering cliffs* **2** of extremely high quality: *a towering performance* **3** (of emotions) extremely strong: *a towering rage*

tow·line /'toʊlaɪn/ *noun* = TOW ROPE

town /taʊn/ *noun*
1 [C, U] a place where people live and work that is smaller than a city but has many houses, stores, etc.: *a college town* ◆ *They live in a rough part of town.* ◆ *The nearest town is ten miles away.* ◆ *the northern Vermont town of Saint Albans* ⊃ see also SMALL-TOWN **HELP** You will find other compounds ending in **town** at their place in the alphabet. **2 the town** [sing.] the people who live in a particular town: *The whole town is talking about it.* **3** [U] the area of a town where most of the stores and businesses are: *Can you give me a lift into town?* ⊃ see also DOWNTOWN, MIDTOWN, OUT-OF-TOWN, UPTOWN **4** [U] a particular town where someone lives and works or one that has just been referred to: *I'll be in town next week if you want to meet.* ◆ *He married a girl from out of town.* ⊃ see also OUT-OF-TOWN **5** [sing., U] life in towns or cities as opposed to life in the country: *Pollution is just one of the disadvantages of living in town.*
IDM **go to town (on sth)** (*informal*) to do something with a lot of energy, enthusiasm, etc., especially by spending a lot of money **(out) on the town** (*informal*) visiting restaurants, clubs, theaters, etc. for entertainment, especially at night: *a night on the town* ◆ *How about going out on the town tonight?* ⊃ more at GAME *n.*, MAN *n.*, PAINT *v.*

TOPIC COLLOCATIONS

Town and Country

town

- **live in** a city/a town/an urban environment/the suburbs/the (housing) projects/shanty towns/ slums/(*informal*) a concrete jungle/the ghetto
- **live downtown/in** the downtown area/uptown/in midtown (Manhattan)
- **enjoy/like** the hectic pace of life/the hustle and bustle of city life
- **cope with** the stress/pressures of urban life

- **get caught up in** the rat race
- **prefer/seek** the anonymity of life in a big city
- **be drawn to/resist** the lure of the big city
- **head for** the bright lights (of the big city/New York)
- **enjoy/love** the vibrant/lively nightlife
- **have/be close to** all the amenities
- **be surrounded by** towering skyscrapers/soulless suburban sprawl
- **use/travel by/rely on** public transportation
- **put up with/get stuck in/sit in** massive/huge/heavy/endless/constant traffic jams
- **tackle/ease/reduce/relieve/alleviate** the heavy/severe (traffic) congestion
- **be affected by/choked with/damaged by** pollution

country
- **live in** a village/the countryside/an isolated area/a rural backwater/(informal) the sticks/the boondocks
- **enjoy/like** the relaxed/slower pace of life
- **enjoy/love/explore** the great outdoors
- **look for/find/get/enjoy** a little peace and quiet
- **need/want** to get back/closer to nature
- **be surrounded by** open/unspoiled/picturesque/peaceful countryside
- **escape/quit/get out of/leave** the rat race
- **seek/achieve** a better/healthy work-life balance
- **downshift** to a less stressful life
- **build/seek/start** a new life in the country
- **pull up stakes** and move to/head for…
- **create/build/foster** a strong sense of community
- **depend on/be employed in/work in** agriculture
- **live off/farm/work** the land
- **tackle/address** the problem of rural/small-town unemployment

ˌtown and ˈgown noun [U] the relationship between the people who live permanently in a town where there is a college or university and the members of the college or university

ˌtown ˈclerk noun a public officer in charge of the records of a town

ˌtown ˈcrier (also crier) noun (in the past) a person whose job was to walk through a town shouting news, official ANNOUNCEMENTS, etc.

ˌtown ˈhall noun a building containing local government offices and often rooms for public meetings, etc.

town·house (also ˈtown house) /ˈtaʊnhaʊs/ noun a house in a town that is one of a row of houses that are joined together on each side, especially a tall, narrow house in a traditional style: an elegant Georgian townhouse ⊃ picture at HOUSE ⊃ compare ROW HOUSE

town·ie /ˈtaʊni/ noun 1 a person who lives in or comes from a town or city, especially someone who does not know much about life in the countryside 2 a person who lives in a town with a college or university but does not attend or work at it

ˌtown ˈmeeting noun a meeting when people in a town come together to discuss problems that affect the town and to give their opinions on various issues

ˌtown ˈplanner noun = CITY PLANNER

ˌtown ˈplanning noun [U] = CITY PLANNING

town·scape /ˈtaʊnskeɪp/ noun 1 what you see when you look at a town, for example from a distance: an industrial townscape 2 (technical) a picture of a town ⊃ compare LANDSCAPE, SEASCAPE

town·ship /ˈtaʊnʃɪp/ noun 1 (in the U.S. or Canada) a division of a county that is a unit of local government 2 (in South Africa in the past) a town or part of a town that black people had to live in, and where only black people lived

towns·peo·ple /ˈtaʊnzˌpipl/ (also towns·folk /ˈtaʊnsfoʊk/) noun [pl.] people who live in towns, not in the countryside; the people who live in a particular town

tow·path /ˈtoʊpæθ/ noun a path along the bank of a river or

CANAL, that was used in the past by horses pulling boats (called BARGES)

ˈtow rope (also tow·line) noun a rope that is used for pulling something along, especially a vehicle

ˈtow truck noun a truck that is used for taking cars away to be repaired when they have had a BREAKDOWN ⊃ picture at TRUCK

tox·e·mi·a /tɑkˈsimiə/ noun [U] (medical) infection of the blood by harmful bacteria SYN BLOOD POISONING

tox·ic /ˈtɑksɪk/ adj. 1 containing poison; poisonous: toxic chemicals/fumes/gases/substances ♦ to dispose of toxic waste ♦ Many pesticides are highly toxic. ANT NONTOXIC 2 ~ debt/loan/asset/investment a level of debt or high-risk investment that causes very serious problems for a bank or other financial institution 3 [usually before noun] (informal) (of a person) having a very unpleasant personality, especially in the way they like to control and influence other people in a dishonest way

tox·ic·i·ty /tɑkˈsɪsəti/ noun (pl. tox·ic·i·ties) (technical) 1 [U] the quality of being poisonous; the extent to which something is poisonous: substances with high levels of toxicity 2 [C] the effect that a poisonous substance has: Minor toxicities of this drug include nausea and vomiting.

tox·i·col·o·gy /ˌtɑksɪˈkɑlədʒi/ noun [U] the scientific study of poisons ▶ tox·i·co·log·i·cal /ˌtɑksɪkəˈlɑdʒɪkl/ adj. tox·i·col·o·gist /ˌtɑksɪˈkɑlədʒɪst/ noun

ˌtoxic ˈshock ˌsyndrome noun [U] a serious illness in women caused by harmful bacteria in the VAGINA, connected with the use of TAMPONS

tox·in /ˈtɑksn/ noun a poisonous substance, especially one that is produced by bacteria in plants and animals

tox·o·plas·mo·sis /ˌtɑksoʊplæzˈmoʊsəs/ noun [U] (medical) a disease that can be dangerous to a baby while it is still in its mother's body, caught from infected meat, soil, or animal FECES

toy /tɔɪ/ noun, adj., verb
- noun 1 an object for children to play with: cuddly/soft toys ♦ The children were playing happily with their toys. ⊃ picture on page 1581 2 an object that you have for enjoyment or pleasure rather than for a serious purpose SYN PLAYTHING: executive toys ♦ His latest toy is the electric drill he bought last week. ⊃ see also BOY TOY
- adj. [only before noun] 1 made as a copy of a particular thing and used for playing with: a toy car ♦ toy soldiers 2 (of a dog) of a very small breed: a toy poodle
- verb
  PHR V ˈtoy with sth 1 to consider an idea or a plan, but not very seriously and not for a long time SYN FLIRT WITH: I did briefly toy with the idea of living in British Columbia. 2 to play with something and move it around carelessly or without thinking: He kept toying nervously with his pen.

ˈtoy boy noun (informal, humorous) a woman's male lover who is much younger than she is

TQM /ˌti kyu ˈɛm/ abbr. TOTAL QUALITY MANAGEMENT

trace ⚷ AWL /treɪs/ verb, noun
- verb 1 ~ sb/sth (to sth) to find or discover someone or something by looking carefully for them/it SYN TRACK DOWN: We finally traced him to an address in Chicago. 2 ~ sth (back) (to sth) to find the origin or cause of something: She could trace her family tree back to the 18th century. ♦ The leak was eventually traced to a broken seal. ♦ The police traced the call (= used special electronic equipment to find out who made the telephone call) to her ex-husband's number. 3 ~ sth (from sth) (to sth) to describe a process or the development of something: Her book traces the town's history from colonial times to the present day. 4 ~ sth (out) to draw a line or lines on a surface: She traced a line in the sand. 5 ~ sth to follow the shape or outline of something: He traced the route on the map. ♦ A tear traced a path down her cheek. 6 ~ sth to copy a map, drawing, etc. by drawing on TRACING PAPER (= transparent paper) placed over it

Toys and Games

toys

teddy bear

stuffed animal

building blocks

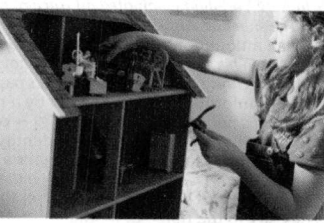

dollhouse

hand puppet

rag doll

rocking horse

games

dominoes

tic-tac-toe

Chinese checkers

queen — king
— pawn
chessboard —

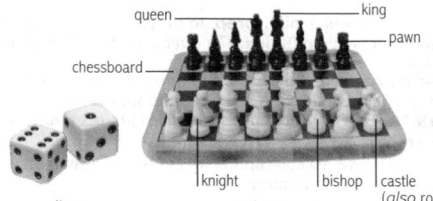

knight   bishop   castle
(also rook)

dice   chess

checkers

backgammon

play equipment

Frisbee™

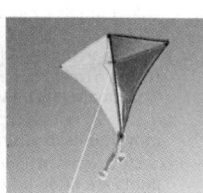

kite

jump rope

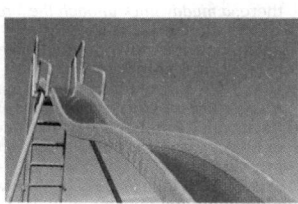

slide

trampoline

swing

sandbox

jungle gym

noun 1 [C, U] a mark, an object, or a sign that shows that someone or something existed or was present: *It's exciting to discover traces of earlier civilizations.* ◆ *Police searched the area but found no trace of the escaped prisoners.* ◆ *Years of living in New York had eliminated all trace of her Southern accent.* ◆ *The ship had vanished without a trace.* **2** [C] ~ **of sth** a very small amount of something: *The autopsy revealed traces of poison in his stomach.* ◆ *She spoke without a trace of bitterness.* **3** [C] (*technical*) a line or pattern on paper or a screen that shows information that is found by a machine: *The trace showed a normal heart rhythm.* **4** [C] ~ **on sb/sth** a search to find out information about the identity of someone or something, especially what number a telephone call was made from: *The police ran a trace on the call.* **5** [C, usually pl.] one of the two long pieces of leather that fasten a CARRIAGE or CART to the horse that pulls it

trace·a·ble `AWL` /ˈtreɪsəbl/ *adj.* ~ **(to sb/sth)** if something is **traceable**, you can find out where it came from, where it has gone, when it began, or what its cause was: *Most telephone calls are traceable.*

trace element *noun* **1** a chemical substance that is found in very small amounts **2** a chemical substance that living things, especially plants, need only in very small amounts to be able to grow well

trac·er /ˈtreɪsər/ *noun* **1** a bullet or SHELL (= a kind of bomb) that leaves a line of smoke or flame behind it **2** (*technical*) a RADIOACTIVE substance that can be seen in the human body and is used to find out what is happening inside the body

trac·er·y /ˈtreɪsəri/ *noun* (*pl.* **trac·er·ies**) **1** [U] (*technical*) a pattern of lines and curves in stone on the top part of some church windows **2** [U, C, usually sing.] (*literary*) an attractive pattern of lines and curves

tra·che·a /ˈtreɪkiə/ *noun* (*pl.* **tra·che·ae** /-kiː/ or **tra·che·as**) (*anatomy*) the tube in the throat that carries air to the lungs ⊃ picture at BODY **SYN** WINDPIPE

tra·che·ot·o·my /ˌtreɪkiˈɑtəmi/ *noun* (*pl.* **tra·che·ot·o·mies**) (*medical*) a medical operation to cut a hole in someone's trachea so that they can breathe

trac·ing /ˈtreɪsɪŋ/ *noun* a copy of a map, drawing, etc. that you make by drawing on a piece of transparent paper placed on top of it

tracing paper *noun* [U] strong transparent paper that is placed on top of a drawing, etc. so that you can follow the lines with a pen or pencil in order to make a copy of it

track 🔊 /træk/ *noun, verb*

noun

> **ROUGH PATH 1** [C] a rough path or road, usually one that has not been built but that has been made by people walking there: *a muddy track through the forest*

> **MARKS ON GROUND 2** [C, usually pl.] marks left by a person, an animal, or a moving vehicle: *We followed the bear's tracks in the snow.* ◆ *tire tracks*

> **FOR TRAIN 3** [C, U] rails that a train moves along: *railroad tracks* ◆ *The country has thousands of miles of track.* **4** [C] a track with a number at a train station that a train arrives at or leaves from: *The train for Chicago is on track 9.* ⊃ note at PLATFORM

> **FOR RACES 5** [C] a piece of ground with a special surface for people, horses, cars, etc. to have races on: *a running track* ◆ *a Formula One Grand Prix track* (= for motor racing) ⊃ see also TRACK AND FIELD **6** the track [sing.] the place where races, especially horse races, are run: *He likes to spend his Saturdays at the track.*

> **DIRECTION/COURSE 7** [C] the path or direction that someone or something is moving in: *Police are on the track of* (= searching for) *the thieves.* ◆ *She is on the fast track to promotion* (= will get it quickly). ⊃ see also ONE-TRACK MIND

> **MUSIC 8** [C] a piece of music or song on a CD, tape, or record: *a track from their latest album* **9** [C] part of a tape or computer disk that music or information can be recorded

on: *a sixteen-track recording studio* ◆ *She sang on the backing track.* ⊃ see also LAUGH TRACK, SOUNDTRACK

> **FOR CURTAIN 10** [C] a pole or rail that a curtain moves along

> **ON LARGE VEHICLE 11** [C] a continuous belt of metal plates around the wheels of a large vehicle such as a BULLDOZER that allows it to move over the ground

IDM back on track going in the right direction again after a mistake, failure, etc.: *I tried to get my life back on track after my divorce.* **be on track** to be doing the right thing in order to achieve a particular result: *Curtis is on track for the gold medal.* **keep/lose track of sb/sth** to have/not have information about what is happening or where someone or something is: *Bank statements help you keep track of where your money is going.* ◆ *I lost all track of time* (= forgot what time it was). **make tracks** (*informal*) to leave a place, especially to go home **on the right/wrong track** thinking or behaving in the right/wrong way **stop/halt sb in their tracks | stop/halt/freeze in your tracks** to suddenly make someone stop by frightening or surprising them; to suddenly stop because something has frightened or surprised you: *The question stopped Anna in her tracks.* ⊃ more at BEAT *v.*, COVER *v.*, HOT, JUMP *v.*, WRONG *adj.*

verb

> **FOLLOW 1** [T, I] ~ **(sb/sth)** to find someone or something by following the marks, signs, information, etc., that they have left behind them: *hunters tracking and shooting bears* **2** [T] ~ **sb/sth | ~ where, how, etc....** to follow the movements of someone or something, especially by using special electronic equipment: *We continued tracking the plane on our radar.* **3** [T] ~ **sb/sth | ~ where, how, etc....** to follow the progress or development of someone or something: *The research project involves tracking the careers of 400 graduates.* ⊃ see also FAST-TRACK

> **SCHOOL STUDENTS 4** [T, usually passive] ~ **sb** (in schools) to put school students into groups according to their ability

> **LEAVE MARKS 5** [T] ~ **sth** (+ adv./prep.) to leave dirty marks behind you as you walk: *Don't track mud on my clean floor.*

> **OF CAMERA 6** [I] + adv./prep. to move in relation to the thing that is being filmed: *The camera eventually tracked away.*

PHR V track sb/sth↔down to find someone or something after searching in several different places **SYN** TRACE: *The police have so far failed to track down the attacker.*

track and field *noun* sports that people compete in, such as running and jumping

track·ball /ˈtrækbɔl/ *noun* (*computing*) a device containing a ball that is used instead of a mouse to move the CURSOR around the screen

track·er /ˈtrækər/ *noun* a person who can find people or wild animals by following the marks that they leave on the ground

track event *noun* [usually pl.] a sports event that is a race run on a track, rather than jumping or throwing something ⊃ compare FIELD EVENT ⊃ picture at SPORT

tracking station *noun* a place where people follow the movements of aircraft, etc. in the sky by RADAR or radio

track lighting *noun* [U] a LIGHTING system in which the lights are fitted onto tracks, allowing the position of the lights to be varied

track record *noun* all the past achievements, successes, or failures of a person or an organization: *He has a proven track record in marketing.*

track·suit /ˈtræksut/ (also **jogging suit**) *noun* a warm loose pair of pants and matching jacket worn for sports practice or as informal clothes

tract /trækt/ *noun* **1** (*biology*) a system of connected organs or TISSUES along which materials or messages pass: *the digestive tract* ◆ *a nerve tract* **2** an area of land, especially a large one **SYN** STRETCH: *vast tracts of forest* **3** (sometimes *disapproving*) a short piece of writing, especially on a

t tea   ţ butter   d did   k cat   g got   tʃ chin   dʒ June   f fall

religious, moral, or political subject, that is intended to influence people's ideas

trac·ta·ble /ˈtræktəbl/ *adj.* (*formal*) easy to deal with or control **SYN** MANAGEABLE **ANT** INTRACTABLE ▸ **trac·ta·bil·i·ty** /ˌtræktəˈbɪləti/ *noun* [U]

'tract house (also **'tract home**) *noun* a modern house built on an area of land where a lot of other similar houses have also been built

trac·tion /ˈtrækʃn/ *noun* [U] **1** the force that stops something, for example the wheels of a vehicle, from sliding on the ground: *The car couldn't get traction on the icy road.* **2** a way of treating a broken bone in your body that involves using special equipment to pull the bone gradually back into its correct place: *He spent six weeks **in traction** after he broke his leg.* **3** the action of pulling something along a surface; the power that is used for doing this **4** the support that is needed in order for a plan, idea, etc. to succeed: *The needed traction to get the bill passed just wasn't there.*

'traction ˌengine *noun* a vehicle, driven by steam or DIESEL oil, used in the past for pulling heavy loads

trac·tor /ˈtræktər/ *noun* **1** a powerful vehicle with two large and two smaller wheels, used especially for pulling farm machinery ➔ picture at TRUCK **2** the front part of a tractor-trailer, where the driver sits

ˌtractor-'trailer (also **'trailer ˌtruck**) (also *informal* **rig, sem·i**) *noun* a large truck with two sections, one in front where the driver sits and one behind for carrying goods. The sections are connected by a FLEXIBLE joint so that the tractor-trailer can turn corners more easily. ➔ picture at TRUCK ➔ see also ARTICULATED

trad·a·ble (also **trade·a·ble**) /ˈtreɪdəbl/ *adj.* (*technical*) that you can easily buy and sell or exchange for money or goods **SYN** MARKETABLE

trade 🔑 /treɪd/ *noun, verb*

• *noun* **1** [U] the activity of buying and selling or of exchanging goods or services between people or countries: *international/foreign trade* ◆ *Trade between the two countries has increased.* ◆ *the international trade in oil* ◆ *the arms, drug, etc. trade* ➔ see also BALANCE OF TRADE, FAIR-TRADE, FREE TRADE ➔ collocations at BUSINESS, INTERNATIONAL **2** [C] a particular type of business: *the building/food/tourist, etc. trade* ◆ *He works in the retail trade* (= selling goods in stores). ➔ see also RAG TRADE **3** **the trade** [sing.] a particular area of business and the people or companies that are connected with it: *They offer discounts to the trade* (= to people who are working in the same business). ◆ *a trade magazine/journal* ➔ see also STOCK-IN-TRADE **4** [U,C] the amount of goods or services that you sell **SYN** BUSINESS: *Trade was very good last month.* **5** [U,C] a job, especially one that involves working with your hands and that requires special training and skills: *He was a carpenter **by trade**.* ◆ *When she leaves school, she wants to learn a trade.* ◆ *She was surrounded by **the tools of her trade*** (= everything she needs to do her job). ➔ thesaurus box at WORK **6** [C] (in sports) the act of exchanging a player on one team for a player on another team **IDM** see JACK *n.*, PLY *v.*, ROARING, TRICK *n.*

• *verb* **1** [I, T] to buy and sell things: **~ (in sth) (with sb)** *The firm openly traded in arms.* ◆ *Early explorers traded directly with the Native Americans.* ◆ *trading partners* (= countries that you trade with) ◆ **~ sth (with sb)** *Our products are now traded worldwide.* **2** [I, T] **~ (sth)** to be bought and sold, or to buy and sell something, on a STOCK EXCHANGE: *Shares were trading at under half their usual value.* **3** [T] to exchange something that you have for something that someone else has: **~ (sb) sth** *to trade secrets/insults/jokes* ◆ **~ sth for sth** *She traded her posters for his DVD.* ◆ **~ sth with sb** *I wouldn't mind **trading places** with her for a day.* **4** [T] **~ sb (for sb)** (in sports) to exchange a player on one team for a player on another team: *He was traded to the Astros for a pair of rookies.* **PHRV** ˌtrade 'down to spend less money on things than you used to: *Shoppers are trading down and looking for bargains.* ˌtrade sth↔'in to give something used as part of the payment for something new: *He traded in his old car for a*

new Mercedes. ➔ related noun TRADE-IN ˌtrade sth↔'off (against/for sth) to balance two things or situations that are opposed to each other: *They were attempting to trade off inflation against unemployment.* ➔ related noun TRADE-OFF 'trade on sth (*disapproving*) to use something to your own advantage, especially in an unfair way **SYN** EXPLOIT: *They trade on people's insecurity to sell them insurance.* ˌtrade 'up **1** to sell something in order to buy something more expensive: *We're going to trade up to a larger house.* **2** to give something you have used as part of the payment for something more expensive

'trade ˌbalance *noun* = BALANCE OF TRADE

'trade ˌdeficit (also **'trade gap**) *noun* [usually sing.] a situation in which the value of a country's imports is greater than the value of its exports

'trade fair *noun* = TRADE SHOW

'trade-in *noun* a method of buying something by giving a used item as part of the payment for a new one; the used item itself: *the trade-in value of a car* ◆ *Do you have a trade-in?*

trade·mark /ˈtreɪdmɑrk/ *noun* (*abbr.* TM) **1** a name, symbol, or design that a company uses for its products and that cannot be used by anyone else: *"Big Mac" is McDonald's best-known trademark.* **2** a special way of behaving or dressing that is typical of someone and that makes them easily recognized

'trade name *noun* **1** = BRAND NAME **2** a name that is taken and used by a company for business purposes

'trade-off *noun* **1** **~ (between sth and sth)** the act of balancing two things that are opposed to each other: *a trade-off between increased production and a reduction in quality* **2** something bad that you have to accept, or something of value that you have to lose, in order to have something good: *We love living in the country, but the trade-off is the long commute to work.* ◆ **~ for sth** *Being popular is sometimes a trade-off for better grades in school.*

trad·er /ˈtreɪdər/ *noun* a person who buys and sells things as a job: *small/independent/local traders* ◆ *bond/currency traders*

'trade route *noun* (in the past) the route that people buying and selling goods used to take across land or ocean

'trade school *noun* a school where students go to learn a trade

ˌtrade 'secret *noun* a secret piece of information that is known only by the people at a particular company: *The recipe for their drink is a closely guarded trade secret.*

'trade show (also **'trade fair**) *noun* an event at which many different companies show and sell their products

trades·man /ˈtreɪdzmən/ *noun* (*pl.* **trades·men** /-mən/) **1** a person who sells goods, especially in a shop/store **SYN** SHOPKEEPER **2** a person whose job involves training and special skills, for example a PLUMBER or an ELECTRICIAN

trades·peo·ple /ˈtreɪdzˌpipl/ *noun* [pl.] people whose job involves training and special skills, for example CARPENTERS

ˌtrade 'surplus *noun* a situation in which the value of a country's exports is greater than the value of its imports

'trade-up *noun* a sale of an object in order to buy something similar but better and more expensive

'trade winds *noun* [pl.] strong winds that blow all the time toward the EQUATOR and then to the west ➔ compare ANTITRADES

trad·ing /ˈtreɪdɪŋ/ *noun* [U] the activity of buying and selling things: *Chicago has long been a trading center for agricultural products of the Midwest.* ◆ *Shares worth $8 million changed hands during a day of hectic trading.* ➔ see also INSIDER TRADING

'trading ˌcard *noun* one of a set of cards, often showing sports players or other famous people on them, that children collect and exchange with one another

'trading ˌfloor *noun* an area in a STOCK EXCHANGE or bank where shares and other securities (SECURITY) are bought and sold

'trading ˌpost *noun* a small place in an area that is a long way from any town, used as a center for buying and selling goods

tra·di·tion 🔑 **AWL** /trəˈdɪʃn/ *noun* [C, U]
a belief, custom, or way of doing something that has existed for a long time among a particular group of people; a set of these beliefs or customs: *religious/cultural, etc. traditions* ◆ *This region is steeped in tradition.* ◆ *The company has a long tradition of fine design.* ◆ *The British are said to love tradition* (= to want to do things in the way they have always been done). ◆ *They broke with tradition* (= did things differently) *and got married quietly.* ◆ *By tradition, children dress up in costumes and go trick-or-treating on Halloween.* ◆ *There's a tradition in our family that we have a party on New Year's Eve.* ◆ *He's a politician in the tradition of* (= similar in style to) *Kennedy.*

tra·di·tion·al 🔑 **AWL** /trəˈdɪʃənl/ *adj.*
1 being part of the beliefs, customs, or way of life of a particular group of people, that have not changed for a long time: *traditional dress* ◆ *It's traditional for Americans to eat turkey on Thanksgiving Day.* **2** (sometimes *disapproving*) following older methods and ideas rather than modern or different ones **SYN** CONVENTIONAL: *traditional methods of teaching* ◆ *Their marriage is very traditional.* **ANT** NONTRADITIONAL ▸ **tra·di·tion·al·ly** **AWL** /-ʃənəli/ *adv.*: *The festival is traditionally held in May.* ◆ *Housework has traditionally been regarded as women's work.*

tra·di·tion·al·ism /trəˈdɪʃənəˌlɪzəm/ *noun* [U] the belief that customs and traditions are more important for a society than modern ideas

tra·di·tion·al·ist **AWL** /trəˈdɪʃənəlɪst/ *noun* a person who prefers tradition to modern ideas or ways of doing things ▸ **tra·di·tion·al·ist** *adj.*

tra·duce /trəˈdus/ *verb* ~ **sb** (*formal*) to say things about someone that are unpleasant or not true **SYN** SLANDER

traf·fic 🔑 /ˈtræfɪk/ *noun, verb*
● *noun* [U] **1** the vehicles that are on a road at a particular time: *heavy/rush-hour traffic* ◆ *local/through traffic* ◆ *There's always a lot of traffic at this time of day.* ◆ *They were stuck in traffic and missed their flight.* ◆ *a plan to reduce traffic congestion* ◆ *traffic police/cops* (= who control traffic on a road or stop drivers who are breaking the law) ◆ *The delay is due simply to the volume of traffic.* ⊃ collocations at DRIVING **2** the movement of ships, trains, aircraft, etc. along a particular route: *transatlantic traffic* ◆ *air traffic control* **3** the movement of people or goods from one place to another: *commuter/freight/passenger traffic* ◆ *the traffic of goods between one country and another* **4** the movement of messages and signals through an electronic communication system: *the computer servers that manage global Internet traffic* **5** ~ **(in sth)** illegal trade in something: *the traffic in firearms*
● *verb* (-ck-)
PHR V **'traffic in sth** to buy and sell something illegally: *to traffic in drugs* ▸ **traf·fick·er** *noun*: *a drug trafficker* **traf·fick·ing** *noun* [U]: *drug trafficking*

'traffic ˌcircle (also **ro·ta·ry**) *noun* a place where two or more roads meet, forming a circle that all traffic must go around in the same direction

'traffic ˌcone (also **cone**) *noun* a plastic object shaped like a CONE and often orange in color, used on roads to show where vehicles are not allowed to go, for example while repairs are being done **SYN** PYLON

'traffic ˌisland *noun* an area in the middle of a road where you can stand and wait for cars to go past until it is safe for you to cross

'traffic ˌjam *noun* a long line of vehicles on a road that cannot move or that can only move very slowly: *We were stuck in a traffic jam.* ⊃ collocations at DRIVING

'traffic ˌlight *noun* [C] (also **'traffic ˌlights** [pl.], **'stop·lights** [pl.]) a signal that controls the traffic on a road, by means of red, yellow, and green lights that show when you must stop and when you can go: *Turn left at the traffic light.*

tra·ge·di·an /trəˈdʒidiən/ *noun* (*formal*) **1** a person who writes tragedies for the theater **2** an actor in tragedies

trag·e·dy /ˈtrædʒədi/ *noun* (*pl.* **trag·e·dies**) [C, U] **1** a very sad event or situation, especially one that involves death: *It's a tragedy that she died so young.* ◆ *Tragedy struck the family when their son was hit by a car and killed.* ◆ *The whole affair ended in tragedy.* **2** a serious play with a sad ending, especially one in which the main character dies; plays of this type: *Shakespeare's tragedies* ◆ *Greek tragedy* ⊃ compare COMEDY

trag·ic /ˈtrædʒɪk/ *adj.* **1** making you feel very sad, usually because someone has died or suffered a lot: *He was killed in a tragic accident at the age of 24.* ◆ *Cuts in Medicare coverage could have tragic consequences for patients.* ◆ *It would be tragic if her talent remained unrecognized.* **2** [only before noun] connected with tragedy (= the style of literature): *a tragic actor/hero* ▸ **trag·i·cally** /-kli/ *adv.*: *Tragically, his wife was killed in a car accident.* ◆ *He died tragically young.*

ˌtragic 'irony *noun* [U] (*technical*) a technique in literature in which a character's actions or thoughts are known to the reader or audience but not to the other characters in the story

trag·i·com·e·dy /ˌtrædʒɪˈkɑmədi/ *noun* [C, U] (*pl.* **trag·i·com·e·dies**) **1** a play or movie that is both funny and sad; plays or movies of this type **2** an event or a situation that is both funny and sad ▸ **trag·i·com·ic** /-ˈkɑmɪk/ *adj.*

trail /treɪl/ *noun, verb*
● *noun* **1** a long line or series of marks that is left by someone or something: *a trail of blood* ◆ *tourists who leave a trail of litter everywhere they go* ◆ *The hurricane left a trail of destruction behind it.* **2** a track, sign, or smell that is left behind and that can be followed, especially in hunting: *The hounds were following the fox's trail.* ◆ *The police are still on the trail of the escaped prisoner.* ◆ *Fortunately the trail was still warm* (= clear and easy to follow). ◆ *The trail had gone cold.* **3** a path through the countryside **SYN** FOOTPATH: *a trail through the woods* ⊃ see also NATURE TRAIL **4** a route that is followed for a particular purpose: *a tourist trail* (= of famous buildings and places) ◆ *politicians on the campaign trail* (= traveling around to attract support) **IDM** see BLAZE *v.*, HIT *v.*, HOT
● *verb* **1** [T, I] to pull something behind someone or something, usually along the ground; to be pulled along in this way: ~ **sth** *A jeep trailing a cloud of dust was speeding in my direction.* ◆ *I trailed my hand in the water as the boat moved along.* ◆ **(+ adv./prep.)** *The bride's dress trailed behind her.* **2** [I] **+ adv./prep.** to walk slowly because you are tired or bored, especially behind someone else: *The kids trailed along after us while we shopped for clothes.* **3** [I, T] (used especially in the progressive tenses) to be losing a game or other contest: *The Bulls were trailing 40–35 at halftime.* ◆ ~ **by sth** *We were trailing by five points.* ◆ ~ **in sth** *This country is still trailing badly in scientific research.* ◆ ~ **sb/sth** *Most Democrats are trailing their Republican rivals in the polls.* **4** [T] ~ **sb/sth** to follow someone or something by looking for signs that show you where they have been: *The police trailed Dale for days.* **5** [I] to grow or hang downward over something or along the ground: *trailing plants* **6** [I] **+ adv./prep.** to move or flow slowly in a thin line behind, away from, or over something: *Smoke trailed up from the chimney.* ◆ *He had tears trailing down his cheeks.*
PHR V **ˌtrail a'way/'off** (of sb's speech) to become gradually quieter and then stop: *His voice trailed away to nothing.* ◆ **+ speech** *"I only hope…," she trailed off.*

trail·blaz·er /ˈtreɪlˌbleɪzər/ *noun* a person who is the first to do or discover something and so makes it possible for

trains

freight train

passenger train

steam train

funicular
(*also* funicular railway)

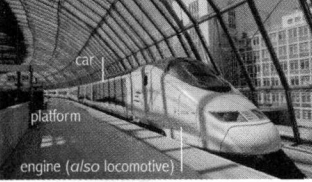

high-speed train

streetcar (*also* trolley car)

others to follow ⊃ compare BLAZE A TRAIL at BLAZE
▶ **trail·blaz·ing** *adj.* [usually before noun]: *trailblazing scientific research*

trail·er /ˈtreɪlər/ *noun* **1** a truck, or a container with wheels, that is pulled by another vehicle: *a car towing a trailer with a boat on it* ⊃ see also TRACTOR-TRAILER **2** a vehicle without an engine, that can be pulled by a car or truck or used as a home or an office when it is parked: *a trailer park* (= an area where trailers are parked and used as homes) ⊃ compare CAMPER, MOBILE HOME **3** a series of short scenes from a movie or television program, shown in advance to advertise it **SYN** PREVIEW

'trailer ˌtrash *noun* [U] (*informal, offensive*) a way of referring to poor white people from a low social class

'trailer ˌtruck *noun* = TRACTOR-TRAILER

'trailing ˌedge *noun* (*technical*) the rear edge of something moving, especially an aircraft wing

train /treɪn/ *noun, verb*
- *noun* **1** a railroad engine pulling a number of cars, taking people and goods from one place to another: *to get on/off a train* ◆ *I like traveling by train.* ◆ *a passenger/commuter/freight/subway train* ◆ *to catch/take/get the train to London* ◆ *a train trip/engineer* ◆ *You have to change trains in Chicago.* ⊃ see also GRAVY TRAIN, WAGON TRAIN **2** a number of people or animals moving in a line: *a camel train* **3** [usually sing.] a series of events or actions that are connected: *His death set in motion a train of events that led to the outbreak of war.* **4** the part of a long formal dress that spreads out on the floor behind the person wearing it
IDM **bring sth in its train** (*formal*) to have something as a result: *Unemployment brings great difficulties in its train.* **in sb's train** (*formal*) following behind someone: *In the train of the rich and famous came the journalists.* **a train of thought** the connected series of thoughts that are in your head at a particular time: *The phone ringing interrupted my train of thought.*
- *verb* **1** [T, I] to teach a person or an animal the skills for a particular job or activity; to be taught in this way: ~ **sb/sth** *badly trained staff* ◆ ~ **sb/sth to do sth** *They train dogs to sniff out drugs.* ◆ ~ **(sb) (as/in/for sth)** *He trained as a teacher before becoming an actor.* ◆ *All members of the team have been trained in first aid.* ◆ ~ **to do/be sth** *Sue is training to be a doctor.* **2** [I, T] to prepare yourself/someone for a particular activity, especially a sport, by doing a lot of exercise; to

prepare a person or an animal in this way: ~ **(for/in sth)** *athletes training for the Olympics* ◆ ~ **sb/sth (for/in sth)** *She trains horses.* ◆ *He trains the Olympic team.* **3** [T] to develop a natural ability or quality so that it improves: ~ **sth** *An expert with a trained eye will spot the difference immediately.* ◆ ~ **sth to do sth** *You can train your mind to think positively.* **4** [T] ~ **sth (around/along/up, etc.)** to make a plant grow in a particular direction: *Roses were trained around the door.*
PHR V **'train sth at/on sb/sth** to aim a gun, camera, light, etc. at someone or something

train·ee /treɪˈni/ *noun* a person who is being taught how to do a particular job: *a management trainee* ◆ *Six months after starting out as a trainee, she was managing the business.* ⊃ collocations at JOB

train·er /ˈtreɪnər/ *noun* **1** a person who teaches people or animals to perform a particular job or skill well, or to do a particular sport: *teacher trainers* ◆ *a racehorse trainer* ◆ *Her trainer decided she shouldn't run in the race.* ⊃ see also CROSS-TRAINER, PERSONAL TRAINER **2** a person whose job is to provide medical help and treat minor injuries for sports teams

train·ing /ˈtreɪnɪŋ/ *noun* [U]
1 ~ **(in sth/in doing sth)** the process of learning the skills that you need to do a job: *staff training* ◆ *Few applicants had received any training in management.* ◆ *a training course* ⊃ collocations at EDUCATION, JOB **2** the process of preparing to take part in a sports competition by doing physical exercises: *to be in training for a race*

'training ˌwheels *noun* [pl.] small wheels that are attached to each side of the back wheel on a child's bicycle to stop it from falling over ⊃ picture at BICYCLE

train·man /ˈtreɪnmən/ *noun* (*pl.* **train·men** /-mən/) a member of the team of people operating a train

'train set *noun* a toy train, together with the track that it runs on, a toy station, etc.

traipse /treɪps/ *verb* [I] + **adv./prep.** (*informal*) to walk somewhere slowly or without a specific aim

trait /treɪt/ *noun* a particular quality in your personality: *personality traits*

trai·tor /ˈtreɪtər/ *noun* ~ **(to sb/sth)** a person who gives away secrets about their friends, their country, etc.: *He was seen as a traitor to the socialist cause.* ◆ *She denied that she had turned traitor* (= become a traitor).

trai·tor·ous /ˈtreɪtərəs/ adj. (formal) giving away secrets about your friends, your country, etc. ▶ **trai·tor·ous·ly** adv.

tra·jec·to·ry /trəˈdʒɛktəri/ noun (pl. **tra·jec·to·ries**) (technical) the curved path of something that has been fired, hit, or thrown into the air: a missile's trajectory ♦ (figurative) My career seemed to be on a downward trajectory.

tram /træm/ noun **1** = CABLE CAR (2) **2** a vehicle that runs automatically on tracks and transports groups of people over short distances: I took the airport tram from the main terminal to the gates.

tram·mel /ˈtræml/ verb (-l-, CanE usually -ll-) [often passive] ~ **sb/sth** (formal) to limit someone's freedom of movement or activity SYN RESTRICT ⊃ compare UNTRAMMELED

tramp /træmp/ noun, verb
● noun **1** (also ho·bo) [C] a person with no home or job who travels from place to place, usually asking people in the street for food or money **2** [sing.] **the ~ of sb/sth** the sound of someone's heavy steps: the tramp of marching feet **3** [C, usually sing.] a long walk SYN TREK: We had a long tramp home.
● verb (also informal tromp) [I, T] to walk with heavy or noisy steps, especially for a long time: (+ adv./prep.) We tramped across the wet grass to look at the statue. ♦ the sound of tramping feet ♦ ~ **sth** He's been tramping the streets looking for a job.

tram·ple /ˈtræmpl/ verb **1** [T, I] to step heavily on someone or something so that you crush or harm them/it with your feet: ~ **sb/sth** People were **trampled underfoot** in the rush for the exit. ♦ He was **trampled to death** by a runaway horse. ♦ ~ **sb/sth down** The campers had trampled the grass down. ♦ ~ **on/over sth** Don't trample on the flowers! **2** [I, T] ~ **(on/over) sb/sth** to ignore someone's feelings or rights and treat them as if they are not important: He felt that big government was trampling on the views of ordinary people.

tram·po·line /ˈtræmpəˈlin; ˈtræmpəlin/ noun, verb
● noun a piece of equipment that is used in GYMNASTICS for doing jumps in the air. It consists of a sheet of strong material that is attached by springs to a frame. ⊃ picture at TOY
● verb [I] to jump on a trampoline ▶ **tram·po·lin·ing** noun [U]

tram·way /ˈtræmweɪ/ noun the rails that form the route for a STREETCAR

trance /træns/ noun **1** [C] a state in which someone seems to be asleep but is aware of what is said to them, for example if they are HYPNOTIZED: to go/fall into a trance **2** [C] a state in which you are thinking so much about something that you do not notice what is happening around you SYN DAZE **3** (also ˈtrance ˌmusic) [U] a type of electronic dance music with HYPNOTIC rhythms and sounds

tran·nie (also **tran·ny**) /ˈtræni/ noun (pl. **tran·nies**) (informal) **1** [C] a TRANSSEXUAL or TRANSVESTITE **2** [U, C] a vehicle's TRANSMISSION

tran·quil /ˈtræŋkwəl/ adj. (formal) quiet and peaceful SYN SERENE: a tranquil scene ♦ the tranquil waters of the lake ♦ She led a tranquil life in the country. ▶ **tran·quil·li·ty** (also **tran·quil·i·ty**) /trænˈkwɪləti/ noun [U] **tran·quil·ly** /ˈtræŋkwəli/ adv.

tran·quil·ize /ˈtræŋkwəˌlaɪz/ verb ~ **sb/sth** to make a person or an animal calm or unconscious, especially by giving them a drug (= a tranquilizer)

tran·quil·iz·er /ˈtræŋkwəˌlaɪzər/ noun a drug used to reduce anxiety: She's on (= is taking) tranquilizers.

trans- /træns; trænz/ prefix **1** (in adjectives) across; beyond: transatlantic ♦ transcontinental **2** (in verbs) into another place or state: transplant ♦ transform

trans·act /trænˈzækt; -ˈsækt/ verb [T, I] ~ **(sth) (with sb)** (formal) to do business with a person or an organization: buyers and sellers transacting business

trans·ac·tion /trænˈzækʃn; -ˈsæk-/ noun **1** [C] ~ **(between A and B)** a piece of business that is done between people,

especially an act of buying or selling SYN DEAL: financial transactions between companies ♦ commercial transactions **2** [U] ~ **of sth** (formal) the process of doing something: the transaction of government business

trans·at·lan·tic /ˌtrænsətˈlæntɪk; ˌtrænz-/ adj. [only before noun] **1** crossing the Atlantic Ocean: a transatlantic flight **2** connected with countries on both sides of the Atlantic Ocean: a transatlantic alliance **3** on or from the other side of the Atlantic Ocean: my transatlantic cousins

trans·ceiv·er /trænˈsivər/ noun a radio that can both send and receive messages

tran·scend /trænˈsɛnd/ verb ~ **sth** (formal) to be or go beyond the usual limits of something SYN EXCEED

tran·scend·ent /trænˈsɛndənt/ adj. (formal) going beyond the usual limits; extremely great ▶ **tran·scend·ence** /-dəns/ noun [U]: the transcendence of God

tran·scen·den·tal /ˌtrænsɛnˈdɛntl; -sən-/ adj. [usually before noun] going beyond the limits of human knowledge, experience, or reason, especially in a religious or spiritual way: a transcendental experience

ˌTranscenˌdental Mediˈtation™ noun [U] (abbr. TM) a method of making yourself calm by thinking deeply in silence and repeating a special phrase to yourself many times

trans·con·ti·nen·tal /ˌtrænsˌkɑntəˈnɛntl; -ˌkɑntnˈɛntl/ adj. crossing a continent: a transcontinental railroad

tran·scribe /trænˈskraɪb/ verb **1** to record thoughts, speech, or data in a written form, or in a different written form from the original: ~ **sth** Clerks transcribe everything that is said in court. ♦ The interview was recorded and then transcribed. ♦ ~ **sth into sth** How many official documents have been transcribed into Braille for blind people? **2** ~ **sth** (technical) to show the sounds of speech using a special PHONETIC alphabet **3** ~ **sth (for sth)** to write a piece of music in a different form so that it can be played by another musical instrument or sung by another voice: a piano piece transcribed for the guitar

tran·script /ˈtrænskrɪpt/ noun **1** (also **tran·scrip·tion**) a written or printed copy of words that have been spoken: a transcript of the interview **2** an official record of a student's work that shows the courses they have taken and the grades they have achieved

tran·scrip·tion /trænˈskrɪpʃn/ noun **1** [U] the act or process of representing something in a written or printed form: errors made in transcription ♦ phonetic transcription **2** [C] = TRANSCRIPT (1): The full transcription of the interview is attached. **3** [C] something that is represented in writing: This dictionary gives phonetic transcriptions of all headwords. **4** [C] a change in the written form of a piece of music so that it can be played on a different instrument or sung by a different voice

trans·duc·er /trænzˈdusər; træns-/ noun (technical) a device for producing an electrical signal from another form of energy such as pressure

tran·sept /ˈtrænsɛpt/ noun (architecture) either of the two wide parts of a church shaped like a cross, that are built at RIGHT ANGLES to the main central part ⊃ compare NAVE

ˌtrans-fatty ˈacid (also **ˌtrans-fat**) noun [C, U] a type of fat produced when oils are changed by a chemical process into solids, for example to make MARGARINE. Trans-fatty acids are believed to encourage the harmful development of CHOLESTEROL: foods that are low in trans-fatty acids ⊃ see also MONOUNSATURATED FAT, POLYUNSATURATED FAT, SATURATED FAT, UNSATURATED FAT

trans·fer ✎ AWL verb, noun
● verb /ˈtrænsfər; trænsˈfər/ (-rr-)
▷ TO NEW PLACE **1** [I, T] to move from one place to another; to move something or someone from one place to another: ~ **(from...) (to...)** The TV show is transferring its location from Los Angeles to New York. ♦ If I spend a semester in Madrid, will my credits transfer? ♦ ~ **sth/sb (from...) (to...)** How can I transfer money from my bank account to his? ♦ The patient was

ʌ cup   ə about   eɪ say   aɪ five   ɔɪ boy   aʊ now   oʊ go   ər bird

transferred to another hospital. ♦ I couldn't transfer all my credits from the community college.
▷ TO NEW JOB/SCHOOL/SITUATION **2** [I, T] to move from one job, school, situation, etc. to another; to arrange for someone to move: **~ (from...) (to...)** He transferred to UCLA after his freshman year. ♦ **~ sb (from...) (to...)** Ten employees are being transferred from the sales department.
▷ FEELING/DISEASE/POWER **3** [T, I] **~ (sth) (from...) (to...)** if you **transfer** a feeling, a disease, or power, etc., or if it **transfers** from one person to another, the second person has it, often instead of the first: Joe had already transferred his affections from Lisa to Cleo. ♦ This disease is rarely transferred from mother to baby (= so that the baby has it as well as the mother).
▷ PROPERTY **4** [T] **~ sth (to sb)** to officially arrange for something to belong to someone else or for someone else to control something **SYN** SIGN OVER: He transferred the property to his son.
▷ TO NEW VEHICLE **5** [I, T] to change to a different vehicle during a trip; to arrange for someone to change to a different vehicle during a trip: **~ (from...) (to...)** We transferred from the train to a bus at the Canadian border. ♦ **~ sb (from...) (to...)** Hotel guests will be transferred from the airport to the hotel by van.
▷ INFORMATION/MUSIC, ETC. **6** [T, I] to copy information, music, an idea, etc. from one method of recording or presenting it to another; to be recorded or presented in a different way: You can transfer data to a memory stick in a few seconds. ♦ **~ (from sth) (to sth)** The novel does not transfer well to the screen.
● **noun** /ˈtrænsfər/
▷ CHANGE OF PLACE/JOB/SITUATION **1** [U, C] the act of moving someone or something from one place, group, or job to another; an occasion when this happens: electronic data **transfer** ♦ the transfer of currency from one country to another ♦ He has asked for a transfer to the company's Minneapolis branch. ♦ After the election there was a swift **transfer of power**. ⊃ see also CASH TRANSFER
▷ CHANGE OF VEHICLE **2** [U, C] an act of changing to a different place, vehicle, or route when you are traveling: The transfer from the airport to the hotel is included in the price.
▷ TRAIN/BUS TICKET **3** [C] a ticket that allows a passenger to continue their trip on another bus or train
▷ PICTURE **4** [C] = DECAL
▷ PSYCHOLOGY **5** [U] (psychology) the process of using behavior that has already been learned in one situation in a new situation ⊃ see also LANGUAGE TRANSFER

trans·fer·a·ble **AWL** /trænsˈfərəbl/ adj. that can be moved from one place, person, or use to another: This ticket is not transferable (= it may only be used by the person who bought it). ♦ We aim to provide our students with transferable skills (= that can be used in different jobs). ▸ **trans·fer·a·bil·i·ty** /ˈbɪləti/ noun [U]

trans·fer·ence **AWL** /ˈtrænsfərəns; trænsˈfərəns/ noun [U] (technical or formal) the process of moving something from one place, person, or use to another: the transference of heat from the liquid to the container

trans·fer·ral /trænsˈfərəl/ noun [U] the action of transferring something or someone

ˈtransfer student noun a student at a college or university who has completed classes at another college or university after leaving high school

trans·fig·ure /trænsˈfɪgyər/ verb [often passive] **~ sb/sth** (literary) to change the appearance of a person or thing so that they look more beautiful ▸ **trans·fig·u·ra·tion** /ˌtrænsˌfɪgyəˈreɪʃn/ noun [U]

trans·fix /trænsˈfɪks/ verb [usually passive] **~ sb** to make someone unable to move because they are afraid, surprised, etc. **SYN** PARALYZE: Luisa stood transfixed with shock.

trans·form ✎ **AWL** /trænsˈfɔrm/ verb
1 **~ sth/sb (from sth) (into sth)** to change the form of something **SYN** CONVERT: The photochemical reactions transform the light into electrical impulses. **2** **~ sth/sb (from**

sth) (into sth) to completely change the appearance or character of something, especially so that it is better: A new color scheme will transform your bedroom. ♦ It was an event that would transform my life.

trans·for·ma·tion **AWL** /ˌtrænsfərˈmeɪʃn/ noun [C, U] a complete change in someone or something: The way in which we work has **undergone a complete transformation** in the past decade. ♦ What a transformation! You look great. ♦ **~ (from sth) (to/into sth)** the country's transformation from dictatorship to democracy ▸ **trans·for·ma·tion·al** /ˈʃənl/ adj.

ˌtransforˌmational ˈgrammar noun [U] (abbr. TG) (linguistics) a type of grammar that describes a language as a system that has a deep structure which changes in particular ways when real sentences are produced

trans·form·er /trænsˈfɔrmər/ noun a device for reducing or increasing the VOLTAGE of an electric power supply, usually to allow a particular piece of electrical equipment to be used

trans·fu·sion /trænsˈfyuʒn/ noun [C, U] **1** = BLOOD TRANSFUSION **2** **~ of sth** the act of investing extra money in a place or an activity that needs it: The project badly needs a transfusion of cash. ▸ **trans·fuse** /trænsˈfyuz/ verb: **~ sth (into sb/sth)** to transfuse blood into a patient

trans·gen·der /trænsˈdʒɛndər; trænz-/ adj. relating to TRANSSEXUALS and TRANSVESTITES: transgender issues ▸ **trans·gen·dered** adj.

trans·gen·ic /trænsˈdʒɛnɪk/ adj., noun (biology)
● **adj.** (of a plant or an animal) having GENETIC material introduced from another type of plant or animal: transgenic crops **SYN** GENETICALLY MODIFIED ▸ **trans·gen·i·cally** /ˈkli/ adv.
● **noun 1** **trans·gen·ics** [pl.] the study or practice of creating transgenic plants or animals **2** [C] a transgenic plant or animal

trans·gress /trænsˈgrɛs/ verb **~ sth** (formal) to go beyond the limit of what is morally or legally acceptable ▸ **trans·gres·sion** /trænsˈgrɛʃn/ noun [C, U] **trans·gres·sor** /trænsˈgrɛsər/ noun

trans·hu·mance /trænsˈhyuməns; trænz-/ noun [U] (technical) the practice of moving animals to different fields in different seasons, for example to higher fields in summer and lower fields in winter

tran·sient /ˈtrænziənt; -ʒənt; -ʃənt/ adj., noun
● **adj.** (formal) **1** continuing for only a short time **SYN** FLEETING, TEMPORARY: the transient nature of speech **2** staying or working in a place for only a short time, before moving on: a city with a large transient population (= of students, temporary workers, etc.) ▸ **tran·sience** /ˈtrænziəns; -ʒəns; -ʃəns/ noun [U]: the transience of human life
● **noun** a person who stays or works in a place for only a short time, before moving on

tran·sis·tor /trænˈzɪstər/ noun **1** a small electronic device used in computers, radios, televisions, etc. for controlling an electric current as it passes along a CIRCUIT **2** (also tranˌsistor ˈradio) a small radio with transistors

tran·sit **AWL** /ˈtrænzət; -sət/ noun, verb
● **noun 1** [U] the process of being moved or carried from one place to another: The cost includes transit. ♦ goods damaged **in transit 2** [U] the system of buses, trains, etc. that people use to travel from one place to another: the transit system ⊃ see also MASS TRANSIT, RAPID TRANSIT **3** [U, C, usually sing.] the act of going through a place on the way to somewhere else: a transit visa (= one that allows a person to pass through a country but not to stay there)
● **verb** [T, I] **~ (sth)** to pass across or through an area: The ship is currently transiting the Gulf of Mexico.

tran·si·tion ✎ **AWL** /trænˈzɪʃn/ noun [U, C]
the process or a period of changing from one state or condition to another: **~ (from sth) (to sth)** the transition from school to full-time work ♦ He will remain head of state

during the **period of transition** to democracy. ♦ **~ (between A and B)** *We need to ensure a smooth transition between the old system and the new one.* ♦ *This course is useful for students who are **in transition** (= in the process of changing) from one field of study to another.* ▶ **tran·si·tion·al** **AWL** /-ʃənl/ *adj.: a transitional period* ♦ *a transitional government*

tran'sition ˌmetal (also **tran'sition ˌelement**) *noun* (*chemistry*) one of the group of metals in the center of the PERIODIC TABLE (= a list of all the chemical elements) that form colored COMPOUNDS and often act as CATALYSTS (= substances that make chemical reactions happen faster)

tran·si·tive /ˈtrænsətɪv; ˈtrænzə-/ *adj.* (*grammar*) (of verbs) used with a DIRECT OBJECT: *In "She wrote a letter," the verb "wrote" is transitive and the word "letter" is the direct object.* **ANT** INTRANSITIVE ▶ **tran·si·tive·ly** *adv.: The verb is being used transitively.*

tran·si·tiv·i·ty /ˌtrænsəˈtɪvəti; ˌtrænzə-/ *noun* [U] (*grammar*) the fact of whether a particular verb is TRANSITIVE or INTRANSITIVE

tran·si·to·ry **AWL** /ˈtrænsəˌtɔri; ˈtrænzə-/ *adj.* (*formal*) continuing for only a short time **SYN** FLEETING, TEMPORARY: *the transitory nature of his happiness*

trans·late 🔑 /ˈtrænsleɪt; ˈtrænz-/ *verb*
1 [T, I] to express the meaning of speech or writing in a different language: **~ sth (from sth) (into sth)** *He translated the letter into English.* ♦ *Her books have been translated into 24 languages.* ♦ *Can you help me translate this legal jargon into plain English?* ♦ **~ sth (as sth)** *"Suisse" had been wrongly translated as "Sweden."* ♦ **~ (from sth) (into sth)** *I don't speak Greek, so Dina offered to translate for me.* ♦ *My work involves translating from German.* **2** [I] to be changed from one language to another: *Most poetry does not translate well.* ♦ **~ as sth** *The name of the town of Fond du Lac translates as "Bottom of the Lake."* **3** [T, I] to change something, or to be changed, into a different form: **~ sth (into sth)** *It's time to translate words into action.* ♦ **~ into sth** *I hope all the hard work will translate into profits.* **4** [T, I] **~ (sth) (as sth)** to understand something in a particular way or give something a particular meaning **SYN** INTERPRET: *the various words and gestures that we translate as love*

trans·la·tion 🔑 /ˈtrænsleɪʃn; ˈtrænz-/ *noun*
1 [U] **~ (from sth) (into sth)** | **~ (of sth) (into sth)** the process of changing something that is written or spoken into another language: *an error in translation* ♦ *He specializes in translation from Danish into English.* ♦ *The book loses something **in translation.*** ♦ *The irony is **lost in translation.*** **2** [C, U] a text or work that has been changed from one language into another: *The usual translation of "glasnost" is "openness."* ♦ *a **rough translation** (= not translating everything exactly)* ♦ *a **literal translation** (= following the original words exactly)* ♦ *a **free translation** (= not following the original words exactly)* ♦ *a **word-for-word translation*** ♦ *I have only read Tolstoy in translation.* ♦ *a copy of Dryden's translation of the Aeneid* **3** [U] **~ (of sth) into sth** the process of changing something into a different form: *the translation of theory into practice*

trans·la·tor /ˈtrænsleɪtər; ˈtrænz-/ *noun* a person who translates writing or speech into a different language, especially as a job: *She works as a translator of technical texts.* ⊃ compare INTERPRETER

trans·lit·er·ate /trænsˈlɪtəˌreɪt/ *verb* **~ sth (into/as sth)** (*formal*) to write words or letters using letters of a different alphabet or language ▶ **trans·lit·er·a·tion** /ˌtrænsˌlɪtəˈreɪʃn/ *noun* [C, U]

trans·lu·cent /trænsˈlusnt/ *adj.* (*formal*) allowing light to pass through but not transparent ▶ **trans·lu·cence** /-ˈlusns/ (also **trans·lu·cen·cy** /-ˈlusnsi/) *noun* [U]

trans·mi·gra·tion /ˌtrænsmaɪˈɡreɪʃn/ *noun* [U] the passing of a person's soul after their death into another body

trans·mis·sion **AWL** /trænsˈmɪʃn; trænz-/ *noun* (*formal*) **1** [U] the act or process of passing something from one person, place, or thing to another **SYN** TRANSFER: *the*

transmission of the disease ♦ *the risk of transmission* **2** [U] the act or process of sending out an electronic signal or message or of broadcasting a radio or television program: *the transmission of computer data along telephone lines* ♦ *a break in transmission* (= of a radio or television broadcast) *due to a technical fault* **3** [C] a radio or television message or broadcast: *a live transmission from Honolulu* **4** [U, C] the system in a vehicle by which power is passed from the engine to the wheels

trans·mit **AWL** /trænsˈmɪt; trænz-/ *verb* (-tt-) **1** [T, I] **~ (sth) (from…) (to…)** to send an electronic signal, radio or television broadcast, etc.: *signals transmitted from a satellite* ♦ *The ceremony was transmitted live by satellite to over fifty countries.* ♦ *a shortwave radio that can transmit as well as receive* **2** [T] to pass something from one person to another **SYN** TRANSFER: **~ sth** *sexually transmitted diseases* ♦ **~ sth to sb** *Parents can unwittingly transmit their own fears to their children.* **3** [T] **~ sth** (*technical*) to allow heat, light, sound, etc. to pass through **SYN** CONDUCT

trans·mit·ter /trænsˈmɪtər; trænz-/ *noun* **1** a piece of equipment used for sending electronic signals, especially radio or television signals ⊃ compare RECEIVER **2 ~ of sth** (*formal*) a person or thing that transmits something from one person or thing to another: *Emphasis was placed on the school as a transmitter of moral values.*

trans·mog·ri·fy /trænsˈmɑɡrəˌfaɪ; trænz-/ *verb* (trans·mog·ri·fies, trans·mog·ri·fy·ing, trans·mog·ri·fied, trans·mog·ri·fied) **~ sb/sth** (often *humorous*) to change someone or something completely, especially in a surprising way **SYN** TRANSFORM ▶ **trans·mog·ri·fi·ca·tion** /ˌtrænsˌmɑɡrəfəˈkeɪʃn; trænz-/ *noun* [U]

trans·mute /trænsˈmyut/ *verb* [T, I] **~ (sth) (into sth)** (*formal*) to change, or make something change, into something different **SYN** TRANSFORM: *It was once thought that lead could be transmuted into gold.* ▶ **trans·mu·ta·tion** /ˌtrænsmyuˈteɪʃn/ *noun* [C, U]

trans·na·tion·al /ˌtrænsˈnæʃənl/ *adj.* (*business*) existing in or involving many different countries: *transnational corporations*

tran·som /ˈtrænsəm/ *noun* **1** a bar of wood or stone across the top of a door or window **2** = FANLIGHT

trans·par·en·cy /trænsˈpærənsi/ *noun* (*pl.* trans·par·en·cies) **1** [C] a picture printed on a piece of film, usually in a frame, that can be shown on a screen by shining light through the film **SYN** SLIDE: *an overhead transparency* (= used with an OVERHEAD PROJECTOR) **2** [U] the quality of something, such as glass, that allows you to see through it **3** [U] the quality of something, such as an excuse or a lie, that allows someone to see the truth easily: *They were shocked by the transparency of his lies.* **4** [U] the quality of something, such as a situation or an argument, that makes it easy to understand: *a need for greater transparency in legal documents*

trans·par·ent 🔑 /trænsˈpærənt/ *adj.*
1 (of glass, plastic, etc.) allowing you to see through it: *The insect's wings are almost transparent.* **ANT** OPAQUE **2** (of an excuse, a lie, etc.) allowing you to see the truth easily **SYN** OBVIOUS: *a man of transparent honesty* ♦ *a transparent attempt to buy votes* ♦ *Am I that transparent* (= are my intentions that obvious)? **3** (of language, information, etc.) easy to understand: *a campaign to make official documents more transparent* **ANT** OPAQUE ▶ **trans·par·ent·ly** *adv.: transparently obvious*

tran·spi·ra·tion /ˌtrænspəˈreɪʃn/ *noun* [U] (*biology*) the process of water passing out from the surface of a plant or leaf

tran·spire /trænˈspaɪər/ *verb* (*formal*) **1** [T] (not usually used in the progressive tenses) **~ that…** if it **transpires that** something has happened or is true, it is known or has been shown to be true: *It transpired that the gang had a contact inside the bank.* ♦ *This story, it later transpired, was untrue.* **2** [I] to happen: *You're meeting him tomorrow? Let me know what*

| t **t**ea | t̮ bu**tt**er | d **d**id | k **c**at | g **g**ot | tʃ **ch**in | dʒ **J**une | f **f**all

transpires. **3** [I, T] **~ (sth)** (*biology*) when plants or leaves **transpire**, water passes out from their surface

trans·plant *verb, noun*
● **verb** /træns'plænt/ **1 ~ sth** to move a growing plant and plant it somewhere else **2 ~ sth (from sb/sth) (into sb/sth)** to take an organ, skin, etc. from one person, animal, part of the body, etc. and put it into or onto another: *Surgeons have successfully transplanted a liver into a four-year-old boy.* ◆ *Patients often reject transplanted organs.* ⊃ compare IMPLANT **3 ~ sb/sth (from…) (to…)** (*formal*) to move someone or something to a different place or environment: *The company has transplanted some of its factories overseas.* ▶ **trans·plan·ta·tion** /ˌtrænsplæn'teɪʃn/ *noun* [U]: *liver transplantation* ◆ *the transplantation of entire communities off the islands*
● **noun** /'trænsplænt/ **1** [C, U] a medical operation in which a damaged organ, etc. is replaced with one from another person: *to have a heart transplant* ◆ *a transplant operation* ◆ *a shortage of suitable kidneys for transplant* **2** [C] an organ, etc. that is used in a transplant operation: *There is always a chance that the body will reject the transplant.* ⊃ compare IMPLANT

tran·spon·der /træn'spɒndər/ *noun* (*technical*) a piece of equipment that receives radio signals and automatically sends out another signal in reply

trans·port 🖉 **AWL** *verb, noun*
● **verb** /træns'pɔːt; 'trænspɔːt/ **1 ~ sth/sb (+ adv./prep.)** to take something or someone from one place to another in a vehicle: *to transport goods/passengers* **2 ~ sth (+ adv./prep.)** to move something somewhere by means of a natural process **SYN** CARRY: *The seeds are transported by the wind.* ◆ *Blood transports oxygen around the body.* **3 ~ sb (+ adv./prep.)** to make someone feel that they are in a different place, time, or situation: *The book transports you to another world.* **4 ~ sb (+ adv./prep.)** (in the past) to send someone to a far away place as a punishment: *British convicts were transported to Australia for life.* ▶ **trans·port·er** *noun*
● **noun** /'trænspɔːt/ **1** [U] = TRANSPORTATION (1) **2** [U] = TRANSPORTATION (2) **3** [U] = TRANSPORTATION (3) **4** [C] a ship, plane, or truck used for carrying soldiers, supplies, etc. from one place to another: *on board a troop transport* **5 transports** [pl.] **~ of sth** (*literary*) strong feelings and emotions: *to be in transports of delight*

trans·port·a·ble /træns'pɔːtəbl/ *adj.* [not usually before noun] that can be carried or moved from one place to another, especially by a vehicle ▶ **trans·port·a·bil·i·ty** *noun* [U]

trans·por·ta·tion 🖉 **AWL** /ˌtrænspɔr'teɪʃn/ *noun* [U]
1 (also **trans·port**) a system for carrying people or goods from one place to another using vehicles, roads, etc.: *air/freight/bus transportation* ◆ *the transportation industry* ◆ *The city is providing free transportation to the stadium from downtown.* ◆ *the transportation of heavy loads* ◆ *transportation costs* ⊃ see also PUBLIC TRANSPORTATION **2** (also **trans·port**) a vehicle or method of travel: *Applicants must have their own transportation.* ◆ *Transportation to and from the airport is included in the price.* ◆ *His bike is his only **means of transportation**.* **3** (also **trans·port**) the activity or business of carrying goods from one place to another using trucks, trains, etc.: *controls on the transportation of nuclear waste* **4** (in the past) the act of sending criminals to a place that is far away as a form of punishment

trans·pose /træns'pəʊz/ *verb* [often passive] **1 ~ sth** (*formal*) to change the order of two or more things **SYN** REVERSE **2 ~ sth (from sth) (to sth)** (*formal*) to move or change something to a different place or environment or into a different form **SYN** TRANSFER: *The director transposes Shakespeare's play from 16th century Venice to present-day California.* **3 ~ sth** (*music*) to write or play a piece of music or

a series of notes in a different key ▶ **trans·po·si·tion** /ˌtrænspə'zɪʃn/ *noun* [C, U]

trans·sex·u·al /ˌtræns'sekʃuəl; træn'sek-/ (also *informal* **tran·nie, tran·ny**) *noun* a person who feels emotionally that they want to live, dress, etc. as a member of the opposite sex, especially one who has a medical operation to change their sex

tran·sub·stan·ti·a·tion /ˌtrænsəbˌstænʃi'eɪʃn/ *noun* [U] the belief that the bread and wine of the COMMUNION service become the actual body and blood of Jesus Christ after they have been BLESSED, even though they still look like bread and wine

trans·verse /ˈtrænsˌvɜːrs; trænz-; ˈtrænsvərs; ˈtrænz-/ *adj.* [usually before noun] (*technical*) placed across something **SYN** DIAGONAL: *A transverse bar joins the two posts.*

transverse 'wave *noun* (*technical*) a wave that VIBRATES at 90° to the direction in which it is moving ⊃ compare LONGITUDINAL WAVE

trans·ves·tite /træns'vestaɪt; trænz-/ (also *informal* **tran·nie, tran·ny**) *noun* a person, especially a man, who enjoys dressing as a member of the opposite sex ▶ **trans·ves·tism** /træns'vestɪzəm/ *noun* [U]

trap 🖉 /træp/ *noun, verb*
● **noun**
⊳ FOR ANIMALS **1** a piece of equipment for catching animals: *a beaver with its leg in a trap* ◆ *A trap was laid, with fresh bait.* ⊃ see also MOUSETRAP
⊳ TRICK **2** a plan designed to trick someone, either by capturing them or by making them do or say something that they did not mean to do or say: *She had **set a trap** for him and he walked straight into it.* ⊃ see also BOOBY TRAP, RADAR TRAP, SAND TRAP, TOURIST TRAP
⊳ BAD SITUATION **3** [usually sing.] an unpleasant situation from which it is hard to escape: *the unemployment trap* ◆ *Some women see marriage as a trap.* ⊃ see also DEATH TRAP, POVERTY TRAP
⊳ CARRIAGE **4** a light CARRIAGE with two wheels, pulled by a horse: *a pony and trap*
⊳ MOUTH **5** (*slang*) mouth: *Shut your trap!* (= a rude way of telling someone to be quiet) ◆ *to keep your trap shut* (= to not tell a secret)
⊳ IN GOLF **6** = BUNKER *n.* (3) ⊃ picture at HOBBY
IDM **to fall into/avoid the trap of doing sth** to do/avoid doing something that is a mistake but which seems at first to be a good idea: *Parents often fall into the trap of trying to do everything for their children.* ⊃ more at SPRING *v.*
● **verb** (-pp-)
⊳ IN DANGEROUS/BAD SITUATION **1** [often passive] **~ sb (+ adv./prep.)** to keep someone in a dangerous place or bad situation that they want to get out of but cannot: *Help! I'm trapped!* ◆ *They were trapped in the burning building.* ◆ *We became trapped by the rising floodwater.* ◆ *He was trapped in an unhappy marriage.* ◆ *I feel trapped in my job.*
⊳ CATCH **2 ~ sth** to catch or keep something in a place and prevent it from escaping, especially so that you can use it: *Solar panels trap energy from the sun.* **3 ~ sb/sth (+ adv./prep.)** to force someone or something into a place or situation that they cannot escape from, especially in order to catch them: *The escaped prisoners were eventually trapped in an underground garage and recaptured.* **4 ~ sth** to catch an animal in a trap: *Raccoons used to be trapped for their fur.*
⊳ TRICK **5 ~ sb (into sth/into doing sth)** to trick someone into something: *He felt he had been trapped into accepting the terms of the contract.*

trap·door /ˌtræp'dɔːr/ *noun* a small door in a floor or ceiling

tra·peze /træ'piːz/ *noun* a wooden or metal bar hanging from two pieces of rope high above the ground, used especially by CIRCUS performers: *a trapeze artist*

tra·pe·zi·um /trə'piːziəm/ *noun* (*pl.* **tra·pe·zi·ums** or **tra·pe·zi·a** /-ziə/) (*geometry*) a flat shape with four straight sides, none of which are parallel ⊃ picture at SHAPE

trap·e·zoid /'træpəˌzɔɪd/ *noun* (*geometry*) a flat shape with four straight sides, one pair of opposite sides being parallel and the other pair not parallel ⊃ picture at SHAPE

trap·per /'træpər/ noun a person who traps and kills animals, especially for their fur

trap·pings /'træpɪŋz/ noun [pl.] ~ (of sth) (especially disapproving) the possessions, clothes, etc. that are connected with a particular situation, job, or social position: *They enjoyed all the trappings of wealth.*

Trap·pist /'træpɪst/ adj. belonging to a group of MONKS who have very strict rules, including a rule that they must not speak ▶ **Trap·pist** noun

trash 🔊 /træʃ/ noun, verb
• noun [U] **1** things that you throw away because you no longer want or need them **2** (informal, disapproving) objects, writing, ideas, etc. that you think are of poor quality: *What's that trash you're watching?* ◆ *He's talking trash* (= nonsense). **3** (informal) an offensive word used to describe people that you do not respect ⊃ see also TRAILER TRASH, WHITE TRASH
• verb (informal) **1** ~ sth to damage or destroy something: *The band was famous for trashing hotel rooms.* **2** ~ sth/sb to criticize something or someone very strongly **3** ~ sth to throw away something that you do not want: *I'm leaving my old toys here—if you don't want them, just trash them.*

trash can noun **1** a container for people to put garbage in, in the street or in a public building **2** = GARBAGE CAN

trash talk (also **trash talking**) noun [U] (informal) a way of talking that is intended to make someone, especially an opponent, feel less confident

trash·y /'træʃi/ adj. (informal) (trash·i·er, trash·i·est) of poor quality; with no value: *trashy TV shows*

trat·to·ri·a /ˌtrɑtəˈriə/ noun (from Italian) an Italian restaurant serving simple food

trau·ma /'trɔmə; 'traumə/ noun **1** [U] (psychology) a mental condition caused by severe shock, especially when the harmful effects last for a long time **2** [C, U] an unpleasant experience that makes you feel upset and/or anxious: *She felt exhausted after the traumas of recent weeks.* **3** [U, C] (medical) an injury: *The patient suffered severe brain trauma.*

trau·mat·ic /trəˈmætɪk; trɔ-; trau-/ adj. **1** extremely unpleasant and causing you to feel upset and/or anxious: *a traumatic experience* ◆ *Divorce can be traumatic for everyone involved.* **2** [only before noun] (psychology or medical) connected with or caused by trauma: *traumatic amnesia* ⊃ see also POST-TRAUMATIC STRESS DISORDER ▶ **trau·mat·i·cally** /-kli/ adv.

trau·ma·tize /'trɔmə.taɪz; 'trau-/ verb [usually passive] ~ sb to shock and upset someone very much, often making them unable to think or work normally

tra·vail /trəˈveɪl/ noun [U, pl.] (old use or literary) an unpleasant experience or situation that involves a lot of hard work, difficulties, and/or suffering

trav·el 🔊 /'trævl/ verb, noun
• verb (-l-, CanE usually -ll-) **1** [I, T] to go from one place to another, especially over a long distance: *to travel around the world* ◆ *I go to bed early if I'm traveling the next day.* ◆ *I love traveling by train.* ◆ *We always travel first class.* ◆ *We traveled to California for the wedding.* ◆ *When I finished college I went traveling for six months* (= spent time visiting different places). ◆ *~ sth He traveled the Yukon River in a canoe.* ◆ *I travel 40 miles to work every day.* **2** [I] (+ adv./prep.) to go or move at a particular speed, in a particular direction, or a particular distance: *to travel at 65 miles an hour* ◆ *Messages travel along the spine from the nerve endings to the brain.* ◆ *News travels fast these days.* **3** [I] (of food, wine, an object, etc.) to be still in good condition after a long trip: *Some wines do not travel well.* **4** [I] to go fast: *Their car can really travel!* **5** [I] (in BASKETBALL) to move while you are holding the ball, in a way that is not allowed ⊃ compare DRIBBLE
  IDM **travel light** to take very little with you when you go on a trip

• noun **1** [U] the act or activity of traveling: *air/rail/space, etc. travel* ◆ *travel expenses* ◆ *The job involves a considerable amount of foreign travel.* ◆ *the travel industry* ◆ *travel sickness* ◆ *a travel bag/clock* (= for use when traveling) ◆ *The pass allows unlimited travel on all public transportation in the city.* **2** **travels** [pl.] time spent traveling, especially in foreign countries and for pleasure: *The novel is based on his travels in India.* ◆ *When are you off on your travels* (= going traveling)?

Travel and Tourism

vacations
- have/take a vacation/a break/a day off/a year off/time off
- go on/be on vacation/leave/honeymoon/safari/sabbatical/a trip/a tour/a cruise/a pilgrimage
- go backpacking/camping/sightseeing
- plan a trip/a vacation/your itinerary
- reserve a hotel room/a flight/tickets
- have/make/cancel a reservation
- rent a condo/a vacation home/a cabin
- rent a car/bicycle/moped/scooter/Jet Ski
- stay in a hotel/a bed and breakfast/a youth hostel/a villa/a trailer/a vacation home/a resort/a timeshare
- cost/charge $100 a/per night for a suite/a single/double/twin room
- check into/out of a hotel/a motel/your room
- pack/unpack your suitcase/bags
- call/order room service
- cancel/cut short a trip/vacation

foreign travel
- apply for/get/renew a/your passport
- take out/buy/get travel insurance
- catch/miss your plane/train/ferry/connecting flight
- fly (in)/travel (in) first/business/economy class
- make/have a brief/two-day/twelve-hour layover/stopover in Hong Kong
- experience/cause/lead to delays
- check (in)/collect/get/lose your baggage/luggage
- be charged for/pay excess baggage fees
- board/get on/leave/get off the aircraft/plane/ship/ferry
- taxi down/leave/approach/hit/overshoot the runway
- experience/hit/encounter (mild/severe) turbulence
- suffer from/recover from/get over your jet lag/motion sickness
- be seasick/carsick

the tourist industry
- attract/draw/bring tourists/visitors
- encourage/promote/hurt tourism
- promote/develop ecotourism
- build/develop/visit a tourist/tropical/beach/ski resort
- work for/be operated by a major hotel chain
- be served by/compete with low-fare/low-cost/budget airlines
- use/go to/have a travel agent
- contact/check with your travel agent/tour operator
- buy/be on/go on a package deal/vacation/tour
- buy/bring back (tacky/overpriced) souvenirs

travel agency noun a company that arranges travel and/or hotels for people going on a vacation or a trip

travel agent noun a person or business whose job is to make arrangements for people wanting to travel, for example buying tickets or arranging hotel rooms ⊃ collocations at TRAVEL ⊃ see also TRAVEL AGENCY

trav·eled (CanE usually **trav·elled**) /'trævld/ adj. (usually in compounds) **1** (of a person) having traveled the amount mentioned: *a much-traveled man* **2** (of a road, etc.) used the amount mentioned: *The path was steeper and less traveled than the previous one.*

trav·el·er 🔑 (*CanE usually* **trav·el·ler**) /ˈtrævələr/ *noun* a person who is traveling or who often travels: *She is a frequent traveler to the Southwest.* ◆ *He passed the time chatting with fellow travelers.*

traveler's ˌcheck (*CanE* **ˈtraveller's ˌcheque**) *noun* a check for a fixed amount, sold by a bank or TRAVEL AGENT, that can be exchanged for cash in foreign countries

trav·el·ing (*CanE usually* **trav·el·ling**) /ˈtrævəlɪŋ/ *adj., noun*
• *adj.* [only before noun] going from place to place: *a traveling circus/exhibition/performer, etc.* ◆ *to ensure the safety of the traveling public* (= people who are traveling)
• *noun* [U] **1** the act of traveling: *The job requires a lot of traveling.* ◆ *a traveling companion* **2** (in BASKETBALL) the act of moving while you are holding the ball, in a way that is not allowed

ˌtraveling ˈsalesman *noun* (*old-fashioned*) = SALES REPRESENTATIVE

trav·e·logue (*also* **trav·e·log**) /ˈtrævəlɔg; -ˌlɑg/ *noun* a movie, broadcast, speech, or piece of writing about travel

trav·erse *verb, noun*
• *verb* /trəˈvɜrs/ ~ **sth** (*formal or technical*) to cross an area of land or water
• *noun* /ˈtrævərs/ (in mountain climbing) an act of moving sideways or walking across a steep slope, not climbing up or down it; a place where this is possible or necessary

trav·es·ty /ˈtrævəsti/ *noun* (*pl.* **trav·es·ties**) ~ **(of sth)** something that does not have the qualities or values that it should have, and as a result is often shocking or offensive **SYN** PARODY: *The trial was a travesty of justice.*

trawl /trɔl/ *verb, noun*
• *verb* **1** [I] ~ **(for sth)** to fish for something by pulling a large net with a wide opening through the water **2** [T, I] to search through a large amount of information or a large number of people, places, etc. looking for a particular thing or person: ~ **sth (for sth/sb)** *She trawled the thrift shops looking for bargains.* ◆ ~ **(through sth) (for sth/sb)** *The police are trawling through their files for similar cases.*
• *noun* **1** (*also* **ˈtrawl net**) a large net with a wide opening, that is dragged along the bottom of the ocean by a boat in order to catch fish **2** a search through a large amount of information, documents, etc.: *A quick trawl through a few Internet sources yielded five promising job ads.*

trawl·er /ˈtrɔlər/ *noun* a fishing boat that uses large nets that it drags through the ocean behind it

tray /treɪ/ *noun* **1** a flat piece of wood, metal, or plastic with raised edges, used for carrying or holding things, especially food: *He brought her breakfast in bed on a tray.* ◆ *She came in with a tray of drinks.* **2** (often in compounds) a shallow plastic box, used for various purposes: *a seed tray* (= for planting seeds in) ◆ *an ice cube tray* ⊃ picture at PACKAGING

treach·er·ous /ˈtrɛtʃərəs/ *adj.* **1** that cannot be trusted; intending to harm you **SYN** DECEITFUL: *He was weak, cowardly, and treacherous.* ◆ *lying, treacherous words* **2** dangerous, especially when seeming safe: *The ice on the roads made driving conditions treacherous.* ▶ **treach·er·ous·ly** *adv.*

treach·er·y /ˈtrɛtʃəri/ *noun* [U, C] (*pl.* **treach·er·ies**) behavior that involves not being loyal to someone who trusts you; an example of this: *an act of treachery*

trea·cle /ˈtrikl/ *noun* [U] (*disapproving*) a way of talking about emotions that is annoying because it is too SENTIMENTAL: *Hollywood treacle* ▶ **trea·cly** /ˈtrikli/ *adj.*: *treacly sentimentality*

tread /trɛd/ *verb, noun*
• *verb* (**trod** /trɑd/, **trod·den** /ˈtrɑdn/ *or* **trod**, **trod** *or* **tread·ed**, **tread·ed**) **1** [I] ~ **(on/in/over sth/sb)** (*old-fashioned*) to put your foot down while you are stepping or walking: *Careful you don't tread in that puddle.* **2** [T] ~ **sth (+ adv./prep.)** to crush or press something with your feet

SYN TRAMPLE: *The wine is still made by treading grapes in the traditional way.* **3** [T, I] ~ **(sth)** (*formal or literary*) to walk somewhere: *Few people had trod this path before.* ◆ *He was treading quietly and cautiously.*
IDM **tread carefully, warily, etc.** to be very careful about what you do or say: *The administration will have to tread very carefully in handling this issue.* **tread a difficult, dangerous, solitary, etc. path** to choose and follow a particular way of life, way of doing something, etc.: *A restaurant has to tread the tricky path between maintaining quality and keeping prices down.* **tread water 1** to keep yourself vertical in deep water by moving your arms and legs **2** to make no progress while you are waiting for something to happen **IDM** see FOOL *n.*, LINE *n.*, TIGHTROPE
• *noun* **1** [C, U] the raised pattern on the surface of a tire on a vehicle: *The treads on the tires were badly worn.* **2** [sing.] the way that someone walks; the sound that someone makes when they walk: *I heard his heavy tread on the stairs.* **3** [C] the upper surface of a step or stair ⊃ compare RISER

trea·dle /ˈtrɛdl/ *noun* (especially in the past) a device worked by the foot to operate a machine

tread·mill /ˈtrɛdmɪl/ *noun* **1** [C] an exercise machine that has a moving surface that you can walk or run on while remaining in the same place ⊃ picture at EXERCISE **2** [sing.] work or a way of life that is boring or tiring because it involves always doing the same things: *I'd like to escape the office treadmill.* **3** [C] (especially in the past) a large wheel turned by the weight of people or animals walking on steps around its inside edge, and used to operate machinery

trea·son /ˈtrizn/ (*also* ˌhigh ˈtreason) *noun* [U] the crime of doing something that could cause danger to your country, such as helping its enemies during a war ▶ **trea·son·able** /ˈtrizənəbl/ *adj.*: *a treasonable act*

treas·ure /ˈtrɛʒər/ *noun, verb*
• *noun* **1** [U] a collection of valuable things such as gold, silver, and jewelry: *buried treasure* ◆ *a pirate's treasure chest* **2** [C, usually pl.] a highly valued object: *the priceless art treasures of the Metropolitan Museum* **3** [sing.] a person who is much loved or valued
• *verb* ~ **sth** to have or keep something that you love and that is extremely valuable to you **SYN** CHERISH: *I treasure his friendship.* ◆ *This ring is my most treasured possession.*

ˈtreasure ˌhouse *noun* a place that contains many valuable or interesting things: *The area is a treasure house of archeological relics.*

ˈtreasure ˌhunt *noun* a game in which players try to find a hidden prize by answering a series of questions that have been left in different places

treas·ur·er /ˈtrɛʒərər/ *noun* a person who is responsible for the money and accounts of a club or an organization

ˈtreasure ˌtrove *noun* **1** [U, C, usually sing.] valuable things that are found hidden and whose owner is unknown **2** [C, usually sing.] a place, book, etc. containing many useful or beautiful things: *This town is a treasure trove of antique stores.*

treas·ur·y /ˈtrɛʒəri/ *noun* (*pl.* **treas·ur·ies**) **1 the Treas·ury** [sing.] (in the U.S. and some other countries) the government department that controls public money **2** [C] a place in a castle, etc. where valuable things are stored

ˈtreasury ˌbill (*also informal* 'T-bill) *noun* a type of investment sold by the U.S. government in which a fixed amount of money is paid back on a certain date

treat 🔑 /trit/ *verb, noun*
• *verb*
▷ BEHAVE TOWARD SOMEONE OR SOMETHING **1** to behave in a particular way toward someone or something: ~ **sb/sth (with sth)** *to treat people with respect/consideration/suspicion, etc.* ◆ *Treat your keyboard with care and it should last for years.* ◆ ~ **sb/sth like sth** *My parents still treat me like a child.* ◆ ~ **sb/sth as sth)** *He was treated as a hero on his release from prison.*
▷ CONSIDER **2** ~ **sth as sth** to consider something in a

particular way: *I decided to treat his remark as a joke.* **3 ~ sth + adv./prep.** to deal with or discuss something in a particular way: *The question is treated in more detail in the next chapter.*

> ILLNESS/INJURY **4 ~ sb (for sth) (with sth)** to give medical care or attention to a person, an illness, an injury, etc.: *She was treated for sunstroke.* ◆ *The condition is usually treated with drugs and a strict diet.* ⊃ collocations at INJURY

> USE CHEMICAL **5 ~ sth (with sth)** to use a chemical substance or process to clean, protect, preserve, etc. something: *to treat crops with insecticide* ◆ *wood treated with preservative*

> PAY FOR SOMETHING ENJOYABLE **6 ~ sb/yourself (to sth)** to pay for something that someone/you will enjoy and that you do not usually have or do: *She treated him to lunch.* ◆ *Don't worry about the cost—I'll treat you.* ◆ *I'm going to treat myself to a new pair of shoes.*

▶ **treat·a·ble** /ˈtriːtəbl/ *adj.*: *a treatable infection*

IDM **treat sb like dirt** (*informal*) to treat someone with no respect at all

PHR V **'treat sb to sth** to entertain someone with something special: *The crowd were treated to a superb display of tennis.*

● *noun* something very pleasant and enjoyable, especially something that you give someone or do for them: *We took the kids to the zoo as a special treat.* ◆ *You've never been to this area before? Then you're in for a real treat.* ◆ *When I was young, chocolate was a treat.* ◆ *Let's go out for lunch—my treat* (= I will pay). ⊃ thesaurus box at PLEASURE ⊃ see also TRICK OR TREAT

trea·tise /ˈtriːtɪs/ *noun* **~ (on sth)** a long and serious piece of writing on a particular subject

treat·ment 🔊 /ˈtriːtmənt/ *noun*
1 [U, C] **~ (for sth)** something that is done to cure an illness or injury, or to make someone look and feel good: *He is receiving treatment for shock.* ◆ *She is responding well to treatment.* ◆ *to require hospital/medical treatment* ◆ *There are various treatments available for this condition.* ◆ *Guests at the health spa receive a range of beauty treatments.* **2** [U] a way of behaving toward or dealing with a person or thing: *the brutal treatment of political prisoners* ◆ *Certain areas of the city have been singled out for special treatment.* **3** [U, C] a way of dealing with or discussing a subject, work of art, etc.: *Shakespeare's treatment of madness in "King Lear"* **4** [U, C] a process by which something is cleaned, or protected against something: *a sewage treatment plant* ◆ **~ for sth** *an effective treatment for dry rot*

trea·ty /ˈtriːti/ *noun* (*pl.* **trea·ties**) a formal agreement between two or more countries: *the Treaty of Rome* ◆ *a peace treaty* ◆ *to draw up/sign/ratify a treaty* ◆ *Under the terms of the treaty, the land was to be divided equally between the warring groups.* ⊃ collocations at WAR

tre·ble /ˈtrebl/ *noun, verb, det., adj.*
● *noun* **1** [U] the high tones or part in music or a sound system: *to turn up the treble on the stereo* ⊃ compare BASS¹ **2** [C] a child's high voice; a boy who sings with a treble voice ⊃ compare SOPRANO **3** [sing.] a musical part written for a treble voice
● *verb* [I, T] to become, or to make something, three times as much or as many **SYN** TRIPLE: *Cases of food poisoning have trebled in the last two years.* ◆ **~ sth** *He trebled his earnings in two years.*
● *det.* [usually before noun] three times as much or as many: *Capital expenditure was treble the 2007 level.*
● *adj.* [only before noun] high in tone: *a treble voice* ◆ *the treble clef* (= the symbol in music showing that the notes following it are high) ⊃ compare BASS¹

tree 🔊 /triː/ *noun*
a tall plant that can live a long time. Trees have a thick central wooden TRUNK from which branches grow, usually with leaves on them: *an oak tree* ◆ *to plant a tree* ◆ *to chop/cut down a tree* ◆ *They followed a path through the trees.* ⊃ picture

on page 1593 ⊃ collocations at LIFE ⊃ compare BUSH, SHRUB ⊃ see also BAY TREE, CHRISTMAS TREE, FAMILY TREE, PHONE TREE, PLANE TREE, SHADE TREE

IDM **be out of your tree** (*informal*) to be behaving in a crazy or stupid way, perhaps because of drugs or alcohol ⊃ more at APPLE, BARK *v.*, FOREST, GROW

'tree ˌdiagram *noun* a diagram with lines that divide more and more as you move to lower levels to show the relationships between processes, people etc.

'tree house *noun* a structure built in the branches of a tree, usually for children to play in

'tree-ˌhugger *noun* (*informal*, *usually disapproving*) a person who cares very much about the environment and tries to protect it

tree·less /ˈtriːləs/ *adj.* without trees: *a treeless plain*

tree·line /ˈtriːlaɪn/ *noun* [sing.] a level of land, for example on a mountain, above which trees will not grow

'tree ˌstructure *noun* (*computing*) a diagram that uses lines that divide into more and more lines to show the various levels of a computer program, and how each part relates to a part in the level above

'tree ˌsurgeon (also *formal* **ar·bor·ist**) *noun* a person whose job is treating trees that are damaged or have a disease, especially by cutting off branches, to try to preserve them ▶ **'tree ˌsurgery** *noun* [U]

tree·top /ˈtriːtɑp/ *noun* [usually pl.] the branches at the top of a tree: *birds nesting in the treetops*

tre·foil /ˈtriːfɔɪl/ *noun* **1** (*technical*) a plant whose leaves are divided into three similar parts, for example CLOVER **2** a decoration or a design shaped like a trefoil leaf

trek /trek/ *verb, noun*
● *verb* (**-kk-**) **1** [I] (**+ adv./prep.**) (*informal*) to make a long or difficult journey, especially on foot: *I hate having to trek up that hill with all the groceries.* **2** also **go trekking** [I] (**+ adv./prep.**) to spend time walking, especially in mountains and for enjoyment and interest: *We went trekking in Nepal.* ◆ *During the expedition, they trekked ten to thirteen hours a day.*
● *noun* **1** a long, hard walk lasting several days or weeks, especially in the mountains **2** (*informal*) a long walk **SYN** TRAMP: *It's a long trek into town.*

Trek·kie /ˈtreki/ *noun* a person who is very interested in the television series *Star Trek* and in space travel

trel·lis /ˈtreləs/ *noun* [C, U] a light frame made of long narrow pieces of wood that cross each other, used to support climbing plants

trem·ble /ˈtrembl/ *verb, noun*
● *verb* **1** [I] **~ (with sth)** to shake in a way that you cannot control, especially because you are very nervous, excited, frightened, etc.: *My legs were trembling with fear.* ◆ *Her voice trembled with excitement.* ◆ *He opened the letter with trembling hands.* **2** [I] to shake slightly **SYN** QUIVER: *leaves trembling in the breeze* **3** [I] to be very worried or frightened: *I trembled at the thought of having to make a speech.*
● *noun* [C, usually sing.] (also **trem·bling** [C, U]) a feeling, movement or sound of trembling: *a tremble of fear* ◆ *She tried to control the trembling in her legs.*

trem·bly /ˈtrembli/ *adj.* (*informal*) shaking from fear, cold, excitement, etc.

tre·men·dous /trəˈmendəs/ *adj.* **1** very great **SYN** HUGE: *a tremendous explosion* ◆ *A tremendous amount of work has gone into the project.* **2** extremely good **SYN** REMARKABLE: *It was a tremendous experience.* ▶ **tre·men·dous·ly** *adv.*: *tremendously exciting*

trem·o·lo /ˈtremə.loʊ/ *noun* (*pl.* **trem·o·los**) (*music*) a special effect in singing or playing a musical instrument made by repeating the same note or two notes very quickly

trem·or /ˈtremər/ *noun* **1** a small EARTHQUAKE in which the ground shakes slightly: *an earth tremor* **2** a slight shaking movement in a part of your body caused, for example, by cold or fear **SYN** QUIVER: *There was a slight tremor in his voice.*

Trees

tree

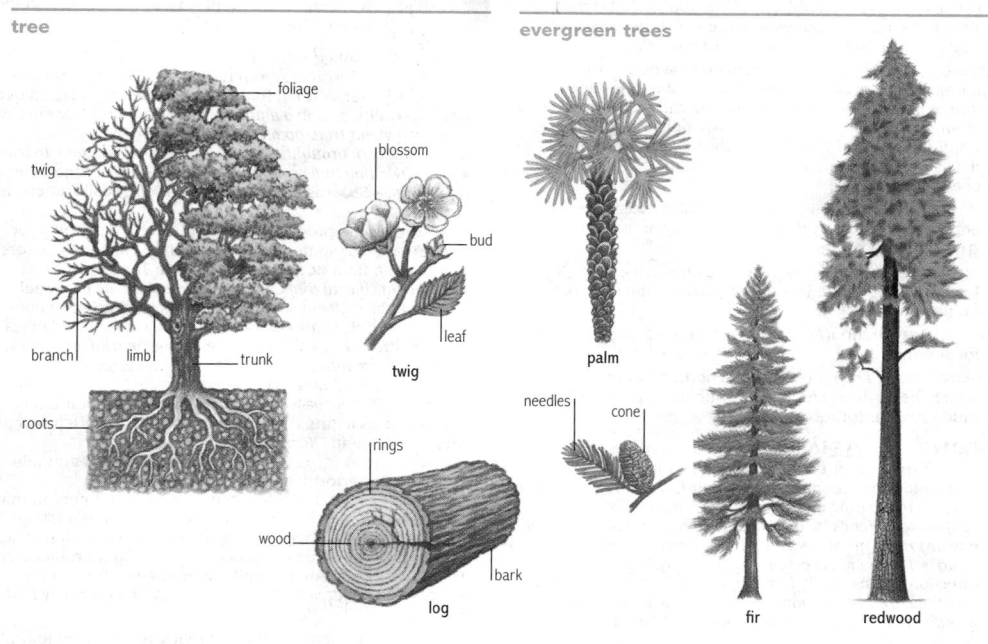

foliage

twig

blossom

bud

branch | limb | trunk

leaf

roots

twig

rings

wood

bark

log

evergreen trees

palm

needles | cone

fir

redwood

deciduous trees

seeds

maple

acorn

oak

birch

blossom

horse chestnut

horse chestnut

beech nut

beech

seeds

ash

trem·u·lous /'tremjələs/ adj. (literary) shaking slightly because you are nervous; causing you to shake slightly **SYN** TREMBLING: a tremulous voice ◆ He was in a state of tremulous excitement. ▶ **trem·u·lous·ly** adv.

trench /trentʃ/ noun **1** a long, deep hole dug in the ground, for example for carrying away water **2** a long, deep hole dug in the ground in which soldiers can be protected from enemy attacks (for example, in northern France and Belgium in World War I): life in the trenches ◆ trench warfare **3** (also ocean 'trench) a long, deep, narrow hole in the ocean floor

trench·ant /'trentʃənt/ adj. (formal) (of criticism, remarks, etc.) expressed strongly and effectively, in a clear way **SYN** INCISIVE ▶ **trench·ant·ly** adv.

'trench coat noun a long, loose coat, worn especially to keep off rain, with a belt and pockets in the style of a military coat

trench·er /'trentʃər/ noun a wooden plate used in the past for serving food

'trench foot noun [U] a painful condition of the feet, in which the flesh begins to decay and die, caused by being in mud or water for too long

trend 🔑 **AWL** /trend/ noun, verb
● **noun** a general direction in which a situation is changing or developing: economic/social/political trends ◆ ~ (toward sth) There is a growing trend toward earlier retirement. ◆ ~ (in sth) current trends in language teaching ◆ a downward/an upward trend in sales ◆ You seem to have set (= started) a new trend. ◆ This trend is being reversed (= is going in the opposite direction). ◆ One region is attempting to buck (= oppose or resist) the trend of economic decline. ◆ The underlying trend of inflation is still upward. ⊃ language bank at FALL
● **verb** [I] + adv./prep. to change or develop in a general direction: Unemployment has been trending upward.

trend·set·ter /'trend,setər/ noun (often approving) a person who starts a new fashion or makes it popular ▶ **trend-set·ting** adj. [only before noun]

trend·y /'trendi/ adj. (trend·i·er, trend·i·est) (informal) very fashionable: trendy clothes ▶ **trend·i·ly** /-dəli/ adv. **trend·i·ness** /-dinəs/ noun [U]

trep·i·da·tion /,trepə'deɪʃn/ noun [U] (formal) great worry or fear about something unpleasant that may happen

tres·pass /'trespæs; -pəs/ verb, noun
● **verb 1** [I] ~ (on sth) to enter land or a building that you do not have permission or the right to enter: He told me I was trespassing on private land. **2** [I] (old use) to do something wrong
PHR V 'trespass on sth (formal) to make unfair use of someone's time, help, etc. **SYN** ENCROACH ON: I mustn't trespass on your time any longer.
● **noun 1** [U, C] an act of trespassing on land **2** [C] (old use) something that you do that is morally wrong **SYN** SIN

tres·pass·er /'trespæsər; -pəsər/ noun a person who goes onto someone's land without their permission: The notice read: "Trespassers will be prosecuted."

tres·ses /'tresəz/ noun [pl.] (literary) a woman's long hair **SYN** LOCK

tres·tle /'tresl/ noun a wooden or metal structure with two pairs of sloping legs. Trestles are used in pairs to support a flat surface, for example the top of a table.

'trestle table noun a table that consists of a wooden top supported by trestle

trey /treɪ/ noun **1** (in card games) a playing card with the number 3 or three repeated marks on it **2** (informal) (in basketball) a shot that scores three points

tri- /traɪ/ combining form (in nouns and adjectives) three; having three: tricycle ◆ triangular

tri·ad /'traɪæd/ noun **1** (formal) a group of three related people or things **2** also Triad a Chinese secret organization involved in criminal activity

tri·age /'triɑʒ; tri'ɑʒ/ noun [U] (in a hospital) the process of deciding how seriously ill or injured a person is, so that the most serious cases can be treated first

tri·al 🔑 /'traɪəl/ noun
▷ LAW **1** [U, C] a formal examination of evidence in court by a judge and often a JURY, to decide if someone accused of a crime is guilty or not: a murder trial ◆ He's on trial for murder. ◆ She will stand trial/go on trial for fraud. ◆ The men were arrested but not brought to trial. ◆ The case never came to trial. ◆ She is awaiting trial on corruption charges. ◆ He did not receive a fair trial. ◆ She was detained without trial. ⊃ collocations at JUSTICE
▷ TEST **2** [C, U] the process of testing the ability, quality, or performance of someone or something, especially before you make a final decision about them: The new drug is undergoing clinical trials. ◆ She agreed to hire me for a trial period. ◆ The system was introduced on a trial basis for one month. ◆ a trial separation (= of a couple whose marriage is having difficulties) ◆ We had the machine on trial for a week. ◆ a trial of strength (= a contest to see who is stronger) ⊃ collocations at SCIENTIFIC
▷ IN SPORTS **3** [C, usually pl.] (also try·out) a competition or series of tests to find the best players for a sports team or an important event: Olympic trials
▷ FOR ANIMALS **4** [C, usually pl.] an event at which animals compete or perform: horse trials
▷ DIFFICULT EXPERIENCE **5** [C] an experience or a person that causes difficulties for someone: the trials and tribulations of married life ◆ ~ to sb She was quite a trial to her family at times.
IDM trial and error the process of solving a problem by trying various methods until you find a method that is successful: Children learn to use computer programs by trial and error.

'trial bal'loon noun something that you say or do to find out what people think about a course of action before you take it

'trial 'run (also 'test run) noun a test of how well something new works, so that you can see if any changes are necessary

tri·an·gle 🔑 /'traɪæŋgl/ noun
1 a flat shape with three straight sides and three angles; a thing in the shape of a triangle: a right triangle ◆ Cut the dough into triangles. **2** a simple musical instrument that consists of a long piece of metal bent into the shape of a triangle, which you hit with another piece of metal ⊃ picture at INSTRUMENT **3** a situation involving three people in a complicated relationship: a love triangle ⊃ see also ETERNAL TRIANGLE **4** an instrument for drawing straight lines and angles, made from a flat piece of plastic or metal in the shape of a triangle with one angle of 90°

tri·an·gu·lar /traɪ'æŋgyələr/ adj. **1** shaped like a triangle **2** involving three people or groups: a triangular contest in an election

tri·an·gu·la·tion /traɪ,æŋgyə'leɪʃn/ noun [U] (technical) a method of finding out distance and position, usually on a map, by measuring the distance between two fixed points and then measuring the angle from each of these to the third point

tri·ath·lete /traɪ'æθlit/ noun a person who competes in a triathlon

tri·ath·lon /traɪ'æθlɑn; -lən/ noun a sporting event in which people compete in three different sports, usually swimming, cycling, and running ⊃ compare BIATHLON, DECATHLON, HEPTATHLON, PENTATHLON, TETRATHLON

trib·al /'traɪbl/ adj. [usually before noun] connected with a tribe or tribes: tribal art ◆ tribal leaders ▶ **trib·al·ly** adv.

trib·al·ism /'traɪbə,lɪzəm/ noun [U] **1** behavior, attitudes, etc. that are based on being loyal to a tribe or other social group **2** the state of being organized in a tribe or tribes

'tri-band adj. (of a cell phone) able to use three different ranges of radio waves so that it can be used in different regions of the world

t tea   ţ butter   d did   k cat   g got   tʃ chin   dʒ June   f fall

tribe /traɪb/ *noun* **1** (sometimes *offensive*) a group of people consisting of families that are related to each other and who have the same customs, language, religion, etc., and often live in a particular area: *tribes living in remote areas of the Amazonian rainforest* **2** (usually *disapproving*) a group or class of people, especially of one profession: *He had a sudden outburst against the whole tribe of actors.* **3** (*biology*) a group of related animals or plants: *a tribe of cats* **4** (*informal* or *humorous*) a large number of people: *One or two of the grandchildren will be there, but not the whole tribe.*

tribes·man /ˈtraɪbzmən/, **tribes·wom·an** /ˈtraɪbzˌwʊmən/ *noun* (*pl.* tribes·men /-mən/, tribes·wom·en /-ˌwɪmən/) a member of a tribe

tribes·peo·ple /ˈtraɪbzˌpipl/ *noun* [pl.] the people who belong to a particular tribe

trib·u·la·tion /ˌtrɪbyəˈleɪʃn/ *noun* [C, U] (*literary* or *humorous*) great trouble or suffering: *the tribulations of modern life*

tri·bu·nal /traɪˈbyunl; trɪ-/ *noun* a type of court with the authority to deal with a particular problem or disagreement: *an international war crimes tribunal* ◆ *a military tribunal*

trib·une /ˈtrɪbyun/ *noun* an official elected by the people in ancient Rome to defend their rights; a popular leader

trib·u·tar·y /ˈtrɪbyəˌteri/ *noun* (*pl.* trib·u·tar·ies) a river or stream that flows into a larger river or a lake ▶ **trib·u·tar·y** *adj.* [only before noun]: *a tributary stream*

trib·ute /ˈtrɪbyut/ *noun* **1** [U, C] ~ (to sb) an act, a statement, or a gift that is intended to show your respect or admiration, especially for a dead person: *At her funeral, her oldest friend **paid tribute to** her life and work.* ◆ *This book is a fitting tribute to the bravery of the pioneers.* ◆ *floral tributes* (= gifts of flowers at a funeral) ◆ *The students presented a musical tribute to their beloved teacher upon his retirement.* **2** [sing.] ~ to sth/sb showing the good effects or influence of something or someone: *His recovery is a tribute to the doctors' skill.* **3** [U, C] (especially in the past) money given by one country or ruler to another, especially in return for protection or for not being attacked

tribute band *noun* a group of musicians who play the music of a famous band and copy the way they look and sound

trice /traɪs/ *noun*
IDM **in a trice** very quickly or suddenly **SYN** IN AN INSTANT: *He was gone in a trice.*

tri·ceps /ˈtraɪseps/ *noun* (*pl.* tri·ceps) the large muscle at the back of the top part of the arm ⊃ compare BICEPS

tri·cer·a·tops /traɪˈserəˌtaps/ *noun* (*pl.* tri·cer·a·tops or tri·cer·a·tops·es) a large DINOSAUR with two large horns and one small horn on its very large head

trick 🔎 /trɪk/ *noun, verb, adj.*
● *noun*
▷ SOMETHING TO CHEAT SOMEONE **1** something that you do to make someone believe something that is not true, or to annoy someone as a joke: *They had to think of a trick to get past the guards.* ◆ *The kids are always **playing tricks on** their teacher.* ⊃ see also DIRTY TRICK
▷ SOMETHING CONFUSING **2** something that confuses you so that you see, understand, remember, etc. things in the wrong way: *One of the problems of aging is that your memory can start to **play tricks on** you.* ◆ *Was there someone standing there, or was it **a trick of the light**?*
▷ ENTERTAINMENT **3** a skillful action that someone or something performs as a way of entertaining people: *He amused the kids with conjuring tricks.* ◆ *a card trick* ⊃ see also HAT TRICK
▷ GOOD METHOD **4** [usually sing.] a way of doing something that works well; a good method: *The trick is to pick the animal up by the back of its neck.* ◆ *He used the old trick of attacking in order to defend himself.*
▷ IN CARD GAMES **5** the cards that you play or win in a single part of a card game: *I won six tricks in a row.*

IDM **be up to your (old) tricks** (*informal, disapproving*) to be behaving in the same bad way as before **do the trick** (*informal*) to succeed in solving a problem or achieving a particular result: *I don't know what it was that did the trick, but I am definitely feeling much better.* **every trick in the book** every available method, whether it is honest or not: *He'll use every trick in the book to keep you from winning.* **have a trick, some more tricks, etc. up your sleeve** to have an idea, some plans, etc. that you keep ready to use if it becomes necessary **the tricks of the trade** skillful ways of doing things that are known and used by people who do a particular job or activity ⊃ more at BAG *n.*, MISS *v.*, TEACH

● *verb* ~ sb to make someone believe something that is not true, especially in order to cheat them: *I was tricked and I felt stupid.* ⊃ thesaurus box at CHEAT
PHRV trick sb ˈinto sth/into doing sth to make someone do something by means of a trick: *He tricked me into lending him $100.* trick sb ˈout of sth to get something from someone by means of a trick: *She was tricked out of her life savings.* trick sb/sth↔ˈout (in/with sth) (*literary*) to dress or decorate someone or something in a way that attracts attention

● *adj.* [only before noun] **1** intended to trick someone: *It was a trick question* (= one to which the answer seems easy but actually is not). ◆ *It's all done using trick photography* (= photography that uses clever techniques to show things that do not actually exist or are impossible). **2** (of part of the body) weak and not working well: *a trick knee*

trick·er·y /ˈtrɪkəri/ *noun* [U] the use of dishonest methods to trick people in order to achieve what you want
SYN DECEPTION

trick·le /ˈtrɪkl/ *verb, noun*
● *verb* **1** [I, T] to flow, or to make something flow, slowly in a thin stream: (+ adv./prep.) *Tears were trickling down her cheeks.* ◆ ~ sth (+ adv./prep.) *She trickled the sand slowly through her fingers.* **2** [I, T] ~ (sth) + adv./prep. to go, or to make something go, somewhere slowly or gradually: *People began trickling into the auditorium.* ◆ *News is starting to trickle out.*
PHRV trickle ˈdown (especially of money) to spread from rich to poor people through the economic system of a country
● *noun* **1** a small amount of liquid, flowing slowly **2** [usually sing.] ~ (of sth) a small amount or number of something, coming or going slowly: *a steady trickle of visitors*

trickle-down *adj.* [only before noun] connected with the theory that if the richest people in society become richer, this will have a good effect on poorer people as well, for example by creating more jobs: *trickle-down economics* ◆ *the trickle-down effect*

trick or ˈtreat *noun* [U] a custom on Halloween when children wear costumes and visit people's houses and say "trick or treat" to ask for candy ▶ trick-or-ˈtreating *noun* [U]: *to go trick-or-treating*

trick·ster /ˈtrɪkstər/ *noun* a person who tricks or cheats people

trick·y /ˈtrɪki/ *adj.* (trick·i·er, trick·i·est) **1** difficult to do or deal with: *a tricky situation* ◆ *Getting it to fit exactly is a tricky business.* ◆ *The equipment can be tricky to install.* **2** (of people) intelligent and skillful but likely to trick you **SYN** CRAFTY

tri·col·or (*CanE usually* tri·col·our) /ˈtraɪˌkʌlər/ *noun* a flag that has three bands of different colors, for example the French national flag

tri·cy·cle /ˈtraɪsɪkl/ (also *informal* trike) *noun* a vehicle, used especially by small children, that is similar to a bicycle, but with one wheel at the front and two at the back ⊃ picture at BICYCLE

tri·dent /ˈtraɪdnt/ *noun* a weapon used in the past that looks like a long fork with three points

tried /traɪd/ *adj.* ⊃ see also TRY *v.*
IDM **tried and true** that you have used or relied on in the

past successfully: *a tried and true method for solving the problem*

tri·en·ni·al /traɪˈɛniəl/ *adj.* happening every three years

tri·er /ˈtraɪər/ *noun* a person who tries very hard at what they are doing and does their best

tri·fle /ˈtraɪfl/ *noun, verb*
• *noun* **1** [C] something that is not valuable or important: *$1,000 is a mere trifle to her.* **2 a trifle** [sing.] (used as an adverb) (*formal* or *humorous*) slightly: *She seemed a trifle anxious.*
• *verb*
  PHR V '**trifle with sb/sth** (*formal*) (used especially in negative sentences) to treat someone or something without genuine respect: *He is not a person to be trifled with.*

tri·fling /ˈtraɪflɪŋ/ *adj.* (*formal*) small and not important **SYN** TRIVIAL: *trifling details*

trig·ger **AWL** /ˈtrɪgər/ *noun, verb*
• *noun* **1** the part of a gun that you press in order to fire it: *to pull/squeeze the trigger* ◆ *He kept his finger on the trigger.* **2** ~ (for sth) | ~ (to sth/to do sth) something that is the cause of a particular reaction or development, especially a bad one: *The trigger for the strike was the closure of yet another factory.* **3** the part of a bomb that causes it to explode: *nuclear triggers*
• *verb* **1** ~ sth (off) to make something happen suddenly **SYN** SET OFF: *Nuts can trigger off a violent allergic reaction.* **2** ~ sth to cause a device to start functioning **SYN** SET OFF: *to trigger an alarm*

'trigger–happy *adj.* (*informal, disapproving*) too willing and quick to use violence, especially with guns

trig·o·nom·e·try /ˌtrɪgəˈnɑmətri/ (also *informal* **trig** /trɪg/) *noun* [U] the type of mathematics that deals with the relationship between the sides and angles of triangles
▶ **trig·o·no·met·ric** /ˌtrɪgənəˈmɛtrɪk/ (also **trig·o·no·met·ri·cal** /-ˈmɛtrɪkl/) *adj.*

tri·graph /ˈtraɪgræf/ *noun* (*linguistics*) a combination of three letters representing one sound, for example "sch" in German

trike /traɪk/ *noun* (*informal*) = TRICYCLE

tri·lat·er·al /traɪˈlætərəl/ *adj.* involving three groups of people or three countries: *trilateral talks* ⭢ compare BILATERAL, MULTILATERAL, UNILATERAL

tril·by /ˈtrɪlbi/ *noun* (*pl.* **tril·bies**) a man's soft hat with a narrow BRIM and the top part pushed in from front to back ⭢ picture at HAT

tri·lin·gual /traɪˈlɪŋgwəl/ *adj.* **1** able to speak three languages equally well: *He is trilingual in English, Spanish, and French.* **2** using three languages; written in three languages: *trilingual education* ◆ *a trilingual menu*

trill /trɪl/ *noun, verb*
• *noun* **1** a repeated short high sound made, for example, by someone's voice or by a bird **2** (*music*) the sound made when two notes next to each other in the musical SCALE are played or sung quickly several times one after the other **3** (also **roll**) (*phonetics*) a sound, usually a /r/, produced by making the tongue VIBRATE against a part of the mouth
• *verb* **1** [I] to make repeated short high sounds **SYN** WARBLE: *An electronic device trilled in the next room.* ◆ *The canary was trilling away happily.* **2** [T] + **speech** to say something in a high cheerful voice **SYN** WARBLE: *"How wonderful!" she trilled.* **3** [T] ~ sth (*phonetics*) to pronounce an "r" sound by making a trill ⭢ compare ROLL

tril·lion /ˈtrɪlyən/ *number* (*plural verb*) **1** 1,000,000,000,000; one million million **HELP** You say **a, one, two, several,** etc. **trillion** without a final "s" on "trillion." **Trillions (of…)** can be used if there is no number or quantity before it. Always use a plural verb with **trillion** or **trillions. 2 a trillion** or **trillions (of…)** (*informal*) a very large amount **HELP** There are more examples of how to use numbers at the entry for **hundred**.

tri·lo·bite /ˈtraɪləˌbaɪt/ *noun* a small sea creature that lived millions of years ago and is now a FOSSIL

tril·o·gy /ˈtrɪlədʒi/ *noun* (*pl.* **tril·o·gies**) a group of three books, movies, etc. that have the same subject or characters

trim /trɪm/ *verb, noun, adj.*
• *verb* (-mm-) **1** ~ sth to make something neater, smaller, better, etc., by cutting parts from it: *to trim your hair* ◆ *to trim a hedge (back)* ◆ (*figurative*) *The training budget was trimmed by $15,000.* **2** ~ sth (off sth) | ~ sth (off/away) to cut away unnecessary parts from something: *Trim any excess fat off the meat.* ◆ *I trimmed two inches off the bottom of the skirt.* **3** [usually passive] ~ sth (with sth) to decorate something, especially around its edges: *gloves trimmed with fur*
  IDM **trim your sails** to arrange the sails of a boat to suit the wind so that the boat moves faster
  PHR V ,**trim** '**down** | ,**trim** sth↔'**down** to become smaller in size; to make something smaller: *Since he went on a diet, he's trimmed down from 190 pounds to 170.*
• *noun* **1** [C, usually sing.] an act of cutting a small amount off something, especially hair: *Don't cut off a lot—I just need a trim.* **2** [U, sing.] material that is used to decorate clothes, furniture, cars, etc., especially along the edges, by being a different color, etc.: *The car is available with black or red trim* (= the color of a stripe along the side). ◆ *a blue jacket with white trim*
• *adj.* **1** (of a person) looking thin, healthy, and attractive: *She has kept very trim.* ◆ *a trim figure* **2** neat and well cared for **SYN** WELL KEPT: *a trim lawn*

tri·ma·ran /ˈtraɪməˌræn/ *noun* a fast sailing boat like a CATAMARAN, but with three HULLS instead of two

tri·mes·ter /traɪˈmɛstər; ˈtraɪmɛs-/ *noun* **1** (*medical*) a period of three months during the time when a woman is pregnant: *the first trimester of pregnancy* **2** one of the three periods in the year during which classes are held in schools, universities, etc.: *The school year is divided into three trimesters.* ⭢ compare SEMESTER

trim·mer /ˈtrɪmər/ *noun* a machine for cutting the edges of bushes, grass, and HEDGES: *a hedge trimmer*

trim·ming /ˈtrɪmɪŋ/ *noun* **1** **trimmings** (also **fix·ings**) [pl.] the extra things that it is traditional to have for a special meal or occasion: *a Thanksgiving meal of turkey with all the trimmings* **2** **trimmings** [pl.] the small pieces of something that are left when you have cut something: *hedge trimmings* **3** [U, C, usually pl.] material that is used to decorate something, for example along its edges: *a white blouse with blue trimming*

trin·i·ty /ˈtrɪnəti/ *noun* [sing.] **1 the Trinity** (in Christianity) the union of Father, Son, and HOLY SPIRIT as one God **2** (*formal*) a group of three people or things

trin·ket /ˈtrɪŋkət/ *noun* a piece of jewelry or a small decorative object that is not worth much money

tri·o /ˈtrioʊ/ *noun* (*pl.* **tri·os**) **1** a group of three people or things ⭢ compare DUO **2** a group of three musicians or singers who play or sing together **3** a piece of music for three musicians or singers: *a trio for piano, oboe, and bassoon* ⭢ compare DUET

trip 🔑 /trɪp/ *noun, verb*
• *noun* **1** a journey to a place and back again, especially a short one for pleasure or a particular purpose: *Did you have a good trip?* ◆ *We went on a trip out west.* ◆ *a day trip* (= lasting a day) ◆ *a boat/bus trip* ◆ *a business/school/shopping trip* ◆ *They took a trip down the river.* ◆ *We had to make several trips to bring all the equipment over.* ⭢ collocations at TRAVEL ⭢ see also EGO TRIP, FIELD TRIP, ROUND TRIP **2** (*slang*) the experience that someone has if they take a powerful drug that affects the mind and makes them imagine things: *an acid* (= LSD) *trip* **3** an act of falling or nearly falling down, because you hit your foot against something **IDM** see GUILT *n.*
• *verb* (-pp-) **1** [I] to catch your foot on something and fall or almost fall: *She tripped and fell.* ◆ ~ **over/on sth** *Someone will*

trip on that cable. ♦ **~ over/up** *She tripped over and skinned her knee.* **2** [T] **~ sb** (also **trip sb up**) to catch someone's foot and make them fall or almost fall: *As I passed, he stuck out a leg and tried to trip me up.* **3** [I] **+ adv./prep.** (*literary*) to walk, run, or dance with quick light steps: *She said goodbye and tripped off along the road.* **4** [T] **~ sth** to release a switch, etc. or to operate something by doing so: *to trip a switch* ♦ *Any intruders will trip the alarm.* **5** [I] (*informal*) to be under the influence of a drug that makes you HALLUCINATE **IDM** see MEMORY LANE, TONGUE

PHR V ,trip 'up | ,trip sb⟷'up to make a mistake; to deliberately make someone do this: *Read the questions carefully, because the wording can sometimes trip you up.*

trip

journey ♦ tour ♦ commute ♦ expedition ♦ excursion ♦ outing

These are all words for an act of traveling to a place.

trip an act of traveling from one place to another, and usually back again: *a business trip* ♦ *a five-minute trip by taxi*

journey an act of traveling from one place to another, especially when they are far apart: *a long and difficult journey across the mountains*

TRIP OR JOURNEY?

A **trip** usually involves you going to a place and back again; a **journey** is usually one-way. A **trip** is often shorter than a **journey**, although it does not have to be: *a trip to New York* ♦ *a round-the-world trip.* It is often short in time, even if it is long in distance. **Journey** is more often used when the traveling takes a long time and is difficult.

tour a journey made for pleasure during which several different places are visited: *a tour of California*

commute the regular trip that a person makes when they travel to work and back home again: *a two-hour commute into downtown Washington*

expedition an organized journey with a particular purpose, especially to find out about a place that is not well known: *the first expedition to the South Pole*

excursion a short trip made for pleasure, especially one that has been organized for a group of people: *We went on an all-day excursion to the island.*

outing a short trip made for pleasure or education, usually with a group of people and lasting no more than a day: *My project team organized an afternoon outing to celebrate.*

PATTERNS

- an **overseas** trip/journey/tour/expedition
- a **bus/train** trip/journey/tour
- to **go on** a(n) trip/journey/tour/expedition/excursion/outing
- to **set out/off on** a(n) trip/journey/tour/expedition/excursion
- to **take** a(n) trip/journey/expedition/excursion

tri·par·tite /ˌtraɪˈpɑrtaɪt/ *adj.* [usually before noun] (*formal*) having three parts or involving three people, groups, etc.

tripe /traɪp/ *noun* [U] **1** the LINING of a cow's or pig's stomach, eaten as food **2** (*informal*) something that someone says or writes that you think is nonsense or not of good quality **SYN** GARBAGE, RUBBISH

'trip hop *noun* [U] a type of electronic music that is a mixture of HIP-HOP and HOUSE MUSIC, has a slow beat, and is intended to create a relaxed atmosphere

tri·ple /ˈtrɪpl/ *adj.*, *verb*
● *adj.* [only before noun] **1** having three parts or involving three people or groups: *a triple heart bypass operation* ♦ *a*

triple alliance ♦ *They're showing a* **triple bill** *of horror movies* (= three horror movies one after the other). **2** three times as much or as many as something: *The library will be triple the size of the existing main library.* ♦ *Its population is about triple that of St. Louis.* ▶ **trip·ly** /ˈtrɪpli/ *adv.*

● *verb* [I, T] **~ (sth)** to become, or to make something, three times as much or as many **SYN** TREBLE: *Output should triple by next year.*

the 'triple ˌjump *noun* [sing.] a sporting event in which people try to jump as far forward as possible with three jumps. The first jump lands on one foot, the second on the other, and the third on both feet.

trip·let /ˈtrɪplət/ *noun* **1** one of three children born at the same time to the same mother **2** (*music*) a group of three equal notes to be played or sung in the time usually taken to play or sing two of the same kind

trip·li·cate /ˈtrɪplɪkət/ *noun*
IDM in triplicate **1** done three times: *Each sample was tested in triplicate.* **2** (of a document) copied twice, so that there are three copies in total ⊃ compare DUPLICATE

tri·pod /ˈtraɪpɑd/ *noun* a support with three legs for a camera, TELESCOPE, etc. ⊃ picture at LABORATORY

trip·tych /ˈtrɪptɪk/ *noun* (*technical*) a picture that is painted or CARVED on three pieces of wood placed side by side, especially one over an ALTAR in a church

trip·wire /ˈtrɪpˌwaɪər/ *noun* a wire that is stretched close to the ground as part of a device for catching someone or something if they touch it

tri·reme /ˈtraɪrim/ *noun* a long, flat ship with three rows of OARS on each side, used in war by the ancient Greeks and Romans

trite /traɪt/ *adj.* (of a remark, an opinion, etc.) dull and boring because it has been expressed so many times before; not original **SYN** BANAL ▶ **trite·ly** *adv.* **trite·ness** *noun* [U]

trit·i·um /ˈtrɪtiəm/ *noun* [U] (*symb.* T) an ISOTOPE (= a different form) of HYDROGEN with a mass that is three times that of the usual isotope

tri·umph /ˈtraɪʌmf/ *noun*, *verb*
● *noun* **1** [C, U] a great success, achievement, or victory: *one of the greatest triumphs of modern science* ♦ **~ over sb/sth** *It was a personal triumph over her old rival.* **2** [U] the feeling of great satisfaction or joy that you get from a great success or victory: *a shout of triumph* ♦ *The winning team returned home in triumph.* **3** [sing.] **a ~ (of sth)** an excellent example of how successful something can be: *Her arrest was a triumph of international cooperation.*

● *verb* [I] **~ (over sb/sth)** to defeat someone or something; to be successful: *As is usual in this kind of movie, good triumphs over evil in the end.* ♦ *France triumphed 3–0 in the final.*

tri·um·phal /traɪˈʌmfl/ *adj.* [usually before noun] done or made in order to celebrate a great success or victory

tri·um·phal·ism /traɪˈʌmfəˌlɪzəm/ *noun* [U] (*disapproving*) behavior that celebrates a victory or success in a way that is too proud and intended to upset the people you have defeated ▶ **tri·um·phal·ist** /-lɪst/ *adj.*

tri·um·phant /traɪˈʌmfənt/ *adj.* **1** very successful in a way that causes great satisfaction: *They emerged triumphant in the September election.* **2** showing great satisfaction or joy about a victory or success: *a triumphant smile* ▶ **tri·um·phant·ly** *adv.*

tri·um·vi·rate /traɪˈʌmvərət/ *noun* (*formal*) a group of three powerful people or groups who control something together

triv·et /ˈtrɪvət/ *noun* a metal stand that you can put a hot dish, etc. on

triv·i·a /ˈtrɪviə/ *noun* [U] **1** unimportant matters, details, or information: *We spent the whole evening discussing domestic trivia.* **2** (usually in compounds) facts about many subjects that are used in a game to test people's knowledge: *a trivia quiz*

triv·i·al /ˈtrɪviəl/ *adj.* not important or serious; not worth considering: *a trivial detail* ◆ *I know it sounds trivial, but I'm worried about it.* ◆ *I'll try to fix it—but it's not trivial* (= it may be difficult to fix). ▶ **triv·i·al·ly** *adv.*

triv·i·al·i·ty /ˌtrɪvi'æləti/ *noun* (*pl.* **triv·i·al·i·ties**) (*disapproving*) **1** [C] a matter that is not important: *I don't want to waste time on trivialities.* **2** [U] the state of being unimportant or dealing with unimportant things: *His speech was one of great triviality.*

triv·al·ize /ˈtrɪviəˌlaɪz/ *verb* ~ **sth** (usually *disapproving*) to make something seem less important, serious, difficult, etc. than it really is ▶ **triv·i·al·i·za·tion** /ˌtrɪviələˈzeɪʃn/ *noun* [U]

tro·chee /ˈtroʊki/ *noun* (*technical*) a unit of sound in poetry consisting of one strong or long syllable followed by one weak or short syllable ▶ **tro·cha·ic** /troʊˈkeɪɪk/ *adj.*

trod *pt of* TREAD

trod·den *pp of* TREAD

trog·lo·dyte /ˈtrɑgləˌdaɪt/ *noun* a person living in a CAVE, especially in PREHISTORIC times **SYN** CAVE DWELLER

troi·ka /ˈtrɔɪkə/ *noun* (*formal*) a group of three politicians or countries working together

Tro·jan /ˈtroʊdʒən/ *noun, adj.* a person from the ancient city of Troy in Asia Minor
IDM **work like a Trojan** (*old-fashioned*) to work very hard

Trojan horse *noun* **1** a person or thing that is used to trick an enemy in order to achieve a secret purpose **2** (*computing*) a computer program that seems to be helpful but that is, in fact, designed to destroy data, etc. **ORIGIN** From the story in which the ancient Greeks hid inside a hollow wooden statue of a horse in order to enter the city of their enemies, Troy.

troll /troʊl/ *noun, verb*
● *noun* **1** (in Scandinavian stories) a creature that looks like an ugly person. Some trolls are very large and evil, others are small and friendly but like to trick people. **2** (*informal*) a message to a discussion group on the Internet that someone deliberately sends to make other people angry; a person who sends a message like this
● *verb* **1** [I] ~ (**for sth**) to catch fish by pulling a line with BAIT on it through the water behind a boat **2** [T, I] (*informal*) to search for or try to get something: ~ **sth for sth** *He trolled the Internet for advice on the disease.* ◆ ~ **for sth** *Both candidates have been trolling for votes.*

trol·ley /ˈtrɑli/ (also **trolley car**) *noun* = STREETCAR

trol·lop /ˈtrɑləp/ *noun* (*old-fashioned, offensive*) **1** a woman who has many sexual partners **2** a woman who is very messy

trom·bone /trɑmˈboʊn/ *noun* a large BRASS musical instrument that you blow into, with a sliding tube used to change the note ➔ picture at INSTRUMENT

trom·bon·ist /trɑmˈboʊnɪst/ *noun* a person who plays the trombone

tromp /trɑmp/ *verb* (*informal*) = TRAMP

trompe l'œil /ˌtrɑmp ˈlɔɪ/ *noun* (*pl.* **trompe l'œils** /ˌtrɑmp ˈlɔɪ/) (from *French*) a painting or design intended to make the person looking at it think that it is a real object

troop 🔑 /trup/ *noun, verb*
● *noun* **1** **troops** [pl.] soldiers, especially in large groups: *They announced the withdrawal of 12,000 troops from the area.* ◆ *The president decided to send in the troops.* ◆ *Russian troops* ➔ collocations at WAR **2** [C] one group of soldiers, especially in tanks or on horses: (*figurative*) *A troop of guests was moving toward the house.* **3** [C] a local group of SCOUTS ▶ **troop** *adj.* [only before noun]: *troop movements* (= of soldiers)
● *verb* [I] + **adv./prep.** (used with a plural subject) to walk somewhere together as a group: *After lunch we all trooped down to the beach.*

troop·er /ˈtrupər/ *noun* **1** a soldier of low rank in the part of

an army that uses tanks or horses **2** = STATE TROOPER
IDM see SWEAR

troop·ship /ˈtrupʃɪp/ *noun* a ship used for transporting soldiers

trop ➔ DE TROP

trope /troʊp/ *noun* (*technical*) a word or phrase that is used in a way that is different from its usual meaning in order to create a particular mental image or effect. METAPHORS and SIMILES are tropes.

troph·ic /ˈtroʊfɪk/ *adj.* (*biology*) **1** relating to feeding, and to the food necessary for growth **2** (of a HORMONE or its effect) causing the release of another HORMONE or other substance into the blood

trophic level *noun* (*technical*) each of several levels in an ECOSYSTEM (= all the plants and animals in a particular area and their relationship with their surroundings). Each level consists of living creatures that share the same function in the FOOD CHAIN and get their food from the same source.

tro·phy /ˈtroʊfi/ *noun, adj.*
● *noun* (*pl.* **tro·phies**) **1** an object such as a silver cup that is given as a prize for winning a competition ➔ picture at MEDAL **2 Trophy** used in the names of some competitions and races in which a trophy is given to the winner **3** an object that you keep to show that you were successful in something, especially hunting or war
● *adj.* [only before noun] ~ **building/art/girlfriend, etc.** (*informal, disapproving*) an impressive or beautiful thing or person that you have in order to make other people admire you: *We don't need a trophy building for our business.*

trophy wife *noun* (*informal, disapproving*) a young attractive woman who is married to an older man and thought of as a trophy (= something that shows that you are successful and impresses other people)

trop·ic /ˈtrɑpɪk/ *noun* **1** [C, usually sing.] one of the two imaginary lines drawn around the world 23° 26′ north (**the Tropic of Cancer**) or south (**the Tropic of Capricorn**) of the EQUATOR **2 the tropics** [pl.] the area between the two tropics, which is the hottest part of the world **SYN** THE TORRID ZONE

trop·i·cal 🔑 /ˈtrɑpɪkl/ *adj.* coming from, found in or typical of the tropics: *tropical fish* ◆ *tropical Africa* ◆ *a tropical island*

tro·pism /ˈtroʊpɪzəm/ *noun* [U] (*biology*) the action of a living thing turning all or part of itself in a particular direction, toward or away from something such as a source of light

the trop·o·sphere /ˈtroʊpəˌsfɪr; ˈtrɑpə-/ *noun* [sing.] (*technical*) the lowest layer of the earth's atmosphere, between the surface of the earth and about 4–12 miles above the surface

trot /trɑt/ *verb, noun*
● *verb* (**-tt-**) **1** [I] (of a horse or its rider) to move forward at a speed that is faster than a walk and slower than a CANTER **2** [T] ~ **sth** to ride a horse in this way: *She trotted her pony around the field.* **3** [I] + **adv./prep.** (of a person or an animal) to run or walk fast, taking short quick steps: *The children trotted into the room.* **4** [I] + **adv./prep.** (*informal*) to walk or go somewhere: *The guide led the way and we trotted along behind him.* **IDM** see HOT
PHR V **trot sth**↔**'out** (*informal, disapproving*) to give the same excuses, facts, explanations, etc. for something that have often been used before: *They trotted out the same old excuses for the lack of jobs in the area.*
● *noun* **1** [sing.] a trotting speed, taking short quick steps: *The horse slowed to a trot.* ◆ *The girl broke into a trot and disappeared around the corner.* **2** [C] a period of trotting

troth /troʊθ; trɑθ; troʊð/ *noun* **IDM** see PLIGHT

Trot·sky·ist /ˈtrɑtskiɪst/ (also **Trot·sky·ite** /ˈtrɑtskiˌaɪt/) *noun* a supporter of the political ideas of Leon Trotsky, especially that SOCIALISM should be introduced all over the world by means of revolution ▶ **Trot·sky·ist** (also **Trot·sky·ite**) *adj.*

trot·ter /ˈtrɑtər/ *noun* **1** a horse that has been trained to

ʌ **cup**   ə **about**   eɪ **say**   aɪ **five**   ɔɪ **boy**   aʊ **now**   oʊ **go**   ər **bird**

TROT fast in races **2** a pig's foot, especially when cooked and eaten as food

trou·ba·dour /ˈtruːbəˌdɔr/ *noun* (*literary*) a writer and performer of songs or poetry (after the French traveling performers of the 11th-13th centuries)

trou·ble 🔑 /ˈtrʌbl/ *noun, verb*

● **noun**
> **PROBLEM/WORRY 1** [U, C] a problem, worry, difficulty, etc. or a situation causing this: *We have trouble getting staff.* ◆ *He could make trouble for me if he wanted to.* ◆ **~ (with sb/sth)** *The trouble with you is you don't really want to work.* ◆ *We've never had much trouble with vandals around here.* ◆ *Her trouble is she's incapable of making a decision.* ◆ *The trouble is* (= what is difficult is) *there aren't any trains at that time.* ◆ *The only trouble is we won't be here then.* ◆ *No, I don't know his number— I have enough trouble remembering my own.* ◆ *financial troubles* ◆ *She was on the phone for an hour telling me her troubles.* ◆ *Our troubles aren't over yet.*
> **ILLNESS/PAIN 2** [U] illness or pain: *back trouble* ◆ *I've been having trouble with my knee.*
> **WITH MACHINE 3** [U] something that is wrong with a machine, vehicle, etc.: *mechanical trouble*
> **DIFFICULT/VIOLENT SITUATION 4** [U] a situation that is difficult or dangerous; a situation in which you can be criticized or punished: *The company ran into trouble early on, when a major order was canceled.* ◆ *A yachtsman got into trouble off the coast and had to be rescued.* ◆ *If I don't get this finished in time, I'll be in trouble.* ◆ *He's in trouble with the police.* ◆ *My brother was always getting me into trouble with my parents.* **5** [U] an angry or violent situation: *The police were expecting trouble after the match.* ◆ *If you're not in by midnight, there'll be trouble* (= I'll be very angry). ◆ *He had to throw out a group of men who were causing trouble in the bar.*
> **EXTRA EFFORT 6** [U] **~ (to sb)** extra effort or work **SYN** BOTHER: *I don't want to put you to a lot of trouble.* ◆ *I'll get it if you like, that will save you the trouble of going out.* ◆ *Making your own yogurt is more trouble than it's worth.* ◆ *She went to a lot of trouble to find the book for me.* ◆ *He thanked me for my trouble and left.* ◆ *Nothing is ever too much trouble for her* (= she's always ready to help). ◆ *I can call back later—it's no trouble* (= I don't mind). ◆ *I hope the children weren't too much trouble.*
IDM **get sb into trouble** (*old-fashioned*) to make a woman who is not married pregnant **give (sb) (some, no, any, etc.) trouble** to cause problems or difficulties: *My back's been giving me a lot of trouble lately.* ◆ *The children didn't give me any trouble at all when we were out.* **look for trouble** to behave in a way that is likely to cause an argument, violence, etc.: *Drunken youths hang around outside looking for trouble.* **take trouble over/with sth | take trouble doing/to do sth** to try hard to do something well: *They take a lot of trouble to find the right person for the right job.* **take the trouble to do sth** to do something even though it involves effort or difficulty **SYN** MAKE THE EFFORT: *She didn't even take the trouble to find out how to spell my name.* ⊃ more at ASK

● **verb**
> **MAKE SOMEONE WORRIED 1** [T] **~ sb** to make someone worried or upset: *What is it that's troubling you?*
> **DISTURB 2** [T] (*often used in polite requests*) to disturb someone because you want to ask them something **SYN** BOTHER: **~ sb** *Sorry to trouble you, but could you tell me the time?* ◆ **~ sb with sth** *I don't want to trouble the doctor with such a small problem.* ◆ (*formal*) **~ sb to do sth** *Could I trouble you to open the window, please?*
> **MAKE EFFORT 3** [I] **~ to do sth** (*formal*) (usually used in negative sentences) to make an effort to do something **SYN** BOTHER: *He rushed into the room without troubling to knock.*
> **CAUSE PAIN 4** [T] **~ sb** (of a medical problem) to cause pain: *My back's been troubling me again.*

trou·bled /ˈtrʌbld/ *adj.* **1** (of a person) worried and anxious: *She looked into his troubled face.* **2** (of a place, situation, or time) having a lot of problems: *a deeply troubled marriage* ◆ *We live in troubled times.*

trou·ble·mak·er /ˈtrʌblˌmeɪkər/ *noun* a person who often causes trouble, especially by involving others in arguments or encouraging them to complain about people in authority

trou·ble·shoot /ˈtrʌblˌʃut/ *verb* **1** [I, T] **~ (sth)** to analyze and solve serious problems for a company or other organization **2** [I, T] **~ (sth)** (*computing*) to identify and correct faults in a computer system ▶ **trou·ble·shoot·ing** *noun* [U]

trou·ble·shoot·er /ˈtrʌblˌʃutər/ *noun* a person who helps to solve problems in a company or an organization

trou·ble·some /ˈtrʌblsəm/ *adj.* causing trouble, pain, etc. over a long period of time **SYN** ANNOYING: *a troublesome cough/child/problem*

'trouble ˌspot *noun* a place or country where trouble often happens, especially violence or war

trough /trɔf/ *noun* **1** [C] a long, narrow, open container for animals to eat or drink from **2** the trough [sing.] (*informal*) if you say that people have their noses **in the trough**, you mean that they are trying to get a lot of money for themselves **3** [C] (*technical*) a long, narrow region of low air pressure between two regions of higher pressure ⊃ compare RIDGE **4** [C] a period of time when the level of something is low, especially a time when a business or the economy is not growing: *There have been peaks and troughs in the long-term trend of unemployment.* **5** [C] a low area between two waves in the ocean, or two hills

trounce /traʊns/ *verb* **~ sb** (*formal*) to defeat someone completely: *Brazil trounced Italy 5–1 in the final.*

troupe /trup/ *noun* a group of actors, singers, etc. who work together

troup·er /ˈtrupər/ *noun* (*informal*) an actor or other person who has a lot of experience and who you can depend on **IDM** **a real trouper** someone who is reliable and does not complain

trou·sers /ˈtraʊzərz/ *noun* [pl.] = PANTS ▶ **trou·ser** *adj.* [only before noun]: *trouser pockets*

trous·seau /ˈtrusoʊ; truˈsoʊ/ *noun* (*pl.* **trous·seaus** or **trous·seaux** /-soʊz; -ˈsoʊz/) (*old-fashioned*) the clothes and other possessions collected by a woman who is soon going to get married, to begin her married life with

trout /traʊt/ *noun* **1** [C, U] (*pl.* **trout**) a common FRESHWATER fish that is used for food: *rainbow trout* ◆ *trout fishing* ◆ *Should we have trout for dinner?* ⊃ picture at ANIMAL **2** [C, usually sing.] usually **old trout** (*informal, disapproving*) a bad-tempered or annoying old woman

trove /troʊv/ *noun* ⊃ TREASURE TROVE

trow·el /ˈtraʊəl/ *noun* **1** a small garden tool with a curved blade for lifting plants and digging holes ⊃ picture at TOOL **2** a small tool with a flat blade, used in building for spreading CEMENT or PLASTER **IDM** **lay it on with a trowel** (*informal*) to talk about someone or something in a way that makes them or it seem much better or much worse than they really are; to exaggerate something: *He was laying the flattery on with a trowel.*

troy /trɔɪ/ *noun* [U] a system for measuring PRECIOUS METALS and PRECIOUS STONES

tru·an·cy /ˈtruənsi/ *noun* [U] the practice of staying away from school without permission

tru·ant /ˈtruənt/ *noun* a child who stays away from school without permission

truce /trus/ *noun* an agreement between enemies or opponents to stop fighting for an agreed period of time; the period of time that this lasts: *to call/break a truce* ⊃ collocations at WAR

truck 🔑 /trʌk/ *noun, verb*

● **noun 1** a large vehicle for carrying heavy loads by road: *a truck driver* ⊃ collocations at DRIVING **2** a vehicle that is open at the back, used for carrying goods, soldiers,

trucks

cement mixer
(*also* concrete mixer)

tractor
tractor-trailer
(*also* trailer truck)

van

pickup (*also* pickup truck)

tow truck

car transporter

tractor

tanker

forklift (*also* forklift truck)

fire engine (*also* fire truck)

animals, etc.: *a delivery/garbage/farm truck* **3** a vehicle for carrying things, that is pulled or pushed by hand ⊃ see also PICKUP, SALT TRUCK
IDM have/want no truck with sb/sth to refuse to deal with someone; to refuse to accept or consider something: *We in this party will have no truck with illegal organizations.* ⊃ more at BACK *n*.

• **verb** ~ **sth (+ adv./prep.)** to take something somewhere by truck ▶ **truck·ing** *noun* [U]: *trucking companies*

truck·er /ˈtrʌkər/ *noun* a person whose job is driving a truck

truck farm *noun* a type of farm where vegetables are grown for sale ▶ **truck farmer** *noun* **truck farming** *noun* [U]

truck·load /ˈtrʌkloʊd/ *noun* ~ **(of sb/sth)** the amount of someone or something that fills a truck (often used to express the fact that an amount is large)

truck stop *noun* a place at the side of a main road where truck drivers can stop for a time and can rest, get something to eat, etc.

truc·u·lent /ˈtrʌkyələnt/ *adj.* (*formal*, *disapproving*) tending to argue or be bad-tempered; slightly aggressive ▶ **truc·u·lence** /-ləns/ *noun* [U] **truc·u·lent·ly** *adv.*

trudge /trʌdʒ/ *verb*, *noun*
• **verb** [I] to walk slowly or with heavy steps, because you are tired or carrying something heavy: **+ noun** *He trudged the last two miles to the town.* ◆ **+ adv./prep.** *The men trudged up the hill, laden with supplies.*

• **noun** [sing.] a long, tiring walk

true 🔑 /tru/ *adj.*, *adv.*, *noun*
• **adj.** (**tru·er, tru·est**)
▷ **CORRECT 1** connected with facts rather than things that have been invented or guessed: *Indicate whether the following statements are **true** or **false**.* ◆ *Is it true she's leaving?* ◆ *All the rumors turned out to be true.* ◆ *That's not strictly (= completely) true.* ◆ *The novel is based on a **true** story.* ◆ *His excuse just doesn't ring (= sound) **true**.* ◆ *Unfortunately, these findings do not hold **true** (= are not valid) for women and children.* ◆ *The music is dull and uninspiring, and*

WORD FAMILY
true *adj.* (≠ untrue)
truth *noun* (≠ untruth)
truthful *adj.* (≠ untruthful)
truthfully *adv.*
truly *adv.*

the same is true of the acting. ◆ *You never spoke a truer word* (= used to emphasize that you agree with what someone has just said). **ANT** UNTRUE
▷ **REAL 2** real or exact, especially when this is different from how sth seems: *the true face of war* (= what it is really like rather than what people think it is like) ◆ *The true cost of these experiments to the environment will not be known for years to come.* ◆ *He reveals his true character to very few people.*
3 [usually before noun] having the qualities or characteristics of the thing mentioned: *It was true love between them.* ◆ *He's a true gentleman.* ◆ *The painting is a masterpiece in the truest sense of the word.* ◆ *He is credited with inventing the first true helicopter.*
▷ **ADMITTING FACT 4** used to admit that a particular fact or statement is correct, although you think that something else is more important: *It's true that he could do the job, but would he fit in with the rest of the team?* ◆ *"We could get it cheaper." "True, but would it be as good?"* ⊃ language bank at NEVERTHELESS
▷ **LOYAL 5** showing respect and support for a particular person or belief in a way that does not change, even in different situations: *a true friend* ◆ ~ **to sb/sth** *She has always been true to herself* (= done what she thought was good, right, etc.). ◆ *He was true to his word* (= did what he promised to do).
▷ **ACCURATE 6** ~ **(to sth)** being an accurate version or copy of something: *The movie is not true to the book.* **7** [not usually before noun] (*old-fashioned* or *literary*) straight and accurate: *His aim was true* (= he hit the target).
IDM come true (of a hope, wish, etc.) to become reality: *Winning the medal was like **a dream come true**.* too good to be true used to say that you cannot believe that something is as good as it seems: *"I'm afraid you were quoted the wrong price." "I thought it was too good to be true."* your true colors (often *disapproving*) your real character, rather than the one that you usually allow other people to see true to form used to say that someone is behaving in the way that you expect them to behave, especially when this is annoying true to life (of a book, movie, etc.) seeming real rather than invented ⊃ more at RING² *v.*, TRIED

• **adv.** (*old-fashioned* or *literary*)
▷ **STRAIGHT 1** in a direct line: *The arrow flew straight and true to the target.*

t **t**ea   t **b**utter   d **d**id   k **c**at   g **g**ot   tʃ **ch**in   dʒ **J**une   f **f**all

> CORRECTLY **2 speak ~** to tell the truth: *He had spoken truer than he knew.*
- **noun**
  IDM out of true if an object is **out of true**, it is not straight or in the correct position

true-'blue *adj.* being a loyal supporter of a particular person, group, principle, etc.; being a typical example of something: *a true-blue Californian*

true-'life *adj.* [only before noun] a **true-life** story is one that actually happened rather than one that has been invented

true 'north *noun* [U] north according to the earth's AXIS (= the imaginary line through the earth's center from north to south) ⊃ compare MAGNETIC NORTH

truf·fle /'trʌfl/ *noun* **1** an expensive type of FUNGUS that grows underground, used in cooking **2** a soft, round candy made of chocolate

trug /trʌg/ *noun* a shallow BASKET used for carrying garden tools, plants, etc.

tru·ism /'truɪzəm/ *noun* a statement that is clearly true and does not therefore add anything interesting or important to a discussion

tru·ly 🔑 /'truli/ *adv.*
1 used to emphasize that a particular statement, feeling, etc. is sincere or genuine: *I'm truly sorry that things had to end like this.* **2** used to emphasize a particular quality: *a truly memorable occasion* **3** used to emphasize that a particular description is accurate or correct: *a truly democratic system of government* ♦ (*informal*) *Well, **really and truly**, things were better than expected.*
IDM Yours truly (*formal*) used at the end of a formal letter before you sign your name ⊃ more at WELL *adv.*

trump /trʌmp/ *noun, verb*
- **noun 1** (also **'trump card**) [C] (in some card games) a card that belongs to the SUIT (= one of the four sets in a DECK of cards) that has been chosen for a particular game to have a higher value than the other three suits: *I played a trump and won the trick.* **2 trumps** [U] (in some card games) the SUIT that has been chosen for a particular game to have a higher value than the other three suits: *What's trumps?* ♦ *Clubs are trumps.*
  IDM come up/turn up trumps to do what is necessary to make a particular situation successful, especially when this is sudden or unexpected: *I didn't honestly think he'd pass the exam, but he came up trumps on the day.*
- **verb 1 ~ sth (with sth)** (in some card games) to play a trump card that beats someone else's card **2 ~ sth/sb** to

beat something that someone says or does by saying or doing something even better
  PHR V ,trump sth↔'up to make up a false story about someone or something, especially accusing them of doing something wrong: *She was arrested on a trumped-up charge.*

'trump card *noun* **1** = TRUMP **2** something that gives you an advantage over other people, especially when they do not know what it is and you are able to use it to surprise them

trump·er·y /'trʌmpəri/ *noun* [U] (*old-fashioned*) objects of little value ▶ **trump·er·y** *adj.*

trum·pet /'trʌmpət/ *noun, verb*
- **noun 1** a BRASS musical instrument made of a curved metal tube that you blow into, with three VALVES for changing the note ⊃ picture at INSTRUMENT **2** a thing shaped like a trumpet, especially the open flower of a DAFFODIL
- **verb 1** [T] **~ sth (as sth)** | **+ speech** to talk about something publicly in a proud or enthusiastic way: *to trumpet someone's achievements* ♦ *Their marriage was trumpeted as the society wedding of the year.* **2** [I] (especially of an ELEPHANT) to make a loud noise

trum·pet·er /'trʌmpətər/ *noun* a person who plays a trumpet

trun·cate /'trʌŋkeɪt/ *verb* [usually passive] **~ sth** (*formal*) to make something shorter, especially by cutting off the top or end: *My article was published in truncated form.* ▶ **trun·ca·tion** /trʌŋ'keɪʃn/ *noun* [U, C]

trun·dle /'trʌndl/ *verb* **1** [I, T] **~ (sth) + adv./prep.** to move or roll somewhere slowly and noisily; to move something slowly and noisily, especially something heavy, with wheels: *A train trundled across the bridge.* **2** [I] **+ adv./prep.** (of a person) to walk slowly with heavy steps

'trundle ,bed *noun* a low bed that can be stored under a higher bed

trunks

trunk of a tree   elephant's trunk

trunk

trunk /trʌŋk/ *noun* **1** [C] the thick main STEM of a tree, that the branches grow from ⊃ picture at TREE **2** [C] the space at the back of a car that you put bags, cases, etc. in ⊃ picture at CAR **3** [C] the long nose of an ELEPHANT ⊃ picture at ANIMAL **4 trunks** [pl.] = SWIMMING TRUNKS **5** [C] a large strong box with a lid used for storing or transporting clothes, books, etc. **6** [C, usually sing.] the main part of the human body apart from the head, arms, and legs ⊃ see also TORSO

truss /trʌs/ *noun, verb*
- **noun 1** a special belt with a thick piece of material, worn by someone suffering from a HERNIA in order to support the muscles **2** a frame made of pieces of wood or metal

used to support a roof, bridge, etc.
• *verb* **1** ~ sb/sth (up) to tie up someone's arms and legs so that they cannot move **2** ~ sth to tie the legs and wings of a chicken, etc. before it is cooked

trust

depend on sb/sth • rely on sb/sth • count on sb/sth • believe in sb

These words all mean to believe that someone or something will do what you hope or expect of them, or that what someone tells you is correct or true.

trust to believe that someone is good, honest, sincere, etc. and that they will do what you expect of them or do the right thing; to believe that something is true or correct: *You can trust me not to tell anyone.* ♦ *Don't trust what you read in the newspapers!*

depend on/upon sb/sth (often used with *can/cannot/could/could not*) to trust someone or something to do what you expect or want, to do the right thing, or to be true or correct: *He was the sort of person you could depend on.* ♦ *I can't depend on my own strength ever since I got sick.*

rely on/upon sb/sth (used especially with *can/cannot/could/could not* and *should/should not*) to trust someone or something to do what you expect or want, or to be honest, correct, or good enough: *Can I rely on you to keep this secret?* ♦ *You can't rely on any data you get from them.*

TRUST, DEPEND, OR RELY ON/UPON SB/STH?

You can **trust** someone's *judgment* or *advice*, but not their support. You can **depend on** someone's *support*, *judgment*, or *advice*. **Rely on/upon sb/sth** is used especially with *you can/could* or *you should* to give advice or a promise: ~~*I don't really rely on his judgment.*~~ ♦ *You can't really rely on his judgment.*

count on sb/sth (often used with *can/cannot/could/could not*) to be sure that someone will do what you need them to do, or that something will happen as you want it to happen: *I'm counting on you to help me.* ♦ *We can't count on the weather.*

believe in sb to feel that you can trust someone and/or that they will be successful: *They need a leader they can believe in.*

PATTERNS
- to trust/depend on/rely on/count on **sb/sth** to do sth
- to trust/believe **in** sb/sth
- to trust/depend on/rely on/count on **sb's** advice/ judgment
- to depend on/rely on/count on **sb's** support
- to trust/depend on/rely on/believe in sb/sth **completely**

trust /trʌst/ *noun, verb*
• *noun* **1** [U] ~ (in sb/sth) the belief that someone or something is good, sincere, honest, etc. and will not try to harm or trick you: *Her trust in him was unfounded.* ♦ *a partnership based on trust* ♦ *It has taken years to earn their trust.* ♦ *If you put your trust in me, I will not let you down.* ♦ *She will not betray your trust* (= do something that you have asked her not to do). ♦ *He was appointed to a position of trust* (= a job involving a lot of responsibility, because people trust him). **2** [C, U] (*law*) an arrangement by which an organization or a group of people has legal control of money or property that has been given to someone, usually until that person reaches a particular age; an amount of money or property that is controlled in this way: *He set up a trust for his children.* ♦ *The money will be held in trust until she is 18.* ♦ *Our fees depend on the value of the trust.* **3** [C] (*law*) an organization or a group of people that invests money that is given or lent to it and uses the profits to help a charity: *a charitable trust* **4** [C] (*business*) a group of companies that work together

illegally to reduce competition, control prices, etc.: *antitrust laws*
IDM in sb's trust| in the trust of sb being taken care of by someone: *The family pet was left in the trust of a neighbor.* **take sth on trust** to believe what someone says even though you do not have any proof or evidence to show that it is true
• *verb* **1** to have confidence in someone; to believe that someone is good, sincere, honest, etc.: ~ **sb** *She trusts Alan implicitly.* ♦ ~ **sb** to do sth *You can trust me not to tell anyone.* **2** ~ sth to believe that something is true or correct or that you can rely on it: *He trusted her judgment.* ♦ *Don't trust what the newspapers say!* **3** ~ (that)... (*formal*) to hope and expect that something is true: *I trust (that) you have no objections to our proposals?*
IDM not trust sb an inch to not trust someone at all **trust you, him, her, etc. (to do sth)** (*informal*) used when someone does or says something that you think is typical of them: *Trust John to forget Sue's birthday!*
PHR V 'trust in sb/sth (*formal*) to have confidence in someone or something; to believe that someone or something is good and can be relied on: *She needs to trust more in her own abilities.* '**trust to sth** [no passive] to put your confidence in something such as luck, chance, etc. because there is nothing else to help you: *I stumbled along in the dark, trusting to luck to find the right door.* '**trust sb with sth/sb** to give something or someone to a person to take care of because you believe they would be very careful with it/them: *I'd trust her with my life.*

trust·ee /trʌˈstiː/ *noun* **1** a person or an organization that has control of money or property that has been put into a TRUST for someone **2** a member of a group of people that controls the financial affairs of a charity or other organization

trust·ee·ship /trʌˈstiːʃɪp/ *noun* [U, C] **1** the job of being a trustee **2** the responsibility for governing a particular region, given to a country by the United Nations Organization; a region that is governed by another country in this way

'**trust fund** *noun* money that is controlled for someone by an organization or a group of people

trust·ing /ˈtrʌstɪŋ/ *adj.* tending to believe that other people are good, honest, etc.: *If you're too trusting, other people will take advantage of you.* ▶ **trust·ing·ly** *adv.*

'**trust ˌterritory** *noun* a region governed by the United Nations Organization or by another country that has been chosen by the United Nations Organization

trust·wor·thy /ˈtrʌstˌwɜːrði/ *adj.* that you can rely on to be good, honest, sincere, etc. **SYN** RELIABLE ▶ **trust·wor·thi·ness** *noun* [U]

trust·y /ˈtrʌsti/ *adj., noun*
• *adj.* [only before noun] (*old use* or *humorous*) that you have had a long time and have always been able to rely on **SYN** RELIABLE: *a trusty friend* ♦ *She spent years touring Europe with her trusty old camera.*
• *noun* (*pl.* **trust·ies**) (*informal*) a prisoner who is given special advantages because of good behavior

truth /truːθ/ *noun* (*pl.* **truths** /truːðz; truːθs/)
1 the truth [sing.] the true facts about something, rather than the things that have been invented or guessed: *Do you think she's telling the truth?* ♦ *We are determined to get at* (= discover) *the truth.* ♦ *The truth (of the matter) is we can't afford to keep all the staff on.* ♦ *I don't think you are telling me the whole truth about what happened.* **2** [U] the quality or state of being based on fact: *There is no truth in the rumors.* ♦ *There is not a grain of truth in what she says.* **ANT** FALSITY **3** [C] a fact that is believed by most people to be true: *universal truths* ♦ *She was forced to face up to a few unwelcome truths about her family.* ⊃ see also HALF-TRUTH, HOME TRUTH ⊃ compare UNTRUTH
IDM if (the) truth be known/told used to tell someone the true facts about a situation, especially when these are not known by other people **in truth** (*formal*) used to

emphasize the true facts about a situation: *She laughed and chatted but was, in truth, not having much fun.* **nothing could be further from the truth** used to say that a fact or comment is completely false **to tell (you) the truth** (*informal*) used when admitting something: *To tell you the truth, I'll be glad to get home.* **truth is stranger than fiction** (*saying*) used to say that things that actually happen are often more surprising than stories that are invented **(the) truth will out** (*saying*) used to say that people will find out the true facts about a situation even if you try to keep them secret ➲ more at BEND *v.*, ECONOMICAL, MOMENT

'**truth drug** *noun* a drug that is believed to be able to put someone into a state where they will answer questions with the truth

truth·ful /'truːθfl/ *adj.* **1** ~ **(about sth)** (of a person) saying only what is true **SYN** HONEST: *They were less than truthful about their part in the crime.* ◆ *Are you being completely truthful with me?* **2** (of a statement) giving the true facts about something: *a truthful answer* **ANT** UNTRUTHFUL ▶ **truth·ful·ly** /-fəli/ *adv.*: *She answered all their questions truthfully.* **truth·ful·ness** *noun* [U]

try /traɪ/ *verb, noun*

● *verb* (tries, try·ing, tried, tried) **1** [I, T] to make an attempt or effort to do or get something: *I don't know if I can come but I'll try.* ◆ ~ **to do sth** *What are you trying to do?* ◆ *I tried hard not to laugh.* ◆ ~ **your best/hardest (to do something)** *She tried her best to solve the problem.* ◆ *Just try your hardest.* **HELP** In spoken English **try** can be used with **and** plus another verb, instead of with **to** and the infinitive: *I'll try and get you a new one tomorrow.* ◆ *Try and finish quickly.* In this structure, only the form **try** can be used, not **tries, trying,** or **tried.** **2** [T] to use, do, or test something in order to see if it is good, suitable, etc.: ~ **sth** *Have you tried this new coffee? It's very good.* ◆ *"Would you like to try some raw fish?" "Why not? I'll try anything once!"* ◆ *Have you ever tried windsurfing?* ◆ *Try these shoes for size —they should fit you.* ◆ *She tried the door, but it was locked.* ◆ ~ **doing sth** *John isn't here. Try calling his home number.* **HELP** Notice the difference between **try to do something** and **try doing something**: *You should try to eat more fruit.* means "You should make an effort to eat more fruit." *You should try eating more fruit.* means "You should see if eating more fruit will help you" (to feel better, for example). **3** [T] to examine evidence in court and decide whether someone is innocent or guilty: ~ **sb (for sth)** *He was tried for murder.* ◆ ~ **sth** *The case was tried before a jury.* **IDM** **not for want/lack of trying** used to say that although someone has not succeeded in something, they have tried very hard: *They haven't won a game yet, but it isn't for want of trying.* **try your hand (at sth)** to do something such as an activity or a sport for the first time **try your luck (at sth)** to do something that involves risk or luck, hoping to succeed: *My grandparents emigrated to Canada to try their luck there.* **try sb's patience** to make someone feel impatient ➲ more at DAMNEDEST, LEVEL *adj.* **PHR V** '**try for sth** to make an attempt to get or win something ,**try sth**↔'**on** to put on a piece of clothing to see if it fits and how it looks: *Try the shoes on before you buy them.* ,**try 'out for sth** to compete for a position or place in something, or to be a member of a team: *She's trying out for the school play.* ➲ related noun TRYOUT ,**try sb/sth**↔'**out (on sb)** to test or use someone or something in order to see how good or effective they are: *They're trying out a new host for the show.* ➲ related noun TRYOUT

● *noun* (*pl.* tries) [usually sing.] an act of trying to do something **SYN** ATTEMPT: *I doubt they'll be able to help but it's worth a try* (= worth asking them). ◆ ~ **(at sth/at doing sth)** *Why don't you have a try at convincing him?* ◆ *The U.S. negotiators decided to make another try at reaching a settlement.* ◆ *I don't think I'll be any good at tennis, but I'll give it a try.* ◆ (*informal*) *"What's that behind you?" "Nice try* (= at making me turn around), *but you'll have to do better than that!"*

,**try-and-'buy** *adj.* [only before noun] (especially of computer programs and equipment) that can be used free

for a limited period of time, during which you can decide whether you want to buy it or not

try·ing /'traɪɪŋ/ *adj.* annoying or difficult to deal with: *These are trying times for all of us.*

try·out /'traɪaʊt/ *noun* **1** an act of testing how good or effective someone or something is before deciding whether to use them in the future **2** a competition or series of tests to find the best players for a sports team or an important event

tryst /trɪst/ *noun* (*literary* or *humorous*) a secret meeting between lovers

tsar, tsa·ri·na, tsar·ism = CZAR, CZARINA, CZARISM

tset·se fly /'tsitsi ˌflaɪ; 'sitsi-/ *noun* an African fly that bites humans and animals and sucks their blood and can spread a disease called SLEEPING SICKNESS

'**T-shirt** (also '**tee shirt**) *noun* an informal shirt with short sleeves and no COLLAR or buttons, or just a few buttons at the top ➲ picture at CLOTHES

tsk tsk /ˌtɪsk 'tɪsk/ *exclamation* used in writing to represent the sound you make with your tongue when you disapprove of something: *So you were out drinking again last night were you? Tsk tsk!*

tsp. *abbr.* (*pl.* **tsp.** or **tsps.**) TEASPOONFUL: *1 tsp. chili powder*

'**T-square** *noun* a plastic or metal instrument in the shape of a T for drawing or measuring RIGHT ANGLES (= of 90°)

tsu·na·mi /tsu'nɑmi/ *noun* (from *Japanese*) an extremely large wave in the ocean caused, for example, by an EARTHQUAKE **SYN** TIDAL WAVE

tub /tʌb/ *noun* **1** (*informal*) = BATHTUB: *They found her lying in the tub.* ➲ see also HOT TUB **2** a large round container without a lid, used for washing clothes in, growing plants in, etc.: *There were tubs of flowers on the balcony.* **3** a small, wide, usually round, plastic or paper container with a lid, used for food, etc.: *a tub of margarine* ➲ picture at PACKAGING

tu·ba /'tubə/ *noun* a large BRASS musical instrument that you play by blowing, and that produces low notes ➲ picture at INSTRUMENT

tub·al /'tubl/ *adj.* (*medical*) connected with the FALLOPIAN TUBES: *a tubal pregnancy*

tub·by /'tʌbi/ *adj.* (*informal*) (of a person) short and slightly fat **SYN** STOUT

tube /tub/ *noun*
> PIPE **1** [C] a long hollow pipe made of metal, plastic, rubber, etc., through which liquids or gases move from one place to another ➲ see also CATHODE RAY TUBE, INNER TUBE, TEST TUBE **2** [C] a hollow object in the shape of a pipe or tube: *a bike's inner tube* ◆ *the cardboard tube from the center of a toilet roll*
> CONTAINER **3** [C] ~ **(of sth)** a long narrow container made of soft metal or plastic, with a lid, used for holding thick liquids that can be squeezed out of it: *a tube of toothpaste* ➲ picture at PACKAGING
> PART OF BODY **4** [C] a part inside the body that is shaped like a tube and through which air, liquid, etc. passes: *bronchial tubes* ➲ see also FALLOPIAN TUBE
> TELEVISION **5** the tube [sing.] (*informal*) the television
> IN EAR **6** [C] a small tube placed in a child's ear in order to DRAIN liquid from it
IDM **go down the tube/tubes** (*informal*) (of a plan, company, situation, etc.) to fail: *The education system is going down the tubes.*

tu·ber /'tubər/ *noun* the short, thick, round part of an underground STEM or root of some plants, such as potatoes, which stores food and from which new plants grow ▶ **tu·ber·ous** /'tubərəs/ *adj.*

tu·ber·cle /'tubərkl/ *noun* **1** (*anatomy, biology*) a small round lump, especially on a bone or on the surface of an animal or plant **2** (*medical*) a small swollen area in the lung caused by tuberculosis

---

tu·ber·cu·lo·sis /tʊˌbərkyəˈloʊsəs/ *noun* [U] (*abbr.* TB) a serious infectious disease in which swellings appear on the lungs and other parts of the body ▶ **tu·ber·cu·lar** /tʊˈbɑːrkyələr/ *adj.*: *a tubercular infection*

ˈtube top *noun* a piece of women's clothing that is made of cloth that stretches and covers the chest

ˈtube well *noun* a pipe with holes in the sides near the end, that is put into the ground and used with a PUMP operated by hand to bring water up from under the ground

tub·ing /ˈtubɪŋ/ *noun* [U] metal, plastic, etc. in the shape of a tube: *a length of copper tubing*

tu·bu·lar /ˈtubyələr/ *adj.* **1** made of tubes or of parts that are shaped like tubes: *a tubular metal chair* **2** shaped like a tube

ˌtubular ˈbells *noun* [pl.] a musical instrument that sounds like a set of bells, consisting of a row of hanging metal tubes that are hit with a stick

tuck /tʌk/ *verb, noun*
● *verb* **1** ~ **sth + adv./prep.** to push, fold, or turn the ends or edges of clothes, paper, etc. so that they are held in place or look neat: *She tucked up her skirt and waded into the river.* ◆ *The sheets should be tucked in neatly* (= around the bed). ◆ *Tuck the flap of the envelope in.* **2** ~ **sth + adv./prep.** to put something into a small space, especially to hide it or keep it safe or comfortable: *She tucked her hair (up) under her cap.* ◆ *He sat with his legs tucked up under him.* ◆ *The letter had been tucked under a pile of papers.* **3** ~ **sth + adv./prep.** to cover someone with something so that they are warm and comfortable: *She tucked a blanket around his legs.*
PHR V ˌtuck sth↔aˈway **1 be tucked away** to be located in a quiet place, where not many people go: *The shop is tucked away down a backstreet.* **2** to hide something somewhere or keep it in a safe place: *She kept his letters tucked away in a drawer.* ◆ *They have thousands of dollars tucked away in a savings account.* ˌtuck sb ˈin to make someone feel comfortable in bed by pulling the covers up around them: *I tucked the children in and said goodnight.*
● *noun* **1** a fold that is sewn into a piece of clothing or cloth, either for decoration or to change the shape of it **2** (*informal*) a medical operation in which skin and/or fat is removed to make someone look younger or thinner

Tu·dor /ˈtudər/ *adj.* connected with the time when kings and queens from the Tudor family ruled England (1485–1603): *Tudor architecture*

Tues·day 🔊 /ˈtuzdeɪ; -di/ *noun* [C, U] (*abbr.* Tue., Tues.) the day of the week after Monday and before Wednesday **HELP** To see how **Tuesday** is used, look at the examples at **Monday. ORIGIN** Originally translated from the Latin for "day of Mars" *dies Marti* and named after the Germanic god Tiw.

tuft /tʌft/ *noun* ~ **(of sth)** a number of pieces of hair, grass, etc. growing or held closely together at the base

tuft·ed /ˈtʌftəd/ *adj.* [usually before noun] having a tuft or tufts; growing in tufts: *a tufted carpet* ◆ *a tufted duck*

tug /tʌɡ/ *verb, noun*
● *verb* (-gg-) **1** [I, T] to pull something hard, often several times: ~ **(at/on sth)** *She tugged at his sleeve to get his attention.* ◆ (*figurative*) *a sad story that tugs at your heartstrings* (= makes you feel sad) ◆ ~ **sth** *The baby was tugging her hair.* ◆ ~ **sth + adj.** *He tugged the door open.* **2** [T] ~ **sth + adv./prep.** to pull something hard in a particular direction: *He tugged the hat down over his head.* ⊃ thesaurus box at **PULL**
IDM see **FORELOCK**
● *noun* **1** = TUGBOAT **2** a sudden hard pull: *I felt a tug at my sleeve.* ◆ *She gave her sister's hair a sharp tug.* **3** [usually sing.] a sudden, strong, emotional feeling: *a tug of attraction*

tug·boat /ˈtʌɡboʊt/ (also **tug**) *noun* a small powerful boat for pulling ships, especially into a HARBOR or up a river ⊃ picture at **BOAT**

ˌtug of ˈwar *noun* [sing., U] **1** a sports event in which two teams pull at opposite ends of a rope until one team drags the other over a line on the ground **2** a situation in which

two people or groups try very hard to get or keep the same thing

tu·i·tion /tuˈɪʃn/ *noun* [U] **1** the money that you pay to be taught, especially in a college or university **2** ~ **(in sth)** (*formal*) the act of teaching something, especially to one person or to people in small groups: *She received private tuition in French.*

tu·lip /ˈtuləp/ *noun* a large, brightly colored spring flower, shaped like a cup, on a tall STEM ⊃ picture at **PLANT**

tulle /tul/ *noun* [U] a type of soft, fine cloth made of silk, NYLON, etc. and full of very small holes, used especially for making VEILS and dresses

tum·ble /ˈtʌmbl/ *verb, noun*
● *verb* **1** [I, T] ~ **(sb/sth) + adv./prep.** to fall downward, often hitting the ground several times, but usually without serious injury; to make someone or something fall in this way: *He slipped and tumbled down the stairs.* **2** [I] ~ **(down)** to fall suddenly and in a dramatic way: *The scaffolding came tumbling down.* ◆ (*figurative*) *World records tumbled at the last Olympics.* ⊃ see also TUMBLEDOWN **3** [I] to fall rapidly in value or amount: *The price of oil is still tumbling.* **4** [I] + **adv./prep.** to move or fall somewhere in a relaxed, uncontrolled or noisy way: *A group of noisy children tumbled out of the bus.* ◆ *Thick golden curls tumbled down over her shoulders.* **5** [I] to perform ACROBATICS on the floor, especially SOMERSAULTS (= a jump in which you turn over completely in the air)
● *noun* **1** [C, usually sing.] a sudden fall: *The jockey took a nasty tumble at the third fence.* ◆ *Share prices took a sharp tumble following news of the merger.* ⊃ see also ROUGH AND TUMBLE **2** [sing.] ~ **(of sth)** a messy group of things: *a tumble of blond curls*

tum·ble·down /ˈtʌmbldaʊn/ *adj.* [usually before noun] (of a building) old and in a poor condition so that it looks as if it is falling down **SYN** DILAPIDATED

ˌtumble-ˈdry *verb* ~ **sth** to dry clothes in a DRYER

tum·bler /ˈtʌmblər/ *noun* **1** a glass for drinking out of, with a flat bottom, straight sides, and no handle or STEM ⊃ picture at **CUP 2** (also **tum·bler·ful** /-ˌfʊl/) the amount held by a tumbler **3** (*old-fashioned*) an ACROBAT who performs SOMERSAULTS (= a jump in which you turn over completely in the air)

tum·ble·weed /ˈtʌmblˌwid/ *noun* [U] a plant that grows like a bush in the desert areas of N. America and Australia. In the fall, it breaks off just above the ground and is blown around like a ball by the wind.

tum·bril /ˈtʌmbrəl/ *noun* an open vehicle used for taking people to their deaths at the GUILLOTINE during the French Revolution

tu·mes·cent /tuˈmɛsnt/ *adj.* (*formal*) (especially of parts of the body) larger than normal, especially as a result of sexual excitement **SYN** SWOLLEN ▶ **tu·mes·cence** /-sns/ *noun* [U]

tum·my /ˈtʌmi/ *noun* (*pl.* **tum·mies**) (*informal*) (used especially by children or when speaking to children) the stomach or the area around the stomach: *Mom, my tummy hurts.* ◆ *to have a tummy ache*

tu·mor (*CanE usually* **tu·mour**) /ˈtumər/ *noun* a mass of cells growing in or on a part of the body where they should not, usually causing medical problems: *a brain tumor* ◆ *a benign/malignant* (= harmless/harmful) *tumor*

tu·mult /ˈtumʌlt; ˈtʌ-/ *noun* [U, C, usually sing.] (*formal*) **1** a confused situation in which there is usually a lot of noise and excitement, often involving large numbers of people **2** a state in which your thoughts or feelings are confused

tu·mul·tu·ous /tuˈmʌltʃuəs/ *adj.* [usually before noun] **1** very loud; involving strong feelings, especially feelings of approval: *tumultuous applause* ◆ *a tumultuous reception/welcome* **2** involving a lot of change and confusion and/or violence **SYN** TEMPESTUOUS: *the tumultuous years of the Civil War*

tu·mu·lus /ˈtumyələs/ *noun* (*pl.* **tu·mu·li** /-ˌlaɪ/) (*technical*) a large pile of earth built over the grave of an important person in ancient times

tun /tʌn/ *noun* (*old-fashioned*) a large, round, wooden container for beer, wine, etc. **SYN** BARREL

tu·na /'tunə/ *noun* (*pl.* **tu·na** or **tu·nas**) [C, U] a large ocean fish that is used for food: *fishing for tuna* ♦ *tuna steaks* ♦ *a can of tuna in vegetable oil*

'tuna ˌfish *noun* [U] cooked tuna sold in a can: *tuna-fish sandwiches*

tun·dra /'tʌndrə/ *noun* [U] the large, flat, Arctic regions of northern Europe, Asia, and N. America where no trees grow and where the soil below the surface of the ground is always frozen

tune 🔊 /tun/ *noun, verb*

● **noun** a series of musical notes that are sung or played in a particular order to form a piece of music: *He was humming a particular tune.* ♦ *I don't know the title but I recognize the tune.* ♦ *It was a catchy tune* (= song). ♦ *The team's song is sung to the tune of* (= using the tune of) *"When the Saints Go Marching In."* ⊃ collocations at MUSIC
IDM be in/out of tune (with sb/sth) to be/not be in agreement with someone or something; to have/not have the same opinions, feelings, interests, etc. as someone or something: *These proposals are perfectly in tune with our own thoughts on the subject.* ♦ *The President is out of tune with public opinion.* in/out of tune to be/not be singing or playing the correct musical notes to sound pleasant: *None of them could sing in tune.* ♦ *The piano is out of tune.* to the tune of sth (*informal*) used to emphasize how much money something has cost: *The hotel has been refurbished to the tune of a million dollars.* ⊃ more at CALL *v.*, CARRY, CHANGE *v.*, DANCE *v.*, PAY *v.*, SING

● **verb 1** ~ sth to adjust a musical instrument so that it plays at the correct PITCH: *to tune a guitar* **2** ~ sth to adjust an engine so that it runs smoothly and as well as possible **3** [usually passive] ~ sth (in) (to sth) to adjust the controls on a radio or television so that you can receive a particular program or channel: *The radio was tuned (in) to a classical music station.* ♦ (*informal*) **Stay tuned** for the news coming up next. **4** ~ sth (to sth) to prepare or adjust something so that it is suitable for a particular situation: *His speech was tuned to what the audience wanted to hear.*
PHRV ˌtune 'in (to sth) to listen to a radio program or watch a television program ˌtune 'in to sb/sth to become aware of other people's thoughts and feelings, etc. ˌtune 'out | ˌtune sb/sth↔'out to stop listening to something: *When she started talking about her job, he just tuned out.* ˌtune 'up | ˌtune sth↔'up to adjust musical instruments so that they can play together: *The orchestra was tuning up as we entered the hall.*

ˌtuned 'in *adj.* [not before noun] ~ (to sth) aware of what is happening in a particular situation: *The resort is tuned in to the tastes of young and old alike.*

tune·ful /'tunfl/ *adj.* having a pleasant tune or sound **ANT** TUNELESS ▶ **tune·ful·ly** /-fəli/ *adv.* **tune·ful·ness** *noun* [U]

tune·less /'tunləs/ *adj.* not having a pleasant tune or sound **ANT** TUNEFUL ▶ **tune·less·ly** *adv.*

tun·er /'tunər/ *noun* **1** (especially in compounds) a person who tunes musical instruments, especially pianos **2** the part of a radio, television, etc. that you move in order to change the signal and receive the radio or television station that you want **3** an electronic device that receives a radio signal and sends it to an AMPLIFIER so that it can be heard

tune·smith /'tunsmɪθ/ *noun* (*informal*) a person who writes popular music

tung·sten /'tʌŋstən/ *noun* [U] (*symb.* **W**) a chemical element. Tungsten is a very hard silver-gray metal, used especially in making steel and in FILAMENTS for BULBS.

tu·nic /'tunɪk/ *noun* **1** a loose piece of clothing covering the body down to the knees, usually without sleeves, as worn in ancient Greece and Rome **2** a piece of women's clothing like a tunic, that reaches to the hips and is worn over pants or a skirt

'tuning ˌfork *noun* a small metal instrument with two long parts joined together at one end, that produces a particular musical note when you hit it and is used in tuning (TUNE) musical instruments

'tuning ˌpeg *noun* = PEG ⊃ picture at PEG

tun·nel 🔊 /'tʌnl/ *noun, verb*

● **noun 1** a passage built underground, for example to allow a road or railroad to go through a hill, under a river, etc.: *a railway/railroad tunnel* ♦ *the Lincoln Tunnel* ⊃ see also WIND TUNNEL **2** an underground passage made by an animal **IDM** see LIGHT *n.*

● **verb** (-l-, *CanE* usually -ll-) [I, T] to dig a tunnel under or through the ground: + **adv./prep.** *The engineers had to tunnel through solid rock.* ♦ ~ **your way** + **adv./prep.** *The rescuers tunneled their way in to the trapped miners.*

'tunnel ˌvision *noun* [U] **1** (*medical*) a condition in which someone cannot see things that are not straight ahead of them **2** (*disapproving*) an inability to see or understand all the aspects of a situation, an argument, etc. instead of just one part of it

Tup·per·ware™ /'tʌpərˌwɛr/ *noun* [U] plastic containers used mainly for storing food

tuque (*CanE*) = TOQUE (2)

tur·ban /'tərbən/ *noun* **1** a long piece of cloth wound tightly around the head, worn, for example, by Muslim or Sikh men **2** a woman's hat that looks like a turban ▶ **tur·baned** /'tərbənd/ *adj.*: *turbaned Sikhs*

tur·bid /'tərbəd/ *adj.* (*formal*) (of liquid) full of mud, dirt, etc. so that you cannot see through it **SYN** MUDDY ▶ **tur·bid·i·ty** /tər'bɪdəti/ *noun* [U]

tur·bine /'tərbaɪn; -bən/ *noun* a machine or an engine that receives its power from a wheel that is turned by the pressure of water, air, or gas ⊃ see also WIND TURBINE

tur·bo·charg·er /'tərbouˌtʃɑrdʒər/ *noun* (also **tur·bo** *pl.* **tur·bos**) a system driven by a turbine that gets its power from an engine's EXHAUST gases. It sends the mixture of gas and air into the engine at high pressure, making it more powerful. ▶ **tur·bo·charge** *verb*: ~ **sth** *turbocharged engines*

tur·bo·jet /'tərbouˌdʒɛt/ *noun* **1** a TURBINE engine that produces forward movement by forcing out a stream of hot air and gas behind it **2** a plane that gets its power from this type of engine

tur·bo·prop /'tərbouˌprɑp/ *noun* **1** a TURBINE engine that produces forward movement by turning a PROPELLER (= a set of spinning blades) **2** a plane that gets its power from this type of engine

tur·bot /'tərbət/ *noun* (*pl.* **tur·bot** or **tur·bots**) [C, U] a large, flat, European, ocean fish that is used for food

tur·bu·lence /'tərbyələns/ *noun* [U] **1** a situation in which there is a lot of sudden change, confusion, disagreement, and sometimes violence **SYN** UPHEAVAL **2** a series of sudden and violent changes in the direction that air or water is moving in: *We experienced severe turbulence during the flight.* ⊃ collocations at TRAVEL

tur·bu·lent /'tərbyələnt/ *adj.* [usually before noun] **1** in which there is a lot of sudden change, confusion, disagreement, and sometimes violence: *a short and turbulent career in politics* ♦ *a turbulent part of the world* **2** (of air or water) changing direction suddenly and violently: *The aircraft is designed to withstand turbulent conditions.* ♦ *a turbulent sea/storm* (= caused by turbulent water/air) **3** (of people) noisy and/or difficult to control **SYN** UNRULY: *a turbulent crowd*

tu·reen /tə'rin/ *noun* a large deep dish with a lid, used for serving vegetables or soup

---

turf /tərf/ *noun, verb*

• *noun* **1** [U, C] short grass and the surface layer of soil that is held together by its roots; a piece of this that has been cut from the ground and is used especially for making LAWNS (= the area of grass in a yard): *newly laid turf* **2** [U, C] PEAT that is cut to be used as fuel; a piece of this **3 the turf** [sing.] the sport of horse racing **4** [U] **sb's ~** (*informal*) the place where someone lives and/or works, especially when they think of it as their own: *He feels more confident on home turf.*

• *verb* **~ sth** to cover an area of ground with turf

'turf war *noun* a violent disagreement between two groups of people about who should control a particular area, activity, or business: *a vicious turf war between rival gangs*

tur·gid /'tərdʒəd/ *adj.* (*formal*) **1** (of language, writing, etc.) boring, complicated, and difficult to understand **2** swollen; containing more water than usual: *the turgid waters of the Missouri River*

tu·ris·ta /tʊ'ristə/ *noun* [U] (*informal*) DIARRHEA that is suffered by someone who is visiting a foreign country

tur·key /'tərki/ *noun* **1** [C] a large bird that is often kept for its meat, eaten especially on Thanksgiving ⊃ picture at ANIMAL **2** [U] meat from a turkey: *roast turkey* **3** [C]·(*informal*) a failure: *His latest movie is a real turkey.* **4** [C] (*informal*) a stupid or useless person ⊃ see also COLD TURKEY **IDM** see TALK *v.*

'turkey ˌshoot *noun* (*informal*) a battle or contest in which one side is much stronger than the other and able to win very easily

Turk·ish /'tərkɪʃ/ *adj., noun*

• *adj.* from or connected with Turkey

• *noun* [U] the language of Turkey

ˌTurkish 'bath *noun* a type of bath in which you sit in a room full of hot steam, have a MASSAGE, and then a cold shower or bath; a building where this treatment takes place

ˌTurkish 'coffee *noun* [U, C] very strong, usually very sweet, black coffee

ˌTurkish de'light *noun* [U, C] a candy made from a substance like jelly that is flavored with fruit and covered with fine white sugar

tur·mer·ic /'tərmərɪk/ *noun* [U] a yellow powder made from the root of an Asian plant, used in cooking as a spice, especially in CURRY ⊃ picture at HERB

tur·moil /'tərmɔɪl/ *noun* [U, sing.] a state of great anxiety and confusion **SYN** CONFUSION: *emotional/mental/political turmoil* ◆ *His statement threw the court into turmoil.* ◆ *Her mind was in (a) turmoil.*

turn /tərn/ *verb, noun*

• *verb*

> MOVE AROUND **1** [I, T] to move or make something move around a central point: *The wheels of the car began to turn.* ◆ *I can't get the screw to turn.* ◆ **~ sth (+ adv./prep.)** *He turned the key in the lock.* ◆ *She turned the wheel sharply to the left.*

> CHANGE POSITION/DIRECTION **2** [I, T] to move your body or part of your body so as to face or start moving in a different direction: *We turned and headed for home.* ◆ *She turned to look at me.* ◆ **+ adv./prep.** *He turned back to his work.* ◆ *I turned away and looked out of the window.* ◆ **~ sth (+ adv./prep.)** *He turned his back to the wall.* ◆ *She turned her head away.* ◆ see also TURN OVER **3** [T] **~ sth + adv./prep.** to move something so that it is in a different position or facing a different direction: *She turned the chair on its side to repair it.* ◆ *Turn the sweater inside out before you wash it.* ⊃ see also TURN OVER **4** [I, T] to change the direction you are moving or traveling in; to make something change the direction it is moving in: **~ (into sth)** *He turned into a narrow street.* ◆ **~ sth** *The man turned the corner and disappeared.* ◆ **~ sth into sth** *I turned the car into the garage.* **5** [I] **(+ adv./prep.)** (of a road or river) to curve in a particular direction: *The road turns to the left after the church.*

> AIM/POINT **6** [T, I] to aim or point something in a particular direction: **~ sth (on/to sb/sth/yourself)** *Police turned a*

water cannon on the rioters. ◆ *He turned the gun on himself.* ◆ *She looked at him then turned her attention back to me.* ◆ **~ to sb/sth/yourself** *His thoughts turned to his dead wife.*

> OF TIDE IN OCEAN **7** [I] to start to come in or go out: *The tide is turning—we'd better get back.*

> LET SOMEONE OR SOMETHING GO **8** [T] to make or let someone or something go into a particular place or state: **~ sth + adv./prep.** *They turned the horse into the field.* ◆ **~ sth + adj.** *to turn the dogs loose*

> FOLD **9** [T] **~ sth + adv./prep.** to fold something in a particular way: *She turned down the blankets and climbed into bed.* ◆ *He turned up the collar of his coat and hurried out into the rain.*

> CARTWHEEL/SOMERSAULT **10** [T, no passive] **~ sth** to perform a movement by moving your body in a circle: *to turn cartwheels/somersaults*

> PAGE **11** [T, I] if you **turn** a page of a book or magazine, you move it so that you can read the next page: **~ sth** *He sat turning the pages idly.* ◆ **~ to sth** *Turn to p. 23.*

> GAME **12** [I, T] **~ (sth) (around)** if a game **turns** or someone **turns** it, it changes the way it is developing so that a different person or team starts to win

> BECOME **13** *linking verb* to change into a particular state or condition; to make something do this: **+ adj.** *The leaves were turning brown.* ◆ *The weather has turned cold.* ◆ *He turned nasty when we refused to give him the money.* ◆ *He decided to turn professional.* ◆ **~ sth + adj.** *The heat turned the milk sour.* ◆ **+ noun** *She turned a deathly shade of white when she heard the news.* ◆ *He's a lawyer turned politician* (= he used to be a lawyer but is now a politician). ⊃ note at BECOME

> AGE/TIME **14** *linking verb* (not used in the progressive tenses) **+ noun** to reach or pass a particular age or time: *She turns 21 in June.* ◆ *It's turned midnight.*

> STOMACH **15** [I, T] **~ (your stomach)** when your stomach **turns** or something **turns** your stomach, you feel as though you will VOMIT

> WOOD **16** [T] **~ sth** to shape something on a LATHE: *to turn a chair leg* ◆ *turned boxes and bowls*

IDM Most idioms containing **turn** are at the entries for the nouns and adjectives in the idioms. For example, **not turn a hair** is at **hair**. **as it/things turned out** as was shown or proved by later events: *I didn't need my umbrella, as it turned out* (= because it didn't rain). **be well, badly, etc. turned out** to be well, badly, etc. dressed **turn around and do sth** (*informal*) used to report what someone says or does, when this is surprising or annoying: *How could she turn around and say that, after all I've done for her?*

PHR V ˌturn a'gainst sb | ˌturn sb a'gainst sb to stop or make someone stop being friendly toward someone: *She turned against her old friend.* ◆ *After the divorce he tried to turn the children against their mother.*

ˌturn a'round | ˌturn sb/sth a'round to change position or direction so as to face the other way; to make someone or something do this: *Turn around and let me look at your back.* ◆ *I turned my chair around to face the fire.* ˌturn a'round | ˌturn sth↔a'round if a business, economy, etc. **turns around** or someone **turns it around**, it starts being successful after it has been unsuccessful for a time ⊃ related noun TURNAROUND

ˌturn sb↔a'way (from sth) to refuse to allow someone to enter a place: *Hundreds of people were turned away from the stadium* (= because it was full). ◆ *They had nowhere to stay so I couldn't turn them away.*

ˌturn 'back | ˌturn sb/sth↔'back to return the way you have come; to make someone or something do this: *The weather became so bad that they had to turn back.* ◆ (*figurative*) *We said we would do it—there can be no turning back.* ◆ *Our car was turned back at the border.* ⊃ thesaurus box at RETURN ˌturn sth↔'down to reject or refuse to consider an offer, a proposal, etc. or the person who makes it: *Why did she turn down your invitation?* ◆ *He has been turned down for ten jobs so far.* ◆ *He asked her to marry him but she turned him down.* ˌturn sth↔'down to reduce the noise, heat, etc. produced by a piece of equipment by moving its controls: *Please turn the volume down.* ◆ **+ adj.** *He turned the lights down low.*

| t tea | ţ butter | d did | k cat | g got | tʃ chin | dʒ June | f fall |

,turn 'in **1** to face or curve toward the center: *Her feet turn in.* **2** (*old-fashioned*) to go to bed ,turn sb↔'in (*informal*) to take someone to the police or someone in authority because they have committed a crime: *She threatened to turn him in to the police.* ◆ *He decided to turn himself in.* ,turn sth↔'in **1** to give back something that you no longer need: *You must turn in your pass when you leave the building.* **2** to give something to someone in authority: *They turned in a petition with 80,000 signatures.* ◆ *I haven't even turned in Monday's work yet.* **3** to achieve a score, performance, profit, etc.: *The champion turned in a superb performance to retain her title.* ,turn 'in on yourself to become too concerned with your own problems and stop communicating with others

,turn (from sth) 'into sth to become something: *Our dream vacation turned into a nightmare.* ◆ *In one year she turned from a problem child into a model student.* ,turn sb/sth (from sth) 'into sth to make someone or something become something: *Ten years of prison had turned him into an old man.* ◆ *The prince was turned into a frog by the witch.*

,turn 'off | ,turn 'off sth [no passive] to leave a road in order to travel on another: *Is this where we turn off?* ◆ *The jet began to turn off the main runway.* ,turn 'off (*informal*) to stop listening to or thinking about someone or something: *I couldn't understand the lecture so I just turned off.* ,turn sb↔'off **1** to make someone feel bored or not interested: *People had been turned off by both candidates in the election.* **2** to stop someone feeling sexually attracted; to make someone have a feeling of disgust ⊃ related noun TURN-OFF ,turn sth↔'off to stop the flow of electricity, gas, water, etc. by moving a switch, button, etc.: *to turn off the light* ◆ *Please turn the television off before you go to bed.*

'turn on sb to attack someone suddenly and unexpectedly: *The dogs suddenly turned on each other.* ◆ *Why are you all turning on me* (= criticizing or blaming me)? 'turn on sth [no passive] **1** to depend on something: *Much turns on the outcome of the current peace talks.* **2** [no passive] to have something as its main topic: *The discussion turned on the need to raise standards.* ,turn sb↔'on (*informal*) to make someone excited or interested, especially sexually: *Jazz has never really turned me on.* ◆ *She gets turned on by men in uniform.* ⊃ related noun TURN-ON ,turn sb 'on (to sth) (*informal*) to make someone become interested in something or use something for the first time: *He turned her on to jazz.* ,turn sth↔'on to start the flow of electricity, gas, water, etc. by moving a switch, button, etc.: *to turn on the heat* ◆ *I'll turn the television on.* ◆ (*figurative*) *He really knows how to* **turn on the charm** (= suddenly become pleasant and attractive)

,turn 'out **1** to be present at an event: *A vast crowd turned out to watch the procession.* ⊃ related noun TURNOUT **2** (used with an adverb or adjective, or in questions with *how*) to happen in a particular way; to develop or end in a particular way: *Despite our worries everything turned out well.* ◆ *You never know how your children will turn out.* ◆ + **adj.** *If the day turns out wet, we may have to change our plans.* **3** to point away from the center: *Her toes turn out.* **4** to be discovered to be; to prove to be: ~ **that...** *It turned out that she was a friend of my sister.* ◆ ~ **to be/have sth** *The job turned out to be harder than we thought.* ◆ *The house they had offered us turned out to be a tiny apartment.* ,turn sb/sth↔'out to produce someone or something: *The factory turns out 900 cars a week.* ,turn sb 'out (of/from sth) to force someone to leave a place ,turn sth↔'out **1** to switch a light or a source of heat off: *Remember to turn out the lights when you go to bed.* **2** to empty something, especially your pockets **3** to make something point away from the center: *She turned her toes out.*

,turn 'over **1** to change position so that the other side is facing toward the outside or the top: *If you turn over you might find it easier to get to sleep.* ◆ *The car skidded and turned over.* ◆ (*figurative*) *The smell made my stomach turn over* (= made me feel sick). **2** (of an engine) to start or to continue to run ,turn 'over sth to do business worth a particular amount of money in a particular period of time: *The company turns over $3.5 million a year.* ⊃ related noun TURNOVER ,turn

sth↔'over **1** to make something change position so that the other side is facing toward the outside or the top: *Brown the meat on one side, then turn it over and brown the other side.* **2** to think about something carefully: *She kept turning over the events of the day in her mind.* **3** (of a store) to sell goods and replace them: *A supermarket will turn over its stock very rapidly.* ⊃ related noun TURNOVER **4** to make an engine start running ,turn sb↔'over to sb to deliver someone to the control or care of someone else, especially someone in authority: *Customs officials turned the man over to the police.* ,turn sth↔'over to sb to give the control of something to someone: *He turned the business over to his daughter.* ,turn sth↔'over to sth to change the use or function of something: *The factory was turned over to the manufacture of aircraft parts.*

'turn to sb/sth to go to someone or something for help, advice, etc.: *She has nobody she can turn to.*

,turn 'up **1** to be found, especially by chance, after being lost: *Don't worry about the letter—I'm sure it'll turn up.* **2** (of a person) to arrive: *We arranged to meet at 7:30, but she never turned up.* **3** (of an opportunity) to happen, especially by chance: *He's still hoping something* (= for example, a job or a piece of luck) *will turn up.* ⊃ related noun TURN-UP ,turn sth↔'up **1** to increase the sound, heat, etc. of a piece of equipment: *Could you turn the TV up?* ◆ + **adj.** *The music was turned up loud.* **2** to find something: *Our efforts to trace him turned up nothing.*

● ***noun*** [C]
▷ **MOVEMENT 1** an act of turning someone or something around: *Give the handle a few turns.*
▷ **OF ROAD/VEHICLE 2** a change in direction in a vehicle: *Make a left/right turn into West Street.* ⊃ see also THREE-POINT TURN, U-TURN **3** a place where a road leads away from the one you are traveling on **4** a bend or corner in a road: *a lane full of* **twists and turns**
▷ **TIME 5** the time when someone in a group of people should or is allowed to do something: *When it's your turn, take another card.* ◆ *Please* **wait your turn.** ◆ *Whose* **turn is it** *to cook?* ◆ *Steve* **took a turn** *driving while I slept.*
▷ **CHANGE 6** an unusual or unexpected change in what is happening: *a surprising* **turn of events** ◆ *His health has* **taken a turn for the worse** (= suddenly got worse). ◆ *Events took a dramatic turn in the weeks that followed.* ◆ *The book is,* **by turns,** *funny and very sad.*
▷ **PERFORMANCE 7** a short performance or piece of entertainment such as a song, etc.: *Everyone got up on stage to do a turn.* ⊃ see also STAR TURN
▷ **WALK 8** (*old-fashioned*) a short walk: *We took a turn around the park.*
▷ **ILLNESS 9** (*old-fashioned*) a feeling of illness: *a funny turn* (= a feeling that you may faint)
IDM **at every turn** everywhere or every time you try and do something: *At every turn I met with disappointment.* **(do sb) a good turn** (to do) something that helps someone: *Well, that's my good turn for the day.* **done to a turn** cooked for exactly the right amount of time **give sb a turn** (*old-fashioned*) to frighten or shock someone **in turn 1** one after the other in a particular order: *The children called out their names in turn.* **2** as a result of something in a series of events: *Increased production will, in turn, lead to increased profits.* **one good turn deserves another** (*saying*) you should help someone who has helped you **speak/talk out of turn** to say something that you should not because it is the wrong situation or because it offends someone **take turns (in sth/to do sth)** if people **take turns** to do something, they do it one after the other to make sure it is done fairly: *The male and female birds take turns in sitting on the eggs.* **the turn of the century/year** the time when a new century/year starts: *It was built at the turn of the century.* **a turn of mind** a particular way of thinking about things **a turn of phrase** a particular way of describing something **a turn of the screw** an extra amount of pressure, CRUELTY, etc. added to a situation that is already difficult to bear or understand

turn·a·bout /'tɜrnəˌbaʊt/ *noun* [sing.] ~ **(in sth)** a sudden and complete change in someone or something **SYN** REVERSAL

turn·a·round /'tərnə,raʊnd/ *noun* [usually sing.] **1** the amount of time it takes to unload a ship or plane at the end of one journey and load it again for the next one **2** the amount of time it takes to do a piece of work that you have been given and return it **3** a situation in which something changes from bad to good: *a turnaround in the economy* **4** a complete change in someone's opinion, behavior, etc.

turn·coat /'tərnkoʊt/ *noun* (*disapproving*) a person who leaves one political party, religious group, etc. to join one that has very different views

'turning ,circle *noun* the smallest circle that a vehicle can turn around in

'turning ,point *noun* ~ (in sth) the time when an important change takes place, usually with the result that a situation improves: *The promotion marked a turning point in her career.*

tur·nip /'tərnəp/ *noun* [C, U] a round white, or white and purple, root vegetable ⊃ picture at FRUIT

turn·key /'tərnki/ *adj.* (especially of computer systems) complete and ready to use immediately

'turn-off *noun* **1** a place where a road leads away from another larger or more important road: *We missed the turn-off for the airport.* **2** [usually sing.] (*informal*) a person or thing that people do not find interesting, attractive, or sexually exciting: *The city's crime rate is a serious turn-off to potential investors.* ♦ *I find beards a real turn-off.*

'turn-on *noun* [usually sing.] (*informal*) a person or thing that people find sexually exciting

turn·out /'tərnaʊt/ *noun* [C, usually sing., U] **1** the number of people who attend a particular event: *This year's festival attracted a record turnout.* **2** the number of people who vote in a particular election: *a high/low/poor turnout* ♦ *a 60% turnout of voters*

turn·o·ver /'tərn,oʊvər/ *noun* **1** [C, usually sing., U] ~ (of sth) the total amount of goods or services sold by a company during a particular period of time: *an annual turnover of $75 million* ♦ *a fall in turnover* ⊃ collocations at BUSINESS **2** [sing.] ~ (of sb) the rate at which employees leave a company and are replaced by other people: *a high turnover of staff* **3** [sing.] ~ (of sth) the rate at which goods are sold in a store and replaced by others: *a fast turnover of stock* **4** [C] a small PIE in the shape of a triangle or half a circle, filled with fruit or jelly **5** [C] (in football or basketball) an occasion when the team that has the ball loses it to the other team

turn·pike /'tərnpaɪk/ (also **pike**) *noun* a wide road, where traffic can travel fast for long distances and that drivers must pay a TOLL to use

'turn ,signal (also *informal* **blink·er**) *noun* a light on a vehicle that flashes to show that the vehicle is going to turn left or right ⊃ picture at CAR

turn·stile /'tərnstaɪl/ *noun* a gate at the entrance to a public building, STADIUM, etc. that turns in a circle when pushed, allowing one person to go through at a time ⊃ picture at STILE

turn·ta·ble /'tərn,teɪbl/ *noun* **1** the round surface on a RECORD PLAYER that you place the record on to be played **2** a large round surface that is able to move in a circle and onto which a railroad engine is driven in order to turn it to go in the opposite direction

tur·pen·tine /'tərpən,taɪn/ *noun* [U] a clear liquid with a strong smell, used especially for making paint thinner and for cleaning paint from brushes and clothes

tur·pi·tude /'tərpə,tud/ *noun* [U] (*formal*) very immoral behavior **SYN** WICKEDNESS

tur·quoise /'tərkɔɪz; -kwɔɪz/ *noun* **1** [C, U] a blue or green-blue SEMIPRECIOUS STONE: *a turquoise brooch* **2** [U] a green-blue color ▶ **tur·quoise** *adj.*: *a turquoise dress*

tur·ret /'tərət/ *noun* **1** a small tower on top of a wall or

building, especially a castle ⊃ picture at BUILDING **2** a small metal tower on a ship, plane, or TANK that can usually turn around and from which guns are fired

tur·ret·ed /'tərətəd/ *adj.* [usually before noun] having one or more turrets

tur·tle /'tərtl/ *noun* **1** (also **sea ,turtle**) a large REPTILE with a hard round shell, that lives in the ocean ⊃ picture at ANIMAL **2** (*informal*) any REPTILE with a large shell, for example a TORTOISE or TERRAPIN
IDM **turn turtle** (of a boat) to turn over completely while sailing

'turtle ,dove *noun* a wild DOVE¹ (= a type of bird) with a pleasant soft call, thought to be a very loving bird

tur·tle·neck /'tərtl,nɛk/ *noun* **1** a high round COLLAR made when the neck of a piece of clothing is folded over **2** (also **turtleneck 'sweater**) a sweater or shirt with a turtleneck ⊃ picture at CLOTHES ⊃ see also MOCK TURTLENECK

tush /tʊʃ/ *noun* (*informal*) the part of the body that you sit on ⊃ compare BUTTOCK

tusk /tʌsk/ *noun* either of the long curved teeth that stick out of the mouth of ELEPHANTS and some other animals ⊃ picture at ANIMAL ⊃ see also IVORY

tus·sle /'tʌsl/ *noun, verb*
● *noun* ~ (for/over sth) a short struggle, fight, or argument especially in order to get something: *He was injured during a tussle for the ball.*
● *verb* [I] ~ (with sb/sth) to fight or compete with someone or something, especially in order to get something: *The children were tussling with one another for the ball.*

tus·sock /'tʌsək/ *noun* a small area of grass that is longer and thicker than the grass around it ▶ **tus·sock·y** *adj.*: *tussocky grass*

tut /tʌt/ (also **tut-'tut**) *exclamation, noun* used as the written or spoken way of showing the sound that people make with their tongues when they disapprove of something: *Tut-tut, I expected better of you.* ♦ *tut-tuts of disapproval* ▶ **tut** (also **tut-'tut**) *verb* (-tt-) [I]: *He tut-tutted under his breath.*

tu·tee /tu'ti/ *noun* a person who is taught or given advice by a TUTOR

tu·te·lage /'tutl·ɪdʒ/ *noun* [U] (*formal*) **1** the teaching and instruction that one person gives to another **SYN** TUITION **2** the state of being protected or controlled by another person, organization, or country: *parental tutelage*

tu·tor /'tutər/ *noun, verb*
● *noun* **1** a private teacher, especially one who teaches an individual student or a very small group **2** an assistant LECTURER in a college **3** a book of instruction in a particular subject, especially music: *a violin tutor*
● *verb* **1** [T] ~ sb (in sth) to be a tutor to an individual student or a small group; to teach someone, especially privately: *He tutors students in mathematics.* **2** [I] to work as a tutor: *Her work was divided between tutoring and research.*

tu·to·ri·al /tu'tɔriəl/ *noun, adj.*
● *noun* **1** a short book or computer program that gives information on a particular subject or explains how something is done: *An online tutorial is provided.* **2** a period of teaching that involves discussion between an individual student or a small group of students and a tutor
● *adj.* connected with the work of a tutor: *tutorial staff*

tut·ti-frut·ti /,tuti 'fruti/ *noun* [U] a type of ice cream that contains pieces of fruit of various kinds

tu·tu /'tutu/ *noun* a BALLET dancer's skirt made of many layers of material. Tutus may be either short and stiff, sticking out from the waist, or long and bell-shaped.

tu-whit, tu-whoo /tə,wɪt tə'wu/ *noun* used to represent the sound that an OWL makes

tux·e·do /tʌk'sidoʊ/ *noun* (*pl.* **tux·e·dos**) (also *informal* **tux** /tʌks/) **1** a black or white jacket and pants, worn with a BOW TIE at formal occasions in the evening **2** a black or white jacket worn with a BOW TIE at formal occasions in the evening **ORIGIN** From Tuxedo Park in New York, where it was first worn.

TV 🔊 /ˌti ˈvi/ noun [C, U]
television: *What's on TV tonight?* ♦ *We're buying a new TV with the money.* ♦ *Almost all homes have at least one TV set.* ♦ *All rooms have a bathroom and color TV.* ♦ *a TV series/show/program* ♦ *satellite/cable/digital TV* ♦ *She's a highly paid TV talk show host.* ➋ collocations at TELEVISION ➋ see also PAY TV

ˌTV ˈdinner noun a meal that you can buy already cooked and prepared, that you only have to heat up before you can eat it

TVP /ˌti ˌvi ˈpi/ abbr. TEXTURED VEGETABLE PROTEIN

TW abbr. (pl. TW) TERAWATT(S)

twad·dle /ˈtwɑdl/ noun [U] (old-fashioned, informal) something that has been said or written that you think is stupid and not true **SYN** NONSENSE

twain /tweɪn/ number (old use) two
IDM **never the twain shall meet** (saying) used to say that two things are so different that they cannot exist together

twang /twæŋ/ noun, verb
● **noun** [usually sing.] **1** used to describe a way of speaking, usually one that is typical of a particular area and especially one in which the sounds are produced through the nose as well as the mouth **2** a sound that is made when a tight string, especially on a musical instrument, is pulled and released
● **verb** [I, T] to make a sound like a tight wire or string being pulled and released; to make something do this: *The bed springs twanged.* ♦ ~ **sth** *Someone was twanging a guitar in the next room.*

ˈtwas /twʌz; twɑz; twəz/ abbr. (old use) it was

tweak /twik/ verb, noun
● **verb 1** ~ **sth** to pull or twist something suddenly: *She tweaked his ear playfully.* **2** ~ **sth** to make slight changes to a machine, system, etc. to improve it: *I think you'll have to tweak these figures a little before you show them to the boss.*
● **noun 1** a sharp pull or twist: *She gave his ear a tweak.* **2** a slight change that you make to a machine, system, etc. to improve it

tweed /twid/ noun **1** [U] a type of thick, rough cloth made of wool that has small spots of different colored thread in it: *a tweed jacket* **2** **tweeds** [pl.] clothes made of tweed

Twee·dle·dum and Twee·dle·dee /ˌtwidlˈdʌm ən ˌtwidlˈdi/ noun [pl.] two people or things that are not different from each other **ORIGIN** From two characters in *Through the Looking Glass* by Lewis Carroll, who look the same and say the same things.

tweed·y /ˈtwidi/ adj. **1** made of or looking like tweed: *a tweedy jacket* **2** (informal, often disapproving) used to describe the sort of person who often wears tweed and behaves in a way thought to be typical of a college professor, writer, etc.

tween /twin/ (also tween·er, tween·ag·er /ˈtwineɪdʒər/) noun a child between the ages of about 10 and 12 **SYN** PRETEEN

tween·er /ˈtwinər/ noun **1** = TWEEN **2** a person or thing that is between two categories, classes, or age groups: *The film is a tweener, neither indie nor mainstream.*

tweet /twit/ noun, verb
● **noun 1** the short high sound made by a small bird **2** (also twit·ter) a message sent using the TWITTER™ SOCIAL NETWORKING service
● **verb** = TWITTER

tweet·er /ˈtwitər/ noun **1** a LOUDSPEAKER for reproducing the high notes in a SOUND SYSTEM ➋ compare WOOFER **2** someone who sends and reads tweets using the TWITTER™ SOCIAL NETWORKING service

tweez·ers /ˈtwizərz/ noun [pl.] a small tool with two long,

thin parts joined together at one end, used for picking up very small things or for pulling out hairs: *a pair of tweezers*

ˌTwelfth ˈNight noun [U] **1** January 6th, the day of the Christian festival of EPIPHANY **2** the evening of January 5th, the day before EPIPHANY, which traditionally marks the end of Christmas celebrations

twelve /twɛlv/ number 12 ▶ **twelfth** /twɛlfθ/ ordinal number, noun **HELP** There are examples of how to use ordinal numbers at the entry for **fifth**.

ˈtwelve·month /ˈtwɛlvmʌnθ/ noun [sing.] (old use) a year

ˈtwelve-note (also do·dec·a·phon·ic, ˈtwelve-tone) adj. [only before noun] (music) used to describe a system of music which uses the twelve notes in the scale equally rather than using a particular KEY

twen·ty /ˈtwɛnti; ˈtwɛni; ˈtwʌni/ **1** number 20 **2** noun **the twenties** [pl.] numbers, years, or temperatures from 20 to 29 ▶ **twen·ti·eth** /ˈtwɛntiəθ; ˈtwɛni-; ˈtwʌni-/ ordinal number, noun **HELP** There are examples of how to use ordinal numbers at the entry for **fifth**.
IDM **in your twenties** between the ages of 20 and 29

ˌtwenty-ˌfour ˈseven (also **24/7**) adv. (informal) twenty-four hours a day, seven days a week (used to mean "all the time"): *He's on duty twenty-four seven.*

ˈtwere /twər/ abbr. (old use) it were

twerp /twərp/ noun (old-fashioned, informal) a stupid or annoying person

twice 🔊 /twaɪs/ adv.
1 two times; on two occasions: *I don't know him well; I've only met him twice.* ♦ *They go there twice a week/month/year.* ♦ *a twice-monthly/yearly newsletter* **2** double in quantity, rate, etc.: *an area twice the size of New Jersey* ♦ *Cats sleep twice as much as people.* ♦ *At 56 he's twice her age.*
IDM **twice over** not just once but twice: *By one estimate, he's a billionaire at least twice over.* ➋ more at LIGHTNING, ONCE adv., THINK n.

twid·dle /ˈtwɪdl/ verb, noun
● **verb** [I, T] to twist or turn something with your fingers, often because you are nervous or bored: ~ **with sth** *He twiddled with the radio knob until he found the right program.* ♦ ~ **sth** *She was twiddling the ring on her finger.*
IDM **twiddle your thumbs 1** to move your thumbs around each other with your fingers joined together **2** to do nothing while you are waiting for something to happen
● **noun** **1** a twist or turn: *a twiddle of the knob* **2** a decorative twist in a pattern, piece of music, etc.: *twiddles on the clarinet*

twig /twɪg/ noun a small, very thin branch that grows out of a larger branch on a bush or tree ➋ picture at TREE

twi·light /ˈtwaɪlaɪt/ noun, adj.
● **noun** [U] **1** the faint light or the period of time at the end of the day after the sun has gone down: *It was hard to see him clearly in the twilight.* ♦ *We went for a walk along the beach at twilight.* **2** **the ~ (of sth)** the final stage of something when it becomes weaker or less important than it was: *the twilight years* (= the last years of your life)
● **adj.** [only before noun] **1** (formal) used to describe a state in which things are strange and mysterious, or where things are kept secret and do not seem to be part of the real world: *the twilight world of the occult* ♦ *They lived in the twilight zone on the fringes of society.* **2** used to describe a situation or area of thought that is not clearly defined

twi·lit /ˈtwaɪlɪt/ adj. (literary) lit by twilight

twill /twɪl/ noun [U] a type of strong cloth that is made in a particular way to produce a surface of raised DIAGONAL lines: *a cotton twill skirt*

ˈtwill /twɪl/ abbr. (old use) it will

twin 🔊 /twɪn/ noun, verb, adj.
● **noun 1** one of two children born at the same time to the same mother: *She's expecting twins.* ➋ collocations at CHILD ➋ see also CONJOINED TWIN, FRATERNAL TWIN, IDENTICAL

TWIN, SIAMESE TWIN **2** one of two similar things that make a pair

- **verb** (-nn-) ~ **sth (with sth)** to join two people or things closely together: *The opera twins the themes of love and death.*
- **adj.** [only before noun] **1** used to describe one of a pair of children who are twins: *twin boys/girls* ◆ *a twin brother/ sister* **2** used to describe two things that are used as a pair: *a ship with twin propellers* **3** used to describe two things that are connected, or present or happening at the same time: *The prison service has the twin goals of punishment and rehabilitation.*

twin ˈbed *noun* **1** [usually pl.] one of a pair of single beds in a room: *Would you prefer twin beds or a double?* ⟳ picture at BED **2** (also ˌsingle ˈbed) a bed big enough for one person: *sheets to fit a twin bed*

twin ˈbedroom *noun* a room in a hotel, etc. that has two single beds

twine /twaɪn/ *noun, verb*
- **noun** [U] strong string that has two or more STRANDS (= single thin pieces of thread or string) twisted together
- **verb** [I, T] ~ **(sth) around/through/in sth** to wind or twist around something; to make something do this: *ivy twining around a tree trunk* ◆ *She twined her arms around my neck.*

twin-ˈengined *adj.* (of an aircraft) having two engines

twinge /twɪndʒ/ *noun* **1** a sudden short feeling of pain: *He felt a twinge in his knee.* **2** ~ **(of sth)** a sudden short feeling of an unpleasant emotion: *a twinge of disappointment*

Twin-kie™ /ˈtwɪŋki/ *noun* a small, sweet, yellow cake with a soft mixture like cream in the middle

twin-kle /ˈtwɪŋkl/ *verb, noun*
- **verb** **1** [I] to shine with a light that keeps changing from bright to faint to bright again: *Stars twinkled in the sky.* ◆ *twinkling lights in the distance* ⟳ thesaurus box at SHINE **2** [I] ~ **(with sth)** | ~ **(at sb)** if your eyes **twinkle**, you have a bright expression because you are happy or excited: *twinkling blue eyes* ◆ *Her eyes twinkled with merriment.*
- **noun** [sing.] **1** an expression in your eyes that shows you are happy or amused about something: *He looked at me with a twinkle in his eye.* **2** a small light that keeps changing from bright to faint to bright again: *the twinkle of stars* ◆ *the twinkle of the harbor lights in the distance*

twin-kling /ˈtwɪŋklɪŋ/ *noun* [sing.] (*old-fashioned, informal*) a very short time
  IDM **in the twinkling of an eye** very quickly **SYN** IN AN INSTANT

twin-set /ˈtwɪnset/ *noun* a woman's matching sweater and CARDIGAN that are designed to be worn together

twin-size (also ˈtwin-sized) *adj.* (of beds, sheets, etc.) big enough for one person, or for a bed for one person

twirl /twɜrl/ *verb, noun*
- **verb** **1** [I, T] ~ **(sb) (around)** to move or dance around and around; to make someone do this: *She twirled around in front of the mirror.* ◆ *He held her hand and twirled her around.* **2** [T] ~ **sth (around/about)** to make something turn quickly and lightly around and around **SYN** SPIN: *He twirled his hat in his hand.* ◆ *She sat twirling the stem of the glass in her fingers.* **3** [T] ~ **sth** to twist or curl something with your fingers: *He kept twirling his mustache.*
- **noun** the action of a person spinning around once: *Kate did a twirl in her new dress.*

twist 🔑 /twɪst/ *verb, noun*
- **verb**
- ▷ BEND INTO SHAPE **1** [T] ~ **sth (into sth)** to bend or turn something into a particular shape: *Twist the wire to form a circle.* **2** [T, I] to bend or turn something into a shape or position that is not normal or natural; to be bent or turned in this way: ~ **sth (+ adv./prep.)** *He grabbed me and twisted my arm behind my back.* ◆ (+ adv./prep.) *Her face twisted in anger.*
- ▷ TURN BODY **3** [T, I] to turn part of your body around while the rest stays still: ~ **sth (+ adv./prep.)** *He twisted his head*

around to look at her. ◆ (+ adv./prep.) *She twisted in her chair when I called her name.* **4** [I, T] to turn your body with quick, sharp movements and change direction often: *I twisted and turned to avoid being caught.* ◆ + adv./prep. *She tried unsuccessfully to twist free.* ◆ ~ **sth/yourself** + adv./prep. *He managed to twist himself around in the restricted space.*
- ▷ TURN WITH HAND **5** [T] ~ **sth (+ adv./prep.)** to turn something around in a circle with your hand: *Twist the knob to the left to open the door.* ◆ *Nervously I twisted the ring on my finger.*
- ▷ OF ROADS/RIVERS **6** [I] to bend and change direction often: *The road twists and turns along the coast.* ◆ *narrow twisting streets* ◆ *a twisting staircase*
- ▷ ANKLE/WRIST/KNEE **7** [T] ~ **sth** to injure part of your body, especially your ankle, wrist, or knee, bending it in an awkward way: *She fell and twisted her ankle.*
- ▷ WIND AROUND **8** [T] ~ **sth (+ adv./prep.)** to wind something around or through an object: *She twisted a scarf around her head.* ◆ *The telephone cable has gotten twisted* (= wound around itself). **9** [I] ~ **(around sth)** to move or grow by winding around something: *A snake was twisting around his arm.*
- ▷ FACTS **10** [T] ~ **sth** to deliberately change the meaning of what someone has said, or to present facts in a particular way, in order to benefit yourself or harm someone else **SYN** MISREPRESENT: *You always twist everything I say.* ◆ *The newspaper was accused of twisting the facts.*
- ▷ THREADS **11** [T] ~ **sth (into sth)** to turn or wind threads, etc. together to make something longer or thicker: *They had twisted the sheets into a rope and escaped by climbing down it.*
  IDM **twist sb's arm** (*informal*) to persuade or force someone to do something ⟳ more at KNIFE, LITTLE FINGER **PHR V** ˌtwist sth↔ˈoff to turn and pull something with your hand to remove it from something: *I twisted off the lid and looked inside.* ◆ *a twist-off top*
- **noun**
- ▷ ACTION OF TURNING **1** [C] the action of turning something with your hand, or of turning a part of your body: *She gave the lid another twist and it came off.* ◆ *He gave a shy smile and a little twist of his head.*
- ▷ UNEXPECTED CHANGE **2** [C] an unexpected change or development in a story or situation: *the twists and turns of his political career* ◆ *The story has taken another twist.* ◆ *The disappearance of a key witness added a new twist to the case.* ◆ *By a curious twist of fate we met again only a week or so later.*
- ▷ IN ROAD/RIVER **3** [C] a sharp bend in a road or river: *The car followed the twists and turns of the mountain road.*
- ▷ SHAPE **4** [C] a thing that has been twisted into a particular shape: *mineral water with a twist of lemon*
- ▷ DANCE **5** the twist [sing.] a fast dance that was popular in the 1960s, in which you twist from side to side

twist-ed 🔑 /ˈtwɪstəd/ *adj.*
  1 bent or turned so that the original shape is lost: *After the crash the car was a mass of twisted metal.* ◆ *a twisted ankle* (= injured by being turned suddenly) ◆ *She gave a small twisted smile.* ⟳ picture at CURVED **2** (of a person's mind or behavior) not normal; strange in an unpleasant way: *Her experiences had left her bitter and twisted.*

twist-er /ˈtwɪstər/ *noun* (*informal*) a violent storm that is caused by a powerful spinning column of air **SYN** TORNADO

ˈtwist tie *noun* a piece of wire covered with plastic or paper that you twist in order to keep a plastic bag closed

twist-y /ˈtwɪsti/ *adj.* (especially of a road) having many bends or turns **SYN** WINDING, ZIGZAG

twit /twɪt/ *noun* (*informal*) a silly or annoying person

twitch /twɪtʃ/ *verb, noun*
- **verb** **1** [I, T] ~ **(sth)** if a part of your body **twitches**, or if you **twitch** it, it makes a sudden quick movement, sometimes one that you cannot control: *Her lips twitched with amusement.* ◆ *The cats watched each other, their tails twitching.* **2** [T, I] ~ **(sth)** to give something a short sharp pull; to be pulled in this way: *He twitched the package out of my hands.* ◆ *The curtains twitched as she rang the doorbell.*

● **noun 1** a sudden quick movement that you cannot control in one of your muscles: *She has a twitch in her left eye.* ◆ *a nervous twitch* **2** a sudden quick movement or feeling: *He greeted us with a mere twitch of his head.* ◆ *At that moment she felt the first twitch of anxiety.*

twitch·y /'twɪtʃi/ *adj.* (*informal*) **1** nervous or anxious about something **SYN** JITTERY **2** making sudden quick movements

Twit·ter™ /'twɪtər/ *noun* [U] a SOCIAL NETWORKING service that allows you to send out short regular messages about what you are doing, that people can access on the Internet or on their cell phones ⊃ compare MICROBLOGGING, TWEET *n.*

twit·ter /'twɪtər/ *verb, noun*
● **verb 1** [I] when birds **twitter**, they make a series of short high sounds **2** [I, T] **~ (on) (about sth)** | **+ speech** to talk quickly in a high excited voice, especially about something that is not very important **3** (also **tweet**) [I] to send a message using the Twitter™ SOCIAL NETWORKING service
● **noun** [sing.] **1** (also **twit·ter·ing**) a series of short high sounds that birds make **2** (*informal*) a state of nervous excitement **3** = TWEET

'**twixt** /twɪkst/ *prep.* (*old use*) between **IDM** see SLIP

two /tu/ *number* **2 HELP** There are examples of how to use numbers at the entry for **five**.
IDM a day, moment, pound, etc. or two one or a few days, moments, pounds, etc.: *May I borrow it for a day or two?* **be of two minds about sth/about doing sth** to be unable to decide what you think about someone or something, or whether to do something or not: *I was of two minds about the book* (= I didn't know if I liked it or not). ◆ *She's of two minds about accepting his invitation.* **in two** in or into two pieces or halves: *He broke the bar of chocolate in two and gave me half.* **in twos and threes** two or three at a time; in small numbers: *People arrived in twos and threes.* **it takes two to do sth** (*saying*) one person cannot be completely responsible for something: *You can't put all the blame on him. It takes two to make a marriage.* **not have two nickles, brain cells, etc. to rub together** (*informal*) to have no money; to be very stupid, etc. **(there are) no two ways about it** (*saying*) used to show that you are certain about something: *It was the wrong decision—there are no two ways about it.* **put two and two together** to guess the truth from what you see, hear, etc.: *He's inclined to put two and two together and make five* (= reaches the wrong conclusion from what he sees, hears, etc.). **that makes two of us** (*informal*) I am in the same position or I agree with you: *"I'm tired!" "That makes two of us!"* **two can play (at) that game** (*saying*) used to tell someone who has played a trick on you that you can do the same thing to them **two's company (, three's a crowd)** (*saying*) used to suggest that it is better to be in a group of only two people than have a third person with you as well **two sides of the same coin** to talk about two ways of looking at the same situation ⊃ more at SHAKE *n.*

'**two-bit** *adj.* [only before noun] (*informal*) not good or important: *She wanted to be more than just a two-bit secretary.*

ˌtwo '**bits** *noun* [pl.] (*old-fashioned, informal*) 25 cents

ˌtwo-di'**mensional** *adj.* flat; having no depth; appearing to have only two DIMENSIONS: *a two-dimensional drawing* ◆ (*figurative*) *The novel was criticized for its two-dimensional characters* (= that did not seem like real people).

ˌtwo-'**edged** *adj.* **1** (of a blade, knife, etc.) having two sharp edges for cutting **2** having two possible meanings or results, one good and one bad: *a two-edged remark* ◆ *Fame can be a two-edged sword.*

'**two-faced** *adj.* (*informal, disapproving*) not sincere; not acting in a way that supports what you say that you believe; saying different things to different people about a particular subject

two·fold /'tufoʊld/ *adj.* (*formal*) **1** consisting of two parts: *The problem was twofold.* **2** twice as much or as many: *a twofold increase in demand* ► **two·fold** /ˌtu'foʊld/ *adv.*: *Her original investment has increased twofold.*

ˌtwo-'**four** *noun* (*CanE, informal*) a case holding 24 cans or bottles of beer

ˌtwo-'**handed** *adj.* using or needing both hands: *a two-handed backhand* (= in TENNIS) ◆ *a two-handed catch*

ˌtwo-'**hander** *noun* a play that is written for only two actors

ˌtwo-'**piece** *noun* a set of clothes consisting of two matching pieces of clothing, for example a skirt and jacket or pants and a jacket ► '**two-piece** *adj.*: *a two-piece suit*

ˌtwo-'**ply** *adj.* (of wool, wood, or other material) with two threads or thicknesses

ˌtwo-'**seater** *noun* a vehicle, an aircraft, or a piece of furniture with seats for two people

two·some /'tusəm/ *noun* a group of two people who do something together **SYN** PAIR

'**two-star** *adj.* [usually before noun] **1** having two stars in a system that measures quality. The highest standard is usually represented by four or five stars: *a two-star hotel* **2** having the fourth-highest military rank, and wearing a uniform that has two stars on it

'**two-stroke** *adj.* (of an engine or vehicle) with a PISTON that makes two movements, one up and one down, in each power CYCLE ⊃ compare FOUR-STROKE

'**two-time** *verb* **~ sb** (*informal*) to not be faithful to a person you have a relationship with, especially a sexual one, by having a secret relationship with someone else at the same time: *Are you sure he's not two-timing you?* ► '**two-ˌtimer** *noun*

'**two-tone** *adj.* [only before noun] having two different colors or sounds

'**twould** /twʊd/ *abbr.* (*old use*) it would

ˌtwo-'**way** *adj.* [usually before noun] **1** moving in two different directions; allowing something to move in two different directions: *two-way traffic* ◆ *two-way trade* ◆ *a two-way switch* (= that allows electric current to be turned on or off from either of two points) **2** (of communication between people) needing equal effort from both people or groups involved: *Friendship is a two-way process.* ◆ *Learning is a two-way street. What lessons have you learned from students?* **3** (of radio equipment, etc.) used both for sending and receiving signals

ˌtwo-way '**mirror** *noun* a piece of glass that is a mirror on one side, but that you can see through from the other

TX *abbr.* (in writing) Texas

ty·coon /taɪ'kun/ *noun* a person who is successful in business or industry and has become rich and powerful: *a business/property/media tycoon*

ty·ing ⊃ TIE *v.*

tyke (also **tike**) /taɪk/ *noun* (*informal*) a small child, especially one who behaves badly

tym·pa·num /'tɪmpənəm/ *noun* (*pl.* **tym·pa·nums** or **tym·pa·na** /-nə/) (*anatomy*) the EARDRUM

type 🔑 /taɪp/ *noun, verb*
● **noun 1** [C] **~ (of sth)** a class or group of people or things that share particular qualities or features and are part of a larger group; a kind or sort: *different racial types* ◆ *a rare blood type* ◆ *There are three main types of contracts.* ◆ *Saltboxes are a type of house.* ◆ *She is friendly with all types of people.* ◆ *She is friendly with people of all types.* ◆ *I love this type of book.* ◆ *I love these types of books.* ◆ (*informal*) *I love these type of books.* ◆ *What do you charge for this type of work?* ◆ *What do you charge for work of this type?* ◆ *It is the first car of its type to have this design feature.* ⊃ note at KIND **2** [sing.] (*informal*) a person of a particular character, with particular features, etc.: *She's the artistic type.* ◆ *He's not the type to be unfaithful.* ◆ *She's not my type* (= not the kind of person I am usually attracted to). **3** **-type** (in adjectives) having the qualities or features of the group, person, or thing mentioned: *a police-type badge* ◆ *a continental-type café* **4** [U] letters that are printed or typed: *The type was too small for me to read.* ◆ *The important words are in bold type.*

• **verb 1** [I, T] to write something using a computer or TYPE-WRITER: *How fast can you type?* ♦ *typing errors* ♦ **~ sth (out/in/up)** *This letter will need to be typed (out) again.* ♦ *Type (in) the filename, then press "Return."* ♦ *Has that report been typed up yet?* **2** [T] **~ sb/sth** (*technical*) to find out the group or class that a person or thing belongs to: *Blood samples were taken from patients for typing.*

type·cast /'taɪpkæst/ *verb* (type·cast, type·cast) [usually passive] **~ sb (as sth)** if an actor is **typecast**, he or she is always given the same kind of character to play: *She didn't want to be typecast as a dumb blonde.*

type·face /'taɪpfeɪs/ *noun* a set of letters, numbers, etc. of a particular design, used in printing: *I'd like the heading to be in a different typeface from the text.*

type·script /'taɪpskrɪpt/ *noun* [C, U] a copy of a text or document that has been typed

type·set·ter /'taɪpˌsɛtər/ *noun* a person, machine, or company that prepares a book, etc. for printing ▶ **type·set** *verb* (type·set·ting, type·set, type·set): **~ sth** *Pages can now be typeset on-screen.* **type·set·ting** *noun* [U]: *computerized typesetting*

type·writ·er /'taɪpˌraɪtər/ *noun* a machine that produces writing similar to print. It has keys that you press to make metal letters or signs hit a piece of paper through a strip of cloth covered with ink. ⊃ **see also** TYPIST

type·writ·ing /'taɪpˌraɪtɪŋ/ *noun* = TYPING

type·writ·ten /'taɪpˌrɪtn/ *adj.* written using a typewriter or computer

ty·phoid /'taɪfɔɪd/ (also *less frequent* ˌtyphoid 'fever) *noun* [U] a serious infectious disease that causes fever, red spots on the chest, and severe pain in the BOWELS, and sometimes causes death: *a typhoid epidemic*

ty·phoon /taɪ'fun/ *noun* a violent tropical storm with very strong winds ⊃ **compare** CYCLONE, HURRICANE

ty·phus /'taɪfəs/ *noun* [U] a serious infectious disease that causes fever, headaches, purple marks on the body, and often death

typ·i·cal 🖉 /'tɪpɪkl/ *adj.*
1 having the usual qualities or features of a particular type of person, thing, or group **SYN** REPRESENTATIVE: *a typical Italian café* ♦ *This is a typical example of Roman pottery.* ♦ **~ of sb/sth** *This meal is typical of local cuisine.* ♦ **~ for sb/sth** *The weather at the moment is not typical for July.* **ANT** ATYPICAL **2** happening in the usual way; showing what something is usually like **SYN** NORMAL: *A typical working day for me begins at 7:30.* **ANT** UNTYPICAL **3 ~ (of sb/sth)** (often *disapproving*) behaving in the way that you expect: *It was typical of her to forget.* ♦ *He spoke with typical enthusiasm.* ♦ (*informal*) *She's late again—typical!*

typ·i·cal·ly 🖉 /'tɪpɪkli/ *adv.*
1 used to say that something usually happens in the way that you are stating: *The factory typically produces 500 chairs a week.* ♦ *A typically priced meal will be around $10.* **2** in a way that shows the usual qualities or features of a particular type of person, thing, or group: *typically American hospitality* ♦ *Mothers typically worry about their children.* **3** in the way that you expect someone or something to behave: *Typically,*

she couldn't find her keys. ♦ *He was typically modest about his achievements.*

typ·i·fy /'tɪpəˌfaɪ/ *verb* (typ·i·fies, typ·i·fy·ing, typ·i·fied, typ·i·fied) (not usually used in the progressive tenses) **1 ~ sth** to be a typical example of something: *clothes that typify the 1960s* ♦ *the new style of politician, typified by the President* **2 ~ sth** to be a typical feature of something: *the haunting guitar melodies that typify the band's music*

typ·ing /'taɪpɪŋ/ (also *less frequent* type·writ·ing) *noun* [U] **1** the activity or job of using a TYPEWRITER or computer to write something: *to do the typing* ♦ *typing errors* ♦ *a* **typing pool** (= a group of people who share a company's typing work) **2** writing that has been done on a TYPEWRITER or computer

typ·ist /'taɪpɪst/ *noun* **1** a person who works in an office typing letters, etc. **2** a person who uses a TYPEWRITER or computer keyboard: *I'm a pretty fast typist.*

ty·po /'taɪpoʊ/ *noun* (*pl.* ty·pos) (*informal*) a small mistake in a typed or printed text

ty·pog·ra·pher /taɪ'pɑgrəfər/ *noun* a person who is skilled in typography

ty·pog·ra·phy /taɪ'pɑgrəfi/ *noun* [U] the art or work of preparing books, etc. for printing, especially of designing how text will appear when it is printed ▶ **ty·po·graph·i·cal** /ˌtaɪpə'græfɪkl/ (also **ty·po·graph·ic** /ˌtaɪpə'græfɪk/) *adj.*: *a typographical error* ♦ *typographic design* **ty·po·graph·i·cal·ly** /-kli/ *adv.*

ty·pol·o·gy /taɪ'pɑlədʒi/ *noun* (*pl.* ty·pologies) (*technical*) a system of dividing things into different types

ty·ran·ni·cal /tə'rænɪkl/ (also *formal* **ty·ran·nous** /'tɪrənəs/) *adj.* using power or authority over people in an unfair and cruel way **SYN** DICTATORIAL

tyr·an·nize /'tɪrəˌnaɪz/ *verb* [T, I] to use your power to treat someone in a cruel or unfair way: **~ sb/sth** *a father tyrannizing his children* ♦ **~ over sb/sth** *a political leader who tyrannizes over his people* ⊃ **see also** TYRANT

ty·ran·no·saur /tə'rænəˌsɔr; taɪ-/ (also **ty·ran·no·saur·us** /tə.rænə'sɔrəs/) *noun* a very large DINOSAUR that stood on two legs and that had large powerful JAWS and two short front legs

tyr·an·ny /'tɪrəni/ *noun* (*pl.* tyrannies) [U, C] **1** unfair or cruel use of power or authority: *a victim of oppression and tyranny* ♦ *The children had no protection against the tyranny of their father.* ♦ *the tyrannies of Nazi rule* ♦ (*figurative*) *These days it seems we must all submit to the tyranny of the automobile.* **2** the rule of a tyrant; a country under this rule **SYN** DICTATORSHIP: *Any political system refusing to allow dissent becomes a tyranny.*

ty·rant /'taɪrənt/ *noun* a person who has complete power in a country and uses it in a cruel and unfair way **SYN** DICTATOR: *The country was ruled by a succession of tyrants.* ♦ (*figurative*) *His boss is a complete tyrant.*

ty·ro /'taɪroʊ/ *noun* (*pl.* ty·ros) a person who has little or no experience of something or is beginning to learn something **SYN** NOVICE

tzar, tza·ri·na, tzar·ism = CZAR, CZARINA, CZARISM

U u

U /yu/ noun also **u** (pl. **Us, U's, u's** /yuz/) [C, U] the 21st letter of the English alphabet: *"Under" begins with (a) U/"U."* ➔ see also U-BOAT, U-TURN

U-bend noun a section of pipe shaped like a U, especially one that carries away used water

uber- (also **über-**) /ˈubər/ combining form (from German, informal) (in nouns and adjectives) of the greatest or best kind; to a very large degree: *His girlfriend was a real uber-babe, with long blonde hair and a big smile.* ◆ *The movie stars the uber-cool Jean Reno.*

u·biq·ui·tous /yuˈbɪkwətəs/ adj. [usually before noun] (formal or humorous) seeming to be everywhere or in several places at the same time; very common: *the ubiquitous bicycles of university towns* ◆ *the ubiquitous movie star, Tom Hanks* ▶ **u·biq·ui·tous·ly** adv. **u·biq·ui·ty** /yuˈbɪkwəti/ noun [U]: *the ubiquity of the mass media*

U-boat noun a German SUBMARINE (= a ship that can travel underwater)

u.c. abbr. (in writing) UPPERCASE

ud·der /ˈʌdər/ noun an organ shaped like a bag that produces milk and hangs underneath the body of a cow, GOAT, etc.

UFO (also **ufo**) /ˌyu ɛf ˈou/ noun (pl. **UFOs**) the abbreviation for "Unidentified Flying Object" (a strange object that some people claim to have seen in the sky and believe is a SPACECRAFT from another planet) ➔ compare FLYING SAUCER

u·fol·o·gy /yuˈfalədʒi/ noun [U] the study of UFOs

ugh /ʌg; ʌh; ʊx/ exclamation the way of writing the sound that people make when they think something is disgusting or unpleasant: *Ugh! How can you eat that stuff?*

Ug·li™ /ˈʌgli/ (also **Ug·li fruit**) noun a large CITRUS fruit with a rough, yellowish-orange skin and sweet flesh with a lot of juice

ug·ly /ˈʌgli/ adj. (**ug·li·er, ug·li·est**)
1 unpleasant to look at SYN UNATTRACTIVE: *an ugly face* ◆ *an ugly building* **2** (of an event, a situation, etc.) unpleasant or dangerous; involving threats or violence: *an ugly incident* ◆ *There were ugly scenes in the streets last night as rioting continued.* **IDM** see REAR v., SIN n. ▶ **ug·li·ness** noun [U]

ugly duckling noun a person or thing that at first does not seem attractive or likely to succeed but that later becomes successful or much admired **ORIGIN** From the title of a story by Hans Christian Andersen, in which a young swan thinks it is an ugly young duck until it grows up into a beautiful adult swan.

uh /ʌ/ exclamation the way of writing the sound that people make when they are not sure about something, when they do not hear or understand something you have said, or when they want you to agree with what they have said: *Uh, yeah, I guess so.* ◆ *"Are you ready yet?" "Uh? Oh. Yes."* ◆ *We can discuss this another time, uh?*

UHF /ˌyu eɪtʃ ˈɛf/ abbr. ultra-high frequency (a range of radio waves used for high-quality radio and television broadcasting)

uh-huh /ʌ ˈhʌ; ã ˈhã/ exclamation the way of writing the sound that people make when they understand or agree with what you have said, when they want you to continue, or when they are answering "Yes": *"Did you read my note?" "Uh-huh."*

uh-oh /ˈʌ ou/ (also ˈoh-oh) exclamation the way of writing the sound that people make when they want to say that they have done something wrong or that they think there will be trouble: *Uh-oh. I forgot to write that letter.* ◆ *Uh-oh! Turn the TV off. Here comes Dad!*

uh-uh exclamation the way of writing the sound that people make when they are answering "No" to a question

U-ie /ˈyui/ noun (informal) a turn of 180° that a vehicle makes so that it can move forward in the opposite direction SYN U-TURN

U.K. /ˌyu ˈkeɪ/ abbr. UNITED KINGDOM

u·ku·le·le /ˌyukəˈleɪli/ noun a musical instrument with four strings, like a small GUITAR

ul·cer /ˈʌlsər/ noun a sore area on the outside of the body or on the surface of an organ inside the body which is painful and may BLEED or produce a poisonous substance: *a stomach ulcer* ➔ see also MOUTH ULCER

ul·cer·ate /ˈʌlsəˌreɪt/ verb [I, T, usually passive] ~ **(sth)** (medical) to become, or make something become, covered with ulcers ▶ **ul·cer·a·tion** /ˌʌlsəˈreɪʃn/ noun [U, C]

ul·na /ˈʌlnə/ noun (pl. **ul·nae** /-ni/) (anatomy) the longer bone of the two bones in the lower part of the arm between the elbow and the wrist, on the side opposite the thumb ➔ picture at BODY ➔ see also RADIUS

ul·te·ri·or /ʌlˈtɪriər/ adj. [only before noun] (of a reason for doing something) that someone keeps hidden and does not admit: *She must have some ulterior motive for being nice to me —what does she really want?*

ul·ti·mate 🔑 **AWL** /ˈʌltəmət/ adj., noun
● **adj.** [only before noun] **1** happening at the end of a long process SYN FINAL: *our ultimate goal/aim/objective/target* ◆ *We will accept ultimate responsibility for whatever happens.* ◆ *The ultimate decision lies with the parents.* **2** most extreme; best, worst, greatest, most important, etc.: *This race will be the ultimate test of your skill.* ◆ *Silk sheets are the ultimate luxury.* **3** from which something originally comes SYN BASIC, FUNDAMENTAL: *the ultimate truths of philosophy and science*
● **noun 1** [sing.] **the ~ in sth** (informal) the best, most advanced, greatest, etc. of its kind: *the ultimate in modern design* **2 Ultimate** [U] = ULTIMATE FRISBEE

ultimate ˈfighting (also exˈtreme ˈfighting) noun [U] a sport that combines different styles of fighting such as BOXING, WRESTLING, and MARTIAL ARTS and in which there are not many rules

Ultimate ˈFrisbee (also ˌultimate ˈfrisbee) (also Ul·ti·mate) noun [U] a sport like football that is played by throwing a FRISBEE™ or similar light plastic disk

ul·ti·mate·ly 🔑 **AWL** /ˈʌltəmətli/ adv.
1 in the end; finally: *Ultimately, you'll have to make the decision yourself.* ◆ *A poor diet will ultimately lead to illness.* **2** at the most basic and important level: *All life depends ultimately on oxygen.*

ul·ti·ma·tum /ˌʌltəˈmeɪtəm/ noun (pl. **ul·ti·ma·tums** or **ul·ti·ma·ta**) a final warning to a person or country that if they do not do what you ask, you will use force or take action against them: *to issue an ultimatum*

ul·tra /ˈʌltrə/ noun a person who holds extreme views, especially in politics

ultra- /ˈʌltrə/ prefix (in adjectives and nouns) extremely; beyond a particular limit: *ultra-modern* ◆ *ultraviolet* ➔ compare INFRA-

ˌultra-high ˈfrequency noun [U] = UHF

ul·tra·light /ˈʌltrəˌlaɪt/ noun a very small light aircraft for one or two people

ul·tra·ma·rine /ˌʌltrəməˈrin/ noun [U] a bright blue color

ul·tra·short /ˌʌltrəˈʃɔrt/ adj. (of radio waves) having a very short WAVELENGTH (shorter than 10 meters), with a FREQUENCY greater than 30 MEGAHERTZ ➔ compare LONG WAVE, MEDIUM WAVE, SHORTWAVE

---

ul·tra·son·ic /ˌʌltrəˈsɑnɪk/ adj. [usually before noun] (of sounds) higher than humans can hear: *ultrasonic waves*

ul·tra·sound /ˈʌltrəˌsaʊnd/ noun **1** [U] sound that is higher than humans can hear **2** [U, C] a medical process that produces an image of what is inside your body: *Ultrasound showed she was expecting twins.* ➔ compare SONOGRAM

ul·tra·vi·o·let /ˌʌltrəˈvaɪələt/ (abbr. UV) adj. [usually before noun] (physics) of or using ELECTROMAGNETIC waves that are just shorter than those of VIOLET light in the SPECTRUM and that cannot be seen: *ultraviolet rays* (= that cause the skin to go darker) ◆ *an ultraviolet lamp* ➔ compare INFRARED

ul·u·late /ˈʌlyəˌleɪt; ˈyulyə-/ verb [I] (literary) to give a long cry **SYN** WAIL ▶ **ul·u·la·tion** /ˌʌlyəˈleɪʃn; ˌyulyə-/ noun [U, C]

um /ʌm; m/ exclamation the way of writing the sound that people make when they hesitate, or do not know what to say next: *Um, I'm not sure how to ask you this....*

u·ma·mi /uˈmɑmi/ noun [U] a taste found in some foods that is neither sweet, sour, bitter, nor salty: *Tomatoes have lots of umami.*

um·ber /ˈʌmbər/ noun [U] a dark brown or yellowish-brown color used in paints

um·bil·i·cal cord /ʌmˈbɪlɪkl ˈkɔrd/ noun a long piece of TISSUE that connects a baby to its mother before it is born and is cut at the moment of birth

um·bil·i·cus /ʌmˈbɪlɪkəs/ noun (pl. um·bil·i·ci /ʌmˈbɪləˌsaɪ; -ˌkaɪ/ or um·bil·i·cus·es) (technical) the NAVEL

um·bra /ˈʌmbrə/ noun (pl. um·bras or um·brae /-bri/) (technical) **1** the darkest part of a shadow **2** the area on the earth or the moon that is the darkest during an ECLIPSE ➔ compare PENUMBRA

um·brage /ˈʌmbrɪdʒ/ noun
IDM **take umbrage (at sth)** (formal or humorous) to feel offended, insulted, or upset by something, often without a good reason **SYN** TAKE OFFENSE

um·brel·la /ʌmˈbrelə/ noun
1 an object with a round folding frame of long, straight pieces of metal covered with material, that you use to protect yourself from the rain or from hot sun: *I put up my umbrella.* ◆ *colorful beach umbrellas* ➔ compare PARASOL, SUNSHADE **2** a thing that contains or includes many different parts or elements: *Many previously separate groups are now operating under the umbrella of a single authority.* ◆ *an umbrella organization/group/fund* ◆ *"Contact sports" is an umbrella term for a variety of different sports.* **3** a country or system that protects people

um·laut /ˈʊmlaʊt/ noun the mark placed over a vowel in some languages to show how it should be pronounced, as over the *u* in the German word *für* ➔ compare ACUTE ACCENT, CIRCUMFLEX, GRAVE¹, TILDE

UMPC /ˌyu ɛm pi ˈsi/ noun (computing) a very small computer that is easy to carry, often with a touch screen and sometimes without a physical keyboard (the abbreviation for "ultra-mobile personal computer")

um·pire /ˈʌmpaɪər/ noun, verb
● **noun** (also informal **ump**) (in sports such as TENNIS and baseball) a person whose job is to watch a game and make sure that rules are not broken ➔ picture at BASEBALL ➔ compare REFEREE

● **verb** [I, T] to act as an umpire: *We need someone to umpire.* ◆ ~ **sth** *to umpire a game of baseball*

ump·teen /ˈʌmptin/ det. (informal) very many: *I've told this story umpteen times.* ▶ **ump·teen** pron.: *Umpteen of them all arrived at once.* **ump·teenth** /ˈʌmptinθ/ det.: *"This is crazy," she told herself for the umpteenth time* (= she had done it many times before).

UN (also **U.N.**) /ˌyu ˈɛn/ abbr. United Nations (an association of many countries that aims to help economic and social conditions improve and to solve political problems in the world in a peaceful way): *the UN Security Council* ◆ *a UN peacekeeping plan*

un- /ʌn/ prefix **1** (in adjectives, adverbs, and nouns) not; the opposite of: *unable* ◆ *unconsciously* ◆ *untruth* ◆ *an un-American concept such as subsidized medical treatment* (= not typical of the U.S.) **2** (in verbs that describe the opposite of a process): *unlock* ◆ *undo*

un·a·bashed /ˌʌnəˈbæʃt/ adj. not ashamed, embarrassed, or affected by people's disapproval, when other people would be **ANT** ABASHED ▶ **un·a·bash·ed·ly** /ˌʌnəˈbæʃədli/ adv.

un·a·bat·ed /ˌʌnəˈbeɪtəd/ adj. [not usually before noun] (formal) without becoming any less strong: *The rain continued unabated.*

un·a·ble /ʌnˈeɪbl/ adj. [not before noun] ~ **to do sth** (somewhat formal)
not having the skill, strength, time, knowledge, etc. to do something: *He lay there, unable to move.* ◆ *I tried to contact him but was unable to.* **ANT** ABLE

un·a·bridged /ˌʌnəˈbrɪdʒd/ adj. (of a novel, play, speech, etc.) complete, without being made shorter in any way **ANT** ABRIDGEd

un·ac·cent·ed /ʌnˈæksɛntəd/ adj. **1** (of someone's speech) having no regional or foreign accent **2** (phonetics) (of a syllable) having no stress

un·ac·cept·a·ble /ˌʌnəkˈsɛptəbl/ adj.
that you cannot accept, allow, or approve of: *Such behavior is totally unacceptable in a civilized society.* ◆ *Noise from the factory has reached an unacceptable level.* **ANT** ACCEPTABLE ▶ **un·ac·cept·a·bly** /-bli/ adv.: *unacceptably high levels of unemployment*

un·ac·com·pa·nied /ˌʌnəˈkʌmpənid/ adj. **1** (formal) without a person going together with someone or something: *No unaccompanied children allowed.* ◆ *unaccompanied luggage/baggage* (= traveling separately from its owner) **2** (music) performed without anyone else playing or singing at the same time: *a sonata for unaccompanied violin* **3** (formal) ~ **by sth** not together with a particular thing: *Mere words, unaccompanied by any violence, cannot amount to an assault.*

un·ac·count·a·ble /ˌʌnəˈkaʊntəbl/ adj. (formal) **1** impossible to understand or explain **SYN** INEXPLICABLE: *For some unaccountable reason, the letter never arrived.* **2** ~ **(to sb/sth)** not having to explain or give reasons for your actions to anyone: *Too many government departments are unaccountable to the general public.* **ANT** ACCOUNTABLE

un·ac·count·a·bly /ˌʌnəˈkaʊntəbli/ adv. (formal) in a way that is very difficult to explain; without any obvious reason: *He has been unaccountably delayed.*

un·ac·count·ed for /ˌʌnəˈkaʊntəd ˌfɔr/ adj. [not before noun] **1** a person or thing that is **unaccounted for** cannot be found and people do not know what has happened to them or it: *At least 300 civilians are unaccounted for after the bombing raids.* **2** not explained: *In the story he gave the police, half an hour was left unaccounted for.*

un·ac·cus·tomed /ˌʌnəˈkʌstəmd/ adj. (formal) **1** ~ **to sth/to doing sth** not in the habit of doing something; not used to something: *He was unaccustomed to hard work.* ◆ *I am unaccustomed to being told what to do.* **2** [usually before noun] not usual, normal, or familiar: *The unaccustomed heat made him weary.* **ANT** ACCUSTOMED

un·a·chiev·a·ble /ˌʌnəˈtʃivəbl/ adj. that you cannot manage to reach or obtain: *unachievable goals*

un·ac·knowl·edged /ˌʌnəkˈnɑlɪdʒd/ adj. **1** not receiving the thanks or praise that is deserved: *Her contribution to the research went largely unacknowledged.* **2** that people do not admit as existing or true; that people are not aware of: *unacknowledged feelings* **3** not publicly or officially recognized: *the unacknowledged leader of the group*

un·ac·quaint·ed /ˌʌnəˈkweɪntəd/ adj. ~ **(with sth/sb)** (formal) not familiar with something or someone; having no experience of something: *visitors unacquainted with local customs* **ANT** ACQUAINTED

un·ad·just·ed /ˌʌnəˈdʒʌstəd/ adj. (statistics) (of figures) not

h **hat**   m **man**   n **no**   ŋ **sing**   l **leg**   r **red**   y **yes**   w **wet**

adjusted according to particular facts or circumstances: *Unadjusted figures which do not take tourism into account showed that unemployment fell in July.*

un·a·dorned /ˌʌnəˈdɔrnd/ *adj.* (*formal*) without any decoration **SYN** SIMPLE: *The walls were plain and unadorned.*

un·a·dul·ter·at·ed /ˌʌnəˈdʌltəˌreɪtəd/ *adj.* **1** [usually before noun] you use **unadulterated** to emphasize that something is complete or total **SYN** UNDILUTED: *For me, the vacation was sheer, unadulterated pleasure.* **2** not mixed with other substances; not ADULTERATED **SYN** PURE: *unadulterated foods*

un·ad·ven·tur·ous /ˌʌnədˈventʃərəs/ *adj.* not willing to take risks or try new and exciting things **SYN** CAUTIOUS **ANT** ADVENTUROUS

un·af·fect·ed **AWL** /ˌʌnəˈfektəd/ *adj.* **1** ~ (**by sth**) not changed or influenced by something; not affected by something: *People's rights are unaffected by the new law.* ◆ *Some members of the family may remain unaffected by the disease.* **2** (*approving*) (of a person or their behavior) natural and sincere **ANT** AFFECTED

un·af·fil·i·at·ed /ˌʌnəˈfɪliˌeɪtəd/ *adj.* ~ (**with sth**) not belonging to or connected with a political party or a large organization **SYN** INDEPENDENT **ANT** AFFILIATED

un·af·ford·a·ble /ˌʌnəˈfɔrdəbl/ *adj.* costing so much that people do not have enough money to pay for it: *Health insurance is now unaffordable for many people.*

un·a·fraid /ˌʌnəˈfreɪd/ *adj.* [not before noun] (*formal*) not afraid or nervous; not worried about what might happen: ~ (**of sth**) *She was unafraid of conflict.* ◆ ~ (**to do sth**) *He's unafraid to speak his mind.*

un·aid·ed **AWL** /ʌnˈeɪdəd/ *adj.* without help from anyone or anything: *He can now walk unaided.*

un·al·ien·a·ble /ʌnˈeɪliənəbl; -ˈeɪlyə-/ *adj.* = INALIENABLE

un·al·loyed /ˌʌnəˈlɔɪd/ *adj.* (*formal*) not mixed with anything else, such as negative feelings **SYN** PURE: *unalloyed joy*

un·al·ter·a·ble **AWL** /ʌnˈɔltərəbl/ *adj.* (*formal*) that cannot be changed **SYN** IMMUTABLE: *the unalterable laws of the universe*

un·al·tered **AWL** /ʌnˈɔltərd/ *adj.* that has not changed or been changed: *This practice has remained unaltered for centuries.*

un·am·big·u·ous **AWL** /ˌʌnæmˈbɪgyuəs/ *adj.* clear in meaning; that can only be understood in one way: *an unambiguous statement* ◆ *The message was clear and unambiguous—"Get out!"* **ANT** AMBIGUOUS ► **un·am·big·u·ous·ly** **AWL** *adv.*

un·am·bi·tious /ˌʌnæmˈbɪʃəs/ *adj.* **1** (of a person) not interested in becoming successful, rich, powerful, etc. **2** not involving a lot of effort, time, money, etc. or anything new: *an unambitious plan* **ANT** AMBITIOUS

ˌun-Aˈmerican *adj.* against American values or interests

u·na·nim·i·ty /ˌyunəˈnɪməti/ *noun* [U] complete agreement about something among a group of people

u·nan·i·mous /yuˈnænəməs/ *adj.* **1** if a decision or an opinion is **unanimous**, it is agreed or shared by everyone in a group: *a unanimous vote* ◆ *unanimous support* ◆ *The decision was not unanimous.* **2** ~ (**in sth**) if a group of people are **unanimous**, they all agree about something: *Local people are unanimous in their opposition to the proposed new road.* ► **u·nan·i·mous·ly** *adv.*: *The motion was passed unanimously.*

un·an·nounced /ˌʌnəˈnaʊnst/ *adj.* happening without anyone being told or warned in advance: *She just turned up unannounced on my doorstep.* ◆ *an unannounced increase in bus fares*

un·an·swer·a·ble /ʌnˈænsərəbl/ *adj.* **1** an **unanswerable** argument, etc. is one that nobody can question or disagree with **SYN** IRREFUTABLE: *They presented an unanswerable case for more investment.* **2** an **unanswerable** question is one that has no answer or that you cannot answer

un·an·swered /ʌnˈænsərd/ *adj.* **1** (of a question, problem, etc.) that has not been answered: *Many questions about the crime remain unanswered.* **2** (of a letter, telephone call, etc.) that has not been replied to: *unanswered letters*

un·an·tic·i·pat·ed **AWL** /ˌʌnænˈtɪsəˌpeɪtəd/ *adj.* (*formal*) that you have not expected or predicted; that you have not anticipated: *unanticipated costs*

un·a·pol·o·get·ic /ˌʌnəˌpɑləˈdʒetɪk/ *adj.* not saying that you are sorry about something, even in situations in which other people might expect you to **ANT** APOLOGETIC ► **un·a·pol·o·get·i·cal·ly** /-kli/ *adv.*

un·ap·peal·ing /ˌʌnəˈpilɪŋ/ *adj.* not attractive or pleasant: *The room was painted in an unappealing shade of brown.* ◆ *The prospect of studying for another five years was distinctly unappealing.* **ANT** APPEALING

un·ap·pe·tiz·ing /ˌʌnˈæpəˌtaɪzɪŋ/ *adj.* (of food) unpleasant to eat; looking as if it will be unpleasant to eat **ANT** APPETIZING

un·ap·pre·ci·at·ed **AWL** /ˌʌnəˈpriʃiˌeɪtəd/ *adj.* [not usually before noun] not having your work or your qualities recognized and enjoyed by other people; not appreciated: *He was in a job where he felt unappreciated and undervalued.*

un·ap·proach·a·ble **AWL** /ˌʌnəˈproʊtʃəbl/ *adj.* (of a person) unfriendly and not easy to talk to **ANT** APPROACHABLE

un·ar·gu·a·ble /ʌnˈɑrgyuəbl/ *adj.* (*formal*) that nobody can disagree with: *unarguable proof* ⊃ compare ARGUABLE ► **un·ar·gu·a·bly** /-bli/ *adv.*: *She is unarguably one of the country's finest athletes.*

un·armed /ʌnˈɑrmd/ *adj.* **1** not carrying a weapon: *unarmed civilians* **2** not involving the use of weapons: *The soldiers were trained in unarmed combat.* **ANT** ARMED

un·a·shamed /ˌʌnəˈʃeɪmd/ *adj.* feeling no shame or embarrassment about something, especially when people might expect you to ⊃ compare ASHAMED ► **un·a·sham·ed·ly** /ˌʌnəˈʃeɪmədli/ *adv.*: *She wept unashamedly.* ◆ *an unashamedly sentimental song*

un·asked /ʌnˈæskt/ *adj.* **1** an **unasked** question is one that you have not asked even though you would like to know the answer **2** without being invited or asked: *He came to the party unasked.* ◆ *She brought him, unasked, the relevant file.*

unˈasked-for *adj.* that has not been asked for or requested: *unasked-for advice*

un·as·sail·a·ble /ˌʌnəˈseɪləbl/ *adj.* (*formal*) that cannot be destroyed, defeated, or questioned: *The party now has an unassailable lead.* ◆ *Their ten-point lead puts the team in an almost unassailable position.*

un·as·signed **AWL** /ˌʌnəˈsaɪnd/ *adj.* not given to or reserved for any particular person or purpose

un·as·sist·ed **AWL** /ˌʌnəˈsɪstəd/ *adj.* not helped by anyone or anything **SYN** UNAIDED: *She could not move unassisted.*

un·as·sum·ing /ˌʌnəˈsumɪŋ/ *adj.* (*approving*) not wanting to draw attention to yourself or to your abilities or status **SYN** MODEST

un·at·tached **AWL** /ˌʌnəˈtætʃt/ *adj.* **1** not married or involved in a romantic relationship **SYN** SINGLE: *He was still unattached at the age of 34.* **2** not connected with or belonging to a particular group or organization ⊃ compare ATTACHED

un·at·tain·a·ble **AWL** /ˌʌnəˈteɪnəbl/ *adj.* impossible to achieve or reach: *an unattainable goal* **ANT** ATTAINABLE

un·at·tend·ed /ˌʌnəˈtendəd/ *adj.* without the owner present; not being watched or cared for: *unattended vehicles* ◆ *Never leave young children unattended.*

un·at·trac·tive /ˌʌnəˈtræktɪv/ *adj.* **1** not attractive or pleasant to look at: *an unattractive brown color* **2** not good, interesting, or pleasant: *one of the unattractive aspects of the free market economy* **ANT** ATTRACTIVE ► **un·at·trac·tive·ly** *adv.*

un·au·thor·ized /ˌʌnˈɔθəˌraɪzd/ adj. without official permission: No access for unauthorized personnel.

un·a·vail·a·ble **AWL** /ˌʌnəˈveɪləbl/ adj. [not usually before noun] ~ (to sb/sth) 1 that cannot be obtained: Such luxuries are unavailable to ordinary people. 2 not able or not willing to see, meet, or talk to someone: The Vice President was *unavailable for comment*. **ANT** AVAILABLE ▶ **un·a·vail·a·bil·i·ty** /ˌʌnəˌveɪləˈbɪləti/ noun [U]

un·a·vail·ing /ˌʌnəˈveɪlɪŋ/ adj. (formal) without success **SYN** UNSUCCESSFUL: Their efforts were unavailing.

un·a·void·a·ble /ˌʌnəˈvɔɪdəbl/ adj. impossible to avoid or prevent: unavoidable delays **ANT** AVOIDABLE ▶ **un·a·void·a·bly** /-bli/ adv.: I was unavoidably delayed.

un·a·ware **AWL** /ˌʌnəˈwɛr/ adj. [not before noun] not knowing or realizing that something is happening or that something exists: ~ of sth He was completely unaware of the whole affair. ◆ ~ that... She was unaware that I could see her. **ANT** AWARE ⟳ collocations at AWARE ▶ **un·a·ware·ness** noun [U]

un·a·wares /ˌʌnəˈwɛrz/ adv. 1 when not expected: The camera had *caught her unawares*. ◆ The announcement *took me unawares*. ◆ She came upon him unawares when he was searching her room. 2 (formal) without noticing or realizing: He slipped unawares into sleep.

un·bal·ance /ʌnˈbæləns/ verb 1 ~ sth to make something no longer balanced, for example by giving too much importance to one part of it 2 ~ sb/sth to make someone or something unsteady so that they are likely to fall down 3 ~ sb to make someone slightly crazy or mentally ill

un·bal·anced /ʌnˈbælənst/ adj. 1 [not usually before noun] (of a person) slightly crazy; mentally ill 2 [usually before noun] giving too much or too little importance to one part or aspect of something: an unbalanced article ◆ an unbalanced diet

un·ban /ʌnˈbæn/ verb (-nn-) ~ sth to allow something that was banned before **ANT** BAN

un·bear·a·ble /ʌnˈbɛrəbl/ adj. too painful, annoying, or unpleasant to deal with or accept **SYN** INTOLERABLE: The heat was becoming unbearable. ◆ unbearable pain ◆ He's been unbearable since he won that prize. **ANT** BEARABLE ▶ **un·bear·a·bly** /-bli/ adv.: unbearably hot

un·beat·a·ble /ʌnˈbitəbl/ adj. 1 (of a team, player, etc.) impossible to defeat **SYN** INVINCIBLE 2 (of prices, value, etc.) impossible to improve: unbeatable offers

un·beat·en /ʌnˈbitn/ adj. (sports) not having been defeated: The Raptors are unbeaten in their last four games. ◆ They will be putting their unbeaten record to the test next Saturday.

un·be·com·ing /ˌʌnbɪˈkʌmɪŋ/ adj. (formal) 1 not suiting a particular person **SYN** UNFLATTERING: She was wearing an unbecoming shade of purple. 2 ~ (to/of sb) not appropriate or acceptable **SYN** INAPPROPRIATE: He was accused of conduct unbecoming to an officer. **ANT** BECOMING

un·be·fit·ting /ˌʌnbɪˈfɪtɪŋ/ adj. ~ (of/for/to sb/sth) (formal) not suitable or good enough for someone or something: His behavior is unbefitting of a university professor. ◆ The amount of litter in the streets is unbefitting for a historic city.

un·be·knownst /ˌʌnbɪˈnoʊnst/ (also **un·be·known** /ˌʌnbɪˈnoʊn/) adj. ~ to sb (formal) without the person mentioned knowing: Unbeknown to her they had organized a surprise party.

un·be·lief /ˌʌnbɪˈlif/ noun [U] (formal) lack of belief, or the state of not believing, especially in God, a religion, etc. ⟳ compare BELIEF, DISBELIEF

un·be·liev·a·ble /ˌʌnbɪˈlivəbl/ adj. 1 used to emphasize how good, bad, or extreme something is **SYN** INCREDIBLE: We had an unbelievable (= very good) time in Paris. ◆ Conditions in the prison camp were unbelievable (= very bad). ◆ The cold was unbelievable (= it was extremely cold). ◆ It's **unbelievable that** (= very shocking) they have permitted this trial to go ahead. 2 very difficult to believe and unlikely to be true **SYN** INCREDIBLE: I found the whole story bizarre, not to say

unbelievable. **ANT** BELIEVABLE ▶ **un·be·liev·a·bly** /-bli/ adv.: unbelievably bad/good ◆ Unbelievably it actually works.

un·be·liev·er /ˌʌnbɪˈlivər/ noun a person who does not believe, especially in God, a religion, etc. **ANT** BELIEVER ⟳ compare NONBELIEVER

un·be·liev·ing /ˌʌnbɪˈlivɪŋ/ adj. (formal) feeling or showing that you do not believe someone or something: She stared at us with unbelieving eyes. ◆ He gazed at the letter, unbelieving.

un·bend /ʌnˈbɛnd/ verb (un·bent, un·bent /-ˈbɛnt/) 1 [I] to relax and become less strict or formal in your behavior or attitude 2 [T, I] ~ (sth) to make something that was bent become straight; to become straight

un·bend·ing /ʌnˈbɛndɪŋ/ adj. (often disapproving) unwilling to change your opinions, decisions, etc. **SYN** INFLEXIBLE

un·bi·ased **AWL** /ʌnˈbaɪəst/ adj. fair and not influenced by your own or someone else's opinions, desires, etc. **SYN** IMPARTIAL: unbiased advice ◆ an unbiased judge **ANT** BIASED

un·bid·den /ʌnˈbɪdn/ adj. (literary) (usually used after the verb) without being asked, invited, or expected **SYN** UNASKED: He walked into the room unbidden.

un·bleached /ʌnˈblitʃt/ adj. not made whiter by the use of chemicals; not bleached: unbleached flour

un·blem·ished /ʌnˈblɛmɪʃt/ adj. (formal) not spoiled, damaged, or marked in any way: He had an unblemished reputation. ◆ her pale unblemished skin

un·blink·ing /ʌnˈblɪŋkɪŋ/ adj. (formal) if someone has an **unblinking stare** or looks with **unblinking eyes**, they look very steadily at something and do not BLINK ▶ **un·blink·ing·ly** adv.

un·block /ʌnˈblɑk/ verb ~ sth to clean something, for example a pipe, by removing something that is blocking it

un·born /ʌnˈbɔrn/ adj. [usually before noun] not yet born: her unborn baby

un·bound·ed /ʌnˈbaʊndəd/ adj. (formal) having, or seeming to have, no limits **SYN** BOUNDLESS, INFINITE: her unbounded energy

un·bowed /ʌnˈbaʊd/ adj. (literary) not defeated or not ready to accept defeat: The losing team left the field **bloody but unbowed**.

un·break·a·ble /ʌnˈbreɪkəbl/ adj. impossible to break **SYN** INDESTRUCTIBLE: This new material is virtually unbreakable. **ANT** BREAKABLE

un·bridge·a·ble /ʌnˈbrɪdʒəbl/ adj. an **unbridgeable** gap or difference between two people or groups or their opinions is one that cannot be closed or made less wide

un·bri·dled /ʌnˈbraɪdld/ adj. [usually before noun] (formal) not controlled and therefore extreme: unbridled passion

un·bro·ken /ʌnˈbroʊkən/ adj. 1 not interrupted or disturbed in any way: a single unbroken line ◆ 30 years of virtually unbroken peace ◆ my first night of unbroken sleep since the baby was born 2 (of a record in a sport, etc.) that has not been improved on

un·buck·le /ʌnˈbʌkl/ verb ~ sth to undo the BUCKLE of a belt, shoe, etc.

un·bur·den /ʌnˈbərdn/ verb 1 ~ yourself/sth (of sth) (to sb) (formal) to talk to someone about your problems or something you have been worrying about, so that you feel less anxious: She needed to unburden herself to somebody. 2 ~ sb/sth (of sth) to take something that causes a lot of work or worry away from someone or something **ANT** BURDEN

un·but·ton /ʌnˈbʌtn/ verb ~ sth to undo the buttons on a piece of clothing: He unbuttoned his shirt. **ANT** BUTTON (UP)

un·but·ton·ed /ʌnˈbʌtnd/ adj. informal and relaxed: Staff respond well to her unbuttoned style of management.

uncalled for /ʌnˈkɔld fɔr/ adj. (of behavior or remarks) not fair or appropriate **SYN** UNNECESSARY: His comments were uncalled for. ◆ uncalled-for comments

un·can·ny /ʌnˈkæni/ adj. strange and difficult to explain **SYN** WEIRD: I had an uncanny feeling I was being watched. ◆ It

ʌ **cup**   ə **about**   eɪ **say**   aɪ **five**   ɔɪ **boy**   aʊ **now**   oʊ **go**   ər **bird**

was really uncanny, almost as if she knew what I was thinking. ▶ **un·can·ni·ly** /-ˈkænl·i/ adv.: He looked uncannily like someone I knew.

un'cared for /ʌnˈkɛrd fɔr/ adj. not taken care of **SYN** NEGLECTED: The garden looked uncared for. ◆ an uncared-for garden

un·car·ing /ʌnˈkɛrɪŋ/ adj. (disapproving) not sympathetic about the problems or suffering of other people **SYN** CARING

un·ceas·ing /ʌnˈsisɪŋ/ adj. (formal) continuing all the time **SYN** INCESSANT: unceasing efforts ◆ Planes passed overhead with unceasing regularity. ▶ **un·ceas·ing·ly** adv.: Snow fell unceasingly.

un·cen·sored /ʌnˈsɛnsərd/ adj. (of a report, movie, etc.) not CENSORED (= having had parts removed that are not considered suitable for the public): an uncensored newspaper article

un·cer·e·mo·ni·ous /ˌʌnsɛrəˈmoʊniəs/ adj. (formal) done roughly and rudely: He was bundled out of the room with unceremonious haste. ⊃ compare CEREMONIOUS **un·cer·e·mo·ni·ous·ly** /ˌʌnsɛrəˈmoʊniəsli/ adv. (formal) in a rough or rude way, without caring about a person's feelings: They dumped his belongings unceremoniously on the floor.

un·cer·tain 🔑 /ʌnˈsərtn/ adj.
1 [not before noun] **~ (about/of sth)** feeling doubt about something; not sure: They're both uncertain about what to do. ◆ I'm still uncertain of my feelings for him. **ANT** CERTAIN **2** likely to change, especially in a negative or unpleasant way: Our future looks uncertain. ◆ a man of uncertain temper **3** not definite or decided **SYN** UNCLEAR: It is uncertain what his role in the company will be. **4** not confident **SYN** HESITANT: The baby took its first uncertain steps.
IDM **in no uncertain terms** clearly and strongly: I told him what I thought of him in no uncertain terms.

un·cer·tain·ly /ʌnˈsərtnli/ adv. without confidence **SYN** HESITANTly: They smiled uncertainly at one another.

un·cer·tain·ty /ʌnˈsərtnti/ noun (pl. un·cer·tain·ties) **1** [U] the state of being uncertain: There is considerable uncertainty about the company's future. ◆ He had an air of uncertainty about him. **2** [C] something that you cannot be sure about; a situation that causes you to be or feel uncertain: life's uncertainties ◆ the uncertainties of war

un·chal·lenge·a·ble /ʌnˈtʃæləndʒəbl/ adj. that cannot be questioned or argued with; that cannot be challenged: unchallengeable evidence

un·chal·lenged /ʌnˈtʃæləndʒd/ adj. **1** not doubted; accepted without question; not challenged: She could not allow such a claim to **go unchallenged**. **2** (of a ruler or leader, or their position) not opposed by anyone: He is in a position of unchallenged authority. ◆ an unchallenged candidate for an election **3** without being stopped and asked to explain who you are, what you are doing, etc.: I walked into the building unchallenged.

un·change·a·ble /ʌnˈtʃeɪndʒəbl/ adj. that cannot be changed: unchangeable laws ⊃ compare CHANGEABLE

un·changed /ʌnˈtʃeɪndʒd/ adj. [not usually before noun] that has stayed the same and not changed: My opinion remains unchanged.

un·chang·ing /ʌnˈtʃeɪndʒɪŋ/ adj. that always stays the same and does not change: unchanging truths

un·char·ac·ter·is·tic /ˌʌnkærəktəˈrɪstɪk/ adj. **~ (of sb)** not typical of someone; not the way someone usually behaves: The remark was totally uncharacteristic of her.
ANT CHARACTERISTIC ▶ **un·char·ac·ter·is·ti·cal·ly** /-kli/ adv.: The children had been uncharacteristically quiet.

un·char·i·ta·ble /ʌnˈtʃærətəbl/ adj. unkind and unfair in the way that you judge people: uncharitable thoughts **ANT** CHARITABLE ▶ **un·char·i·ta·bly** /-bli/ adv.

un·chart·ed **AWL** /ʌnˈtʃɑrtəd/ adj. [usually before noun]
1 that has not been visited or investigated before; not

familiar: They set off into the country's uncharted interior.
◆ (figurative) The party is sailing in **uncharted waters** (= a situation it has not been in before). ◆ (figurative) I was moving into **uncharted territory** (= a completely new experience) with this relationship. **2** not marked on a map: The ship hit an uncharted rock.

un·checked /ʌnˈtʃɛkt/ adj. if something harmful is **unchecked**, it is not controlled or stopped from getting worse: The fire was allowed to burn unchecked. ◆ The rise in violent crime must not **go unchecked**. ◆ The plant will soon choke ponds and waterways if **left unchecked**.

un·chris·tian /ʌnˈkrɪstʃən; -ˈkrɪʃtʃən/ adj. not showing the qualities you expect of a Christian; not kind or thinking about other people's feelings **ANT** CHRISTIAN

un·civ·il /ʌnˈsɪvl/ adj. (formal) not polite **ANT** CIVIL ⊃ see also INCIVILITY

un·civ·i·lized /ʌnˈsɪvəˌlaɪzd/ adj. (disapproving) **1** (of people or their behavior) not behaving in a way that is acceptable according to social or moral standards **2** (of people or places) not having developed a modern culture and way of life: I have worked in the wildest and most uncivilized parts of the world. **ANT** CIVILIZED

un·claimed /ʌnˈkleɪmd/ adj. that nobody has claimed as belonging to them or being owed to them

un·clas·si·fied /ʌnˈklæsəˌfaɪd/ adj. **1** (of documents, information, etc.) not officially secret; available to everyone **ANT** CLASSIFIED **2** (technical) that has not been CLASSIFIED as being the member of a particular group

un·cle 🔑 /ˈʌŋkl/ noun
1 the brother of your mother or father; the husband of your aunt: Uncle John ◆ I'm going to visit my uncle. ◆ I've just become an uncle (= because your brother/sister has had a baby).
2 used by children, with a first name, to address a man who is a close friend of their parents
IDM **cry/say uncle** (informal) to admit that you have been defeated in a fight and want to give up: The older boys made Jimmy cry uncle.

un·clean /ʌnˈklin/ adj. **1** (formal) dirty and therefore likely to cause disease: unclean water **ANT** CLEAN **2** considered to be bad, immoral, or not pure in a religious way, and therefore not to be touched, eaten, etc. **SYN** IMPURE: unclean thoughts ◆ unclean food

un·clear /ʌnˈklɪr/ adj. **1** not clear or definite; difficult to understand or be sure about: His motives are unclear. ◆ It is unclear whether there is any damage. ◆ Your diagrams are unclear. **2 ~ (about sth)** | **~ (as to sth)** not fully understanding something **SYN** UNCERTAIN: I'm unclear about what you want me to do.

Uncle Sam /ˌʌŋkl ˈsæm/ noun (informal) a way of referring to the United States of America or the U.S. government (sometimes shown as a tall man with a white beard and a tall hat): He owed $20,000 in taxes to Uncle Sam.

Uncle Tom noun (offensive) sometimes used in the past to refer to a black man who wants to please or serve white people **ORIGIN** From a character in the novel Uncle Tom's Cabin by Harriet Beecher Stowe.

un·clog /ʌnˈklɑg; -ˈklɔg/ verb (-gg-) **~ sth** to clear something, for example a pipe, by removing something that is blocking it: How do I unclog a sink pipe?

un·clothed /ʌnˈkloʊðd/ adj. (formal) not wearing any clothes **SYN** NAKED **ANT** CLOTHED

un·clut·tered /ʌnˈklʌtərd/ adj. (approving) not containing too many objects, details, or unnecessary items **SYN** TIDY **ANT** CLUTTERED

un·coil /ʌnˈkɔɪl/ verb [I, T] to become or make something straight after it has been wound or twisted around in a circle: The snake slowly uncoiled. ◆ **~ sth/itself** to uncoil a rope

un·col·ored (CanE usually **un·col·oured**) /ʌnˈkʌlərd/ adj. with no color; with no color added

un·combed /ʌnˈkoʊmd/ adj. (of hair) that has not been brushed or COMBED; very messy

un·com·fort·a·ble 🔑 /ʌnˈkʌmftərbl; -ˈkʌmfərtəbl/ *adj.*
1 (of clothes, furniture, etc.) not letting you feel physically comfortable; unpleasant to wear, sit on, etc.: *uncomfortable shoes* ◆ *I couldn't sleep because the bed was so uncomfortable.* **ANT** COMFORTABLE **2** not feeling physically relaxed, warm, etc.: *I was sitting in an extremely uncomfortable position.* ◆ *She still finds it uncomfortable to stand without support.* **ANT** COMFORTABLE **3** anxious, embarrassed, or afraid and unable to relax; making you feel like this: *He looked distinctly uncomfortable when the subject was mentioned.* ◆ *There was an uncomfortable silence.* **ANT** COMFORTABLE **4** unpleasant or difficult to deal with: *an uncomfortable fact* ◆ *I had the uncomfortable feeling that it was my fault.*

un·com·fort·a·bly /ʌnˈkʌmftərbli; -ˈkʌmfərtəbli/ *adv.* **1** in a way that makes you feel anxious or embarrassed; in a way that shows you are anxious or embarrassed: *I became uncomfortably aware that no one else was laughing.* ◆ *Her comment was uncomfortably close to the truth.* ◆ *He shifted uncomfortably in his seat when I mentioned money.* **2** in a way that is not physically comfortable: *I was feeling uncomfortably hot.* ◆ *She perched uncomfortably on the edge of the table.*

un·com·mit·ted /ʌnkəˈmɪtəd/ *adj.* ~ **(to sb/sth)** not having given or promised support to a particular person, group, belief, action, etc.: *The party needs to canvass the uncommitted voters.* ⊃ compare COMMITTED

un·com·mon /ʌnˈkɑmən/ *adj.* **1** not existing in large numbers or in many places **SYN** RARE, UNUSUAL: *an uncommon occurrence* ◆ *Side effects from the drug are uncommon.* ◆ *It is not uncommon for college students to live at home.* ◆ *Red squirrels are not uncommon in this area.* **ANT** COMMON **2** (*formal* or *literary*) unusually large in degree or amount; great **SYN** REMARKABLE: *She showed uncommon pleasure at his arrival.*

un·com·mon·ly /ʌnˈkɑmənli/ *adv.* (*formal*) **1** to an unusual degree; extremely: *an uncommonly gifted child* **2** not often; not usually: *Not uncommonly, there is a great deal of rain in August.*

un·com·mu·ni·ca·tive **AWL** /ʌnkəˈmyunɪkəṭɪv; -kə-ˈmyunəˌkeɪṭɪv/ *adj.* (*disapproving*) (of a person) not willing to talk to other people or give opinions **SYN** TACITURN **ANT** COMMUNICATIVE

un·com·pet·i·tive /ʌnkəmˈpɛṭɪtɪv/ *adj.* (*business*) not cheaper or better than others and therefore not able to compete equally: *an uncompetitive industry* ◆ *uncompetitive prices* **ANT** COMPETITIVE

un·com·plain·ing /ʌnkəmˈpleɪnɪŋ/ *adj.* (*approving*) not saying that you are unhappy about a difficult or unpleasant situation; not saying that you are in pain ▶ **un·com·plain·ing·ly** *adv.*

un·com·plet·ed /ʌnkəmˈpliṭəd/ *adj.* that has not been finished: *an uncompleted project*

un·com·pli·cat·ed /ʌnˈkɑmpləˌkeɪṭəd/ *adj.* simple; without any difficulty or confusion **SYN** STRAIGHTFORWARD: *an easygoing, uncomplicated young man* ◆ *Why can't I have an uncomplicated life?* **ANT** COMPLICATED

un·com·pli·men·ta·ry /ʌnˌkɑmpləˈmɛntri; -ˈmɛntəri/ *adj.* rude or insulting: *uncomplimentary remarks* ⊃ compare COMPLIMENTARY

un·com·pre·hend·ing /ʌnkɑmprɪˈhɛndɪŋ/ *adj.* (*formal*) (of a person) not understanding a situation or what is happening ▶ **un·com·pre·hend·ing·ly** *adv.*: *She looked at him uncomprehendingly.*

un·com·pro·mis·ing /ʌnˈkɑmprəˌmaɪzɪŋ/ *adj.* unwilling to change your opinions or behavior: *an uncompromising attitude* ◆ *He has a reputation for being tough and uncompromising.* ▶ **un·com·pro·mis·ing·ly** *adv.*

un·con·cealed /ʌnkənˈsild/ *adj.* [usually before noun] (of an emotion, etc.) that you do not try to hide **SYN** OBVIOUS: *unconcealed curiosity*

un·con·cern /ʌnkənˈsərn/ *noun* [U] (*formal*) a lack of care, interest, or worry about something that other people would care about **SYN** INDIFFERENCE: *She received the news with apparent unconcern.* ⊃ compare CONCERN

un·con·cerned /ʌnkənˈsərnd/ *adj.* **1** ~ **(about/by sth)** not worried or anxious about something because you feel it does not affect you or is not important: *He drove on, apparently unconcerned about the noise the engine was making.* **2** ~ **(with sb/sth)** not interested in something: *Young people are often unconcerned with political issues.* **ANT** CONCERNED ▶ **un·con·cern·ed·ly** /-ˈsərnədli/ *adv.*

un·con·di·tion·al /ʌnkənˈdɪʃənl/ *adj.* without any conditions or limits: *the unconditional surrender of military forces* ◆ *She gave her children unconditional love.* **ANT** CONDITIONAL ▶ **un·con·di·tion·al·ly** /-ʃənəli/ *adv.*

un·con·di·tioned /ʌnkənˈdɪʃnd/ *adj.* (*psychology*) (of behavior) not trained or influenced by experience; natural: *an unconditioned response*

un·con·fined /ʌnkənˈfaɪnd/ *adj.* (*formal*) not limited in space, range, or amount: *The animals have unconfined access to pasture.* ◆ *When the news came through, joy was unconfined.*

un·con·firmed /ʌnkənˈfərmd/ *adj.* that has not yet been proved to be true or confirmed: *unconfirmed rumors* ◆ *Unconfirmed reports said that at least six people were killed.*

un·con·gen·ial /ʌnkənˈdʒinyəl/ *adj.* (*formal*) **1** (of a person) not pleasant or friendly; not like yourself: *uncongenial company* **2** ~ **(to sb)** (of a place, job, etc.) not pleasant; not making you feel relaxed; not suitable for your personality: *an uncongenial atmosphere* **3** ~ **(to sth)** not suitable for something; not encouraging something: *The religious climate at the time was uncongenial to new ideas.* **ANT** CONGENIAL

un·con·nect·ed /ʌnkəˈnɛktəd/ *adj.* not related or connected in any way: *The two crimes are apparently unconnected.* ◆ ~ **with/to sth** *My resignation was totally unconnected with recent events.*

un·con·quer·a·ble /ʌnˈkɑŋkərəbl/ *adj.* too strong to be defeated or changed **SYN** INVINCIBLE

un·con·scion·a·ble /ʌnˈkɑnʃənəbl/ *adj.* [usually before noun] (*formal*) **1** (of an action, etc.) so bad, immoral, etc. that it should make you feel ashamed **2** (often *humorous*) too great, large, long, etc. **SYN** EXCESSIVE

un·con·scious 🔑 /ʌnˈkɑnʃəs/ *adj., noun*
● *adj.* **1** in a state like sleep because of an injury or illness, and not able to use your senses: *She was knocked unconscious.* ◆ *They found him lying unconscious on the floor.* **2** (of feelings, thoughts, etc.) existing or happening without you realizing or being aware; not deliberate or controlled: *unconscious desires* ◆ *The brochure is full of unconscious humor.* ⊃ compare SUBCONSCIOUS **3** ~ **of sb/sth** not aware of someone or something; not noticing something; not conscious **SYN** OBLIVIOUS TO: *She is unconscious of the effect she has on people.* ◆ *He was quite unconscious of the danger.* **ANT** CONSCIOUS
● *noun* **the unconscious** [sing.] (*psychology*) the part of a person's mind with thoughts, feelings, etc. that they are not aware of and cannot control but which can sometimes be understood by studying their behavior or dreams ⊃ compare SUBCONSCIOUS

un·con·scious·ly /ʌnˈkɑnʃəsli/ *adv.* without being aware: *Perhaps, unconsciously, I've done something to offend her.*

un·con·scious·ness /ʌnˈkɑnʃəsnəs/ *noun* [U] a state like sleep caused by injury or illness, when you are unable to use your senses: *He had lapsed into unconsciousness.*

un·con·sid·ered /ʌnkənˈsɪdərd/ *adj.* (*formal*) not thought about, or not thought about with enough care: *I came to regret my unconsidered remarks.*

un·con·sol·a·ble /ʌnkənˈsoʊləbl/ *adj.* = INCONSOLABLE ▶ **un·con·sol·a·bly** /-bli/ *adv.*

un·con·sti·tu·tion·al **AWL** /ʌnkɑnstəˈtuʃənl/ *adj.* not allowed by the CONSTITUTION of a country, a political

| t tea | ṭ butter | d did | k cat | g got | tʃ chin | dʒ June | f fall |

system, or an organization **ANT** CONSTITUTIONAL ▶ un·con·sti·tu·tion·al·ly /-'tuʃənəli; -'tuʃnəli/ adv.

un·con·strained **AWL** /ˌʌnkən'streɪnd/ adj. (formal) not restricted or limited: unconstrained growth ⊃ see also CON-STRAIN

un·con·tam·i·nat·ed /ˌʌnkən'tæməˌneɪtəd/ adj. not harmed or spoiled by something (for example, dangerous substances): uncontaminated water

un·con·ten·tious /ˌʌnkən'tɛnʃəs/ adj. (formal) not likely to cause disagreement between people: The proposal is relatively uncontentious. **ANT** CONTENTIOUS

un·con·test·ed /ˌʌnkən'tɛstəd/ adj. without any opposition or argument: an uncontested election/divorce ◆ These claims have not gone uncontested.

un·con·trol·la·ble /ˌʌnkən'troʊləbl/ adj. that you cannot control or prevent: an uncontrollable temper ◆ uncontrollable bleeding ◆ I had an uncontrollable urge to laugh. ◆ The ball was uncontrollable. ◆ He's an uncontrollable child (= he behaves very badly and cannot be controlled). ▶ un·con·trol·la·bly /-bli/ adv.: She began shaking uncontrollably.

un·con·trolled 🔑 /ˌʌnkən'troʊld/ adj.
1 (of emotions, behavior, etc.) that someone cannot control or stop: uncontrolled anger ◆ The thoughts rushed into my mind uncontrolled. **2** that is not limited or managed by law or rules: the uncontrolled growth of cities ◆ uncontrolled dumping of toxic wastes ⊃ compare CONTROLLED

un·con·tro·ver·sial **AWL** /ˌʌnkɑntrə'vərʃl/ adj. not causing, or not likely to cause, any disagreement: an uncontroversial opinion ◆ He chose an uncontroversial topic for his speech. **ANT** CONTROVERSIAL ⊃ compare NONCONTRO-VERSIAL

un·con·ven·tion·al **AWL** /ˌʌnkən'vɛnʃənl/ adj. (often approving) not following what is done or considered normal or acceptable by most people; different and interesting **SYN** UNORTHODOX: an unconventional approach to the problem ◆ unconventional views **ANT** CONVENTIONAL ▶ un·con·ven·tion·al·i·ty /ˌʌnkənˌvɛnʃə'næləti/ noun [U] un·con·ven·tion·al·ly /-'vɛnʃənəli/ adv.

un·con·vinced **AWL** /ˌʌnkən'vɪnst/ adj. not believing or not certain about something despite what you have been told: ~ (of sth) I remain unconvinced of the need for change. ◆ ~ (by sth) She seemed unconvinced by their promises. ◆ ~ (that...) The jury was unconvinced that he was innocent. **ANT** CONVINCED

un·con·vinc·ing /ˌʌnkən'vɪnsɪŋ/ adj. not seeming true or real; not making you believe that something is true: I find the characters in the book very unconvincing. ◆ She managed a weak, unconvincing smile. **ANT** CONVINCING ▶ un·con·vinc·ing·ly adv.

un·cooked /ʌn'kʊkt/ adj. not cooked **SYN** RAW: Eat plenty of uncooked fruit and vegetables.

un·cool /ʌn'kul/ adj. (informal) not considered acceptable by fashionable young people **SYN** UNHIP **ANT** COOL

un·co·op·er·a·tive /ˌʌnkoʊ'ɑprətɪv/ adj. not willing to be helpful to other people or do what they ask **SYN** UNHELPFUL **ANT** COOPERATIVE

un·co·or·di·nat·ed /ˌʌnkoʊ'ɔrdnˌeɪtəd/ adj. **1** if a person is uncoordinated, they are not able to control their movements well, and are therefore not very skillful at some sports and physical activities **2** (of movements or parts of the body) not controlled; not moving smoothly or together **3** (of plans, projects, etc.) not well organized; with no thought for how the different parts work together

un·cork /ʌn'kɔrk/ verb ~ sth to open a bottle by removing the CORK from the top **ANT** CORK

un·cor·rob·o·rat·ed /ˌʌnkə'rɑbəˌreɪtəd/ adj. (of a statement or claim) not supported by any other evidence; not having been CORROBORATED **SYN** UNCONFIRMED

un·count·a·ble /ʌn'kaʊntəbl/ (also non·count) adj. (grammar) a noun that is **uncountable** cannot be made

plural or used with a or an, for example water, bread, and information **ANT** COUNTABLE ⊃ compare COUNTLESS

un·count noun /ˌʌnkaʊnt 'naʊn/ noun (grammar) an uncountable noun **ANT** COUNT NOUN

un·cou·ple /ʌn'kʌpl/ verb ~ sth (from sth) to remove the connection between two vehicles, two parts of a train, etc.

un·couth /ʌn'kuθ/ adj. (of a person or their behavior) rude or socially unacceptable **SYN** COARSE: uncouth laughter ◆ an uncouth young man

un·cov·er /ʌn'kʌvər/ verb **1** ~ sth to remove something that is covering something: Uncover the pan and let the soup simmer. **2** ~ sth to discover something that was previously hidden or secret: Police have uncovered a plot to kidnap the President's son.

un·cov·ered /ʌn'kʌvərd/ adj. not covered by anything: His head was uncovered.

un·crit·i·cal /ʌn'krɪtɪkl/ adj. (usually disapproving) not willing to criticize someone or something or to judge whether someone or something is right or wrong: Her uncritical acceptance of everything I said began to irritate me. **ANT** CRITICAL ▶ un·crit·i·cally /-kli/ adv.

un·crowd·ed /ʌn'kraʊdəd/ adj. not full of people: The beach was pleasantly uncrowded. **ANT** CROWDED

un·crowned /ʌn'kraʊnd/ adj. (of a king or queen) not yet CROWNED
IDM the uncrowned king/queen (of sth) the person considered to be the best, most famous, or most successful in a particular place or area of activity

unc·tion /'ʌŋkʃn/ noun [U] **1** the act of pouring oil on someone's head or another part of their body as part of an important religious ceremony ⊃ see also EXTREME UNCTION **2** (formal, disapproving) behavior or speech that is not sincere and that expresses too much praise or admiration of someone

unc·tu·ous /'ʌŋktʃuəs/ adj. (formal, disapproving) friendly or giving praise in a way that is not sincere and that is therefore unpleasant ▶ unc·tu·ous·ly adv.

un·cul·ti·vat·ed /ʌn'kʌltəˌveɪtəd/ adj. (of land) not used for growing crops **ANT** CULTIVATED

un·cul·tured **AWL** /ʌn'kʌltʃərd/ adj. (of people) not well educated; not able to understand or enjoy art, literature, etc. **ANT** CULTURED

un·curl /ʌn'kərl/ verb [I, T] to become straight, or to make something become straight, after being in a curled position: The snake slowly uncurled. ◆ ~ sth/itself The cat uncurled itself and jumped off the wall. **ANT** CURL UP

un·cut /ʌn'kʌt/ adj. **1** left to grow; not cut short: The uncut grass came up to her waist. **2** (of a book, movie, etc.) left in its complete form; without any parts removed; not CENSORED: the original uncut version **3** (of a PRECIOUS STONE) not shaped by cutting: uncut diamonds **4** not cut into separate pieces: an uncut loaf of bread

un·dam·aged /ʌn'dæmɪdʒd/ adj. not damaged or spoiled: There was a slight collision but my car was undamaged. ◆ He emerged from the court case with his reputation undamaged.

un·dat·ed /ʌn'deɪtəd/ adj. **1** without a date written or printed on it: an undated letter **2** of which the date is not known: undated archaeological remains ⊃ compare DATED

un·daunt·ed /ʌn'dɔntəd/ adj. [not usually before noun] (formal) still enthusiastic and determined, despite difficulties or disappointment **SYN** UNDETERRED: He seemed undaunted by all the opposition to his idea.

un·de·cid·ed /ˌʌndɪ'saɪdəd/ adj. [not usually before noun] **1** not having made a decision about someone or something: ~ (about sb/sth) I'm still undecided (about) who to vote for. ~ (as to sth) He was undecided as to what to do next. **2** not having been decided: The venue for the annual shareholders' meeting remains undecided. ⊃ compare DECIDED

un·de·clared /ˌʌndɪ'klɛrd/ adj. not admitted to; not stated in an open way; not having been declared: *No income should remain undeclared.* ◆ *Undeclared goods* (= that the customs are not told about) *may be confiscated.*

un·de·feat·ed /ˌʌndɪˈfiːtəd/ *adj.* (especially in sports) not having lost or been defeated: *They are undefeated in 13 games.* ◆ *the undefeated world champion*

un·de·fend·ed /ˌʌndɪˈfɛndəd/ *adj.* **1** not protected or guarded **SYN** UNPROTECTED: *undefended borders* **2** if a case in court is **undefended**, no defense is made against it

un·de·fined **AWL** /ˌʌndɪˈfaɪnd/ *adj.* not made clear or definite: *The money was lent for an undefined period of time.*

un·de·lete /ˌʌndɪˈliːt/ *verb* [T, I] ~ **(sth)** (*computing*) to cancel an action of deleting (DELETE) a document, a file, text, etc. on a computer, so that it appears again

un·de·mand·ing /ˌʌndɪˈmændɪŋ/ *adj.* **1** not needing a lot of effort or thought: *an undemanding job* **2** (of a person) not asking for a lot of attention or action from other people **ANT** DEMANDING

un·dem·o·crat·ic /ˌʌndɛməˈkrætɪk/ *adj.* against or not acting according to the principles of democracy: *undemocratic decisions* ◆ *an undemocratic regime* **ANT** DEMOCRATIC ▶ **un·dem·o·crat·i·cally** /-kli/ *adv.*: ◆ *He was accused of acting undemocratically.*

un·de·mon·stra·tive /ˌʌndəˈmɑnstrətɪv/ *adj.* not showing feelings openly, especially feelings of affection **ANT** DEMONSTRATIVE

un·de·ni·a·ble **AWL** /ˌʌndɪˈnaɪəbl/ *adj.* true or certain; that cannot be denied **SYN** INDISPUTABLE: *He had undeniable charm.* ◆ *It is an undeniable fact that crime is increasing.* **ANT** DENIABLE ▶ **un·de·ni·a·bly** /-bli/ *adv.*: *undeniably impressive*

un·der 🔑 /ˈʌndər/ *prep., adv., adj.*
● *prep.* **1** in, to, or through a position that is below something: *Have you looked under the bed?* ◆ *She placed the ladder under* (= just lower than) *the window.* ◆ *The dog squeezed under the gate and ran into the road.* **2** below the surface of something; covered by something: *The boat lay under several feet of water.* **3** less than; younger than: *an annual income of under $10,000* ◆ *It took us under an hour.* ◆ *Nobody under 21 is allowed to buy alcohol.* ◆ *children aged 12 and under* **4** used to say who or what controls, governs, or manages someone or something: *The country is now under martial law.* ◆ *The coinage was reformed under Elizabeth I* (= when she was queen). ◆ *She has a staff of 19 working under her.* ◆ *Under its new conductor, the orchestra has established an international reputation.* **5** according to an agreement, a law or a system: *Six suspects are being held under the Computer Fraud and Abuse Act.* ◆ *Under the terms of the lease you had no right to sublet the property.* ◆ *Is the television still under guarantee?* **6** experiencing a particular process: *The hotel is still under construction.* ◆ *The matter is under investigation.* **7** affected by something: *The wall collapsed under the strain.* ◆ *I've been feeling under stress lately.* ◆ *I'm under no illusions about what hard work this will be.* ◆ *You'll be under anesthetic, so you won't feel a thing.* **8** using a particular name: *She also writes under the pseudonym of Barbara Vine.* **9** found in a particular part of a book, list, etc.: *If it's not under "sports," try looking under "games."*
● *adv.* **1** below something: *He pulled up the covers and crawled under.* **2** below the surface of water: *She took a deep breath and stayed under for more than a minute.* ◆ *The boat was going under fast.* **3** less; younger: *prices of ten dollars and under* ◆ *children aged 12 and under* **4** in or into an unconscious state: *He felt himself going under.*
● *adj.* [only before noun] lower; underneath: *the under layer* ◆ *the under surface of a leaf*

un·der- /ˈʌndər/ *prefix* **1** (in nouns and adjectives) below; beneath: *undergrowth* ◆ *undercover* **2** (in nouns) lower in age or rank: *the under-fives* ◆ *an undergraduate* **3** (in adjectives and verbs) not enough: *underripe* ◆ *undercooked*

un·der·a·chieve /ˌʌndərəˈtʃiːv/ *verb* [I] to do less well than you could do, especially in SCHOOLWORK ▶ **un·der·a·chieve·ment** /-mənt/ *noun* [U]

un·der·a·chiev·er /ˌʌndərəˈtʃiːvər/ *noun* a person who does not do as well as they could do, especially in SCHOOLWORK: *How can we identify the underachievers in our classrooms?*

un·der·age /ˌʌndərˈeɪdʒ/ *adj.* [only before noun] done by people who are too young by law: *underage drinking* ➔ see also AGE

un·der·arm /ˈʌndərˌɑrm/ *adj.*
● *adj.* [only before noun] connected with a person's ARMPIT: *underarm hair/deodorant/sweating*
● *noun* the part of the body under the arm where it joins the shoulder ➔ see also ARMPIT

un·der·bel·ly /ˈʌndərˌbɛli/ *noun* [sing.] **1** the weakest part of something that is most easily attacked: *The trade deficit remains the **soft underbelly** of the U.S. economy.* **2** the underneath part of an animal: (*figurative*) *He became familiar with the dark underbelly of life in the city* (= the parts that are usually hidden)

un·der·bid /ˌʌndərˈbɪd/ *verb* (un·der·bid·ding, un·der·bid, un·der·bid) ~ **sb/sth** to make a lower bid than someone else, for example when trying to win a contract

un·der·brush /ˈʌndərˌbrʌʃ/ *noun* [U] a mass of bushes and plants that grow close together under trees in woods and forests **SYN** UNDERGROWTH

un·der·car·riage /ˈʌndərˌkærɪdʒ/ (also ˈlanding ˌgear) *noun* the part of an aircraft, including the wheels, that supports it when it is landing and taking off ➔ picture at PLANE

un·der·charge /ˌʌndərˈtʃɑrdʒ/ *verb* [I, T] ~ **(sb) (for sth)** to charge too little for something, usually by mistake **ANT** OVERCHARGE

un·der·class /ˈʌndərˌklæs/ *noun* [sing.] a social class that is very poor and has no status: *The long-term unemployed are becoming a new underclass.*

un·der·class·man /ˌʌndərˈklæsmən/, **un·der·class·wom·an** /ˌʌndərˈklæsˌwʊmən/ *noun* (*pl.* **un·der·class·men** /-mən/, **un·der·class·wom·en** /-ˌwɪmən/) a student in the first or second year of high school or college ➔ compare UPPERCLASSMAN

un·der·clothes /ˈʌndərˌkloʊz; -ˌkloʊðz/ *noun* [pl.] (also **un·der·cloth·ing** /ˈʌndərˌkloʊðɪŋ/ [U]) (*formal*) = UNDERWEAR

un·der·coat /ˈʌndərˌkoʊt/ *noun* [C, U] a layer of paint under the final layer; the paint used for making this ➔ compare TOPCOAT

un·der·cook /ˌʌndərˈkʊk/ *verb* [usually passive] ~ **sth** to not cook something for long enough, with the result that it is not ready to eat

un·der·count /ˌʌndərˈkaʊnt/ *verb* ~ **sb/sth** to count fewer than the actual number of people or things in a particular group: *The census undercounts low-income people and children.*

un·der·cov·er /ˌʌndərˈkʌvər/ *adj.* [usually before noun] working or done secretly in order to find out information for the police, a government, etc.: *an undercover agent* ◆ *an undercover operation/investigation* ▶ **un·der·cov·er** *adv.*: *The illegal payments were discovered by a journalist **working undercover**.*

un·der·cur·rent /ˈʌndərˌkərənt/ *noun* ~ **(of sth)** a feeling, especially a negative one, that is hidden but whose effects are felt **SYN** UNDERTONE: *I detect an undercurrent of resentment toward the new proposals.*

un·der·cut *verb, noun*
● *verb* /ˌʌndərˈkʌt/ (un·der·cut·ting, un·der·cut, un·der·cut) **1** ~ **sb/sth** to sell goods or services at a lower price than your COMPETITORS: *to undercut someone's prices* ◆ *We were able to undercut our overseas rivals by 5%.* **2** ~ **sb/sth** to make something weaker or less likely to be effective **SYN** UNDERMINE: *Some members of the board were trying to undercut the chairman's authority.*
● *noun* /ˈʌndərˌkʌt/ a way of cutting someone's hair in which

the hair is left quite long on top but the hair on the lower part of the head is cut much shorter

un·der·de·vel·oped /ˌʌndərdɪˈvɛləpt/ adj. (of a country, society, etc.) having few industries and a low standard of living ⊃ compare DEVELOPED, DEVELOPING, UNDEVELOPED **HELP** "A developing country" is now the usual expression. ▶ **un·der·de·vel·op·ment** /-dɪˈvɛləpmənt/ noun [U]

un·der·dog /ˈʌndərˌdɔg/ noun a person, team, country, etc. that is thought to be in a weaker position than others and therefore not likely to be successful, win a competition, etc.: *Before the game we were definitely the underdogs.* ◆ *In politics, he was a champion of the underdog* (= always fought for the rights of weaker people). **ANT** OVERDOG

un·der·done /ˌʌndərˈdʌn/ adj. not completely cooked ⊃ compare OVERDO, WELL DONE

un·der·dressed /ˌʌndərˈdrɛst/ adj. (usually disapproving) wearing clothes that are too informal for a particular occasion: *Aren't you a little underdressed for the interview?* **ANT** OVERDRESSED

un·der·em·ployed /ˌʌndərɪmˈplɔɪd/ adj. not having enough work to do; not having work that makes full use of your skills and abilities

un·der·es·ti·mate [AWL] verb, noun
- **verb** /ˌʌndərˈɛstəˌmeɪt/ **1** ~ sth | ~ what, how, etc.... to think or guess that the amount, cost, or size of something is smaller than it really is: *to underestimate the cost of the project* ◆ *We underestimated the time it would take to get there.* ⊃ collocations at ESTIMATE **2** ~ sb/sth to not realize how good, strong, determined, etc. someone really is: *Never underestimate your opponent.* **ANT** OVERESTIMATE ⊃ compare UNDERRATE
- **noun** /ˌʌndərˈɛstəmət/ (also un·der·es·ti·ma·tion /ˌʌndərˌɛstəˈmeɪʃn/ [C, U]) an estimate about the size, cost, etc. of something that is too low: *My guess of 400 proved to be a serious underestimate.* **ANT** OVERESTIMATE

un·der·ex·pose /ˌʌndərɪkˈspoʊz/ verb [usually passive] ~ sth to allow too little light to reach the film when you take a photograph **ANT** OVEREXPOSE

un·der·fed /ˌʌndərˈfɛd/ adj. having had too little food to eat **SYN** MALNOURISHED

un·der·floor /ˈʌndərˌflɔr/ adj. [only before noun] placed underneath the floor: *underfloor heating*

un·der·foot /ˌʌndərˈfʊt/ adv. under your feet; on the ground where you are walking: *The ground was dry and firm underfoot.* ◆ *I was nearly trampled underfoot by the crowd of people rushing for the door.*

un·der·funded /ˌʌndərˈfʌndəd/ adj. (of an organization, a project, etc.) not having enough money to spend, with the result that it cannot function well: *seriously/chronically underfunded*

un·der·gar·ment /ˈʌndərˌgɑrmənt/ noun (old-fashioned or formal) a piece of underwear

un·der·go [AWL] /ˌʌndərˈgoʊ/ verb (un·der·went /-ˈwɛnt/, un·der·gone /-ˈgɔn; -ˈgɑn/) ~ sth to experience something, especially a change or something unpleasant: *to undergo tests/trials/repairs* ◆ *My mother underwent major surgery last year.* ◆ *Some children undergo a complete transformation when they become teenagers.*

un·der·grad·u·ate /ˌʌndərˈgrædʒuət/ (also informal un·der·grad /ˈʌndərˌgræd/) noun a college student who is studying for their first degree: *a first-year undergraduate* ◆ *an undergraduate course/student/degree* ⊃ note at STUDENT

un·der·ground ⚷ adj., adv., noun
- **adj.** /ˈʌndərˌgraʊnd/ [only before noun] **1** under the surface of the ground: *underground passages/caves/streams* ◆ *underground cables* ⊃ compare OVERGROUND **2** operating secretly and often illegally, especially against a government: *an underground resistance movement*
- **adv.** /ˌʌndərˈgraʊnd/ **1** under the surface of the ground: *Rescuers found victims trapped several feet underground.* ◆ *toxic waste buried deep underground* **2** in or into a secret place in

order to hide from the police, the government, etc.: *He went underground to avoid arrest.*
- **noun** /ˈʌndərˌgraʊnd/ [sing.] **1 the underground** a secret political organization, usually working against the government of a country **2** an underground railroad system, especially in London: *underground stations* ⊃ compare METRO, SUBWAY

the ˌunderground eˈconomy noun [sing.] business activity or work that is done without the knowledge of the government or other officials so that people avoid paying tax on the money they earn

un·der·growth /ˈʌndərˌgroʊθ/ noun [U] a mass of bushes and plants that grow close together under trees in woods and forests **SYN** UNDERBRUSH: *They used their knives to clear a path through the dense undergrowth.* ◆ *The murder weapon was found concealed in undergrowth.*

un·der·hand /ˈʌndərˌhænd/ adj., adv.
- **adj.** an **underhand** throw of a ball is done with the hand kept below the level of the shoulder ⊃ compare OVERHAND
- **adv.** if you throw, etc. **underhand**, you throw keeping your hand below the level of your shoulder ⊃ compare OVERHAND

un·der·hand·ed /ˌʌndərˈhændəd/ (also less frequent un·der·hand) adj. (disapproving) secret and dishonest: *I would never have expected her to behave in such an underhanded way.*

un·der·in·sured /ˌʌndərɪnˈʃʊrd/ adj. not having enough insurance protection

un·der·lay [AWL] /ˈʌndərˌleɪ/ noun [U, C] a layer of thick material placed under a carpet to protect it

un·der·lie [AWL] /ˌʌndərˈlaɪ/ verb (un·der·ly·ing, un·der·lay /-ˈleɪ/, un·der·lain /-ˈleɪn/) [no passive] ~ sth (formal) to be the basis or cause of something: *These ideas underlie much of his work.* ◆ *It is a principle that underlies all the party's policies.* ⊃ see also UNDERLYING

un·der·line /ˈʌndərˌlaɪn/ (also un·der·score) verb **1** ~ sth to draw a line under a word, sentence, etc. **2** to emphasize or show that something is important or true: ~ sth *The report underlines the importance of preschool education.* ◆ ~ how, what, etc.... *Her question underlined how little she understood him.* ◆ ~ that... *The report underlined that the project enjoyed considerable support in both countries.* ◆ **it is underlined that...** *It should be underlined that these are only preliminary findings.*

un·der·ling /ˈʌndərlɪŋ/ noun (disapproving) a person with a lower rank or status **SYN** MINION

un·der·ly·ing [AWL] /ˈʌndərˌlaɪŋ/ adj. [only before noun] **1** important in a situation but not always easily noticed or stated clearly: *The underlying assumption is that the amount of money available is limited.* ◆ *Unemployment may be an underlying cause of the rising crime rate.* **2** existing under the surface of something else: *the underlying rock formation* ⊃ see also UNDERLIE

un·der·manned /ˌʌndərˈmænd/ adj. (of a hospital, factory, etc.) not having enough people working in order to be able to function well **SYN** UNDERSTAFFED **ANT** OVERMANNED

un·der·mine /ˈʌndərˌmaɪn; ˌʌndərˈmaɪn/ verb **1** ~ sth to make something, especially someone's confidence or authority, gradually weaker or less effective: *Our confidence in the team has been seriously undermined by their recent defeats.* ◆ *This crisis has undermined his position.* **2** ~ sth to make something weaker at the base, for example by digging under it

un·der·neath ⚷ /ˌʌndərˈniθ/ prep., adv., noun
- **prep., adv. 1** under or below something else, especially when it is hidden or covered by the thing on top: *The coin rolled underneath the piano.* ◆ *This jacket's too big, even with a sweater underneath.* **2** used to talk about someone's real feelings or character, as opposed to the way they seem to be: *Underneath her cool exterior she was really very frightened.* ◆ *He seems grumpy, but he's very soft-hearted underneath.*
- **noun the underneath** [sing.] the lower surface or part of

---

| i see | ɪ sit | ɛ ten | æ cat | ɑ hot | ɔ saw | ʊ put | u too | 1621 |

something: *She pulled the drawer out and examined the underneath carefully.*

un·der·nour·ished /ˌʌndər'nɜrɪʃt/ *adj.* in bad health because of a lack of food or a lack of the right type of food **SYN** MALNOURISHED: *severely undernourished children* ► **un·der·nour·ish·ment** /-'nɜrɪʃmənt/ *noun* [U]

un·der·paid /ˌʌndər'peɪd/ *adj.* not paid enough for the work you do: *Nurses complain of being overworked and underpaid.*

un·der·pants /'ʌndər,pænts/ *noun* [pl.] a piece of underwear worn by men or women under pants, a skirt, etc.

un·der·pass /'ʌndər,pæs/ *noun* a road or path that goes under another road or railroad track **⊃** compare OVERPASS

un·der·pay /ˌʌndər'peɪ/ *verb* (un·der·paid, un·der·paid /-'peɪd/) [usually passive] **~ sb** to pay someone too little money, especially for their work **ANT** OVERPAY

un·der·per·form /ˌʌndərpər'fɔrm/ *verb* [I] to not be as successful as was expected

un·der·pin /ˌʌndər'pɪn/ *verb* (-nn-) **1 ~ sth** (*formal*) to support or form the basis of an argument, a claim, etc.: *The report is underpinned by extensive research.* **2 ~ sth** (*technical*) to support a wall by putting metal, concrete, etc. under it ► **un·der·pin·ning** /'ʌndər,pɪnɪŋ/ *noun* [C, U]

un·der·play /ˌʌndər'pleɪ; 'ʌndər,pleɪ/ *verb* **~ sth** to make something seem less important than it really is **SYN** DOWNPLAY, PLAY DOWN **ANT** OVERPLAY

un·der·pre·pared /ˌʌndərprɪ'perd/ *adj.* not having done enough preparation for something you have to do

un·der·priced /ˌʌndər'praɪst/ *adj.* something that is **underpriced** is sold at a price that is too low and less than its real value

un·der·priv·i·leged /ˌʌndər'prɪvəlɪdʒd; -'prɪvlɪdʒd/ *adj.* **1** [usually before noun] having less money and fewer opportunities than most people in society **SYN** DISADVANTAGED: *underprivileged sections of the community ♦ educationally/socially underprivileged groups* **⊃** compare PRIVILEGED **2 the underprivileged** *noun* [pl.] people who are underprivileged

un·der·rate /ˌʌndər'reɪt/ *verb* **~ sb/sth** to not recognize how good, important, etc. someone or something really is: *He's seriously underrated as a writer. ♦ an underrated movie* **⊃** compare OVERRATE, UNDERESTIMATE

un·der·re·hearsed /ˌʌndərrɪ'hɜrst/ *adj.* (of a play or other performance) that has not been prepared and practiced enough

un·der·rep·re·sent·ed /ˌʌndər,reprɪ'zentəd/ *adj.* not having as many representatives as would be expected or needed: *Women are underrepresented at senior levels in business.*

under-resourced **AWL** /ˌʌndər'rɪsɔrst; -rɪ'sɔrst/ *adj.* not provided with as much money or as many staff, materials, etc. as are needed: *Nurses are overstretched and the hospital is seriously under-resourced.*

un·der·score /'ʌndər,skɔr/ *verb, noun*
• *verb* = UNDERLINE
• *noun* (*computing*) the symbol (_) that is used to draw a line under a letter or word and used in computer commands and in Internet addresses

un·der·sea /'ʌndər,si/ *adj.* [only before noun] found, used, or happening below the surface of the ocean: *undersea cables/earthquakes*

un·der·sec·re·tar·y /ˌʌndər'sekrə,teri/ *noun* (*pl.* un·der·sec·re·tar·ies) an official of high rank in a government department, directly below a member of a cabinet

un·der·sell /ˌʌndər'sel/ *verb* (un·der·sold, un·der·sold /-'sould/) **1 ~ sth** to sell goods or services at a lower price than your COMPETITORS **2 ~ sth** to sell something at a price lower than its real value **3 ~ sb/sth/yourself** to make people think that someone or something is not as good or

as interesting as they really are: *Don't undersell yourself at the interview.*

un·der·served /ˌʌndər'sərvd/ *adj.* (of an area or group of people) not getting enough help, products, or services: *improving access to healthcare in underserved areas*

un·der·shirt /'ʌndər,ʃərt/ *noun* a piece of underwear worn under a shirt, etc. next to the skin

un·der·shoot /ˌʌndər'ʃut/ *verb* (*pt, pp* un·der·shot) [I, T] **~ (sth)** (of an aircraft) to land before reaching the RUNWAY ► **un·der·shoot** *noun*

un·der·shorts /'ʌndər,ʃɔrts/ *noun* [pl.] UNDERPANTS that are worn by men

un·der·side /'ʌndər,saɪd/ *noun* the side or surface of something that is underneath **SYN** BOTTOM

the un·der·signed /'ʌndər,saɪnd/ *noun* (*pl.* the un·der·sign·ed) (*formal*) the person who has signed that particular document: *We, the undersigned, agree to…*

un·der·sized /'ʌndər,saɪzd/ *adj.* not as big as normal

un·der·skirt /'ʌndər,skərt/ *noun* a skirt that is worn under another skirt as underwear

un·der·sold *pt, pp* of UNDERSELL

un·der·spend /ˌʌndər'spend/ *verb* (un·der·spent, un·der·spent) [I, T] to not spend enough money on something: **~ (on sth)** *The inquiry found that the company had seriously underspent on safety equipment. ♦ ~ sth We've underspent our budget this year.*

un·der·staffed /ˌʌndər'stæft/ *adj.* [not usually before noun] not having enough people working and therefore not able to function well **SYN** UNDERMANNED **ANT** OVERSTAFFED

un·der·stand 🔑
/ˌʌndər'stænd/ *verb*
(un·der·stood, un·der·stood /-'stʊd/) (not used in the progressive tenses)
▸ MEANING **1** [T, I] to know or realize the meaning of words, a language, what someone says, etc.: **~ (sth)** *Can you understand French? ♦ Do you understand the instructions? ♦ She didn't understand the form she was signing. ♦ I'm not sure that I understand. Go over it again. ♦ I don't want you doing that again. Do you understand? ♦* **~ what…** *I don't understand what he's saying.*
▸ HOW SOMETHING WORKS/HAPPENS **2** [T, I] to know or realize how or why something happens, how it works, or why it is important: **~ (sth)** *Doctors still don't understand much about the disease. ♦ No one is answering the phone — I can't understand it. ♦* **~ why, what, etc.…** *I could never understand why she was fired. ♦* **~ sb/sth doing sth** *I just can't understand him taking the money. ♦* (*formal*) *I just can't understand his taking the money. ♦* **~ that…** *He was the first to understand that we live in a knowledge economy.*
▸ KNOW SOMEONE **3** [T, I] to know someone's character, how they feel, and why they behave in the way they do: **~ sb** *Nobody understands me. ♦ He doesn't understand women at all. ♦* **~ what, how, etc.…** *They understand what I have been through. ♦* **~ (that…)** *I understand that you need some time alone. ♦ If you want to leave early, I'm sure he'll understand. ♦* **~ sb doing sth** *I understand you needing some time alone.*
▸ THINK/BELIEVE **4** [T] (*formal*) to think or believe that something is true because you have been told that it is: **~ (that)** *… I understand (that) you wish to see the manager. ♦ Am I to understand that you refuse? ♦* **~ sb/sth to be/have sth** *The senator is understood to have been extremely angry about the report. ♦* **it is understood that…** *It is understood that the band is working on their next album.*
▸ BE AGREED **5** [T] **it is understood that…** to agree something with someone without it needing to be said: *I thought it was understood that my expenses would be paid.*
▸ MISSING WORD **6** [T, usually passive] **~ sth** to realize that a word in a phrase or sentence is not expressed and to supply it in your mind: *In the sentence "I can't drive," the object "a car" is understood.*

WORD FAMILY
understand *verb* (≠ misunderstand)
understandable *adj.*
misunderstood *adj.*
understanding *adj.*, *noun* (≠ misunderstanding)

IDM make yourself understood to make your meaning clear, especially in another language: *He doesn't speak much Japanese, but he can make himself understood.* ⊃ **more at** GIVE

understand

see ◆ get ◆ follow ◆ grasp ◆ comprehend

These words all mean to know or realize something, for example why something happens, how something works, or what something means.

understand to know or realize the meaning of words, a language, what someone says, etc.; to know or realize how or why something happens, how it works, or why it is important: *I don't understand the instructions.* ◆ *Doctors are just beginning to understand the causes of the disease.*

see to understand what is happening, what someone is saying, how something works, or how important something is: *Aha—I see how it works now.* ◆ *Oh yes, I see what you mean.*

get (*informal*) to understand a joke, what someone is trying to tell you, or a situation that they are trying to describe: *She didn't get the joke.* ◆ *I don't get you.*

follow to understand an explanation, a story, or the meaning of something: *Sorry—I don't quite follow what you're saying.* ◆ *The plot is almost impossible to follow.*

grasp to come to understand a fact, an idea, or how to do something: *They failed to grasp the importance of his words.*

UNDERSTAND OR GRASP?

You can use **understand** or **grasp** for the action of realizing the meaning or importance of something for the first time: *It's a difficult concept for children to understand/grasp.* Only **understand** can be used to talk about languages, words, or writing: ~~I don't grasp French/the instructions.~~

comprehend (often used in negative statements) (*formal*) to understand a fact, an idea, or a reason: *The concept of infinity is almost impossible for us to comprehend.*

PATTERNS

- to understand/see/get/follow/grasp/comprehend **what**...
- to understand/see/get/grasp/comprehend **why/how**...
- to understand/see/grasp/comprehend **that**...
- to understand/see/get/grasp **the point/idea** (of sth)
- to be **easy/difficult/hard** to understand/see/follow/grasp/comprehend
- to **fully** understand/see/grasp/comprehend sth

un·der·stand·a·ble /ˌʌndərˈstændəbl/ *adj.* **1** (of behavior, feelings, reactions, etc.) seeming normal and reasonable in a particular situation **SYN** NATURAL: *Their attitude is perfectly understandable.* ◆ *It was an understandable mistake to make.* **2** (of language, documents, etc.) easy to understand **SYN** COMPREHENSIBLE: *Warning notices must be readily understandable.*

un·der·stand·a·bly /ˌʌndərˈstændəbli/ *adv.* in a way that seems normal and reasonable in a particular situation **SYN** NATURALLY: *They were understandably disappointed with the result.*

un·der·stand·ing /ˌʌndərˈstændɪŋ/ *noun, adj.*

- *noun* **1** [U, sing.] ~ **(of sth)** the knowledge that someone has about a particular subject or situation: *The committee has little or no understanding of the problem.* ◆ *The existence of God is beyond human understanding* (= humans cannot know whether God exists or not). **2** [C, usually sing.] an informal agreement: *We finally came to an understanding about what hours we would work.* ◆ *We have this understanding that no one talks about work over lunch.* **3** [U, sing.] the ability to under-

stand why people behave in a particular way and the willingness to forgive them when they do something wrong: *We must tackle the problem with sympathy and understanding.* ◆ *We are looking for a better understanding between the two nations.* **4** [U, C] ~ **(of sth)** the particular way in which someone understands something **SYN** INTERPRETATION: *My understanding of the situation is...* ◆ *The statement is open to various understandings.*
IDM on the understanding that... (*formal*) used to introduce a condition that must be agreed before something else can happen: *They agreed to the changes on the understanding that they would be introduced gradually.*

- *adj.* showing sympathy for other people's problems and being willing to forgive them when they do something wrong **SYN** SYMPATHETIC: *She has very understanding parents.* ▶ un·der·stand·ing·ly *adv.*

un·der·state /ˌʌndərˈsteɪt/ *verb* ~ **sth** to state that something is smaller, less important, or less serious than it really is: *It would be a mistake to understate the seriousness of the problem.* **ANT** OVERSTATE

un·der·stat·ed /ˌʌndərˈsteɪtəd/ *adj.* (*approving*) if a style, color, etc. is **understated**, it is pleasing and elegant in a way that is not too obvious **SYN** SUBTLE

un·der·state·ment /ˌʌndərˈsteɪtmənt/ *noun* **1** [C] a statement that makes something seem less important, impressive, serious, etc. than it really is: *To say we were pleased is an understatement* (= we were extremely pleased). ◆ *"These figures are a bit disappointing." "That's got to be the understatement of the year."* **2** [U] the practice of making things seem less impressive, important, serious, etc. than they really are: *typical British understatement* ◆ *He always goes for subtlety and understatement in his movies.*

un·der·stood pt, pp of UNDERSTAND

un·der·stud·y /ˈʌndərˌstʌdi/ *noun, verb*
- *noun* (*pl.* un·der·stud·ies) ~ **(to sb)** an actor who learns the part of another actor in a play so that they can play that part if necessary
- *verb* (un·der·stud·ies, un·der·stud·y·ing, un·der·stud·ied, un·der·stud·ied) ~ **sb/sth** to learn a part in a play as an understudy; to act as an understudy to someone

un·der·take **AWL** /ˌʌndərˈteɪk/ *verb* (un·der·took /-ˈtʊk/, un·der·tak·en /-ˈteɪkən/) (*formal*) **1** ~ **sth** to make yourself responsible for something and start doing it: *to undertake a task/project* ◆ *College professors both teach and undertake research.* ◆ *The company has announced that it will undertake a full investigation into the accident.* **2** ~ **to do sth** | ~ **that**... to agree or promise that you will do something: *He undertook to finish the job by Friday.*

un·der·tak·er /ˈʌndərˌteɪkər/ *noun* = FUNERAL DIRECTOR

un·der·tak·ing **AWL** /ˈʌndərˌteɪkɪŋ/ *noun* **1** [C] a task or project, especially one that is important and/or difficult **SYN** VENTURE: *He is interested in buying the club as a commercial undertaking.* ◆ *In those days, a cross-country trip was a dangerous undertaking.* **2** [C] (*formal*) an agreement or a promise to do something: ~ **(to do sth)** *a government undertaking to spend more on education* ◆ ~ **(that...)** *The landlord gave a written undertaking that the repairs would be carried out.* **3** /ˈʌndərˌteɪkɪŋ/ [U] the business of an undertaker

ˌunder-the-ˈcounter *adj.* (*informal*) illegal

un·der·tone /ˈʌndərˌtoʊn/ *noun* ~ **(of sth)** a feeling, quality, or meaning that is not expressed directly but is still noticeable from what someone says or does **SYN** UNDERCURRENT: *His soft words contained an undertone of warning.* ◆ *The play does not have the political undertones of the novel.* ⊃ compare OVERTONE
IDM in an undertone | in undertones in a quiet voice

un·der·took **AWL** pt of UNDERTAKE

un·der·tow /ˈʌndərˌtoʊ/ *noun* [usually sing.] **1** a current in the ocean that moves in the opposite direction to the water near the surface: *The children were carried out to sea by the strong undertow.* **2** ~ **(of sth)** a feeling or quality that influences people in a particular situation even though they may not really be aware of it

un·der·used /ˌʌndər'yuzd/ (also formal **un·der·u·ti·lized**) adj. not used as much as it could or should be ▶ **un·der·use** /ˌʌndər'yus; 'ʌndərˌyus/ (also formal **un·der·u·ti·li·za·tion**) noun [U]

un·der·val·ue /ˌʌndər'vælyu/ verb [usually passive] ~ **sb/sth** to not recognize how good, valuable, or important someone or something really is: *Education is currently undervalued in this country.* ◆ *He believes his house has been undervalued.* **ANT** OVERVALUE

un·der·wa·ter 🔑 /ˌʌndər'wɔtər; -'wɑtər/ adj. [only before noun] found, used, or happening below the surface of water: *underwater creatures* ◆ *an underwater camera* ▶ **un·der·wa·ter** adv.: *Take a deep breath and see how long you can stay underwater.*

un·der·way /ˌʌndər'weɪ/ adj. [not before noun] = UNDER WAY at WAY

un·der·wear 🔑 /'ʌndərˌwɛr/ noun [U] (also formal **un·der·clothes**, **un·der·cloth·ing**) clothes that you wear under other clothes and next to the skin: *She packed one change of underwear.*

un·der·weight /ˌʌndər'weɪt; 'ʌndərˌweɪt/ adj. (especially of a person) weighing less than the normal or expected weight: *She is a few pounds underweight for* (= in relation to) *her height.* **ANT** OVERWEIGHT ➔ collocations at DIET

un·der·went **AWL** pt of UNDERGO

un·der·whelmed /ˌʌndər'wɛlmd/ adj. (informal, humorous) not impressed with or excited about something at all: *We were distinctly underwhelmed by the director's speech.* ➔ compare OVERWHELM

un·der·whelm·ing /ˌʌndər'wɛlmɪŋ/ adj. (informal, humorous) not impressing or exciting you at all: *the contrast between his overwhelming guitar-playing and his underwhelming singing*

un·der·wire /'ʌndərˌwaɪər/ adj. (of a BRA) having a thin metal strip sewn into the bottom half of each CUP to provide support for a woman's breasts

un·der·world /'ʌndərˌwɜrld/ noun [sing.] **1** the people and activities involved in crime in a particular place: *the criminal underworld* ◆ *the Glasgow underworld* **2** the underworld (in MYTHS and LEGENDS, for example those of ancient Greece) the place under the earth where people are believed to go when they die

un·der·write /'ʌndərˌraɪt; ˌʌndər'raɪt/ verb (**un·der·wrote** /-ˌroʊt; -'roʊt/, **un·der·writ·ten** /-ˌrɪtn; -'rɪtn/) (technical) **1** ~ **sth** to accept financial responsibility for an activity so that you will pay for special costs or for losses it may make **2** ~ **sth** to accept responsibility for an insurance policy so that you will pay money in case loss or damage happens **3** ~ **sth** to agree to buy shares that are not bought by the public when new shares are offered for sale

un·der·writ·er /'ʌndərˌraɪtər/ noun **1** a person or organization that underwrites insurance policies, especially for ships **2** a person whose job is to estimate the risks involved in a particular activity and decide how much someone must pay for insurance

un·de·scend·ed /ˌʌndɪ'sɛndəd/ adj. (medical) (of a TESTICLE) staying inside the body instead of moving down normally into the SCROTUM

un·de·served /ˌʌndɪ'zɜrvd/ adj. that someone does not deserve and is therefore unfair: *The criticism was totally undeserved.* ◆ *an undeserved victory* ▶ **un·de·serv·ed·ly** /-'zɜrvədli/ adv.

un·de·serv·ing /ˌʌndɪ'zɜrvɪŋ/ adj. ~ **(of sth)** (formal) not deserving to have or receive something: *He was undeserving of her affections.* **ANT** DESERVING

un·de·sir·a·ble /ˌʌndɪ'zaɪrəbl/ adj., noun
● **adj.** not wanted or approved of; likely to cause trouble or

problems: *undesirable consequences/effects* ◆ *It would be highly undesirable to increase class sizes further.* **ANT** DESIRABLE ▶ **un·de·sir·a·bly** /-bli/ adv.
● **noun** [usually pl.] a person who is not wanted in a particular place, especially because they are considered dangerous or criminal: *petty criminals and other undesirables*

un·de·tect·a·ble /ˌʌndɪ'tɛktəbl/ adj. impossible to see or find: *The sound is virtually undetectable to the human ear.*

un·de·tect·ed /ˌʌndɪ'tɛktɛd/ adj. not noticed by anyone: *How could anyone break into the palace undetected?* ◆ *The disease often goes/remains undetected for many years.*

un·de·terred /ˌʌndɪ'tɜrd/ adj. if someone is **undeterred** by something, they do not allow it to stop them from doing something

un·de·vel·oped /ˌʌndɪ'vɛləpt/ adj. **1** (of land) not used for farming, industry, building, etc. **2** (of a country) not having modern industries, and with a low standard of living **3** not grown to full size: *undeveloped limbs* ➔ compare UNDER-DEVELOPED

un·did pt of UNDO

un·dies /'ʌndiz/ noun [pl.] (informal) underwear

un·dif·fer·en·ti·at·ed /ˌʌndɪfə'rɛnʃiˌeɪtəd/ adj. having parts that you cannot distinguish between; not split into different parts or sections: *a view of society as an undifferentiated whole* ◆ *an undifferentiated target audience*

un·dig·ni·fied /ʌn'dɪgnəˌfaɪd/ adj. causing you to look silly and to lose the respect of other people: *There was an undignified scramble for the best seats.* **ANT** DIGNIFIED

un·di·lut·ed /ˌʌndaɪ'lutəd; ˌʌndɪ-/ adj. **1** (of a liquid) not made weaker by having water added to it; not having been DILUTED **2** (of a feeling or quality) not mixed or combined with anything and therefore very strong **SYN** UNADULTERATED

un·di·min·ished **AWL** /ˌʌndɪ'mɪnɪʃt/ adj. that has not become smaller or weaker: *They continued with undiminished enthusiasm.*

un·dis·ci·plined /ʌn'dɪsəplənd/ adj. lacking control and organization; behaving badly **ANT** DISCIPLINED

un·dis·closed /ˌʌndɪs'kloʊzd/ adj. not made known or told to anyone; not having been DISCLOSED: *He was paid an undisclosed sum.*

un·dis·cov·ered /ˌʌndɪ'skʌvərd/ adj. that has not been found or noticed; that has not been discovered: *a previously undiscovered talent*

un·dis·guised /ˌʌndɪs'gaɪzd/ adj. (especially of a feeling) that you do not try to hide from other people; not DISGUISED: *a look of undisguised admiration*

un·dis·mayed /ˌʌndɪs'meɪd/ adj. [not before noun] (formal) not worried or frightened by something unpleasant or unexpected **SYN** UNDAUNTED

un·dis·put·ed /ˌʌndɪ'spyutəd/ adj. **1** that cannot be questioned or proved to be false; that cannot be DISPUTED **SYN** IRREFUTABLE: *undisputed facts* **2** that everyone accepts or recognizes: *the undisputed world champion*

un·dis·tin·guished /ˌʌndɪ'stɪŋgwɪʃt/ adj. not very interesting, successful, or attractive: *an undistinguished career* **ANT** DISTINGUISHED

un·dis·turbed /ˌʌndɪ'stɜrbd/ adj. **1** [not usually before noun] not moved or touched by anyone or anything **SYN** UNTOUCHED: *The treasure had lain undisturbed for centuries.* **2** not interrupted by anyone **SYN** UNINTERRUPTED: *She succeeded in working undisturbed for a few hours.* **3** [not usually before noun] ~ **(by sth)** not affected or upset by something **SYN** UNCONCERNED: *He seemed undisturbed by the news of her death.* ➔ compare DISTURBED

un·di·vid·ed /ˌʌndə'vaɪdəd/ adj. **1** not split into smaller parts; not divided: *an undivided country* **2** [usually before noun] total; complete; not divided: *undivided loyalty* ◆ *You must be prepared to give the speaker your undivided attention.*

un·do /ʌnˈdu/ verb (un·does /-ˈdʌz/, un·did /-ˈdɪd/, un·done /-ˈdʌn/)
1 ~ sth to open something that is fastened, tied or wrapped: *to undo a button/knot/zip, etc.* ◆ *to undo a jacket/shirt, etc.* ◆ *I undid the package and took out the books.* **ANT** DO UP **2** ~ sth to cancel the effect of something: *He undid most of the good work of the previous manager.* ◆ *It's not too late to try and undo some of the damage.* ◆ *UNDO* (= a command on a computer that cancels the previous action) **3** [usually passive] ~ sb/sth (formal) to make someone or something fail: *The team was undone by the speed and strength of their opponents.*

un·dock /ʌnˈdɑk/ verb ~ sth (computing) to remove a computer from a DOCKING STATION **ANT** DOCK

un·do·cu·ment·ed /ʌnˈdɑkyəˌmɛntəd/ adj. **1** not supported by written evidence: *undocumented accusations* **2** not having the necessary documents, especially permission to live and work in a foreign country: *undocumented immigrants*

un·do·ing /ʌnˈduɪŋ/ noun [sing.] the reason why someone fails at something or is unsuccessful in life **SYN** DOWNFALL: *That one mistake was his undoing.*

un·done /ʌnˈdʌn/ adj. [not usually before noun] **1** (especially of clothing) not fastened or tied: *Her shoelace had come undone.* **2** (especially of work) not finished: *Most of the work had been left undone.* **3** (old use) (of a person) defeated and without any hope for the future

un·doubt·ed /ʌnˈdaʊtəd/ adj. [usually before noun] used to emphasize that something exists or is definitely true: *She has an undoubted talent as an organizer.* ▶ **un·doubt·ed·ly** adv.: *There is undoubtedly a great deal of truth in what he says.*

un·dreamed-of /ʌnˈdrimd ʌv/ (also **un·dreamt-of** /ʌnˈdrɛmt ʌv/) adj. much more or much better than you thought was possible: *undreamed-of success*

un·dress /ʌnˈdrɛs/ verb, noun
● verb [I, T] to take off your clothes; to remove someone else's clothes: *She undressed and got into bed.* ◆ ~ **sb** to undress a child ◆ *He got undressed in the locker room.* **ANT** DRESS
● noun [U] (formal) the fact of someone wearing no, or few, clothes: *He appeared at the window in a state of undress.*

un·dressed /ʌnˈdrɛst/ adj. [not usually before noun] not wearing any clothes: *She began to get undressed* (= remove her clothes). **ANT** DRESSED

un·drink·a·ble /ʌnˈdrɪŋkəbl/ adj. not good or pure enough to drink **ANT** DRINKABLE

un·due /ʌnˈdu/ adj. [only before noun] (formal) more than you think is reasonable or necessary **SYN** EXCESSIVE: *They are taking undue advantage of the situation.* ◆ *The work should be carried out without undue delay.* ◆ *We did not want to put any undue pressure on them.* ➔ compare DUE

un·du·late /ˈʌndʒəˌleɪt/ verb [I] (formal) to go or move gently up and down like waves: *The tall grasses undulated in the breeze.*

un·du·la·tion /ˌʌndʒəˈleɪʃn/ noun [C, U] a smooth curving shape or movement like a series of waves

un·du·ly /ʌnˈduli/ adv. (formal) more than you think is reasonable or necessary **SYN** EXCESSIVEly: *He did not sound unduly worried at the prospect.* ◆ *The levels of pollution in this area are unduly high.* ◆ *The thought did not disturb her unduly.* ➔ compare DULY

un·dy·ing /ʌnˈdaɪŋ/ adj. [only before noun] lasting for ever **SYN** ETERNAL: *undying love*

un·earned /ʌnˈərnd/ adj. [usually before noun] used to describe money that you receive but do not earn by working: *Declare all unearned income.*

un·earth /ʌnˈərθ/ verb **1** ~ sth to find something in the ground by digging: *to unearth buried treasures* **2** ~ sth to discover or find something by chance or after searching for it: *I unearthed my old diaries when we moved house.* ◆ *The newspaper has unearthed some disturbing facts.*

un·earth·ly /ʌnˈərθli/ adj. [usually before noun] very strange; not natural and therefore frightening: *an unearthly cry* ◆ *an unearthly light*
IDM **at an unearthly hour** (informal) very early, especially when this is annoying: *The job involved getting up at some unearthly hour to catch the first train.*

un·ease /ʌnˈiz/ (also **un·eas·i·ness** /ʌnˈizinəs/) noun [U, sing.] the feeling of being worried or unhappy about something **SYN** ANXIETY: *a deep feeling/sense of unease* ◆ *There was a growing unease about their involvement in the war.* ◆ *He was unable to hide his unease at the way the situation was developing.*

un·eas·y /ʌnˈizi/ adj. **1** feeling worried or unhappy about a particular situation, especially because you think that something bad or unpleasant may happen or because you are not sure that what you are doing is right **SYN** ANXIOUS: *an uneasy laugh* ◆ ~ **about sth** *He was beginning to feel distinctly uneasy about their visit.* ◆ ~ **about doing sth** *She felt uneasy about leaving the children with them.* ➔ thesaurus box at WORRIED **2** not certain to last; not safe or settled: *an uneasy peace* ◆ *The two sides eventually reached an uneasy compromise.* **3** that does not enable you to relax or feel comfortable: *She woke from an uneasy sleep to find the house empty.* **4** used to describe a mixture of two things, feelings, etc. that do not go well together: *an uneasy mix of humor and violence* ◆ *Old farmhouses and new condos stood together in uneasy proximity.* ▶ **un·eas·i·ly** /ʌnˈizəli/ adv.: *I wondered uneasily what he was thinking.* ◆ *She shifted uneasily in her chair.* ◆ *His socialist views sit uneasily with his huge fortune.*

un·eat·a·ble /ʌnˈiṭəbl/ adj. (of food) not good enough to be eaten ➔ see also INEDIBLE

un·eat·en /ʌnˈitn/ adj. not eaten: *Bill put the uneaten food away.*

un·ec·o·nom·ic /ˌʌnɛkəˈnɑmɪk; ˌʌnikə-/ adj. **1** (of a business, factory, etc.) not making a profit **SYN** UNPROFITABLE: *uneconomic industries* **ANT** ECONOMIC **2** = UNECONOMICAL

un·ec·o·nom·i·cal **AWL** /ˌʌnɛkəˈnɑmɪkl; ˌʌnikə-/ (also **un·ec·o·nom·ic**) adj. ~ **(to do sth)** using too much time or money, or too many materials, and therefore not likely to make a profit: *It soon proved uneconomical to stay open 24 hours a day.* **ANT** ECONOMICAL

un·ed·i·fy·ing /ʌnˈɛdəˌfaɪŋ/ adj. (formal) unpleasant in a way that makes you feel disapproval: *the unedifying sight of the two party leaders screeching at each other* ➔ compare EDIFYING

un·ed·u·cat·ed /ʌnˈɛdʒəˌkeɪṭəd/ adj. having had little or no formal education at a school; showing a lack of education: *an uneducated workforce* ◆ *an uneducated point of view* ➔ compare EDUCATED

un·e·lect·ed /ˌʌnɪˈlɛktəd/ adj. not having been chosen by people in an election: *unelected bureaucrats*

un·e·mo·tion·al /ˌʌnɪˈmoʊʃənl/ adj. not showing your feelings: *an unemotional speech* ◆ *She seemed very cool and unemotional.* **ANT** EMOTIONAL ▶ **un·e·mo·tion·al·ly** /-ʃənəli/ adv.

un·em·ploy·a·ble /ˌʌnɪmˈplɔɪəbl/ adj. lacking the skills or qualities that you need to get a job **ANT** EMPLOYABLE

un·em·ployed /ˌʌnɪmˈplɔɪd/ adj.
without a job although able to work **SYN** JOBLESS: *How long have you been unemployed?* ◆ *an unemployed lawyer* ➔ collocations at UNEMPLOYMENT ▶ **the unemployed** noun [pl.]: *a program to get the **long-term unemployed** back to work* ◆ *I've joined the ranks of the unemployed* (= I've lost my job).

un·em·ploy·ment /ˌʌnɪmˈplɔɪmənt/ noun [U]
1 the fact of a number of people not having a job; the number of people without a job: *an area of **high/low** unemployment* ◆ *rising/falling unemployment* ◆ *It was a time of **mass** unemployment.* ◆ *measures to help reduce/tackle unemployment* ◆ *the level/rate of unemployment* ◆ *unemployment benefits/statistics* ➔ collocations at

ECONOMY **2** the state of not having a job: *Thousands of young people are facing long-term unemployment.* ⊃ compare EMPLOYMENT **3** = UNEMPLOYMENT BENEFITS: *Since losing his job, Mike has been collecting unemployment.*

unem·ploy·ment ˌbenefits *noun* [pl.] (also **unemˈploy·ment compenˌsation**, **un·em·ploy·ment** [U]) money paid by the government to someone who is unemployed: *people on* (= receiving) *unemployment benefits* ◆ *Applications for unemployment benefits dropped last month.*

un·en·cum·bered /ˌʌnɪnˈkʌmbərd/ *adj.* (*formal*) **1** not having or carrying anything heavy or anything that makes you go more slowly **2** (of property) not having any debts left to be paid

un·end·ing /ʌnˈendɪŋ/ *adj.* seeming to last for ever: *a seemingly unending supply of money*

un·en·dur·a·ble /ˌʌnɪnˈdʊrəbl/ *adj.* (*formal*) too bad, unpleasant, etc. to bear **SYN** UNBEARABLE: *unendurable pain*

un·en·vi·a·ble /ʌnˈenviəbl/ *adj.* [usually before noun] difficult or unpleasant; that you would not want to have: *She was given the **unenviable** task of informing the losers.* **ANT** ENVIABLE

un·e·qual /ʌnˈikwəl/ *adj.* **1** [usually before noun] in which people are treated in different ways or have different advantages in a way that seems unfair **SYN** UNFAIR: *an unequal distribution of wealth* ◆ *an unequal contest* **2** ~ **(in sth)** different in size, amount, etc.: *The sleeves are unequal in length.* ◆ *The rooms upstairs are of unequal size.* **3** ~ **to sth** (*formal*) not capable of doing something: *She felt unequal to the task she had set herself.* **ANT** EQUAL ▶ **un·e·qual·ly** *adv.*

un·e·qualed /ʌnˈikwəld/ *adj.* better than all others **SYN** UNPARALLELED: *an unequaled record of success*

un·e·quiv·o·cal /ˌʌnɪˈkwɪvəkl/ *adj.* (*formal*) expressing your opinion or intention very clearly and firmly **SYN** UNAMBIGUOUS: *an unequivocal rejection* ◆ *The answer was an unequivocal "no."* **ANT** EQUIVOCAL ⊃ thesaurus box at PLAIN ▶ **un·e·quiv·o·cally** /-kli/ *adv.*

un·err·ing /ʌnˈerɪŋ; -ˈərɪŋ/ *adj.* always right or accurate **SYN** UNFAILING: *She had an unerring instinct for a good business deal.* ▶ **un·err·ing·ly** *adv.*

UNESCO (also **Unesco**) /yuˈnɛskoʊ/ *abbr.* United Nations Educational, Scientific, and Cultural Organization (an organization that works to promote international peace and security through educational, scientific, and cultural projects)

un·eth·i·cal **AWL** /ʌnˈɛθɪkl/ *adj.* not morally acceptable: *unethical behavior* **ANT** ETHICAL ▶ **un·eth·i·cally** /-kli/ *adv.*

un·e·ven /ʌnˈivən/ *adj.* **1** not level, smooth, or flat: *The floor felt uneven under his feet.* **ANT** EVEN **2** not following a

regular pattern; not having a regular size and shape **SYN** IRREGULAR: *Her breathing was quick and uneven.* ◆ *uneven teeth* **ANT** EVEN **3** not having the same quality in all parts: *an uneven performance* (= with some good parts and some bad parts) **4** (of a contest or match) in which one group, team, or player is much better than the other **SYN** UNEQUAL **ANT** EVEN **5** organized in a way that is not regular and/or fair **SYN** UNEQUAL: *an uneven distribution of resources* **ANT** EVEN ▶ **un·e·ven·ly** *adv.* **un·e·ven·ness** *noun* [U]

unˈeven ˌbars *noun* [pl.] two bars on posts of different heights that are used by women for doing exercises on

un·e·vent·ful /ˌʌnɪˈvɛntfl/ *adj.* in which nothing interesting, unusual, or exciting happens: *an uneventful life* **ANT** EVENTFUL ▶ **un·e·vent·ful·ly** /-fəli/ *adv.*: *The day passed uneventfully.*

un·ex·cep·tion·a·ble /ˌʌnɪkˈsɛpʃənəbl/ *adj.* **1** (*formal*) not giving any reason for criticism: *a man of unexceptionable character* **2** (*informal*) not very new or exciting

un·ex·cep·tion·al /ˌʌnɪkˈsɛpʃənl/ *adj.* not interesting or unusual **SYN** UNREMARKABLE ⊃ compare EXCEPTIONAL

un·ex·cit·ing /ˌʌnɪkˈsaɪtɪŋ/ *adj.* not interesting; boring **ANT** EXCITING

un·ex·pect·ed 🔑 /ˌʌnɪkˈspɛktəd/ *adj.*
if something is **unexpected**, it surprises you because you were not expecting it: *an unexpected result* ◆ *an unexpected visitor* ◆ *The announcement was not entirely unexpected.* ▶ **the unexpected** *noun* [sing.]: *Police officers must be prepared for the unexpected.* **un·ex·pect·ed·ly** *adv.*: *They had arrived unexpectedly.* ◆ *an unexpectedly large bill* ◆ *The plane was unexpectedly delayed.* ◆ *Not unexpectedly, most local business depends on tourism.* **un·ex·pect·ed·ness** *noun* [U] ⊃ compare EXPECT, EXPECTED

un·ex·pired /ˌʌnɪkˈspaɪərd/ *adj.* [usually before noun] (of an agreement or a period of time) still valid; not yet having come to an end or expired (EXPIRED)

un·ex·plained /ˌʌnɪkˈspleɪnd/ *adj.* for which the reason or cause is not known; that has not been explained: *an unexplained mystery* ◆ *He died in unexplained circumstances.*

un·ex·plod·ed /ˌʌnɪkˈsploʊdəd/ *adj.* [only before noun] (of a bomb, etc.) that has not yet exploded

un·ex·plored /ˌʌnɪkˈsplɔrd/ *adj.* **1** (of a country or an area of land) that no one has investigated or put on a map; that has not been explored **2** (of an idea, a theory, etc.) that has not yet been examined or discussed thoroughly

un·ex·pressed /ˌʌnɪkˈsprɛst/ *adj.* (of a thought, a feeling, or an idea) not shown or made known in words, looks, or actions; not expressed

un·ex·pur·gat·ed /ʌnˈɛkspərˌgeɪtəd/ *adj.* (of a text) complete and containing all the original material, even if it is offensive: *This is the full, unexpurgated version of the diaries.*

un·fail·ing /ʌnˈfeɪlɪŋ/ *adj.* that you can rely on to always be there and always be the same **SYN** UNERRING: *unfailing support* ◆ *She fought the disease with **unfailing** good humor.* ▶ **un·fail·ing·ly** *adv.*: *unfailingly loyal/polite*

un·fair 🔑 /ʌnˈfɛr/ *adj.*
not right or fair according to a set of rules or principles; not treating people equally **SYN** UNJUST: *unfair criticism* ◆ **~ (on/to sb)** *It seems unfair on him to make him pay for everything.* ◆ *It would be unfair not to let you have a choice.* ◆ *They had been given an **unfair advantage**.* ◆ *measures to prevent **unfair competition** between member countries* ◆ *Life seems so unfair sometimes.* ◆ *It's so unfair!* **ANT** FAIR ▶ **un·fair·ly** *adv.*: *She claims to have been unfairly dismissed.* ◆ *The tests discriminate unfairly against older people.* **un·fair·ness** *noun* [U]

un·faith·ful /ʌnˈfeɪθfl/ *adj.* **~ (to sb)** having sex with someone who is not your husband, wife, or usual partner: *Have you ever been unfaithful to him?* **ANT** FAITHFUL ▶ **un·faith·ful·ness** *noun* [U]

un·fa·mil·iar /ˌʌnfəˈmɪlyər/ *adj.* **1** that you do not know or recognize: *She felt uneasy in the unfamiliar surroundings.* ◆ **~ to sb** *Please highlight any terms that are unfamiliar to you.* **2 ~ with sth** not having any knowledge or experience of something: *an introductory course for students who are unfamiliar with computers* **ANT** FAMILIAR ▶ **un·fa·mil·i·ar·i·ty** /ˌʌnfəˌmɪliˈærəti; -ˌmɪlˈyær-/ *noun* [U]

un·fash·ion·a·ble /ʌnˈfæʃənəbl/ *adj.* not popular or fashionable at a particular time: *an unfashionable part of the city* ◆ *unfashionable ideas* **ANT** FASHIONABLE ▶ **un·fash·ion·a·bly** /-bli/ *adv.*: *a man with unfashionably long hair*

un·fas·ten /ʌnˈfæsn/ *verb* **~ sth** to undo something that is fastened: *to unfasten a belt/button, etc.* **ANT** FASTEN

un·fath·om·a·ble /ʌnˈfæðəməbl/ *adj.* (*formal*) **1** too strange or difficult to be understood: *an unfathomable mystery* **2** if someone has an **unfathomable** expression, it is impossible to know what they are thinking

un·fa·vor·a·ble (*CanE usually* **un·fa·vour·a·ble**) /ʌnˈfeɪvərəbl; -ˈfeɪvrəbl/ *adj.* **1 ~ (for/to sth)** (of conditions, situations, etc.) not good and likely to cause problems or make something more difficult: *The conditions were unfavorable for agriculture.* ◆ *an unfavorable exchange rate* **2** showing that you do not approve of or like someone or something: *an unfavorable comment* ◆ *The documentary presents him in a very unfavorable light.* ◆ *an unfavorable comparison* (= one that makes one thing seem much worse than another) **ANT** FAVORABLE ▶ **un·fa·vor·a·bly** (*CanE usually* **un·fa·vour·a·bly**) /-bli/ *adv.*: *In this respect, Germany compares unfavorably with other European countries.*

un·fazed /ʌnˈfeɪzd/ *adj.* (*informal*) not worried or surprised by something unexpected that happens

un·fea·si·ble /ʌnˈfizəbl/ *adj.* not possible to do or achieve **ANT** FEASIBLE

un·feel·ing /ʌnˈfilɪŋ/ *adj.* not showing care or sympathy for other people

un·feigned /ʌnˈfeɪnd/ *adj.* (*formal*) real and sincere **SYN** GENUINE: *unfeigned admiration*

un·fenced /ʌnˈfɛnst/ *adj.* (of a road or piece of land) without fences beside or around it

un·fet·tered /ʌnˈfɛtərd/ *adj.* (*formal*) not controlled or restricted: *an unfettered free market*

un·filled /ʌnˈfɪld/ *adj.* **1** if a job or position is **unfilled**, no one has been chosen for it **2** if a pause in a conversation is **unfilled**, no one speaks **3** if an order for goods is **unfilled**, the goods have not been supplied

un·fin·ished /ʌnˈfɪnɪʃt/ *adj.* not complete; not finished: *We have some unfinished business to settle.*

un·fit /ʌnˈfɪt/ *adj.* **1** not of an acceptable standard; not suitable: **~ (for sth)** *The housing was unfit for human habitation.* ◆ *The food on offer was unfit for human consumption.* ◆ **~ (to eat, drink, live in, etc.)** *This water is unfit to drink.* ◆ *Most of the buildings are unfit to live in.* ◆ **~ (to do sth)** *They described him as unfit to govern.* ◆ (*technical*) *Many of the houses were condemned as unfit.* ◆ (*technical*) *The court claims she is an unfit mother.* **2** not capable of doing something, for example because of illness: **~ for sth** *He's still unfit for work.* ◆ **~ to do sth** *The company's doctor found that she was unfit to carry out her normal work.* **3** (of a person) not in good physical condition; not fit, because you have not taken exercise: *Wilson reported to training camp overweight and unfit.* **ANT** FIT ▶ **un·fit·ness** *noun* [U]

un·fit·ted /ʌnˈfɪtəd/ *adj.* **~ for sth | ~ to do sth** (*formal*) not suitable for something: *She felt herself unfitted for marriage.*

un·flag·ging /ʌnˈflægɪŋ/ *adj.* [usually before noun] remaining strong; not becoming weak or tired **SYN** TIRELESS: *unflagging energy*

un·flap·pa·ble /ʌnˈflæpəbl/ *adj.* (*informal*) able to stay calm in a difficult situation **SYN** IMPERTURBABLE

un·flat·ter·ing /ʌnˈflætərɪŋ/ *adj.* making someone or something seem worse or less attractive than they really are: *an unflattering dress* ◆ *unflattering comments* **ANT** FLATTERING

un·flinch·ing /ʌnˈflɪntʃɪŋ/ *adj.* remaining strong and determined, even in a difficult or dangerous situation **SYN** STEADFAST: *unflinching loyalty* ◆ *an unflinching stare* ▶ **un·flinch·ing·ly** *adv.* ⊃ see also FLINCH

un·fo·cused (also **un·fo·cussed**) /ʌnˈfoʊkəst/ *adj.* **1** (especially of eyes) not looking at a particular thing or person; not having been focused: *an unfocused look* **2** (of plans, work, etc.) not having a clear aim or purpose; not well organized or clear: *The research is too unfocused to have any significant impact.* ◆ *unfocused questions*

un·fold /ʌnˈfoʊld/ *verb* **1** [T, I] **~ (sth)** to spread open or flat something that has previously been folded; to become open and flat: *to unfold a map* ◆ *She unfolded her arms.* **ANT** FOLD **2** [I, T] to be gradually made known; to gradually make something known to other people: *The audience watched as the story unfolded before their eyes.* ◆ **~ sth (to sb)** *She unfolded her tale to us.*

un·forced /ʌnˈfɔrst/ *adj.* **1** (especially in sports) an **unforced** error is one that you make by playing badly, not because your opponent has caused you to make a mistake by their skillful play **2** natural; done without effort: *unforced humor*

un·fore·see·a·ble /ˌʌnfərˈsiəbl; -fɔr-/ *adj.* that you cannot predict or FORESEE: *Building a dam here could have unforeseeable consequences for the environment.* **ANT** FORESEEABLE

un·fore·seen /ˌʌnfərˈsin; -fɔr-/ *adj.* that you did not expect to happen **SYN** UNEXPECTED: *unforeseen delays/problems* ◆ *The project was running late owing to unforeseen circumstances.* ⊃ compare FORESEE

un·for·get·ta·ble /ˌʌnfərˈgɛtəbl/ *adj.* if something is **unforgettable**, you cannot forget it, usually because it is so beautiful, interesting, enjoyable, etc. **SYN** MEMORABLE ⊃ compare FORGETTABLE

un·for·giv·a·ble /ˌʌnfərˈgɪvəbl/ *adj.* if someone's behavior is **unforgivable**, it is so bad or unacceptable that you cannot forgive the person **SYN** INEXCUSABLE **ANT** FORGIVABLE ▶ **un·for·giv·a·bly** /-bli/ *adv.*

un·for·giv·ing /ˌʌnfərˈgɪvɪŋ/ *adj.* (*formal*) **1** (of a person) unwilling to forgive other people when they have done something wrong **ANT** FORGIVING **2** (of a place, situation, etc.) unpleasant and causing difficulties for people

un·formed /ʌnˈfɔrmd/ *adj.* (*formal*) not fully developed: *unformed ideas*

un·forth·com·ing /ˌʌnfɔrθˈkʌmɪŋ/ *adj.* not wanting to help or give information about something **SYN** RETICENT: *He was very unforthcoming about what had happened.* **ANT** FORTHCOMING

un·for·tu·nate 🔊 /ʌnˈfɔrtʃənət/ *adj., noun*

● *adj.* **1** having bad luck; caused by bad luck **SYN** UNLUCKY: *He was unfortunate to lose in the final round.* ◆ *It was an unfortunate accident.* **ANT** FORTUNATE **2** (*formal*) if you say that a situation is **unfortunate**, you wish that it had not happened or that it had been different **SYN** REGRETTABLE: *She described the decision as "unfortunate."* ◆ *It was unfortunate that he couldn't speak English.* ◆ *You're putting me in a most unfortunate position.* ⊃ language bank at IMPERSONAL **3** embarrassing and/or offensive: *It was an unfortunate choice of words.*

● *noun* (*literary*) a person who does not have much luck, money, etc.: *one of life's unfortunates*

un·for·tu·nate·ly 🔊 /ʌnˈfɔrtʃənətli/ *adv.* used to say that a particular situation or fact makes you sad or disappointed, or gets you into a difficult position: *Unfortunately, I won't be able to attend the meeting.* ◆ *I can't make it, unfortunately.* ◆ *Unfortunately for him, the police had been informed and were waiting outside.* ◆ *It won't be finished for a few weeks. Unfortunately!* **ANT** FORTUNATELY

un·found·ed **AWL** /ʌnˈfaʊndəd/ *adj.* not based on reason or fact: *unfounded allegations/rumors, etc.* ◆ *Speculation about a divorce **proved** totally **unfounded**.*

un·freeze /ʌnˈfriz/ *verb* (**un·froze** /-ˈfroʊz/, **un·fro·zen** /-ˈfroʊzn/) **1** [T, I] ~ **(sth)** if you **unfreeze** something that has been frozen or very cold, or it **unfreezes**, it melts or warms until it reaches a normal temperature ➔ **compare** DEFROST, DE-ICE, THAW **2** [T] ~ **sth** to remove official controls on money or an economy: *The party plans to unfreeze some of the cash held by local government.* **ANT** FREEZE

un·friend·ly 🔑 /ʌnˈfrɛndli/ *adj.*
not kind or pleasant to someone: *an unfriendly atmosphere* ◆ ~ **(to/toward sb)** *There's no need to be so unfriendly toward them.* ◆ *the use of **environmentally unfriendly** products* (= that harm the environment) **ANT** FRIENDLY ▶ **un·friend·li·ness** *noun* [U]

un·ful·filled /ˌʌnfʊlˈfɪld/ *adj.* **1** (of a need, wish, etc.) that has not been satisfied or achieved: *unfulfilled ambitions/hopes/promises, etc.* **2** if a person feels **unfulfilled**, they feel that they could achieve more in their life or work **ANT** FULFILLED

un·ful·fill·ing /ˌʌnfʊlˈfɪlɪŋ/ *adj.* not causing someone to feel satisfied and useful: *an unfulfilling job*

un·fund·ed /ʌnˈfʌndəd/ *adj.* not provided with money or funds; not funded: *The new education program remains unfunded.*

un·fun·ny /ʌnˈfʌni/ *adj.* not funny or amusing, especially when something is supposed to be funny: *The show was deeply unfunny.*

un·furl /ʌnˈfərl/ *verb* [I, T] when something that is curled or rolled tightly **unfurls**, or you **unfurl** it, it opens: *The leaves slowly unfurled.* ◆ ~ **sth** *to unfurl a flag/sail*

un·fur·nished /ʌnˈfərnɪʃt/ *adj.* without furniture: *We rented an unfurnished apartment.* **ANT** FURNISHED

un·gain·ly /ʌnˈgeɪnli/ *adj.* moving in a way that is not smooth or elegant **SYN** AWKWARD: *He was a tall, ungainly boy of 15.*

un·gen·tle·man·ly /ʌnˈdʒɛntlmənli/ *adj.* (of a man's behavior) not polite or pleasant; not acceptable **ANT** GENTLEMANLY

un·glam·or·ous /ʌnˈɡlæmərəs/ *adj.* not attractive or exciting; dull: *an unglamorous job* **ANT** GLAMOROUS

un·glued /ʌnˈɡlud/ *adj.*
IDM **come unglued** (*informal*) **1** to become very upset **2** if a plan, etc. **comes unglued**, it does not work successfully

un·god·ly /ʌnˈɡɑdli/ *adj.* **1** (*old-fashioned*) not showing respect for God; evil **ANT** GODLY **2** [only before noun] (*informal*) shocking and unacceptable: *The dessert had an ungodly amount of fat and calories.*
IDM **at an ungodly hour/time** very early or very late and therefore annoying

un·gov·ern·a·ble /ʌnˈɡʌvərnəbl/ *adj.* **1** (of a country, region, etc.) impossible to govern or control **2** (*formal*) (of a person's feelings) impossible to control **SYN** UNCONTROLLABLE: *ungovernable rage*

un·gra·cious /ʌnˈɡreɪʃəs/ *adj.* (*formal*) not polite or friendly, especially toward someone who is being kind to you **ANT** GRACIOUS ▶ **un·gra·cious·ly** *adv.*

un·gram·mat·i·cal /ˌʌnɡrəˈmætɪkl/ *adj.* not following the rules of grammar **ANT** GRAMMATICAL

un·grate·ful /ʌnˈɡreɪtfl/ *adj.* not showing or expressing thanks for something that someone has done for you or given to you **ANT** GRATEFUL ▶ **un·grate·ful·ly** /-fəli/ *adv.*

un·guard·ed /ʌnˈɡɑrdəd/ *adj.* **1** not protected or watched: *The museum was unguarded at night.* ◆ *an unguarded fire* (= that has nothing to stop people from burning themselves on it) **2** (of a remark, look, etc.) said or done carelessly, at a time when you are not thinking about the effects of your words or are not paying attention: *an unguarded remark* ◆ *It was something I'd let out **in an unguarded moment**.* ➔ compare GUARDED

un·guent /ˈʌŋɡwənt/ *noun* [C, U] (*formal*) a soft substance that is used for rubbing onto the skin to heal it

un·gu·late /ˈʌŋɡyələt; -ˌleɪt/ *noun* (*technical*) any animal which has HOOFS, such as a cow or horse

un·hand /ʌnˈhænd/ *verb* ~ **sb** (*old-fashioned* or *humorous*) to release a person that you are holding

un·hap·pi·ly /ʌnˈhæpəli/ *adv.* **1** in an unhappy way: *He sighed unhappily.* **2** used to say that a particular situation or fact makes you sad or disappointed **SYN** UNFORTUNATELY: *Unhappily, such good luck is rare.* ◆ *His wife, unhappily, died five years ago.* **ANT** HAPPILY

un·hap·py 🔑 /ʌnˈhæpi/ *adj.*
(**un·hap·pi·er**, **un·hap·pi·est**) **HELP** more unhappy and most unhappy are also common **1** not happy; sad: *to be/look/seem/sound unhappy* ◆ *an unhappy childhood* ◆ *I didn't realize, but he was **deeply unhappy** at that time.* **2** ~ **(about/at/with sth)** not pleased or satisfied with something: *They were unhappy with their hotel room.* ◆ *He was unhappy at being left out of the team.* **3** (*formal*) unfortunate or not suitable: *an unhappy coincidence* ◆ *It was an unhappy choice of words.*
▶ **un·hap·pi·ness** *noun* [U]

un·harmed /ʌnˈhɑrmd/ *adj.* not injured or damaged; not harmed **SYN** UNHURT

UNHCR /ˌyu ɛn eɪtʃ si ˈɑr/ *abbr.* United Nations High Commission for Refugees (an organization whose function is to help and protect REFUGEES)

un·health·y /ʌnˈhɛlθi/ *adj.* **1** not having good health; showing a lack of good health: *They looked poor and unhealthy.* ◆ *unhealthy skin* ◆ *His eyeballs were an unhealthy yellow.* **2** harmful to your health; likely to make you sick: *unhealthy living conditions* ◆ *an unhealthy diet/lifestyle* **3** not normal and likely to be harmful **SYN** UNWHOLESOME: *He had an unhealthy interest in disease and death.* **ANT** HEALTHY
▶ **un·health·i·ly** /-θəli/ *adv.*

un·heard /ʌnˈhərd/ *adj.* **1** that no one pays attention to: *Their protests **went unheard**.* **2** not listened to or heard: *a previously unheard tape of their conversations*

un·heard-of /ʌnˈhərd ʌv/ *adj.* that has never been known or done; very unusual: *He had dyed his hair, which was almost unheard-of in the 1960s.* ◆ *It is almost unheard-of for a new band to be offered such a deal.*

un·heat·ed /ʌnˈhitəd/ *adj.* having no form of heating: *an unheated bathroom* **ANT** HEATED

un·heed·ed /ʌnˈhidəd/ *adj.* (*formal*) that is heard, seen, or noticed but then ignored: *Her warning **went unheeded**.*
➔ compare HEED

un·help·ful /ʌnˈhɛlpfl/ *adj.* not helpful or useful; not willing to help someone: *an unhelpful response* ◆ *The taxi driver was being very unhelpful.* **ANT** HELPFUL ▶ **un·help·ful·ly** /-fəli/ *adv.*

un·her·ald·ed /ʌnˈhɛrəldəd/ *adj.* (*formal*) **1** not previously mentioned; happening without any warning **2** not recognized or publicly praised as good or important: *an unheralded athlete* ◆ *an unheralded factor in our success*

un·hes·i·tat·ing /ʌnˈhɛzəˌteɪtɪŋ/ *adj.* done or given immediately and confidently: *He gave an unhesitating "yes" when asked if he would go through the experience again.* ▶ **un·hes·i·tat·ing·ly** *adv.*

un·hin·dered /ʌnˈhɪndərd/ *adj.* without anything stopping or preventing the progress of someone or something: *She had unhindered access to the files.* ◆ *He was able to **pass unhindered** through several military checkpoints.* ➔ see also HINDER

un·hinge /ʌnˈhɪndʒ/ *verb* [usually passive] ~ **sb/sth** to make someone very upset or mentally ill

un·hip /ʌnˈhɪp/ *adj.* (*informal*) not following or knowing what is fashionable **SYN** UNCOOL: *He's so unhip!* **ANT** HIP

un·hitch /ʌnˈhɪtʃ/ *verb* ~ **sth** to undo something that is tied to something else: *to unhitch a trailer* ➔ see also HITCH

un·ho·ly /ʌnˈhoʊli/ *adj.* **1** dangerous; likely to be harmful:

ʌ **cup**   ə **about**   eɪ **say**   aɪ **five**   ɔɪ **boy**   aʊ **now**   oʊ **go**   ər **bird**

an **unholy alliance** between the medical profession and the pharmaceutical industry **2** not respecting the laws of a religion **ANT** HOLY **3** [only before noun] (*informal*) used to emphasize how bad something is: *She wondered how she had gotten into this unholy mess.*

un·hook /ʌnˈhʊk/ *verb* **~ sth (from sth)** to remove something from a hook; to undo the hooks on clothes, etc.: *He unhooked his coat from the door.* ◆ *She unhooked her bra.*

un·hur·ried /ʌnˈhərid/ *adj.* (*formal*) relaxed and calm; not done too quickly **ANT** HURRIED ▶ **un·hur·ried·ly** /ʌnˈhərədli; -ˈhərid-/ *adv.*: *Lynn walked unhurriedly into the kitchen.*

un·hurt /ʌnˈhərt/ *adj.* [not before noun] not injured or harmed **SYN** UNHARMED: *He escaped from the crash unhurt.* **ANT** HURT

un·hy·gien·ic /ˌʌnhaɪˈdʒɛnɪk; -ˈdʒinɪk; -dʒiˈɛnɪk/ *adj.* not clean and therefore likely to cause disease or infection **ANT** HYGIENIC

uni- /ˈyunə/ *combining form* (in nouns, adjectives, and adverbs) one; having one: *uniform* ◆ *unilaterally*

u·ni·cam·er·al /ˌyuniˈkæmərəl/ *adj.* (*technical*) (of a LEGISLATURE) that has only one main governing body

UNICEF /ˈyunəˌsɛf/ *abbr.* United Nations Children's Fund (an organization within the United Nations that helps to take care of the health and education of children all over the world)

u·ni·cel·lu·lar /ˌyunəˈsɛlyələr/ *adj.* (*biology*) (of a living thing) consisting of only one cell: *unicellular organisms*

u·ni·corn /ˈyunɪˌkɔrn/ *noun* (in stories) an animal like a white horse with a long straight horn on its head

u·ni·cy·cle /ˈyunəˌsaɪkl/ (also **mon·o·cy·cle**) *noun* a vehicle that is similar to a bicycle but that has only one wheel
⊃ picture at BICYCLE

un·i·den·ti·fi·a·ble **AWL** /ˌʌnaɪˌdɛntəˈfaɪəbl; -aɪˈdɛntəˌfaɪ-/ *adj.* impossible to identify: *He had an unidentifiable accent.* ◆ *Many of the bodies were unidentifiable except by dental records.* **ANT** IDENTIFIABLE

un·i·den·ti·fied /ˌʌnaɪˈdɛntəˌfaɪd/ *adj.* not recognized or known; not identified: *an unidentified virus* ◆ *The painting was sold to an unidentified New York dealer* (= his or her name was not given).

Unifi·cation Church *noun* a religious and political organization begun in Korea in 1954 by Sun Myung Moon

u·ni·form 🔑 **AWL** /ˈyunəˌfɔrm/ *noun, adj.*

• *noun* **1** [C, U] the special set of clothes worn by all members of an organization or a group at work, or by children at school: *a military/police/nurse's uniform* ◆ *soldiers in uniform* ◆ *The hat is part of the school uniform.* ◆ *Do you have to wear a uniform?* **2** [C, usually sing., U] the clothes worn by the members of a sports team when they are playing: *a striped baseball uniform* ◆ *the team's road uniform* (= that they use when playing games away from home) ⊃ picture at SPORT **3** [sing., U] the type of clothes that a person or group usually wears: *my standard teenage uniform of sweatshirt and jeans*

• *adj.* not varying; the same in all parts and at all times: *uniform rates of pay* ◆ *The walls were a uniform gray.* ◆ *Growth has not been uniform across the country.* ◆ *uniform lines of apartment houses* (= they all looked the same) ▶ **u·ni·form·i·ty** **AWL** /ˌyunəˈfɔrməti/ *noun* [U, sing.]: *They tried to ensure uniformity across the different departments.* ◆ *the drab uniformity of the houses* **u·ni·form·ly** **AWL** /ˈyunəˌfɔrmli/ *adv.*: *The principles were applied uniformly across all the departments.* ◆ *The quality is uniformly high.* ◆ *Pressure must be uniformly distributed over the whole surface.*

u·ni·formed /ˈyunəˌfɔrmd/ *adj.* wearing a uniform: *a uniformed chauffeur*

u·ni·fy **AWL** /ˈyunəˌfaɪ/ *verb* (**u·ni·fies**, **u·ni·fy·ing**, **u·ni·fied**, **u·ni·fied**) **~ sth** to join people, things, parts of a country, etc. together so that they form a single unit: *The new leader hopes to unify the country.* ◆ *the task of unifying the North and*

South ◆ *a unified transport system* ▶ **u·ni·fi·ca·tion** **AWL** /ˌyunəfəˈkeɪʃn/ *noun* [U]: *the unification of Germany*

u·ni·lat·er·al /ˌyunəˈlætərəl/ *adj.* done by one member of a group or an organization without the agreement of the other members: *a unilateral decision* ◆ *a unilateral declaration of independence* ◆ *They were forced to take unilateral action.* ◆ *They had campaigned vigorously for* **unilateral nuclear disarmament** (= when one country gets rid of its nuclear weapons without waiting for other countries to do the same). ⊃ compare BILATERAL, MULTILATERAL, TRILATERAL ▶ **u·ni·lat·er·al·ly** *adv.*

u·ni·lat·er·al·ism /ˌyunəˈlætərəˌlɪzəm/ *noun* [U] belief in or support of unilateral action, especially military action ▶ **u·ni·lat·er·al·ist** /-lɪst/ *noun*: *the defeat of the unilateralists on nuclear disarmament* **u·ni·lat·er·al·ist** *adj.*: *unilateralist defense policy*

u·ni·lin·gual /ˌyunəˈlɪŋgwəl/ *adj.* (*CanE*) = MONOLINGUAL

un·im·ag·i·na·ble /ˌʌnɪˈmædʒənəbl/ *adj.* (*formal*) impossible to think of or to believe exists; impossible to imagine: *unimaginable wealth* ◆ *This level of success would have been unimaginable just last year.* **ANT** IMAGINABLE ▶ **un·im·ag·i·na·bly** /-bli/ *adv.*

un·im·ag·i·na·tive /ˌʌnɪˈmædʒənətɪv/ *adj.* lacking in original or new ideas **SYN** DULL: *an unimaginative solution to a problem* ◆ *a boring, unimaginative man* **ANT** IMAGINATIVE

un·im·ag·ined /ˌʌnɪˈmædʒənd/ *adj.* [usually before noun] that you had not imagined or thought of as possible: *new and unimagined freedom* ◆ *Things could change in ways that are unimagined.*

un·im·paired /ˌʌnɪmˈpɛrd/ *adj.* (*formal*) not damaged or spoiled: *Although he's ninety, his mental faculties remain unimpaired.* **ANT** IMPAIRED

un·im·peach·a·ble /ˌʌnɪmˈpitʃəbl/ *adj.* (*formal, approving*) that you cannot doubt or question: *evidence from an unimpeachable source*

un·im·ped·ed /ˌʌnɪmˈpidəd/ *adj.* (*formal*) with nothing blocking or stopping someone or something: *an unimpeded view of the bay* ◆ *free and unimpeded trade*

un·im·por·tant 🔑 /ˌʌnɪmˈpɔrtnt/ *adj.* not important: *unimportant details* ◆ *relatively/comparatively unimportant* ◆ *They dismissed the problem as unimportant.* ◆ *This consideration was not unimportant.* ◆ *I was just a nobody from a small town and I felt very unimportant.* ▶ **un·im·por·tance** /-tns/ *noun* [U]

un·im·pressed /ˌʌnɪmˈprɛst/ *adj.* **~ (by/with sb/sth)** not thinking that someone or something is particularly good, interesting, etc.; not impressed by someone or something

un·im·pres·sive /ˌʌnɪmˈprɛsɪv/ *adj.* ordinary; not special in any way: *His academic record was unimpressive.* **ANT** IMPRESSIVE

un·im·proved /ˌʌnɪmˈpruvd/ *adj.* **1** (of land) that has not been changed in a way that would make it more useful, for example by putting buildings on it: *The property is unimproved.* **2** (of someone's medical condition or health) not showing an improvement: *The patient's condition remains unimproved.*

un·in·cor·po·rat·ed /ˌʌnɪnˈkɔrpəˌreɪtəd/ *adj.* (of an area of land) not part of a particular city or town: *an unincorporated community governed by the county*

un·in·flect·ed /ˌʌnɪnˈflɛktəd/ *adj.* (*linguistics*) (of a word or language) not changing its form to show different functions in grammar

un·in·form·a·tive /ˌʌnɪnˈfɔrmətɪv/ *adj.* not giving enough information: *The reports of the explosion were brief and uninformative.* **ANT** INFORMATIVE

un·in·formed /ˌʌnɪnˈfɔrmd/ *adj.* having or showing a lack of knowledge or information about something: *an uninformed comment/criticism* ◆ *The public is generally uninformed about these diseases.* **ANT** INFORMED

un·in·hab·it·a·ble /ˌʌnɪnˈhæbətəbl/ *adj.* not fit to live in;

impossible to live in: *The building was totally uninhabitable.*
ANT HABITABLE

un·in·hab·it·ed /ˌʌnɪnˈhæbətəd/ *adj.* with no people living
there; not **INHABITED**: *an uninhabited island*

un·in·hib·it·ed /ˌʌnɪnˈhɪbətəd/ *adj.* behaving or expressing
yourself freely without worrying about what other people
think **SYN** UNRESTRAINED: *uninhibited dancing*
ANT INHIBITED

the un·in·i·ti·at·ed /ˌʌnɪˈnɪʃiˌeɪtəd/ *noun* [pl.] people who
have no special knowledge or experience of something: *To
the uninitiated the system seems too complicated.* ▶ **un·in·i-
ti·at·ed** *adj.*

un·in·jured **AWL** /ʌnˈɪndʒərd/ *adj.* [not usually before noun]
not hurt or injured in any way **SYN** UNHURT: *They escaped
from the crash uninjured.*

un·in·spired /ˌʌnɪnˈspaɪərd/ *adj.* not original or exciting
SYN DULL **ANT** INSPIRED

un·in·spir·ing /ˌʌnɪnˈspaɪərɪŋ/ *adj.* not making people
interested or excited: *The view from the window was uninspiring.* **ANT** INSPIRING

un·in·stall /ˌʌnɪnˈstɔl/ *verb* ~ **sth** (*computing*) to remove a
program from a computer: *Uninstall any programs that you
no longer need.* **ANT** INSTALL (2)

un·in·sur·a·ble /ˌʌnɪnˈʃʊrəbl/ *adj.* something that is
uninsurable cannot be given insurance because it involves
too much risk

un·in·sured /ˌʌnɪnˈʃʊrd/ *adj.* not having insurance; not
covered by insurance: *an uninsured driver* ◆ *an uninsured
claim*

un·in·tel·li·gent **AWL** /ˌʌnɪnˈtɛlədʒənt/ *adj.* not intelligent:
He was not unintelligent, but he was lazy.

un·in·tel·li·gi·ble /ˌʌnɪnˈtɛlədʒəbl/ *adj.* impossible to understand **SYN** INCOMPREHENSIBLE: *She turned away and
muttered something unintelligible.* ◆ ~ **to sb** *A lot of the jargon
they use is unintelligible to outsiders.* **ANT** INTELLIGIBLE
▶ **un·in·tel·li·gi·bly** /-bli/ *adv.*

un·in·tend·ed /ˌʌnɪnˈtɛndəd/ *adj.* an **unintended** effect,
result, or meaning is one that you did not plan or intend to
happen

un·in·ten·tion·al /ˌʌnɪnˈtɛnʃənl/ *adj.* not done deliberately,
but happening by accident: *Perhaps I misled you, but it really
was unintentional* (= I did not mean to). **ANT** INTENTIONAL
▶ **un·in·ten·tion·al·ly** /-ʃənəli/ *adv.*: *They had unintentionally provided the wrong information.*

un·in·ter·est·ed /ʌnˈɪntrəstəd; -ˈɪntəˌrɛs-; -ˈɪntrɛs-/ *adj.* ~ (**in
sb/sth**) not interested; not wanting to know about
someone or something: *He was totally uninterested in sports.*
◆ *She seemed cold and uninterested.* ⊃ note at INTERESTED

un·in·ter·est·ing /ʌnˈɪntrəstɪŋ; -ˈɪntəˌrɛs-; -ˈɪntrɛs-/ *adj.* not
attracting your attention or interest; not interesting ⊃ note
at INTERESTED

un·in·ter·rupt·ed /ˌʌnɪntəˈrʌptəd/ *adj.* not stopped or
blocked by anything; continuous and not interrupted: *We
had an uninterrupted view of the stage.* ◆ *eight hours of
uninterrupted sleep* ◆ *We managed to eat our meal uninterrupted by phone calls.*

un·in·vit·ed /ˌʌnɪnˈvaɪtəd/ *adj.* doing something or going
somewhere when you have not been asked or invited to,
especially when someone does not want you to: *uninvited
guests at a party* ◆ *He showed up uninvited.*

un·in·vit·ing /ˌʌnɪnˈvaɪtɪŋ/ *adj.* not attractive or pleasant:
The water looked cold and uninviting. **ANT** INVITING

un·in·volved **AWL** /ˌʌnɪnˈvɑlvd/ *adj.* ~ (**in /with sth**) not
taking part in something; not connected with someone or
something, especially on an emotional level: *My mom was
distant and cold and very uninvolved in my life.* **ANT** INVOLVED

un·ion 🔑 /ˈyunyən/ *noun*
1 (also ˈlabor ˌunion) [C] an organization of workers,
usually in a particular industry, that exists to protect their
interests, improve conditions of work, etc.: *I've joined the*

union. ◆ *a union member* **2** [C] an association or a club for
people or organizations with the same interest ⊃ see also
STUDENT UNION **3** [C] a group of states or countries that
have the same central government or that agree to work
together: *the former Soviet Union* ◆ *the European Union*
4 Union [sing.] the U.S. (especially at the time of the
Civil War): *the Union and the Confederacy* ◆ *the State of the
Union address by the President* **5** [U, sing.] the act of joining
two or more things together; the state of being joined
together; the act of two people joining together: *a summit to
discuss economic and monetary union* ◆ *a union with one of the
big banks* **6** [C] (*old-fashioned*) a marriage: *Their union was
blessed with six children.*

un·ion·ist /ˈyunyənɪst/ *noun* Unionist a supporter of the
Union during the Civil War in the U.S. ▶ **un·ion·ism**
/ˈyunyəˌnɪzəm/ *noun* [U]

un·ion·ize /ˈyunyəˌnaɪz/ *verb* [T, I] ~ (**sth**) to organize
people to become members of a LABOR UNION; to become a
member of a labor union: *a unionized workforce* ◆ *They were
forbidden to unionize.* ▶ **un·ion·i·za·tion** /ˌyunyənəˈzeɪʃn/
noun [U]

the ˌUnion ˈJack *noun* [sing.] the name for the national flag
of the United Kingdom

u·nique 🔑 **AWL** /yuˈnik/ *adj.*
1 being the only one of its kind: *Everyone's fingerprints are
unique.* **HELP** You can use **absolutely**, **totally**, or **almost**
with **unique** in this meaning. **2** very special or unusual: *a
unique talent* ◆ *The preview offers a unique opportunity to see
the show without the crowds.* ◆ *The deal will put the company in
a unique position to export goods to Asia.* **HELP** You can use
more, **very**, etc. with **unique** in this meaning. **3** ~ (**to sb/
sth**) belonging to or connected with one particular person,
place, or thing: *an atmosphere that is unique to New York* ◆ *The
koala is unique to Australia.* ▶ **u·nique·ly** **AWL** *adv.*: *Her past
experience made her uniquely suited to lead the campaign.* ◆ *The
U.K., uniquely, has not had to face the problem of mass
unemployment.* ◆ *He was a uniquely gifted teacher.* **u·nique-
ness** **AWL** *noun* [U]: *The author stresses the uniqueness of the
individual.*

u·ni·sex /ˈyunəˌsɛks/ *adj.* intended for or used by both men
and women: *a unisex hair salon* ◆ *unisex jeans*

u·ni·son /ˈyunəsn/ *noun*
IDM in unison (with sb/sth) **1** if people do or say something **in unison**, they all do it at the same time **2** if people
or organizations are working **in unison**, they are working
together, because they agree with each other **3** (*music*) if
singers or musicians sing or play **in unison**, they sing or
play notes at the same PITCH or at one or more OCTAVES
apart

u·nit 🔑 /ˈyunət/ *noun*
▷ SINGLE THING **1** a single thing, person, or group that is
complete by itself but can also form part of something
larger: *The cell is the unit of which all living organisms are
composed.* ◆ *The basic unit of society is the family.* **2** (*business*)
a single item of the type of product that a company sells:
The game's retail price was $15 per unit. ◆ *What's the unit cost?*
▷ GROUP OF PEOPLE **3** a group of people who work or live
together, especially for a particular purpose: *army/
military/police units* ◆ *Medical units were operating in the
disaster area.*
▷ MEASUREMENT **4** ~ (**of sth**) a fixed quantity, etc. that is used
as a standard measurement: *a unit of time/length/weight* ◆ *a
unit of currency, such as the euro or the dollar*
▷ FURNITURE **5** a piece of furniture, especially a cupboard,
that fits with and matches others of the same type: *a custom
kitchen with white units* ◆ *floor/wall units* ◆ *bedroom/kitchen/
storage units*
▷ SMALL MACHINE **6** a small machine that has a particular
purpose or is part of a larger machine: *a waste disposal unit*
◆ *the central processing unit of a computer*
▷ IN TEXTBOOK **7** one of the parts into which a TEXTBOOK or a
series of lessons is divided: *The present perfect is covered in
Unit 8.*

| t tea | ţ butter | d did | k cat | g got | tʃ chin | dʒ June | f fall |

> APARTMENT **8** one of the parts or sections that a large building is divided into

> IN A HOSPITAL **9** a department, especially in a hospital, that provides a particular type of care or treatment: *the intensive care unit* ♦ *a trauma unit*

> NUMBER **10** any whole number from 0 to 9: *a column for the tens and a column for the units*

U·ni·tar·i·an Uni·ver·sal·ist /ˌyunəˈtɛriən ˌyunəˈvərsəlɪst/ *noun* a member of a Christian Church that does not believe in the TRINITY and has no formal teachings ▶ **U·ni·tar·i·an Uni·ver·sal·ist** *adj.* **U·ni·tar·i·an Uni·ver·sal·ism** /ˌyunə-ˈvərsəˌlɪzəm/ *noun* [U]

u·ni·tar·y /ˈyunəˌtɛri/ *adj.* **1** (*technical*) (of a country or an organization) consisting of a number of areas or groups that are joined together and are controlled by one government or group: *a single unitary state* **2** (*formal*) single; forming one unit

u·nite 🔊 /yuˈnaɪt/ *verb*
1 [I] to join together with other people in order to do something as a group: **~ in sth** *Local resident groups have* **united in opposition** *to the plan.* ♦ **~ in doing sth** *We will unite in fighting crime.* ♦ **~ (behind/against sb/sth)** *Will they unite behind the new leader?* ♦ *Nationalist parties united to oppose the government's plans.* **2** [T, I] to make people or things join together to form a unit; to join together: **~ (sb/sth)** *A special bond unites our two countries.* ♦ *His aim was to unite the North and South.* ♦ *The two countries united in 1887.* ♦ **~ (sb/sth) (with sb/sth)** *She unites good business skills with a charming personality.*

u·nit·ed 🔊 /yuˈnaɪtəd/ *adj.*
1 (of countries) joined together as a political unit or by shared aims: *the United States of America* ♦ *efforts to build a united Europe* **2** (of people or groups) in agreement and working together: *We need to become a more united team.* ♦ *They are united in their opposition to the plan.* ♦ *We should present a* **united front** (= an appearance of being in agreement with each other).

the U·nited 'Kingdom *noun* [sing.] (*abbr.* (the) U.K.) England, Scotland, Wales, and Northern Ireland (considered as a political unit)

the U·nited 'Nations *noun* (*abbr.* (the) UN) an association of many countries that aims to improve economic and social conditions and to solve political problems in the world in a peaceful way

the ˌUnited ˌNations Se'curity ˌCouncil *noun* = SECURITY COUNCIL

ˌUnited ˌPress Inter'national *noun* (*abbr.* UPI) a company that collects news and sells it to newspapers and radio and television stations

the U·nited 'States (also the U·nited ˌStates of A'merica) *noun* (*abbr.* the U.S., the U.S.A.) a large country in N. America consisting of 50 states and the District of Columbia ⟳ note at AMERICAN

u·ni·ty /ˈyunəti/ *noun* (*pl.* **u·ni·ties**) **1** [U, sing.] the state of being in agreement and working together; the state of being joined together to form one unit: *European unity* ♦ *a plea for unity within the party* ♦ *unity of purpose* **ANT** DISUNITY **2** [U] (in art, etc.) the state of looking or being complete in a natural and pleasing way: *The design lacks unity.* **3** [C] (in literature and theater) any of the principles of CLASSICAL or NEOCLASSICAL theater that restrict the action of a play to a single story, day, and place: *the unities of action, time, and place* **4** [sing.] (*formal*) a single thing that may consist of a number of different parts: *If society is to exist as a unity, its members must have shared values.* **5** [U] (*mathematics*) the number one

Univ. *abbr.* (in writing) University

u·ni·ver·sal 🔊 /ˌyunəˈvərsl/ *adj.*
1 done by or involving all the people in the world or in a particular group: *Such problems are a universal feature of old age.* ♦ *Agreement on this issue is almost universal.* ♦ *universal*

suffrage (= the right of all the people in a country to vote) **2** true or right at all times and in all places: *universal facts about human nature* ▶ **u·ni·ver·sal·i·ty** /ˌyunəvərˈsæləti/ *noun*: *the universality of religious experience*

ˌuni'versal 'grammar *noun* [U, C] (*linguistics*) the set of rules that is thought to be able to describe all languages

ˌuni'versal 'indicator *noun* (*chemistry*) a substance that changes color when another substance touches it, indicating whether it is an acid or an ALKALI

u·ni·ver·sal·ly /ˌyunəˈvərsəli/ *adv.* **1** by everyone: *to be universally accepted* **2** everywhere or in every situation: *This treatment is not universally available.* ♦ *The theory does not apply universally.*

Uni'versal ˌTime *noun* [U] = GMT

u·ni·verse 🔊 /ˈyunəˌvərs/ *noun*
1 the universe [sing.] the whole of space and everything in it, including the earth, the planets, and the stars: *theories of how the universe began* **2** [C] a system of stars, planets, etc. in space outside our own: *The idea of a parallel universe is hard to grasp.* ♦ *He lives in a little universe of his own.* **3** [sing.] a set of experiences of a particular type: *the moral universe*

u·ni·ver·si·ty 🔊 /ˌyunəˈvərsəti/ *noun* (*pl.* **u·ni·ver·si·ties**) [C, U] (*abbr.* Univ.)
an institution at the highest level of education where you can study for a degree or do research: *Penn State University* ♦ *the University of Michigan* ♦ *Harvard University* ♦ *a university degree/professor* ⟳ note at COLLEGE ⟳ see also STATE UNIVERSITY

IDM **the university of 'life** (*informal*) the experience of life thought of as giving someone an education, instead of the person gaining formal qualifications

U·nix™ (also **U·NIX**) /ˈyunɪks/ *noun* [U] (*computing*) an OPERATING SYSTEM that can be used by many people at the same time

un·just /ʌnˈdʒʌst/ *adj.* not deserved or fair: *an unjust law* **ANT** JUST ▶ **un·just·ly** *adv.*: *She felt that she had been unjustly treated.*

un·jus·ti·fi·a·ble /ˌʌndʒʌstəˈfaɪəbl; -ˈdʒʌstəˌfaɪ-/ *adj.* (of an action) impossible to excuse or accept because there is no good reason for it **SYN** INDEFENSIBLE: *an unjustifiable delay* **ANT** JUSTIFIABLE ▶ **un·jus·ti·fi·a·bly** /-bli/ *adv.*

un·jus·ti·fied **AWL** /ʌnˈdʒʌstəˌfaɪd/ *adj.* not fair or necessary **SYN** UNWARRANTED: *The criticism was wholly unjustified.* **ANT** JUSTIFIED

un·kempt /ʌnˈkɛmpt/ *adj.* (especially of someone's hair or general appearance) not well cared for; messy **SYN** DISHEVELED: *greasy, unkempt hair*

un·kind 🔊 /ʌnˈkaɪnd/ *adj.* **~ (to sb/sth) (to do sth)** unpleasant or unfriendly; slightly cruel: *an unkind remark* ♦ *He was never actually unkind to them.* ♦ *It would be unkind to go without him.* **ANT** KIND ▶ **un·kind·ly** *adv.*: *"That's your problem," she remarked unkindly.* **un·kind·ness** *noun* [U]

un·know·a·ble /ʌnˈnoʊəbl/ *adj.* (*formal*) that cannot be known: *a distant, unknowable, divine power*

un·know·ing /ʌnˈnoʊɪŋ/ *adj.* [usually before noun] (*formal*) not aware of what you are doing or what is happening: *He was the unknowing cause of all the misunderstanding.* ⟳ compare KNOWING ▶ **un·know·ing·ly** *adv.*: *She had unknowingly broken the rules.*

un·known 🔊 /ʌnˈnoʊn/ *adj., noun*
● *adj.* **1 ~ (to sb)** not known or identified: *a species of insect previously unknown to science* ♦ *He was trying,* **for some unknown reason**, *to count the stars.* ♦ *The man's identity remains unknown.* **2** (of people) not famous or well known: *an unknown actor* ♦ *The author is virtually unknown outside Poland.* **3** never happening or existing: *The disease is as yet unknown in Europe* (= there have been no cases there). ♦ *It was* **not unknown** *for people to have to wait several hours* (= it happened sometimes).

IDM **an unknown quantity** a person or thing whose qualities or abilities are not yet known **unknown to sb** without the person mentioned being aware of it: *Unknown to me, he had already signed the agreement.*

• **noun 1 the unknown** [sing.] places or things that are not known about: *a journey into the unknown* ◆ *a fear of the unknown* **2** [C] a person who is not well known: *A young unknown played the leading role.* **3** [C] a fact or an influence that is not known: *There are so many unknowns in the proposal.* **4** [C] (*mathematics*) a quantity that does not have a known value: *X and Y in the equation are both unknowns.*

the ¡Unknown 'Soldier *noun* [sing.] a soldier who has been killed in a war, whose body has not been identified, and who is buried in special ceremony. The **Unknown Soldier** is a symbol for all the soldiers killed in a particular war or in wars generally: *the tomb of the Unknown Soldier*

un·lace /ʌnˈleɪs/ *verb* ~ **sth** to undo the LACES of shoes, clothes, etc. **ANT** LACE

un·lad·en /ʌnˈleɪdn/ *adj.* (*technical*) (of a vehicle) not loaded: *a vehicle with an unladen weight of 5,000 lbs.* ◐ compare LADEN

un·law·ful /ʌnˈlɔːfl/ *adj.* (*formal*) not allowed by the law **SYN** ILLEGAL **ANT** LAWFUL ▶ **un·law·ful·iy** /-fəli/ *adv.*

un¡lawful 'killing *noun* (*law*) a murder or other killing that is considered a crime, for example when a person dies because someone is careless: *The two police officers were accused of unlawful killing.*

un·lead·ed /ʌnˈlɛdəd/ *adj.* (of gas) not containing LEAD 2 and therefore less harmful to the environment **ANT** LEADED ▶ **unleaded** *noun* [U]: *Unleaded is cheaper than diesel.*

un·learn /ʌnˈlɜːrn/ *verb* ~ **sth** to deliberately forget something that you have learned, especially something bad or wrong: *You'll have to unlearn all the bad habits you picked up with your last piano teacher.*

un·leash /ʌnˈliːʃ/ *verb* ~ **sth (on/upon sb/sth)** to suddenly let a strong force, emotion, etc. be felt or have an effect: *The government's proposals unleashed a storm of protest in the press.*

un·leav·ened /ʌnˈlɛvnd/ *adj.* (of bread) made without any YEAST and therefore flat ◐ see also LEAVEN

un·less 🔑 /ənˈlɛs/ *conj.*
1 used to say that something can only happen or be true in a particular situation: *You won't get paid for time off unless you have a doctor's note.* ◆ *I won't tell them — not unless you say I can.* ◆ *Unless I'm mistaken, she was back at work yesterday.* ◆ *He hasn't got any hobbies — unless you call watching TV a hobby.* **2** used to give the only situation in which something will not happen or be true: *I sleep with the window open unless it's really cold.* ◆ *Unless something unexpected happens, I'll see you tomorrow.* ◆ *Have a cup of tea — unless you'd prefer a cold drink?* **HELP** Unless is used to talk about a situation that could happen, or something that could be true, in the future. If you know that something has not happened or that something is not true, use if… not: *If you weren't always in such a hurry (= but you are), your work would be much better.* ◆ ~~Your work would be much better unless you were always in such a hurry.~~

un·let·tered /ʌnˈlɛtərd/ *adj.* (*formal*) unable to read

un·li·censed **AWL** /ʌnˈlaɪsnst/ *adj.* without a license: *an unlicensed vehicle* **ANT** LICENSED

un·like 🔑 /ʌnˈlaɪk/ *prep., adj.*
• **prep. 1** different from a particular person or thing: *Music is quite unlike any other art form.* ◆ *The sound was not unlike that of birds singing.* **2** used to contrast someone or something with another person or thing: *Unlike most systems, this one is very easy to install.* ◐ language bank at CONTRAST **3** not typical of someone or something: *It's very unlike him to be so late.* **ANT** LIKE
• **adj.** [not before noun] (of two people or things) different

from each other: *They are both teachers. Otherwise they are quite unlike.* ◐ compare ALIKE, LIKE

un·like·ly 🖉 /ʌnˈlaɪkli/ *adj.* (**un·like·li·er, un·like·li·est**) **HELP** more unlikely and most unlikely are the usual forms **1** not likely to happen: ~ **(to do sth)** *The project seemed unlikely to succeed.* ◆ ~ **(that…)** *It's most (= very) unlikely that she'll arrive before seven.* ◆ *In the unlikely event of a problem arising, please contact the hotel manager.* **2** [only before noun] not the person, thing, or place that you would normally think of or expect: *He seems a most unlikely candidate for the job.* ◆ *They have built hotels in the most unlikely places.* **3** [only before noun] difficult to believe **SYN** IMPLAUSIBLE: *She gave me an unlikely explanation for her behavior.* **ANT** LIKELY ▶ **un·like·li·hood** /ʌnˈlaɪkliˌhʊd/ (also **un·like·li·ness**) *noun* [U]

un·lim·it·ed /ʌnˈlɪmətəd/ *adj.* as much or as many as is possible; not limited in any way: *The ticket gives you unlimited travel for seven days.* ◆ *The court has the power to impose an unlimited fine for this offense.* ◆ *You will be allowed unlimited access to the files.*

un·lined /ʌnˈlaɪnd/ *adj.* **1** not marked with lines: *unlined paper/skin* **2** (of a piece of clothing, etc.) made without an extra layer of cloth on the inside **ANT** LINED

un·list·ed /ʌnˈlɪstəd/ *adj.* **1** not on a published list, especially of STOCK EXCHANGE prices: *an unlisted company* **2** (of a telephone number) not listed in the public telephone book or available from DIRECTORY ASSISTANCE, at the request of the owner of the telephone

un·lit /ʌnˈlɪt/ *adj.* **1** dark because there are no lights or the lights are not switched on: *an unlit passage* **2** not yet burning: *an unlit cigarette* **ANT** LIGHTED

un·load 🖉 /ʌnˈloʊd/ *verb*
1 [T, I] to remove things from a vehicle or ship after it has taken them somewhere: ~ **sth from sth** *Everyone helped to unload the luggage from the car.* ◆ ~ **(sth)** *This isn't a suitable place to unload the van.* ◆ *The truck driver was waiting to unload.* **ANT** LOAD **2** [T] ~ **sth** to remove the contents of something after you have finished using it, especially the bullets from a gun or the film from a camera **ANT** LOAD **3** [T] ~ **sth/sb (on/onto sb)** (*informal*) to pass the responsibility for someone or something to someone else: *It's his problem, not something he should unload onto you.* **4** [T] ~ **sth (on/onto sb/sth)** (*informal*) to get rid of or sell something, especially something illegal or of bad quality: *They want to unload their shares at the right price.* **5** [I, T] (*informal*) to express strong feelings or worries: *Give her a chance to unload.* ◆ ~ **sth (on sb)** *He's just unloading his anger on us.*

un·lock 🖉 /ʌnˈlɑk/ *verb* **1** ~ **sth** to undo the lock of a door, window, etc., using a key: *to unlock the door* **ANT** LOCK **2** ~ **sth** to discover something and let it be known: *The divers hoped to unlock some of the secrets of the ocean.*

un·locked /ʌnˈlɑkt/ *adj.* not locked: *Don't leave your bike unlocked.*

un·looked-for /ʌnˈlʊkt fɔr/ *adj.* (*formal*) not expected: *unlooked-for developments*

un·loose /ʌnˈlus/ (also **un·loos·en** /ʌnˈlusn/) *verb* ~ **sth** (old-fashioned or *formal*) to make something loose: *He unloosed his tie.*

un·loved /ʌnˈlʌvd/ *adj.* (*formal*) not loved by anyone: *unloved children*

un·love·ly /ʌnˈlʌvli/ *adj.* (*formal*) not attractive: *an unlovely building*

un·luck·i·ly /ʌnˈlʌkəli/ *adv.* unfortunately; as a result of bad luck: *He was injured in the first game and unluckily missed the final.*

un·luck·y 🖉 /ʌnˈlʌki/ *adj.* (**un·luck·i·er, un·luck·i·est**) **HELP** You can also use more unlucky and most unlucky. **1** ~ **(to do sth)** having bad luck or happening because of bad luck; not lucky **SYN** UNFORTUNATE: *He was very unlucky not to win.* ◆ *By some unlucky chance, her name was left off the* list. **2** ~ **(to do sth)** causing bad luck: *Some people think it's unlucky to walk under a ladder.* ◆ *Thirteen is often considered an unlucky number.* **ANT** LUCKY

un·made /ʌnˈmeɪd/ *adj.* an **unmade** bed is not ready for sleeping in because the sheets, etc. have not been arranged neatly

un·man·age·a·ble /ʌnˈmænɪdʒəbl/ *adj.* difficult or impossible to control or deal with **ANT** MANAGEABLE

un·man·ly /ʌnˈmænli/ *adj.* (*formal*) not having the qualities that are admired or expected in a man **ANT** MANLY

un·manned /ʌnˈmænd/ *adj.* if a machine, a vehicle, a place, or an activity is **unmanned**, it does not have or need a person to control or operate it **ANT** MANNED: *an unmanned spacecraft* ◆ *an unmanned Mars mission*

un·man·ner·ly /ʌnˈmænərli/ *adj.* (*formal*) not having or showing good manners; not polite

un·marked /ʌnˈmɑrkt/ *adj.* **1** without a sign or words to show what or where something is: *an unmarked police car* ◆ *He was buried in an unmarked grave.* ⭢ compare MARKED **2** (*linguistics*) (of a word or form of a word) not showing any particular feature or style, such as being formal or informal **ANT** MARKED

un·mar·ried /ʌnˈmærid/ *adj.* not married **SYN** SINGLE: *an unmarried mother*

un·mask /ʌnˈmæsk/ *verb* ~ **sb/sth** to show the true character of someone, or a hidden truth about something **SYN** EXPOSE: *to unmask a spy*

un·matched /ʌnˈmætʃt/ *adj.* ~ **(by sb/sth)** (*formal*) better than all others: *He had a talent unmatched by any other politician of this century.*

un·me·di·at·ed /ʌnˈmidiˌeɪtəd/ *adj.* happening or done without any people, actions, etc. in between; direct: *unmediated face-to-face collaboration* ◆ *spelling errors in unmediated blogs* (= that have not been edited or corrected) ◆ *pure unmediated experiences*

un·mem·o·ra·ble /ʌnˈmɛmərəbl/ *adj.* that cannot be remembered because it was not special **ANT** MEMORABLE

un·men·tion·a·ble /ʌnˈmɛnʃənəbl/ *adj.* [usually before noun] too shocking or embarrassing to be mentioned or spoken about: *an unmentionable disease*

un·men·tion·a·bles /ʌnˈmɛnʃənəblz/ *noun* [pl.] (*old-fashioned, humorous*) = UNDERWEAR

un·met /ʌnˈmɛt/ *adj.* (*formal*) (of needs, etc.) not satisfied: *a report on the unmet needs of elderly people*

un·mind·ful /ʌnˈmaɪndfl/ *adj.* ~ **of sb/sth** (*formal*) not giving thought or attention to someone or something **ANT** MINDFUL

un·miss·a·ble /ʌnˈmɪsəbl/ *adj.* that you must not miss because it is so good: *an unmissable opportunity*

un·mis·tak·a·ble (also *less frequent* **un·mis·take·a·ble**) /ˌʌnmɪˈsteɪkəbl/ *adj.* that cannot be mistaken for someone or something else: *Her accent was unmistakable.* ◆ *the unmistakable sound of gunfire* ▸ **un·mis·tak·a·bly** (also *less frequent* **un·mis·take·a·bly**) /-bli/ *adv.*: *His accent was unmistakably British.*

un·mit·i·gat·ed /ʌnˈmɪtəˌgeɪtəd/ *adj.* [only before noun] used to mean "complete," usually when describing something bad **SYN** ABSOLUTE: *The evening was an unmitigated disaster.* ⭢ see also MITIGATE

un·mod·i·fied **AWL** /ʌnˈmɑdəˌfaɪd/ *adj.* not modified (MODIFY)

un·mo·lest·ed /ˌʌnməˈlɛstəd/ *adj.* [not usually before noun] (*formal*) not disturbed or attacked by someone; not prevented from doing something

un·mo·ti·vat·ed **AWL** /ʌnˈmoʊtəˌveɪtəd/ *adj.* **1** not having interest in or enthusiasm for something, especially work or study: *unmotivated students* **2** without a reason or MOTIVE: *an unmotivated attack*

un·moved /ʌnˈmuvd/ *adj.* ~ **(by sth)** not feeling sympathy or emotions, especially in a situation where it would be normal to do so: *Alice seemed totally unmoved by the whole experience.* ◆ *She pleaded with him but he remained unmoved.*

un·mov·ing /ʌnˈmuvɪŋ/ *adj.* (*formal*) not moving: *He stood, unmoving, in the shadows.*

un·mu·si·cal /ʌnˈmyuzɪkl/ *adj.* **1** (of a sound) unpleasant to listen to: *His voice was harsh and unmusical.* **2** (of a person) unable to play or enjoy music **ANT** MUSICAL

un·named /ʌnˈneɪmd/ *adj.* whose name is not given or not known: *information from an unnamed source* ◆ *Two casualties, as yet unnamed, are still in the local hospital.*

un·nat·u·ral /ʌnˈnætʃrəl; -ˈnætʃərəl/ *adj.* **1** different from what is normal or expected, or from what is generally accepted as being right: *It seems unnatural for a child to spend so much time alone.* ◆ *There was an unnatural silence and then a scream.* ◆ *He gave an unnatural smile* (= that did not seem genuine). **2** different from anything in nature: *Her leg was bent at an unnatural angle.* ◆ *an unnatural death* (= one not from natural causes) **ANT** NATURAL ▸ **un·nat·u·ral·ly** *adv.*: *She was, not unnaturally, very surprised at the news.* ◆ *His eyes were unnaturally bright.*

un·nec·es·sar·y 🔑 /ʌnˈnɛsəˌsɛri/ *adj.*
1 not needed; more than is needed **SYN** UNJUSTIFIED: *unnecessary expense* ◆ *They were found guilty of causing unnecessary suffering to animals.* ◆ *All this fuss is totally unnecessary.* **ANT** NECESSARY **2** (of remarks, etc.) not needed in the situation and likely to be offensive **SYN** UNCALLED FOR: *That last comment was a little unnecessary, wasn't it?* ▸ **un·nec·es·sar·i·ly** /ˌʌnnɛsəˈsɛrəli/ *adv.*: *There's no point worrying him unnecessarily.* ◆ *unnecessarily complicated instructions*

un·nerve /ʌnˈnərv/ *verb* ~ **sb** to make someone feel nervous or frightened or lose confidence: *His silence unnerved us.* ◆ *She appeared strained and a little unnerved.* ▸ **un·nerv·ing** *adj.* **un·nerv·ing·ly** *adv.*

un·no·ticed /ʌnˈnoʊtəst/ *adj.* [not before noun] not seen or noticed: *His kindness did not go unnoticed by his staff.*

un·num·bered /ʌnˈnʌmbərd/ *adj.* not marked with a number; not NUMBERED: *unnumbered seats*

UNO /ˌyu ɛn ˈoʊ; ˈyunoʊ/ *abbr.* United Nations Organization ⭢ see also UNITED NATIONS

un·ob·jec·tion·a·ble /ˌʌnəbˈdʒɛkʃənəbl/ *adj.* (*formal*) (of an idea, etc.) that you can accept **SYN** ACCEPTABLE

un·ob·served /ˌʌnəbˈzərvd/ *adj.* without being seen: *It's not easy for somebody to get into the building unobserved.*

un·ob·tain·a·ble **AWL** /ˌʌnəbˈteɪnəbl/ *adj.* [not usually before noun] that cannot be obtained **ANT** OBTAINABLE

un·ob·tru·sive /ˌʌnəbˈtrusɪv/ *adj.* (*formal, often approving*) not attracting unnecessary attention: *The service at the hotel is efficient and unobtrusive.* **ANT** OBTRUSIVE ▸ **un·ob·tru·sive·ly** *adv.*: *Daria slipped unobtrusively in through the back door.*

un·oc·cu·pied /ʌnˈɑkyəˌpaɪd/ *adj.* **1** empty, with no one living there or using it: *an unoccupied house* ◆ *I sat down at the nearest unoccupied table.* **2** (of a region or country) not controlled by foreign soldiers: *unoccupied territory* **ANT** OCCUPIED

un·of·fi·cial /ˌʌnəˈfɪʃl/ *adj.* **1** that does not have permission or approval from someone in authority: *an unofficial agreement/strike* ◆ *Unofficial estimates put the figure at over two million.* **2** that is not part of someone's official business: *The former president paid an unofficial visit to China.* **ANT** OFFICIAL ▸ **un·of·fi·cial·ly** /-ʃəli/ *adv.*

un·o·pened /ʌnˈoʊpənd/ *adj.* not opened yet: *The letter was returned unopened.*

un·op·posed /ˌʌnəˈpoʊzd/ *adj.* [not usually before noun] not opposed or stopped by anyone: *The party leader was re-elected unopposed.*

un·or·gan·ized /ʌnˈɔrgəˌnaɪzd/ *adj.* **1** (of workers) without a LABOR UNION or other organization to represent or support them **2** = DISORGANIZED **3** not having been organized: *unorganized data* ➔ compare ORGANIZED

un·or·tho·dox /ʌnˈɔːrθəˌdɑks/ *adj.* different from what is usual or accepted: *unorthodox methods* **ANT** ORTHODOX ➔ compare HETERODOX

un·pack /ʌnˈpæk/ *verb* **1** [T, I] ~ (sth) to take things out of a bag, SUITCASE, etc.: *I unpacked my bags as soon as I arrived.* ♦ *She unpacked all the clothes she needed and left the rest in the case.* ♦ *She went to her room to unpack.* **ANT** PACK **2** [T] ~ sth to separate something into parts so that it is easier to understand: *to unpack a theory*

un·paid /ʌnˈpeɪd/ *adj.* **1** not yet paid: *unpaid bills* **2** done or taken without payment: *unpaid work* ♦ *unpaid leave* **ANT** PAID **3** (of people) not receiving payment for work that they do: *unpaid volunteers* **ANT** PAID

un·pal·at·a·ble /ʌnˈpælətəbl/ *adj.* ~ (to sb) **1** (of facts, ideas, etc.) unpleasant and not easy to accept **SYN** DISTASTEFUL: *Only then did I learn the unpalatable truth.* **2** not pleasant to taste: *unpalatable food* **ANT** PALATABLE

un·par·al·leled **AWL** /ʌnˈpærəˌlɛld/ *adj.* (formal) used to emphasize that something is bigger, better, or worse than anything else like it **SYN** UNEQUALED: *It was an unparalleled opportunity to develop her career.* ♦ *The book has enjoyed a success unparalleled in recent publishing history.* ➔ compare PARALLEL

un·par·don·a·ble /ʌnˈpɑrdnˌəbl/ *adj.* that cannot be forgiven or excused **SYN** INEXCUSABLE, UNFORGIVABLE **ANT** PARDONABLE

un·pa·tri·ot·ic /ʌnˌpeɪtriˈɑtɪk/ *adj.* not supporting your own country **ANT** PATRIOTIC

un·paved /ʌnˈpeɪvd/ *adj.* (of a road) not covered with a hard, smooth surface; not PAVED

un·per·turbed /ˌʌnpərˈtɜːrbd/ *adj.* not worried or anxious: *She seemed unperturbed by the news.*

un·pick /ʌnˈpɪk/ *verb* ~ sth to take out STITCHES from a piece of sewing or KNITTING

un·placed /ʌnˈpleɪst/ *adj.* not one of the first three to finish in a race or competition

un·planned /ʌnˈplænd/ *adj.* not planned in advance: *an unplanned pregnancy*

un·play·a·ble /ʌnˈpleɪəbl/ *adj.* not able to be played; impossible to play on or with: *The ball was unplayable (= it was hit so well that it was impossible to hit it back).* ➔ compare PLAYABLE

un·pleas·ant 🔑 /ʌnˈplɛznt/ *adj.*
1 not pleasant or comfortable **SYN** DISAGREEABLE: *an unpleasant experience* ♦ *The minerals in the water made it unpleasant to drink.* **2** ~ (to sb) not kind, friendly or polite: *He was very unpleasant to me.* ♦ *She said some very unpleasant things about you.* **ANT** PLEASANT ▶ **un·pleas·ant·ly** *adv.*: *The drink is very sweet, but not unpleasantly so.* ♦ *He laughed unpleasantly.*

un·pleas·ant·ness /ʌnˈplɛzntnəs/ *noun* [U] bad feeling or arguments between people

un·plug /ʌnˈplʌg/ *verb* (-gg-) ~ sth to remove the plug of a piece of electrical equipment from the electricity supply **ANT** PLUG STH IN

un·plugged™ /ʌnˈplʌgd/ *adj.* (sometimes after noun) (of pop or ROCK music or musicians) performed or performing with ACOUSTIC rather than electric instruments: *an unplugged concert* ♦ *Eric Clapton unplugged*

un·pol·lut·ed /ˌʌnpəˈluːtəd/ *adj.* that has not been POLLUTED (= made dirty by harmful substances)

un·pop·u·lar /ʌnˈpɑpyələr/ *adj.* not liked or enjoyed by a person, a group, or people in general: *an unpopular choice* ♦ *an unpopular government* ♦ ~ with/among sb *The proposed increase in income tax proved deeply unpopular with the electorate.* **ANT** POPULAR ▶ **un·pop·u·lar·i·ty** /ˌʌnpɑpyəˈlærəti/ *noun* [U]: *the growing unpopularity of the military regime*

un·prec·e·dent·ed **AWL** /ʌnˈprɛsəˌdɛntəd/ *adj.* that has never happened, been done, or been known before: *The situation is unprecedented in modern times.* ▶ **un·prec·e·dent·ed·ly** *adv.*: *a period of unprecedentedly high food prices*

un·pre·dict·a·ble **AWL** /ˌʌnprɪˈdɪktəbl/ *adj.* that cannot be predicted because it changes a lot or depends on too many different things: *unpredictable weather* ♦ *The result is entirely unpredictable.* ➔ collocations at PREDICT **2** if a person is **unpredictable**, you cannot predict how they will behave in a particular situation **ANT** PREDICTABLE ▶ **un·pre·dict·a·bil·i·ty** **AWL** /ˌʌnprɪˌdɪktəˈbɪləti/ *noun* [U]: *the unpredictability of Seattle weather* **un·pre·dict·a·bly** /ˌʌnprɪˈdɪktəbli/ *adv.*

un·prej·u·diced /ʌnˈprɛdʒədəst/ *adj.* not influenced by an unreasonable fear or dislike of something or someone; willing to consider different ideas and opinions **ANT** PREJUDICED

un·pre·med·i·tat·ed /ˌʌnprɪˈmɛdəˌteɪtəd/ *adj.* (formal) (of a crime or bad action) not planned in advance **ANT** PREMEDITATED

un·pre·pared /ˌʌnprɪˈpɛrd/ *adj.* **1** ~ (for sth) not ready or not expecting something: *She was totally unprepared for his response.* **2** ~ (to do sth) (formal) not willing to do something: *She was unprepared to accept that her marriage was over.* **ANT** PREPARED

un·pre·pos·ses·sing /ˌʌnpriːpəˈzɛsɪŋ/ *adj.* (formal) not attractive; not making a good or strong impression **SYN** UNATTRACTIVE ➔ compare PREPOSSESSING

un·pre·ten·tious /ˌʌnprɪˈtɛnʃəs/ *adj.* (approving) not trying to appear more special, intelligent, important, etc. than you really are **ANT** PRETENTIOUS

un·prin·ci·pled **AWL** /ʌnˈprɪnsəpld/ *adj.* without moral principles **SYN** DISHONEST **ANT** PRINCIPLED

un·print·a·ble /ʌnˈprɪntəbl/ *adj.* (of words or comments) too offensive or shocking to be printed and read by people **ANT** PRINTABLE

un·prob·lem·at·ic /ˌʌnprɑbləˈmætɪk/ (also less frequent **un·prob·lem·at·i·cal** /ˌʌnprɑbləˈmætɪkl/) *adj.* not having or causing problems **ANT** PROBLEMATIC ▶ **un·prob·lem·at·i·cally** /-kli/ *adv.*

un·pro·duc·tive /ˌʌnprəˈdʌktɪv/ *adj.* not producing very much; not producing good results: *unproductive land* ♦ *an unproductive meeting* ♦ *I've had a very unproductive day.* **ANT** PRODUCTIVE ▶ **un·pro·duc·tive·ly** *adv.*

un·pro·fes·sion·al /ˌʌnprəˈfɛʃnl/ *adj.* not reaching the standard expected in a particular profession: *She was found guilty of unprofessional conduct.* **ANT** PROFESSIONAL ➔ compare NONPROFESSIONAL ▶ **un·pro·fes·sion·al·ly** /-ʃənəli/ *adv.*

un·prof·it·a·ble /ʌnˈprɑfətəbl/ *adj.* **1** not making enough financial profit: *unprofitable companies* **2** (formal) not bringing any advantage **ANT** PROFITABLE ▶ **un·prof·it·a·bly** /-bli/ *adv.*

un·prom·is·ing /ʌnˈprɑməsɪŋ/ *adj.* not likely to be successful or show good results **ANT** PROMISING

un·prompt·ed /ʌnˈprɑmptəd/ *adj.* said or done without someone asking you to say or do it: *Unprompted, Sam started telling us exactly what had happened that night.* ➔ see also PROMPT

un·pro·nounce·a·ble /ˌʌnprəˈnaʊnsəbl/ *adj.* (of a word, especially a name) too difficult to pronounce **ANT** PRONOUNCEABLE

un·pro·tect·ed /ˌʌnprəˈtɛktəd/ *adj.* **1** not protected against being hurt or damaged **2** not covered to prevent it from causing damage or injury: *Machinery was often unprotected and accidents were frequent.* **3** (of sex) done without using a CONDOM

un·prov·en /ʌnˈpruːvn/ *adj.* not proved or tested: *unproven theories* ➔ compare PROVEN

un·pro·voked /ˌʌnprəˈvʊkt/ adj. (especially of an attack) not caused by anything the person being attacked has said or done: *an act of unprovoked aggression* ◆ *Her angry outburst was totally unprovoked.* ➔ see also PROVOKE

un·pub·lished **AWL** /ʌnˈpʌblɪʃt/ adj. not published: *an unpublished novel*

un·pun·ished /ʌnˈpʌnɪʃt/ adj. not punished: *He promised that the murder would not go unpunished.*

un·put·down·a·ble /ˌʌnpʊtˈdaʊnəbl/ adj. (informal) (of a book) so exciting or interesting that you cannot stop reading it

un·qual·i·fied /ʌnˈkwɑlɪˌfaɪd/ adj. **1** not having the right knowledge, experience, or qualifications to do something: *an unqualified instructor* ◆ *~ to do sth I feel unqualified to comment on the subject.* ◆ *~ for sth He was totally unqualified for his job as a senior manager.* **2** /ʌnˈkwɑləfaɪd/ [usually before noun] complete; not limited by any negative qualities: *The event was not an unqualified success.* ◆ *I gave her my unqualified support.* **ANT** QUALIFIED

un·quench·a·ble /ʌnˈkwɛntʃəbl/ adj. (formal) that cannot be satisfied: *He had an unquenchable thirst for life.* ➔ see also QUENCH

un·ques·tion·a·ble /ʌnˈkwɛstʃənəbl/ adj. that cannot be doubted: *a man of unquestionable honesty* **ANT** QUESTIONABLE ▶ **un·ques·tion·a·bly** /-bli/ adv.: *It was unquestionably a step in the right direction.*

un·ques·tioned /ʌnˈkwɛstʃənd/ adj. (formal) **1** so obvious that it cannot be doubted: *His courage remains unquestioned.* **2** accepted as right or true without really being considered: *an unquestioned assumption*

un·ques·tion·ing /ʌnˈkwɛstʃənɪŋ/ adj. (formal) done or given without asking questions, expressing doubt, etc.: *unquestioning obedience* ▶ **un·ques·tion·ing·ly** adv.

un·qui·et /ʌnˈkwaɪət/ adj. [usually before noun] (literary) not calm; anxious and RESTLESS

un·quote /ˈʌnkwoʊt; ʌnˈkwoʊt/ noun **IDM** see QUOTE v.

un·rat·ed /ʌnˈreɪtəd/ adj. an **unrated** movie has not been given a RATING (= a letter that shows which groups of people it is suitable for), usually for marketing reasons

un·rav·el /ʌnˈrævl/ verb (-l-, CanE usually -ll-) **1** [T, I] ~ (sth) if you **unravel** threads that are twisted, WOVEN, or KNIT, or if they **unravel**, they become separated: *I unraveled the string and wound it into a ball.* **2** [I] (of a system, plan, relationship, etc.) to start to fail or no longer stay together as a whole **3** [T, I] ~ (sth) to explain something that is difficult to understand or is mysterious; to become clearer or easier to understand: *The discovery will help scientists unravel the mystery of the Ice Age.*

un·read /ʌnˈrɛd/ adj. (of a book, etc.) that has not been read: *a pile of unread newspapers*

un·read·a·ble /ʌnˈridəbl/ adj. **1** (of a book, etc.) too dull or difficult to be worth reading **2** = ILLEGIBLE **3** if someone's face or expression is **unreadable**, you cannot tell what they are thinking or feeling **4** (computing) (of a computer file, disk, etc.) containing information that a computer is not able to read

un·re·al /ʌnˈril; -ˈriəl/ adj. **1** so strange that it is more like a dream than reality: *The party began to take on an unreal, almost nightmarish quality.* **2** not related to reality **SYN** UNREALISTIC: *Many people have unreal expectations of what marriage will be like.* **3** (informal) used to say that you like something very much or that something surprises you: *"That's unreal!" she laughed.* ▶ **un·re·al·i·ty** /ˌʌnriˈæləti/ noun [U]

un·re·al·is·tic /ˌʌnriəˈlɪstɪk/ adj. not showing or accepting things as they are: *unrealistic expectations* ◆ *It is unrealistic to expect them to be able to solve the problem immediately.* **ANT** REALISTIC ▶ **un·re·al·is·ti·cally** /-kli/ adv.: *These prices are unrealistically high.*

un·re·al·ized /ʌnˈriəˌlaɪzd/ adj. **1** not achieved or created: *an unrealized ambition* ◆ *Their potential is unrealized.*

2 (finance) not sold or changed into the form of money: *unrealized assets*

un·rea·son·a·ble 🔑 /ʌnˈrizənəbl; -ˈriznəbl/ adj. not fair; expecting too much: *The job was beginning to make unreasonable demands on his free time.* ◆ *The fees they charge are not unreasonable.* ◆ *It would be unreasonable to expect somebody to come at such short notice.* ◆ *He was being totally unreasonable about it.* **ANT** REASONABLE ▶ **un·rea·son·a·ble·ness** noun [U] **un·rea·son·a·bly** /-bli/ adv.

un·rea·son·ing /ʌnˈrizənɪŋ/ adj. [usually before noun] (formal) not based on facts or reason **SYN** IRRATIONAL: *unreasoning fear*

un·rec·og·niz·a·ble /-rɛkəgˈnaɪ-/ adj. (of a person or thing) so changed or damaged that you do not recognize them or it: *He was unrecognizable without his beard.* **ANT** RECOGNIZABLE

un·rec·og·nized /ʌnˈrɛkəgˌnaɪzd/ adj. **1** that people are not aware of or do not realize is important: *The problem of ageism in the workplace often goes unrecognized.* **2** (of a person) not having received the admiration they deserve for something that they have done or achieved

un·re·con·struct·ed /ˌʌnrikənˈstrʌktəd/ adj. [only before noun] (disapproving) (of people and their beliefs) not having changed, although the situation they are in has changed

un·re·cord·ed /ˌʌnrɪˈkɔrdəd/ adj. not written down or recorded: *Many crimes go unrecorded.*

un·re·fined /ˌʌnrɪˈfaɪnd/ adj. **1** (of a substance) not separated from the other substances that it is combined with in its natural form: *unrefined sugar* **2** (of a person or their behavior) not polite or educated **ANT** REFINED

un·re·gen·er·ate /ˌʌnrɪˈdʒɛnərət/ adj. (formal) not trying to change your bad habits or bad behavior

un·reg·is·tered /ʌnˈrɛdʒəstərd/ adj. not listed in an official or public record; not registered: *That region has a high number of unregistered births.*

un·reg·u·lat·ed **AWL** /ʌnˈrɛgyəˌleɪtəd/ adj. not controlled by laws or regulations: *unregulated industries*

un·re·lat·ed /ˌʌnrɪˈleɪtəd/ adj. **1** not connected; not related to something else **SYN** UNCONNECTED: *The two events were totally unrelated.* **2** (of people, animals, etc.) not belonging to the same family **ANT** RELATED

un·re·lent·ing /ˌʌnrɪˈlɛntɪŋ/ adj. (formal) **1** (of an unpleasant situation) not stopping or becoming less severe **SYN** RELENTLESS: *unrelenting pressure* ◆ *The heat was unrelenting.* **2** if a person is **unrelenting**, they continue with something without considering the feelings of other people **SYN** RELENTLESS: *He was unrelenting in his search for the truth about his father.* ▶ **un·re·lent·ing·ly** adv.

un·re·li·a·ble **AWL** /ˌʌnrɪˈlaɪəbl/ adj. that cannot be trusted or depended on: *The trains are notoriously unreliable.* ◆ *He's totally unreliable as a source of information.* **ANT** RELIABLE ➔ collocations at RELY ▶ **un·re·li·a·bil·i·ty** /ˌʌnrɪˌlaɪəˈbɪləti/ noun [U]: *the unreliability of some statistics*

un·re·lieved /ˌʌnrɪˈlivd/ adj. (formal) (of an unpleasant situation) continuing without changing

un·re·mark·a·ble /ˌʌnrɪˈmɑrkəbl/ adj. ordinary; not special or remarkable in any way: *an unremarkable life*

un·re·marked /ˌʌnrɪˈmɑrkt/ adj. (formal) not noticed: *His absence went unremarked.*

un·re·mit·ting /ˌʌnrɪˈmɪtɪŋ/ adj. (formal) never stopping: *unremitting hostility* ▶ **un·re·mit·ting·ly** adv.: *unremittingly gloomy weather*

un·re·peat·a·ble /ˌʌnrɪˈpitəbl/ adj. **1** too offensive or shocking to be repeated: *He called me several unrepeatable names.* **2** that cannot be repeated or done again: *an unrepeatable experience* **ANT** REPEATABLE

un·re·pent·ant /ˌʌnrɪˈpɛntənt/ adj. showing no shame about your actions or beliefs **ANT** REPENTANT ▶ **un·re·pent·ant·ly** adv.

un·re·port·ed /ˌʌnrɪˈpɔrtəd/ adj. not reported to the police or someone in authority or to the public: *Many cases of bullying* **go unreported**.

un·rep·re·sent·a·tive /ˌʌnreprɪˈzentətɪv/ *adj.* ~ **(of sb/sth)** not typical of a group of people or things and therefore not useful as a source of information about that group **SYN** UNTYPICAL: *an unrepresentative sample* **ANT** REPRESENTATIVE

un·re·quit·ed /ˌʌnrɪˈkwaɪtəd/ *adj.* (*formal*) (of love) not returned by the person that you love ⊃ **compare** REQUITE

un·re·served /ˌʌnrɪˈzɜrvd/ *adj.* **1** (of seats in a theater, etc.) not paid for in advance; not kept for the use of a particular person **2** (*formal*) complete and without any doubts: *He offered us his unreserved apologies.*

un·re·serv·ed·ly /ˌʌnrɪˈzɜrvədli/ *adv.* completely; without hesitating or having any doubts: *We apologize unreservedly for any offense we have caused.*

un·re·solved **AWL** /ˌʌnrɪˈzalvd/ *adj.* (*formal*) (of a problem or question) not yet solved or answered; not having been resolved

un·re·spon·sive **AWL** /ˌʌnrɪˈspansɪv/ *adj.* ~ **(to sth)** (*formal*) not reacting to someone or something; not giving the response that you would expect or hope for: *a politician who is unresponsive to the mood of the country* **ANT** RESPONSIVE

un·rest /ʌnˈrest/ *noun* [U] a political situation in which people are angry and likely to protest or fight: *civil/social/political/popular/industrail unrest* ◆ *There is* **growing unrest** *in the south of the country.* ⊃ **collocations** at WAR

un·re·strained **AWL** /ˌʌnrɪˈstreɪnd/ *adj.* (*formal*) not controlled; not having been RESTRAINED: *unrestrained aggression*

un·re·strict·ed **AWL** /ˌʌnrɪˈstrɪktəd/ *adj.* not controlled or limited in any way **SYN** UNLIMITED: *We have unrestricted access to all the facilities.* **ANT** RESTRICTED

un·re·ward·ed /ˌʌnrɪˈwɔrdəd/ *adj.* not receiving the success that you are trying to achieve: *Real talent often* **goes unrewarded**.

un·re·ward·ing /ˌʌnrɪˈwɔrdɪŋ/ *adj.* (of an activity, etc.) not bringing feelings of satisfaction or achievement **ANT** REWARDING

un·ripe /ʌnˈraɪp/ *adj.* not yet ready to eat: *unripe fruit* **ANT** RIPE

un·ri·valed /ʌnˈraɪvld/ *adj.* (*formal*) better or greater than any other **SYN** UNSURPASSED

un·roll /ʌnˈroʊl/ *verb* **1** [T, I] ~ **(sth)** if you **unroll** paper, cloth, etc. that was in a roll or if it **unrolls**, it opens and becomes flat: *We unrolled our sleeping bags.* ⊃ **compare** ROLL **2** [I] (of events) to happen one after another in a series: *We watched the events unroll before the cameras.*

un·round·ed /ʌnˈraʊndəd/ *adj.* (*phonetics*) (of a speech sound) pronounced with the lips not forming a narrow round shape **ANT** ROUNDED

un·ruf·fled /ʌnˈrʌfld/ *adj.* (of a person) calm **SYN** UNPERTURBED: *He remained unruffled by their accusations.*

un·ruled /ʌnˈruld/ *adj.* (of paper) not having printed lines on it

un·ru·ly /ʌnˈruli/ *adj.* difficult to control or manage **SYN** DISORDERLY: *an unruly class* ◆ *unruly behavior* ◆ *unruly hair* (= difficult to keep looking neat) ▶ **un·ru·li·ness** *noun* [U]

un·sad·dle /ʌnˈsædl/ *verb* **1** [T, I] ~ **(sth)** to take the saddle off a horse **2** [T] ~ **sb** to throw a rider off **SYN** UNSEAT

un·safe /ʌnˈseɪf/ *adj.* **1** (of a thing, a place, or an activity) not safe; dangerous: *The roof was declared unsafe.* ◆ *It was considered unsafe to release the prisoners.* ◆ *unsafe sex* (= for example, sex without a CONDOM) **2** (of people) in danger of being harmed: *He felt unsafe and afraid.* **ANT** SAFE

un·said /ʌnˈsed/ *adj.* [not before noun] thought but not spoken: *Some things are better* **left unsaid**.

un·sal·a·ble (also **un·sale·a·ble**) /ʌnˈseɪləbl/ *adj.* that cannot be sold, because it is not good enough or because no one wants to buy it **ANT** SALABLE

un·salt·ed /ʌnˈsɔltəd/ *adj.* (especially of food) without added salt: *unsalted butter*

un·san·i·tar·y /ʌnˈsænəˌteri/ (also **in·san·i·tar·y**) *adj.* dirty and likely to spread disease **ANT** SANITARY

un·sat·is·fac·to·ry /ˌʌnsætəsˈfæktəri/ *adj.* not good enough **SYN** INADEQUATE, UNACCEPTABLE **ANT** SATISFACTORY ▶ **un·sat·is·fac·to·ri·ly** /-tərəli/ *adv.*

un·sat·is·fied /ʌnˈsætəsˌfaɪd/ *adj.* **1** (of a need, demand, etc.) not dealt with **2** (of a person) not having gotten what you hoped; not having had enough of something ⊃ **compare** DISSATISFIED, SATISFIED

un·sat·is·fy·ing /ʌnˈsætəsˌfaɪɪŋ/ *adj.* not giving you any satisfaction **ANT** SATISFYING: *a shallow, unsatisfying relationship*

un·sat·u·rat·ed fat /ʌnˌsætʃəreɪtəd ˈfæt/ *noun* [U, C] a type of fat found in nuts, seeds, and vegetable oils that does not encourage the harmful development of CHOLESTEROL: *Avocados are high in unsaturated fat.* ⊃ **see also** MONO-UNSATURATED FAT, POLYUNSATURATED FAT, SATURATED FAT, TRANS-FATTY ACID

un·sa·vor·y (*CanE* usually **un·sa·vour·y**) /ʌnˈseɪvəri/ *adj.* unpleasant or offensive; not considered morally acceptable: *an unsavory incident* ◆ *Her friends are all pretty unsavory characters.*

un·scathed /ʌnˈskeɪðd/ *adj.* [not before noun] not hurt **SYN** UNHARMED: *The hostages* **emerged from their ordeal unscathed**.

un·sched·uled **AWL** /ʌnˈskɛdʒuld; -dʒəl-/ *adj.* that was not planned in advance **SYN** UNPLANNED: *an unscheduled stop*

un·sci·en·tif·ic /ˌʌnsaɪənˈtɪfɪk/ *adj.* (often *disapproving*) not scientific; not done in a careful, logical way: *an unscientific approach to a problem* ⊃ **compare** NONSCIENTIFIC

un·scram·ble /ʌnˈskræmbl/ *verb* **1** ~ **sth** to change a word, message, television signal, etc. that has been sent in a code so that it can be read or understood **ANT** SCRAMBLE **2** ~ **sth** to arrange something that is confused or in the wrong order in a clear correct way

un·screw /ʌnˈskru/ *verb* **1** [T, I] ~ **(sth)** to undo something by twisting or turning it; to become undone in this way: *I can't unscrew the lid of this jar.* **2** [T] ~ **sth** to take the screws out of something: *You'll have to unscrew the handles to paint the door.*

un·script·ed /ʌnˈskrɪptəd/ *adj.* (of a speech, broadcast, etc.) not written or prepared in detail in advance **ANT** SCRIPTED

un·scru·pu·lous /ʌnˈskrupyələs/ *adj.* without moral principles; not honest or fair **SYN** UNPRINCIPLED: *unscrupulous methods* **ANT** SCRUPULOUS ▶ **un·scru·pu·lous·ly** *adv.* **un·scru·pu·lous·ness** *noun* [U]

un·sea·son·a·ble /ʌnˈsizənəbl/ *adj.* unusual for the time of year: *unseasonable weather* **ANT** SEASONABLE ▶ **un·sea·son·a·bly** /-bli/ *adv.*: *unseasonably warm*

un·sea·son·al /ʌnˈsizənl/ *adj.* not typical of or not suitable for the time of year: *unseasonal weather* **ANT** SEASONAL

un·seat /ʌnˈsit/ *verb* **1** ~ **sb** to remove someone from a position of power **2** ~ **sb** to make someone fall off a horse or bicycle: *The horse unseated its rider at the first fence.*

un·se·cured /ˌʌnsɪˈkyʊrd/ *adj.* **1** (of a debt or loan) entered into without legally agreeing to give someone valuable property if you cannot pay the money back ⊃ **see also** SECURITY (5) **2** not locked, guarded, or protected: *unsecured windows*

un·seed·ed /ʌnˈsidəd/ *adj.* not chosen as a SEED in a sports competition, especially in TENNIS: *unseeded players* **ANT** SEEDED

un·see·ing /ʌnˈsiɪŋ/ *adj.* (*literary*) not noticing or really looking at anything although your eyes are open ▶ **un·see·ing·ly** *adv.*: *They stared unseeingly at the wreckage.*

un·seem·ly /ʌnˈsimli/ *adj.* (*old-fashioned* or *formal*) (of behavior, etc.) not polite or suitable for a particular situation **SYN** IMPROPER **ANT** SEEMLY

un·seen /ʌnˈsin/ adj. **1** that cannot be seen: *unseen forces* ◆ *He was killed by a single shot from an unseen soldier.* ◆ *I managed to slip out of the room unseen.* **2** not previously seen: *unseen dangers* ◆ *The exam consists of an essay and an unseen translation.* **IDM** see SIGHT n.

un·self·con·scious /ˌʌnsɛlfˈkɑnʃəs/ adj. not worried about or aware of what other people think of you **ANT** SELF-CONSCIOUS ▶ **un·self·con·scious·ly** adv.

un·sel·fish /ʌnˈsɛlfɪʃ/ adj. willing to give more time or importance to other people's needs, wishes, etc. than to your own **SYN** SELFLESS: *unselfish motives* **ANT** SELFISH ▶ **un·self·ish·ly** adv. **un·self·ish·ness** noun [U]

un·sen·ti·men·tal /ˌʌnsɛntəˈmɛntl/ adj. not having or expressing emotions such as love or sympathy; not allowing such emotions to influence what you do **ANT** SENTIMENTAL

un·ser·vice·a·ble /ʌnˈsɜrvəsəbl/ adj. not suitable to be used **ANT** SERVICEABLE

un·set·tle /ʌnˈsɛtl/ verb ~ **sb** to make someone feel upset or worried, especially because a situation has changed: *Changing schools might unsettle the kids.*

un·set·tled /ʌnˈsɛtld/ adj. **1** (of a situation) that may change; making people uncertain about what might happen: *These were difficult and unsettled times.* ◆ *The weather has been very unsettled* (= it has changed a lot). **2** not calm or relaxed: *They all felt restless and unsettled.* **3** (of an argument, etc.) that continues without any agreement being reached **SYN** UNRESOLVED **4** (of a bill, etc.) not yet paid

un·set·tling /ʌnˈsɛtl·ɪŋ, -ˈsɛtlɪŋ/ adj. making you feel upset, nervous, or worried

un·shad·ed /ʌnˈʃeɪdəd/ adj. (of a source of light) without a SHADE or other covering: *an unshaded light bulb*

un·shak·a·ble (also **un·shake·a·ble**) /ʌnˈʃeɪkəbl/ adj. (of a feeling or an attitude) that cannot be changed or destroyed **SYN** FIRM

un·shak·en /ʌnˈʃeɪkən/ adj. ~ **(in sth)** not having changed a particular feeling or attitude: *They remain unshaken in their loyalty.*

un·shav·en /ʌnˈʃeɪvn/ adj. not having shaved or been shaved recently: *He looked pale and unshaven.* ◆ *his unshaven face* ⊃ compare SHAVEN

un·sight·ly /ʌnˈsaɪtli/ adj. not pleasant to look at **SYN** UGLY

un·signed /ʌnˈsaɪnd/ adj. **1** without a signature: *an unsigned letter to the editor* **2** not having a contract with a company or team: *an unsigned band/player*

un·skilled /ʌnˈskɪld/ adj. not having or needing special skills or training: *unskilled manual workers* ◆ *unskilled work* **ANT** SKILLED

un·smil·ing /ʌnˈsmaɪlɪŋ/ adj. (formal) not smiling; looking unfriendly: *His eyes were hard and unsmiling.* ▶ **un·smil·ing·ly** adv.

un·so·cia·ble /ʌnˈsoʊʃəbl/ adj. not enjoying the company of other people; not friendly **ANT** SOCIABLE

un·sold /ʌnˈsoʊld/ adj. not bought by anyone: *Many of the houses remain unsold.*

un·so·lic·it·ed /ˌʌnsəˈlɪsətəd/ adj. not asked for and sometimes not wanted: *unsolicited advice*

un·solved /ʌnˈsɑlvd, -ˈsɔlvd/ adj. not having been solved: *an unsolved murder/mystery/problem*

un·so·phis·ti·cat·ed /ˌʌnsəˈfɪstəˌkeɪtəd/ adj. **1** not having or showing much experience of the world and social situations: *unsophisticated tastes* **2** basic and simple; not complicated **SYN** CRUDE: *unsophisticated equipment* **ANT** SOPHISTICATED

un·sort·ed /ʌnˈsɔrtəd/ adj. not sorted, or not arranged in any particular order: *a pile of unsorted papers*

un·sound /ʌnˈsaʊnd/ adj. **1** not acceptable; not holding acceptable views: *ideologically unsound* ◆ *The use of dispos-*

able products is considered ecologically unsound. **2** containing mistakes; that you cannot rely on **SYN** UNRELIABLE: *The methods used were unsound.* **3** (of a building, etc.) in poor condition; weak and likely to fall down: *The roof is structurally unsound.* **ANT** SOUND ▶ **un·sound·ness** noun [U]

IDM **of unsound mind** (law) not responsible for your actions because of a mental illness

un·spar·ing /ʌnˈspɛrɪŋ/ adj. ~ **(in sth)** (formal) **1** not caring about people's feelings: *She is unsparing in her criticism.* ◆ *an unsparing portrait of life in the slums* **2** giving or given generously: *He won his mother's unsparing approval.* ⊃ compare SPARING ▶ **un·spar·ing·ly** adv.

un·speak·a·ble /ʌnˈspikəbl/ adj. (literary, usually disapproving) that cannot be described in words, usually because it is so bad **SYN** INDESCRIBABLE ▶ **un·speak·a·bly** /-bli/ adv.

un·spec·i·fied **AWL** /ʌnˈspɛsəˌfaɪd/ adj. not stated clearly or definitely; not having been specified (SPECIFY): *The story takes place at an unspecified date.*

un·spec·tac·u·lar /ˌʌnspɛkˈtækyələr/ adj. not exciting or special: *He had a steady but unspectacular career.*

un·spoiled /ʌnˈspɔɪld/ adj. (approving) **1** (of a place) beautiful because it has not been changed or built on **2** (of a person) not affected or made unpleasant, badly behaved, etc. by being praised too much **ANT** SPOILED

un·spo·ken /ʌnˈspoʊkən/ adj. (formal) not stated; not said in words but understood or agreed between people **SYN** UNSTATED: *an unspoken assumption* ◆ *Something unspoken hung in the air between them.*

un·sports·man·like /ʌnˈspɔrtsmənˌlaɪk/ adj. (disapproving) not behaving in a fair, generous, and polite way, especially when playing a sport or game: *unsportsmanlike conduct*

un·sta·ble **AWL** /ʌnˈsteɪbl/ adj. **1** likely to change suddenly **SYN** VOLATILE: *The political situation remains highly unstable.* **2** if people are **unstable**, their behavior and emotions change often and suddenly because their minds are upset ⊃ thesaurus box at MENTALLY ILL **3** likely to move or fall **4** (technical) (of a substance) not staying in the same chemical or ATOMIC state: *chemically unstable* **ANT** STABLE ⊃ see also INSTABILITY

un·stat·ed /ʌnˈsteɪtəd/ adj. (formal) not stated; not said in words but understood or agreed between people **SYN** UNSPOKEN: *Their reasoning was based on a set of unstated assumptions.*

un·stead·y 🔑 /ʌnˈstɛdi/ adj. **1** not completely in control of your movements so that you might fall: *She is still a little unsteady on her feet after the operation.* **2** shaking or moving in a way that is not controlled: *an unsteady hand* **ANT** STEADY ▶ **un·stead·i·ly** /-ˈstɛdl·i/ adv. **un·stead·i·ness** /-ˈstɛdinəs/ noun [U]

un·stint·ing /ʌnˈstɪntɪŋ/ adj. given or giving generously: *unstinting support* ◆ ~ **in sth** *They were unstinting in their praise.* ▶ **un·stint·ing·ly** adv.

un·stop·pa·ble /ʌnˈstɑpəbl/ adj. that cannot be stopped or prevented: *an unstoppable rise in prices* ◆ *This year's team is simply unstoppable.*

un·stressed **AWL** /ʌnˈstrɛst/ adj. (phonetics) (of a syllable) pronounced without emphasis **ANT** STRESSED

un·struc·tured **AWL** /ʌnˈstrʌktʃərd/ adj. without structure or organization

un·stuck /ʌnˈstʌk/ adj.
IDM **come unstuck** to become separated from something it was stuck or fastened to: *The flap of the envelope had come unstuck.*

un·sub·scribe /ˌʌnsəbˈskraɪb/ verb [I, T] ~ **(from sth)** | ~ **sb/sth** (computing) to remove your e-mail address from an Internet MAILING LIST

un·sub·stan·ti·at·ed /ˌʌnsəbˈstænʃiˌeɪtəd/ adj. (formal) not proved to be true by evidence **SYN** UNSUPPORTED: *an unsubstantiated claim/rumor, etc.*

un·suc·cess·ful ♪ /ˌʌnsəkˈsesfl/ *adj.*
not successful; not achieving what you wanted to: *His efforts to get a job proved unsuccessful.* ♦ *They were unsuccessful in meeting their objectives for the year.* ♦ *She made several unsuccessful attempts to see him.* **ANT** SUCCESSFUL
▶ **un·suc·cess·ful·ly** /-fəli/ *adv.*

un·suit·a·ble /ʌnˈsutəbl/ *adj.* ~ **(for sb/sth)** not right or appropriate for a particular person, purpose, or occasion: *He was wearing shoes that were totally unsuitable for climbing.* **ANT** SUITABLE ▶ **un·suit·a·bil·i·ty** /ˌʌnˌsutəˈbɪləti/ *noun* [U] **un·suit·a·bly** /ʌnˈsutəbli/ *adv.*: *They were unsuitably dressed for the occasion.*

un·suit·ed /ʌnˈsutəd/ *adj.* **1** ~ **(to/for sth)** | ~ **(to do sth)** not having the right or necessary qualities for something: *He is unsuited to academic work.* ♦ *She was totally unsuited for the job.* **2** if two people are **unsuited** to each other, they do not have the same interests, etc. and are therefore not likely to make a good couple **ANT** SUITED

un·sul·lied /ʌnˈsʌlid/ *adj.* (*literary*) not spoiled by anything; still pure or in the original state **SYN** UNSPOILED

un·sung /ʌnˈsʌŋ/ *adj.* [usually before noun] (*formal*) not praised or famous but deserving to be: *the unsung heroes of the war*

un·sup·port·ed /ˌʌnsəˈpɔrtəd/ *adj.* **1** (of a statement, etc.) not proved to be true by evidence **SYN** UNSUBSTANTIATED: *Their claims are unsupported by research findings.* **2** not helped or paid for by someone or something else: *She has brought up three children unsupported.* **3** not physically supported: *Sections of the structure have been left unsupported.*

un·sure /ʌnˈʃʊr; -ˈʃər/ *adj.* [not before noun] **1** not certain of something; having doubts: ~ **about/of sth** *There were a lot of things I was unsure about.* ♦ ~ **how, what, etc....** *I was unsure how to reply to this question.* ♦ ~ **of/as to how, what, etc....** *He was unsure of what to do next.* ♦ *They were unsure as to what the next move should be.* **2** ~ **(of yourself)** lacking confidence in yourself: *Like many women, deep down she was unsure of herself.* **ANT** SURE

un·sur·passed /ˌʌnsərˈpæst/ *adj.* (*formal*) better or greater than any other **SYN** UNRIVALED

un·sur·prised /ˌʌnsərˈpraɪzd; -səˈpraɪzd/ *adj.* [not usually before noun] not surprised: *She appeared totally unsurprised at the news.*

un·sur·pris·ing /ˌʌnsərˈpraɪzɪŋ; -səˈpraɪ-/ *adj.* not causing surprise **ANT** SURPRISING ▶ **un·sur·pris·ing·ly** *adv.*: *Unsurprisingly, the plan failed.*

un·sus·pect·ed /ˌʌnsəˈspektəd/ *adj.* not predicted or known; that you were not previously aware of

un·sus·pect·ing /ˌʌnsəˈspektɪŋ/ *adj.* [usually before noun] feeling no suspicion; not aware of danger or of something bad: *He had crept up on his unsuspecting victim from behind.*

un·sus·tain·a·ble **AWL** /ˌʌnsəˈsteɪnəbl/ *adj.* that cannot be continued at the same level, rate, etc.: *unsustainable growth* **ANT** SUSTAINABLE

un·sweet·ened /ʌnˈswitnd/ *adj.* (of food or drinks) without sugar or a similar substance having been added

un·swerv·ing /ʌnˈswɜrvɪŋ/ *adj.* (*formal*) strong and not changing or becoming weaker: *unswerving loyalty/support, etc.*

un·sym·pa·thet·ic /ˌʌnsɪmpəˈθetɪk/ *adj.* **1** ~ **(to/toward sb)** not feeling or showing any sympathy: *I told him about the problem but he was totally unsympathetic.* **2** ~ **(to/toward sth)** not in agreement with something; not supporting an idea, aim, etc.: *The government was unsympathetic to public opinion.* **3** (of a person) not easy to like; unpleasant **ANT** SYMPATHETIC ▶ **un·sym·pa·thet·i·cally** /-kli/ *adv.*: *"You've only got yourself to blame," she said unsympathetically.*

un·sys·tem·at·ic /ˌʌnsɪstəˈmætɪk/ *adj.* not organized into a clear system **ANT** SYSTEMATIC ▶ **un·sys·tem·at·i·cally** /-kli/ *adv.*

un·taint·ed /ʌnˈteɪntəd/ *adj.* ~ **(by sth)** (*formal*) not damaged or spoiled by something unpleasant; not TAINTED

un·tal·ent·ed /ʌnˈtæləntəd/ *adj.* without a natural ability to do something well **ANT** TALENTED

un·tamed /ʌnˈteɪmd/ *adj.* allowed to remain in a wild state; not changed, controlled, or influenced by anyone; not TAMED

un·tan·gle /ʌnˈtæŋgl/ *verb* **1** ~ **sth (from sth)** to undo string, hair, wire, etc. that has become twisted or has knots in it **2** ~ **sth** to make something that is complicated or confusing easier to deal with or understand

un·tapped /ʌnˈtæpt/ *adj.* available but not yet used: *untapped reserves of oil*

un·ten·a·ble /ʌnˈtenəbl/ *adj.* (*formal*) (of a theory, position, etc.) that cannot be defended against attack or criticism: *His position had become untenable and he was forced to resign.* **ANT** TENABLE

un·test·ed /ʌnˈtestəd/ *adj.* not tested; of unknown quality or value

un·think·a·ble /ʌnˈθɪŋkəbl/ *adj.* ~ **(for sb) (to do sth)** | ~ **(that...)** impossible to imagine or accept **SYN** INCONCEIVABLE: *It was unthinkable that she could be dead.* **ANT** THINKABLE ▶ **the un·think·a·ble** *noun* [sing.]: *Suddenly the unthinkable happened and he pulled out a gun.* ♦ *The time has come to* **think the unthinkable** (= consider possibilities that used to be unacceptable).

un·think·ing /ʌnˈθɪŋkɪŋ/ *adj.* (*formal*) not thinking about the effects of what you do or say; not thinking much about serious things **SYN** THOUGHTLESS ▶ **un·think·ing·ly** *adv.*

un·ti·dy /ʌnˈtaɪdi/ *adj.* (un·ti·di·er, un·ti·di·est) **1** not neat or well arranged; in a state of confusion: *an untidy desk* ♦ *untidy hair* **2** (of a person) not keeping things neat or well organized: *Why do you have to be so untidy?* **ANT** TIDY ▶ **un·ti·di·ly** /-ˈtaɪdɪ-i/ *adv.* **un·ti·di·ness** /-ˈtaɪdinəs/ *noun* [U]

un·tie /ʌnˈtaɪ/ *verb* ~ **sth** to undo a knot in something; to undo something that is tied: *to untie a knot* ♦ *I quickly untied the package and peeped inside.* ♦ *He untied the rope and pushed the boat into the water.*

un·til ♪ /ənˈtɪl; ʌn-/ *conj., prep.* (also *informal* till, til, 'til) up to the point in time or the event mentioned: *Let's wait until the rain stops.* ♦ *Until she spoke I hadn't realized she wasn't American.* ♦ *You're not going out until you finish this.* ♦ *Until now I have always lived alone.* ♦ *They moved here in 2009. Until then they'd always been in the Denver area.* ♦ *He continued working* **up until** *his death.* ♦ *The street is full of traffic* **from morning till night.** ♦ *You can stay on the bus until Dallas* (= until you reach Dallas).

un·time·ly /ʌnˈtaɪmli/ *adj.* (*formal*) **1** happening too soon or sooner than is normal or expected **SYN** PREMATURE: *She met a tragic and untimely death at 25.* **2** happening at a time or in a situation that is not suitable **SYN** ILL-TIMED: *His interruption was untimely.* **ANT** TIMELY

un·tir·ing /ʌnˈtaɪərɪŋ/ *adj.* (*approving*) continuing to do something for a long period of time with a lot of effort and/ or enthusiasm **SYN** TIRELESS

un·ti·tled /ʌnˈtaɪtld/ *adj.* (of a work of art) without a title

un·to /ˈʌntu; ˈʌntə/ *prep.* (*old use*) **1** to or toward someone or something: *The angel appeared unto him in a dream.* **2** until a particular time or event: *The knights swore loyalty unto death.*

un·told /ʌnˈtoʊld/ *adj.* **1** [only before noun] used to emphasize how large, great, unpleasant, etc. something is **SYN** IMMEASURABLE: *untold misery/wealth* ♦ *These gases cause untold damage to the environment.* **2** (of a story) not told to anyone

un·touch·a·ble /ʌnˈtʌtʃəbl/ *adj., noun*
● *adj.* **1** a person who is **untouchable** is in a position where they are unlikely to be punished or criticized: *Given his political connections, he thought he was untouchable.* **2** that cannot be equaled or matched: *We took the silver medal behind the untouchable Italian team.* **3** (in India in the past) belonging to or connected with the Hindu social class (or CASTE) that was considered by other classes to be the lowest

• **noun** often **Untouchable** (in India in the past) a member of a Hindu social class (or CASTE) that was considered by other classes to be the lowest

un·touched /ʌnˈtʌtʃt/ *adj.* [not usually before noun] **1 ~ (by sth)** not affected by something, especially something bad or unpleasant; not damaged: *The area has remained relatively untouched by commercial development.* **2** (of food or drink) not eaten or drunk: *She left her meal untouched.* **3** not changed in any way: *The final clause in the contract will be left untouched.*

un·to·ward /ʌnˈtɔrd; -ˈtwɔrd; -ˈtouərd/ *adj.* unusual and unexpected, and usually unpleasant: *That's the plan—unless anything untoward happens.* ◆ *He had noticed nothing untoward.*

un·trained /ʌnˈtreɪnd/ *adj.* **~ (in sth)** not trained to perform a particular job or skill; without formal training in something: *untrained in keyboard skills* ◆ *To the untrained eye, the products look remarkably similar.*

un·tram·meled (CanE usually **un·tram·melled**) /ʌnˈtræmld/ *adj.* **~ (by sth)** (*formal*) not restricted or limited by something ⊃ compare TRAMMEL

un·treat·ed /ʌnˈtritəd/ *adj.* **1** not receiving medical treatment: *If untreated, the illness can become severe.* **2** (of substances) not made safe by chemical or other treatment: *untreated sewage* **3** (of wood) not treated with substances to preserve it

un·tried /ʌnˈtraɪd/ *adj.* **1** without experience of doing a particular job: *She chose two untried actors for the leading roles.* **2** not yet tried or tested to discover if it works or is successful **SYN** UNTESTED: *This is a new and relatively untried procedure.*

un·true /ʌnˈtru/ *adj.* **1** not true; not based on facts: *These accusations are totally untrue.* ◆ *an untrue claim* ◆ *It is untrue to say that something like this could never happen again.* ⊃ thesaurus box at WRONG **2 ~ (to sb/sth)** (*formal*) not loyal to someone or something **SYN** UNFAITHFUL: *If he agreed to their demands, he would have to be untrue to his own principles.* **ANT** TRUE

un·trust·wor·thy /ʌnˈtrʌstwɜrði/ *adj.* that cannot be trusted **ANT** TRUSTWORTHY

un·truth /ʌnˈtruθ/ *noun* (*pl.* **un·truths** /-ˈtruðz; -ˈtruθs/) **1** [C] (*formal*) a lie. People often say "untruth" to avoid saying "lie." ⊃ compare TRUTH **2** [U] the state of being false

un·truth·ful /ʌnˈtruθfl/ *adj.* saying things that you know are not true **ANT** TRUTHFUL ▶ **un·truth·ful·ly** /-fəli/ *adv.*

un·turned /ʌnˈtɜrnd/ *adj.* **IDM** see STONE *n.*

un·tu·tored /ʌnˈtutərd/ *adj.* (*formal*) not having been formally taught about something

un·typ·i·cal /ʌnˈtɪpɪkl/ *adj.* **~ (of sb/sth)** not typical: *an untypical example* ◆ *Schools in this area are untypical of schools in the rest of the country.* ◆ *All in all, it had been a not untypical day* (= it had been very like other days). **ANT** TYPICAL ⊃ compare ATYPICAL ▶ **un·typ·i·cally** /-kli/ *adv.*

un·us·a·ble /ʌnˈyuzəbl/ *adj.* in such a bad condition or of such low quality that it cannot be used **ANT** USABLE

un·used¹ /ʌnˈyuzd/ *adj.* not being used at the moment; never having been used ⊃ compare DISUSED

un·used² /ʌnˈyust/ *adj.* not having much experience of something and therefore not knowing how to deal with it; not used to something: **~ to sth** *This is an easy routine, designed for anyone who is unused to exercise.* ◆ **~ to doing sth** *She was unused to talking about herself.* **ANT** USED¹

un·u·su·al 🔊 /ʌnˈyuʒuəl; -ʒəl/ *adj.*
1 different from what is usual or normal **SYN** UNCOMMON: *It's unusual for the trees to flower so early.* ◆ *She has a very unusual name.* ◆ *It's not unusual for young doctors to work a 70-hour week* (= it happens often). **2** different from other similar things and therefore interesting and attractive: *an unusual color*

un·u·su·al·ly 🔊 /ʌnˈyuʒuəli; -ʒəli/ *adv.*
1 used before adjectives to emphasize that a particular quality is greater than normal: *unusually high levels of radiation* ◆ *an unusually cold winter* **2** used to say that a particular situation is not normal or expected: *Unusually for him, he wore a tie.*

un·ut·ter·a·ble /ʌnˈʌtərəbl/ *adj.* [only before noun] (*formal*) used to emphasize how great a particular emotion or quality is: *unutterable sadness* ▶ **un·ut·ter·a·bly** /-bli/ *adv.*

un·var·nished /ʌnˈvɑrnɪʃt/ *adj.* **1** [only before noun] (*formal*) with nothing added: *It was the plain, unvarnished truth.* **2** (of wood, etc.) not covered with VARNISH

un·var·y·ing /ʌnˈvɛriɪŋ/ *adj.* (*formal*) never changing: *an unvarying routine*

un·veil /ʌnˈveɪl/ *verb* **1 ~ sth** to remove a cover or curtain from a painting, statue, etc. so that it can be seen in public for the first time: *The mayor unveiled a plaque to mark the official opening of the hospital.* **2 ~ sth** to show or introduce a new plan, product, etc. to the public for the first time **SYN** REVEAL: *They will be unveiling their new models at the Car Show.*

un·voiced /ʌnˈvɔɪst/ *adj.* **1** thought about but not expressed in words **2** (*phonetics*) (of consonants) produced without moving your VOCAL CORDS; not VOICED **SYN** VOICELESS: *unvoiced consonants such as "p" and "t"*

un·want·ed /ʌnˈwɑntəd; -ˈwɔn-; -ˈwʌn-/ *adj.* that you do not want: *unwanted advice* ◆ *unwanted pregnancies* ◆ *It is very sad when children feel unwanted* (= feel that other people do not care about them).

un·war·rant·ed /ʌnˈwɔrəntəd; -ˈwar-/ *adj.* (*formal*) not reasonable or necessary; not appropriate **SYN** UNJUSTIFIED: *Much of the criticism was totally unwarranted.*

un·war·y /ʌnˈwɛri/ *adj.* **1** [only before noun] not aware of the possible dangers or problems of a situation and therefore likely to be harmed in some way ⊃ compare WARY **2 the unwary** *noun* [pl.] people who are unwary: *The stock market is full of traps for the unwary.*

un·washed /ʌnˈwɑʃt; -ˈwɔʃt/ *adj.* not washed; dirty: *a pile of unwashed dishes* ◆ *Their clothes were dirty and their hair was unwashed.*

un·wa·ver·ing /ʌnˈweɪvərɪŋ/ *adj.* (*formal*) not changing or becoming weaker in any way: *unwavering support* ▶ **un·wa·ver·ing·ly** *adv.*

un·wed /ʌnˈwɛd/ *adj.* not married **SYN** UNMARRIED: *unwed mothers*

un·wel·come /ʌnˈwɛlkəm/ *adj.* not wanted: *an unwelcome visitor* ◆ *To avoid attracting unwelcome attention he kept his voice down.* **ANT** WELCOME

un·wel·com·ing /ʌnˈwɛlkəmɪŋ/ *adj.* **1** (of a person) not friendly toward someone who is visiting or arriving **2** (of a place) not attractive; looking uncomfortable to be in **ANT** WELCOMING

un·well /ʌnˈwɛl/ *adj.* [not before noun] (somewhat *formal*) sick: *She said she was feeling unwell and went home.* **ANT** WELL

un·whole·some /ʌnˈhoulsəm/ *adj.* **1** harmful to health; not looking healthy **2** that you consider unpleasant or not natural **SYN** UNHEALTHY **ANT** WHOLESOME

un·wield·y /ʌnˈwildi/ *adj.* **1** (of an object) difficult to move or control because of its size, shape, or weight **SYN** CUMBERSOME **2** (of a system or group of people) difficult to control or organize because it is very large or complicated

un·will·ing 🔊 /ʌnˈwɪlɪŋ/ *adj.*
1 [not usually before noun] **~ (to do sth)** not wanting to do something and refusing to do it: *They are unwilling to invest any more money in the project.* ◆ *She was unable, or unwilling, to give me any further details.* **2** [only before noun] not wanting to do or be something, but forced to by other people **SYN** RELUCTANT: *an unwilling hero* ◆ *He became the unwilling*

object of her attention. **ANT** WILLING ▶ **un·will·ing·ly** adv. **un·will·ing·ness** noun [U]

un·wind /ʌnˈwaɪnd/ verb (**un·wound, un·wound** /-ˈwaʊnd/) **1** [T, I] ~ **(sth) (from sth)** to undo something that has been wrapped into a ball or around something: *to unwind a ball of string* ♦ *He unwound his scarf from his neck.* ♦ *The bandage gradually unwound and fell off.* **2** [I] to stop worrying or thinking about problems and start to relax **SYN** RELAX: *Music helps me unwind after a busy day.*

un·wise /ʌnˈwaɪz/ adj. ~ **(to do sth)** showing a lack of good judgment **SYN** FOOLISH: *It would be unwise to comment on the situation without knowing all the facts.* ♦ *an unwise investment* **ANT** WISE ▶ **un·wise·ly** adv.: *Perhaps unwisely, I agreed to help.*

un·wit·ting /ʌnˈwɪtɪŋ/ adj. [only before noun] not aware of what you are doing or of the situation you are involved in: *He became an unwitting accomplice in the crime.* ♦ *She was the unwitting cause of the argument.*

un·wit·ting·ly /ʌnˈwɪtɪŋli/ adv. without being aware of what you are doing or the situation that you are involved in: *She had broken the law unwittingly, but she had still broken it.* **ANT** WITTINGLY

un·wont·ed /ʌnˈwɒntəd; -ˈwʌn-; -ˈwoʊn-/ adj. (formal) not usual or expected: *He spoke with unwonted enthusiasm.*

un·work·a·ble /ʌnˈwɜrkəbl/ adj. not practical or possible to do successfully: *an unworkable plan* ♦ *The law as it stands is unworkable.* **ANT** WORKABLE

un·world·ly /ʌnˈwɜrldli/ adj. **1** not interested in money or the things that it buys **2** lacking experience of life **SYN** NAIVE **ANT** WORLDLY **3** having qualities that do not seem to belong to this world: *The landscape had a stark, unworldly beauty.*

un·wor·ried /ʌnˈwɜrid/ adj. [not usually before noun] (formal) not worried; calm; relaxed: *She appeared unworried by criticism.*

un·wor·thy /ʌnˈwɜrði/ adj. (formal) **1** ~ **(of sth)** not having the necessary qualities to deserve something, especially respect: *He considered himself unworthy of the honor they had bestowed on him.* **ANT** WORTHY **2** ~ **(of sb)** not acceptable from someone, especially someone who has an important job or high social position **SYN** UNBEFITTING: *Such opinions are unworthy of educated people.* ▶ **un·wor·thi·ness** noun [U]: *feelings of unworthiness*

un·wound pt, pp of UNWIND

un·wrap /ʌnˈræp/ verb (-pp-) ~ **sth** to take off the paper, etc. that covers or protects something: *Don't unwrap your present until your birthday.* **ANT** WRAP UP

un·writ·ten /ʌnˈrɪtn/ adj. **1** ~ **law, rule, agreement, etc.** a law, etc. that everyone knows about and accepts even though it has not been made official: *an unwritten understanding that nobody leaves before five o'clock* **2** (of a book, etc.) not yet written: *The photographs were to be included in his as yet unwritten autobiography.*

un·yield·ing /ʌnˈyildɪŋ/ adj. (formal) **1** if a person is **unyielding**, they are not easily influenced and they are unlikely to change their mind **SYN** INFLEXIBLE **2** an **unyielding** substance or object does not bend or break when pressure is put on it

un·zip /ʌnˈzɪp/ verb (-pp-) **1** [T, I] ~ **(sth)** if you **unzip** a piece of clothing, a bag, etc., or if it **unzips**, you open it by undoing the ZIPPER that fastens it **ANT** ZIP UP **2** [T] ~ **sth** (computing) to return a computer file to its original size after it has been COMPRESSED (= made smaller) **SYN** DECOMPRESS **ANT** ZIP

up ✐ /ʌp/ adv., prep., adj., verb, noun

• **adv. HELP** For the special uses of **up** in phrasal verbs, look at the entries for the verbs. For example, **break up** is in the phrasal verb section at **break**. **1** toward or in a higher position: *He jumped up from his chair.* ♦ *The sun was already up (= had risen) when they set off.* ♦ *They live up in the mountains.* ♦ *It didn't take long to put the tent up.* ♦ *I pinned the notice up on*

the wall. ♦ *Lay the cards face up (= facing upward) on the table.* ♦ *You look nice with your hair up (= arranged on top of or at the back of your head).* ♦ *Up you go! (= said when lifting a child).* **2** to or at a higher level: *She turned the volume up.* ♦ *Prices are still going up (= rising).* ♦ *The Mets were 4 runs up in the top of the 7th inning.* ♦ *The wind is getting up (= blowing more strongly).* ♦ *Sales are up on last year.* ⟳ **language bank at** INCREASE **3** to the place where someone or something is: *A car drove up and he got in.* ♦ *She went straight up to the door and knocked loudly.* **4** to or at an important place, especially a large city: *We're going up to New York for the day.* **5** to a place in the north of a country: *They've moved up north.* ♦ *We drove up to Maine to see my father.* **6** into pieces or parts: *She tore the paper up.* ♦ *How shall we divide up the work?* **7** completely: *We ate all the food up.* ♦ *The stream has dried up.* **8** so as to be formed or brought together: *The government agreed to set up a committee of inquiry.* ♦ *She gathered up her belongings.* **9** so as to be finished or closed: *I have some paperwork to finish up.* ♦ *Do your coat up; it's cold.* **10** (of a period of time) finished; over: *Time's up. Stop writing and hand in your papers.* **11** out of bed: *I stayed up late (= did not go to bed until late) last night.* **12** (informal) used to say that something is happening, especially something unusual or unpleasant: *I could tell something was up by the looks on their faces.* ♦ *What's up? (= What is the matter?)* ♦ *What's up with him? He looks furious.* ♦ *Is anything up? You can tell me.* **HELP** **What's up?** can just mean "What's new?" or "What's happening?" There may not be anything wrong. **IDM** **be up to sb** to be someone's duty or responsibility; to be for someone to decide: *It's not up to you to tell me how to do my job.* ♦ *Shall we eat out or stay in? It's up to you.* **up against sth** (informal) facing problems or opposition: *Teachers are up against some major problems these days.* ♦ *She's really up against it (= in a difficult situation).* **up and down 1** moving upward and downward: *The boat bobbed up and down on the water.* **2** in one direction and then in the opposite direction: *She was pacing up and down in front of her desk.* **3** sometimes good and sometimes bad: *My relationship with him was up and down.* **4** (informal) if you swear **up and down** that something is true, you say that it is definitely true **up and running** (of a system, for example a computer system) working; being used: *By that time the new system should be up and running.* **up before sb/sth** appearing in front of someone in authority for a judgment to be made about something that you have done: *He came up before the judge for speeding.* **up for sth 1** on offer for something: *The house is up for sale.* **2** being considered for something, especially as a candidate: *Two candidates are up for election.* **3** (informal) willing to take part in a particular activity: *We're going clubbing tonight. Are you up for it?* **up there** (informal) among or almost the best, worst, most important, etc.: *It may not have been the worst week of my life but it's up there.* ♦ *OK, it's not my absolute dream, but it's up there.* **up to sth 1** as far as a particular number, level, etc.: *I can take up to four people (= but no more than four) in my car.* ♦ *The temperature went up to 95°F.* **2** (also **up until sth**) not further or later than something; until something: *Read up to page 100.* ♦ *Up to now he's been very quiet.* **3** as high or as good as something: *Her latest book isn't up to her usual standard.* **4** (also **up to doing sth**) physically or mentally capable of something: *He's not up to the job.* ♦ *I don't feel up to going to work today.* **5** (informal) doing something, especially something bad: *What's she up to?* ♦ *What've you been up to?* ♦ *I'm sure he's up to no good (= doing something bad).*

• **prep. 1** to or in a higher position somewhere: *She climbed up the flight of steps.* ♦ *The village is further up the valley.* **2** along or further along a road or street: *We live just up the road, past the post office.* **3** toward the place where a river starts: *a cruise up the Hudson* **IDM** **up and down sth** in one direction and then in the opposite direction along something: *I looked up and down the corridor.*

• **adj. 1** [only before noun] directed or moving upward: *an up stroke* ♦ *the up escalator* **2** [not before noun] (informal) cheerful; happy or excited: *The mood here is really up.* **3** [not before noun] having your turn at something; taking its place in the order of things: *Are you ready? You're up next.* ◆ *First up, a report on baseball's bright new star Stephen Strasburg.* **4** [not before noun] (of a computer system) working: *Our system should be up by this afternoon.*

● **verb** (-pp-) **1** [I] **up and…** (*informal* or *humorous*) to suddenly move or do something unexpected: *He up and left without telling anyone.* **2** [T] **~ sth** to increase the price or amount of something **SYN** RAISE: *The buyers upped their offer by $1,000.* **IDM** see ANTE

● **noun**
IDM **on the up** increasing or improving: *Business confidence is on the up.* **on the up and up** (*informal*) = ON THE LEVEL at LEVEL *n.*: *The offer seems to be on the up and up.* **ups and downs** the mixture of good and bad things in life or in a particular situation or relationship

up- /ʌp/ *prefix* (in adjectives, verbs, and related nouns) higher; upward; toward the top of something: *upland* ◆ *upturned* ◆ *upgrade* ◆ *uphill*

up·anchor *verb* [I] (of a ship or its CREW) to raise the ANCHOR from the water in order to be ready to sail

up-and-coming *adj.* likely to be successful and popular in the future: *up-and-coming young actors*

up·beat /ˈʌpbit/ *adj.* (*informal*) positive and enthusiastic; making you feel that the future will be good **SYN** OPTIMISTIC: *The tone of the speech was upbeat.* ◆ *The meeting ended on an upbeat note.* **ANT** DOWNBEAT

up·braid /ʌpˈbreɪd/ *verb* **~ sb (for sth/for doing sth)** (*formal*) to criticize someone or speak angrily to them because you do not approve of something that they have said or done **SYN** REPROACH

up·bring·ing /ˈʌpˌbrɪŋɪŋ/ *noun* (sing., U) the way in which a child is cared for and taught how to behave while it is growing up: *to have had a sheltered upbringing* ◆ *He was a Catholic by upbringing.*

UPC /ˌyu pi ˈsi/ *abbr.* (*technical*) Universal Product Code: *The Universal Product Code symbol, also known as the "bar code," is printed on products for sale and contains information that a computer can read.*

up·chuck /ˈʌptʃʌk/ *verb* [I, T] **~ (sth)** (*informal*) to VOMIT

up·com·ing /ˈʌpˌkʌmɪŋ/ *adj.* [only before noun] going to happen soon: *the upcoming presidential election* ◆ *a single from the band's upcoming album*

up·coun·try /ˈʌpˌkʌntri/ *adj.* [only before noun] connected with an area of a country that is not near large towns ▶ **up·country** *adv.*

up·date /ˈʌpdeɪt; ˌʌpˈdeɪt/ *verb, noun*
● **verb** **1** **~ sth** to make something more modern by adding new parts, etc.: *It's about time we updated our software.* **2** to give someone the most recent information about something; to add the most recent information to something **SYN** BRING UP TO DATE: **~ sb (on sth)** *I called the office to update them on the day's developments.* ◆ **~ sth** *Our records are regularly updated.*
● **noun** /ˈʌpdeɪt/ **1** **~ (on sth)** a report or broadcast that gives the most recent information about something; a new version of something containing the most recent information: *a news update* **2** (*computing*) the most recent improvements to a computer program that are sent to users of the program

up·draft /ˈʌpdræft/ *noun* an upward movement of air: *hawks riding the thermal updrafts* **ANT** DOWNDRAFT

up·end /ʌpˈɛnd/ *verb* **~ sb/sth** to turn someone or something upside down: *The bicycle lay upended in a ditch.*

up·field /ˌʌpˈfild/ *adv.* (*sports*) toward your opponent's end of the playing field

up·front /ˌʌpˈfrʌnt/ *adj.* **1** **~ (about sth)** not trying to hide what you think or do **SYN** FRANK, HONEST: *He's been upfront about his intentions since the beginning.* **2** [only before noun] paid in advance, before other payments are made: *There will be an upfront fee of 4%.* ⊃ see also UP FRONT at FRONT

up·grade /ˈʌpgreɪd; ʌpˈgreɪd/ *verb* [often passive] **1** **~ sth** to make a piece of machinery, computer system, etc. more powerful and efficient **2** **~ sb (to sth)** to give someone a better seat on a plane, room in a hotel, etc. than the one that they have paid for **3** **~ sth** to improve the condition of a building, etc. in order to provide a better service: *to upgrade the town's public facilities* ⊃ compare DOWNGRADE **4** **~ sb (to sth)** to give someone a more important job **SYN** PROMOTE ▶ **up·grade** /ˈʌpgreɪd/ *noun*

up·heav·al /ʌpˈhivl/ *noun* [C, U] a big change that causes a lot of confusion, worry, and problems **SYN** : *the latest upheavals in the education system* ◆ *I can't face the upheaval of moving house again.* ◆ *a period of emotional upheaval*

up·hill *adj., adv.*
● **adj.** /ˌʌpˈhɪl; ˈʌphɪl/ **1** sloping upward: *an uphill climb/slope* ◆ *The last part of the race is all uphill.* **ANT** DOWNHILL **2** **~ battle, struggle, task, etc.** an argument or a struggle that is difficult to win and takes a lot of effort over a long period of time
● **adv.** /ˌʌpˈhɪl/ toward the top of a hill or slope: *We climbed uphill for over an hour.* ◆ *The path slopes steeply uphill.* **ANT** DOWNHILL

up·hold /ʌpˈhoʊld/ *verb* (**up·held, up·held** /-ˈhɛld/) **1** **~ sth** to support something that you think is right and make sure that it continues to exist: *We have a duty to uphold the law.* **2** **~ sth** (especially of a court of law) to agree that a previous decision was correct or that a request is reasonable: *to uphold a conviction/an appeal/a complaint* ▶ **up·hold·er** *noun*: *an upholder of traditional values*

up·hol·ster /əˈpoʊlstər/ *verb* [usually passive] **~ sth (in sth)** to cover a chair, etc. with soft material (= PADDING) and cloth

up·hol·ster·er /əˈpoʊlstərər/ *noun* a person whose job is to upholster furniture

up·hol·ster·y /əˈpoʊlstəri/ *noun* [U] **1** soft covering on furniture such as ARMCHAIRS and SOFAS **2** the process or trade of UPHOLSTERING

UPI /ˌyu pi ˈaɪ/ *abbr.* UNITED PRESS INTERNATIONAL

up·keep /ˈʌpkip/ *noun* [U] **1** **~ (of sth)** the cost or process of keeping something in good condition **SYN** MAINTENANCE: *Tenants are responsible for the upkeep of rented property.* **2** **~ (of sb/sth)** the cost or process of giving a child or an animal the things that they need: *He makes payments to his ex-wife for the upkeep of their children.*

up·land /ˈʌplənd; -lænd/ *noun* [usually pl.] an area of high land that is not near the coast ▶ **up·land** *adj.* [only before noun]: *upland agriculture*

up·lift *noun, verb*
● **noun** /ˈʌplɪft/ [U, sing.] **1** the fact of something being raised or of something increasing: *an uplift in sales* **2** a feeling of hope and happiness: *The news gave them a much needed uplift.* **3** (also **up·thrust**) (*geology*) the process or result of land being moved to a higher level by movements inside the earth
● **verb** /ʌpˈlɪft/ **~ sb** (*formal*) to make someone feel happier or give someone more hope

up·lift·ed /ʌpˈlɪftəd/ *adj.* **1** [not before noun] feeling happy and full of hope **2** (*literary*) lifted upward: *a sea of uplifted faces*

up·lift·ing /ʌpˈlɪftɪŋ/ *adj.* making you feel happier or giving you more hope: *an uplifting experience/speech*

up·light /ˈʌplaɪt/ *noun* a lamp in a room that is designed to send light upward ⊃ compare DOWNLIGHT

up·link /ˈʌplɪŋk/ *noun* (*technical*) a communications link to a SATELLITE

up·load /ˈʌploʊd/ *verb, noun*
● **verb** **~ sth** (*computing*) to move data to a larger computer system from a smaller one ⊃ collocations at E-MAIL **ANT** DOWNLOAD
● **noun** (*computing*) data that has been moved to a larger computer system from a smaller one **ANT** DOWNLOAD

up·mar·ket /ˌʌpˈmɑrkɪt/ adj. [usually before noun], adv. = UPSCALE

up·on 🔑 /əˈpɑn; əˈpɔn/ prep.
1 (formal) = ON: The decision was based upon two considerations. **HELP** Although the word **upon** has the same meaning as **on**, it is usually used in more formal contexts or in phrases such as: once upon a time and: row upon row of seats. **2** ...upon... used to emphasize that there is a large number or amount of something: mile upon mile of dusty road ◆ thousands upon thousands of letters
IDM (almost) upon you if something in the future is **almost upon you**, it is going to arrive or happen very soon: The summer season was almost upon them again. ⊃ more at ONCE adv.

up·per 🔑 /ˈʌpər/ adj., noun
• adj. [only before noun] **1** located above something else, especially something of the same type or the other of a pair: the upper lip ◆ the upper deck **2** at or near the top of something: the upper arm ◆ the upper slopes of the mountain ◆ a member of the upper middle class ◆ salaries at the upper end of the pay scale ◆ There is an upper limit of $20,000 spent on any one project. **3** (of a place) located away from the coast, on high ground or toward the north of an area: the upper reaches of the river **ANT** LOWER[1]
IDM gain, get, have, etc. the ˌupper ˈhand to get an advantage over someone so that you are in control of a particular situation ⊃ more at STIFF
• noun [usually pl.] **1** the top part of a shoe that is attached to the SOLE: shoes with leather uppers **2** (informal) a drug that makes you feel excited and full of energy ⊃ compare DOWNER

up·per·case (also ˌupper ˈcase) /ˌʌpərˈkeɪs/ noun [U] capital letters (= the large form of letters, for example A, B, C rather than a, b, c): Headings should be in uppercase. ⊃ compare LOWERCASE ▸ **up·per·case** adj.: uppercase letters

ˌupper ˈchamber noun = UPPER HOUSE

the ˌupper ˈclass noun the groups of people that are considered to have the highest social status, and that have more money, and/or power than other people in society: a member of the upper class/upper classes ▸ ˌupper-ˈclass adj.: Her family is very upper class. ◆ an upper-class accent ⊃ compare LOWER CLASS, MIDDLE CLASS, WORKING CLASS

up·per·class·man /ˌʌpərˈklæsmən/, **up·per·class·wom·an** /ˌʌpərˈklæsˌwʊmən/ noun (pl. up·per·class·men /-mən/, up·per·class·wom·en /-ˌwɪmən/) a student in the last two years of high school or college ⊃ compare UNDERCLASSMAN

the ˌupper ˈcrust noun [sing.] (informal) the people who belong to the highest social class **SYN** ARISTOCRACY ▸ ˌupper-ˈcrust adj.

up·per·cut /ˈʌpərˌkʌt/ noun (in boxing) a way of hitting someone on the chin, in which you bend your arm and move your hand upward

ˌupper ˈhouse (also ˌupper ˈchamber) noun [sing.] one of the two parts of a LEGISLATURE or parliament. In the U.S. it is the Senate. ⊃ compare LOWER HOUSE

up·per·most /ˈʌpərˌmoʊst/ adj., adv.
• adj. **1** [usually before noun] (formal) higher or nearer the top than other things: the uppermost branches of the tree **2** [not usually before noun] more important than other things in a particular situation: These thoughts were uppermost in my mind.
• adv. (formal) in the highest or most important position; facing upward: Investors put environmental concerns uppermost on their list.

up·pi·ty /ˈʌpəti/ adj. (informal) behaving as if you are more important than you really are, especially when this means that you refuse to obey orders

up·raised /ˌʌpˈreɪzd/ adj. lifted upward: She strode toward them, her fist upraised.

up·right /ˈʌpraɪt/ adj., adv., noun
• adj. **1** (of a person) not lying down, and with the back straight rather than bent: an upright posture ◆ Gradually raise your body into an upright position. **2** placed in a vertical position: Keep the bottle upright. ◆ an upright freezer (= one that is taller than it is wide) ◆ an upright piano (= one with vertical strings) **3** (of a person) behaving in a moral and honest way **SYN** UPSTANDING: an upright citizen **IDM** see BOLT adv.
• adv. in or into a vertical position: She sat upright in bed. ◆ He managed to pull himself upright.
• noun **1** a long piece of wood, metal, or plastic that is placed in a vertical position, especially in order to support something **2** = UPRIGHT PIANO

up·right·ness /ˈʌpraɪtnəs/ noun [U] behavior or attitudes that are very moral and honest

ˌupright piˈano (also up·right) noun a piano in which the strings are vertical ⊃ compare GRAND PIANO, SPINET

up·ris·ing /ˈʌpˌraɪzɪŋ/ noun ~ (against sth) a situation in which a group of people join together in order to fight against the people who are in power **SYN** REBELLION, REVOLT: an armed uprising against the government ◆ a popular uprising (= by the ordinary people of the country) ◆ to crush/ suppress an uprising

up·riv·er /ˌʌpˈrɪvər/ adv. = UPSTREAM

up·roar /ˈʌprɔr/ noun [U, sing.] **1** a situation in which people shout and make a lot of noise because they are angry or upset about something: The room was in (an) uproar. ◆ Her comments provoked (an) uproar from the audience. **2** a situation in which there is a lot of public criticism and angry argument about something that someone has said or done **SYN** OUTCRY: The article caused (an) uproar.

up·roar·i·ous /ʌpˈrɔriəs/ adj. [usually before noun] **1** in which there is a lot of noise, and people laugh or shout a lot: an uproarious party **2** extremely funny: an uproarious story ▸ **up·roar·i·ous·ly** adv.: The audience laughed uproariously. ◆ uproariously funny

up·root /ʌpˈrut; -ˈrʊt/ verb **1** [T] ~ sth to pull a tree, plant, etc. out of the ground **2** [I, T] to leave a place where you have lived for a long time; to make someone do this: We decided to uproot and head for Florida. ◆ ~ yourself/sb If I accept the job, it will mean uprooting my family and moving to Hong Kong.

up·rush /ˈʌprʌʃ/ noun [sing.] ~ of sth (formal) a sudden feeling of something such as joy or fear: an uprush of joy

ups-a-dai·sy /ˈʌpsəˌdeɪzi/ exclamation = UPSY-DAISY

up·scale /ˈʌpskeɪl/ (also up·mar·ket) adj., adv. [usually before noun] designed for or used by people who belong to a high social class or have a lot of money: an upscale restaurant/ neighborhood **ANT** DOWNSCALE ▸ **up·scale** (also up·mar·ket) adv.

up·sell /ˈʌpsɛl/ verb (up·sold, up·sold /-ˈsoʊld/) [I] (business) to persuade a customer to buy more products or a more expensive product than they originally intended: You can usually upsell to about half the customers. ▸ **up·sell·ing** noun [U] (business): You can make great profits from upselling.

up·set 🔑 verb, adj., noun
• verb /ʌpˈsɛt/ (up·set·ting, up·set, up·set) **1** to make someone/something feel unhappy, anxious, or annoyed **SYN** DISTRESS: ~ sb/yourself This decision is likely to upset a lot of people. ◆ Don't upset yourself about it — let's just forget it ever happened. ◆ it upsets sb that... It upset him that no one had bothered to tell him about it. ◆ it upsets sb to do sth It upsets me to think of her all alone in that big house. ⊃ thesaurus box at ANGRY **2** ~ sth to make a plan, situation, etc. go wrong: He arrived an hour late and upset all our arrangements. **3** ~ someone's stomach to make someone feel sick after they have eaten or drunk something **4** ~ sth to make something fall over by hitting it by accident: She stood up suddenly, upsetting a glass of wine.

t tea   ṭ butter   d did   k cat   g got   tʃ chin   dʒ June   f fall

IDM **upset the apple cart** to cause problems for someone or spoil their plans, arrangements, etc.

● **adj.** /ʌpˈsɛt/ **1** [not before noun] **~ (about sth)** | **~ (that…)** unhappy or disappointed because of something unpleasant that has happened: *There's no point getting upset about it.* **2** [not before noun] **~ (about sth)** | **~ (that…)** | **~ with sb (for doing sth)** somewhat angry or annoyed: *I was quite upset with him for being late.* ➲ thesaurus box at ANGRY **3 an ˌupset ˈstomach** an illness in the stomach that makes you feel sick or have DIARRHEA

● **noun** /ˈʌpsɛt/ **1** [C] (in a competition) a situation in which a person or team beats the person or team that was expected to win **2** [C] an illness in the stomach that makes you feel sick or have DIARRHEA: *a stomach upset* **3** [U] a situation in which there are problems or difficulties, especially when these are unexpected: *The company has survived the recent upset in share prices.* ◆ *His health has not been improved by all the upset at home.* **4** [U, C] feelings of unhappiness and disappointment caused by something unpleasant that has happened: *It had been the cause of much emotional upset.*

up·set·ting /ʌpˈsɛtɪŋ/ *adj.*
making you feel unhappy, anxious, or annoyed: *an upsetting experience*

up·shift /ˈʌpʃɪft/ *verb* [I] to change into a higher gear in a vehicle

the up·shot /ˈʌpʃɑt/ *noun* [sing.] the final result of a series of events **SYN** OUTCOME: *The upshot of it all was that he left college and got a job.*

up·side /ˈʌpsaɪd/ *noun, prep.*
● **noun** [sing.] the more positive aspect of a situation that is generally bad **ANT** DOWNSIDE
● **prep.** (*informal*) on the side of a part of the body: *She slapped him upside the head.*

ˌupside ˈdown 🔊 *adv.*
in or into a position in which the top of something is where the bottom is normally found and the bottom is where the top is normally found: *The canoe floated upside down on the lake.* **ANT** RIGHT SIDE UP ▶ **ˌupside ˈdown** *adj.* [not usually before noun]: *The painting looks like it's upside down to me.* **IDM** **turn sth upside down 1** to make a place messy when looking for something: *The police turned the whole house upside down looking for clues.* **2** to cause large changes and confusion in a person's life: *His sudden death turned her world upside down.*

up·si·lon /ˈʊpsəˌlɑn; ˈyup-; ˈʌp-/ *noun* the 20th letter of the Greek alphabet (Υ, υ)

up·stage /ʌpˈsteɪdʒ/ *adv., adj., verb*
● **adv., adj.** at or toward the back of the stage in a theater **ANT** DOWNSTAGE
● **verb** **~ sb** to say or do something that makes people notice you more than the person that they should be interested in: *She was furious at being upstaged by her younger sister.*

up·stairs 🔊 *adv., noun*
● **adv.** /ˌʌpˈstɛrz/ **1** up the stairs; on or to a floor of a house or other building higher than the one that you are on: *The cat belongs to the people who live upstairs.* ◆ *I carried her bags upstairs.* ◆ *She went upstairs to get dressed.* **ANT** DOWNSTAIRS **2** (*informal*) in the mind; mentally: *She works hard, but she doesn't have much upstairs* (= she is not intelligent). ▶ **upstairs** *adj.* /ˈʌpstɛrz/ [only before noun]: *an upstairs room* **IDM** see KICK *v.*
● **noun** /ˈʌpstɛrz/ [sing.] the floor or floors in a building that are above the ground floor: *We've converted the upstairs into an office.* **ANT** DOWNSTAIRS

up·stand·ing /ˌʌpˈstændɪŋ/ *adj.* [usually before noun] (*formal*) behaving in a moral and honest way **SYN** UPRIGHT: *an upstanding member of the community*

up·start /ˈʌpstɑrt/ *noun* (*disapproving*) a person who has just started in a new position or job but who behaves as if they are more important than other people, in a way that is annoying

up·state /ˌʌpˈsteɪt/ *adv.* in or to a part of a state that is far from its main cities, especially a northern part: *They retired and went to live upstate.* ▶ **up·state** /ˈʌpsteɪt/ *adj.* [only before noun]: *upstate New York*

up·stream /ˌʌpˈstrim/ (also *less frequent* **up·riv·er**) *adv.* **~ (of/from sth)** along a river, in the opposite direction to the way in which the water flows: *The nearest town is about ten miles upstream.* ◆ *upstream of/from the bridge* **ANT** DOWNSTREAM

up·surge /ˈʌpsərdʒ/ *noun* [usually sing.] (*formal*) a sudden large increase in something: **~ (in sth)** *an upsurge in violent crime* ◆ **~ (of sth)** *a recent upsurge of interest in his movies*

up·swell /ˈʌpswɛl/ (also **up·swell·ing** /ˈʌpˌswɛlɪŋ/) *noun* [sing.] **~ of sth** (*formal*) an increase in something, especially a feeling: *a huge upswell of emotion*

up·swept /ˈʌpswɛpt/ *adj.* curved or sloping upward: *an upswept hairdo*

up·swing /ˈʌpswɪŋ/ *noun* [usually sing.] **~ (in sth)** a situation in which something improves or increases over a period of time **SYN** UPTURN: *an upswing in economic activity* ◆ *an upswing in the team's wins*

up·sy-dai·sy /ˈʌpsi ˌdeɪzi/ (also **ups-a-daisy, oops-a-daisy**) *exclamation* said when you have made a mistake, dropped something, fallen down, etc., or when someone else has

up·take /ˈʌpteɪk/ *noun* [U, sing.] **1 ~ (of sth)** (*technical*) the process by which something is taken into a body or system; the rate at which this happens: *the uptake of oxygen by muscles* **2 ~ (of sth)** the use that is made of something that has become available: *a recent uptake in music downloads* **IDM** **be quick/slow on the uptake** (*informal*) to be quick/slow to understand something: *Is he always this slow on the uptake?*

up·tem·po /ˈʌpˌtɛmpoʊ/ *adj.* (especially of music) fast: *uptempo dance tunes*

up·thrust /ˈʌpθrʌst/ *noun* [U] **1** (*physics*) the force with which a liquid or gas pushes up against an object that is floating in it **2** (*geology*) = UPLIFT

up·tick /ˈʌptɪk/ *noun* (*economics*) a small increase in the level or value of something, especially in the price of shares: *The futures market is showing an uptick.* **ANT** DOWNTICK

up·tight /ˌʌpˈtaɪt/ *adj.* **~ (about sth)** (*informal*) **1** anxious and/or angry about something: *Relax! You're getting too uptight about it.* **2** nervous about showing your feelings: *an uptight teenager*

up·time /ˈʌptaɪm/ *noun* [U] the time during which a machine, especially a computer, is working **ANT** DOWNTIME

ˌup to ˈdate *adj.* **1** modern; fashionable: *This technology is very up to date* (= completely modern). ◆ *up-to-date fashions* ◆ *up-to-date equipment* **2** having or including the most recent information: *We are keeping up to date with the latest developments.* ◆ *up-to-date records* ◆ *She brought him up to date with what had happened.* ➲ see also OUT OF DATE

ˌup-to-the-ˈminute *adj.* [usually before noun] **1** having or including the most recent information: *up-to-the-minute news* **2** modern; fashionable: *up-to-the-minute designs* ➲ see also UP TO THE MINUTE at MINUTE *n.*

up·town /ˌʌpˈtaʊn/ *adv., adj.*
● **adv.** in or to the parts of a town or city that are away from the center, where people live: *They live in an apartment uptown.* ◆ *We walked uptown a couple of blocks until we found a cab.* ➲ compare DOWNTOWN, MIDTOWN
● **adj.** **1** [only before noun] in, to, or typical of the parts of a town or city that are away from the center, where people live: *an uptown train* **2** typical of an area of a town or city where people have a lot of money: *uptown prices* ◆ *an uptown girl*

up·trend /ˈʌptrɛnd/ *noun* [sing.] a situation in which business activity or performance increases or improves over a period of time **ANT** DOWNTREND

up·turn /ˈʌptərn/ noun [usually sing.] ~ (in sth) a situation in which something improves or increases over a period of time SYN UPSWING: *an upturn in the economy* ◆ *The restaurant trade is on the upturn.* ANT DOWNTURN

up·turned /ˈʌptərnd/ adj. [usually before noun] **1** pointing or facing upward: *an upturned nose* (= that curves upward at the end) ◆ *She looked down at the sea of upturned faces.* **2** turned upside down: *She sat on an upturned box.*

uPVC /ˌyu pi vi ˈsi/ noun [U] the abbreviation for "unplasticized polyvinyl chloride" (a strong plastic used to make window frames and pipes)

up·ward ♪ /ˈʌpwərd/ adj., adv.
● *adj.* [only before noun] **1** pointing toward or facing a higher place: *an upward gaze* **2** increasing in amount or price: *an upward movement in property prices* ANT DOWNWARD
● *adv.* (also **up·wards** /ˈʌpwərdz/) **1** toward a higher place or position: *A flight of steps led upward to the front door.* ◆ *Place your hands on the table with the palms facing upward.* ANT DOWNWARD **2** toward a higher amount or price: *Bad weather forced the price of fruit upward.* ◆ *The budget has been revised upward.* ANT DOWNWARD **3 ~ of sth** more than the amount or number mentioned: *You should expect to pay upward of $90 for a hotel room.*

ˌupwardly ˈmobile adj. moving toward a higher social position, usually in which you become richer: *upwardly mobile immigrant groups* ◆ *an upwardly mobile lifestyle* ▶ ˌupward moˈbility noun [U]

up·wind /ˌʌpˈwɪnd/ adv. in the opposite direction to the way in which the wind is blowing: *to sail upwind* ◆ *The house was upwind of the factory and its smells* (= the wind did not blow the smells toward the house). ANT DOWNWIND ▶ **up·wind** adj.

ur- /ʊr/ prefix (formal) earliest or original

u·ra·ni·um /yʊˈreɪniəm/ noun [U] (symb. **U**) a chemical element. Uranium is a heavy, silver-white, RADIOACTIVE metal, used mainly in producing nuclear energy.

U·ran·us /ˈyʊrənəs; yʊˈreɪnəs/ noun the planet in the SOLAR SYSTEM that is 7th in order of distance from the sun ⊃ picture at EARTH

ur·ban ♪ /ˈərbən/ adj. [usually before noun]
1 connected with a town or city: *damage to both urban and rural environments* ◆ *urban areas* ◆ *urban life* ◆ *urban development* (= the process of building towns and cities or making them larger) ◆ *urban renewal/regeneration* (= the process of improving the buildings, etc. in the poor parts of a town or city) ◆ *efforts to control urban sprawl* (= the spread of city buildings into the countryside) ⊃ compare RURAL **2** connected with types of music such as RHYTHM AND BLUES and REGGAE that are played by black musicians: *today's urban music scene* ◆ *urban radio shows*

ur·bane /ərˈbeɪn/ adj. (especially of a man) good at knowing what to say and how to behave in social situations; appearing relaxed and confident ▶ **ur·bane·ly** adv. **ur·ban·i·ty** /ərˈbænəti/ noun [U]

ur·ban·ite /ˈərbəˌnaɪt/ noun a person who lives in a town or city

ur·ban·ized /ˈərbəˌnaɪzd/ adj. **1** (of an area, a country, etc.) having a lot of towns, streets, factories, etc. rather than countryside **2** (of people) living and working in towns and cities rather than in the country: *an increasingly urbanized society* ▶ **ur·ban·i·za·tion** /ˌərbənəˈzeɪʃn/ noun [U]

ˌurban ˈlegend (also ˌurban ˈmyth) noun a story about an amusing or strange event that is supposed to have happened, which is often repeated and which many people believe is true

ur·chin /ˈərtʃən/ noun **1** (old-fashioned) a young child who is poor and dirty, often one who has no home: *a dirty little street urchin* **2** = SEA URCHIN

Ur·du /ˈʊrdu; ˈərdu/ noun [U] the official language of Pakistan, also widely used in India

-ure /yər; ər/ suffix (in nouns) the action, process, or result of: *closure* ◆ *failure*

u·re·a /yʊˈriə/ noun [U] (technical) a clear substance containing NITROGEN that is found especially in URINE

u·re·thra /yʊˈriθrə/ noun (anatomy) the tube that carries liquid waste out of the body. In men and male animals SPERM also flows along this tube. ▶ **u·re·thral** /-θrəl/ adj. [only before noun]

u·re·thri·tis /ˌyʊrəˈθraɪtəs/ noun [U] (medical) infection of the urethra

urge ♪ /ərdʒ/ verb, noun
● *verb* **1** to advise or try hard to persuade someone to do something: ~ **sb to do sth** *She urged him to stay.* ◆ ~ **that…** *The report urged that all children be taught to swim.* ◆ ~ **(sb) + speech** *"Why not give it a try?" she urged (him).* ⊃ thesaurus box at RECOMMEND **2** ~ **sth (on/upon sb)** to recommend something strongly: *The situation is dangerous and the UN is urging caution.* **3** ~ **sb/sth + adv./prep.** (formal) to make a person or an animal move more quickly and/or in a particular direction, especially by pushing or forcing them: *He urged his horse forward.*
PHR V ˌurge sb↔ˈon to encourage someone to do something or support them so that they do it better: *She could hear him urging her on as she ran past.*
● *noun* a strong desire to do something: *sexual urges* ◆ ~ **to do sth** *I had a sudden urge to hit him.*

ur·gent ♪ /ˈərdʒənt/ adj.
1 that needs to be dealt with or happen immediately SYN PRESSING: *an urgent appeal for information* ◆ *a problem that requires urgent attention* ◆ *"Can I see you for a moment?" "Is it urgent?"* ◆ *Mark the message "urgent," please.* ◆ *The law is in urgent need of reform.* **2** showing that you think that something needs to be dealt with immediately: *an urgent whisper* ▶ **ur·gen·cy** /ˈərdʒənsi/ noun [U, sing.]: *This is a matter of some urgency.* ◆ *The attack added a new urgency to the peace talks.* **ur·gent·ly** adv.: *New equipment is urgently needed.* ◆ *I need to speak to her urgently.* ◆ *"We must find him," she said urgently.*

u·ri·nal /ˈyʊrənl; ˈyər-/ noun a type of toilet for men that is attached to the wall

u·ri·nary /ˈyʊrəˌneri; ˈyər-/ adj. [usually before noun] (medical) connected with URINE or the parts of the body through which it passes

u·ri·nate /ˈyʊrəˌneɪt; ˈyər-/ verb [I] (formal or technical) to get rid of URINE from the body ▶ **u·ri·na·tion** /ˌyʊrəˈneɪʃn; ˌyər-/ noun [U]

u·rine /ˈyʊrən; ˈyər-/ noun [U] the waste liquid that collects in the BLADDER and that you pass from your body

URL /ˌyu ar ˈɛl/ abbr. (computing) uniform/universal resource locator (the address of a Web site)

urn /ərn/ noun **1** a tall decorated container, especially one used for holding the ASHES of a dead person **2** a large metal container with a tap, used for making and/or serving tea or coffee: *a tea urn*

u·rol·o·gy /yʊˈrɑlədʒi/ noun [U] (medical) the scientific study of the URINARY system ▶ **u·ro·log·i·cal** /ˌyʊrəˈlɑdʒɪkl/ adj. **u·rol·o·gist** /yʊˈrɑlədʒɪst/ noun

Ur·sa Ma·jor /ˌərsə ˈmeɪdʒər/ (also the ˌGreat ˈBear) noun [sing.] (astronomy) a large group of stars that can be clearly seen from the northern HEMISPHERE

Ur·sa Mi·nor /ˌərsə ˈmaɪnər/ (also the ˌLittle ˈBear) noun [sing.] a group of stars that can be clearly seen from the northern HEMISPHERE and that includes the POLE STAR

ur·sine /ˈərsaɪn/ adj. [usually before noun] (technical or literary) connected with BEARS; like a bear

ur·ti·car·i·a /ˌərtəˈkeriə/ noun [U] (medical) = HIVE (3)

us /əs; strong form ʌs/ pron.
(the object form of we) used when the speaker or writer and another or others are the object of a verb or preposition, or after the verb be: She gave us a picture as a wedding present. ◆ We'll take the dog with us. ◆ Please let us in.

U.S. (also **US**) /ˌyu ˈɛs/ abbr. UNITED STATES: She became a U.S. citizen. ◆ the U.S. dollar

U.S.A. (also **USA**) /ˌyu ɛs ˈeɪ/ abbr. UNITED STATES OF AMERICA: Do you need a visa for the U.S.A.?

us·a·ble /ˈyuzəbl/ adj. that can be used; in good enough condition to be used: The bike is rusty but usable. ◆ How can we display this data in a usable form? **ANT** UNUSABLE

U.S.A.F. (also **USAF**) /ˌyu ɛs eɪ ˈɛf/ abbr. United States Air Force

us·age /ˈyusɪdʒ/ noun **1** [U, C] the way in which words are used in a language: current English usage ◆ It's not a word in common usage. **2** [U] the fact of something being used; how much something is used: land usage ◆ Car usage is predicted to increase.

USB /ˌyu ɛs ˈbi/ abbr. (computing) universal serial bus (the system for connecting other pieces of equipment to a computer): All new PCs now have USB sockets. ◆ a USB port ⊃ picture at COMPUTER

USˈB drive (also informal USˈB stick) noun = FLASH DRIVE

USCIS /ˌyu ɛs ˌsi aɪ ˈɛs/ abbr. United States Citizenship and Immigration Services (the U.S. government department that deals with people from other countries who want to visit or live in the U.S. or to become a U.S. citizen, part of the Department of Homeland Security)

use verb, noun
● **verb** /yuz/ (**used, used** /yuzd/) **1** [T] to do something with a machine, a method, an object, etc. for a particular purpose: ~ **sth** Can I use your phone? ◆ Have you ever used this software before? ◆ How often do you use (= travel by) the bus? ◆ They were able to achieve a settlement without using military force. ◆ I have some information you may be able to use (= to get an advantage from). ◆ ~ **sth for sth/for doing sth** The blue files are used for storing old invoices. ◆ ~ **sth to do sth** Police used tear gas to disperse the crowds. ◆ ~ **sth as sth** The building is currently being used as a warehouse. ◆ You can't keep using your bad back as an excuse. **2** [T] ~ **sth** to take a particular amount of a liquid, substance, etc. in order to achieve or make something: This type of heater uses a lot of electricity. ◆ I hope you haven't used all the milk. **3** [T] ~ **sth** to say or write particular words or a particular type of language: The poem uses simple language. ◆ That's a word I never use. ◆ You have to use the past tense. **4** [T] ~ **sb** (disapproving) to be kind, friendly, etc. to someone with the intention of getting an advantage for yourself from them **SYN** EXPLOIT: Can't you see he's just using you for his own ends? ◆ I felt used. **5** [T, I] ~ (**sth**) to take illegal drugs: Most of the inmates have used drugs at some point in their lives. ◆ (slang) She's been using since she was 13.
IDM **I, you, etc. could use sth** (informal) used to say that you would like to have something very much: I think we could all use a drink after that! **use your head** (informal) used to tell someone to think about something, especially when they have asked for your opinion or said something stupid: "Why don't you want to see him again?" "Oh, use your head!"
PHRV **use sth↔'up** to use all of something so that there is none left: Making soup is a good way of using up leftover vegetables.
● **noun** /yus/ **1** [U, sing.] the act of using something; the state of being used: A ban was imposed on the use of chemical weapons. ◆ The software is designed for use in schools. ◆ I'm not sure that this is the most valuable use of my time. ◆ The chapel was built in the 18th century and is still in use today. ◆ The pool is for the use of members only. **2** [C, U] a purpose for which something is used; a way in which something is or can be used: I'm sure you'll think of a use for it. ◆ This chemical has a wide range of industrial uses. ⊃ see also SINGLE-USE **3** [U] ~ (**of sth**) the right or opportunity to use something, for

example something that belongs to someone else: I have the use of the car this week. **4** [U] the ability to use your mind or body: He lost the use of his legs (= became unable to walk) in an accident.
IDM **be no use (to sb)** (also formal be of no use) to be useless: You can throw those away — they're no use to anyone. **be of use (to sb)** (formal) to be useful: Can I be of any use (= can I help)? **come into/go out of, etc. use** to start/stop being used: When did this word come into common use? **have its/their/your uses** (informal, often humorous) to be useful sometimes: I know you don't like him, but he has his uses. **have no use for sb** to dislike someone: I have no use for people who don't make an effort. **have no use for sth** to not need something **it's no use (doing sth) | what's the use (of doing sth)?** used to say that there is no point in doing something because it will not be successful or have a good result: What's the use of worrying about it? ◆ It's no use — I can't persuade her. **make use of sth/sb** to use something or someone, especially in order to get an advantage: We could make better use of our resources. **put sth to good use** to be able to use something for a purpose, and get an advantage from doing so: She'll be able to put her languages to good use in her new job.

used¹ /yust/ adj.
familiar with something because you do it or experience it often: ~ **to doing sth** I'm not used to eating so much at lunchtime. ◆ ~ **to sth** I found the job tiring at first but I soon got used to it. ⊃ note at USED TO

used² /yuzd/ adj. [usually before noun]
that has belonged to or been used by someone else before **SYN** SECONDHAND: used cars

used to /ˈyustə; finally and often before vowels ˈyustu/ modal verb
used to say that something happened continuously or frequently during a period in the past: I used to live in London. ◆ We used to go sailing on the lake in the summer. ◆ I didn't use to like him much when we were in school. ◆ You used to see a lot of her, didn't you? ⊃ note at MODAL

WHICH WORD?

used to / be used to
- Do not confuse **used to do sth** with **be used to sth**.
- You use **used to do sth** to talk about something that happened regularly or was the case in the past, but is not now: I used to smoke, but I gave up a couple of years ago.
- You use **be used to sth/to doing sth** to talk about something that you are familiar with so that it no longer seems new or strange to you: We're used to the noise from the traffic now. ◆ I'm used to getting up early. You can also use **get used to sth**: Don't worry—you'll soon get used to his sense of humor. ◆ I didn't think I could ever get used to living in a big city after living in the country.

GRAMMAR

used to
- Except in negatives and questions, the correct form is **used to**: I used to go there every Saturday. ◆ ~~I use to go there every Saturday.~~
- To form questions, use **did**: Did she use to have long hair? Note that the correct spelling is **use to**, not "used to."
- The negative form is usually **didn't use to**, but this is informal and is not usually used in writing.

use·ful /ˈyusfl/ adj.
that can help you to do or achieve what you want: a useful gadget ◆ ~ (**to do sth**) It can be useful to write a short summary of your argument first. ◆ ~ (**to sb**) He might be useful to us.

◆ ~ (for sth/for doing sth) *These plants are particularly useful for brightening up shady areas.* ◆ *Don't just sit watching TV — make yourself useful!* ◆ *This information could prove useful.* ◆ *Your knowledge of German may come in useful* (= be useful in a particular situation). ◆ *Some products can be recycled at the end of their useful life.* **ANT** USELESS ▶ **use·ful·ly** /-fəli/ *adv.*: *The money could be more usefully spent on new equipment.*

use·ful·ness /'yusfəlnəs/ *noun* [U] the fact of being useful or possible to use: *There are doubts about the usefulness of these tests.* ◆ *The building has outlived its usefulness.*

use·less 🔑 /'yusləs/ *adj.*
1 not useful; not doing or achieving what is needed or wanted: *This pen is useless.* ◆ ~ (to do sth) *He knew it was useless to protest.* ◆ ~ (doing sth) *It's useless worrying about it.* ◆ *She tried to work, but it was useless* (= she wasn't able to). **ANT** USEFUL **2** ~ (at sth/at doing sth) (*informal*) not very good at something; not able to do things well: *I'm useless at French.* ◆ *Don't ask her to help. She's useless.* ▶ **use·less·ly** *adv.* **use·less·ness** *noun* [U]

Use·net /'yuznɛt/ *noun* [U] (*computing*) a service on the Internet used by groups of users who e-mail each other because they share a particular interest

us·er 🔑 /'yuzər/ *noun*
1 a person or thing that uses something: *road users* ◆ *computer software users* ◆ *a user manual* ⟹ see also END-USER **2** (*slang*) a person who uses illegal drugs

'user ˌfee *noun* a tax on a service that is provided for the public

ˌuser-'friendly *adj.* easy for people who are not experts to use or understand ▶ **ˌuser-'friendliness** *noun* [U]

'user ˌgroup *noun* a group of people who use a particular thing and who share information about it, especially people who share information about computers on the Internet

ˌuser I'D *noun* = USERNAME

us·er·name /'yuzərˌneɪm/ *noun* (also **ˌuser I'D**) (*computing*) the name you use in order to be able to use a computer program or system: *Please enter your username.*

ush·er /'ʌʃər/ *noun, verb*
● *noun* **1** a person who shows people where to sit in a church, public hall, etc. **2** a friend of the BRIDEGROOM at a wedding, who has special duties
● *verb* ~ sb + adv./prep. to politely escort or take or show someone where you want them to be, especially within a building: *The secretary ushered me into his office.* ⟹ thesaurus box at TAKE
PHRV **usher sth⟷'in** (*formal*) to be the beginning of something new or to make something new begin: *The change of management ushered in fresh ideas and policies.*

ush·er·ette /ˌʌʃə'rɛt/ *noun* a woman whose job is to lead people to their seats in a theater

U.S.N. (also USN) /ˌyu ɛs 'ɛn/ *abbr.* United States Navy

USO /ˌyu ɛs 'ou/ *abbr.* United Service Organizations (an organization that provides entertainment and activities to members of the U.S. military)

the U.S. of A. /ˌyu ɛs əv 'eɪ/ *noun* [sing.] (*informal, humorous*) UNITED STATES OF AMERICA: *It's nice to be back in the U.S. of A.*

USP /ˌyu ɛs 'pi/ *noun* (*business*) a feature of a product or service that makes it different from all the others that are available and is a reason for people to choose it (the abbreviation for "unique selling proposition" or "unique selling point"): *You need to come up with a USP.*

USPS (also **U.S.P.S.**) /ˌyu ɛs pi 'ɛs/ *abbr.* United States Postal Service

U.S.S. (also USS) /ˌyu ɛs 'ɛs/ *abbr.* United States Ship (used before the name of a ship in the U.S. navy): *U.S.S. Oklahoma*

USSR (also **U.S.S.R.**) /ˌyu ɛs ɛs 'ɑr/ *abbr.* (the former) Union of Soviet Socialist Republics

u·su·al 🔑 /'yuʒuəl; -ʒəl/ *adj.*
1 that happens or is done most of the time or in most cases **SYN** NORMAL: *She made all the usual excuses.* ◆ *He came home later than usual.* ◆ *She sat in her usual seat at the back.* ◆ *He didn't sound like his usual happy self.* ◆ ~ (for sb/sth) (to do sth) *It is usual to start a speech by thanking everyone for coming.* ⟹ compare UNUSUAL **2** the usual *noun* [sing.] (*informal*) what usually happens; what you usually have, especially the drink that you usually have
IDM as usual in the same way as what happens most of the time or in most cases: *Steve, as usual, was the last to arrive.* ◆ *As usual at that hour, the place was deserted.* ◆ *Despite her problems, she continued to work as usual.* ⟹ more at BUSINESS, PER

u·su·al·ly 🔑 /'yuʒuəli; -ʒəli/ *adv.* in the way that is usual or normal; most often: *I'm usually home by 6 o'clock.* ◆ *We usually go by car.* ◆ *How long does the trip usually take?*

u·su·rer /'yuʒərər/ *noun* (*old-fashioned, disapproving*) a person who lends money to people at unfairly high rates of interest

u·su·ri·ous /yu'ʒʊriəs/ *adj.* (*formal*) lending money at very high rates of interest

u·surp /yu'sərp/ *verb* ~ sb/sth (*formal*) to take someone's position and/or power without having the right to do this ▶ **u·sur·pa·tion** /ˌyusər'peɪʃn/ *noun* [U, C] **u·surp·er** *noun*

u·su·ry /'yuʒəri/ *noun* [U] (*old-fashioned, disapproving*) the practice of lending money to people at unfairly high rates of interest

UT *abbr.* (in writing) Utah

Ute /yut/ *noun* (*pl.* Ute or Utes) a member of a Native American people, many of whom live in the states of Colorado and Utah

u·ten·sil /yu'tɛnsl/ *noun* a tool that is used in the house: *cooking/kitchen utensils*

u·ter·o ⟹ IN UTERO

u·ter·us /'yutərəs/ *noun* (*anatomy*) the organ in women and female animals in which babies develop before they are born **SYN** WOMB ▶ **u·ter·ine** /'yutərən; -ˌraɪn/ *adj.* [only before noun] ⟹ see also INTRAUTERINE DEVICE

u·til·i·tar·i·an /yuˌtɪlə'tɛriən/ *adj.* **1** (*formal*) designed to be useful and practical rather than attractive **2** (*philosophy*) based on or supporting the ideas of utilitarianism

u·til·i·tar·i·an·ism /yuˌtɪlə'tɛriəˌnɪzəm/ *noun* [U] (*philosophy*) the belief that the right course of action is the one that will produce the greatest happiness of the greatest number of people

u·til·i·ty **AWL** /yu'tɪləti/ *noun, adj.*
● *noun* (*pl.* **u·til·i·ties**) **1** [C] a service provided for the public, for example an electricity, water, or gas supply: *the administration of public utilities* **2** [U] (*formal*) the quality of being useful **SYN** USEFULNESS **3** [C] (*computing*) a piece of computer software that performs a particular task
● *adj.* [only before noun] that can be used for several different purposes: *an all-around utility player* (= one who can play equally well in several different positions in a sport)

u'tility ˌroom *noun* a room, especially in a private house, that contains large pieces of equipment such as a WASHING MACHINE, FREEZER, etc.

u'tility ˌvehicle (also u'tility ˌtruck) *noun* a small truck with low sides designed for carrying light loads

u·ti·lize **AWL** /'yutlˌaɪz/ *verb* ~ sth (as sth) (*formal*) to use something, especially for a practical purpose **SYN** MAKE USE OF: *The Romans were the first to utilize concrete as a building material.* ◆ *The resources at our disposal could have been better utilized.* ▶ **u·ti·li·za·tion** **AWL** /ˌyutlə'zeɪʃn/ *noun* [U]

ut·most /'ʌtmoust/ *adj., noun*
● *adj.* (also *less frequent* ut·ter·most /'ʌtərˌmoust/) [only before noun] greatest; most extreme: *This is a matter of the utmost*

importance. ◆ *You should study this document with the utmost care.*

● **noun** [sing.] the greatest amount possible: *Our resources are strained to the utmost.* ◆ *He **did his utmost** (= tried as hard as possible) to persuade me not to go.*

u·to·pi·a /yu'toʊpiə/ *noun* also **Utopia** [C, U] an imaginary place or state in which everything is perfect **ORIGIN** From the title of a book by Sir Thomas More, which describes a place like this.

u·to·pi·an /yu'toʊpiən/ *adj.* also **Utopian** having a strong belief that everything can be perfect, often in a way that does not seem to be realistic or practical: *utopian ideals* ◆ *a utopian society* ▶ **u·to·pi·an·ism** /yu'toʊpiəˌnɪzəm/ *noun* also **Utopianism** [U]

ut·ter /'ʌtər/ *adj., verb*

● **adj.** [only before noun] used to emphasize how complete something is: *That's complete and utter nonsense!* ◆ *To my utter amazement she agreed.* ◆ *He felt like an utter fool.* ▶ **ut·ter·ly** *adv.*: *We're so utterly different from each other.* ◆ *She utterly failed to convince them she was right.*

● **verb** ~ **sth** (*formal*) to make a sound with your voice; to say something: *to utter a cry* ◆ *She did not **utter a word** during lunch* (= said nothing).

ut·ter·ance /'ʌtərəns/ *noun* (*formal*) **1** [U] the act of expressing something in words: *to give utterance to your thoughts*

2 [C] something that you say: *one of her few recorded public utterances*

ˈU-turn *noun* **1** a turn of 180° that a vehicle makes so that it can move forward in the opposite direction: *to do/make a U-turn* **2** (*informal*) a complete change in policy or behavior, usually one that is embarrassing

UV /ˌyu 'vi/ *abbr.* ULTRAVIOLET: *UV radiation*

UVA /ˌyu vi 'eɪ/ *noun* [U] ULTRAVIOLET RAYS that are relatively long: *UVA rays*

UVB /ˌyu vi 'bi/ *noun* [U] ULTRAVIOLET RAYS that are relatively short: *UVB rays*

UVC /ˌyu vi 'si/ *noun* [U] ULTRAVIOLET RAYS that are very short and do not get through the OZONE LAYER: *UVC radiation*

u·vu·la /'yuvyələ/ *noun* (*pl.* **u·vu·lae** /-li/) (*anatomy*) a small piece of flesh that hangs from the top of the inside of the mouth just above the throat ➲ picture at BODY

u·vu·lar /'yuvyələr/ *adj.* (*phonetics*) (of a consonant) produced by placing the back of the tongue against or near the uvula

ux·o·ri·al /ʌk'sɔriəl/ *adj.* (*formal*) connected with a wife

U·zi™ /'uzi/ *noun* a type of SUBMACHINE GUN designed in Israel

Vv

V /viː/ *noun, abbr., symbol*

● *noun* (*pl.* Vs, V's /viːz/) **1** also **v** (*pl.* **v's**) [C, U] the 22nd letter of the English alphabet: *"Violin" begins with (a) V/"V."* **2** a thing shaped like a V: *Ahead was the deep V of a gorge with water pouring down it.* ➔ see also V-CHIP, V-NECK, V-SIGN

● *abbr.* (in writing) VOLT(S): *a 1.5 V battery*

● *symbol* also **v** the number 5 in ROMAN NUMERALS

v. *abbr.* **1** (also **vs.**) (in sport or in a legal case) VERSUS (= against): *Miranda v. Arizona* (= a case in a court of law) ◆ *Yankees vs. Red Sox* **2** VIDE

VA *abbr.* (in writing) Virginia

va·can·cy /ˈveɪkənsi/ *noun* (*pl.* **va·can·cies**) **1** [C] a job that is available for someone to do: *job vacancies* ◆ *a temporary vacancy* ◆ *~ (for sb/sth)* *vacancies for bar staff* ◆ *to fill a vacancy* ➔ thesaurus box at JOB **2** [C] a room that is available in a hotel, etc.: *I'm sorry, we have no vacancies.* **3** [U] lack of interest or ideas SYN EMPTINESS: *the vacancy of her expression*

va·cant /ˈveɪkənt/ *adj.* **1** (of a seat, hotel room, house, etc.) empty; not being used SYN UNOCCUPIED: *vacant properties* ◆ *The seat next to him was vacant.* ◆ *a vacant lot* (= a piece of land in a city that is not being used) ➔ compare ENGAGED, OCCUPIED **2** (*formal*) if a job in a company is **vacant**, no one is doing it and it is available for someone to take: *When the post finally fell* (= became) *vacant, they offered it to Natasha.* **3** (of a look, an expression, etc.) showing no sign that the person is thinking of anything: *a vacant look* ▶ **va·cant·ly** *adv.*: *to stare vacantly*

va·cate /ˈveɪkeɪt/ *verb* (*formal*) **1** *~ sth* to leave a building, seat, etc., especially so that someone else can use it: *Guests are requested to vacate their rooms by noon on the day of departure.* **2** *~ sth* to leave a job, position of authority, etc. so that it is available for someone else

va·ca·tion 🔑 /veɪˈkeɪʃn/ *noun, verb*

● *noun* **1** [U, C] a period of time spent traveling or resting away from home: *They're on vacation in Hawaii right now.* ◆ *You look tired — you should take a vacation.* ◆ *The job includes two weeks of paid vacation.* ◆ *a vacation home* ➔ collocations at TRAVEL **2** [C] one of the periods of time when schools, colleges, or courts of law are closed: *the Christmas/Easter/summer vacation*

● *verb* [I] to spend a vacation somewhere: *They are currently vacationing in Florida.*

va·ca·tion·er /veɪˈkeɪʃənər/ *noun* a person who is visiting a place on vacation

vac·ci·nate /ˈvæksəneɪt/ *verb* [often passive] *~ sb (against sth)* to give a person or an animal a vaccine, especially by INJECTING it, in order to protect them against a disease: *I was vaccinated against tetanus.* ➔ compare IMMUNIZE, INOCULATE ▶ **vac·ci·na·tion** /ˌvæksəˈneɪʃn/ *noun* [C, U]: *Make sure your vaccinations are up to date.* ◆ *vaccination against typhoid*

vac·cine /vækˈsiːn/ *noun* [C, U] a substance that is put into the blood and that protects the body from a disease: *a measles vaccine* ◆ *There is no vaccine against HIV infection.*

vac·il·late /ˈvæsəleɪt/ *verb* [I] (*formal*) to keep changing your opinion or thoughts about something, especially in a way that annoys other people SYN WAVER ▶ **vac·il·la·tion** /ˌvæsəˈleɪʃn/ *noun* [U, C]

va·cu·i·ty /væˈkyuəti/ *noun* [U] (*formal*) lack of serious thought or purpose

vac·u·ole /ˈvækyuoʊl/ *noun* **1** (*biology*) a small space within a cell, usually filled with liquid **2** (*medical*) a small hole in the TISSUE of the body, usually caused by disease

vac·u·ous /ˈvækyuəs/ *adj.* (*formal*) showing no sign of intelligence or sensitive feelings: *a vacuous expression* ▶ **vac·u·ous·ly** *adv.* **vac·u·ous·ness** *noun* [U]

vac·u·um /ˈvækyuəm/ *noun, verb*

● *noun* **1** a space that is completely empty of all substances, including all air or other gas: *a vacuum pump* (= one that creates a vacuum) ◆ *vacuum-packed foods* (= in a package from which most of the air has been removed) **2** a vacuum cleaner **3** [usually sing.] a situation in which someone or something is missing or lacking: *His resignation has created a vacuum which cannot easily be filled.*
IDM **in a vacuum** existing separately from other people, events, etc. when there should be a connection: *This kind of decision cannot ever be made in a vacuum.*

● *verb* [T, I] *~ (sth)* to clean something using a vacuum cleaner: *Have you vacuumed the stairs?*

ˈvacuum ˌbottle *noun* = THERMOS™

ˈvacuum ˌcleaner (also **vac·u·um**) *noun* an electric machine that cleans floors, carpets, etc. by sucking up dirt and dust ➔ picture at CLEANING

va·de me·cum /ˌvɑːdi ˈmeɪkəm/ *noun* (from *Latin, formal*) a book or written guide which you keep with you all the time, because you find it helpful

vag·a·bond /ˈvægəbɑːnd/ *noun* (*old-fashioned, disapproving*) a person who has no home or job and who travels from place to place

va·gar·ies /ˈveɪgəriz/ *noun* [pl.] (*formal*) changes in someone or something that are difficult to predict or control

va·gi·na /vəˈdʒaɪnə/ *noun* the passage in the body of a woman or female animal between the outer sex organs and the WOMB ▶ **vag·i·nal** /ˈvædʒənl/ *adj.* **vag·i·nal·ly** /-nəli/ *adv.*

va·gran·cy /ˈveɪgrənsi/ *noun* [U] (*law*) the crime of living on the streets and BEGGING (= asking for money) from people

va·grant /ˈveɪgrənt/ *noun* (*formal* or *law*) a person who has no home or job, especially one who BEGS (= asks for money) from people ▶ **va·grant** *adj.*

vague /veɪg/ *adj.* (**vaguer**, **vaguest**) **1** not clear in a person's mind: *to have a vague impression/memory/recollection of something* ◆ *They had only a vague idea where the place was.* **2** *~ (about sth)* not having or giving enough information or details about something: *She's a little vague about her plans for next year.* ◆ *The politicians made vague promises about tax cuts.* ◆ *He was accused of being deliberately vague.* ◆ *We had only a vague description of the attacker.* **3** (of a person's behavior) suggesting a lack of clear thought or attention SYN ABSENTMINDED: *His vague manner concealed a brilliant mind.* **4** not having a clear shape SYN INDISTINCT: *In the darkness they could see the vague outline of a church.* ▶ **vague·ness** *noun* [U]

vague·ly /ˈveɪgli/ *adv.* **1** in a way that is not detailed or exact: *a vaguely worded statement* ◆ *I can vaguely remember my first day at school.* **2** slightly: *There was something vaguely familiar about her face.* ◆ *He was vaguely aware of footsteps behind him.* **3** in a way that shows that you are not paying attention or thinking clearly: *He smiled vaguely, ignoring her questions.*

vain /veɪn/ *adj.* **1** that does not produce the result you want SYN USELESS: *She closed her eyes tightly in a vain attempt to hold back the tears.* ◆ *I knocked loudly in the vain hope that someone might answer.* **2** (*disapproving*) too proud of your own appearance, abilities, or achievements SYN CONCEITED: *She's too vain to wear glasses.* ➔ see also VANITY
IDM **in vain** without success: *They tried in vain to persuade her to go.* ◆ *All our efforts were in vain.* ➔ more at NAME *n.*

vain·glo·ri·ous /ˌveɪnˈglɔːriəs/ *adj.* (*literary, disapproving*) too proud of your own abilities or achievements ▶ **vain·glo·ry** /ˈveɪnˌglɔːri/ *noun* [U]

vain·ly /ˈveɪnli/ *adv.* without success: *He shouted after them, vainly trying to attract their attention.*

val·ance /ˈvæləns/ *noun* **1** a strip of wood or cloth above a

---

t tea   ʈ butter   d did   k cat   g got   tʃ chin   dʒ June   f fall

window that hides the curtain rail **2** a narrow piece of cloth like a short curtain that hangs around the frame of a bed, under a shelf, etc.

vale /veɪl/ *noun* (*old use* or *literary*) (also used in modern place names) a valley: *a wooded vale ◆ the Vale of the White Horse*

val·e·dic·tion /ˌvælə'dɪkʃn/ *noun* [C, U] (*formal*) the act of saying goodbye, especially in a formal speech

val·e·dic·to·ri·an /ˌvælədɪk'tɔːriən/ *noun* the student who has the highest grades in a particular group of students and who gives the valedictory speech at a GRADUATION ceremony ⊃ compare SALUTATORIAN

val·e·dic·to·ry /ˌvælə'dɪktəri/ *adj.* [usually before noun] (*formal*) connected with saying goodbye, especially at a formal occasion: *a valedictory speech*

va·len·cy /'veɪlənsi/ *noun* (*pl.* **va·len·cies**) [C, U] (also **va·lence** /'veɪləns/) **1** (*chemistry*) a measurement of the power of an atom to combine with others, by the number of HYDROGEN atoms it can combine with or DISPLACE: *Carbon has a valency of 4.* **2** (*linguistics*) the number of GRAMMATICAL elements that a word, especially a verb, combines with in a sentence

val·en·tine /'væləntaɪn/ *noun* **1** (also **valentine card**) a card that you send to someone that you love on Valentine's Day (= February 14) **2** a person that you send a valentine to

Valentine's Day the day (February 14), when people send a card or presents to the person that they love

va·le·ri·an /və'lɪriən/ *noun* [U] a drug obtained from the root of a plant with the same name, used to make people feel calmer

val·et /væ'leɪ; 'væleɪ/ *noun, verb*

- **noun 1** a person who parks your car for you at a hotel or restaurant **2** a man's personal servant who takes care of his clothes, serves his meals, etc. **3** a hotel employee whose job is to clean the clothes of hotel guests
- **verb** [I] to perform the duties of a valet

valet parking (also **valet service**) *noun* [U] the service of having an employee park your car for you at a hotel or restaurant

Val·hal·la /væl'hælə/ *noun* [U] (in ancient Scandinavian stories) a palace in which some chosen men who had died in battle went to live with the god Odin for ever

val·iant /'væliənt/ *adj.* (especially *literary*) very brave or determined **SYN** COURAGEOUS: *valiant warriors ◆ She made a valiant attempt not to laugh.* ▶ **val·iant·ly** *adv.*

val·id 🔑 **AWL** /'væləd/ *adj.*

1 that is legally or officially acceptable: *a valid passport ◆ a bus pass valid for 1 month ◆ They have a valid claim to compensation.* **2** based on what is logical or true: *She had valid reasons for not supporting the proposals. ◆ The point you make is perfectly valid.* **3** (*computing*) that is accepted by the system: *a valid password* **ANT** INVALID[1] ▶ **val·id·ly** **AWL** *adv.*: *The contract had been validly drawn up.*

AWL COLLOCATIONS

valid

valid *adj.*

officially or legally acceptable; logical or true

- clinically, empirically, experimentally, scientifically, statistically | externally, legally | deductively | equally | universally
  An argument either way could be equally valid.
- assumption, generalization | hypothesis, theory | methodology, model | instrument | test | finding, result | conclusion, inference | argument, reason | criticism
  There were some potential flaws in the study design that made it difficult to draw valid conclusions from these data.
- seem | remain | consider sth, deem sth | accept sth as, regard sth as

---

The conclusions of these studies remain valid for both large and small numbers of molecules.

validate *verb*

- assumption | hypothesis, theory | methodology, model | instrument | test | finding, result | conclusion, inference | argument | accuracy
  This study validated findings from earlier studies.
- clinically, empirically, experimentally, scientifically, statistically | externally | extensively | rigorously
  A similar procedure had been scientifically validated.

validation *noun*

- clinical, empirical, experimental, scientific, statistical | external | extensive | rigorous
  This lack of empirical validation has led to psychology's dismissal of Toman's theory.

validity *noun*

- challenge, dispute, doubt, question | assess, evaluate, test | affirm, attest to, confirm, demonstrate, verify
  The author questions the validity and reliability of standardized tests.
- assumption | hypothesis, theory | model | instrument | test | finding, result | conclusion, inference | argument
  Two tests were performed to assess the validity of this theory.
  Consistent results emerged across the study, which attests to the validity of the findings.

val·i·date **AWL** /'vælədeɪt/ *verb* (*formal*) **1** ~ sth to prove that something is true: *to validate a theory* **ANT** INVALIDATE ⊃ collocations at VALID **2** ~ sth to make something legally valid: *to validate a contract* **ANT** INVALIDATE **3** ~ sth to state officially that something is useful and of an acceptable standard: *Check that their courses have been validated by a reputable organization.* ▶ **val·i·da·tion** **AWL** /ˌvælə'deɪʃn/ *noun* [U, C]

va·lid·i·ty **AWL** /və'lɪdəti/ *noun* [U] **1** the state of being legally or officially acceptable: *The period of validity of the agreement has expired.* **2** the state of being logical and true: *We had doubts about the validity of their argument.* ⊃ collocations at VALID

va·lise /və'liːs/ *noun* (*old-fashioned*) a small bag for carrying clothes, used when you are traveling

Val·i·um™ /'væliəm/ *noun* [U] a drug used to reduce anxiety

Val·kyr·ie /væl'kɪri; 'vælkəri/ *noun* (in ancient Scandinavian stories) one of the twelve female servants of the god Odin, who selected men who had been killed in battle and took them to VALHALLA

val·ley 🔑 /'væli/ *noun*

an area of low land between hills or mountains, often with a river flowing through it; the land that a river flows through: *a small town set in a valley ◆ a wooded valley ◆ the valley floor ◆ the Shenandoah Valley*

Valley Girl *noun* (*informal*) a girl from a rich family who is only interested in things like shopping, thought to be typical of one of those living in the San Fernando Valley of California

val·or (*CanE usually* **val·our**) /'vælər/ *noun* [U] (*literary*) great courage, especially in war **SYN** BRAVERY ▶ **val·or·ous** /'vælərəs/ *adj.* **IDM** see DISCRETION

val·u·a·ble 🔑 /'væljəbl; -juəbl/ *adj.*

1 ~ (to sb/sth) very useful or important: *a valuable experience ◆ The book provides valuable information on recent trends. ◆ This advice was to prove valuable.* **2** worth a lot of money: *valuable antiques ◆ Luckily, nothing valuable was stolen.* **ANT** VALUELESS, WORTHLESS ⊃ compare INVALUABLE, PRICELESS

---

val·u·a·bles /ˈvælyəblz; -yuəblz/ *noun* [pl.] things that are worth a lot of money, especially small personal things such as jewelry, cameras, etc. ⊃ thesaurus box at THING

val·u·a·tion /ˌvælyuˈeɪʃn/ *noun* [C, U] **1** a professional judgment about how much money something is worth; its estimated value: *Surveyors carried out a valuation of the property.* ◆ *Experts set a high valuation on the painting.* ◆ *land valuation* **2** (*formal*) a judgment about how useful or important something is; its estimated importance: *She puts a high valuation on trust between colleagues.*

val·ue 🔊 /ˈvælyu/ *noun, verb*

- **noun**
> HOW MUCH SOMETHING IS WORTH **1** [U, C] how much something is worth in money or other goods for which it can be exchanged: *to go up/rise/increase in value* ◆ *to go down/fall/drop in value* ◆ *rising property values* ◆ *Sports cars tend to hold their value well.* ⊃ see also MARKET VALUE, STREET VALUE ⊃ thesaurus box at PRICE **2** [C, U] how much something is worth compared with its price: *to be a good/an excellent value* (= worth the money it costs) ◆ *to be a bad/a poor value* (= not worth the money it costs) ◆ *Larger sizes give the best value for your money.*
> BEING USEFUL/IMPORTANT **3** [U] the quality of being useful or important **SYN** BENEFIT: *The value of regular exercise should not be underestimated.* ◆ *The arrival of canals was of great value to many industries.* ◆ *to be of little/no value to someone* ◆ *This ring has great sentimental value for me.* ◆ *I suppose it has a certain novelty value* (= it's interesting because it's new). ◆ *food with a high nutritional value* ◆ *The story has very little news value.*
> BELIEFS **4** values [pl.] beliefs about what is right and wrong and what is important in life: *moral values* ◆ *a return to traditional values in education, such as firm discipline* ◆ *The young have a completely different set of values and expectations.*
> MATHEMATICS **5** [C] the amount represented by a letter or symbol: *Let x have the value 33.*

- **verb**
> CONSIDER IMPORTANT **1** (not used in the progressive tenses) to think that someone or something is important: ~ sb/sth (as sth) *I really value him as a friend.* ◆ ~ sb/sth (for sth) *The area is valued for its vineyards.* ◆ *a valued member of the staff*
> DECIDE WORTH **2** [usually passive] ~ sth (at sth) to decide that something is worth a particular amount of money: *The property has been valued at over $2 million.*

WORD FAMILY
value *noun, verb*
valuable *adj.*
invaluable *adj.* (≠ valueless)
valuables *noun*

value-ˈadded ˌtax (*abbr.* VAT) *noun* [U] a tax that is added to the price of goods and services

value-ˈfree *adj.* not influenced by personal opinions

ˈvalue ˌjudgment (*CanE usually* **ˈvalue ˌjudgement**) *noun* [C, U] (sometimes *disapproving*) a judgment about how good or important something is, based on personal opinions rather than facts

ˈvalue-ˌladen *adj.* influenced by personal opinions: *"Freedom fighter" is a value-laden word.*

val·ue·less /ˈvælyuləs/ *adj.* (*formal*) without value or worth **SYN** WORTHLESS **ANT** VALUABLE

val·u·er /ˈvælyuər/ *noun* a person whose job is to estimate how much property, land, etc. is worth

valve /vælv/ *noun* **1** a device for controlling the flow of a liquid or gas, letting it move in one direction only ⊃ picture at BICYCLE **2** a structure in the heart or in a VEIN that lets blood flow in one direction only **3** a device in some BRASS musical instruments for changing the note ⊃ picture at MUSIC

va·moose /væˈmus/ *verb* [I] (*old-fashioned, informal*) to leave quickly

vamp /væmp/ *noun, verb* (*old-fashioned, disapproving*)
- **noun** a sexually attractive woman who tries to control men
- **verb** [I, T] ~ (sb) to act like a vamp; to try to attract and control men: *She vamps in her role as a Broadway star.* ◆ *vamping him with her dark eyes* ◆ *She likes to vamp it up for the camera.*

vam·pire /ˈvæmpaɪər/ *noun* (in stories) a dead person who leaves his or her grave at night to suck the blood of living people

ˈvampire ˌbat *noun* a S. American BAT (= an animal like a mouse with wings) that sucks the blood of other animals

vam·pir·ism /ˈvæmpaɪəˌrɪzəm; -pəˌrɪzəm/ *noun* [U] the behavior or practices of VAMPIRES

van 🔊 /væn/ *noun*
1 a covered vehicle with no side windows in its back half, usually smaller than a truck, used for carrying goods: *a moving van* ◆ *a police van* (= for carrying police officers or prisoners) ◆ *a delivery van* ◆ *a van driver* ⊃ picture at TRUCK **2** a covered vehicle with side windows, smaller than a bus, that can carry about twelve passengers ⊃ picture at BUS **IDM** in the van (*formal*) at the front or in the leading position

va·na·di·um /vəˈneɪdiəm/ *noun* [U] (*symb.* V) a chemical element. Vanadium is a soft, poisonous, silver-gray metal that is added to some types of steel to make it stronger.

ˈvan conˌversion *noun* = CONVERSION VAN

van·dal /ˈvændl/ *noun* a person who deliberately destroys or damages public property

van·dal·ism /ˈvændlˌɪzəm/ *noun* [U] the crime of destroying or damaging something, especially public property, deliberately and for no good reason: *an act of vandalism* ⊃ collocations at CRIME

van·dal·ize /ˈvændlˌaɪz/ *verb* [usually passive] ~ sth to damage something, especially public property, deliberately and for no good reason

vane /veɪn/ *noun* a flat blade that is moved by wind or water and is part of the machinery in a WINDMILL, etc. ⊃ see also WEATHERVANE

van·guard /ˈvængɑrd/ *noun* usually **the vanguard** [sing.] **1** the leaders of a movement in society, for example in politics, art, industry, etc.: *The company is proud to be in the vanguard of scientific progress.* **2** the part of an army, etc. that is at the front when moving forward to attack the enemy **ANT** REARGUARD

va·nil·la /vəˈnɪlə/ *noun, adj.*
- **noun** [U] a substance obtained from the BEANS of a tropical plant, also called vanilla, used to give flavor to sweet foods, for example ice cream: *vanilla extract* ◆ *a vanilla bean*
- **adj.** **1** flavored with vanilla: *vanilla ice cream* **2** (*informal*) ordinary; not special in any way: *The city is pretty much plain vanilla.*

va·nil·lin /vəˈnɪlən/ *noun* [U] a strong-smelling chemical which gives VANILLA its smell

---

h **hat**   m **man**   n **no**   ŋ **sing**   l **leg**   r **red**   y **yes**   w **wet**

van·ish /'vænɪʃ/ verb **1** [I] to disappear suddenly and/or in a way that you cannot explain: *The magician vanished in a puff of smoke.* ♦ *My glasses seem to have vanished.* ♦ *He vanished without a trace.* **2** [I] to stop existing: *the vanishing woodlands of California* ♦ *All hopes of a peaceful settlement had now vanished.* **IDM** see ACT *n.*, FACE *n.*

'**vanishing** ,**point** noun [usually sing.] (*technical*) the point in the distance at which parallel lines appear to meet

van·i·ty /'vænəti/ noun (*pl.* **van·i·ties**) **1** [U] (*disapproving*) too much pride in your own appearance, abilities, or achievements: *She had no personal vanity* (= about her appearance). ⊃ see also VAIN **2** [U] (*literary*) the quality of being unimportant, especially compared with other things that are important: *the vanity of human ambition in the face of death* **3** vanities [pl.] behavior or attitudes that show people's vanity: *Politics is too often concerned only with the personal vanities of politicians.* **4** [C] = DRESSING TABLE **5** [C] a SINK fixed into a flat surface with cupboards underneath

'**vanity** ,**case** noun a small bag or case with a mirror in it, used for carrying makeup

'**vanity** ,**plate** noun a LICENSE PLATE on a vehicle that shows a combination of letters and numbers chosen by the vehicle's owner: *a vanity plate on his truck that says ZEN*

van·quish /'væŋkwɪʃ/ verb ~ **sb/sth** (*literary*) to defeat someone completely in a competition, war, etc. **SYN** CONQUER

the van·quished /'væŋkwɪʃt/ noun [pl.] (*literary*) people who have been completely defeated in a competition, war, etc.

van·tage point /'væntɪdʒ ,pɔɪnt/ (also *formal* **van·tage**) noun a position from which you watch something; a point in time or a situation from which you consider something, especially the past: *The café was a good vantage point for watching the world go by.* ♦ *From the vantage point of the present, the war seems to have achieved nothing.*

vap·id /'væpəd/ adj. (*formal*) lacking interest or intelligence **SYN** DULL ▶ **va·pid·i·ty** /væ'pɪdəti/ noun [U]

va·por (*CanE usually* **va·pour**) /'veɪpər/ noun [C, U] a mass of very small drops of liquid in the air, for example steam: *water vapor*

va·por·ize /'veɪpə,raɪz/ verb [I, T] ~ **(sth)** (*technical*) to turn into gas; to make something turn into gas ▶ **va·por·i·za·tion** /,veɪpərə'zeɪʃn/ noun [U]

va·por·ous /'veɪpərəs/ adj. (*formal*) full of vapor; like vapor: *clouds of vaporous air*

'**vapor** ,**trail** (*CanE usually* '**vapour** ,**trail**) noun the white line that is left in the sky by a plane

va·por·ware (*CanE usually* **va·pour·ware**) /'veɪpər,wɛr/ noun [U] (*computing*) a piece of software or other computer product that has been advertised but is not available to buy yet, either because it is only an idea or because it is still being written or designed

var·i·a·bil·i·ty **AWL** /,veriə'bɪləti/ noun [U] the fact of something being likely to vary: *climatic variability* ♦ *a degree of variability in the exchange rate* ⊃ collocations at VARY

var·i·a·ble **AWL** /'veriəbl/ adj., noun
● **adj. 1** often changing; likely to change **SYN** FLUCTUATE: *variable temperatures* ♦ *The acting is of variable quality* (= some of it is good and some of it is bad). ⊃ compare INVARIABLE **2** able to be changed: *The drill has variable speed control.* ♦ *variable lighting* ▶ **var·i·a·bly** **AWL** /-bli/ adv.
● **noun** a situation, number, or quantity that can vary or be varied: *With so many variables, it is difficult to calculate the cost.* ♦ *The temperature remained constant while pressure was a variable in the experiment.* **ANT** CONSTANT ⊃ collocations at VARY

var·i·ance **AWL** /'veriəns/ noun [U, C] (*formal*) the amount by which something changes or is different from something else: *variance in temperature* ♦ *a note with subtle variances of pitch* **IDM** **at variance (with sb/sth)** (*formal*) disagreeing with or opposing someone or something: *These conclusions are totally at variance with the evidence.*

var·i·ant **AWL** /'veriənt/ noun ~ **(of/on sth)** a thing that is a slightly different form or type of something else: *This game is a variant of baseball.* ▶ **var·i·ant** adj.: *variant forms of spelling* ♦ *a variant form of oxygen known as ozone*

var·i·a·tion 🔊 **AWL** /,veri'eɪʃn/ noun
1 [C, U] ~ **(in/of sth)** a change, especially in the amount or level of something: *The dial records very slight variations in pressure.* ♦ *Currency exchange rates are always subject to variation.* ♦ *regional/seasonal variation* (= depending on the region or time of year) ⊃ collocations at VARY **2** [C] ~ **(on sth)** a thing that is different from other things in the same general group: *This soup is a spicy variation on a traditional favorite.* **3** [C] ~ **(on sth)** (*music*) any of a set of short pieces of music based on a simple tune repeated in a different and more complicated form: *a set of variations on a theme by Mozart* ♦ (*figurative*) *His numerous complaints are all variations on a theme* (= all about the same thing).

var·i·cose vein /,værəkoʊs 'veɪn/ noun a VEIN, especially one in the leg, which has become swollen and painful

var·ied 🔊 **AWL** /'verid/ adj. (usually *approving*)
1 of many different types: *varied opinions* ♦ *a wide and varied selection of cheeses* ⊃ collocations at VARY **2** not staying the same, but changing often: *He led a full and varied life.*

var·i·e·gat·ed /'veriə,geɪtəd; 'verə,geɪ-/ adj. **1** (*technical*) having spots or marks of a different color: *a plant with variegated leaves* **2** (*formal*) consisting of many different types of things or people

va·ri·e·ty 🔊 /və'raɪəti/ noun (*pl.* **va·ri·e·ties**)
1 [sing.] ~ **(of sth)** several different kinds of the same thing: *There is a wide variety of patterns to choose from.* ♦ *He resigned for a variety of reasons.* ♦ *This tool can be used in a variety of ways.* ♦ *I was impressed by the variety of dishes on offer.* **2** [U] the quality of not being the same or not doing the same thing all the time **SYN** DIVERSITY: *We all need variety in our diet.* ♦ *We want more variety in our work.* **3** [C] ~ **(of sth)** a type of a thing, for example a plant or language, that is different from the others in the same general group: *Apples come in a great many varieties.* ♦ *a rare variety of orchid* ♦ *different varieties of English* ♦ *My cooking is of the "quick and simple" variety.* **4** (also **vaude·ville**) [U] a form of theater or television entertainment that consists of a series of short performances, such as singing, dancing, and funny acts: *a variety show/theater* **IDM** **variety is the spice of life** (*saying*) new and exciting experiences make life more interesting

va'**riety** ,**meats** noun [pl.] = OFFAL

va'**riety** ,**store** noun (*old-fashioned*) a store that sells a wide range of goods at low prices

var·i·fo·cals /'veri,foʊklz/ noun [pl.] a pair of glasses in which each LENS varies in thickness from the upper part to the lower part. The upper part is for looking at things at a distance, and the lower part is for looking at things that are close to you. ⊃ compare BIFOCALS ▶ **var·i·fo·cal** adj.

var·i·ous 🔊 /'veriəs/ adj.
1 several different **SYN** DIVERSE: *Tents come in various shapes and sizes.* ♦ *She took the job for various reasons.* ♦ *There are various ways of doing this.* **2** (*formal*) having many different features **SYN** DIVERSE: *a large and various country*

var·i·ous·ly /'veriəsli/ adv. (*formal*) in several different ways, usually by several different people: *He has been variously described as a hero, a genius, and a bully.* ♦ *The cost has been variously estimated at between $10 million and $20 million.*

var·mint /'vɑrmənt/ noun (*old-fashioned, informal*) **1** a person, especially a child, who causes trouble **2** a wild animal, especially a FOX, that causes problems

var·nish /'vɑrnɪʃ/ noun, verb
● **noun** [U, C] a liquid that is painted onto wood, metal, etc.

and that forms a hard, shiny, transparent surface when it is dry

● **verb** to put varnish on the surface of something: **~ sth** The doors are then stained and varnished.

var·si·ty /ˈvɑrsəti/ noun (pl. **var·si·ties**) [C, U] the main team that represents a college or high school, especially in sports competitions

vary

vary verb
to be different from each other; to become different or to change
■ estimate, opinion, pricing, ratio, result | rate, size
Estimates vary because measurement techniques differ from study to study.
■ considerably, greatly, significantly, substantially | widely | inversely | seasonally
Spanish is spoken with an accent that varies considerably according to region.
The cost of cattle varies inversely with supply.
■ varying degrees
There are a wealth of resources on the World Wide Web, containing information with varying degrees of accuracy and reliability.

variable noun
■ independent, predictor | dependent, outcome | continuous, categorical
One predictor variable of early reading success is vocabulary knowledge.
In this study, age was measured as a continuous variable ranging from 18 to 70 years.
The categorical variables were gender and marital status.

variation noun
■ considerable, slight | spatial, temporal | genetic, geographic, seasonal
There is considerable variation; what works for one patient does not necessarily work for another.
The area has spatial variations in rainfall, with the southern areas receiving more rainfall than central locations.

variability noun
■ considerable, substantial | climatic, genetic
Considerable variability in all aspects of testing practices was evident.
Wild plant species usually have a great deal of genetic variability.
■ within | across, among, between
There is considerable variability within the group, with some students reading at grade level, and others demonstrating significant reading problems.

varied adj.
■ widely | immensely, infinitely, richly
Fibers may be derived from paper, metal, nylon, and other materials having widely varied physical properties.
The judicial systems of the rest of the world are immensely varied.

variable adj.
■ highly
Rainfall is highly variable, and the start and end of the two rainy seasons are unreliable.

var·y 🔑 **AWL** /ˈvɛri/ verb
(var·y·ing, var·ied, var·ied) **1** [I] **~ (in sth)** (of a group of similar things) to be different from each other in size, shape, etc. **SYN** DIFFER: *The students' work varies consider-*

ably in quality. ◆ *The quality of the students' work varies considerably.* ◆ *New techniques were introduced with varying degrees of success.* **2** [I] to change or be different according to the situation: **~ with sth** *The menu varies with the season.* ◆ **~ according to sth** *Prices vary according to the type of room you need.* ◆ **~ from sth to sth** | **~ (between A and B)** *Class numbers vary between 25 and 30.* ◆ *"What time do you start work?" "It varies."* **3** [T] **~ sth** to make changes to something to make it slightly different: *The job enables me to vary the hours I work.*

vas·cu·lar /ˈvæskyələr/ adj. [usually before noun] (technical) of or containing VEINS (= the tubes that carry liquids around the bodies of animals and plants)

vas de·fe·rens /ˌvæs ˈdɛfəˌrɛnz/ noun (pl. **va·sa de·fe·ren·ti·a** /ˌveɪsə dɛfəˈrɛnʃiə/) (anatomy) the tube through which SPERM pass from the TESTICLES on their way out of the body

vase /veɪs; veɪz; vɑz/ noun a container made of glass, etc., used for holding cut flowers or as a decorative object: *a vase of flowers*

vas·ec·to·my /vəˈsɛktəmi/ noun (pl. **vas·ec·to·mies**) (medical) a medical operation to remove part of each of the tubes in a man's body that carry SPERM, after which he is not able to make a woman pregnant

Vas·e·line™ /ˈvæsəˌlin; ˈvæsəˌlin/ noun [U] a thick, soft, clear substance that is used on skin to heal or protect it, or as a LUBRICANT to stop surfaces from sticking together

vas·o·con·stric·tion /ˌveɪzoʊkənˈstrɪkʃn/ noun [U] (biology or medical) a process in which BLOOD VESSELS become narrower, which tends to increase BLOOD PRESSURE

vas·o·di·la·tion /ˌveɪzoʊdaɪˈleɪʃn/ noun [U] (biology or medical) a process in which BLOOD VESSELS become wider, which tends to reduce BLOOD PRESSURE

vas·sal /ˈvæsl/ noun **1** a man in the Middle Ages who promised to fight for and be loyal to a king or other powerful owner of land, in return for being given land to live on **2** a country that depends on and is controlled by another country: *a vassal state*

vast 🔑 /væst/ adj.
extremely large in area, size, amount, etc. **SYN** HUGE: *a vast area of forest* ◆ *a vast crowd* ◆ *a vast amount of information* ◆ *At dusk bats appear in vast numbers.* ◆ *His business empire was vast.* ◆ *In the vast majority of cases, this should not be a problem.* ▶ **vast·ness** /ˈvæstnəs/ noun [U, C]

vast·ly /ˈvæstli/ adv. very much: *I'm a vastly different person now.* ◆ *The quality of the training has vastly improved.*

VAT /ˌvi eɪ ˈti; væt/ abbr. VALUE-ADDED TAX

vat /væt/ noun a large container for holding liquids, especially in industrial processes: *distilling vats* ◆ *a vat of whiskey*

Vat·i·can /ˈvætɪkən/ noun the Vatican [sing.] **1** the group of buildings in Rome where the POPE lives and works **2** the center of government of the Roman Catholic Church

vaude·ville /ˈvɔdvɪl; ˈvad-/ noun [U] **1** = VARIETY **2** a type of entertainment popular in the late 19th and early 20th centuries, including singing, dancing, and comedy ▶ **vaude·vill·i·an** /ˌvɔdˈvɪlyən; ˌvad-/ noun: *Fred is an old vaudevillian who still longs for the spotlight.* **vaude·vill·i·an** adj.: *old vaudevillian routines*

vault /vɔlt/ noun, verb
● **noun 1** a room with thick walls and a strong door, especially in a bank, used for keeping valuable things safe **2** a room under a church or in a CEMETERY, used for burying people **3** a roof or ceiling in the form of an ARCH or a series of ARCHES **4** a jump made by vaulting ➔ see also POLE VAULT
● **verb** [I, T] **1** to jump over an object in a single movement, using your hands or a pole to push you: **~ sth** *to vault a fence*

♦ **~ over sth** *She vaulted over the gate and ran up the path.* ⊃ see also POLE VAULT **2** to rise suddenly to a higher level, rank, or position; to cause someone to rise in this way: **~ (sb) to/into sth** *She vaulted to stardom in Paris in the 1920s.* ♦ *The election vaulted him into power.*

vault·ed /'vɔltəd/ *adj.* (*architecture*) made in the shape of an ARCH or a series of ARCHES; having a ceiling or roof of this shape: *a vaulted ceiling/roof*

vault·ing /'vɔltɪŋ/ *noun* [U] (*architecture*) a pattern of ARCHES in a ceiling or roof

'**vaulting** ˌhorse (also **horse**) *noun* a large object with legs, and sometimes handles, that GYMNASTS use to vault over

vaunt·ed /'vɔntəd/ *adj.* [usually before noun] (*formal*) proudly talked about or praised as being very good, especially when this is not deserved: *Their much vaunted reforms did not materialize.*

va-va-voom /ˌva va 'vum/ *noun* [U] (*informal*) the quality of being exciting or sexually attractive **ORIGIN** First used in the 1950s to represent the sound of a car engine running.

'**V-chip** *noun* a computer chip in a television RECEIVER that can be programmed to block material that contains sex and violence

VCR /ˌvi si 'ar/ *noun* the abbreviation for "video cassette recorder" (a machine which is used to play videos or to record programs from a television): *Don't forget to program the VCR.*

VD /ˌvi 'di/ *abbr.* VENEREAL DISEASE

VDT /ˌvi di 'ti/ *noun* the abbreviation for "video display terminal" (a machine with a screen like a television that displays information from a computer)

veal /vil/ *noun* [U] meat from a CALF (= a young cow)

vec·tor /'vɛktər/ *noun* **1** (*mathematics*) a quantity that has both size and direction: *Acceleration and velocity are both vectors.* ⊃ compare SCALAR **2** (*biology*) an insect, etc. that carries a particular disease from one living thing to another **3** (*technical*) a course taken by an aircraft

Ve·da /'veɪdə/ *noun* an ancient holy text of Hinduism

Ve·dic /'veɪdɪk/ *adj., noun*
● *adj.* relating to the Veda
● *noun* [U] the language of the Veda

vee·jay /'vidʒeɪ/ *noun* = VIDEO JOCKEY

veep /vip/ *noun* (*informal*) VICE PRESIDENT

veer /vɪr/ *verb* **1** [I] + *adv./prep.* (especially of a vehicle) to change direction suddenly **SYN** SWERVE: *The bus veered onto the wrong side of the road.* **2** [I] + *adv./prep.* (of a conversation or way of behaving or thinking) to change in the way it develops: *The debate veered away from the main topic of discussion.* ♦ *His emotions veered between fear and anger.* **3** [I] + *adv./prep.* (*technical*) (of the wind) to change direction: *The wind veered to the west.*

veg /vɛdʒ/ *verb* (-gg-)
PHR V ˌveg '**out** (*informal*) to relax by doing something that needs very little effort, for example watching television

veg·an /'vigən/ *noun* a person who does not eat any animal products such as meat, milk, or eggs. Some vegans do not use animal products such as silk or leather.

veg·e·ta·ble 🖉 /'vɛdʒtəbl/ *noun*
1 (also *informal* **veg·gie**) a plant or part of a plant that is eaten as food. Potatoes, BEANS, and onions are all vegetables: *green vegetables* (= for example SPINACH) ♦ *root vegetables* (= for example CARROTS) ♦ *a salad of raw vegetables* ♦ *a vegetable garden/patch/plot* ♦ *vegetable matter* (= plants in general) ⊃ compare ANIMAL, FRUIT, MINERAL **2** a person who is physically alive but not capable of much mental or physical activity, for example because of an accident or illness: *Severe brain damage turned him into a vegetable.*

veg·e·tal /'vɛdʒətl/ *adj.* (*formal*) connected with plants

veg·e·tar·i·an /ˌvɛdʒə'tɛriən/ (also *informal* **veg·gie**) *noun* a person who does not eat meat or fish: *Is she a vegetarian?*

⊃ compare FRUITARIAN, HERBIVORE, VEGAN ▶ **veg·e·tar·i·an** *adj.*: *Are you vegetarian?* ♦ *a vegetarian diet* (= with no meat or fish in it) ♦ *a vegetarian restaurant* (= that serves no meat or fish) **veg·e·tar·i·an·ism** /ˌvɛdʒə'tɛriə,nɪzəm/ *noun* [U]

veg·e·tate /'vɛdʒə,teɪt/ *verb* [I] (of a person) to spend time doing very little and feeling bored

veg·e·tat·ed /'vɛdʒə,teɪtəd/ *adj.* having the amount of plant life mentioned: *a densely/sparsely vegetated area*

veg·e·ta·tion /ˌvɛdʒə'teɪʃn/ *noun* [U] plants in general, especially the plants that are found in a particular area or environment: *The hills are covered in lush green vegetation.*

veg·e·ta·tive /'vɛdʒə,teɪtɪv/ *adj.* **1** relating to plant life **2** (*medical*) (of a person) alive but showing no sign of brain activity ⊃ see also PERSISTENT VEGETATIVE STATE

veg·gie /'vɛdʒi/ *noun* (*informal*) **1** = VEGETABLE **2** = VEGETARIAN: *He's a veggie now* (= become a vegetarian). ▶ **veg·gie** *adj.*

'**veggie** ˌburger *noun* a BURGER made with vegetables, especially BEANS, instead of meat

ve·he·ment /'viəmənt/ *adj.* showing very strong feelings, especially anger **SYN** FORCEFUL: *a vehement denial/attack/protest, etc.* ♦ *He had been vehement in his opposition to the idea.* ▶ **ve·he·mence** /-məns/ *noun* [U] **ve·he·ment·ly** *adv.*: *The charge was vehemently denied.*

ve·hi·cle 🖉 **AWL** /'viɪkl; 'vihɪkl/ *noun*
1 (somewhat *formal*) a thing that is used for transporting people or goods from one place to another, such as a car or truck: *motor vehicles* (= cars, buses, trucks, etc.) ♦ *Are you the driver of this vehicle?* ♦ *rows of parked vehicles* **2** ~ **(for sth)** something that can be used to express your ideas or feelings or as a way of achieving something: *Art may be used as a vehicle for propaganda.* ♦ *The play is an ideal vehicle for her talents.*

ve·hic·u·lar /vi'hɪkyələr/ *adj.* (*formal*) intended for vehicles or consisting of vehicles: *vehicular access* ♦ *The road is closed to vehicular traffic.*

veil /veɪl/ *noun, verb*
● *noun* **1** a covering of very thin, transparent material worn, especially by women, to protect or hide the face, or as part of a hat, etc.: *a bridal veil* **2** a piece of cloth worn by NUNS over the head and shoulders **3** [sing.] (*formal*) something that stops you from learning the truth about a situation: *Their work is carried out behind a veil of secrecy.* ♦ *It would be better to draw a veil over what happened next* (= not talk about it). **4** [sing.] (*formal*) a thin layer that stops you from seeing something: *The mountain tops were hidden beneath a veil of mist.* **5** the veil [sing.] the religious system under which Muslim women must wear head coverings in public: *the history of the veil in Islam* **SYN** HIJAB
IDM take the veil (*old-fashioned*) to become a NUN
● *verb* **1** ~ **sth/yourself** to cover your face with a veil **2** ~ **sth** (*literary*) to cover something with something that hides it partly or completely **SYN** SHROUD: *A fine drizzle began to veil the hills.*

veiled /veɪld/ *adj.* **1** not expressed directly or clearly because you do not want your meaning to be obvious: *a thinly veiled threat* ♦ *She made a veiled reference to his past mistakes.* **2** wearing a veil: *a mysterious veiled woman*

vein /veɪn/ *noun* **1** [C] any of the tubes that carry blood from all parts of the body toward the heart: *the jugular vein* ⊃ compare ARTERY ⊃ see also DEEP VEIN THROMBOSIS, VARICOSE VEIN **2** [C] any of the very thin tubes that form the frame of a leaf or an insect's wing **3** [C] a narrow strip of a different color in some types of stone, wood, and cheese **4** [C] a thin layer of minerals or metal contained in rock: *a vein of gold* **SYN** SEAM **5** [sing.] ~ **(of sth)** an amount of a particular quality or feature in something: *They had tapped a rich vein of information in his secretary.* **6** [sing., U] a particular style or manner: *A number of other people commented in a similar vein.* ♦ *"And that's not all," he continued in angry vein.*

veined /veɪnd/ *adj.* having or marked with veins or thin lines: *thin blue-veined hands* ♦ *veined marble*

vein·ing /'veɪnɪŋ/ noun [U] a pattern of veins or thin lines: *the blue veining in Gorgonzola cheese*

vein·ous /'veɪnəs/ adj. *(technical)* having VEINS that are very noticeable

ve·lar /'viːlər/ noun *(phonetics)* a speech sound made by placing the back of the tongue against or near the back part of the mouth, for example /k/ or /g/ in the English words *key* and *go* ▶ **ve·lar** adj.

Vel·cro™ /'velkroʊ/ noun [U] a material for fastening clothes, etc. with two different surfaces, one rough and one smooth, that stick to each other when they are pressed together ⊃ picture at CLOSURE

veld (also **veldt**) /velt/ noun [U] (in South Africa) flat, open land with grass and no trees ⊃ compare PAMPAS, PRAIRIE, SAVANNAH, STEPPE

vel·lum /'veləm/ noun [U] **1** material made from the skin of a sheep, GOAT, or CALF, used for making book covers and, in the past, for writing on **2** smooth cream-colored paper used for writing on

ve·loc·i·rap·tor /və'lɒsəˌræptər/ noun a small DINOSAUR that moved fairly quickly

ve·loc·i·ty /və'lɑsəti/ noun [U, C] *(pl.* **ve·loc·i·ties)** **1** *(technical)* the speed of something in a particular direction: *the velocity of light* ◆ *to gain/lose velocity* ◆ *a high-velocity rifle* **2** *(formal)* high speed: *Jaguars can move with an astonishing velocity.*

ve·lo·drome /'velədroʊm/ noun a track or building used for cycle racing

ve·lour /və'lʊr/ noun [U] a type of silk or cotton cloth with a thick soft surface like velvet

ve·lum /'viləm/ noun *(pl.* **ve·la** /'vilə/) *(anatomy)* a layer of TISSUE that covers something, especially the soft PALATE inside the mouth

vel·vet /'velvət/ noun [U] a type of cloth made from silk, cotton, or NYLON, with a thick soft surface: *a velvet dress* ◆ *velvet curtains/drapes*

vel·vet·een /ˌvelvə'tin; ˌvelvə'tin/ noun [U] a type of cotton cloth that looks like VELVET but is less expensive

vel·vet·y /'velvəti/ adj. pleasantly smooth and soft: *velvety skin* ◆ *a velvety red wine*

ve·na ca·va /ˌvinə 'keɪvə; -'kɑvə/ noun *(pl.* **ve·nae ca·vae** /ˌvini 'keɪvi; -'kɑvi/) *(anatomy)* either of the two VEINS that take blood without OXYGEN in it toward the heart

ve·nal /'vinl/ adj. *(formal)* prepared to do dishonest or immoral things in return for money SYN CORRUPT: *venal journalists* ▶ **ve·nal·i·ty** /vi'næləti/ noun [U]

vend /vend/ verb ~ **sth** *(formal)* to sell something

ven·det·ta /ven'detə/ noun **1** a long and violent disagreement between two families or groups, in which people are murdered in return for previous murders SYN FEUD **2** ~ **(against sb)** a long argument or disagreement in which one person or group does or says things to harm another: *He has accused the media of pursuing a vendetta against him.* ◆ *She conducted a **personal** vendetta against me.*

'vending ma·chine noun a machine from which you can buy candy, drinks, etc. by putting coins into it

ven·dor /'vendər/ noun **1** a person who sells things, for example food or newspapers, usually outside on the street: *street vendors* **2** *(formal)* a company that sells a particular product: *software vendors* **3** *(law)* a person who is selling a house, etc. ⊃ compare SELLER

ve·neer /və'nɪr/ noun, verb
● noun **1** [C, U] a thin layer of wood or plastic that is glued to the surface of cheaper wood, especially on a piece of furniture **2** [sing.] ~ **(of sth)** *(formal)* an outer appearance of a particular quality that hides the true nature of someone or something: *Her veneer of politeness began to crack.*
● verb ~ **sth (with/in sth)** *(formal)* to cover the surface of something with a veneer of wood, etc.

ven·er·a·ble /'venərəbl/ adj. **1** *(formal)* **venerable** people or

things deserve respect because they are old, important, wise, etc.: *a venerable old man* ◆ *a venerable institution* **2** **the Venerable...** [only before noun] (in the Roman Catholic Church), a title given to a dead person who is very holy but who has not yet been made a SAINT

ven·er·ate /'venəˌreɪt/ verb ~ **sb/sth (as sth)** *(formal)* to have and show a lot of respect for someone or something, especially someone or something that is considered to be holy or very important SYN REVERE ▶ **ven·er·a·tion** /ˌvenə'reɪʃn/ noun [U]: *The relics were objects of veneration.*

ve·ne·re·al /və'nɪriəl/ adj. [only before noun] relating to diseases spread by sexual contact: *a venereal infection*

ve'nereal di,sease noun [C, U] *(abbr.* VD) a disease that is caught by having sex with an infected person

ve·ne·tian blind /vəˌniʃn 'blaɪnd/ noun a BLIND for a window that has flat, horizontal, plastic or metal strips going across it that you can turn to let in as much light as you want ⊃ picture at BLIND

venge·ance /'vendʒəns/ noun [U] *(formal)* the act of punishing or harming someone in return for what they have done to you, your family, or your friends SYN REVENGE: *a desire for vengeance* ◆ ~ **on/upon sb** *to take vengeance on someone* ◆ *He swore vengeance on his child's killer.*
IDM **with a vengeance** *(informal)* to a greater degree than is expected or usual: *She set to work with a vengeance.*

venge·ful /'vendʒfl/ adj. *(formal)* showing a desire to punish someone who has harmed you ▶ **venge·ful·ly** /-fəli/ adv.

ve·ni·al /'viniəl/ adj. [usually before noun] *(formal)* (of a SIN or mistake) not very serious and therefore able to be forgiven

ven·i·son /'venəsn/ noun [U] meat from a DEER

Venn diagram

Venn di·a·gram /ˌven 'daɪəˌgræm/ noun *(mathematics)* a picture showing SETS (= groups of things that have a shared quality) as circles that cross over each other, to show which qualities the different sets have in common

ven·om /'venəm/ noun [U] **1** the poisonous liquid that some snakes, spiders, etc. produce when they bite or sting you **2** *(formal)* strong bitter feeling; hatred and a desire to hurt someone: *a look of pure venom* ⊃ see SPIT

ven·om·ous /'venəməs/ adj. **1** (of a snake, etc.) producing venom **2** *(formal)* full of bitter feeling or hatred: *a venomous look* ▶ **ven·om·ous·ly** adv.

ve·nous /'vinəs/ adj. *(technical)* of or contained in VEINS (= the tubes that carry liquids around the bodies of animals and plants): *venous blood*

vent /vent/ noun, verb
● noun **1** an opening that allows air, gas, or liquid to pass out of or into a room, building, container, etc.: *air/heating vents* ⊃ picture at CAR, VOLCANO **2** *(technical)* the opening

| t tea | ṭ butter | d did | k cat | g got | tʃ chin | dʒ June | f fall |

in the body of a bird, fish, REPTILE, or other small animal, through which waste matter is passed out **3** a long thin opening at the bottom of the back or side of a coat or jacket **IDM** **give vent to sth** (*formal*) to express a feeling, especially anger, strongly: *She gave vent to her feelings in a violent outburst.*

● *verb* ~ **sth (on sb)** (*formal*) to express feelings, especially anger, strongly: *He vented his anger on the referee.*

ven·ti·late /ˈvɛntlˌeɪt/ *verb* **1** ~ **sth** to allow fresh air to enter and move around a room, building, etc.: *a well-ventilated room* ◆ *The bathroom is ventilated with an extractor fan.* **2** ~ **sth** (*formal*) to express your feelings or opinions publicly **SYN** AIR ▶ **ven·ti·la·tion** /ˌvɛntlˈeɪʃn/ *noun* [U]: *a ventilation shaft* ◆ *Make sure that there is adequate ventilation in the room before using the paint.*

ven·ti·la·tor /ˈvɛntlˌeɪtər/ *noun* **1** a device or an opening for letting fresh air come into a room, etc. **2** a piece of equipment with a PUMP that helps someone to breathe by sending air in and out of their lungs: *He was put on a ventilator.*

ven·tral /ˈvɛntrəl/ *adj.* [only before noun] (*biology*) on or connected with the part of a fish or an animal that is underneath (or that in humans faces forward): *a fish's ventral fin*

ven·tri·cle /ˈvɛntrɪkl/ *noun* (*anatomy*) **1** either of the two lower spaces in the heart that PUMP blood to the LUNGS or around the body ⊃ compare AURICLE **2** any hollow space in the body, especially one of four main hollow spaces in the brain

ven·tril·o·quism /vɛnˈtrɪləˌkwɪzəm/ *noun* [U] the art of speaking without moving your lips and of making it look as if your voice is coming from another person ▶ **ven·tril·o·quist** /-kwɪst/ *noun*: *Entertainment included a ventriloquist.* ◆ *a ventriloquist's dummy*

ven·ture ♪ /ˈvɛntʃər/ *noun, verb*

● *noun* a business project or activity, especially one that involves taking risks **SYN** UNDERTAKING: *A disastrous business venture lost him thousands of dollars.* ⊃ see also JOINT VENTURE

● *verb* **1** [I] + *adv./prep.* to go somewhere even though you know that it might be dangerous or unpleasant: *They ventured nervously into the water.* ◆ *He has never ventured far from his hometown.* **2** [T] (*formal*) to say or do something in a careful way, especially because it might upset or offend someone: ◆ ~ **sth** *She hardly dared to venture an opinion.* ◆ ~ **to do sth** *I ventured to suggest that she might have made a mistake.* ◆ + **speech** *"And if I say no?" she ventured.* ◆ ~ **that…** *He ventured that the data might be flawed.* **3** [T] ~ **sth (on sth)** to risk losing something valuable or important if you are not successful at something **SYN** GAMBLE: *It was wrong to venture his financial security on such a risky deal.* **IDM** **nothing ventured, nothing gained** (*saying*) used to say that you have to take risks if you want to achieve things and be successful **PHRV** ˈ**venture into/on sth** to do something, even though it involves risks: *This is the first time the company has ventured into movie production.*

ˌventure ˈcapital *noun* [U] (*business*) money that is invested in a new company to help it develop, which may involve a lot of risk ⊃ compare WORKING CAPITAL

ven·ture·some /ˈvɛntʃərsəm/ *adj.* (*formal* or *literary*) willing to take risks **SYN** DARING

ven·ue /ˈvɛnyu/ *noun* a place where people meet for an organized event, for example a concert, sporting event, or conference: *The band will be playing at 20 different venues on their East Coast tour.* ◆ *Please note the change of venue for this event.* ⊃ thesaurus box at PLACE

Ve·nus /ˈvinəs/ *noun* the planet in the SOLAR SYSTEM that is second in order of distance from the sun, between Mercury and the earth ⊃ picture at EARTH

Ve·nus ˈfly·trap /ˌvinəs ˈflaɪtræp/ *noun* a small carnivorous

(CARNIVORE) (= flesh-eating) plant with leaves that trap insects by closing quickly around them

ve·rac·i·ty /vəˈræsəti/ *noun* [U] (*formal*) the quality of being true; the habit of telling the truth **SYN** TRUTH: *They questioned the veracity of her story.*

ve·ran·da (also **ve·ran·dah**) /vəˈrændə/ *noun* a platform with an open front and a roof, built onto the side of a house on the ground floor: *After dinner, we sat talking on the veranda.* **SYN** PORCH

verb /vɜrb/ *noun* (*grammar*) a word or group of words that expresses an action (such as *eat*), an event (such as *happen*), or a state (such as *exist*): *regular/irregular verbs* ◆ *transitive/intransitive verbs* ⊃ see also PHRASAL VERB

ver·bal /ˈvɜrbl/ *adj.* **1** relating to words: *The job candidate must have good verbal skills.* ◆ *nonverbal communication* (= expressions of the face, GESTURES, etc.) **2** spoken, not written: *a verbal agreement/warning* ◆ *verbal instructions* ⊃ compare ORAL **3** (*grammar*) relating to verbs: *a verbal noun*

ver·bal·ize /ˈvɜrbəˌlaɪz/ *verb* [T, I] ~ **(sth)** (*formal*) to express your feelings or ideas in words **SYN** PUT INTO WORDS: *He's a real genius but he has difficulty verbalizing his ideas.*

ver·bal·ly /ˈvɜrbəli/ *adv.* in spoken words and not in writing or actions: *The company had received complaints both verbally and in writing.*

ver·ba·tim /vərˈbeɪtəm/ *adj., adv.* exactly as spoken or written **SYN** WORD FOR WORD: *a verbatim report* ◆ *He reported the speech verbatim.*

ver·be·na /vərˈbinə/ *noun* [U, C] a garden plant with bright flowers

ver·bi·age /ˈvɜrbiɪdʒ/ *noun* [U] (*formal, disapproving*) the use of too many words, or of more difficult words than are needed, to express an idea

ver·bose /vərˈboʊs/ *adj.* (*formal, disapproving*) using or containing more words than are needed **SYN** LONG-WINDED: *a verbose speaker/style* ▶ **ver·bos·i·ty** /vərˈbɑsəti/ *noun* [U]

ver·bo·ten /vərˈboʊtn, fɜr-/ *adj.* (from *German, humorous*) not allowed: *Cake and cookies are strictly verboten in my house.*

ver·dant /ˈvɜrdnt/ *adj.* (*literary*) (of grass, plants, fields, etc.) fresh and green

ver·dict /ˈvɜrdɪkt/ *noun* **1** a decision that is made by a JURY in court, stating if someone is considered guilty of a crime or not: *Has the jury reached a verdict?* ◆ *The jury returned a verdict* (= gave a verdict) *of guilty.* ⊃ collocations at JUSTICE ⊃ see also MAJORITY VERDICT **2** ~ **(on sth/sb)** a decision that you make or an opinion that you give about something, after you have tested it or considered it carefully: *The coroner recorded a verdict of accidental death.* ◆ *The panel will give their verdict on the latest video releases.* ◆ *Well, what's your verdict?*

ver·di·gris /ˈvɜrdəˌgris; -ˌgri/ *noun* [U] the greenish substance which forms, for example on roofs, when COPPER reacts with the air

ver·dure /ˈvɜrdʒər/ *noun* [U] (*literary*) thick green plants growing in a particular place

verge /vɜrdʒ/ *noun, verb*

● *noun* **IDM** **on/to the verge of sth/of doing sth** very near to the moment when someone does something or something happens: *He was on the verge of tears.* ◆ *They are on the verge of signing a new contract.*

● *verb* **PHRV** ˈ**verge on sth** to be very close to an extreme state or condition **SYN** BORDER ON STH: *Some of his suggestions verged on the outrageous.*

ver·i·fy /ˈvɛrəˌfaɪ/ *verb* (**ver·i·fies, ver·i·fy·ing, ver·i·fied, ver·i·fied**) **1** to check that something is true or accurate: ~ **sth** *We have no way of verifying his story.* ◆ ◆ ~ **that…** *Please verify that there is sufficient memory available before loading the program.* ◆ ~ **whether, what, etc.…** *I'll leave you to verify* whether these claims are true. **2** ~ sth | ~ that... to show or say that something is true or accurate **SYN** CONFIRM: *Her version of events was verified by neighbors.* ▶ **ver·i·fi·a·ble** /ˌvɛrəˈfaɪəbl/ *adj.*: *a verifiable fact* **ver·i·fi·ca·tion** /ˌvɛrəfəˈkeɪʃn/ *noun* [U]: *the verification of hypotheses*

ver·i·ly /ˈvɛrəli/ *adv.* (*old use*) really; truly

ver·i·si·mil·i·tude /ˌvɛrəsəˈmɪləˌtud/ *noun* [U] (*formal*) the quality of seeming to be true or real **SYN** AUTHENTICITY: *To add verisimilitude, the stage is covered with sand for the desert scenes.*

ver·i·ta·ble /ˈvɛrətəbl/ *adj.* [only before noun] (*formal* or *humorous*) a word used to emphasize that someone or something can be compared to someone or something else that is more exciting, more impressive, etc. **SYN** POSITIVE: *The meal that followed was a veritable banquet.*

ver·i·ty /ˈvɛrəti/ *noun* (*pl.* **ver·i·ties**) **1** [usually pl.] (*formal*) a belief or principle about life that is accepted as true: *the eternal verities of life* **2** [U] (*old use*) truth

ver·mi·cel·li /ˌvɜrməˈtʃɛli/ *noun* [U] PASTA in the shape of very thin sticks, often broken into small pieces and added to soups

ver·mil·ion /vərˈmɪlyən/ *adj.* bright red in color ▶ **ver·mil·ion** *noun* [U]

ver·min /ˈvɜrmən/ *noun* [pl.] **1** wild animals or birds that destroy plants or food, or attack farm animals and birds: *On farms the fox is considered vermin and treated as such.* **2** insects that live on the bodies of animals and sometimes humans: *The room was crawling with vermin.* **3** (*disapproving*) people who are very unpleasant or dangerous to society

ver·min·ous /ˈvɜrmənəs/ *adj.* (*formal*) covered with vermin

ver·mouth /vərˈmuθ/ *noun* [U] a strong wine, flavored with HERBS and spices, often mixed with other drinks as a COCKTAIL

ver·nac·u·lar /vərˈnækyələr/ *noun* **1** usually **the vernacular** [sing.] the language spoken in a particular area or by a particular group, especially one that is not the official or written language **2** [U] (*technical*) a style of ARCHITECTURE concerned with ordinary houses rather than large public buildings ▶ **ver·nac·u·lar** *adj.*

ver·nal /ˈvɜrnl/ *adj.* [only before noun] (*formal* or *literary*) connected with the season of spring: *the vernal equinox*

ver·nis·sage /ˌvɜrnəˈsɑʒ/ *noun* (*pl.* **ver·nis·sages** /ˌvɜrnəˈsɑʒ/) an occasion when a few invited people can look at paintings before they go on show to the public

ver·sa·tile /ˈvɜrsətl/ *adj.* (*approving*) **1** (of a person) able to do many different things: *He's a versatile actor who has played a wide variety of parts.* **2** (of food, a building, etc.) having many different uses: *Eggs are easy to cook and are an extremely versatile food.* ▶ **ver·sa·til·i·ty** /ˌvɜrsəˈtɪləti/ *noun* [U]: *She is a designer of extraordinary versatility.*

verse /vɜrs/ *noun* **1** [U] writing that is arranged in lines, often with a regular rhythm or pattern of RHYME **SYN** POETRY: *Most of the play is written in verse, but some of it is in prose.* ⮊ see also BLANK VERSE, FREE VERSE **2** [C] a group of lines that form a unit in a poem or song: *a hymn with six verses* **3** verses [pl.] (*old-fashioned*) poetry: *a book of romantic verses* **4** [C] any one of the short NUMBERED divisions of a chapter in the Bible **IDM** see CHAPTER

versed /vɜrst/ *adj.* ~ in sth having a lot of knowledge about something, or skill at something **SYN** EXPERT IN, PRACTICED IN: *He was well versed in employment law.*

ver·si·fi·ca·tion /ˌvɜrsəfəˈkeɪʃn/ *noun* [U] (*formal*) the art of writing poetry in a particular pattern; the pattern in which poetry is written

ver·si·fy /ˈvɜrsəˌfaɪ/ *verb* (**ver·si·fies**, **ver·si·fy·ing**, **ver·si·fied**, **ver·si·fied**) ~ sth (*formal*, sometimes *disapproving*) to write something in verse ▶ **ver·si·fi·er** /-ˌfaɪər/ *noun*

ver·sion 🔑 **AWL** /ˈvɜrʒn/ *noun*
1 a form of something that is slightly different from an earlier form or from other forms of the same thing: *There are* two versions of the game, a long one and a short one. ◆ *the latest version of the software package* ◆ *the deluxe/luxury version* ⮊ see also BETA VERSION **2** a description of an event from the position of a particular person or group of people: *She gave us her version of what had happened that day.* ◆ *Their versions of how the accident happened conflict.* ⮊ **thesaurus** box at REPORT **3** a movie, play, piece of music, etc. that is based on a particular piece of work but is in a different form, style, or language: *the film version of War and Peace* ◆ *The English version of the novel is due for publication next year.* ⮊ see also COVER VERSION

ver·so /ˈvɜrsoʊ/ *noun* (*pl.* **ver·sos**) (*technical*) the page on the left side of an open book **ANT** RECTO

ver·sus /ˈvɜrsəs; -səz/ *prep.* (*abbr.* **v.**, **vs.**) **1** (*sports* or *law*) used to show that two teams or sides are against each other: *It is Texas versus Nebraska in the championship game.* ◆ *in the case of Roe versus Wade* **2** used to compare two different ideas, choices, etc.: *It was the promise of better job opportunities versus the inconvenience of moving away and leaving her friends.*

ver·te·bra /ˈvɜrtəbrə/ *noun* (*pl.* **ver·te·brae** /-ˌbreɪ; -ˌbri/) any of the small bones that are connected together to form the SPINE ⮊ picture at BODY ▶ **ver·te·bral** /ˈvɜrtəbrəl/ *adj.* [only before noun]

ver·te·brate /ˈvɜrtəbrət; -ˌbreɪt/ *noun* (*technical*) any animal with a BACKBONE, including all MAMMALS, birds, fish, REPTILES, and AMPHIBIANS ⮊ compare INVERTEBRATE ▶ **ver·te·brate** *adj.*

ver·tex /ˈvɜrtɛks/ *noun* (*pl.* **ver·ti·ces** /ˈvɜrtəsiz/ or **ver·tex·es**) **1** (*geometry*) a point where two lines meet to form an angle, especially the point of a triangle or CONE opposite the base ⮊ picture at SHAPE **2** (*technical*) the highest point or top of something

ver·ti·cal 🔑 /ˈvɜrtɪkl/ *adj.*, *noun*
● *adj.* **1** (of a line, pole, etc.) going straight up or down from a level surface or from top to bottom in a picture, etc. **SYN** PERPENDICULAR: *the vertical axis of the graph* ◆ *The cliff was almost vertical.* ◆ *There was a vertical drop to the ocean.* ⮊ picture at LINE ⮊ compare HORIZONTAL **2** having a structure in which there are top, middle, and bottom levels: *a vertical flow of communication* ▶ **ver·ti·cal·ly** /-kli/ *adv.*
● *noun* usually **the vertical** a vertical line or position **SYN** PERPENDICULAR: *The wall is several degrees off the vertical.*

ver·tig·i·nous /vərˈtɪdʒənəs/ *adj.* (*formal*) causing a feeling of vertigo **SYN** DIZZYING: *From the path there was a vertiginous drop to the valley below.*

ver·ti·go /ˈvɜrtɪˌgoʊ/ *noun* [U] the feeling of dizziness (DIZZY) and fear, and of losing your balance, that is caused in some people when they look down from a very high place

verve /vɜrv/ *noun* [U, sing.] energy, excitement, or enthusiasm **SYN** GUSTO: *It was a performance of verve and vitality.*

ver·y 🔑 /ˈvɛri/ *adv.*, *adj.*
● *adv.* **1** used before adjectives, adverbs, and determiners to mean "in a high degree" or "extremely": *very small* ◆ *very quickly* ◆ *Very few people know that.* ◆ *Thanks very much.* ◆ *"Do you like it?" "Yeah, I do. Very much."* ◆ *"Is it what you expected?" "Oh yes, very much so."* ◆ *"Are you busy?" "Not very."* ◆ *The new building has been very much admired.* ◆ *I'm not very* (= not at all) *impressed.* ◆ *I'm very very grateful.* **2** used to emphasize a superlative adjective or before own: *They wanted the very best quality.* ◆ *Be there by six at the very latest.* ◆ *He finally got his very own car* (= belonging to him and to no one else). **3** the ~ same exactly the same: *Mario said the very same thing.* **4** ~ good/well (*formal*) used to say that you agree to something or give your permission, usually unwillingly: *Very good - we'll meet at 8:00.* ◆ *Very well. Stay out as late as you want.*
● *adj.* [only before noun] **1** used to emphasize that you are talking about a particular thing or person and not about another **SYN** ACTUAL: *Those were her very words.* ◆ *He might be phoning her at this very moment.* ◆ *That's the very thing I*

h hat   m man   n no   ŋ sing   l leg   r red   y yes   w wet

need. **2** used to emphasize an extreme place or time: *It happens at the very beginning of the book.* ◆ *We stayed till the very end of the party.* **3** used to emphasize a noun **SYN** MERE: *The very thought of a drink made him feel sick.* ◆ *"I can't do that!" she gasped, shocked at the very idea.* **IDM** see EYE *n.*

very ◆ very much

- **Very** is used with adjectives, past participles used as adjectives, and adverbs: *I am very hungry.* ◆ *I was very happy to get your letter.* ◆ *You played very well.* But notice this use: *I'm very much afraid that your son may be involved in the crime.*
- **Very** is not used with past participles that have a passive meaning. **Much, very much,** or **greatly** (*all formal*) are usually used instead: *Your help was very much appreciated.* ◆ *He was much loved by everyone.* ◆ *She was greatly admired.*
- **Very** is used to emphasize superlative adjectives: *my very best work* ◆ *the very youngest students.* However, with comparative adjectives, **much, very much, a lot,** etc. are used: *Your work is a lot better.* ◆ *much younger students*
- **Very** is not used with adjectives and adverbs that already have an extreme meaning. You are more likely to use an adverb such as *absolutely, completely,* etc: *She was absolutely furious.* ◆ *I'm completely exhausted.* ◆ *You played really flawlessly.*
- **Very** is not used with verbs. Use **very much** instead: *We enjoyed staying with you very much.*

ˌvery high ˈfrequency *noun* [U] = VHF

Very light /ˈvɛri ˌlaɪt/ *noun* a bright colored light that is fired from a gun as a signal from a ship that it needs help

ve·si·cle /ˈvɛsɪkl/ *noun* **1** (*biology*) a small bag or hollow structure in the body of a plant or an animal **2** (*medical*) a small swelling filled with liquid under the skin **SYN** BLISTER

ves·pers /ˈvɛspərz/ *noun* [U] the service of evening prayer in some Christian Churches ⊃ compare MATINS

ves·sel /ˈvɛsl/ *noun* **1** (*formal*) a large ship or boat: *ocean-going vessels* **2** a tube that carries blood through the body of a person or an animal, or liquid through the parts of a plant ⊃ see also BLOOD VESSEL **3** (*old use* or *technical*) a container used for holding liquids, such as a bowl, cup, etc.: *a Bronze Age drinking vessel*

vest /vɛst/ *noun, verb*
- *noun* **1** a short piece of clothing with buttons down the front but no sleeves, usually worn over a shirt and under a jacket, often forming part of a man's suit ⊃ picture at CLOTHES **2** an informal piece of clothing without sleeves that is pulled over the head or has buttons down the front: *knitted vests for women* ◆ *a V-neck sweater vest* **3** a special piece of clothing that covers the upper part of the body: *a bulletproof vest* ◆ *a down vest*
- *verb*
  PHR V ˈvest in sb/sth (*law*) (of power, property, etc.) to belong to someone or something legally ˈvest sth in sb | ˈvest sb with sth [often passive] (*formal*) **1** to give someone the legal right or power to do something: *Overall authority is vested in the Supreme Court.* ◆ *The Supreme Court is vested with overall authority.* **2** to make someone the legal owner of land or property

ˌvested ˈinterest *noun* ~ (in sth) a personal reason for wanting something to happen, especially because you get some advantage from it: *They have a vested interest in keeping the club as exclusive as possible.* ◆ *Vested interests* (= people with a vested interest) *are opposing the plan.*

ves·ti·bule /ˈvɛstəˌbyul/ *noun* **1** (*formal*) an entrance hall of a large building, for example where hats and coats can be left **2** (*technical*) a space at the end of a car on a train that connects it with the next car

ves·tige /ˈvɛstɪdʒ/ *noun* (*formal*) **1** a small part of something that still exists after the rest of it has stopped existing **SYN** TRACE: *the last vestiges of the old political regime* **2** usually used in negative sentences, to say that not even a small amount of something exists: *There's not a vestige of truth in the rumor.*

ves·tig·i·al /vɛˈstɪdʒəl; -dʒiəl/ *adj.* [usually before noun] (*formal* or *technical*) remaining as the last small part of something that used to exist: *vestigial traces of an earlier culture* ◆ *It is possible to see the vestigial remains of rear legs on some whales.*

vest·ment /ˈvɛstmənt/ *noun* [usually pl.] a piece of clothing worn by a priest during church services

ves·try /ˈvɛstri/ *noun* (pl. **ves·tries**) a room in a church where a priest prepares for a service by putting on special clothes and where various objects used in worship are kept **SYN** SACRISTY

vet /vɛt/ *noun, verb*
- *noun* **1** = VETERINARIAN **2** the place where a VETERINARIAN works: *I have to take the dog to the vet tomorrow.* **3** (*informal*) = VETERAN: *a Vietnam vet*
- *verb* (-tt-) **1** ~ sb to find out about a person's past life and career in order to decide if they are suitable for a particular job **SYN** SCREEN: *All candidates are carefully vetted for security reasons.* **2** ~ sth to check the contents, quality, etc. of something carefully **SYN** SCREEN: *All reports are vetted before publication.*

vetch /vɛtʃ/ *noun* [U] a plant of the PEA family. There are several types of vetch, one of which is used as food for farm animals.

vet·er·an /ˈvɛtərən/ *noun* **1** (also *informal* **vet**) a person who has been a soldier, sailor, etc. in a war: *war veterans* ◆ *a Vietnam vet* **2** a person who has a lot of experience in a particular area or activity: *veteran actor Dustin Hoffman*

ˈVeterans ˌDay *noun* a holiday on November 11 in the U.S., in honor of members of the armed forces and others who have died in war ⊃ see also MEMORIAL DAY, REMEMBRANCE DAY

vet·er·i·nar·i·an /ˌvɛtərəˈnɛriən/ (also **vet**) *noun* a person who has been trained in the science of animal medicine, whose job is to treat animals that are sick or injured

vet·er·i·nar·y /ˈvɛtərəˌnɛri/ *adj.* [only before noun] connected with caring for the health of animals: *veterinary medicine/science*

ve·to /ˈvitoʊ/ *noun, verb*
- *noun* (pl. **ve·toes**) **1** [C, U] the right to refuse to allow something to be done, especially the right to stop a law from being passed or a decision from being made: *The governor used his veto to block the proposal.* ◆ *to have the power/right of veto* ◆ *the use of the presidential veto* **2** [C] ~ (on sth/on doing sth) an occasion when someone refuses to allow something to be done **SYN** BAN: *For months there was a veto on hiring new staff.* ⊃ see also LINE-ITEM VETO
- *verb* (**ve·toes, ve·to·ing, ve·toed, ve·toed**) **1** ~ sth to stop something from happening or being done by using your official authority (= by using your veto): *Plans for the dam have been vetoed by the Environmental Protection Agency.* ⊃ collocations at POLITICS **2** ~ sth to refuse to accept or do what someone has suggested **SYN** RULE OUT: *I wanted to go camping but the others quickly vetoed that idea.*

vex /vɛks/ *verb* ~ sb (*old-fashioned* or *formal*) to annoy or worry someone ▶ **vex·ing** *adj.*: *a vexing problem*

vex·a·tion /vɛkˈseɪʃn/ *noun* (*old-fashioned* or *formal*) **1** [U] the state of feeling upset or annoyed **2** [C] a thing that upsets or annoys you

vex·a·tious /vɛkˈseɪʃəs/ *adj.* (*old-fashioned* or *formal*) making you feel upset or annoyed

vexed /vɛkst/ *adj.* **1** ~ (at/with sb/sth) (*old-fashioned*) upset or annoyed **2** ~ question/issue a problem that is difficult to deal with **SYN** THORNY: *The conference spent days discussing the vexed question of border controls.*

VHF /ˌviː eɪtʃ ˈef/ *abbr.* very high frequency (a range of radio waves used for high-quality broadcasting)

VHS™ /ˌviː eɪtʃ ˈes/ *abbr.* video home system (a system used by VIDEO CASSETTE RECORDERS and some CAMCORDERS)

via 🔑 **AWL** /ˈviːə; ˈvaɪə/ *prep.*
1 through a place: *We flew home via Dubai.* **2** by means of a particular person, system, etc.: *I heard about the sale via Jane.* ◆ *The news program came to us via satellite.*

vi·a·ble /ˈvaɪəbl/ *adj.* **1** that can be done; that will be successful **SYN** FEASIBLE: *a viable option/proposition* ◆ *There is no viable alternative.* ◆ *to be commercially/ politically/financially/economically viable* **2** (*biology*) capable of developing and surviving independently: *viable organisms* ▶ **vi·a·bil·i·ty** /ˌvaɪəˈbɪləti/ *noun* [U]: *commercial viability*

vi·a·duct /ˈvaɪədʌkt/ *noun* a long high bridge, usually with ARCHES, that carries a road or railroad across a river or valley

vi·al /ˈvaɪəl/ (also **phial**) *noun* a small glass container, for medicine or PERFUME

vibes /vaɪbz/ *noun* [pl.] **1** (also *formal* **vi·bra·tions**) (also **vibe** [sing.]) (*informal*) a mood or an atmosphere produced by a particular person, thing, or place: *good/bad vibes* ◆ *The vibe of the place just wasn't right.* **2** = VIBRAPHONE: *a jazzy vibes backing*

vi·brant /ˈvaɪbrənt/ *adj.* **1** full of life and energy **SYN** EXCITING: *a vibrant city* ◆ *Thailand is at its most vibrant during the New Year celebrations.* **2** (of colors) very bright and strong **SYN** BRILLIANT: *The room was decorated in vibrant reds and yellows.* ⊃ **thesaurus box** at BRIGHT **3** (of music, sounds, etc.) loud and powerful: *vibrant rhythms* ▶ **vi·bran·cy** /-brənsi/ *noun* [U] **vi·brant·ly** *adv.*

vi·bra·phone /ˈvaɪbrəfoʊn/ *noun* [C] (also *informal* **vibes** [pl.]) a musical instrument used especially in JAZZ, that has two rows of metal bars that you hit, and a motor that makes them vibrate

vi·brate /ˈvaɪbreɪt/ *verb* [I, T] to move or make something move from side to side very quickly and with small movements: *~ (sth) Every time a train went past the walls vibrated.* ◆ *~ with sth The atmosphere seemed to vibrate with tension.*

vi·bra·tion /vaɪˈbreɪʃn/ *noun* **1** [C, U] a continuous shaking movement or feeling: *We could feel the vibrations from the trucks passing outside.* ◆ *a reduction in the level of vibration in the engine* **2 vibrations** [pl.] (*formal*) = VIBES

vi·bra·to /vɪˈbrɑːtoʊ/ *noun* [U, C] (*pl.* **vi·bra·tos**) (*music*) a shaking effect in singing or playing a musical instrument, made by rapid, slight changes in PITCH (= how high or low a sound is)

vi·bra·tor /ˈvaɪbreɪtər/ *noun* an electrical device that produces a continuous shaking movement, used in MASSAGE or for sexual pleasure

vic·ar /ˈvɪkər/ *noun* **1** a priest in the Episcopal Church **2** an Anglican priest who is in charge of a church and the area around it (called a PARISH) **3** a Catholic priest who can take the place of a BISHOP or the Pope ⊃ **compare** CURATE[1], MINISTER, PRIEST, RECTOR

vic·ar·age /ˈvɪkərɪdʒ/ *noun* a vicar's house

vi·car·i·ous /vaɪˈkɛriəs/ *adj.* [only before noun] felt or experienced by watching or reading about someone else doing something, rather than by doing it yourself: *He got a vicarious thrill out of watching his son score the winning goal.* ▶ **vi·car·i·ous·ly** *adv.*

vice /vaɪs/ *noun, combining form*
● *noun* **1** [U] criminal activities that involve sex or drugs: *plain-clothes detectives from the vice squad* **2** [U, C] evil or immoral behavior; an evil or immoral quality in someone's character: *The film ended most satisfactorily: vice punished and virtue rewarded.* ◆ *Greed is a terrible vice.* ◆ (*humorous*) *Cigarettes are my only vice.* **3** = VISE
● *combining form* also **vice-** (in nouns and related adjectives)

next in rank to someone and able to represent them or act for them: *vice captain*

ˌvice ˈadmiral *noun* an officer of very high rank in the navy

ˌvice ˈpresident *noun* (*abbr.* VP) **1** the person below the president of a country in rank, who takes control of the country if the president is not able to **2** a person in charge of a particular part of a business company: *the vice president of sales* ▶ **ˌvice presiˈdential** *adj.* [usually before noun]

vice·roy /ˈvaɪsrɔɪ/ *noun* (often used as a title) (in the past) a person who was sent by a king or queen to govern a COLONY

ˌvice verˈsa /ˌvaɪs ˈvərsə; ˌvaɪsə-/ *adv.* used to say that the opposite of what you have just said is also true: *You can cruise from Cairo to Aswan or vice versa (= also from Aswan to Cairo).*

the vi·cin·i·ty /vəˈsɪnəti/ *noun* [sing.] the area around a particular place: *Crowds gathered in the vicinity of Times Square.* ◆ *There is no hospital in the immediate vicinity.*

vi·cious /ˈvɪʃəs/ *adj.* **1** violent and cruel **SYN** BRUTAL: *a vicious attack* ◆ *a vicious criminal* ◆ *She has a vicious temper.* **2** (of animals) aggressive and dangerous: *a vicious dog* **3** (of an attack, criticism, etc.) full of hatred and anger: *She wrote me a vicious letter.* **4** (*informal*) very bad or severe: *a vicious headache* ◆ *a vicious spiral of rising prices* ▶ **vi·cious·ly** *adv.* **vi·cious·ness** *noun* [U]: *Police were shocked by the viciousness of the assault.*

ˌvicious ˈcircle (also **ˌvicious ˈcycle**) *noun* [sing.] a situation in which one problem causes another problem that then makes the first problem worse ⊃ **compare** VIRTUOUS CIRCLE

vi·cis·si·tude /vəˈsɪsətud/ *noun* [usually pl.] (*formal*) one of the many changes and problems in a situation or in your life, that you have to deal with

vic·tim 🔑 /ˈvɪktəm/ *noun*
1 a person who has been attacked, injured, or killed as the result of a crime, a disease, an accident, etc.: *murder/rape, etc. victims* ◆ *accident/earthquake/famine, etc. victims* ◆ *AIDS/cancer/stroke, etc. victims* ◆ *victims of crime* ◆ *She was the innocent victim of an arson attack.* ◆ *Schools are the latest victims of cuts in public spending.* **2** a person who has been tricked **SYN** TARGET: *They were the victims of a cruel hoax.* ⊃ **see also** FASHION VICTIM **3** an animal or a person that is killed and offered as a SACRIFICE: *a sacrificial victim* **IDM** **fall victim (to sth)** (*formal*) to be injured, damaged, or killed by something

vic·tim·ize /ˈvɪktəmaɪz/ *verb* [often passive] *~ sb* to make someone suffer unfairly because you do not like them, their opinions, or something that they have done: *For years he had been victimized by neighborhood bullies.* ◆ *The union claimed that some of its members had been victimized for taking part in the strike.* ▶ **vic·tim·i·za·tion** /ˌvɪktəməˈzeɪʃn/ *noun* [U]

vic·tim·less /ˈvɪktəmləs/ *adj.* a **victimless** crime is one in which no one seems to suffer or be harmed

ˌvictim supˈport *noun* [U] a service provided by the police that helps people who are victims of crime

vic·tor /ˈvɪktər/ *noun* (*literary*) the winner of a battle, competition, game, etc.

Vic·to·ri·a Day /vɪkˈtɔriə ˌdeɪ/ (also **Queen's ˈBirthday**) *noun* (*CanE*) a public holiday on the Monday before May 25

Vic·to·ri·an /vɪkˈtɔriən/ *adj., noun*
● *adj.* **1** connected with the period from 1837 to 1901 when Queen Victoria ruled Britain: *Victorian architecture* ◆ *the Victorian age* **2** having the attitudes that were typical of society during Queen Victoria's REIGN: *Victorian attitudes to sex (= being easily shocked by sexual matters)* ◆ *She advocated a return to Victorian values (= hard work, pride in your country, etc.).*
● *noun* **1** a house built during Queen Victoria's REIGN **2** a British person who was alive during the period from 1837 to 1901, when Queen Victoria ruled

vic·to·ri·ous /vɪkˈtɔriəs/ *adj.* having won a victory; that ends in victory **SYN** SUCCESSFUL, TRIUMPHANT: *the victori-*

ʌ cup   ə about   eɪ say   aɪ five   ɔɪ boy   aʊ now   oʊ go   ər bird

ous army/team ♦ **~ in sth** *He emerged victorious in the elections.* ▶ **vic·to·ri·ous·ly** *adv.*

vic·to·ry /ˈvɪktəri/ *noun* (*pl.* **vic·to·ries**) [C, U] **~ (over/against sb/sth)**
success in a game, an election, a war, etc.: *the team's 10–7 victory against Cleveland* ♦ *to* **win a victory** ♦ *a* **decisive/narrow victory** ♦ *an election victory* ♦ *She is confident of victory in Saturday's game.* ♦ *victory celebrations/parades* ⊃ see also MORAL VICTORY
IDM **roar, romp, sweep, etc. to victory** to win something easily: *He swept to victory in the final of the championship.*

vic·tu·als /ˈvɪtlz/ *noun* [pl.] *(old-fashioned)* food and drink

vi·cu·ña /vɪˈkunjə/ *noun* a wild animal with a long neck and very soft wool, which lives in S. America. Vicuñas are related to LLAMAS.

vi·de /ˈvaɪdeɪ/ *verb* (*abbr.* v.) **~ sth** used (meaning "see") as an instruction in books to tell the reader to look at a particular book, passage, etc. for more information

vid·eo /ˈvɪdioʊ/ *noun*
(*pl.* **vid·e·os**) **1** (also **vid·e·o·tape**) [U, C] a type of MAGNETIC tape used for recording television pictures and sound; a box containing this tape, also called a **video cassette**: *The movie was released* **on video** *almost immediately.* ♦ *Do we have a blank video?* **2** [C] a copy of a movie, program, etc. that is recorded on VIDEOTAPE: *a video of "ET"* ♦ *a* **home video** (= not a professional one) ♦ *a video store* **3** [U] the process of recording and showing movies and programs using a special camera and a television set: *A wedding is the perfect subject for video.* ♦ *the use of video in schools* **4** (also ˈmusic ˈvideo) [C] a short film made by a pop or rock band to be shown with a song when it is played on television **5** (also ˈvideo ˌclip) [C] a short film or recording of an event, made using DIGITAL technology and viewed on a computer, especially over the Internet: *The school made a short promotional video.* ♦ *Upload your videos and share them with friends and family online.*

ˈvideo arcˌade *noun* a place where you can play video games on machines that you use coins to operate

ˈvideo ˌcamera *noun* a special camera for making video films ⊃ see also CAMCORDER

ˈvideo ˌcard (also ˈgraphics ˌcard) *noun* (*computing*) a device that allows images to be shown on a computer screen

ˌvideo casˈsette reˌcorder *noun* (*abbr.* VCR) a piece of equipment that you use to record and play movies and TV programs on video

ˈvideo ˌclip *noun* = VIDEO (5)

vid·e·o·con·fer·enc·ing /ˈvɪdioʊˌkɑnfrənsɪŋ/ *noun* [U] a system that enables people in different parts of the world to have a meeting by watching and listening to each other using video screens

ˈvideo ˌdiary *noun* a series of video recordings made by someone over a period of time, in which they record their experiences, thoughts, and feelings

vid·e·o·disc /ˈvɪdioʊˌdɪsk/ *noun* [U, C] a plastic disk that you can record movies and programs on, for showing on a television screen ⊃ see also DVD

ˈvideo ˌgame *noun* a game in which you press buttons to control and move images on a screen

ˈvideo ˌjockey (also VJ, vee·jay) *noun* a person who introduces music videos on television

vid·e·o·phone /ˈvɪdioʊˌfoʊn/ *noun* a type of telephone with a screen that enables you to see the person you are talking to

vid·e·o·tape /ˈvɪdioʊˌteɪp/ *noun, verb*
● *noun* [U, C] = VIDEO
● *verb* **~ sth/sb** (*formal*) to record a television program using a VIDEO CASSETTE RECORDER; to film something/someone using a video camera: *a videotaped interview*

vid·e·o·tex /ˈvɪdioʊˌtɛks/ *noun* [U] = VIEWDATA

vie /vaɪ/ *verb* (**vy·ing** /ˈvaɪɪŋ/, **vied, vied**) [I] (*formal*) to compete strongly with someone in order to obtain or achieve something **SYN** COMPETE: **~ (with sb) (for sth)** *She was surrounded by men all vying for her attention.* ♦ *a row of restaurants vying with each other for business* ♦ **~ (to do sth)** *Screaming fans vied to get closer to their idol.*

view /vyu/ *noun, verb*
● *noun*
▷ OPINION **1** [C] a personal opinion about something; an attitude toward something: *to have* **different/conflicting/opposing views** ♦ *to have* **strong** *political views* ♦ **~ (about/on sth)** *His views on the subject were well known.* ♦ *This evidence* **supports the view** *that there is too much violence on television.* ♦ *We* **take the view** *that it would be wrong to interfere.* ♦ **In my view** *it was a waste of time.* ♦ *What is needed is a frank* **exchange of views.** ⊃ see also POINT OF VIEW ⊃ language bank at ACCORDING TO, OPINION
▷ WAY OF UNDERSTANDING **2** [sing.] **~ (of sth)** a way of understanding or thinking about something: *He has an optimistic view of life.* ♦ *the Christian view of the world* ♦ *The traditional view was that marriage was meant to last.* ⊃ see also WORLD VIEW
▷ WHAT YOU CAN SEE **3** [U, sing.] used when you are talking about whether you can be seen in a particular situation: *The lake soon* **came into view.** ♦ *The sun disappeared* **from view.** ♦ *There was no one* **in view.** ♦ *Sit down — you're blocking my view.* ♦ *I didn't* **have a good view** *of the stage.* ⊃ thesaurus box at SIGHT **4** [C] what you can see from a particular place or position, especially beautiful countryside: *There were magnificent views of the surrounding countryside.* ♦ *The view from the top of the tower was spectacular.* ♦ *an ocean/mountain view* ♦ *I'd like a room with a view.*
▷ PHOTOGRAPH/PICTURE **5** [C] a photograph or picture that shows an interesting place or scene: *a book with views of Paris*
IDM **have, etc. sth in view** (*formal*) to have a particular aim, plan, etc. in your mind **SYN** HAVE STH IN MIND **in full view (of sb/sth)** completely visible, directly in front of someone or something: *He was shot in full view of a large crowd.* **in view of sth** (*formal*) considering something: *In view of the weather, the event will now be held indoors.* **on view** being shown in a public place so that people can look at it **with a view to sth/to doing sth** (*formal*) with the intention or hope of doing something: *He's painting the house with a view to selling it.* ⊃ more at BIRD, DIM *adj.*, HEAVE *v.*, LONG *adj.*, PLAIN *adj.*
● *verb*
▷ THINK ABOUT SOMETHING **1** to think about someone or something in a particular way: **~ (sb/sth as sth)** *When the car was first built, the design was viewed as highly original.* ♦ *How do you view your position within the company?* ♦ **~ sb/sth with sth** *She viewed him with suspicion.* ⊃ thesaurus box at REGARD
▷ LOOK AT SOMETHING **2 ~ sth** to look at something, especially when you look carefully: *People came from all over the world to view her work.* ♦ *A viewing platform gave stunning views over the valley.* ⊃ thesaurus box at LOOK **3 ~ sth** to visit a house, etc. with the intention of buying or renting it: *The property can only be viewed by appointment.*
▷ WATCH TV, MOVIE **4 ~ sth** (*formal*) to watch television, a movie, etc.: *The show has a viewing audience of six million* (= six million people watch it). ♦ *an opportunity to view the movie before it goes on general release* ⊃ note at LOOK

┌─────────────────────────────────┐
│ **THESAURUS** │
│ │
│ **view** │
│ │
│ sight ♦ scene ♦ panorama │
│ These are all words for a thing that you can see, │
│ especially from a particular place. │
│ │
│ **view** what you can see from a particular place or │
│ position, especially beautiful natural scenery: *The │
│ cottage had an amazing ocean view.* │
└─────────────────────────────────┘

view·da·ta /ˈvyuˌdeɪtə; -ˌdætə/ (also **vid·e·o·tex**) *noun* [U] an information system in which computer data is sent along telephone lines and shown on a television screen

view·er /ˈvyuər/ *noun* **1** a person watching television: *The program attracted millions of viewers.* ⟳ collocations at TELE-VISION **2** a person who looks at or considers something: *Some of her art is intended to shock the viewer.* ♦ *viewers of the current political scene* **3** a device for looking at SLIDES (= photographs on special film), for example a small box with a light in it

view·er·ship /ˈvyuərˌʃɪp/ *noun* [usually sing.] the number or type of people who watch a particular television program or television channel

view·find·er /ˈvyuˌfaɪndər/ *noun* the part of a camera that you look through to see the area that you are photographing

view·point /ˈvyupɔɪnt/ *noun* **1** ~ **(on sth)** a way of thinking about a subject **SYN** POINT OF VIEW: *Try looking at things from a different viewpoint.* ♦ *She will have her own viewpoint on the matter.* ♦ *From a practical viewpoint, I'd advise you not to go.* **2** a direction or place from which you look at something **SYN** ANGLE: *The artist has painted the scene from various viewpoints.* ⟳ see also POINT OF VIEW

view·port /ˈvyupɔrt/ *noun* **1** (*computing*) an area inside a frame on a screen, for viewing information **2** a window in a SPACECRAFT

vig·il /ˈvɪdʒəl/ *noun* [C, U] a period of time when people stay awake, especially at night, in order to watch a sick person, say prayers, protest, etc.: *His parents kept a round-the-clock vigil at his bedside.*

vig·i·lant /ˈvɪdʒələnt/ *adj.* (*formal*) very careful to notice any signs of danger or trouble **SYN** ALERT, WATCHFUL: *A pilot must remain vigilant at all times.* ▶ **vig·i·lance** /-ləns/ *noun* [U] **SYN**: *She stressed the need for constant vigilance.* **vig·i·lant·ly** *adv.*

vig·i·lan·te /ˌvɪdʒəˈlænti/ *noun* (sometimes *disapproving*) a member of a group of people who try to prevent crime or punish criminals in their community, especially because they think the police are not doing this ▶ **vig·i·lan·tism** /ˌvɪdʒəˈlæntɪzəm/ *noun* [U]

vi·gnette /vɪnˈyɛt/ *noun* (*formal*) **1** a short piece of writing or acting that clearly shows what a particular person, situation, etc. is like **2** a small picture or drawing, especially on the first page of a book

vig·or (*CanE usually* **vig·our**) /ˈvɪgər/ *noun* [U] energy, force, or enthusiasm **SYN** VITALITY: *He worked with renewed vigor and determination.*

vig·or·ous /ˈvɪgərəs/ *adj.* **1** very active, determined, or full of energy **SYN** ENERGETIC: *a vigorous campaign against tax fraud* ♦ *a vigorous opponent of the government* ♦ *Do vigorous exercise for several hours a week.* **2** strong and healthy: *a vigorous young man* ♦ *This plant is a vigorous grower.* ▶ **vig·or·ous·ly** *adv.*

Vi·king /ˈvaɪkɪŋ/ *noun* a member of a race of Scandinavian people who attacked and sometimes settled in parts of N.W. Europe, including Britain, in the 8th to the 11th centuries

vile /vaɪl/ *adj.* (**vil·er**, **vil·est**) **1** (*informal*) extremely unpleasant or bad **SYN** DISGUSTING: *a vile smell* ♦ *The weather was really vile most of the time.* ♦ *He was in a vile mood.* **2** (*formal*) morally bad; completely unacceptable **SYN** WICKED: *the vile practice of taking hostages* ▶ **vile·ly** /ˈvaɪlli/ *adv.* **vile·ness** *noun* [U]

vil·i·fy /ˈvɪləˌfaɪ/ *verb* (**vil·i·fies**, **vil·i·fy·ing**, **vil·i·fied**, **vil·i·fied**) ~ **sb/sth (as sth)** | ~ **sb/sth (for sth/for doing sth)** (*formal*) to say or write unpleasant things about someone or something so that other people will have a low opinion of them **SYN** MALIGN, REVILE ▶ **vil·i·fi·ca·tion** /ˌvɪləfəˈkeɪʃn/ *noun* [U]: *the vilification of single parents by right-wing politicians*

vil·la /ˈvɪlə/ *noun* **1** a house in the country with a large garden **2** (in Roman times) a country house or farm with land attached to it

vil·lage /ˈvɪlɪdʒ/ *noun* [C] a very small town located in a country area, usually outside the United States: *We visited towns and villages all over Spain.* ♦ *a fishing/mountain/seaside village* ♦ *Her books are about village life.*

village ˈidiot *noun* a person in a village who is thought to be stupid; a stupid person

vil·lag·er /ˈvɪlɪdʒər/ *noun* a person who lives in a village

vil·lain /ˈvɪlən/ *noun* **1** the main bad character in a story, play, etc.: *He often plays the part of the villain.* **2** a person who is morally bad or responsible for causing trouble or harm: *the heroes and villains of the 20th century* ♦ *Industrialized nations are the real environmental villains.* **3** (*informal*) a criminal

vil·lain·ous /ˈvɪlənəs/ *adj.* [usually before noun] (*formal*) very evil; very unpleasant

vil·lain·y /ˈvɪləni/ *noun* [U] (*formal*) immoral or cruel behavior

vil·lein /ˈvɪlən; -lein/ *noun* (in the Middle Ages) a poor man who had to work for a richer man in return for a small piece of land to grow food on

vil·lus /ˈvɪləs/ *noun* (*pl.* **vil·li** /ˈvɪlaɪ; -li/) (*biology*) any one of the many small thin parts shaped like fingers that stick out from some surfaces on the inside of the body (for example in the INTESTINE). Villi increase the area of these surfaces so that substances can be absorbed by the body more easily.

vim /vɪm/ *noun* [U] (*old-fashioned*, *informal*) energy

vin·ai·grette /ˌvɪnɪˈgrɛt/ *noun* [U] a mixture of oil, VINEGAR, and various HERBS, etc., used to add flavor to a salad

vin·da·loo /ˈvɪndəˌlu/ *noun* [U, C] (*pl.* **vin·da·loos**) a very spicy Indian dish, usually containing meat or fish: *lamb vindaloo*

vin·di·cate /ˈvɪndəˌkeɪt/ *verb* (*formal*) **1** ~ **sth** to prove that something is true or that you were right to do something, especially when other people had a different opinion **SYN** JUSTIFY: *I have every confidence that this decision will be fully vindicated.* **2** ~ **sb** to prove that someone is not guilty when they have been accused of doing something wrong or illegal: *New evidence emerged, vindicating him completely.* ▶ **vin·di·ca·tion** /ˌvɪndəˈkeɪʃn/ *noun* [U, sing.]: *Antinuclear protesters regarded the Chernobyl accident as a clear vindication of their campaign.*

vin·dic·tive /vɪnˈdɪktɪv/ *adj.* trying to harm or upset someone, or showing that you want to, because you think that they have harmed you **SYN** SPITEFUL: *He accused her of being vindictive.* ♦ *a vindictive comment* ▶ **vin·dic·tive·ly** *adv.* **vin·dic·tive·ness** *noun* [U]

vine /vaɪn/ *noun* **1** a climbing plant that produces GRAPES: *grapes on the vine* ♦ *vine leaves* ⟳ see also GRAPEVINE **2** any climbing plant with long thin STEMS; one of these STEMS

vin·e·gar /ˈvɪnɪgər/ *noun* [U] a liquid with a sour taste made from wine or apples, used to add flavor to food or to preserve it: *cider/wine vinegar* ⟳ see also BALSAMIC VINEGAR

| t **t**ea | t̯ bu**tt**er | d **d**id | k **c**at | g **g**ot | tʃ **ch**in | dʒ **J**une | f **f**all |

vin·e·gar·y /ˈvɪnɪɡəri/ adj. having a taste or smell that is typical of vinegar: a vinegary wine

vine·yard /ˈvɪnyərd/ noun a piece of land where GRAPES are grown in order to produce wine; a business that produces wine from the GRAPES it grows in a vineyard ⊃ compare WINERY

vi·no /ˈvinou/ noun [U] (informal, humorous) wine

vin·tage /ˈvɪntɪdʒ/ noun, adj.
● noun 1 the wine that was produced in a particular year or place; the year in which it was produced: the 1999 vintage ◆ 2005 was a particularly fine vintage. 2 [usually sing.] the period or season of gathering GRAPES for making wine: The vintage was later than usual.
● adj. [only before noun] 1 vintage wine is of very good quality and has been stored for several years 2 typical of a period in the past and of high quality; the best work of the particular person: a collection of vintage designs ◆ vintage cars ◆ The opera is vintage Rossini. 3 ~ year a particularly good and successful year: 2008 was not a vintage year for the movies.

vint·ner /ˈvɪntnər/ noun (old-fashioned, formal) a person whose business is buying and selling wines or a person who grows GRAPES and makes wine

vi·nyl /ˈvaɪnl/ noun [U] 1 a strong plastic that can bend easily, used for making wall, floor, and furniture coverings, book covers, and, especially in the past, records 2 records made of vinyl, in contrast to CDs: My dad had to buy CDs of all the albums he already owned on vinyl.

vi·ol /ˈvaɪəl/ noun an early type of musical instrument with strings, shaped like a VIOLIN

vi·o·la /viˈoulə/ noun a musical instrument with strings, that you hold under your chin and play with a BOW 2. A viola is larger than a VIOLIN and plays lower notes: a viola player ⊃ picture at INSTRUMENT

vi·o·late **AWL** /ˈvaɪəˌleɪt/ verb 1 ~ sth (formal) to go against or refuse to obey a law, an agreement, etc. **SYN** FLOUT: to violate international law 2 ~ sth (formal) to disturb or not respect someone's peace, PRIVACY, etc.: She accused the press photographers of violating her privacy. 3 ~ sth to damage or destroy a holy or special place **SYN** DESECRATE: to violate a grave 4 ~ sb (literary or old-fashioned) to force someone to have sex **SYN** RAPE ▶ **vi·o·la·tion** **AWL** /ˌvaɪə-ˈleɪʃn/ noun [U, C]: They were in open violation of the treaty. ◆ gross violations of human rights **vi·o·la·tor** /ˈvaɪəˌleɪtər/ noun

vi·o·lence 🔊 /ˈvaɪələns/ noun [U]
1 violent behavior that is intended to hurt or kill someone: crimes/acts/threats of violence ◆ ~ (against sb) He condemned the protesters' use of violence against the police. ◆ domestic violence (= between family members) ◆ Why do they always have to resort to violence? ◆ Violence broke out/erupted inside the prison last night. ◆ Is there too much sex and violence on TV? 2 physical or emotional force and energy: The violence of her feelings surprised him.

vi·o·lent 🔊 /ˈvaɪələnt/ adj.
1 involving or caused by physical force that is intended to hurt or kill someone: violent crime ◆ Students were involved in violent clashes with the police. ◆ He met with a violent death (= he was murdered, killed in a fight, etc.) ◆ Her husband was a violent man. ◆ The crowd suddenly turned violent. ◆ Children should not be allowed to watch violent movies (= that show a lot of violence). 2 showing or caused by very strong emotion: There was a violent reaction from the public. 3 very strong and sudden **SYN** INTENSE, SEVERE: I took a violent dislike to him. ◆ a violent explosion ◆ a violent change ◆ a violent headache 4 (of a color) extremely bright: Her dress was a violent pink.

vi·o·lent·ly 🔊 /ˈvaɪələntli/ adv.
1 with great energy or strong movement, especially caused by a strong emotion such as fear or hatred: She shook her head violently. ◆ to shiver violently 2 very strongly or severely: He was violently sick. ◆ They are violently opposed

to the idea. 3 in a way that involves physical violence: The crowd reacted violently.

vi·o·let /ˈvaɪələt/ noun 1 [C] a small wild or garden plant with purple or white flowers with a sweet smell that appear in spring 2 [U] a blue-purple color: dressed in violet ▶ **vi·o·let** adj.: violet eyes **IDM** see SHRINK v.

vi·o·lin /ˌvaɪəˈlɪn/ noun a musical instrument with strings, that you hold under your chin and play with a BOW 2: Brahms' violin concerto ⊃ picture at BOW2, INSTRUMENT ⊃ compare VIOLA ⊃ see also FIDDLE

vi·o·lin·ist /ˌvaɪəˈlɪnɪst/ noun a person who plays a violin

vi·o·list noun 1 /viˈoulɪst/ a person who plays a VIOLA 2 /ˈvaɪəlɪst/ a person who plays a VIOL

vi·o·lon·cel·lo /ˌvaɪələnˈtʃɛlou/ noun (pl. vi·o·lon·cel·los) (formal) = CELLO

VIP /ˌvi aɪ ˈpi/ noun the abbreviation for "Very Important Person" (a famous or important person who is treated in a special way) **SYN** CELEBRITY, DIGNITARY: the VIP lounge ◆ to get the VIP treatment

vi·per /ˈvaɪpər/ noun 1 a small poisonous snake 2 (formal) a person who harms other people

vi·ra·go /vəˈragou/ noun (pl. vi·ra·gos) (literary, disapproving) a woman who is aggressive and tries to tell people what to do

vi·ral /ˈvaɪrəl/ adj. like or caused by a virus: a viral infection ◆ a viral e-mail (= that is sent on from one person to others, who then send it on again)

viral ˈmarketing noun [U] a way of advertising in which information about a company's products or services is sent by e-mail to people who then send it on by e-mail to other people they know

vir·gin /ˈvərdʒən/ noun, adj.
● noun 1 [C] a person who has never had sex 2 the (Blessed) Virgin [sing.] the Virgin Mary, mother of Jesus Christ 3 [C] a person who has no experience of a particular activity: a political virgin ◆ an Internet virgin
● adj. 1 [usually before noun] in its original, pure, or natural condition and not changed, touched, or spoiled: virgin forest/land/territory ◆ virgin snow (= fresh and not marked) 2 [only before noun] with no sexual experience: a virgin bride ◆ the virgin birth (= the belief that Mary was a virgin before and after giving birth to Jesus)

vir·gin·al /ˈvərdʒənl/ adj. of or like a virgin; pure and innocent: She was dressed in virginal white.

Vir·gin·ia creep·er /vərˌdʒɪnyə ˈkripər/ noun [U, C] a climbing plant, often grown on walls, with large leaves that turn red in the fall

vir·gin·i·ty /vərˈdʒɪnəti/ noun [U] the state of being a virgin

Vir·go /ˈvərgou/ noun 1 [U] the 6th sign of the ZODIAC, the VIRGIN 2 [C] (pl. Vir·gos) a person born under the influence of this sign, that is between August 23 and September 23, approximately

vi·rid·i·an /vəˈrɪdiən/ noun [U] (technical) a blue-green PIGMENT used in art; the color of this pigment

vir·ile /ˈvɪrəl/ adj. (usually approving) 1 (of men) strong and full of energy, especially sexual energy 2 having or showing the strength and energy that is considered typical of men: a virile performance ◆ virile athleticism

vi·ril·i·ty /vəˈrɪləti/ noun [U] 1 sexual power in men: displays of male virility ◆ a need to prove his virility 2 strength or energy: economic virility

vi·rol·o·gy /vaɪˈrɑlədʒi/ noun [U] the scientific study of viruses and the diseases caused by them ▶ **vi·rol·o·gist** /-dʒɪst/ noun

vir·tu·al **AWL** /ˈvərtʃuəl/ adj. [only before noun] 1 almost or very nearly the thing described, so that any slight difference is not important: The country was sliding into a state of virtual civil war. ◆ The company has a virtual monopoly in this area of trade. ◆ He married a virtual stranger. 2 made to appear to exist by the use of computer software, for example on the Internet: *New technology has enabled development of an online "virtual library."*

vir·tu·al·ly 🔑 AWL /'vərtʃuəli; -tʃəli/ *adv.*
1 almost or very nearly, so that any slight difference is not important: *to be virtually impossible* ◆ *Virtually all students will be exempt from the tax.* ◆ *He virtually admitted he was guilty.* ◆ *This year's results are virtually the same as last year's.* **2** (*computing*) by the use of computer software that makes something appear to exist; using VIRTUAL REALITY technology

,**virtual 'memory** (also ,**virtual 'storage**) *noun* [U] (*computing*) extra memory that is automatically created when all the normal memory is being used

,**virtual re'ality** *noun* [U] (*abbr.* **VR**) images created by a computer that appear to surround the person looking at them and seem almost real

,**virtual 'world** *noun* images, sounds, and text used by a computer to create a world where people can communicate with each other, play games, and pretend to live another life

vir·tue /'vərtʃu/ *noun* **1** [U] (*formal*) behavior or attitudes that show high moral standards: *He led a life of virtue.* ◆ *She was certainly no **paragon** of virtue!* **2** [C] a particular good quality or habit: *Patience is not one of her virtues, I'm afraid.* **3** [C, U] an attractive or useful quality **SYN** ADVANTAGE: *The plan **has** the virtue of simplicity.* ◆ *He was extolling the virtues of the Internet.* ◆ *They could see **no virtue** in discussing it further.* **IDM** **by/in virtue of sth** (*formal*) by means of or because of something: *She got the job by virtue of her greater experience.* **make a virtue of necessity** to manage to gain an advantage from something that you have to do and cannot avoid **virtue is its own reward** (*saying*) the reward for acting in a moral or correct way is the knowledge that you have done so, and you should not expect more than this, for example praise from other people or payment ⊃ more at EASY *adj.*

vir·tu·os·i·ty /ˌvərtʃuˈasəti/ *noun* [U] (*formal*) a very high degree of skill in performing or playing: *technical virtuosity* ◆ *a performance of breathtaking virtuosity*

vir·tu·o·so /ˌvərtʃuˈousou/ *noun, adj.*
● *noun* (*pl.* **vir·tu·o·sos** or **vir·tu·o·si** /-si/) a person who is extremely skillful at doing something, especially playing a musical instrument: *a piano virtuoso*
● *adj.* [only before noun] showing extremely great skill: *a virtuoso performance* ◆ *a virtuoso pianist*

vir·tu·ous /'vərtʃuəs/ *adj.* **1** (*formal*) behaving in a very good and moral way **SYN** IRREPROACHABLE: *a wise and virtuous man* ◆ *She lived an entirely virtuous life.* **2** (*disapproving* or *humorous*) claiming to behave better or have higher moral standards than other people: *He was feeling virtuous because he had finished and they hadn't.* ▶ **vir·tu·ous·ly** *adv.*

,**virtuous 'circle** *noun* (*formal*) a series of events in which each one seems to increase the good effects of the previous one ⊃ compare VICIOUS CIRCLE

vir·u·lent /'vɪrələnt; 'vɪryə-/ *adj.* **1** (of a disease or poison) extremely dangerous or harmful and quick to have an effect **2** (*formal*) showing strong negative and bitter feelings: *virulent criticism* ◆ *virulent nationalism* ▶ **vir·u·lence** /-ləns/ *noun* [U] **vir·u·lent·ly** *adv.*

vi·rus 🔑 /'vaɪrəs/ *noun*
1 a living thing, too small to be seen without a MICROSCOPE, that causes infectious disease in people, animals, and plants: *the flu virus* ◆ *a virus infection* ⊃ collocations at LIFE **2** (*informal*) a disease caused by a virus: *There's a virus going around the office.* **3** instructions that are hidden within a computer program and are designed to cause faults or destroy data ⊃ collocations at E-MAIL ⊃ see also VIRAL

vi·sa /'vizə; -sə/ *noun* a stamp or mark put in your passport by officials of a foreign country that gives you permission to enter, pass through, or leave their country: *to **apply for** a visa* ◆ *an entry/tourist/transit/exit visa*

vis·age /'vɪzɪdʒ/ *noun* (*literary*) a person's face

vis-à-vis /ˌvizaˈvi/ *prep.* (from *French*) **1** in relation to: *Britain's role vis-à-vis the United States* **2** in comparison with: *It was felt that the corporation had an unfair advantage vis-à-vis smaller companies elsewhere.*

vis·cer·a /'vɪsərə/ *noun* [pl.] (*anatomy*) the large organs inside the body, such as the heart, lungs, and stomach

vis·cer·al /'vɪsərəl/ *adj.* **1** (*literary*) resulting from strong feelings rather than careful thought: *She had a visceral dislike of all things foreign.* **2** (*technical*) relating to the viscera

vis·cid /'vɪsɪd/ *adj.* (*formal* or *technical*) sticky and SLIMY: *the viscid lining of the intestine*

vis·cose /'vɪskous/ *noun* [U] a chemical made from CELLULOSE, used to make FIBERS which can be used to make clothes, etc.

vis·count /'vaɪkaunt/ *noun* (in Britain) a NOBLEMAN of a rank below an EARL and above a BARON

vis·count·ess /'vaɪˌkauntəs/ *noun* **1** a woman who has the rank of a VISCOUNT **2** the wife of a VISCOUNT

vis·cous /'vɪskəs/ *adj.* (*technical*) (of a liquid) thick and sticky; not flowing freely ▶ **vis·cos·i·ty** /vɪˈskasəti/ *noun* [U]

vise (also **vice**) /vaɪs/ *noun* [C] a tool with two metal blocks that can be moved together by turning a screw. The vise is used to hold an object firmly while work is done on it: *He held my arm in a vise-like* (= very firm) *grip.* ⊃ picture at TOOL

vis·i·bil·i·ty AWL /ˌvɪzəˈbɪləti/ *noun* [U] **1** how far or well you can see, especially as affected by the light or the weather: *good/poor/bad/zero visibility* ◆ *Visibility was down to about 100 yards in the fog.* ◆ *The car has excellent all-around visibility* (= you can see what is around you very easily from it). **2** the fact or state of being easy to see: *high visibility equipment for cyclists* ◆ *The advertisements were intended to increase the company's visibility in the marketplace* (= to make people more aware of their products and services).

vis·i·ble 🔑 AWL /'vɪzəbl/ *adj.*
1 that can be seen: *The house is **clearly visible** from the beach.* ◆ *Most stars are not **visible to the naked eye**.* **2** that is obvious enough to be noticed **SYN** OBVIOUS: *visible benefits* ◆ *a visible police presence* ◆ *He showed no visible sign of emotion.* ◆ *She made a visible effort to control her anger.* ⊃ compare INVISIBLE

,**visible mi'nority** *noun* (*CanE*) a group whose members are clearly different in race from those of the majority race in a society

vis·i·bly AWL /'vɪzəbli/ *adv.* in a way that is easily noticeable: *He was visibly shocked.* ◆ *She paled visibly at the news.*

vi·sion 🔑 AWL /'vɪʒn/ *noun*
1 [U] the ability to see; the area that you can see from a particular position: *to have good/perfect/poor/blurred/normal vision* ◆ *20–20 vision* (= the ability to see perfectly) ◆ *Cats have good night vision.* ◆ *The couple moved out of her field of vision.* ◆ *He glimpsed something on the edge of his vision.* ⊃ see also TUNNEL VISION ⊃ thesaurus box at SIGHT **2** [C] an idea or a picture in your imagination: *He had a vision of a world in which there would be no wars.* ◆ *I had visions of us getting hopelessly lost.* **3** [C] a dream or similar experience, especially of a religious kind: *The idea came to her in a vision.* **4** [U] the ability to think about or plan the future with great imagination and intelligence **SYN** FORESIGHT: *a leader of vision* **5** [C] **a ~ (of sth)** (*literary*) a person of great beauty or who shows the quality mentioned: *She was a vision in white lace.* ◆ *a vision of loveliness* **6** [U] the picture on a television or movie theater screen: *We apologize for the loss of vision.*

vi·sion·ar·y /'vɪʒəˌnɛri/ *adj., noun*
● *adj.* **1** (*approving*) original and showing the ability to think about or plan the future with great imagination and intelligence: *a visionary leader* **2** relating to dreams or strange experiences, especially of a religious kind: *visionary experiences*
● *noun* (*pl.* **vi·sion·ar·ies**) (usually *approving*) a person who

has the ability to think about or plan the future in a way that is intelligent or shows imagination

vis·it 🔑 /ˈvɪzət/ *verb, noun*
- *verb* **1** [T] ~ **sb/sth** to go to see a person or a place for a period of time: *She went to visit relatives in Phoenix.* ◆ *The president is visiting Japan at the moment.* ◆ *You should visit your dentist at least twice a year.* **2** [T] ~ **sth** (*computing*) to go to a Web site on the Internet: *For more information, visit our Web site.* **3** [I, T] to stay somewhere for a short time: *We don't live here. We're just visiting.* ◆ ~ **sth** *The lake is also visited by seals in the summer.* **4** [T] ~ **sth** to make an official visit to someone, for example to perform checks or give advice: *government inspectors visiting schools*
  PHRV '**visit sth on/upon sb/sth** (*old use*) to punish someone or something: *The sins of the fathers are visited upon the children* (= children are blamed or suffer for what their parents have done). '**visit with sb** to spend time with someone, especially talking socially: *Come and visit with me some time.*
- *noun* **1** ~ **(to sb/sth) (from sb)** an occasion or a period of time when someone goes to see a place or person and spends time there: *It's my first visit to New York.* ◆ *If you have time, pay a visit to the local museum.* ◆ *We had a visit from the police last night.* ◆ *Is this a social visit, or is it business?* ◆ *a visit to the doctor* **2** (*computing*) an occasion when someone looks at a Web site on the Internet: *Visits to our Web site have doubled in a year.* **3** ~ **(with sb)** (*informal*) an occasion when two or more people meet to talk in an informal way

vis·it·a·tion /ˌvɪzəˈteɪʃn/ *noun* **1** [U] the right of a parent who is divorced or separated from his or her partner to visit a child who is living with the partner: *She is seeking more liberal visitation with her daughter.* ◆ *visitation rights* **2** [C, U] ~ **(of/from sb/sth)** (*formal*) an official visit, especially to check that rules are being obeyed and everything is as it should be **3** [C] ~ **(of/from sb/sth)** (*formal*) an unexpected appearance of something, for example a GHOST **4** [C] ~ **(of sth)** (*formal*) a disaster that is believed to be a punishment from God: *a visitation of plague*

ˌvisiting 'nurse *noun* a nurse who visits and treats patients in their homes

ˌvisiting pro'fessor *noun* a professor who is teaching for a fixed period at a particular university or college, but who normally teaches at another one

vis·i·tor 🔑 /ˈvɪzətər/ *noun*
~ **(to…)** a person who visits a person or place: *We've got visitors coming this weekend.* ◆ *Do you get many visitors?* ◆ *She's a frequent visitor to the U.S.* ◆ *The theme park attracts 2.5 million visitors a year.* ◆ *How can we attract more visitors to our website?*

'visitors' ˌbook *noun* a book in which visitors write their names, addresses, and sometimes comments, for example, at a hotel or place of public interest

vi·sor /ˈvaɪzər/ *noun* **1** a part of a HELMET that can be pulled down to protect the eyes and face ⊃ picture at HAT **2** a curved piece of plastic, etc. worn on the head above the eyes to protect them from the sun **3** a small piece of plastic, etc. inside the front window of a car that can be pulled down to protect the driver's eyes from the sun ⊃ picture at CAR **4** = BILL *n.* (8)

vis·ta /ˈvɪstə/ *noun* **1** (*literary*) a beautiful view of the countryside, a city, etc. **SYN** PANORAMA **2** (*formal*) a range of things that might happen in the future **SYN** PROSPECT: *This new job could open up whole new vistas for her.*

vis·u·al **AWL** /ˈvɪʒuəl/ *adj., noun*
- *adj.* of or connected with seeing or sight: *I have a very good visual memory.* ◆ *the visual arts* ◆ *The building makes a tremendous visual impact.* ▶ **vis·u·al·ly** **AWL** *adv.*: *visually handicapped/impaired* ◆ *visually exciting*
- *noun* a picture, map, piece of film, etc. used to make an article or a talk easier to understand or more interesting: *He used striking visuals to get his point across.*

ˌvisual 'aid *noun* [usually pl.] a picture, video, etc. used in teaching to help people to learn or understand something

ˌvisual dis'play ˌunit *noun* (*computing*) = VDU

ˌvisual 'field *noun* (*technical*) = FIELD OF VISION

vis·u·al·ize **AWL** /ˈvɪʒuəˌlaɪz/ *verb* to form a picture of someone or something in your mind **SYN** IMAGINE: ~ **sb/sth/yourself (as sth)** *Try to visualize him as an old man.* ◆ ~ **what, how, etc.…** *I can't visualize what this room looked like before it was decorated.* ◆ ~ **sb/sth/yourself doing sth** *It can help to visualize yourself making your speech clearly and confidently.* ◆ ~ **doing sth** *She couldn't visualize climbing the mountain.* ▶ **vis·u·al·i·za·tion** **AWL** /ˌvɪʒuələˈzeɪʃn/ *noun* [U, C]

vi·ta /ˈvitə; ˈvaɪtə/ *noun* = CURRICULUM VITAE

vi·tal 🔑 /ˈvaɪtl/ *adj.*
1 necessary or essential in order for something to succeed or exist: ~ **(for sth)** *the vitamins that are vital for health* ◆ ~ **(to sth)** *Good financial accounts are vital to the success of any enterprise.* ◆ *Reading is of vital importance in language learning.* ◆ *The police play a vital role in our society.* ◆ ~ **that…** *It is vital that you keep accurate records when you are self-employed.* ◆ ~ **to do sth** *It was vital to show that he was not afraid.* ⊃ thesaurus box at ESSENTIAL ⊃ language bank at EMPHASIS, IMPERSONAL **2** [only before noun] connected with or necessary for staying alive: *the vital organs* (= the brain, heart, lungs, etc.) **3** (*of a person*) full of energy and enthusiasm **SYN** DYNAMIC

LANGUAGE BANK

vital
saying that something is necessary

- It is vital that journalists are able to verify the accuracy of their reports.
- Journalists play a **vital/crucial** role in educating the public.
- Public trust is a **crucial** issue for all news organizations.
- The ability to write well is **essential** for any journalist.
- The Internet has become an **indispensable** tool for reporters.
- In journalism, accuracy is **paramount**. / …is **of paramount importance**.
- It is **imperative** that journalists maintain the highest possible standards of reporting.
  ⊃ Thesaurus at ESSENTIAL
  ⊃ Language Banks at EMPHASIS, IMPERSONAL

vi·tal·i·ty /vaɪˈtæləti/ *noun* [U] energy and enthusiasm **SYN** VIGOR: *She is bursting with vitality and new ideas.*

vi·tal·ly /ˈvaɪtl.i/ *adv.* extremely; in an essential way: *Education is vitally important for the country's future.*

vit·als /ˈvaɪtlz/ *noun often* the vitals [pl.] **1** = VITAL SIGNS **2** (*old-fashioned or humorous*) the organs of the body that are essential for staying alive, for example the brain, heart, lungs, etc.

ˌvital 'signs (also vi·tals) *noun* [pl.] (*medical*) measurements that shows that someone is alive, such as the rate of their breathing, their body temperature, or their HEARTBEAT

ˌvital sta'tistics *noun* [pl.] figures that show the number of births and deaths in a country

vi·ta·min /ˈvaɪtəmən/ *noun* **1** a natural substance found in food that is an essential part of what humans and animals eat to help them grow and stay healthy. There are many different vitamins: *breakfast cereals enriched with vitamins* ◆ *vitamin deficiency* ◆ *vitamin pills* ◆ *Broccoli is high in Vitamins C, K, and A.* **2** a pill containing vitamins: *I take my vitamin with breakfast.* ⊃ collocations at DIET

ˌvitamin 'C (also as·corbic 'acid) *noun* [U] a vitamin found in fruits such as oranges and lemons, and in green vegetables: *Oranges are rich in vitamin C.*

vi·ti·ate /ˈvɪʃiˌeɪt/ *verb* [usually passive] ~ **sth** (*formal*) to spoil or reduce the effect of something

vit·i·cul·ture /'vɪtəˌkʌltʃər/ noun [U] (technical) the science or practice of growing GRAPES

vit·re·ous /'vɪtriəs/ adj. (technical) hard, shiny, and transparent like glass: vitreous enamel

vitreous 'humor (CanE usually **vitreous 'humour**) noun [U] (anatomy) the transparent jelly-like substance inside the eye ➔ compare AQUEOUS HUMOR

vit·ri·fy /'vɪtrəˌfaɪ/ verb (vit·ri·fies, vit·ri·fy·ing, vit·ri·fied, vit·ri·fied) [I, T] ~ (sth) (technical) to change or make something change into glass, or a substance like glass ▶ **vit·ri·fi·ca·tion** /ˌvɪtrəfə'keɪʃn/ noun [U]

vit·ri·ol /'vɪtriəl; -ˌɑl/ noun [U] (formal) very cruel and bitter comments or criticism SYN ABUSE

vit·ri·ol·ic /ˌvɪtri'ɑlɪk/ adj. (formal) (of language or comments) full of anger and hatred SYN BITTER: The newspaper launched a vitriolic attack on the president.

vi·tro ➔ IN VITRO

vi·tu·per·a·tion /vaɪˌtupə'reɪʃn/ noun [U] (formal) cruel and angry criticism SYN ABUSE ▶ **vi·tu·per·a·tive** /vaɪ-'tupərətɪv; -ˌreɪtɪv/ adj.: a vituperative attack

vi·va /'vivə/ exclamation used for expressing support for someone or something

vi·va·ce /vɪ'vatʃeɪ/ noun (music) (from Italian) a piece of music to be played in a quick, lively way ▶ **vi·va·ce** adv., adj.

vi·va·cious /vɪ'veɪʃəs; vaɪ-/ adj. (approving) (especially of a woman) having a lively, attractive personality: He had three pretty, vivacious daughters. ▶ **vi·va·cious·ly** adv. **vi·vac·i·ty** /vɪ'væsəti; vaɪ-/ noun [U]: He was charmed by her beauty and vivacity.

vi·var·i·um /vaɪ'veriəm; vɪ-/ noun (pl. vi·var·i·a /-'veriə/) a container for keeping live animals in, especially for scientific study

vi·va vo·ce /ˌvivə 'voʊtʃeɪ; ˌvaɪvə 'voʊsi/ noun (from Latin) a spoken exam

vive la dif·fe·rence /ˌviv la ˌdɪfə'rɑns; ˌvivə-/ exclamation (from French, humorous) used to show that you think it is good that there is a difference between two people or things, especially a difference between men and women

viv·id /'vɪvəd/ adj. 1 (of memories, a description, etc.) producing very clear pictures in your mind SYN GRAPHIC: vivid memories ◆ He gave a vivid account of his life as a fighter pilot. 2 (of light, colors, etc.) very bright: vivid blue eyes ➔ thesaurus box at BRIGHT 3 (of someone's imagination) able to form pictures of ideas, situations, etc. easily in the mind ▶ **viv·id·ly** adv.: I vividly remember the day we first met. **viv·id·ness** noun [U]: the vividness of my dream

vi·vip·a·rous /vaɪ'vɪpərəs/ adj. (biology) (of an animal) producing live babies from its body rather than eggs ➔ compare OVIPAROUS, OVOVIVIPAROUS

viv·i·sec·tion /ˌvɪvə'sekʃn; 'vɪvəˌsek-/ noun [U] the practice of doing experiments on live animals for medical or scientific research

vi·vo ➔ IN VIVO

vix·en /'vɪksn/ noun 1 a female FOX (= a wild animal of the dog family) 2 (old-fashioned) an unpleasant and bad-tempered woman

viz. /vɪz/ adv. (formal) used to introduce a list of things that explain something more clearly or are given as examples SYN NAMELY: Ivy league schools, viz. Dartmouth, Yale, Harvard, and Brown

vi·zier /və'zɪr/ (also wa·zir) noun an important official in some Muslim countries in the past

VJ /'vi dʒeɪ/ abbr. = VIDEO JOCKEY

'V-neck noun an opening for the neck in a piece of clothing, shaped like the letter V; a piece of clothing with a V-neck: a V-neck sweater ◆ a navy V-neck ▶ **'V-necked** adj.: a V-necked sweater ➔ picture at CLOTHES ➔ picture at NECK

VOA /ˌvi oʊ 'eɪ/ abbr. VOICE OF AMERICA

vo·cab·u·lar·y 🔑 /voʊ'kæbyəˌleri; və-/ noun [C, U] (pl. vo·cab·u·lar·ies)
1 all the words that a person knows or uses: to have a wide/ limited vocabulary ◆ your active vocabulary (= the words that you use) ◆ your passive vocabulary (= the words that you understand but don't use) ◆ Reading will increase your vocabulary. ◆ The word "failure" is not in his vocabulary (= for him, failure does not exist). ➔ see also DEFINING VOCABULARY ➔ note at LANGUAGE **2** all the words in a particular language: When did the word "bungalow" first enter the vocabulary? ➔ note at LANGUAGE **3** the words that people use when they are talking about a particular subject: The word has become part of advertising vocabulary. ➔ thesaurus box at LANGUAGE **4** (also informal vo·cab /'voʊkæb/) a list of words with their meanings, especially in a book for learning a foreign language

vo·cal /'voʊkl/ adj., noun
● adj. **1** [only before noun] connected with the voice: vocal music ◆ the vocal organs (= the tongue, lips, etc.) ➔ thesaurus box at SPOKEN **2** telling people your opinions or protesting about something loudly and with confidence: He has been very vocal in his criticism of the government's policy. ◆ The protesters are a small but vocal minority.

● noun [usually pl.] the part of a piece of music that is sung, rather than played on a musical instrument: backing vocals ◆ In this recording Armstrong himself is on vocals.

'vocal ˌcords noun [pl.] the thin strips of TISSUE in the throat that are moved by the flow of air to produce the voice

vo·cal·ic /voʊ'kælɪk/ adj. (phonetics) relating to or consisting of a vowel or vowels ➔ compare CONSONANTAL

vo·cal·ist /'voʊkəlɪst/ noun a singer, especially in a pop, ROCK, or JAZZ band: a lead/guest/backing vocalist ➔ compare INSTRUMENTALIST

vo·cal·i·za·tion /ˌvoʊkələ'zeɪʃn/ noun (formal) **1** [C] a word or sound that is produced by the voice: the vocalizations of animals **2** [U] the process of producing a word or sound with the voice

vo·cal·ize /'voʊkəˌlaɪz/ verb (formal) **1** [T] ~ sth to use words to express something SYN ARTICULATE, EXPRESS: Showing children pictures sometimes helps them to vocalize their ideas. **2** [I, T] ~ (sth) to say or sing sounds or words: Your baby will begin to vocalize long before she can talk.

vo·cal·ly /'voʊkəli/ adv. **1** in a way that uses the voice: to communicate vocally **2** by speaking in a loud and confident way: They protested vocally.

vo·ca·tion /voʊ'keɪʃn/ noun **1** [C] a type of work or way of life that you believe is especially suitable for you SYN CALLING: Nursing is not just a job — it's a vocation. ◆ She believes that she has found her true vocation in life. ◆ You missed your vocation — you should have been an actor. ➔ collocations at JOB **2** [C, U] ~ (for sth) a belief that a particular type of work or way of life is especially suitable for you: He has a vocation for teaching. ◆ She is a doctor with a strong sense of vocation. **3** [C, U] a belief that you have been chosen by God to be a priest or NUN: a vocation to the priesthood

vo·ca·tion·al /voʊ'keɪʃənl/ adj. connected with the skills, knowledge, etc. that you need to have in order to do a particular job: vocational education/qualifications/training

vo'cational ˌschool noun [C, U] a school that teaches skills that are necessary for particular jobs

voc·a·tive /'vɑkətɪv/ noun (grammar) (in some languages) the form of a noun, a pronoun, or an adjective used when talking to a person or thing ➔ compare ABLATIVE, ACCUSATIVE, DATIVE, GENITIVE, NOMINATIVE ▶ **voc·a·tive** adj.: the vocative case

vo·cif·er·ous /voʊ'sɪfərəs/ adj. (formal) expressing your opinions or feelings in a loud and confident way SYN STRIDENT: vociferous protests ◆ a vociferous critic of the president's stance ▶ **vo·cif·er·ous·ly** adv.: to complain vociferously

vod·ka /'vɑdkə/ noun **1** [U] a strong, clear, alcoholic drink, made from grain, originally from Russia **2** [C] a glass of vodka: *I'll have a vodka and lime.*

vogue /voʊɡ/ *noun* [C, usually sing., U] **~ (for sth)** a fashion for something: *the vogue for child-centered education* ♦ *Black is in vogue again.* ➔ collocations at FASHION

voice 🖉 /vɔɪs/ *noun, verb*

● *noun*
> **SOUND FROM MOUTH 1** [C, U] the sound or sounds produced through the mouth by a person speaking or singing: *I could hear voices in the next room.* ♦ *to speak in a deep/soft/loud/quiet, etc. voice* ♦ *"I promise," she said in a small voice* (= a quiet, shy voice). ♦ *to raise/lower your voice* (= to speak louder/more quietly) ♦ *Keep your voice down* (= speak quietly). ♦ *Don't take that tone of voice with me!* ♦ *Her voice shook with emotion.* ♦ *"There you are," said a voice behind me.* ♦ *When did his voice change* (= become deep like a man's)? ♦ *He was suffering from flu and had lost his voice* (= could not speak). ♦ *She has a good singing voice.* ♦ *She was in good voice* (= singing well) *at the concert tonight.*
> **-VOICED 2** (in adjectives) having a voice of the type mentioned: *low-voiced* ♦ *squeaky-voiced*
> **OPINION 3** [sing.] **~ (in sth)** the right to express your opinion and influence decisions: *Employees should have a voice in the decision-making process.* **4** [C] a particular attitude, opinion, or feeling that is expressed; a feeling or an opinion that you become aware of inside yourself: *He pledged that his party would listen to the voice of the people.* ♦ *Very few dissenting voices were heard on the right of the party.* ♦ *the voice of reason/sanity/conscience* ♦ *"Coward!" a tiny inner voice insisted.*
> **GRAMMAR 5** [sing.] **the active/passive ~** the form of a verb that shows whether the subject of a sentence performs the action (*the active voice*) or is affected by it (*the passive voice*)
> **PHONETICS 6** [U] sound produced by movement of the VOCAL CORDS used in the pronunciation of vowels and some consonants ➔ see also VOICED, VOICELESS
> **IDM** give voice to sth to express your feelings, worries, etc. make your voice heard to express your feelings, opinions, etc. in a way that makes people notice and consider them with one voice as a group; with everyone agreeing: *The various opposition parties speak with one voice on this issue.* ➔ more at FIND v., SOUND n., STILL adj., TOP n.

● *verb*
> **GIVE OPINION 1 ~ sth** to tell people your feelings or opinions about something: *to voice complaints/criticisms/doubts/objections, etc.* ♦ *A number of parents have voiced concern about their children's safety.*
> **PHONETICS 2 ~ sth** to produce a sound with a movement of your VOCAL CORDS as well as your breath ➔ compare UNVOICED, VOICELESS

voice box *noun* the area at the top of the throat that contains the VOCAL CORDS **SYN** LARYNX

voiced /vɔɪst/ *adj.* (phonetics) (of consonants) produced by moving your VOCAL CORDS. For example, the consonants /b/, /d/, and /ɡ/, are voiced. **ANT** UNVOICED

voice·less /ˈvɔɪsləs/ *adj.* (phonetics) (of consonants) produced without moving your VOCAL CORDS. For example, the consonants /p/, /t/ and /k/ are voiceless. **SYN** UNVOICED **ANT** VOICED

voice mail *noun* [U] an electronic system which can store telephone messages, so that someone can listen to them later ➔ compare ANSWERING MACHINE

the ˌVoice of Aˈmerica *noun* [sing.] (abbr. VOA) an official government service that broadcasts news and other programs in English and many other languages around the world

voice-ˌover *noun* information or comments in a movie, television program, etc. that are given by a person who is not seen on the screen: *She earns a lot of money doing voice-overs for TV commercials.*

voice·print /ˈvɔɪsprɪnt/ *noun* (technical) a printed record of a person's speech, showing the different frequencies (FREQUENCY) and lengths of sounds as a series of waves

ˈvoice recogˌnition *noun* [U] **1** technology that allows a computer to identify a voice **2** = SPEECH RECOGNITION

void /vɔɪd/ *noun, adj., verb*
● *noun* [usually sing.] (formal or literary) a large empty space: *Below him was nothing but a black void.* ♦ (figurative) *The void left by his mother's death was never filled.*
● *adj.* **1 ~ of sth** (formal) completely lacking something **SYN** DEVOID: *The sky was void of stars.* **2** (law) (of a contract, an agreement etc.) not valid or legal: *The agreement was declared void.* **3** (formal) empty: *void spaces* **IDM** see NULL
● *verb* **1 ~ sth** (law) to state officially that something is no longer valid **SYN** INVALIDATE, NULLIFY **2 ~ sth** (formal) to empty waste matter from the BLADDER or BOWELS

voi·là /vwɑˈlɑ/ *exclamation* (from French) used to say "there it is!" when you show something to someone, or something appears suddenly: *"Voilà!" she said, producing a pair of strappy white sandals.*

voile /vɔɪl/ *noun* [U] a type of cloth made of cotton, wool, or silk that is almost transparent, used for making clothes

VoIP /vɔɪp/ (also ˌIP teˈlephony) *noun* [U] the abbreviation for "voice over Internet protocol" (a telephone system that allows users to make and receive calls using the Internet)

vol. **AWL** *abbr.* VOLUME: *the Complete Works of Byron Vol. 2*

vol·a·tile /ˈvɑlətl/ *adj.* **1** (often disapproving) (of a person or their moods) changing easily from one mood to another: *a highly volatile personality* **2** (of a situation) likely to change suddenly; easily becoming dangerous **SYN** UNSTABLE: *a highly volatile situation from which riots might develop* ♦ *a volatile exchange rate* **3** (technical) (of a substance) that changes easily into a gas: *Gas is a volatile substance.* ▶ **vol·a·til·i·ty** /ˌvɑləˈtɪləti/ *noun* [U]

vol·can·ic /vɑlˈkænɪk; vɔl-/ *adj.* caused or produced by a volcano: *volcanic rocks* ♦ *volcanic eruptions*

volcano

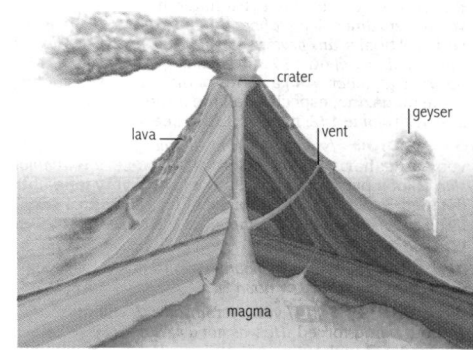

vol·ca·no /vɑlˈkeɪnoʊ; vɔl-/ *noun* (pl. **vol·ca·noes** or **vol·ca·nos**) a mountain with a large opening at the top through which gases and LAVA (= hot liquid rock) are forced out into the air, or have been in the past: *An active volcano may erupt at any time.* ♦ *a dormant volcano* (= one that is not active at present) ♦ *an extinct volcano* (= one that is no longer active)

vol·can·ol·o·gy /ˌvɑlkəˈnɑlədʒi; ˌvɔl-/ (also **vul·can·ol·o·gy**) *noun* [U] the scientific study of volcanoes

vole /voʊl/ *noun* a small animal like a mouse or RAT that lives in fields or near rivers

vo·li·tion /vəˈlɪʃn/ *noun* [U] (formal) the power to choose something freely or to make your own decisions **SYN** FREE WILL: *They left entirely of their own volition* (= because they wanted to).

vol·ley /ˈvɑli/ *noun, verb*
● *noun* **1** (in some sports, for example TENNIS or SOCCER) a hit or kick of the ball before it touches the ground: *She hit a forehand volley into the net.* **2** a lot of bullets, stones, etc. that

are fired or thrown at the same time: *A volley of shots rang out.* ◆ *Police fired a volley over the heads of the crowd.* **3** a lot of questions, comments, insults, etc. that are directed at someone quickly one after the other **SYN** TORRENT: *She faced a volley of angry questions from her mother.*

● *verb* [T, I] ~ (sth) (in some sports, for example TENNIS or SOCCER) to hit or kick the ball before it touches the ground: *He volleyed the ball into the back of the net.*

vol·ley·ball /ˈvɑliˌbɔl/ *noun* [U] a game in which two teams of six players use their hands to hit a large ball backward and forward over a high net while trying not to let the ball touch the ground on their own side ⊃ see also BEACH VOLLEYBALL

volt /voʊlt/ *noun* (*abbr.* V) a unit for measuring the force of an electric current: *a high security fence with 5,000 volts passing through it*

volt·age /ˈvoʊltɪdʒ/ *noun* [U, C] electrical force measured in volts: *high/low voltage*

volte-face /ˌvɔlt ˈfɑs; ˌvalt-/ *noun* [sing.] (*formal*) a complete change of opinion or plan **SYN** ABOUT-FACE: *This represents a volte-face in government thinking.*

volt·me·ter /ˈvoʊltˌmitər/ *noun* an instrument for measuring VOLTAGE

vol·u·ble /ˈvɑlyəbl/ *adj.* (*formal*) **1** talking a lot, and with enthusiasm, about a subject: *Evelyn was very voluble on the subject of women's rights.* **2** expressed in many words and spoken quickly: *voluble protests* ▶ **vol·u·bly** /-bli/ *adv.*

vol·ume 🔑 **AWL** /ˈvɑlyəm; -yum/ *noun*

1 [U, C] the amount of space that an object or a substance fills; the amount of space that a container has: *How do you measure the volume of a gas?* ◆ *jars of different volumes* **2** [U, C] the amount of something: *the **sheer volume** (= large amount) of business* ◆ *This work has grown in volume recently.* ◆ *New roads are being built to cope with the increased volume of traffic.* ◆ *Sales volumes fell 0.2% in June.* **3** [U] the amount of sound that is produced by a television, radio, etc.: *to turn the volume up/down* **4** [C] (*abbr.* vol.) a book, that is part of a series of books: *an encyclopedia in 20 volumes* **5** [C] (*formal*) a book: *a library of over 50,000 volumes* ◆ *a slim volume of poetry* **6** [C] (*abbr.* vol.) a series of different issues of the same magazine, especially all the issues for one year: *New Scientist volume 142, number 3* **IDM** see SPEAK

vo·lu·mi·nous /vəˈlumənəs/ *adj.* (*formal*) **1** (of clothing) very large; having a lot of cloth **SYN** AMPLE: *a voluminous skirt* **2** (of a piece of writing, a book, etc.) very long and detailed **3** (of a container, piece of furniture, etc.) very large: *I sank down into a voluminous armchair.* ▶ **vo·lu·mi·nous·ly** *adv.*

vol·u·mize /ˈvɑlyuˌmaɪz/ *noun* ~ sth to make hair look thicker ▶ **vol·um·iz·er** *noun*

vol·un·tar·i·ly **AWL** /ˌvɑlənˈtɛrəli/ *adv.* **1** willingly; without being forced: *He was not asked to leave — he went voluntarily.* **2** without payment; free: *The fund is voluntarily administered.*

vol·un·tar·y **AWL** /ˈvɑlənˌtɛri/ *adj., noun*

● *adj.* **1** done willingly, not because you are forced: *a voluntary agreement* ◆ *Attendance at the meetings is purely voluntary.* ◆ *to pay **voluntary contributions** into a pension fund* **ANT** COMPULSORY **2** [usually before noun] (of work) done by people who choose to do it without being paid: *I do some voluntary work at the local hospital.* ◆ *She works there on a **voluntary basis**.* ◆ ***voluntary services/bodies/agencies/organizations*** (= organized, controlled, or supported by people who choose to do this and are usually not paid) ◆ ***the voluntary sector*** (= organizations that are set up to help people and that do not make a profit, for example charities) **3** [only before noun] (of a person) doing a job without wanting to be paid for it: *a voluntary worker* **4** (*technical*) (of movements of the body) that you can control **ANT** INVOLUNTARY

● *noun* (*pl.* **vol·un·tar·ies**) a piece of music played before, during, or after a church service, usually on an organ

vol·un·teer **AWL** /ˌvɑlənˈtɪr/ *noun, verb*

● *noun* **1** a person who does a job without being paid for it: *volunteer helpers* ◆ *Schools need volunteers to help children learn to read.* **2** a person who offers to do something without being forced to do it: *Are there any volunteers to help clean up?* **3** a person who chooses to join the armed forces without being forced to join ⊃ compare CONSCRIPT

● *verb* **1** [I, T] to offer to do something without being forced to do it or without getting paid for it: ~ to do sth *Jill volunteered to start a petition.* ◆ ~ (for/as sth) *Several staff members volunteered for early retirement.* ◆ ~ sth (for/as sth) *He volunteered his services as a driver.* **2** [T] ~ sth | + speech to suggest something or tell someone something without being asked: *to volunteer advice* **3** [I] ~ (for sth) | ~ to do sth to join the army, etc. without being forced to: *to volunteer for military service* **4** [T] ~ sb (for/as sth) | ~ sb to do sth to suggest someone for a job or an activity, even though they may not want to do it: *They volunteered me for the job of interpreter.*

vol·un·teer·ism /ˌvɑlənˈtɪrɪzəm/ *noun* [U] **1** the practice of working as a volunteer, especially in community service **2** (also **vol·un·tar·ism** /ˈvɑlənˌtrɪzəm/) the practice of using or relying on volunteers rather than paid workers

vo·lup·tu·ary /vəˈlʌptʃuˌɛri/ *noun* (*pl.* **vo·lup·tu·ar·ies**) (*formal*, usually *disapproving*) a person who enjoys physical, especially sexual, pleasures very much

vo·lup·tu·ous /vəˈlʌptʃuəs/ *adj.* **1** (*formal*) (of a woman) attractive in a sexual way with large breasts and hips **SYN** BUXOM: *a voluptuous woman* ◆ *a voluptuous body* **2** (*literary*) giving you physical pleasure **SYN** SENSUAL: *voluptuous perfume* ▶ **vo·lup·tu·ous·ly** *adv.* **vo·lup·tu·ous·ness** *noun* [U]

vom·it /ˈvɑmət/ *verb, noun*

● *verb* (also *informal* **throw** ˈup) [I, T] to bring food from the stomach back out through the mouth **SYN** BE SICK: *The smell made her want to vomit.* ◆ ~ sth up *He had vomited up his supper.* ◆ ~ sth *The injured man was vomiting blood.* ⊃ see also SICK

● *noun* [U] food from the stomach brought back out through the mouth

voo·doo /ˈvudu/ *noun* [U] a religion that is practiced especially in Haiti and involves magic and WITCHCRAFT

ˈvoodoo ˌdoll *noun* a kind of DOLL that some people believe you can stick pins in to cast a magic spell on someone

vo·ra·cious /vəˈreɪʃəs/ *adj.* (*formal*) **1** eating or wanting large amounts of food **SYN** GREEDY: *a voracious eater* ◆ *to have a **voracious appetite*** **2** wanting a lot of new information and knowledge **SYN** AVID: *a voracious reader* ◆ *a boy with a voracious and undiscriminating appetite for facts* ▶ **vo·ra·cious·ly** *adv.* **vo·rac·i·ty** /vəˈræsəti/ *noun* [U]

vor·tex /ˈvɔrtɛks/ *noun* (*pl.* **vor·tex·es** or **vor·ti·ces** /ˈvɔrtəsiz/) **1** (*technical*) a mass of air, water, etc. that spins around very fast and pulls things into its center **SYN** WHIRLPOOL, WHIRLWIND **2** (*literary*) a very powerful feeling or situation that you cannot avoid or escape from: *They were caught up in a whirling vortex of emotion.*

vo·ta·ry /ˈvoʊtəri/ *noun* (*pl.* **vo·ta·ries**) ~ of sb/sth (*formal*) a person who worships or loves someone or something: *a votary of John Keats*

vote 🔑 /voʊt/ *noun, verb*

● *noun* **1** [C] ~ (for/against sb/sth) a formal choice that you make in an election or at a meeting in order to choose someone or decide something: *There were 21 votes for and 17 against the motion, with 2 abstentions.* ◆ *The motion was passed by 6 votes to 3.* ◆ *The chairperson has the **casting/deciding vote**.* ◆ *The Independent candidate won over 3,000 of the 14,000 votes cast.* **2** [C] ~ (on sth) an occasion when a group of people vote on something: *to take a vote on an issue* ◆ *The issue was **put to a vote**.* ◆ *The vote was unanimous.* ⊃ thesaurus box at ELECTION **3** **the vote** [sing.] the total number of votes in an election: *She obtained 40% of the vote.* ◆ *The party increased their share of the vote.* **4** **the vote** [sing.]

the vote given by a particular group of people, or for a particular party, etc.: *the student vote* ◆ *the Hispanic vote* **5** **the vote** [sing.] the right to vote, especially in political elections: *In the U.S., people get the vote at 18.* ⊃ see also BLOCK VOTE

● **verb 1** [I, T] to show formally by marking a paper, raising your hand, etc. which person you want to win an election, or which plan or idea you support: **~ (for/against sb/sth)** *Did you vote for or against her?* ◆ *How did you vote in the last election?* ◆ **~ in favor of sth** *Over 60% of members voted in favor of* (= for) *the motion.* ◆ **~ (on sth)** *We'll listen to the arguments on both sides and then vote on it.* ◆ *Only about half of the electorate bothered to vote.* ◆ **~ sth** *We voted Democratic in the last election.* ◆ **~ to do sth** *The board voted to set up an independent investigation into the matter.* ⊃ collocations at POLITICS **2** [T, usually passive] **~ sb/sth + noun** to choose someone or something for a position or an award by voting: *He was voted most promising new director.* **3** [T, usually passive] **~ sth + noun** to say that something is good or bad: *The event was voted a great success.* **4** [T] **~ sb/yourself sth** to agree to give someone/yourself something by voting: *The politicians have just voted themselves a huge pay raise.* **5** [T] **~ (that)…** to suggest something or support a suggestion that someone has made: *I vote (that) we go out to eat.*

IDM **vote with your feet** to show what you think about something by going or not going somewhere: *Shoppers voted with their feet and avoided the store.*

PHR V ˌvote sb/sth↔'down to reject or defeat someone or something by voting for someone or something else ˌvote sb 'in | ˌvote sb 'into/'onto sth to choose someone for a position by voting: *He was voted in as treasurer.* ◆ *She was voted onto the board of directors.* ˌvote sb 'out | ˌvote sb 'out of/'off sth to dismiss someone from a position by voting: *He was voted out of office.* ˌvote sth↔'through to bring a plan, etc. into effect by voting for it: *A proposal to merge the two companies was voted through yesterday.*

TOPIC COLLOCATIONS

Voting in Elections

running for election

- **conduct/hold** an election/a referendum
- **run for** office/election/governor/mayor/president/ the White House
- **enter/run in/withdraw from** the primary/Senate/ gubernatorial race
- **represent** the Democrats/the Republican Party
- **hold/contest** a local/mid-term/primary/national election
- **launch/run** a presidential (election) campaign
- **support/back** a candidate
- **sway/convince/persuade** voters/the electorate
- **appeal to/attract/woo/target/pander to** swing voters
- **fix/rig/steal** an election/the vote

voting

- **go to/be turned away from** a polling place/station
- **cast a/your** vote/ballot (for sb)
- **vote for** the Republican candidate/the Democratic ticket
- **mark/spoil** your ballot paper
- **count** the early/absentee ballots
- **go to/be defeated at** the ballot box
- **get/win/receive/lose** votes
- **get/win** (60% of) the popular/black/Hispanic/Latino vote
- **win** power/the election/the primary/a senate seat/a majority
- **lose** an election/the vote/your majority/your seat
- **win/come to power in** a landslide (victory) (= with many more votes than any other party)
- **elect/reelect sb (as)** mayor/president/congress-man/congresswoman/a Senator/a Representative

taking power

- **be sworn** into office/in as president
- **take/administer** the oath of office
- **give/deliver** the inaugural address
- **take/enter/hold/leave** office
- **appoint sb (as)** ambassador/governor/minister/a federal judge/a Supreme Court justice
- **form** a government/a cabinet
- **serve** two terms as president/in office
- ⊃ more collocations at ECONOMY, POLITICS

ˌvote of ˈconfidence *noun* [usually sing.] a formal vote to show that people support a leader, a political party, an idea, etc.

ˌvote of ˌno ˈconfidence *noun* [usually sing.] a formal vote to show that people do not support a leader, a political party, an idea, etc.

ˌvote of ˈthanks *noun* [usually sing.] a short formal speech in which you thank someone for something and ask other people to join you in thanking them

vot·er /ˈvoʊtər/ *noun* a person who votes or has the right to vote, especially in a political election: *A clear majority of voters were in favor of the motion.* ◆ *Only 60% of eligible voters actually used their vote.* ⊃ collocations at VOTE ⊃ see also SWING VOTER

vot·ing /ˈvoʊtɪŋ/ *noun* [U] the action of choosing someone or something in an election or at a meeting: *He was eliminated in the first round of voting.* ◆ *Voting will take place on May 1.* ◆ *to be of voting age*

ˈvoting ˌbooth *noun* a small place in a POLLING PLACE, separated from the surrounding area, where people vote by marking a card, etc.

ˈvoting maˌchine *noun* a machine in which votes can be recorded automatically

vo·tive /ˈvoʊtɪv/ *adj., noun* (*technical*)
● *adj.* [usually before noun] presented to a god as a sign of thanks: *votive offerings*
● *noun* = VOTIVE CANDLE

ˈvotive ˌcandle (also vo·tive) *noun* a small CANDLE, usually one that is used in churches: *Votive candles were lit in front of the statue of Jesus.*

vouch /vaʊtʃ/ *verb*
PHR V ˈvouch for sb/sth to say that you believe that someone will behave well and that you will be responsible for their actions: *Are you willing to vouch for him?* ◆ *I can vouch for her ability to work hard.* ˈvouch for sth to say that you believe that something is true or good because you have evidence for it **SYN** CONFIRM: *I was in bed with the flu. My wife can vouch for that.*

vouch·er /ˈvaʊtʃər/ *noun* a printed piece of paper that can be used instead of money to pay for something: *a voucher for a free meal* ◆ *a housing voucher*

vouch·safe /ˌvaʊtʃˈseɪf; ˈvaʊtʃseɪf/ *verb* **~ sth (to sb)** | **~ sb sth** | **~ that…** | **+ speech** (*old-fashioned* or *formal*) to give, offer, or tell something to someone, especially in order to give them a special advantage: *He vouchsafed to me certain family secrets.*

vow /vaʊ/ *noun, verb*
● *noun* a formal and serious promise, especially a religious one, to do something: *to make/take a vow* ◆ *to break/keep a vow* ◆ *to break your marriage/wedding vows* ◆ *Nuns take a vow of chastity.* ⊃ collocations at MARRIAGE
● *verb* to make a formal and serious promise to do something or a formal statement that is true: **~ to do sth** *She vowed never to speak to him again.* ◆ **~ (that)…** *He vowed (that) he had not hurt her.* ◆ **~ sth** *They vowed eternal friendship.* ◆ **+ speech** *"I'll be back," she vowed.*

vow·el /ˈvaʊəl/ *noun* (*phonetics*) **1** a speech sound in which the mouth is open and the tongue is not touching the top of the mouth, the teeth, etc., for example /ɑ, ɛ, ɔ/ : *vowel sounds* ◆ *Each language has a different vowel system.* ⊃ see also

CARDINAL VOWEL **2** a letter that represents a vowel sound. In English the vowels are a, e, i, o, and u. ⊃ compare CONSONANT ⊃ see also DIPHTHONG

voy·age /ˈvɔɪɪdʒ/ *noun, verb*
- *noun* a long journey, especially by ocean or in space: *an around-the-world voyage* ◆ *a voyage in space* ◆ *The Titanic sank on its **maiden voyage*** (= first journey). ◆ (*figurative*) *Going to college can be a voyage of self-discovery.*
- *verb* [I] + adv./prep. (*literary*) to travel, especially in a ship and over a long distance

voy·ag·er /ˈvɔɪɪdʒər/ *noun* (*old-fashioned* or *literary*) a person who goes on a long journey, especially by ship to unknown parts of the world

vo·yeur /vɔɪˈɜr; vwaˈjɜr/ *noun* (*disapproving*) **1** a person who gets pleasure from secretly watching other people have sex **2** a person who enjoys watching the problems and private lives of others ▶ **vo·yeur·ism** /ˈvɔɪɜrɪzəm; ˈvɔɪəˌrɪzəm/ *noun* [U] **voy·eur·is·tic** /ˌvɔɪəˈrɪstɪk/ *adj.*: *a voyeuristic interest in other people's lives*

VP /ˌviˈpi/ *abbr.* VICE PRESIDENT

VR /ˌviˈɑr/ *abbr.* VIRTUAL REALITY

vroom /vrum; vrʊm/ *noun* [U] used to represent the loud sound made by a vehicle moving very fast: *Vroom! A sports car roared past.*

vs. *abbr.* VERSUS

ˈV-sign *noun* a sign that you make to mean "victory" by holding up your hand and making a V-shape with your first and second fingers, with the inside part of your hand facing out

VT *abbr.* (in writing) Vermont

VTOL /ˈvitɒl; -tɑl/ *abbr.* vertical takeoff and landing (used to refer to an aircraft that can take off and land by going straight up or straight down)

vul·can·ized /ˈvʌlkəˌnaɪzd/ *adj.* (*technical*) (of rubber) treated with SULFUR at great heat to make it stronger

vul·can·ol·o·gy /ˌvʌlkəˈnɑlədʒi/ *noun* [U] = VOLCANOLOGY

vul·gar /ˈvʌlgər/ *adj.* **1** not having or showing good taste; not polite, elegant, or well behaved **SYN** COARSE, TASTE: *a vulgar man* ◆ *vulgar decorations* ◆ *She found their laughter and noisy games coarse and rather vulgar.* **2** rude and likely to offend, especially because it is connected with sex or bodily functions **SYN** CRUDE: *vulgar jokes* **3** (*old use*) connected with or characteristic of the ordinary people in society, usually people who are not educated: *the vulgar speech of ancient Rome* ▶ **vul·gar·ly** *adv.*: *He eyed her vulgarly.*

vul·gar·i·an /vʌlˈɡeriən/ *noun* (*formal*) a person who does not have polite manners or good taste

vul·gar·ism /ˈvʌlɡəˌrɪzəm/ *noun* (*formal*) a rude word or expression, especially one relating to sex

vul·gar·i·ty /vʌlˈɡɛrəti/ *noun* (*pl.* **vul·gar·i·ties**) [U, C] the fact of being rude or not having good taste; a rude object, picture, etc.: *She was offended by the vulgarity of their jokes.* ◆ *a pornographic magazine full of vulgarities*

vul·gar·ize /ˈvʌlɡəˌraɪz/ *verb* ~ sth (*formal, disapproving*) to spoil something by changing it so that it is more ordinary than before and not of such a high standard ▶ **vul·gar·i·za·tion** /ˌvʌlɡərəˈzeɪʃn/ *noun* [U]

ˌvulgar ˈLatin *noun* [U] the spoken form of Latin which was used in the western part of the Roman Empire

the ˈVul·gate /ˈvʌlɡeɪt; -ɡət/ *noun* [sing.] the main Latin version of the Bible prepared in the late 4th century

vul·ner·a·ble /ˈvʌlnərəbl/ *adj.* ~ (to sb/sth) weak and easily hurt physically or emotionally: *to be vulnerable to attack* ◆ *She looked very vulnerable standing there on her own.* ◆ *In cases of food poisoning, young children are especially vulnerable.* ◆ *The sudden resignation of the financial director put the company in a very **vulnerable position.*** ▶ **vul·ner·a·bil·i·ty** /ˌvʌlnərəˈbɪləti/ *noun* [U]: ~ (of sb/sth) (to sth) *financial vulnerability* ◆ *the vulnerability of newborn babies to disease* **vul·ner·a·bly** /ˈvʌlnərəbli/ *adv.*

vul·pine /ˈvʌlpaɪn/ *adj.* (*formal*) of or like a FOX

vul·ture /ˈvʌltʃər/ *noun* **1** a large bird, usually without feathers on its head or neck, that eats the flesh of animals that are already dead: *vultures circling/wheeling overhead* ⊃ picture at ANIMAL **2** a person who hopes to gain from the troubles or sufferings of other people

vul·va /ˈvʌlvə/ *noun* (*anatomy*) the outer opening of the female sex organs

vy·ing *pres part of* VIE

Ww

W /'dʌbl,yu; -yə/ *noun, abbr.*

● **noun** also **w** [C, U] (*pl.* **Ws, W's, w's** /-yuz; -yəz/) the 23rd letter of the English alphabet: *"Water" begins with (a) W/"W."*

● **abbr.** (in writing) **1** usually **W.** west; western **2** WATT: *a 100W light bulb*

W-2 form /,dʌblyu 'tu fɔrm; ,dʌblyə-/ *noun* an official document that an employer gives to an employee that shows the amount of pay and tax for the year

WA *abbr.* (in writing) Washington

wack /wæk/ *adj.* (*informal*) **1** very bad; not of good quality: *That movie was really wack.* **2** (also **whack, whacked**) very strange

wack·o /'wækoʊ/ *adj., noun* (*informal*)
● **adj.** crazy; not sensible: *wacko opinions*
● **noun** (*pl.* **wack·os** or **wack·oes**) a crazy person

wack·y /'wæki/ *adj.* (**wack·i·er, wack·i·est**) (*informal*) funny or amusing in a slightly crazy way SYN ZANY: *wacky ideas* ◆ *Some of his friends are pretty wild and wacky characters.*

wad /wad/ *noun, verb*
● **noun 1** a thick pile of pieces of paper, paper money, etc. folded or rolled together: *He pulled a thick wad of $20 bills out of his pocket.* **2** a mass of soft material, used for blocking something or keeping something in place: *The nurse used a wad of gauze to stop the bleeding.* IDM see SHOOT *v.*
● **verb** (**-dd-**) **1 ~ sth (up)** to fold or press something into a tight wad **2 ~ sth** to fill something with soft material for warmth or protection

wad·ding /'wadɪŋ/ *noun* [U] soft material that you wrap around things to protect them

wad·dle /'wadl/ *verb* [I] (**+ adv./prep.**) to walk with short steps, swinging from side to side, like a DUCK ▶ **waddle** *noun* [sing.]: *She walked with a waddle.*

wade /weɪd/ *verb* **1** [I, T] to walk with an effort through something, especially water or mud: (**+ adv./prep.**) *He waded into the water to push the boat out.* ◆ *Sometimes they had to wade waist-deep through mud.* ◆ *They waded the river at a shallow point.* **2** [I] to walk or stand with no shoes or socks in shallow water in the ocean, a lake, etc.
PHR V **wade 'in** | **wade 'into sth** (*informal*) to enter a fight, a discussion, or an argument in an aggressive or not very sensitive way: *The police waded into the crowd with batons.* ◆ *You shouldn't have waded in with all those unpleasant accusations.* **wade 'through sth** [no passive] to deal with or read something that is boring and takes a lot of time: *I spent the whole day wading through the paperwork on my desk.*

wad·er /'weɪdər/ *noun* **1** (also **wading bird**) [C] any of several different types of birds with long legs that feed in shallow water **2 waders** [pl.] long rubber boots that reach up to your THIGHS, that you wear for standing in water, especially when fishing: *a pair of waders*

wa·di /'wadi/ *noun* (in the Middle East and N. Africa) a valley or channel that is dry except when it rains

'wading ˌpool *noun* a shallow swimming pool for children to play in, especially a small plastic one that you fill with water

wa·fer /'weɪfər/ *noun* **1** a thin, crisp, light cookie, sometimes eaten with ice cream **2** a very thin round piece of special bread given by the priest during COMMUNION **3 ~ (of sth)** a very thin piece of something

ˌwafer-'thin *adj.* very thin ⊃ compare PAPER-THIN

waf·fle /'wafl/ *noun, verb*
● **noun** [C] a crisp flat cake with a pattern of squares on both sides, often eaten for breakfast with sweet sauce, etc. on

top: *a waffle iron* (= for making waffles with)
● **verb** [I] **~ (on/over sth)** (*informal*) to be unable to decide what to do about something or what you think about something: *The senator was accused of waffling on major issues.*

waft /waft; wæft/ *verb, noun*
● **verb** [I, T] to move, or make something move, gently through the air SYN DRIFT: **+ adv./prep.** *The sound of their voices wafted across the lake.* ◆ *Delicious smells wafted up from the kitchen.* ◆ **~ sth + adv./prep.** *The scent of the flowers was wafted along by the breeze.*
● **noun** (*formal*) a smell or a line of smoke carried through the air: *wafts of perfume/smoke*

wag /wæg/ *verb, noun*
● **verb** (**-gg-**) **1** [T, I] **~ (sth)** if a dog wags its tail, or its tail wags, its tail moves from side to side several times **2** [T] **~ sth** to shake your finger or your head from side to side or up and down, often as a sign of disapproval IDM see TAIL *n.*, TONGUE *n.*
● **noun 1** (*old-fashioned*) a person who enjoys making jokes SYN JOKER **2** a wagging movement

wage 🔑 /weɪdʒ/ *noun, verb*
● **noun** [sing.] also **wages** [pl.] a regular amount of money that you earn, usually every week, for work or services: *wages of $500 a week* ◆ *a weekly wage of $500* ◆ *wage cuts* ◆ *a wage increase of 3%* ◆ *wage demands/claims/settlements* ◆ *Wages are paid on Fridays.* ⊃ see also LIVING WAGE, MINIMUM WAGE ⊃ compare SALARY ⊃ thesaurus box at INCOME
● **verb** to begin and continue a war, a battle, etc.: **~ sth** *The rebels have waged a guerrilla war since 2007.* ◆ **~ sth against/on sb/sth** *He alleged that a press campaign was being waged against him.*

'wage ˌearner *noun* a person who earns money, especially a person who works for wages: *We have two wage earners in the family.*

wa·ger /'weɪdʒər/ *noun, verb*
● **noun** (*old-fashioned* or *formal*) an arrangement to risk money on the result of a particular event SYN BET
● **verb** (*old-fashioned* or *formal*) **1** [I, T] to bet money SYN BET: **~ on sth** *She always wagered on the underdog.* ◆ **~ sth (on sth)** *to wager $50 on a horse* ◆ **~ sth/sb that…** *I had wagered a great deal of money that I would beat him.* **2** [T] **~ (that)…** used to say that you are so confident that something is true or will happen that you would be willing to bet money on it SYN BET: *I'll wager that she knows more about it than she's saying.*

wag·ish /'wægɪʃ/ *adj.* (*old-fashioned*) funny, smart, and not serious: *waggish remarks*

wag·gle /'wægl/ *verb* [T, I] **~ (sth)** (*informal*) to make something move with short movements from side to side or up and down; to move in this way: *Can you waggle your ears?* ▶ **waggle** *noun*

Wag·ne·ri·an /vɑɡ'nɪriən/ *adj.* **1** related to the music of the German COMPOSER Richard Wagner; typical of this music **2** (*humorous*) very big or great, or in a style that is too serious or exaggerated: *a hangover of Wagnerian proportions*

wag·on /'wægən/ *noun* **1** a small vehicle with wheels that can be pulled or pulled along and is used for carrying things **2** a vehicle with four wheels, pulled by horses or OXEN and used for carrying heavy loads ⊃ see also BAND-WAGON, CHUCK WAGON **3** = STATION WAGON
IDM **be/go on the wagon** (*informal*) to not drink alcohol, either for a short time or permanently **fall off the wagon** (*informal*) to start drinking alcohol again after stopping

wag·on·load /'wægən,loʊd/ *noun* an amount of goods carried on a wagon

'wagon ˌtrain *noun* a long line of WAGONS and horses, used by people traveling west in N. America in the 19th century

wah-wah /'wa wa/ *noun* [U] (*music*) a special effect made on electric musical instruments, especially the GUITAR, which varies the quality of the sound

waif /weɪf/ *noun* a small thin person, usually a child, who looks as if they do not have enough to eat: *the waifs and strays of our society* (= people with no home) ▶ **waif·like** *adj.*: *waiflike young girls*

wail /weɪl/ *verb, noun*
• *verb* **1** [I] to make a long, loud, high cry because you are sad or in pain: *The little girl was wailing miserably.* ◆ *women wailing and weeping* **2** [T, I] to cry or complain about something in a loud high voice **SYN** MOAN: + speech *"It's broken," she wailed.* ◆ ~ **(about sth)** *There's no point in wailing about something that happened so long ago.* **3** [I] (of things) to make a long high sound: *Ambulances raced by with sirens wailing.* ▶ **wail·ing** *noun* [sing., U]: *a high-pitched wailing*
• *noun* a long, loud, high cry expressing pain or sadness; a sound similar to this **SYN** MOAN: *a wail of despair* ◆ *the distant wail of sirens*

wain·scot·ing (also **wain·scot·ting**) /ˈweɪnˌskɔtɪŋ; -ˌskoʊtɪŋ/ *noun* wood that is attached along the lower part of the walls in a house

waist /weɪst/ *noun*
1 the area around the middle of the body between the RIBS and the hips, often narrower than the areas above and below: *He put his arm around her waist.* ◆ *She was paralyzed from the waist down* (= in the area below her waist). ◆ *The workmen were stripped to the waist* (= wearing no clothes on the top half of their bodies). ⊃ picture at BODY ⊃ collocations at PHYSICAL **2** the part of a piece of clothing that covers the waist: *a skirt with an elasticized waist* **3** -waisted (in adjectives) having the type of waist mentioned: *a high-waisted dress*

waist·band /ˈweɪstbænd/ *noun* the strip of cloth that forms the waist of a piece of clothing, especially at the top of a skirt or pants: *an elasticized waistband*

waist·coat /ˈwɛskət; ˈweɪskoʊt/ *noun* = VEST

waist-ˈdeep *adj., adv.* up to the waist: *The water was waist-deep.* ◆ *We waded waist-deep into the muddy water.*

waist-ˈhigh *adj., adv.* high enough to reach the waist: *waist-high grass* ◆ *The grass had grown waist-high.*

waist·line /ˈweɪstlaɪn/ *noun* **1** the amount that a person measures around the waist, used to talk about how fat or thin they are: *an expanding waistline* **2** the place on a piece of clothing where your waist is **SYN** WAIST

wait /weɪt/ *verb, noun*
• *verb* **1** [I, T] to stay where you are or delay doing something until someone or something comes or something happens: *She rang the bell and waited.* ◆ + adv./prep. *Have you been waiting long?* ◆ *I've been waiting (for) twenty minutes.* ◆ *I'll wait outside until the meeting's over.* ◆ ~ **for sb/sth** *Wait for me!* ◆ ~ **for sb/sth to do sth** *We're waiting for the rain to stop before we go out.* ◆ ~ **to do sth** *Hurry up! We're waiting to go.* ◆ ~ **your turn** *You'll just have to wait your turn* (= wait until your turn comes). **2** [I, T] to hope or watch for something to happen, especially for a long time: ~ **(for sth)** *This is just the opportunity I've been waiting for.* ◆ ~ **for sb/sth to do sth** *He's waiting for me to make a mistake.* **3** be waiting [I] (of things) to be ready for someone to have or use: ~ **(for sb)** *There's a letter waiting for you at home.* ◆ ~ **to do sth** *The hotel had a taxi waiting to pick us up.* **4** [I] to be left to be dealt with at a later time because it is not urgent: *I've got some calls to make but they can wait until tomorrow.*
IDM **an accident/a disaster waiting to happen** a thing or person that is very likely to cause danger or a problem in the future because of the condition it is in or the way they behave **I, they, etc. can't wait/can hardly wait** used when you are emphasizing that someone is very excited about something or keen to do it: *The children can't wait for Christmas to come.* ◆ *I can hardly wait to see him again.* **keep sb waiting** to make someone have to wait or be delayed, especially because you arrive late: *I'm sorry to have kept you waiting.* **wait and see** used to tell someone that they must be patient and wait to find out about something later: *We'll just have to wait and see — there's nothing we can do at the moment.* ◆ *a wait-and-see policy* ◆ *"Where are we going?" "Wait and see!"* **wait a minute/moment/second 1** to wait for a short time: *Can you wait a second while I make a call?* **2** used when you have just noticed or remembered something, or had a sudden idea: *Wait a minute — this isn't the right key.* **wait on sb hand and foot** (*disapproving*) to take care of someone's needs so well that they do not have to do anything for themselves **wait tables** to work serving food to people in a restaurant **wait till/until…** (*informal*) used to show that you are very excited about telling or showing something to someone: *Wait till you see what I found!* **what are we waiting for?** (*informal*) used to suggest that you should all start doing what you have been discussing **what are you waiting for?** (*informal*) used to tell someone to do something now rather than later: *If the car needs to be cleaned, what are you waiting for?* **(just) you wait** used to emphasize a threat, warning, or promise: *I'll be famous one day, just you wait!* ⊃ more at DUST *n.*, WING *n.*
PHR V **wait aˈround** to stay in a place, with nothing particular to do, for example because you are expecting something to happen or someone to arrive **ˈwait on sb** to act as a servant to someone, especially by serving food to them **ˈwait on sth/sb** (*informal*) to wait for something to happen before you do or decide something: *She is waiting on the results of a blood test.* **ˌwait sth↔ˈout** to wait until an unpleasant event has finished: *We sheltered in a doorway to wait out the storm.* **ˌwait ˈup** used to ask someone to stop or go more slowly so that you can join them **wait ˈup (for sb)** to wait for someone to come home at night before you go to bed
• *noun* [usually sing.] ~ **(for sb/sth)** an act of waiting; an amount of time waited: *We had a long wait for the bus.* ◆ *He now faces an agonizing two-month wait for the test results.*
IDM see LIE¹

wait·er /ˈweɪtər/ (*feminine* **wait·ress**) *noun* a person whose job is to serve customers at their tables in a restaurant, etc.: *I'll ask the waitress for the bill.* ⊃ see also DUMB WAITER, SERVER ⊃ note at GENDER

wait·ing /ˈweɪtɪŋ/ *noun* [U] **1** the fact of staying where you are or delaying doing something until someone or something comes or something happens **2** the fact of working as a waiter or waitress ⊃ see also WAITRESSING

ˈwaiting ˌgame *noun* [sing.] a policy of waiting to see how a situation develops before you decide how to act

ˈwaiting ˌlist (also **ˈwait list**) *noun* a list of people who are waiting for something such as a service that is not yet available: *There are no places available right now, but I'll put you on the waiting list.* ◆ *There's a waiting list to join the golf club.*

ˈwaiting ˌroom *noun* a room where people can sit while they are waiting, for example for a bus or train, or to see a doctor or dentist

ˈwait list *noun* = WAITING LIST: *She was on a wait list for a liver transplant.*

ˈwait-list *verb* ~ **sb** to put someone's name on a WAITING LIST: *He's been wait-listed for admission to Stanford.*

wait·per·son /ˈweɪtˌpərsn/ *noun* (*pl.* **wait·per·sons**) a person whose job is to serve customers at their tables in a restaurant, etc.

wait·ress /ˈweɪtrəs/ *noun* ⊃ WAITER ⊃ see also COCKTAIL WAITRESS

wait·ress·ing /ˈweɪtrəsɪŋ/ *noun* [U] the job of being a waitress: *I did some waitressing when I was a student.*

wait·staff /ˈweɪtstæf/ *noun* [U] the people whose job is to serve customers at their tables in a restaurant, etc.

waive /weɪv/ *verb* ~ **sth** to choose not to demand something in a particular case, even though you have a legal or official right to do so **SYN** FORGO

waiv·er /ˈweɪvər/ *noun* (*law*) a situation in which someone

ʌ cup   ə about   eɪ say   aɪ five   ɔɪ boy   aʊ now   oʊ go   ər bird

gives up a legal right or claim; an official document stating this

wake 🔊 /weɪk/ *verb, noun*

• **verb** (woke /woʊk/, wok·en /ˈwoʊkən/) **1** [I, T] to stop sleeping; to make someone stop sleeping: ~ **(up)** *What time do you usually wake up in the morning?* ◆ *I always wake early in the summer.* ◆ *Wake up! It's eight o'clock.* ◆ ~ **to sth** (*formal*) *They woke to a clear blue sky.* ◆ ~ **from** (*formal*) *She had just woken from a deep sleep.* ◆ ~ **to do sth** *He woke up to find himself alone in the house.* ◆ ~ **sb (up)** *Try not to wake the baby up.* ◆ *I was woken by the sound of someone moving around.* ⊃ note at AWAKE **2** [T] ~ **sth** (*literary* or *formal*) to make someone remember something or feel something again: *The incident woke memories of his past sufferings.*
IDM **wake up and smell the coffee** (*informal*) (usually in orders) used to tell someone to become aware of what is really happening in a situation, especially when this is something unpleasant
PHR V ,wake ˈup to become more lively and interested: *Wake up and listen!* ⊃ see also WAKE ,wake sb↔ˈup to make someone feel more lively: *A cold shower will wake you up.* ◆ *The class needs to wake up.* ⊃ see also WAKE v. (1) ,wake ˈup to sth to become aware of something; to realize something: *He hasn't yet woken up to the seriousness of the situation.*

• **noun 1** an occasion before or after a funeral when people gather to remember the dead person, traditionally held the night before the funeral to watch over the body before it is buried **2** the track that a boat or ship leaves behind on the surface of the water
IDM **in the wake of sb/sth** coming after or following someone or something: *There have been demonstrations on the streets in the wake of the recent bomb attack.* ◆ *A group of reporters followed in her wake.* ◆ *The storm left a trail of destruction in its wake.*

wake·board·ing /ˈweɪkˌbɔːrdɪŋ/ *noun* [U] the sport of riding on a short wide board called a **wakeboard** while being pulled along through the water by a fast boat ▶ **wake·board** *verb* [I]

wake·ful /ˈweɪkfl/ *adj.* (*formal*) **1** not sleeping; unable to sleep **SYN** SLEEPLESS: *He lay wakeful all night.* **2** (of a period at night) spent with little or no sleep **SYN** SLEEPLESS: *She had spent many wakeful nights worrying about him.* ▶ **wake·ful·ness** *noun* [U].

wak·en /ˈweɪkən/ *verb* (*formal*) **1** [I, T] to wake, or make someone wake, from sleep: ~ **(up)** *The child had just wakened.* ◆ ~ **sb (up)** *I was wakened by a knock at the door.* ⊃ note at AWAKE **2** [T] ~ **sth** to make someone remember something or feel something again: *The dream wakened a forgotten memory.*

ˈwake-up ˌcall *noun* **1** a telephone call that you arrange to be made to you at a particular time, for example in a hotel, in order to wake you up: *I asked for a 6:30 a.m. wake-up call.* **2** an event that makes people realize that there is a problem that they need to do something about: *These riots should be a wake-up call for the government.*

wak·ing /ˈweɪkɪŋ/ *adj.* [only before noun] used to describe time when you are awake: *She spends all her waking hours caring for her mother.* ▶ **wak·ing** *noun* [U]: *the dreamlike state between waking and sleeping*

Wal·dorf sal·ad /ˌwɔːldɔːrf ˈsæləd/ *noun* [U, C] a salad made from apples, nuts, CELERY, and MAYONNAISE (= sauce made with egg and oil)

walk 🔊 /wɔːk/ *verb, noun*

• **verb 1** [I, T] to move or go somewhere by putting one foot in front of the other on the ground, but without running: *The baby is just learning to walk.* ◆ *"How did you get here?" "I walked."* ◆ + *adv./prep. He walked slowly away from her.* ◆ *The door opened and Jo walked in.* ◆ *She missed the bus and had to walk home.* ◆ *The school is within easy walking distance of the train station.* ◆ ~ **sth** *Children here walk several miles to school.* **2** [T] ~ **sb** + *adv./prep.* to go somewhere with someone on foot, especially in order to make sure they get there safely: *He always walked her home.* **3** [T] ~ **sth** + **adv./prep.** to take an animal for a walk; to make an animal walk somewhere: *They walk their dogs every day.* ⊃ thesaurus box at TAKE **4** [T] ~ **sth** to move a large or heavy object along the ground while walking with it: *He walked the bookcase to the other end of the room.* ◆ *We walked our bikes up the hill.* **5** [I, T] ~ **(sb)** (in baseball) to go to FIRST BASE after four PITCHES are thrown outside the STRIKE ZONE; to allow a BATTER to do this: *The pitcher walked the first batter in the fifth inning.* **6** [I] (*informal*) to disappear; to be taken away: *Lock up any valuables. Things in this office tend to walk (= be stolen).* **7** [I] (*literary*) (of a GHOST) to appear
IDM **run before you can walk** to do things that are difficult, without learning the basic skills first **walk a/the beat** (of police officers) to walk around the area that they are responsible for **walk free** to be allowed to leave court, etc., without receiving any punishment **walk it** (*informal*) to go somewhere on foot instead of in a vehicle **walk sb off their feet** (*informal*) to make someone walk so far or so fast that they are very tired **walk off the job** to stop working in order to go on strike **walk the plank** (in the past) to walk along a board placed over the side of a ship and fall into the ocean, as a punishment **walk the streets** to walk around the streets of a town or city: *Is it safe to walk the streets alone at night?* **walk tall** to feel proud and confident **walk the walk** (*informal, approving*) to act in a way that shows people you are really good at what you do, and not just good at talking about it: *You can talk the talk but can you walk the walk?* ⊃ more at AIR *n.*, AISLE, LINE *n.*, THIN *adj.*, TIGHTROPE
PHR V ,walk aˈway (from sb/sth) to leave a difficult situation or relationship, etc. instead of staying and trying to deal with it ,walk aˈway with sth (*informal*) to win or obtain something easily: *She walked away with the gold medal.* ,walk ˈin on sb/sth to enter a room when someone in there is doing something private and does not expect you ,walk ˈinto sth (*informal*) **1** to become involved in an unpleasant situation, especially because you were not sensible enough to avoid it: *I realized I'd walked into a trap.* **2** to succeed in getting a job very easily ,walk ˈinto sth/sb to crash into something or someone while you are walking, for example because you do not see them ,walk ˈoff to leave a person or place suddenly because you are angry or upset ,walk sth↔ˈoff **1** to go for a walk after a meal so that you feel less full: *We walked off a heavy Sunday lunch.* **2** to go for a walk in order to make yourself feel better: *Is your foot OK? Come on, let's walk it off.* ,walk ˈoff with sth (*informal*) **1** to win something easily **2** to take something that is not yours; to steal something ,walk ˈout (*informal*) (of workers) to stop working in order to go on strike ⊃ related noun WALKOUT ,walk ˈout (of sth) to leave a meeting, performance, etc. suddenly, especially in order to show your disapproval ,walk ˈout (on sb) (*informal*) to suddenly leave someone that you are having a relationship with and that you have a responsibility for **SYN** DESERT: *How could she walk out on her kids?* ,walk ˈout (on sth) (*informal*) to stop doing something that you have agreed to do before it is completed: *I never walk out on a job that's half done.* ,walk (all) ˈover sb (*informal*) **1** to treat someone badly, without considering them or their needs: *She'll always let him walk all over her.* **2** to defeat someone easily ⊃ related noun WALKOVER ,walk sb ˈthrough sth to help someone learn or become familiar with something, by showing them each stage of the process in turn: *She walked me through a demonstration of the software.* ⊃ related noun WALK-THROUGH ,walk ˈup (to sb/sth) to walk toward someone or something, especially in a confident way

• **noun 1** [C] a journey on foot, usually for pleasure or exercise: *Let's go for a walk.* ◆ *I like to take a walk in the evenings.* ◆ *She took the dog for a walk.* ◆ *He set out on the long walk home.* ◆ *The office is ten minutes' walk from here.* ◆ *a ten-minute walk* ◆ *It's only a short walk to the beach.* **2** [C] a path or route for walking, usually for pleasure; an organized event when people walk for pleasure: *a circular walk* ◆ *There are some interesting walks in the area.* ◆ *a guided walk around the farm* **3** [sing.] a way or style of walking; the act or speed of walking rather than running: *I recognized him by his walk.*

◆ *The horse slowed to a walk.* **4** [C] a SIDEWALK or PATH (1)
5 [C] (in baseball) a move by a BATTER to FIRST BASE after
four PITCHES are thrown outside the STRIKE ZONE: *He
pitched six innings, allowing one hit and one walk.*
IDM **a walk in the park** (*informal*) a thing that is very easy to
do or deal with: *The role isn't exactly a walk in the park.* **walk
of life** a person's job or position in society
SYN BACKGROUND: *She has friends from all walks of life.*
⊃ more at MEMORY LANE

VOCABULARY BUILDING

---

ways of walking

- **creep** *He could hear someone creeping around down-stairs.*
- **limp** *One player limped off the field with a twisted ankle.*
- **pace** *I found him in the corridor, nervously pacing up and down.*
- **pad** *She spent the morning padding around the house in her slippers.*
- **plod** *They wearily plodded home through the rain.*
- **shuffle** *The people waiting in line shuffled slowly forward.*
- **stagger** *They staggered out of the bar, completely drunk.*
- **stomp** *She stomped out of the room, slamming the door behind her.*
- **stroll** *Families were strolling around the park.*
- **tiptoe** *They tiptoed upstairs so they wouldn't wake up the baby.*
- **trudge** *We trudged up the hill.*

walk·a·thon /'wɔkəˌθɑn/ *noun* an event in which a lot of
people participate in a long-distance walk to raise money
for a charity: *an annual walkathon for breast cancer*

walk·er /'wɔkər/ *noun* **1** a person who walks, usually for
pleasure or exercise: *The coastal path is a popular route for
walkers.* **2 a fast, slow, etc. ~** a person who walks fast,
slow, etc. **3** a metal frame that people use to help them to
walk, for example people who are old or who have
something wrong with their legs: *He now needs a walker to
get around.* **4** a frame with wheels and a HARNESS for a
baby, which allows them to walk around a room, supported
by the frame

walk·ie-talk·ie /ˌwɔki 'tɔki/ *noun* (*informal*) a small radio
that you can carry with you and use to send or receive
messages

walk-in *adj.* [only before noun] **1** large enough to walk into:
a walk-in closet **2** not arranged in advance; where you do
not need to arrange a time in advance: *a walk-in interview* ◆ *a
walk-in clinic*

walk·ing /'wɔkɪŋ/ *noun, adj.*
● *noun* [U] **1** the activity of going for walks in the countryside for exercise or pleasure: *to go walking* ◆ *walking shoes*
⊃ see also POWER WALKING **2** the sport of walking a long
distance as fast as possible without running
● *adj.* [only before noun] (*informal*) used to describe a human
or living example of the thing mentioned: *She's a walking
dictionary* (= she knows a lot of words).

walking ˌpapers *noun* [pl.] (*informal*) the letter or notice
dismissing someone from a job: *She got her walking papers
on Friday.*

walking ˌstick *noun* **1** a stick that you carry and use as a
support when you are walking **2** a large insect with a long
thin body that looks like a stick

the ˌwalking ˈwounded *noun* [pl.] people who have been
injured in a battle or an accident but who are still able to
walk

Walk·man™ /'wɔkmən; -mæn/ *noun* (*pl.* **Walk·mans** /-mənz;
-mænz/) a type of PERSONAL STEREO

walk-on *adj.* **~ part/role** used to describe a very small part
in a play or movie, without any words to say

walk·out /'wɔkaʊt/ *noun* **1** a sudden strike by workers

2 the act of suddenly leaving a meeting as a protest against
something

walk·o·ver /'wɔkˌoʊvər/ *noun* an easy victory in a game or
competition

walk-through *noun* **1** an occasion when you practice a
performance, etc. without an audience being present **2** a
careful explanation of the details of a process **3** a written
guide that gives advice on how to play and complete a
computer game

walk-up *noun* a tall building with stairs but no elevator; an
office or a apartment in such a building

walk·way /'wɔkweɪ/ *noun* a passage or path for walking
along, often outside and raised above the ground

wall /wɔl/ *noun, verb*
● *noun* **1** a long, vertical, solid structure, made of stone,
brick, or concrete, that surrounds, divides, or protects an
area of land: *The fields were divided by stone walls.* ◆ *He sat on
the wall and watched the others playing.* ⊃ see also SEA
WALL **2** any of the vertical sides of a building or room: *I'm
going to paint the walls white and the ceiling pink.* ◆ *Hang the
picture on the wall opposite the window.* ◆ *She leaned against
the wall.* ⊃ picture at HOUSE ⊃ collocations at DECORATE
3 something that forms a barrier or stops you from making
progress: *The boat struck a solid wall of water.* ◆ *The
investigators were confronted by a wall of silence.* **4** the outer
layer of something hollow such as an organ of the body or a
cell of an animal or a plant: *the abdominal wall* ◆ *the wall of an
artery*
IDM **go to the wall** (*informal*) (of a company or an
organization) to fail because of lack of money **off the wall**
(*informal*) unusual and amusing; slightly crazy: *Some of his
ideas are really off the wall.* ◆ *off-the-wall ideas* **up the wall**
(*informal*) crazy or angry: *That noise is driving me up the wall.*
walls have ears (*saying*) used to warn people to be careful
what they say because other people may be listening **the
writing is on the wall | see the writing on the wall | the
handwriting on the wall** (*saying*) used when you are
describing a situation in which there are signs that
something is going to have problems or that it is going to
be a failure: *It is amazing that not one of them saw the writing
on the wall.* **ORIGIN** From the Bible story in which strange
writing appeared on a wall during a feast given by King
Belshazzar, predicting Belshazzar's death and the fall of his
city. ⊃ more at BACK *n.*, BOUNCE *v.*, BRICK *n.*, FLY *n.*, FOUR
number., HEAD *n.*, HIT *v.*,
● *verb* [usually passive] **~ sth** to surround an area, a town, etc.
with a wall or walls: *a walled city*
PHR V **wall sth↔'in** [usually passive] to surround something or someone with a wall or barrier **wall sth↔'off**
[usually passive] to separate one place or area from another
with a wall **wall sb↔'up** [usually passive] to keep someone
as a prisoner behind walls **wall sth↔'up** [usually passive]
to fill an opening with a wall, bricks, etc. so that you can no
longer use it

wal·la·by /'wɑləbi/ *noun* (*pl.* **wal·la·bies**) an Australian
animal like a small KANGAROO, that moves by jumping on
its strong back legs and keeps its young in a POUCH (= a
pocket of skin) on the front of the mother's body

wall ˌanchor *noun* a small plastic tube, closed at one end,
that you put into a wall to hold a screw

wall·board /'wɔlbɔrd/ *noun* [U] a building material used to
cover walls and ceilings, usually made of sheets of heavy
paper with GYPSUM between them ⊃ compare PLASTER-
BOARD

wall·chart /'wɔltʃɑrt/ *noun* a large piece of paper on which
there is information, fixed to a wall for people to look at

wall ˌcovering *noun* [U, C] WALLPAPER or cloth used to
decorate the walls in a room

wal·let /'wɑlət; 'wɔ-/ (also **bill·fold**) *noun*
a small, flat, folding case made of leather or plastic used for
keeping paper money and credit cards in ⊃ picture at BAG

wall·eye /ˈwɔlaɪ/ *pl.* **wall·eye**) (also **wall·eyed pike** /ˌwɔlaɪd ˈpaɪk/) *noun* a N. American FRESHWATER fish with large eyes

wall·flow·er /ˈwɔlˌflaʊər/ *noun* **1** a garden plant with yellow, orange, or red flowers with a sweet smell that appear in late spring **2** (*informal*) a person who does not dance at a party because they do not have someone to dance with or because they are too shy

wall·ing /ˈwɔlɪŋ/ *noun* [U] **1** material from which a wall is built: *stone walling* **2** the act or skill of building a wall or walls: *a firm that does paving and walling*

wall-ˌmounted *adj.* fixed onto a wall: *wall-mounted lights*

wal·lop /ˈwɑləp/ *noun, verb*
- *noun* [sing.] (*informal*) a heavy, powerful hit
- *verb* (*informal*) **1** ~ sb/sth to hit someone or something very hard **SYN** THUMP **2** ~ sb/sth to defeat someone completely in a contest, match, etc.: *We walloped them 6–0.*

wal·lop·ing /ˈwɑləpɪŋ/ *noun, adj.* (*informal*)
- *noun* [usually sing.] **1** a heavy defeat: *Our team got a real walloping last week.* **2** an act of hitting someone very hard several times, often as a punishment
- *adj.* [only before noun] very big: *They had to pay a walloping fine.*

wal·low /ˈwɑloʊ/ *verb, noun*
- *verb* **1** [I] ~ (in sth) (of large animals or people) to lie and roll about in water or mud, to keep cool or for pleasure: *hippos wallowing in the river* ◆ *He loves to wallow in a hot bath after a game.* **2** [I] ~ in sth (often *disapproving*) to enjoy something that causes you pleasure: *She wallowed in the luxury of the hotel.* ◆ *to wallow in despair/self-pity* (= to think about your unhappy feelings all the time and seem to be enjoying them)
- *noun* [sing.] an act of wallowing: *a wallow in nostalgia*

wall ˌpainting *noun* a picture painted straight onto the surface of a wall

wall·pa·per /ˈwɔlˌpeɪpər/ *noun, verb*
- *noun* [U] **1** thick paper, often with a pattern on it, used for covering the walls and ceiling of a room: *wallpaper paste* ◆ *a roll of wallpaper* ◆ *to hang wallpaper* ⊃ collocations at DECORATE **2** (*computing*) the background pattern or picture that you choose to have on the screen of your computer, cell phone, etc.
- *verb* (also **paper**) [T, I] ~ (sth) to put wallpaper onto the walls of a room

ˈWall Street *noun* [U] the financial center and STOCK EXCHANGE in New York City (used to refer to the business that is done there): *Share prices fell on Wall Street today.* ◆ *Wall Street responded quickly to the news.*

ˈwall tent *noun* a large tent with a roof and walls that do not slope much ⊃ compare A-FRAME TENT, DOME TENT

ˌwall-to-ˈwall *adj.* [only before noun] **1** covering the floor of a room completely: *wall-to-wall carpets/carpeting* **2** (*informal*) continuous; happening or existing all the time or everywhere: *wall-to-wall TV sports coverage*

wal·nut /ˈwɔlnʌt/ *noun* **1** [C] the light brown nut of the walnut tree that has a rough surface and a hard round shell in two halves ⊃ picture at NUT **2** (also **ˈwalnut tree**) [C] the tree on which walnuts grow **3** [U] the brown wood of the walnut tree, used in making furniture

wal·rus /ˈwɔlrəs; ˈwɑl-/ *noun* an animal like a large SEAL (= an ocean animal with thick fur, that eats fish and lives around coasts), that has two long outer teeth called TUSKS and lives in Arctic regions

ˌwalrus ˈmustache *noun* (*informal*) a long thick MUSTACHE that hangs down on each side of the mouth

Wal·ter Mit·ty /ˌwɔltər ˈmɪti/ *noun* a person who imagines that their life is full of excitement and adventures when it is in fact just ordinary **ORIGIN** From the name of the main character in James Thurber's story *The Secret Life of Walter Mitty.*

waltz /wɔlts/ *noun, verb*
- *noun* a dance in which two people dance together to a regular rhythm; a piece of music for this dance: *to dance a/ the waltz* ◆ *a Strauss waltz*
- *verb* **1** [I, T] to dance a waltz: (+ adv./prep.) *I watched them waltzing across the floor.* ◆ ~ sb + adv./prep. *He waltzed her around the room.* **2** [I] + adv./prep. (*informal*) to walk or go somewhere in a very confident way: *I don't like him waltzing into the house like he owns it.* **3** [I] ~ (through sth) to complete or achieve something without any difficulty: *The recruits have waltzed through their training.*
  PHR V ˌwaltz ˈoff (with sth/sb) (*informal*) to leave a place or person in a way that is annoying, often taking something that is not yours: *He just waltzed off with my umbrella!*

WAN /wæn/ *noun* (*pl.* **WANs**) (*computing*) the abbreviation for "wide area network" (a system in which computers in different places are connected, usually over a large area) ⊃ compare LAN

wan /wɑn/ *adj.* looking pale and weak: *his gray, wan face* ◆ *She gave me a wan smile* (= showing no energy or enthusiasm). ▶ **wan·ly** *adv.*: *He smiled wanly.*

wand /wɑnd/ *noun* **1** (also ˌmagic ˈwand) a straight thin stick that is held by someone when performing magic or magic tricks: *The fairy waved her wand and the table disappeared.* ◆ *You can't expect me to just wave a (magic) wand and make everything all right again.* **2** any object in the shape of a straight thin stick: *a mascara wand* ⊃ picture at MAKEUP

wan·der 🔑 /ˈwɑndər/ *verb, noun*
- *verb* **1** [I, T] to walk slowly around or to a place, often without any particular sense of purpose or direction: + adv./prep. *She wandered aimlessly around the streets.* ◆ *We wandered back toward the car.* ◆ ~ sth *The child was found wandering the streets alone.* **2** [I] to move away from the place where you should be or the people you are with **SYN** STRAY: ~ away/off *The child wandered off and got lost.* ◆ ~ from/off sth *They had wandered from the path into the woods.* **3** [I] (of a person's mind or thoughts) to stop being directed on something and to move without much control to other ideas, subjects, etc. **SYN** DRIFT: *It's easy to be distracted and let your attention wander.* ◆ *Try not to let your mind wander.* ◆ ~ away, back, to, etc. sth *Her thoughts wandered back to her youth.* **4** [I] (of a person's eyes) to move slowly from looking at one thing to looking at another thing or in other directions: *She let her gaze wander.* ◆ + adv./prep. *His eyes wandered toward the photographs on the wall.* **5** [I] (+ adv./prep.) (of a road or river) to curve instead of following a straight course: *The road wanders along through the hills.*
- *noun* [sing.] a short walk in or around a place, usually with no special purpose: *I went to the park and had a wander around.*

wan·der·er /ˈwɑndərər/ *noun* a person who keeps traveling from place to place with no permanent home

wan·der·ings /ˈwɑndərɪŋz/ *noun* [pl.] (*literary*) journeys from place to place, usually with no special purpose

wan·der·lust /ˈwɑndərˌlʌst/ *noun* [U] (from *German*) a strong desire to travel

wane /weɪn/ *verb, noun*
- *verb* **1** [I] to become gradually weaker or less important **SYN** DECREASE, FADE: *Her enthusiasm for the whole idea was waning rapidly.* **2** [I] (of the moon) to appear slightly smaller each day after being round and full **ANT** WAX *v.* **IDM** see WAX *v.*
- *noun* [sing.]
  IDM on the wane becoming smaller, less important, or less common **SYN** DECLINE: *Her popularity has been on the wane for some time.*

wan·gle /ˈwæŋɡl/ *verb* (*informal*) to get something that you want by persuading someone or by tricking them: ~ sth *She had wangled an invitation to the opening night.* ◆ *We should be able to wangle it so that you can start tomorrow.* ◆ *He managed to wangle his way into the class.* ◆ ~ sth from/out of

---

ν **v**oice   θ **th**in   ð **th**en   s **s**o   z **z**oo   ʃ **sh**e   ʒ vi**s**ion   x **Ch**anukah

sb *I'll try to wangle some money out of my parents.* ◆ **~ sb sth** *He had wangled her a seat on the plane.*

wan·na /'wɒnə; 'wɔnə; 'wʌnə/ *(informal, non-standard)* the written form of the word some people use to mean "want to" or "want a," which is not considered to be correct: *I wanna go.* ◆ *Wanna drink?* (= Do you want…) **HELP** You should not write this form, unless you are copying somebody's speech.

wan·na·be /'wɒnəbi; 'wɔnə-/ *noun (informal, disapproving)* a person who behaves, dresses, etc. like someone famous because they want to be like them

want 🔑 /want; wɔnt/ *verb, noun*

● *verb* (not usually used in the progressive tenses)
> **WISH 1** [T] to have a desire or a wish for something: **~ sth** *Do you want some more tea?* ◆ *She has always wanted a large family.* ◆ *All I want is the truth.* ◆ *Thanks for the present — it's just what I wanted.* ◆ *I can do whatever I want.* ◆ *The last thing I wanted was to upset you.* ◆ *The committee wants her as chairperson.* ◆ **~ (to do sth)** *What do you want to do tomorrow?* ◆ *"It's time you do your homework." "I don't want to!"* ◆ *There are two points that I wanted to make.* ◆ *I just wanted to know if everything was all right.* ◆ *(informal) You can come too, if you want.* ◆ **~ sb/sth to do sth** *Do you want me to help?* ◆ *We didn't want this to happen.* ◆ *I want it (to be) done as quickly as possible.* **HELP** Notice that you cannot say "want that…": *I want that you do it quickly.* When the infinitive is used after want, it must have to: *I want study in America.*: **~ sb/sth doing sth** *I don't want you coming home so late.* ◆ **~ sb/sth + adj.** *Do you want your coffee black or light?*
> **NEED 2** [T] *(informal)* to need something: **~ sth** *On these trails, you'll want a mountain bike.* **3** [T, usually passive] **~ sb (+ adv./prep.)** to need someone to be present in the place or for the purpose mentioned: *She is wanted immediately in the principal's office.* ◆ *Excuse me, you're wanted on the phone.* ⊃ see also WANTED
> **SHOULD 4** [T] **~ to do sth** *(informal)* used to give advice to someone, meaning "should": *If possible, you want to avoid alcohol.* ◆ *You don't want to do it like that.*
> **FEEL SEXUAL DESIRE 5** [T] **~ sb** to feel sexual desire for someone
> **LACK 6** [T] **~ sth** *(formal)* to lack something **SYN** BE SHORT OF: *He doesn't want courage.*
> **IDM** not want to know (about sth) *(informal)* to take no interest in something because you do not care about it or it is too much trouble: *I've tried to ask her advice, but she doesn't want to know* (= about my problems). ◆ *"How much was it?" "You don't want to know"* (= it is better if you don't know). what do you want? used to ask someone in a rude or angry way why they are there or what they want you to do ⊃ more at NONE *pron.*, PART *n.*, TRUCK *n.*, WASTE *v.*, WAY *n.*
> **PHRV** 'want for sth (especially in negative sentences) *(formal)* to lack something that you really need: *He made sure that his children will want for nothing* (= will have everything they need). want sth from/out of sth/sb to hope to get something from a particular experience or person: *I had to discover what I really wanted out of life.* ◆ *What do you want from me?* ˌwant 'in/'out *(informal)* to want to come in or out of a place: *The dog wants in.* ˌwant 'in/ˌinto sth *(informal)* to want to be involved in something: *He wants in on the deal.* ˌwant 'out | ˌwant 'out of sth *(informal)* to want to stop being involved in something: *Jenny was fed up. She wanted out.*

● *noun (formal)*
> **SOMETHING YOU NEED 1** [C, usually pl.] something that you need or want: *She spent her life pandering to the wants of her children.*
> **LACK 2** [U, sing.] **~ of sth** *(formal)* a situation in which there is not enough of something; a lack of something: *a want of adequate medical facilities*
> **BEING POOR 3** [U] *(formal)* the state of being poor, not having food, etc.: *Visitors to the slums were clearly shocked to see so many families living in want.*
> **IDM** for (the) want of sth because of a lack of something; because something is not available: *The project failed for*

want of financial backing. ◆ *We call our music "postmodern" for the want of a better word.* in want of sth *(formal)* needing something: *The present system is in want of a total review.* not for (the) want of doing sth used to say that if something is not successful, it is not because of a lack of effort: *If he doesn't manage to convince them, it won't be for want of trying.*

'**want ads** *noun* [pl.] = CLASSIFIED ADVERTISEMENTS

want·ed /'wɒntəd; 'wɔn-/ *adj.* being searched for by the police, in connection with a crime: *He is wanted by the police in connection with the deaths of two people.* ◆ *Italy's most wanted man*

want·ing /'wɒntɪŋ; 'wɔn-/ *adj.* [not before noun] *(formal)* **1 ~ (in/for sth)** not having enough of something **SYN** LACKING: *The students were certainly not wanting in enthusiasm.* **2 ~ (in sth)** not good enough: *This explanation is wanting in many respects.* ◆ *The new system was tried and found wanting.*

wan·ton /'wɒntən; 'wɔn-/ *adj. (formal)* **1** [usually before noun] causing harm or damage deliberately and for no acceptable reason: *wanton destruction* ◆ *a wanton disregard for human life* **2** *(old-fashioned, disapproving)* (usually of a woman) behaving in a very immoral way; having many sexual partners ▶ **wan·ton·ly** *adv.* **wan·ton·ness** *noun* [U]

WAP /wæp/ *abbr.* wireless application protocol (a technology that links devices such as cell phones to the Internet): *a WAP-enabled phone*

wap·i·ti /'wɒpəti/ *noun (pl. wap·i·ti)* = ELK (1)

fighting

- **join/serve** in the Army/Navy/Air Force/Marines/ Coast Guard/reserves
- **be/go/remain/serve** on active duty
- **do/complete/return from** a tour of duty
- **be sent to the front** (line)
- **attack/strike/engage/defeat/kill/destroy** the enemy
- **witness/see/report/be engaged in** heavy fighting
- **call for/be met with** armed resistance
- **come under** heavy/machine-gun/mortar fire
- **fire** a machine gun/mortar shells/rockets (at sb/sth)
- **shoot** a rifle/a pistol/bullets/missiles
- **launch/fire** a(n) cruise/ballistic/anti-tank missile
- **use** biological/chemical/nuclear weapons
- **inflict/suffer/sustain** heavy losses/casualties
- **be hit/killed by** enemy/friendly/artillery fire
- **become/be held as/be taken as** a prisoner of war

civilians in war

- **harm/kill/target/protect** innocent/unarmed civilians
- **cause/avoid/limit/minimize** civilian casualties/ collateral damage
- **impose/enforce/lift** a curfew
- **engage in/be a victim of** ethnic cleansing
- **be sent to** a concentration/an internment camp
- **accept/house/resettle/turn away** refugees fleeing from war
- **fear/threaten** military/violent reprisals
- **commit/be accused of** war crimes/crimes against humanity/genocide

making peace

- **make/bring/win/achieve/maintain/promote** peace
- **call for/negotiate/broker/declare** a ceasefire/a temporary truce
- **sign** a ceasefire agreement
- **call for/bring/put an end to** hostilities
- **demand/negotiate/accept** the surrender of sb/sth
- **establish/send (in)** a peacekeeping force
- **negotiate/conclude/ratify/sign/accept/reject/ break/violate** a peace treaty

war 🔧 /wɔr/ *noun*

1 [U, C] a situation in which two or more countries or groups of people fight against each other over a period of time: *World War II* ◆ *the threat of (a) nuclear war* ◆ *to* **win/lose** *a/the war* ◆ *the war* **between** *England and the American Colonies* ◆ *England's war* **with/against** *the American Colonies* ◆ *It was the year Britain* **declared war on** *Germany.* ◆ *Social and political problems led to* **the outbreak** (= the beginning) *of war.* ◆ *Where were you living when war* **broke out**? ◆ *The government does not want to* **go to war** (= start a war) *unless all other alternatives have failed.* ◆ *How long have they been* **at war**? ◆ *a* **war hero** ◆ (*formal*) *The Greeks* **waged war** *on Troy for ten years.* ◆ *More troops are being dispatched to the* **war zone**. ◆ (*formal*) *the* **theater of war** (= the area in which fighting takes place) ⊃ *see also* CIVIL WAR, COLD WAR, POSTWAR, PRISONER OF WAR, WARRING, WORLD WAR **2** [C, U] a situation in which there is aggressive competition between groups, companies, countries, etc.: *the class war* ◆ *a trade war* ⊃ *see also* PRICE WAR **3** [U, sing.] ~ **(against/on sb/sth)** a fight or an effort over a long period of time to get rid of or stop something unpleasant: *The government* **has declared war on** *drug dealers.* ◆ *We seem to be winning the war against crime.* ⊃ **thesaurus box at** CAMPAIGN

IDM **a war of nerves** an attempt to defeat your opponents by putting pressure on them so that they lose courage or confidence **a war of words** a bitter argument or disagreement over a period of time between two or more people or groups: *the political war of words over tax* ⊃ **more at** FAIR *adj.*, MEAN *v.*

war·ble /'wɔrbl/ *verb* **1** [T, I] ~ **(sth)** | + **speech** (*humorous*) to sing, especially in a high voice that is not very steady: *He warbled his way through the song.* **2** [I, T] ~ **(sth)** (of a bird) to sing with rapidly changing notes ▶ **war·ble** *noun*

war·bler /'wɔrblər/ *noun* a small bird. There are many types of warblers, some of which have a musical call.

'war bride *noun* a woman who meets a soldier during a war and marries him: *My mother, a war bride, came to the U.S. from Italy in 1946.*

war·chalk·ing /'wɔrˌtʃɔkɪŋ/ *noun* [U] (*informal*) the action of drawing a symbol on the wall of a building to show that you can get a free Internet connection near that place

'war chest *noun* an amount of money that a government or an organization has available to spend on a particular plan, project, etc.

'war crime *noun* a cruel act that is committed during a war and is against the international rules of war

'war ˌcriminal *noun* a person who has committed war crimes

'war cry *noun* a word or phrase that is shouted by people fighting in a battle in order to give themselves courage and to frighten the enemy

ward /wɔrd/ *noun, verb*
- *noun* **1** a separate room or area in a hospital for people with the same type of medical condition: *a maternity/ surgical/psychiatric/children's, etc. ward* ◆ *He worked as a nurse* **on the** *children's* **ward**. **2** one of the areas into which a city is divided for local government elections **3** (*law*) a person, especially a child, who is under the legal protection of a court or another person (called a GUARDIAN): *The child was made a* **ward of the court**.
- *verb*
 PHR V ˌward sb/sth↔'off to protect or defend yourself against danger, illness, attack, etc.: *to ward off criticism* ◆ *She put up her hands to ward him off.*

-ward /wɔrd/ (also *less frequent* **-wards**) *suffix* (in adjectives) in the direction of: *backward* ◆ *eastward* ◆ *homeward* ▶ **-ward** (also **-wards**) (in adverbs): *onward* ◆ *forward*

'war dance *noun* a dance that is performed by members of some peoples, for example before battle or to celebrate a victory

war·den /'wɔrdn/ *noun* **1** the person in charge of a prison **2** a person who is responsible for taking care of a particular place and making sure that the rules are obeyed: *a forest warden* ⊃ *see also* GAME WARDEN

ward·robe /'wɔrdroʊb/ *noun* **1** [usually sing.] the clothes that a person has: *everything you need for your summer wardrobe* ⊃ **collocations at** FASHION **2** a large piece of furniture like a cupboard for hanging clothes in **3** [usually sing.] the department in a theater or television company that takes care of the clothes that actors wear

'wardrobe ˌmistress, **'wardrobe ˌmaster** *noun* a person whose job is to take care of the clothes that the actors in a theater company, etc. wear on stage

ward·room /'wɔrdrum; -rʊm/ *noun* a room in a ship, especially a WARSHIP, where the officers live and eat

-wards /wɜrdz/ ⊃ -WARD

ward·ship /'wɔrdʃɪp/ *noun* [U] (*law*) the fact of a child being cared for by a GUARDIAN (= a person who is not his or her parent) or of being protected by a court ⊃ *see also* WARD *n.* (3)

ware /wɛr/ *noun* **1** [U] (in compounds) objects made of the material or in the way or place mentioned: *ceramic ware* ◆ *crystal ware* ⊃ *see also* EARTHENWARE, FLATWARE, GLASSWARE, SILVERWARE **2** [U] (in compounds) objects used for the purpose mentioned or in the room mentioned: *ovenware* ◆ *homewares* ⊃ *see also* KITCHENWARE, TABLEWARE **3** [U] (in compounds) computer equipment and programs ⊃ *see also* HARDWARE (1), SOFTWARE **4** wares [pl.] (*old-fashioned*) things that someone is selling, especially in the street or at a market: *He traveled from town to town selling his wares.*

ware·house /ˈwɛrhaʊs/ *noun* a building where large quantities of goods are stored, especially before they are sent to stores to be sold ⊃ **picture at** BUILDING

ˈwarehouse ˌclub (also **ˈwarehouse ˌstore**) *noun* a type of store that sells goods in large quantities at low prices and usually charges an annual membership fee

ware·hous·ing /ˈwɛrˌhaʊzɪŋ/ *noun* [U] the practice or business of storing things in a warehouse

war·fare /ˈwɔrfɛr/ *noun* [U] **1** the activity of fighting a war, especially using particular weapons or methods: *air/naval/guerrilla, etc. warfare* ◆ *countries engaged in warfare* ⊃ collocations at WAR ⊃ see also BIOLOGICAL WARFARE, CHEMICAL WARFARE, **2** the activity of competing in an aggressive way with another group, company, etc.: *class/gang warfare* ◆ *The debate soon degenerated into open warfare.* ⊃ see also PSYCHOLOGICAL WARFARE

war·fa·rin /ˈwɔrfərən/ *noun* [U] a substance that is used as a poison to kill RATS and also for people as a medicine to make the blood thinner, for example in the treatment of THROMBOSIS

ˈwar game *noun* **1** a practice battle that is used to test military plans and equipment **2** a game or activity in which imaginary battles are fought, for example by moving models of soldiers, ships, etc. around on a table, or on a computer

ˈwar ˌgaming *noun* [U] the activity of playing war games

war·head /ˈwɔrhɛd/ *noun* the EXPLOSIVE part of a MISSILE: *nuclear warheads*

war·horse /ˈwɔrhɔrs/ *noun* **1** (*informal*) an old soldier or politician who has a lot of experience **2** (in the past) a large horse used in battle

war·i·ly, war·i·ness ⊃ WARY

war·like /ˈwɔrlaɪk/ *adj.* (*formal*) **1** aggressive and wanting to fight SYN BELLIGERENT: *a warlike nation* **2** connected with fighting wars SYN MILITARY: *warlike preparations*

war·lock /ˈwɔrlak/ *noun* a man who is believed to have magic powers, especially evil ones

war·lord /ˈwɔrlɔrd/ *noun* (*disapproving*) the leader of a military group that is not official and that fights against other groups within a country or an area

warm 🔑 /wɔrm/ *adj., verb, noun, adv.*

● *adj.* (**warm·er, warm·est**)
▷ AT PLEASANT TEMPERATURE **1** at a fairly high temperature in a way that is pleasant, rather than being hot or cold: *a warm breeze* ◆ *Wash the blouse in warm soapy water.* ◆ *It's nice and warm in here.* ◆ *Are you warm enough?* ◆ *The children jumped up and down to keep warm.* ◆ *You'll be toasty warm in here.*
▷ CLOTHES/BUILDINGS **2** keeping you warm or staying warm in cold weather: *a warm pair of socks* ◆ *This sleeping bag is very warm.* ◆ *a warm house*
▷ FRIENDLY **3** showing enthusiasm and/or affection; friendly: *His smile was warm and friendly.* ◆ *The speaker was given a warm welcome/reception.* ◆ *Please send her my warmest congratulations.*
▷ COLORS **4** (of colors) containing red, orange, or yellow, which creates a pleasant, comfortable, and relaxed feeling or atmosphere: *The room was decorated in warm shades of red and orange.*
▷ IN GAME **5** [not before noun] used to say that someone has almost guessed the answer to something or that they have almost found someone or something that has been hidden: *Keep guessing — you're getting warmer.*
▶ **warm·ly** *adv.*: *They were warmly dressed in coats and scarves.* ◆ *The play was warmly received by the critics.* ⊃ see also WARMTH

● *verb*
▷ MAKE/BECOME WARM **1** [T, I] to make something or someone warm or warmer; to become warm or warmer: *~ sth/sb/yourself (up)* *I'll warm up some milk.* ◆ *Come in and warm yourself by the fire.* ◆ *The hot cocoa warmed and relaxed him.* ◆ *~ (up)* *As the climate warms (up) the ice caps will melt.*

▷ BECOME FRIENDLY **2** [I, T] *~ (sb)* to become more friendly, loving, etc.; to make someone feel or become more friendly, loving, etc. ⊃ see also GLOBAL WARMING, HOUSEWARMING IDM see DEATH
PHR V **ˌwarm ˈdown** to do gentle exercises to help your body relax after doing a particular sport or activity ⊃ related noun WARM-DOWN **ˈwarm to/toward sb** to begin to like someone: *I warmed to her immediately.* **ˈwarm to/toward sth** to become more interested in or enthusiastic about something: *The speaker was now warming to her theme.* **ˌwarm ˈup 1** to prepare for physical exercise or a performance by doing gentle exercises or practice ⊃ related noun WARM-UP **2** (of a machine, an engine, etc.) to run for a short time in order to reach the temperature at which it will operate well **ˌwarm ˈup** | **ˌwarm sb/sth↔ˈup** to become more lively or enthusiastic; to make someone or something more lively or enthusiastic: *The party soon warmed up.* **ˌwarm sth↔ˈup** to heat previously cooked food again for eating

● *adv.* (**warm·er, warm·est**) (*informal*) in a way that makes you feel warm SYN WARMLY: *Wrap up warm before you go outside!*

ˌwarm-ˈblooded *adj.* (of animals) having a warm blood temperature that does not change if the temperature around them changes ⊃ compare COLD-BLOODED, HOT-BLOODED

ˈwarm-down *noun* [usually sing.] a series of gentle exercises that you do to help your body relax after doing a particular sport or activity

ˌwarmed-ˈover *adj.* **1** warmed-over food has been cooked and heated again after getting cold: *warmed-over chicken and rice* **2** (*disapproving*) a **warmed-over** idea or product has been used too many times before and is no longer interesting or exciting: *There's not much drama in the warmed-over plot.*

warm·er /ˈwɔrmər/ *noun* (especially in compounds) a piece of clothing, a device, etc. that warms someone or something: *a plate warmer* ⊃ see also LEG WARMER

ˈwarm fuzzies /wɔrm ˈfʌziz/ *noun* [pl.] (*informal*) feelings of affection, comfort, and support, or things that give you these feelings: *The memories fill me with warm fuzzies.*

ˌwarm-ˈhearted *adj.* (of a person) kind, friendly, and sympathetic ⊃ compare COLD-HEARTED

warm·ing /ˈwɔrmɪŋ/ *noun* [U] the process of making something, or of becoming, warm or warmer: *atmospheric warming* ⊃ see also GLOBAL WARMING ▶ **warm·ing** *adj.*: *the warming rays of the sun* ◆ *a warming drink*

ˈwarming ˌpan *noun* a metal container with a long handle that, in the past, was filled with hot coals and used to warm beds

ˈwarming ˌtrend *noun* a period of time when the temperature increases in a particular region: *There is a warming trend over the past few decades.*

war·mon·ger /ˈwɔrˌmʌŋgər; -ˌmʌŋgər/ *noun* (*formal, disapproving*) a person, especially a politician or leader, who wants to start a war or encourages people to start a war ▶ **war·mon·ger·ing** *noun* [U] **war·mon·ger·ing** *adj.* [only before noun]

warmth 🔑 /wɔrmθ/ *noun* [U]
1 the state or quality of being warm, rather than hot or cold: *She felt the warmth of his arms around her.* ◆ *The animals huddled together for warmth.* ◆ *He led the child into the warmth and safety of the house.* **2** the state or quality of being enthusiastic and/or friendly: *They were touched by the warmth of the welcome.*

ˈwarm-up *noun* [usually sing.] **1** a short practice or a series of gentle exercises that you do to prepare yourself for doing a particular sport or activity: *warm-up exercises* **2** a short performance of music, comedy, etc. that is intended to prepare the audience for the main show: *a warm-up act*

ʌ **cup**   ə **about**   eɪ **say**   aɪ **five**   ɔɪ **boy**   aʊ **now**   oʊ **go**   ər **bird**

warn /wɔrn/ verb

1 [T, I] to tell someone about something, especially something dangerous or unpleasant that is likely to happen, so that they can avoid it: **~ sb** *I tried to warn him, but he wouldn't listen.* ♦ *If you're thinking of getting a dog, be warned — they take a lot of time and money.* ♦ **~ (sb) about/against sb/sth** *He warned us against pickpockets.* ♦ **~ (sb) of sth** *Police have warned of possible delays.* ♦ **~ (sb) that…** *She was warned that if she did it again she would lose her job.* ♦ **~ sb what, how, etc.…** *I had been warned what to expect.* ♦ **~ (sb) + speech** *"Beware of pickpockets," she warned (him).* **2** [I, T] to strongly advise someone to do or not to do something in order to avoid danger or punishment **SYN** ADVISE: **~ (sb) against/about sth** *The guidebook warns against walking alone at night.* ♦ **~ sb (to do sth)** *He warned Billy to keep away from his daughter.* **3** [T] **~ sb (for sth)** (in sports, etc.) to give someone an official warning after they have broken a rule: *The referee warned him for dangerous play.*

PHR V ,warn sb 'off (sth) **1** to tell someone to leave or stay away from a place or person, especially in a threatening way: *The farmer warned us off his land when we tried to camp there.* **2** to advise someone not to do something or to stop doing something: **~ doing sth** *We were warned off buying the house.*

warn·ing /'wɔrnɪŋ/ noun

1 [C, U] a statement, an event, etc. telling someone that something bad or unpleasant may happen in the future so that they can try to avoid it: *Doctors issued a warning against eating any fish caught in the river.* ♦ *to give someone fair/advance/adequate warning of something* ♦ *The bridge collapsed without (any) warning.* ♦ *Let me give you a word of warning.* ⊃ see also EARLY WARNING **2** [C] a statement telling someone that they will be punished if they continue to behave in a particular way **SYN** CAUTION: *to give someone a verbal/written/final warning* ▶ **warn·ing** adj. [only before noun]: *She had ignored the warning signs of trouble ahead.* ♦ *Police fired a number of warning shots.* ♦ *Warning bells began to ring* (= it was a sign that something was wrong) *when her letters were returned unopened.*

warp /wɔrp/ verb, noun

● verb **1** [I, T] **~ (sth)** to become, or make something become, twisted or bent out of its natural shape, for example because it has become too hot, too damp, etc.: *The window frames had begun to warp.* **2** [T] **~ sth** to influence someone so that they begin to behave in an unacceptable or shocking way: *His judgment was warped by prejudice.*

● noun the warp [sing.] (technical) the threads on a LOOM (= a machine used for making cloth) that other threads are passed over and under in order to make cloth ⊃ compare WEFT ⊃ see also TIME WARP

war·paint /'wɔrpeɪnt/ noun [U] **1** paint that some peoples, for example Native American peoples, put on their bodies and faces before fighting a battle **2** (informal, humorous) makeup, especially when it is thick or bright

war·path /'wɔrpæθ/ noun

IDM (be/go) on the warpath (informal) (to be) angry and wanting to fight or punish someone

warped /wɔrpt/ adj. **1** (disapproving) (of a person) having ideas that most people think are strange or unpleasant: *a warped mind* ♦ *a warped sense of humor* **2** bent or twisted and not in the normal shape

war·plane /'wɔrpleɪn/ noun a military plane that is designed for fighting in the air or dropping bombs

warp speed noun [sing.] (informal, humorous) a very fast speed **ORIGIN** From the television series *Star Trek*, in which a "warp drive" allowed space travel at speeds faster than the speed of light.

war·rant /'wɔrənt; 'wɑr-/ noun, verb

● noun **1** [C] a legal document that is signed by a judge and gives the police authority to do something: *an arrest warrant* ♦ **~ for sth** *They issued a warrant for her arrest.* ♦ **~ to do sth**

They had a warrant to search the house. ⊃ see also DEATH WARRANT, SEARCH WARRANT **2** [U] **~ (for sth/for doing sth)** (formal) (usually in negative sentences) an acceptable reason for doing something: *There is no warrant for such criticism.* **3** [C] **~ (for sth)** a document that gives you the right to receive money, services, etc.

● verb (formal) to make something necessary or appropriate in a particular situation **SYN** JUSTIFY: **~ sth** *Further investigation is clearly warranted.* ♦ **~ (sb/sth) doing sth** *The situation scarcely warrants their/them being dismissed.* ⊃ see also UNWARRANTED

IDM I/I'll warrant (you) (old-fashioned) used to tell someone that you are sure of something and that they can be sure of it too

'warrant ,officer noun a member of one of the middle ranks in the U.S. military: *Warrant Officer Gary Owen*

war·ran·ty /'wɔrənti; 'wɑr-/ noun (pl. war·ran·ties) [C, U] a written agreement in which a company selling something promises to repair or replace it if there is a problem within a particular period of time **SYN** GUARANTEE: *The television comes with a full two-year warranty.* ♦ *Is the car still under warranty?*

war·ren /'wɔrən; 'wɑr-/ noun = RABBIT WARREN: (figurative) *The office was a warren of small rooms and passages.*

war·ring /'wɔrɪŋ/ adj. [only before noun] involved in a war: *A cease-fire has been agreed by the country's three warring factions.*

war·ri·or /'wɔriər; 'wɑr-/ noun (formal) (especially in the past) a person who fights in a battle or war: *a warrior nation* (= whose people are skilled in fighting) ♦ *a Zulu warrior*

war·ship /'wɔrʃɪp/ noun a ship used in war

wart /wɔrt/ noun a small hard lump that grows on your skin and that is caused by a virus ⊃ see also PLANTAR WART

IDM warts and all (informal) including all the bad or unpleasant features of someone or something: *She still loves him, warts and all.*

wart·hog /'wɔrthɔg; -hɑg/ noun an African wild pig with two large outer teeth called TUSKS and lumps like warts on its face

war·time /'wɔrtaɪm/ noun [U] the period during which a country is fighting a war: *Different rules applied in wartime.* ▶ **war·time** adj. [only before noun]: *Meat was a luxury in wartime America.* ⊃ compare PEACETIME

'war-torn adj. [only before noun] a **war-torn** country or area is severely affected by the fighting that is taking place there

wart·y /'wɔrti/ adj. covered with WARTS

'war ,widow noun a woman whose husband was killed in a war

war·y /'wɛri/ adj. (comparative war·i·er, no superlative) careful when dealing with someone or something because you think that there may be a danger or problem **SYN** CAUTIOUS: **~ (of sb/sth)** *Be wary of strangers who offer you a ride.* ♦ **~ (of doing sth)** *She was wary of getting involved with him.* ♦ *He gave her a wary look.* ♦ *The police will need to keep a wary eye on this area of town* (= watch it carefully, in case there is trouble). ⊃ compare UNWARY ▶ **war·i·ly** /'wɛrəli/ adv.: *The cat eyed him warily.* **war·i·ness** /'wɛrinəs/ noun [U]: *feelings of wariness* ♦ *There was a wariness in her tone.*

'war zone noun a region in which a war is being fought

was /wəz; wʌz/ ⊃ BE

wa·sa·bi /wə'sɑbi/ noun [U] (from *Japanese*) a root vegetable with a strong taste like HORSERADISH, used in Japanese cooking, especially with raw fish

wash /wɑʃ; wɔʃ/ verb, noun

● verb **1** [T] to make something or someone clean using water and usually soap: **~ sth/sb** *These jeans need to be washed.* ♦ *to wash the car* ♦ *to wash your hands* ♦ *Wash the fruit thoroughly before eating.* ♦ **~ sth from sth** *She washed the blood from his face.* ♦ **~ sth/sb + adj.** *The beach had been* *washed clean by the tide.* ⊃ thesaurus box at CLEAN **2** [I, T] to make yourself clean using water and usually soap: *I washed and changed before going out.* ♦ **~ yourself** *She was no longer able to wash herself.* **3** [I] (**+ adv./prep.**) (of clothes, cloth, etc.) to be able to be washed without losing color or being damaged: *This sweater washes well.* **4** [I, T] (of water) to flow or carry something or someone in a particular direction: **+ adv./prep.** *Water washed over the deck.* ♦ **~ sth/sb + adv./prep.** *Pieces of the wreckage were washed ashore.* ♦ *He was washed overboard by a huge wave.*

IDM **wash your hands of sb/sth** to refuse to be responsible for or involved with someone or something: *When her son was arrested again she washed her hands of him.* **sth won't/doesn't wash (with sb)** used to say that someone's explanation, excuse, etc. is not valid or that you or someone else will not accept it: *That excuse simply won't wash with me.*
PHR V ˌwash sb/sth↔ˈaˈway (of water) to remove or carry someone or something away to another place: *Part of the path had been washed away by the sea.* ˌwash sth↔ˈdown (with sth) **1** to clean something large or a surface with a lot of water: *Wash down the walls before painting them.* **2** to drink something after, or at the same time as, eating something: *For lunch we had bread and cheese, washed down with beer.* ˌwash ˈoff to be removed from the surface of something or from clothes by washing: *Those grease stains won't wash off.* ˌwash sth↔ˈoff (sth) to remove something from the surface of something or from clothes by washing: *Wash that mud off your boots before you come in.* ˌwash ˈout (of a dirty mark) to be removed from clothes by washing: *These ink stains won't wash out.* ˌwash sth↔ˈout **1** to wash the inside of something to remove dirt, etc.: *to wash out empty bottles* **2** to remove a substance from something by washing: *Wash the dye out with shampoo.* **3** (of rain) to make a game, an event, etc. end early or prevent it from starting: *The game was completely washed out.* ⊃ related noun WASHOUT ˌwash ˈover sb **1** (also ˌwash ˈthrough sb) (*literary*) (of a feeling) to suddenly affect someone strongly, so that they are not aware of anything else: *Waves of nausea washed over him.* **2** to happen to or around someone without affecting them: *She manages to let criticism just wash over her.* ˌwash ˈup to wash your face and hands: *Go and get washed up.* ˌwash sth↔ˈup (of water) to carry something onto land: *The body was found washed up on a beach.*

• *noun* **1** [C] clothes that need to be cleaned, or clothes that have just been cleaned: *I'm doing a dark wash* (= washing all the dark clothes together). ♦ *Your shirt's in the wash* (= being washed or waiting to be washed). ♦ *My sweater shrank in the wash.* ♦ *Please put the wash in the dryer.* **2** [C] an act of cleaning something using water and usually soap: *My hair color shouldn't have faded so much after only two washes.* ⊃ see also CAR WASH **3** the wash [sing.] an area of water that has waves and is moving a lot, especially after a boat has moved through it; the sound made by this: *The dinghy was rocked by the wash of a passing ferry.* ♦ *They listened to the wash of waves on the beach.* **4** [C] a thin layer of a liquid, especially paint, that is put on a surface: *The walls were covered with a pale yellow wash.* ⊃ see also WHITEWASH **5** [C, U] a liquid containing soap, used for cleaning your skin: *an antiseptic skin wash* ⊃ see also MOUTHWASH **6** a wash (*informal*) a situation that stays the same because bad and good factors are equal: *Our earnings are up, but so are our costs, so it's a wash.*

IDM it will (all) come out in the wash (*informal*) **1** used to say that the truth about a situation will be made known at some time in the future **2** used to make someone less anxious by telling them that any problems or difficulties will be solved in the future

wash·a·ble /ˈwɑʃəbl; ˈwɔ-/ *adj.* that can be washed without being damaged: *machine washable* (= that can be washed in a washing machine)

wash·ba·sin /ˈwɑʃˌbeɪsn; ˈwɔʃ-/ *noun* a large bowl that can be filled with water and used for washing your hands and face in ⊃ see also SINK

wash·board /ˈwɑʃbɔrd; ˈwɔʃ-/ *noun* a board with a surface with RIDGES on it, used in the past for rubbing clothes on

when washing them; a similar board played as a musical instrument

wash·cloth /ˈwɑʃklɔθ; ˈwɔʃ-/ *noun* a small piece of cloth used for washing yourself

wash·day /ˈwɑʃdeɪ; ˈwɔʃ-/ (also ˈwashing ˌday) *noun* the day in someone's house when the clothes, etc. are washed, especially when this happens on the same day each week

ˌwashed ˈout *adj.* **1** (of cloth, clothes, or colors) no longer brightly colored, often as a result of frequent washing: *She didn't like jeans that looked too washed out.* ♦ *a pair of washed-out old jeans* ♦ *The walls were a washed-out blue color.* **2** (of a person) pale and tired **SYN** EXHAUSTED: *He always looks washed out at the end of the week.*

ˌwashed ˈup *adj.* (*informal*) no longer successful and unlikely to succeed again in the future: *In this game he needs to prove he isn't washed up.*

wash·er /ˈwɑʃər; ˈwɔ-/ *noun* **1** a small flat ring made of rubber, metal, or plastic placed between two surfaces, for example under a NUT to make a connection tight ⊃ picture at TOOL **2** (*informal*) a WASHING MACHINE ⊃ see also DISH-WASHER

ˌwasher-ˈdryer *noun* an electric machine that washes and dries clothes, etc.

wash·er·wom·an /ˈwɑʃərˌwumən; ˈwɔʃər-/ *noun* (*pl.* wash·er·wom·en /-ˌwɪmən/) a woman in the past whose job was to wash clothes, etc. for other people

wash·ing /ˈwɑʃɪŋ; ˈwɔ-/ *noun* [U] the act of cleaning something using water and usually soap: *a gentle shampoo for frequent washing*

ˈwashing ˌday *noun* = WASHDAY

ˈwashing ma·chine *noun* an electric machine for washing clothes

ˈwashing ˌsoda *noun* [U] = SODIUM CARBONATE

wash·out /ˈwɑʃaut; ˈwɔʃ-/ *noun* (*informal*) an event, etc. that is a complete failure, especially because of rain

wash·room /ˈwɑʃrum; ˈwɔʃ-; -rʊm/ *noun* (*especially CanE*) a bathroom, especially one that is in a public building

wash·stand /ˈwɑʃstænd; ˈwɔʃ-/ *noun* (especially in the past) a special table in a bedroom that holds a BASIN for washing yourself in

wash·tub /ˈwɑʃtʌb; ˈwɔʃ-/ *noun* (in the past) a large metal container for washing clothes, etc. in

was·n't /ˈwʌznt/ ⊃ BE

Wasp also **WASP** /wɑsp; wɔsp/ *noun* (usually *disapproving*) the abbreviation for "White Anglo-Saxon Protestant" (a white American whose family originally came from northern Europe and is therefore thought to be from the most powerful section of society): *a privileged WASP background*

wasp /wɑsp; wɔsp/ *noun* a black and yellow flying insect that can sting: *a wasp sting* ♦ *a wasps' nest* ⊃ picture at ANIMAL

wasp·ish /ˈwɑspɪʃ; ˈwɔs-/ *adj.* (*formal*) bad-tempered and unpleasant **SYN** IRRITABLE ▶ **wasp·ish·ly** *adv.*

was·sail /ˈwɑsl; -seɪl/ *verb* (old use) **1** [I] to enjoy yourself by drinking alcohol with others **2** [I] to go from house to house at Christmas time singing CAROLS ▶ **was·sail·er** *noun*

wast·age /ˈweɪstɪdʒ/ *noun* **1** [U, sing.] **~ (of sth)** the fact of losing or destroying something, especially because it has been used or dealt with carelessly: *It was a new production technique aimed at minimizing wastage.* **2** [U] the amount of something that is wasted: *There is little wastage from a lean cut of meat.*

waste /weɪst/ *verb, noun, adj.*

• *verb*

▸ NOT USE WELL **1** to use more of something than is necessary or useful: **~ sth** *to waste time/food/energy* ♦ **~ sth on sth** *Why waste money on clothes you don't need?* ♦ **~ sth (in) doing sth** *She wasted no time in rejecting the offer* (= she rejected it immediately). ◆ *You're **wasting your time** trying to explain it to him* (= because he will not understand). **2** ~ **sth (on sb/sth)** to give, say, use, etc. something good where it is not valued or used in the way that it should be: *Don't waste your sympathy on him — he got what he deserved.* ◆ *Her comments were not wasted on Chris* (= he understood what she meant). **3** [usually passive] to not make good or full use of someone or something: ~ **sb/sth** *It was a wasted opportunity.* ◆ ~ **sb/ sth as sth** *You're wasted as a sales manager — you should have been an actor.*

> KILL SOMEONE **4** ~ **sb** (*informal*) to get rid of someone, usually by killing them
> DEFEAT SOMEONE **5** ~ **sb** (*informal*) to defeat someone very easily in a game or competition

IDM waste your breath to say something that no one takes any notice of waste not, want not (*saying*) if you never waste anything, especially food or money, you will always have it when you need it

PHR V waste a'way (of a person) to become thin and weak, especially because of illness **SYN** BECOME EMACIATED

● *noun*
> NOT GOOD USE **1** [U, sing.] ~ **(of sth)** the act of using something in a careless or unnecessary way, causing it to be lost or destroyed: *I hate unnecessary waste.* ◆ *It seems such a waste to throw good food away.* ◆ *I hate to see good food go to waste* (= be thrown away). ◆ *The report is critical of the department's waste of resources.* ◆ *What a waste of paper!* **2** [sing.] a situation in which it is not worth spending time, money, etc. on something: *These meetings are a complete waste of time.* ◆ *They believe the statue is a waste of taxpayers' money.*
> MATERIALS **3** [U] also wastes [pl.] materials that are no longer needed and are thrown away: *household/industrial waste* ◆ *toxic wastes* ◆ **waste disposal** (= the process of getting rid of waste) **4** (also **waste 'matter**) [U] material that the body gets rid of as solid or liquid material: *The farmers use both animal and human waste as fertilizer.*
> LAND **5** wastes [pl.] (*formal*) a large area of land where there are very few people, animals, or plants: *the frozen wastes of Siberia*

IDM a waste of space (*informal*) a person who is useless or no good at anything

● *adj.* [usually before noun]
> LAND **1** not suitable for building or growing things on and therefore not used **SYN** DERELICT: *The car was found on a piece of waste ground.*
> MATERIALS **2** no longer needed for a particular process and therefore thrown away: *Waste water is pumped from the factory into a nearby river.*

IDM lay sth waste | lay waste (to) sth (*formal*) to destroy a place completely

waste·bas·ket /ˈweɪstˌbæskət/ (also **'wastepaper ˌbasket**) *noun* a BASKET or other container for waste paper, etc. ➔ picture at BASKET

wast·ed /ˈweɪstɪd/ *adj.* **1** [only before noun] (of an action) unsuccessful because it does not produce the result you wanted: *It was a wasted trip — the store was already closed.* **2** (*slang*) strongly affected by alcohol or drugs **3** too thin, especially because of illness: *thin, wasted legs*

waste·ful /ˈweɪstfl/ *adj.* using more of something than is necessary; not saving or keeping something that could be used: *The whole process is wasteful and inefficient.* ◆ ~ **of sth** *an engine that is wasteful of fuel* ▶ **waste·ful·ly** /-fəli/ *adv.* **waste·ful·ness** *noun* [U]

waste·land /ˈweɪstlænd/ *noun* [C, U] an area of land that cannot be used or that is no longer used for building or growing things on: *industrial wasteland* ◆ *the desert waste-lands of Arizona* ◆ (*figurative*) *The mid 1970s are seen as a cultural wasteland for rock music.*

'waste ˌpaper *noun* [U] paper that is not wanted and is thrown away

wastepaper basket /ˈweɪstpeɪpər ˌbæskət/ *noun* = WASTEBASKET

'waste ˌproduct *noun* a useless material or substance produced while making something else

wast·er /ˈweɪstər/ *noun* **1** (often in compounds) a person or thing that uses too much of something in an unnecessary way: *He's a time-waster.* **2** (*informal, disapproving*) a person who is useless or no good at anything

waste·wa·ter /ˈweɪstˌwɔtər; -ˌwɑtər/ *noun* [U] used water that contains waste substances from homes, factories, and farms: *municipal water and wastewater systems* ◆ *a wastewater treatment plant* ➔ compare SEWAGE

wast·ing /ˈweɪstɪŋ/ *adj.* a **wasting** disease or illness is one that causes someone to gradually become weaker and thinner

wast·rel /ˈweɪstrəl/ *noun* (*literary*) a lazy person who spends their time and/or money in a careless and stupid way

watch 🔑 /wɑtʃ/ *verb, noun*

● *verb* **1** [T, I] to look at someone or something for a time, paying attention to what happens: ~ **sb/sth** *to watch television/a football game* ◆ ~ **sth for sth** *He watched the house for signs of activity.* ◆ ~ **(for sth)** *He watched for signs of activity in the house.* ◆ *"Would you like to play?" "No thanks—I'll just watch."* ◆ *We watched to see what would happen next.* ◆ ~ **what, how, etc....** *Watch what I do, then you try.* ◆ ~ **sb/sth doing sth** *She watched the kids playing in the yard.* ◆ ~ **sb/sth do sth** *They watched the bus disappear into the distance.* ➔ thesaurus box at LOOK **2** [T] ~ **sb/sth (for sb)** to take care of someone or something for a short time: *Could you watch my bags for me while I buy a paper?* **3** [T] (*informal*) to be careful about something: ~ **sth/yourself** *Watch yourself* (= be careful, because you are in a dangerous situation)*!* ◆ *Watch your bag—there are thieves around.* ◆ *I have to watch every penny* (= be careful what I spend). ◆ *Watch your head on the low ceiling.* ◆ ~ **where, what, etc....** *Hey, watch where you're going!*

IDM watch the clock (*disapproving*) to be careful not to work longer than the required time; to think more about when your work will finish than about the work itself a watched pot never boils (*saying*) used to say that when you are impatient for something to happen, time seems to pass very slowly watch it (*informal*) used as a warning to someone to be careful watch your language/mouth/ tongue to be careful what you say in order not to offend someone or make them angry: *Watch your language, young man!* watch the time to be sure that you know what the time is, so that you finish something at the correct time, or are not late for something: *I'll have to watch the time. I need to leave early today.* watch this space (*informal*) used in orders, to tell someone to wait for more news about something to be announced: *I can't tell you any more right now, but watch this space.* watch your step **1** to walk carefully **2** to behave in a careful and sensible way watch the world go by to relax and watch people in a public place: *We sat outside a café, watching the world go by.*

PHR V 'watch for sb/sth to look and wait for someone or something to appear, or for something to happen: *The cat was on the wall, watching for birds.* ˌwatch 'out (*informal*) used to warn someone about something dangerous: *Watch out! There's a car coming!* ˌwatch 'out for sb/sth **1** to make an effort to be aware of what is happening, so that you will notice if anything bad or unusual happens: *The cashiers were asked to watch out for forged banknotes.* **2** to be careful of something: *Watch out for the stairs—they're steep.* ˌwatch 'over sb/sth (*formal*) to take care of someone or something; to guard and protect someone or something

● *noun* **1** [C] a type of small clock that you wear on your wrist, or (in the past) carried in your pocket: *She kept looking anxiously at her watch.* ◆ *My watch is fast/slow.* ➔ picture at CLOCK ➔ see also STOPWATCH, WRISTWATCH **2** [sing., U] the act of watching someone or something carefully in case of possible danger or problems: *The police have mounted a watch outside the hotel.* ◆ *I'll keep watch while you go through his papers* (= watch and warn you if someone is coming). ◆ *The government is keeping a close watch on how the situation develops.* ➔ see also NEIGHBORHOOD WATCH **3** [C, U] a fixed period of time, usually while other people are asleep, during which someone watches for any danger so that they can warn others, for example on a ship; the person or people who do this: *I'm on first watch.* ◆ *I go on watch in an hour.* ➔ see also NIGHT WATCHMAN

IDM **be on the watch (for sb/sth)** to be looking carefully for someone or something that you expect to see, especially in order to avoid possible danger: *Be on the watch for thieves.* ➔ more at CLOSE² *adj.*

watch·a·ble /'wɒtʃəbl/ *adj.* (*informal*) entertaining or pleasant to watch

watch·band /'wɒtʃbænd/ (also 'watch strap) *noun* a thin strip of leather, etc. for fastening your watch around your wrist

watch·dog /'wɒtʃdɔg; -dag/ *noun* a person or group of people whose job is to check that companies are not doing anything illegal or ignoring people's rights: *a consumer watchdog* ➔ compare GUARD DOG

watch·er /'wɒtʃər/ *noun* (often in compounds) a person who watches and studies someone or something regularly: *an industry/a market watcher* ➔ see also BIRDWATCHER, CLOCK-WATCHER

watch·ful /'wɒtʃfl/ *adj.* paying attention to what is happening in case of danger, accidents, etc.: *Her expression was watchful and alert.* ◆ *His mother kept a watchful eye on him.* ◆ *The children played under the watchful eye of their teacher.* ▶ **watch·ful·ly** /-fəli/ *adv.* **watch·ful·ness** *noun* [U]

watch·mak·er /'wɒtʃmeɪkər/ *noun* a person who makes and repairs watches and clocks as a job

watch·man /'wɒtʃmən/ *noun* (*pl.* **watch·men** /-mən/) (*old-fashioned*) a man whose job is to guard a building, for example a bank, an office building, or a factory, especially at night ➔ see also NIGHT WATCHMAN

'**watch strap** *noun* = WATCHBAND

watch·tow·er /'wɒtʃtaʊər/ *noun* a tall tower from which soldiers, etc. watch when they are guarding a place

watch·word /'wɒtʃwərd/ *noun* a word or phrase that expresses someone's beliefs or attitudes, or that explains what someone should do in a particular situation: *Quality is our watchword.*

wa·ter 🔑 /'wɒtər; 'wɑ-/ *noun, verb*

● *noun* **1** [U] a liquid without color, smell, or taste that falls as rain, is in lakes, rivers, and oceans, and is used for drinking, washing, etc.: *a glass of water* ◆ **drinking water** ◆ *water pollution* ◆ **clean/dirty water** ◆ *water shortages* ◆ *There is hot and cold running water in all the bedrooms.* ➔ see also BATHWATER **2** [U] an area of water, especially a lake, river, or ocean: *We walked down to the water's edge.* ◆ *She fell into the water.* ◆ **shallow/deep water** ◆ *In the lagoon the water was calm.* ➔ see also BACKWATER, BREAKWATER **3** waters [pl.] the water in a particular lake, river, or ocean: *the gray waters of the Mississippi* ◆ *This species is found in coastal waters around the Indian Ocean.* **4** [U] the surface of a mass of water: *She dived under the water.* ◆ *The leaves floated on the water.* ➔ see also UNDERWATER **5** waters [pl.] an area of ocean belonging to a particular country: *We were still in American waters.* ◆ *fishing in international waters* ➔ see also TERRITORIAL WATERS **6** waters [pl.] **murky, uncharted, stormy, dangerous, etc. ~** used to describe a situation, usually one that is difficult, dangerous, or not familiar: *The conversation got into the murky waters of jealousy and relationships.* ◆ *The government has warned of stormy waters ahead.* **HELP** There are many other compounds ending in **water.** You will find them at their place in the alphabet. **IDM** **by water** (*formal*) using a boat or ship **it's (all) water under the bridge** used to say that something happened in the past and is now forgotten or no longer important **like water** (*informal*) in large quantities: *He spends money like water.* **not hold water** (*informal*) if an argument, an excuse, a theory, etc. does not **hold water**, you cannot believe it **sb's water breaks** when a pregnant woman's **water breaks,** the liquid in her WOMB passes out of her body just

before the baby is born **(like) water off a duck's back** (*informal*) used to say that something, especially criticism, has no effect on someone or something: *I can't tell my son what to do; it's water off a duck's back with him.* ➔ more at BLOOD, BLOW, COLD, DEAD, DEEP, DIP, DUCK, FISH, HEAD, HELL, HORSE, HOT, MUDDY, PASS, STILL, TEST, TREAD

● *verb* **1** [T] **~ sth** to pour water on plants, etc.: *to water the plants/garden* **2** [I] (of the eyes) to become full of tears: *The smoke made my eyes water.* **3** [I] (of the mouth) to produce SALIVA: *The smells from the kitchen made our mouths water.* **4** [T] **~ sth** to give water to an animal to drink: *to water the horses* ◆ (*humorous*) *After a tour of the grounds, the guests were fed and watered.* **5** [T, usually passive] **~ sth** (*technical*) (of a river, etc.) to provide an area of land with water: *The valley is watered by a stream.* **6** [T] **~ sth** to add water to an alcoholic drink: *watered wine*

PHR V **water sth↔'down** **1** to make a liquid weaker by adding water **SYN** DILUTE **2** [usually passive] to change a speech, a piece of writing, etc. in order to make it less strong or offensive **SYN** DILUTE

the '**Water ˌBearer** *noun* [sing.] = AQUARIUS

wa·ter·bed /'wɒtərˌbɛd; 'wɑ-/ *noun* a bed with a rubber or plastic MATTRESS that is filled with water

wa·ter·bird /'wɒtərˌbərd; 'wɑ-/ *noun* a bird that lives near and walks or swims in water, especially rivers or lakes

wa·ter·board·ing /'wɒtərˌbɔrdɪŋ; 'wɑ-/ *noun* [U] a way of trying to force someone to give you information by pouring water onto their face while making them lie on their back, so that they feel as if they are DROWNING

wa·ter·borne /'wɒtərˌbɔrn; 'wɑ-/ *adj.* spread or carried by water: *cholera and other waterborne diseases* ◆ *waterborne goods* ➔ compare AIRBORNE

'**water ˌbuffalo** *noun* (*pl.* '**water ˌbuffalo** or '**water ˌbuffaloes**) a large Asian animal of the cow family, used for pulling vehicles and farm equipment in tropical countries

'**water ˌbug** (also **wa·ter·bug**) *noun* an insect that lives in or near water

'**water ˌcannon** *noun* a machine that produces a powerful flow of water, used by the police to control crowds of people

the '**Water ˌCarrier** *noun* [sing.] = AQUARIUS

'**water ˌchestnut** *noun* the thick, round, white root of a tropical plant that grows in water, often used in Chinese cooking

'**water ˌclock** *noun* (in the past) a clock that used the flow of water to measure time

'**water ˌcloset** *noun* (*abbr.* WC) (*old-fashioned*) a toilet

wa·ter·col·or (*CanE usually* **wa·ter·col·our**) /'wɒtərˌkʌlər; 'wɑ-/ *noun* **1** watercolors [pl.] paints that you mix with water, not oil, and use for painting pictures ➔ collocations at ART **2** [C] a picture painted with these paints

wa·ter·col·or·ist /'wɒtərˌkʌlərɪst; 'wɑ-/ *noun* a person who paints with watercolors

'**water-ˌcooled** *adj.* (of machines, etc.) cooled using water

'**water ˌcooler** *noun* **1** a machine, for example in an office, that cools water and supplies it for drinking **2** used when referring to a place where office workers talk in an informal way, for example near the water cooler: *It was a story they'd shared around the water cooler.*

wa·ter·course /'wɒtərˌkɔrs; 'wɑ-/ *noun* (*technical*) a stream or an artificial channel for water

wa·ter·cress /'wɒtərˌkrɛs; 'wɑ-/ *noun* [U] a water plant with small, round, green leaves and thin STEMS. It has a strong taste and is often eaten raw in salads.

ˌwatered-'down *adj.* **1** a watered-down speech, piece of writing, etc. is changed in order to make it less strong or offensive **2** a watered-down drink is made weaker by adding water

ˌwatered 'silk *noun* [U] a type of shiny silk cloth with a pattern on it that looks like water in waves

wa·ter·fall /ˈwɔtərˌfɔl; ˈwɑ-/ *noun* a place where a stream or river falls from a high place, for example over a CLIFF or rock

ˈwater ˌfeature *noun* an artificial area of water, or structure with water flowing through it, which is intended to make a garden more attractive and interesting

ˈwater ˌfountain (also **ˈdrinking ˌfountain**) *noun* a device that supplies water for drinking in public places

wa·ter·fowl /ˈwɔtərˌfaʊl; ˈwɑ-/ *noun* (*pl.* **wa·ter·fowl**) [usually pl.] a bird that can swim and lives near water, especially a DUCK or GOOSE

wa·ter·front /ˈwɔtərˌfrʌnt; ˈwɑ-/ *noun* [usually sing.] a part of a town or an area that is next to water, for example in a HARBOR: *an apartment on the waterfront*

ˈwater ˌgun *noun* = WATER PISTOL

wa·ter·hole /ˈwɔtərˌhoʊl; ˈwɑ-/ (also **ˈwatering ˌhole**) *noun* a place where animals go to drink

ˈwater ˌice *noun* [U, C] = SORBET

ˈwatering ˌcan *noun* a metal or plastic container with a handle and a long SPOUT, used for pouring water on plants ⊃ picture at TOOL

ˈwatering ˌhole *noun* **1** = WATERHOLE **2** (*informal, humorous*) a bar or place where people go to drink

ˈwatering ˌplace *noun* (*old-fashioned*) a town with a natural supply of MINERAL WATER where people go for their health **SYN** SPA

ˈwater ˌjump *noun* an area of water that horses or runners have to jump over in a race or competition

wa·ter·less /ˈwɔtərləs; ˈwɑ-/ *adj.* with no water: *a waterless, barren region*

ˈwater ˌlevel *noun* [U, C] the height that the surface of a mass of water rises or falls to, or the height it is at

ˈwater ˌlily *noun* a plant that floats on the surface of water, with large, round, flat leaves and white, yellow, or pink flowers

wa·ter·line /ˈwɔtərˌlaɪn; ˈwɑ-/ *noun* **the waterline** [sing.] the level that the water reaches along the side of a ship

wa·ter·logged /ˈwɔtərˌlɔgd; ˈwɑtər-; -ˌlɑgd/ *adj.* **1** (of soil, a field, etc.) so full of water that it cannot hold any more water and becomes flooded: *They couldn't play because the field was waterlogged.* **2** (of a boat, etc.) so full of water that it can no longer float

Wa·ter·loo /ˌwɔtərˈlu; ˌwɑtər-; ˈwɔtərˌlu; ˈwɑtər-/ *noun* [sing.] **sb's ~** a final defeat for someone: *This was the point at which he was to meet his Waterloo.* **ORIGIN** From the battle of **Waterloo** in 1815, in which the British (under the Duke of Wellington) and the Prussians finally defeated Napoleon.

ˈwater ˌmain *noun* a large underground pipe that supplies water to buildings, etc.

wa·ter·mark /ˈwɔtərˌmɑrk; ˈwɑ-/ *noun* a symbol or design in some types of paper that can be seen when the paper is held against the light ⊃ see also HIGH-WATER MARK, LOW-WATER MARK

wa·ter·mel·on /ˈwɔtərˌmɛlən; ˈwɑ-/ *noun* [C, U] a type of large MELON with hard, dark green skin, red flesh, and black seeds ⊃ picture at FRUIT

wa·ter·mill /ˈwɔtərˌmɪl; ˈwɑ-/ *noun* a MILL next to a river in which the machinery for GRINDING grain into flour is driven by the power of the water turning a wheel

ˈwater ˌmoccasin *noun* = COTTONMOUTH

ˈwater ˌpark (also **wa·ter·park**) *noun* an AMUSEMENT PARK that has activities involving water: *The main attraction at the water park is a really tall water slide.*

ˈwater ˌpipe *noun* **1** a pipe for carrying water **2** a pipe for smoking TOBACCO, MARIJUANA, etc. that draws the smoke through water to cool it

ˈwater ˌpistol (also **ˈwater ˌgun**, **ˈsquirt gun**) *noun* a toy gun that shoots water

ˈwater ˌpolo *noun* [U] a game played by two teams of people swimming in a swimming pool. Players try to throw a ball into the other team's goal.

ˈwater ˌpower *noun* [U] power produced by the movement of water, used to drive machinery or produce electricity

wa·ter·proof /ˈwɔtərˌpruf; ˈwɑ-/ *adj., verb*
● *adj.* that does not let water through or that cannot be damaged by water: *waterproof clothing* ◆ *a waterproof camera*
● *verb* ~ **sth** to make something waterproof

ˈwater ˌrat *noun* an animal like a RAT that swims and lives in a hole beside a river or lake

water-reˌpellent *adj.* a material, etc. that is **water-repellent** is specially treated so that water runs off it rather than going into it: *a water-repellent coating*

water-reˌsistant *adj.* that does not let water through easily: *a water-resistant jacket*

wa·ter·shed /ˈwɔtərˌʃɛd; ˈwɑ-/ *noun* [C] **1** ~ **(in sth)** an event or a period of time that marks an important change: *The middle decades of the 19th century marked a watershed in Russia's history.* **2** a line of high land where streams on one side flow into one river, and streams on the other side flow into a different river

wa·ter·side /ˈwɔtərˌsaɪd; ˈwɑ-/ *noun* [sing.] the area at the edge of a river, lake, etc.: *They strolled down to the waterside.* ◆ *a waterside café*

wa·ter·ski /ˈwɔtərˌski; ˈwɑ-/ *verb, noun*
● *verb* [I] to SKI on water while being pulled by a fast boat ▶ **wa·ter·ski·ing** *noun* [U]: *We snorkeled and did some waterskiing.* ⊃ picture at SPORT
● *noun* either of the pair of long, flat boards on which a person stands in order to waterski

ˈwater ˌslide *noun* a SLIDE (= a structure with a steep slope) with water flowing down it, used for sliding down into a swimming pool: *a water slide with lots of twists and turns*

ˈwater ˌsoftener *noun* [U, C] a device or substance that removes particular minerals, especially CHALK, from water

water-ˌsoluble *adj.* able to be dissolved in water: *The paint is water-soluble.*

ˈwater ˌsports *noun* [pl.] sports that are done on or in water, for example sailing and WATERSKIING

wa·ter·spout /ˈwɔtərˌspaʊt; ˈwɑ-/ *noun* a column of water that is pulled up from the ocean during a storm by a rapidly spinning column of air

ˈwater ˌstrider *noun* an insect which moves quickly across the surface of water

ˈwater supˌply *noun* [C, U] the water provided for a town, an area, or a building; the act of or system for supplying water to a town, etc.: *a clean/contaminated water supply* ◆ *to improve the water supply to rural villages*

ˈwater ˌtable *noun* [C, usually sing.] (*technical*) the level at and below which water is found in the ground

wa·ter·tight /ˈwɔtərˌtaɪt; ˈwɑ-/ *adj.* **1** that does not allow water to get in or out: *a watertight container* **2** (of an excuse, a plan, an argument, etc.) carefully prepared so that it contains no mistakes, faults, or weaknesses: *a watertight alibi* ◆ *The case has to be made watertight.*

ˈwater ˌtower *noun* a tall structure with a tank of water at the top from which water is supplied to buildings in the area around it

wa·ter·way /ˈwɔtərˌweɪ; ˈwɑ-/ *noun* a river, CANAL, etc. along which boats can travel: *inland waterways* ◆ *a navigable waterway*

wa·ter·wheel /ˈwɔtərˌwil; ˈwɑ-/ *noun* a wheel turned by the movement of water, used, especially in the past, to drive machinery

ˈwater ˌwings *noun* [pl.] (*old-fashioned*) a pair of plastic bags filled with air that children wear on their arms when they learn to swim

wa·ter·works /ˈwɔtərˌwɔrks; ˈwɑ-/ *noun* (*pl.* **wa·ter·works**) **1** [C] a building with machinery for supplying water to an

area **2** [pl.] (*informal* or *humorous*) the organs of the body through which URINE (= waste water) is passed
> **IDM** **turn on the waterworks** (*informal, disapproving*) to start crying, especially in order to get sympathy or attention

wa·ter·y /ˈwɔtəri; ˈwɑ-/ *adj.* **1** of or like water; containing a lot of water: *a watery fluid* ◆ *His eyes were red and watery.* ◆ (*literary*) *She was rescued from a watery grave* (= saved from DROWNING). **2** weak and/or pale: *a watery sun* ◆ *His eyes were a watery blue.* ◆ *a watery smile* (= weak and without much feeling) **3** (of food, drink, etc.) containing too much water; thin and having no taste: *watery soup*

watt /wɑt/ *noun* (*abbr.* W.) a unit for measuring electrical power: *a 60-watt light bulb*

watt·age /ˈwɑtɪdʒ/ *noun* [U] (*technical*) an amount of electrical power expressed in watts

wat·tle /ˈwɑtl/ *noun* **1** [C] a piece of red skin that hangs down from the throat of a bird such as a TURKEY **2** [U] sticks twisted together as a material for making fences, walls, etc.: *walls made of **wattle and daub***

wave 🔑 /weɪv/ *noun, verb*
● *noun*
> OF WATER **1** [C] a raised line of water that moves across the surface of the ocean, etc.: *Huge **waves were breaking** on the shore.* ◆ *Surfers flocked to the beach to **ride the waves**.* ◆ *the gentle sound of **waves lapping*** ◆ *Children were playing **in the waves**.* ◆ *Seagulls bobbed **on the waves**.* ◆ *The wind made little waves on the pond.* ➔ see also TIDAL WAVE
> OF ACTIVITY/FEELING **2** [C] a sudden increase in a particular activity or feeling: *a **wave of opposition/protest/violence**, etc.* ◆ *a crime wave* ◆ *A wave of fear swept over him.* ◆ *Guilt and horror flooded her **in waves**.* ◆ *A wave of panic spread through the crowd.* ➔ see also BRAINWAVE, HEATWAVE
> LARGE NUMBER **3** [C] a large number of people or things suddenly moving or appearing somewhere: *Wave after wave of aircraft passed overhead.* ➔ see also NEW WAVE
> MOVEMENT OF ARM/HAND/BODY **4** [C] a movement of your arm and hand from side to side: *She declined the offer with a wave of her hand.* ◆ *He gave us **a wave** as the bus drove off.* **5 the wave** [sing.] a continuous movement that looks like a wave on the ocean, made by a large group of people, especially people watching a sports game, when one person after another stands up, raises their arms, and then sits down again
> OF HEAT/SOUND/LIGHT **6** [C] the form that some types of energy such as heat, sound, light, etc. take as they move: *radio/sound/ultrasonic waves* ➔ see also AIRWAVES, LONG WAVE, MEDIUM WAVE, MICROWAVE, SHOCK WAVE, SHORTWAVE, SOUND WAVE
> IN HAIR **7** [C] if a person's hair has **a wave** or **waves**, it is not straight, but curls slightly ➔ see also PERMANENT WAVE, WAVY
> SEA **8 the waves** [pl.] (*literary*) the ocean
> **IDM** **make waves** (*informal*) to be very active in a way that makes people notice you, and that may sometimes cause problems ➔ more at CREST, RIDE *v.*
● *verb*
> MOVE HAND/ARM **1** [I, T] to move your hand or arm from side to side in the air in order to attract attention, say hello, etc.: *The people on the bus waved and we waved back.* ◆ *~ at/to sb Why did you wave at him?* ◆ *~ sth (about/around) A man in the water was shouting and waving his arms around frantically.* ◆ *~ sth at sb She waved her hand dismissively at the housekeeper.* ◆ *~ sth to sb My mother was crying as I waved goodbye to her.* ◆ *~ sb sth My mother was crying as I **waved her goodbye**.* **2** [I, T] to show where something is, show someone where to go, etc. by moving your hand in a particular direction: *~ + adv./prep. She waved vaguely in the direction of the house.* ◆ *~ sth/sb + adv./prep. "He's over there," said Ali, **waving a hand** toward some trees.* ◆ *I showed my pass to the security guard and he waved me through.* **3** [T] to hold something in your hand and move it from side to side: *~ sth Crowds lined the route, waving flags and cheering.* ◆

~ sth + adv./prep. "I'm rich!" she exclaimed, waving the money under his nose.
> MOVE FREELY **4** [I] to move freely and gently, for example in the wind, while one end or side is held in position: *The flag waved in the breeze.*
> HAIR **5** [I] to curl slightly: *His hair waves naturally.*
> **IDM** **like waving a red flag in front of a bull** something that is likely to make someone very angry ➔ more at FLAG *n.*
PHR V **wave sth↔aˈside/aˈway** to not accept something because you do not think it is necessary or important **SYN** DISMISS: *My objections to the plan were waved aside.* **ˌwave sth/sbˈdown** to signal to a vehicle or its driver to stop, by waving your hand **ˌwave sb↔ˈoff** to wave goodbye to someone as they are leaving

wave·band /ˈweɪvbænd/ *noun* = BAND: *a radio set with medium and short wavebands*

ˌwave-cut ˈplatform *noun* (*technical*) an area of land between the CLIFFS and the ocean that is covered by water when the ocean is at its highest level

wave·form /ˈweɪvfɔrm/ *noun* (*physics*) a curve showing the shape of a wave at a particular time

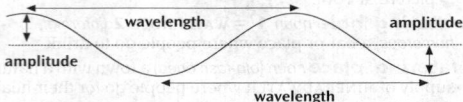

wave·length /ˈweɪvlɛŋkθ; -lɛŋθ/ *noun* **1** the distance between two similar points on a wave of energy, such as light or sound **2** the size of a radio wave that is used by a particular radio station, etc. for sending signals or broadcasting programs
> **IDM** **be on the same wavelength | be on sb's wavelength** (*informal*) to have the same way of thinking or the same ideas or feelings as someone else

wave·let /ˈweɪvlət/ *noun* (*literary*) a small wave on the surface of a lake or the ocean

ˈwave maˌchine *noun* a machine that makes waves in the water in a swimming pool

wa·ver /ˈweɪvər/ *verb* **1** [I] to be or become weak or unsteady: *His voice wavered with emotion.* ◆ *Her determination never wavered.* ◆ *She never wavered in her determination to succeed.* **2** [I] *~ (between A and B)* | *~ (on/over sth)* to hesitate and be unable to make a decision or choice **SYN** HESITATE: *She's wavering between buying a house in the city and moving away.* **3** [I] (especially of light) to move in an unsteady way ▶ **wa·ver·er** /ˈweɪvərər/ *noun*: *The strength of his argument convinced the waverers.*

wav·y /ˈweɪvi/ *adj.* (**wav·i·er, wav·i·est**) having curves; not straight: *brown wavy hair* ◆ *a pattern of wavy lines* ➔ picture at CURVED, HAIR, LINE

wax /wæks/ *noun, verb*
● *noun* [U] **1** a solid substance that is made from BEESWAX or from various fats and oils, used for making CANDLES, polish, models, etc. It becomes soft when it is heated: *styling wax for the hair* ◆ *floor wax* ◆ *wax crayons* ◆ *wax polish* ➔ see also PARAFFIN WAX, SEALING WAX **2** a soft, sticky, yellow substance that is found in your ears **IDM** see BALL
● *verb* **1** [T] *~ sth* to polish something with wax **2** [T, usually passive] *~ sth* to cover something with wax: *waxed paper* ◆ *a waxed jacket* **3** [T, often passive] *~ sth* to remove hair from a part of the body using wax: *to wax your legs/to have your legs waxed* **4** [I] (of the moon) to seem to get gradually bigger until its full form is visible **ANT** WANE **5** [I] *~ + lyrical, eloquent, sentimental, etc.* (*formal*) to become LYRICAL, etc. when speaking or writing: *He waxed lyrical on the food at the new restaurant.*
> **IDM** **wax and wane** (*literary*) to increase then decrease in strength, importance, etc. over a period of time

ˈwax bean *noun* a type of BEAN that is a long, thin, yellow POD, cooked and eaten whole as a vegetable

waxed paper (also **wax paper**) *noun* [U] paper covered with a thin layer of wax, used to wrap food or when cooking

wax·en /ˈwæksn/ *adj.* **1** (*formal*) made of wax: *waxen images* **2** (*literary*) pale and looking sick: *a waxen face*

wax museum *noun* a museum where you can see wax models of famous people

wax paper *noun* = WAXED PAPER

wax·work /ˈwækswɜrk/ *noun* a model of a person that is made of wax

wax·y /ˈwæksi/ *adj.* made of wax; looking or feeling like wax

way /weɪ/ *noun, adv.*

● **noun**

> METHOD/STYLE **1** [C] a method, style, or manner of doing something: *~ to do sth That's not **the right way** to hold a pair of scissors.* ♦ (*informal, disapproving*) **That's no way** to speak to your mother! ♦ *~ of doing sth I'm not happy with this way of working.* ♦ *~ (that…) It's not what you say, it's the way that you say it.* ♦ *I hate the way she always criticizes me.* ♦ *I told you we should have done it my way!* ♦ *Infectious diseases can be acquired in several ways.* ♦ *I generally get what I want **one way or another** (= by some means).* ⟳ see also THIRD WAY

> BEHAVIOR **2** [C] a particular manner or style of behavior: *They grinned at her **in a friendly way**.* ♦ *It was not his way to admit that he had made a mistake.* ♦ *Don't worry if she seems quiet—it's just her way.* ♦ *He was showing off, **as is the way** with adolescent boys.* **3 ways** [pl.] the typical way of behaving and living of a particular group of people: *After ten years I'm used to the strange British ways.*

> ROUTE/ROAD **4** [C, usually sing.] *~ (from…) (to…)* a route or road that you take in order to reach a place: *the best/quickest/shortest way from A to B* ♦ *Can you **tell me the way** to Times Square?* ♦ *to **ask someone the way*** ♦ *We went the **long way around**.* **5** [C, usually sing.] the route along which someone or something is moving; the route that someone or something would take if there was nothing stopping them/it: ***Get out of my way!** I'm in a hurry.* ♦ *Riot police with shields were blocking the demonstrators' way.* ♦ *We fought our way through the dense vegetation.* ♦ *Unfortunately they ran into a snowstorm along the way.* ⟳ see also RIGHT OF WAY **6** [C] a road, path, or street for traveling along: *There's a way across the fields.* ⟳ see also FREEWAY, HIGHWAY, RAILWAY, WATERWAY **7 Way** used in the names of streets: *106 Headley Way*

> DIRECTION **8** [C, usually sing.] **which, this, that, etc.** *~* a particular direction; in a particular direction: *Which way did they go?* ♦ *We just missed a car going **the other way**.* ♦ *Look **both ways** (= look left and right) before crossing the road.* ♦ *Make sure that sign is **the right way up**.* ♦ *Kids were running **this way and that** (= in all directions).* ♦ *They decided to split the money four ways (= between four different people).* ♦ (*figurative*) *Which way (= for which party) are you going to vote?* ⟳ see also ONE-WAY, THREE-WAY, TWO-WAY

> FOR ENTERING/LEAVING **9** [C, usually sing.] a means of going into or leaving a place, such as a door or gate: *the **way in/out*** ♦ *They escaped out the back way.* ⟳ see also COMPANIONWAY

> DISTANCE/TIME **10** [sing.] (also *informal* **ways**) a distance or period of time between two points: *A little way up on the left is the Museum of Modern Art.* ♦ *September was **a long way off**.* ♦ (*figurative*) *The area's wine industry still has **a way to go** to full maturity.* ♦ *You came **all this way** to see us?* ♦ (*informal*) *We still have **a ways to go**.*

> AREA **11** [sing.] (*informal*) an area, a part of a country, etc.: *I think he lives somewhere **over** Chicago **way**.* ♦ *I'll stop by and see you next time I'm **down your way**.*

> ASPECT **12** [C] a particular aspect of something
   SYN RESPECT: *I have changed in every way.* ♦ *It's been quite a day, **one way and another** (= for several reasons).*

> CONDITION/STATE **13** [sing.] a particular condition or state: *The economy's **in a bad way**.* ♦ *I don't know how we're going to manage, **the way things are**.*

   IDM **across the way** on the other side of the street, etc.: *Music blared from the open window of the house across the way.* **all the way 1** (also **the whole way**) during the whole journey/period of time: *She didn't speak a word to me all the*

way back home. **2** completely; as much as it takes to achieve what you want: *I'm fighting him all the way.* ♦ *You can feel that the audience is with her all the way.* **(that's/it's) always the way** (*informal*) used to say that things often happen in a particular manner, especially when it is not convenient **any way you slice it** (*informal*) however you choose to look at a situation **be/be born/be made that way** (of a person) to behave or do things in a particular manner because it is part of your character: *It's not his fault he's so pompous—he was born that way.* **be set in your ways** to have habits or opinions that you have had for a long time and that you do not want to change **by the way** (also **by the by/bye**) (*informal*) used to introduce a comment or question that is not directly related to what you have been talking about: *By the way, I found that book you were looking for.* ♦ *What time is it, by the way?* ♦ *Oh, by the way, if you see Jackie, tell her I'll call her tonight.* **by way of sth** by a route that includes the place mentioned **SYN** VIA: *The artist recently arrived in Paris from Bulgaria by way of Vienna.* ♦ *She came to TV by way of drama school.* **by way of/in the way of sth** as a form of something; for something; as a means of something: *He received $6000 by way of compensation from the company.* ♦ *She rolled her eyes by way of an answer and left.* **come your way** to happen to you by chance, or when you were not expecting it: *He took whatever came his way.* **cut both/two ways** (of an action, argument, etc.) to have two opposite effects or results **either way | one way or the other** used to say that it does not matter which one of two possibilities happens, is chosen, or is true: *Was it his fault or not? Either way, an explanation is due.* ♦ *We could meet today or tomorrow—I don't mind one way or the other.* **every which way** (*informal*) in all directions: *Her hair tumbled every which way.* **get in the way of** to prevent someone from doing something; to prevent something from happening: *He wouldn't allow emotions to get in the way of him doing his job.* **get/have your own way** to get or do what you want, especially when someone has tried to stop you: *She always gets her own way in the end.* **give way** to break or fall down: *The pillars gave way and a section of the roof collapsed.* ♦ *Her numb leg gave way beneath her and she stumbled clumsily.* **give way (to sb/sth)** to stop resisting someone or something; to agree to do something that you do not want to do: *He refused to give way on any of the points.* **give way to sth 1** to allow yourself to be very strongly affected by something, especially an emotion: *Flinging herself on the bed, she gave way to helpless misery.* **2** to be replaced by something: *The storm gave way to bright sunshine.* **go all the way (with sb)** (*informal*) to have full SEXUAL INTERCOURSE with someone **go a long/some way toward doing sth** to help very much/a little in achieving something: *The new law goes a long way toward solving the problem.* **go out of your way (to do sth)** to make a special effort to do something: *He would always go out of his way to be friendly toward her.* **go your own way** to do as you choose, especially when someone has advised you against it: *It's best to let her go her own way if you don't want a fight.* **go sb's way 1** to travel in the same direction as someone: *I'm going your way—I'll walk with you.* **2** (of events) to go well for you; to be in your favor: *By the third round he knew the fight was going his way.* **go the way of all flesh** (*saying*) to die **have it your (own) way!** (*informal*) used to say in an angry manner that although you are not happy about something that someone has said, you are not going to argue: *Oh OK, then. Have it your own way.* **have it/things/everything your own way** to have what you want, especially by opposing other people **have a way of doing sth** used to say that something often happens in a particular manner, especially when it is out of your control: *First love affairs have a way of not working out.* **have a way with sb/sth** to be good at dealing with someone or something: *He has a way with small children.* ♦ *She has a way with words (= is very good at expressing herself).* **have/want it both ways** to have or want to have the advantages of two different situations or types of behavior that are impossible to combine: *You can't have it both ways. If you can afford to go out all the time, you can afford to pay off some of your debts.* **in a big/small way** on a large/small scale: *The new delivery* *service has taken off in a big way.* ♦ *Many people are investing in a small way in the stock market.* **in more ways than one** used to show that a statement has more than one meaning: *With the first goal he used his head in more ways than one.* **in her, his, its, etc. (own) way** in a manner that is appropriate to or typical of a person or thing but that may seem unusual to other people: *I expect she does love you in her own way.* **in a way | in one way | in some ways** to some extent; not completely: *In a way it was one of our biggest mistakes.* **in the/ sb's way** stopping someone from moving or doing something: *You'll have to move—you're in my way.* ♦ *I left them alone, as I felt I was in the way.* **in the way of sth** used in questions and negative sentences to talk about the types of something that are available: *There isn't much in the way of entertainment in this place.* **keep/stay out of sb's way** to avoid someone **look the other way** to deliberately avoid seeing someone or something: *Prison officers know what's going on, but look the other way.* **lose your way** **1** to become lost: *We lost our way in the dark.* **2** to forget or move away from the purpose or reason for something: *I feel that the project has lost its way.* **make your way (to/toward sth)** to move or get somewhere; to make progress: *Will you be able to make your own way to the airport* (= get there without help, a ride, etc.)? ♦ *Is this your plan for making your way in the world?* **make way (for sb/sth)** to allow someone or something to pass; to allow someone or something to take the place of someone or something: *Make way for the governor!* ♦ *Tropical forest is felled to make way for grassland.* **my way or the highway** (*informal*) used to say that someone else has either to agree with your opinion or to leave **(there is) no way** (*informal*) used to say that there is no possibility that you will do something or that something will happen: *"Do you want to help?" "No way!"* ♦ *No way am I going to drive them there.* ♦ *There's no way we could afford that sort of money.* **on your/ the/its way** **1** going or coming: *I'd better be on my way* (= I must leave) *soon.* ♦ *The letter should be on its way to you.* **2** during the journey: *He stopped for breakfast on the way.* ♦ *She grabbed her camera and bag on her way out.* **3** (of a baby) not yet born: *They've got three kids and one on the way.* **the other way around** **1** in the opposite position, direction, or order: *I think it should go on the other way around.* **2** the opposite situation: *I didn't leave you. It was the other way around* (= you left me). **out of the way** **1** no longer stopping someone from moving or doing something: *I moved my legs out of the way so that she could get past.* ♦ *I didn't say anything until Dad was out of the way.* **2** finished; dealt with: *Our region is poised for growth once the election is out of the way.* **3** used in negative sentences to mean "unusual": *She had obviously noticed nothing out of the way.* ○ see also OUT-OF-THE-WAY **out of your way** on the route that you planned to take: *I'd love a ride home—if it's not out of your way.* **see your way (clear) to doing sth/to do sth** to find that it is possible or convenient to do something: *Small companies cannot see their way clear to taking on many interns.* **see which way the wind is blowing** to get an idea of what is likely to happen before doing something **(not) stand in sb's way** to (not) prevent someone from doing something: *If you believe you can make her happy, I won't stand in your way.* **that's the way the cookie crumbles** (*informal*) that is the situation and we cannot change it, so we must accept it **there's more than one way to skin a cat** (*saying, humorous*) there are many different ways to achieve something **to my way of thinking** in my opinion **under way** (also **un·der·way**) having started: *Preparations are well under way for a week of special events in May.* **a/the/sb's way of life** the typical pattern of behavior of a person or group: *the American way of life* **the way of the world** the way that most people behave; the way that things happen, which you cannot change: *The rich and powerful make the decisions— that's the way of the world.* **ways and means** the methods and materials available for doing something: *ways and means of raising money* **a way into sth** (also **a way in to sth**) something that allows you to join a group of people, an industry, etc. that it is difficult to join, or to understand something that is difficult to understand **the way to sb's heart** the way to make someone like or love you: *The way to*

a man's heart is through his stomach (= by giving him good food). **way to go!** (*informal*) used to tell someone that you are pleased about something they have done: *Good work, guys! Way to go!* **work your way through college, around the world, etc.** to have a job or series of jobs while studying, traveling, etc. in order to pay for your education, etc. **work your way through sth** to do something from beginning to end, especially when it takes a lot of time or effort: *She worked her way through the pile of documents.* **work your way up** to move regularly to a more senior position in a company: *He worked his way up from messenger boy to account executive.* ○ more at CHANGE *v.*, CLAW *v.*, CLEAR *v.*, DOWNHILL *adj.*, EASY *adj.*, ERROR, FAMILY *n.*, FEEL *v.*, FIND *v.*, HARD *adj.*, HARM *n.*, KNOW *v.*, LAUGH *v.*, LIE² *v.*, LONG *adj.*, MEND *v.*, MIDDLE *adj.*, OPEN *v.*, PARTING *n.*, PAVE, PAY *v.*, PICK *v.*, RUB *v.*, SEPARATE *adj.*, SHAPE *n.*, SHOW *v.*, SMOOTH *v.*, SWEET *adj.*, TALK *v.*, TWO, WELL *adv.*, WILL *n.*, WRONG *adj.*

● **adv.** **1** (used with a preposition or an adverb) very far; by a large amount: *She finished the race way ahead of the other runners.* ♦ *I have to get home; it's way past my bedtime.* ♦ *The price is way above what we can afford.* ♦ *They live way out in the suburbs.* ♦ *This skirt is way* (= a lot) *too short.* ♦ *I guessed that there would be a hundred people there, but I was way out* (= wrong by a large amount). **2** (used with an adjective) (*informal*) very: *Things just got way difficult.* ♦ *I'm way glad to hear that.*
  IDM way back (in...) a long time ago: *I first met him way back in the 80s.*

way·far·er /ˈweɪˌfɛrər/ *noun* (*old-fashioned* or *literary*) a person who travels from one place to another, usually on foot

way·lay /ˈweɪleɪ/ *verb* (way·laid, way·laid /-leɪd/) **~ sb** to stop someone who is going somewhere, especially in order to talk to them or attack them: *I got waylaid on my way here.*

way ˈout *noun* a way of escaping from a difficult situation: *She was in a mess and could see no way out.*
  IDM on the way out 1 as you are leaving **2** going out of fashion

way-ˈout *adj.* (*old-fashioned, informal*) unusual or strange **SYN** WEIRD: *way-out ideas*

way·point /ˈweɪpɔɪnt/ *noun* **1** a place where you stop during a trip **2** (*technical*) the COORDINATES, checked by a computer, of each stage of a flight or trip by ocean

-ways /weɪz/ *suffix* (in adjectives and adverbs) in the direction of: *lengthways* ♦ *sideways*

the ˌWays and ˈMeans Comˌmittee *noun* [*sing.*] a group of members of the U.S. House of Representatives that makes suggestions about laws concerning tax and trade in order to provide money for the U.S. government

way·side /ˈweɪsaɪd/ *noun* [*sing.*] the area at the side of a road or path: *a wayside inn* ♦ *wild flowers growing by the wayside*
  IDM fall by the wayside to fail or be unable to make progress

ˈway ˌstation *noun* a place where people stop to eat or rest during a long journey

way·ward /ˈweɪwərd/ *adj.* (*formal*) difficult to control **SYN** HEADSTRONG: *a wayward child* ♦ *wayward emotions*
  ▶ **way·ward·ness** *noun* [U]

wa·zir /wəˈzɪr/ *noun* = VIZIER

wa·zoo /wɑˈzu/ *noun* (*slang*) the part of the body that you sit on
  IDM out/up the wazoo in large numbers or amounts

Wb *abbr.* WEBER

WC /ˌdʌblyuˈsi/ *noun* (*old-fashioned*) (on signs and doors in public places) toilet (the abbreviation for "water closet")

we 🔑 /wi/ *pron.*
(used as the subject of a verb) **1** I and another person or other people; I and you: *We've moved to Atlanta.* ♦ *We'd* (= the company would) *like to offer you the job.* ♦ *Why don't we go and see it together?* **2** people in general: *We should take more care of our historic buildings.*

t tea   ţ butter   d did   k cat   g got   tʃ chin   dʒ June   f fall

weak /wik/ adj. (weak·er, weak·est)
> NOT PHYSICALLY STRONG **1** not physically strong: *She is still weak after her illness.* ◆ *His legs felt weak.* ◆ *She suffered from a weak heart.*
> LIKELY TO BREAK **2** that cannot support a lot of weight; likely to break: *That bridge is too weak for heavy traffic.*
> WITHOUT POWER **3** easy to influence; not having much power: *a weak and cowardly man* ◆ *In a weak moment* (= when I was easily persuaded) *I said she could borrow the car.* ◆ *a weak leader* ◆ *The unions have always been weak in this industry.*
> POOR/SICK PEOPLE **4 the weak** noun [pl.] people who are poor, sick, or without power
> CURRENCY/ECONOMY **5** not strong or successful: *a weak currency* ◆ *The economy is very weak.*
> NOT GOOD AT SOMETHING **6** not good at something: *a weak team* ◆ ~ **in sth** *I was always weak in the science subjects.*
> NOT CONVINCING **7** that people are not likely to believe or be persuaded by **SYN** UNCONVINCING: *weak arguments* ◆ *I enjoyed the movie but I thought the ending was very weak.*
> HARD TO SEE/HEAR **8** not easily seen or heard: *a weak light/signal/sound*
> WITHOUT ENTHUSIASM **9** done without enthusiasm or energy: *a weak smile* ◆ *He made a weak attempt to look cheerful.*
> LIQUID **10** a weak liquid contains a lot of water: *weak tea*
> POINT/SPOT **11** ~ **point/spot** the part of a person's character, an argument, etc. that is easy to attack or criticize: *The team's weak points are in defense.* ◆ *He knew her weak spot where Steve was concerned.*
> GRAMMAR **12** a weak verb forms the past tense and past participle by adding a regular ending and not by changing a vowel. In English this is done by adding *-d*, *-ed* or *-t* (for example *walk*, *walked*)
> PHONETICS **13** (of the pronunciation of some words) used when there is no stress on the word. For example, the weak form of *and* is /ən/ or /n/, as in *bread and butter* /ˌbrɛd n ˈbʌtər/ **ANT** STRONG
IDM **weak at/in the knees** (*informal*) hardly able to stand because of emotion, fear, illness, etc.: *His sudden smile made her go weak in the knees.* **the weak link (in the chain)** the point at which a system or an organization is most likely to fail

weak·en /ˈwikən/ verb **1** [T, I] ~ **(sb/sth)** to make someone or something less strong or powerful; to become less strong or powerful: *The team has been weakened by injury.* ◆ *The new evidence weakens the case against her.* ◆ *His authority is steadily weakening.* **ANT** STRENGTHEN **2** [T, I] ~ **(sb/sth)** to make someone or something physically less strong; to become physically less strong: *The explosion had weakened the building's foundations.* ◆ *She felt her legs weaken.* **3** [I, T] to become or make someone become less determined or certain about something: *You must not agree to do it. Don't weaken.* ◆ ~ **sth** *Nothing could weaken his resolve to continue.*

weak force noun (*technical*) one of the four FUNDAMENTAL FORCES in the universe, which is produced between PARTICLES in an atom ⊃ see also ELECTROMAGNETISM, GRAVITY, STRONG FORCE

weak-kneed adj. (*informal*) lacking courage or strength

weak·ling /ˈwiklɪŋ/ noun (*disapproving*) a person who is not physically strong

weak·ly /ˈwikli/ adv. in a weak way: *She smiled weakly at them.* ◆ *"I'm not sure about it," he said weakly.*

weak·ness /ˈwiknəs/ noun
1 [U] lack of strength, power, or determination: *The sudden weakness in her legs made her stumble.* ◆ *the weakness of the dollar against the pound* ◆ *He thought that crying was a sign of weakness.* **ANT** STRENGTH **2** [C] a weak point in a system, someone's character, etc.: *It's important to know your own strengths and weaknesses.* ◆ *Can you spot the weakness in her argument?* **ANT** STRENGTH **3** [C, usually sing.] ~ **(for sth/sb)** difficulty in resisting something or someone that you like very much: *He has a weakness for chocolate.*

weal /wil/ noun a sore red mark on someone's skin where they have been hit

wealth /wɛlθ/ noun
1 [U] a large amount of money, property, etc. that a person or country owns: *a person of wealth and influence* ◆ *His personal wealth is estimated at around $100 million.* ◆ *the distribution of wealth in Asia* **2** [U] the state of being rich: *The purpose of industry is to create wealth.* ◆ *Good education often depends on wealth.* **3** [sing.] ~ **of sth** a large amount of something: *a wealth of information* ◆ *The new manager brings a great wealth of experience to the job.* ⊃ compare RICHNESS

wealth·y /ˈwɛlθi/ adj. (wealth·i·er, wealth·i·est) **1** having a lot of money, possessions, etc. **SYN** RICH: *a wealthy nation* ◆ *The couple is said to be fabulously wealthy.* ◆ *They live in a wealthy suburb of Chicago.* ⊃ thesaurus box at RICH **2 the wealthy** noun [pl.] people who are rich

wean /win/ verb ~ **sb/sth (off/from sth)** to gradually stop feeding a baby or young animal with its mother's milk and start feeding it with solid food
PHR V **'wean sb off/from sth** to make someone gradually stop doing or using something: *The doctor tried to wean her off sleeping pills.* **'wean sb on sth** [usually passive] to make someone experience something regularly, especially from an early age: *He was weaned on a diet of rigid discipline and duty.*

weap·on /ˈwɛpən/ noun
1 an object such as a knife, gun, bomb, etc. that is used for fighting or attacking someone: *nuclear weapons* ◆ *a lethal/deadly weapon* ◆ *The police still haven't found the murder weapon.* ◆ *He was charged with carrying an offensive weapon.* ⊃ collocations at WAR ⊃ see also BIOLOGICAL WEAPON, CHEMICAL WEAPON **2** something such as knowledge, words, actions, etc. that can be used to attack or fight against someone or something: *Education is the only weapon to fight the spread of the disease.* ◆ *Guilt is the secret weapon for controlling children.* **IDM** see DOUBLE-EDGED

weap·on·ize /ˈwɛpəˌnaɪz/ verb ~ **sth** to make something suitable for use as a weapon: *They may have weaponized quantities of anthrax.* ▶ **weap·on·i·za·tion** /ˌwɛpənəˈzeɪʃn/ noun [U]

weapon of mass de'struction noun (abbr. WMD) a weapon such as a nuclear weapon, a CHEMICAL WEAPON, or a BIOLOGICAL WEAPON that can cause a lot of destruction and kill many people

weap·on·ry /ˈwɛpənri/ noun [U] all the weapons of a particular type or belonging to a particular country or group: *high-tech weaponry* ◆ *U.S. weaponry*

wear /wɛr/ verb, noun
● verb (wore /wɔr/, worn /wɔrn/)
> CLOTHING/DECORATION **1** [T] ~ **sth** to have something on your body as a piece of clothing, a decoration, etc.: *She was wearing a new coat.* ◆ *Do I have to wear a tie?* ◆ *Was she wearing a seat belt?* ◆ *He wore glasses.* ◆ *All delegates must wear a badge.* ◆ *She always wears black* (= black clothes). ⊃ collocations at FASHION
> HAIR **2** [T] to have your hair in a particular style; to have a beard or MUSTACHE: ~ **sth + adj.** *She wears her hair long.* ◆ ~ **sth** *to wear a beard*
> EXPRESSION ON FACE **3** [T] ~ **sth** to have a particular expression on your face: *He wore a puzzled look on his face.* ◆ *His face wore a puzzled look.*
> DAMAGE WITH USE **4** [I, T] to become or make something become thinner, smoother, or weaker through continuous use or rubbing: *The carpets are starting to wear.* ◆ ~ **+ adj.** *The sheets have worn thin.* ◆ ~ **sth + adj.** *The stones have been worn smooth by the constant flow of water.* **5** [T] ~ **sth + adv./prep.** to make a hole, path, etc. in something by continuous use or rubbing: *I've worn holes in all my socks.*
> STAY IN GOOD CONDITION **6** [I] ~ **well** to stay in good condition after being used for a long time: *That carpet is wearing well, isn't it?* ◆ (*figurative, humorous*) *You're wearing well—only a few gray hairs!*

IDM wear your heart on your sleeve to allow your feelings to be seen by other people wear the pants (often *disapproving*) (especially of a woman) to be the person in a marriage or other relationship who makes most of the decisions wear thin to begin to become weaker or less acceptable: *These excuses are wearing a little thin* (= because we've heard them so many times before). ⊃ more at SHOE

PHR V wear a'way | wear sth↔a'way to become, or make something become, gradually thinner or smoother by continuously using or rubbing it: *The inscription on the coin had worn away.* ◆ *The steps had been worn away by the feet of thousands of pilgrims.* wear 'down | wear sth↔'down to become, or make something become, gradually smaller or smoother by continuously using or rubbing it: *Notice how the tread on this tire has worn down.* wear sb/sth↔'down to make someone or something weaker or less determined, especially by continuously attacking or putting pressure on them or it over a period of time: *Her persistence paid off and she eventually wore me down.* wear 'off to gradually disappear or stop: *The effects of the drug will soon wear off.* wear 'on (of time) to pass, especially in a way that seems slow: *As the evening wore on, she became more and more nervous.* wear 'out | wear sth↔'out to become, or make something become, thin or no longer able to be used, usually because it has been used too much: *He wore out two pairs of shoes last year.* wear yourself/sb 'out to make yourself/someone feel very tired: *The kids have totally worn me out.* ◆ *You'll wear yourself out if you go on working so hard.*

● **noun** [U]
>CLOTHING **1** (usually in compounds) used especially in stores to describe clothes for a particular purpose or occasion: *casual/evening, etc. wear* ◆ *children's/ladies' wear* ⊃ see also FOOTWEAR, MENSWEAR, SPORTSWEAR, UNDER-WEAR **2** the fact of wearing something: *casual clothes for everyday wear* ◆ *These wool suits are not designed for wear in hot climates.* ⊃ thesaurus box at CLOTHES
>USE **3** the amount or type of use that something has over a period of time: *You should get years of wear out of that carpet.*
>DAMAGE **4** the damage or loss of quality that is caused when something has been used a lot: *His shoes were beginning to show signs of wear.*
IDM wear and tear the damage to objects, furniture, property, etc. that is the result of normal use: *The insurance policy does not cover damage caused by normal wear and tear.* ⊃ more at WORSE

wear·a·ble /'werəbl/ *adj.* (of clothes, etc.) pleasant and comfortable to wear; suitable to be worn

wear·er /'werər/ *noun* the person who is wearing something; a person who usually wears the thing mentioned: *The straps can be adjusted to suit the wearer.* ◆ *contact lens wearers*

wear·ing /'werɪŋ/ *adj.* that makes you feel very tired mentally or physically **SYN** EXHAUSTING

wear·i·some /'wɪrisəm/ *adj.* (*formal*) that makes you feel very bored and tired **SYN** TEDIOUS

wear·y /'wɪri/ *adj., verb*
● *adj.* (wear·i·er, wear·i·est) **1** very tired, especially after you have been working hard or doing something for a long time: *a weary traveler* ◆ *She suddenly felt old and weary.* ◆ *a weary sigh* **2** (*literary*) making you feel tired or bored: *a weary journey* **3** ~ of sth/of doing sth (*formal*) no longer interested in or enthusiastic about something: *Students soon grow weary of listening to a parade of historical facts.*
▶ **wea·ri·ly** /'wɪrəli/ *adv.*: *He closed his eyes wearily.* **wea·ri·ness** /'wɪrinəs/ *noun* [U]
● *verb* (wear·ies, wea·ry·ing, wear·ied, wear·ied) **1** [T] ~ sb (*formal*) to make someone feel tired **SYN** TIRE **2** [I] ~ of sth/of doing sth to lose your interest in or enthusiasm for something **SYN** TIRE: *She soon wearied of his stories.*

wea·sel /'wizl/ *noun, verb*
● *noun* a small wild animal with red-brown fur, a long thin body, and short legs. Weasels eat smaller animals.

● *verb*
PHR V weasel 'out (of sth) (*informal, disapproving*) to avoid doing something that you ought to do or have promised to do: *He's now trying to weasel out of our agreement.*

weasel word *noun* [usually pl.] (*informal, disapproving*) a word that has little meaning, or more than one meaning, that you use when you want to avoid saying something in a clear or direct way

weath·er /'weðər/ *noun, verb*
● *noun* [U] **1** the condition of the atmosphere at a particular place and time, such as the temperature, and if there is wind, rain, sun, etc.: *hot/cold/wet/fine/summer/windy, etc. weather* ◆ *Did you have good weather on your trip?* ◆ *I'm not going out in this weather!* ◆ *There's going to be a change in the weather.* ◆ *if the weather holds/breaks* (= if the good weather continues/changes) ◆ *The weather is very changeable at the moment.* ◆ *"Are you going to the beach tomorrow?" "It depends on the weather."* ◆ *We'll have the party outside, weather permitting* (= if it doesn't rain). ◆ *a weather map/chart* ◆ *a weather report* **2** the weather (*informal*) a report of what the weather will be like, that is on the radio or television, or in the newspapers: *to listen to the weather* ⊃ see also WEATHER FORECAST
IDM in all weathers in all kinds of weather, good and bad: *She goes out jogging in all weathers.* keep a weather eye on sb/sth to watch someone or something carefully in case you need to take action under the weather (*informal*) if you are or feel under the weather, you feel slightly sick and not as well as usual ⊃ more at HEAVY *adj.*
● *verb* [I, T] to change, or make something change, color or shape because of the effect of the sun, rain, or wind: *This brick weathers to a warm pinkish-brown color.* ◆ ~ sth *Her face was weathered by the sun.* **2** [T] ~ sth to come safely through a difficult period or experience: *The company just managed to weather the recession.* ◆ *She refuses to resign, intending to weather the storm* (= wait until the situation improves again).

TOPIC COLLOCATIONS

The Weather

good weather
- be bathed in/bask in/be blessed with/enjoy bright/brilliant/glorious sunshine
- the sun shines/warms sth/beats down (on sth)
- the sunshine breaks/streams through sth
- fluffy/wispy clouds drift across the sky
- a gentle/light/stiff/cool/warm breeze blows in/comes in off the sea
- the snow crunches beneath/under sb's feet/boots

bad weather
- thick/dark/storm clouds form/gather/roll in/cover the sky/block out the sun
- the sky darkens/turns black
- a fine mist hangs in the air
- a dense/heavy/thick fog rolls in
- the rain falls/comes down (in buckets/sheets)/pours down
- snow falls/comes down/covers sth/blankets sth
- the wind blows/whistles/howls/picks up/whips through sth/sweeps across sth
- strong/gale-force winds blow/gust (up to 80 mph)
- a storm is approaching/is moving inland/hits/strikes/rages
- thunder rolls/rumbles/sounds
- (forked/sheet) lightning strikes/hits/flashes
- a (blinding/snow) blizzard hits/strikes/blows/rages
- a tornado touches down/hits/strikes/destroys sth/rips through sth
- forecast/expect/predict rain/snow/a category-four hurricane
- rain pours (down)
- get caught in/seek shelter from/escape the rain
- be covered/shrouded in mist/a blanket of fog

---

h hat   m man   n no   ŋ sing   l leg   r red   y yes   w wet

- be in for/brave/shelter from a/the storm
- hear rolling/distant thunder
- be battered/buffeted by strong winds
- battle against/brave the elements

the weather improves
- the sun breaks through the clouds
- the sky clears/brightens (up)/lightens (up)
- the clouds part/clear
- the rain stops/lets up/holds off
- the wind dies down
- the storm passes
- the mist/fog lifts/clears

'weather bal,loon *noun* a BALLOON that carries instruments into the atmosphere to measure weather conditions

'weather-,beaten *adj.* [usually before noun] (especially of a person or their skin) rough and damaged because the person spends a lot of time outside

'weather ,bureau *noun* a place where information about the weather is collected and reports are prepared

weath·er·cock /ˈwɛðərˌkɑk/ *noun* a WEATHERVANE in the shape of a male chicken (a ROOSTER)

weath·ered /ˈwɛðərd/ *adj.* changed in color or shape because of the effect of the sun, rain, or wind: *smooth, weathered rocks*

'weather ,forecast (also fore·cast) *noun* a description, for example on the radio or television, of what the weather will be like tomorrow or for the next few days

weath·er·ing /ˈwɛðərɪŋ/ *noun* [U] the action of sun, rain, or wind on rocks making them change shape or color

weath·er·ize /ˈwɛðəˌraɪz/ *verb* ~ sth to protect a building against the effects of cold weather, for example by providing INSULATION

weath·er·man /ˈwɛðərˌmæn/ (*pl.* weath·er·men /-ˌmɛn/), **weath·er·girl** /ˈwɛðərˌgərl/ *noun* (*informal*) a person on radio or television whose job is describing the weather and telling people what it is going to be like

'weather ,map *noun* a map showing the weather conditions over a large area at a particular time

weath·er·proof /ˈwɛðərˌpruf/ *adj.* that is not affected by weather; that protects someone or something from wind and rain: *The finished roof should be weatherproof for years.* ◆ *a weatherproof jacket*

'weather ,station *noun* a place where weather conditions are studied and recorded

weath·er·strip·ping /ˈwɛðərˌstrɪpɪŋ/ *noun* [U] material that helps to prevent cold air coming through a door, window, etc. ▶ weath·er·strip *verb*: ~ sth *Weatherstrip all doors and windows that leak air.*

weath·er·vane /ˈwɛðərˌveɪn/ *noun* a metal object on the roof of a building that turns easily in the wind and shows which direction the wind is blowing from ⊃ see also WEATHERCOCK

weave /wiv/ *verb, noun*
● *verb* (wove /woʊv/, wo·ven /ˈwoʊvən/) **HELP** In sense 4 **weaved** is used for the past tense and past participle.
1 [T, I] to make cloth, a carpet, a BASKET, etc. by crossing threads or strips over and under each other by hand or on a machine called a LOOM: ~ A from B *The baskets are woven from strips of willow.* ◆ ~ B into A *The strips of willow are woven into baskets.* ◆ ~ sth together *threads woven together* ◆ ~ (sth) *Most spiders weave webs that are almost invisible.* ◆ *She is skilled at spinning and weaving.* **2** [T] ~ A (out of/from B) | ~ B (into A) to make something by twisting flowers, pieces of wood, etc. together: *She deftly wove the flowers into a garland.* **3** [T] to weave facts, events, details, etc. together to make a story or a closely connected whole: ~ (sth into) sth *to weave a narrative* ◆ ~ sth together *The biography weaves together the various strands of Einstein's life.* **4** (weaved, weaved) [I, T] to move along by running and changing direction continuously to avoid things that are in your way:

+ *adv./prep. She was weaving in and out of the traffic.* ◆ *The road weaves through a range of hills.* ◆ ~ your way + adv./ prep. *He had to weave his way through the milling crowds.*
IDM **weave a spell (over sb)** to perform or behave in a way that is attractive or interesting, or that makes someone behave in a particular way: *Her storytelling wove a spell over the children.*
● *noun* the way in which threads are arranged in a piece of cloth that has been woven; the pattern that the threads make

weav·er /ˈwivər/ *noun* a person whose job is weaving cloth

'weaver ,bird *noun* a tropical bird that builds large nests by weaving sticks and pieces of grass together in a complicated way

web /wɛb/ *noun*
1 [C] = SPIDER WEB: *A spider had spun a perfect web outside the window.* ⊃ picture at ANIMAL **2** [C] a complicated pattern of things that are closely connected to each other: *a web of streets* ◆ *We were caught in a tangled web of relationships.* **3** the Web (also the web) [sing.] = WORLD WIDE WEB: *I found the information on the Web.* ⊃ collocations at E-MAIL **4** [C] a piece of skin that joins the toes of some birds and animals that swim, for example DUCKS and FROGS

Web 2.0 /ˌwɛb tu pɔɪntˈoʊ/ *noun* [U] the developments in the way that people use the Internet that allow users free access and give them more control over the information

webbed /wɛbd/ *adj.* [only before noun] a bird or an animal (such as a DUCK or FROG) that has webbed feet has pieces of skin between the toes

web·bing /ˈwɛbɪŋ/ *noun* [U] strong strips of cloth that are used to make belts, etc., and to support the seats of chairs, etc.

web·cam /ˈwɛbkæm/ *noun* a video camera that is connected to a computer so that what it records can be seen on a Web site as it happens ⊃ picture at COMPUTER

web·cast /ˈwɛbkæst/ *noun* a live broadcast that is sent out on the Internet

'Web-enabled *adj.* able to be connected to and used with the Internet: *a Web-enabled interface*

we·ber /ˈwɛbər; ˈveɪbər/ *noun* (*abbr.* Wb) (*physics*) a unit for measuring MAGNETIC FLUX

'Web feed (also web feed) *noun* a way of sending data over the Internet that provides users with content that changes often, especially on a BLOG

web·head /ˈwɛbhɛd/ *noun* (*informal*) a person who uses the Internet a lot

web·i·nar /ˈwɛbəˌnɑr/ *noun* a presentation or SEMINAR (= a meeting for discussion or training) that is conducted over the Internet: *Our company uses webinars to develop leadership skills.*

web·li·og·ra·phy /ˌwɛbliˈɑgrəfi/ *noun* (*pl.* web·li·og·ra·phies) a list of Web sites or electronic works about a particular subject that have been used by a person writing an article, etc.: *a Hemingway webliography* ◆ *a selected webliography on new Irish poetry*

web·log /ˈwɛblɔg; -lɑg/ *noun* = BLOG

web·mas·ter /ˈwɛbˌmæstər/ *noun* (*computing*) a person who is responsible for particular pages of information on the World Wide Web

'Web page (also 'web page) *noun* a document that is connected to the World Wide Web and that anyone with an Internet connection can see, usually forming part of a Web site: *We learned how to create and register a new Web page.*

'Web site (also 'web site, web-site) /ˈwɛbsaɪt/ *noun* a place connected to the Internet, where a company or an organization, or an individual person, puts information: *I found this information on their Web site.* ◆ *For current prices please visit our Web site.* ⊃ collocations at E-MAIL

| i see | ɪ sit | ɛ ten | æ cat | ɑ hot | ɔ saw | ʊ put | u too | 1687 |

web·zine /ˈwɛbzin/ *noun* a magazine published on the Internet, not on paper

wed /wɛd/ *verb* (**wed·ded, wed·ded** or **wed, wed**) [I, T] (not used in the progressive tenses) (*old-fashioned* or used in newspapers) to marry: *The couple plans to wed next summer.* ♦ **~ sb** *Rock star to wed supermodel* (= in a HEADLINE)

we'd /wid/ *short form* **1** we had **2** we would

wed·ded /ˈwɛdəd/ *adj.* **1 ~ to sth** (*formal*) if you are **wedded** to something, you like or support it so much that you are not willing to give it up: *She's wedded to her job.* **2** [usually before noun] (*old-fashioned* or *formal*) legally married: *your lawfully wedded husband* ♦ *to live together in wedded bliss* **3** [not before noun] **~ (to sth)** (*formal* or *literary*) combined or united with something

wed·ding 🔑 /ˈwɛdɪŋ/ *noun*
a marriage ceremony, and the party that usually follows it: *a wedding present* ♦ *a wedding ceremony/reception* ♦ *Were you invited to their wedding?* ♦ *She looked beautiful on her wedding day.* ♦ *All her friends could hear wedding bells* (= they thought she would soon get married). ➔ collocations at MARRIAGE ➔ see also SHOTGUN WEDDING

ˈwedding anniˌversary *noun* the celebration every year of the date when two people were married: *Today's our wedding anniversary.* ➔ see also DIAMOND ANNIVERSARY, GOLDEN ANNIVERSARY, SILVER ANNIVERSARY

ˈwedding ˌband *noun* a wedding ring in the form of a plain band, usually of gold

ˈwedding ˌcake *noun* [C, U] a cake covered with ICING, and usually with several layers, eaten at a wedding party

ˈwedding ˌdress *noun* a dress that a woman wears at her wedding, especially a long white one

ˈwedding ˌring *noun* a ring that is given during a marriage ceremony and worn afterward to show that you are married ➔ picture at JEWELRY

wedge /wɛdʒ/ *noun, verb*
● *noun* **1** a piece of wood, rubber, metal, etc. with one thick end and one thin pointed end that you use to keep a door open, to keep two things apart, or to split wood or rock: *He hammered the wedge into the crack in the stone.* ♦ (*figurative*) *I don't want to drive a wedge between the two of you* (= to make you start disliking each other). **2** something that is shaped like a wedge or that is used like a wedge: *a wedge of cheese* ➔ picture at SHOE **3** a GOLF CLUB that has the part you hit the ball with shaped like a wedge
● *verb* **1 ~ sth + adv./prep.** to put or squeeze something tightly into a narrow space, so that it cannot move easily **SYN** JAM: *The boat was now wedged between the rocks.* ♦ *She wedged herself into the passenger seat.* **2 ~ sth (+ adj.)** to make something stay in a particular position, especially open or shut, by placing something against it: *to wedge the door open*

ˈwedge ˌissue *noun* an important and difficult political issue, used by a political party to draw supporters away from an opposing party

wedg·ie /ˈwɛdʒi/ *noun* (*informal*) an act of lifting someone up by their underwear, usually done as a joke

wed·lock /ˈwɛdlɑk/ *noun* [U] (*old-fashioned* or *law*) the state of being married: *children born in/out of wedlock* (= whose parents are/are not married)

Wednes·day 🔑 /ˈwɛnzdeɪ, -di/ *noun* [C, U] (*abbr.* **Wed., Weds.**)
the day of the week after Tuesday and before Thursday **HELP** To see how **Wednesday** is used, look at the examples at **Monday**. **ORIGIN** Originally translated from the Latin for "day of Mercury" *Mercurii dies* and named after the Germanic god *Odin*.

wee /wi/ *adj.* (*informal*) **1** (*old-fashioned*) very small in size: *a wee girl* **2** small in amount; little: *Just a wee drop of milk for me.* ♦ *I felt a wee bit guilty about it.*
IDM **the wee hours** = HOUR

weed /wid/ *noun, verb*
● *noun* **1** [C] a wild plant growing where it is not wanted, especially among crops or garden plants: *The yard was overgrown with weeds.* **2** [U] any wild plant without flowers that grows in water and forms a green floating mass **3** [U] (*informal*) the drug CANNABIS **4 the weed** [sing.] (*humorous*) TOBACCO or cigarettes: *I wish I could give up the weed* (= stop smoking).
● *verb* [T, I] **~ (sth)** to take out weeds from the ground: *I've been weeding the flower beds.*
PHR V **weed sth/sb↔ˈout** to remove or get rid of people or things from a group because they are not wanted or are less good than the rest

weed·kil·ler /ˈwidˌkɪlər/ *noun* [U, C] a substance that is used to destroy weeds

weed·y /ˈwidi/ *adj.* (**weed·i·er, weed·i·est**) **1** full of or covered with weeds **2** (*informal, disapproving*) having a thin weak body: *a weedy little man*

Wee·juns™ /ˈwidʒənz/ *noun* [pl.] MOCCASIN style shoes

week 🔑 /wik/ *noun* (*abbr.* **wk.**)
1 a period of seven days, either from Monday to Sunday or from Sunday to Saturday: *last/this/next week.* ♦ *What day of the week is it?* ♦ *He comes to see us once a week.* **2** any period of seven days: *a two-week vacation* ♦ *The course lasts five weeks.* ♦ *a week ago today* (= seven days ago) ♦ *She'll be back in a week.* **3** the five days other than Saturday and Sunday: *They live in town during the week and go to the country for the weekend.* **4** the part of the week when you go to work: *a 35-hour week* ➔ see also WORKWEEK
IDM **a week (from) today, etc.** seven days after the day that you mention: *I'll see you a week from Thursday.* **week after week** (*informal*) continuously for many weeks: *Week after week the drought continued.* **week by week** as the weeks pass: *Week by week he grew a little stronger.* **week in, week out** happening every week: *Every Sunday, week in, week out, she goes to her parents for lunch.* ➔ more at OTHER

week·day /ˈwikdeɪ/ *noun* any day except Saturday and Sunday: *The center is open from 9 a.m. to 6 p.m. on weekdays.* ▶ **week·days** *adv.*: *open weekdays from 9 a.m. to 6 p.m.*

week·end 🔑 /ˈwikɛnd/ *noun, verb*
● *noun* **1** Saturday and Sunday: *Are you doing anything over the weekend?* ♦ *Have a good weekend!* ♦ *It happened on the weekend of April 24.* ♦ *The office is closed on the weekend.* ♦ *We go skiing most weekends in winter.* ➔ see also LONG WEEK-END **2** Saturday and Sunday, or a slightly longer period, as a vacation: *He won a weekend for two in Florida.*
● *verb* [I] **+ adv./prep.** to spend the weekend somewhere: *They're weekending in New York.*

week·end·er /ˈwikˌɛndər/ *noun* a person who visits or lives in a place only on Saturdays and Sundays

ˌweekend ˈwarrior *noun* a person who works all week, especially in an office or other indoor job, and uses the weekends to go out and do more active and/or dangerous physical activities

week·long /ˈwiklɔŋ/ *adj.* [only before noun] lasting for a week: *a weeklong visit to Rome* ♦ *weeklong courses*

week·ly 🔑 /ˈwikli/ *adj., noun*
● *adj.* (*abbr.* **wkly.**) happening, done, or published once a week or every week: *weekly meetings* ♦ *a weekly magazine* ▶ **week·ly** *adv.* (*abbr.* **wkly.**): *Employees are paid weekly.* ♦ *The newspaper is published twice weekly.*
● *noun* (*pl.* **week·lies**) a newspaper or magazine that is published every week

week·night /ˈwiknaɪt/ *noun* any night of the week except Saturday, Sunday, and sometimes Friday night: *I have to stay home on weeknights.*

wee·nie /ˈwini/ *noun* (*informal*) **1** (*disapproving*) a person who is not strong, brave, or confident **SYN** WIMP: *Don't be such a weenie!* **2** = FRANKFURTER

ʌ **cup**   ə **about**   eɪ **say**   aɪ **five**   ɔɪ **boy**   aʊ **now**   oʊ **go**   ər **bird**

wee·ny /ˈwini/ adj. (**wee·ni·er, wee·ni·est**) (informal) extremely small **SYN** TINY: Weren't you just a weeny bit scared? ⊃ see also TEENY

weep /wip/ verb (**wept, wept** /wɛpt/) **1** [I, T] (formal or literary) to cry, usually because you are sad: She started to weep uncontrollably. ◆ **I could have wept** thinking about what I'd missed. ◆ **~ for/with sth** He wept for joy. ◆ **~ at/over sth** I do not weep over his death. ◆ **~ sth** She wept bitter tears of disappointment. ◆ **~ to do sth** I wept to see him looking so sick. ◆ + speech "I'm so unhappy!" she wept. **2** [I] (usually used in the progressive tenses) (of a wound) to produce liquid: His legs were covered with weeping sores (= sores that had not healed).

weep·ing /ˈwipɪŋ/ adj. [only before noun] (of some trees) with branches that hang downward: a weeping willow/fig/birch

weep·y /ˈwipi/ adj., noun
● adj. (informal) sad and tending to cry easily: She was feeling tired and weepy.
● noun (also **weep·ie**) (pl. **weep·ies**) (informal) a sad film/movie or play that makes you want to cry **SYN** TEARJERKER

wee·vil /ˈwivl/ noun a small insect with a hard shell, that eats grain, nuts, and other seeds and destroys crops

ˈwee-wee = URINE

the weft /wɛft/ (also less frequent **the woof**) noun [sing.] the threads that are twisted under and over the threads that are held on a LOOM (= a frame or machine for making cloth) ⊃ compare WARP

weigh /weɪ/ verb

1 linking verb (+ noun) to have a particular weight: How much do you weigh (= how heavy are you)? ◆ She weighs 130 pounds. ◆ These cases weigh a ton (= are very heavy). **2** [T] **~ sb/sth/yourself** to measure how heavy someone or something is, usually by using a SCALE: He weighed himself on the bathroom scale. ◆ She weighed the stone in her hand (= estimated how heavy it was by holding it.). **3** [T] to consider something carefully before making a decision: **~ sth** You must weigh the pros and cons (= consider the advantages and disadvantages of something). ◆ She weighed all the evidence. ◆ **~ sth against sth** I weighed the benefits of the plan against the risks involved. **4** [I] **~ (with sb) (against sb/sth)** to have an influence on someone's opinion or the result of something: His past record weighs heavily against him. **5** [T] **~ anchor** to lift an ANCHOR out of the water and into a boat before sailing away
IDM **weigh your words** to choose your words carefully so that you say exactly what you mean
PHR V **ˌweigh sb↔ˈdown** to make someone feel worried or anxious **SYN** BURDEN: The responsibilities of the job were weighing him down. ◆ He is weighed down with guilt. **ˌweigh sb/sth↔ˈdown** to make someone or something heavier so that they are not able to move easily: I was weighed down with baggage. **ˌweigh ˈin (at sth)** to have your weight measured, especially before a contest, race, etc.: Both boxers weighed in at several pounds below the limit. ⊃ related noun WEIGH-IN **ˌweigh ˈin (with sth)** (informal) to join in a discussion, an argument, an activity, etc. by saying something important, persuading someone, or doing something to help: We all weighed in with our suggestions. ◆ Finally the government weighed in with financial aid. **ˌweigh on sb/sth** to make someone anxious or worried: The responsibilities weigh heavily on him. ◆ Something was weighing on her mind. **ˌweigh sth↔ˈout** to measure an amount of something by weight: She weighed out a pound of grapes. **ˌweigh sb↔ˈup** to form an opinion of someone by watching or talking to them

ˈweigh-in noun the occasion when the weight of a BOXER, JOCKEY, etc. is checked officially

weight /weɪt/ noun, verb

● noun
▷ BEING HEAVY **1** [U, C] how heavy someone or something is, which can be measured in, for example, pounds or kilograms: It is about 76 pounds **in weight**. ◆ Bananas are sold **by weight**. ◆ In the wild, this fish can reach a weight of 5 lbs. ◆ She is trying to **lose weight** (= become less heavy and less fat). ◆ He's **put on/gained weight** (= become heavier and fatter) since he gave up smoking. ◆ Sam has a **weight problem** (= is too fat). ◆ No more for me. I have to **watch my weight**. ⊃ collocations at DIET ⊃ see also OVERWEIGHT, UNDERWEIGHT **2** [U] the fact of being heavy: He staggered a little **under the weight of** his backpack. ◆ I just hoped the branch would **hold my weight**. ◆ The pillars have to support the weight of the roof. ◆ Don't put any weight on that ankle for at least a week. ⊃ see also DEAD WEIGHT
▷ HEAVY OBJECT **3** [C] an object that is heavy: The doctor said he should not lift heavy weights. **4** [C] an object used to keep something in position or as part of a machine: weights on a fishing line ⊃ see also PAPERWEIGHT
▷ RESPONSIBILITY/WORRY **5** [sing.] **~ (of sth)** a great responsibility or worry **SYN** BURDEN: The full weight of responsibility falls on her. ◆ The news was certainly a **weight off my mind** (= I did not have to worry about it any more). ◆ Finally telling the truth was **a great weight off my shoulders**.
▷ INFLUENCE/STRENGTH **6** [U] importance, influence, or strength: The many letters of support **added weight** to the campaign. ◆ The president has now offered to **lend his weight** to the project. ◆ Your opinion **carries weight** with the boss. ◆ How can you ignore the **sheer weight** of medical opinion? ◆ The weight of evidence against her is overwhelming.
▷ FOR MEASURING/LIFTING **7** [C, U] a unit or system of units by which weight is measured: tables of weights and measures ◆ imperial/metric weight **8** [C] a piece of metal that is known to weigh a particular amount and is used to measure the weight of something, or lifted by people to improve their strength and as a sport: a set of weights ◆ She lifts weights as part of her training. ◆ He does a lot of **weight training**.
IDM **throw your weight around** (informal) to use your position of authority or power in an aggressive way in order to achieve what you want **throw/put your weight behind sth** to use all your influence and power to support something **weight of numbers** the combined power, strength, or influence of a group: They won the argument by sheer weight of numbers. ⊃ more at GROAN v., PULL v., PUNCH v., WORTH adj.
● verb
▷ ATTACH HEAVY OBJECT **1 ~ sth (down) (with sth)** to attach a weight to something in order to keep it in the right position or make it heavier: The fishing nets are weighted with lead.
▷ GIVE IMPORTANCE **2** [usually passive] **~ sth** to give different values to things to show how important you think each of them is compared with the others: The results of the survey were weighted to allow for variations in the sample. ◆ a **weighted vote** (= one that is worth more than a single vote) ◆ a **weighted grade** (= given at school for a course that is more advanced or harder and so has a higher value)

weight·ed /ˈweɪtəd/ adj. [not before noun] arranged in such a way that a particular person or thing has an advantage or a disadvantage **SYN** BIASED: **~ toward sb/sth** The proposal is weighted toward smaller businesses. ◆ **~ against sb/sth** Everything seemed weighted against them. ◆ **~ in favor of sb/sth** The course is heavily weighted in favor of engineering.

weight·ing /ˈweɪtɪŋ/ noun [C, U] a value that you give to each of a number of things to show how important it is compared with the others: Each of the factors is given a weighting on a scale of 1 to 10. ◆ Each question in the exam has equal weighting.

weight·less /ˈweɪtləs/ adj. having no weight or appearing to have no weight, for example because there is no GRAVITY: Astronauts work in weightless conditions. ▸ **weight·less·ness** noun [U]

weight·lift·ing /ˈweɪt lɪftɪŋ/ noun [U] the sport or activity of lifting heavy weights ▸ **weight·lift·er** noun

weight·y /ˈweɪti/ adj. (**weight·i·er, weight·i·est**) (formal) **1** important and serious: weighty matters **2** heavy: a weighty volume/tome ▸ **weight·i·ly** /ˈweɪtl·i/ adv. **weight·i·ness** /ˈweɪtinəs/ noun [U]

weir /wɪr/ *noun* a low wall or barrier built across a river in order to control the flow of water or change its direction

weird 🔑 /wɪrd/ *adj., verb*

- **adj.** (weird·er, weird·est) **1** very strange or unusual and difficult to explain: *a weird dream* **SYN** STRANGE: *She's a really weird girl.* ◆ *He's got some weird ideas.* ◆ *It's really weird seeing yourself on television.* ◆ *the weird and wonderful creatures that live beneath the sea* **2** strange in a mysterious and frightening way **SYN** EERIE: *She began to make weird inhuman sounds.* ▶ **weird·ly** *adv.*: *The town was weirdly familiar.* **weird·ness** *noun* [U]

- **verb**
  PHR V **weird sb 'out** (*informal*) to seem strange or worrying to someone and make them feel uncomfortable: *The whole concept really weirds me out.*

weird·o /ˈwɪrdoʊ/ *noun* (*pl.* **weird·os** /-doʊz/) (*informal, disapproving*) a person who looks strange and/or behaves in a strange way

welch /wɛltʃ; wɛlʃ/ *verb* = WELSH

wel·come 🔑 /ˈwɛlkəm/ *verb, adj., noun, exclamation*

- **verb 1** [T, I] to say hello to someone in a friendly way when they arrive somewhere: **~ (sb)** *They were at the door to welcome us.* ◆ *a welcoming smile* ◆ **~ sb to sth** *It is a pleasure to welcome you to our home.* **2** [T] **~ sb** to be pleased that someone has come or has joined an organization, activity, etc.: *They welcomed the new volunteers with open arms* (= with enthusiasm). **3** [T] **~ sth** to be pleased to receive or accept something: *I'd welcome any suggestions.* ◆ *I warmly welcome this decision.* ◆ *In general, the changes they had made were to be welcomed.*

- **adj. 1** that you are pleased to have, receive, etc.: *a welcome sight* ◆ *Your letter was very welcome.* ◆ *The fine weather made a welcome change.* **2** (of people) accepted or wanted somewhere: *Children are always welcome at the hotel.* ◆ *Our neighbors made us welcome as soon as we arrived.* ◆ *I had the feeling we were not welcome at the meeting.* **3** **~ to do sth** (*informal*) used to say that you are happy for someone to do something if they want to: *They're welcome to stay here as long as they like.* **4** **~ to sth** (*informal*) used to say that you are very happy for someone to have something because you definitely do not want it: *It's an awful job. If you want it, you're welcome to it!*
  IDM **you're welcome** used as a polite reply when someone thanks you for something: *"Thanks for your help." "You're welcome."*

- **noun 1** [C, U] something that you do or say to someone when they arrive, especially something that makes them feel you are happy to see them: *Thank you for your warm welcome.* ◆ *The winners were given an enthusiastic welcome when they arrived home.* ◆ *a speech/smile of welcome* ◆ *to receive a hero's welcome* **2** [C] the way that people react to something, which shows their opinion of it: *This new comedy deserves a warm welcome.* ◆ *The proposals were given a cautious welcome by the trade unions.*
  IDM **outstay/overstay your welcome** to stay somewhere as a guest longer than you are wanted

- **exclamation** used as a GREETING to tell someone that you are pleased that they are there: *Welcome home!* ◆ *Welcome to Columbus!* ◆ *Good evening everybody. Welcome to the show!*

welcome mat *noun*
  IDM **lay, put, roll, etc. out the welcome mat (for sb)** to make someone feel welcome; to try to attract visitors, etc.

wel·com·ing /ˈwɛlkəmɪŋ/ *adj.* **1** (of a person) friendly toward someone who is visiting or arriving **2** (of a place) attractive and looking comfortable to be in
  ANT UNWELCOMING

weld /wɛld/ *verb, noun*

- **verb 1** [T, I] to join pieces of metal by heating their edges and pressing them together: **~ (sth)** *to weld a broken axle* ◆ **~ A (on) (to B)** *The car has had a new wing welded on.* ◆ **~ A and B (together)** *All the parts of the sculpture have to be welded together.* **2** [T] to unite people or things into a strong

and effective group: **~ sb/sth into sth** *They had welded a bunch of untrained recruits into an efficient fighting force.* ◆ **~ sth together** *The crisis helped to weld the party together.*

- **noun** a joint made by welding

weld·er /ˈwɛldər/ *noun* a person whose job is welding metal

wel·fare **AWL** /ˈwɛlfɛr/ *noun* [U] **1** money that the government pays regularly to people who are poor, unemployed, sick, etc.: *They would rather work than live on welfare.* ⊃ collocations at UNEMPLOYMENT **2** practical or financial help that is provided, often by the government, for people or animals that need it: *child welfare* ◆ *a social welfare program* ◆ *welfare provision/services/work* **3** the general health, happiness, and safety of a person, an animal, or a group **SYN** WELL-BEING: *We are concerned about the child's welfare.*

welfare state *noun* **1** often **the welfare state** [usually sing.] a system by which the government provides a range of free services to people who need them, for example medical care, money for people without work, care for old people, etc. **2** [C] a country that has such a system

wel·kin /ˈwɛlkɪn/ *noun* [U] (*literary or old use*) the sky or heaven
  IDM **let/make the welkin ring** to make a very loud noise

well 🔑 /wɛl/ *adv., adj., exclamation, noun, verb*

- **adv.** (bet·ter /ˈbɛtər/, best /bɛst/) **1** in a good, right, or acceptable way: *The kids all behaved well.* ◆ *The conference was very well organized.* ◆ *His campaign was not going well.* ◆ *These animals make very good pets if treated well* (= with kindness). ◆ *People spoke well of* (= spoke with approval of) *him.* ◆ *She took it very well* (= did not react too badly), *all things considered.* ◆ *They lived well* (= in comfort and spending a lot of money) *and were generous with their money.* ◆ *Well done!* (= expressing admiration for what someone has done) ◆ *She was determined to marry well* (= marry someone rich and/or with a high social position). **2** thoroughly and completely: *Add the lemon juice and mix well.* ◆ *The surface must be well prepared before you start to paint.* ◆ *How well do you know Carla?* ◆ *He's well able to take care of himself.* **3** to a great extent or degree: *He was driving at well over the speed limit.* ◆ *a well-loved tale* ◆ *The castle is well worth a visit.* ◆ *He liked her well enough* (= to a reasonable degree) *but he wasn't going to make a close friend of her.* **4** **can/could well** easily: *She could well afford to pay for it herself.* **5** **can/could/may/might well** probably: *You may well be right.* ◆ *It may well be that the train is delayed.* **6** **can/could/may/might well** with good reason: *I can't very well leave now.* ◆ *I couldn't very well refuse to help them, could I?* ◆ *"What are we doing here?" "You may well ask"* (= I don't really know either)*.*
  IDM **as well (as sb/sth)** (somewhat *formal*) in addition to someone or something; too: *Will your husband be attending as well?* ◆ *They sell books as well as newspapers.* ◆ *She is a talented musician as well as being a photographer.* ⊃ note at ALSO **be doing well** to be getting healthier after an illness; to be in good health after a birth: *Mother and baby are doing well.* **be well on the way to sth/doing sth** to have nearly achieved something and be going to achieve it soon: *She is well on the way to recovery.* ◆ *He is well on the way to establishing himself among the top ten players in the world.* **be well up on/in sth** to know a lot about something: *He's well up on all the latest developments.* **do well** to be successful: *Jack is doing very well at school.* **do well by sb** to treat someone generously **do well for yourself** to become successful or rich **do well to do sth** to be sensible or wise to do something: *He would do well to concentrate more on his work.* ◆ *You did well to sell when the price was high.* **leave/let well enough alone** to not get involved in something that does not concern you: *When it comes to other people's arguments, it's better to leave well enough alone.* **may/might (just) as well do sth** to do something because it seems best in the situation that you are in, although you may not really want to do it: *If no one else wants it, we might as well give it to him.* **well and truly** (*informal*) completely: *By that time we were well and truly lost.* **well in (with sb)** (*informal*) to be good friends with someone, especially someone important: *She*

seems to be well in with all the right people. ⊃ more at KNOW, MEAN v., PRETTY

well

good • all right • OK • fine • healthy • strong • in shape

These words all describe someone who is not sick and is in good health.

well [not usually before noun] (*somewhat informal*) in good health: *Is he well enough to travel?* **NOTE** Well is used especially to talk about your own health, to ask someone about their health, or to make a comment on it.

good [not usually before noun] (*somewhat informal*) in good health: *I don't feel good.* ◆ *She's looking much better these days.*

all right [not before noun] (*somewhat informal*) not feeling ill; not injured: *Are you feeling all right?*

OK [not before noun] (*informal*) not feeling ill; not injured: *She says that she's OK now, and will be back at work tomorrow.*

ALL RIGHT OR OK?

These words are slightly less positive than the other words in this group. They are both used in spoken English, to talk about not actually being sick or injured, rather than being positively in good health. Both are somewhat informal but **OK** is slightly more informal than **all right**.

fine [not before noun] (not used in negative statements) (*somewhat informal*) completely well: "*How are you?*" "*Fine, thanks.*" **NOTE** Fine is used especially to talk about your health, especially when someone asks you how you are. It is also used to talk about someone's health when you are talking to someone else.

healthy in good health and not likely to become sick: *Stay healthy by exercising regularly.*

strong in good health and not suffering from an illness: *After a few weeks, she was feeling stronger.* **NOTE** Strong is often used to talk about becoming healthy again after an illness.

in shape in good physical health, especially because you take regular physical exercise: *I go swimming every day in order to stay in shape.*

PATTERNS

- all right/OK/in shape **for** sth
- all right/OK **to do** sth
- to **feel/look** well/good/all right/OK/fine/healthy/strong
- to **keep (sb)** well/healthy/in shape
- **perfectly** well/all right/OK/fine/healthy
- **physically** well/healthy/strong

● **adj.** (bet·ter /ˈbɛtər/, best /bɛst/) **1** [not usually before noun] in good health: *I don't feel very well.* ◆ *Is she well enough to travel?* ◆ *Get well soon!* (= said when someone is sick) ◆ *I'm better now, thank you.* ◆ (*informal*) *He's not a well man.* **2** [not before noun] in a good state or position: *It seems that all is not well at home.* ◆ *All's well that ends well* (= used when something has ended happily, even though you thought it might not). **3** [not before noun] **(as) ~ (to do sth)** sensible; a good idea: *It would be just as well to call and say we might be late.* ◆ (*formal*) *It would be well to start early.* **IDM** all very well (for sb) (to do sth) (*informal*) used to criticize or reject a remark that someone has made, especially when they were trying to make you feel happier about something: *It's all very well for you to say it doesn't matter, but I've put a lot of work into this and I want it to be a success.* all well and good (*informal*) quite good, but not

exactly what is wanted: *That's all well and good, but why didn't he call her to say so?*

● **exclamation 1** used to express surprise, anger, or relief: *Well, well —I would never have guessed it!* ◆ *Well, really! What a thing to say!* ◆ *Well, thank goodness that's over!* **2** used to show that you accept that something cannot be changed: *Well, it can't be helped.* ◆ "*We lost.*" "*Oh, well. Better luck next time.*" **3** used to agree to something, rather unwillingly: *Well, I suppose I could fit you in at 3:45.* ◆ *Oh, very well, then, if you insist.* **4** used when continuing a conversation after a pause: *Well, as I was saying…* **5** used to say that something is uncertain: "*Do you want to come?*" "*Well, I'm not sure.*" **6** used to show that you are waiting for someone to say something: *Well? Are you going to tell us or not?* **7** used to mark the end of a conversation: *Well, I'd better be going now.* **8** used when you are pausing to consider your next words: *I think it happened, well, toward the end of last summer.* **9** used when you want to correct or change something that you have just said: *There were thousands of people there—well, hundreds, anyway.* **IDM** well I never (did)! (*old-fashioned*) used to express surprise ⊃ more at SAY

● **noun 1** a deep hole in the ground from which people obtain water. The sides of wells are usually covered with brick or stone and there is usually some covering or a small wall at the top of the well. **2** = OIL WELL **3** a narrow space in a building that drops down from a high to a low level and usually contains stairs or an elevator ⊃ see also STAIRWELL

● **verb 1** [I] **~ (up)** (of a liquid) to rise to the surface of something and start to flow: *Tears were welling up in her eyes.* **2** [I] **~ (up)** (*literary*) (of an emotion) to become stronger: *Hate welled up inside him as he thought of the two of them together.*

we'll /wil; wɪl/ *short form* **1** we will **2** we shall

well

- Compound adjectives beginning with **well** are generally written with no hyphen when they are used after a verb, but with a hyphen when they come before a noun: *She is well dressed.* ◆ *a well-dressed woman* The forms with hyphens are given in the entries in the dictionary, but forms without hyphens can be seen in some examples.
- The comparative and superlative forms of these are usually formed with **better** and **best**: *better-known poets* ◆ *the best-dressed person in the room*

ˌwell-adˈjusted *adj.* (of a person) able to deal with people, problems, and life in general in a normal, sensible way ⊃ compare MALADJUSTED

ˌwell-adˈvised *adj.* [not before noun] **~ (to do sth)** acting in the most sensible way: *You would be well advised to tackle this problem urgently.* ⊃ compare ILL-ADVISED

ˌwell-apˈpointed *adj.* (*formal*) having all the necessary equipment; having comfortable and attractive furniture, etc.

ˌwell-atˈtended *adj.* attended by a lot of people: *a well-attended conference*

ˌwell-ˈbalanced *adj.* **1** containing a sensible variety of the sort of things or people that are needed: *a well-balanced diet* ◆ *The team was not well balanced.* **2** (of a person or their behavior) sensible and emotionally in control: *His response was well balanced.*

ˌwell-beˈhaved *adj.* behaving in a way that other people think is polite or correct: *a well-behaved child* ◆ *The audience was surprisingly well behaved.*

ˌwell-ˈbeing *noun* [U] general health and happiness: *emotional/physical/psychological well-being* ◆ *to have a sense of well-being*

ˌwell-ˈborn *adj.* (*formal*) from a rich family or a family of high social class

---

v voice   θ thin   ð then   s so   z zoo   ʃ she   ʒ vision   x Chanukah   1691

well-'bred *adj.* (*old-fashioned, formal*) having or showing good manners; typical of a high social class: *a well-bred young lady* ◆ *She was too well bred to show her disappointment.* **ANT** ILL-BRED

well-'built *adj.* **1** (of a person) with a solid, strong body **2** (of a building or machine) strongly made

well-con'nected *adj.* (*formal*) (of a person) having important or rich friends or relatives

well-'cut *adj.* (of clothes) made well and therefore probably expensive

well-de'fined *adj.* easy to see or understand: *well-defined rules* ◆ *These categories are not well defined.* **ANT** ILL-DEFINED

well-de'veloped *adj.* fully developed; fully grown: *He had a well-developed sense of his own superiority.*

well-dis'posed *adj.* ~ **(toward/to sb/sth)** having friendly feelings toward someone or a positive attitude toward something **ANT** ILL-DISPOSED

well-'documented *adj.* having a lot of written evidence to prove, support, or explain it: *The problem is well documented.* ◆ *well-documented facts*

well-'done *adj.* (of food, especially meat) cooked thoroughly or for a long time: *He prefers his steak well done.* ⊃ **compare** RARE, UNDERDONE

well-'dressed *adj.* wearing fashionable or expensive clothes: *This is what today's well-dressed man is wearing.*

well-'earned *adj.* much deserved: *a well-earned rest*

well-en'dowed *adj.* **1** (*informal, humorous*) (of a woman) having large breasts **2** (*informal, humorous*) (of a man) having a large PENIS **3** (of an organization) having a lot of money: *well-endowed colleges*

well-es'tablished *adj.* having a respected position, because of being successful, etc. over a long period: *a well-established firm* ◆ *He is now well established in his career.*

well-'fed *adj.* having plenty of good food to eat regularly: *well-fed family pets* ◆ *The animals all looked well fed and cared for.*

well-'formed *adj.* (of sentences) written or spoken correctly according to the rules of grammar

well-'founded (also *less frequent* ,well-'grounded) *adj.* having good reasons or evidence to cause or support it: *well-founded suspicions* ◆ *His fear turned out to be well founded.* **ANT** ILL-FOUNDED

well-'groomed *adj.* (of a person) looking clean, neat, and carefully dressed

well-'grounded *adj.* **1** ~ **in sth** having a good training in a subject or skill **2** = WELL FOUNDED

well-'heeled *adj.* (*informal*) having a lot of money **SYN** RICH, WEALTHY

well-'hung *adj.* (of meat) having been left for several days before being cooked in order to improve the flavor

well-in'formed *adj.* having or showing knowledge or information about many subjects or about one particular subject: *a well-informed decision* **ANT** ILL-INFORMED

well-in'tentioned *adj.* intending to be helpful or useful, but not always succeeding very well **SYN** WELL MEANING

well-'kept *adj.* **1** kept neat and in good condition: *well-kept gardens* **2** (of a secret) known only to a few people

well-'known 🔑 *adj.*
1 known about by a lot of people **SYN** FAMOUS: *a well-known actor* ◆ *His books are not well known.* **2** (of a fact) generally known and accepted: *It is a well-known fact that caffeine is a stimulant.*

well-'mannered *adj.* (*formal*) having good manners **SYN** POLITE **ANT** ILL-MANNERED

well-'matched *adj.* able to live together, play or fight each other, etc. because they are similar in character, ability, etc.: *a well-matched couple* ◆ *The two teams were well matched.*

well-'meaning *adj.* intending to do what is right and helpful, but often not succeeding **SYN** WELL INTENTIONED: *a well-meaning attempt to be helpful* ◆ *He's very well meaning.*

well-'meant *adj.* done, said, etc. in order to be helpful but often not succeeding: *well-meant comments* ◆ *His offer was well meant.*

well·ness /'wɛlnəs/ *noun* [U] the state of being healthy

well-'nigh *adv.* (*formal*) almost: *Defense was well-nigh impossible against such opponents.*

well-'off *adj.* **1** (*comparative* ,better-'off) having a lot of money **SYN** RICH: *a well-off family* ◆ *They are much better off than us.* ⊃ **thesaurus box at** RICH **2** (*comparative* ,better-'off, *superlative* ,best-'off) in a good situation: *I've got my own room so I'm well off.* ◆ *You'll be better off if you leave before rush hour.* **ANT** BADLY OFF

well-'oiled *adj.* operating smoothly and well: *The company ran like a well-oiled machine.*

well-'ordered *adj.* carefully planned or neatly organized: *a well-ordered home*

well-'paid *adj.* earning or providing a lot of money: *well-paid managers* ◆ *The job is very well paid.*

well-pre'served *adj.* not showing many signs of age; kept in good condition

well-read /,wɛl 'rɛd/ *adj.* having read many books and therefore having gained a lot of knowledge

well-'rounded *adj.* **1** having a variety of experiences and abilities and a fully developed personality: *well-rounded individuals* **2** providing or showing a variety of experience, ability, etc.: *a well-rounded education* **3** (of a person's body) pleasantly round in shape

well-'run *adj.* managed smoothly and well: *a well-run hotel*

well-'spoken *adj.* having a way of speaking that is considered correct or elegant

well·spring /'wɛlsprɪŋ/ *noun* (*literary*) a supply or source of a particular quality, especially one that never ends

well-'thought-of *adj.* respected, admired, and liked: *Their family has always been well thought of around here.*

well-thought-'out *adj.* carefully planned

well-'thumbed *adj.* a **well-thumbed** book has been read many times

well-'timed *adj.* done or happening at the right time or at an appropriate time **SYN** TIMELY: *a well-timed intervention* ◆ *Your remarks were certainly well timed.* **ANT** ILL-TIMED

well-to-'do *adj.* having a lot of money **SYN** RICH, WEALTHY: *a well-to-do family* ◆ *They're very well-to-do.*

well-'traveled (*CanE usually* ,well-'travelled) *adj.* **1** (of a person) having traveled to many different places **2** (of a route) used by a lot of people

well-'trodden *adj.* (*formal*) (of a road or path) much used

well-'turned *adj.* (*formal*) expressed in an elegant way: *a well-turned phrase*

well-'used *adj.* used a lot: *a well-used path*

well-'versed *adj.* having a lot of knowledge about something, or skill at something: *She's not a well-versed cook.*

'well-,wisher *noun* a person who wants to show that they support someone and want them to be happy, successful, etc.

well-'worn *adj.* **1** worn or used a lot or for a long time: *a well-worn jacket* ◆ *Most British visitors beat a well-worn path to the same tourist areas of the U.S.* **2** (of a phrase, story, etc.) heard so often that it does not sound interesting anymore **SYN** HACKNEYED

Welsh /wɛlʃ/ *noun, adj.*
• *noun* **1** [U] the Celtic language of Wales: *Do you speak Welsh?* **2** **the Welsh** [pl.] the people of Wales
• *adj.* of or connected with Wales, its people, or its language: *Welsh poetry*

welsh /wɛlʃ/ (also **welch**) *verb* [I] ~ **(on sb/sth)** (*disapproving, informal*) to not do something that you have promised to do,

h hat   m man   n no   ŋ sing   1 leg   r red   y yes   w wet

for example to not pay money that you owe: *"I'm not in the habit of welshing on deals,"* said Don.

ˌWelsh ˈrarebit (also **rare·bit**, ˌWelsh ˈrabbit) *noun* [U] a hot dish of cheese melted on TOAST

welt /wɛlt/ *noun* a raised mark on the skin where something has hit or rubbed you **SYN** WEAL

Welt·an·schau·ung /ˈvɛltanˌʃaʊʊŋ/ *noun* (*pl.* **Welt·an·schau·ung·en** /-ˌʃaʊʊŋən/) (from *German, formal*) a particular philosophy or view of life

wel·ter /ˈwɛltər/ *noun* [sing.] **~ of sth** (*formal*) a large and confusing amount of something: *a welter of information*

wel·ter·weight /ˈwɛltərˌweɪt/ *noun* a BOXER weighing from 140 to 147 pounds (63-67 kg), heavier than a LIGHTWEIGHT: *a welterweight champion*

wench /wɛntʃ/ *noun* (*old use* or *humorous*) a young woman

wend /wɛnd/ *verb* [T, I] **~ (your way) (+ adv./prep.)** (*old use* or *literary*) to move or travel slowly somewhere: *Leo wended his way home through the wet streets.*

went pt of GO

wept pt, pp of WEEP

were /wər/ ➔ BE

we're /wɪr/ *short form* we are

weren't /wɑrnt; ˈwɑrənt/ *short form* were not

were·wolf /ˈwɛrwʊlf/ *noun* (*pl.* **were·wolves** /-wʊlvz/) (in stories) a person who sometimes changes into a WOLF, especially at the time of the full moon

Wer·nick·e's ar·e·a /ˈvɛrnɪkəz ˌɛriə; -kɪz-/ *noun* (*anatomy*) an area in the brain concerned with understanding language

west 🔊 /wɛst/ *noun, adj., adv.*

• *noun* [U, sing.] (*abbr.* **W.**, **W**) **1** (also **the west**) the direction that you look toward to see the sun go down; one of the four main points of the COMPASS: *Which way is west?* ✦ *Rain is spreading from the west.* ✦ *He lives to the west of (= further west than) the town.* ➔ picture at COMPASS ➔ compare EAST, NORTH, SOUTH **2** **the West** the countries of North America and western Europe: *I was born in Japan, but I've lived in the West for some years now.* **3** **the West** the western side of the U.S.: *the history of the American West* ➔ see also THE MID-WEST, THE WILD WEST **4** **the West** (in the past) Western Europe and N. America, when contrasted with the Communist countries of Eastern Europe: *East-West relations*

• *adj.* [only before noun] **1** (*abbr.* **W.**, **W**) in or toward the west: *West Africa* ✦ *the west coast of Scotland* **2** a **west wind** blows from the west ➔ compare WESTERLY

• *adv.* toward the west: *This room faces west.*

west·bound /ˈwɛstbaʊnd/ *adj.* traveling or leading toward the west: *westbound traffic* ✦ *the westbound lane of the highway*

the ˌWest ˈCoast *noun* [sing.] the states on the west coast of the U.S., especially California

west·er·ly /ˈwɛstərli/ *adj., noun*

• *adj.* **1** [only before noun] in or toward the west: *traveling in a westerly direction* **2** [usually before noun] (of winds) blowing from the west: *westerly gales* ➔ compare WEST

• *noun* (*pl.* **west·er·lies**) a wind that blows from the west: *light westerlies*

west·ern 🔊 /ˈwɛstərn/ *adj., noun*

• *adj.* **1** [only before noun] (*abbr.* **W.**, **W**) also **Western** located in the west or facing west: *western Alaska* ✦ *Western Europe* ✦ *the western slopes of the mountain* **2** usually **Western** connected with the west part of the world, especially Europe and N. America: *Western art* ➔ see also COUNTRY AND WESTERN

• *noun* a movie or book about life in the western U.S. in the 19th century, usually involving COWBOYS

west·ern·er /ˈwɛstərnər/ *noun* **1** a person who comes from or lives in the western part of the world, especially western Europe or N. America **2** **Westerner** a person who was born in or who lives in the western U.S. or western Canada

west·ern·i·za·tion /ˌwɛstərnəˈzeɪʃn/ *noun* [U] the process of becoming westernized

west·ern·ize /ˈwɛstərˌnaɪz/ *verb* [usually passive] **~ sth** to bring ideas or ways of life that are typical of western Europe and N. America to other countries: *The islands have been westernized by the growth of tourism.* ▶ **west·ern·ized** *adj.*: *a westernized society*

ˌWestern ˈmedicine *noun* [U] the type of medical treatment that is standard in Europe and N. America and that relies on scientific methods: *the drugs used in Western medicine*

west·ern·most /ˈwɛstərnˌmoʊst/ *adj.* located furthest west: *the westernmost tip of the island*

the West In·dies /ˌwɛst ˈɪndiz/ *noun* [pl.] (*abbr.* **WI**) a group of islands between the Caribbean and the Atlantic that includes the Antilles and the Bahamas ▶ ˌWest ˈIndian *adj.* ˌWest ˈIndian *noun*

ˌwest-northˈwest *noun* [sing.] (*abbr.* **W.N.W.**, **WNW**) the direction at an equal distance between west and northwest ▶ ˌwest-northˈwest *adv.*

the ˈWest Side *noun* [sing.] the western part of Manhattan in New York City, which includes Broadway

ˌwest-southˈwest *noun* [sing.] (*abbr.* **W.S.W.**, **WSW**) the direction at an equal distance between west and southwest ▶ ˌwest-southˈwest *adv.*

west·ward /ˈwɛstwərd/ (also **west·wards**) *adv.* toward the west: *to turn westward* ▶ **west·ward** *adj.*: *in a westward direction*

wet 🔊 /wɛt/ *adj., verb, noun*

• *adj.* (**wet·ter**, **wet·test**) **1** covered with or containing liquid, especially water: *wet clothes* ✦ *wet grass* ✦ *You'll get wet* (= in the rain) *if you go out now.* ✦ *Try not to get your shoes wet.* ✦ *His face was wet with tears.* ✦ *We were all soaking wet* (= extremely wet). ✦ *Her hair was still dripping wet.* ✦ *My shirt was wet through* (= completely wet). **2** (of weather, etc.) with rain: *a wet day* ✦ *a wet climate* ✦ *It's wet outside.* ✦ *It's going to be wet tomorrow.* ✦ *It was the wettest October for many years.* **3** (of paint, ink, etc.) not yet dry: *Keep off! Wet paint.* **4** if a child or its DIAPER is **wet**, its diaper is full of URINE ▶ **wet·ly** *adv.* **wet·ness** *noun* [U]

IDM **all wet** (*informal*) completely wrong (still) wet behind the ears (*informal, disapproving*) young and without much experience **SYN** NAIVE ➔ more at FOOT

• *verb* (**wet·ting**, **wet**, **wet** or **wet·ting**, **wet·ted**, **wet·ted**) **~ sth** to make something wet: *Wet the brush slightly before putting it in the paint.*

IDM **wet the/your bed** [no passive] to URINATE in your bed by accident: *It is quite common for small children to wet their beds.* **wet yourself| wet your pants** [no passive] to URINATE in your underwear by accident

• *noun* **1** **the wet** [sing.] wet weather; rain: *Come in out of the wet.* **2** [U] liquid, especially water: *The dog shook the wet from its coat.*

THESAURUS

wet

moist ✦ **damp** ✦ **soaked** ✦ **drenched** ✦ **saturated**

These words all describe things covered with or full of liquid, especially water.

wet covered with or full of liquid, especially water: *The car skidded on the wet road.* ✦ *You'll get wet* (= in the rain) *if you go out now.*

moist slightly wet, often in a way that is pleasant or useful: *a rich, moist cake*

damp slightly wet, often in a way that is unpleasant: *The cabin was cold and damp.*

soaked (*somewhat informal*) very wet: *You're soaked through!* (= completely wet)

drenched very wet: *We got caught in the storm and were drenched to the skin.*

'**wet bar** *noun* a counter with a SINK that is used for serving alcoholic drinks at home or in a hotel room

ˌwet '**blanket** *noun* (*informal, disapproving*) a person who is not enthusiastic about anything and who stops other people from enjoying themselves

'**wet dock** *noun* a place for ships to stay in order to be repaired, have goods put onto them, etc., in which there is enough water for the ship to float ⊃ compare DRY DOCK

'**wet dream** *noun* a sexually exciting dream that a man has that results in an ORGASM

wet·land /'wetlænd; -lənd/ *noun* [C, U] also **wet·lands** [pl.] an area of wet land: *The wetlands are home to a large variety of wildlife.* ▶ **wetland** *adj.* [only before noun]: *wetland birds*

'**wet nurse** *noun* (usually in the past) a woman employed to feed another woman's baby with her own breast milk

wet·suit /'wetsut/ *noun* a piece of clothing made of rubber that fits the whole body closely, worn by people playing water sports or DIVING ⊃ picture at HOBBY

wet·ware /'wetwer/ *noun* [U] (*humorous, computing*) the human brain, considered as a computer program or system

we've /wiv/ *short form* we have

whack /wæk/ *verb, noun*
- *verb* **1** ~ **sb/sth** (*informal*) to hit someone or something very hard: *She whacked him with her handbag.* ◆ *James whacked the ball over the net.* **2** ~ **sb** (*slang*) to murder someone
- *noun* [usually sing.] (*informal*) the act of hitting someone or something hard; the sound made by this: *He gave the ball a good whack.* ◆ *I heard the whack of the bullet hitting the wood.* **IDM out of whack** (*informal*) **1** no longer correct or working correctly: *The system is clearly out of whack.* ◆ *All the traveling had thrown my body out of whack.* **2** not agreeing with or not the same as something else: *Expectations and reality got out of whack.*

whacked /wækt/ (also **whack**) *adj.* (*informal*) = WACK: *I have a really whacked family.*

ˌwhacked '**out** *adj.* (*informal*) **1** under the influence of drugs or alcohol: *The kid is obviously whacked out.* **2** [not usually before noun] very tired: *I'm whacked out!*

whale /weɪl/ *noun* a very large animal that lives in the ocean and looks like a very large fish. There are several types of whales, some of which are hunted: *whale meat* ⊃ see also BLUE WHALE, KILLER WHALE, PILOT WHALE, SPERM WHALE ⊃ picture at ANIMAL **IDM have a whale of a time** (*informal*) to enjoy yourself very much; to have a very good time

whale·bone /'weɪlboʊn/ *noun* [U] a thin, hard substance found in the upper JAW of some types of whales, used in the past to make some clothes stiffer

whal·er /'weɪlər/ *noun* **1** a ship used for hunting whales **2** a person who hunts whales

whal·ing /'weɪlɪŋ/ *noun* [U] the activity or business of hunting and killing WHALES

wham /wæm/ *exclamation* (*informal*) **1** used to represent the sound of a sudden, loud hit: *The bombs went down — wham! — right on target.* **2** used to show that something that is unexpected has suddenly happened: *I saw him yesterday and — wham! — I realized I was still in love with him.*

wham·my /'wæmi/ *noun* (*pl.* **wham·mies**) (*informal*) an unpleasant situation or event that causes problems for someone or something: *With this government we've had a double whammy of tax increases and benefit cuts.* **ORIGIN** From the 1950s American cartoon *Li'l Abner*, in which one of the characters could **shoot a whammy** (put a curse on someone) by pointing a finger with one eye open, or a **double whammy** with both eyes open.

wharf /wɔrf/ *noun* (*pl.* **wharves** /wɔrvz/ or **wharfs**) a flat structure built beside the ocean or a river, where boats can be tied up and goods unloaded SYN DOCK

what /wʌt; wɑt; *weak form* wət/ *pron., det.*
1 used in questions to ask for particular information about someone or something: *What is your name?* ◆ *What* (= what job) *does he do?* ◆ *What time is it?* ◆ *What kind of music do you like?* ⊃ compare WHICH **2** the thing or things that; whatever: *What you need is a good meal.* ◆ *Nobody knows what will happen next.* ◆ *I spent what little time I had with my family.* **3** used to say that you think that something is especially good, bad, etc.: *What awful weather!* ◆ *What a beautiful house!* **IDM and what not | and what have you** (*informal*) and other things of the same type: *It's full of old toys, books, and what not.* **get/give sb what for** (*informal*) to be punished/punish someone severely: *I'll give her what for if she does that again.* **or what** (*informal*) **1** used to emphasize your opinion: *Is he stupid or what?* **2** used when you are not sure about something: *I don't know if he's a teacher or what.* ◆ *Are we going now or what?* **what?** (*informal*) **1** used when you have not heard or have not understood something: *What? I can't hear you.* **2** used to show that you have heard someone and to ask what they want: *"Mommy!" "What?" "I'm thirsty."* **3** used to express surprise or anger: *"It will cost $500." "What?"* ◆ *"I asked her to marry me." "You what?"* **what about…?** (*informal*) **1** used to make a suggestion: *What about a trip to Mexico?* **2** used to introduce someone or something into the conversation: *What about you, Joe? Do you like football?* **what-d'you-call-him/-her/-it/-them | what's-his/-her/-its/-their-name** used instead of a name that you cannot remember: *I spoke to what's-his-name, you know, Sue's math teacher.* **what for?** for what purpose or reason?: *What is this tool for?* ◆ *What did you do that for* (= why did you do that)? ◆ *"I need to see a doctor." "What for?"* **what if…?** what would happen if?: *What if the train is late?* ◆ *What if she forgets to bring it?* **what of it?** (*informal*) used when admitting that something is true, to ask why it should be considered important: *Yes, I wrote the article. What of it?* **what's it to you?** (*informal*) used as a slightly rude reply to a question about something you think is private : *"What's in the package?" "What's it to you?"* **what's up with that?** used to suggest that something you have heard is a stupid idea or does not make sense: *They benched their best player. What's up with that?* **what's what** (*informal*) what things are useful, important, etc.: *She certainly knows what's what.* **what's with sb?** (*informal*) used to ask why someone is behaving in a strange way: *What's with you? You haven't said a word all morning.* **what's with sth?** (*informal*) used to ask the reason for something: *What's with all this walking? Can't we take a cab?* **what with sth** used to list the various reasons for something: *What with the cold weather and my bad leg, I haven't been out for weeks.*

what·cha·ma·call·it /'wʌtʃəməˌkɔlɪt; 'wɑ-/ *noun* (*informal*) used when you cannot think of the name of something: *Have you got a whatchamacallit? You know… a screwdriver?*

what·ev·er /wət'evər; wʌt-/ *det., pron., adv.*
- *det., pron.* **1** any or every; anything or everything: *Take whatever action is needed.* ◆ *Do whatever you like.* **2** used

when you are saying that it does not matter what someone does or what happens, because the result will be the same: *Whatever decision he made I would support it.* ♦ *You have our support, whatever you decide.* **3** (*informal, ironic*) used as a reply to tell someone that you do not care what happens or that you are not interested in what they are talking about: *"You should try an herbal remedy." "Yeah, whatever."*
4 (*informal*) used to say that you do not mind what you do, have, etc. and that anything is acceptable: *"What would you like to do today?" "Oh, whatever is fine with me."*
IDM or whatever (*informal*) or something of a similar type: *It's the same in any situation: in a prison, hospital, or whatever.* **whatever you do** used to warn someone not to do something under any circumstances: *Don't tell Paul, whatever you do!*

● *adv.* (also **what·so·ev·er** /ˌwʌtsouˈɛvər; ˌwɑt-/) **no…, nothing, none, etc.** ~ not at all; not of any kind: *They received no help whatever.* ♦ *"Is there any doubt about it?" "None whatsoever."*

what·not /ˈwʌtnɑt; ˈwɑt-/ *noun* [U] **and** ~ (*informal*) used when you are referring to something, but are not being exact and do not mention its name: *It's a new store. They sell toys and whatnot.*

wheat /wit/ *noun* [U] a plant grown for its grain that is used to produce the flour for bread, cakes, PASTA, etc.; the grain of this plant: *wheat flour* ⊃ picture at CEREAL ⊃ collocations at FARMING
IDM sort out/separate the wheat from the chaff to distinguish useful or valuable people or things from ones that are not useful or have no value

the ˈWheat Belt *noun* [sing.] the western central region of the U.S. including the Great Plains, where wheat is an important crop

ˈwheat germ *noun* [U] the center of the wheat grain, which is especially good for your health

whee /wi/ *exclamation* used to express excitement

whee·dle /ˈwidl/ *verb* (*disapproving*) to persuade someone to give you something or to do something by saying nice things that you do not mean **SYN** COAX: ~ *sth (out of sb)* *The kids can always wheedle money out of their father.* ♦ ~ *sb into doing sth* *She wheedled me into lending her my new coat.* ♦ + *speech* *"Come on, Em," he wheedled.*

wheel 🔊 /wil/ *noun, verb*
● *noun*
▷ON/IN VEHICLES **1** [C] one of the round objects under a car, bicycle, bus, etc. that turns when it moves: *He braked suddenly, causing the front wheels to skid.* ♦ *One of the boys was pushing the other along in a little box on wheels.* **2** [C, usually sing.] the round object used to steer a car, etc. or ship: *This is the first time I've sat behind the wheel since the accident.* ♦ *A car swept past with Laura at the wheel.* ♦ *Do you want to take the wheel* (= drive) *now?* ⊃ see also HELM, STEERING WHEEL **3** wheels [pl.] (*informal*) a car: *At last he had his own wheels.*
▷IN MACHINE **4** [C] a flat, round part in a machine: *gear wheels* ⊃ see also CARTWHEEL, FERRIS WHEEL, MILL WHEEL, SPINNING WHEEL, WATERWHEEL
▷ORGANIZATION/SYSTEM **5** wheels [pl.] ~ (of sth) an organization or a system that seems to work like a complicated machine that is difficult to understand: *the wheels of bureaucracy/commerce/government, etc.* ♦ *It was Rob's idea. I merely set the wheels in motion* (= started the process).
▷-WHEELER **6** (in nouns) a car, bicycle, etc. with the number of wheels mentioned: *a three-wheeler*
IDM wheels within wheels a situation which is difficult to understand because it involves complicated or secret processes and decisions: *There are wheels within wheels in this organization—you never really know what is going on.* ⊃ more at COG, GREASE, REINVENT, SHOULDER
● *verb*
▷MOVE SOMETHING WITH WHEELS **1** [T] ~ sth (+ adv./prep.) to push or pull something that has wheels: *She wheeled her bicycle across the road.* **2** [T] ~ sb/sth (+ adv./prep.) to

move someone or something that is in or on something that has wheels: *The nurse wheeled him down the hallway.*
▷MOVE IN CIRCLE **3** [I] (+ adv./prep.) to move or fly in a circle: *Birds wheeled above us in the sky.*
▷TURN QUICKLY **4** [I, T] to turn quickly or suddenly and face the opposite direction; to make someone or something do this: (+ adv./prep.) *She wheeled around and started running.* ♦ ~ sb/sth (+ adv./prep.) *He wheeled his horse back to the gate.*
IDM wheel and deal (usually used in the progressive tenses) to do a lot of complicated deals in business or politics, often in a dishonest way
PHR V wheel sth↔ˈout to show or use something to help you do something, even when it has often been seen or heard before: *They wheeled out the same old arguments we'd heard so many times before.*

ˈwheel arch *noun* a space in the body of a vehicle over a wheel, shaped like an ARCH

wheel·bar·row /ˈwilˌbæroʊ/ (also bar·row) *noun* a large open container with a wheel and two handles that you use outside to carry things ⊃ picture at TOOL

wheel·base /ˈwilbeɪs/ *noun* [sing.] (*technical*) the distance between the front and back wheels of a car or other vehicle

wheel·chair /ˈwiltʃɛr/ *noun* a special chair with wheels, used by people who cannot walk because of illness, an accident, etc.: *Does the hotel have wheelchair access?* ♦ *He's been confined to a wheelchair since the accident.* ♦ *wheelchair users* ⊃ picture at CHAIR

-wheeled /wild/ *adj.* (usually in compounds) having the number or type of wheels mentioned: *a sixteen-wheeled truck*

wheeler–dealer /ˌwilər ˈdilər/ *noun* (*informal*) a person who does a lot of complicated deals in business or politics, often in a dishonest way

wheel·house /ˈwilhaʊs/ *noun* a small CABIN with walls and a roof on a ship where the person steering stands at the wheel

wheel·ie /ˈwili/ *noun* (*informal*) a trick that you can do on a bicycle or motorcycle by balancing on the back wheel, with the front wheel off the ground: *to do a wheelie*

wheel·wright /ˈwilraɪt/ *noun* a person whose job is making and repairing wheels, especially wooden ones

wheeze /wiz/ *verb, noun*
● *verb* [I, T] to breathe noisily and with difficulty: *He was coughing and wheezing all night.* ♦ + *speech* *"I have a chest infection," she wheezed.*
● *noun* [usually sing.] the high whistling sound that your chest makes when you cannot breathe easily

wheez·y /ˈwizi/ *adj.* making the high whistling sound that your chest makes when you cannot breathe easily: *I'm wheezy today.* ♦ *a wheezy cough* ▶ wheez·i·ly /-zəli/ *adv.* wheez·i·ness /-zinəs/ *noun* [U]

whelk /wɛlk/ *noun* a small SHELLFISH that can be eaten

whelp /wɛlp/ *noun, verb*
● *noun* (*technical*) a young animal of the dog family; a PUPPY or CUB
● *verb* [I, T] ~ (sth) (*formal*) (of a female dog) to give birth to a PUPPY or puppies

when 🔊 /wɛn; weak form wən/ *adv., pron., conj.*
● *adv.* **1** (used in questions) at what time; on what occasion: *When did you last see him?* ♦ *When can I see you?* ♦ *When* (= in what circumstances) *would such a solution be possible?*
2 used after an expression of time to mean "at which" or "on which": *Sunday is the only day when I can relax.* ♦ *There are times when I wonder why I do this job.* **3** at which time; on which occasion: *The last time I went to Florida was in May, when the weather was beautiful.*
● *pron.* what/which time: *Until when can you stay?* ♦ *"I got a new job." "Since when?"*
● *conj.* **1** at or during the time that: *I loved history when I was at*

school. **2** after: *Call me when you've finished.* **3** at any time that; whenever: *Can you spare five minutes when it's convenient?* **4** just after which: *He had just drifted off to sleep when the phone rang.* **5** considering that: *How can they expect to learn anything when they never listen?* **6** although: *She claimed to be 18, when I know she's only 16.* **IDM** see AS

whence /wɛns/ *adv.* (*old use*) from where: *They returned whence they had come.*

when·ev·er 🔑 /wɛn'ɛvər; wən-/ *conj., adv.*
- **conj. 1** at any time that; on any occasion that: *You can ask for help whenever you need it.* **2** every time that: *Whenever she comes, she brings a friend.* ◆ *The roof leaks whenever it rains.* ◆ *We try to help whenever possible.* **3** used when the time when something happens is not important: *"When do you need it by?" "Saturday or Sunday. Whenever."* ◆ *It's not urgent—we can do it next week or whenever.*
- **adv.** (in) in questions to mean "when," expressing surprise: *Whenever did you find time to do all that cooking?*

where 🔑 /wɛr/ *adv., conj.*
- **adv. 1** in or to what place or situation: *Where do you live? I wonder where they will take us.* ◆ *Where* (= at what point) *did I go wrong in my calculations?* ◆ *Where* (= in what book, newspaper, etc.) *did you read that?* ◆ *Just where* (= to what situation or final argument) *is all this leading us?* **2** used after words or phrases that refer to a place or situation to mean "at," "in," or "to which": *It's one of the few countries where people drive on the left.* **3** the place or situation in which: *We then moved to Chicago, where we lived for six years.*
- **conj.** (in) the place or situation in which: *This is where I live.* ◆ *Sit where I can see you.* ◆ *Where people were concerned, his threshold of boredom was low.* ◆ *That's where* (= the point in the argument at which) *you're wrong.*

where·a·bouts *noun, adv.*
- **noun** /'wɛrəˌbaʊts/ [U, pl.] the place where someone or something is: *His whereabouts is/are still unknown.*
- **adv.** /'wɛrəˌbaʊts; ˌwɛrə'baʊts/ used to ask the general area where someone or something is: *Whereabouts did you find it?*

where·as 🔑 **AWL** /wɛr'æz; 'wɛrəz/ *conj.*
1 used to compare or contrast two facts: *Some of the studies show positive results, whereas others do not.* ⊃ language bank at CONTRAST **2** (*law*) used at the beginning of a sentence in an official document to mean "because of the fact that…"

where·by **AWL** /wɛr'baɪ; 'wɛrbaɪ/ *adv.* (*formal*) by which; because of which: *They have introduced a new system whereby all employees must undergo regular training.*

where·fore /'wɛrfɔr/ *noun* **IDM** see WHY

where·in /wɛr'ɪn/ *adv., conj.* (*formal*) in which place, situation, or thing; in what way: *Wherein lies the difference between conservatism and liberalism?*

where·of /wɛr'ʌv/ *conj.* (*old use or humorous*) of what or which: *I know whereof I speak* (= I know a lot about what I am talking about).

where·up·on /ˌwɛrə'pan; -'pɔn; 'wɛrəˌpan; -ˌpɔn/ *conj.* (*formal*) and then; as a result of this: *He told her she was a liar, whereupon she walked out.*

wher·ev·er 🔑 /wɛr'ɛvər; wər-/ *conj., adv.*
- **conj. 1** in any place: *Sit wherever you like.* ◆ *He comes from Boula, wherever that may be* (= I don't know where it is). **2** in all places that **SYN** EVERYWHERE: *Wherever she goes, there are crowds of people waiting to see her.* **3** in all cases that **SYN** WHENEVER: *Use whole grain breakfast cereals wherever possible.*
  IDM **or wherever** (*informal*) or any other place: *tourists from Spain, France, or wherever*
- **adv.** used in questions to mean "where," expressing surprise: *Wherever can he have gone to?*

the where·with·al /'wɛrwɪˌðɔl; -ˌθɔl/ *noun* [sing.] **~ (to do sth)** the money, things, or skills that you need in order to be able to do something: *They lacked the wherewithal to pay for the repairs.*

whet /wɛt/ *verb* (-tt-) **~ sth** to increase your desire for or interest in something: *The book will whet your appetite for more of her work.*

wheth·er 🔑 /'wɛðər/ *conj.*
1 used to express a doubt or choice between two possibilities: *He seemed undecided whether to go or stay.* ◆ *It remains to be seen whether or not this idea can be put into practice.* ◆ *I asked him whether he had done it all himself or whether someone had helped him.* ◆ *I'll see whether she's at home* (= or not at home). ◆ *It's doubtful whether there'll be any seats left.* ⊃ note at IF **2** used to show that something is true in either of two cases: *You are entitled to a free gift whether you accept our offer of insurance or not* ◆ *I'm going whether you like it or not.* ◆ *Whether or not we're successful, we can be sure that we did our best.*

whet·stone /'wɛtstoʊn/ *noun* a stone that is used to make cutting tools and weapons sharp

whew /hwyu; hyu; fyu/ *exclamation* a sound that people make to show that they are surprised or RELIEVED about something, or that they are very hot or tired: *Whew—and I thought it was serious!* ◆ *Ten grand? Whew!* ⊃ compare PHEW

whey /weɪ/ *noun* [U] the thin liquid that is left from sour milk after the solid part (called CURD) has been removed

which 🔑 /wɪtʃ/ *pron., det.*
1 used in questions to ask someone to be exact about one or more people or things from a limited number: *Which is better exercise—swimming or tennis?* ◆ *Which of the applicants got the job?* ◆ *Which of the patients have recovered?* ◆ *Which way is the wind blowing?* ⊃ compare WHAT **2** used to give more information about something, or make a comment on something: *His best movie, which won several awards, was about the life of Gandhi.* ◆ *We had to wait 16 hours for our plane, which was really annoying.* ◆ *Your claim should succeed, in which case the damages will be substantial.* **HELP** That cannot be used instead of which in this meaning. **3** used to be exact about the thing or things that you mean: *It was a crisis for which she was totally unprepared.* **HELP** In this meaning which is usually used after a preposition; it can be used when there is no preposition, but that is usually preferred: *Houses that overlook the lake cost more.* That is not used immediately after a preposition: *It was a crisis that she was totally unprepared for.*
IDM **which is which** used to talk about distinguishing one person or thing from another: *The twins are so alike I can't tell which is which.*

which·ev·er /wɪtʃ'ɛvər/ *det., pron.* **1** used to say what feature or quality is important in deciding something: *Choose whichever brand you prefer.* ◆ *Pensions should be increased annually in line with earnings or prices, whichever is the higher.* ◆ *Whichever of you gets here first will get the prize.* **2** used to say that it does not matter which, as the result will be the same: *It takes three hours, whichever route you take.* ◆ *The situation is an awkward one, whichever way you look at it.* ◆ *Whichever they choose, we must accept their decision.*

whiff /wɪf/ *noun, verb*
- **noun** [usually sing.] **1 ~ (of sth)** a smell, especially one that you only smell for a short time: *a whiff of cigar smoke* ◆ *He caught a whiff of perfume as he leaned toward her.* **2 ~ (of sth)** a slight sign or feeling of something: *a whiff of danger* **3** (in GOLF or baseball) an unsuccessful attempt to hit the ball
- **verb** [I] (in GOLF or baseball) to try without success to hit the ball

Whig /wɪg/ *noun* **1** an American who supported the American Revolution and wanted to have independence from England **2** a member of a 19th-century political party that was formed to oppose the Democrats and later became the Republican Party

   t **tea**   t̬ **butter**   d **did**   k **cat**   g **got**   tʃ **chin**   dʒ **June**   f **fall**

while /waɪl/ *conj., noun, verb*

● **conj.** (also *formal* **whilst** /waɪlst/) **1** during the time that something is happening **SYN** WHEN: *We must have been robbed while we were asleep.* ◆ *Her parents died while she was still in school.* ◆ *While I was waiting at the bus stop, three buses went by in the opposite direction.* **2** at the same time as something else is happening: *You can go swimming while I'm having lunch.* ◆ *shoes repaired while you wait* **3** used to contrast two things: *While Tom's very good at science, his brother is absolutely hopeless.* ⊃ language bank at CONTRAST **4** (used at the beginning of a sentence) although; despite the fact that…: *While I am willing to help, I do not have much time available.* ⊃ language bank at NEVERTHELESS **IDM** **while you're/I'm etc. at it** used to suggest that someone could do something while they are doing something else: *"I'm just going to buy some postcards." "Can you get me some stamps while you're at it?"*

● **noun** [sing.] a period of time: *They chatted for a while.* ◆ *I'll be back in a little while* (= a short time). ◆ *I haven't seen him for quite a while* (= a long time). ◆ *They walked back together, talking all the while* (= all the time). **IDM** see ONCE, WORTH

● **verb**
PHR V **while sth↔a'way** to spend time in a pleasant, lazy way: *We whiled away the time reading and playing cards.*

whim /wɪm/ *noun* [C, U] a sudden wish to do or have something, especially when it is something unusual or unnecessary: *He was forced to pander to her every whim.* ◆ *We bought the house on a whim.* ◆ *My duties seem to change daily at the whim of the boss.* ◆ *the whims of fashion* ◆ *She hires and fires people at whim.*

whim·per /ˈwɪmpər/ *verb, noun*
● **verb** [I, T] to make low, weak crying noises; to speak in this way: *The child was lost and began to whimper.* ◆ **+ speech** *"Don't leave me alone," he whimpered.*
● **noun** a low, weak cry that a person or an animal makes when they are hurt, frightened, or sad

whim·si·cal /ˈwɪmzɪkl/ *adj.* unusual and not serious in a way that is either amusing or annoying: *to have a whimsical sense of humor* ◆ *Much of his writing has a whimsical quality.* ▶ **whim·si·cally** /-kli/ *adv.*

whim·sy /ˈwɪmzi/ *noun* [U] a way of thinking or behaving, or a style of doing something, that is unusual and not serious, in a way that is either amusing or annoying

whine /waɪn/ *verb, noun*
● **verb** **1** [I, T] (+ speech) | ~ that… to complain in an annoying, crying voice: *Stop whining!* ◆ *"I want to go home," whined Toby.* ⊃ thesaurus box at COMPLAIN **2** [I] to make a long, high, unpleasant sound because you are in pain or unhappy: *The dog whined and scratched at the door.* **3** [I] (of a machine) to make a long, high, unpleasant sound ▶ **whin·y** /ˈwaɪni/ *adj.*: *a whiny voice/tone* ◆ *a whiny kid/brat*
● **noun** [usually sing.] **1** a long, high sound that is usually unpleasant or annoying: *the steady whine of the engine* **2** a long, high cry that a child or dog makes when it is hurt or wants something **3** a high tone of voice that you use when you complain about something

whin·ny /ˈwɪni/ *verb* (whin·nies, whin·ny·ing, whin·nied, whin·nied) [I] (of a horse) to make a quiet NEIGH ▶ **whin·ny** *noun* (*pl.* whin·nies)

whip /wɪp/ *noun, verb*
● **noun** **1** [C] a long, thin piece of rope or leather, attached to a handle, used for making animals move or punishing people: *He cracked his whip and the horse leapt forward.* **2** [C] an official in a political party who is responsible for making sure that party members attend and vote in important government debates: *the Senate Minority Whip* **3** [U, C] a sweet dish made from cream, eggs, sugar, and fruit mixed together **IDM** **have/hold, etc. the whip hand (over sb/sth)** to be in a position where you have power or control over someone or something ⊃ more at CRACK
● **verb** (-pp-) **1** [T] ~ sb/sth to hit a person or an animal hard

with a whip, as a punishment or to make them go faster or work harder **2** [I, T] to move, or make something move, quickly and suddenly or violently in a particular direction: **+ adv./prep.** *A branch whipped across the car window.* ◆ *Her hair whipped around her face in the wind.* ◆ ~ **sth** *The waves were being whipped by 50 mile an hour winds.* **3** [T] ~ **sth** **+ adv./prep.** to remove or pull something quickly and suddenly: *She whipped the mask off her face.* ◆ *The man whipped out a knife.* **4** [T] to stir cream, etc. very quickly until it becomes stiff: ~ **sth** *Serve the pie with whipped cream.* ◆ ~ **sth up** *Whip the egg whites up into stiff peaks.* ⊃ picture at COOKING **5** [T] ~ **sb/sth** (*informal*) to defeat someone very easily in a game: *The team whipped its opponents by 35 points.* **SYN** THRASH **IDM** see SHAPE *n.*
PHR V **,whip 'through sth** (*informal*) to do or finish something very quickly: *We whipped through customs in ten minutes.* **,whip sb/sth↔'up 1** to deliberately try and make people excited or feel strongly about something **SYN** ROUSE: *The advertisements were designed to whip up public opinion.* ◆ *He was a speaker who could really whip up a crowd.* **2** to quickly make a meal or something to eat: *She whipped up a delicious lunch for us in 15 minutes.*

whip·lash /ˈwɪplæʃ/ *noun* **1** [C, usually sing.] a hit with a whip **2** [U] a neck injury caused when your head moves forward and back suddenly, especially in a car accident: *He was very bruised and suffering from whiplash.*

whip·per·snap·per /ˈwɪpərˌsnæpər/ *noun* (*old-fashioned, informal*) a young and unimportant person who behaves in a way that others think is too confident and rude

whip·pet /ˈwɪpət/ *noun* a small thin dog, similar to a GREYHOUND, that can run very fast and is often used for racing

whip·ping /ˈwɪpɪŋ/ *noun* [usually sing.] an act of hitting someone with a whip, as a punishment

'whipping ˌboy *noun* a person who is often blamed for or punished for things other people have done

'whipping ˌcream *noun* [U] cream that becomes thicker when it is WHIPPED (= stirred quickly)

whip·poor·will /ˈwɪpərˌwɪl/ *noun* a brown N. American bird with a cry that sounds like its name

whip·saw /ˈwɪpsɔ/ *noun, verb*
● **noun** a SAW with a narrow blade and a handle at both ends, used by two people together
● **verb** **1** [T] ~ **sth** to cut something with a whipsaw: *They were whipsawing lumber.* **2** [T] ~ **sb/sth** to expose someone or something to two difficult situations or opposing forces at the same time: *The public has been whipsawed by good and bad news about vitamins.* **3** [I, T] ~ **(sth)** to rise or fall or move back and forth; to cause something to do this **SYN** FLUCTUATE: *Gold has whipsawed, falling from a peak of $1,000 an ounce.* **4** [T] ~ **sb** to cheat or beat someone in two ways at once: *The champions whipsawed them with equally effective running and passing for a 24-7 victory.*

whir (also **whirr**) /wər/ *verb, noun*
● **verb** (-rr-) [I] to make a continuous low sound like the parts of a machine moving: *The clock began to whir before striking the hour.*
● **noun** (also **whir·ring**) [usually sing.] a continuous low sound, for example the sound made by the regular movement of a machine or the wings of a bird: *the whir of a motor* ◆ *There was a whirring of machinery.*

whirl /wərl/ *verb, noun*
● **verb** **1** [I, T] to move, or make someone or something move, around quickly in a circle or in a particular direction **SYN** SPIN: (+ adv./prep.) *Leaves whirled in the wind.* ◆ *She whirled around to face him.* ◆ *the whirling blades of the helicopter* ◆ ~ **sb/sth** (+ adv./prep.) *Tom whirled her across the dance floor.* **2** [I] if your mind, brain, etc. **whirls**, you feel confused and excited and cannot think clearly **SYN** REEL: *I couldn't sleep—my mind was whirling from all that had happened.* ◆ *So many thoughts whirled around in her mind.*
● **noun** [sing.] **1** a movement of something spinning around

and around: *a whirl of dust* ◆ (*figurative*) *Her mind was in a whirl* (= in a state of confusion or excitement). **2** a number of activities or events happening one after the other: *Her life was one long whirl of parties.* ◆ *It's easy to get caught up in the social whirl.*

IDM **give sth a whirl** (*informal*) to try something to see if you like it or can do it

whirl·i·gig /ˈwɜːrlɪˌgɪg/ *noun* **1** something that is very active and always changing: *the whirligig of fashion* **2** (*old-fashioned*) a MERRY-GO-ROUND at a FAIRGROUND for children to ride on

whirl·pool /ˈwɜːrlpuːl/ *noun* **1** a place in a river or the ocean where currents of water spin around very fast **SYN** EDDY: (*figurative*) *She felt she was being dragged into a whirlpool of emotion.* **2** a special BATHTUB or swimming pool for relaxing in, in which the water moves in circles ⊃ see also JACUZZI™

whirl·wind /ˈwɜːrlwɪnd/ *noun, adj.*
● *noun* **1** a very strong wind that moves very fast in a spinning movement and causes a lot of damage **2** a situation or series of events where a lot of things happen very quickly: *To recover from the divorce, I threw myself into a whirlwind of activities.*
● *adj.* [only before noun] happening very fast: *a whirlwind romance* ◆ *a whirlwind tour of Europe*

whirr = WHIR

whisk /wɪsk/ *verb, noun*
● *verb* **1** ~ **sth** to mix liquids, eggs, etc. into a stiff light mass, using a fork or special tool ⊃ picture at COOKING **SYN** BEAT : *Whisk the egg whites until stiff.* **2** ~ **sb/sth** + **adv./prep.** to take someone or something somewhere very quickly and suddenly: *Jamie whisked her off to Hawaii for the weekend.* ◆ *The waiter whisked away the plates before we had finished.*
● *noun* a kitchen UTENSIL (= a tool) for stirring eggs, etc. very fast: *an electric whisk* ⊃ picture at KITCHEN

whisk·er /ˈwɪskər/ *noun* **1** [C] any of the long stiff hairs that grow near the mouth of a cat, mouse, etc. **2** **whisk·ers** [pl.] (*old-fashioned* or *humorous*) the hair growing on a man's face, especially on his cheeks and chin
IDM **be, come, etc. within a whisker of sth/doing sth** to almost do something: *They came within a whisker of being killed.* **by a whisker** by a very small amount

whisk·ered /ˈwɪskərd/ (also **whisk·er·y** /ˈwɪskəri/) *adj.* having whiskers

whis·key (also **whis·ky**) /ˈwɪski/ *noun* (*pl.* **whis·keys, whis·kies**) **1** [U, C] a strong alcoholic drink made from MALTED grain. It is sometimes drunk with water and/or ice: *a bottle of whiskey* ◆ *Scotch whisky* ◆ *highland whiskies* ⊃ see also BOURBON, SCOTCH **2** [C] a glass of whiskey: *a whiskey and soda* ◆ *Two whiskies, please.* ⊃ see also SCOTCH

whis·per 🔊 /ˈwɪspər/ *verb, noun*
● *verb* **1** [I, T] to speak very quietly to someone so that other people cannot hear what you are saying **SYN** MURMUR: *Don't you know it's rude to whisper?* ◆ ~ **about sth** *What are you two whispering about?* ◆ + **speech** *"Can you meet me tonight?" he whispered.* ◆ ~ **sth (to sb)** *She leaned over and whispered something in his ear.* ◆ ~ **(to sb) that...** *He whispered to me that he was afraid.* **2** [T, often passive] ~ **that...** | **it is whispered that...** to say or suggest something about someone or something in a private or secret way: *It was whispered that he would soon die and he did.* **3** [I] (+ **adv./prep.**) (*literary*) (of leaves, the wind, etc.) to make a soft, quiet sound
● *noun* **1** [C] a low, quiet voice or the sound it makes **SYN** MURMUR: *They spoke in whispers.* ◆ *Her voice dropped to a whisper.* ⊃ see also STAGE WHISPER **2** (also **whis·per·ing**) [sing.] (*literary*) a soft sound **SYN** MURMUR: *I could hear the whispering of the sea.* **3** [C] a piece of news that is spread by being talked about but may not be true **SYN** RUMOR: *I've heard whispers that he's leaving.*

whispering cam·paign *noun* an attempt to damage

someone's reputation by saying unpleasant things about them and passing this information from person to person

whist /wɪst/ *noun* [U] a card game for two pairs of players in which each pair tries to win the most cards

whis·tle 🔊 /ˈwɪsl/ *noun, verb*
● *noun* **1** a small metal or plastic tube that you blow to make a loud, high sound, used to attract attention or as a signal: *The referee finally blew the whistle to stop the game.* ⊃ see also TIN WHISTLE **2** the sound made by blowing a whistle: *He scored the winning goal just seconds before the final whistle.* **3** the sound that you make by forcing your breath out when your lips are closed: *a shrill whistle* ⊃ see also WOLF WHISTLE **4** the high, loud sound produced by air or steam being forced through a small opening, or by something moving quickly through the air **5** a piece of equipment that makes a high, loud sound when air or steam is forced through it: *The train whistle blew as we left the station.* ◆ *a factory whistle* **IDM** see BLOW, CLEAN
● *verb* **1** [T, I] to make a high sound or a musical tune by forcing your breath out when your lips are closed: ~ **(sth)** *to whistle a tune* ◆ *He whistled in amazement.* ◆ *The crowd booed and whistled as the player came onto the field.* ◆ ~ **to sb/sth** *She whistled to the dog to come back.* ◆ ~ **at sb/sth** *Workmen whistled at her as she walked past.* **2** [I] to make a high sound by blowing into a whistle: *The referee whistled for a foul.* **3** [I] (of a KETTLE or other machine) to make a high sound: *The kettle began to whistle.* ◆ *The microphone was making a strange whistling sound.* **4** [I] + **adv./prep.** to move quickly, making a high sound: *The wind whistled down the chimney.* ◆ *A bullet whistled past his ear.* **5** [I] (of a bird) to make a high sound

whistle-blower *noun* (used especially in newspapers) a person who informs people in authority or the public that the company they work for is doing something wrong or illegal

whistle-stop *adj.* [only before noun] visiting a lot of different places in a very short time: *to go on a whistle-stop tour* of Europe ◆ *politicians on a whistle-stop election campaign*

whit /wɪt/ *noun* [sing.] (*old-fashioned*) (usually in negative sentences) a very small amount **SYN** JOT
IDM **not a whit| not one whit** not at all; not the smallest amount

white 🔊 /waɪt/ *adj., noun*
● *adj.* (**whit·er, whit·est**) **1** having the color of fresh snow or of milk: *a crisp white shirt* ◆ *white bread* ◆ *a set of perfect white teeth* ◆ *His hair was as white as snow.* ◆ *The horse was almost pure white* in color. **2** belonging to or connected with a race of people who have pale skin: *white middle-class families* ◆ *She writes about her experiences as a black girl in a predominantly white city.* **3** (of the skin) pale because of emotion or illness: *white with shock* ◆ *She went white as a sheet when she heard the news.* ▶ **white·ness** *noun* [U, sing.]
● *noun* **1** [U] the color of fresh snow or of milk: *the pure white of the newly painted walls* ◆ *She was dressed all in white.* **2** [C, usually pl.] a member of a race or people who have pale skin **3** [U, C] white wine: *Would you like red or white?* ◆ *a very dry white* **4** [C, U] the part of an egg that surrounds the YOLK (= the yellow part): *Use the whites of two eggs.* **5** [C, usually pl.] the white part of the eye: *The whites of her eyes were bloodshot.* ⊃ picture at BODY **6** **whites** [pl.] white clothes, sheets, etc. when they are separated from colored ones to be washed: *Don't wash whites and colors together.* **7** **whites** [pl.] white clothes worn for playing some sports: *tennis whites* **IDM** see BLACK
IDM **whiter than white** (of a person) completely honest and morally good: *The government must be seen to be whiter than white.*

white·bait /ˈwaɪtbeɪt/ *noun* [pl.] very small young fish of several types that are fried and eaten whole

white 'blood cell (also **'white cell**) (also *technical* **leu·co·cyte**) *noun* (*biology*) any of the clear cells in the blood that help to fight disease

white·board /ˈwaɪtbɔːrd/ *noun* a large board with a smooth

h **hat**	m **man**	n **no**	ŋ **sing**	l **leg**	r **red**	y **yes**	w **wet**

white surface that teachers, etc. write on with special pens ⊃ compare BLACKBOARD

'white 'bread noun [U] bread made with WHITE FLOUR

'white-bread adj. [only before noun] (informal) ordinary and traditional: a white-bread town

'white·caps /'waɪtkæps/ noun [pl.] waves in the ocean with white tops on them

,white 'chocolate noun [U] a yellow-white candy that is flavored with COCOA BUTTER ⊃ compare DARK CHOCOLATE, MILK CHOCOLATE

,white 'Christmas noun a Christmas during which there is snow on the ground

,white-'collar adj. [usually before noun] working in an office, rather than in a factory, etc.; connected with work in offices: white-collar workers ♦ a white-collar job ♦ white-collar crime (= in which office workers steal from their company, etc.) ⊃ compare BLUE-COLLAR, PINK-COLLAR

,white 'dwarf noun (astronomy) a small star that is near the end of its life and is very DENSE (= solid and heavy)

,white 'elephant noun [usually sing.] a thing that is useless and no longer needed, although it may have cost a lot of money: The new office building has become an expensive white elephant. **ORIGIN** From the story that in Siam (now Thailand) the king would give a white elephant as a present to someone that he did not like. That person would have to spend all their money on looking after the rare animal.

white·fish /'waɪtfɪʃ/ noun [C, U] (pl. white·fish) a mainly FRESHWATER fish of the SALMON family, widely used as food

,white 'flag noun [usually sing.] a sign that you accept defeat and wish to stop fighting: to raise/show/wave the white flag

,white 'flight noun [U] a situation where white people who can afford it go to live outside the cities because they are worried about crime in city centers

,white 'flour noun [U] flour made from WHEAT grains, from which most of the BRAN (= outer covering) and WHEAT GERM (= center part) have been removed

,white 'heat noun [U] the very high temperature at which metal looks white

,white-'hot adj. **1** (of metal or something burning) so hot that it looks white **2** very strong and INTENSE

the 'White House noun [sing.] **1** the official home of the President of the U.S. in Washington, D.C. **2** the U.S. President and his or her officials: The White House has issued a statement. ♦ White House aides

,white 'knight noun a person or an organization that rescues a company from being bought by another company at too low a price

,white-knuckle 'ride noun **1** a ride at an AMUSEMENT PARK that makes you feel very excited and frightened at the same time **2** an experience that makes you feel nervous or frightened: (figurative) The flight was a real white-knuckle ride.

,white 'lie noun a harmless or small lie, especially one that you tell to avoid hurting someone

,white 'light noun [U] ordinary light that has no color

'white meat noun [U] **1** meat that is pale in color, such as chicken ⊃ compare RED MEAT **2** pale meat from the breast of a chicken or other bird that has been cooked ⊃ compare DARK MEAT

whit·en /'waɪtn/ verb [I, T] to become white or whiter; to make something white or whiter: He gripped the wheel until his knuckles whitened. ♦ ~ sth Snow had whitened the tops of the trees.

,white 'noise noun [U] unpleasant noise, like the noise that comes from a television or radio that is turned on but not TUNED IN

white-out /'waɪtaʊt/ noun weather conditions in which there is so much snow or cloud that it is impossible to see anything

the 'white ,pages noun [pl.] a telephone book (on white

paper), or a section of a book, that lists the names, addresses, and telephone numbers of people living in a particular area

,white 'pepper noun [U] a grayish-brown powder made from the inside of dried berries (BERRY) (called PEPPER-CORNS), used to give flavor to food

'white sauce noun [U] a thick sauce made from butter, flour, and milk **SYN** BECHAMEL

,white su'premacist noun a person who believes that white people are better than other races and should be in power ► ,white su'premacy noun [U]

,white-tailed 'deer noun (pl. white-tailed deer) a N. American DEER with a tail that is white underneath

,white-'tie adj. (of social occasions) very formal, when men are expected to wear white BOW TIES and jackets with TAILS: Is it a white-tie affair? ► ,white 'tie noun: dressed in white tie and tails

,white 'trash noun [U] (informal, offensive) a way of referring to poor white people, especially those living in the southern U.S.

white·wall /'waɪtwɔl/ noun **1** (also ,whitewall 'tire) a tire with a white line going around it for decoration **2** white-walls [pl.] the shaved area at the sides of the head when the hair is cut in a very short style

white·wash /'waɪtwɑʃ; -wɔʃ/ noun, verb
• noun **1** [U] a mixture of CHALK or LIME and water, used for painting houses and walls white **2** [U, sing.] (disapproving) an attempt to hide unpleasant facts about someone or something **SYN** COVER-UP: The opposition claimed the report was a whitewash.
• verb **1** ~ sth to cover something such as a wall with whitewash **2** ~ sb/sth (disapproving) to try to hide un-pleasant facts about someone or something; to try to make something seem better than it is: His wife had wanted to whitewash his reputation after he died.

white·wa·ter /'waɪt,wɔtər; -,wɑtər/ noun [U] (also ,white 'water) **1** a part of a river that looks white because the water is moving very fast over rocks: a stretch of whitewater ♦ whitewater rafting **2** a part of the ocean that looks white because it is very rough and the waves are high

,white 'wine noun **1** [U, C] pale yellow wine: a bottle of dry white wine ♦ chilled white wine **2** [C] a glass of white wine ⊃ compare BLUSH WINE, RED WINE, ROSE

whith·er /'wɪðər/ adv., conj. **1** (old use) where; to which: Whither should they go? ♦ They did not know whither they should go. ♦ the place whither they were sent **2** (formal) used to ask what is likely to happen to something in the future: Whither modern architecture?

whit·ing /'waɪtɪŋ/ noun [C, U] (pl. whit·ing) a small ocean fish with white flesh that is used for food

whit·ish /'waɪtɪʃ/ adj. fairly white in color: a bird with a whitish throat

Whit·sun /'wɪtsn/ noun [U, C] the 7th Sunday after Easter and the days close to it

whit·tle /'wɪtl/ verb to form a piece of wood, etc. into a particular shape by cutting small pieces from it: ~ A (from B) He whittled a simple toy from the piece of wood. ♦ ~ B (into A) He whittled the piece of wood into a simple toy. **PHR V** ,whittle sth↔a'way to make something gradually decrease in value or amount ,whittle sth↔'down to reduce the size or number of something: I finally managed to whittle down the names on the list to only five.

whiz /wɪz/ verb, noun
• verb (-zz-) **1** [I] + adv./prep. to move very quickly, making a high continuous sound: A bullet whizzed past my ear. ♦ He whizzed down the road on his motorcycle. **2** [I] + adv./prep. to do something very quickly: She whizzed through the work.
• noun (informal) a person who is very good at something: She's a whiz at crosswords.

'whiz kid noun (informal) a person who is very good at and successful at something, especially at a young age: *financial whiz kids*

whiz·zy /ˈwɪzi/ *adj.* (**whiz·zi·er, whiz·zi·est**) (*informal*) having features that make use of advanced technology: *a whizzy new hand-held computer*

WHO /ˌdʌblyu eɪtʃ ˈoʊ/ *abbr.* World Health Organization (an international organization that aims to fight and control disease)

who 🔊 /hu/ *pron.*
1 used in questions to ask about the name, identity, or function of one or more people: *Who is that woman?* ◆ *I wonder who that letter was from.* ◆ *Who are you calling?* ◆ *Who's the money for?* **2** used to show which person or people you mean: *The people who called yesterday want to buy the house.* ◆ *The people who we met on vacation have sent us a card.* **3** used to give more information about someone: *Mrs. Smith, who has a lot of teaching experience at all grade levels, will be joining the school in September.* ◆ *And then Mary, who we had been talking about earlier, walked in.* ⊃ compare WHOM
IDM **who am I, who are you, etc. to do sth?** used to ask what right or authority someone has to do something: *Who are you to tell me I can't park here?* **who's who** people's names, jobs, status, etc.: *You'll soon find out who's who in the office.*

whoa /woʊ/ *exclamation* used as a command to a horse, etc. to make it stop or stand still

who'd /hud/ *short form* **1** who had **2** who would

who·dun·it /ˌhuˈdʌnɪt/ *noun* (*informal*) a story, play, etc. about a murder in which you do not know who did the murder until the end

who·ev·er 🔊 /huˈɛvər/ *pron.*
1 the person or people who; any person who: *Whoever says that is a liar.* ◆ *Send it to whoever is in charge of sales.* **2** used to say that it does not matter who, since the result will be the same: *Come out of there, whoever you are.* ◆ *I don't want to see them, whoever they are.* **3** used in questions to mean "who," expressing surprise: *Whoever heard of such a thing!*

whole 🔊 /hoʊl/ *adj., noun, adv.*
● *adj.* **1** [only before noun] full; complete: *He spent the whole day writing.* ◆ *We drank a whole bottle each.* ◆ *The whole country (= all the people in it) mourned her death.* ◆ *Let's forget the **whole thing**.* ◆ *She wasn't telling the **whole truth**.* **2** [only before noun] used to emphasize how large or important something is: *We offer a whole variety of weekend breaks.* ◆ *I can't afford it—that's **the whole point**.* **3** not broken or damaged **SYN** IN ONE PIECE: *Owls usually swallow their prey whole (= without chewing it).* ⊃ note at HALF ▶ **whole·ness** *noun* [U] ⊃ see also WHOLLY
IDM Most idioms containing **whole** are at the entries for the nouns and verbs in the idioms. For example, **go the whole hog** is at hog. **a whole lot** (*informal*) very much; a lot: *I'm feeling a whole lot better.* **a whole lot (of sth)** (*informal*) a large number or amount: *There were a whole lot of people I didn't know.* ◆ *I lost a whole lot of money.* **the whole lot** everything; all of something: *I've sold the whole lot.*
● *noun* **1** [C] a thing that is complete in itself: *Four quarters make a whole.* ◆ *The subjects of the curriculum form a coherent whole.* **2** [sing.] **the ~ of sth** all that there is of something: *The effects will last for the whole of his life.* ⊃ note at HALF
IDM **as a whole** as one thing or piece and not as separate parts: *The festival will be great for our city and for the country as a whole.* **on the whole** considering everything; in general: *On the whole, I'm in favor of the idea.*
● *adv.* **~ new/different/other...** (*informal*) completely new/different: *It's a whole new world out here.* ◆ *That's a whole other story.*

whole ˈfood *noun* [U] (also **whole ˈfoods** [pl.]) food that is considered healthy because it is in a simple form, has not been REFINED, and does not contain artificial substances

whole-grain *adj.* made with or containing whole grains, for example of WHEAT

whole·heart·ed /ˌhoʊlˈhɑrt̬əd/ *adj.* (*approving*) complete and enthusiastic: *The plan was given wholehearted support.* ▶ **whole·heart·ed·ly** *adv.*: *to agree wholeheartedly*

whole milk *noun* [U] milk from which fat has not been removed

whole note *noun* (*music*) a note that lasts as long as four QUARTER NOTES ⊃ picture at MUSIC

whole ˈnumber *noun* (*mathematics*) a number that consists of one or more units, with no FRACTIONS (= parts of a number less than one)

whole·sale /ˈhoʊlseɪl/ *adj.* [only before noun] **1** connected with goods that are bought and sold in large quantities, especially so they can be sold again to make a profit: *wholesale prices* ⊃ compare RETAIL¹ **2** (especially of something bad) happening or done to a very large number of people or things: *the wholesale slaughter of innocent people* ▶ **whole·sale** *adv.*: *We buy the building materials wholesale.* ◆ *These young people die wholesale from heroin overdoses.*

whole·sal·ing /ˈhoʊlˌseɪlɪŋ/ *noun* [U] the business of buying and selling goods in large quantities, especially so they can be sold again to make a profit ⊃ compare RETAILING ▶ **whole·sal·er** *noun*: *fruit and vegetable wholesalers*

whole·some /ˈhoʊlsəm/ *adj.* **1** good for your health: *fresh, wholesome food* **2** morally good; having a good moral influence: *It was clean wholesome fun.* **ANT** UNWHOLESOME ▶ **whole·some·ness** *noun* [U]

whole step (*US*) *noun* (*music*) one of the five longer INTERVALS in a musical SCALE, for example the INTERVAL between C and D or between E and F♯

whole-wheat *adj.* **whole-wheat** bread or flour contains the whole grains of WHEAT, etc. including the HUSK

who'll /hul/ *short form* who will

whol·ly /ˈhoʊli/ *adv.* (*formal*) completely **SYN** TOTALLY: *wholly inappropriate behavior* ◆ *The government is not wholly to blame for the recession.*

whom 🔊 /hum/ *pron.* (*formal*)
used instead of "who" as the object of a verb or preposition: *Whom did they invite?* ◆ *To whom should I write?* ◆ *The author whom you criticized in your review has written a reply.* ◆ *Her mother, in whom she confided, said she would support her unconditionally.*

GRAMMAR

whom

- **Whom** is not always used in spoken English. **Who** is often used as the object pronoun, especially in questions: *Who did you invite to the party?*
- **Whom** is used as the pronoun after prepositions in written English and formal spoken English: *To whom should I address the letter?* ◆ *He asked me with whom I had discussed it.* In spoken English, it is more accepted to use **who** and put the preposition at the end of the sentence: *Who should I address the letter to?* ◆ *He asked me who I had discussed it with.*
- In defining relative clauses, the object pronoun **whom** is often replaced in speaking or informal writing with **who**, or you might leave out the pronoun completely: *The family (who/that/whom) I met at the airport were very kind.*
- In nondefining relative clauses, **whom** is used and the pronoun cannot be left out: *Our doctor, whom we all liked very much, retired last week.* In speaking and informal writing, **who** is sometimes used instead.

---

whom·ev·er /huˈmɛvər/, **whom·so·ev·er** /ˌhumsoʊˈɛvər/ *pron.* (*literary*) used instead of "whoever" as the object of a verb or preposition: *He was free to marry whomever he chose.*

whoop /wup; wʊp/ *noun, verb*
● *noun* a loud cry expressing joy, excitement, etc.: *whoops of delight*
● *verb* [I] to shout loudly because you are happy or excited

IDM **whoop it up** (*informal*) **1** to enjoy yourself very much with a noisy group of people **2** to make people excited or enthusiastic about something

whoop-de-do /ˌwʊp di ˈdu; ˌwʊp-; ˌhup-/ *exclamation* (*informal*, *ironic*) used to tell someone that something they have just said does not impress you very much: *So she runs five miles a day. Whoop-de-do!*

whoop·ee *exclamation*, *noun*
● *exclamation* /ˌwʊˈpi; ˈwʊpi/ used to express happiness: *Whoopee, we've won!*
● *noun* /ˈwʊpi/ [U]
IDM **make whoopee** (*old-fashioned*, *informal*) to celebrate in a noisy way

whoopee cushion *noun* a rubber CUSHION that makes a noise like a FART when someone sits on it, used as a joke

whoop·ing cough /ˈhupɪŋ ˌkɔf/ (also *medical* **per·tus·sis**) *noun* [U] an infectious disease, especially of children, that makes them cough and have difficulty breathing

whoops /wʊps; wups/ *exclamation* **1** used when someone has almost had an accident, broken something, etc.: *Whoops! Careful, you almost spilled coffee everywhere.* **2** used when you have done something embarrassing, said something rude by accident, told a secret, etc.: *Whoops, you weren't supposed to hear that.*

whoosh /wʊʃ; wuʃ/ *noun*, *verb*
● *noun* [usually sing.] (*informal*) the sudden movement and sound of air or water rushing past: *a whoosh of air* ◆ *There was a whoosh as everything went up in flames.*
● *verb* [I] + **adv./prep.** (*informal*) to move very quickly with the sound of air or water rushing

whop·per /ˈwɑpər/ *noun* (*informal*) **1** something that is very big for its type: *Pete has caught a whopper* (= a large fish). **2** a lie: *She's told some whoppers about her past.*

whop·ping /ˈwɑpɪŋ/ *adj.* [only before noun] (*informal*) very big: *The company reported a whopping 75 million dollar loss.*

whore /hɔr/ *noun* (*old-fashioned*, *offensive*) a female PROSTI-TUTE

who're /ˈhuər/ *short form* who are

whorl /wɔrl; wɔrl/ *noun* **1** a pattern made by a curved line that forms a rough circle, with smaller circles inside bigger ones: *the whorls on your fingertips* **2** (*technical*) a ring of leaves, flowers, etc. around the STEM of a plant

who's /huz/ *short form* **1** who is **2** who has

whose /huz/ *det.*, *pron.*
1 used in questions to ask who something belongs to: *Whose house is that?* ◆ *I wonder whose this is.* **2** used to say which person or thing you mean: *He's a man whose opinion I respect.* ◆ *It's the house whose door is painted red.* **3** used to give more information about a person or thing: *Isaac, whose brother he was, had heard the joke before.*

who·so·ev·er /ˌhusoʊˈɛvər/ *pron.* (*old use*) = WHOEVER

who's who a list or book of facts about famous people: *The list of delegates attending read like a who's who of the business world.* **ORIGIN** From the reference book *Who's Who*, which gives information about many well-known people and what they have done.

who've /huv/ *short form* who have

whup /wʌp; wʊp/ *verb* (-pp-) ~ **sb/sth** (*informal*) to defeat someone easily in a game, a fight, an election, etc.

why /waɪ/ *adv.*, *exclamation*, *noun*
● *adv.* **1** used in questions to ask the reason for or purpose of something: *Why were you late?* ◆ *Tell me why you did it.* ◆ *"I would like you to go." " Why me? "* ◆ (*informal*) *Why oh why do people keep leaving the door open?* **2** used in questions to suggest that it is not necessary to do something: *Why get upset just because you got one bad grade?* ◆ *Why bother to write? We'll see him tomorrow.* **3** used to give or talk about a reason: *That's why I left so early.* ◆ *I know you did it—I just want to know why.* ◆ *The reason why the injection needs repeating*

every year is that the virus changes.
IDM **why ever** used in questions to mean "why," expressing surprise: *Why ever didn't you tell us before?* **why not?** used to make or agree to a suggestion: *Why not write to her?* ◆ *"Let's eat out." " Why not? "* ◆ *Why don't we go together?*
● *exclamation* used to express surprise, lack of patience, etc.: *Why Jane, it's you!* ◆ *Why, it's easy—a child could do it!*
● *noun*
IDM **the whys and (the) wherefores** the reasons for something: *I had no intention of going into the whys and the wherefores of the situation.*

WI *abbr.* (in writing) **1** West Indies **2** Wisconsin

Wic·ca /ˈwɪkə/ *noun* [U] a modern form of WITCHCRAFT, practiced as a religion ▶ **Wic·can** /ˈwɪkən/ *adj.*

wick /wɪk/ *noun*, *verb*
● *noun* **1** the piece of string in the center of a CANDLE, which you light so that the candle burns **2** the piece of material in an oil lamp that absorbs the oil and that you light so that the lamp burns
● *verb* ~ **sth (away)** (of a material) to take small drops of liquid from an area and move them away: *Wool socks wick away sweat.*

wick·ed /ˈwɪkəd/ *adj.*, *adv.*, *noun*
● *adj.* (**wick·ed·er**, **wick·ed·est**) **HELP** You can also use **more wicked** and **most wicked**. **1** morally bad **SYN** EVIL: *a wicked deed* ◆ *stories about a wicked witch* **2** (*informal*) slightly bad but in a way that is amusing and/or attractive **SYN** MISCHIEVOUS: *a wicked grin* ◆ *Jane has a wicked sense of humor.* **3** dangerous, harmful, or powerful: *He has a wicked punch.* ◆ *a wicked-looking knife* **4** (*slang*) very good: *This song's wicked.* ▶ **wick·ed·ly** *adv.*: *Martin grinned wickedly.* ◆ *a wickedly funny comedy* ◆ *a wickedly sharp blade* **wick·ed·ness** *noun* [U]
● *adv.* (*slang*) + **adj./adv.** very: *That kid is wicked cute!*
● *noun* **the wick·ed** [pl.] people who are wicked
IDM **(there's) no peace/rest for the wicked** (usually *humorous*) used when someone is complaining that they have a lot of work to do

wick·er /ˈwɪkər/ *noun* [U] thin sticks of wood twisted together to make BASKETS, furniture, etc.: *a wicker chair*

wick·er·work /ˈwɪkərˌwərk/ *noun* [U] BASKETS, furniture, etc. made from wicker

wicket gate *noun* a small gate, especially one at the side of a larger one

wide /waɪd/ *adj.*, *adv.*
● *adj.* (**wid·er**, **wid·est**)
▷ **FROM ONE SIDE TO THE OTHER** **1** measuring a lot from one side to the other: *a wide river* ◆ *Sam has a wide mouth.* ◆ *a jacket with wide lapels* ◆ *Her face broke into a wide grin.* **ANT** NARROW **2** measuring a particular distance from one side to the other: *How wide is that stream?* ◆ *It's about 2 yards wide.* ◆ *The road was just wide enough for two vehicles to pass.* ⟳ see also WIDTH
▷ **LARGE NUMBER/AMOUNT** **3** including a large number or variety of different people or things; covering a large area: *a wide range/choice/variety of goods* ◆ *Her music appeals to a wide audience.* ◆ *Jenny has a wide circle of friends.* ◆ *a manager with wide experience of industry* ◆ *It's the best job in the whole wide world.* ◆ *The incident has received wide coverage in the press.* ◆ *The festival attracts people from a wide area.*
▷ **DIFFERENCE/GAP** **4** very big: *There are wide variations in prices.*
▷ **GENERAL** **5** (only used in the comparative and superlative) general; not only looking at details: *the wider aims of the project* ◆ *We are talking about education in its widest sense.*
▷ **EYES** **6** fully open: *She stared at him with wide eyes.*
▷ **NOT CLOSE** **7** ~ **(of sth)** far from the point aimed at: *Her shot was wide of the target).*
▷ **-WIDE** **8** (in adjectives and adverbs) happening or existing in the whole of a country, etc.: *a nationwide search* ◆ *We need to act on an industry-wide scale.*

WORD FAMILY		
wide *adj.*, *adv.*		
widely *adv.*		
widen *verb*		
width *noun*		

IDM **give sb/sth a wide berth** to not go too near someone or something; to avoid someone or something: *He gave the dog a wide berth.* **wide of the mark** not accurate: *Their predictions turned out to be wide of the mark.*

● *adv.* (wid·er, wid·est) as far or fully as possible: *The door was wide open.* ◆ *The championship is still wide open* (= anyone could win). ◆ *She had a fear of wide-open spaces.* ◆ *He stood with his legs wide apart.* ◆ *In a few seconds she was wide awake.* ◆ *Open your mouth wide.* **IDM** see CAST v., FAR

wide-angle 'lens *noun* a camera LENS that can give a wider view than a normal lens

'wide-eyed *adj.* **1** with your eyes fully open because of fear, surprise, etc.: *She stared at him in wide-eyed amazement.* **2** having little experience and therefore very willing to believe, trust, or accept someone or something **SYN** NAIVE

wide·ly /'waɪdli/ *adv.*
1 by a lot of people; in or to many places: *a widely held belief* ◆ *The idea is now widely accepted.* ◆ *He has traveled widely in Asia.* ◆ *Her books are widely read* (= a lot of people read them). ◆ *He's an educated, widely-read man* (= he has read a lot of books). **2** to a large degree; a lot: *Standards vary widely.*

wid·en /'waɪdn/ *verb* **1** [I, T] to become wider; to make something wider **SYN** BROADEN: *Her eyes widened in surprise.* ◆ *~ into sth Here the stream widens into a river.* ◆ *~ sth They may have to widen the road to cope with the increase in traffic.* **2** [I, T] to become larger in degree or range; to make something larger in degree or range **SYN** BROADEN: *the widening gap between rich and poor* ◆ *~ sth We plan to widen the scope of our existing activities by offering more language courses.* ◆ *The legislation will be widened to include all firearms.*

wide-'ranging *adj.* including or dealing with a large number of different subjects or areas: *The commission has been given wide-ranging powers.* ◆ *a wide-ranging discussion*

wide re'ceiver *noun* (in football) a RECEIVER, usually one who starts a play in a position near the edge of the field

wide·screen /'waɪdskrin/ *noun* [U] a way of presenting images on television with the width a lot greater than the height **SYN** LETTERBOX

wide·spread **AWL** /'waɪd'sprɛd; 'waɪdsprɛd/ *adj.* existing or happening over a large area or among many people: *widespread damage* ◆ *The plan received widespread support throughout the country.*

widg·eon = WIGEON

widg·et /'wɪdʒət/ *noun* **1** (*informal*) used to refer to any small device that you do not know the name of **2** (*business*) a product that does not exist, used as an example of a typical product when making calculations: *Company A produces two million widgets a year.* **3** (*computing*) a small box on a web page that delivers changing information, such as news items or weather reports, while the rest of the page remains the same

wid·ow /'wɪdoʊ/ *noun, verb*
● *noun* a woman whose husband has died and who has not married again
● *verb* **be wid·owed** if someone **is widowed**, their husband or wife has died: *She was widowed when she was 35.*
▶ **wid·owed** *adj.*: *his widowed father*

wid·ow·er /'wɪdoʊər/ *noun* a man whose wife has died and who has not married again

wid·ow·hood /'wɪdoʊˌhʊd/ *noun* [U] the state or period of being a widow or widower

'widow's ˌpeak *noun* hair growing in the shape of a V on someone's FOREHEAD ⊃ picture at HAIR

width /wɪdθ; wɪtθ/ *noun*
1 [U, C] the measurement from one side of something to the other; how wide something is: *It's about 10 yards in width.* ◆ *The terrace runs the full width of the house.* ◆ *The carpet is available in different widths.* ⊃ picture at DIMENSION **2** [C] a piece of material of a particular width: *You'll need two widths of fabric for each curtain.* **3** [C] the distance between the two long sides of a swimming pool: *How many widths can you swim?* ⊃ compare LENGTH

width·wise /'wɪdθwaɪz; 'wɪtθ-/ *adv.* (also **width·ways** /'wɪdθweɪz/) along the width and not the length: *Cut the cake in half widthwise.* ⊃ compare LENGTHWISE

wield /wild/ *verb* **1** *~ sth* to have and use power, authority, etc.: *She wields enormous power within the party.* **2** *~ sth* to hold something, ready to use it as a weapon or tool **SYN** BRANDISH: *He was wielding a large knife.*

wie·ner /'winər/ *noun* **1** = FRANKFURTER **2** (*slang*) a word for a PENIS, used especially by children

wife /waɪf/ *noun* (*pl.* wives /waɪvz/)
the woman that a man is married to; a married woman: *the doctor's wife* ◆ *She's his second wife.* ◆ *an increase in the number of working wives* ⊃ collocations at MARRIAGE ⊃ see also FISHWIFE, HOUSEWIFE, MIDWIFE, TROPHY WIFE **IDM** see HUSBAND, OLD

wife·ly /'waɪfli/ *adj.* (*old-fashioned* or *humorous*) typical or expected of a wife: *wifely duties*

'wife-ˌswapping *noun* [U] (*informal*) the practice of exchanging sexual partners between a group of married couples

Wi-Fi /'waɪ faɪ/ *noun* [U] (*computing*) the abbreviation for "wireless fidelity" (a system for sending data over computer networks using radio waves instead of wires)

wig /wɪg/ *noun, verb*
● *noun* a piece of artificial hair that is worn on the head, for example to hide the fact that a person is BALD, or to cover someone's own hair
● *verb* (-gg-)
PHR V **wig 'out** (*informal*) to become very excited, anxious, or angry about something; to go crazy

wig·eon (also **widg·eon**) /'wɪdʒən/ *noun* (*pl.* wig·eon, widg·eon) a type of wild DUCK

wig·gle /'wɪgl/ *verb, noun*
● *verb* [I, T] (*informal*) to move from side to side or up and down in short, quick movements; to make something move in this way **SYN** WRIGGLE: *The puppy wiggled in my arms.* ◆ *~ sth He removed his shoes and wiggled his toes.*
● *noun* a small movement from side to side or up and down

'wiggle ˌroom *noun* [U] (*informal*) the chance to change something or to understand it in a different way: *The* amendment leaves no wiggle room for lawmakers. ♦ There is some wiggle room in the budget.

wig·gly /ˈwɪgli/ adj. (informal) (of a line) having many curves in it; **SYN** WAVY

wight /waɪt/ noun (literary or old use) **1** a GHOST or other spirit **2** (especially following an adjective) a person, considered in a particular way: a poor wight

wig·wam /ˈwɪgwɑm/ noun a type of tent, shaped like a DOME or CONE, used by Native Americans in the past ⊃ see also TEPEE

wi·ki /ˈwɪki/ noun a Web site that allows any user to change or add to the information it contains: There's a wiki page hosted by the conference where you can share ideas and information.

wil·co /ˈwɪlkoʊ/ exclamation people say Wilco! in communication by radio, to show that they agree to do something

wild /waɪld/ adj., noun

● **adj.** (wild·er, wild·est)
> ANIMALS/PLANTS **1** living or growing in natural conditions; not kept in a house or on a farm: wild animals/flowers ♦ a wild rabbit ♦ wild strawberries ♦ The plants **grow wild** along the banks of rivers.
> SCENERY/LAND **2** in its natural state; not changed by people: wild prairies
> OUT OF CONTROL **3** lacking discipline or control: The boy is wild and completely out of control. ♦ He had a wild look in his eyes.
> FEELINGS **4** full of very strong feeling: wild laughter ♦ The crowd went wild. ♦ It makes me wild (= very angry) to see such waste.
> NOT SENSIBLE **5** not carefully planned; not sensible or accurate: He made a wild guess at the answer. ♦ wild accusations
> EXCITING **6** (informal) very good, enjoyable, or exciting: We had a wild time in New York.
> ENTHUSIASTIC **7** ~ about sb/sth (informal) very enthusiastic about someone or something: She's totally wild about him. ♦ I'm not wild about the idea.
> WEATHER/SEA **8** affected by storms and strong winds **SYN** STORMY: a wild night ♦ The sea was wild.
> ▶ **wild·ness** noun [U] ⊃ see also WILDLY
IDM **beyond sb's wildest dreams** far more, better, etc. than you could ever have imagined or hoped for **not/never in sb's wildest dreams** used to say that something has happened in a way that someone did not expect at all: Never in my wildest dreams did I think I'd meet him again. **run wild 1** to grow or develop freely without any control: The ivy has run wild. ♦ Let your **imagination run wild** and be creative. **2** if children or animals **run wild**, they behave as they like because no one is controlling them **wild horses would not drag, make, etc. sb (do sth)** used to say that nothing would prevent someone from doing something or make them do something they do not want to do ⊃ more at HOG, SOW¹

● **noun 1 the wild** [sing.] a natural environment that is not controlled by people: The bird is too tame now to survive **in the wild. 2 the wilds** [pl.] areas of a country far from towns or cities, where few people live: the wilds of Alaska ♦ (humorous) They live on a farm somewhere out **in the wilds.**

ˌwild ˈboar noun = BOAR

ˈwild card noun **1** (in card games) a card that has no value of its own and takes the value of any card that the player chooses **2** a person or thing whose behavior or effect is difficult to predict **3** (sports) an opportunity for a player or a team to play in a competition when they have not qualified in the usual way; a player or team that enters a competition in this way **4** (computing) a symbol that has no meaning of its own and can represent any letter or number

wild·cat /ˈwaɪldkæt/ adj., verb, noun
● **adj.** [only before noun] **1** a **wildcat strike** happens suddenly and without the official support of a LABOR UNION **2** (of a business or project) that has not been carefully

planned and that will probably not be successful; that does not follow normal standards and methods
● **verb** (-tt-) [I] to look for oil in a place where no one has found any yet ▶ **wild·cat·ter** noun
● **noun** a type of small wild cat that lives in mountains and forests

wil·de·beest /ˈwɪldəˌbist/ noun (pl. **wil·de·beest**) (also **gnu**) a large ANTELOPE with curved horns: a herd of wildebeest

wil·der·ness /ˈwɪldərnəs/ noun [usually sing.] **1** a large area of land that has never been developed or used for growing crops because it is difficult to live there: The Antarctic is the world's last great wilderness. ♦ a **wilderness area** (= one where it is not permitted to build houses or roads) ♦ (figurative) the barren wilderness of modern life **2** a place that people do not take care of or control: Their yard is a wilderness of grass and weeds.
IDM **in the wilderness** no longer in an important position, especially in politics

ˈwild-eyed adj. **1** having eyes that express strong and uncontrolled emotion: a wild-eyed gunman ♦ wild-eyed deer **2** too extreme; not sensible or realistic: wild-eyed activists ♦ a wild-eyed plot

wild·fire /ˈwaɪldˌfaɪər/ noun [U] a fire that spreads quickly over a large area and is difficult to control **IDM** see SPREAD

wild·flower /ˈwaɪldˌflaʊər/ noun a flower growing freely where it has not been deliberately planted

wild·fowl /ˈwaɪldfaʊl/ noun [pl.] birds that people hunt for sport or food, especially birds that live near water such as DUCKS and GEESE

ˌwild ˈgoose chase noun a search for something that is impossible for you to find or that does not exist, that makes you waste a lot of time

wild·life /ˈwaɪldlaɪf/ noun [U] animals, birds, insects, etc. that are wild and live in a natural environment: Development of the area would endanger wildlife. ♦ a **wildlife habitat/sanctuary**

wild·ly /ˈwaɪldli/ adv.
1 in a way that is not controlled: She looked wildly around for an escape. ♦ His heart was beating wildly. **2** extremely; very: The story had been wildly exaggerated. ♦ It is not a wildly funny play.

ˌwild ˈrice noun [U] a grain that is produced by a type of North American grass and is used as food; the plant that produces this grain

the ˌWild ˈWest noun [sing.] the western states of the U.S. in the late 19th century, used especially to refer to the fact that there was not much respect for the law there

wiles /waɪlz/ noun [pl.] tricks that someone uses in order to get what they want or to make someone behave in a particular way

wil·ful = WILLFUL

will /wɪl/ modal verb, verb, noun
● **modal verb** /wəl; əl; l; strong form wɪl/ (short form ˈll /l/, negative will not, short form won't /woʊnt/, pt would /wəd; əd; d; strong form wʊd/, short form ˈd /d/, negative would not, short form would·n't /ˈwʊdnt/) **1** used for talking about or predicting the future: You'll be in time if you hurry. ♦ How long will you be staying in Paris? ♦ Fred said he'd be leaving soon. ♦ By next year all the money will have been spent. **2** used for showing that someone is willing to do something: I'll check this letter for you, if you want. ♦ They won't lend us any more money. ♦ He wouldn't come—he said he was too busy. ♦ We said we would keep them. **3** used for asking someone to do something: Will you send this letter for me, please? ♦ You'll water the plants while I'm away, won't you? ♦ I asked him if he wouldn't mind calling later. **4** used for ordering someone to do something: You'll do it this minute! ♦ Will you be quiet! **5** used for stating what you think is probably true: That'll be the doctor now. ♦ You'll have had dinner already, I suppose. **6** used for stating what is generally true: If it's made of wood

it will float. ♦ *Engines won't run without lubricants.* **7** used for stating what is true or possible in a particular case: *This jar will hold a pint.* ♦ *The door won't open!* **8** used for talking about habits: *She'll listen to music, alone in her room, for hours.* ♦ *He would spend hours on the telephone.* **HELP** If you put extra stress on the word **will** or **would** in this meaning, it shows that the habit annoys you: *He 'will talk with his mouth full, even though he knows I don't like it.* ⊃ note at MODAL, SHALL

● *verb* /wɪl/ (*third person sing.pres.t.* **will**) [I] (only used in the simple present tense) (*old-fashioned* or *formal*) to want or like: *Call it what you will, it's still a problem.*

● *verb* /wɪl/ **1** to use the power of your mind to do something or to make something happen: *~ sth As a child he had thought he could fly, if he willed it enough.* ♦ *~ sb/sth to do sth She willed her eyes to stay open.* ♦ *He willed himself not to panic.* **2** *~ sth* | *~ that…* (*old use*) to intend or want something to happen: *They thought they had won the war because God had willed it.* **3** to formally give your property or possessions to someone after you have died, by means of a WILL: *~ sb sth Joe had willed them everything he possessed.* ♦ *~ sth (to sb) Joe had willed everything he possessed to them.*

● *noun* /wɪl/ **1** [C, U] the ability to control your thoughts and actions in order to achieve what you want to do; a feeling of strong determination to do something that you want to do: *to have a strong will* ♦ *to have an iron will/a will of iron* ♦ *Her decision to continue shows great strength of will.* ♦ *In spite of what happened, he never lost the will to live.* ♦ *The meeting turned out to be a clash of wills.* ♦ *She always wants to impose her will on other people* (= to get what she wants). ⊃ see also FREE WILL, WILLPOWER **2** [sing.] what someone wants to happen in a particular situation: *I don't want to go against your will.* ♦ (*formal*) *It is God's will.* **3** (also tes·ta·ment) [C] a legal document that says what is to happen to someone's money and property after they die: *I ought to make a will.* ♦ *My father left me the house in his will.* ⊃ see also LIVING WILL **4** **-willed** (in adjectives) having the type of will mentioned: *a strong-willed young woman* ♦ *weak-willed greedy people* **IDM** **against your will** when you do not want to: *I was forced to sign the agreement against my will.* **at will** whenever or wherever you like: *They were able to come and go at will.* **sth has a will of its own** used to say that something can move or act in ways that we cannot control: *Mother Nature has a will of its own.* **where there's a will there's a way** (*saying*) if you really want to do something then you will find a way of doing it **with a will** in a willing and enthusiastic way

will·ful (also **wil·ful**) /'wɪlfl/ adj. (*disapproving*) **1** [usually before noun] (of a bad or harmful action) done deliberately, although the person doing it knows that it is wrong: *willful damage/misconduct/neglect* **2** determined to do what you want; not caring about what other people want **SYN** HEADSTRONG: *a willful child* ▶ **will·ful·ly** /-fəli/ adv. **will·ful·ness** noun [U]

the wil·lies /'wɪliz/ noun [pl.] (*informal*) if something **gives you the willies**, you are frightened by it or find it unpleasant

will·ing 🔎 /'wɪlɪŋ/ adj.

1 [not usually before noun] *~ (to do sth)* not objecting to doing something; having no reason for not doing something: *They keep a list of people (who are) willing to work nights.* ♦ *I'm perfectly willing to discuss the problem.* **2** [usually before noun] ready or pleased to help and not needing to be persuaded; done or given in an enthusiastic way: *willing helpers/volunteers* ♦ *willing support* ♦ *She's very willing.* **ANT** UNWILLING ▶ **will·ing·ly** adv.: *People would willingly pay more for better services.* ♦ "*Will you help me?*" "*Willingly.*" **will·ing·ness** noun [U, sing.] **IDM** see GOD, READY, SPIRIT

will-o'-the-wisp /ˌwɪl ə ðə 'wɪsp/ noun [usually sing.] **1** a thing that is impossible to obtain; a person that you cannot depend on **2** a blue light that is sometimes seen at night on soft wet ground and is caused by natural gases burning

wil·low /'wɪloʊ/ noun **1** [C] a tree with long, thin branches and long, thin leaves, that often grows near water ⊃ see also PUSSY WILLOW ⊃ picture at TREE **2** [U] the wood of the willow tree

wil·low·y /'wɪloʊi/ adj. (*approving*) (of a person, especially a woman) tall, thin, and attractive

will·pow·er /'wɪlˌpaʊər/ noun [U] the ability to control your thoughts and actions in order to achieve what you want to do

wil·ly-nil·ly /ˌwɪli 'nɪli/ adv. (*informal*) **1** in a careless way without planning: *Don't use your credit card willy-nilly.* **2** whether you want to or not: *She was forced willy-nilly to accept the company's proposals.*

wilt /wɪlt/ verb **1** [I, T] *~ (sth)* if a plant or flower **wilts**, or something **wilts** it, it bends toward the ground because of the heat or a lack of water **SYN** DROOP **2** [I] (*informal*) to become weak or tired or less confident **SYN** FLAG: *The spectators were wilting visibly in the hot sun.* ♦ *He was wilting from all the pressure at work.* **3** thou wilt (*old use*) used to mean "you will," when talking to one person

wilt·ed /'wɪltəd/ adj. **wilted** vegetable leaves, for example SPINACH leaves, have been cooked for a short time and then used in a salad

wil·y /'waɪli/ adj. (**wil·i·er, wil·i·est**) skillful at getting what you want, especially by tricking people **SYN** CUNNING: *The boss is a wily old fox.*

wimp /wɪmp/ noun, verb
● *noun* (*informal, disapproving*) a person who is not strong, brave, or confident ▶ **wimp·ish** (also **wimp·y**) adj.: *wimpish behavior*
● *verb* **PHR V** **wimp 'out (of sth)** (*informal, disapproving*) to not do something that you intended to do because you are too frightened or not confident enough to do it

wim·ple /'wɪmpl/ noun a head covering made of cloth folded around the head and neck, worn by women in the past and now by some NUNS

win 🔎 /wɪn/ verb, noun

● *verb* (**win·ning, won, won** /wʌn/) **1** [I, T] to be the most successful in a competition, race, battle, etc.: *Which team won?* ♦ *~ at sth to win at cards/chess, etc.* ♦ *~ against sb/sth The Penguins won by six goals to two against the Devils.* ♦ *~ sth to win an election/a game/a war, etc.* ♦ *She loves to win an argument.* **2** [T] to get something as the result of a competition, race, election, etc.: *~ sth The ski team won five gold medals.* ♦ *He won $3,000 in the lottery.* ♦ *How many trophies did you win?* ♦ *~ sth from sb The Democrats won control of Congress from the Republicans in the last election.* ♦ *~ yourself/sb sth You've won yourself a trip to New York.* **3** [T] *~ sth* to achieve or get something that you want, especially by your own efforts: *They are trying to win support for their proposals.* ♦ *The company has won a contract to supply books and materials to schools.* ♦ *She won the admiration of many people in her battle against cancer.* ⊃ see also NO-WIN, WINNER, WINNING, WIN-WIN **IDM** **you, he, etc. can't win** (*informal*) used to say that there is no acceptable way of dealing with a particular situation **you can't win them all** | **you win some, you lose some** (*informal*) used to express sympathy for someone who has been disappointed about something **you win** (*informal*) used to agree to what someone wants after you have failed to persuade them to do or let you do something else: *OK, you win, I'll admit I was wrong.* **win (sth) hands down** (*informal*) to win something very easily **win sb's heart** to make someone love you **win or lose** whether you succeed or fail: *Win or lose, we'll know we've done our best.* ⊃ more at DAY, SPUR **PHR V** **win sth/sb↔'back** to get or have again something or someone that you had before: *The party is struggling to win back voters who have been alienated by recent scandals.* **win 'out** (*informal*) to be successful despite difficulties: *It won't be easy, but we'll win out in the end.* **win sb↔'over (to sth)** to get someone's support or approval by persuading them

---

| h **hat** | m **man** | n **no** | ŋ **sing** | l **leg** | r **red** | y **yes** | w **wet** |

that you are right: *She's against the idea, but I'm sure I can win her over.*

● **noun** a victory in a game, contest, etc.: *two wins and three losses* ◆ *They have not had a win so far this season.* ◆ *The Eagles swept the Steelers in a 23–7 win.*

wince /wɪns/ *verb* [I] **~ (at sth)** to suddenly make an expression with your face that shows that you are feeling pain or embarrassment: *He winced as a sharp pain shot through his left leg.* ◆ *I still wince when I think about that stupid thing I said.* ▶ **wince** *noun* [usually sing.]: *a wince of pain*

winch /wɪntʃ/ *noun, verb*
● **noun** a machine for lifting or pulling heavy objects using a rope or chain
● **verb ~ sb/sth + adv./prep.** to lift someone or something up into the air using a winch

Win·ches·ter /'wɪntʃəstər/ (also **Winchester 'rifle**) *noun* a type of long gun that fires several bullets one after the other

wind¹ 🔊 /wɪnd/ *noun, verb* ⊃ see also WIND²
● **noun 1** [C, U] also **the wind** air that moves quickly as a result of natural forces: *strong/high winds* ◆ *gale-force winds* ◆ *a light wind* ◆ *a north/south/east/west wind* ◆ *a bitter/cold/biting wind from the north* ◆ *The wind is blowing from the south.* ◆ *The trees were swaying in the wind.* ◆ *A gust of wind blew my hat off.* ◆ *The wall gives some protection from the prevailing wind.* ◆ *The wind is getting up* (= starting to blow strongly). ◆ *The wind has dropped* (= stopped blowing strongly). ◆ **wind speed/direction** ⊃ collocations at WEATHER ⊃ see also CROSSWIND, DOWNWIND, HEADWIND, TAILWIND, TRADE WINDS, WINDY **2** [U] breath that you need when you do exercise or blow into a musical instrument: *I need time to get my wind back after that run.* ◆ *He kicked Gomez in the stomach, knocking the wind out of him.* ⊃ see also SECOND WIND **3** [U] (also **winds** [pl.]) one of the group of musical instruments in an ORCHESTRA that produce sounds when you blow into them; the musicians who play those instruments: *music for wind and strings* ◆ *the wind section* ◆ *The winds played beautifully.* ⊃ compare WOODWIND
IDM **break wind** to release gas from your BOWELS through your ANUS **get wind of sth** (*informal*) to hear about something secret or private **in the wind** about to happen soon, although you do not know exactly how or when **like the wind** very quickly **take the wind out of sb's sails** (*informal*) to make someone suddenly less confident or angry, especially when you do or say something that they do not expect **the winds of change** (used especially by journalists) an event or a series of events that has started to happen and will cause important changes or results: *The winds of change were blowing through the banking world.* ⊃ more at CAUTION, FOLLOWING, ILL, SAIL *v.*, WAY *n.*

● **verb** [usually passive] **~ sb** to make someone unable to breathe easily for a short time: *He was momentarily winded by the blow to his stomach.* ⊃ see also LONG-WINDED

wind² 🔊 /waɪnd/ *verb*
⊃ see also WIND¹ (**wound, wound** /waʊnd/) **1** [I, T] (of a road, river, etc.) to have many bends and twists: **+ adv./prep.** *The path wound down to the beach.* ◆ **~ its way + adv./prep.** *The river winds its way between two meadows.* ⊃ see also WINDING **2** [T] **~ sth + adv./prep.** to wrap or twist something around itself or something else: *He wound the wool into a ball.* ◆ *Wind the bandage around your finger.* **3** [T, I] to make a clock or other piece of machinery work by turning a KNOB, handle, etc. several times; to be able to be made to work in this way: **~ sth (up)** *He had forgotten to wind his watch.* ◆ **~ up** *It was one of those old-fashioned gramophones that winds up.* ⊃ see also WINDUP **4** [T, I] to operate a tape, film, etc. so that it moves nearer to its ending or starting position: **~ sth forward/back** *He wound the tape back to the beginning.* ◆ **~ forward/back** *Wind forward to the part where they discover the body.* **5** [T] **~ sth** to turn a handle several times: *You operate the trap door by winding this handle.* **IDM** see LITTLE FINGER ▶ **wind** *noun*: *Give the handle another couple of winds.*
PHRV **,wind 'down 1** (of a person) to rest or relax after a

period of activity or excitement **SYN** UNWIND **2** (of a piece of machinery) to go slowly and then stop **,wind sth↔'down 1** to bring an activity, etc. to an end gradually over a period of time: *The government is winding down its nuclear program.* **2** to make something such as the window of a car move downward by turning a handle, pressing a button, etc.: *Can I wind my window down?* **,wind 'up** (*informal*) (of a person) to find yourself in a particular place or situation: *I always said he would wind up in prison.* ◆ **~ doing sth** *We eventually wound up staying in a little hotel a few miles from town.* ◆ **+ adj.** *If you take risks like that you'll wind up dead.* **,wind 'up | ,wind sth↔'up 1** to bring something such as a speech or meeting to an end: *The speaker was just winding up when the door was flung open.* ◆ *If we all agree, let's wind up the discussion.* **2** to make something such as the window of a car move upward by turning a handle, pressing a button, etc.

wind·bag /'wɪndbæg/ *noun* (*informal, disapproving*) a person who talks too much, and does not say anything important or interesting

wind-blown /'wɪnd bloʊn/ *adj.* **1** carried from one place to another by the wind **2** made messy by the wind: *wind-blown hair*

wind·break /'wɪndbreɪk/ *noun* a row of trees, a fence, etc. that provides protection from the wind

wind·break·er /'wɪnd,breɪkər/ *noun* a jacket designed to protect you from the wind ⊃ picture at CLOTHES

wind·burn /'wɪndbɜrn/ *noun* [U] the condition of having painful red skin, caused by cold or a very strong wind

wind chill /'wɪnd tʃɪl/ *noun* [U] the effect of low temperature combined with wind on someone or something: *Take the wind-chill factor into account.*

wind chimes /'wɪnd tʃaɪmz/ *noun* [pl.] a set of hanging pieces of metal, etc. that make a pleasant ringing sound in the wind

wind–down /'waɪnd daʊn/ *noun* [sing.] a gradual reduction in activity as something comes to an end: *The wind-down of the party took longer than we would have liked.*

wind·er /'waɪndər/ *noun* a device or piece of machinery that winds something, for example something that winds a clock or the film in a camera

wind·fall /'wɪndfɔl/ *noun* **1** an amount of money that someone or something wins or receives unexpectedly: *The hospital got a sudden windfall of $900,000.* ◆ *windfall profits* ◆ *The government imposed a windfall tax* (= a tax on profits to be paid once only, not every year) *on some industries.* **2** a fruit, especially an apple, that the wind has blown down from a tree

wind farm /'wɪnd fɑrm/ *noun* an area of land on which there are a lot of WINDMILLS or WIND TURBINES for producing electricity ⊃ collocations at ENVIRONMENT

wind gauge /'wɪnd geɪdʒ/ *noun* = ANEMOMETER

wind·ing /'waɪndɪŋ/ *adj.* having a curving and twisting shape: *a long and winding road*

wind·ing sheet /'waɪndɪŋ ʃit/ *noun* (especially in the past) a piece of cloth that a dead person's body was wrapped in before it was buried **SYN** SHROUD

wind in·stru·ment /'wɪnd ,ɪnstrəmənt/ *noun* any musical instrument that you play by blowing ⊃ compare BRASS, WOODWIND

wind·lass /'wɪndləs/ *noun* a type of WINCH (= a machine for lifting or pulling heavy objects)

wind·less /'wɪndləs/ *adj.* (*formal*) without wind: *a windless day* **ANT** WINDY

wind ma·chine /'wɪnd məʃin/ *noun* **1** a machine used in the theater or in movies that blows air to give the effect of wind **2** a machine used in ORCHESTRAS to produce the sound of wind

wind·mill /'wɪndmɪl/ *noun* **1** a building with machinery for GRINDING grain into flour that is driven by the power of the wind turning long arms (called SAILS) **2** a tall thin structure with parts that turn around, used to change the power of the wind into electricity **IDM** see TILT

win·dow /ˈwɪndoʊ/ noun

1 [C] an opening in the wall or roof of a building, car, etc., usually covered with glass, that allows light and air to come in and people to see out; the glass in a window: *She looked out the window.* ♦ *to open/close the window* ♦ *the bedroom/car/kitchen, etc. window* ♦ *a broken window* ⊃ picture at HOUSE ⊃ see also BAY WINDOW, PICTURE WINDOW, ROSE WINDOW, SASH WINDOW **2** [C] = STORE WINDOW: *I saw the dress I wanted in the window.* ♦ *a window display* **3** [C] an area within a frame on a computer screen, in which a particular program is operating or in which information of a particular type is shown: *to create/open a window* **4** [C] a small area of something that you can see through, for example to talk to someone or to read something: *There was a long line of people at the box-office window.* ♦ *The address must be clearly visible through the window of the envelope.* **5** [sing.] ~ **on/into sth** a way of seeing and learning about something: *Television is a sort of **window on the world**.* ♦ *It gave me an intriguing window into the way people live.* **6** [C] a time when there is an opportunity to do something, although it may not last long: *We now have a small **window of opportunity** in which to make our views known.*
IDM **fly/go (right) out the window** (*informal*) to stop existing; to disappear completely: *As soon as the kids arrived, peace went out the window.* **throw/toss sth out the window** (*informal*) to stop caring about or considering something: *I think he's thrown hope out the window.* ♦ *I suggested some changes, but she just tossed them out the window.*

ˈwindow ˌbox noun a long narrow box outside a window, in which plants are grown ⊃ picture at HOUSE

ˈwindow ˌcleaner noun **1** [U] a liquid substance used for cleaning windows **2** [C] = WINDOW WASHER

ˈwindow ˌdressing noun [U] **1** the art of arranging goods in store windows in an attractive way **2** (*disapproving*) the fact of doing or saying something in a way that creates a good impression but does not show the real facts: *The reforms are seen as window dressing.*

ˈwindow ˌledge noun = WINDOWSILL

win·dow·less /ˈwɪndoʊləs/ adj. without a window: *a tiny, windowless cell*

win·dow·pane /ˈwɪndoʊˌpeɪn/ noun a piece of glass in a window ⊃ picture at HOUSE

ˈwindow ˌseat noun **1** a seat below a window **2** a seat next to a window in an aircraft, train, or other vehicle

ˈwindow ˌshade noun = BLIND

ˈwindow-ˌshopping noun [U] the activity of looking at the goods in store windows, usually without intending to buy anything: *to go window-shopping* ⊃ collocations at SHOPPING ▶ **ˈwindow-ˌshop** verb (-pp-) [I] **ˈwindow-ˌshopper** noun

win·dow·sill /ˈwɪndoʊˌsɪl/ (also sill, **ˈwindow ˌledge**) noun a narrow shelf below a window, either inside or outside: *Place the plants on a sunny windowsill.* ⊃ picture at HOUSE

ˈwindow ˌwasher (also **ˈwindow ˌcleaner**) noun a person whose job it is to clean windows

wind·pipe /ˈwɪndpaɪp/ noun the tube in the throat that carries air to the lungs **SYN** TRACHEA ⊃ picture at BODY

wind·shield /ˈwɪndʃild/ noun **1** the window across the front of a vehicle ⊃ picture at CAR ⊃ collocations at DRIVING **2** a glass or plastic screen that provides protection from the wind, for example at the front of a motorcycle

ˈwindshield ˌwiper (also wip·er) noun a blade with a rubber edge that moves across a windshield to make it clear of rain, snow, etc. ⊃ picture at CAR

wind·sock /ˈwɪndsɑk/ noun a tube made of soft material, open at both ends, that hangs at the top of a pole, to show the direction of the wind

wind·storm /ˈwɪndstɔrm/ noun a storm where there is very strong wind but little rain or snow

wind·surf·er /ˈwɪndˌsɜrfər/ noun **1** (also **Wind·surf·er™**) (also sail·board) a long, narrow board with a sail, that you stand on and sail across water on ⊃ picture at SPORT **2** a person on a windsurfer

wind·surf·ing /ˈwɪndˌsɜrfɪŋ/ (also board·sail·ing) noun [U] the sport of sailing on water standing on a windsurfer: *to go windsurfing* ⊃ picture at SPORT ▶ **wind·surf** verb [I]: *Most visitors come to sail or windsurf.*

wind·swept /ˈwɪndswɛpt/ adj. **1** (of a place) having strong winds and little protection from them: *the windswept Atlantic coast* **2** looking as though you have been in a strong wind: *windswept hair*

ˈwind ˌtun·nel /ˈwɪnd ˌtʌnl/ noun a large tunnel where aircraft, etc. are tested by forcing air past them

ˈwind tur·bine /ˈwɪnd ˌtɜrbaɪn; -bən/ noun a type of modern WINDMILL used for producing electricity

wind·up /ˈwaɪndʌp/ adj., noun
• *adj.* [only before noun] **1** that you operate by turning a key or handle: *an old-fashioned windup gramophone* **2** intended to bring something to an end: *a windup speech*
• *noun* (in baseball) the movements of a PITCHER immediately before throwing the ball: *The pitcher goes/moves into his windup and delivers the pitch.*

wind·ward /ˈwɪndwərd/ adj., noun
• *adj.* on the side of something from which the wind is blowing: *the windward side of the boat* **ANT** LEEWARD ⊃ see also LEE ▶ **wind·ward** adv. **ANT** LEEWARD
• *noun* [U] the side or direction from which the wind is blowing: *to sail to windward* ⊃ compare LEEWARD

wind·y /ˈwɪndi/ adj. (wind·i·er, wind·i·est) **1** (of weather, etc.) with a lot of wind: *a windy day* **ANT** WINDLESS **2** (of a place) getting a lot of wind: *windy hills* **3** (*informal*, *disapproving*) (of speech) involving speaking for longer than necessary and in a way that is complicated and not clear

the ˌWindy ˈCity noun [sing.] a name for the city of Chicago

wine /waɪn/ noun, verb

• *noun* **1** [U, C] an alcoholic drink made from the juice of GRAPES that has been left to FERMENT. There are many different kinds of wine: *a bottle of wine* ♦ *a glass of dry/sweet wine* ♦ *red/white wine* ♦ *rosé/blush wine* ♦ *sparkling wine* ⊃ see also TABLE WINE **2** [U, C] an alcoholic drink made from plants or fruits other than GRAPES: *strawberry/rice wine* **3** [U] (also ˌwine ˈred) a dark red color
• *verb*
IDM **wine and dine (sb)** to go to restaurants, etc. and enjoy good food and drink; to entertain someone by buying them good food and drink: *The firm spent thousands wining and dining potential clients.*

ˈwine bar noun a bar or small restaurant where wine is the main drink available

ˈwine ˌcellar (also cel·lar) noun an underground room where wine is stored; the wine stored in this room

ˈwine ˌcooler noun **1** a drink made with wine, fruit juice, ice, and SODA WATER **2** a container for putting a bottle of wine in to cool it

wine·glass /ˈwaɪnglæs/ noun a glass for drinking wine from

wine·grow·er /ˈwaɪnˌɡroʊər/ noun a person who grows GRAPES for wine

ˈwine list noun a list of wines available in a restaurant ⊃ collocations at RESTAURANT

wine·mak·er /ˈwaɪnˌmeɪkər/ noun a person who produces wine ▶ **wine·mak·ing** /ˈwaɪnˌmeɪkɪŋ/ noun [U]

win·er·y /ˈwaɪnəri/ noun (pl. win·er·ies) a place where wine is made ⊃ compare VINEYARD

ˈwine ˌtasting noun an event at which people taste and compare a number of wines: *The local liquor store hosted a wine tasting.*

ˈwine ˌvinegar noun [U] VINEGAR which is made from wine rather than from grain or apples

wing /wɪŋ/ noun, verb

● **noun**
▷ OF BIRD/INSECT **1** [C] one of the parts of the body of a bird, insect, or bat that it uses for flying: *The swan flapped its wings noisily.* ◆ *wing feathers* ⊃ picture at ANIMAL
▷ OF PLANE **2** [C] one of the large, flat parts that stick out from the side of a plane and help to keep it in the air when it is flying ⊃ picture at PLANE
▷ OF BUILDING **3** [C] one of the parts of a large building that sticks out from the main part: *the east wing* ◆ *the new wing of the hospital*
▷ OF ORGANIZATION **4** [C] one section of an organization that has a particular function or whose members share the same opinions **SYN** ARM: *the radical wing of the party* ◆ *the political wing of the National Resistance Army* ⊃ see also LEFT WING, RIGHT WING
▷ IN SOCCER/HOCKEY **5** [C] = WINGER ⊃ see also LEFT WING, RIGHT WING **6** [C] the far left or right side of the sports field: *He plays on the wing.*
▷ IN THEATER **7 the wings** [pl.] the area at either side of the stage that cannot be seen by the audience
IDM get your wings to pass the exams that mean you are allowed to fly a plane **(waiting) in the wings** ready to take over a particular job or be used in a particular situation when needed **on a wing and a prayer** with only a very slight chance of success **on the wing** (*literary*) (of a bird, insect, etc.) flying **take sb under your wing** to take care of and help someone who has less experience of something than you **take wing** (*literary*) (of a bird, insect, etc.) to fly away: (*figurative*) *Her imagination took wing.* ⊃ more at CLIP v., SPREAD v.

● **verb**
▷ FLY **1** [T, I] ~ **(its way) + adv./prep.** (*literary*) to fly somewhere: *A solitary seagull winged its way across the bay.*
▷ GO QUICKLY **2** [T] ~ **its way + adv./prep.** to be sent somewhere very quickly: *An application form will be winging its way to you soon.*
IDM wing it (*informal*) to do something without planning or preparing it first **SYN** IMPROVISE: *I didn't know I'd have to make a speech—I just had to wing it.*

'**wing back** noun (in soccer) a player who plays near the edge of the field and who both attacks and defends

'**wing chair** noun a comfortable chair that has a high back with pieces pointing forward at the sides

ˌ**wing 'collar** noun a high stiff shirt COLLAR for men, worn with formal clothes

wing·ding /'wɪŋdɪŋ/ noun (*old-fashioned, informal*) a party

winged /wɪŋd/ adj. **1** having wings: *winged insects* **ANT** WINGLESS **2** -**winged** (in adjectives) having the number or type of wings mentioned: *a long-winged bird*

wing·er /'wɪŋər/ noun (also **wing**) (*sports*) either of the attacking players who play toward the side of the playing area in sports such as soccer or HOCKEY

wing·less /'wɪŋləs/ adj. (especially of insects) without wings **ANT** WINGED

'**wing nut** noun a NUT for holding things in place, which has parts that stick out at the sides so that you can turn it easily

wing·span /'wɪŋspæn/ noun the distance between the end of one wing and the end of the other when the wings are fully stretched: *a bird with a two-foot wingspan*

wing·tips /'wɪŋtɪps/ noun [pl.] strong leather shoes that fasten with LACES and have an extra piece of leather with small holes in it over the toe ⊃ picture at SHOE

wink /wɪŋk/ verb, noun
● **verb 1** [I] ~ **(at sb)** to close one eye and open it again quickly, especially as a private signal to someone, or to show something is a joke: *He winked at her and she knew he was thinking the same thing that she was.* ⊃ compare BLINK **2** [I] to shine with an unsteady light; to flash on and off **SYN** BLINK: *We could see the lights of the ship winking in the distance.*

PHR V 'wink at sth to pretend that you have not noticed something, especially something bad or illegal
● **noun** an act of winking, especially as a signal to someone: *He gave her a knowing wink.* ⊃ see also FORTY WINKS **IDM not get/have a wink of sleep| not sleep a wink** to not be able to sleep: *I didn't get a wink of sleep last night.* ◆ *I hardly slept a wink.* ⊃ more at QUICK adv.

Win·ne·ba·go™ /ˌwɪnə'beɪgoʊ/ noun (pl. **Win·ne·ba·go** or **Win·ne·ba·go·gos**) a large vehicle designed for people to live and sleep in when they are camping; a type of RV

win·ner /'wɪnər/ noun
1 a person, a team, an animal, etc. that wins something: *The winners of the competition will be announced next month.* ◆ *There are no winners in a divorce* (= everyone suffers). **2** [usually sing.] (*informal*) a thing or person that is successful or likely to be successful: *I think your idea is a winner.* ◆ *Did you see that touchdown? Manning is a real winner!* **3** [sing.] (*sports*) a goal or point that causes a team or a person to win a game: *Bonds finally hit the winner in the bottom of the 9th inning.* ⊃ compare LOSER **IDM** SEE PICK

win·ning /'wɪnɪŋ/ adj.
1 [only before noun] that wins or has won something, for example a race or competition: *the winning horse* ◆ *the winning run* **2** [usually before noun] attractive in a way that makes other people like you: *a winning smile* ▶ **win·ning·ly** adv. **IDM** SEE CARD

win·ning·est /'wɪnɪŋəst/ adj. (*informal*) having won the most games, races, or competitions: *the winningest coach in the history of the Michigan team*

win·nings /'wɪnɪŋz/ noun [pl.] money that someone wins in a competition or game or by gambling

win·now /'wɪnoʊ/ verb ~ **sth** to blow air through grain in order to remove its outer covering (called the CHAFF) **PHR V** ˌ**winnow sb/sth 'out (of sth)** | ˌ**winnow (sb/sth) 'down** (*formal*) to remove people or things from a group so that only the best ones are left **SYN** SIFT

win·o /'waɪnoʊ/ noun (pl. **win·os**) (*informal*) a person who drinks a lot of cheap alcohol and who has no home

win·some /'wɪnsəm/ adj. (*formal*) (of people or their manner) pleasant and attractive **SYN** ENGAGING: *a winsome smile* ▶ **win·some·ly** adv.

win·ter /'wɪntər/ noun, verb
● **noun** [U, C] the coldest season of the year, between fall and spring: *a mild/severe/hard winter* ◆ *Our house can be very cold in the winter.* ◆ *They worked on the building all through the winter.* ◆ *We went to New Zealand last winter.* ◆ *the winter months* ◆ *a winter coat* **IDM** SEE DEAD n.
● **verb** [I] (+ adv./prep.) to spend the winter somewhere: *Many birds winter in the South.* ⊃ compare OVERWINTER

ˌ**winter 'sports** noun [pl.] sports that people do on snow or ice

win·ter·time /'wɪntərˌtaɪm/ noun [U] the period of time when it is winter: *The days are shorter in the wintertime.*

win·try /'wɪntri/ adj. **1** typical of winter; cold: *wintry weather* ◆ *a wintry landscape* ◆ *wintry showers* (= of snow) **2** not friendly **SYN** FROSTY: *a wintry smile*

ˌ**win-'win** adj. [only before noun] (of a situation) in which there is a good result for each person or group involved: *This is a **win-win situation** all around.*

wipe /waɪp/ verb, noun
● **verb 1** to rub something against a surface, in order to remove dirt or liquid from it; to rub a surface with a cloth, etc. in order to clean it: ~ **sth (on sth)** *Please wipe your feet on the mat.* ◆ *He wiped his hands on a clean towel.* ◆ ~ **sth with sth** *She was sniffling and wiping her eyes with a tissue.* ◆ ~ **sth + adj.** *He wiped his plate clean with a piece of bread.* **2** to remove dirt, liquid, etc. from something by using a cloth, your hand, etc.: ~ **sth (from/off sth)** *He wiped the sweat from his forehead.* ◆ (*figurative*) *Wipe that stupid smile off your face.* ◆ ~ **sth away/off/up** *She wiped off her makeup.* ◆ *Use that*

cloth to wipe up the mess. **3** to remove information, sound, images, etc. from a computer, tape, or video **SYN** ERASE: ~ **sth off (sth)** *You must have wiped off that program I recorded.* ◆ ~ **sth** *Somebody had wiped all the tapes.* **4** to deliberately forget an experience because it was unpleasant or embarrassing **SYN** ERASE: ~ **sth from sth** *I tried to wipe the whole episode from my mind.* ◆ ~ **sth out** *You can never wipe out the past.*

IDM **wipe sb/sth off the face of the earth** | **wipe sth off the map** to destroy or remove someone or something completely **wipe the slate clean** to agree to forget about past mistakes or arguments and start again with a relationship ⊃ more at FLOOR *n.*

PHR V ‚**wipe sth**↔'**down** to clean a surface completely, using a wet cloth: *She took a cloth and wiped down the kitchen table.* ‚**wipe sth** '**off sth** to remove something from something: *Billions of dollars were wiped off share prices today.* ‚**wipe** '**out** (*informal*) to fall over, especially when you are doing a sport such as SKIING or SURFING ‚**wipe sb**↔'**out** (*informal*) to make someone extremely tired: *All that traveling has wiped her out.* ⊃ see also WIPED OUT ‚**wipe sb/sth**↔'**out** [often passive] to destroy or remove someone or something completely: *Whole villages were wiped out by the earthquake.* ◆ *Last year's profits were virtually wiped out.* ◆ *a campaign to wipe out malaria* ⊃ related noun WIPEOUT

● **noun** **1** an act of cleaning something using a cloth: *Can you give the table a quick wipe?* **2** a special piece of thin cloth or soft paper that has been treated with a liquid and that you use to clean away dirt and bacteria: *Remember to take diapers and baby wipes.*

‚**wiped** '**out** *adj.* [not before noun] (*informal*) extremely tired: *You look wiped out.*

wipe·out /'waɪpaʊt/ *noun* (*informal*) **1** [U, C] complete destruction, failure, or defeat: *The party faces virtual wipeout in the election.* ◆ *a 5-0 wipeout* **2** [C] a fall from a SURFBOARD, bicycle, etc.

wip·er /'waɪpər/ *noun* = WINDSHIELD WIPER

wire 🔑 /'waɪər/ *noun, verb*
● **noun** **1** [U, C] metal in the form of thin thread; a piece of this: *a coil of copper wire* ◆ *a wire basket* ◆ *The box was fastened with a rusty wire.* ⊃ picture at CORD ⊃ see also BARBED WIRE, HIGH WIRE, TRIPWIRE **2** [C, U] a piece of wire that is used to carry an electric current or signal: *overhead wires* ◆ *fuse wire* ◆ *The telephone wires had been cut.* ⊃ see also HOT-WIRE **3** the wire [sing.] a wire fence: *Three prisoners escaped by crawling under the wire.* **4** [C] (*informal*) = TELEGRAM: *We sent a wire asking him to join us.* ⊃ see also WIRY

IDM **get your wires crossed** (*informal*) to become confused about what someone has said to you so that you think they meant something else **go, come, etc. (right) down to the wire** (*informal*) if you say that a situation goes **down to the wire**, you mean that the result will not be decided or known until the very end ⊃ more at LIVE², PULL
● **verb** **1** ~ **sth (up)** to connect a building, piece of equipment, etc. to an electricity supply using wires: *Make sure the plug is wired up correctly.* **2** ~ **sb/sth up (to sth)** | ~ **sb/sth to sth** to connect someone or something to a piece of equipment, especially a TAPE RECORDER or computer system: *He was wired up to a police tape recorder.* **3** ~ **sth (for sth)** to put a special device somewhere in order to listen secretly to other people's conversations **SYN** BUG: *The room had been wired for sound.* **4** to send someone a message by TELEGRAM: ~ **sth (to sb)** *He wired the news to us.* ◆ ~ **sb (sth)** *He wired us the news.* **5** to send money from one bank to another using an electronic system: ~ **sth (to sb)** *The bank wired the money to her.* ◆ ~ **sb sth** *The bank wired her the money.* **6** ~ **sth** to join things together using wire

wire-‚cutters *noun* [pl.] a tool for cutting wire: *a pair of wire-cutters*

wired /'waɪərd/ *adj.* **1** connected to a system of computers: *Many colleges now have wired dormitories.* **2** (*informal*) excited or nervous; not relaxed: *I was so wired after the concert that I*

couldn't get to sleep. **3** (*informal*) under the influence of alcohol or an illegal drug **4** (of glass, material, etc.) containing wires that make it strong or stiff

'**wire fraud** *noun* [U, C] FRAUD (= dishonest ways of getting money) using computers and telephones

wire·less /'waɪərləs/ *adj., noun*
● *adj.* not using wires: *Is there a wireless Internet connection in my room?* ▶ **wire·less·ly** *adv.*
● *noun* **1** [C] (*old-fashioned*) a radio: *I heard it on the wireless.* **2** [U] a system of sending and receiving signals: *a message sent by wireless*

‚**wire** '**netting** *noun* [U] wire that is twisted into a net, used especially for fences

wire-pull·er /'waɪər‚pʊlər/ *noun* a person who is able to control or influence events without people realizing it

'**wire ‚service** *noun* an organization that supplies news to newspapers and to radio and television stations

'**wire ‚strippers** *noun* [pl.] a tool for removing the plastic covering from electric wires

wire-tap·ping /'waɪər‚tæpɪŋ/ *noun* [U] the act of secretly listening to other people's telephone conversations by attaching a device to the telephone line ▶ **wire·tap** *verb* (-pp-) ~ **sth wire·tap** *noun*: *the use of illegal wiretaps* ⊃ see also TAP

wir·ing /'waɪərɪŋ/ *noun* [U] the system of wires that is used for supplying electricity to a building or machine: *to check the wiring* ◆ *a wiring diagram*

wir·y /'waɪəri/ *adj.* (wir·i·er, wir·i·est) **1** (of a person) thin but strong **SYN** SINEWY: *a wiry little man* **2** (of hair, plants, etc.) stiff and strong; like wire

wis·dom /'wɪzdəm/ *noun* [U] **1** the ability to make sensible decisions and give good advice because of the experience and knowledge that you have: *a woman of great wisdom* ◆ *words of wisdom* **2** ~ **of sth/of doing sth** how sensible something is: *I question the wisdom of giving a child so much money.* **3** the knowledge that a society or culture has gained over a long period of time: *the collective wisdom of the Native American people*

IDM **conventional/received wisdom** the view or belief that most people hold: *Conventional wisdom has it that riots only ever happen in cities.* **in his/her/its, etc. (infinite) wisdom** used when you are saying that you do not understand why someone has done something: *The government in its infinite wisdom has decided to support the ban.* ⊃ more at PEARL

'**wisdom ‚tooth** *noun* any of the four large teeth at the back of the mouth that do not grow until you are an adult

wise 🔑 /waɪz/ *adj., verb*
● *adj.* (wis·er, wis·est) **1** (of people) able to make sensible decisions and give good advice because of the experience and knowledge that you have: *a wise old man* ◆ *I'm older and wiser after ten years in the business.* **2** (of actions and behavior) sensible; based on good judgment: *a wise decision* **SYN** PRUDENT: *It was very wise to leave when you did.* ◆ *The wisest course of action is just to say nothing.* ◆ *I was grateful for her wise counsel.* ▶ **wise·ly** *adv.*: *She nodded wisely.* ◆ *He wisely decided to tell the truth.*

IDM **be none the wiser** | **not be any the wiser** **1** to not understand something, even after it has been explained to you: *I've read the instructions, but I'm still none the wiser.* **2** to not know or find out about something bad that someone has done: *If you put the money back, no one will be any the wiser.* **be wise after the event** (often *disapproving*) to understand something, or realize what you should have done, only after something has happened **be wise in the ways of sth** having knowledge in the subject mentioned: *We're wise in the ways of hurricane survival.* **be/get wise to sb/sth** (*informal*) to become aware that someone is being dishonest: *He thought he could fool me but I got wise to him.* **put sb wise (to sth)** (*informal*) to inform someone about something ⊃ more at PENNY

t **tea** ‚t **butter** d **did** k **cat** g **got** tʃ **chin** dʒ **June** f **fall**

• **verb**

PHR V ‚wise 'up (to sth) (*informal*) to become aware of the unpleasant truth about a situation

-wise /waɪz/ *suffix* (in adjectives and adverbs) **1** in the manner or direction of: *likewise* ◆ *clockwise* **2** (*informal*) concerning: *Things aren't too good businesswise.*

wise·a·cre /'waɪzˌeɪkər/ *noun* (*old-fashioned*, *informal*) a person who is annoying because they are very confident and think they know a lot

wise·crack /'waɪzkræk/ *noun* (*informal*) a smart remark or joke ▶ **wise·crack** *verb* [I, T]: **(+ speech)** *He plays a wisecracking detective.*

'**wise guy** *noun* **1** (*informal*, *disapproving*) a person who speaks or behaves as if they know more than other people **SYN** KNOW-IT-ALL: *OK, wise guy, what do we do now?* **2** (*slang*) a member of the Mafia

'**wise ‚woman** *noun* (*old use*) a woman with knowledge of traditional medicines and magic

wish ✏ /wɪʃ/ *verb, noun*

• **verb 1** [T] (not usually used in the present progressive tense) to want something to happen or to be true even though it is unlikely or impossible: **~ (that)…** *I wish I were taller.* ◆ *I wish I was taller.* ◆ *I wish I hadn't eaten so much.* ◆ *"Where is he now?" "I only wish I knew!"* ◆ *I wish you wouldn't leave your clothes all over the floor.* **HELP** "That" is almost always left out, especially in speech.: **~ sb/sth/yourself + adj.** *He's dead and there's no point in wishing him alive again.* ◆ **~ sb/sth/yourself + adv./prep.** *She wished herself a million miles away.* **2** [I, T] (*formal*) to want to do something; to want something to happen: *You may stay until the morning, if you wish.* ◆ *"I'd rather not talk now." "(Just) as you wish."* ◆ **~ to do sth** *This course is designed for people wishing to update their computer skills.* ◆ *I wish to speak to the manager.* ◆ *I don't wish (= I don't mean) to be rude, but could you be a little quieter?* ◆ **~ sb sth** *She could not believe that he wished her harm.* ◆ **~ sb/sth to do sth** *He was not sure whether he wished her to stay or go.* **3** [I] **~ (for sth)** to think very hard that you want something, especially something that can only be achieved by good luck or magic: *She shut her eyes and wished for him to get better.* ◆ *If you wish really hard, maybe you'll get what you want.* ◆ *There's no use in wishing for the impossible.* ◆ *He has everything he could possibly wish for.* ◆ *Be careful what you wish for. You just might get it* (= and find that you really don't want it). **4** [T] to say that you hope that someone will be happy, lucky, etc.: **~ sb sth** *I wished her a happy birthday.* ◆ *Wish me luck!* ◆ **~ someone well** *We wish them both well in their retirement.*

IDM **I wish!** (*informal*) used to say that something is impossible or very unlikely, although you would like it to be possible **SYN** IF ONLY: *"You'll be finished by tomorrow." "I wish!"* **you wish!** (*informal*) used to tell someone that something is impossible or very unlikely, although that person might want it to be possible: *Sell that junk? You wish!* **PHR V** ‚wish sth a'way to try to get rid of something by wishing it did not exist 'wish sb/sth on sb (*informal*) (used in negative sentences) to want someone to have something unpleasant: *I wouldn't wish something like that on my worst enemy.*

• **noun 1** [C] a desire or a feeling that you want to do something or have something: **~ (to do sth)** *She expressed a wish to be alone.* ◆ *He had no wish to start a fight.* ◆ *His dearest wish* (= what he wants most of all) *is to see his grandchildren again.* ◆ **~ for sth** *I can understand her wish for secrecy.* ◆ **~ that…** *It was her dying wish that I should have it.* **2** [C] a thing that you want to have or to happen: *to carry out someone's wishes* ◆ *I'm sure that you will get your wish.* ◆ *She married against her parents' wishes.* ⊃ see also DEATH WISH **3** [C] an attempt to make something happen by thinking hard about it, especially in stories when it often happens by magic: *Throw some money in the fountain and make a wish.* ◆ *The genie granted him three wishes.* ◆ *The prince's wish came true.* **4** wishes [pl.] **~ (for sth)** used especially in a letter or card to say that you hope that someone will be happy, well,

or successful: *We all send our best wishes for the future.* ◆ *Give my good wishes to the family.* ◆ *With best wishes* (= for example, at the end of a letter)

IDM **if wishes were horses, beggars would/might ride** (*old-fashioned*, *saying*) wishing for something does not make it happen **your wish is my command** (*humorous*) used to say that you are ready to do whatever someone asks you to do **the wish is father to the thought** (*saying*) we believe a thing because we want it to be true

GRAMMAR

wish

- After the verb **wish** in sense 1, a past tense is always used in a *that* clause: *Do you wish (that) you had a better job?* In more formal English many people use *were* after *I, he, she, it* instead of *was*: *I wish he were here tonight.*

wish·bone /'wɪʃboʊn/ *noun* a V-shaped bone between the neck and breast of a chicken, DUCK, etc. When the bird is eaten, this bone is sometimes pulled apart by two people, and the person who gets the larger part can make a wish.

wish·ful think·ing /ˌwɪʃfl 'θɪŋkɪŋ/ *noun* [U] the belief that something that you want to happen is happening or will happen, although this is actually not true or is very unlikely: *I've got a feeling that Alex likes me, but that might just be wishful thinking.*

'**wishing ‚well** *noun* a WELL that people drop a coin into and make a wish

'**wish list** *noun* (*informal*) all the things that you would like to have, or that you would like to happen

wish·y-wash·y /'wɪʃi ˌwɒʃi; -ˌwɔʃi/ *adj.* (*informal*, *disapproving*) **1** not having clear or firm ideas or beliefs: *a wishy-washy liberal* **2** not bright in color: *a wishy-washy blue*

wisp /wɪsp/ *noun* **~ (of sth) 1** a small, thin piece of hair, grass, etc. **2** a long, thin line of smoke or cloud

wisp·y /'wɪspi/ *adj.* consisting of small, thin pieces; not thick ones: *wispy hair/clouds* ◆ *a wispy beard*

wis·te·ri·a /wɪˈstɪriə/ (also **wis·ta·ri·a** /wɪˈstɛriə/) *noun* [U] a climbing plant with bunches of pale purple or white flowers that hang down

wist·ful /'wɪstfl/ *adj.* thinking sadly about something in the past that you would like to have, especially something that you can no longer have: *a wistful smile* ▶ **wist·ful·ly** /-fəli/ *adv.*: *She sighed wistfully.* ◆ *"If only I had known you then," he said wistfully.* **wist·ful·ness** *noun* [U]

wit /wɪt/ *noun* **1** [U, sing.] the ability to say or write things that are both smart and amusing: *to have a quick/sharp/dry/ready wit* ◆ *a woman of wit and intelligence* ◆ *a book full of the wit and wisdom of his 30 years in politics* **2** [C] a person who has the ability to say or write things that are both smart and amusing: *a well-known wit and raconteur* **3** wits [pl.] your ability to think quickly and clearly and to make good decisions: *He needed all his wits to find his way out.* ◆ *The game was a long battle of wits.* ◆ *Kate paused and gathered her wits.* ◆ *a chance to pit your wits against our quiz champion* **4 -witted** (in adjectives) having the type of intelligence mentioned: *a quick-witted group of students* **5** [U] **~ to do sth** the intelligence or good sense to know what is the right thing to do: *At least you had the wit to ask for help.* ◆ *It should not be beyond the wit of man to resolve this dispute.* ⊃ see also WITLESS

IDM **be at your wits' end** to be so worried by a problem that you do not know what to do next **be frightened/scared/terrified out of your wits** to be very frightened **have/keep your wits about you** to be aware of what is happening around you and ready to think and act quickly **to wit** (*old-fashioned*, *formal*) you use *to wit* when you are about to be more exact about something that you have just

WORD FAMILY
wit *noun*
witty *adj.*
witticism *noun*
outwit *verb*

---

referred to: *Pilot error, to wit, failure to follow procedures, was the cause of the accident.* ⊃ more at LIVE¹

witch /wɪtʃ/ *noun* **1** a woman who is believed to have magic powers, especially to do evil things. In stories, she usually wears a black, pointed hat and flies on a BROOMSTICK. **2** (*disapproving*) an ugly, unpleasant, old woman

witch·craft /'wɪtʃkræft/ *noun* [U] the use of magic powers, especially evil ones

'witch ,doctor *noun* (especially in Africa) a person who is believed to have special magic powers that can be used to heal people ⊃ compare MEDICINE MAN

'witch ,hazel *noun* [U] a liquid that is used for treating injuries on the skin

'witch-hunt *noun* (usually *disapproving*) an attempt to find and punish people who hold opinions that are thought to be unacceptable or dangerous to society

the 'witching ,hour *noun* [sing.] the time, late at night, when it is thought that magic things can happen

Wite-out™ /'waɪtaʊt/ *noun* [U] a white liquid that you use to cover mistakes that you make when you are writing or typing, and that you can write on top of; a type of CORRECTION FLUID ⊃ see also WHITEOUT

with 🔑 /wɪθ; wɪð/ *prep.*
> **HELP** For the special uses of **with** in phrasal verbs, look at the entries for the verbs. For example, **bear with sb/sth** is in the phrasal verb section at **bear**. **1** in the company or presence of someone or something: *She lives with her parents.* ◆ *I have a client with me right now.* ◆ *a nice steak with a bottle of red wine* **2** having or carrying something: *a girl with* (= who has) *red hair* ◆ *a jacket with a hood* ◆ *He looked at her with a hurt expression.* ◆ *They're both in bed with the flu.* ◆ *a man with a suitcase* **3** using something: *Cut it with a knife.* ◆ *It is treated with acid before being analyzed.* **4** used to say what fills, covers, etc. something: *The bag was stuffed with dirty clothes.* ◆ *Sprinkle the dish with salt.* **5** in opposition to someone or something; against someone or something: *to fight with someone* ◆ *to play tennis with someone* ◆ *at war with a neighboring country* ◆ *I had an argument with my boss.* **6** concerning; in the case of: *Be careful with the glasses.* ◆ *Are you pleased with the result?* ◆ *Don't be angry with her.* ◆ *With these students it's pronunciation that's the problem.* **7** used when considering one fact in relation to another: *She won't be able to help us with all the family commitments she has.* ◆ *It's much easier compared with last time.* **8** including: *The meal with wine came to $20 each.* ◆ *With all the lesson preparation I have to do, I work 12 hours a day.* **9** used to show the way in which someone does something: *He behaved with great dignity.* ◆ *She sleeps with the window open.* ◆ *Don't stand with your hands in your pockets.* **10** because of; as a result of: *She blushed with embarrassment.* ◆ *His fingers were numb with cold.* **11** because of something and as it happens: *The shadows lengthened with the approach of sunset.* ◆ *Skill comes with practice.* **12** in the same direction as something: *Marine mammals generally swim with the current.* **13** used to show who has possession of or responsibility for something: *The keys are with reception.* ◆ *Leave it with me.* **14** employed by; using the services of: *She acted with a touring company for three years.* ◆ *I bank with HSBC.* **15** showing separation from something or someone: *I could never part with this ring.* ◆ *Can we dispense with the formalities?* **16** despite something: *Even with all her faults, I still love her.* **17** used in exclamations: *Off with her head!* ◆ *Down with school!*
> **IDM** **be with me/you** (*informal*) to be able to understand what someone is talking about: *Are you with me?* ◆ *I'm afraid I'm not quite with you.* **be with sb (on sth)** to support someone and agree with what they say: *We're all with you on this one.* **with it** (*informal*) **1** understanding what is happening around you SYN ALERT: *You don't seem very with it today.* **2** knowing about current fashions and ideas SYN TRENDY: *Don't you have anything more with it to wear?* **with that** straight after that; then: *He muttered a few words of apology and with that he left.*

with·draw 🔑 /wɪθ'drɔ; wɪð-/ *verb* (with·drew /-'dru/, with·drawn /-'drɔn/)
1 [I, T] to move back or away from a place or situation; to make someone or something do this SYN PULL OUT: *Government troops were forced to withdraw.* ◆ ~ **(sb/sth) (from sth)** *Both powers withdrew their forces from the region.* ◆ *She withdrew her hand from his.* **2** [T] to stop giving or offering something to someone: ~ **sth** *Workers have threatened to withdraw their labor* (= go on strike). ◆ *He withdrew his support for our campaign.* ◆ ~ **sth from sth** *The drug was withdrawn from sale after a number of people suffered serious side effects.* **3** [I, T] to stop taking part in an activity or being a member of an organization; to stop someone or something from doing these things: ~ **(from sth)** *There have been calls for the candidate to withdraw from the presidential race.* ◆ ~ **sb/sth (from sth)** *The horse had been withdrawn from the race.* **4** [T] ~ **sth (from sth)** to take money out of a bank account: *I'd like to withdraw $250, please.* **5** [T] ~ **sth** (*formal*) to say that you no longer believe that something you previously said is true SYN RETRACT: *The newspaper withdrew the allegations the next day.* **6** [I] ~ **(from sth) (into sth/yourself)** to become quieter and spend less time with other people: *She's beginning to withdraw into herself.*

with·draw·al /wɪθ'drɔəl; wɪð-/ *noun* **1** [U, C] the act of moving or taking something away or back: *the withdrawal of support* ◆ *the withdrawal of the UN troops from the region* ◆ *the withdrawal of a product from the market* **2** [U] the act of no longer taking part in something or being a member of an organization: *his withdrawal from the election* **3** [C] the act of taking an amount of money out of your bank account: *You can make withdrawals of up to $250 a day.* **4** [U] the period of time when someone is getting used to not taking a drug that they have become ADDICTED to, and the unpleasant effects of doing this: *I got withdrawal symptoms after quitting smoking.* **5** [C, usually sing., U] the act of saying that you no longer believe that something you have previously said is true SYN RETRACTION: *The newspaper published a withdrawal the next day.* **6** [U] (*psychology*) the behavior of someone who wants to be alone and does not want to communicate with other people

with·drawn /wɪθ'drɔn; wɪð-/ *adj.* not wanting to talk to other people; extremely quiet and shy

with·er /'wɪðər/ *verb* **1** [I, T] ~ **(sth)** if a plant withers or something withers, it, it dries up and dies: *The grass had withered in the warm sun.* **2** [I] ~ **(away)** to become less or weaker, especially before disappearing completely: *All our hopes just withered away.*

with·ered /'wɪðərd/ *adj.* [usually before noun] **1** (of plants) dried up and dead SYN SHRIVELed: *withered leaves* **2** (of people) looking old because they are thin and weak and have very dry skin **3** (of parts of the body) thin and weak and not fully developed because of disease: *withered limbs*

with·er·ing /'wɪðərɪŋ/ *adj.* (of a look, remark, etc.) intended to make someone feel silly or ashamed: *She gave him a withering look.* ◆ *withering criticism* ▶ **with·er·ing·ly** *adv.*

with·ers /'wɪðərz/ *noun* [pl.] the highest part of a horse's back, between its shoulders ⊃ picture at HORSE

with·hold /wɪθ'hoʊld; wɪð-/ *verb* (with·held, with·held /-'held/) ~ **sth (from sb/sth)** (*formal*) to refuse to give something to someone SYN KEEP: *She was accused of withholding information from the police.*

with'holding ,tax *noun* [C, U] an amount of money that an employer takes out of someone's income and pays directly to the government as tax

with·in 🔑 /wɪ'ðɪn; wɪ'θɪn/ *prep., adv.*
● ***prep.*** **1** before a particular period of time has passed; during a particular period of time: *You should receive a reply within seven days.* ◆ *The ambulance arrived within minutes of the call being made.* ◆ *Two elections were held within the space of a year.* **2** not further than a particular distance from something: *a house within a mile of the station* ◆ *Is it within walking distance?* **3** inside the range or limits of some-

| h hat | m man | n no | ŋ sing | l leg | r red | y yes | w wet |

thing: *That question is not within the scope of this talk.* ◆ *We are now within range of enemy fire.* ◆ *He finds it hard to live within his income* (= without spending more than he earns). **4** (*formal*) inside something or someone: *The noise seems to be coming from within the building.* ◆ *There is discontent within the farming industry.* **ANT** OUTSIDE

● *adv.* (*formal*) inside: *Server needed. Apply within.* (= on a sign)

with·out /wɪˈðaʊt; wɪˈθaʊt/ *prep., adv.* (*abbr.* w/o)

● *prep.* **1** not having, experiencing, or showing something: *They had gone two days without food.* ◆ *He found the place without difficulty.* ◆ *She spoke without much enthusiasm.* **2** not in the company of someone: *Don't go without me.* **3** not using or taking something: *Can you see without your glasses?* ◆ *Don't go out without your coat.* **4** not doing the action mentioned: **~ doing sth** *He left without saying goodbye.* ◆ *You can't make an omelet without breaking eggs.* ◆ *Without wanting to criticize, I think you could have done better.* (= used before you make a critical comment) ◆ **~ sb doing sth** *The party was planned without her knowing anything about it.*

● *adv.* not having or showing something: *Do you want a room with a bath or one without?* ◆ *If there's none left we'll have to do without.* ◆ *I'm sure we'll manage without.*

with·stand /wɪθˈstænd; wɪð-/ *verb* (with·stood, with·stood /-ˈstʊd/) **~ sth** (*formal*) to be strong enough not to be hurt or damaged by extreme conditions, the use of force, etc. **SYN** RESIST, STAND UP TO: *The materials used have to be able to withstand high temperatures.* ◆ *They had withstood siege, hunger, and deprivation.*

wit·less /ˈwɪtləs/ *adj.* silly or stupid; not sensible **SYN** FOOLISH
IDM **be scared witless** (*informal*) to be extremely frightened

wit·ness /ˈwɪtnəs/ *noun, verb*

● *noun*
> **PERSON WHO SEES SOMETHING 1** (also **eye·wit·ness**) [C] a person who sees something happen and is able to describe it to other people: *Police have asked witnesses to the accident to come forward.* ◆ *a witness to the killing* ⊃ collocations at CRIME, JUSTICE
> **IN COURT 2** [C] a person who gives evidence in court: *a defense/prosecution witness* ◆ *to appear as (a) witness for the defense/prosecution* ⊃ see also HOSTILE WITNESS
> **OF SIGNATURE 3** [C] a person who is present when an official document is signed and who also signs it to prove that they saw this happen: *He was one of the witnesses at our wedding.*
> **OF RELIGIOUS BELIEFS 4** [U] evidence of a person's strong religious beliefs, that they show by what they say and do in public ⊃ see also JEHOVAH'S WITNESS
IDM **be (a) witness to sth 1** (*formal*) to see something take place: *He has been witness to a terrible murder.* **2** to show that something is true; to provide evidence for something: *His good health is a witness to the success of the treatment.* **bear/give witness (to sth)** to provide evidence of the truth of something

● *verb*
> **SEE SOMETHING 1** [T] **~ sth** to see something happen (typically a crime or an accident): *She was shocked by the violent scenes she had witnessed.* ◆ *Police have asked for anyone who witnessed the incident to contact them.* ◆ *We are now witnessing an unprecedented increase in violent crime.* ⊃ thesaurus box at NOTICE
> **OF TIME/PLACE 2** [T] **~ sth** to be the place, period, organization, etc. in which particular events take place: *Recent years have witnessed a growing social mobility.* ◆ *The retail trade is witnessing a sharp fall in sales.*
> **SIGNATURE 3** [T] **~ sth** to be present when an official document is signed and sign it yourself to prove that you saw this happen: *to witness a signature*
> **BE SIGN/PROOF 4** [T, usually passive, I] to be a sign or proof of something: **~ sth** *There has been increasing interest in her life and work, as witnessed by the publication of two new biographies.* ◆ **~ to sth** *The huge attendance figures for the*

exhibition witness to a healthy interest in modern art. **5** [T] **~ sth** (*formal*) used when giving an example that proves something you have just said: *Authentic Italian cooking is very healthy—witness the low incidence of heart disease in Italy.*
> **TO RELIGIOUS BELIEFS 6** [I] **~ (to sth)** to speak to people about your strong religious beliefs **SYN** TESTIFY

ˈwitness ˌstand (also **stand**) *noun* the place in court where people stand to give evidence ⊃ collocations at JUSTICE

wit·ti·cism /ˈwɪtəˌsɪzəm/ *noun* a smart and amusing remark

wit·ting·ly /ˈwɪtɪŋli/ *adv.* (*formal*) in a way that shows that you are aware of what you are doing **SYN** INTENTIONALLY: *It was clear that, wittingly or unwittingly, he had offended her.* **ANT** UNWITTINGLY

wit·ty /ˈwɪti/ *adj.* (wit·ti·er, wit·ti·est) able to say or write smart, amusing things: *a witty speaker* ◆ *a witty remark* ⊃ thesaurus box at FUNNY ► **wit·ti·ly** /ˈwɪtl̩i/ *adv.* **wit·ti·ness** /ˈwɪtinəs/ *noun* [U]

wives pl. of WIFE

wiz·ard /ˈwɪzərd/ *noun* **1** (in stories) a man with magic powers **2** a person who is especially good at something: *a computer/financial, etc. wizard* **3** (*computing*) a program that makes it easy to use another program or perform a task by giving you a series of simple choices

wiz·ard·ry /ˈwɪzərdri/ *noun* [U] a very impressive achievement; great skill: *electronic wizardry* ◆ *The second goal was sheer wizardry.*

wiz·ened /ˈwɪznd/ *adj.* looking smaller and having many folds and lines in the skin, because of being old **SYN** SHRIVELED: *a wizened little man* ◆ *wizened apples*

wk. *abbr.* (in writing) WEEK

wkly. *abbr.* (in writing) WEEKLY

WLTM *abbr.* would like to meet (used in personal advertisements)

WMD /ˌdʌblyu ɛm ˈdi/ *abbr.* WEAPON OF MASS DESTRUCTION

w/o *abbr.* (in writing) WITHOUT

woad /woʊd/ *noun* [U] a blue substance that people used to paint their bodies and faces with in ancient times

wob·ble /ˈwɑbl/ *verb, noun*

• *verb* **1** [I, T] to move from side to side in an unsteady way; to make something do this: *This chair wobbles.* ♦ (*figurative*) *Her voice wobbled with emotion.* ♦ ~ **sth** *Don't wobble the table —I'm trying to write.* **2** [I] + **adv./prep.** to go in a particular direction while moving from side to side in an unsteady way: *He wobbled off on his bike.* **3** [I] to hesitate or lose confidence about doing something: *Yesterday the president showed the first signs of wobbling over the issue.*

• *noun* **1** [usually sing.] a slight unsteady movement from side to side: *The handlebars developed a wobble.* **2** a moment when you hesitate or lose confidence about something: *The team is experiencing a mid-season wobble.*

wob·ble·board /ˈwɑblˌbɔrd/ *noun* a musical instrument consisting of a piece of board that is shaken to produce low sounds, originally played by Australian Aborigines

wob·bly /ˈwɑbli/ *adj.* (*informal*) **1** moving in an unsteady way from side to side: *a chair with a wobbly leg* ♦ *a wobbly tooth* ♦ *He's still a little wobbly after the operation* (= not able to stand firmly). **2** not firm or confident **SYN SHAKY**: *the wobbly singing of the choir* ♦ *The evening got off to a wobbly start.*

woe /woʊ/ *noun* (*old-fashioned* or *humorous*) **1** woes [pl.] the troubles and problems that someone has: *financial woes* ♦ *Thanks for listening to my woes.* **2** [U] great unhappiness **SYN MISERY**: *a tale of woe*

IDM **woe betide sb**| **woe to sb** (*formal* or *humorous*) a phrase that is used to warn someone that there will be trouble for them if they do something or do not do something: *Woe betide anyone who gets in her way!* **woe is me!** *exclamation* (*old use* or *humorous*) a phrase that is used to say that you are very unhappy

woe·be·gone /ˈwoʊbɪˌɡɔn; -ˌɡɑn/ *adj.* (*formal*) looking very sad **SYN MISERABLE**: *a woebegone expression*

woe·ful /ˈwoʊfl/ *adj.* **1** [usually before noun] very bad or serious; that you disapprove of **SYN DEPLORABLE**: *She displayed a woeful ignorance of the rules.* **2** (*literary* or *formal*) very sad: *a woeful face* ♦ *woeful tales of failed romances* ▶ **woe·ful·ly** /-fəli/ *adv.*

wok /wɑk/ *noun* (from *Chinese*) a large pan shaped like a bowl, used especially for cooking Chinese food ⊃ picture at COOKING

woke pt of WAKE

wok·en pp of WAKE

wolf /wʊlf/ *noun, verb*

• *noun* (*pl.* wolves /wʊlvz/) a large wild animal of the dog family, that lives and hunts in groups: *a pack of wolves*

wolf

IDM **keep the wolf from the door** (*informal*) to have enough money to avoid going hungry; to stop someone feeling hungry **throw sb to the wolves** to leave someone to be roughly treated or criticized without trying to help or defend them **a wolf in sheep's clothing** a person who seems to be friendly or harmless but is really an enemy ⊃ more at CRY, LONE

• *verb* ~ **sth (down)** (*informal*) to eat food very quickly, especially by putting a lot of it in your mouth at once **SYN GOBBLE**

wolf·hound /ˈwʊlfhaʊnd/ *noun* a very large, tall dog with long hair and long legs, originally used for hunting wolves: *an Irish wolfhound*

wolf·ish /ˈwʊlfɪʃ/ *adj.* (*formal*) like a wolf: *wolfish yellow eyes* ♦ (*figurative*) *a wolfish grin* (= showing sexual interest in someone) ▶ **wolf·ish·ly** *adv.*

ˈwolf ˌwhistle *noun* a whistle with a short rising note and a long falling note, used by someone, usually a man, to show that they find someone else attractive, especially someone

passing in the street: *She was fed up with the construction workers' wolf whistles every morning.* ▶ **ˈwolf-ˌwhistle** *verb* [I, T] ~ **(sb)**

wol·ver·ine /ˌwʊlvəˈrin; ˈwʊlvəˌrin/ *noun* a wild animal that looks similar to a small bear, with short legs, long brown hair, and a long tail. Wolverines live in cold, northern areas of Europe and North America.

wolves pl. of WOLF

wom·an 🔑 /ˈwʊmən/ *noun*(*pl.* wom·en /ˈwɪmən/) **1** [C] an adult female human: *men, women, and children* ♦ *a 24-year-old woman* ♦ *I prefer to see a woman doctor.* **2** [U, sing.] female humans in general: (*informal*) *She's all woman!* (= has qualities that are typical of women) ♦ *These days, a woman should not have to do everything her husband demands.* **3** [C] (in compounds) a woman who comes from the place mentioned or whose job or interest is connected with the thing mentioned: *a businesswoman* ♦ *a Congresswoman* ♦ *a horsewoman* ⊃ note at GENDER **4** [C] a female worker, especially one who works with her hands: *We used to have a woman to do the cleaning.* **5** [sing.] (*old-fashioned*) a rude way of addressing a female person in an angry or important way: *Be quiet, woman!* **6** [C] (sometimes *disapproving*) a wife or sexual partner: *He's got a new woman in his life.* ⊃ see also FALLEN WOMAN, KEPT WOMAN, OTHER WOMAN

IDM **be your own man/woman** to act or think independently, not following others or being ordered: *Working for herself meant that she could be her own woman.* ⊃ more at HEART, HELL, HONEST, LEISURE, MAN, PART, POSSESSED, SUBSTANCE, WORLD

wom·an·hood /ˈwʊmənˌhʊd/ *noun* [U] (*formal*) **1** the state of being a woman, rather than a girl: *He watched his daughters grow to womanhood.* **2** women in general: *the womanhood of this country* ⊃ compare MANHOOD

wom·an·ish /ˈwʊmənɪʃ/ *adj.* (*disapproving*) (especially of a man) behaving in a way that is more suitable for a woman; more suitable for women than men: *He has a womanish manner.* ♦ *a womanish novel*

wom·an·iz·ing /ˈwʊməˌnaɪzɪŋ/ *noun* [U] (*disapproving*) the fact of having sexual relationships with many different women **SYN PHILANDERING** ▶ **wom·an·iz·er** *noun*

wom·an·kind /ˈwʊmənˌkaɪnd/ *noun* [U] (*old-fashioned*, *formal*) women in general ⊃ compare MANKIND

wom·an·ly /ˈwʊmənli/ *adj.* (*approving*) behaving, dressing, etc. in a way that people think is typical of or very suitable for a woman **SYN FEMININE**: *womanly qualities* ♦ *a soft, womanly figure* ▶ **wom·an·li·ness** *noun* [U]

womb /wum/ *noun* the organ in women and female animals in which babies develop before they are born **SYN UTERUS**

wom·bat /ˈwɑmbæt/ *noun* an Australian animal like a small BEAR, that carries its young in a POUCH (= a pocket of skin) on the front of the mother's body

wom·en·folk /ˈwɪmənˌfoʊk/ *noun* [pl.] (*old-fashioned* or *humorous*) all the women in a community or family, especially one that is led by men: *The male hunters brought back the food for their womenfolk to cook.* ⊃ compare MENFOLK

wom·en's lib·ber /ˌwɪmənz ˈlɪbər/ *noun* (*old-fashioned*, *informal*, often *disapproving*) a person who supports Women's Liberation

ˌwomen's libeˈration *noun* [U] (*old-fashioned*) **1** (also *informal* ˌwomen's ˈlib) the freedom of women to have the same social and economic rights as men **2 Women's Liberation** (also *informal* Women's Lib) the movement that aimed to achieve equal social and economic rights for women

ˌwomen's ˈrights *noun* [pl.] legal, economic, and social rights for women that are equal to those of men: *supporting women's rights in the workplace* ♦ *a women's rights speech*

ˈwomen's ˌroom *noun* = LADIES' ROOM

ˈwomen's ˌstudies *noun* [U] the study of women and their role in history, literature, and society: *to major in women's studies*

wom·ens·wear /'wɪmənzˌwɛr/ *noun* [U] (used especially in stores) clothes for women

won *pt, pp of* WIN

won·der 🎵 /'wʌndər/ *verb, noun*

- *verb* **1** [T, I] to think about something and try to decide what is true, what will happen, what you should do, etc.: ~ **who, where, etc.…** *I wonder who she is.* ♦ *I was just beginning to wonder where you were.* ♦ ~ **(about sth)** *"Why do you want to know?" "No particular reason. I was just wondering."* ♦ *We were wondering about next April for the wedding.* ♦ + **speech** *"What should I do now?" she wondered.* **2** [T] ~ **if, whether…** used as a polite way of asking a question or asking someone to do something: *I wonder if you can help me.* ♦ *I was wondering whether you'd like to come to a party.* **3** [I, T] to be very surprised by something: ~ **(at sth)** *She wondered at her own stupidity.*

- *noun* **1** [U] a feeling of surprise and admiration that you have when you see or experience something beautiful, unusual, or unexpected **SYN** AWE: *He retained a childlike sense of wonder.* ♦ *She gazed down **in wonder** at the city spread below her.* **2** [C] something that fills you with surprise and admiration **SYN** MARVEL: *The Grand Canyon is one of the natural wonders of the world.* ♦ *the wonders of modern technology* ♦ *That's the wonder of poetry—you're always discovering something new.* ♦ *the **Seven Wonders of the World*** (= the seven most impressive structures of the ancient world) **3** [sing.] (*informal*) a person who is very good at doing something; a person or thing that seems very good or effective: *Jeff, you're a wonder! I would never have thought of doing that.* ♦ *Have you seen the **boy wonder** play yet?* ♦ *a new wonder drug* **IDM** **do wonders (for sb/sth)** to have a very good effect on someone or something: *The news has done wonders for our morale.* **(it's) no/little/small wonder (that)…** it is not surprising: *It's no small wonder (that) she was so upset.* ♦ (*informal*) *No wonder you're tired, you've been walking for hours.* **it's a wonder (that)…** (*informal*) it is surprising or strange: *It's a wonder (that) more people weren't hurt.* **wonders will never cease** (*informal*, usually *ironic*) a phrase used to express surprise and pleasure at something: *"I cleaned my room." "Wonders will never cease!"* **work wonders** to achieve very good results: *Her new diet and exercise program has worked wonders for her.*

won·der·ful 🎵 /'wʌndərfl/ *adj.* **1** very good, pleasant, or enjoyable: *a wonderful surprise* ♦ *We had a wonderful time last night.* ♦ *You've all been absolutely wonderful!* ♦ *It's wonderful to see you!* **2** making you feel surprise or admiration **SYN** REMARKABLE: *It's wonderful what you can do when you have to.*

won·der·fully /'wʌndərfli/ *adv.* (*formal*) **1** very; very well: *The hotel is wonderfully comfortable.* ♦ *Things have worked out wonderfully (well).* **2** unusually; in a surprising way: *He's wonderfully fit for his age.*

won·der·ing·ly /'wʌndərɪŋli/ *adv.* (*formal*) in a way that shows surprise and/or admiration: *She gazed at him wonderingly.*

won·der·land /'wʌndərˌlænd/ *noun* [usually sing.] **1** an imaginary place in children's stories **2** a place that is exciting and full of beautiful and interesting things

won·der·ment /'wʌndərmənt/ *noun* [U] (*formal*) a feeling of pleasant surprise or admiration

won·drous /'wʌndrəs/ *adj.* (*literary*) strange, beautiful, and impressive **SYN** WONDERFUL ▶ **won·drous·ly** *adv.*

wonk /wɑŋk/ *noun* (*informal*, *disapproving*) **1** a person who works too hard and is considered boring **2** a person who takes too much interest in the details of political policy: *the President's chief economic **policy wonk***

won·ky /'wɑŋki/ *adj.* (*informal*) **1** not working or made correctly **2** involving a great deal of complex detail **3** interested in a great deal of complex detail which other people find boring **4** not steady; not straight: *a wonky chair*

wont /wɔnt; wɑnt/ *adj., noun*

- *adj.* [not before noun] ~ **(to do sth)** (*old-fashioned*, *formal*) in the habit of doing something **SYN** ACCUSTOMED: *He is wont to fall asleep after a big meal.*

- *noun* [sing.] (*old-fashioned*, *formal*) something a person often does **SYN** HABIT: *She got up early, as was her wont.*

won't /woʊnt/ *short form* will not

won·ton /'wɑntɑn/ *noun* (from *Chinese*) a small piece of food wrapped in DOUGH, often served in Chinese soup or as DIM SUM

woo /wu/ *verb* **1** ~ **sb** to try to get the support of someone: *Voters are being wooed with promises of lower taxes.* **2** ~ **sb** (*old-fashioned*) (of a man) to try to persuade a woman to love him and marry him **SYN** COURT

wood 🎵 /wʊd/ *noun* **1** [U, C] the hard material that the TRUNK and branches of a tree are made of; this material when it is used to build or make things with, or as a fuel: *He chopped some wood for the fire.* ♦ *a plank of wood* ♦ *All the furniture was made of wood.* ♦ *a wood floor* ♦ *furniture made of a variety of different woods* ⊃ picture at TREE ⊃ see also DEADWOOD, HARDWOOD, SOFTWOOD, WOODEN, WOODY **2** [C] **woods** [pl.] an area of trees, smaller than a forest: *a large wood* ♦ *a walk in the woods* ⊃ see also WOODED **3** [C] a GOLF CLUB with a large head, that usually made of wood in the past ⊃ compare IRON **IDM** **not out of the woods** (*informal*) not yet free from difficulties or problems ⊃ more at KNOCK, NECK

wood·block /'wʊdblɑk/ *noun* **1** a piece of wood with a pattern cut into it, used for printing **2** each of the small, flat pieces of wood that are fitted together to cover a floor: *a woodblock floor* ⊃ compare PARQUET

wood·carv·ing /'wʊdˌkɑrvɪŋ/ *noun* [U, C] the process of shaping a piece of wood with a sharp tool; a decorative object made in this way ⊃ picture at HOBBY ▶ **wood·carv·er** *noun*

wood·chuck /'wʊdtʃʌk/ (also **ground·hog**) *noun* a small N. American animal of the SQUIRREL family

wood·cock /'wʊdkɑk/ *noun* (pl. **wood·cock** or **wood·cocks**) a brown bird with a long straight beak, short legs, and a short tail, hunted for food or sport

wood·cut /'wʊdkʌt/ *noun* a print that is made from a pattern cut in a piece of wood

wood·cut·ter /'wʊdˌkʌtər/ *noun* (*old-fashioned*) a person whose job is cutting down trees

wood·ed /'wʊdəd/ *adj.* (of land) covered with trees

wood·en 🎵 /'wʊdn/ *adj.* **1** [usually before noun] made of wood: *a wooden box* **2** not showing enough natural expression, emotion, or movement **SYN** STIFF: *The actor playing the father was too wooden.* ▶ **wood·en·ly** *adv.*: *She speaks her lines very woodenly.* **wood·en·ness** *noun* [U]

wooden spoon *noun* a spoon made of wood, used in cooking for stirring and mixing ⊃ picture at KITCHEN

wood·land /'wʊdlænd; -lænd/ *noun* [U, C] (also **wood·lands** [pl.]) an area of land that is covered with trees: *ancient woodland* ♦ *The house is fringed by fields and woodlands.* ♦ *woodland walks*

wood louse *noun* (pl. **wood lice**) a small gray creature like an insect, with a hard shell, that lives in decaying wood or damp soil ⊃ picture at ANIMAL

wood·peck·er /'wʊdˌpɛkər/ *noun* a bird with a long beak that it uses to make holes in trees when it is looking for insects to eat

wood·pile /'wʊdpaɪl/ *noun* a pile of wood that will be used for fuel

wood pulp *noun* [U] wood that has been broken into tiny pieces and crushed until it is soft. It is used for making paper.

wood·shed /'wʊdʃɛd/ noun a small building for storing wood in, especially for fuel

woods·man /'wʊdzmən/ noun (pl. **woods·men** /-mən/) a person who works or lives in a forest, taking care of and sometimes cutting down trees, etc.

woods·y /'wʊdzi/ adj. (informal) covered with trees; connected with woods

wood·turn·ing /'wʊdˌtɜrnɪŋ/ noun [U] the process of shaping a piece of wood by turning it against a sharp tool on a machine (called a LATHE) ► **wood·turn·er** noun

wood·wind /'wʊdwɪnd/ noun one of the group of musical instruments in an ORCHESTRA that are mostly made of wood or metal and are played by blowing. FLUTES, CLARINETS, and BASSOONS are all woodwind instruments: the woodwind section of the orchestra ⊃ compare BRASS, PERCUSSION, STRING, WIND¹, WIND INSTRUMENT

wood·work /'wʊdwɜrk/ noun [U] things made of wood in a building or room, such as doors and stairs: The woodwork needs painting.
IDM **blend/fade into the woodwork** to behave in a way that does not attract any attention; to disappear or hide **come/crawl out of the woodwork** (informal, disapproving) if you say that someone **comes/crawls out of the woodwork**, you mean that they have suddenly appeared in order to express an opinion or to take advantage of a situation: When he won the lottery, all sorts of distant relatives came out of the woodwork.

wood·work·ing /'wʊdˌwɜrkɪŋ/ noun [U] the activity or skill of making things from wood

wood·worm /'wʊdwɜrm/ noun **1** [C] a small WORM that eats wood, making a lot of small holes in it **2** [U] the damage caused by woodworms: The beams are riddled with woodworm.

wood·y /'wʊdi/ adj. **1** (of plants) having a thick, hard STEM like wood **2** covered with trees: a woody valley **3** having a smell like wood

woof /wʊf/ exclamation, verb, noun
● **exclamation** (informal) a word used to describe the loud noise that a dog makes: "Woof! Woof!" he barked. ► **woof** verb [I]

● **noun** = WEFT

woof·er /'wʊfər/ noun a LOUDSPEAKER for reproducing the low notes in a SOUND SYSTEM ⊃ compare TWEETER

woo hoo /ˌwu 'hu/ exclamation (informal) used when you are glad because something happens that you enjoy: Woo hoo! The weekend is here.

wool 🔑 /wʊl/ noun [U]
1 the soft, fine hair that covers the body of sheep, GOATS, and some other animals **2** long, thick thread made from animal's wool, used for KNITTING: a ball of wool ⊃ picture at HOBBY **3** cloth made from animal's wool, used for making clothes, etc.: This scarf is 100% wool. ◆ pure new wool ◆ a wool blanket ⊃ see also DYED IN THE WOOL, LAMBSWOOL, STEEL WOOL **IDM** see PULL v.

wool·en /'wʊlən/ adj. **1** [usually before noun] made of wool: a woolen blanket ◆ woolen cloth **2** [only before noun] involved in making cloth from wool: the woolen industry

wool·ens /'wʊlənz/ noun [pl.] clothes made of wool, especially clothes that are KNITTED

wool·ly /'wʊli/ adj. (also **wool·y**) (wool·li·er, wool·li·est) **1** covered with wool or with hair like wool: woolly monkeys **2** (of people or their ideas, etc.) not thinking clearly; not clearly expressed **SYN** CONFUSED: woolly arguments ► **wool·li·ness** noun [U]

wooz·y /'wuzi/ adj. (informal) **1** feeling unsteady, confused, and unable to think clearly **2** feeling as though you might VOMIT

Worces·ter·shire sauce /'wʊstərʃɪr ˌsɔs/ noun [U] a dark thin sauce made of VINEGAR, SOY SAUCE, and spices

word 🔑 /wɜrd/ noun, verb, exclamation
● **noun**
> UNIT OF LANGUAGE **1** [C] a single unit of language that means something and can be spoken or written: Do not write more than 200 words. ◆ Do you know the words to this song? ◆ What's the Spanish word for "table"? ◆ He was a true friend **in all senses of the word**. ◆ Tell me what happened **in your own words**. ◆ I could hear every word they were saying. ◆ He couldn't **find the words** to thank her enough. ◆ **Words fail me** (= I cannot express how I feel). ◆ There are no words to say how sorry we are. ◆ I can't remember her exact words. ◆ Angry **is not the word for it** —I was furious. ⊃ see also BUZZWORD, FOUR-LETTER WORD, SWEAR WORD
> SOMETHING YOU SAY **2** [C] a thing that you say, a remark or statement: **Have a word** with Pat and see what she thinks. ◆ Could I **have a quick word** with you (= speak to you quickly)? ◆ A **word of warning**: read the instructions very carefully. ◆ words of love ◆ She left **without a word** (= without saying anything). ◆ I don't believe **a word of** his story (= I don't believe any of it). ◆ a **man of few words** (= who doesn't talk very much) ◆ I'd like to say a few words about future plans. ◆ Remember— **not a word to** (= don't tell) Peter about any of this. ◆ He never **breathed a word** of this to me.
> PROMISE **3** [sing.] a promise or guarantee that you will do something or that something will happen or is true: **I give you my word** that this won't happen again. ◆ I give you my **word of honor** (= my sincere promise) ... ◆ We never doubted her word. ◆ We only **have** his **word for it** that the check is in the mail. ◆ to **keep your word** (= do what you promised) ◆ He promised to help and **was as good as his word** (= did what he promised). ◆ He's a **man of his word** (= he does what he promises). ◆ I trusted her not to **go back on her word** (= break her promise). ◆ I can't prove it—you'll **just have to take my word for it** (= believe me).
> INFORMATION/NEWS **4** [sing.] a piece of information or news: There's been no word from them since before Christmas. ◆ She **sent word** that she would be late. ◆ If **word gets out** about the affair, he will have to resign. ◆ **Word has it that** she's leaving. ◆ **The word is** they split up. ◆ He likes to **spread the word** about the importance of healthy eating.
> BIBLE **5** the **Word** (also the **Word of God**) [sing.] the Bible and its teachings
IDM **by word of mouth** because people tell each other and not because they read about it: The news spread by word of mouth. **(right) from the word go** (informal) from the very beginning **(not) get a word in edgewise** (not) to be able to say anything because someone else is speaking too much: When Mary starts talking, no one else can get a word in edgewise. **have/exchange words (with sb) (about sth)** to have an argument with someone: We've had words. ◆ Words were exchanged. **in other words** used to introduce an explanation of something: They asked him to leave—in other words he was fired. ⊃ language bank at I.E. **(not) in so/as many words** (not) in exactly the same words as someone says were used: "Did she say she was sorry?" "Not in so many words." ◆ He didn't approve of the plan and said so in as many words. **in a word** (informal) used for giving a very short, usually negative, answer or comment: "Would you like to help us?" "In a word, no." **the last/final word (on sth)** the last comment or decision about something: He always has to **have the last word** in any argument. **(upon) my word** (old-fashioned) used to show that you are surprised about something **not have a good word to say about/for sb/sth** (informal) to never say anything good about someone or something: Nobody had a good word to say about him. **put in a (good) word for sb** to praise someone to someone else in order to help them get a job, etc. **put words into sb's mouth** to suggest that someone has said something when in fact they have not **say/give the word** to give an order or make a request: Just say the word, and I'll go. **take sb at their word** to believe exactly what someone says or promises **take the words right out of sb's mouth** to say what someone else was going to say **too funny, silly, ridiculous, etc. for words** extremely funny, silly, ridiculous, etc. **word for word** in exactly the same words or (when translated) exactly equivalent words: She repeated their conversation word for word to me. ◆ a word-for-word translation

sb's word is their bond someone's promise can be relied on completely **words to that effect** used to show that you are giving the general meaning of what someone said rather than the exact words: *He told me to leave—or words to that effect.* ⊃ more at ACTION, BANDY *v.*, DIRTY *adj.*, EAT, FAMOUS, FIGHT *v.*, HANG *v.*, LAST¹, LOST, MINCE *v.*, MUM *adj.*, OPERATIVE *adj.*, PLAY *n.*, PRINT *v.*, WAR *n.*, WEIGH, WRITTEN

- **verb** [often passive] **~ sth** to write or say something using particular words: *How was the letter worded* (= what did it say exactly)*?* ▶ **word·ed** *adj.*: *a carefully worded speech* ♦ *a strongly worded letter of protest*
- **exclamation word!** (*slang*) used to show that you accept or agree with what someone has just said

---

THESAURUS

word

term • phrase • expression • idiom

These are all words for a unit of language used to express something.

word a single unit of language that means something and can be spoken or written: *Do not write more than 200 words.* ♦ *He uses a lot of long words.*

term (*somewhat formal*) a word or phrase used as the name of something, especially one connected with a particular type of language: *technical/legal/scientific terms* ♦ *"Old man" is a slang term for "father."*

phrase a group of words that have a particular meaning when used together: *Who coined the phrase "desktop publishing"* (= used it for the first time)*?* **NOTE** In grammar, a **phrase** is a group of words without a finite verb, especially one that forms part of a sentence: "the green car" and "on Friday morning" are phrases.

expression a word or phrase: *He tends to use lots of new expressions that I've never heard before.*

idiom a group of words whose meaning is different from the meanings of the individual words: *"To let the cat out of the bag" is an idiom meaning to tell a secret by mistake.*

PATTERNS

- a(n) word/term/expression **for** sth
- a **new** word/term/phrase/expression
- a **technical/colloquial/slang** word/term/phrase/expression
- an **idiomatic** phrase/expression
- to **use** a(n) word/term/phrase/expression/idiom
- to **coin** a(n) word/term/phrase/expression
- a(n) word/term/phrase/expression/idiom **means** sth

---

word break (also **word division**) *noun* (*technical*) a point at which a word is split between two lines of text

word class *noun* (*grammar*) one of the classes into which words are divided according to their grammar, such as noun, verb, adjective, etc. **SYN** PART OF SPEECH

word family *noun* **1** a group of related words that are formed from the same word: *a word family consisting of "help," "helper," and "helpful"* **2** a group of words with particular features in common: *"Cat" and "hat" are in the same word family.*

word·ing /'wərdɪŋ/ *noun* [U, C, usually sing.] the words that are used in a piece of writing or in speech, especially when they have been carefully chosen: *The wording was deliberately ambiguous.* ⊃ thesaurus box at LANGUAGE

word·less /'wərdləs/ *adj.* (*formal* or *literary*) **1** [usually before noun] without saying any words; silent: *a wordless cry/prayer* **2** (of people) not saying anything ▶ **word·less·ly** *adv.*

word·play /'wərdpleɪ/ *noun* [U] making jokes by using words in a smart or amusing way, especially by using a word that has two meanings, or different words that sound the same ⊃ compare PUN

---

word processing *noun* [U] the use of a computer to create, store, and print a piece of text, usually typed in from a keyboard

word processor *noun* a computer that runs a word processing program and is usually used for writing letters, reports, etc.

word·search /'wərdsərtʃ/ *noun* a game consisting of letters arranged in a square, containing several hidden words that you must find ⊃ picture at PUZZLE

word·smith /'wərdsmɪθ/ *noun* a person who is skillful at using words

word·y /'wərdi/ *adj.* (usually *disapproving*) using too many words, especially formal ones **SYN** VERBOSE: *a wordy and repetitive essay* ▶ **word·i·ness** *noun* [U]

wore *pt of* WEAR

work 🔑 /wərk/ *verb, noun*

- **verb**

> **DO JOB/TASK 1** [I] to do something that involves physical or mental effort, especially as part of a job: *I can't work if I'm cold.* ♦ **~ at sth** *I've been working at my assignment all day.* ♦ **~ on sth** *He is working on a new novel.* ♦ *She's outside, working on the car.* ♦ **+ noun** *Doctors often work very long hours.* **2** [I] to have a job: *Both my parents work.* ♦ **~ for sb/sth** *She works for an engineering company.* ♦ **~ in sth** *I've always worked in education.* ♦ **~ with sb/sth** *Do you enjoy working with children?* ♦ **~ as sth** *My son is working as a teacher.*

> **MAKE EFFORT 3** [T] **~ yourself/sb + adv./prep.** to make yourself/someone work, especially very hard: *She works herself too hard.* **4** [I] to make efforts to achieve something: **~ for sth** *She dedicated her life to working for peace.* ♦ **~ to do sth** *The committee is working to get the prisoners freed.*

> **MANAGE 5** [T] **~ sth** to manage or operate something to gain benefit from it: *to work the land* (= grow crops on it, etc.) ♦ *He works a large area* (= selling a company's goods, etc.). ♦ (*figurative*) *She was a skillful speaker who knew how to work a crowd* (= to excite them or make them feel something strongly).

> **MACHINE/DEVICE 6** [I] to function; to operate: *The phone isn't working.* ♦ *It works by electricity.* ♦ *Are they any closer to understanding how the brain works?* **7** [T] **~ sth** to make a machine, device, etc. operate: *Do you know how to work the coffee machine?* ♦ *The machine is worked by wind power.*

> **HAVE RESULT/EFFECT 8** [I] to have the result or effect that you want: *The pills the doctor gave me aren't working.* ♦ *My plan worked, and I got them to agree.* ♦ **~ on sb/sth** *His charm doesn't work on me* (= does not affect or impress me). **9** [I] to have a particular effect: **~ against sb** *Your age can work against you in this job.* ♦ **~ in sb's favor** *Speaking Italian should work in his favor.* **10** [T] **~ sth** to cause or produce something as a result of effort: *You can work miracles with very little money if you follow our home decoration tips.*

> **USE MATERIAL 11** [T] to make a material into a particular shape or form by pressing, stretching, hitting it, etc.: **~ sth** *to work clay* ♦ *to work gold* ♦ **~ sth into sth** *to work the mixture into a paste* **12** [I] **~ (in/with sth)** (of an artist, etc.) to use a particular material to produce a picture or other item: *an artist working in oils* ♦ *a craftsman working with wood*

> **OF PART OF FACE/BODY 13** [I] (*formal*) to move violently: *He stared at me in horror, his mouth working.*

> **MOVE GRADUALLY 14** [I, T] to move or pass to a particular place or state, usually gradually: **+ adv./prep.** *It will take a while for the drug to work out of your system.* ♦ **~ your way + adv./prep.** (*figurative*) *He worked his way to the top of his profession.* ♦ **~ yourself/sth + adj.** *I was tied up, but managed to work myself free.* ♦ **+ adj.** *The screw had worked loose.*

IDM Most idioms containing **work** are at the entries for the nouns and adjectives in the idioms. For example, **work your fingers to the bone** is at **finger**. **work it/things** (*informal*) to arrange something in a particular way, especially by being smart: *Can you work it so that we get free tickets?* **PHR V** **work a'round to sth/sb** to gradually turn a conversation toward a particular topic, subject, etc.: *It was some time before he worked around to what he really wanted to say.* **'work at sth** to make great efforts to achieve some-

---

thing or do something well: *He's working at losing weight.* ◆ *Learning to play the piano isn't easy. You have to* **work at it.** ,work sth 'in | work sth into sth **1** to try to include something: *Can't you work a few more jokes into your speech?* **2** to add one substance to another and mix them together: *Gradually work in the butter.* ,work sth↔'off **1** to get rid of something, especially a strong feeling, by using physical effort: *She worked off her anger by going for a walk.* **2** to earn money in order to be able to pay a debt: *They had a large bank loan to work off.* 'work on sb to try to persuade someone to agree to something or to do something: *He hasn't said he'll do it yet, but I'm working on him.* 'work on sth to try hard to improve or achieve something: *You need to work on your pronunciation a bit more.* ◆ *"Have you gotten a babysitter for Friday yet?" "No, but I'm working on it."* ,work 'out **1** to train the body by physical exercise: *I work out regularly to stay in shape.* ⊃ related noun WORKOUT **2** to develop in a successful way: *My first job didn't work out.* ◆ *Things have worked out really well for us.* ,work 'out (to sth) if something **works out** to something, you calculate that it will be a particular amount: **+ adj.** *It'll work out cheaper to travel by bus.* ,work sth↔'out **1** to calculate something: *to work out the answer* **2** to find the answer to something SYN SOLVE: *to work out a problem* ◆ *~ what, where, etc.... Can you work out what these squiggles mean?* ◆ *I couldn't work out where the music was coming from.* **3** to plan or think of something: *I've worked out a new way of doing it.* **4** [usually passive] to remove all the coal, minerals, etc. from a mine over a period of time: *a worked-out silver mine* ,work sb↔'over (*slang*) to attack someone and hit them, for example to make them give you information 'work to sth to follow a plan, schedule, etc.: *to work to a budget* ◆ *We're working to a very tight deadline* (= we have very little time to do the work). 'work toward sth to try to reach or achieve a goal ,work sth↔'up to develop or improve something with some effort: *I can't work up any enthusiasm for his idea.* ◆ *She went for a long walk to work up an appetite.* ,work sb/ yourself 'up (into sth) to make someone/yourself reach a state of great excitement, anger, etc.: *Don't work yourself up into a state about it. It isn't worth it.* ◆ *What are you so worked up about?* ,work sth 'up into sth to bring something to a more complete or more acceptable state: *I'm working my notes up into a dissertation.* ,work 'up to sth to develop or move gradually toward something, usually something more exciting or extreme: *The music worked up to a rousing finale.*

● **noun**

▶ JOB/TASK **1** [U] the job that a person does, especially in order to earn money SYN EMPLOYMENT: *She had been out of work* (= without a job) *for a year.* ◆ *He started work as a security guard.* ◆ *It is difficult to find work in the present economic climate.* ◆ *I'm still looking for work.* ◆ *She's planning to return to work once the children start school.* ◆ *What line of work are you in* (= what type of work do you do)? ◆ *before/after work* (= in the morning/evening each day) ◆ *full-time/part-time/ unpaid/volunteer work* ⊃ collocations at JOB, UNEMPLOY-MENT **2** [U] the duties that you have and the activities that you do as part of your job: *Police work is mainly routine.* ◆ *The accountant described his work to the sales staff.* ⊃ see also PIECEWORK, SOCIAL WORK **3** [U] tasks that need to be done: *There is plenty of work to be done in the garden.* ◆ *Taking care of a baby is hard work.* ◆ *I have some work for you to do.* ◆ *Stop talking and finish your work.* ⊃ see also HOMEWORK, SCHOOLWORK **4** [U] materials needed or used for doing work, especially books, papers, etc.: *She often brings work* (= for example, files and documents) *home with her from the office.* ◆ *His work was spread all over the floor.* ⊃ see also PAPERWORK

▶ PLACE OF JOB **5** [U] (used without *the*) the place where you do your job: *I go to work at 8 o'clock.* ◆ *When do you leave for work?* ◆ *The new legislation concerns health and safety at work.* ◆ *I have to leave work early today.* ◆ *Her friends from work came to see her in the hospital.*

▶ EFFORT **6** [U] the use of physical strength or mental power in order to do or make something: *She earned her grades through sheer hard work.* ◆ *We started work on the project in 2009.* ◆ *Work continues on renovating the hotel.* ◆ *The work of*

building the bridge took six months. ◆ *The art collection was his life's work.* ◆ *She set them to work painting the fence.* ⊃ see also DONKEY WORK, FIELDWORK

▶ PRODUCT OF WORK **7** [U] a thing or things that are produced as a result of work: *She's an artist whose work I really admire.* ◆ *Is this all your own work* (= did you do it without help from others)? ◆ *The book is a detailed and thorough piece of work covering all aspects of the subject.*

▶ RESULT OF ACTION **8** [U] the result of an action; what is done by someone: *The damage is clearly the work of vandals.*

▶ BOOK/MUSIC/ART **9** [C] a book, piece of music, painting, etc.: *the collected/complete works of Tolstoy* ◆ *works of fiction/ literature* ◆ *Beethoven's piano works* ⊃ see also WORK OF ART ⊃ compare OPUS

▶ BUILDING/REPAIRING **10** works [pl.] (often in compounds) activities involving building or repairing something: *They expanded the shipyards and started engineering works.* ⊃ see also PUBLIC WORKS

▶ FACTORY **11** works (*pl.* works) [C] (often in compounds) a place where things are made or industrial processes take place: *a brickworks* ⊃ thesaurus box at FACTORY

▶ PARTS OF MACHINE **12** the works [pl.] the moving parts of a machine, etc. SYN MECHANISM

▶ EVERYTHING **13** the works [pl.] (*informal*) everything: *I want a pizza with the works: pepperoni, sausage, mushrooms, and anchovies.*

▶ PHYSICS **14** [U] the use of force to produce movement ⊃ see also JOULE

IDM all work and no play (makes Jack a dull boy) (*saying*) it is not healthy to spend all your time working; you need to relax too at work **1** having an effect on something: *She suspected that secret influences were at work.* **2** ~ (on sth) busy doing something: *He is still at work on the painting.* ◆ *Danger—men at work.* get (down) to/set to work to begin; to make a start: *We got to work on the outside of the house* (= for example, painting it). good works kind acts to help others go/set about your work to do/start to do your work: *She went cheerfully about her work.* have your work cut out (for you) (*informal*) to be likely to have difficulty doing something: *You have your work cut out for you if you want to get there on time.* in the works/pipeline something that is in the works or in the pipeline is being discussed, planned, or prepared and will happen or exist soon the work of a moment, second, etc. (*formal*) a thing that takes a very short time to do ⊃ more at DAY, DEVIL, DIRTY *adj.*, HAND *n.*, HARD *adj.*, LIGHT *adj.*, MONKEY WRENCH, NICE, SHORT *adj.*

occupation (*somewhat formal*) a job or profession: *Please state your name, age, and occupation.*

trade a job, especially one that involves working with your hands and requires special training and skills: *Carpentry is a highly skilled trade.*

PATTERNS

- (a) **full-time/part-time** work/employment/career/occupation
- **permanent/temporary** work/employment
- (a) **well-paid** work/employment/profession/occupation
- (a) **low-paid** work/employment/occupation
- to **look for/seek/find/have** work/employment/a career/an occupation
- to **get/obtain/give sb/offer sb/create/generate/provide** work/employment

work·a·ble /ˈwɜrkəbl/ *adj.* **1** (of a system, an idea, etc.) that can be used successfully and effectively **SYN** PRACTICAL: *a workable plan* **2** that you can shape, spread, dig, etc.: *Add more water until the dough is workable.* **3** (of a mine, etc.) that can still be used and will make a profit

work·a·day /ˈwɜrkəˌdeɪ/ *adj.* [usually before noun] (*formal*) ordinary; not very interesting **SYN** EVERYDAY

work·a·hol·ic /ˌwɜrkəˈhɔlɪk; -ˈhɑlɪk/ *noun* (*informal*, usually *disapproving*) a person who works very hard and finds it difficult to stop working and do other things

work·a·round /ˈwɜrkəˌraʊnd/ *noun* (*computing*) a way in which you can solve or avoid a problem when the most obvious solution is not possible

work·bench /ˈwɜrkbɛntʃ/ (also **bench**) *noun* a long heavy table used for doing practical jobs, working with tools, etc.

work·book /ˈwɜrkbʊk/ (also **exercise book**) *noun* a book with exercises in it, often with spaces for students to write answers in, to help them practice what they have learned

work·day /ˈwɜrkdeɪ/ *noun* **1** (also **working day**) the part of a day during which you work: *an 8-hour workday* ◆ *I spend most of my workday sitting at a desk.* **2** = WORKING DAY

worked up *adj.* [not before noun] ~ **(about sth)** (*informal*) very excited or upset about something: *There's no point in getting worked up about it.*

work·er /ˈwɜrkər/ *noun*

1 (often in compounds) a person who works, especially one who does a particular kind of work: *farm/factory/office workers* ◆ *rescue/aid/research workers* ◆ *temporary/part-time/freelance workers* ◆ *manual/skilled/unskilled workers* ➔ collocations at JOB ➔ see also GUEST WORKER, SEX WORKER, SOCIAL WORKER **2** [usually pl.] a person who is employed in a company or industry, especially someone who does physical work rather than organizing things or managing people: *Conflict between employers and workers intensified and the number of strikes rose.* ◆ *talks between workers and management* **3** (usually after an adjective) a person who works in a particular way: *a hard/fast/quick/slow worker* **4** a female BEE that helps do the work of the group of bees but does not reproduce ➔ compare DRONE, QUEEN BEE

workers' compen·sation (also **workers' comp**) *noun* [U] a type of insurance that provides payments to employees who get injured or sick as a direct result of their job: *He filed a claim for workers' compensation.*

work ethic *noun* [sing.] the principle that hard work is a good habit and should be rewarded

work ex·perience *noun* [U] the work or jobs that you have done in your life so far: *The opportunities available will depend on your previous work experience and qualifications.*

work·fare /ˈwɜrkfɛr/ *noun* [U] a system in which unemployed people have to work in order to get money for food, rent, etc. from the government

work·force /ˈwɜrkfɔrs/ *noun* [sing.] **1** all the people who work for a particular company, organization, etc. **SYN** STAFF: *The factory has a 1000-strong workforce.* ◆ *Two thirds of the workforce is women.* ➔ collocations at UNEMPLOYMENT **2** all the people in a country or an area who are available for work: *A quarter of the local workforce is unemployed.*

work·horse /ˈwɜrkhɔrs/ *noun* a person or machine that you can rely on to do hard and/or boring work

work·house /ˈwɜrkhaʊs/ (also **poor·house**) *noun* (in the past) a building where very poor people were sent to live and given work to do

work·ing /ˈwɜrkɪŋ/ *adj., noun*

● *adj.* [only before noun] **1** having a job for which you are paid **SYN** EMPLOYED: *the working population* ◆ *a working mother* ➔ see also HARD-WORKING **2** connected with your job and the time you spend doing it: *long working hours* ◆ *poor working conditions* ◆ *I have a good working relationship with my boss.* ◆ *She spent most of her working life as a teacher.* ◆ *recent changes in working practices* **3** a working breakfast or lunch is one at which you discuss business **4** used as a basis for work, discussion, etc. but likely to be changed or improved in the future: *a working theory* ◆ *Have you decided on a working title for your thesis yet?* **5** if you have a working knowledge of something, you can use it at a basic level **6** the working parts of a machine are the parts that move in order to make it function **7** a working majority is a small majority that is enough to enable a government to win votes in the government and make new laws **IDM** see ORDER *n.*

● *noun* [usually pl.] **1** ~ **(of sth)** the way in which a machine, a system, an organization, etc. works: *an introduction to the workings of Congress* ◆ *the workings of the human mind* ◆ *the machine's inner workings* **2** the parts of a mine or QUARRY where coal, metal, stone, etc. is or has been dug from the ground

working capital *noun* [U] (*business*) the money that is needed to run a business rather than the money that is used to buy buildings and equipment when starting the business ➔ compare VENTURE CAPITAL

the working class *noun* the social class whose members do not have much money or power and are usually employed to do MANUAL work (= physical work using their hands): *the political party of the working class* ◆ *The working class has rejected them in the elections.* ➔ compare MIDDLE CLASS, UPPER CLASS ▶ **working-class** *adj.*: *a working-class background*

working day *noun* **1** = WORKDAY **2** (also *less frequent* **work·day**) a day on which you usually work or on which most people usually work: *Sunday is a normal working day for me.* ◆ *Thousands of working days were lost through strikes last year.*

working girl *noun* (*informal*) **1** (becoming *old-fashioned*) a PROSTITUTE. People say "working girl" to avoid saying "prostitute." **2** (sometimes *offensive*) a woman who has a paid job

working group *noun* a group of people chosen to study a particular problem or situation in order to suggest ways of dealing with it

working papers *noun* [pl.] an official document that enables someone under 16 years old or born outside the U.S. to have a job

the working poor *noun* [pl.] people who work at low-paid jobs and still have very little money

working stiff *noun* (*informal*) an ordinary person whose job is not very interesting

work-life balance *noun* [sing.] the number of hours per week you spend working, compared with the number of hours you spend with your family, relaxing, etc.: *Part-time work is often the best way to improve your work-life balance.*

work·load /ˈwɜrkloʊd/ *noun* the amount of work that has to be done by a particular person or organization: *a heavy*

workload ◆ *We have taken on extra staff to cope with the increased workload.* ⊃ collocations at JOB

work·man /'wɜrkmən/ *noun* (*pl.* **work·men** /-mən/) a man who is employed to do physical work

work·man·like /'wɜrkmənˌlaɪk/ *adj.* done, made, etc. in a skillful and thorough way but not usually very original or exciting

work·man·ship /'wɜrkmənˌʃɪp/ *noun* [U] the skill with which someone makes something, especially when this affects the way it looks or works: *Our buyers insist on high standards of workmanship and materials.*

work of art *noun* (*pl.* **works of art**) **1** a painting, statue, etc.: *A number of priceless works of art were stolen from the gallery.* **2** something that is attractive and skillfully made: *The bride's dress was a work of art.*

work·out /'wɜrkaʊt/ *noun* a period of physical exercise that you do to keep fit: *She does a 20-minute workout every morning.*

work permit *noun* an official document that someone needs in order to work in a particular foreign country

work·place /'wɜrkpleɪs/ *noun* often **the workplace** [sing.] the office, factory, etc. where people work: *the introduction of new technology into the workplace*

work re·lease *noun* [U] a system that allows prisoners to leave prison during the day to go to work

work·room /'wɜrkrum; -rʊm/ *noun* a room in which work is done, especially work that involves making things: *The jeweler has a workroom at the back of his shop.*

works *noun* ⊃ WORK ⊃ thesaurus box at FACTORY

work·sheet /'wɜrkʃit/ *noun* **1** a piece of paper on which there is a series of questions and exercises to be done by a student **2** a piece of paper on which work that has been done or has to be done is recorded

work·shop /'wɜrkʃap/ *noun* **1** (also **shop**) a room or building in which things are made or repaired using tools or machinery ⊃ thesaurus box at FACTORY **2** a period of discussion and practical work on a particular subject, in which a group of people share their knowledge and experience: *a drama workshop* ◆ *a poetry workshop* ⊃ collocations at EDUCATION

work·space /'wɜrkspeɪs/ *noun* **1** [U, C] a space in which to work, especially in an office **2** [C] (*computing*) a place where information that is being used by one person on a computer network is stored

work·sta·tion /'wɜrkˌsteɪʃn/ *noun* the desk and computer at which a person works; one computer that is part of a computer network

work·week /'wɜrkwik/ *noun* the total amount of time that you spend at work during the week: *a 40-hour workweek*

world 🔊 /wɜrld/ *noun*

> **THE EARTH/ITS PEOPLE 1 the world** [sing.] the earth, with all its countries, peoples, and natural features: *to sail around the world* ◆ *traveling (all over) the world* ◆ *a map of the world* ◆ *French is spoken in many parts of the world.* ◆ *Which is the largest city in the world?* ◆ *He's the world's highest paid entertainer.* ◆ *a meeting of world leaders* ◆ *campaigning for world peace* **2** [C, usually sing.] a particular part of the earth; a particular group of countries or people; a particular period of history and the people of that period: *the Arab world* ◆ *the English-speaking world* ◆ *the industrialized and developing worlds* ◆ *the ancient/modern world* ⊃ see also THE FIRST WORLD, THE NEW WORLD, THE OLD WORLD, THE THIRD WORLD

> **ANOTHER PLANET 3** [C] a planet like the earth: *There may be other worlds out there.*

> **TYPE OF LIFE 4** [C] the people or things belonging to a particular group or connected with a particular interest, job, etc.: *the animal/plant/insect world* ◆ *the world of fashion* ◆ *stars from the sporting and artistic worlds* **5** [usually sing.] (usually used with an adjective) everything that exists of a particular kind; a particular kind of life or existence: *the*

---

natural world (= animals, plants, minerals, etc.) ◆ *They are a couple in the real world as well as in the movie.* ◆ *The island is a world of brilliant colors and dramatic sunsets.* ◆ *They had little contact with the outside world* (= people and places that were not part of their normal life).

> **PERSON'S LIFE 6** [sing.] a person's environment, experiences, friends and family, etc.: *Parents are the most important people in a child's world.* ◆ *When his wife died, his entire world was turned upside down.*

> **SOCIETY 7** [sing.] our society and the way people live and behave; the people in the world: *We live in a rapidly changing world.* ◆ *He's too young to understand the ways of the world.* ◆ *The whole world was waiting for news of the astronauts.* ◆ *She felt that the world was against her.* ◆ *The eyes of the world are on the president.* **8 the world** [sing.] a way of life where possessions and physical pleasures are important, rather than spiritual values: *monks and nuns renouncing the world* ⊃ see also OLD-WORLD

> **HUMAN EXISTENCE 9** [sing.] the state of human existence: *this world and the next* (= life on earth and existence after death)

IDM **the best of both/all possible worlds** the benefits of two or more completely different situations that you can enjoy at the same time: *If you enjoy the coast and the country, you'll get the best of both worlds on this walk.* **be worlds apart** to be completely different in attitudes, opinions, etc. **come/ go down/up in the world** to become less/more important or successful in society **come into the world** (*literary*) to be born **do sb/sth a world of good** to make someone feel much better; to improve something: *A change of job would do you a world of good.* **for all the world as if/though…** | **for all the world like sb/sth** (*formal*) exactly as if…; exactly like someone or something: *She behaved for all the world as if nothing unusual had happened.* ◆ *He looked for all the world like a cat that just ate a bird.* **have the world at your feet** to be very successful and admired **how, why, etc. in the world** (*informal*) used to emphasize something and to show that you are surprised or annoyed: *What in the world did they think they were doing?* **in an ideal/a perfect world** used to say that something is what you would like to happen or what should happen, but you know it cannot: *In an ideal world we would be recycling and reusing everything.* **in the world** used to emphasize what you are saying: *There's nothing in the world I'd like more than to visit New York.* ◆ *Don't rush—we've got all the time in the world.* ◆ *You look as if you haven't got a care in the world!* **(be/live) in a world of your own** if you are **in a world of your own**, you are so concerned with your own thoughts that you do not notice what is happening around you **a man/woman of the world** a person with a lot of experience of life, who is not easily surprised or shocked **mean the world to sb** to be loved by and very important to someone **not for (all) the world** used to say that you would never do something: *I wouldn't hurt you — not for all the world.* **the… of this world** (*informal*) used to refer to people of a particular type: *We all envy the Bill Gateses of this world* (= the people who are as rich and successful as Bill Gates). **out of this world** (*informal*) used to emphasize how good, beautiful, etc. something is: *That meal was out of this world.* **see the world** to travel widely and gain wide experience **set the world on fire** (*informal*) (usually used in negative sentences) to be very successful and gain the admiration of other people: *He's never going to set the world on fire with his paintings.* **what is the world coming to?** used to express disapproval, surprise, or shock, especially at changes in people's attitudes or behavior: *When I listen to the news these days, I sometimes wonder what the world is coming to.* **a world away (from sth)** used to emphasize how different two things are: *His new luxury mansion was a world away from the tiny house where he was born.* **the world is your oyster** there is no limit to the opportunities open to you **a world of difference** (*informal*) used to emphasize how much difference there is between two things: *There's a world of difference between liking someone and loving them.* **the (whole) world over** everywhere in the world: *People are* basically *the same the world over.* ➔ more at BRAVE, DEAD, END, LOST, PROMISE, SMALL, TOP, WATCH *v.*, WAY, WORST

the ˌWorld ˈBank *noun* [sing.] an international organization that lends money to countries who are members at times when they are in difficulty and need more money

ˌworld-ˌbeater *noun* a person or thing that is better than all others ▶ ˈworld-ˌbeating *adj.*

ˌworld-ˈclass *adj.* as good as the best in the world: *a world-class athlete*

the ˌWorld ˈCup *noun* (in sports) a competition between national teams from all over the world, usually held every few years: *The World Cup in soccer takes place every four years.*

ˌworld ˈEnglish *noun* [U] the English language, used throughout the world for international communication, including all of its regional varieties, such as Australian, Indian, and South African English

ˌworld-ˈfamous *adj.* known all over the world: *a world-famous scientist* ◆ *His books are world-famous.*

ˌWorld ˈHeritage ˌSite *noun* a natural or MAN-MADE place that is recognized as having great international importance and is therefore protected

ˌworld ˈlanguage *noun* a language that is known or spoken in many countries

world·ly /ˈwɜrldli/ *adj.* (*literary*) 1 [only before noun] connected with the world in which we live rather than with spiritual things: *worldly success* ◆ *your worldly goods* (= the things that you own) ANT SPIRITUAL 2 having a lot of experience of life and therefore not easily shocked: *At 15, he was more worldly than his older cousins who lived in the country.* ANT UNWORLDLY ▶ world·li·ness *noun* [U]

ˌworldly-ˈwise *adj.* having a lot of experience of life and therefore not easily shocked

ˌworld ˈmusic *noun* [U] 1 traditional music from non-Western countries 2 Western popular music that includes aspects of traditional music from non-Western countries

ˌworld ˈpower *noun* a powerful country that has a lot of influence in international politics

the ˌWorld ˈSeries *noun* a series of baseball games played every year between the winners of the American League and the National League

ˌworld ˈview *noun* a person's way of thinking about and understanding life, which depends on their beliefs and attitudes: *Your education is bound to shape your world view.*

ˌworld ˈwar *noun* [C, U] a war that involves many countries

ˌWorld ˌWar ˈI /ˌwɜrld wɔr ˈwʌn/ (also the ˌFirst World ˈWar) *noun* a war that was fought from 1914 to 1918, mainly between France, the U.K., Russia, and the U.S. on one side, and Germany, Austria-Hungary, and Turkey on the other side

ˌWorld ˌWar ˈII /ˌwɜrld wɔr ˈtu/ (also the ˌSecond ˌWorld ˈWar) *noun* a war that was fought from 1939 to 1945, mainly between the U.S., the U.K., and the Soviet Union on one side, and Germany, Japan, and Italy on the other side

ˌworld-ˈweary *adj.* no longer excited by life; showing this SYN JADED ▶ ˌworld-ˌweariness *noun* [U]

world·wide /ˌwɜrldˈwaɪd/ *adj.* [usually before noun] affecting all parts of the world: *an increase in worldwide sales* ◆ *The story has attracted worldwide attention.* ▶ ˌworldˈwide *adv.*: *We have 2,000 members worldwide.*

the ˌWorld Wide ˈWeb (also the ˌWeb) *noun* (*abbr.* WWW) a system for finding information on the Internet, in which documents are connected to other documents using HYPERTEXT links: *to browse a site on the World Wide Web*

worm /wɜrm/ *noun, verb*
• *noun* 1 [C] a long, thin creature with no bones or legs, that lives in soil: *birds looking for worms* ➔ see also EARTHWORM, LUGWORM 2 worms [pl.] long, thin creatures that live inside the bodies of humans or animals and can cause illness: *The dog has worms.* ➔ see also HOOKWORM, TAPEWORM 3 [C] the young form of an insect when it looks like a

short worm: *This apple is full of worms.* ➔ see also GLOW-WORM, SILKWORM, WOODWORM 4 [C] (*computing*) a computer program that is a type of virus and that spreads across a network by copying itself 5 [C, usually sing.] (*informal*, *disapproving*) a person you do not like or respect, especially because they have a weak character and do not behave well toward other people
IDM the worm will turn (*saying*) a person who is normally quiet and does not complain will protest when the situation becomes too hard to bear ➔ more at CAN², EARLY
• *verb* 1 ~ your way + *adv./prep.* to use a twisting and turning movement, especially to move through a narrow or crowded place: *She wormed her way through the crowd to the reception desk.* 2 ~ sth to give an animal medicine that makes worms pass out of its body in the FECES
PHR V ˌworm your way/yourself ˈinto sth (*disapproving*) to make someone like you or trust you, in order to gain some advantage for yourself SYN INSINUATE: *He managed to worm his way into her life.* ˌworm sth ˈout of sb (*informal*) to gradually get someone to tell you something that they do not want to tell you: *We eventually wormed the secret out of her.*

ˌworm-ˌeaten *adj.* full of holes made by WORMS or WOOD-WORMS

worm·hole /ˈwɜrmhoʊl/ *noun* 1 a hole made by a worm or young insect 2 (*physics*) a possible connection between regions of SPACE-TIME that are far apart

worm·wood /ˈwɜrmwʊd/ *noun* [U] a plant with a bitter flavor, used in making alcoholic drinks and medicines

worm·y /ˈwɜrmi/ *adj.* containing WORMS: *a wormy apple*

worn /wɔrn/ *adj.* 1 [usually before noun] (of a thing) damaged or thinner than normal because it is old and has been used a lot: *an old pair of worn jeans* ◆ *The stone steps were worn and broken.* ➔ see also WELL WORN 2 (of a person) looking very tired SYN WEARY: *She came out of the ordeal looking thin and worn.* ➔ see also WEAR
IDM be worn to a frazzle (*informal*) to be extremely tired

ˌworn ˈout *adj.* 1 (of a thing) badly damaged and/or no longer useful because it has been used a lot: *These shoes are worn out.* ◆ *the gradual replacement of worn-out equipment* ◆ *a speech full of worn-out old clichés* 2 [not usually before noun] (of a person) looking or feeling very tired, especially as a result of hard work or physical exercise: *Can we sit down? I'm worn out.* ➔ compare OUTWORN

wor·ried 🔊 /ˈwɜrid/ *adj.*
thinking about unpleasant things that have happened or that might happen and therefore feeling unhappy and afraid: *Don't look so worried!* ◆ ~ about sb/sth *I'm not worried about her—she can take care of herself.* ◆ *Doctors are worried about the possible spread of the disease.* ◆ ~ by sth *We're not too worried by these results.* ◆ ~ (that...) *The police are worried that the man may be armed.* ◆ *I was worried you wouldn't come.* ◆ *Where have you been? I've been worried sick* (= extremely worried). ◆ *Try not to get worried.* ◆ *She gave me a worried look.* ▶ wor·ried·ly *adv.*: *He glanced worriedly at his father.*
IDM you had me worried (*informal*) used to tell someone that you were worried because you had not understood what they had said correctly: *You had me worried for a moment—I thought you were going to resign!*

THESAURUS

worried

concerned ◆ nervous ◆ anxious ◆ uneasy

These words all describe feeling unhappy and afraid because you are thinking about unpleasant things that might happen or might have happened.

worried thinking about unpleasant things that might happen or might have happened and therefore feeling unhappy and afraid

concerned worried and feeling concern about something

ɪr near   ɛr hair   ɑr car   ɔr north   ʊr tour   ɑ̃ denouement   p pen   b bad

wor·ri·er /'wəriər/ *noun* a person who worries a lot about unpleasant things that have happened or that might happen

wor·ri·some /'wərisəm/ *adj.* that makes you worry

wor·ry 🔑 /'wəri/ *verb, noun*

- *verb* (wor·ries, wor·ry·ing, wor·ried, wor·ried) **1** [I] to keep thinking about unpleasant things that might happen or about problems that you have: *Don't worry. We have plenty of time.* ◆ ~ **about sb/sth** *Don't worry about me. I'll be all right.* ◆ *He's always worrying about his weight.* ◆ ~ **over sb/sth** *There's no point in worrying over things you can't change.* ◆ ~ **(that)…** *I worry that I won't get into college.* **2** [T] to make someone/yourself anxious about someone or something: ~ **sb/yourself (about sb/sth)** *What worries me is how I am going to get another job.* ◆ ~ **sb/yourself + adj. (about sb/sth)** *He worried himself sick* (= become extremely anxious) *about his daughter.* ◆ **it worries sb that…** *It worries me that he hasn't come home yet.* ◆ **it worries sb to do sth** *It worried me to think what might happen.* **3** [T] to annoy or disturb someone: ~ **sb** *The noise never seems to worry her.* ◆ ~ **sb with sth** *Don't keep worrying him with a lot of silly questions.* **IDM** not to worry (*informal*) it is not important; it does not matter: *Not to worry — I can fix it.* ◆ *Not to worry — no harm done.* **PHR V** 'worry at sth **1** to think about a problem a lot and try and find a solution **2** to bite something and shake or pull it: *Rebecca worried at her lip.* ◆ *He began to worry at the knot in the cord.*

- *noun* (*pl.* wor·ries) **1** [U] the state of worrying about something **SYN** ANXIETY: *The threat of losing their jobs is a constant source of worry to them.* ◆ *to be frantic with worry* **2** [C] something that worries you: *family/financial worries* ◆ ~ **(about/over sth)** *worries about the future* ◆ ~ **(for/to sb)** *Mugging is a real worry for many old people.* ◆ *My only worry is that…* **IDM** no worries! (*informal*) it's not a problem; it's all right

(often used as a reply when someone thanks you for something)

'worry ₁beads *noun* [pl.] small BEADS on a string that you move and turn in order to keep calm

wor·ry·ing 🔑 /'wəriiŋ/ *adj.* that makes you worry: *a worrying development* ◆ *It must be worrying for you not to know where he is.* ◆ *It is particularly worrying that nobody seems to be in charge.* ◆ *It's been a worrying time for us all.* ▶ **wor·ry·ing·ly** /'wəriiŋli/ *adv.*: *worryingly high levels of radiation* ◆ *Worryingly, the plan contains few details on how spending will be cut.*

wor·ry·wart /'wəri₁wɔrt/ *noun* (*informal*) a person who worries about unimportant things

worse 🔑 /wərs/ *adj., adv., noun*

- *adj.* (comparative of *bad*) **1** of poorer quality or lower standard; less good or more unpleasant: *The rooms were awful and the food was worse.* ◆ *The weather got worse during the day.* ◆ *I've been to far worse places.* ◆ ~ **than sth** *The interview was much worse than he had expected.* ◆ ~ **than doing sth** *There's nothing worse than going out in the cold with wet hair.* **2** ~ **(than sth/doing sth)** more serious or severe: *They were trying to prevent an even worse tragedy.* ◆ *The crisis was getting worse and worse.* ◆ *Don't tell her that — you'll only make things worse.* ◆ *Never mind — it could be worse* (= although the situation is bad, it is not as bad as it might have been). **3** [not before noun] more sick or unhappy: *If he gets any worse we'll call the doctor.* ◆ *He told her she'd let them down and she felt worse than ever.* **IDM** come off worse to lose a fight, competition, etc. or suffer more compared with others go from bad to worse (of a bad condition, situation, etc.) to get even worse ⊃ more at BARK, FATE

- *adv.* (comparative of *badly*) **1** ~ **(than sth)** less well: *I didn't do it very well, but, if anything, he did it worse than I did.* **2** ~ **(than sth)** more seriously or severely: *It's raining worse than ever.* **3** ~ **(than sth)** used to introduce a statement about something that is more serious or unpleasant than things already mentioned: *She lost her job. Even worse, she lost her house and her children, too.* **IDM** be worse off (than sb/sth) to be poorer, unhappier, etc. than before or than someone else: *The increase in taxes means that we'll be $30 a month worse off than before.* you can/could do worse than do sth used to say that you think something is a good idea: *If you want a safe investment, you could do a lot worse than putting your money in bonds.*

- *noun* [U] more problems or bad news: *I'm afraid there is worse to come.* **IDM** be none the worse (for sth) to not be harmed by something: *The kids were none the worse for playing in the mud.* the worse for wear (*informal*) **1** in a poor condition because of being used a lot **2** drunk ⊃ more at BETTER *n.*, CHANGE *n.*

wors·en /'wərsn/ *verb* [I, T] to become or make something worse than it was before **SYN** DETERIORATE: *The political situation is steadily worsening.* ◆ *Her health has worsened considerably since we last saw her.* ◆ ~ **sth** *Staff shortages were worsened by the flu epidemic.* ▶ **wors·en·ing** *noun* [sing.]: *a worsening of the international debt crisis* **wors·en·ing** *adj.*: *worsening weather conditions*

wor·ship 🔑 /'wərʃəp/ *noun, verb*

- *noun* [U] **1** the practice of showing respect for God or a god, by saying prayers, singing with others, etc.; a ceremony for this: *an act/a place of worship* ◆ *ancestor worship* ◆ *morning worship* (= a church service in the morning) **2** a strong feeling of love and respect for someone or something **SYN** ADORATION ⊃ see also HERO WORSHIP

- *verb* (-p-, *CanE usually* -pp-) **1** [T] ~ **sb/sth** to show respect for God or a god, especially by saying prayers, singing, etc. with other people in a religious building ⊃ collocations at RELIGION **2** [I] to go to a service in a religious building: *We worship at St. Mary's.* ◆ *He worshiped at the local mosque.*

| t **t**ea | ṭ **butt**er | d **d**id | k **c**at | g **g**ot | tʃ **ch**in | dʒ **J**une | f **f**all |

3 [T] ~ **sb/sth** to love and admire someone very much, especially so much that you cannot see their faults: *She worships her children.* ◆ *He worshiped her from afar* (= he loved her but did not tell her his feelings). ◆ *She worships the ground he walks on.*

wor·ship·er (*CanE usually* **wor·ship·per**) /ˈwərʃəpər/ *noun* a person who worships God or a god: *regular worshipers at St. Andrew's Church* ◆ (*figurative*) *sun worshipers lying on the beach*

wor·ship·ful /ˈwərʃəpfl/ *adj.* [only before noun] (*formal*) showing or feeling respect and admiration for someone or something

worst 🔎 /wərst/ *adj., adv., noun, verb*

- *adj.* (superlative of *bad*) of the poorest quality or lowest standard; worse than any other person or thing of a similar kind: *It was by far the worst speech he had ever made.* ◆ *What's the worst thing that could happen?* ◆ *What she said confirmed my worst fears* (= proved they were right).
  IDM be your own worst enemy to be the cause of your own problems

- *adv.* (superlative of *badly*) most badly or seriously: *He was voted the worst dressed celebrity.* ◆ *The manufacturing industry was worst affected by the fuel shortage.* ◆ *Worst of all, I lost the watch my father had given me.*

- *noun* the worst [sing.] the most serious or unpleasant thing that could happen; the part, situation, possibility, etc. that is worse than any other: *The worst of the storm was over.* ◆ *When they did not hear from her, they feared the worst.* ◆ *The worst of it is that I can't even be sure if they received my letter.* ◆ *He was always optimistic, even when things were at their worst.*
  IDM at (the) worst used for saying what is the worst thing that can happen: *At the very worst, he'll have to pay a fine.* bring out the worst in sb to make someone show their worst qualities: *Pressure can bring out the worst in people.* do your worst (of a person) to do as much damage or be as unpleasant as possible: *Let them do their worst—we'll fight them every inch of the way.* get the worst of it to be defeated: *He'd been in a fight and had obviously got the worst of it.* if worst comes to worst if the situation becomes too difficult or dangerous: *If worst comes to worst, we'll just have to sell the house.* the worst of all (possible) worlds all the disadvantages of every situation

- *verb* ~ **sb** (*old-fashioned* or *formal*) [usually passive] to defeat someone in a fight, a contest, or an argument **SYN** GET THE BETTER OF

worst-case *adj.* [only before noun] involving the worst situation that could happen: *In the worst-case scenario, more than ten thousand people might be affected.*

wor·sted /ˈwʊstəd; ˈwərstəd/ *noun* [U] a type of cloth made of wool with a smooth surface, used for making clothes: *a gray worsted suit*

worth 🔎 /wərθ/ *adj., noun*

- *adj.* [not before noun] (used like a preposition, followed by a noun, pronoun, or number, or by the *-ing* form of a verb) **1** ~ **sth** having a value in money, etc.: *Our house is worth about $100,000.* ◆ *How much is this painting worth?* ◆ *to be worth a fortune* (= a lot of money) ◆ *It isn't worth much.* ◆ *If you answer this question correctly, it's worth five points.* ⊃ the-saurus box at PRICE **2** used to recommend the action mentioned because you think it may be useful, enjoyable, etc.: ~ **sth** *The museum is certainly worth a visit.* ◆ ~ **doing sth** *This idea is well worth considering.* ◆ *It's worth making an appointment before you go.* **3** ~ **sth/doing sth** important, good, or enjoyable enough to make someone feel satisfied, especially when difficulty or effort is involved: *Was it worth the effort?* ◆ *The new house really wasn't worth all the expense involved.* ◆ *The job involves a lot of hard work but it's worth it.* ◆ *The trip was expensive but it was worth every penny.* ⊃ see also WORTHWHILE **4** ~ **sth** (of a person) having money and possessions of a particular value: *He's worth $10 million.*
  IDM for all sb/it is worth **1** with great energy, effort, and determination: *He was rowing for all he was worth.* **2** in order

to get as much as you can from someone or something: *She is milking her success for all it's worth.* for what it's worth (*informal*) used to emphasize that what you are saying is only your own opinion or suggestion and may not be very helpful: *I prefer this color, for what it's worth.* not worth the paper it's written/printed on (of an agreement or official document) having no value, especially legally, or because one of the people involved has no intention of doing what they said they would worth your/its salt deserving respect, especially because you do your job well: *Any teacher worth her salt knows that.* worth your/its weight in gold very useful or valuable: *A good mechanic is worth his weight in gold.* worth sb's while interesting or useful for someone to do: *It will be worth your while to come to the meeting.* ◆ *He'll do the job if you make it worth his while* (= pay him well). ⊃ more at BIRD

- *noun* [U] **1 ten dollars', $40, etc. ~ of something** an amount of something that has the value mentioned: *We lost $2,000 worth of furniture in the flood.* ◆ *a dollar's worth of change* **2 a week's, month's, etc. ~ of something** an amount of something that lasts a week, etc. **3** the financial, practical, or moral value of someone or something: *Their contribution was of great worth.* ◆ *The activities help children to develop a sense of their own worth.* ◆ *A good interview enables candidates to prove their worth* (= show how good they are). ◆ *a personal net worth of $10 million* **IDM** see CENT, MONEY

worth·less /ˈwərθləs/ *adj.* **1** having no practical or financial value: *Critics say his paintings are worthless.* **ANT** VALUABLE **2** (of a person) having no good qualities or useful skills: *a worthless individual* ◆ *Constant rejections made him feel worthless.* ▶ **worth·less·ness** *noun* [U]: *a sense of worthlessness*

worth·while /ˌwərθˈwaɪl/ *adj.* important, enjoyable, interesting, etc.; worth spending time, money, or effort on: *It was in support of a worthwhile cause* (= a charity, etc.) ◆ *The smile on her face made it all worthwhile.* ◆ ~ **for sb to do sth** *High prices at home make it worthwhile for buyers to look overseas.* ◆ ~ **to do sth** *It is worthwhile to include really high-quality illustrations.* ◆ ~ **doing sth** *It didn't seem worthwhile writing it all out again.* **HELP** This word can be written **worth while**, except when it is used before a noun.

wor·thy /ˈwərði/ *adj., noun*

- *adj.* (**wor·thi·er, wor·thi·est**) **1** ~ (**of sb/sth**) (*formal*) having the qualities that deserve someone or something: *to be worthy of attention* ◆ *A number of the report's findings are worthy of note.* ◆ *No composer was considered worthy of the name until he had written an opera.* ◆ *a worthy champion* (= one who deserved to win) ◆ *He felt he was not worthy of her.* **ANT** UNWORTHY **2** [usually before noun] having qualities that deserve your respect, attention, or admiration **SYN** DESERVING: *The money we raise will be going to a very worthy cause.* ◆ *a worthy member of the team* **3** having good qualities but not very interesting or exciting: *her worthy but dull husband* **4** ~ **of sb/sth** typical of what a particular person or thing might do, give, etc.: *He gave a speech that was worthy of Martin Luther King.* **5 -worthy** (in compounds) deserving, or suitable for, the thing mentioned: *trustworthy* ◆ *roadworthy* ▶ **wor·thi·ly** /-ðəli/ *adv.* **wor·thi·ness** /-ðinəs/ *noun* [U]

- *noun* (*pl.* **wor·thies**) (often *humorous*) an important person: *a meeting attended by local worthies*

would 🔎 /wəd; əd; d; *strong form* wʊd/ *modal verb* (*short form* **'d** /d/, *negative form* **would not**, *short form* **would·n't** /ˈwʊdnt/) **1** used as the past form of *will* when reporting what someone said or thought: *He said he would be here at eight o'clock* (= His words were: "I will be here at eight o'clock."). ◆ *She asked if I would help.* ◆ *They told me that they probably wouldn't come.* **2** used for talking about the result of an event that you imagine: *She'd look better with shorter hair.* ◆ *If you went to see him, he would be delighted.* ◆ *Hurry up! It would be a shame to miss the beginning of the play.* ◆ *She'd be a fool to accept it* (= if she accepted it). **3** used for describing a possible action or event that did not in fact happen, because something else did not happen first: *If I had seen*

the advertisement in time I would have applied for the job. ♦ They would never have met if she hadn't gone to Emma's party. **4 so that/in order that sb/sth ~** used for saying why someone does something: *She burned the letters so that her husband would never read them.* **5 wish (that) sb/sth ~** used for saying what you want to happen: *I wish you'd be quiet for a minute.* **6** used to show that someone or something was not willing or refused to do something: *She wouldn't change it, even though she knew it was wrong.* ♦ *My car wouldn't start this morning.* **7** used to ask someone politely to do something: ***Would you mind*** *leaving us alone for a few minutes?* ♦ *Would you open the door for me, please?* **8** used in polite offers or invitations: *Would you like a sandwich?* ♦ *Would you have dinner with me on Friday?* **9 ~ like, love, hate, prefer, etc. sth/(sb) to do something | ~ rather do sth/sb did something** used to say what you like, love, hate, etc.: *I'd love some coffee.* ♦ *I'd be only too glad to help.* ♦ *I'd hate you to think I was criticizing you.* ♦ *I'd rather come with you.* ♦ *I'd rather you came with us.* **10 ~ imagine, say, think, etc. (that)…** used to give opinions that you are not certain about: *I would imagine the job will take about two days.* ♦ *I'd say he was about fifty.* **11 I would…** used to give advice: *I wouldn't have any more to drink, if I were you.* **12** used for talking about things that often happened in the past SYN USED TO: *When my parents were away, my grandmother would take care of me.* ♦ *He'd always be the first to offer to help.* **13** (usually disapproving) used for talking about behavior that you think is typical: *"She said it was your fault." "Well, **she would say that,** wouldn't she? She's never liked me."* **14 ~ that…** (literary) used to express a strong wish: *Would that he had lived to see it.* ⊃ note at MODAL, SHOULD

'**would-be** adj. [only before noun] used to describe someone who is hoping to become the type of person mentioned: *a would-be actor* ♦ *advice for would-be parents*

'**wound**[1] 🔑 /wuːnd/ noun, verb ⊃ see also WOUND[2]
• *noun* **1** an injury to part of the body, especially one in which a hole is made in the skin using a weapon: *a leg/head, etc. wound* ♦ *a bullet/knife/gunshot/stab wound* ♦ *an old war wound* ♦ *The nurse **cleaned** the wound.* ♦ *The **wound healed** slowly.* ♦ *He died from the wounds he had received to his chest.* ⊃ see also FLESH WOUND ⊃ thesaurus box at INJURE ⊃ collocations at INJURY **2** mental or emotional pain caused by something unpleasant that has been said or done to you: *After a serious argument, it can take some time for the wounds to heal.* ♦ *Seeing him again **opened up old wounds**.* IDM see LICK, REOPEN, RUB
• *verb* [often passive] **1 ~ sb/sth** to injure part of the body, especially by making a hole in the skin using a weapon: *He had been wounded in the arm.* **2 ~ sb** to hurt someone's feelings: *She felt **deeply wounded** by his cruel remarks.*

wound[2] /waʊnd/ pt, pp of WIND ⊃ see also WOUND[1]

wound·ed 🔑 /ˈwuːndəd/ adj.
1 injured by a weapon, for example in a war: *wounded soldiers* ♦ *seriously wounded* ♦ *There were 79 killed and 230 wounded.* **2** feeling emotional pain because of something unpleasant that someone has said or done: *wounded pride* **3 the wounded** noun [pl.] people who are wounded, for example in a war

wound·ing /ˈwuːndɪŋ/ adj. that hurts someone's feelings: *He found her remarks deeply wounding.*

wove pt of WEAVE

wo·ven pp of WEAVE

wow /waʊ/ exclamation, verb, noun
• *exclamation* (also **wow·ee** /ˌwaʊˈiː/) (informal) used to express great surprise or admiration: *Wow! You look terrific!*
• *verb* **~ sb (with sth)** (informal) to impress someone very much, especially with a performance: *He wowed audiences around the country with his new show.*
• *noun* [U] (technical) gradual changes in the PITCH of sound played on a record or tape ⊃ compare FLUTTER

'**wow** ˌ**factor** noun [sing.] (informal) the quality something

has of being very impressive or surprising to people: *If you want to sell your house quickly, it needs the wow factor.*

wpm abbr. words per minute: *to type at 60 wpm*

wrack = RACK

wraith /reɪθ/ noun the GHOST of a person that is seen a short time before or after that person dies SYN SPECTER: *a wraith-like figure* (= a very thin, pale person)

wran·gle /ˈræŋɡl/ noun, verb
• *noun* **~ (with sb)(over sth) | ~ (between A and B)** an argument that is complicated and continues over a long period of time: *a legal wrangle between the company and their suppliers* ▶ **wran·gling** noun [U, C]
• *verb* [I] **~ (with sb) (over/about sth)** to argue angrily and usually for a long time about something: *They're still wrangling over the financial details.*

wran·gler /ˈræŋɡlər/ noun (informal) a COWBOY or a COWGIRL, especially one who takes care of horses

wrap 🔑 /ræp/ verb, noun
• *verb* (-pp-) **1** [T] **~ sth (up) (in sth)** to cover something completely in paper or other material, for example when you are giving it as a present: *He spent the evening wrapping up the Christmas presents.* ♦ *individually wrapped chocolates* ⊃ see also GIFT-WRAP **2** [T] to cover something or someone in material, for example in order to protect it/them: **~ A (up) in B** *Wrap the meat in foil before you cook it.* ♦ *I wrapped the baby (up) in a blanket.* ♦ **~ B around A** *I wrapped a blanket around the baby.* ⊃ see also SHRINK-WRAPPED **3** [T] **~ sth around sb/sth** to put something firmly around something or someone: *A scarf was wrapped around his neck.* ♦ *His arms were wrapped around her waist.* **4** [T, I] (computing) to cause text to be carried over to a new line automatically as you reach the end of the previous line; to be carried over in this way: **~ sth (around)** *How can I wrap the text?* ♦ **~ (around)** *The text wraps around if it is too long to fit the screen.* ⊃ compare UNWRAP
IDM **be wrapped up in sb/sth** to be so involved with someone or something that you do not pay enough attention to other people or things SYN ABSORBED, ENGROSSED ⊃ more at LITTLE FINGER
PHR V ˌ**wrap** '**up** | ˌ**wrap it** '**up** (slang) usually used as an order to tell someone to stop talking or causing trouble, etc. ˌ**wrap** '**up** | ˌ**wrap sb/yourself** '**up** to put warm clothes on someone/yourself: *She told them to wrap up warm/warmly.* ˌ**wrap sth↔**'**up** (informal) to complete something such as an agreement or a meeting in an acceptable way: *That just about wraps it up for today.*
• *noun* **1** [U] paper, plastic, etc. that is used for wrapping things in: *We stock a wide range of cards and gift wrap.* ⊃ see also PLASTIC WRAP, SHRINK-WRAPPED **2** [C] used when making a movie to say that filming has finished: *Cut! That's a wrap.* **3** [C] a type of SANDWICH made with a cold TORTILLA rolled around meat or vegetables **4** [C] (old-fashioned) a piece of cloth that a woman wears around her shoulders for decoration or to keep warm
IDM **under wraps** (informal) being kept secret until some time in the future: *Next year's collection is still being kept under wraps.*

'**wrap-around** adj. **1** curving or stretching around at the sides: *wrap-around sunglasses* **2** (of a piece of clothing) having one part that is pulled over to cover another part at the front and then loosely fastened: *a wrap-around skirt*

wrap·a·rounds /ˈræpəˌraʊndz/ noun [pl.] a pair of SUN-GLASSES that fit closely and curve around the sides of the head

wrap·per /ˈræpər/ noun a piece of paper, plastic, etc. that is wrapped around something, especially food, when you buy it and keep it to protect it and keep it clean: *candy wrappers*

wrap·ping /ˈræpɪŋ/ noun [U] paper, plastic, etc. used for covering something in order to protect it: *She tore the cellophane wrapping off the box.* ♦ *shrink wrapping* (= plastic designed to SHRINK around objects so that it fits them tightly) ♦ *The painting was still in its wrapping.*

| h **hat** | m **man** | n **no** | ŋ **sing** | l **leg** | r **red** | y **yes** | w **wet** |

wrapping paper noun [U] colored paper used for wrapping presents: *a piece/sheet/roll of wrapping paper*

wrasse /ræs/ noun (*pl.* **wrasse** or **wrass·es**) an ocean fish with thick lips and strong teeth

wrath /ræθ/ noun [U] (*old-fashioned* or *formal*) extreme anger: *the wrath of God* ▶ **wrath·ful** /'ræθfl/ *adj.* **wrath·ful·ly** /-fəli/ *adv.*

wreak /rik/ verb **~ sth (on sb)** (*formal*) to do great damage or harm to someone or something: *Their policies would wreak havoc on the economy.* ◆ *He swore to wreak vengeance on those who had betrayed him.*

wreath /riθ/ noun (*pl.* **wreaths** /riðz/ /riθz/) **1** an arrangement of flowers and leaves, especially in the shape of a circle, placed on graves, etc. as a sign of respect for someone who has died: *The president laid a wreath at the war memorial.* **2** an arrangement of flowers and/or leaves in the shape of a circle, traditionally hung on doors as a decoration at Christmas: *a holly wreath* **3** a circle of flowers or leaves worn on the head, and used in the past as a sign of honor: *a laurel wreath* **4** (*literary*) a circle of smoke, cloud, etc.

wreathe /rið/ verb (*formal*) **1** [T, usually passive] **~ sth (in/with sth)** to surround or cover something: *The mountain tops were wreathed in mist.* ◆ (*figurative*) *Her face was wreathed in smiles* (= she was smiling a lot). **2** [I] **+ adv./prep.** to move slowly and lightly, especially in circles **SYN** WEAVE: *smoke wreathing into the sky*

wreck /rɛk/ noun, verb
● noun **1** a ship that has sunk or that has been very badly damaged ➔ see also SHIPWRECK **2** a car, plane, etc. that has been very badly damaged in an accident: *Two passengers are still trapped in the wreck.* ➔ note at CRASH **3** [usually sing.] (*informal*) a person who is in a bad physical or mental condition: *Physically, I was a total wreck.* ◆ *The interview reduced him to a nervous wreck.* **4** (*informal*) a vehicle, building, etc. that is in very bad condition: *The house was a wreck when we bought it.* ◆ (*figurative*) *They still hoped to salvage something from the wreck of their marriage.* **5** = CRASH: *a car/train wreck*
● verb **1** **~ sth** to damage or destroy something: *The building had been wrecked by the explosion.* ◆ *The mob wrecked twenty-four cars.* ➔ thesaurus box at CRASH **2** **~ sth (for sb)** to spoil something completely: *The weather wrecked all our plans.* ◆ *A serious injury nearly wrecked his career.* **3** [usually passive] **~ sth** to damage a ship so much that it sinks or can no longer sail: *The ship was wrecked off the coast of France.* ➔ see also SHIPWRECK

wreck·age /'rɛkɪdʒ/ noun [U] the parts of a vehicle, building, etc. that remain after it has been badly damaged or destroyed: *A few survivors were pulled from the wreckage.* ◆ *Pieces of wreckage were found ten miles away from the scene of the explosion.* ◆ (*figurative*) *Could nothing be rescued from the wreckage of her dreams?*

wrecked /rɛkt/ *adj.* **1** [only before noun] having been wrecked: *a wrecked ship/marriage* **2** [not before noun] (*slang*) very drunk

wreck·er /'rɛkər/ noun **1** a person who ruins another person's plans, relationship, etc.: *a home-wrecker* **2** a vehicle used for moving other vehicles that have been damaged in an accident

wrecking ball noun a heavy metal ball that swings from a CRANE and is used to hit a building to make it fall down

wren /rɛn/ noun a very small brown bird

wrench /rɛntʃ/ verb, noun
● verb **1** [T, I] to pull or twist something or someone/yourself suddenly and violently **SYN** JERK: **~ (sth/sb/yourself) + adv./prep.** *The bag was wrenched from her grasp.* ◆ *He grabbed Ben, wrenching him away from his mother.* ◆ (*figurative*) *Guy wrenched his mind back to the present.* ◆ **~ (sth/sb/yourself) + adj.** *They wrenched the door open.* ◆ *She managed to wrench herself free.* **2** [T] **~ sth** to twist and injure a part of your body, especially your ankle or

shoulder **SYN** TWIST: *She wrenched her knee when she fell.* **3** [T, I] (*formal*) to make someone feel great pain or unhappiness, especially so that they make a sound or cry: **~ (sth) (from sb)** *His words wrenched a sob from her.* ◆ **~ at sth** *Her words wrenched at my heart.* ➔ see also GUT-WRENCHING
● noun **1** [C] a metal tool with a specially shaped end for holding and turning things, including one that can be adjusted to fit objects of different sizes, also called a MONKEY WRENCH ➔ picture at TOOL **2** [sing.] pain or unhappiness that you feel when you have to leave a person or place that you love: *Leaving home was a terrible wrench for me.* **3** [C, usually sing.] a sudden and violent twist or pull: *She stumbled and gave her ankle a painful wrench.*
IDM **throw a (monkey) wrench in/into the works** (*informal*) to do something to spoil someone's plans

wrest /rɛst/ verb
PHR V **'wrest sth from sb/sth** (*formal*) **1** to take something such as power or control from someone or something with great effort: *They attempted to wrest control of the town from government forces.* **2** to take something from someone that they do not want to give, suddenly or violently **SYN** WRENCH: *He wrested the gun from my grasp.*

wres·tle /'rɛsl/ verb **1** [I, T] to fight someone by holding them and trying to throw or force them to the ground, sometimes as a sport: *As a boy he had boxed and wrestled.* ◆ **~ with sb** *Armed guards wrestled with the intruder.* ◆ **~ sb (+ adv./prep.)** *Officers wrestled the gunman to the ground.* **2** [I, T] to struggle to deal with something that is difficult **SYN** BATTLE, GRAPPLE: **~ (with) sth** *She had spent the whole weekend wrestling with the problem.* ◆ *He wrestled with the controls as the plane plunged.* ◆ **~ to do sth** *She has been wrestling to raise the money all year.*

wres·tler /'rɛslər/ noun a person who takes part in the sport of wrestling

wres·tling /'rɛslɪŋ/ noun [U] a sport in which two people fight by holding each other and trying to throw or force the other one to the ground

wretch /rɛtʃ/ noun **1** a person that you feel sorry for: *a poor wretch* **2** (*often humorous*) an evil, unpleasant or annoying person

wretch·ed /'rɛtʃəd/ *adj.* **1** (of a person) feeling sick or unhappy: *You look wretched—what's wrong?* ◆ *I felt wretched about the way things had turned out.* **2** (*formal*) extremely bad or unpleasant **SYN** AWFUL: *She had a wretched time at school.* ◆ *The animals are kept in the most wretched conditions.* **3** (*formal*) making you feel sorry for someone or something **SYN** PITIFUL: *She finally agreed to have the wretched animal put down.* **4** [only before noun] (*informal*) used to show that you think that someone or something is extremely annoying: *Is it that wretched woman again?* ▶ **wretch·ed·ly** *adv.* **wretch·ed·ness** noun [U]

wrig·gle /'rɪgl/ verb, noun
● verb **1** [I, T] to twist and turn your body or part of it with quick short movements **SYN** WIGGLE: **~ (about/around)** *The baby was wriggling around on my lap.* ◆ **~ sth** *She wriggled her toes.* **2** [I, T] to move somewhere by twisting and turning your body or part of it **SYN** SQUIRM: **(+ adv./prep.)** *The fish wriggled out of my fingers.* ◆ **+ adj.** *She managed to wriggle free.* ◆ **~ your way/yourself + adv./prep.** *They wriggled their way through the tunnel.* ▶ **wrig·gly** /'rɪgli/ *adj.*: *a wriggly worm*
PHR V **,wriggle 'out of sth/out of doing sth** (*informal, disapproving*) to avoid doing something that you should do, especially by thinking of a good excuse: *He tried desperately to wriggle out of giving a clear answer.*
● noun [usually sing.] an act of wriggling

wring /rɪŋ/ verb (wrung, wrung /rʌŋ/) **1** **~ sth (out)** to twist and squeeze clothes, etc. in order to get the water out of them ➔ picture at SQUEEZE **2** **~ sth** if you wring a bird's neck, you twist it in order to kill the bird
IDM **wring sb's hand** to squeeze someone's hand very tightly when you shake hands **wring your hands** to hold

your hands together, and twist and squeeze them in a way that shows you are anxious or upset, especially when you cannot change the situation つ see also HANDWRINGING **wring sb's neck** (*informal*) when you say that you will **wring someone's neck**, you mean that you are very angry or annoyed with them

PHR V ,wring sth from/out of sb | 'wring sth from sb to obtain something from someone with difficulty, especially by putting pressure on them **SYN** EXTRACT

wring·er /'rɪŋər/ *noun* = MANGLE
IDM go through the wringer (*informal*) to have a difficult or unpleasant experience, or a series of them

,wringing 'wet *adj.* (especially of clothes) very wet

wrin·kle /'rɪŋkl/ *noun, verb*
• *noun* **1** a line or small fold in your skin, especially in your face, that forms as you get older: *There were fine wrinkles around her eyes.* つ collocations at PHYSICAL **2** [usually pl.] a small fold that you do not want in a piece of cloth or paper **SYN** CREASE
• *verb* **1** [T, I] to make the skin on your face form into lines or folds; to form lines or folds in this way: *~ sth (up) She wrinkled up her nose in distaste.* ◆ *He wrinkled his brow in concentration.* ◆ *~ (up) His face wrinkled in a grin.* **2** [I, T] *~ (sth)* to form raised folds or lines in a messy way; to make something do this: *Her stockings were wrinkling at the knees.*

wrin·kled /'rɪŋkld/ *adj.* (of skin, clothing, etc.) having wrinkles

wrin·kling /'rɪŋklɪŋ/ *noun* [U] the process by which WRINKLES form in the skin

wrin·kly /'rɪŋkli/ *adj.* (*informal*) (of skin, clothing, etc.) having WRINKLES

wrist 🔧 /rɪst/ *noun*
the joint between the hand and the arm: *She broke her wrist.* ◆ *He wore a copper bracelet on his wrist.* つ picture at BODY
IDM see SLAP

wrist·band /'rɪstbænd/ *noun* a strip of material worn around the wrist, as a decoration, to absorb sweat during exercise, or to show support for something: *He was wearing a Save the Children wristband.*

wrist·watch /'rɪstwɒtʃ/ *noun* a watch that you wear on your wrist

writ /rɪt/ *noun, verb*
• *noun* *~ (for sth) (against sb)* a legal document from a court telling someone to do or not to do something: *The company has been served with a writ for breach of contract.* ◆ *We fully intend to issue a writ against the newspaper.* つ see also HOLY WRIT
• *verb* (*old use*) pp of WRITE
IDM writ large (*literary*) **1** easy to see or understand: *Mistrust was writ large on her face.* **2** (used after a noun) being a large or obvious example of the thing mentioned: *This is deception writ large.*

write 🔧 /raɪt/ *verb* (wrote /rəʊt/, writ·ten /'rɪtn/)
> LETTERS/NUMBERS **1** [I, T] to make letters or numbers on a surface, especially using a pen or a pencil: *In some countries children don't start learning to read and write until they are six.* ◆ *~ in/on/with sth Please write in pen on both sides of the paper.* ◆ *I haven't got anything to write with.* ◆ *~ sth Write your name at the top of the page.* ◆ *The teacher wrote the answers on the board.* ◆ *The "b" had been wrongly written as a "d."*
> BOOK/MUSIC/PROGRAM **2** [T, I] to produce something in written form so that people can read, perform, or use it, etc.: *~ sth to write a novel/a song/an essay/a computer program, etc.* ◆ *Who was "The Grapes of Wrath" written by?* ◆ *Which opera did Verdi write first?* ◆ *~ sth about/on sth He hopes to write a book about his experiences one day.* ◆ *She had to write a report on the project.* ◆ *~ (about sth) I wanted to travel and then write about it.* ◆ *He writes for the "The New Yorker."* (= works as a writer) ◆ *No decision has been made at the time of writing.* ◆ *~ sb sth She wrote him several poems.*
> A LETTER **3** [I, T] to put information, a message of good

wishes, etc. in a letter and send it to someone: *Bye! Don't forget to write.* ◆ *Can you write and confirm your reservation?* ◆ *I'm writing to inquire about language classes* ◆ *~ to sb She wrote to him in France.* ◆ *~ sth (to sb) I wrote a letter to the Publicity Department.* ◆ *~ sb sth I wrote the Publicity Department a letter.* ◆ *~ that... She wrote that they were all fine.* ◆ *~ sb Write me while you're away.* ◆ *~ sb that... He wrote me that he would be arriving Monday.* ◆ *~ doing sth They wrote thanking us for the present.*
> STATE IN WRITING **4** [T, I] to state the information or the words mentioned: *~ that... In his latest book he writes that the theory has since been disproved.* ◆ *~ of sth Ancient historians wrote of a lost continent beneath the ocean.* ◆ *+ speech "Of all my books," wrote Dickens, "I like this the best."*
> CHECK/FORM **5** [T] to put information in the appropriate places on a check or other form: *~ sth (out) to write out a check* ◆ *~ sb (out) sth I'll write you a receipt.*
> COMPUTING **6** [T, I] *~ (sth) to/onto sth* to record data in the memory of a computer: *An error was reported when he tried to write data to the file for the first time.*
> OF PEN/PENCIL **7** [I] to work correctly or in the way mentioned: *This pen won't write.*
IDM be written all over sb's face (of a feeling) to be very obvious to other people from the expression on someone's face: *Guilt was written all over his face.* have sth/sb written all over it/sb (*informal*) to show clearly the quality mentioned or the influence of the person mentioned: *It was a performance with star quality written all over it.* ◆ *This essay has got Mike written all over it.* nothing (much) to write home about (*informal*) not especially good; ordinary that's all she wrote (*informal*) used when you are stating that there is nothing more that can be said about something or that something is completely finished つ more at WORTH *adj.*
PHR V ,write a'way = WRITE ,write 'back (to sb) to write someone a letter replying to their letter **SYN** REPLY: *I'm afraid I never wrote back.* ◆ *She wrote back saying that she couldn't come.* ,write sth↔'down **1** to write something on paper, especially in order to remember or record it: *Write down the address before you forget it.* **2** (*business*) to reduce the value of ASSETS when stating it in a company's accounts つ related noun WRITE-DOWN ,write 'in (to sb/sth) (for sth) to write a letter to an organization or a company, for example to ask about something or to express an opinion: *I'll write in for more information.* ,write sb/sth↔'in (*politics*) to add an extra name to your voting paper in an election in order to be able to vote for them つ related noun WRITE-IN ,write sth 'into sth to include a rule or condition in a contract or an agreement when it is made ,write 'off/a'way (to sb/sth) (for sth) to write to an organization or a company, usually in order to ask them to send you something **SYN** SEND: *I've written off for the catalog.* ,write sth↔'off **1** (*business*) to cancel a debt; to recognize that something is a failure, has no value, etc.: *to write off a debt/ an investment* つ related noun WRITE-OFF **2** to take away an amount of money from the total you must pay in tax: *Charitable donations can be written off on your taxes.* ,write sb/ sth↔'off (as sth) to decide that someone or something is a failure or not worth paying any attention to **SYN** DISMISS つ related noun WRITE-OFF ,write sth↔'out to write something on paper, including all the details, especially a piece of work or an account of something つ see also WRITE (5) ,write sb↔'out (of sth) to remove a character from a regular series on television or radio ,write sth↔'up to record something in writing in a full and complete form, often using notes that you made earlier: *to write up your notes/the minutes of a meeting* つ related noun WRITE-UP

'**write-back** *noun* [C, U] (*business*) a situation where an ASSET gets a value that it was thought to have lost; an amount of money entered in the financial records because of this

'**write-down** *noun* (*business*) a reduction in the value of ASSETS, etc.

'**write-in** *noun* a vote for someone who is not an official candidate in an election, in which you write their name on your BALLOT

ʌ cup   ə about   eɪ say   ɪə near   aɪ five   ɔɪ boy   aʊ now   oʊ go   ər bird

write-off noun **1** [sing.] (*informal*) a period of time during which you do not achieve anything: *With meetings and phone calls, yesterday was a complete write-off.* **2** ~ (of sth) (*business*) an act of canceling a debt and accepting that it will never be paid **3** an amount by which the money you have to pay can be reduced: *You can get a tax write-off for some home improvements.*

write-pro|tect *verb* ~ **sth** (*computing*) to protect the information on a computer disk from being changed or DELETED (= destroyed)

writ·er 🔊 /ˈraɪtər/ *noun*
1 a person whose job is writing books, stories, articles, etc.: *writers of poetry* ♦ *a travel/food, etc. writer* **2** a person who has written a particular thing: *the writer of this letter* **3** (with an adjective) a person who forms letters in a particular way when they are writing: *a messy writer*

writer's |block *noun* [U] a problem that writers sometimes have when they cannot think of what to write and have no new ideas

writer's |cramp *noun* [U] a pain or stiff feeling in the hand caused by writing for a long time

write-up *noun* an article in a newspaper or magazine in which someone writes what they think about a new book, play, product, etc.

writhe /raɪð/ *verb* [I] ~ (about/around) (in/with sth) to twist or move your body without stopping, often because you are in great pain: *She was writhing around on the floor in agony.* ♦ *The snake writhed and hissed.* ♦ (*figurative*) *He was writhing* (= suffering a lot) *with embarrassment.*

writ·ing 🔊 /ˈraɪtɪŋ/ *noun*
1 [U] the activity of writing, in contrast to reading, speaking, etc.: *Our son's having problems with his reading and writing* (= at school) **2** [U] the activity of writing books, articles, etc., especially as a job: *Only later did she discover a talent for writing.* ♦ *He is leaving the band to concentrate on his writing.* ♦ *creative writing* ♦ *feminist/travel, etc. writing* ⬥ see also SONGWRITING **3** [U] books, articles, etc. in general: *The review is a brilliant piece of writing.* **4** writings [pl.] a group of pieces of writing, especially by a particular person or on a particular subject: *His experiences in India influenced his later writings.* ♦ *the writings of Hegel* **5** [U] words that have been written or painted on something: *There was writing all over the desk.* **6** [U] the particular way in which someone forms letters when they write **SYN** HANDWRITING: *Who's this from? I don't recognize the writing.*
IDM in writing in the form of a letter, document, etc. (that gives proof of something): *All telephone reservations must be confirmed in writing.* ♦ *Could you put your complaint in writing?* ♦ *You must get it in writing.* ⬥ more at WALL *n.*

writing |desk *noun* a piece of furniture with a surface for writing on and separate sections for pens and paper

writing |paper *noun* [U] = NOTEPAPER

writ·ten 🔊 /ˈrɪtn/ *adj.*
1 [usually before noun] expressed in writing rather than in speech: *written instructions* **2** [usually before noun] (of an exam, a piece of work, etc.) involving writing rather than speaking or practical skills: *a written test* ♦ *written communication skills* **3** [only before noun] in the form of a letter, document, etc. and therefore official: *a written apology* ♦ *a written contract* ⬥ see also WRITE
IDM the written word language expressed in writing rather than in speech: *the permanence of the written word*

wrong 🔊 /rɔŋ/ *adj., adv., noun, verb*
● *adj.*
▷ NOT CORRECT **1** not right or correct: *I got all the answers wrong.* ♦ *He was driving on the wrong side of the road.* ♦ *Sorry, I must have dialed the wrong number.* ♦ *You're holding the camera the wrong way up!* ♦ *That picture is the wrong way around.* **ANT** RIGHT **2** [not before noun] (of a person) not right about something or someone **SYN** MISTAKEN: *I think she lives at number 44, but I could be wrong.* ♦ ~ (about sth/sb) *You were wrong about Tom; he's not married after all.* ♦

~ (to do sth) *We were wrong to assume that she'd agree.* ♦ *She would prove him wrong* (= prove that he was wrong) *whatever happened.* ♦ (*informal*) *You think you've beaten me but that's where you're wrong.* ♦ (*informal*) *Correct me if I'm wrong* (= I may be wrong) *but didn't you say you two knew each other?*
▷ CAUSING PROBLEMS **3** [not before noun] causing problems or difficulties; not as it should be: *Is anything wrong? You look worried.* ♦ *" What's wrong?" "Oh, nothing."* ♦ ~ with sb/sth *There's something wrong with the printer.* ♦ *The doctor could find nothing wrong with him.* ♦ *I have something wrong with my foot.*
▷ NOT SUITABLE **4** [usually before noun] not suitable, right or what you need: ~ (sth) (for sth) *He's the wrong person for the job.* ♦ ~ (sth to do) *I realized that it was the wrong thing to say.* ♦ *We don't want this document falling into the wrong hands.* ♦ *It was his bad luck to be in the wrong place at the wrong time* (= so that he got involved in trouble without intending to).
▷ NOT MORALLY RIGHT **5** [not usually before noun] not morally right or honest: *This man has done nothing wrong.* ♦ ~ (of/for sb) (to do sth) *It is wrong of me to get so angry.* ♦ *It was wrong of me to get so angry.* ♦ *It is wrong to tell lies.* ♦ ~ with sth/with doing sth *What's wrong with eating meat?* ♦ ~ that... *It is wrong that he should not be punished for what he did.*
▶ **wrong·ness** *noun* [U] (*formal*)
IDM from/on the wrong side of the tracks from or living in a poor area or part of town on the wrong side of the law in trouble with the police take sth the wrong way to be offended by a remark that was not intended to be offensive ⬥ more at BARK *v.*, BED *n.*, FAR, NOTE *n.*, RUB *v.*, SIDE *n.*, TRACK *n.*

THESAURUS

wrong

false ♦ mistaken ♦ incorrect ♦ inaccurate ♦ misguided ♦ untrue

These words all describe something that is not right or correct, or someone who is not right about something.

wrong not right or correct; (of a person) not right about something: *I got all the answers wrong.* ♦ *We were wrong to assume that she'd agree.*

false not true or correct; wrong because it is based on something that is not true or correct: *A whale is a fish. True or false?* ♦ *She gave false information to the insurance company.*

mistaken wrong in your opinion or judgment; based on a wrong opinion or bad judgment: *You're completely mistaken about Jane.*

incorrect (*somewhat formal*) wrong according to the facts; containing mistakes: *Many of the statistics were incorrect.*

inaccurate wrong according to the facts; containing mistakes: *The report was badly researched and fairly inaccurate.*

INCORRECT OR INACCURATE?

A fact, figure, or spelling that is wrong is **incorrect**; information, a belief, or a description based on incorrect facts can be **incorrect** or **inaccurate**; something that is produced, such as a film, report, or map, that contains incorrect facts is **inaccurate**.

misguided wrong because you have understood or judged a situation badly: *In her misguided attempts to help, she only made the situation worse.*

untrue not based on facts, but invented or guessed: *These accusations are totally untrue.*

PATTERNS
- to be wrong/mistaken **about** sth
- wrong/false/mistaken/incorrect/inaccurate **information**
- a(n) false/mistaken/incorrect/inaccurate/misguided **belief**
- a(n) wrong/incorrect **answer**

● **adv.** (used after verbs) in a way that produces a result that is not correct or that you do not want: *My name is spelled wrong.* ◆ *The program won't load. What am I doing wrong?* ◆ *I was trying to apologize but it came out wrong* (= what I said sounded wrong). ◆ *"I thought you were going out." "Well you must have thought wrong, then!"* **ANT** RIGHT

IDM **get sb wrong** (*informal*) to not understand correctly what someone means: *Don't get me wrong* (= do not be offended by what I am going to say), *I think he's doing a good job, but...* **get sth (all) wrong** (*informal*) **1** to not understand a situation correctly: *No, you've got it all wrong. She's his wife.* **2** to make a mistake with something: *I must have gotten the figures wrong.* **go wrong 1** to make a mistake: *If you do what she tells you, you can't go wrong.* ◆ *Where did we go wrong with those kids* (= what mistakes did we make for them to behave so badly)? **2** to experience problems or difficulties: *The relationship started to go wrong when they moved abroad.* ◆ *What else can go wrong* (= what other problems are we going to have)? **you can't go wrong (with sth)** (*informal*) used to say that something will always be acceptable in a particular situation: *For a quick lunch you can't go wrong with pasta.*

WHICH WORD?

wrong ◆ wrongly ◆ wrongfully

- In informal language, **wrong** can be used as an adverb instead of **wrongly** when it means "incorrectly" and comes after a verb or its object: *My name was spelled wrong.* ◆ *I'm afraid you guessed wrong.* **Wrongly** is used before a past participle or a *that* clause: *He was wrongly targeted by the media.* ◆ *She guessed wrongly that he was a teacher.*
- **Wrongfully** is often used in a formal legal situation with words like *convicted, dismissed,* and *imprisoned.*

● **noun 1** [U] behavior that is not honest or morally acceptable: *Children must be taught the difference between right and wrong.* ◆ *Her son can do no wrong in her eyes.* **2** [C] (*formal*) an act that is not legal, honest, or morally acceptable: *It is time to forgive past wrongs if progress is to be made.* **ANT** RIGHT

IDM **in the wrong** responsible for an accident, a mistake, an argument, etc.: *The cab driver was clearly in the wrong.* **two wrongs don't make a right** (*saying*) used to say that if someone does something bad to you, the situation will not be improved by doing something bad to them ➔ more at RIGHT

● **verb** [usually passive] **~ sb** (*formal*) to treat someone badly or in an unfair way: *He felt deeply wronged by the allegations.*

wrong·do·er /ˈrɔŋˌduər/ *noun* (*formal*) a person who does something dishonest or illegal **SYN** CRIMINAL, OFFENDER

wrong·do·ing /ˈrɔŋˌduɪŋ/ *noun* [U, C] (*formal*) illegal or dishonest behavior **SYN** CRIME, OFFENSE

wrong·ful /ˈrɔŋfl/ *adj.* [usually before noun] (*law*) not fair, morally right, or legal: *She decided to sue her employer for wrongful termination.* ▶ **wrong·ful·ly** /-fəli/ *adv.*: *to be wrongfully convicted/terminated* ➔ note at WRONG

wrong-ˈheaded *adj.* having or showing bad judgment: *wrong-headed beliefs*

wrong·ly /ˈrɔŋli/ *adv.*
in a way that is unfair, immoral, or not correct: *She was wrongly accused of stealing.* ◆ *He assumed, wrongly, that she did not care.* ◆ *The sentence had been wrongly translated.* ◆ *They knew they had acted wrongly.* ◆ *Rightly or wrongly, they felt they should have been better informed* (= I do not know whether they were right to feel this way). ➔ note at WRONG

wrote pt of WRITE

wrought /rɔt/ *verb* **~ sth** (*formal* or *literary*) (used only in the past tense) caused something to happen, especially a change: *This century wrought major changes in our society.* ◆ *The storm wrought havoc in the south.* **HELP** Wrought is an old form of the past tense of **work**.

wrought iron *noun* [U] a form of iron used to make decorative fences, gates, etc.: *The gates were made of wrought iron.* ◆ *wrought-iron gates* ➔ compare CAST IRON

wrung pt, pp of WRING

wry /raɪ/ *adj.* [usually before noun] **1** showing that you are both amused and disappointed or annoyed: *"At least we got one vote," she said with a wry smile.* **2** amusing in a way that shows IRONY: *a wry comedy about family life* ◆ *a wry comment* ◆ *wry humor* ▶ **wry·ly** *adv.*: *to smile wryly* **wry·ness** /ˈraɪnəs/ *noun* [U]

WTO /ˌdʌblyu ti ˈoʊ; ˌdʌblyə-/ *abbr.* World Trade Organization (an international organization that encourages international trade and economic development, especially by reducing restrictions on trade)

Wu /wu/ *noun* [U] a form of Chinese spoken in Jiangsu, Zhejiang and Shanghai

wun·der·kind /ˈvʊndərˌkɪnd; ˈwʌndər-/ *noun* (*pl.* wun·der·kind·er /-ˌkɪndər/ or wun·der·kinds) (from *German*, sometimes *disapproving*) a person who is very successful at a young age

Wur·litz·er™ /ˈwɜrlɪtsər/ *noun* a large musical organ, especially one used in the movie theaters of the 1930s

wuss /wʊs/ *noun* (*slang*) a person who is not strong or brave: *Don't be such a wuss!*

WV *abbr.* (in writing) West Virginia

WWW /ˌdʌblyu ˌdʌblyu ˈdʌblyu; ˌdʌblyə ˌdʌblyə ˈdʌblyə/ *abbr.* = WORLD WIDE WEB: *several useful WWW addresses*

WY *abbr.* (in writing) Wyoming

WYSIWYG /ˈwɪziˌwɪg/ *abbr.* (*computing*) what you see is what you get (what you see on the computer screen is exactly the same as what will be printed)

t tea   ṭ butter   d did   k cat   g got   tʃ chin   dʒ June   f fall

Xx

X /ɛks/ *noun, symbol*
● *noun* also **x** (*pl.* **Xs, X's, x's** /'ɛksəz/) **1** [C, U] the 24th letter of the English alphabet: *"Xylophone" begins with (an) X/"X."* **2** [U] (*mathematics*) used to represent a number whose value is not mentioned: *The equation is impossible for any value of x greater than 2.* **3** [U] a person, a number, an influence, etc. that is not known or not named: *Let's suppose X knows what Y is doing.* ➔ see also X CHROMOSOME, X-RATED, X-RAY
● *symbol* **1** also **x** the number 10 in ROMAN NUMERALS **2** used to represent a kiss at the end of a letter, etc.: *Love from Kathy xxx.* **3** used to show a vote for someone in an election: *Write an X beside the candidate of your choice.* **4** used to show that a written answer is wrong **5** used to show position, for example on a map: *X marks the spot.* **6** used in the past to show that no one younger than 17 was allowed to see a particular movie; now used in an unofficial way to describe a movie that contains a lot of sex ➔ compare NC-17

'X ˌchromosome *noun* (*biology*) a SEX CHROMOSOME. Two X chromosomes exist in the cells of human females. In human males each cell has one X chromosome and one Y chromosome.

xe·non /'zinɑn; 'zɛ-/ *noun* [U] (*symb.* **Xe**) a chemical element. Xenon is a gas that is found in very small quantities in the air and is used in some special electric lamps.

xen·o·pho·bi·a /ˌzɛnə'foʊbiə; ˌzinə-/ *noun* [U] (*disapproving*) a strong feeling of dislike or fear of people from other countries: *a campaign against racism and xenophobia*
► **xen·o·pho·bic** /-'foʊbɪk/ *adj.*

xen·o·trans·plan·ta·tion /ˌzɛnəˌtrænsplæn'teɪʃn; ˌzinə-/ *noun* [U] (*medical*) the process of taking organs from animals and putting them into humans for medical purposes

Xerox™ /'zɪrɑks/ *noun* a process for producing copies of letters, documents, etc. using a special machine; a copy made using this process: *a Xerox machine*

xerox /'zɪrɑks/ *verb* ~ **sth** to make a copy of a letter, document, etc. by using Xerox™ or a similar process **SYN** PHOTOCOPY: *Could you xerox this letter, please?*

'X ˌfac·tor *noun* [sing.] a special quality, especially one that is essential for success and is difficult to describe: *She certainly has the X factor that all great singers have.*

Xho·sa /'koʊsə/ *noun* [U] a language spoken by the Xhosa people in South Africa

xi /zaɪ; ksaɪ/ *noun* the 14th letter of the Greek alphabet (Ξ, ξ)

Xi·ang (also **Hsi·ang**) /ʃi'ɑŋ/ *noun* [U] a form of Chinese spoken mainly in Hunan

XL *abbr.* (in writing) extra large (used for sizes of things, especially clothes): *an XL T-shirt*

Xmas /'krɪsməs; 'ɛksməs/ *noun* [C, U] (*informal*) used as a short form of "Christmas," usually in writing: *A merry Xmas to all our readers!*

XML /ˌɛks ɛm 'ɛl/ *abbr.* (*computing*) Extensible Mark-up Language (a system used for marking the structure of text on a computer, for example when creating Web site pages)

'X-ˌrated *adj.* (especially of a movie) not considered suitable for children and young people because it contains sex and/or violence

X-ray /'ɛks reɪ/ *noun, verb*
● *noun* **1** [usually pl.] a type of RADIATION that can pass through objects that are not transparent and make it possible to see inside them: *an X-ray machine* (= one that produces X-rays) **2** a photograph made by X-rays, especially one showing bones or organs in the body: *a chest X-ray* ◆ *The doctor studied the X-rays of her lungs.* ◆ *to take an X-ray* **3** a medical examination using X-rays: *I had to go for an X-ray.*
● *verb* ~ **sth** to photograph and examine bones and organs inside the body, using X-rays: *He had to have his chest X-rayed.*

XS *abbr.* (in writing) extra small (used for sizes of things, especially clothes)

xy·lem /'zaɪləm/ *noun* [U] (*biology*) the material in plants that carries water and minerals upward from the root ➔ compare PHLOEM

xy·lo·phone /'zaɪlə.foʊn/ *noun* a musical instrument made of two rows of wooden bars of different lengths that you hit with two small sticks ➔ picture at INSTRUMENT ➔ compare GLOCKENSPIEL

Y y

Y /waɪ/ *noun, abbr.*
- *noun* also **y** (*pl.* **Ys, Y's, y's** /waɪz/) **1** [C, U] the 25th letter of the English alphabet: *"Year" begins with (a) Y/"Y."* **2** [U] (*mathematics*) used to represent a number whose value is not mentioned: *Can the value of y be predicted from the value of x?* **3** [U] a person, a number, an influence, etc. that is not known or not named: *Let's suppose X knows what Y is doing.* ⊃ see also Y CHROMOSOME
- *abbr.* **the Y** (*informal*) = YMCA, YWCA
- *symbol* the symbol for the chemical element YTTRIUM

-y /i/ *suffix* **1** (also **-ey, -ie**) (in adjectives) full of; having the quality of: *dusty* ♦ *cakey* ♦ *girlie* **2** (in adjectives) tending to: *runny* ♦ *sticky* **3** (in nouns) the action or process of: *inquiry* **4** (also **-ie**) (in nouns, showing affection): *daddy* ♦ *doggie*

ya /jə/ *pron., det.* (*informal, non-standard*) used in writing as a way of showing the way people sometimes pronounce the word "you" or "your": *He said, "I got something for ya."* ♦ *See ya later!*

yacht /jɑt/ *noun* a large sailing boat, often also with an engine and a place to sleep on board, used for pleasure trips and racing: *a yacht club/race* ♦ *a motor yacht* ♦ *a luxury yacht* ⊃ picture at BOAT ⊃ compare DINGHY, SAILBOAT

yacht·ing /ˈjɑtɪŋ/ *noun* [U] the sport or activity of sailing or racing yachts

yachts·man /ˈjɑtsmən/, **yachts·wom·an** /ˈjɑtsˌwʊmən/ *noun* (*pl.* **yachts·men** /-mən/, **yachts·wom·en** /-ˌwɪmən/) a person who sails a yacht for pleasure or as a sport: *a round-the-world yachtsman*

yad·da yad·da yad·da (also **yad·a yad·a yad·a**) /ˌjɑdə ˈjɑdə ˈjɑdə/ *exclamation* (*informal*) used when you are talking about something to show that some of the details are not worth saying because they are not important or are boring or obvious: *His new girlfriend is attractive, funny, smart, yadda yadda yadda.*

ya·hoo *noun, exclamation*
- *noun* /ˈjɑhu/ (*pl.* **ya·hoos**) (*disapproving*) a rude, noisy, or violent person
- *exclamation* /jɑˈhu/ (*informal*) used to show that you are very happy: *Yahoo, we did it!*

Yah·weh /ˈjɑweɪ/ *noun* = JEHOVAH

yak /jæk/ *noun, verb*
- *noun* an animal of the cow family, with long horns and long hair, that lives in central Asia
- *verb* (**-kk-**) (also **yack**) [I] (*informal, often disapproving*) to talk continuously about things that are not very serious or important: *She just kept yakking on.*

ya·ku·za (also **Ya·ku·za**) /ˈjɑkuˌzɑ; -zə/ *noun* often **the ya·ku·za** [sing.] a secret organization of criminals in Japan that is similar to the MAFIA: *The yakuza is involved in gambling and sports.*

y'all /jɔl/ *pron.* = YOU-ALL

yam /jæm/ *noun* [C, U] the large root of a tropical plant that is cooked as a vegetable ⊃ picture at FRUIT

yam·mer /ˈjæmər/ *verb* [I] ~ **(on/away) (about sth)** (*informal*) to talk continuously, especially in an annoying way: *He was yammering on about his new job.*

yang /jæŋ/ *noun* [U] (from *Chinese*) (in Chinese philosophy) the bright active male principle of the universe ⊃ compare YIN

Yank /jæŋk/ *noun* (also **Yan·kee**) *noun* (*informal, often disapproving*) a slightly offensive word for a person from the U.S.; an American

yank /jæŋk/ *verb* [T, I] (*informal*) to pull something or someone hard, quickly and suddenly: ~ **sth/sb (+ adv./prep.)** *He yanked her to her feet.* ♦ ~ **sth (+ adj.)** *I yanked the door open.* ♦ **(+ adv./prep.)** *Liz yanked at my arm.* ▶ **yank** *noun*: *She gave the rope a yank.*

Yan·kee /ˈjæŋki/ *noun* **1** a person who comes from or lives in any of the northern states of the U.S., especially New England **2** a soldier who fought for the Union (= the northern states) in the American Civil War **3** (*informal*) = YANK

yap /jæp/ *verb* (**-pp-**) **1** [I] ~ **(at sb/sth)** (especially of small dogs) to BARK a lot, making a high, sharp, and usually irritating sound: *The dogs yapped at his heels.* ♦ *yapping dogs* **2** [I] (*informal*) to talk in a silly, noisy, and usually irritating way ▶ **yap** *noun*

yard /jɑrd/ *noun*
1 a piece of land next to or around your house where you can grow flowers, fruit, vegetables, etc., usually with an area of grass (called a LAWN) ⊃ see also BACKYARD **2** (*abbr.* **yd.**) a unit for measuring length, equal to 3 feet (36 inches) or 0.9144 of a meter **3** an area outside a building, usually with a hard surface and a surrounding wall: *the prison yard* ♦ *The children were playing in the yard at the front of the school.* ⊃ see also BACKYARD **4** (usually in compounds) an area of land used for a special purpose or business: *a boat yard* **HELP** You will find other compounds ending in **yard** at their place in the alphabet. ⊃ thesaurus box at FACTORY **5** (*technical*) a long piece of wood fastened to a MAST that supports a sail on a boat or ship **IDM** see NINE

yard·age /ˈjɑrdɪdʒ/ *noun* [C, U] (*technical*) **1** size measured in yards or square yards **2** (in football) the number of yards that a team or player has moved forward

yard·arm /ˈjɑrdɑrm/ *noun* (*technical*) either end of the long piece of wood fastened to a ship's MAST that supports a sail

yard·bird /ˈjɑrdbərd/ *noun* (*informal*) **1** a soldier of low rank, especially one who does outdoor tasks **2** someone who is in prison

yard sale *noun* a sale of things from someone's house, held in their yard ⊃ see also GARAGE SALE, RUMMAGE SALE, TAG SALE

yard·stick /ˈjɑrdstɪk/ *noun* **1** a ruler for measuring one yard **2** a standard used for judging how good or successful something is: *a yardstick by which to measure something* ♦ *Exam results are not the only yardstick of a school's performance.*

yard·work /ˈjɑrdwərk/ *noun* the work involved in taking care of the plants, trees, paths, etc. in your yard

yar·mul·ke (also **yar·mul·ka**) /ˈjɑməkə; ˈjɑrməlkə/ (also **kip·pa**) *noun* a small round cap worn on top of the head by Jewish men; a type of SKULLCAP

yarn /jɑrn/ *noun* **1** [U] thread that has been spun, used for KNITTING, making cloth, etc. ⊃ picture at HOBBY **2** [C] (*informal*) a long story, especially one that is exaggerated or invented: *He used to spin yarns* (= tell stories) *about his time in the army.* **IDM** see PITCH v.

yar·row /ˈjæroʊ/ *noun* [U, C] a plant with flat groups of many small white or pink flowers that have a strong smell

yash·mak /jɑʃˈmɑk; ˈjɑʃmæk/ *noun* a piece of cloth covering most of the face, worn by some Muslim women

yaw /jɔ/ *verb* [I] (*technical*) (of a ship or plane) to turn to one side, away from a straight course, in an unsteady way ▶ **yaw** *noun* [C, U]

yawl /jɔl/ *noun* **1** a type of boat with sails **2** a ROWBOAT carried on a ship

yawn /jɔn/ *verb, noun*
- *verb* **1** [I] to open your mouth wide and breathe in deeply through it, usually because you are tired or bored: *He stood up, stretched and yawned.* **2** [I] (of a large hole or an empty space) to be very wide and often frightening and difficult to get across **SYN** GAPE: *A crevasse yawned at their feet.*

♦ (*figurative*) *There's a **yawning gap** between rich and poor.*
● **noun 1** an act of yawning: *She stifled another yawn and tried hard to look interested.* **2** [usually sing.] (*informal*) a boring event, idea, etc.: *The meeting was one big yawn from start to finish.*

yaws /jɔːz/ *noun* [U] a tropical skin disease that causes large red swellings

yay /jeɪ/ *exclamation, adv.* (*informal*)
● **exclamation** used to show that you are very pleased about something: *I won! Yay!*
● **adv. 1** to this degree **SYN** SO: *The fish I caught was yay big.* **2** to a high degree **SYN** EXTREMELY: *Yay good movie!*

'Y ˌchromosome *noun* (*biology*) a SEX CHROMOSOME. In human males each cell has one X chromosome and one Y chromosome. In human females there is never a Y chromosome.

yd. *abbr.* (*pl.* **yds.**) YARD: *12 yds. of silk*

ye *pron., det.*
● **pron.** /jiː/ (*old use* or *dialect*) a word meaning "you," used when talking to more than one person: *Gather ye rosebuds while ye may.*
● **det.** /jiː; ðiː; ðə/ a word meaning "the," used in the names of bars, shops, etc. to make them seem old: *Ye Olde Sweet Shoppe*

yea /jeɪ/ *adv., noun* (*old use* or *politics*) yes: *How many senators voted yea on the bill?* ⟳ compare NAY

yeah 🔊 /jɛə/ *exclamation* (*informal*)
yes
IDM **oh yeah?** used when you are commenting on what someone has just said: *"We're off to France soon." "Oh yeah? When's that?"* ♦ *"I'm going to be rich one day." "Oh yeah?"* (= I don't believe you.) **yeah, right** used to say that you do not believe what someone has just said, disagree with it, or are not interested in it: *"You'll be fine." "Yeah, right."*

year 🔊 /jɪr/ *noun* (*abbr.* **yr.**)
1 (also ˌcalendar 'year) [C] the period from January 1 to December 31, that is 365 or 366 days, divided into 12 months: *in the year 1865* ♦ *I lost my job earlier this year.* ♦ *Elections take place every year.* ♦ *The museum is open all year round* (= during the whole year). ⟳ see also LEAP YEAR, NEW YEAR **2** [C] a period of 12 months, measured from any particular time: *It's exactly a year since I started working here.* ♦ *She gave up teaching three years ago.* ♦ *in the first year of their marriage* ♦ *the prewar/war/postwar years* (= the period before/during/after the war) ♦ *I have happy memories of my years in Paris* (= the time I spent there). ⟳ see also GAP YEAR, LIGHT YEAR, OFF YEAR **3** [C] a period of 12 months connected with a particular activity: *the academic/school year* ♦ *the tax year* ⟳ see also FISCAL YEAR **4** [C, usually pl.] age; time of life: *He was 14 years old when it happened.* ♦ *She looks young for her years.* ♦ *They were both only 20 years of age.* ♦ *a twenty-year-old man* ♦ *He died in his sixtieth year.* ♦ *She's getting on in years* (= is no longer young). **5** years [pl.] (*informal*) a long time: *It's years since we last met.* ♦ *They haven't seen each other for years.* ♦ *That's the best movie I've seen in years.* ♦ *We've had a lot of fun over the years.*
IDM **man, woman, car, etc. of the year** a person or thing that people decide is the best in a particular field in a particular year **not/never in a hundred, etc. years** (*informal*) used to emphasize that you will/would never do something: *I'd never have thought of that in a million years.* **put years on sb** to make someone feel or look older **take years off sb** to make someone feel or look younger **year after year** every year for many years **year by year** as the years pass; each year: *Year by year their affection for each other grew stronger.* **(the) year one** (*informal*) a very long time ago: *I've been going there every summer since the year one.* **year in, year out** every year **year of grace** | **year of our Lord** (*formal*) any particular year after the birth of Christ **year on year** (used especially when talking about figures, prices, etc.) each year, compared with the last year:

Spending has increased year on year. ♦ *a year-on-year increase in spending* ⟳ more at ADVANCED, DECLINE, TURN *n.*

year·book /'yɪrbʊk/ *noun* **1** a book that is produced by the senior class in a school or college, containing photographs of students and details of school activities **2** a book published once a year, giving details of events, etc. of the previous year, especially those connected with a particular area of activity

ˌyear 'end (also ˌyear's 'end) *noun* [U] the end of the year: *We will discuss additional budget cuts at year end* ▸ 'year-end *adj.* [only before noun]: *year-end donations to charity*

year·ling /'yɪrlɪŋ/ *noun* an animal, especially a horse, between one and two years old

year-long *adj.* [only before noun] continuing for a whole year: *a year-long dispute*

year·ly /'yɪrli/ *adj.* **1** happening once a year or every year: *Pay is reviewed on a yearly basis.* **2** paid, valid, or calculated for one year: *yearly income/interest* ▸ **year·ly** *adv.*: *The magazine is issued twice yearly* (= twice every year).

yearn /yɜrn/ *verb* [I] (*literary*) to want something very much, especially when it is very difficult to get **SYN** LONG: **~ (for sth/sb)** *The people yearned for peace.* ♦ *There was a yearning look in his eyes.* ♦ **~ to do sth** *She yearned to escape from her office job.*

yearn·ing /'yɜrnɪŋ/ *noun* [C, U] (*formal*) a strong and emotional desire **SYN** LONGING: **~ (for sb/sth)** *a yearning for a quiet life* ♦ **~ (to do sth)** *She had no great yearning to go back.* ▸ **yearn·ing·ly** *adv.*

ˌyear-'round *adj.* all through the year: *an island with year-round sunshine*

yeast /yist/ *noun* [U, C] a FUNGUS used in making beer and wine, or to make bread rise ▸ **yeast·y** *adj.*: *a yeasty smell*

'yeast inˌfection *noun* an infectious disease that affects the VAGINA

yech (also **yecch**) /yʌx; yɛx; yʌk; yɛk/ *exclamation* (*informal*) used to show that you think something is disgusting or unpleasant **SYN** YUCK: *This tastes like dog food! Yech!*

yell /yɛl/ *verb, noun*
● **verb** [I, T] to shout loudly, for example because you are angry, excited, frightened, or in pain: **~ (at sb/sth)** *He yelled at the other driver.* ♦ **~ at sb to do sth** *She yelled at the child to get down from the wall.* ♦ **~ with sth** *They yelled with excitement.* ♦ **~ out (in sth)** *She yelled out in pain.* ♦ + **speech** *"Be careful!" he yelled.* ♦ **~ sth (at sb/sth)** *The crowd yelled encouragement at the players.* ♦ **~ out sth** *He yelled out her name.* ⟳ thesaurus box at SHOUT
● **noun 1** a loud cry of pain, excitement, etc.: *to let out/give a yell* ♦ *a yell of delight* **2** an organized shout of support for a team at a sports event

yel·low 🔊 /'yɛloʊ/ *adj., noun, verb*
● **adj.** (**yel·low·er, yel·low·est**) **1** having the color of lemons or butter: *pale yellow flowers* ♦ *a bright yellow rain jacket* **2** (*informal, disapproving*) easily frightened **SYN** COWARDLY ▸ **yel·low·ness** *noun* [U, sing.]
● **noun** [U, C] the color of lemons or butter: *She was dressed in yellow.* ♦ *the reds and yellows of the trees*
● **verb** [I, T] **~ (sth)** to become yellow; to make something become yellow

ˌyellow-ˌbelly *noun* (*old-fashioned, informal, disapproving*) a COWARD (= someone who is not brave) ▸ **ˌyellow-ˌbellied** *adj.* [usually before noun]

ˌyellow 'card *noun* (in SOCCER) a card shown by the REFEREE to a player as a warning about bad behavior ⟳ compare RED CARD

ˌyellow 'fever *noun* [U] an infectious tropical disease that makes the skin turn yellow and often causes death

yel·low·fin /'yɛloʊˌfɪn/ *noun* (*pl.* **yel·low·fin** or **yel·low·fins**) (also ˌyellowfin 'tuna) [C, U] a type of TUNA (= a large sea fish used for food) that has yellow FINS on its back

ˌyellow 'flag *noun* **1** a yellow flag on a ship showing that someone has or may have an infectious disease **2** a type of yellow IRIS (= a flower) that grows near water

yel·low·ish /ˈjɛlouʃ/ (also *less frequent* **yel·low·y** /ˈjɛloui/) *adj.* fairly yellow in color: *The paper had a yellowish tinge because it was so old.*

ˈyellow ˈjacket (also **yel·low·jack·et**) /ˈjɛlouˌdʒækət/ *noun* a type of small WASP (= a black and yellow flying insect)

ˌyellow ˈjournalism *noun* [U] newspaper reports that are exaggerated and written to shock readers **ORIGIN** From a comic strip *The Yellow Kid* that was printed in yellow ink to attract readers' attention.

ˈYellow ˈPages (also **ˈyellow ˌpages**) *noun* [pl.] a book with yellow pages that gives a list of companies and organizations and their telephone numbers, arranged according to the type of services they offer

ˌyellow ˈribbon *noun* a piece of yellow material that someone ties around a tree as a sign that they are thinking about someone who has gone away, especially a soldier fighting in a war, or someone taken as a HOSTAGE or prisoner, and that they hope that the person will soon return safely

yelp /jɛlp/ *verb* [I, T] **(+ speech)** to give a sudden short cry, usually of pain: *She yelped when I stepped on her foot.* ▶ **yelp** *noun*

yen /jɛn/ *noun* **1** (*pl.* **yen**) [C] the unit of money in Japan **2 the yen** [sing.] (*finance*) the value of the yen compared with the value of the money of other countries **3** [C, usually sing.] **~ (for sth/to do sth)** a strong desire **SYN** LONGING: *I've always had a yen to travel around the world.*

yeo·man /ˈjoumən/ *noun* (*pl.* **yeo·men** /-mən/) **1** an officer in the navy who does mainly office work **2** (in the past) a farmer who owned and worked on his land

yeow /yiˈau; yau/ *exclamation* (*informal*) used to express sudden pain

yep /jɛp/ (also **yup**) *exclamation* (*informal*) used to say "yes": *"Are you ready?" "Yep."*

yer /yər/ *pron., det.* (*informal, non-standard*) used in writing as a way of showing the way people sometimes pronounce the word "you" or "your": *See yer when I get back.* ♦ *What's yer name?*

yes 🔊 /yɛs/ *exclamation, noun*
● *exclamation* **1** used to answer a question and say that something is correct or true: *"Is this your car?" "Yes, it is."* ♦ *"Are you coming? Yes or no?"* **2** used to show that you agree with what has been said: *"I enjoyed her latest novel." "Yes, me too."* ♦ *"It's an excellent hotel." "Yes, but (= I don't completely agree) it's too expensive."* **3** used to disagree with something negative that someone has just said: *"I've never met her before." "Yes, you have."* **4** used to agree to a request or to give permission: *"Dad, can I borrow the car?" "Yes, but be careful."* ♦ *We're hoping that they will say yes to our proposals.* **5** used to accept an offer or invitation: *"Would you like a drink?" "Yes, please/thanks."* **6** used for asking someone what they want: *Yes? How can I help you?* **7** used for replying politely when someone calls you: *"Waiter!" "Yes, sir?"* **8** used to show that you have just remembered something: *Where did I put the keys? Oh, yes—in my pocket!* **9** used to encourage someone to continue speaking: *"I'm going to Paris this weekend." "Yes…"* **10** used to show that you do not believe what someone has said: *"Sorry I'm late—the bus didn't come." "Oh yes?"* **11** used to emphasize what you have just said: *Mrs. Smith has just won $2 million—yes!—$2 million!* **12** used to show that you are excited or extremely pleased about something that you have done or something that has happened: *"They've scored another goal." "Yes!!"* **13 yes, yes** used to show that you are impatient or irritated about something: *"Hurry up—it's late." "Yes, yes—I'm coming."*
IDM **yes and no** used when you cannot give a clear answer to a question: *"Are you enjoying it?" "Yes and no."*
● *noun* (*pl.* **yes·ses** or **yes·es** /ˈyɛsəz/) an answer that shows that you agree with an idea, a statement, etc.; a person who

says "yes": *I need a simple yes or no to my questions.* ♦ *There will be two ballot boxes—one for yesses and one for noes.* ♦ *I'll put you down as a yes.*

ye·shi·va /yəˈʃivə/ *noun* a college or school for Orthodox Jews

ˈyes-man *noun* (*pl.* **ˈyes-men** /-mɛn/) (*disapproving*) a person who always agrees with people in authority in order to gain their approval

ˌyes-ˈno ˌquestion *noun* (*grammar*) a question to which the answer can be either "yes" or "no," for example "Do you like dogs?" ⊃ compare WH-QUESTION

yes·sir /ˈyɛsər/ *exclamation* (*informal*) used to emphasize your opinion or say that you agree very strongly: *Yessir, she was beautiful.*

yes·ter·day 🔊 /ˈyɛstərˌdei; -di/ *adv., noun, adj.*
● *adv.* on the day before today: *They arrived yesterday.* ♦ *I can remember our wedding as if it were yesterday.* ♦ *Where were you yesterday morning?* ♦ *To think I was lying on a beach only **the day before yesterday**.* **IDM** see BORN
● *noun* [U] **1** the day before today: *Yesterday was Sunday.* ♦ *What happened at yesterday's meeting?* **2** (also **yes·ter·days** [pl.]) the recent past: *Yesterday's students are today's employees.* ♦ *All her yesterdays had vanished without a trace.* ♦ *This is already yesterday's news* (= no longer of interest).
● *adj.* [not before noun] (*informal, often humorous*) no longer fashionable or new: *E-mail—that's so yesterday!*

yes·ter·year /ˈyɛstərˌyir/ *noun* [U] (*old-fashioned* or *literary*) the past, especially a time when attitudes and ideas were different: *the Hollywood stars of yesteryear*

yet 🔊 /yɛt/ *adv., conj.*
● *adv.* **1** used in negative sentences and questions to talk about something that has not happened but that you expect to happen: *I haven't received a letter from him yet.* ♦ *I didn't receive a letter from him yet.* ♦ *"Are you ready?" "No, not yet."* ♦ *We have yet to decide what action to take* (= We have not decided what action to take). ⊃ note at ALREADY **2** (used in negative sentences) now; as soon as this: *Don't go yet.* ♦ *We don't need to start yet.* **3** from now until the period of time mentioned has passed: *He'll be busy for ages yet.* ♦ *They won't arrive for at least two hours yet.* **4 could, might, may, etc. do something ~** used to say that something could, might, etc. happen in the future, even though it seems unlikely: *We may win yet.* ♦ (*formal*) *She could yet surprise us all.* **5 the best, longest, etc. something ~ (done)** the best, longest, etc. thing of its kind made, produced, written, etc. until now/then: *the most comprehensive study yet of his music* ♦ *It was the highest building yet constructed.* **6 ~ another/more | ~ again** used to emphasize an increase in number or amount or the number of times something happens: *snow, snow and yet more snow* ♦ *yet another diet book* ♦ *Prices were cut yet again* (= once more, after many other times). **7 ~ worse, more importantly, etc.** used to emphasize an increase in the degree of something (= how bad, important, etc. it is) **SYN** EVEN, STILL: *a recent and yet more improbable theory*
IDM **as yet** until now or until a particular time in the past: *an as yet unpublished report* ♦ *As yet little was known of the causes of the disease.*
● *conj.* despite what has just been said **SYN** NEVERTHELESS: *It's a small car, yet it's surprisingly spacious.* ♦ *He has a good job, and yet he never seems to have any money.*

yet·i /ˈyɛti/ (also **Aˌbominable ˈSnowman**) *noun* a large creature with a BEAR or a man covered with hair, that some people believe lives in the Himalayan mountains

yew /yu/ *noun* **1** [C, U] (also **ˈyew tree**) a small tree with dark green leaves and small red berries (BERRY) **2** [U] the wood of the yew tree

YHA /ˌwai eitʃ ˈei/ *abbr.* Youth Hostels Association (an organization that exists in many countries and provides cheap places to stay for young people)

Yid·dish /ˈyidiʃ/ *noun* [U] a language, originally used by Jews in central and eastern Europe, based on a form of

ʌ **cup**   ə **about**   eɪ **say**   aɪ **five**   ɔɪ **boy**   aʊ **now**   oʊ **go**   ər **bird**

German with words from Hebrew and several modern languages ▶ **Yiddish** *adj.*

yield /yild/ *verb, noun*

● *verb* **1** [T] **~ sth** to produce or provide something, for example a profit, result, or crop: *Higher-rate deposit accounts yield good returns.* ♦ *The research has yielded useful information.* ♦ *trees that no longer yield fruit* **2** [I] to stop resisting something or someone; to agree to do something that you do not want to do **SYN** GIVE WAY: *After a long siege, the town was forced to yield.* ♦ **~ to sth/sb** *He reluctantly yielded to their demands.* ♦ *I yielded to temptation and had a chocolate bar.* **3** [T] **~ sth/sb (up) (to sb)** *(formal)* to allow someone to win; to have or take control of something that has been yours until now **SYN** SURRENDER: *He refused to yield up his gun.* ♦ *(figurative) The universe is slowly yielding up its secrets.* **4** [I] to move, bend, or break because of pressure: *Despite our attempts to break it, the lock would not yield.* **5** [I] **~ (to sb/sth)** to allow vehicles on a bigger road to go first: *Yield to oncoming traffic.* ♦ *a yield sign*

PHR V 'yield to sth *(formal)* to be replaced by something: *Barges yielded to road vehicles for transporting goods.*

● *noun* [C, U] the total amount of crops, profits, etc. that are produced: *a high crop yield* ♦ *a reduction in milk yield* ♦ *This will give a yield of 10% on your investment.*

yield·ing /ˈyildɪŋ/ *adj. (formal)* **1** (of a substance) soft and easy to bend or move when you press it **2** (of a person) willing to do what other people want **3** (used with an adverb) giving the amount of crops, profits, etc. mentioned: *high/low yielding crops*

yikes /yaɪks/ *exclamation (informal)* used to show that you are surprised or suddenly afraid

yin /yɪn/ *noun* [U] *(from Chinese)* (in Chinese philosophy) the dark, not active, female principle of the universe ⊃ compare YANG

yip·pee /ˈyɪpi; yɪˈpi/ *exclamation (old-fashioned, informal)* used to show that you are pleased or excited

y·lang-y·lang (also **i·lang-i·lang**) /ˌilɑŋ ˈilɑŋ/ *noun* **1** [U] an oil from the flowers of a tropical tree, used in PERFUMES and AROMATHERAPY **2** [U, C] a tree with yellow flowers from which this oil is obtained

YMCA /ˌwaɪ ɛm si ˈeɪ/ (also *informal* **the Y**) *abbr.* Young Men's Christian Association (an organization that exists in many countries and provides a place to stay and social and sports activities): *We stayed at the YMCA.* ⊃ see also YWCA

yo /youˈ/ *exclamation (slang)* used in very informal situations to get someone's attention, or as a greeting when you meet someone, or as a response when someone calls your name: *Yo, Mike! Over here!*

yo·del /ˈyoudl/ *verb, noun*

● *verb* [I, T] **~ (sth)** to sing or call in the traditional Swiss way, changing your voice frequently between its normal level and a very high level

● *noun* a song or musical call in which someone yodels

yo·ga /ˈyougə/ *noun* [U] **1** a system of exercises for your body and for controlling your breathing, used by people who want to become fitter or to relax ⊃ picture at EXERCISE **2** a Hindu philosophy that teaches you how to control your body and mind in the belief that you can become united with the spirit of the universe in this way ▶ **yo·gic** /ˈyougɪk/ *adj.*: *yogic techniques*

yo·gi /ˈyougi/ *noun* (*pl.* **yo·gis**) an expert in, or teacher of, the philosophy of yoga

yo·gurt (also **yo·ghurt**) /ˈyougərt/ *noun* [U, C] a thick white liquid food, made by adding bacteria to milk, served cold and often flavored with fruit; an amount of this sold in a small pot: *natural yogurt* ♦ *There's a yogurt left if you're still hungry.* ♦ *a strawberry yogurt*

yoke /youk/ *noun, verb*

● *noun* **1** [C] a long piece of wood that is fastened across the necks of two animals, especially OXEN, so that they can pull heavy loads **2** [sing.] *(literary or formal)* rough treatment or something that restricts your freedom and makes your life

very difficult to bear: *the yoke of imperialism* **3** [C] a piece of wood that is shaped to fit across a person's shoulders so that they can carry two equal loads **4** [C] a part of a dress, skirt, etc. that fits around the shoulders or hips and from which the rest of the cloth hangs

● *verb* **1** to join two animals together with a yoke; to attach an animal to something with a yoke: **~ A and B together** *A pair of oxen, yoked together, was used.* ♦ **~ sth to sth** *an ox yoked to a plow* **2** [usually passive] **~ A and B together** | **~ sth to sth** *(formal)* to bring two people, countries, ideas, etc. together so that they are forced into a close relationship: *The Hong Kong dollar was yoked to the American dollar for many years.*

yo·kel /ˈyoukl/ *noun (often humorous)* if you call a person a **yokel**, you are saying that they do not have much education or understanding of modern life, because they come from the country

yolk /youk/ *noun* [C, U] the round yellow part in the middle of an egg: *Separate the whites from the yolks.*

Yom Kip·pur /ˌyoum kɪˈpur; ˌyam-; -ˈkɪpər/ *noun* [U] a Jewish religious holiday in September or October when people eat nothing all day and say prayers of PENITENCE, also known as the Day of Atonement

yon /yɑn/ *det., adv.*

● *det.* (*old use* or *dialect*) that: *There's an old farm over yon hill.*

● *adv.* **IDM** SEE HITHER

yon·der /ˈyɑndər/ *det.* (*old use* or *dialect*) that is over there; that you can see over there: *Let's rest under yonder tree.* ▶ **yonder** *adv.*: *Whose is that farm over yonder?*

yoo-hoo /ˈyu hu/ *exclamation (informal,* becoming *old-fashioned)* used to attract someone's attention, especially when they are some distance away

yore /yɔr/ *noun*

IDM of yore (*old use* or *literary*) long ago: *in days of yore*

York·shire ter·ri·er /ˌyɔrkʃər ˈtɛriər/ (also **York·ie** /ˈyɔrki/) *noun* a very small dog with long brown and gray hair

Yo·ru·ba /ˈyɔrəbə/ *noun* [U] a language spoken by the Yoruba people of S.W. Nigeria and Benin

you 🔑 /yə; *strong form* yu/ *pron.*

1 used as the subject or object of a verb or after a preposition to refer to the person or people being spoken or written to: *You said you knew the way.* ♦ *I thought she told you.* ♦ *Can I sit next to you?* ♦ *I don't think that hairstyle is you* (= it doesn't suit your appearance or personality). **2** used with nouns and adjectives to speak to someone directly: *You girls, stop talking!* ♦ *You stupid idiot!* **3** used for referring to people in general: *You learn a language better if you visit the country where it is spoken.* ♦ *It's a friendly place — people come up to you in the street and start talking.*

you-all /yu ˈɔl; yɔl/ (also **y'all**) *pron. (informal)* used especially in the southern U.S. to mean *you* when talking to more than one person: *Have you-all brought swimsuits?*

you'd /yəd; *strong form* yud/ *short form* **1** you had **2** you would

you-know-'what *pron. (informal)* used when you want to talk about something without mentioning its name, although the person you are speaking to knows what it is: *Our neighbor was finally arrested for you-know-what.*

you-know-'who *pron. (informal)* used when you want to avoid mentioning someone's name, although the person you are speaking to knows who it is: *You-know-who called me three times today.*

you'll /yəl; *strong form* yul; yʊl/ *short form* you will

young 🔑 /yʌŋ/ *adj., noun*

● *adj.* (**young·er** /ˈyʌŋgər/, **young·est** /ˈyʌŋgəst/) **1** having lived or existed for only a short time; not fully developed: *young babies* ♦ *a young country* ♦ *Caterpillars eat the young leaves of this plant.* ♦ *a young wine* ♦ *The night is still young* (= it has only just started). **ANT** OLD **2** not yet old; not as old as others: *young people* ♦ *talented young football players* ♦ *I am* the youngest of four sisters. ◆ *In his younger days* he played baseball for the Mets. ◆ *I met the young Bill Clinton at Georgetown.* ◆ *Her grandchildren keep her young.* ◆ *My son is thirteen, but he's young for his age* (= not as developed as other boys of the same age). ◆ *They married young* (= at an early age). ◆ *My mother died young.* **ANT** OLD **3** suitable or appropriate for young people **SYN** YOUTHFUL: *young fashion* ◆ *The clothes she wears are much too young for her.* **4** consisting of young people or young children; with a low average age: *They have a young family.* ◆ *a young audience* **5** ~ **man/lady** used to show that you are angry or annoyed with a particular young person: *I think you owe me an apology, young lady!* **6** **the younger** used before or after a person's name to distinguish them from an older relative: *the younger Kennedy* ◆ (*formal*) *William Pitt the Younger* ⟳ compare ELDER, JUNIOR

IDM **be getting younger** (*informal*) used to say that people seem to be doing something at a younger age than they used to, or that they seem younger because you are now older: *The band's fans are getting younger.* ◆ *Why do police officers seem to be getting younger?* **not be getting any younger** (*informal*) used when you are commenting that time is passing and that you, or someone else, is growing older **young at heart** thinking and behaving like a young person even when you are old ⟳ more at ONLY

● *noun* [pl.] **1** often **the young** young people considered as a group: *It's a movie that will appeal to the young.* ◆ *It's a book for young and old alike.* **2** young animals of a particular type or that belong to a particular mother: *a mother bird feeding her young*

young·ish /ˈyʌŋɪʃ/ *adj.* fairly young: *a youngish president*

young·ster /ˈyʌŋstər/ *noun* (*informal*) a young person or a child: *The camp is for youngsters aged 8 to 14.*

young thing *noun* (*informal*) a young adult: *bright young things working in the computer business*

young Turk /ˌyʌŋ ˈtərk/ *noun* (*old-fashioned*) a young person who wants great changes to take place in the established political system

your /yər; *strong form* yɔr; yʊr/ *det.* (the possessive form of *you*) **1** of or belonging to the person or people being spoken or written to: *I like your dress.* ◆ *Excuse me, is this your seat?* ◆ *The bank is on your right.* **2** of or belonging to people in general: *Dentists advise you to have your teeth checked every six months.* ◆ *In Japan you are taught great respect for your elders.* **3** (*informal*) used to show that someone or something is well known or often talked about: *This is your typical dive bar.* ◆ (*ironic, disapproving*) *You and your bright ideas!* **4** **Your** used in some titles, especially those of royal people: *Your Majesty* ◆ *Your Excellency*

you're /yər; *strong form* yɔr; yʊr/ *short form* you are

yours /yɔrz; yʊrz; yərz/ *pron.*
1 of or belonging to you: *Is that book yours?* ◆ *Is she a friend of yours?* ◆ *My hair is very fine. Yours is much thicker.* **2** usually **Yours** used at the end of a letter before signing your name: *Sincerely Yours* ◆ *Yours Truly*

your·self /yərˈsɛlf/ *pron.* (*pl.* **your·selves** /-ˈsɛlvz/) **1** (the reflexive form of *you*) used when the person or people being spoken to both cause and are affected by an action: *Did you hurt yourself?* ◆ *You don't seem like yourself today* (= you do not seem well or do not seem as happy as usual). ◆ *Enjoy yourselves!* **2** used to emphasize the fact that the person who is being spoken to is doing something: *Do it yourself—I don't have time.* ◆ *You can try it out for yourselves.* **3** (*informal, non-standard*) you: *We sell a lot of these to people like yourself.* ◆ *"And yourself," he replied, "How are you?"* **HELP** Yourself is sometimes used in this way as a polite way of saying "you," but some people think this is incorrect.

IDM **(all) by yourself/yourselves 1** alone; without anyone else: *How long were you by yourself in the house?* **2** without help: *Are you sure you did this work by yourself?* **(all) to yourself/yourselves** for only you to have, use, etc.: *I'm*

going to be away next week, so you'll have the office to yourself. **be yourself** to act naturally: *Don't try to act sophisticated — just be yourself.*

youse /yəz; *strong form* yuz/ *pron.* (*non-standard*) a word meaning "you," used when talking to more than one person

youth /yuθ/ *noun* (*pl.* **youths** /yuðz; yuθs/) **1** [U] the time of life when a person is young, especially the time before a child becomes an adult: *He had been a talented musician in his youth.* **2** [U] the quality or state of being young: *She brings to the job a rare combination of youth and experience.* **3** [C] (often *disapproving*) a young man: *The fight was started by a gang of youths.* **4** also **the youth** [pl.] young people considered as a group: *the nation's youth* ◆ *the youth of today* ◆ *youth culture* ◆ *youth unemployment*

youth club *noun* a club where young people can meet each other and take part in various activities

youth·ful /ˈyuθfl/ *adj.* **1** typical of young people: *youthful enthusiasm/energy/inexperience* **2** young or seeming younger than you are: *She's a very youthful 65.* ◆ *a youthful appearance* ▶ **youth·ful·ly** /-fəli/ *adv.* **youth·ful·ness** *noun* [U]

youth hostel *noun* a building that provides a cheap place to stay and meals, especially to young people who are traveling ⟳ collocations at TRAVEL

you've /yəv; *strong form* yuv/ *short form* you have

yowl /yaʊl/ *verb* [I] to make a long loud cry that sounds unhappy **SYN** WAIL ▶ **yowl** *noun*

yo-yo /ˈyoʊ yoʊ/ *noun, verb, adj.*
● *noun* (*pl.* **yo-yos**) a toy that consists of two round pieces of plastic or wood joined together, with a piece of string wound between them. You put one end of the string around your finger and make the yo-yo go up and down: *He kept bouncing up and down like a yo-yo.*
● *verb* [I] (+ **adv./prep.**) to change repeatedly in size, amount, quality, etc. from one extreme to another: *When I was young, my weight yo-yoed between 140 and 190 pounds.*
● *adj.* [only before noun] changing repeatedly in size, amount, quality, etc. from one extreme to another: *She worries about her pattern of yo-yo dieting.*

yr. *abbr.* **1** (*pl.* **yrs.**)YEAR: *children aged 4–11 yrs.* **2** YOUR

yt·ter·bi·um /ɪˈtərbiəm/ *noun* [U] (*symb.* **Yb**) a chemical element. Ytterbium is a silver-white metal used to make steel stronger and in some X-RAY machines.

yt·tri·um /ˈɪtriəm/ *noun* [U] (*symb.* **Y**) a chemical element. Yttrium is a gray-white metal used in MAGNETS.

yu·an /yuˈɛn; -ˈɑn/ *noun* (*pl.* **yu·an**) the unit of money in China ⟳ see also RENMINBI

yuc·ca /ˈyʌkə/ *noun* a tropical plant with long stiff pointed leaves on a thick straight STEM, often grown indoors

yuck (also **yuk**) /yʌk/ *exclamation* (*informal*) used to show that you think something is disgusting or unpleasant **SYN** YECH

yuck·y (also **yuk·ky**) /ˈyʌki/ *adj.* (*informal*) disgusting or very unpleasant: *yucky food*

Yue /yuˈeɪ/ /yuˈeɪ/ *noun* = CANTONESE

yuks /yʌks/ *noun* [pl.] (*informal*) loud laughs: *The comedian only got a few yuks.*

Yule /yul/ *noun* [C, U] (*old use* or *literary*) the festival of Christmas

yule log *noun* **1** a large LOG of wood traditionally burned on Christmas Eve **2** a chocolate cake in the shape of a LOG, traditionally eaten at Christmas

Yule·tide /ˈyultaɪd/ *noun* [U, C] (*old use* or *literary*) the period around Christmas Day: *Yuletide food and drink*

yum /yʌm/ (also **yum-ˈyum**) *exclamation* (*informal*) used to show that you think something tastes or smells very nice

yum·my /ˈyʌmi/ *adj.* (*informal*) very good to eat **SYN** DELICIOUS: *a yummy cake*

yup /yʌp/ *exclamation* = YEP

| t tea | t̬ butter | d did | k cat | g got | tʃ chin | dʒ June | f fall |

yup·pie (also **yup·py**) /ˈyʌpi/ *noun* (*pl.* **yup·pies**) (*informal, often disapproving*) a young professional person who lives in a city and earns a lot of money that they spend on expensive and fashionable things **ORIGIN** Formed from the first letters of the words "young urban professional."

yup·pi·fy /ˈyʌpəˌfaɪ/ *verb* (**yup·pi·fies, yup·pi·fy·ing, yup·pi·fied, yup·pi·fied**) [often passive] ~ **sth** (*informal, disapproving*) to make something such as an area of a city more expensive and fashionable, and attractive to yuppies: *a yuppified area of Brooklyn* ▶ **yup·pi·fi·ca·tion** /ˌyʌpəfə-ˈkeɪʃn/ *noun* [U]

yurt /yərt/ *noun* a type of traditional tent used in Mongolia and Siberia

YWCA /ˌwaɪ ˌdʌblyu si ˈeɪ; -ˌdʌblyə-/ (also *informal* **the Y**) *abbr.* Young Women's Christian Association (an organization that exists in many countries and provides a place to stay and social and sports activities): *members of the YWCA* ➔ **see also** YMCA

Zz

Z also **z** /zi/ noun (pl. Zs, Z's, z's /ziz/) **1** [C, U] the 26th and last letter of the English alphabet: *"Zebra" begins with (a) Z/"Z."* **2** Z's [pl.] (informal, humorous) sleep: *I need to catch some Z's.* **IDM** see A

zaf·tig /ˈzɑftɪg/ adj. (informal) (of a woman) slightly fat, in a way that is attractive **SYN** PLUMP

za·ny /ˈzeɪni/ adj. (za·ni·er, za·ni·est) (informal) strange or unusual in an amusing way **SYN** WACKY: *zany humor*

zap /zæp/ verb (-pp-) (informal) **1** [T] to destroy, kill, or hit someone or something suddenly and with force: *~ sb/sth The monster got zapped by a flying saucer* (= in a computer game). ♦ *It's vital to zap stress fast.* ♦ *~ sb/sth with sth He jumped like a man who'd been zapped with 1,000 volts.* **2** [I] **+ adv./prep.** to do something very fast: *I'm zapping through* (= reading very fast) *some modern novels at the moment.* **3** [I, T] *~ (sth)* to use the REMOTE CONTROL to change television channels quickly **4** [I, T] *~ (sb/sth) + adv./prep.* to move, or make someone or something move, very fast in the direction mentioned **SYN** ZIP: *The racing cars zapped past us.*

zap·per /ˈzæpər/ noun (informal) **1** = REMOTE CONTROL **2** a device or weapon that attacks or destroys something quickly: *a bug zapper*

zeal /zil/ noun [U, C] *~ (for/in sth)* (formal) great energy or enthusiasm connected with something that you feel strongly about: *her missionary/reforming/religious/political zeal*

zeal·ot /ˈzɛlət/ noun (often disapproving) a person who is extremely enthusiastic about something, especially religion or politics **SYN** FANATIC

zeal·ot·ry /ˈzɛlətri/ noun [U] (often disapproving) the attitude or behavior of a zealot: *religious zealotry*

zeal·ous /ˈzɛləs/ adj. (formal) showing great energy and enthusiasm for something, especially because you feel strongly about it: *a zealous reformer* ▸ **zeal·ous·ly** adv.

ze·bra /ˈzibrə/ noun (pl. ze·bra or ze·bras) an African wild animal like a horse with black and white stripes on its body

ze·bu /ˈzibu/ noun (pl. ze·bus or ze·bu) an animal of the cow family with long horns and a HUMP (= high part) on its back, kept on farms especially in hot climates

zeit·geist /ˈzaɪtgaɪst; ˈtsaɪt-/ noun [sing.] (from German, formal) the general mood or quality of a particular period of history, as shown by the ideas, beliefs, etc. common at the time **SYN** SPIRIT OF THE TIMES

Zen /zɛn/ noun [U] a Japanese form of Buddhism

ze·nith /ˈzinəθ/ noun **1** the highest point that the sun or moon reaches in the sky, directly above you **2** (formal) the time when something is strongest and most successful **SYN** PEAK **ANT** NADIR

zeph·yr /ˈzɛfər/ noun (old-fashioned or literary) a soft, gentle wind

Zep·pe·lin /ˈzɛpələn/ noun a German type of large AIRSHIP

ze·ro 🔑 /ˈzɪroʊ; ˈzɪroʊ/ number, verb
● **number 1** (pl. ze·ros) 0: *Five, four, three, two, one, zero… We have liftoff.* **2** a temperature, pressure, etc. that is equal to zero on a scale: *It was ten degrees below zero last night* (= −10°C). ♦ *The thermometer had fallen to zero.* **3** the lowest possible amount or level; nothing at all: *I rated my chances as zero.* ♦ *zero inflation*
● **verb** (ze·roes, ze·ro·ing, ze·roed, ze·roed) *~ sth* to turn an instrument, control, etc. to zero
  PHR V ,zero 'in on sb/sth **1** to fix all your attention on the person or thing mentioned: *They zeroed in on the key issues.* **2** to aim guns, etc. at the person or thing mentioned

,zero-'carbon adj. in which the amount of CARBON DIOXIDE produced has been reduced to nothing or is balanced by actions that protect the environment **SYN** CARBON NEUTRAL: *a zero-carbon house that uses no energy from external sources*

,zero 'gravity noun [U] (abbr. ,zero 'G) a state in which there is no GRAVITY, or where gravity has no effect, for example in space

,zero 'grazing noun [U] a farming method that involves keeping cows inside and bringing them cut grass, rather than letting them feed in the fields

'zero ,hour noun [U] the time when an important event, an attack, etc. is planned to start

,zero-sum 'game noun a situation in which what is gained by one person or group is lost by another person or group

,zero 'tolerance noun [U] the policy of applying laws very strictly so that people are punished even for offenses that are not very serious

zest /zɛst/ noun **1** [sing., U] *~ (for sth)* enjoyment and enthusiasm **SYN** APPETITE: *He had a great zest for life.* **2** [U, sing.] the quality of being exciting, interesting, and enjoyable: *The slight risk added zest to the experience.* **3** [U] the outer skin of an orange, a lemon, etc., when it is used to give flavor in cooking ⊃ compare PEEL, RIND, SKIN ▸ **zest·ful** /ˈzɛstfl/ adj. **zest·y** adj.

ze·ta /ˈzeɪtə/ noun the 6th letter of the Greek alphabet (Z, ζ)

zeug·ma /ˈzugmə/ noun [C, U] (technical) the use of a word which must be understood in two different ways at the same time in order to make sense, for example "The bread was baking, and so was I."

zig·gu·rat /ˈzɪgəˌræt/ noun in ancient Mesopotamia, a tower with steps going up the sides, sometimes with a TEMPLE at the top

zig·zag /ˈzɪgzæg/ noun, verb
● **noun** a line or pattern that looks like a series of letter W's as it bends to the left and then to the right again: *The path descended the hill in a series of zigzags.* ⊃ picture at LINE ▸ **zig·zag** adj. [only before noun]: *a zigzag line/path/pattern*
● **verb** (-gg-) [I] (+ adv./prep.) to move forward by making sharp sudden turns first to the left and then to the right: *The narrow path zigzags up the cliff.*

zilch /zɪltʃ/ noun [U] (informal) nothing: *I arrived in this country with zilch.*

zil·lion /ˈzɪljən/ noun (informal) a very large number: *There was a bunch of kids waiting and zillions of reporters.*

zinc /zɪŋk/ noun **1** [U] (symb. Zn) a chemical element. Zinc is a blue-white metal that is mixed with COPPER to produce BRASS and is often used to cover other metals to prevent them from RUSTING. **2** [C] (informal) a sheet of CORRUGATED IRON that is used to make a roof, shelter, etc.: *They built a temporary home out of zincs.*

,zinc 'oxide noun [U] (symb. ZnO) a substance used in creams as a treatment for certain skin conditions

'zine (also zine) /zin/ noun (informal) a magazine, especially a FANZINE

Zin·fan·del /ˈzɪnfənˌdɛl/ noun [U, C] a type of dry red or white wine from California

zing /zɪŋ/ verb, noun
● **verb** (informal) **1** [I, T] *~ (sth) + adv./prep.* to move or to make something move very quickly, often with a high whistling sound: *electrical pulses zinging down a wire* **2** [T] *~ sb/sth (for/on sth)* to criticize someone strongly
● **noun** [U] (informal) interest or excitement ▸ **zing·y** /ˈzɪŋi/ adj.

zing·er /'zɪŋər/ noun (informal) a smart or amusing remark that criticizes or insults someone: *She opened the speech with a real zinger.*

zin·ni·a /'zɪniə/ noun an American plant with brightly colored flowers

Zi·on·ism /'zaɪə,nɪzəm/ noun [U] a political movement that was originally concerned with establishing an independent state for Jewish people, and is now concerned with developing the state of Israel ▶ **Zi·on·ist** /'zaɪənɪst/ noun, adj.

zip /zɪp/ noun, verb
- **noun 1** [U] (informal) energy or speed **2** (also **zip·po**) [sing.] (informal) nothing: *We won four zip (4–0).* ♦ *He said zip all evening.*
- **verb** (-pp-) **1** [T] to fasten clothes, bags, etc. with a zipper: ~ **sth** *I zipped and buttoned my jacket.* ♦ ~ **sb/yourself into sth** *The children were safely zipped into their sleeping bags.* ♦ ~ **sth** + **adj.** *He zipped his case shut.* ⊃ compare UNZIP **2** [I] ~ **(up/together)** to be fastened with a zipper: *The sleeping bags can zip together.* **3** [I, T] ~ **(sth)** + **adv./prep.** (informal) to move very quickly or to make something move very quickly in the direction mentioned: *A sports car zipped past us.* **4** [T] ~ **sth** (computing) to COMPRESS a computer file (= make it smaller) **ANT** UNZIP
  PHRV **zip 'up** | **zip sb/sth 'up** to be fastened with a zipper; to fasten something with a zipper: *This jacket zips up right to the neck.* ♦ *Should I zip you up (= fasten your dress, etc.)?* ⊃ compare UNZIP

zip code noun also **ZIP code** a group of numbers that is used as part of an address so that mail can be separated into groups and delivered more quickly

zip file (also **ZIP file**) (also **zipped file**) noun a computer file that has been COMPRESSED (= made smaller) to make it easier to store and send

zip gun noun (informal) a simple gun that a person has made him or herself

Zip·lock (also **Zip·loc™**) /'zɪplɑk/ noun a small plastic bag for storing food, that has edges that seal when you press them together in order to keep the air out

zip·per /'zɪpər/ noun a thing that you use to fasten clothes, bags, etc. It consists of two rows of metal or plastic teeth that you can pull together to close something or pull apart to open it. ⊃ picture at CLOTHES

zip·po /'zɪpoʊ/ noun [sing.] (informal) = ZIP n. (2)

zip·py /'zɪpi/ adj. (zip·pi·er, zip·pi·est) (informal) **1** able to move very quickly: *a zippy little car* **2** lively and exciting, especially in flavor: *a wine with a zippy tang*

zir·co·ni·um /zər'koʊniəm/ noun [U] (symb. **Zr**) a chemical element. Zirconium is a hard silver-gray metal that does not CORRODE very easily.

zit /zɪt/ noun (informal) a spot on the skin, especially on the face **SYN** PIMPLE

zith·er /'zɪðər; 'zɪθər/ noun a musical instrument with a lot of metal strings stretched over a flat wooden box, that you play with your fingers or a PLECTRUM

zo·di·ac /'zoʊdi,æk/ noun **1 the zodiac** [sing.] the imaginary area in the sky in which the sun, moon, and planets appear to lie, and which has been divided into twelve equal parts each with a special name and symbol: *the signs of the zodiac* **2** [C] a diagram of these twelve parts, and signs that some people believe can be used to predict how the planets will influence our lives ▶ **zo·di·a·cal** /zoʊ'daɪəkl/ adj.

zom·bie /'zɑmbi/ noun **1** (informal) a person who seems only partly alive, without any feeling or interest in what is happening **2** (in some African and Caribbean religions and in horror stories) a dead body that has been made alive again by magic

zon·al /'zoʊnl/ adj. (technical) connected with zones; arranged in zones

zone 🔑 /zoʊn/ noun, verb
- **noun 1** an area or a region with a particular feature or use: *a security/demilitarized, etc. zone* ♦ *an earthquake/danger, etc. zone* ♦ *a pedestrian zone* (= where vehicles may not go) ⊃ see also NO-FLY ZONE, TIME ZONE, TWILIGHT **2** one of the areas that a larger area is divided into for the purpose of organization: *postal charges to countries in zone 2* **3** an area or a part of an object, especially one that is different from its surroundings: *When the needle enters the red zone, the engine is too hot.* ♦ *the erogenous zones of the body* ⊃ see also CRUMPLE ZONE **4** one of the parts that the earth's surface is divided into by imaginary lines that are parallel to the EQUATOR: *the northern/southern temperate zone*
  IDM **in the zone** (informal) in a state in which you feel confident and are performing at your best: *When I'm in the zone, writing is the most satisfying thing in the world.*
- **verb** [usually passive] **1** ~ **sth (for sth)** to keep an area of land to be used for a particular purpose: *The town center was zoned for office development.* **2** ~ **sth** to divide an area of land into smaller areas
  PHRV **zone 'out** (informal) to fall asleep, become unconscious, or stop paying attention: *Sorry, I just zoned out for a moment.*

zoned /zoʊnd/ adj. **1** divided into areas designed for a particular use: *zoned housing land* **2** (also **zoned 'out**) (informal) not behaving or thinking normally because you are tired or because of the effects of a drug such as MARIJUANA or alcohol

zon·ing /'zoʊnɪŋ/ noun [U] a system of laws restricting how particular areas of land can be used and what can be built on the land: *violation of the city's zoning laws* ♦ *zoning for residential use*

zonk /zɑŋk; zɔŋk/ verb (slang) **1** [I, T] to fall asleep quickly or become unconscious; to make someone do this: ~ **out** *After two drinks, I usually zonk out.* ♦ ~ **sb (out)** *Rowing always zonks me.* **2** [T] ~ **sb** to hit someone very hard: *The book fell and zonked me on the head.*

zonked /zɑŋkt; zɔŋkt/ adj. [not before noun] ~ **(out)** (slang) extremely tired or suffering from the effects of alcohol or drugs

zoo /zu/ noun (pl. zoos) (also formal **zoological 'garden**) a place where many kinds of wild animals are kept for the public to see and where they are studied, bred, and protected

zoo·keep·er /'zu,kipər/ noun a person who works in a zoo, taking care of the animals

zo·o·log·i·cal /,zoʊə'lɑdʒɪkl; ,zuə-/ adj. connected with the science of ZOOLOGY

zoological 'garden noun (formal) = ZOO

zo·ol·o·gist /zoʊ'ɑlədʒɪst; zu-/ noun a scientist who studies zoology

zo·ol·o·gy /zoʊ'ɑlədʒi; zu-/ noun [U] the scientific study of animals and their behavior ⊃ compare BIOLOGY, BOTANY

zoom /zum/ verb, noun
- **verb 1** [I] + **adv./prep.** to move or go somewhere very fast **SYN** RUSH, WHIZ: *Traffic zoomed past us.* ♦ *For five weeks they zoomed around Europe.* **2** [I] ~ **(up) (to…)** (of prices, costs, etc.) to increase a lot, quickly, and suddenly: *House prices have zoomed up this year.*
  PHRV **zoom 'in/'out** (of a camera) to show the object that is being photographed from closer/farther away, with the use of a ZOOM LENS: *The camera zoomed in on the actor's face.*
- **noun 1** [C] = ZOOM LENS: *a zoom shot* **2** [sing.] the sound of a vehicle moving very fast

zoom lens (also **zoom**) noun a camera LENS that you use to make the thing that you are photographing appear nearer to you or further away from you than it really is ⊃ picture at HOBBY

zoo·plank·ton /'zoʊə,plæŋktən/ noun [U] the very small forms of animal life that live in water and are part of PLANKTON

---

zoot suit /ˈzut sut/ *noun* a man's suit with wide pants and a long loose jacket with wide shoulders that was popular in the 1940s

zorb·ing /ˈzɔrbɪŋ/ *noun* [U] a sport in which someone is put inside a large transparent plastic ball that is then rolled along the ground or down hills

Zo·ro·as·tri·an·ism /ˌzɔroʊˈæstriəˌnɪzəm/ *noun* [U] a religion started in ancient Persia by Zoroaster, that teaches that there is one God and a continuing struggle in the world between forces of light and dark ▶ **Zo·ro·as·tri·an** /ˌzɔroʊˈæstriən/ *noun, adj.* ⊃ see also PARSEE

zuc·chi·ni /zuˈkini/ *noun* (*pl.* **zuc·chi·ni** or **zuc·chi·nis**) a long vegetable with dark green or yellow skin and white flesh ⊃ picture at FRUIT

Zu·lu /ˈzulu/ *noun* **1** [C] a member of a race of black people who live in South Africa **2** [U] the language spoken by Zulus and many other black South Africans ▶ **Zu·lu** *adj.*

Zu·ni /ˈzuni/ *noun* (*pl.* **Zu·ni** or **Zu·nis**) a member of a Native American people many of whom live in western New Mexico

zwie·back /ˈzwaɪbæk/ *noun* [U] (from *German*) slices of sweet bread that are cooked again until they are dry and hard

zy·de·co /ˈzaɪdəˌkoʊ/ *noun* [U] a type of dance music, originally played by black Americans in Louisiana

zy·gote /ˈzaɪɡoʊt/ *noun* (*biology*) a single cell that develops into a person or animal, formed by the joining together of a male and a female GAMETE (= a cell that is provided by each parent)

Reference Section Contents

Oxford Writing Tutor

Irregular Verbs

This appendix lists all the verbs with irregular forms that are included in the dictionary, except for the modal verbs (for example, **can**, **must**). Irregular forms that are only used in certain senses are marked with an asterisk (for example,*abode).

Full information on usage, pronunciation, etc. is given at the entry.

Infinitive	Past Tense	Past Participle	Infinitive	Past Tense	Past Participle
abide	abided, *abode	abided, *abode	cost	cost, *costed	cost, *costed
arise	arose	arisen	creep	crept, *creeped	crept, *creeped
awake	awoke	awoken	cut	cut	cut
babysit	babysat	babysat	deal	dealt	dealt
bear	bore	borne	dig	dug	dug
beat	beat	beaten	dive	dived, dove	dived
become	became	become	draw	drew	drawn
befall	befell	befallen	dream	dreamed,	dreamed,
beget	begot, *begat	begot,		dreamt	dreamt
		*begotten	drink	drank	drunk
begin	began	begun	drive	drove	driven
behold	beheld	beheld	dwell	dwelled, dwelt	dwelled, dwelt
bend	bent	bent	eat	ate	eaten
beseech	beseeched,	beseeched,	fall	fell	fallen
	besought	besought	feed	fed	fed
beset	beset	beset	feel	felt	felt
bespeak	bespoke	bespoken	fight	fought	fought
bet	bet, betted	bet	find	found	found
betake	betook	betaken	fit	fitted, fit	fitted, fit
bid¹	bid	bid	flee	fled	fled
bid²	bade, bid	bidden, bid	fling	flung	flung
bind	bound	bound	floodlight	floodlit	floodlit
bite	bit	bitten	fly	flew, *flied	flown, *flied
bleed	bled	bled	forbear	forbore	forborne
blow	blew	blown	forbid	forbade	forbidden
break	broke	broken	forecast	forecast,	forecast,
breastfeed	breastfed	breastfed		forecasted	forecasted
breed	bred	bred	foresee	foresaw	foreseen
bring	brought	brought	foretell	foretold	foretold
broadcast	broadcast,	broadcast,	forget	forgot	forgotten
	broadcasted	broadcasted	forgive	forgave	forgiven
browbeat	browbeat	browbeaten	forgo	forwent	forgone
build	built	built	forsake	forsook	forsaken
burn	burned, burnt	burned, burnt	forswear	forswore	forsworn
burst	burst	burst	freeze	froze	frozen
buy	bought	bought	gainsay	gainsaid	gainsaid
cast	cast	cast	get	got	got, gotten
catch	caught	caught	give	gave	given
choose	chose	chosen	go	went	gone, *been
cleave	cleaved, *cleft,	cleaved, *cleft,	grind	ground	ground
	*clove	*cloven	grow	grew	grown
cling	clung	clung	hamstring	hamstrung	hamstrung
come	came	come	hang	hung, *hanged	hung, *hanged

Infinitive	Past Tense	Past Participle	Infinitive	Past Tense	Past Participle
hear	heard	heard	overcome	overcame	overcome
heave	heaved, *hove	heaved, *hove	overdo	overdid	overdone
hew	hewed	hewed, hewn	overdraw	overdrew	overdrawn
hide	hid	hidden	overeat	overate	overeaten
hit	hit	hit	overfeed	overfed	overfed
hold	held	held	overfly	overflew	overflown
hurt	hurt	hurt	overhang	overhung	overhung
inlay	inlaid	inlaid	overhear	overheard	overheard
input	input, inputted	input, inputted	overlay	overlaid	overlaid
inset	inset	inset	overlie	overlay	overlain
intercut	intercut	intercut	overpay	overpaid	overpaid
interweave	interwove	interwoven	override	overrode	overridden
keep	kept	kept	overrun	overran	overrun
kneel	knelt, kneeled	knelt, kneeled	oversee	oversaw	overseen
knit	knitted, *knit	knitted, *knit	oversell	oversold	oversold
know	knew	known	overshoot	overshot	overshot
lay	laid	laid	oversleep	overslept	overslept
lead	led	led	overspend	overspent	overspent
leap	leaped, leapt	leaped, leapt	overtake	overtook	overtaken
leave	left	left	overthrow	overthrew	overthrown
lend	lent	lent	overwrite	overwrote	overwritten
let	let	let	partake	partook	partaken
lie¹	lay	lain	pay	paid	paid
light	lit, *lighted	lit, *lighted	plead	pleaded, pled	pleaded, pled
lose	lost	lost	preset	preset	preset
make	made	made	proofread	proofread	proofread
mean	meant	meant	/ˈpruːfriːd/	/ˈpruːfrɛd/	/ˈpruːfrɛd/
meet	met	met	prove	proved	proved, proven
miscast	miscast	miscast	put	put	put
mishear	misheard	misheard	quit	quit	quit
mishit	mishit	mishit	read /riːd/	read /rɛd/	read /rɛd/
mislay	mislaid	mislaid	rebuild	rebuilt	rebuilt
mislead	misled	misled	recast	recast	recast
/mɪsˈliːd/	/ˌmisˈlɛd/	/ˌmisˈlɛd/	redo	redid	redone
misread	misread	misread	redraw	redrew	redrawn
/mɪsˈriːd/	/ˌmisˈrɛd/	/ˌmisˈrɛd/	rehear	reheard	reheard
misspell	misspelled, misspelt	misspelled, misspelt	relay²	relaid	relaid
			remake	remade	remade
misspend	misspent	misspent	rend	rent	rent
mistake	mistook	mistaken	repay	repaid	repaid
misunderstand	misunderstood	misunderstood	rerun	reran	rerun
mow	mowed	mown, mowed	resell	resold	resold
offset	offset	offset	reset	reset	reset
outbid	outbid	outbid	resit	resat	resat
outdo	outdid	outdone	restring	restrung	restrung
outgrow	outgrew	outgrown	retake	retook	retaken
output	output	output	retell	retold	retold
outrun	outran	outrun	rethink	rethought	rethought
outsell	outsold	outsold	retread	retreaded, *retrod	retreaded, *retrodden
outshine	outshone	outshone			

Infinitive	Past Tense	Past Participle	Infinitive	Past Tense	Past Participle
rewind	rewound	rewound	stand	stood	stood
rewrite	rewrote	rewritten	stave	staved, *stove	staved, *stove
rid	rid	rid	steal	stole	stolen
ride	rode	ridden	stick	stuck	stuck
ring²	rang	rung	sting	stung	stung
rise	rose	risen	stink	stank, stunk	stunk
run	ran	run	strew	strewed	strewed, strewn
saw	sawed	sawed, sawn	stride	strode	–
say	said	said	strike	struck	struck, *stricken
see	saw	seen	string	strung	strung
seek	sought	sought	strive	strove, *strived	striven, *strived
sell	sold	sold	sublet	sublet	sublet
send	sent	sent	swear	swore	sworn
set	set	set	sweep	swept	swept
sew	sewed	sewn, sewed	swell	swelled	swollen, swelled
shake	shook	shaken	swim	swam	swum
shear	sheared	shorn, sheared	swing	swung	swung
shed	shed	shed	take	took	taken
shine	shone, shined	shone, shined	teach	taught	taught
shoe	shod	shod	tear	tore	torn
shoot	shot	shot	telecast	telecast	telecast
show	showed	shown, *showed	tell	told	told
shrink	shrank, shrunk	shrunk, shrunken	think	thought	thought
shut	shut	shut	throw	threw	thrown
simulcast	simulcast	simulcast	thrust	thrust	thrust
sing	sang	sung	tread	trod, treaded	trodden, trod,
sink	sank, *sunk	sunk			treaded
sit	sat	sat	typecast	typecast	typecast
slay	slew	slain	typeset	typeset	typeset
sleep	slept	slept	unbend	unbent	unbent
slide	slid	slid	underbid	underbid	underbid
sling	slung	slung	undercut	undercut	undercut
slink	slunk	slunk	undergo	underwent	undergone
slit	slit	slit	underlie	underlay	underlain
smite	smote	smitten	underpay	underpaid	underpaid
sneak	sneaked, snuck	sneaked, snuck	undersell	undersold	undersold
sow	sowed	sown, sowed	understand	understood	understood
speak	spoke	spoken	undertake	undertook	undertaken
speed	speeded, *sped	speeded, *sped	underwrite	underwrote	underwritten
spell	spelled, spelt	spelled, spelt	undo	undid	undone
spend	spent	spent	unfreeze	unfroze	unfrozen
spill	spilled, spilt	spilled, spilt	unwind	unwound	unwound
spin	spun	spun	uphold	upheld	upheld
spit	spat, spit	spat, spit	upset	upset	upset
split	split	split	wake	woke	woken
spotlight	spotlit,	spotlit,	waylay	waylaid	waylaid
	*spotlighted	*spotlighted	wear	wore	worn
spread	spread	spread	weave	wove, *weaved	woven, *weaved
spring	sprang, sprung	sprung	wed	wedded, wed	wedded, wed

Infinitive	Past Tense	Past Participle
weep	wept	wept
wet	wet, wetted	wet, wetted
win	won	won
wind² /waɪnd/	wound /waʊnd/	wound /waʊnd/
withdraw	withdrew	withdrawn

Infinitive	Past Tense	Past Participle
withhold	withheld	withheld
withstand	withstood	withstood
wring	wrung	wrung
write	wrote	written

Full Forms	Short Forms	Negative Short Forms

be present tense

I am	I'm	I'm not
you are	you're	you aren't / you're not
he is	he's	he isn't / he's not
she is	she's	she isn't / she's not
it is	it's	it isn't / it's not
we are	we're	we aren't / we're not
you are	you're	you aren't / you're not
they are	they're	they aren't / they're not

be past tense

I was	—	I wasn't
you were	—	you weren't
he was	—	he wasn't
she was	—	she wasn't
it was	—	it wasn't
we were	—	we weren't
you were	—	you weren't
they were	—	they weren't

have present tense

I have	I've	I haven't
you have	you've	you haven't
he has	he's	he hasn't
she has	she's	she hasn't
it has	it's	it hasn't
we have	we've	we haven't
you have	you've	you haven't
they have	they've	they haven't

have past tense (all persons)

had	I'd, he'd, etc.	hadn't

do present tense

I do	—	I don't
you do	—	you don't
he does	—	he doesn't
she does	—	she doesn't
it does	—	it doesn't
we do	—	we don't
you do	—	you don't
they do	—	they don't

do past tense (all persons)

did	—	didn't

	be	do	have
present participle	being	doing	having
past participle	been	done	had

be, do, have

- The negative full forms are formed by adding **not**.

- Questions in the present and past are formed by placing the verb before the subject:
  - ➤ *am I?*   *isn't he?*   *was I?*   *weren't we?*
  - ➤ *do I?*   *don't you?*   *did I?*   *didn't I?*
  - ➤ *have I?*   *haven't they?* etc.

- Questions using the negative full form are more formal:
  - ➤ *has he not?*   *do you not?* etc.

- The short negative question form for **I am** is **aren't**:
  - ➤ *aren't I?*

- When **do** or **have** is used as a main verb, questions and negative statements can be formed with **do/does/doesn't** and **did/didn't**:
  - ➤ *How did you do it?*
  - ➤ *I don't do any teaching now.*
  - ➤ *Do you have any money on you?*
  - ➤ *We didn't have much time.*

- The short forms *'ve*, *'s*, and *'d* are not usually used when **have** is a main verb:
  - ➤ *I have three children.*
  - ➤ NOT *I've three children.*

- The short form *'s* can be added to other subjects:
  - ➤ *Sally's sick.*
  - ➤ *The car's been damaged.*

- The other tenses of **be**, **do**, and **have** are formed in the same way as those of other verbs:
  - ➤ *will be*   *would be*   *has been*
  - ➤ *will do*   *would do*   *has done*
  - ➤ *will have*   *would have*   *have had*; etc.

- The **pronunciation** of each form of **be**, **do**, and **have** is given at its entry in the dictionary.

Verbs

Transitive and Intransitive

- ≻ *He sighed.*
  ≻ *She cut her hand.*
  The soup tastes salty.

Each of these sentences has a subject (**he, she, the soup**) and a verb (**sigh, cut, taste**).

In the first sentence, **sigh** stands alone. Verbs like this are called INTRANSITIVE.

In the second sentence, **cut** is TRANSITIVE because it is used with an object (**her hand**).

In the third sentence, **taste** has no object but it cannot be used alone without an adjective. An adjective like **salty** that gives more information about the subject of a verb is called a COMPLEMENT. Verbs that take complements are called LINKING VERBS.

Verb Codes

- In the dictionary, grammatical codes at the beginning of each meaning show you whether a verb is always transitive or always intransitive, or whether it can be sometimes transitive and sometimes intransitive.

  The code [I] shows you that in this meaning, **change** is always intransitive.

  change 🔊 /tʃeɪndʒ/ *verb, noun*
  • *verb*
  ≻ **BECOME/MAKE DIFFERENT 1** [I] to become different: *Rick hasn't changed. He looks exactly the same as he did at school.* ♦ *changing attitudes toward education* ♦ *Her life changed completely when she won the lottery.* **2** [T] ~ sb/sth to make someone or something different: *Fame hasn't really changed him.* ♦ *Computers have changed the way people work.* **3** [I, T] to pass or make someone or something pass from one state or form into another: *Wait for the traffic lights to change.* ♦ ~ **(from A) to/into B** *The lights changed from red to green.* ♦ *Caterpillars change into butterflies.* ♦ ~ **sb/sth (from A) to/into B** *With a wave of her magic wand, she changed the frog into a handsome prince.* **4** [T] ~ sth to stop having one state, position, or direction and start having another: *Leaves change color in the fall.* ♦ *The wind has changed direction.* ♦ *Our ship changed course.*

  The code [T] shows you that in this meaning, **change** is always transitive.

  The code [I, T] shows you that in this meaning, **change** is sometimes intransitive and sometimes transitive.

Transitive verbs are the most common type of verb. A verb that is always transitive in all its meanings is just marked *verb*, and no other verb code is given.

Verb Frames

- Transitive verbs can take different types of objects – a noun, phrase, or clause. Both transitive and intransitive verbs can combine with different prepositions or adverbs. Different linking verbs can take either adjectives or nouns as complements.

  pro·vide 🔊 /prəˈvaɪd/ *verb*
  1 to give something to someone or make it available for them to use **SYN** SUPPLY: ~ **sth** *The hospital has a commitment to provide the best possible medical care.* ♦ *The report was not expected to provide any answers.* ♦ *Please answer questions in the space provided.* ♦ ~ **sth for sb** *We are here to provide a service for the public.* ♦ ~ **sb with sth** *We are here to provide the public with a service.* **2** ~ **that...** (*formal*) (of a law or rule) to state that something will or must happen **SYN** STIPULATE: *The final section provides that any work produced for the company is thereafter owned by the company.* ⊃ **see also** PROVISION

  In the dictionary, the different patterns (or "verb frames") in which a verb can be used are shown in **bold type**, usually just before an example showing that pattern in context.

  If a particular verb, or one particular meaning of a verb, is always used in the same pattern, this pattern is shown in **bold type** before the definition.

Intransitive Verbs [I]

- Intransitive verbs do not take an object. When they are used alone after a subject, there is no verb frame.

  The example showing this use will usually appear first, before any other patterns and examples.

  shiv·er 🔊 /ˈʃɪvər/ *verb, noun*
  • *verb* [I] (of a person) to shake slightly because you are cold, frightened, excited, etc.: *Don't stand outside shivering—come inside and get warm!* ♦ *He shivered at the thought of the cold, dark sea.* ♦ ~ **with sth** *to shiver with cold/excitement/pleasure, etc.*

  Some intransitive verbs are often used with a particular preposition or adverb. This pattern will be shown in bold type, usually before an example.

- Some intransitive verbs are always or usually used with a preposition or adverb, but not always the same one. These are often verbs showing movement in a particular direction:
  ≻ *A runaway car came **hurtling toward** us.*
  ≻ *A group of swans **floated by**.*

In the dictionary this use will be shown by the frame + **adv./prep.** If a preposition or adverb is often used, but not always, there will be parentheses around the frame: (+ **adv./prep.**)

hur·tle 🔊 /ˈhɜrtl/ *verb* [I] + **adv./prep.** to move very fast in a particular direction **SYN** CAREEN: *A runaway car came **hurtling** toward us.*

Transitive Verbs [T]

- Transitive verbs must have an object. The object can be a noun or a pronoun, a noun phrase, or a clause.

For information on verbs that take a clause as the object, see page **R8**.

The frames used to show a transitive verb with a noun, pronoun, or noun phrase as object are ~ **sb**, ~ **sth**, and ~ **sb/sth**.

> **ac·com·mo·date** **AWL** /əˈkɒməˌdeɪt/ verb **1** [T] ~ **sb** to provide someone with a room or place to sleep, live, or sit: *The hotel can accommodate up to 500 guests.* **2** [T] ~ **sb/sth** to provide enough space for someone or something: *The old town hall now accommodates a Folk Museum.* **3** [T] ~ **sth** (*formal*) to consider something, such as someone's opinion or a fact, and be influenced by it when you are deciding what to do or explaining something: *Our proposal tries to accommodate the special needs of the disabled.*

~ **sb** is used when the object is a person.

~ **sth** is used when the object is a thing.

~ **sb/sth** is used when the object can be a person or a thing.

As with intransitive verbs, some transitive verbs are often used with a preposition or an adverb.

If there is a wide range of possible prepositions or adverbs, a frame such as **sb/sth + adv./prep.** is used.

> **hack** /hæk/ verb, noun
> ● **verb 1** [T, I] to cut someone or something with rough, heavy blows: ~ **sb/sth + adv./prep.** *I hacked the dead branches off.* ◆ *They were hacked to death as they tried to escape.* ◆ *We had to hack our way through the jungle.* ◆ **+ adv./prep.** *We hacked away at the bushes.* **2** [I, T] (*computing*) to secretly find a way of looking at and/or changing information on someone else's computer system without permission: ~ **into sth** *He hacked into the bank's computer.* ◆ ~ **sth** *They had hacked secret data.*

If a particular preposition or adverb is used, then it is given in the frame.

Transitive Verbs with Two Objects

- Some verbs, like **sell** and **buy**, can be used with two objects. This is shown by the frame ~ **sb sth**:
  > I sold Jim a car.
  > I bought Mary a book.

You can often express the same idea by using the verb as an ordinary transitive verb and adding a prepositional phrase starting with **to** or **for**:
  > I **sold** a car **to** Jim.
  > I **bought** a book **for** Mary.

These will be shown by the frames ~ **sth to sb** and ~ **sth for sb**.

> **bake** 🔑 /beɪk/ verb
> **1** [T, I] to cook food in an oven without extra fat or liquid; to be cooked in this way: ~ **(sth)** *baked apples* ◆ *the delicious smell of baking bread* ◆ ~ **sth for sb** *I'm baking a birthday cake for Alex.* ◆ ~ **sb sth** *I'm baking Alex a cake.* ⊃ picture at COOKING ⊃ collocations at COOKING

A pair of examples, with different frames, shows the same idea expressed in two different ways.

Linking Verbs

- > His voice sounds hoarse.
  > Elena became a doctor.

In these sentences, the linking verb (**sound, become**) is followed by a complement, an adjective (**hoarse**), or a noun phrase (**a doctor**) that tells you more about the subject.

Verbs that have an adjective as the complement have the frame + **adj.**, and verbs with a noun phrase as the complement have the frame + **noun**. Verbs that can take either an adjective or a noun phrase as the complement may have the frame + **adj./ noun**, or the two frames may be shown separately with an example for each.

> **be·come** 🔑 /bɪˈkʌm/ verb (be·came /bɪˈkeɪm/, be·come)
> **1** *linking verb* to start to be something: ~ **+ adj.** *It was becoming more and more difficult to live on his salary.* ◆ *It soon became apparent that no one was going to come.* ◆ *She was becoming confused.* ◆ **+ noun** *Obama became president in 2009.* ◆ *The bill will become law next year.*

The linking verb **become** can be used with either an adjective or a noun phrase.

There are also verbs that take both an object and a complement:
  > She considered herself lucky.
  > They elected him president.

The complement (**lucky, president**) tells you more about the object (**herself, him**) of the verb. The frames for these verbs are ~ **sb/ sth + adj.**, **sb/sth + noun**, or **sb/sth + adj./ noun**.

Verbs Used with "that clauses"

- The frame ~ **that...** shows that a verb is followed by a clause beginning with **that**:
  > She **replied that** she would prefer to walk.

However, it is not always necessary to use the word **that** itself:
  > I **said that** he would come.
  > I **said** he would come.

These two sentences mean the same. In the dictionary, they are shown by the frame

~ (that)... and a single example is given, using parentheses:

> *I said (that) he would come.*

Some verbs can be used with both a noun phrase and a "that clause." The frame for verbs used like this is **~ sb that...** or **~ sb (that)...**:

> *Can you **remind me that** I need to buy some milk?*
> *I **told her (that)** I would be late.*

Verbs Used with "wh- clauses"

■ A "wh- clause" (or phrase) is a clause or phrase beginning with one of the following words: **wh**ich, **wh**at, **wh**ose, **wh**y, **wh**ere, **wh**en, **wh**o, **wh**om, **h**ow, **if**, **wh**ether:

> *I **wonder what** the new job will be like.*
> *He doesn't **care how** he looks.*
> *Did you **see which** way they went?*

In the dictionary, verbs used like this have a frame such as **~ how, what, etc....** or **~ why, where, etc....**

The particular "wh- words" given in each frame will be words that are typical for that verb, but the "etc." shows that other "wh- clauses" are possible.

won·der 🔊 /ˈwʌndər/ *verb, noun*
• *verb* **1** [T, I] to think about something and try to decide what is true, what will happen, what you should do, etc.: **~ who, where, etc....** *I wonder who she is.* • *I was just beginning to wonder where you were.* • **~ (about sth)** *"Why do you want to know?" "No particular reason. I was just wondering."* • *We were wondering about next April for the wedding.* • **+ speech** *"What should I do now?" she wondered.* **2** [T] **~ if, whether...** used as a polite way of asking a question or asking someone to do something: *I wonder if you can help me.* • *I was wondering whether you'd like to come to a party.*

If there is no "etc." in the frame, then this verb or meaning can only take the particular "wh- words" that are listed.

Some verbs can be used with both a noun phrase and a "wh- clause." Verbs used like this have a frame such as **~ sb where, when, etc....**

> *I **asked him where** the library was.*
> *I **told her when** the baby was due.*
> *He **teaches his students how** to research a subject thoroughly.*

Verbs with Infinitive Phrases

■ **Eat** and **to eat** are both the infinitive form of the verb. **Eat** is called a BARE INFINITIVE and **to eat** is called a TO-INFINITIVE. Most verbs that take an infinitive are used with the to-infinitive. The frame for these verbs is **~ to do sth:**

> *The goldfish **need to be fed**.*
> *She never **learned to read**.*

Some verbs can be used with both a noun phrase and a to-infinitive. The frame for these is **~ sb to do sth, ~ sth to do sth,** or **~ sb/ sth to do sth.** The noun phrase can be the object of the main verb:

> *Can you **persuade Sheila** to chair the meeting?*

or the noun phrase and the infinitive phrase together can be the object:

> *I **expected her to pass** her driving test the first time.*
> *We'd love **you to come** and visit us.*

Only two groups of verbs are used with a bare infinitive (without **to**). One is the group of MODAL VERBS. These are the special verbs like **can, must,** and **will** that go before a main verb and show that an action is possible, necessary, etc. These verbs have special treatment in the dictionary and are labeled *modal verb.*

A small group of ordinary verbs, for example **see** and **hear**, can be used with a noun phrase and a bare infinitive. The frame for these is **~ sb do sth, ~ sth do sth,** or **~ sb/sth do sth:**

> *She **watched him eat** his lunch.*
> *Did you **hear the phone ring** just then?*

Verbs with Present Participles

■ The PRESENT PARTICIPLE (OR GERUND) is the form of the verb that ends in **–ing**, for example **doing, eating,** or **catching**. Some verbs can be followed by a present participle on its own or by a phrase beginning with a present participle. The frame for a verb that takes a present participle is **~ doing sth:**

> *She never **stops talking**!*
> *I **started looking** for a job two years ago.*

Some verbs can be used with both a noun phrase and a present participle. The frame for this is **~ sb doing sth, ~ sth doing sth,** or **~ sb/sth doing sth.** The noun phrase can be the object of the main verb:

> *His comments got **me thinking**.*
> *I can smell **something good cooking**.*

or the noun phrase and the present participle together can be the object:

> *I hate **him joking** (= the fact that he jokes) about serious things.*

In this pattern, you can replace **him** with the possessive pronoun **his:**

> *I hate **his joking** about serious things.*

However, sentences with a possessive pronoun sound very formal and the object pronoun is more common. In cases where the verb itself is formal and the possessive pronoun may well be used, this is shown in the dictionary entry.

Verbs with Direct Speech

- Verbs like **say**, **answer**, and **demand** can be used either to report what someone has said using a "that clause" or to give their exact words in DIRECT SPEECH, using quotation marks (" "). Verbs that can be used with direct speech have the frame + **speech**. Compare these two sentences:
  - ➤ **+ speech** *"It's snowing," she said.*
  - ➤ **~ (that)...** *She said (that) it was snowing.*

Some verbs can be used with both direct speech and a noun phrase, to show who is being spoken to. The frame for this is **~ sb + speech**:
  - ➤ *"Tom's coming to lunch," she **told him**.*

Verbs in the Passive

- Most transitive verbs can be used in the passive:
  - ➤ *Jill's behavior **annoyed** me.*
  - ➤ *I **was annoyed** by Jill's behavior.*

If a verb can be active or passive, the same verb frame is used. If the verb is often passive, there will be an example in the passive.

con·firm 𝒫 **AWL** /kənˈfɜːrm/ *verb*
1 to state or show that something is definitely true or correct, especially by providing evidence: *~ sth Rumors of job losses were later confirmed.* ◆ *His guilty expression confirmed my suspicions.* ◆ *Please write to confirm your reservation* (= say that it is definite). ◆ *~ (that)... Has everyone confirmed (that) they're coming?* ◆ *~ what/when, etc.... Can you confirm what happened?* ◆ **it is confirmed that...** *It has been confirmed that the meeting will take place next week.*

If a pattern is *only* used in the passive, then the frame is put in the passive. This happens especially with verbs that take "it" and a "that clause."

If a transitive verb cannot be used in the passive, the label [no passive] appears before the definition.

Verbs in Different Patterns

- Many verbs, for example **watch**, can be used in a number of different ways:
  - ➤ *~ sb/sth do sth I watched him eat.*
  - ➤ *~ sb/sth doing sth I watched him eating.*
  - ➤ *~ sb/sth I watched the pianist's left hand.*
  - ➤ *~ how, what, etc. ... I watched how the pianist used her left hand.*

The dictionary entry for each verb shows the different ways in which it can be used by giving a range of example sentences. The

frame before each example shows what type of grammatical pattern is being used. When an example follows another one illustrating the same pattern, the frame is not repeated.

Sometimes patterns can combine with each other to form a longer pattern. This happens especially with patterns involving particular prepositions or adverbs. Sometimes there is a choice of two or three different prepositions or adverbs:
  - ➤ *~ sth We shared the pizza.*
  - ➤ *~ sth among sb We shared the pizza among the four of us.*
  - ➤ *~ sth between sb We shared the pizza between the four of us.*

In cases like this, the dictionary does not always give a separate frame and example for each different combination. It may use brackets to show where part of a long frame can be left out, and slashes to show where there is a choice between two or three different words in the frame:

> **DIVIDE BETWEEN PEOPLE 2** [T] **~ sth (among/between sb)** to divide something between two or more people: *We shared the pizza between the four of us.* ➲ see also JOB-SHARING, POWER-SHARING

The frame **~ (sb)**, **~ (sth)**, or **~ (sb/sth)** may also be used, where a verb can be used without an object (that is, it can be intransitive), but is more commonly used with a noun phrase as an object. In these cases the more common, transitive, use is given in the first example(s), and any intransitive examples are placed after that:

broad·cast 𝒫 /ˈbrɔːdkæst/ *verb, noun*
● *verb* (broad·cast, broad·cast or broad·cast·ed, broad·cast·ed) **1** [T, I] **~ (sth)** to send out programs on television or radio: *The concert will be broadcast live* (= at the same time as it takes place) *tomorrow evening.* ◆ *They began broadcasting in 1922.* ➲ collocations at TELEVISION

Sb and **sth** may also appear within brackets within longer frames, for example to show a verb that can take a preposition, adverb, or "that clause" either with or without a noun phrase as another object:

warn 𝒫 /wɔːrn/ *verb*
1 [T, I] to tell someone about something, especially something dangerous or unpleasant that is likely to happen, so that they can avoid it: *~ sb I tried to warn him, but he wouldn't listen.* ◆ *If you're thinking of getting a dog, be warned — they take a lot of time and money.* ◆ *~ (sb) about/against sb/sth He warned us against pickpockets.* ◆ *~ (sb) of sth Police have warned of possible delays.* ◆ *~ (sb) that... She was warned that if she did it again she would lose her job.* ◆ *~ sb what, how, etc.... I had been warned what to expect.* ◆ *~ (sb) + speech "Beware of pickpockets," she warned (him).*

Phrasal Verbs

What are Phrasal Verbs?

> Jan **turned down** the job offer.
> Buying that new car has really **eaten into** my savings.
> I don't think I can **put up with** his behavior much longer.

PHRASAL VERBS (sometimes called MULTI-WORD VERBS) are verbs that consist of two, or sometimes three, words. The first word is a verb, and it is followed by an adverb (turn **down**), or a preposition (eat **into**), or both (put **up with**). These adverbs or prepositions are sometimes called PARTICLES.

- In this dictionary, phrasal verbs are listed at the end of the entry for the main verb in a section marked **PHRV**. They are listed in alphabetical order of the particles following them:

> **PHRV** ˌfight ˈback (against sb/sth) to resist strongly or attack someone who has attacked you: *Don't let them bully you. Fight back!* ♦ *It is time to fight back against street crime.* ˌfight sth↔ˈback to try hard not to do or show something, especially not to show your feelings: *I was fighting back the tears.* ˌfight sb/sth↔ˈoff to resist someone or something by fighting against them/it: *The jeweler was stabbed as he tried to fight the robbers off.* ˌfight ˈout sth | ˌfight it ˈout to fight or argue until an argument has been settled: *The conflict is still being fought out.* ♦ *They hadn't reached any agreement so we left them to fight it out.*

Meaning of Phrasal Verbs

> He **sat down** on the bed.

The meaning of some phrasal verbs, such as **sit down**, is easy to guess because the verb and the particle keep their usual meaning. However, many phrasal verbs have idiomatic meanings that you need to learn. The separate meanings of **put**, **up**, and **with**, for example, do not add up to the meaning of **put up with** (= tolerate).

- Some particles have particular meanings that are the same when they are used with a number of different verbs:

> I didn't see the point of **hanging around** waiting for him, so I went home.
> I wish you wouldn't leave all those books **lying around**.

Around adds the meaning of "with no particular purpose or aim" and is also used in a similar way with many other verbs, such as **play**, **sit**, and **wait**.

- The meaning of a phrasal verb can sometimes be explained with a one-word verb. However, phrasal verbs are frequently used in spoken English and, if there is a one-word equivalent, it is usually more formal in style:

> I wish my ears didn't **stick out** so much.
> The garage **projects** five feet beyond the front of the house.

Both **stick out** and **project** have the same meaning – "to extend beyond a surface" – but they are very different in style. **Stick out** is used in informal contexts, and **project** in formal or technical contexts.

Grammar of Phrasal Verbs

- Phrasal verbs can be TRANSITIVE (they take an object) or INTRANSITIVE (they have no object). Some phrasal verbs can be used in both ways:

> Try not to **wake** the baby **up**. (transitive)
> **Wake up!** It's eight o'clock. (intransitive)

- INTRANSITIVE phrasal verbs are written in the dictionary without **sb** (somebody) or **sth** (something) after them. This shows that they do not have an object:

> **PHRV** ˌeat ˈout to have a meal in a restaurant, etc. rather than at home: *Do you feel like eating out tonight?*

Eat out is intransitive, and the two parts of the verb cannot be separated by any other word. You can say:

> Should we eat out tonight?
> BUT NOT Should we eat tonight out?

- In order to use TRANSITIVE phrasal verbs correctly, you need to know where to put the object. With some phrasal verbs (often called SEPARABLE verbs), the object can go either between the verb and the particle or after the particle:

> She **tore** the letter **up**.
> She **tore up** the letter.

- When the object is a long phrase, it usually comes after the particle:

> She **tore up** all the letters he had sent her.

- When the object is a pronoun (for example **it** standing for "the letter"), it must always go between the verb and the particle:

> She read the letter and then **tore** it **up**.

- In the dictionary, verbs that are separable are written like this:
tear sth ↔ up

- The double arrow between the object and the particle shows that the object may come either before or after the particle:

> ,call sth↔'off to cancel something; to decide that something will not happen: *to call off a trip/strike* ♦ *They have called off their engagement* (= decided not to get married). ♦ *The game was called off because of bad weather.*

You can say:

> They **called** the game **off**.

AND They **called off** the game.

- With other phrasal verbs (sometimes called INSEPARABLE verbs), the two parts of the verb cannot be separated by an object:
  > I didn't really **take to** her husband.
  NOT *I didn't really take her husband to.*
  > I didn't really **take to** him.
  NOT *I didn't really take him to.*

- In the dictionary, verbs that are inseparable are written like this:
  take to sb

  When you see **sb** or **sth** after the two parts of a phrasal verb, and there is no double arrow, you know that they cannot be separated by an object:

> ,run 'into sb (*informal*) to meet someone by chance: *Guess who I ran into today!*

You can say:

> I ran **into** Joe yesterday.

BUT NOT *I ran Joe into.*

- There are a few phrasal verbs in which the two parts of the verb must be separated by the object. You can say:
  > She was bossy and **pushed** everyone **around**.
  BUT NOT *She was bossy and pushed around everyone.*

- In the dictionary, these verbs are written like this:
  push sb around

  When you see **sb** or **sth** between the two parts of a phrasal verb and there is no double arrow, you know that they must be separated by the object.

- Some transitive phrasal verbs can be made passive:
  > The game **has been called off**.

  When this is common, you will find an example at the dictionary entry.

Phrasal Verbs Used with Phrases and Clauses

Like other verbs, some phrasal verbs can be used with another phrase or clause. The different types of clauses and phrases are explained on pages **R8–9**. When a phrasal verb can be used with a particular type of clause or phrase, an example is given in the dictionary entry, labeled with a special frame:

~ that	We **found out** later **that** we had gone to the same school.
~ how, what, etc. ...	I can't **figure out how** to do this.
~ to do sth	It didn't **occur to** her **to** ask for help.
~ doing sth	I didn't **count on finding** Matthew there as well.
+ speech	"Help!" he **cried out**.

Related Nouns

A particular phrasal verb may have a noun related to it. This noun will be mentioned at the verb entry:

> ,break 'in to enter a building by force: *Burglars had broken in while we were away.* ⊃ related noun BREAK-IN ,break sb/sth 'in **1** to train someone or something in something new that they must do: *to break in new recruits* ♦ *The young horse was not yet broken in* (= trained to carry a rider). **2** to wear something, especially new shoes, until they become comfortable ,break 'in (on sth) to interrupt or disturb something: *She longed to break in on their conversation, but didn't want to appear rude.* ♦ [+ **speech**] *"I didn't do it!" she broke in.*
> ,break 'into sth **1** to enter a building by force; to open a car, etc. by force: *Our car was broken into last week.* ⊃ related noun BREAK-IN **2** to begin laughing, singing, etc. suddenly: *As the president's car pulled up, the crowd broke into loud applause.*

> ,break 'out (of war, fighting, or other unpleasant events) to start suddenly: *They had escaped to America shortly before war broke out in 1939.* ♦ *Fighting had broken out between rival groups of fans.* ♦ *Fire broke out during the night.* ⊃ related noun OUTBREAK ,break 'out (of sth) to escape from a place or situation: *Several prisoners broke out of the jail.* ♦ *She needed to break out of her daily routine and do something exciting.* ⊃ related noun BREAKOUT

A noun is often related in meaning to only one or two of the phrasal verbs using a particle. **Break-in** is related to **break in** and the first meaning of **break into sth**, but not to **break sb/sth in** or **break in (on sth)**. **Breakout** is related to **break out (of sth)**, whereas the noun **outbreak** relates to **break out**.

Nouns

Countable and Uncountable

The two biggest groups of nouns are COUNTABLE nouns (or COUNT nouns) and UNCOUNTABLE nouns (also called NONCOUNT nouns or MASS nouns). Most countable nouns are words for separate things that can be counted, like **apples**, **books**, or **teachers**. Uncountable nouns are usually words for things that are thought of as a quantity or mass, like **water** or **time**.

However, there are some nouns in English that you might expect to be countable but are not. For example, **furniture**, **information**, and **equipment** are all uncountable nouns in English, although they are countable in some other languages.

Countable Nouns [C]

A countable noun has a singular form and a plural form. When it is singular, it must always have a DETERMINER (a word such as **a**, **the**, **both**, or **each**) in front of it. In the plural it can be used with or without a determiner:

> I have *a* driving *lesson* this afternoon.
> I had *several lessons* already.
> *Lessons* cost $40 an hour.

Countable nouns are the most common type of noun. If they have only one meaning, or if all the meanings are countable, they are just marked *noun*. For nouns that have a number of meanings, some of which are not countable, each meaning that is countable is marked [C].

Uncountable Nouns [U]

An uncountable noun has only one form, not a separate singular and plural. It can be used with or without a determiner:

> Can we make *space* for an extra chair?
> There isn't *much space* in this room.

If an uncountable noun is the subject of a verb, the verb is singular:

> Extra money *has been found* for this project.

With nouns such as **furniture**, **information**, and **equipment**, you can talk about amounts of the thing or separate parts of the thing by using phrases like **a piece of**, **three items of**, **some bits of**:

> I picked up *some information* that might interest you.
> I picked up *two pieces of information* that might interest you.

Plural Nouns [pl.]

Some nouns are always plural and have no singular form. Nouns that refer to things that have two parts joined together, for example **glasses**, **jeans**, and **scissors**, are often plural nouns. You can usually also talk about **a pair of jeans**, **a pair of scissors**, etc.

> I'm going to buy *some* new jeans.
> I'm going to buy *a* new *pair of* jeans.

An example is given in the entry for the noun to show that it can be used in this way.

Some plural nouns, such as **police** and **cattle**, look as if they are singular. Nouns like this usually refer to a group of people or animals of a particular type, when they are considered together as one unit. They also take a plural verb:

> **Police are searching** for a man who escaped from Sing Sing prison today.
> The **cattle are fed** on barley and grass.

Singular Nouns [sing.]

Some nouns are always singular and have no plural form. Many nouns like this can be used in only a limited number of ways. For example, some singular nouns must be or are often used with a particular determiner in front of them or with a particular preposition after them. The correct determiner or preposition is shown before the definition. In the case of **cutting edge** the pattern given is **the ~ (of sth)**:

,cutting 'edge *noun* [sing.] **1 the ~ (of sth)** the newest, most advanced stage in the development of something: *working at the cutting edge of computer technology* ➔ compare BLEEDING EDGE

Patterns with Nouns

Many nouns are followed by a particular preposition, adverb, or other pattern:

> My comments were taken as an allegation of negligence.

The correct pattern to use is shown in **bold type**, either before the definition or before an individual example. Where any part of a pattern is optional, it is given in parentheses.

---

al·le·ga·tion /ˌæləˈgeɪʃn/ *noun* a public statement that is made without giving proof, accusing someone of doing something that is wrong or illegal **SYN** ACCUSATION: *to investigate/deny/withdraw an allegation* ◆ ~ **of sth** *Several newspapers made allegations of corruption in the city's police department.* ◆ ~ **(of sth) against sb** *allegations of dishonesty against him* ◆ ~ **about sb/sth** *The committee has made serious allegations about interference in its work.* ◆ ~ **that...** *an allegation that he had been dishonest* ➔ thesaurus box at CLAIM

The example sentences show the patterns in use.

Adjectives

Comparative and Superlative

- Adjectives of one syllable form their comparative with **-er** and their superlative with **-est**:
  > tall   taller   tallest

- When the adjective ends in **-e**, the comparative and superlative are formed by adding **-r** and **-st**:
  > nice   nicer   nicest

- Sometimes the final consonant must be doubled:
  > wet   wetter   wettest
  > big   bigger   biggest

- Adjectives with three syllables, and some with two syllables, form their comparative with **more** and their superlative with **most**:
  > beautiful, more beautiful, most beautiful

- However, many two-syllable adjectives, especially those that end in **-er**, **-y**, or **-ly**, behave like adjectives of one syllable (note that a final **-y** changes to an **i** before the endings are added):
  > clever   cleverer   cleverest
  > sunny   sunnier   sunniest
  > kindly   kindlier   kindliest

- A few adjectives have irregular comparative and superlative forms:
  > good   better   best

- All comparative and superlative forms are shown in the dictionary, except those with **more** and **most**. When a one-syllable adjective is not used in the comparative or superlative forms, these are not shown.

Attributive and Predicative

- Many adjectives can be used both before a noun:
  > a serious expression
  > gray hair

  and after a LINKING VERB:
  > She looked serious.
  > His hair had turned gray.

- However, some adjectives, or particular meanings of adjectives, are always used before a noun, and cannot be used after a linking verb. They are called ATTRIBUTIVE adjectives:
  > the chief reason

- Others are only used after a linking verb. They are called PREDICATIVE adjectives:
  > The baby is awake.

→ For more information about linking verbs, look at page **R6**.

[only before noun] [usually before noun]

Attributive adjectives are labeled [only before noun]. The label [usually before noun] is used when it is rare but possible to use the adjective after a verb.

> Senses **1** and **2** can only be used before a noun.

> **con·ti·nen·tal** /ˌkɑntəˈnɛntl; ˌkɑntnˈɛntl/ adj. **1** [only before noun] connected with the main part of the N. American continent: Prices are often higher in Hawaii than in the continental United States. **2** [only before noun] forming part of, or typical of, any of the seven main land masses of the earth: continental Antarctica/Asia/Europe ◆ to study continental geography **3** typical of the main part of Europe: The restaurant serves excellent continental fare. ◆ The shutters and balconies make New Orleans look continental.

> Sense **3** has no grammar label because it can be used both before a noun and after a linking verb.

[not before noun] [not usually before noun]

Predicative adjectives, labeled [not before noun], are used only after a linking verb, never before a noun. The label [not usually before noun] is used when it is rare but possible to use the adjective before a noun.

> The grammar label right after the adj. label shows that both meanings must be used after a linking verb.

> **rife** /raɪf/ adj. [not before noun] **1** if something bad or unpleasant is **rife** in a place, it is very common there **SYN** WIDESPREAD: It is a country where corruption is rife. ◆ Rumors are rife that he is going to resign. **2** ~ (with sth) full of something bad or unpleasant: Los Angeles is rife with gossip about the stars' private lives.

[after noun]

A few adjectives always follow the noun they describe. This is shown in the dictionary by the label [after noun]:

> **ga·lore** /gəˈlɔr/ adj. [after noun] (informal) in large quantities: There will be games and prizes galore.

Idioms

What are Idioms?

An idiom is a phrase whose meaning is difficult or sometimes impossible to guess by looking at the meanings of the individual words it contains. For example, the phrase **be in the same boat** has a literal meaning that is easy to understand, but it also has a common idiomatic meaning:

> I found the job difficult at first. But we were all in the same boat; we were all learning.

Here, **be in the same boat** means "to be in the same difficult or unfortunate situation."

Some idioms are imaginative expressions such as proverbs and sayings:

> Too many cooks spoil the broth.
> (= If too many people are involved in something, it will not be done well.)

If the expression is well known, part of it may be left out:

> Well, I knew everything would go wrong – it's the usual story of too many cooks!

Other idioms are short expressions that are used for a particular purpose:

> Hang in there! (used to encourage someone in a difficult situation)

Many idioms, however, are not vivid in this way. They are considered idioms because their form is fixed:

> for certain   > in any case

Idioms in the Dictionary

Idioms are defined at the entry for the first "full" word (a noun, a verb, an adjective, or an adverb) that they contain. This means ignoring any grammatical words such as articles and prepositions. Idioms follow the main senses of a word, in a section marked **IDM**:

> **IDM** **in the blink of an eye** very quickly; in a short time **on the blink** (*informal*) (of a machine) no longer working correctly

The words **in**, **the**, and **on** in these idioms do not count as "full" words, so the idioms are not listed at the entries for these words.

Deciding where idioms start and stop is not always easy. If you hear the expression:

> They decided to bury the hatchet and try to be friends again.

you might think that **hatchet** is the only word you do not know and look that up. In fact, **bury**

the hatchet is an idiomatic expression and it is defined at **bury**. At **hatchet** you will find a cross reference directing you to **bury**:

> **hatch·et** /ˈhætʃət/ *noun* a small AX (= a tool with a heavy blade for chopping things) with a short handle **IDM** see **BURY**

Sometimes one "full" word of an idiom can be replaced by another. For example, in the idiom **be common knowledge**, **common** can be replaced by **public**. This is shown as **be common/public knowledge** and the idiom is defined at the first full fixed word, **knowledge**. If you try to look the phrase up at either **common** or **public** you will find a cross reference to **knowledge** at the end of the idioms section.

> **IDM** **the common touch** the ability of a powerful or famous person to talk to and understand ordinary people **make common cause with sb** (*formal*) to be united with someone about something that you both agree on, believe in, or wish to achieve ⊃ **more at** KNOWLEDGE

A few very common verbs and the adjectives **bad** and **good** have so many idioms that they cannot all be listed in the entry. Instead, there is a note telling you to look at the entry for the next noun, verb, adjective, etc. in the idiom:

> **IDM** Most idioms containing **go** are at the entries for the nouns and adjectives in the idioms. For example, **go it alone** is at **alone**.

In some idioms, many alternatives are possible. In the expression **disappear into thin air**, you could replace **disappear** with **vanish**, **melt**, or **evaporate**. In the dictionary this is shown as **disappear, vanish, etc. into thin air**, showing that you can use other words with a similar meaning to disappear in the idiom. Since the first "full" word of the idiom is not fixed, the expression is defined at **thin** with a cross reference only at **air**.

If you cannot find an idiom in the dictionary, look it up at the entry for one of the other main words in the expression.

Some idioms only contain grammatical words such as **one**, **it**, or **in**. These idioms are defined at the first word that appears in them. For example, the idiom **one up on sb** is defined at the entry for **one**.

Idioms are given in alphabetical order within the idioms sections. Grammatical words such as **a/an** or **the**, **sb/sth**, and the possessive forms **your**, **sb's**, **his**, **her**, etc., as well as words in parentheses ( ) or after a slash (/), are ignored.

Collocation

What is Collocation?

COLLOCATION is the way in which particular words tend to occur or belong together.
For example, you can say:

> Meals will be served outside on the terrace, **weather permitting**.
>
> BUT NOT ~~Meals will be served outside on the terrace, weather allowing~~.

Both these sentences seem to mean the same thing: **allow** and **permit** have very similar meanings. But in this combination, only **permitting** is correct. It COLLOCATES with **weather**, and **allowing** does not.

Types of Collocation

In order to write and speak natural and correct English, you need to know, for example:

- which adjectives are used with a particular noun
- which nouns a particular adjective is used with
- which verbs are used with a particular noun
- which adverbs are used to intensify a particular adjective

Collocation in this Dictionary

To find out which adjectives to use with a particular noun, look at the examples at the entry for the noun. Typical adjectives used with the noun are separated by a slash (/):

Can you say "pink wine"?

> **wine** /waɪn/ noun, verb
> • noun 1 [U, C] an alcoholic drink made from the juice of GRAPES that has been left to FERMENT. There are many different kinds of wine: *a bottle of wine* ♦ *a glass of dry/sweet wine* ♦ *red/white wine* ♦ *rosé /blush wine* ♦ *sparkling wine* ⊃ see also TABLE WINE

(No, **rosé** or **blush**)

If you look up an adjective, you will see which nouns are commonly used with it:

Which words can be used with the adjective heady?

> **head·y** /'hedi/ adj. (**head·i·er, head·i·est**) 1 [usually before noun] having a strong effect on your senses; making you feel excited and confident **SYN** INTOXICATING: *the heady days of youth* ♦ *the heady scent of hot spices* ♦ *a heady mixture of desire and fear*

(**days, scent, mixture**)

Look at the examples in a noun entry to find out which verbs can be used with it:

Which verbs are used with mortgage?

> **mort·gage** /'mɔːrgɪdʒ/ noun, verb
> • noun (also informal ˌhome 'loan) a legal agreement by which a bank or similar organization lends you money to buy a house, etc., and you pay the money back over a particular number of years; the sum of money that you borrow: *to apply for/take out/pay off a mortgage* ♦ *mortgage rates* (= of interest) ♦ *a mortgage on the house* ♦ *a mortgage of $260,000* ♦ *monthly mortgage repayments*

(**apply for, take out, pay off**)

If you look up an adjective, you will see which adverbs you can use to intensify it:

Strongly or bitterly disappointed?

> **dis·ap·point·ed** /ˌdɪsə'pɔɪntəd/ adj.
> upset because something you hoped for has not happened or been as good, successful, etc. as you expected: ~ **(at/by sth)** *They were bitterly disappointed at the result of the game.* ♦ *I was disappointed by the quality of the wine.* ♦ ~ **(in/with sb/sth)** *I'm disappointed in you—I really thought I could trust you!* ♦ *I was very disappointed with myself.* ♦ ~ **(to see, hear, etc.)** *He was disappointed to see she wasn't at the party.* ♦ ~ **(that...)** *I'm disappointed (that) it was sold out.* ♦ ~ **(not) to be...** *She was disappointed not to be chosen for the team.*

(**bitterly**)

Important collocations are printed in bold type within the examples. If the meaning of the collocation is not obvious, there is a short explanation after it in parentheses.

having unexpected luck

hoping you will be lucky

> **luck** /lʌk/ noun, verb
> • noun [U] 1 good things that happen to you by chance, not because of your own efforts or abilities: *With (any) luck, we'll be home before dark.* ♦ *So far I have had no luck with finding a job.* ♦ *I could hardly believe my luck when he said yes.* ♦ *It was a stroke of luck that we found you.* ♦ *By sheer luck no one was hurt in the explosion.* ♦ *We wish her luck in her new career.* ♦ *You're in luck* (= lucky)—*there's one ticket left.* ♦ *You're out of luck. She's not here.* ♦ *What a piece of luck!* ⊃ see also BEGINNER'S LUCK

being lucky

not being lucky

hoping someone else will be lucky

The Academic Word List and Collocations

Averil Coxhead, Victoria University of Wellington, New Zealand

Vocabulary is a key area of language knowledge for second language learners. Learners need to know not only which words to learn, but what it really means to know a word. This dictionary highlights 3,000 words (**the Oxford 3000™**) as a basic or core vocabulary that learners need. It also highlights words from the **Academic Word List** (AWL), which was developed to help second language learners decide which words to learn to prepare for academic studies in English, and help their teachers decide which words to teach. Knowing a word includes understanding its meaning, as well as other factors such as how it is spelled or pronounced, whether it is an everyday or more formal word, or if we use it more in speaking than in writing. This dictionary focuses on these and other aspects of knowing a word, but it also emphasizes knowing which words commonly occur together. In other words, which words co-occur, or are *collocates* for each other.

The Academic Word List (AWL)[1]

In this dictionary, words in the AWL are marked **AWL**, like the entry for the word *anlayze* in the example below.

> **an·a·lyze** 🔑 **AWL** (*CanE also* an·a·lyse) /ˈænlˌaɪz/ *verb*
> **1** to examine the nature or structure of something, especially by separating it into its parts, in order to understand or explain it: **~ sth** *The job involves gathering and analyzing data.* ◆ *He tried to analyze his feelings.* ◆ **~ what, how, etc....** *We need to analyze what went wrong.* ➔ thesaurus box at EXAMINE

The AWL was developed to help answer the question, "Which words do these learners need to prepare them for their academic studies?" It was created by analyzing the vocabulary in a corpus (a body of written academic texts) from 28 subject areas, including Accounting, Biology, Chemistry, Computer Science, Criminal Law, Economics, History, International Law, Mathematics, Management, and Politics. The AWL words were selected on their range, frequency, and whether they occurred regularly across four academic disciplines (Arts, Commerce, Law, and Science). Words that are in the first 2,000 words of English were not included in the list. In written academic texts on average, ten words in every hundred are in this list.

[1] For more details and the AWL words, see this Web site: **www.victoria.ac.nz/lals/resources/academicwordlist**. You can also find the AWL words on the CD-ROM of this dictionary.

The AWL is used in many English for Academic Purposes programs, textbooks, and classroom materials. But because the AWL is a list of words on their own, we need to know more about the words that collocate with them. Doing so will help us develop our understanding and knowledge of these words even further.

AWL Collocation Boxes

While all of the AWL words are marked in this dictionary, some of them have been selected for an in-depth analysis of their most important collocations. Highlighting the collocations draws our attention to them. Also, the boxes include example sentences so we can see the full context of the collocations. This means we know more about both how the collocations work and how we might use them in our own writing and speaking. The collocations have been selected by examining the AWL words in context in a large corpus of academic writing.

AWL COLLOCATIONS

conclude

conclude *verb*
to reach a belief or an opinion as a result of thought or study
- article, paper, report, study, survey | author, researcher, scientist | court
  Lee's study concluded that rewarding employees who repeatedly try new things leads to more innovation.
- reasonably, safely
  Direct evidence is needed before safely concluding that the drug is not effective.

conclusion *noun*
a belief or an opinion that you reach after considering something carefully
- arrive at, come to, draw, reach | reinforce, support
  There are too many exceptions to draw any firm conclusions on this point.
- be based on, derive from
  Their conclusion derives from a survey carried out in five countries.
- definitive, firm | logical, valid | tentative | erroneous
  Without careful examination, erroneous conclusions can result.

conclusive *adj.*
- evidence, proof
  Despite the lack of conclusive evidence, the claims were accepted.
- far from
  Despite years of study, the results from empirical research are far from conclusive.

inconclusive *adj.*
- evidence, findings, result
  The inconclusive findings of these studies indicate the need for additional research.

You can see in the collocation box for *conclude* that the meaning of the word is given, along with common collocations for that word. Sometimes quite common words are collocations for the AWL words, for example *come to a conclusion*. Learners need to make sure the sequence of words is right when using these words together. Other collocations are other words from the AWL, for example *derive* in the sentence *Their conclusion derives from a survey…*. In this case, the collocation word *derive* might not be well known. Learners need to be careful to make sure they know the meaning of the collocation word well. Remember to think about these words as a unit.

Which words collocate with each other?
It helps to know about the grammatical patterns of words when we look at collocations. The collocation box for the verb *investigate* shows us common adverbs that occur with this verb, such as *systematically* and *further*. The noun *investigation* appears with adjectives that describe it (for example *empirical* and *scientific*) as well as verbs that take the noun as object (*conduct* and *undertake*).

AWL COLLOCATIONS

investigate

investigate *verb*

- **empirically**, **experimentally** | **theoretically** | **rigorously**, **systematically**, **thoroughly** | **extensively**, **further**
  This theory has been investigated experimentally by heating volcanic rock.
  This speculation needs to be investigated further.
- **influence**, **interaction**, **relationship**, **role** | **effect**, **efficacy** | **hypothesis**
  Our study aims to investigate the role of optimism in preventing illness.
  To investigate our hypothesis, we will present two analyses.

investigation *noun*

- **empirical**, **scientific** | **thorough** | **further**, **ongoing**
  Proposals for scientific investigations will probably increase as new discoveries are made.
  A thorough investigation of the evidence confirms this conclusion.
- **conduct**, **undertake**
  We conducted a follow-up investigation to determine whether or not the students enrolled in French the following year.
- **demonstrate**, **reveal**, **show**, **uncover**, **yield**
  Investigations showed no chemical contamination of the air or water.
  Recent investigations have yielded new insight into sleep's role in memory and learning.

Another pattern to look for is adverbs with adjectives, for example *seemingly significant*. Drawing attention to these patterns might help you develop your own skills in finding and using common collocations.

Word Families of the AWL
The AWL contains 570 word families. Word families from the AWL are included in the dictionary for some words, such as *conceive*. Sometimes word families contain members that have different spellings, and so the words don't always occur one after the other in the dictionary. *Conception*, for example, does not occur directly after *conceive*.

WORD FAMILY
conceive *verb*
conceivable *adj.*
 (≠ inconceivable)
conceivably *adv.*
concept *noun*
conception *noun*
conceptual *adj.*

These word family boxes can help develop our understanding of how words are connected. For example, you might know the noun *theory*, but might not know the adjective, *theoretical*. Then you might see in the collocation box that collocates for *theoretical* include the adverbs *highly* and *purely* as well as the nouns *framework* and *approach*. It is important to know that some words might have different grammatical categories, for example *variable* can be a noun or an adjective. Watch out also for prefixes that change the meaning of a word, for instance *overestimate* versus *estimate*. Finally, sometimes word family members might carry slightly or very different meanings from each other, for example *evident* and *evidence*.

Conclusion
At times, the amount of knowledge we need about a word and the number of words we need to know might seem too much. Tools such as the Academic Word List can help us decide which words to spend valuable time learning. Using a dictionary to support our learning can help us add to our knowledge bit by bit. If we know more about which words to use alongside each other, it helps our reading because we can read groups of words faster if we already know which words will be used together. There are benefits for our writing also, because we know more about which words can be used together. And there are benefits for our general language learning as we start to focus on developing our existing knowledge of a word to include collocations. Collocations are not the only aspect of word knowledge we need, but they are an important part of learning more about a word.

The Oxford 3000™

The keywords of the **Oxford 3000** have been carefully selected by a group of language experts and experienced teachers as the words that should receive priority in vocabulary study because of their importance and usefulness. The selection is based on three criteria.

The words that occur most **frequently** in English are included, based on the information in the American English section of the Oxford English Corpus. A corpus is an electronically held collection of written or spoken texts, and this corpus contains more than 2 billion words. However, being frequent in the corpus alone is not enough for a word to qualify as a keyword. Some words may be used very frequently, but only in a narrowly defined area, such as in newspapers or scientific articles. In order to avoid including these restricted words, we include as keywords only those words which are frequent across a **range** of different types of text. In other words, keywords are both frequent and used in a variety of contexts.

In addition, the list includes some very important words that are very **familiar** to most users of English, even though they are not used very frequently. These include, for example, words for parts of the body, words used in travel, and words that are useful for explaining what you mean when you do not know the exact word for something. These words were identified by consulting a panel of over seventy experts in the fields of teaching and language study.

The words of the **Oxford 3000** are shown in the main section of the dictionary in larger print and in a different color from the other words, and are marked with a key symbol 🔑.

¡**sharp-'eyed** *adj.* able to see very well and quick to notice things **SYN** OBSERVANT: *A sharp-eyed reader spotted the mistake in yesterday's paper.*

sharp·ly 🔑 /ˈʃɑrpli/ *adv.*
1 in a critical, rough, or severe way: *The report was sharply critical of the police.* ◆ *"Is there a problem?" he asked sharply.*
2 suddenly and by a large amount: *Profits fell sharply following the takeover.* ◆ *The road fell sharply to the sea.* **3** in a way that clearly shows the differences between two things: *Their experiences contrast sharply with those of other children.*
4 quickly and suddenly, or loudly: *She moved sharply across the room to block his exit.* ◆ *He rapped sharply on the window.*

The entries for keywords often have extra information in the form of more examples of use, special notes explaining synonyms or related words, or helpful illustrations. This means that the keywords make an excellent starting point for expanding your vocabulary. With most keywords, there is far more to learn about them than the first meaning in the entry. These words often have many meanings, have a large family of words derived from them, or are used in a variety of patterns.

The list covers American English only. Some basic phrases are also included. Proper names (names of people, places, etc. beginning with a capital letter) are not included in the list.

In order to make the definitions in this dictionary easy to understand, we have written them using the keywords of the **Oxford 3000**. All words used in normal definition text are keywords, or are on the list of language study terms, shown on page **R19**. Numbers and proper names are also used in definitions. When it has been necessary to use a specialist term that is not in the **Oxford 3000**, the word is shown in SMALL CAPITALS. If you do not know the meaning of this word, look it up in the dictionary: it will help you to understand the definition that you are interested in, and will probably be a useful word to learn because it will be related to the original word you looked up.

There is a full list of the **Oxford 3000** on the CD-ROM of this dictionary.

Language Study Terms

Knowing these words will be useful in your study of English and will also help you to use the *Oxford Advanced American Dictionary* more effectively. This list includes words to do with grammar, pronunciation, and punctuation.

abbreviation *n.*
active *adj., n.*
adjective *n.*
adverb *n.*
antonym *n.*
apostrophe *n.*
article *n.*
auxiliary (*also* auxiliary verb) *n.*
clause *n.*
colon *n.*
comma *n.*
comparative *adj., n.*
compound *n., adj.*
conditional *adj., n.*
conjunction *n.*
consonant *n.*
contraction *n.*
countable *adj.*
count noun *n.*
continuous
   ⊃progressive
derivative *n.*
determiner *n.*
dialect *n.*
entry *n.*
exclamation *n.*
exclamation point *n.*
figurative *adj.*
gerund *n.*
hyphen *n.*
idiom *n.*
imperative *adj., n.*
indirect speech
   ⊃reported speech
infinitive *n.*
interjection *n.*
intransitive *adj.*
ironic *adj.*
irregular *adj.*
literal *adj.*
literary *adj.*
mass noun *n.*
modal *n.*
noncount adj.
   ⊃uncountable
noun *n.*
object *n.*

ordinal *n.*
paragraph *n.*
parenthesis *n.*
part of speech (*also* word class) *n.*
participle *n.*
particle *n.*
passive *adj., n.*
perfect *adj.*
period *n.*
phrasal verb *n.*
plural *n., adj.*
possessive *adj., n.*
prefix *n.*
preposition *n.*
progressive (*also* continuous) *adj.*
pronoun *n.*
punctuation *n.*
question mark *n.*
question tag (*also* tag question) *n.*
quotation marks *n.*
reflexive *adj.*
register *n.*
regular *adj.*
relative *adj.*
reported speech (*also* indirect speech) *n.*
saying *n.*
semicolon *n.*
simple *adj.*
singular *n., adj.*
slang *n.*
slash *n.*
subject *n.*
suffix *n.*
superlative *adj., n.*
syllable *n.*
synonym *n.*
taboo *adj.*
tag question
   ⊃question tag
tense *n.*
transitive *adj.*
uncountable *adj.*
verb *n.*
vowel *n.*
word class
   ⊃part of speech

Canadian English

Katherine Barber, editor of the *Canadian Oxford Dictionary*

There are many English-speaking countries in the world, and in each of them the variety of English spoken has some of its own characteristics. The two biggest, most influential varieties are American English and British English. There are many differences in vocabulary and pronunciation between these two varieties, and some differences in spelling and grammar. Because Canadian English grew out of a mixture of these two varieties, it shares some things with American English and others with British English. There are also some features that are unique to Canadian English.

In pronunciation, vocabulary, and grammar, Canadian English is very similar to General American English as it is spoken in the northern United States, but there are some differences. The differences are more noticeable in spelling, where British spellings for many words are preferred by Canadians to American spellings. In fact, many Canadians get quite upset if other Canadians use American spellings.

Spelling

Both American and British spellings are used in Canada. For some words, the British spelling is much more common; for others, the American spelling is more common. In this dictionary, the Canadian spelling variant is listed after the American spelling.

Some words that end in *-or* (**color**, **labor**, **neighbor**, etc.) are more commonly spelled with the *-our* than with *-or* in Canadian English: **colour**, **labour**, **neighbour**. It is not wrong to spell these words with *-or*, but many Canadians think it is "un-Canadian" to do so. Be careful: some words are always spelled with *-or* in all varieties of English: **director**, **actor**, **monitor**, **error**, etc.

Some words that end in *-ter* (**center**, **theater**, **liter**, etc.) are more commonly spelled *-tre* in Canadian English: **centre**, **theatre**, **litre**. Be careful: some words are spelled with *-ter* in all varieties of English: **enter**, **thermometer**, etc.

In verbs ending in *l* or *p* that are not stressed on the final syllable, the *l* or *p* is doubled in Canadian English in the present participle, the past participle, and when forming a noun: **cancelling**, **worshipped**, **traveller**. Recently, however, Canadians are opting more for the American spelling, which does not double the last consonant, for these words. This is especially true for the word **dial**: **dialing**, **dialed**, **dialer**.

For words ending in *-dge*, the *-e* is kept when the suffix *-ment* is added, as in British English: **judgement**, **acknowledgement**.

In American English many verbs are spelled with *-ize* or *-yze* (**organize**, **analyze**). In Canadian English they are most commonly spelled the same way, although from time to time you may see them spelled with *-ise* or *-yse*, as in British English.

In Canadian English, **licence** and **practice** are nouns, while **license** and **practise** are verbs. American English uses **license** and **practice** for both noun and verb.

For certain specific words, Canadian English prefers the British spelling. The piece of paper you use to pay someone money out of your bank account is a **cheque** in Canadian English (American English **check**). A book that contains information about all the things you can buy from a company is a **catalogue** (American English usually **catalog**). Rings, brooches, and necklaces are spelled **jewellery** more often than **jewelry**. **Grey** is much more common than **gray**.

For other words, Canadians prefer the American spelling. Cars have **tires** (not **tyres** as in British English), and they park at the **curb** (not the **kerb** as in British English).

Pronunciation

Generally, west of the Atlantic Provinces, Canadian pronunciation is very similar to pronunciation in the northern United States, with some differences.

The short "o" is more open in American English, so that an American saying the word **hot** sounds to a Canadian as if they are saying **hat**.

The sound in the word **caught** is exactly the same as the word **cot** in Canadian English (and likewise in words like **daughter**, **ought**, etc.).

The sound in words ending in *-arry* is the same as in words ending in *-erry*, so that **marry** and **merry** sound exactly the same.

Jewellery is most commonly pronounced /ˈdʒuləri/.

For a very few words, Canadians all use the British pronunciation:

Shone, the past tense of **shine**, rhymes with *on*. (For Americans, it sounds like **shown**.)

The vowel in **roof** is the same as the vowel in *boot* (Americans use the same vowel as in *book*.)

The second syllable in **anti-** and **multi-** rhymes with *tea*. (Some Americans say *tie*.)

Most Canadians say **route** like *root*, though some say it to rhyme with *out* (as many Americans also do).

About half of Canadians pronounce the "h" in **herb** while the other half don't. (Americans don't.)

About half start the word **schedule** with a "sh" and the other half with a "sk." (Americans say "sk.")

More Canadians say the first syllable of **lieutenant** as /lɛf/ than as /lu/. (Americans say /lu/.)

Some say the word **been** like *bean* and others like *bin*. Some use both of these pronunciations. (Americans say *bin*.)

Vocabulary

The vocabulary of Canadian English is mostly the same as that of American English, but there are some differences.

Canadians use some British English words that are not found in American English:

- Most Canadians call the letter Z **zed**, and tend to get upset with Canadians who call it **zee** like the Americans.
- **constable** for a police officer of the lowest rank

- **icing sugar** (American English **confectioner's sugar**)
- **semi-detached** for a house that is joined to another house and **detached** for one that stands on its own
- **tea towel** as well as the American **dish towel**
- **serviette** for a table napkin, especially one made of paper
- The favorite tag ending for Canadians is **eh** (rather than the American **huh**), as in "*Nice day, eh?*")

There are also many words that only Canadians use, or which have one meaning that only Canadians use. Some examples are:

- A **toque** (also spelled **tuque**) is a knitted cap.
- **Washroom** is the polite word for a toilet; *go to the washroom* means to use the toilet.
- The **humidex** is a number that weather forecasters use to tell you how much hotter than the actual temperature it really feels on a hot, humid day.
- A **seat sale** is when an airline offers reduced fares for a limited time.
- The native peoples of Canada are called **First Nations** (formerly called Indians), **Inuit** (formerly called Eskimos), and **Métis** (people who have both European and native ancestors).
- **Hydro** is electricity.
- A **loonie** is a one-dollar coin; a **toonie** is a two-dollar coin.
- A type of apartment that is one big room for sleeping, eating, cooking, and sitting is a **bachelor**.
- Something you give a baby to suck on is a **soother** (also called a **pacifier**, as in American English).

Grammar

There are not many grammatical differences between Canadian and American English, but one notable one is that many Canadians say that someone is taken **to hospital** or is **in hospital** like the British, rather than **to the hospital** and **in the hospital** like the Americans.

ATLANTIC OCEAN

0   50   100   150 miles
0   100   200 km

MAINE
Augusta
Portland
NEW HAMPSHIRE
Manchester
VERMONT
Sherbrooke
Montreal
Burlington
Montpelier
Concord
Cambridge
Boston
Providence
MASSACHUSETTS
Cape Cod
RHODE ISLAND
CONNECTICUT
Long Island
Gatineau
Hudson
Albany
Hartford
Bridgeport
Ottawa
Syracuse
NEW YORK
New York
ONTARIO
Rochester
Newark
Princeton
Trenton
NEW JERSEY
Niagara Falls
Buffalo
Philadelphia
Wilmington
DELAWARE
Lake Ontario
PENNSYLVANIA
Harrisburg
Baltimore
Annapolis
Toronto
Hamilton
London
Pittsburgh
Washington D.C.
Chesapeake Bay
Windsor
Cleveland
OHIO
WEST VIRGINIA
VIRGINIA
Greater Sudbury
Detroit
Toledo
Columbus
Allegheny Mountains
MICHIGAN
Lansing
Dayton
Cincinnati
Charleston
Sault Sainte Marie
Grand Rapids
Milwaukee
INDIANA
Indianapolis
Lake Huron
Lake Michigan
Green Bay
Chicago
Lake Superior
Lake Erie

Labrador Sea

NEWFOUNDLAND & LABRADOR
St. John's
Smallwood Reservoir
La Grande Rivière

Iqaluit

Baffin Island
Bylot Island

Hudson Bay
Belcher Islands

Southampton Island

C A N A D A

MANITOBA

Ellesmere Island
Devon Island
Somerset Island
Prince of Wales Island

ARCTIC OCEAN

Queen Elizabeth Islands

Victoria Island

Banks Island

NUNAVUT

Melville Island

Beaufort Sea

Great Bear Lake

NORTHWEST TERRITORIES

Yellowknife

Great Slave Lake

Lake Athabasca

SASKATCHEWAN

Mackenzie

Mackenzie Mts.

Peace

ALBERTA

R O C

BRITISH COLUMBIA

Liard

Fraser

Coast Mountain

YUKON TERRITORY

Klondike

Whitehorse

Juneau

Mt. Logan 18 008 △19 524

Brooks Range

Mt. McKinley △20 320

ALASKA
U.S.A.

Alaska Range
Mt. Saint Elias

Yukon

Gulf of Alaska

Anchorage

Bering Sea

U.S.A.

ALASKA
Yukon
Anchorage

Aleutian Islands

0   100   200   300 miles
0   250   500 km

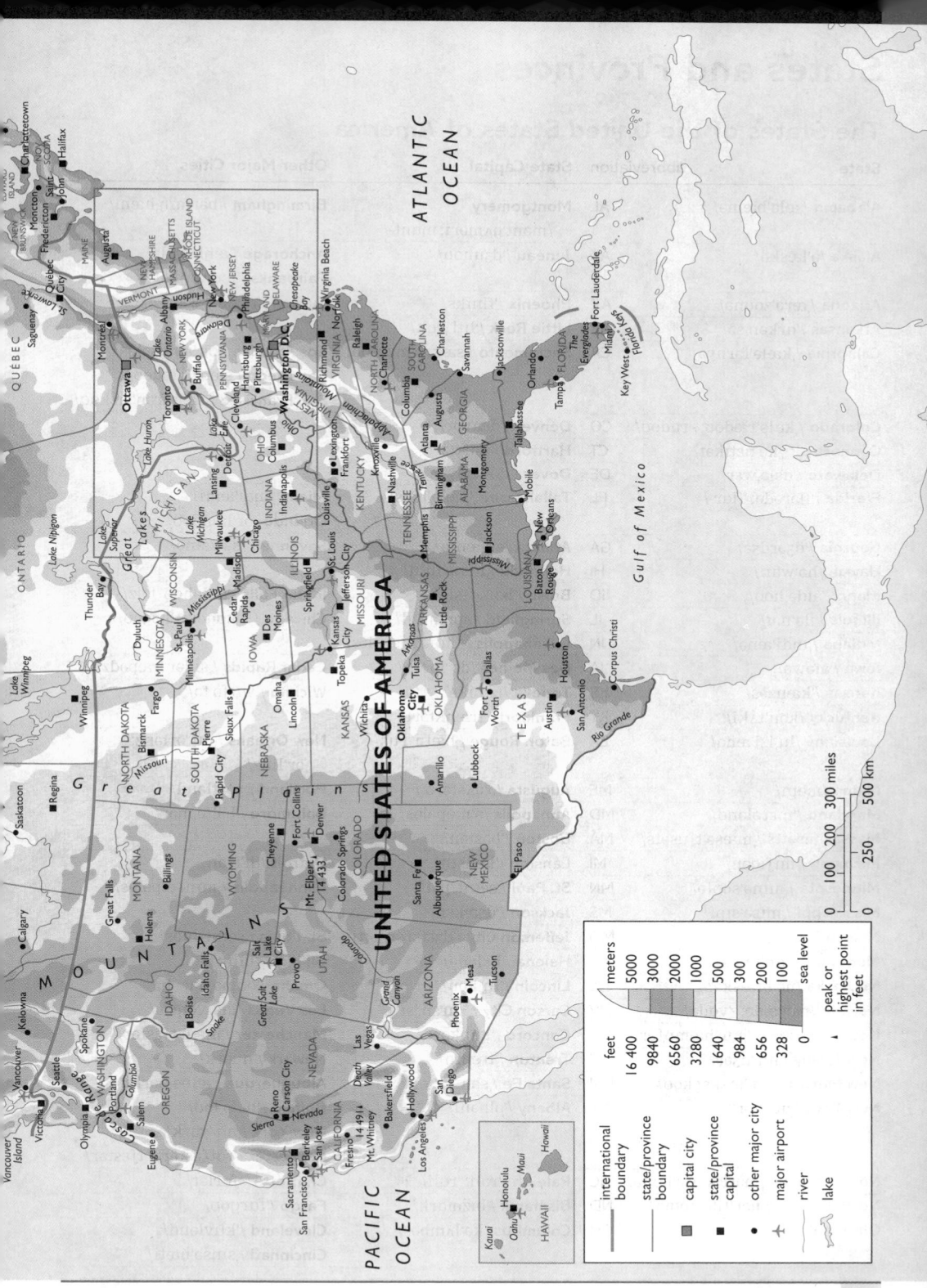

ATLANTIC OCEAN

PACIFIC OCEAN

Gulf of Mexico

UNITED STATES OF AMERICA

international boundary		
state/province boundary		
◼	capital city	
■	state/province capital	
●	other major city	
✛	major airport	
	river	
	lake	

feet		meters
16 400		5000
9840		3000
6560		2000
3280		1000
1640		500
984		300
656		200
328		100
0		sea level

▲ peak or highest point in feet

0   100   200   300 miles
0   250   500 km

R23

States and Provinces

The States of the United States of America

State	abbreviation	State Capital	Other Major Cities
Alabama /ˌæləˈbæmə/	AL	Montgomery /mənt'gʌməri; mɑnt-/	Birmingham /ˈbərmɪŋˌhæm/
Alaska /əˈlæskə/	AK	Juneau /ˈdʒunoʊ/	Anchorage /ˈæŋkərɪdʒ/ Fairbanks /ˈfɛrbæŋks/
Arizona /ˌærəˈzoʊnə/	AZ	Phoenix /ˈfinɪks/	Tucson /ˈtusɑn/
Arkansas /ˈɑrkənˌsɔ/	AR	Little Rock /ˈlɪtl̩ ˌrɑk/	
California /ˌkæləˈfɔrnyə/	CA	Sacramento /ˌsækrəˈmɛntoʊ/	Los Angeles /lɔs ˈændʒələs/ San Diego /ˌsæn diˈeɪgoʊ/ San Francisco /ˌsæn frənˈsɪskoʊ/
Colorado /ˌkɑləˈrædoʊ; -ˈrɑdoʊ/	CO	Denver /ˈdɛnvər/	
Connecticut /kəˈnɛt̬ɪkət/	CT	Hartford /ˈhɑrtfərd/	
Delaware /ˈdɛləˌwɛr/	DE	Dover /ˈdoʊvər/	
Florida /ˈflɔrədə; ˈflɑr-/	FL	Tallahassee /ˌtæləˈhæsi/	Miami /maɪˈæmi/ Orlando /ɔrˈlændoʊ/
Georgia /ˈdʒɔrdʒə/	GA	Atlanta /ətˈlæntə/	Savannah /səˈvænə/
Hawaii /həˈwaɪi/	HI	Honolulu /ˌhɑnəˈlulu/	
Idaho /ˈaɪdəˌhoʊ/	ID	Boise /ˈbɔɪzi; -si/	Idaho Falls /ˌaɪdəhoʊ ˈfɔlz/
Illinois /ˌɪləˈnɔɪ/	IL	Springfield /ˈsprɪŋfild/	Chicago /ʃɪˈkɑgoʊ; -ˈkɔgoʊ/
Indiana /ˌɪndiˈænə/	IN	Indianapolis /ˌɪndiəˈnæpələs/	
Iowa /ˈaɪəwə/	IA	Des Moines /də ˈmɔɪn/	Cedar Rapids /ˌsidər ˈræpədz/
Kansas /ˈkænzəs/	KS	Topeka /təˈpikə/	Wichita /ˈwɪtʃəˌtɔ/
Kentucky /kənˈtʌki/	KY	Frankfort /ˈfræŋkfərt/	
Louisiana /luˌiziˈænə/	LA	Baton Rouge /ˌbætn̩ ˈruʒ/	New Orleans /nu ˈɔrlənz; -ɔrˈlinz/
Maine /meɪn/	ME	Augusta /ɔˈgʌstə; ə-/	Portland /ˈpɔrtlənd/
Maryland /ˈmɛrələnd/	MD	Annapolis /əˈnæpələs/	Baltimore /ˈbɔltəˌmɔr/
Massachusetts /ˌmæsəˈtʃusəts/	MA	Boston /ˈbɔstən/	
Michigan /ˈmɪʃɪgən/	MI	Lansing /ˈlænsɪŋ/	Detroit /dɪˈtrɔɪt/
Minnesota /ˌmɪnəˈsoʊt̬ə/	MN	St. Paul /ˌseɪnt ˈpɔl/	Minneapolis /ˌmɪniˈæpələs/
Mississippi /ˌmɪsəˈsɪpi/	MS	Jackson /ˈdʒæksn̩/	
Missouri /məˈzʊri/	MO	Jefferson City /ˌdʒɛfərsn ˈsɪt̬i/	St. Louis /ˌseɪnt ˈluəs/
Montana /mɑnˈtænə/	MT	Helena /ˈhɛlənə/	Billings /ˈbɪlɪŋz/
Nebraska /nəˈbræskə/	NE	Lincoln /ˈlɪŋkən/	Omaha /ˈoʊməˌhɑ; -ˌhɔ/
Nevada /nəˈvædə; -ˈvɑdə/	NV	Carson City /ˌkɑrsn ˈsɪt̬i/	Las Vegas /lɑs ˈveɪgəs/
New Hampshire /ˌnu ˈhæmpʃər/	NH	Concord /ˈkɑŋkərd/	Manchester /ˈmænˌtʃɛstər/
New Jersey /ˌnu ˈdʒɜrzi/	NJ	Trenton /ˈtrɛntn̩/	Newark /ˈnuərk/
New Mexico /ˌnu ˈmɛksɪˌkoʊ/	NM	Santa Fe /ˌsæntə ˈfeɪ/	Albuquerque /ˈælbəˌkərki/
New York /ˌnu ˈyɔrk/	NY	Albany /ˈɔlbəni/	Buffalo /ˈbʌfəˌloʊ/ New York /ˌnu ˈyɔrk/ Rochester /ˈrɑtʃəstər; -ˌtʃɛstər/
North Carolina /ˌnɔrθ kærəˈlaɪnə/	NC	Raleigh /ˈrɔli; ˈrɑli/	Charlotte /ˈʃɑrlət/
North Dakota /ˌnɔrθ dəˈkoʊt̬ə/	ND	Bismarck /ˈbɪzmɑrk/	Fargo /ˈfɑrgoʊ/
Ohio /oʊˈhaɪoʊ/	OH	Columbus /kəˈlʌmbəs/	Cleveland /ˈklivlənd/ Cincinnati /ˌsɪnsəˈnæt̬i/

State	abbreviation	State Capital	Other Major Cities
Oklahoma /ˌoʊkləˈhoʊmə/	OK	Oklahoma City /ˌoʊkləhoʊmə ˈsɪt̬i/	Tulsa /ˈtʌlsə/
Oregon /ˈɔrəgən; ˈɑr-; -ˌgɑn/	OR	Salem /ˈseɪləm/	Portland /ˈpɔrtlənd/
Pennsylvania /ˌpɛnslˈveɪnyə/	PA	Harrisburg /ˈhærəsˌbərg/	Philadelphia /ˌfɪləˈdɛlfiə/ Pittsburgh /ˈpɪtsbərg/
Rhode Island /ˌroʊd ˈaɪlənd/	RI	Providence /ˈprɑvədəns/	
South Carolina /ˌsaʊθ kærəˈlaɪnə/	SC	Columbia /kəˈlʌmbiə/	Charleston /ˈtʃɑrlstən/
South Dakota /ˌsaʊθ dəˈkoʊt̬ə/	SD	Pierre /pɪr/	Sioux Falls /ˌsu ˈfɔlz/
Tennessee /ˌtɛnəˈsi/	TN	Nashville /ˈnæʃvɪl/	Memphis /ˈmɛmfəs/
Texas /ˈtɛksəs/	TX	Austin /ˈɔstən/	Dallas /ˈdæləs/ Fort Worth /ˌfɔrt ˈwərθ/ Houston /ˈhyustən/ San Antonio /ˌsæn ænˈtoʊnioʊ/
Utah /ˈyutɔ; ˈyutɑ/	UT	Salt Lake City /ˌsɔlt leɪk ˈsɪt̬i/	Provo /ˈproʊvoʊ/
Vermont /vərˈmɑnt/	VT	Montpelier /mɑntˈpilyər/	
Virginia /vərˈdʒɪnyə/	VA	Richmond /ˈrɪtʃmənd/	Norfolk /ˈnɔrfək/
Washington /ˈwɑʃɪŋtən; ˈwɔ-/	WA	Olympia /əˈlɪmpiə/	Seattle /siˈæt̬l/
West Virginia /ˌwɛst vərˈdʒɪnyə/	WV	Charleston /ˈtʃɑrlstən/	
Wisconsin /wɪsˈkɑnsn/	WI	Madison /ˈmædəsn/	Milwaukee /mɪlˈwɔki/
Wyoming /waɪˈoʊmɪŋ/	WY	Cheyenne /ʃaɪˈæn/	

The Great Lakes

Lake Erie /ˌleɪk ˈɪri/
Lake Ontario /ˌleɪk ɑnˈtɛrioʊ/
Lake Huron /ˌleɪk ˈhyʊrɑn; -ən/
Lake Superior /ˌleɪk səˈpɪriər/
Lake Michigan /ˌleɪk ˈmɪʃɪgən/

The Provinces and Territories of Canada

Province/Territory	Provincial/Territorial Capital	Other Major Cities
Alberta /ælˈbərt̬ə/	Edmonton /ˈɛdməntən/	Calgary /ˈkælgəri/
British Columbia /ˌbrɪtɪʃ kəˈlʌmbiə/	Victoria /vɪkˈtɔriə/	Vancouver /vænˈkuvər/
Manitoba /ˌmænəˈtoʊbə/	Winnipeg /ˈwɪnəˌpɛg/	
New Brunswick /ˌnu ˈbrʌnzwɪk/	Fredericton /ˈfrɛdrɪktən/	
Newfoundland and Labrador /nufəndlənd ən ˈlæbrədɔr/	St. John's /ˌseɪnt ˈdʒɑnz/	
Northwest Territories /ˌnɔrθwɛst ˈtɛrətɔriz/	Yellowknife /ˈyɛloʊˌnaɪf/	
Nova Scotia /ˌnoʊvə ˈskoʊʃə/	Halifax /ˈhæləˌfæks/	
Nunavut /ˈnunəˌvʊt/	Iqaluit /ɪˈkæluət/	
Ontario /ɑnˈtɛrioʊ/	Toronto /təˈrɑntoʊ/	Ottawa /ˈɑt̬əwə/
Prince Edward Island /ˌprɪns ˌɛdwərd ˈaɪlənd/	Charlottetown /ˈʃɑrlətˌtaʊn/	
Québec /kwɪˈbɛk; kəˈbɛk/	Québec City /kwɪˌbɛk ˈsɪt̬i; kəˌbɛk-/	Montréal /ˌmɑntriˈɔl/
Saskatchewan /sæˈskætʃəwən; -ˌwɑn/	Regina /rɪˈdʒaɪnə/	Saskatoon /ˌsæskəˈtun/
Yukon Territory /ˌyukɑn ˈtɛrətɔri/	Whitehorse /ˈwaɪthɔrs/	

Geographical Names

This list shows the English spelling and pronunciation of geographical names.

If a country has different words for the country, adjective, and person, all are given (for example **Denmark**; **Danish**, **a Dane**). To make the plural of a word for a person from a particular country, add **-s**, except for **Swiss** and for words ending in **-ese** (for example **Japanese**), which stay the same, and for words that end in **-man** or **-woman**, which change to **-men** or **-women**.

Inclusion in this list does not imply status as a sovereign nation.

Noun	Adjective, Person
Afghanistan /æfˈɡænəˌstæn/	Afghan /ˈæfɡæn/
Africa /ˈæfrɪkə/	African /ˈæfrɪkən/
Albania /ælˈbeɪniə/	Albanian /ælˈbeɪniən/
Algeria /ælˈdʒɪriə/	Algerian /ælˈdʒɪriən/
America /əˈmɛrɪkə/	American /əˈmɛrɪkən/
Andorra /ænˈdɔrə/	Andorran /ænˈdɔrən/
Angola /æŋˈɡoʊlə/	Angolan /æŋˈɡoʊlən/
Antarctica /æntˈɑrktɪkə; -ˈɑrtɪkə/	Antarctic /æntˈɑrktɪk; -ˈɑrtɪk/
Antigua and Barbuda /ænˌtiɡə ən barˈbudə/	Antiguan /ænˈtiɡən/, Barbudan /barˈbudn/
(the) Arctic /ˈɑrktɪk; ˈɑrtɪk/	Arctic /ˈɑrktɪk; ˈɑrtɪk/
Argentina /ˌɑrdʒənˈtinə/	Argentine /ˈɑrdʒənˌtin; -taɪn/ Argentinian /ˌɑrdʒənˈtɪniən/
Armenia /ɑrˈminiə/	Armenian /ɑrˈminiən/
Asia /ˈeɪʒə/	Asian /ˈeɪʒn/
Australasia /ˌɔstrəˈleɪʒə/	Australasian /ˌɔstrəˈleɪʒən/
Australia /ɔˈstreɪlyə/	Australian /ɔˈstreɪlyən/
Austria /ˈɔstriə/	Austrian /ˈɔstriən/
Azerbaijan /ˌæzərbaɪˈdʒan; ˌazər-/	Azerbaijani /ˌæzərbaɪˈdʒani; ˌazər-/
(the) Bahamas /bəˈhaməz/	Bahamian /bəˈheɪmiən/
Bahrain /baˈreɪn/	Bahraini /baˈreɪni/
Bangladesh /ˌbaŋɡləˈdɛʃ; ˌbæŋ-/	Bangladeshi /ˌbaŋɡləˈdɛʃi; ˌbæŋ-/
Barbados /barˈbeɪdoʊs/	Barbadian /barˈbeɪdiən/
Belarus /ˌbɛləˈrus/	Belarusian /ˌbɛləˈrusiən/, Belorussian /ˌbɛləˈrʌʃn/
Belgium /ˈbɛldʒəm/	Belgian /ˈbɛldʒən/
Belize /bəˈliz/	Belizean /bəˈliziən/
Benin /bəˈnin/	Beninese /ˌbɛnəˈniz; -ˈnis/
Bhutan /buˈtan/	Bhutanese /ˌbutnˈiz; -ˈis/
Bolivia /bəˈlɪviə/	Bolivian /bəˈlɪviən/
Bosnia and Herzegovina /ˌbazniə ən ˌhɛrtsəɡoʊˈvinə/	Bosnian /ˈbazniən/, Herzegovinian /ˌhɛrtsəɡəˈvɪniən/
Botswana /batˈswanə/	Botswanan /batˈswanən/, **a Motswana** /moʊtˈswanə; mat-/ plural **Batswana** /batˈswanə; bæt-/
Brazil /brəˈzɪl/	Brazilian /brəˈzɪlyən/
Brunei /bruˈnaɪ /	Bruneian /bruˈnaɪən/
Bulgaria /bʌlˈɡɛriə/	Bulgarian /bʌlˈɡɛriən/
Burkina Faso /bərˌkinə ˈfasoʊ/	Burkinabe /bərˌkinəˈbeɪ/
Burma /ˈbərmə/ **(now officially Myanmar)**	Burmese /ˌbərˈmiz; -ˈmis/
Burundi /bʊˈrʊndi; -ˈrun-/	Burundian /bʊˈrʊndiən; -ˈrun-/
Cambodia /kæmˈboʊdiə/	Cambodian /kæmˈboʊdiən/
Cameroon /ˌkæməˈrun /	Cameroonian /ˌkæməˈruniən/
Canada /ˈkænədə/	Canadian /kəˈneɪdiən/
Cape Verde /ˌkeɪp ˈvərd/	Cape Verdean /ˌkeɪp ˈvərdiən/

Noun	Adjective, Person
(the) Central African Republic /ˌsɛntrəl ˌæfrɪkən rɪˈpʌblɪk/	Central African /ˌsɛntrəl ˈæfrɪkən/
Chad /tʃæd/	Chadian /ˈtʃædiən/
Chile /ˈtʃɪli/	Chilean /ˈtʃɪliən; tʃɪˈleɪən/
China /ˈtʃaɪnə/	Chinese /ˌtʃaɪˈniz; -ˈnis/
Colombia /kəˈlʌmbiə/	Colombian /kəˈlʌmbiən/
Comoros /ˈkɑməˌroʊz/	Comoran /ˈkɑmərən; kəˈmɔrən/
Congo /ˈkɑŋgoʊ/	Congolese /ˌkɑŋgəˈliz; -ˈlis/
Costa Rica /ˌkoʊstə ˈrikə; ˌkɑstə-/	Costa Rican /ˌkoʊstə ˈrikən; ˌkɑstə-/
Côte d'Ivoire /ˌkoʊt diˈvwɑr/	Ivorian /aɪˈvɔriən/
Croatia /kroʊˈeɪʃə/	Croatian /kroʊˈeɪʃn/
Cuba /ˈkyubə/	Cuban /ˈkyubən/
Cyprus /ˈsaɪprəs/	Cypriot /ˈsɪpriət/
(the) Czech Republic /ˌtʃɛk rɪˈpʌblɪk/	Czech /tʃɛk/
(the) Democratic Republic of the Congo /ˌdɛməˌkrætɪk rɪˌpʌblɪk əv ðə ˈkɑŋgoʊ/	Congolese /ˌkɑŋgəˈliz; -ˈlis/
Denmark /ˈdɛnmɑrk/	Danish /ˈdeɪnɪʃ/, **a Dane** /deɪn/
Djibouti /dʒɪˈbuṭi/	Djiboutian /dʒɪˈbuṭiən/
Dominica /ˌdɑməˈnikə/	Dominican /ˌdɑməˈnikən/
(the) Dominican Republic /dəˌmɪnɪkən rɪˈpʌblɪk/	Dominican /dəˈmɪnɪkən/
East Timor /ˌist ˈtimɔr/	East Timorese /ˌist ˌtimɔˈriz; -ˈris/
Ecuador /ˈɛkwəˌdɔr/	Ecuadorian, Ecuadorean /ˌɛkwəˈdɔriən/
Egypt /ˈidʒɪpt/	Egyptian /ɪˈdʒɪpʃn/
El Salvador /ɛl ˈsælvəˌdɔr/	Salvadoran /ˌsælvəˈdɔrən/
England /ˈɪŋglənd/	English /ˈɪŋglɪʃ/
Equatorial Guinea /ˌikwəˌtɔriəl ˈgɪni; ˌɛkwə-/	Equatorial Guinean /ˌikwəˌtɔriəl ˈgɪniən; ˌɛkwə-/
Eritrea /ˌɛrəˈtriə/	Eritrean /ˌɛrəˈtriən/
Estonia /ɛˈstoʊniə/	Estonian /ɛˈstoʊniən/
Ethiopia /ˌiθiˈoʊpiə/	Ethiopian /ˌiθiˈoʊpiən/
Europe /ˈyʊrəp/	European /ˌyʊrəˈpiən/
Fiji /ˈfidʒi/	Fijian /ˈfidʒiən; fɪˈdʒiən/
Finland /ˈfɪnlənd/	Finnish /ˈfɪnɪʃ/, **a Finn** /fɪn/
France /fræns/	French /frɛntʃ/, **a Frenchman** /ˈfrɛntʃmən/, **a Frenchwoman** /ˈfrɛntʃˌwʊmən/
(the) Former Yugoslav Republic of Macedonia /ˌfɔrmər ˌyugəslav rɪˈpʌblɪk əv ˌmæsəˈdoʊniə/	Macedonian /ˌmæsəˈdoʊniən/
Gabon /gæˈboʊn/	Gabonese /ˌgæbəˈniz; -ˈnis/
(the) Gambia /ˈgæmbiə/	Gambian /ˈgæmbiən/
Georgia /ˈdʒɔrdʒə/	Georgian /ˈdʒɔrdʒən/
Germany /ˈdʒərməni/	German /ˈdʒərmən/
Ghana /ˈgɑnə/	Ghanaian /gɑˈneɪən/
Great Britain /ˌgreɪt ˈbrɪtn/	British /ˈbrɪtɪʃ/
Greece /gris/	Greek /grik/
Grenada /grəˈneɪdə/	Grenadian /grəˈneɪdiən/
Guatemala /ˌgwɑṭəˈmɑlə/	Guatemalan /ˌgwɑṭəˈmɑlən/
Guinea /ˈgɪni/	Guinean /ˈgɪniən/
Guinea-Bissau /ˌgɪni bɪˈsaʊ/	Guinean /ˈgɪniən/
Guyana /gaɪˈænə; -ˈɑnə/	Guyanese /ˌgaɪəˈniz; -ˈnis/
Haiti /ˈheɪṭi/	Haitian /ˈheɪʃn/
Holland /ˈhɑlənd/ → (the) Netherlands	
Honduras /hɑnˈdʊrəs/	Honduran /hɑnˈdʊrən/
Hungary /ˈhʌŋgəri/	Hungarian /hʌŋˈgɛriən/
Iceland /ˈaɪslənd/	Icelandic /aɪsˈlændɪk/, **an Icelander** /ˈaɪsˌlændər; -ləndər/

Noun	Adjective, Person
India /ˈɪndiə/	Indian /ˈɪndiən/
Indonesia /ˌɪndəˈniʒə/	Indonesian /ˌɪndəˈniʒn/
Iran /ɪˈrɑn; ɪˈræn/	Iranian /ɪˈreɪniən; ɪˈrɑ-/
Iraq /ɪˈrɑk; ɪˈræk/	Iraqi /ɪˈrɑki; ɪˈræki/
Israel /ˈɪzriəl; ˈɪzreɪl/	Israeli /ɪzˈreɪli/
Italy /ˈɪt̬l•i/	Italian /ɪˈtælyən/
(the) Ivory Coast /ˌaɪvri ˈkoʊst; ˌaɪvəri-/ → Côte d'Ivoire	
Jamaica /dʒəˈmeɪkə/	Jamaican /dʒəˈmeɪkən/
Japan /dʒəˈpæn/	Japanese /ˌdʒæpəˈniz; -ˈnis/
Jordan /ˈdʒɔrdn/	Jordanian /dʒɔrˈdeɪniən/
Kazakhstan /ˌkazakˈstɑn/	Kazakh /kəˈzak/, Kazakhstani /ˌkazakˈstɑni/
Kenya /ˈkɛnyə; ˈkin-/	Kenyan /ˈkɛnyən; ˈkin-/
Kiribati /ˈkɪrəˌbæs; ˌkɪrəˈbɑt̬i/	I-Kiribati /ˌi ˈkɪrəˌbæs; ˌi ˌkɪrəˈbɑt̬i/
Korea /kəˈriə/ → North Korea, South Korea	Korean /kəˈriən/
Kuwait /kʊˈweɪt/	Kuwaiti /kʊˈweɪt̬i/
Kyrgyzstan /ˈkɪrgɪstæn; -ˌstɑn/	Kyrgyz /kɪrˈgiz/, Kyrgyzstani /ˌkɪrgɪˈstɑni; -ˈstæni/
Laos /laʊs; ˈlaoʊs/	Laotian /leɪˈoʊʃn/, Lao /laʊ/
Latvia /ˈlætviə/	Latvian /ˈlætviən/
Lebanon /ˈlɛbəˌnɑn; -nən/	Lebanese /ˌlɛbəˈniz; -ˈnis/
Lesotho /ləˈsoʊtoʊ; ləˈsutu/	Basotho /bəˈsoʊtoʊ; -ˈsutu/, a Mosotho /məˈsoʊtoʊ; -ˈsutu/, plural Basotho /bəˈsoʊtoʊ; -ˈsutu/
Liberia /laɪˈbɪriə/	Liberian /laɪˈbɪriən/
Libya /ˈlɪbiə/	Libyan /ˈlɪbiən/
Liechtenstein /ˈlɪktənˌstaɪn; -ˌʃtaɪn/	Liechtenstein /ˈlɪktənˌstaɪn; -ˌʃtaɪn/, a Liechtensteiner /ˈlɪktənˌstaɪnər; -ˌʃtaɪnər/
Lithuania /ˌlɪθuˈeɪniə/	Lithuanian /ˌlɪθuˈeɪniən/
Luxembourg /ˈlʌksəmˌbərg/	Luxembourg /ˈlʌksəmˌbərg/, a Luxembourger /ˈlʌksəmˌbərgər/
Macedonia /ˌmæsəˈdoʊniə/	Macedonian /ˌmæsəˈdoʊniən/
Madagascar /ˌmædəˈgæskər/	Madagascan /ˌmædəˈgæskən/
Malawi /məˈlɑwi/	Malawian /məˈlɑwiən/
Malaysia /məˈleɪʒə/	Malaysian /məˈleɪʒn/
(the) Maldives /ˈmɔldivz; -daɪvz/	Maldivian /mɔlˈdɪviən/
Mali /ˈmɑli/	Malian /ˈmɑliən/
Malta /ˈmɔltə/	Maltese /ˌmɔlˈtiz; -ˈtis/
(the) Marshall Islands /ˌmɑrʃl ˈaɪləndz/	Marshallese /ˌmɑrʃəˈliz; -ˈlis/
Mauritania /ˌmɔrəˈteɪniə/	Mauritanian /ˌmɔrəˈteɪniən/
Mauritius /mɔˈrɪʃəs/	Mauritian /mɔˈrɪʃn/
Mexico /ˈmɛksɪˌkoʊ/	Mexican /ˈmɛksɪkən/
Micronesia /ˌmaɪkrəˈniʒə/	Micronesian /ˌmaɪkrəˈniʒn/
Moldova /mɑlˈdoʊvə; mɔl-/	Moldovan /mɑlˈdoʊvn, mɔl-/
Monaco /ˈmɑnəˌkoʊ/	Monegasque /ˌmɑnɪˈgæsk/, Monacan /ˈmɑnəkən/
Mongolia /mɑŋˈgoʊliə/	Mongolian /mɑŋˈgoʊliən/
Montenegro /ˌmɑntəˈnɛgroʊ; -ˈnigroʊ/	Montenegrin /ˌmɑntəˈnɛgrən; -ˈnigrən/
Morocco /məˈrɑkoʊ/	Moroccan /məˈrɑkən/
Mozambique /ˌmoʊzæmˈbik; -zəm-/	Mozambican /ˌmoʊzæmˈbikən; -zəm-/
Myanmar /ˈmyanmɑr; ˈmyæn-/	Burmese /ˌbərˈmiz; -ˈmis/
Namibia /nəˈmɪbiə/	Namibian /nəˈmɪbiən/
Nauru /nɑˈuru/	Nauruan /nɑˈuruən/
Nepal /nəˈpɔl; nəˈpɑl/	Nepalese /ˌnɛpəˈliz; -ˈlis/

Noun	Adjective, Person
(the) Netherlands /'nɛðərləndz/	Dutch /dʌtʃ/, a Dutchman /'dʌtʃmən/, a Dutchwoman /'dʌtʃ,wʊmən/
New Zealand /,nu 'zilənd/	New Zealand /,nu 'zilənd/, a New Zealander /,nu'ziləndər/
Nicaragua /,nɪkə'rɑgwə/	Nicaraguan /,nɪkə'rɑgwən/
Niger /ni'ʒɛr; 'naɪdʒər/	Nigerien /ni'ʒɛriən; naɪ,dʒiri'ɛn/
Nigeria /naɪ'dʒɪriə/	Nigerian /naɪ'dʒɪriən/
Northern Ireland /,nɔrðərn 'aɪərlənd/	Northern Irish /,nɔrðərn 'aɪrɪʃ/
North Korea /,nɔrθ kə'riə/	North Korean /,nɔrθ kə'riən/
Norway /'nɔrweɪ/	Norwegian /nɔr'widʒən/
Oceania /,oʊʃi'æniə/	Oceanian /,oʊʃi'æniən/
Oman /oʊ'mɑn/	Omani /oʊ'mɑni/
Pakistan /'pækə,stæn; 'pɑkə,stɑn/	Pakistani /,pækə'stæni; ,pɑkə'stɑni/
Palau /pə'laʊ/	Palauan /pə'laʊən/
Panama /'pænə,mɑ/	Panamanian /,pænə'meɪniən/
Papua New Guinea /,pæpyuə nu 'gini; ,pæpuə-/	Papua New Guinean /,pæpyuə nu 'giniən; ,pæpuə-/
Paraguay /'pærə,gwaɪ; -,gweɪ/	Paraguayan /,pærə'gwaɪən; -'gweɪ-/
Peru /pə'ru/	Peruvian /pə'ruviən/
(the) Philippines /'fɪlə,pinz; ,fɪlə'pinz/	Philippine /'fɪlə,pin/, a Filipino /,fɪlə'pinoʊ/, a Filipina /,fɪlə'pinə/
Poland /'poʊlənd/	Polish /'poʊlɪʃ/, a Pole /poʊl/
Portugal /'pɔrtʃəgl/	Portuguese /,pɔrtʃə'giz; -'gis; 'pɔrtʃə,giz; -,gis/
Qatar /'katar; -tər/	Qatari /kə'tari/
(the) Republic of Ireland /rɪ,pʌblɪk əv 'aɪərlənd/	Irish /'aɪrɪʃ/
Romania /rʊ'meɪniə; roʊ-/	Romanian /rʊ'meɪniən; roʊ-/
Russia /'rʌʃə/	Russian /'rʌʃn/
Rwanda /ru'ɑndə/	Rwandan /ru'ɑndən/
Saint Kitts and Nevis /seɪnt ,kɪts ən 'nivəs/	Kittitian /kə'tɪʃn/, Nevisian /nə'vɪʒn/
Saint Lucia /,seɪnt 'luʃə/	Saint Lucian /seɪnt 'luʃən/
Saint Vincent and the Grenadines /seɪnt vɪnsnt ən ðə 'grɛnədinz/	Saint Vincentian /,seɪnt vɪn'sɛnʃn/, Vincentian /vɪn'sɛnʃn/
Samoa /sə'moʊə/	Samoan /sə'moʊən/
San Marino /,sæn mə'rinoʊ/	Sammarinese /,sæm,mærə'niz; -'nis/
São Tomé and Principe /,saʊ tə'meɪ ən 'prɪnsəpi; ,saʊn-/	São Tomean /,saʊ tə'meɪən; ,saʊn-/
Saudi Arabia /,saʊdi ə'reɪbiə; ,sɔdi-/	Saudi /'saʊdi; 'sɔdi/, Saudi Arabian /,saʊdi ə'reɪbiən; ,sɔdi-/
Scandinavia /,skændə'neɪviə/	Scandinavian /,skændə'neɪviən/
Scotland /'skɑtlənd/	Scottish /'skɑtɪʃ/, Scots /skɑts/, a Scot /skɑt/
Senegal /'sɛnəgɔl; -gɑl/	Senegalese /,sɛnəgə'liz; -'lis/
Serbia /'sərbiə/	Serbian /'sərbiən/, a Serb /sərb/
(the) Seychelles /seɪ'ʃɛlz; -'ʃɛl/	Seychellois /,seɪʃɛl'wɑ/
Sierra Leone /si,ɛrə li'oʊn/	Sierra Leonean /si,ɛrə li'oʊniən/
Singapore /'sɪŋə,pɔr/	Singaporean /,sɪŋə'pɔriən/, Singapore /'sɪŋə,pɔr/
Slovakia /sloʊ'vakiə/	Slovak /'sloʊvɑk/, Slovakian /sloʊ'vakiən/
Slovenia /sloʊ'viniə/	Slovenian /sloʊ'viniən/
(the) Solomon Islands /,sɑləmən 'aɪləndz/	a Solomon Islander /,sɑləmən 'aɪləndər/
Somalia /sə'mɑliə/	Somali /sə'mɑli/
South Africa /,saʊθ 'æfrɪkə/	South African /,saʊθ 'æfrɪkən/
South Korea /,saʊθ kə'riə/	South Korean /,saʊθ kə'riən/
Spain /speɪn/	Spanish /'spænɪʃ/, a Spaniard /'spænyərd/
Sri Lanka /,sri 'laŋkə; ,ʃri-/	Sri Lankan /,sri 'laŋkən; ,ʃri-/
Sudan /su'dæn/	Sudanese /,sudn'iz; -'is/

Noun	Adjective, Person
Suriname /ˈsʊrəˌnɑm; -ˌnæm; ˌsʊrəˈnɑmə/	Surinamese /ˌsʊrənəˈmiz; -ˈmis/
Swaziland /ˈswɑziˌlænd/	Swazi /ˈswɑzi/
Sweden /ˈswidn/	Swedish /ˈswidɪʃ/, **a Swede** /swid/
Switzerland /ˈswɪtsərlənd/	Swiss /swɪs/
Syria /ˈsɪriə/	Syrian /ˈsɪriən/
Tajikistan /təˈdʒikəˌstæn; -ˈdʒɪkə-; -ˌstɑn/	Tajik /tɑˈdʒik; tɑˈdʒɪk/, Tajikistani /təˌdʒikəˈstɑni; -ˌdʒɪkə-; -ˈstæni/
Tanzania /ˌtænzəˈniə/	Tanzanian /ˌtænzəˈniən/
Thailand /ˈtaɪlænd/	Thai /taɪ/
Togo /ˈtoʊɡoʊ/	Togolese /ˌtoʊɡəˈliz; -ˈlis/
Tonga /ˈtɑŋɡə/	Tongan /ˈtɑŋɡən/
Trinidad and Tobago /ˌtrɪnədæd ən təˈbeɪɡoʊ/	Trinidadian /ˌtrɪnəˈdædiən/, Tobagonian /ˌtoʊbəˈɡoʊniən/
Tunisia /tuˈniʒə/	Tunisian /tuˈniʒn/
Turkey /ˈtərki/	Turkish /ˈtərkɪʃ/, **a Turk** /tərk/
Turkmenistan /tərkˈmɛnəstæn; -stɑn/	Turkmen /ˈtərkmɛn; -mən/
Tuvalu /tuˈvɑlu/	Tuvaluan /tuˈvɑluən/
Uganda /yuˈgændə/	Ugandan /yuˈgændən/
Ukraine /yuˈkreɪn; ˈyukreɪn/	Ukrainian /yuˈkreɪniən/
(the) United Arab Emirates /yʊˌnaɪṭəd ˌærəb ˈɛmərəts/	Emirati /ˌɛməˈrɑṭi/
(the) United Kingdom /yʊˌnaɪṭəd ˈkɪŋdəm/	British /ˈbrɪtɪʃ/
(the) United States of America /yʊˌnaɪṭəd ˌsteɪts əv əˈmɛrɪkə/	American /əˈmɛrɪkən/
Uruguay /ˈyʊrəˌgwaɪ; -ˌgweɪ/	Uruguayan /ˌyʊrəˈgwaɪən; -ˈgweɪ-/
Uzbekistan /ʊzˈbɛkəstæn; -stɑn/	Uzbek /ˈʊzbɛk/, Uzbekistani /ʊzˌbɛkəˈstɑni; -ˈstæni/
Vanuatu /ˌvɑnuˈɑtu; ˌvænu-/	Ni-Vanuatu /ˌni ˌvɑnuˈɑtu; -ˌvænu-/
(the) Vatican City /ˌvæṭɪkən ˈsiṭi/	—
Venezuela /ˌvɛnəˈzweɪlə/	Venezuelan /ˌvɛnəˈzweɪlən/
Vietnam /ˌviɛtˈnɑm; -ˈnæm/	Vietnamese /ˌviɛtnəˈmiz; viˌɛt-; -ˈmis/
Wales /weɪlz/	Welsh /wɛlʃ/
(the) West Indies /ˌwɛst ˈɪndiz/	West Indian /ˌwɛst ˈɪndiən/
Yemen /ˈyɛmən/	Yemeni /ˈyɛməni/
Zambia /ˈzæmbiə/	Zambian /ˈzæmbiən/
Zimbabwe /zɪmˈbɑbweɪ; -wi/	Zimbabwean /zɪmˈbɑbweɪən; -wiən/

Expressions Using Numbers

Writing and Saying Numbers

Numbers over 20
- are written with a hyphen:
  35 thirty-five
  67 sixty-seven
- When writing a check, we often use words for the dollars and figures for the cents:
  $79.30 seventy-nine dollars (and) $^{30}/_{100}$

Numbers over 100
329 three hundred and twenty-nine (also *informal* three twenty-nine)
- The **and** is pronounced /n/ and the stress is on the final number.
- The **and** is sometimes left out.
- The **hundred** can also be left out in more informal speech.

Numbers over 1,000
1,100 one thousand one hundred (also *informal* eleven hundred)
2,500 two thousand five hundred (also *informal* twenty-five hundred)
- These informal forms are most common for whole hundreds between 1,100 and 1,900.
- A comma is often used to divide large numbers into groups of 3 figures:
  > *33,423 (thirty-three thousand, four hundred and twenty-three)*
  > *2,768,941 (two million, seven hundred and sixty-eight thousand, nine hundred and forty-one)*

A or One?
130   a/one hundred and thirty
1,000,000 a/one million
- **one** is more formal and more precise, and can be used for emphasis:
  > *The total cost was one hundred and sixty-three dollars exactly.*
  > *It cost about a hundred and fifty dollars.*
- **a** can only be used at the beginning of a number:
  1,000 a/one thousand
  2,100 two thousand, one hundred
          ~~two thousand a hundred~~
- **a** is not usually used between 1,100 and 1,999
  1,099 a/one thousand and ninety-nine
  1,100 one thousand, one hundred
  1,340 one thousand, three hundred and forty
          ~~a thousand three hundred and forty~~

Ordinal Numbers

1st	first	4th	fourth	12th	twelfth
2nd	second	5th	fifth	21st	twenty-first,
3rd	third	9th	ninth		etc.

Fractions

½	a/one half		$^1/_{16}$	one sixteenth
⅓	a/one third		$^2/_3$	two thirds
¼	a/one quarter *or* a/one fourth		¾	three quarters *or* three fourths
	(for emphasis, use **one** instead of **a**)		$^9/_{10}$	nine tenths
$^1/_{12}$	one twelfth			

More Complex Fractions
- Use **over**:
  $^{19}/_{56}$ nineteen **over** fifty-six $^{31}/_{144}$ *thirty-one **over** one forty-four*

Whole Numbers and Fractions

- Link with **and**:
  - 2½   two and a half
  - 5⅔   five and two thirds

- **one** plus a fraction is followed by a plural noun:
  - 1½ lbs   one and a half pounds

Fractions/Percentages and Noun Phrases

- Use **of**:
  - > *a fifth* **of** *the women questioned*
  - > *three-quarters* **of** *the population*
  - > *75%* **of** *the population*

- With **half** do not use **a**, and **of** can sometimes be omitted:
  - > *Half (of) the work is already finished.*

- Do not use **of** in expressions of measurement or quantity:
  - > *How much is half a pound of cheese?*
  - > *It takes me half an hour by bus.*

- Use **of** before pronouns:
  - > *We can't start – only half* **of** *us are here.*

Fractions/Percentages and Verbs

- If a fraction/percentage is used with an uncountable or a singular noun, the verb is generally singular:
  - > *Fifty percent of the land is cultivated.*
  - > *Half (of) the land is cultivated.*
  - > *75% of the workforce is against the strike.*

- If the noun is plural, the verb is plural:
  - > *One-third of the children play sports regularly.*

Decimals

- Write and say with a point (.)
- Say each figure after the point separately:
  - 79.3   seventy-nine point three
  - 3.142 three point one four two
  - 0.67 (zero) point six seven

Mathematical Expressions

+	plus	%	percent
−	minus	3^2	three squared
×	times/multiplied by	5^3	five cubed
÷	divided by	6^{10}	six to the tenth power / six to the power of ten
=	equals	√	square root of

Zero

- used to talk about a number, age, etc.:
  - > *A million is written with six zeros.*
  - > *The car goes from zero to sixty in ten seconds.*
  - > *clothes for children aged zero to six*

- used in precise scientific, medical, and economic contexts and to talk about temperature:
  - > *zero inflation/growth/profit*
  - > *It was ten degrees below zero last night.*

- used to talk about the score in a team game, for example in soccer:
  - > *The final score was one-zero. (1-0)*

Telephone Numbers

- You say each number separately, often with a pause after the first three numbers. 0 is pronounced like "oh" /oʊ/:
  > *731-5037 seven three one, five oh three seven*
- If you are calling a number in a different area or on a cell phone, you have to use the area code first:
  > *(212) 569-2236 two one two, five six nine, two two three six*
- Numbers containing 00 are pronounced like this:
  > *1 (800) 555-1212 one eight hundred, five five five, one two one two*
  > *589-2300 five eight nine, two three hundred*

Temperature

- The Fahrenheit (°F) scale is usually used to measure temperature in the U.S.:
  > *Temperatures went up to over a hundred (=100°F).*
  > *You'll need a hat and gloves – it's three below (= -3°F) outside today!*
  > *She's sick in bed with a temperature of a hundred and two (=102°F).*
- The Celsius or Centigrade scale (°C) is used in scientific contexts:
  > *Water freezes at 0°C (= zero degrees Celsius) and boils at 100°C (= one hundred degrees Celsius).*

Money

1¢	one cent	a penny
5¢	five cents	a nickel
10¢	ten cents	a dime
25¢	twenty-five cents	a quarter
$1.00	one dollar	a dollar bill
$20.00	twenty dollars	a twenty-dollar bill *or* a twenty

- In informal speech, dollars are sometimes called **bucks** and a thousand dollars is called a **grand**:
  > *This shirt cost fifty bucks.*
  > *Her car cost over fifty grand!*

Writing and Saying Dates

> *October 14, 1998 (10/14/98)*
> *Her birthday is December 9th.*
> *Her birthday is on **the ninth of** December.*

Years

1999	nineteen ninety-nine
1608	sixteen o eight
1700	seventeen hundred
2000	(the year) two thousand
2002	two thousand and two
2015	twenty fifteen

A.D. 76   A.D. seventy-six
76 C.E.   seventy-six C.E.
(Both these expressions mean "76 years after the beginning of the Christian calendar." The period of the Christian calendar is now usually referred to as the "Common Era" (C.E.).)

1000 B.C.   one thousand B.C.
1000 B.C.E.   one thousand B.C.E.
(Both these expressions mean "1,000 years before the beginning of the Common Era.")

Age

- When saying a person's age, use only numbers:
  > Sue is ten and Tom is six.
  > She left home at sixteen.
- In writing, in descriptions, or to emphasize someone's age, use **... years old**:
  > She was thirty-one years old and a lawyer by profession.
  > He is described as white, 5 feet ten inches tall, and about 50 years old.
  > You're forty years old – stop behaving like a teenager!
- **... years old** is also used for things:
  > The monument is 120 years old.
- You can also say **a ... year-old/month-old/week-old**, etc.:
  > Job training is available to all eighteen-year-olds.
  > a ten-week-old baby
  > a remarkable 1,000-year-old tomb
- Use **... years of age** in formal or written contexts:
  > not applicable to people under eighteen years of age
- Use **the ... age group** to talk about people between certain ages:
  > He won first prize in the 10-16 age group.
- To give the approximate age of a person:
13-19	in his/her teens
21-29	in his/her twenties
31-33	in his/her early thirties
34-36	in his/her mid thirties
37-39	in his/her late thirties
- To refer to a particular event, you can use at/by/before, etc. the age of...
  > Most smokers start smoking cigarettes before the age of sixteen.

Numbers in Time

6:05	six o five	five after six
8:10	eight ten	ten after eight
4:15	four fifteen	(a) quarter after four
11:30	eleven thirty	half past eleven
9:45	nine forty-five	(a) quarter to/of ten
12:55	twelve fifty-five	five to/of one

- With 5, 10, 20, and 25 the word **minutes** is not necessary, but it is used with other numbers:
10:25	twenty-five after ten
10:17	seventeen **minutes** after ten
- Use **o'clock** only for whole hours:
  > It's three o'clock.
- The 12-hour clock is usually used in the U.S., so sometimes you need to specify the time of day:
  > He gets up at **4 a.m.** to deliver the mail (= in the morning).
  > The meeting will begin at **8 p.m.** sharp (= in the evening).
  > My plane leaves at six in the morning/three in the afternoon/six in the evening/eleven at night.
- Do not use **o'clock** with **a.m.** or **p.m.**:
  > He gets up at 4 o'clock a.m.
- The twenty-four hour clock is used for military purposes and in some other particular contexts, for example for air travel:
13:52	thirteen fifty-two (1:52 p.m.)
22:30	twenty-two thirty (10:30 p.m.)
- For military purposes, whole hours are said as **hundred hours**:
0400	(o) four hundred hours (4 a.m.)
2400	twenty-four hundred hours (midnight)

Weights and Measures

	U.S. Standard System	Metric System

Weight

	1 ounce (oz.)	= 28.35 grams (g)
16 ounces	= 1 pound (lb.)	= 0.454 kilogram (kg)
2,000 pounds	= 1 ton	= 907 kilograms

> *I weigh 195 pounds.*
> *Their new baby weighs 7 pounds, 12 ounces.*
> *The truck weighs over four tons.*
> *We added eight ounces of nuts to the cookies.*

Length/Distance/Height

	1 inch (in.)	= 2.54 centimeters (cm)
12 inches	= 1 foot (ft.)	= 30.48 centimeters
3 feet	= 1 yard (yd.)	= 0.9144 meter (m)
1,760 yards	= 1 mile	= 1.609 kilometers (km)

> *The bus stop is only 30 yards away from our house.*
> *The frame is 5 inches by 7 inches.*
> *There are 5,280 feet in one mile.*
> *He's only five feet four (inches).*
> *He's only five foot four.*

Area

	1 square inch (sq. inch)	= 6.45 square centimeters (cm^2)
144 square inches	= 1 square foot (sq. foot)	= 929.03 square centimeters
9 square feet	= 1 square yard (sq. yard)	= 0.836 square meter (m^2)
4,840 square yards	= 1 acre	= 0.405 hectare
640 acres	= 1 square mile	= 2.59 square kilometers (km^2) or 259 hectares

> *Our backyard measures 700 square feet.*
> *How many square inches are in a square yard?*
> *The farm has four acres of corn fields.*
> *Population density is only 24 people per square mile.*

Capacity

	1 fluid ounce (fl. oz.)	= 29.573 milliliters (ml)
16 fluid ounces	= 1 pint (pt.)	= 0.473 liter (l)
2 pints	= 1 quart (qt.)	= 0.946 liter
4 quarts	= 1 gallon (gal.)	= 3.785 liters
	1 teaspoon (tsp.)	= 5 milliliters
1 tablespoon (tbsp.)	= 3 teaspoons	= 15 milliliters
1 cup (c.)	= 8 ounces	= 237 milliliters
2 cups	= 1 pint	= 473 milliliters

> *I need to buy a gallon of milk and some bananas at the supermarket.*
> *How many pints are there in a gallon?*
> *To make bread, you will need 4 cups of flour and 1 tablespoon of yeast.*
> *My new car gets more than 50 miles to the gallon (= of gasoline/diesel).*

Punctuation

🔴 Period

- at the end of a sentence that is not a question or an exclamation:
  - ➤ *I knocked at the door. There was no reply.*
  - ➤ *I knocked again.*

- in abbreviations:
  - ➤ *Jan.   e.g.   etc.*

- in Internet and e-mail addresses (said "dot"):
  - ➤ *www.oup.com*

❓ Question Mark

- at the end of a direct question:
  - ➤ *Where's the car?*
  - ➤ *Are you leaving already?*

  Do not use a question mark at the end of an indirect question:
  - ➤ *He asked if I was leaving.*

- especially with a date, to express doubt:
  - ➤ *John Marston (?1575-1634)*

❗ Exclamation Point

- at the end of a sentence expressing surprise, joy, anger, shock, or another strong emotion:
  - ➤ *That's amazing!*
  - ➤ *"Never!" she cried.*

, Comma

- to separate items in a series:
  - ➤ *a bouquet of red, pink, and white roses*
  - ➤ *Do you want coffee, tea, or orange juice?*
  - ➤ *She was a tall, slim, beautiful woman.*

- to separate phrases or clauses:
  - ➤ *If you keep calm, take your time, concentrate, and think ahead, then you're likely to pass your test.*
  - ➤ *Worn out after all the excitement of the party, the children soon fell asleep.*

- before and after a clause or phrase that gives additional, but not essential, information about the noun it follows:
  - ➤ *Michael Jackson, the American pop star, was famous all over the world.*
  - ➤ *They don't like our dog, which barks all day.*

  Do not use commas before and after a clause that **defines** the noun it follows:
  - ➤ *The river that separates New York from New Jersey is called the Hudson.*

- to separate main clauses, especially long ones, linked by a conjunction such as *and, as, but, for, or*:
  - ➤ *We had been looking forward to our vacation all year, but unfortunately it rained every day.*

- to separate an introductory word or phrase, or an adverb or adverbial phrase that applies to the whole sentence, from the rest of the sentence:
  - ➤ *Oh, so that's where it was.*
  - ➤ *As it happens, however, I never saw her again.*
  - ➤ *By the way, did you hear about Joe's car?*

- to separate a tag question from the rest of the sentence:
  - ➤ *It's really expensive, isn't it?*
  - ➤ *You live in Chicago, right?*

- before or after "he said," etc. when writing down conversation:
  - ➤ *"Come back soon," she said.*
  - ➤ *She said, "Come back soon."*

- before or after a name when a person is being spoken to directly:
  - ➤ *Stuart, would you like to go?*
  - ➤ *I'm sorry, Jess.*

- to separate cities and towns from states:
  - ➤ *Des Moines, Iowa*
  - ➤ *Juneau, Alaska*

: Colon

- to introduce a list of items:
  - ➤ *These are our options: we go by train and leave before the end of the show, or we take the car and see the whole thing.*

- to introduce a quotation:
  - ➤ *As Thomas Jefferson said: "All men are born equal."*

- in formal writing, before a clause or phrase that gives more information about the main clause. (You can use a semicolon or a period, but not a comma, instead of a colon here):
  - ➤ *The garden had been neglected for a long time: It was overgrown and full of weeds.*

ℹ Semicolon

- instead of a comma to separate parts of a sentence that already contain commas:
  > *She was determined to finish cleaning the house; she had to fold the laundry; vacuum the rugs; and dust the furniture, lamps, and pictures.*

- in formal writing, to separate two main clauses, especially those not joined by a conjunction:
  > *The sun was already low in the sky; it would soon be dark.*

❷ Apostrophe

- with *s* to indicate that a person or thing belongs to someone:
  > *my friend's brother*
  > *James's car* or *James' car*
  > *the students' books*
  > *the women's coats*

- in short forms, to indicate that letters or figures have been omitted
  > *I'm* (I am)
  > *they'd* (they had/they would)
  > *the summer of '99* (1999)

- sometimes, with *s*, to form the plural of a letter, a figure, or an abbreviation:
  > *roll your r's*
  > *count up all the 3's*

❻❾ Quotation Marks

- to enclose words and punctuation in direct speech:
  > *"Why on earth did you do that?" he asked.*
  > *"I'll get it," she replied.*

- to draw attention to a word that is unusual for the context, for example a slang expression, or to a word that is being used for special effect, such as irony:
  > *He told me in no uncertain terms to "get lost."*
  > *Thousands were imprisoned in the name of "national security."*

- around the titles of articles, songs, poems, etc.:
  > *Keats's "Ode to Autumn"*
  > *I was listening to "Sweet Caroline."*

- around short quotations or sayings:
  > *Do you know the origin of the saying: "A little learning is a dangerous thing"?*

➖ Hyphen

- to form a compound from two or more other words:
  > *hard-hearted*
  > *ice-skating rink*
  > *mother-to-be*

- to form a compound from a prefix and a proper name
  > *pre-Raphaelite*
  > *pro-American*

- when writing compound numbers between 21 and 99 in words:
  > *seventy-three*
  > *thirty-one*

- after the first section of a word that is divided between one line and the next:
  > *Decide what to do in order to avoid mis-takes of this kind in the future.*

➖ Dash

- in informal English, instead of a colon or semicolon, to indicate that what follows is a summary or conclusion of what has gone before:
  > *Men were shouting, women were screaming, children were crying – it was chaos.*
  > *You admitted that you lied to me – how can I trust you again?*

- singly or in pairs to separate a comment or an afterthought from the rest of the sentence:
  > *He knew nothing about it – or so he said.*

⋯ Dots/Ellipsis

- to indicate that words have been omitted, especially from a quotation or at the end of a conversation:
  > *…challenging the view that Chicago… had not changed all that fundamentally.*

／ Slash

- to separate alternative words or phrases:
  > *have dessert and/or cheese*
  > *single/married/widowed/divorced*

- in Internet and e-mail addresses to separate the different elements (often said "forward slash")
  > *www.oup.com/us/*

① Parentheses

- to separate extra information or a comment from the rest of a sentence:
  - > *Mount Robson (12,972 feet) is the highest mountain in the Canadian Rockies.*
  - > *He thinks that modern music (i.e., anything written after 1900) is garbage.*
- to enclose cross-references:
  - > *This moral ambiguity is a feature of Shakespeare's later works (see Chapter Eight).*
- around numbers or letters in text:
  - > *Our objectives are (1) to increase output, (2) to improve quality, and (3) to maximize profits.*

① Brackets

- around words inserted to make a quotation grammatically correct:
  - > *Roosevelt in [these] years was without…*

Italics

- to show emphasis:
  - > I'm not going to do it – *you are.*
  - > … proposals that we cannot accept *under any circumstances…*
- to indicate the titles of books, plays, etc.:
  - > Joyce's *Ulysses*
  - > the title role in Puccini's *Tosca*
  - > a letter in *The New York Times*
- for foreign words or phrases
  - > the sugar maple (*Acer saccharum*)
  - > I had to renew my *permesso di soggiorno* (residence permit).

Quoting Conversation

When you write down a conversation, you normally begin a new paragraph for each new speaker.

- Quotation marks enclose the words spoken:
  - > *"You're sure of this?"* I asked.
  - > He nodded grimly.
  - > *"I'm sure."*
- Verbs used to indicate direct speech, for example *he said, she complained,* are separated by commas from the words spoken, unless a question mark or an exclamation point is used:
  - > *"That's all I know,"* said Nick.
  - > Nick said, *"That's all I know."*
  - > *"Why?"* asked Nick.
- Single quotation marks are used to indicate direct speech being quoted by someone else within direct speech:
  - > *"But you said you loved me! 'I'll never leave you, Beth, as long as I live.' That's what you said, isn't it?"*

Oxford Writing Tutor

Using the Oxford Advanced American Dictionary
to improve your writing

Whether you are writing a business e-mail or a long research essay, your dictionary can be a powerful tool to assist you in becoming a better writer in English.

1 Using the main part of the dictionary

You can use the main A–Z of the dictionary to help you:

- **Choose your words carefully.** Many words in English have similar or related meanings but are used in different contexts or situations.

  Look carefully at the example sentences provided in the entries for words you want to use. Also, look at **vocabulary notes** to help you choose the most appropriate word. If you need academic vocabulary, look for the **AWL** symbol.

- **Combine words naturally and effectively.** In English, certain pairs of words go together and sound natural to native speakers (for example, *heavy rain*) – and others do not (*strong rain*). This is called **collocation**. Information on which words collocate with one another can be found in the example sentences in the dictionary entries.

  Look up the key nouns you have used in your writing to check which verbs or adjectives are usually used with them.

  Also, look at the **Topic Collocations** notes and the **AWL Collocations** notes.

- **Become more flexible.** Rather than repeating the same word or phrase many times in your work, try to find other ways to express your ideas.

  Look for the **SYN** symbol to find synonyms and also study the **Thesaurus Boxes**. Look for word families and try using words in the same family that are different parts of speech (e.g., *different*, adjective and *differ*, verb). For example, you could write: *French **is different from** English in this respect.* You could also write: *French **differs from** English in this respect.*

- **Edit and check your work.** You can use your dictionary to check any problem areas such as as spelling, parts of speech, irregular forms, grammar, phrasal verbs, and prepositions.

2 Using the Writing Tutor

In the following pages you will find examples of essays and practical types of writing that you can use as models for your own work. You will also find advice about planning, organizing, and writing each type of text.

- **Examples of written texts**
  Look carefully at:
  - the structure and organization of the text
  - the way ideas and paragraphs are linked
  - the language and style
  - the notes on particular points

- **Tips** These are quick reminders and advice to help when you are writing.

- **Language Banks** give you some useful phrases that you can use in each type of writing.

  Check that you are familiar with these phrases and know how to use them correctly.

You can add other phrases as you come across them in your reading. In the main part of the dictionary you will find more notes like this which give you further phrases and examples to show you how to use them.
(*For example, see the note at "however."*)

Contents

The Writing Process

Each individual writer has their own aims and needs and their own way of approaching various parts of the writing process. However, whether you are writing a short essay, an article, a report, or a research paper, the overall process is generally the same.

1 Preliminary Phase

Ask yourself some planning questions that will help guide the rest of the process.

What is the purpose of this piece of writing?

For example:
- To answer a specific essay, examination, or research question
- To convince others of your point of view
- To communicate your knowledge or understanding to others, such as a teacher or an admissions board

Who is my audience?

For example:
- A teacher or professor
- Fellow students or colleagues
- An employer
- The general public

These answers (you may have more than one purpose or type of audience) will help you to choose the appropriate level of formality. They will also help you make decisions about the amount of research required, as well as the kinds of examples and supporting evidence you will use.

2 Pre-Writing Phase

Explore

Brainstorm ideas using whatever method suits you best:
- Mind maps
- Lists of interesting concepts, facts, questions, etc.
- Conversations with colleagues

Research

Next, research your topic and gather information from a variety of sources:
- Books and journals
- The media
- Web sites
- Interviews or questionnaires
- Scientific studies

When you read sources, take detailed notes and keep an accurate record of each source. (*See page WT11.*)

Organize

After carrying out your research, you can draft a thesis statement (your main argument or idea) to guide you.

Then, using your notes, make a detailed outline of the logical plan of your essay, article, or report to support this thesis, giving a structure to your writing *before* you begin to write.

- Decide roughly how many words you will give to each part of your essay/report.
- Collect or prepare any visual aids such as graphics, charts, or diagrams that you might need.

3 Writing Phase

In this phase, you will draft and revise several times until you have what you consider to be a final draft.

Draft

Write your draft in sentences and paragraphs.

- Remain focused on your thesis statement. If you do change this, go back and adapt your original plan to ensure that your essay/report continues to support the new thesis.
- Follow your outline, modifying it if necessary as you write.
- In early drafts, concentrate on structure rather than spelling and punctuation.

Review/Edit

In this step, read your writing with a critical eye.

In early drafts, ask yourself:
- Have you answered the question or achieved your original purpose?
- Have you introduced your subject, developed it logically, and come to a conclusion?
- Is your supporting evidence appropriate and complete? Do you need more examples, statistics, or quotes?
- Have you used headings to help the reader, if appropriate?
- Are the relationships between ideas clear and clearly signaled to the reader?
- Is each part the right length for the demands of the topic?

In later drafts, ask yourself:
- Have you used paragraph breaks well?
- Is the level of formality appropriate for your readers?
- Have you chosen your words carefully, using correct collocations?
- Have you avoided repeating the same words or phrases too often (except technical terms)?
- Have you met any word count requirements?

If possible, ask someone else to read your text.

After each review, return to the drafting step, revising and editing your writing as necessary.

Using Sources in Essays

Ask yourself:
- Have you quoted or mentioned sources to support your points?
- Have you used the citation style recommended by your teachers or institution?
- Have you listed your references in the style recommended?

(Look also at page WT11.)

4 Presentation Phase

Proofread

When you have a final draft of your writing, you will need to read it once more to find and correct surface errors.

Try to leave some time between your final draft and proofreading. This will make it easier to see your mistakes.

Check for:
- Spelling
- Punctuation
- Grammatical correctness

You may find it helpful to ask someone else to proofread your final draft as a last step.

Format

Check how you should present your work in terms of:
• Font size • Margins • Line spacing

Examinations

In an exam, you will not have time for all these stages, but you can usually:
- brainstorm ideas
- organize and plan
- reread, check, and edit

What Makes Writing Formal?

Whatever type of text you are writing, your aim should always be to express your ideas clearly and in a way that your readers can easily understand.

When you read, notice the kind of language that is used in the type of writing you need to do.

To make your writing more formal, consider:

1 Word Choice
- It is usually best to use standard English words and phrases. Avoid anything marked *informal*, *slang*, *offensive*, etc.
- Only use words and phrases marked *formal* if you are sure they are appropriate.
- Use suitable synonyms for simple verbs such as *do*, *put*, *get*, *make*. (e.g., *Several operations* **were carried out/performed** – not *done*).

2 Short Forms
- Avoid contracted forms (e.g., *haven't*, *I'm*) and abbreviations (e.g., *ad – advertisement*)

3 Sentence Structure
- To express complex ideas, you will need to write sentences using relative pronouns (e.g., *which*, *that*), subordinating conjunctions (e.g., *although*, *because*, *if*), and coordinating conjunctions (e.g., *and*, *but*, *or*).
- Very long sentences with many clauses can be difficult to understand. Aim for **clarity**.

Academic Writing

This tends to be impersonal in style in order to sound more objective and formal. When you read in your subject, notice how the writers express themselves. The following points may help you in your writing:
- Limit the use of the **first person pronouns** (*I* and *we*). Rather than *In this study I aim to…*, write: *This study aims to…* or *The aim of this study is to…* Avoid using *you*.
- **Passive forms** are often used as they focus attention on the action, not the person: *A study was conducted to see…*; *It can be argued that…*
- Patterns with **it is + adjective** are often used: *It is clear that…*; *It is necessary to…*
- **Nouns** for things are often used as subjects of active verbs: *The results show that…*

Answering the Question

At all times, you must ensure that you understand the examination question or assignment title and address all the required parts.

Questions can be considered in terms of three main components:

- **Topic**
- **Scope and Focus**
- **Question Type**

Topic

The topic(s) of the question will usually be clear from the question itself. For example:
Explain the process of photosynthesis.
When you write your answer, think about why the examiner has chosen to ask about this topic.

Scope and Focus

Often, the wording of the question will include a word or phrase that either limits or expands the topic in a very specific way. These phrases show you the focus of the question. Try to avoid common mistakes, such as:

- **Covering too broad an area.** For example, if the question asks about textile mills in the American South in the 1930s, think very carefully before including information about the 1920s or 1940s, or about textile mills in other parts of the country.

- **Writing with too narrow a focus.** For example, if you are asked about the impact of climate change on South America, you should not write about its impact only on Brazil.

- **Including irrelevant information.** For example, if you are asked about nuclear power, you should not write about wind or solar power.

- **Answering only half of the question.** For example, if the question asks *What effects will a reduction in air travel have, and will the advantages outweigh the disadvantages?* you need to answer both points: the effects and your opinion about the end result.

Question Type

The depth and type of information that you provide in your answer depend on the kind of question being asked. The table on the next page shows the key words that might appear in different types of questions.

1 **Knowledge Questions**

These ask you to recall important facts and are the simplest questions.

2 **Comprehension Questions**

These ask you to demonstrate your understanding of concepts. You must clearly show that you understand the ideas and theories that underlie the facts.

3 **Application Questions**

Here you use your knowledge of facts and concepts to address a specific problem. These questions require you to move beyond simple recollection.

4 **Analysis Questions**

These examine relationships between/among various facts and concepts.

5 **Synthesis Questions**

These ask you to create a new product or structure in written form.

6 **Evaluation Questions**

These ask you to make value judgments and present your own opinions. This kind of question is very common in academic work. It is important to support your opinions by citing the work and views of experts in the field, if possible.

Question Types

4 Analysis Questions

Key Verbs
- analyze
- compare
- contrast
- distinguish
- differentiate
- subdivide

Example:

Compare the merits of "renting" and "squatting" as solutions to housing problems for the poor in cities in the developing world.

5 Synthesis Questions

Key Verbs
- design
- plan
- construct
- create
- compose
- produce
- develop
- invent
- combine

Example:

Design an experiment to investigate whether listening to music improves students' performance in their studies.

6 Evaluation Questions

Key Verbs
- discuss
- evaluate
- compare
- consider
- examine
- explore
- comment (on)
- justify
- appraise
- weigh
- support
- recommend

Example:

Discuss the argument that the use of force in self-defense is justifiable.

3 Application Questions

Key Verbs
- apply
- show
- solve
- choose
- organize
- generalize
- prepare
- relate (X to Y)

Example:

Show how a "public option" for health insurance will affect small businesses.

2 Comprehension Questions

Key Verbs
- explain
- summarize
- illustrate
- restate
- paraphrase
- give examples
- express
- distinguish (between)
- trace
- match

Example:

Give three examples of human activities that have major effects on our climate.

1 Knowledge Questions

Key Verbs
- outline
- define
- describe
- give
- state
- summarize
- label
- identify
- name
- list

Example:

Define the term "muscle tone" and describe how it can help good posture.

Level of Difficulty

WT5

Writing a Comparison Essay

You are often asked to **compare** and **contrast** two things, ideas, places, or people in exams, essays, work, and everyday life. Here is an example of a comparison essay.

Paragraph 1 – Introduction
Sentences 1 and 2 capture the reader's attention.
The next two sentences give a definition of the two types of card. (Note: a definition is optional.)
The fifth sentence indicates the scope of the essay and leads into the first body paragraph.

**Paragraph 2 –
First Difference**
How the cards are used.
The writer notes an obvious difference.

Qualifying adverbs such as *usually* and *often* allow you to generalize without going into too much detail about exceptions.

**Paragraph 3 –
Second Difference**
Profitability for merchants and banks.
The writer notes a less obvious but significant difference.

Again, *some* allows you to write about trends or possibilities.

Paragraph 4 – Similarities
The writer notes one way in which the cards are similar.

Modal verbs like *can* and *may* allow you to write about possibilities and interesting facts without over-generalizing.

Paragraph 5 – Conclusion
The first sentence summarizes the information in paragraphs 2–3.
The final sentences give the writer's personal opinion and recommendation.

Blue shows ways of introducing similarities.

Pink shows ways of introducing contrasts.

Green shows ways of connecting or summarizing the different points of your argument.

Compare and contrast debit and credit cards as methods of payment.

1 Debit or credit? It is a much more complex question than most people realize. Credit cards allow you to build up a total balance that you can pay off with cash either at the end of each month or over time, with interest charges added. Debit cards are like electronic checks; cash for each transaction is immediately taken out of the bank account to which the card is linked. When deciding whether to use a debit card or a credit card, it helps to know the basic similarities and differences between these two methods of paying for purchases.

2 One of the most obvious differences between the two cards is how they are used. Merchants will usually ask you to sign for credit card transactions. In contrast, debit cards usually require you to enter a PIN.

3 Hidden behind this seemingly insignificant feature, however, is the key to why banks prefer credit cards and merchants prefer debit cards. Banks charge merchants more for signature transactions, which therefore bring the banks higher profits. This is why some merchants charge an extra fee for signature transactions, especially for small amounts. On the other hand, PIN transactions cost merchants less; indeed, some banks charge their customers fees for debit card transactions in order to discourage their use.

4 Still, debit and credit cards are similar in many ways. For example, both can cost you a lot of money in penalty fees if you fail to track your spending accurately. A credit card comes with an overall spending limit, and your bank can charge you as much as $40 for each transaction that causes you to exceed this limit. Similarly, debit cards usually have daily spending limits of around $300. If you attempt to use the card for purchases in excess of this amount, your bank can charge you a substantial fee. Also, if your debit card causes the cash balance of your bank account to drop below zero, your bank may charge you overdraft fees for each attempted transaction, just as if you had written a bad check.

5 In short, both credit cards and debit cards have been designed to increase convenience – for customers and merchants – as well as bank profits. For people with a good credit history, the best plan is probably to use a credit card with a high spending limit, check your total balance regularly online, pay off the balance completely each month, and use cash as needed for small transactions. This way, you can keep your retail spending separate from your bills, and you will not accrue penalty fees, pay interest charges, or lose track of your checking account balance.

Explore and Research

Brainstorm ideas about similarities and differences, and then research the topic as needed. You might arrange the points in a table, in columns, or in a mind map. You will then need to choose which points to include and which to leave out (for example, the writer did not include the point about "Risk" from the table below).

Aspect	Debit Card	Credit Card
How it works	Enter PIN	Signature
	Funds come out of bank account immediately	Total monthly bill of charges – may be paid over time
Fees	Fees charged for exceeding bank account balance	Fees charged for going over limit
	Some banks & merchants charge fees for transactions	Some merchants charge fees, especially for small transactions
Spending limits	Daily limit on spending	Overall limit on total balance – no daily limit
Risk	More risk if card stolen	Risk for stolen cards limited to $50
Profitability	Cheaper for merchants if PIN is used – banks make less profit	Costs merchants more in fees – banks make more profit

Organize

Choose an organization structure that best presents your selected points.

Emphasizing the Similarities 1 Introduction 2 Differences between X and Y 3 Similarities of X and Y 4 Conclusion This structure can be used for either long or short essays.	**By Topic** 1 Introduction 2 Characteristics of X 3 Characteristics of Y 4 Conclusion This simplistic structure is usually used only for very short essays.
Emphasizing the Differences 1 Introduction 2 Similarities of X and Y 3 Differences between X and Y 4 Conclusion This structure can be used for either long or short essays.	**By Aspect** 1 Introduction 2 Aspect 1: compare X and Y 3 Aspect 2: compare X and Y (etc.) 4 Conclusion This structure can be expanded as much as necessary to be used for longer essays.

Language Bank

Being More Precise

Similarities
X is almost/nearly/virtually/exactly/precisely *the same as Y.*
X and Y are very/somewhat *similar.*

Differences
X is slightly/a little/somewhat *smaller than Y.*
X is much/considerably *smaller than Y.*
X and Y are completely/totally/entirely *different.*
X and Y are not exactly/entirely *the same.*

Writing an Argument Essay

Many essays that you have to write, whether in school or college or in an examination, will require you to present a reasoned argument on a particular issue. This will often be based on your research into the topic, but some questions may ask you simply to give your opinion. In both cases, your argument must be clearly organized and supported with information, evidence, and reasons. The language tends to be formal and impersonal.

Paragraph 1 – Introduction
[1] Introduces the topic.
[2] States the focus of the essay.

Paragraph 2 – Introduces the argument
The first point (manned missions are not cost-effective) with a quote from an expert to give authority.
[1] This is a useful way to introduce a quotation.

Paragraph 3 – Development
Reasons and data are given to support the writer's point of view.

Paragraph 4 – Development
Introduces the second point (unmanned projects are more scientifically productive).

Paragraph 5 – Counterargument
[1] Presents the argument. *Some may argue* suggests that the writer will go on to argue against this position.
[2] Refutes it. *However* introduces the argument against [1].

Paragraph 6 – Conclusion
Summarizes the writer's points and states his/her conclusion on the title.
[1] *Thus* introduces the conclusion.
[2] *I would argue that* clearly shows the writer's position.

"Manned space missions should now be replaced with unmanned missions." Discuss.

1 [1]It is clear that the study of space and the planets is by nature expensive. Scientists and politicians must constantly attempt to balance costs with potential research benefits. [2]A major question to be considered is whether the benefits of manned space flight are worth the costs.

2 For Nobel Prize-winning physicist Steven Weinberg, the answer is clear. As he noted in 2007[1] in a lecture at the Space Telescope Science Institute in Baltimore: "Human beings don't serve any useful function in space. They radiate heat, they're very expensive to keep alive, and unlike robotic missions, they have a natural desire to come back."

3 Unmanned missions are much less expensive, having no requirement for airtight compartments, food, or life support systems. They are also lighter and therefore require less fuel and launch equipment. According to NASA, the 1992 manned Space Shuttle Endeavor cost $1.7 billion to build and approximately $450 million for each launch. In contrast, the entire unmanned Voyager mission from 1972 until 1989 cost only $865 million.

4 In addition to their relative cost-effectiveness, unmanned projects generally yield a much greater volume of data. While manned flights have yet to extend beyond the orbit of Earth's moon, unmanned missions have explored almost our entire solar system. Manned missions would not be able to travel so far, be away so long, or collect so much data while at the same time guaranteeing the astronauts' safe return.

5 [1]Some may argue that only manned space flight has the ability to inspire and engage people, providing much-needed momentum for continued governmental funding and educational interest. [2]However, media coverage of recent projects such as the Mars rover and the Titan moon lander demonstrates that unmanned missions clearly have the ability to attract and hold public interest.

6 [1]Thus, taking into account the lower cost, the greater quantity of data, and widespread popular support, [2]I would argue that unmanned space missions undoubtedly yield the most value in terms of public spending.

Linking words and phrases guide the reader through the argument and show the writer's opinion.

Adverbs can be used to show your opinion.

These phrases make the argument less personal and more objective.

Experts are quoted to support the argument.

Explore and Research

- Brainstorm your ideas on the question, read, and research the topic (unless in an examination). Which do you think are the strongest arguments? Decide what your viewpoint will be, and write a thesis statement.
- Select 2 or 3 strong points on each side, with supporting examples, ideas, or evidence. For some questions, you can use evidence from your personal experience.
- Note down some useful vocabulary on the topic.

Organize

- Decide how to organize your essay to persuade readers of your case.

Structure 1 (used in the model essay)	Structure 2
1 Introduction	1 Introduction
2 Arguments **for** your case + supporting evidence, examples, or reasons	2 Argument 1:+ supporting evidence, examples, or reasons
3 Arguments **against** + evidence	3 Counterargument
4 Evaluation of arguments	4 Argument 2: + supporting evidence, examples, or reasons
5 Summary and conclusion	5 Counterargument (and so on)
It is possible to reverse arguments for and against.	6 Evaluation of arguments
	7 Summary and conclusion

Tips

- Look carefully at the **title** or **question** and make sure you really answer it.
- Use your **stronger points** at the beginning and end, and put weaker points in the middle.
- Use **general statements** to convey the main ideas, and then provide **evidence**, **examples**, **details**, and **reasons** to support these statements.
- Use **paragraph divisions** and **connecting words and phrases** to make the structure of your essay clear to your readers.
- For language to help you structure your argument, look at the notes at "addition" and "first."

Showing Your Position

When you write an argument essay, you can show what your opinion is on the issue or question without using personal phrases such as *I think...* or *In my opinion,....* You can do this by choosing words carefully as you write. Some examples are given below. Look out for more in your reading.

Language Bank

Adjectives	Verbs
important, major, serious, significant	**It + verb**: It appears that, It seems that...
*An **important** point to consider is...*;	**It + passive verb**: It can be seen that...; It should/
*This was a **highly significant** discovery.*	must be noted/emphasized that...
	Showing Verbs: show, indicate, demonstrate,
It is + adjective	suggest, imply (*These have a non-human subject.*)
clear, likely, possible, surprising, evident,	**Arguing Verbs**: argue, suggest, consider, conclude
important, difficult, necessary, possible, interesting	(*These can have a human subject.*)
*It is **clear** that the study of space is expensive.*	
Adverbs and Adverbial Phrases	**Linking Words and Phrases**
clearly, indeed, in fact, of course	Firstly, (= *I have several points to make*)
generally, usually, mainly, widely	Furthermore,...; In addition,...; Moreover,...
perhaps, probably, certainly, possibly	(= *I have another important point*)
rarely, sometimes, often	However,... (*to introduce a counterargument*)
Clearly, this is a serious issue that deserves further study.	Thus,... Therefore,... (*to introduce a conclusion*)

Writing a Longer Essay or Dissertation

When you have a longer essay or dissertation to write, you will go through the same process of preparing and writing as for shorter essays. (*Look at page WT2.*) However, you will also want to bear in mind a few additional points.

The Title

If your title or a question has been given to you, check that you understand exactly what it means. (*Pages WT4–5*). If you are writing the title yourself, choose a clear title with definite boundaries.

Ask yourself:

- How can I define my subject so that it is not too wide or too narrow in scope?

  For example: **Not** *How does Faulkner reflect southern society in his novels?* **but** *How does* Light In August *reflect Faulkner's view of southern society?*

Reading and Research: Evaluate Your Sources

The quality of your research will play a vital part in the success of your writing. Keep the question or title in mind when you look for source material in books, journals, or Web sites.

Ask yourself:

- Is the content relevant?
- Is it reliable? Is it written by someone who is an expert in the field?
- Is it biased in any way?
- Is there evidence to support information on Web sites?

If you are using surveys, questionnaires, market research, or other studies, look carefully at the statistics and consider whether the results are valid and the conclusions justified.

Making Notes

When you are reading, make clear, accurate notes which summarize the key points and main information. Keep a note of the full reference for your source (title, author, date, publisher, and page numbers).

Ask yourself:

- Have I summarized the information accurately?
- Is this part particularly useful? If so, have I written down the exact words used and the page number, so that I can quote it?

Planning and Organizing

A long text is usually divided into sections with subheadings and has a list of references or a bibliography at the end.

When you plan your work, ask yourself:

- How long should my text and each part be?
- Have I organized my notes, grouping together writers who have made similar points?
- Do I agree or disagree with their opinions?
- What is the point I want to make to my readers?
- What do I want my readers to know by the end?
- Have I planned what to write in the introduction, body, and conclusion?

Using Other People's Ideas

When you have finished writing, look carefully at how you have used other people's words and ideas.

Ask yourself:

- Have I considered and discussed other people's ideas adequately?
- Have I paraphrased their ideas accurately?
- Have I made it clear which words/ideas are mine and whose words/ideas I have quoted or referenced?
- Have I included in my list of references all the works I have used and referred to?

Dissertations

A dissertation may differ from a long essay in the way in which it is organized. Check with your instructor. A dissertation will usually have all or some of the following chapters or parts:

- Title
- Contents
- Abstract (*a short text summarizing your dissertation*)
- Introductory chapter (broad to narrow focus: *to give the background, justify your research, explain your approach, give major arguments and current ideas on your topic, and show the structure of your dissertation*)
- Review of the literature
- Methodology (*how you carried out any empirical research*)
- Results/findings
- Discussion
- Conclusion (narrow to broad focus: *a summary of your arguments and an evaluation of your work; further research needed*)
- Bibliography or list of references

Citation Styles

If you use or refer to the words or ideas of another person, you must always say where these have come from. If you do not, you might be accused of **plagiarism** (= copying another person's ideas or words and pretending that they are yours).

Many different citation styles are used in North America, so be sure to confirm which style you need to use in your research paper. Each discipline has its own generally preferred style, but some instructors or publications will require that a different style be used.

Four commonly-used citation styles are:

- Social Sciences: APA (American Psychological Association)
- Humanities: MLA (Modern Language Association)
- History: Chicago Manual of Style
- Sciences: CSE (Council of Science Editors)

Each citation style includes two components.

Inline or In-text Citations

This refers to how you specify the source of a quote or idea within the text you are writing. The APA style, for example, uses the author's name and publication date in parentheses immediately following each quotation or reference. MLA style uses the author's name and a page number in parentheses. The Chicago and CSE styles use either footnotes or endnotes.

References, Works Cited, or Bibliography

Like inline citations, each style has its own rules for the list of works that you cite, refer to, or use in your research. Dozens of different formats are used for the items in this list, which usually appears at the very end of your paper.

Each item's format will be different, for example, depending on the number of authors, the publication medium (e.g., print or electronic), and whether the source stands alone or is part of a series. Just a few examples are as follows:

APA style, for a magazine article
Parker, I. (2010, May 17). The Poverty Lab. *The New Yorker*, 78-89.

MLA style, for a book
Gert, Bernard. *Common Morality: Deciding What to Do*. New York: Oxford University Press, 2004. Print.

Chicago style, for a Web site
Footnote/Endnote:
5. Janine Jackson, "NYT Grades Charter Schools on the Curve," *Fairness and Accuracy in Reporting*, August 2009, www.fair.org/index.php?page=3894.
Bibliographic entry:
Jackson, Janine. "NYT Grades Charter Schools on the Curve." *Fairness and Accuracy in Reporting*. August 2009. www.fair.org/index.php?page=3894.

CSE style, for a government report
19. Centers for Disease Control and Prevention (U.S.). HIV/AIDS Surveillance Report, 2007. Vol. 19. Atlanta: U.S. Department of Health and Human Services, Centers for Disease Control and Prevention; 2009: [p. 17]. Available from: www.cdc.gov/hiv/topics/surveillance/resources/reports

For More Information

Although citation styles and formats can be extremely complicated, the rules for the style you are using must be followed with precision. Detailed information about specific styles can be found in various print publications as well as on the Web.

- www.apastyle.org
- www.mla.org
- www.chicagomanualofstyle.org
- www.councilscienceeditors.org/publications/citing_internet.cfm
- owl.english.purdue.edu/owl/

Oral Presentations

You may have to give an oral presentation or talk as part of your studies, for an examination, or at work. In many ways, preparing a talk is similar to preparing an essay. The guidelines below apply to most types of talk.

Preparing an Oral Presentation

Good preparation is the most important factor for a successful presentation.

1 Explore and Research

- Check the **time** allowed for your talk and any **guidelines** you have been given.
- Think about the **purpose** of your talk: is it to inform, to entertain, or to persuade your audience?
- Think about the **audience**. Who are they? How much do they already know? How much do you need to tell them? What will interest them?
- Decide on the topic if you do not know this already. If you do, decide on the specific area that you will present. Be realistic about how much you can cover in the time allowed.
- **Collect** your ideas and gather more information if you need to.

2 Organize

- Make notes on what you want to include. Think about what you *must* tell the audience, what you *should* tell them, and what you *would like* to tell them if you have time.
- Produce an outline or a plan of your talk.

Tips
■ Structure your talk as you would an essay: have an introduction, a middle, and a conclusion.
■ Use headings to show the different sections of your talk.
■ Open with an introduction to the title and an overview of what you want to say.
■ Try to get the attention of your audience at the beginning (e.g., with a story, joke, or surprising fact).
■ Close with a summary and an invitation for people to ask questions.

Some people prefer to write out the whole talk like an essay. If you do this, it is better not to read this when you give your talk, but make notes or slides as below and talk from those.

3 Producing Notes

Make notes in English that you can refer to while you are speaking on paper cards or electronically attached to your slides.

The benefits of learning a foreign language 1	The benefits of learning a foreign language 2	
Show Slide 1	Show Slide 2	**Number** note cards.
Intro: **Good morning. My talk today examines** the benefits of learning a foreign language. Overview: I intend to outline 3 imp. benefits of learning another lang.	**The first benefit I'll describe is** practical – communicating with other nationalities **Another benefit is** increased cultural understanding – breaking down barriers / bridging gap between cultures **The final benefit that I'll discuss is** improved cognitive skills – research shows → brain power	Note the **number** of the visual you will show. Write out and **highlight** key words and phrases to **guide** your audience through your talk.

Some people find it helpful to write out the whole introduction and conclusion.

4 Preparing Visual Aids

If they are prepared carefully and used well, visual aids help you to communicate your talk to the audience.

The benefits of learning a foreign language	2
Three main benefits:	
• Practical uses	
• Increased cultural understanding	
• Improved cognitive skills	

Leave lots of white space.

Use headings and bullets to show the relationships between ideas.

Use notes, not sentences.

The benefits of learning a foreign language	3
1 Practical uses for:	
• Travel	
• Work	
• Study	

5 Practicing Your Talk

The more you practice, the more confident you will feel and the better your talk will be.

- First, practice your talk alone several times until you can speak fluently and confidently from your notes and keep to the time allowed.
- Then practice with one or more friends listening. Is the talk clear? Is your voice loud and clear? Are you looking at the audience?
- If you can, practice at least once with the equipment you will use.
- Use your dictionary or dictionary CD-ROM to check pronunciation, vocabulary, and grammar.

6 Preparing for Questions

Try to predict some of the questions your audience may ask you and practice your answers.

Language Bank

Introduction	Changing the Subject
Good morning. My talk today examines...	*So, I have discussed...*
The subject/title of my talk/paper is...	*Now I'd like to turn to...*
Hello. Today I'm going to talk about/discuss...	*Moving on to the next/second/last benefit...*
Explaining Structure	**Concluding**
In this talk, I intend to outline...	*So, I have talked about...*
In my talk, I will discuss the main features of....	*To sum up/summarize: today I have...*
I am going to examine three benefits/advantages of...	*In conclusion, I believe it is clear that...*
	To conclude: the benefits I have described here/ today are important and therefore I consider that...
Introducing Each Point	**Answering Difficult Questions**
The first/second/next/last point/area... I would like to discuss is...	*I'm sorry, I don't quite understand your question. Could you repeat it?*
I want to begin by looking at...	*Well, I'm not sure about that, but I think...*
I'd now like to look at another/the second benefit of...	*That's an interesting point, but I think...*

Writing a Summary

A summary is a shortened version of a text containing only the key information. The aim is to present readers with a short, clear account of the ideas in the text. Summary writing is an important skill in both academic and business contexts.

Preparing to Write

Select the key information:

- Read the text carefully, looking up words you don't know. It is important to understand the whole sequence of the argument. Ask yourself what the text is about. Think about the purpose of your summary and what your readers need to know.
- Highlight the **key information** (the main ideas). Omit details such as examples, quotations, information in parentheses, repetitions, figures of speech, and most figures and statistics.
- Underline any information which you are not sure about. Include it in your summary if you have space.
- Make notes on the key information in your own words.

Are we living in a surveillance society?

The number of surveillance cameras in America has grown enormously in recent years. There are now thousands of visible cameras in Manhattan, monitored by both the police and private businesses. Police in Washington, D.C. have access to a network of over 5,000 cameras, more than three times the number that were active in 2001.

Surveillance cameras have been used for many years to monitor public areas associated with an obvious security risk, such as military installations, airports, casinos, and banks. However, since September 11, 2001, there has been a huge increase in the surveillance of everyday locations such as downtowns, parking lots, stores, and highways. Added to this, more and more individuals are buying their own consumer security systems for personal or commercial use. The most common function of these systems is to survey the area in front of a house or business and record any suspicious or criminal behavior. People who buy these systems range from wealthy individuals who are afraid of being targeted by burglars, to people who are not wealthy at all but who live in high-crime areas and are trying to protect themselves.

For some people, the huge increase in public surveillance is a threat to the individual's civil liberties and is a sign that society is becoming increasingly authoritarian. They argue that the individual's right to privacy and right to live anonymously is an important aspect of being American. They also fear that present or future governments might abuse the information gathered by surveillance in order to manipulate, control, or persecute the population, as happens in George Orwell's novel *1984*.

Individuals and groups in favor of surveillance cameras, including the police, believe that they are a valuable weapon against crime. In fact, there is no strong evidence that surveillance cameras reduce crime overall. They may act as a deterrent in certain locations, but the crime is displaced to another location. They are not even always a good deterrent. Many criminals aren't afraid of surveillance cameras because they know that the cameras may not be running, or that no one is likely to be watching the screens. Few crimes are solved through surveillance videos. Sometimes footage is analyzed retrospectively to identify criminals after a crime has taken place, but even this process is enormously time-consuming and expensive. One promising new development is the computer monitoring of surveillance cameras, where computers are programmed to notice unusual movements, such as those of a car thief in a supermarket parking lot, and sound an alarm. Meanwhile, we can expect the argument about the rights and wrongs of surveillance cameras to continue.

Writing the Summary

Write a first draft of your summary using the key information you have selected.

- **Organize** the main ideas in your notes into a logical order. This need not be the same order as in the original text, but must show the same argument.
- **Condense** the information where possible.
- **Express the ideas in your own words.** This will usually be shorter than the original. Rewrite phrases in the text, but keep any **key terms** from the subject area.
- Do not give your own opinion on the topic.

Your own words:
try using synonyms or rephrasing words and expressions such as adjective + noun phrases. Use the dictionary to help you.
- *everyday* → *ordinary*
- *their own consumer security systems for personal ... use* → *private systems*
- *no strong evidence* → *no clear proof*
- *promising* → *that may be more effective*

Introduce **new terms** and concepts to condense and clarify the argument. For example, **opponents** and **supporters** can be used to refer to those against, and those in favor of, surveillance cameras.

America has a very high number of surveillance cameras. **Originally** used for locations with an obvious security risk, video surveillance has **now** spread to ordinary public areas, **while** individuals are **also** buying private systems to protect themselves from crime.

Opponents of the growth in video surveillance base their arguments on the threat to civil liberties and the danger of government misuse of the data acquired by surveillance.

Supporters of surveillance cameras argue that they reduce crime, although there is no clear proof of this. If they act as deterrents, crime probably moves to another area. Often they are not a deterrent and do not solve many crimes. However, the technology is developing in ways that may be more effective.

Combine sentences in new ways to condense the argument, (e.g., by linking the key ideas with different conjunctions and adverbs from those in the original text).

Rephrase information to shorten it: try changing the verb form or the part of speech. Examples and word families in the dictionary can help.
E.g., **passive → active verb**: *Few crimes are solved through surveillance videos →* *they do not solve many crimes*
noun → verb: *One promising new development is ...* → *the technology is developing*

Working on the Draft

Ask yourself these questions:

- **Is it the right length?**
  If there is a word limit, try to stay as close to it as possible. If your summary is too long, you can usually reduce it further by:
  - cutting adjectives, (e.g., *locations with an obvious security risk* → *locations with a security risk; no clear proof* → *no proof*)
  - replacing phrases with shorter versions, (e.g., *a lot of/not a lot of* → *many/few*)
  If it is still too long, go back and reduce your key information.
- **Does it contain all the important points from the text?**
- **Does it read well?**
- **Are the grammar and spelling correct?**

Writing a Report

A report describes a study, an investigation, or a project. Its purpose is to provide recommendations or updates, and sometimes to persuade the readers to accept an idea. It is written by a person or group who has investigated the issue. It is read by people who require the information.

Think About the Readers

You need to make the objective of the report clear so that the people who are reading the report know why they are reading. Thinking about the readers and what they need to know will help improve your report.
- Is the purpose of the report clear throughout?
- Can the readers find the information they need?
- Would diagrams or tables make the information clearer?
- Should I just present the facts or include recommendations as well?

Organizing Your Report

A typical report should follow the structure outlined below. Shorter reports might not need all the sections, but they should include at least the highlighted sections.

1 Title

Your title should tell the reader exactly what the report is about.

2 Contents List

If your report has a number of sections it is important to include a table of contents so that the readers can find the information they want. A good way to structure a report is to use numbered headings:

2.0 Research
2.1 Focus Groups
2.2 Technology for Accessing the Web

3 Summary

This section is often called an **Executive Summary**. It tells the readers what the objectives of the report are, as well as the main findings, conclusions, and any recommendations.

4 Introduction

This section may include the following:
- A statement of the report's objective(s)
- The scope of the report (i.e., what it will and will not cover)
- How you obtained the information upon which the report is based

5 Body of the Report

The main body of the report will follow the structure in the Contents List. It will give precise information about the research you have carried out and what you have discovered from it. The information here should be mainly factual and not based on opinion. Tables, charts, and bullet points can make the information clearer. Very detailed information can go into Appendices.

6 Conclusions

This is where you give your opinions on the facts that you have discovered.

7 Recommendations

If you have been asked to give recommendations, they should be based on your conclusions. You should also let the reader know what you predict will happen if your recommendations are followed.

8 Appendices

In a long report, you should put very detailed information in the Appendices with cross references to them in the body of the report.

9 Bibliography

If your report refers to a number of other publications, you should list these in a Bibliography.

Executive Summary

The summary below gives some useful language in context. In the Language Bank are some other phrases that you can use in reports. Notice that the language used should be **clear**, **accurate**, and **formal**. *We* and *I* are often used in internal reports, for example for describing research.

Web Page Design

The purpose of this report is to compare two different Web designs. The reason for this is to decide what kind of Web page is most likely to attract new customers and to encourage existing customers to buy more products from us.

We asked two developers to produce alternative Web pages for our company. We asked Developer A to produce a simple, easy-to-use design, and we asked Developer B to produce a more sophisticated design with lots of eye-catching graphics. We conducted our research by asking a group of twenty existing customers and twenty non-customers to use the Web page over a month. The group was made up of people with a range of ages, professions, incomes, and computer expertise. We divided the group in two and asked one subgroup to use Design A and the other to use Design B. We asked each subgroup to log on once a day and to use the Web page to perform certain tasks, including: buying products, getting information, returning damaged products, and tracking deliveries. We also asked the subgroups to assess how attractive they found the designs and whether they would be encouraged to return to the Web page.

In addition, we researched the technology that people had available for accessing the Internet, including the devices people used and the connection speeds available.

We found that, on the whole, people preferred to be able to purchase products quickly and easily. In conclusion, users do not visit a site such as ours for entertainment. While they initially enjoyed some of the aspects of Design B, these often took a long time to load, and users eventually became impatient.

We recommend that we adopt Design A with two or three of the more practical features from Design B.

Language Bank

Stating Objectives *The purpose/aim/objective of this report is to...* *This report aims to...* *This reports presents/gives information on...*	**Giving Conclusions** *In conclusion...* *The research shows/demonstrates (that)...* *The research shows/demonstrates + noun* *(e.g., the effect of...)* *Based on the research/the evidence, we conclude that...*
Outlining Research *We asked (two developers) to...* *We conducted our research by... (e.g., asking a group of...)* *We examined/looked at/researched... (e.g., the problem/the cost/several companies)* *We surveyed... (e.g., a total of 250 employees)* *We compared A and B.* *The group was made up of/comprised...*	**Giving Recommendations** *We recommend that...* *It is recommended that...* *The best solution is/would be to...* *(e.g., to adopt design A)* *The best solution is/would be + noun* *(e.g., a reduction in office hours)* *If we do A, we will see B.* *This will have an impact on + noun* *(e.g., costs/productivity/the business)*
Presenting Findings *We found that, on the whole,...* *According to the majority of respondents...* *Overall, people preferred...* *50% of those surveyed said (that)...*	

Writing a Review of a Book or Movie

The main purpose of a review is to give information to a potential reader or viewer so that they can decide whether or not they want to read the book or see the movie.

Asking a question is one way to engage the reader. Or you could start with a personal opinion.

The title and **author's name** should appear in the introductory paragraph.

Adventures of Huckleberry Finn by Mark Twain

Is it the tale of an epic journey? Or is it a biting piece of social commentary? The classic novel *Adventures of Huckleberry Finn* by Mark Twain is, in my opinion, a unique and gripping blend of these genres. Published in 1885, it is the tale of "Huck" Finn's travels with his friend Jim, an escaped slave. The rough and wild setting of the great Mississippi River cleverly reflects the often unconventional nature of the characters' opinions and behavior.

Information about the **setting** and **era** can be useful.

This is one of many **synonyms** of "interesting." Look at the note at the dictionary entry "interesting."

Not long after escaping from first his elderly guardian and then his alcoholic father in Missouri, Huck discovers the fugitive slave Jim hiding on an island. In spite of his feeling a moral and legal obligation to turn Jim over to the authorities, Huck eventually decides to travel with him. Together, they encounter a number of shrewd, unsavory, and deceitful characters and narrowly avoid disaster several times before finally coming to rest in southern Arkansas.

It is usual to use the present tense to describe the story.

The hypocrisy and moral failings of many of the characters whom Huck and Jim meet along the river provide a richly satirical critique of the postwar South, and American society in general. Throughout their adventures, Jim clearly demonstrates his kindness and integrity. Huck finally chooses to face the potential consequences of defying both the law and social convention rather than to betray his friend.

The brilliant satire, the authentic portrayals of the many colorful characters, and the ambitious themes of racism and moral conflict all combine to propel the reader from the first page to the last. Some modern readers may find some of Huck's expressions and opinions to be shocking and difficult to understand. However, the reader readily sympathizes with Huck's feisty attitude, Jim's desperate search for his family, and both of the runaways' pursuit of freedom.

Including information on the **style of writing** can be helpful.

The vernacular dialogue in this novel makes it far from an "easy read." Indeed, many readers will very likely struggle with the southern idioms and dialects. In addition, a basic knowledge of the geography of the Mississippi River is useful in following the plot and understanding certain references in the narrative. Nevertheless, this classic and compelling story is sure to remain with the persevering reader for a lifetime.

Linking words aid organization and can also give your opinion.

Conclusion. Restate your opinion of the book as a recommendation to read it or not to read it.

Writing Your Review
Reviewing Works of Fiction

Read or reread the book and make notes. Try to answer the questions a reader might have:

- What kind of book is it?
- What happens in the story?
- Who are the main characters?
- What is the main theme of the book?
- Is it well written?
- Would you recommend this book?

You can use the same plan as the model review. A successful review will contain these elements, but the order can be changed.

Paragraph 1 – Introduction
General comments about the book and its genre. Use your dictionary to help you find synonyms for words such as *story*.

Paragraph 2 – Plot
A brief summary of what happens. Remember not to include too many details and don't give away the ending of the book. Keep in mind that your reader has probably **not** read the book!

Paragraph 3 – Characters
Use your dictionary to find a range of adjectives to describe the main characters.

Paragraph 4 – Literary devices and other information
You may want to comment on themes, symbolism, and any particular techniques used by the author.

Paragraph 5 – Conclusion
Include your personal recommendation here. It is a good idea to try and write about both positive and negative aspects of the book.

Reviewing Works of Nonfiction

When reading a nonfiction review, your readers will have different questions:

- What is the author's reason for writing the work?
- Is it well organized? Can you follow the argument easily and find important information?
- Does the author of the work support their findings well?
- How does the work compare with other literature on the same subject?

Language Bank

Beginnings
It is a fascinating tale of... (e.g., *rural life*)
This moving account of... (e.g., *a young man's experiences*)
I found this story far-fetched and unconvincing.

Details/Plot
Written in..., the story begins with...
The events unfold in...
The tale is set in...

Characters
The writer introduces us to...
The principal characters are...
My favorite character is undoubtedly...
The story focuses on...
We experience all this through the eyes of...

Giving Your Opinion
The writer excels at... (e.g., *describing...*)
I was impressed by...
One aspect I found a little disappointing was...
One possible flaw is that...

Conclusions
I would highly recommend this rewarding book.
I thoroughly enjoyed this book. In fact I couldn't put it down!
By the end of this book, you feel...
I was left unmoved by this story.
I would strongly advise against reading this book.

Writing a Formal Letter

The important things to remember about writing formal letters are the layout, which follows particular conventions, and the language, which must be formal or semiformal and polite.

A Letter of Complaint

August 2, 2010

28 Lee Street
Brevard, NC 28712

Customer Services Manager
Old South Airlines
419 Meeting Street
Charleston, SC 29413

To Whom It May Concern:

My husband and I and our two children, aged 2 and 4, were passengers in flight OS238 from Charlotte to Orlando on July 23, 2010. I am writing to complain about a number of aspects of the service that we received.

First, when the flight was delayed due to mechanical problems, the staff at the airline's information desk were very unhelpful. We were not given any vouchers for drinks or meals, even though it was clear very early on that the delay would last for several hours. This meant that we had to spend a considerable amount of money in a nearby restaurant.

Then, when we were finally able to board the plane, families were not allowed to board first, although we had paid extra for this service. As a result, we were not able to sit together, further upsetting our already exhausted children.

I am aware that airlines are under no legal obligation to provide refreshments to travelers in the event of a long delay. However, as a regular customer, a gold-level member of your frequent flyer program, and a passenger who paid extra for priority boarding that I did not receive, I would expect some sort of compensation for the problems that we experienced.

I am enclosing copies of our boarding passes and restaurant receipts and look forward to hearing from you soon.

Sincerely,

Hillary Allan

Hillary Allan

Date
The date appears at the top in month, day, year format.

Sender's Address
Your address may appear either one line below the date or directly below your closing.

Inside Address
Try to address your letter to a specific person, and/or their job title.

Salutation
If you do not know the person's name, you can use "To Whom It May Concern:" instead.

Paragraph 1
Explain clearly why you are writing.

Paragraph 2
Explain the problem and how you were affected.

Paragraph 3
Explain any further problem and the consequences.

Paragraph 4
Clearly state what action you wish the company to take.

Ending
Say that you would like a quick reply.

Closing
Sign your name, followed by your name typewritten (and your full address, if you did not include it at the top of your letter).

Blue = layout and conventions	Green = structure and content	Pink = key language

A Letter to the Editor

A letter to the editor of a newspaper or other publication should show your opinion clearly and tell people something interesting or new. It can be direct and have a personal tone—you can use *I*, *we*, and *you*.

Format your letter as a formal or semiformal letter (as seen here).

If possible, try to reference and reply directly to a recent article in the publication to which you are writing.

Strong adjectives, rhetorical questions, and exclamation marks are all appropriate to show how you feel.

A challenge to readers can be effective.

Include your contact details, including a telephone number and an e-mail address. Also include your job title or other affiliation if you are writing for professional reasons.

April 9, 2010

Editor
The Seattle Post-Intelligencer
101 Elliott Avenue West
Suite 540
Seattle, WA 98119

Dear Editor:

As a student in my early twenties, I am part of a key demographic for TV networks. Why, then, do I find so little to interest or entertain me? One trend I find particularly disturbing is the increase in "reality" TV shows such as *Survivor*, *The Real Housewives*, and *Jersey Shore*, to name but a few ("Jersey Shore headed back to New Jersey," April 8, 2010).

"Reality" TV shows involve "real" people performing ridiculous and often dangerous acts and generally behaving horribly toward each other. These shows appeal to that part of us that takes pleasure in watching the humiliation of others, and I believe that networks are being irresponsible by promoting this. It is demeaning to both the participants and the viewers.

It is time we took a stand against reality TV in favor of quality TV! How can we do it? Start by changing the channel.

Sincerely,

Kim Brissey

Kim Brissey

18 Main Street North
Coupeville, WA 98239
Telephone (515) 555 1212
E-mail kimb@whidbeyadventures.com

Writing a Résumé

A well-written, well-produced, appropriate résumé is vital for getting you to the interview stage for a job. Use the example and advice here to help you.

Tips

- Adapt your résumé so that it is appropriate for the job you are applying for.
- Present yourself positively and accurately.
- Keep your résumé short – no more than 2 pages if possible, or 1 page for new graduates.
- Make your résumé attractive and easy to read: use capitals, bold type, spacing, and underlining.
- Choose a typeface such as Times New Roman, Arial, or Verdana. Use at least 10 point font size.
- Describe your work experience in terms of self-motivation, teamwork, organization, problem-solving, and enthusiasm.

Personal Information
There is no need to mention your age, gender, nationality, race, religion, or marital status. Don't send a photo unless you are asked to.

Objective To summarize your goals and customize your résumé for specific positions. State a realistic short-term goal and/or a job for which you are currently qualified.

Education Put the most recent first. Omit elementary and middle school.

Experience Put the most recent first. Experienced candidates: put this before Education and write more about your most recent position.

Jane Q. Student
jqstudent@mba.nau.edu

Present Address:
508 Blackbird's Roost
Flagstaff, AZ 86011, U.S.A.
Tel. +1 929 555 1212

Permanent Address:
50, rue de Vaugirard
Saint-Sulpice, France 75006
Tel. +33 1234 567 890

OBJECTIVE To obtain an entry-level management position within an international hospitality organization.

EDUCATION **Masters in Business Administration** (M.B.A.), 2008-2010 Northern Arizona University, Flagstaff, Arizona, U.S.A.
B.A. in International Hospitality, 2004-2008 Université de Savoie, Chambéry, France

EXPERIENCE **Travel Agent**, Sep. 2008-Present **Kokopelli Extreme Tours**, Sedona, Arizona, U.S.A.
Organized adventure package tours for large student groups, trained and supervised new staff members, and maintained partner relationships.
Camp Counselor, Jun. 2004-Aug. 2008 **Voyageurs Summer Camp**, Voglans, France
Group leader for children aged 10-15. Developed curriculum for campers and led overnight hiking trips.

HONORS Agent of the Month, Kokopelli Extreme Tours, March 2010
Voted "Most Popular Counselor," Voyageurs, 2006 & 2007

SKILLS & INTERESTS Fluent in French and English; conversational Spanish
Enjoy Web design in HTML and Flash

Writing a Cover Letter

A one-page cover letter accompanies a résumé or an application form. A good letter uses formal language and presents some key arguments for why your application should be taken seriously.

April 18, 2010

112 Columbia Street
Cambridge, MA 02139

Ms. Alice Griffin
Director of Software Development
Prescott Cryptosoft, Incorporated
513 West 54th Street
New York, NY 10019

Dear Ms. Griffin:

I am writing to apply for the entry-level developer position in your software group (Job ID: NNG-SR-NY) advertised on Dice.com.

I am currently a senior studying computer engineering at MIT, with a specialization in security and encryption. I have a 3.9 overall GPA and have interned for the past two summers at Mesa Rosa Software in San Jose, where I worked on several projects related to digital rights management (DRM) and other access control technologies.

The skills list for this position includes experience with content security, digital signatures, and certificates. I feel that I am particularly well-qualified for this position. In addition to my experience at Mesa Rosa, my senior project explored a new approach to DRM for computer software, based on an algorithm that I designed and implemented myself. In terms of teamwork, I am extremely dependable, organized, and deadline-oriented. In addition to my technical background and abilities, I would also hope to bring to the team my sincere enthusiasm for the field of security.

In short, I am confident that my experience and education make me an ideal candidate for this position. I would very much welcome the opportunity discuss the position in more detail and would be available for an interview over the phone or in person at your convenience. Thank you for your time and consideration.
Sincerely,

Asok Chaudary

Asok Chaudary
Encl. Résumé
      Three letters of reference

For advice on layout, see WT20–WT21.

In a cover letter, use the more formal words *position*, *internship*, or *vacancy*, not the less formal word *job*.

Try to address your letter to a specific person, preferably the hiring manager for the position. You may need to do some research to find a name, perhaps by asking someone in the company's Human Resources department.

Paragraph 1 states your purpose for writing. Say which job you are applying for and how/where you heard about it. Include a Job ID if one is provided.

Paragraph 2 outlines your current or most recent job (or educational situation) and responsibilities. Make it clear how your current position is relevant to the job you are applying for.

Paragraph 3 says why you want the job and what you can bring to the company. It is very important to say what you can do for them.

Paragraph 4 gives other relevant information and when you are available for an interview.

Closing
"Sincerely" is always an appropriate closing, followed by a comma.

Encl. indicates that you have enclosed something.

Blue = layout and conventions

Green = structure and content

Pink = key language

Writing E-mails

- E-mails **vary in formality** depending on how well you know the reader and what your status is in relation to them.
- All e-mails should be polite, but they **vary in level of politeness** depending on who you are writing to and what you are asking them.
- Writers use a level of formality and politeness to achieve an appropriate **tone**.
- E-mails between colleagues of a similar status can be informal and personal, but should still be polite and friendly.

Writing Business E-mails

An inquiry to a company – *formal, polite*

Notice the use of periods and commas in these e-mails. Use periods after abbreviations.

Clear **subject** line

To:	kmiller@charitytrainers.org
From:	risai@newgreenspaces.com
Date:	08/19/2010
Subject:	Request for customized training

Dear Mr. Miller:

I am writing to ask about the possibility of organizing a customized training program for a group of five of our mid-level managers. We would be interested in having them learn more about staff recruitment, project management, and fundraising practices. Could you please let me know what scheduling and pricing options are available for a week-long course fulfilling these requirements? FYI, the first week in December is our winter retreat and would not be a good time for us.

I look forward to hearing from you at your earliest convenience.

Sincerely,
Risa Inyaka

Learning and Development Coordinator
New Green Spaces, Inc.

Greeting: Title plus last name, since this is the first contact with this person.

Direct but polite questions using "you" are fine.

Closing: *Sincerely*, or *Sincerely yours*, are good ways to close a business e-mail. Include your job title as well as your name.

Some abbreviations are acceptable in formal e-mails.
ad = advertisement
ASAP = as soon as possible
FYI = for your information

A reply – *less formal (semiformal), polite*

Greeting and closing: Kareem chooses to use first names – correspondence will now tend to be less formal. "Dear Risa" is followed by a comma.

Opening: a formal, polite opening sentence is appropriate for the first reply.

Contracted forms can be used as the language is less formal.

To: risai@newgreenspaces.com
Subject:Re: Request for customized training

Dear Risa,

Thank you for your interest in our training programs. We would be happy to provide you with a customized management course. Attached you'll find a detailed proposal for the program you requested, along with a contract for you to sign and return (along with a 10% deposit) if you would like to accept the proposal. I'm also attaching a PDF brochure providing brief biographies of the instructors for the course.

If you have any questions or would like to modify any of the details of this program, please feel free to contact me directly.

Regards,
Kareem

Kareem Miller, Marketing Manager
Charity Trainers U.S.A.
kmiller@charitytrainers.org
Tel 800-555-1212, ext. 27

Language sets a polite, semi-formal, friendly tone:
▶ *We would be happy to...*
or
We would be pleased to...
not:
~~We would be delighted to...~~
– too formal for e-mails
▶ *Please feel free to...*
not:
~~Please don't hesitate to~~
– too formal

Say what's in the **attachment**.

Language Bank

Greetings		
Formal	**Semiformal**	**Informal**
Dear Ms. Klein/Dear Professor Smith/Dear Chris White (if you don't know the gender). Do not use title and first name	*Dear Risa*	*Hi/Hi Renata/ Hello/ Hello Risa*
Dear All (to a group)	*Dear All*	*Hi everyone/Hello all*
Attention:/For the attention of the Sales Manager	—	—

Closings		
Sincerely/Sincerely yours + your full name. Add position and contact details.	*Regards/Best Wishes/All the best/ Best/Thank you* + your first name or your full name. (or formal closings)	*Thanks/Thx/Speak to you soon* + your first name.

Requesting Action		
Very Polite	**Polite**	**Informal Request**
Would it be possible (for you) to send me...?	*Could you (please) send me...?*	*Can you send me...?/ Pls can you let me have...?*
Would it be possible for me to come...?	*Could I come...?*	*Can I come...?*
I would really appreciate your help./I would be very grateful for your help.	*Thank you.*	*Thanks*

Writing Academic E-mails

- Academic e-mails are usually **personal**, not official. You are writing to a specific, named individual, not to someone in their official role.
- The level of **politeness** you need will vary. If you are asking a favor of an academic outside your university, you need to express a higher level of politeness than if you are asking your own teacher for a meeting. E-mails between colleagues can be very informal.
- Remember to use a level of formality and politeness to achieve an appropriate tone.

Formal – a request from a student to an academic from a different department
Low status writer to high status reader whom he does not know.

Tone: *personal, very formal, very polite*

Greeting: use *Dear* + academic title and family name, or *Mr.*, *Ms.*, etc. and family name

Clear **subject** line

Introduce yourself by giving your position in the university.

Say **why you are writing**. Mention any academic contact. **Be specific** about what you would like the reader to do. Give **supporting details**.

Would it be possible... Very polite. or *Could I possibly...* (not *I kindly request* – too official)

```
Subject:  Request for statistical help

Dear  Dr. Barr:

I am a first year Ph.D. student in the
department of linguistics and my
research topic is a quantitative study
of verb forms in academic writing.
Since I need to use advanced
statistical tools for processing the
data, my supervisor, Dr. John Pugh,
suggested that I contact you to ask for
advice.
Would it be possible for me to come and
see you to discuss what I need?
I'm attaching a copy of my draft
research proposal to give you an idea
of the scope of my study.

I would be very grateful for your help.

Best wishes,
David Samuels
```

Ending: very polite or: *I would really appreciate your help.* (not: *Thank you for your time* – official. not: *Thank you for your attention* – very formal spoken)

Closing: or *Sincerely*, or *Regards*. Give your full name. Add position and contact details if necessary.

Less formal – request from a student to their own supervisor
Lower status writer to higher status reader whom she knows well.

Tone: *personal, polite, less formal*

Attachments should be no larger than 2MB, if possible.

Short, clear subject line

Use periods after short titles. A comma after the greeting is less formal than a colon.

```
Subject:    Proposed meeting this week
Attachments: mif.doc

Dear Dr. Jacobi,

I'm planning to submit the attached paper
to "Markets in Focus" next week. I wonder
if it might be possible for us to meet to
discuss it before I send it off? I'd be
very grateful for your comments and advice.
I'm available every day after 3 p.m., or in
the morning on either Tuesday or Thursday.

Thank you,
Emily Wagner
```

Closing: courteous and fairly formal

ACKNOWLEDGMENTS

Illustrations and photographs by: A Levenson 318 (backhoe); AA Reps 1461 (stethoscope); Alamy Ltd. 67 (gargoyle), 99 (clutch bag), 133 (scooter), 155 (catamaran, container ship, ferry, hovercraft, liner, speedboat, yacht), 196 (school bus, tour bus), 215 (Jeep™, SUV, hatchback, sedan, sports car, taxi), 264 (ironing board), 273 (dress, suit), 302 (flash drive, PDA, digital camera), 318 (dump truck), 329 (grate, steam, stew, stir-fry), 691 (sou'wester), 719 (bowling, caving, embroidery, ice skating, model making, photography, scuba diving) , 735 (duplex, mobile home), 830 (dry measuring cups, kitchen scissors, paring knife), 1116 (biplane, blimp, light aircraft), 1195 (sudoku), 1363 (jelly shoe, platform, wedge, high-tops), 1438 (archery, field hockey), 1439 (hang-gliding), 1456 (glue), 1573 (bradawl), 1581 (Frisbee™, backgammon, dominoes, slide), 1600 (pickup, tanker, tractor); Anton Balazh 279 (teakettle); Blend Images 719 (stamp collecting); Brand X Pictures 302 (headset), 1438 (the pole vault); CAMP/ RelaXimages/ Photolibrary Group Ltd. 155 (rowboat); Corbis 133 (unicycle), 155 (raft), 215 (RV), 719 (painting, pottery, woodcarving), 735 (row house), 830 (measuring spoons), 837 (tubes), 1116 (glider), 1195 (jigsaw puzzle), 1438 (basketball, gymnastics, Ping-Pong™), 1439 (bungee jumping, breaststroke, butterfly, jet-skiing, windsurfing), 1581 (dice, stuffed animal); Corel 67 (cloister), 155 (submarine), (189 (amphitheater, castle, greenhouse, hut, lighthouse, log cabin, mansion, oil rig, portico, pyramid, skyscraper, warehouse), 442 (donkey), 573 (flashlight), 642 (baseball glove), 1438 (boxing), 1561 (tiger), 1585 (freight train, passenger train, steam train), 1600 (fire engine); Creatas 1121 (a hand of cards); Creatas Images/ Jupiterimages (UK) Ltd 1116 (seaplane); Creativ Studio Heinemann 329 (mash); D Laurens 1581 (swing); Dennis Kitchen Studio 99 (backpack, purse), 264 (bucket, sponge, vacuum cleaner), 273 (T-shirt), 302 (printer), 812 (chain, engagement ring, pin), 1286 (rope), 1363 (Loafers™), 1456 (calculator, stapler, staples), 1480 (baby carriage, stroller), 1573 (nails, screwdriver, screws, tape measure); Dex Image 1581 (sandbox); Digital vision 1438 (bobsled, skydiving); Duomo TIPS RF/ Tips Italia RF 1438 (hockey); E Calderoni 1438 (the hammer); FCM Graphic 1439 (paragliding); Frazier Photolibrary, Inc. 155 (hydrofoil), 196 (van), 1600 (car transporter); Getty Images, Inc. 719 (darts), 1438 (horse racing), 1581 (tic-tac-toe); Getty/ Buccina Studios/PhotoDisc 133 (mountain bike), 329 (slice), 518 (jogging), 787 (glockenspiel), 1438 (cycling), 1439 (cross-country skiing, the high jump), 1581 (dollhouse); Glowimages Inc. 133 (dirt bike), 329 (fry), 1439 (backstroke); Hemera CD 189 (barn), 207 (camel), 264 (broom, dustpan and brush, paintbrushes, roller, squeegee), 273 (bow ties, fleece vest, silk scarf, turtleneck sweater), 279 (French press, coffee maker), 286 (comb, hairbrush), 364 (beer mug, cup and saucer, wine glass), 573 (battery), 642 (rubber gloves), 691 (cap, mortarboard, panama, trilby), 787 (French horn, acoustic guitar, balalaika, banjo, castanets, drum kit, harmonica, mandolin, maracas, steel drum, tambourine, triangle), 812 (cuff links, hoop earring, medallion, signet ring, wedding ring), 825 (flute), 830 (blender, bottle opener, bread knife, carving knife, cleaver, cutting board, food processor, grater, hand mixer, hand blender, juicer, mortar and pestle, nutcracker, pastry brush, peeler, pepper mill, rolling pin, spatulas, timer, tongs, wooden spoon, zester), 901 (mailboxes), 1061 (panda), 1363 (kitten heels, moccasins, sandal, slippers, sneakers, stiletto, wingtips), 1395 (sleigh), 1456 (card index, clipboard,

files, folders, paper clips, pushpins), 1526 (tarantula), 1573 (a pair of scissors, coping saw, drill, file, fork, hacksaw, hammer, hose, ladder, lawn mower, mallet, pliers, tools, watering can, wrench), 1581 (chess, hand puppet), 1601 (trunk); Hemera Technologies Inc. 9 (accordion, concertina), 47 (anchor), 55 (antelope), 92 (axes), 99 (briefcase, duffel bag, fanny pack, grocery bag, suitcase), 121 (pump), 126 (bellows), 133 (U-lock, helmet, light, motorcycle), 138 (binoculars, telescope), 187 (buffalo), 235 (armchair, bench, chair, chaise longue, deck chair, director's chair, recliner, sofa, stool, swivel chair, wheelchair), 269 (alarm clock, clock, digital watch, grandfather clock, watch), 273 (bathrobe, cardigan, denim jacket, leather jacket, man in blue shirt, hoody, man in red shirt, polo shirt, raincoat, red blouse, scarf, shorts, vest, windbreaker, zipper), 297 (compass, pair of compasses), 364 (champagne flute, mug, sippy cup, tumbler), 441 (dolphin), 540 (fans), 642 (glove, mitten), 691 (baseball cap, beanie, beret, boater, cowboy hat, derby, hard hat, hood, knitted hat, crash helmet, sun hat, top hat), 714 (hinge), 787 (bass guitar, cello, clarinet, congas, electric guitar, flute, harp, piano recorder, saxophone, trombone, trumpet, viola), 812 (bangle, bracelet, charm bracelet, pendant), 830 (can opener, colander, corkscrew, garlic press, ice-cream scoop, ladle, sieve, whisk), 917 (Halloween mask, surgical mask), 926 (medals, trophy), 928 (megaphone), 937 (metronome), 1057 (padlock), 1111 (jug, pitcher), 1121 (deck of cards, face cards, playing cards), 1286 (ball of string, chain, ribbon, thread), 1359 (clam, lobster, mussel, oyster), 1363 (clogs, cowboy boot, flip-flops, mule, rubber boots, slingback), 1395 (sled, snowmobile), 1456 (fountain pen, marker, notebook, pencil, punch, rubber stamp), 1494 (sundial), 1505 (swan), 1511 (dagger, spear, sword), 1573 (ax, handsaw, hoe, pocket knife, rakes, shears, shovel, spade, spirit level, stepladder, trowel, hand fork, wheelbarrow), 1600 (cement mixer, tractor, tractor-trailer, van), 1601 (elephant's trunk, trunk of a tree), 1734 (zebra); Hemera Technologies Inc./ OUP 273 (overcoat); I MacDonald 155 (paddle wheeler); Iconotec 1571 (toolbox); Illustration Ltd. 958 (bill), 1456 (ballpoint pen, eraser, pencil sharpener), 958 (money); Image Source 329 (bake, barbecue, chop), 518 (barbell, dumbbell, push-up, yoga), 719 (Rollerblade™, snorkeling), 1116 (hot-air balloon), 1195 (wordsearch), 1438 (fencing, squash), 1439 (rappelling); Ingram Publishing 67 (arch); JB Illustrations 69 (armadillo), 338 (cougar), 346 (coyote), 468 (globe, the seasons), 598 (fox), 715 (hippopotamus), 858 (leopard), 1033 (opossum), 1062 (panther), 1116 (plane), 1138 (porcupine), 1203 (raccoon), 1269 (rhinoceros), 1282 (beaver, chipmunk, gopher, mouse, rat, squirrel), 1392 (skunk), 1712 (wolf); Jae Wagoner Artists Rep. 1581 (checkers); James Oliver/ Digital Vision/ Getty Images, Inc./ Photolibrary Group Ltd. 1438 (sprinting); Janet Baker & Julian Baker (JB Illustrations) 111 (all baskets), 157 (the eye, the face, the hand), 215 (convertible), 453 (dreamcatcher), 626 (gazebo), 730 (horse), 1465 (stile, turnstile), 1663 (volcano); Jupiterimages (UK) Ltd 189 (pagoda), 273 (bow ties), 329 (roll out), 719 (gardening, pool), 1438 (badminton); K Hiscock 52 (lion), 53 (beetle, frog, octopus, trout), 232 (barley, corn, ear of wheat, millet, oats, rice, rye, wheat), 611 (chili), 707 (bay, black peppercorns, cardamom, chives, cilantro, coriander seeds, cumin seeds, dill, ginger, nutmeg, oregano, paprika, rosemary, saffron, sage, star anise, tarragon, turmeric), 1011 (macadamia), 1118 (bluebell, bulrush, buttercup, carnation, chrysanthemum, daisy, dandelion, flower, lotus, nettle, poppy, primrose, reed, sweet pea, thistle), 1593 (ash, horse chestnut); KAKIMAGE/ Alamy Ltd. 735 (apartment building); KJA-artists.com 273 (buckle, button, drawstring, hook and eye, safety pin, shoelace, toggle, Velcro™), 1056 (aerosol can, bags, blister pack, bottles, boxes, cans, cartons, jars, juice box, matchbox, multipack, package, packets, packs, plastic bag, rolls, shopping basket, shopping cart, shopping bag, stick, tin, tray, tubs); Kevin Jones 144 (blade of a knife); Luminis/ Alamy Ltd. 215 (minivan, station wagon); M Mason 1581 (rag doll); M Milbradt/Brand X Pictures/Jupiterimages (UK) Ltd 67 (obelisk); Meiklejohn Illustrations 106 (all bars); 121 (air mattress, bunk beds, cot, cradle, crib, four-poster bed, futon, hammock, sofa bed, travel crib) 147 (roller blind, Venetian blind), 169 (all bows), 179 (all bridges), 227 (cat's cradle), 367 (bent, curled up, curly, curved, twisted, wavy), 609 (bubbles, froth), 677 (all hairstyles), 728 (all hooks), 837 (beaker, Bunsen burner, crucible, dropper, evaporating dish, graduated cylinder, magnet, microscope, Petri dish, pipette, powder, retort, spatula, stand, syringe, tongs), 866 (all lamps), 905 (blush, concealer, eyeliner, eyeshadow, foundation, lip gloss, lipliner, lipstick, mascara, nail polish), 988 (all necks), 1053 (oxbow), 1275 (boxing ring, diamond ring, key ring), 1351 (shade), 1398 (slingshot), 1440 (spring), 1445 (crumple, crush, press, squash, squeeze, wring), 1456 (ring binder, staple remover); Moodboard/Mike Watson Images Limited 1438 (soccer); NB Illustration 99 (wallets); O Drew/National Geographic 1581 (jungle gym); OUP 45 (ammonite), 52 (albatross, bald eagle, barn owl, bat, buck, chicken, chimpanzee, dog, duck, elephant, goat, gull, kangaroo, koala, monkey, pheasant, puffin, sperm whale, spider monkey, talons, turkey, vulture, webbed foot), 53 (alligator, ant, bumblebee, butterfly, cobra, crab, crocodile, dragonfly, flea, fly, grasshopper, ladybug, mosquito, moth, salamander, scorpion, sea turtle, shrimp, slug, snail, spider, tick, toad, trout, turtle, wasp, wood louse), 82 (atom, molecule), 92 (graph axes), 99 (change purse, tote bag, trash bag), 102 (ball-and-socket joint, ball bearing), 106 (barbed wire, barcode), 110 (baseball), 121 (full-size bed, twin bed), 131 (beveled), 144 (all blades), 149 (block and tackle), 157 (the body, the internal organs, the skeleton), 163 (boomerang), 215 (cars), 235 (car seat, high chair, rocking chair), 264 (cloths, dish towel, dishwashing liquid, feather duster, scrub brush), 273 (snaps), 279 (cogwheel), 303 (concentric circles), 327 (convex), 332 (all cords), 415 (dimensions), 447 (all joints), 588 (football, football player), 610 (apples, apricot, avocados, banana, blackberries, blueberries, cantaloupe, cherries, coconut, cranberries, figs, grapefruit, grapes, honeydew melon, kiwis, lemon, lime, lychee, mango, orange, passion fruit, peaches, pear, pineapple, plum, pomegranate, raspberries, starfruit, strawberries, watermelon), 611 (artichoke, asparagus, bean sprouts, beet, broccoli, butternut squash, cabbage, carrot, cauliflower, celery, corn on the cob, cucumber, eggplant, fennel, garlic, green beans, green onions, kidney beans, leek, lettuce, mushrooms, okra, onion, parsnip, peas, peppers, pumpkin, radishes, rutabaga, shallots, spinach, tomatoes, turnip, zucchini), 652 (gorilla), 657 (all graphs and charts), 703 (helices), 707 (basil, cinnamon, cloves, mint, parsley, thyme), 728 (picture hooks), 735 (house), 749 (ideograms), 811 (jellyfish), 812 (clip earrings, locket, pearl necklace,

pierced earrings), 830 (potato masher, spatula), 833 (bow, coil, knot, loop), 836 (label, price tag, ticket), 871 (lines), 878 (lizard), 926 (plaque), 958 (credit card, dollar, half dollar), 962 (moose), 975 (music), 1011 (almond, Brazil nut, cashew, chestnut, hazelnut, peanut, pecan, pistachio, walnut), 1034 (optical illusions), 1049 (overhanging branches, overlapping dates, overlapping tiles), 1085 (penguin), 1106 (pigeon), 1110 (piston), 1118 (bamboo, cactus, daffodil, fern, iris, ivy, lichen, lily, log, moss, orchid, plant, rose, sunflower, tulip), 1125 (plugs), 1203 (hare, rabbit), 1213 (ratchet), 1223 (rebus), 1276 (ripple), 1312 (bathroom scale, the scale of C), 1354 (shapes, solids and angles), 1356 (shark), 1358 (sheep), 1363 (boots, flats, hiking boots, oxfords, pumps), 1441 (sprocket wheel), 1456 (correction fluid, highlighter, rubber bands, ruler, tape dispenser, thumbtacks), 1571 (chisel, monkey wrench, plane, plunger, sandpaper, vise), 1593 (beech, birch, fir, maple, oak, palm, redwood, tree, twig), 1654 (Venn diagram), 1682 (wavelength); OUP (OXED) 1547 (thermometers); Photo Agency EYE 329 (boil), 1581 (teddy bear); PhotoLink/ PhotoDisc/ Getty Images, Inc./ Photolibrary Group Ltd 1438 (hurdling); Photodisc/Getty 67 (colonnade, rotunda, vaulted ceiling), 133 (bicycle, tandem, tricycle), 155(canoe, kayak, sailboat), 189 (fort), 719 (crochet), 787 (bassoon, double bass, kettledrum, oboe, piccolo, sitar, tuba, xylophone), 830 (liquid measuring cup), 1581 (trampoline); Photolibrary Group Ltd. 133 (bikes, quad bike), 273 (crew neck sweater), 302 (PC, laptop), 329 (flambé, knead, whip), 518 (exercise bike, rowing machine, sit-up, treadmill), 719 (knitting, sewing, skateboarding), 735 (townhouses), 830 (ramekin), 1116 (fighter, helicopter), 1438 (crawl, golf, tennis, the discus, the javelin), 1439 (downhill skiing, rock climbing, surfing, the luge waterskiing), 1456 (envelope), 1600 (forklift truck); Photolink Ltd. 302 (MP3 player, flatbed scanner), 1456 (notepad); Photostock-israel 1581 (Chinese checkers); Pixoi Ltd 318 (bulldozer), 1585 (funicular, high-speed train, streetcar); Q2A Solutions 50 (ankh), 183 (broken, chipped, cracked), 336 (corrugated), 473 (edge), 599 (all frames), 682 (all handles), 710 (hieroglyphics), 825 (all keys), 954 (Möbius strip), 1083 (all pegs), 1204 (all racks), 1312 (fish scales, kitchen scale); Q2AMedia 468 (The earth and the solar system); R Kaestner/ Corbis Corporation 189 (palace); Reppans 1195 (crossword puzzle); RubberBall 273 (pajamas and nightgown), 1581 (jump rope); S Nicolas/ICONOTEC 67 (dome); Steve Cole/ PhotoDisc/ Getty Images, Inc./ Photolibrary Group Ltd. 691 (sombrero); Stockbyte/ Getty 264 (mop, sponge mop), 302 (Webcam TM, router), 329 (toast), 830 (cake server), 1456 (Post-it TM), 1581 (kite, rocking horse); Tetra Images LLC 1573 (sprinkler); Thinkstock Images/ Jupiterimages (UK) Ltd. 1438 (snowboarding); Thinkstock Images/ Jupiterimages (UK) Ltd. 1600 (tow truck); Comstock 1581 (building blocks); graficart.net 67 (geodesic dome); iStockphoto.com 279 (espresso machine), 735 (bungalow, condominium).

Maps © Oxford University Press

Minimum system requirements

Windows XP®, Windows Vista®, Windows® 7; 350 MHz, 256 MB RAM

Macintosh OSX 10.4 or higher; 500 MHz, 256 MB RAM

Full installation of the software requires 250 MB available on hard disk.

Macintosh users must perform a complete installation of the software.

Oxford University Press
Software Licence

Please read these terms before using the CD-ROM

This CD-ROM contains copyright material and by using it you agree to be bound by the terms of this Licence. If you do not accept the terms set out below then do not use the CD-ROM.

The literary material and computer software programs in this CD-ROM ('the Software') and any associated documentation are protected by copyright laws worldwide. The copyright is owned or licensed to Oxford University Press ('OUP').

1   Licence

OUP grants you the non-exclusive non-transferable right to use the Software on a single computer of the type specified in the packaging. You may not network the Software.

2   Use of the Software

2.1 Without prejudice to any statutory rights so to do and except as expressly permitted by this licence, you must not modify, adapt, distribute, transmit, transfer, publish, reproduce or alter any of the Software or any associated documentation.

2.2 Recognising the damage to OUP's business which would flow from unauthorized use of the Software and any associated documentation, you will make every effort to keep the CD-ROM and associated documentation secure both during the continuance of this licence and after its termination.

3   Termination

You may terminate this licence at any time by destroying the Software and any associated documentation. This licence will also terminate if you breach any of its terms.

4   Warranties

4.1 OUP warrants that the Software will be free from defects in materials and workmanship under normal use and will conform to the published specification for 90 days from the date you receive it.

4.2 The above warranty is in lieu of all other warranties express or implied and representations and in particular but without limitation to the foregoing:

4.2.1   OUP gives no warranties and makes no representations that the Software will be suitable for any particular purpose or for use under any specific conditions notwithstanding that such purpose or conditions may be known either to OUP or the dealer from whom you acquired the CD-ROM;

4.2.2   OUP accepts no responsibility for any mathematical or technical limitations of the Software;

4.2.3   OUP does not warrant that the operation of the Software will be uninterrupted or free from errors.

5   Limitation of liability

5.1 The entire liability of OUP and its suppliers and your exclusive remedy shall at OUP's option be replacement of the CD-ROM disc.

5.2 Save in the case of death or personal injury, in no circumstances will OUP or its suppliers be liable for any damages whatsoever (including without limitation damages for loss of data, loss of business, loss of profit, goodwill or any other consequential losses of any nature) arising out of the use or inability to use the Software or any associated documentation.

5.3 Links to any third party websites are provided by OUP for information only and OUP disclaims any responsibility for any materials contained in any third website to which a link is provided.

6   Law

This licence is governed by English law and the English Courts shall have jurisdiction.